Implementing Reforms in the Telecommunications Sector

Lessons from Experience

WORLD BANK

REGIONAL AND

SECTORAL STUDIES

Implementing Reforms in the Telecommunications Sector

Lessons from Experience

EDITED BY

BJORN WELLENIUS

AND

PETER A. STERN

The World Bank
Washington, D.C.

The World Bank Regional and Sectoral Studies series provides an outlet for work that is relatively limited in its subject matter or geographical coverage but that contributes to the intellectual foundations of development operations and policy formulation. Some sources cited in this paper may be informal documents that are not readily available.

The findings, interpretations, and conclusions expressed in this publication are those of the authors and should not be attributed in any manner to the World Bank, to its affiliated organizations, or to the members of its Board of Executive Directors or the countries they represent.

The material in this publication is copyrighted. Requests for permission to reproduce portions of it should be sent to the Office of the Publisher at the address shown in the copyright notice above. The World Bank encourages dissemination of its work and will normally give permission promptly and, when the reproduction is for noncommercial purposes, without asking a fee. Permission to copy portions for classroom use is granted through the Copyright Clearance Center, Suite 910, 222 Rosewood Dr., Danvers, Massachusetts 01923, U.S.A.

The complete backlist of publications from the World Bank is shown in the annual *Index of Publications*, which contains an alphabetical title list and indexes of subjects, authors, and countries and regions. The latest edition is available free of charge from Distribution Unit, Office of the Publisher, The World Bank, 1818 H Street, N.W., Washington, D.C. 20433, U.S.A., or from Publications, The World Bank, 66, avenue d'Iéna, 75116 Paris, France.

Björn Wellenius is telecommunications adviser in the Industry and Energy Department of the World Bank; Peter A. Stern is director of government and international affairs at Teleglobe, Inc., Canada.

Cover design by Sam Ferro; globe design developed by Robert Walker from an idea by André Stern.

Library of Congress Cataloging-in-Publication Data

Wellenius, Bjorn,
    Implementing reforms in the telecommunications sector : lessons
from experience / Bjorn Wellenius, Peter A. Stern.
       p.   cm. — (World Bank regional and sectoral studies)
    ISBN 0-8213-2606-6
    1. Telecommunication policy—Developing countries—Case studies.
    2. Telecommunication policy—Europe—Case studies.
    3. Telecommunication policy—Case studies.   I. Stern, Peter A.,
1941–   . II. Title. III. Series.
HE8635.W45   1994
384'.068—dc20   94-7423
                                                  CIP

Contents

Foreword

THE MOVEMENT TOWARD STRUCTURAL REFORM of the telecommunications sector, which began in the 1980s, has become a veritable worldwide wave of change. Most Organization for Economic Cooperation and Development (OECD) countries, and a growing number of developing countries, have by now either completed major reforms or have these well under way. The reforms are driven by growing awareness of the importance of telecommunications in an increasingly integrated and competitive world economy, coupled to continued technological innovation leading to new network and market structures as well as dramatically lower costs. This is a good time to take stock of the considerable volume and diversity of accumulated experience, and to draw some lessons of practical significance for countries still at the early stages of change.

The time to take stock is also right from the standpoint of international institutions as they evolve in the early 1990s in response to rapid change in the global telecommunications scene. For example, the International Telecommunication Union upgraded the development function to an equal footing with well-established activities in the areas of standards and radio communications. The World Bank integrated its telecommunications and information technology experts within a new central vice presidency responsible for financial and private sector development, with a mandate to innovate in the Bank's approach in these broad thematic areas. The International Finance Corporation established a specialized unit to help mobilize capital for private investment in telecommunications in developing countries. For the first time since the creation of the General Agreement on Trade and Tariffs, telecommunications have been included in negotiations on trade liberalization.

In the context of these sectoral and institutional changes, in 1991, the World Bank, the International Telecommunication Union, and the Commonwealth Telecommunications Organisation jointly hosted a seminar in Washington, DC, to examine the experience of implementing reforms in the telecommunications sector. This highly successful event brought together over one hundred participants involved in telecommunications reform in some forty countries.

The message from the seminar was clear. In order to overcome persistent shortfalls in telecommunications development, it is necessary to attract private investment and new entrants to the telecommunications business as well as to shift the role of governments from ownership and management of operations to sector policy formulation and regulation. The impact of initial reforms along these lines has been generally very positive: accelerated growth, better and new services, higher productivity, and gains by most or all stakeholders. There are, however, no standard blueprints for sectoral reform. Sector designs and implementation strategies must be crafted to fit the specific economic, political, and institutional features of each country. Imperfect solutions are often the best that can be achieved in practice. From inception to maturity, sector reform is typically a long process. Although some components of reform, including privatizing state enterprises, can be successfully completed fairly quickly, other components, notably developing regulatory capabilities and competition, require more time and sustained government attention. Some developing countries can successfully go most or all the way on their own, but many others will need substantial financial and technical assistance to help them along.

The book you now have in your hands is the product of a collective undertaking to make available the main findings of the Washington seminar to a larger audience. As the reform debate moves from principles to practice, we trust this book will provide readers with valuable insights on the process of reform as well as contribute to the design and implementation of solutions for the telecommunications sector throughout the developing world.

> Jean-François Rischard
> Vice President
> Financial and Private Sector Development
> The World Bank
>
> Pekka Tarjanne
> Secretary General
> International Telecommunication Union
>
> B. K. Syngal
> Chairman
> Commonwealth Telecommunications Council

Preface

DRIVEN BY TECHNOLOGICAL CHANGE AND MARKET DEMAND, a wave of change in the organization of the telecommunications sector began in the early 1980s in a few highly industrialized countries, gradually extended throughout the Organization for Economic Cooperation and Development (OECD), and by the early 1990s had reached a number of developing countries. Traditional state monopolies are giving way to more complex sector structures that seek to overcome past constraints on telecommunications development through commercialization of operations, competition, and private sector participation.

Organizations such as the International Telecommunication Union (ITU), the Commonwealth Telecommunications Organization (CTO), OECD, the Agence de Coopération Culturelle et Technique (ACCT), and the World Bank have become increasingly involved in helping governments address the complex policy, regulatory, financial, institutional, and management issues that arise in such a process of change. In particular, since 1985 the World Bank, along with ITU, CTO, and ACCT, has organized a series of gatherings that focused on management and reform in the telecommunications sector. Seminars in Nairobi and Harare were followed by others in Barbados; Kuala Lumpur; Windsor, England; Washington, DC; and most recently Tunis.

The Kuala Lumpur seminar, organized in November 1987 by the World Bank and CTO, examined the forces driving sector reform, as well as the main policy issues and options. The experiences presented were mainly those of precursor industrialized countries. The United States was well advanced in the transition toward a highly competitive environment, and the United Kingdom and Japan had recently restructured their telecommunications sectors. Several developing countries in Asia and Latin America were preparing for change. Four years later, in April 1991, when the World Bank, ITU, and CTO organized a similar seminar in Washington, DC the base of experience had widened substantially. Many more countries, including several from the developing world, had completed reform or were well advanced in the process. Many more were seriously examining their options. The Washington, DC, seminar and a follow-up in the French language organized by the World Bank with ITU and ACCT in Tunis a year later, gave policymakers, operators, regulators, strategic and market investors, international bankers, representatives of the international development community, professionals, academics, and other key players the opportunity to share their experiences on the actual design and implementation of telecommunications reforms and to learn from others.

This book brings together material on the practical experiences of sector reform from a wide range of viewpoints, which attests to the varying interest of a worldwide pool of experts who have actually participated in reforms in the telecommunications sector. Most of the material is derived from contributions to the Washington, DC, seminar, expanded and updated by the original authors. In addition, a number of new contributions were invited. All contributions were then extensively revised and reorganized to ensure a logical flow and bring out common themes and contrasts. Reference material was prepared on telecommunications sector organization and regulatory framework in some eighty countries. A substantial glossary was developed.

Thus, the experience and knowledge of nearly fifty experts in reform in the telecommunications sector are gathered in one volume. It offers readers an up-to-date account of approaches to major policy and structural issues, describes practical experiences in Latin America, Asia and the Pacific, and Europe, and discusses issues related to investment, regulation, and implementation. Whereas each of the book's eight parts is intended to elaborate on a particular aspect or area of experience in sector reform, several recurrent themes are brought out, and a number of countries' experiences are examined successively from different angles sustained by various players. We expect this volume will provide valuable reference information on how reforms have actually been carried out, give some insight into how well these reforms have worked and what main areas remain for further improvement, draw lessons that may be useful to those now embarking on similar processes of change, and stimulate further reflection and discussion of related policy and implementation issues.

The value and success of this book rests largely on the work of the experts who contributed to it. Their patience and the great deal of personal time they devoted to preparing and revising their material confirms the enormous interest that the subject of this book has generated among an ever-increasing audience.

Mark Fowler, former chairman of the U.S. Federal Communications Commission and Janice Obuchowski, then head of the U.S. National Telecmmunications and Information Administration added their valuable insight through keynote speeches during the Washington seminar. This is reflected in the contents of this book although their speeches have not been transcribed.

Ahmed Laouyane and Anthony Odeh of the ITU, Ana Martinez, Carmel Charles, and Johanna Klaus of the World Bank, and Peter Chang of Teleglobe Canada helped organize the Washington seminar. Many people helped research and prepare material for the Annex and Glossary. Martine des Lauriers of Teleglobe Inc. provided invaluable assistance patiently word-processing successive versions of the book manuscript. Jenepher Moseley of the World Bank managed production of the book, and Beverly Logan Associates was responsible for copyediting and processing.

This book would not have been possible without the support of Charles Sirois, president and chief executive officer of Teleglobe Inc.

Implementing Reforms in the Telecommunications Sector: Background, Overview, and Lessons

Björn Wellenius and Peter A. Stern

DRIVEN BY UNRELENTING TECHNOLOGICAL and market forces, telecommunications is today one of the world's most dynamic economic sectors. Until not long ago a relatively obscure territory of interest mainly to engineers, telecommunications today seem to be everybody's proper playing field. Large and small businesses, user groups, investment banks, policymakers, development organizations, legislators, economists, political scientists, and lawyers, among others, are now also actively and visibly involved in telecommunications. Hardly a day goes by without telecommunications events making news in the international and local press—ask anyone who reads, for example, the *Economist,* the *Financial Times,* the *New York Times,* the *Asian Economic Review, El Mercurio,* or the *China Daily.*

How did this change come to be? What are the broad directions in which telecommunications are evolving? How are the developing countries faring? What are the practical lessons that emerge from the experience of recent years? Those are the main questions around which this chapter, and to a large extent this book, is centered.

This opening chapter provides a background, an overview, and a synthesis of the rich material contributed to the book from the viewpoints of different stakeholders and on a wide range of countries. The chapter is organized in five parts. The first gives a brief account of how the perceptions about the development role of telecommunications have evolved from the 1960s. In the second, the changes under way in telecommunications sector organization and ownership worldwide are outlined, and some lessons are drawn from the early experience of sector reform in industrial countries. The third part takes a closer look at what is happening in the developing countries, from past shortfalls and constraints to the beginnings of structural change and the special problems of implementing reforms in these countries. In the fourth, the reader is given an annotated walk through the various parts and chapters of the book. Along this walk, selected common themes and contrasting views are pulled together. Lastly, some lessons from cross-country experiences are drawn. These lessons highlight the complexity of designing and implementing effective sector reforms, and also identify areas in which a better understanding is needed of the underlying processes and factors.[1]

Telecommunications and the Economy: Changing Views

Traditionally, telecommunications was regarded as a relatively straightforward public utility. Economies of scale, political and military sensitivities, and large externalities made telecommunications a typical public service believed to be a natural monopoly. In this environment, telecommunications development focused mainly on extending standard service, building basic networks, and improving the performance of the operating entities.[2] The main issues were technological, and management of telecommunications enterprises was largely oriented toward engineering.

Research in the 1960s and 1970s documented the importance of telecommunications as infrastructure for economic and social development. It was shown that telecommunications services are used in connection with a wide range of economic production and distribution activities, delivery of social services, and government administration. They also contribute to the quality of life and to social, political, and security objectives. Where available, telecommunications benefit a broad cross-section of the urban and rural population by income, education, and occupation. These features result in high social and (with appropriate tariffs) private returns from telecommunications investment, as well as in a considerable financial resource mobilization capacity.[3]

Information is regarded today as a fundamental factor of production, alongside capital and labor. The information economy accounted for one-third to one-half of gross domestic product (GDP) and of employment in Organization for Economic Cooperation and Development (OECD) countries in the 1980s and is expected to reach 60 percent for the European Community in the year 2000. Information also accounts for a substantial proportion of GDP in the newly industrialized economies and the modern sectors of developing countries.[4]

This increasing information intensity of economic activity, coupled with the globalization of capital flows, trade, manufacturing, and other activities, resulted in strong demand for better, more varied, and less costly communication and information services. Demand growth has been intertwined with rapid changes in telecommunications technology fueled by advances in microelectronics, software, and optics. These changes have greatly reduced the cost of information transmission and processing, changed the cost structures of telecommunications and many other industries, made possible new ways of meeting a wider range of communication needs at lower cost, reduced user dependence on established operating entities, and increasingly integrated information and telecommunications technologies and services.[5] These interrelated market and technological processes show no signs of abating.

In this context, telecommunications is now widely considered a strategic investment to maintain and develop competitive advantage at all levels—national, regional, firm. Telecommunications constitute the core of, and provide the infrastructure for, the information economy as a whole. Telecommunications facilitate market entry, improve customer service, reduce costs, and increase productivity. They are an integral part of financial services, commodities markets, media, transportation, and the travel industry, and provide vital links among manufacturers, wholesalers, and retailers.

Moreover, industrial and commercial competitive advantage is now not only influenced by availability of telecommunications facilities, but also by choice of network alternatives and control to reconfigure and manage networks in line with changes in corporate objectives. Countries and firms that lack access to modern telecommunications systems cannot effectively participate in the global economy. This applies to the least-developed countries of Africa and Asia as much as to middle-income countries, such as those in Latin America, East Asia, and Central and Eastern Europe that aspire to become industrial countries in the next decade or so.

The Telecommunications Sector in Transition

In most industrial countries, telecommunications services were provided by government departments or state enterprises.[6] These entities generally succeeded in building and profitably operating countrywide infrastructures, meeting the demand for basic telephone service, and starting to introduce more advanced services.

In the 1980s, however, driven by the twin forces of technological innovation and growing demand discussed above, a wave of liberalization and privatization led to major changes in telecommunications sector structure in most industrial countries. Deregulation and divestiture of the Bell System in the United States was followed by privatization and introduction of competition in the United Kingdom, Japan, and, more recently, in Australia and New Zealand. By the early 1990s, virtually all OECD countries were at some stage and form of restructuring the telecommunications sector. These reforms have accelerated investment, increased responsiveness to user needs, greatly broadened user choices, and reduced prices.

Main Directions of Structural Change

Although the policy issues and options faced by governments in reforming the telecommunications sector are fairly universal, the relative importance of the issues, the package of sectoral solutions chosen, and especially the strategy to implement it, are turning out to be highly country-specific.[7] Yet, all telecommunications reforms so far mainly involve some degree of change along each of four directions: commercializing and separating operations from government; increasing the participation of private enterprise and capital; containing monopolies, diversifying supply of services, and developing competition; and shifting government responsibility from ownership and management to policy and regulation. This is true for developing as well as industrial countries.

COMMERCIALIZING OPERATIONS. Telecommunications operations are being reorganized along the lines of commercial companies. Agreement is widespread that telecommunications operating entities, irrespective of who owns them, perform best when run as profit-driven businesses.[8]

Achieving this with state-owned entities involves transforming them into companies or otherwise placing them in conditions that approximate the freedoms, incentives, and discipline of commercial enterprises. In particular, state operating entities are being distanced from governments by reorganizing government depart-ments into state enterprises, state-owned joint-stock companies, mixed state/private companies, or private companies. All reforms are moving in this direction, although only some go the whole way to privatizing state operations.

At the same time, improvements are also undertaken in internal organization and management, such as reorganizing the enterprise into cost and profit centers, subcontracting functions that can be undertaken efficiently by other organizations,[9] establishing or improving commercial accounting and management information systems, as well as emphasizing customer service, cost awareness, financial disci-pline, and staff performance.

INCREASING PRIVATE SECTOR PARTICIPATION. The private sector is playing a much larger role than in the past. Increased private sector participation can attract new sources of capital, management, and technology to the telecommunications sector; it also contributes to the development of the private sector overall.

A number of countries are considering the option of privatizing the state telecom-munications enterprises by transferring a controlling interest to the private sector, and several have already done so. Privatization may take a number of different forms. For example, ownership control can be transferred through the sale of shares of an existing enterprise to strategic investors or in public markets, or may involve setting up state/private joint ventures, possibly with experienced foreign operators. Alter-natively, one or more new companies can be set up by taking over parts of the assets of the existing enterprise and then sold separately. Evidence is mounting that privatization in this sector as well as others, when correctly conceived and imple-mented, is accompanied by accelerated investment and growth, increased efficiency, and gains by most or all stakeholders (consumers, labor, government, investors).[10] Telecommunications privatizations are also generating large government revenues[11] and helping reduce sovereign debt.[12]

Besides privatization of state enterprises, there are many other avenues for private participation in existing telecommunications operations. Some options involve an increased role of the private sector in the operation of state enterprises; for example:

- Existing state enterprises may divest or outsource construction, maintenance, transportation, routine design, billing and collection, directory services, operator assistance, and other functions traditionally undertaken internally.

- Experienced private operating companies can be retained under management contracts to run the state enterprises.

- State enterprises can be reorganized as joint-stock companies and some shares sold to institutional investors and the public while the state retains a controlling interest.

Other options involve alternative forms of private sector financing, such as:

• Bonds and other commercial debt instruments can be floated in domestic and sometimes foreign markets.

• Private financial entities can be attracted to invest in developing profitable extensions of the public telecommunications networks to new areas.[13]

• Subscriber financing schemes can raise a large proportion of the local funds needed for expansion in situations of severe supply shortage.[14]

One of the most important avenues to attract private sector participation, however, is new entry.

DEVELOPING COMPETITION. The number of providers of telecommunications services and networks is rapidly increasing. A single monopoly operating enterprise, whether state-owned or private, is increasingly unable to meet equally well the large, varied, and rapidly changing demands of all types of users.

In the context of broad economic liberalization, an essential element of sector reform is developing competition. Competition, or a credible threat of competition, is likely to spur established operating enterprises to focus attention on customers, improve service, accelerate network expansion, reduce costs, and lower prices. Competition also widens user choices and accelerates the introduction of new services and facilities. Elements of competition can be effectively introduced in the early stages of sector reform and extended by stages to most or all market segments.[15]

Technological changes are making competition possible in a widening range of market segments. Competition in the provision and maintenance of customer premises equipment and value added services is beneficial in virtually all countries. The introduction of elements of competition in the long-distance networks makes sense as increasing traffic volumes reduce the importance of economies of scale. In several countries, industrial and developing alike, licensing private company networks and regulating their interconnection to the public network and provision of service to third parties has been used to build up competition in this market segment. At present, large economies of scale make competition in the provision of wired local services viable only in exceptional situations (for example, highly developed urban business districts); however, new radio technologies (such as cellular, public communication networks, and mobile satellite), although still more costly than wired telephones, already offer competing alternatives to business and high-income residences when conventional telephone lines are very scarce or perform poorly, and when time to provide service is highly valued.[16]

In addition to measures that promote competition, there are various other ways to diversify and expand the provision of services and networks. Diversifying supply can attract new sources of capital and management to the telecommunications sector, develop rivalry among service providers regarding performance and price, and generate cost benchmarks to guide pricing of monopoly suppliers. The following are some options:

- Dividing monopolies by regions

- Setting up joint ventures for the provision of specific new services or facilities (such as very small aperture terminal (VSAT), packet-switched data, cellular)

- Leasing, build-operate-transfer (BOT), and related arrangements with other operating companies, equipment manufacturers, and investors for developing parts of the public network

- Licensing selected specialized networks to meet the needs of major communication-intensive sectors of the economy (for example, banking, tourism, mining)

- Franchising independent public telephone companies in unattended areas (for example, rural communities, new industrial estates, residential developments)

- Licensing extensions of the public telephone network (for example, public call offices)

- Articulating rules for voluntary commercial relationships between dedicated and public telecommunications networks.

DEVELOPING REGULATION. Operations are being separated from the functions of sector policy and regulation. While operations remain in the public sector, the political system provides, however imperfectly, for reconciling diverse objectives such as those of commercial efficiency and broader national and regional development. As operations move away from government and the number of participants in the telecommunications business increases, this arrangement breaks down and the functions of policy and regulation must be developed separately from operation.[17]

The nature and extent of sector reforms that can be undertaken are conditioned by the existence of institutions capable of effectively formulating policy and regulating its implementation. Irrespective of the particular sector and ownership structures adopted, regulation is needed to enhance economic efficiency of markets, contain monopoly power, and create market rules to encourage investor and consumer confidence. In particular, regulation is essential when public sector monopolies are privatized.[18] It is generally politically intolerable to substitute private for public ownership of monopoly services unless there is effective government oversight of the new owners' prices and behavior.[19]

Telecommunications and International Trade

Industrialized countries which have substantially liberalized their telecommunications sectors, such as the United States and the United Kingdom, are actively promoting similar market openings in other countries. They are doing this through multilateral and bilateral negotiations to establish new international trade and regulatory regimes. For example, the 1988 World Administrative Telegraph and

Telephone Conference (WATTC-88), which resulted in new International Tele-communication Regulations (ITR), removed certain international regulatory re-strictions on the provision of nonbasic services which are not generally provided to the public. With respect to trade rules, the 1989 Canada-U.S. Free Trade Agree-ment was the first bilateral agreement to embody services and, more particularly, the liberalization of trade in enhanced telecommunications services.

In 1985 the United States was instrumental in having services included for the first time in multilateral trade negotiations under the General Agreement on Tariffs and Trade (GATT) Uruguay Round, whose final act contains, in addition to a number of other trade related texts, a General Agreement on Trade in Services (GATS) made up of three parts: a framework setting out the basic rules for trade in all services; some sectoral annexes which clarify the application of the framework with respect to specific sectors; and schedules of market access commitments for sectors and subsectors. Annexes have been developed for financial services, air transport, and telecommunications, with the latter being by far the most compre-hensive, confirming its overall importance in the information economy. The dual role of telecommunications as a *tradable service* and as a *mode of delivery* of other services is set out in the statement of the objectives of the telecommunications annex. The North American Free Trade Agreement (NAFTA), which was signed among Canada, the United States, and Mexico in December 1992, and which went into effect on January 1, 1994, contains provisions pertaining to telecommu-nications similar to those of the GATS.

Why this emphasis on having others liberalize their telecommunications mar-kets? At least two factors are relevant: the changing production and marketing environment of the firm, and the growing importance of services and services trade in the economy.

Slower economic growth and the entry of new suppliers have increased competi-tion in certain world-scale industries such as automobile, banking, textiles, and electronics. These industries are adopting new production and marketing methods through which they can better confront the new competitive environment. Produc-tion is decentralized and globalized. Similar products are differentiated for divers markets rather than produced undifferentiated in large numbers to cater for all markets at the same time. Production is more rapidly adapted to changing demand in quantity, color, size, and other distinguishing characteristics. Timing of produc-tion is brought closer to the receipt of actual orders.

This new production and marketing environment requires continuous communica-tion and interaction among productive units, suppliers, design and sales teams, distributors, and customers around the world. Telecommunications are essential, and to make most effective use of them large multinational firms in these industries are increasingly calling for the freedom to configure, manage, and control their networks. They want to be able to dynamically allocate bandwidth and to dimension their networks in accordance with rapidly changing requirements and circumstances. They want the flexibility to use the most suitable mix of public and private facilities and, in sum, to have at their disposal the right capacity and facilities when they need them without having to pay for excess capacity and unused facilities when they do not need them.[20] The United States has probably the most open market structure in this respect. Multinationals are, however, hampered in their global aspirations by varying regulatory regimes around the world. They would naturally want to have the same freedoms that they enjoy in the United States and in a few other countries with relatively open telecommunications structures. They are therefore pressuring governments to agree to more liberal trade and regulatory regimes. These pressures are being felt by governments of both industrialized and developing countries, which may otherwise be reluctant to allow such extensive market openings.

Another important factor causing pressure for countries to liberalize the sector is the growing importance of services in national economies and in trade. This has been especially important for countries such as the United States with persistent merchandise trade deficits, which have, however, been offset by surpluses in services trade. For example, in 1991 the United States had a negative trade balance in merchandise of US$73.6 billion. In absolute terms this was nearly double the positive services trade balance (US$52.2 billion). Yet, in spite of a growing positive services trade balance, the United States continues to have an overall negative trade balance, as figure 1 shows.[21] These amounts do not take into account the substantial sale of services through foreign affiliates of U.S. firms.

Given its comparative advantage in services and the growing importance of its services industry relative to the production of goods, it is of little wonder that the U.S. government and industry groups are actively promoting services trade liberalization and the opening of other countries' markets in the services sectors, of which the most significant are travel and tourism, business and professional services (such as consulting), financial services, education, maritime shipping, and, of course, telecommunications.[22]

In spite of the large net settlements outpayments associated with U.S. international telephone traffic, which in 1992 reached US$4 billion, the liberalization of telecommunications remains high on U.S. trade negotiators' agenda because of its increasing importance in delivering the other services where the United States continues to have surpluses.[23] Given the additional benefits derived from services provided by affiliates of U.S. companies in other countries, there is a strong incentive to open these markets to both basic and enhanced telecommunications services provision either through local affiliates, branches, or across the border.

Some Early Lessons from Industrial Countries

Significant early milestones in telecommunications sector reform in industrial countries were the consent decree of 1982 which led to the divestiture of AT&T in 1984, the establishment of a facilities-based duopoly and privatization of British Telecom and Cable & Wireless in the United Kingdom in 1981 and 1984, respectively, and the introduction of competition and privatization of NTT in Japan in 1985. These were followed in 1987 by the corporatization of the New Zealand Post Office and the privatization of Teleglobe Canada, Canada's international

Figure 1. U.S. Services and Merchandise Trade Balance 1981 - 92

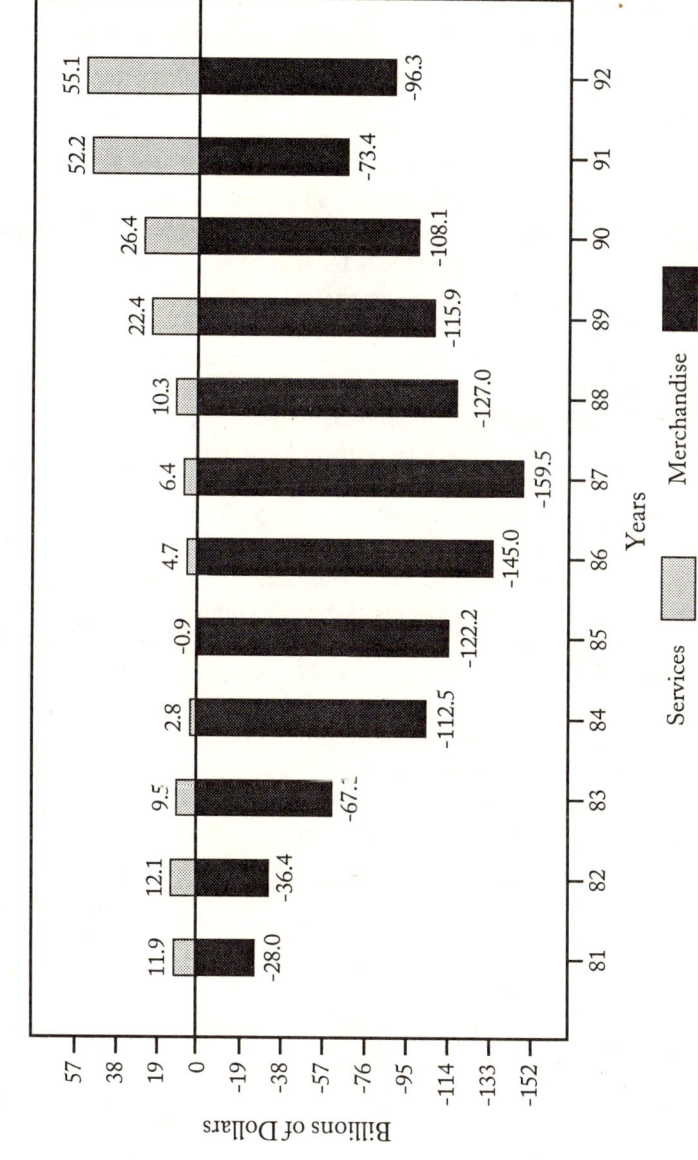

telecommunications operator. In 1987 also the European Commission issued its Green Paper, which has paved the way for sector reform not only within the European Community but also in most of the rest of Europe, including states of Central and Eastern Europe.[24] By the end of the 1980s many more OECD countries were in the process of reforming or were planning it. A review of how the process was undertaken, the structures selected, the regulatory issues raised, and the way state enterprises were commercialized and privatized serves as a source of early lessons from industrial country experiences with sector reform. It should, however, be underlined that because the situation has been different in each country, one cannot generalize these experiences.

THE PROCESS. One of the most important conclusions that can be drawn from observing these experiences in industrial countries is that the process is complex and there is no single model or design. This is because of the multitude of factors, conflicting interests, and interrelated events that are involved.

Industrial countries with parliamentary systems have, for example, learned to appreciate the benefits of a transparent process which involves consultation with stakeholders at all stages of policy and law making. The experiences in the United Kingdom, France, and Canada have been particularly revealing in this respect. Responsive governments have taken criticisms raised during such consultations into account when redrafting their initial proposals.[25]

When reform has also included privatization of a state enterprise, governments have sometimes been able to convince the population of the benefits of reform by encouraging them to become shareholders of the new company and by facilitating their doing so. This was done effectively in the United Kingdom when British Telecom was first privatized in 1985, at a time when it was the policy of the Thatcher government to encourage more Britons to become shareholders.[26]

Governments in industrial countries have come to appreciate and take into account the concerns of the employees of a state enterprise which is to be privatized. These employees, who generally had job security, generous pensions, and other advantages which were as good as, if not better than, those in the private sector, were, therefore, brought into the consultations and encouraged to participate in privatizations through employee stock ownership plans. In addition, conditions of sale have required, as they did in Canada, that the new owners offer existing employees conditions equal to those that they enjoyed as civil servants.[27] Privatization has brought with it improved labor productivity; this has meant reducing the former state enterprise's labor force. Although some of the former state enterprise employees have been able to find jobs with competitors or subcontractors, this has not been the case for all.[28] On the other hand, it has resulted in better salaries for those who have continued because they have been able to adapt and contribute to the new commercially-oriented operations.

THE POLICY DECISIONS. Design of more liberalized sector structures has required policymakers to select among a complex array of interrelated parameters. Among other matters, they have had to decide on which areas to open to competition and which to maintain for monopoly provision; how many competitors to allow to enter into the competitive domain; how long to maintain restrictions on entry into the monopoly domain or further entry into a partially opened competitive domain; what sorts of regulatory safeguards to put into place to guarantee fair practices; and what sort of regulatory mechanism to select.

Establishing a boundary line between monopoly and competitive domains or between different competitive domains is no easy task. With time these boundary lines have become untenable since those who are allowed to operate or compete in one domain will soon find ways to transgress boundaries, which are never absolute. Attempts to distinguish between *basic* and *enhanced* in the United States and Canada, *Type I* and *Type II* in Japan, *reserved service* and others in Europe, *domestic* and *international* in Japan and the United Kingdom, have either failed or have come under untenable pressure.[29]

Policymakers in industrial countries have also had to deal with the difficult issues of cross-subsidization and rebalancing of tariffs. To what extent will subscribers in rural or remote areas of the country be asked to pay for the higher price that it costs the operator to bring the service to them? To what extent should the new entrants have to contribute to the incumbent's cost of continuing to supply services in these areas to which newcomers are not particularly attracted, that is, to maintain universal service? These questions have become particularly important in countries such as Japan, Canada, and the United Kingdom after the introduction of competition.

Governments have also had to weigh the benefits of a privatization against the costs. Sales of telecommunications enterprises have resulted in substantial one-time cash infusions into the treasury at the cost, however, of a lost income stream and perhaps also a convenient instrument for economic and social policy implementation.

REGULATION. Regulatory structures after reform have become more involved and complex. This is particularly true when reform also included privatization of a state enterprise. Prior to privatization social control of the company had been achieved through public ownership with the government appointing the board of directors and approving the company's budgets, tariffs, construction program, and general policy direction.[30] This simple and fairly straightforward relationship between the telecommunications operator and the state changed substantially with reform, which introduced a whole new set of issues, including how to:

- Prevent the incumbent operator from abusing its dominant position to prevent competition

- Ensure that a private monopoly does not make monopoly profits

- Continue to promote certain economic and social goals, including universal service

- Ensure adherence to certain technical standards

- Ensure that quality-of-service standards are maintained

- Monitor license conditions and ensure that laws and regulations are respected

- Deal with interconnection problems

- Regulate tariffs and contribution payments for network development.

These issues are complex, interrelated, and sometimes conflicting. The regulatory mechanisms developed in industrialized countries as a result of reform have had to deal with these unequivocally but fairly. Thus, to facilitate the development of competition, regulations for new entrants have had to be more lenient than for the incumbent without, however, disadvantaging the latter unduly. The Federal Communications Commission (FCC) in the United States has, for example, regulated the long-distance carrier AT&T more rigorously than its new competitors, including MCI and Sprint.[31] In Japan the new entrants received favorable pricing conditions with respect to access to the local network of the former monopoly's (NTT). In Canada the new entrant in the long-distance market (Unitel) will be able to charge 15 percent less than the incumbent (Stentor).

Important in the United States, Canada, and the United Kingdom is the flexibility which has been built into the regulatory framework to deal with rapidly changing and unforeseen circumstances. Indeed, the law which regulates telecommunications in the United States and which applies even today was drafted in 1934. The Canadian law, which only now is being redrafted, was adopted in 1906. Although there has been no lack of suggestions, proposals, and even pressure to change these laws, politically, change has proven to be far too difficult and therefore has been avoided. Yet even in the absence of up-to-date legislation, policymakers and regulators in these and other industrialized countries are dealing with new and even more complex issues of how the new entrants should be permitted to access the incumbent carrier's local networks, what the most appropriate form of price regulation should be, and what level of subsidy the new entrants should have to contribute to network development.

The distinction between the policymaking responsibilities of the government and the regulatory functions of an independent regulator in countries where this distinction exists, such as the United States, Canada and the United Kingdom, has not always been as clear-cut as may have been intended. Indeed, it has sometimes been convenient for governments to let the independent regulator make difficult policy decisions on its behalf.

Countries that have carried out reforms have discovered that the cost of regulation is not negligible. Independent regulatory bodies have had to hire substantial numbers of highly qualified experts. Operating companies have also had to dedicate substantial resources to satisfying the requirements of the regulators, and armies of lawyers, economists, accountants, engineers, and others are involved every day in a complex regulatory process in countries such as the United States and Canada. These did not exist under the old monopoly PTT-type structures.

COMMERCIALIZING AND PRIVATIZING STATE ENTERPRISES. In the United Kingdom, Canada, and New Zealand, when the government decided to privatize their state-owned telecommunications operations they proceeded first to prepare them structurally, financially, and commercially in order to optimize the proceeds from the sale; government departments such as the British and New Zealand Post Offices first had to be corporatized to allow them to develop proper commercial management, accounting, and legal practices.[32] They were given boards of directors (often with members from the private sector), management structures, balance sheets, profit and loss statements, and business plans, which made them look very much like their private counterparts. Governments knew that potential buyers would look very closely at the historical development of the company, its growth, its cash flow, and its return on assets in deciding whether and how much to offer. In Canada the capital structure of the corporatized international operator, Teleglobe Canada, had to be changed to give it a ratio of debt to equity which potential buyers would find attractive. Also the value of the company's assets and goodwill had to be properly evaluated for regulation and sale. Corporatization was sometimes accompanied by a separation of telecommunications from the nontelecommunications activities of the entity. This was the case in both the United Kingdom and New Zealand.

The Canadian government chose outright sale of its international telecommunications carrier to one buyer; others, for reasons mentioned earlier, chose the issuing of shares to the general public and the employees. The United Kingdom, which chose the latter, privatized British Telecom in tranches over a period of several years. This had the advantage of the government's maintaining control (initially, majority) over a transition period as the company adjusted to both a competitive and a commercial environment. Furthermore, the government was able to benefit in each subsequent flotation from an appreciated value of the shares of the partially privatized company.

Governments that have chosen flotations have had to prepare the necessary prospectuses and procedures and, most important, have had to price the shares so as to maximize the benefits to the state but also to attract a large number of buyers.[33] The New Zealand government chose to avoid the complexities of a flotation by selling to a consortium of a few buyers with the condition that the buyers had to offer a part of the company for sale at a later stage through a flotation that they had the responsibility of organizing.[34]

Governments have learned from experience that the conditions of sale of a state enterprise have to be clearly defined and unambiguous. This includes terms of exclusivity granted to the newly privatized company as well as other privileges and obligations. There have been cases where initial calls for tender have failed precisely because such conditions were not clearly stated. Bidders came back with so many questions and with such demanding conditions of their own that the sale had to be canceled.

Because the process is so dynamic and constantly evolving there is still no set of well-defined models of sector reform in industrial countries to which one could specifically refer. New, unforeseen problems arise daily and there are no set formulas for dealing with them. The countries must improvise and define and redefine structures continuously.

One can, however, draw an initial conclusion with respect to who has benefitted in industrial countries. So far, at least, all the stakeholders have come out ahead as a result of reform, including the governments, the operators and service providers, the consumers, and the employees. Governments have benefitted from the sale of state-owned telecommunications entities which in turn have gained greater commercial and financial freedom. Employees have gained with better salaries, and the consumer has seen an increase in choice along with a substantial reduction in the price of telecommunications services.

Telecommunications in the Developing World

In developing countries, telecommunications services were initially run by foreign private companies and colonial government agencies. In the 1960s, most telecommunications operations were nationalized and taken over by the public sector. This reflected the emergence and consolidation of independent nations in Asia and Africa, widespread adoption of development strategies based on increasing state participation in economic production and distribution, and concerns about the security and development significance of telecommunications.

Persistent Shortfalls

State telecommunications monopolies in most developing countries, unlike in industrial countries, generally fell short of meeting the service requirements. That is still mostly the case today:[35]

LARGE UNMET DEMAND FOR CONNECTIONS. Outstanding applications for telephone connections are numerous, and people often wait several years to obtain service. In the late 1980s it was estimated that the supply of about 60 million telephone connections in the developing world was about 20 million lines short of expressed demand, and total unmet demand was maybe 30 million to 40 million lines.[36] By 1993, the estimated unmet demand in China and India alone exceeded 50 million lines. In addition, more advanced services (such as cellular, data transmission, electronic mail, access to information and data-processing services) are in their infancy or nonexistent.

CALL TRAFFIC CONGESTION. The limited telecommunications infrastructure is heavily congested. During peak business hours communicating by telephone is often impossible. International service is ultimately constrained by congestion at the local and interexchange levels. Congestion partly reflects insufficient traffic capacity of switching and transmission equipment but ultimately derives from the shortage of lines in service.

POOR SERVICE. Reliability and quality of service tend to be inconsistent and generally substandard. Cities are often left without telephone service when it rains. Individual lines break down frequently and can take weeks or even months to repair.

LIMITED TERRITORIAL COVERAGE. Much remains to be done to complete a countrywide infrastructure of basic telephone service. Most facilities are concentrated in a small number of cities, and a large proportion of the population lives in places without even a public telephone. Lack of a countrywide infrastructure of basic telephone service also impedes development of more advanced business services.

USER WILLINGNESS TO PAY MORE. Many users clearly value the service more than they are charged for. One way or another, they often pay in excess of official tariffs to obtain service, for example, by acquiring telephone connections in secondary markets (legal or otherwise) or by paying premium rentals for properties with telephones.

USER PRESSURE TO DEVELOP OWN FACILITIES. As public service fails to meet their needs, major users tend to set up their own networks. Modern technologies have substantially reduced the cost of bypassing public networks.

Main Constraints

The annual rate of return of telecommunications investment to a developing country's economy as a whole is often in the range of 20 to 30 percent or more, well above the 10 to 14 percent threshold returns used to screen public sector investments in general. With adequate tariffs, telecommunications are also a profitable business. Investments often yield annual financial rates of return of 15 percent or more. Given these high social and private returns, why do telecommunications services lag so far behind demand? There are three main constraints:

INVESTMENT CAPITAL. The level of investment has consistently been much lower than that needed to meet demand. Although overall telecommunications investment in the developing world grew in the last twenty years at 10 to 12 percent per annum in real terms, to about US$11 billion in the late 1980s, this averaged only 0.4 to 0.6 percent of gross national product (GNP).[37] Developing countries that succeeded in rapidly modernizing their economies invested in telecommunications a much larger share of GNP (for example, Singapore 1.1 percent, Malaysia 2.3 percent). On average, about US$1,800 is needed to provide one additional telephone line,[38] of which in most countries 50 to 80 percent is in foreign currency.

Underinvestment reflects capital and foreign currency shortages in the public sector generally, many competing demands, government appropriation of telecommunications operating surpluses to the detriment of reinvestment within the sector, and limited or no access of the operating enterprises to other sources of capital. Furthermore, like other public or parastatal entities, telecommunications enterprises are subject to investment ceilings to contain public sector spending and attain broader macroeconomic objectives (for example, to contain inflation).[39]

In the 1970s, attempts to accelerate telecommunications growth and modernization focused on obtaining for this sector a larger share of the countries' limited public funds and external development credit and aid. This, combined with borrowing by enterprises in creditworthy countries, and in some cases by mandatory subscriber financing and surtaxes on telecommunications bills earmarked for reinvestment, resulted in sustained rapid growth and modernization of telecommunications services in several countries.

Overall, however, the telecommunications operating entities did not have access to enough capital for investment. Deteriorating national economies and tighter international credit in the early 1980s further constrained investment and led to escalating supply shortages and lower service quality, even in countries that earlier had done fairly well.

In the late 1980s it was estimated that for developing countries in Asia-Pacific, Latin America, and Africa to catch up with the demand for basic telephone service by the year 2000, as a group they would have to invest in the 1990s about US$25 billion to US$30 billion per annum, or about five times the average achieved in the 1980s in real terms. To this must be added at least US$10–15 billion per annum for upgrading facilities in Central and Eastern Europe and in the former U.S.S.R., and an unknown but rapidly growing amount for more advanced business services and facilities. By 1993 all these numbers appeared to have been underestimated by a wide margin.

ORGANIZATION AND MANAGEMENT. The operating entities are often organized and managed in ways that may be appropriate for government administration but not for running a high-technology commercial service in a rapidly changing business environment. Common problems include inadequate organization structure, financial management, accounting and information systems, procurement, and personnel development.

These weaknesses result in high cost of operation and expansion, poor maintenance, slow response to changing demands and business opportunities, and limited capacity to prepare and implement development programs and projects. Project preparation and implementation capacity are often the ultimate constraints on telecommunications expansion and improvement in the least-developed countries.

SECTOR POLICIES. The telecommunications operating entities generally lack the freedoms and incentives to perform as efficient businesses. Capital shortages and poor enterprise performance can ultimately be traced to inadequate government policies for the telecommunications sector.

Specific problems include insufficient financial and administrative autonomy, little incentive to contain costs and improve customer service, noncompetitive salaries and career opportunities for staff and managers, tariffs that do not reflect the entity's financial requirement and cost structure, limited or no access to capital markets, and political interference.

Forces of Change

From the mid–1980s, a growing number of developing country governments realized that, in order to overcome these persistent constraints, the prevailing sector arrangements would have to be overhauled. This movement was driven by the same factors underlying reforms in the industrial world, namely, technological change and demand, amplified by six additional factors:

- The limits of state monopoly of telecommunications supply had been reached and were increasingly recognized. In particular, it became clear that the governments would be unable to provide the huge amounts of capital required to meet outstanding and rapidly growing demand. Also, although organization and management improvements within the telecommunications operating enterprises resulted in more efficient use of scarce resources in several developing countries, in the context of sector policies that did not provide the necessary freedoms and incentives for these entities to perform better, internal changes alone had proved to be of limited value.

- Developing countries began to adopt economic strategies including measures to liberalize trade, promote competition, deregulate financial and capital markets, reduce restrictions on foreign investment, and restructure public enterprises. Rapid growth in developing countries in the 1960s and 1970s came to a halt in the late 1970s and early 1980s, the result of excessive external debt, rising energy costs, overgrown public sectors, and inefficient import-substitution industries. The turnaround in economic policy gave renewed urgency to developing telecommunications as required for the broader economic reforms to be effectively implemented. The constituency for telecommunications development quickly grew to include a whole crowd of powerful and vocal users, including multinational corporations, domestic and foreign investors, industrialists, traders, and bankers, demanding telecommunications services required for them to succeed under the new economic strategies. Telecommunications became a central theme in multilateral and bilateral trade in services negotiations. Suddenly, governments started to feel pressure to do something definitive about telecommunications.[40] The new economic strategies also provided a framework in which new models of sector organization became politically acceptable. In several countries, telecommunications were chosen to lead government efforts in state enterprise restructuring.

- Popularly elected governments found that public dissatisfaction with service and, in many countries, extensive corruption of telephone company personnel, resulted in widespread support for major reform initiatives.

- Telecommunications reforms in industrial countries raised international awareness of a wide range of sector policy issues and options, and demonstrated the viability and increasing political desirability of alternatives to state monopoly.

- Telecommunications operating companies in industrial countries, repositioning themselves in their own changing domestic markets, aggressively started to pursue new business opportunities in developing countries.

- Commercial banks sought to shift their exposure in highly indebted developing countries from nonperforming loans to new investment opportunities, among which telecommunications were particularly promising.

Beginnings of Reform in the Developing World

The wave of telecommunications reforms that began in the 1980s in a few highly developed economies has quickly spread and is reaching worldwide dimensions. By 1993, major reforms had been completed or were well under way in at least fifteen developing countries, and a comparable number were in preparation. The pace and scope of structural change has varied considerably among regions.

LATIN AMERICA. The reform movement got to an early start in Latin America. Privatizations of state telecommunications enterprises were completed in Chile (1987), Argentina (1990), Mexico (1990), and Venezuela (1991). By 1993 reforms were at various stages of preparation in Bolivia, Ecuador, Panama, Peru, and Uruguay, and being considered in Brazil, El Salvador, Honduras, Nicaragua, and other countries.[41]

FORMER U.S.S.R. AND EASTERN BLOC. Following the collapse of the communist regimes in Central and Eastern Europe and in the former U.S.S.R., rapid progress was initially made in outlining broad sector reform strategies to deal with the huge service and technology gaps relative to the rest of Europe. By 1993 all governments were developing the details of implementation, and several of them (for example, Hungary, Poland, Ukraine) were already building state-of-the-art business networks and extending service to rural areas through joint ventures and innovative investment and management modalities.

ASIA. Reforms were initially slower and of more limited scope in Asia: corporatization in Malaysia (1987) and subsequent partial privatization (1990), corporatization and liberalization of nonbasic services in Indonesia (1990), decentralization of operations in India (1985, partial) and China (1988, extensive), government initiatives to accelerate development outside the main urban centers in the Philippines (from the late 1980s), and reorganization from telecommunications departments to state enterprises in Sri Lanka and Fiji (1990). The pace picked up, however, with Pakistan preparing for privatization, Thailand embarking on major build-transfer-operate (BTO) ventures, the Philippines government taking steps to develop competition (international services, 1993), Indonesia having established a new, partially state-owned competing international operator (1993), the Malaysian government issuing several new international gateway licenses (1993), the Indian government exploring options for sector reform (1992) which may include restructuring the state operating entity and opening up parts of the market to new service providers, and China moving toward sweeping reforms including competition and possible private investment.

AFRICA. It could be argued that, in relative terms, the least-developed countries have the most to gain from sector reforms. Yet in sub-Saharan Africa the efforts to overcome telecommunications shortages have so far been largely confined to trying to improve the performance of existing telecommunications state entities.

Although some African countries have explored possible new modalities, including joint ventures with PTTs and introducing some competition, most governments still hesitate to consider broader reforms and privatization. This mainly reflects their concern for limited available resources, especially skills to prepare and implement such programs. Compounded by small markets, extreme paucity of existing facilities, disproportionate size of social needs, and sometimes unfriendly economic policies, getting involved in Africa appears less attractive to foreign operators and investors than opportunities in other regions. In many developing countries, concerns about national security, which loomed large in telecommunications policy discussions of the 1960s and 1970s, are waning as telecommunications facilities become widespread and are viewed as production and consumption items commercially available to all buyers; yet in Africa, national security is still a politically significant issue, compounded by a broader concern about foreign control of key factors of economic production and distribution.

Nevertheless, telecommunications privatization is now under way in Côte d'Ivoire and Guinea. Some other governments have expressed interest in privatization experiences. There are success stories of small private ventures (for example, cellular) led by local entrepreneurs in a few countries, and regional organizations are starting to examine the broader prospects for telecommunications restructuring.[42]

Special Issues of Reform in Developing Countries

Developing countries offer exceptional opportunities for telecommunications reform. Large pent-up demands make attractive markets. Major efficiency gains can be achieved quickly through separation from government, improved management, technological innovation, and accelerated growth. Substantial operating surpluses can be generated from the beginning to help finance expansion. Telecommunications reform, however, faces some unique difficulties in developing countries, as outlined below.

INCOMPLETE INFRASTRUCTURES. Developing countries have very incomplete telecommunications infrastructures. Changes in technology and markets are driving governments to undertake profound sector reforms well before countrywide networks have been built. Existing facilities are of insufficient capacity and have yet to be extended to many places that lack even basic services. At the same time, more advanced services must be quickly introduced to meet the needs of the modern sectors of the economy, but the infrastructure that would make these new services viable is not in place. Reforms are thus likely to require the restructured operating companies to meet demanding growth targets, placing large burdens on cash flow to finance large up-front investments that can only be recovered over long periods. In contrast, industrial countries have entered the current wave of sector reforms equipped with extensive and generally well-functioning infrastructures, and the demand for basic services is largely met.

SCARCE HUMAN RESOURCES. There is a limited base of educated professionals. In particular, whereas most developing countries have cadres of competent and well-educated telecommunications engineers and technicians, many are short of experienced managers, accountants, and computer specialists needed to run telecommunications as commercial operations.[43] Likewise, it may not be possible to assemble a sufficient number of qualified professionals to build up even a minimum core of expertise in all basic regulatory functions.[44] The problem is compounded since other sectors are likely to be reformed at about the same time as telecommunications, creating further pressure on the small human resource base. These shortages limit the range of sector designs that are viable, especially in the least developed countries of sub-Saharan Africa and some parts of Asia.

PAUCITY OF INFORMATION. Limited information is available on the telecommunications operating enterprises. Accounts often do not follow internationally accepted practices. Financial statements are audited late or never. Information on liabilities, especially regarding debt and pensions, tends to be unreliable. Information on plant, particularly on cable network utilization and customer connections, is often out of date and incomplete. Prospective strategic investors thus have little to go by to assess the financial and physical condition of the enterprise.

UNDEVELOPED LOCAL CAPITAL MARKETS. Few developing countries have well-established local capital markets. Stock markets are usually small or nonexistent. Institutional investors (such as insurance companies, pension funds) that can pool small savings are seldom in place. Wealthy families and large companies are few and tend to demand high rates of return to invest in the country. Local markets for debt instruments, if they exist, tend to be narrow, and the private sector is crowded out by public sector borrowing. Long-term debt is seldom available, and short-term debt is unreliable and expensive.[45] Thus, although in many developing countries the potential for domestic savings is substantial, the market mechanisms to channel these savings towards the large investments required by telecommunications are rarely in place. Privatization may thus be tantamount to foreign ownership, and domestic ownership is likely to be highly concentrated, which may raise political issues.

WEAK LEGAL, REGULATORY, AND INSTITUTIONAL FRAMEWORK. Many developing countries are still struggling to replace legal and institutional arrangements geared to a state-dominated economy by a framework in which a competitive, open, market economy, based increasingly on private enterprise and capital, can effectively function. Examples of inadequacies of the legal and regulatory framework include lack of or ineffective laws and enforcement mechanisms to protect private property; absent or outmoded trade laws; no antitrust law in most countries; a complex tax regime that is often antibusiness; and controls on access to foreign exchange. The telecommunications law is often too old to provide meaningful reference in the context of contemporary technologies and markets; or telecommunications is covered by laws primarily designed for other sectors which it no longer resembles (for example, transport *and* communications, or electricity, gas, *and* telecommunications). The institutional arrangements are also often quite weak. Examples include a judiciary that lacks independence from the executive power or is prone to manipulation by interest groups; a legislative that is either captured by the executive or paralyzed by party fragmentation; unstable governments; and slow, ineffective, and sometimes corrupt government administration. There are generally no effective telecommunications regulatory institutions separate from the main operating enterprises, and there is little or no regulatory tradition of any public service.

LIMITED INTEREST OF FOREIGN INVESTORS AND BANKS. Although many developing countries now profess to be open to private investment in telecommunications, including foreign, the conditions are still seldom right to attract investors. Foreign firms are deterred from investing particularly by political risk, possibility of expropriation of assets or profits, foreign exchange controls, discretional taxation, and restrictions on capital repatriation. Although multinationals invest in their subsidiaries, they do so only in small amounts. Foreign portfolio investment, although growing in some countries, remains overall very limited. Also, following a borrowing binge in the 1970s and early 1980s, many developing countries are saddled with relatively large sovereign and private external debts that leave little room for new debt financing. International commercial bank lending is now rarely available without external guarantees or political risk insurance.[46]

Outline and Highlights of This Book

Sectoral reform, which began in only a few countries in the early 1980s, has intensified and become widespread in the 1990s. This book presents these experiences from a diverse and broad perspective, describing not only the forces that caused change but also the problems, solutions, successes, failures, and the lessons of reform.

The book has eight parts. The first reviews the current state of telecommunications policy and structural issues in industrialized countries as well as assesses their impact on, and implications for, developing countries. Experiences in Latin America, the Asia-Pacific region, and Europe are presented in the next three parts. This is followed by two parts on investment, giving the perspectives of both strategic and market investors and the various modes of raising private capital. The last two parts cover issues related to regulation and implementation of sector reform. An annex summarizes the sectoral structures and regulatory arrangements in over 80 countries as of the beginning of 1994. A glossary explains in plain English many of the specialized terms used throughout the book.

Current Policy and Structural Issues

Part I of the book provides a background to the discussion of telecommunications reforms by outlining how they relate to the countries' broader economic development strategy and to events and current issues in the industrial countries.

The case for telecommunications reform in developing countries is made by Peter R. Scherer (chapter 1). Reform, he suggests, is essential if countries are to succeed in an increasingly globalized, competitive, and information-based world economy. He shows how business activity in many sectors is becoming critically dependent on users having access to and control of telecommunications and information. Modern and inexpensive telecommunications have become a key determinant of economic competitiveness. Yet, argues Scherer, successful restructuring of telecommunications can only be achieved in the environment of national economic strategies that favor a stable business environment, prudent fiscal and exchange rate policies, effective competition, price and foreign trade liberalization, and sound financial and capital markets. Conversely, reform of telecommunications could be used as a catalyst to engender changes in the role of government and in other sectors that would go beyond the direct role of telecommunications in enhancing a country's economic performance. Scherer postulates that the economywide incentive system is more important than ownership for effective modernization of telecommunications. Contrary to Richard J. Schultz (40), however, he believes that few state-owned telecommunications enterprises can successfully change as radically as needed. The solution generally must be sought through disengagement from government intervention. This can be achieved initially through corporatization of the public telecommunications company, preferably with the simultaneous introduction of competition by allowing private sector entry. Change in ownership, another policy instrument, may or may not be part of the restructuring process and is neither strictly necessary nor sufficient for good performance, unless important additional conditions are met. Although advocating that governments disengage from direct management of telecommunications, Scherer calls for a continued role of governments focused on policymaking and regulation. Lastly, he proposes that developing countries planning to undertake reforms should recognize that:

- A balance must be struck between investment in telecommunications and in other sectors.

- Quality of reform is considered a test for the country's ability to improve the domestic business climate.

- Judicious choice of sector structure and regulatory framework is critical.

- Business demand for advanced services must be attended at the same time as basic services are extended to unattended populations.

- Efficiency is the overriding objective of reform.

- Plant development must be accompanied by organization and management changes that improve performance.

- Competition is an effective policy tool to promote growth and efficiency.

- Tying telecommunications development to domestic equipment manufacturing results in high costs to the economy.

- Policy and regulation must be separated from operations.

- The participation of foreign capital and expertise need not compromise national sovereignty.

Countries contemplating sectoral restructuring can benefit from the experiences of industrial countries. Robert R. Bruce (2) presents an overview and critical analysis of recent experiences in those countries, with special attention to the European Community (EC), Japan, and the United States. A dominant theme is the need to keep policies moving forward. Telecommunications policies and structures in EC member states are being harmonized in accordance with the 1987 Green Paper, which seeks to achieve a single European telecommunications market. Bruce argues, however, that despite enormous progress, reform must now proceed further. For example, the performance of telecommunications is already being constrained by lack of competition in facilities and in voice services. In particular, the Open Network Provision (ONP), which describes the terms and conditions under which leased-line capabilities are offered to new service providers, does not allow local switching and network management capabilities to be offered to third parties, placing EC users at a disadvantage relative to the United States, where a more pro-competitive open network architecture (ONA) policy is in place. Furthermore, EC policy does not provide for a sufficiently independent and well-developed regulatory authority that can deal effectively with issues related to interconnection (access) charges and tariff rebalancing.

According to Bruce, Japan also needs to reassess elements of the 1984 Telecommunications Business Law and other policy developments. Current Japanese policy does not allow the dominant domestic and international operators to compete with each other; more formal and transparent regulation is needed; and the separation between facilities-based and services-based competition is increasingly difficult to maintain. The U.S. experience, despite important shortcomings, shows how policy and regulatory changes have resulted in diversified and unbundled service offerings, cost-oriented prices, a spectacular demand-driven expansion of network capacity, the development of safeguards for new entrants through (complex) regulation of access charges, the development of elements of price-cap regulation, a well-developed even if intricate (and costly) regulatory process, and a division of regulatory responsibilities between federal and state authorities.

There is also valuable experience to be gained from smaller industrialized countries. In Finland, local telephone cooperatives are poised to compete in long-distance and new services with Telecom Finland, the newly corporatized former PTT. New Zealand presents a unique experiment in privatization, with foreign participation, open entry, and reliance on competition law rather than sector-specific regulation. Australia provides an example of privatization accompanied by the opening of markets to competition.

Lessons drawn from these and other experiences in the industrial world suggest that successful reforms are likely to include:

- Liberalizing both facilities-based and service-based markets—at least at the margins

- Rebalancing tariffs to help users become globally more competitive and as a means to attract investment

- Reorganizing the PTT to separate it from the government and to allow it to operate independently and in a commercial manner

- Decentralizing the operator's functions to separate out new business activities and perhaps local, long-distance, and international services

- Using novel approaches to encourage investment and develop effective competition.

Many issues, however, will have no straightforward answer, including:

- Determining the appropriate procedure for rebalancing rates

- Parameters of price-cap schemes

- Interconnection arrangements

Background, Overview, and Lessons

- Cost-accounting and allocation criteria

- Means of introducing competition and using it as a regulatory tool

- How to structure the regulatory and policy functions.

Bruce concludes with a warning. The process of restructuring telecommunications is very complex, requiring a variety of skills and expertise, and time must be allowed to prepare the operating entity and the legal and regulatory framework.

Recent Experiences in Latin America

Latin America has taken the lead in reforming telecommunications in the developing world. First Chile, then Argentina and Mexico, and most recently Venezuela, have undergone profound changes in sector structure and ownership. These experiences, and lessons that may apply to future reforms in this region as well as elsewhere, are discussed in part II of the book. An overview and synthesis of these experiences and lessons (Wellenius, 3) is followed by more detailed analyses of the experiences of Chile (Melo, 4), Argentina (Mairal, 5), Mexico (Casasús, 6) and Venezuela (Pisciotta, 7). Aspects of the Latin American experience are also discussed later in this book, from the viewpoint of strategic and market investors (for example, Massari, 25, on Argentina; Vallimarescu, 29, on Chile; Watkins, 30, on reduction of sovereign debt) and the relationship of sector reform and the political system (Cowhey, 38, on Mexico and Argentina).

Like developing countries generally, telecommunications in Latin America have lagged far behind demand. Compared with the rest of the developing world, however, this region generally has more advanced telecommunications systems and better institutional and human resource bases. One after another, by the late 1980s most Latin American countries had returned to democratic forms of government and started to put in place new economic strategies that emphasized competition, private enterprise, and openness. This has provided a favorable political and economic environment for telecommunications reform.

The reforms undertaken in Latin America have similarities and also significant differences. They are similar in that in all cases so far, reform has revolved around privatization of state enterprises; privatization has been realized through international competitive bidding; elements of competition in nonbasic services and networks were introduced immediately; protection of the dominant operator from competition in the core business has assured for a limited time; and international capital markets were willing to invest in the privatized companies. There are also important differences. The process of reform was very focused and rapid in Argentina, Mexico, and Venezuela, where privatizations were completed in less than two years, and somewhat indecisive and much slower in Chile, where it took over ten years. Important improvements were made in Mexico's enterprise before privatization, whereas those in the other countries were sold "as is" (ranging from good to

25

poor), and internal changes were left to the new owners. In all countries, the privatized companies were granted operating concessions, but the role and scope of these varied. For example, the concessions in Argentina, Mexico, and Venezuela, but not in Chile, defined monopoly privileges as well as quantitative service development targets. In Argentina, the basic rules of the game were set mainly in the terms and conditions of sale of the state enterprise and in the sales contracts, rather than in the concession. Pricing policies and rules for marginal cost pricing were set in the law in Chile, while price-cap regulation was adopted elsewhere with capping formulas defined in the concessions or sales contracts. Both approaches to pricing have run into problems, including implementation difficulties in Chile and the government's reneging on indexation in Argentina (Massari). In all cases markets were initially structured as multiple monopolies (Cowhey), and then split up in rather different ways. In Chile, where monopoly is not granted by legislation or contract, local telephone service is provided by two de facto monopoly operators, one covering a small region and the other, the rest of the country. A third company operates most long-distance services and facilities. In Argentina, local and domestic long-distance telephone services were divided into two regional companies of about equal size. Here the government granted them monopoly privileges for seven years with a possible extension of up to ten years, subject to exceptionally good performance. In Mexico, the main operator has a six-year monopoly of basic services and networks, but another enterprise exercises the satellite facilities monopoly granted to the state by the Constitution. In Venezuela the concession granted to the privatized Compañía Anónima Nacional de Teléfonos de Venezuela (CANTV) was granted exclusivity for basic services for nine years. In most cases the state enterprises were sold to consortia that include experienced foreign operators who have responsibility for running the companies (the exception being the Chilean long-distance company, in which none of the investors has a controlling interest). These controlling consortia, however, own varying proportions of the company, ranging from 20 percent to over 50 percent. Likewise, requirements varied among countries regarding the extent of domestic ownership. Where needed, capital structures were modified before the sale to allow minority (including foreign) owners to have administrative control. In all cases, although a single buyer was given controlling interest, ownership of the companies was widely dispersed among domestic and foreign investors, company employees, and the public at large.

In general, initial results from reform in Latin America have been very positive. Investment has accelerated, service has expanded rapidly, and new services have been introduced. There are indications that the countries' economies gained considerably from privatization, and in some cases all major stakeholders (customers, foreign and domestic investors, employees, government) have benefitted.[47] The operating companies are much better positioned for sustained development. In particular, new management teams have been put in place, unfavorable contracts with domestic suppliers renegotiated, corruption reduced, improved work practices introduced, and urgent technical problems addressed; however, many problems remain to be solved. In particular, regulatory institutions remain weak. In Venezuela a temporary regulatory entity had to be established by presidential decree because it was not possible to promulgate a new telecommunications law before the privatization of CANTV. Like the original Argentine regulatory agency, it lacks funding. In Argentina and Mexico the regulatory agencies got off to a very slow start. In Chile the reliance on a mix of sector-specific regulation and antitrust law has been rather slow in dealing with critical issues.

A well-designed concession can, however, as Björn Wellenius shows, serve as an effective means of regulating the privatized operator's network expansion, quality, pricing, and other obligations. This is the case in Mexico. Developing competition at the margins and the necessary skills are also very important.

Comparing the major privatizations in Latin America (those of Argentina, Mexico, Venezuela, and Chile), Wellenius draws the following conclusions:

- There is a pattern of selling controlling interest in the state enterprise to private owners, giving them a limited-term monopoly, and opening immediately some segments to competition (such as cellular).

- There has been considerable interest of domestic and foreign investors in Latin American telecommunications privatizations.

- Privatizations in Argentina, Mexico, and Venezuela were achieved quickly and generally effectively because there was political support at the highest level.

- Employees were persuaded to support reform.

Recent Experiences in the Asia-Pacific Region

Part III of the book examines the experience with telecommunications sector reform in the Asia and Pacific region. An extensive regional overview by Robert R. Bruce and Jeffrey P. Cunard (8) is followed by more detailed analyses of events in two industrial countries: Australia (Hutchinson, 9; Ergas, 10) and New Zealand (Donaldson, 11). Two developing countries at different stages of reform are also discussed: Sri Lanka (Watson, 12), and Malaysia (Syed, 13).

The Australian telecommunications reforms must be understood in the context of broader economic reforms begun in 1983, including the financial, manufacturing, transport, and communication sectors, which involved changes in government policy regarding competition, regulation, and state enterprises. The telecommunications reform announced in 1990 sought to enhance competition by setting up a duopoly of all services and networks between a merger of the existing domestic and international state companies (AOTC, now Telstra) and a new private company, to be built starting from the sale of state's satellite company (AUSSAT);[48] taking specific steps to increase competition in cellular and other specific market segments; and establishing pro-competitive safeguards. Michael J. Hutchinson discusses the main issues raised in connection with reform, including the need to continue ensuring universal service, attract private domestic and foreign investment, promote Australian telecommunications manufacturing, develop a regulatory framework, and ensure interconnection and equal access. The resulting policy requires that both Telstra and the new carrier cross-subsidize the universal provision of services, at an estimated annual cost of some A\$250 million. AUSSAT was sold to a consortium including 49 percent interest of two foreign operating companies. Australia is pursuing telecommunications liberalization through both bilateral and multilateral negotiations—including the GATT Uruguay Round on trade in services—as a means to promote domestic telecommunications manufacturing, software, and service industries. The role of the independent regulator (AUSTEL) has been strengthened and consolidated; its functions now include monitoring competition, protecting new entrants from potential abuse by the dominant carrier, reviewing interconnection and equal access arrangements, promoting carrier efficiency, setting standards, preventing misuse of market power by international entrants, protecting consumers, and acting as arbitrator between carriers where their commercial negotiation is unsuccessful. Telstra, the dominant carrier, is required to provide to new carriers interconnection with the main network at a directly attributable incremental cost and on an equal access basis.

Henry Ergas is critical of Australia's approach, especially of the government's continued involvement in the sector after the reform, and suggests that the sector is mature enough for competition to develop without direct government involvement, which he believes is constraining and delaying competition. In particular, the government's power to set prices and the conditions for community service obligations are contrary to the objective of increasing aggregate welfare. There is also the risk that the government will use state ownership of the dominant carrier to promote its own investment, human resources, and service interests rather than leaving these to market forces. Ergas highlights the burden on the carriers of financing community service obligations and the continued reliance on the treasury to finance the dominant carrier's investments, especially in international ventures.

New Zealand's approach is closer to the model Ergas would have preferred for Australia. Like Australia, New Zealand was characterized until the early 1980s by a large and pervasive public sector judged to be inefficient, inflexible, and subject to political interference. Hunter Donaldson describes the process of reform. In the mid–1980s the government decided to corporatize a number of state-owned enterprises, including the Post Office, which was responsible for telecommunications. Posts and telecommunications were separated, as were the regulatory and operational functions. This was, however, only the first step to what is now regarded as the most radical liberalization and deregulation of any telecommunications market to date. By 1991 all restrictions to market entry and ownership were removed, and any new network operators could be established on proof that they met certain criteria specified in the Telecommunications Act. With the 1990 sale of Telecom Corporation of New Zealand (TCNZ, the corporatized successor of the Post

Office's telecommunications operations) to a consortium of local and foreign investors, including two foreign operating companies, the government was wholly out of the business of providing telecommunications services. The New Zealand government does, however, retain veto power on specified matters, particularly to ensure that TCNZ meets agreed service obligations. Unlike Australia, New Zealand does not have a telecommunications regulatory agency. Rather, the policy is to rely on various provisions of the commerce, antitrust, and telecommunications laws to regulate the market. Allocation of use of the radio spectrum is subject to a tendering process. The initial results of reform in New Zealand, according to Donaldson, have been generally positive in terms of accelerated investment as well as better and more services at lower prices. The world continues to watch eagerly.

In contrast, progress toward telecommunications reforms in the developing countries of Asia and the Pacific have been scattered and achieved mixed success. In 1987 the government of Sri Lanka decided to reorganize the telecommunications department into a separate state-owned company with the possibility of foreign private participation at a later date. Despite good progress toward setting up a regulatory authority and drafting new legislation and a corporate charter, this attempt at reform was abandoned by a new government in 1988. This, according to Vernon Watson, resulted largely from management, labor, and political opposition. In 1991 the government adopted a more modest reform program and created Sri Lanka Telecom (SLT) as a fully government-owned corporation to be run on a commercial basis but controlled by the government through a board of directors. A ministerial regulatory authority, less independent than originally envisaged, was also established. The initial adjustments to the new structure are still under way, and it is too early to assess whether they will result in substantial change in behavior and performance. Restructuring in Malaysia has been more consistent. As Syed Hussein Mohamed points out, it was driven by government policy to turn the private sector into the engine of economic growth. The government's telecommunications department was first corporatized in 1987 and then partially privatized through sale of shares in 1990. As in Sri Lanka, staff were offered job security and improved conditions if they chose to move into the new company. Restructuring was accompanied by the inculcation of a new commercial approach through training and emphasis on marketing, customer services, and quality of service. The former telecommunications department remains responsible for regulatory matters, including issuing of operating licenses, establishing of network standards, type approval of terminal equipment, and spectrum management. Reform in Malaysia has resulted in improved operating and financial performance, reflected in more than tripling of share prices by mid–1993.

In their survey of reform in twelve countries, Bruce and Cunard make some general observations about the experiences in the region:

* The Four Tigers (Singapore, Hong Kong, Korea, and Taiwan) should liberalize further by allowing greater competition in nonvoice services.

- Corporatization and privatization need to be pursued in these countries and foreign ownership rules need to be relaxed.

- All countries of the region can learn from the Thai example of bringing in private investors through new arrangements such as build-operate-transfer (BOT).

- Private parallel networks can be developed as a means of competing with the existing operator.

- Strong political commitment to reform needs to be maintained as well as large investment programs supported, at least partially, by tariff structures designed to generate necessary investment capital.

- Allowing in new competitors can also be a means to attract investment.

- Adequate regulatory structures, which are still lacking to a large extent in the region, need to be put in place.

Recent Experiences in Western, Central, and Eastern Europe

Europe has a unique mix of telecommunications sector development situations. While the countries of Western Europe, which have some of the world's most advanced telecommunications facilities, are moving toward a single telecommunications market, no part of the world has been so abruptly exposed to accumulated weaknesses of its telecommunications facilities and skills as Central and Eastern Europe (CEE). Attempts to catch up with the West in a few years place huge burdens on financial resources and on the emerging market-oriented policies and institutions. Part III of the book looks at some pieces of this European kaleidoscope. A concise regional overview by Herbert Ungerer (14) is followed by more detailed analyses of three Western countries with very different sector approaches within a common European Community (EC) policy framework: Bruce Laidlaw (15) summarizes the United Kingdom's pioneering progress in privatization and liberalization; Eric Huret (16) and Gerard J. van Velzen (17) examine the different approaches followed by France and the Netherlands toward increasing commercialization and competition without privatization. The unique case of Germany following reunification is presented by Karl-Heinz Neumann and Thomas Schnöring (18). The situation of other Central and Eastern European countries following the collapse of communist governments are discussed by Timothy E. Nulty (19), Jürgen Müller and Emilia Nyevrikel (20), and Krisztina Heller (21).

EC telecommunications policy is reflected in the 1987 Green Paper on telecommunications, the 1990 Green Paper on satellite communications, and various sectoral directives, all of which are part of a wider process of building a single European market. Telecommunications, as Ungerer points out, have a vital role to play in Europe's services market, and liberalization of telecommunications structures is essential if these markets are themselves to be liberalized and thereby allowed to develop. Sector reform in progress mainly comprises liberalization of terminal equipment supply (including Europe-wide type approval) and most services except the telephone; separation of regulatory and operational functions; opening and harmonization of access to the network for new services providers through open network provision (ONP); transborder provision of services; and opening of domestic markets to foreign suppliers of major equipment. Ungerer concludes with a review of current work and challenges of the European Commission in areas of the liberalization of satellite communications, frequency coordination for various mobile services, numbering plans, and the future integration of Eastern Europe.

Within the framework of EC policy, the United Kingdom and France have approached reform in two completely different ways. The U.K. liberalization process, described by Laidlaw, began in 1981 with the corporatization of British Telecom (BT) and the creation of Mercury, the first potential competitor to BT's core business. The corporatization of BT and creation of Mercury were followed by the liberalization of mobile services and cable television markets and by the privatization of BT through sale of a majority of shares in the United Kingdom and foreign markets. Concurrently, a regulatory framework and agency, the Office of Telecommunications (OFTEL) were put into place, and a duopoly was established (BT and Mercury). Markets were further liberalized in 1991 following a review of the duopoly policy. Although there are still shortcomings, such as the limited competition in international basic services and the continuing dominance of BT, the United Kingdom has the most liberal telecommunications market in Europe. The approach to reform in France was quite different. Whereas in the United Kingdom many of the early decisions were made by Parliament without much input from the public,[49] the French government undertook a wide-ranging consultative process involving PTT employees and unions, civil servants, and the general public. "Le débat public," described by Huret, involved hundreds of thousands of people expressing their views at meetings, national conferences, broadcast debates, by mail and videotext, and through questionnaires. The resulting reforms reflect the diversity of inputs, striking a balance between competition and the provision of a public service, and between regulatory control and market forces—competition within a public service framework. State-owned France Télécom, the monopoly provider of basic services and networks, obtained a large degree of financial and management autonomy but at the same time has strict public service obligations established by contract. This duality is reflected in the government's having functions of both a public regulator and a supervisor of France Télécom's service responsibilities.

The usual pressures to liberalize and deregulate the telecommunications sector were augmented in the Netherlands by the country's dominant position as a regional and international center for transport, financial services, and other communication-intensive sectors. Van Velzen discusses reform in Dutch telecommunications from the point of view of the operator. Following promulgation of a new telecommunications law in 1989, PTT Telecom Netherlands was corporatized, its postal and banking facilities spun off, and the regulatory function left with the ministry. The main thrust of reorganizing PTT Telecom Netherlands has been to make it more commercially-oriented by developing a new corporate culture focused on service quality, setting specific customer-oriented investment objectives, adopting a new organizational structure with greater management flexibility, and emphasizing internationalization of the business activities of PTT Telecom Netherland via joint ventures and the creation of specialized subsidiaries.

After long studies and the recommendations of a government-appointed commission, the telecommunications sector was restructured in the Federal Republic of Germany on January 1, 1990. Consistent with EC policy, regulatory and operational functions were separated, telecommunications were separated from posts and banking, and DBP Telekom maintained exclusive rights over the telephone service and network. The new structure was hardly in place when the unification of East and West Germany took place in October 1990. The consequent merger of the two telecommunications entities presented a much more substantial challenge. East and West had very different structures and levels of development, as Neumann and Schnöring point out. In the former the government was responsible not only for policy, regulation, frequency allocation, and operation but also for manufacturing, installation, and export promotion. The network was outdated, penetration rates were one-fourth those of the West, and data and other new services were virtually nonexistent. Neumann and Schnöring describe the ambitious plans and massive investments (about DM 60 billion) under way to bring telecommunications performance in the eastern states to Western standards by 1997, with priority for business customers.

The task is even more daunting in the other CEE countries, which have no ready access to the huge amounts of capital needed. There had earlier been isolated attempts to develop the telecommunications infrastructure in Bulgaria, East Germany, and Hungary. As Müller and Nyevrikel show, however, only Bulgaria achieved significant growth, with financing and help from local municipalities, agricultural cooperatives, and user networks. All these countries, according to Nulty, face a particularly difficult challenge to bring their telecommunications infrastructures and services up to the level of those in Western Europe. They will have to develop their network at an accelerated pace using the newest of technology, under unfamiliar commercial conditions, in the absence of well-developed financial markets, and with a lack of adequate skills. Nulty estimates a total requirement of about US$60 billion over ten years (of which 40 to 50 percent will be in acutely short hard currency) or 2 percent of GNP. He discusses possible strategies that CEE countries might employ to overcome these challenges. These include establishing joint ventures with Western firms, developing digital or cellular overlay networks, exploiting the rights of way and infrastructures of other public utilities, and franchising independent operators. The CEE countries also need to develop a regulatory framework that strikes a balance between protecting commercial interests of private operators and the obligations of public service providers. There is, furthermore, the problem of dealing with domestic manufacturers which have hitherto been protected but whose technological level is inadequate. Finally, Nulty reviews possible sources of financing which may be available to countries of CEE, including internal generation through retained earnings, issuance of subscriber bonds, outside financing, including direct foreign investment (for example, share equity, joint ventures, franchises), multilateral development financing, and bilateral and supplier loans. Müller and Nyevrikel discuss several other measures, including implementing tariffs that reflect costs as well as improving network management and work practices.

Heller shows that in Hungary, since World War II at least, the political situation and the structure of the telecommunications sector have been closely linked. Liberalization of the political regime in 1989 and 1990 led to legislation which will substantially reform the sector through the introduction of competition, privatization, and more open markets.

Privatization: Foreign Operators' Perspective

What makes a particular business opportunity in developing countries attractive to a foreign telecommunications operating company? That is what part V of the book seeks to elucidate, especially regarding privatization of state telecommunications enterprises. Judith D. O'Neill (22) suggests that a balance must be struck between the objectives of the government and those of the private investor-operators (also referred to as active or strategic investors) that is good for both and that enhances the value of the investment opportunities. Following O'Neill's overview of the elements that go into such a balance, three major operators (Bell Atlantic, Cable & Wireless, and Societá Finanziaria Telefonica Spa (STET)) describe what they seek in a privatization and also what they perceive to be a government's goals in privatizing a telecommunications company. In presenting their views, frequent cross-reference is made to specific country experiences discussed earlier in this book (for example, Tucker on New Zealand, Massari on Argentina), and the reader will doubtless note many stimulating complementary as well as contrasting opinions.

A strategic investor's prime motive is the creation of additional revenue at minimal risk. The choice of time and place to invest varies. As Bell Atlantic's Hyde Tucker (23) points out, there are more telecommunications investment opportunities today than there is global investment capacity. As home markets are being liberalized and the potential for growth decreases, operators seek new opportunities in untapped, emerging markets. They have the know-how, the strength, and often also the financial and human resources. In addition, sometimes cultural reasons have a bearing on a decision to where to invest, as Telefónica and STET (Massari, 25) have shown in Latin America. The potential investor-operator will take many factors into consideration. He will, as Tucker states, look at the revenue-generating capabilities of the company to be purchased and how this may be affected by government pricing, market regulation, taxation, and foreign exchange policies. Control is most important, says Joseph E. Pilcher (24), for an investor such as Cable & Wireless (C&W) which is a telecommunications operating company, not a financial investor, and seeks therefore to control the company in which it has invested. STET, on the other hand, sought both foreign (France Télécom) and local partners to share the risk and

33

the financial burden of its investment in Argentina. The local partner, says Francesco Massari, is important because of its intimate knowledge of the local market conditions. For C&W, in contrast, joint ventures with local partners are purely marriages of convenience.

Another set of factors which interests foreign operators is what Tucker calls productivity improvement opportunities, including the freedom to reduce staff if necessary, to introduce new labor-saving technologies, and to tie salaries to performance. For Pilcher, it would be unreasonable for the government to expect foreign operators to meet demanding service obligations, refrain from rationalizing the labor force, and at the same time confront new competitors that have neither obligations.

The legal and regulatory structure, which for O'Neill includes the appropriate enabling legislation, creation of an independent regulatory body, a new telecommunications law, and the sector-specific regulations, must be well defined and transparent so that the investors can assess the political and legal risk of their investments. Most important, since the privatization of a public utility raises a number of social welfare concerns, there must be a clear understanding of what the potential buyer's obligations with respect to these are (Pilcher).

Political stability and a strong government commitment to reform are also very important. Given the size of investment and the time required to realize benefits, the foreign operator seeks both political and economic stability, safety for its assets and employees, and freedom from corruption and other pressures (Tucker, Pilcher). The foreign operator must have assurances that the conditions of the sale will not change once a deal is struck. Massari and Pilcher refer specifically to uncertainty regarding the government's commitment to honor tariff agreements.

Just as important as the conditions of the privatization are those of the process. It must be well managed, clearly defined, consistent with the government's objective and timetable, and it must allow sufficient time for the investor-operators to carry out the necessary research (Pilcher), yet not be excessively long to discourage them (O'Neill). The process must, furthermore, be free of corruption and inappropriate influences. All relevant information must be made available to all potential bidders. Pilcher suggests that involvement of potential bidders in establishing the conditions of the sale during the pre-bid negotiations will ensure that the best interests of both the government and the investor-operator are taken into account. Also a telecommunications company which has been put in order and improved before the sale, for instance through corporatization, will be much more attractive to potential strategic investors (O'Neill).

Governments are perceived by potential foreign operators to have a wide range of motives for wanting to sell off their telecommunications enterprises (Massari). These include:

- The need to rapidly build up a network that is key to economic development

- The need to attract private (especially foreign) capital for this purpose

- Recognition that privatization provides the sector with flexibility to meet rapidly changing requirements

- User pressure

- Reducing public foreign debt

- Developing a domestic capital market

- Safeguarding the company management from political influence

- Motivating management and employees through employee stock ownership plans (ESOPs)

- Achieving a commitment by the company to maximize profits

- Desirability of associating foreign investors with the necessary expertise, experience, and pride in operating a telecommunications undertaking.

Mobilizing Capital for Privatization

Market investors, which include commercial and investment banks as well as both institutional and retail public equity investors, invest in emerging markets for reasons somewhat different to those of strategic investors. According to François J. Grossas (26), the former invest in emerging markets because they want to:

- Diversify their portfolios and enhance the potential for long-term returns

- Find venture capital alternatives to mature industrialized country markets where investment opportunities have become more scarce

- Invest in markets whose performances are not strongly correlated to those of the European, North American, and developed Asian markets

- In the case of commercial banks, find opportunities to exchange sovereign debt for equity which has potential for growth.

Like strategic investors, market investors are attracted to these markets because they see potential for high yields and returns on their investments and certain conditions being met which tend to reduce their risks. Strategic investors have longer-term perspectives and are, therefore, usually willing to sacrifice near-term earnings and pay a higher price to build up the value of their investments in the long term. Market investors, on the other hand, want stable earnings and high dividend yields. They want shares which are accessible and easy to trade, generally facilitated through a large equity flotation and, in order to attract foreign equity investors, the issuing of share certificates such as American Depositary Receipts (ADRs) in major international stock exchanges (Harland, 27). Listing requirements imposed by the latter and their financial regulators are, as Dan Vallimarescu (29) point out, a comforting stamp of approval to most investors.

The 1990 flotation of shares of Compañía de Teléfonos de Chile (CTC) was, in this respect, a success, as were the sales of shares of TELMEX, Telecom Corporation of New Zealand (TCNZ), and British Telecom shares. These privatizations through public share issues on domestic and international markets were successful because a number of favorable attributes, described by Grossas, Harland, and Vallimarescu, were present, including:

- A stable political and economic environment

- High potential for economic growth

- A well-defined and transparent legal and regulatory structure

- A viable company with high potential for growth

- A competent and stable labor force

- Fair and neutral tax treatment

- Evidence of a capital market and financial regulations which are favorable to foreign investment

- Financial statements using internationally recognized accounting standards

- Potential to finance network expansion through internally generated funds

- A fair and predictable tariff-setting structure

- Attractive share price/earnings ratio

- Association of strategic investors and local partners.

In addition, market and strategic investors both want a well-defined and effectively managed process which is simple, transparent, predictable, and absent of bureaucracy, and which gives them enough time to assess the company being offered for sale.

Dean Lewis (28) discusses five options for selling a telecommunications company, in order of increasing complexity, and examines the relative merits of each. The negotiated sale of the company to a single buyer is relatively straightforward and may maximize the sale price, but most likely no single domestic buyer who is large enough can be found or the company's management or board may not be supportive of a particular buyer, especially if foreign. As a second option, sale of a partial stake to a single buyer or group of buyers may be easier to achieve and can be used to restrict the level of foreign participation, to allow the state to retain a share in the ownership if so desired. Proceeds can approach those from an outright sale. The third option, privatization through public share offerings in domestic or international markets, details of which are discussed by Vallimarescu, can attract a wide range of investors. Domestic markets tend to be too small, however; few companies from developing countries meet the strict standards required by major foreign markets; transaction costs are high; and the potential benefits to the government depend on the price at which the shares can be sold. The fourth option is to sell a controlling stake to a single strategic buyer combined with one or a sequence of public offerings. Involvement of a single major shareholder enhances the public offering by instilling confidence and stability in the market and encouraging competitive bidding among strategic financial investors. The fifth option, break up and sale of components of the company, is the most difficult and time-consuming and may result in lower overall benefit to the government. (A hybrid between the last two options, however, has potential advantages in terms of developing competitive markets and has been successfully utilized, for example, in Argentina).

Vallimarescu also discusses a number of factors which governments should consider in privatizing through the issuing of shares in domestic or international markets, whether or not accompanied by the sale of a significant package to a single buyer. Initially, the legal and corporate status of the company to be privatized must be clearly defined. Restructuring and operational changes might be required before the privatization can take place. The government must decide if it will maintain a majority or a minority ownership share or if, alternatively, it wishes to retain a "golden share" giving it effective control when, for example, issues of a nationally sensitive nature arise. It must put in place a predictable, disciplined, and fair tariff-setting process free from arbitrary political involvement. The share issue must be large enough to ensure liquidity, equity research, and a large secondary market. The government must, furthermore, structure the flotation to the type of investors (for example, domestic institutional and retail; nonresident national, foreign institutional retail; experienced utility; or "country play") which it wishes to attract. It must not overlook national sensitivities, and it must be able to price properly the shares to be issued so as to maximize proceeds while achieving widespread investor interest.

Privatization through public share issues may be hampered because of the limited availability of both local and foreign equity capital. Desmond Watkins (30) discusses the conditions under which foreign commercial banks may be prepared to exchange sovereign debt for the assets of a telecommunications operator. Countries employing debt exchange programs can not only reduce their foreign debt exposure (for example, privatization of Empressa Nacional de Telecomunicaciones (ENTel) in Argentina) but also help develop a viable and successful private sector through the participation of foreign commercial banks. This in turn can bring debtors and creditors back together in the marketplace and stimulate foreign and domestic capital markets. The banks do this by bringing along their financial, managerial, and other skills and also by associating themselves with foreign operators and local investors who contribute sector-specific technical and commercial expertise. Successful sovereign debt exchange programs applicable to various sectors, such as those in Argentina, Venezuela, and Chile, were characterized by:

- Projects large enough to interest commercial banks and other potential investors (the privatization of ENTel) involved US$5 billion in debt exchanges and over US$0.5 billion in cash

- Relatively small fixed discount on the debt (such as 15 to 30 percent in Venezuela, depending on the project) or discount determined through auction or negotiation

- Clearly defined rules and conditions regarding the portions of a project that can be financed through debt exchange as distinct from new funds

- Attractive foreign investment legislation, including conditions for repatriating earnings and capital

- Clear commitment of government to the targeted sectors

- Fast and efficient execution

- Flexibility of process and possibility to negotiate on a case-by-case basis

- Noninflationary mechanism achieved through debt-for-debt or direct exchange of debt for assets rather than governments printing money to finance debt-for-equity programs

- Equality of treatment of commercial banks with other market and strategic investors.

Important for the commercial bank which seeks to redeploy sovereign debt is that the debt exchange program must be perceived as a more attractive alternative to continuing to hold the debt.

For a variety of reasons it may not be initially possible to privatize a telecommunications company through any of the above mechanisms. In such cases governments might consider, among others, the approaches suggested by Robert R. Bruce, Jeffrey P. Cunard, and Lothar A. Kneifel (31) for attracting private capital to the telecommunications company. Under an asset-based financing scheme, private entities build and own infrastructure facilities which they then lease to the telecommunications company. The entities raise the necessary financing in domestic and international capital markets and eventually exchange their assets for shares in the telecommunications company. An alternative approach is for private entities to construct and operate segments of the network in terms of a franchise agreement with the telecommunications company. Eventually these franchises can be repurchased by the telecommunications company in exchange for shares. Such franchising schemes could be applied to rural telephone systems, VSAT networks, private automatic branch exchanges (PBX), and small business exchanges. These relatively small, decentralized, and low-risk investments can attract small and medium investors. They can also help develop entrepreneurial skills and provide opportunity for introducing rational pricing and billing mechanisms that may gradually be extended to the existing network.

Issues of Regulation

The authors in part VII of the book underline the need to have a well-developed regulatory framework in place well before any major reform of the sector takes place. The task is complex, must balance a number of competing interests and objectives, and takes considerably more time than other components of a reform program, such as sale of a state enterprise.

Richard J. Schultz (32) explores the complexities of economic regulation. Although some prescriptions suggest that regulation is relatively straightforward, Schultz argues otherwise. He describes the multiple goals now being pursued in regulatory systems and how those goals need to be specified as clearly as possible and then ranked, to avoid confusion and unnecessary conflict. He then discusses the need to refine the various regulatory instruments available, both because traditional instruments have not been useful in promoting certain objectives, especially regulated firm productivity, and because of the new economic circumstances, such as competition, within which regulatory instruments must operate. Finally, Schultz describes some of the major institutional alternatives for implementing regulatory control that have developed.

Privatization of a telecommunications company raises issues of public policy, economic development objectives, social justice, and the boundary between government and private roles. Because competition is still not generally possible in some major market segments (especially the local telephone network), monopoly provision is, as Nicholas P. Miller (33) points out, often the only option for privatization. This entails continued government intervention. Also, as David N. Townsend (34) shows, telecommunications monopolies, because of their declining marginal costs and the inelastic demand for their services, will tend to maximize profits in a way which does not maximize social welfare. A private operator will be interested in investing in areas where the short-run demand and potential for profits are high rather than throughout the network (as needed for economic development) where the investment can be profitable only in the long run. Tariffs must allow the private monopoly to expand the network and earn a reasonable return on its investment yet offer service at affordable rates.

For Paul Waterschoot (35), application of competition or antitrust rules is often a more effective way to regulate the provision of a monopoly service than through sector-specific measures. A regulator, he suggests, will be more reluctant than the courts to challenge aspects of a regulatory framework in which he also operates. Furthermore, application of antitrust rules by the courts only when required is less burdensome than the continuous and detailed surveillance which a priori regulation of a monopoly entails. The reluctance of the monopolist to provide relevant information does not make the regulator's task easier. Miller agrees that the threat of competition is the best form of regulation but argues that because competition is not feasible in a large part of the network, the government must intervene to ensure that its social and economic goals are met. John J. Collings (39) also prefers regulation of structure by a regulatory authority based on well-defined rules rather than regulation of conduct as implied in Waterschoot's approach. Collings is critical of the European Commission's use of antitrust rules to achieve policy goals. In contrast to Waterschoot, Miller believes that an independent regulatory agency is more effective than legislatures and courts.

Waterschoot would admit a monopoly only in cases where a public service cannot be provided in competition with other service providers. Where privatization is accompanied by the introduction of competition, conditions must exist which allow an appropriate and viable competition to develop; that is, new entrants must not be crowded out of the market by the dominant operator. For Waterschoot the functions of a regulator can be summarized as preventing the monopoly operator's discriminating among different categories of users; preventing abuse of the operator's monopoly power where, for example, it can use the benefits from its monopoly services to subsidize its competitive services; ensuring the maintenance of a prescribed quality of service; and avoiding monopoly profits. Collings suggests that the protection of the established operator from economic harm to allow it to meet its network expansion and service obligations is also an important role for the regulator. Miller adds to this the need to ensure that a number of sector development and government policy objectives are met, including expansion of the network; bringing prices in line with costs; stable or reduced prices; maintenance of limited, occasional, but explicit subsidies; and facilitating the introduction of more open markets where the regulator must act as arbitrator among conflicting interests involving the role of the monopoly operator (Waterschoot). This can be achieved only if the regulator is independent of the operator.

Although Miller and Collings argue that the regulator should also be independent of the government, Waterschoot suggests that a regulatory agency responsible to a government department can act in a much more pro-competitive manner because it has to be less concerned about being neutral. Indeed, this was the option the French government chose when it reformed the sector in 1990. This decision was based less on a desire to use the regulator (Direction de la Réglementation Générale) as a vehicle to promote greater competition than, as Dominique Garnier (36) points out, to ensure continued close government involvement in telecommunications matters related to national sovereignty and independence as well as the development of France's public sector infrastructure. Having the regulator within the government has, according to Garnier, the added advantage that the regulator is able to participate in decisionmaking processes of international bodies such as the European Commission and the International Telecommunication Union (ITU). Decisions of these bodies, be they directives, regulations, or other have a direct impact on France's national telecommunications policy. In the United Kingdom, as Donald Mason (37) points out, independence of the regulator is embodied in the post of director general of telecommunications, the head of OFTEL. The Telecommunications Act of 1984 clearly defines his role and responsibilities with respect to that of Parliament and the secretary of state for trade and industry, the minister responsible in the United Kingdom for telecommunications. In Venezuela, as Aileen A. Pisciotta (7) shows, the government wanted to establish an independent agency but could not because it was neither contemplated nor permitted under the government structure.

For Miller a regulatory agency should have expertise in four general areas:

- Developing and implementing regulatory policy

- Financial analysis of prices and costs

- Capability to assess quality of service, investment programs, technical standards, and conformity of terminal equipment

- The administrative, legal, and information support necessary to carry out its functions.

The structure of the FCC, given as one example, is based largely on these functions. In France, where the regulator mainly grants licenses, approves terminal equipment, manages the spectrum, and settles disputes arising between network operators, a capability in detailed financial analysis or quality of service standards is not needed. Properly staffed and funded, strong, independent, imbued with a definite legal mandate and clear objectives are, according to Miller, some of the attributes of a successful regulator. OFTEL, the U.K. regulatory, satisfies these criteria. The act which established it clearly defines the role of its director general with respect to granting, enforcing, and modifying licenses, handling complaints, and appointing staff. OFTEL's functions are, as Mason shows, clearly defined with respect to, among others, universal service obligation, competitive safeguards, regulation of tariffs (via price caps), quality of service, interconnection, standards, numbering and public consultation. Mason also shows the staffing and organization of OFTEL and indicates the main sources of its £8 million annual budget. This was not the case in Venezuela where a regulatory agency had to be established in haste by presidential decree to allow the privatization of the telephone company to go ahead in the absence of telecommunications legislation which was being held up for political reasons (Pisciotta).

Conclusions: Strategic Issues of Implementation

The book ends by looking at telecommunications reforms from two viewpoints that cut across many aspects dealt with earlier, namely, the relationship between reform and the political system (Cowhey, 38) and the process of reform (Collings, 39), and also by challenging some of the underlying concepts (Schultz, 40).

The telecommunications reforms that are most likely to succeed depend on the country's political system and institutions. The political aspects of reform, however, have been dealt with largely through common sense and the intuition of key players. Results have been mixed. It could be argued that some of the problems—for instance the collapse of the otherwise well-crafted first attempt at reform in Sri Lanka (12) and the failure to start up the regulatory agency in Argentina (3)—could have been averted through more deliberate and knowledgeable consideration of political and institutional factors. Only very recently have the relationships between reform and political systems begun to be examined more systematically.

Peter F. Cowhey sketches the beginnings of a theory of regulation of telecommunications systems in developing countries; in that light he revisits the experience of Mexico and Argentina and briefly discusses Singapore, Japan, and Canada. He proposes a typology of restructuring models, ranging from improving the monopoly to full competition. Examples illustrate how the political institutions—that is, the electoral and party system, the degree of federalism, and the division of power within the government—have a bearing on the model that is selected. For example, Singapore, which has a parliamentary system with a strong centralized leadership, adopted the monopoly modernization model with close political oversight and strong government influence on the board of directors. That model suited the government's policy to use its influence in all key sectoral activities toward developing Singapore as the preeminent commercial center in Southeast Asia. Mexico and Argentina, in contrast, have presidential systems within federalist structures. The strength and influence of the dominant political parties play an important role in the way the governments act, and sector policy as well as the timing and modality of privatization can be explained in terms of party strategies and changing political constituencies. Heller (21) in her historical sketch of reform in Hungary illustrates how closely this has been tied to the political situation of the time.

Although each country has gone about reforming the telecommunications sector in its own way, some common lessons on how to manage the process of change are highlighted by John J. Collings. There are four broad policy variables that any government contemplating sector reform must take into consideration. These involve determining the appropriate:

- Degree of competition

- Sector structure, including separation of regulatory, policy, and operating functions, determining boundaries between competitive and noncompetitive domains, and other market structures

- Regulatory framework consistent with the degree of competition, the sector structure, the social obligations, and other conditions established

- Ownership structure.

Collings suggests that the approaches to sector reform which have so far been adopted can be classified into four types, and he agrees with Cowhey that choice will depend on each country's political, institutional, economic, and sector-specific circumstances:

- The piecemeal approach, as in the United States, where change is achieved through regulatory rule making and adjudication at both the federal and state levels as well as application of antitrust law

- The gradualist approach, as in the United Kingdom, with a managed transition to competition over many years

- The goal-oriented approach, as in Argentina, where reform was driven by the government's decision to privatize public enterprises while ensuring that public service obligations were not neglected

- The strategic approach, such as adopted by the European Commission as part of its policy to develop a single European market in all sectors.

Collings discusses the relative merits of these options; he favors a strategic approach which he believes an increasing number of countries will adopt, but notes it may not be applicable in some political environments, for the reasons explained by Cowhey. Collings offers a procedural checklist of items to be considered in the formulation of a strategy for sector restructuring:

- Situation analysis to provide factual basis for policy development

- Defining the government's primary policy aims

- Identifying specific sector goals and constraints

- Translating critical goals and constraints into specific sector objectives and performance measures.

Finally, Collings argues that realistic timing is essential for effective privatization and setting up a regulatory framework. Timing and the approach and model chosen are closely related.

Richard Schultz takes exception to five views widely held across this book. The first he labels "the gospel of globalization," and he argues that even in many industrialized countries development of the domestic infrastructure takes precedence over ensuring interconnection with the advanced networks of other countries. This is not the view of Scherer (1), for whom countries which fail to adopt their telecommunications infrastructure to the global, information-based economy will fall behind. Second, Schultz challenges the image of poor performance by public enterprises. He argues that in countries with a long-established public service ethic, the road to greater efficiency and productivity, better performance, and more ethical corporate practices is not necessarily through privatization, but more likely through better regulation, incentives, and management tools. Huret (16) had indicated that the French, when consulted on their preferences for reform, came to a similar conclusion. Bruce (2) and Scherer would probably agree on the need for an effective regulatory framework and organization but are less confident that the public service is up to the difficult task of implementing and carrying through the required improvements. Third, Schultz disagrees with the notion that divestiture of ownership reduces government involvement. The state, he points out, simply reappears in another form. Direct control through full ownership of the operating company is replaced by minority or golden share ownership or the privatized company's public service, network expansion, tariff, and other obligations. Fourth, like Bruce (2), Wellenius (3), and others, Schultz emphasizes that countries contemplating reform cannot merely copy solutions in place elsewhere. But he makes the point that many of the contributors to this book, while subscribing to this view, do not understand or bring out the shortcomings and implicit limitations of the systems they are putting forward as examples. Finally, Schultz believes that sensitivity to foreign ownership of telecommunications operations is often exaggerated and inconsistent with policies of globalization. Donaldson (11) and Laidlaw (15) would no doubt agree that this was the case in New Zealand and the United Kingdom.

Some Lessons from Cross-Country Experience

Although it is too early to assess the extent to which reforms in the developing countries will in the long run overcome past constraints and provide a basis for sustained sector growth and performance, the initial experience in implementing reforms is generally encouraging. In particular, telephone service has expanded and improved at a faster pace, productivity has increased, new services have become available, and in some cases the international capital markets have been effectively tapped to finance subsequent investment. Sector reform, however, is not without pitfalls and difficulties, nor is it a singular event that can be taken care of in one stroke and then left to itself. Some of the lessons drawn in different ways by a number of the contributors to this book are highlighted below.

Privatization—Ownership Matters But Is No Panacea

The significance of privatization is to obtain for the public the full range of benefits of the incentives that drive competitive private enterprise—innovation, efficiency, responsiveness to user needs.[50] Privatization has demonstrated considerable potential for attracting capital and management resources as well as overcoming administrative and other public sector constraints. Privatization is not always a feasible option, however, nor does it by itself guarantee improved sector performance. The following summarizes some of the main issues of privatization.

FACETS AND SEQUENCING OF PRIVATIZATION. Privatization is a complex process of introducing private capital and know-how in telecommunications operations, and there is more than one way to time and sequence this process effectively.

Various facets of the privatization process can be distinguished:

- Separating operations from government and nontelecommunications activities (for example, posts, manufacturing)

- Restructuring telecommunications operations as an independent state enterprise charged with being financially self-sufficient and placing its financial relationship with government at arm's length

- Internally reorganizing the enterprise in ways that are suited for running it as a business

- Reorganizing the telecommunications enterprise under private company law

- Devising a privatization strategy including decisions on controlling interest, employee stock ownership, tranching of stock sales, and residual state ownership, as well as changing the company's capital structure to enable implementation of this strategy.

- Carrying out the sale.

A number of these facets may be dealt with over a relatively short time (as in Argentina, Mexico, Venezuela) or they may evolve in stages over longer periods (as in Chile, Malaysia). There are also various ways of sequencing these changes. For example, internal reorganization of the enterprise may be undertaken before privatization to enhance the company's value (for example, Mexico) or left to the new owners (for example, Argentina, Venezuela). Management contracts could be used to run the enterprise along private business lines, followed later by privatization of assets.

FACTORS OF SUCCESSFUL PRIVATIZATION. Successful privatization of a state telecommunications enterprise depends on a number of factors falling into place.

Privatization must be inserted in the political process. The timing and modality of privatization in a given country is largely conditioned by relatively narrow and somewhat unpredictable windows of political opportunity and by broader developments in economic strategy. At an early stage, the government must clarify its position regarding trade-offs among conflicting interests arising from privatization, such as among existing operators, workers, prospective buyers, potential competitors, investment bankers, the treasury, equipment suppliers, large users, and the public at large.[51] Of particular importance is addressing from the start the concerns of organized labor.

Privatization also requires creating a market structure and a regulatory environment that provides the new owners incentives and obligations to invest and perform as well as an institutional arrangement that frees the operators from unwarranted controls yet safeguards users and reconciles commercial interests with broader development objectives. The regulatory framework for privatizing a monopoly must separate out potentially competitive activities, establish the tariff and interconnection regimes, clarify service goals, develop cost containment targets and incentives, and create or strengthen a regulatory capability to oversee implementation.[52] In particular, privatization brings to the fore central issues of pricing policy and regulation. Of special importance is sorting out to what extent, if at all, it is necessary to continue charging prices well above costs for some services (such as international) in order to finance expansion of the basic network. A closely related issue is that of the scope and duration of monopoly privileges. Initial practice has been to give the dominant operator exclusive rights to provide basic telephone services and networks during up to ten years, largely on grounds that this was needed to enable investors to undertake the large initial investments needed to modernize and expand facilities. The trend, however, is likely to be toward more pro-competitive sector designs, including narrower scope of protection (for example, more liberal licensing of private networks and interconnection to the public network) and shorter duration (for example, up to three years).[53]

International market considerations are also increasingly important. A large number of sales of telecommunications enterprises are planned in both industrial and developing countries. Only a limited number of experienced operating companies, however, are interested in these opportunities.[54] Timing and preparation will influence the extent to which privatization offerings by developing countries succeed. Commercialization of operations, organizational and financial restructuring of enterprises, renegotiation of labor contracts, and improvement of available enterprise information are examples of actions that can make a particular offering more attractive. Some of the most visible and promising privatizations, however, have been carried out very quickly (in little over one year), which limited opportunity for preparatory work to the bare essentials.

Proper design and implementation of the complex process of privatization and related sector reforms require strong and visible high-level political commitment, clear allocation of authority and resources to manage the process, and expert assistance (including foreign) on policy, regulatory, legal, and financial matters. Although sectoral solutions are highly country-specific and individual models cannot readily be transplanted, the experience of other countries (including industrial countries) in dealing with related issues and options has proven to be highly relevant.

CONCERNS ABOUT FUTURE PRIVATIZATIONS. Initial results from privatizing state telecommunications enterprises are generally very encouraging. Governments have successfully sold to consortia led by experienced foreign operating companies capable of providing expert managers, specialized management tools, and continued access to the latest technologies.[55] Good financial performance, reflecting both major tariff adjustments and lower costs, is allowing privatized companies to initially finance accelerated investments largely from internally generated funds. Also, international markets have been increasingly willing to provide large amounts of capital for privatized companies in countries with sound macroeconomic and regulatory frameworks (for example, Chile, Mexico, Argentina).

Some concerns have been raised, however, about the longer-term prospects. Privatization is now being considered in a number of countries perceived by investors as posing higher political risk or offering less attractive markets. In several of these countries, even after sector-specific steps are taken to improve the investment environment, raising post-privatization capital may be a problem. The companies may be unable to attract enough private foreign capital, find themselves cut off from traditional sources of development financing, and lack sufficiently developed domestic capital markets on which to fall back.[56]

The importance of foreign operators will increase as privatization reaches the less-developed enterprises. Some analysts, however, worry that the incentives and obligations of the operators as set by the government at the time of privatization are not strong enough to secure their permanence for the rather long periods that are needed to turn around some of these companies.[57]

Some observers also believe that only five or six major operating companies will dominate the world market in which state telecommunications enterprises are sold. If such is the case, dealing with cartel-like proposals will become an issue. Other analysts, however, believe that in the long run, at least twelve to fifteen companies will be in this business and that the market will continue to be vigorously competitive. Under that scenario, design of the privatization process should emphasize the use of competition to the selling country's advantage.

Although so far these problems are largely hypothetical, they do raise questions that must be examined in designing the reforms. Experience will show to what extent these concerns are justified, and how reform strategies might be modified to deal with them.

Competition and Regulation—Essential Twin Pillars of Reform

Besides increased private sector participation, all major reforms involve two other key elements: competition and regulation. These elements are closely intertwined, and are essential for success of the reforms in terms of the long-run ability to overcome past constraints on telecommunications development. Yet in practice they have been largely shortchanged. Partly this reflects the fact that building up competition and regulation is an inherently slower and more laborious process than selling state enterprises, requiring sustained action over a number of years. It also reflects less political will and sometimes inadequate management of the emerging regulatory institutions.

REGULATORY SHORTFALLS. The single most troubling issue in recent reforms is slow progress in developing regulatory capabilities. All major reforms have been based on the expectation that effective public regulation of the privatized monopolies, especially with respect to prices, service obligations, interconnection, competitive behavior, and access to the public domain (including use of the radio spectrum), can be developed fairly quickly.

Yet building up regulatory institutions where none exist, in countries with little or no regulatory tradition in any sector, is proving to be an arduous and slow task. Whereas some developing countries have carried out satisfactory privatization in little over one year, the telecommunications regulatory systems are only in their infancy. The initial operation of the largest privatized companies is taking place with little or no competition and in a regulatory vacuum in which critical regulatory responsibilities regarding licensing, pricing, technical and accounting standards and performance monitoring, for example, are not properly discharged. In a market dominated by one operator, and lacking effective and proactive regulation, competitors are unlikely to emerge and become firmly established, and numerous forms of anticompetitive behavior may become entrenched. The impact and cost resulting from slow start-up of regulation has not been assessed, but there is a growing volume of anecdotal evidence that lends support to these concerns.[58]

FACTORS OF SUCCESSFUL REGULATION.[59] Whatever the specific regulatory structure, successful regulation requires:

- Political will in the government to make it work

- Strong regulatory leadership committed to serving the public interest

- Good management of the regulatory process, including knowledge of the industry

- Qualified professional staff in the various related disciplines

- Fair and open decisionmaking mechanisms accessible to all the parties affected

- Actions that respond to the broad political goals of the government.

Effective regulation can only develop where there is strong government support and understanding of its goals. Lack of progress in building up effective regulatory institutions and processes is seen by some observers as symptomatic of a lack of government will to regulate the sector. This is basically a political problem. A government will find the will to regulate when it faces a political penalty for not regulating. Such will is typically created by interests within the economy demanding that the government define transparent rules to govern the marketplace. In an economy emerging from government domination, as is the case in most of the developing countries where telecommunications reforms have been undertaken, typically the only economic interests coalesced at the beginning of reform are those of the entrenched suppliers and the new owners that have purchased the privatized assets. Those groups will not generally favor strong regulation, at least not initially.

LOCATION AND INDEPENDENCE OF THE REGULATORY FUNCTION. Regulation requires both a political mandate and freedom from narrow political agendas. An effective regulator must mediate among competing interests seeking to appropriate rents and understand how this affects sector performance. In particular, the regulator must issue and implement decisions that provide incentives for investment while it also must protect customers from potential monopoly abuses. Given the high sunken costs that characterize the telecommunications sector, an effective regulator must also produce credible and stable regulatory policies that promote investment by reducing the risk of expropriation of profits through regulation.

This regulatory capacity can be organized in a variety of institutional ways, ranging from dependence on antitrust legislation and tribunals and courts, to independent regulatory agencies, to locating telecommunications regulatory authority in a ministry. There is no unique formula for success. For example, locating the regulatory function in or under a ministry, as is the case in a number of countries (industrial as well as developing), rather than in an autonomous agency, makes regulation more responsive to broad government policy directions; this advantage, however, has to be balanced against the risk that the ruling powers may co-opt the regulator for self-serving political purposes, which may not be consistent with developing truly open and competitive markets or with effectively controlling the new owners of monopoly services. Nevertheless, locating telecommunications regulatory authority in an agency that is at least partly insulated from party politics and changes of government is more likely to be conducive to reducing investor risk and, thereby, to promoting investment to meet demand. Autonomy can be enhanced by full public exposure of all regulatory action, rules of engagement that restrict channels for the government to insert its political will in the regulatory agency's decisions, and financing that is independent from the annual budgetary cycle.

STEPS TOWARD BETTER REGULATION. The search for better regulatory solutions merits high priority in the design of sector reforms. The following partial steps can help.

Development of regulation is closely intertwined with that of market structure. Designing the sector reforms in ways that set up strong competitors in key market segments from the outset generates a demand by both the new entrants and the dominant operators for regulatory action and shifts the regulatory focus from economic issues to the more technical issues of interconnection and standards. There are, however, limits to how much competition a particular market can sustain.

There are important complementarities and trade-offs between telecommunications-specific regulation and broad regulation of commercial activities. Where effective antitrust legislation and enforcement mechanisms are in place, they may be relied upon to handle some of the matters that otherwise need sector-specific regulation. Some countries (such as New Zealand) have chosen initially to leave all telecommunications regulation to the latter mechanisms, while others (for example, Chile) resort to a mix of both. The jury is still out on the relative effectiveness of these arrangements.

Government action on regulation can be encouraged by creating political incentives through the creation of new constituencies. Of particular significance are building up competitors, consumer groups, and commercial user groups which will benefit economically from effective regulation, and giving these groups a forum to express their interests to the government and to the regulatory body.

Major regulatory decisions can be built into sales contracts, concessions, or licenses granted to the operators rather than left to the incipient regulatory process. For example, the concession can define the terms and limits of competition, the required capital expansion of the network, and the prices or rules to set the prices to be charged. In particular, setting caps for real prices of baskets of services has the potential of simplifying price regulation, providing the operator with incentives to contain costs as well as a degree of freedom to rebalance tariffs to reflect changing factors, and affording some protection to consumers. Some self-enforcement can be expected to follow. Substantial implementation and oversight problems, however, typically remain. For example, tariff rebalancing and the regulation of the interface between competitive and monopoly segments of the businesses cannot be left to self-enforcement alone, partly because there is a large imbalance in resources and information between the dominant operators and other players. Also, key parameters must be changed over time. For example, the targets for service growth and quality cannot be set in advance for the duration of a concession (typically twenty years or more) but may have to be revised, say, every five years. The productivity gain factor in a price-cap formula has to be adjusted from time to time in the light of actual evolution of costs.[60] Lastly, contracts are not particularly effective in some countries.

The regulatory function could be divided into discrete tasks, some of which may be subcontracted. Possibilities (so far untested) include retaining internationally reputable audit firms to monitor compliance with franchise and other obligations (or requiring the main operating companies to retain such firms to report periodically to the regulator); contracting out recurrent regulatory procedures and conflict resolution to local management or legal consultants, probably with foreign associates for specialized assistance; adopting technical standards and type approvals from another country; and retaining the spectrum management agency of another country to set up a local branch backed up by the agency's established norms, practices, processing hardware and software, and expertise.

Other possibilities to improve regulation include arbitration of disputes, government's appointing a public counsel to press for and assist in regulatory actions, and establishing an advisory board representing users and other key interests and charged with setting an agenda for the regulator.

PRACTICAL LIMITS TO REGULATORY DESIGN. Development of regulation, like privatization, is not a one-shot affair but rather a political process, and it will struggle with the same problems as the broader government. The quality and progress of the telecommunications sector will be tied to those of the country as a whole. Structures that are possible and necessary in the more advanced developing economies that have vigorous participation in competitive global markets may be neither affordable nor really necessary in lesser ones.

In many cases, regulatory arrangements that seem optimal from a sectoral viewpoint may not be feasible, and compromise solutions become necessary. In particular, the economic benefits of improved services following privatization of a state enterprise may well outweigh the rents captured by an imperfectly regulated monopoly. In some countries, having to pay high prices for communication, which accounts for only a small proportion of total cost of most businesses, may be less of a handicap to users than lack of good services. As an extreme example, entrusting services to an experienced foreign investor-operator may quickly remove communication bottlenecks in critical productive sectors, even if the absence of competition and effective regulation may keep prices high and compromise the pace of future innovation.

In all situations, earlier and more prominent attention to the regulatory component of sector reform is an essential anticipatory response to such inevitable difficulties. Increasingly, this is also signaling the need for more pro-competitive reform designs.

Telecommunications Reform and the Political System

Telecommunications reforms do not occur in isolation from the broader economic and social changes taking place in developing countries. The linkages to economic policy and strategy have already been briefly noted. More generally, it is increasingly recognized that the timing and drive for telecommunications reforms, several key features of the sector solutions, and the ways governments go about preparing and implementing reforms, are all closely related to the country's political environment. In particular, a country's political institutions and electoral arrangements, the interests of constituent groups, and the role of the judiciary and of the government bureaucracy, are likely to be key determinants of policy outcomes and reform features.[61] Conversely, the effectiveness of particular sectoral solutions, and indeed, whether they are at all viable, are largely conditioned by country- and time-specific political factors.

Yet the political dimension of sector reform, in telecommunications as much as in other public services, is given only casual attention by practitioners. In recent years, however, valuable research has begun that should help improve on this state of affairs.

One approach of recent research is based on the modern theory of institutions, which emphasizes informational, commitment, and transaction cost considerations in understanding the role of economic and political institutions. In this framework, Brian Levy and Pablo Spiller have focused on the credibility of arrangements that limit arbitrary change of the "rules of the game" by the government, which is necessary to attract large and sustained private investment.[62] A comparative analysis of five industrial and developing countries with private telecommunications operations suggests that the design of regulatory systems can usefully be viewed at two distinct levels: the "basic engineering" of the regulatory system establishes the mechanisms to constrain regulatory discretion and resolve conflicts that arise in relation to these constraints, while the "detailed engineering" defines the rules governing pricing, market entry, interconnection, and other regulatory decisions. The study suggests that, in order to limit administrative discretion, the basic engineering must include substantive restraints on the regulator embedded in the regulatory system, formal or informal constraints on changing the regulatory system, and institutions that enforce these constraints. A country's institutional endowment is therefore an important determinant of whether it can credibly put in place a regulatory system that meets these requirements. Of particular importance are the judiciary's structure, organization, and tradition of independence; the nature and structure of the legislative and executive; and informal norms.[63] Some countries will only be able to restrain arbitrary administrative action by erecting institutions that substantially limit regulatory flexibility and hence narrow the range of possible detailed engineering solutions. For example, efficient regulatory rules, such as price-cap regulation, require institutional foundations which are likely to be absent in many low-income countries. Rules that appear optimal from a sectoral viewpoint may require a basic engineering that is not feasible in a particular country, and thus the country may have to settle for less than optimal solutions.[64] In the absence of an institutional endowment required for workable regulation, however, a country may find it possible to commit to stable rules of the game through the use of certain modalities of privatization,[65] or perhaps by using international substitutes for the missing national foundations.[66]

Another research approach looks at telecommunications regulation from the viewpoint of allocation of property rights and competition as the main determinants of investment and of allocative and technical efficiency in a private economy. By focusing on the linkages between political incentives and institutions, the reallocation of property rights implied in sector reform, and changes in the regulatory regime, Cowhey has sketched the beginnings of a theory of telecommunications regulation in developing countries. Observations in several countries suggest that the regulatory arrangements that can be expected in different countries are closely tied to the forms of government.[67]

The results of these lines of inquiry are very promising. The analysis of telecommunications development, which in the 1960s emphasized engineering and finance, in the 1970s discovered economics and institution building, and in the 1980s again expanded its scope to include sector policy and regulation driven by global technology and demand, might in the 1990s encompass the practical links of all this with the countries' political and institutional realities. The research illustrates the value of so doing. It also provides some guidance on what to look for during the design of sector reforms: a checklist of political and institutional aspects could be produced momentarily, for use in the course of sector analysis.

Further research would be well justified. For example, creating conditions that attract investment (the central concern of Levy and Spiller) is a necessary, but not sufficient, condition of successful reform. Economic efficiency and equity, however, which are equally important objectives of reform, have so far received only passing attention. The research illustrates that these objectives are to an important extent in conflict with one another. For example, in one of the countries studied by Levy and Spiller, a sector structure and regulatory design explained by the need to establish government credibility with investors has been accompanied by large economic inefficiencies—lack of incentives or controls to contain capital and operating costs, very distorted price structure, large and growing cross-subsidies, and sweeping and permanent monopoly privileges. The argument that this was the only possible sectoral solution in that country's political and institutional environment capable of attracting sustained private investment to ensure badly needed network growth and modernization, and that there was at best space for marginal improvements, is not convincing. Closer examination of the trade-offs among the growth, efficiency, and equity objectives of reform would probably show that a substantially better balance was possible. Also, recognition that sectoral designs are subject to changing forces would say something on reform as a dynamic process. For example, in the current world technological and market context, the country solution discussed above is unsustainable—the structure creates powerful incentives for bypass by users and for entry of new providers.[68] This will inevitably lead to the government's initiating further reforms despite its credible assurances of stability. The initial sector solution will largely determine the negotiating positions of government and the investors in this next round.

The test of the practical value of these new lines of inquiry will lie in their operational significance. Although research so far has been quite successful in explaining past events, it has had little to say on how things could have been done better, or how they could be improved in the future, or how they could be done well elsewhere. The road toward operationalizing the findings of research could start by including political economic analysis in the early stages of reform design in a small number (say, two or three) of countries[69] and in regional telecommunications reform studies.[70] In addition to testing the practical significance of adding a new dimension to sector analysis, these countries' experiences would surely be of value in setting the agenda for further research.

Endnotes

1. In a number of places this chapter draws (often verbatim) on Björn Wellenius and others, "Telecommunications: World Bank Experience and Strategy," World Bank Discussion Paper (Washington, DC: World Bank, March 1993). Both were developed more or less in parallel, and improvements in one were incorporated in the other. Thus, this chapter owes much to many Bank staff and managers who participated in the discussion of successive drafts of the strategy paper. Cross-references and quotations are omitted from both documents.

2. Timothy E. Nulty, "Emerging Issues in World Telecommunications," in *Restructuring and Managing the Telecommunications Sector*, ed. B. Wellenius, P. A. Stern, T. E. Nulty, and R. D. Stern, A World Bank Symposium (Washington, DC: World Bank, 1989).

3. Efforts to study the relationships between telecommunications and economic development began in the mid–1960s, peaked probably in the late 1970s, and tailed off rapidly in the early 1980s. By that time a fragmented but fairly comprehensive picture of the development role of telecommunications had been pieced together, and new studies largely confirmed earlier findings without breaking new ground. For a comprehensive overview of analytic techniques and results, as well as an extensive bibliography, see R. J. Saunders, J. J. Warford, and B. Wellenius, *Telecommunications and Economic Development* (Baltimore and London: The Johns Hopkins University Press, 1983; rev. ed. 1993).

Nonetheless, in contrast with, say, power and transportation, telecommunications were never fully integrated into the development debate (Jan Bjerninger, Swedish International Development Authority, Seminar on Economic and Financial Analysis of Telecommunications Projects, Uppsala, Sweden, March 1991) and received only spotty attention from government planners and development agencies.

From the mid–1980s, the shift toward economic development strategies that increasingly emphasize domestic and international competitiveness resulted in business and political forces bringing government attention to telecommunications. In this context, the interest of analysts has shifted from questions of resource allocation (what should be telecommunications' share of scarce government and aid resources?) to questions of creating an environment in which telecommunications can be effectively run as a business capable of attracting the necessary capital, management, and technology.

Questions on the development role of telecommunications, however, are being revisited in terms of the potential of information technologies for redeveloping rural areas and regions based on declining industries in the United States and other highly industrial countries. See, for example, Edwin B. Parker, Heather E. Hudson, Don A. Dillman, and Andrew D. Roscoe, *Rural America in the Information Age— Telecommunications Policy for Rural Development* (Lanham, MD and London, England: The Aspen Institute and University Press of America, 1989).

4. Loosely speaking, the information sector comprises all activities that involve the production, processing, and distribution of information and knowledge, as distinct from physical goods. It includes activities that primarily comprise the handling of information, such as banking and government, as well as the information components of other activities, such as accounting in a factory and management of a farm. The information sector thus includes activities traditionally counted under the primary, secondary, and tertiary sectors. The information sector has been quantified by a number of researchers in the U. S., Europe, and Japan, from the 1950s. Data for developing countries are more limited. Several studies in the Asia and Pacific region in the early 1980s, using data of the late 1970s, however, give some indicative figures of the information sector as proportion of GDP, for example, Singapore 25 percent, Indonesia 19 percent, Malaysia 14 percent. See, for example, Meheroo Jussawalla, Donald M. Lamberton, and Neil D. Karunaratne, *The Cost of Thinking—Information Economies of Ten Pacific Countries* (Norwood, N.J.: Ablex Publishing Corporation, 1988).

5. Timothy E. Nulty, "Emerging Issues in World Telecommunications," in *Restructuring and Managing the Telecommunications Sector,* ed. B. Wellenius, P. A. Stern, T. E. Nulty, and R. D. Stern, A World Bank Symposium (Washington, DC: World Bank, 1989).

6. The main exceptions being the United States, Canada, and Finland.

7. A checklist of matters that need to be addressed through sector policies, regulation, and legislation, is given in International Telecommunication Union, "The Changing Telecommunications Environment: Policy Considerations for the Members of the ITU" (Geneva, Switzerland: International Telecommunication Union, February 1989), p. 37.

8. Although this is fairly obvious in industrial countries, only in recent years has it begun to be widely accepted in the developing world. One of the main contributions of the ITU's advisory group on telecommunications policy was to send this message unambiguously. The ITU's Plenipotentiary Conference of 1989 endorsed the group's recommendations and brought them to the attention of all member governments. See ITU, "The Changing Telecommunications Environment: Policy Considerations for the Members of the ITU" (Geneva, Switzerland: International Telecommunication Union, February 1989).

9. It has been proposed that subcontracting can also be an effective tool among different organizational units of the same operating company. See Robert R. Bruce, "Franchising and Subcontracting for Services and Facilities: New Options for Attracting New Sources of Investment," Roundtable on Eastern European Telecommunications, Badacsonytomaj, Hungary, May 1991. This concept is also developed in this book's chapters by Bruce (2), and by Bruce, Cunard, and Kneifel (31).

10. S. Kikeri, J. Nellis, and M. Shirley, *Privatization: the Lessons of Experience* (Washington, DC: World Bank, 1992).

11. For example, the sale of state-owned shares in Teléfonos de Mexico yielded about US$4 billion. Annual net flows of funds from TELMEX to the treasury have also increased, despite abolition of the special telephone tax, as a result of ending government contributions to investment and rapidly growing taxable profits.

12. For example, sale of the telephone company allowed the Argentine government to recover about US$5 billion of state bonds from foreign markets.

13. The new facilities can be operated by the private investor, by the existing telecommunications company under lease, revenue sharing, or other arrangements, or by new operators created for this purpose.

14. Subscriber financing can also be used to diversify company ownership or as a price mechanism to allocate scarce supply efficiently.

15. *Competition* is a big word that includes a wide range of possible modalities, from competitive award of time-limited monopoly or duopoly to minimally regulated entry to unrestricted competition. The following are examples: (a) international competitive bidding for a ten-year license to provide cellular services in a given region (more than one or two cellular operators are seldom possible in terms of market size and radio spectrum capacity); (b) competitive supply of subscriber terminal equipment (for example, telephone sets, PBXs) subject to technical standards and type

approval to ensure network compatibility; (c) unrestricted competition in the provision of shared data processing, information, electronic mail, packet-switched data, and store-and-forward facsimile, and telex.

16. For example, to quickly upgrade existing networks (as in Eastern Germany following unification) and for disaster relief.

17. Timothy E. Nulty and Eric Schneidewinde, "Regulatory Policy for Telecommunications," in *Restructuring and Managing the Telecommunications Sector,* ed. B. Wellenius, P. A. Stern, T. E. Nulty, and R. D. Stern, A World Bank Symposium (Washington, DC: World Bank, 1989).

18. Early development of regulatory frameworks and institutional arrangements are needed to monitor operator performance, prevent abuses of market power, and promote the development of competition. Alternatively, temporary arrangements could be made to overview the transition from public to private ownership and deal with regulatory matters that require attention while a more permanent capability is built up.

19. This appears to be the case even in New Zealand, where government policy was to have no sector-specific regulation. In late 1991 the minister responsible for telecommunications warned that he would intervene and change this policy if the country's rival operators did not resolve their differences. Two new operators were complaining that Telecom New Zealand, the former state company sold in 1990 to a consortium led by two U.S. regional telephone companies (Bell Atlantic and Ameritech), was not upholding its obligations and was trying to use its near-monopoly position to crowd them out. Specific disagreements related to interconnection and billing information.

20. For an excellent analysis of the requirement of large multinationals in the automotive, banking, electronics, and other industries to configure, manage, and control their own telecommunications capabilities to adapt to a more competitive international environment, see François Bar and Michael Borrus, "Information Networks and Competitive Advantages: The Issues for Government Policy and Corporate Strategy," presented at a seminar on Information Networks and Business Strategies, Berkeley Roundtable on the International Economy (BRIE), Paris, October 19–20, 1989. One of the key findings of this OECD-BRIE user group study was the need for countries to achieve an optimal balance of regulation and competition to realize flexibility as well as integration and diversity. Too much regulation sacrifices flexibility, but too little regulation leads to network fragmentation, network incompatibility, and needless redundancy.

21. Source: "The Service Economy," Coalition of Service Industries (CSI), April 1992, Washington, DC, and additional information provided by Marie Eli of CSI and Zaharo Sofianou of the Boston Company Economic Advisors Inc., New York. These statistics, however, pertain only to cross-border sales of services. Sales of services through affiliates of U.S. companies in other countries are not considered balance of payments transactions and are not included in normal trade figures. They are, however, significant and important. For example, in 1989 (the last year for which statistics are available), sales of services through foreign affiliates of U.S. firms

amounted to nearly US$100 billion, which is nearly five times the positive services trade balance for that year.

22. The contribution of each of these key sectors to the overall positive U.S. cross-border services trade balance in 1991 was as follows:

Sector	Balance (US$ billion)
Royalties and License Fees	13.8
Travel	11.8
Business, Professional and Technical Services	7.8
Education	5.0
Passenger Fares	5.0
Financial Services	2.3
Other Transportation	0.3
Insurance	-0.6
Telecommunications	-2.8
Other	9.6
Overall U.S. Cross-border Services Trade Balance	52.2

The negative figure for telecommunications is due in large part to the net outpayments of U.S. international carriers in their telephone traffic with the rest of the world and which were between US$2 billion and US$3 billion. (Source: Coalition of Service Industries, Washington, DC, the Boston Company Economic Advisors Inc., New York, and the Bureau of Economic Analysis, New York.) Lester Thurow of MIT does not believe there is much scope for growth of services trade in the U.S. economy. He does not feel that services are worth fighting for in the Uruguay Round. See Lester Thurow, *Head to Head: The Coming Economic Battle Among Japan, Europe and America* (New York: William Morrow, 1992).

23. The U.S. government and U.S. international carriers have unrelentingly been pursuing the reduction of accounting rates, the tariff permit of traffic applied between international carriers in each bilateral relations. Above-cost accounting rates accompanied by large traffic imbalances result in net settlement outpayments by the international carrier which sends out more traffic than it receives. The U.S. government in support of its international carriers has lobbied other governments through the OECD, the European Commission, the ITU, and the GATT to have their international carriers agree to substantial lowering of accounting rates in their relations with U.S. international carriers.

24. Descriptions of reform in the United States, the United Kingdom, Japan, and New Zealand can be found in Henry Geller, "U.S. Telecommunications Policy: Increasing Competition and Deregulation"; John A. C. King, "The Privatization of Telecommunications in the United Kingdom"; Nubuyoshi Mutoh, "Deregulation of Japan's Telecommunications Business and the Role of Kokusai Denshin Denwa"; and

Donald E. Murphy, "New Zealand: From Post Office to Telecommunications Corporation," respectively, in *Restructuring and Managing the Telecommunications Sector,* ed. B. Wellenius, P. A. Stern, T. E. Nulty, and R. D. Stern, A World Bank Symposium (Washington, DC: World Bank, 1989). See also chapter 15 of this book by Bruce Laidlaw, "The Evolution of Telecommunications Policy in the United Kingdom," for a discussion of the U.K. experience, and chapter 14 by Herbert Ungerer, "The European Situation: An Overview," for a discussion of the EC Green Paper.

25. Eric Huret in chapter 16 of this book, "Restructuring Telecommunications: The French Experience," describes the extensive consultation process undertaken by the French government before reforming its telecommunications sector. The United Kingdom and European Commission have used discussion papers and invited comment before finalizing policy. In Canada, after a proposed new telecommunications law was introduced in the House of Commons in February 1992, it was referred to a Standing Committee of the Senate for "pre-study." Over a two-month period, the committee heard from more than ninety witnesses representing thirty organizations from all parts of the Canadian telecommunications industry and users. As a result of these consultations, the committee recommended that a number of changes be made to the draft law. Most of these recommended changes were taken into account when the draft law was sent to the House of Commons for Second Reading more than one year later. A good review of the Canadian legislative process and discussion of the proposed new law can be found in Hudson N. Janisch, "New Federal Telecommunications Legislation and Federal-Provincial Arrangements," The National Conference on the Future of Telecommunications Policy in Canada, Toronto, April 1–2, 1993.

26. Share prices in some privatizations, like that of British Telecom in the United Kingdom, have been deliberately underpriced to allow shareholders to make some initial capital gains. This has been used effectively to attract a public which has not traditionally bought and traded shares to become shareholders in private companies.

27. In a letter announcing the choice of the successful bidder for the purchase of Teleglobe Canada, Canada's international telecommunications carrier, the minister of state for privatization stated that the government had taken the necessary dispositions concerning the conditions of the sale to take into account the employees' concerns with respect to employment security, union collective agreements, a new pension plan equivalent at least to that in the rest of the industry, an ESOP offering at least a 5 percent share in the new company, and the maintaining of the headquarters of the company in the city of Montreal (Privatization of Teleglobe Canada, letter by Barbara McDougall, Minister of State for Privatization, dated February 11, 1987). Memotec, the successful bidder, offered existing employees a pension plan equivalent to that of the federal civil service as well as 5 percent of the shares of the company with a 10 percent reduction off the purchase price of the company and a five-year interest-free loan to facilitate purchase of the shares.

28. See, for example, Hunter Donaldson, "Telecommunications Liberalization and Privatization: The New Zealand Experience," chapter 11 of this book. In Japan NTT has reduced its staff by 70,000 since it was privatized in 1985. There are similar

examples of staff reductions in the United Kingdom, Canada, the United States, and other countries. When the president of AGT Ltd., the privately owned telecommunications company in the Canadian province of Alberta, recently announced that the company was laying off 1,200 people out of a total of 8,000, he said, "It's never going to be the same again as it was in the old monopoly days. We can no longer afford to be all things to all people" (The *Globe and Mail,* Toronto, April 16, 1993).

29. See for example, Henry Geller, "U.S. Telecommunications Policy: Increasing Competition and Deregulation," in *Restructuring and Managing the Telecommunications Sector,* ed. B. Wellenius, P. A. Stern, T. E. Nulty, and R. D. Stern, A World Bank Symposium (Washington, DC: World Bank, 1989), for a discussion of the failure of boundary lines in the United States. Robert Bruce, "Restructuring the Telecommunications Sector: Experience in Some Industrialized Countries and Implications for Policymakers," chapter 2 of this book, discusses some of the issues raised by the market segmentation policy in Japan. A very detailed analysis of the boundary line issues in the United States, the United Kingdom, Japan, France, the Netherlands, Canada, and a number of other industrial countries in relation to enhanced and value added services can be found in R. R. Bruce, J. P. Cunard, M. D. Director, *The Telecom Mosaic, Assembling the New International Structure* (London: Butterworths, 1988).

30. See discussion on the regulatory role of the state in chapter 32 of this book by Richard J. Schultz.

31. Following the divestiture of AT&T in 1984 the FCC treated competitors to AT&T such as MCI and Sprint as "nondominant"; that is, they were not subject to the same regulatory obligations (such as the requirement to file tariffs) as was AT&T. AT&T appealed this practice, and in November 1992 the U.S. Court of Appeals ruled that the Communications Act of 1934 did not give the FCC the authority to adopt such a policy. MCI, Sprint, and other nondominant carriers have since then been required to file tariffs with the FCC, which is now, in the light of the court's ruling, proposing to streamline their filing requirements.

32. Teleglobe Canada was a state enterprise (Crown Corporation) for thirty-seven years before it was privatized in 1987. It was set up as a corporation when the assets of Cable & Wireless and Marconi were nationalized in 1950 to form the Canadian Overseas Telecommunications Corporation, the predecessor to Teleglobe Canada.

33. See note 26 above.

34. This was the case with the privatization of Telecom Corporation of New Zealand; see chapters by Tucker (23) and Donaldson (11) in this book. In Canada, Teleglobe Canada was sold to a single buyer, Memotec, which was, however, a publicly held share company.

35. For further details and numerical examples from the late 1980s, see R. J. Saunders, J. J. Warford, and B. Wellenius, *Telecommunications and Economic Development* (Baltimore and London: The Johns Hopkins University Press, second edition, 1993).

36. Expressed demand is the sum of connected line plus outstanding applications. Total demand is generally much higher, as prospective customers do not bother to apply when they are aware that service takes years to be provided, and telephone

companies usually do not accept applications in areas where service expansion is not planned.

37. Total telecommunications investment in the developing world is estimated to have grown from about US$3 billion in the 1970s to US$7 billion in the 1980s and to US$11 billion in the late 1980s, all in 1990 dollars. These are tentative figures based on international statistics on growth in telephone lines and average investment cost per line under World Bank projects.

38. This is the total investment in public telecommunications divided by the net addition of telephone lines in the same period. It provides some indication of the average cost of adding one line, including all parts of the network—subscriber set and installations, cable network, local exchanges, interexchange and long-distance transmission and switching, international facilities. The average varies considerably among countries and enterprises, from less than US$1,000 to over US$5,000 per line, depending on the size, density, and coverage of the network, procurement and financing arrangements, quality of management, and other factors.

39. The inflationary impact of increases in telecommunications tariffs is likely to be negligible, since telecommunications accounts for only a small fraction of production costs. Government measures to combat inflation, however, often do not distinguish among individual public services, and telecommunications tariffs are controlled together with those of transportation, water, electricity, and other services which, taken together, do have a significant impact on inflation.

40. Björn Wellenius, "Telecommunications in the Developing World: Current Trends and New Issues," paper presented at a symposium to honor Professor Kenneth Cattermole, University of Essex, Colchester, Essex, England, September 1990.

41. Several countries in the Caribbean have also gone through substantial changes in the ownership of their telecommunications sectors, but these continue to be organized as traditional monopolies. For example, in Jamaica in 1967 the foreign-owned domestic telephone company was taken over by the state, in 1971 the separate foreign-owned international services company was reorganized as a joint venture with the state, and in 1987 all services were merged into a state/private joint venture with complete monopoly for the duration of the franchise. In several other countries the state monopolies were sold to foreign private operators without much other change (for example, Belize).

42. The seminar on which this book is largely based included a number of participants from Africa but did not specifically address the particular concerns of Africa. Follow-up seminars have subsequently been organized to respond to that interest. The first one, for francophone countries, took place in Tunis, Tunisia, in May 1992.

43. It has sometimes been said that underdevelopment is largely a matter of lack of management capability. This point was made, probably not for the first time, by Radomiro Tomic, a candidate to the presidency of Chile in 1970. (He lost.)

44. About thirty economists, engineers, accountants, and lawyers is probably the minimum needed to staff all basic regulatory functions. See Nulty and Schneidewinde, "Regulatory Policy for Telecommunications" in *Restructuring and Managing the Telecommunications Sector,* ed. B. Wellenius, P. A. Stern, T. E. Nulty, and R. D.

Stern, A World Bank Symposium (Washington, DC: World Bank, 1989). When this was pointed out to a team designing a reform plan for a relatively small Latin American country in 1992, experts who knew the country well commented that there probably were fewer than thirty economists in the whole country!

45. Abstracted from Desmond Watkins, "Debt Exchange: Financing Privatization and Reducing Country Debt," chapter 30 of this book.

46. This paragraph is partly taken from Desmond Watkins, *op. cit.*

47. In Argentina, Telefónica de Argentina, the southern regional company owned by a consortium led by Telefónica de España, earned taxable profits during the 1991–92 financial year of US$293.2 million, 81 percent higher than the year before. During the same period the net profits of Telecom Argentina, the northern regional company owned by a consortium led by France Télécom and the Italian STET, were US$150.3 million, a 172 percent increase over the previous year. Profits at Telefónica de Argentina during the first half of the 1992–93 financial year were up 53 percent. Telefónica de Argentina has been able to finance 80 percent of its investment program from retained earnings ("Profits at Argentine Telecoms Group Soar," *Financial Times,* May 18, 1993).

48. AOTC and AUSSAT are now known as Telstra and Optus, respectively.

49. Subsequently the 1990–91 duopoly review did involve a consultative process in which interested parties and some individuals participated.

50. Mark Fowler, "Privatization as an Objective: The Case of Telecommunications," keynote address of the closing dinner of the seminar which originated this book.

51. For example, sale price can be enhanced by giving the new owners extended monopoly privileges, whereas reducing service costs and promoting responsiveness and innovation requires competition and regulation.

52. S. Kikeri, J. Nellis, and M. Shirley, *Privatization: The Lessons of Experience* (Washington, DC: World Bank, 1992).

53. It is often said, correctly, that today's extensive networks in industrial countries were built with the help of extensive cross-subsidies facilitated by integrating all services under monopoly operators. This is one of the arguments given in favor of limiting competition in basic services and networks for a long initial protection period following privatization. On the other hand, in increasingly market-oriented international and domestic environments, rebalancing monopoly tariffs to reflect costs becomes a major objective of sector policy along the way toward creating conditions for effective and sustainable competition. Moreover, these two objectives are not mutually exclusive and can be reconciled, for instance, by a mix of tariff rebalancing to render local services profitable, attracting new entrants to the basic networks business, and allowing interconnection charges that reflect the value of basic network expansion to other operators.

54. A growing number of major telecommunications operating companies from industrial countries are getting into ventures in developing countries as part of strategies to globalize their business. Some of them are already now involved in several developing countries, and the trend is likely to continue. There are limits, however, to the pace at which these companies can divert internal human and

financial resources to foreign ventures, and in the context of a growing number of opportunities, the companies can be increasingly selective.

55. The size and relative importance of the presence of experienced foreign operators varies considerably, from rather marginal in the companies that already were good performers before privatization (such as Chile's CTC) to critical where major overhauls are required (such as Argentina), with the middle ground occupied by companies where foreign experts play an important advisory role but are not centrally involved in management (for example, Mexico).

56. International capital markets may have little interest in emerging companies located in relatively risky countries, where many future privatizations will be attempted, or they may require returns so high as to be politically unacceptable. Developing-country capital markets already appear to be too small to meet the requirements of several privatized companies. Although in the initial years internally generated funds are likely to meet most of a company's investment requirements, a better mix of sources of funds, including fresh equity capital and long-term debt, will be essential to sustain growth in the longer run. And in most developing countries, a large proportion of telecommunications equipment will continue to be imported, posing a burden on the balance of payments. The problems of raising capital may be especially acute for telecommunications companies, given this sector's high capital intensity, large initial investments required to modernize and expand facilities, and mainly local currency revenues.

57. The government's expectation of sustained commitment by foreign operators is often reflected in the new sector laws and regulations, the terms and conditions of sale, and the transfer contracts and franchises, all of which provide for medium- and long-term incentives and obligations. In certain cases, however, it can be argued that the foreign operator has mainly secured a profitable management contract supplemented by a minor equity interest, and that under those conditions the cost of exiting could be lower than that of staying if things get rough. Others, however, point out that major operating companies, intent on building up an international presence, are unlikely to walk out or do less than their best.

58. For example, in Chile issues of new entry to the basic services market have been under review by the telecommunications regulatory agency and litigated in the antitrust and regular courts for several years without coming to closure. This has delayed new service offerings to customers who would benefit from competition and has immobilized substantial amounts of equipment purchased by one of the operating companies. In Argentina, lack of resolution by the regulator regarding clarifications of the scope of the concessions of the two regional privatized operating companies reportedly has resulted in slower investment than would otherwise have been the case.

59. Much of this and the following two sections draw on World Bank staff discussion of alternative regulatory schemes, and on a summary note prepared by Nicholas Miller in early 1992.

60. It is difficult to estimate before the fact how quickly productivity can improve following reform. Experience in Mexico, for example, only a little over one year after

privatization, suggested that the price-cap formula underestimated widely the initial gains from accelerated growth, technological change, and competitive procurement. In the United Kingdom, successive increases in the productivity offset of the price cap may be interpreted along similar lines.

61. Pablo T. Spiller, "Regulation, Institutions and Economic Efficiency: Promoting Regulatory Reform and Private Sector Participation in Developing Countries," research proposal submitted to the World Bank, December 5, 1991.

62. This paragraph is adapted from B. Levy and P. Spiller, "Regulation, Institutions and Commitment in Telecommunications: A Comparative Analysis of Five Country Studies," World Bank Seminar on The Institutional Foundations of Utility Regulation: Research Results and Their Operational Implications, Washington, DC, April 16, 1993.

63. The institutional endowment of a country comprises (a) the legislative and executive institutions of government, including formal mechanisms for appointing legislators, making and implementing laws and regulations, and determining the relations between the legislative and executive; (b) the judicial institutions, including formal mechanisms for appointing judges, determining the structure of the judiciary, and impartially resolving disputes among private parties as well as between private parties and the government; (c) custom and other informal but widely accepted norms that tacitly constrain the actions of individuals and institutions; (d) administrative capabilities; and (e) contending social interests, the balance among them, and the role of ideology.

64. This emphasizes the difficulty of transplanting regulatory designs from one country to another.

65. For example, wide distribution of share ownership limits the opportunity and increases the political cost to government of reneging on commitments made to the newly privatized company (for example, the United Kingdom). Also, the credibility of the terms and conditions of a telecommunications privatization that is the flagship of a broader public sector reform program is protected by the government's need to be seen to meet its obligations as a factor of success of the remainder of the program (for example, Argentina).

66. For example, international guarantees against noncommercial risk, underwritten by the government.

67. For further details, see Peter F. Cowhey's chapter, "The Political Economy of Telecommunications Reform in Developing Countries," later in this book.

68. Including spurious businesses that are only viable while the factors of inefficiency remain in place.

69. The choice of countries could usefully be in terms of *a priori* likelihood that political economic analysis will have a significant impact in the outcomes. (It is unclear, however, what are the relevant selection criteria.)

70. Such as a World Bank study under way on the prospects for telecommunications reform in Africa, or partial reinterpretation of a similar study being finalized in Asia.

Part I

Current State of

Telecommunications Policy

and Structural Issues

1

Telecommunications Reform in Developing Countries: Importance and Strategy in the Context of Structural Change

Peter R. Scherer

TECHNOLOGICAL PROGRESS IS CHANGING the ways of communicating and doing business at breathtaking speed. This process constitutes an opportunity for and a threat to governments and businesses alike. Those who use the process effectively will enhance economic growth and gain markets; those who fail to do so simply will lose out. Modern telecommunications systems and user flexibility have become important parameters in promoting economic development. Governments in developing countries in particular are faced with the challenge of harnessing effectively a complex array of technologies and systems which have tremendous potential for enhancing social welfare but pose heavy demands on organizational and financial capabilities. Surprisingly though, telecommunications reforms in many developing countries are being driven more by myopic fiscal and debt management concerns than considerations of strategic development.

The purpose of this chapter is to analyze key elements of telecommunications reform in the broader context of interlocking structural changes for enhancing economic efficiency and growth in developing countries. The chapter is based on the following presuppositions:

- The quality and range of telecommunications services has become a strategic element in determining a country's competitiveness in an increasingly globalized economy.

- The success of developing countries in improving telecommunications services, and in reaping the benefits from such improvements, is linked intrinsically to progress in broader reforms in the macroeconomic environment and in public enterprises.

- Telecommunications reform can be used effectively as a spearhead for changing contractual relationships and improving business practices in the economy at large.

• Although developing countries can choose from a menu of strategic options in sequencing the reform of telecommunications, they will not make much progress unless they unshackle the sector from the constraints that typically are imposed on government-managed public utilities and introduce competition.

The chapter concludes by setting forth a number of premises devised from institutional experience as a framework for designing telecommunications sector reform.

Global Competition: Challenge and Opportunities

Business is going global. The output of transnational corporations and international trade has been growing at more than twice the rate of world output. Aggregate telecommunications output and productivity growth have outpaced corresponding macroeconomic parameters by a multiple of three. International telephone traffic has grown at five times the rate of world output. It is estimated that the information sector now accounts for more than one-third of gross domestic product in most countries of the Organization for Economic Cooperation and Development. The high quality of telecommunications systems and services has become a critical determinant of economic competitiveness. Farsighted policymakers therefore are increasingly focusing on telecommunications, and more broadly, on information technology not merely as an element of supporting infrastructure but as a driving force of economic growth.

Information technology capability (commonly defined as the integration of computing and telecommunications hardware and software) is being used increasingly as a strategic instrument for gaining market share and for entering new markets. Improved communications and computational capabilities enable firms to grow larger, become more complex, and enter into joint production and servicing arrangements. In the process, national labels and boundaries are losing meaning and importance. National economies are becoming increasingly interdependent; telecommunications is a major driving force in this development, leading to global markets, global competitors, and global marketing strategies. Hence, decisions on the location of manufacturing plants, design studies, and research facilities increasingly are made with a view to gaining advantages from a global reach.

Business activities that depend on telecommunications and information-processing facilities go beyond financial services, commodity markets, media, transportation, and tourism. Communication services by now have become vital links between manufacturers, wholesalers, and retailers. Some examples are manufacturers who link to a worldwide web of suppliers by means of electronic data interchange (EDI); retailers who coordinate fashion decisions for their stores through video and electronic mail; and service-oriented firms that receive customer complaints and dispatch service personnel from single command stations. Advanced information processing also has paved the way for introducing new work methods such as simultaneous engineering, synchronous manufacturing, and justin-time procurement; it provides strategic capabilities to achieve vertical integration of companies in the areas of manufacturing and marketing systems, inventory adjustment and reconciliation of purchase orders, capture of point-of-sale information, and analysis of market trends.

The ability to use information technology effectively will be among the determining factors in separating leaders from laggards in the world economy during the coming decade. As advances in information technology are driving the globalization of capital flows, trade, and manufacturing, opportunities for creating competitive advantage in international trade are being offered. These opportunities are not determined merely by the physical configuration of the telecommunications network. Firms need to have access to a broad choice of network alternatives, from integrated public services to private facilities and dedicated applications. Firms also need sufficient management and control flexibility to configure and reconfigure network choices in line with changes in corporate objectives.

As information networks have become the central nervous system of the global economy, they have developed into policy instruments to attract economic activities on a regional or national scale. The capacity of telecommunications services and the rules governing their use have become crucial factors for transnational corporations in locating regional headquarters as well as service and production sites. The government of Singapore, for example, has been using reliable, efficient, and sophisticated telecommunications facilities as a major incentive to develop the country into a center for international commerce, financial and banking services, transportation, and electronic publishing. Many transnationals have set up regional headquarters in Singapore. Singapore's container port has become number one worldwide, mainly because it is using advanced information technology to cut turnaround time to a fraction of that of competitor ports. In Europe, the United Kingdom and the Netherlands have been successful, through telecommunications liberalization and deregulation, in attracting increasing numbers of information-sensitive industries, as well as transport and financial services. These institutions and services have been acquired at the expense, among others, of Germany, which had maintained an entrenched and rigid structural service monopoly.

Gaining Competitiveness: Need for Structural Reform

Virtually all developing countries are undertaking structural reforms of some kind—varying in scope and depth—to enhance economic efficiency as a prerequisite toward increasing national welfare. The range and impact of telecommunications reform are intrinsically linked to this broader reform agenda. Successful restructuring toward international competitiveness typically would include actions in the following areas:

- Macroeconomic policies geared toward providing a stable business environment based on prudent fiscal, monetary, and exchange rate policies

- Effective competition policies combining phased import liberalization, changes in regulations to reduce barriers to entry and exit, and promotion of export rivalry

- Liberalization of factor and output prices combined with competitive deregulation of financial and capital markets

- Provision of effective institutional and infrastructure services, including the establishment of a credible administration, sound governance, and development of human resources, power, transport, and telecommunications.

A change in the role of government from predominantly selective (including direct management of utilities) to functional intervention has been a core element of the more successful reforms.

In a broad strategic sense, the conceptual framework for structural reform can be characterized as follows. Strengthening the competitiveness of a country's economy requires improvements in productivity, financial viability, and service quality of enterprises. Achieving these objectives, in turn, requires changes in the organization of enterprises, their incentive framework, and their way of doing business. The policy instruments for achieving these objectives seek to change both the enabling environment and the corporate domain of the enterprise. Changes in the environment focus on establishing efficiency prices to reflect economic scarcities through effective competition and regulation. Changes in the corporate domain focus on improving the capability of enterprises to respond to price signals and improvements in infrastructure through rational decisionmaking and organizational strengthening.

Government disengagement from direct intervention in the economy through control of strategic industries and infrastructure toward a system driven by market forces and competitive regulation would seem to be among the main conditions for successful restructuring in most developing countries. In theory a state-owned firm can operate as efficiently as a private firm if both function according to the same set of rules, regulations, and incentives. All too often, however, this is not the case in practice. On the one hand, governments tend to provide special protection and incentives to the state-owned companies. On the other hand, private enterprises with clearly defined profit incentives are more likely to emphasize discipline in imposing cost control, flexibility in responding to user demand, and new technology to increase efficiency.

Slow progress, and in many cases outright failure, in improving public sector services has put pressure on governments in developing as well as in industrial countries to disengage from managing industrial, commercial, and infrastructure activities. Public enterprises typically display some or all of the following characteristics: poor operating performance, unresponsive service, weak financial positions, bloated work force, inadequate capital investment, a cumbersome decisionmaking process, and distorted prices and tariffs. Generally it has been recognized that changes in the contractual relationships among stakeholders of state-owned companies are key to overcoming these deficiencies and that these changes can be achieved more effectively through private sector participation.

Contractual arrangements and business practices determine, within the context of a country's regulatory norms, the extent to which price signals reflect efficiency levels and to which companies respond effectively. Successful restructuring typically entails contractual changes in the following areas:

ADMINISTRATION. Central public administrations tend to interfere in core business transactions of public enterprises without having the requisite expertise and without having to account for mistakes. Overriding concerns with social objectives are often used to camouflage inefficiency and justify the absence of good business practices.

LABOR MANAGEMENT. Public officials tend to be less willing than private managers to face labor conflicts simply because of differences in the incentives for increasing labor productivity. As a consequence, labor union leaders typically have a tremendous grip on the management of public enterprises that frequently goes beyond salary issues to encompass personnel decisions and organizational, technological, and operational issues.

SUPPLIERS AND BUYERS. Suppliers want to sell at high prices and buyers want to purchase at low prices. Although this axiom applies generally, the scope for abuse is highest in a noncompetitive environment; it is higher in public than in private enterprises, where rents can be built into contracts more easily.

A rather solid body of international evidence would suggest that a commitment to change contractual relationships throughout the economy is a critical prerequisite in most developing countries for making full use of technological advances in offering better, wider, and more varied telecommunications services. The political and economic environment of a developing country thus essentially sets the stage for the design of telecommunications reform. The degree of political commitment to broad multisector restructuring, the ability to enhance factor mobility and supply response, and the suitability of the political process for reaching decisions on issues with economy-wide implications are the principal parameters that define the scope of sector reforms. Hence, the options for organizational and structural changes in telecommunications cannot be seen in isolation. Ultimately, the pace of reform and the extent to which its potential benefits can be harnessed will be contingent on the capability of governments to create an environment that promotes efficiency and enables private investment and initiative.

Modernizing Telecommunications: Effects of Technological Change

Rapidly developing information technologies are cause and consequence of the drive for global competitiveness. They are ushering in innovative types of telecommunications services that bring opportunities for business to reduce costs, to increase supply flexibility, and to gain advantage in the marketplace. As such, they are creating dynamics for organizational and institutional changes that have been taxing the management capabilities of industrial and developing countries alike. Basically, technological developments have altered the conditions of entry into the telecommunications sector and the role governments have been playing in the development of the sector.

Key among the technological changes which have been shaping the structure of telecommunications operators and the introduction of competition are the following:

- Microwave and signal-processing technology have led to a significant increase in private network capacity, with a concomitant differentiation in some countries between wholesalers who own networks and retailers who rely on the facilities of other carriers.

- Digital exchange technology allows users to route calls selectively through networks owned by different operators and to bill these calls appropriately.

- Advances in switching technology have resulted in lower costs of switching relative to transmission. This has paved the way for increasing decentralization by prompting users to install their own switches and manage their own networks.

- Similarly, synchronous digital hierarchy transmission systems are enhancing the commercial attractiveness of smaller networks by allowing the entry and exit of individual data streams from within broadband systems at a reasonable cost.

- Finally, satellite technology (using very small aperture terminals) and dramatic advances in cutting the costs of wireless radio-based telephony are effectively competing in basic telephone service with the traditional wireline facilities in both urban and rural areas.

These technological advances have made it possible for telecommunications service providers to enter the sector efficiently on a smaller scale than in the past. Although this development is made possible by the fall in the cost of equipment, it is also affected by the increased diversity in demand for telecommunications services. This is making it profitable for suppliers to offer specialized network services and features. Hence, new service providers can, using new technology, now enter on a smaller scale more cheaply than they could in the past on a larger scale using the older technology.

Technological advances cast a new light on the traditional argument for a proactive government role in telecommunications. This argument rests on the assumption that telecommunications is an infrastructure with inherent externalities; that is, benefits derived from telecommunications services cannot be captured fully by their provider. It is generally agreed that the telecommunications infrastructure serves a broad public interest because its existence promotes development of the economy at large. Yet a private owner of a basic network may not be willing (or able) to deploy speedily advanced technologies—such as an integrated services digital network (ISDN)—throughout the public network. Advanced technologies are needed to transmit sophisticated intracompany applications beyond company limits to partners or subcontractors in a network-based production process. Accelerated development of the public-switched network thus would seem necessary to meet this requirement. Seen from a different angle, individual corporate strategies, articulated around privately controlled networks, do not necessarily add up to optimal economy-wide exploitation of information networking technologies.

The challenge facing decisionmakers of developing countries in deciding on a development strategy for telecommunications is perhaps best exemplified in the different approaches adopted by France and the United States. In France, the strategic objective has centered on providing an integrated network through a government monopoly that features one of the world's highest rates of network digitization, the largest packet-switching network, and the national availability of ISDN service. To a large extent these services have been provided in anticipation of user demand. Thus, the telecommunications network in France is being used as a spearhead to promote economic activities and harness associated benefits that otherwise would have materialized only later, or not at all. In contrast, the overarching goal in the United States has been the competitive provision of a wide choice of networks and network services by the private sector. Competition is being relied upon as the driving force to bring down costs and to foster dynamic innovation in telecommunications equipment and services. As a result, large telecommunications users have unmatched access to a wide array of telecommunications resources and substantial freedom to control their deployment and use. The different approaches followed in the United States and France have resulted in significantly different telecommunications infrastructures and regulations in the two countries.

In deciding on the merits of selective intervention to develop an infrastructure that the private sector would not provide, governments in developing countries need to carefully ascertain their administrative, financial, and technical capabilities to take on this task. Although there is a risk of market failure, notably in the early stages of telecommunications development (when the coverage of the system has to be expanded rapidly to meet demand and social objectives), there also is a risk that government failure may exacerbate problems rather than solve them. Rapid technological evolution in telecommunications has brought great opportunities for expanding penetration, lowering costs, and upgrading services, thus affording developing countries an opportunity to leapfrog the stages of network development in industrial countries. At the same time these changes have added tremendous complexities to the work of designing, procuring, and managing telecommunications systems which are likely to overtax the capabilities of governments, and domestic private sectors for that matter, in most developing countries.

The need to go global in order to take advantage of the opportunities embodied in technological progress is manifest in the transformation of the traditional state telecommunications operating entities in industrial countries towards global business consortia with increasing transborder investment that aim at providing one-stop shopping for the client. This development is in large measure the result of pressure on competitive efficiency and greater productivity, which require the design of systems that stimulate service innovation, accelerate diffusion of technical innovation, and improve responsiveness to customer needs. This movement toward global networking appears to be proceeding at an inexorable and accelerating pace. Similarly, the increase in worldwide competition is causing communications equipment suppliers to polarize because of increasingly low margins, even on products such as packet switches and large multiplexers that were launched not that long ago. Suppliers are moving out of the pure product business and into services—systems integration, operation and management, and eventually facilities management. The effectiveness with which developing countries are able to tap into this world of fast-moving changes, protocols, architectures, and standards, and of transforming telecommunications service providers and equipment suppliers, will significantly affect their ability to carve out international-product market shares.

Defining a Telecommunications Strategy: Choice of Policy Instruments

It seems that developments are turning full circle from the early days of telephony, when telecommunications companies were in private hands. The arguments that led to their transformation into noncommercial utilities under government monopoly were based on the need to (a) realize the scale economies of the basic telecommunications network, (b) use revenues from profitable services to subsidize universal domestic service and perhaps other government activities, and (c) retain control of a strategic infrastructure for political, social, economic, and defense programs. Developments in the last decade have changed this scenario drastically. On the one hand, quantum jumps in technology have rendered these presumptions largely obsolete; on the other hand, traditional government-operated telephone utilities have not performed well in the face of surging consumer demand for new, better, and faster telecommunications services.

The options for organizational and structural changes in telecommunications cannot be seen in isolation from the plans for change in other sectors. Still, success in reforming telecommunications may well accelerate developments in sectors with more mature technology in which the need for change may not be that obvious but in which substantial efficiency gains could be achieved nonetheless.

Drawing on the paradigm of telecommunications reform, four closely related yet distinct policy instruments to transform public telecommunications monopolies can be identified: corporatization, competition, privatization, and regulation.

The mix and sequencing of these instruments, as well as the speed of their deployment, depend on country characteristics. There are examples of private ownership yet limited competition, corporatization without private sector entry, and privatization without effective regulation. In the same vein, examples of cautious incrementalism contrast with cases of bold structural and organizational leapfrogging.

Well-documented evidence indicates that effective corporatization of state telecommunications operations can result in significant improvements in operational efficiency, consumer responsiveness, diversification of services, and accelerated investments. Corporatization aims at moving the telecommunications service provider out of the civil service, subjecting it to the discipline of commercial law, and vesting its management with the authority that is common in a private company. Corporatization also typically implies a change in accounting standards and the publication of balance sheets and profit and loss statements. Increased transparency and changes in management incentives have proved to be powerful instruments in promoting efficiency improvements. Furthermore, corporatization enlarges the scope for revenue-sharing arrangements and build-operate-transfer (BOT) schemes to access private sector technical expertise and capital.

International experience suggests that typically the benefits of corporatization are significantly expanded with the introduction of competition or a pending threat of competition. Indeed, competition policies have become the main instruments in modernizing telecommunications sectors. There is ample evidence that monopolies are not well suited to adapt to increasingly dynamic and globalized markets. Pointing to the actual performance of the monopoly operators, potential competitors are pressing the case that they would be in a position to provide many telecommunications services more efficiently. Indeed, technological progress has substantially increased the scope for competition, even in the local loop, provided the authorities permit interconnection and leasing of lines on reasonable terms. There are various options for introducing competition, often starting with customer premises equipment while maintaining network facilities under a monopoly, expanding to value added services including mobile telephones, to fully competitive networks. It is difficult to say a priori which option is most suitable in the context of a given country. There are tradeoffs between market efficiency and economies of scale, as well as considerations of regulatory effectiveness, maturity of the existing telecommunications network, and a country's attractiveness for foreign investment.

Privatization, narrowly defined as a change in the ownership of telecommunications infrastructure, is seen by many as the most important vehicle for sector restructuring. However, it is not a sufficient condition for improvement unless important side conditions are met. It could be argued that privatization may not even be a necessary condition. There are many inefficiently operated private telecommunications companies. Yet some state-owned companies are among the world's top performers, such as Sweden's Telia AB and Singapore Telecom. In reviewing the conditions for successful transformation, it could plausibly be postulated that the economy-wide incentive system is more important than ownership. To the extent that incentives are distorted, however, ownership indeed would matter in most developing countries. Although many developing countries are sensitive to a change in ownership, they have shown themselves to be quite amenable to privatization, defined broadly as allowing participation of nongovernment parties in the telecommunications sector. Although it may be possible to create competition among fully government-owned entities, it is unlikely that it will bring the complete range of benefits (capital, management expertise, technical skills) that would result from the participation of private sector interests.

Because privatization is a process (one that transfers some or all of the operations, management and ownership of state-owned telecommunications facilities to the private sector), it can be initiated and expanded in a variety of ways, including use of management contracts, revenue sharing, joint ventures, and diverse forms of BOT. Considerable experience has now been gained in managing privatization. Issues involve the timing and integration of policy design (competition, structure, pricing, performance targets) with social considerations (employment, early retirement, work rules, pensions), as well as the modalities of sale. All these issues will need to be considered by decisionmakers in the broader, economy-wide context of government role and regulations. Similarly, there are many options for private sector participation short of the outright sale of shares to private operators and the public. These options in turn can be applied to conventional local networks, cellular radio systems, satellite systems, or long-distance terrestrial and submarine links. Most of these schemes are attractive in that they do not require changes in legislation. Their drawback is that desirable legislative modifications involving changes in competition policies and sector regulation may not be introduced.

Sector restructuring addresses only one side of inadequate telecommunications services. The other side is effective government control over the various players to ensure that restructuring does indeed achieve the intended purposes. Regulation is essential for optimizing the performance of the telecommunications sector as long as competition is limited, natural monopoly characteristics prevail, and standards and norms change frequently. Regulations of the sector typically address issues of network interconnection, network expansion targets, pricing and use of leased lines, and cross-subsidies to achieve social objectives. There are various models of regulation, depending on the degree of government intervention in the economy. A fundamental principle in designing regulatory functions is to separate those functions from both policy and management functions. Setting up an effective regulator is indeed a daunting challenge in countries where a tradition of independent administration tribunals does not exist. Transitional solutions may have to be found.

The process of telecommunications reform evidently will be most effective in an institutional structure that clearly defines separate and distinct roles for policymaking, regulation, and management. Although the importance of removing operating functions from the central government has been widely accepted, the need for separating the policymaking and the regulating functions has not been generally recognized. The policymaker concentrates on long-term objectives, the structure of the telecommunications sector, its importance in relation to other sectors, and the financing of its investment. Specifically, the policymaker sets rules with respect to the scope of competition, pricing, quality and condition of service, network interconnection, provision of leased lines for resale, approval of network facilities, application of technical standards, and sale of terminal equipment. In contrast, the regulator is responsible for implementing government policy, ensuring that the operator is accountable for responding to economic and social objectives, resolving disputes between competitors and between consumers and operators, and monitoring the cost efficiency and tariff adequacy of different services. Thus the regulator acts as a buffer between telecommunications operators and policymakers.

Developing Telecommunications: Catalyst for Broader Reforms

High-quality telecommunications service is only one among various factors that determine a country's competitiveness and its attractiveness for investment. There is no conclusive evidence either way in the debate on the potential catalytic role of telecommunications in accelerating economic development. There are examples of both fast-and-slow growing countries that have emphasized telecommunications as a spearhead for gaining competitive advantage in manufacturing and services, and there are examples of fast-and-slow growing countries that have developed telecommunications in response to consumer demand. Limited technical and administrative capabilities would seem to advise against government directly intervening in providing telecommunications services in developing countries; rather, emphasis should be on setting incentives that are most conducive to the development of the sector. Generally, governments in developing countries should aim at minimizing investment outlays for the public telecommunications network while ensuring that the range and quality of service required for reasons of competitiveness and social equity are met.

Even though the macroincentive environment sets the framework for scope, pace, and ultimately the achievements of telecommunications reform, changes in structure and operation of the telecommunications sector may prove to be an effective catalyst in engendering reforms in other sectors. More broadly, these changes may reform business practices in the economy at large, which could go beyond the direct role of telecommunications in enhancing a country's economic performance. There are technological arguments and considerations of political economy that would support this proposition, as well as tangible evidence of the substantial benefits from telecommunications reform.

The demands of export-oriented sectors and of the service industry for a wide and sophisticated telecommunications menu, clearer transparency in measuring the performance of telecommunications, and technical possibilities to bypass the public network are leaving governments little choice but to restructure the sector. The challenge is to use this restructuring as an opportunity for initiating reforms on a broader scale, because introducing the best international practices in telecommunications will require overcoming many issues of a generic nature that likewise constrain the development of other sectors.

The scope of telecommunications reform obviously will be determined by the financial health of the sector and its relative efficiency in satisfying demand; the externalities of reform will depend on the extent to which the economies are already market-oriented and governments have shifted to the role of facilitator and regulator. Demonstrable improvements in the performance of the telecommunications sector can be seen as a general test of the ability of governments in developing countries to overcome vested interests in modernizing their economies. In order to overcome opposition from these interests, governments may be able to form stronger alliances with user groups and with parts of the administration in telecommunications than they could with other sectors. Yet the signal effect of allowing competition in a previously protected public domain, the application of commercial principles in a market segment with significant social connotations, and the introduction of accountability in a more transparent regulatory framework most likely will have implications on the way business is done elsewhere in the economy.

The task of forming coalitions for change seems easier and the benefits of extending competition to other sectors more obvious when looking at successful examples of overhauling traditional telecommunications structures. Two examples may suffice to make the point. Both New Zealand and Japan are among the industrial countries, but there is no apparent reason why developing countries could not make similar relative progress. After all, the issue is not national mastery of technology but national commitment to a process of change. First, a look at New Zealand, which has introduced virtually open competition in its telecommunications market, including basic network services and the allocation of slots in the radio spectrum. This environment has led to some impressive achievements: within eighteen months, price for the basket of telecommunications services was reduced by 31 percent in real terms. Similarly, the efficiency of the Telecom Corporation of New Zealand (TCNZ), measured in lines per staff, improved by more than 20 percent in less than one year. Generally, time for installation was cut, new technology was introduced (the proportion of customers served by digital lines was raised from 35 percent to 70 percent), tariff rates were rebalanced, and profits increased. These results were achieved during a period (1989-90) when the government was still the single shareholder of TCNZ and there was merely a threat that competition would be introduced.

Japan is another telling example of the benefits of competition to the consumer and of the speed with which reforms can be introduced. Until twenty years ago, Japan prohibited the connection of computers to the telecommunications network, and it was only in 1985 that the monopolistic structure of telecommunications service was dismantled. By March 1993 some 80 facilities-based (Type I) carriers and more than 1,200 carriers provided specialized services to their customers by leasing lines (Type II). Fierce competition among the various service providers has led to significantly reduced telephone charges. Between 1985 and 1991, average tariffs for domestic long-distance telephone service were reduced by one-half, whereas international rates fell by one-third. Monthly service charges for cellular telephone service were cut to nearly one-fourth and the pulse rate by one-third. Similarly, paging charges were reduced by one-third. Price reduction and increased choice have dramatically expanded privately owned customer premise equipment. The number of cordless telephones has grown 40 times, and the number of cellular telephones 20 times. Sales of facsimile equipment have been rising by 23 percent per year and telephone sets by 56 percent per year.

Whereas telecommunications sector reforms in New Zealand and Japan were undertaken in the context of broader economic reforms, Argentina is the clearest example of a government using restructuring of telecommunications as a lever to initiate broad reform programs (that is, to change the traditional way of doing business) and to gain credibility with foreign investors. In reorganizing and privatizing telecommunications, Argentina's government demonstrated its commitment and ability to overcome the opposition of public enterprise managers, labor unions, equipment suppliers, political organizations, and large segments of the public bureaucracy. By succeeding against the odds of a highly unfavorable economic and fragmented political environment, the government of Argentina was able to start establishing new rules of the game that ultimately translated into consumer confidence, macroeconomic stability, and a resurgence of direct foreign investment. Even though it would be misleading to qualify telecommunications reform in Argentina as the single causal factor for the economic turnaround, the powerful effects of reform demonstrate that the government was well advised to choose telecommunications as the battleground for establishing a new economic paradigm.

The Argentina example, no doubt, is an extreme case because of the adversity of the starting position regarding the performance of telecommunications, the state of the economy, and the credibility of the government as well as the degree of change and the speed of its implementation. Yet, it provides an interesting lesson on how full commitment to telecommunications reform (which, although part of a more comprehensive reform package, preceded reforms in other sectors), can change, among other things, administrative procedures, labor legislation, public enterprise management responsiveness, and regulatory practices. This occurred despite flaws in implementation that were rooted in the country's exogenous endowments.

Planning for Change: Frame of Reference

Based on the foregoing considerations and drawing on international experience, some premises can be formulated that may be useful as a frame of reference for planning telecommunications reform in developing countries.

Premises

- Advanced telecommunications capability is a tremendously important factor in determining a country's competitiveness, but a nation's development has to be seen in the context of other factors that constitute the enabling environment for economic growth. There is a strong correlation between high telecommunications investment and high rates of economic growth, but there is no evidence of a causal relationship. Although telecommunications may be an engine of growth under certain circumstances, it is possible to overbuild the physical infrastructure in relation to the needs of service. The challenge to policymakers is to find the right incentive framework and to ensure the balanced development of skills and physical endowments and the efficient deployment of productive factors in the economy.

- Reform of telecommunications has acquired added importance as it is considered both a test for the ability of governments more generally to overcome vested interests opposed to economic modernization and a catalyst for engendering changes in a country's traditional way of doing business, thus improving the domestic business climate and gaining credibility with foreign investors.

- The resource envelope for telecommunications financing is finite. There are limits to a nation's domestic savings effort and to its ability to borrow abroad, and there is competition for resources from other sectors. The enormous investment requirements for developing telecommunications and the wide array of technological options put a premium on the judicious choice of sector structure and the regulatory framework.

- There can be a conflict between the objectives of rapidly achieving high rates of coverage at affordable prices and of providing sophisticated services to the business community at cost-based tariffs. There is no right answer to determine the appropriate balance; it is essentially an issue for the policymaker to use judgment in deciding. However, in assessing balances, the relative contribution of telecommunications compared with other basic services in enhancing social welfare and in relation to other policy variables in promoting competitiveness has to be taken into account. Ultimately, lost business also means social welfare costs in terms of lost income for wage earners. Thus, there is a limit to cross-subsidization, on the one hand, and an imperative to use capacity economically on the other hand.

- Organizational and management changes are at least as important, if not more so, as the expansion of physical facilities. Simply put, the basic issue is how to structure the telecommunications environment so that telecommunications facilities are used most effectively. In fact, there are indications of wide variations in management performance among developing and industrial countries alike. In this sense, telecommunications mirrors a broader economic challenge: how to design a system of incentives and penalties to ensure that both capital and human resources are employed so as to achieve the highest returns to society.

- Competition policy is the most powerful instrument to expand and manage the telecommunications sector with a high degree of efficiency. The threat of losing business, or the risk of not getting it, does wonders to motivate those involved to give the maximum effort; it even promotes changes in behavior which are at the grass roots of development. Competition essentially means eliminating monopolistic rents, be they of the government or the private sector, by removing barriers to entry. Thus, competition means a broader participation of the private sector, not necessarily privatization in terms of ownership change.

- Structure, organization, and the rules of the sector should be designed to meet overall market needs in the most effective way. An essential condition for achieving this objective is the selection of additional players who demonstrably make the greatest contribution to sector performance. Hence, a decision on private sector participation in telecommunications development should, whatever the specific arrangement, be based on a thorough assessment of the real value added, that is, the tangible contribution to overcoming financial, technical, and managerial constraints. Avoiding free riders is essential for gaining efficiency.

- Subsidizing domestic telecommunications manufacturing capability by setting restrictive standards, imposing reserve procurement, or providing tariff protection has shown limited benefits at best. International experience suggests that the opportunity cost of high-priced services and constraints on technological offerings far outweigh the benefits associated with the development of domestic telecommunications manufacturing. Examples in Eastern Europe, Brazil, and even Korea indicate that the development of switches, just to pick an item with some national appeal, has had either negative rates of return or rates below the opportunity cost of capital, if strict economic calculations are applied. There is ample evidence, however, that developing countries can establish domestic production capability in important market segments (such as peripheral equipment and software) under competitive conditions.

- An efficient, high-quality telecommunications sector requires a clear separation of policy, regulatory, and operational functions. The policymaker ought to concentrate on setting objectives and defining strategies. The regulator should ensure compliance with these parameters in a transparent and equitable manner, taking account of the needs of consumers as well as those of operators. The facilities and service providers, operating under commercial principles even if government owned, ought to focus on delivering needed services at the lowest cost.

- National sovereignty is not tantamount to monopolistic public ownership of basic facilities or restrictions on foreign participation. Rather, sovereignty calls for deciding the rules of the game that are best suited to the country and enforcing them transparently and effectively. The telecommunications sector is a good example. Exclusion of foreign capital and expertise can limit the ability of a developing country to compete, ultimately weakening its position in the global economy. Similarly, whereas monopolistic public ownership would seem to ensure that rents accrue to the treasury, the probability of inadequate service response that comes with a monopoly implies less business and thus, ultimately erodes the government's ability to use the monopoly to achieve social objectives.

2

Restructuring the Telecommunications Sector: Experience in Some Industrial Countries and the Implications for Policymakers

Robert R. Bruce

THE DEBATE AND DIALOGUE ABOUT THE restructuring of the telecommunications sector has grown increasingly sophisticated and complex. Proposals for reform and liberalization that just a few years ago might have seemed radical are now considered to be part of the conventional wisdom of policy reformers. Although there is no consensus about any ideal approach to sectoral restructuring, there is broad acceptance of the idea that existing policies cannot go unexamined. There is also an increasing perception that maintaining a state telecommunications monopoly unchallenged by competition is no longer a viable option.

Policymakers have also grown increasingly sophisticated about the distinctions between policy options favoring liberalization and privatization; they are more sensitive to the potential conflicts between these objectives. They are beginning to appreciate, as well, that privatization can involve a myriad of different mechanisms and timetables for introducing private capital into state posts, telegraphs, and telephone (PTT) operating entities and modifying the structure of governance. It is better recognized that policy reform is a long and arduous process—with no prompt and painless solutions—that is likely to test severely the patience and resolve of political leaders. Pressure has increased for sectoral strategies tailored to the unique institutional, economic, and political context of each country; formulaic solutions are unacceptable.

As attention to telecommunications reform from political leaders has grown, so has the interest in privatization from finance ministries and the financial community. This interest often results in an orientation toward policies that might lead to privatizing a state telecommunications operating entity in a sheltered competitive environment, a scheme that might maximize returns in the short run. It can sometimes be difficult to assure a full hearing for policy options favoring not merely privatization but an aggressive approach to the introduction of competition that may in the long run contribute most reliably to sustained economic growth.

What follows is not a comprehensive updating of sectoral reforms in major industrial and developing countries. This chapter offers an assessment of recent experience with reform in the telecommunications sector. The perspective may be somewhat unconventional, even radical, in perspective. Change begets more changes. Policy determinations in the telecommunications sector do not occur in a vacuum; they are a product of political compromise. Hard-won reforms in one country not only create an impetus for further changes in that country but also create an impetus for more rapid and more radical reform in countries that have delayed initiating the process of sectoral reform.

Incremental reforms may have been successfully implemented in countries that have permitted new entrants on the peripheries or in the use of the network infrastructure. Incremental reforms may not, however, be the right prescription for sectoral reform in countries where the technical and institutional infrastructure has collapsed, huge backlogs of demand have accumulated, and business users desperately need new services. More far-reaching reforms that contemplate a role for new entities in the provision of core infrastructure—that find some parallels in smaller industrial countries—should not necessarily be viewed as a radical program for reform. Such reforms may involve a sensible, even a conservative, response to a desperate need for new investment in telecommunications infrastructures.

Future debates about sectoral reform will not necessarily be led by policymakers from industrial countries. New options for privatizing and for introducing new sources of private investment into telecommunications sectors are being much more freely explored in discussions about sectoral reform in Latin America, Asia, and Eastern Europe than in the heart of the European Community. Ironically, innovative techniques for financing new network infrastructures in developing countries might well provide the models and mechanisms for implementing broadband or intelligent networking capabilities in countries with developed infrastructures. This chapter assesses in particular some of the conventional wisdom about how to privatize and identifies possible new options for introducing private sector investment into the telecommunications sector.

Because of the rapid evolution of the telecommunications environment, policy prescriptions must be based on new and empirically derived concepts as well as on assessments of future trends. This applies particularly to the likely future evolution of telecommunications policies of countries that have been undergoing restructuring; policies cannot be drawn merely on the patterns of past policy determinations. This chapter attempts to anticipate some of these new policy directions.

Sectoral Restructuring in Some Major Industrial Countries: An Assessment of Trends and Future Developments

Examined below are important issues being confronted in the reform of the telecommunications sector in the European Community (EC) as well as in Japan and the United States. Sector reforms in three smaller countries—Finland, New Zealand, and Australia—are also the focus of attention. The bold and innovative thrust of reform initiatives warrants close scrutiny by countries still deciding on future sectoral policies.

The discussion that follows is not intended as a detailed primer on reforms in the above-mentioned countries; such background information is available elsewhere. Instead, the focus is on identifying trends and likely future developments. Important lessons for policymakers now weighing options for sectoral reform may often lie less in a factual account of what has happened than in an interpretative assessment of the direction in which developments are headed and what revisions of past reform initiatives might be anticipated. Interpreting and predicting future trends is inherently a controversial, subjective, and risky undertaking. However, such an effort, provides an important underpinning in determining policy prescriptions for countries faced with decisions concerning how to develop their telecommunications infrastructure in the future.

Countries still developing their infrastructure or attempting to effectuate a rapid and smooth transition from centrally managed to market-driven economies need not slavishly imitate the reform initiatives of countries that earlier started down the road to reforming their telecommunications sectors. Policy reforms must, of course, be tailored to unique national circumstances. Moreover, policy reforms of late starters can also leapfrog the first tentative initiatives of early reform efforts. They can and should reflect changes in conventional wisdom and any new synthesis of ideas about restructuring telecommunications sectors that emerge from the experience of other countries. The following assessment of the experiences of the European Community, Japan, the United States, and several small industrial countries is thus intended as a backdrop for the later discussion on some implications of recent sectoral restructuring efforts that focuses on a number of new or unconventional approaches to telecommunications sector reform.

Sectoral Reform in the European Community

The EC Commission's 1987 Green Paper represented a brilliant synthesis, both in political and policy terms, of telecommunications policy discussions that had been taking place in Europe, the United States, and Japan. It defined a new consensus—European response to developments in the United States and Japan—that both was influenced by, and has influenced, policy debates under way in various EC member states.

This European consensus drew largely on efforts by the Japanese in their business telecommunications law to distinguish between the provision of facilities and the provision of services. The consensus, however, was distinguished from the predilections of both American and Japanese policymakers to favor facilities-based competition in its consideration that network infrastructure, public-switched voice services, and potentially certain public-switched data services should all be considered "reserved services" of the PTTs. Nevertheless, the Green Paper left the door open for limited facilities-based competition from satellite services. At the same time, it acknowledged the right of some EC member states, such as the United Kingdom, to pursue a more open-handed approach to facilities competition.

The Community has had remarkable success in defining a policy consensus among twelve member states with vastly different institutional structures and stages of development. It has been effectively implementing that consensus through its terminal equipment and services directives, as well as through a number of other initiatives. The Community efforts have, moreover, crystallized policy debates on a continent-wide basis. The Green Paper has become a starting point for discussions about telecommunications reform both in European Free Trade Area (EFTA) countries and in Eastern Europe. As such, the paper may well be one of the most influential statements of telecommunications policy that has ever been formulated.

The EC's approach to telecommunications reform as first articulated in its Green Paper includes four main elements. First, it endorsed the liberalization of the provision of all services utilizing existing infrastructure with the exception of certain previously described reserved services. Second, through its Open Network Provision (ONP) initiative, the European Community has been encouraging harmonization among EC member states with respect to the terms and conditions of access to network-based services essential for the provision of service-based competition. Third, although not rejecting the policy preference of the United Kingdom for facilities-based competition, the Green Paper left the door open for limited facilities-based competition from satellite services. Through its Satellite Green Paper the Community is pressing for consensus on liberalizing satellite-based services (at least those services permissible under its services directive). Fourth, the Green Paper has forcefully advocated the separation of the operational and regulatory roles of PTTs. In so doing, it has created an environment within which ongoing policy reforms can be pursued at the national level. Nevertheless, each of these important elements of the EC's consensus approach to telecommunications reform is being severely eroded by new developments and pressures in the telecommunications sector. The core elements of the European consensus may have to be re-evaluated relatively soon.

WIDENING THE SCOPE OF THE EC SERVICES DIRECTIVE. The EC services directive's limited focus on nonvoice services may not adequately recognize growing pressures from large and middle-size users for managed network offerings of both voice and data services. PTTs will no doubt be keen to respond to these pressures; however, it will be difficult for them to do so unless service providers unaffiliated with PTTs do not have comparable opportunities to offer such services. Pressures for integrated data and voice service offerings are both technology and market driven.

In the United States and, more recently, in the United Kingdom as a consequence of white paper recommendations resulting from the U.K. duopoly review, large carriers are offering specialized services to large users based on discounted tariffs. Users are insisting on enhanced capabilities to manage and configure their own networks. Sophisticated network management capabilities make it harder to differentiate public and private network services; however, this growth in demand for managed network services will generate pressures to differentiate the regulatory and business arrangements through which such services are offered. From a strategic standpoint it may thus be advantageous for large carriers to differentiate services provided on overlay networks or those with specialized network management capabilities from those services that are routinely offered to long-distance customers.

To compete with modern facilities and networks installed by new entrants, PTTs may have to create new business organizations within their corporate structures to offer specialized networking services. Faced with claims by new entrants that pricing for large users is predatory or not cost justified, an established carrier may find it useful to establish a separate business enterprise to offer services for large business users. Such a business unit would provide a basis for establishing cost accounting and cost allocation systems necessary to justify pricing for new services in response to complaints to regulators of unfair competition made by new entrants.

From a technological standpoint, as well, the emergence in the coming decade of intelligent network architectures may result in a separation, driven by business considerations, of the capabilities and resources necessary to manage and operate networks from the operational level of a PTT consisting of its switching and transmission capabilities. It is likely that PTTs will begin to shift the strategic center of their business to separate business units that manage and control transmission and switching resources wherever they might be located (in a PTT's national market or overseas).

The essential capabilities for devising and managing all types of future telecommunications services will thus be increasingly distinguishable from the PTTs' physical network infrastructure. Moreover, the primary hardware and software capabilities for managing and controlling future networks is likely to be supplied from outside the traditional telephone industry by firms in the computer and information-processing fields that have been developing network management capabilities for data services. Such firms are not likely to accept a permanent exclusion from becoming suppliers of both data and voice services, because distinctions between voice and data services are rendered obsolete by advances in digital techniques. Users will reinforce this trend toward competitive provision of managed network services. They are not likely to agree to the packaging and management of their networks by PTTs unless third parties or users themselves can engage in similar network management services. A package price will probably not be acceptable unless parts of the package can be separately provided and priced.

Necessity has become the mother of policy innovation. The scope of services open to competition will expand as a consequence of the EC's promotion of satellite-based networking and from the urgent need to utilize such services to speed the integration of Germany and of Eastern and Western Europe. For example, the gross inadequacy of telecommunications links between the eastern and western regions of Germany has forced the German Ministry of Post and Telecommunications to lift restrictions it had imposed on the utilization of satellite networks to provide switched voice services. Although undertaken as a temporary measure, this move may be difficult to retract because users may not easily surrender their freedom to use satellite services on a flexible basis.

The Community has proposed in its Satellite Green Paper to limit the use of satellite networks to services that can be offered subject to restrictions in its services directive. However, like the German Ministry of Post and Telecommunications, the Community will have no incentive to block the use of switched voice services on satellite links between Eastern and Western Europe when adequate terrestrial services are not available. Moreover, it is not likely to be a sustainable policy option to permit switched voice services on satellite links into Eastern Europe but not into EC member states such as Portugal or Greece, where terrestrial networking is not as yet fully developed. In short, the scope of services reserved under the EC services directive seems likely to narrow substantially.

EXPANDING THE SCOPE OF THE ONP INITIATIVE TO INCLUDE OPTIONS FOR UNBUNDLING LOCAL EXCHANGE CAPABILITIES. The Community is likely to have to take into greater account the real differences between its ONP initiative and the Federal Communications Commission's (FCC) Open Network Architecture (ONA) efforts in the United States. The EC's ONP initiative has yet to wrestle with hard questions concerning the local switching capabilities that should be offered to third-party providers of services and at what price. These policy concerns are finally being addressed in the context of the EC's investigation of future intelligent network architectures. However, to date the European Community has seen its ONP effort primarily as a means of achieving greater harmonization concerning the terms and conditions under which leased-line capabilities are offered to new service providers. In the United States such harmonization of service offerings was largely achieved because of the unifying influence of American Telephone and Telegraph Corporation (AT&T) prior to its divestiture.

Neither the European Community nor its member states, except for the United Kingdom, have really addressed how to structure and price access arrangements for new entrants. The United Kingdom's duopoly review focused attention on some difficult issues that the Office of Telecommunications (OFTEL), the UK telecommunications regulatory agency, must face in establishing competitive safeguards applicable not merely to Mercury, but to all new competitors dependent on British Telecom's (BT) local exchange capabilities. As the debate over formulating access arrangements grows more sophisticated and intense in the United Kingdom, there will inevitably be some spillover of the consequences and outcomes of these discussions elsewhere in Europe. Users of leased-line services and providers of value added services will also be driving the debate forward as they seek from PTTs access to the same sets of local network capabilities that are available to them in the United States.

PERMITTING FACILITIES-BASED COMPETITION IN THE COMMUNITY. The cautious approach of the EC Green Paper, and European policy generally, toward facilities-based competition is likely to come under increasing pressure for a variety of reasons. The U.K. duopoly review established the basis for more far-reaching and unrestricted competition in the United Kingdom. Inevitably, the widening gap between the liberal approach to authorizing new facilities-based competitors in the United Kingdom and policies favoring an infrastructure monopoly seems likely to undermine the legitimacy of, and political support for, status quo-oriented policies in Europe.

The opening for limited facilities-based competition that will be created by the Satellite Green Paper will accelerate changes in the current policy environment. It has not escaped the notice of business users of telecommunications services in Europe that European policymakers are still in the process of implementing liberal policies toward satellite networks almost four years after the issuance of the 1987 Green Paper and two decades after the adoption of the FCC's Open Skies policy that stimulated the development of satellite services in the United States. Moreover, there seems to be growing interest on the part of large users and some European railway companies in exploring options for the construction of new fiber-optic networks. Although the legal and practical barriers to the entry of new facilities-based competitors are substantial, large users seem quite convinced that they lack access to the wide range of transmission options available to their competitors in the United States and Japan.

In the long term, PTTs that perceive an irreversible trend toward further liberalization of services-based competition may see their incentives to be the exclusive investors in transmission and switching facilities significantly reduced. Moreover, as PTTs begin to center their business strategies around the management of networks and the development of service applications, they may conclude that being the exclusive provider of infrastructure need not necessarily be an essential part of their business strategy. In addition, the joint-venture business model utilized in constructing transoceanic fiber-optic cables might begin to influence the business arrangements through which trans-European networks are constructed. Finally, the possibility of a global credit crunch and the resulting shortages of capital necessary to construct new networks and new switching infrastructure might encourage PTTs to become more open to a new role for intermediaries in the financing and construction of telecommunications infrastructures.

What might be decisive, however, in tilting the balance in Europe toward policies more receptive to facilities-based competition could be the view that the absence of competitive pressures from new facilities-based entrants has slowed down the process of rate rebalancing in Europe. One of the major consequences of divestiture in the United States has been to compel the regional Bell operating companies (RBOCs) to base their long-term profitability on efficiently priced and regulated local exchange services. Vigorous competition in the interexchange market in the United States has guaranteed that efforts to remove embedded subsidies between local and long-distance services have moved at a vigorous pace. Indeed, perhaps the most significant consequence of the major restructuring of U.S. telecommunications policies in the past decade has been to turn first AT&T—through the FCC's initial deregulatory initiatives—and then the RBOCs—through divestiture—into the prime movers of price reform in the U.S. telecommunications sector. It has been U.S. carriers as interested parties, and not U.S. regulators, that have been the engine behind the introduction of highly efficient pricing arrangements in the U.S. telecommunications sector.

Surely arguments persist over whether embedded cross-subsidies have been eliminated in the United States. No doubt European PTTs have also initiated their own rebalancing efforts. These rebalancing initiatives, however, have lacked the strong impetus that facilities-based competition inevitably provides. Moreover, as the price-rebalancing process proceeds in the United States, it undermines the case that facilities-based competition necessarily results in "cream skimming" and loss of revenue necessary to meet universal service goals.

European business and economic policymakers may begin to perceive that Europe is at a strategic disadvantage because of deeply embedded disparities in the pricing of telecommunications services and infrastructure between Europe and the United States and Japan. Bulk transmission capacity is not only much more expensive in Europe than in the United States, but there is also much less diversity of supply with respect to the unbundled capabilities of local exchange facilities. Thus, for all the reasons discussed above, it may be reasonable to expect a steady and possibly rapid erosion of support in Europe for policies disfavoring facilities-based competition.

SHARPENING DEBATE IN EUROPE ON REGULATION. One of the most important elements of the EC's telecommunications reform initiatives is the impetus for the separation of the policy and regulatory responsibilities of the PTTs from their operational responsibilities. New regulatory bodies are springing up throughout Europe in the aftermath of the 1987 Green Paper—most notably in France, the Netherlands, Portugal, and Spain. However, in Italy, with its byzantine and apparently reform-resistant industry structure, it has proved difficult even to identify an individual or institution that is a pretender to becoming an Italian regulatory body.

There are considerable differences in the structure of new regulators. Only in the United Kingdom is the regulatory body significantly independent of the operator or the ministry that maintains control of the state's ownership stake in the operator. Although it is true that in Germany there is separation of operational and regulatory responsibilities, there is not that same degree of separation between regulatory and ownership responsibilities. Ultimately, the German Minister of Post and Telecommunications has responsibility for the German regulatory body and for Deutsche Bundespost Telekom (DBP Telekom). However, the German experience demonstrates that an effective and vigorous regulatory mechanism can be established notwithstanding the dual entrepreneurial and regulatory responsibilities of the minister. One of the most impressive aspects of the German regulatory initiatives is its extraordinary openness; public comment has been sought on significant policy initiatives both from Germans and foreign interests. Such openness is an important antidote against both the perception or the reality that a regulatory mechanism is likely to favor an established competitor.

In spite of the impressive progress in recent years in developing new regulatory mechanisms in Europe, European regulators have not yet been fully tested. They have not had to confront difficult controversies generated by the emergence of facilities-based competition and by pressures for unbundling local exchange capabilities.

United Kingdom regulatory officials were quite insistent on being able to regulate with a light hand, often contrasting their intended approach with the burdensome and litigious aspects of regulation in the United States and Canada. The United Kingdom's duopoly white paper and, in particular, the OFTEL director general's commentary in an appendix on BT's pricing policies suggests that overseeing the British competitive scene will become much more complex as a result of initiatives favoring a more open competitive environment. One illustration of this likely complexity is the white paper's discussion of how to deal with BT's evident frustration at not being able to rebalance its local exchange tariffs on a more accelerated basis. OFTEL has agreed to a limited rebalancing of local tariffs; one of the concessions for continued restraint on local pricing increases has been to accord BT more flexibility to introduce special discounted services for large users. Such flexibility will come with the caveat that pricing reductions cannot be predatory or be set below long-run incremental costs. However, pricing for large users need not, according to the OFTEL director general, *have* to be based on fully distributed costing principles.

How OFTEL, BT and its competitors will determine whether specific pricing proposals conform with these benchmarks remains to be seen. OFTEL evidently intends to demand more from BT in the way of transparent accounting and cost allocation principles. It is also apparent that OFTEL will become increasingly embroiled in the process of establishing access charge arrangements. What seems inevitable in the United Kingdom—and perhaps ultimately in the European Community—is that both new entrants and users will see themselves having a greater and greater stake in the process of rate rebalancing and structuring access tariffs. However, the necessary tools and regulatory skills to oversee this complex process are not readily available. European regulators may have to begin a serious exploration of new procedures for the resolution of disputes arising from intensified levels of competition.

Replication of the institutional structure and procedures of American or Canadian agencies is certainly no answer to the difficult challenges that European regulators will be facing. Truly novel institutional arrangements will have to be devised in order to be responsive to the structure of competition that is introduced into each different national market. Regulators in Europe are being drawn into an increasingly contentious debate over the high level of international tariff charges and the long-term viability of international settlement mechanisms. It is not likely that either national regulators or competition authorities in Brussels, who have been undertaking an investigation of international rates and settlements, can or should deal with the restructuring of the international settlement mechanism. However, political and regulatory pressures, as well as new competitive policies, will eventually reduce subsidies for local services from international services. As these subsidies are drained away, PTTs will find themselves in the position of having to make significant rate level and structure changes in order to finance adequately future infrastructure investments.

These international price pressures are significant indeed in the long run. The dependency of PTTs in Europe and beyond on international revenues will be reduced, and preparations for radical pricing changes must be undertaken. Regulators in Europe will find themselves having to deal more frequently with PTT-devised rate rebalancing proposals.

Recent Developments in Japan

Telecommunications policies in Japan, like those adopted in the United States, have relied heavily on a strong commitment to competition on an across-the-board basis. However, Japanese policy has been based on establishing a clear demarcation between competition in the provision of facilities and competition in the provision of services. Providers of facilities are designated as Type I service providers, providers of services as Type II service providers.

Japanese policy has also endeavored to maintain a distinction between the policies applicable to the provision of services domestically and internationally. In particular, one of the most distinctive aspects of the Japanese telecommunications scene has been the effort to compartmentalize the roles of domestic and international providers of telecommunications service. As discussed in detail below, some critical elements of Japanese telecommunications policy may undergo some re-evaluation in the next several years.

LOOKING AT THE CONSEQUENCES OF COMPETITION. Since the enactment of the Telecommunications Business Law in 1984, Japanese policymakers have permitted far-reaching competition in both the domestic and international sectors of their telecommunications market. However, the consequences of such competition in the international and domestic segments of the Japanese market have been quite different; changes initiated since 1984 are likely to set in motion even more far-reaching changes in the coming years.

Both Kokusai Denshin Denwa Company Limited (KDD) and Nippon Telegraph and Telephone Corporation (NTT)—which had traditionally dominated the international and domestic segments of the Japanese markets—were confronted with new entrants but were not permitted or encouraged to compete with each other. KDD was confronted with two new Type I facilities-based competitors, International Telecom Japan Incorporated (ITJ) and International Digital Communications (IDC), as well as with a number of service-based special Type II carriers known as international value added network providers, or IVANs. NTT now confronts three Type I competitors that have constructed terrestrial networks within Japan, as well as two other Type I facilities-based competitors utilizing satellite services. Literally hundreds of new entrants have been authorized to compete with NTT in providing value added network services.

In the international segment of the Japanese telecommunications market, KDD has been able to respond rather dramatically to price reductions introduced by the new entrants ITJ and IDC. The rationale for such a competitive response, which convinced the Ministry of Posts and Telecommunications (MPT) officials wary of permitting NTT to respond in a similarly vigorous way to its domestic competitors, was provided by dramatic evidence of loss of market share by KDD. KDD's ability to react strongly to new entries, has, however, had some disruptive consequences for new competitors. In the longer run, it may require these entrants, or Japanese policymakers, to question whether fusion between domestic and international new entrants should be permitted. Alternatively, it may open a new debate, even in the extraordinarily cautious Japanese environment, about whether NTT should be permitted to become a provider of international services.

The introduction of competition in the Japanese domestic sector is also somewhat of a mixed success. In some ways, all the players in the market may be dissatisfied with the status quo. New Type I entrants were encouraged to discount their prices significantly below those of NTT; however, they were discouraged from competing with one another. NTT, for its part, was often constrained from responding to new entrants by lowering or restructuring its own prices.

Two years ago the MPT deferred any decision on the restructuring of NTT for five years; it imposed on NTT a number of competitive safeguards intended to assure fair competition in the Japanese market. NTT has been required, for example, to convert its powerful data subsidiary into a separate independent entity. It has also been required to keep separate accounts for its different lines of business. Nevertheless, NTT has generally been subject to less stringent or explicit regulatory safeguards than were applied in the United States to AT&T before the divestiture.

The result of Japanese policy has been to leave new domestic entrants in a position in which they are highly vulnerable to competitive forays by NTT. In turn, NTT has been, at least until recently, significantly inhibited from responding vigorously in the new competitive environment. Many observers believe that the lack of a formal regulatory process in Japan has significantly impaired the emergence of a vigorous competitive environment.

DEVELOPING MORE FORMAL AND TRANSPARENT REGULATION. It is often observed that significant changes in industry structure and competition policy inevitably require changes in legal and regulatory arrangements. The Japanese experience with telecommunications reform is, however, a significant exception to this rule. The traditional mechanisms for government oversight have tended to linger on and have changed only in limited ways compared with the radical shift in Japanese policy toward new entry that were mandated by the Telecommunications Business Law.

Only time will tell whether pressures will grow for a more formal and transparent regulatory process in Japan. Japanese observers repeatedly point out that the mechanisms utilized in the United Kingdom are not well suited to the administrative and cultural style of Japan. The Japanese MPT, however, is beginning to deal in a more open manner with controversies over access issues and the future development of open network architectures. Foreign entrants in the Japanese market, and even new Japanese competitors, have criticized the closed mandarin-style decisionmaking of the past as being insufficiently open and responsive in coping with the difficult transitional issues and disputes created by a competitive telecommunications sector. Japanese policymakers will soon be forced to address head-on some of the difficult questions faced in the U.K. duopoly white paper. In particular, they will have to decide how NTT can be more effectively permitted to respond to pricing initiatives of the new domestic common carriers.

REASSESSING INDUSTRY ARRANGEMENTS. Although the Japanese MPT was not scheduled to revisit fundamental questions about NTT's structure until 1993, pressure certainly existed to consider the implications and results of the far-reaching sectoral restructuring undertaken in Australia, where the role of international and domestic service providers had historically been kept separate; however, Australian policymakers decided to merge Telecom Australia and Overseas Telecommunications Commission (OTC) and to permit duopolistic competition by privatizing and opening to foreign investors the Australian satellite provider, AUSSAT.

Although it is certainly risky to make predictions about the future direction of Japanese telecommunications policy, the results of the U.K. duopoly review and the major restructuring under way in Australia seem likely to make a substantial impression on the thinking of Japanese policymakers. Because the Japanese are already committed to the open-entry policies permitted in the U.K. following the duopoly review, the review's tough-minded recognition of the problems of overseeing competition between BT and Mercury is bound to become a benchmark for evaluating the status and effectiveness of current Japanese policies toward umpiring competition between new and established entrants. Moreover, the Australian decision to blur distinctions between domestic and international service providers is likely to be studied carefully in Japan by competitors and policymakers concerned with the viability of the current industry structure.

Ultimately, it seems reasonable to predict some significant changes in the Japanese approach to structuring its telecommunications sector in the next few years. Advocates of divestiture within NTT may grow in number and significance. Many key decisionmakers in Japan are not convinced that all parts of NTT are of equal strategic significance. During the last review of NTT's structure, there was a substantial body of opinion that the overall value of NTT would be increased through restructuring and divestiture. There is certainly a respectable case to be made that NTT would become a more efficient and a more effective competitor if it were not so constrained by the MPT. The dilemma of Japanese policymakers is that there may be no significant way to increase NTT's competitiveness without further major structural reforms.

Such reforms might well seek to ensure that any step to break or at least to formalize ties between NTT's local exchange and interexchange businesses would be accompanied by increased flexibility for NTT to operate as an international service provider. In turn, if NTT is permitted to integrate outward to become an international service provider, KDD is sure to be allowed to integrate inward and become a provider of domestic services. It would seem, however, that some of the solutions rejected in Australia—permitting the former international carrier, OTC, to become a domestic competitor of the established domestic carrier, Telecom Australia— would be more viable in the Japanese context than permitting the established carriers to merge in order to compete against some configuration of new entrants.

REVISITING REGULATORY DISTINCTIONS IN THE INTERNATIONAL ARENA. Other elements of the reforms adopted in the 1985 Telecommunications Business Law have also proved less workable than the Japanese might have anticipated or hoped. For example, as might have been predicted, the distinction adopted in the international arena between facilities-based Type I carriers, (such as ITJ and IDC) and the IVANs, has turned out to be a difficult one to maintain in practice. The primary difference has been that Type I carriers negotiate directly with cable consortia owners and with International Telecommunications Satellite Organization (INTELSAT) and IVANs do not. Moreover, Type I carriers can offer switched voice services, whereas IVANs cannot; however, as pressures grow for managed network voice and data services, the Type I—Type II distinction may prove to be untenable internationally.

Because of pressures from U.S. trade negotiators, the Japanese have also had to relent and permit more leeway for flexible use of leased international circuits by entities that are not classified as IVANs. The U.S.-Japan IVAN agreement negotiated in 1992 established that customers of leased circuits had certain leeway to offer intracorporate networks and were not required to be treated as carriers. Overall, however, the Japanese have adamantly insisted that the CCITT's (Comité Consultatif International Télégraphique et Téléphonique) D Series Recommendations did not permit various types of third party activities that have been freely authorized in a European country such as the Netherlands that has a liberal and flexible approach to the use of international circuits. Given this posture, the Japanese have insisted on negotiating carrierlike interconnection agreements with the United Kingdom and a number of other European countries, as well as with Hong Kong and countries in Southeast Asia.

Ultimately, movement toward liberalizing the D Series Recommendations, along with pressures from large users, may require the Japanese to further relax their insistence on formal interconnection agreements for IVANs. Their stance internationally has tended to confuse the distinction between customers and carriers. It has placed the Japanese squarely in the camp of not permitting third-party uses by customers of leased circuits that clearly are not carriers unless such nontelecommunications entities are subjected to MPT regulatory licensing.

Not surprisingly, such a rigid licensing policy is better suited to the consortium-oriented approach taken by Japanese companies that have emerged as providers of international value added services than to the interests of foreign financial or other service organizations seeking to gain access to the Japanese market. In spite of the fact that the Japanese IVAN policy framework has proved resilient in response to criticism from Japan's trading partners, the heavily regulation-oriented policy toward IVANs does not seem likely to be sustainable in the long run. The Japanese may eventually be required to collapse their distinction between Type I and Type II international carrier. In turn, there should be more receptivity to allowing ordinary users of leased circuits more freedom to operate without being subject to MPT regulation.

REASSESSING FACILITIES-SERVICES DISTINCTION. In 1985 when the Telecommunications Business Law was adopted, Japanese policymakers proudly proclaimed that their distinction between service-based and facilities-based competition was more progressive and less prone to definitional ambiguity than the FCC's distinction between basic and enhanced. Slowly but surely the Japanese have had to retreat from this posture. For example, they have had to add a gloss to their typology for international services to permit, in effect, only enhanced facsimile services. As noted above, the facilities-services distinction has proved difficult to apply internationally.

As useful as this important distinction proved to be in the years immediately following the adoption of the Telecommunications Business Law, it now seems apparent that a more defined and sophisticated approach to definitional boundary lines will be required in Japan and in other countries as well. It has turned out, in fact, that the Japanese never meant to imply that domestic Type II service providers could offer *all* services. The resale of switched voice services never proved to be a practical option for Type II providers because of NTT's refusal to permit such practices and the MPT's acquiescence in such a carrier-imposed gloss on the definition of the services opened to competition.

Japanese telecommunications reform has tended to enshrine the distinction between services and facilities. For reasons set forth in detail below, it may also be important for policymakers to take a closer look at the concept of a provider of facilities or infrastructure. It might well be useful to develop a new concept of the role of an infrastructure provider. Such a new approach might distinguish between the ownership and operation of transmission and switching assets when provided to carriers and when provided to the public at large. Establishing such a distinction might create flexibility for new sources of investment, either private or foreign, in countries that have been cautious about preserving control over the telecommunications sector. The real lesson of the Japanese experience—and indeed a lesson of the experience with telecommunications reform in other countries—is that sectoral structuring is a highly dynamic process. Stability is not one of the hallmarks of the telecommunications policymaking process. Policymakers must be prepared to deal not with a static environment, but with one that is likely to change in kaleidoscopic fashion.

Experiences with Divestiture and Deregulation in the United States

The American experience with telecommunications reform is almost inevitably written off as unique and of limited relevance to countries that are geographically smaller or are still in the process of developing their infrastructure. Nevertheless, there are a number of aspects of the American experience with deregulation and divestiture that are likely to be important for policymakers in other countries to take fully into account.

Commentators on the American scene, especially those who view it from abroad, inevitably focus on the fervor with which American policymakers have sought to open to competition virtually every sector of the telecommunications industry. Indeed, much attention is directed at what is often viewed as an excessively zealous, even misguided, effort to sever—through the modified final judgment (MFJ) that ended the Department of Justice's antitrust suit against AT&T—the nexus between the provision of local exchange and interexchange services on the part of the seven RBOCs that emerged from the MFJ. Whatever the merits of continuing in place the MFJ's restrictions on the RBOCs, some important practical consequences of the restrictions imposed are often overlooked, especially by foreign observers of the American scene.

RESTRUCTURING OF TELECOMMUNICATIONS PRICING. Perhaps the most significant impact of divestiture has been its acceleration of the pace of the restructuring of telecommunications pricing in the United States. The RBOCs have been given a significant impetus to make their local exchange businesses profitable. Their desire to stimulate new utilization of their networks by offering the functionalities of the local network to third-party service providers and their desire to escape the line of business restrictions of the MFJ have led the RBOCs to play a constructive and leading role in developing the FCC's ONA initiative. Pricing of local access capabilities has become very cost oriented, and service offerings have become increasingly diversified and unbundled.

ADOPTING DEMAND-DRIVEN POLICIES. Another important consequence of policies adopted in the United States over the past two decades is that the country has evolved a truly demand-driven approach to the marketing of infrastructure. The FCC has reported that there is now four times the network transmission capacity that existed in 1984 at the time of the AT&T divestiture. Price reductions over the past seven years have demonstrated dramatically that there is significant elasticity of demand for long-distance service. The experience of the past decade illustrates that the market has extraordinary capability to absorb new transmission capacity that is provided both through carriers and through intermediaries who have installed transmission capacity to lease to carriers.

COPING WITH DISPARITIES. The FCC has wrestled with disparities in market position between established and newer entrants, a problem that besets or will beset regulators around the world as competition is opened up in the sector. The FCC is exploring in particular how to deal with special discount offerings for large customers and whether to allow AT&T significant new degrees of freedom to price its services. The FCC's energies are now being focused as well on complex issues involved in properly setting the level and structure of access charges for new providers of interexchange and local exchange services. It is also concerned with

97

how the pricing in FCC tariffs of separate service elements available as a result of the FCC's ONA initiative might affect comparable service capabilities available under state tariffs.

INTRODUCING PRICE-CAP REGULATION. Along with OFTEL in the United Kingdom, the FCC has had a pioneering role in developing effective new ways of overseeing rates of interexchange and local carriers. In shifting its focus from rate of return to price-cap regulation, the FCC has differentiated, at least in terms of the timing of implementation of its new approach to rate regulation, between AT&T's interexchange services and RBOC's local exchange services. In its price-cap proceeding, the FCC confronted enormously difficult issues that are often glossed over in discussions about price-cap regulation in European regulatory forums. The agency has addressed the difficult question of whether it would be appropriate to cap existing rates without determining how related to cost they might be. It focused on whether there should be one or several different price caps for different sets of services. And finally, the FCC addressed the need for periodic review and readjustment of results as a consequence of the application of the new regulatory regime.

FACING THE TRANSITION TO COMPETITIVE MARKETS. For all the criticism hurled at the American regulatory process, it cannot really be denied that American regulators have devised workable solutions to some intractable problems that their counterparts in the United Kingdom and Australia, in particular, are just beginning to confront. The American experience suggests that regulatory proceedings ought to be conducted in a less onerous and litigious way. It also suggests, however, that there is no escape from confrontation over the hard task of overseeing the major transformation of a once monopoly-dominated sector into one that is effectively competitive. Policymakers elsewhere who hope to effectuate similar sectoral changes will have to steel themselves to the fact that competition cannot be introduced without more complex regulatory oversight of the telecommunications sector, at least in a transition period.

DEALING WITH FRAGMENTED REGULATORY JURISDICTION. A final important aspect of the American regulatory process is the persistent and successful effort at sharing regulatory responsibilities between federal and state authorities. The FCC has grown adept at this process in the face of an increasingly hostile legal environment that has required the agency to negotiate with state public utility commissioners rather than mandate important regulatory initiatives that affect the states.

This aspect of the FCC's experience may be of particular interest and relevance in the few but important situations around the world in which the sharing of regulatory power among central and local authorities is an important issue. The American experience has parallels in Europe, where the Community is striving to integrate telecommunications policies on a national and regionwide basis. In the former Soviet republics, the People's Republic of China, and Canada procedures and protocols for allocating regulatory and policymaking responsibility are of critical importance as well.

SPILLING OVER OF U.S. DEVELOPMENTS IN THE INTERNATIONAL ARENA. The American regulatory experience is less important for policymakers overseas because it may be a model for restructuring than because changes in the U.S. telecommunications sector have a way of affecting the dynamics of other important national markets and the international telecom market as a whole. The most important such impact has been, and will continue to be, the extraordinary pressure exerted by U.S. price levels and structures on the level of international tariffs. Pricing reductions for international services have become a fact of life. Telecommunications administrations around the world that historically depended on international tariffs will have to adjust to this reality.

The other major trend that is likely to evolve out of the American scene is an increasing tendency for international services to be provided on an end-to-end basis with the assistance of sophisticated network management techniques. Traditional correspondent relationships will not disappear, but they will be supplemented by a new range of business relationships between foreign and local carriers. As will be discussed subsequently , there may be a new impetus for international carriers to become more involved in the construction of infrastructure for international services in overseas markets. There may be techniques for facilitating these new roles that minimize interference and involvement by major international carriers in the operations of their overseas partners in smaller markets.

Sectoral Reform in Smaller Markets: Finland, New Zealand, Australia

Because of the large scale and developed status of the telecommunications sector in many industrial countries, it may be tempting to conclude that any lessons derived from the experience of such countries have limited applicability to smaller countries that are still developing their infrastructure. Hence, it may be of particular interest to consider the situations of three small industrial countries—Finland, New Zealand, and Australia—that are in varying stages of introducing highly competitive industry structures.

REFORMING TELECOMMUNICATIONS IN FINLAND. For many years Finland has had a highly complex industry structure in which public and private sector entities have had important roles. The Finnish PTT has been in recent years converted from a government ministry into a public corporation, Telecom Finland, whose shares are held by the government. It is responsible for interexchange services within Finland as well as internationally. It is also a provider of local exchange services in many small communities.

The largest local telephone companies, those serving the cities of Helsinki, Tampere, and Turku, as well as many other local telephone companies are operated by cooperatives of the local companies' subscribers. These local companies have been able to form an independent carrier, Datatie, which can offer leased-line and private network services for customers. It is likely that Datatie may soon be authorized as an interexchange carrier for the second Global System for Mobile Communications (GSM) cellular carrier in Finland. As a result of competition from Datatie, Telecom Finland has engaged in a major rebalancing of its tariffs, which has resulted in significant price reductions for Finnish subscribers. The competition between Datatie and Telecom Finland is the basis for full competition in switched voice services at all levels, which will be allowed in 1994. The complex competitive environment is overseen by an independent regulatory agency, the Telecommunications Administration Centre, in the Ministry of Telecommunications. This body is responsible for ensuring the evolution of a fair and effective competitive environment.

DEVELOPING COMPETITION IN NEW ZEALAND. In New Zealand the government moved aggressively to privatize Telecom Corporation of New Zealand Limited (TCNZ). In 1990 Bell Atlantic and Ameritech acquired the shares of TCNZ with an expectation that their stake in the company would be reduced to less than a 50 percent interest within two years.

Policymakers in New Zealand opted for an entirely open market. New entrants are able to offer either interexchange or local exchange services. Instead of creating a new regulatory body, New Zealand officials have taken the unusual step of relying on the country's Commerce Act, its basic competition law, to oversee the evolution of competition. In practical terms, the absence of a regulatory process may place TCNZ in the difficult position of determining how far it can go in rebalancing its pricing in response to competition. New Zealand authorities have not mandated the development of any specific accounting standards or cost allocation principles. Consequently, the company has had to take the initiative itself to justify the various rate packages it hopes to implement. Moreover, as a practical matter TCNZ has been constrained from increasing its local tariffs; instead, it has proposed and justified reductions in long-distance tariffs.

TCNZ's ability to adjust to a competitive climate is clearly a result of its privatization, which has produced a substantial reduction in its work force. Increasingly, TCNZ has been contracting out for all but the most essential services. New Zealand thus is a fascinating and important laboratory in which the effects of both privatization and open-entry policies in small markets can be assessed. In particular, the process of sectoral reform in New Zealand will illustrate how well government officials can seek to oversee a competitive environment with only a minimal regulatory regime centered around competition law principles.

REFORMING THE SECTOR IN AUSTRALIA. After extended debate over a number of different restructuring options, the Australian government decided to merge the two major players on the Australian telecommunications scene, Telecom Australia and OTC into a single new entity now called Telstra. This new entity combined the small but highly market-oriented international carrier OTC with its gigantic domestic counterpart Telecom Australia, which many observers viewed as slow moving and overstaffed. It was to face across-the-board competition from the heavily debt-ridden and money-losing national satellite carrier AUSSAT, which was offered for sale to consortia of Australian and foreign interests.

Prior to the sale, the Australian government had to simultaneously wrestle with two difficult and interrelated concerns: (1) which consortium was to be permitted to buy AUSSAT and on what terms and conditions, and (2) what arrangements for combining OTC and Telecom Australia would be adopted and what competitive safeguards for the introduction of competition would be implemented. In particular, government policymakers—along with the Australian Telecommunications Authority (AUSTEL), the independent regulatory body—had to devise a set of access arrangements through which the new entrant and perhaps even Telstra could utilize local exchange capabilities. Undoubtedly, potential purchasers took a keen interest in what flexibility Telstra had in order to respond to offerings by its newly privatized competitor.

To establish a yardstick to assess Telstra's response to competition, Australian policymakers may have to mandate Telstra to conduct extensive cost-accounting and cost-allocation analyses. Thus, the recent experience of American regulators and OFTEL's recent policy determinations in its duopoly white paper are likely to be of great relevance to Australian policymakers. Policymakers in Australia also had to grapple with the reality that they could not easily attract new investors without a clearly defined set of regulatory initiatives setting forth the basic parameters in which competition is likely to occur.

The balances that ultimately were struck in Australia should be of interest to policymakers around the world who are contemplating, or are in the process of, privatization. The Australian experience should fundamentally test the tolerance of investors for arrangements where privatization and vigorous competition coexist. A well-structured competitive environment may offer the best possible assurance to investors that both new players on the Australian scene are well motivated to structure their operations in the most efficient way.

CONSIDERING OPTIONS BEYOND THE EC CONSENSUS. The important lesson that can be drawn from the experience of all three of these countries is that a full range of restructuring options going well beyond the consensus embedded in the 1987 EC Green Paper are practical and worthy of careful consideration. That the national markets of these three countries are small by comparison should not alter policymakers' analysis as to how much competition may be viable.

Some Implications of Recent Sectoral Restructuring Efforts

The following summarizes a number of observations about the sectoral restructuring processes under way in industrial countries around the world that may have some relevance to countries still developing their infrastructure.

Options for Reform

Policymakers should not necessarily limit the range of options to those that have evolved in countries with well-developed infrastructures. Where there is a pressing need for new infrastructure to serve the needs of users, a full range of options for encouraging new investment should be fully explored. In particular, telecommunications users and new service providers with access to foreign-exchange resources should be permitted to invest in facilities that can be utilized in connection with a PTT's facilities. Very small aperture terminals (VSAT) satellite networks may be one way to provide services rapidly in the face of facilities shortages. The experience of German regulatory officials in encouraging voice telephony services between the eastern and western regions of Germany should be carefully studied. In general, satellite networks should not be limited to nonvoice services and precluded from offering switched voice services where reliable transmission links are urgently needed.

As is more fully set forth below, there may be other effective ways of meeting demand and encouraging independent entrepreneurs to become retailers of services marketed through a PTT's network. The experience of smaller industrial countries also suggests that there is room for new providers of infrastructure and that fair terms and conditions of competition can be structured between new and established service providers. Overall, PTTs are likely to be well served by liberalizing arrangements through which telecommunications users can utilize leased circuits and add their own switching and application-related information processing capabilities. Telecommunications carriers should permit broad flexibility for users to tailor the networks and capabilities that are necessary for key sectors of the national economy, such as banking, transportation and tourism, and manufacturing activities. Carriers should recognize that such specialized networks often will entail third party or shared use of networks and may even involve the resale of pure telecommunications transmission services.

The practical effect of liberalizing the provision of value added networks and of ancillary transmission facilities such as VSATs will be primarily to attract new sources of investment and to put PTTs in the position of becoming more oriented to the needs of their customers. Permitting new entrants and new services should help in tapping new sources of investment necessary to develop telecom infrastructures.

Options for Increasing Self-Financing Capabilities

Telecommunications operators should recognize the crucial importance of improving their capability of financing new infrastructure investment through measures that increase revenues and cut costs.

RESTRUCTURING TARIFFS. One of the most critical steps is for a PTT to begin to redress historic tariff imbalances which have generally resulted in local tariffs being too low and interexchange tariffs being too high. Raising local tariffs does not generally appear politically expedient. However, the experience of countries that have been restructuring their telecommunications sectors strongly suggests that repricing local services is imperative.

One of the consequences of liberalization and deregulation around the world has been the reduction of interexchange and international tariffs. Maintaining international and interexchange tariffs at traditional levels places national telecommunications users at a competitive disadvantage in an increasingly globalized economy. Pricing policies that are not set on an efficient basis and are not consistent with international benchmarks are also likely to place the telecommunications operator at a competitive disadvantage in seeking to raise financing in international capital markets. The efficiency of telecommunications pricing may often be a determining factor in foreign investors' decisions about where to locate plants as well as service industries dependent on computer-processing capabilities.

Another reason for moving promptly to adjust tariff structures is that both collection and settlement rates for international services are steadily being reduced as a result of pressures in the international arena. Such services have traditionally contributed a disproportionately high percentage of PTT profits. Failure to put in place new tariff structures to offset expected lost international revenues could place a PTT at a serious disadvantage.

Reductions in international and interexchange tariffs may often contribute to significantly higher levels of calling. Although profit margins may decrease, a PTT may have opportunities to maintain the current level of contribution to its profits from international services through increased calling volumes. Such a strategy requires, however, that a PTT take increased demand into account in its facilities planning.

A PTT may also be able to identify means of increasing local tariffs on a selective basis. For example, if an overlay network of new digital facilities is implemented, users of these new facilities might be expected to pay local exchange charges that are set at international levels.

INCREASING EFFICIENCY THROUGH ORGANIZATIONAL REFORM. There are a number of approaches to reducing costs at a PTT. Such initiatives often involve fundamental changes in organizational or management structure. Privatization may, of course, create significant incentives for cost cutting. Private investors inevitably will demand substantially more information about operating results and will expect management to follow through on its cost and revenue projections. Improvements in management performance can also be obtained through more limited measures that transform a PTT from a government department into a corporate entity whose shares are owned by the government.

Corporatization usually results in a complete reexamination of a PTT's relations with the state. Commercial considerations will weigh more heavily in determining how funds are invested by the state or borrowed from public or private lenders. A PTT's dividend policy might be restructured to conform with the practices of private corporations. A PTT might also expect to pay both corporate and excise taxes in the same way as private corporations. In addition, a PTT might be given leeway to collect accounts payable without taking into account the governmental status of its debtors. In this way, a PTT could be prevented from making de facto transfer payments to support the operations of entities responsible for other areas of governmental activity.

Mere changes in the legal status of a PTT may not make it more aware of the profitability of its various lines of business. A PTT may also have to improve its cost accounting systems to make it possible to measure the performance and profitability of its various lines of business.

DECENTRALIZING OPERATIONS OF PTTs. One useful technique for increasing the awareness of managers of the profitability of a PTT's business is to decentralize its organizational structure. A first step can usually be taken with respect to new business activities such as the provision of data networking, terminal equipment, or cellular services. Such activities can be set up as separate subsidiaries incorporated under private law (usually even where a PTT operates as a public corporation). The creation of subsidiaries also facilitates the establishment of joint ventures and investment in a PTT's business by domestic or foreign entities. It may also be useful to consider breaking a PTT down into core businesses such as local exchange, domestic interexchange, and international services. The implementation of cost accounting and allocation systems should facilitate the identification of specific business initiatives necessary to increase profits or to reduce operating deficits.

Another approach might be to begin the process of reorganization and restructuring within the existing organizational structure but establish a parallel corporate structure that could be utilized as a vehicle for attracting new investment in infrastructure. New entities could be created to own and potentially manage new infrastructure assets and would be established with up-to-date management systems. A PTT could also be reformed by gradually shifting more and more operational responsibilities from the old PTT structure into a parallel new business unit. In effect, a new institutional structure might be established as an overlay on the traditional structure. In a similar way, new network facilities would be added as overlays to the existing network infrastructure.

One important advantage of decentralizing existing organizational structures is that managers would be required to negotiate explicit transfer prices for services provided within a PTT. Services that could not be performed efficiently by PTT staff could be contracted out. The operators of interexchange services would have to contract with local exchange service providers to terminate circuits; however, if transfer prices were set too high, an interexchange business unit could be permitted to make independent arrangements for local loops, in effect bypassing the local exchange operating unit. Through such a strategy, policymakers would be, in effect, setting in motion institutional rivalries within a PTT that might spur more efficient performance. These efficiency producing benefits could be obtained even where no decision had been taken to permit competition by entities other than a PTT.

ENCOURAGING INFRASTRUCTURE DEVELOPMENT THROUGH COOPERATIVE ARRANGEMENTS. In addition to decentralizing existing business units within a PTT, it may also be appropriate in some countries where a great unmet demand exists to encourage new entities or suppliers to build out the ends of a PTT's network. Under such arrangements, described in greater detail in chapter 31 a PTT would authorize private entities to construct segments of the local network. These would be connected to the PTT's network, subject to a franchise agreement that would set out technical interface standards and the division of revenue between the PTT and the new entity. The franchise agreement might provide for the PTT to purchase the assets of the franchise in exchange for stock in a privatized PTT at a later stage. Local cooperatives might be established to take on such franchises.

This approach could facilitate the raising of investment capital for infrastructure development, offer a training ground for a new class of entrepreneurs and managers, and stimulate the development of specialized equipment and billing systems. The development of new local cooperative companies would thus become an important mechanism for preparing a PTT for privatization.

UTILIZING NEW METHODS FOR FINANCING INFRASTRUCTURE. As already discussed, there may be novel mechanisms for attracting private investment into a PTT even without initially selling shares in it. For example, a structure of financing entities that would enable a PTT to attract sources of private or foreign investment capital for the construction of new infrastructure might be established. These entities could be structured to finance the construction of local exchange facilities in particular cities or regions or in the country as a whole and then lease these facilities to the PTT. They could also be utilized as a vehicle for attracting capital for particular business initiatives such as the development of cellular services or packet-switching networks. Such an asset-based financing approach is also discussed in detail in chapter 31.

DEVELOPING A COMPREHENSIVE PLAN FOR FINANCIAL RECOVERY OF A PTT. Both the utilization of a separate financing mechanism and initiatives to encourage new investment on the peripheries of a PTT's network should help establish the necessary groundwork for a PTT to privatize. Investors should view these as significant and useful steps, which should increase the success of the privatization process.

It makes little sense to rush toward privatization without addressing a number of threshold problems, including most of the issues that must be confronted in the process of corporatizing a PTT. Certainly among the most important concerns are reassessing the structure of government-held debt, defining dividend expectations of the government with respect to shares retained, and delineating the ongoing control relationships between a PTT and the state (including board representation and mechanisms for holding and voting shares).

The timing and sequence of privatization thus become matters of crucial importance. The incumbent management of a PTT and the state may not be ideally suited to undertake the important initial steps involved in privatization. Still, moving too quickly may ultimately diminish the value of the government's stake in a PTT. This could leave few options other than replacing government control with control by one or more outside investors.

Overall Approach to Sectoral Reform

Any consideration of privatization as an option must be undertaken in the context of a thorough review of options for restructuring the telecommunications sector as a whole. Modernizing and privatizing a PTT alone is seldom likely to provide the necessary impetus for the full development of the telecommunications sector as an engine for economic growth. It is a mistake to conclude that a PTT, or even a privatized PTT, can meet all the needs of all the industry sectors dependent on telecommunications services; thus, diversification in supply of equipment and service capabilities is essential. Moreover, the careful introduction of competition into the telecommunications sector is likely to prod a PTT into performing more effectively and efficiently; competitive pressures in the sector also minimize the burden on regulators to assure that, once privatized, a PTT does not abuse its advantageous position in the market.

Notwithstanding the important benefits of competition in the sector, the privatization process can often create pressure from those responsible for selling a PTT to maintain it as an exclusive provider of certain services, such as switched voice services. It is not always clear, however, that these concerns about limiting competition are well founded. The real and legitimate concern of investors is, or should be, that the parameters for future regulatory and competitive arrangements are explicitly and clearly delineated and provide for a level playing field. Investors should not necessarily be concerned about competition in the sector; rather, their concern should be that the regulatory and competitive environment will not be capricious and unpredictable.

Regulatory Mechanisms for the Sector

Often it is easier for policymakers to maintain the regulatory status quo than to attempt to undertake the daunting task of defining a new regulatory environment. It is beyond the scope of this discussion to detail fully the issues that must be addressed in structuring a new regulatory framework. Nevertheless, some of the most difficult issues center around how to oversee the pricing of a PTT that is to undergo restructuring and face competition for the first time.

OVERSEEING THE PROCESS OF RATE REBALANCING. There is usually no easy way to initiate the process of rate rebalancing. Policymakers can know with confidence the direction in which rates must be revised; usually, local rates must be increased by a factor of three or four and international rates must be lowered. How this process is initiated can be an important and controversial issue, especially in nonmarket economies that concurrently are introducing principles of the free market and of democratic control. In such countries it may often be politically unacceptable simply to accede, without analysis and deliberation, to a new rate prescription developed by a former or soon-to-be former state monopoly. Ministry officials or even legislators will insist that a PTT provide information justifying rate changes; they will want to be involved in the process of developing new rates. Insistence on public control can, however, easily lead to populist resistance to the unpleasant consequences of necessary price restructuring. Thus, it is necessary to devise new procedures that not only permit public participation and input but also expert analysis of complex pricing issues.

ASSESSING THE PITFALLS OF PRICE-CAP REGULATION. Introducing a form of price-cap regulation can often be an important step forward. However, price-cap regulation can be counterproductive if the proper prices are not set before the application of a price cap. Policymakers in some countries have sought to develop a scheme of international benchmark prices. Devising these benchmarks may be an extraordinarily difficult task and may not adequately reflect conditions unique to a national market. Nevertheless, reference to pricing levels and practices in industrial countries can be a good starting point for rate-rebalancing proposals.

In implementing price-cap regulation in an environment where a PTT has been a monopoly and may remain an exclusive supplier of some essential services such as local exchange services, two particularly difficult policy issues are (1) how many price-cap baskets to structure and what services to include in them, and (2) how to deal with the special problem of setting prices for access to the local network. In the United States, a number of different baskets were created to differentiate among AT&T's various interexchange services in which AT&T was viewed as having differing market shares and potential for cross-subsidization. Similarly, an even larger group of separate price-cap baskets were implemented for local exchange services provided by RBOCs.

STRUCTURING INTERCONNECTION ARRANGEMENTS. Although it is a difficult task to devise interconnection arrangements, a good start is to base such arrangements initially upon contractual negotiations between a PTT and the competitive entity or the users requiring network access. Policymakers, can, however, insist on some basic principles, such as nondiscrimination by the PTT among similarly situated users and between entities affiliated and unaffiliated with the PTT. Whether interconnection arrangements must be equal or merely comparably efficient is a question with which policymakers have grappled in many industrial countries, especially the United States.

DEVELOPING COST-ACCOUNTING AND ALLOCATION SYSTEMS. Assuring that pricing is cost based or cost oriented is difficult to achieve in practice. PTTs often have inadequate business accounting systems that are based on functional rather than on line-of-business accounting principles. Deciding on proper cost-accounting and allocation systems is an inexact process. However, it may be useful for officials responsible for overseeing a PTT to encourage the adoption of business accounting schemes that permit an assessment of the profitability of different business activities of a PTT. One of the advantages of creating separate subsidiaries is that costs and revenues can be effectively accounted for.

UTILIZING COMPETITIVE ENTRY AS A REGULATORY TOOL. Implementing effective cost-accounting schemes is a process that cannot take place in isolation from a well-focused effort to introduce competition into the telecommunications sector. Competitive entry will tend to encourage a PTT to take a closer look at its operational costs and its pricing practices. There is, of course, substantial potential for predatory pricing by a PTT anxious to maintain its traditional market share when first confronted with new competition. Regulators may be inclined to assure the viability of new competitive entrants; thus, they may hesitate to approve a PTT's efforts to meet competition with new pricing plans, particularly discount pricing targeted at large users. As noted above, NTT has been quite constrained in its ability to respond to new entrants. In the United Kingdom, the duopoly white paper addressed for the first time a concrete scheme for allowing BT increased flexibility in offering discounted pricing options for its customers.

As much as regulators may wish to shy away from the quagmire of addressing cost accounting, cost allocation, and pricing issues, they may avoid facing these issues only at the risk of impairing the rapid and effective emergence of competition in the telecommunications sector. Regulators must be able to devise dispute-resolution mechanisms that permit carriers and users affected by price changes to accommodate their differences. PTTs in the process of restructuring must be allowed leeway to implement pricing structures that will encourage new investment. However, these policies must also permit a competitive environment to flourish.

It is important to ensure that when new and established entrants are competing in the same market, they are subject to comparable licensing schemes and regulatory burdens. However, regulators must also recognize that special importance attaches to the negotiation of a regulatory framework or concession for the operation of a PTT. Such a framework must explicitly address competitive safeguards or special obligations essential to ensure the viability of any new competitive initiatives that are to be adopted.

SEPARATING REGULATORY FUNCTIONS AND ESTABLISHING OPEN PROCEDURES. As discussed, questions concerning regulatory structure and process are extraordinarily important and will affect policy outcomes. There are many ways of approaching the separation of regulatory, operational, and ownership functions that have, in many countries, been centered in the same institution. The core concern of policymakers should be to assure that these separate roles are kept in separate hands as fully as possible.

A vigorous and aggressive competitor cannot be a fair umpire. Likewise, the role of devising effective regulation for a PTT involves quite different concerns than must be addressed by a chairman of the board of a large enterprise. Overlapping responsibilities may result in ineffective regulation as well as in ineffective corporate governance. Ultimately, devising new regulatory mechanisms is less about establishing new institutions than it is about establishing new procedures that permit the issues and disputes generated by a transition to a new industry structure to be effectively addressed and resolved. Those procedures must assure an openness that allows all affected interests to have their views heard.

Overseeing the Process of Sectoral Reform

It is appropriate to make some concluding observations about the role of multilateral lending institutions and private enterprisebanks in the process of sectoral reform.

A Multidimensional Process

The process of sectoral restructuring is clearly an extraordinarily complex one with many dimensions. There are at least four major elements in this process: (1) a plan for modernizing the organizational structure of a PTT, reforming its pricing, and setting new strategic priorities, (2) a scheme for financing the development of a PTT's infrastructure, including an assessment of options for introducing new sources of investment from the private sector into a PTT, (3) a design for the future market structure and for competitive arrangements in the telecommunications sector as a whole, and (4) a mechanism for setting policy and regulating a PTT and others in the sector.

Managing the restructuring process requires a diverse array of skills and expertise. Attention must be focused both on the future of a PTT and of the sector as a whole. One of the risks implicit in any restructuring process is that there will be too much of a rush to sell the assets of a PTT and not enough time given to the arduous process of preparing a PTT and the telecommunications sector for the privatization process. Policymakers must keep in mind that investors have to be convinced of both the viability of a PTT and the overall regulatory and competitive arrangements for the sector.

Conflicts between Short-Term and Long-Term Objectives

Policymakers must make some basic decisions about their objectives. In particular, they must decide whether they want to maximize proceeds from the sale of a PTT or whether they want to create a competitive environment that will benefit telecommunications users and even a PTT in the long run. It is certainly not at all clear that the shareholders of a state-owned PTT will be better off by limiting competition in critical sectors of a PTT's business. Permitting competitive pressures may force a PTT to become more efficient and profitable. Over time, the state may benefit from increased tax revenues derived from a well-run PTT, as well as from economic activity stimulated by diverse and widely available telecommunications services.

In order to transform the functioning of a PTT and the telecommunications sector as a whole, the contributions of private investment bankers and multilateral lending agencies are required. Multilateral lenders have an essential role in devising new regulatory and institutional arrangements. They are often, however, less able to contribute to the identification of new financing methods and strategies for organizational reform. The utilization of conditions on sectoral readjustment loans may sometimes be too blunt and ineffective an instrument to bring about rapid sectoral changes.

Entrepreneurially Oriented Restructuring

Another approach for multilateral lending agencies is to consider making loans for initiatives that involve new technique for infrastructure financing or organizational reform. Such loans would not be centered around a project investment in the traditional sense. Rather they would be intended to achieve quite focused objectives in terms of organizational reform or sectoral organization.

For example, the utilization of a separate financing mechanism as described above would require a PTT and sector policymakers to reach agreements on crucial new institutional and regulatory arrangements. A financing entity that is established to build an overlay network might only become viable if restructured pricing arrangements were put in place for services to be offered through the overlay network. The new operating entity would have to enter into negotiations with local exchange providers to obtain access services. In the process, steps would be taken to reform existing mechanisms for settlement of revenues among different parts of a PTT.

New private sector investment could not be feasibly introduced unless some agreement on future regulatory arrangements was reached among national policymakers and those developing a new overlay network. In short, the process of developing both a business and a strategic plan for a new enterprise should inevitably result in important steps toward sectoral restructuring.

Need for Incremental Options

Some observers believe that the potential sellers of PTTs may now be outnumbering the potential buyers. Investors may be becoming increasingly wary of the risks involved in a major restructuring and in the privatization of an entire PTT. It may thus be important to begin actively exploring techniques that allow an incremental approach to introducing new private investment into the telecommunications sector but involve important steps toward overall sectoral reform.

Conclusion

The lessons of recent experience with sectoral reform and privatization are no doubt valuable ones. However, the most critical ingredient for the success of future sectoral restructuring may be the ability to devise solutions that are unique to each national setting and that involve new and imaginative approaches to financing and institutional reform.

Part II

Recent Experiences

in Latin America

3

Telecommunications Restructuring in
Latin America : An Overview

Björn Wellenius

NOWHERE IN THE DEVELOPING WORLD has the movement toward restructuring the telecommunications sector been as rapid and vigorous as in Latin America. First in Chile, then in rapid succession in Argentina, Mexico, and Venezuela, and by 1993 under way at various stages in Bolivia, Brazil, Colombia, Ecuador, El Salvador, Honduras, Panama, Peru, and Uruguay, profound changes have been sweeping through this region, especially since the late 1980s. Governments are replacing the traditional model of state telecommunications monopoly embraced in the 1960s with solutions that largely rely on services provided by the private sector, growing competition, and a shift of government role from ownership and operation to policy and regulation. These changes seek to overcome long-standing constraints on economic and social development imposed by telecommunications services that are in short supply, unreliable, of poor quality, and slow to respond to changing demand patterns and technology choices.[1]

The reforms in Chile, Argentina, Mexico, and Venezuela are outlined and discussed below, and progress so far in other Latin American countries is briefly described in the Annex. The rest of this chapter presents some lessons on implementation of reforms drawn from the Latin American experience, including a tentative assessment of how well these reforms have met the governments' objectives. This chapter concludes by raising some concerns about the long-term success of reforms in overcoming past constraints on telecommunications development. The following chapters discuss in more detail selected aspects of the reforms in Chile (chapter 4), Argentina (chapter 5), Mexico (chapter 6), and Venezuela (chapter 7).

The Beginnings of Sector Reform in Latin America

Chile was the first country in Latin America to undertake major reforms of the telecommunications sector and the first to complete privatization of its state enterprises in 1987. Argentina and Mexico did likewise by 1990, at what was then regarded as an exceptionally fast pace. By the time Venezuela followed suit in 1991, a pattern had been established.

Chile

Reform of the telecommunications sector in Chile started in 1975 and was substantially completed in 1987. At the time reforms began, telecommunications were dominated by two joint-stock companies, mainly state-owned. Compañía de Teléfonos de Chile (CTC) had about 95 percent of the local telephone market, and Empresa Nacional de Telecomunicaciones (ENTEL) operated most long-distance and all international facilities. CTC had been a private, foreign-owned company until 1964, when it became jointly owned by the state, which injected substantial amounts of capital for expansion and modernization. In 1970 CTC was taken over by the government, and in 1974 the foreign partner was bought out. ENTEL had been established as a state-owned company in 1964 with the mandate of building a countrywide, modern long-distance network and, shortly after, satellite facilities for international services.[2]

Early reform attempts had mixed results. For example, several new small companies were licensed in the mid-1970s to provide local telephone service in competition with CTC in areas where there was large unmet demand. Although these companies initially thrived developing overlay local networks wholly financed by high subscriber connection fees, none of them ever achieved anywhere near efficient size; one went bankrupt, and the rest became involved in protracted litigation with CTC over revenue sharing, predatory practices, and other regulatory problems which the government was not well equipped to handle. On the other hand, telex services were successfully reorganized from a stagnant section of the government's posts and telegraphs administration into a dynamic commercial state enterprise that was then sold to Chilean private investors.

Concurrently, however, a reform process got under way comprising a relatively slow but ultimately consistent sequence of changes that transformed the sector overall very successfully. In the context of the government's adoption in 1975 of a strong market-oriented economic development strategy favoring private enterprise and foreign investment, a series of steps was taken to create a policy and regulatory framework specifically for telecommunications. In 1977, Subsecretaría de Telecomunicaciones (SUBTEL) was established in the Ministry of Transport and Telecommunications, with responsibility for mainly technical regulation. An executive decree of 1978 promulgated a telecommunications policy which set the basic principles that guided all subsequent liberalization and privatization. In 1982 a telecommunications law was passed which enabled enforcement of specific actions to implement the government's policy and abrogated preexisting, conflicting statutes. An amendment to the law in 1987 established specific means to implement privatization. In particular, it defined mechanisms for investment financing and a system for regulating the tariffs of monopoly services. In 1986 the government began to sell some of its shares in CTC and ENTEL to company employees and the public.[3] In 1987 international bids were invited for a controlling interest in CTC and awarded to Alan Bond, an Australian investor; the balance of the state's ENTEL shares were sold to various domestic and foreign investors and to the public at large.

In 1989 the government sold its remaining CTC shares to employees and the public. In 1990, Bond sold CTC to Telefónica de España, which by then also held a 25 percent interest in ENTEL.

The reforms have greatly revitalized the telecommunications sector. Telephone lines, which had been growing at about 5 percent in the 1970s and 1980s, expanded at over 20 percent per annum in 1990 and 1991. Digitalization accelerated from around 35 percent to over 70 percent. Modern optical-fiber networks, digital microwaves, and satellite systems were or are being built. Labor productivity, already rather good for developing countries at around 13 staff per 1,000 lines, improved further to 7 in 1991, which is within the range of industrial countries.[4] New services were introduced and there is substantial competition in nonbasic services and networks. Three companies (including one subsidiary each of CTC and ENTEL) compete in providing cellular service in the main cities. Business users can choose between the public-switched telephone system and network solutions offered by several new carriers besides CTC and ENTEL. The deregulated market for customer premises equipment offers a wide variety of telephones, private automatic branch exchanges (PABXs), fax machines, and other goods. CTC and ENTEL are operating very profitably, new sources of financing have been developed (including CTC's breakthrough placement of US$100 million in new shares in the U.S. market in 1990), and share values of both CTC and ENTEL roughly doubled in 1991. There are also the beginnings of competition in long-distance voice service. CTC negotiated with a new company to carry about 20 percent of the traffic earlier handled through ENTEL.

From a broader economic viewpoint, moreover, there is some evidence that the Chilean telecommunications reforms have resulted in substantial benefits to *all* stakeholders. A study shows that with the privatization of CTC, aggregate welfare has been enhanced by some US$600 million, of which 94 percent accrues to Chilean parties.[5] Consumers were the biggest winners, capturing 90 percent of the gain in domestic welfare, largely resulting from accelerated investment leading to a greatly increased stock of telephone lines in service, and from the introduction of new services.[6] The government, CTC's domestic shareholders and employees, and ENTEL[7] share the balance. Privatization with foreign participation thus created a non–zero-sum game which benefited both nationals and foreigners.[8]

The regulatory arrangement is also overall successful. Chile's stable political institutions and the independence of the judiciary result in contracts (for example, government licenses to private operators) that are credible and enforceable. The relative difficulty of passing or amending legislation gives stability to the sector's legal framework, making it less vulnerable to policy changes from one government to the next. In particular, pricing rules for monopoly services are spelled out in the telecommunications law in considerable detail, including a five-year cycle for revisions. This allows investment decisions based on revenue forecasts that are fairly robust, while allowing for periodic reassessment in the light of changes in technology and other factors. SUBTEL has clearly defined functions, including the authority to verify compliance by service producers and users of legal, procedural, and technical resolutions. Deciding whether a service is not subject to effective competition, and thus its prices should be regulated, is left to the antitrust tribunal in the context of well-established general commerce law. Disputes on sharing costs and revenues among operating companies are resolved through arbitration.[9]

Nevertheless, not all is well. The market is still dominated by CTC and ENTEL. As for quality of service, the results have been mixed. Faults are being cleared faster, and CTC appears to be more responsive to customer complaints; however, the fault rate has not continued to decrease, call completion rate has actually dropped, and the increased percentage of busy signal suggests growing network congestion.[10] No practical solution has been found to ensure service in rural and other areas that are less profitable than cities, and mechanisms for direct government subsidy, where needed, have proven ineffective.[11]

There are also critical regulatory issues that remain unresolved despite several years' litigation in the antitrust tribunals and ordinary courts of justice. One issue is of particular importance in terms of competition. CTC's plans to become itself a long-distance carrier and develop its own optical-fiber and satellite long-distance network have been challenged by ENTEL, which holds a virtual monopoly of these facilities over many routes. A court order has restrained CTC from putting into service new equipment and satellite leases already purchased. In turn, ENTEL's attempts to expand its base of direct access to final business users has been contested by CTC. Another issue has a major bearing on sector structure and thus also on competition. From the viewpoint of Chilean antitrust policy and law, Telefónica's substantial although minority stake in ENTEL conflicts with its ownership of CTC. This is further complicated by ENTEL employees' intention to sell their shares, and by the possibility of financial restructuring of ENTEL that would reportedly allow Telefónica to take administrative control. Whatever is the right solution to these regulatory problems, the fact that they have not been sorted out definitively within a reasonable period of time points to significant weaknesses of the Chilean regulatory system.

As for SUBTEL, it is not fully equipped to discharge its regulatory responsibilities effectively. In particular, relatively low government remunerations make it difficult for SUBTEL to attract and retain qualified specialists who are also in high demand in the private sector. Being part of a ministry largely dominated by the much larger transportation sector, SUBTEL's problems tend to receive rather limited attention at the higher levels of government.[12] Solutions under consideration include reorganizing SUBTEL as a more independent "superintendencia," similar to the successful banking regulatory agency, or along the lines of the widely acclaimed energy commission.

Argentina

In early 1989 the president of Argentina announced his decision to privatize Empresa Nacional de Telecomunicaciones (ENTel), the state telecommunications monopoly. A prominent politician was appointed as trustee of ENTel with mandate to sell it in about twelve months. The trustee retained a small number of experienced managers and professionals from the private sector to prepare and carry out this task.

In January 1990 an executive decree outlined the government's new sector policies and structure and set forth the terms and conditions for the sale of ENTel. These provisions were designed to enhance competition and diversify ownership. In particular, ENTel was to be divided into two regional companies, each including about half of the lucrative Buenos Aires market.[13] The regional companies would have the monopoly of basic telephone services and networks for seven years, or up to ten years subject to meeting higher performance targets. Sixty percent of the shares of each regional company would be sold under competition to foreign telecommunications operating enterprises responsible for managing the new companies, associated with local and foreign investors. Bidding and evaluation were designed to give preference to different owners-operators for each regional company, partly in order to facilitate subsequent performance comparisons and to give credibility to the potential for competition between them. Two separate companies, jointly owned by the regional companies, would provide international and competitive services, respectively. Franchises for cellular services would be awarded under competition, the first franchise in each locality being adjudicated to a company other than the regional telephone operator. The supply of subscriber terminal equipment, private networks, and data and value added services, would be liberalized immediately. Three independent companies, licensed during a short-lived liberalization effort by the previous government, were to continue developing competing data networks and services using satellite technology.

Privatization was completed close to schedule. In early November 1990 the new owners-operators took over the two regional companies. Telecom Argentina, the northern regional company, is owned by a consortium led by France Télécom and STET (Italy). Telefónica de Argentina, the southern regional company, is owned by a consortium led by Telefónica (Spain). The remaining 40 percent of shares were sold by tranches in 1991 and early 1992 to the employees, subscribers, existing rural telephone cooperatives, and the public at large. The public sales, in Argentina and through agents abroad, were several times oversubscribed.

The new owners-operators got off to a good start. Six months after taking over, new organization structures were in place in both regional companies, and about 100 specialists had been brought over from the parent operating companies to occupy senior management positions and assist in a wide range of tasks at middle-management and supervisory technical levels. The companies were renegotiating labor contracts and introducing improved work practices and had taken initial steps to control fraud. Urgent technical problems were being addressed, service was starting to improve for large users, and investments worth about US$700 million were under way in 1991, mostly financed from operating surpluses.

A tentative assessment two years after privatization confirms that the new owners-operators have been successful in rationalizing the two regional companies and meeting the performance and investment targets set forth in the terms and conditions of sale. The labor force has shrunk by 20 percent, from a combined total of 41,000 workers at the end of 1990 to 33,000 in early 1993, mostly through voluntary retirements for which the companies made incentive payments. The combination of sharply reduced work force and modest system growth resulted in an improvement of labor productivity from 13 to 10 workers per 1,000 lines in the first year of operation. Improved systems for internal information and control were put in place, especially in the areas of billing and collection, payroll, contracting, and purchasing. Contracts with equipment suppliers inherited from ENTel were renegotiated, resulting in price reductions of up to 50 percent. All contracts in excess of US$0.5 million were awarded through international competitive bidding, further reducing investment costs.[14] Already in 1991, the first year of operation after privatization, the regional companies averaged a modest 4 percent return on equity. The return on investment was much larger for the foreign operator partners who, including management contracts, netted 17 percent for STET and France Télécom and 83 percent for Telefónica. The regional companies' investment plans for 1991–96 are well in excess of what would be required to meet the targets agreed at the time of purchase.[15]

Progress on the regulatory front, however, has been slow. An executive decree of June 1990 established Comisión Nacional de Telecomunicaciones (CNT), a semi-autonomous telecommunications regulatory agency, and outlined its functions and organization. Although the CNT chairman and six directors were appointed and took office at around the time the ENTel sale was completed, in mid-1991 government administrative decisions were still pending regarding temporary organization, staffing, salary scales, and budget and accounting rules. Whereas the sector reform schedule called for a core regulatory capacity to be in place by the time the regional companies were transferred to the new owners-operators, in practice this did not materialize. Urgent regulatory matters, including establishing guidelines for interconnection pricing between the regional companies and their international and competitive services subsidiaries, specifying the basic flows of information from the regulated companies to enable CNT to monitor compliance with service and performance obligations, and establishing regulations for competitive services, were not given timely attention.

Lack of effective regulation immediately after privatization is likely to have had a significant, albeit unquantifiable, negative impact on sector development. The following are some examples. CNT has been unable to verify the regional companies' compliance with service and performance obligations. CNT failed to act when, five months after privatization, the government reneged on its contractual agreement to let the regional companies adjust their tariffs for inflation, a key determinant of the viability of the companies; eventually the issue was resolved, but through direct negotiation between the companies and the Ministry of Economy, not CNT. Unregulated marketing of calling card services by international operators may have violated the temporary exclusivity rights of the incumbents and may result in significant revenue losses to them. The introduction of new services, as well as the extension of basic services by cooperatives to new areas, were delayed by CNT's failure to develop standards and processes for issuing licenses. Consumers found CNT unable to handle complaints.[16]

The reasons for CNT's initial failure are not entirely clear, but several contributing factors can be identified. First, although CNT was designed to be accountable directly to the president, eventually it was placed under the Ministry of Public Works and Services (MPWS). Furthermore, soon after the CNT directors took office, the MPWS was abolished and CNT came under the authority of an undersecretary of the Ministry of Economy who also was responsible for a number of other sectors.

Second, some observers also point out that quality of management was a factor. A motivated, strong manager could, it is argued, have broken through the government's indifference and got CNT working. Also, for want of qualified staff, the directors took upon themselves responsibility for day-to-day professional work divided among them by lines of business (for example, broadcasting, satellites), thus forgoing the benefits of collective decisionmaking detached from technical preparation, and also resulting in weak technical work, since only two of the directors had any telecommunications experience.

Third, although funds were available, CNT lacked access to them. A levy of 0.5 percent on gross operating revenues of Telecom Argentina and Telefónica de Argentina, established by the same decree that created CNT, generated sufficient funds to meet CNT's operating costs, including competitive remunerations. CNT, however, never got the government to approve its budget and administrative procedures and was unable to tap these funds, which accumulated in a non-interest-earning account. CNT was unable to hire qualified staff as prescribed in the decree or retain local consultants to assist on a temporary basis. Some of the directors were based in the provinces and CNT was unable to fund their commuting to Buenos Aires. Although a substantial amount was also available from a World Bank loan to the government for consultants, seconded experts, equipment and software needed to jump-start CNT, they were not used, partly due to CNT's inability to assemble a qualified local counterpart team.

Lastly, some observers interpret these events as clear indication of weak government commitment to the new regulatory framework. This framework had been established largely at the insistence of consultants and financial advisers rather than in response to the government's own political interests.[17]

By early 1992, pressure for the government to do something about CNT had built up from several sides, including new consumer advocacy groups, emerging new service providers, and the regional operators themselves. The government responded by appointing an energetic new undersecretary for communications (a position that had earlier been abolished) with a clear mandate to turn CNT into an effective regulator. In the following three months, trustees appointed to take over temporarily the positions of CNT commissioners achieved more than had been done in the fifteen months since CNT's creation. During 1992, CNT issued licenses to regularize the operation of 140 of 300 independent new telephone cooperatives; initiated bidding for cellular licenses outside Buenos Aires; established norms for competitive provision of domestic data transmission, private mobile radio, and videoconferencing; established norms for the use of the radio spectrum, resumed monitoring and greatly improved collection of fees; took important steps to protect customers;[18] and retained a firm of international consultants to prepare a development plan for CNT.

There is still a long way to go, however, before Argentina can claim to have a stable, credible telecommunications regulatory regime. For example, the rules of the game (and investor confidence) were undermined when the revitalized CNT undertook to negotiate with the regional companies tariffs below those guaranteed in existing contracts, which it regarded as excessive. CNT made lower tariffs a condition for granting the regional companies the second cellular license in Buenos Aires, an essentially unrelated regulatory matter.[19]

CNT's institutional development outlook also remains unsettled. The current managers are political appointees unlikely to remain in office for long, and plans to staff and equip CNT on a more permanent basis are not being implemented. Contrary to what was established in the decree that created CNT, the agency does not have effective control over the fees it collects from the regulated companies but instead depends on government allocations to meet its expenses. CNT's authority and enforcement capability remains compromised by being ascribed to an undersecretary of economy with numerous other responsibilities. The very existence of CNT is at the mercy of the government, as it was created by executive decree, which can be readily revoked, rather than by law of Congress.[20]

Mexico

As of 1989, Teléfonos de México S.A. de C.V. (TELMEX), a 51 percent state-owned parastatal company, provided local, long-distance, and international telephone service throughout Mexico.[21] The Secretaría de Comunicaciones y Transporte (SCT), through its Subsecretaría de Comunicaciones y Desarrollo Tecnológico, was the government's policy and regulatory agency. SCT also owned and operated a national microwave network, the domestic satellite system, a small packet-switched network, aeronautical and maritime stations, and other facilities. The postal administration operated the telex and telegraph services. Although Mexico's was the second largest telecommunications system in the developing world (after Brazil's) and TELMEX was one of the country's best-run parastatals, Mexico exhibited all the telecommunications deficiencies typical of developing countries.

In August 1989 the government published a program for the modernization of telecommunications. It identified four main structural obstacles to better sector performance: complex labor and administrative arrangements that limited technological innovation and service quality improvements; tax and tariff distortions that resulted in excessive dependence of TELMEX on long-distance revenues and, consequently, limited possibility of introducing competition;[22] insufficient management and financial autonomy of the operating enterprises; and inadequate regulation of TELMEX's monopoly operations. The modernization plan sought to improve service to reach internationally competitive levels; expand service coverage in rural and urban areas; diversify and modernize services; establish competitive tariffs at the international level and achieve financial self-sufficiency; and promote greater private investment and competition. To achieve these objectives, the modernization plan proposed a new regulatory framework that would promote efficiency, competition, and private investment; abolish the telephone tax and restructure tariffs; privatize TELMEX and subject it to price and service quality regulation; introduce competition in the provision of local and long-distance services as well as in new services; and franchise competing regional cellular operators.

These far-reaching policy proposals were, to a very substantial degree, implemented during 1990 and 1991. Tariffs were increased to ensure profitable operations and rebalanced to reduce distortions. The tax on telephone bills was replaced by a special tax on profits that could be offset by accelerated investment. Two licenses for cellular services were awarded in each of nine regions, one to a TELMEX subsidiary and the other to independent operators. SCT became solely the sector regulatory agency after its operating functions were reorganized as an autonomous state enterprise.[23] The telecommunications regulations were extensively revised. The supply of customer premises equipment, provision of value added and information services, and ownership and operation of private networks, all were liberalized. A controlling interest in TELMEX was sold to a consortium of national and foreign investors associated with France Télécom and Southwestern Bell. The privatized TELMEX was granted a concession that provided for price-cap tariff regulation, serious obligations for network expansion in urban and rural areas, as well as progressively demanding targets for quality of service, and exclusivity for basic services and networks until 1996, after which competition will be allowed.[24]

Some fifteen months after TELMEX's privatization, the sector appeared to be making good progress along the lines sought by the government's modernization program. TELMEX had overall met its obligations under the concession regarding growth, quality, and price of basic telephone service;[25] had improved availability and quality of service for large business users; was building a sound organizational, physical, and financial base for sustained expansion and improvement of service; and yielded high returns to its investors.[26] Independent operating companies were successfully competing with TELMEX's cellular subsidiary in each of the nine zones; were providing business and high-income residential customers cellular alternatives to the scarce and unreliable wired telephone service at prices close to the U.S. average; and as a group were becoming a force to be contended with when TELMEX's monopoly privileges end in 1996.[27] Private corporate networks using satellite, microwave, and other own and leased facilities continue to develop, providing cost-effective solutions to meet the needs of large business users and specific communications-intensive sectors of the economy.

Progress in developing regulation receives mixed reviews. Significant successes were achieved in preparing for and following privatization. TELMEX's concession is a carefully crafted contract that provides essential government assurances to the operator while imposing important service obligations. The new telecommunications regulations established in Mexico for the first time a comprehensive, modern framework with policy formulation, licensing, and regulatory functions exercised by the government, with telecommunications networks and services largely provided by the private sector in an increasingly competitive marketplace. In several instances, SCT has responded effectively to important regulatory issues. For example, a wide divide between TELMEX and the independent cellular operators regarding interconnection charges was successfully settled through SCT intervention.

On the other hand, progress in developing SCT as a regulatory agency with strong professional staff capability has been slower than expected. Although SCT prepared, with the assistance of consultants, a comprehensive development plan, SCT's new organization did not come into effect until April 1992. Moreover, implementation of the development plan has been constrained by a shortage of authorized management positions (related to the government's austerity program). There is also an acute shortage of experienced senior professional staff. As of mid-1992, SCT was not well equipped to deal with a number of regulatory issues likely to arise in the near future. For example, competitive pressures were building up rapidly, from within Mexico[28] as well as across the U.S. border, raising issues such as possible cross-subsidy between TELMEX's monopoly and competitive services, and possible preferential provision of scarce leased lines by TELMEX to its own subsidiaries. Some observers believe that TELMEX's monopoly will break down well before it expires in 1996, particularly regarding long-distance networks and services, bringing forward a full range of regulatory matters to be handled by SCT. Also, discussions on telecommunications are under way in the context of the proposed North American Free Trade Agreement,[29] which requires a substantial level of regulatory competence in Mexico to deal with the implementation issues likely to follow, perhaps as early as 1993. SCT does not have a sufficient number of appropriately qualified management and professional staff to deal with these issues as well as complex calculations of TELMEX performance with respect to its price cap, quality of service, and growth obligations. The question does arise whether, in the longer run, a quasi-independent commission, outside any ministry, could provide a more effective means for regulating the sector.

Venezuela

Approximately 1.6 million lines were in service in Venezuela at the end of 1990.[30] This was the fourth largest telecommunications system in Latin America (after Brazil, Mexico, and Argentina), and with 8.2 lines per 100 inhabitants it was also among the largest relative to population size. Service, however, was very poor: call completion rates were less than 30 percent for long distance and international calls and waiting periods exceeded 18 months for new lines. Unmet demand for new telephone connections was estimated at up to 3 million. Local tariffs were far below cost, with the result that total revenue per subscriber (for all services) averaged only $250 in 1990.

In mid-1990, the government appointed a new Minister of Transport and Communications and also a new president of Compañía Anónima Nacional de Teléfonos de Venezuela (CANTV), the state-owned monopoly providing local and long-distance service throughout the country. A Telecommunications Restructuring Group was established to manage the reform of the sector and the privatization of CANTV. Consulting firms were hired in early 1991 to analyze the competition regime, develop a new tariff structure, prepare a new telecommunications law and regulations, and design the regulatory institutional regime. An investment banking consortium was also hired to prepare the sales memorandum and bidding documents.

In March 1991, the government published pre-qualification criteria for the privatization. The criteria included six financial and technical benchmarks. Based on these criteria, eight international operators were pre-qualified. Draft bidding documents were distributed and discussed with the pre-qualified firms. Following these discussions and the due diligence period, the government issued the final bidding documents in September 1991. The government established a base price of US$900 million for the sale of 40 percent of CANTV's shares. An additional 11 percent was to be sold to CANTV employees on the same terms and conditions. The government's remaining shares (49 percent) were to be progressively sold in the future through global share issue(s).

The public tender process took place on November 15, 1991. Two consortia participated, including one consortia led by GTE and one led by Bell Atlantic. The GTE consortia won the tender with a bid of US$1,885 million ($2,930 per line in service). The company was formally transferred to the new owners-operators the following month.

Privatization was accompanied by the preparation of a new telecommunications law (still before congress), the establishment of a new regulatory agency (CONATEL), major tariff adjustments, and the introduction of competition in cellular, private networks, and value added services. One cellular band was granted to CANTV (and transferred to the new operator following the privatization). The second band was awarded through competitive bidding to TELCEL (A Bell-South consortium) at a price of roughly US$100 million.

Key features of the privatization of CANTV included:

- The new operator would have a 9-year monopoly on basic service, including long distance and international. This essentially followed the Mexican and Argentinian examples. The exclusivity period was deemed essential to ensure sufficient financial incentive and cashflow to finance the ambitious expansion program for the basic network.

- The concession requires an aggressive investment program: 3,000,000 new lines in addition to 640,000 replacement lines over 9 years (or 400,000 lines annually). The concession also included a number of service performance targets to be achieved during the exclusivity period.

- Tariffs were increased in mid-1991 (prior to privatization) and again on January 1, 1992 (upon transfer to the new operator). This included major increases in local tariffs, as well as the introduction of a new surcharge for digitalization and modernization. As a result, revenue per subscriber line increased from US$250 in 1990 to an estimated US$500 in 1992. Tariffs were grouped into three baskets, to be regulated on a price-cap basis, with full inflation indexing on a quarterly basis until end-1996, followed by partial indexing for the remainder of the exclusivity period (end-2000).

- The new operator was required to adhere to the collective labor contracts (which were to expire at end-1993). The government did not implement any work force reductions in CANTV prior to privatization. At the time of privatization, CANTV productivity was 12.3 employees/1000 lines, about average for Latin America.

Some Features and Lessons of Recent Reforms

Although the Latin American reforms are country-specific, some common features and preliminary lessons can be noted.

Scope and Pace of Reforms

The authorities entrusted with the design and implementation of the reforms succeeded in identifying and addressing a wide range of key policy, regulatory, managerial, and financial issues. Although the governments' decisions to restructure initially focused narrowly on transferring ownership of state enterprises to the private sector, the teams in charge of this process responded rapidly to signals from consultants and financial advisers that a broader range of issues needed to be tackled. Reflecting this comprehensive approach to policy issues, the reforms completed or under way have four main components:

- Selling a controlling interest in the state enterprises to private owners (generally led by foreign operating companies) and the balance to employees and a large number of investors. This places administrative control and management responsibility on a single owner group with experience in telecommunications operations. At the same time, this scheme creates a large number of new stakeholders by distributing ownership widely among domestic and foreign investors. Transfer of shares to the operating companies' workers in largely concessional terms contributes to bringing labor on board the privatization program.

- Reducing the scope and duration of monopoly privileges formerly held by the state companies. The privatized companies are granted exclusivity privileges for the core telephony business, including the necessary networks, for up to ten years as a maximum, and in most cases less than that. At the end of the exclusivity periods, competition may be introduced in any and all segments of the business.

- Opening immediately to competition important segments of the telecommunications business. Various degrees of competition are allowed (indeed, in some measure actively pursued by the governments) in many nonbasic services and facilities, including cellular telephony, customer premises equipment, value added and information services, as well as private networks with various degrees of resale and interconnection to the public network.

- Establishing public regulation separate from the operating entities. Although specific institutional arrangements vary, the regulatory agencies so far are either parts of ministries or are under the authority or direct intervention of ministries.

Possibly the most striking feature of telecommunications reforms in Latin America has been their speed. Contrary to belief widely held on the basis of the experiences of industrial countries (for example, United Kingdom and Japan), the state telecommunications enterprises of Argentina, Mexico, and Venezuela were privatized in little over one year. Although the timetables set by the governments for privatization often appeared to be unrealistically tight, in the event they proved feasible.

Regulatory Development

Not all components of the reform packages, however, progressed at the same pace. In particular, development of regulatory capacity has lagged far behind privatization of the state enterprises. In Chile, despite an overall good regulatory design, little was done to develop the specialized telecommunications regulatory authority. Repeated rounds at various levels of the ministries and the judiciary over a period of several years failed to resolve major issues of market structure and competition policy, at high cost to the operating enterprises, the users, and the economy at large. In both Argentina and Mexico, privatization included careful regulatory designs, and telecommunications regulatory agencies were competently outlined and formally set up or redefined at about the time the state enterprises were transferred to the new owners. However, three years later, these agencies (subject to the same public sector constraints that earlier afflicted the operating companies) were still struggling to get organized and build up a basic core of expertise which should have been in place at the time of privatization or earlier. In Venezuela the government had planned to establish a temporary regulatory authority to overview the transition from state to private operation and act on urgent regulatory matters such as licensing new networks and services. A more permanent regulatory structure would be developed and take over later. Almost two years after privatization, however, the new telecommunications law still had not been passed by Congress.

Given the difficulty of getting regulation off the ground, it is important to identify partial measures that help, even if they do not offer comprehensive solutions. First, in the political and institutional environment of Latin America, a carefully crafted concession can be an important instrument of self-regulation by the dominant operator. In Mexico, for example, even if SCT is not yet equipped to monitor compliance thoroughly, TELMEX takes the obligations under the concession very seriously. Several features contribute to make the concession an effective instrument of self-regulation. One is that the obligations are not unreasonable: they strike a good balance between what the government wanted for development and public interest reasons, on the one hand, and, on the other, what can be achieved in practice by a commercial operator. Another feature is that major actions (such as the introduction of cost accounting) required of the operator for reasons of sound policy and regulation (for example, to contain cross-subsidies between the competitive and monopoly businesses) are also wanted by the operator (as tools for good business management).

Second, a well-designed concession provides a framework for negotiations between the operator and the regulator. This helps keep negotiations largely in the technical arena, containing the risk of undue politicization which, in turn, would weaken the power of the concession as an instrument to define the terms of business of the operator. For example, SCT and TELMEX agreed in 1991 and 1992 on tariff adjustments that differed somewhat from the mechanism defined by the concession but followed very closely the principles established therein.

Third, steps to introduce competition at the margin can spearhead the development of a competitive marketplace. Again in Mexico, the independent cellular operators are building up a credible threat of competition to TELMEX beyond the limits of the cellular business. An important contributing factor is the existence of an association of cellular companies which groups all cellular operators that are not subsidiaries of the dominant operator. This association has successfully helped the independent operators face the dominant operator on critical issues such as interconnection standards and prices. Another factor is the network strategies chosen by the cellular operators. For example, they have already built some 2,200 kilometers of digital microwave networks, which may give them a head start in becoming a second long-distance carrier in the future.[31]

Lastly, although regulation may get off to a slow start, countries can make the transition from very basic to fairly sophisticated regulatory capabilities in about one decade—much longer than the time needed to sell a state enterprise, but well within the planning horizon of a broad reform agenda. In Chile, a number of economists, engineers, and lawyers in government, academia, and the consulting business have developed from the mid-1980s considerable regulatory skill and insight. These competencies have been clearly noted by analysts of the Chilean regulatory environment and are visible through the participation of some of these experts in international regulatory roundtables and conferences. In Mexico, small pockets of regulatory expertise and culture are quickly emerging where none existed only two or three years ago. These pockets are found in local consulting firms, the cellular operators' association, major users, academia, and of course, SCT and TELMEX.

An important factor seems to have been the government's decision to open the cellular market to competitive entry at an early stage of the reform process. This started to create a constituency for regulation. A related factor may have been the pressure by large users, and the favorable response of the regulator in the mid-1980s (well before the government decided to reform the sector), to allow users to build their own satellite earth stations and microwave links. This has resulted in a wide mix of technologies and combinations of own and leased facilities, and in an environment in which diversity of supply and user choice are increasingly the accepted norm.

Strong Competition for Private Entry

Despite the considerable (and growing) number of similar business opportunities in other parts of the world (notably Asia and Eastern Europe), the Latin American reforms have attracted considerable interest among foreign operators, investors, and manufacturers. For example, seven consortia of foreign operators and banks associated with domestic investors prequalified to bid for ENTel in Argentina, and three bids (involving four operators) were eventually received. Over 100 bids were received in Mexico for the licenses to provide cellular services in nine regions. In 1990, CTC's first international issue of stock (US$100 million in the New York Stock Exchange was oversubscribed. The sale of shares in Telefónica de Argentina and Telecom Argentina in 1991 and 1992 were also several times oversubscribed. The price of TELMEX ADRs, which for years have been traded in the U.S., more than quadrupled in one year as preparation for privatization got under way, and again roughly doubled following the first earnings report under private ownership.[32]

The bidding and award processes were designed to enhance credibility and price competition. However, it could be argued that the procedures followed in the event did not always take full advantage of competition. For example, in Chile (1987) only three firms were invited to bid for CTC, without competitive prequalification, and eventually the sale was negotiated with one of them (Australian investor Alan Bond) after all bids were rejected. Opposition to a privatization effort of the previous Argentine government may have been related partly to the government's having entered into negotiations with a single prospective buyer, without the benefit of a transparent bidding process. By announcing the winning bids before the contracts were negotiated in substance, and having cornered itself into a tight deadline to conclude the sales, the Menem government may have weakened its bargaining position in the late stages of privatization.

The prices paid for the various state telecommunications enterprises varied considerably. Although what the investor buys is the future business rather than the existing plant, the price paid per telephone line in service at the time of purchase, corrected for the different shares of the total equity bought in each case, provides a rough measure of value. The unit prices, shown in Table 3–1 for Chile, Argentina, Mexico, and Venezuela, have varied over a 4:1 range among countries and over time.

Observers differ in their interpretations of this wide range. The level of tariffs and other terms of business, as well as the rules for adjusting them, are key determinants of company value. The market growth prospect—which relates to the current service deficits, population income distribution, and the country's expected economic development potential—is also a major factor. Country risk, in terms of the government's commitment to sector rules (for example, on changing tariffs), broad economic policy (such as treatment of foreign investment), and overall political prospects, is often mentioned (but may be more significant in deciding whether to buy rather than how much to pay). Lastly, the transparency and competitiveness of the sale process itself affects the price.

This long list of factors leaves considerable latitude for explaining the wide differences in unit prices. For example, the low price at which CTC was sold in 1987, compared to 1990, could be attributed to limited transparency and competition in the initial sale. An alternative explanation, however, is that the higher price of 1990 largely reflected increased investor confidence in the government's by-then proven resolve to sustain the rules of the game in this sector. Another factor may have been that the 1987 sale was the first among sizable telecommunications companies in developing countries, whereas by 1990 the market for such transactions was well developed. In most cases, however, the investments have proven to be highly profitable, at least in the short run. CTC and TELMEX shares have appreciated considerably with privatization. The Mexican and Argentine governments made large gains by deferring the sale of the balance of their equity until the privatized companies had increased in value.[33]

Political Will and Leadership

The breakneck pace of reform in Argentina, Venezuela and, to a lesser extent, Mexico, was both necessary and possible because a clear political decision was taken

Table 3–1. Approximate Purchase Price per Line

Country	Company (year)	US$ per line
Chile	CTC (1988)	700
Argentina	ENTel (1990)	700
Chile	CTC (1990)	1,100
Mexico	TELMEX (1990)	1,700
Venezuela	CANTV (1991)	3,200

Note: In 1988 Bond purchased 35 percent of CTC shares for US$140 million; the company had about 550,000 lines in service. In 1990, Bond sold to Telefónica 50 percent of CTC shares for US$390 million; the company by then had about 700,000 lines. In Argentina, for both regions taken together Telefónica de España/STET/France Télécom in 1990 paid US$214 million cash, US$380 million in promissory notes, and US$5 billion face value of government debt, for 60 percent of shares; ENTel had about 3.3 million lines; the calculation assumes the government debt was worth 17 percent of face value (in line with marginal transactions at the time, for want of a better indicator). Carso/Southwestern Bell/France Télécom in 1990 paid US$1.76 billion for 20.4 percent of TELMEX, which had about 5.2 million lines. In 1991, GTE/Telefónica de España/Electricidad de Caracas/Cima/AT&T paid US$1.9 billion for 40 percent of CANTV, which had about 1.5 million lines.

at the highest level of government authority. Necessary, because these high-level decisions had implications that went well beyond the telecommunications sector alone. In particular, the privatizations of ENTel, TELMEX, and CANTV were flagships of broad public sector reform programs. Prompt success in such lead operations was needed to demonstrate (to both domestic and foreign constituencies, including the international financial community) the governments' resolve and effectiveness. Also, although the decisions to restructure telecommunications were made from positions of political strength, such strength, and therefore the likelihood of completing the task, could be expected to erode with time. Possible, because in the wake of high-powered political decisions, the persons charged with implementing reforms were able to cut many bureaucratic corners and mobilize support from a wide range of sources. Also, the fact that government credibility for a much larger reform program was at stake reduced the political risk to investors in telecommunications.

Restructuring has been largely driven by the finance and economic authorities, not by those responsible for telecommunications. Whereas the lead players therefore mostly lacked telecommunications experience, they brought to the reform process direct access to the highest levels of political and government authority, consistency with broader economic reform programs, ability to put together teams with strong business backgrounds, and skill to liaise with the main relevant players in the telecommunications sector and business community. The leaders also recognized the need for specialist advice and were quick to bring on board consultants as well as investment and development bankers to provide expert inputs. In this manner, the teams quickly developed an understanding of the essential concepts as well as considerable sophistication in dealing with the issues and options in hand.

These observations are consistent with the experience in situations where top-level political decisions were or are lacking. Although Chile was the first Latin American country to fully privatize telecommunications and start to develop significant competition, it took more than ten years from the government's initial attempts at liberalization to final privatization of CTC and ENTEL. The previous Argentine government's attempt to privatize ENTel ran into political deep water as deteriorating country economic conditions and approaching presidential elections weakened the government earlier than expected. In the absence of clear political definition, the pace, direction, and ultimate extent of telecommunications restructuring in Brazil, Panama, and Uruguay, for example, are still uncertain.[34]

Organized Labor

Labor organizations have eventually supported the reforms. The underlying process, however, is not well documented. Very little was ever made public on discussions and negotiations with labor unions. Replies by government officials to questions on this subject were generally inconclusive. Some observations, however, are generally applicable. First, labor unions are very concerned about prospective major changes that may result in loss of acquired worker privileges and union power. Any reform process must be prepared and carried out in a manner that brings worker organizations on board. This emphasizes that reform is not merely a technocratic exercise but also a political process and needs to be managed accordingly.

Second, worries about possible massive layoffs ultimately proved to have been exaggerated. It is not necessary to reduce total employment in order to increase productivity. Major gains result from rapid growth in connections and traffic as the operating enterprise accelerates investment, modernizes facilities and adopts modern management methods. Furthermore, reforms lead to rapidly expanding new business opportunities which create attractive employment alternatives. The new management needs, however, to change the mix of skills. Although some workers can be retrained, others must be eased out and new talent brought into the company. In practice, this does not appear to have been an insurmountable problem. Attrition, early retirement, and other incentive schemes well within what the company can manage without undue financial burden, seem to have sufficed.[35]

Third, worker participation in company ownership has played an important role in securing labor support for reform. Employee stock ownership plans have been an integral part of the capital restructuring of all state telecommunications enterprises privatized in Latin America so far. In all cases, they have involved transfer of shares to workers under favorable terms with a substantial grant element.

Country-Specific Solutions

The Latin American experience confirms that the sector solutions adopted, and especially the strategies to implement them, are highly country-specific. Sector structures and institutional arrangements cannot be readily transplanted from one country to another.

Despite this country-specificity, the Latin American experience also confirms that the main issues, as well as the elements of solutions, are rather universal.[36] Thus, knowledge gained in one country can be reinterpreted usefully in others. In Latin America, consultants, investment bankers, and development bankers contributed to the understanding of the issues and options at play, drawing on the experience of other countries. In particular, the experience of industrial countries in North America, Europe, and Asia, where related matters had been assiduously debated and studied for years, proved relevant and valuable.

An international body of expertise in telecommunications restructuring is thus gradually building up, on which countries embarking in telecommunications reforms can increasingly draw.

Concluding Remarks

The pace and scope of telecommunications reforms in Latin America show that with political will and management skill, major structural changes can be undertaken rather effectively in a short period of time. Initial results suggest that under appropriate terms and conditions, the newly privatized companies are starting to be rebuilt and managed in ways consistent with the governments' expectations. The longer-term outlook is less certain. Questions are already being asked regarding the extent of commitment of the foreign operators and investors, access to foreign capital for sustained investment, and the ultimate prospects of regulation. Other issues are likely to emerge.

Have the reforms secured long-term access to management and technology? A primary objective of privatization has been to turn around the former state telecommunications enterprises into modern, efficient, well-run businesses. That is why Latin American governments have chosen to sell to consortia led by well-established foreign operating companies capable of providing expert managers, specialized management tools, and access to the latest technologies. Turning around these enterprises, however, is in many cases a formidable task that can only be accomplished over a number of years and therefore requires a long-term commitment by the new owners. The terms and conditions of sale of the enterprises in most cases reflect this. For example, franchises have been awarded for twenty or more years, monopoly privileges granted for up to ten years, and service development objectives and performance targets initially specified for about five years, subject to periodic renewal.

The issue is whether the new owners have sufficient incentives to address the painstaking, long, and costly task of overall enterprise reorganization, modernization, and expansion, rather than limit their intervention to short-term exploitation of the more profitable segments of the market. This question received, of course, considerable attention at the time of preparing the new sector regulations, the terms and conditions of sale, the transfer contracts, and the licenses, all of which include incentives and obligations. The views are divided, however, as to whether these incentives and obligations will prove strong enough in practice. For example, in some cases it can be argued that the foreign operator has mainly secured a profitable management contract supplemented by a relatively minor equity interest, and that under these conditions the cost of exiting could be less than that of staying on if things get harder than expected. Also, short-term transactional profits could prove more attractive than longer-term business gains, giving the whole exercise a rather speculative character.[37] Others argue, however, that foreign operators move into developing countries as part of broader strategies to diversify their markets and develop a global business presence, have their international reputation at stake, and thus can be counted upon to do a serious job.

How important is the role of the foreign operator? The answer to this question surely varies among countries and over time. Partly it depends on how well run the telecommunications enterprise was before privatization. There are only three Telefónica people in Chile's CTC (the chief executive officer, an adviser, and a member of the board of directors). CTC's improved performance has been largely achieved by Chilean staff and managers, mostly the same people who ran the company under state ownership. Nonetheless, this does not tell the whole story. Through the ownership link, CTC gained ready access to modern tools for management, quality assurance, and operation, as well procurement experience and cost information, which are well established in Telefónica de España, the parent company. Conversely, Telefónica gained an environment with highly qualified professionals who can contribute to adapting and further developing these tools in ways that Telefónica can then apply in other countries. A different situation prevails in Argentina, where the companies needed major overhaul. There, Telefónica, STET, and France Télécom have about 100 people who occupy the key senior management positions as well as middle-level management and specialized technical posts. Yet there is no reason why not to believe that in a few years these numbers could be reduced to a barely nominal presence, once the companies are running well and Argentine managers and staff have gained enough experience in the context of modern operations. The situation in Mexico is somewhere in between. A team of about thirty professionals from France Télécom and Southwestern Bell joined TELMEX in an advisory capacity and are assigned to different tasks as needed. The parent companies are also available for consultation at their headquarters. The partners have tended to divide their support along lines that reflect their different business and regulatory environments. For example, Southwestern Bell is assisting in the areas of marketing, information systems, and tariffs, while France Télécom concentrates on outside plant construction and maintenance, development of new services, and planning. Since all these services could alternatively have been secured through contracts with suppliers and consultants, it may well be that in Latin America the main role of the foreign operators was to reduce the risk of the main investors by ensuring competent management of their assets.

Will privatization give the new companies sustained access to foreign capital? This was also a primary reason for selling to consortia including foreign partners. Some argue that, in common with other privatized state enterprises, some of the new companies may become financial orphans—unable in the long run to attract foreign private capital, being cut off from traditional sources of long-term development financing that require state guarantees, and not having sufficiently developed domestic markets from which to obtain adequate debt and equity financing. Although in the initial years most or all of the funds needed for investment are being internally generated, a better mix of sources of funds—including fresh equity capital and long-term debt—will be essential to sustain growth in the longer run. If a foreign operator or investor has or develops only a limited interest in staying on, it is unlikely to contribute such new equity.[38] Likewise, the foreign bank partners, goes the argument, have at best a medium-term interest, and at worst are in the venture only to recover some of the losses from holding highly devalued government debt paper by transforming them into equity in a promising business, and in either case are also unlikely to bring in fresh capital. Foreign capital markets might have little interest in emerging companies located in fairly high-risk countries (several of the Latin American countries currently preparing for privatization are in this category), or require returns so high as to become politically unacceptable. The successful experiences of CTC and TELMEX may be exceptions, in terms of both low country risk and high company quality, that prove this rule.[39] Domestic capital markets may be too small to meet the capital requirements of several large privatized companies (as is the case of Chile). Also, mostly domestic financing of telecommunications investments with large import requirements would adversely affect the countries' balance of payments.

Will future reforms in Latin America follow the established pattern? Not necessarily. The next wave of reforms is likely to include significant departures from recent trends. For example, in contrast with the wholesale top-down privatizations of Chile, Argentina, Mexico, and Venezuela, events starting to unfold in Brazil seem to favor bottom-up development of private sector participation, as well as regionalization, growing autonomy, and possible participation in capital markets of mainly state-owned operations. In Colombia, provincial and municipal telephone companies may develop new enterprise structures and lines of business in competition with the central state-owned company, now slated for privatization. There is some experience in Latin America (and in some industrial countries) with subscriber ownership of telecommunications operating enterprises through shareholding and cooperatives, which may be further developed as a reform modality.[40]

Some observers say that Latin America is merely returning eventually to where it was forty years ago—private, foreign-owned telecommunications monopolies. If this is all there is to the reform movement, it would be unfortunate indeed. After all, telecommunications companies were taken over by the Latin American governments in the 1960s not only because of the wave of nationalistic fervor and inward-looking economic development strategies sweeping the region, but primarily because the telephone companies were increasingly unable to meet the countries' development needs. True, this had come to be for much the same reasons that lead to restructuring and privatization today, namely, inadequate sector policies.

It is unlikely that reforms are merely repeating history. At least three conditions are very different today than in the 1950s and 1960s. First, technological change has made it possible and increasingly cost-effective to have a highly diversified supply of telecommunications services. The argument for natural monopolies has largely faded away.[41] Second, with increasing globalization and information intensity of world economic activity, numerous economic agents demand more, better, and lower cost services and networks, well beyond what any single enterprise can effectively provide. Third, driven by these forces, structural changes in telecommunications worldwide are subjecting developing countries to a wide range of new demands and business opportunities. Lastly, the developing countries are increasingly turning to economic policies and strategies that advocate competition as well as diversified domestic and foreign investment.

In this very changed environment, the major reforms of telecommunications taking place in Latin America constitute important improvements. Undoubtedly, as time goes by, it will be clear that some things could have been done better. But so far everything seems to confirm that, with reforms, telecommunications are finally moving from a constraint to becoming a leading factor of Latin American economic development.

Annex: Beginnings of Telecommunications Reforms in Other Latin American Countries

Major restructuring of the telecommunications sector has been completed in Chile, Argentina, Mexico, and Venezuela. These are discussed in the main text and following chapters. A number of other countries have made some moves toward revising the established policies and structures. Events as of mid-1993 are summarized below.

Bolivia

With only 174,000 telephone lines, or about 2.7 lines per 100 inhabitants, Bolivia has one of the least-developed telecommunications systems in Latin America. ENTEL, a state-owned enterprise, operates the domestic and international long-distance network for telephony, telex, telegraph, television networking, and other services. Seventeen cooperatives provide local residential, business, and public telephone service, primarily in the main cities. About 40 percent of telephone lines are in the capital city of La Paz, 25 percent in Santa Cruz, 15 percent in Cochabamba, and the balance in smaller localities. Although this scheme superficially resembles the successful structure of Finland, and some parts function rather well (for example, COTAS, the local cooperative of Santa Cruz de la Sierra, Bolivia's second largest city), the Bolivian network remains highly fragmented and inefficient.

Partly seeking to emulate the relatively good performance of COTAS, the government decreed in 1985 the reorganization of all other local operating entities—at the time mostly poorly performing municipal enterprises—into subscriber-owned cooperatives. This by itself, however, has not resulted in substantial improvements. In particular, most operators are unable to raise the capital needed for sustained expansion and modernization. Major constraints on telecommunications development are the inadequate regulatory framework and institutional arrangements, tariffs unrelated to costs and expansion requirements, ineffective sector and enterprise management, and interference by various interest groups in the management of the operating entities.

The government seeks to expand basic telephone service in urban and rural areas to an average of 5.2 telephone lines per 100 inhabitants by the year 2000, as well as introduce data and other services for specific market segments where there is demand; improve service quality and reliability; improve operating efficiency across the board; and mobilize sufficient capital from operating surpluses as well as domestic and foreign investment.

In 1992 and 1993, a team including representatives from various branches of government, the cooperatives, and ENTEL, supported by international telecommunications consultants and lawyers, developed a strategic plan for sector reforms that would overcome constraints and enable the sector to move toward these targets. The plan mainly envisages (a) making the local cooperatives the engines of sector growth through voluntary merger into a small number (possibly three) of regional operating enterprises restructured as joint-stock companies, and (b) privatizing ENTEL to attract capital and management expertise. Policy options include giving the regional companies equity interests in ENTEL, to strengthen the companies' balance sheets and to facilitate network integration.

The team also drafted a new telecommunications law that outlines the new sector structure and regulatory framework as well as enables privatization. The plan and the draft law have been extensively discussed with various political groups and other constituents and appear to have fairly broad support. The next step is to send the draft law to Congress.

Brazil

Brazil has the second largest telecommunications system in the developing world (after China), with about 10 million telephone lines in service.[42] Telecommunications services and networks are mainly provided by Telecomuniçacoes Brasileiras S.A. (TELEBRÁS), a federal state holding of twenty-nine operating companies, one in each state plus Empresa Brasileira de Telecomunicaçoes (EMBRATEL), the interstate and international long-distance company. Established in the late 1960s, TELEBRÁS had been remarkably successful in consolidating over 1,000 scattered telephone operations, quickly building up a modern and fast-growing countrywide telecommunications infrastructure. However, in the context of Brazil's deteriorating overall economic conditions in the 1980s, including constraints on public sector investment and on international credit, TELEBRÁS was unable to keep up the pace of growth and innovation. Major contributing factors were government price controls that did not allow TELEBRÁS to fully recover costs and generate surpluses for reinvestment, an increasingly outdated policy of industrial autarky resulting in high cost of equipment and slow technological change in the network, and TELEBRÁS's organizational structure that gives the individual state enterprises insufficient managerial and financial autonomy to be run as modern businesses. Large backlogs developed for basic telephone service, service quality deteriorated, and new services increasingly required by Brazil's dynamic modern business sectors have been slow to develop.

Although until now there has been no concerted attempt to overhaul the telecommunications sector, a number of partial measures have been adopted by the government. Several ministerial decrees issued in 1990 were aimed at alleviating these constraints by opening the doors to private participation in the telecommunications business. Users were allowed to build and operate their own networks, and private entities were allowed to offer value added services, in parallel with TELEBRÁS's public-switched network. Satellite, data, and cellular services were opened to private provision. New modalities were authorized to finance investment in the public network by private parties.[43] At the same time, broad trade and industrial policy reforms are under way that would promote domestic and international competition in the supply of telecommunications equipment to TELEBRÁS and others, leading to lower costs and accelerated technological innovation. In particular, the informatics law was revised, relaxing restrictions on trade in telecommunications equipment. For the longer run, the government reportedly has also considered restructuring the twenty-eight TELEBRÁS state enterprises into eight large regional companies and exploring possibilities of attracting private capital to some of these. A constitutional reform, currently planned for 1993, would seek to modify the article that reserves to TELEBRÁS and its subsidiaries all public telecommunications networks and services except for limited services offered to closed groups with common activities and interests.

Progress, however, has been slower than initially planned by the government. In particular, implementing regulations for the 1990 telecommunications decrees were only finalized more than one year later. Moreover, the government's past tendency to overregulate TELEBRÁS now seems to have extended to the new players as well. For example, the implementing regulations of the 1990 decrees focus largely on interconnection between the new networks and TELEBRÁS, with emphasis on preserving the public network rather than facilitating and promoting development of new networks.

Colombia

Local telephone services are provided by some forty municipal or provincial telephone companies. Several of the larger ones, such as Teléfonos de Bogotá in the nation's capital, and Empresas Públicas de Medellín (which also provides electricity, water, sewer, and trash collection services) in the capital of the province of Antioquía, are veritable regional operating companies. Empresa Nacional de Telecomunicaciones (TELECOM), a state enterprise, operates most domestic long-distance and all international facilities.[44] TELECOM has also over the years acquired some twenty small local telephone operations in various provinces and has developed an extensive rural network.

As elsewhere in Latin America, there is a persistent shortage of telecommunications services. The performance of the operating enterprises varies considerably from one to another, ranging from highly efficient operation by some of the larger municipals to stagnation and decay in many of the smaller ones. Overall, the sector has lagged behind rapid modernization and growth of the economy.

Four decrees enacted in September 1990 provide the basis for potentially sweeping reforms of the telecommunications sector. In particular, these decrees would allow the Ministry of Communications to license existing regional telephone companies, alone or in association with foreign partners, to build and operate domestic long-distance networks in competition with TELECOM. The decrees also allow the regional operating companies to provide new services, including cellular and nonbasic services. In 1991, as part of an effort to improve public sector enterprises generally, the government entered into a performance contract with TELECOM, which was also asked to undertake a revision of its internal organization and management. In 1992, these events were overtaken by the government's decision to privatize TELECOM. There has been, however, little progress in any of these directions.

Ecuador

A new telecommunications law passed by the Congress in August 1992 gave Empresa Estatal de Telecomunicaciones (EMETEL), the state monopoly telecommunications enterprise (formerly Instituto Ecuatoriano de Telecomunicaciones, IETEL), considerably more autonomy to be run as a business. In particular, the enterprise was given control of its revenues and expenditures independent of the national budget; it is no longer subject to civil service rules on staff hiring and remunerations; and it can undertake procurement independently of the cumbersome central government procedures. EMETEL is, however, still subject to a number of controls as a public sector enterprise. In particular, it needs approval from the Ministry of Finance to undertake new foreign debt. Also, a number of key policy issues remain to be resolved before EMETEL can be run as a fully commercial enterprise. For example, major adjustments in tariff level and structure are needed to better reflect costs.

The 1992 law also established Superintendencia de Telecomunicaciones as the specialized telecommunications regulatory agency. The agency is independent of EMETEL, from which it took over management of the radio spectrum.

The two political parties facing a second round of presidential elections in June 1992 considered options for further restructuring Ecuador's telecommunications sector, including privatizing EMETEL. The government had already taken steps toward inviting competitive bids for a franchise to provide cellular services countrywide.

Although during the electoral campaign the now-president of Ecuador had advocated privatizing EMETEL, in his inaugural address he announced that EMETEL would be given "a second chance." It appears that the government seeks to improve the enterprise before privatizing it in 1994 or 1995. The Consejo de Modernización del Estado (CONAM), established by the president under the direction of a prestigious private sector industrialist, is the lead agency for public sector reform, including EMETEL.

Panama

The vice president of Panama announced in April 1991 the government's intention to restructure Instituto Nacional de Telecomunicaciones (INTEL), the state telecommunications monopoly, as a company owned 51 percent by the private sector and 49 percent by the state. Consultants assisted in defining a new sector policy, structure, and regulatory regime, and in preparing a plan for privatizing INTEL. The consultants also drafted a new telecommunications law which would establish the framework for private provision of telecommunications services, setting a time limit for INTEL's monopoly, issuing cellular licenses to independent operators, and opening up other market segments to competition.

Subsequent progress, however, was slower than expected. A general law of privatization of public enterprises was passed by Congress but excluded INTEL. A draft law that would enable the government to privatize INTEL was not submitted to Congress until December 1992, for lack of sufficient congressional support to pass. Discussion of this law in Congress began in March 1993. Cellular services are still not available.

Peru

The government of Peru has been moving since 1991 to address major weaknesses in the telecommunications sector, the least-developed in Latin America except for Bolivia's.

A telecommunications law passed by the Congress in November 1991 established a broadly liberalized framework for the provision of services, allowing competition in all market segments, subject to concessions and licenses.

In early 1992 the Comité de Privatización (CPRI) was established by the president of Peru to privatize all state enterprises, a key component of the government's program. This includes divesting the state's 22 percent interest in Compañía Peruana de Teléfonos (CPT), the mainly subscriber-owned local telephone monopoly in metropolitan Lima, with about 300,000 lines including most of the high-traffic business users. It also includes the state's 100 percent ownership of Empresa Nacional de Telecomunicaciones (ENTEL), which runs all long-distance and international services as well as about 220,000 telephone lines in the provinces.

Privatization of ENTEL and CPT is scheduled to be completed by December 1993. International firms of telecommunications consultants, lawyers, and investment bankers have been retained by CPRI to help prepare a strategic plan for sector reform, outline a regulatory framework and institution, restate financial information in line with international accounting standards, draft terms and conditions of sale, contracts, and licenses, as well as carry out the sales.

Policy options include selling the state's shares of ENTEL and CPT as a single package, leaving it up to the new owners to decide on possible merger or other restructuring. Alternatively, the government may decide to divide ENTEL into long-distance and local operating companies, then sell these and CPT separately. Other critical issues to be sorted out include the scope and duration of any monopoly privileges of the privatized companies as well as a protracted conflict between ENTEL and CPT on sharing of long-distance revenues.

At the same time, steps are being taken to improve ENTEL's performance before the sale. The company's labor force has been reduced by one-third, from about 11,500 to 7,500 workers. Reportedly, these cuts mainly affected former operators rendered redundant by automatization and redeployed to make-work community telephone offices now privatized; excess labor hired in response to past governments' employment objectives; and persons on the payroll who did not actually perform any functions. These labor reductions, together with tariff adjustments predating CPRI, have turned ENTEL into a highly profitable operation.

Uruguay

With about 10 telephone lines per 100 inhabitants, Uruguay's telecommunications system is (in relative terms) one of the most developed in Latin America.

However, there is still substantial unmet demand for basic telephone service, especially outside Montevideo, and service is often unreliable and of poor quality. Despite digitalization of part of Montevideo's exchanges, much of the plant countrywide is antiquated and in disrepair. More advanced services required by the modern economic sectors (which account for a large part of Uruguay's economy) have been slow to arrive.

In 1990 the Congress of Uruguay passed two public sector reform laws that sought to end monopoly privileges of all state entities and privatize the national telecommunications, air transport, ports, gas, and liquor enterprises. In principle, this legislation opened the way to introduce competition in the provision of telecommunications services and private participation in Administración Nacional de Telecomunicaciones (ANTEL), the state telecommunications monopoly. A study of options for restructuring the telecommunications sector, carried out in 1991 with the assistance of consultants, recommended substantial reforms, including privatization of ANTEL.

Opposition groups, however, succeeded in defeating these initiatives by calling for and winning a national referendum on the government's plans. In Uruguay, the government is obligated to hold a referendum on any matter for which a petition can collect a number of signatures equal to at least 25 percent of the number of votes cast in the immediately preceding presidential election. The referendum, held in December 1992, mustered a substantial majority of voters opposing privatization of ANTEL. Some observers interpret this result more as a no-confidence vote on the government rather than specific opposition to telecommunications reform. The setback may also reflect lack of private sector involvement in managing the privatization initiative and insufficient attention to inserting this initiative in the political process. Whichever is the right reading, no further action toward telecommunications reform is likely, at least until after the next presidential election in 1994.

Central America and Paraguay

Telecommunications reform has been talked about from time to time in Central America from the late 1980s, but little action has followed. By mid-1993 the main exception is El Salvador. In the wake of the end of civil strife which had severely damaged the country's already modest telecommunications facilities, the government, with the assistance of consultants, carried out a review of Administración Nacional de Telecomunicaciones (ANTEL), the state telecommunications enterprise. Whereas initially the focus was on improving ANTEL, it subsequently broadened to consider a wider range of sector options. Consultants will help prepare detailed plans for reform. There is also some movement in Honduras. In early 1993, the president of Honduras announced the privatization of Empresa Hondureña de Telecomunicaciones (HONDUTEL), the state telecommunications company. Action may follow the presidential elections of late 1993. Also, bids have been invited from independent operators for a national license to provide cellular services. In Nicaragua, in 1992, the government examined options for telecommunications reform as part of a broad economic strategy review, but in the context of deteriorating economic and political situations no decisions have been announced. Scattered initiatives toward private sector participation in Costa Rica and Guatemala were quickly defeated by various interest groups.

In 1991 the government of Paraguay expressed interest in revising the telecommunications sector arrangements. So far, however, action has been limited mainly to introducing cellular services.

Endnotes

1. These characteristics and constraints are discussed for developing countries in general in the first chapter of this book.

2. Several other smaller companies, including a few private ones, provided telephone service in parts of the country, and domestic and international telex.

3. Employees were offered 50 percent of future severance payments provided they invested 80 percent of the amount received in purchasing CTC shares. Eighty-four percent of employees thus acquired 6.4 percent of CTC by the end of 1987. Pension funds acquired a further 7.6 percent. By end 1987, 25 percent of CTC was privately owned.

4. This figure is comparable to Europe (for example, British Telecom 9) and close to the U.S. average of about 5.

5. These results are based on subtracting from the social net present value of CTC under private operation from what would have been its value had it continued under public ownership. The methodology and detailed analysis of various cases can be found in Galal and others, World Bank, forthcoming. The analysis for CTC is given in Ahmed Galal and Clemencia Torres, "Compañía de Teléfonos de Chile," World Bank, 1992, processed.

6. Lower tariffs would further increase consumer gains, but CTC privatization did not result in tariffs changing either way.

7. ENTEL's gains from CTC privatization followed from the prevailing sector structure in which most of the highly profitable long-distance and international traffic was carried by ENTEL. As competition builds up in these market segments, ENTEL's gains will be shared with new entrants.

8. This is in contrast with the initial results of similar studies in Mexico and Argentina, which suggest that the gain in welfare was captured mainly by foreigners while nationals were actually left worse off. These findings, however, may relate to the fact that since the studies were done soon after privatization, data on actual service growth and improvement, which are the main source of user gains, were not yet in hand.

9. For a detailed discussion of the evolution and features of the Chilean telecommunications regulatory regime, and its impact on sector development, see Ahmed Galal, "Regulation, Commitment and Development of Telecommunications in Chile," World Bank, December 1992, processed.

10. Since Galal's study did not include quality of service in the measure of welfare changes, this means that the figures for consumers (and the total) are somewhat overstated.

11. Although the discussion of the provision of telephone service in rural areas is often cast in terms of the need for subsidy, the problem probably has more to do with

rural areas being less profitable than meeting unmet demands in cities. A number of commercially successful rural telephone services operate in Chile, including that promoted by a small regional operating company in the south of the country as well as telephone and power cooperatives.

12. In a sense it could be said that SUBTEL suffers the weaknesses of ministerial regulatory arrangements but enjoys few of the advantages.

13. The government decided at an early stage that ENTel had to be divided before sale, on a regional or services basis. The consultants' initial proposition—to break up ENTel into three regional companies (Buenos Aires, north, and south)—proved highly controversial in terms of market structure. In particular, the Buenos Aires company would have most of the revenue-earning potential but little of the network, which would be mostly in the other two companies. This imbalance was thought to exacerbate issues of division of revenues and also to limit the threat of competition in the lucrative Buenos Aires market at the end of the exclusivity period. Eventually the government agreed to have only two regional companies, splitting Buenos Aires in the middle—along Avenida Cordoba. It was considered that the technical difficulties of untangling the two companies' network in Buenos Aires were not unduly intractable, could be largely done by the companies themselves after taking over from ENTel, and the costs would be more than offset by the gain in market dynamics.

14. In mid-1992, the two regional companies also consolidated operations in their respective territories by purchasing the assets of Compañía Argentina de Telefónos (CAT). CAT, an Argentine company related to L. M. Ericsson of Sweden, was a residual from much earlier sector structures. Nonetheless, with about 290,000 telephone lines (9 percent of Argentina's total) in Mendoza and several other provinces, CAT was not an insignificant operation. CAT's operating authorization, however, had expired several years before ENTel was privatized, and it had been agreed that the successors to ENTel would negotiate directly the purchase of CAT assets in their respective coverage areas. It may be noted that the combined sale price of US$120 million, or about $400 per line, paid for CAT amounts to little over one-half the price per line paid for ENTel two years earlier (see Table 3-1 in the main text), and an even lower fraction of the share value of the regional companies at the time they took over CAT.

15. This paragraph draws heavily on Alice Hill and Manuel Abdala, "Regulation, Institutions and Commitment: Privatization and Regulation of the Argentine Telecommunications Sector," World Bank, January 1993, processed.

16. See Alice Hill and Manuel Abdala, "Regulation, Institutions and Commitment: Privatization and Regulation of the Argentine Telecommunications Sector," World Bank, January 1993, processed.

17. The consultants who helped the government draw up the terms and conditions for sale of ENTel, the World Bank, which financed preparation of the privatization and awarded the government a large balance-of-payments support loan partly on condition of good progress in this process, as well as the local and international investment bankers who led the actual sale, all insisted on the need to establish clear regulatory foundations. They regarded this as essential to provide assurances to the

new operators-investors as well as to safeguard the public interest and that of emerging competitors. The government went along with this but, with hindsight, never took much interest. In particular, the World Bank went as far as meeting President Carlos Saúl Menem to press the point of setting CNT directly under his office, but failed to achieve this goal.

18. CNT now pays an independent consumer defense group to receive and process customer complaints. In response, Telefónica retained an international accounting and management firm to provide computerized service centers to handle customer billing and complaints.

19. Licenses for cellular services in the provinces (that is, outside Buenos Aires, where a subsidiary of BellSouth and Motorola has been in operation since 1990) will be awarded under competition. TELECOM and Telefónica de Argentina will be allowed to provide a second cellular service in the provinces only two years later, to allow the new entrants to get started.

20. This and the preceding paragraph draw mainly on Alice Hill and Manuel Abdala, "Regulation, Institutions and Commitment: Privatization and Regulation of the Argentine Telecommunications Sector," World Bank, January 1993, processed.

21. This section draws extensively on Peter Smith and Björn Wellenius, "Mexico Telecommunications: One Year (Plus) After the Reform Program," World Bank, May 1, 1992 mimeo.

22. In general, compared with practice in the U.S. and other countries where tariffs are closer to costs, TELMEX's rental and local call charges were low, and connection fees and international call charges high. This was compounded by a telephone tax averaging over 30 percent of telephone bills, with higher tax rates for international and long-distance than for local use. This was perceived to cause substantial economic inefficiencies, including a competitive disadvantage to Mexican businesses.

23. Telecomunicaciones de Mexico (TELECOMM) took over SCT's former operating functions as well as the telex and packet-switched data services of the postal administration. Subsequently, TELECOMM sold the microwave network to TELMEX. TELECOMM, which does not receive government funding, is now almost solely in the satellite business, mainly leasing facilities to TELMEX and a substantial number of private networks. TELECOMM owns and operates the domestic Morelos satellites, is building a new satellite system (Solidaridad) for domestic and subregional coverage in Latin America, and provides access to the INTELSAT system for international services. An article in the Mexican constitution has been interpreted to mean that only the state can own and operate satellite systems.

24. It should not be assumed that reforms proceeded entirely along a smooth sequence as might be inferred from the text. For example, the modernization program went through successive drafts and was finalized only after TELMEX had been privatized. The franchises to independent cellular operators were awarded before the reform package was fully defined and at the time appeared to some as premature and preempting some policy choices as well as potentially undermining TELMEX's sale price. The franchise for cellular services in the federal district of

Mexico City, the largest single cellular market, was not awarded through competition but rather granted as an extension to an existing license for mobile radio.

25. For example, in 1991 the number of connected public-switched telephone lines increased by 12.5 percent (670,000 lines), exceeding the minimum 12 percent per annum required in 1991–94 by the concession. It was also above the 11 percent actual growth in 1990 and 1989 and the paltry 5 to 7 percent since the early 1980s. Quality and continuity of service targets (defined by composite indexes, including fault rate and proportion of faults cleared in one and three days, time to obtain dial tone, local and long-distance completion rates, operator response times, and number of public telephones in service) were met in all regions except the capital city, where a massive improvement program was under way. Tariff levels were adjusted from time to time for inflation and remained below the aggregate cap established in the concession while further rebalancing individual service charges (higher rental and local call charges, lower long-distance and international call charges), bringing them closer to international practice.

26. TELMEX has done very well financially. In real terms, during 1991 revenues increased 21 percent while operating expenses rose only 7 percent. Net income after cost of financing, taxes, and workers' profit sharing increased by a whopping 78 percent, yielding a healthy 28.7 percent return on stockholders' equity, up from 20.3 percent in 1990. In 1991, about 75 percent of total investment was financed with internally generated funds.

27. For example, several of the cellular companies have built about 2,000 kilometers of digital microwave routes for interconnecting cellular facilities, but this may also provide a starting point for developing a second long-distance carrier in the future.

28. For example, cellular operators seeking to expand the scope of business, private networks selling excess capacity.

29. Center for Strategic and International Studies (CSIS), June 1991, "Telecom and Mexico: The New Bilateral Menu," The International Communications Studies Program, Washington, DC.

30. This section was kindly contributed by Robert R. Taylor.

31. Another factor is the relative homogeneity of cellular technology. The nine Mexican independents use equipment supplied by only two manufacturers, which minimizes the technical problems of network integration.

32. American Depository Receipts (ADRs) represent ownership of shares held in other countries by U.S. banks or their agents. They are traded in the U.S. as regular stock.

33. Nonetheless, some analysts believe that the price paid for CANTV, and maybe for TELMEX, will in the long run prove to have been excessive, in terms of the investors' exposure and credit rating, if not in terms of initial returns on equity. Recent events lend some support to these views. For example, in a single week in June 1992, TELMEX's shares lost almost one-third of their value, ending three years of uninterrupted appreciation that made TELMEX one of the most sought-after stock market investments.

34. There is related experience in other regions. For example, the case of Sri Lanka will be discussed in a later part of this book.

35. The government's accrued pension liabilities are often large, insufficiently documented, and highly valued by the workers. The tendency so far has been for these liabilities to stay with the state rather than be passed on to the new owners. This gives assurance to the workers as well as facilitates the buyers' evaluation of the company.

36. For a checklist of policy, legal, and regulatory issues see International Telecommunication Union, "The Changing Telecommunications Environment— Policy Considerations for Members of the ITU," chapter 5, Geneva, February 1989.

37. For example, Bond's sale of CTC, after contributing little to the company apart from carrying it across the threshold between the state to private sectors, could with hindsight be interpreted this way. This is not to say that the privatization had no effect on CTC's performance. It did, but mostly resulting from freeing CTC from the constraints it had been subjected to as a state-owned enterprise, and from profit-seeking pressure by the foreign owners on CTC's local management, rather than due to any contribution of management or technical resources.

38. The operators do not view themselves as financial investors and have so far kept their equity participation at a minimum. See, for example, the views of STET and Bell Atlantic in a later part of this book.

39. Also note that although the flotation of US$100 million by CTC in the U.S. market was a breakthrough, it contributed but a small fraction of the capital required for investment.

40. For example, there are successful cases of rural telephone cooperatives in Brazil, Argentina, and Chile. Telephone service in the city of Santa Cruz, Bolivia, is successfully provided by a cooperative, COTAS (but similar arrangements in other cities have been less satisfactory). Finland's highly efficient telecommunications sector is largely structured in terms of small local cooperatives. A study completed in 1992 by TELECON (the Finnish PTT's international consulting arm) and the World Bank has examined the Finnish experience and drawn lessons for developing countries that are relevant to Latin America.

41. Some technological developments, however, work in the opposite direction. It could be argued that the advent of wide-band optical-fiber transmission, for example, reintroduces large economies of scale.

42. In 1992 China's telecommunications system became the largest in the developing world. Relative to population, Brazil with about 8 lines per 100 inhabitants is somewhat above average for Latin America and several times the average for the developing world. China has about 1 line per 100 inhabitants, the lowest in Asia and one of the lowest in the world.

43. In particular, local communities and real estate developers may now invest in and build local telephone facilities interconnected with TELEBRÁS.

44. In one province, telecommunications are organized as a provincial company, providing both local services and intraprovincial long-distance service.

4

Liberalization and Privatization in Chile

José Ricardo Melo

THE PROCESS OF LIBERALIZATION AND PRIVATIZATION of the telecommunications sector in Chile began about fifteen years ago. The legal, economic, technical, administrative, and political components of reform were dealt with in stages. New policy, law, regulatory arrangement, and pricing rules were designed and successively introduced. The government then sold its shares in the major telecommunications operating companies. Although it has gone a long way, the reform process is still not complete. Currently, a reevaluation of the whole process is likely to lead to further policy and regulatory adjustments. This chapter describes the main features of the Chilean telecommunications reform, focusing on changes in regulation and ownership.

The Preliberalization Scene

Until the mid-1970s, the telecommunications scene in Chile was one that was quite common in developing countries. The accepted view was that for infrastructure sectors, such as telecommunications, the government should not only direct and oversee the development and operation of the sector but also be directly involved in planning and operating the facilities and services. Even if the law did not rule out private operating companies, in practice the government-owned enterprises dominated the field. Although the resulting system was overall technically sound, development was constrained especially regarding financing and management of the dominant operating enterprises. The sector organization came to be perceived as clearly unable to catch up with demand and face the growing requirements of the emerging information era.

The Legal Framework

There was no specific law for telecommunications. The Electric Utilities Law was deemed to apply to telecommunications, even if the resemblance between both sectors was quite limited. Actually, only two provisions of this law were enforced in the telecommunications sector. First, any user or supplier interested in establishing and operating a public or private (that is, dedicated) telecommunications facility or service had to apply for a government license. In practice, monopoly operation, although not established either by law or the terms of the concessions, was the norm. The government did not authorize new public service operators in areas already covered by existing concessions, irrespective of whether the existing operator met user needs. Licenses for dedicated networks (for instance, for use among sites of large mining and farming companies) were granted, provided the public operators could not meet the users' requirements.

The second aspect of the Electric Utilities Law that was applied to telecommunications was pricing. Tariffs of public telecommunications services were set by the government so as to allow each operating enterprise to make a 10 percent rate of return on fixed assets. Approved tariffs, however, often were lower than those applied for by the operators. This led to company accounting practices that overstated the value of fixed assets. The government agency responsible for reviewing the applications for tariff changes largely lacked the accounting standards, analytic skills, access to information, and independent regulatory power to deal with tariffs in any depth. In this context, tariffs were largely decided on a political basis.

Technical standards issued by the government were all but nonexistent, as were the control procedures for their enforcement. Standards were mostly issued by the monopoly companies themselves as internal norms which thus became the de facto national standards.

The Operating Enterprises

In this period there were two main public telecommunications enterprises and a number of smaller ones. These two main companies, both state-owned, had the power to control almost every significant development in the telecommunications sector, since for every new project it was normally necessary to request some local or long-distance capacity from them, the sole providers.

Compañía de Teléfonos de Chile (CTC) was the largest of these enterprises. CTC provided local telephone service to about 300,000 subscribers, accounting for 95 percent of the country's total. CTC resulted from mergers among a large number of small private local telephone companies set up around the turn of the century, consolidated in 1930 into a company owned by International Telephone and Telegraph Corporation (ITT). In 1967 the government invested in an ambitious program to expand and modernize CTC, which thus became jointly owned by ITT and the Chilean state. In 1971 the government unilaterally intervened and took over CTC's management and assets. Finally in 1974 a compensation agreement was reached with ITT, and CTC became a mostly state-owned company under the control of Corporación de Fomento de la Producción (CORFO), the state development corporation.[1] Despite accelerated growth in the 1960s, service penetration remained very low (about 3 telephone lines per 100 inhabitants in 1976) and showed no signs of growing. Unsatisfied expressed demand (waiting list) had reached over 50 percent of lines in service, and hidden demand probably amounted to a similar or even higher figure.[2] Although local service in most locations was automatic, new technologies coexisted with old and service innovation was slow. In particular,

CTC's outdated long-distance network using mainly open wire lines and a single short microwave link between the capital city Santiago, and the main port Valparaiso, had not kept up with development of local facilities; all calls required operator assistance, and service was often of poor quality and subject to long delays.

Empresa Nacional de Telecomunicaciones S.A. (ENTEL), the other large operator, was a mainly state-owned company established by CORFO in 1964. Together with government investment in and joint ownership of CTC, the advent of ENTEL represented the culmination of years of public debate—largely led by the professional engineering associations and academia—and increasing government awareness of the extent to which inadequate telecommunications was constraining economic and social development.[3] ENTEL built a modern, countrywide microwave network including terrestrial links to neighboring countries and in 1969 was first in South America to introduce international service by satellite. ENTEL's main business was leasing domestic long-distance capacity to CTC, other local telephone companies, television broadcasting networks, and corporate users, as well as operating international services. CTC was not authorized to expand or modernize its own long-distance facilities; the old network was largely segmented to provide spurs into low-traffic centers, while circuits leased from ENTEL provided the main trunks. Although the new facilities greatly improved service, protracted conflicts between CTC and ENTEL impeded introducing subscriber trunk dialing, data transmission, and other services and facilities. Also, although long-distance revenues were to be split, theoretically, in proportion to each operating company's share of costs, in practice greatly overpriced long-distance and international services cross-subsidized underpriced, flat-rate local services; this, however, did not result in sustained extension of service to new areas.

There were also two smaller telephone companies: Compañía Nacional de Teléfonos (CNT) provided local and intraregional long-distance telephone service in the south of continental Chile to about 12,000 subscribers, accounting for about 4 percent of the country's total[4]; Compañía de Teléfonos de Coyhaique (CTY) provided telephone service in the main towns of the province of Aysen, with about 1,000, or less than 1 percent of all subscribers. Both companies were privately owned until they were taken over by the government in 1971. Domestic and international telex service was provided to about 1,500 subscribers across the country by the telegraph branch of Correos y Telégrafos, the government post office administration. Three small privately owned companies competed with the post office to provide international cable, and later telex in major cities.[5]

Deregulation

In 1975, a new national development strategy was implemented in Chile, encompassing almost every sector of the economy. It was based on encouraging a free market economy, stressing the roles of domestic and international competition and of private investment. Efficiency in the allocation of resources and in business management was strongly advocated. One of the first steps was to liberalize sectors that were highly regulated, thus opening the way for new investments and more efficient operation. Moreover, better management in government-owned corporations was sought.[6]

First Openings

In the telecommunications sector, only partial measures were initially taken. Resale of telephone lines by subscribers was made legal, overriding objections by the operating companies, resulting in a more efficient allocation of available lines, reduced pressures on company management, and in market transaction prices that better reflected the real scarcities of service.[7] Likewise, telephone companies were required to accept the transfer of telephone service with rental or sale of real estate. Shortly after, telephone companies were also required to interconnect terminal equipment—especially telephone sets and private branch exhanges (PBXs)—obtained by the subscribers from independent suppliers. The absolute power of the main telecommunications companies started to decline.

Establishment of a Regulatory Agency

The first important change in telecommunications legislation established in 1977 a government agency responsible for telecommunications regulation. This was the Subsecretaría de Telecomunicaciones (SUBTEL, or Office of the Undersecretary of Telecommunications) under the Ministry of Transport and Telecommunications. SUBTEL was put in charge of granting licenses and franchises, developing and enforcing technical standards, and overseeing the operation of all telecommunications networks and services. Clearly, the government was establishing an institutional basis for a new legal structure of the telecommunications sector.

Telecommunications Policy

The next important step was the promulgation, in 1978, of a national telecommunications policy. This was a public statement of principles and intentions, a rather uncommon step in the Chilean legal and political system. The policy statement introduced the principle of economic efficiency and established that telecommunications services would normally be provided by parties other than government. The policy, however, had limited legal standing (it was an executive decree, not a law) and was operationally inconclusive (general principles with no specific rules). Therefore, it was unsuitable for direct enforcement and most probably was not intended for that purpose. Nevertheless, it was on the policy's principles that sector reform was subsequently built.

The process of change was not without legal problems in the first years. As old regulations based on the electric utilities law had still not been abrogated, they frequently conflicted with the new principles espoused in the policy. It was well known that the government was trying to follow the latter, but legally the old regulations had to be complied with. Important decisions were not made because of insufficient legal basis, and others ran the risk of being challenged in courts by those interested in maintaining the status quo.

Even if not directly enforceable, the policy encouraged aggressive entrepreneurs, who started investing in telecommunications almost as soon as the policy was promulgated. Of course, these were not isolated initiatives: private investors had noted and felt supported by the fact that the whole economic regime was moving in the same direction, and that the telecommunications policy was just one among several related economic and legal initiatives taken by the government.

The 1982 Telecommunications Law

In 1982, a new telecommunications law was finally passed, one that reflected the 1978 policy statement very closely. The old Electric Utilities Law was explicitly abrogated for telecommunications.

In broad terms, the 1982 Telecommunications Law included a classification of different services; a system of concessions and licenses whereby any person or entity, national or alien, can apply to provide telecommunications services; the requirement that all telecommunications operators comply with basic technical and operational standards (defined through subsequent ministerial decrees); the reinforcement of SUBTEL's regulatory powers; and penalties for infringements of the law.

One important point on which the law elaborated very little, however, was tariffs. Only a general statement was included, indicating that monopoly services could have their tariffs set by the government, tariffs for other services being set without restriction. This did not provide enough information for prospective investors to assess the returns that could be obtained in most telecommunications businesses. Nonetheless, given that the government still exercised ownership control of the main operating companies and that its general pricing policy was that tariffs should reflect costs, tariffs were gradually adjusted toward decreasing cross-subsidies.

The 1987 Additional Telecommunications Law

In 1987 a major addition to the 1982 law was introduced, focusing mainly on three matters: procedure for setting monopoly tariffs, service obligations for public telephone companies, and subscriber financing of new investment.

On the issue of tariffs, the Fiscalía Nacional Económica (Office of the National Economic Prosecutor) was empowered to decide whether a service was offered under monopoly conditions and thus the government should set its tariffs. A tariff-setting procedure was specified for such cases, based on incremental costs subject to review every five years. Regarding service obligations, the additional law required the telephone companies to provide a telephone line to any applicant within two years of filing for service in listed urban areas within the company's concession territory.[8] The list would be revised from time to time until eventually all urban areas were included. New operating companies would be licensed to offer service in areas where the existing companies had failed to meet this obligation. Lastly, the telephone companies were given the option of requiring that new subscribers contribute capital up to the average investment cost per line, in exchange for which the company must give the subscriber shares in the company's capital stock, or bonds or other debt instruments.

The 1987 law also established a fee to be paid to the government by every licensee who holds a band in the radio frequency spectrum, according to the kind of service, bandwidth, and radiated power. The 1982 and 1987 laws were followed by several decrees that detailed technical standards for different services and networks.

At present, the overall framework established by the policy, laws, and decrees, is legally in full force: the concessions and licenses system, the standards-setting system, the supervisory system, and the rate-setting system, are effectively in operation (the latter since 1989). This framework, even if far from being perfect, has provided the basis for major changes in the supply of telecommunications services which are generally well regarded by users. It has been also the basis for very significant changes in the ownership of the largest telecommunications companies.

Privatization

Abandoning the traditional view that state ownership was essential for telecommunications development, the 1978 telecommunications policy advocated private ownership of the telecommunications operating companies.

Emerging New Operators

In 1978 and 1980, two small privately owned telephone companies were established and granted concessions overlapping parts of CTC's service areas. These companies took advantage of the severe shortage in the supply of telephone lines, especially in affluent residential and commercial districts. CTC was required to interconnect to the new networks, which partly duplicated CTC's own networks. Later, a new small private company, a joint venture with a foreign operator, was established to provide mobile telephone service. By then, several small firms represented and distributed foreign telecommunications equipment manufacturers; the terminal equipment market in particular flourished.

Sale of State-Owned Enterprises

By 1982, the government started selling its shares in telecommunications companies. First it sold CNT and CTY, the two small telephone companies in southern Chile. Both were bought through private bids by VTR, one of the existing private telex companies.

A struggle had started by that time within and outside the government on the eventual privatization of the two largest state-owned companies, namely CTC and ENTEL. Several voices (including the military) opposed total or significant privatization, on political, economic, labor, and security grounds. However, the government went ahead with its plans. In 1986, Telex-Chile, the successor to Correos y Telégrafos's telex operations which had been restructured as a state-owned company and prepared for privatization under commercial management, was put up for sale by the government and awarded to a consortium of Chilean investors and telecommunications professionals. That same year the government began selling limited amounts of stock in CTC and ENTEL through the Santiago stock exchange and private sales. The principal buyers were several Chilean private pension funds and other national and foreign investors. A significant percentage of ENTEL stock was sold to the company's employees.

In 1987, the government identified three consortia interested in CTC and invited them to bid for a controlling package of CTC shares. The very simple terms and conditions of sale required the buyer to increase the company's capital by US$100 million within twelve months of the sale but did not include any obligations regarding service expansion or quality improvement. At this time, however, the 1987 additional law was passed, including provisions concerning tariffs and service obligations. The terms and conditions of sale allowed bidders to make their offers partly payable in Chilean sovereign debt outstanding in the international financial markets. The selected bid was disqualified by the State Comptroller's Office (Controloría General de la República), however, on administrative grounds. The government subsequently negotiated with the previously selected bidder, Australian investor Alan Bond, who paid US$140 million for 35 percent of CTC's shares and took control of the company in early 1988. Two years later, after investing the required US$100 million in CTC and collecting about US$90 million in dividends, Bond sold his share of CTC stock, now about 50 percent, through direct negotiation to Telefónica de España for US$390 million. In mid-1990, US$100 million of new CTC's stock was sold in the U.S., the first transaction of this kind by a Chilean company.[9]

In 1989 Telefónica de España, which had unsuccessfully bid for CTC in 1987, bought from CORFO 10 percent of ENTEL's shares, and a further 10 percent in 1990. Although this did not give Telefónica a controlling interest in ENTEL, it was the largest single holding and allowed it to exercise considerable power.

By mid-1991, the state retained no significant ownership of any telecommunications company. Telefónica, with a strong minority interest in ENTEL and majority ownership of CTC, had become the largest single investor in Chilean telecommunications. By the end of the year, ENTEL's employees sold a small percentage of the shares they held in the company, dismantled the association they had set up for jointly managing their stock, and distributed the remaining shares among the employees individually; however, the ownership pattern may not be fully settled: in April 1993, the Supreme Court decided that on anticompetitive grounds Telefónica must sell its stock in either CTC or ENTEL. In the meantime, the market prices of CTC and ENTEL shares have increased above the average increase of the index of the Chilean stock market.

Pricing Policy and Tariffs

Throughout the liberalization and privatization process, one ever-present issue has been that of tariffs. At the beginning of reform, the average level of telecommunications tariffs was too low to provide an adequate return on investment, and the tariff structure (that is, the relative prices of the various services) bore little relationship to the cost structure.

Initial Tariff Corrections

Despite general agreement that these imbalances should be ended as soon as possible, there were different opinions on the timing of tariff adjustments. A particular difficulty was the lack of reliable cost data by types of service. Nonetheless, the government decided that the direction of adjustments was clear enough, and that initial adjustments could be safely undertaken even if the exact cost figures were not yet known. The first corrections were introduced in 1983 and 1984. At the same time, the first service-based cost studies ever conducted in Chilean telecommunications companies were started. These studies were expected to provide a better basis for the next round of tariff review.

Experience with these tariff changes showed that they could be implemented quickly and that demand was rather inelastic, at least initially. However, as service expanded to lower-income groups, incremental demand slowly became more elastic, especially in relation to the initial connection charge.

Theoretical Model for Telecommunications Tariffs

In 1987, a rate model for telecommunications was developed. Its theoretical basis was the determination of long-term incremental costs for each service, in each part of the country, and for each operating company. Rather than actual costs, those of ideally efficient companies were used, reflecting what would result from using the most appropriate new technologies available. Since these incremental costs most probably would not be enough to cover total costs, they would be corrected in such a way as to minimize distortions [*sic*], thus obtaining a set of tariffs that ensured near-maximum economic efficiency as well as self-financing for every service, every region, and every company. Profits were indirectly set since capital costs were included; the exact applicable figure for capital cost would be calculated considering basic risk-free investments, market risk, and telecommunications industry risk.

An indexation formula was included in the model for each company. The whole tariff system was built on a plan for services development that each operator was to submit to the government in advance of the tariff-adjusting process.

Practical Simplifications of the Model

Even if theoretically appropriate, this model was too elaborate for practical purposes, and some simplifications became necessary. Not enough information on the cost of capital was available in Chile, and so a proxy had to be adopted. Then, clearly, the model could not solve the classic problem of irrefutably apportioning common costs among different services of regions. Moreover, it could not determine unambiguously which was the ideal efficient network design. And finally, the process assigned to the regulated companies the dominant role in the process of setting its own tariffs. But the model at least provided a reasonable general framework, and it was put to work.

It also became apparent that even if the avowed goal was to eliminate all cross-subsidies in five years, that would not be possible in some cases. A small distant city in the far south of the country, for example, linked only by satellite to the rest of the country, would have its long-distance rates multiplied several times if it were to pay for all its costs. The definition of a very large service area became necessary to allow some averaging out of singularly high cost elements.

Finally, decisions were made, simplifications were introduced, and numerical results came out of the model, setting the tariff framework for a term of five years; however, this term has been shown to be one of the most critical parts of the system. On the one hand, it is desirable that frameworks such as this be kept as stable as possible, in order to allow for adequate evaluation of possible investments by private companies. On the other, it is also desirable to keep open the option of introducing some changes in the model if it reveals itself as inadequate or too tight, especially when being applied for the first time.

In this case, the model, although too rigid, was embodied in the law, making it therefore extremely difficult to modify. As the end of the first five-year term approaches, both the government and the companies are interested in modifying some parts of the tariff system, even if each side has different opinions on which parts should be revised. Moreover, introduction of competition in the long-distance area will necessarily change some of the assumptions made when the tariff system was first set up.

The Telecommunications Companies in the New Environment

In Chile, telecommunications liberalization has shown that dismantling monopoly powers is a rewarding but long and difficult task. New companies have been established, and of course, many of the old monopoly powers have all but vanished. Nevertheless, the two old big companies, CTC and ENTEL, now private and partly subject to competition, are still the strongest controlling powers on the Chilean telecommunications scene. One can only wonder what the results would have been had there been just one big company. Before privatizing CTC, the government debated whether to first break it up into smaller regional companies; it became convinced, however, that significant economies of scale continued to prevail and that the regional pieces would eventually have been merged into a new single company.

It is evident that in any liberalized sector, companies try to keep their old monopoly niches and simultaneously try to erode those of other companies and advance into new markets. Their credo might well be "My area is a natural monopoly, but yours is a competitive one." No company likes to be labeled a monopoly, but it dreams of having a market niche for itself.

Long-Distance and New Services

In the aftermath of liberalization in Chile, the most interesting opportunities are perceived to be in the long-distance market. Both CTC, the mainly local services company, and at least one of the smaller operators, Telex-Chile, have shown themselves to be very aggressive in disputing this market with ENTEL. CTC has also entered or is trying to enter other markets, including cellular, consultancy, customer premises equipment, and even investment in telecommunications abroad. For the time being, CTC is not fearful of having its original local services market invaded: with current technology, this market is still largely a natural monopoly, even if cellular telephony could become a strong challenger (it is therefore no coincidence that CTC is investing heavily in cellular service).

Other companies are trying to position themselves in new emerging markets. Telex-Chile has been very active exploring and developing technically more sophisticated markets, because the demand for telex is quickly disappearing. In fact, Telex-Chile has established an independent domestic and international long-distance satellite network (which CTC is still not allowed to do). A contract has been signed between Telex-Chile and CTC through which a significant portion of the public international traffic is managed by this network. This contract has been denounced by ENTEL and VTR as monopolistic (VTR has established a network similar to that of Telex-Chile, but it has not been able to reach a similar agreement with CTC). Other smaller companies are still looking for an appropriate place in the market.

Even if initially the different companies were interested in entering domestic long-distance, now clearly the focus of interest is international long-distance. The present tariff system, recognizing the benefits of imbalances in international traffic, permits exceptions to the general criteria of cost-based tariffs. The exceptionally high returns thus produced are now attracting several competitors, but the outcome of competition in this area is still not clear: Who should be accepted into this very profitable market? What tariff-setting system should be applied, if any? Is uneconomic entry into the market being promoted by the present conditions? If this is the case, how can it be avoided?

This is just the point where a strong dispute has arisen, shaking the whole new regulatory system. Even before it had requested the corresponding concessions, CTC bought some US$50 million worth of the latest long-distance equipment and is now at least temporarily prevented from installing and operating it by a restraining court order. ENTEL argued that a captive market could be developed by CTC with its local subscribers and requested that if a competitive market is established for long-distance services, CTC should be excluded from it. In the meantime, other companies such as Telex-Chile and VTR have already established their systems; yet it has been impossible to reach a stable agreement for operation during the more than three years that this dispute has lasted. Up to now, the only point acknowledged by everyone is that the most adequate structure for competition is the so-called dialled multicarrier (whereby every long-distance call would include a special digit through which the caller would select its preferred carrier); however, there is still dissent on how and when this system should be introduced (and who would be the competitors).

The Government's Position in the New Environment

The reform process has deliberately changed, in a major way, the role of the government in the telecommunications sector. Traditionally, the government determined its sectoral policies and implemented them through the enterprises that were directly under its control. Liberalization, and especially privatization, extinguished this path. Moreover, sectoral policy today is conceptually quite a different subject: more orientation than direct action, more emphasis on services than on systems and networks.

The government is still developing the exact idea of what a sectoral policy should be in this new environment. Very important issues, such as under what conditions could or should the regulator reject an application for a concession, have not yet been solved. Even if all the operational activities are now in private hands, there is general agreement that this is a sector where the government must keep a supervisory and possibly an orientation role. However, the exact extent of these remain to be defined. At the same time, the institutional means to discharge these duties must be determined.

One of the most important lessons from the reform process is that the government did not adequately foresee the need of a specific institution to take over the role of developing and overseeing implementation of sectoral policy. Between 1977, when SUBTEL was established, and 1987, when privatization was largely under way, the state-owned companies were still the most important institutions in terms of sectoral policy. During this time SUBTEL devoted itself mostly to technical and administrative matters. But then, after 1987, the government found itself with no locus for sectoral policy formulation, and this is clearly a point that must be changed.

Also, long-standing conflicts among telecommunications companies call for important additional policy guidelines and regulatory decisions, but the current allocation of responsibilities has resulted in protracted debate with no firm decision in sight. Two cases in point are the conflict between CTC and ENTEL regarding competitive provision of long-distance services discussed above, and the question of whether Telefónica should divest itself of either CTC or ENTEL to avert the risk of anticompetitive practices and possible monopoly consolidation of the two dominant operating companies. For more than three years, both these issues had been subject to successive rounds of review, decisions, revision, and referral to other agencies, by SUBTEL, the antitrust tribunals, and the ordinary courts of justice. Irrespective of what each player thinks is right, a system that takes several years in settling these crucial matters badly needs improvement.[10] Independently of whether CTC overstepped its authority when it purchased new long-distance equipment, as some observers argue, the fact is that it has been impossible to define the final destination for a substantial amount of equipment; this results in economic loss not only to the companies involved but also to the economy at large.

Overall Evaluation of Results

Almost fifteen years after the beginning of the reform process, the results seem to be considered, overall, quite positive, but major weaknesses remain to be addressed.

Successes

Evidently, the telecommunications sector is currently far more active than it was in the old times of state-owned monopoly. Many new services have been introduced, including data transmission, cellular telephony, radio paging, and cable television. Even though supply still lags behind demand, public-switched telephony has been growing at more than 10 percent per annum (especially in these last years), more than twice the rate of the preceding two decades.

Besides the increase in the volume and variety of services being offered, a significant improvement in the ease of transactions must be emphasized. The market has replaced a centralized scheme where almost every sale or purchase was made to one of the large monopolies. Now resale is possible in almost every situation, and normally one can find several providers for different service needs. Many third parties contract freely among themselves and transfer the facilities they have at their disposal.

The equipment market has also developed. Terminal equipment and the number of providers have increased dramatically in number and variety. The big telecommunications companies have also increased the variety of equipment they buy, and now do business with numerous manufacturers of many different countries. Chile is no longer the territory of any particular supplier.

Moreover, the public seems to judge positively the changes that the sector has undergone. A limited survey, conducted in 1989, showed that users rated service as generally good, even if some aspects were mentioned as deserving improvement.

Weaknesses

On the other hand, the reform process itself also shows some weaknesses. First, and despite the increase in number and variety of service providers, the two large traditional carriers, CTC and ENTEL, still have much power in the overall system. Of course CTC, as the local distribution company, controls much of the access to the final users, and it still has not been possible to balance this power to guarantee a real, open network for other providers. It is not that CTC's network is totally closed, but neither is it totally open; would-be competitors tend to distrust CTC, which happens also to own the basic means to access the users, as it tries entering almost every other market. Even if much weaker, ENTEL is in a similar situation in the long-distance market, where economies of scale seem to have decreased much faster than in local distribution. In fact, in the area of domestic long-distance ENTEL is no longer the only alternative; it may soon be losing its controlling position in the international long-distance market as well.

An additional problem is the limited real capacity of the regulatory system to control the supervised companies and services as indicated by law. Besides the lack of institutional locus for policy formulation and overview, the regulatory agency has very limited human and financial resources to carry out its functions. Any effective control of compliance with standards and service regulations has been all but impossible; procedures for testing and approving equipment to be connected to the network are still not wholly defined; the tariffs for monopoly services are largely determined by the regulated companies, while the regulator is unable to fully probe or challenge them. Finally, some aspects of regulation are under other jurisdictions, more specifically the ordinary courts of justice and the antitrust tribunals. This adds confusion and delay in dealing with regulatory problems.

One special point still not resolved is the difficulty currently faced by the government in promoting telecommunications projects of social interest, such as rural services, when these projects are not sufficiently profitable to attract the interest of the private operators. The feasibility of direct government subsidies was initially investigated, and this approach worked reasonably well in limited situations for some time; however, the administrative procedure proved to be too cumbersome, involving authorities in many different areas of government, and had little practical capacity to verify the extent of subsidies actually justified. Direct subsidy has been all but discontinued, and the prospects for getting a predictable flow of capital for this purpose from the central government budget are not encouraging. Probably some kind of limited cross-subsidy within the telecommunications sector would offer an acceptable compromise, but current rules do not provide for this.

Next Steps

A government evaluation of the whole telecommunications policy and of the present condition of systems and services was initiated in 1991. As a result, some amendments to the telecommunications law were proposed to Congress by the end of 1992, dealing mainly with the policy of competition in this sector, some refinements of the concession-granting procedure, and changes in the price-setting system. Evaluation of the most adequate institutional form for the regulatory agency is still ongoing. This could lead to further proposals of change in 1994. However, the most widely accepted opinion is that the fundamental basis of the sector policy should be kept and that only a few adjustments for better guaranteeing the basic goals of a liberalized system should be introduced.

On the other hand, feeling is widespread that the present state of relations among the main operating companies does not favor development. Of course, competition means some degree of confrontation, but at this time it seems that too many aspects of the market remain still undefined, and that this situation has lasted for too long. Legal conflicts among the companies are recurrent and the associated juridical procedures can take years. Challenges of governmental decisions in court frequently immobilize regulatory action, and practical capacity of the regulatory institution is still very limited.

Unquestionably, these conditions must change. The government would expect to find a way out of this, for itself and for the companies, through modifications in the law or other means; but then, in a liberalized system such as the one that is being built, it is not clear up to which point the government can actually intervene in affairs that can be considered private or that are currently subject to decisions of the courts. The proposals for modifications of the law will be a crucial test for the government's capacities in dealing with these problems.

Clearly, some aspects of reform still remain to be resolved. Most probably they have to do with some kind of re-regulation; that is, a regulation specially suited for a liberalized system. Probably one of the most important results that has become apparent in the Chilean process is that deregulation, liberalization, and privatization should not be considered synonymous with elimination of regulation but rather with adapting regulation to a new environment.

Endnotes

1. Throughout this process CTC was a company incorporated under the Chilean companies law. A small proportion of shares was normally traded in the Santiago stock exchange. CTC's franchise covered 76 percent of Chile's territory and 92 percent of its population.

2. A study carried out by the University of Chile in the late 1960s documented, for the first time in a developing country, that with supply shortage the number of outstanding applications for new telephone connections largely understated unmet demand. In Santiago, the capital city, the study found that residential telephone connections demand at prevailing tariffs was about four times the number of outstanding applications. The existence of large hidden demands has since been repeatedly observed in other countries.

3. An important role in this process was played by Empresa Nacional de Electricidad (ENDESA), the highly successful and prestigious national state-owned power utility. ENTEL was eventually organized along the lines of ENDESA, which also provided its first generation of senior managers.

4. CNT was a joint venture by Chilean investors and Siemens, the main source of equipment and technical support. CNT served the main cities from Valdivia to Puerto Montt and extensive rural areas, developed its own long-distance regional network, and was the first to introduce subscriber trunk dialing in Chile.

5. These companies were subsidiaries of, or joint ventures with, foreign companies. ITT Comunicaciones Mundiales was part of ITT's world radio telegraph network. VTR was a joint venture between RCA, several European manufacturers, and Chilean investors. Both provided international cable, and then telex service, to customers in major cities using their own transmission and switching facilities connected to users through lines leased from the local telephone companies. A subsidiary of Cable and Wireless offered cable services and later specialized in press services until it closed down in the 1970s.

6. Certainly it is ironic that this liberalizing policy could be enforced only by resorting to the powers of the military regime then in office.

7. Small businesses sprang up specializing in brokerage of telephone lines by individual local exchange areas. Individual buyers and sellers advertised in the main newspapers. Transaction prices typically were in the range of US$500 to US$2,000. Even higher prices prevailed for some time in certain business and high-income residential areas where shortages were particularly acute. Potential buyers were encouraged to check with CTC to ensure the change was technically feasible and paid CTC the standard fee levied to any subscriber for moving to a new location.

8. However, this provision would be fully enforced only at the end of a ten-year period, that is, in 1997.

9. See also chapter 29 by Dan Vallimarescu, "Privatization Through Public Issue of Shares."

10. On April 20, 1993, Chile's Supreme Court ruled that Telefónica must divest itself of its holding in either ENTEL or CTC. The court left the decision up to Telefónica. Also on April 20, 1993, Chile's antitrust tribunal decided that Chile's telecommunications market should not be segmented and that CTC and ENTEL should be permitted to enter each other's markets which are open also to other service providers.

5

The Argentine Telephone Privatization

Hector A. Mairal

ON FEBRUARY 6, 1991, THE PRIVATE GROUPS that had purchased a controlling interest in the Argentine telephone system from the Argentine state paid the last installment of the purchase price. The first stage of the privatization process begun in September of 1989 was thereby successfully concluded.

The previous Argentine government[1] had endeavored to privatize the telephone system in 1988 by selling a 40 percent participation to Telefónica de España S.A. Lack of competitive bidding was the main objection raised by the opposition to block this effort; however, given the swing in public opinion in favor of the privatization of state-owned public utilities, it was not surprising that when the opposition was elected as the new government in 1989, it announced from the start that it would pursue the same objective.

Most of the Argentine telephone system was nationalized in 1946–48. Until then, the main operator had been a subsidiary of ITT which functioned under a never-well-legislated regime of authorizations.[2] In six of the twenty-two provinces, the service was owned and operated by the Compañía Argentina de Telefónos (CAT, a subsidiary of L. M. Ericsson), which was never nationalized and was still operating in 1989. Telephone cooperatives operating services in small communities also existed.

The telephone system acquired by the state was put under the ownership and operation of Empresa Nacional de Telecomunicaciones (ENTel), a wholly state-owned enterprise subject to the law of state enterprises.[3] The main services provided by ENTel were: (a) public-switched telephone (local, long-distance, and international); (b) national and international telex; (c) packet-switched data; and (d) leased circuits. Prior to privatization, ENTel operated approximately 3,300,000 lines, comprising over 90 percent of all public network subscribers (CAT had 6 percent, and the balance was provided by local cooperatives). Argentina had only 8.8 telephone lines per 100 inhabitants, compared with 25 and 16 for Spain and Portugal, respectively. Quality of service was low: telephone call completion rates were estimated at 49 percent for urban calls and 29 percent for long-distance calls; there was a backlog of over four years to connect a new line; and the average repair time was fourteen days. Tariffs were low in comparison with neighboring countries; they were one-fourth of those in Chile and one-third of those in Uruguay. ENTel had 47,000 employees in 1989, most of them unionized.

The Legal Framework

The legal basis for the privatization program was provided by the State Reform Law 23,696 enacted by the National Congress in September 1989, and by its implementing regulation, Executive Decree 1105 of October 1989,[4] whose main features were:

- According to Law 23,696 Congress decides which state enterprises may be privatized; however, the law identifies some state enterprises and companies which are to be privatized, including ENTel.

- Once a state enterprise or company is declared by Congress to be subject to privatization, the executive is empowered to carry out the privatization process.

- Privatization may be implemented through a sale of assets or shares, as well as by means of the granting of licenses or concessions.

- In principle, the new owner is to be selected through competitive bidding.

- The executive may choose to accept payment of part of the purchase price through the redemption of Argentine public debt.

As soon as the State Reform Law was enacted, the Executive issued Decree 731/89 to implement the privatization of ENTel. Successive decrees approved and amended the terms and conditions of the competitive bidding process, set its calendar, approved the awards, and finally approved the transfer agreements and granted the licenses to the new operators.[5]

The Dramatis Personae

The State Reform Law gave the minister of public works and services the responsibility for implementing the privatization program.[6] Responsibility for the privatization of ENTel was vested in an interventor[7] appointed by the executive with all the chief executive powers granted by ENTel's charter to the board of directors.[8] Key roles were also to be played by the secretary and the undersecretary of communications.

One of the first decisions of the interventor was to appoint technical and financial advisers. This was achieved through a shortlist selection process, which proved essential to maintain the required professionalism of the privatization within the limits imposed by the general political and economic environment and the situation of ENTel itself. The management consulting firm Coopers & Lybrand, which drew on its experience in the privatization of British Telecom, was appointed technical adviser, while Morgan Stanley, a U.S. investment bank, and Banco Roberts, an Argentine bank, were appointed financial advisers.

The Key Initial Decisions

The State Reform Law provided for privatizations by means of competitive bidding, thereby excluding, in principle, direct negotiations with possible interested parties. Although this enhanced the transparency of the process, it imposed limitations on the discretion of the people in charge of the process; this was because Argentine rules on competitive bidding, at least as generally construed, tend to emphasize formal aspects and accept only a static comparison of offers instead of a more dynamic competitive *cum* negotiation process allowed, for example, by rules in the United States on negotiated procurement procedures.[10] It became necessary, therefore, to draft the conditions so as to include all points which the bidders would need to know to be able to make a firm offer. Thus, most of the terms which normally would be included in a license granted to a telephone operator (as is the case with the license of British Telecom), were now included in the conditions provided to bidders. Initially, also, it had been expected that the text of the transfer agreements were to be firmed up by ENTel prior to the date for presentation of offers so that no subsequent discussions on this point would take place, but this did not prove possible.

The State Reform Law had also provided for the total privatization of ENTel, instead of the partial approach tried by the previous government. This ruled out a retention of partial ownership by the state, either as a simple shareholder or enjoying special rights through a mechanism of a golden share.[11] The law did not specify whether the new operator(s) would enjoy a quasi-monopoly status, such as did ENTel's.

Conflict among public objectives soon became evident. The interest of bidders in the privatization and consequently the price of the offering clearly favored extending the monopoly. Also, a high sales price and high investment requirements would have meant high rates for users. Furthermore, the higher the protection enjoyed by local equipment suppliers, the lesser would be the chances of attracting efficient operators or ensuring low costs and tariffs.

One aspect of the decision was easy: the privatization was to be final; that is, there would be no reversion of the telephone operation to the state. This called for a sale and not a mere concession to operate the assets of ENTel. It also called for a license to be granted to the new operator, instead of the public service concession, an instrument taken from French administrative law and heretofore prevalently used in Argentina for privately operated public utilities; the main difference between these two concepts is that in a concession of public service the state is supposed to delegate or transfer the operation of the public service to a private party and may thus reassume such operation at the end of the term of the concession (and even during its course when so dictated by public interest),[12] whereas when a license expires, the natural consequences are either its renewal to the existing operator or the granting of a new license to a different operator.

Given these conditions the following characteristics of the privatization emerged:

- The country was divided into two regions (north and south) of almost equal importance,[13] with the Greater Buenos Aires area split between the two.

- The personnel and the assets of ENTel (but only a few of its liabilities) were transferred to two new corporations set up by the interventor of ENTel. These were to become the licensees for each region (provisionally called Telco Norte and Telco Sur and now called Telecom Argentina and Telefónica de Argentina, respectively).

- The personnel and the assets pertaining to the international service were transferred to a third corporation; those pertaining to all services provided by ENTel in competition with private firms, to a fourth. The shares of both these corporations were allocated, equally, to the two newly formed licensees.

- The initial objective of the privatization was the sale by ENTel of 60 percent of the shares of Telco Norte and Telco Sur to one investor group each. The remaining 40 percent was to be sold at a later stage to the personnel of the Telcos, the local telephone cooperatives, and to the general public in proportions of 10 percent, 5 percent, and 25 percent, respectively.

- The Telcos were to enjoy monopoly rights during an initial seven-year period (the first two years of which were considered a transition period in which the Telcos were be reorganized by the new owners) and, provided certain exceptionally demanding investment and tariff objectives were met, for a subsequent three years. After this period, competition was to be allowed.

Although it caused complex problems of area definition and assets and personnel allocation, the division of the country into two regions was considered advantageous for two main reasons: first, it would allow the government to analyze the performance of both licensees and obtain valuable comparative information; second, it would set the basis for effective competition when the monopoly status ended and each Telco (as well as any newcomer) was free thereafter to enter the other Telco's region.

The Main Problems

The privatization team was faced with problems common to all sectors and with additional ones specific to ENTel. The former had to do with the economic, political, and legal environment of Argentina. The new government had taken office in July 1989 in the midst of a bout of hyperinflation: the retail price index had risen by 114 percent in June 1989, 197 percent in July, and then subsided to 38 percent in August. (A second bout occurred in early 1990: in January the retail price index rose by 79 percent, in February by 62 percent, and in March by 96 percent.) This caused a rapid reduction in real income of wage earners, played havoc with tariff levels, and forced bidders to make offers in a context of high uncertainty. Complicating this were the arrears since April 1988 on Argentina's interest payments on its foreign bank debt, including that of ENTel. This debt had been renegotiated in 1985 and 1987, resulting in a General Refinancing Agreement, the terms of which required the consent of a certain proportion of the creditor banks for some major decisions of the debtor entities.

The political environment was more favorable, with all but a minority of the political spectrum in favor of the privatization. However, Congress had reserved for itself a monitoring role in the State Reform Law,[14] and at least on one occasion it became necessary to obtain informal congressional approval for some key financial decisions.

Finally, there had been in the legal history of Argentina several annulments of government contracts with foreign investors decided unilaterally by the executive. Although compensation was finally paid to the foreign investors in all cases, memories of those actions were still fresh in the minds of the legal profession.[15] Furthermore, the fiscal problems of the Argentine government had forced Congress to include in the State Reform Law a two-year moratorium on the enforcement of money judgments against the state, thereby giving rise to doubts about the effectiveness of future contractual commitments of the government.[16]

Problems specific to ENTel were also important. First of all, there was a lack of reliable accounting information. ENTel did not have international auditors, and its financial statements, audited by a government agency, were two to three years old and were, in addition, qualified.[17] This created great difficulties for the listing and valuation of ENTel's assets. The situation of work contracts in force, which were to be assumed by the privatized Telcos, was not precisely known. Union troubles, including a major strike, arose during the privatization process. In addition to defaulting on the interest payments of its external debt, ENTel was in arrears in payments to its local creditors, one of whom tried, without success, to attach the proceeds of the sale.[18] Poor maintenance and lack of investments, the results of low tariffs and political mismanagement over many years, had produced a low standard of service and a huge backlog of unfilled installation requests. The new licensees would, therefore, have to make substantial investments to bring the service up to more acceptable levels.

Another area of concern was that of local equipment supply. Argentina had two main manufacturers of telephone equipment and a local manufacturer of cables and other materials. Although the privatization was conducted within a general economic policy of opening up of the economy after almost fifty years of protectionism, there was concern that new operators could maintain, or set up, their own links with suppliers, which might increase costs and limit technological choice.

Lastly, after many years of state-operated telephones, there was no experience in the regulation of this activity. Practice had shown that, although regulatory powers were retained by the central government during those years, the government seldom had exercised a zealous control over state-run public utilities except to set their tariffs, with political considerations often gaining the upper hand. Existing laws and regulations applicable to the telecommunications services[19] were drafted with the concept that a state enterprise would be the main operator of the telephone system. Thus, a new regulatory framework for a privately run system had to be drafted and a new agency created to enforce the new regulations.

Some of the Solutions

The conditions and the transfer agreements were therefore drafted in order to provide at least partial answers to some of these problems, namely:

- The lack of reliable information was tackled by establishing a two-step procedure whereby at the outset only the more basic information was provided to the purchasers of the conditions. Interested parties which met the required standards of net worth (US$1.5 billion for the operator and US$4 billion jointly for each bidding group) and experience in operating were to be prequalified prior to any submission of bids. The parties thus selected were then to have access to more detailed information provided through a data room and direct consultations with ENTel in order to prepare their bids, which they were then free to present or not without penalty.

- This two-step procedure had the added advantage that it allowed for a distinction between the selection of qualified bidders and the selection of the winners, with the latter based solely on a comparison of the amounts bid for purchase of the shares of the Telcos. This was deemed important since it eliminated a complicated and long, drawn out award procedure as well as subjective decisions, which are always open to suspicion. Accordingly, and also to avoid setting a value to the Argentine debt to be tendered (a request posed by the banks), the price was set with a cash portion which had to be met by all bidders and which was the same for all bidders. The debt portion was therefore the deciding factor with only a minimum having been set. In this respect, all foreign debt was to be computed at face value regardless of the technical differences between different types of government foreign debt.

- The gradual approach was also confirmed in the setting of a relatively low bid bond (1 percent of the cash portion of the price, or about US$1 million for each bidder). This allowed hesitant selected parties to submit bids with the knowledge that, if in the meantime dramatic changes in the Argentine economy occurred, they would be able to withdraw at a nominally fixed cost.

- To avoid the uncertainties concerning hidden or contingent liabilities, only the assets of ENTel (with a few specific liabilities) were transferred to the Telcos. According to one opinion this infringed upon the Argentine law on transfer of businesses, which required publication of the sale and allowed creditors of the seller to oppose any such transfer unless paid or guaranteed.[20] Given the size of foreign and local debt of government enterprises, this point of view would have prevented most privatizations, including that of ENTel. A federal court of appeals, however, confirmed that the reorganization of ENTel was authorized by the State Reform Law and, furthermore, since it concerned the reorganization of a state entity, it was subject to administrative law and not to the rules applicable to private business entities.[21]

- With respect to tariffs, the conditions stated that the Telcos would be delivered to the winners with a tariff level that allowed a reasonable return on assets to an efficient operator and would thereafter be adjusted by the cost-of-living index. Were the new operators to deem such return insufficient, they were entitled to seek, during the transition period (that is, the first two years), biannual readjustments in order to reach a 16 percent return on a value of assets to be set prior to the date of submission of the bids. Following the transition period, the rates had to decrease 2 percent in real terms each year during the remaining five years of the monopoly. This annual reduction had to reach 4 percent during the optional three-year extension of the monopoly. This was similar to the price-cap system used in the privatization of British Telecom.[22]

- To cope with the requirements of foreign creditors, the transfer agreements provided in their initial drafts that obtaining the waiver required by the General Refinancing Agreement was a condition of closing. As the signature of the transfer agreements was delayed until after this waiver was granted, the point became moot. The fact that debt conversion was allowed went a long way to ensure favorable reception of this request by the international banking community.

- The uncertainty over the existence and working conditions of the assets of ENTel led to the adoption of the following provisions:

  1. The sale of the shares was not accompanied by a warranty on the working conditions of the assets; that is, the assets were to be taken on an "as is" basis.

  2. The failure to transfer certain major assets such as facilities, the lack of which caused an interruption of service for more than thirty consecutive days and affected at least 1 percent of the lines in the region above the prevailing average rate of interruption, was to be compensated by a cash payment, return of Telco notes (see following section on financial returns), and delivery of government debt of similar terms to that surrendered in payment, in the same proportion as that existing between the aggregates of each component of the price (that is, 3.75 percent in cash, 6.65 percent in Telco notes, and the balance in government debt).

  3. With respect to other assets, the obligation of ENTel was limited to the nonretention of any asset included in the inventories.

  4. Damages and other harmful events occurring between the act of signing of the transfer agreements and the closing were to be covered by insurance.

- A covenant on the part of ENTel not to exceed certain ceilings on new work and service contracts, both in time and amount, was included in the conditions. In the transfer agreements, the assignment of contracts in the course of performance at closing was made dependent on the consent of the contractors not to hold the Telcos liable for the debt accrued prior to closing and to accept the ceilings reported by ENTel, both as to the subsequent time of performance and as to the amount still to be invoiced.

- The value of the assets of ENTel, on which the 16 percent rate of return would be based, was to be set at a level which would allow an annual profit sufficient to generate the investments needed to meet the high improvement of quality and penetration standards set by the conditions. This annual profit was set at US$557 million in the aggregate for both Telcos during the second year of the transition period.

- The conditions included a rule whereby all purchases in excess of US$500,000 in any given year had to be made on a competitive bidding basis. This rule was subsequently watered down in the transfer agreement negotiated by the minister.

- The conditions forbade the Telcos to provide telephone equipment (for example, telephone sets, PABXs to subscribers.

Finally, prior to the submission of bids, a new regulatory agency framework was established by executive decree.[23]

The Financial Terms

According to the conditions of sale, the financial terms for both Telcos were as follows:

- Total cash price: US$214 million.

- The minimum amount of sovereign debt to be retired was US$3,500 million of principal face value. All interest accrued on this amount and unpaid as of June 26, 1990, was to be forgiven as well.

- In order to provide some leverage, the Telcos were to jointly recognize a debt to ENTel of US$380 million, to be evidenced in promissory notes and reimbursed over six years, with three years' grace, at an annual rate of interest equal to the LIBOR plus 0.8125 percent.

- On closing, and against delivery of 60 percent of Telcos' shares, the buyers were required to pay the cash part of the price and deliver the sovereign debt instruments. The latter was rendered more flexible in the transfer agreements as the buyers irrevocably undertook to provide the sovereign debt instruments within ninety days of closing.

- Also on closing, the Telcos, under their new boards of directors, were to execute the notes and deliver them to ENTel.

Other Features

Other features of the conditions were that:

- Each winning bidder group was to establish a local company to act on its behalf as the buyer and holder of the shares in the respective Telco. Thirty percent of the shares in this local investment company had to belong to a core of up to three shareholders, including one or two operators whose own participation had to be at least 4.9 percent.

- The operator of the winning group was to enter into a management agreement with the respective Telco.

- The name of each Telco was to include the identifying part of the name of the respective operator.

- After closing, any sale of more than 49 percent of the shares of the investment company would require the approval of the regulatory agency. Members of the core group could not reduce their holdings without such approval.

- No minimum local participation was required.

The Timetable

The decision to privatize ENTel was made in September 1989. Table 5–1 compares the initial, rather ambitious timetable and the actual dates at which the main stages were carried out.

Although there was some telescoping of the intermediate dates, the process was completed only one month later than scheduled. This delay was caused by the withdrawal of one of the winning bidders and the consequent need to negotiate the respective transfer agreement with another bidder group.

The largest deviation from the planned timetable occurred in the dates planned for the signing of the transfer agreements. This occurred because it had been planned to provide the selected parties with the text of the transfer agreements prior to the date of submission of bids and to sign it two months prior to closing; however, the first deadline could not be met because the prospective bidders would not agree on the sections regulating the eventual transfer of CAT's assets, an issue that had been the subject of a separate agreement between the government and CAT negotiated by the minister. This inability forced the privatization team into long negotiations

Table 5–1. Planned and Actual Implementation Dates

Stages	Plan	Actual
Executive approval of terms and conditions of sale of ENTel	December 31, 1989	January 5, 1990
Submission of requests for prequalification	March 21, 1990	April 27, 1990
Announcement of selected parties	March 28, 1990	May 2, 1990
Submission of bids	June 11, 1990	June 25, 1990
Executive approval of awards	June 28, 1990	June 28, 1990
Signature of transfer agreements	August 6, 1990	November 8, 1990
Closing	October 8, 1990	November 8, 1990

with the winners over the terms of the transfer agreement. These were only finalized on the day of closing. Thus, the signing of the transfer agreement and closing took place on the same day.

The Controversy over Rates

The amount initially contemplated as the value of the assets on which the 16 percent rate of return was to be based during the transition period, was an estimated market value of US$3,900 million, an amount which was below ENTel's book value and which yielded the required revenue to fund annual investments in excess of US$500 million. At a congressional inquiry held in March 1990, the minister of public works agreed to reduce this to US$1,900 million.[24] Since this amount was insufficient to generate the cash necessary for the required investments, the bidders lost interest in the rate-of-return formula and sought another alternative, namely, the actual tariffs which were to be in effect at closing. These had already been set by a resolution of ENTel's interventor on March 5, 1990, and were subject to adjustment thereafter by the increase in the cost of living; however, the cost-of-living increase for the month of March 1990 was 96 percent. A debate ensued in the last stages of the privatization on whether the cost-of-living adjustment of the rate set on March 5, 1990, had to include the 96 percent increase for that month. Finally, the minister negotiated a different approach: the buyers were to forgo the increase that they had claimed and in its place accept a new formula for adjustments which had a dollar component to temper the effect of devaluation, which greatly exceeded the increase in the cost of living at a given time. The transfer agreement included this new formula and deleted the 16 percent rate-of-return rule. This change seriously weakened the powers of the regulatory agency to control the financial performance of the licensees, since the rules granting such power were predicated on a rate-of-return system and not on a cap on an inflation-adjusted tariff.

The Participants and Winners

All seven groups which requested to participate were prequalified. They were:

- Telefónica de España, with Citibank and a local group led by Techint

- The Italian state-owned STET, with Morgan Stanley and a local group led by Perez Companc

- France Cable et Radio, a wholly owned subsidiary of the French state telephone company, France Télécom

- Bell Atlantic, with Manufacturers Hanover and a local group

- Cable & Wireless PLC

- GTE

- NYNEX.

Only four of these, however, presented offers. They were placed in the following order by bid amount:[25]

Telco Sur:	(i)	Telefónica de España
	(ii)	STET/France Cable et Radio
Telco Norte:	(i)	Telefónica de España
	(ii)	Bell Atlantic
	(iii)	STET/France Cable et Radio

The conditions were designed to avoid awarding both Telcos to the same bidder, provided the runner-up was prepared to match the highest bid. Consequently, Bell Atlantic was invited to match Telefónica's bid for Telco Norte, which it agreed to do, and was awarded this Telco, with Telefónica being awarded Telco Sur.

After three months of hard negotiations, however, the Bell Atlantic group was unable to sign the transfer agreement when called to do so on October 4, 1991. Telefónica, on the other hand, was by then prepared to sign for Telco Sur. Bell Atlantic's bid was rejected and Telco Norte was awarded to the STET/France Cable et Radio group, which also matched Telefónica's offer. This group had one month to sign the transfer agreement and pay the cash portion of the price. It was able to do so on November 8, 1990, at the same time as Telefónica, when 60 percent of the shares in the two Telcos were delivered to the buyers, who assumed management control on the same date. Delivery of the sovereign debt portion of the price took place on February 6, 1991, ninety days after closing.

Aftermath

In the last quarter of 1991, a group of four Argentine and eight international banks undertook to make a global offering of the 30 percent of the Telcos shares still owned by the government. This 30 percent included the 5 percent to be sold to the cooperatives as initially contemplated.

The sale was made by a private offer in the United States under Rule 144A of the SEC and by a public offer in Argentina. The 30 percent was divided into (a) a wholesale competitive tranche (15 percent) which set the price through a "Dutch auction" mechanism; (b) a wholesale noncompetitive tranche (7.5 percent) to be allocated on a pro rata basis at the price set by the competitive tranche; and (c) a retail tranche (7.5 percent) to be sold to Argentine residents at the same prices less 5 percent, also on a pro rata basis.

Although it was initially contemplated that both stockholdings were to be sold simultaneously, in the end Telefónica's 30 percent was sold in December 1991 and Telecom's 30 percent in March 1992. In both sales all shares were sold. Total proceeds were US$838 million for Telefónica de Argentina's (Telco Sur) and US$1,266 million for Telecom Argentina's (Telco Norte) shares.

Two noticeable developments during 1991 and 1992 were:

- The reorganization of the Comisión Nacional de Telecomunicaciones (CNT), the semiautonomous telecommunications regulatory agency, through the appointment of an interventor and three subinterventors to replace the board.

- The "dollarization" of the telephone tariffs as a result of an agreement reached by the government with the licensees at the time of the placement of Telefónica's 30 percent stockholding and which had been made necessary by the passing of the Convertibility Law in March of 1991,[27] making all inflation adjustment clauses referring to local currency thereafter invalid: tariffs are now fixed in dollars and adjusted in line with the U.S. consumer price index.[28]

Conclusion

Given the obstacles faced and the time constraint, the privatization of ENTel can be considered a success. ENTel received US$214 million in cash and US$380 million in promissory notes issued by the Telcos. A total of US$5,028 million of face value of Argentine foreign debt principal and interest was canceled.[26] Additional proceeds were to be generated by the later sale of the remaining 40 percent of the shares still held by ENTel.

Although it is too soon to expect a material improvement of service, the Telcos have begun to correct some of the practices which accounted for ENTel's lackluster performance. Full management teams comprising both local and foreign professionals have been put in place. Contracts with domestic suppliers have been renegotiated, reportedly reducing the purchase price of major equipment by about one-third. Illegal practices are being eradicated; for example, phony salary recipients have been weeded out, and the large clandestine telephone network which charged its customers reduced rates and then had the differences billed to other unsuspecting users has been uncovered and dismantled.

It is to be hoped that future improvements of the service and an adequate level of tariffs will lead the Argentine public to share this conclusion and that the path thus opened may be followed by other major public utilities still operated by the government in Argentina.

Endnotes

1. The government of President Raul Alfonsin of the Radical party, which had been elected in 1983 and which served up to July 1989, when the newly elected president, Carlos S. Menem, of the Peronist party, took office.

2. Telephone service was subject to the Telegraph Law 750 1/2 of 1875. The main regulation specifically concerning the telephone service was Executive Decree 91.698 of 1936. See, in general, Manuel M. Diez, *Servicio Publico de los Teléfonos*, Buenos Aires, 1942.

3. Law 13,653 as amended and restated. Its implementing regulation is Executive Decree 5883 of 1955. ENTel's current charter was granted by Executive Decree 2748 of 1978.

4. A "decree" or "executive decree" is a decision issued by the executive, either of an individual or general nature. They shall be referred to hereafter simply as "decree."

5. Decree 731 of September 12, 1989, was amended by decree 59 of January 5, 1990. The terms and conditions of the competitive bidding, which also included the terms of the licenses to be granted to the new operators were approved by decree 62, also of January 5, 1990, and subsequently amended by Decrees 575, 636 and 677 and 1130 of March 28, April 4, April 11, and June 14, 1990, respectively. The awards were approved by Decrees 1229 and 1230 of June 28, 1990, and, due to the withdrawal of one of the winners, the new award was approved by Decree 2096 of October 4, 1990. The transfer agreements were approved by Decree 2332 of November 8, 1990. The licenses to the Telcos were granted by Decrees 2344, 2345, 2346 and 2347 also of November 8, 1990, respectively. The incorporation of the new telephone companies was approved by Decrees 60 and 61 of January 5, 1990. Other executive decrees which regulated certain aspects of the competitive process were Decrees 420, 1948, 1967, and 1968 of February 28, September 21, 1990, and, the last two, September 26, 1990. In addition, several decisions of the Ministry of Public Works and Services and of the intervention of ENTel were issued along the privatization process to govern other aspects thereof.

6. Throughout the privatization of ENTel the minister was Dr. José Roberto Dromi.

7. *Interventor* is an officer appointed by the executive to act as the interim head of an agency, often after the removal of the executive of the collegiate body which is the head of such an agency.

8. The interventor, Engineer María Julia Alsogaray, was appointed by Executive Decree 191 of July 12, 1989.

9. The secretary of communications was Engineer Raul Otero and his undersecretary was Engineer Raul Parodi. During the privatization the administration was reorganized and all secretaries were eliminated. Eng. Otero then became undersecretary, and Eng. Parodi continued as a high officer of the undersecretary of communications.

10. See J. Cibinic and R. C. Nash, *Formation of Government Contracts*, pp. 522-704 (2nd ed., 1986).

11. See, for example, Graham and Prosser, "Golden Shares, Industrial Policy by Stealth?" *Public Law* 413-431 (Autumn 1988), and "Privatizing Nationalized Industries: Constitutional Issues and New Legal Techniques," 50 MOD L. REV. 16-51 (1987).

12. See A. de Laubadere, 2 *Traité des contrats administratifs*, pp. 678, 704-740 (2nd ed., F. Moderne and P. Delvolve, 1984). For Argentina, see 3-B M. Marienhoff, *Tratado de Derecho Administrativo*, pp. 582-85, 631 (1983).

13. The proportion set between the two regions for purposes of the cash part of the price and the minimum debt amount to be surrendered was 53.3 percent for the south and 46.7 percent for the north.

14. Section 14 of Law 23,696 established a bicameral commission to liaise with the executive and keep Congress informed on the implementation of the privatization process.

15. See Mairal, *Foreign Investments and Municipal Laws: The Argentine Experience*, 4 CONN.J.INT.LAW 635 (1989).

16. Sections 50 to 56 of Law 23,696 governed this issue.

17. One of the Offering Memoranda of the investment companies formed by the bidders included this paragraph: "No historical financial information is available for the years 1988 and 1989 or for any period during 1990. The historical financial statements that are available and included in this Memorandum for the years 1983 to 1987 have not been audited by an independent recognized accounting firm. In addition, the governmental accounting body that audited such statements would not provide an opinion with respect to the financial statements for 1983 through 1985, and qualified its opinion for 1986 and 1987 due to the lack of independent verification of the existence, ownership and value of ENTel's fixed assets. Moreover, other accounting practices and lack of audit controls make the existing historical financial information inadequate or unreliable. Consequently, investors should not rely on historical financial information in making their decision to participate in the Exchange."

18. Guia de la Industria v. ENTel, decision of the 2d Chamber of the Federal Administrative Court of Appeals, dated November 6, 1990.

19. Law 19,798 of 1972 was the Telecommunications Law in force during the privatization of ENTel. Pursuant to the authority granted by sec. 10 of the State Reform Law, the executive excluded the application of some of the rules of law 19,798 (see Decree 731 of September 12, 1989, sec. 5).

20. See Boggiano, "La Protección de los Acreedores en el Proceso de Privatización de las Empresas del Estado." E.D., August 28, 1990.

21. Decision cited at 19, *supra.*

22. See Prosser, "Regulation of Privatized Enterprises: Institutions and Procedures," in *Capitalism, Culture and Economic Regulation,* ed. L. Hancher and M. Moran (Oxford: Clarendon Press, 1989), 136.

23. Decree 1185 of June 22, 1990, which created the Comisión Nacional de Telecomunicaciones.

24. See sec. 5 of Decree 575 of March 28, 1990.

25. According to the conditions of sale, operators who had been qualified as selected parties could submit a joint bid.

26. Plus interest accrued from June 26, 1990, until the date of actual delivery of the debt instruments.

27. Law 23,928.

28. Decree 2585/91.

6

Privatization of Telecommunications: The Case of Mexico

Carlos Casasús

AS IN MANY OTHER DEVELOPING COUNTRIES, Mexico's telecommunications state monopoly was characterized by serious shortcomings in service delivery, reliability, and quality. By all usual measures of performance, basic services were far below the standards expected in a newly industrialized country, and value added services were virtually nonexistent. Day-to-day management of the operating company was often guided by political objectives instead of broad public goals and sound business practice. The company was regarded by the government largely as a source of revenue. Tariffs, rather than reflecting costs, were used as indirect tools of macroeconomic policy. Expansion was constrained by government limitations on public spending. At the time of the devastating 1985 earthquake in Mexico City, telecommunications in Mexico had reached a state of near crisis. Recognition of these problems, and growing awareness of the experience of developed countries with liberalization and privatization, led the government to announce in 1989 a comprehensive modernization plan for the telecommunications sector. In this chapter we shall examine how successive earlier Mexican governments from 1925 had handled the sector, the measures introduced from 1989 to achieve structural change, and an assessment of the process of change as viewed shortly after privatization of the state operating company.

Past Governments and Telecommunications Policies

Telecommunications policy in Mexico has been closely linked to the general strategy of the governments that have run Mexico since the Revolution of 1910. Four periods of government, and the effects they had on telecommunications policy, can be distinguished.

Post-Revolution (1925–1948)

After the period of armed struggle, in which telecommunications played a key role in ensuring military control of the country, a regulatory framework was established by President Cárdenas that gave extraordinary powers to the government for intervening in the telecommunications sector. This framework is embodied in the Law of General Means of Communications, which dates from 1938. The highly interventionist framework, and the fact that the country had two competitive telephone service concessions that were not interconnected, impeded accelerated development of the sector. In 1950 the country had only 141,000 telephone lines for a population of 26 million people (0.5 lines per 100 people).

Desarrollo Estabilizador (1948–1970)

For a period that runs from the 1950s through the 1970s, Mexico had a succession of governments that made inflation control a central policy goal. This period is known as "desarrollo estabilizador," or development with stability. Government participation in economic activities was limited. Public finances were kept under control and, as a result, inflation was kept at single-digit levels. Rapid economic growth followed, averaging more than 6 percent per year for the twenty-two-year period.

During this period, telecommunications developed within the private sector, but with the active support of government. In 1950 the government induced the two competing telephone companies to merge, approved adequate tariffs, and provided soft financing for accelerated network development. Following the merger of the two networks, growth accelerated. From 1955 until 1976, Teléfonos de México (TELMEX), the merged company, grew at an average rate of 10 percent per year, well above the growth rates achieved by most other developing countries in that period.

Populism (1970–1982)

The period of "desarrollo estabilizador" started showing signs of stress in 1968. Extreme presidential power and lack of democratic alternatives for participation led to serious political disturbances, including widespread student unrest immediately prior to the Olympic Games that took place in Mexico in 1968. When President Luis Echeverría was elected in 1970, he responded to political pressure with a macroeconomic strategy based on populism. The government started spending heavily on programs that subsidized special interest groups and that promoted greater public sector participation in the economy. As a result, public finances, which had been kept under strict control in the "desarrollo estabilizador" period, showed growing deficits. Money supply, in turn, grew at an accelerated rate. Inflation set in, and by 1976 the country had a serious balance of payments problem, which led to the first currency devaluation in twenty-two years. The next government (of President López Portillo) maintained the populist policies of his predecessor, but this time with the support of oil discoveries that helped public finances momentarily in the late 1970s. Nevertheless, public spending increased. Inflation accelerated even further, and when oil prices tumbled in 1982, the country found itself in the midst of a foreign debt crisis that was to burden its development for years to come.

In the telecommunications sector, populism translated into the nationalization of the telephone company. In August 1976 TELMEX entered into an agreement with the Mexican government through which the government became majority owner of the company. Nationalization created a series of new obstacles for continuing sector development. The government became, at the same time, owner, competitor, and regulator. Regulation of the telephone company reflected the government's pursuit of short-term political goals rather than of sector performance. Short-sighted tariff policies resulted in serious deterioration of revenues and profitability as well as the worsening of cross-subsidies from long-distance to local service. The government was politically unable to stand up to strong labor pressures, which led to deteriorating labor relations and an increasingly unproductive work force. Growth slowed down because inadequate internal funding was coupled to growing difficulty in obtaining external financing.

The telecommunications system became increasingly unable to meet demand. Insufficient plant capacity caused growing congestion in the network, and quality of service deteriorated. Scarcity and low prices induced corruption in the relationship between customers and telephone company employees.

Recovery (1982–Present)

Mexico's recovery started during President De la Madrid's government from 1982 to 1988. Macroeconomic policy focused on reestablishing public finance control. President De la Madrid was able to reduce the fiscal deficit from the high level of 18 percent of GDP which prevailed in the last years of his predecessor to nearly zero in 1988. This government opened the Mexican economy to foreign trade, eliminated quantitative trade barriers, and joined the General Agreement on Tariffs and Trade (GATT). President De la Madrid also opened the door to more democratic electoral processes and allowed for the irreversible development of opposition democratic forces within the political system, making opposition parties, for the first time, credible alternatives to the ruling party.

This period was very difficult for the telecommunications sector. The government, strapped for fiscal resources, increased taxes on telephone services. Simultaneously, it reduced the levels of its yearly investments in telecommunications, further stretching the company's capacity for financing growth. The lowest point in the company's recent history was probably reached when the 1985 earthquake of Mexico City destroyed the nucleus of the long-distance network and left the country's capital without communications with the outside world for two weeks. In 1985 Mexico, despite being one of the fifteen largest economies in the world, ranked eighty-third in telephone density. Average waiting time for a telephone line was in excess of three years. The country had no cellular telephones or data transmission services, and the tariff structure was severely distorted with relation to costs. In order to modernize the network, massive investments on the order of US$2 billion per year needed to be undertaken.

President De la Madrid's economic team, headed by Mr. Carlos Salinas (the current president) and Mr. Pedro Aspe (the current finance minister), realized that the telecommunications situation was no longer tenable and started a series of measures that culminated with the privatization of the company.

Systemic Change in the Telecommunications Sector

These measures have to be thought of as a systemic change. The measures taken would have been insufficient if they had been implemented individually, but because they were taken jointly, they reinforced each other, creating very favorable conditions for the development of a modern telecommunications sector.

Tariff and Fiscal Reform

First and foremost was tariff and fiscal reform. Tariffs, which had deteriorated significantly with inflation, had to be adjusted to reflect the cost of providing each service. Accordingly, substantial increases in local service and national long-distance tariffs went into effect, and international long-distance prices, which were well above international norms, were reduced. The tax on telephone services, averaging about 35 percent and among the highest in the world, was substituted for a tax on profits that does not penalize the company if investment programs of the magnitude required are undertaken. As a result of the tariff and tax reforms, revenues per line, which had deteriorated to approximately half their peak value, rose again to approximately US$860 per line in 1991.

Regulatory Framework

The Law of General Means of Communication of 1938 is still the basic legal instrument. It gives extraordinary faculties to the state for intervention in company affairs, reflecting the determinant impact that telecommunications had during the postrevolutionary period in national security. The company's license was extremely simple and reflected the ease with which the government could influence the company, given its dual role of regulator and owner.

In order to modernize the sector, the government began a reform of the regulatory framework along three main directions. First, there has been an effort to reform the Ministry of Communications, which besides policy and regulation functions also operated certain networks and services in competition with the main regulated telephone company. The government sold to TELMEX the federal microwave network that the ministry operated directly. The government also privatized, or restructured under a separate state enterprise, other services that it earlier provided directly. As a result, the ministry now is exclusively a policymaker and regulator, and not a service provider.

The second main avenue for regulatory reform involved revision of the concession under which TELMEX operates. The new concession establishes telephone tariffs subject to a price cap which keeps an index of prices of a basket of different telephone services constant in real terms until 1996. Nevertheless, the price formula allows for local service to increase and international long-distance to decrease in such a way that by the end of the period, local service will cover its costs and rates of return will be roughly similar for all services. The new concession also forces a gradual opening to competition of all telecommunication services. It prohibits competition, however, in local and long-distance services and networks during the six-year period in which prices will be rebalanced.

The concession requires the company to grow at least at a rate of 12 percent per year in installed telephone lines and requires that the company provide service to all towns of more than 500 inhabitants by 1996. The concession establishes quality-of-service goals and penalties in case these goals are not met. TELMEX has also been granted a national cellular concession. This concession, however, has been granted on a duopoly basis making TELMEX one of two competing suppliers in each region. Lastly, the government published a new implementing regulation for the Law of General Means of Communications, specifying the conditions for competition and limiting the intervention faculties of the government.

Company Reorganization

The company's structure was modified to allow greater decentralization. The organization along functional lines was replaced by a corporate structure based on profit centers responsible for financial results by specific geographic area or by service. This change accelerated decisionmaking, clarified responsibility, helped allocate capital more efficiently, and focused service strategies on the needs of TELMEX's different customer groups.

Labor Renegotiation

In April 1989, TELMEX negotiated a major settlement with its union. The amended contract greatly simplified the old bargaining process by reducing the number of different job categories and provided management with flexibility to introduce new technology and allocate the labor force as required. This agreement allowed TELMEX to achieve significant economies by permitting the implementation of its capital expenditure program with only modest growth in total employment.

Privatization

In September 1989, the government announced its intention to privatize TELMEX, selling a majority position in the company's equity, thereby facilitating the evolution toward more efficient and competitive telecommunications. President Salinas announced the following objectives of privatization:

• To maintain government sovereignty over the sector

• To guarantee the rights of the existing workers and give them opportunity to participate in the company's ownership

- To raise service quality to international levels

- To retain Mexican majority control of the company

- To assure sustained network growth

- To strengthen research and development.

To ensure rapid progress towards privatization, in October 1989, Mr. Pedro Aspe, by then secretary of finance and public credit, was appointed chairman of the board of directors of TELMEX, and Mr. Alfredo Baranda, previously governor of the State of Mexico and ambassador to Spain, was appointed president. The new management team was fully committed to privatization and had the clout to make it come about.

In order to comply with the restriction of keeping the control of TELMEX in Mexican hands and simultaneously allowing a wide participation of foreign investment in its equity, the capital structure of the company was changed. At that time, TELMEX had two classes of shares: series AA, in which ownership was restricted to the Mexican government and represented approximately 56 percent of the shares, and series A shares, which were publicly traded and had no ownership restriction. On June 15, 1990, a stockholders meeting adopted a new capital structure. AA shares can now be owned not only by the Mexican government but by any person or corporation of Mexican nationality. A new class of limited voting shares, denominated L shares, were distributed as a dividend to AA and A shareholders at a rate of 1.5 L shares for each existing share. L shares have no ownership restrictions and have identical economic rights as common shares.

As a result of this reform, the new capital structure is as follows:

- 20.4 percent AA shares that have full voting rights and can only be owned by Mexican nationals

- 19.6 percent A shares that have full voting rights and no ownership restrictions

- 60.0 percent L shares with limited voting rights and no ownership restrictions

As a consequence of these measures, the government ended up with 20.4 percent of the company's capital in AA shares, approximately 5 percent in A shares, and 31 percent in L shares.

These holdings would be sold to the private sector in three steps. First, the government announced the sale of 4.4 percent of its A shares to the company's employees. Employees paid for these shares using an eight-year credit provided by NAFINSA, the government's development bank, on very favorable conditions. Second, the 20.4 percent AA shares were auctioned to Mexican-led consortia, in which foreign operating companies were allowed to participate as minority partners. After an initial evaluation period in which twenty-three companies made visits to TELMEX, three groups headed by Mexican investors submitted bids by November 15, 1990. In strict accordance with the schedule of privatization, the winning group was announced on December 19, 1990. The new controlling consortium was led by Grupo Carso, a diversified Mexican group, in association with Southwestern Bell and France Télécom. Lastly, 31 percent of L shares were sold in several public and private offerings in the world capital markets. The government filed a registration statement for the L shares before the U.S. Securities and Exchange Commission, and the L shares were approved for trading in the New York Stock Exchange.

Results So Far

The fiscal and tariff reforms had a dramatic impact on TELMEX's financial results. Revenues increased 44 percent, from US$2.66 billion in 1989 to US$3.84 billion in 1990. Profits increased 82 percent from 1989, to US$1.1 billion in 1990. TELMEX expects to generate internally nearly 80 percent of the funds needed for its US$13.9 billion five-year investment program. In addition, the company has once again been able to participate in the world capital market and has been placing new debt issues with extraordinary success.

The network is growing again at rates that exceed 10 percent. As a result of taking advantage of the latest equipment, it will leapfrog technological stages and, in five years' time, will be one of the world's most modern.

The winning consortium appointed a new president of the company on December 19, 1990, and a new board of directors on January 9, 1991. The management change took place with a minimum of outside appointments, and TELMEX is well on the way to making the transition to a private telecommunications company.

These results were reflected in spectacular appreciation of share value. The share price rose from US31¢ in January 1989 to nearly US$3 dollars in April 1990, an increase of 460 percent. In the same period, the Mexican Stock Exchange grew 123 percent in dollar terms, and the Dow Jones only 16 percent. As a consequence of the rapid appreciation of the shares, the government will receive approximately US$5 billion from the TELMEX privatization.

Privatization of Telecommunications in a Global Context

Not surprisingly, privatization of telecommunications is now in vogue. In 1991, for example, more than eighteen countries were contemplating the privatization of their telephone companies. Governments that adopt a privatization policy generally expect to accomplish specific objectives, such as to improve service delivery, develop new services, improve public finances, and stimulate local capital markets. However, unless a systemic approach is adopted, the results can be less than satisfactory and may in fact hinder development efforts.

To achieve the desired results, governments would benefit from adopting simultaneous measures that create snowball effects in the sector's modernization. Namely, measures to:

- Create or reform the regulatory framework, addressing issues such as how to adjust tariffs, which standards to adopt, rules for how competition will be allowed, and the structure and role of regulatory bodies

- Reorganize the telecommunications company to improve its performance, therefore obtaining a better price when it is privatized

- Establish guidelines for privatizing the enterprise, specifying the capital structure, the bidding process, the valuation criteria, and managing of the bids and public equity offerings

Well-planned telecommunications sector reform will certainly entice potential investors. Cross-border investments in telecommunications have boomed in the last few years. At least forty major acquisitions have occurred between 1984 and 1990. In 1991 there were perhaps US$20 billion of public offerings by governments privatizing telephone companies. Most of these transactions occurred in the industrial world. However, the potential reward from investing in developing countries can be very considerable. To be able to attract investors and convince them that despite the multiple risks involved, they can achieve an attractive return, authorities need to address the following areas:

LINK BETWEEN MACROECONOMIC STRATEGY AND TELECOMMUNICATIONS POLICY. It is paramount to convince investors about the soundness of the economic and political dynamics of each country, because these will be the key to understanding how profound and systematic the reform of the telecommunications sector will be.

REGULATORY ENVIRONMENT. Another key issue is the regulatory environment that a privatized company will find. Particularly important is that ground rules must be clear and that pricing guidelines and decisions have sufficient permanence to ensure that potential returns on long-term investments can effectively materialize.

TRANSPARENCY OF INFORMATION. Investors should be given a clear understanding of the company. Its network infrastructure, the staff's technical capability, and the organizational design of the company will be key to its future profitability.

FINANCING CONSIDERATION. The investment vehicle per se has to be well understood and, it is hoped, will be an instrument that is registered in major capital markets. That will ensure that the security will become easily tradable in the future.

In the Mexican case the privatization process addressed all these issues adequately. That is why TELMEX has been such an extraordinarily attractive investment and why the privatization process guarantees that the telecommunications sector of Mexico will transform itself from being an obstacle for development to being one of its major propellants.

7

Privatization of Telecommunications: The Case of Venezuela

Aileen A. Pisciotta

THE PRIVATIZATION OF THE TELEPHONE COMPANY of Venezuela, Compañía Anónima Nacional de Teléfonos de Venezuela (CANTV), finalized in December 1991, is probably most commonly noted for its unexpectedly successful financial outcome. Although the total value of CANTV had been estimated at approximately US$2 billion, a controlling 40 percent share was sold to a GTE-led consortium for the surprising sum of US$1.885 billion. There were, however, other significant aspects of the transaction which will be far more telling of the prospects for long-term success and sustainability of the privatization.

One of the most important of these aspects is the approach taken in Venezuela to the establishment of a regulatory process. Much attention was paid by the government of Venezuela during the privatization process to the establishment of a regulatory entity, Consejo Nacional de Telecomunicaciones (CONATEL). Nonetheless, long after the institutionalization of CONATEL, many issues remain concerning the ability of the Venezuelan regulatory process to meet expectations of successfully steering the course toward a private market. After briefly summarizing the "vital statistics" of the CANTV privatization, this chapter reviews and comments on the process and constraints in Venezuela in the creation of a regulatory authority and suggests lessons to be learned for future privatizations.

Background and Legal Framework

Founded in 1930 by Felix A. Guerrero, a private investor, CANTV grew through acquisition of preexisting private concessions and eventually competed directly with other telephone, telegraph, and telex systems owned and operated by the government.

In 1940, the Telecommunications Law was enacted, specifying the exclusive powers of the government with respect to telephone and other telecommunications services, as well as radio and television broadcast services. Under the 1940 law, which is still in effect, the government is exclusively responsible for the "establishment and exploitation" of telecommunications services. However, the executive branch has the power to grant concessions and permits to private entities for the provision of such services. The 1940 law also authorizes the government to promulgate regulations concerning telecommunications and requires the executive branch to approve tariffs.

In the early 1960s, the government began to acquire private concessions, some held by foreign companies. In 1964, CANTV and all of the competing government systems were consolidated into one national operating company. In 1965, the Law for Reorganization of Telecommunications Services was enacted, granting to CANTV an exclusive concession to operate telecommunications systems in Venezuela for twenty-five years. The 1965 law left open the possibility that concessions might be granted to other private parties, but no such concessions were actually granted.[1]

The 1965 law provided that regulatory functions were to be assumed by the Ministry of Transportation and Communications (MTC) and that all operational functions were to be performed by CANTV. In practice, however, MTC dealt mainly with radio and television issues, while telecommunications tariffs, technical standards, and frequency allocations were left largely to CANTV's determination, with MTC's nominal approval.

The Privatization Process

Work on the privatization of CANTV began in early 1991. Initially, it was planned that a private operator would enter into a management contract for the operation of the telephone company, with an option to buy up to 30 percent of the stock of CANTV in two years. The remainder of the stock ultimately would be sold in national and international capital markets, with a portion reserved for CANTV employees and with a share retained by the government of Venezuela to safeguard national security interests. It was believed that this plan would permit swift improvements in the quality of service and would maximize the value of the stock for sale. Later, upon further analysis, the plan was changed to permit a direct sale at the outset of 40 percent of the stock to an international telephone operator and 11 percent to employees.

Pursuant to contracts financed by the World Bank, the Venezuela Investment Fund and the Telecommunications Restructuring Group of the MTC hired consultants to develop a strategic plan for the telecommunications sector, design a regulatory framework, develop procedures and documents for the sale of CANTV, prepare financial projections, and establish a valuation of the enterprise. Pursuant to separate contracts financed by the U.S. Trade and Development Program, MTC hired other consultants to design a regulatory entity.[2]

Prior to the completion of work by these consultants, a proposed new telecommunications law was drafted with the assistance of the MTC and CANTV and introduced into the Venezuelan Congress. Key features of the proposed law included the promotion of competition in certain services and the establishment of clear criteria for the control of noncompetitive services. Most significantly, the legislation contemplated the establishment of an autonomous regulatory authority. Critically, the proposed law was addressed only to changes in the provision and administration of telecommunications and did not address any issues concerning radio and television broadcasting. It was expected that the legislation would pass Congress by

October 1991, well before the closing of the sale. As recounted further below, however, the law did not pass on schedule.

It was determined that the grant of authorization to the newly privatized company should be by concession rather than by license.[3] Therefore, a central part of the privatization process was the drafting and negotiation of the concession agreement, including proposed regulations for basic services and establishment of criteria for the suspension or termination of the concession rights granted.

On March 6, 1991, a dozen companies filed prequalification statements. In order to prequalify, companies were required to have (in non-Venezuelan systems) more than 6 million installed lines, over 25 percent digitalization of local exchanges, over 65 percent completion of international calls, 1-month average waiting time for new lines, and 16-hour average time for line repair. Candidates also had to have gross annual income of over US$5 billion. On April 18, 1991, the government announced that eight firms had prequalified, namely, Ameritech, Bell Atlantic, Bell Canada, France Télécom, GTE, Nippon Telephone & Telegraph, Southwestern Bell, and US West.

On November 15, 1991, two final bids were submitted. The GTE-led consortium was the clear winner with a bid for a 40 percent share of CANTV of nearly $1.85 billion. The consortium members were GTE Telephone Operations (51 percent), Telefónica de España (16 percent), Electricidad de Caracas (16 percent), the Venezuelan Consorcio Inversionista Mercantil Cima (12 percent) and AT&T (5 percent). The losing consortium, which bid $1.4 billion, included Bell Atlantic, Bell Canada, Italcable, Nippon Telephone & Telegraph, and the Venezuelan groups Banco Provincial, Finalven, and Organización Diego Cisneros. In addition to their cash payment, the GTE consortium assumed $125 million out of the $600 million owed by CANTV in foreign debt. Of the remaining 60 percent of stock, 11 percent was placed in trust for CANTV employees and 49 percent was retained by the government, ultimately to be offered for sale in the Venezuelan stock market.

Market Structure

The main impetus for the privatization of CANTV in Venezuela was the urgent need to improve the quality of basic telephone service. With a lack of sufficient investment in infrastructure, switching equipment had become obsolete and transmission systems had deteriorated. This resulted in high levels of congestion, difficulty in obtaining dial tone, and interrupted connections. Prior to privatization, call completion was only 54 percent, with interruption running at 23 percent. Excessive redialing for basic services further burdened the system, while requirements for new services, including fax and value added services, were increasingly leading to intolerable congestion. At the same time, although Venezuela's density of telephone lines, at 7.3 percent, was slightly higher than the Latin American average of 6 percent, subscribers still waited an average of eight years for a new telephone line.[4]

Privatization was intended to create incentives and opportunities for private sector management of and investment in the basic telephone network. The concession agreement governing the newly privatized CANTV is for an initial duration of thirty years and includes a period of exclusivity for the provision of basic services for nine years. The concession also establishes a price-cap system of tariff regulation to encourage and reward efficiency.

The concession contract also sets forth certain specific requirements for service quality improvement. For example, in 1992 CANTV must install over 169,000 new digital lines and modernize over 40,000 lines. Until the year 2000, CANTV must provide 355,000 new digital lines per year and modernize 75,000 lines per year. CANTV must also establish a plan for the development of basic services in rural areas with inhabitants of 5,000 or less. Other important service quality requirements include:

- Improvement in dial tone (obtained within 3 seconds) from 78 percent in 1992 to 98 percent in the year 2000

- Improvement in call completion for local, interurban, and international calls from 52 percent, 38 percent, and 25 percent respectively in 1992 to 68 percent, 68 percent, and 65 percent respectively in the year 2000

- Improvement in operator response from 10 seconds in 1992 to 5 seconds in 1993

- Improvement in repair response time, including repairs within 48 hours and successful completion of repairs per visit, from 70 percent for each in 1992 to 90 percent and 96 percent respectively in the year 2000

- Improvement in waiting time for obtaining a new line. Between January 1, 1994, and December 31, 1995, 70 percent of requests for new service must be satisfied in less than 180 days. After January 1, 1998, 98 percent of all requests for new service must be satisfied in less than 5 days

- User satisfaction must increase from 15 percent in 1992 to 98 percent in the year 2000.

In addition to providing for the improvement of basic telephone service, the privatization of CANTV was intended to permit development of certain competitive services. In this respect, the Venezuela privatization was more aggressive than certain others have been. At the same time that the government endeavored to encourage the development and improvement of the basic telephone network, it attempted to move aggressively to encourage competition, not only in value added services, but also in private network services, which in some respects are substitutes for basic services. This was seen to be a necessary strategy to satisfy unmet demand and service requirements, particularly for large business users.

Specifically, competition was introduced in cellular telephone services with the awarding of a twenty-year renewable competitive cellular concession on May 31, 1991, to TELCEL Celular, C.A., a private consortium led by BellSouth with minority participation by Comtel, owned by Venezuelan businessman Oswaldo Cisneros, Bancor, a Venezuelan bank, and Telecomunicaciones BBS, a Venezuelan engineering group.[5] TELCEL's winning bid was US$107 million for nationwide concession for cellular voice and data transmission. At the time of the privatization, CANTV operated the "wireline" band of cellular service but had only 4,000 subscribers in Caracas. Starting in Caracas, TELCEL quickly signed up 8,000 subscribers.

Competition in value added services was specified as part of the privatization plan, and special regulations for such services, including for VSAT (very small aperture terminal) satellite data networks were adopted in October 1991. In May 1992, CONATEL also announced plans to grant concessions for private trunking and paging operations to provide mobile radio services for taxi companies, ambulances, contractors, and building security services.

Satellite services were also liberalized in connection with the privatization. Under Decrees 1876 and 1877, adopted in October 1991, the provision of satellite services was officially opened to competition. Private entities may apply for licenses for utilization of any satellite for either private networks or public services. Satellites operating in Venezuela include the international consortium INTELSAT and the U.S. licensed private international satellite operated by Alpha Lyracom/Pan American Satellite (PamAmSat).

Most significantly, the new market structure implemented at the time of privatization included authorization for private networks. The notion of authorizing private networks created a quandary, as such networks can serve as "bypass" systems that drain revenues from the basic switch network. Nonetheless, it was determined that authorization of private networks was important in Venezuela. Such authorizations would provide continuity of services already established through major private networks utilized by the oil companies and others, as well as relief from service quality problems for large users during the period of service improvement by CANTV. Thus, the government established policies and procedures for authorization of private networks by either permit (for networks restricted to internal company use) or concession (networks for third-party service). The authorizations included restrictions on interconnection with the public-switched network.

In anticipation of the establishment of private network regulations, numerous parties filed applications with CONATEL. By early 1992, CONATEL had awarded several concessions for private domestic and international business services, including teleports, VSAT networks, and other voice and data networks.

Regulatory Process

The success of an implementation of a new regulatory regime in connection with privatization depends not just on the wisdom of substantive regulatory policies, but also on the structural elements of the regulatory process.[6] In particular, it is critical to the success of a new regulatory authority that its jurisdiction and powers be clearly established, that it be guaranteed some degree of insulation from political processes, that significant funding be assured, and the mechanisms be provided for access to special experts and advisory services, particularly in the early stages when significant training is required. Each regulatory authority in every individual country will have to resolve these issues within the context of that country's own legal system. Necessarily, the instrumentalities of regulation, as well as the goals and objectives of the regulatory process, must be uniquely tailored for every situation. The critical aspects mentioned here, however, are fundamental elements of the essential survivability of a regulatory process, particularly for countries that have had no recent or well-established tradition of regulation and must quickly marshal resources to address complex issues.

At the outset of the privatization process in Venezuela, it was the intention of the government of Venezuela to establish an independent regulatory agency, reflective of the powers and capabilities of model regulatory authorities in other countries, such as the Federal Communications Commission (FCC) in the United States. The governmental structure of Venezuela, however, neither contemplates nor permits the establishment of an "independent" regulatory agency.

In particular, the Constitution of Venezuela, adopted in 1965, provides that authority over telecommunications is reserved exclusively to the federal government. Telecommunications services were established, in the 1940 law, as "public services" which are the responsibility of the government to provide, either directly or through concession to private parties. Jurisdiction over telecommunications public services is delegated to the MTC. Thus, any regulatory authority with oversight in telecommunications matters had to be developed within, or in a structure related to, MTC. This is in strong contrast to the U.S. governmental structure which, through the U.S. Constitution, delegates powers over interstate commerce to the Congress, which has delegated jurisdiction over interstate and international communications to the FCC.

Moreover, under the organizational law of the government of Venezuela, there are only limited options for the structuring of a "regulatory authority." One option was to continue with a separate general directorate for communications within the ministry. This, however, was deemed not to provide the desired political and economic independence for the regulatory authority. The second option was to create an "autonomous service," again within the ministry. This is a form of governmental entity which has intermediate autonomy. It does not have a legal identity separate from the ministry, but unlike a general directorate, it may maintain a budget and assets separate from the ministry.

Some interpretations of Venezuelan law indicated that an autonomous service, even though formed as part of a ministry, had to be established by law. In fact, the Venezuelan attorney general had issued formal opinions in other cases to that effect. The attorney general had also, however, accepted certain other cases in which autonomous services had been established through presidential decree.

A third option for a regulatory entity was the establishment of an "autonomous institute." Unlike an autonomous service, an autonomous institute would have a separate legal identity and could directly receive its own revenues. An autonomous institute would have to be "ascribed" to or connected with the ministry, but would be essentially independent. It could maintain its own administration and could directly receive revenues from license fees, and appeals from its decision could be made directly to the courts.

The draft telecommunications law being considered by the Venezuelan Congress in the spring and summer of 1991 provided for the establishment of an autonomous institute: the Instituto Nacional de Telecomunicaciones (INATEL) which was to be ascribed to MTC but would be given full and complete authority for actual regulatory functions, including development of policy proposals, promulgation of regulations and technical standards, issuing of permissions and concessions, administering the radio frequency spectrum, entering into international agreements, and overseeing tariffs. INATEL was to be directed by a board of seven members with staggered terms, each member to be selected by the heads of different government departments. The president of INATEL was to be selected by the Minister of Transportation and Communications.

The draft legislation also provided for the creation of another entity called the Consejo Nacional de Telecomunicaciones (CONATEL), which was intended to be organized within MTC and led by the Minister of Transportation and Communications. The role contemplated for CONATEL was as adviser to the government on objectives and policies. CONATEL was to be composed of twenty-one members representing various governmental and commercial interests, including labor unions and users.

Unfortunately, the progress of the telecommunications law ran into unexpected political impediments. The primary difficulty was that, although the 1940 law addressed both telecommunications and broadcasting issues, the proposed new telecommunications law created a new regime only for telecommunications. Certain interests in the government desired new legislation to govern broadcasting. The resistance of broadcasters to this development resulted in an impenetrable deadlock. Consequently, the privatization of CANTV had to proceed without a new telecommunications law and without the benefit of the establishment of an independent regulatory entity.

As a result, on September 5, 1991, President Perez issued Decree 1826, which formed CONATEL as an autonomous service within MTC. CONATEL was constituted through the reorganization of a department of engineering which had reported to the General Directorate for the Sector of Telecommunications. CONATEL is now responsible for all regulatory functions, including the following:

- Planning, directing, and supervising telecommunications services

- Regulating telecommunications services

- Keeping abreast of the execution of plans and programs in the telecommunications area

- Recommending and granting concessions, permits, and other authorizations

- Promoting investment and technological innovation

- Applying administrative sanctions permitted under law to enforce technical and service regulations

- Ensuring that regulated entities respect the rights of the users

- Coordinating with national and international organizations on technical aspects of telecommunications

- Administration of the radio frequency spectrum

- Developing criteria for administration of tariffs; and

- Any other functions that may be assigned by law.

A separate consultant or advisory council (Consejo Asesor) also was created to help advise CONATEL on regulatory policy.

Although the telecommunications law remains pending in Congress as of early 1993, passage would require resolution of very intricate political issues, and such resolution does not appear likely in the near future.

The consequence of these developments is that Venezuela is faced with very significant and intricate regulatory issues but is severely handicapped with respect to regulatory resources that it can apply. CONATEL has no independent base of continued funding and is completely dependent upon allocations from MTC and whatever assistance it can obtain through sympathetic foreign or multilateral sources, such as U. S. Trade and Development Program (TDP). Whereas at one time it had been contemplated that CONATEL would receive a percentage allocation from the substantial concession fee payments made by TELCEL and GTE, those funds have been absorbed into the general treasury without any mechanism provided for direction of a portion of the revenues to the regulatory effort. Also, whereas it was originally expected that CONATEL would be able to impose and collect regulatory processing and license fees, it now cannot do so.

The Venezuela market is a particularly complicated one, as it is characterized by a particularly progressive combination of monopoly and competition elements. It is in such mixed markets that regulatory issues become most complex. CONATEL is faced with the need to address very sophisticated regulatory policy issues in the areas of interconnection, frequency allocation, pricing and tariff oversight, service quality monitoring, consumer responsiveness, international cooperation, and establishment of subsidy for rural telephony. The paucity of resources available do not bode well for optimum regulatory attention to these issues.

Lessons Learned

The first lesson learned from Venezuela is that the regulatory process itself is a critical element of the success of a privatization, both before and after the closing of the transaction. The success of the privatization must be measured not only in terms of the price paid, but also in the ability of the participants in the process to achieve established goals and objectives. In Venezuela it is clear that the goals have been to improve the quality of basic services quickly while moving expeditiously to a competitive market model. These objectives require regulatory authorities to deal with the most sophisticated regulatory issues. The stability and rationality of the regulatory process, therefore, was an important element in attracting investors to Venezuela. The degree of success achieved in meeting established goals for improvement of service quality and reduction of barriers to entry, however, will not be apparent for some time and will depend upon the continuous effectiveness of the regulatory process, long after the privatization itself has been completed.

The second lesson is that, although we may take from foreign models the best that alternative systems have to offer, foreign systems can never be successfully grafted on to a different legal system. In Venezuela, as has been the case in other privatizations, it was tempting to try to apply notions of U.S. regulatory processes. The unique structure of the Venezuelan government, however, as dictated by the Constitution and other domestic laws, as well as the fact that Venezuela is a civil law country, requires that unique regulatory structures be devised.[7]

The third lesson is that no matter how attentive advisers are to domestic legal structures and requirements, and no matter how elegant the plans may be for the implementation of an effective regulatory structure uniquely suited to that particular country, such plans may fail. In the case of Venezuela, the best laid plans for an "independent" regulatory entity were sidetracked with the unexpected failure of the passage of the telecommunications law. The resulting structure, established by presidential decree, along with the limitations on funding and lack of insulation from political shifts, is by no means optimum. Therefore, it is very important to develop contingency plans for the establishment of a regulatory process and to provide, to the greatest extent possible, for the most critical elements of regulatory structure, namely clarity of jurisdiction, political insulation, and adequate funding.

The fourth lesson is that, of all of the fundamental elements of an effective regulatory process, funding is perhaps the most important, at least in the early stages. Significant funding is needed to hire and train competent staff and, where desirable, to hire expert advisers. It is important for privatizing governments to ensure that certain financial resources, perhaps earmarked from concession fees, be directed to the regulatory effort. It is also important for international agencies supporting privatization programs to commit resources to follow through in ensuring the effective implementation of regulatory programs long after the closing of the sale.

Finally, another lesson is that expert advisers working on different aspects of regulatory processes and substantive issues should be closely coordinated. The structure of advisory contracts varies from one privatization to the next. In some cases, only one legal adviser is appointed to handle the transactional and regulatory issues. In other cases, separate contracts may be awarded under the same funding source. In still other cases, as was true in Venezuela, separate contracts may be awarded and funded by separate agencies. This favors diversity of viewpoints which is a valuable asset in the privatization process. Ineffective coordination, however, results in duplication of effort, tremendous waste, and ineffective advice. For example, substantive regulatory policy issues, raised for the purpose of drafting bidding documents by one firm must be closely related to assumptions in the organizational structure of a regulatory entity designed by a different firm. For lack of effective coordination, some important opportunities to share and take best advantage of diverse expert resources were lost.

Conclusion

In spite of the problems that Venezuela inevitably will face, the privatization of CANTV has opened the door to a new era of market-based telecommunications systems in that country. There certainly will be many fits and starts as policies evolve and the market adjusts to new participants and developments in services and technologies. It is hoped that the new regulatory process in Venezuela, though not the structure originally envisioned, will survive and prosper and serve as a positive force in fostering market developments.

Endnotes

1. CANTV's concession under the 1965 law expired in 1990. Prior to that expiration, however, the Venezuelan Supreme Court ruled that the concession actually was not necessary, and that CANTV operated as an instrument of the state pursuant to the obligations and powers already established for the government in the Constitution and the 1940 Law.

2. The author, international communications counsel for Latham & Watkins, was legal adviser to MTC under the TDP contract granted to Teleconsult, Inc., for the design of a telecommunications regulatory entity.

3. A concession is a form of delegation, to a private party, of rights and obligations that legally remain with the government. A license or permit is a governmental authorization of a private sector activity.

4. U.S. Department of Commerce, International Trade Administration, *A Guide to Telecommunications Markets in Latin America and the Caribbean,* May 1992, p. 144. See also "Venezuela," unpublished paper presented by Aileen A. Pisciotta and Philip L. Gordon at "Latin American Telecommunications Reforms: A Workshop on New Industry Structures and Regulatory Frameworks," presented by the Organization of American States and Latham & Watkins, April 20–May 1, 1991, Washington, DC.

5. Another initial participant in the consortium, Racal Telecom of the U.K., subsequently pulled out.

6. See, for example, Aileen A. Pisciotta, "Effective Regulatory Procedures: The Foundation of Successful Telecommunications Reform," published in proceedings of 1992 Pacific Telecommunications Conference. Honolulu, Hawaii, January 1992.

7. In contrast to the U.S. common law legal system derived from England, which is based on judicial precedent reflective of basic principles, Latin American countries generally have civil law systems derived from Western Europe and based on legislatively enacted codes which establish comprehensive sets of rules. One of the key distinguishing features between modern common law and civil law systems is the role of the judiciary.

Part III

Recent Experiences

in the Asia-Pacific Region

8

Restructuring the Telecommunications Sector in Asia: An Overview of Approaches and Options

Robert R. Bruce and Jeffrey P. Cunard

THE PROCESS OF DEVELOPING AND RESTRUCTURING the telecommunications sector in emerging and developing countries and economies in Asia has been as complex and diverse as the myriad economic, political, and social milieus of the region. This chapter is not a comprehensive analysis of sectoral reform in each country or economy in Asia. Rather, it is highly selective and impressionistic and is intended to highlight several of the varying approaches to sectoral reform being explored. Notably, this chapter does not discuss the Japanese experience because of its complexity and because Japan is much further along the path toward competition and reform. It concludes with some perspectives concerning possible future policies in the region.

Overall, the restructuring process in Asia has, so far, been distinctly different from reform in Latin America, Europe, or North America. In Latin America the process is characterized by efforts to privatize state enterprises at a very accelerated pace. In connection with this effort, Latin Americans have sought significant amounts of foreign investment while, at least temporarily, limiting competitive entry into basic service sectors.

In Asia, by contrast, a mixed set of strategies for the telecommunications sector is being pursued. It is not surprising that this is so, given the aggressive approach to economic development in Malaysia, the Republic of Korea, Singapore, Taiwan, and Hong Kong. In Malaysia, privatization of the telecommunications operator has been implemented in a deliberate, carefully staged process without significant involvement by foreign investors. Singapore Telecom, a company serving a thriving city-state with an abundance of resources, has been restructured; the first stock offering is anticipated for 1994. Latin American-style privatization is an approach being pursued in Pakistan.

Economies such as Korea, Singapore, and Taiwan have been able to generate substantial investment resources for basic infrastructure. For them, cutting-edge debates have focused on how to permit new services and service providers to use the infrastructure. In Hong Kong, the debate also has focused on the nature and viability of future infrastructure and service-based competition.

In other countries, where it is often difficult to establish basic connections, service-based competition, though no less important from the standpoint of telecom users, may be an elusive goal. In those environments, policymakers may well have to confront the significance of permitting new providers of core infrastructure, either directly, as competitors to the existing operator, or as contractors to that operator.

Thus, the future evolution of the telecommunications sector in Asia may be characterized by dynamically new scenarios for the evolution of industry structure. The fact that many of the newly industrial economies of the region have been able to make substantial investment in infrastructure without new entrants or competition may not necessarily mean that others, with more limited resources, can afford to follow a similar path for development of their telecom infrastructure.

Beyond those economies that have already achieved significant telephone penetration, policymakers are wrestling with difficult choices concerning steps that might be more limited than immediate privatization of the operator. They are seeking ways to introduce private investment into the sector. They are attempting to focus on rearranging existing organizational and institutional structures to lay the groundwork for sectoral reform. They are also addressing issues of whether regulatory reform ought to precede—or is a consequence of introducing—competition in or the privatization or reorganization of operators in the telecommunications sector.

Regional Pacesetters: In the Footsteps of the Four Tigers

In each of the rapidly emerging economies of Korea, Taiwan, Hong Kong, and Singapore, there is significant penetration of the telecommunications infrastructure. Korea has approximately 35 subscriber lines per 100 population. Taiwan has over 33, Hong Kong has 45, and Singapore has 47. In each one of these environments, the existing operators are confronting a wide range of issues and competitive challenges from diverse quarters.

Republic of Korea

Korea has achieved a remarkably high level of telephone penetration through an aggressive program of sectoral investment initially managed through the Korea Telecommunications Authority (KTA). Telephone penetration expanded from 2.8 million access lines in 1980 to over 15 million in 1990, and in the same period the telecommunications sector's share of national fixed assets jumped from 3 to 7 percent. With 35 telephone subscribers per 100 population by April 1991, Korea now has among the highest telephone penetrations in Asia, and the ninth-largest telephone network in the world, measured in terms of access lines.

On January 1, 1991, KTA was converted from a governmental authority to a joint-stock company, Korea Telecom, that the government plans to privatize. It is anticipated that the majority of the shares of Korea Telecom will remain in the hands of the government. The plan had been to offer shares in Korea Telecom to Korean investors, beginning with an initial tranche of 25 percent of the shares, followed by the sale of another 24 percent over the following two-year period. Privatization plans have been delayed for several reasons, including the downturn in the Korean stock market.

The Korean government has remained wary of removing restrictions on foreign ownership of Korea Telecom's shares. As part of the much broader economic objective of trying to diversify the country's industrial base beyond the few large, highly diversified business conglomerates, or *chaebol*, the government has been cautious about major Korean industrial or trading firms obtaining a significant ownership stake in Korea Telecom. The privatization plans would bar any single shareholder from owning more than 10 percent of Korea Telecom.

Notwithstanding the very deliberate pace with which Korea Telecom is being restructured, major changes have taken place in the structure and organization of the Korean telecommunications sector. These changes are largely the result of a) a recognition by Korean policymakers that further industrial development is predicated on a modern and efficient telecommunications sector; b) pressures from major telecommunications users in Korea; c) intense trade pressure from Korea's major trading partners—principally the United States—for a more liberal and open telecommunications regime.

In August 1991, Korea enacted a new telecommunications law that establishes lines of demarcation between various service categories: General Service Providers (basic telephony and data services), Special Service Providers (cellular, paging, and other regional or wireless services), and Value Added Service Providers. The new legal framework also establishes the regulatory framework for authorizing new service providers. As a result, competition is now emerging in various subsectors of the Korean telecommunications sector.

For example, for many years all data communications services were provided through the Data Communications Corporation of Korea (DACOM), which was created in 1982. DACOM has been a private-sector entity organizationally independent of—but partially (33 percent) owned by—Korea Telecom. Among its remaining twenty-seven private corporate shareholders are a number of Korea's major firms. To a significant extent, DACOM saw itself as competing with (at least at the margins)—and more entrepreneurial than—Korea Telecom, which was limited to a monopoly in domestic and international voice services. Recently, the Korean government has lowered the barriers between markets to sanction a less segmented approach to the provision of services.

First, DACOM's monopoly with respect to data services was ended in 1992. Korea Telecom has been allowed to offer data as well as voice services. Second, to ensure that fair and viable competition develops between DACOM and Korea Telecom, the latter was required to transfer its shares in DACOM to the government by 1993. Third, as of December 3, 1991, DACOM has been able to provide international voice services, which had been the exclusive preserve of Korea Telecom. DACOM has moved aggressively into this market; with a 5 percent rate advantage over the services of Korea Telecom and the ability to provide bypass services, DACOM has substantial shares of traffic on major international routes. Fourth, DACOM is eagerly pursuing a license to provide domestic long-distance services by 1995. This initiative is opposed by Korea Telecom, in part because rates are not yet rebalanced.

The services that Korea Telecom and DACOM can provide will remain somewhat partitioned, at least for the next several years. The opportunities for direct head-to-head competition in the domestic market are still limited, though competition internationally is quite vigorous. Korea is now headed toward a competitive industry structure with full duopolistic competition between Korea Telecom and DACOM.

The Koreans are also moving aggressively to introduce competition in mobile services in the Special Service Provider category. Significant foreign investment in the provision of mobile services is expected; several of the U.S. regional operating companies and equipment suppliers are actively pursuing opportunities in Korea as they become available. No foreign entity can, however, own more than one-third of the voting stock of such a provider.

Again, in an attempt to diversify the sector, the government has decided to exclude Korea Telecom and DACOM from the mobile sector. Korea Telecom is, in fact, in the process of divesting its stake in Korea Mobile Telecommunications Corporation (KMTC); in October 1989, KMTC sold 35 percent of its shares to its employees and the general public. In a further attempt to encourage competition, individual companies may not own more than one-third of a Special Service Provider's voting stock.

As a consequence of several years of tough trade negotiations with the United States, the Korean government has been yielding ground stubbornly with respect to long-standing restrictions on the competitive provision of value added services. Over time, and in phases, restrictions have been lifted on the offering of such services. First, information processing was opened up. Then, group value added network (VAN) operations were permitted. Next, private companies could participate in certain local area networks and group VAN services.

Private companies and Korea Telecom are permitted to provide a wide array of domestic value added services. As a result of the 1991 law, a registration requirement has been adopted for authorizing providers of certain value added services; views differ on the simplicity or automaticity of registration. Providers of domestic database and remote computer services are not required to register. Over time, it is expected that the registration requirement will be further liberalized.

Also in 1991, Korea and the United States, and later Korea and Japan, entered into arrangements to permit the international provision of value added services (the so-called IVANs). These services could include electronic data interchange (EDI) and other message-handling services.

The Koreans continue to resist lifting the remaining restrictions on foreign ownership of providers of value added services. Currently, foreign investors can hold no more than 50 percent of the shares of a Korean provider of value added services (but there is no restriction on database and remote computer services). Largely as a result of trade pressure, in February 1992 the Koreans agreed to lift this restriction by January 1, 1994. Restrictions on foreign investment will not be lifted, however, with respect to General Service Providers.

Taiwan

Change in the telecommunications sector in Taiwan is coming about very deliberately, and with increasing impatience from large users and Taiwan's trading partners. For several years Taiwanese policymakers have recognized the need for reform . Various structural options have been evaluated and advisory groups have been formed. Currently, a draft law that would reform the telecommunications sector is being circulated.

Given the size and growth of that economy, the relatively slow movement in Taiwan is somewhat surprising, but it may be the result of several factors. Taiwan has been subject to less significant external and internal pressures than other countries to open the telecommunications sector. In addition, widely felt concerns over national security issues have delayed consideration of steps that would permit competition and encourage reform in a sector as vital to the national interest as that of telecommunications. Moreover, the overall pace of change—not just in telecommunications, but in the capital markets and financial services area, for example—is far more deliberate and cautious than in other countries in Asia. The deliberate approach toward introducing reform has not been without its frustrations, for both Taiwanese and foreign industries.

At the same time, many believe that the telecommunications operator, the Directorate General for Telecommunications (DGT), has done a reasonable job. The DGT recently launched a twelve-year, US$22 billion investment plan. In 1991, Taiwan ranked thirteenth in the world in total telecommunications expenditures, behind Korea (ranked eleventh) but ahead of the Netherlands (fourteenth) and Sweden (nineteenth).

The DGT is part of the Taiwanese Ministry of Transportation and Communications and has not yet been corporatized, although there have been various proposals to corporatize or otherwise transform the DGT. The most recent proposal is wending its way through the government in parallel with the draft law that would, if enacted, create a new, competitive structure for the telecommunications sector. Operational and regulatory responsibilities remain bundled in the ministry. For example, in spite of significant demand for cellular telephony, the DGT has maintained control over such services. The existing cellular service, installed with Ericsson equipment, grew from 38,500 subscribers in 1990 to over 210,000 subscribers currently. An additional contract to install another 220,000 lines has been awarded. Likewise, with respect to paging services, foreign firms have been restricted to supplying systems and equipment, even though demand for paging services is burgeoning. (In 1991, the demand for a second paging system increased 41 percent over the previous year, nearly filling the 1 million line capacity of the system.)

The Taiwanese approach to the provision of value added services also has been incremental. Certain value added services can be provided on a competitive basis domestically; to date, those services that can be provided competitively have been quite limited, focusing on information storage and retrieval, information processing, remote transaction services, and electronic mail. Additional restrictions are imposed on the extent to which international value added services can be provided. The Taiwanese are, however, taking some steps to liberalize the use of leased circuits by large users.

The most significant limitation to date has been the absolute bar on any foreign investment in providers of telecommunications services, including value added services. Under current Taiwanese law, even a single foreign shareholder could disqualify a company from being able to provide such services, whether domestically or internationally. The draft law would permit some—perhaps up to one-third—limited foreign ownership of providers of value added services. The stated intention of some in the government is that over time the restriction might be lifted altogether.

The first steps toward structural reform may involve instituting more liberal arrangements for the use of DGT infrastructure. For the foreseeable future, the DGT will probably remain under relatively tight government control. There is little talk about permitting competition in wireline infrastructure, though cellular telephone and other mobile services are seen as presenting significant potential opportunities for foreign investors.

The draft law contemplates dividing the telecommunications sector into two categories of service, a hybrid of the approaches pursued in Japan (Type I and Type II) and the United States ("basic" and "enhanced" services). Category II services—intended to be value added services that use the facilities of a Category I enterprise—could be provided on a relatively competitive basis. Presumably, Category I services—defined as the installation of telecommunications facilities that provide telecommunications services—would (aside from mobile services) remain a monopoly of the corporate successor to the DGT.

The draft law contemplates that the DGT would be transformed into a state-run company, Chinese Telecommunications Company (CTC), which would be permitted to provide both Category I and II services, subject to the requirement that there be no cross-subsidies. Much thinking has gone into this law to alter the status of the DGT, with considerable attention to personnel and retirement issues. CTC shareholders could include only Taiwanese entities or those of Taiwanese nationality; foreigners could hold up to one-third of the shares of any such shareholding entity, however.

In short, the government in Taiwan remains concerned about maintaining control over what is obviously considered a strategic sector. There is already a relatively high level of investment by the DGT. Telephone penetration is significant, amounting to over 33 main lines per 100 population. Telephone subscription increased to 6.7 million in 1991, an 8.1 percent increase over the previous year. Accordingly, there is little pressure to introduce private investment to accelerate the expansion of infrastructure. Nevertheless, the government's investment program for the period 1991–1996 is highly ambitious. It calls for:

- The installation of 12 million lines of digital local switching equipment by the end of 1996—with 92 percent of these lines digitalized by that time

- 100 percent digitalization of toll switching lines by 1994

- Construction of 23,000 kilometers of fiber-optic network

- Significant investment in international transmission projects and in the development of ISDN capabilities in the national network.

There is growing concern that the Taiwanese government has not made a sufficiently adequate investment in a range of basic infrastructure. As pressures grow for increased investment, Taiwanese government officials may become more open to permitting increased participation by private investors, including foreigners, in the telecommunications sector. Such a step may well be a prerequisite to any effort to accelerate the process of reforming DGT's existing structure.

Hong Kong

In Hong Kong, Cable & Wireless (C&W), through its holding company, Hong Kong Telecommunications Ltd. (Hong Kong Telecom), has a monopoly on the provision of both domestic (Hong Kong Telephone Company) and international (Hong Kong Telecom International) services. Given that these monopolies expire in 1995 and 2006, respectively, policymakers have spent the last couple of years exploring models for encouraging facilities-based competition in Hong Kong. In the abortive effort to franchise a cable television system in Hong Kong, which collapsed in late 1990, it was made clear that such a system should have the capability to provide telecommunications services as well.

Competition in mobile services is exceptionally vigorous. In cellular telephony the Hong Kong-based conglomerate Hutchison Whampoa is a major player, in competition with Hong Kong Telecom. Three licensees operate four cellular networks with the second-highest rate of subscribers in the world. Other radio-based systems also serve as viable competitors to Hong Kong Telecom's wireline network. With thirty paging licensees, Hong Kong has the highest penetration of pagers in the world (650,000 subscribers for a population of 5.9 million) and two operators of CT 2-type cordless telephone or telepoint services have together built up a customer base of 50,000 in a year.

In 1991, Hong Kong concluded bilateral agreements to provide international value added network services with the United States and Japan. These arrangements carefully delimit what services can be provided, excluding, for example, basic voice and facsimile services. Over time, they will undoubtedly apply pressure on C&W's monopoly to provide international switched voice services. Due to Hong Kong's status as an essential node on emerging global networks, it seems likely that C&W will have to cede some control over the provision of international switched voice services into Hong Kong if it wishes to have operational flexibility in and access to other major international markets.

A new price-cap regulatory scheme has been put in place for Hong Kong Telephone Company, which elected to shift from a traditional scheme of price regulation based on reliance on rate-of-return regulation. Under the new scheme, Hong Kong Telephone will be allowed to increase its prices by a rate equal to the rate of inflation, minus a factor x. This factor will be fixed at 4 percent for the last three years of the company's franchise.

Telecommunications policy in Hong Kong is driven in significant part by the recognition that telecommunications services of every sort are needed to maintain the growth and vigor of Hong Kong as a trading and financial center. This is particularly true as Hong Kong aggressively competes with Singapore and Tokyo to be the economic epicenter of the world's fastest-growing region. Accordingly, value added services can be provided within Hong Kong on a liberal and competitive basis. The licensing scheme is straightforward and various service providers are thriving. Hong Kong Telephone has moved smartly to meet competition and introduce new services tailored to the dynamism of the market, including the provision of very sophisticated facsimile services over a separate, dedicated network.

How fast Hong Kong will open up its telecommunications sector will depend on various external factors. To a significant extent, it may be determined by the pace at which other relatively closed markets in continental Europe are opened in the 1990s. If competition in infrastructure becomes a broadening phenomenon on the Continent, it may be difficult for Hong Kong to remain isolated from what could become an international trend.

Sector developments in Hong Kong must also be understood in the context of the changes that will take place in 1997. Already, China has a powerful and growing political and economic presence, including a 20 percent shareholding in Hong Kong Telecom through China International Trust and Investment Corporation (CITIC). Combined with intensifying pressures from international users and service providers, these changes will have a profound—and still uncertain—impact on the dynamic Hong Kong market.

Prompted by these factors and the general worldwide trend to liberalization, the Hong Kong government conducted a telecommunications policy review. As a result of this review, the government decided that Hong Kong Telephone Company's exclusive franchise would be replaced in 1995 by a nonexclusive license which would include a universal services obligation. In addition, in September 1992 the government invited proposals for competing providers of local service. By the closing date of February 1, 1993, it had received seven proposals, some involving the world's major telecommunications operators. The government undertook to assess each proposal on its merits and a priori not set a limit to the number of competitors it would license. It promised a decision by mid-1993 to allow adequate transition to competition at the conclusion of Hong Kong Telephone Company's monopoly in 1995. At the end of November 1993 the Hong Kong government announced that it had awarded three licences to provide domestic fixed telecommunications network services. These were awarded to: Hutchison Communications Ltd. owned by Hutchison Whampoa (80 percent) and Telstra of Australia (20 percent); New T&T

Hong Kong Ltd. owned 100 percent by Warf Holdings Ltd. of Hong Kong; and New World Telephone Ltd. which is owned by New World Development Ltd. of Hong Kong (66.5 percent), US West (25 percent), Shanghai Long Distance (5 percent) and Infa Telecom Asia Ltd. of Hong Kong (3.5 percent). Also, a newly established regulatory body will be given the power to arbitrate between a new competitor and Hong Kong Telephone Company on appropriate interconnection arrangements and access charges if the two are unable to agree through negotiation. If the Hong Kong government accepts one or more of the competing proposals, Hong Kong will become an important laboratory within the Asian region to test how competition might be introduced into the major "city-states" of the Asian region.

The government of Hong Kong is continuing to review core elements of its regulatory framework. By mid-1993 it had put in place a new regulatory entity known as the Office of the Telecommunications Authority (OFTA). Interestingly, the director-general of the OFTA is a former senior staff member of the Australian regulatory body AUSTEL; this demonstrates that not only new competitive policies, but even regulatory officials attuned to overseeing procompetitive policies, are on the move in the Asian region.

The government is likely to proceed carefully, especially in the international arena. Pressures are mounting for further liberalization; at the same time, the government is reluctant to take any action that would be construed as a unilateral termination of an existing franchise agreement, given the general climate of concern about the transition to occur in 1997. The overall pace of change in Hong Kong may well be governed by the pressures from the United States and Japan, which have open markets and where C&W has been permitted to offer services competitively. It is likely that these two trading partners will argue, both to C&W and to officials in Hong Kong, that their firms are entitled to reciprocal market access in Hong Kong.

Finally, additional international competitive pressures—an inevitable consequence of Hong Kong's continuing participation in commercial and financial markets—will dictate the future direction of events in Hong Kong. Hong Kong is less insulated from and more vulnerable to external pressures than is Singapore. Consequently, it seems possible to imagine that Hong Kong will be the gateway through which developments from other regions are passed on to and adapted for the Asian environment.

Singapore

The telecommunications scene in Singapore has been dominated by the pervasive presence of Singapore Telecom (ST). The extraordinary success and the visible and concerted orientation of ST toward becoming a global player are emblematic of Singapore's status as an economic powerhouse in the region.

Singapore is locked in a competitive dynamic with the other major economic centers of the region: Tokyo and Hong Kong. The intensity of this competition and the jockeying for international business are likely to ensure that Singapore will take steps to liberalize the use of telecommunications infrastructure at least to the level of Hong Kong.

The status of Singapore and, derivatively, that of ST are unique in the region. Officials in the Singaporean government and within ST (the de facto policymaker and regulator in the telecommunications sector in Singapore) are sufficiently savvy to be able to react swiftly to pressures from abroad. Singapore may not need to lead the region in the process of restructuring the sector, given the uncertainties of Hong Kong's status after 1997 and the developing state of Malaysia's economy.

Conversely, ST may increasingly be exposed to insistent pressures from Singapore's major international trading partners to open up the Singaporean market. Following the highly successful example of Singapore Airlines, ST is seeking to enter the international arena more actively as a competitor (and as a provider of managed network services for large business users). As it moves outward, ST may confront demands to loosen its stranglehold over the telecommunications sector in its home market. For example, although there is now in place a regulatory body, the Telecommunications Authority of Singapore (TAS), and a regulatory regime for international value added services, Singapore's approach to service-based competition is much more restrictive than that permitted under the EC Services Directive. For example, applicants for licenses for international value added network services are required to show a substantial "value added" element to the proposed service. Any services that purport to involve any element of resale of ST's services are not permitted.

TAS undertakes to evaluate new applications for service on an ad hoc basis; however, the regulatory regime in Singapore is much more restrictive than in most major industrial countries. Thus, many service providers that are able to implement services within the European Community under its Services Directive and hope to connect such services to the United States, Japan, and Australia will find that Singapore has become a restrictive bottleneck where emerging international managed network services cannot be provided. ST has attempted to accommodate large private line subscribers within the existing regulatory framework; increasingly, ST will be expected to accommodate international providers of value added and managed network services, especially as it seeks increased presence in international markets as a service provider.

On April 1, 1992, ST was corporatized as Singapore Telecommunications Pte. Ltd., which is wholly government owned through a holding company (MinCom Holdings Pte. Ltd.). At the same time a reconstituted TAS was given the responsibility to regulate telecommunications and postal services. Privatization itself is being undertaken principally to enhance ST's global competitiveness and to improve the incentives for its management.

About 11 percent of Singapore Telecommunications was floated in November 1993 in three tranches. Two of the three tranches (approximately 550 million shares) were reserved for Singaporeans including employees of ST. The third (approximately 550 million shares) was open to bidding by Singaporeans and foreigners. The basic sale price per share was S$2.

The corporatization-privatization project follows the privatization of the telecommunications operator in Malaysia and of Singapore Airlines. ST seems to understand that it may need to present a more commercial, corporate face to the world to venture with partners abroad. Indeed, it is for this reason that foreign partners ultimately may be invited to make equity investments in ST. ST also recognizes the strategic importance of realigning the balance between local and international revenues. Singapore has been quite successful in attracting large users to route their traffic through its facilities, notwithstanding its controversial volume-based orientation to charging for leased circuits. Consequently, revenues from international services have long been the economic engine behind the success of ST.

ST's financial results are almost unimaginable for others in less developed markets. In the year ending March 31, 1991, ST reported a surplus of US$1.1 billion on revenues of US$2.1—representing a rate of return of 36.7 percent of operating income. (By comparison, Hong Kong Telephone's after-tax return is reported to be 30.8 percent.) Profits in the first six months ending in September 1993 were S$0.78 billion (a 20 percent rise over the same period the previous year) on revenues of S$1.53 billion. As is true of its counterparts in Korea and Taiwan, ST has been able to reinvest surpluses aggressively into its operations. Of the US$1.1 billion surplus, only US$217 million was turned over to the Singapore government treasury. It is believed that ST's profits from the offering of international services are sufficient to completely subsidize the expansion and costs of the services provided over the domestic network. ST has an accumulated surplus of US$4.9 billion, out of which US$2.4 billion is earmarked for investment in new assets. Investments of US$3.2 billion are planned over the next five years. Once privatized, ST would pay a government corporate tax of 32 percent and be required to pay dividends to the state, to the extent it remains at least a partial shareholder.

At the end of 1991, substantial controversy was generated when the government proposed to begin charging on a usage basis (Singapore ¢1.4 or US¢0.8 per minute during business hours and half that rate the rest of the time). Annual subscriber fees of US$190 for a residence line and US$290 for a business line were to be reduced to US$100 and US$150, respectively. Despite these reductions in monthly fees, policymakers elsewhere in the region might take note of the extent to which local exchange tariffs are structured to recover investment costs.

Privatization is focusing attention on the economic dynamics of providing telephone service in Singapore and other major urban centers in Asia. Singapore's experience provides a fascinating benchmark for other Asian markets that aspire to follow in its footsteps. According to ST's own statistics, the top 30 percent of users account for 74 percent of all traffic; the bottom 30 percent generate 2.2 percent of all calls.

Singapore's successful strategy for developing its telecommunications sector has several important components. First, Singapore has maintained a tariff structure for local access that has supported investment in the sector. It is now modernizing that tariff structure to take into account increased use of local plants for data and facsimile transfer as well as to respond to pressures to lower international accounting rates and prices for international calls. Second, ST has been able to accumulate significant cash reserves to finance new investment. The government has resisted the temptation to siphon off revenues to support other areas of activity, and ST has generated huge cash reserves for future plant improvements. This strategy of aggressive reinvestment certainly should be given careful consideration by economic planners elsewhere as they assess how best to keep up with the fastest moving economies in the region.

Developing Economies in Rapid Pursuit: The Cases of Malaysia, Thailand, Indonesia, and the Philippines

Countries that have lagged behind the Four Tigers in the pace of overall economic development have been pursuing various approaches to sectoral reform. These countries' economies are pressing hard to follow the lead of the four economies that have sprinted ahead. To varying degrees, development of the telecommunications infrastructure, coupled with structural change, is perceived as critical to realizing sectoral reform.

Malaysia

The approach to privatization in the telecommunications sector in Malaysia has been lengthy and deliberate. It has also been consistent with Prime Minister Mahathir's views that the private sector should take the lead in developing the country's economy and that the effort should be to move as quickly as possible to follow Singapore. Although the government has focused on restructuring and reorganization, the telecommunications sector has been marked by substantial investment plans to increase the number of main lines and to modernize and digitalize the network. The goal is to have a telephone penetration rate of 15 percent by the middle of this decade and 40 percent by the year 2005. In the meantime, mobile communications is growing quickly, with four cellular telephone companies, thirty-two paging licenses, and other licenses granted for new mobile technologies (such as CT 2).

In 1984, the government began the process of privatization by separating the regulatory and operational roles of the Ministry of Energy, Posts and Telecommunications. It did this on January 1, 1987 by transferring the telecommunications operating function to a new entity, Syarikat Telekom Malaysia Berhad (STM), a wholly owned government company incorporated under the companies Act of Malaysia, and now known simply as Telekom Malaysia. Regulatory functions were retained in the telecommunications department (Jabatan Telekom Malaysia or JTM) of the Ministry. As a first priority, policymakers focused on how best to introduce private investment into Telekom Malaysia, the operating entity rather than on setting up elaborate regulatory procedures within the Ministry. Telekom Malaysia began operations on January 1, 1987. The company's structure was reorganized and steps leading to its privatization proper were taken.

In November 1990, the government offered a block of approximately 23 percent of Telekom Malaysia's shares on the basis of a private placement to various Malaysian institutions. It also effected a public offering of a portion of these shares on the Malaysian stock exchange. Of the 470,000 shares offered by the government, 70,000 were reserved for employees and managers of Telekom Malaysia. Moreover, as part of the government's policy of developing the Malay population of the country, 100,000 shares were reserved for Bumiputera institutions. Another 152,000 shares were reserved for "designated institutions"—financial institutions and pension funds.

Although they are allowed to own up to 25 percent of the shares of Telekom Malaysia, foreign investors now hold a total of about 15 percent of the privately held shares. In this first tranche of the public offering, the government did not rely on substantial investment by foreign institutional or strategic investors. Thus, in sharp contrast with the first wave of privatizations in Latin America, no foreign operator was involved in the privatization of Telekom Malaysia.

The thrust of the privatization process in Malaysia has been to accord the operator more operational autonomy and independence to finance its operations. The goal has not been necessarily to reduce foreign debt or to inspire confidence for those who would invest directly in the economy. (Despite some recent economic difficulties, Malaysia has had little difficulty attracting foreign investment.) Rather, the government's objective has been to widen and deepen the liquidity of the Malaysian capital market through the flotation of Telekom Malaysia's shares.

Recently, the telecommunications scene in Malaysia has grown more complex, with the government's issuing a number of facilities-based, cellular, and paging licenses.

Technology Resource Industries (TRI), a holding company, divested itself of all its nontelecommunications business, purchased the remaining 49 percent of Celcom Sdn Bhd, the independent mobile cellular operator, and obtained an international gateway license. (TRI had previously purchased 51 percent of Celcom from Telekom Malaysia, which had been required by the government to divest itself of this cellular operation.) Initially TRI plans to provide international services to its own mobile cellular customers which, at the end of 1992, numbered 160,000 and were increasing at a rate of 6,000 to 8,000 new subscribers a month; its long-term plan, however, is to establish itself as a competitor in international services to Telekom Malaysia.

Binariang Sdn Bhd, a privately held company with diverse interests, also obtained licenses to operate an international gateway, to provide local public network services, to operate a nationwide GSM mobile cellular service, and to launch and operate Malaysia's geostationary orbit satellite, MEASAT. Binariang intends to develop its local network using fixed wireless rather than fixed wireline facilities and to compete aggressively with Telekom Malaysia and TRI in international services. Its GSM mobile cellular service, due to start in mid-1994, will compete with TRI's Celcom, Telekom Malaysia's ATUR, and the new Mobikom, which is jointly owned by Telekom Malaysia (30 percent), the Bumiputera Bank (30 percent), Malaysia's automobile manufacturer EON (30 percent), and Sapura Holdings, a manufacturer of telecommunications equipment (10 percent).

A third potential competitor to Telekom Malaysia in domestic long-distance and international services is Time Telecommunications, which is currently laying a 1,000-kilometer fiber-optic cable along the new north-south expressway and hopes to obtain an international gateway license and the right to interconnect its facility into the public network. Time sold its 49 percent interest in the Celcom mobile cellular operation to TRI.

The government has issued thirty-two paging licenses. Not all of these are operational or nationwide; there are, however, five to six large, nationwide competitors. The provision of pay phones has also been liberalized, with Sapura Holdings being both a supplier and operator of pay phones as well as the country's largest paging operator.

Malaysian officials have not yet developed a regulatory institution that could address all the issues arising from a more competitive environment. It would appear that the possible emergence of a competitive challenge—rather than the privatization of Telekom Malaysia itself—will create the impetus for new regulations. Malaysian government officials have stressed the importance of developing an overall policy for the development of the telecommunications sector—a policy that was not adopted at the time that Telekom Malaysia was privatized. They have also focused on the relatively antiquated nature of the basic legislative framework for the telecommunications sector which, in their view, is lacking with respect to:

- Policies on competition, licensing, foreign equity participation, and type of technology as well as a policy on how to implement competition, especially for basic services

- An adequate procedure for revocation of licenses, disputes settlement, license fees, use of rights-of-way, etc.

- Provisions for the control and supervision of new value added and computer-based services

- An adequate regulatory framework for developing competition in both the basic and value added services and the new personal communications system (PCS) type services

- A sufficient number of qualified persons to regulate the sector

- Policies on interconnection of competing networks.

Thus, in Malaysia, regulation will evolve as competition evolves. In this regard, the Malaysian experience may offer some useful insights for countries beginning the process of reform and trying to decide what degree of emphasis or priority should be given to formulating new regulations and regulatory institutions in the crucible of the privatization process. Malaysia has left some leeway for refinement of its national telecommunications policies. Having been one of the first countries in the region to privatize its telecommunications operator, it may be one of the first countries in the region, excluding Australia, Japan, or New Zealand, to implement real competition.

New policy initiatives in Malaysia are not being driven by ideological consider-ations; rather there is a very pragmatic concern with how to attract the necessary investment to develop the telecommunications infrastructure further. Though Telekom Malaysia has been expanding the number of local access lines at almost 10 percent a year, the size of the waiting list for new telephones in Malaysia's fast-growing economy has trebled. The government recognizes that new mechanisms for attracting private investment, and perhaps new service providers, will be needed to keep the telecommunications infrastructure growing at the pace required to sustain Malaysia's future economic expansion.

Thailand

In Thailand, perhaps to a greater extent than for any other country in the region, the telecommunications sector has been unable to remain entirely insulated from politics. This may be due to the greater political stability elsewhere and because other economies historically have been controlled by single parties.

The web of relationships between the Communications Authority of Thailand (CAT) and the Telephone Organization of Thailand (TOT) has been complex and difficult to unravel. TOT is the primary provider of domestic telecommunications services in Thailand; CAT provides international telecommunications services as well as telex, telegraph, packet-switching, and domestic satellite services.

Telephone penetration remains low. Currently, there are only about 3 main lines per 100 persons, and these largely in Bangkok. Although the number of lines doubled between 1986 to 1991, the waiting list almost quadrupled over the same period. As of 1991, the installation backlog was over 900,000 lines in an economy that has become one of the fastest-growing in the world, with 11 percent average growth between 1987 and 1991. TOT is required to add 3 million lines by 1996, for a total of 5.3 million lines or a penetration rate of 10.

There are, accordingly, very substantial investment projects under way. Mobile services, including cellular telephony and paging services, are becoming quite widespread. Both CAT and TOT have entered into concessions with private investors to develop both services.

For example, in 1990 the Shinawatra Computer Group, a Thai computer and communications equipment consortium, was granted a concession to offer data communications service. It later sold 49 percent of its holdings in the franchise to Singapore Telecom. Shinawatra was also awarded a concession by CAT to offer a digital paging service; another paging franchise was granted to a joint venture between the Hong Kong-based Hutchinson Telecommunicaions and Loxley Com-pany. A thirty-year concession to operate a national satellite system was awarded by the Ministry of Transport and Communications to the Shinawatra group. The 12-transponder satellite should be operational by 1994. The Post and Telegraph Department has also awarded franchises for data transmission. TOT and CAT have major plans to develop integrated services digital network (ISDN), teleports, and international submarine optical-fiber systems. TOT and the State Railway of

Thailand plan to jointly install 3000 kilometers of optical-fiber cable along four railway lines by 1995.

The lack of a clear-cut regulatory mechanism has resulted in a concession-granting process that mixes what might be viewed as traditional licensing of third-party service providers with the process of subcontracting services by telecommunications operators.

Both TOT and CAT have large work forces entangled with public sector unions, political parties, and other interests powerful in Thai society. Policymakers recognize that the telecommunications sector in Thailand must become an impetus for, and not a barrier to, further growth in the rapidly developing Thai economy. Nonetheless, neither CAT nor TOT necessarily has the dynamism to channel new resources into the telecommunications sector.

Largely in response to rigidities in the existing sectoral arrangements, several years ago the Ministry of Transport and Communications began exploring the possibility of constructing new lines and facilities through a build-transfer-and-operate arrangement (BTO) with an outside contractor. Discussions were begun with several consortia of private investors and, eventually, with the successful bidder, a large Thai conglomerate, Charoen Pokphand (CP). The bid was to install 2 million lines in Bangkok and another 1 million lines outside Bangkok.

CP, which did not have substantial expertise in the telecommunications sector, initially identified a foreign operator, British Telecom (BT), which was to take responsibility for management of the construction project. CP and its foreign partner were to take responsibility for raising construction funds through the international capital market; they hired a financial adviser to take the lead in this process. CP's agreement with the Thai ministry ensured CP a percentage of revenues collected by TOT in compensation for the services provided by CP in installing new lines, raising capital, and providing certain operational and managerial capabilities as well.

This initiative of the Thai government encountered considerable resistance. It was a major point of contention in the spring of 1991 when the Thai military staged a coup. After a long and contentious review process, the agreement with CP was restructured so that CP would take responsibility only for installing the 2 million lines in Bangkok. NYNEX replaced British Telecom as the outside contractor, and the new venture was renamed Telecom Asia. As of fall 1992, Telecom Asia had begun the installation of lines in Bangkok under a renegotiated agreement calling for Telecom Asia to channel 16 percent of its revenues to TOT. The project is estimated to cost US$4 billion. Lines outside Bangkok would be provided through a separate contractor, a partnership of Loxley Bangkok and Jasmine International that is now known as Thai Telephone & Telecommunications (TT&T), which agreed to provide TOT with 43.1 percent of its revenues, reflecting the fact that the services offered by TT&T in rural Thailand are expected to involve a significant percentage of profitable long-distance and international calls.

From the Thai experience it is clear that the BTO option has considerable promise but also presents potential pitfalls. Using contractors permits the mobilization of new sources of capital and expertise to develop badly needed infrastructure. It permits, in particular, new partnerships between the telecommunications operator and private investors, both domestic and foreign. The option allows construction of not only specialized services such as cellular telephone networks, but also of core local switching services. New ventures can be targeted at different segments of the telecommunications operator's network infrastructure.

The scope of ventures to contract for new construction or the operation of new service providers must be carefully delineated. There is no single best way to address such fundamental issues as (a) the scope of the venture; (b) the role of the private contractor in providing operational capabilities; (c) the timing of transfer of new assets to existing entities; and (d) methods of financing the transaction. The most difficult issues are how to integrate new and established operators from an operational and technical standpoint.

Tensions between any new contracting entity and the existing operator can, of course, present serious problems and create opportunities. A new entity could use management and accounting systems for greater efficiency in operation; it can serve as a benchmark for measuring the performance of the existing operator.

As is all too well illustrated in the Thai situation, the successful implementation of an initiative to contract out construction requires a high degree of political support. When this political support falters, so, too, will the new venture. Thus, although the incentive for using new entities might be to bypass existing institutional structures, they can precipitate a political or institutional crisis. In this way, policymakers will be forced to contend with the very forces, those resistant to changes in the status quo, that the new structures were to bypass.

The process of contracting out services to third parties in Thailand has been very much complicated by the government's very ad hoc approach to the task of sectoral restructuring. CAT and TOT continue to encompass a mix of operational and regulatory responsibilities; this confusion of roles will ultimately make more difficult the task of third-party contractors like Telecom Asia and TT&T. The potentially rivalrous relationship between new service providers and existing organizations could create paralysis and indecision as contractor and contractee attempt to work out potentially differing approaches to their respective business objectives. Since TOT and CAT will retain responsibility for setting tariffs, they will continue to have considerable leverage over Telecom Asia and TT&T.

By the fall of 1992, the Thai government had added another element of complexity by requesting advice concerning the eventual privatization of TOT and CAT. Privatization of these two entities will inevitably ensure a more intensive review of the long-term relationship of TOT and CAT as well as of their respective relationships with Telecom Asia and TT&T.

Potential investors in TOT and CAT will certainly insist on a full delineation of sector relationships and policies. Investors in Telecom Asia and TT&T may end up regretting that their significant financial commitments were not made in light of an overview of future sectoral arrangements.

Notwithstanding these concerns, the use of new techniques for infusing private capital and expertise into the telecommunications sector in Thailand and elsewhere in the region may hold substantial promise for rapidly upgrading the infrastructure. Contracting initiatives can be flexible and diverse. Many different operational relationships are available, especially where policymakers hope to mobilize new sources of capital quickly. As sector arrangements in Thailand unfold, it is likely to become ever more apparent that the benefits of contracting out to attract new investment can be thwarted if future sectoral policies are not carefully delineated on a concurrent basis.

Indonesia

Policymakers recognize that the challenge of developing new infrastructure in Indonesia is immense. With a population of 180 million people, Indonesia has a telephone penetration of only 0.7 per 100, far below that in neighboring Malaysia (11.6) and Singapore (47). Telephone density in Jakarta is ten times the national average; however, the waiting list is 80 percent of existing lines.

The Indonesian government has set an investment goal of about US$7.5 billion over the five-year 1994–1998 period in hopes of increasing telephone penetration to 3.2 per 100. Nevertheless, the barriers to achieving this target are very formidable. With an area stretching 5,000 kilometers from west to east and 2,000 kilometers from north to south, only 50 percent of its subdistrict capitals and 25 percent of its 65,000 villages are now served by telephone service.

In Indonesia, as in Thailand, policymakers have been exploring the prospects for developing new infrastructure through contracting out with private entities. These discussions have had some false starts; initial efforts were too limited in scope and involved too many outside contractors. Indonesian officials now appear prepared to address how to structure a relationship with an outside contractor to expand and develop the infrastructure.

The government has taken the position that constitutional and national security considerations require all telecommunications services to be provided by government-owned service providers; however, leeway has been opened for private investment in cellular and satellite services; the government remains committed to finding new ways to increase private investment in the telecommunications sector.

In addition to focusing on new techniques for financing development, Indonesian officials are trying to reform existing institutional arrangements. In 1991, Perumtel, the government department which, until then, had provided telecommunications services, was organized into a wholly government-owned joint-stock company called, PT Telekomunikasi Indonesia (PT Telkom). Any effort to involve new entities in installing infrastructure will be implemented in a framework in which PT Telkom functions as a holding company with ultimate responsibility for providing service to the public.

PT Telkom is exploring a variety of ways of increasing its efficiency and attracting new sources of investment capital. The holding company is being organized into a series of regional companies as well as a long-distance operating company. Each of these companies would have increased responsibility to manage its costs and revenues; central management functions would be reduced and decentralized.

Strategic investors are being sought to participate in these subsidiary companies with an expectation of increased competition among the regional operators. There is also much focus on other financing activities such as issuance of bonds, formation of joint ventures, requiring bonds from subscribers, and even enhanced build-operate-and-transfer schemes.

One of the primary difficulties of various contracting schemes is that they have not provided real impetus to managerial reforms within PT Telkom. As is the case in Thailand, there is an urgent need to integrate effectively the utilization of new techniques for contracting out with a coherent program to restructure the existing telecommunications operator.

PT Indosat, also a wholly government-owned joint-stock company, provides international services via the INTELSAT satellite network and various undersea cable systems. Currently, cellular and paging services are being provided through joint ventures between PT Telkom and two private investors, Elektrindo Nusantara (EN) and Centralindo Panca Sakti (CPS).

In January 1993 a new company, PT Satelindo, was established to provide international, cellular, and satellite services using existing satellite capacity and developing additional capacity for the latter. PT Satelindo is owned by PT Telkom (30 percent), PT Indosat (10 percent), and PT Bima Graha (60 percent), a private company. By 1995 PT Satelindo will take over the operation of the Palalpa domestic and regional satellite system (PT Telkom will continue to operate the earth stations). In its first five years PT Satelindo plans to invest US$800 million, half to develop its domestic cellular business and half to purchase satellite and international facilities, including earth stations and capacity in undersea cable systems. In April 1993 it signed a US$128 million contract with Hughes Aerospace to launch two satellites with regional coverage in 1995. There are no immediate plans to allow foreign participation in PT Satelindo nor for the two (competing) state enterprises, PT Telkom and PT Indosat, to divest themselves of their interests in the new company.

Although the future direction of policy developments in Indonesia remains clouded, some observers believe that a combination of contracting out and competitive entry will be necessary to accelerate investment in a country where overall telephone penetration lags well behind other countries in the region. Such pressures may be an effective way to stir PT Telkom into becoming a more efficient enterprise and to ensure greater responsiveness to the needs of telecommunications users.

Only limited steps have been taken to formulate a new regulatory framework. Some believe it might be preferable to have the emergence of competition control the tempo of regulatory developments. Of immediate concern is the development of programs for overseeing tariffs that create incentives for new investment. Tariff and investment policies in the sector must be freed from political interference through the creation of more independent and stable regulatory arrangements. Multiyear financing plans are essential to increasing efficiency and reducing costs. The government needs a well-concerted plan to exploit new radio-based services to increase local access capabilities.

Another crucial area where reform is required concerns procurement policies. Traditionally, protective government policies kept the cost of service excessively high through import controls and market allocations to existing suppliers. Recently, new suppliers have gained a foothold in the Indonesia market and hold promise for significantly reducing the cost of new installations. As might be the case elsewhere in Asia, regulatory functions and capabilities will evolve in response to sectoral developments; it may not be wise to implant all at once a framework that could overly limit innovation and new entry.

The Philippines

The Philippines is unique in Asia in that its industry structure has been quite fragmented. Other countries in the region have had rather centralized industry structures dominated by government-owned telecom operators. Fragmentation in the Philippines has, along with broader economic difficulties, posed special problems for Filipino policymakers.

Some observers note parallels between the tradition of private ownership and reliance on regulation in the Philippines, on the one hand, and the sectoral arrangements in the United States, on the other; however, the performances of the telecommunications sectors of the two countries are obviously hardly comparable owing to a wide variety of factors beyond the differences in overall economic and political development. There are significant differences as well in both the entrepreneurial and regulatory cultures of the two countries. In the Philippines, private entrepreneurs are deeply entangled in a web of close-knit relationships among well-placed groups with great economic and political influence. Inevitably, such relationships affect both the governance arrangements and the performance of firms within the telecommunications sector.

Telephone penetration is low, with only 1.4 main lines per 100 across the 7,100 islands in the Philippine archipelago. In Manila, the penetration is better, with 8 subscribers per 100, and there are at least 400,000 people on the waiting list. This penetration level is lower than in other major urban centers in the region such as Bangkok; moreover, there appears to be a chronic failure of the dominant provider of domestic telecommunications in the Philippines, the privately owned Philippines Long Distance Telephone Company (PLDT), to make any dent in the backlog, even in urban areas where demand is strong and subscribers have the resources to pay for telephone service. (Penetration in rural areas, by contrast, is only 0.4 per 100.)

In the Philippines, there are several providers of telecommunications service. PLDT operates more than 94 percent of the telephones in the country, mostly in urban areas. Overall, there are more than seventy telecommunications companies in the country; some do not have access to the main network.

Seven domestic record carriers provide domestic telex, facsimile, and leased-line services. Four international record carriers have been authorized to provide international services.

Two international gateways have been authorized to Eastern Telecommunications Philippines, Inc. (ETPI), a company that is 40 percent owned by C&W, and Philippine Global Communications Corporation. ETPI, however, cannot serve customers in most areas of the Philippines, including, in particular, Manila, without interconnection with PLDT. It does have a subsidiary, Digitel, that provides services in several localities, however.

Competition is emerging in satellite services as well. Five companies have been granted permits to provide domestic satellite services. The Philippines Communications Satellite Corporation (Philcomsat) is confined to being a wholesaler of satellite circuits and to dealing with PLDT and other authorized carriers.

C&W, Telstra of Australia, Benpres, and a number of small Philippine investors are considering establishing a US$3 billion joint venture to enter the Philippine domestic market.

Until recently, competition among the various service providers has been highly segmented. Competition has only recently emerged in the provision of mobile telephone services. Other service providers have been seeking to broaden the scope of their franchises to compete in the provision of switched voice services. PLDT, however, has met these moves to reduce its dominance by resisting interconnecting with new service providers. Moreover, controversies over the scope of existing franchises have been hard fought, not only through the regulatory process but into the legislative process as well.

Policymakers in the Department of Transport and Communications created an independent regulatory body, the National Telecommunications Commission (NTC), which is responsible for authorizing new licenses and use of the radio spectrum. Nonetheless, given that the most significant issues are not technical but concern the definition of operational and financial relationships among PLDT and other service providers, the most pressing concerns are beyond the NTC's legal competence. Consequently, the present institutional relationships pose unresolved questions regarding the respective roles of the department and the NTC.

Existing regulatory mechanisms are not strong enough or independent enough to provide an effective forum to precipitate the emergence of competition. In turn, as competition has evolved only slowly, there has been only a limited constituency to convert existing regulatory mechanisms into effective dispute resolution bodies.

As a privately owned venture, PLDT primarily is subject to regulatory and policy guidance from the department and the NTC. PLDT has, however, been plagued by allegations of entanglements with former President Ferdinand Marcos and of affiliations between its shareholders and President Corazon Aquino.

PLDT has been coming under increased pressure to eliminate the growing backlog of requests for service in relatively affluent areas of the Philippines. It has begun to seek increased financial resources in international capital markets. In this process, it is likely that its operations will receive intensive scrutiny from potential investors who are likely to compare the financial performance of PLDT with other telecommunications operators in the region and around the world.

These pressures, along with the challenge presented by new entrants in the Philippine telecommunications sector, will force PLDT to look more critically at its existing tariff structures and internal operations. As pressures increase on the revenue streams generated by international services, PLDT will have to prune its operations and rebalance its tariffs, reducing its dependence on international revenues and seeking new ways to install local access lines very rapidly.

The critical concern for the country is how to create incentives to develop the core infrastructure in the Philippines. The government has had an ambitious investment plan to increase telephone density to 3.5 main lines per 100.

One significant question is how to create incentives for PLDT to invest in rural areas. The company has an economic incentive to focus its attention on serving the large metropolitan centers, such as Manila; it asserts that over 70 percent of its revenues derive from toll calls and, in particular, from international calls. Policymakers are keen to encourage PLDT to extend service to more remote or rural areas served by government-owned telephone enterprises.

Even though PLDT faces a great challenge in serving rural areas, its greatest challenge may be in meeting demand in major urban centers. The overall economic recovery of the Philippines may depend heavily on making modern telecommunications capabilities available to highly educated and entrepreneurially-oriented groups in the Philippines.

There are some interesting parallels between PLDT and TELMEX in Mexico prior to its privatization. Like the preprivatization TELMEX, PLDT is structured as a joint-stock company with significant private investment; has begun to access international capital markets; is highly dependent on revenues from international services and is hobbled by excessively low local tariffs; operates in a political environment highly sensitive about maintaining sovereignty with respect to strategic parts of the national economy. Unlike TELMEX prior to its privatization, PLDT is already nominally in private control, despite its long-standing and significant entanglements with the executive and legislative branches of the government of the Philippines.

One of the future challenges for policymakers in the Philippines is likely to be how to make PLDT more responsive to user needs and more open to external competitive pressures. One option is surely to steadily increase competitive pressures on PLDT and at the same time to recognize the importance of permitting PLDT to restructure itself to deal with these pressures. The difficult transition faced by PLDT might also be facilitated by encouraging it to seek out strategic investment partners; such partners might play a significant role in PLDT, as have foreign strategic investors in TELMEX, within a corporate governance structure that leaves control in the hands of investors from the Philippines.

One of the key roles for strategic investors might be to mobilize resources to ensure the rapid installation of local access lines in major urban centers. Any effort to expand local access lines rapidly might require a resort to innovative financing techniques. For example, PLDT and any new strategic investors might be able to structure new and opportunistic arrangements providing for the installation of local lines through contracting out or franchising arrangements. Policymakers might permit as well the utilization of two-tier pricing for local access lines (or in effect allowing new access lines to be priced on the same basis as cellular telephone services until backlog is reduced).

PLDT has been involved in several exploratory discussions concerning joint ventures or joint investments with foreign operators. In addition, foreign suppliers have been actively pressing to enter into turnkey construction projects outside PLDT's operating territories. Subsidized export funding from their home countries would be managed by the department; broader strategies for encouraging development in the sector have, however, been hindered by the turbulence, both political and economic, through which the Philippines has been passing in the past several years.

As new competitive entrants are established on the scene and as new investors take a stake within PLDT, there may be a new impetus behind efforts to change traditional arrangements through which policy in the telecommunications sector is developed and overseen. There is an inevitable linkage between regulatory reform and increased performance within the telecommunications sector; however, it is very difficult to put an end to old arrangements and begin anew. New competitive structures and influences are likely to beget new governance arrangements, but effective entry cannot occur without new policies in the telecommunications sector.

The challenge for policymakers in the Philippines will be to break a vicious circle of traditional and self-defeating policies. A new consensus among all concerned participants in the sector—among new entrants and PLDT—will be required; PLDT will have to conclude that new policies will benefit it as well as new entrants.

PLDT faces, in fact, enormous challenges that are likely to require basic structural and policy changes. It must meet unfulfilled demand for telephone service to remain the preeminent service provider in the Philippines. To do so, it must compete with other fast-moving telecommunications operators in the region for scarce resources in international capital markets. Simply maintaining the status quo within the Philippines may not effectively enable PLDT to confront the challenges it faces.

Telecommunications Sectors of the Indian Subcontinent

Adding to the complexity of sectoral strategies to reform in the Asian region are the differing situations of the Indian subcontinent. The following discussion touches on approaches being followed in three countries: India, Pakistan, and Bangladesh. In doing so, however, it does not intend to diminish the value of a provocative proposal considered some years back in Sri Lanka, before the present political turmoil and civil strife there, or to ignore early efforts to consider issues of infrastructure development and sectoral reform in Nepal.

India

Over the years, policymakers in India have struggled with the enormous challenge of increasing telephone penetration to the immense and diverse Indian populace and of developing an industrial base in the sector. The results of years of innovative and focused attention on the problems of the telecommunications sector have been quite mixed. Telephone penetration is extremely low (in 1987, there were 0.4 telephone lines per 100 population), and service is not considered to be of high quality. A vigorous debate continues over the extent to which government resources should be devoted to the sector.

In India, the Department of Telecommunications (DOT) both sets the rules for and provides telecommunications services. At the same time, it encourages the manufacture of domestic telecommunications equipment. The issues of sectoral reform are now being reviewed intensively at the highest levels in the Indian government.

More than any other country in the region, India has devoted attention to nurturing the manufacturing capabilities in the telecommunications sector. In particular, Indian policymakers have given the highest priority to developing an innovative switching technology, through its research and manufacturing organization, C-DOT, which is intended for smaller, rural exchanges. In this way, the DOT has encouraged the development of telecommunications services and of manufacturing capabilities. Doing so has fostered favorable conditions for producing equipment domestically, at the expense, however, of constricting the importation of switching and other technologies from abroad.

In the view of many observers, intermingling industrial and telecommunications policies has significantly held back investment and innovation in the sector. They believe that an important first step for the future development of Indian policy is to separate quite sharply the responsibilities for industrial policy and for telecommunications policy. Further, and within that overall approach, the DOT's responsibility for making policies and developing regulations must be segregated from its operation and management of telecommunications services.

For several years, policymakers have attempted to delegate operational responsibility to independent business units within the DOT. Mahanagar Telephone Nigam, Ltd. (MTNL) was established as a corporate entity within the DOT to operate telephone services in Bombay and New Delhi; it was also charged with generating financing through the issuance of bonds. Similarly, Videsh Sanchar Nigam, Ltd. (VSNL) was established to operate international telecommunications services.

These steps toward creating autonomous business units within the DOT have hardly been an unqualified success. Indeed, some observers believe that MTNL has been unable to achieve real operational autonomy and that it has remained subject to close oversight by officials of the DOT. Moreover, MTNL has not been able to retain earnings independently for reinvestment.

VSNL, like its predecessor, Overseas Communications Service (OCS), which was responsible for India's international services, has had a longer tradition of independent operation than that of MTNL. VSNL, however, must provide service to its customers through MTNL and through the DOT in areas outside of Bombay and New Delhi. Thus, despite its regular contacts with the largest Indian and foreign telecommunications users, VSNL has not been able to function along the lines of an entirely independent private sector entity.

Against the background of these only partially successful steps, the Arethyea Committee, a high-level government committee made up of diverse constituencies concerned about the future of the telecommunications sector, submitted its recommendations in March 1991. These recommendations were designed to encourage more regionalization and decentralization in the DOT. The committee recommended that the DOT's operational function be separated into five regional operating companies; a separate group within the DOT would offer services on an interregional basis. The committee also recommended a restructuring of regulatory and policymaking functions within the DOT.

The committee's recommendations, however, have encountered some stiff resistance from employees of the DOT. They have asserted that corporatizing the DOT would oblige the government to incur immediate obligations for accumulated pension rights of the DOT's employees.

Recently, as a result of a new government's coming to power, in June 1991, there has been a broader policy examination of options for the Indian telecommunications sector. These included the possibility of introducing private investment for cellular telephony and value added services. In 1992 the Indian government moved ahead with the process of attracting private investment in cellular telephony systems throughout India; however, after operating rights were awarded to potential new cellular operators, this important new initiative has become seriously bogged down in litigation over alleged improprieties and lack of transparency in the concession granting process.

Several years ago, the DOT had been considering creating an overlay network intended to serve large business users. The objective had been to have users finance the network with up-front subscription fees. This initiative became bogged down and was never implemented.

Currently, the Indian National Railways and the Oil and Natural Gas Commission are developing more sophisticated private networks. Other state-owned enterprises in the manufacturing and services sectors have funneled substantial capital into developing private networks to meet their needs.

In the coming years, policymakers will want to examine how to exploit effectively the need or willingness of large users to invest in telecommunications infrastructure. Certainly private investors would have an interest in investing in ancillary telecommunications services such as cellular telephone networks. Avenues for direct investment in core infrastructure are less clear, however.

For some time, the government of the State of Maharashtra (in which Bombay is located) has been exploring how to attract major Indian or foreign private investment in infrastructure. To date, initiatives to bring new investors into the Indian telecommunications sector have not borne fruit.

Nonetheless, officials in India are more conscious of the fact that many economies in Southeast Asia are growing at a very fast pace, and they realize that telecommunications infrastructure makes an important contribution to this growth. An across-the-board approach to sectoral reform may not work, however, because it might take too long to implement and could stymie initiatives of the most progressive users of the key sectors of the Indian economy. Thus, to the extent that Indian policy recognizes the importance of certain Indian industrial sectors not falling further behind the dynamic economies of the region, the government and the private sector will want to explore seriously how to increase infrastructure investment targeted at high-growth regions and sectors in India.

Policymakers in India will be faced with a serious dilemma of deciding how to get the process of sectoral restructuring under way. The India telecommunications sector is immense; the potential political obstacles to reform seem intractable. An entirely ad hoc approach to sectoral reform may result in a serious misallocation of scarce resources; reform initiatives may not contribute toward the realization of a future workable structure for the telecommunications sector. On the other hand, if immediate steps are not taken and new investment is not attracted into the sector, the policymakers' best vision of well-structured future arrangements may be entirely unattainable; the economic penalty of delay and indecision in adopting new sectoral policies may be incalculable.

Indian policymakers might be well advised to assess carefully some innovative initiatives beginning to be taken in China as a result of administrative decentralization. In China, as the superstructure of administrative arrangements is being reformed on a top-down basis, various initiatives at the local and provincial level are being allowed to flourish. In India, a careful blend of restructuring on a top-down basis—emphasizing more entrepreneurial autonomy and full separation of regulatory and operational responsibilities—and a flowering of new entrepreneurial initiatives within and outside the DOT may be the required prescription for real sectoral reform. Policymakers in India will have to devise an innovative mix of policies to achieve success. There is much in the rich experience of telecommunications restructuring in the Asian region—in the initiatives of policymakers in China, Malaysia, and Thailand—that could contribute toward a workable set of future policies for the Indian telecommunications sector.

Pakistan

As of mid-1991, Pakistan's national telephone company, Pakistan Telecommunications Corporation (PTC), provided access to a telephone to only about 1 percent of Pakistan's population of 110 million. By the end of 1992, telephone density had increased to about 1.5 main lines per 100 inhabitants; density at a level of 1.8 per 100 is projected for the end of 1993. Many observers attribute the increased pace of infrastructure expansion to the conversion of PTC into a corporate entity.

In 1989 the Pakistani government granted two cellular telephone system licenses to two consortia of private companies, the first awards of major telecommunications projects in Pakistan to private entities. A third license was awarded to provide cellular telephony in 1992. Other licenses have been issued to private firms to install card pay phones and paging systems.

Currently, there is active exploration of options to privatize the PTC. In this regard, the approach of the government has resembled that of Latin America: a top-down sale of shares in PTC. It is reported that the government is considering the sale of 25 percent or so of PTC's equity to a private investor.

Until 1992 the government had shown much interest in attracting investors to install infrastructure on a contractual basis. In 1992 the government authorized a special scheme for the installation of 500,000 lines under a contracting arrangement now being implemented. Various turnkey projects are being supported by supplier credits and government guarantees.

Consistent with the path being followed, Pakistani officials are focusing on how to define Pakistan's regulatory framework in detail. Options for structuring a regulatory entity are under review; Pakistani officials seem to be leaning in the direction of establishing a multimember commission rather than an entity like OFTEL in the United Kingdom. One possible result of steps to delineate future regulatory arrangements is that potential investors in PTC may try to limit the scope of potential competition in the telecommunications sector.

As in Latin America, the purchasers of a privatized PTC may seek a significant period of exclusivity for PTC, at least with respect to the provision of switched voice services. Nonetheless, an overly restrictive approach to authorizing entrants may be unwise, in that it could limit the possibilities for attracting investors to build telecom infrastructure.

Pakistani officials must, however, develop schemes for aggregating and deploying capital to build infrastructure. They may wish to avail themselves of the various techniques for infusing new capital and expertise into the telecommunications sector through joint ventures, or through BTO- or BOT-like arrangements, such as are being explored in Thailand and Indonesia.

Bangladesh

Currently, Bangladesh has one of the lowest telephone densities in the world, with 0.2 main lines per 100 population, ranking below China with 0.3, India with 0.5, and Indonesia with 0.5. It is estimated that US$1 billion will be required to raise telephone density over the coming decade by 0.3.

Service is currently provided by the Bangladesh Telegraph and Telephone Board (BTTB). Recent efforts to reorganize BTTB into a fully government-owned public corporation foundered along with efforts to attract private investors.

Policymakers have explored several approaches to encouraging new investment. They had sought to establish a joint venture, known as Banglatel, with C&W to provide international services. Due to resistance within the government, the joint venture could not be effectuated. The government has also attempted to establish three separate privately owned entities to provide telecommunications services in rural areas as well as a private company to provide cellular services.

Notwithstanding these efforts to restructure and reorganize the means by which service is provided, policymakers in Bangladesh have been unable to overcome some severe and fundamental impediments to attract new investment. In particular, an unstable political environment has undermined efforts to encourage private investment into the sector. In Bangladesh neither top-down institutional reform nor initiatives for private investment have been successful.

The Special Case of China

A detailed description of the complex structural arrangements and potential reforms under consideration in China is beyond the scope of this paper. Some observations may highlight a few of the major issues facing China.

The Ministry of Posts and Telecommunications (MPT) provides all public domestic and international telecommunications services, primarily through about thirty provincial posts and telecommunications administrations which coordinate the approximately 350 city Post and Telecommunications (P&T) enterprises. Thirty of these city enterprises are located in the provincial capitals; however, the provincial P&T administrations are separated and distinct from the provincial city P&T enterprises which provide services in the provincial capital. One further step down, around 2,150 county P&T enterprises provide local service in the county capital. These county-level enterprises are grouped, sets of six to eight of them reporting to each city P&T enterprise. Each one of the 2,500 city and country enterprises has rural branches, which together with all kind of cooperatives and Township and Village Enterprises, are in charge of providing services to urban centers lower than county capitals. (Centers administratively lower than county capitals, irrespective of size or population, are termed *rural* in China.)

The telecommunications system is large but consists of mainly obsolete technology, with wide variations among large cities (some of which have the latest technology) and small centers (many county-level installations are old manual exchanges). In 1991, there were about 8.5 million main lines plus around 4.0 million lines in the rural network, giving an overall telephone density of 1.29 percent.

Mobile service is being introduced into China. Competing cellular and radio paging services serve many cities across the country. As to cellular services, a roaming function serves Guangdong, Beijing, and Hong Kong.

The MPT began to reorganize in 1988. The objectives of the reorganization program included decentralization of the MPT in favor of the provincial administrations, accountability for financial performance, separation of regulatory and operational functions, as well as separation of Posts and Telecommunications. The separation of government and enterprise responsibilities is being implemented through the creation of a Directorate General for Telecommunications, which will be in charge of all telecommunications operating activities, a Directorate General for Posts, which will be in charge of all post-related services, and several departments in the central MPT which will be in charge of the governmental responsibilities (regulation, policy, monitoring, etc.). These objectives have been only partially met. Central planning and complex lines of control govern the telecommunications sector. Certain of the wealthier provinces have achieved more independence from central control than have other provinces.

The telecommunications system grew rapidly in the 1980s, reaching a growth rate of 16 percent in the latter part of the decade. The number of main lines grew by 23 percent from 1990 to 1991. Investment in the system reached US$1.5 billion in 1988. In 1989, the MPT achieved an annual rate of return of about 12 percent on net fixed assets in operation. In 1992, the total investment will be Yuan 10.5 billion (US$1.84 billion). The performance of different services and regions varies considerably, with large cross-subsidies both within the telecommunications system and between the telecommunications system and the postal system.

The projected growth of the telecommunications systems during the 1990s is by far the most ambitious development program in the world; the ongoing five-year plan includes an expansion of local networks in the range of 20 million to 25 million main lines, together with around 50,000 kilometers of new fiber-optic transmission lines, and 50,000 kilometers of new digital microwave lines.

In China, as in India, important state enterprises, such as the national railway system, have been channeling significant investment into the telecommunications sector. These efforts are parallel to the investments of the MPT.

The Chinese have taken significant steps to decentralize the provision of telecommunications services. Provincial governments and telecommunications administrations have more responsibility for new infrastructure investment. Special efforts are being made to stimulate telecommunications investment in Special Economic Zones.

At the same time, various management incentives have been put in place to increase staff initiative. Revenues are distributed in accordance with the contribution of particular provincial posts and telecommunications enterprises. Salary is related to total traffic volume of each province. The director of the provincial administration signs a contract—which includes rewards and penalty provisions—with the MPT. Given the system, these measures may be an effective way of stimulating the responsiveness of and growth in the telecommunications sector in China.

Institutional reform has gained increased momentum in recent years. Chinese officials have been open to limited reforms intended to increase the efficiency of the existing operational activities of the MPT. They are becoming more open to considering the introduction of more business-oriented arrangements in the telecommunications sector. Such arrangements could include encouraging the joint development and exploitation of infrastructure by the MPT and other ministries that require high-capacity telecommunications services.

It is possible, in the long term, to imagine that the MPT's operational activities might be organized into a corporate structure. Relationships between the operating entity responsible for long-distance services and providers of local exchange services might be structured through specific tariff arrangements rather than a general division-of-revenues formula. Conceivably, the major regional entities, charged with providing local telecommunications services, might begin to offer services to subscribers in their regions on a countrywide basis.

Recently, prospects for foreign investment in the sector have revived significantly. Decentralization in the Chinese telecommunications sector has opened the door for many innovative arrangements between local operators and foreign suppliers. As of now, foreign participation in the provision of services has been foreclosed, however.

More flexible arrangements for the construction of telecommunications networks and the provision of nonbasic services, such as paging, dedicated business networks, and domestic VSAT services, are now emerging. The MPT, in turn, is becoming more focused on studying tariff arrangements to ensure better alignment of tariffs and the costs of providing different services, including specifically local, long-distance, and postal services. The introduction of commercial accounting principles is being carefully considered. Enterprise and regulatory responsibilities within the MPT are becoming more sharply differentiated. Within individual administrative units, employees are being given greater managerial autonomy and responsibility for expanding the services that they manage.

All of these changes cumulatively are accelerating the pace of change within the Chinese telecommunications sector and enhancing the interest of foreign suppliers and investors in being part of the process of restructuring that is now beginning to gain significant momentum. The immense program of investment in the telecommunications sector of the world's most populous country is being watched with keen interest around the world by suppliers, investors, and other telecommunications administrations.

A Survey of Developments and Suggested Policy Options in Asia

Several observations can be made about the diversity of approaches to reform and restructuring being pursued in Asia. These are not meant to be an exhaustive catalogue of options for reform. They do, however, suggest some trends that observers may wish to follow more closely in the years ahead.

Focus on Service-Based Competition in the Four Tigers

First, it may be appropriate to focus on the most highly developed economies (other than Japan) in the region. In Korea, Singapore, Hong Kong, and to a lesser extent, Taiwan, where significant investment in infrastructure already has been made, the cutting-edge issues will center around opportunities for service-based competition. Businesses have more flexibility in how they may use leased circuits. Providers of service to third parties increasingly will be able to offer a wider range of nonvoice services. Nevertheless, restrictions on foreign investment, even with respect to value added services, remain in place in Korea and Taiwan. The Koreans have committed to lifting their restriction. The restrictions in Taiwan will unquestionably become the subject of tough, trade-based demands for further liberalization.

Global competition for managed data and voice services will continue to evolve in the 1990s. As they seek to provide such services, the well-entrenched and capable telecommunications operators of Singapore and Hong Kong will be subject to intense pressures to permit the provision of a wider spectrum of services, including public-switched voice services, in their home markets.

Steps toward Corporatization and Privatization

Second, the globalization of the telecommunications business will force profound changes in the very organizational and financial makeup of the most advanced players. In particular, telecommunications operators such as Singapore Telecom, Korea Telecom, and the Taiwanese DGT (or CTC, its corporate successor) will aggressively seek to overhaul their institutional and capital structures.

Currently, Singapore Telecom is the furthest along the road to privatization. Korea Telecom, to a much greater extent than the Taiwanese DGT, continues to operate in a climate unreceptive to the establishment of global operating companies with international capital structures. Even Telekom Malaysia operates in an environment that accords first priority to generating private investment capital from domestic sources.

Investment in Asia by strategic investors, such as the Bell operating companies or the major European PTTs, has been spotty to date. Obviously, very significant investments have been made in the non-Asian, Pacific countries of New Zealand and Australia. NYNEX has a very significant project in Thailand. Other foreign companies are actively pursuing opportunities for cellular service in Korea, Taiwan, and elsewhere in the region. Equipment suppliers are seeking to extend their reach into the construction of networks or the provision of service. Foreign investors are, no doubt, eyeing with great interest the opportunities and strategic advantages that a potential investment in Singapore Telecom or, to a lesser extent, Telekom Malaysia might present.

If investment opportunities in the economies of the Four Tigers or Malaysia do materialize for foreign investors, they would probably be made available on a restricted basis. Unlike the Latin American (or Australian or New Zealand) cases, it is unlikely that operators in any of those countries would surrender control to a single foreign investor, or even to a consortium of investors. Instead, privatization will be seen as a mechanism for strengthening emerging domestic capital markets.

New Techniques for Introducing Private Investment

Third, countries such as Thailand and Indonesia have shown themselves to be more open to foreign investment. They have very low rates of telephone penetration, however. In such countries, officials are exploring techniques for introducing private investment through various contracting initiatives. Such techniques are not yet fully developed, and they have generated substantial political controversy, in Thailand, for example. Contracting initiatives confront policymakers with a significant set of issues: how to define the scope of new ventures; the relationships between new and established entities; and the techniques for dividing revenues among existing service providers and new operators.

There may be promise in using these new techniques in tandem with efforts to reform existing arrangements on a top-down basis. In Indonesia, Perumtel has been converted from a public corporation into a limited liability company; however, it is a truism that a mere change in legal status does not necessarily result in changes in the performance of the institution.

In Thailand, rationalizing the operational functions of CAT and TOT is a formidable task. Consequently, using a contracting arrangement may be an effective mechanism to implement a new investment program while encouraging the introduction of management practices and techniques from the "bottom up." Time will tell, in India, for example, whether the government will rely on private firms to accelerate investment in the sector.

New Approaches to Infrastructure Development: The Tinkertoy Model

Fourth, where existing institutional arrangements are not efficient at attracting the investment capital required to increase network penetration, policymakers may choose to explore new techniques for introducing investment in the sector. What may work in one country, where infrastructure has been developed through a single provider, is not necessarily optimal for other countries in the region.

In India, China, and other countries, large public and private sector enterprises are channeling resources into developing and maintaining parallel private networks. Hence, one method for encouraging investment may be to permit use of private networks on a more liberal basis. In other words, infrastructure might be developed in a "Tinkertoy" fashion—by adopting liberal policies regarding the interconnection of those private networks with one another, and with the basic network provider.

Top-Down and Transitional Techniques for Reform

Fifth, a top-down approach to sectoral reform can be quite successful. This much is evident from the Malaysian experience with privatization. Nevertheless, the process of institutional reform obviously cannot be accomplished overnight; full implementation can take years. Thus, interim or transitional arrangements to accelerate investment into the sector may have substantial merit.

Importance of Maintaining a Political Commitment to the Reform Process

Sixth, sectoral reform requires political commitment and will, and it can be difficult to implement. The Malaysian experience strongly suggests how deeply rooted economic policies favoring across-the-board privatization are able to assist in effectuating reforms in the telecommunications sector. The turbulence in Bangladesh is striking evidence of how even incremental reforms favoring limited private sector investment can be thwarted without political consensus.

Thus, in countries where private investors can invest in the telecommunications sector, a high-level political commitment is usually needed to sustain the effort. Critical to the success of reforms, therefore, is the leadership not just of officials in the telecommunications sector, but also of economic advisers and others concerned about overall economic performance. Undoubtedly, a broader approach to reform of the sector is important to ensure that privatization initiatives do not inadvertently result in policies that are overly protective of the existing provider, unnecessarily limiting the potential for new entrants and investment in the sector.

Pricing and Sectoral Investment Policies

Seventh, Asia has some truly striking examples of countries that initiated massive investment programs in the telecommunications sector. Korea doubled the percentage of its national output devoted to the telecommunications sector. Taiwan has doubled its level of sectoral investment in the past year. Singapore Telecom has generated huge surpluses that are being reinvested in the telecommunications sector. Its successful investment program is closely related to the careful structuring of tariffs to generate necessary investment capital.

Policies to Promote Competition as a Pragmatic Tool to Increase Investment and the Efficiency of the Existing Operator

Eighth, an important implication of the foregoing discussion is that new entry and the prospect of competition may be promising tools for attracting new investment and encouraging increased efficiency by established providers. To date, experience in Asia (essentially, in Japan) with vigorous, across-the-board, facilities-based competition is quite limited.

In Malaysia, where the government has issued a number of local service and international gateway licenses, there is scope for some facilities-based competition to develop. Foreign investment in the new facilities-based providers as in the various cellular and paging operations is not excluded; however, there are no clearly defined rules for the time being on the limits of foreign participation. In Indonesia, the new international and cellular operator PT Satelindo is poised to compete aggressively with PT Indosat internationally and PT Telkom (through an extensive cellular network) domestically, even though the latter owns 40 percent of Satelindo itself.

In India, international and domestic services are served by separate operating entities within the DOT. There, too, it is conceivable that eventually VSNL, the international provider, could be permitted to diversify and become an alternative carrier serving, in particular, large business users.

The rationale for greater reliance on competition in Asia might well be pragmatic rather than ideological. New entrants are an attractive source of capital and expertise. Moreover, competitive pressure on existing operators may accelerate the process of institutional and sectoral reform.

Here, a further point might be noted with respect to some of the new techniques—such as contracting out to other entities—for introducing private investment into the telecommunications sector. Established operators may principally choose to use outside contractors as sources of capital and expertise. Policymakers may choose to restrict such contractors from offering service directly to end users; contractors' lines and facilities would be absorbed by existing operators. Conversely, contractors ultimately might be permitted to provide services directly and independently to end users. Given the possibility of their providing such services directly to users, new contractors may well be seen as, or actually become, a form of potential competition to the existing operator.

The Structure and Timing of Regulatory Reform: Getting the Horse in Front of the Cart

Finally, it might be appropriate to offer a few observations about the evolution of regulatory procedures and policies in Asia. In hardly any of the economies of Asia can it be said that new regulatory mechanisms have fully or effectively developed. In the Philippines, there is the NTC; however, the NTC has not demonstrated that it is capable of coping effectively with structural difficulties in the telecommunications sector.

In Malaysia, which has successfully moved ahead with a privatization program and established a regulatory body within the Ministry of Energy, Posts and Telecommunications, the regulatory scheme is not yet fully articulated. As new service providers emerge, a more fully-developed regulatory scheme may also evolve.

Clearly, if competitive entry is to become an important tool for developing new infrastructure and encouraging existing operators to become more efficient, officials will have to think through and develop effective frameworks for regulation. Policymakers have several regulatory models from which to choose. The contrasting situations in Australia and New Zealand present illustrative paradigms.

In New Zealand, a laissez-faire approach toward the development of new regulatory institutions has been adopted. A consciously pro-regulatory stance was adopted in Australia with the creation of AUSTEL. Until the emergence of recent disputes over such matters as interconnection arrangements between TCNZ and the new entrant, Clear Communications, New Zealand policymakers had been quite content to rely on the more general principles of competition law embedded in the Commerce Act; they had felt no need to create a new regulatory body. As competition is burgeoning in New Zealand, however, pressures are growing for more specialized mechanisms for resolving the inevitable disputes that arise (and that have arisen).

Putting in place adequate regulatory arrangements in Asia does not, however, necessarily mean that great emphasis should be placed on establishing new regulatory institutions. Institution building need not necessarily precede or displace the development of new regulatory procedures and techniques for dispute resolution.

Careful attention must also be paid to the timing of creating new regulatory arrangements. It is by now conventional wisdom that privatization cannot be implemented successfully without clarifying the basic regulatory framework. In the most successful recent privatizations in the telecommunications sector, all the details of a future regulatory scheme have not been spelled out in detail. This was certainly true in Malaysia. In Mexico as well, the government shied away from immediately creating a new regulatory body.

Some of the major lines of policy must, of course, clearly be identified in the privatization process. Investors must know what the future ground rules for the sector will be. Clarity and transparency are critically important in privatizing.

Nonetheless, all this is not to say that a successful privatization requires a guaranteed fixed term of exclusivity for the existing operator. Potential investors may ask for such exclusivity to shore up their investment; the government's outside advisers may find it in their own and their client's interests to advocate such protection to enhance the price at which shares in a to-be-privatized entity can be sold. Granting excessively long periods of exclusivity to an operator—or, arguably, any period of exclusivity—may not represent sound sectoral policy.

Perhaps more important than delineating every last element of a regulatory scheme is creating a predictable process for the evolution of future regulations. Thus, one could question whether countries now beginning to explore options for privatization, Pakistan being one example, are well advised in seeking to create, at the outset, an entirely new and complete regulatory entity as an essential component of the privatization strategy.

Conclusion

From a telecommunications point of view, Asia certainly is full of promise and great diversity. There are, most obviously, considerable differences among the economies of Asia. Some have robust economies. Others are among the poorest on earth. Some have modern and rapidly expanding telecommunications infrastructures. Others have extremely low rates of penetration.

The most advanced economies will continue to become fully integrated into the global economy. As such, they will face increasingly strong pressure to allow ever more liberal arrangements for service-based as well as facilities-based competition.

Elsewhere in the region, pressures to keep pace with the Four Tigers—and to the economies in close pursuit—will create a climate that could be quite favorable to innovative techniques for attracting new investment into the sector. In this regard, Asia could well become a dynamic testing ground for new approaches to privatization. Although there will be top-down privatizations in Asia, such as Malaysia and, potentially, Pakistan, Asian countries are unlikely to follow blindly the models that have been used in Latin America.

Means of encouraging new actual or potential competitors in the sector will be important to accelerate development. At the same time, policymakers will have to devise appropriate regulatory initiatives for the new financing techniques or approaches to competitive entry.

Regulatory structures for Asia in the 1990s cannot be lifted from a hornbook based on the experience of the United States or other Western countries that have taken steps to introduce competition. Innovation and creativity in developing new regulatory and institutional arrangements will be essential to the success of sectoral reform in Asia.

At the end of the day, Asia will develop its own techniques for and unique approaches to sectoral reform. What was done in Latin America, Europe, or North America in recent years will not be the only models for the region. Rather, in Asia the emergence of an extraordinarily diverse set of economies will test the mettle of government officials, existing operators, would-be and new entrants and investors throughout the coming decade.

9

Telecommunications Reform in Australia

Michael J. Hutchinson

IT IS AN ACCEPTED FACT THAT TELECOMMUNICATIONS are now an essential component of any country's infrastructure as well as an important contributor to economic growth and well-being in both developing and industrial countries. This is true both for the domestic economy and in relation to international competitiveness. There is also a common perception that national access to basic voice telephony is not so much a privilege, or even a discretionary commercial service, but a right. Finally, telecommunications is an important and growing service and equipment industry in itself. All countries of the Asia-Pacific region, including Australia, have these issues in common.

In Australia, far-reaching and major decisions on the future structure of the telecommunications sector have recently been made and are currently being implemented. These are the latest in a series of structural reforms in telecommunications designed to bring price and service benefits to both business and residential users as well as to increase Australia's capacity for participation in regional and global telecommunications activity.

This chapter explains what these reforms are and why Australia has made such significant changes at this time. Its perspective is that of a policy adviser to the government.

Telecommunications in Australia: Background

Until 1975, domestic telecommunications services were provided in Australia by a traditional PTT, the Postmaster-General's Department. International services were provided by a separate government-owned authority, the Overseas Telecommunications Commission (later OTC Ltd.), which had been formed in 1946 through the government's acquiring the overseas-controlled entities that had previously provided the service.

Postal and telecommunications functions were separated in 1975. Two statutory authorities, Australia Post and Telecom Australia (Telecom), were established in recognition of the need to manage separately the distinctly different requirements of the two sectors for capital, labor, and technology. Both organizations were placed outside the direct administrative structure of the government. At this time, and for some time subsequently, the principal telecommunications policy focus was extension of universal service. This posed particular problems for Australia outside the major urban centers. Population is sparse, distances are vast, and climate and terrain can be unfriendly.

The next major structural change occurred in 1983, with the establishment of an independent, government-owned national satellite system, AUSSAT. For the first time, many residents in rural and remote areas of Australia gained access to radio and television broadcasting services. Telecom faced limited competition on its trunk telephone and data services from the private network services now made possible by AUSSAT which also had the scope to operate internationally within and between third countries.

At the time of these institutional and structural changes, in the mid–1970s and early 1980s, the need and scope for anything more than limited competition in telecommunications did not appear great. Recommendations in the Davidson Report of 1982 for limited competition were not proceeded with.

Since then, however, the perceptions of all industry participants—government, carriers, users, private service providers, manufacturers—have changed significantly. This has been due to rapid changes in technology, an increase in quantity and diversity of demand (essentially a shift from a seller's to a buyer's market), the increasingly international nature of the industry, and the rapid economic growth of the Asia-Pacific region.

Since 1983, the Australian government has placed the highest priority on restructuring key areas of the economy, including financial markets, manufacturing, transport, and communications. In general, the approach to economic reform has involved:

- Institutional reform of government business enterprises through:

  - Corporatization

  - Changes to incentives

  - Changes to performance measures

- Structural or policy reform through:

  - Regulatory changes

  - Changes to the competitive environment

- Industry policy.

The Department of Transport and Communications has policy responsibility for a significant part of the economic reform agenda, including telecommunications and postal policy, broadcasting, aviation, as well as maritime and land transport.

Telecommunications Reform: 1987–1989

By 1987, basic telephone access had been achieved on a near Australia-wide basis, and the domestic and international networks were well developed in terms of facilities. Policy change focused on the broader significance of telecommunications was (and is) still a key concern of the government. Some of these newer issues were referred to by the managing director of Telecom Australia, Mr. Mel Ward, at the World Bank Seminar on Restructuring and Managing the Telecommunications Sector, held in Kuala Lumpur in 1987.[1] At that time Australia had just embarked on a major review of telecommunications policy.

The outcome of this review in 1988 was a series of measures to:

- Clarify government policy objectives for the sector

- Separate the policy, regulatory, and operational functions, and place them with the Department of Transport and Communications, a new independent regulatory authority, and the carriers, respectively

- Increase the commercial focus of the carriers through new accountability measures and removal of unnecessary constraints

- Provide for competition in value added services and customer equipment, but not, at this time, in network infrastructure or basic services.

Regulatory arrangements at this point were largely concerned with clarifying and maintaining the boundary between monopoly services reserved to the carriers and other services. Central to these arrangements was the establishment of the Australian Telecommunications Authority (AUSTEL) as an independent regulatory. AUSTEL commenced operations on July 1, 1989. It has a chairman and two members, all government appointees. AUSTEL operates under the general policy direction of the minister for transport and communications, but is otherwise an independent authority.

The major functions of AUSTEL at present are: technical regulation, particularly in relation to customer equipment and cabling; policing of the boundary between monopoly and competitive services; protection of competitors from any unfair practices of carriers; consumer protection; and promotion of carrier efficiency. AUSTEL has also undertaken, at the direction of the government, a number of specific investigations into areas of possible policy change, including third-party resale and public mobile telecommunications services.

Overall, the existence and activities of AUSTEL have received industry support, and have helped to keep telecommunications reform an issue of general interest.

New Export Focus

In parallel with this more commercial emphasis, both major carriers and the private sector had begun to increase export and offshore activities. Telecom and OTC established international marketing arms as subsidiary companies: Telecom Australia (International) in 1986, and OTC International in 1987. These subsidiaries were established to concentrate on export of world-class telecommunications services and facilities from or through Australia. They operate on a fully commercial basis, but their activities have also had a significant positive impact on technology transfer for developing countries. This occurred outside the traditional aid framework and is operating to the mutual benefit of Australia and other countries in the Asia-Pacific region.

Telecom Australia (International) is active in major facilities installation and management projects in Saudi Arabia and Pakistan, the latter in conjunction with Australian manufacturers. OTC International participates in projects ranging from network management, equity investment and development (for example, the Pacific Area Cooperative Telecommunications Network and a ten-year development program in Vietnam) to joint venture participation in major markets such as Thailand (digital satellite data) and Hong Kong (telepoint services). These activities have been complemented by the regionally-oriented export work of Australian manufacturers. Close relationships have been established with telecommunications enterprises throughout the world, but especially in the Asia-Pacific region.

Telecommunications Reform: 1990–91

It was never envisaged that the reforms of 1987–89 would mean a fixed regulatory environment. In particular, the 1987–89 package recognized that the separation of satellite and terrestrial telecommunications facilities, as well as that of domestic and international, in separate enterprises would be increasingly unsustainable in the face of technological developments and market demands. The pressures for change continued, and the government initiated a comprehensive review of structural arrangements. Australia was mindful of the increasing investment requirements of the telecommunications sector and the need to remove barriers to participating in the growing regional and global markets. It has become evident over the last two years or so that many other Asia-Pacific countries have also moved to address these issues, although of course each country has different needs and circumstances and hence will tailor its approach to these.

As Australia sought lessons from the experiences of other countries, it became clear that concepts such as deregulation and privatization had relevance only as elements of a comprehensive set of policy measures—in particular, the appropriate change mechanisms for an entrenched market structure. The acceleration of efficiency gains and sustaining of ongoing modernization on a commercial basis would not occur without genuine scope for competition, hence the need for stringent safeguards and requirements for equal access, at least in the initial phase. The interests of ordinary consumers would also require special regulatory attention.

In November 1990 the Australian government announced its intention to introduce wide-ranging network competition into the telecommunications industry. There are several important elements in the move to full competition by 1997:

- To establish, by the end of 1991, a transitional facilities duopoly based on a merged Telecom/OTC (known initially as AOTC and now as Telstra) and a privatized AUSSAT (now known as Optus)

- To provide procompetitive safeguards, including equal access and interconnection between the carriers

- To issue three public mobile telephone service licenses, one each to Telecom/OTC and the second carrier, and a third to be issued by the end of 1992

- To remove restrictions on third-party resale

- To introduce full competition in the provision of public access cordless telephone (telepoint) services.

Reasons for Australia's Policy Changes

A number of factors were taken into account by the Australian government before the changes described above were taken.

Universal Service

Considerations of universal service and equity remain very important. Australia was fortunate enough to achieve a high level of basic telephony coverage at a time when the monopoly operator could concentrate on that task and ordinary telephony services were overwhelmingly dominant in the service repertoire. The continued provision of such services to all users remains a key government policy, so that some noncommercial element will continue to be involved for the carriers. This noncommercial element comprises the community service obligations (CSOs), which must now be managed in a competitive environment. The annual cost of such CSOs in Australia is estimated at A$250 million. This compares with total annual telecommunications revenue of A$9.4 billion.

Australia has explicitly recognized and accepted the economic costs of continuing universal service policies through cross-subsidy funding. Although we have determined that this is affordable and sustainable within a competitive industry at our established high level of telephone ownership, such conclusions may differ depending on the geographic structure and national development level in other countries. Burdening commercially viable customers with unduly onerous charges to sustain disproportionate cross-subsidy costs in extending universal service from a lower basis or at higher costs might actually serve to inhibit overall network development by retarding the achievement of economies of scale among economically viable connections.

Australia has examined several possible approaches to funding the delivery of the various types of CSOs (universal service, concessions to disadvantaged groups, and emergency services). With regard to universal service, the government decided that Telecom/OTC would be obligated to continue providing a standard telephone service (including pay phones) between places within Australia. The cost of universal service would be met by the carriers, with the second carrier being required to pay Telecom/OTC a fee which covers an equitable pro rata share of the cost of fulfilling the universal service obligation.

This is an area where Australia has carried out a considerable volume of research and analysis, including a 1990 Bureau of Transport and Communications Economics study on the funding of Telecom's CSOs. Some further background material on a related decision is attached (see the Annex included in this chapter).

Investment Sourcing and Resource Allocation

Like many countries in the Asia-Pacific region (both developing and industrial), Australia recognizes that the requirements of the telecommunications sector are now so great, and the global market so influenced by very large-scale players, that previous approaches to funding of expansion must change. Australia's liberalization of its policy regime is aimed in large part at attracting world-class expertise and capital to ensure continued growth in services and facilities. Although Telecom/OTC is and will remain a world-class operation, it needs a competitive domestic commercial environment to stimulate expansion. The task is to keep pace with a global market increasingly dominated by large carriers, some of the largest of which, according to recent reports, are examining further strategic alliances for the purpose of attracting outsourcing of international corporate networks.

The resource allocation issues involved in an industry of the size and complexity of telecommunications are, in the Australian case, only capable of resolution through competitive market mechanisms. This represents a logical evolution of the industry and is consistent with international and regional trends.

Put simply, the capital needs of a modern telecommunications system are now such that prudent allocation from public sector sources requires augmentation from equity capital raised in the private sector. Such sources are available from both domestic and international capital markets. If they are not tapped to develop public, common carrier, networks, they will be tapped to develop private networks to meet business needs. Australia's policy allows for appropriate access to such capital through the privatization of AUSSAT as the seedbed for the second network provider. It welcomes international investment, while retaining the incumbent carrier in public sector ownership and assuming eventual majority national ownership of the second carrier.

Development of Australian Manufacturing

Government policy aims at developing an Australian telecommunications manufacturing industry which is world competitive. We already have a sound manufacturing base covering transmission and switching equipment (including optical-fiber cable) and terminal equipment. Development of the value added services sector, where Australia has established comparative advantages in software applications and network management, is a complementary priority. The export activities of the carriers have been referred to previously. A competitive environment which removes any restrictions on access to the world's best technology will ensure that the current trend in the Australian industry to increased exports, as well as research and development, continues on the scale (qualitative as much as quantitative) necessary to be internationally viable.

Acceleration through Trade

There is growing international recognition that the main barriers to increased trade in telecommunications services and goods are the telecommunications policy regimes that apply. Australia is conscious of being a part of the fastest-growing telecommunications market in the world, the Asia-Pacific region, and is approaching the issue at several levels.

First, we are mindful of the potential benefits which would flow from a successful outcome to the current GATT Uruguay Round negotiations. Australia is prepared to work toward an appropriate international framework for telecommunications market access within this context, but such a framework will clearly depend on progress within the Uruguay Round as a whole.

Second, Australia will continue to pursue regional and bilateral policy consultations with a focus on the benefits of liberalization.

Finally, from the perspective of Australia as exporter, we believe that the unilateral policy liberalization undertaken will mean that the benefits of a competitive domestic market flow on to Australia's export activity in terms of pricing and product innovation. To this end, Australia supports liberalization in both the bilateral and multilateral contexts.

The public debate that preceded the government's recent major decisions was extensive and focused on a wide range of factors. Inevitably, the question of telecommunications reform became a sensitive political issue. Although the nature of the debate may have reflected Australia's unique political, social, and institutional structure, its intensity also reflected the importance of telecommunications to the whole community in a situation of near-universal availability of service.

Implementation Issues

The implementation of the major reforms announced in 1990 is proceeding according to plan. The first stage, involving legislation to put in place the new regulatory framework and to merge Telecom and OTC (AOTC)[2], was completed on July 1, 1991.[3] The second stage, involving the sale of AUSSAT and licensing of the second carrier, Optus Communications, was decided on November 22, 1991, and finalized on February 2, 1992. Some particular issues of implementation are noted below.

Strengthening the Independent Regulator

AUSTEL was established in 1989 as an independent statutory authority with overall responsibility for economic and technical regulation of Australia's telecommunications industry. The chairman and members are government appointees. AUSTEL currently has a staff of approximately 140. Its major functions to date have been technical regulation, promotion of fair and efficient market conduct, and consumer protection. The general industry perception is that the independent regulator model has worked successfully in Australia to date.

AUSTEL has a specific mandate to promote competition within the regulatory framework established by the government. This includes a detailed monitoring role and arbitration between the carriers where commercial negotiation is unsuccessful. AUSTEL will ensure that arrangements for interconnection, access to network and customer information, billing practices, and other level-playing-field practicalities are equitable between the carriers, and that the incumbent carrier does not derive unfair market advantage from its dominant position.

AUSTEL has recently assumed primary responsibility for managing Australia's input to the setting of international telecommunications standards and will have the role of preventing the misuse of market power by international carriers supplying services to and from Australia.

Interconnection and Equal Access

AOTC is required to provide the second carrier with interconnection on a directly attributable incremental cost and equal access basis. AUSTEL, at government direction, is currently inquiring into the economic, commercial, and technical considerations of this requirement. The importance of this part of the reform package is evident from the fact that the merger of Telecom and OTC was not permitted to proceed until AUSTEL had certified that interconnection and equal access arrangements were fully in place in all capital cities and that there was an agreed timetable for finalizing such arrangements in provincial cities.

There appears to be general agreement that charges for the use of network facilities should be separated from those for actual interconnection; that charges should reflect underlying costs; and that pricing principles should encourage the second carrier to invest in new facilities where such facilities could be provided at costs which are lower than those presently being achieved. The basis for assessing directly attributable incremental costs and cost categories to be included have been set out in the Telecommunications (Interconnection and Related Charging Principles) Determination No. 1 of 25 November 1991.

Australia is determined that experience elsewhere, where effective competition has been delayed by legal and commercial disputes about efficient equal access and interconnection arrangements, will not be repeated. Much effort was therefore devoted toward having fair and efficient equal access arrangements in place, ready for the second carrier to take up in accordance with its proposed network rollout program. On January 14, 1992, AUSTEL certified to the minister for transport and communications that interconnection and equal access were either in place or sufficiently advanced. The AOTC network was conditioned to allow Optus to provide competitive dial code access using the "1" prefix. Network modernization is being implemented to provide for universal equal access and preselection. AOTC and Optus have made substantial progress in developing an access agreement, and AOTC has been instructed to resolve remaining issues in a time frame suited to Optus' plans to provide services.

Powers and Immunities

Government-owned monopoly carriers generally have a range of legal powers and immunities that have been granted to them in recognition of their public service role and the need to install facilities expeditiously. Although in principle having as few special provisions as possible applying to telecommunications, it can be argued that specific powers and immunities are needed in the short term to facilitate the building of a network by the second carrier and to enable AOTC to adjust to the new environment. Significant issues include application of planning, development, and environmental laws; limitations on liability in tort; and powers of land acquisition and access. In the transition to competition, the question arose of whether to remove or modify such powers and immunities or whether to extend some or all of them to the second and subsequent carriers. This is particularly relevant in Australia with respect to state and local government laws and immunity from suit. Australia has now adopted a unique approach to these issues, by balancing the carriers' immunities from state and local planning laws with a national planning code. This is intended to ensure that carriers give appropriate consideration to environmental and other factors when engaging in network rollout activity. The government has also removed the wide immunities that the carriers enjoyed with respect to the general tort and contract law. This has been replaced with a simple cap on tort liability to be determined by AUSTEL.

Selection of the Second Carrier

The process of selecting the second carrier began in earnest during the first quarter of 1991. A preliminary stocktaking of expressions of interest during November 1990 to January 1991 allowed the government to take into account interested parties' views before finalizing the policy framework. The list of interested parties included some of the world's leading telecommunications companies as well as some enterprises new to the industry.

The government then issued an information memorandum and an invitation to submit detailed proposals. Following assessment of these, shortlisted parties were invited to negotiate contracts and submit tenders for the acquisition of AUSSAT and the right to operate the second carrier. This process was finalized on January 31, 1992, with the winning consortium, Optus Communications, taking control of AUSSAT and beginning to offer services shortly thereafter.

The Optus consortium, which has been guaranteed a duopoly environment for noncellular services until mid-1997, consists of BellSouth (24.5 percent), Cable & Wireless (24.5 percent), and Optus Pty Ltd. (51 percent), in which the principal shareholder is Australia's Mayne Nickless Ltd.

The consortium paid the government an up-front amount of US$395 million, with payment of US$120 million due in 1995 and 1996. Optus has also estimated a total expenditure of A$3 billion over the next five years to build and operate a domestic and international telecommunications network to compete with AOTC. Optus has planned to offer initial service in the Sydney-to-Melbourne corridor, with nationwide coverage promised by 1996. Optus will also offer resale cellular services in 1992 and then move to its own network in 1993.

Australia and the Asia-Pacific Region

The Australian approach to telecommunications reform must be seen in its regional context. The Asia-Pacific region is an area of significant real and potential growth. This is a region where the total telecommunications market is expected to grow to US$178 billion by 1995, with an annual growth rate of nearly 10 percent. It is a region where international call traffic within the region and to other parts of the world is expected to grow by more than 25 percent per annum over the next few years. Total traffic growth is estimated to be in the order of 33 percent per annum at present.

What are the policy implications of this for governments? At a recent conference in Bangkok organized by the Asian Development Bank and the Asia Pacific Telecommunity,[4] it was apparent that many Asia-Pacific countries, some at widely differing stages of economic development, are focusing on similar policy issues. Australia sees itself as integrally involved in this regional movement.

It can be argued that the more traditional approach to telecommunications development—first building up basic telephone services and only then moving on to more sophisticated infrastructure, boosted by development assistance and differential accounting rates for international calls—is no longer a sufficient model. On this view, the financial and human capital needs of the sector are so great in both quantitative and qualitative terms that government policy measures will increasingly need to focus on the benefits of a competitive regulatory environment and scope for private sector development, but always tailored to specific country needs. Complementary to this would be a continuing need for targeted aid to assist sectoral restructuring, of the type currently provided so successfully by the Asian Development Bank, the Asia Pacific Telecommunity, the International Telecommunication Union, and the World Bank.

The key to maximizing the region's growth potential in telecommunications is greater trade in services and equipment through policy liberalization as well as the freer flow of capital and management skills which will follow. The countries of the Asia-Pacific region are moving to develop their own approaches. Some current examples of this might include the Philippine approach to private sector participation; Indonesia's provision for cooperative ventures in basic services; and the managed transition to competition in the Republic of Korea.

As part of this process, Australia is involved with its neighbors in the region in mutually developing this industry, both government-to-government and at the commercial level. Telecommunications policy issues are increasingly on the agenda of regional forums such as the Asia Pacific Telecommunity (APT), the Asia Pacific Economic Cooperation forum (APEC), and the ASEAN-Australia Forum. Australia has taken a significant role in structural reforms of the APT to ensure that its activities are of value to developing countries within the region.

The recent visit of the Australian minister for transport and communications to Japan and the Republic of Korea emphasizes the complementary role of bilateral policy relationships in this area. Telecommunications policy issues will be an important agenda item for the forthcoming Australia-Japan Ministerial Council.

The objective of both multilateral and bilateral policy consultations is discussion and analysis of common issues and exploration of the areas in which growth can be encouraged through the ongoing policy change in which all countries are engaged.

Annex: Main Findings of the Interdepartmental Committee on CSOs in Telecommunications

The main findings of the committee were as follows:

1. In a number of public policy statements during 1990, the government reaffirmed its commitment to meeting the present level of delivery of community service obligations (CSOs), particularly to rural and remote areas, to pensioners and to people with disabilities.

2. The government's decision on the continued application of price caps to Telecom Australia (Telecom) provides the means of ensuring that connections and call charges continue to be available at generally affordable levels. To the extent that there are groups within the community which the government believes should receive additional financial assistance for their telephone costs, these can be most effectively and appropriately assisted through the welfare system.

3. CSOs provided by Telecom can be divided into three broad groups: universal service (that is, access to a standard telephone service, including pay phones); emergency services; and concessions (to the disabled and charitable organiza-

tions). Government-provided CSOs involve telephone rental concessions to pensioners and a telephone interpreter service.

4. There are four broad approaches to ensuring the future delivery of CSOs:

    - Imposing a requirement on carriers to fulfil obligations as a condition of license *without* compensation

    - Imposing a requirement on carriers to fulfill obligations as a condition of license *with* compensation

    - Competitive tendering for the provision of CSOs

    - Allowing carriers to charge for all services, including CSOs, on a full cost recovery basis, and compensating subscribers through the provision of direct or indirect financial assistance.

    These options are not mutually exclusive.

5. It is not axiomatic that Telecom would discontinue the provision of loss-making CSOs in a competitive duopoly market. There are sound commercial reasons for supplying loss-making services (provided the losses can be absorbed):

    - To support a good corporate citizen image

    - As a "loss leader," that is, for strategic marketing reasons.

6. The committee, however, took the view that, to ensure delivery of CSOs that government felt were vital for national policy reasons, it would be necessary to provide a general authority in legislation with detailed requirements specified in carrier licenses.

7. The concessions currently provided by Telecom to people with disabilities and charitable organizations may be continued by Telecom in the new competitive environment, either to support a good corporate citizen image or because of clear marketing advantages. The continuation of specific concessions, however, could be ensured by government through legislative provision or license conditions or through directly targeted assistance via, for example, welfare or social programs. Action to make them an obligation on Telecom may then require the recognition of direct or indirect compensation for those concessions specified.

8. Given that Telecom may choose to continue to provide many of the currently available concessions without any explicit obligations, it is preferable that the

specification of concessions as a condition of license be minimized in the first instance. Further concessions could be specified as obligations should Telecom choose to drop those regarded as socially important by the government, or alternative means of provision investigated (for example, through social welfare programs).

9. Telecom and the second carrier should both have obligations placed on them as part of their license conditions to ensure that emergency-service-related activities continue. Compensation should not be provided to either carrier for this activity; it should be regarded as a standard function of a carrier.

10. With respect to the universal service obligation, the committee noted that, should a carrier not be compensated for loss-making services, it will seek to cross-subsidize those services. It recognized that there are drawbacks to continued funding of CSOs by cross-subsidy.

11. The best available information indicates that the annual net cost of continuing to maintain obligations currently provided by Telecom would be around A\$250 million (A\$237 million for loss-making services [that is, access to the standard telephone service], A\$8 million to A\$10 million for concessions, A\$4.5 million for emergency services). Considerably more work needs to be done by Telecom, however, to properly identify loss-making services and their actual net costs.

12. Two broad options for funding CSOs, which are not mutually exclusive, are largely independent of the delivery options:

    •   Funding from general revenues, and

    •   Industry funding (carrier levy, user levy, or cross-subsidy).

13. Some form of carrier levy is the most obvious mechanism for ensuring that the second carrier contributes directly to the cost of CSOs on a pro rata basis (as required by the government's decisions). Imposing a levy on interconnection from trunk routes to customer access networks is one practical alternative. A levy based on revenue from each carrier's reserved areas may constitute a more competitively neutral form of funding. Adoption of the broadest possible base would also minimize distortions to the pricing of particular services.

14. A carrier levy imposed by the government would be considered a tax and may therefore need to be paid into consolidated revenue in the first instance, with subsidies to Telecom/OTC then being provided through appropriation of consolidated revenue funds. As a consequence, budget revenues and expenditure would be increased.

15. In the longer term there may be a need to review delivery and funding arrangements for CSOs adopted by the government during this phase of implementing carrier competition, in light of the impact of competition on consumer prices and carrier behavior. This would ensure that the arrangements remain consistent with the government's social and economic policy objectives.

16. Before any compensation is given, Telecom must be required to specifically identify any loss-making services. The onus of proof must be placed on Telecom, and the costing procedure would need to be consistent with the long-term avoidable cost approach which has been adopted by government as the best measure of costs. The option for the government to put the provision of any individual or combination of services to competitive contract should be explicitly kept open in order to give Telecom an incentive to minimize costs. The timing and implementation of such contracting should be decided by government, following advice from AUSTEL. Although competitive contracting may not be practical until significantly more information is available and the second carrier is established, equivalent information should still be required from Telecom before any compensation is paid.

17. The introduction of carrier competition will not affect the Telephone Rental Concession Scheme, which is funded on budget (A$48 million per annum). This scheme should continue to be funded in this way.

Endnotes

1. Mel K. Ward, "The Australian Perspective," in *Restructuring and Managing the Telecommunications Sector,* ed. B. Wellenius, P. A. Stern, T. E. Nulty, and R. D. Stern, A World Bank Symposium, Washington, DC, 1989.

2. In April 1993 AOTC changed its name to Telstra.

3. The legislative basis for the regulatory framework, which came into operation on 1 July 1991, comprises seven Acts of Parliament. These are the:
Telecommunications Act 1991
Australian and Overseas Telecommunications Corporations Act 1991
Telecommunications (Carrier Licence Fees) Act 1991
Telecommunications (Applications Fees) Act 1991
Telecommunications (Number Fees) Act 1991
Telecommunications (Universal Service Levy) Act 1991
Telecommunications (Transitional Provisions and Consequential Amendments) Act 1991.

Subsequently, a range of subordinate legislation was also made, including the carrier licenses and ministerial determination on interconnect pricing principles.

4. "The Information Age: Challenges for the Telecommunications Sector in the Asia Pacific Region," Bangkok, Thailand, March 19–22, 1991.

10

An Alternative View of Australian Telecommunications Reforms

Henry Ergas

THERE ARE MANY SIMILARITIES BETWEEN the path taken in Australia and that taken by other countries engaged in telecommunications reform.[1] But there are also important differences, and while learning from the mistakes of others, we have made mistakes of our own. It is worthwhile to try to draw out the pattern of our experience and place against the context it defines the issues and choices which are still open.

One feature dominates this pattern, and that is the progressive disengagement of the Commonwealth of Australia from responsibility for providing telecommunications service. The Commonwealth, while retaining ownership of the telecommunications carriers, has sought to distance operating responsibility for these entities from direct ministerial and departmental control. This process of disengagement has operated at three fundamental levels.

A first step in this respect was taken in the mid-1970s, with the creation of Telecom Australia and of Australia Post as statutory authorities out of what had been the Postmaster-General's Department. Since then attempts have been made to replace *ex ante* administrative controls over individual decisions taken by the carriers with *ex post* accountability for performance, judged in terms of the objectives set down by legislation and the commitments entered into between the Commonwealth and the carriers' boards. Second, while shifting from controls over the carriers' day-to-day decisions to controls over their outputs, the Commonwealth has increasingly viewed competitive markets as the best judge of what these outputs should be and as the best gauge of the carriers' efficiency. Here too, the process began well before the latest round of reform, with the liberalization of several terminal equipment markets in the early 1980s. Lastly, as the carriers have been thrust into competitive markets, the Commonwealth has acted to strip them of responsibility for market regulation, largely by transferring the relevant powers to independent regulatory agencies, most notably AUSTEL.

Though analytically distinct, these three layers have in practice been interdependent, and it is their interaction which has most powerfully shaped the change process. Four factors have been at work. The first is that the Commonwealth, by distancing itself from the carriers, made it easier to expose them to the disciplines of competition. Once these entities were separated from the central machinery of public administration, the commercial elements in their charter gained greater prominence, reducing any claim they might have on exclusive access to consumers. The Commonwealth could, after all, hardly stress that the carriers were and would be judged as businesses, while at the same time denying their consumers the freedom to choose. The decentralizing impetus of developments in telecommunications technology therefore found a receptive environment.

Second, competition, once allowed, developed a momentum of its own, straining at the boundaries initially imposed upon it. In retrospect, it is difficult to see how it could have been otherwise. The technology was steadily blurring the regulatory distinctions between service classes and making a nonsense of the fine lines drawn between public and private networks, while its impact was reinforced by a normal commercial dynamic in which firms, struggling to establish themselves in the difficult markets open to competition, sought the comfort of those larger and more lucrative markets still reserved to the established carriers.

Third, these pressures to further liberalization were more readily accommodated because of the change in regulatory arrangements, notably the setting up of AUSTEL as an independent authority. This, in effect, made it more difficult for the carriers to stop the market-opening process (and it is certain that they would otherwise have come under intense pressure from the unions to do so), while also placing at least a bit of distance between the government and the sometimes difficult choices which needed to be made. And there were, here too, important elements of mutual reinforcement: each successive liberalizing step increased the desirability and legitimacy of truly independent regulation, strengthened the constituency for further change, and though perhaps too slowly, boosted the confidence of the regulators in the change process.

Fourth and lastly, and closing our feedback loop, liberalization made it all the more urgent for the government to review, and where possible relax, those remaining direct controls which limited the carriers' flexibility and hence their ability to survive and prosper in a competitive environment; in equal measure, liberalization also seemed to reduce the need for these controls, since the carriers' decisions would be tested by performance in the market, surely a better standard than that set by administrative fiat.

The interaction of these forces has created powerful pressures, but from the outset, the response has hardly been smooth or continuous. Governments have, in particular, found it difficult to strike a balance between a genuine intellectual commitment to standing back from the carriers' day-to-day decisionmaking on the one hand, and their desire to retain a significant degree of control over the carriers on the other.

Three factors largely explain this discrepancy. The first is what Professor Max Corden, a distinguished Australian economist, has described as the "conservative social welfare function." This phenomenon, hardly specific either to Australia or to telecommunications, refers to the reluctance of communities to accept changes which, though they may increase aggregate or total welfare, will make, or threaten to make, some individuals absolutely worse off. In the specific circumstances of Australia's telecommunications system, the desire to avoid these changes, or to assure the community that they will be avoided, has led governments to intervene in management decisions, notably as regards pricing, which appeared justified on commercial grounds.

The second factor underpinning the Australian government's difficulty is conflict in policy objectives. This involves differences both between the government's macroeconomic and microeconomic goals, and among its microeconomic goals. The macro/micro conflict is straightforward and centers on access to resources: the government faces continuing pressure to reduce its call on national savings and to moderate the growth of labor costs; it wants to ensure that the states discipline the behavior of their statutory authorities in these respects; and it believes that the states will only curb their authorities if the Commonwealth does the same. The Commonwealth has therefore retained a high degree of control over the carriers' borrowing levels and labor practices and has, in a number of instances, used these controls to impose outcomes quite different from those which the carriers, acting freely, would have chosen. At the heart of the micro/macro economic conflict lies the tension between promoting competition on the one hand, and protecting individual competitors on the other. Established carriers enter competitive markets with considerable advantages which only a long period as an incumbent monopolist can confer, most notably control over the essential facilities associated with the customer access network. The normal protections which trade practices legislation provide to competitors may well seem too weak to avoid the misuse of this market power so that special safeguards, and associated regulatory mechanisms, are required to allow competition to develop. This, in turn, implies a network of controls which primarily limit the behavior of the established carriers, controls which at best sit uneasily, and at worst conflict, with the goal of encouraging the carriers to act in a robustly competitive way. The strains this creates have, most recently, been accentuated by the specific manner in which competition is being introduced. The decision to link the selection of a second carrier with the privatization of AUSSAT forces difficult choices about how the government's continuing role as owner of Telecom and OTC, and the powers and responsibilities inherent in that role, can be reconciled with the understandable desire to see this privatization succeed. These are, inevitably, troubled waters, and though they will doubtless settle once the process is complete, they have great potential to damage the goal of statutory independence and board accountability highlighted above. In short, the government has retained elements of its hands-on role both so as to protect itself from community backlash, and because it has proved useful in advancing its sometimes conflicting policy goals; but there is also a third factor at work.

This third factor is the natural reluctance of government to relax administrative controls before competitive forces are sufficiently well established to act as an effective alternative source of discipline. The perceived risk is that management, freed from any real constraints, could waste the community's resources in capacity expansion schemes which, though superficially appealing, would, at best, fail to cover their opportunity costs and might, at worst, make it more difficult for competition to establish itself in the market.

Taken on its own, each of these factors involves a good deal of common sense, and their interaction creates formidable obstacles to advancing toward greater real independence for the established carriers. Yet progress in this respect is both possible and desirable; indeed, it could be argued that it is central to the next stage in our telecommunications evolution.

Further progress is indeed possible. Competition is likely to establish itself relatively quickly in significant parts of the Australian market, thus reducing the rationale for continuing controls over the established carriers. This is for three primary reasons. The first is that the government has put in place a framework of competitive safeguards which anticipates and solves in advance many of the difficulties which have hindered the establishment of competition in the other markets where liberalization has been attempted. Taken together with the strongly liberalizing provisions of the legislation, notably the requirement on the carriers to unbundle a broad range of the services they provide, this framework should significantly reduce the lead time involved in the transition to competition and allow an early move to a fully commercial market. A second reason has to do with the selection of the competing carrier. In the United Kingdom and the United States, the transition to competition involved entry by players with little experience of major common carrier markets and whose financial resources were slight relative to the task they were taking on. In contrast, the winning consortium in Australia involves major foreign carriers, which, though they are generally monopolists in their own markets, have similar or even greater technical resources than the incumbent carrier and (partly thanks to their monopoly cash flows) ready access to finance. It is only natural to expect that this will be reflected in a more rapid erosion of the incumbents' bottleneck control, an erosion made all the surer by the government's decision to allow full and unrestricted resale, at least in the domestic market. Finally, the fact is that the Australian market involves relatively powerful and sophisticated major customers, well aware of the range of services and service options available in competitive markets overseas, and who are already gearing up to shift suppliers should this prove worthwhile. And though Australia's own carriers have significantly improved their performance in recent years, there remains considerable scope for a new provider to offer attractive packages to these customers and hence gain a solid foothold in the market.

Taken together, these factors mean that the development of workable competition in Australian telecommunications will be measured in years rather than, as in the United Kingdom and the United States, decades. The discipline this provides will, in turn, erode the three primary grounds for retaining direct controls, namely the desire to avoid a community backlash, the need to check the abuse of market power, and the concern about possible wasteful use of resources by the carriers.

All of this makes a further move away from direct government involvement in the industry not only possible, but also increasingly desirable. This is primarily because the greatest benefits of liberalization come not from the inroads made by the entrants but from the improved performance by the incumbent. In no country have the entrants secured more than 15 to 20 percent of the market as a whole, and even in the Australian circumstances they are unlikely to secure much more. What really counts for improved economic performance are, consequently, the efficiency gains made in the remaining 80 percent, that is, in the market held by the established carrier. Securing these gains requires not only effective competitive pressures but also that the incumbent carriers be free to respond to the incentives competition creates. This is hardly possible in an environment of extensive regulation and of direct government controls.

How, then, should the government respond to this changing environment? What are the priority areas for action and the concrete implications for policy? Any realistic answer to these questions must distinguish two levels of government involvement, namely as regulator and as owner. As regulator, the government should exercise restraint, regulating only where competitive forces are too weak to provide the disciplines needed. This principle is well reflected in our new telecommunications legislation; it needs to be fully built into the regulatory arrangements now being devised. The goal should be to move as quickly as possible from a regime of special regulation for telecommunications to reliance on the general, economywide protection of competition policy.

Inevitably, the government's role as owner is more controversial. The logic of the argument above implies a need for a more hands-off stance, one closer to that which generally characterizes the governance of large corporations. Yet it is appropriate to ask whether the government as owner can or legitimately should act in that way. Doubts as to whether it can are consistent with our experience. It is not to be cynical to recognize that governments will use all the policy levers at their disposal to achieve their dominant objectives and that the enterprises they own inevitably form part of the armory on which they can rely. Even when they recognize the long-run costs this entails, these costs often seem outweighed by the stakes which immediately confront them.

But there are also broader issues involved, issues which will increasingly come to the fore as the industry's environment evolves. The commanding factor here is the changing nature of the carriers' capital requirements. Two elements are fundamental. To begin with, the arrangements now being defined, notably for the financing of community service obligations (CSOs), socialize the supply of the capital needed for the noncommercial parts of the infrastructure, transferring the primary funding burden from the Commonwealth to the users.[2] Thus, even in this extreme area, the argument that provision of the social infrastructure requires continued public ownership will therefore lose the force it may once have had.

At the same time, it will prove increasingly difficult to justify relying on taxpayer-provided equity for many of the investments the carriers will quite rightly want to carry out. Competition will increase the risk these investments entail, and it is by no means obvious that these risks should be borne by taxpayers rather than by investors freely choosing to take them on. Nowhere is this dilemma likely to be greater than in the international sphere. It is clearly desirable for our carriers to invest overseas, just as we are welcoming foreign investment into the Australian market. But can taxpayers be asked to supply the equity needed for the carriers to do so? As the industry globalizes, these questions will inevitably become more pressing.

Conclusion

It is no easy task to try to look at the picture of our telecommunications environment as a whole. The processes I have described are still under way, and as complex and uncertain as ever. But I would venture one lesson and one forecast.

The lesson is that in the longer run, the market, like love, laughs at locksmiths. In Australia, as elsewhere, much time and effort was devoted to trying to delineate sharp boundaries between areas open to competition and those reserved to the carriers. Far more quickly than any of us could have imagined, those graphite fine lines proved as fragile as they were elegant, a fate which, I would suggest, history reserves for those who follow in our ways.

The forecast is that the next five years of our telecommunications policy will be dominated by the need to allow our carriers the freedom to compete and the resources required to do so. Unless this issue is resolved, we will not reap the full benefits of the competitive environment we have labored so hard to obtain.

Endnotes

1. This chapter is an edited version of a paper, "Australian Telecommunications: Four Years On," presented by the author at the July 1991 International Institute of Communications Telecommunications Forum in Sydney.

2. Much remains to be done in the field of community service obligations, most urgently to continue and extend the efforts Telecom has already made to ensure an acceptable level of service provision to the Aboriginal community.

11

Telecommunications Liberalization and Privatization: The New Zealand Experience

Hunter Donaldson

DURING THE LAST FEW YEARS, NEW ZEALAND has undertaken a major program of regulatory reform of its telecommunications sector. The objective of this program has been to promote economic efficiency by exposing the telecommunications sector to increased competition. Although implementation of reform has not been without its difficulties, there is clear evidence of benefits being gained by both residential and business consumers.

Economic Environment

During the 1960s and 1970s, the New Zealand economy was characterized by a wide range of controls, regulations, and interventions. The effect of these was to encourage investment by the private sector in areas that were not always the most valuable from a national perspective. In addition, direct government involvement in the economy had increased to unprecedented levels. The performance of the state trading activities, which included such diverse activities as coal mining, banking, forestry, and postal and telecommunications services, was in general very poor. In particular, the 1986 Mason/Morris Report found that the New Zealand Post Office, which provided postal, telecommunications, and banking services, had an inefficient operating structure, inadequate information systems, and a tendency for tariffs to be influenced by political considerations. In 1986, the net return to the government on its NZ$20 billion investment in all productive sectors was zero. Given the size of the government sector, increased efficiency was necessary if the state of the economy as a whole was to be improved.

In 1986, the government announced plans to corporatize a number of government trading departments. The new corporations, known as state-owned enterprises, were set up with independent boards of directors, adequate capital structures, and a proper level of indebtedness. Most importantly, they were required to operate on a fully commercial basis, capable of earning profits and of paying dividends and tax to the government. Social considerations became the direct responsibility of the government, not the enterprises; where appropriate, the government paid explicit

253

subsidies to the enterprises to maintain a social service. At the same time, regulatory and commercial functions were separated.

The largest department affected, the Post Office, was split into three state-owned enterprises: New Zealand Post Limited, Telecom Corporation of New Zealand Limited (TCNZ), and Post Office Bank Limited. Policy and regulatory functions, previously handled by the Post Office, were transferred to the newly established Communications Division of the Department of Trade and Industry (now Ministry of Commerce).

Following corporatization and a major sectoral review by consultants, in December 1987 the government announced the progressive and full deregulation of the New Zealand telecommunications sector. This process, which had begun in October 1987 with the liberalization of residential wiring and continued with that of telephone sets in May 1988, culminated in April 1989 with the abolition of the statutory telecommunications monopoly. In 1989 the possibility of privatizing TCNZ was examined and the regulatory regime was revised. TCNZ was fully privatized in 1990.

Regulatory Reform

In order to maximize the efficiency of the telecommunications sector, an environment was created that would facilitate fair and open competition throughout this sector. To this end the telecommunications sector has been fully deregulated.

Prior to 1987, the Post Office enjoyed a statutory monopoly for the provision of all telecommunications services. The Telecommunications Act 1987 provided that from April 1, 1987, the telecommunications sector would be subject to progressive and extensive deregulation, including the market for customer premises equipment. To ensure that equipment connected to the TCNZ network will not interfere with the performance of the network, TCNZ requires users to obtain a TCNZ permit. Equipment is independently tested in accordance with a series of Comité Consultatif International Téléphonique-based standards (CCITT Recommendations) before a permit is issued.

The Telecommunications Amendment Act 1988 removed the statutory monopoly held by TCNZ for the provision of public-switched network services from April 1, 1991. Competition is now permitted in the provision of all telecommunications services. There are no restrictions on the number of entrants to the market. With the exception of specific provisions relating to TCNZ, there are no specific controls on foreign shareholding in telecommunications entities in New Zealand.

The Telecommunications Act 1987, as amended, provides designated network operators with certain rights of access to land, and in particular the road reserve, to lay or construct lines where this is required to commence and carry on a telecommunications business. Companies are declared network operators by means of a statutory process, once they have met the criteria specified in the Act.[1] The Broadcasting Act 1989 extended the scope of the network operator designation to include cable broadcasting operations.

New Zealand does not have a telecommunications regulatory body. The approach is rather to rely on general competition law, the Commerce Act 1986[2], the consumer protection provisions of the Fair Trading Act 1986, and two industry-specific measures established by the Telecommunications Act 1987 to promote competition. These measures are the Telecommunications (International Services) Regulations 1989 and the Telecommunications (Disclosure) Regulations 1990. The Commerce Commission has the responsibility for the enforcement of the Commerce and Fair Trading acts. Both acts also provide for private legal action.

Under the Telecommunications (Disclosure) Regulations 1990, TCNZ is required to disclose information relating to prices, terms, and conditions of the provision of certain specified services, and is also required to publish financial accounts for its regional operating companies as if they were separate and unrelated companies. The purpose of the regulations is to provide potential and actual competitors with the level of information that is generally available in a competitive market and that is necessary to make a decision about entry into the market. This information also assists the monitoring of TCNZ's conduct.

The Telecommunications (International Services) Regulations 1989, which apply to operators providing international services in New Zealand, require uniform accounting and proportional returns of traffic. In this way, the regulations ensure that overseas operators with monopoly privileges in their own domestic markets do not play off one New Zealand carrier against another to the detriment of New Zealand customers (also known as whipsawing).

The government's involvement as the main provider of telecommunications services ended on September 12, 1990, when it sold TCNZ to a consortium of New Zealand and American buyers for NZ$4.25 billion. Bell Atlantic and Ameritech were the American partners in this consortium. The two U.S. companies which purchased 100 percent of TCNZ were joined in the consortium by Freightways Limited and private interests associated with Fay, Richwhite Limited undertook to purchase nearly 9.70 percent of TCNZ by September 1993. At the time of the sale the government established two specific conditions on the future shareholding in the corporation. These conditions were:

- A ceiling of 49.9 percent on the shareholding of any foreign buyer (although provision was made for a larger shareholding to be acquired, provided it was reduced to 49.9 percent within three years, with allowance for an extension of one additional year. This extension was agreed upon in 1993).

- A requirement that at least NZ$500 million worth of shares must be made available by public offering on the New Zealand market.

In July 1991, a large parcel of TCNZ stock was released on the New York, London, Sydney, and New Zealand markets. Interest was high and the stock issue was substantially oversubscribed. In the period July to August 1991, the TCNZ shares, which had a New Zealand issue price of NZ$2.00 per share, were traded in the range of NZ$2.25 to NZ$2.37. By the beginning of February 1992 their price had risen to NZ$2.64.

In March 1993, Bell Atlantic reduced its shareholding from 34.17 to 29.56 percent with the sale of 108.9 million shares to the sharebroking firm Barclays de Zoete Wedd (BZW) for NZ$2.56 per share. BZW undertook to sell a portion of these shares on the New Zealand share market. Bell Atlantic was required to reduce its shareholding to 24.95 percent by September 12, 1994. The sale of the remaining 4.61 percent shareholding necessary to achieve this, was accomplished when Fay, Richwhite and Freightways took up their remaining shareholdings in September 1993, as agreed at the time of privatization.

BZW undertook to offer at least NZ$17 million worth of the shares on the New Zealand stockmarket. In fact, it offered NZ$29 million worth thereby fulfilling the condition established by the New Zealand government at the time of privatization that at least NZ$500 million worth of stock had to be publicly offered on the New Zealand stockmarket. At the time of the public float in 1991, NZ$483 million worth had been offered in New Zealand. Thus, total New Zealand stockmarket sales exceeded NZ$500 million.

In March 1993, Ameritech's shareholding remained at 34.17 percent and it had until September 12, 1994 to reduce its shareholding to 24.95 percent. In July 1993, it sold 4.61 percent, or $108.9 million shares, to U.S. interests (the Capital Group) at NZ$2.86 per share. In September 1993, a further 4.61 percent was sold to Freightways and Fay Richwhite which in turn sold a significant portion of their shareholding in the same month at NZ$3.82 per share to institutional buyers including the American fund manager, the Capital Group, which now owns more than 5 percent of TCNZ.

The resulting shareholdings in TCNZ were as follows:

24.95%	Ameritech
24.95%	Bell Atlantic
1.24%	Fay Richwhite
2.06%	Freightways
46.80%	Other parties
100.00%	

Although the New Zealand government is no longer a shareholder in TCNZ as such, it has retained a "Kiwi" or golden share. This has special voting rights enabling the government to control the maximum shareholding of any single foreign party and to ensure that TCNZ's Articles of Association obligations relating to residential services remain in place. Under its Articles of Association, TCNZ is required to ensure that:

- Free local calls (that is, included in the fixed rental) remain a tariff option available to all residential callers

- Standard residential line rentals do not rise faster than the rate of the consumer price index, unless the profits of the Telecom regional operating companies are unreasonably impaired

- Line rentals to residential customers in rural areas will not be higher than in city areas

- The residential service will be as widely available as it is at present.

In order to facilitate competitive entry in telecommunications and broadcasting, and to promote efficiency in spectrum use, the government has established a new regime for the management of the radio spectrum. The Radiocommunications Act 1989 provides for market-based allocation of spectrum management rights of up to twenty years, and for the transfer and subdivision of such rights.[3] It is the government's general policy that where the demand for such rights or licenses exists, supply of these rights will be tendered. The Ministry of Commerce is responsible for the planning and creation of these rights and, where necessary, for the tendering process. The Ministry of Commerce recently tendered the spectrum bands available for cellular telephony and is planning to tender frequencies suitable for land mobile services.

Effects of Deregulation

The benefits of competition to the consumer are evident in terms of lower prices and a greater variety and better quality of service. The impact of competition can be seen in the increased level of productivity by TCNZ, in the emergence of a number of entrants into the telecommunications markets, and in the overall increase in the level of economic activity in this sector. The government itself has benefitted in terms of dividends and taxes paid by TCNZ as well as from the proceeds of the sale of what is now a modern and efficient company.

Effects on Consumers

Overall, consumer's telephone bills have markedly declined in real terms. In accordance with TCNZ's policy of aligning its charges to cost, TCNZ has in the period since deregulation increased the standard residential rental while reducing domestic long-distance charges. According to the Department of Statistics telecommunications price index, between December 1986 and March 1991 residential telephone rentals (including purchase and connection fees) have risen in real terms by 23 percent, while residential call charges have fallen by 43 percent. At the same time, greater flexibility in charging has been introduced by replacing the three-minute minimum charge for toll calls with a one-minute minimum charge with one-second rounding for subsequent time periods; offering greater discounts for off-peak toll calls; basing tariffs on traffic volumes rather than on distances; and introducing off-peak rates for a number of international destinations.

Businesses in most areas now face charges for local calls on a timed basis and this is to be extended to remaining areas. Local call charging may also be introduced as an option for residential calls. However, under the terms of the sale, free local calls must remain an option for residential customers. TCNZ is also to begin a concessional service for the elderly.

Consumer benefits have also been derived from a better performance by TCNZ in the maintenance and repair of the network. Fault rates in Wellington are down from 11 faults per 100 circuits per month to 4. Directory assistance answering times are down from an average of several minutes to an average of 17 seconds, while handling times have also dropped from several minutes to 30 seconds or less.

Installation times are another factor in customer satisfaction. In 1985, an average of 15,000 customers were waiting, at any one time, for a new connection, and the average waiting period was six weeks. Today, there is virtually no queue and the average waiting time is usually three working days.

Effects on TCNZ

The formation of TCNZ as a state-owned enterprise had an initial significant impact. TCNZ was established with commercial objectives quite different from those prevailing in the old Post Office. Accordingly, TCNZ was restructured with a modern and accountable corporate structure. To this end four regional telephone companies were formed as well as an international company and a number of new venture companies. TCNZ became a holding company for these new operating companies.

The likelihood of increased competition in the initial phase of the deregulation process, and latterly with the emergence of real competition, prompted TCNZ to undertake a program to lower its costs, rebalance its tariffs, and improve its quality of service.

In order to reduce costs, TCNZ embarked on streamlining the company's operations. Staff levels have been reduced from nearly 26,000 in the old Post Office days to the current level of less than 12,700. TCNZ announced at the beginning of 1993 that it will reduce staff levels further, down to 7,500 by 1997. Many of the maintenance and support services which TCNZ previously provided in-house are now supplied by contractors (many of them former employees). The inventory levels have also been greatly reduced.

TCNZ has undertaken a heavy program of investment in new cabling and equipment to upgrade its network, including in provincial and rural areas. Between 1987 and 1993, NZ$3,500 million has been spent on this program, with the result that a very high proportion of the network is now digital and the overall service performance has risen dramatically. This program has also resulted in the introduction of new services, including an 800 toll-free direct dialing service, cellular services, and electronic paging. TCNZ now operates one of the most modern telecommunications networks in the world.

Competition in Customer Premises Equipment

The number of suppliers of telecommunications equipment has grown rapidly, which has resulted in an increase in the variety of models available and a substantial decline in prices. In 1986, the Post Office was the sole purchaser of telecommunications equipment in New Zealand, and the range of equipment made available to consumers was extremely limited. Following deregulation on April 1, 1987, the customer premises equipment market has developed into a very competitive sector. The price of a basic handset has more than halved since early 1988. Car phones have fallen in price dramatically since 1988, to levels which are at least 10 to 15 percent cheaper than similar equipment available in Australia and the United Kingdom.

Network Competition

Currently four companies have been designated as network operators under the provisions of the Telecommunications Act of 1987, as amended. Of these, Clear Communications has emerged as the leading competitor for the provision of network services. Clear Communications, a consortium of local and two North American companies (MCI and Bell Canada International), commenced its business of providing national and international telephone service in early 1991. The company utilizes facilities owned by New Zealand Rail Limited and Broadcast Communications Limited (BCL), two of the local owners, and is investing in its own facilities. It expects to gain a substantial market share of both residential and business customers from TCNZ, due to its more flexible charging systems and its price discounts. Securing interconnection to the TCNZ network is a test of the effectiveness of the regulatory environment. To this end, a Memorandum of Agreement, signed between TCNZ and Clear Communications setting out the broad principles of interconnection to TCNZ's network, has been working effectively in practice.

Competitive pressure is also emerging from the providers of a number of other telecommunications services. For instance a number of suppliers are offering packet-switched services, data services, and electronic mail, using both TCNZ's and their own facilities.

Cellular Services

At present TCNZ is the sole provider of cellular services. Despite this, the market for the provision of mobile services is strong because TCNZ sells radio spectrum utilization time to a number of wholesalers who in turn sell it to their customers. As of February 1993, 97,000 subscribers were connected to this network, which has been growing at the rate of 1500 per month.

A further development has been the interest shown by potential competitors in the cellular telephone market. The recent tender of cellular spectrum resulted in Bell South's acquiring the TACS A band, with which it intends to provide a digital GSM (Groupe Speciale Mobile) system when the technology becomes available. TCNZ is currently providing analog services on the AMPS A and B bands, and it has recently also introduced a digital AMPS service. In accordance with the provisions of the Radiocommunications Act 1989, TCNZ holds the management rights over these bands. The Ministry of Commerce is currently tendering the management rights for the TACS B Band.

Effects on Telecommunications Manufacturing

Faced with reductions in the level of tariff protection as part of general industry deregulation and the end of compulsory local purchasing by TCNZ, domestic telecommunications manufacturing has been substantially reoriented. This has resulted in a leaner, more efficient, competitive export-oriented industry. The value of telecommunications equipment exports in 1990-91 was three times as high as in the preceding year.

Conclusion

Overall, the New Zealand experience with regulatory reform of its telecommunications sector has been positive and, with the emergence of real competition, this is expected to continue. The program of regulatory reforms in telecommunications undertaken in New Zealand has provided significant benefits to consumers and to the economy in general. Although the process is complete in terms of legislation, not all of its impact has been felt as yet. To date the major effect has been through the improved efficiency of TCNZ due to the prospect of competition. Now, with the sale of TCNZ and the emergence of competition in network services as well as other areas, other improvements in price and quality of service can be expected.

Although the reform process has clearly provided positive gains, there have been certain costs. Jobs have been lost as TCNZ rapidly streamlined its operation, although other jobs have been opened up in competing companies and within the industry, but to a lesser degree. Also, many consumers feared a loss of services, such as free residential local calls and universal access to the telephone network. Undertakings such as those provided in TCNZ's Articles of Association have to a large part allayed such fears, and consumers overall now enjoy a cheaper telephone service than they did prior to reform. Businesses are enjoying benefits in terms of lower prices, a more reliable service, and the introduction of advanced telecommunications services.

Endnotes

1. The Telecommunications Act 1987 contains sector-specific powers necessary for the conduct of business. With amendments it constitutes a rather modest document of fewer than twenty pages.
2. The Commerce Act 1986 is New Zealand's general competition law. Part II of this act prohibits (a) contracts, arrangements, and understandings that substantially lessen competition; (b) exclusionary provisions and price fixing; and (c) use of a dominant position for the purpose of restricting, preventing, or deterring or eliminating a person from a market.
3. This method was chosen to bring in market forces in determining the most valuable use of radio frequencies as well as to allow rapid response to changes in technology and consumer demand.

12

Restructuring the Telecommunications Sector in Sri Lanka: Review of Progress 1988–91

Vernon Watson

THE RESTRUCTURING OF THE TELECOMMUNICATIONS sector in Sri Lanka has been under way since 1985, following the recommendations of a Presidential Commission of Inquiry to report on the reorganization of the Sri Lanka Department of Telecommunications (SLTD) to meet the demand for improved and expanded services. The principal recommendations of the commission were to reorganize the operating functions of SLTD into an autonomous enterprise, establish a regulatory body for telecommunications, and permit other operators to offer services to the public under license by the regulatory body.

Initial Steps toward Sector Reform (1985–89)

In 1986 the government decided to proceed along these lines and pass responsibility for providing telecommunications services on to the private sector. In early 1986 it established the Telecommunications Board of Sri Lanka to implement these decisions. After extensive analysis of various options, the board recommended setting up a company wholly owned by the state, with the possibility of foreign private participation at a later date. This was to allow the company to develop on its own and be better positioned for seeking foreign partners. The board also recommended preparing new legislation, as required for restructuring a government department into a company, instead of amending the existing Telecommunications Ordinance. A draft act, approved by the cabinet in early 1987, provided for the divestiture of SLTD's operating functions and the transfer of its assets and liabilities to the new company. It also provided for setting up a National Telecommunications Commission (NTC) as an independent regulatory body. NTC was to oversee and regulate all operators, ensuring that they perform in accordance with the act and within the terms of their licenses. Licenses to operate telecommunications networks and services were to be issued to the new company and others by the minister of communications on recommendation of the NTC. To ensure the autonomy of the NTC, its chairman and other members were to be appointed by the head of state.

International experts assisted the board throughout this process, supported by several multilateral and bilateral development agencies.[1]

Subsequent events, however, brought the reform process to a standstill. In mid-1988, the dialogue between the board, SLTD management, and the trade unions broke down. SLTD management was particularly concerned that with privatization, senior posts would be filled from outside the organization. The trade unions were opposed to privatization; despite financial and other benefits that would accrue to their members, they worried that privatization would result in retrenchment and deprive workers of existing rights and privileges. There was also some political opposition to privatization in general and to the possible foreign ownership of national assets. Concurrently, internal security conditions in parts of the country deteriorated, and a new government was elected in December 1988. The new government abandoned the proposal for privatization, and the board was dissolved in March 1989.

During this period, however, a degree of liberalization had already been introduced. Subscribers were authorized to obtain their own terminal equipment, including telephone sets, telex and facsimile machines, and PABXs, from private suppliers. Private companies also introduced some new services, such as cellular telephones and radio paging, which previously were provided exclusively by SLTD. This trend continued under the new government, which has already issued licenses for two data networks and an additional cellular network. As a result the successor of SLTD will be competing with the private providers in all these new markets. Liberalization, however, has not found favor with the staff of SLTD and the trade unions, who see the gradual erosion of the government's monopoly in the provision of telecommunications services and networks as leading to a reduction in the strategic importance of the organization. Yet competition should have the effect of promoting and stimulating efficiency.

Revised Restructuring Proposal–1990

In July 1989 the government, having abandoned its earlier proposal to privatize the main network and introduce foreign participation, decided to transfer SLTD's operating functions to a fully government-owned corporation, Sri Lanka Telecom (SLT). The main objective was to provide the autonomy required for telecommunications services to be run efficiently on a commercial basis, while retaining overall government control over the enterprise. In February 1990, SLT was legally established under the State Industrial Corporations Act and the board of directors was appointed. In July 1991 a new Telecommunications Act was passed by Parliament, transferring the operating assets and liabilities of SLTD to SLT, giving staff the option of joining SLT, and establishing a regulatory authority.

SLT Corporate Structure

SLT has been structured as a large commercial business. This gives it greater financial and administrative autonomy than was the case of SLTD, but not to the same degree as would have been exercised by the company that was proposed under the Companies Act in 1988. The overall objectives of SLT are to expand access to telecommunications throughout the country, improve service quality, satisfy 80 percent of demand for services by 1995, introduce new services, and increase productivity and efficiency.

As a step toward transforming SLTD into a commercial organization, a new management structure had been defined, with a managing director as chief executive supported by three directors (one each for operations, finance, and corporate affairs) and a general manager for human resources. The managing director is responsible to the board of directors. The new organization took over operations on September 1, 1991.

Greater importance has been given to the disciplines of finance, human resources development, marketing and materials management than in the previously existing SLTD organization. Key posts in those disciplines were accordingly advertised to attract the best available talent in the market, and selections were made from qualified candidates with wide experience. The need to open these posts to candidates from outside the organization was made known to the senior staff of SLTD, who were eligible to apply if they had the qualifications and experience. Appointments to all senior engineering management positions were made from the existing staff of SLTD. For all other levels and grades the existing structure was retained at the time of the changeover. Changes are being introduced gradually as part of a general reorganization exercise to be undertaken. At the operational level, the regional offices are being reorganized and upgraded, with a larger measure of delegated authority than at present with respect to technical, financial, and administrative functions. This is intended to provide better customer services. Furthermore, the regional centers are becoming cost centers for the purpose of monitoring performance, based on which annual bonuses for staff in the region will be determined. With increased wages and welfare benefits, SLT expects to increase staff productivity and efficiency. The present cadre will not be increased over the next five years, while the total number of subscribers will be nearly tripled. This will improve the staffing ratio from about 75 per 1,000 lines at present to about 20.

Addressing Labor Issues

As a major public organization, labor issues have loomed large in the restructuring of SLTD. The original policy decision for privatization of the telecommunications sector had to be modified largely because of serious opposition encountered from the work force at all levels. The consequent delay in implementing the amended policy of corporatization gave time for a fruitful dialogue with the staff and union leaders which led to fairly widespread acceptance of the changes proposed. The main concerns of staff and the trade unions were:

SECURITY OF EMPLOYMENT. The unions feared that commercialization, and especially privatization, would lead to massive layoffs.

PERFORMANCE AND COMPENSATION. Stricter discipline and higher productivity would be expected from staff in a commercial organization, including promotions based on efficiency and merit rather than the established seniority system.

PENSION RIGHTS. There was a potential loss of government pension privileges, including those of widows.

STATUS. There was to be a loss of social standing and prestige traditionally associated in Sri Lanka with employment in the public service.

Following the decision to convert SLTD into a corporation, the government discussed with the unions how the revised structural changes being proposed would deal with these issues. In particular, assurances were given for the continued employment of all existing staff. According to the provisions regarding employment security and compensation, the new act gave SLTD employees the choice of three options. These were:

- To continue to work for SLT and opt to continue as public officers under the existing terms and conditions regarding salaries and wages, benefits, pensions, and disciplinary procedures

- To join SLT on its new terms and conditions of service. These terms provided for enhanced salaries, new allowances and welfare benefits, and staff participation in the Employees Provident Fund instead of the government pension scheme

- To retire and draw their pension.

If at the time of joining SLT they held a pensionable post and had completed ten years of public service on the date of transfer, their pension would have been frozen and become payable on reaching retirement age. If they had between eight and ten years of service, they could have opted to continue as public officers until they completed ten years and then opted to join SLT, the pension so earned becoming payable on retirement.[2]

Staff were invited to participate in the process of formulating the package of salaries, benefits, and allowances that will apply in SLT. In so doing, the SLT board took into consideration the need to attract and retain qualified staff and, accordingly, while increasing salaries across the board by one-third, it granted increases of up to 40 percent for middle-level technical staff, engineers, and accountants.

Developing Human Resources

It is recognized that at middle and top management levels, training is required to prepare staff for the change from a government organization to a commercial business. SLT will need to develop a different work culture than that of SLTD, including new objectives and operating standards and procedures to meet the needs of a modern commercial telecommunications service. New management skills must be acquired. These requirements are to be initially addressed through two management training projects, one for senior management staff and the other for middle management staff, funded by the United Nations Development Program (UNDP) and executed by the International Telecommunication Union (ITU). In particular, the firm of consultants engaged to develop the accounting system will also train staff to use the system. SLT also will be placing considerable emphasis on the training and retraining of nonmanagement staff at all levels and in all disciplines. Comprehensive training facilities have been established by SLTD under a UNDP-ITU project. As incentive, SLT proposes to pay a training allowance for attendance. Satisfactory completion of specified training programs will also be made a mandatory requirement for promotion.

Post-Corporatization Experience

As a corporation Sri Lanka Telecom has the autonomy to utilize its financial resources; however, its capital expenditure is governed by a finance act and other financial controls of the Ministry of Finance, resulting in many bottlenecks in executing its upgrading and expansion program. Similar constraints apply to administrative matters such as the recruitment of personnel.

During the first year of operations it was very clear to the management that further autonomy was necessary to enable SLT to accelerate the pace of growth and development, and several representations were made to the government seeking this increased autonomy. As a solution the government decided that Sri Lanka Telecom should set up a subsidiary company which will be given the autonomy, free of controls, required for executing major projects and undertaking procurement on behalf of SLT. The subsidiary company should be established by June 1993.

The alternative of inviting foreign investors to undertake the development of the network, on a BOT basis as a parallel operator, was also pursued by government in 1992. This was abandoned after the government analyzed the offers received.

Developing Regulation

With some liberalization of the telecommunications business and the conversion of SLTD to a corporation run on commercial lines, the regulatory responsibility of the state increases. This function is to be undertaken by the Telecommunications Authority, the regulatory authority established under the Telecommunications Act of 1991 and headed by a director general appointed by and accountable to the minister of posts and telecommunications. The Telecommunications Authority has similar powers and responsibilities as proposed in 1988 for the NTC; however, it is a somewhat less independent agency than originally envisaged. The general objectives to be achieved by the Authority are to ensure the provision of reliable and efficient national and international telecommunications services meeting all reasonable demand; to ensure that the operators have adequate technical, financial, and managerial resources to provide the services specified in their license; to protect the interests of all parties; and to promote rapid development and competition. For these purposes, the Authority has been vested with wide-ranging powers and duties. Licenses to operate telecommunications services and networks will be issued by the minister on application by an operator, subject to recommendation by the Authority based on an assessment of the applicant's financial and technical capabilities, and under terms and conditions set by the Authority. Complaints by the public regarding telecommunications services will be investigated by the Authority, which will stipulate remedial measures and financial redress where appropriate. The Authority was appointed on July 3, 1991, the date on which the new Telecommunications Act became effective.[3]

The Authority has the powers and duties to establish methods for determining telecommunications tariffs, taking into account government policy and the requirements of the operators concerning the telecommunications services provided by them. The operators will propose changes in tariffs which in their commercial judgment are best suited to promote their business objectives while fulfilling the conditions of the license. The proposed changes in tariffs must be supported by documenting actual investment, maintenance, and operating costs, and shall be subject to the approval of the Authority.

Endnotes

1. For further details of this stage of reform see Vernon L. B. Mendis, "Phased Privatization with Proposed Foreign Participation: The Sri Lanka Experience," in *Restructuring and Managing the Telecommunications Sector,* ed. B. Wellenius, P. A. Stern, T. E. Nulty, and R. D. Stern, A World Bank Symposium, Washington, 1989.
2. Only about 17 percent of SLTD employees opted to remain as public officers; less than 3 percent retired, and the remaining 80 percent joined the new corporation under the new terms and conditions which were offered. Those who opted to remain as public officers have the option to join the corporation under the new terms and conditions at a later date. The corporation has received several applications from this category of employees who have seen the benefit of being a corporation employee.
3. The Authority had to be in place before SLT took over because it had to issue the license to SLT to operate the telecommunications service.

13

Corporatization and Partial Privatization of Telecommunications in Malaysia

Syed Hussein Mohamed

IN THE 1980s, DRIVEN BY THE NEED TO TURN the private sector into the engine of economic growth, the Malaysian government decided to transfer a number of government-run activities to private ownership. Two of the largest early privatizations were those of Malaysian International Shipping Corporation (MISC), in 1985, and Malaysian Airlines System (MAS), in 1986, both of which are now traded on the Kuala Lumpur Stock Exchange. In 1987, Syarikat Telekom Malaysia Berhad (STM), a fully state-owned corporation established under private company law, took over the telecommunications services formerly provided by Jabatan Telekom Malaysia (JTM), the government's telecommunications department.[1] In November 1990, less than four years later, STM made its debut in the Kuala Lumpur Stock Exchange, becoming the largest listed company with a capitalization of over US$5 billion, more than twice the value of the next largest listed company.

The decision to corporatize and gradually privatize telecommunications operations largely followed from the need to mobilize new sources of financing for the sector's rapidly growing capital requirements. JTM's annual telecommunications investments had grown from an average of Malaysian $0.4 billion in 1976–80 to M$1.1 billion in 1981–85, exceeding total operating revenues. The long-term debt swelled to M$4.6 billion, or 2.3 times equity, well above prudent limits. The decline of the domestic economy in 1985–86 made it impossible for the government to sustain this level of investment and borrowing.

Privatizing telecommunications, however, was a more complex affair than that of MISC or MAS. Whereas the latter had been run as profit-oriented corporations for years, telecommunications had to be transformed first from a government department into a corporation and then establish itself as a profitable business before it could successfully attract private capital.

Corporatization

In order to shift the responsibility of providing telecommunications services from JTM to a company, a series of changes in legislation were required. The Telecommunications Services (Successor Company) Act of 1985 was the centerpiece. Among other things, the act provided for transfer of telecommunications operating assets and liabilities from JTM to STM, under the authority of the minister of finance. It also provided for the transfer of JTM staff "… on terms and conditions of service not less favorable than … [those prevailing] … before the transfer date … " Other important legislation was amended: the Telecommunications Act of 1950, to enable setting up a regulatory body; the Pensions Act of 1980, to enable pensionable civil servants to be transferred to the private sector without loss of rights; and the Malaysian Constitution, to allow the disposal of state land and assets to a private company.

Restructuring JTM operations as a company also involved important internal changes. Following a study by international consultants, a major reorganization was launched. This involved refocusing management and staff efforts toward marketing, customer service, and more effective network management. The terms of employment were reviewed, bringing them into line with those of comparable businesses. Most of STM's 28,000 staff are former JTM employees who, despite initial reluctance to focus on profits and customer service, chose to join the new company. The commercial approach also demanded a new company philosophy and work culture as well as new skills and practices, all of which take time to develop. New work standards were set. Closer accountability was established. Time for decisions was cut down and individuals were given greater decisionmaking power to replace the slow, collective processes of the past. Crash training programs were put in place. Some new talent was externally recruited, carefully balanced with internal reassignments as needed to maintain staff morale.

Lastly, as responsibility for telecommunications operations shifted to STM, the government's regulatory activities were reorganized. A much reduced JTM, with about 200 staff under a director general answerable to the minister for telecommunications, is now responsible only for regulatory matters. This mainly comprises issuing of operating licenses, setting of network standards, type approval of equipment for connection to the public network, and management of the radio spectrum. Legal changes are being made to strengthen JTM in monitoring compliance with regulations and with the terms and conditions of licenses. JTM issued a license to STM giving it the right to operate the basic telecommunications network for twenty years from 1987. Licenses have also been granted to other companies to operate mobile, public pay phone, and paging services in competition with STM. Increasing competition is expected to develop, but not in basic telephone services and networks, in the near future.

Performance Improvements from Corporatization

Corporatization led to rapid improvements in service access and quality. Growth in telephone subscriber lines accelerated from less than 10 percent per annum in 1984–87 to 11 percent in 1988, 12 percent in 1989, and 14 percent in 1990. In 1987 a total of 1.4 million customer complaints were received, or 1.2 complaints per line per annum; two years later, despite rapid growth in connected lines, the number of complaints decreased, in absolute terms to 1.2 million and in relative terms to 0.8 per line per annum. Likewise, the proportion of telephone faults cleared in 24 hours rose from 84 percent in 1987 to 93 percent in 1989. Operator response also improved markedly; for example, the proportion of directory assistance calls answered within 20 seconds rose from 85 percent in 1987 to 99 percent in 1989, and the standard was then changed to 10 seconds.

Financial performance also improved markedly. Operating revenues increased by 12 percent in 1988, 13 percent in 1989, and 17 percent in 1990. In 1988 STM made US$180 million profit before tax, which rose to US$360 million in 1989, and US$560 million in 1990. The latter figure was equivalent to 17 percent of revenue and resulted in a 14 percent return on assets; as illustrated in Table 13-1, these ratios are comparable to those of telecommunications companies in industrial countries. At the same time, the long-term debt-to-equity ratio improved from a high 2.3 in 1987 to 1.5 in 1989, which was at the high end of the range considered normal elsewhere.

Labor productivity increased at about 13 percent per annum. As the number of lines in service as well as revenues expanded by more than 40 percent from 1987 to 1990 while the number of staff remained roughly constant, the ratio of staff per 1,000 lines decreased from 25 to 18.

Partial Privatization

Although initially it appeared that it would take at least five years before STM could be publicly listed, rapid improvement of performance and a favorable econom-

Table 13-1. Comparison of Financial and Other Performance Indicators of Selected Telecommunications Companies

Category	NTT (Japan)	BT (U.K.)	TCNZ (New Zealand)	STM (Malaysia)
Financial (in US$ MM)				
Revenue	40,960	18,930	1,300	800
Profit before Taxes (PBT)	3,650	4,170	260	130
Long-Term Loans	25,720	6,190	430	1,410
Shareholders Fund	27,780	15,130	1,450	1,000
Ratios				
Debt/Equity	0.9	0.4	0.3	1.5
Return on Equity	0.13	0.28	0.18	0.14
PBT/Revenue	0.09	0.22	0.20	0.17
Penetration (telephones/100 population)	42	43	44	8

ic climate led the board of directors to move this stage forward. A prospectus for the sale of 25 percent of STM stock was published in September 1990, and receipt of offers closed two weeks later. The shares were listed on November 7, 1990.

The issue netted the company over M\$2 billion. Despite the Gulf War and a nervous equity market, on the first day of listing STM's shares were priced 20 percent above the offering price of M\$5; six months later, in March 1991, they traded at around M\$10. By May 1993 they had risen to M\$15. By 1991 STM's market capitalization reached about US\$7 billion, making STM the largest listed company in the Association of South East Asian Nations (ASEAN). STM accounts for 12 percent of the total value of the Kuala Lumpur Stock Exchange; in February 1991, STM was included in the stock exchange composite index, of which it accounts for 20 percent.

The government still owns 75 percent of STM's stock which, at M\$10 per share had a market value of more than US\$5 billion, five times the net value of assets transferred to STM in 1987.

Conclusion

Corporatization and partial privatization of telecommunications in Malaysia has been a win-win situation for all stakeholders. The customers have more and better services at about the same prices. The value of the government's equity increased fivefold even as its share decreased by 25 percent. Through the sale of shares, the company raised a large amount of capital which it credited against STM debt; combined with increased market value, STM's long-term debt-to-equity ratio is now at only 0.3, which gives management ample margin to incur new debt in the future if desired—a major turnaround from excessive indebtedness only five years ago. The employees benefit from better remunerations and a forthcoming employee stock option plan. Accelerated network expansion and modernization have increased contractor and supplier business volume at an unprecedented pace. And lastly, STM has added to the prestige and renewed interest of investors in the Malaysian capital market.

Endnote

1. For a discussion of the transfer of the telecommunications operating functions from the government to Syarikat Telekom Malaysia (STM), see Daud bin Isahak, "Meeting the Challenges of Privatization in Malaysia," in *Restructuring and Managing the Telecommunications Sector*, ed. B. Wellenius, P. A. Stern, T. E. Nulty, and R. D. Stern, A World Bank Symposium, Washington, 1989, pp. 118-121.

Part IV

Recent Experiences

in Western, Central, and

Eastern Europe

14

The European Situation: An Overview

Herbert Ungerer

AGAINST A BACKGROUND OF WORLDWIDE dramatic reform of telecommunications structures, Europe is entering a decade of fundamental change. Since these changes are mirrored on a worldwide scale, Europe provides a window on recent telecommunications development. The main trend in telecommunications reform across the European Community's (EC) 340 million inhabitants continues to be strongly influenced by the blueprint for future market structures sketched out in the European Commission's 1987 EC Green Paper on the Development of the Common Market for Telecommunications and Services (the "The EC Green Paper")[1] and subsequent Community legislation. Member states have continued or initiated moves toward liberalization and reform of the sector. Liberalization and privatization have accelerated in the United Kingdom following the Duopoly White Paper and may turn the United Kingdom into the most liberal and competitive market in the world. There have been the profound reforms in Germany and France, and changes are under way or planned in all other member states.

A number of factors continue to add dynamics to the evolution of telecommunications in Europe. These include:

- The increasing role of European telecommunications operators in the international arena, especially their growing involvement in the developing parts of the world such as Latin America, adding to the worldwide orientation which has been characteristic of the European telecommunications manufacturing industry

- The inclusion of telecommunications as an important element in the current discussions between the EC and the European Free Trade Association (EFTA) on a common European Economic Area (EEA)

- The new needs in Central and Eastern Europe (CEE) to rapidly build up the networks starting from a disastrously low level, underlining the importance of telecommunications for Europe as a whole

- The EC Green Paper on satellite telecommunications (Satellite Green Paper) which articulates, for the first time, the promise of true Europe-wide service across the whole region.

Given its diversified structure, its very different national characteristics, and its aim of building one single harmonized area of fundamental unity, Europe can be looked upon as an indicator of possible development lines of future regulatory reform in the sector. It is therefore worthwhile to look at European development at the level of both the European Community and the individual countries. Major country developments are reviewed in the following chapters. This overview concentrates on the developments concerning European Community policy and on issues characteristic of the evolution in the European region as a whole.

The Impact of the European Single Market Objective of 1992

The Community's telecommunications policy is meant as part of the wider process of building the single European Community market of 1992 which, in fact, exerts a strong unifying effect well beyond the frontiers of the EC members, particularly with regard to the countries of the European Free Trade Association and, more recently, Central and Eastern Europe. It is worth recalling the major goals set by this wider task and examining their impact on telecommunications in Europe.

The reform of the Treaty of Rome, the so-called Single European Act, means that achieving a Europe-wide market by the end of 1992 is now a legally binding obligation on all twelve EC member state governments. The Europe-wide market in 1992 will mean free movement of people, capital, goods, and services throughout Europe. In particular, among the many profound changes which these goals imply, the common market will be fully implemented for some sectors which have been the most regulated and protected at the national level in the European economy: financial and insurance markets, transport, and telecommunications. Within this broad range of services, which represents a large share of the potential for the future growth of the European services economy, telecommunications plays, in a more and more communications-based society, a key supportive role. Free circulation of services in the European Community will mean more trade. Trade in services means more freedom of choice for the user. More freedom of choice for the user requires the liberalization of structures.

Building a single market will, therefore, inevitably expose telecommunications in Europe to a new competitive environment and will introduce new demands for a reorganization of telecommunications. Europe's industrial and service enterprises will depend critically on the Europe-wide telecommunications infrastructure for their international operations. This represents a major political and economic spur for current telecommunications reform in Europe.

The European Commission's Green Paper on Telecommunications

In the context of the single market plan but based on the analysis of worldwide technical and market facts as well as telecommunications reforms, the Green Paper on the development of telecommunications in the European Community, issued in June 1987, launched a broad discussion on the future of telecommunications in the Community. In February 1988, after an in-depth public debate, the Commission published a schedule for the implementation of the EC Green Paper,[2] which has since developed into the common reference point for Europe-wide telecommunications reform.

The EC Green Paper sets out a common framework for the future development of open market conditions in Europe, while accepting that telecommunications networks will continue to develop in Europe under different forms of ownership and national regimes. Although recognizing continuing diversity, the EC Green Paper insists on the commonality of a number of fundamental goals, critical to the development of cross-border, free, open markets in the European Community. These goals are:

- An open Community-wide market for terminal equipment

- An open Community-wide market for value added services and progressive liberalization for data services, while accepting, subject to political review in 1992–93, national choice with regard to exclusive rights in the field of the public network infrastructure and the public voice telephony service

- Separation of regulation and operation

- The development of European standards and the mutual recognition of type approval to permit a single terminal market to emerge

- The mutual recognition of service licensing, to allow a single services market to emerge

- The definition of Open Network Provision (ONP), to give new service providers fair access to the facilities of the network infrastructure and basic services.

The broad consensus achieved in the Europe-wide discussion around the EC Green Paper was reflected in the unanimous support given by the EC Council of Ministers in their Resolution of 30 June 1988 to the proposals of the EC Green Paper and its overall policy approach.

The regulatory actions at European Community level since that time can best be summed up as the implementation of this program. This complex process has involved terminal equipment, services, standards, procurement and type approval, and regulatory structures. It culminated in December 1989 with a unanimous agreement between the

Commission and the EC Council of Ministers on how to proceed in the liberalization of the services market, the most important market in telecommunications.

Fundamentals of the Concept

Three key areas are driving action at EC level (and across the whole of the European region) as well as driving the national reform debates in all the member states.

LIBERALIZATION OF USE. Europe-wide, and indeed worldwide, all countries are confronted with enormous new technological possibilities offering a broad range of new activities for users and the public telecommunications operators, in both the terminals and the services field. Clear regulatory answers are required as to whether those involved should be restricted in the use of this vast new potential, or whether they should be allowed to make full use of it for economic and social growth. In accordance with the general trend in the European debate on this basic issue, the EC Green Paper clearly favors liberalization of the market for terminal equipment, far-reaching liberalization of the services market, and participation of both the new private operators and the traditional telecommunications organizations in the new markets without restrictions regarding lines of business.

SEPARATION OF REGULATION AND OPERATIONS. The creation of genuine competition requires a full separation between the functions of regulation and operation, on the one hand, and the building up of effective regulatory procedures, independent of the network operator, on the other. As competition emerges, the national telecommunications administrations that now compete with new service providers cannot at the same time set the rules of these new competitive markets. They cannot set mandatory standards, allocate frequencies, or define conditions for access to services, as has been the case in the past. The creation of transparent market rules calls for a full separation of regulation from operations, which in turn generally requires the establishment of new regulatory functions or bodies.

TRANSBORDER PROVISION. Although the first two fundamentals apply worldwide, the emphasis on transborder provision is explained by the particular situation of the European Community of 340 million people, or in the wider European context, a region of more than 500 million moving rapidly toward close economic and political integration. The aim of producing one single market means that allowing competitors to enter the twelve markets of the different member states is not enough. New service providers and equipment vendors must be free to supply across the whole of the Community.

National Reforms in Europe

National reforms are moving in parallel and in close relation with Europe-wide reforms, discussed in detail later. Some major events can be highlighted:

- In the Netherlands a new law broadly liberalizing the telecommunications sector entered into force at the beginning of 1989.

- In the Federal Republic of Germany reform of the sector was adopted in July 1989, with the reorganization of the Deutsche Bundespost and extensive introduction of competition as well as the liberalization of mobile communications. In July 1990, satellite liberalization was implemented, and the procedures for further licensing of mobile systems are proceeding currently.

- France adopted its regulatory reform in December 1990, and new legislation with regard to the organization of the sector in June 1990, giving full independence to France Télécom and separating the operations and regulatory functions.

- In March 1991, a new law was adopted in Belgium and greater autonomy extended to Belgacom, the newly-named national telecommunications operator.

- Spain is currently adjusting its telecommunications law, and in Italy and Portugal the reform legislation is proceeding.

- Denmark has recently liberalized mobile communications.

- In March 1991, the Secretary of State for Trade and Industry presented to parliament a white paper entitled, Competition and Choice: Telecommunications Policy for the 1990s. This white paper, also known as the Duopoly White Paper, announced broad competition in all areas of network activity, satellite, and mobile communications. Subsequently, a number of other companies have been issued licenses to compete with BT and Mercury. The white paper also clearly sets out the major regulatory issues, all of which also have a substantial international perspective, such as the future regulation of interconnection, coordination, as well as equal opportunity in numbering and frequency planning.[3]

Other countries of the region have also initiated important telecommunications reforms, including Switzerland, Sweden, Norway, and Finland, and with the revolutionary events in Central and Eastern Europe since 1989, the countries of the former central state economies.

The Current Status of EC Legislation

Implementation of the framework described in the EC Green Paper required certain EC legislation. The status of this legislation with respect to terminal equipment, liberalization of services, ONP and procurement can be summarized as follows:

Open Market for Terminals

In May 1988 the EC Commission issued a directive (a law binding on all EC member states) to open up Community-wide competition in the market for terminal equipment within its mandate under EC competition law. On March 19, 1991, the European Court of Justice rendered a historic ruling which fully confirmed the approach adopted, that is, the principle of eliminating all monopoly rights in the sector, the legal instrument used, and the principle of separation of the operating and regulatory functions, while requesting modifications on some minor points. The court ruling gives a firm legal basis to much of European telecommunications policy. By now over 95 percent in value of the EC market for terminal equipment, including PABXs, is open to competition. With the court giving full backing to the directive, the remaining difficulties are likely to be overcome very rapidly.

In April 1991, the EC Council of Ministers adopted a directive concerning the next major step needed in this area: Europe-wide type approval. The full mutual recognition of type approval for terminal equipment is the necessary complement of liberalization of terminal equipment to ensure that equipment, once approved according to European standards, can then be freely sold across the Community.

Open Market for Services

The Commission's directive on competition in the markets for telecommunications services, adopted on the same basis as the terminal liberalization directive, follows an agreement reached in December 1989 by the EC Council of Ministers and the Commission on the approach to be taken to the introduction of competition into this market. It is based on a differentiated approach to three categories of services: value added services, data, and voice. Competition will be introduced across the whole of the Community rapidly and fully for all value added services. Data communications services will be progressively liberalized with simple resale of capacity being allowed from January 1, 1993. This deadline may be extended up to the beginning of 1996 for those member states that have underdeveloped public data networks. For public voice telephony to the general public and network infrastructure, it is up to each country to decide whether or not to introduce competition. The directive called for the Commission to conduct a review of remaining monopoly positions in 1992. This is further discussed below.

The immediate impact of the directive is substantial. It lifts a large number of current restrictions. In particular, the market for value added services such as electronic data interchange and electronic funds transfer is being fully liberalized, with a substantial impact on the service sectors of the economy at large. The ruling of the European Court of Justice on the terminal case was endorsed by its subsequent ruling on the services directive case in November 1992. The court upheld the abolition of exclusive rights granted by member states for the provision of so-called nonreserved telecommunications services, while annulling the directive's references to special rights.

Open Network Provision—Interconnection Issues

In Europe, access issues are covered by the principle of ONP and a related program. A key element of the ONP program, the ONP framework directive, was adopted by the EC Council of Ministers in July 1990.[4] ONP must be seen in the context of the open network concepts which seem currently to be developing worldwide into a core issue of future telecommunications regulation. The basic principles of ONP are to open and to harmonize the conditions of access to the network infrastructure for new service providers and for users across the European Community.

The ONP framework directive is now being followed by specific implementation directives. The conditions for the remaining, very limited, number of access regulations are set by the so-called essential requirements related to various aspects of public interest, namely, network security, network integrity, interoperability, confidentiality of communications and protection of privacy. The ONP framework directive includes specific provisions for participation of industry and users in the process, in order to ensure that access and interconnection conditions are worked out in an open way. The directive states that the advisory committee assisting the Commission, "shall, in particular, consult the representatives of the telecommunications organizations, the users, the consumers, the manufacturers, and the service providers."

In the meantime, major progress has been made in the implementation of the ONP program. In June 1992, the ONP directive for the provision of leased lines[5] was adopted by the EC Council. The directive reforms profoundly the provision of leased lines in Europe. It guarantees, among other things, the provision of a basic set of voice grade and digital circuits up to 2 Mbps. Provisions for higher bandwidths will be incorporated as demand develops. Also ONP Recommendations are now in force; one of these is for the application of ONP to the integrated services digital network (ISDN) and the other, for packet-switched data services. Together with the ONP leased-line directive, these initiatives give a new basis for competitive service operations in Europe.

Opening of Procurement

In October 1990, the EC Council adopted a directive on the procurement procedures of entities operating in the water, energy, transport, and telecommunications sectors. For telecommunications this implied opening of procurement by the telecommunications organizations to bidders from other EC member states from January 1, 1993 onwards.

GATT Uruguay Round Negotiations

The current Uruguay Round negotiations will set, together with the reforms going on in the context of the International Telecommunication Union (ITU), the future conditions for worldwide telecommunications and international relations between countries in this area. The EC negotiating position on telecommunications services and market access is based on the open network concept. It is hoped that, in spite of the current difficulties, a stable open environment for worldwide telecommunications development will emerge from the current negotiations and the telecommunications annex to the agreement, which sets guidelines relating to access to and use of the network for the provision of services.

Future Challenge

A number of issues raised in the European region clearly will have a wider impact on future telecommunications reform:

Satellite Communications

In November 1990 the Commission adopted a new green paper on satellite communications.[6] The paper aims at a fundamental reform and liberalization of the sector in Europe and, in fact, of the worldwide satellite system. Following an extensive period of public consultation, the Telecommunications Council adopted a resolution which defines as major objectives:

- Harmonization and liberalization of the earth segment, including where applicable the abolition of all exclusive and special rights in this area in Europe.

- In the future, removal of restrictions on procurement and use of satellite terminal dishes for direct reception across Europe, as well as two-way satellite terminals, subject to type approval and licensing procedures, in order to avoid, in particular, harmful interference and to ensure frequency coordination.

- Improved access to space segment capacity, subject to adequate licensing procedures. In conformity with these procedures, service providers will be able to obtain the transmission capacity they need through contracts with satellite providers, and these service providers will themselves be able to transmit signals via satellite.

- Commercial freedom for space segment providers. The objective is to move toward the direct sale of satellite transmission capacity to service providers and users by satellite providers, in particular, the European Telecommunications Satellite Organisation (EUTELSAT), International Telecommunications Satellite Organization (INTELSAT), and International Maritime Satellite Organization (INMARSAT), while taking full account also of the interests of the developing countries.

- Adoption of harmonization measures, as required to facilitate the provision of Europe-wide services. This concerns, in particular, the mutual recognition of licensing and type approval procedures, frequency coordination, and matters related to the coordination of services provided to and from countries outside the

European Community, as well as the definition of standards to ensure compatibility of equipment and techniques.

Specific legislation will follow to implement these principles, thus allowing full use of the satellite medium in the European region and, in fact, beyond and, at the same time, creating an appropriate framework for liberalization of the sector. Satellites have a particularly vital role in meeting the needs of areas currently underserved by network infrastructure. It is to be hoped, therefore, that rapid progress can be made in realizing their potential worldwide.

Pricing

For the EC Commission, interest concentrates naturally on international tariffs in Europe, a first priority for efficient Europe-wide services.

In Europe, international telephone tariffs are still on average 2.5 times more expensive than the highest national long-distance calls, even though some countries have narrowed this gap substantially or even eliminated it. In some cases, tariffs from country A to country B are still three times higher than those from B to A. These anomalies are, of course, not restricted to the European region but are characteristic of the international telecommunications tariffs. Current accounting rules and the rapid changes of the underlying cost structures are leading to broad divergences and imbalance which have now stirred a worldwide debate. In July 1992 the EC Commission produced a communication outlining the nature of the tariff problem, which was taken up in the Services Review.

Frequency Coordination and Numbering Plans

As mobile communications now enter the center stage of telecommunications with the development of personal communications systems, a common Europe-wide perspective is essential in order to respond to the important regulatory questions which are emerging.

The major regulatory involvement of the EC Commission in mobile communications up to now has been in designating frequency bands, underpinning with binding EC law the recommendations of the Conference of European Postal and Telecommunications Administrations (CEPT) in key areas within the framework of ITU international frequency coordination. A directive on the reservation of radio frequencies for the new pan-European digital mobile system, GSM, has provided the firm basis for the development of the system. Other initiatives are addressing the new pan-European digital radiopaging system and the introduction of the Digital European Cordless Telecommunications Standard (DECT).

With their rapid development and with the Europe-wide dimension inherent in mobile systems, European coordination in this area will develop substantially further. A profound reform of radio frequency coordination has started. A European Radiocommunications Committee (ERC) has been created, and a European Radiocommunications Office (ERO) has been established in Copenhagen. In 1992, the ERO's announcement on detailed spectrum investigations marked the beginning of the development of a common European Table of Frequency Allocations. These reforms should make frequency coordination in Europe more effective and make radio frequency planning an open process, with consultation of users, industry, and service providers.

Besides the growing role of the radio spectrum and its planning as a key regulatory activity, another major resource is now entering the center stage: fair sharing of numbering plans is becoming a key element of efficient operation and fair competition. Therefore, the management of numbering plans will now become a major regulatory task for the future, in Europe as elsewhere. In November 1992, the EC Council adopted a resolution on the promotion of Europe-wide cooperation on numbering of telecommunications services and proposing the creation of a European numbering office to be known as European Telecommunications Office-Numbering (ETO-N), under the auspices of the CEPT, along the lines of the ERO. Given the requirement for global mobility in future telecommunications, this area will need substantial development both in the European region as well as worldwide.

Central and Eastern Europe

Due to forty-five years of neglect of the communications infrastructure of the industrial and civil sectors, the investment requirements in the countries now transforming into market economies are enormous. Globally speaking, telecommunications development in the countries of Central and Eastern Europe is twenty to thirty years behind that in the western part of Europe. One estimate suggests that ECU 55 billion (approximately US$74 billion) must be invested in Poland, Czechoslovakia, Hungary, Romania, and Bulgaria for these countries to reach a level of telecommunications by the year 2000 equivalent to the current level in Spain, and this excludes requirements in the former U.S.S.R., which are substantially larger.

The EC Commission has published a communication on the role of telecommunications and the Community's relations with the countries in Central and Eastern Europe. This communication sets out the instruments available to help in the current change in Central and Eastern Europe, including coordinated assistance by the Community and the Organization for Economic Cooperation and Development (OECD), the World Bank, the European Investment Bank (EIB), and the European Bank for Reconstruction and Development (EBRD) financing; and joint ventures and other kinds of access to private capital.

In the face of these enormous investment requirements, it is not surprising that thinking has started again across Europe on the best way to attract the vast amounts of capital needed for this development, including the future sharing of responsibility in this regard between the public and private sector. It seems obvious that new imaginative ways are needed in order to provide for rapid satisfaction of the requirements emerging in the east of the continent. It is likely that the experiences made in this context will also be of high interest for the developing countries.

Outlook

The new experience in Central and Eastern Europe, and the reforms in European countries such as the United Kingdom, Germany, France, and the Netherlands, have set forth a vision of the future regulation of telecommunications in a competitive environment which without doubt will have substantial impact beyond Europe. At the same time, EC telecommunications policy aims at creating a telecommunications market which may become the world's largest during this decade, and which may lead development worldwide in key fields of technologies such as mobile communications.

European countries face very different situations in the difficult process of reform. Although in a number of Community member states the main topic of reform was to extend the usage of the existing, already built, telephone network, in others the main focus was, and still is, on building up the network. The Commission has set in motion programs such as STAR,[7] which make an important contribution to network buildup in the less developed regions of these countries.

A major objective of EC telecommunications policy is to provide for an even telecommunications development across the Community and the region as a whole. It is the management of this diversity which gives originality to the European approach and which makes it a unique example of the creation of a common liberal market in telecommunications across a whole region, without imposing any particular national model. It is this creation of a common market across the entire Community that is at the heart of the Services Review which began in 1992. In a communication adopted in October of that year, a number of remaining bottlenecks were identified, including the surcharge associated with telephone services between member states. The communication put forward four options for the future these involved varying degrees of further liberalization or more extensive regulatory control on tariffs. The options formed the basis of an extensive public consultation, and the results of this are now forming the basis of proposals which the Commission will submit to the EC Council.

This decade will be one of challenge for the telecommunications sector in Europe. Large numbers of new market entries and new regulatory schemes at work are likely. Mobile and satellite communications will become major leaders of development. Intense cooperation must be further developed on key issues such as interconnection, frequency management, and numbering plans. True Europe-wide services must further develop to support the 1992 single market. A number of European countries, particularly in the central and eastern part of the continent, will have to build up their networks. Others will have to manage the fundamental transformation of their network resource, as telecommunications moves into the age of intelligent networks. But Europe can, and must, provide a sound market base for this time of change. With the rapidly expanding mobile and satellite communications markets as well as growing capital needs for network development and transformation, discussion on the regulation of future network infrastructure and the merits of different ownership schemes as the best way to attract capital will be reopened.

In this phase of broad expansion undertaken on a common basis, the European region can be expected to be a pacesetter of telecommunications reform during the decade. Telecommunications reforms are under way worldwide and particularly now in the developing countries. Institutions such as the International Telecommunication Union, the World Bank, the Commonwealth Telecommunications Organization, and others are furthering this transformation. European telecommunications operators, as they turn into full-scale international operators and investors, are more and more playing a direct key role in this process.

From the European experience, worldwide telecommunications projects can be assessed according to some of the following key criteria:

- Are free-market reforms being undertaken to ensure long-term viability? In the European Community the EC Green Paper has developed into a key point of reference in this respect.

- Are standards being implemented to ensure easy interconnection in a future multi-actor international environment?

- Are the telecommunications plans viable by themselves? This includes, in particular, developing efficient management methods, separation of regulatory and operational interest, sound financial structures, and realistic tariff policies.

Given its current exposure to regulatory changes, Europe will be able to offer valuable experience from its own reforms in the area.

Endnotes

1. *Towards a Dynamic European Economy: Green Paper on the Development of the Common Market for Telecommunications Services and Equipment,* Commission of the European Communities, COM(87)290 final, Brussels, June 30, 1987.

2. *Towards a Competitive Community-wide Telecommunications Market in 1992, Implementing the Green Paper,* COM(88)48, February 1988.

3. *Competition and Choice: Telecommunications Policy for the 1990s,* Department of Trade and Industry, London, HMSO, Con 1461, March 1991.

4. *Directive on the Establishment of the Internal Market for Telecommunications Services through the Implementation of Open Network Provision,* European Council, 1990.

5. *Directive on the Application of Open Network Provision to Lease Lines,* 92/44/EEC, June 5, 1992.

6. *Towards Europe-wide Systems and Services—Green Paper on a Common Approach in the Field of Satellite Communications in the European Community,* COM (90) 490 final, Brussels, November 20, 1990.

7. STAR is an EC development program (1987–1991) to promote the use of advanced telecommunications in the developing regions of the European Community. The second phase will be launched in 1993. Another program, Telematique, will bridge the two phases.

15

The Evolution of Telecommunications Policy in the United Kingdom

Bruce Laidlaw

NO BRIEF ACCOUNT OF POLICY DEVELOPMENTS in telecommunications can fail to be highly selective. This chapter, therefore, examines two principal themes drawn from the U.K. experience which serve to illustrate the evolution of telecommunications sector policy in the United Kingdom over the last ten years:

- Restructuring of the telecommunications sector has multiple objectives, which should ideally be ordered in time and in priority. The practical difficulty in so doing is that the objectives may conflict; the resolution of such conflict is almost bound to disturb the smooth evolution of policy.

- Restructuring involves the government in choosing a commercial partner or partners with whom jointly to achieve policy objectives. Once chosen, these partners help policy formulation as well as implementation. The incumbent network operator is obviously one such partner; a key issue is whether it is to be the only one and, if not, who else will be chosen?

The prospects for success in restructuring will be improved if these issues are recognized.

Commercialization

At the outset of the 1980s, the newly elected Conservative government changed the priorities of policy in the telecommunications sector. From 1968 to 1980, there had been bipartisan agreement on the need to commercialize the activities of the national network operator. To this end, the Post Office had been separated from the civil service and, within the new corporation, postal and telecommunications services were separated into distinct business units, up to managing director level.

The pace of change was slow, but the ultimate intention was to divest the Post Office of its telecommunications business. In 1981, this was achieved with the creation of

British Telecommunications plc (BT) which, for convenience, is here referred to as BT even for what was initially the Telecommunications Division of the Post Office.

Liberalization

The change of policy priority in 1980 was to liberalize the telecommunications market, that is, to offer it to private sector competitors. To an extent, the shift took place in response to complaints from customers that BT was being restrictive in neither providing the latest subscriber apparatus itself nor allowing importation; however, on the more fundamental level, the policy was driven by an ideological conviction that a nationalized industry with a monopoly would be inefficient.

The policy shift had important implications:

• Whereas commercialization had been largely under the control of, and was proceeding at a pace largely dictated by, senior managers in BT, liberalization was from the outset led by the sector ministry (the Department of Industry, which later became the Department of Trade and Industry, or DTI). The government wanted quick results and was in the position to ensure that it got them.

• The domestic manufacturing industry had been geared increasingly to meeting BT's requirements in a cartel-like arrangement. Liberalization meant dismantling the sponsorship of the domestic industry by BT and its replacement by a formal system of standards and type approval. This in turn gave increased opportunities to importers.

A modest element of liberalization of the subscriber apparatus market had been considered by the previous Labour government but not pursued in the face of trade union opposition. The main innovation, at least in a European context, was that the scope for liberalization was not limited a priori to subscriber apparatus or value added services. From the outset, the government set up a Network Liberalisation Study Group to consider the potential for opening up the operation of networks. The willingness to allow commercial interests to determine as far as possible the scope for market entry in network operation has led the United Kingdom toward a unique sector structure. Three main events followed.

First, Cable & Wireless (C&W) reappeared on the scene, putting itself forward as a potential partner that could help deliver competition in the operation of public telephone networks. C&W, although British, did not operate in the United Kingdom; its main interests were in operating international networks and cable routes overseas. Together with British Petroleum (BP) and Barclays Merchant Bank, C&W proposed to lay a digital transmission network, with right of access in principle to BT's public-switched telephone network, connecting the main business centers in England (the Mercury project). Their proposal was accepted in 1981, marking the start of the government's duopoly policy (discussed below). From that date, C&W has played a central role in policy on voice telephony—particularly on the timing of developments.

Second, in addition to licensing Mercury Communications to compete with BT's telephone network, the government decided to establish cellular radio services on a competitive basis from the outset. In this market, Racal was selected as the vehicle for developing a mobile radio network operation to rival BT's (called Cellnet and run in conjunction with Securicor). It was considered that the spectrum available would permit the development of only two national cellular radio networks. Recognizing that licensing two networks was insufficient in itself to ensure competition rather than tacit collusion, the DTI devised a regulatory regime in which the network operators were barred from retailing both the handsets and the connection to a network ("airtime"). As might have been predicted, free entry into airtime reselling produced intense rivalry, reflected in steep discounts on handset prices and connection charges. On the other hand, the price of calls to and from cellular handsets remained high. This price structure was reinforced by the failure of the regulatory authorities to insist on interoperability of the two networks, which meant that customers were effectively tied into the network they first joined. The overall effectiveness of the policy may be judged from the fact that Racal now operates the largest single cellular radio network in the world.

The third area where the U.K. government experimented with a competitive market structure in network operation concerned cable television. From the outset, policy toward cable television was driven by the idea that such networks might develop an interactive (that is, a telecommunications) capability. In general, these hopes have not been realized, although it has been demonstrated that the sharing of facilities between telephony and TV distribution can be the basis for competitive entry into local networks. At this time, only four local TV networks offer a telecommunications service, and these on a small scale. Among the many reasons for the slow development of cable TV is the fact that the effort has until recently been fragmented among a large number of commercial interests. None were able to deal effectively with the government to secure the regulatory provisions necessary for success, in the way that C&W and Racal did. In part, this failure resulted from a lack of understanding on the part of the licensing authorities; in part the fragmentation was deliberately arranged as part of the duopoly policy. As explained below, the ending of the duopoly and the recent concentration of ownership of cable TV interests in the hands of North American telephone companies appear to have corrected this deficiency.

Privatization

The decision of the U.K. government to privatize BT, announced in July 1982, may be explained as part of the same ideological predisposition as underlay the drive to liberalize the telecommunications market. After all, C&W itself had been privatized in 1980, and it was soon clear that the company was prospering under new management; however, the BT privatization was an unexpected turn in government policy which virtually no one, not even the closest observers of developments in the U.K. telecommunications scene nor most of BT's management, expected. This sudden change in policy required specific explanation.

The problem to which privatization was put forward as a solution was how to finance BT's massive investment program to modernize its network while maintaining strict controls over public sector spending. The DTI tried to find a way of securing private sector finance for BT's investment, but the effort foundered on the refusal of the Treasury to provide a guarantee. The government then gave BT a limited exemption to the general controls on borrowings by nationalized industries. It was probably the subsequent failure of BT's management actually to spend the sums set aside, at great political costs, for its modernization program which led directly to the decision in favor of privatization.

It was clear from the outset that the decision to privatize BT would have profound implications for the liberalization policy. First, the market entrants were not yet sufficiently well established to provide by themselves a bulwark against abuse by BT of its monopoly position. A strong regulatory framework was needed. On the other hand, if regulatory restraint was too tight, the expected benefits from privatization might not emerge. Second, the potential investors in BT would require assurance of policy stability in the period following privatization. These conflicting considerations resulted in an acceleration in liberalization in the year after the decision to privatize, from which C&W was the main beneficiary, followed by a relatively long period in which no new licenses were issued.

Whether privatization itself produced a significant improvement in BT's performance still remains moot. The clearest gains appear to have been the absence of Treasury interference with the pace of modernization and the avoidance of any major strategic errors in investment or diversification (at least in the United Kingdom, since BT's investments in North America have not looked very clever). The productivity performance has improved, but only at about the same rate as was being achieved before privatization. Not until 1990 did BT begin seriously to tackle its overstaffing; by that date, it is reasonable to infer that the prospect of intensifying competition was the motivating factor.

The Duopoly Policy

At the time the decision to privatize BT was made, it was still not clear which of the experiments in network liberalization were going to be successful. The government took the view that Mercury needed to be given a boost so that it could take on the role of second national network. By stimulating competition from that source, it was hoped that it would become feasible to design a framework of relatively light regulatory controls for BT; however, the commercial risk being taken by C&W (which by 1984 had become the sole owner of Mercury) was thereby greatly increased. C&W as much as the investors in BT, now urged caution in licensing policy.

The outcome of these pressures was the duopoly policy. Broadly, Mercury was given the chance to develop its challenge to BT in whatever direction it felt best, supported by the assurance that the government would not license any other competitor until 1990 at the earliest. As part of this, resale opportunities were also deferred. In effect, Mercury was given the task of carrying through the experiment in network liberalization initiated by the government.

What Mercury did with this responsibility can best be summarized by saying that it focused on providing digital communications for business customers. For this purpose, Mercury constructed local optical-fiber networks in business districts as well as a long-distance network to connect major cities. It also sought direct international links to countries with major telecommunications traffic flows with the United Kingdom. Mercury also introduced services for single-exchange line customers, directly and via the cable television networks, but these were not a priority. Mercury established a tariff with relatively high fixed charges but an average discount on BT's call charges of around 20 percent.

Gradually, Mercury's service has become available virtually throughout England as well as in the more populated parts of Scotland and Wales. Mercury has also been able to acquire a position in mobile radio services, being granted a personal communications networks license in 1989. Rather more slowly than the government had hoped, Mercury has established itself as a second national network.

Predictably, Mercury's business focus induced in BT the response of reorienting its service offerings more toward the perceived needs of business. The price controls on BT restricted the pace but did not prevent the rebalancing of tariffs. Long-distance charges fell and rental and local call charges rose. Similarly, BT's network modernization strategy shifted so that those areas more exposed to competition from Mercury were modernized first.

Initial Terms of Interconnection

The key to Mercury's entry into public network operation was the terms it could secure for interconnection with the BT network. This was understood from an early stage; BT was unwilling to accept its new license without a clear basis for interconnection. Heads of Agreement were signed by BT and Mercury in June 1984, just before the BT privatization. In the event, this agreement did not last, and Mercury sought and obtained better terms from the new regulatory body, the Office of Telecommunications (OFTEL). With all this maneuvering, however, Mercury's entry into switched voice services was delayed until May 1986.

The principles on which OFTEL settled the interconnection issue have never been made explicit, and disputes have continued ever since. It would appear that the terms initially determined by OFTEL were not so much related to BT's costs but rather set to ensure that Mercury could operate profitably with discounted call charges. In this respect, Professor Bryan Carsberg, at the time the head of OFTEL, essentially made a commercial judgment in negotiation with C&W and then imposed these terms on BT.

The Duopoly Review

Despite the accelerating pace of change in telecommunications, the government stuck to its original timetable and allowed the duopoly period to run its course. In November 1990 it reviewed the policy and concluded that although market entry was feasible in all aspects of network operation, much more needed to be done to make competition a reality. The slow pace of evolution of competition under the duopoly had led to a gradual tightening of controls on BT, a tendency with which the government was clearly unhappy. The strategy that emerged in the review was to:

- Open fully the domestic telecommunications market, while restraining competition in international services

- Maintain price controls on BT for a further period

- Revise interconnection terms to establish a level playing field among competitors.

Opening the domestic market would mean reducing restrictions on entry into long-distance and local networks as well as licensing new mobile services such as personal communications networks (PCN) on terms that would enable them in due course to become competitive with fixed services. In the light of the remarks above, it may be noted that merely removing regulatory restrictions is insufficient to ensure entry. For commercial interests to undertake the risks of network construction in the face of the established monopoly enjoyed by BT probably requires positive encouragement and the promise of protection from retaliation. Moreover, with so many opportunities now on offer, it is possible that the efforts of entrants will be dissipated.

It is notable that no one entrant has been singled out for favorable attention in the way C&W was. Apparently, the government did not receive any offers. Many companies have indicated an intention to invest in new networks, but the experience of Mercury in taking on the burden of demonstrating the feasibility of competition has been discouraging. Although now profitable, and producing additional benefits for all telephone users through the impact on BT, the Mercury project cannot be regarded as a successful commercial investment.

OFTEL, though not the government, has stated that benefits for the consumer would be maximized if further market entry were concentrated at local level; however, little is being done to achieve this, beyond the decision to go slow on opening up international services. The reluctance to liberalize international services, where prices charged are well above cost, is rationalized as being due to the difficulty of securing bilateral agreements; however, the basic reason appears to be to give Mercury some residual protection during the transition to full domestic competition since Mercury's profits come disproportionately from its international services.

Maintaining price controls on BT is essential so long as its market share remains so high (about 95 percent in voice telephony). Although the price-cap method of regulation has the merit of allowing flexibility in setting individual tariff elements, in the United Kingdom, as elsewhere, the residential rental charge is a matter of critical importance. A separate limit is being maintained on the rate at which residential rental charges can increase as part of tariff rebalancing.

Revised Interconnection Terms

The revision of interconnection terms is explicitly linked to this control on residential rentals. While BT's costs have not been made public, competitors and others have argued that the prices that BT charges for residential exchange connections are below their cost. To subsidize these below cost prices BT must, it is therefore argued, charge above cost for local, long distance or international calls. If competitors who do not need to charge above cost for such calls were able to connect into BT's residential exchanges at cost, they would obtain an unfair advantage over BT. This argument was at first accepted by OFTEL, which, in March 1991, proposed a system of supplementary interconnection payments per call, termed "contributions to the access deficit," to remove this imbalance.

Although formally correct, these arrangements had a fatal flaw. If required to pay the contributions, new entrants might well be deterred from entering altogether and the new competitive policy would be stillborn. In the face of a chorus of opposition, OFTEL's proposals have been revised effectively to postpone the idea of contributions indefinitely. However, BT will still receive more per call minute in interconnection payments in future than in the past from Mercury. This is because payments will be explicitly based on fully allocated costs, rather than on an ex cathedra judgment by OFTEL.

Another major proposal to revise interconnection terms has been to allow equal access for customers of competitive long-distance networks. Although the principle is clear from U.S. practice, in application in the United Kingdom there are two practical difficulties. First, neither BT's nor Mercury's local and long-distance networks are under separate management, so there must be doubts as to whether equal access could be implemented satisfactorily. Second, ensuring long-distance competitors access to established local networks on equal terms may act to the commercial disadvantage of new local networks. For this reason, OFTEL has conceded that it will undertake a cost-benefit study of the effects of equal access before allowing it to be introduced.

In short, equal access raises in acute form the problem of conflicting policy priorities. There is no desire in government to divest BT of its local networks, even though this measure, more than any other, would encourage competition. To do so would mean postponing once again the sale of the government's remaining shareholdings in BT. It now seems clear that equal access was proposed mainly at the urging of Mercury. Mercury has since had a change of heart, presumably realizing that specialist long-distance competitors might gain relatively more than it would. The cable TV interests have been flatly opposed throughout the policy review. The most likely outcome of these conflicting priorities and interests is that equal access, while remaining a theoretical possibility, will not be taken up on a wide scale in the United Kingdom.

Conclusion

Because the policy review is still continuing, it is too early to draw conclusions as to whether or not it will result in further market entry on a significant scale. The relatively open nature of the U.K. market in European terms has attracted many North American telephone and cable TV companies to take strategic positions. Which of them will stay the course and what exactly they will choose to do are not known. The future structure of the industry is genuinely uncertain. This uncertainty may be claimed to be a measure of the success of sector policy. More than in any other country, the United Kingdom has avoided letting regulatory bodies determine sector structure; instead, this task is shared with commercial interests.

16

Restructuring Telecommunications: The French Experience

Eric Huret

THREE QUESTIONS WOULD SEEM APPROPRIATE in this review of France's experience of restructuring its telecommunications sector. One is obvious: *What did we do?* In the most complete yet concise way possible this chapter endeavors to outline a reform that constituted a cultural revolution of sorts in a sector that has a long history, that is associated with very high expectations from the public, and in which the economic stakes are considerable. Another important question must, however, be answered: *Why did we do it?* This chapter underscores why a thorough reform of the sector was indispensable, given the escalating rate of technological development over the past fifteen or twenty years, the increasing convergence of data processing and telecommunications, and the worldwide movement toward deregulation, an important issue in the move toward a single European market. Finally, the question that this chapter will concentrate on most, as it involves the most innovative part of our experience in France: *How did we do it?*

The success of this sort of restructuring process presupposes the involvement of all the parties concerned at all levels; however, that involvement was by no means self-evident at the outset.

Why Was the Restructuring of Telecommunications Essential?

The last fifteen years have been marked by profound changes of various sorts that have led to structured reforms in the telecommunications industry. Three of these are:

NEW TECHNOLOGY. Technological development supported by the development of microprocessors brought telecommunications and data processing much closer; telephone exchanges have become powerful computers specialized for one specific function. Also, telecommunications networks are particularly important, and complex, data processing networks. This technological convergence opened the way to a real boom in the telecommunications-based services market, including radiocommunications services, airline reservation and management services, stock ordering and inventory management, invoicing and payment services, and, more generally, the huge area of electronic data interchange (EDI) and value added services.

Obviously monopolies were not the most appropriate structures for the rapid exploitation of these new markets.

LIBERAL IDEOLOGY. At the same time, since the beginning of the eighties, through the impetus of President Reagan and Mrs. Thatcher, deregulation and privatization appeared to many as the solution to all the problems resulting from inefficiency. This concerned every sector: banks, air transport, health, and telecommunications.

GLOBALIZATION OF MARKETS. Large-scale customers, and more particularly multinationals—for which networks had progressively become the nervous system on which their decisionmaking, production management, and competitiveness are dependent—increased pressure on operators for international services which are as coherent, homogeneous, well adapted to their needs, and economical as the services provided by the best domestic operators. The telecommunications market was destined to burst its national frontiers and become globalized.

The convergence of these three impulses—data transport and data processing technologies, the triumph of the liberal ideology, and the globalization of the market—resulted in the opening of new markets to be exploited. These same impulses are also the three main reasons an administration or a monopoly cannot be a satisfactory regulator of the telecommunications sector.

The decisive milestone in this development was the dismantling of AT&T, which took place on January 1, 1984, after a long process that had begun ten years earlier within the framework of U.S. antitrust legislation. That decision, known as the Modified Final Judgment (MFJ), had a considerable snowball effect.

AT&T, which could no longer operate local U.S. networks (responsibility for which had been turned over to the Regional Bell Operating Companies, or RBOCs) and was no longer obliged to restrict its activities to telephone services, was now able to turn toward international markets. On the other hand, the relative opening of the U.S. equipment market favored the start of foreign competition (essentially Canadian and Asian), which resulted in a shift from a trade surplus of US$800 million in 1981 to a deficit of US$2.5 billion in 1987. This led the U.S. to launch a strategy to regain the market and push for the opening of foreign service and equipment markets through bilateral discussions and multilateral forums such as the GATT. All the necessary conditions were met for the globalization of telecommunications (which, until then, had been characterized by a very rigid partitioning of national markets, centered on traditional operators and their suppliers) and a change in regulatory structures in most industrial countries (Japan and the United Kingdom were the first to adopt reforms).

Another important and determining factor was the move toward a single European market. The need to create an inter-European telecommunications market led to the publication of the EC Commission's Green Paper on the Development of the Common Market for Telecommunications and Services (EC Green Paper) in 1987, the overall objective of which was to provide European users with the largest possible range of services under the most favorable conditions possible while maintaining coherence and uniformity among the networks and services provided in member countries.

The EC Green Paper articulated ten proposals to attain this objective:

- The possibility of maintaining exclusive or special rights over network infrastructures

- The possibility of maintaining exclusive or special rights over the supply of a limited number of basic services (telephone and telex)

- Unrestricted offering of all other services within and among member countries

- Stringent standards pertaining to network infrastructure and primary services in order to preserve or allow for interconnectivity throughout Europe

- Uniform conditions imposed on network users and services providers

- Unrestricted offering of terminal equipment within and among member countries, subject to the approval and agreement procedures stipulated in the Treaty of Rome

- Separation of regulatory and operating activities

- Application of Treaty of Rome articles that pertain to competition guidelines and the limitation of cross-subsidization by public telecommunications operating companies

- Application of Treaty of Rome articles that pertain to competition guidelines and the abuse of a dominant position over private telecommunications service providers

- Application of the European Community's common trade policy to the telecommunications sector.

The EC Green Paper thus established a general framework which took into account the unquestionable specificity of telecommunications and, in a sense, brought it into the realm of the common law regulating the exchange of services, while also recognizing the globalization of the sector and putting an end to the protectionist context in which it had developed.

This evolution was confirmed in multilateral discussions outside the Community. Telecommunications were introduced into the GATT forum as negotiations began in 1986 under the Uruguay Round to liberalize trade in services. Moreover, the ITU recognized the reality of this upheaval when, in December 1988 at the World Administrative Telegraph and Telephone Conference (WATTC-88) in Melbourne, it adopted international regulations which liberalized the exchange of international telecommunications services.

Main Elements of the French Posts and Telecommunications Reform

Technological development, the evolution of ideas, globalization, and competition were all new and important challenges to be faced. Yet the concept of public service, which is intrinsically linked to the telecommunications sector, had, at the same time, to be preserved. Such was the international and EC context under which the process of reform began in France in 1989.

Three principal issues were raised:

- What regulatory framework should be established?

- What status should the public operating company be given?

- How can a monopoly be made competitive (a question that may initially appear paradoxical)?

The new legislative and regulatory framework of telecommunications in France is based on two texts: the first is the Law of July 2, 1990 (Loi du 2 juillet 1990), which took effect on January 1, 1991, and which defines a new statutory framework for the French postal and telecommunications services (Postes et Télécommunications). This law modified the status of France Télécom, granting it the means to become a competitive public service (*service public entreprenant*). We shall return to the statutory issue later. The second is the Law of December 29, 1990 (Loi du 29 décembre 1990), which defines the regulatory control over telecommunications in France by stipulating how networks and services may be established and operated.

Law on the Regulation of Telecommunications

France was the first EC country to bring its national regulatory structure in line with the EC Green Paper. Although the Law of December 29, 1990 conforms to the provisions of the Green Paper and the various EC guidelines and directives already adopted, it further reflects the original approach adopted by the French administration, which wanted, above all, to find an appropriate balance between government regulatory control and the law of supply and demand, on the one hand, and between public service and competition, on the other.

Table 1 shows how the Law of December 29, 1990, divides the provision of telecommunications services into three areas: monopoly; structured and controlled competition; and full competition.

The new law, therefore, provides for competition within a public service framework within the three areas, ranging from the conservation of a monopoly, in the case of activities or resources that are unquestionably strategic or decisive in the establishment of structures (for terrestrial infrastructures, voice telephone services, public telephone services, etc.), to open competition (for value added services and terminals) and, in between the two, structured and controlled competition (for support services and radiotelephony).

A thriving market has developed in the value added service sector, which has been open to competition since 1987. Conversely, the objective of maintaining a monopoly over the network and voice telephony is to preserve a basic framework for the French national infrastructure and to ensure optimal efficiency at both the economic and technical levels, while guaranteeing a concern for public service and the fundamental interests of the state.

The New Status of France Télécom

Under the Law of July 2, 1990, which took effect on January 1, 1991, France Télécom severed its traditional ties with the French administration and became an independent operating company, established as a public corporation.

France Télécom, like all other telecommunications service providers in France, must follow the guidelines set out by the Ministry of Posts and Telecommunications (*Ministère des Postes et Télécommunications*), now the Ministry of Industry, Posts and Telecommunications and Foreign Trade (*Ministère de l'Industrie, des Postes et Télécommunications et du Commerce Extérieure*); however, it is no longer required to submit its budgets for government approval. The management of France Télécom is responsible to its board of directors, president, and chief executive officer.

France Télécom's financial autonomy, which is comparable to that of similar organizations in neighboring countries, is essential if it is to continue to progress in

Table 16-1. Market Entry Provisions of the Telecommunications Law of December 29, 1990

Regime	Domain	Objectives
Monopoly	Public terrestrial infrastructures Telephone Telex	Public Service Strategic resource Cost optimization Coherence of basic networks
Structured and controlled competition	Bearer services[a] Radio services Independent networks[b]	Dynamic market Not to harm public service provision
Full competition	Valued added services Terminals	To create a dynamic force in multifarious markets

a. Data transmission services which do not include processing other than that necessary to transport data

b. Telecommunications infrastructures reserved for private or shared use as, for example, a cable linking two sites of the same company or the network belonging to the French national railway company (SNCF)

times of rapid technological development and to meet the increasingly complex needs of its clientele, both in France and abroad, whether alone or in partnerships. It must therefore be able to quickly adapt to the dynamic conditions of the market. Its status as a state-owned public corporation guarantees that its public service responsibilities will continue to be taken into account and that its concerns for defense, security, and research are maintained, as are its efforts to provide technical assistance to foreign countries, especially in the developing world.

The corporation s relationship with the Ministère des Postes et Télécommunications also reflects a duality and a balance. In areas where it does not have exclusive rights, France Télécom is subject to the same regulations that the Direction de la Réglementation Générale (DRG) has established for all other telecommunications service providers. For areas open to competition, the corporation, as a public operating company, is subject to the same regulations as its competitors except in the case of data transmission services. The Direction du Service Public (DSP) has a supervisory role over the corporation which is characterized by proprietary functions (notably the approval of its strategy) and by the protection of specific state interests. The relationship between France Télécom and the state is defined contractually in a plan implementation agreement (known as a "*contrat de plan*"). The current agreement, the first, covers the period from 1991 to 1994.

Supervisory Authority and Monopoly Efficiency

The new status of France Télécom and La Poste, the postal service, required restructuring of the Ministry of Posts and Telecommunications as well as the definition of a new framework for the relationship between the state and these operators.

The new ministry has two directorates:

- *Direction de la Réglementation Générale* (Directorate of General Regulatory Affairs, or DRG) is responsible for defining the regulatory framework for the activities of France Télécom and the other telecommunications service operators. This framework is defined in accordance with EC directives.

- *Direction du Service Public* (Public Service Directorate, or DSP) is responsible for exercising state supervision over France Télécom and La Poste. In this respect, it participates in the definition of their main strategic choices and defines, in cooperation with the other ministries concerned, the main economic and financial objectives which the operators must reach.

These economic and financial guiding principles are reflected in the *contrat de plan*, which, as mentioned, is a genuine contract between the operator and the state. France Télécom's contractual plan for 1991–1994 stipulates that:

- Its prices can only increase by an amount which is 3 percent lower than the yearly general increase of consumer prices.

- Its investments over the period may reach an amount to FF 150 billion.

- The level of its debt over the period must be significantly reduced.

- Personnel productivity should increase by at least 4.6 percent per year.

In addition to these economic objectives there are a certain number of quality service objectives.

The contractual plan reflects the supervisory role of the state, the owner of France Télécom, by recognizing the role of the state in:

- Exercising the necessary control over France Télécom in all areas not regulated naturally by market forces

- At the same time, vigorously protecting the operator's management autonomy from the unavoidable and powerful, long-standing and ingrained temptations of the state

- Ensuring that the operator continues to take into account the public service requirements and specific interests of the state with respect to defense, civil security, research, and cooperation with other countries.

This is a difficult task given this complex relationship between the state and the operators; it is, nevertheless, an essential prerequisite for the establishment and development of a public operator that is responsible and efficient.

How Did We Do It?

As important as the results of the reform and the reason for having undertaken it, is the process which the government chose to follow.

Dialogue as a Means of Carrying Out a Restructuring Process

Even though most factors such as technological developments, worldwide movement toward deregulation, and globalization of the telecommunications markets underlined the need for a profound restructuring of the sector, the proposed changes were perceived as a veritable cultural revolution. Also, in view of the very close link between the French postal service and France Télécom, it appeared impossible to deal with changes in the status of France Télécom without considering that of the postal service. Reform of the sector, therefore, concerned not 150,000 but 450,000 civil servants, those most opposed to change. Discussions between the government and the civil service unions did not advance beyond each side's fixed positions for a long time. It was necessary to find a way out of this stalemate and bring public opinion, customers, and all the personnel to discuss the problems of the sector and to engage in the most open reflections on the possible future directions.

Moreover, rather than trying to explain and sell a completely finalized reform package after the fact, Paul Quilès, the minister of posts and telecommunications, decided to conduct a large-scale nationwide public debate on the future of the postal and telecommunications services in France. This debate, referred to as *"Le Débat Public,"* was unique in terms of its purpose and scope.

In December 1988, Paul Quilès invited Hubert Prévot, former general commissioner of national plans (*Commissaire Général du Plan*) and former secretary of one of the three most important French unions, to conduct *Le Débat Public.* The debate was to involve both internal and external stakeholders in the most open and participatory way possible.

During the first phase, from December 1988 to March 1989, Prévot held private meetings with those most directly involved from both within the sector and outside. On the basis of these initial meetings, an interim report was prepared that included a list of the major issues to be dealt with during the second phase, the public debate.

Principles of the Public Debate

In order to successfully carry out this exceptional initiative, certain fundamental principles had to be respected. These included:

TRANSPARENCY. The complete interim report was distributed to all civil servants in the sector to allow them to familiarize themselves with the issues of the upcoming debate and to express their points of view. Throughout the debate, internal and external communication channels were used extensively.

THE NEED FOR INTERNAL AND EXTERNAL DEBATE. To allow for participation of everyone involved, simultaneous debates were held both inside and outside the sector. All participants were kept informed through *Le journal du débat public,* a bulletin created especially for the occasion. Six issues, with a distribution of over 500,000, were published.

A DEMOCRATIC APPROACH. Everyone, whether individually or collectively, was able to address Prévot, the chairman of the public debate. The unions were also able to take full part in the debate and voice their opinions and make suggestions.

The Topics of the Public Debate

The debate, which ran from April to the end of June 1989, covered the following subjects:

* *The Role and Mandate of a Public Service* from the point of view of users and from the perspective of economic modernization and competitiveness of companies.

* *Competition, Monopoly, and Regulatory Control* for both the postal and the telecommunications services. The debate examined the conditions for a public

corporation as well as the status of civil servants and the reevaluation of their careers and qualifications. Another consideration was the need to conduct a debate on autonomous management and the form it should take.

How the Public Debate Was Conducted

THE INTERNAL DEBATE: PRESENTATIONS, DEBATES, AND VIDEO BROADCASTS. Most civil servants responded by mail (6,400 sent their responses to a special post office box), by videotex, or by means of a detailed questionnaire. In addition, 8,000 meetings were organized in all postal and telecommunications departments. In total, more than 200,000 civil servants from the postal and telecommunications services were able to participate in the debate at their workplace on the future of their public service.

An internal video network was used to conduct five live debates from a broadcast center in Paris to six interactive centers and 150 television monitors throughout France and in overseas French territories. The average number of participants in each of these videoconference debates was 15,000. The same network was used to organize a number of meetings with union representatives.

THE EXTERNAL DEBATE: PRESENTATIONS, NATIONAL CONFERENCES AND PUBLIC HEARINGS. Ten million questionnaires were made available to the public through post offices and the commercial outlets of France Télécom. Seven national conferences were organized with public service representatives, allowing numerous participants throughout the country to debate the issues that concerned them. These conferences debated issues such as "The Expectations of the Business Sector," "The Stakes in Europe," "What Are the Expectations of the French People?" and "Instruments of Decentralization."

At the same time, a hundred or so public hearings provided a means for discovering the opinions of all parties involved in the debate, including the political view of parliamentary groups, representatives of industry and finance, banks, professional federations, heads of companies, the views of consumer and user organizations, and of prominent figures from university and research sectors.

In sum there was an unprecedented effort to involve as many participants as possible in reflection on the restructuring to be done.

The debate led to a number of clear conclusions, specifically, that:

• On the whole, the public (the customers) was satisfied with the services provided by France Télécom and La Poste.

• It wanted to have the concept of public service, which it deemed essential, maintained.

• There was general hostility to privatization.

- Most of the personnel wanted to retain the status of civil servant.

On the basis of these conclusions, Paul Quilès carried out a new phase of direct consultations with the union, at the end of which he proposed to the government a reform in three points:

- A restructuring leading to the creation of two public corporations (La Poste and France Télécom) with the status of civil servant for the personnel being maintained

- The introduction of either free or regulated competition compatible with a strong public service

- The adoption of a package of social measures for the personnel of the two new public corporations resulting in a reduction in the number of categories of P&T civil servants from 45 to 6, and the number of grades from 111 to 11.

Conclusions

This is the essence of the reform carried out in the French postal and telecommunications sector between 1988 and 1990. Its success is due first to the strong determination of the politicians in charge, namely, the minister of posts and telecommunications and the whole government, including the personal commitment of the prime minister. It is also due to the method adopted, which consisted in talking frankly with all the stakeholders, listening to them, and taking their views into account. Yet this reform is not a model; rather it was adapted to the actual situation in France at that time and carried out in an atmosphere of social peace. It corresponds to a phase of much broader developments; the rapid changes which affect the sector will undoubtedly require further reform and adaptations where each must find the way which best suits its situation and history. The best reform is one that is successful!

17

PTT Telecom Netherlands: Civil Servant or Entrepreneur?

Gerard J. van Velzen

APART FROM NATURAL DECAY AND PURELY random processes, most changes are reactions, that is, adaptations to other changes in the corporate or social environment. Let us turn first to these external factors and then to our reactions and responses. An example from the air transport industry will illustrate the point. It is well known that most airlines operate similar types of aircraft on the same routes to the same destinations, that they use the same type of fuel from the same suppliers, and that they charge about the same fare. And yet most people have a preference. Service—measured in terms of reliability and punctuality, friendliness, and the ability to improvise in unusual situations—makes the difference. Probably the biggest change in modern business—and this is especially relevant to the telecommunications and information sectors—is the current shift away from pure technology to the service business. But that is not all.

Markets and suppliers are going global at an increasingly rapid rate for several reasons. Economies of scale imply a minimum level of production, leading often to a need to expand beyond the limitations of a domestic market. Specific know-how and specialization fit well with international demand. Combining the product and service activities of two or more companies often yields a more complete package that is better suited to a discerning market and to the apparent need for one-stop shopping. Economic internationalization is also reflected in and stimulated by international cooperation at a structural level and within alliances such as the European Community. The synergistic effects may even transcend the sphere of economics; those who trade, do not fight wars!

Increasingly firms are going international by launching joint ventures or other forms of cooperation. The trend toward globalization applies to an increasing number of commodities and services, and especially to the information and telecommunications sectors. The role of information has changed dramatically over the last centuries. The invention of the printing press ushered in the end of the Middle Ages. Today we find ourselves in the middle of a comparable information revolution. The use of computer and telecommunications technologies has become widespread, becoming an integral part of almost all production processes and increasingly influential in our daily lives.

Importance of Information and Telecommunications to Other Sectors

Information, and therefore its transmission, has become essential for all transport flows of goods around the world and is, indeed, a crucial factor of production. This is illustrated by the percentage of the total work force employed in the information sector, the percentage of information costs in total corporate expenditure, and the fact that some specialized firms and sectors deal in information and information only. These factors, which cannot generally be influenced by the market players, will largely determine the environment within which the suppliers and transmitters of information operate; there are, however, other important determinants over which suppliers and transporters of information can exert considerable influence. These are quality, price, and added value, and it is in these areas that companies will seek a high profile and where they will compete. It is here, too, where the customers' priorities lie.

Changing regulations within the different markets are also of great significance to the information sector. The deregulation of the telecommunications industry has increasingly gained momentum over the last few years and shows no sign of abating. Indeed, one could go so far as to predict that the process of legislative change will be ongoing, reflecting not only the changes in market forces and technology but also the customers' constantly changing needs and desires.

The reasons for deregulation are varied. In the first place, we are faced with a mature market encompassing today's hardware, clients, and operators. The regulation of this market requires a structure other than that of the traditional monopoly. Allied to this, the performance of a telecommunications operator—or rather the price-to-performance ratio—may prompt a government to allow or encourage competition by opening up the market as a whole or in part. Taking the view that telecommunications are essential to the functioning of a modern economy, the government may also wish to create the essential production factors.

The Dutch Experience

The latter, positive approach lies at the heart of the deregulation of the Dutch telecommunications market. The Dutch economy is characterized by a high degree of specialization in the trade, transport, and service sectors, where information and the transmission of information are of special importance. More than half of all Dutch companies are active in these sectors. In addition, the Netherlands has traditionally been an open, internationally-oriented society situated at the crossroads of major trade routes and international connections. Although the country is home to just 5 percent of Europe's population, its accounts for over 25 percent of intra-European Community road transport. The Netherlands fulfills its function as gateway to Europe in various ways at the port of Rotterdam, one of the busiest in the world, at Amsterdam's Schiphol Airport, and in its role in the international transport of information. This background to the Netherlands' service-oriented economic structure was a decisive influence in the far-reaching deregulation of the telecommunications sector in 1989 and the broad consensus that supported it.

More and more companies are internationalizing their business, a trend that will be reinforced by the lifting of most trade barriers within Europe. The quality and reliability of the services offered in the Netherlands will reflect the growing importance of moving information from country to country.

Deregulation in Europe will start with data transport and mobile communications. Views and developments in the Netherlands are in keeping with the open market approach. Regulatory changes are expected in the near future as part of the overall aim of broadening and deepening the choice of services available to customers. In the Netherlands a second mobile operator will enter the market in 1994. Most satellite services are already offered in a competitive environment, and the market for data transport services were opened up in 1993.

The government announced that it will sell up to two-thirds of its shares in Royal PTT Nederland NV (KPN), the parent of PTT Telecom Netherlands; the first tranche, about 30 percent of the two-thirds will be sold during the first half of 1994. KPN was turned into a wholly government-owned joint stock company at the time of the 1989 reform.

The New PTT Telecom Netherlands

On the face of it, the current situation as envisaged in the legislation has resulted in an optimal business environment for the information industry. More than that, the current order offers PTT Telecom Netherlands an optimal sphere of operations. This can be illustrated with reference to some important corporate parameters, including corporate culture, capital, flexibility, organization (personnel), and quality.

Corporate Culture

The question of corporate culture pertains particularly to the strategic base of business operations and the obvious long-term aspects. One can compare an old-style civil service organization with a leading company by reference to specific points that illustrate the change: from political satisfaction to satisfied customers, from the avoidance of political problems to the prevention of corporate problems, and from occasionally nonexplicit to clearly delineated standards of output. The system is no longer leading the population but is controlled by it. Corporate decisions are made without regard to political timetables. Risk avoidance has been replaced by entrepreneurial behavior that weighs the risks and is service-oriented. And finally, employees are no longer exclusively regarded as a cost factor but first and foremost as an asset.

Capital

As to capital formation the new situation offers far greater freedom than that permitted by a state budget. The implementation of new technologies, the expansion of traffic capacity, and the continued rise in the level of quality, all require additional funds. Therefore in recent years PTT Telecom has roughly doubled its scale of investment, from some 1.5 billion guilders to around 3 billion guilders a year. Changes in PTT Telecom Netherlands' performance and investment levels are shown in Table 17–1 and Figure 17–1.

Organization

To achieve the necessary organization to enable PTT Telecom Netherlands to operate in today's and tomorrow's telecommunications service market required a clear external reorientation of the company and a concomitant internal regrouping of resources. Improved market orientation was achieved through the creation of five so-called business areas which ensure that the services and products are closely attuned to the needs of their particular markets (coherent product-market combinations). The managers of these business areas and the managers of the Netherlands' thirteen telecommunications districts are personally responsible for the operating profit. By 1992 a new accounting scheme had to be introduced. Clear goals with regard to investments, returns, quality, profit, and market share are formulated on a contract basis. The basic structure of PTT Telecom Netherlands is illustrated in Figure 17–2. At present PTT Telecom Netherlands is further subdividing its structure of districts with the introduction of some thirty regional units which will provide integrated services to customers in their areas. These will form the cutting edge of the organization and will be able to enlist the assistance of support units when necessary. Each telecommunications district will have some of these regional units, while some districts will share a support unit. The planning, construction, and management of the infrastructure will be rearranged to enable a flexible response to changing capacity requirements.

Table 17-1. PTT Telecom Netherlands, Key Performance Figures, 1990 and 1992

Parameter	1990	1992
Net turnover (billion guilders)	9.6	11.1
Operating result (billion guilders)	2.6	2.8
Operating profit (billion guilders)	1.3	1.3
Total investment (billion guilders)	2.7	2.9
Employees	29,000	31,000
Total lines (millions)	7	7.4
Penetration (lines)	46	48

Figure 17-1. Investments PTT Telecom

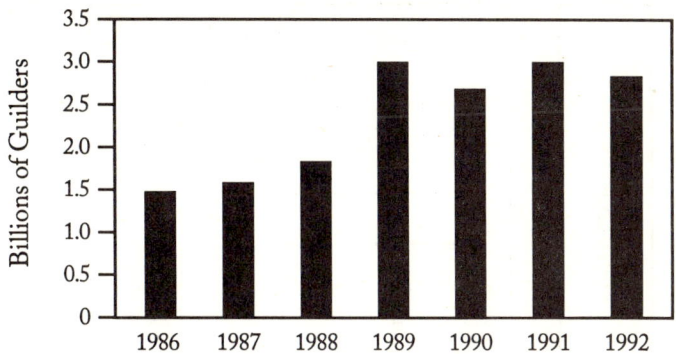

Quality

The most important factor in the entire operation and in the current management of the business has turned out to be quality. Quality stands for a customer-oriented approach and flexibility; quality affects the culture and organization mentioned earlier and, in relation to the price, quality is a decisive factor in the service business. The overall importance of quality to an organization is best illustrated by comparing the profile of a normal business with that of a quality company as illustrated in Table 17-2.

An active response to the changing business environment entails more than optimal performance in individual cases. The company must be geared structurally to the market as a whole and be prepared for future developments. PTT Telecom Netherlands strategy therefore includes a sweeping quality improvement program, intensified cooperation with other companies, reinforcement of its international position, and further streamlining of the organization.

PTT Telecom Netherlands has set itself some of the highest performance targets in the world and is on course to meeting them within a few years. Independent customer surveys are conducted every three months to determine performance in a number of key areas, including directory assistance, the time taken to respond to customer requests, the condition of pay phones, and other items that customers indicate as being crucial to their perception of good service. The comprehensive total quality management program, started in 1989, continues. All parts of the company have since become involved in the program, and the entire workforce is receiving training in quality.

A series of measures produced noticeable improvements in directory assistance, pay phones, the response to complaints, and the provision of information to customers about their telephone bills and other matters. PTT Telecom Netherlands obtained an International Standards Organization (ISO) quality of service certificate in 1992 for efficient and economic provision of telephone shops, other outlets, and

Figure 17-2. PTT Telecom Netherlands Organization Structure

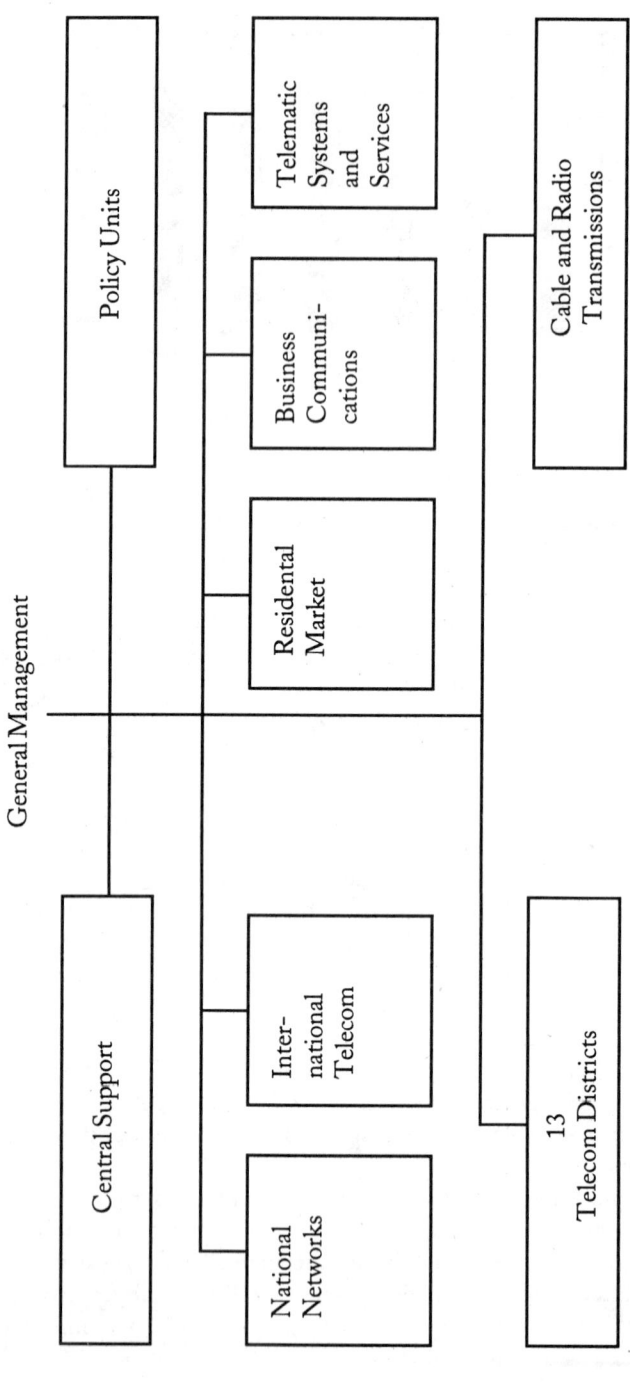

Table 17-2. Importance of Quality to an Organization: Normal vs. Quality Company

Normal Company	Quality Company
First profit, then satisfied customers	Profit results from satisfied customers
Problem tracking	Problem prevention
Cost control by limitation	Cost control through the coordination of activities and supplies
Limited training budget	Large training budget
No clear goals, roles, or style	Clear view on goals, own role, and style at all levels
Complaints are a nuisance	One can learn from complaints
Emphasis on technology	Selectively applied technology under management supervision
Controlled by systems	Controlled by cooperative people
Quality, productivity, cost control are separate items	Managed simultaneous improvement

production units. This international approval of quality and reliability confirms for PTT Telecom Netherlands—and, consequently, for its customers—the efficiency and effectiveness of its vital, nationwide distribution network. More customer-oriented processes in the core business are now under review and will be certified in the near future. ISO-certificates fit into PTT Telecom Netherlands customer-oriented marketing strategy.

PTT Telecom Netherlands international telecommunications position follows naturally from the Dutch economic position and specialization in the service industry, the relatively small size of our home market, and the large number of multinational companies operating in the Netherlands. To offer them and others a high-quality international access port, one-stop shopping, and a complete range of services, PTT Telecom Netherlands is establishing its own international telecommunications circuits, setting up its own network of foreign offices, and maintaining a highly favorable price-to-performance ratio that is one of the best in Europe. For purposes of comparison, independent data such as those illustrated in Figures 17-3 to 17-6 show that both business and private customers consistently spend less in the Netherlands than almost anywhere else in Europe for comparable services and products.

Considerations of size, core activities, and a rapidly changing market mean that suppliers are unable to provide a total package of services single-handedly. As a

Figure 17-3. Installed Main Lines Per Employee

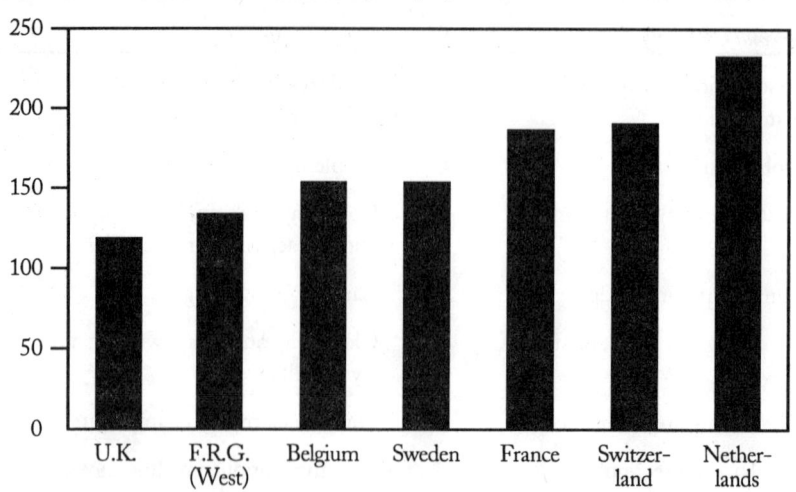

privatized company, PTT Telecom can respond more quickly to market opportunities, since only business aspects need to be taken into account in the decision-making process.

Cooperation and Joint Ventures

PTT Telecom Netherlands is actively seeking forms of cooperation with other operators and companies. It has acquired interests in both domestic and foreign companies and has set up forms of cooperation in those areas requiring specialized knowledge of the market or where new services and products must be marketed with exceptional speed. In addition, partnerships are regarded as both necessary and desirable for the provision of services on a European or worldwide scale. PTT Telecom Netherlands specializes in the networks field.

PTT Telecom Netherlands has interests in more than twenty companies, including: Surfnet which develops and operates a value added network for universities and research centers; INTIS, an electronic data interchange services for the port of Rotterdam; Satellite Business Television; and Infonet, a worldwide supplier of network services. In addition, PTT Telecom participates in: Dutch Videotex; Transponet, a value added services and electronic data interchange for the European road haulage sector; and Medimatica which provides networks and services for the health sector.

A strategic alliance with our Swedish partner Televerket (transformed on July 1, 1993, from a government agency into a limited liabililty company called Telia AB), in a joint venture called Unisource, took shape in 1992. In 1993 the company welcomed the Swiss telecommunications operator as a new partner. Unisource

Figure 17-4. Charges for Outgoing Calls from the Netherlands

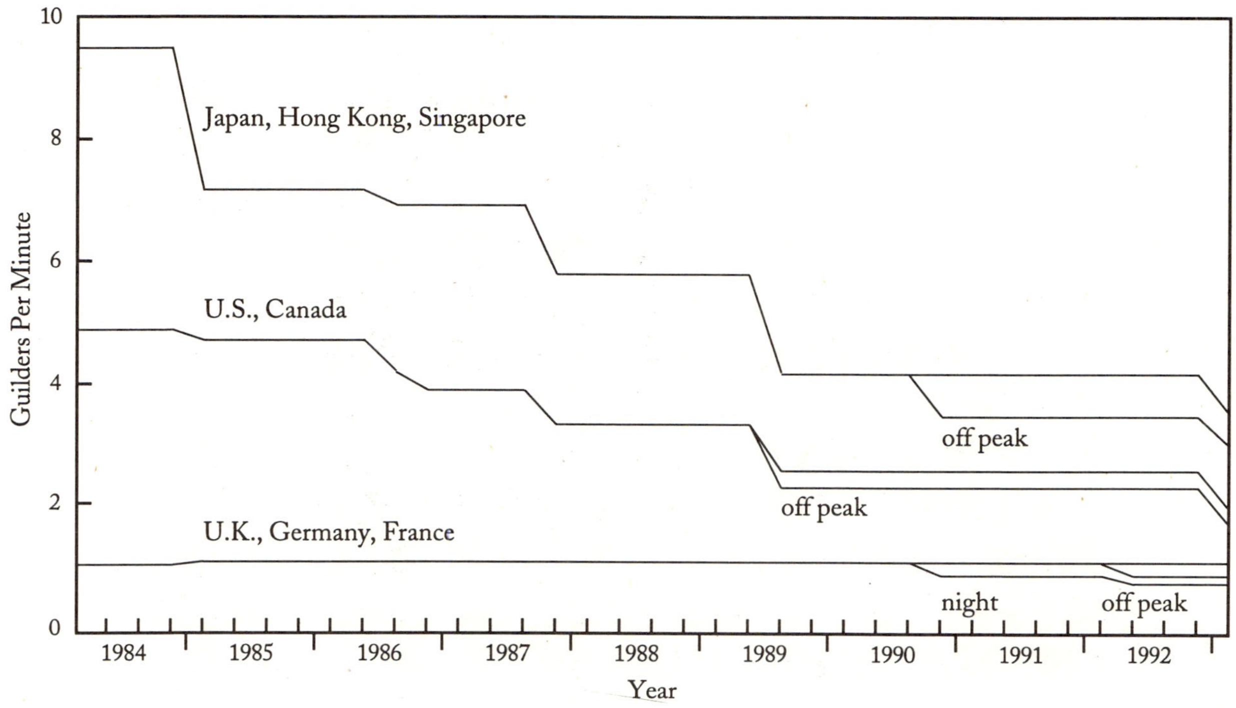

Figure 17-5. Residential Telephone Costs (February 1, 1993)

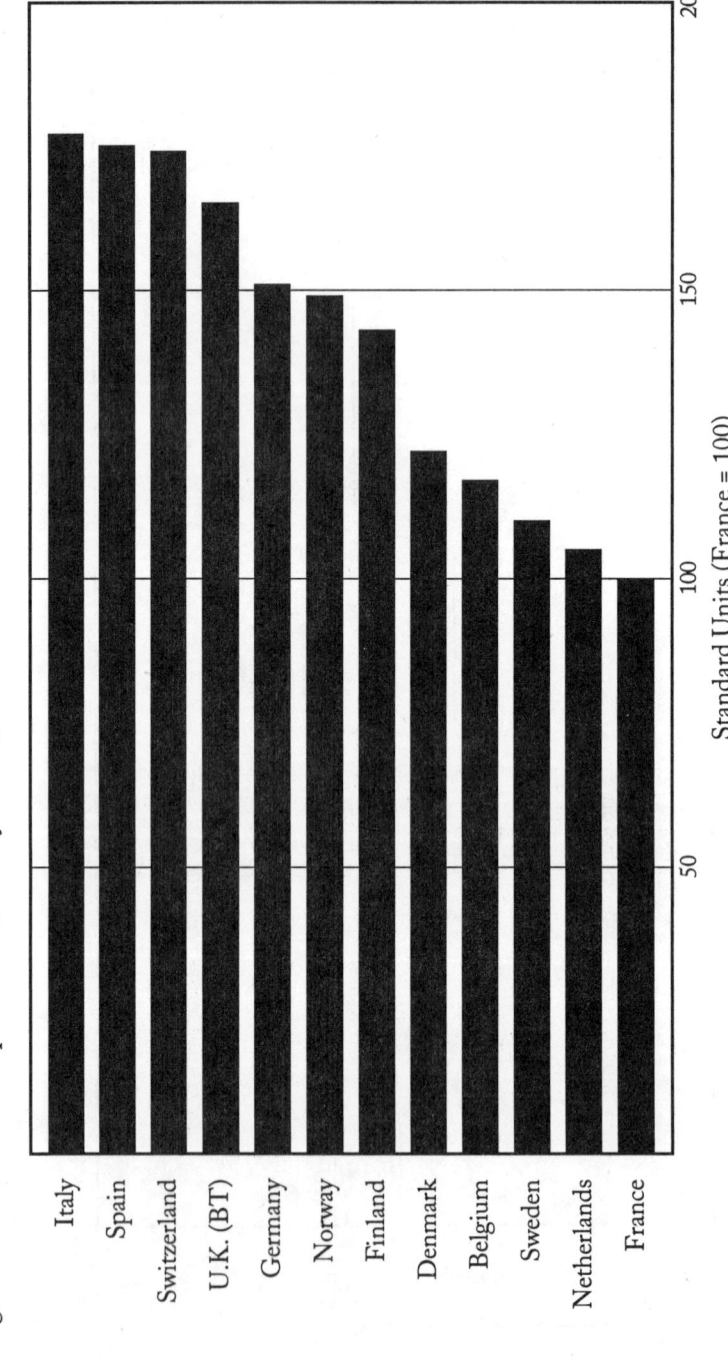

Standard Units (France = 100)

Source: Tarifica Service, Intelidata Ltd

312

Figure 17-6. Business Telephone Costs (February 1, 1993)

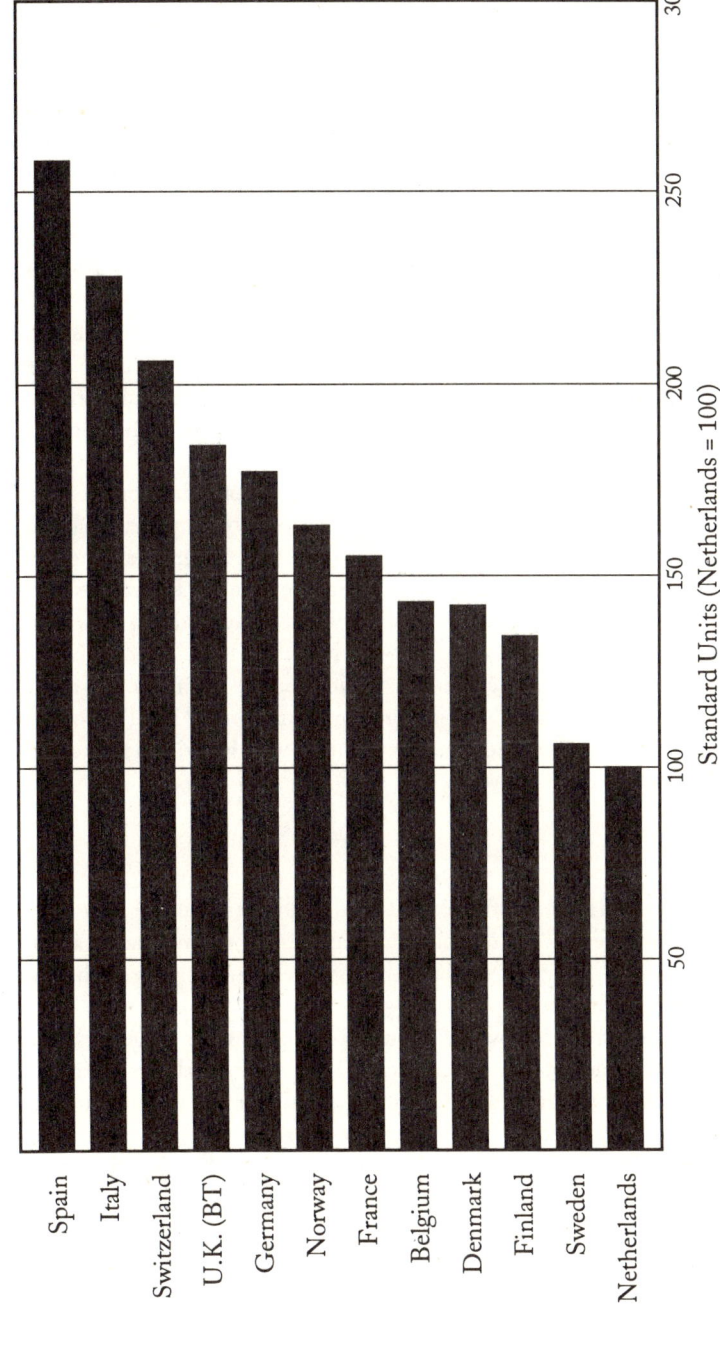

Standard Units (Netherlands = 100)

Source: Tarifica Service, Intelidata Ltd

313

Business Networks (UBN) and Unisource Satellite Services (USS) are now ready to provide their customers with a wide range of services and products. Unisource is establishing subsidiaries in several countries.

PTT Telecom Netherlands launched a joint venture with the Czech and Slovak telecommunications operators and is looking into acquiring a Caribbean interest.

Business activities have been developed in Eastern Europe, notably in the Ukraine, with the Ukrainian Telecom (UTEL) and Ukrainian Mobile Communications (UMC) joint ventures. In UTEL PTT Telecom Netherlands joined forces with Deutsche Bundespost Telekom (DBP Telekom) of Germany, AT&T of the United States, and the Ukrainian government. This cooperation is aimed at establishing, modernizing, and operating Ukraine's international telecommunications services as well as installing and managing a long-haul trunk network.

UMC, which has a twenty-year license, is a joint venture of the Ukrainian government, DBP Telekom, Telecom Denmark, and PTT Telecom Netherlands. In the coming seven years, UMC will install a mobile telecommunications network for the twenty-one largest cities in the Ukraine. It will be ready for use in the five principal cities within three years.

Using satellite links PTT Telecom Netherlands is handling some of Bulgaria's international traffic and examining the scope for modernizing and expanding local facilities. PTT Telecom Netherlands has entered into a cooperative venture with US Sprint, Cable & Wireless, Unitel, and Teleglobe Canada to provide worldwide private company networks using the public-switched international network, known as virtual private networks (VPNs). Through Nepostel, PTT Telecom Netherlands contributes know-how and assistance to developing countries. In addition to cooperation with established international organizations, PTT Telecom Netherlands has intensified its contacts and cooperation with individual telecommunications companies all over the world.

Conclusion

Having redefined its core activities, changed its corporate culture, reconfigured its organization, established partnerships, and emphasized the international context of its operations, PTT Telecom Netherlands must ask how all this affects the customer, the company's raison d'être.

The discerning client is now able to choose from a wider range of services and products. This is true not only of peripherals but applies equally to new services and tailor-made service contracts. Increasing competition is putting pressure on prices, as for instance, international traffic. In addition, the customer has more points of access to PTT Telecom Netherlands via the countrywide chain of Primafoon shops, business centers, and, of course, improved telephone access.

Service is improving. Customers who are being connected more quickly and the rapidly growing number of telephone booths are but two examples of this. In addition, PTT Telecom Netherlands maintains close ties with business user groups and consumer organizations and regularly conducts customer surveys.

These changes are also of interest to other, highly important market players, and particularly the telecommunications operators beyond the Netherlands' borders. These are PTT Telecom Netherlands' natural partners. After all, their basic service is seamlessly compatible with PTT Telecom Netherland's, which is why the international telecommunications community became one of the first organizations to encompass the entire world. Against this background of globalizing services and the ever-more important role of information and its transportation, cross-border cooperation is increasingly in the common and general interest. In addition, foreign operators' areas of expertise hold out interesting possibilities for the combination of complementary skills and the provision of tailor-made services and products for a differentiated market.

PTT Telecom Netherlands' relations with other operators are characterized by a more businesslike but also more open approach than in the past. In many respects these relations are more differentiated. On the one hand, they offer possibilities for cooperation at a number of levels, from joint ventures for single projects to preferred partnerships; on the other, it has become clear that within an otherwise good relationship there may be several opposing points of contact which need not be mutually exclusive. One's partner in one area may be a rival in another. The demarcation of such areas is subject to change over time and, naturally, always open to discussion; however, a lasting relationship requires mutual investment in terms of time, attention, and the exchange of know-how, and it should be based on a clear foundation of trust. PTT Telecom Netherlands adopts an open attitude in these matters.

18

Reform and Unification of Telecommunications in Germany

Karl-Heinz Neumann and Thomas Schnöring

TELECOMMUNICATIONS, LIKE THE POSTAL SERVICE, developed in Germany in a stable PTT environment managed by the government under the Ministry of Posts and Telecommunications. The Deutsche Bundespost (DBP), which offered postal, telecommunications, and postal banking services, was endowed with far-reaching monopoly rights. Interestingly enough, the scope of reserved services was much broader for telecommunications than for the posts, and there was no regulation in an economic sense of the dominant supplier. The DBP itself was responsible for regulation of private service providers and users.

The old structure, however, started to become inefficient, and conflicts of interest began to appear. By the early 1980s it became evident that this structure could not meet the challenges of market forces and technological developments and, therefore, that it could not be expected to survive. Reform models were discussed in the mid-1980s, and a final political and parliamentary decision to restructure the telecommunications system was made in the first half of 1989. On January 1, 1990 the telecommunications, post, and postal banking functions of the Deutsche Bundespost were split into three separate state entities. Deutsche Bundespost Telekom (DBP Telekom) is the entity responsible for telecommunications. The first part of this chapter discusses the outcome of this reform process.

By late 1989 discussion of German unification dominated the political debate. It also became the major event in the telecommunications sector, and the merger of the East and the West German PTTs occurred just as DBP Telekom, the restructured public telecommunications service provider, was beginning operation in a new organizational environment. Developing telecommunications in East Germany became the most important challenge in German telecommunications. A large part of this chapter deals with the policies and strategies of meeting this challenge.

Telecommunications Reform in Germany

Reform of the German telecommunications sector began with a governmental commission which developed a new telecommunications policy model. Table 18–1

Table 18-1. Time Table of the German Telecommunications Sector Reform Process

Time	Event
1984	First decision of the government to reform the structure and policy of the telecommunications sector.
1985–1987	Government commission on telecommunications prepares analysis and recommendations.
September 1987	Report presented by the commission to the government.
September 1987– March 1988	Drafting of the new legislation in the Ministry of Posts and Telecommunications.
May 1988	Government adopts a new telecommunications policy and drafts new legislation.
May 1988– May 1989	Parliamentary debate on the new legislation.
July 1, 1989	Enactment of the new law (Poststrukturgesetz).
July 1989– December 1989	Separation of the DBP from the Ministry of Posts and Telecommunications; separation of the three DBP enterprises (post, telecommunications, banking).
January 1, 1990	New organizational structure becomes effective.
July 1, 1990	Liberalization of the telephone equipment market.
October 3, 1990	Merger of East and West German PTTs.
July 1, 1991	Change in the legal relationship between the three DBP enterprises and their customers. This is now subject to private rather than public law.

indicates the key milestones in the reform process, which extended over several years. Although Germany was a latecomer among major countries to reform, the rather lengthy time schedule should not be a surprise since the political reform package in Germany was larger than that in other Western countries. This was because of two major steps that had to be taken. The first (in many countries, the only) step was the formulation and implementation of a competitive environment in the telecommunications markets. The second involved putting into place a new regulatory structure and the organizational restructuring of the major supplier.

The reform process consisted of four major elements:

1. Separation of the regulatory from the business functions in the sector

2. Separation of posts from telecommunications

3. Definition of regulatory models, instruments, and policies

4. Establishment of a new managerial structure within the Deutsche Bundespost to improve internal efficiency.

The new legislation produced an organizational structure where the Ministry of Posts and Telecommunications no longer has the managerial authority but maintains the regulatory function for the sector (see Figure 18-1).

The German Parliament did not open all segments of the telecommunications market to competition. Major areas of reserved services remain. DBP Telekom, for example, remains the only provider of transmission facilities (network monopoly) and of voice telephony. All other services, including data communications and value added services, are open to unregulated competition. There are two major and significant exemptions from the general network monopoly. These are all segments of mobile communications and the whole satellite communications area, which are open to competition. Market access is possible on the basis of licensing. Free and unrestricted competition exists in all aspects of the customer premises equipment market.

DBP Telekom, the dominant supplier in the German market, is now subject to regulatory measures to ensure a fair and efficient competitive environment in services.

Unification and the Challenge to Develop Telecommunications in East Germany

The rest of this chapter deals with the poor state of the telecommunications sector in East Germany and the undertaking to integrate it into DBP Telekom's West German network following unification in October 1990.

The Organizational Structure of East German Telecommunications before Unification

In the German Democratic Republic (GDR), as in West Germany before restructuring in 1989, the Ministry of Posts and Telecommunications (Ministerium für Post- und Fernmeldewesen, or MPF) was in charge of postal and telecommunications services. These were provided by the East German PTT which also distributed all newspapers and journals. This involved not only physical delivery but also billing and marketing functions, which usually represent a publisher's main economic risk. In addition, the MPF was responsible for manufacturing all telecommunications equipment through the Kombinat Nachrichtenelekronik, the parent organization of fourteen production units or firms (VEBs). Cabling and installation of switching equipment was carried out by the VEB Fernmeldebau, a subsidiary of the PTT.

The telecommunications industry, which had previously been under the control of one of the manufacturing industry ministries, came under the control of the

Figure 18-1. The New Regulatory Framework of German Posts and Telecommunications

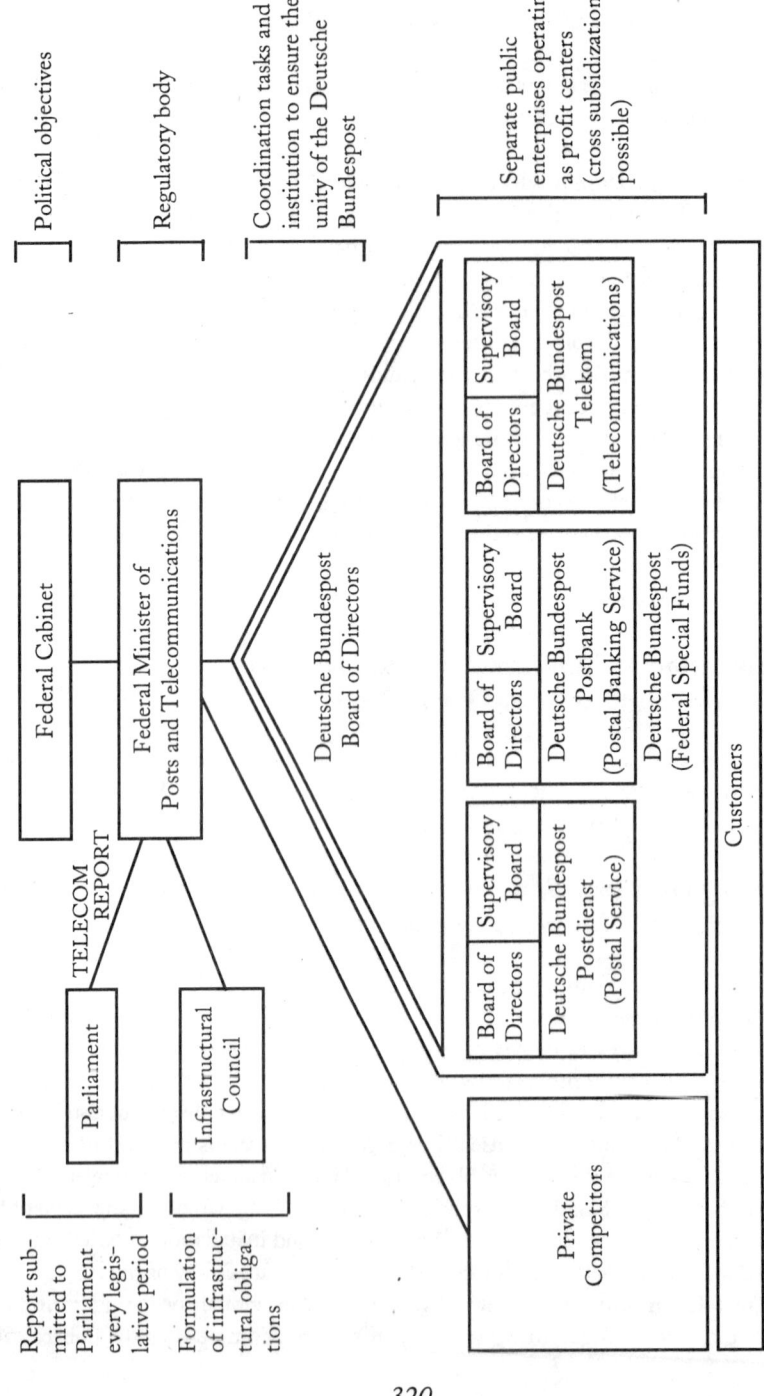

MPF in 1989. This change, seen as one of the last attempts of the PTT management to improve the poor economic performance of the telecommunications system within the old organizational and political framework, was controversial. In the planned economic system of the GDR, the PTT could not expand the telecommunications system on the basis of its own financial viability. It had to report its investment needs to a central planning bureaucracy which made investment decisions based on its own priorities rather than the economic needs and financial performance of the sector. Foremost among these was the export of telecommunications equipment, mainly to other East European countries. In 1987, 80 percent of the national production of switching equipment was exported, 13 percent went to other national users, and just 7 percent to the East German PTT. In an industry where, on average, 40 percent of all production was for export, the threat that a PTT in charge of its own investment decisions would divert consumption to national use was obvious. The merger of the East German PTT with DBP Telekom has resulted in a complete separation of service provision from manufacturing, along the lines of the arrangement in the Federal Republic.

Broadcast and television matters had a high priority in the East German political system and, therefore, in the East German telecommunications system. The East German PTT had an influential department for broadcast and television with far-reaching responsibilities. Not only did the East German PTT operate all receiver and transmitter stations, it also controlled and ran all studio aspects. If, for instance, a private citizen, wanted to use a microphone for public purposes, he had to rent it from the PTT, which was in all respects a comprehensive communications company. For obvious political reasons, broadcasting and television have now, like manufacturing, been separated from the telecommunications services business and put under the control of a totally reorganized broadcasting and television system.

Structurally, the East German PTT had a rather broad monopoly. In 1985 the Law on Posts and Telecommunications gave the state the sovereign right to operate posts and telecommunications traffic. This right was exercised by the MPF and the PTT, with the minister responsible for ensuring uniformity of control, management, and planning. The government as a whole decided on basic policy matters. The law distinguished between public and nonpublic telecommunications. The PTT operated all public telecommunications systems and services. Nonpublic telecommunications was defined as traffic within a private telecommunications system and within a leased-line network; leased lines, however, could be rented only from the PTT, which had a comprehensive services and network monopoly. Only other state institutions such as the armed forces and the police were allowed to run their own telecommunications networks.

The minister of posts and telecommunications was head of a government commission responsible for coordinating the various state-owned telecommunications networks and for controlling their integration with the public telecommunications network. The East German PTT provided leased lines to business users to run their own private networks. Operating private networks, however, required a waiver by the MPF. Private networks were one way out of the poor public network performance.

Sectors which had a high priority on the political agenda could claim investment funds for telecommunications equipment in the central budgeting process, and the East German PTT had to provide leased lines for these private networks. Roughly 20 percent of the lines at the upper level of the telecommunications network were leased lines. This led, as one can imagine, to a substantial waste of network capacity.

The state regulated the use of the radio frequency spectrum through a public frequency commission headed by the MPF.

Generally, any private operation of a telecommunications service or equipment required authorization by the MPF. There was no private market for telecommunications equipment. All terminals were provided by the PTT. The few exceptions concerned some private PABXs where the PTT had to authorize their connection to the public network.

The Situation and Performance of the East German Telecommunications System

The telecommunications system in East Germany provided only basic services consisting of telephony, telex, and, to a very limited extent, data communications and leased lines. Mobile communications and value added services were virtually unknown.

There were 1.8 million main exchange lines before unification. This was about double that in 1969 (see Figure 18-2) and represented an installed base of about 4 million telephones. Approximately 1.1 million, or 60 percent of main stations, belonged to private households, the majority of whom had to rely on party lines. Only one out of seven private households could make use of a telephone. On average, there were 11 main lines per 100 population.

The telephone network exhibited enormous regional differences in density. While in East Berlin nearly every second household was connected to the network, in cities such as Dresden and Rostock only every ninth household was connected. These differences were due only in very small part to differences in income and demand. Political priorities were determinate.

The level of telephone penetration obviously did not reflect the demand for telephones in East Germany. In 1990 there was a waiting list for main exchange lines of 1.2 million. Nearly as many private households wanted access to the network as were connected to it. Given that the delay in obtaining a telephone connection was ten to twenty years, the official waiting list probably represented only a fraction of total demand. During the last years before unification, the size of the waiting list increased twice as fast as the number of newly installed main stations (Figure 18–2).

Nearly all main exchange lines were connected to automatic exchanges, but only about 20 percent had access to international direct dialing. The East German network consisted of 1,500 local networks and 2,700 local switching centers, and the two-level trunking network consisted of 182 switching centers. All local and trunk switches were analog and electromechanical and only 25 percent of these were crossbar. Table 18–2 shows the age distribution of local switches. Trunk switches exhibited a similar age structure. Most switches were, in fact, totally depreciated, some more than twice.

Figure 18-2. East German Main Lines and Waiting Lists, 1963–88

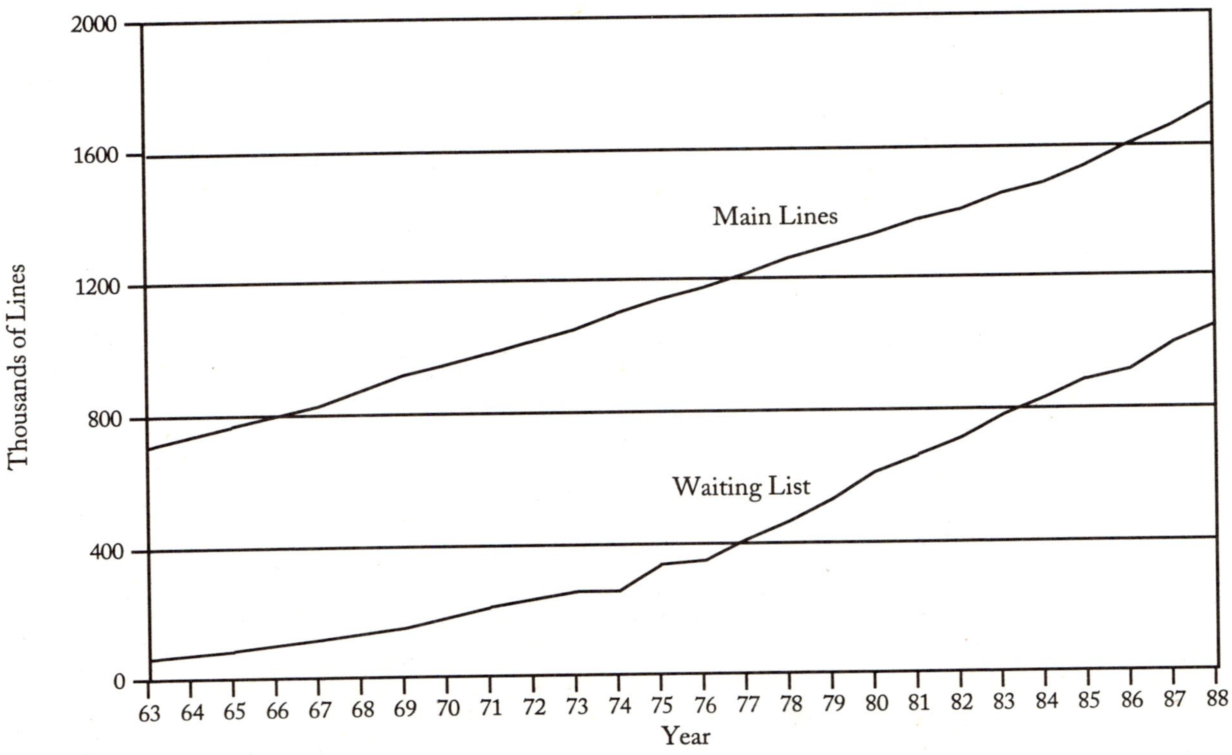

Main Lines

Waiting List

Thousands of Lines

Year

2000
1600
1200
800
400
0

63 64 65 66 67 68 69 70 71 72 73 74 75 76 77 78 79 80 81 82 83 84 85 86 87 88

Table 18-2. Age Distribution of Local Switches in East Germany

Year Built	Percent of all Local Switches
1922 to 1934	23.1
1935 to 1950	42.6
1953 to 1958	6.1
1963 to 1965	28.1

The situation and performance of the transmission network was better. Pulse Code Modulation (PCM) systems had been implemented since the mid-seventies, but a large part of all transmission systems was still analog. Less than 1 percent of all cables used optical-fiber technology, which was mainly introduced in larger local networks.

The poor technical performance of the telephone network did not permit facsimile or data communications. Only a few hundred facsimile machines and data modems with very low transmission rates were connected to the network.

The East German PTT operated neither a circuit-switched nor a packet-switched data communications network. It had 3,000 leased-line subscribers for data communications and another 1,500 subscribers connected to an operator-handled data communications network. The waiting list for data connections exceeded 10,000.

There had been plans since the mid-eighties to set up a packet-switched data network based on Western technology. A contract signed with Siemens, however, could not be realized because of the restrictions on the export of high technology equipment to the former Soviet block countries, the so-called CoCom restrictions. The telex network, with about 20,000 subscribers, also consisted mainly of technology of the fifties. Only one international switching center was digital.

Services in general and telecommunications in particular had a rather low priority in the political budgeting process of the East German economic system. The East German government had for a very long time underestimated the importance of a modern telecommunications infrastructure for economic and social development. The share of telecommunications investments during the seventies and eighties was around 0.7 percent—1.3 percent of the total national investment—and the percentage of depreciated equipment increased from 50 percent in 1971 to 57 percent in 1989.[2]

Figure 18–3 illustrates the poor performance and underdevelopment of East German telecommunications with respect to other countries. East Germany's telephone penetration of 10.6 was one of the lowest in Europe. Table 18–3 compares the situation in East and West Germany before unification.

East Germany was, in fact, underprovided in telecommunications services relative to other goods and services. This was neither rational nor justified even under the economic system of the former East Germany, where not even the centrally planned economic system could explain the poor performance in the sector. Underdevelopment in telecommunications must, therefore, have been due to political rather than economic factors.

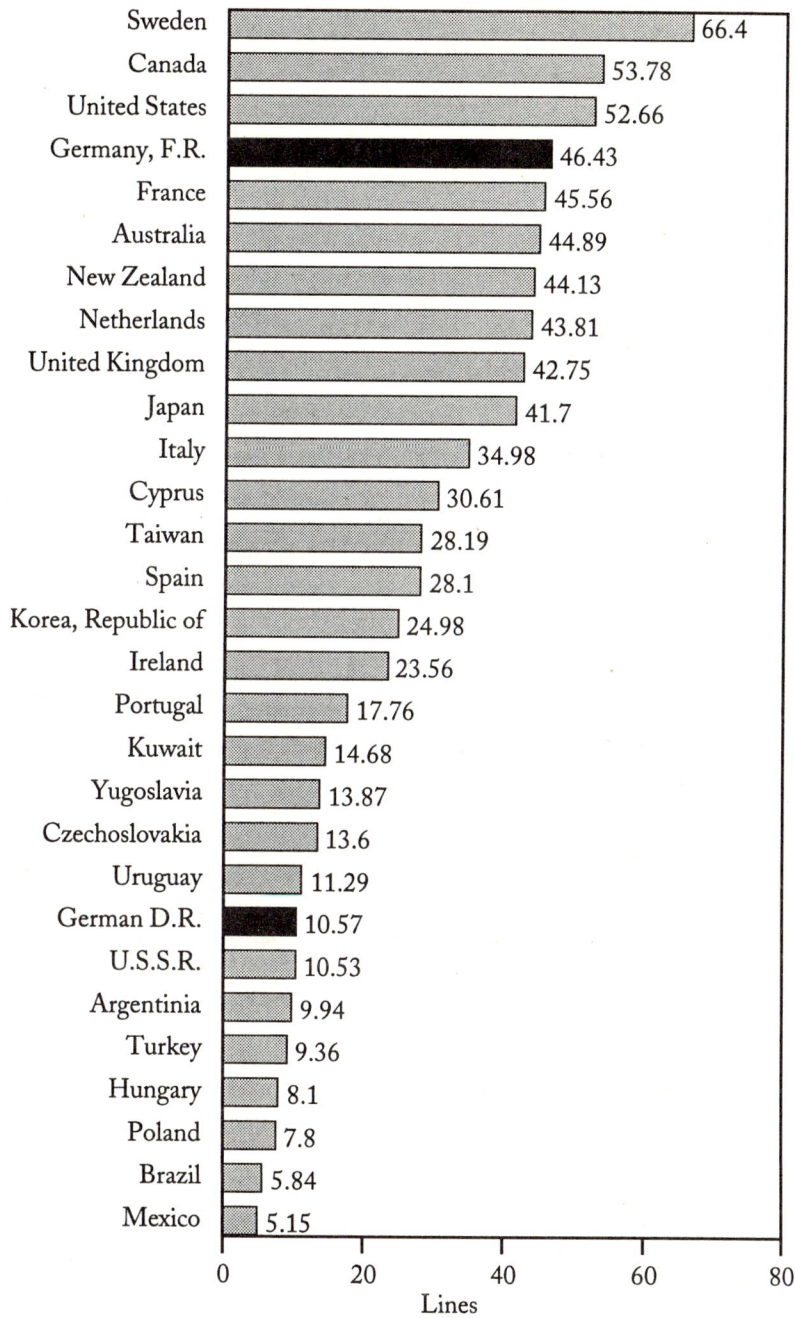

Figure 18-3. Main Lines per 100 Inhabitants 1989

Country	Lines
Sweden	66.4
Canada	53.78
United States	52.66
Germany, F.R.	46.43
France	45.56
Australia	44.89
New Zealand	44.13
Netherlands	43.81
United Kingdom	42.75
Japan	41.7
Italy	34.98
Cyprus	30.61
Taiwan	28.19
Spain	28.1
Korea, Republic of	24.98
Ireland	23.56
Portugal	17.76
Kuwait	14.68
Yugoslavia	13.87
Czechoslovakia	13.6
Uruguay	11.29
German D.R.	10.57
U.S.S.R.	10.53
Argentinia	9.94
Turkey	9.36
Hungary	8.1
Poland	7.8
Brazil	5.84
Mexico	5.15

Source: UIT

325

Table 18-3. Telecommunications in East and West Germany 1989: The Starting Point

Category	East	West
Main telephone lines (millions)	1.8	28.4
Waiting list (millions)	1.2	~0
Main lines per 100 inhabitants	11	47
Fax subscribers	2,500	500,000
Packet-switching users	0	50,000
Telex subscribers	20,000	133,000
Telephone lines between East and West Germany (international lines)	1,461	
Population (millions)	15	60
GNP per capita	DM 18,200	DM 38,500

One such political factor was the need for the totalitarian regime to control communications and information flow among its citizens, a task made more difficult when the telecommunications system is well developed and widespread. The fewer the phone calls, the easier to monitor and control communications. In addition, from an economic point of view there was the economic doctrine of socialist governments, which generally regard the services sector as less productive and consequently assign it a lower priority in the central investment planning. This argument is fortified, in particular, in sectors which, like telecommunications, are not able to earn foreign exchange.

The poor performance and status of telecommunications are two of many factors which explain the generally poor overall economic performance in Eastern Europe. Underdevelopment of the sector has caused and continues to cause significant overall economic losses.

The role of telecommunications in providing a basic infrastructure of successful economies stands out in this situation. In East Germany, as in other Central and Eastern European countries, it became obvious that telecommunications is a prerequisite for private and public investment in many instances. Therefore, a fast improvement of the East German telecommunications infrastructure became a top-level political issue in the unification process and thereafter.

Transitional Organization and Policy Development up to the Unification

The process of unification of the two German states began in November 1989 and ended on October 3, 1990, when the federal states of the former German Democratic Republic joined the Federal Republic of Germany and became part of the political and legal system of West Germany.

The new cooperation between the East and the West German PTTs began at the end of 1989, with short-term measures to increase communications capacity for the enormously growing telephone demand between East and West Germany. This was followed by requests from the East German PTT to support the development of telecommunications in its territory. Starting in December 1989 a joint commission of the East and West German governments dealt with all questions and aspects of telecommunications of mutual interest.

By early 1990 the MPF had concluded that the only feasible way to develop and to get the necessary support was to adopt West German structures in both posts and telecommunications. The (East German) Modrow government had already decided in favor of a financially independent PTT ("Sondervermögen") and consequently to transform it into a public enterprise. Initial plans to restructure it into a private company had been dropped.

The new (and last) East German government, elected in March 1990, then made far-reaching posts and telecommunications organizational decisions, including the decision to separate the Deutsche Post from the ministry and posts from telecommunications; the original plans, however, still maintained the concept of a unified PTT. To facilitate the future merger of the PTTs, the West German three-public-enterprises structure for posts, telecommunications, and postal banking was adopted.

While the two governments were negotiating a basic contract for economic and currency union (Staatsvertrag), the two ministers of posts and telecommunications dealt with the unification of posts and telecommunications. Their Joint Declaration of May 17, 1990, was the result of these negotiations. Basically, this document defined how the West German organizational and regulatory structure, in place since the reform of 1989–90, was to be introduced in East Germany. The aim was to adopt West Germany's telecommunications legislation step by step.

Cooperation between both sides was thereafter separated at the ministry and the management levels. The Joint Government Commission, in its various working groups, dealt with all policy and regulatory aspects of telecommunications, while the Joint Management Committee of the DBP Telekom and Deutsche Post discussed and drafted a shared management and business policy. As mentioned, the basic policy decision in the Joint Declaration was the gradual introduction of West German legislation into East Germany in anticipation of unification, which occurred on October 3, 1990.

The basic objective and consequent business policy decision was the creation of a common market for telecommunications in Germany through the integration of services, network planning, and business policy. DBP Telekom was to provide the financial support necessary to realize the agreed investment program by way of loans prior to the merger and subsequently through direct investments.

Telecommunications Modernization in East Germany

Modernization of the East German telecommunications network and its integration into the existing network of West Germany has raised a number of important policy, infrastructure development, financing, tariff and other issues.

TELECOMMUNICATIONS POLICY. The basic policy decision of German unification was the introduction of West German legislation into East Germany. In telecommunications this meant the adoption of the West German organizational and regulatory structure in place since the reform of 1989–90. The public debate about the appropriateness of this approach focused on the question of whether DBP Telekom as a state-owned monopoly would be able to achieve substantial improvements of the telecommunications infrastructure fast enough or whether the introduction of some kind of network competition with private competitors would achieve better results. The German Monopolkommission (monopolies and merger commission) argued strongly in favor of more competition and private investment, but overall the adoption of the West German regulatory structure was widely accepted.[3] In the meantime it became obvious that any private network operator would have had great problems and disadvantages in building a telecommunications network in East Germany. The numerous locations of the Deutsche Post and special rights of way of DBP Telekom put the latter in a much better position to do the job faster than any private competitor.

The Ministry of Posts and Telecommunications decided to extend satellite licenses for voice communication between East and West Germany as well as within East Germany up to 1997. The license of the private mobile communications carrier Mannesmann Mobilfunk was extended to East Germany, with the obligation to reach 90 percent coverage by the end of 1994. In 1991 the ministry issued four licenses for private trunk mobile radio networks within four regions of the East. In 1992 four more licenses were issued for East Germany.

Unification has had an enormous impact on the state budget. The net financial transfer from the West to the East for 1991 is estimated to be in the order of DM 150 billion. In face of these financial burdens the Ministry of Finance forced the Ministry of Posts and Telecommunications to levy an extra tax on DBP Telekom and telecommunications users. In 1991–92 DBP Telekom had to pay DM 2 billion extra to the state. Unification, therefore, put pressure on DBP Telekom's financial situation, through not only the supplementary tax but also the huge investment program, TELEKOM 2000.

PLANS AND ACTIONS FOR IMPROVING TELECOMMUNICATIONS INFRASTRUCTURE. Unification was significant in two ways for DBP Telekom. First, the company took over full responsibility for the telecommunications infrastructure in the new federal states and, second, it involved the merger of two big telecommunications operators with totally different backgrounds and corporate cultures.

There were high expectations on the speed of the integration of the East and West German networks and the improvement of the telecommunications infrastructure in the new federal states. Private investors in particular compared the poor situation in the East with that in the West. Therefore time was, and still is, the critical factor for DBP Telekom.

The time available to prepare for the merger of the two PTTs and for the huge investment program was rather short. Until July 1990, it was thought that the merger would not take place until 1993, yet, it occurred only three months later. The planning process for the infrastructure modernization program started in the spring of 1990, under a joint project of the two companies known as TELEKOM 2000. By the middle of 1990 DBP Telekom provided a loan of DM 2 billion to the Deutsche Post to allow it to procure and install modern digital equipment. With unification in October of that year, the framework of TELEKOM 2000 changed. Plans had to be accelerated.

TELEKOM 2000 is a strategic plan, announced in May 1990, covering DBP Telekom's activities in Eastern Germany in the eight-year period from 1990 and 1997. Its goal is to raise the level of telecommunications performance in the five new federal states to that currently found in West Germany. This is very much a political, rather than a purely commercial goal. From an economic perspective it is very doubtful that the demand for telecommunications services will increase that rapidly in the new states, so that DBP Telekom clearly runs the risk of building up overcapacity. Figure 18–4 shows some objectives and investment figures of the original TELEKOM 2000.

Shortly after unification DBP Telekom came under public pressure, in particular from the business community, to accelerate the development of the network in the new federal states. It was suggested that private investors could not wait until 1997 to get a telephone, even though the original TELEKOM 2000 program would have gradually improved the situation.

DBP Telekom therefore sought ways to speed up development. Because of the bottlenecks due to shortages of planning and managerial resources, it was decided to award turnkey contracts to private enterprises. These were to be aimed at business customers and entailed comprehensive projects involving construction of a whole local network, including cabling, switching equipment, and building, with projects being handed over to DBP Telekom on completion in a fully operational state. In order to ensure technical interoperability and to minimize transaction costs, DBP Telekom decided to limit the number of contractors to four companies which were

Figure 18–4. Objectives of the TELEKOM 2000 Program

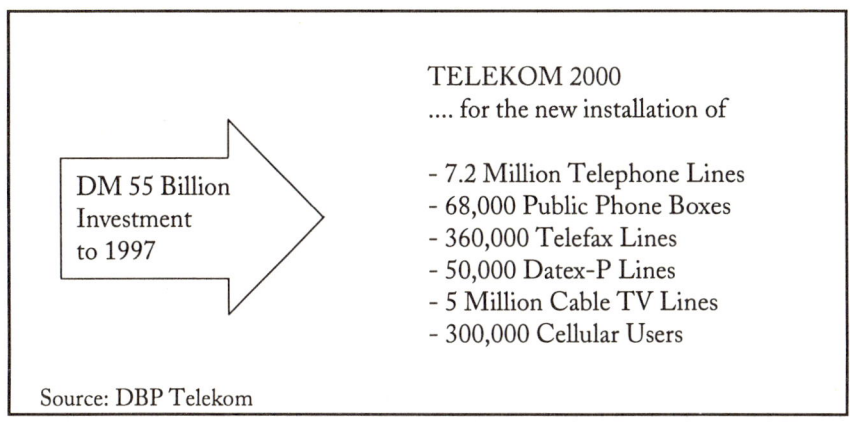

TELEKOM 2000
.... for the new installation of

DM 55 Billion
Investment
to 1997

- 7.2 Million Telephone Lines
- 68,000 Public Phone Boxes
- 360,000 Telefax Lines
- 50,000 Datex-P Lines
- 5 Million Cable TV Lines
- 300,000 Cellular Users

Source: DBP Telekom

already supplying the company with switching and transmission systems. The risk of bringing new technology into the network and of working with companies not familiar with DBP Telekom's procedures was felt to be too high compared with the potential benefits of bringing in new suppliers.

Overall, therefore, the very tight schedule favored well-known technologies, network structures, and suppliers. This increased costs and may be a burden for the future. There were, for example, those who believed that DBP Telekom should have taken a chance and implemented only optical fiber for the local network; however, the risk of installing new, untried technology such as fiber to the home was judged to be too high. Instead, DBP Telekom decided to run some field trials and in December 1991 announced plans to connect 1.2 million homes and businesses in Eastern Germany with optical fiber. For some observers this was in itself a bold move.[4] In July 1992 DBP Telekom invited its four suppliers to build the world's first commercial local optical-fiber telecommunications networks, and thereby took a major network initiative.

The original TELEKOM 2000 program of May 1990 planned to increase the number of main telephone lines by 300,000 during 1991. With the additional turnkey projects this goal was raised to 500,000, ten times the number of new lines the Deutsche Post had installed in recent years. Figure 18–5 shows the objectives announced in the spring of 1991 for telephone lines for the coming years. After one year the objective for 1992 was increased further, to 600,000 new lines, of which 400,000 were to be installed by DBP Telekom and 200,000 by means of turnkey projects.

The investment budget for the TELEKOM 2000 program up to 1997 was originally estimated at DM 55 billion, of which about DM 35 billion was for equipment and DM 20 billion for construction. In 1991 the estimated investment was increased to DM 60 billion.

At the beginning of the unification process DBP Telekom was the largest single investor in East Germany. This investment was having a positive effect on the tumbling economic situation in the new federal states. In 1991, roughly 8 percent of the total investment in East Germany was due to DBP Telekom.

WHAT HAS BEEN ACHIEVED SINCE 1989? Prior to unification there were only 1500 international circuits connected between East and West Germany. This resulted in a major bottleneck. Demand had been increasing significantly, and customers sometimes had to wait and redial for hours to get a connection. This became an important political issue. By the end of 1990 the capacity of East-West German communications increased by a factor of four. Switches on both sides of the old East-West border were connected directly to each other; however, initially technical adjustments had to be made because the two networks used different signaling systems, which made a direct integration impossible.

Satellite capacity is being used to give customers from East Germany direct access to the western network for voice and data communication and vice versa. Licenses have been awarded for private voice communications services, even though these would not normally be allowed under current German regulation. Despite all this, the number of private competitors and customers remained surprisingly small. By

Figure 18-5. Projected Telephone Main Lines in East Germany

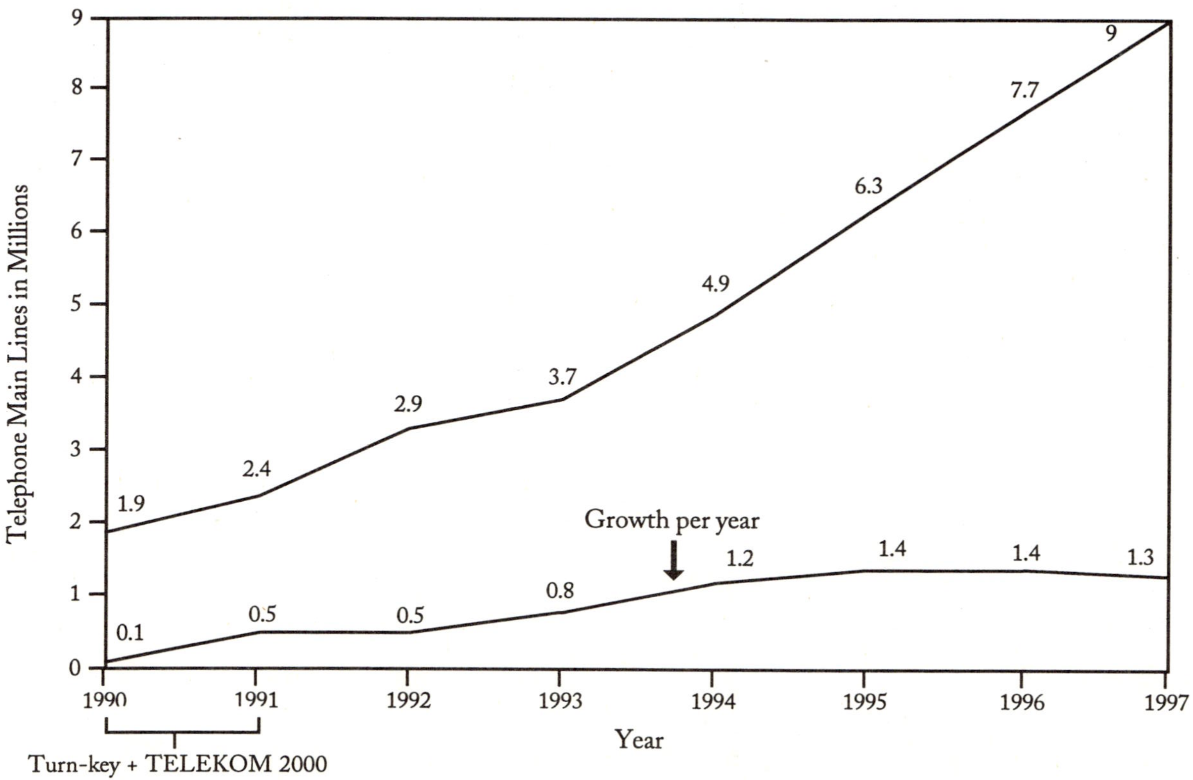

331

the summer of 1991 DBP Telekom's DIVA (Direkte Verbindungen über Ausnahmehauptanschlüsse) service for satellite voice communications had only about 280 customers, with the number of customers of the private systems estimated to be even smaller. The market for VSAT data communications services seems to be influenced to a greater extent by the poor terrestrial network in eastern Germany. It is estimated that 80 to 90 percent of the VSAT stations installed in Germany are located in the East. The number of VSAT stations is increasing but remains relatively small. By the summer of 1991 there were about 1,000 VSAT stations.[5]

One of the key projects under the TELEKOM 2000 program is the installation, over existing analog network, of a digital overlay network which will form the backbone of the future digitized network (Figure 18-6). The first stage of this overlay network went into operation in July 1991. Built in nine months it uses optical-fiber cable, copper cable with PCM, and digital radio links. It brought 70,000 additional lines for telephone calls within East Germany and increased the number of lines between West and East from 8,000 to 34,000.

Completion of the first stage of the overlay network resulted in a significant improvement in quality of service. The era of the constant busy signal and redialing was over. The effect of the overlay network on customer satisfaction is evident in the results of various polls (Figure 18-7).[6]

Given the exceptionally difficult structural situation in East Germany, the TELEKOM 2000 program set ambitious objectives for the development of the telecommunications infrastructure. Taking into account the various elements of this situation—namely, the merger of Deutsche Post and DBP Telekom, the organizational restructuring of the company, the need to educate and train 40,000 former Deutsche Post employees, and the severe bottlenecks in almost every type of infrastructure, the results appear quite good, despite a continuing large excess demand for telecommunications services within the new federal states.

The number of telephone lines increased substantially, increasing by 80,000 main lines in 1990, by 450,000 main lines in 1991, and by 760,000 main lines in 1992. DBP Telekom's objective for 1993 was an increase to 850,000 main lines. The total number of telephone main lines has increased from 1.9 million in 1990 to 3.1 million in 1992. Despite these achievements, the waiting list has continued to increase and was well above 2 million at the beginning of 1993. DBP Telekom's vision is to normalize the waiting list by 1994, a very ambitious objective indeed.

BUSINESS CUSTOMERS. TELEKOM 2000 was designed as a comprehensive program for all telecommunications services, including cable TV. While this reflects the broad responsibility of DBP Telekom, it also indicates one of its major problems, namely, how to set priorities. As mentioned, the business community began in late 1990 and early 1991 to take a very active interest in the reform process. This led to DBP Telekom's setting a clear priority for business customers and the development of the telephone network. Polls have indicated that this priority has been widely accepted by private customers in the East.

Figure 18-6. Development of Digital Overlay Network in East Germany to 1993

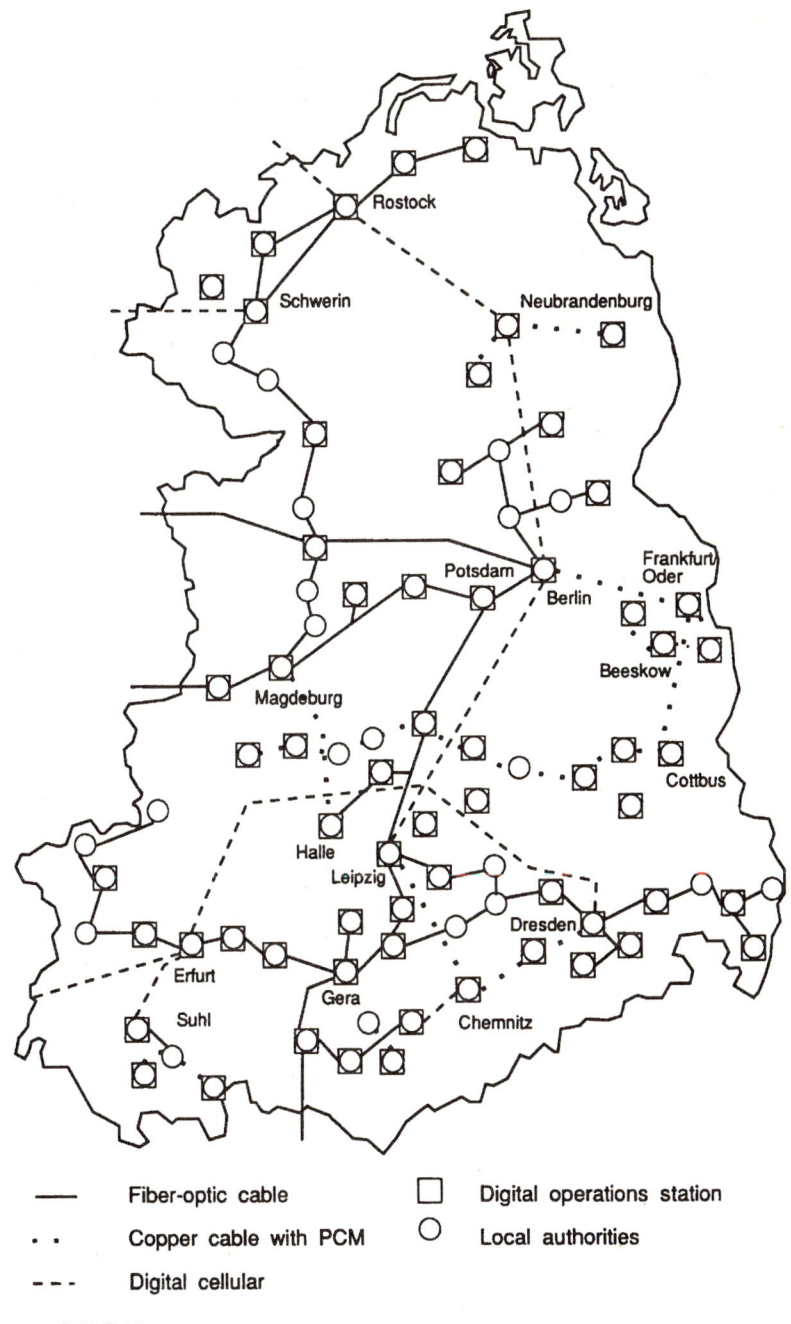

Fiber-optic cable — Digital operations station

Copper cable with PCM · · — Local authorities

Digital cellular - - -

Source: DBP Telekom

333

Figure 18-7. Measure of Business Customer Satisfaction I

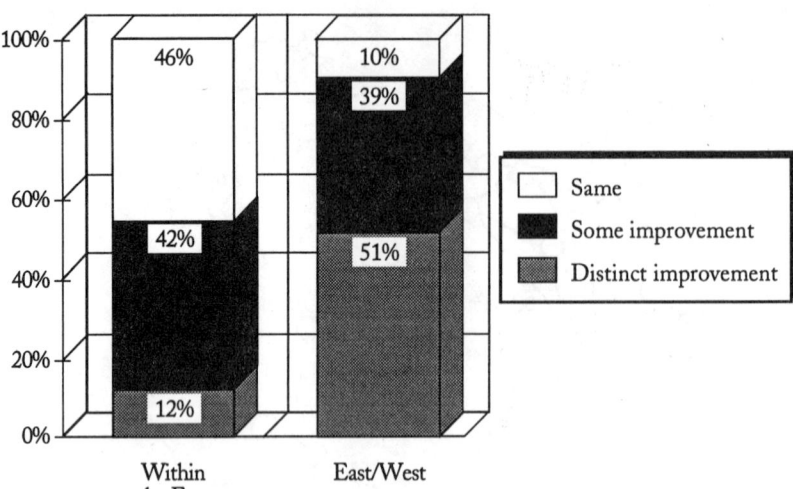

Source: Schnöring, Szafran 1991

Priority must be given to construction of the terrestrial local network in order to overcome a bottleneck because free access lines in one local loop cannot be transferred to another. Under this strategy business customers are served first in areas with free access capacity, through connections to neighboring local switching centers if possible. The density of potential business customers is, therefore, a major criterion for the allocation of construction work in the local loop. All 1991 turnkey projects were targeted at areas with a high share of business customers. In the spring of 1991 DBP Telekom started to procure radio-based systems for the connection of business customers to distant local switching centers. These systems will be used in areas where the terrestrial network cannot be developed immediately. They provide telephony, facsimile, and data communication services, and came into operation during the first half of 1992. Even though these radio-based connections involve higher costs to DBP Telekom than conventional terrestrial connections, all customers are charged the same tariffs.

Under strong public pressure, the board of DBP Telekom announced its goal that every business customer should have a telephone by the end of 1991; however, given the structural problems and the nature of telephone networks, this goal was not realistic from the beginning. At that time, in the spring of 1991, the company had no computer-based information about its customers. The old waiting lists had been handwritten and were totally out of date, especially with respect to businesses. Furthermore, the business sector had changed dramatically and many new businesses had been established. As a consequence, even though it provided telephones to 153,000 businesses during 1991, DBP Telekom could not meet its objective of satisfying all business customers in 1991. At the beginning of 1992 very many business customers were still on the waiting list;

Figure 18-8. Measure of Business Customer Satisfaction II

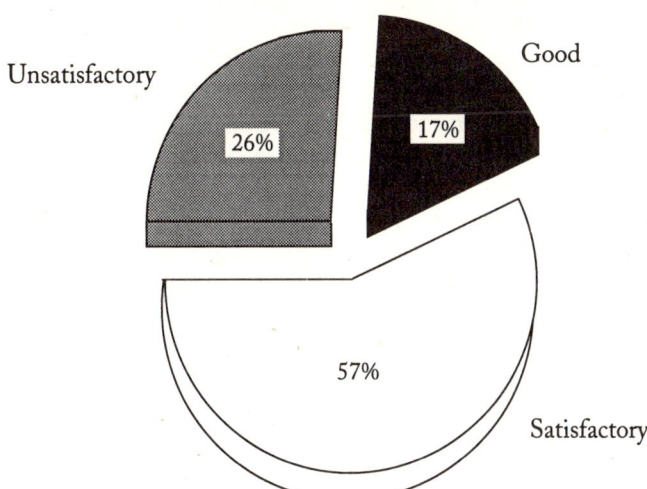

Source: Schnöring, Szafran 1991

however, questionnaires showed that already more than 95 percent of all businesses of the manufacturing and the building sectors had at least one main telephone line. Overall the business community in the new federal states was reasonably satisfied with the development of the telecommunications infrastructure (Figure 18-8).[6] At the beginning of 1993 there were still business customers waiting for a telephone due to shortages in the local network, but ongoing surveys showed that almost all businesses had one telephone and more than 70 percent had facsimile. Customer satisfaction was increasing despite ongoing shortages for additional telephone lines.

In this transitional phase, mobile services have become particularly important for business customers. Since they can be used as substitutes for nonexistent terrestrial lines, the development of DBP Telekom's C-network was given a high priority. By the end of 1991 this network was available in all major cities and on all major highways, covering 60 percent of the area of the new federal states and 80 percent of the population. The number of subscribers from East Germany increased dramatically and network capacity was being used heavily all day long. By the end of 1992 the C-network was available over 80 percent of the territory and to 90 percent of the population.

The number of data communications access points increased from 3,400 to 27,000 in 1992. It was expected to increase by an additional 30,000 in 1993.

TARIFF POLICY. From the beginning, DBP Telekom's policy was to adopt the same tariff for the same service in East and West Germany as quickly as possible. Although this was easy to implement for installation and rental charges, it required technical adjustments in the network for call charges and could therefore not be realized immediately. Major tariff elements were harmonized in mid–1991, with remaining differences to disappear by 1994.[7]

From an economic point of view, harmonization of tariffs between East and West is inefficient because the market situation in the East is very different from that in the West. Given the huge excess demand in Eastern Germany, tariffs should be used to allocate scarce supply capacities and, therefore, should be orientated toward demand. In West Germany where supply more or less equals demand, tariffs should be more cost-oriented. The lowering of East German tariffs to the West German level increased demand in Eastern Germany and created additional bottlenecks. This argument is especially valid for installation and rental charges and less so for call charges, where reverse calling is always possible.

In Germany, a large element of politics is still involved in the setting of prices for the telephone services. It would have been politically difficult, if not impossible, to convince the general public that installation and rental charges should be higher in the East than in the West. DBP Telekom, therefore, established administrative rules indicating that, for example, business customers should be served first. Such rules create many problems and do not necessarily result in those customers who could best use the lines being served first. Such a policy gives private customers the incentive to be classified as business customers and, furthermore, removes from DBP Telekom the economic incentive to invest in more expensive temporary solutions such as radio-connected lines. With higher and differentiated rental charges, the number of radio-connected lines probably would be higher than what is now planned. The tariff policy chosen is just one of many examples which illustrates the strong political influence in the transformation of the former centrally planned East German economy to a market-driven economy. Although this is necessary in many cases, it is a problem and burden in others.

Conclusion

The unification of East and West Germany just two years after the reform of the telecommunications sector in the Federal Republic of Germany heavily burdened the process of restructuring the telecommunications sector in Germany. The merger of DBP Telekom and Deutsche Post and the massive infrastructure development program for Eastern Germany have been absorbing a substantial share of scarce managerial and financial resources within DBP Telekom. This has slowed down the necessary transformation process of the organization from a national public administration to an internationally-oriented company. This is a disadvantage for DBP Telekom, at least in the short run. On the other hand, DBP Telekom is building up experience and a reputation for modernizing the telecommunications infrastructure in Eastern Europe, and this clearly is giving it a competitive advantage in those markets.

The modernization of the telecommunications infrastructure in the new federal states is well under way. Improvements are faster than in many other parts of the public infrastructure, such as roads and public administration. A rapid and massive transfer of financial resources and know-how from the western to the eastern part of the country stimulates the development and makes the situation in the former German Democratic Republic in many respects much different from the development in the rest of Central and Eastern Europe.

Endnotes

1. Source G. Pfeiffer and B. Wieland, *Telecommunications in Germany,* Springer-Verlag, Berlin, 1990.

2. See G. Tenzer and H. Uhlig, "Ausgangssituation und Entwicklungsstrategie," in *Telekom 2000,* ed. G. Tenzer and H. Uhlig (Heidelberg: R. v. Decker's Verlag, 1991), pp. 1–42.

3. See Monopolkommission, *Zur Neuordnung der Telekommunikation,* (Köln: Sondergutachten der Monopolkommission, gemäß 24b Abs. 5 Satz 4 GWB, 1991).

4. See *Communications Week International,* December 10, 1991.

5. See J. Drescher, "Welchen Beitrag leisten Satelliten-Telefondienste bei der Verbesserung der Telekommunikation zwischen alten und neuen Bundesländern?" *WIK-Newsletter* Nr. 4, Bad Honnef 1991, pp. 19–21.

6. See Thomas Schnöring and U. Szafran, "Telekommunikativer Aufschwung Ost," *WIK Newsletter* Nr. 5, Bad Honnef 1991, pp. 5–8.

7. H. Schön, E. Auer, and W. Hummel, "Aufbau des Telefonnetzes in den neuen Bundesländern und die Integration der Teilnetze Ost und West," in *Telekom 2000,* ed. G. Tenzer and H. Uhlig (Heidelberg: R. v. Decker's Verlag, 1991), pp. 113–166.

19

Challenges and Issues in Central and Eastern European Telecommunications

Timothy E. Nulty

THE COUNTRIES OF CENTRAL AND EASTERN Europe (CEE),[1] handicapped by peculiarities of their unique history and the need to transform their economies, must confront simultaneously three difficult challenges to their telecommunications sectors: they have to develop their networks at an accelerated pace; they must implement the newest technology; and they have to adapt to the new competitive commercial environment. Although many other middle-income developing countries face one or two of these challenges, none faces all three on such a magnitude or with such urgency. Together, they make the overall circumstances and problems of CEE telecommunications quite different from those found elsewhere in the world. Yet despite the extent of the difficulties and the short time which has elapsed since the revolutions of 1989 and 1990, a consensus is beginning to emerge on the most appropriate strategies to pursue, and progress is already being made on execution of these strategies. Obviously, not all have followed the same policy nor achieved the same degree of progress. Nevertheless, a substantial beginning has been made, which augurs well for the future of the telecommunications sectors in these countries, the political situation willing.

The Need for Accelerated Growth of the Networks

Telecommunications was relatively neglected by CEE governments until well into the 1980s. Overall investment was low and the little new investment that was forthcoming was used to connect new lines rather than maintain, replace, and strengthen the underlying infrastructure. As a result, countries of the region have inherited underdeveloped, worn out, and unbalanced networks.

CEE has about 100 million inhabitants and approximately 11 million connected direct exchange lines, giving an average penetration of 11 lines per 100 population. Poland, Romania, Hungary, and Czechoslovakia are fairly similar in this regard: penetrations range from 8 to 13 in the order listed. Bulgaria is something of an exception; having started to increase investment in telecommunications some time ago, it now has a penetration of over 25.

This is far below what their economies need. The GNP per capita for the CEE countries averages about US$2500 (official government figures reconciled with international methods by the World Bank).[2] If we assume that during the next decade CEE economies move strongly toward mixed market structures similar to those of Western Europe, that GNP levels become progressively more comparable, and that real growth averages around 1.5 percent to 2 percent per annum over the decade, then GNP per capita can be expected to rise to about US$6000 (in today's dollars) by the year 2000. Historical experience in the West suggests that telephone penetration associated with this level of development should at the very least be 25 lines per 100 inhabitants to support a comparable level of economic activity.

The foregoing analysis does not, however, take into account that telecommunications services play a far greater role in modern economies than they did when today's industrialized countries had GNPs per capita of around US$6000. Taking account of this additional importance of telecommunications in modern economies, CEE governments and PTTs are aiming to reach penetrations around 30 per 100 by the year 2000 (and 40 by 2010). Assuming the current low rates of population growth continue, this implies a stock of 31 to 32 million connected lines by the year 2000, requiring an annual growth rate of 11 percent. This is a major acceleration in the growth of telecommunications networks in countries which have seen rates in the order of 3 percent over the last thirty years and have only reached 6 percent per annum during the second half of the 1980s. Again, Bulgaria is something of an exception. It grew faster than the others in the 1980s and may not need to increase the overall growth rate in the 1990s.

Achieving such growth will be difficult and costly, but failing to achieve it will perpetuate the environment of acute shortage and poor service which in turn imposes even higher costs on the economy as a whole.

The Need to Introduce New Technology

All CEE networks are overwhelmingly analog. Although there is some early-vintage digital equipment, some electronic PBXs, and some very recently installed modern equipment, all forms of digital electronic equipment account for less than 5 percent of all facilities. Many switches are of very old step-by-step technology which is not only inflexible and ill-suited to modern demands but also worn out and unreliable.

The economics and technology of modern telecommunications dictate that virtually all new equipment must be digital and that existing equipment should be replaced as rapidly as economically possible. This requires massive implementation of a technology with which telecommunications operators in CEE have little experience and which is very different from that currently in place. All Western countries, even the relatively less developed, have many years of experience implementing digital technology. CEE countries have practically none, having been effectively locked out until very recently by Western export restrictions and the failure to develop digital technology in the former Eastern bloc. Their telecommunications sectors must now be developed more rapidly than any has ever been before in order to catch up with the digitalization process which has been in progress in the West over the past fifteen years.

The Need to Adapt to the New Commercial Competitive Environment

Demand is increasing rapidly, especially from business users (including highly desired foreign investors), for better telephone service than is generally available, for data and other new services, for more and better dedicated facilities, and for discounted bulk rates. As in Western countries, aggressive demand from major users will become a major force which will drive the sector in the near and medium term. It already manifests itself in intense pressure on CEE telecommunications operators and governments to redirect operators' resources away from traditional balanced network development toward targeted investment for special user groups, and to permit alternative providers to enter the market.

At the same time that operators are being pressured to provide target services for special groups, there is a desperate need and intense political pressure to build a general, nationwide public network. But doing this requires (especially in an era of severe stringency on government budgets) the ability to utilize surpluses from profitable services and customer groups to finance extension of the network, since the latter is costly up front and only yields returns slowly.

These sometimes conflicting challenges have created a new and exceedingly difficult climate for the telecommunications operators in these countries. It will require them to change their attitudes and modus operandi from traditional state public utilities to commercial, cost- and customer-sensitive, enterprises.

Special Complications Facing CEE Telecommunications

Complicating these challenges are some special conditions which arise from the region's unique history and which make the CEE predicament quite unlike that found elsewhere in the world. Foremost among these are:

CoCom Restrictions.[3] These restrictions on the export of high technology equipment to the former Soviet block are being relaxed but have not yet disappeared. The spirit of euphoria which dominated 1990 cooled following the events in the Gulf in early 1991 and the dramatic events in the former U.S.S.R. Although the eventual disappearance of export controls to CEE is virtually certain, the nuts-and-bolts reality of CoCom restrictions will continue to complicate investment and modernization for some time yet.

Telecommunications Manufacturing Industries. Most developing countries have little or no telecommunications manufacturing industry. Of those that do, several have built them recently and, therefore, with modern technology. CEE countries have telecommunications manufacturing industries which are unusually large relative to their traditional domestic markets (partly due to exports to the former U.S.S.R.). All of these industries are based on outmoded technology. Although CoCom restrictions prevented them from acquiring new technology, they also protected them. Hidden from competition behind the CoCom barrier, they were slow to adopt or develop new technology or to improve efficiency. Now, suddenly, they are faced with a dramatic increase in competition from much more advanced and efficient Western companies. Many are in danger of going under completely. On the other hand, faced with rapid contraction in many other sectors, CEE governments are loath to see their telecommunications manufacturing industries collapse as well. Their reluctance stems not only from potential employment and output loss but also, faced with the necessity of expanding telecommunications networks, they know there will be a large demand for manufacturing output and a shortage of foreign exchange with which to purchase Western equipment. Therefore, one can already observe substantial pressure on telecommunications operators to purchase as much as they can from domestic manufacturers; however, if the operators are forced to purchase equipment which is inferior, overly expensive, or antiquated, their network development plans will be affected, resulting in a drag on the economy.

All CEE countries want to short-circuit this dilemma by joint ventures or licensing arrangements with Western firms. In principle, this can yield good solutions; there is, however, also a danger that these arrangements could saddle countries with (relatively) obsolete equipment, tied procurement, and high costs. This is particularly so if each country insists on maintaining its entire line of equipment production and isolates itself from neighboring countries which face the same dilemma by dealing solely with one or two Western firms. Much depends on the details of the strategies and arrangements adopted.

UNPOPULARITY OF TELECOMMUNICATIONS ENTERPRISES. Although telephone companies are rarely loved anywhere, those of CEE are particularly unpopular. Working, universal telephone service is seen as a hallmark of advanced democracies and, conversely, its absence in the region is seen by most as a symbol of the failure of the old regime. Telecommunications operators suffer from some of the stigma of the previous governments, and opposition to them carries an overtone of opposition to the entire previous political and economic system. Consequently, there is more widespread popular political support for liberalization and competition in the sector than is typical in the West, where such pressure comes primarily from large users and where popular sentiment is ambivalent because of the fear of increased residential prices and lost jobs.

ABSENCE OF FINANCIAL AND COMMERCIAL INFRASTRUCTURE AND SKILLS. Virtually all middle-income Western countries have long experience with market systems and well-developed infrastructures to support them, including accounting systems and professionals, laws dealing with contracts, property, corporate structure, behavior, fraud, and antitrust, as well as courts to enforce the laws. Furthermore, most such countries have a sizable cadre of people who are knowledgeable and skillful in commercial management and enterprise. Indeed, these are so necessary for a market system and so ubiquitous that they are often taken for granted; in CEE, however, they are extremely scarce. The infrastructure, knowledge, and experience which took decades, even centuries, to build up elsewhere, are having to be created in the CEE almost overnight.

Strategy for Meeting the Challenges

Despite the enormous challenges facing CEE telecommunications, much has been accomplished in the short time since the revolutions of 1989 and 1990. Despite a good deal of fluidity and confusion in the overall political and economic climate, the picture in the sector is beginning to clarify and, more specifically, the leadership structure is starting to be better defined. Also, a consensus is beginning to emerge throughout the region on the best direction and strategy for reforming the sector. This strategy is composed of several elements:

NETWORK STRATEGY. In the long term, all CEE countries are aiming to double or treble the rate of investment and network growth with a view to achieving a penetration of about 30 lines per 100 inhabitants by the year 2000. Second, all countries plan to start installing digital equipment immediately and to cease all new installations of analog equipment within two or three years.

In the short term, a combination of actions is contemplated to provide rapid relief. These include (a) installing new digital international switches to decongest a critical bottleneck and generate income; (b) constructing overlay digital networks to relieve congestion in the trunk networks, provide high-quality services to large users, and build the skeleton for long-term network modernization; (c) licensing one or more cellular operators to provide service quickly to those willing and able to pay (and generate income via the franchise fee); and (d) licensing or building packet-switched data networks for large data users.

TELECOMMUNICATIONS ENTERPRISE INTERNAL REORGANIZATION. This generally involves separating telecommunications from posts and other activities, reorganizing of internal operations to focus on reducing costs, increasing quality of service, marketing and customer service, and measurement and accountability of management.

TELECOMMUNICATIONS ENTERPRISE CORPORATE GOVERNANCE. Governmental regulatory and policy functions are being separated from telecommunications operations and being vested in the ministry. Telecommunications operations are being recognized as independent, financially self-supporting, commercial companies which neither give nor receive any government subsidies, and will eventually be transformed into joint-stock companies.

SECTOR STRUCTURE AND COMPETITION. The CEE countries intend to broadly follow the framework outlined in the EC Green Paper,[4] but with some differences among countries. In general, they will (a) completely liberalize terminal equipment and value added services provision; (b) continue to maintain monopoly over some core definition of basic facilities; (c) allow a gradual opening of markets for a variety of other network facilities which both the PTT and other companies may operate (chiefly in peripheral networks such as cellular and private networks); and (d) allow foreign participation at a minority level in some areas and unrestricted in others.

TELECOMMUNICATIONS MANUFACTURING INDUSTRY. All CEE countries appear to have decided to promote their domestic telecommunications manufacturing industries mainly through joint ventures with Western firms and to link at least part of their telecommunications purchases to these firms.

These elements of an overall strategy seem to have gained broad acceptance. They represent a rational and realistic approach framework for effective action. As such, to have gotten this far in so short a time and in difficult circumstances is a considerable accomplishment for telecommunications authorities in these countries.

Implementation of the Telecommunications Strategy

Implementation of this strategy has barely begun. Relatively few elements have been put into detailed plans, and few concrete actions have been taken. This is, of course, not surprising given the short time period. Nevertheless, it is important to keep up the momentum. A sensible set of broad principles and objectives has been reasonably well agreed on in CEE, and now the more difficult task of concrete implementation must be accelerated. To do so requires addressing the problems discussed below.

Liberalization and Privatization

The explosion of demand for telecommunications services of all kinds is so great that it is virtually impossible for the traditional telecommunications operators to meet all of it alone. Hence, there is large and growing pressure to permit new enterprises into the market. In response, numerous enterprises, foreign and domestic, are pushing to set up business in the telecommunications market in countries of CEE. Examples include plans for MAV, the Hungarian railroad, to build a fiber-optic network whose spare capacity could be made available to provide telecommunications facilities and services; the Cable & Wireless franchise in Gdansk; proposals for a fiber-based network to offer data and electronic mail in Poland; joint ventures for cellular networks in Czechoslovakia and Hungary as well as efforts in that direction in the other countries; the joint venture for a packet-switched network in Czechoslovakia; efforts to set up independent local telephone companies in Hungary and Poland; and the banking network in Poland which will be able to offer service to a limited number of large subscribers.

In principle, although such liberalization is beneficial and can lead to faster growth, new and better services, and competitive discipline on costs and quality, it also raises a number of serious issues. For example, how will it be done? Who can enter which markets and under what terms and conditions? How should the telecommunications operators respond? Central to these issues are questions of PTT joint ventures with other enterprises (especially foreign) and awarding of franchises (concessions) to enterprises other than the telecommunications operators. As many have discovered already, it is much easier to agree in principle that these are good ideas than it is to put them into practice. For example: What should be the scope and duration of a franchise? How does one organize fair and efficient bidding for a franchise? How does one select a joint venture partner? How does one arrive at a good deal with partners who are far more expert?

In part these are business decisions to be made by the new telecommunications entrants and by the PTT, after it has been restructured as an independent commercial entity without government interference except via the overall regulatory framework which sets the rules of the game and referees them.

Regulation

The process of liberalization makes it increasingly clear how critical a well-structured regulatory framework is. First, liberalization cannot and should not be permitted to proceed completely unchecked and unregulated. The telecommunications sector is not like restaurants or textile factories; it cannot be completely unregulated. The liberalization process in telecommunications must be managed in a coherent fashion or it will not work at all. Second, a regulatory framework must ensure that social values, such as universal service provision, and scarce natural resources such as the radio spectrum, are protected. Third, regulation must prevent monopoly abuse of prices and service quality. Lastly, regulation must ensure fair competition via nondiscriminatory interconnection, signaling systems, and protocols. Such regulation is, properly and preeminently, the work of the government. Although very important, regulation is not the same as running the telecommunications enterprise, the only function which governments in CEE have experience performing.

There is significant danger if key questions are not handled well. For instance, most new applicants, including foreigners, often want an exclusive franchise (which would eliminate competition); the freedom not to have to pay taxes or other concessions, which are expensive to the government; and minimal (if any) regulation of tariffs, service, or performance. In addition, new entrants usually seek only the most profitable markets and prefer not to serve the others, while at the same time undermining the profits of the PTT which it needs to extend service to underserved areas. If granted in full, such conditions could lead to monopoly abuse, distorted investment, and drain on government treasuries, which would be inimical to sectoral and national development.

On the other hand, in the face of competition, the main telecommunications operator typically seeks to control all protocols, set interconnection tariffs so as to disadvantage competitors, overcharge those customers who have no choice, and undercharge those customers who have competitive alternatives. Clearly a difficult balance must be struck between the assurances and protection which telecommunications businesses legitimately want if they are to make large investments, and national goals of fiscal responsibility, efficiency, competition, and economic reform.

Striking this balance is a complex and difficult political task. Rules of the game covering franchising arrangements, interconnection, tariffs, taxation, standardization, frequency allocation, enforcement, and dispute resolution must all be clarified in law, regulation, and administrative responsibility. This is one of the most urgent tasks facing those in charge of policy and sector reform. Little or no development—except traditional (and inadequate) forms of investment—will be possible until significant progress is made on these key issues. This is what governments, especially telecommunications ministries, should be focusing their attention on, rather than choosing switching systems or entering joint venture deals with foreign companies, which in any case should be the business of these companies and PTTs.

None of the CEE governments has gotten far in this crucial area. Hungary has done the most work on devising a serious, modern regulatory scheme and has recently enacted a telecommunications law to put the scheme into effect (see chapter 21). In Poland a new law which permits liberalization but provides very few details was passed in 1991. Serious work on the details of a regulatory framework to implement liberalization has begun. Czechoslovakia has only started to think about these matters and to draft a law. In Romania the government appears to have formulated a broad policy, but little work has been done on the details either of a law or of the regulatory scheme to implement it. In the other countries the issue has barely been raised.

Relations with Equipment Suppliers (Foreign and Domestic)

Traditionally telecommunications operators had no choice but to take whatever the domestic telecommunications manufacturing industries had to offer, regardless of quality, price, delivery delays, or technology. Now that these operators are being told to be businesslike, that is, to improve quality, to cut costs, to accelerate investment using their own finance by making a profit, and to respond to increasing competition, they can no longer afford to be slaves to the domestic telecommunications manufacturing industries. They must get the best, cheapest, state of the art equipment possible.

At the same time, CEE governments are faced with increasing unemployment and collapsing industries. Their telecommunications manufacturing industries, while far below world level, are not their worst industries. Indeed, unlike most regional industries, telecommunications manufacturers face a rising domestic demand from accelerating telecommunications investment. Together these provide strong reasons for governments to try to save them. This, in turn, depends on finding foreign partners or licensers from which modern technology and know-how can be obtained and also on the domestic telecommunications enterprises' buying from domestic manufacturers.

The interests of all three players in this process differ. The telecommunications operator wants the best, cheapest, and most reliable equipment. The government wants jobs, added value, and technology. The manufacturer (especially the foreign manufacturer) wants to charge the highest possible price and put the least possible number of jobs, investment, and technology into another country because these undermine and compete with his home factories.

Although none of these three interested groups can get its way completely, none can be ignored either; however, reconciling them in a manner which gives all three a reasonable deal is difficult. Several countries in the region have made some progress; others have barely begun to think about it. The problem is made even more difficult because each country is talking independently to the same few foreign suppliers, who, in contrast, know the situation in all countries of the region. This points to the need for CEE governments to consult with each other on common problems in order to be able to confront potential foreign suppliers and domestic manufacturers with more and better information about the whole regional situation.

Financing

Although now the most difficult issue of all, financing did not cause serious problems in the past for telecommunications authorities because politicians set the goals and, having done so, were obliged to provide the financing and the necessary inputs. Telecommunications managers themselves had little responsibility. They merely translated the targets delivered from the top into a detailed program for installation and a list of inputs required. It was the government's responsibility to ensure that the necessary goods and financing were available. If it failed, the government and the suppliers, not the telecommunications managers, took the blame for not fulfilling the plan. In the future, telecommunications operators will have to stand on their own. The government may set ostentatious public targets, but it will definitely not be able to pay for them. PTTs will have to find the financing for their own investments and will have to set only those targets which they can realistically hope to finance. Already it is clear that financing the stated targets of achieving penetration levels of 30 lines per 100 inhabitants by the year 2000 will be very difficult on several counts.

VOLUME OF FINANCING. A number of countries (mostly the ambitious newly industrialized countries, or NICs, such as Korea, Singapore, Taiwan, Malaysia) have, for sustained periods, achieved telecommunications network growth rates as high as CEE countries would need to attain; however, this was usually accomplished in the context of faster overall economic growth rates than are likely for the countries of CEE, and without having to contend with massive simultaneous restructuring of the entire economy. For CEE countries to finance 10 to 12 percent per annum growth in telecommunications while their real GNPs are growing by 1 to 2 percent will be difficult. To illustrate, assume that the countries of the region are able to get the cost of an added line down to something in the order of US$2000, from the current level of about US$2500 to US$2600 (at world market prices). Achieving a penetration of around 30 lines per 100 (including replacement of 5 percent per annum) will then cost in the range of US$55 billion to US$60 billion in 1990 dollars over the next decade, or US$5.5 billion to US$6.0 billion per year. This is approximately three to four times what these countries have spent over the last decade, even after adjusting for previous, unrealistic prices of equipment. If real GNP growth is 1.5 to 2.0 percent p.a., such a rate of investment would absorb around 2.0 percent of GNP over the decade.

SHORTAGE OF CONVERTIBLE CURRENCY. A much higher proportion of investment will have to be paid for in convertible currency than in the past. Previously about 90 to 95 percent of CEE telecommunications investment was with domestic or soft currencies. About half of this was for construction and civil works, and the rest for locally produced equipment. Even with optimistic assumptions about modernization of domestic telecommunications manufacturing industries, the proportion of equipment purchased with hard currency will rise to 40 to 50 percent in the next five years and probably remain at 30 percent for the rest of the decade. This implies a hard currency bill for telecommunications equipment in the region of at least US$5 billion to US$6 billion over each of the coming five years and US$4 billion to US$5 billion in the following five years. If domestic manufacturers fail to modernize, reduce costs, and improve quality, these countries will have to spend an even higher amount of hard currency or curtail their telecommunications investments or both. This will be doubly difficult for those countries with large hard currency debt burdens. Even countries with low debt have limited ability to earn hard currency. The difficulty of financing the large amount of imported telecommunications equipment which will be needed by these countries will make them vulnerable to disadvantageous terms and conditions.

UNDERDEVELOPED CAPITAL MARKETS. Traditionally, the government financed any expansion which it authorized. In the future, severe budget constraints will prevent this. CEE telecommunications operators can rely on their own revenues for a large part of the domestic currency financing they need, but only if they get costs down, increase efficiency, increase traffic, and maintain economic tariffs. These are difficult tasks, and even if they are successful, they will still need substantial outside domestic financing in order to meet their investment targets. Normal financing sources such as banks and the stock and bond markets, are extremely rudimentary in all countries of the region, if they exist at all.

Sources of Finance

Traditionally, financial considerations were secondary in the decision schemes of CEE telecommunications operators. Financial planning consisted primarily of negotiations over the share of the government budget to be allocated to the sector. Tactics were those of bureaucracies the world around and included (a) overstating needs and overdesigning systems in anticipation of blanket cutbacks by budget authorities; (b) overbuilding whenever possible, since the government could often be forced to pay after the fact, and having capacity in reserve whenever possible; (c) if forced to cut, threatening to cut the most valuable or politically sensitive parts of the network in order to apply leverage to the budget bargaining process; (d) resisting any genuine exploration of alternatives, since that might undermine one's bargaining position; (e) spending all allocated funds in an allotted period, regardless of economic justification, in order to avoid turning the money back to the treasury.

These traditions are deeply embedded and must now be radically altered. In relatively short order telecommunications operators must become fully responsible for their own financing. At the same time they must accelerate investment. The two imperatives will require radical reorientation of institutional attitudes toward financing. Development of financial strategies which closely integrate physical and technical planning with financial planning are top priorities.

Chief among the financial resources to which Central and Eastern European telecommunications operators must look are the following options.

Internal Generation

This will necessarily be the main source of funds for the foreseeable future because of the weakness in the capital markets, national macroeconomic limits on overall credit creation, uncertainty, and riskiness of the overall economy. Internal generation of a large percentage of required investment (at least 50 percent on average during the period 1990–95, rising to 85 to 90 percent by the end of the decade) should, in principle, be possible. These entities are actually, or potentially, profitable. Demand for telecommunications and willingness to pay (and ability to collect bills) are high, and telecommunications entities are relatively strong institutions; however, this level of internal generation requires a thorough reevaluation of tariff policy, investment priorities, cost reduction, and marketing.

Domestic Outside Finance

In the current environment of extreme excess demand coupled with rudimentary development of normal Western capital market mechanisms (that is, stock markets, commercial and investment banking), promising sources of domestic outside finance are instruments which are tied in some way to service connection, such as subscriber bonds, subscriber subscriptions, and telecommunications associations. The conceptual line between subscriber subscriptions, subscriber bonds, and connection charges can be blurred at times; however, in all of them, a preferential place in the queue for connection is exchanged for or associated with the purchase by the subscriber of a financial asset. A potential subscriber may pay for this by a straight subscription or deposit (which may or may not be repaid by discounting his monthly bill after connection), or he may be issued a bond of some sort which may or may not be transferrable.

The Hungarian telecommunications operator, MTV, has experimented with various forms of this type of financing for several years with considerable success. From 1986 through 1989 subscriber deposits raised approximately 7.9 percent of the total amount of capital expenditure during that period. Municipal contributions, which are somewhat similar in that municipalities would contribute to the cost of network construction in their localities on behalf of their citizens, raised 9 percent, and the sale of bonds, 8 percent. Recent and imminent changes in the law will make it possible to expand the scope of these mechanisms into equity instruments (both general and attached to service hookup) and more general debt instruments. If MTV proceeds with its current intention to build a digital overlay network to provide high-quality service to business customers (and, simultaneously, to unblock the national long-distance network), it would have the opportunity to expand this mechanism still further by charging these business customers a substantial initial hookup fee. In addition, it would have substantial scope for financing development from connection-related financial instruments.

Foreign Outside Finance

So far the only significant foreign sources have been the World Bank and a certain amount of supplier credit. It is desirable and likely that this will change, although the speed and magnitude of new sources is unlikely to match the more sanguine hopes of potential recipients.

INTERNATIONAL INSTITUTIONS. Institutions such as the World Bank, the European Investment Bank (EIB), and the European Bank for Reconstruction and Development (EBRD), will remain central players for the foreseeable future, both on their own accounts and as catalysts for other sources through co-financing arrangements. It is not possible to say with any precision how much the international institutions will be able to commit during the next ten years. Much depends on imponderables but the amount will be based on the likely size of available resources, concerns about exposure, and the many demands from other sectors which will be made on these institutions; however, it is unlikely that they can contribute more than 40 to 50 percent of the total foreign exchange financing required. More likely they will be able to contribute less. This leaves roughly US$3 billion to US$6 billion of hard currency imports for the region to be financed from other sources.

DIRECT FOREIGN INVESTMENT. Direct foreign investment is desirable both because it is equity and also because it may bring foreign management expertise. Direct foreign investment can come in many forms, including foreign purchase of share equity in existing telecommunications entities after their transformation into joint-stock companies, equity (or quasi-equity) participation in new ventures with CEE telecommunications enterprises, direct purchase of specified subunits of the networks (for example, local or rural networks), and construction of entirely new wholly or partially owned enterprises to provide packet-switched data, private, or mobile networks. Although Western companies have expressed considerable interest in all of these, and there appears to be a great deal of opportunity, little concrete progress has been made to date. In large part, this is due to the lack of legal (and political) clarity regarding ownership of existing entities; assets and mechanisms for transferring them; and of regulatory frameworks governing franchises, tariffs, service obligations, frequency allocation, and interconnection. There is also considerable ambivalence in CEE (as elsewhere), despite the professed desire for Western management expertise, about granting ownership control of telecommunications networks to foreigners.

COMMERCIAL BANKS AND SIMILAR LENDERS. These have been a relatively small source of telecommunications financing in the past, but this may change if opportunities expand for co-financing, either with international agencies or as syndicated packages put together in the context of direct foreign investment.

TIED BILATERAL AND SUPPLIER FINANCING. More promising in terms of potential volume are various forms of tied and semi-tied financing, bilateral government grants and credits, and supplier or contractor credits. The current political pressure to help CEE, and the highly competitive nature of the telecommunications equipment market, virtually guarantee that financing of this sort will be available. Under the right terms and conditions these sources are highly beneficial. The right terms and conditions are, however, an important caveat. Financing of this sort often carries limitations in choosing technologies which can deflect the recipients from their own optimal development strategies. Furthermore, apparently attractive terms are often balanced by higher equipment prices and servicing costs. Also too many different systems may get installed, which complicates (and increases the cost of) maintenance and operations.

Currently, the sheer magnitude of Western interest is a problem. Large numbers of companies, consultants, investment bankers, and government officials are inundating CEE governments and telecommunications operators, which have little experience in dealing with such a flood. Currently, clear, orderly, and enforceable frameworks for considering and comparing offers, awarding franchises, and allocating frequency are rare. Establishing such frameworks is a critical priority if the situation is to remain under control, in the sense that excessive entry takes place without any order or process, contrary to national interests, and possibly with considerable corruption—which in turn can lead to a backlash against foreign participation per se. Alternatively, a number of qualified potential entrants will be so discouraged as to be unwilling to come back for some time to come, resulting in important opportunities lost.

In conclusion, therefore, financing will become a central problem in the coming years. CEE telecommunications sectors should, in theory, be able to find the necessary domestic and foreign financing to accomplish their development goals without having to rely on government budget contributions. Success, however, will not be easy. It will depend on the performance of the overall economy, the government's ability to implement a stable regulatory regime (including ownership, corporate structure, franchise, and tariff policy), and finally, the performance of the telecommunications operators themselves.

Regarding the latter, CEE telecommunications operators must begin serious financial planning to have any chance of meeting the ambitious goals they are setting for themselves. These goals are just barely feasible, and this only if operators use every means available to reduce costs, increase revenues, attract outside debt and equity, and tightly control financial planning. In April 1991 the World Bank conducted a course in Czechoslovakia on financial analysis and management of telecommunications for strategic planners from all CEE countries. That was only the very beginning. In May 1991 at a roundtable in Badacsonytomaj, Hungary, telecommunications policymakers and government officials discussed concrete options for raising finance. The World Bank has no particular view as to the best method of raising finance. All have their advantages and disadvantages, and it is up to each country to critically examine each option and pick those that best fit their own situation.

Endnotes

1. Central and Eastern Europe (CEE) comprises the former Warsaw Pact countries excluding the former Soviet republics, the former Yugoslavia, and Albania.

2. Official CEE GNP figures have well-known flaws. Efforts to correct for these have their own deficiencies and produce results which differ widely, from low estimates of about double to high estimates of four times the official numbers.

3. CoCom restrictions continue to apply to transmission equipment operating at 565 Mbps and higher.

4. *Towards a Dynamic European Economy: Green Paper on the Development of the Common Market for Telecommunications Services and Equipment,* Commission of the European Communities, COM(87)290 final, Brussels, June 30, 1987.

20

Closing the Capacity and Technology Gaps in Central and Eastern European Telecommunications

Jürgen Müller and Emilia Nyevrikel

FOR FORTY YEARS THE COUNTRIES OF CENTRAL and Eastern Europe (CEE) neglected investment in infrastructure, including telecommunications. Only on rare occasions did they attempt to bring their telecommunications systems up to Western European levels. (Even the relatively high telephone penetration of 17 DELs (direct exchange lines) per 100 population in Bulgaria is low in comparison with other West European countries; Table 20–1.)

The Capacity, Technology, and Quality Gaps in Telecommunications

It is very difficult to estimate the extent of the current capacity gap and the pent-up demand for telephone connections in CEE. In most of these countries, waiting lists which, if fulfilled, would double the number of current lines may in fact understate pent-up demand. Until the end of 1989, telephones and the telephone services in these countries were primarily meant for the commercial sector, the government, and the ruling cadre rather than for the general population. Available waiting lists from the private sector therefore did not always represent the total demand. Often those who got their names on them were in the party or had bribed officials. Also telephone usage, especially for private households, was very low, even at unrealistically low prices.

Before World War II Czechoslovakia, East Germany, and Hungary were among the richest regions of Central Europe. A considerable neglect of public infrastructure, including telecommunications, resulted from the destruction of the war and the socialist reconstruction afterwards. (The railways were something of an exception.) The development of the telecommunications infrastructure in CEE, therefore, fell behind that of Western Europe. Average growth rates for expansion also remained relatively low, thereby widening the capacity gap. Often, the telephone network was more developed in the major cities and administrative centers than in the outlying regions, which had much lower telephone penetration rates than suggested by the national average figures.[1] Only a very few outlying regions had direct dialing

Table 20-1. Comparison of Eastern European Telecommunications Performance, 1989

Country	Inhabitants (in mill.)	Main lines (in mill.)	ML penetration/ 100 pers.	Waiting list (in 1,000)	Waiting list per 100 pers.	Direct dialing (in percent)	Public phones (in 1,000)	Telex connections (in 1,000)
Hungary	10.6	0.9	8.7	552 (85)	5.2	85.6	24.4	13.5
Poland	38.0	3.0	7.9	2000	5.2	91.5	25.6	33.5
Former Yugoslavia	23.9	3.2	13.6	142	0.6	(88.0)	7.9	13.0
Bulgaria	8.9	1.5	17.0	168	7.9	99.7	9.7	6.0
Former CSFR	15.6	2.1	13.6	372	2.4	(96.0)	n.a.	n.a.
Romania	23.0	2.6	10.4	800	3.5	67.5	n.a.	n.a.
Total	120.0	13.2	12.0					
EC (1987)	320.0	122.7	37.0					
EFTA (1987)	32.0	16.3	51.0					

n.a. Not applicable.

Source: MDIS, World Bank

facilities, making the gap between the city and the countryside in terms of technology and availability even larger.[2]

The telecommunications systems in all of CEE are, in sum, substantially underdeveloped. They are characterized by exponentially increasing waiting lists, a growing technology gap, obsolete equipment, few if any nationwide dialing facilities (and even fewer international), low service quality with a high proportion of failed calls, slow fault clearance, high noise and distortion ratios, and frequent disconnections.

The technology gap between Eastern and Western Europe increased substantially during the late seventies and eighties, due to the advances in digital technology which Western economies (and many developing countries) used to modernize and digitalize their networks but which was, to a large extent, unavailable in Eastern Europe. This was partially due to the CoCom restrictions on the export of certain high-technology equipment with potential military use to the countries of the former Soviet block but also to the insistence on autarkic production and the lack of competition in the supply of equipment. In the fall of 1989 the CoCom restrictions were somewhat eased. Pre-1984 digital equipment (except common channel signaling no. 7, packet switching, and high-speed—above 45 Mbps—transmission equipment) could now be imported. Integrated services digital network (ISDN) techniques, 1350-nanometer optical fiber, and radio transmission equipment using the sophisticated 16-QAM modulation technique continue to be restricted and will likely only be available after further easing of CoCom restrictions.

The reasons for the large gap between Eastern and Western European technology in telecommunications can be summarized as follows:

- Although firms and public enterprises had a workable level of telecommunications infrastructure (except, of course, for a lack of new services), telecommunications were not seen as a necessary basic household need.

- Public investment funds were always scarce, so that the telephone companies were severely stretched, both for extension and replacement investment.

- The rapid technological changes in the sector over the last two decades has widened the gap as Eastern European countries have fallen further and further behind. CoCom restrictions extended and enlarged this gap.

- Equipment markets were largely protected. As a consequence production costs in terms of resource needs were relatively high, exhausting investment funds earlier than would have been the case under a more competitive situation.

Isolated Attempts to Decrease the Capacity Gap

The recent economic and political changes in Eastern Europe have led the authorities to realize that the problems facing the telecommunications sectors are more complex than just closing the capacity and technology gaps. The experience in the West showed that the widening of telecommunications applications and the emerging new service needs not only were adding to demand in the sector, but also making the institutional implementation of this demand more complex. Policies of liberalization and deregulation are therefore being considered in a number of these countries. Given the dissatisfaction with centrally planned solutions and excessive state intervention, there is now a greater willingness in Eastern Europe to experiment with alternative institutional arrangements. At the same time, however, the level of discussion and the problems of implementation are evidence of an additional gap, namely that of institutional knowledge and administrative flexibility in dealing with these issues. As many of these countries are currently also confronted with a period of fundamentally changing economies and political restructuring, of which telecommunications is only a small part, the enormous task of restructuring the sector should not be underestimated.

Bulgaria

While Hungary undertook to boost its telecommunications infrastructure on several occasions in the seventies and eighties, but not as part of an integrated, ambitious plan, Bulgaria implemented an accelerated development program which could, however, not be sustained. The Bulgarian example is interesting because it illustrates what could be achieved even with the limited resources and institutional constraints described above. In 1973 the government announced a nationwide program to improve service industries and put special emphasis on telecommunications. In a ten-year period it was able to triple its main line penetration through annual growth rates of 10 to 20 percent, during a period in which Hungary and Poland were only able to double theirs (Tables 20–2 and 20–3).

Financing of this program was achieved through the operational income of the PTT, which had been the main source of investment in the past as well as an increasing amount of credit, accounting for 20 to 22 percent of total investment. The PTT also enlisted the

Table 20–2. Effects of Bulgarian Investment in Telecommunications, 1970–1983

Year	Total exchange capacity	Increase in percent	Automated exchange capacity	Increase in percent
1970	387,768	—	295,156	—
1975	617,532	59.3	522,838	77.0
1980	1,181,656	91.4	1,121,603	114.5
1983	1,524,285	29.0	1,481,056	32.0

— Not available.
Source: Nyevrikel

Table 20–3. *Comparison of Main Line Densities in Bulgaria, Hungary, and Poland, 1974–1989*

Year	Bulgaria		Hungary		Poland	
	Density	Percent increase	Density	Percent increase	Density	Percent increase
1974	5.8*	—	4.7	—	3.8	—
1975	6.4*	10.3	4.8	2.2	4.1	7.8
1976	6.9*	7.8	4.9	2.1	4.3	4.9
1977	7.8*	13.0	4.9	0.0	4.6	7.0
1978	8.5*	9.0	5.0	2.0	4.8	4.3
1979	9.3*	9.1	5.2	4.0	5.0	4.2
1980	10.3*	10.8	5.8	11.5	5.2	4.0
1981	10.3	0.0	6.0	3.4	5.5	5.8
1982	12.7	24.2	6.1	1.7	5.8	5.5
1983	15.1	18.7	6.3	4.9	6.0	3.5
1984	16.9*	11.7	6.6	4.8	6.3	5.0
1985	17.4	3.3	7.0	6.1	6.7	6.3
1986	n.a.	—	7.3	4.3	7.0	4.5
1987	n.a.	—	7.7	3.5	7.4	5.7
1988	21.0	—	8.1	5.2	7.4	5.7
1989	22.2	5.7	8.7	7.4	7.3	5.4

* estimate from telephone density and extensions/main lines ratio

n.a. Not applicable.

— Not available.

Source: Poland: ITU Statistical Yearbook

Hungary: Statistical Yearbook of the Hungarian PTT

Bulgaria: ITU Statistical Yearbook (1974–1987 and Danka Zafiratou: Telecommunications in Bulgaria, OECD Seminar with Central and Eastern European countries. The Hague, April 22–24, 1991 (1988–1989)

help of local municipalities, agriculture cooperatives, and enterprises which helped in the construction of the local networks. Once completed, the local networks, buildings, and land became the property of the PTT; the local organizations, however, benefitted from an early access to a more developed and denser national telephone network.

Also, the Bulgarian program was associated with increased technology transfer and a general upgrading of the Bulgarian telecommunications industry. Siemens A-29 cross-point quasi-electronic exchanges were initially imported and later produced under a license. In 1976 this license was amended to also cover cross-point electronic telephone exchanges, mainly for the trunk-switching centers. In 1981, a digitalization program was implemented, with the objective of installing eleven digital trunk exchanges by 1990 and reducing the network hierarchies from four to three levels; however, problems in technology transfer and cutbacks in funds diminished the growth potential of the program by 1983. Nevertheless, the push up to 1983 gave Bulgaria a large infrastructure jump to put it ahead of all the other Eastern European countries. The total cost for the program was estimated at Leva 1.607 billion.

In the 1980s the Hungarians pursued a similar but less ambitious program. Given the ever-increasing waiting list and the limited funds available from internal sources, the PTT sought new ways of increasing telecommunications investment. One form of financing was a "partnership with local communities," similar to that which had been implemented earlier in Bulgaria but much more formalized. Another was the issuing of telephone bonds, complemented by increased borrowing, essentially through access to funds from the World Bank. These new funding mechanisms permitted more than a doubling of the number of main lines being connected per year in Hungary, from between 15,000 to 20,000 in 1981–82 to 43,000 by 1989.

The other CEE countries were unable to deviate from a long-term network expansion rate of 2 to 3 percent per annum, a very unsatisfactory rate given increasing telecommunications applications and the low level of basic infrastructure investment.

East Germany

The impact of the capacity and technology gaps was particularly felt in Eastern Germany, which was left with an outdated, old-fashioned network, 60 percent of which had already been written off. The age structure of the switches was particularly bad. Almost two-thirds of the switches were of the prewar Strowger type; the most recent were only 1963–65 models. Seventy percent of switching equipment, 60 percent of underground cables, and a full 98 percent of outside cables had already been written off. Yet, given the past rate of replacement, some of these outside cables (38,000 kilometers in 1989) will still be in use in 2050.[3]

In 1989 there were only about 950 kilometers of fiber-optical cable in use and some 133,000 kilometers of digital trunks.[4] There was no digital microwave system.

Data transmission could be provided only through the normal telephone network, which had only 700 data connections. An additional 226 data connections were provided via the telex network. A manual-switched data network operating at 2400 Hz provided 8000 connections, and there were 2,900 leased lines operating at 48 Kbps. In 1989 there were between 10,000 and 12,000 unfulfilled requests for data connections. There was no packet-switched network and no line-switched data network available. Facsimile transmission was not possible because of the bad transmission quality. Mobile communications was not publicly available, even though they were used to a large extent on a private basis and in large manufacturing and public utility firms.

Hungary

The Hungarian network resembled the one in Eastern Germany. It had equally low penetration with very large regional imbalances. Budapest, with only 20 percent of the population, had 50 percent of the country's telephones. Its 35 lines per 100 population compared with 9 for the rest of the country. Only 89 percent of local exchanges were automated (100 percent in Budapest and 77 percent elsewhere). The long-distance network had a lower degree of automation. While 90 percent of exchange lines in Budapest had subscriber trunk dialing (STD), only 61 percent had it elsewhere, giving a nationwide average of 79 percent. Only one in three towns and villages was connected to the STD network; the rest, with manual trunk exchanges, accounted for 32 percent of the traffic in 1985. International direct dialing (IDD) was available to eighty-four countries by 1985.[5]

A 1985 report from the Hungarian Ministry of Post and Telecommunications showed that 28 percent of exchanges and 20 percent of outside facilities required immediate replacement. Call completion rates were 45 percent for local calls, 50 percent for long-distance, and 35 percent for subscriber-dialed international calls.[5] To reduce overload of the network the ministry introduced partial or complete restrictions on new connections in more than 100 of 344 exchanges.

There was almost a complete absence of modern business services such as data transmission services, fiber-optical networks, and modern multifunctional terminal equipment, all of which were becoming increasingly important for business.[6]

The Increased Importance of the Telecommunications Sector

The political changes and restructuring efforts in CEE countries, from centrally planned to market economies, have also changed the priority for the telecommunications sector. The number of business firms is growing as a result of this restructuring and the special emphasis on creating small and medium-size enterprises. As a result the number of business access lines being demanded is increasing significantly. In addition, there is a growth in private households demanding access to the telephone network.

Foreign trade is also receiving a higher priority. Many of these countries are trying to reorient their trading patterns, which in the past relied to a large extent on the trading relations with the West and the member countries of the U.S.S.R.-based Council for Mutual Economic Assistance (CMEA) or Comecon. Furthermore, to upgrade the outdated capital infrastructure in the manufacturing sector, increased foreign investment and technology transfer are needed. All this requires a functioning telecommunications system, an aspect which is giving further importance to a properly functioning telecommunications infrastructure.

Not only are telecommunications being given increasing priority these days, but given the financial constraints of these countries and the disappointing performance of centrally planned systems, there is also an increasing willingness to experiment with new institutional structures. Telephone companies are being moved out of government departments into separate public companies. In some instances, privatization is envisaged, in whole or in part. This is being done not only to reduce political influence on the telephone companies but also to increase performance and to attract foreign capital to meet the investment needs of the 1990s. A reorganization of the telecommunications sector, including the possibilities of direct foreign investment, is increasingly being considered not only as a means of transfer of capital but also as a method for the transfer of technology and organizational know-how.

Short-Term Solutions

These increasing demands on the telecommunications network cannot be easily met, and especially not in the short term. As a consequence, administrations' main priorities are to try to keep the existing network working, to replace outdated equipment in major bottleneck areas, and to improve quality of service. Only in the medium term is a larger capacity increase achievable. Nevertheless, a number of short-term measures can be taken immediately, including:

- More realistic pricing of telephone services

- Relieving of bottlenecks in the network

- Improved efficiency in the operation of the network.

Longer-term goals, to which we will turn later, involve both institutional and financial reform.

Tariff Reform

Most telephone companies in CEE were not allowed to raise tariffs even though their costs rose. It should not be forgotten that in these planned economies, no one spoke about inflation. The result is that current tariffs often do not cover costs. An increase in tariffs, perhaps with a move toward some form of peak load pricing, is therefore inevitable. Although experience in countries with high excess demand indicates that demand for telecommunications services remains relatively price inelastic until penetration rates rise very much above current CEE levels, some rationing of demand through higher tariffs might still be expected. Poland has recently increased the prices for its infrastructure goods (mainly transportation) by more than 100 percent. A price rise of similar magnitude could certainly be envisaged for telecommunications services, at least for local and trunk calls. If such a price rise were coupled with a less pronounced increase during the off-peak period, some of the social tensions related to increases in telephone prices could be reduced along with demand on the network.

In addition, an increase in connection charges should be envisaged to reduce access to the limited telecommunications network in the short term, since such access has high opportunity cost. Such a policy could be coupled with new financing instruments, such as the issuing of telecommunications bonds in Hungary. An access charge in the order of DM 2,000 (US$1,400), which would indicate to existing telephone subscribers the opportunity cost of their own access, could be envisaged. This might in some cases even lead to a market for access.

Relief of Network Congestion

A second priority of telecommunications operators should be to relieve some of the current network congestion, to reduce the high fault rates, and speed up fault clearance. This would not only improve the usefulness of the present network but also help to raise more revenues. Such a network improvement program implies more investment in fault-monitoring, traffic-measuring, and traffic-engineering activities, as well as investments in the short term to relieve some of the bottlenecks in the long-distance network. Given the expected reduction in network congestion and the associated revenue growth, increased automation, especially in the long-distance network, could be an important and profitable area for such short-term investment.

Our discussions with some officials suggest that small investments for improving traffic-handling capacity in the network, especially in bottleneck areas, would help to relieve the most urgent needs of customers and yield relatively high rates of return. At the same time such a policy would help to better fulfill demand of old and new business customers, who are pressing hardest for capacity expansion.

Intermediate solutions

There are a number of additional measures which are somewhat slower to implement than immediate relief but play critical roles bridging the gap to long-term sustained development. Of particular interest are measures to improve efficiency of the incumbent operator and construction of overlay networks.

Improving Efficiency of the Telecommunications Operators

Telecommunications operators in CEE did not generally see themselves as service providers, namely, businesses which provide a functioning telecommunications infrastructure quickly and reliably at cost-effective prices. They had little interest in utilizing their capacity better, to reduce costs, or to respond to wishes of customers. Productivity in the network was low, as the number of main lines per employee in comparison to Western European standards indicates (Table 20–4) and, as previously indicated, tariffs were not usually used as a rationing or financing instrument. Demand management tools and network optimization techniques were and are still missing, resulting in relatively high-cost organizations.

In many cases the operator has already been separated out of the ministries and set up as a separate organization, with increased responsibilities and a clearer objective. The old telecommunications ministries, on the other hand, have had to learn how to regulate and oversee the sector. Given the increasing emphasis on telecommunications as a crucial tool in the restructuring of the economy, this reorganization of the sector is often being planned in consultation with foreign administrations and advisers. Hungary has already proceeded quite far in this process. Poland and the Czech and Slovak Republics will follow.[7]

If this reorganization is effective, productivity should improve and there should be higher capacity utilization of the existing network in the intermediate term. Although this will not solve the capacity and technology gaps, it is an attempt to reduce some of its shortcomings.

Overlay Networks

Short-term solutions can only help to better administer shortages and temporarily relieve some bottlenecks. Longer-term solutions to upgrade the networks to required standards take time and enormous financial resources. As a result, many administrations are seeking to install modern overlay networks, mainly for business users as an intermediate solution. Some of these are based on short-term measures, like VSAT technology to quickly upgrade certain communications islands; in the intermediate term, however, all major business centers should be connected with a modern network, either through an fiber-optical overlay network, as is currently being planned in Poland and Hungary, or with modern microwave technology. These overlay networks help link the major business centers among themselves and to the international networks, thereby upgrading service quality and access to modern services.[8]

The introduction of modern mobile services is a further intermediate step. In most countries of CEE, mobile services were available almost exclusively for military and some business applications. Now some of these countries are moving to a rapid introduction of mobile services as a way of coping with the telephone shortage. In 1990 Hungary (within the Budapest area) and Croatia (for the Zagreb area) implemented modern analog mobile systems. Other systems were implemented in 1991 in Ljubljana, Slovenia, in Prague, Brno, and Brastislava in the Slovak Republic, as well as Warsaw in Poland (Table 20–5). Over the next two to three years, these systems will be extended to most of the important business centers in each country. Mobile services have, therefore, become an important means of access to the overlay networks.

The introduction of overlay networks is not only a practical way to solve the technology and capacity shortages in the short term; it also allows for a degree of tariff

Table 20–4. Telecommunications Labor Productivity
Main Lines per Employee, 1974–1988/89

Year	1974	1981	1984	1988/89
USA	89	99	n.a.	n.a.
Canada	89	94	113	135
Finland	n.a.	83	101	125
Denmark	109	114	141	158
Italy	93	133	152	?
Spain	67	107	124	136
Sweden	107	122	127[1]	136
Great Britain	50	75	83	99[3]
France	70[2]	109	132	171
West Germany	64	110	118	130
Netherlands	122	182	203	222
Belgium	60	89	104	148
Austria	87	130	145	169
Norway	56	70	93	127
Hungary*	24	28	30	44
Former CSFR	n.a.	n.a.	n.a.	n.a.
Poland	23	33	38	46
Former Yugoslavia	37	56	67[1]	100
GDR	n.a.	n.a.	n.a.	n.a.

[1]1983, [2]1977, [3]1987; Source: ITU Statistics,
*   Hungarian Post Statistics
n.a. Not applicable.

Table 20–5. Eastern European Mobile Radio Projects, 1992

Country	System	Operator	Coverage	Start
Hungary	NMT 450MHz	WESTEL 51% Hungarian 49% U.S. West	Budapest	October 1990
Hungary	890–898 MHz	HTC 50% Hungarian 50% Contel Cellular	Budapest	Postponed because of license dispute
Croatia	NMT 410 MHz	Croation PTT	Zagreb	August 1990
Slovenia	NMT 410 MHz	Slovenian PTT	Ljubljana	1991
Czech & Slovak Republics	NMT 450 MHz	FMPT 51% Czech & Slovak Rep. 49% U.S. West/Bell Atlantic	Prague Brno Bratislava	1991
Poland	NMT 450 MHz	Polish PTT 51% France Telecom 49% Ameritech	Warsaw	1991/92
Hungary	NMT 450 MHz	WESTEL	Lake Balaton	August 1991

Source: Pyramid Research, 1991, internal data

differentiation which is not possible in most other countries.[9] Ideally, given the capacity shortage on the traditional network, access and usage tariffs should be increased throughout the network. Instead, higher charges are being demanded only for use and access to qualitatively better overlay networks as, for example, via mobile services. Although this policy may be a way of delaying the necessary tariff reform on the regular network, it gives business customers quicker access to modern and qualitatively superior communications products. Tariff differentiation violates the principle of uniform national tariffs, but it is a price most administrations seem to be willing to pay.

Longer-Term Solutions

In the long term, if the countries of Central and Eastern Europe wish to bring telephone services to a level comparable to that in Western European, they will have to implement a more integrated planning approach and carry out a number of more radical institutional changes. Table 20–6 shows the order of magnitude of investment needed if these countries are to attain half the Western European levels. It is based on some preliminary data and calculations of the investment required over the next decade to bring telecommunications penetration up to 27 lines per 100 inhabitants in six countries of the region (equivalent to the present level of telephone penetration in Spain), based on a full-cost-per-main-line figure of US$2,000. According to these calculations US$3.5 billion per year (at 1991 prices) would be needed, most of it in Poland and Romania.

Investment Needs

An examination of the resources involved puts these figures into perspective. Most CEE countries have official GNPs per capita in the order of US$2,000 to US$2,500. If, optimistically, GNP grows at a rate of 2 to 2.5 percent per year, it would reach US$2,800 to US$3,200 (in 1991 dollars) by the end of the decade. (This is similar to Portugal's 1990 GNP and Austria's 1960 GNP.) To achieve the present level of the Spanish telephone penetration by the year 2000, these countries would have to divert a significant amount of resources to the telecommunications sector or seek a substantial increase in outside financing. To reach a higher growth level would require investments in the neighborhood of 2 to 2.5 percent of GNP. Yet in most of these countries past growth rates were only about a third of that which would be required (Table 20–6). These would, therefore, have to increase significantly. To achieve this without outside help is an unrealistic proposition, especially given the higher foreign currency content required to overcome the technology gap.

Examples

Current Hungarian and Polish development plans illustrate the investment problem. The Hungarian Telecommunications Company (HTC) completed a ten-year development plan, according to which penetration should reach 28 DELs per 100 population by

Table 20-6. Central and Eastern European Investment Levels Needed to Reach a Penetration Level of 27 by 2000

Country	Main Lines (ML) in millions (1988–89)	(2000)	Needed growth in percent p.a.	Previous growth rates p.a. (1965–1983)	Total cost (U.S. $ billion)	Cost per annum (U.S. $ million)
Bulgaria	1.5	2.4	4.5	9.7	1.8	169
Former CSFR	2.1	4.2	6.5		4.2	382
Hungary	0.8	2.9	12.3	3.8	4.1	375
Poland	3.0	10.2	11.8	4.4	14.4	1,311
Romania	2.6	6.2	8.2	2.8	7.2	651
Former Yugoslavia	3.2	6.3	6.4	6.2		567
Total	13.2	32.2		38.0		3,455

Source: ITU, authors own research

the year 2000. This implies an investment of up to US$4.5 billion for 2.5 million to 3 million new subscriber lines (one-third of which would be for replacement of the present network). This plan is to be supplemented by a three-year crash program in which an overlay network is to be built to decongest the present network and to satisfy the needs of the business community, especially with respect to international links. This overlay network is to be interconnected with the existing analog network in which some old electromechanical local exchanges are also to be replaced with digital switches. According to a preliminary estimate for the three-year crash program there is an investment need of US$1 billion, with one-third of this to be financed by foreign exchange lending through the World Bank.

Poland is planning a similar type of crash program but even more oriented toward overcoming short-term bottlenecks. Its current emergency program consists of measures to decongest the international, long-distance, and local telephone networks; to install an international digital exchange; to lay a fiber-optic undersea cable to Denmark; and to link Poland to the West with a new EUTELSAT satellite earth station. Simultaneously, a digital overlay network is being planned to connect the major urban centers. Some local exchanges are also to be digitalized. A separate overlay network with local tandem exchanges interconnected by fiber-optic transmission systems are also to be constructed in Warsaw to improve traffic flow.[10] The Polish program, like the Hungarian short-term crash program, is being co-financed by the World Bank, at least for the foreign exchange component.

A somewhat different picture (in terms of finance and speed) is presented by East Germany as a result of unification. In addition to a crash program, which is aimed mainly at relieving network congestion between East and West Germany, there is an intermediate plan to establish a digital overlay trunk network, on which 95,000 digital connections were already available by the end of 1991. This overlay network should be fully available throughout East Germany by 1995. In addition data networks and mobile services are to be introduced and network penetration is to be increased by a factor of four. The quantum increase in investment in East Germany (with only 20 percent of West Germany's population) shown in Tables 20–7 and 20–8 results in a one-third increase in investment volume in telecommunications in the unified Germany.[11]

Table 20-7. Forecast Telecommunications Investment in East Germany 1990-1995

Period	Past Investment (Mark billion)	Investment for 3 Scenarios (DM billion)		
		1	2	3
1971-1975	2.1			
1976-1980	2.9			
1981-1985	2.4			
1986-1990	3.9			
1991-1995		15.6	30.0	60.0

Source: Jahn, 1990

Table 20-8. East German Investment Goals to 1995

Service	Current Demand	Expected Increase and Scenario		
		1	2	3
Main lines	1,200,000	1,100,000	2,000,000	6,000,000
Public phones		10,000	25,000	60,000
Telefax	1,200	15,000	25,000	200,000
Data connection	13,000	19,000	35,000	60,000
Telex	4,000	5,000	8,000	8,000
Videotex		5,000	10,000	10,000
Mobile radio			15,000	50,000

Source: Jahn, 1990

Can the Equipment Manufacturing Sector Overcome the Technology and Productivity Lags?

For telecommunications operators, current "world market" investment costs per DEL are in the order of US$1,600 to US$2,000.[12] Given local manufacturing conditions and present exchange rates, operators in CEE sometimes have higher investment costs. This is due partly to the technology gap, since much of the equipment is still of the electromechanical type, and partly to a lack of competitive pressure. Open procurement policy was unheard of in the past and even today is not often favored because of the lack of foreign exchange and the need to use large public investments in telecommunications to stimulate the restructuring of an important manufacturing sector. At present, the large CEE telecommunications equipment exporters, such as East Germany, Bulgaria, and Hungary, are facing a declining market in the former Comecon countries, due to payment difficulties and economic reorganization. As a result some of these countries have adopted protectionist policies for domestic industries as, for example, in Hungary where manufacturers can obtain a 10 to 15 percent price advantage on tenders in international bids. Given their technology and productivity lags this may not, however, be enough for domestic firms to obtain orders.

The case of Germany illustrates the problem created by the backwardness of the Eastern European equipment manufacturing sector. Here, in spite of increased demand, inefficient East German firms with their old products cannot compete with their EC counterparts. Instead, these firms have had to close most of their plants and seek extended production orders from the West. Of the 35,000 employees in East German telecommunications manufacturing in 1989, no more than 10,000 will probably remain, even in spite of the short-term new production and assembly capacity which is being built up. Difficulties arise not only because of the lower labor requirement for electronic equipment but also because of the cheaper source of switching, microwave transmission, and fiber-optical equipment from existing equipment manufacturing plants in the West.

Other CEE manufacturers may be spared such a rude shock because of their often undervalued currencies as well as the foreign exchange and borrowing constraints of their governments (unless of course this constraint is broken through foreign direct investment); they must, however, rationalize and improve production and product technology. If the process of technology transfer is successful, much of the equipment needed in these countries could continue to be met through domestic production. At present, only 20 percent of telecommunications procurement of the Hungarian PTT is made up of imports (Table 20-9). With a move to more modern exchanges, fiber optics, and mobile equipment, this ratio is expected to increase to 40 percent; however, given the expected expansion in the Hungarian network this increased import share should still leave enough demand for the domestic manufacturing sector, even though it is facing smaller markets in its traditional Comecon export area. How can one ensure that these firms are able to quickly reduce the present technology gap? Nulty and Holcer have estimated that with the exception of ordinary metallic cable, the domestic

Table 20-9. Expected Changes in the Value of Imports and Domestic Production of Telecommunications Equipment for HTC 1989-2000

Category	1989 (current)		2000 (estimate)	
	Domestic	*Imported**	*Domestic*	*Imported**
Switching	90%	10%	30%	70%
Transmission Equipment				
wire	80%	20%	60%	40%
microwave (analog)	80%	20%	80%	20%
microwave (digital)	60%	40%	60%	40%
Cables	50%	50%	80%	20%
Telephone sets	100%	0	100%	0
Power Supplies and Batteries	80%	20%	80%	20%
Average	80%	20%	60%	40%

* Note: The "Import" category is made up of: (1) MP expenditures on finished equipment, and (2) industry expenditures on imported inputs. It *excludes* industry investment in imported machinery and capital goods. All figures are estimated.

Source: Nulty and Holcer (1990)

industry in these countries is anywhere from five to fifteen years or one to three equipment generations behind its Western counterparts.[13] The relaxation of CoCom restrictions should make the task of catching up easier, but this will probably not be possible without joint ventures or direct technology licensing.

This analysis indicates that a viable procurement policy related to the long-term policy of network expansion cannot be carried out without a long-term industrial policy, developed in close consultation with the governments and possibly the old Comecon trading partners. Which companies will in the long run maintain a competitive advantage as trade flows are redirected? Who are the obvious losers? How fast can the necessary restructuring be carried out? What financial and technical support programs are necessary? These questions must be answered before the telecommunications equipment manufacturing sector can be made competitive in terms of product quality and price. Otherwise its long-term viability is in serious doubt, even in spite of the pent-up demand confronting service providers in all CEE countries.

Institutional Change

As users are demanding increased infrastructure availability, a broader range of service offerings, as well as more innovation and responsiveness in service provision, the pressure on the operators is growing to abandon the traditional monopoly service provision policies and to allow for alternative provisions of network services. This pressure has increased with the concurrent economic reform, which is characterized by moves away from the old form of state-planned activities.

Joint Ventures and Private Networks

Initially, as mentioned, telecommunications administrations are being separated from the old PTT ministries and transformed into public corporations. This allows them to participate in joint ventures at least on subsections of the networks such as mobile, international, and overlay, or to be at least partially privatized, or both. There are a number of institutional options being considered at present.

The implications of these institutional changes on performance and financial viability should not be overlooked. The ability to attract direct foreign investment in this way relieves the government of an important foreign exchange constraint. At the same time joint ventures with foreign partners facilitate technology transfer in the form of human capital as well as the important organizational know-how to deliver new telecommunication services, an area in which these PTTs have little experience.

Although the carving out of parts of the market for new entrants or joint ventures can be positive in increasing the availability of scarce foreign resources and expertise, such a policy deprives the traditional PTT of its ability to cross-subsidize low-density, high-cost areas of the network. Deregulation in the telecommunications sector in the highly industrialized Western economies such as Japan, USA, and the U.K. is taking place, with these countries already having attained high penetration levels with marginal regions well served. In CEE, on the other hand, institutional reform and deregulation must be implemented in conjunction with an accelerated development of the basic network. This means that if regional imbalances are to be avoided, significant policy changes (that is, explicit regional subsidies) must take place alongside the implementation of new telecommunication policies.

These policies have to answer the following question:

- Given the associated financial and organizational needs, what new institutional structure best fits an accelerated infrastructure development program?

- How is this development to be financed?

- How can extreme regional imbalances be avoided?

- What technology strategy should the accelerated infrastructure development follow?

- What is the best procurement and technology policy for supplying the service provider with the required equipment and installation capacity?

The Hungarian Case

In Hungary in 1989, the regulatory function was transferred from the PTT to the Ministry of Transport, Communication and Watermanagement. As of January 1, 1990, telecommunications operation have been separated from the postal and broadcasting functions. The new telephone company, MTV, is to become a joint-stock company, opening the possibility to seek private (including foreign) equity participation. The state will, however, retain majority ownership.

Development of the future Hungarian telecommunications policy led to two institutional alternatives concerning the technical strategy to be pursued. Under the first, the so-called island strategy, a given area was to be targeted for large-scale expansion, thereby reducing investment costs per area and access line while allowing the operator to increase access lines rapidly and maintain the network economically because of the uniform technology that each chosen priority area would have obtained. The drawbacks of this alternative were the lower revenue-generating capability in a given area (because a proportionally larger number of private households would have been included right away) and an uneven regional development, since other, nonpriority areas may not have been served for a long time. The strategy could therefore not provide an efficient nationwide infrastructure quickly for all those who wanted it, nor could it provide access to trunk transmission for the new services like mobile telecommunications.

The alternative technical strategy considered was that of an overlay network similar to that being implemented in East Germany and Poland. This option would generate more revenue by concentrating on new business subscribers and pent-up demand, while at the same time freeing up access line for households in the old network. This strategy was also preferable from a rate-of-return point of view, even if the speed of increasing nationwide residential connections was slower.

The current Hungarian ten-year telecommunications program is based on the second alternative; however, to overcome the associated infrastructure expansion problem, especially in the rural areas, this program is to be complemented by one of regional liberalization. Local franchise areas or "telephone development partnerships," which can run local networks policy, are to be created. This is a change from the past practice of using local development partnerships only to construct the network and then hand it over to the PTT. Experience with the first of such local companies shows, however, that the revenues in a given partnership region may not be enough to cover costs, so that some averaging across companies and regions will be necessary to avoid large differences in local telephone rates.

This institutional change is similar in ways to those in the West; however, it also highlights the need for a proper regulatory structure to ensure that a proper balance can be achieved between uneven development, on the one hand, and optimal resource use, on the other, while attracting a maximum amount of private investment.

Preliminary Conclusions

Although this analysis is based on preliminary data, it does nevertheless permit drawing some initial conclusions:

- CEE is recognizing the growing importance of telecommunications for economic development.

- To upgrade the CEE networks to at least half the typical level of Western European penetration levels requires a large resource transfer to the sector and to the countries concerned. Institutional structures must be found in which this transfer can be brought about effectively; it cannot be achieved without significant financial help from the West.

- With the (untypical) exception of East Germany, the institutional changes necessary to bring about more effective resource transfer are being pursued rather slowly. On the other hand, more radical solutions are being considered, including privatization and large-scale liberalization.

- An important issue in this process is the restructuring of the telecommunications equipment sector, which could become a crucial strategic industry for most of these countries.

- As a consequence an integrated approach must be sought, with appropriate trade-offs between short-term gain, long-term growth potential, and macroeconomic implications.

This difficult adjustment process must be coupled with Western help at several levels. More room for private incentive must be found, since successful restructuring of the networks also provides an entry for foreign participants into what may be a very lucrative market and service area in the next century.

Endnotes

1. For example, in Hungary 20 percent of the population has access to 50 percent of the available telephones.

2. In Poland 7,500 villages have no telephones, while 65 percent of villages with telephones have manual switching. In Hungary 86 percent of 2,226 local exchanges still have manual switching. For international switching, the level of manual switching is sometimes even higher (90 percent in Romania).

3. W. Gülzow and J. Jahn, "Entwicklung des Telekommunikation in der DDR," in *Nachrichtentechnik* (Berlin: 1990), 40/9.

4. This was on the basis of PCM 30 and PCM 120. The use of PCM 480 started only in 1989.

5. Timothy E. Nulty and N. Holcer, *Telecommunication Strategies in Eastern Europe*, World Bank, 1989.

6. Most of this business demand is still being met by an equally deteriorating telex network.

7. Ignoring for the moment that East Germany, after unification, adopted the administrative structure of West Germany.

8. Many of these countries had in the past actually used some kind of separate overlay network for business users. In East Germany, for example, a number of private networks within the major conglomerates were used to facilitate communication within. These private networks could reach up to 36,000 connections. In Poland, there is a separate network which can reach 4,000 customers. Neither of these networks are, however, linked to the PSTN network.

9. This is especially possible with mobile services which are introduced as a higher-grade, more expensive access service.

10. Nulty and Holcer, p. 23.

11. Based on a current investment level for West Germany of about DM 18 billion to DM 20 billion per annum.

12. Nulty and Holcer, p. 9.

13. Nulty and Holcer, p. 20.

21

Restructuring in Hungary

Krisztina Heller

BY THE END OF 1992 THE HUNGARIAN PARLIAMENT passed a Telecommunications Act and a number of other pieces of legislation which will lead to reforms in the sector through privatization, introduction of competition, and liberalization of markets. Transformation of telecommunications in Hungary has been closely tied to the political situation of the times. A highly structured sectoral regime which was in place from after the war until the late 1960s was replaced with a somewhat more liberal regime which coincided with the cautious political and economic opening that the Kadar government began in the early 1970s. The level and quality of service which Hungarian telecommunications could provide can virtually be correlated with the extent to which the sector itself began to open. The most substantial steps in reform have taken place since 1988. This chapter describes the evolution of the telecommunications sector in Hungary since the war. Although the process has generally been in the direction of greater liberalization, there have been reversals along the way. This chapter shows how these have been related to political realities of the time.

The Pre- and Immediate Postwar Years

During the early part of this century and up to the Second World War, telephone penetration in Hungary—where the world's first telephone exchange was installed, in Budapest, before the turn of the century—was comparable to that of most European countries. Although there was no shortage of telephones in the years immediately after the war, this changed with the advent of a communist regime in 1948. With it came a very hierarchically organized society, with a strong political dictatorship and a "planned economy" in which all resources were directed to serve the political needs of those in power and to maintain them. This was the period of "hard" communism, which in Hungary lasted from 1948 to 1968.

Telecommunications, postal, and broadcast signal transmission services were provided by Magyar Posta, a single entity with an ambiguous legal status: it was both a state-owned enterprise like others in the planned economy and a department of the Ministry of Transport and Communication which was reorganized in 1989 into the Ministry of Transport, Communication, and Construction and in 1990 into the Ministry of Transport, Communication and Watermanagement. Prices of telecommunications services, like those of other goods and services, were set by the state, and funds for investment were "awarded" or distributed by the National Planning Office, which also determined the number of new lines to be built.

In 1964 the government enacted a Post Law which gave the state the legal basis to allocate frequencies as well as to operate the postal and telecommunications services and the networks on an exclusive basis. Telephones, however, like other resources, continued to be distributed through a centrally controlled mechanism. There was a separate world of various closed and dedicated networks serving strategic industries and constituencies such as water, energy supply, railways, mining, network, and the political corps. The total combined size of these networks was almost as large as the public network. Political preferences prevailed even in the distribution of residential telephones. People with key positions in the political apparatus, in the basic industries, and those with political merit decorations were put high on the priority list. Telephone penetration in the basic industries was much higher than in others. State and party administrations were also well equipped while the agricultural sector was essentially deprived. As a result, the overall telephone penetration rate at the end of the period of hard communism in 1968 was only 3.5 main lines per 100 population.

The Period of Soft Communism, 1968–87

Around 1968, which was characterized by student demonstrations in Europe and North America as well as the Prague Spring, there emerged in Hungary a new economic liberalism which attempted to create a real marketplace. Although Soviet policy at the time soon put an end to this liberalism, specific markets were allowed to remain open. Limited private undertakings became legal. Foreign trade increased. This period of soft communism was, however, unable to overcome previous shortcomings since there was neither capital nor a labor market. There was no unemployment until 1990. The distribution channels for resources (that is, material, investment, and labor) were governed by the so-called planned economy and remained close to what could be considered one-directional. Nevertheless, some newly emerging companies and industries such as financial services became wealthy and politically powerful, while traditional industries began to lose an increasing amount of their resources due to their inefficiency.

During the first half of the 1980s the relationship between the United States and the U.S.S.R. cooled, and CoCom restrictions prevented Hungary from buying electronic exchanges. Burdened with a gap between economy and policy, Hungary began to take cautious political steps toward the West. This was contrary to Soviet policy, but the political credibility of Hungary increased in Western eyes. This opened new lending possibilities, but because internal policy remained unchanged these loans were used not to implement new infrastructure but to maintain the old economic structure with the dominance of primary industry. By the mid–1980s Hungary's debt had increased to a level which would later lead to an economic crisis, and subsequently, to political changes. Toward 1968 growing discrepancies between supply and demand in the telecommunications sector became apparent. Studies to determine the negative impact on the economy resulting from shortages in the sector were inconclusive.

The Hungarian PTT continued in its dual role as a state-owned enterprise and a government department until 1985, when it was separated from the Ministry of Transport and Communication and transformed into a stand-alone government entity which, however, retained its dual role. Under its new status it was expected to have greater freedom in pursuing its telecommunications interests, and it was expected to modernize its structure as well as to separate its regulatory and operating functions. It survived four years in this state with mixed results. The separation of regulatory and operating functions proved impossible, due to the lack of an appropriate legislative framework.

In an attempt to reduce the level of unsatisfied demand, various new types of financing methods, including the issuing of subscriber bonds, were tried. Communities which were keen to develop their telephone networks were allowed to fund their construction. They were the source of a quarter of all telecommunications investment during this period. In 1987 the Hungarian government signed a loan agreement with the World Bank for US$70 million to expand the telecommunications network. As a result, telephone density, which had been increasing at a rate of 3.8 percent between 1980 and 1986, began to accelerate. By 1988 the penetration rate had reached 8. Yet one-third of all villages continued to have outdated manual switches with only eight hours of service a day. The network was overloaded and the quality of service was very poor.

The loan agreement with the World Bank had far-reaching organizational and administrative consequences for the modernization of the Hungarian PTT. Tele-communications began to be accounted separately from the other lines of business, and the government began to give the PTT a subsidy equivalent to that by which telecommunications had been cross-subsidizing the postal services. As a result of the World Bank loan agreement, Hungarian telecommunications have had audited financial statements since 1988. Procurement has been put on a public bidding basis. Western consultant firms were hired to advise on tariff policy, network management, and other matters. The principle of tariff increases, especially to keep pace with inflation, was accepted by the government.

The Removal of Communism

The process of liberalizing the economy was irreversible. The growing indebtedness of the economy affected central distribution because there were fewer and fewer resources to be distributed.

Important steps were taken to modernize the economy from 1988 to early 1990: a two-tier banking system was established, with commercial banks separated from the central bank; some securities became legal and a small stock exchange was established; a value added tax regime was adopted; a newly enacted company law opened the way for creating limited companies under legal circumstances similar to those in Western countries; privatization became legally possible and an independent Privatization

Agency was created; a newly enacted law on foreign investments proved to be one of the most liberal in the world; and borders were opened to most foreign trade.

In 1989 a law was passed giving Hungary a multiparty policy system, and an agreement was concluded on the departure of Soviet troops.

During these years the government also began reforming the telecommunications sector, making Hungary the first Central and Eastern European country to modernize its telecommunications institutional structure. In 1989 the regulatory and operational functions were separated, with regulation moving to the Ministry of Transport, Communication and Construction. The Post Law of 1964 was amended to allow private investors to take a minority stake in the telecommunications company which was established in 1990 as the Hungarian Telecommunications Company (HTC), with the separation of the postal, telecommunications, and broadcast signal transmission functions into three different companies. Activities not directly related to telecommunications, such as building, installation, and others, were assigned to subsidiary companies.

In 1990 two regulatory bodies were established: one for spectrum management and one for regulating technical aspects of posts and telecommunications (such as standardization and type approval). A further amendment in the Post Law provided for liberalization of wireless telecommunications such as paging, VSAT, and mobile telephones; however, licenses could be given only to companies in which the state had a majority holding. As a result Westel, a joint venture between HTC and the U.S. regional Bell operating company US West, was given a license to provide cellular services in the 450 MHz band. The venture proved quite successful. At the same time, a license was awarded on a trial basis to a state-owned company to build and operate a telephone network consisting of some 1,000 lines in a village near Budapest.

Growing liberalism in economy led to similar tendencies in political life, where advocates of major reform gained momentum. Privatization of HTC and elaboration of a regulatory framework were put on the political agenda; rapid political changes, however, temporarily halted the process.

The Newly Emerging Democracy

Free elections in May 1990 gave Hungary a right-wing government which continued the general policies of the previous government. The task of the new government was very complex: it had not only to construct a democratic society and a market economy but also remove the old monolithic ones. The Russian troops left in 1991, and Hungary was struck from the CoCom list in 1992. In 1991 Hungary, along with Poland and Czechoslovakia, signed an Association Agreement with the European Community with a view to their joining the Community around 2000. Ratification of this agreement is pending.

In order to build up a private economy, the government had as an objective the reduction of its assets holdings by one-half in the medium term. In order to allow the market economy to develop, much legislation needed to be replaced or, at least, substantially amended. This could not be achieved overnight. The Parliament has been creating and amending more then a hundred laws a year, including basic laws such as the Constitution and the civil code; these were, however, no substitute for having a telecommunications act which could stand the test of time.

The new democratic legislation emerged slower than expected because of unrealistic expectations, untrained politicians, and the lack of well-formed political and professional views about which way and how to proceed. Old practices were difficult to change. Recession set in, due in part to the breakup of the Comecon, an almost totally liberalized foreign trade, and a reduction in government subsidies. Unemployment reached 10 percent. The national budget became exhausted. Inflation climbed to 30 percent but started to decrease in 1992.

During this period, foreign debt decreased, the volume of hard currency reserves increased, the balance of payments became positive, and after more than a decade the balance of foreign trade turned positive.

Between the spring of 1990 and the end of 1992 the government created and passed some very important pieces of legislation. Among these were a Western-type competition law which provides for an independent Competition Office to report directly to Parliament; a price law which liberalizes almost all prices, except those of public utilities; a budget law which modernizes the national budget; an amendment to the civil code which spells out the equality of the state and private ownership; and a concession law which establishes rules for running activities where the state retains special rights (specifically in public utilities and energy supply). Also, the government established the independence of the courts and redefined the rights and duties of local governments. New laws for banking and financial activities were created, and a new accounting law, which provides for internationally accepted financial statements and a legal framework for state property management and privatization, was created.

There was consensus that neither democracy nor the marketplace can function properly without telecommunications. The shortage in telephones became critical as it had never been before, as did the need for new enhanced services due to the emergence of joint ventures with foreign investors. The public was impatient and keen to see continued reforms in the telecommunications sector. It became strongly opposed to all types of monopolies and state intervention. The change in mood was also felt at the HTC, where younger managers replaced some of the older. The monopolistic position of HTC started to erode, but the government still did not have adequate regulatory tools in place for regulating the sector. Domestic entrepreneurs, looking for new investment opportunities in the midst of a recession, supported by promises of foreign would-be investors, called for the opening of investment possibilities in telecommunications.

As a result the government began to prepare the terrain for privatization and to create a telecommunications regulatory framework in conjunction with the underlying Telecommunications Act. This turned out to be quite a lengthy process because of the ever-changing political and legislative environment.

In the meantime HTC, almost free from regulation, attempted to develop and expand the network as quickly as possible in order to strengthen its position. Further loans were obtained from the World Bank, EIB, EBRD, as well as other international institutions, and HTC was able to raise a total of US$40 million. It also issued bonds on domestic money markets. This initiative proved to be quite successful, and since these loans reduced the self-financing ratio of its investments to 50 percent, HTC was able to formulate a policy of creating subsidiaries with domestic partners to construct local networks. The largest of these will construct 100,000 main lines by 1993.

As a result the telecommunications network has been expanding at rates never seen before. The rate of increase in telephone lines reached 13 percent in 1991, bringing the penetration rate up to 11 main lines per 100 population. Waiting time for telephone lines dropped from twelve years to five years. Construction of a digital overlay network was expected to be completed in 1993.

Due to extended projects for the modernization of operation and organization, labor productivity improved considerably (by 9 percent in 1991 alone). The profit of the HTC in 1991 reached Ft 10 billion (US$135 million). A nation-wide, high-performance packet-switched data transmission system was launched, and together with VSAT connections, data transmission demand can now be met everywhere in the country. These, like other noncore activities, are provided by subsidiaries of HTC.

HTC, whose assets were now being valued by an internationally renowned auditing firm, was being prepared for privatization. New injection of money was needed. Investment plans were drawn up and being implemented, taking into account additional external financing in the form of equity.

The draft Telecommunications Act was submitted to Parliament in January 1992. After long debate the government resubmitted a modified, more liberalized version and gave municipalities and domestic investors a greater role. The new act, which supplements the Post and Frequency Acts as well as existing and new regulations and which entered into force in mid-1993, was approved by Parliament in November 1992 by an outstanding 75 percent majority. As a result and immediately upon its approval, a tender was issued for two GSM licenses. These were awarded in October 1993 to Pannon GSM, a consortium of operators from the Netherlands, Denmark, Sweden and Finland and to the consortium of US West and HTC. Also the first stage of the privatization of HTC was completed in December 1993 with the government's selling of an initial 30 percent of HTC's shares to DBP Telekom and the U.S. RBOC Ameritech for US$875 million. The government will retain 51 percent. The 1992 Law also provides for the creation of 56 local regions, each of which is to be handled by an operating concession to be awarded by end-1994, potentially in competition with HTC. Local or regional telephone companies covering one or more of the 56 primary areas have to be awarded concessions based on a public tendering process. Of these, 25 have been offered in such a process closed on December 29, 1993.

The New Regulatory Framework of Telecommunications

The regulatory framework for telecommunications in Hungary is designed to be as consistent as possible with the policy of the European Community.

According to the Telecommunications Act, as of April 1994 the provision of public-switched telephone, mobile telephone, nationwide paging, and broadcast signal transmission services will require a concession from the state. All other services have been liberalized. It will be possible to provide them subject only to a technical license based on objective criteria having been issued. Concessions are not required for closed user group networks or network construction. If a new entity has constructed a network under more favorable economic and technical conditions than the existing organization, the latter must conclude a commercial contract including terms, price, and other conditions of the usage of this network. This will promote network construction but it will also make maintaining of network integrity and interoperability more difficult.

A concession is a civil-type agreement between the state and the concessioner. It can be awarded in a public bidding where the state is represented by the minister of Transport, Communication and Watermanagement. Concurrent concessions can be issued provided that nonexclusivity is included in the first concession agreement. A privatization agreement can be regarded as a concession agreement. Service obligations and quality-of-service targets will also be included in the concession agreements and related regulations.

If local governments are not satisfied with the service provided, municipalities have the right to initiate a public bidding for concessions. The minister is obliged to go along if more than half the municipalities in a given primary area join such an action and if they are ready to cover the costs of an unsuccessful tendering.

Details of the industry structure and the principles of privatization are contained in a telecommunications policy statement which was to be submitted to the Parliament in early 1993. (A policy statement was submitted to Parliament in January 1993, but then withdrawn by the new minister in March.) International, long-distance, and local telephone services were expected to remain a monopoly for about five years, by which time near-universal coverage was expected to be achieved. Local and regional telecommunications companies covering one or more of fifty-six primary areas must be awarded concessions based on a tendering process. Given the level of demand and the general state of the economy, near-universal coverage will require a doubling or tripling of the existing number of telephones. This would result in a telephone density of 25 to 35 main lines per 100 population, a figure equal to that in Western Europe ten or twenty years ago.

The 1992 law on the property of the state provides for the state's ownership in telecommunications to be held by the State Property Management Holding Company. The state, through this company, will retain a 51 percent majority stake in HTC. The Ministry of Transport Communication and Watermanagement will regulate the sector.

Tariffs will be subject to price-cap regulation. There will be no other form of economic and financial regulation. The Telecommunications Act establishes a Telecommunications Fund for subsidizing underprivileged areas. Terms-and-conditions contracts between operators and users of networks as well as for interconnection will be specified in a government decree.

Next Steps and Lessons

The transition from a state-owned to a privatized sector began about five years ago and should soon be finalized. Two lessons can be learned from early experience in telecommunications sector restructuring in Hungary. The first is that the appropriate political, economic and legal conditions have to be in place. The second is that, governments of new democracies like the one in Hungary have to develop the necessary political skills to implement such ambitious national modernization programs whether they are initiated "from the top down" or "from the bottom up"— the latter through appropriate consensus building among opposing factions. Arriving at a viable compromise requires the government's time and effort.

Part V

Privatizations: Foreign

Operators' Perspectives

22

Privatization of Telecommunications Enterprises: The Viewpoints of Foreign Operators

Judith D. O'Neill

PRIVATIZATION IS A VERY BIG BUSINESS. It was estimated that privatizations in all sectors in Latin America alone would reach a potential of US$50 billion in 1991. In Eastern Europe, in Czechoslovakia it was estimated in 1992 that there would be at least 70,000 privatizations. In the Pacific Rim in the telecommunications sector already we have seen successful transactions worth billions of dollars in Malaysia and New Zealand, and opportunities are emerging in multiples of that value in Singapore, Thailand, Hungary, the Netherlands, Germany and possibly France.

Privatizations of state telecommunications enterprises are business deals and service opportunities from the point of view of the foreign operating companies who participate in them. The norms and analyses that apply to the pursuit of international investment opportunities in general apply as well to telecommunications privatizations. Similarly, telecommunications, like any other economic sector, has its sectoral peculiarities which must be evaluated within the specific set of applicable national attributes and incorporated into the risk-reward formula. In essence, the process and the concepts of how a potential foreign operator analyzes an opportunity are neither esoteric nor unpredictable. Common business sense prevails, together with the desire to be in an environment which allows the foreign operator the realistic opportunity to have a positive impact on service.

Foreign telecommunications operators are mostly concerned with three categories of features of prospective privatizations. Whether these items are classified in sets of deal attributes, as the bankers tend to do, or as a package of revenue-operational-environmental-procedural features, as operating companies tend to do, the ultimate information needed to make a sound business decision rarely changes. These categories are:

NATIONAL ATTRIBUTES. The extent to which the history as well as the economic and political situation of the country add to or detract from the privatization opportunity.

LEGAL-REGULATORY ENVIRONMENT. The articulation by the government of how it plans to restructure its telecommunications sector, and what it is doing through legislative and regulatory efforts to accomplish its objectives.

MANAGEMENT OF THE PROCESS. Whether a perceptible organization and deliberate plan for a transparent process is implemented through an organized government team and a small but expert group of outside advisers.

National Attributes

The state of the national economy, stability and convertibility of its currency, perceived and real stability of the political system, demography, history, and culture are all attributes of great interest to a foreign operator-investor. Nevertheless, other than to make the information available at the time of the privatization and articulate whatever commitments it has made to improve any negative elements, the government has little control over these factors during the investment opportunity analysis period.

The government does have control, however, over another factor in this category: its demonstrated commitment to the privatization. This factor is potentially very important to help propel the foreign operator-investor's pursuit of the opportunity. This commitment often includes governmental salesmanship of the concept before and during the process. In Venezuela, for example, industry surveys were conducted before the privatization of CANTV commenced, polling selected user groups and lending an air of openness and demonstration of government sensitivity to the desires of the end users.

Other aspect of national attributes is the government's handling of labor issues. The government must strike a balance between the desires of the labor market and the economic realities of the foreign operator-investor. In Puerto Rico, for example, the government issued a decree at the outset of the first privatization attempt of PRTC, announcing that telephone company employees could not be discharged for two years. The combination of a legislated purchase price (US$3 billion) and employee mandates caused all interested purchasers to abandon the opportunity. Later a more relaxed environment allowed the successful sale of the long-distance company Telefónica Larga Distancia de Puerto Rico (TLD) to Telefónica de España.

Finally, as with the sale of any property, the more it is put in order and improved before the sale, the more likely it is to sell and the higher the price will be. From the point of view of the investor, therefore, the recent corporate history of the telecommunications company is meaningful. The ideal opportunity, from a foreign operator's point of view, is a company which has been corporatized before its sale. That is, to prepare for privatization, the government has dedicated some period of time to restructuring the telecommunications sector and the telephone company. Preprivatization corporatization is beneficial to the potential purchaser in that it allows a more accurate evaluation of cost, revenue, and market projections than may otherwise be possible. This, in turn, is beneficial to the government, since it enhances the value of the company and is a clear indicator of government resolve.

In the United Kingdom, the government began the restructuring process by separating the telecommunications services from the British Post Office and creating British Telecom in 1981, and then in 1984 establishing the Office of Telecommunications (OFTEL) as an independent regulator. In 1982, it licensed Mercury as a second carrier. In 1983 it granted a seven-year duopoly to the pair, and in 1984 it privatized British Telecom. In Chile, a similar, though longer process, occurred which began with a telecommunications policy decree in 1978, followed by a new law in 1982 and an amendment in 1987, then the privatization of the two dominant carriers Compañia de Teléfonos de Chile (CTC) and Empresa Nacional de Telecommunicaciones (ENTEL) in 1988. In Mexico, TELMEX was restructured in 1987 into three regional (North, South, and Mexico City) and two service (large user and long-distance) divisions designed to monitor costs and revenues and to control cross-subsidies. In November 1990, the Department of Transportation and Communications (Secretaria de Comunicaciones y Transportes) was relieved of its operating responsibilities and given the job of full-time regulator, and on January 1, 1990, Telecomunicaciones de Mexico (TELECOMM), an autonomous state enterprise, began operating the government's satellite and microwave services as an autonomous state enterprise. In August 1991 the privatization of TELMEX formally began. In New Zealand, the government spent approximately two years corporatizing the Telecom Corporation of New Zealand (TCNZ) before its privatization in 1990.

In some countries, however, for a variety of reasons, this preparation for privatization may not be possible. Argentina, and Venezuela are cases in point. The state enterprises were sold with minimal restructuring about one year after reforms began.

Legal and Regulatory Structure

Some form of government intervention into commercial enterprise is often necessary to direct sector growth and protect the interests of the population at large; however, where there is government intervention, it necessarily will impact on the structure and profitability of the commercial enterprise. In the micro sense, its impact will be on the day-to-day cost to the company of compliance with whatever policy and regulatory obligations the government imposes. In the macro sense, its impact will be from the type and timing of market entry of any potential competitors which the government permits, as well as from whatever fiscal control the government is inclined to impose on the business, such as tariff controls, investment-performance obligations, and partnering-consortia rules.

The government's decisions will be based on commercial and political dynamics. Ideally, the government will be knowledgeable regarding what decisions are optimum for the commercial success of the privatization and will accommodate those optimum commercial desires to national goals and needs as well as to political realities. The result should be reached in an expeditious, thorough, deliberate manner, based on organized and experienced input, and published as quickly as feasible. Accurate, reliable information which industry can use is crucial.

A balance which serves the needs of both government and private operator-investors is best for both and maximizes the value of the investment opportunity.

Where any form of a multioperator system (including cellular or value added services) is contemplated in the short or long run, the relevant legal and regulatory bases are as follows:

- Drafting and enacting of legislation necessary to allow for the restructuring

- Creation of an independent regulatory body, with enabling legislation and a structural-functional description

- Drafting and enacting the rules of the game:

  1. A new telecommunications law, if necessary, to pursue the government's objectives and to assure purchasers of the government's commitment

  2. As much of a base of specific sector regulations as is feasible

- A regulatory design oriented toward carriers (rather than services) so as to give potential investors a clear picture of the intended structure of the sector so as to allow reliable financial projections and so as to give the government the ability to control the speed with which the sector opens up.

Regulatory Infrastructure

In most countries undergoing restructuring, particularly in the developing world, the regulatory scheme is either nonexistent or loosely managed by the dominant or monopoly carrier itself. This creates insecurity for potential foreign operators because certain future market factors cannot be evaluated.

Passive regulation is logical and even efficient when the sector and the law of the country allow for only one carrier owned by the government. Also, regulation is not important where fiscal accountability is not a major concern of the telecommunications provider, and where broad social issues rather than corporate profit or efficiency in the management of the telecommunications system are the main responsibility of the government.

With privatization, roles have changed dramatically. Generally, governments have relieved themselves of the responsibility to provide telecommunications service. Private or corporatized government operators have assumed the responsibility of profitability and service improvement. The government or a specialized agency has stepped into the role of regulator.

When telecommunications become commercialized and responsibilities change, that process needs to be regulated. Government has a public welfare interest in regulating dominant carriers who can otherwise control their own market, and potential foreign operators need to know in advance what the rules of the game will be in the environment in which their investment is sought.[1]

The regulatory cliché that one should fully regulate monopolies and not fully regulate competitive services is often sound, but most countries do not find themselves in such clear extremes, particularly in the developing world. Thus, it is in everyone's interest to make and publicize decisions about the kind and amount of regulation appropriate to achieve the government's goals and the potential investor's aspirations.

In general, when a regulatory scheme focuses on the carrier rather than the service, a government is better able to encourage healthy economic growth of the telecommunications sector in a developing economy, and an investor is better able to evaluate when and where competition will be imposed; however, there are no absolutes in telecommunications policy and there is always some need for regulatory regimes to address specific services, such as cellular. Nevertheless, in conceiving and drafting the guidelines of a macroregulatory scheme for the sector, a developing economy is more likely to achieve the customary government and operator goals of universality and quality of service, variety of offerings, and reasonable price, through a scheme where the carrier is the focus of regulation. Similarly, the investor is likely to be better able to predict his future.

Corporate Structure

On the corporate side of the legal issues, investors naturally will be interested in the capital structure established by the government. This will provide critical input to the risk-reward formula, such as how much investment will be required, when, and in what form, what amount of control the investors will have over the operation of the company, and how the balance of the company's stock will be distributed. In this area, there are perhaps as many models as there are privatizations. The chapters by Hector A. Mairal (5) and Carlos Casasús (6) discuss the capital structures following privatization in Argentina and Mexico, respectively.

Management of the Privatization Process

An exchange between speakers at a conference on telecommunications privatization in Latin America illustrates the complexity of the privatization process. Following the speech by a U.S. lawyer who proposed a logical, orderly set of steps for a privatization process, the next speaker, one of the last employees of ENTel Argentina and a key participant in its privatization, praised the tidy steps articulated by that lawyer. He added, however, that such a process would be possible only if governments in general, and human beings in particular, were not involved.

Indeed, to the outside viewer, and particularly to the potential investor pressured by a sometimes multibillion dollar decision, the privatization often seems more like a fire drill than a business school exercise. Nevertheless, as much order as is reasonably possible should be a priority of the government to attract and keep foreign operator interest.

The Privatization Team

The investor wants as much information as possible, in as much detail as possible, as quickly as possible, about the privatization attributes. There is, indeed, a delicate balance in timing a privatization. Political, labor union, economic, and service pressures require a rapid announcement of the privatization decision. Once it has been made by the government the announcement attracts a series of private sector inquiries which government often is not prepared to answer. If wrong answers are given, or answers change as the governmental decisionmaking process matures, potential investors may lose interest.

It is not in the investor's interest to provoke ill-contemplated, rapid replies to long-term issues. Nor is it in the government's interest to discourage foreign operators by excessive delay or the inability to make the necessary decisions reasonably expeditiously once the decisionmaking tools are in place.

As to the latter, in most privatizations the government looks to outside experts to provide the input and experience it needs to make its decisions. Organizing and coordinating the efforts of outside assistance is important to the stability and efficiency of the privatization process. From the investor's point of view, it is best to have one continuous source of information from the government. From the government's point of view, too many assistants, or groups with overlapping responsibilities, could generate inefficiencies or even conflicting conclusions.

In general, outside assistance serving in privatizations mainly includes technical consultants, accountants-appraisers, lawyers, and bankers. A small, well-organized government team should be in place to work with these experts and coordinate their activities.

Process Transparency

The conduct of the privatization process must be, and must appear to be, free of inappropriate influences, free of corruption, and dedicated exclusively to the articulated objectives of the government. Proper procedures must be established and announced for all activities in the privatization, from the invitation to prequalify to the ultimate selection of an operator, where a new operator is a contemplated element of the privatization.

Although all processes vary slightly, they share many attributes in common, and certain norms have come to be expected by investors. These include, by way of example, provision of sufficient data room information and analyses; corporate debt instrument review; analysis of the salient laws of the country; reasonable timetables and articulated requirements for prequalification; a regulatory "house in order"; the issuance of a statement of terms and conditions of the sale which define the elements of the risk-reward formula; an offering statement; the requirement of a deadlined bidder proposal; a bidder selection, negotiation, and execution of a concession agreement.

The chapters that follow expand on these and related issues from the viewpoints of some of the main operating companies from developed countries that have already established a presence in the developing world.

Endnote

1. In some regions where the economy has been controlled substantially by the government via a system of government-owned parastatal corporations, broad-based price controls, and the like, a review of the entire legal structure as it impacts entry into and exist from the marketplace may be appropriate. For example, in Kenya, as part of a program to privatize nonstrategic parastatal corporations and restructure strategic ones (like the telecommunications company), an entire legal review has been done with suggested changes in parts of the commercial legal-regulatory infrastructure to facilitate the achievement of the move toward a market-driven private commercial sector within the framework of the government's goals.

23

Evaluating Investment Opportunities: Bell Atlantic's Approach and the New Zealand Experience

Hyde Tucker

THERE ARE MORE TELECOMMUNICATIONS investment opportunities today than there is global investment capacity. Examples include corporatization, privatization, joint ventures for the development of landline infrastructure, second and third licenses for cellular and other wireless systems, and the licensing of alternative full-service carriers.

We know of more than twenty telecommunications privatizations under way or being considered. Right behind them, corporatizations are creating opportunities for management and consulting contracts to help streamline operations, improve service, and modernize assets to fetch a higher price if the telecommunications enterprises are eventually privatized. At least a dozen countries are already in or about to start the tender process for second and third licenses for cellular mobile telephone or other wireless systems. Democracy and market reform in Eastern Europe and the strong economies in South Asia are creating exciting investment opportunities in infrastructure development.

This wealth of opportunities is good news for Bell Atlantic[1] and other foreign operators pursuing a global vision, because it will result in downward pressure on the current price of opportunities and lead governments to create more favorable terms and conditions surrounding foreign investment in telecommunications projects in order to attract interested parties and spur aggressive competition among them. Bell Atlantic evaluates each and every privatization opportunity. We are more likely to participate and compete aggressively when foreign governments put in place the right set of conditions to help us improve the value of the asset.

In the process, Bell Atlantic companies have been consultants as well as software and systems integrators for leading telephone administrations in Western Europe and in the Asia-Pacific region; partners in cellular consortia, with projects under way in the Czech and Slovak Republics, and agreements announced in Norway, Poland, and the former U.S.S.R.; exploring ventures for infrastructure development in several countries in Asia, Latin America, and Eastern Europe; a partner in a consortium that may bid for the second carrier's license in Australia; and participants in two telecommunications privatizations. In 1990, the company acquired Telecom

New Zealand in a partnership with Ameritech and two New Zealand firms. In Argentina, we would have managed a new regional telephone company under contract, as part of a consortium that ultimately was disqualified because it could not obtain the financing necessary to close the transaction. From these experiences, we have developed rigorous screening criteria to evaluate privatizations and other investment opportunities created by telecommunications sector reforms.

Value Added Analysis

When considering investment opportunities, we ask two fundamental questions: Can we add value to the investment? In doing so, can we increase Bell Atlantic shareowner value? The specific analyses we undertake to determine if and how we will participate in an international telecommunications investment opportunity fall into four broad areas. We will apply them here to the case of privatization of state enterprises.

Revenue Opportunities

We evaluate the country's economy—as it is today and as it is likely to be tomorrow. Our investment threshold certainly does not require economies as robust as Germany or Japan, but we do look at trends and developments, including the opportunity the telecommunications sector has to influence economic growth.

The overall environment surrounding the privatization also affects revenue generation:

- Is there pricing freedom or price regulation?

- What are the competitive dynamics in the country's telecommunications sector?

- What is the country's tax structure? Are there limitations on foreign ownership and dividend treatment?

- Are there opportunities to improve existing products or introduce new ones?

Bell Atlantic fully subscribes to the benefits of competitive markets and has, indeed, prospered in them. Each country must evaluate, however, whether the managed introduction of competition would better meet its early stage objectives of sector reform, to allow the foreign operator to implement changes that will lead to long-term efficiencies. The greater the degree of competition on high-margin products and services, the slower the development of basic services because the telephone company will have fewer resources to apply to access line penetration.

Throughout the analysis, we carefully balance the opportunities against the risks. For example, low telephone penetration could mean significant future revenue streams. On the other hand, major network modernization or expansion represents enormous capital costs and earnings requirements.

Productivity Improvement Opportunities

Second, we evaluate the prospects for adding value by increasing productivity:

- Can we streamline operations through consolidation and restructuring?

- Will the government and labor unions allow reduction of the telephone company workforce?

- Will we be permitted to develop incentive pay plans that tie compensation to performance?

- What are the opportunities to deploy new technology in switching and transmission as well as software-based operating support systems?

Political Environment

Next, we look at political, monetary, and other environmental conditions:

- Is there stability in the current government and in the national political system?

- Will our employees and assets be safe?

- Will there be calls or other pressures on our investment, as in a nationalization of foreign-owned assets?

- Is the currency convertible?

- Is the procurement process free from corruption or other pressures? Will we be permitted to make independent decisions on product sourcing and vendor selection?

Transaction Features

Finally, we identify and evaluate a host of other considerations—internal and external—tied directly to the bid process or the transaction:

- The expected size of the transaction against our investment capacity

- The strengths and goals of our joint venture partners, if any

- The structure of the transaction, including requirements and opportunities to sell shares

- Language or other cultural barriers and the costs of overcoming them

- Legal matters, including property titles, assumed liabilities and, in our case, restrictions imposed on Bell Atlantic's participation in certain lines of business by the 1982 Consent Decree which resulted in the divestiture of AT&T and the creation of seven regional Bell operating companies including Bell Atlantic.

The New Zealand Experience

As we applied our value added analysis to the privatization of Telecom Corporation of New Zealand Limited (TCNZ), we were attracted to the stability of the government and the political system, the long-term economic prospects, and our belief that telecommunications could give New Zealand an important competitive edge in attracting service industries.

TCNZ is the principal supplier of domestic and international telecommunications services in that country, serving approximately 1.5 million access lines. The company also provides its customers with a full range of other services: cellular mobile communications and radio paging, leased circuits, data communications and information services, telephone equipment sales and repair, and telephone directories.

In 1990 Bell Atlantic, Ameritech, and two New Zealand companies, Fay Richwhite and Freightways, purchased 100 percent of TCNZ from the New Zealand government for NZ$4.25 billion (approximately US$2.4 billion). It was a cash transaction, funded entirely by the investment team.

TCNZ was already a modern, well-capitalized company. Today, its network is 87 percent digital, with wide-scale deployment of fiber-optic systems. Future capital expenditures, therefore, will be more focused on business development opportunities than on core network modernization requirements. Another important element in determining revenue potential was that New Zealand is a largely untapped market for enhanced services such as Yellow Pages and international toll, cellular, and other wireless systems such as intelligent network services.

On the productivity improvement issues, TCNZ was acquired under the terms of New Zealand's ongoing privatization of state-owned enterprises. It had been corporatized two years earlier to begin its transition to a competitive, market-driven telecommunications company. For example, TCNZ's workforce decreased from nearly 26,000 employees in 1987 to fewer than 15,000 today. The company is committed to cost performance leadership, and we anticipate a force reduction of several thousand more over the next few years. Today, Bell Atlantic and Ameritech have a small team in New Zealand working with TCNZ management to identify opportunities to add value through the transfer of technology, operating support, and management systems as well as through marketing and other programs.

The absence of rate-of-return regulation in New Zealand means that cost reductions and revenue stimulation directly affect the company's bottom line and, therefore, its return to its owners.

Apart from the financial advantages, our position in TCNZ enables us to participate in the international services market, and it is a platform from which we can monitor and participate in other regional investment opportunities. One such opportunity is our recent purchase of a 51 percent interest in a pay television company in New Zealand, in a partnership with Ameritech, Time Warner, and Tele-Communications, Inc.

Benefits to Government and Customers

In deciding to sell TCNZ, the government had two key objectives:

* To obtain the best possible price in order to reduce public debt and debt servicing costs

* To give New Zealand the best possible telecommunications system in the world to help improve that nation's ability to compete effectively worldwide.

To meet those objectives the government set certain conditions for the sale:

* A ceiling of 49.9 percent ownership by any foreign strategic buyer or buyers

* A requirement that a public stock offering worth at least NZ$500 million be made to the New Zealand public

* The government would retain a "Kiwi share," which included service and rate pledges to residential customers.

The proceeds from the sale alone reduced New Zealand's public debt by nearly 12 percent in one hit and lowered annual debt service charges by NZ$430 million. A side benefit was that, unlike most other privatizations in New Zealand, most of the money came from overseas. The economy received an injection of about 7 percent of its gross domestic product (GDP) of approximately NZ$60 billion.

Our 100 percent purchase of TCNZ also relieved New Zealand taxpayers of the cost and risk of a public stock offering. The sale also relieved government of the responsibility and distraction of running a large complex company, and it was an outward and visible sign that New Zealand was moving to a market-based economy.

Bell Atlantic and Ameritech have three years to reduce their combined position in TCNZ to the 49.9 percent ceiling. We expect the ultimate ownership structure will have investors in New Zealand, in the United States, and in other markets owning 40 percent; Bell Atlantic and Ameritech each owning just under 25 percent; and the present New Zealand partners owning 10 percent.

Although the benefits to the government were obvious, the benefits to TCNZ customers were less so, at least at first. Just weeks before the final bids for TCNZ were due, a national poll indicated that some 90 percent of the public opposed the sale.

The dissatisfaction centered on two issues: foreign ownership and fear of increased prices. When we agreed to the terms of the Kiwi share, residential customers benefitted from our commitments to rate stability, uniform pricing, and the continued availability of phone service. Specifically, we agreed to maintain an option for flat rate local calling for residential customers, limit residential line rate increases to that of the cost of living, maintain uniform residential line rental rates for rural and urban customers, and not withdraw from any areas that TCNZ already served. It was important that we agreed to these service and rate pledges against the backdrop of a fully competitive telecommunications market. In New Zealand, an alternative telecommunications company has begun operations, and there are few regulatory barriers there for others to enter the telecommunications market.

On the foreign ownership issue, we helped the public understand that we would attempt to maximize New Zealand ownership of TCNZ through a public stock offering, and that through Bell Atlantic and Ameritech, TCNZ was gaining the skills and experience of two of the world's top performing telephone companies.

In the end, our commitment to the Kiwi share provisions and the foreign operators' records of innovation, efficiency, and customer service helped reassure the public. Immediately following the bid award, opposition to new ownership dropped to 53 percent, and it is only 39 percent today.

The Promise and Challenge of Privatization

In closing, we believe privatization holds enormous promise—for the foreign operator and its shareholders, for government, and for telephone customers. Our experience in New Zealand supports that proposition. But for all its promise, privatizations also present enormous challenges:

- For companies like Bell Atlantic, to select wisely from the range of international telecommunications investment opportunities available

- For governments, to create the right conditions and climate for privatization in order to spur aggressive competition to purchase the asset

- And finally, for owners, customers, and public policymakers alike, the biggest challenge is turning the long-term promise of information technology into a strategic competitive advantage in a global marketplace.

Endnote

1. Bell Atlantic is one of the seven regional U.S. telephone companies that resulted from the restructuring of the telecommunications industry in the 1980s. It serves 17.5 million telephone access lines in the six mid-Atlantic states of the United States and in Washington, D.C. With a population of 28.4 million, this economically vital

and communications-intensive region of the country also is home to the U.S. federal government and headquarters for eighty of the Fortune 500 companies.

Bell Atlantic meets the communications needs of residence, business, and government customers in this region with an intelligent network that is the most efficient in the United States (256 access lines per employee) and one of the most advanced in the world. Besides telephony, the company offers its customers high-quality cellular, mobile, and other wireless communications services, and provides a range of support services for computers and other business systems as well as leasing and financial services throughout North America and in selected overseas markets. Outside the United States, Bell Atlantic actively markets its core telephone business and related skills and technologies, and it has been exploring investment opportunities with a view to reaching its strategic goal of being a leading international communications and information management company.

24

The Point of View of a Global Operator: Cable & Wireless

Joseph E. Pilcher

ABOUT $150 BILLION OF TELECOMMUNICATIONS assets are reputed to be in line for privatization worldwide. A sound appreciation by governments of the operating companies to which these vital assets will be entrusted, and of the global telecommunications environment, is essential for charting the course of privatization and ensuring success.

Cable & Wireless plc (C&W) has over one hundred years' experience in investing in the developing world and existing operations in forty countries. After thirty-five years as a nationalized British company, C&W was privatized in 1981. It thus became the world's first private basic services telecommunications company with worldwide operations. As a private operating company, C&W's commercial freedom is firmly linked to accountability. No excuses can be advanced to our shareholders if our investment strategies are not coherent and based on sound financial principles. C&W seeks to maximize the return on its investments. To this end, four factors are critically important as C&W examines potential participation in new privatizations.

A carefully structured privatization process with adequate time given for preselected operators to carry out a proper risk assessment

The large investments associated with privatizations, and the fact that often it is not politically acceptable to carry out large tariff corrections overnight, result in cash flows which are invariably back-loaded. The long periods needed to recover the investment costs accentuate the risk of political and economic disruption, for example, renationalizations, devaluations, exchange controls, and shortage of hard currencies. It is therefore important for multinational operators to be given sufficient time during the privatization process to research these risks so that these can be properly factored into the decisionmaking process and associated risk premiums.

Suitable time during the due diligence process given to establishing the terms and conditions, as required by both governments and operators

A factor of concern from recent experiences is the absence of a pre-bid negotiation to establish suitable terms and conditions. The due diligence processes we have encountered are more geared to the operator's establishing a price and placing a bid than to recognizing the issues most likely to result in the development of a prosperous company, a necessity if the country is to avoid possibly facing renationalization after privatization. C&W would like to see suitable time being given during the privatization process to the government's reaching agreement with a shortlist of operators on such important issues as pricing denominated in hard currencies, government guarantees on foreign exchange, tax holidays on reinvested profits, and management of debtors. These are but some of the issues that require consideration. No one will gain if the operator bids for the business on false pretenses or due to unclear understanding of what can be really achieved.

Majority voting control vested in the operator

A contributing factor to an investment by C&W is the ownership structure sought by the government. C&W is a telecommunications operating company, not a financial investor. It brings to the developing world unmatched experience in the operation of telecommunications companies outside our own frontiers. If the objective of the privatization process is to ensure that the country's telecommunications networks and services reach the highest standards, then control must be with the operator(s). They must have the right to manage operations as well as to control its board of directors. This is imperative so as to drive through investment strategies and management structures. Any shareholding structure that reduces C&W's ownership below 51 percent of the voting shares rapidly reduces our interest in the project. There are a number of ways of ensuring control while still keeping ownership of the voting shares below 51 percent. Some of these structures have necessitated joint ventures with local partners which are purely marriages of convenience and do not necessarily bring partnership strength to the consortium. The question is whether these arrangements with local partners will benefit the single-mindedness that is required to engineer the change of these nationalized entities into profitable companies capable of facing competition in the future. Furthermore, due to the accounting treatment in the United Kingdom for associated companies, any equity position below 20 percent would again reduce our potential interest in the project.

A clearly defined regulatory scheme

Finally, there is the thorny issue of establishing the regulatory framework not normally in place at the time of privatization. It is our experience that telecommunications companies in line for privatization in developing countries are not well managed, profitable concerns and are, furthermore, suffering from years of gross underinvestment. No operator of sound logic will be prepared to take on such onerous responsibilities as investing in these companies, having to honor labor contractual obligations as well as not being able to rationalize the work force if, at the same time, it is having to confront new competitors that are not subject to such constraints or to universal service obligations.

With long-distance revenues a less prominent proportion of local revenues in the developing world than in the industrial world, and with international tariffs under pressure, the often-stated political need of keeping local charges down through cross-subsidization is clearly a dangerous road to travel. If this problem is compounded by introducing competition in the long-distance and international areas, the market distortion instituted by the cross-subsidy will weigh heavily against the privatized operator as it seeks to implement a large investment program geared to the development of the network to the nonurban population. C&W would, therefore, seek a period during which competition would be limited to domestic value added services. Governments, therefore, need to decide on a strategy to either introduce competition in long-distance and international services or to maintain the cross-subsidy. Whatever the answer, the objective must be clearly visible to those who may seek to invest.

25

Internationalizing Telecommunications Operations: STET and the Argentina Experience

Francesco Massari

WHAT DO FOREIGN OPERATORS EXPECT WHEN they take part in a process of privatization? STET's answer is, in the end, consistent with the direction being taken by most international operators: to participate in meeting the rising demand for increasingly sophisticated services in the context of deregulation, and to benefit from the opportunities offered by the privatization processes now under way in many countries around the world. These opportunities prompt the more enterprising companies to step outside their national boundaries and extend their range of action. This maneuver is at once an onslaught and a defense (a defense to the extent that expansion into the international market tends to compensate a possible redimensioning of the former standing income offered by their own home market). Elaborating on this general theme, this chapter attempts to formulate several more specific considerations on the basis of the experiences of the STET Group, a group which is active across the whole telecommunications sector, not only in services but also in the manufacturing industry.[1] A good starting point is STET's new project in Argentina, its first experience in an overseas venture in the field of basic telephone service management.

The Argentina Experience

To understand the rationale of our recent move into Argentina, we must answer two questions. First, why Argentina? and, second, why team up with another operator and with Argentine partners?

Italy has close ties with Argentina. Suffice it to recall that nearly 60 percent of Argentina's population is of Italian origin and that many Argentineans of Italian extraction still retain dual nationality. This close link means heavy two-way traffic in telecommunications. Italy ranks second in Argentina's international traffic (after the United States). STET's international carrier, Italcable, originally was an Argentine company formed after World War I by Italians living in Argentina to secure direct links with their native land. STET looked upon the Argentinean project as a way to protect and promote the position Italcable holds in that country. We also felt that it would be an advantage if our first major experience as managers of a public service abroad were to take place in a country with which we are naturally so familiar. This situation definitely simplifies our approach to the problems of relationship with the local environment.

With respect to the second question, STET now helps manage the northern part of the former ENTel together with France Télécom, the Argentine group Pérez Companc, and the J. P. Morgan Bank (the latter was our consortium's financial adviser, and in the end decided to take a stake in the investment, evidently convinced of its prospect of success). Our decision to join forces with another leading telephone company, France Télécom, was motivated by our wish to share the financial and other burdens of the undertaking; we prefer not to commit too great a share of our resources to one single operation. France Télécom seems to us an ideal associate, because we are both European companies and because more and more integration is developing in Europe; we are both convinced that this shared experience in the international field will also serve to increase our capacity for teamwork within Europe. Then, the fact that we are both European appeared to play an important role in Argentina, a country conscious of a certain nostalgia for Europe at every turn. The local partner, finally, is very important, not only because it is a financially solid company, but particularly because this company's knowledge of the operating conditions of the Argentine market makes a fundamental contribution to the success of our initiative.

Turning to the organizational aspect, our objective is to transfer our know-how as quickly as possible to the Argentine personnel, to share knowledge which will enable them to make the most of their own valuable professional skills. The reports arriving from the technical team which STET and France Télécom sent to the site are, in this regard, very encouraging.

At the operational level, the situation five months after the takeover was even more complex than it appeared at the outset. Countless things needed to be done, on the organizational, technical, and commercial sides, to restart an enterprise that had been on hold for several years and to reshape it into a modern, efficient company. This was to be a long and arduous task which had to be done in the context of great expectations for renewal under the privatization process. This is why the consortium asked, and continues to ask its new Argentine clients for trust, patience, and understanding.

Moreover, the problems associated with getting the project off the ground have been compounded by others deriving from the new economic laws passed by the government of Argentina. At the beginning of April 1991, the minister of economy issued a strong anti-inflationary law which eliminated all forms of indexation of regulated prices, including telecommunications, while the prices of products traded on the free market could fluctuate without any constraint.

STET, of course, is sympathetic toward energetic, disciplined strategies to normalize the economic situation. But our presence in Argentina and the price paid for the acquisition of the telecommunications company were based on economic estimates dependent on a set of mutual obligations. These obligations cannot be unilaterally modified: they are the rules of the game, on the basis of which the efficiency and reliability of each party is gauged. Maintaining tariffs in real terms is one of these rules, as is our commitment to carry out investments up to a certain amount. If the rules change, the players are entitled to review their position. If we are not allowed to adjust tariffs to keep up with general price inflation, as agreed at the time of purchase, a hard blow would be inflicted on our investment in Argentina, and the entire privatization process initiated by the government would lose credibility. We are confident, however, that a solution can be found. In the entire world, the principles underlying telecommunications tariffs are rapidly evolving toward greater autonomy for the carriers while also complying with the users' interests. Within the context of this conviction we intend to search for a rational solution with the Argentine government.

Toward a Generalized Model

These considerations regarding Argentina provide a basis for outlining what may be a general framework for STET's overseas initiatives.

The scene of contemporary telecommunications business is largely set by two particularly significant events: the integration of national markets into broader aggregates virtually on a global scale and the increasing use of telecommunications networks to provide computer-based services to the public or telematics in a wide range of economic activities. National telecommunications systems, however, differ considerably with regard to efficiency and quality of service. Moreover, until only a few years ago they have evolved in an atmosphere of natural monopoly and isolation.

Demand for Experienced Operator Assistance

One focal point in the revolution we are considering is the gap between the demand for services posed by the most qualified and internationalized business users, on the one hand, and many telecommunications companies' insufficient supply, on the other. This gap is leading the companies to seek external assistance from more efficient carriers in order to improve performance. The requirement for assistance is the more urgent the larger the gap between the supply and demand for services, and as technology increasingly enables users to satisfy their requirements by themselves. Thus, one of the first reasons for STET's foreign initiatives comes to light: to meet a new type of market demand which originates from the contrast between modern and advanced business users, on the one hand, and less developed national carriers, on the other.

Business users, however, are not the only force driving the carriers' demand for assistance; after all, problems of this type could be solved by private networks. More generally, the role of basic services and the public network in promoting development is recognized. Efficiency gaps thus trigger government interest in foreign assistance. Moreover, broader macroeconomic considerations also come into play. In particular, the problem of foreign debt and the desire to obtain public funds through the sale of state property are especially strong motives. The whole world manifests this trend, which has practical as well as neoliberal ideological dimensions and follows a long period of public planning and state intervention in economic affairs.

In summary, operating companies of countries with economic difficulties seek foreign operators to assist in managing their telecommunications networks, attempting thus to solve the problem of the efficiency gap, which is dramatically worsened by the globalization of economic systems and the wider use of telematics. Through these initiatives the countries also aim to help solve financial problems and move along neoliberal economic paths. In a way, these operators are doing what those of the more industrialized countries have already done or are in the process of doing: privatizing and liberalizing their telecommunications systems.

Objectives of Foreign Operators

The foreign carriers invited to share management responsibilities in other countries are themselves involved, to varying degrees, in a process of liberalization and privatization in their home countries. Therefore, some competition, actual or prospective, is pervading their systems. Parts of their market, either at present or in the future, are wearing away. Their tariff structures are being adjusted on the basis of the individual services' costs. Moreover, the majority of these telecommunications systems are approaching saturation levels as far as basic services are concerned.

In general, these carriers are tending to respond with competitive strategies (such as described in the works of Professor Michael Porter of the Harvard Business School) consisting of moves and countermoves to ensure their survival and growth in the face of aggressive strategies from competitors. Obviously not all of the industrial countries are at this stage; some are merely concerned with future possibilities, which, however, already have a bearing on present strategies. In any case, telecommunications carriers are starting to behave as if they were firms operating in free markets, somehow replicating the latter's strategic behavior.

An initial tentative interpretation can therefore be outlined: operators in the industrial countries are reacting to the liberalization, actual or prospective, of their own markets, like free economic agents in a competitive environment, gaining elsewhere the space which is being worn away at home. STET, like the carriers of other industrial countries, is seizing the strategic opportunities offered, with a logic of both defense and development in a competitive environment. The objective is to protect and enhance economic margins where possible, to ensure the most appropriate use of resources, both human and otherwise, and to realize, eventually, economies of scale.[2]

Conflict between Global and Domestic Strategies

As might reasonably have been expected, this internationalization strategy was initially met with lively discussion within the STET Group.

One of the objections concerned possible inconsistencies with our priority internal objectives of growth and completion of the national network. It was eventually decided to proceed with the envisaged strategy, mainly for two reasons. First, the financial and human resources to be diverted toward foreign countries would be relatively small and unlikely to slow down STET's domestic development. This does not mean that we would have held back the means and energies needed to properly carry out our foreign initiatives; on the contrary, our managers and specialists were to be first-rate and our investments, financially sound. Second, these external operations were to involve mainly the transfer of know-how, management techniques, and control methods. This sharing of knowledge would not diminish resources at the home operation but merely extend them to our new partners abroad.

The Main Constraint: Human Resources

It would be a great mistake, however, to underestimate the importance of human resources in this type of initiative. After all, transfer of knowledge consists, essentially, in assigning the appropriate managers to key positions. It is this kind of resource which allows objectives to be reached, abroad as well as in the country of origin. The mix of qualities of a successful senior manager (for example, experience, personality, discipline) alongside particular features necessary to operate internationally is rare; moreover, not everybody is willing to move to a foreign country for a long period. This is a considerable problem to which the top management of the large carriers of industrialized countries must apply their creativity. A standard solution is not at hand. Probably, both time and increasing familiarity with these initiatives will play an important role in developing effective ways of dealing with the question of human resources.

Long-Term Perspectives of These Initiatives

We can, and indeed we must ask ourselves the question: What will happen when the objectives of these initiatives abroad have been reached? In other words, what will happen when the gap between telecommunications systems has been closed?

Very probably, the past tendency of countries to maintain control over their own telecommunications network will reassert itself. This would be consistent with the behavior of industries that operate in a competitive framework. For example, when transferring know-how, a manufacturing company knows that the receiving end will attempt, when possible and convenient, to become self-reliant in research and development. The reappropriation of control of telecommunications networks is part of the risk posed by our overseas initiatives. But, in the world of economics and business, nothing is eternal and immutable; it is, indeed, a changing world. It is essential, however, that enough time be allowed to reach the institutional and financial objectives of these initiatives.

Endnotes

1. STET, Società Finanziaria Telefonica Spa, is the 70 percent IRI held and controlled provider and manufacturer of telecommunications facilities and services. While STET focuses on telephone and telex, its subsidiaries SIP and Italcable focus on local and long-distance and on intercontinental services, respectively. Its industrial activities (production of installation of telecommunications and distributing systems) are mainly the concern of Italcable and SIRTI. STET is also active in publishing and communications through its subsidiary SEAT. Instituto Ricostruzione Industriale Spa, (IRI) is Italy's largest industrial and financial holding company which is fully controlled by the Italian State.

2. Economies of scale are at stake when the managing of a foreign network entails the transfer of methods, software, know-how with more advanced research, introduction and maintenance costs.

Part VI

Mobilizing Capital

for Privatization

26

Privatization of Telecommunications Enterprises: The Viewpoints of Investors

François J. Grossas

DURING THE PAST TEN YEARS, A NUMBER OF INDUSTRIAL and developing countries have transferred the ownership of dominant telecommunications enterprises from the state to private hands. Many more privatizations are under way or being considered. Not all privatizations, however, are viable and attractive to private investors. In order to succeed, a privatization must offer a good deal to all parties. In particular, it must respond to the concerns and selection criteria of the investor community. This chapter provides an overview of the considerations of investors as they assess how attractive a particular privatization opportunity is for them.

Different Classes of Investors

The examples of privatization discussed in this book illustrate the differences between two main types of investors, namely strategic investors and market investors.

Strategic Investors

In several countries, privatization has revolved around selling a controlling interest in the company to one or more multinational operating companies. That was the case, for example, in Argentina, Mexico, New Zealand, and Venezuela. Ownership of the privatized company becomes closely held by hands-on operating investors. This arrangement is preferred particularly when the company to be privatized is in poor shape and requires remedial management by an experienced, committed, and responsible shareholder group (for example, in Argentina, Venezuela). For the multinational companies, acquiring controlling interests in formerly state-owned enterprises in a number of key countries is a means to implement long-term telecommunications business development strategies, such as building up a regional or global market presence. This theme is explored from the viewpoint of the multinational operators in more detail in Part V of this book.

Market Investors

Other countries, including Chile (initially), Japan, Malaysia, and the United Kingdom, sold shares of their telecommunications companies only to equity market investors, both domestic and foreign. Market investors also provided a substantial part of the financing for privatizations involving multinational operators. Companies privatized in this way are generally strong, professionally managed entities which do not require the intervention of a particular shareholder group. Market investors include banks and institutional investors such as pension funds, equity mutual funds, and individuals. Ownership, in this case, is widely dispersed among investors that are essentially looking for opportunities to earn a stable return on their assets, often have a shorter time horizon than strategic investors, and are not interested in the telecommunications business per se.

Objectives of Privatization

Governments privatize state-owned telecommunications and other utilities mainly for financial, economic, and developmental reasons.[1] Although often differing in priority, these objectives are common to most privatizations.

Financial objectives essentially consist of raising government revenues and reducing future government outlays. Privatization revenues can be considerable. In the United Kingdom, for example, thirteen privatizations between 1982 and 1989 generated over £26 billion in governmental proceeds. In Argentina, the sale of ENTel in 1990 helped the government reduce its foreign debt by over US$5 billion.

Economic objectives relate to the improved efficiency, innovation, and performance which can result when privatized companies are freed from political constraints and exposed to the discipline and competitive pressures of the market. Empirical evidence suggests that privatizations can indeed contribute to these objectives. Since its privatization in 1984, British Telecom has expanded services and products considerably while at the same time showing increased dividends and profits. Nonetheless, the privatization of monopolies without a corresponding introduction of competitive pressures and regulation will not necessarily optimize or result in desired efficiencies. The Argentine government, aware of this, divided ENTel into two regional companies before selling it, thereby creating opportunities to compare performances and a credible competitive threat by the end of an exclusivity period which was limited to seven to ten years.

Developmental objectives relate to enhancing the domestic capital markets and encouraging widespread company ownership among the public at large. These objectives include expanding the retail ownership of shares and contributing to the depth and liquidity of the local market. Fostering foreign investor interest in the local market is often an equally desired goal. Privatized companies, often large, have traditionally been ideal vehicles for promoting these objectives. In the United Kingdom, only 2 percent of the population (1.4 million individuals) owned securities in 1984; the British Telecom issue alone resulted in 2.3 million new shareholders. In Spain, the flotations of Empresa Nacional de Electricidad S.A. (ENDESA) and Telefónica on international markets

(United States, Europe, Japan) led to virtually continuous trading in these shares, a first for the Spanish securities market; in addition, these listings contributed to a surge of foreign investor interest in the Spanish market.

Investment Opportunities in Telecommunications Privatizations

The telecommunications industry in developing countries should offer increasing investment opportunities throughout the 1990s. After years of pent-up demand, the need to expand and modernize telephone networks has created such an enormous appetite for capital that governments, struggling with budgetary constraints, are opening their telecommunications industry to private investment. In most developing countries, however, the need for capital exceeds the domestic resources available, and many governments are now encouraging foreign private investment.

Government interest in foreign capital has been paralleled by the development of equity markets. In a number of developing countries, particularly in Latin America and Asia, local stock exchanges have come to play a significant role in mobilizing capital for the local economies. These emerging markets, which essentially developed from the mid–1980s, have been attracting foreign investors in substantial numbers.[2] This contrasts with the deteriorating debt situation which continues to result in negative net transfers to developing countries. Several factors account for the success of emerging markets. First, in an effort to reduce the volatility of their returns and increase profitability, fund managers for large institutional investors are increasingly looking for diversification across national borders. Most emerging markets do not follow closely the variations of the major world stock markets, and therefore offer good choices for portfolio diversification. Second, both the information available on stock markets and government attitudes toward the private sector have improved in developing countries, and investors feel generally more comfortable than in the past dealing with emerging markets. Third, as investment opportunities in industrialized countries, and especially in the United States, became somewhat scarce in the 1980s, investors began to turn to the newer, less developed markets. Lastly, investors are attracted to emerging markets because they perceive them to be undervalued relative to industrial country markets, with many companies showing strong fundamentals and excellent growth prospects.[3]

Most telecommunications companies are potentially attractive investments. With appropriate tariffs, returns are usually above the average for investments of comparable risk. Domestic and international traffic growth in most countries is consistently higher than GNP growth. And because the industry is treated as a utility, telecommunications companies typically retain a monopoly, if only temporarily. This allows investors to enjoy downside protection while making investments with high-growth potential. For many investors, these advantages outweigh the political risk associated with developing countries. Current trends in strategic and market investment in telecommunications are further discussed by Harland (chapter 27). The main mechanisms for selling shares of a telecommunications company, and some of their relative merits, are discussed by Lewis (chapter 28). The sale through the public issue of shares is further discussed by Vallimarescu (chapter 29). Alternative ways of attracting private capital to telecommunications enterprises are explored by Bruce and others. (chapter 31).

Prospective investors assess particular telecommunications privatization opportunities from enterprise- and sector-specific viewpoints as well as in terms of broader country considerations. Privatizations in developing countries present investors with a different set of issues than in industrialized countries, with which they may have greater familiarity. For example, accounts often do not conform to internationally accepted standards, technical and particularly management expertise may be in scarce supply, and the governments' objectives and attitudes may be unclear or unreliable.

Enterprise and Sector Considerations

Investors look at prospective privatizations from a number of (interrelated) viewpoints. The main ones are the prospects for turning the company into a viable business, the conditions under which the company will operate in the future, the price at which it will be sold, and the likely returns on investment. These are briefly outlined below.

Company Viability

Investors look closely into the financial condition and outlook of the enterprise. State-owned telecommunications enterprises in developing countries, however, often are undercapitalized, perform poorly, and are both overstaffed and lacking specific skills. Most of them must be reorganized as companies under commercial law and their capital restructured before they are offered to investors. Debt may have to be rescheduled or assumed by the government. This also happens in industrial countries—for example, some of the debt from loans made by the British government to British Telecom prior to privatization was not transferred so as to improve the company's capital structure.

It is the company's potential for cash flow generation that will ultimately determine how attractive the company is to prospective investors. In many cases the enterprises perform poorly and need major internal improvements to render them profitable. Some governments may postpone public offerings until the privatization candidate starts showing steady profits. This, however, may not be necessary; some investors may be attracted by the opportunity to buy into a loss-making enterprise with turnaround potential.

The investors attach great importance to securing peaceful relations with labor. Company viability will depend to a large extent on the support of employees and trade unions. State telecommunications enterprises are usually overstaffed (while lacking specific skills). Most privatizations have initially been opposed by labor, primarily because of fears of layoffs. Offering employees a stake in the company's future through employee stock ownership plans is one of the tools successfully used to bring labor on board the privatization initiative.

Future Operating Conditions

Investors look closely at the conditions under which the newly privatized company will operate. They are likely to be particularly concerned with the quality of management, the potential for competitive entry, the future service requirements imposed on the company by the government as part of the privatization, and regulatory restrictions that may affect profitability.

Investors will want experienced and efficient management able to operate a complex telecommunications company in a market environment. Foreign operators that have bought a controlling interest in a newly privatized company will need to demonstrate that they can succeed in an environment that may be very different from that in their own country.

The potential for competitive entry is also important. A continuation of certain monopoly privileges, which reduce investment risk by guaranteeing a stable flow of revenues, is generally sought by investors. This, however, presents developing countries with a dilemma: on the one hand, governments want to provide incentives for new investment, as foreign investors will demand high returns to compensate for country risks; on the other, liberalization and competition may be essential to promote efficiency and introduce high-quality services. One possible solution is to guarantee exclusivity for a limited number of years, as has been done in most Latin American countries so far (with the main exception of Chile, where the incumbents do not have statutory monopoly).

Investors also need to know how much growth and what scope of services will be required from the newly privatized company. For example, committing the company to an ambitious capital investment program to rapidly increase the number of telephone lines may create a drain on cash flow.

Investors feel more secure when national telecommunications policy is clearly defined, allowing for the orderly growth of the industry. Simple and transparent industry regulations are important to investors. The treatment of tariffs is of singular importance. Profitability of the privatized company will depend critically on the level and structure of tariffs. To the extent that in most cases the company will retain a legal or de facto market dominance or exclusivity for at least some time, it will not be wholly free to set and change the prices it charges for its services. The applicable regulatory rules and procedures are therefore of the greatest interest to the investor. The company must be able to negotiate objectively with the regulators, and this process must be protected by law and free from contingent political considerations.

Company Valuation

Establishing a fair and competitive valuation for the telecommunications entity is critical to the success of a public offering. Price is one of the principal factors determining whether the privatization is attractive to potential investors. It also plays an important role in making the proposed privatization politically acceptable. Determining a fair price is a difficult task in industrial countries, and far more so in developing countries. Expected revenue growth is the main determinant, but a number of other factors also intervene (for example, level of technology in use, investment cost per additional telephone line). The privatization process must allow enough time for both market and strategic investors to closely examine the company being offered as well as its potential market.

Return on Investment

A crucial consideration for investors is the expected return on their investment. This is an area where market and strategic investors may have quite different objectives. Market investors mainly seek stable, competitive, risk-adjusted returns. To attract market investors, governments may need to underprice the initial public offering. Strategic investors have a long-term interest in the telecommunications sector. They may be prepared to pay a higher price, and accept lower initial returns on their investments and less stable earnings, in exchange for building up a regional or global market presence.

Debt exchanges (or "swaps") have been used in connection with privatizations in a number of countries as a way to improve returns and attract foreign investors. Enterprise or government debt can be exchanged at a discount for equity in the privatized company. The investors get a financially unencumbered enterprise at a lower price, and the government reduces total outstanding debt. Watkins discusses three successful debt swap systems, including one used in conjunction with the privatization of the Argentine telecommunications companies (chapter 30).

Country Considerations

However viable and promising the investment may look, successful privatization of the telecommunications enterprise will also depend on features of the country as a whole. Local capital markets are expected to play important roles. Investors, especially market investors, are sensitive to how their money will be treated, especially regarding taxation of profits and dividends, and repatriation of capital. General political conditions also have an impact on investors' decisions.

Capital Markets

The success of a public offering depends to a large extent on how well organized the local capital markets are. Adequate and accurate information on financial markets and on potential investments must be readily available. Authorities must ensure the openness and transparency of market transactions by requiring appropriate disclosure standards and accounting systems for publicly quoted companies and by strictly prohibiting malpractices such as insider trading.

The availability of professional investment advice and facilities, such as brokerage houses for processing orders, is also an important factor influencing market investors. Also the existence of a strong secondary market may be critical to the success of a public offering, since investors will want to be able to trade their shares quickly and inexpensively. The larger the initial offering the more liquid the secondary market is likely to be. In general, the weaker the local financial markets, the more intensive the information campaign must be for public offerings to succeed.

One way to attract foreign investors is to list the securities in the investors' home country. U.S. investors, for example, have shown considerable interest in American Depositary Receipts (ADRs), which represent ownership of securities in non-U.S. companies. ADRs are listed and traded in the United States. Compared with the alternative of directly purchasing equities in foreign markets, ADRs provide a convenient and cost-effective means of investing in non-U.S. securities. Vallimarescu discusses the experience of Chile's main telecommunications company and others in placing new share issues in the U.S. market through ADRs (chapter 29).

The growing reliance of telecommunications companies in developing countries on market investors to finance modernization and growth should bring additional benefits to the local economy, such as the development of modern capital markets. In addition the market discipline that results from the public listing of a company's shares, through continuous valuation of the share price, should make a positive contribution to the growth and performance of the companies themselves.

Taxation and Repatriation

Investors tend to shy away from countries where their money is not well treated or is overtaxed. They favor countries with neutral tax systems that treat all financial instruments equally. In particular, taxing capital gains and dividend income more heavily than other income, still common practice in many countries, discourages investors.

Governments must also guarantee repatriation of dividends. Not surprisingly, equity financing has taken off in countries that have lifted restrictions on repatriation. For example, Mexico's 1989 tax reforms and its favorable treatment of dividends have helped reduce foreign reluctance to invest and encouraged the return of Mexican flight capital.

Political Environment

The government must show a clear, unequivocal commitment to privatization and remove the telecommunications company from the national political process. Privatization should be led by a politically secure leader and be written into law. The legal framework must provide a favorable climate for private investment and protect the interests of both domestic and foreign investors. If the government retains a stake in the company, it must clearly define the terms of its shareholding.

Endnotes

1. This section, and some statements in the next section, were originally in the draft of the chapter by Dan Vallimarescu and in material originally contributed by Vallimarescu and Teng-Hong Cheah.

2. In 1985, foreigners invested about US$200 million in emerging stock markets; this figure grew to about US$8.2 billion in 1989. In 1991 total foreign portfolio investment in emerging stock markets exceeded US$20 billion, accounting for roughly 3.3 percent of capitalization in those markets. It is estimated that such investments could grow to US$170 billion by the year 2000, which would represent 4 percent of the expected capitalization of emerging markets and 5 percent of all internationally invested funds. While representing a substantial increase, that amount would remain low relative to the percentage or worldwide GNP which those markets represent. Data for Latin America are perhaps more striking: Mexico, Venezuela, and Chile attracted US$5 billion of international capital market financing between 1989 and 1991. There were close to thirty international public and private sector bond issues from Latin America during that period, and fourteen in just the last six months of the same period. Yields on these debt issues have dropped from about 17 percent per year initially to between 11.5 percent to 14.5 percent per year. These developments would have been virtually inconceivable just a few years ago.

3. Investment returns from emerging markets can be very—often spectacularly—high. For example, in 1990, as measured in U.S. dollar terms, eight of the ten best-performing stock markets in the world were from emerging markets. The best performer, Venezuela, was up by over 550 percent, followed by 91 percent from Zimbabwe, 90 percent for Greece, 31 percent for Chile, and 27 percent for Colombia. Four of the five worst-performing markets in 1990, however, were also from the emerging world, with, for example, Brazil down almost 70 percent, the Philippines down 52 percent, and Argentina down 38 percent.

27

Trends in Strategic and Market Equity Investments

Christopher M. Harland

THIS CHAPTER DISCUSSES CURRENT TRENDS in the demand for investment opportunities in telecommunications. It distinguishes between strategic and public equity market investors. The viewpoint is that of an investment banker.

Strategic Investors

Strategic investors have played a leading role in the privatization of telecommunications companies in recent years, in both industrial and developing countries. They have mainly been North American and European telecommunications operating companies, including the Southwestern Bell and France Télécom investment in TELMEX; Bell Atlantic and Ameritech's acquisition of Telecom Corporation of New Zealand (TCNZ); Telefónica de España's investments in Chile (CTC and ENTEL) and Argentina (Telefónica de Argentina); STET and France Télécom's investment in Argentina (Telecom Argentina); BellSouth and Cable & Wireless's investment in AUSSAT, Australia's second operator; and GTE, AT&T, and Telefónica de España's investment in Venezuela (CANTV).

We foresee a continued interest on the part of the major strategic investors in telecommunications privatizations. This interest is driven by, among other factors, a desire to:

- Achieve more rapid access line growth than what is available in their mature home markets

- Participate in a more favorable regulatory environment than that which exists in their home markets

- Achieve earnings leverage from the significant productivity gains that can be realized in many of these situations

- Utilize surplus skilled manpower that increasingly is available within their own companies.

Although we believe these factors will continue to prompt strategic investors to look at international telecommunications privatization opportunities, we sense that the leverage in these operations is shifting toward the buyers and that the possibility of a failed auction is increasing. For example, because some of the more aggressive strategic buyers have recently completed transactions, they may not be as eager to take on additional projects, given the finite management and capital resources as well as limited international experience. A bunching of opportunities is also taking place which could negatively impact availability of investors interested in a particular operation. This becomes apparent when we look at forthcoming privatizations: the Netherlands, Germany, France, Singapore, the Czech Republic, Ecuador, Hungary, Pakistan, Peru, and Portugal, among others, are all considering, or rumored to be considering, selling stakes in their state telecommunications operations to strategic investors. Investor interest in new privatizations could also be constrained by the fact that a number of potential investors believe they are better off investing in a second or third cellular license rather than in existing telephone operations because of the lower capital required and reduced risk.

As strategic investors become increasingly selective, they are likely to attach importance to:

- Having a clear understanding of what the required investment will be

- Ensuring that any capital required beyond the initial investment can be financed on a stand-alone basis

- Teaming up with strong local investors who can, among other things, share in the investment and provide guidance on the political and regulatory front

- Teaming up with other international telecommunications companies (most of the examples cited earlier already manifest this trend).

Public Market Investors

The overall market for U.S. and international equities is very robust, and market investors have already found good opportunities in established telecommunications companies. For example, although U.S. telecommunications service stocks have not always kept pace with the broad market average, they are very attractively valued from an investor's perspective. For example, in mid–1991 the regional Bell operating companies (RBOCs) traded at an estimated price/earnings multiple of 14.2x, compared with 23.4x for the Standard & Poor (S&P) 500 average. Many non-U.S. telecommunications service companies trade at a premium to their U.S. counterparts due to their more attractive growth prospects. In 1991 Cable & Wireless traded at 16.3x estimated earnings.

In recent years we have seen a large volume of new equity issue activity by telecommunications service companies. For example, in March 1991 Morgan Stanley, together with Rashed Hussein Securities, lead-managed a US$110 million issue of sovereign bonds for the government of Malaysia exchangeable into Telekom Malaysia common stock. Also in 1991, the British government sold more than half of its remaining 49 percent stake in British Telecom. This represented one of the largest equity offerings ever attempted, aggregating approximately US$9.5 billion. Bell Atlantic and Ameritech sold 40 percent of TCNZ and then a further 11 percent in 1992. In December 1991, Telefónica de Argentina sold 3.5 billion shares, representing 30 percent of its capitalization in a global competitive offering. These companies subsequently did very well, their share overall appreciating substantially, as shown in Figure 27-1. In addition, several telecommunications privatizations that may take place in the near future are rumored to involve an equity flotation, including Singapore Telecom, Swedish Telecom, Telecom Eireann, and TELEBRÁS.

So, as with privatizations directed at strategic investors, the argument could be made that there is some risk that abundant supply of investment opportunities could adversely affect investors' demand over time. Nevertheless, in the near term we are confident that there is strong demand for high-quality new stock offerings by international telecommunications service companies.

International equity flotations, however, are clearly not a viable source of capital for all government-owned telecommunications service companies. In particular, the absence of a vibrant local equity market, the presence of significant political risk, the existence of restrictions on foreign ownership of common stock, and a poor operating track record are all factors that could impede a successful international offering from a developing country. As with strategic investors, public market investors are attracted to countries where the overall economic situation and the regulatory, political, and competitive environments are favorable, significant potential for access line growth and margin/earnings improvement exist, and, perhaps most important, the valuation is attractive. TELMEX was an excellent example of an opportunity that met all of these criteria.

When analyzing an opportunity, public market investors also seek stability of earnings and cash flow. Inconsistent earnings performance penalize the companies in terms of their relative price/earnings multiples. In contrast, a strategic investor's focus with regard to the value of his investment may be longer-term in nature; the strategic investor, therefore, may be more willing to sacrifice near-term earnings in order to build the long-term value of the enterprise. Therefore, in planning for international public offerings, government-owned telecommunications companies should seek to develop the systems required to project and manage their earnings growth over time.

Public market equity investors need to be distinguished between institutional and retail investors. In the United States, institutional investors currently account for approximately 80 percent of the total available pool of equity. U.S. telecommunications companies, however, tend to have a much higher retail ownership profile. For example, the average RBOC ownership is 33 percent institutional and 67 percent retail.

Figure 27-1. Privatized Issue Trading Performance

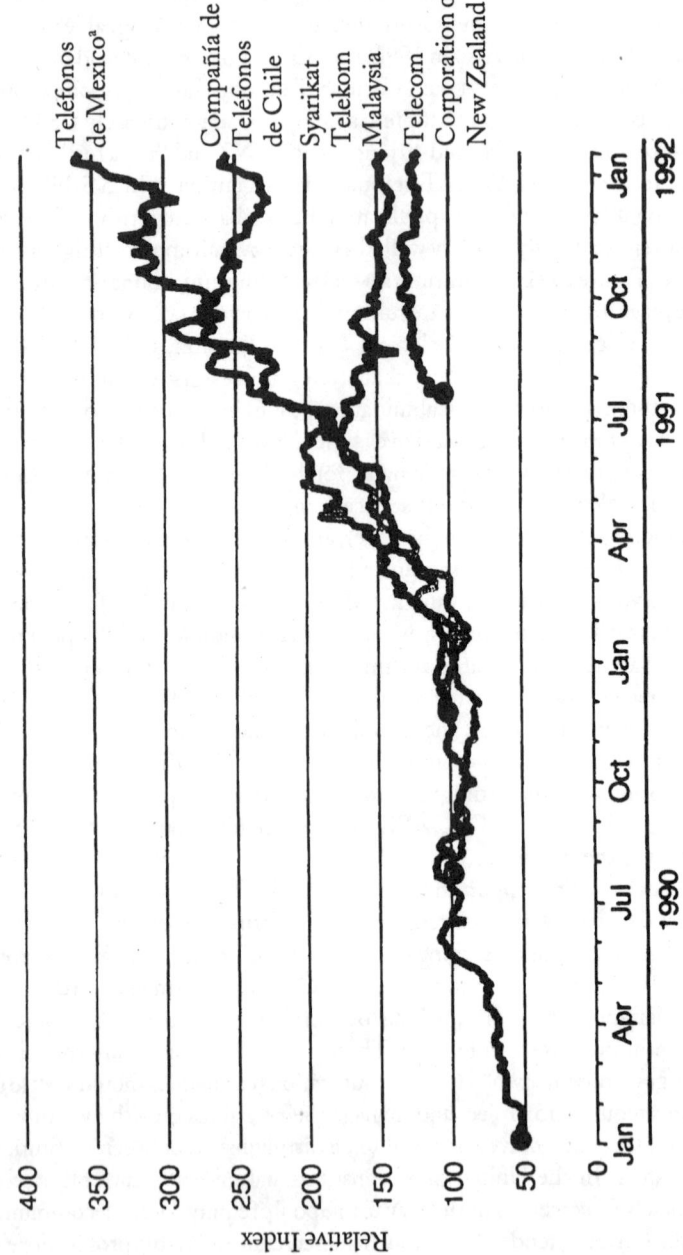

a. Price indexed to 12/20/90, date that consortium received voting control. Secondary public offering took place 5/14/91.

When one decides to access the public equity market it is important to consider each of these constituencies. Although elements of the institutional equity community are so-called yield-motivated buyers, the dividend rate set by an entity contemplating a privatization has particularly important ramifications for the retail buyers and, hence, is an important factor governing the investment decision. The average dividend yield for the RBOCs is 5.4 percent, whereas for non-U.S. telecommunications companies yields range from 0.1 percent (TELMEX) to 5.2 percent (Bell Canada).

Another important consideration for public market investors is the liquidity of their investment. The public market investor is typically adding to a broader portfolio and will want to have the flexibility to change weightings within that portfolio at his/ her discretion. The ideal equity flotation from an international investor's viewpoint is one that is large enough to ensure adequate aftermarket trading and thereby a healthy level of liquidity.

Conclusion

The best managed telecommunications service companies, no matter how tough the overall equity market environment, will probably be able to access these markets. Companies that do not have strong service reputations and operate in countries lacking a developed local equity market, however, will most likely have to seek out strategic partners for outside investment and operational assistance. Once these companies have developed a reasonable track record, the public markets will be receptive investors. Historically, telecommunications service companies have been a major component of the total equity market capitalization. This situation will no doubt continue to be the case, given the size of these companies, their importance to the economy and everyday life, and their ability to generate consistent earnings over time.

28

Options for Selling a Telecommunications Company

Dean Lewis

THIS CHAPTER DISCUSSES FIVE OPTIONS FOR SELLING all or part of a major state-owned telecommunications enterprise. How the enterprise is sold will be determined largely by the government's objectives for the privatization program and by the commercial and policy constraints surrounding the transaction. An important set of objectives consists of maximizing proceeds, limiting exposure to the impediments of the sale, and keeping the execution as simple as possible. The five basic options are examined in terms of the extent to which each of these three objectives is likely to be met. There often are also other objectives, which may conflict with maximizing sale proceeds. The method of analysis used in this chapter can be extended to include other objectives.

Sale Options and Assessment Criteria

The five options are:

- Negotiated sale of 100 percent of the company to a single buyer

- Sale of a minority stake to a single buyer or group of buyers

- Public offerings in the domestic market or international markets or both

- Sale of a minority stake to a single purchaser combined with a public offering

- Breakup and sale of components.

Each is examined in terms of three criteria:

MAXIMIZING PROCEEDS. How likely is the sale to maximize the net proceeds of the transaction to the government? This criterion incorporates judgments about the likely maximum size of the transaction, the price obtained, and the transaction costs.

MINIMIZING EXPOSURE TO KNOWN IMPEDIMENTS TO SALE. How sensitive is the sale to known impediments such as the availability of financial information, economic and market factors, board and management preferences, and the government's policy on foreign ownership of key economic activities?

MINIMIZING COMPLEXITY OF EXECUTION. How complex is the sale from a legal and logistical point of view, including the time required to complete the transaction? Although these considerations are, to a large degree, reflected in the transaction costs taken into account in the assessment of the maximization of net proceeds, for some options the logistical complexities are significant. Given the limited amount of historical financial information available and the commercial sensitivity of releasing profit projections, this criterion evaluates the options in terms of the amount of financial information which would need to be disclosed as part of the sales process and reviews other factors that will add to the complexity of the transaction.

Option 1—Negotiated Sale of 100 Percent to a Single Buyer

In all likelihood, the negotiated sale of 100 percent of a telecommunications operating company to a single purchaser will result in proceeds significantly higher than any other option; however, it is unlikely that any domestic company will be large enough to buy the company outright. Thus, if prospective overseas purchasers are not prepared to put in a bid, outright sale may not be realistic.

The sale price will be influenced substantially by the buyers' perceptions of the certainty of the regulatory regime. Buyers will need to be comfortable that the regulatory environment will not be subject to arbitrary review which adversely affects the expected financial performance of the telecommunications company. In addition, the imposition of restrictions on the company's operation, such as any noncommercial service obligations, will detract from the value achieved.

Typically, the realization of value under a negotiated sale will be driven by the generation of buyer interest. This will be influenced both by the process adopted and the ability to create a competitive environment. It is generally preferable to undertake a controlled auction process rather than an exclusive negotiation with a selected party. The auction process creates competition and provides alternative potential buyers.

Given the inability of domestic entities to undertake such a large transaction, in order to reach a maximum price the universe of buyers would need to include international parties. The likely buyers primarily include the major international telephone companies. These entities are familiar with the auction process and should be able to react relatively quickly. The auction process needs to be well managed to maximize value, and prospective buyers need to have confidence in the integrity of the process.

An impediment to sale that often arises in an exclusive sales process is management's or the company board's own preference as to the buyer. Many buyers, particularly foreign, will be reluctant to purchase a business unless they feel satisfied that management will be supportive.

A negotiated sales process is usually relatively straightforward to execute. The process involves an initial valuation by the advisers, preparation of a sales memorandum, selection of and approach to interested parties, buyer due diligence, and negotiation of a final contract of sale. Government involvement tends to be less than in the other options due to the controlled nature of the process. Issues do tend to arise relating to the preservation of confidentiality as against disclosure, which must be managed carefully in order to protect the company's business.

Normally a negotiated sale can be completed within six months once the regulatory environment is established. The most time-consuming aspect of the sale is initial buyer evaluation and due diligence.

Option 2—Sale of Minority Stake (to a Single Buyer or Group of Buyers)

The sale of a minority stake in a telecommunications operating company, although still requiring a significant outlay, would probably result in a greater number of interested parties participating in the auction process. This option reduces control concerns and, depending on the proportion of the equity sold, is consistent with government policy restricting the level of foreign ownership by a single investor. It enables the government to structure a transaction that involves a domestic-international and active-passive investor mix. This could enhance the business. The universe of investors could include domestic conglomerates and large domestic companies.

This option requires a determination to be made of the maximum level of participation by any one investor. There is generally a correlation between the size of the stake sold and the control premium that would be captured by the sale. A sale of, say, five 5 percent stakes is likely to be more complicated and result in significantly lower proceeds than a sale of one 25 percent stake. Value will be enhanced by the absence of limitations imposed on the investor and flexibility of an investor to further increase or dispose of his investment. It is expected that investor interest would be greater if there were a prospect of achieving influence, board representation, or eventual control of the company. Related to this is the need for the government to provide some indication of its intentions with respect to its remaining shares. By selling a minority stake to a single purchaser, the government potentially limits its options in dealing with its remaining interest.

Overall, the price received for the sale of a significant minority shareholding should achieve a premium over the price obtained by a public offering. In ideal circumstances this premium could approach that of the 100 percent sale option. The sale of multiple but smaller minority stakes is likely to result in a price comparable to the public market value, due to the lack of control.

The impediments to sale under this option are broadly similar to those discussed under option 1 but are potentially less severe, depending on the size of the minority stake. For example, if a small stake were sold to a number of different buyers, it could be expected that management would be supportive. As with any partial sale, ongoing government monitoring may present problems.

The process and timetable for the execution of a minority sale to a single buyer is similar to option 1, although possibly slightly more complicated due to the necessary resolution of the factors highlighted above. Such issues would include whether a right of first refusal is granted on the sale of the stake to third parties and the extent of operating influence or board representation granted to a shareholder. The maintenance of majority government ownership, however, does potentially simplify the regulatory issues, as government would still have ultimate control over the company's actions. In conclusion, the complexity of this option is likely to be neutral although the sale of multiple stakes to parties with different objectives could complicate the process significantly.

Option 3—Public Offerings in Domestic or International Markets

The critical factor in maximizing proceeds under a public offering is the capacity of, and the valuation ascribed by, the local market and the degree to which this value can be enhanced through international markets.

Under this option, an aggressive marketing strategy would need to be developed to maximize sales revenue. This could be supplemented by the issue of vouchers to retail investors, providing price reductions on telephone services, or other incentives to encourage interest from individual investors in the domestic market.

The transaction costs related to a public offering will exceed those of the other options because of the additional marketing needed to develop the market.

Given the likelihood of a limited domestic public market and the likely attractiveness to foreign investors, an international offering in conjunction with a domestic offering could be pursued. Recent U.K., French, Spanish, and U.S. privatizations of significant size have involved some form of simultaneous international offering to increase the offering size and to maximize value. British privatizations have targeted investors in the United States and Europe, and have resulted in stable, long-term shareholdings being developed in such areas. The choice of international markets to access depends on both likely potential demand and registration requirements. The United States has a well-developed and highly educated telecommunications sector investor base but requires complex Securities and Exchange Commission (SEC) registration prior to accessing the public market. The European markets have less restrictive issuing requirements and a more developed interest in emerging market stocks.

The allocation among various international markets depends on the relative demand that could be developed and would need to be carefully coordinated to ensure minimal flow-back and a high level of liquidity. The benefits to the overall value of a company to be privatized results from accessing a potentially more sophisticated investor base and by encouraging international comparisons and analyst following. Again, structural issues, such as simultaneous or sequential access and single or multiple tranches, would need to be reviewed in light of government's objectives and market conditions, both public and private, at the time of the offering.

An impediment to this option is the limited capacity of the domestic market to underwrite and absorb any large public equity offering.

If combined with an international public offering, the degree of complexity increases considerably. The conformity of disclosure, underwriting conditions, marketing, execution, and structural considerations need to be carefully coordinated. As such, the timetable would need to allow sufficient time to resolve such issues and to develop the marketing program. Once the company is publicly listed, additional ongoing information requirements and investor programs are required.

Option 4—Sale of a Minority Stake to a Single Purchaser Combined with a Public Offering

In addition to the issues outlined in options 2 and 3 above, a number of issues are inherent in a combination of these options.

Care is required in executing this option, which if successful, could result in the sale of 100 percent of a telecommunications operating company, if so desired. Given the probable size of the sale, it is likely that each transaction would need to be carried out sequentially. Proceeds would be maximized by the initial sale of a minority stake to a strategic buyer at a premium to the anticipated public offering value. In addition, by placing the shares with a single purchaser prior to the public offering, the government can enhance the public offering price by giving an increased degree of comfort and leadership to public investors. Alternatively, a placement of shares with a single purchaser after the public offering could provide stability in the market and encourage competitive bidding among financial buyers looking to build a significant stake.

Option 4 has no real disadvantages apart from a minor increase in complexity, yet it could lead to the realization of greater proceeds. On balance, depending on the size of the shareholding purchased, some degree of control premium could be obtained. This should achieve higher overall proceeds than a public issue in isolation.

Similar impediments could arise to those outlined under options 2 and 3 but, because of the involvement of a new major shareholder, the success of a public offering could be enhanced. It is, however, likely that the new major shareholder will want board representation and possible management involvement.

Overall, the execution of this option is more complicated than those already discussed, primarily due to the coordination required between the two separate sale processes. The time required to complete both transactions could be in the order of six to nine months.

Option 5—Breakup and Sale of Components

The sale of a telecommunications operating company following a breakup of its core businesses would generally result in a lower value for the business as a whole because of the additional overheads of the individual operations and the loss of operating synergies. In addition, the breaking up of the core business would likely lead to lower value due to reduced international investor interest and result in a reduction in the proceeds from sale due to the negative impact on aggregate profitability.

In terms of public benefit, however, there is a trade-off between the loss of operational efficiency caused by the breakup and the potential benefits flowing from the development of rivalry and competition. (This is an example of some other conflicting objectives of privatization, which this chapter generally does not cover.) It could be possible to sell off certain noncore businesses, such as the cellular service, without the loss of operational efficiencies, but the resulting impact on aggregate value is likely to be immaterial.

The breakup could be time-consuming and strongly opposed by the company's board and management. The breaking up of the core activities could also significantly reduce investor appeal. The separate sale of certain noncore businesses could be more readily achieved on satisfactory terms, probably by way of a sale in the private market.

Given the complexity of trying to identify and separate the boundaries of the various businesses as well as to differentiate the assets and liabilities, this option could be the most difficult and time-consuming to execute if core activities were split up. Equally, the legislative requirements required to implement this alternative could, quite possibly, be the most complex. By comparison, divestment of noncore activities could be handled relatively easily.

Conclusion

Table 28-1 summarizes ratings of the five possible options against the three assessment criteria.

Table 28-1. The Five Possible Options Rated Against Assessment Criteria

Option	Maximization of proceeds	Minimization of sensitivity to known impediments	Minimization of complexity of execution
1. Sale of 100% of a single buyer	●	○	●
2. Sale of minority stake	◕	◑	◕
3. Public offerings domestic/inter-national	◑	●	◑
4. Combination of 2 and 3	◕	◔	◔
5. Break-up sale	○	○	○

Compliance with criteria

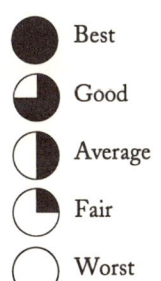

● Best

◕ Good

◑ Average

◔ Fair

○ Worst

29

Privatization through Public Issue of Shares

Dan Vallimarescu

THIS CHAPTER EXPLORES THE USE OF PUBLIC share issues in the privatization process. It examines a sample of six European utility companies (including two telecommunications companies) which have been privatized in this way, focusing on the international component of these public offerings. It then discusses the flotation of Compañía de Teléfonos de Chile (CTC) in the U.S. security market.[1]

Main Flotation Methods

When privatizing via the public issuance of shares, governments often access the domestic and international markets simultaneously, as shown in Table 29-1. This is common when issues are deemed too large for the domestic market, the domestic market is of interest to foreign investors, and the privatized entity is itself demonstrably attractive from an international perspective. Such integrated offerings can help reduce the cost of capital, establish a diversified and stable investor base, and enhance the recognition and prestige of the issuer and its domestic market.

These elements were evident in the 1984 landmark privatization of British Telecom, which was achieved through a domestic and international public issuance of shares. The privatization was, at the time, the largest equity offering ever in the London market. The market value of that offering represented, by some estimates, a full 20 percent of funds budgeted for portfolio investment that year by institutions in the United Kingdom. In light of the potential difficulties in placing all of the shares on the domestic market and given foreign investor interest, an international tranche was deemed realistic and advisable. The British Telecom issue was indeed successfully placed largely with institutional investors in the United States, Europe, and Japan.

Purely domestic issues are usually employed when the offering is too small for an international offering, nationalistic concerns preclude foreign involvement, or the country or company is not yet positioned to attract significant foreign interest. For example, due to its relatively small size, the privatization of the British Airports Authority was accomplished through a domestic-only public offering. In most of Latin America, until several years ago, international offerings would generally not have elicited sufficient foreign investor interest, although this would no longer necessarily be the case today. In Japan, NTT was privatized through a domestic-only private issue. Although a foreign offering has been promised, some analysts believe the Japanese authorities prefer minimizing foreign investment and trading in such a nationally sensitive concern.

Some governments have opted to issue shares internationally only after an initial domestic issue. This is meant to satisfy the domestic market's initial appetite for shares, as well as to establish a domestic market price from which to value the international flotation. The public issuance of shares in TELMEX is a good example.

Structural Considerations

The following discussion focuses on privatizations implemented through widely distributed integrated domestic and foreign public offerings. The analysis, based mainly on the six company privatizations listed in Table 29-1, reveals a number of important considerations in the privatization process.

Legal and Corporate Framework

Significant legal and corporate restructuring is often required to transform a government entity into a privatizable company. Investors must be assured they are purchasing shares of legally and operationally autonomous entities. This restructuring need is particularly acute today in Central and Eastern Europe. Companies targeted for privatization have, in several Central and Eastern European countries, been transformed into joint-stock entities via governmental decree; however, lingering concerns remain in some of these countries as to the clear and unencumbered ownership of privatized assets.

An important consideration which governments face is whether to privatize the enterprise as a whole or segment it for sale into smaller entities. British Telecom was sold as a vertically integrated whole; this was deemed preferable in light of economies of scale, the value of maintaining a nationwide franchise, and lingering benefits of cross-subsidization. In contrast the National Bus Company was splintered into

Table 29-1. Domestic and International Share: Offerings in Selected Privatizations (in US$ millions)

Company	Total offering	International Tranche (% of total)	
British Telecom (U.K.), 1984	4,855	670	(13.8%)
British Gas (U.K.), 1987	8,746	1,618	(18.5%)
Telefónica (Spain), 1987	591	136	(23.0%)
Endesa (Spain), 1988	453	172	(38.0%)
Verbund (Austria)	115	15	(13.0%)
British Water Authority (U.K.)	5,103	944	(18.5%)

seventy separate companies, since economies of scale were deemed less important than the potential benefits of competition. Furthermore, the value of the parts was arguably greater than the whole: the government raised £325 million by privatizing the company in this way, considerably more than might have been raised by privatizing it intact. Argentine's ENTel was divided into two regional companies, a jointly owned international, and several value added services companies.

Governments must also decide whether to undertake necessary operational reforms prior to privatization or, alternatively, leave this task to the new shareholders and competitive forces of the market. Some analysts argue that by implementing difficult operational restructuring when necessary—such as reducing payroll and closing unprofitable lines—the government will attract more investors at a substantially enhanced price. Other privatization analysts argue that governments privatize precisely because they cannot efficiently implement substantive change on their own. They believe that market forces should be relied on to adequately value and implement operational change. In our sample, privatized companies were often restructured from a legal or corporate standpoint prior to sale; however, wholesale operational changes were not made. In Argentina, in the case of ENTel, virtually all agreed that the company required major operational restructuring to reduce costs and improve service; nonetheless, the government left this task—under its general supervision—to the acquiring shareholders.

Residual State Ownership

Governments must equally decide how much, if any, ownership stake they wish to retain in the privatized company. As shown in Table 29-2, government ownership initially retained in our sample of companies ranged from zero, for the British Water Authority, to 75 percent for Endesa, the Spanish electricity company.

Various considerations impact the percentage of governmental ownership retained. These include investor preference and expectations, the market's ability to absorb

Table 29-2. Residual State Ownership after Initial Privatization

Company	Percent government ownership retained
British Telecom	49.8% plus golden share[a]
British Gas	3.0% plus golden share
Telefónica de España	36.0%
Endesa	75.6%
Verbund	51.0%
British Water Authority	0%

a. Reduced to 22 percent at the end of 1991 after a subsequent sale of an additional 27 percent of the company. The government's remaining 22 percent of the shares were sold in mid–1993.

shares, and the profit potential of maintaining shares for resale at a what could eventually be a higher price. The most critical factor, however, is often the perceived need to safeguard the independence and viability of activities deemed to be of national interest. British Telecom and British Gas are good examples. U.K. authorities sold the majority of shares for both vitally important companies in the open market. Nonetheless, by retaining so-called golden shares, the government maintained ultimate authority as regards the independence and integrity of both companies.

Golden shares enable the government to prevent changes in a company's articles of association, limit the percentage of foreign ownership, limit the percentage of total ownership by any one individual or group, restrict the liquidation of assets, and prevent a potentially disruptive concentration of voting rights. These shares can eventually be used to recapture control should a company's autonomy be at risk. As opposed to cumbersome legislation, golden shares can be flexibly used to privatize a nationally sensitive entity without fully abdicating control. The shares, valid indefinitely or for a predetermined amount of time, are essentially passive instruments triggered only by clearly defined developments and acts. Consequently, investor concerns regarding arbitrary government involvement are minimized.

Rate Regulation

Rate regulation is perhaps the key determinant of success for a utility company. Along with country risk and share price, it is a critical element in any investor's decision to buy shares. Investors must believe that the rate-setting process is predictable, disciplined, and fair. A good regulatory framework achieves this, while at the same time ensuring that consumers receive satisfactory service at competitive rates. In order to attain this balance, some degree of continued governmental involvement appears inevitable. Regardless of the methods used, investors must be confident that the rate-setting mechanism will enable the company to prosper relatively free from arbitrary political involvement. In the international community, perceptions as regards country risk obviously influence this degree of confidence. At the time of Telefónica's privatization, international concerns regarding the rate-setting mechanism appeared to be more prevalent than for British Telecom. This reflected the relative unfamiliarity with and increased wariness which investors felt as regards Spain's country risk. Similar elements of concern often influence investor perceptions of privatizations in Latin America and elsewhere.

Size of the Issue

Investors generally prefer large public issues which offer liquidity, equity research, and ample trading. Foreign investors, in particular, can be comforted by an issue's size. As evidenced by the continuous trading of Telefónica shares through American Depositary Receipts (ADRs), the international component can itself contribute to an issue's liquidity and trading success. In general, an international tranche in excess of US$100 million to US$150 million, with a total issue several times that size, appears to be an optimal structure for a major securities issue.

Investors

An important aspect of the privatization process is determining which investors, both domestically and internationally, the equity offering should target. Factors which influence this choice are the offering's size, the underlying company's fundamentals, and investor perception of risk in the privatized company's home market. Furthermore, governmental objectives such as development of the retail market or the fostering of foreign investment play an important role. Finally, financial imperatives—placing the requisite number of shares, maximizing the share price, establishing a diversified and stable investor base—contribute to determining the most appropriate investor mix.

Domestic investors can be broadly segmented into institutional and retail buyers. In our sample, indeed in most privatizations, developmental issues influence the allotment of shares between the two. The British government used its privatization program to promote the acquisition of shares by retail buyers, such as households and employees. The government's deliberate appeal to the retail market was particularly evident in the privatization of British Telecom. Mass market publicity, acquisition financing, pricing incentives, and limitations on the bulk purchase of shares were all used to encourage household investment. The campaign was a success; domestic retail buyers purchased 40 percent of the total issue, as indicated in Table 29-3.

Internationally, investor segmentation is somewhat more complex. The government's intent in accessing these foreign buyers is to augment demand, encourage investment by a diversified and stable base of relatively passive long-term investors, and generate overall foreign investor interest in the domestic market.

As in the case of the domestic market, the most fundamental distinction among international investors is between institutional and retail investors. In the United States, institutional investors account for roughly 40 percent of share ownership; however, they account for a full 70 percent of share trading, over 50 percent of which is in large block trades. In contrast, in Japan, although 70 percent of shares are owned

Table 29-3. Privatization of British Telecom, 1984: Initial Distribution of Shareholders

Buyer type	Amount purchased
Domestic retail	30%
Domestic employees	10%
Domestic institutional investors	45%
International	13%
Other	2%

by corporations and institutional investors, approximately 40 percent of secondary market trading is done by individuals. In Europe, principal investors are typically banks, insurance companies, and investment trusts. When dealing with foreign securities, a further distinction must be made between investors who usually, occasionally, or never, purchase foreign shares or shares from a particular foreign market. Some institutional investors invest predetermined percentages of their portfolio in foreign equities. Others, including so-called country funds, dedicate the entirety of their investments to one or several specific foreign markets. Individuals are usually much less of a factor in the purchase of foreign shares. Nonetheless flight capital (offshore funds held by residents of the issuer's home country) can be an important source of financing for certain emerging market issues. Finally, for utility stocks, a distinction can be made between traditional utility investors, who examine the company's fundamentals on a comparative basis, and country-play investors, who consider the foreign utility a proxy for the underlying country's economy as a whole.

By and large, institutional investors—due to their experience and resources—account for the bulk of foreign investment in the international issuance of shares. These investors purchase shares internationally in an effort to diversity risk and maximize returns. They invest in utility shares specifically because of the relatively high yields and insulation from recession which these securities can provide. Some investors apply a bottom-up approach to investment in foreign shares. They examine the company's fundamentals on an internationally comparative basis first and then, second, consider the issuer's domestic market environment. Others apply a top-down approach, first determining their interest in the issuer's domestic market and, if comfortable, investing in the most prominent or obvious equity plays in that market. Shares of utility companies are deemed to be highly correlated to the economic and market evolution of their domestic market. Consequently, an investor's decision to buy into a country almost always leads, at least initially, to the utilities sector. For example, by investing in utility stocks of certain emerging markets, investors are often hoping to purchase high growth, recession-resistant stock.

The international issuance of shares of two telecommunications companies, Compañía de Telefónos de Chile (CTC) and TELMEX, offer interesting perspectives on the approach to foreign markets. CTC issued a US$100 million share offering in 1991 on the New York Stock Exchange (discussed below in more detail). Buyers were largely emerging market investors as well as more traditional utility and generalist fund managers who allocate a portion of their holdings to international shares. Roughly 75 percent of the shares were placed in the United States, with the remainder purchased by investors in Europe and Asia. TELMEX launched a several-billion-dollar issue. That amount greatly exceeded the investment capacity of specialist Latin American or emerging market buyers. The mainstream investor community had to be made comfortable with Mexican country risk for the issue to succeed.

A final note of importance in targeting foreign investors is the ease with which the investment decision and implementation can be made. The preparation of comprehensive, understandable financial statements is of obvious importance. Financial statements prepared in conformity with international accounting standards will, clearly, attract a wider range of investor interest than those presented using purely local accounting practice. Country- or industry-specific investors will make the effort to understand foreign financial statements; the majority of generalist investors probably will not. Furthermore, the investment decision—once made—should be easy to implement. Generalist investors are often reluctant to purchase shares of a foreign company directly abroad. Brokerage fees, communication barriers, and timing constraints all contribute to this reluctance. On the other hand, a listing in the investor's own market—or, alternatively, on a readily accessible worldwide exchange—will considerably facilitate the investment decision and expand the universe of foreign buyers. In the United States, for example, investors undoubtedly prefer foreign shares issued in the form of ADRs and listed on one of the major U.S. exchanges. Established to facilitate foreign portfolio investment by U.S. companies, ADRs are negotiable certificates, traded in U.S. dollars, which entitle the holder to a specific number of shares in a foreign company. The actual shares are held in the issuer's home market by a custodian bank. ADRs and their international equivalent IDRs remove much of the complexity which U.S. or other international investors face in accessing the shares of a company in a foreign market.

Share Price Valuation

Perhaps one of the most difficult considerations is how to price the offered shares. For a de novo listing, for which a market price does not exist, the valuation process can be complex. Several methods are used to establish a share price in any listing: discounted cash flow, book value, and comparative price/earnings and other ratios. Investors will examine the offered price for a new listing with other comparable investment opportunities; that price must clearly incorporate a relative discount or premium as a function of investor perceptions of the issuer's country risk.

In light of the importance and complexity of correctly pricing an initial public offering, it is important for the government and issuer to assemble a coordinated syndicate of domestic and international underwriting banks. This syndicate should structure, price, promote, and place the issue as well as provide adequate trading support. Furthermore, it is often advisable for the government and issuer to have separate advisers, to incorporate the legitimate if sometimes conflicting concerns of both parties.

In general, initial public offerings are deliberately underpriced to ensure sufficient investor interest at and following the issue date. This discount can be relatively substantial in privatizations. Initial public offerings in the private sector are often underpriced by between 5 percent and 10 percent. In the privatization of state companies, discounts have often been much higher, particularly in the early stages of a privatization program. For example, the shares of British Telecom traded at an 85 percent premium from the offer price on the issue date. Clearly, the pricing of shares is an imprecise science; the price at which shares will just clear the market is often exceedingly difficult to predict. Nonetheless, deliberate underpricing by governments is often evident in order to successfully encourage retail investor interest and to create a success dynamic for the privatization program as a whole.

Table 29-4 compares the current and listing share price of some of the New York Stock Exchange-listed ADRs in our sample. The comparative pricing information is somewhat misleading in light of the time elapsed and currency fluctuations since issue date. Nonetheless, more comprehensive data indicate that the price performance of privatized utility companies has generally been good. This success is attributable to relative underpricing at issue date, the attractiveness of candidates chosen, and, in many respects, the privatization methods used.

Domestic National Interests

Finally, national interests, as defined by public opinion and the governmental authorities, must be secured in any privatization. Most privatizations seek to ensure that domestic investors are privileged in the purchase of shares and that foreign investors do not unduly influence or control the privatization process. These concerns can be well addressed by an appropriate structuring of the offering. The offering can be structured to include clawback provisions, restrictions on foreign ownership and voting rights, a so-called loyalty bonus to encourage employee purchases, and installment payments or discounts to help domestic retail investors finance the purchase of shares.

Clawback provisions allow the issuer, through its underwriting-placement banks, to recall part of the international share offering for resale in the domestic market should the domestic offering be oversubscribed; such provisions can equally be used for "clawing back" from institutional to individual buyers or from any one investor group to another in order of priority. Individual investor or employee investment schemes or both are used to facilitate the purchase of shares by retail investors; employee incentives, such as shares reserved for employees at a discounted price, are often used to encourage employee participation; finally, discounts and related benefits are often given to utility consumers to encourage them to buy utility shares.

Table 29-4. Trading Performance of Shares

Category	British Telecom	British Gas	Telefónica	Endesa
Issue date	Nov. 1984	Feb. 1987	Oct. 1987	May 1988
Issue price	$15.50	$19.18	$19.62	$12.29
Recent Price[a]	$62.86	$43.50	$29.50	$28.13
Year high/low[a]	$68/$40	$49/$30	$30/$22	$26/$18
P/E Ratio[a]	12	11	6	10
Dividend Yield[a]	5.0%	5.5%	6.1%	4.6%

a. Data for the period ending April 14, 1991

The Experience of Compañía de Teléfonos de Chile

Compañía de Teléfonos de Chile (CTC), the largest Chilean telephone company, placed a public issue of shares worth almost US$100 million on the New York Stock Exchange in July 1990. This transaction was the first internationally listed equity issue for a Latin American company since 1963. The oversubscribed issue was a success.

CTC was privatized by the Chilean government in 1988. Following a competitive bidding process, the Australian financier Alan Bond acquired 49 percent and, via special "B" shares, majority voting rights of the company.[2] The remainder of the shares were, at the time, held by institutional investors and individuals and were publicly traded on the Chilean stock exchange. In light of his financial difficulties outside of Chile, Mr. Bond sold the entirety of his holdings in CTC to Telefónica de España, the Spanish telephone company, in April 1990. Mr. Bond had initiated the idea of issuing CTC shares on the international capital markets; the Telefónica acquisition delayed but did not stop that process.

CTC chose to access the international capital markets for two reasons. First, a consent agreement with the government stipulated that Bond—and his successor Telefónica—could not own more than 45 percent of the shares of CTC; dilution was thus required. Second, the company was engaged in a US$1.7 billion long-term expansion program which the domestic markets alone could not finance.

In July 1990, CTC issued approximately US$100 million in American Depositary Shares (ADS), evidenced by American Depositary Receipts (ADRs) publicly listed on the New York Stock Exchange. Salomon Brothers and the International Finance Corporation (IFC)[3] led a syndicate which underwrote and placed the securities issue. The ADRs were issued at a price of US$15.125 per share, a roughly 1.4 percent premium to the underlying share price on the Chilean stock market on this issue date. The share issue represented about 12 percent of the capital structure of CTC and raised almost US$85 million in net proceeds for the company.

In almost every respect, the CTC share issue was a success. It was the first international public offering of shares for a Latin American company since 1963; it raised substantial and much needed financing for the company; it established CTC as a recognized name in the international capital markets. Furthermore, investors have done well. Ten months after the issue, CTC shares were trading at roughly US$26 a share, up almost 75 percent from the issue price (see Figure 29-1).[4]

The CTC issue was substantially oversubscribed. Buyers comprised emerging market investors as well as traditional utility investors and generalist fund managers. Approximately 75 percent of the shares were placed in the United States, with the remainder purchased by investors in Europe and Asia.

Why was the CTC share offering a success? More generally, what do investors look for when they invest in emerging markets? An initial answer appears easy. Investors look for profitable, well-managed growth companies in markets where the political risk is low, economic prospects are high, and the stock market is liquid and transparent. The reality, however, is more complex. When investing in emerging markets, investors will sacrifice one or more of these criteria in the expectation of a substantial upside gain.

Emerging market investors use a combination of two conceptual approaches. Top-down investors examine the economic fundamentals of a country first. If they conceptually buy into a country (in other words, if they believe the political, economic, and market prospects of a country are good, yet the stock market is undervalued), they will invest in shares which are most likely to prosper should expectations of country and market growth be realized. Utility companies, which offer protection from the downside but are highly leveraged to economic growth, are probably the first place such investors look. Alternatively, bottom-up investors examine the fundamentals of a company first, usually on an internationally comparable basis, and consider the country environment on a secondary basis only.

CTC was attractive from both perspectives. As regards country risk, Chile, in 1990 and today, was and is perceived by investors as being an attractive growth market. Three basic elements were particularly appealing:

- Investors were cautiously optimistic that the political environment would remain stable and, in any case, that a political consensus as regards free markets and foreign investment would continue to exist.

- Chile was perceived as having a well-managed growth economy; the country's GNP, driven by export-oriented sectors, had grown by an average of around 6.0 percent per annum since 1984.

- Almost all indicators suggested the Chilean stock market was undervalued on an internationally comparable basis. As shown in Figures 29-2 through 29-5, the market had grown rapidly over the past few years and had comparatively high average dividend yields.

Figure 29-1. Value of CTC Shares on the New York Stock Exchange

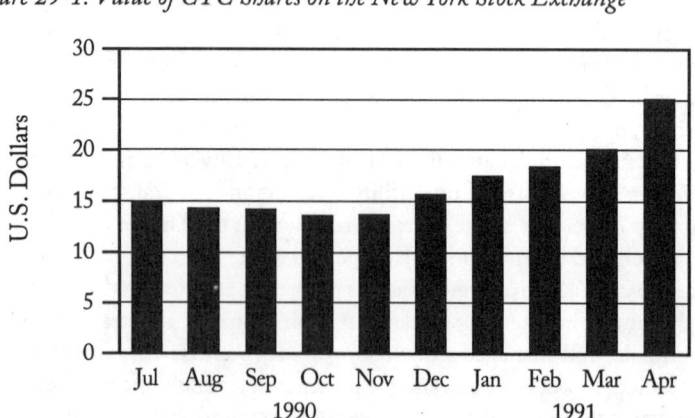

Latest share price: April 23, 1991

Figure 29-2. Comparative Price/Earnings Ratios

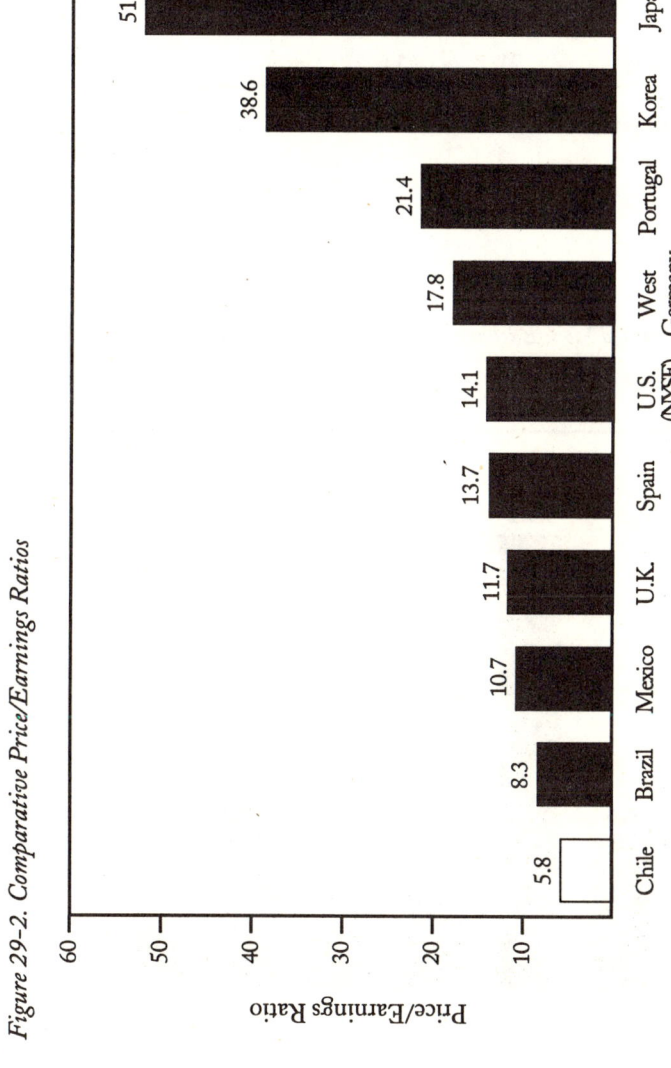

Price/earnings reflect each country's accounting standards
Source: IFC, as of December 31, 1989

Table 29-5. Operating Results Comparisons (Percent)

Category	CTC	TELMEX	Telefónica de España	British Telecom	U.S. Regional Bells
Operating margin	43	33	33	25	19
Net margin	45	21	21	14	12
Return on operations	15	12	19	21	11
Return on equity	21	11	15	18	14

Source: Annual reports

Figure 29-3. Santiago Stock Exchange: Market Index Performance in US$ Terms

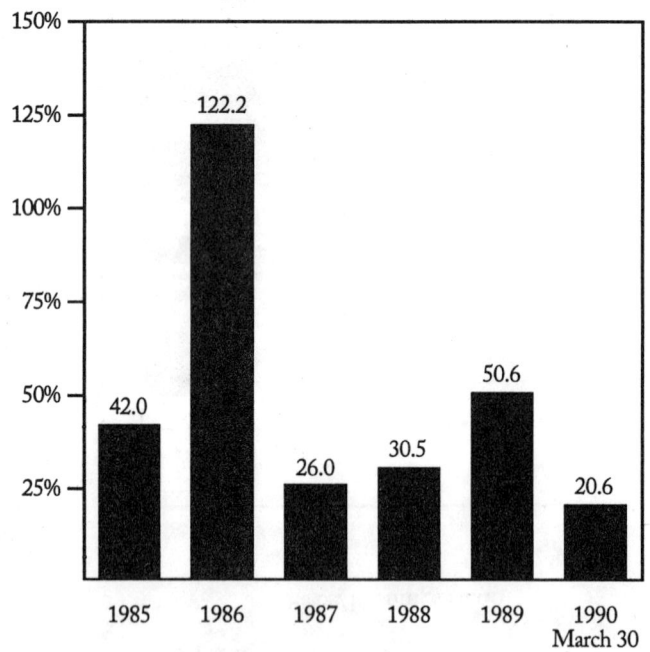

Source: Bolsa de Comercil de Santiago

444

Figure 29-4. Comparative Stock Markets Performance

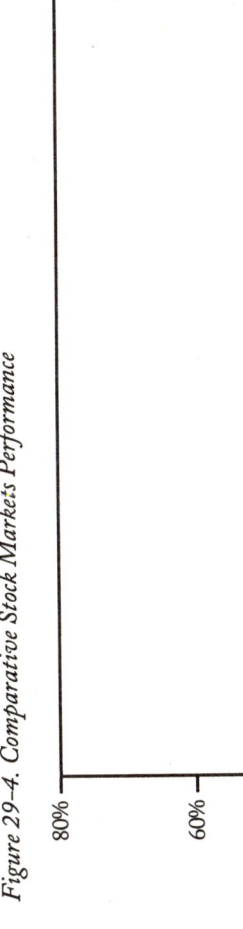

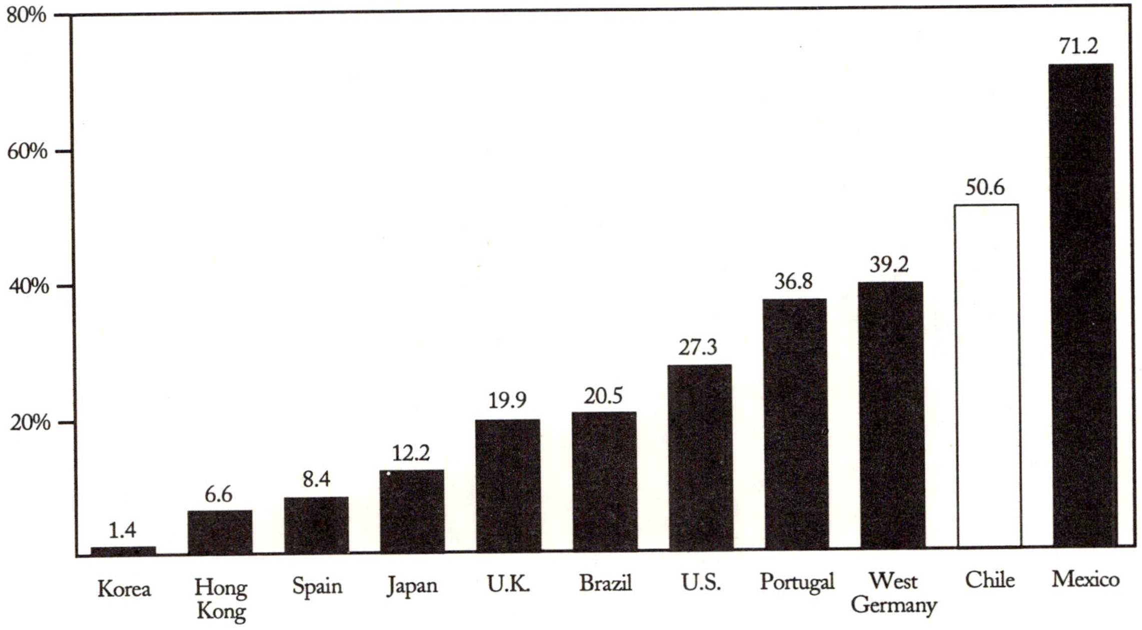

Korea 1.4
Hong Kong 6.6
Spain 8.4
Japan 12.2
U.K. 19.9
Brazil 20.5
U.S. 27.3
Portugal 36.8
West Germany 39.2
Chile 50.6
Mexico 71.2

80%
60%
40%
20%

U.S. is based on the S&P 500 Index.
Source: IFC, index performance in US$ terms in 1989

Figure 29-5. Comparative Dividend Yields

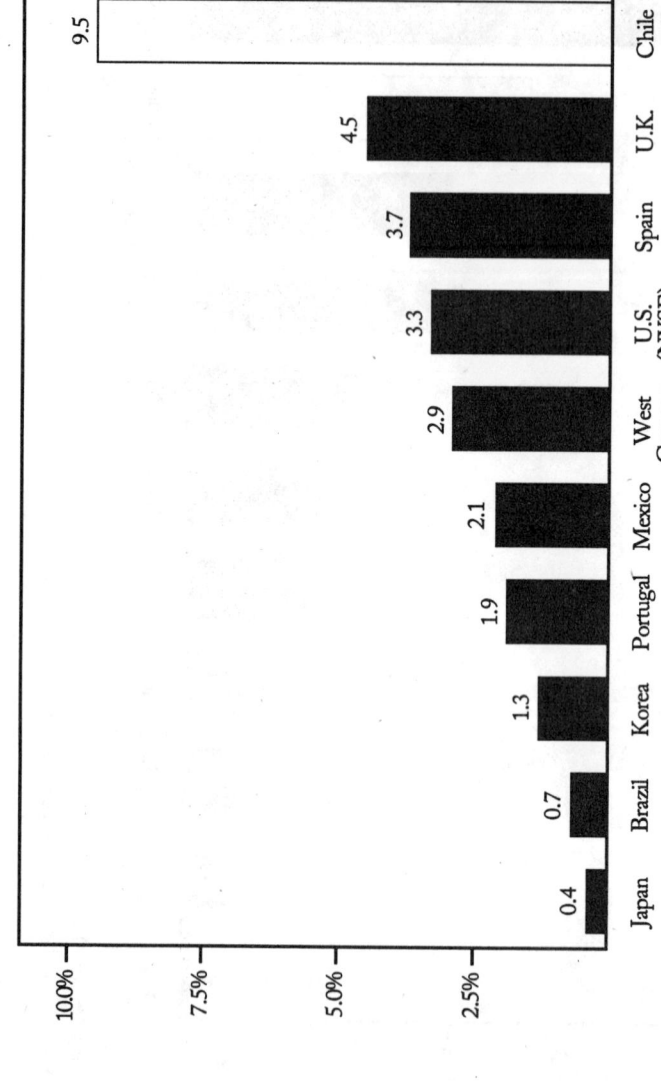

Source: IFC, as of December 31, 1989

- In addition, investor confidence in the CTC offering was boosted by the Central Bank, which explicitly granted CTC shareholders access to the official foreign exchange market. Although this did not eliminate foreign exchange risk, it went a long way toward demonstrating the government's commitment to the repatriation of funds by foreign investors.

As regards company risk, CTC was itself viewed positively because of the following key corporate attributes:

- From a profitability and financial standpoint, the company compared favorably with its international telecommunications peer group (see Table 29-5).

- The company presented its financial statements using internationally recognized accounting standards.

- Management was viewed as competent.

- Relations with the skilled work force were relatively good.

- CTC shares were already listed on the Chilean market and were one of the most actively traded shares in Chile; liquidity was relatively high.

- CTC shares were attractively priced on a comparative price/earnings basis (see Figure 29-6).

- CTC's dividend yield was high (see Figure 29-7). Historically the company had paid 100 percent of profits in dividends. This was to be reduced to 80 percent; however, this reduction, rather than disillusioning investors, was viewed as a positive sign of the company's commitment to financing growth.

- The company's growth prospects, in line with the projected growth of the Chilean economy as a whole, were extremely high; perhaps the single most telling statistic, used by some international investors as an investment "mantra," was the lines-per-capita comparison (see Figure 29-8). This was viewed by some investors as an assurance that, even if the company did almost everything wrong, growth in the subscriber base and revenues was inevitable.

- Competition for CTC in its core local telecommunications business was expected to be slight.

- CTC had an ambitious but detailed and realistic US$1.7 billion modernization and expansion plan. This entailed potentially significant cost savings and, more important, substantial subscriber growth.

447

Figure 29-6. Comparative Price/Earnings Ratios: March 30, 1990

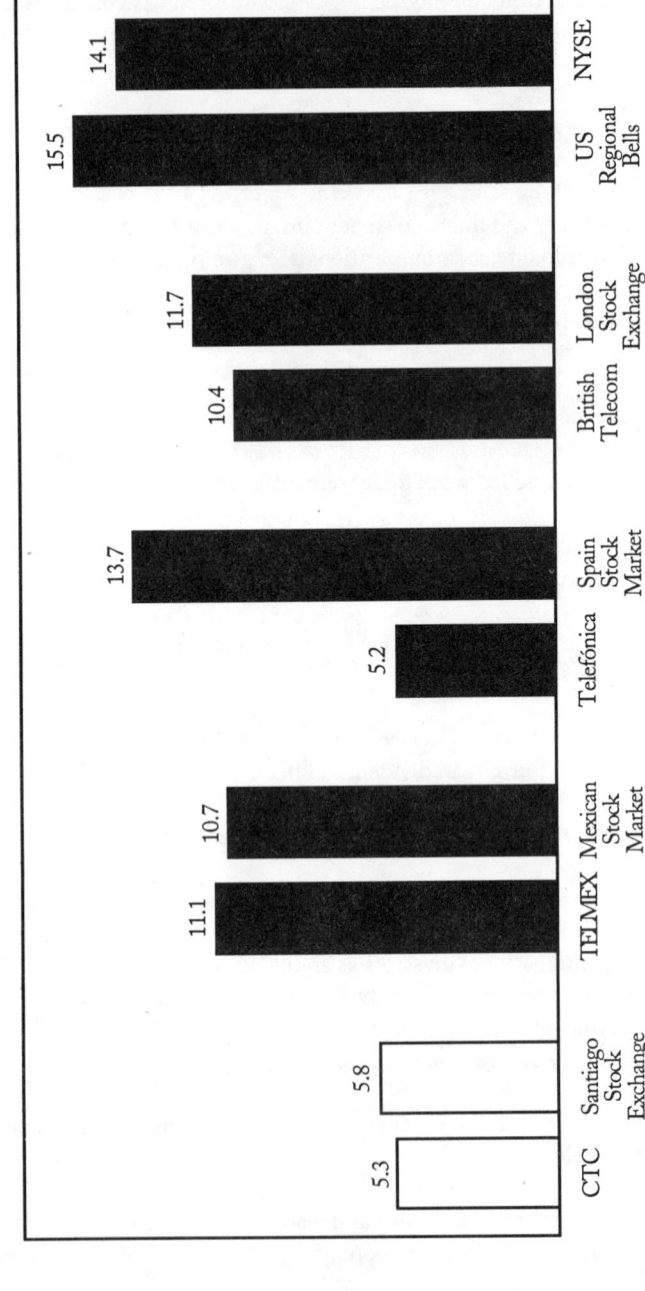

CTC	5.3
Santiago Stock Exchange	5.8
TELMEX	11.1
Mexican Stock Market	10.7
Telefónica	5.2
Spain Stock Market	13.7
British Telecom	10.4
London Stock Exchange	11.7
US Regional Bells	15.5
NYSE	14.1

Source: IFC, December 31, 1989; company annual reports and March 30, 1990 market data

Figure 29-7. Dividend Yield Comparisons (Percent)

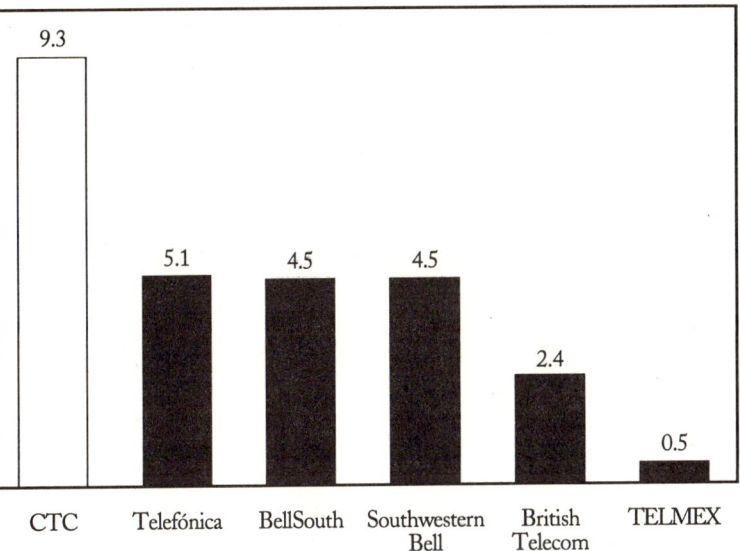

Dividend yield to U.S. holder after withholding tax
Based on 1989 financial results and March 30, 1990 price.

Figure 29-8. Comparison of Telephone Penetration: Lines in Service per 100 Inhabitants

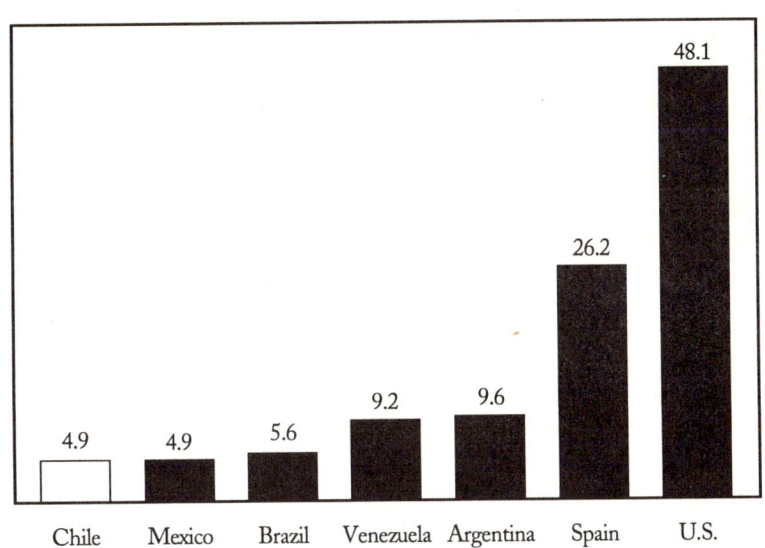

Source: The World's Telephones, 1988

- As important, investors believed CTC would be able to finance that plan through internally generated funds and via the domestic and international capital markets. As part of this financing, IFC had itself made a US$80 million financing commitment.

- Although scheduled for periodic review, CTC's operating concessions were viewed as essentially secure.

- Finally, and perhaps most important, the Chilean tariff structure and rate-setting mechanism were perceived as being fair and relatively safe from unpredictable political influence. We come back, in this key component of investor confidence, to the generally positive view taken by investors as regards Chilean country risk.

There was one additional element of importance to investors. Even if they are comfortable with the investment fundamentals of a company, most international investors will not buy a company's shares unless the shares are readily accessible. CTC's ADRs were available on the New York Stock Exchange. ADRs are negotiable certificates, traded in dollars and settled in the United States, which entitle the holder to a specific number of shares in a foreign company. The actual shares are held in by a custodian bank in the issuer's home market. ADRs, very commonly used, make the purchase and ownership of foreign shares extremely easy. Furthermore, CTC issued its ADRs on the New York Stock Exchange, perhaps the most visible and liquid stock market in the world. Listing requirements, imposed by the exchange and by the U.S. Securities and Exchange Commission, were a comforting stamp of approval to most investors.

Although CTC went through a time-consuming, expensive, and complex process, it raised much-needed financing and created new financing options by establishing itself as a credible name in the international capital markets.

There is a strong demand for international telecommunications issues from emerging markets. Upcoming issues, some valued at several billion dollars, will test just how deep that interest is.

Conclusion

Many of the objectives of the flotations examined above appear to have been met. Financial objectives as regards the raising of funds and cessation of government expenditures occurred. The privatizations helped deepen and broaden domestic capital markets. Financial results and service generally improved. Foreign investor interest was sparked. And domestic national interests were preserved.

In light of the above, what are the implications for the privatization of telecommunications companies through the public issuance of shares, particularly in emerging markets? A larger foreign tranche than in the examples given above might be desirable should the domestic market be too small to absorb the privatization. Clawback provisions can be used to ensure that domestic demand is not frustrated by an international overallotment. For an ongoing privatization program, flotation of the most attractive companies first, at a somewhat discounted price to expected market value, can help create a success dynamic. Establishing a predictable and fair legal and regulatory environment is critical for international investor interest. To encourage the retail ownership of shares, incentive schemes such as installment plans, loyalty bonuses, discounts, and employee stock offers should be used. Finally, concerns about protecting the national interest can be satisfactorily addressed through an appropriate structuring of the share issue.

Endnotes

1. The experience of CTC was written by Vallimarescu. The rest of this chapter is by Vallimarescu and Cheah. Introductory sections on the objectives and modalities of privatization, originally in Vallimarescu and Cheah's paper, were merged by the editors into the chapter by Grossas to reduce duplication.

2. Bond acquired 35 percent of existing CTC stock from the government, and undertook the obligation to bring in new investment as a capital expansion that took his holding to a total of 45 percent.

3. The IFC's mandate is to foster private sector economic growth in the developing world. This has traditionally involved making loans and equity investments to the private sector as well as encouraging financial and operating partners to co-invest in projects with IFC. On the average, for every dollar invested in a project by the IFC, another five dollars are raised from operating and financial partners. More recently, the IFC has tried to expand that resource mobilization role by encouraging international portfolio investors to purchase private sector securities from emerging markets.

4. By the end of May 1993 the share's value had risen to over US$65 (more than four times the July 1990 issue price).

30

Debt Exchange: Financing Privatization and Reducing Country Debt

Desmond Watkins

DEBT EXCHANGE INCLUDES BOTH SPECTACULAR success stories and disappointments. In this chapter we examine the rationale for, and features of, successful debt exchange programs from the viewpoint of a commercial banker. Three examples are discussed. Venezuela's program has illustrative value for the readers of this book even if it was not actually used in the privatization of CANTV. The second example explains debt exchange in the privatization of Argentina's state telecommunications enterprise in 1991. Lastly, some features of the Chilean debt exchange program, a leader in its class, provide additional insights of general applicability.

The Government's Rationale for Debt Exchange

Privatizations may be financed from essentially four types of sources: local equity, foreign equity, local debt, and foreign debt. Developing countries, however, often have difficulty in drawing on these sources.

LOCAL EQUITY. Stock markets in developing countries are usually small or nonexistent. There is no significant pool of small savers through insurance companies, pension funds, and others. In some developing countries a limited number of wealthy private individuals or companies are prepared to take local equity. In general, investors are few and they require a significant premium or high rate of return to be persuaded to invest. Also, many such potential investors prefer to diversify their political and currency risk by investing their funds in other havens, even at substantially lower returns.

FOREIGN EQUITY. Political risk, absence of free currency convertibility, and foreign exchange exposure cause most foreign firms to minimize their equity investment in developing countries. Very large multinationals may invest in their own business subsidiaries but usually only in some (lesser) proportion of the size of that business to their worldwide portfolio. Foreign portfolio investment is extremely limited.

LOCAL DEBT. The local markets for debt instruments (if they exist) are extremely narrow and the private sector is crowded out. Almost invariably a large public sector debt problem makes the whole situation highly unstable. Long-term debt is usually not available and short-term debt is unreliable and expensive.

FOREIGN DEBT. Bank lending involves foreign exchange and cross-border exposure and is now rarely available without parent guarantee or cross-border/political risk insurance. Most developing countries are already struggling or failing to service a sizable foreign debt.

Given these constraints, a number of developing countries have established some form of voluntary mechanisms involving exchange of sovereign debt for equity, assets, or private sector debt, as a means to attract foreign investment and at the same time reduce government foreign debt. Debt exchange usually takes place in one of two forms:

DEBT-TO-EQUITY. The foreign commercial banks are given local currency for their foreign-denominated debt which they then invest in a local project. Governments usually set limits on eligible projects and the repatriation of dividends and principal.

DEBT-FOR-DEBT. The foreign commercial bank exchanges a government debt for a debt owed to the government by a private sector or a government corporation (this could be part of a privatization). The private sector or government corporation then undergoes a capital restructuring so that the debt becomes common equity.

Countries where the debt exchange programs have succeeded in attracting additional investment exhibit two features. First, government policy places emphasis on creating a successful private sector, particularly for export-driven growth projects. Beyond divesting government of a poorly run business, privatization is used to create a sector of the economy which is viable and well run, and which, through managerial and technical skills as well as investment, provides a service or a product that is internationally competitive and upon which the society can rely. Second, beyond debt exchange as an opportunity to reduce external debt, successful governments pursue export-driven growth by developing world-class industries and do so by attracting both international capital and expertise.

The key to good debt exchange projects of a significant size is the involvement of foreign banks who are debt holders, whereby the banks provide capital for projects in developing countries against some form of partnership interest in these projects. Many international banks are overexposed to the governments of developing countries, and the governments have difficulty in providing the foreign exchange to service those debts. Unable to reduce their exposure, short of selling their debt at a very deep discount, some banks are prepared to redeploy this exposure toward private sector risks.

Governments sometimes stay away from offering debt-to-equity programs, arguing that they are inflationary. Indeed, such programs must be accompanied by fiscal discipline—governments should not simply print the extra local currency required. Countries such as Chile have successfully developed debt-to-equity programs. One route followed has been for the government to exchange the debt for its own local currency—denominated debt, which the banks then sell in the market to raise the local currency, thereby taking the local currency out of the existing system. Inflationary impact is not an issue in the case of debt-for-debt programs since there is no monetary transaction. The companies' balance sheets, however, can be transformed, giving them a stronger equity base, freeing them from the burden of high local interest rates on their debt, and opening up the possibility of taking on more debt as the equity is increased.

The real argument in favor of developing debt exchange schemes is, however, more subtle: these schemes provide an incentive for the banks to develop a viable and successful private sector. Banks take a lead in structuring and putting projects together. Into their projects they invite capable technical and commercial companies (often their customers elsewhere) who probably would not be able, or would not wish, to take the whole risk of the project themselves. These banks obtain political or exchange risk insurance and export credits as well as advise on the financial and legal structure of the company. They make available a whole range of experience and skills from modern management techniques to available export opportunities. They must insist on high ethical, safety, and environmental standards in the project. They will insist on proper accounting and recording of all transactions. They will pay the proper taxes to the government. Furthermore, they will compete for the government's assets and therefore raise their value. They will seek to make the companies they invest in profitable, competitive, and if possible, foreign exchange earners. Acting in their own self-interest they will do much to create a genuine, viable private sector that meets the government's objectives.

The role of a commercial bank such as Citibank as an investor can be crucial, not just because of the financial considerations but because it gives confidence and shares risks with partners who, on their own, would not be prepared to accept the risk of the whole venture, and who may therefore not even consider the opportunity carefully—particularly if they do not have experience of the country concerned.

The Commercial Banks' Interest in Telecommunications Privatizations

Commercial banks are not telecommunications companies. In the normal course of business, banks may make investments in telecommunications companies, for example, as part of an overall diversified portfolio. Banks also make venture capital investments in various industries and countries. In general, the central reason for a bank to hold more than a portfolio investment in a foreign telecommunications company being privatized is the opportunity to redeploy some of the sovereign debt it holds.

Although the commercial bank's investment decision is largely driven by the exchange of existing sovereign debt, this does not lead to desperate investments. Exchanging one piece of debt paper with impaired value for another piece of paper of questionable worth is unacceptable. The proposed investment must be attractive relative to the alternative of continuing to hold the sovereign debt. The secondary market price of debt is no indication of its value to those who intend to stay in a country and who are being asked to reinvest their funds in another long-term venture, such as a privatization.

The investment, therefore, must stand on its own merits. The bank looks for good management, sound strategy, a country and an industry with favorable potential, investment returns commensurate with risk, a risk suitable to the investor's risk tolerance framework, defined exit mechanism allowing the investor to actually realize capital appreciation, and goal congruence with partners. The bank requires a company which is not encumbered by legal problems or a backlog of unresolved issues such as debt, taxes, or other claims. It needs to be sure that the government has the necessary agreement of other parties or lenders to carry out these transactions. For a bank, there is somewhat less emphasis on sovereign or cross-border risk because the debt conversion does not involve incremental exposure to this risk. In addition, for a bank there is a more indirect emphasis on operational characteristics and a commensurately greater emphasis on a strong technical and commercial partner.

Commercial banks attach great importance to finding the right partners. The banks look not just for technical skills and financial strength, but for parties who have experience in upgrading networks from a state similar to the targeted investment and who have the human resources available to do so effectively, including language and compatibility both with the bank and with the country concerned. That means the bank must share, among many other things, the same standards as regards environmental concerns, safety, and, say, integrity of accounts. The bank looks for the partnership to provide a balance of skills. It does not seek to be the majority partner but neither is it usually a passive investor. It provides help and expertise in the areas of its specialty, such as financial controls, foreign exchange transactions, loans, supplier credits, and guarantees, tasks to which the Citibank has, for example, assigned employees in Telefónica de Argentina in which it is an important shareholder.

A number of other factors contribute to making a particular debt exchange opportunity attractive:

- Opportunity to use a significant proportion of debt in hand

- Attractive discount rate and conditions for the debt conversion. A large fixed discount is a disincentive because the banks must then take an immediate loss on the transaction into their books, which only those banks that wish to exit the country are prepared to do

- Bid in terms of face value of debt to be exchanged for particular assets. This avoids valuing the debt in local currency, gives a transparent market value for the assets sold, and often also results in a discount for the government

- Clearly defined rules of debt exchange financing. Debt exchange on specified terms should be available if the project put together by the bank is approved. A process whereby banks submit their investment projects and subsequently bid for the right to convert debt to finance these investments does not meet this criterion

- Attractive foreign investment legislation, including dividend and capital repatriation, and fiscal incentives

- Export or offshore hard currency revenues (for telecommunications companies, net revenue from overseas calls) as the sovereign debt being exchanged is denominated in hard currency

- Maximum tenor of ten years and defined exit mechanism, consistent with regulations in the banker's home country and with viewing the investment as part of a time-bound recovery process

- Upside potential with recovery of 100 percent or more of the value of the paper exchanged

- Large investment which justifies the high fixed (legal, accounting, regulatory) costs of an equity investment via debt exchange

- Participating preferred equity with a minimum dividend. This is often more attractive than straight common equity, particularly when the sovereign debt being exchanged is current on interest

- Equality of treatment with other participating banks and investors, regardless of whether investment is being made via a debt exchange.

Debt-to-Equity Exchange in Venezuela

In the 1980s, the government of Venezuela had a debt-to-equity exchange program based on a set amount of conversion rights being auctioned at regular intervals (approximately US$50 million per month) with a maximum set per project and an approval process for the project allowed to benefit from the program. Although the auctions attracted both foreign and domestic investors, the discounts rapidly became large, with only a limited premium over the market value of the paper. Also, neither banks nor large-scale projects, which the government most wanted to encourage, actually participated. A revised program became effective in late 1990. The discount on the debt was set at a low 15 percent of face value. Only projects with capital cost of $300 million or more were eligible. Up to one-third of the project cost could be financed with debt-to-equity exchange. Another one-third of capital cost had to be financed through equity contributions by the sponsors.

A special debt exchange program was created for investments in priority sectors—petrochemicals, aluminum, pulp and paper, tourism, and infrastructure. Projects were individually approved by the President and the cabinet. Minimum eligible capital cost was set at $150 million for petrochemical, aluminum, and pulp and paper projects, $50 million for tourism, and no minimum for infrastructure. The discount was set at 30 percent for one particular sovereign debt issue with a secondary market price approximately 50 percent, and lower for most other issues. The debt/equity exchange funds had to be invested against project expenditure incurred in local currency. Up to 30 percent of the capital cost of the project could be financed with debt/equity exchanges (50 percent for tourism, exceptions granted for infrastructure). Public sector foreign debt exchanged for central bank bonds was converted at 100 percent of face value. Prospective investors were required to deposit a 5 percent surety bond to guarantee that the proceeds from the conversion were invested as planned. During each of the first three years of the foreign investment undertaken through the debt/equity exchange program, the foreign investor was allowed to remit abroad dividends of up to 10 percent of the debt/equity exchange investment; no limits were set for subsequent years, or for dividend payouts in local currency in any year. Capital repatriation was not allowed during the first five years, and limited to 12.5 percent per annum thereafter.

In the first year of operation of this special program, the government selected about a dozen large projects, including aluminum smelters (costing from US$700 million to US$1 billion each), petrochemical projects (US$300 million each), a pulp and paper project, and large integrated tourism projects.

By implementing this program, the government made possible some large and economically beneficial projects that had been talked about but not acted upon for a long time. Lack of sponsors and financing had for years prevented these projects from moving to the implementation stage. The new program turned major international banks into active promoters and committed financiers of these large projects. In the aluminum sector, nine consortia were competing to obtain the available projects, including the major U.S., Japanese, and Korean companies. In the petrochemical area, international chemical companies joined with the banks and with the Venezuelan state-owned company to finance and compete for the projects.

For the banks, the new debt-to-equity program brought the opportunity to convert the existing sovereign debt into common or preferred shares of attractive private sector projects with exporting earning potential, without having to take large amounts of losses into their books. Banks were particularly attracted by four features of the program: large project size; demonstrable commitment of the government to the sectors targeted; debt/equity exchange approved in conjunction with project approval early in the planning stage; and small fixed discount on face value of debt.

Results at the implementation have been mixed. Despite the downturn of the petrochemical markets, the petrochemical projects went ahead successfully. In contrast, two years later the aluminum projects had not yet materialized.

Argentina: Debt Exchange in the Privatization of the Telephone Company

When the government of Argentina made the decision to privatize the telephone company, ENTel, it realized that given the general condition of that company, it was likely that few, if any, experienced telephone companies would bid and that the price offered would be unattractive from a political point of view. To help remedy those problems, the government resorted to the international banks and their large relationship network as the marketing and structuring vehicle.

The basic idea was to accept a large part of the payment for the shares of the company in the form of sovereign debt and to have the bidders (not the government) put a price on that debt. The government decided that the shares of the company would go to the one bidder that offered a set amount in cash and the highest amount of face value of sovereign debt. At the same time, the bid included conditions regarding future capital expenditure levels and the upgrading of the telephone network by the consortium and the commercial partner. The commercial partner, who had to be an established successful telephone operator, accepted responsibility to carry out operations and extensive upgrading of facilities.

In August 1989, the Argentine Congress authorized the President to proceed with the total or partial privatization of government-owned companies operating in a number of areas, including petrochemicals, transportation, communications, and energy. ENTel was among the most substantial entities to be privatized. Subsequently, the Argentine government issued decrees setting the terms of the privatization of ENTel, including a requirement that it be implemented through an international public bid procedure. The equity of the two regional companies into which ENTel was divided was to be placed 60 percent through an international public bid procedure, 25 percent through a public offering in Argentina, 10 percent with employees of ENTel, and 5 percent with private cooperatives which, prior to the bid, provided certain telecommunications services to ENTel. The two regional companies were to assume only specific liabilities of ENTel, such as payments for construction in progress and purchases of equipment and obligations to install telecommunications lines for which payments had been made. Additionally, the southern regional company was to issue a US$202 million promissory note to be paid to ENTel in six semiannual installments commencing three and a half years after the transfer date. The promissory note would bear interest at the six-month London Inter-Bank Offered Rate (LIBOR) plus 0.8125 percent, payable semiannually in arrears. A similar note would be issued by the northern regional company. ENTel was not to transfer to the southern company any outstanding receivables from customers. Both regional companies would be responsible to act as connection agents for ENTel's receivables which were outstanding on the transfer date.

The international public bid procedure to privatize ENTel set minimum prices US$114 million in cash and US$1,865 million of face value of Argentine debt instruments for the southern company, and US$100 million in cash and US$1,500 million of Argentine debt instruments for the northern company. The bidders submitting the highest bid in Argentine debt instruments were to be awarded 60 percent of the common stock of each company. Interest accruing after June 26, 1990, and the Argentine debt instruments which were tendered would be the property of ENTel and would not be considered in computing the bid in Argentine debt instruments.

The privatization was successfully concluded at a price far above the minimum price for debt paper set by the government. The foreign commercial banks, eager to convert their sovereign debt into securities with a more attractive profile in the private sector, took it upon themselves to identify potential partners, both international operators and local corporations, and bring them together in the bidding. Under the leadership of three major international banks, including Citibank, three consortia were created and participated in the bidding. Bids for the two regional companies topped US$5 billion. Apart from the price paid in debt paper, the new owners paid US$214 million in cash up front and another US$387 million in installments over a six-year period. The takeover was effective on October 8, 1990.

Telefónica de España, teaming up with Citicorp and the local group Techint, took over the southern company, which includes the profitable Buenos Aires financial district. In addition to Telefónica, Citibank brought in a group of Spanish private banks. Telefónica now has an equity interest together with other Spanish investors to ensure their continuing interest in the successful operation of the network. The pressure of the private investors removes the possibility that the Argentine network would be handed over to another government entity. The second major equity partner brought to the venture was Techint, the preeminent local engineering company that will carry out the supervision of much of the engineering and construction of the network. Telefónica and Techint both seconded highly qualified and experienced personnel to the venture, and Citibank itself seconded seventeen highly qualified staff members to help establish the new systems and final arrangements. Local private investors and a syndicate of banks, both local and foreign, also participated in the consortia with both common and preferred shares.

The two regional telephone companies are now managed by operators of international renown, together with major local corporations; the government has canceled more than US$5 billion in sovereign debt; and the banks have been able to exchange their sovereign debt against common equity and preferred shares in the newly privatized telephone company, written into their books at a price agreed with the auditors. The Argentine government intends to follow this model for privatizing other publicly owned companies.

The banks were particularly attracted by the absolute size of the transaction, which was large enough to warrant the interest of international banks and telephone companies; by the minimum bid specification of a large utilization of debt paper; and by the structure of the auction as a direct exchange of debt for assets, providing investors the ability to place their own value on the debt paper.

The Chilean Model

Chile's debt-to-equity conversion program is often acknowledged as a model of success. This is in large part attributable to key structural attributes specific to the country: favorable foreign investment regulations; attractive investment opportunities; a stable economic environment; the existence of a significant portion of private sector debt; relatively high price of the debt on the secondary market; and a well-developed and relatively efficient local capital market. Critical to the formation of the local capital markets was the government's policy to allow individuals to transfer their pensions from state funds to private sector funds, thus creating a body of institutional investors with an appetite for long-term, private investments—in essence, a pool of local capital.

The debt-to-equity exchange program is tailored to these structural conditions. The approval process functions very fast, giving results generally within one to two months of submission. Investments are approved on a case-by-case basis and are most liberal in terms of investments allowed, although the rules target certain industries and restrict some types of investments. To mitigate the inflationary impact, the investor of private sector debt negotiates the conversion rate directly with the debtor, who in turn has the capability to refinance in the local capital markets. An investor exchanging public sector debt with the government receives a note denominated in local currency, which is then sold in the local capital market to raise cash. In both cases, money creation (and therefore, inflation) from the exchange itself is avoided.

Reliance on the well-developed local capital markets is what makes the Chilean program unique, primarily because most developing countries have neither a similar split of private and public sector debt nor a well-developed local capital market. Privatization does not have inflationary, money creation impact; however, for debt exchange programs not associated with privatization, certain stabilizing mechanisms are required, along with continued monitoring of the money creation impact. In many countries, the potential inflationary impact of excess money supply creation is addressed by establishment of quotas. Other approaches need to be considered when quotas are eased or exceeded by larger projects. In successful situations, compensating public sector budgetary adjustments have been made. In addition, investors have been issued local currency—denominated bonds in exchange for the tendered foreign currency bonds. Where there is a very liquid secondary market as in Chile, these bonds may then be resold by the investor to raise the actual local currency with little price risk to the investor. In the absence of a well-developed and liquid secondary market, some price protection mechanism is provided to the investor; in the context of a project financing, this might most appropriately take the form of a series of local currency bonds with maturity dates corresponding to the planned investment schedule.

Conclusion

The privatization and large-project debt exchange programs used in Argentina and Venezuela have in general succeeded in accomplishing investment goals of government that otherwise would not have been achieved. They did so because the governments had clear objectives and structured the programs to attract participation by financial institutions; the terms were clear and predictable; the market forces were allowed to work through specific types of competitive bidding; and the amounts of government debt involved were significant. The Chilean experience demonstrates the advantage of a broadly based program available to a wide range of projects to stimulate the development of the private sector. As time has passed we can now see that Argentina and Chile have also reduced their inflation to low levels. Their currencies have been strong so that remittance is now no problem for investors.

What distinguishes privatizations in countries such as Argentina, Chile, and Venezuela (as well as others in Latin America) is the extent to which foreign investors have come not only with capital but also with management, technical, commercial, and other necessary expertise to make such an undertaking successful. This is sadly lacking in many countries, especially those of the former U.S.S.R. and in Central and Eastern Europe, where privatizations are often being attempted by the simple distribution of vouchers or shares to ordinary citizens and foreign ownership has at least initially been limited. This does not, unfortunately, bring in the required expertise on how to set up and run a private company, let alone on how to establish a viable private sector.

31

Exploring New Ways to Attract Capital for Privatization

Robert R. Bruce, Jeffrey P. Cunard, and Lothar A. Kneifel

IMPROVING THE TELECOMMUNICATIONS INFRASTRUCTURE in countries with underdeveloped infrastructures will consume enormous resources over the next decade. Few countries will be in a position to marshal the necessary funds out of their domestic capital market. Instead, they will have to look to international sources, competing among countries to fashion solutions that will attract investor interest.

A well-accepted approach to attracting new investment capital is to authorize joint ventures between local and foreign telecommunications operators. For example, telecommunications operators in Central and Eastern Europe (CEE) have been actively involved in joint ventures for the provision of cellular services and overlay networks for business users. Joint ventures, however, while useful for new services, may not be particularly well suited for investment in the core telecommunications infrastructure, such as major urban telephone switching and distribution facilities. Another traditional approach to obtaining private investment in the telecommunications area is through corporatization and sale of a significant or controlling equity stake in the operator. There is, however, a large number of such potential offerings in international capital markets; investors, both foreign operators and institutional investors, are likely to be increasingly selective about the nature, size, and risk of the investments they make. Also, the recession in Western industrialized countries, together with other factors, have constricted the supply of capital available for portfolio investment.

Given these limitations, a government might alternatively open up parts of the telecommunications system for development by private investors. Although it would not initially dispose of any of its equity stake in the existing telecommunications operator, it would encourage private entities to invest directly in building additional core infrastructure. The financing options explored below would constitute a sort of bottom-up privatization in which private operators would obtain an equity interest in the infrastructure they construct, but not necessarily in the entity responsible for providing service to the public. Such a notion, which would have been radical a few years ago, raises fewer eyebrows today. In Eastern Germany, for example, DBP Telekom has waived its telephone service monopoly until 1997 to allow private entities to offer voice service via their VSAT links, thus greatly accelerating development. Variants of this approach could be employed elsewhere to mobilize private capital and expertise in response to user needs. An expanding range of new technologies can be used to develop these solutions through unconventional network structures. This chapter discusses two novel approaches for reorganizing and financing the development of the telecommunications sector in emerging market countries. These are asset-based financing and franchising.

Asset-based Financing

Private entities could be engaged to construct and own infrastructure facilities and then lease these assets to telecommunications operators. A variant might be to establish such entities separately for each main line of the telecommunications operator's business (for example, local exchange, national interexchange, and international services). Such separate entities could raise debt or equity in domestic and international markets. The lease arrangement with the telecommunications operator might be structured to relate lease payments to the operating results of the business unit in which the leased assets are deployed. In a sense, investors would thus be offered a de facto equity stake in the telecommunications operator.

If lease payments are based in part on income earned by the telecommunications operator's business in which the new assets are utilized, it may be possible to increase the interest of investors and the marketability of securities of the financing entities. This financing technique was utilized by France Télécom in the mid–1970s when France initiated a major effort to reduce backlogs and improve the quality of service.[1] The establishment of such new intermediaries that finance and install new telecommunications infrastructure could effectively establish the groundwork for a later effort to sell control or a substantial ownership stake in the telecommunications operator. Investors in such financing entities would require some assurances and guarantees. They might be more interested, for example, in an investment in new facilities utilized in an overlay network where prices for business users—both local and international—are set at international levels. Investors would also need to know in very clear terms the regulatory and legal framework applicable to such facilities' leasing arrangements. The negotiation of these understandings might well accelerate the process of overall sectoral reform.

These efforts to create new investment opportunities in the telecommunications operator would offer an opportunity for investors and the telecommunications operator to gain experience in accessing capital markets. Privatization would thus occur in stages. Investors in packages of assets might, for example, be afforded the option to exchange their interest in such limited investment vehicles for shares in the telecommunications operator once it is privatized.

If new entities are allowed to own infrastructure that can be leased to operators, policymakers will have the option of deciding whether an intermediary could also use its own infrastructure to offer services directly to third parties and, if so, what range of services. Under one approach, an intermediary, such as an electric utility or a railway company, might retain for its own use all capacity not made available to a telecommunications operator. Alternatively, a facilities provider might have the option of selling off capacity to other large users. A final option would be to permit the lease or resale of unutilized capacity.

An initiative to permit private ownership and operation of core assets might also operate quite successfully in tandem with a franchising initiative, described below. For example, in order to accommodate new traffic loads generated by franchisees, the telecommunications operator might have to construct a ring network to collect traffic generated by franchisees. Such a network might be separately capitalized by private investors or by such investors and a group of franchisees.

Many of the details of such a scheme for attracting new investment need to be refined. They suggest, however, some new and promising avenues for new investment and warrant careful assessment in the context of the experience of different countries.

Franchising

Under a franchising scheme, telecommunications operators might authorize private entities to construct segments of the local network and connect these facilities with the telecommunications operator in accordance with a specific business agreement. This agreement would establish technical standards for franchisees as well as a formula for dividing revenues. The agreement could provide the telecommunications operator with the option of acquiring its franchisees in exchange for stock. This financing technique would permit increased access to capital and foreign exchange resources held by telecommunications users, both residential and business.

For example, telecommunications operators could establish a franchising program to encourage small firms to construct new local telephone plant. These entrepreneurs would not operate as independently licensed local companies. Instead, they would operate utilizing the existing license of the telephone company.

In some rural areas, cooperative associations might be formed to undertake the construction of telephone infrastructure, consisting of small-scale switching systems (possibly radio-based) or of novel new technical configurations, for example, utilizing telepoint technology with handsets designed for use with prepaid telephone cards that would virtually eliminate the need for customer billing.[2] To overcome the fact that telepoint systems might be used only to originate calls, rural subscribers could be equipped with paging equipment to notify them of incoming calls.

Another idea is to implement a franchising program involving small scale VSAT systems with built-in signaling and billing functions, such as those now available for connection to EUTELSAT and other satellite systems. In particular, EUTELSAT will provide satellite capability through duly authorized telecommunications entities even in countries that are not now members of EUTELSAT. Thus, in office or apartment complexes a VSAT terminal could be utilized to provide direct access to the public-switched network in the same country or on a cross-border basis. The use of a VSAT system which could bypass terrestrial networks would not necessarily result in a loss of revenue to the main telecommunications provider if such systems operate as franchisees of such an operator. The originating VSAT terminal could generate information concerning the called and calling number that would provide a basis for proper billing of the customer and for a division of revenues between the originating company and the telecommunications operator-franchiser.

New service providers need not, however, be dependent on new technological capabilities or systems. A variety of different systems capabilities, ranging from advanced electronic digital PBXs to small exchanges adapted for use in meeting needs for limited groups of public subscribers, could be utilized. Indeed, the emergence of new franchising arrangements might well stimulate equipment manufacturers to offer cost-effective packages of equipment.

In establishing franchising schemes, policymakers would have the option of permitting new tariffing schemes to apply to facilities installed by franchisees. It might be possible to make arrangements through outside suppliers to obtain various billing or customer information system software capabilities. Enhanced billing capabilities would also be required to assure the efficient settlement of accounts between the new service providers and the telecommunications operator. For example, calls could be billed on an individual basis utilizing calling and called-party number identification rather than on the basis of pulses. In this way, it might be possible with new rate structures to better recover the cost of local networks and to stimulate higher interexchange and international calling volumes. Effective transparent management systems will ultimately be essential if new operators are to be successful in obtaining new sources of investment capital.

Establishing a demarcation between a telecommunications operator's existing retail services provided directly to customers and those offered on a wholesale basis through intermediaries could provide important incentives for the construction of new networks. Centralized state-run companies have not offered incentive-based compensation, nor have they developed the marketing and business skills that will be needed in the future. A web of small-scale, entrepreneurially-oriented firms might be better than any business school course in training the new managers needed for the future.

The implementation of a franchising scheme could create attractive opportunities for new investors—either in establishing the franchising scheme or in running franchises. These new investments would be on a smaller scale and may be perceived as less risky than a direct investment in a former state-run company.

The telecommunications operator may also be able to facilitate the financing of new service providers by establishing payment and settlement mechanisms that provide adequate security for lenders. Funds payable to new service providers by the telecommunications operator might be channeled through special trust accounts; these receivables would provide a financial basis and security for loans by third-party lenders. The telecommunications operator might be able to establish financing arrangements for new service providers by financial institutions participating in the new franchising program.

The new operators might be organized in a variety of different ways. Some might be owned by individual entrepreneurs. Others might be cooperative associations of telephone subscribers managed by employees of the cooperative or by a separate management company. In some cases the new service providers would own their own equipment and facilities; in others they might lease such equipment from third parties or even from the telecommunications operator. Foreign investors might be permitted to participate in the new franchising scheme in a variety of different ways—as investors in new operators, in entities established to own assets or facilities needed to provide services, or in service companies offering billing or other logistical capabilities to service providers.

Giving the telecommunications operator an option to acquire its franchisees in the future minimizes the risk that the operator would be balkanized and reduced to a group of uncooperative and contentious small-scale companies. The telecommunications operator—or an outside firm brought in to establish such a franchising company—would have responsibility for setting standards and assuring the smooth provision of service on an integrated basis. It would also retain control over the billing mechanisms within the franchising scheme.

It is conceivable, of course, that new service providers could be set up as separate carriers with their own licenses rather than as companies operating under the umbrella of a telecommunications operator's license. Policymakers should, however, recognize the significant differences between franchising new business units and licensing new independent operators with their own licenses. Licensing new local carriers certainly adds a layer of complexity to any regulatory process that might be in the process of being established. A franchising program, by contrast, would result in certain potential disputes between the telecommunications operator and local companies in being treated as business contract questions, not regulatory questions requiring independent adjudication. Policymakers would anyhow retain the option to license new carriers.

In establishing a franchising program, there is no reason for new local companies to be limited to rural areas. Underserved parts of an urban area could become a target for a well-focused marketing campaign coordinated by new service providers. The new companies would, in fact, take on responsibility from the telecommunications operator for selling services and dealing with customer service concerns.

Utilizing new entities to meet unmet demand would appear to have many advantages:

- Many existing telecommunications operators are not merely limited in the amount of capital to meet unmet customer demand, but also in the managerial resources required to install and oversee new systems.

- New entities might well become vehicles for developing managerial and entrepreneurial talent necessary for the future development of a telecommunications operator. Large centralized organizations, in particular, those that have operated in centrally directed economies, have not generally been able to produce managers prepared for the rigors of a profit-and loss-oriented, market-driven environment.

- A decentralized approach to building up local infrastructure might actually facilitate the process of raising investment capital, since the risk and scale of necessary loans are well within the capabilities of traditional commercial lending organizations.

- New service providers might become a vehicle for the development and deployment of new sophisticated billing or other software-based logistical capabilities. These entities could become a proving ground for new management capabilities and systems that might eventually be deployed in the telecommunications operator itself.

These new entities that are intended to build out the ends of the operator's network need not always remain small-scale and entrepreneurially separate from the telecommunications operator. It might be feasible, after a transition period, to merge separate new local companies into larger business units or to consolidate new entities with parts of the telecommunications operator's local exchange businesses that have been decentralized into separate business units.

One particularly attractive option might be to provide in a franchise agreement for downstream consolidation, involving the exchange of an ownership interest in new local companies for stock in a telecommunications operator that is to undergo privatization. In this way, managers who expand the telecommunications operator's base of subscribers would be rewarded in proportion to their contribution to the operator's profitability. The development of new local cooperative companies would thus become an important mechanism for preparing a telecommunications operator for privatization.

A franchising initiative would produce a group of indigenous entrepreneurs who, in exchanging the stock of franchisees for stock in the telecommunications operator, could become a significant part of the governance structure of a restructured telecommunications operator. This plan could be an avenue for rewarding a telecommunications operator's employees not for their past years of service with the company, but for their future contributions to its growth.

More important, by stimulating the growth of new connections and revenues, the implementation of a franchising scheme would improve the prospects of the telecommunications operator to attract investment. Investors will ultimately prefer to base their decisions on trends concerning emerging new income streams than on evaluations of the great enigma that telecommunications operators' current accounts now generally represent.

Conclusion

Both the utilization of separate financing mechanisms and initiatives to encourage new investment on the peripheries of the telecommunications operator's network could help establish the necessary groundwork for a telecommunications operator to privatize. They would constitute significant and useful steps by investors and increase the likelihood of success of the privatization process.

It makes little sense to rush toward privatization without addressing a number of threshold problems, including most of the issues that must be confronted when corporatizing a state enterprise. Certainly among the most important concerns are reassessing the structure of government-held debt, defining dividend expectations of the government with respect to shares retained, and delineating the ongoing control relationships between the telecommunications operator and the state (including board representation and mechanisms for holding and voting shares).

The timing and sequence of privatization thus become matters of crucial importance. The incumbent management of the telecommunications operator and the state may not be ideally suited to undertake the important initial steps involved in privatization; however, interim steps toward introducing private investment into the telecommunications sector buy time to undertake the tough institutional and regulatory reforms necessary to assure the success of any privatization initiative. Moving too quickly to privatize a telecommunications operator on a top-down basis may ultimately diminish the value of the government's stake in the telecommunications operator. It may leave few options other than replacing government control with control by one or more outside investors.

Endnotes

1. A good discussion of the types of financing techniques which were used in France to catch up can be found in J. C. Deniaud, "Le rôle prioritaire des investissements en télécommunications pour le développement socio-économic," presented at the European Regional Telecommunications Development Conference, Prague, November 19–23, 1991.

2. Cooperative telephone companies have long had an important role in the Finnish telecommunications sector, which provides an interesting case study concerning how private telephone companies can coexist in a dynamic way with a traditional PTT. The Finnish cooperative movement is strong and influential; the Finnish cooperative form of organization may provide an interesting model for countries seeking to diversify the organizational structure of their telecommunications sectors and to create new opportunities for small-scale, market-driven enterprises. Such new enterprises might prod the traditional telecommunications organization into performing more efficiently; they might also provide a breeding ground for new cadres of entrepreneurially minded telecommunications managers. See also J. Taurianinen, "Cooperative Movement in Finland," *Fin Coop Pellervo*, 1990.

Part VII

Issues of Regulation

32

Regulation and Telecommunications Reform: Exploring the Alternatives

Richard J. Schultz

POLICYMAKERS CONTEMPLATING TELECOMMUNICATIONS sector reform must consider at least three distinct but interrelated and increasingly complex processes, namely, corporatization of a state enterprise; privatization; and establishing of a regulatory framework. Although not a prerequisite for restructuring that entails only corporatization, creating some form of regulatory system is unavoidable if privatization is undertaken, regardless of the extent or nature of competition, if any, that is to be permitted. No country to date has been prepared to transfer a public corporation into the private sector without imposing some degree of continuing public or social control over its activities.

The introduction or transformation of regulation is the most complex, and consequently controversial, of the reform processes because of the wide range of interrelated issues that must be resolved. These involve: fundamental questions about the nature of the regulatory role for the state in telecommunications; the objectives or purposes of that role; the specific regulatory instruments to be employed to perform that role; and, finally, questions about the appropriate public institutions and their interrelationships, both within the state and between the state and the private sector. This chapter presents a survey of the conceptual and analytical issues involved and describes some of the major alternative approaches employed by the countries which have undertaken the reform of their telecommunications sectors and which are discussed in this volume. No attempt is made either to evaluate these reforms or to offer particular prescriptions based on the experience of individual countries.

The Regulatory Role of the State

All economic systems, except perhaps the most primitive, require some regime for the social control of economic decisionmaking. The range of such regimes can be conceptualized as a continuum with markets at one end and public ownership at the other. Such a continuum is relevant to economic systems generally or to individual sectors of economic activity such as telecommunications. Our concern in this chapter is with the latter.

For markets, the social control regime is highly decentralized and dependent on voluntary private relations between buyers and sellers to determine which goods and services are produced and at what price and quality they are made available. There is no presumption that markets are derived from some state of economic "grace" or that the market is anything but a regime highly dependent on very sophisticated state or public initiatives, such as contract and patent law, to ensure that market control can operate effectively.[1]

Public ownership of the means of production of goods and services is a vastly different social control regime. Public ownership entails public, centralized, compulsory relations directed by the state, which determines the production of goods and services, the prices to be charged, and the quality of the specific transactions.

For most of the world, telecommunications services have traditionally been provided through public instruments, normally state monopolies. The assumption has been that, for a variety of reasons ranging from the high capital cost to the fundamental economic and social importance of the sector as one of society's infrastructures, telecommunications—like other comparable sectors such as transportation, broadcasting, and energy—is too important to rely on market or private forces, even if such forces could work effectively.

In North America, especially the United States, there has been much greater, indeed almost exclusive, reliance on markets as a economic social control system. The United States and Canada, however, confronted problems common to the rest of the world, namely, that markets could not effectively control some economic activities, such as telecommunications, because of the presumption that certain sectors were "natural monopolies" where it did not make economic sense to have more than one firm providing the service in a specific geographical area. Although North Americans had the choice of public ownership available to them (three Canadian provinces availed themselves of this option), an alternative to public ownership in the face of "market failure" had to be devised. This option was public regulation, wherein public authorities did not own the services but subjected private owners to detailed public scrutiny and surveillance. Private decisions on price, quality, and availability were regulated or subject to public approval.

Nations that are restructuring their telecommunications sectors, particularly if that involves privatization or the introduction of some competition, must come to grips with the complex world of regulation. It is complex because, despite all the discussion of regulation and deregulation, the basic concepts and issues are often not clearly understood even by those familiar with regulation as an instrument for social control.[2]

Evidence of the underlying confusion can be found in the commonplace description of regulation as "a substitute for competition where competition cannot presumably work" or alternatively as a "halfway house" between markets and public ownership; however, regulation has been both more and less than both these phrases suggest. It is vitally important that nations introducing regulation understand the multiple objectives, some at fundamental cross-purposes, that have been or can be pursued through regulatory controls. Failure to do so can frustrate or undermine the restructuring or reform process.

In the conventional North American view, regulation was introduced because markets could not work to discipline the economic actors—the telephone companies—providing telecommunications services. According to this perspective, absent regulation, privately owned telephone companies would be able to exploit their customers to earn monopoly profits and to engage in socially unacceptable forms of discrimination. Where the rest of the world generally opted for public ownership to address such problems, North American governments opted instead for the creation of an "economic policeman" to protect the interests of society. This, however, assigns regulation a much lesser role than that assumed by the phrase "substitute for competition."

Competition is expected to play a more comprehensive role, particularly with respect to promoting static and dynamic efficiency. From this perspective regulation was expected to act at best as a very partial, limited substitute for competition, inasmuch as it was really only supposed to prevent the more egregious abuses of monopoly power. Regulation's failure or intrinsic inability to perform a more positive role vis-à-vis productivity and efficiency has been a focus for attention in North America in recent years. This has resulted in a search for improvements or, increasingly, alternatives to replace regulation to compensate for this shortcoming.

If economic policing were the only objective of the regulatory system, introduction of regulation in other countries which opt for privatization would be relatively straightforward. Unfortunately, neither the North American regulatory tradition nor the contemporary circumstances within which most countries are contemplating the creation of a regulatory regime allow for such a one-dimensional appreciation of the nature of regulatory objectives. In particular, two issues are germane to any discussion of the regulatory role of the state in any restructured telecommunications sector. The first is an appreciation of the multiple objectives of traditional economic regulation. The second is an understanding of the need to adapt such regulation to the complex policy and economic environment confronting contemporary telecommunications, most notably the mix of monopoly and varying degrees of competitive provisioning of telecommunications services.

Turning to the first issue, although it is true that originally telecommunications regulation was introduced in both Canada and the United States, when it was presumed that competitive markets could not work, for the essentially negative reason of policing the behavior of the private companies, subsequently regulation was employed for more positive reasons—for promoting certain economic and social objectives. In particular, as a result of technological factors that dramatically lowered the cost of long-distance service, regulation became a central, if not the primary, instrument for the attainment of social policy objectives, notably universal service and subsidized local rates. Regulation in effect became the instrument for the taxation of some subscribers in order to confer benefits on others.[3] Where other countries used public ownership to accomplish this and other public policies, North America used economic regulation. This fact helps explain why reform of such regulation has been such a complex political undertaking. An appreciation of the multifaceted objectives pursued through regulatory means shows that regulation is neither neutral, impartial, nor even nonpolitical. Regulation in North America, to paraphrase von Clausewitz, has always been "politics by other means."

Notwithstanding the perspective of many economists who believe that regulation should be used only where competition cannot work, in Canada and the United States regulation in a number of sectors, most notably transportation, has historically been used because political actors did not want competition to work. Consequently they used regulation to promote the interests of particular producers or consumers.[4] Perhaps the clearest and most extensive example of this is found in Canadian regulation of the broadcasting sector where—in combination with public ownership of the largest broadcaster, the Canadian Broadcasting Corporation—the Canadian state has for more than six decades attempted to plan the roles and relationships for broadcasting to promote, among other things, national unity and, more recently, so-called cultural sovereignty.

The significance of the foregoing discussion in the context of contemporary debates about introducing regulation to other countries is that one should be wary of overly simplistic descriptions of regulation, and particularly prescriptions about its supposedly nonpolitical, impartial, limited role in those economies where regulation has been a cornerstone of the state's role in the telecommunications sector.

The multifaceted role of regulation as a primary instrument for achieving economic and social objectives in North America is especially relevant in current debates about reforming national telecommunications sectors worldwide. Most countries today face simultaneously a complex set of interrelated problems and issues that North American governments were able to address individually over a prolonged period of time.

The first is how to discipline or police the market power of dominant firms, especially those that have been or are in the process of being privatized. The second is how to provide for or encourage the widespread availability of telecommunications services. The third problem arises from the now conventional perspective that telecommunications is the modern railroad or "nervous system" of the economy and society at large. No society, even the most advanced, if the current American administration's concern about promoting the "economic telecommunications highway" is an indication, is prepared to rely solely or even primarily on market forces to produce economic results deemed to be so crucial to economic modernization.

Finally, to the extent that competition is permitted as part of a set of telecommunications reforms, states must come to grips with the complications resulting from the mix of monopoly and competitive services, particularly when the dominant firm provides both.[5] In such a situation the objectives of regulation are particularly complicated. One problem is how to prevent the incumbent firm from exploiting its market position to cross-subsidize from its monopoly to its competitive services and thereby undermine the introduction and spread of competition. A related problem is how to prevent the regulator from being drawn into the competitive battle by new entrants who want to exploit what in North America is known as "the regulation game" so as to strategically handicap the incumbent from effectively competing.[6] Because of their fear that such circumstances might hamper competition, some countries, most notably the United Kingdom and Australia, have legislatively imposed a positive function on their newly created regulatory agencies to promote competition.

OFTEL, for example, in the United Kingdom is required, in regulating telecommunications firms subject to its jurisdiction, to take due regard to "the desirability of maintaining and promoting competition. . . ."[7] This will inevitably lead to charges and countercharges of regulatory preference and partisanship, as it has in the United Kingdom among British Telecom, Mercury, and OFTEL. More important, it imposes on the regulator the complex task, even if it wishes to be neutral with respect to individual firms, of considering and seeking to balance a wide range of social, economic, and, unavoidably, political factors in its decisionmaking.

The purpose of the preceding survey of the complexities of regulation is not to be definitive nor to argue that regulation is the most appropriate governmental instrument to accomplish the wide-ranging objectives that have been and increasingly are asked of it. The most important point is to establish a recognition that regulation is far more complex than many assume. Policymakers should be cautioned against a too-easy acceptance of recommendations that presume that regulation is automatically or intrinsically nonpolitical, objective, or impartial. Although these are laudable goals, the record of regulation suggests that the purity some would advocate for regulatory regimes as instruments for the control of economic decisionmaking may be more apparent than real.

Alternative Regulatory Instruments

Choosing regulatory objectives and establishing some degree of balance or rank among them are only the first regulatory stages in reforming the telecommunications structure. The next stages are selecting the appropriate regulatory instruments and then establishing the desired institutional mix to pursue those regulatory objectives. In this section we address the former set of concerns.

When regulation had as its primary, if not sole, objective the control of monopoly abuses, the selection of regulatory instruments was relatively straightforward. Public authorities sought to control against abuse in three ways. Overall profit levels were established through the use of detailed scrutiny of the firm's rate or cost base. The instrument was some variant of rate-of-return, rate-base regulation where regulators examined the expenses of the firm, including a specified profit level, and then set a revenue requirement for the firm. The next stage was the approval of individual categories of rates to be charged the firm's customers to ensure that they were "just and reasonable" and did not involve any "undue discrimination." The third method was to permit customers of the monopoly firm to file complaints; the regulator would investigate these and issue a decision.

Although a few analysts maintain that monopoly regulation does not and cannot protect consumers from abuse, this is distinctly a minority position.[8] From the perspective of availability, reliability, and affordability, rate-of-return regulation appears to have served customers reasonably well. In addition to the lack of persuasive evidence that telephone companies in North America have earned excessive monopoly profits, a further measure of reasonable effectiveness is the fact that local residential rates, if the Canadian experience is any measure, have consistently increased more slowly than the inflation rate.

If traditional regulatory instruments have performed as a satisfactory constraint against corporate abuse, there is less persuasive evidence that they have adequately served as a "substitute for competition." As S.C. Littlechild noted in his report on possible forms of regulation for a privatized British Telecom (which led to the most significant innovation in regulatory instruments, namely price caps), regulation "is essentially a means for preventing the worst excesses of monopoly; it is not a substitute for competition."[9]

In particular, regulatory instruments have performed very badly in providing checks or incentives for regulated firms to be efficient, innovative, or improve their productivity. The central criticism of rate-of-return regulatory instruments has been that they are wholly inadequate for such tasks, in part because they are essentially negative in character. More important, they rest on "heroic assumptions" about the capacity of external actors, who have limited resources and are dependent on the regulated firm for information, to determine where and in what measure the firm could be induced to become more productive.

It is important to emphasize that negative assessments of regulatory instruments from the perspective of corporate productivity performance coincided over the past two decades with the introduction and extension of competition in traditionally monopolistic telecommunications markets. This resulted in the complex mix of objectives or public policy purposes discussed above and the search for means to reconcile conflicts among such objectives. Consequently, the search for alternative regulatory instruments has become intertwined with the larger questions of how to improve regulatory performance and how to design and implement new techniques for mixed monopoly-competitive sectors.

In particular, public policymakers have had to address the question of how to regulate telecommunications firms which have some monopoly markets and are active simultaneously in competitive markets. The issues involved are twofold. In the first place, the concern is how to protect monopoly subscribers from being forced to cross-subsidize competitive services. The second issue flows from the first, namely, how to protect competitors from anticompetitive conduct which will undermine the emerging competitive markets. Simultaneously, of course, the traditionally constrained regulated monopolist must be allowed to engage in legitimate competitive responses and not be handicapped by regulation.

A number of alternatives have been introduced in various jurisdictions in North America with varying success. For our purposes here, no attempt can be made to assess their success, and we will limit ourselves to providing a brief survey of some of the major instrumental responses. One has been outright prohibitions imposed on the incumbent firms from participating in specific markets. The most notable example of this was the line-of-business restrictions placed on AT&T after the 1956 antitrust settlement as well as those which followed the 1982 Consent Decree. In

Canada, for example, telephone companies have been prohibited from holding broadcasting licenses, including those for cable television.

Two other instruments have been structural separation and cost allocation systems. The former allows a traditional monopolist to enter competitive markets, but only through completely separate subsidiaries or separate corporate divisions within the firm. The use of such separation has been common in equipment sales as well as in the provision of cellular services by the telephone companies. Cost allocation systems have been developed in both Canada and the United States as an alternative to structural separations. These systems are designed to allocate costs among and between service categories as a means of ensuring that competitive services are not being subsidized by monopoly services.

Another new regulatory instrument is forbearance.[10] Although traditionally all companies providing telecommunications services have been subject to detailed regulatory surveillance, in some markets there has been a recognition that new entrants may possess no market power. Consequently regulators have opted to forbear or, at a minimum, place only the lightest of regulatory controls on these firms. This has subsequently led to the extension in some instances of light-handed regulation, even to the incumbent firms, when it is concluded that market forces offer an effective regulatory alternative to protect customers and competitors. Such forbearance is usually introduced in association with other instruments, such as separation and especially cost allocation systems.

Over the last twenty years, an attempt has been made to address the failure of traditional regulatory instruments to provide appropriate incentives for regulated firms to be as efficient as possible. The criticism is that since rate-of-return regulation is cost-plus regulation, firms have no incentive to reduce their costs or to use their available resources as productively as possible. Such regulation is said to send the wrong signals and encourages firms to overinvest in order to inflate their rate base.

Concerns over regulated firm productivity have been aggravated by privatizations because of the widespread perception that public sector firms are notoriously inefficient and that subjecting them to traditional regulation would only exacerbate the problems. Certainly this was a primary consideration in the U.K. government's rejection of traditional regulation for British Telecom and the search for new regulatory instruments. More recently, with the introduction of long-distance competition, even new entrants have argued that regulation must address the productivity of incumbents. The reason for their concern is straightforward. As long as the local telephone service remains a monopoly and new entrants must pay for interconnection to this service, they want their payments to be as low as possible. Encouraging the reduction of local service costs through productivity gains reduces the amount they must pay, especially when their interconnection costs include some element of cross-subsidy to keep local telephone rates at levels below their costs.

To respond to the productivity issues as well as to the recognition that traditional profit regulation may no longer be necessary to protect residential telephone customers from monopoly exploitation, a variety of so-called incentive regulatory instruments have been introduced. These normally involve some degree of rate freeze or moratorium to protect local subscribers with the firms allowed pricing flexibility on competitive services. The assumption is that if the firms can keep all or most of the benefits from cost cutting and efficiency gains, then they will seek to be as efficient as possible. These instruments have the added attraction of removing both the incentive and the opportunity of cross-subsidizing competitive services from monopoly service revenues.

The most imaginative new instrument to address the productivity issue is the price-cap mechanism, originally introduced for British Telecom and subsequently adapted for American and other telecommunications companies. Unlike other incentive schemes, which simply provide an incentive for productivity improvements, price caps make such improvements a mandatory part of the regulatory system.[11]

Although oversimplified, the essential features of any price-cap system are fourfold. First, services are divided into regulated and unregulated categories, with the latter not subject to regulatory control. Second, regulated services are subdivided into individual baskets according to some established criteria, such as relatedness and degree of competition. Third, the firm is given considerable but not necessarily complete freedom to price the services within individual baskets subject to an overall cap or maximum annual increase on the average price of the services in the basket. The fourth characteristic is the most significant: any increase is limited to the rate of increase in the designated rate of inflation, less a specified annual productivity adjustment to reflect the gains in productivity expected for the telecommunications sector over a period of time.

Regulatory Institutions

The third major area of telecommunications reform has been in the design of regulatory institutions. The growth and complexity of regulatory objectives and the experimentation with regulatory instruments have arisen at a time of continuing political saliency as a result of privatization and especially the introduction of varying degrees of competition in the provision of telecommunications. This has meant that what were once mundane concerns of regulatory structure have become hotly contested issues.

In North America, where regulation was the chosen instrument of public control, a standard institutional framework has been employed. This framework involves a courtlike, collegial, or collective agency whose members are to act impartially in balancing the interests of the regulated firm and its customers. Given the original limited public objectives, this framework worked reasonably satisfactorily in meeting the demands for transparent, nonpolitical, and, most important for private firms, stable and predictable regulation.

The independent regulatory agency continues to be the instrument of choice for North America, although subject to increasing political scrutiny and involvement as a result of the growing politicization of the telecommunications sector. Two particular innovations have been debated. One, reflecting the compound set of policies to be pursued through regulatory initiatives, has been the political directive. This instrument, which was introduced in Canada, enables political authorities such as the cabinet to issue instructions to the regulatory agency not on individual cases but on the interpretation or ranking of the broad set of legislative objectives. The other innovation is to transfer actual licensing decisions to political authorities such as the minister of communications and to confine the regulatory body to an advisory role. Both adjustments in the relationship between traditionally independent regulators and their political masters have been controversial because of the fear of partiality and political interference which may ensue. On the other hand, it should be noted that ministerial regulation has continued to be the arrangement for countries such as Germany, France, and Japan.

Three major institutional innovations in regulation in other countries are worth noting insofar as they represent alternatives to addressing the problems of multiple objectives and the need for experimentation in regulatory instruments. The first is the British model where a single regulator, OFTEL, has been appointed to oversee the sector. In the British case a government minister continues to have licensing authority but the director general of telecommunications has advisory and enforcement powers. Of particular significance in the British approach is that the North American quasi-judicial public model has given way to a private or confidential negotiating role for the regulator. The significance of this, especially combined with OFTEL's statutory duty to promote competition, is that it has led to charges and countercharges that OFTEL is partisan and prone to interfering in corporate activities.

The United Kingdom has also introduced another modification in the regulatory structure by establishing what has been described as competition between regulators.[12] In the British case, not only is regulatory authority shared between a minister and OFTEL, but if the latter wishes to amend a condition of license for British Telecom, the company may lodge an appeal with the Monopolies and Mergers Commission. This is one check against arbitrary behavior on the part of OFTEL.

Australia has introduced a variant of the British model, employing a more collegial independent regulatory agency similar to that found in North America to directly oversee its telecommunications sector. Instead of competition between different agencies, Australia has sought to impose a more collaborative approach by making cross-appointments between AUSTEL, its telecommunications regulatory body, and the Trade Practices Commission, the agency responsible for enforcing its competition policies. This model seeks to have a specialized telecommunications regulator, but one that is institutionally required to give appropriate emphasis to the promotion and protection of competition in telecommunications.

The third institutional approach is that adopted by New Zealand following the privatization of its telecommunications company and opening up the sector to competitive entry. New Zealand rejected both the North American independent agency and the British single regulator models and opted to rely solely on its competition authorities, in this case the Commerce Commission, to regulate the emerging marketplace. Recently this approach has been criticized by both new entrants and by the Commerce Commission itself on the grounds that both the competition law and the commission are inadequate.

Conclusion

Reforms to the telecommunications sector of any country that include privatization or the introduction of competition to segments of the sector inevitably lead to regulatory issues. These are complex and controversial and involve not only the most basic questions about the purposes and roles of the state but also about the most appropriate instruments and institutional arrangements to pursue those roles. Although some commentators have suggested that the resolution of these issues can be relatively straightforward, namely that governments must create objective, impartial, transparent regulatory regimes, the experience of countries familiar with regulatory forms of economic control argues against assumptions that these objectives are easily attained. Regulatory forms and processes operative in one country may not be easily transferred to others with different institutional, political, and economic histories.

Governments that seek or are compelled to adopt regulatory control systems must come to appreciate that the determination of regulatory objectives is now much more complex than when regulation was introduced in North America. Many of the contemporary objectives are in conflict with one another, and the first task is to develop some means to reconcile such conflicts and establish an appropriate ranking. Similarly, traditional regulatory instruments must be subject to a critical assessment to determine their relevance to contemporary regulatory needs. Finally, the classic North American regulatory institution, the quasi-judicial collective regulatory agency, is not the only alternative available as countries experiment with new institutional designs.

The diversity of circumstances facing the multitude of countries attempting to reform their telecommunications sectors to confront contemporary issues and realities argues against single, and especially simple, solutions. The complexity of the problems of telecommunications reform and restructuring, combined with an acceptance of the imperfections associated with any form of social control, should encourage caution. In searching for regulatory reforms that can meet the needs of diverse national circumstances, those who seek to introduce reform, and those who would urge specific courses on them, should heed the following advice from an experienced and perceptive observer of the regulatory process:

> The right mix of regulation and competition is not easily determined. . . . Good policy decisions turn more on common sense than on the unthinking transference of precedents. Certainly emotional attachments to either free markets or to regulatory processes stand in the way of good policy decisions. The most sagacious of us will err, and it is well that we occasionally acknowledge mistakes and plot new courses.[13]

Endnotes

1. See, for example, Richard R. Nelson, "Roles of Government in a Mixed Economy," *Journal of Policy Analysis and Management*, vol. 6, no. 4 (1987); and Roderick A. Macdonald, "Understanding Regulation by Regulations," in *Regulations, Crown Corporations and Administrative Tribunals*, ed. Ivan Bernier and Andree Lajoie (Toronto: University of Toronto Press, 1985).

2. For a discussion of some of the conceptual ambiguities and conflicts surrounding even basic terms such as *privatization* and *deregulation*, see Richard J. Schultz, "Privatization, Deregulation and the Changing Role of the State," *Business in the Contemporary World*, autumn 1990, pp. 25–32.

3. This is a basic point made by R. A. Posner in "Taxation by Regulation," *The Bell Journal of Economics and Management Science*, vol. 2, no. 1 (1971).

4. This is explored in much greater detail in Richard J. Schultz and Alan Alexandroff, *Economic Regulation and the Federal System* (Toronto: University of Toronto Press, 1985).

5. See, for example, Giandomenico Majone, ed., *Deregulation or Re-regulation? Regulatory Reform in Europe and the United States* (New York: St. Martin's Press, 1990), especially the chapter by John Kay and John Vikers, "Regulatory Reform: An Appraisal."

6. The term was popularized by B. M. Own and R. Braeutigam, *The Regulation Game: Strategic Use of the Administrative Process* (Cambridge, Mass.: Bassinger Publishing Co., 1978).

7. M. E. Beesley and S. C. Littlechild, "The Regulation of Privatized Monopolies in the United Kingdom," *RAND Journal of Economics*, vol. 20, no. 3 (autumn 1989), pp. 454–72.

8. The strongest criticism of rate-of-return regulation is found in Nina W. Cornell and Douglas W. Webbink, "Public Utility Rate-of-Return Regulation: Can It Ever Protect Customers?" in *Unnatural Monopolies: The Case for De-regulating Public Utilities*, ed. Robert W. Pool, Jr. (Lexington, Mass: Lexington Books, 1985).

9. S. C. Littlechild, *Regulation of British Telecommunication's Profitability* (London: Department of Industry, 1983).

10. See Hudson N. Janisch and Bohdan S. Romaniuk, "The Quest for Regulatory Forbearance in Telecommunications," *Ottawa Law Review*, 1985.

11. The most useful introduction to the principles and mechanism of price-cap regulation as it pertains to British privatized firms is found in M. E. Beesley and S. C. Littlechild, "The Regulation of Privatized Monopolies in the United Kingdom," *RAND Journal of Economics*, vol. 20, no. 3 (autumn 1989), pp. 454–72.

12. See John Kay and John Vickers, "Regulatory Reform: An Appraisal," in *Deregulation or Re-regulation? Regulatory Reform in Europe and the United States*, ed. Giandomenico Majone (New York: St. Martin's Press, 1990).

13. Almarin Phillips, "Antitrust Principles and Regulatory Needs," *The Antitrust Bulletin*, 1990.

33

Regulation: Reconciling Policy Objectives

Nicholas P. Miller

TELECOMMUNICATIONS RESTRUCTURING IN the 1990s is a worldwide phenomenon. Faced with serious consumer and competitive demands on telephone enterprises, governments are struggling to find answers. The traditional government-operated telephone utility has not performed well in the face of rapidly changing technology, rapidly changing prices for competitive alternatives, and a revolution of increasing consumer and private sector demands for new, better, and faster telecommunications services. Under this pressure, many governments are restructuring their telecommunications sectors. Developing countries are examining a range of alternatives to improve incentives for efficiency and consumer responsiveness in their telecommunications sectors. The restructuring actions fall within two broad categories: opening the sector to additional participants besides the traditional monopoly telephone company; and reorganizing the traditional telephone company itself to make it more commercial in character.[1] It is the thesis of this chapter that whatever the form of restructuring, the government must implement appropriate regulatory oversight of the restructured sector and company.

Restructuring Alone Is Insufficient

Restructuring the telecommunications sector, including commercializing the telephone enterprise, addresses only half the problem. The other half is to maintain appropriate government controls over the telecommunications sector to ensure that the new structure achieves the purposes intended by the government.

In general, privatization of government-owned enterprises and withdrawal of government intervention in an economic sector has worked well in sectors and industries traditionally operated by nongovernmental entities and subject to normal marketplace competitive forces. Telecommunications are different. Competition does not exist in the local telephone distribution facility.[2] This is true whether the telephone enterprise is privately or publicly owned, whether it holds a legally mandated monopoly or is legally subject to competition. A law opening a sector to competition does not create competition. It only permits competition if the economics of the marketplace will sustain more than one operator. No one today seriously argues that any local telephone company is threatened by a competitor's building a duplicate local switching and wire distribution network. In other words, there is no evidence that the local exchange distribution facilities are subject to effective competition, no matter how much government policymakers might wish otherwise.

This lack of effective competition in the local telephone distribution network may change in time,[3] but effective competition for basic local telephone service remains a hope for the future, not a reality of the present. As long as full and fair competition with open market entry and exit for local exchange distribution remains a hope for the future, there is no alternative to continued government intervention in the market for telephony. The marketplace alone cannot drive the local exchange telephone company to provide fair competition, fair prices, and high-quality service. As an economist would say, the local telephone network is still a natural monopoly with declining marginal costs to provide additional services. Therefore, there are no marketplace incentives forcing the company toward economically efficient allocation of resources.

Restructuring Requires Regulation External to the Company

The country seriously considering restructuring will typically display a set of common characteristics. The government-owned telephone company will have generally poor operating characteristics (in the form of unresponsive service, under-capitalized investment, and an inefficient work force). Its pricing structure for services will be badly distorted by political considerations to favor certain users, equipment manufacturers, or labor groups. Normally, the central economic planners will have identified the underdevelopment of the telecommunications sector as a major drag on general economic development, and the business community and local subscribers will have expressed high levels of frustration with the inadequate service.

This set of circumstances leads to the real need to commercialize the company— to restructure so it operates like a business, not a government bureaucracy. Not every alternative will be better than the status quo. Restructuring is pointless unless it holds the prospect of better serving several important and simultaneous goals. The country has a right to expect the following benefits from commercialization:

- Improved management and operational efficiency in the company resulting in reduced operating costs

- Improved strategic business planning and implementation of new technologies

- Accelerated investment in high-capacity, high-revenue services, and improved services to business users

- Maintaining and expanding the asset value of the company

- Removing day-to-day operations from the national political process

- Reducing financial demands on the company to support the national budget.

The country has additional expectations for its telephone service. Presumably, most countries will want:

- Aggressive reinvestment of earned capital to expand the geographical reach and quality of the basic network

- Individual service prices to reflect the cost of that service

- Limited and occasional explicit subsidies to particular user groups, such as low-density rural areas, where necessary to achieve an important national developmental or social equity goal

- Stable or reduced prices to all classes of customers

- Expansion of competition throughout the telecommunications sector wherever possible to assure economically efficient allocation of resources by the sector.

This list is interesting because each item, including the expansion of competition, promises to reduce the profitability of the operating monopoly. One would assume that a well-managed, strategically minded company would not voluntarily undertake such actions which promise to reduce its net cash flow and its value to its owners.[4]

Adding efficiencies to the internal operations of the company by itself will not remove the monopoly power of the local exchange operator. Commercialization may provide the company the ability to generate greater profits. But the company has no incentive to apply those profits to broadly improved service or to reduce its prices to levels reflected by the cost of serving monopoly customers. As a result, commercialization without outside incentives to the company to be socially responsible can turn an inefficient operation into a politically intolerable one.[5]

This dilemma must be acknowledged and addressed in telecommunications restructuring. Otherwise a country is doomed to swing between the pendulum extremes of socially unresponsive private operators and nationalized services. Governments must create a system of dual incentives. The company must be commercialized and given internal incentives to improve its operating efficiency as a business enterprise. The government must accept its responsibility to set appropriate limits and guidelines for the company through external incentives which force actions by the company that will reduce the company's overall potential profitability as a monopoly. In other words, the company must be regulated on two fronts—internally through profit maximization incentives, and externally through government-imposed restrictions wherever internal profit maximization incentives do not correspond with the country's or the telecommunications sector's overall interests.

External Regulation Comes in Two Forms

The best form of regulation of any business enterprise is the threat of effective competition in the marketplace.[6] But an essential portion of the telecommunications sector, the local telephone distribution facility, is not subject to effective competition. Where the marketplace cannot establish and enforce social equity and economically efficient resource allocation, the only alternative is for the government to establish the rules directly and then resolve complaints of violations of those rules. This substitutes, albeit imperfectly, for the discipline of competition.

Expressed in these terms, government regulation sounds like normal governmental action: adopt the law and then enforce it. But government, in the form of legislatures and courts, are slow moving, unable to draw narrow distinctions, and reactive to the loudest and most powerful political forces in the society. This is not a formula likely to be a close substitute for competition in compelling economically efficient behavior in the high-technology, fast-moving, consumer-driven world of telecommunications.

Telecommunications regulation requires a new, lighter-handed government agent to exercise the traditional governmental powers of rule making and adjudication. The agent should:

- Be independent of day-to-day government political pressure

- Be independent of the telephone company and the users of the telephone company's services (including the government)

- Provide a transparent, open, honest, and accessible process for considering new rules and resolving disputes

- Perform competent analysis of all the relevant facts

- Be subject to the discipline of the national goals as expressed in statutes

- Give quick decisions consistent with the fast-changing nature of the telecommunications sector

- Engage in consistent and predictable behavior that removes unnecessary risk and uncertainty from the sector.

Every nation that currently has a serious and credible independent regulatory agency overseeing the telecommunications sector, such as Great Britain, the United States, Canada, and Australia, has chosen somewhat different ways for achieving these goals.

The successes, however, show significant common denominators. The successful countries have created agencies that have a professional, politically independent staff who are paid adequate salaries, are given adequate training, and hold to the highest standards of civil service integrity and efficiency. The agencies are fully competent in the necessary disciplines of policy analysis, financial and accounting analysis, and economic, legal, and engineering analysis. These agencies have created processes for receiving public comment and resolving complaints which both are fair and appear to be fair to the carriers and to the user community. These agencies have complete access to the information required to reach sound decisions and have mechanisms to assure this information is presented to the decisionmaker in a manner that does not give unfair advantage to the economically most powerful parties in the dispute.

However, the best laboratories and computer analyses, the best salaries and working circumstances do not always guarantee quality results. Only quality decisionmakers, given quality support, will perform reasonably well. As personnel change, even the best agencies ebb and flow in quality. Therefore, ultimately, the sine qua non of good regulation is a political commitment by the national government to appoint good people to run the regulatory agency and then to stay out of the way.

Crucial Organization and Decision Elements Necessary for Successful Regulation

Several crucial organization and decision elements are necessary for successful regulation. First, the agency must be properly staffed and funded. It must be given strong, independent leadership by a credible and politically secure leader of national stature. Regulation of a national telephone company is a very complex political problem, and progressive decisions are impossible unless properly equipped persons of integrity and stature make the tough decisions independent of day-to-day political pressures.

Second, the agency must be given a definite legal mandate with stated national goals. This mandate should define the basic objectives for the telecommunications sector, the general sector framework, and the scope of discretion allowed the agency. The law should empower the agency to enforce its decisions and should command the fairest of procedures and processes.

Third, there are difficult decisions as to the scope of monopoly and competition to be implemented as part of any restructuring. The typical developing country has significant problems associated with inadequate capitalization and an undeveloped basic network. The policy dilemma is how to get high-quality, business-oriented services up and operating quickly, relying on the forces of competition, while leaving enough of the core business available to the new telephone company to be able to generate the capital to expand and develop the entire network. In other words, a bright line between monopoly and competitive services is not self-evident. The regulator must be given discretion to move this line as needed to take advantage of the benefits of competition, consistent with network development.

Fourth, specific devices should be created to prevent the agency from being captured by the interests of the telephone company, which will push for less regulation and less competition to achieve higher cash flows and a higher telephone company value.[7] The regulation process has to balance this pressure with the need to truly protect consumers and to protect competitors of the telephone company from unfair business practices.

And finally, countries setting up new regulatory agencies should use the advice and experience of others. Countries with regulatory experience can help an interested country avoid most of the typical mistakes. The problems are common to all. The solutions will be unique to each country, its political culture, its legal processes, its size and level of telecommunications development, and the scope of activities it assigns the agency. For example, an agency responsible for broadcasting and electronic media regulations as well as frequency management will require a different organization and skill mix than one looking solely at telephone issues. Annexes A and B to this chapter provide useful examples of two United States regulatory agencies. The Federal Communications Commission (FCC) operates on a budget of about US$70 million and regulates all electronic media, telecommunications licenses, and equipment certifications in the United States. It has created relatively efficient and transparent decisionmaking processes to handle the most complex telecommunications regulatory questions in the world. The much smaller Public Service Commission of the District of Columbia regulates all the public utilities (electric, gas, and telephone) serving the city of Washington, DC, with a resident population of 350,000. Its telephone responsibilities are exclusively to oversee the rates and service of a single local exchange company of annual revenues of US$500 million. Annex B describes the level of detail and types of actions this commission finds necessary to execute on its responsibilities.

The Task of Regulation

Effective regulation is a daunting task. The following is a sample and partial listing of necessary projects a country will face in organizing and starting up a new telecommunications regulatory agency:

- Prepare the proposed telecommunications sector rules with respect to:

  - Pricing of services

  - Quality and conditions of service

  - Network interconnection

  - Provision of leased lines for resale

  - Approval of network facilities

  - Approval of resellers

- Application of technical standards

- Sale of terminal equipment.

• Identify the procedures, activities, functions, and information necessary to undertake the above regulatory tasks.

• Build a minimum core of expertise in four areas, namely: regulatory policy; price, cost, and financial analysis; quality of service, investment program, technical equipment; and administrative, legal, and information systems.

• Build a capability to develop and implement regulatory policies with respect to:

- Licensing of telecommunications networks facilities

- Licensing of resellers and other competitive service providers

- Provision of leased lines

- Anticompetitive or unduly discriminatory behavior by facilities-based service providers

- Network interconnection and revenue settlement arrangements

- Other regulatory issues.

• Build a financial analytical capability to:

- Monitor, analyze, and approve or reject tariff proposals

- Review financial projections of service providers and develop a financial model of the operating companies to forecast rates of return and other financial indicators; and review methodologies and estimate the costs of providing telecommunications services.

• Build a capability to set criteria for service, investment program, technical standards, and terminal equipment:

- Establish performance indicators and systems to monitor results

- Assess the operating companies' investment program, depreciation, and procurement policies

- Establish, monitor, and enforce technical standards for networks (including national fundamental technical plans) and terminal equipment.

- Build the necessary administrative, legal, and information systems:

  - Operate modern administrative systems for both externally-oriented needs (for example, processing of license applications, regulatory proceedings) and internal requirements (such as personnel, finance, supplies)

  - Provide in-house legal advice and undertake legal actions in support of agency operations

  - Establish and maintain information systems to support the agency's operations.[8]

Conclusion

Restructuring requires creating internal and external incentives for improving service in the telecommunications sector. Commercialization, and possibly privatization, promises substantial managerial improvements in a telephone company. Expansion of competition wherever possible in the telecommunications sector promises additional economic efficiency by the sector's service providers; however, important facilities are, and will probably remain, a monopoly for the relevant future regardless of government action to expand competition. This requires government regulation as a substitute for the discipline of competition. Industrial countries have had successful experiences with telecommunications sector regulation. No single model is perfect, but integrity, skill, adequate resources, specific national goals, reasonable regulatory discretion, and unbiased decisionmaking processes are common denominators of success. These are the principles to measure a country's success in restructuring its telecommunications sector.

In the words of one U.S. regulator:

> It is no secret to any of us that regulation is not glamorous. . . . Organizational effectiveness is concerned with doing the right things. . . . Regulators need to be taking steps now to build an effective organization, one that is responsive to the changes coming in the next decade. Regulators must create an organizational vision and structure that will enrich and sustain the organization throughout the next decade. The process of organizational development is slow; results take time to generate. Steps which are taken now may not pay off for five or six years. However, if those steps are not taken, there will be a price to pay.[9]

Annex A: The Federal Communications Commission*

Composition and Functions

The Federal Communications Commission (FCC) is an independent federal administrative agency created by the U.S. Congress, and empowered under the Communications Act of 1934 to regulate U.S. interstate and international telecommunications. Prior to 1934, U.S. telecommunications was regulated by the Interstate Commerce Commission. The FCC consists of five commissioners, four divisional bureaus (Common Carrier, Mass Media, Private Radio, and Field Operations), eight offices and a Review Board. It has a staff of about 1,800. FCC commissioners are appointed to five-year terms by the President of the United States, subject to Senate approval. No more than three commissioners may be from a single political party. While the President also designates the chairman, the agency is not bound to support administration positions and occasionally refuses to do so.

FCC commissioners may raise issues on their own initiative, while other policies are suggested by studies of the Office of Plans and Policy, or by the main bureaus often in response to stakeholders' requests. The commissioners may act through Rule Making, Notices of Inquiry (NOIs), Notices of Proposed Rule Makings (NPRMs), adjudication, or even speeches. The primary sources of policy are the Policy and Program Planning Division within the Common Carrier Bureau, the Policy and Rules Division within the Mass Media Bureau, and the Office of International Communications. The commissioners and their bureaus and offices also serve as enforcers and adjudicators of rules and regulations.

Because they can be overruled by Congressional legislation and, more important, because they depend on Congressional funding, FCC commissioners have traditionally been very sensitive to the wishes of Congress. Nevertheless, they have opposed Congressional will on occasion when they believed that the President or the courts would support their decisions.

Many have complained that the FCC has been captured by the industries it regulates. However, this may only reflect the superior quantity and quality of information that industries are able to present to it to justify their positions. Despite the existence of the Office of Plans and Policy, some complain that the agency does not have the funding to carry out the necessary long-range policy planning. Another criticism is that the predominance of legal and administrative backgrounds of the FCC commissioners leads the FCC to view regulatory activities in a legal and administrative way, rather than in broader social and economic terms.

---

*Mark S. Nadel, Attorney, Policy Division, FCC Common Carrier Bureau, "US Communications Policy Making: Who and Where," *Hastings Communications and Entertainment Law Journal*, vol. 13, no. 2 (Winter 1991), pp. 273–323.

Figure 33–1. Federal Communications Commission Organization Chart

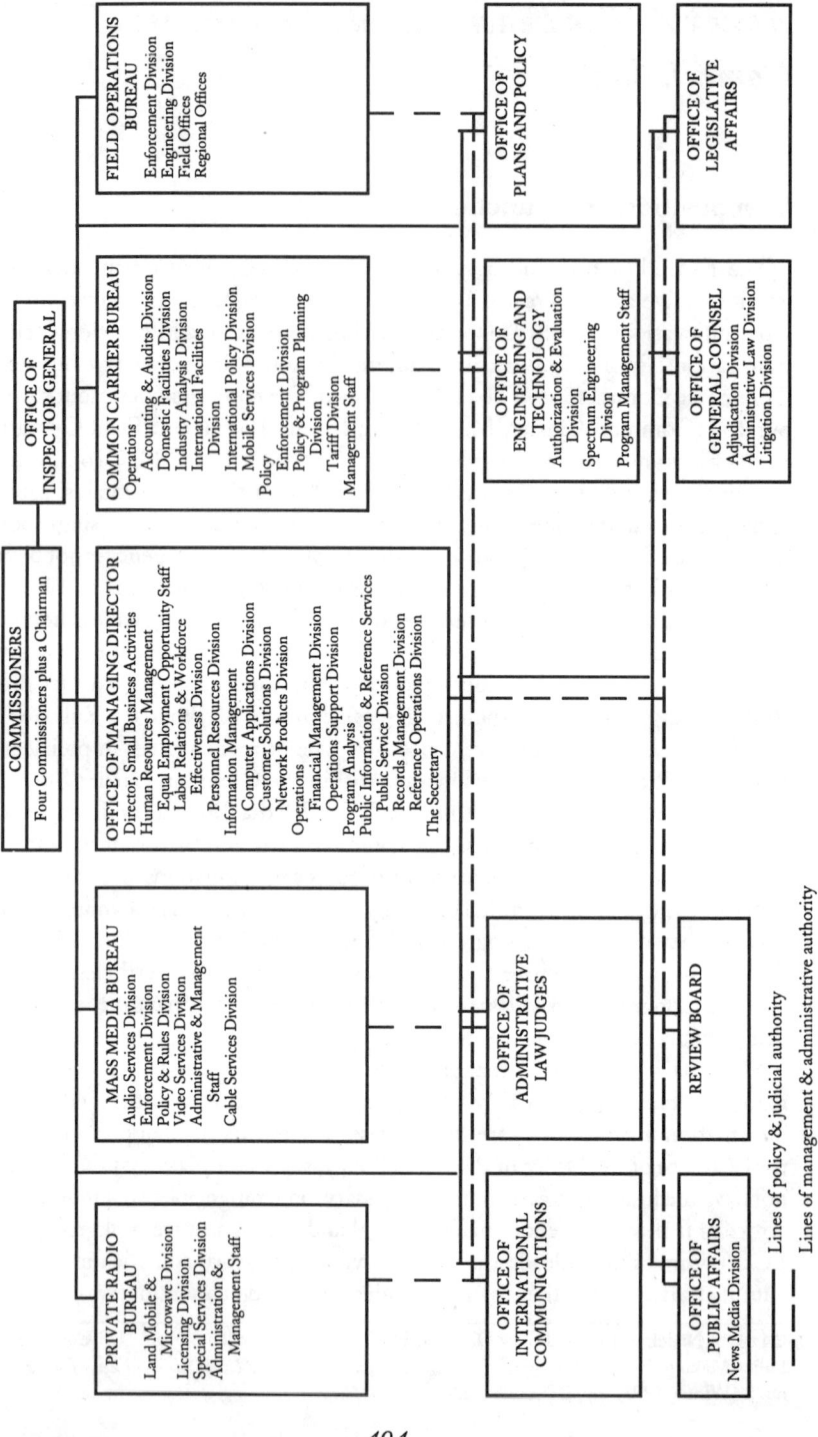

COMMISSIONERS
Four Commissioners plus a Chairman

OFFICE OF INSPECTOR GENERAL

PRIVATE RADIO BUREAU
Land Mobile & Microwave Division
Licensing Division
Special Services Division
Administration & Management Staff

MASS MEDIA BUREAU
Audio Services Division
Enforcement Division
Policy & Rules Division
Video Services Division
Administrative & Management Staff
Cable Services Division

OFFICE OF MANAGING DIRECTOR
Director, Small Business Activities
Human Resources Management
  Equal Employment Opportunity Staff
  Labor Relations & Workforce Effectiveness Division
  Personnel Resources Division
Information Management
  Computer Applications Division
  Customer Solutions Division
  Network Products Division
Operations
  Financial Management Division
  Operations Support Division
Program Analysis
Public Information & Reference Services
  Public Service Division
  Records Management Division
  Reference Operations Division
The Secretary

COMMON CARRIER BUREAU
Operations
  Accounting & Audits Division
  Domestic Facilities Division
  Industry Analysis Division
  International Facilities Division
  International Policy Division
  Mobile Services Division
Policy
  Enforcement Division
  Policy & Program Planning Division
  Tariff Division
Management Staff

FIELD OPERATIONS BUREAU
Enforcement Division
Engineering Division
Field Offices
Regional Offices

OFFICE OF INTERNATIONAL COMMUNICATIONS

OFFICE OF ADMINISTRATIVE LAW JUDGES

REVIEW BOARD

OFFICE OF ENGINEERING AND TECHNOLOGY
Authorization & Evaluation Division
Spectrum Engineering Division
Program Management Staff

OFFICE OF PLANS AND POLICY

OFFICE OF PUBLIC AFFAIRS
News Media Division

OFFICE OF GENERAL COUNSEL
Adjudication Division
Administrative Law Division
Litigation Division

OFFICE OF LEGISLATIVE AFFAIRS

———— Lines of policy & judicial authority

– – – – Lines of management & administrative authority

494

How Rules are Made at the FCC

Suggestions for changes to the FCC rules and regulations can come from sources outside of the Commission either by formal petition, legislation, court decision, or informal suggestion.[10] In addition, a bureau or office within the FCC can initiate a rule making proceeding on its own.

When a petition for rule making is received, it is sent to the appropriate bureau(s) or office(s) for evaluation. If a bureau or office decides a particular petition is meritorious, it can request that Dockets assign a rule making number to the petition. A similar request is made when a bureau or office decides to initiate a rule making procedure on its own. A weekly notice is issued listing all accepted petitions for rule making: the public has thirty days to submit comments. The bureau or office then has the option of generating an agenda item requesting one of four actions by the Commission. If a Notice of Inquiry (NOI) or a Notice of Proposed Rule Making (NPRM) is issued, a Docket is instituted, and a Docket number is assigned.

Major changes to the rules are presented to the public as either an NOI or an NPRM. The Commission will issue an NOI when it is simply asking for information on a broad subject or trying to generate ideas on a given topic: an NPRM is issued when a specific change to the rules is being proposed. If an NOI is issued, it must be followed by either an NPRM or a Memorandum Order & Opinion (MO&O) concluding the inquiry.

When an NOI or NPRM has been issued, the public is given the opportunity to present comments and then to reply to the comments made by others. If the Commission does not receive sufficient comments to make a decision, a further NOI or NPRM may be issued, again calling for comments and replies. On rare occasions the Commission conducts an open en banc hearing on a major issue.

After the Commission has issued on Order the proceeding may be terminated. Petitions for reconsideration may be filed by the public within thirty days after an Order is released. These petitions are reviewed by the appropriate bureau(s)/office(s) and/or by the Commission. As a result of its review of a petition for reconsideration, the Commission may issue a MO&O modifying its initial decision or denying the petition for reconsideration. The Commission may, on its own initiative, also issue additional Orders in the Docket.

Figure 33-2. Federal Communications Commission Flow Chart

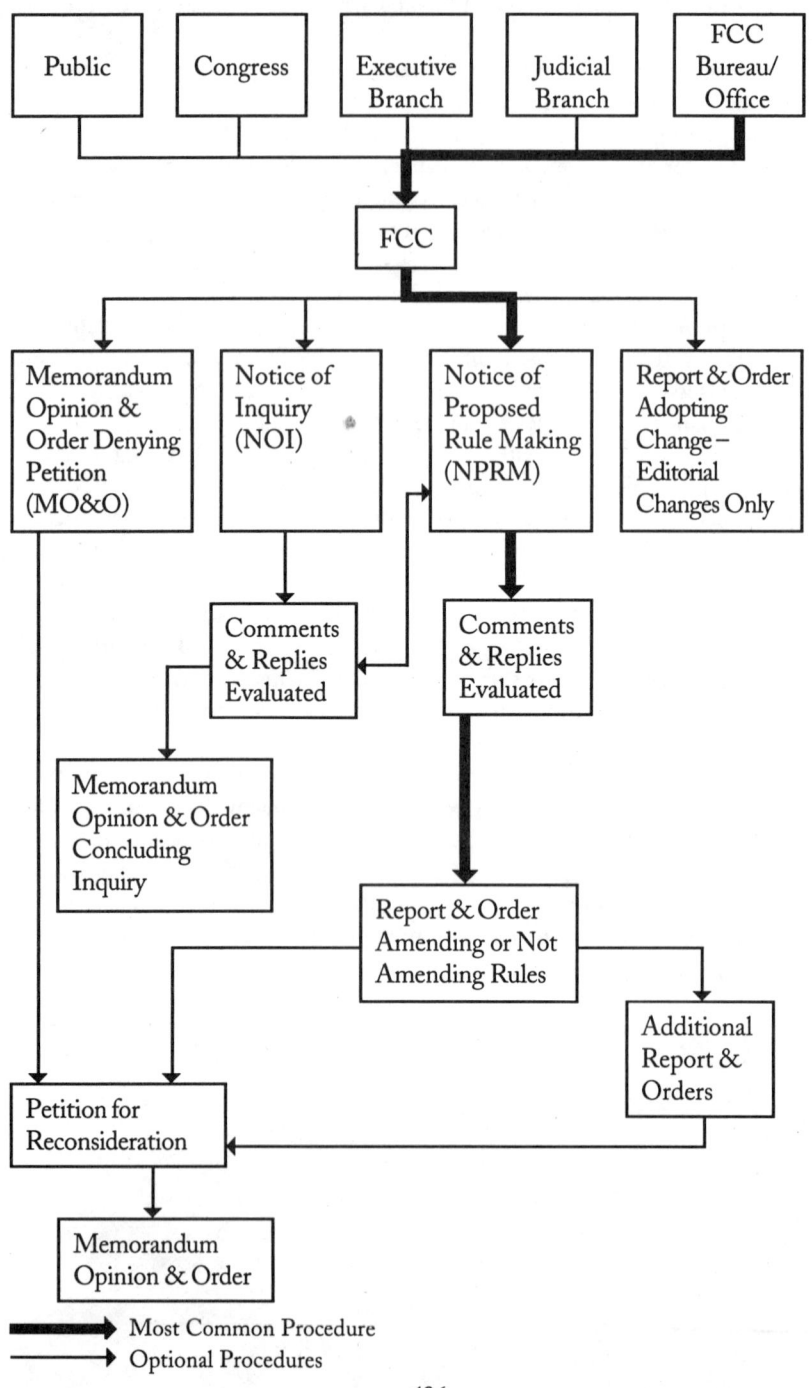

Annex B: Public Service Commission of the District of Columbia (Washington, DC)

Functions of the Commission

The District of Columbia Public Service Commission is an independent regulatory agency established by Congress in 1913. By law, the Commission has ratemaking and other regulatory authority over the electric, natural gas, and telephone companies. It also regulates tourist vehicles for hire, all securities transactions taking place in the District of Columbia, and customer-owned coin-operated telephones.

The Commission is headed by three full-time commissioners appointed to four-year terms by the mayor, with the advice and consent of the Council of the District of Columbia. The commissioners sit as a body in hearings upon applications for rate and service changes proposed by the utility companies. A support staff of over seventy technical, legal, professional, and clerical employees assists the commissioners in conducting research and investigations and in analyzing financial and operating data.

The primary responsibility of the Commission is to ensure safe, reliable, and quality utility service at the lowest possible cost. It conducts hearings and investigations into utility company charges and operations in order to determine just and reasonable rates in accordance with the needs of District utility consumers.

In order to carry out its responsibilities the Commission performs three types of functions—legislative, judicial, and administrative. First, the Commission legislates or authorizes utility rates and sets rules and guidelines for the regulated companies. Second, the Commission acts in a quasi-judicial capacity, deciding whether existing rates are no longer adequate, by conducting formal rate and investigatory cases, and by holding hearings on consumer complaints. Third, the Commission's administrative functions include analyzing regularly filed utility company reports and implementing Commission orders.

The bulk of the Commission's work relates to formal matters such as rate cases, utility bond and stock offerings, construction plans of the utilities, civil proceedings on the licensing of securities broker-dealers and agents in the District of Columbia, and investigatory cases such as management and conservation audits.

Informal consumer complaint cases also account for an important part of the Commission's dockets. These cases usually arise from consumer grievances regarding the quality of service or billing problems. In 1979, the Commission instituted a Consumer Bill of Rights. This Bill of Rights expanded consumers' rights and set up a model for the relationship between the utility company and the ratepayers. The Commission also promulgated uniform rules which govern the standards of conduct and billing practices of the gas, electric, and telephone companies in the provision of residential and commercial utility service in the District of Colombia.

Departmental Responsibilities

The executive director plans, directs, coordinates, and manages the internal affairs of the Commission on a day-to-day basis under the broad direction of the chairman.

This office coordinates and supervises staff activities in rate cases and generic proceedings; plans and implements policies and directives of the Commission; prepares budgets to the mayor, Council of the District of Columbia, and United States Congress; and is responsible for personnel and fiscal operations.

The *Office of the General Council* consists of the general counsel, staff counsels, and support staff. It serves as the legal adviser to the Commission, which entails many functions. It represents the Commission staff in formal cases (those proceedings involving major utility ratemaking, financial, and other investigatory issues), and tariff proceedings (such as filings by the Chesapeake and Potomac Telephone Company, the single local exchange company that the Commission regulates, to amend certain aspects of telephone service); represents the Commission before federal agencies, including the Federal Energy Regulatory Commission and the Federal Communications Commission, and the federal courts; advises and makes recommendations to the Commission with respect to proposed legislation in the U.S. Congress and the Council of the District of Columbia; interprets federal statutes and regulations affecting the Commission; prepares notices of proposed and final rule making for the Commission; and performs all other legal functions.

The *Office of the Commission Secretary* has the responsibility of maintaining the formal case system for the Commission. This includes the receipt and distribution of Commission orders, notices and press releases, and maintenance of an up-to-date information referral system.

The Commission relies on the *Office of Accounting and Finance* for professional accounting and financial expertise. The responsibilities of this office include the examination and audits of the books, records, financial statements, and other information filed by the following three jurisdictional utility companies: The Chesapeake and Potomac Telephone Company (C&P); District of Columbia Natural Gas, a division of Washington Gas Light Company (DCNG); and the Potomac Electric Power Company (PEPCO).

The Office of Accounting and Finance is required to verify and attest to the accuracy and the compliance of all accounting and financial filings with the respective Uniform System of Accounts, the Generally Accepted Accounting Principles (GAAP), the District of Columbia Public Utilities Municipal Regulations, and the directives of the Commission. The routine financial reports filed by the three jurisdictional utility companies include (a) monthly and annual financial statements, (b) depreciation studies, (c) cost allocation studies, and (d) special studies requested by the Commission.

One of the most time-consuming tasks of this office is the review and analysis of financial data submitted by the utility companies when requesting changes in jurisdictional utility rates. Staff perform detailed reviews of all accounting and financial data in the company's application for rate changes. A report of staff's findings, conclusions, and recommendations is submitted to the Commission when staff are advisers in a case, or incorporated in staff's direct testimony and exhibits filed as a part of such rate case proceedings on those issues in which the Commission orders staff participation. As a case witness, staff prepare data requests on the direct testimony filed by the jurisdictional companies and other parties and submits data responses to the data requests on its direct testimony. Staff also assist legal counsel in the preparation of cross-examination questions for the accounting and financial witnesses testifying on behalf of other parties to the case. Rebuttal testimony is written and filed, when necessary. During the rate case hearings, staff are cross-examined on the direct and rebuttal testimony filed by all the accounting and financial witnesses.

The auditing activities of this office include a detailed audit of the monthly Fuel Adjustment Clause (FAC) filed by PEPCO and the monthly Purchased Gas Adjustment (PGA) filed by DCNG. These Commission-authorized fuel clauses adjust the base charge for each unit of electric or gas service billed to DC customers to reflect the current, actual costs of the fuel purchased by the utility company. Upon recommendation of this office, the Commission approves each of the proposed adjustment factors calculated by the company.

Staff are required to analyze each telephone tariff, attend data conferences, file data requests, review data responses, and provide legal counsel with technical information which is used in staff's comments filed on the record. Another area of responsibility is the monitoring of the customer-owned coin-operated telephones. Staff continuously review and submit comments to the Commission on the customer-owned coin-operated telephone applications, the annual reports, and reports on the connections and disconnections of such telephones.

In addition to the duties outlined above, the accounting and financial staff are involved in the ongoing process of monitoring the utility companies' operations, construction programs, management efficiency programs, transactions with affiliated companies, etc.

The *Office of Consumer Services,* serving as the public relations arm of the Public Service Commission, provides complaint and informational services to utility consumers. It investigates, adjudicates, and negotiates customer complaints and disputes that cannot be resolved informally between the customer and the utility company. Office staff is responsible for providing public information and education regarding utility consumers' rights and responsibilities as well as other Commission matters.

Office staff inform the Commission of local and national utility-related trends and provide the Commission with information on how well the utility companies serve the customers. This office participates in the consumer hearing process by collecting data, providing the consumer with information, and coordinating the hearing schedule. A quarterly newsletter is published by the Office of Consumer Services, covering utility-related matters and activities at the Commission. Office staff implement a community outreach project for the Commission which includes a speaker's bureau and the development and distribution of informational literature (that is, the Consumer Bill of Rights and an energy conservation booklet).

The primary duties and responsibilities of the *Office of Economics* are to represent Commission staff on economics issues in formal cases that are being litigated actively and those that are in the postlitigation stage. These duties involve critiquing studies and reports filed by the three utility companies and conducting independent studies. This office also advises the Commission on economics issues, conducts Commission-sponsored studies, and prepares papers and articles for presentation at economics and regulatory conferences as well as for publication in economics and regulatory journals and periodicals.

The responsibilities of the *Office of Engineering* center on participation in formal cases which have a technical dimension and the administration of the Natural Gas Pipeline Safety Program. The Office of Engineering is responsible for providing engineering review and analysis in (a) formal rate cases, investigations, and rule making; (b) informal studies and investigations; (c) matters related to customer service; and (4) gas pipeline safety.

Special Programs Authorized by the Public Service Commission to Customers of the Chesapeake and Potomac Telephone Company

- *Link Up America:* Helps make telephone service available to people who cannot afford all the costs. Persons who are eligible for public assistance are eligible for Link Up America, if there has been no telephone in the home for at least three months; if the individual has not been claimed as a dependent for federal income tax purposes; or if the individual meets certain DC Energy Office criteria.

- *Audiotex Blocking:* Customers may elect to receive or block the audiotex (976) calls from their telephone lines.

- *Economy I:* A service available to all C&P residential customers who are charged a flat 6.8 cents per outgoing call and have unlimited incoming calls.

- *Economy II:* A low-cost telephone service to residents of the District of Columbia who meet specific eligibility requirements. Customers must be sixty-five years of age or older and qualify for DC energy assistance. The service permits the customer to make 60 calls per month in the DC area (Maryland and Virginia) for a flat monthly fee of $4.00. Any additional calls cost 7 cents each.

Endnotes

1. There is confusion in the literature and in professional discussions over the terms *commercialization, restructuring,* and *privatization.* The author uses the term *restructuring* to refer to any reorganization of either the monopoly telephone

enterprise or the telecommunications sector. *Commercialization* refers to any reorganization of a monopoly telephone enterprise intended to improve its responsiveness to consumer preferences. *Privatization* is used only when a restructuring includes the transfer of government property to the control and ownership of private individuals or enterprises. Restructuring alternatives range from the government's separating the post office function from the telephone enterprise to redefining the scope of the monopoly of the telephone enterprise and permitting other entities to enter telecommunications businesses. Commercialization can range from creating a separate government-owned company, hiring private individuals as consultants and contract managers, sharing profits with a foreign telephone company to manage the system, to selling part ownership of the company to raise capital or to selling controlling interest and management responsibility for the company to a foreign operator while retaining partial ownership for the benefit of employees and other domestic interests. Only these latter two examples can be properly referred to as privatizations.

2. Again, careful terminology is essential. The author does not argue that telephone companies are free from competition, nor that all telecommunications services are monopolies. In fact, much of the business of telephone companies is subject to substantial competition. The problem is that the essential facility which most telecommunications services must use is available only from the local telephone company and is not subject to effective competition. That element is the local switch and local distribution wire pair. This local telephone distribution facility is an essential bottleneck facility which most telecommunications services and service providers who compete with the telephone company must use to reach their customers. See, for example, Order, Civil Action No. 82-0192, U.S. District Court, District of Columbia (September 10, 1987). In that opinion reviewing the effect of the divestiture of AT&T, Judge Harold Greene rejected the Bell operating companies' (BOCs') claim that competitors were bypassing the local telephone distribution facility to a significant extent. The judge concluded that the local telephone facility remained a bottleneck monopoly whose control gave the BOCs the ability to manipulate and monopolize the entire telecommunications sector:

> The complete lack of merit of arguments that economic, technological, or legal changes have substantially eroded or impaired the Regional Company bottleneck monopoly power is demonstrated by the fact that only one-tenth of one percent of interLATA [author's note: non-local] traffic volume, generated by one customer out of one million, is carried through non-Regional Company facilities to reach an inter-exchange carrier.... The Department of Justice found only twenty-four customers in the entire United States who managed to deliver their interexchange traffic directly to their interexchange carriers, bypassing the Regional Companies.... It is clear, therefore, and the Court finds, that no substantial competition exists at the present time in the local

exchange service, and that the Regional Companies have retained control of the local bottlenecks.

Use of this bottleneck facility and the price paid for that access is subject to the discretion of the local telephone company. If the would-be service provider is unhappy with the terms of access or the price imposed by the telephone company, there is no alternative competitor ready and able to provide equivalent access at an equivalent price to the customer's premises. The local loop is very different from long distance facilities in the United States, or packet-switched networks in Europe, or database services in Japan. Each of these is a competitive service offering or facility. But each must use the local telephone distribution facility to reach its customers.

3. The literature is full of speculation that new technologies may soon become effective economic substitutes for the local telephone distribution facility. If this develops, policymakers will enjoy the luxury of seeing the breakdown of the de facto telephone monopoly. Broadband fiber networks serving homes and businesses, microcellular digital radio systems, and even high-capacity digital cellular systems may, in time, offer substitute two-way, switched, point-to-point transmission alternatives to bypass the local telephone distribution facility at prices competitive with the marginal costs of operating those facilities. But this remains to develop. Until proven otherwise, government policymakers must assume the local telephone distribution facility will remain a bottleneck monopoly which must be used by all telecommunications services, whether competitive or monopoly offering.

Policymakers must adopt a wait-and-see attitude as to whether the local telephone distribution facility will remain an unchallenged monopoly for two reasons. First, none of these potential sources of competition are projected to be widely available before the turn of the century. And second, the experience to date with so-called competitive or bypass alternatives to local exchange service is disquieting. Analog cellular radio systems, coaxial cable television systems, two-way VSAT satellite services, and high-capacity private line business networks which connect directly to a long-distance carrier, were each expected to challenge the local telephone bottle-neck monopoly in the United States. Each, in turn, has failed this prediction. Without question, each of these technologies has found a profitable market niche and is offering a new, special service that was not previously available on the traditional telephone network. But they have not challenged the local telephone company's core business. Even the most avid VSAT customer or private network multinational company has kept its local telephone service and remains connected to the local telephone network. And overall revenues, and profits, of local telephone companies have continued to grow. This evidence suggests the marginal costs for new technologies may never equal the extremely low marginal costs of an in-place wire telephone facility to provide universal, switched, point-to-point interconnectivity.

4. This point was graphically illustrated at an early point in the Argentine effort to privatize its national telephone company, ENTel. Originally the government had

intended only to sell the company and did not intend to provide for effective continued regulation of the company after the sale. The government assumed its continued presence on the board of directors of the new company would assure compliance with the national interest in telecommunications sector development. In particular, all decisions on revisions of the new company's strategic plan, reinvestment, and profit distribution, were to be at the sole discretion of its board, making the board responsible for reconciling the company and national interests, a direct conflict with the board's main obligation of managing the company. Nobody independent of the company was to be given authority to restrain the company's overall profitability. Even the accounting system, particularly regarding depreciation and cost allocation among services, was to be the sole discretion of the company, allowing it to play enormous games with tariffs and book values. Fortunately, the government, accepting the advice of consultants, corrected this deficiency before announcing the eventual terms of sale. Today, Argentina is moving to establish a strong, independent regulatory agency overseeing the restructured telecommunications sector and the two new privatized telephone companies formed out of ENTel.

5. Increasing the company's internal efficiency does not ensure the company will share these benefits with the customers. Left to its own devices, the company will maximize profits through monopoly-pricing behavior. It will invest limited capital to improve service to the small percentage of its customers, such as business users, willing to pay premium prices for quality facilities in the local exchange. It will avoid further investment and attempt to reduce operating expenditures associated with other customers less willing or able to pay these premium prices. The result can be a dramatic increase in the rate of return on the limited amount of company-invested capital. A few valued customers will get greatly improved service if they are willing to pay an extremely high price. But this price will not be economically efficient, that is, it will be well above the actual costs of providing the service, and these inflated rates of return will not induce competitive entry because of the monopoly characteristics of the local exchange. All other customers will experience deteriorating service as the company refuses to invest capital that will not earn the same inflated rate of return. See Bolter, McConnaughey, *Telecommunications Policy for the 1990s and Beyond: New Markets, Technology & Global Competitive Trends*, 1990, Armonk, New York: M.E. Sharpe. pp. 15–16. The obvious social and economic inequities illustrate the problem. It is this monopolistic service and pricing behavior that created the pressure in the 1930s to nationalize public utilities, including telephone companies. It is important that countries avoid repeating the same mistake.

6. This chapter takes this statement as a proven theorem that is broadly accepted throughout the marketplace economies of the world. The reader is referred to a wide selection of economic literature explaining price theory. See Bolter, pp. 8–45, for an excellent summary of the economic literature and a compilation of market theories and their weaknesses.

7. The economist and Nobel laureate George Stigler developed a theory of regulatory capture, where regulators end up serving the interests of the regulated firms because those firms overwhelm opposing interests in the regulatory process

with superior resources, familiarity with the process, and political power. The major defense against the threat of capture is to protect the agency's independence rigorously and to equip all sides in a dispute with equivalent ability to argue before the agency. Then the agency will retain its power to decide hard cases critically and independently.

8. This list is the product of extensive work performed by Peter Smith and others at the World Bank. It provides the reader a sense of the complexity and range of activity even the smallest regulatory agency will face, but it is not a complete checklist.

9. Remarks by Sharon L. Nelson, chairman, Washington Utilities and Transportation Commission, and president, National Association of Regulatory Utility Commissioners, before the National Convention of NARUC, 1990.

10. This brief account of how rules are made at the FCC merely highlights the major components of the process.

34

The Vital Role of Regulation in the Telecommunications Sector

David N. Townsend

THE DRIVE TO REFORM THE TELECOMMUNICATIONS sector in many countries throughout the world is motivated by a conviction that telecommunications can and ought to contribute much more to national prosperity than the sector currently does. Low penetration rates, poor quality of service, large operating and management inefficiencies, and imbalanced development are the norm in a majority of developing countries. Even where telecommunications technology and services have made strong advances recently, the industry's performance tends to fall far short of its potential.

Typically, the blame for these failings is laid upon the fact that telecommunications remain in the control of the government bureaucracy, interwoven with the postal services as part of a PTT or otherwise operated according to public sector incentives, restrictions, and goals. Among the often misdirected and inconsistent motivations influencing operating decisions are political pressures to maintain artificially low local tariffs; cross-subsidies of the posts and other areas; civil service commitments to telephone company staff; employee rewards and incentives unrelated to performance; and shifting mandates and obligations tied to changes in administrations and political alliances.

The increasing consensus for a solution points toward removing the government from the business of running the telephone company, either entirely, by means of privatization, or in principle, through some type of commercialization that allows the operator to act according to private market standards. Among the key anticipated effects of such reforms are a rebalancing of prices for telephone services, bringing down above-cost long-haul and international tariffs, and raising subsidized local charges. Such a policy, in an environment of high unserved demand, promises to increase overall revenues, generating new capital which can be used to finance network expansion. The theory is that, in a private market, the operator will naturally move toward such a rebalancing since the profit motive will imply revenue maximizing prices. Indeed, in practice, such tariff changes are often explicitly mandated as part of the reform process.

This picture is not complete, however. There is a risk that, in the rush to introduce market forces into the telecommunications sector, reformers may leap to the conclusion that government involvement in telephone service operation and policy is inherently counterproductive and should be minimized. Such an extreme swing of the pendulum should be avoided. An active public role in the telecommunications sector should in fact be a central element of any reform effort if the overriding objectives of economic development and social justice are to be maintained. The key is to define the appropriate parameters of public versus private responsibility.

Regulation, in the literal sense of the word, implies maintaining a steady balance or flow, preventing disruptions or extremes, or diversion from a preferred path of activity. This function, the regulatory function, becomes the new challenge of the government when direct operation of the telecommunications utility is transferred from public to private or semiprivate hands. In many cases, where operation has been very centrally controlled, the notion of indirect regulation may be a comparatively new one, requiring a different perspective and a new set of skills. Indeed, overregulation can be almost as stifling as central management; however, these concerns do not take away from the importance of maintaining government involvement in the industry. This is especially the case for those major segments of the industry that operate as monopolies, such as the local communications access infrastructure. But even where some degree of competition may be introduced, such as in long-distance or value added markets, the government must regulate that competition. The consequences of ignoring this critical element of telecommunications sector reform could be grave, especially given the stakes involved in large-scale privatization.

In this context, it is worth recalling the classic case for government regulation of a monopoly: telecommunications, like other utilities that rely upon a ubiquitous and interconnected infrastructure, exhibits declining marginal (and average) supply costs over nearly all potential volumes of service output; this is especially true of the basic local network infrastructure. At the same time, demand for telecommunications services tends to be extremely inelastic, which is one reason the industry is classified as a utility in the first place. Thus, at a given level of service, price increases will not tend to drive down demand; similarly, it is not necessary to decrease prices while expanding the network in order to attract a large volume of new customers—the demand is out there, waiting to be served even at higher prices. In this situation, a pure monopolist will establish service levels and prices that maximize profits, the margin of total revenues above total costs. In theory, this price-production point will occur at the point at which marginal revenue (price) equals marginal cost; beyond that point, each new customer would cause the company to lose money, since his willingness to pay would be less than the cost to serve him; however, this profit-maximizing supply point will not typically be the social welfare-maximizing point. Prices will tend to be higher and output lower than society as a whole would prefer. A lower average price would allow additional customers to subscribe and would increase the consumer surplus of all customers.

As abstract concepts, consumer surplus and social welfare may not be easy to visualize. But in the real world, in an underdeveloped rural area, these concepts could take the form of the ability to use a public telephone to call a doctor in a medical emergency, a timely early warning system in the event of natural disasters, or the ability of low-income and illiterate citizens to learn about and participate in democratic politics. If monopoly pricing and investment practices were to prevail, these forms of consumer benefits would be transferred largely to producer surplus, that is, to greater retained profits for the new private (and often foreign) owners of the telephone company.

In addition to the objective of preserving social equity, there may be more fundamental long-run net economic gains (that is, accruing to the economy as whole) to be achieved through telecommunications development that a monopolist, focusing on pecuniary short-run profits, would not pursue. In the theoretical model, the loss of such concrete economic benefits is known as deadweight loss. As a practical matter, deadweight loss translates into slower growth and the potential reversal of progress in many sectors. Consider the example of a farmer who harvests a particular crop and then must transport his produce by cart some fifty kilometers over bad roads to sell or trade in the nearest village. With no access to modern communications, the farmer can have no advance knowledge if, for whatever reason, demand for his crop will not materialize in the village: perhaps another farmer has already been there selling the same crop; perhaps needs are changing; perhaps a flood has washed out the only bridge and he will be unable to reach the village before the crop spoils. With access to a telephone, at least in theory, the farmer could learn of these problems in advance and either travel to another village or make other contingency plans; however, it is often unlikely that the farmer could afford to pay up front the capital cost of installing telephone service or even that a community would collectively be able to anticipate these types of benefits enough to gather the resources to create their own access connections.

The difference in concrete economic value between the two scenarios is obvious, and quite large. By extension, the effects of telecommunications development in rural areas is likely to have a very important direct economic impact upon those areas; over time these gains could certainly contribute to national growth, and thus (at least indirectly) could support the costs of the network investment itself. Yet since these types of gains will not show up in villagers' short-term ability to pay for telephone services themselves, the prospect of rural investments will not seem appealing to a private carrier operating entirely on its own. Instead, it will choose to invest only where short-run demand is capable of paying the cost of network expansion and to charge prices that will prevent most rural and poor citizens from subscribing, even where service is made available.

Still, it might be argued that these are long-run, theoretical considerations, since in the short run, price increases for local service are what are most necessary to support the development of the network, whether in rural or urban areas, and the private monopolist will surely agree to higher prices, even in exchange for specific commitments to investment in unprofitable areas. Simply increasing prices to generate revenue to support expansion, however, is not an end in itself; even achieving this goal successfully only means that the relatively wealthy can get access, but the poor will still be shut out. Eventually, the government must come to grips with the affordability of service for the bulk of the population that is to be served by the expanding network.

In the long run, therefore, some form of price regulation will always be required, as increasing volumes of investment allow the carrier to achieve greater economies of scale. Returning to the classic declining cost model of the monopoly utility, this suggests that a pure price-cap model, for example, for a newly privatized carrier, would allow permanent and increasing margins above costs, since while prices would increase with inflation, unit costs would actually be declining. A price-cap model with offsets for productivity would be more appropriate, but it is important that the productivity measures be based upon actual experience. In the United States and the United Kingdom, productivity offsets to price caps have hovered in the low single digits; however, those networks are near full development and further scale economies will be relatively slight. In a severely underdeveloped network, on the other hand, the carrier will begin expansion at the most steep portion of the cost curve and productivity gains in just a few short years could be of a magnitude of 50 percent to 75 percent or more. A U.K.-style productivity offset of 6 to 7 percent in such an environment would be entirely inappropriate and lead to outrageous profit margins before long, thereby frustrating the goal of making service affordable to the majority of the population.

Beyond price regulation, the regulator must play an active role in monitoring and promoting compliance with network expansion agreements. Left alone, carriers will invariably find means of meeting the most minimal obligations for unprofitable expansion, while avoiding the most high-cost investments. For example, in Mexico, the recent TELMEX concession requires expansion to rural areas and remote villages according to certain general parameters. One requirement is that TELMEX must install service, through a manual or electronic exchange, in any village with 2,500 or more inhabitants whenever at least one hundred applications for service are received from such a village. Think of the regulatory questions this requirement raises:

- What constitutes an application for service?

- Who monitors, and counts, such requests?

- Will the government take the initiative to inform villagers of these provisions and encourage them to submit applications and facilitate the application process?

- How will the scope and timing of TELMEX's response be overseen?

Finally, and most important, consider the interaction of expansion obligations with pricing decisions. According to the concession, an application for service requires a deposit payment of three months' service fees for the application to be officially processed and the applicant to be placed on the waiting list. How much impact, then, will a substantial increase in the prices of local services have upon villagers' ability to make such deposits and thus to apply formally for service? If the ninety-ninth or hundredth person in the village cannot afford the deposit, the village may not get service for several more years.

The point is that only the regulatory authority is in the position to assure that telephone network resources are adequately and fairly distributed. The impact of tariff increases will always have two conflicting sides: on the one hand, more capital for expansion will be available; on the other, the affordability of service will be increasingly shifted toward the wealthier segments of the population. A private telephone company, naturally seeking profits and efficiency according to the laws of the marketplace, can help maximize the potential resources available within the sector, but it cannot be expected to strike the balance between growth and allocation, in effect, between market efficiency and distributional justice. This is the role, the vital role, of the regulator.

Thus, in the process of reforming the telecommunications sector, the function of regulation must not only be maintained, and maintained at the center of the industry, but must typically be strengthened as well. At present, most developing country telecommunications administrations or PTT operators (and many of those in industrialized countries as well) do not even have enough basic knowledge of their own national industry to begin assessing realistic policy choices. The questions of how much to invest, how much to cross-subsidize, how efficient is the sector, cannot be answered until more fundamental information gaps are closed. Especially in a situation of planned privatization, these types of data are vital before any reliable concession agreement can be achieved. For example, in order to consider cross-subsidies, it is necessary to know the levels of current costs and related revenues on a service-by-service basis. Many administrations, indeed many carriers, do not maintain or study this information except in the most aggregated form. Such considerations as long-run incremental costs, scale economies, demand elasticities, and the like, should all be central to public policymaking as well as private investment planning.

It is therefore apparent that the greatest emphasis in the area of regulatory sector reform should be on developing the basic tools and information sources necessary to begin considering alternative development policies. Ideally, these types of programs should precede any large-scale privatization effort, so that the cooperation of the government-controlled PTT can be assured, before the lure of market forces begins to conflict with public regulation of the telecommunications utility.

35

Regulation and Competition Policy

Paul Waterschoot

THE INFLUENCE OF UNITED STATES ANTITRUST legislation in shaping the structure of telecommunications cannot be questioned. Divestiture of AT&T, rather than control over rates applied by the dominant carriers, was the main regulatory feature leading to increased competition in long-distance telecommunications services. The antitrust suit brought by the Justice Department, based on the Sherman Act, has been more determining than decades of regulation by the Federal Communications Commission (FCC) based on the 1934 Telecommunications Act. Antitrust law was a predominant factor in the process of regulating the United States telecommunications industry, overshadowing the work of the designated regulator.

But even in the United States, antitrust legislation does not generally have such an important role in regulating utilities. It is commonly accepted that the Sherman Act does not apply to the United States Postal Service (USPS), although it has a dominant position in several postal services provided to the public in competition with private operators. One of the main tasks of the Postal Rate Commission (PRC) is to avoid cross-subsidies between the monopoly services and the services provided in competition with the private operators; however, the PRC clearly lacks the impetus provided by the antitrust legislation.

In the electric power sector there seems to be, at least in theory, some scope for the application of the antitrust laws to utilities, but in practice this has hardly been of any relevance. It is a paradox that the Federal Energy Regulatory Commission (FERC) is more concerned with the dominant position of the generators of electricity than by the considerable market power retained by the owners of the transmission grid. The Ottor Tail case[1] was hardly of any future relevance for regulation of the industry, and the electricity brotherhood largely continued to restrict access to the transmission grid as before. The leverage provided by the legislation implemented by the FERC[2] in the context of wholesale transactions has mainly led to increased transmission among utilities but not to any real competition in providing electricity to the users.

In the EC context the situation is likely to develop differently in the sense that, under the Treaty of Rome, competition law applies to utilities in a similar way as to any other provider of goods or services. The behavior of a monopoly is submitted to scrutiny under the competition rules and as such can be challenged when the monopoly abuses its dominant position in extending the scope of the monopoly to new services, for example, or when it distorts competition in services also provided by private operators. The European Court of Justice has ruled that, even in a case where a monopoly has a legal franchise but where the designated service is not all provided by the monopoly or only provided in an unsatisfactory manner, the application of the EC competition rules allow private operators to challenge the monopoly services[3].

The implementation of competition rules has in several instances proved to constitute an extremely powerful tool to challenge franchised monopolies more effectively than does the regulatory framework established to regulate the state monopoly. In some instances it has, however, occurred that the implementation of a new regulatory framework for a specific monopoly has led to protecting it from the direct application of antitrust rules. This process is often prompted by the legislative framework within which the regulator is operating because his primary task is to ensure that the relevant service is provided in a satisfactory manner. The objective of antitrust rules, on the other hand, is mainly to ensure that competition is not distorted and is less concerned with the protection of the monopoly service. A question of utmost importance for the public at large and for private business operating at the fringes of the monopoly service is to what extent the legislation regulating a franchised monopoly leaves scope for the implementation of antitrust rules as regards the behavior of the monopoly operator.

The complex nature of the relationship between regulation of a public utility and application of antitrust rules often stems from the issue of responsibility for the contested action. On some occasions the franchised monopoly operator acts on the instigation of the legislator within the framework of the monopoly service. But often this operator has a rather large scope of discretionary power within this framework and can on its own behalf discriminate against certain categories of users of the monopoly service or against private competitors in the liberalized parts of the market.

In the latter case there seems to be no reason to protect the monopoly operator from the full application of the relevant antitrust rules because in this case it acts on its own behalf. In the first case, however, the responsibility of the contested action lies with the state, which has instructed the monopoly operator to act in a certain way, leaving no scope for any choice. Such a case falls outside the possible action of the regulator because he will not be able to overtly challenge the framework within which he also operates; however, it is the regulator's task to deal with the frequent cases regarding the limits of the monopoly franchise. Moreover, in a federal structure the central regulator can apply antitrust principles to the behavior of the decentralized regulatory instances. Examples are issues of preemption of the state's legal prerogative in the United States.

Although in most countries the legislation establishing the tasks of the regulator is the result of a political compromise and often only specifies the objectives of such regulation in a rather general way, it is possible, at least theoretically, to consider some of the main tasks involved in regulating the telecommunications industry. This chapter examines the borderlines of such regulation and the link with competition policy.

Competition Principles as They Relate to the Tasks of the Regulator

The main task of a regulator can be summarized as avoiding monopoly profits, ensuring that satisfactory service is provided, avoiding discrimination between users of the monopoly service, and preventing the operator from using its monopoly power in related activities. In each of these tasks competition principles are relevant. We shall now examine how the task of the regulator can be influenced by such considerations.

It is important to stress from the outset that in all of the above tasks the regulator acts as arbitrator among conflicting interests involving the role of the monopoly operator. It would therefore not be acceptable that the regulator form part of the monopoly administration. If this were the case, it would be impossible for the regulator to have a balanced view between diverging interests. Thus, one of the main concerns of competition policy in the area of utility regulation generally, and more particularly in the telecommunications sector, is that the regulator should be an independent entity at least as regards the monopoly operator. In the United States, the FCC is not directly linked to other parts of the federal administration. In other countries, however, the regulator often falls under the direct responsibility of a government department. This structure can in some cases lead to a strong procompetitive behavior of the regulator as he is liable to be less concerned with a totally neutral stand.

Monopoly Profits

We come now to the first task of the regulator—avoiding monopoly profits. This is directly linked to the market protection given to the franchised monopoly. It is generally considered that the monopoly operator has to fulfill a task of providing a service of general economic interest. In the case of a telecommunications monopoly this obligation is to provide adequate telecommunications services to all citizens over the whole of the national territory; however, this is often not possible if some market protection is not provided through restraining market entry of other potential service providers. The reason generally given is that the monopoly must provide the designated service by applying averaged tariffs, thus allowing all citizens to have access to this service for the same price. The cost of providing such a service can, however, vary substantially in the telecommunications sector, say between high-density routes and those in rural areas. Allowing market entry by other operators would make cream-skimming of the more profitable high-density routes possible and would probably require increasing the price of the monopoly service in rural areas. A monopoly service is often a way to cross-subsidize the provision of such services in rural areas. A franchised monopoly benefits from an exemption from the competition rules as it is granted total market protection. Such a situation may however only be granted as far as such a large exemption from competition is justified by the provision of a public service which could not be provided in competition with other operators. Market protection given to the franchised monopoly should, however, not go beyond what is demonstrably strictly necessary to provide the designated public service.

The market protection given to the monopoly is liable to give rise to monopoly profits as the relevant market cannot be contested by other operators. Higher tariffs for the monopoly service would be to the detriment of the users of the service and would lead to a less than optimum allocation of the productive resources at the national level. In the case of telecommunications services, for example, higher tariffs for such services increase the communications bill for industry and service providers in general and lead to a lower level of use of technologically advanced services; as such, they reduce the competitiveness of industry and the service sector.

Price-cap and rate-of-return regulation are instruments applied by the regulator to contain monopoly profits. They are generally a poor substitute for market forces as they often lead to distorting effects of their own. For example, rate-of-return regulation, which is generally linked to artificial cost allocation methods between different monopoly services, influences investment decisions by the monopoly operator, who emphasizes investments in traditional services (gold-plating) to the detriment of new, more risky services.

Service Quality

Avoiding monopoly profits is also linked to the second task of the regulator, namely, to ensure that the monopoly service is provided in an adequate manner to the users. Service price is but one element of quality of service as a whole. The absence of market pressure leading to low-quality service and long waiting time for installing new telephone connections is a well-known example in many countries. It is a rather difficult task for the regulator to prompt the franchised monopoly to provide a high-quality service. Regulatory action is generally insufficient, and in some instances the most efficient sanction is to allow the relevant service to be provided under competition. This is the means envisaged by the European Court of Justice whereby an inefficient monopoly can be legally challenged by private operators[4].

Discrimination

The third task of the regulator is to ensure that the monopoly operator does not discriminate among different users of the service. Tariffs applied to different categories of users should reflect the relevant costs. This concept is, however, rather difficult to implement in practice, and some degree of cross-subsidy (as between urban and rural areas) is often considered part of providing public service. On the other hand, cross-subsidies between households and business users of telecommunications services should normally not occur. In this context tariffs for international calls, which were estimated to be too high in the EC, have been challenged, even if to some extent the additional revenues had allowed for lower tariffs for domestic calls. The full implementation of this concept is rendered difficult because of the problem of cost allocation among services using the shared equipment for a large number of services (for example, allocation of fixed costs related to local loops in the United States).

Participation in Competitive Markets

The regulatory task of ensuring that the franchised monopoly does not discriminate among users of the monopoly service is closely linked to ensuring that the monopoly does not abuse its market power flowing from the monopoly sector by distorting competition in other markets. This is also an area where the task of the regulator is more directly related to competition policy.

It is often considered acceptable that the monopoly operator is allowed to provide goods and services outside the designated monopoly. This can be explained by the fact that common investments can be used or that the nonmonopoly services can contribute to pay the costs for the public service provided under monopoly. Recently Judge Greene allowed the U.S. regional Bell operating companies (RBOCs) to provide information services in competition with private service providers. In another context, the United States Postal Service provides parcel services in competition with private operators such as United Parcel Service (UPS). It is the task of the regulator to ensure that the franchised monopoly does not use resources coming from the monopoly market in the competitive part of the market. This concept was central in the second antitrust case against AT&T, in which Judge Greene decided that AT&T used its market power in local monopoly telecommunications services to distort the market in long-distance services and the supply of telecommunications equipment.

The problem of the possible transfer of resources from the monopolized area to the competitive sector is mainly dealt with through rate regulation. Rates should be determined such that the services provided by the monopoly operator in the areas subject to competition reflect all the relevant costs and are not subsidized by the monopoly services. Rate regulation is, however, extremely complex as the allocation of the relevant costs is very difficult in the context of a multiproduct operator. Moreover, the allocation of institutional costs leads to protracted debates. The importance of this issue can be illustrated by the problem of access charges for the interconnection between telecommunications networks, where considerable costs are involved. In the United States, one-third of long-distance carrier revenues (US$15 billion) are transferred to the local network operators annually. Only a fraction of this amount is justified by additional costs of delivering or initiating long-distance calls. In the United Kingdom the problem of rebalancing local charges and rates for leased lines, mainly used by the business community, is at the center of debates on the future, more competitive structure of the industry. The relevance of this issue in the context of the application of competition rules is evident. The FCC was to a large extent involved in regulating AT&T's long-distance rates, although this was never a franchised monopoly. Moreover, after divestiture, AT&T's long-distance services were no longer part of the same entities providing local monopoly telecommunications services. FCC, in regulating AT&T's long-distance services, was not involved in regulating a franchised monopoly but implemented competition principles to a dominant operator in the long-distance telecommunications market.

Regulation vs. Antitrust Policies

Although antitrust policies can be implemented by the designated regulator of the franchised monopoly, it has to be stressed that the legal context and the procedures will be drastically different from the situation where such rules are applied by the courts. A regulator will generally act on an a priori basis, systematically scrutinizing all the new action the monopoly intends to undertake. This leads to a very heavy regulatory burden for all parties involved, including a large number of submissions and hearings. The regulated enterprise has to provide, on a permanent basis, information allowing the regulator to have a constant view of the monopoly's operations. The implementation of antitrust rules by the courts is, on the contrary, generally done on a case-by-case basis as problems occur and complaints are filed. This often leads to a lesser regulatory burden for the parties concerned.

It can be argued that an essential task of the regulator of a monopoly should be to ensure efficiency gains by the relevant operator. In this instance regulation should be seen as a substitute for market forces not sanctioning inefficient behavior of the managers of the franchised monopoly. The choice of regulatory tools is very important in this context, as well as the degree of competition allowed in some areas where the monopoly also provides its services.

The regulator's task is complicated by the fact that he is often at a disadvantage acquiring information from the regulated enterprise. Generally the managers of the monopoly have access to all the relevant information and are reluctant to give the regulator access to data which might make his activities more efficient. A solution might be to break up the monopoly into several parts so as to allow the regulator to compare data for different parts of the monopoly. In the telecommunications area, for example, it is easier for the FCC to assess some of the activities exercised by the RBOCs, because data is comparable for local monopoly operators, than to evaluate some of AT&T's activities, since this is the only long-distance carrier whose rates are regulated. In this case, it is not the antitrust principles themselves which give rise to better information and more efficient regulation, but the existence of several comparable monopolies, which can lead to an incentive for more transparent behavior by the monopoly operators.

Endnotes

1. The refusal, in the early 1970s, by a public utility (Ottor Tail) to wheel power to municipalities which had formerly been served by it. *United States v. Ottor Tail*, Co 331 F Supp 54 60-61. The Supreme Court upheld the conclusion that an abuse of monopoly power had occurred. *Ottor Tail Power v. United States*, 410 US 366 (1973).
2. The Federal Power Act of 1935 (FPA).
3. *Bundesanstalt für Arbeit*, Case C-41/90 of April 23, 1991; not yet published.
4. Ibid.

36

The Strategic Role of Regulation in France

Dominique Garnier

THE VAST MOVEMENT TOWARDS DEREGULATION that began in the United States in the 1970s has gradually spread to all industrialized nations over the past decade. As far as Europe is concerned, the 1987 Green Paper of the European Commission (EC Green Paper) broadly outlined an ambitious EC policy, which has been applied in the form of a number of very important guidelines, essentially contained in two texts adopted in December 1989, while the Commission was chaired by France: the ONP Framework and the Services Directives. The two documents strike a balance between two factors:

- A harmonization of European networks (because the development of heterogeneous national systems was seen as a hindrance to building a single European market).

- The progressive liberalization of the telecommunications services market (because the growing diversification of the demand among users created a need for a more flexible market).[1]

France, however, had already introduced greater competition into the telecommunications industry before the EC directives were drafted. The sale of terminal equipment was liberalized as early as the mid–1980s, and value added services, paging, and radiocommunications services were opened to competition in 1987. The largely discretionary character of the minister's powers over the licensing of telecommunications networks and services, however, by virtue of the Code des Postes et Télécommunications (essentially based on legislation dating back to 1837, the period of King Louis-Philippe), was not particularly well suited to a liberalization policy. Therefore, it was decided that a major regulatory reform would be undertaken as soon as an EC policy was adopted.

The reform, legislated in 1990 following a lengthy consultation period, consists of two essential facets that comprise a coherent whole:

- On the institutional level, it provides a restructuring, and a change in the relationships among organizational levels.

- On the regulatory level, it adopts a totally new framework that was directly inspired by the EC documents.

This brief overview is intended to present the essential features of both facets of the reform, as well as the primary reasons behind the choices that were ultimately made.

Institutional and Organizational Reforms

The principle of the separation of regulatory and operating functions, outlined in the 1987 EC Green Paper, was implemented in France in several stages. It might be useful to review briefly the factors that led the European Commission to make this issue a priority in the various member countries.

The Separation of Regulatory and Operating Functions

It was essentially the introduction of new players in the terminal-equipment-and-services market that made the separation of functions absolutely essential. Until quite recently, public carriers in most EC member countries were fully state-run; the government's decisionmaking role in the telecommunications sector was therefore fused with its role as carrier, in which it was responsible for supplying telecommunications networks and services (formerly limited exclusively to telephone and telex).

Furthermore, in most cases, it was the public carrier that authorized the connection of terminal equipment to its network. Although the carrier was generally not the manufacturer of the terminal equipment, it was often the exclusive distributor and the only source of telephone equipment for the user.

France was one of the first European countries to liberalize the distribution of telephone equipment in the mid–1980s; however, the responsibility of approving telephone equipment for sale remained in the hands of the Direction Générale des Télécommunications (DGT), as it was called at the time—a situation not fully compatible with the concept of true freedom of choice where public carriers were concerned.

Moreover, the proliferation of players on the telecommunications scene no longer allowed the dominant carrier (which in most countries enjoyed a monopoly over a good portion of the services) to have full rein and set the ground rules for its own competitors. That is why the Direction de la Réglementation Générale (DRG) was created in France in May 1989, under the Ministère des Postes et Télécommunications (changed in 1993 to Ministère de l'Industrie, des Postes et Télécommunications, et du Commerce Extérieur). Its mission is twofold: to approve terminal equipment and to define the ground rules for the telecommunications industry on a case-by-case basis.

The next step was the reform legislated in the statute of July 2, 1990, which declared France Télécom a legal entity by making it separate from the government administration of which it had been a part until then. France Télécom's new status, which took effect January 1, 1991, made it a type of public institution, with full administrative autonomy, its own assets, and a board of directors in charge of defining policy.

It was at that point that the separation of functions took full effect, as France Télécom and the Direction de la Réglementation Générale became separate entities—not only functionally, as had been the case, but legally as well.

The role of the state as shareholder was, at the same time, delegated to another section within the Ministère des Postes et Télécommunications: the Direction du Service Public, which is responsible for overseeing France Télécom's activities.

The Organization and Status of the DRG

During parliamentary discussions on the new law, the question of the status of the regulatory body was raised. Certain parties wanted the regulatory function to be entrusted to an independent authority, like OFTEL in Britain or the FCC in the United States, because they were afraid there might be some confusion between the state's concurrent roles of owner of the public carrier and the party responsible for defining the guidelines for competition between the carrier and the new entrants into the market.

This type of independent authority is not unique in France—notably in the audiovisual sector, with the Conseil Supérieur de l'Audiovisuel (CSA); however, the parliamentary debates raised a number of arguments for dealing with the audiovisual and telecommunications sectors differently:

• In the audiovisual sector, regulatory matters pertain essentially to program content; the preservation of freedom and plurality of information fully justifies the idea of an independent regulatory body.

• Conversely, in the case of telecommunications, regulatory matters are often directly linked to issues of national sovereignty and autonomy, the development of public infrastructures, and territorial planning, all aspects that largely stem from the state's decisionmaking role.

Furthermore, it should be noted that almost all European countries (except the United Kingdom with OFTEL and Portugal with the ICP) have chosen to delegate regulatory authority to a government department—either a department exclusively in charge of postal and telecommunications services, or a department such as the Ministry of Transport and Public Works in the Netherlands or Spain's Ministry of Public Works and Transportation.

One of the great advantages of giving responsibility to a government department is that the national regulatory body serves as an international representative. This aspect is particularly important for EC countries, since it enables the national regulatory bodies to participate in establishing regulatory guidelines in the telecommunications sector, whereas independent authorities generally do not fully participate in international talks.

Thus, the DRG is directly involved in the work of intergovernmental organizations, such as the International Telecommunication Union (ITU), and satellite organizations, such as EUTELSAT, INTELSAT, and INMARSAT, in which the distribution of functions is determined in distinct proceedings (the Assembly of Parties for government representatives and the Meeting of Signatories or the equivalent for the representatives of carriers.)

This unified method of representation on both the national and international levels allows for fully coherent positions and analyses; it also allows for ongoing adaptation to the evolution of the regulatory environment worldwide. Analysis and coordination are carried out primarily by the Sous-direction de la Prospective et des Affaires Internationales, in close collaboration with other ministry subsections and, if necessary, with the other government departments concerned.

Regulatory Choices

The Law of December 29, 1990, was an important milestone in the history of the regulation of telecommunications in France, as it involved a complete restructuring of an embryonic regulatory system. The restructuring was based on four main principles:

- Separation of regulatory and operating functions (as noted previously)

- Establishment of conditions that ensure fair competition within a framework of stability and objectivity

- Transparency of decisions (publications, etc.)

- Ongoing consultation among all telecommunications professionals and users.

The law clearly distinguishes between regulatory matters pertaining to networks, services, and terminal equipment, and clarifies the distribution of responsibilities between the DRG and the CSA in cases in which the growing convergence of telecommunications and audiovisual activities might lead to an overlapping of responsibilities.

Network Infrastructures

The law defines a network infrastructure as the physical elements of a network. The regulatory framework makes an important distinction between networks that are open to the general public and independent networks.

Networks Open to the General Public

In accordance with the EC guidelines adopted in 1989, the establishment and operation of an open network remains the exclusive responsibility of the public carrier, as a general rule, as part of the carrier's obligations to ensure universal and nondiscriminatory service.

The high cost of such infrastructures, as well as the lengthy period preceding return on investments and the recognized importance of economies of scale, would suggest that the duplication of basic networks would definitely generate more secondary costs for society than benefits resulting from competition. Therefore, the issue at hand—as parliamentary consensus has demonstrated—is the result of a pragmatic rather than an ideological approach to the problem. Moreover, it has been concluded that excellent quality and a high level of development in a public carrier's network does not justify the introduction of a competitive stimulus.

Conversely, the same reasoning has led to a departure from the monopoly, as provided for in the law, over radiocommunications networks such as car telephone service, paging, and new mobile services. The infrastructures required for such networks are, in effect, less cumbersome, with fewer physical constraints than wireline networks, lower civil engineering costs, etc. It was thought that competition would foster the development of such services—an area in which France has not been in the forefront.

Permission to set up and operate such networks is granted subject to the conditions of a public telecommunications operating license or *cahier des charges*. These conditions ensure fair competition and maximum benefit for the public interest. The approval granted for the new GSM service (a digital cellular radio service that conforms to EC standards) meets both concerns, as the two competitors involved, France Télécom and the Société Française du Radiotéléphone (SFR), were chosen according to their technical expertise and were subject to strictly identical conditions in terms of the granting of frequency bands and commercial and technical obligations. France Télécom is thus required to keep separate accounts for this line of products and to submit to the same conditions as its competitor with respect to interconnection with its own network and the payment of user fees for leased lines.

Independent Networks

Independent networks, which can be reserved for private use (for example, by a company) or shared by a closed user group, must be licensed by the Ministère des Postes et Télécommunications.

Among the independent networks in France, there are currently approximately 60,000 private radiocommunications networks, which connect some 450,000 mobile telephones. In addition, there are wireline networks, which are essentially private, linking a company with its subsidiaries, or units with common interests; a certain number of independent satellite networks (VSAT or mobile satellite service) exist as well.

Although independent networks are, by definition, not primarily designed to be connected to the public-switched telephone network, they can be in exceptional cases, according to stipulations contained in the specific licensing agreements issued by the DRG.

Unregulated Independent Networks

Unregulated independent networks are generally internal wireline networks which use neither public facilities nor those of a third party. Government licensing is not required in order to set up an independent network, as long as it is low-power and short-range.

Services

In France, only services that are available to the general public are regulated. Those limited to closed user groups are totally unregulated.

The exclusive rights of the public carrier over services available to the public are limited to telephone service between fixed points, telex, and public telephones on state property. The restrictions to competition are motivated, as in the case of basic network infrastructures, only by the requirements of universal and nondiscriminatory service to all users. The monopoly is, in effect, considered a balance to the obligations imposed on the public carrier by the regulator.

Bearer Services

The law defines a bearer service as "... the commercial provision to the public of a simple data transmission, meaning a service including either the transmission, or the transmission and routing, of signals between telecommunications network terminals without these data being subject to any processing other than that required to ensure their transmission and the routing and processing associated with the control of these functions."[2]

In concrete terms, bearer services essentially involve the provision of leased lines and basic data transmission service (for example, when a customer who leases lines from a public carrier installs his own switching equipment and provides services made possible by such an interconnection to third parties) as well as resale of capacity on leased lines from the public carrier.

In conformity with the Services Directive, the provision of bearer services was opened to competition by January 1, 1993. Providers of bearer services are subject to the conditions contained in a *cahier des charges*. These conditions are intended to protect the public service mandate of the public carrier, that is, to provide such services in a universal and nondiscriminatory manner. It is clear, however, that a general license is in no way intended to hinder competition and that the conditions stipulated in the general license will be strictly proportionate to the requirement of preserving the carrier's public service mandate.

Telecommunications Services on Cable Networks

The provision of telecommunications services on a cable network requires a license, as such services involve a modification in the initial destination of such networks. The licensing procedure for setting up cable networks, however, remains unchanged: licensing is still the responsibility of the *commune* (that is, the local administrative body).

Other Services

The provision of services other than those outlined previously is unregulated. The minister needs be notified of such services (generally referred to as value added services) only if lines are leased from the public carrier, and a class license is required only if the user capacity exceeds 5 Mbps. A consultative committee, which advises the Directeur de la Réglementation Générale, may be consulted, if necessary, to interpret the notion of value added.

Terminal Equipment

The market for terminal equipment is open to free competition. Approval is required, however, if the equipment is intended for connection to a public network, and approval is required for all radiocommunications equipment. The approval is intended to ensure that the essential requirements are met—particularly the safety of users and representatives of the public carrier as well as protection of the public network.

One of the EC directives contains a provision for mutual recognition of approved equipment, which allows for a single approval procedure for all EC countries for equipment that meets standardized European technical specifications. The EC directive has been carried over to French law, in the statute of February 4, 1992, in keeping with the deadline of November 6, 1992, stipulated in the directive.

Practical Implications of Regulation

The role of the regulatory body is twofold. First, it must ensure the proper application of the current legislative and regulatory guidelines. Second, it must ensure a dynamic adaptation of those guidelines to current situations and technical developments in the telecommunications industry.

Transparent Application of Regulatory Guidelines

On behalf of the minister, the Direction de la Réglementation Générale is responsible for licensing various networks and services according to the guidelines stipulated in the law and the prescribed means of applying them.

All licenses granted must be listed in the *Journal Officiel de la République Française* (official gazette of the French government). For each type of network or service, a standard set of licensing conditions is established and is identical for all competing carriers. This procedure is therefore a transparent means of ensuring fair competition among all the parties involved.

Calls for tenders are published regularly, especially for the establishment of independent radiocommunications networks, such as trunked radio networks (such as 3RP) and dedicated data radio networks (such as 3RD), or public networks, such as Pointel (the French term for telepoint [CT 2] service). The objective is to heighten general interest by reaching a broad range of candidates in order to ensure high-quality services and the most efficient use of radio frequencies.

Optimal management of rare resources is yet another primary function of the regulating body. The range of frequencies, in addition to numbering resources, is among the essential elements that require action, or at least careful monitoring of how they are used.

The DRG is also responsible for approving terminal equipment on the basis of testing by the accredited laboratory to determine whether they meet minimum requirements.

When necessary, the DRG can also be called upon to arbitrate any disputes between network operators (particularly in the case of problems related to interconnection conditions) or service providers, if the market guidelines do not adequately safeguard the best interests of users and the requirement of fair competition.

The DRG publishes a widely distributed yearly report on its activities which includes appendixes containing its primary decisions.

Dialogue

In view of ongoing developments in the telecommunications sector, regulatory matters cannot remain static. The regulating body must constantly adapt and interpret guidelines according to innovations that come to light.

In order to do so, the French government has implemented a means of dialogue among users and professionals in the telecommunications industry by setting up two consultative committees which advise the Directeur de la réglementation générale. One is responsible for radiocommunications, the other is concerned with telecommunications services. Both committees consist of representatives from three groups—users, service providers, and independent specialists—and are assisted by technical groups that are largely outward looking.

The committees especially allow for a pragmatic, jurisprudential approach to certain topics, such as criteria for distinguishing value added services from bearer services and defining the concept of closed user groups. Moreover, they constitute a forum for reflecting on future developments—an activity that the DRG wanted to promote even further by means of a public consultation procedure for certain topics. The first public consultation, on the introduction of personal communication systems in France, has just been completed. The process reached a large sector, which enabled the DRG to compile a significant number of responses from industrialists, users, and service providers.

Conclusion

The introduction of competition has by no means weakened the role of the regulatory body; on the contrary, it has strengthened it. Regulatory policy, both present and future, must be guided essentially by a concern for the general interest, in a context in which historically dominant carriers have made it necessary to be especially watchful of fair competition with new entrants on the market, and in which the proliferation of services calls for management that pays ever greater attention to resources, in an environment that is becoming increasingly international.

International cooperation is, in fact, one of the new characteristics of the telecommunications industry. It will be a major factor in the sector's activities over the next few years, not only on the regional level, as has been the European experience, but on a global level as well.

International conferences enable interested parties to observe the growing convergence of policies, in which institutions such as the ITU can play a major role alongside multilateral organizations such as the GATT, while leaving participants the option of what approach to take, according to their own situation and their own analysis of the strategic role that regulation will play over the next few decades.

Endnotes

1. See 90/387/EEC: Council Directive of 28 June 1990 on the establishment of the internal market for telecommunications services through the implementation of open network provision and 90/338/EEC: Commission Directive of 28 June 1990 on competition in the markets for telecommunications services.

2. English translation of Law no. 90-1170 (Dec. 29, 1990) supplied by the Ministère des Postes et Télécommunications.

37

Telecommunications Regulation in the United Kingdom and the Role of OFTEL

Donald Mason

TELECOMMUNICATIONS IN THE UNITED KINGDOM became a legal state monopoly in 1880 and an effective operational monopoly in 1913 under the control of the Post Office, the government department which operated the postal service. In 1965 the Post Office became a state corporation, and British Telecommunications (BT) was created out of it as a separate state corporation in 1981.

Since then the telecommunications sector in the United Kingdom has moved from being one in which all services were provided by a state-owned monopoly (BT) to one in which there is competition in all areas and no significant state ownership: BT and Mercury Communications Ltd. provide fixed national and international services; four new providers of fixed public services are developing plans to enter the market; cable TV companies provide local telephone service in more than twenty areas; two cellular mobile operators are well established; and two PCN (personal communication network, that is to say, microcellular mobile) operators have well-advanced market entry plans.

Originally competition was seen (as it continues to be seen) as the best way of ensuring adequate services, responsiveness on the part of operators to developing technology, and customer choice. The restructuring of BT as a private limited company in 1984 and its immediate privatization was a development which occurred in parallel with the introduction of competition. One of its major aims was to free the company from the constraints of government accounting methods and changeable financial policy so that it would be able to raise, on a commercially rational basis, the capital needed for large-scale investment in digital technology and optical-fiber links.

In the initial privatization the government sold 51 percent of the shares to the general public by way of a stock market issue. As a matter of policy the government has not since exercised the voting rights associated with its remaining shareholding; that is, it has not in any way used its votes as a means of controlling the company. The government has, however, retained a golden share which entitles it to attend and speak at shareholders meetings and to block changes to certain of the company's Articles of Association, including that which limits any shareholder to 15 percent of the shares. The golden share also entitles the government to appoint two directors who, when appointed, have no special position or powers. The government has so far appointed only one. The government sold a further 27 percent of BT's shares in 1991 and the remaining 22 percent in 1993.

Privatization and the development of competition both imply the need for independent regulation, the function today of OFTEL, the U.K. regulatory agency.

The Telecommunications Act 1984

Telecommunications in the United Kingdom today is governed by the Telecommunications Act 1984, which was passed at the time of the privatization of BT. It created the post of Director General of Telecommunications, established a coherent and comprehensive licensing system, and gave separate regulatory roles to the Director General and the secretary of state for trade and industry, who also has the title of President of the Board of Trade. The main provisions of the Act have remained unchanged since 1984.

General Duties of the Secretary of State and the Director General

The Act sets out certain policy goals to guide the secretary of state and the Director General in their functions. The most important of these are:

- The provision of telecommunications services throughout the United Kingdom such as to satisfy all reasonable demands for them.

- The promotion of the interests of consumers, purchasers, and other users in respect of the price, quality, and variety of the telecommunications services provided to them.

- The maintenance and promotion of effective competition in telecommunications activities.

Role of the Secretary of State

The Act allows the secretary of state to grant licenses, after consultation with the Director General, and gives guidelines on the content of these licenses; however, the Act does not specify how many licenses should be granted, to whom they should be granted, nor what they should permit. There is no definition of a monopoly area. All these matters are within the discretion of the secretary of state. The granting of licenses, together with the initial determination of their terms and conditions, is the secretary of state's main vehicle for pursuing the policy goals of the Act. As a government minister with telecommunications as one of his responsibilities, the secretary of state is guided by general government policy.

There are both individual and class licenses. The former is granted to a single legal or natural person as, for example, BT. A class license is granted to persons of a class, which often means all persons, in which case it functions as a general authorization for which no individual application or notification is needed. Examples are the Telecommunication Services Licence, under which the vast majority of value added and data service providers are licensed, and the Self-Provision Licence, under which people operate systems for their own use such as domestic telephones and other private systems, where there are no services provided to third parties.

According to the Act it is an offense, subject to certain exceptions, to run a telecommunications system in the United Kingdom without a license; that is, almost all use of telecommunications equipment in the United Kingdom must be covered by some license or other. Regulation of telecommunications operators has to be incorporated into the conditions of licenses granted under the Act. New regulations are imposed through the granting of new licenses by the secretary of state or the modification of conditions in existing licenses by the Director General.

Role of the Director General

The Act gives the Director General many duties and powers including:

- Advising the secretary of state on the granting of licenses and on any other matter where he considers it expedient or where his advice is requested.

- Taking enforcement action when license conditions are not respected by licensees.

- Allowing him to modify the conditions in licenses. Such license modification is the Director General's main vehicle for pursuing the policy goals of the Act.

- Considering any matter which is the subject of a representation. In practice this amounts largely to investigating consumer complaints.

Additional powers have been given to the Director General under the Competition and Service (Utilities) Act 1992 (see below).

OFTEL

The Act allows the Director General to appoint staff, subject to the approval of the Treasury (the government department responsible for finance) with respect to numbers as well as terms and conditions of service. The staff he appoints assists him in carrying out his functions under the Act and form the Office of the Director General of Telecommunications, commonly shortened to Office of Telecommunications, or OFTEL.

The Work of the Director General of Telecommunications and of OFTEL

The post of Director General of Telecommunications embodies the notion of independent regulation. He is totally independent of the telecommunications industry which he regulates and is to a very large extent independent of the government. The Director General is appointed by the secretary of state for a fixed term of up to five years and may be reappointed. He may be removed by the secretary of state on the grounds of "incapacity or misbehaviour." During his term of office he is responsible to Parliament for carrying out his duties under the Act. He does not lose his post on a change of government, nor is he subject to control by the secretary of state except in a small number of well-defined circumstances related to national security and international relations. Historically, this control by the secretary of state has been exercised only in order to assist in the implementation of European Community legislation by giving the Director General new duties.

In addition to direct intervention by Parliament (by act of Parliament) or control by the secretary of state in the limited circumstances in which this is possible, actions of the Director General may be subject to "judicial review," a court procedure which enables the reasonableness of official decisions to be challenged.

The Director General may come to the post from any area of national life, as for example, business, law, the financial world, or academic life. OFTEL's first Director General, Professor Sir Bryan Carsberg, held the office initially from 1984 to 1987, after which he was reappointed for a five-year term. In 1992 he became Director General of Fair Trading, a similar type of post but with broader responsibilities. The current Director General is Mr. Don Cruickshank.

The Director General's staff, that is to say, the staff of OFTEL, are civil servants. They work under the same terms and conditions as in government departments. All OFTEL action is in the name of the Director General, and no action can legally be taken if there is no Director General in post.

Advice to the Secretary of State

New licenses are normally drafted by the Department of Trade and Industry (DTI) and then sent to OFTEL for comment. On occasion the final form of a license is only agreed after lengthy informal discussion at official level. Normally, the Director General becomes personally involved in this process only with respect to its broad lines.

On general issues of policy, on request or on his own initiative, the Director General advises the secretary of state personally, after consultations within OFTEL. Such advice may be published.

Enforcement of License Conditions

The Director General is required to enforce licenses. The Act requires him to issue an order if he is satisfied that a licensee is contravening or has contravened and is likely again to contravene any of the conditions of his license. Contravention of a license condition is not in itself an offense, but subsequent refusal to comply with an order from the Director General is. The licensee may challenge the validity of an order in court.

It is generally difficult to establish sufficient, legally admissible evidence of a license contravention to meet the conditions for issuing an order laid down in the Act. Since 1984 very few such orders have been issued; this, however, does not mean that the process of license enforcement is ineffective. OFTEL investigates all suspected contraventions. The normal pattern is for the investigation to end when it is clear that no contravention is continuing or likely to occur. Thus, the powers of the Director General ensure in practice that license compliance is achieved effectively and without recourse to legal process.

The Act gives the Director General the important power to require any person to provide information that is relevant to the investigation of a suspected license contravention.

Modification of License Conditions

The Director General has the power (which the secretary of state does not) to modify license conditions. This is important mainly in relation to the licenses of the major individual operators, such as those of BT, Mercury, and the mobile and cable operators. The Act lays down the procedure.

The Director General must publish his proposed modifications, allowing a period of at least twenty-eight days in which anyone who reads his published proposals may comment. He must "consider" any representations or objections received. The modifications can then go ahead only if the licensee agrees. In practice this generally means that there is a period of discussion between OFTEL and the licensee in order to establish whether agreement is possible.

If agreement is reached, the license conditions are duly modified. If no agreement is reached, the Director General may simply withdraw his proposals, or he may, according to the Act, refer the matter to the Monopolies and Mergers Commission (MMC), which then conducts an independent and thorough investigation which may take as long as a year. The MMC, whose conclusions are binding on the Director General and on the licensee, is not bound by the preceding discussions between OFTEL and the licensee; its conclusions may be in accord with the Director General's original proposals, the licensee's views, or neither.

In practice, agreement on the modification of license conditions is normally reached. In making his proposals, the Director General is governed by the policy goals in the Act which also govern the MMC. Discussions about proposed modifications are therefore guided by an objective measure of reasonableness and legitimacy.

In fact, the Director General has so far referred only one matter, that of certain audiotex services (premium rate services), to the MMC.

Regulation for the Provision of Telecommunications Services

BT's license area extends over the whole of the United Kingdom except for the city of Kingston upon Hull and its environs of some 200 square kilometers, in the northeast of the country. Kingston Communications (Hull) plc, which is owned by the municipality, has for historical reasons the license to provide telecommunications services in the Hull district instead of BT. Thus Kingston, in Hull, and BT, elsewhere in the United Kingdom, have similarly dominant positions.

Condition 1 of both BT's and Kingston's licenses requires them to provide voice telephony services everywhere in their license areas. Most services provided under the universal service obligation are subject to price control. In the absence of other provisions, it could be regarded, in a competitive situation, as an unfair burden on BT and Kingston which their competitors do not have to carry. In fact, the licenses allow a fair proportion of the cost of the universal service obligation to be recovered from competitors. Thus, there is no incompatibility between the provision of universal service and a competitive situation in voice telephony. Hitherto BT has not sought to recover these costs.

The licenses of new providers of public telecommunications services also contain service obligations, but which are much more limited in their scope.

Asymmetric Regulation

Although competition is permitted in all telecommunications services in the United Kingdom, BT retains over 90 percent of the market overall and, correspondingly, a considerable degree of market power. As a consequence, regulation for the interests of consumers and regulation for competition mean to a significant extent regulation to prevent the abuse by BT of its dominant position. The regulation expressed in conditions in BT's license has as a broad objective to mimic the results that effective competition would have, were it present.

At the same time, regulation aims at promoting effective competition. This implies at times giving new market entrants assistance in the form of conditions which take account of the difficulties they face in becoming established.

Regulation for the Interests of Consumers

PRICE CONTROL: RPI MINUS X. Through an appropriate license condition, modified from time to time, OFTEL exercises control over the general level of BT's prices but not over the prices of other operators. Control is not over individual prices but over the weighted average of a group or "basket" of prices. The prices in the basket are weighted according to contribution the services make to BT's revenues. The form of the control is a price cap, which is a limit to the annual rate at which the weighted average of the basket of prices may increase. It is expressed by the formula *RPI minus X* (or *RPI-X*), where *RPI* stands for "retail price index," a measure of inflation which is published monthly, and *X* is a preset number.

The broad principles on which price-cap regulation are based are that, in an situation of effective competition, there would be a limit on the overall return on capital employed that BT could expect. BT would derive benefits, in the form of higher profits, from increases in efficiency beyond what was normal for the industry. According to these principles, the setting of a price cap begins with an assessment of what is a reasonable rate of return on capital employed for BT, based on an analysis of its activities and structure and on relevant comparisons with other industries. There is then an attempt to estimate what improvements in efficiency may reasonably be expected in the light of factors such as BT's unit costs, again based on comparisons with relevant companies in the United Kingdom and elsewhere.

These estimates, combined with BT's actual current rate of return, enable a price cap to be calculated which will bring BT's actual rate of return into line with its allowable rate of return at the end of a price control period, if expected progress is made in improving efficiency. The price cap is set for a period of four or five years. If in that time BT increases its efficiency more quickly than has been predicted, its profits are correspondingly greater. These extra profits are not clawed back. Each year during the period of the price cap, individual price changes in the basket are weighted according to the contribution the service in question made to BT's revenues in the previous year in order to calculate whether the overall cap is being adhered to.

The first price cap, set in 1984 at RPI-3, lasted until the middle of 1989. It covered exchange line rentals as well as local and national call charges. Connection charges were not, and are not, included in the basket of controlled services, but they have been subject to a separate control since 1989. In 1989 the cap was tightened to RPI -4.5. This regime was intended to last until 1993, but concern about the level of international call charges led to the Director General's introducing the latter into the basket in 1991 and at the same time discussed and agreed with BT a corresponding adjustment to the price cap to RPI -6.25. A new level, RPI -7.5 , came into force for a four-year period in August 1993.

Outside the main price cap there has since 1989 been, and will continue to be, a cap of RPI -0 on private circuit prices, and within the main price cap there has been subsidiary cap, since 1989, of RPI +2 on domestic line rentals. The same cap was originally applied to business line rentals; since 1990 business multiline rentals have been allowed to increase at RPI +5.

With the low inflation of the early 1990s, the price cap means that BT's prices must fall in monetary as well as in real terms. The overall effect of the price-cap regime in the eight years since 1984 has been a real decrease in BT's prices of some 30 percent. Within this figure business customers have benefited considerably more than residential customers. A new feature of the regime which came into force in 1993 is that, apart from line rentals, no individual price in the basket may increase by more than the RPI. This is expected in the future to increase the benefit of the regime to residential customers.

The price cap which took effect in 1993 assumes a rate of return on BT's capital in the range 16.5 to 18.5 percent (calculated on the basis of BT's method of historical cost accounting) and efficiency increasing at a rate of 3 percent a year on average.

Quality of Service

OFTEL has not in the past set quality-of-service targets but has encouraged BT to do so and to publish quality-of-service information. This was a result of considerable public dissatisfaction with the state of public telephone boxes, of which at one stage only about 75 percent were in working order at any one time, with the proportion in some areas much lower. BT now publishes reports every six months on quality of service covering public telephones (some 95 percent were working in September 1992), speed in meeting orders, speed in dealing with faults, call success rates, speed of operator response, accessibility of the directory assistance service, and speed in providing and repairing private circuits. Mercury publishes a similar report. In addition, an independent survey of the quality of service offered by the cellular networks, commissioned by OFTEL, commenced in 1992.

Also on a voluntary basis after encouragement from OFTEL, BT operates a customer compensation scheme where the quality of service provided does not meet certain levels.

COMPLAINTS HANDLING. The Act requires the Director General to "consider" any matter which is the subject of a "representation," meaning, in practice, any letter or telephone call to OFTEL on any subject relevant to the Director General's duties. In line with this requirement, all written representations are investigated, with a view to establishing, in the case of complaints, whether the organization complained of has been at fault.

In 1992 OFTEL handled some 9,500 letters and 33,300 telephone calls. Most of these concerned BT. Telephone callers (if OFTEL is in fact the right organization to deal with them and if the inquiry cannot be dealt with immediately) are asked to put their complaints in writing. The Director General's duty to consider representations does not depend on the complainant first having approached the operator concerned but, if that has not been done, OFTEL's first action is to pass the complaint on to the operator and only take it up again if the problem has not been resolved.

OFTEL's investigation of complaints involves correspondence, sometimes extensive, with the operator and the complainant. In some 35 percent of the cases investigated it becomes reasonably clear that the operator has been at fault. The operator is then usually willing to offer the customer a rebate or other form of compensation. In other cases OFTEL can only advise the complainant that redress for an unsatisfied grievance has to be sought either through arbitration or the courts.

Such complaints handling occupies more than 25 percent of OFTEL staff. It has a value beyond the resolution, where that is possible, in particular disputes, to provide information on the underlying causes of subscriber and customer concern.

THE COMPETITION AND SERVICE (UTILITIES) ACT 1992 amended the Telecommunications Act 1984 by giving the Director General explicit powers to set standards of service for BT and Kingston and to set compensation if they fail to meet the standards set. The Director General now also has powers to approve BT's and

Kingston's complaints-handling procedures and deposit-taking criteria and to resolve certain kinds of disputes (that is, those relating to billing, quality of service to the individual, discrimination in charging and deposits) in a legally enforceable way. Procedures under these new provisions are in the course of being set up, including the appointment by the Director General of arbitrators to act on his behalf.

Regulation for Competition

OFTEL regulates for competition by ensuring that:

- There is no cross-subsidy between those of BT's services of which provision is required by its license and those services it offers solely on the grounds of their commercial attractiveness.

- BT does not link the provision of services in the latter category in any way to the provision of services in the former category.

- BT does not offer services at prices below cost in such a way as to harm smaller competitors.

- BT does not discriminate unduly.

- All networks have access at fair and reasonable terms to all other networks.

The last two of these deserve some elaboration.

NONDISCRIMINATION. The licenses of operators who are obliged to provide services require them not to discriminate unduly in favor of, or against, any person or class of persons; that it, they are required, among other things, to offer a service which is offered at a particular price to one person to every other person on the same terms.

The major practical consequence of this to BT is that its connection charges, line rentals and call charges are the same throughout the United Kingdom. Because costs are not the same across the country, this implies a degree of forced subsidy of rural services by the less costly urban services. Although BT is permitted to charge competitors a fair proportion of this subsidy through the terms of interconnect agreements or otherwise, it has not so far done so.

INTERCONNECTION ARRANGEMENTS. Network providers are required in their licenses to agree with other network providers, competitors, or those offering complementary services, on the financial, technical, and information transfer terms of interconnection. If negotiated successfully between the operators, such agreements remain private. If the operators are unable to agree on any aspect of an interconnect agreement, either or both may appeal to Director General for a determination which is then made public.

The financial terms of interconnection may include usage charges; charges to reflect the cost to BT of its universal obligation and the forced equalization of urban and rural charges; and access deficit contributions. Technical terms may include the technical interfaces, where they are to be located, and how many there will be. Information transfer terms involve each operator's providing the other with sufficient information for call routing, billing, and so forth.

ACCESS DEFICIT CONTRIBUTIONS. In common with those of most telephone companies worldwide, BT's connection charges and line rentals have traditionally not covered the cost of providing the lines; that is, BT's call charges are, in general, higher than would otherwise be the case since the profits from calls are required to fund the access deficit. The size of the access deficit depends on how it is defined and measured. According to the method of calculation employed, it is in the range £1 billion to £2 billion; however, whatever the exact size, the consequence is that, other things being equal, the price ceiling for competitors is unnaturally high and market entry is thus, in BT's view, unfairly easy.

Although BT would like to rebalance its charges, by increasing line rentals sharply and making corresponding decreases in its call charges, the Director General is reluctant to permit a rapid rebalancing because of the effect it would have on, in particular, low users of the telephone service. He has therefore agreed only on a gradual rebalancing, under which BT may increase line rentals by RPI +2 within the new overall price cap of RPI -7.5. Over time this will have the effect of eliminating the access deficit.

In the meantime, interconnect agreements may include a fair contribution to the access deficit of BT or, as appropriate, any other operator. In the case of BT, the contribution is calculated for any class of call (local, national, or international) according to the contribution that class of call, when charged by BT, makes to the funding of the access deficit, the contribution being assumed to be proportional to the contribution that that class of call makes to BT's profits. International calls delivered on BT's local network attract, in principle, a substantially higher access deficit contribution than national calls, since their profitability to BT is considerably greater, whereas the access deficit contribution attracted by local calls is lower again.

Liability to pay access deficit contributions at the calculated rate would often make it particularly difficult for new competitors, without the advantages of economies of scale, to enter the market. For this reason the Director General has reserved the power to waive contributions in the case of competitors whose share of a particular market is less than 10 percent.

ACCOUNTING SEPARATION. OFTEL's policy on interconnection has evolved since 1984 and continues to evolve. With the abandonment of the duopoly policy for national and local services, the rapid growth in the provision of local services by cable TV companies, the prospect of further local competition through radio-based services, and the emergence of several competitors to BT and Mercury in national services, a much more complex competitive situation has become evident than was imagined some years ago.

It is reasonable to expect that in a few years there will be several major providers of national services, including BT, and a large number of operators providing local services in competition with BT, either on a national or local basis. This has focused attention on the need for the terms on which BT's local business interconnects with BT's national business to be the same, as are available to other national and local operators. With this in view, the Director General has decided that BT's accounts for each business area should be prepared and reported as though each was operating as a separate business.

At the same time the Director General has concluded that future interconnect agreements should be published, whether or not they have been the subject of a determination by him.

Other Activities

OFTEL also has several other responsibilities, some of which are technical in nature while others facilitate interaction between OFTEL, the public, and international activities.

APPROVALS AND STANDARDS. Although the Act gives responsibility for approvals to the secretary of state, he has delegated this responsibility to the Director General and to the British Approvals Board for Telecommunications (BABT). OFTEL is responsible for policy in general and for general and site-specific approvals. (General approvals cover equipment which does not require type approval testing but is certified as approved by a manufacturer's declaration. Site-specific approvals are approvals that are specific to a particular licensee at a particular location.) Type approval, which covers all other items of apparatus intended for connection to the public network, is handled by BABT.

Standards to which approvals relate are designated by either the Director General or the secretary of state. They may be national standards, or they may be drawn up by BABT for use pending the formal designation of a permanent standard.

NUMBERING. OFTEL is in the process of taking over responsibility for the administration of national numbering from BT, including the development of numbering conventions which will guide the use and allocation of numbers and a numbering scheme which will map out in broad terms the way in which numbers should be used in the United Kingdom both now and in the future.

INTERNATIONAL ACTIVITIES. Under the Act the Director General is required to keep telecommunications developments outside the United Kingdom under review. This becomes important in the case of European Community (EC) legislation, much of which has implications for OFTEL activity. For this reason OFTEL follows the development of EC legislation very closely and advises the Department of Trade and Industry. OFTEL is then involved with the implementation of EC measures, which may entail new duties being given to the Director General.

Figure 37-1. OFTEL Organization Chart

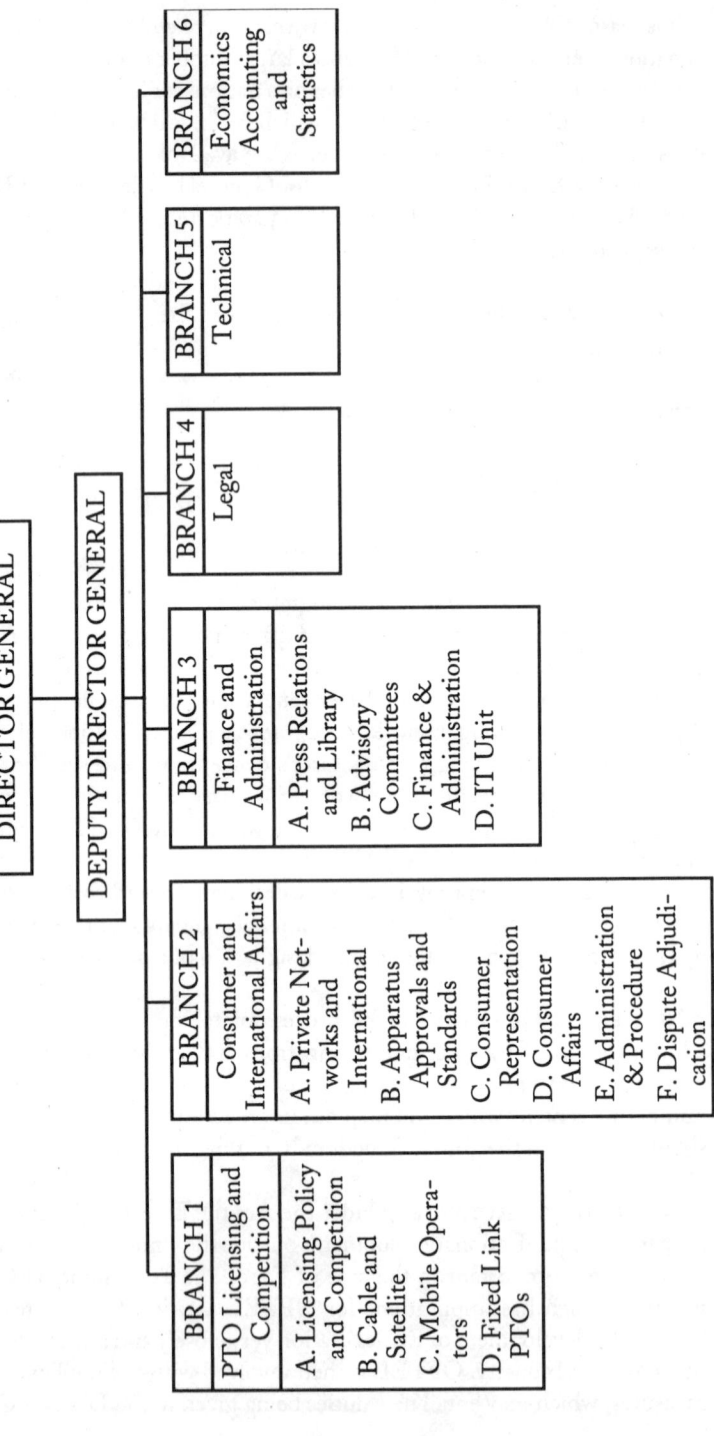

PUBLIC REGISTER. The Director General is required under the Act to keep a register, open to public inspection, of all licenses issued and related orders. This is kept in the OFTEL library. In addition there are public registers of approved apparatus and maintainers.

PUBLIC CONSULTATION. In carrying out many of its activities OFTEL engages in widespread informal public consultation, beyond that which is required by the Act. This always involves the advisory committees and often includes issuing public consultative documents and inviting comments.

Staffing, Financing and Organization of OFTEL

Like ministerial government departments, OFTEL negotiates the number of staff it requires with the Treasury (the ministry of finance) each year. The staff are then appointed by OFTEL on an individual basis. All staff other than the Director General and a few consultants are civil servants loaned from other government departments. They usually serve from two to four years in OFTEL before returning to their "home" departments. During their time at OFTEL their loyalty is solely to the Director General. Their conditions of service and pay are according to the standard civil service arrangements and are determined largely by grade, seniority, and performance.

The running costs and associated capital expenditure costs of OFTEL are provided by Parliament, but the Treasury receives back from the secretary of state a similar amount each year paid by the operators in license fees. Fee conditions are included in licenses and generally involve an initial fee and a variable annual renewal fee. Initial fees are based on the cost to the Department of Trade and Industry and OFTEL of preparing the licenses. Renewal fees are based on the estimated running costs of OFTEL and are related, broadly, to the turnover of the licensees. Thus, far and away the largest license fee is that of BT. This contributes about three-quarters of OFTEL's running costs which, in 1992–93, amounted to £8.0 million.

OFTEL is organized into six branches, as shown in the structure chart (Figure 37–1).

The 168 staff complement at 1 March 1993 has the following specialization.

1	Deputy Director General
3	Economists
1	Statistician
1	Accountant
10	Technical staff (i.e., electronics engineers)
3	Lawyers
3	Information officers
2	Librarians
22	Senior generalists
54	Middle and junior managers
68	Clerical, secretarial, and office support staff
168	Total

Table 37-1. OFTEL Distribution of Staff: March 1, 1993

OFFICE OR BRANCH	POSITIONS	NUMBER
Director General/Deputy Director General's Offices	junior manager	1
	clerical/secretarial staff	3
Branch 1 –PTO Licensing and Competition	senior generalists	10
	middle & junior managers	15
	clerical/secretarial staff	7
Branch 2 –Consumer and International Affairs	senior generalists	7
	middle & junior managers	31
	clerical/secretarial staff	34
Branch 3 –Finance and Administration		
1. Press Office & Library	information officers	3
	librarians	2
	clerical staff	4
2. Advisory Committees Secretariat	senior generalists	2
	middle/junior manager	1
	clerical	1
3. Finance, Administration and Information Technology	senior generalists	3
	middle/junior managers	6
	clerical, secretarial and office support staff	11
Branch 4 –Legal Advice	lawyers	3
	secretaries	2
Branch 5 –Technical Advice	engineers	10
	clerical/secretarial staff	3
Branch 6 –Economics, Accounting and Statistics	economists	3
	statistician	1
	accountant	1
	junior managers/clerical/ secretarial staff	3
TOTAL		168

There are in addition four part-time specialist consultants. The senior specialist staff (such as engineers and lawyers) hold appropriate professional qualifications. The majority of senior generalists are career civil servants on loan to OFTEL mainly from the Department of Trade and Industry. The distribution of staff among the branches is shown in Table 37-1.

Branches 1 and 2 are the operational branches which undertake the tasks of advising on new licenses, license modification, and license enforcement in relation to the various categories of licensee. They also assist the Director General in carrying out his specific duties under the Act, for example, dealing with consumer representations. The large staff numbers in Branch 2 reflect this role. The staff in Branches 1 and 2 are general administrators, not specialists.

Branches 4, 5 and 6, respectively, the legal, technical and economic branches, are staffed by relevant specialists. They have an advisory role, directly to the Director General and to Branches 1 and 2. The number of lawyers is small. This is possible because such a high proportion of OFTEL's work is carried out informally rather than by formal legal process. The number of economists is also small, despite the large part economic regulation plays in OFTEL's work. The work of the staff economists is supplemented by considerable use of consultants, generally major accountancy firms, on individual studies.

Conclusion

The U.K. Telecommunications Act, as with most legislation in most countries, attempted to deal with many issues at the same time. Many of its features would not be appropriate for other countries because the latter's immediate circumstances are different. In one general respect, however, the Act can be recommended unreservedly. It provided a clear administrative framework and laid down broad policy goals. Within these there has been considerable and invaluable scope for the exercise of discretion by the secretary of state and the Director General.

This has enabled OFTEL to evolve over the years and to react flexibly to developments in technology, in the economy, and in the competitive environment. Much of the policy work within OFTEL is devoted to the development of new regulatory approaches and new administrative structures to meet the demands of a rapidly changing world. The legal framework of the Act accommodates this process without strain.

The final goal is that competition will develop to such an extent that regulation will be unnecessary, and OFTEL will be able to be disbanded. The tendency hitherto has been for increasing liberalization to require a larger rather than a smaller regulatory apparatus and for OFTEL staff numbers to increase. In those areas which were liberalized first and have been liberalized most completely, for example, private networks licensing, however, staff numbers have been declining for some years and the decline is set to continue. Under the present regime there is little doubt that this will become the dominant tendency before long and, as well as liberalization, telecommunications deregulation in the United Kingdom will genuinely be on the way to being achieved.

Part VIII

Conclusion: Strategic Issues

of Implementation

38

The Political Economy of Telecommunications Reform in Developing Countries

Peter F. Cowhey

THE ALLOCATION OF PROPERTY RIGHTS AND the regulation of competition are fundamental economic and political tasks of the modern state. This is particularly so for the infrastructure of society, including the rationalization and development of transportation and communications networks. Indeed, the oldest international organization, the International Telecommunication Union (ITU), has its roots in the mid-nineteenth-century agreements in Europe to expedite the exchange of telegraph messages between countries. Each national market was largely a monopoly (frequently owned and operated by governments), and national monopolies worked together to invest jointly in the facilities needed to provide international services across national borders. ITU regulations provided a framework for dividing revenues among countries for international services, working out common technical standards and indirectly limiting new entrants into the market. These arrangements presumably exploited the economies of scale and scope possible in the development of a network for universal service. They also made it easier to cross-subsidize consumer households and rural areas.

So powerful is the idea of natural monopoly that history was even largely rewritten to reflect its premises. Supposedly, only national monopoly permitted the extension of local services by virtue of subsidies from money-making long-distance services. But in countries such as the United States and Canada, and many nations in Europe, a careful reexamination of the historical record shows that local telephone companies were thriving under competition prior to the period of monopoly.[1] In fact, the AT&T system used its patent monopolies for long-distance technology to squeeze local competitors out of business for local telephone service. And many state monopolies were so poorly run that competition might have yielded more service even without optimal economies of scale. The central point is not whether monopoly was the optimal system for telecommunications or not. Rather, the record shows that alternative ways of organizing telephone systems were available. Even if these alternatives to monopoly were not optimal, they would not have collapsed.

Most accounts of telecommunications development and regulation largely ignore the politics of the development of monopoly systems. It is vital, however, to be aware of the ways in which the political roots of the current telecommunications system have been lost from sight. Today, countries are faced by new choices over the organization of their telecommunications system. A simple investigation of the elasticities of supply and demand, the optimal pricing system, or the best plan for the development of new regulations fails to appreciate many of the forces that will decide the next form of organization for national and global communications systems.

This chapter sketches the beginning of a theory of the regulation of telecommunications systems in developing countries. It argues that the structure of political incentives and political institutions in each country powerfully shape how the country will reallocate the property rights and reorganize the regulation of the communications system. Brief examples from Canada, Japan, and Singapore illustrate the argument, and short case studies of Mexico and Argentina spell it out in more detail. The chapter has four parts. First, the common dimensions to the challenges to the current telecommunications systems around the world are noted; technological innovation has made the existing distribution of cost and benefits from traditional monopoly problematic to constituencies that are present in virtually any country of any economic sophistication, including many of the developing countries. Second, the chapter argues that the crises concerning the distribution of cost and benefits have no unique solution. It sketches out several major alternatives available for reformulating telecommunications policy. Third, the chapter suggests how the structure of national political institutions shape countries' preferences concerning reform. Lastly, the argument is developed in relation to Mexico and Argentina.

The Constituency for Change

Developing countries face a double dilemma. They have yet to complete the expensive and logistically difficult task of providing high-quality basic services to large parts of their population, while many are strapped by foreign debt problems that make public financing difficult. At the same time, they have clients demanding even more sophisticated services on new commercial terms. These clients are both multinational firms and domestic commercial enterprises that are starting to become significant global competitors with increasingly sophisticated communication needs. The double challenge of universal service and advanced services makes upgrading the network imperative. But the political story of telecommunications is that large users are highly suspicious of traditional government monopolies.

The growth of digital technology in the telecommunications industry moved one group of players, the large users of telecommunications systems in the business sector, to reexamine the workings of the telecommunications regime.[2] From the viewpoint of these customers, reorganizing monopolies to operate on a commercial basis and introducing some form of competition in the telecommunications system have several virtues. First, in developing countries the users want assurances that operating surpluses from long-distance services are used to upgrade the network overall. Traditional monopolies often spend the money on vested interests without achieving significant modernization. Second, competition provides the large customer with better strategic control over critical input. It is easier to bargain over the terms and conditions of service with a company that is subject to competition than with a monopolist.

A third reason an increasing number of major users favor moving away from traditional monopoly supply of telecommunications services is that they want to leverage their own products and services by providing information services as a supplement to their main lines of business. For example, manufacturing pharmaceuticals is one line of business, providing an information service to order, inventory, and handle billing for those pharmaceuticals is a second business. This is more easily done where there is at least some competition in the telecommunication system. In particular, although users may not want to become telephone companies in themselves, they want the freedom to repackage and supplement standard telecommunications services with their own specialized services. This means in turn that they want to be able to buy the basic technological capacities of the telecommunications networks on a competitive basis and without restrictions on the elements from which they may pick and chose. They also know that in many cases they will get better service at lower prices from their own individual perspective if they can pick and choose among competing communications infrastructures.

Lastly, major customers want better accountability from their telecommunications carriers in an age of the technological innovation. No company truly trusts government regulation in itself to provide adequate oversight over increasingly complex telecommunications networks. In the old days simply knowing if a telephone could be installed, whether it would work, and how much it would cost was enough to regulate the industry. Even then, regulation was far from perfect. In an age of information infrastructure, it is hard even to know what the products are or what their cost structure is. Only competition can help sort this out. Moreover, even efforts to streamline regulation, such as price caps for telephone services, have their own dilemmas. Should there, for example, be compulsory reinvestment in modernization of the network if a company earns massive profits by cost savings under prices caps? More general competition at least allows customers to know that there will be some competitive incentives to modernize the network.

Indeed, perhaps the most important innovation in the regulation of communications technology since competition—namely, the introduction of open network architecture (ONA) and its equivalent in other countries—is a testimony to the attractiveness of private regulation of the communications network. In one sense ONA allows customers to get involved in the design of the network of the future. This is all the more critical to customers because the very architecture of the network of the future is in question. Although there are many blueprints for the future, of which the integrated services digital network (ISDN) is the most prevalent, new technologies raise fundamental questions about even the delivery of local telephone services. For example, personal communications network (PCN) technology opens the possibility of wireless networks challenging the standard wired telephone network in the future. One can easily imagine that a combination of cable television services with PCN cells might well be a rival to the conventional telephone network.

The point is not that users necessarily favor one technology over another. They have such a large stake in the overall telecommunications system that they simply do not want the wrong sort of architectural choice to be made. The special dilemma for public policy is that the right choice from the viewpoint of these large business customers may not be the best choice for the welfare of the country as a whole. Thus, the real moral to the story is that telecommunications carriers and large business users are forcing the series of ever more difficult choices upon public policy. This is reinforced by the growing significance of the drag on the economies of industrialized countries by incomplete universal service.

The Alternatives for Change

There is no unique solution for sorting out the path of change for telecommunications. National policymakers have enormous latitude in how they choose to mix and match policy reforms. But it is useful to have some benchmark by which to compare national policy outcomes. For purposes of simplicity, a fivefold typology of policy alternatives is proposed.

Monopoly Modernization

Countries can elect to modernize the existing monopolies. The model for this strategy is Singapore. Whether the old telecommunications system was a cash cow for the national treasury or a black hole for subsidies from the national treasury, many governments have decided that the financing and upgrading of the national telecommunications network require significant restructuring and rationalization. Investment is significantly stepped up in improving and extending the central public network. Financial benefits are passed through primarily to the users of the system, especially large users. Labor and equipment suppliers are upgraded in quality and efficiency, but they may not be thoroughly rationalized. Some selective competition may be permitted, but the biggest assumption is that the public network will be sufficiently universal and sophisticated to discourage competitive entry.

Modernization requires new devices for introducing innovative management, better regulatory oversight, and raising large amounts of investment capital. But better regulation and innovation are very difficult when fundamental management incentives remain unchanged. Privatization (including foreign ownership) may be one such modernizing device; the creation of independent regulatory agencies may be another. But there are reasons to wonder if they are enough.

Multiple Monopolies

Some countries are implicitly moving toward a multiple monopolies model. This wrinkle on monopoly tries to retain a largely monopolistic system, but it splits up territorial service jurisdictions for the monopoly so as to use the monopolies as yardsticks for checking on each other. Argentina, Hong Kong (until the Cable &

Wireless purchase of Hong Kong Telephone), and Canada illustrate the idea of multiple monopolies. In theory, one might in the same way use new overlay networks, that is networks requiring specialized new infrastructure in addition to the common public infrastructure, as in cellular systems. In practice, however, most countries introducing overlay networks are making them competitive.

Competitive Enhanced Services

Some countries endorse the distinction between monopoly of basic services and competitive supply of enhanced services. This is a direct descendant of U.S. regulatory policies until the end of the AT&T monopoly. Presumably this speeds innovation and lowers prices for the most sophisticated users. It also gives the major telephone company an incentive to boost performance in order to claim a stake in these attractive new market segments. The trick to this approach is defining what constitutes enhanced services. In the case of the United States the definition was quite elastic because it said anything that was not part of basic services (however vaguely defined that was) was enhanced. Most countries have entered the realm of this distinction much more cautiously by developing positive lists of enhanced services. Of course, services change so quickly that it is almost impossible to have an adequate positive list of enhanced services, except as a temporary form of protection. Even if the problem of listing is resolved, this approach requires significant new policies concerning the transparency of network architecture and the rights of interconnection, which are very hard to work out.

Reserved Services

The problems of maintaining a distinction between basic and enhanced services drove the European Community (EC) to the reserved services model. The EC model turns the tables on the enhanced services model by saying that the only monopolistic services should be those that are explicitly reserved. Thus, it is monopoly (rather than competition) that requires a positive policy decision. This has the virtue of focusing attention on a much more easily defined subset of services which may require monopoly in order to produce sufficient economies of scale and scope. But it is not a panacea.

The European Community has struggled over which services should be reserved. Several member countries would prefer that packet-switching networks be monopolies even though they are treated as enhanced services elsewhere. Others would like new services such as facsimile networks to be reserved. They argue for these reservations in order to maintain a broad range of universal services. The crucial struggle is over what should be the definition of universal services. The Community currently favors a more expansive definition than does the United States. It is interested in developing guarantees of modern information services for households whereas the United States tends to believe that this is best left to the marketplace, with perhaps a small helping hand from government. The real issue then becomes how fast and ambitious must the spread of these new information services be.

In addition, the European Community largely treats overlay services as a separate category. For example, new selective network capabilities such as cellular telephones and personal communications networks will be delivered by a small number of competitive licenses. But some of these specialized new services may start to overlap with the capabilities of either reserved services or nonreserved services. In particular, the growing capabilities of wireless networks raise serious questions about how to evaluate traditional telephone franchises.

Full Competition

Countries such as the United States, Japan, the United Kingdom, New Zealand, and Australia are embracing a model of widespread competition. The basic logic is to allow competition among many providers of network facilities on a full range of network services.[3] These countries differ in how they have at least temporarily reserved some areas of the network for monopoly while providing for general competition. For example, the United States made local telephone services a monopoly while long-distance services were competitive. Britain until recently limited the number of long-distance competitors to two. Japan permits competition in both local telephone services and allows multiple long-distance networks; however, the administrative bureaucracy of Japan carefully oversees the total number of entrants into the market in order to manage total network capacity, which in turn reduces downward pressure on prices and allows the government to manipulate the extension of services by its licensing decisions.

In short, no model is without problems. All approaches to policy change retain significant discretionary power to allocate property rights for entry and operation in the market, even in unregulated market segments.

Developing countries have a wide range of choices when they consider departures from traditional communications policies. The question is not monopoly versus competition, but rather which types of reform of monopoly and competition are best for what purposes. The next section lays out the beginnings of a general theory of why different countries chose different telecommunications sector models.

Political Institutions and Policy Incentives

Political scientists have concluded that the key determinants of the policy outcomes in countries are institutional and electoral. The political institutions and constitutional rules of a country shape and constrain what actors want and what they can get.[4] Many of the problems and special interests concerning telecommunications policy are similar in any moderately advanced country, but how those interests are balanced change enormously according to the nature of the political institution. Electoral incentives refer to the rules for the advancement and retention of power (even if the country is not a democracy).

Institutions alone do not tell us about the everyday preferences and incentives of the political leaders of a country; yet this leadership is important, indeed vital, even in countries with strong and highly professional bureaucracies. Political scientists increasingly agree that bureaucracies operate underneath a system of elaborate checks, balances, and incentives created by political leaders. A hidden hand of political control exists even where bureaucrats appear to operate largely on their own reckoning. (This is no different than the way in which the chief executive officer of a large corporation shapes the incentives and controls over his many divisions even though he often has no knowledge of their detailed workings.)[5]

Political leaders are responsive to the basic incentives for how they are selected and how they can exercise power. The study of these political incentives is easier in democracies because the ground rules for the competition and control over power are established by electoral systems. It is harder to figure out the structure of incentives for political leadership where elections either do not take place or their meaning is substantially less important because of other political controls.[6] The purpose in this chapter is not to resolve all these questions, but rather to use a few cases to illustrate the variables that shape the choice of telecommunications regulation.

Recognition that political institutions shape policy choices allows us to make judgments about why, for example, permitting a telephone company to remain a monopoly may have a different implication in a country like Singapore than it does in a country like Argentina. The answer is that the types of political structures and incentives differ in the two countries and so the rewards or the incentives for the monopoly may differ, even though the form of ownership is the same.

In short, political leaders understand how their political institutions change the incentives of the owners of their national telecommunications systems. This underlines a fundamental policy lesson: identifying the model of telecommunications regulatory and ownership system prevailing in a country is only a first step; the second step is to understand this model within the context of the political institutions and incentives of that country.

The case of monopoly modernization in Singapore illustrates this point well. Singapore has a parliamentary system with strong centralized leadership, and it is a small country. Thus, we would expect coherent and centralized policy which (paradoxically) can give skilled bureaucracies considerable latitude in policy implementation. Close political oversight and monitoring of major public bureaucracies will not disappear, although extensive overt control will wane. This is precisely what has happened when the Telecommunication Authority of Singapore (Singapore Telecom) remained a government operating monopoly as well as policymaker. It modernized with a vengeance to satisfy international business and local constituents. Although the economies of this strategy had unique advantages in Singapore, the real key to the strategy was effective accountability.[7] A careful examination of the board controlling Singapore Telecom shows strong input from the government ministries charged with attracting global businesses, especially the powerful Economic Development Board. Moreover, there was indirectly a second monopoly, Cable & Wireless in Hong Kong, by which to measure its performance, because the bulk of Singapore's telecommunications revenues were from international opera-tions. Singapore Telecom was under instruction to match Cable & Wireless on service rates and terms for connection to Tokyo irrespective of the greater distances from Singapore. In short, the telephone company had an unambiguous mandate (to please global business) and a degree of informal but effective political monitoring that is hard for most governments to match. Thus, its incentive structure was appropriate because of the political institutions of Singapore.

The general argument about institutions and political incentives can be explored by focusing on three variables. (All of the following propositions, assuming all other things being equal, tell us the incentives for behavior, but the details of the case are always vital.)

Division of Government Power

The first variable is whether the political system is presidential or parliamentary. Parliamentary systems have no division of control over the government. Therefore, the ruling party and its prime minister can effectively control all parts of government. Party discipline in the legislature means that the majority party cannot prevent the political will of the majority (within broad limits). Therefore, we ought to expect that policy in a parliamentary system will be more coordinated and more centralized at the national level than in other types of democratic systems.

In contrast, presidential systems must deal with the division of power between the executive and the legislative. Particularly when the division arises from different parties controlling each branch of government, there can be a pronounced tendency toward political and policy stalemate. In addition, the struggle over power between the legislative and the executive reduces the national bureaucracy's degree of independence of initiative and willingness to take strong leadership. The legislative and the executive seek to check each other's power over the bureaucracy and thereby lead to a bureaucracy that is far more constrained by formal checks and balances than in a parliamentary system.

Voting and Party System

A further variable of importance is the type of voting system. For example, the U.S. Congress features a single member per district in which the majority wins all. Other election systems apportion multiple members per district according to their percent-age of the vote. These esoteric differences strongly influence the political reality of surviving and advancing politically in these countries.

For example, the Japanese voting system features what is called the single, nontransferable vote for the election of three to five representatives per district. In practice, this means that each member of the Diet wins by cultivating a very small intense base of voters in his or her district. There is simply no effort to win a majority of voters, and as a result the members of the Diet have almost no interest in establishing broad policy positions on issues. They are far better served by empha-sizing very narrow favors for their devoted supporters. This is one reason why protection of industry is so much more popular among Japanese politicians than pro-consumer policies. If one combines the electoral system with long-standing rule by one party and a parliamentary system one would expect, and one does find, that Japanese telecommunications reform has some distinctive features. Introduction of full competition is less disposed to significantly alter winners and losers than in the United States. (After all, the Liberal Democratic Party (LDP) has the same electoral base—it is only fine-tuning it). Moreover, the policy shows much greater reliance on centralized bureaucratic guidance to fine-tune the results of competition than in a presidential system with rotating party rule as in the United States.

Degree of Federalism

Finally, the degree of federalism of the country matters. Some countries are highly federalist, such as the United States, and others have virtually no federal structure. Some countries which formally look federalist, like Mexico, may have much lower degrees of federalism in practice because virtually all key ruling officials at the local level are nominated by the national political party controlled by the President. Nonetheless, we expect a federal structure to have more decentralization of policy than a nonfederal structure.

Canada combines a parliamentary system with a strong form of federalism. The result is a fascinating hybrid in its traditional form of telecommunications regulation. For example, there was virtually no formal regulation of its monopoly long-distance carrier, Stentor. Stentor is jointly operated by the provincial and regional common carriers, and it remained unregulated because there was a de facto unit veto by each individual carrier, which was in return subject to oversight by its province.[8] This peculiar pattern of hidden regulation nicely reflected the priorities of federalist politics in Canada. But, as one might expect in a parliamentary system, the growing national importance of telecommunications policy is leading to a substantial recentralization of decisionmaking.

In summary, the way in which power is divided in the national government, the form of electoral and party system, and the degree of federalism strongly influence the choice of telecommunications policies. The argument can be illustrated in more depth by concentrating on two Latin American countries with presidential systems: Argentina and Mexico.

Presidential Systems and Telecommunications Reform

Latin American governments largely have some form of presidential system. The traditions of one-party rule and military intervention have often modified the normal impact of presidentialism. But it can be argued that the differences between the political structures of Mexico and Argentina made for important policy differences in the road to privatizing and permitting foreign ownership of the telecommunications system.

The Case of Mexico

Presidential systems tied to a federalist structure normally have a hard time coordinating policy. They tend toward decentralization both within the central government and from the central government to local governments and the marketplace. But some factors can modify this tendency to fragmentation. If the electoral system and the existing distribution of power among parties does not pose a significant degree of competition for control of the presidency and the legislature, then there will be less fragmentation. If political parties in control of the central government also have effective control over the choice of offices for regional and local governments, then the effect of federal structures will also be less pronounced.

Mexico, in recent years, has seen the apex of the consolidation of presidential power. But this same consolidation of power was tied to an effort to renovate the political base of support for the Partido Revolucionario Institucional (PRI), the controlling political party. This, in the longer term, may lead to a decline in the coordination of policy. In the short term, it has led to policy which is more willing to change the way the benefits from the major regulated sectors of the economy are distributed. In short, Mexican telecommunications policy exhibits strong centralized coordination, a willingness to redistribute who wins and loses from the policy, and a strong mobilization of policy to reinforce the political realignment of the base of support for the PRI.

The privatization of TELMEX, the introduction of some competition for overlay services, and the fundamental redirection of management practices and commercial policies all reflect the strategy of the Salinas government and the PRI. They favor the middle class over traditional labor, and export-led businesses over traditional manufacturing. Above all, the case shows how the political structure of Mexico permitted effective restructuring of the telephone company before privatization.

Structure of the Mexican Government

The presidential system of Mexico is unusual because a single party, the PRI, has ruled continuously since the 1930s. Many terms describe the PRI—authoritarian, populist, mass mobilizing, and mass patronage—but all draw attention to the party's effort to organize the major parts of the Mexican electorate into an elaborate institutional complex and to its highly centralized control over all nominations of candidates for the party. The President of Mexico is the head of the PRI. By constitutional rule, the President and all elected officials in Mexico can serve only one term. The President is chosen for all practical purposes by the previous President in consultation with the senior party leadership. (The Salinas government instituted a formal rule that 150 senior party officials would officially be chosen to consult with the President.) There were absolutely no formal guidelines concerning who and on what terms the President consulted, but presumably, the President could not simply choose randomly or else the normally passive party would fail to ratify the choice of the candidates. In practice, every presidential nominee of recent years has come from the current cabinet. And because the cabinet ministers represented the political factions of the PRI in their personal bases of power, there was a good deal of infighting at the cabinet level.

Although the last few Presidents have never held a prior elected office, they all were veterans of the PRI internal political system.[9] The emphasis on technocrats in recent years partly reflects the belief of the party elite controlling the presidency that fundamentally new skills are necessary to turn around the Mexican economy and save the PRI's political future. It is probably also true that the emphasis on technical qualifications is one way of showing that the new Presidents are not part of a system often associated with corruption and favoritism. Moreover, the cabinet as a whole is probably more cohesive than in the past as the de la Madrid/Salinas wing of the party tries to solidify control.

The PRI was organized internally around an elaborate system of formal interest groups representing such sources of support as agricultural workers, government employees, and small business. Perhaps first among equals was organized labor. Traditionally, PRI policy was worked out by bargaining among the various interest groups within PRI and the major regional political leaders.

The unusual power of PRI to organize all branches of the government came in part because the power over nomination of candidates was tightly held in closed hands. The PRI at the national level nominated all congressional candidates. The local mayor was nominated for all practical purposes by the senator from the state.

As a consequence of being limited to only one term of office and tight central control over nomination, the legislative wing of the PRI is quite passive compared to a normal legislative branch of a presidential system. The implication for existing and future political reforms in Mexico is that the number of opposition legislators will grow. This will lead to an increased role for the legislature and probably more independent behavior by the PRI members inside the legislature (although they still have fewer incentives to act independently because they are not seeking reelection).[10]

The federal structure of Mexico offers some incentives to articulate policies which speak to special regional interests in the federal system. Local governments in Mexico in theory have considerable power. There is some evidence that they have served as sources for independent power bases within the PRI and are the places where the opposition parties will make their first and strongest mark. Although the national government retains the right to dissolve any state government it finds lacking, any sweeping reform of the telecommunications system should reflect regional political calculations.

The final piece of the political story of Mexico is the effort by the PRI to realign its political support. Traditionally, the government relied upon a policy of import-substitution industrialization to win the support of labor unions, heavy industry protected from foreign and local and much of the domestic competition, and small business. Nationalism was a major theme, and the policy of sharp limits on foreign investments in Mexico reflected the salience of nationalism. Heavy government spending on social welfare programs and many large subsidies for state-owned corporations were other measures to win popular support.

The economic crisis caused by the decline of oil revenues and the growth of foreign debt finally forced the PRI to reexamine its priorities. Economic performance was poor and popular discontent was growing. (There had already been a wave of political crises in 1968, but growing oil revenues temporarily saved the PRI. Now oil could not bail out the PRI.)

The PRI responded by fundamentally changing its economic priorities and therefore its political priorities. It decided to emphasize competition, privatization, and an export-based growth strategy for the economy. Tight fiscal and monetary policies to control inflation and stabilize public finances were also part of the package. The government intended to cut spending and boost revenue. This meant ending many subsidies and, just as important, it meant finding new sources of revenues. One important source of revenue was the sale of public assets, particularly the major state-owned enterprises.

The strategy was potentially attractive to a new mix of supporters for the PRI. Agriculture was declining in importance in Mexico. Labor unions could no longer be wooed with traditional subsidies for inefficient enterprises because the costs to the economy were too high. Large businesses could no longer be compensated for the highly constrained regulatory environment of Mexico by simply offering them quasi-monopolies. Instead, the Salinas government decided to make the very rapidly growing number of professional and white-collar workers (many of them the product of the development of the Mexican educational system and the oil boom) major sources of support. It also hoped to gain new support from business by emphasizing the growth of large industry and companies in a freer market in return for fewer forms of protection. This policy was explicitly designed to outmaneuver the Partido de Acción Nacional (PAN), the right-wing opposition party. It was prepared to accept some losses of support from labor in the short run (although the PRI strongly controlled the unions and so the unions themselves were unlikely to defect), in the hopes that sustained economic growth and low inflation would eventually make union workers once again happy with the government. The strategy also explicitly recognized that many of the long-term sources of political challenge to the PRI were coming from the northern states of Mexico closest to the U.S. border. A successful strategy would provide reasons for these states to see the PRI as a champion of their interests instead of being the protector of Mexico City at their expense.

The Choice of Telecommunications Policy

The leadership of TELMEX readily acknowledged that the telephone network needed substantial new investment. During the 1980s the company had cut back its rate of growth from 14 to 6 percent per year, and Mexico had fewer than 5 telephone lines per 100 people. Domestic service reached only 18 percent of the homes, and 10,000 rural communities were without service. The company in 1988 had revenues of about US$3.5 billion and 50,000 employees. Its labor union was one of the strongest in the country. To a large extent the company was being used as a cash cow for the government and its constituents.[11] At the same time, bickering was endemic between the telecommunications and transport secretariat and TELMEX. The secretariat controlled, for example, the Morelos domestic satellites and the state-owned microwave network. Thus, in some sense the secretariat was in competition with the company that it regulated.

The Salinas government recognized that it needed new sources of revenue to clean up its budget problems and provide monies for social welfare programs during a general austerity economic policy. It also wanted to find some way to quickly improve performance of a government-regulated sector for the middle class in industry in order to show that its reform policies could bring quick results.[12]

Presidents de la Madrid and Salinas chose to make a major effort to privatize TELMEX. Because the President of Mexico controls the PRI and PRI has such extraordinary control over the political leadership of all branches of government, it was possible to move decisively to change communications policy.

The fundamentals of the changes were severalfold. First, there was a process of administrative reform in regulation. The secretariat of communications was taken out of the business of providing services in order to become a more pure regulator. Second, by 1988 the government began a serious restructuring of TELMEX's internal bureaucracy, service priorities, financing, and pricing of its operations. It did so in anticipation of making the company a more attractive asset for sale. Instead of relying upon privatization to remedy TELMEX, the government decided to begin the remedies early on to show that it was serious about allowing TELMEX to grow in an economically efficient manner. Third, the government chose a strategy which combined full privatization involving foreign investment with a strategy of enhanced services and overlay networks.

The sale of TELMEX, on December 20, 1990, involved 20.4 percent of its class AA stock, which, although a minority of total equity, amounted to the majority of all voting stock and thus conferred management control to the purchasers. The price was US$1.758 billion. The majority (51 percent) of the consortium which purchased TELMEX is owned by Grupo Carso (a Mexican company is required by law). The minority is held by a partnership of Southwestern Bell and France Télécom.[13] TELMEX was to remain a national monopoly for basic telecommunications services for six years, including international long-distance services which yield most of its profits. It was given explicit permission to enter into all new forms of advanced telecommunications services through separate subsidiaries. It also holds a national cellular license.

The new ownership has also received major tax concessions which reduced the previous tax rate of 89 percent on local revenues and 40 percent on long-distance revenues. This had already increased income per line from US$425 in 1989 to US$800 in 1990.[14] In addition, the government approved considerable rate rebalancing and introduced something like a price cap which would guarantee a predictable flow of income for the telephone company and price protection for consumers for the next eight years. In return, the new ownership had to undertake a number of pledges. This included increasing the number of new lines by a rate of 12 percent a year, extending service to numerous small communities without telephones, undertaking a massive investment program of US$12 billion, increasing service quality as measured by a set of indicators set down in the contract, and meeting explicit goals for introducing digital switching and optic-fiber networks. In addition, the new owners had to agree to protect labor, including the rights of workers and their economic participation in the new TELMEX, by means of the 4.4 percent of stock allocated to them from the new privatization. (Assuming that TELMEX does well, workers should be able to share in the success.) But much of the labor renegotiation, including a reshuffling of union leadership, had been done prior to privatization.

The structure of competition emphasizes the broad monopoly of the basic public network until 1997. Mexico, however, has granted nine new cellular licenses to competitors of TELMEX and roughly thirty other licenses for paging and other services. Foreign firms may own up to 49 percent of these ventures. As one might expect, many of them are located in industrial regions along the border where there is strong demand for a quick improvement in services from the network and more formidable political opposition locally. It permitted companies to establish private corporate satellite networks over the Mexican national satellite system. Although it has also permitted PanAmSat to establish video services, it has so far rejected two-way digital services.

One last point should be made about the choice of privatization strategies. Because Salinas could take his time in introducing change and make it part of a broader set of policies to revitalize Mexican financial markets, already one of the best developed in Latin America, he was able to reap a special benefit from telecommunications policy. We can call this the "Nippon dividend" in honor of its inventors, the political leaders of Japan's Liberal Democratic Party (LDP), who figured out that properly managing privatization is a financial bonanza for political supporters. It provides the government with funds for specific public works projects (Salinas travels to towns telling people that local projects were paid for by the sale of a state company), and it gives the middle class a big financial dividend through stockholdings. Forty percent of TELMEX stock is reserved for Mexican nationals; the value of the stock has appreciated considerably since privatization. A stock certificate in every household is almost as good as a chicken in every pot when the company is a well-financed monopoly whose new ownership structure assures that its incentives are largely business expansion, not distributive politics.

The Case of Argentina

The Argentine case shows how political dynamics can alter the timing and objectives of reform and possibly compromise some of the normally preferred strategies for restructuring the communications sector. In particular, unlike Mexico, Argentina could not restructure effectively prior to privatization.

Argentina has a presidential system with an independent legislature (a Chamber of Deputies and Senate with relatively equal powers) and a federalist structure: provincial governors are powerful, there is an electoral college for the President, and presidential nominations are strongly influenced by provincial leaderships. Presidents may serve only a single term (of six years).[15]

As a general rule, policy coordination at the national level is more difficult in presidential and federalist systems. Political party structures may make these problems better or worse, and the extraordinary role of Peronism made it worse.

The Peronists won every free election (they were forbidden to participate in some) for some forty years until the 1983 election of the Radical Party candidate, Raul Alfonsin. The Peronist party itself was a vehicle for organizing support for the authoritarian rule of Peron in his initial term in office by creating a corporatist structure of interest groups, especially the labor unions and implicitly import-substitution industries, such as the state firms that were vastly overstaffed and paid well. Corruption was rampant. About 117 state-owned companies represented almost half of the GNP, and 30 percent of their budgets came from budget subsidies. After Peron's personal control declined the corporatist structures and provincial party bosses largely dominated the party, locking it into support for continued patronage and subsidy policies. Their dominance also further reinforced the traditional struggle between agricultural exporters (wheat and cattle) and labor.

Argentina struggled with a multiparty regime subject to frequent bouts of nondemocratic rule. Apparently, the lack of continuity of democratic politics fueled factionalism built around provincial party leaders and made policy innovations difficult to achieve.[16] But the 1983 election (following the end of the fourth period of military rule since 1945) redefined the political landscape. The Radical Party (traditionally a social welfare party in the European fashion) rallied around Alfonsin's new agenda for the party, the promotion of stable democracy, and won over much of the traditional third-party votes for center-right candidates. This turned Argentina into a two-party democracy for the time being and suggested that voter loyalties were volatile.

A further shift in the electoral system was occurring because of demographic change. The continued decline of Argentina's economy had shrunk the ranks of union workers, left the numbers of the middle class about the same, and greatly increased the numbers of self-employed in the formal and informal sectors. Although analysts disagree on how to categorize the preferences of the self-employed, all agree that labor unions do not represent them and their preferences differ from traditional Peronist policies because traditional industry does not support them. At the same time, the economic crisis had highlighted the declining performance of the public sector on other counts. The poor performance of ENTel, the state telephone company, offended large customers such as banks and everyday consumers in the middle class who could not get telephone service.

The 1983 election made both parties aware that some new mix of policies was necessary to attract the middle class and the self-employed. Because of the dual problems of inflation and foreign debt, almost no policy mix could primarily appeal to both the unions and to these groups. So, winning support from export agriculture and the pro-market wing of the business community seemed more attractive for coalition building. Accordingly, the new focus of electoral competition has come in programs to cut inflation, to emphasize jobs by export-led growth, and to privatize state industries, making them more efficient, lowering the financial drag on government, and above all slashing the foreign debt.

As electoral competition under democratic guidelines became more routinized, the electoral rules started to open the possibility of somewhat greater party discipline. The provincial leaders are still vital in the struggle for nomination and election to the presidency. But the national party controls who may run for the Chamber of Deputies, a powerful source of central political control. (The Senate may be more fractious because the terms run for six years.) Thus, one should expect more organized party behavior in the legislature than in the past, which means that significant policy changes will almost surely depend on one party's controlling both branches of the legislature.

All other things being equal there should also be greater sensitivity to regional variations in interest in a federalist system. The political party in power should define many of the secondary characteristics of policy. For example, Peronists should be more pro-labor and more concerned with protecting local industry within the boundaries of the general new program.

The Transformation of ENTel

The Alfonsin administration initially concentrated on normalizing ties with the military and coping with inflation and foreign debt. Its economic stabilization programs failed, and it turned to privatization of state enterprise as a chance for some favorable economic outcome. This was particularly urgent because it lost control of the legislature in the 1987 elections and had to prepare rapidly for the presidential race of 1989. Under the circumstances we should have expected the Radical Party program to put a premium on a quick sale of state properties to slash debt and bring immediate benefits to the middle class and business supporters (such as the banks). It would also have been expected to care less about labor and local and state industrialists than the Peronists.

What the Alfonsin government did not do is significant. Under the 1956 law governing ENTel, the President of Argentina had effective control over ENTel. Not only did he possess official final authority, he also controlled the appointment of the Ministry of Communication subsecretary who served as president of the ENTel board.[17] The company had a debt load of US$2 billion and the government subsidy per new installed line was about 50 percent. So this was a badly financed cash drain with bloated staffing (45,000 employees).

One alternative would have been to entertain monopoly modernization by order of the President. In 1987, seventeen banks joined together to push for new network facilities in Buenos Aires, preferably by a new private operator. The government could have used this as the opening wedge to push for readjusted rates, realigned labor practices (remember that labor mattered less to the Radical Party), and stepped up investment.[18] But this program had several political defects. It cost money just when stabilization and cutting foreign debt were the priorities. Just as vitally, there was no guarantee that continued public ownership would consistently yield reform policies precisely because the office of the President controlled the company. A Peronist victory could have reversed monopoly modernization by a simple directive of the President. (In most presidential systems the current ruling government is likely to suboptimize policy in order to lock in its benefits for its supporters.)[19]

In 1988 the Alfonsin government proposed to privatize ENTel. Its chosen vehicle was selling the company as a single entity, to Telefónica de España. Telefónica was to receive management control and 40 percent of the stock, with 9 percent going to employees and 51 percent to the government. Telefónica was to pay US$750 million: US$250 million for foreign debt relief and US$250 million for investment in the system in the first year. The remainder was due to be spent over thirty months. This total figure was about US$250 million less than the estimated net worth of ENTel seemed to justify. Telefónica was to receive an exclusive twenty-five-year license, and was free to realign and rationalize equipment suppliers for ENTel in order to lower costs.

This package had the virtue of delivering a quick investment of money and new services by virtue of its payment schedule. It also promised a decisive administrative reform. The opinion polls indicated that discontent with ENTel was very high, especially among the middle-class and commercial farm regions that were the Radical Party's electoral base. Privatization and sale to a foreign firm also would make it harder for the next administration to reverse its policy.

The package soon stumbled, however, because the Peronists acted coherently to take advantage of the Radical Party's minority position in the national legislature. Peronists appealed to their traditional constituents in the unions, the large equipment suppliers to ENTel, and other state enterprises. Union strikes were called to oppose the plan, for example. The attack emphasized two issues: first, the negotiation with Telefónica had violated the public bidding process required by law and second, the government was hastily awarding a valuable monopoly to a foreign company. The opposition strategy was carefully orchestrated to leave room for privatization at a later time, when the Peronists controlled the government and could fine-tune the terms as well as claim the popular credit. There was no formal rejection of the bill, simply delay until Menem won the election.[20]

In 1989 the Peronists won the presidential and legislative elections. The legislature quickly gave the President virtually carte blanche to privatize all state companies except the petroleum corporation. The only consultation with Congress required was through a bicameral commission which had no specific powers. But party unity in presidential systems is usually imperfect. So, the President had to act early in the term when his political stock in his own party was highest. Menem did so by relying on presidential decrees and a very tight time schedule for privatization (fourteen months in all). This schedule, for example, gave companies contesting the franchise awards only one week to protest!

As one might expect, the President chose a strategy to avoid his own criticisms of the prior policies and to find a new base of political supporters. The highlights of the new policy were an open auction process and the breakup of the single national monopoly. The policy itself was implemented by a key member of one of the third parties most associated with free-market policies. The ENTel privatization became the symbol of the government's effort to attract these swing voters. Above all, Menem wanted to sell the company quickly to reform it. The government secondarily needed cash to meet the huge debts being run up by ENTel. Later, to build political support, it was also critical to show that Menem could make progress on reducing the strain on public finances by easing the servicing of the foreign debt. Therefore, Menem began to push for a high component of debt relief in the purchase package. At the same time, he worked hard to split the unions so that some factions of the union movement endorsed privatization on the (presumably) less stringent terms of his government. He also obtained a new antistrike law and used troops to man the telephone system when a major strike finally came.

The crux of the reform was that it had to be done quickly before the traditional Peronist wing of the party could rebel and before the next round of legislative elections. Thus, unlike Mexico, the government could not undertake substantial administrative and financial reform of ENTel prior to privatization. This in turn increased the risk level for foreign investors and forced less attractive terms for the transaction. There was always a ticking clock. Because ENTel could not be reformed before the sale, it faced the competition of other, more attractive privatizations in the near future that would seek the same scarce investment funds.

The government decided to split the country into two regional monopolies (after a heated debate over the proper number) with five-year exclusive licenses for local voice services.[21] There were numerous provisos to ensure that the worst political case did not occur, the creation of a de facto national monopoly because the same foreign company won the option in both regions. The government was to sell 60 percent of the stock in two new companies to foreign purchasers. Although there was no absolute agreement on the value of ENTel, the new number being quoted commonly was US\$3.5 billion, a largely arbitrary number because there had been no audit of ENTel since 1988. The government wanted US\$1.807 billion for the 60 percent. The rest of the stock was to go to ENTel employees, publicly traded shares in Argentina, and local telecommunications equipment suppliers.

Before the end of the process the government switched to seven-year licenses with a three-year option to extend, a joint monopoly of the two regional firms for international voice services, and competition permitted only in mobile cellular service (today there are already eight cellular firms), national telex, domestic data services, private satellite systems via PanAmSat.

The plan had to be modified as it progressed because opposition within the Peronist party was strong. In essence, the government boosted the asking price to US\$1.9 billion even though the company was losing US\$50 million per month. It originally assured the winners that tariffs would be tied to the national inflation rates and guaranteed a rate of return of 16 percent on assets of US\$3.2 billion in the first two years. This would have assisted in self-financing the desired US\$5 billion in new investment demanded over the next ten years. But the legislature (led by the Radical Party) got the guarantee reduced to cover only the US\$1.9 billion purchase price, and it legislated a minimum floor for foreign debt to be covered by the purchase price.

The plan also called for the franchise to cut real prices (that is, after inflation) by 2 percent per year for the next five years (and later by 4 percent). When the consortium of Bell Atlantic and Manufacturers Hanover, the winners of the northern zone, had to bow out, the government further modified the terms by including the price of the dollar as a second element in the rate formula. The telephone company also has the right to book its revenues from installing new lines in U.S. dollars.[22]

What are the obligations of the new telephone companies? They must meet goals for new numbers of lines per region annually, quality of service, as well as reliability and repair rates for the infrastructure. The new National Telecommunications Commission may sanction the company if it does not meet the goals, including fines, denial of extension of the minimum franchise period, or revocation of the license.[23] (The commission has five members with five-year terms, but they are appointed and can be removed by the President.) The franchises also have to provide all value added services by separate subsidiaries. The biggest priorities appear to be capping the rate of price increases, much speedier and reliable offering of services, and limited subsidies to households for new telephone lines. (The telephone company can charge a household only half the cost of a new line.)

The final division of ENTel assets was slightly uneven (55 percent went to the southern company, Telco Sur). The total selling price was worth about US$1.2 billion: US$5.028 billion in redeemed foreign debt (purchased at a discount of about 15 cents on the dollar) including accrued interest, US$214 million in cash, and US$380 million in medium-term loans to cover ENTel debts. France Télécom, STET (Italy), and Morgan Stanley (handling the buying of the deeply discounted debt) combined with the local Argentine financial group of Compañía Naviera Perez Companc, bought the northern company, Telco Norte. The southern company went to Telefónica de España, Citicorp, and Techint.

The speed and shifting terms of the process have led many to suggest that the government botched the process. My perspective suggests that it did about all that was possible given the political structure of Argentina. By far the most interesting feature of the system was the deliberate decision to opt for multiple monopolies, especially for basic services, and foreign ownership. This combination had many advantages politically.

Multiple monopolies mean that each monopoly is a benchmark for the other.[24] This is a good check when divisions in the government suggest that regulators may well be limited to their efficacy. Already, the northern company cut rates when demand lagged behind projections, and this put pressure on the southern company to do the same. The regional franchises also permit some measure of responsiveness to variations in regional politics in a federal system.

Foreign ownership has two advantages. On the one hand, the new foreign owners have good incentives to perform well because they are vulnerable to political attack. They cannot play the game of massive pork-barrel politics to anywhere near the same extent as local firms. Improved efficiency is their best card. On the other hand, as long as they perform, it will be harder to reverse policies precisely because their parent governments (and the world financial community in general) are a defensive shield for the new owners.

Conclusion

In summary, Mexico and Argentina are both relatively industrialized countries that needed massive extension of their communications infrastructure. Both chose to privatize and permit foreign ownership. But they split over whether to retain a single company for basic phone services, and the strategy for privatizing differed significantly. Political institutions suggest why the policies diverged. Put differently, economics and technology propose, but politics dispose.

Endnotes

1. For the United States see Garnet, *The Telephone Enterprise* (Baltimore: Johns Hopkins Press). For Canada see Christopher Armstrong and H.V. Nells, *Monopoly's Moment* (Philadelphia: Temple University Press, 1986).

2. For a full discussion see Jonathan David Aronson and Peter F. Cowhey, *When Countries Talk: International Trade in Telecommunications Services* (Cambridge, Massachusetts: Ballinger, 1988); Peter F. Cowhey, "The International Telecommunications Regime: The Political Roots for High Technology Regimes," *International Organization*, Vol. 44, No. 2, Cambridge, Massachusetts, Spring 1990.

3. The international counterpart to this domestic policy is commitment to international competition. Jonathan Aronson and I have pointed toward the growth of a global "greenbelt" for telecommunications that joins London, New York, and Tokyo under a revised set of international competitive rules. See Peter F. Cowhey, Jonathan David Aronson, and Gabriel Szekely, eds., *Changing Networks: Mexico's Telecommunications Options* (San Diego: UC San Diego, Center for U.S–Mexican Studies).

4. Political scientists will recognize that these themes overlap with work in the "statist" tradition. I am not using a statist model.

5. This is true in the United States, long considered an example of uncontrolled bureaucratic fighting. See Mathew D. McCubbins, "The Legislative Design of Regulatory Structure," *American Journal of Political Science*, 29 (1985), pp. 721–48.) A significant new body of work is showing that it is also true in such countries as Japan. See Samuel Kernell, ed., *Parallel Politics* (Washington, DC: Brookings Institution, 1991).

6. For example, Singapore has a parliamentary system, but its leader was so dominant for so long that some questioned whether the parliamentary system election really was a truly meaningful political incentive. I would expect that it was, because the elections were not fraudulent, but some might disagree. A more perplexing case is exemplified by countries like South Korea or Thailand where the political leadership has to contend with frequent military intervention.

7. A dense urban network has the great advantage of little in the way of problems of rural service (and its subsidy). Singapore also has great geographic advantages as a potential communications hub for Asia.

8. This being Canadian federalism, nothing is quite this simple. The federal government directly regulated some provincial carriers (Bell Canada and British Columbia Telecom), but not most provinces. See the works of Richard Schultz and Hudson Janisch; for example, Hudson Janisch, "Telecom 2000: A Glance at Future Trends in Canadian Telecommunications Regulation," *Media and Communications Law Review,* 1990.

9. My thanks to Professor Wayne Cornelius for sharing unpublished papers with me on the current strategy of the PRI.

10. The legislature always has some influence because the presence of a small opposition within meant that the legislature had to have some role in the policymaking system, especially for interest groups bargaining with the PRI. Certainly the PRI has foreseen the possibilities of a growing minority role because it has written the rules for the organization of the legislature in such a way that the PRI could command a minority vote nationally and still control the legislature.

11. Juan Ricardo Perez Escamilla, "Telephone Policy in Mexico: Rates and Investment," in *Changing Networks: Mexico's Telecommunications Options* (UC San Diego, Center for U.S.–Mexican Studies), ed. Peter F. Cowhey, Jonathan David Aronson, and Gabriel Szekely.

12. The government clearly wanted to emphasize rapid, clear performance goals. Some critics charged that this would require sacrificing revenues on the sales price, but the government reform of TELMEX and regulatory policy prior to the sale eased this problem.

13. The breakdown of voting rights to Southwestern Bell, is 12.5 percent each for Southwestern Bell and France Telecom, 26 percent for Grupo Carso and 48 percent for the public. Grupo Carso has 10.5 percent of TELMEX equity, France Telecom and Southwestern Bell each have 5.0 percent. The consortium has the option of buying another 5.1 percent equity in TELMEX over the next four years. Southwestern Bell argues that it paid a 2 percent premium over the market price for TELMEX stock.

14. Carlos Mier y Teran, "Modernization of Telecom in Mexico," *Transnational Data and Communications Report,* March/April 1991, pp.18–22.

15. My entire discussion of telecommunications policy is strongly indebted to a paper by Cynthia Baur of the Department of Communications at UC San Diego. Data on the Argentine political structure are from John Carey and Matthew Shugart, *Presidents and Assemblies: Constitutional Design and Electoral Dynamics* (Cambridge: Cambridge University Press, 1992). The work on elections is reported in Paul Drake and Eduardo Silva, eds., *Elections and Democratization in Latin America, 1980–1985,* (UC San Diego, Center for US–Mexican Studies) Co-publications Sec. No. 2, 1986.

16. This issue requires more research than I have done so far. General theories of electoral dynamics would suggest that the Peronist opposition parties had their incentives misaligned because of the military's implicit veto over Peronist victories.

17. One of the other six seats on the board was reserved for the military. The ENTel general manager was the board vice president. The high rate of turnover of general managers suggest strong outside pressure on a recurring basis.

18. There was even a precedent for raising funds to modernize. A prior program had required customers to put up deposits for new lines to fund the work. Unfortunately, ENTel's chaotic management procedures had lost track of who deposited the monies.

19. Terry M. Moe, "The New Economics of Organization," *American Journal of Political Science*, 26 (1984), pp. 739–77.

20. I should note that President Menem's brother led the Peronist opposition to the Menem plan and his major ally in the Senate would later become Menem's minister of public works and services.

21. Several small phone companies owned by Ericsson of Sweden (serving rural districts) are exempt from the plan. A study by Coopers & Lybrand said that three regions might be an option. Many in the government liked three regions because it meant smaller territories, which would permit more participation by Argentine companies. This was politically attractive but threatened to make the franchises too small to draw the attention of premium foreign investors.

22. I am told that the final formula assured a rate of return on the US$1.9 billion of over 16 percent. The investors calculated that the new tariff levels plus expected levels of demand would yield a cash flow that would largely (but not fully) cover the US$5 billion investment schedule demanded by the contract.

23. In theory, any pattern of having to wait for new lines for more than six months could yield permission for creation of independent private line networks in the territory with their own private infrastructure. Such rules are fairly idle threats absent other rules about the rights of the new entrants.

24. This follows from the logic of the classic article on regulation by Stigler and Friedlander.

39

Managing the Process of Sector Reform

John J. Collings

REFORM OF THE TELECOMMUNICATIONS SECTOR IS under way or in prospect in many countries, both industrial and developing. Over the past decade, the convergence of telecommunications and information technologies has had a profound effect on economic activity. As a result, the availability of a modern and efficient telecommunications sector has grown rapidly in importance as a determinant of national competitive advantage across a range of industries. This has made governments increasingly aware of the dangers of maintaining supply structures that may be unable to adapt to rapid technological and market change. New supply structures are therefore being sought which will enhance the contribution of the telecommunications sector to economic and social development.

The Inherited Supply Structure

Traditionally, the provision of telecommunications has been entrusted in most countries to a telecommunications administration operating on a self-regulating basis under exclusive rights and with access to investment capital determined by government decisions on the allocation of public funds. In many cases, the telecommunications administration has been supplied by a local equipment industry manufacturing under license to meet domestic needs and protected by import duties and other local preference measures. This institutional and legal framework for the provision of telecommunications has shielded the sector from competitive forces in both product markets and capital markets.

This traditional monopoly supply structure has evolved for a number of reasons. In particular, there was a belief that economies of scale and scope were so great in the telecommunications sector, relative to the size of the market, that services could be provided most efficiently by one rather than several operators. Furthermore, governments have attached considerable strategic importance to the national communications infrastructure and have therefore been reluctant to leave development of a vital national asset solely to the influence of market forces. Also, integration of network planning standards and operation have been necessary for the provision of national and international long-distance services. These factors have encouraged the adoption of supply structures characterized by monopoly provision and state ownership.

In many countries, long-standing ties between the telecommunications and postal sectors reflect the historical development of telegraph services followed by telephone service. In these countries, telecommunications have been provided by a posts and telecommunications administration (PTT). In some other countries, telephone service was developed through one or more concessions granted to foreign companies whose operations were subsequently nationalized. Finally, the United States developed a variant of the traditional supply structure in which pervasive regulation of AT&T as a shareholder-owned monopoly operator replaced direct government control of the sector through ownership.

Pressures for Reform

The traditional supply structure endured for many decades, suggesting that it was well suited to the provision of a limited range of basic telecommunications services by means of a mature analog technology. This structure was, of course, subject to wider concerns about the financial and operational performance of public enterprises (or regulated utilities, in the case of the United States). Nonetheless, widespread challenges to the traditional supply structure have only emerged as technological change has redefined sector boundaries and dramatically increased the interdependencies between telecommunications and other sectors. This rapid technological change has impacted both supply and demand conditions in the sector. On the supply side, technological change has transformed network capital and operating cost structures, permitted a wide array of services to be provided by means of a single integrated network, and enabled processing functions to be embedded in the network or sited at customer premises. On the demand side, completely new applications of telecommunications have been made possible, creating user needs of a kind not seen before.

The increasing diversity of services and markets has led to growing pressures for telecommunications sector reform. The traditional supply structure, designed primarily to meet demand for voice telephony, excludes rivalry between competing suppliers as a mechanism for encouraging responsiveness to changing technologies and markets. Limits on access to investment capital imposed as a consequence of government budgetary targets constrain the pace of network modernization and the introduction of new services. They have also left a legacy of past underinvestment in the network infrastructure in many countries.

A further force for change in the telecommunications sector has come from broader economic policies aimed at reducing the size of the public sector and strengthening market forces in the economy. Telecommunications can be viewed as a sector in which conditions particularly favor a shift from public to private provision. As a rapidly growing, technology-based sector, telecommunications is attractive to both domestic and foreign investors. For this reason, the sector has been used in many countries to spearhead programs of privatization of state-owned enterprises and the removal of statutory monopolies.

Policy Instruments

The process of telecommunications sector reform involves four policy variables: competition, regulation, restructuring, and ownership.

Competition

The introduction of competition as a process which encourages innovation and efficiency may be seen as increasingly necessary as the telecommunications sector becomes more dynamic. On the other hand, although it may be desirable to open up the telecommunications sector to market forces, it may be considered inappropriate for the development of the national network infrastructure to be entirely market-led. Furthermore, to the extent that competition drives prices toward costs, it may not be possible to maintain existing pricing structures that incorporate cross-subsidies geared to social policy objectives for affordability and uniformity of charges for basic service.

Regulation

Regulation may be a necessary part of the telecommunications sector reform process in order to achieve political control of market processes. First, the established operating entity is likely to have considerable market power, and regulation may therefore be required to ensure that exploitative or anticompetitive conduct is prevented. Second, regulatory measures may be put in place to secure national coverage of the network infrastructure and uniform tariffs for basic telephone service at affordable levels. Third, regulation may be used to enforce the mandatory provision of certain socially desirable services (such as free emergency service, directory assistance service, and maritime service). Fourth, regulation may be used to prevent undue economic harm to the established operating entity from competition, thereby safeguarding its ability to finance its infrastructural and service obligations.

The regulatory provisions for telecommunications sector reform should replace informal political control of sectoral public policy objectives with enforcement of clearly defined obligations imposed on the established operating entity. This should make the development of the sector less vulnerable to short-term political pressures; however, regulation clearly limits the extent to which sector reform can bring about a shift from monopolistic public provision of services toward a greater reliance on private provision and market forces.

Restructuring

Restructuring of the institutional framework for service provision is an inherent part of the process of telecommunications sector reform. Clear separation of policymaking, regulatory, and operational roles has to be achieved if private enterprise is to be the main driver of sector development rather than government intervention. At the same time, it may be necessary to consider restructuring of the established operating entity where the inherited structure appears likely to act as a barrier to increased efficiency or to the introduction of competition. Possible options could include:

- Divestiture of some activities to reduce the level of involvement of the established operating entity in competitive markets

- Separation of long-distance and international service provision from local service provision to remove structural barriers to competition

- Formation of separate regional operating companies to facilitate performance comparisons, thereby creating rivalry in monopoly local service provision

- Merging fragmented local exchange operations to ensure that networks can be reconfigured to take maximum advantage of the replacement of hardwired networks by electronically defined networks.

Ownership

In order to introduce commercial disciplines into the telecommunications sector, it may be necessary to change the relationship between the established operating entity and its owner. Corporatization does this by replacing the existing administrative relationship by one in which the government acts as shareholder of a telephone company set up on normal private sector lines. Privatization goes beyond this, with the government transferring all or part of its ownership of the established operating entity to the private sector, whether through a public flotation or a trade sale.

Approaches to Sector Reform

The approaches to reform of the telecommunications sector that have been used to date can be broadly classified as either piecemeal, gradualist, goal-oriented, or strategic. Each of these approaches is described below and the choice of approach is then considered.

Piecemeal Approaches

In some countries, institutional factors may take a piecemeal approach to sector reform inevitable. A good example of this is the United States, where the redefinition of telecommunications market structures has been achieved through rule making and adjudication by regulators at both federal and state levels, through frequent court reviews of regulatory action and through court-supervised settlements of antitrust litigation. As a result, regulatory policy development has proceeded through a series of decisions on specific issues with all evidence and reasoning on the public record.

The main danger with this approach is that transparency of decisionmaking and procedural fairness will be achieved at the cost of fragmented and issue-driven policy development and protracted regulatory and legal proceedings.

In other countries, piecemeal approaches to sector reform result from different government departments or agencies having responsibility for telecommunications, information technology, broadcasting, radio spectrum management, trade policy, and competition matters. With many departments making decisions which will shape the structure of telecommunications markets, there are clearly great difficulties of policy coordination to be overcome.

Gradualist Approaches

Sector reform by means of a series of incremental steps has obvious attractions for policymakers aware of the political sensitivity of universal service and affordability issues, concerned by possible labor union hostility, and bewildered by the proliferation of choices resulting from technological change and new market demand.

The United Kingdom provides an example of the gradualist approach. In 1977, the government-appointed Post Office Review Committee recommended that the U.K. Post Office's telecommunications business and data-processing service should be established as a separate telecommunications authority. The committee's report also noted that technological developments then in progress would result in a wide range of new services becoming available and suggested that this might favor a redefinition of the boundaries of the telecommunications monopoly in the United Kingdom. In 1981, legislation was enacted under which British Telecom was separated from the Post Office and government took over responsibility for licensing other telecommunications operators and for setting technical standards for equipment. Over the following ten years, a series of liberalization and privatization measures led in stages to:

- Withdrawal of government from the sector other than in the role of licensing authority

- Independent regulation by a specialist, single-purpose body (OFTEL)

- Fully competitive domestic markets for customer premises equipment and for value added and data services (with unrestricted resale of leased capacity)

- Duopolistic markets for the national provision of fixed public telecommunications networks, cellular radio networks, and private mobile radio networks.

It was not until the completion of a policy review in 1991, however, that the government decided it would consider applications for operating licenses on their merits as opposed to a general presumption that they should be allowed. It also decided that it would issue class licenses for self-provision of circuits and for the provision of satellite services not requiring connection to the public-switched network. This marked the end of the managed transition to full competition in U.K. telecommunications markets, although restrictions remain on competition in international services to avoid harm to national interests by dominant overseas operators.

The advantages of a gradualist approach are that with proper sequencing of measures, it allows time for:

- Perceptions of sector priorities by stakeholders to evolve as intermediate policy objectives are achieved

- Significant contributions to be made to the sector reform process by research into critical empirical questions

- Regulatory capability to be developed in step with the sector reform process

- Adjustment to competition to be made by the established operating entity.

Goal-Oriented Approaches

The pace of reform in the telecommunications sector has been most rapid in those countries where clear political decisions have been made in pursuit of critical policy goals going well beyond the sector itself and demanding immediate attention. Key challenges for the management of the sector reform process under these circumstances are:

- Broadening the scope of the reform process from its initial narrow focus on particular policy goals to ensure that decisions are consistent with a rational strategy for telecommunications sector development

- Quickly identifying the key tasks that have to be undertaken, and mobilizing the necessary resources to do so

- Ensuring that all the critical elements in the reform process are progressing in step.

Argentina provides a good example of rapid reform of the telecommunications sector driven by broader policy goals. In this case, the critical policy goals driving the sector reform process were the privatization and liberalization of the Argentine economy. The result was strong political backing and a tight timetable for the privatization of ENTel and the associated adjustment of the institutional and regulatory framework for the provision of telecommunications in Argentina. The telecommunications sector reform process was initiated by a decree dated September 12, 1989. This specified that the national executive power should approve the terms and conditions for the privatization by the end of the year and established a timetable for an international public tender leading to the new owners taking possession on November 8, 1990. Such tight time-scales clearly had major implications for the management of the process of telecommunications sector reform:

- There was only limited opportunity to overcome information deficiencies and to resolve empirical questions.

- It was difficult to adjust underresourcing of particular tasks that became apparent during the reform process.

- Many of the practicalities of the restructuring of ENTel had to be left for the new owners to sort out.

The Argentine experience shows that the process of sector reform can be managed so as to achieve quick results in terms of privatization without neglecting the need for measures to secure benefits from improvements in the availability and quality of basic telephone service; to provide greater customer choice of advanced telecommunications equipment and services; and to control monopoly prices. The effectiveness of these measures will, however, depend crucially on regulatory capabilities whose development so far significantly lags behind the rest of the sector reform process.

Strategic Approaches

To date there have been few examples of telecommunications sector reform undertaken on the basis of an integrated strategy for sector development. In part this is due to the many unresolved empirical questions facing policymakers, particularly regarding the feasibility and desirability of public network competition. Recently, however, countries such as Panama and Uruguay have commissioned sector strategy studies which are to provide a blueprint for telecommunications development and from which a coherent set of objectives and priorities for sector reform will be identified.

The management of telecommunications sector reform by the European Commission provides one illustration of a strategic approach. The Commission's primary aim has been to establish the conditions necessary for the development of a European Community-wide market for telecommunications services and equipment. Through its Green Papers on telecommunications services and equipment (1987) and on satellite communications (1990), the Commission has established a blueprint for sector development and has backed this with directives to open up to competition the markets for terminal equipment as well as for value added services and data communications. At the same time, the Commission's measures permit diversity in national approaches to the issue of network competition. An interesting aspect of the Commission's approach is that it shows how sector reform may be managed in a federal system. The Commission has succeeded in achieving a consensus of opinion on general principles for the liberalization and reform of the sector in the European Community. Nonetheless, to secure the necessary action by member states, it has been necessary for the Commission to use the competition rules of the Treaty of Rome. This use of competition rules to achieve a policy aim rather than to deal with specific misconduct is controversial, but it has been upheld by the European Court.

Choice of Approach and Strategy Formulation

The choice of approach to sector reform will clearly depend on particular national circumstances—political, institutional, economic, and sector-specific. Where circumstances permit, however, it seems likely that countries will increasingly choose a strategic approach in which aims, objectives, and constraints are clearly identified and the transition to new market structures takes place over a period through the achievement of clearly defined milestones for market, institutional, and regulatory development. In this way the triggering of particular change mechanisms for market structure takes place in step with measures to put in place the institutional framework and regulatory safeguards that are prerequisites for successful strategy implementation. Properly managed, this approach to sector reform combines the advantages of the gradualist approach with those of the strategic approach. The process of sector reform in Australia illustrates how a phased approach underpinned by a clear strategic intent can be implemented.

To provide a strategic framework for the assessment of options for sector reform, it is necessary to identify and prioritize a comprehensive set of objectives, and to define the measures that will be used to monitor their achievement. To do this requires four tasks: situation analysis, definition of aims, identification of goals and constraints, and objective setting.

Successful completion of these tasks will require significant resources and will depend on access to the necessary data and policy guidance to ensure that the sector reform process is geared to particular national circumstances rather than some generic model of sector development.

Situation Analysis

The situation analysis provides the factual basis for policy development and evaluation and needs to cover both supply and demand conditions. In interpreting the results, extensive use is likely to be made of international comparisons. The range of topics to be covered by the situation analysis includes:

- Market conditions, covering the current and prospective levels of demand, service development, and the scope for new service

- Network capability, covering the current and planned size, technical development, and performance of the network

- Financial performance, covering the current financial position and medium-term prospects on current policies for the established provider of infrastructure and telephone service

- Nonfinancial performance, covering key indicators of service quality and efficiency

- Tariff structure, covering the level of tariffs by major service, service profitability, demand elasticity, and the scope for unbundling and de-averaging of the present tariffs.

Definition of Aims

The purpose of this task is to articulate the government's primary policy aims for the sector. This short statement should be derived from and encapsulate the government's vision of market development for telecommunications services and equipment. Depending on national circumstances, the statement of primary aims might be more oriented toward either social policy or economic development. A social policy-based statement of aims would emphasize the achievement of universal availability of basic telephone service at affordable rates and would look to regulatory oversight of prices, service quality, and efficiency to protect the public interest. An economic development-based statement of aims would emphasize the need to enhance national competitive advantage by securing for business users internationally competitive levels of service availability, quality and price, and, possibly, by requiring the telecommunications sector to play a catalytic role in the development of the domestic electronics and information services industries.

Identification of Goals and Constraints

Having identified the primary aims of telecommunications sector policy, it is then possible to identify the critical goals for sector reform and the relevant constraints. The critical goals might include, for example:

- Availability of a modern and efficient network providing services at internationally competitive levels of service availability, quality, and price

- Improvement in access to basic telephone service at the lowest prices consistent with economy and efficiency of use

- Satisfaction of growing demand for innovative services

- Reduction of regional disparities in the availability, quality, and prices of telecommunications services

- Strengthening of the government's budgetary position

- Reduction in the size of the public sector and in the extent to which it competes with the private sector.

Relevant constraints on the sector reform process may include, for example:

- Constitutional or political restrictions on privatization of the national telecommunications infrastructure

- Requirements that any privatization proceeds adequately compensate the public for relinquishing ownership of assets which were previously collectively held

- Avoidance of rate shock to residential and small business users as prices are brought into line with costs

- Restrictions on retrenchment of staff

- Need to ensure that service providers undertake community service obligations.

Recent experience in Puerto Rico illustrates the imposition of constraints on the sector reform process in the national interest. Preconditions for the sale of the Puerto Rico Telecommunications Company (PRTC) were:

- That the proceeds should exceed US$3 billion to cover the company's outstanding debt and that funds of US$1 billion each for education and infrastructure projects be set up

- A three-year price freeze

- No retrenchment of staff.

A clear statement of preconditions does assist potential bidders in their evaluation of the investment opportunity, although it reduces the scope for trading off different elements through negotiation.

Objective Setting

Each of the critical goals and constraints identified have to be translated into a set of objectives and associated performance measures. These can then be used as the basis for comparative assessment of options for sector reform. Thus, if one of the critical goals is to have a modern and efficient network, then the relevant objectives and performance measures might relate to improvements in labor productivity, network digitalization, network performance, fault rates and repair times, waiting lists for connections, and procurement costs.

Where critical goals concern the provision of services at internationally competitive levels of availability, quality, and price, or the satisfaction of demand for innovative services, the objectives are likely to relate not only to the achievement of standards set by key comparator countries but also to securing favorable market entry conditions. This is because the threat of market entry should act as a spur to efficiency, economic pricing, innovation, and responsiveness to user needs, while market entry itself will increase customer choice. Performance measures expressed relative to international standards might include waiting times for network connection, call failure rates, fault clearance times, and price levels by service. Other performance measures might include penetration rates for mobile and data communications services as well as the share of new entrants in sector revenues.

Goals for improvement in access to basic telephone service at affordable rates or reduction of regional disparities will be reflected in objectives for network coverage and density, quality of service, and the price of basic service. Relevant performance measures may include the percentage of communities over a given size with local exchange service, the number of exchange lines per 100 households, the number of coin- or card-operated public telephones per 100 population, waiting times for connection, call failure rates, and the cost (in real terms) of the telecommunications services purchased by the average residential customer and by a representative low user.

Goals for strengthening the government's budgetary position may lead to the setting of objectives for increasing tax and dividend receipts from the sector, for the maximization of privatization proceeds, for development of local capital markets through the sale of shares, and for the attraction of foreign investment.

Among the constraints that may be placed on the sector reform process, the avoidance of rate shock to residential and small business users is often of particular importance. In most countries, the inherited rate structure incorporates substantial cross-subsidies from long-distance and international services to local service. This means that any rebalancing of prices toward cost will tend to affect adversely residential and small business users whose telephone bills comprise mainly charges for line rental and local calls. To avoid rate shock it may therefore be necessary to control the pace of rebalancing by putting a cap on the rate of increase in the charges for local service (in real terms).

Another important constraint on the sector reform process involves the imposition of community service obligations on the providers of telecommunications infrastructure and services. Frequently such obligations apply only to the established operating entity, although competing service providers may be required to contribute to their funding. The most important community service obligation is likely to relate to the maintenance or achievement of universal service at uniform rates. Other obligations may cover the mandatory provision of such services as free calls to fire, police, and ambulance, directory assistance, maritime services, and services to the armed forces and emergency organizations.

Feasibility and Assessment of Options

The assessment of options will usually be underpinned by financial modeling of the established operating entity over the medium term. This is because the achievement of sector policy aims is inescapably bound to the financial health of the dominant player. Thus, combinations of policy instruments which put at risk the continued financial viability of the established operating entity may be ruled out even though they score well in terms of the various objectives and constraints that have been identified.

Another key feasibility issue is the adequacy of regulatory capabilities. Achievement of sector policy aims by means of a given combination of policy instruments will usually depend on effective regulation to manage the transition to new technical and economic structures as well as to protect consumer interests where competition fails to do so. The necessary regulatory skills, administrative procedures, and information systems, however, may be hard to establish.

International experience suggests that options for sector reform which depend on effective regulation of structure rather than conduct are likely to present fewest difficulties. The regulation of conduct is most problematic where it requires the detection of exploitative or anticompetitive behavior and the prescription of remedies by the regulatory authority. Such requirements may be minimized by limiting the regulatory authority's areas of discretion as far as possible through the use of rules that are hard to change and predetermined sanctions as the basis for regulation. Not only will this simplify the task of the regulatory authority, but it will reassure investors in the sector that the rules of the game will not be radically changed and also satisfy customers that an explicitly guaranteed outcome will be delivered. On the other hand, a rule-based approach to regulation of conduct may be too inflexible to deal effectively with an environment characterized by rapid technological and market change.

Considerations of financial viability and regulatory capability are particularly likely to affect the timing of market liberalization measures. Some countries decide to delay market liberalization so that the existing monopoly operator has sufficient time to prepare to face competition. Such preparation may involve tariff rebalancing and network modernization over a number of years, together with organizational development and efficiency improvement. To permit competition before this preparation is complete may require elaborate regulatory mechanisms to inhibit selective entry into market segments that are vulnerable as a result of inherited overpricing, poor service quality, or inefficiency. Without such regulatory mechanisms there is a danger that market entry decisions will be based on misleading signals and may undermine the financial viability of the dominant player. For example, in the United Kingdom Mercury Communications, the company licensed as a network competitor to British Telecom, has focused on the overpriced international and long-distance markets rather than on local service where, if the market is contestable rather than a natural monopoly, there might have been greater benefits from competitive pressures. The New Zealand experience illustrates a different approach, a period of about three years having been allowed for the Telecom Corporation of New Zealand to rebalance tariffs, reduce costs, and develop its organization, at the end of which the market was totally deregulated, subject only to the generally applicable competition law.

There may, of course, be pressing reasons for early market liberalization. These may relate to the need to meet customer expectations or to take advantage of a favorable political climate or to act before the dominant player has secured an unassailable market position. In any case, even if it is decided to delay liberalization of the core voice telephony markets, it may be possible to rapidly open up to competition:

- The supply of all customer premises equipment (with the possible exception of the first telephone)

- The installation and maintenance of customer premises equipment, including inside wiring

- The provision of value added and data services

- The operation of mobile communications and specialized satellite communications

- The self-provision of circuits which do not carry third-party traffic.

Under these conditions of partial liberalization, a key regulatory task is defining and policing the boundary between monopoly and competitive services and preventing anticompetitive cross-subsidy by means of transfers across that boundary. With continuing monopoly supply of the national telecommunications infrastructure, regulation must also secure the necessary degree of openness of the network to other service providers. In most cases the regulatory task will be made more difficult by the excessive market share of the infrastructural monopolist in competitive markets.

In some countries, the inherited situation leaves so much scope for performance improvement that sector reform may be capable of delivering benefits to all stakeholders. For example, prices may be high but financial performance may be poor due to inherited inefficiency, past investment undertaken on noncommercial criteria, and overreliance on debt finance. At the same time, there may be unmet demand for both basic and advanced services as well as poor service quality, despite user willingness to pay for improvements. Against this background, measures such as the transfer of all or part of the government's ownership of infrastructure assets to a strong technical partner may deliver affordable prices, improved supply conditions, and higher service quality for customers; enhanced employment opportunities for the work force; satisfactory sale proceeds to government; and adequate returns to investors.

More usually, however, options for sector reform involve a distribution of gains and losses among stakeholders. In this situation, the results of the assessment of options may need to be presented to decisionmakers in the form of scenarios. The scenarios should be designed to indicate the range of feasible outcomes and the nature of the trade-offs between stakeholder interests that arise as different weight is given to particular objectives within the policy mix. There may well be an iterative process whereby a particular scenario is selected for further elaboration before it is adopted as the basis for implementation of sector reform.

40

Toward the Future: Highlights and Outstanding Issues

Richard J. Schultz

THE OTHER CHAPTERS IN THIS VOLUME discuss recent experiences in restructuring, regulation, private sector participation, financing, and other issues as they pertain to the telecommunications sector in various regions of the world. Five very important issues are both highlights, in the sense that many of the chapters address them, and are also outstanding issues, in that the debates continue to rage over their resolution. These are:

- The gospel of globalization

- The negative images of public enterprise

- The exaggerated claims, and corresponding fears, of state telecommunications restructuring

- The multiple policy alternatives available to pursue restructuring

- The foreign ownership problem.

This closing chapter provides some thoughts on each of these issues.

Globalization

Globalization is simultaneously a concept and a process which is often at the cornerstone of the debates over restructuring. For some advocates of restructuring, globalization is a description of the central driving force for the worldwide phenomenon of restructuring. The world economy is becoming so integrated and telecommunications is the crucial link between individual countries and the world economy that the description of this driving force becomes inevitably a prescription. If countries are to respond effectively to reality, so goes the argument, they must structure, or restructure as the case may be, their telecommunications systems so that they can benefit from globalization.

Although I do not want to deny the reality, and concomitant pressures, of globalization, I would suggest that the case may be greatly overstated, particularly with respect to the advocacy of particular policy responses. Globalization is undoubtedly a compelling force in today's interdependent economy, but is it as compelling for all countries as some of its advocates appear to believe? Surely in countries whose telecommunications infrastructure development is at a relatively early stage, priority must be given to the painful, demanding, and difficult process of creating the most basic telecommunications system to serve pressing internal social, economic, and political needs. Demanding that countries where telecommunications is in such a primitive state of development focus on globalization imperatives rather than domestic priorities is surely inappropriate.

Even in countries with advanced telecommunications systems, blanket prescriptions to tailor their telecommunications development to global developments may seriously distort national planning. What is required, it seems, is an appreciation of the forces of globalization that is finely tuned to the needs and imperatives of individual countries. In fact, before we are overwhelmed by the power of the globalization thesis, we need to specify as concretely as possible which particular segments of a country's economy are linked to external components of the global economy. Once we have specified these linkages, we then can address those aspects of the telecommunications system that may require restructuring so as to maximize the linkages.

Several chapters in this book warn about the dangers of imposing universal solutions that ignore local conditions on individual countries. Such an approach, it is recognized, is rife with potential for failure. Notwithstanding the general support for this admonition, in the equivalent discussion of globalization there is less appreciation for a similar problem. There appears to be an implicit yet widely accepted presumption that the issues and options, if not the individual solutions, arising from globalization are fairly universal. It can be argued, however, that one of the continuing pressing issues facing the telecommunications sector in most countries is to establish the explicit and concrete linkages between domestic and global needs before embarking on reform initiatives.

The (Negative) Images of Public Enterprises

For many advocates of reforming national telecommunications structures, public enterprises are grossly inefficient, patronage-ridden, and overstaffed, and must therefore be swept away as a first and most fundamental step in restructuring.

Although such arguments cannot be ruled out, more precision and a more detailed bill of goods attached to such charges would be needed to confirm their validity. Blanket condemnation of public enterprises, particularly coming as it often does from representatives of countries with little experience with them or especially of the rationales for them, may undercut the efficacy of the argument. There are several problems with the blanket condemnation.

First, such descriptions, even when valid, hardly seem likely to persuade entrenched interests to commit economic suicide. This may apply particularly to the public enterprise labor force, especially where it is unionized. Without addressing the merits of the criticisms, it is important to note that in many countries the public service ethic is deeply ingrained. Indeed, it is an ethic familiar to enterprises such as traditional privately owned telecommunications companies in some countries. Restructuring, particularly one that may involve an attempt to supplant the existing ethic with a private sector ethic in an existing work force, however reduced it may become, is best accomplished by persuasion than denigration.

But what if the claims are not as valid as the proponents claim? Or, alternatively, what if the root problem is not ownership per se but some other aspect of the policy structure of the industry? In North America, for example, in the railroad industry there was ample evidence in the 1970s that productivity deficiencies were not primarily the result of ownership but of state regulation. In the 1970s prior to large-scale American deregulation, Canadian railroads, publicly and privately owned, outperformed their American counterparts when Canadian regulation was relaxed. Similarly, it is important when criticizing public ownership to remember the problems associated with other regulated but privately owned firms. AT&T, for example, although an exemplar of private ownership, was hardly a lean, mean machine prior to divestiture in 1984.

It is important to remember that, notwithstanding profound and fundamental restructuring, much of the existing work force, including the executives, will remain in place after restructuring. This has been true in the United States and appears to be largely true in such countries as Mexico, Argentina, and Australia, which have privatized their telecommunications companies. Although there are problems with public ownership, the point is that reformers must pinpoint those problems and not rely on general denunciations. Restructuring that involves issues such as ownership or regulation entails changing incentive systems for both executives and the general work force. The issue is much more complex than simpleminded assumptions about incompetent public enterprise. Failure to address explicitly the incentive system may easily derail reform initiatives.

The (Exaggerated) Fears of Restructuring

For critics of telecommunications restructuring and those still to be persuaded, privatization, particularly if accompanied by deregulation, however that may be defined, constitutes an inevitable and undesirable shrinking of the state. But does restructuring along these lines mean the substitution of the presumed mean market for the equally presumed beneficent state? Obviously, in part to ask the question is to answer it: No.

Opponents of restructuring, particularly privatization, have greatly misread the results of restructuring. Privatization and regulatory reform in most instances have led not to a reduction of the state but, as several chapters in this book have demonstrated, continuing, indeed enhanced and refurbished, roles for the state in the telecommunications sector. Changing the instrument, such as public for private ownership, does not automatically lead to no role for the state. These chapters have described direct and indirect roles for the state through the form of imposed operating conditions, often of a long-term nature, on the privatized firm. Among examples discussed are continued forms of government participation through minority ownership as well as through what is known in the United Kingdom as the "golden share" or in New Zealand as the "Kiwi share." Similarly the chapter by Carlos Casasús on the Mexican privatization refers to the service quality goals and the growth requirements for the extension of service as publicly mandated requirements, while Michael Hutchinson cited the imposition of community service obligations in the case of the Australian restructuring. Although the efficacy of the continuing state role remains to be assessed, the fact that such a role continues to be a major preoccupation of policymakers should assuage some of the critics' concerns.

Restructuring as a Multidimensional Phenomenon

Notwithstanding the preceding two comments, one of the major strengths of many of the chapters in this volume is the appreciation of the fact that whatever the merits of restructuring the ownership or regulatory regimes, both are complex, multidimensional phenomena.

Although many authors argue for privatization, in itself such a measure tells us little about the appropriate telecommunications market structure for individual countries. Peter Cowhey cogently makes this point with his discussion of the fivefold typology of policy alternatives, namely monopoly modernization, multiple (that is, regional) monopolies, competition for so-called enhanced services, reserved services model, and full competition model. He concludes by noting that the question is not monopoly versus competition, but which types of reform of monopoly and competition for what purposes. In other words, privatization is only the first step, and not necessarily the most important, in restructuring a nation's telecommunications sector.

Although regulatory regimes are also complex, they do not get the degree of attention nor are as thoroughly analyzed as other structural issues. Deregulation, for example, is a term often invoked but seldom defined. Deregulation has become something akin to the Loch Ness monster of current policy debates: something often cited but seldom seen. It is important that there be a much more comprehensive discussion of the forms and nature of regulation as fundamental components of telecommunications restructuring. It can be argued that some authors in this book give far too much credit to regulation in developing the American telecommunications system, particularly its high quality. Other analysts are more inclined to suggest that government regulators were more peripheral, at least until the 1960s and early 1970s.

On the other hand, some of the chapters manifest an almost unquestioning belief in the efficacy and appropriateness of the American model of regulation. This is particularly the case in the papers by representatives of foreign operators seeking entry into other countries as well as by members of the investment community. François Grossas, to cite only one example, states that

> simple and transparent industry regulation are important to investors. The treatment of tariffs is of singular importance. Profitability of the privatized company will depend critically on the level and structure of tariffs. To the extent that in most cases the company will retain a legal or de facto market dominance or exclusivity for at least some time, it will not be wholly free to set and change the prices it charges for its services. The applicable regulatory rules and procedures are therefore of the greatest interest to the investor. The company must be able to negotiate objectively with the regulators, and this process must be protected by law and free from contingent political considerations.

Although all the above is desirable, how realistic a prescription is this? More important, how reasonable is it for other countries just introducing regulation after restructuring when it represents an ideal that other countries more experienced with regulation do not attain? Is American or Canadian regulation, for example, free from political considerations? Hardly. Is British regulation transparent? Doubtful. Does the United States or Canada have a clearly defined national telecommunications policy?

Advocates should be careful about insisting on a model of regulation for other countries that is not employed at home. Furthermore, one reason operating telecommunications companies in both the United States and Canada are pursuing offshore opportunities is in part to escape from onerous, capricious, and politically inspired domestic regulatory constraints. Finally, after all the discussion about how to structure the regulatory system in order to protect the interests of the service providers, simply ask whether nontraditional operators, namely, those new to the telecommunications business, insist on the same regulatory conditions, or do they accept the inherent instability of operating in foreign markets that they have encountered in other lines of business activity?

Foreign Ownership: How Much of an Issue?

Many chapters in this volume refer to real or proposed restrictions on foreign ownership that accompany the restructuring of domestic telecommunications systems. Why is foreign ownership the problem that it universally appears to be? Countries with less-developed governmental policy instruments require what is after all a rather blunt tool—bans or limitations on foreign ownership—but it remains to be shown that advanced industrialized countries such as Australia, Canada, or the United States, with their highly developed and varied panoply of public controls such as taxation, regulation, and antitrust, require such controls. Just exactly what is the problem? Given that restructuring is designed in large part to make telecommunications systems much more responsive to needs arising from global imperatives, does not the restriction on foreign ownership amount to little more than a continued protection for domestic operators from the full blast of external forces? Or is such a restriction little more than an unconscious remnant from the preglobal era? If globalization is the trend and the imperative so many speakers describe it to be, why the leftover?

Annex

Current Sector Structure and
Regulatory Framework in
Selected Countries, Economies, and Regions

(Status, January 1994)

Antigua and Barbuda

Operating Entity(s) Including Ownership	Competition Policy	Legal and Regulatory Framework	Regulatory Agency
The Antigua and Barbuda Public Utilities Authority, a government-owned entity, is the provider of domestic telephone services. Cable & Wireless (C&W) provides the international telephone service. Cellular is provided by BoatPhone Ltd., a subsidiary of C&W.	The domestic and international services are provided on a monopoly basis. Competition is allowed in the provision of value added services (VAS).	Regulations have been recently updated.	Ministry of Public Works and Communications.

Argentina

Operating Entity(s) Including Ownership	Competition Policy	Legal and Regulatory Framework	Regulatory Agency
State-owned telephone company, Empresa Nacional de Telecomunicaciones (ENTel), was privatized in 1990–91 as two separate regional monopolies: Telefónica de Argentina in the south and Telecom Argentina in the north, with Buenos Aires split between the two. Sixty percent of the new companies was sold to new operators (Telefónica de Argentina to Telefónica de España; Telecom Argentina to France Télécom and STET of Italy); 40% was sold in tranches in 1991 and 1992 to employees (10%), and the public (30%). International monopoly operator, Teleintar, is owned by Telefónica de Argentina (50%) and Telecom Argentina (50%). There are some 300 local telephone cooperatives and several private satellite service providers. Two cellular licenses have been granted in the metro Buenos Aires region; two more will be granted by November 1993 in the provinces. They will have a two-year exclusivity clause. There are no foreign ownership restrictions on cellular.	Exclusivity for basic services and networks maintained until 1997 (possible three-year extension depending on performance). Value added services (VAS), data, private networks, cellular, and some satellite services opened to competition.	Telecommunications Law of 1972 still applies, although it has been modified to permit private ownership and competition. Lack of interconnection regulation in 1991–92 created problems for licensed carriers to enter monopoly networks. Price-cap regulation replaced rate-of-return regulation prior to privatization. Tariffs indexed to the U.S. consumer price index. Certain conditions apply pertaining to procurement, equipment manufacturing, sale of more than 49% of company, etc.	Semi-autonomous regulatory agency, Comisión Nacional de Telecomunicaciones (CNT), initially established by decree under Ministry of Public Works and Services. CNT reorganized under telecommunications ministry in 1992. Development plan for CNT is being prepared by international consultants.

Australia

Operating Entity(s) Including Ownership	Competition Policy	Legal and Regulatory Framework	Regulatory Agency
Sector characterized by a facilities duopoly based on a merged Telecom/OTC (Telstra), and a privatized AUSSAT (Optus) established in 1991. Sale of AUSSAT to BellSouth (24.5%), C&W (24.5%), and Optus Pty Ltd. (51%), was finalized Jan. 1992. Three public mobile telephone licenses were issued by end–1992 to Telstra, Optus, and Arena GSM Pty Ltd. (includes U.K.-based Vodafone and AAP Information Services of Australia). The Australian Associated Press (AAP) is the only major reseller. No legal foreign ownership restriction exists.	Duopoly exists in basic services (local, long-distance and international) with six-year exclusivity (to 1997). Restrictions on third-party resale including international were removed in 1992. There is competition in public access cordless telephone service. A community service obligation (CSO) on Telstra ensures universal service. Optus and licensed public mobile operators contribute to cost of CSO.	Relevant legal documents are: • Telecommunications Act 1991 which replaces the Telecommunications Act 1989. • Australia and Overseas Telecommunications Corporations Act, 1991. • Telecommunications (Universal Service Levy) Act, 1991. • Telecommunications (Transitional Provisions and Consequential Amendments) Act, 1991. • Telecommunications (Application Fees) Act, 1991. • Telecommunications (Carrier Licence Fees) Act, 1991. • International code of practice. • National planning code.	Australian Telecommunications Authority (AUSTEL) is a statutory authority independent of the carriers and subject to ministerial direction only in specific instances. It was established by the Telecommunications Act 1989.

Austria

Operating Entity(s) Including Ownership	Competition Policy	Legal and Regulatory Framework	Regulatory Agency
Post-und Telegraphenverwaltung (PTV) is organized as an enterprise but is still part of the Austrian government.	PTV has a monopoly on the operation of the public switched telephone network (PSTN) and the provision of basic services. Value added services can be provided by private operators. Users may install their own terminal equipment after the first handset (which must be supplied by PTV). The provision and installation of equipment for connection to the PSTN was fully liberalized in 1988.	The legal and regulatory framework of telecommunications in Austria will be made to conform with EC Directives. Accordingly, a new telecommunications law, which fulfills these requirements, is under elaboration. It will complement a progressive opening of markets to competition which began in the 1980s, on a "no harm to the network" basis. The separation of PTV's regulatory and operational functions was begun in May 1991.	The new regulatory body will be part of the federal Ministry of Public Economy and Transport.

Bahamas, The

Operating Entity(s) Including Ownership	Competition Policy	Legal and Regulatory Framework	Regulatory Agency
Government-owned telephone company, Bahamas Telecommunications Corporation (BATELCO), was established in 1967. BATELCO provides both domestic and international services, which include high-speed data, radio trunking, paging, cellular, Intelsat Business Services (IBS), and Intermediate Data Rate (IDR) Services.	BATELCO has a monopoly on all telecommunications services.	A Telecommunications Act of 1966 is in effect, along with associated regulations which are modified from time to time.	BATELCO is the regulatory agency. The Bahamas legislature is responsible for approving significant rate changes.

Bangladesh

Operating Entity(s) Including Ownership	Competition Policy	Legal and Regulatory Framework	Regulatory Agency
The public operator Bangladesh Telegraph and Telephone Board (BTTB) was split in 1990 into an autonomous operating company and a regulatory board. The operating company controls local service networks in the areas not covered by private operators as well as domestic and international long-distance. Licenses were issued in 1990 to four private operators to provide local service in rural areas and international long-distance services. With the change in government of 1991 most of these have been canceled or abandoned. Only Bangladesh Rural Telephone Authority (BRTA) continues to operate, providing rural telephony and data services. Telephone Silpa Sangstha Ltd. (TSS), a wholly government-owned national equipment manufacturer, has been licensed and plans to install a pay phone network on a revenue-sharing basis with BTTB.	There is no policy. BTTB has monopoly for provision of urban domestic and international telecommunications services. BRTA provides telecommunications services in rural areas. BTL with joint venture partner, Hutchison Whampoa of Hong Kong, established a limited radio communications services. The license is in dispute.	Under the 1885 Telegraph Act, the Government has the exclusive power to (a) establish and maintain telecommunications apparatus; (b) grant licenses to any other person to establish and maintain apparatus; (c) regulate the sector. Similar provisions were included in the 1933 Wireless Telegraphy Act in relation to wireless telegraphy except that the responsibility for management of frequency spectrum was given to the Director General of the Post Office. By virtue of the 1979 BTTB Ordinance, both the monopoly rights and the power to issue license for both telecommunications and wireless services, were transferred to BTTB. The Industrial Policy of June 1991 opened the telecommunications sector to the private sector.	Under the Telegraph Act of 1885, Ministry of Posts and Telecommunications (MOPT) is responsible for regulation of the sector. The 1979 BTTB Ordinance has given BTTB the power to issue licenses for telecommunications and wireless services.

Barbados

Operating Entity(s) Including Ownership	Competition Policy	Legal and Regulatory Framework	Regulatory Agency
Barbados Telephone Company (Bartel), the exclusive provider of local services, is 85% owned by C&W and 15% privately via shares. Barbados External Telecommunications (BET), exclusive provider of international services, is 75% owned by C&W and 25% through private shares. Barbados Communications Services (BCS), which is owned 50% by Bartel and 50% by BET, is only cellular mobile service provider allowed to interconnect to the PSTN.	Bartel and BET have exclusive franchises for domestic and international, respectively. Competition is allowed only in paging.	Telecommunications Act.	Bartel is regulated by the Public Utilities Board. BET is regulated by the Ministry of International Transport, Telecommunications and Immigration.

Belgium

Operating Entity(s) Including Ownership	Competition Policy	Legal and Regulatory Framework	Regulatory Agency
Belgacom, an autonomous public enterprise, is a state-owned monopoly. The government has decided to turn Belgacom into a limited company and intends to sell a minority stake (size not decided) in 1994.	Activities reserved exclusively to Belgacom include: • Establishment, maintenance, modernization, and operation of public telecommunications infrastructure; • Provision of services to third parties, namely: telephone, telex, mobile, and paging services; packet-switched data communications telegraph services; fixed circuits (leased lines); and establishment, maintenance, and operation of public pay phones.	The Law of 21 March 1991 concerning reform of certain public economic enterprises brings Belgium into compliance with EC Directives on terminal equipment, services, open network provision (ONP), etc.	The Belgium Institute for Postal and Telecommunications Services (BIPT) grants authorizations for services provision and makes declarations of non-reserved services not requiring an authorization. The minister responsible for telecommunications allocates radio frequencies; supervises the BIPT and may annul its decisions.

Belize

Operating Entity(s) Including Ownership	Competition Policy	Legal and Regulatory Framework	Regulatory Agency
Belize Telecommunications Ltd., 25% owned by British Telecommunications plc, 37% by government, with the rest owned by the public (i.e., pension funds, banks, and other local institutions), is sole service provider.	Belize Telecommunications Ltd. has a monopoly for all services.	Belize Telecommunications Act, 1987, amended in 1993 to stop call-back services.	Ministry of Energy and Communications.

Bolivia

Operating Entity(s) Including Ownership	Competition Policy	Legal and Regulatory Framework	Regulatory Agency
Empresa Nacional de Telecomunicaciones (ENTEL) is government-owned; it provides long-distance and international telecommunications. There are plans to privatize ENTEL. Seventeen cooperatives (Federación de Compañías de Teléfonos, FECOTEL) provide local service in urban centers, most important of which are COTEL in La Paz and COTAS in Santa Cruz. The government is considering consolidation of the cooperatives into a single government-owned entity. Telefónica Celular de Bolivia, TELECEL (joint venture between Millicom [USA], 46%; Comvik [Sweden], 23%; Bolivian investors, 31%) provides cellular services in La Paz, Santa Cruz, and Cochabamba. There are no specific restrictions on foreign investment; however, foreign ownership in a privatized ENTEL will be limited to 40%.	Telecommunications services are provided on a monopoly basis	A liberal foreign investment law (September 1990) accorded foreign investors national treatment and removed restrictions on foreign ownership of equipment suppliers and service providers.	Dirección General de Telecomunicaciones (DGT), part of the Ministry of Transport and Communications. DGT regulates prices and tariffs for all domestic and international telecommunications services, allocates frequencies, and authorizes private telecommunications operators. There are plans to establish a new, autonomous regulatory body, Superintendencia de Telecomunicaciones.

Brazil

Operating Entity(s) Including Ownership	Competition Policy	Legal and Regulatory Framework	Regulatory Agency
Telecomunicaçoes Brasileiras S.A. (TELEBRÁS) is a joint-stock (mainly state-owned) holding of 27 state operating enterprises and Empresa Brasileira de Telecomunicaçoes (EMBRATEL, the interstate and international carrier). TELEBRÁS accounts for about 98% of Brazil's telephones, the rest being provided by several small independent operators. With about 10 million lines, TELEBRÁS is the second largest telecommunications enterprise in developing countries (after China).	TELEBRÁS has monopoly of basic voice services. Competition policy has been developing piecemeal since 1990. Some competition and new entry are currently allowed in cellular, leased lines (including satellite, microwave), data services, information services, customer premises equipment, private build-out of telephone infrastructure (e.g., new residential developments, condominiums).	Telecommunications Law No. 4117 of August 27, 1952. Law No. 5792 of June 11, 1972, created TELEBRÁS. Presidential decree of 1990 provided for private entry, subject to limitations established in the Constitution of 1988. Presidential decree No. 177 of July 17, 1991, defines "limited services" and establishes conditions for licensing independent operators. Provisional and definitive regulations are issued as Secretaría Nacional de Comunicaciones (SNC) decrees ("portarias").	Secretaría Nacional de Comunicaciones (SNC) under the Ministry of Infrastructure is the telecommunications policy and regulatory authority. Telecommunications manufacturing policy is partly under SNC, which in the past used TELEBRÁS's purchasing power extensively to promote domestic industry.

Brunei

Operating Entity(s) Including Ownership	Competition Policy	Legal and Regulatory Framework	Regulatory Agency
Jabatan Telekom Brunei is a wholly government-owned state company operated by the Telecommunications Department.	There is no competition in any telecommunications services and the government has no plans to deregulate or privatize the telecommunications sector.		Telecommunications Department.

Bulgaria

Operating Entity(s) Including Ownership	Competition Policy	Legal and Regulatory Framework	Regulatory Agency
Bulgarian Telecommunications Company (BTC), a wholly government-owned corporation separate from the postal service, was formed in 1992 and provides all basic voice services (local, long-distance, and international). BTC is negotiating joint ventures with Cable & Wireless (cellular) and Sprint (data services).	Competition is permitted in value added services (VAS) terminal equipment.	Licensing regime exists under the Committee for Posts and Telecommunications (CPT), which is equivalent to a ministry for the sector. Its capabilities to develop and administer policy are being strengthened.	The Committee for Posts and Telecommunications (CPT) issues licenses to operate in the telecommunications sector. Its regulatory functions are being strengthened to properly oversee BTC and the new competitive environment.

Canada

Operating Entity(s) Including Ownership	Competition Policy	Legal and Regulatory Framework	Regulatory Agency
Sector is characterized by private and governmental operators. The Stentor companies (a national consortium of telephone companies which manages interconnection of the regional networks) have a virtual monopoly on local service provision in their operating areas. They also provide domestic and Canada–U.S. long-distance services, as does Unitel, a privately owned national carrier which entered the market in late 1992. Some independent telephone companies also provide local and long-distance services within the provinces in which they are based. In 1993, AT&T bought 20% of Unitel, and MCI invested the equivalent of 20% in BCE, the main Stentor company. Cellular mobile services are provided on a duopoly basis by Mobility Canada (cellular divisions of the Stentor companies) and Rogers Cantel Mobile Inc. There are many resellers. The 1993 Telecommunications Act restricts foreign ownership of facilities-based carriers to 20%; there are no restrictions on foreign ownership of nonfacilities-based carriers.	Competition in domestic long-distance voice has been permitted since June 1992. Telesat (which is owned by the Stentor member companies) has a monopoly for domestic satellite service. Unitel is now offering (nonsatellite) domestic public long-distance voice services in addition to leased line, data, etc. Teleglobe Canada Inc. has an exclusive mandate for overseas international services until at least 1997. There is a licensed duopoly in each serving area for cellular mobile services. There are no restrictions on competition in the resale of domestic and international long-distance voice.	The crucial regulatory distinction is between Type I (facilities-based) and Type II carriers. CRTC rulings permit resale and sharing of international as well as domestic leased lines for data, fax, voice messaging, interconnected private circuits, and voice services. The 1993 Telecommunications Act replaces the 1908 Railway Act. It allows the CRTC to forbear from regulating where competition levels are sufficient to protect the interests of users; however, the federal Cabinet will be able to "vary or rescind" CRTC decisions. It also places *all* PSTN operators under the jurisdiction of the CRTC, including those previously owned by provincial governments.	The independent federal regulatory agency is the Canadian Radio-television and Telecommunications Commission (CRTC). Some provincial governments also regulate the independent telephone companies. The federal government has primary responsibility for international telecommunications policy, not the CRTC.

Chile

Operating Entity(s) Including Ownership	Competition Policy	Legal and Regulatory Framework	Regulatory Agency
Compañía de Teléfonos de Chile (CTC) is the dominant carrier in local services market. Empresa Nacional de Telecomunicaciones S.A. (ENTEL) is the main domestic and international long-distance service provider. Both are fully private, with Telefónica de España holding 45% of CTC and 20% of ENTEL. There are small local carriers in the southern part of the country. Two small privately held companies have concessions overlapping parts of CTC's service areas. Telex-Chile, a private company provides telex services. There are several other international services license holders in addition to ENTEL which have licenses to provide international services (most prominent are VTR, Chilesat, Cidcom S.A.) which along with CTC (through an affiliate CTC-Mundo), are aggressively trying to enter ENTEL's market as well as other markets (e.g., cellular, information services).	Legal conflicts between CTC and ENTEL have increased dramatically. Government review of telecommunications policy and service conditions initiated in 1991 has resulted in proposals for changes in the law, retaining the basic conditions of liberalization. An April 1993 antitrust tribunal decided that Chile's telecommunications market should not be segmented and that CTC and ENTEL should be permitted to enter each other's markets which are also open to other service providers. The question of whether and on what terms (e.g., separate subsidiaries) CTC and ENTEL should be permitted into each other's markets is a matter of legislative debate. An April 1993 Supreme Court decision requires Telefónica de España to divest itself of its holding in either CTC or ENTEL. There are provisions in the new legislation for an equal access system (multicarrier discado) whereby the subscriber will choose the long distance carrier for each call by dialing a carrier-specific access code.	The 1992 Telecommunications Law includes a classification of services, a system of concessions and licenses, the requirement that all telecommunications operators must comply with basic technical and operational standards, reinforcement of SUBTEL's regulatory powers, and penalties for infringement of the law. The 1987 Additional Telecommunications Law includes procedures for setting monopoly tariffs, service obligations for public telephone companies, and subscriber financing of new investment. There are decrees detailing services of and network standards. A significant overhaul of the telecommunications law is wending its way through the National Assembly and will likely be completed by mid-1994.	Subsecretaría de Telecomunicaciones (SUBTEL), a part of the Ministry for Transportation and Telecommunications. Studies are being conducted to redefine characteristics of the regulatory body and its placement in the government.

China

Operating Entity(s) Including Ownership	Competition Policy	Legal and Regulatory Framework	Regulatory Agency
The Ministry of Posts and Telecommunications (MPT) coordinates telecommunications services provision, including the operation of interprovincial and international services. Thirty provincial administrations coordinate investment planning, network implementation, operation, maintenance, training, etc., of intraprovincial long-distance services. At municipal and county levels 2,500 post and telecommunications (P&T) enterprises provide telecommunications services. Some state enterprises and other ministries have separate dedicated networks. There is no direct foreign investment in the sector, although indirect investments with Chinese partners is possible for value added and nonbasic services.	Monopoly provision of basic services under the MPT, including local, domestic long-distance and international, telegraph, telex, and facsimile. The MPT also has a monopoly for leased lines, videoconferencing, and low- and mid-speed data. There is increasing decentralization of responsibility to provincial administrations and local P&T enterprises as well as emerging competition in selected wireless (e.g., paging, cellular). Value added services likely soon will be opened to competition.	A basic Telecommunications Law has been drafted and regulations are in preparation. In 1993 or 1994, posts and telecommunications will be separated at the national level. At the same time, the MPT's operational and regulatory functions will be separated into: • The Directorate General of Telecommunications, responsible for operations. • The Departments of Policies and Law, and of Communications, will be responsible for regulation and policy development.	Ministry of Posts and Telecommunications (MPT) at national level; provincial P&T administrations at provincial level.

Colombia

Operating Entity(s) Including Ownership	Competition Policy	Legal and Regulatory Framework	Regulatory Agency
Basic services at local level are provided by 26 municipal, district, and departmental enterprises and by Empresa Nacional de Telecomunicaciones (TELECOM). The latter also provides domestic long-distance and international services on an exclusive basis. As a result of a 1992 decree domestic long-distance can be provided by a fully private company, although the state must maintain at least 51% of an international operator. Services in the city of Bogotá will continue to be provided by a state-owned company.	Local and long-distance (domestic and international) basic services are to be provided on a monopoly basis. Value added service provision is open to competition. Cellular mobile services are provided on a duopoly basis in each of three geographic zones. One of the two has to be a wholly or partly state-owned operator. The other can be wholly private.	Decree 1990 (19 August 1990) defines a borderline between basic and value added services and service providers. Value added services can be provided by private companies. Decrees 1901 (1990) and 2122 (1992) restructure the Ministry. Law 37 (6 January 1993) establishes a duopoly for cellular mobile services. Decree 1421 (21 July 1993) provides for public services in the city of Bogotá to continue to be provided by a state-owned company.	Ministry of Communications is the regulator. Tariffs are regulated by the Junta Nacional de Tarifas de Servicios (National Services Tariffs Board).

Côte d'Ivoire

Operating Entity(s) Including Ownership	Competition Policy	Legal and Regulatory Framework	Regulatory Agency
Joint stock company, Côte d'Ivoire Telecommunications (CI-Telcom) 98% owned by state and 2% owned by employees, was created on May 14, 1991. It is planned to sell shares in CI-Telcom to private investors.	Monopoly is maintained for the provision of "reserved" (i.e., telephone and telex) services. These are provided by CI-Telcom. Other services, e.g., VAS, terminal equipment, etc., can be provided in association or in competition with CI-Telcom (Ministerial Decision of March 6, 1991).	Decree 91-72 of February 2, 1991, creates a regulatory agency (Direction de la Réglementation Générale), a technical control agency (Inspection Générale), and a planning agency (Direction de la Planification et du Développement). Decision of Council of Ministers of March 6, 1991, defines monopoly and competitive domaines.	The regulator is the Direction de la Réglementation Générale (DRG) within the Ministry of Posts and Telecommunications.

Denmark

Operating Entity(s) Including Ownership	Competition Policy	Legal and Regulatory Framework	Regulatory Agency
Fixed services are provided by Tele Danmark plc, which is 94% owned by the Danish government. There are plans to reduce the government's interest to 51% by mid–1994	Competition is not allowed for telex, telephone, radio-based mobile services, public-switched telephone network (PSTN) infrastructure, and the radio/ television broadcast networks. Duopoly exists in mobile communications where Tele Danmark and Dansk Mobil Telefon each are licensed to provide mobile services. The terminal equipment market is liberalized.	The Act to Regulate Certain Aspects of the Telecommunications Sector (Act No. 743, 14 November 1990), has resulted in a separation of regulatory and operating functions. Also, a concession was granted to Tele Danmark for installation and operation of PSTN transmission routes and exchanges. The Public Mobile Telecommunications Act gave the Minister of Communications authority to grant a second mobile license in competition with Tele Danmark. The Act on Tele Terminal Equipment gives the Minister of Communications authority to issue directives on telecommunications terminal equipment provision, including rules necessary to apply EC Directives.	Minister of Communications is responsible for telecommunications. The National Telecommunications Agency oversees administrative and regulatory activities. The General Directorate of the Danish P&T attends to the departmental functions of the sector and is responsible for relations with the concessionary sector, i.e., Tele Danmark.

Dominica

Operating Entity(s) Including Ownership	Competition Policy	Legal and Regulatory Framework	Regulatory Agency
C&W, a privately owned company, provides both internal and external telecommunications services.	C&W has exclusive rights to all tele-communications services.	Currently, moves are afoot to imple-ment a Telecommunications Act.	The Telecommunications Department of the Ministry of Communications Works and Housing.

Dominican Republic

Operating Entity(s) Including Ownership	Competition Policy	Legal and Regulatory Framework	Regulatory Agency
The sector is all private. The dominant carrier is CODETEL, a GTE subsidiary. A new second carrier, TRICOM, is licensed for all services.	All services are available for competition, which has, however, been held back for lack of a regulatory structure. Interconnection regulation is lacking. On July 2, 1993, DOMTEL (owned by TRICOM) applied in the USA to provide international telephone, data, video, and private line service between the two countries.		Director General of Telecommunications.

Estonia

Operating Entity(s) Including Ownership	Competition Policy	Legal and Regulatory Framework	Regulatory Agency
Estonian Telephone Company Ltd., a joint-venture between the state holding company, Estonian Telecom (51%), Telia AB Sweden (24.5%), and Telecom Finland (24.5%), has a 25-year concession to provide basic services (i.e., local, national, and international switched voice, telex, and telegraph). The same partners run Estonian Mobile Telephone Company Ltd. which operates NMT-450 and NMT-900 cellular systems. Estonian Paging Co. is owned 60% by Estonian telecom and 40% by Telecom Finland. Data services are provided by a subsidiary of Estonia Telecom.	Concession agreement of 1992 grants Estonian Telephone Company Ltd. exclusivity for provision of basic services for 8 years with a possible extension up to 14 years.	Concession agreement, 1992.	Ministry of Transport and Communications.

European Community

Operating Entity(s) Including Ownership	Competition Policy	Legal and Regulatory Framework	Regulatory Agency
N/A	See Legal and Regulatory Framework	Objectives of 1987 Green Paper have been implemented through the adoption of a number of EC Directives. These liberalize all services except public voice, operation of the basic PSTN network, and supply and provision of network and terminal equipment, including mutual recognition of type approval. They ensure open access; interworking and interconnection via ONP, and the separation of regulatory and operating functions. As a result of the 1992 Review, liberalization of all public voice is foreseen for January 1, 1998. The 1998 liberalization does not, however, include facilities-based competition in voice. Spain, Portugal, Greece, and Ireland, which have "lesser developed networks," will have the right to preserve their monopolies until 2003, while Luxembourg and Belgium, countries with "small" networks, can put off competition until 2000.	N/A

Finland

Operating Entity(s) Including Ownership	Competition Policy	Legal and Regulatory Framework	Regulatory Agency
Local services are provided by 49 concessioned operating companies (mainly cooperatives coming together as the Association of Telephone Companies in Finland or Telegroup), covering 25% of the geographical area of the country (67% of population), and Telecom Finland, which covers 75% of the area (33% of population). Telecom Finland also provides long-distance and international services. Since January 1, 1994 Kankoverkko Oy which is partly owned by the Association has been providing competing public switched domestic long distance services. As of July 1, 1994 Finnet International also owned by TeleGroup will be providing competing international public switched services. Three are five national concessions for cellular mobile. Private networks are also operated by railways and others. Telecom Finland is likely to become a public limited liability company in January 1994.	Competition is allowed in all services, including infrastructure. Customer premises equipment, data, voice, mobile, intracorporate voice, and value added services are fully liberalized. There are no restrictions on resale. Interconnection is mandated by law.	Telecommunications Law of 1987 (revised in 1988, 1990, and 1992) provides for public telecommunications services to be operated either by Telecom Finland, or a Finnish entity which has been granted a concession. It also confirms Telecom Finland's monopoly in national and international public long distance, telex and paging. Licences to build infrastructure and operate services can be granted to a Finnish entity, and to an affiliate of a foreign company.	Ministry of Communications supervises public telecommunications. Telecommunication Administration Centre (TAC), established in 1987, carries out technical inspections, type approves equipment, and manages the radio frequency spectrum.

France

Operating Entity(s) Including Ownership	Competition Policy	Legal and Regulatory Framework	Regulatory Agency
Law of 2 July 1990 transformed France Télécom into a state-owned public corporation with the state maintaining a supervisory role (e.g., approval of tariffs, compliance with public service obligations) through the Direction du Service Public (DSP) of the Ministry of Posts and Telecommunications. France Télécom may be partially or totally privatized. De facto, no foreign ownership.	France Télécom retains monopoly over network open to the public and voice telephony, but there is open competition in VAS and CPE (customer premises equipment) as well as structured and controlled competition in support and mobile services.	Law of 2 July 1990 modified status of France Télécom, turning it into a public service company. Law of 29 December 1990 stipulated how networks and services may be established and operated, and provided for France Télécom to retain monopoly over the network open to the public and voice telephony.	Direction de la Réglementation Générale (DRG) of the Ministry of Posts and Telecommunications was created in 1989. In 1993 it was turned into Direction Générale des Postes et Télécommunications of the Ministry of Industry, Posts and Telecommunications and Foreign Trade.

Germany

Operating Entity(s) Including Ownership	Competition Policy	Legal and Regulatory Framework	Regulatory Agency
On German unification (October 3, 1990), the East German PTT was merged into DBP Telekom. The German government wants to sell 49% of DBP Telekom (25% in 1996 and 24% in 1998). This requires modification of the German Basic Law or Constitution (Grundgesetz); Article 87(1) states that "the federal postal service . . . shall be conducted as matters of direct federal administration with its own administrative substructure." Change of Constitution requires two-thirds majority approval in the German Parliament (Bundestag). There is no foreign ownership of public enterprises.	1989 Law (Poststrukturgesetz) provides for the separated telecommunications entity, DBP Telekom to retain federal monopoly over network and telephone service. Exceptions include satellite networks for all nonvoice services, mobile services, and cellular. Other services, including third-party resale, are liberalized. On January 1, 1992, DBP Telekom's monopoly for terminal equipment was ended.	Law Concerning the Restructuring of the Postal and Telecommunications Sector and of the Deutsche Bundespost (Poststrukturgesetz) enacted July 1, 1989, provided for the reorganization of the Deutsche Bundespost (DBP), including separation of regulatory and business functions as well as and separation of postal, banking, and telecommunications functions. An amendment to 1928 Telecommunications Installation Act (Fernmeldeanlagengesetz, or FAG) introduced new regulatory conditions and created a more competitive telecommunications market. The terminal equipment market was liberalized on July 1, 1990. Legal relations of three DBP enterprises (including Telekom) with their customers became subject to private law on July 1, 1991).	Ministry of Posts and Telecommunications.

614

Ghana

Operating Entity(s) Including Ownership	Competition Policy	Legal and Regulatory Framework	Regulatory Agency
State-owned Ghana Post and Telecommunications Corporation (GPTC) is the monopoly provider of infrastructure as well as basic and enhanced services. Private entrepreneurs provide terminal equipment, enhanced services, cellular (Mobitel), and paging (City Pagers, Anokyema Ventures) services. Government is considering a partial privatization of GPTC.	Ghana Post and Telecommunications Corporation has legal monopoly for all services and infrastructure; however, PABXs, terminal equipment, value added services (e.g., public call offices), cellular mobile, and paging are being provided on an unregulated basis by private operators.	Post and Telecommunications Decree of 1975 grants the state-owned GPTC monopoly over basic and enhanced services and infrastructure.	Ministry of Transport and Communications.

Greece

Operating Entity(s) Including Ownership	Competition Policy	Legal and Regulatory Framework	Regulatory Agency
Hellenic Telecommunications Organization S.A. (OTE), is a state-owned public utility. Parliament approved plans to sell 49% of OTE in 1993. Of this, a strategic 35% was to be sold to an experienced telecommunications operator. Qualified bidders included NTT (Japan), France Télécom, Telefónica de España, STET (Italy), GTE Corp., and Korea Telecom. An additional 10% was to be sold on the stock exchange and 4% was to be offered to OTE employees. The government was to retain 51% and a majority of seats on OTE's board. The new socialist government canceled the partial privatization on October 13, 1993.	Currently in the process of bringing marketplace in line with EC Directives on competition.	Changes in the last three years, have resulted in: • Partial deregulation and strengthening of competition rules (Law 2000/1991) • Provision "to remove OTE from the public sector" (PD 361/1991) • Requirement for type approval before connection and use of terminal equipment • Granting of license to OTE for provision of fixed voice telephony; and an exclusive mandate for installation and development of the public network (LD 1049/1949 and 165/1973) • Obligation imposed on OTE to provide interconnection to any other service providers which may be licensed in the future (Law 1892/1990).	Ministry of Transport and Communications exercises regulatory authority. It does not directly audit or intervene, however, in OTE affairs. A National Telecommunications Committe was to be created by end-1993, empowered to grant licenses and be responsible for the control and observance of competition rules.

Grenada

Operating Entity(s) Including Ownership	Competition Policy	Legal and Regulatory Framework	Regulatory Agency
The provider of domestic and external telephone services is the Grenada Telephone Ltd. (GRENTEL). When established in 1989, the government owned 51% of the company, and C&W 49%. Currently the government has 30% shares, having sold 21% to C&W. Prior to 1989, the domestic services operator was state owned, while external communications were provided by C&W.	GRENTEL has a total monopoly on telecommunications.	The Public Telecommunications Act of 1989.	Ministry of Communications and Works.

Guyana

Operating Entity(s) Including Ownership	Competition Policy	Legal and Regulatory Framework	Regulatory Agency
Guyana Telephone and Telegraph Co. Ltd. (GTTC), privatized in January 1991, is owned by Atlantic Tele-Network (ATN) Inc. of the U.S. (80%) and the Guyana government (20%). The purchase contract contains a blueprint for infrastructure development.	Monopoly exists only on wireline and international telephone and telegraph services.	A Post and Telegraph Act (amended in 1927) regulates all radio-communications, and a Telecommunications Act of 1990 applies to wireline telephony and cable television.	The Guyana Public Utility Commission created in January 1991 approves the rates for GTTC, and in so doing has the authority to look into all the operations of that company. The Ministry of Communications, however, is the overall regulatory agency in Guyana.

Honduras

Operating Entity(s) Including Ownership	Competition Policy	Legal and Regulatory Framework	Regulatory Agency
State-owned Empresa Hondureña de Telecomunicaciones (HONDUTEL) has monopoly for provision of all telecommunications services in the whole territory. HONDUTEL is also responsible for broadcasting of radio and TV signals.	All services are provided on a monopoly basis. Studies are under way with the objective of liberalizing some services by 1997.	Constitution of Honduras confers on HONDUTEL the exclusive right and obligation to provide all telecommunications services and broadcast transmission in the country.	HONDUTEL is the regulator for all telecommunications services and for frequency spectrum management.

Hong Kong

Operating Entity(s) Including Ownership	Competition Policy	Legal and Regulatory Framework	Regulatory Agency
Hong Kong Telecom Ltd. is the privately owned (by Cable & Wireless) holding company for Hong Kong Telephone Co. (HKTC) and Hong Kong Telecom International (HKTI). HKTC has the exclusive right to provide local and long-distance domestic public telephone service. HKTI has a similar exclusive license to provide public international services (i.e., telephone, telex, telegraph, facsimile, data transmission, and leased circuits). Hong Kong has concluded bilateral agreements to provide international value added network (IVAN) services (which however, specifically exclude basic voice and facsimile) with the USA, U.K., and Japan. There are no foreign ownership restrictions.	Hong Kong Telephone Co. has monopoly on domestic telephone service until 1995. Hong Kong Telecom International has monopoly for international services until 2006. Vigorous competition exists in public nonwireline and value added services (VAS): cellular (4 licensees operate 5 networks), paging (31 licenses), CT2 telepoint (3 licenses), and several VAS licenses. HKTC's exclusive license will be replaced in 1995 with a nonexclusive license which will include a universal services obligation. New competitors in local fixed-link voice telephone services market were licensed in 1993.	The Telephone Ordinance requires directors of HKTC to be residents in Hong Kong and the majority to be Commonwealth citizens. The management and staff of HKTI must be British subjects. A price-cap regulatory scheme has been put in place for HKTC, replacing traditional rate-of-return regulation.	New independent regulatory body, Office of the Telecommunications Authority (OFTA), established on July 1, 1993. OFTA assumes responsibility for licensing and regulation from the Telecommunications Branch of the Post Office.

Hungary

Operating Entity(s) Including Ownership	Competition Policy	Legal and Regulatory Framework	Regulatory Agency
State-owned Hungarian Telecommunications Company (HTC) has almost 100% of telephone market. Noncore services are provided by subsidiaries of HTC. Westel, a joint venture of HTC and US West, operates analog mobile services. Newly emerging private companies, with or without HTC stake, are building network infrastructure with or without the intention to operate them. In December 1993 the Hungarian government selected the consortium of DBP Telekom and the U.S. RBOC Ameritech as purchasers of 30% of HTC for US$875 million. The 1992 Law also provides for the creation of 56 local regions, each of which is to be handled by an operating concession to be awarded by end-1994, potentially in competition with HTC. Local or regional telephone companies covering one or more of the 56 primary areas have to be awarded concessions based on a public tendering process. Of these, 25 have been offered in such a process due to close on December 29, 1993. Two GSM licenses (one to Pannon GSM and one to US West/HTC) were awarded in October 1993, with service scheduled to begin in April 1994.	Voice telephony will be subject to monopoly provision until 2002, with several regional, one long-distance, and one international service provider being given monopoly concessions. Building and owning network infrastructure is open to competition, but by law agreement with the service providers is required. Three operators have been awarded concessions for mobile services: one for analog and two for GSM. All other telecommunications services, including data transmission, are open to competition and can be provided by those meeting the licensing requirements.	Post, telecommunications, and broadcast signal transmission were separated in 1990. The Telecommunications Law passed by Parliament in November 1992 provides for exclusive and special rights in telecommunications services. Public telephone, mobile telephone, nationwide paging, and nationwide broadcast signal transmission need concession, which may be either exclusive or concurrent. The 1992 law entered into force with the accompanying regulations in 1993. The industry structure for the public telephone service, along with privatization guidelines, are set out in a telecommunications policy statement approved by the Parliament in 1993.	The Communication Inspectorate, a semiautonomous regulatory body under the Ministry of Transport, Communication and Water-management were established in 1989. State ownership rights were transferred to State Property Management Company.

India

Operating Entity(s) Including Ownership	Competition Policy	Legal and Regulatory Framework	Regulatory Agency
Department of Telecommunications (DOT) provides local network and domestic long-distance services everywhere except in metropolitan Bombay and New Delhi, where Mahanagar Telephone Nigam Ltd. (MTNL) operates the local network. MTNL is 80% government-owned, with the remaining 20% held by institutional investors. International long-distance services are provided by Videsh Sanchar Nigam Ltd. (VSNL), which is 85% government-owned and 15% privately held. Further disinvestment by the government is likely with an international flotation planned in 1994. Eight licenses for cellular have been awarded for four cities, but these are under review following a ruling by the Delhi High Court. In September 1993 the government approved a ten-year joint venture between US West and an Indian partner to install and operate up to 1 million new lines in competition with DOT in the South India town of Tirupur.	There is monopoly provision of basic services (voice telephony, telex, telegraph) in local, domestic, and international long-distance. DOT has expressed interest in private operator offers to provide some corporate services. The government is interested in opening the value added services (VAS) market to competition. Licenses for VAS are subject to open tender, and foreign participation will be permitted where necessary.	The Indian Telegraph Act of 1885 is under review. Recommendations for the creation of a separate regulatory authority are being prepared.	Telecommunications Commission, within the Department of Telecommunications (DOT), is responsible for both planning and operations. Frequency management is the responsibility of the Wireless Planning and Coordination branch of the DOT.

Indonesia

Operating Entity(s) Including Ownership	Competition Policy	Legal and Regulatory Framework	Regulatory Agency
PT Telekomunikasi Indonesia (PT Telkom, formerly Perumtel), is 100% government-owned and responsible for providing domestic telecommunications services. PT Indosat, also 100% government-owned, provides international services. The first mobile telephone system was built by PT RHP, a joint venture between Permutel and a private company; another is operated by PT INTI; PT Elektrindo Nusantara and PT CPS also have been authorized to build additional systems. In 1993, PT Satelindo was formed to operate the Palapa satellite system (from 1995) and to provide cellular, international, and satellite services. It is 60% privately and 40% state-owned (shared between PT Indosat (10%) and PT Telkom (30%)).	Monopoly state-owned enterprises. Emerging competition with the establishment of PT Satelindo and in cellular.	1989 Telecommunications Law (Law No. 3/1989) was passed in order to allow private sector participation in infrastructure development. It permits competition in the provision of non-basic services, but emphasizes that telecommunications must be controlled by government.	The Directorate General of Posts and Telecommunications (DGPT), a department within the Ministry of Tourism, Posts and Telecommunications (Parpostel). DGPT manages policy implementation, regulatory functions, licensing, and use of radio frequencies. Parpostel sets policy guidelines for telecom's development and services provision. The National Telecommunications Board (NTB) is the principal coordinating organization for telecom policy issues involving two or more government and agencies.

623

Ireland

Operating Entity(s) Including Ownership	Competition Policy	Legal and Regulatory Framework	Regulatory Agency
Bord Telecom Eireanns is 100% state-owned. No foreign ownership is permitted.	Bord Telecom Eireanns has an exclusive right to provide public voice telephony, telex services, mobile radio services, and satellite services. Other telecommunications services can be offered on a competitive basis.	European Communities Telecommunications (services) Regulations 1992 (were adopted) for the purpose of implementing EC Directives.	The Department of Tourism, Transport and Communications. It regulates type approval of equipment intended for connection to the PSTN and licenses providers of third-party telecom services.

Italy

Operating Entity(s) Including Ownership	Competition Policy	Legal and Regulatory Framework	Regulatory Agency
The process of reorganizing the telecommunications sector is expected to be completed in 1994. The government has approved plans to consolidate five state-owned carriers controlled by IRI (the agency responsible for managing Italian state industries), through STET (holding company), into a single organization, Telecom Italia. They include: • SIP, local and immediate long-distance, and mobile communications operator • Iritel (formerly ASST), domestic long-distance and European/Mediterranean Basin international operator • Italcable, operator of non-European international services • Telespazio, satellite and space communications operator • SIRM, maritime communications operator. The new carrier, which eventually will be privatized, will remain under STET (51% owned by IRI; 49% by private shareholders).	There is monopoly provision by various state-owned enterprises. Italy has not yet adopted EC Directives to liberalize nonvoice services, although the government is expected to grant a second cellular license in line with EC guidelines. Private networks are technically illegal but, in practice, leased circuits are provided. Interconnection to the PSTN, carriage of third-party traffic, and resale of capacity generally are not allowed, although the carriers have shown some latitude in this area. The terminal equipment market has been liberalized.	Law No. 58 on "Provisions for Reforming the Telecommunications Sector" was adopted in January 1992. A restructuring plan has been submitted by IRI to the Treasury, which also allows for privatization.	Ministry of Posts and Telecommunications. Plans are in place to create an independent regulatory body to be responsible for issuing concessions, authorizations, and licenses. It will also supervise competition, in accordance with EC directives.

Jamaica

Operating Entity(s) Including Ownership	Competition Policy	Legal and Regulatory Framework	Regulatory Agency
The Jamaica Telephone Company (JTC) and JAMINTEL together form Telecommunications of Jamaica, Ltd. (TOJ) and have a common board of directors. TOJ is owned by Cable & Wireless (79%) and public shareholders (21%). JTC provides domestic telephone and telex traffic. JAMINTEL provides international services. Jamaica Digiport International (JDI), a joint venture between TOJ (30%), Cable & Wireless (35%), and AT&T (35%), offers international private-line service for Jamaica's free trade zones.	TOJ has a monopoly for all basic and value added services, including provision of leased lines. Exclusive license for provision of all basic public services is for 25 years. In addition TOJ has a right of first refusal on value added services if and when these are opened to competitive provision. Policy is currently under review.	Radio and Telegraphy Act 1972. New legislation is being drafted.	The Telecommunications Branch of the Ministry of Public Utilities and Transport.

Japan

Operating Entity(s) Including Ownership	Competition Policy	Legal and Regulatory Framework	Regulatory Agency
Nippon Telegraph and Telephone Corporation (NTT), Japan's largest domestic carrier, was partially privatized in 1985. As of March 1993, there were 77 new Type I carriers—including 3 long-distance, 3 international, 3 satellite, 8 regional, 25 cellular, and 36 radio paging operators. New entrants in domestic long-distance market are Daini Denden Inc. (DDI), Japan Telecom Co. (JT), and Teleway Japan Corp. (TWJ). International services are provided by Kokusai Denshin Denwa Company Ltd. (KDD), International Telecom Japan, Inc. (ITJ), and International Digital Communications, Inc. (IDC). On March 1, 1993, there were 1,128 Type II carriers, of which 1,092 were General Type II and 36 were Special Type II. Foreign ownership in Type I carriers is limited to 33%, except for NTT and KDD (initially not permitted; but since 1992, 20% foreign ownership allowed). No foreign ownership restrictions exist for Type II carriers.	Since April 1985, all segments of the market, including local service, are open to competition. Because of the absence of tariff rebalancing and huge deficits in the local service market, only a few competitors have emerged in the local market. By contrast, there have been several entries into long-distance and international markets. New long-distance carriers do not have to pay access charges to NTT, but instead can use NTT's local network at a subsidized price. A universal service obligation is imposed only on NTT. The facilities-based carrier (Type I) is divided between domestic and international. Domestic and international carriers cannot enter each other's markets.	1985 Telecommunications Business Law introduced competition for facilities-based (Type I) carriers, liberalized circuit usage (Type II), deregulated terminal equipment, and led to the privatization of NTT. Type I carriers can construct and operate telecommunications infrastructure. They need MPT permission to operate and authorization for their tariffs. Type II carriers lease facilities from Type I carriers. Only Special (large-scale) Type II carriers need to notify tariffs to MPT; General Type II need not. Special Type II must register, and General Type II must notify MPT when they enter the market. The status of competition and structure of NTT is currently under review, as is the current lack of transparency in tariff setting.	Ministry of Post and Telecommunications (MPT).

Jordan

Operating Entity(s) Including Ownership	Competition Policy	Legal and Regulatory Framework	Regulatory Agency
Telecom Corporation (TCC) is a government-owned public operator of all basic services. The government currently is studying the corporatization of TCC (to be registered under Companies Law). Paging services are provided by a private company. A private company will be granted a mobile cellular license shortly. Customer premises equipment market has been liberalized.	There is no competition in basic services, but competition is allowed in value added services.	The government is studying the possibility of establishing an independent regulatory body.	The Council of Ministers, with support from the public operator (TCC).

Korea

Operating Entity(s) Including Ownership	Competition Policy	Legal and Regulatory Framework	Regulatory Agency
Korea Telecom, 100% government-owned, was converted from a government authority into a joint-stock company on January 1, 1991. DACOM, created in 1982, is owned by Korea Telecom (33%) and 27 private Korean corporations. Korea Telecom must transfer its share to the government in 1993. Korea Mobile Telecommunications Corp. (KMTC) is designated as an independent common carrier for mobile services. No foreign ownership is allowed for General Service Providers; the 50% foreign ownership limitation on value added services providers is to be lifted by January 1, 1994. There is no restriction on database and network computer value added services (VAS). The government has plans to partially privatize Korea Telecom. An initial 25% will be offered to Korean investors; a further 24% will be offered over two years, and no single shareholder will be allowed to own more than 10%. Foreign ownership will likely not be permitted.	Korea Telecom provides domestic voice service on a monopoly basis. DACOM has been allowed to offer international voice services since 1991. Korea Telecom has been allowed to compete with DACOM in data services since 1992. DACOM is pursuing a license to provide domestic long-distance services by 1995. Competition is developing in mobile services, from which both Korea Telecom and DACOM will be excluded. Private companies and Korea Telecom provide a variety of domestic VAS. Korea has entered into international value added network (IVAN) services arrangements with several countries, including Australia, USA, and Japan.	1991 Telecommunications Law defines three service categories: General Service Providers (basic telephony and data services); Special Service Providers (cellular, paging, and other regional or wireless services); and value added services (VAS) providers. The Law also establishes regulatory framework for authorizing new service providers. Registration is required for providers of certain VAS.	Ministry of Communications (MOC).

Kuwait

Operating Entity(s) Including Ownership	Competition Policy	Legal and Regulatory Framework	Regulatory Agency
The state-owned national telecommunications operator has a monopoly for all basic services, domestic and international. The Kuwaiti government has announced plans to privatize the national operator, to create the Kuwait Telecommunications Company (KTC), and to offer shares (51% initially) to the public; later, foreign investors would be allowed to buy another 25%. KTC is to begin operations in 1994, providing domestic and international telephone, fax, and telex services now provided by the government operator. Mobile and paging services are provided by the Mobile Telephone Services Company (MTSC).	There are plans to allow competition in value added but not in mobile initially. Basic services will remain under monopoly provision.	There are plans to establish a regulatory capability within the Ministry of Communications.	Ministry of Communications.

Lithuania

Operating Entity(s) Including Ownership	Competition Policy	Legal and Regulatory Framework	Regulatory Agency
State-owned Lietuvos Telekomas (Lithuanian Telecom), established on January 1, 1992, is responsible for basic telecommunications services (local, long-distance, and international) and data transmission. International 2 Mb/s (120 channel) link to Western countries is provided by LINTEL a joint venture between Lietuvos Telekomas and US West. CITCOM, a joint venture between NERIS of the U.S. and the Lithuanian commodity exchange operates a satellite earth station which provides services to the USA and Canada through Intelsat. A mobile cellular (NMT 450) service joint venture, COMLIET, was established in February 1992. Shareholders are Lietuvos Telekomas, Antena, Millicom, and Telecom Denmark.	There is monopoly provision of public long-distance and international basic services. Local networks in urban and rural areas are open for provision by alternate (private) operators. Two licenses for GSM operators and two licenses for national radio paging services will be issued in 1994. Licenses for local radio paging services will be not limited.	Telecommunications Law of 1991 describes responsibilities of the Ministry of Communications and Informatics and provides for competition in the local network and the establishment of private networks under certain conditions. Regulations of the Ministry of Communications and Informatics of the Republic of Lithuania were ratified by the government of the Republic of Lithuania on March 12, 1992. Rules of State for local telephone network service were approved by the Ministry of Communications and Informatics on December 12, 1992.	Ministry of Communications and Informatics regulates the sector, allocates frequencies, regulates tariffs, issues licenses, and applies standards.

Madagascar

Operating Entity(s) Including Ownership	Competition Policy	Legal and Regulatory Framework	Regulatory Agency
At present, the monopoly telecommunications service provider for domestic services is the Ministry of Posts and Telecommunications, and for international, the Société Internationale des Télécommunications. A new law foresees the creation of Madagascar Télécom, which would be initially (first two years) owned 85% by the state and 15% by France Cable & Radio (currently partner in Société Internationale des Télécommunications). Later the government would sell all but 34% of its share of Madagascar Télécom. Under the newly proposed legislation	Madagascar Télécom would have an exclusive mandate for basic services for seven to ten years. Value added services would be open to competition.	A new telecommunications law was passed on December 15, 1993. A detailed regulatory framework and tariff policy are being prepared under a World Bank loan.	Under the new legislation the Ministry of Posts and Telecommunications will become the regulator.

Malaysia

Operating Entity(s) Including Ownership	Competition Policy	Legal and Regulatory Framework	Regulatory Agency
The main facilities-based operator, Telekom Malaysia Bhd (TMB), was corporatized in 1987 and partially privatized (25%) in 1990. Two private companies, Technology Resource Industries (TRI) and Binariang Sdn Bhd, have been given international gateway licenses. The latter also has licenses to provide local public networks and services as well as to launch Malaysia's geostationary satellite, MEASAT. Time Telecommunications Bhd is seeking licenses to provide long-distance and international services. There are four cellular mobile license holders (Telekom Malaysia, Binariang, TRI, and Mobikom) and 33 regional radio paging licenses. There are no clearly defined foreign ownership restrictions; however, foreign ownership in Telekom Malaysia is limited to 25%.	The policy is not clearly defined, but the government wants to encourage competition. Competition is allowed in cellular and paging. Competition is emerging in facilities-based services, with the government having issued some domestic and international facilities licenses.	The Telecommunications Act (1950) grants the government "exclusive privilege" to provide all domestic and international telecommunications services. "Exclusive privilege" is interpreted as meaning that the government may either provide these services itself or license others to do so.	Jabatan Telekom Malaysia (JTM), the telecommunications department of the Ministry of Energy, Posts and Telecommunications, is the regulator. The Minister grants licenses and approves tariffs. JTM establishes standards, regulates the radio spectrum and use of the geostationary orbit, promotes R&D, protects consumer interests, encourages quality of service, and represents Malaysia in international telecommunications organization.

Malta

Operating Entity(s) Including Ownership	Competition Policy	Legal and Regulatory Framework	Regulatory Agency
Telemalta Corporation is government-owned and has a monopoly for provision of all telecommunications services except cellular mobile, which is provided on a monopoly basis by Telecell Ltd. The latter is owned 80% by Vodaphone (U.K.) and 20% by Telemalta Corporation, which has an option to purchase controlling interest after five years.	There is monopoly provision of all basic telecommunications and mobile services. Legislation on value added services (VAS) is unclear as to what services private operators can provide without infringing on Telemalta's monopoly. Such cases currently are decided on an ad hoc basis.	Framework includes: • Telemalta Act (1975) Chapter 250 • Telephone Service Regulation (1972) • Telegraphic and Telex Service Tariffs Regulations (1977) • Overseas Telephone Service Regulations 911957) • Overseas (Cable Service Regulations) (1957) • Fixed Electrical Power and Telegraphic Connection System Ordinance (1934) Chapter 01	Ministry of Transport and Communications is the regulatory agency. Telemalta's capital and operating budgets are subject to parliamentary approval.

Mexico

Operating Entity(s) Including Ownership	Competition Policy	Legal and Regulatory Framework	Regulatory Agency
TELMEX was privatized in 1990, with controlling interest held by a consortium consisting of Grupo Carso, Southwestern Bell, and France Télécom.	TELMEX has a monopoly for basic services network until 1996 subject to price-cap regulation as well as network expansion and quality-of-service target obligations. There are regional duopolies in the mobile cellular service. In each region a TELMEX subsidiary competes with a new entrant. Private networks, terminal equipment, value added services, and information services markets are liberalized.	Law of General Means of Communications of 1938 is the basic legal instrument. Telecommunications regulations have been revised.	Secretaría (Ministry) de Comunicaciones y Transportes (SCT).
Telecomunicaciones de Mexico (TELECOMM) is a semiautonomous government-owned entity which operates the federal satellite network as well as provides telex and telegraph services.			
TELCEL (a TELMEX subsidiary) provides cellular services in competition with privately owned operators in nine regions. Numerous foreign firms, such as McCaw, Cantel, Motorola, etc., have interests in the regional cellular operators.			

Montserrat

Operating Entity(s) Including Ownership	Competition Policy	Legal and Regulatory Framework	Regulatory Agency
C&W, the sole provider of telecommunications on the domestic and international levels, operates under a 25-year agreement with the government, with five-year revision periods.	Exclusivity for all telecommunications services.	The Telecommunications Ordinance, which is forty years old, is to be revised shortly.	Ministry of Communications and Works.

Morocco

Operating Entity(s) Including Ownership	Competition Policy	Legal and Regulatory Framework	Regulatory Agency
At present the monopoly service provider is the state enterprise, Office National des Postes et Télécommunications (ONPT). A new law being prepared would split ONPT into two separate enterprises, one for telecommunications and one for postal services. For the time being privatization is not envisaged.	Under the proposed legislation the new telecommunications operator (Société des Télécommunications) will have an exclusive mandate for basic services. There is so far no time limit for this mandate. Value added services would be open to competition.	The new telecommunications law is expected to be passed in 1994. At the same time a detailed regulatory framework will be put in place. This is currently being prepared under a World Bank loan. Increases in tariffs for basic services will be tied to the rate of inflation.	Under the proposed legislation the regulatory agency will initially be the Ministry of Posts and Telecommunications.

Myanmar

Operating Entity(s) Including Ownership	Competition Policy	Legal and Regulatory Framework	Regulatory Agency
Myanmar Posts and Telecommunications (MPT) is a wholly government-owned carrier and is responsible for all of Myanmar's domestic and international telecommunications.	There is little private sector activity in Myanmar's telecommunications sector and no indication that the government is planning to privatize MPT or liberalize the telecommunications service markets. Given the political situation in Myanmar, there is no reason to expect any substantial service market liberalization in either the near, medium, or long term.		Ministry of Transport and Communications.

Nepal

Operating Entity(s) Including Ownership	Competition Policy	Legal and Regulatory Framework	Regulatory Agency
Nepal Telecommunications Corporation (NTC), wholly government-owned, provides all telecommunications services.	There are no immediate plans for privatization or segmentation of telecommunications services. The opportunity is further limited by the low demand for specialized services.	Communications Corporation Act (1975). NTC requires Ministry of Communications approval for major acquisitions (exceeding $25,000) or tariff changes.	Ministry of Communications.

Netherlands

Operating Entity(s) Including Ownership	Competition Policy	Legal and Regulatory Framework	Regulatory Agency
PTT Telecom Netherlands provides voice telephony and leased-line services (domestic and international). The Dutch government has announced that it will sell up to two-thirds of its shares in Royal PTT Netherlands NV (KPN), parent of PTT Telecom Netherlands; the first tranche, about 30% of the two-thirds, will be sold during the first half of 1994.	Competition was introduced in packet-switched data services in 1993. Leased-lines resale has been liberalized, and from 1994, licenses for competitive public mobile services will be issued. Competition will be allowed in both services and infrastructure for telephone to closed user groups from January 1, 1995, and for public basic voice on January 1, 1998. There are also plans to license a second fixed network operation in competition with PTT Telecom. This may involve a combination of cable television, electricity utilities, and railway operators' existing infrastructures to allow them to provide leased lines to business customers.	The 1989 Telecommunications Law liberalized customer premises equipment (CPE), value added services, and simple resale of services. Under proposed legislation, foreign companies will be excluded from the liberalization of the nonmobile sector. Foreign companies will be allowed only to compete for permits to establish a new cellular network.	The Telecommunications and Posts Department (HDTP) of the Ministry of Transport and Public Works. HDPT oversees application of the 1989 Telecommunications Law, type-approves CPE, issues licenses, and manages the radio frequency spectrum.

New Zealand

Operating Entity(s) Including Ownership	Competition Policy	Legal and Regulatory Framework	Regulatory Agency
Telecom Corporation of New Zealand (TCNZ) was sold in September 1990 to a consortium of Fay Richwhite and Freightways of New Zealand, Bell Atlantic, and Ameritech for US$2.4 billion, under the condition that the American partners reduce their combined share of TCNZ to 49.9% in three years. At the end of 1993, ownership structure was Bell Atlantic and Ameritech (25.95% each), Fay Richwhite (1.24%), Freightways (2.06%), and others (46.8%). The government maintains golden ("Kiwi") share. On April 1, 1993, TCNZ restructured itself, with its principal operating subsidiary becoming Telecom New Zealand Limited. The main competitor is Clear Communications Ltd. (a consortium involving Bell Canada, MCI, and three NZ companies—the Todd Group, NZ Railway, and NZ Broadcasting; the last two are 100% government-owned). There are no foreign ownership restrictions except for specific provisions pertaining to TCNZ.	Competition permitted in the provision of all services. No market entry restrictions. TCNZ currently is the only provider of cellular services, but BellSouth is establishing a competing service for implementation in 1993, and Telstra has plans to offer service in 1994. TCNZ in its Articles of Association undertook to maintain a) free local calling, b) the price rise of residential rentals within inflation, and c) the price of rural residential rentals the same as in the cities. TCNZ will also publish quality-of-service indicators.	Commerce Act 1986 (antitrust law) and the Fair Trading Act 1986 govern competitive and fair trading behavior in the provision of telecommunications services. The Radiocommunication Act 1989 covers frequency allocation and use. The Telecommunications Act 1987, Telecommunications Amendment Act 1988, and Telecommunications Amendment Act 1990 liberalize the provision of telecommunications services and facilitate competition. The Telecommunications (International Services) Regulations 1989 and Telecommunications (Disclosure) Regulations 1990 pertain to certain registration and disclosure requirements with respect to international services and domestic competition.	The Ministry of Commerce administers the relevant laws and regulations.

Nicaragua

Operating Entity(s) Including Ownership	Competition Policy	Legal and Regulatory Framework	Regulatory Agency
Instituto Nicaragüense de Telecomunicaciones y Correos (TELCOR), a government administration operating under the supervision of a minister-director, provides all telecommunications and postal services except cellular mobile. The latter is provided in Managua and region by NICACEL, an affiliate of Motorola. There are plans to privatize TELCOR in 1994, with a sale of 40% to a foreign strategic investor and 10% to employees.	No competition is allowed today. There are plans to allow competition, but only in the fringe services.		At present, regulator is a division of TELCOR, Dirección General de Telecomunicaciones (Digetel). Plans are to set up an independent regulatory body.

Nigeria

Operating Entity(s) Including Ownership	Competition Policy	Legal and Regulatory Framework	Regulatory Agency
NITEL is an autonomous government-owned company. A joint venture (in which NITEL is a partner) provides mobile cellular service.	Nigerian Telecommunications (NITEL) has a monopoly to provide all basic services, domestic and international. The mobile cellular service is open to competition.	A 1993 law established the Nigeria Communications Commission. A June 1992 law incorporated NITEL as an autonomous, government-owned company.	There is a newly established independent regulatory body, Nigeria Communications Commission (NCC).

Norway

Operating Entity(s) Including Ownership	Competition Policy	Legal and Regulatory Framework	Regulatory Agency
Norwegian Telecom, a fully state-owned limited company (since January 1, 1992), retains exclusive right to provide two-way public telecommunications services. It also has monopoly on leased lines. TBK A/S, fully owned by Norwegian Telecom, provides competitive services, including import, sale, and installation of PABXs and CPEs, supply of security systems, operation of local cable television networks, VANs, etc.	There is monopoly provision of two-way public telecommunications services (telephone, telex, and circuit and packet-switched data transmission). The market for terminal equipment, including modems, PABXs, and user networks was fully liberalized in 1988. Mobile and paging services have been liberalized. Resale of capacity for voice is not allowed.		Independent authority under Ministry of Transport and Communications, Norwegian Telecommunications Regulatory Authority (NTRA) is responsible for type approval of user equipment, authorization of equipment suppliers and installation contractors, radio frequency management, and licensing for cable TV.

Pakistan

Operating Entity(s) Including Ownership	Competition Policy	Legal and Regulatory Framework	Regulatory Agency
The Pakistan Telephone and Telegraph Department was transformed in 1991 into a wholly state-owned company, the Pakistan Telecommunications Corporation (PTC). It provides basic telecommunications services. Cellular services are provided by several private companies: Paktel (owned 80% by Cable & Wireless, 20% by Hassan Associates), and Pakcom (owned 50% by Millicom Int. Cellular; 50% Afreen Int.) were licensed in 1989. A cellular consortium (51% owned by Saif International; 32% by Hutchison; 15% Motorola and 2% British Telecom) also was licensed in 1991, but has not begun network construction. Digitel Communications (privately owned Pakistani corporation) was licensed to provide paging services in 1991. Licenses to provide pay phone services have been issued to 22 private operators. The government had announced its intention to privatize PTC, with foreign participation. The plan was to offer a 51% share to a single foreign investor or consortium and the rest to employees and the public. Political differences have halted the process.	Basic services are provided by PTC on a monopoly basis. The cellular mobile service has been opened to competition.	Legal and regulatory framework is based on a pre-1900 telecommunications law which needs to be updated.	Regulatory is the Pakistan Telecommunications Corporation (PTC) which also issues licenses. There are plans to set up an independent regulator.

Panama

Operating Entity(s) Including Ownership	Competition Policy	Legal and Regulatory Framework	Regulatory Agency
Instituto Nacional de Telecomunicaciones (INTEL) is a private company with shares held by the government. Privatization had been under way but was suspended when the National Assembly rejected the draft law.	Intel is sole provider of wireline local, national, and international services.	A draft telecommunications law has been prepared.	Plans to create a regulatory body (part of the draft telecommunications law) is on hold.

Paraguay

Operating Entity(s) Including Ownership	Competition Policy	Legal and Regulatory Framework	Regulatory Agency
All services are provided by government-owned Administración Nacional de Telecomunicaciones (ANTELCO). There has been discussion of privatizing many state-owned enterprises, including ANTELCO. A consortium led by Millicom (51%) was awarded a cellular concession in 1991.	ANTELCO is the monopoly provider of all services except cellular mobile.		ANTELCO functions as both an operator and a regulatory agency.

Peru

Operating Entity(s) Including Ownership	Competition Policy	Legal and Regulatory Framework	Regulatory Agency
Compañía Peruana de Teléfonos (CPT) operates local service in Lima. Empresa Nacional de Telecomunicaciones (ENTEL) operates in the rest of Peru and provides long-distance and international services. The government plans to sell its stakes in both ENTEL (100%) and CPT (20%), and has invited international operators to public bidding. Telemóvil and CPT provide cellular mobile services in competition with each other in Lima. ENTEL provides cellular mobile services in the rest of the country.	There is a five-year exclusivity for basic services and a duopoly for cellular services. Competition is allowed in all other services.	Law 702 and Decree 26096 promote competition in the telecom sector by private suppliers and operators, regulated by the state.	Regulator is Organismo Superior de Inversión Privada en Telecomunicaciones (OSIPTEL), an autonomous institution, dependent on the President of the Republic.

Philippines

Operating Entity(s) Including Ownership	Competition Policy	Legal and Regulatory Framework	Regulatory Agency
Philippines Long Distance Telephone Company (PLDT) controls 94% of all telephones. Other major carriers are: Eastern Telecommunications Philippines Inc. (ETPI), itself 40% owned by Cable & Wireless), Paptelco, and TELOF (government network serving rural areas). Seven record carriers provide domestic telex, facsimile and leased-line services; four provide international services. PLDT, ETPI, and Philippines Global Communications Corp. (Philcom) operate international gateways. Philippines Telephone Company (subsidiary of PLDT) and Extelcom provide domestic satellite services: DOMSAT, Liberty Broadcasting, Clavecilla, International Communications Corp. (ICC), and IRC Capital Wireless Inc. (CapWire). The Philippines Communications Satellite Corp. (Philcomsat) provides international satellite services.	PLDT had a de facto monopoly for international telephone service until 1990, when ETPI was licensed and installed its own international gateway. Philcom is the third international gateway operator. In 1990, the Department of Transport and Communications (DOTC) mandated the eventual privatization of all government-owned telecommunications facilities. It also awarded digital authority to operate facilities in Luzon under a lease-buy arrangement, and is selling off local networks under a plan to improve services in each municipality. The government is developing policies aimed at increasing competition for the provision of all services as means of overcoming the demand backlog.	Proposed new legislation to clarify and modernize the roles and responsibilities of the DOTC and the National Telecommunications Commission (NTC) is being reviewed, but progress is slow.	National Telecommunications Commission (NTC), an independent regulatory body, is responsible for licensing and radio spectrum management. The Department of Transportation and Communications (DOTC) establishes telecommunications policy, including the definition of operational and financial arrangements among PLDT and other services providers. The respective roles of the DOTC and NTC are not clearly defined.

649

Poland

Operating Entity(s) Including Ownership	Competition Policy	Legal and Regulatory Framework	Regulatory Agency
Polish Telecom (Telekomunikacja Polska, S.A. or TPSA), a 100% government-owned joint-stock company, is expected to be privatized by about 1996. The Ministry of Posts and Telecom (MPT) has issued more than 40 licenses for local, regional, and value added services. There is one cellular mobile operator, which is a joint venture among TPSA, France Télécom and Ameritech. In local (i.e., rural) data and value added service, foreign participation is allowed with no limit on foreign ownership. In intercity network, foreign ownership is allowed up to 49%.	TPSA has a monopoly over international and long-distance trunk networks. The remainder is open to competition. Intercity and local operations are fully liberalized.	Law of 15 January 1991 modified the status of TPSA, turning it into joint-stock public service monopoly. Acts of 28 June 1991 and 9 October 1991 stipulate the use of telecommunications equipment and connection of international services as well as establish a liberalized local environment.	Regulatory agencies are the Ministry of Posts and Telecom (MPT); National Telecom Inspectorate (Panstwowal Telecom Inspectorate (Panstwowa Inspekcja Telekomunikacji, or PIT); and National Radio Committee (Panstwowa Agencja Radiofonii, or PAR). These agencies together determine overall policies for telecommunications development, granting licenses, and supervising and coordinating activities of telecommunications companies.

Portugal

Operating Entity(s) Including Ownership	Competition Policy	Legal and Regulatory Framework	Regulatory Agency
Telecom Portugal, part of the PTT, provides domestic telecommunications except in Lisbon and Oporto, and international telecommunications to European countries. The 100% state-owned Telefones de Lisboa e Porto (TLP) provides local services in Lisbon and Oporto. Companhia Portuguesa de Rádio Marconi (CPRM) is responsible for intercontinental links. Legislation introduced in 1989 turned these operators into public-limited companies under a state-owned holding company, Comunicaçoes Nacionais (CN). Forty-nine percent of the government's shares in Telecom Portugal and TLP are to be sold, with the initial 30% to be sold in late 1994 or early 1995. CPRM is already 49% privately owned. Telcel (in which Pacific Telesis has a stake) is a new provider of cellular services.	Basic network infrastructure, telephone, and data services are provided on a monopoly basis.	1989 legislation separates postal and telecommunications activities and defines the monopoly on basic network infrastructure, telephone service, and data service.	The Portuguese Institute of Communications, Instituto das Comunicaçoes de Portugal (ICP) established in 1989, is responsible for administering competition, issuing licenses, approving equipment, and managing the radio frequency.

Puerto Rico

Operating Entity(s) Including Ownership	Competition Policy	Legal and Regulatory Framework	Regulatory Agency
International services provider Telefónica Larga Distancia de Puerto Rico (TLD) was privatized in December 1992, when the FCC approved sale of 79% of TLD to Telefónica de España through a holding company LD Acquisition Corporation (LD). The government retains 19% via the Puerto Rican Telephone Authority (PRTA). Two percent has been placed in an Employee Stock Option Plan. Common carrier radio licenses (subject to U.S. foreign ownership restrictions) have been assigned to PRTA, a public authority of the Commonwealth of Puerto Rico. Domestic services are provided on a monopoly basis by the Puerto Rico Telephone Company (PRTC), which is 100% owned by PRTA.	There is monopoly provision of domestic and international services.		At the local level, the Local Public Utilities Commission (PUC) was recently established. At the federal level, the regulator is the FCC in Washington, DC.

Romania

Operating Entity(s) Including Ownership	Competition Policy	Legal and Regulatory Framework	Regulatory Agency
ROM TELECOM is a separate, wholly government-owned corporation which resulted from the breakup of the old post and telecommunications operator. The company is wholly autonomous. An NMT 450 mobile cellular service is operated as a joint venture between Telefónica de España and two government operators, ROM TELECOM and ROM RADIOCOM.	Competition is permitted in almost every aspect of telecommunications except basic services, which remain a monopoly for ROM TELECOM. Terminal equipment market is open to competition subject only to type approval.	Regulatory framework has generally been made consistent with that in the European Union.	Ministry of Communications.

Saint Kitts–Nevis

Operating Entity(s) Including Ownership	Competition Policy	Legal and Regulatory Framework	Regulatory Agency
Saint Kitts–Nevis Telecommunications (SKANTEL) is the operating entity. Ownership is shared between C&W (65%), government (17%), and the public (18%). Cellular services are provided by Boatphone, a separate company which is serviced by SKANTEL.	No competition is permitted.	The Telecommunications Ordinance of 1959, Chapter 203 of the laws of Saint Kitts–Nevis. Regulations pertaining to licenses and fees were revised by Order #10 of 1986.	Ministry of Communications and Works through a telecommunications officer.

Saint Vincent and the Grenadines

Operating Entity(s) Including Ownership	Competition Policy	Legal and Regulatory Framework	Regulatory Agency
C&W is the only operating entity on the island. A subsidiary company, Boatphone Ltd., provides cellular services.	Exclusive rights exist for telecommunications and all basic services on the domestic and international levels.	Telecommunications Act of 1988 covers all telecommunications activities.	Ministry of Communications and Works.

Singapore

Operating Entity(s) Including Ownership	Competition Policy	Legal and Regulatory Framework	Regulatory Agency
Singapore Telecom (ST) was corporatized as Singapore Telecommunications Pte Ltd. and Singapore Post Pte Ltd. on April 1, 1992, through a government-owned holding company (MinCom Holdings Pte. Ltd.). About 11% of the government's share in ST was sold in November 1993 in three tranches. Half the shares were reserved for Singaporeans. The government will retain majority control, but plans to sell an additional 25% within five to seven years through public offerings and private placements.	ST has a monopoly for domestic services for an indefinite period, for international services until 2007, and for mobile (paging and cellular) until 1997. Provision of value added services has been liberalized; however, applicants for licenses to provide international value added network (IVAN) services are required to show a substantial "value added" element to the proposed service. Those that would involve resale of any of ST's services are not permitted. The sale of Telecommunications Terminal equipment was liberalized on July 1, 1991. ST is subject to a universal service obligation.	The Telecommunications Authority of Singapore Act 1992 defines the regulatory and licensing functions of the Telecommunications Authority of Singapore (TAS), the regulatory authority for both telecommunications and postal services.	Telecommunications Authority of Singapore (TAS).

Spain

Operating Entity(s) Including Ownership	Competition Policy	Legal and Regulatory Framework	Regulatory Agency
Telefónica de España, in which the government has a minority share (32%) but maintains financial oversight, is monopoly provider of all basic telephone services. Correos y Telégrafos, part of the Ministry of Transportation, Tourism and Communication, provides telex and telegraph services. Radio paging services are provided by four operators, one of which is a subsidiary of Telefónica.	Monopoly provision of all basic services by Telefónica de España and Correos y Telégrafos. Spain has not yet adopted EC Directives to liberalize services markets. Telefónica has discouraged construction of private networks, and digital-leased circuits remain difficult to obtain. Resale of capacity, carriage of third-party traffic, and interconnection to the public-switched network are all prohibited, and no changes are planned. The government has liberalized the provision of data transmission services and will liberalize cellular mobile service in 1994. Following 1993 review of basic telephone services market in the EC, the Council of Ministers has allowed Spain until 2003 to open voice to competition.	Telecommunications Act of 1987 will be amended to give effect to EC Directives.	Ministerio de Transporte, Turismo y Comunicaciones.

657

Sri Lanka

Operating Entity(s) Including Ownership	Competition Policy	Legal and Regulatory Framework	Regulatory Agency
Sri Lanka Telecom (SLT), a wholly government-owned corporation, was created in September 1991. It provides local as well as domestic and international long-distance services. Eventually it will be privatized. Value added services (VAS) are provided by private operators. Cellular licenses have been granted to two private operators (both joint ventures with foreign companies), Celltel and Lanka Cellular Services. Paging licenses have been granted to four private operators: Intercity Paging Service (joint venture with Motorola), Bartleet Electronics Ltd., Wimaladharma Bros Ltd., and Services Trade Ltd.; all operate primarily in the metro Colombo area. Privately owned Lanka Payphones Ltd. was licensed in 1989 to install and operate card and coin pay phones in metropolitan areas.	Basic services (local, long-distance, and international voice) are provided by Sri Lanka Telecom on a monopoly basis. There is competition in cellular and paging services, which are provided by private companies (cellular since 1982, paging since 1989). Private operators also have been licensed to provide store-and-forward fax and trunked mobile radio services.	Relevant legislation is contained in: • Sri Lanka Telecommunications Act No. 25 (1991), which provided for the transfer of assets from the former Sri Lanka Telecommunications Department to the New Sri Lanka Telecom (SLT). It also established the role of Director General of Telecommunications. • Telecommunications Ordinance (1988).	The Director General of Telecommunications (DGT) was appointed in July 1991 by—and is accountable to—the Minister of Posts & Telecommunications (MPT). In 1992, the MPT proposed to convert the functions of the DGT into a com-mission and give it greater autonomy.

Sweden

Operating Entity(s) Including Ownership	Competition Policy	Legal and Regulatory Framework	Regulatory Agency
The fully government-owned, limited liability company, Telia AB (formerly Televerket of Swedish Telecom), has a de facto monopoly. A second operator, Tele2 AB (40% owned by Cable & Wireless), was formed in 1991 and launched an international telephone service in March 1993. Fonotel (owned by U.S. entrepreneur Arne Dunham) also plans to launch a rival public telecommunications service. The government is considering Televerket's partial or full privatization.	Sweden has open competition in telecommunications networks and services. Tele2 has an interconnection agreement with Televerket for international calls, but has failed to reach agreement for domestic service. The terminal equipment market was liberalized in 1988.	Until 1993 Sweden had no telecommunications law. The Telecommunications Act which was passed by Parliament on June 8, 1993, and came into force on July 1, 1993, defines the legal framework for increased competition. It regulates licenses for operators of telephone network services, leased circuits, and mobile communications. It also defines terms of interconnection and tariffs for basic services. A second law passed at the same time as the Telecommunications Act transformed Televerket into a limited liability company fully government-owned (Telia AB). Radio Communications Law (revised July 1, 1993) covers frequency management and the use of radio transmitters.	The National Telecommunications Agency was established July 1, 1992, as the regulatory agency. It administers frequencies, certifies CPEs, licenses operators of basic services, administers numbers, and represents Sweden in international organizations.

659

Switzerland

Operating Entity(s) Including Ownership	Competition Policy	Legal and Regulatory Framework	Regulatory Agency
Entreprise des PTT (Swiss PTT) has been granted monopoly for the establishment of infrastructures and, in principle, is the sole provider of basic services.	Policy is characterized by: • Full liberalization of terminal equipment market • Resale of basic services under certain conditions, and leased lines and value added services (VAS) fully liberalized (no license or registration required) • Licenses may be granted to third parties for radiocommunication and satellite services (except voice telephony) • Network and basic service (telephone, telex, data transmission) provision maintained under state-owned monopoly.	The 1991 Telecommunications Law distinguishes between basic (voice, telex, and data transmission) and value added services. The 1 May 1992 Order sets out conditions under which basic services other than voice can be provided by third parties through leased lines.	Independent body, Office fédéral de la communication (OFCOM), is attached to the Federal Department of Transport, Communications, and Energy, but managed separately from the Swiss PTT. OFCOM is also responsible for radio frequency management and spectrum allocation.

Taiwan

Operating Entity(s) Including Ownership	Competition Policy	Legal and Regulatory Framework	Regulatory Agency
Domestic and international basic services are provided on a monopoly basis by the Directorate General of Telecommunications (DGT), a part of the Ministry of Transportation and Communications (MOTC). Local services (including cellular and radio paging) are provided by Northern Taiwan Telecommunications Administration, Central Taiwan Telecommunications Administration, and Southern Taiwan Telecommunications Administration. Domestic long-distance is provided by DGT through Long-Distance Telecommunications Administration. International services are provided through International Telecommunications Administration. No foreign investment is allowed in providers of telecommunications services, including value added services (VAS).	Domestic and international basic telecommunications services are provided on a monopoly basis. Certain VAS (e.g., information storage and retrieval, information processing, remote transaction services, electronic mail) can be provided competitively, subject to approval by the MOTC. Steps are being taken to liberalize the use of leased circuits by large users.	Legislation being drafted would create a corporatized government entity, Chinese Telecommunications Company (CTC), to assume DGT's operational functions. It would also create an independent regulatory agency. The law would permit foreign ownership of VAS providers (up to 33%) and would divide carrier services into two categories: Category I (installation of facilities that provide telecom services) would remain a monopoly of DGT's corporate successor; Category II (VAS using the facilities of Category I enterprises) could be provided on a relatively competitive basis. CTC would be permitted to provide both Category I and II services without cross-subsidization. CTC eventually would be privatized under the following conditions: Only Taiwanese entities or nationals could hold CTC shares, but foreigners would be allowed to hold up to one-third of the shares of a Taiwanese entity with an interest in CTC.	The Directorate General of Telecommunications, part of the Ministry of Transportation and Communications (MOTC), is currently both the regulator and operator.

Tajikistan

Operating Entity(s) Including Ownership	Competition Policy	Legal and Regulatory Framework	Regulatory Agency
The Ministry of Communication (MOC) operates all public telecommunications (about 270,000 main telephone lines) and posts as well as TV and wireline audio broadcasting systems (but not contents). The armed forces, electric power, railways, and civil aviation ministries operate own telecommunications facilities (about 24,000 lines).	Liberalized provision of customer premises equipment.		MOC is a government department responsible for policy and regulation as well as operation.

Tanzania

Operating Entity(s) Including Ownership	Competition Policy	Legal and Regulatory Framework	Regulatory Agency
Tanzania Posts & Telecommunications Corp. (TPTC), a statutory body, is the monopoly provider of all telecommunications services and facilities.	No competition is allowed for the time being. It is, however, envisaged that competitive provision of value added services will be allowed shortly.	Law is being prepared.	Establishment of an independent regulatory body is envisaged by end–1994.

Thailand

Operating Entity(s) Including Ownership	Competition Policy	Legal and Regulatory Framework	Regulatory Agency
Telephone Organization of Thailand (TOT) operates the domestic network. International services are provided mostly by the Communications Authority of Thailand (CAT). Both TOT and CAT are wholly owned by the government. The Post and Telegraph Department of the Ministry of Transport and Communications (MOTC) provides telegraph, telex, and packet-switching services. Shinawatra Satellite Co. has a 30-year concession to operate the domestic satellite system (operational in 1994). TOT has sought private (including foreign) financing of domestic infrastructure projects through build-transfer-and-operate (BTO) arrangements for Bangkok (2 million lines) and the provincial areas (1 million lines). There is no direct foreign participation in TOT or CAT. Limited indirect foreign investment is, however, possible, as in TOT's BTO arrangement with NYNEX.	There is no clear policy. There is some overlap (cellular, data, and paging), but CAT increasingly provides business-oriented services while TOT is concentrating on expanding the domestic network. Franchised competition has developed for data communications and cellular telephony.	Relevant legislation is contained in: • Postal Services Act (1934) • Telegraph and Telephone Act (1936) stipulates that telecom-munications services destined for the general public be government controlled • Telephone Organization of Thailand Act (1954) established TOT to provide domestic telephone and related services • Communication Radio Act (1955) • Communication Authority Act (1976) • Communications Authority of Thailand Act (1977) established CAT to provide international services and domestic services that are not a monopoly of TOT.	The Ministry of Transport and Communications (MOTC) oversees the operation of TOT and CAT and approves capital investments and tariffs. The Post and Telegraph Dept. (PTC) is responsible for international and regional cooperation in telecommunications on behalf of the Thai government. It also regulates the radio frequency spectrum.

Trinidad and Tobago

Operating Entity(s) Including Ownership	Competition Policy	Legal and Regulatory Framework	Regulatory Agency
Telecommunications Services of Trinidad and Tobago (TSTT), established in 1991, is owned 51% by the government and 49% by C&W. Prior to 1991, the domestic carrier was a 100% government-owned company, TELCO. TEXTEL, a joint venture between C&W and the government, was the external carrier.	There is exclusivity for local and international telephone services and competition in terminal equipment provision.	Telephone Act legislated the telephone company. A Wireless Act, Chapter 36, No. 2 of the Laws of Trinidad and Tobago, applies to all radiocommunications. A 1991 Telecommunications Act has been passed in the legislature but not yet proclaimed.	The Telecommunications Division in the Office of the Prime Minister. The establishment of a telecommunications authority is being planned.

Turkey

Operating Entity(s) Including Ownership	Competition Policy	Legal and Regulatory Framework	Regulatory Agency
Turkish PTT is sole provider of telecommunications services. In late 1992, the Turkish government announced plans to sell 20% of the Turkish PTT. Prior to privatization, the postal and telecommunications operations will be split. There is de facto no foreign ownership.	All telecommunications services are provided under the monopoly of the Turkish PTT.	Telegraph and Telephone Law No. 406 contains the provision for the Turkish PTT's monopoly, which includes telecommunications service installation, operation, and regulation.	The Ministry of Transportation has control over the Turkish PTT.

Ukraine

Operating Entity(s) Including Ownership	Competition Policy	Legal and Regulatory Framework	Regulatory Agency
National and regional (oblast) transmission and microwave companies were inherited from the breakup of the former Soviet network. A major joint venture for international and long-distance service, Ukrainian Telecom (UTEL), is being introduced with the existing Ukrainian service companies, AT&T, and the PTT Telecom Netherlands and DBP Telekom as partners. A second major joint venture for cellular, Ukrainian Mobile Communications (UMC), involves the Dutch, German, and Danish PTTs.	No formal arrangements have yet been developed.	No framework has yet been developed. The Ministry of Communications has concentrated on addressing immediate issues, including the negotiating of the joint ventures listed.	Ministry of Communications.

United Kingdom

Operating Entity(s) Including Ownership	Competition Policy	Legal and Regulatory Framework	Regulatory Agency
The government's remaining 22% share in British Telecommunications plc (BT) was sold to the public in mid–1993. Mercury (a wholly owned subsidiary of Cable & Wireless) entered the switched voice market in 1986. It provides international and domestic voice services. A number of cable television companies—many associated with North American telephone companies—are starting to provide local exchange services. There are no foreign ownership restrictions.	Full competition is allowed in all services except international network (where duopoly remains). Liberalization of CPE, mobile, cellular, VAS, data, and resale markets between 1985 and 1990. Interconnection and contribution issues remain.	The Telecommunications Act (1981) split telecommunications from Post Office and allowed government to establish network competition. Telecommunications Act 1984 led to privatization of BT and setting up of independent regulator, OFTEL. Under the 1984 Act, the two primary duties of DTI and OFTEL are to secure the provision of telecom services throughout the U.K. to meet reasonable demand; and to assure that operators are financially qualified. They also must attend to the protection of consumer interests and promotion of competition. 1991 DTI White Paper further opened network and other markets. The domestic long-distance was opened to competition. Government policy is to streamline licensing and issue a class license whenever possible. Systems using radio spectrum require both a Telecommunications Act license and a license under the Wireless Telegraphy Act.	Independent body, Office of Telecommunications (OFTEL). Regulation of telecommunications is the ultimate responsibility of the Secretary of State for the Department of Trade and Industry (DTI). The Director General of Telecommunications (DGT), who heads OFTEL, together with DTI is responsible for implementing the regulatory regime prescribed in the 1984 Act. DTI has responsibility for licensing and regulation of the radio spectrum. OFTEL has responsibility for monitoring and enforcing license conditions, investigating complaints, and keeping the sector under review generally.

United States

Operating Entity(s) Including Ownership	Competition Policy	Legal and Regulatory Framework	Regulatory Agency
Most local services are still provided on a monopoly basis. Domestic long-distance and international voice services are provided by AT&T, MCI, Sprint, and others. There is a 20% foreign ownership restriction on radio license holders.	Competition is allowed for all services, with a few restrictions. There is no federal segmentation of markets or carrier restrictions except for regional Bell operating companies (RBOCs) as per the 1982 Modified Final Judgment (MFJ). Competition, however, is in varying stages of development for many services—i.e., local access competition is nascent, and the FCC has limited entry in some markets, such as cellular (two licenses per market).	Communications Act of 1934.	An independent agency, the Federal Communications Commission (FCC), regulates interstate and international communications as well as the radio frequency spectrum for commercial radio and television. State public utilities commissions (PUC) regulate intrastate communications.

Uruguay

Operating Entity(s) Including Ownership	Competition Policy	Legal and Regulatory Framework	Regulatory Agency
Administración Nacional de Telecomunicaciones (ANTEL) has monopoly for local, domestic long-distance, and international telecommunications and of cable, microwave, and satellite services. Plan was announced in December 1991 to establish a mixed capital corporation with 51% government and 49% private ownership. This was preceded by legislation (September 1991) allowing private ownership of certain public enterprises, including ANTEL. Foreign ownership was to be limited to 49%, according to the State Enterprise Reform Law. Privatization plans had to be canceled in December 1992 when a national referendum rejected the plan by a 71.2% majority.	Competition is allowed for value added services. Private operators offer cellular, rural networks, and data communications. Competition is not allowed for local, domestic long-distance, and international services.	Law 14325 of July 1974 grants ANTEL a monopoly on local, long-distance, and international as well as regulatory functions. An attempt was made in 1991 to reform the telecommunications sector through the State Enterprise Reform Law (September 1991). It was overruled, however, by a national referendum in December 1992.	The regulator is the National Department of Communications, which is controlled by the Ministry of Defense. State Enterprise Reform Law was to have created a Comisión de Telecomunicaciones.

Uzbekistan

Operating Entity(s) Including Ownership	Competition Policy	Legal and Regulatory Framework	Regulatory Agency
National and regional telecommunications service providers have been established. Some of these have been organized separately from the government, and some of these are administered directly by the Ministry of Communications.	No formal arrangements are in place.	The Ministry of Communications is planning to develop a comprehensive regulatory structure soon.	Ministry of Communications.

Vanuatu

Operating Entity(s) Including Ownership	Competition Policy	Legal and Regulatory Framework	Regulatory Agency
Telecom Vanuatu Ltd., which is owned equally (one-third each) by the Vanuatu government, Cable & Wireless and France Cable et Radio (a branch of France Télécom).	Telecom Vanuatu has an exclusive mandate to provide all domestic and international telecommunications services.	Telecommunications Act of 1990 empowers Telecom Vanuatu to provide all telecommunications services.	Ministry of Communications. The Telecommunications Act (1990) established a telecommunications regulatory authority, but the current government abolished it.

Venezuela

Operating Entity(s) Including Ownership	Competition Policy	Legal and Regulatory Framework	Regulatory Agency
Privatization of CANTV was finalized in December 1991. Forty percent of CANTV sold to consortium of GTE (20.4%); Telefónica de España (6.4%); Electricidad de Caracas (6.4%); Consorcio Inversionista Mercantil Cima (4.8%); and AT&T (2%). The government has retained 49% for later sale and has placed 11% in trust for CANTV employees. The new company has a 35-year concession, renewable for an additional 20 years. It also is authorized to operate a Band B cellular network, under its subsidiary, Movilnet. Telcel operates a Band A cellular network and is owned by a consortium led by BellSouth.	Basic services monopoly has been assured for nine years. In 1991, TELCEL was granted a 20-year concession to compete with CANTV in cellular mobile. Private and public satellite, value added services, VSAT data networks, private line, and certain mobile services also have been liberalized.	The Telecommunications Law of 1940 gives the government the responsibility to provide, either directly or through concession to private parties, telephone and other telecommunications services as well as radio and television broadcast services. The 1940 Law also authorizes the government to promulgate regulations concerning telecommunications and requires the executive branch to approve tariffs. The Constitution adopted in 1965 gives the federal government exclusive authority over telecommunications.

In 1991, the government considered a new telecommunications law which would have created an autonomous regulatory body called INATEL as well as a new policy advisory body within the Ministry of Transportation and Communications. The law was not passed, and CONATEL was created by presidential decree. | Regulator is Consejo Nacional de Telecomunicaciones (CONATEL), an autonomous service within the Ministry of Transportation and Communications. |

Zimbabwe

Operating Entity(s) Including Ownership	Competition Policy	Legal and Regulatory Framework	Regulatory Agency
Zimbabwe Posts and Telecommunications Corporation (ZPTC) is a statutory body and monopoly provider of all telecommunications services.	No competition is allowed for the time being.		Regulator and operator is ZPTC.

Glossary*

access charge. Term used in the United States for the fee imposed by local exchange carriers on interexchange carriers and on end users to defray that portion of the costs of the carriers' facilities that are associated with or otherwise assigned to the provision of interexchange services.

access deficit (U.K.). The annual gap between BT's revenues from providing exchange lines and its attributable or accounting costs which are allocated according to a formula (not in the public domain) which includes profits up to an approved limit (called applicable rate of return).

access deficit (U.S.). The difference between revenues—from connection and rental charges—and the costs of the installation and maintenance of direct exchange lines.

access deficit contribution (U.K.). Supplementary interconnection payments per call proposed by OFTEL, the U.K. regulator, on BT's competitors to help BT subsidize the below-cost price it charges for residential exchange connections.

access line. The wireline or other physical link that connects a customer to a telephone company's central office to allow calls to be made. Also called subscriber line.

---

*Some of the definitions in this glossary have been taken with permission from the *Bilingual Dictionary of International Telecommunications,* Teleglobe Canada, Montreal, Vol. 1 (1983), Vol.2 (1985), Vol. 3 (1988), Vol.4 (1991); from the *Report of the Federal-Provincial-Territorial Task Force on Telecommunications,* Ottawa, December 1988; and from Pierre Guislain, *Divestiture of State Enterprises: An Overview of the Legal Framework,* World Bank Technical Paper, Number 186 (Washington, DC: World Bank 1992). Finally, a number of people helped in researching terms in the glossary. They include Bruce Laidlaw, an independent consultant in the UK; Anton Lenson of the European Parliament; Donald Mason of the UK Office of Fair Trading; Alain Morissette and Jocelyn LeNéal of Teleglobe Canada, Inc.; Hudson Janisch of the University of Toronto, Faculty of Law; A. H. Odeh of the ITU; Brownlee Thomas of Teleglobe Inc., Christopher Devine of McGill University, and many others.

access tariff. Charges imposed by a telephone company to access its local exchange facilities for the origination or termination of interexchange calls.

act (legislative). Term generally used as an abbreviation for *legislative act* or *act of Parliament*, a synonym for *law*.

American Depositary Receipts (ADRs). Receipts issued by a U.S. bank or trust company against certificates of shares in foreign stock registered in their name and held by them for safekeeping. ADRs are traded in the U.S. like shares, and are subject to U.S. regulatory rules. ADRs facilitate investment in foreign securities by overcoming the complications of directly accessing foreign markets.

Ameritech. One of the seven regional Bell operating companies that resulted from the 1984 breakup of the Bell System. Headquartered in Chicago, Ameritech is the parent of the Bell companies serving 12 million customers in the Great Lakes region (comprising the states of Illinois, Indiana, Michigan, Ohio, and Wisconsin), as well as companies providing mobile communications, directory publishing, voice messaging, lease financing, and audiotex services. 1992 revenues were US$11.2 billion, and total corporate assets exceed US$20 billion.

AMPS (advanced mobile phone service). A public cellular land mobile system developed in North America operating in the 800 MHz frequency band, designed to permit automatic exchange of traffic with the public-switched telephone network. It features high voice quality, high reliability, and relatively low cost, and can be used for both voice and data transmission.

analog technology. The means to process and transmit voice, data, or other information by using electric or electromagnetic signals that provide a continuous replica of the information. As opposed to digital technology.

ANTEL (Administración Nacional de Telecomunicaciones). The state telecommunications operating enterprise of Uruguay.

Antitrust II case. Case brought by the U.S. Department of Justice against AT&T and which was settled in 1982 as the Modified Final Judgment which led to divestiture of the Bell operating companies.

antitrust laws (rules). National legislation (regulation) aimed at enhancing competition. For example, in the European Community's rules concerning competition, Article 85 of the Treaty of Rome deals with agreements between companies, and Article 86 with abuse of dominant position.

AOTC. Name given to the 1991 merged Telecom Australia, Australia's domestic operator, and OTC Ltd., Australia's international operator, now know as Telstra. See also **Telstra**.

APEC (Asia Pacific Economic Cooperation). A loosely structured intergovernmental consultative forum established in 1989 to increase multilateral cooperation in the Asia-Pacific region in light of the rapid economic growth and increasing interdependence within the region. APEC's founding members were Australia, Canada, Japan, South Korea, New Zealand, and the United States, along with the six members of the Association of South East Asian Nations (ASEAN): Brunei, Indonesia, Malaysia, Philippines, Singapore, and Thailand. Later, China, Hong Kong, Taiwan, Mexico and Papua New Guinea joined. The chairmanship of APEC rotates on an annual basis, as does the executive director of the APEC Secretariat, which was set up in February 1993 in Singapore. APEC has ten working groups covering data in investment and trade, trade promotion, investment and industrial science and technology, human resources development, energy cooperation, marine resource conservation, telecommunications, transport, tourism, and fisheries.

article of association. A document that sets forth the objectives and rules for the management of an association. In common-law jurisdictions, the formal document evidencing the incorporation of a company.

ASEAN (Association of South East Asian Nations). Economic association comprising Malaysia, Indonesia, Singapore, Thailand, Brunei, and the Philippines.

asset valuation method. Value of a company determined by its net assets, that is, its assets minus its liabilities.

AT&T (American Telephone & Telegraph Company). The largest U.S. provider of domestic and international long-distance communications services.

attributable cost. The share of total costs specifically associated with providing a particular service.

audiotex. A technique that allows users to access computers through a telephone. Audiotex services range from public announcement services in which the same message is disseminated to all those who dial a given number, to interactive services in which callers access specific information in a database or carry out transactions using their telephone keypad to indicate their choices and enter commands. Examples of audiotex services are financial information, airline flight schedule information, electronic funds transfer, and bill-paying services.

AUSSAT (AUSSAT Pty. Ltd.). The operating company of the Australian national satellite system. AUSSAT was sold under provisions of the 1991 Telecommunications Bill and is allowed to compete with the merged Telecom/OTC (now Telstra) as a general carrier. Now called Optus.

AUSTEL (Australian Telecommunications Authority). The independent regulatory body in Australia, established in 1989 under the general policy direction of the Minister for Transport and Communications. AUSTEL is responsible for technical regulation with respect to customer equipment and cabling; setting of technical standards; promotion of competition; ensuring that competitive safeguards are respected; licensing; administering the national numbering plan; protection of public interest and consumers; and administration of universal levy arrangements.

averaged pricing. The regulatory practice of making rates for a regulated service component uniform throughout a nation (or a state) based on average nationwide (statewide) figures for costs and usage. In an averaged rate structure, the rate charged by a specific vendor for a service or service component will be uniform no matter where in the nation (interstate services) or state (intrastate services) a subscriber is located.

Baby Bells. See RBOC.

balanced loading requirement. A former FCC requirement that international record carriers and AT&T use international cable and satellite facilities equally in the North Atlantic region, as a means to support development of satellite service.

bandwidth. The range of frequencies over which a particular communications channel is effective, which determines the maximum rate at which information can be transmitted. Measured in hertz (Hz) and multiples, such as KHz (one thousand Hz), MHz (one million hertz), and GHz (gigahertz, one billion hertz). A single telephone-grade voice signal requires a bandwidth of about 3 KHz, while a color TV picture needs a bandwidth about one thousand times larger.

basic service. A regulatory term in the United States, subsequently adopted by the Canadian Radio-television and Telecommunications Commission and others, for a carrier offering a "pure transmission capability over a communications path that is virtually transparent in terms of its interaction with customer supplied information."

BCE Inc. (Bell Canada Enterprises Inc.). The parent corporation of the Bell group of companies in Canada since the reorganization of Bell Canada in

1983. It has six principal subsidiaries: Bell Canada; Northern Telecom, a major manufacturer of telecommunications equipment; Bell Northern Research, a telecommunications research establishment; BCE Telecom International, BCE Inc.'s international investment and consulting division; BCE Mobile Communications, a provider of cellular, paging, telephone answering, and shared radio services; and Montreal Trust, a financial services company. Its 1992 revenues were Cdn$19.4 billion and assets Cdn$13.6 billion.

Bell Atlantic. One of the seven U.S. regional Bell operating companies created by the AT&T divestiture in 1984. Bell Atlantic provides telecommunications services to 18 million customers in the mid-Atlantic region of the U.S., which includes the states of New Jersey, Pennsylvania, Maryland, Delaware, Virginia, and West Virginia, as well as the District of Columbia. The company has more than 80,000 employees and provides local telephone, cellular mobile, business systems, and financial services. It is one of the largest cellular telephone providers in the U.S., with over half a million customers. Its 1992 assets and operating revenues were US$28.1 and US$12.6 billion, respectively. In October 1993, Bell Atlantic announced a merger with TCI, the largest owner and operator of cable television systems in the U.S.

Bell Canada. Canada's largest telecommunications operating company, with about 7 million customers in the provinces of Ontario and Quebec and in the eastern Arctic.

BellSouth. One of the seven U.S. regional Bell operating companies created by the AT&T divestiture in 1982. Its subsidiaries offer local telephone service in nine southeastern states of the U.S. and mobile communications services; they also market and maintain stand-alone and fully integrated communications systems.

Binariang Sdn Bhd. A privately held Malaysian company with diverse interests which, in 1993, obtained licenses to provide local and international services, a nationwide GSM mobile cellular service, and a geostationary domestic satellite, MEASAT.

bit rate. The rate at which digital information is processed or transmitted. Expressed in bits per second (b/s) or multiples thereof, such as Kb/s (one thousand bits per second) or Mb/s (one million bits per second).

BOC (Bell operating company). Each of the pre-divestiture 22 U.S. telephone companies wholly owned by the AT&T Bell System providing local and intrastate telephone service. Under the terms of the AT&T 1982 Consent

Decree, these 22 companies and their local exchange service and exchange access functions were divested from the Bell System and reorganized into seven regional holding companies (Ameritech, Bell Atlantic, BellSouth, NYNEX, Pacific Telesis, Southwestern Bell Corporation, and US West). The seven regional holding companies each own a one-seventh interest in Bell Communications Research (Bellcore), whose major functions are to furnish technical assistance and serve as a central contact point for national security, emergency preparedness, and natural disaster functions. See also **RBOC**.

bond. A certificate evidencing a debt on which the issuer promises to pay the holder a specified amount of interest for a specified length of time and to repay the loan on its maturity. Strictly speaking, assets are pledged as security for a bond issue, except in the case of government bonds, but the term is often loosely used to describe any funded debt issue.

book value. The value of a share of common stock calculated by subtracting all liabilities from total assets and dividing the result by the number of outstanding common shares. Also the current value of equipment and other capital assets after deducting from their acquisition cost all accumulated depreciation. Book value may be very different from market value, i.e., the price that may be obtained for a share or a capital asset.

British Approvals Board for Telecommunications (BABT). An independent private company appointed by the U.K. Secretary of State to approve telecommunications equipment for connection to the public network. BABT is responsible for evaluating apparatus against published standards and, after testing at one of a number of contracted laboratories, granting type approval where appropriate. BABT also operates a scheme to assess applicants' production facilities. With the emergence of the single European market, the emphasis has shifted from British standards to European standards.

BT. Formerly British Telecommunications plc or British Telecom. The major provider of domestic and international telecommunications services in the United Kingdom. BT operates the fourth largest telecommunications system in the world. In mid–1993 BT announced a strategic alliance with MCI whereby BT would buy 20% of the latter's shares for US$4.3 billion and receive three seats on MCI's 15-member board of directors.

BTTB (Bangladesh Telegraph and Telephone Board). An agency of the government that operates the public telecommunications services in Bangladesh.

build-lease-transfer (BLT). A variant of BOT in which the telecommunications entity, rather than the investor, has responsibility for operating the equipment supplied during the period of the agreement. The revenues are divided between the parties to recognize their respective contributions to service.

build-operate-transfer (BOT). A form of investment financing whereby a private contractor (usually a manufacturer of equipment, an investor group, a foreign operating company, or a consortium of all three) finances and builds a telecommunications facility in exchange for permission to operate the facility for a fixed period, charges customers for use of these facilities, and retains revenues to cover the cost of investment (*b*uild) and service operation (*o*perate). On an agreed date, the contractor *t*ransfers title and operational responsibility of the facilities to the telecommunications entity, thereby completing the arrangement between the two parties. The contractor is entitled to keep any revenues in excess of costs but also assumes the risk that revenues will not cover costs.

build-own-operate (BOO). A variant of BOT in which there is no provision to transfer the assets to the telecommunications operating entity at the end of the agreement period. Under such a scheme, ownership is conceded to the private contractor on a more or less permanent basis. The scheme may be regarded as a form of licensing or franchising.

build-own-operate-transfer (BOOT). A variant of BOT which emphasizes that the investment is owned by the private investors until paid for and transferred to the operating entity.

build-transfer-operate (BTO). A variant of BOT in which a contractor finances and builds a telecommunications facility in exchange for permission to operate the facility for a fixed period of time; however, the contractor agrees to transfer title of the facilities to the telecommunications entity upon having completed their construction and installation.

Bumiputera institutions. Institutions in Malaysia designated to hold Bumiputera interests in trust or to cater specifically to the interests of Bumiputera members (these include companies where Bumiputeras hold the controlling stake). *Bumiputera* literally means "son of the earth" and in the Malaysian context refers to the indigenous people of Malaysia. Certain conditions must be met for a public listed company to be designated a Bumiputera Controlled Public Listed Company. These pertain to percentage of voting shares held by an identified Bumiputera group; the percentage of members of the board that must be Bumiputera; the percentage of management, professional, and supervisor staff that must be Bumiputera; and to the requirement that the chief executive officer be Bumiputera.

bypass. Arrangements or facilities whereby a customer can access long-distance, international, or other services without using the local operating company's switched network, thus avoiding payment of access charges. More generally, any means whereby customers avoid usage of a monopoly service or facility.

C&W (Cable & Wireless plc). A private company based in London that invests in and operates public telecommunications facilities and services in over 40 countries worldwide. C&W was a state-owned company until 1981 when it was privatized. C&W's two largest subsidiaries are Mercury, with about 10% of the U.K. market in competition with BT, and Hong Kong Telephone Company. Other operations comprise national monopoly telecommunications companies (e.g., Jamaica) as well as participation in competitive markets (e.g., one of Pakistan's three cellular companies).

cable television (CATV). A service that distributes a wide range of television programs to the homes of subscribers from a central facility through own networks of optical fiber and coaxial cable. The programs originate in many sources, including national broadcasting networks, a large and growing number of companies producing material (e.g., news, sports, documentaries, movies) especially for cable, and community interest groups (e.g., local government, universities, community colleges). Most cable television networks are unidirectional, but with new technologies they are evolving toward facilities capable of offering increasingly interactive services.

cahier des charges. In France, a set of universal service obligations which are imposed on a public telecommunications operator in its license. At present only France Télécom, the public telecommunications operator, and Société Française du Radiotéléphone (SFR), the mobile cellular operator, have such obligations imposed on them.

CANTV (Compañía Anónima Nacional de Teléfonos de Venezuela). The local, long-distance, and international telecommunications operator in Venezuela, formerly a state enterprise but which is now 40% owned by a consortium led by GTE of the U.S. and Telefónica de España.

capital asset. An asset with a life of more than a specified period of time (say one year) that is not bought and sold in the ordinary course of business.

capital gain (or loss). Income from the sale of a capital asset. The price at which the asset is sold, less the price paid to acquire it, including buying and selling expenses. Capital gains are sometimes treated differently from earned income for purposes of taxation, for example, to encourage investment.

capital market. A market where securities with long-term maturities (generally in excess of one year) are traded. These securities (e.g., most corporate and government bonds, mortgages, some preferred stocks) ultimately represent claims against capital assets.

capital stock. The total value of all shares representing ownership of a company, including preferred as well as common.

capitalization, capital structure. Term used (mostly in North America) to designate the total dollar amount of all debt, preferred and common stock, contributed surplus, and retained earnings of a company.

carrier. Any individual, partnership, association, joint-stock company, trust, or corporation engaged in providing telecommunications facilities or services in exchange for payment.

cartel. A group of firms which enter into an agreement to set mutually acceptable prices for their products, often accompanied by output and investment quotas. The rules of the cartel may be embodied in a formal document, which may be legally enforceable, and penalties will be laid down for firms which violate it. The essence of a cartel is that it is a formal system of collusion, as opposed to a set of informal or tacit agreements to follow certain pricing policies. Cartels are illegal in many countries.

cash flow. A company's net income for a stated period plus any deductions from revenue that are not paid out in actual cash, such as depreciation, deferred income taxes, minority interests, and amortization.

CAT (Communications Authority of Thailand). A state entity established in 1976 to provide international public telecommunications services (except to neighboring countries) as well as telex, telegraph, packet switching, cellular mobile, paging, domestic satellite, and postal services. See also **TOT**.

CATV. See **cable television**.

CCITT (Comité Consultatif International Télégraphique et Téléphonique, or in English **International Telegraph and Telephone Consultative Committee).** The permanent organ of the International Telecommunication Union (ITU) responsible for the development of voluntary international standards for telecommunications. Periodically the CCITT published recommended technical and administrative practices relating to international telecommunications. These generally have the effect of voluntary international telecommunications standards to which most manufacturers and operators adhere. Under the restructured ITU this work is now being carried on by the Standards Sector.

C-DOT (Centre for Development of Telematics). Established by the government of India in 1984 to locally design, develop, and transfer to Indian industries the technology for manufacturing a range of digital switching systems with a capacity of up to 40,000 lines and transmission equipment.

CEE (Central and Eastern Europe). A term generally used to refer to the former Warsaw Pact countries excluding the former U.S.S.R., the former Yugoslavia, and Albania.

Cellnet (U.K.). A company providing cellular telephone services in the United Kingdom, of which BT is the majority shareholder.

cellular service. A terrestrial radio-based service providing two-way communications by dividing the serving area into a regular pattern of sub-areas or cells, each with a base station having a low-power transmitter and receiver. Although cellular radio is primarily a means of providing public mobile telephone service in urban areas, it is also used to provide data services and private voice services, and as an alternative to fixed wired telephone service where this is scarce, such as in developing countries.

central office. Term used in the U.S. to denote a telephone exchange or switch.

CEPT (Conférence Européenne des Administrations des Postes et des Télécommunications, or in English, European Conference of Posts and Telecommunications). An organization formed by the European PTTs to coordinate relevant policies among its members; prepare technical specifications regarding equipment used by its members or connected to their telecommunications networks; and harmonize European positions vis-à-vis international standardization.

chaebol. In Korea, a very large, highly diversified business conglomerate under a common controlling ownership. As a group, chaebols account for a large part of the economy, especially industry.

Chilesat. A competing domestic long-distance and international telecommunications operator in Chile, leasing both satellite and fiber-optic cable facilities. Since 1992 Chilesat has competed with ENTEL and VTR Telecomunicaciones.

CITIC (China International Trust and Investment Corporation). An agency of the government of China that undertakes investments abroad on behalf of the state. It is, for example, a minority shareholder in the parent of Hong Kong Telephone Company.

civil law. A system of law based on a comprehensive written code (as in France, Mexico, and the Canadian province of Quebec, for example), in contrast with a common-law system built up through precedent set by individual judicial decisions (as in the U.K. and U.S).

clawback provision. In a privatization, the provision whereby a certain number of shares sold in or destined for foreign markets can be brought back for sale in the domestic markets.

Clear Communications. A joint venture of BCE Inc. of Canada, MCI International of the U.S., Television New Zealand Ltd., Todd Corporation of New Zealand, and New Zealand Rail Ltd., formed in 1990 to compete with Telecom Corporation of New Zealand in the provision of the full range of telecommunications services in New Zealand. By 1993 Clear had a staff of about 450, had invested more than NZ$120 million in building an all-digital network, had achieved about 15% market share in domestic and international long-distance service, had connected about 112,000 customers to its network, and could be accessed by over 80% of the New Zealand population.

CMEA. Council for Mutual Economic Assistance. See Comecon.

CNT (Companía Nacional de Teléfonos). Private holding company owned 73% by VTR Inversiones providing local telephone services in southern Chile (Telefónica del Sur), long-distance and international (VTR Telecomunicaciones), and cellular services (VTR Celular).

CoCom (Coordinating Committee on Multilateral Export Controls). An informal Paris-based organization of NATO, Japan, and Australia which has controlled export of high technology with potential military uses, primarily to the former U.S.S.R., China, and Central and Eastern Europe. CoCom is now focusing its attention on countries such as Iraq, Iran, North Korea, Cuba, and Libya and may invite Russia and China to join a transformed organization.

COCOT (customer owned coin-operated telephone). A type of pay telephone that may be connected to an ordinary telephone line. The distinction between a COCOT and a regular coin telephone is that the calculation and assignment of charges is performed by a microprocessor inside the CO-COT apparatus, whereas with other coin-operated telephones these functions are performed at the telephone company's central office. COCOTs are also referred to as instrument-implemented phones or private pay phones.

code conversion. The conversion from one representation of coded information to another representation of the same information in another code.

Comecon (Council for Mutual Economic Assistance (CMEA)). Organization founded in 1949 by Bulgaria, the former Czechoslovakia, Hungary, Poland, Romania, and the former U.S.S.R. to improve and extend mutual cooperation in the economic, technological, and industrial development of member countries as well as in the improvement of their labor productivity and the social well-being of their citizens in accordance with socialist economic principles. Later Albania, the German Democratic Republic, Mongolia, Cuba, and Vietnam joined and then Albania withdrew. North Korea, Angola, Ethiopia, Laos, Mozambique, Nicaragua, and Yemen participated as observers at one time or other.

commercialization. Introduction of commercial objectives into the management and operations of a state-owned enterprise. Commercialization does usually not imply a change in legal status. See also **corporatization.**

Commission. See **Commission of the European Communities.**

Commission of the European Communities. The executive organ of the European Union. The Commission has 17 members who are appointed by their governments for four years. The main role of the Commission is to initiate European Union (EU) law, to propose EU action to the Council of Ministers, and to ensure that decisions are implemented. Also referred to as **EC Commission** or the **Commission.**

common carrier. A carrier that provides telecommunications services to the public at large and is generally subject to nondiscrimination requirements. Common carriage is the regulatory status describing any common carrier service.

common stock. Securities which represent ownership in a company and usually carry voting rights and residual claim to the assets and profits of the company.

Community. See **European Community.**

community service obligation (CSO). Term used in Australia and some other countries to indicate the requirement imposed upon a carrier by public policy to provide services which it would choose not to provide on purely commercial grounds. Also sometimes referred to as universal service obligation.

company. A legal entity created by stockholders (whether individuals, companies, or other legal entities) to carry on business activities, which exists independent of such stockholders.

company law. A body of law covering the formation, registration, and operation of companies and setting out legal requirements. Normally, all privately owned businesses in a country are incorporated under such a law.

competitive access provider (CAP). A term in the U.S. which is applied to a provider of local exchange (or access) services in the form of transport services either (a) from an end user to the facilities of a long-distance carrier; (b) from an end user to another end user; or (c) between facilities of long-distance carriers, generally over fiber-optic links or microwave facilities.

Computer I decision (U.S.). An FCC decision which recognized the confluence of telecommunications (regulated) and computer services (not regulated). At the time it allowed AT&T to provide some computer services through a separate subsidiary, even though provision of such services had been generally barred under the 1956 Consent Decree. Computer I clearly indicated that computer services were not regulated. Hybrid services were to be regulated or unregulated depending on the service characteristics and service provider. The vagueness of *hybrid services* forced the FCC to establish a clear demarcation line in its Computer II decision.

Computer II decision (U.S.). An FCC decision that distinguished between basic and enhanced services and determined that enhanced services should not be regulated. The FCC also determined that customer premises equipment should be deregulated. Computer II permitted AT&T to offer enhanced services and customer premises equipment through a subsidiary separate from AT&T's communications services.

Computer III decision (U.S.). An FCC decision that permitted the Bell operating companies to offer enhanced and basic services on an unseparated basis, provided that comparably efficient interconnection procedures are followed pending FCC approval of Bell operating companies' open network architecture plans.

CONATEL (Consejo Nacional de Telecomunicaciones). An autonomous agency, created within the Venezuelan Ministry of Transportation and Communications in 1991, which is responsible for regulating and overseeing telecommunications services. It is also responsible for recommending and granting concessions, permits, and other authorizations; promoting investment and technological innovation; enforcing technical and service regulations; coordinating with national and international organizations on technical aspects of telecommunications; administering the radio frequency spectrum, and developing criteria for the administration of tariffs.

concentrator. A switching system that connects a number of lines to a smaller number of transmission circuits, thereby allowing a few transmission channels to carry traffic from many sources. A wide variety of concentrators is used in telecommunications, including voice concentrators (which take advantage of the silent periods in telephone conversations to increase the capacity of submarine cable or satellite systems) and data concentrators (which permit a common high-speed channel to handle traffic from several low-speed terminals). In telephone switching, however, the term usually refers to a line concentrator or to a line or trunk module that can be remotely located from its host switch.

concession. A form of legal authorization given to an operator to provide a service, including the terms and conditions under which the service is to be provided. A contractual arrangement between the state (or other public entity) and a private operator (called a concessionaire) requiring the latter to build (and finance the construction of) public works, such as a telecommunications network, a road, or water supply system, in the general interest. In exchange, the state grants the concessionaire the right to operate the infrastructure for a specified period time and at its own risk as well as to charge users. A concession of this type is similar to a BOT agreement. Other forms of concessions include concessions to provide a public service on the basis of existing infrastructure and mining concessions.

connection charge. A single payment made by a customer for becoming connected to a communications service provided by an operator. Connection charges (typically around US$50) are expected to cover the nonrecoverable plant and administrative costs of connection. In presence of excess demand, however, higher connection charges (sometimes as high as several thousand U.S. dollars) may be levied to generate additional funds for investment and allocate scarce supply.

Conseil Supérieur de l'Audiovisuel (CSA). Regulatory body responsible for licensing and regulating radio and television (including cable) broadcasting in France. It has nine members appointed in equal shares by the President of the Republic, the Parliament, and the Senate.

consent decree. A form of court settlement utilized by some U.S. federal regulatory agencies and the U.S. Department of Justice to resolve antitrust suits. Under this method of settlement, the accused party makes no admission of guilt; however, it does agree to make changes in its behavior and/or structure. The terms of consent decree are enforced by the U.S. federal court system.

Consent Decree (1956). A judicial settlement between AT&T and the U.S. federal government ending a seven-year antitrust case. It generally limited the Bell System to providing communications services, subject to price regulation, and to manufacturing equipment used to provide such services. Among certain exceptions, it permitted the Bell System to perform any kind of work for the U.S. government and to engage in business incidental to the provision of common carrier communications services. In 1982 the U.S. Department of Justice and AT&T agreed to vacate the 1956 Consent Decree in its entirety and replace it with the new Consent Decree (1982).

Consent Decree (1982). Agreed to by AT&T and the U.S. Department of Justice in 1982 and approved by U.S. District Court Judge Harold Greene, it required that AT&T divest sufficient facilities, personnel, systems, and rights to technical information within Bell operating companies (BOCs) to permit them to perform local telecommunications, local exchange access, and printed Yellow Pages directory functions independent of AT&T. AT&T retained Western Electric (manufacturing), Bell Labs (R&D), and Long Lines (long-distance facilities), and assumed the interLATA long-distance operations of the BOCs as well as their embedded customer premises equipment. License and standard supply contracts with the BOCs, Southern New England Telephone, and Cincinnati Bell were terminated. After AT&T's reorganization, the BOCs were prohibited from discriminating in favor of AT&T and its products and services with respect to local exchange and information access, procurement, dissemination of technical information and standards, interconnection and use of BOC facilities, and in the planning for new services and facilities.

consumer surplus. The difference between the total benefit an individual derives from consuming a particular quantity of a good or service (usually expressed in terms of the amount he is prepared to pay for it) and the amount he actually pays for that good or service (tariffs charged by the operating company as well as any taxes, surcharges, or other levies).

contract. A legally enforceable agreement, either written or oral, between two or more persons or entities, to exchange something of value such as services, goods, money, or legal rights. Contract law is the legal regime that applies to contracts.

CORFO (Corporación de Fomento de la Producción). The Chilean stat development corporation. CORFO held the state-owned shares in Compañía de Teléfonos de Chile (CTC) and Empresa Nacional de Telecomunicaciones (ENTEL), the two main telecommunications operating companies, before they were privatized.

corporation. A legal entity created by or under the laws of a state. Normally classified either as a public corporation, created and owned by the state or another public body, or as a private corporation, created by private persons for private purposes.

corporatization. The transformation of a state-owned enterprise or business asset into a public corporation organized under company law. Also, term loosely used to designate changes in a state enterprise's corporate structure, internal organization and management, and rules linking it to the government, with the objective of providing management with the freedoms and incentives needed to run the enterprise along commercial lines. Corporatization is often the first step in the privatization of a state-owned enterprise.

cost-based pricing. The general principle of charging for services in relation to the cost of providing these services.

cost-benefit analysis. A technique of economic analysis used to compare the cost of carrying out a particular investment with the benefits to be derived from it, both costs and benefits being assessed over the life of the investment. It is used in connection with deciding whether an investment is worth undertaking, or to compare alternative investments. Results are commonly expressed in terms of net present value or of rate of return, and vary depending on whose viewpoint is adopted. In particular, private returns (the balance of costs and benefits to a firm) may be considerably different from social returns (to the economy as a whole).

COTAS (Bolivia). The telephone operating company of Santa Cruz de la Sierra, a city in the highlands of Bolivia. It is fully owned by its subscribers and has a reputation as a well-run operating company.

coupon. A portion of a bond certificate entitling the holder to an interest payment of a specified amount on a specified date when clipped and presented at a bank on or after its due date.

CPE (customer premises equipment). Term used in North America to designate terminal equipment, supplied by either the telephone common carrier or by a competitive supplier, which is connected by the user to the telephone network. Includes, for example, telephone sets, fax and teleprinter machines, data terminals, PBXs, and PABXs.

CPT (Compañía Peruana de Teléfonos). The mainly subscriber-owned local telephone company in Lima, Peru.

cream-skimming. Refers to the concern of traditional carriers, policymakers, or regulators that service providers without broad service obligations may choose to compete in only the most lucrative market segments and will thereby reduce the income which the traditional carrier would normally have used to meet other service obligations, such as in rural and remote high-cost areas.

cross-bar exchange. A common-control electromechanical analog switching system introduced in the 1950s and superseded by electronic technologies in the late 1970s.

cross-subsidization. The practice of using profits generated from one product or service to support another provided by the same operating entity.

CRTC (Canadian Radio-television and Telecommunications Commission). The Canadian federal regulatory authority for commercial radio and television broadcasters, cable system operators, and telecommunications common carriers.

CSFR. The former Czech and Slovak Federal Republic.

CT 2. A cordless telephone technology developed in the United Kingdom. Also known as telepoint.

CTC (Compañía de Teléfonos de Chile). The largest Chilean local telephone company, now privately owned. As of end 1993 it had about 1.2 million telephone customers throughout most of the country, as well as subsidiaries providing cellular and other services in the main cities. CTC also operates some domestic long-distance facilities and plans to build a modern optical-fiber and satellite network once given regulatory approval to compete with ENTEL, the dominant long-distance and international carrier, also private.

CTO (Commonwealth Telecommunication Organisation). An intergovernmental collaborative organization of twenty-nine British Commonwealth countries, which promotes the efficient exploitation and development of the Commonwealth's external telecommunications system through consultation and collaboration on all aspects of Commonwealth international telecommunications policies and practices.

DACOM (Data Communications Corporation of Korea). A provider of data communications services in Korea, created in 1982, which is partially owned by the government of Korea (33%) and a number of Korea's major (private) firms. Since December 1991, DACOM has been allowed to compete with Korea Telecom in international voice services. DACOM's monopoly with respect to data services ended in 1992.

data networking. A term used to describe an assembly of functional units that establishes data circuits among different pieces of data terminal equipment at data stations. More generally, the term describes a network that facilitates the transfer of data among interconnected stations.

data-processing services. Term which refers to processing functions such as (a) general purpose programming and program execution, usually under user control; (b) special purpose numerical data processing for accounting and other business applications; (c) word processing; (d) proprietary information retrieval services; (e) automatic type setting; (f) systems design and programming; and (g) programming turnkey or integrated systems, which combine all of the above.

Datatie Oy. Organization of the independent private operating telephone companies of Finland offering a national data transmission service using their own interconnected facilities in competition with the data services offered by Telecom Finland, the state-owned long-distance company.

DBP Telekom (Deutsche Bundespost Telekom). The public enterprise in Germany responsible for telecommunications. Under the July 1, 1989 Law Concerning the Restructuring of the Postal and Telecommunications Sector and of the Deutsche Bundespost (Poststrukturgesetz), the Deutsche Bundespost (DBP), the public administration previously responsible for posts, telecommunications, and postal banking services, was reorganized into separate regulatory and business functions, with the latter subdivided into three public enterprises corresponding to the post, postal banking, and telecommunications functions. Each is managed by a board of directors and a supervisory board. The 1989 Law gives DBP Telekom a monopoly over transmission facilities and voice telephony. Upon German unification in 1990 the East German PTT was merged into DBP Telekom. The German government is planning partial privatization of DBP Telekom.

DDD (direct distance dialing). See STD.

debenture. A certificate of indebtedness of a government or company backed only by the general credit of the issuer and unsecured by mortgage or lien on any specific asset.

debt financing   The long-term borrowing of money by a business, usually in exchange for debt securities or a note, to obtain working capital or other funds necessary for investment or operations or to retire other debts.

debt-for-debt (swaps).   Exchange of foreign debt against local currency debt.

debt-to-equity (swaps).   Exchange of foreign debt against equity denominated in local currency.

decree.   An executive order, which is usually subordinated to a law. Secondary or derived legislation, as opposed to primary legislation (i.e., law enacted by the legislature). Depending on the legal regime, decrees may be issued by the President, the Council of Ministers, the Prime Minister, or another Cabinet member.

DECT (Digital European Cordless Telecommunications).   The standard adopted by European countries for digital cordless telephones.

DEL (direct exchange line).   Term used in the U.K. to denote the physical connection between a customer and the local telephone exchange. See **main line.demonopolization.** The process of undoing or breaking up a monopoly. See **monopoly.**

demand elasticity.   The change in the demand for a good or service resulting from a change in one of its determining factors, usually price or income. A highly elastic demand is one which is very sensitive to changes of the factors. Demand is said to be inelastic when it changes less than proportionally to the factor. Usually measured by an elasticity coefficient which is approximately equal to the percent change in demand divided by the percent change of the factor. For most goods and services the price elasticity coefficient of demand is negative (i.e., an increase in price results in a drop in demand) while the income elasticity is positive.

demonopolization.   The process of undoing or breaking up a monopoly. See **monopoly.**

de novo listing.   Listing on a stock exchange of a new issue of shares of stock in a company.

deregulation.   Removal of a regulation or regulations governing a service or provider. The deregulated service or provider is principally subject to the rules and practices of the competitive markets. In most countries, costs of a deregulated service may not be covered by profits from regulated operations. Profits from a deregulated service are usually not included in the calculations when figuring the appropriate profit margin to be allowed on a firm's regulated operations.

determination (U.K.). A ruling by the Director General of Telecommunications (OFTEL), the regulatory authority in the United Kingdom.

developed country. Refers to an industrialized nation, most of which are members of the Organization for Economic Cooperation and Development (OECD). The World Bank avoids this term, which is considered value-laden, preferring *industrial country* instead.

developing countries. A broad range of countries that generally lack a high degree of industrialization, infrastructure, and other capital investment or advanced living standards among their populations as a whole. The poorest of such countries are sometimes referred to as the least-developed countries.

DFI (direct foreign investment). Active investment directly in companies (as opposed to commercial loans, indirect purchase of shares purely for financial investment, etc.).

DGT (Directorate General for Telecommunications). Taiwan's monopoly telecommunications service provider, which is part of the Ministry of Transportation and Communications.

dial code access (U.K.). A three-digit code by which a competitive long-distance network can be reached by customers of another network.

Diet. Japanese parliament.

digital technology. Means to process and transmit information by sampling and coding it at discrete intervals by a digital code, usually binary. It is the basis of all contemporary telecommunications and information technology systems.

discount. The amount by which a preferred stock or bond sells below its par or stated value. In the case of a promissory note or bond, the lower price relative to face value at which it is traded before the maturity date. More generally, to take into account the present value of a sum of money or other asset having a known value at a given future time.

disinvestment. Process inverse to the act of investing; action leading to the end or winding up of an investment. See also **divestiture**.

divestiture. Transfer of public or state-owned property (including state-owned enterprises) to the private sector. In the U.S. divestiture generally refers to the breakup of AT&T mandated by the U.S. District Court for the District of Columbia. See **Consent Decree (1982)**.

dividend. An amount distributed out of a company's profits to its shareholders in proportion to the number of shares they hold. Over the years a preferred dividend will remain at a fixed annual amount. Common dividend payout over the years may fluctuate with the company's ability to earn profits.

division of revenues. The allocation of the revenues from jointly used facilities among various kinds of services (such as trunk and local calls) and among the entities providing those services.

docket. A formal U.S. Federal Communications Commission (FCC) procedure.

dominant carrier. A regulatory classification for the telecommunications provider that has the predominant market share or is otherwise able to exercise market power.

DOT (Department of Telecommunications). Regulator and the main domestic telecommunications service provider in India.

Dow Jones Industrial Average (DJIA). Daily average closing prices of a selected number of U.S. industrial stocks, prepared by Dow Jones & Co. and published in the *Wall Street Journal* and other publications which subscribe to this service.

DRG (Direction de la Réglementation Générale). Department of the French Ministry of Industry, Post and Telecommunications and Foreign Trade that regulates the telecommunications sector. The DRG is responsible for licensing networks and services, frequency management, approving terminal equipment, and representing France in international organizations such as the ITU, INTELSAT, and EUTELSAT.

D Series Recommendations. Recommendations of the CCITT concerning general tariff principles, charging, and accounting in international telecommunications services.

DSP (Direction du Service Public). Department of the French Ministry of Industry Post and Telecommunications and Foreign Trade responsible for supervising and protecting the state's interest in France Télécom.

DTI (Department of Trade and Industry). In the U.K., DTI, under the Secretary of State and in accordance with the Telecommunications Act of 1984, is responsible for issuing licenses to operate telecommunications systems. DTI's Telecommunications and Posts Division considers such applications in consultation with OFTEL, the U.K. regulator. In addition, DTI is responsible for the U.K.'s policy on telecommunications regulatory and technical matters at the international level, in particular, within the European Community, ETSI, CEPT, the ITU, and the CTO. DTI also acts as a sponsorship focus for the manufacturing and service sectors of the telecommunications, radiocommunications, and broadcasting industries.

due diligence. A term used to describe the reasonable investigations to be made by officers of a company in order to obtain sufficiently accurate and complete information as needed to undertake a securities offering or other corporate transaction.

duopoly. The market situation in which there are only two sellers of a particular good or service.

duopoly review (U.K.). Review initiated in November 1990 by the Department of Trade and Industry (DTI) and OFTEL, the regulator in the United Kingdom, in the form of a consultative document proposing to open up the U.K. telecommunications market to increased competition and consumer choice. The review culminated in March 1991 with the publication by DTI of *Competition and Choice: Telecommunications Policy for the 1990s* which ended the duopoly policy. This document also allows cable television companies to provide telecommunications services, allows BT and Mercury to apply for fran-chises to provide entertainment services in local areas only, further reduces BT's prices, and provides for equal access. It allows international simple resale but does not foresee the granting of any new international operator licenses.

earnings per share (EPS). Net income of a company, less preferred share dividends, divided by the average number of common shares outstanding for the period.

earth station. Ground-based equipment used to control or provide communication through a satellite. Transmit/receive earth stations can send and receive signals and may be used in two-way communications such as telephony.

EBDIT. Earnings before depreciation, interest, and taxes.

EBIT. Earnings before interest and taxes.

EBRD. See **European Bank for Reconstruction and Development.**

EC. See **European Community.**

EC Commission. See **Commission of the European Communities**.

EC Council of Ministers. One of the institutions of the EC assembling the relevant ministers of the member states dealing with a particular subject. It decides upon proposals from the Commission of the European Communities (the executive body) and shares its legislative powers with the European Parliament, which can amend proposals for legislation. EC telecommunications matters are, for example, dealt with by ministers responsible for telecommunications in their own states.

EC Directive. A form of EC legislation. Directives are binding as to the results to be achieved but leave the form and method to the national authorities. EC Directives cannot take effect until they are transferred into national law.

EC Green Paper. The 1987 document, *Towards a Dynamic European Economy: Green Paper on the Development of the Common Market for Telecommunications Services and Equipment,* published by the Commission of the European Communities, which analyzes the trends in telecommunications policy in the EC and proposes an EC-wide telecommunications policy. It led to EC legislation which is binding on EC members and is generally followed by countries aiming to become members of the EC.

EC Official Journal. A publication of the EC. Legislation is usually published in the "L" (Law) series. Proposals and communications are published in the "C" series.

economic rate of return (ERR). The discount rate that makes equal to zero the present value of project benefits, net of costs, when all costs and benefits are valued to reflect true scarcities in the economy. Economic rate of return differs from internal rate of return in that financial costs are corrected to remove pure transfer payments (such as import duties) and major price distortions (of capital, foreign exchange, or unskilled labor, for example), and benefits are corrected to include payments excluded from the revenue stream (such as taxes on the bills), and sometimes also to include conservative estimates of consumer surplus. Used as a test against investments that are wasteful of scarce national (as opposed to company) resources.

economies of scale. Reductions in the unit cost of production achieved in certain industries when an increase in the volume of production is accompanied by a less than proportional increase in total production costs. Economies of scale may result from sharing fixed costs among a growing number of units produced or from increased efficiency of utilization of plant at higher output volumes.

economies of scope. Reduction in production costs that can be achieved in some industries when the production of a combination of two or more distinct services or products within a single firm results in lower costs than the production of each one separately by individual firms. Economies of scope result from the sharing of facilities, marketing, labor, and/or management between two or more products or services.

ECU (European currency unit). Basket of a majority of the EC currencies. MECU is used to indicate a million ECU.

EDI (electronic data interchange). The transmission, in a standard syntax, of specific information of business or strategic significance, between computers of independent companies or organizations.

EEC (European Economic Community). See **European Community**.

efficiency prices. Prices that, according to economic theory, maximize welfare for the economy as a whole. In perfect markets, it is the price that results from the competitive interplay of supply and demand. In imperfect markets, such as in the presence of monopoly or dominant suppliers, as is commonly the case in telecommunications, approximations to efficiency prices are sought through public regulation. In practice, deviations from efficiency prices are often necessary to reconcile economic efficiency with other objectives, such as meeting the financial requirements of the firm.

EFTA. See **European Free Trade Association**.

electronic banking. See **telebanking**.

electronic funds transfer (EFT). The process through which the banking industry utilizes computer and telecommunications technology to move funds from one banking location and/or account to another.

electronic mail. A means for electronic transmission of text, usually utilizing computers. A system for entering a document and transmitting it by electronic means either to its ultimate destination or to a point near the destination for delivery by post, courier, or some other means.

electronic messaging. The creation, transfer, storage, and retrieval of text, graphics, images, voice, or messages of any nature entirely by electronic means. Messaging implies retrieval at the recipient's discretion, and facilities are generally provided for filing, redirecting, and replying to messages received.

EMBRATEL (Empresa Brasileira de Telcomunicaçoes). The state-owned Brazilian interstate and international telecommunications company. See also **TELEBRÁS**.

emerging markets database (EMD). Data maintained and sold by the International Finance Corporation (IFC) containing information on emerging stock markets around the world.

EMETEL (Empresa Estatal de Telecomunicaciones). The state-owned telecommunications operating enterprise in Ecuador.

employee stock ownership plan (ESOP). One of any number of schemes in which employees acquire a share in the stock of the company where they work. ESOPs are sometimes used to create an interest from organized labor in the privatization of a state enterprise.

ENDESA (Empresa Nacional de Electricidad S.A.). The state-controlled, partially privatized, national electric power producer and distributor in Spain. INI, the Spanish state holding company, owns 67% of ENDESA. Also refers to electric power utilities in several other countries, such as in Chile.

enhanced services. See **VAS (value added services)**.

ENTEL or ENTel (Empresa Nacional de Telecomunicaciones). The name used in various Latin American countries and Spain for a state telecommunications enterprise, as for example, Argentina's state telecommunications monopoly before privatization, and Chile's dominant long-distance and international carrier.

equal access. A principle of interconnection designed to ensure nondiscrimination in the provision of services. For the customer of a public telecommunications network, equal access means that a particular service can be reached in the same way and on the same terms, whether provided by other networks or by the network to which he is connected. For a public telecommunications network operator, equal access means that it has the right to use the facilities of, and services provided by, another network operator on nondiscriminatory terms. In the U.S., equal access refers to a requirement of the Modified Final Judgment (MFJ) in the AT&T case that the divested Bell operating companies offer switched access and other interconnections to all interexchange carriers of a type equivalent to that furnished to AT&T.

equity or shareholders' equity. Ownership interest of common and preferred stockholders in a company. The difference between the assets and liabilities of a company.

equity financing. Raising capital through the issuance of equity shares. In particular, equity flotation is the act of raising equity by selling shares in stock markets.

ESOP. See **employee stock ownership plan.**

ESPRIT (European Strategic Programme for Research and Development in Information Technology). A European research and development program, launched in 1984, which works in collaboration with universities, research institutes, and businesses. It combines projects in micro-electronic and related technologies, information-processing systems, software programming, and industrial automation.

ETPI (Eastern Telecommunications Philippines Inc.). A Philippine international telecommunications service provider which is 40% owned by Cable & Wireless and Philippine Global Communications Corporation.

ETSI (European Telecommunications Standards Institute). An association charged with producing technical specifications relating to telecommunications networks and services and associated terminal equipment. Adoption of these specifications as European Telecommunications Standards is the prerogative of an independent committee of the CEPT called the Technical Recommendations Applications Committee. Similarly, application of the European standards is a matter of national concern. ETSI's permanent secretariat is located in France and is governed by French law.

EU. See **European Union.**

EUREKA. A European program of technical cooperation launched in 1985 with the aim of defining joint projects among European firms and their public counterparts in order to improve the competitiveness of European businesses on a world-scale through technical and commercial alliances.

European Bank for Reconstruction and Development (EBRD). A multilateral development organization with headquarters in London, England, established in 1991 to help finance the modernization of the economies of the former U.S.S.R. and Eastern bloc, with emphasis on building up the private sector.

European Commission. See **Commission of the European Communities.**

European Community (EC). An association of Western European countries established by the Treaty of Rome in 1957 to facilitate the removal of trade barriers and promote the free movement of goods, labor services, and capital between member nations. Formerly known as the European Economic Community (EEC), the EC has grown from its six original members (Belgium, France, Italy, Luxembourg, the Netherlands, and the Federal Republic of Germany) to twelve nations (now also including Denmark, Greece, Ireland, Portugal, Spain, and the United Kingdom). The EC resulted from the merger of the EEC, EURATOM, and the Coal and Steel Community. The main institutions of the EC are the Council of Ministers, the Commission of the European Communities, the Parliament, and the Court of Justice. See **European Union**.

European Council. see **EC Council of Ministers**.

European Court of Justice. The judiciary institution of the EC which interprets community law. It is composed of 13 judges and six advocates general, who are appointed for a period of six years. There is also a Court of First Instance, which deals with competition.

European Economic Area (EEA). Free trade area between the EC and EFTA countries which involves the freedom of movement of goods, services, capital, and persons. The 1991 EEA Agreement extends this to cooperation in competition, research, and standardization policies.

European Free Trade Association (EFTA). Free trade association consisting of Austria, Finland, Iceland, Norway, Sweden, and Switzerland.

European Investment Bank (EIB). Financial institution within the EC created by the Treaty of Rome. It provides loans and guarantees within and outside the Community to finance investment projects.

European Parliament. Directly elected EC institution of 518 members with supervisory powers over the European Commission and Council. It participates in the legislative process (right of amendment) and has budgetary powers.

European Radiocommunications Committee (ERC). The principal regulatory committee on radiocommunications within the Conférence Européenne des Administrations des Postes et des Télécommunications (CEPT) dealing, on a European level, with all regulatory matters concerning radiocommunications and all services requiring the use of the frequency spectrum.

European Radiocommunications Office (ERO). A permanent body of the European Radiocommunications Committee (ERC) which assists the ERC in harmonizing, as far as is necessary, radio regulatory, frequency management, and spectrum engineering activities in consultation with industry, users, operators, administrations, and other organizations.

European Union (EU). Union of the 12 member countries of the European Community (EC) created on November 1, 1993, by the entry into force of the Maastricht Treaty, which strengthens the European Parliament and provides for greater cooperation on foreign and security policy, a move toward a single European currency by 1999, and citizenship of the Union for all citizens of the EC.

EUTELSAT (European Telecommunications Satellite Organization). Organization provisionally established in 1977 by 17 member countries of CEPT to provide the space segment required for international domestic public telecommunications services in Europe. The definitive organization came into force in 1985 with 26 member countries. Thirteen more countries from Central and Eastern Europe joined in 1986–92. By 1992, EUTELSAT had eight satellites, offering around 90 Ku-band transponders providing telephony, business, TV and radio distribution, and land mobile services. Headquarters are in Paris, and its turnover in 1992 was ECU 230 million.

externality. Any benefit from or cost of an action that accrues to persons (or firms) other than those directly involved in the action. For example, when new customers are connected to the telephone network, all existing customers benefit because they can reach a larger number of people (say, customers). In a congested network, when one user makes a call, he imposes a cost on all others whose call attempts are defeated.

facilities. The ensemble of equipment, sites, lines, circuits, software, and other plant used to provide telecommunications services. Also referred to as networks.

facilities-based carrier. A carrier owning, as opposed to leasing, networks used to provide telecommunications services.

facsimile. The communications process in which graphics or text documents are scanned, transmitted via a (typically dial-up) telephone line, and reproduced on paper by a receiver. Facsimile device operation typically follows one of the CCITT standards for information representation and transmission: Group 1, analog, with page transmission in four or six minutes; Group 2, analog, with page transmission in two or three minutes; Group 3, digital, with page transmission in less than one minute; and Group 4, digital, defined for operation in conjunction with teletex.

Federal Communications Commission (FCC). The U.S. federal administrative agency within the executive branch of the U.S. government established under the Communications Act of 1934 to regulate U.S. interstate and international telecommunications.

Federal Energy Regulatory Commission (FERC). A federal regulatory agency of the U.S. established in 1977 by the Department of Energy Organization Act. FERC's primary goal is to ensure that U.S. consumers have adequate energy supplies at just and reasonable rates, while providing incentives for increased productivity, efficiency, and competition. Its primary functions are to regulate certain aspects of the natural gas, electric utility, hydroelectric power, and oil pipeline industries. FERC is composed of five members appointed by the President of the United States with the advice and consent of the Senate. One member is chosen by the President to serve as chairman, and all commissioners serve four-year terms.

fiber-optic cable. A communication cable containing one or more low-loss, highly transparent silica, glass, or plastic fibers used to transmit information in the form of light, that is, using electromagnetic signals in the visible or nearly visible region of the frequency spectrum. Also called optical-fiber cable.

flat rate. Method of pricing local service by which customers pay a regular charge each month for remaining connected to the telephone network, including an unlimited number of local calls or of call pulses.

forbearance. Discretionary authority granted to the regulator to refrain selectively from regulating.

Foreign Corrupt Practices Act (FCPA). A law enacted in the United States in 1977 that makes it a criminal offense for publicly held U.S. firms to offer a bribe to a foreign official, political party, or candidate for foreign political office for the purpose of obtaining preferential treatment in a commercial dealing. The law requires that every company create and maintain a system of internal accounting sufficient to assure that these objectives are achieved.

foreign exchange convertibility. Ability of a certain currency to be freely exchanged for (i.e., converted into) other currencies.

foreign exchange repatriation. The return by a foreign investor of his capital and/ or profits out of the country of investment.

Fortune 500 company. Refers to a listing of the 500 largest U.S. corporations compiled annually by *Fortune* magazine. The companies are ranked in terms of sales volume, assets, number of employees, and other factors, weighted and averaged to produce an overall ranking.

franchise. Authorization given to a company by a regulatory agency to provide a public service, such as a cable or telecommunications service. It usually specifies the geographic area of service and other obligations and privileges.

frequency spectrum. The spectrum or range of radio frequencies available for communication, industrial, and other uses. Frequency bands or segments are assigned to various categories of users for specific purposes, such as commercial radio and television, terrestrial microwave links, satellites, and police. At the international level this is done by the International Frequency Registration Board (IFRB) of the International Telecommunication Union (ITU). Individual national regulatory agencies monitor the occupancy of the radio spectrum and allocate frequencies to individual users or a groups of users so as to enable a large number of services to operate within specified limits of interference. This is also referred to as spectrum management.

fully allocated cost. The result of allocating the total costs of a network among each service provided.

fundamentals. A general term used by the investment community to indicate the basic strengths and weaknesses of a company whose shares are traded.

gateway. A facility that provides a link between two or more networks, as for example the international switching center which links a country's domestic network to the international network.

GATS (General Agreement on Trade in Services). A sub-agreement to the General Agreement on Tariffs and Trade, comprising a series of protocols and agreements which signatory governments agree to respect with regard to the treatment of international trade in services (as opposed to goods), first developed during the Uruguay Round negotiations (1986–93).

GATT (General Agreement on Tariffs and Trade). A set of successive international trade agreements that seeks to promote world trade by abolishing import quotas and other discriminatory constraints on trade and by reducing import duties among the signatory nations. The GATT was first concluded in 1947 in Geneva, Switzerland. The current round of negotiations toward a new agreement is referred to as the Uruguay Round, the first meeting of which took place in Uruguay. GATT also refers to the permanent organization that negotiates and oversees compliance with the agreements. The GATT organization is based in Geneva and comprises a Secretariat, a Council of Representatives (which meets several times a year), an Annual Assembly (called the Sessions), and an International Trade Centre. More than 85 countries are members of the GATT.

GDP (gross domestic product). The money value of the sum of all goods and services produced in a given country in a given year, excluding net income from abroad.

GEN (Global European Network). A project by France, Germany, and others to provide switched broadband services.

GNP (gross national product). The money value of the sum of all goods and services produced in a given country in a given year, including net income from abroad.

golden share. A single share held by the government in a privatized company which conveys controlling voting rights (veto) in a limited number of specified circumstances, such as when selling a large or controlling interest in the company. Referred to as "Kiwi share" in New Zealand.

goodwill. An intangible asset appearing on a company's balance sheet representing nonphysical value such as trademarks, patents, copyrights, and prestige of the company.

Green Paper. See **EC Green Paper.**

gross profit margin. The difference between revenues and costs, before taking account of interest and taxation, expressed as a percentage of revenues.

gross revenue. The total amount of sales revenue, before deductions for returns and allowances but after deductions for trade discounts, sales taxes, excise taxes based on sales, and cash discounts.

Grupo Carso. A diversified private business conglomerate in Mexico which leads the consortium that owns a controlling interest in Teléfonos de México.

GSM (Global System for Mobile Communications or Groupe Spécial Mobile). A pan-European digital cellular mobile communications system which can be utilized in all of the CEPT countries. Loosely used as a generic for the technology and standards used in this system.

GTE. The largest U.S.-based local telephone company, providing telephone service through more than 21 million access lines in 40 states, British Columbia, Quebec, Venezuela, as well as the Dominican Republic, and the second largest cellular service provider in the United States. GTE also provides government and defense communications systems and equipment, satellite and aircraft passenger telecommunications, directories, as well as telecommunications-based services and systems; markets telecommunications products and services; and supplies computer software and data processing. It is based in Irving, Texas, and has about 104,000 employees worldwide. Its 1992 revenues were US$20 billion.

head of agreement. Term used in the U.K. to designate a document setting out the principles of an agreement which the sig-natories intend to enter into at a future date. Generally referred to as a memorandum of understanding (MOU) in North America.

holding company. A company that controls one or more other companies through ownership of stock in those companies, usually without direct participation in their productive activities.

HONDUTEL (Empresa Hondureña de Telecomunicaciones). The state-owned telecommunications enterprise in Honduras.

Hong Kong Telecom. Holding company of Hong Kong Telephone Company and Hong Kong Telecom International, majority owned by Cable & Wireless. Hong Kong Telephone Company is the domestic telecommunications services provider, with a monopoly until 1995. Hong Kong Telecom International is the international operating company, with a monopoly until 2006.

HTC (Hungarian Telecommunications Company). The state telecommunications operating company of Hungary, established in 1990 with the separation of the postal, telecommunications, and broadcasting functions of Magyar Posta, the former Hungarian PTT.

Hutchison Whampoa. A Hong Kong-based diversified multinational corporation. Through its subsidiary Hutchison Telecommunications, the conglomerate has extensive interests in telecommunications, particularly cellular mobile communications, personal communications, and paging networks. Hutchison operates three paging networks in Australia, a joint venture paging network in Thailand, is a member of a consortium operating a paging network in Malaysia, operates a cellular network in the Philippines, and is attempting to become involved in cellular and paging services in India and Korea.

IBS (INTELSAT Business Service). A digital international or domestic private network communications service offered through the INTELSAT system.

IDC (International Digital Communications). One of two new Japanese Type I international telecommunications carriers. It competes with KDD and ITJ and is owned by Japanese and foreign private interests.

IDD (international direct dialing). A telephone service that allows subscribers to make international calls without going through the operator, also referred to as international direct distance dialing (IDDD), international subscriber dialing (ISD), and international trunk dialing.

IDR (Intermediate Data Rate). A digital satellite-based carrier system designed primarily to provide international regional or domestic public-switched telephone and ISDN services.

IFC (International Finance Corporation). The member organization of the World Bank Group that finances investments in private companies for projects of development interest. It is the largest source of direct project financing for private investment in the developing world. The IFC brings together entrepreneurship and investment capital, both foreign and domestic, when conventional financing and technical resources are insufficient to meet the needs of a business venture. On its own account and for others, it has funded nearly 1,000 private enterprises in more than 90 countries. The IFC's business and political-risk-management skills, developed through long experience of international investments and its affiliation with the World Bank, contribute to its success.

industrial country. See **developed country.**

Infonet (Infonet Services Corporation). A consortium established in 1970 which provides international communications services to multinational enterprises in approximately 50 countries. Services provided include international value added network (IVAN), end-to-end data encryption and managed networks. Infonet is owned by France Télécom Transpac (21.6%), Deutsche Bundespost Telekom (21.6%), PTT Telecom Netherlands (7.2%), Telefónica International (7.2%), Belgacom (7.2%), Sweden's Telia International (7.2%), Swiss PTT (7.2%), Kokusai Denshin Denwa (KDD) Co. Ltd. (6.8%), Singapore Telecom International (7.2%), and Australia's Telstra (7.2%). In December 1993 MCI which had a 24.8% share of Infonet agreed to sell its ownership share to the existing shareholders as a consequence of its proposed joint venture with BT.

initial offering. First offering of shares of a company on the market.

INMARSAT (International Maritime Satellite Organization). A commercial nonprofit cooperative of 65 member states (end 1993) that leases, owns, and operates a global telecommunications satellite system that provides maritime, aeronautical, and land mobile satellite services. Headquarters are in London.

insider. All directors and senior officers of a corporation and those who may also be presumed to have access to internal information concerning the company. Also anyone owning more than 10% of the voting shares in a corporation. Insider trading is the purchase or sale of stock or other securities by individuals making use of information not available to the public.

institutional investor. A large investor that pools savings from numerous individuals, such as a pension fund or insurance company, and seeks to invest these funds in low-risk instruments that provide a steady revenue stream.

INTELSAT (International Telecommunications Satellite Organization). A commercial nonprofit cooperative of 129 member states (end 1993) that owns and operates the global communications satellite system used by countries around the world for international communications and by more than 35 countries for domestic communications. Headquarters are in Washington, DC.

interconnection charge. A charge levied by network operators on other service providers to recover the costs of the interconnection facilities (including the hardware and software for routing, signaling, and other basic service functions) provided by the network operators.

interest. The cost of borrowing money; amount paid by the borrower to the lender for using his or her money. Also, ownership participation of an investor in a company.

interexchange (U.S.). Services and channels between or among two or more exchanges, rate centers, or LATAs, or to carriers providing such services and channels. An interexchange carrier is a carrier authorized by the FCC or a state public utility commission to provide long-distance telecommunications services between local access and transport areas (LATAs). Interexchange rates are the rates charged for measured and flat-rate interexchange services based on the distance between rate centers.

interLATA (U.S.). Interexchange service between or among the 161 local telephone serving LATAs in the United States. The 1982 Consent Decree that led to the divestiture in 1984 of AT&T prevents RBOCs from providing interLATA services.

internal rate of return (IRR). The discount rate that makes equal to zero the present value of future revenues resulting from an investment project, net of the costs incurred to produce these revenues. IRR is derived from comparing financial projections with and without the project, and provides a measure of the desirability of the project from the viewpoint of the investor. Sometimes also called financial rate of return (FRR) or internal financial rate of return. See also **economic rate of return (ERR)**.

International Electrotechnical Commission (IEC). Geneva-based international commission representing national governments, manufacturers, users, individuals, and trade associations, whose purpose is to coordinate and unify electric and electronic standards.

International Finance Corporation. See **IFC**.

International Securities Group (ISG). Unit within the capital markets department of the International Finance Corporation (IFC) that is involved in the underwriting and placement of emerging market securities.

INTUG (International Telecommunications Users Group). An organization formed in Brussels in 1974 to promote internationally the interests of telecommunications users.

IRI (Instituto Ricostruzione Industriale Spa). Italy's largest industrial and financial holding company which is fully controlled by the Italian state. IRI owns the majority of shares in the following companies: Finmeccanica (high-tech industries), STET (telecommunications), Finmare (shipping), ILVA (steel), Iritecna (civil works), Fincantiori (ship building), Alitalia (air transport), RAI (TV producer and broadcaster), Banca Commerciale Italiana e Credito Italiano (banking). Other companies are in the food (SME) and industrial restructuring (SPI) sectors. The IRI Group employs about 385,000 people, and the total 1992 value of gross production was 82,988 billion lire.

ISDN (integrated services digital network). A switched network providing end-to-end digital connectivity for simultaneous transmission of voice and/or data over multiple communications channels and employing transmission and out-of-band signaling protocols that conform to internationally defined standards. ISDN is considered by many to be the basis for a future universal network that can support almost any conceivable type of communications device or service, but so far ISDN has been used only to a limited extent in any country. Broader band ISDN standards are being developed.

ISO (International Standards Organization). An international organization that brings together national institutes of standardization from more than 80 countries. The activities of the ISO are aimed at obtaining worldwide agreement on international standards in order to develop trade, improve quality, and reduce costs. The work of the ISO touches every aspect of standardization with the exception of electronic and electrical technology, which is handled by the Commission Electrotechnique Internationale (International Electrotechnical Commission).

Italcable. Company that provides telephone, telex, telegraph, data, and other telecommunications services, including international value added services, between Italy and non-European countries. Italcable is 49% owned by STET and has 3,300 employees. Its 1989 turnover was 664 billion lire.

ITJ (International Telecom Japan Inc.). A new Type I international carrier in Japan that competes with KDD and IDC; it is owned by private interests.

ITU (International Telecommunication Union). The specialized agency of the United Nations responsible for international telecommunications matters. Founded in 1865, it is the oldest existing intergovernmental organization. At the end of 1988 it had 166 members. Its functions include establishing equipment and systems-operating standards, coordinating and disseminating information required for planning and operating telecommunications services, coordinating use of the radio spectrum, and promoting telecommunications growth and modernization in developing countries. The ITU Convention is the basic treaty instrument and addresses, among other things, the composition, purposes, and structure of the ITU. The Plenipotentiary Conference is the fundamental organic meeting of the ITU.

IVAN (international value added network). Facilities used to provide value added services (VAS) on an international basis.

Jabatan Telekom Malaysia. See **JTM.**

joint-stock company. A company having a joint stock or capital which is divided into units of ownership interest, such as shares which may be transferred without consent of the other shareholders. Equivalent to the French *Société Anonyme* or the German *Aktiengesellschaft* (AG). See **company, corporation.**

joint venture. An association of persons or entities jointly undertaking a commercial undertaking. A joint venture may or may not be incorporated. The participants accept duties to one another to act in good faith. A *joint venture agreement* will often define their business relationships. Joint venture is sometimes also used to refer to a company established jointly by the state and private partners, or by domestic and foreign partners.

JTM (Jabatan Telekom Malaysia). The telecommunications department of the Ministry of Energy, Posts, and Telecommunications, which is responsible for telecommunications regulation in Malaysia. Before 1987 it was also responsible for operating Malaysia's telecommunications network.

KDD (Kokusai Denshin Denwa Co. Ltd.). Japan's only international telecommunications carrier until 1985. KDD now faces competition from two other Type I international carriers: ITJ and IDC.

Kiwi share. See golden share.

KMTC (Korea Mobile Telecommunications Corporation). The Korean mobile cellular operator.

Kombinat. The trustlike organization structure which combined and administered all firms in a given industry in the former German Democratic Republic.

KTA (Korea Telecommunications Authority). The Korean government's domestic and international telecommunications operating entity which was reorganized in 1991 into a government-owned joint-stock company, Korea Telecom.

Ku-band. A set of frequencies between 10 and 14 gigahertz used for a variety of fixed and broadcast satellite services. These frequencies enable very small aperture terminal (VSAT) earth stations to be used. Ku-band communications are more affected by weather than C-band communications (which use frequencies between 4 and 6 gigahertz).

La Poste. The public agency in France which provides the postal service in France and which, like France Télécom, comes under the supervision of the Ministry of Industry, Posts and Telecommunications and Foreign Trade.

LAN (local area network). A privately owned digital communications system that provides a high-speed link among a variety of devices (generally computer terminals, microcomputers, or minicomputers) on a single shared medium, usually over a distance of up to two kilometers on the user's premises.

LATA (local access and transport area, U.S.). One of 161 local geographical areas established as a result of the 1984 divestiture of AT&T and within which a local exchange carrier is authorized to provide service. With minor exceptions for urban areas crossing a LATA boundary, local exchange carriers may not provide services between different LATAs.

LDP (Liberal Democratic Party). The former ruling political party in Japan.

lead manager. In an underwritten offering of shares, the managing underwriter responsible for initiating the transaction with the issuer and for organizing (or designating another to organize) the successful syndication and placement of the issue in the primary market.

lease. The conveyance of the right to use an asset by one person (the lessor) to another (the lessee) for a specified period of time in return for rent.

leased line. A permanent connection between two customer premises, provided by a telecommunications carrier—usually for a flat monthly charge—for the exclusive use by a customer. This service may be provided using terrestrial or satellite facilities and generally does not involve central office switching operations. Also called a private line.

least-developed countries. Some 36 of the world's poorest countries, as defined by the United Nations. Sometimes abbreviated LDC, but this is also used by others for *less-developed countries* as synonym of *developing countries*, a much larger group.

legislation. Used in a narrow sense, this term refers to laws, i.e., acts of the legislature. In a broad sense, and in particular in civil-law countries, it refers to laws as well as derived or secondary legal instruments (e.g., decrees, executive orders).

leverage. Use of borrowed funds, margin accounts, or securities which require payment of only a fraction of the underlying security's value (such as rights, warranties, or options) to increase the return from one's own investments. It is also the effect of fixed charges (debt interest, preferred dividends, or both) on per-share earnings of common stock.

liabilities. Debts of a company, usually divided into current liabilities (due and payable within the accounting year) and long-term liabilities (those payable in later years).

LIBOR (London Inter-Bank Offered Rate). The interest rate at which first-class banks in London are prepared to offer deposits to other first-class banks. Different LIBOR rates are applied for different currencies (e.g., US$, £) and repayment periods (e.g., daily, six months).

license. Authorization or permit to carry out a function or use a scarce natural resource, as required by law. For example, licenses are often required to provide certain types of public telecommunications services and for using any part of the radio spectrum. See also **franchise**.

licensee. The party being awarded a license, such as a telecommunications operating company (to provide a public service) or a user building its own microwave link (to use a particular radio frequency).

licensor. Authority that awards a license. Telecommunications licenses are usually granted by a ministry or separate regulatory agency, but in some countries by the cabinet, parliament, or other.

lifeline rates. In the U.S., subsidized telephone rates for selected subscriber groups, e.g., low-income or elderly.

limited liability company. A company in which the owners (stockholders) are liable for the debts of the company only up to the amount of capital contributed by them into the company. In some countries, this term refers to a type of company that has fewer incorporation and legal requirements than joint-stock companies (equivalent in this sense to the French SARL or the German Gmbh).

line-of-business restrictions (U.S.). Lines of business from which regional Bell operating companies (RBOCs) are barred under the 1982 Consent Decree because of their local monopoly position. Includes manufacturing (so that the RBOCs would purchase the best and cheapest and not necessarily their own-made equipment), long-distance (so that RBOCs could not discriminate against competitors in providing access), and information services.

line of credit. An agreement by a creditor, lender, or bank to extend credit or to make a loan up to a maximum specified amount, drawn down when needed by a customer.

Link Up America (U.S.). A program established by the Federal Communications Commission (FCC) and the state public utilities commissions to increase penetration rates by reducing installation and monthly charges for telephone service.

LMS (local measured service). A method for charging customers for local calls on the basis of usage. A charge is made for at least some calls and may be determined on the basis of duration, time of day, and distance of the call. A call allowance may be included in the monthly subscription charge.

local access and transport area (U.S.). See LATA.

local exchange carrier (LEC). In the U.S., the telephone company that provides local service to connect individual business and residential subscribers within its local serving area (LATA). It also provides switched access connections between its subscribers and interexchange carriers as well as long-distance service within each LATA (i.e., intraLATA) that it serves.

local exchange line. A term used to describe the communication channel established between a switching center and a customer, subscriber, or user instrument. Normally established between distribution frames and data terminals, telephone and facsimile units, they consist of a single connection between either a switching center or an individual message distribution point and the user equipment (e.g., telephone). A unique dialing number is associated with each local exchange line. The connection can be maintained by numerous means, such as radio, wire loop, or fiber-optic cable. Called direct exchange line (DEL) in the U.K. and former colonies. Since more than one telephone set may be connected to one line (e.g., in parallel or through a PBX or PABX), the number of telephones is generally higher than the number of lines. The number of lines connected to customers is usually less than the capacity of the exchanges, since the capacity is used up only gradually and some reserve is needed for technical reasons. Both the costs and the benefits of an expansion program are more directly linked to the number of connected lines than to exchange capacity or number of telephones, so the former is preferred when specifying growth targets. Also referred to as *main telephone, main line,* or *line.*

local loop. That part of a telecommunications circuit between the customer's location and the nearest central office.

local network. The network of cables and radio links over which local circuits are provided.

long-distance. Loosely used to denote any telecommunications transmission service, such as telephone service, that connects locations which cannot be reached with a local call, i.e., which lie outside of each other's local exchange area. The locations may be within the same state (intrastate) or in different states (interstate). A long-distance network is any network involved in long-distance communication. Often called toll (North America) and trunk (United Kingdom) networks.

Maastricht Treaty. Treaty signed at Maastricht, the Netherlands, in 1992 among the members of the EC, creating a European Union (EU) with the objective to promote economic and social progress through creating an area without internal frontiers, strengthening economic and social cohesion, establishing economic and monetary union ultimately including a single currency, implementing a common foreign and security policy leading to an eventual common defense policy, introducing a citizenship of the Union, and developing close cooperation on justice and home affairs. The treaty entered into force on November 1, 1993.

Magyar Posta. See **HTC**.

marginal cost. The increment in total production costs needed to produce one additional unit of output. There are several ways of defining marginal cost, depending on the time horizon used. Long-run marginal cost includes concentrated ("lumpy") investments needed from time to time, as in individual telecommunications facilities.

marginal cost pricing. The principle of setting prices equal to marginal cost. According to economic theory, marginal cost pricing maximizes economic efficiency when there are no supply constraints. See **efficiency prices**.

marginal price. A term used to describe the price a person is willing to pay to obtain an additional increment of a commodity. Because the marginal utility of a product diminishes with increased availability of the product or an acceptable substitute, the marginal price will diminish proportionately with increased supply.

marginal revenue. The change in a firm's total revenue resulting from the sale of an additional unit of output.

Mason/Morris Report. A study conducted in New Zealand in 1985 on the telecommunications, postal, and agency services of the then–Post Office. The report highlighted the inadequacies of the Post Office's organizational structure, recommended that it be reorganized into specific business units, and recommended that authority and responsibility for day-to-day operations be decentralized within each enterprise in order to ensure quick response to market conditions. The report drew a distinction between basic network telecommunications services and enhanced services, and recognized the need to open the latter to market competition. It also recommended the eventual deregulation of the customer premises equipment market and identified the need for greater flexibility in pricing and access to sources of capital. Following this report, the government decided to establish Telecom New Zealand as a corporation.

Matav (Magyar Tavkoslesi Vallalat). Hungarian name for Hungarian Telecommunications Company. See **HTC**.

MCI (MCI Communications Corporation). The second largest interexchange carrier in the United States, which provides domestic long-distance and international public and private telecommunications services. MCI employs the most advanced fiber-optic and microwave technologies to provide an all-digital network of nearly 3.5 billion-capacity circuit miles, representing an investment of over US$10 billion. It has developed a number of long-distance and international service offerings to compete effectively with other long-distance carriers in the U.S. such as AT&T and Sprint. These include a number of cost-saving packages for users and value added services. MCI was founded in 1968, is incorporated in the state of Delaware, and is headquartered in Washington, DC, with divisional offices in New York, Atlanta, and Arlington, Va., as well as more than 65 overseas offices in 55 countries and territories. It has over 35,000 employees worldwide. In mid–1993 it announced a strategic alliance with British Telecommunications plc, whereby the latter would buy about 20% of MCI's shares for US$4.3 billion and receive 3 seats on MCI's 15-member board of directors.

MECU. See ECU.

Mercury (Mercury Communications Limited). The United Kingdom's second network operator, a subsidiary of Cable & Wireless plc.

MFJ (Modified Final Judgment). The judicial decree that ended the U.S. Department of Justice's antitrust suit against AT&T in 1982. See also **Consent Decree (1982).**

MFN (most favored nation). Principle of the General Agreement on Tariffs and Trade (GATT), North American Free Trade Agreement (NAFTA), and other similar agreements whereby each party to the agreement accords providers of goods and services of another party treatment no less favorable than that it accords, in like circumstances, to providers of goods and services of another party or nonparty. The principle of MFN which is contained in Article 1 of the GATT has been the cornerstone of the world trading system since 1947.

microwave link. A radio transmission system operating in the range above 1 gigahertz (GHz) capable of carrying large numbers of telecommunications circuits using line-of-sight beams relayed by means of highly directive antennas.

MIGA (Multilateral Investment Guarantee Agency). The member of the World Bank Group that is dedicated to helping developing countries attract productive foreign investment through (1) guarantees against specified noncommercial risks perceived by investors in economically sound projects in developing member countries, and (b) consultative and advisory services to members on means of improving their attractiveness to foreign investment. Both these facilities complement the work of the World Bank, the IFC, and other agencies in encouraging and facilitating investment in developing countries. MIGA was inaugurated in 1988 by an initial group of 42 member countries that subscribed 63% of the agency's authorized capital of US$1.08 billion. Since then, membership has grown to over 60 and is expected to continue to expand.

MITI. Ministry of International Trade and Industry, in Japan.

MMC. Monopolies and Mergers Commission, U.K.

mobile services. Radiocommunications services between ships, aircraft, road vehicles, or other stations for use while in motion or between such stations and fixed points on land.

Modified Final Judgment. See **MFJ** or **Consent Decree (1982)**.

money market. That part of the capital market in which short-term financial obligations are bought and sold. These include Treasury bills and other government securities maturing in three years or less as well as commercial paper, banker's acceptances, trust company guaranteed investment certificates, and other instruments with a year or less left to maturity. Longer-term securities, when their term shortens to the limits mentioned, are also traded in the money markets.

Monopolies and Mergers Commission (MMC). A statutory body in the U.K. set up to inquire into and report on questions relating to specific mergers, monopolies, anticompetitive practices, the performance of public sector bodies, and the regulation of certain privatized industries including telecommunications. Such references generally are made by the Secretary of State for Trade and Industry, the Director General of Fair Trading or, in the case of the privatized industries, by the appropriate regulator. MMC is independent of the government and other reference-making bodies in both its conduct of inquiries and in its conclusions. Its reports are all published.

monopoly. A market structure with only one firm selling a given good or service and no other firms selling closely related goods or services. *Natural monopoly* is a service or facility which, because of large economies of scale and/or scope, is produced at the lowest cost when provided by a single supplier. Most public utilities, including telecommunications, were traditionally considered to be natural monopolies. With rapid technological innovation, however, telecommunications is no longer a natural monopoly, except perhaps for the wired local network which, in turn, is being challenged by the decreasing cost of new radio technologies. The natural monopoly concept is also questioned in terms of dynamic efficiency gains resulting from competition offsetting the losses in scale or scope.

MPF (Ministerium für Post-und Fernmeldewesen). The Ministry of Posts and Telecommunications in the former German Democratic Republic.

MPT. Ministry of Posts and Telecommunications in various countries.

MTNL (Mahanagar Telephone Nigam Ltd.). A wholly-owned corporation of the government of India which provides the telecommunications services in Bombay and Delhi.

MTV (Magyar Tavkoslesi Vallalat). Hungarian name and initials for Hungarian Telecommunications Company. See **HTC.**

Multilateral Investment Guarantee Agency. See **MIGA.**

multiplexer. A device that combines two or more signals for transmission over a shared path by allocating to each a distinctive frequency range or time slot in a common spectrum or bit stream.

NAFIN (Nacional Financiera S.A.). The Mexican federal government's state development bank.

NAFTA. See **North American Free Trade Agreement.**

national treatment. Principle of the General Agreement on Tariffs and Trade (GATT), North American Free Trade Agreement (NAFTA), Canada-U.S. Free Trade Agreement and similar agreements whereby each party to the agreement accords providers of goods and services of another party treatment no less favorable than that it accords, in like circumstances, to its own providers of such goods and services.

net asset value. Total assets of a company less its liabilities.

net earnings. That part of a company's profits remaining after all expenses and taxes have been paid and out of which dividends may be paid.

net present value (NPV). The value today of all future benefits resulting from a specific investment or business activity, net of all initial and future costs incurred to produce these benefits, discounted at the appropriate rate.

network. A combination of switches, terminals, and circuits in which transmission facilities interconnect user stations, usually by means of a single switching or service center.

network architecture. The overall structure of a network; it details the format the data must take, specific operating procedures, the design principles followed, the physical structure, and the functional organization utilized.

NIC (newly industrialized country). One of a group of countries (such as the Republic of Korea and Singapore) that have experienced accelerated economic growth and modernization in recent years, reaching levels of income, industrialization, and other indicators that rank them somewhere between the typical developing country and the economies of OECD member countries. The number of NICs is growing, and countries such as Brazil, Indonesia, Malaysia, Mexico, and Thailand are increasingly included. Alternatively, NICs are sometimes referred to as *newly industrialized economies* (NIE) to include territories (such as Hong Kong and Taiwan) for which the term *country* is sometimes politically sensitive.

NIE (newly industrialized economy). See NIC.

NMT (Nordic Mobile Telephone System). An international public land mobile system developed jointly by Denmark, Finland, Norway, and Sweden, operating in the 450 MHz (NMT-450) and 900 MHz (NMT-900) frequency bands. It features roaming between countries and full access to the international public-switched telephone network and its services.

NOI (Notice of Inquiry). Refers to a public notice issued by the U.S. Federal Communications Commission (FCC) or National Telecommunications and Information Administration (NTIA) soliciting information and comment from interested parties with respect to policy options, rule modifications, or new rules being considered.

noncommon carrier (U.S.). A carrier in the U.S. that offers telecommunications services on a highly individualistic basis.

nondiscrimination. In trade terms, nondiscrimination means that parties to a trade agreement (e.g., GATT) shall accord to providers of goods and services of any other party treatment that is no less favorable than that accorded to the provider of goods and services of any other party.

nondominant carrier (U.S.). A telecommunications carrier in the U.S. that does not have market power, that is, does not have the ability to restrict output or increase prices.

non-tariff-based circuits. Telecommunications transmission capacity obtained by negotiation between an international telecommunications operator and the operator of an IVAN; used to distinguish the terms and conditions of such circuits from tariff-based (usually leased-line) circuits.

non-traffic-sensitive costs. Investment and operating costs (including depreciation and return on investment) associated with telephone company facilities which do not vary with the aggregate level of usage (number of calls, minutes of use) of the telephone system. The principal component is the subscriber line connecting each customer's home or business premise with the local telephone company's central office.

North American Free Trade Agreement (NAFTA). A trade liberalization agreement among Canada, the United States, and Mexico signed in December 1992 and which went into effect on January 1, 1994. NAFTA aims to eliminate barriers to trade in, and facilitate the cross-border movement of, goods and services between the territories of the parties; promote conditions of fair competition in the free trade area; increase substantially investment opportunities in the territories of the parties; provide adequate and effective protection and enforcement of intellectual property rights in each party's territory; create effective procedures for the implementation and application of this agreement, for its joint administration, and for the resolution of disputes; and establish a framework for further trilateral, regional, and multilateral cooperation to expand and enhance the benefits of the agreement, in a manner consistent with article XXIV (Territorial Application-Frontier Traffic-Customs Unions and Free-Trade Areas) of the General Agreement on Tariffs and Trade (GATT).

NPRM (Notice of Proposed Rule Making). A public notice issued by the Federal Communications Commission (FCC) in the U.S. inviting comment from interested parties on a proposed new regulatory policy or modification to an existing one.

NTC. National Telecommunications Commission, the regulatory body in the Philippines.

NTIA (National Telecommunications and Information Administration). Established in the U.S. in 1978 to replace the President's Office of Telecommunications Policy (OTP), the NTIA is responsible for fostering the development and growth of communications industries and their customers. It also has primary responsibility for managing the use of the electromagnetic spectrum by the U.S. government and acts as chief telecommunications policy adviser to the President. NTIA makes studies of both broad and narrow communications policy topics. It occasionally makes proposals to the FCC on specific issues, comments on most FCC proceedings, and provides testimony on such issues to Congress.

NTT (Nippon Telegraph and Telephone Corporation). Formerly Japan's only domestic carrier, NTT was privatized in 1985 and now competes as a Type I domestic carrier.

NYNEX. One of the seven regional Bell operating companies resulting from the 1984 breakup of the Bell System, NYNEX is a leading provider of information networks and telecommunications services, with 1992 operating revenues of US$13.2 billion and total assets of US$27.5 billion. In NYNEX's domestic markets, its two operating telephone companies—New York Telephone and New England Telephone—provide telephone services to more than 12 million customers in the northeastern United States. Through their computers and switching facilities, NYNEX's operating telephone companies handle 185 million calls daily. In addition, NYNEX offers telecommunications services in selected markets around the world. Through NYNEX's Worldwide Services Group of companies, a full range of services, such as integrated voice and data services, cellular mobile telephone service, telephone directory publishing, database management, and software and consulting services, are provided to NYNEX's diverse and competitive markets. These global business initiatives include international activities in Australia, Belgium, Canada, Czech Republic, Gibraltar, Greece, Hong Kong, Indonesia, Ireland, Japan, Korea, Malaysia, Mexico, Poland, the Philippines, Taiwan, Thailand, and the United Kingdom.

OECD (Organization for Economic Cooperation and Development). A forum for the highly industrialized countries whose aims are to encourage economic growth and high employment with financial stability among member countries, as well as to contribute to the economic development of the less advanced member and nonmember countries and the expansion of world multilateral trade. The OECD has provided an important forum for the discussion of international monetary problems and for promoting aid to developing countries.

offering. Offering of securities for sale to the public or a restricted group.

Office of Fair Trading (OFT). The U.K. agency responsible for protecting consumers by monitoring unfair and uncompetitive business practices as well as taking steps to correct them. OFT keeps watch on the effects of trading practices and may suggest changes to the law in problem areas. In certain circumstances, it can take legal action against businesses that cause problems for consumers. As lack of competition in business may act against the public interest, OFT also keeps a watch on monopolies, mergers, and trade practices which may be restrictive or anticompetitive. In some cases, the issue may be referred to the MMC for deeper investigation.

OFTA (Office of the Telecommunications Authority). The telecommunications regulatory body of Hong Kong, established in 1993.

OFTEL (Office of Telecommunications). The regulatory body set up to supervise the implementation of telecommunications policies, competition, and licenses in the United Kingdom.

ONA (open network architecture). A telecommunications network configuration and regulatory scheme adopted by the Federal Communications Commission (FCC) in the United States. Upon approval of the Bell operating companies' ONA plans by the FCC, the BOCs may provide both basic and enhanced services on condition that they offer certain basic network functions on an unbundled, equivalent basis to all affiliated and unaffiliated enhanced service providers. Cross-subsidization between monopoly (basic) and enhanced services is prohibited, and accounting and reporting schemes are to be implemented.

online database services. The provision of electronically published machine-readable information that can be accessed directly by the researcher over a telecommunications network.

ONP. See **open network provision**.

open network provision (ONP). Proposal by the Commission of the European Communities for standardizing telecommunications transport service offerings, network interfaces, and access arrangements among member states. Basic principles include nondiscriminatory access to networks, transparent network configuration, and the prohibition of cross-subsidization.

OPIC (Overseas Private Investment Corporation). A self-sustaining U.S. government agency established in 1969 to promote economic growth in developing countries by encouraging U.S. private investment in those nations. OPIC assists U.S. investors by financing investment projects through direct loans and/or loan guarantees, and by insuring investment projects against a broad range of political risks. All of OPIC's guaranty and insurance obligations are backed by the U.S. government as well as by OPIC's own substantial financial reserves. OPIC will not provide assistance for any project that adversely affects the U.S. economy or domestic employment, is financially unsound, or does not promise significant benefits to the social and economic development of the host country. It is structured like a private corporation and does not receive government funds.

opportunity cost. The cost of a good or service measured in terms of benefits forgone by others. The opportunity cost may be very different from the actual price charged for the good or service. For example, the opportunity cost of scarce investment funds can be measured by the returns from the best alternative project in which these funds could be invested. This cost could be much higher than the interest rate charged (or paid) for funds by banks. The opportunity cost of labor may be lower than the salaries and wages paid, when there is a combination of minimum wages mandated by law and unemployment.

Optus. See AUSSAT.

OTC (Overseas Telecommunications Commission). The former state-owned Australian international telecommunications carrier, which was merged with Telecom Australia under the 1991 Telecommunications Bill and is now known as Telstra.

overlay network. A separate network for a particular service or market segment covering most or part of the same geographical locations as an existing basic network. Increasingly used in Central and Eastern Europe, the Commonwealth of Independent States, and other countries where there is urgent need to overcome critical communication shortages while the overall network is expanded and modernized at a slower pace consistent with modest capital and management capabilities.

PABX (private automatic branch exchange). A PBX which makes possible some or all connections from extensions without the services of an attendant or operator.

packet switching. A data communications service in which a data stream is divided into units called *packets* (typically composed of approximately 200 characters) that are separately routed to a destination where the original message is then reconstituted.

paging. See **radio paging service.**

PAN (Partido de Acción Nacional). Right-wing opposition party in Mexico.

PanAmSat. The first privately owned international satellite system, PanAmSat launched its first satellite, PAS–1, in June 1988 and currently offers a range of specialized broadcast and data services to the Western Hemisphere and Europe. PAS–2 will offer similar services to the Asia-Pacific region and is scheduled for launch in May 1994; PAS–3 will cover the Atlantic Ocean region and is scheduled for launch in late 1994; PAS–4 will cover the Indian Ocean region and is scheduled for launch in early 1995, completing PanAmSat's global coverage.

Pannon GSM. The consortium of national telecommunications operators from the Netherlands, Denmark, Sweden, and Finland which was awarded one of two (the other going to a consortium of US West and the Hungarian Telecommunications Company) 15-year, pan-European standard GSM licenses in Hungary in October 1993.

par value. The stated face value of a bond or stock expressed as a currency (e.g., dollar) amount. The par value of a common stock usually has little relationship to the current market value and so *no par value* stock is now more common. The par value of a preferred stock is significant because it indicates the dollar amount of assets each preferred share would be entitled to in the event of liquidating the company.

PBX (private branch exchange). A manually operated switching system owned or leased by a customer and generally installed on its premises, which provides lines for internal communication between local extensions and provides a smaller number of trunk lines that give access to the public network.

PCN (personal communications network). The generic term to describe a digital cellular radio service that is universally available, working indoors as well as while on the move.

PCO (public call office). A telephone station available for the use of the public, generally on payment of a fee to an attendant or a coin box.

penetration level. The percentage of households with local telephone service, a widely used measure of telephone service accessibility. (A national penetration level of 100% would indicate that every household in the country had telephone service.) Alternatively, *telephone density*, or number of main telephone lines per 100 inhabitants, is a common measure of a country or region's telecommunications development.

PEPCO (Potomac Electric Power Company). The electric power generation and distribution utility serving the District of Columbia and most of Prince Georges County and Montgomery County in Maryland.

Philcomsat (Philippines Communications Satellite Corporation). Wholesale provider of domestic satellite services in the Philippines.

plc or Plc (public limited company, U.K.). A limited company with broad share ownership to which higher standards of financial reporting apply.

PLDT (Philippines Long Distance Telephone Company). The privately owned dominant provider of domestic telecommunications services in the Philippines. PLDT operates more than 94% of the telephones in the Philippines, mainly in urban areas.

portfolio investment. Passive investment in securities by fund managers.

Postal Rate Commission (PRC). A federal government commission in the U.S. which, along with a board of governors, manages the U.S. Postal Service (USPS). The President appoints all five members of the PRC, which recommends rates and classifications for approval by the board of governors. The President also appoints nine members of the board who select a Postmaster General as the tenth member. These ten board members then appoint the Deputy Postmaster General as an eleventh member. In addition to regulating postal rates, the board also sets policy for USPS entry into or out of new services, such as electronic mail, and the permissible areas of entry by private delivery services. The Postal Rate Commission and board of governors were established by the 1971 Postal Reorganization Act, which transformed the USPS from a Cabinet-level department to an independent agency.

predatory pricing. The setting of prices so far below costs that competitors will be driven out of business.

presubscription. In the U.S., an arrangement whereby an individual telephone customer may designate one long-distance carrier over whose facilities interLATA calls normally will be routed. Under the terms of the MFJ, BOCs are required to offer presubscription choices in all central offices equipped for equal access.

PRI (Partido Revolucionario Institucional). The dominant political party which has been in power in Mexico since the 1930s.

price-cap regulation. A method of regulating the tariffs charged by a monopoly or dominant telecommunications operator, whereby a *cap* is placed by the regulator or by contract (e.g., license) on the prices of a basket of services, with annual increases usually tied to a measure of inflation. Under certain conditions, price-cap regulation provides an incentive for the operators to cut costs and is relatively simple to administer. The method was first used extensively in telecommunications in the U.K. to regulate BT. In the U.S., the FCC similarly has proposed price-cap regulation of AT&T and the BOCs, to replace rate-of-return regulation.

price/earning ratio (P/E ratio). A common stock's current market price divided by its annual per-share earnings.

Primafoon shop. Telephone and subscription outlet for PTT Telecom Netherlands which offers various telecommunications customer services.

primary offering. An issue of new shares or securities by a company, typically in the case of a capital increase; proceeds of the offering go to the issuing company.

private company. A company owned by private parties (individuals or legal entities), and not by the state or another public body. A company with mixed ownership (some private and some public owners) may be considered a private company if the public sector owns less than a controlling interest in it. A private company is to be contrasted with a public enterprise or state-owned enterprise, which are owned and controlled by a state or other public entity. See **public company**.

private line. See **leased line**.

private network. Any network used to communicate within an organization (as distinct from providing service to the public), based on a configuration of own or leased facilities. The term includes networks used by private companies, state enterprises, or government entities.

private offering. See **private placement**.

private placement or **private offering**. An offering made only to a limited number of persons and not to the public at large. Securities laws may or may not regulate such offerings.

privatization. Transfer of control of ownership of a state enterprise to private parties, generally by organizing the enterprise as a share company and selling shares to investors. More generally, the term is sometimes used to refer to a wide range of modalities whereby business is opened to private enterprise and investment.

producer surplus. The difference between the sale price of goods or services and the cost of providing it.

promissory note. A note documenting a promise to pay. See also **bond**.

prospectus. A legal document that describes securities being offered for sale to the public and which must be prepared in conformity with requirements of applicable securities regulations.

protocol. A collection of agreements permitting the exchange of information between the user and a network, or among different networks. There currently exist several levels of telecommunications protocols sponsored by national and international standards-making bodies and manufacturers, consisting of electrical (ex. RS-232-C), character encodage (ASCII, BCD), linkage (XModem, HASP, HD2C), network (SNA, X.25), and equipment (3270, VT-100) protocols.

protocol conversion. Exchange of information between terminals or networks using incompatible communication protocols. Example: asynchronous-to-X.25 conversion provided by a packet assembler-disassembler to allow character-mode terminals to exchange information over a packet-switched network. Protocol conversion is considered to be not only a technique but also a separately tariffed service in countries that have promoted the unbundling of telecommunications services. It is often classified as a value added service.

PSTN (public-switched telephone network). A country's telephone system, including local loops, exchanges, trunks, international links, and, in some countries, the telephone apparatus.

PTC (Pakistan Telecommunications Corporation). Pakistan's state-owned telephone company.

PT Indosat. A government-owned joint-stock company which provides international telecommunications services in Indonesia.

PTO (public telephone operator). A term sometimes used for the organization that has sole responsibility for the provision of telecommunications services in a particular country.

PT Satelindo. Telecommunications service provider established in Indonesia in 1993, which is owned by PT Telkom (30%), PT Indosat (10%), and PT Bima Graha, a private company (60%), to provide international, cellular mobile, and satellite services in Indonesia. PT Satelindo will take over operation of Indonesia's domestic satellite system, Palapa, in 1995.

PTT (post, telephone, and telegraph). Generic name used to designate a government department or agency that operates the public telecommunications and postal networks, usually as a monopoly, and sets standards and policies. Until recently, telecommunications and postal services were organized as PTTs in most European countries, and from there the form was exported to a number of other countries, especially in Africa and Asia. In recent years the trend has been toward breaking up PTTs, leaving the policy and regulatory functions with the government or specialized agencies and restructuring the operating functions as separate enterprises or companies.

PTT Telecom Netherlands. The telecommunications operating subsidiary of Royal PTT Nederland NV, due to be floated on the Amsterdam stock exchange in several tranches starting in 1994. It provides all types of telecommunications services in the 32 telecommunications regions of the Netherlands. Basic services and infrastructure are provided on a monopoly basis; however, regulatory changes are expected in the near future with the aim of creating a duopoly. PTT Telecom Netherlands has joined forces with several Dutch and foreign companies so as to offer a full range of services in line with market demand. Unisource, the joint venture in which PTT Telecom Netherlands and Telia AB of Sweden (formerly Televeket) are concentrating a significant proportion of their activities, has been strengthened by the participation of Swiss PTT Telecom as of July 1, 1993. Net turnover in 1992 was Dfl 10.487 million, and 1992 operating profit was Dfl 2.789 million.

PT Telkom (PT Telekomunikasi Indonesia). A government-owned joint-stock company responsible for the provision of domestic telecommunications services in Indonesia. PT Telkom also provides cellular mobile and paging services in joint ventures with private investors. Prior to the establishment of PT Satelindo, PT Telkom operated Indonesia's domestic satellite system, Palapa.

public company. A company whose shares are held by the public or a group of persons who do not otherwise have a common business interest. The shares are often traded on a securities market.

public enterprise. Enterprise owned by the public sector. This term includes state-owned enterprises, as well as enterprises owned by other state-owned enterprises, municipalities, or other public bodies.

public offering. An offering of stock or securities to the public at large, in which any member of the public may participate, as opposed to a private offering or placement. Public offerings are generally regulated by law.

public utility commission (PUC). An agency charged with regulating telecommunications and other public utility services within a state of the United States. Sometimes called a public service commission.

pulse code modulation (PCM). A form of modulation in which an analog signal is sampled, and the sample is quantized and then converted at regular intervals to a digital code to represent the absolute amplitude of each sampled pulse.

QAM (quadrature amplitude modulation). A sophisticated modulation technique using variations in signal amplitude that allows data-encoded symbols to be represented as any of 16 or 32 different states. The modulation is achieved through the impression of two independent signals on carriers of the same frequency that are 90 degrees out of phase with respect to one another. In 16-QAM each quadrature signal uses four-level coding to achieve a combination of 16 phase and amplitude states.

RACE (Research and Development in Advanced Communications Technologies in Europe). A European R&D program for information technologies and telecommunications, adopted in 1987 to facilitate progressive evolution toward an EC-wide broadband integrated communications system.

Radiocommunications Agency (U.K.). The government authority responsible for the use of radio spectrum in the United Kingdom. The Radiocommunications Agency issues licenses for specific use of radio frequencies for aeronautical, marine, land, satellite, microwave, and hobby uses. It also produces specifications for radio equipment, is responsible for overseeing type approval of equipment, and monitors the use of the radio spectrum. The Radiocommunications Agency has satellite and terrestrial radio-monitoring stations and a radio laboratory. Agency staff investigate cases of radio interference and misuse of radio frequencies.

radio paging service. A service that allows transmitting a signal, usually only an alarm tone, via radio from any telephone in the public-switched network to a personal, portable receiving device in a defined operating area. More sophisticated systems provide audible or visual display messages.

radio spectrum. See **frequency spectrum**.

rate averaging. A regulatory practice of setting uniform rates for the same service rather than having different rates based on the differing costs of, for example, different locations or traffic routes. See also **rate de-averaging**.

rate base regulation. A method of regulation in which a common carrier is limited in its operations to a revenue level that will recover no more than its expenses plus an allowed rate of return on the carrier's investment or rate base. See also **price-cap regulation**.

rate de-averaging. The regulatory practice of setting different rates for a regulated service or service component in response to differences in costs and usage from one route to another, one city to another, or one state to another. In a de-averaged rate structure, the rate a subscriber pays for a particular service from a specific vendor will vary according to the subscriber's geographic location.

rate of return. The profit shown by an investment, expressed as percentage of the total money invested. The rate of return varies depending on behalf of whom it is calculated. In particular, costs and benefits to a telecommunications operating company ("private returns") can be quite different from those to the economy as a whole ("social returns"). See also **cost-benefit analysis** and **economic rate of return.**

rate rebalancing. Moving telecommunications service rates closer to their associated costs, as needed when an incumbent provider prepares to face competition from new entrants or when a regulator seeks to increase economic efficiency of a monopoly operator. In most countries, monopoly provision of telecommunications services has resulted in subscription (rental) and local charges that are below costs, and long-distance and international charges that are above costs.

RBOC (regional Bell operating company). One of seven U.S. regional companies created by the 1984 divestiture of AT&T to take over ownership of the Bell operating companies within their region. The seven RBOCs and their respective operating company subsidiaries are (1) NYNEX Corporation (New York Telephone Company and New England Telephone Company); (2) Bell Atlantic Corporation (New Jersey Bell, Bell of Pennsylvania, Diamond State Telephone, and the Chesapeake and Potomac Telephone Companies of Maryland, Virginia, West Virginia and the District of Columbia); (3) BellSouth Corporation (Southern Bell and South Central Bell); (4) Ameritech Corporation (Michigan Bell, Ohio Bell, Indiana Bell, Illinois Bell, and Wisconsin Telephone Company); (5) Southwestern Bell Corporation (Southwestern Bell Telephone Company); (6) US West (Northwestern Bell, Mountain Bell, and Pacific Northwest Bell); and (7) Pacific TELESIS Group (Pacific Bell and Nevada Bell). Two other former Bell System operating companies, Southern New England Telephone and Cincinnati Bell, Inc., were not majority owned by AT&T and are not considered BOCs for the purposes of the various line-of-business restrictions imposed by the antitrust settlement. The RBOCs also have set up numerous unregulated subsidiaries engaged in a variety of communications-related and noncommunications businesses. The divestiture agreement barred RBOCs from engaging in certain business activities, such as providing long-distance service, but provided mechanisms for review, waiver, modification, or removal of the prohibitions.

regulation. The process ensuring that public utilities such as common carriers operate in accordance with specific rules and fair competition principles. Also the body of rules in a tariff governing the offering of service by a carrier and including practices, classifications, and definitions. A regulator is an agency empowered to control and monitor the commercial activities of radio and television broadcasters, cable system operators, telecommunications carriers, or any other public utility in the public interest.

resale. The subsequent sale or lease on a commercial basis, with or without adding value, of a service provided by a telecommunications carrier. A resale carrier or reseller is a company that leases bulk-rated plant (e.g., transmission) capacity from facilities-based carriers and uses that capacity to provide services to individual customers or groups of customers at prices high enough to make a profit yet sufficiently below the equivalent rates of the facilities-based carriers to attract customers.

reserved service. A term used by the Commission of the European Communities to describe telecommunications services that may be provided only by the existing public telecommunications operator and a limited number of others under license.

restructuring. Major changes in sectoral organization, enterprise organization, or enterprise ownership. Also may refer to a change in the structure of rate components for an existing service.

retail investor. An expression used in the investment community to refer to an individual who is investing on his or her own behalf, in contrast to an institutional investor, who invests on behalf of large organizations.

return on assets (ROA). Net income of a company expressed as a percentage of average total assets. ROA is used, along with ROE (return on equity), as a measure of profitability and as a basis for intra-industry performance comparison.

return on equity (ROE). Net income less preferred share dividends, expressed as a percentage of average common shareholders' equity.

right of first refusal. A contractual term providing that one party to the contract has a right to acquire certain rights or privileges, such as to buy or sell shares, before they are offered to others.

risk. The potential costs, monetary or otherwise, resulting from uncertain future events. *Credit risk* refers to the possibility that borrowers and others to whom a bank has made commitments to extend credit will be unable to repay their obligations when due. *Liquidity risk* refers to potential demands on a bank for cash resulting from commitments to extend credit, deposit maturities, and many other transactions. *Market risk* refers to possible losses resulting from price changes, such as a decrease in the value of a portfolio of common shares (or, more generally, from failure of an enterprise to sell goods and services as expected). *Interest rate risk* refers to possible losses resulting from changes in interest rates. *Foreign exchange risk* refers to possible losses resulting from exchange rate movements.

roaming. An expression that describes mobile cellular telephone use which involves passing from the local service area of one company to that of another.

RPOA (recognized private operating agency). A private or government-controlled corporation (such as AT&T, BT, France Télécom, Telefónica de España, Swiss PTT) that provides telecommunications services in adherence to international telecommunications conventions. RPOAs participate as nonvoting members of the ITU and its organs.

Rural Electrification Administration (REA). Agency created in the U.S. in 1935 to support the development of electricity and telephone facilities in rural areas by granting self-liquidating loans and providing technical assistance. About 1,000 rural electric and 900 rural telephone utility systems in 47 states have received loans from the REA.

Satellite Green Paper (EC). Communication published by the Commission of the European Communities in 1990 on a common approach in the field of satellite communications in the EC. The Satellite Green Paper extends the application of the generally agreed upon principles of EC telecommunications policy to satellite communications, taking into account its specificities. It proposes (a) full liberalization of the earth segment, including both receive-only and transmit/receive terminals; (b) free (unrestricted) access to space segment capacity; (c) full commercial freedom for space segment providers, including direct marketing of satellite capacity to service providers and users; and (d) harmonization measures as far as required to facilitate the provision of Europe-wide services, all subject to the appropriate licensing and type approval procedures.

SCT (Secretaría de Comunicaciones y Transporte). The government department in Mexico responsible for telecommunications policy and regulation.

secondary market. A market for the purchase and sale of outstanding issues following the initial distribution. Shares sold on the various exchanges and in the over-the-counter market are secondary trades.

secondary offering. An offering of a large block of existing stock in a company, where the proceeds of the sale go to the owner-seller of the stock, i.e., typically to the government in the case of state-owned enterprise divesture.

Secondary offerings are in contrast to primary offerings, which are issues of new stock.

Securities and Exchange Commission (SEC). The U.S. regulatory body which supervises the issuance of securities.

Services Directive (EC). Directive issued by the Commission of the European Communities in 1990 on competition in the markets for telecommunications services. It requires member states of the European Community to (a) withdraw all special exclusive rights for the supply of telecommunications services other than voice; (b) make the conditions of access to the public networks nondiscriminatory and transparent; (c) publish information on the characteristics of the technical interfaces necessary for the use of public networks; (d) end restrictions on processing of signals before and after transmission over the public network; (e) separate regulatory and operating functions by July 1, 1991. It allowed member states to prohibit simple (voice) resale until December 31, 1992, and contains provisions to avoid abuse of dominant position.

Sherman Act. The main United States antitrust law under whose Section 2 the Antitrust II case was brought against AT&T. The complaint charged that AT&T had abused its power as a monopolist supplying equipment, thus excluding competition from the terminal equipment market and denying access to its network by long-distance competitors.

Single European Act. A revision of the Treaty of Rome which entered into force in 1987. It streamlined EC decision procedures, particularly for internal market proposals.

SITA (Société Internationale de Télécommunications Aéronautiques, or in English **Airline Telecommunications and Information Services).** A nonprofit organization that is owned by 350 member airlines and provides a variety of essential communications and data-processing services to its members via a global telecommunications network.

'SLT (Sri Lanka Telecom). The government-owned corporation responsible for providing domestic and international telecommunications services in Sri Lanka, established by the Telecommunications Act of 1991.

Société Française du Radiotéléphone (SFR). One of two licensed providers of GSM-type digital cellular mobile services in France, the other being France Télécom.

sovereign debt. Foreign debt owed or guaranteed by a national government.

SPC (stored-program controlled exchange). A generic switching system in which the control logic is stored in software form in the memory of one or more digital computers. Changes can readily be made to such a system—to provide new services, for instance—by altering or replacing the software rather than rewiring components or paths.

Sprint. A global telecommunications carrier based in the United States. It operates the world's largest all-digital, fiber-optic communications network (45,000 kilometers in length), which provides long-distance voice, data, and videoconferencing services throughout the United States. Sprint also provides local exchange service to more than 4 million subscribers in 17 states, operates one of the world's largest telecommunications equipment distributors, publishes telephone directories, and provides local and long-distance operator services. The company also has experience in cellular telephone and CATV system operations. Through Sprint International, the company offers, from the U.S., direct-dial voice service to 220 countries and locations, provides packet-switched data service to more than 100 countries, and has the world's largest videoconferencing network, serving 35 nations.

Standard & Poor's 500 Index. An index of the share prices of 500 key public corporations, divided into 87 industry groups, which is maintained on a continual basis by the Standard & Poor's bond-rating agency. Of these equities, 90% are traded on the New York Stock Exchange, with the balance traded over-the-counter. This index is considered a representative barometer of overall economic health, and of equity markets in particular. See also **Dow Jones Industrial Average.**

STAR Program. EC development program initiated in 1987 to promote the use of advanced telecommunications in the developing regions of the EC.

state holding company. A state-owned enterprise confining its activities to the ownership and holding of other companies (typically, though not necessarily, state-owned enterprise) and to the management and control thereof.

statute. Law or act of Parliament, as opposed to court-made law. Binding rule enacted by the sovereign authority in a society and laying down the fundamental principles for relations between the members of that society.

STD (Subscriber trunk dialing or direct distance dialing (DDD). A telephone exchange service that enables the customer to call other subscribers outside his local area without operator assistance.

Stentor. Formerly Telecom Canada. A consortium consisting of Telesat Canada and the nine major telephone companies across Canada: British Columbia Telephone Company (BC Tel), AGT Ltd., Saskatchewan Telecommunications, Manitoba Telephone System (MTS), Bell Canada, New Brunswick Telephone Company, Island Telephone Company, Maritime Telegraph and Telephone Company Limited (MT&T), and Newfoundland Telephone Company Limited. The consortium originally was formed in 1931 to facilitate the provision of coast-to-coast telephone service.

STET (Società Finanziaria Telefonica Spa). A provider and manufacturer of telecommunications facilities and services, 70% owned by the Italian state-controlled IRI-Group. While STET focuses on telephone and telex, its subsidiaries SIP and Italcable provide local and short-range long-distance and intercontinental services, respectively. STET's industrial activities (production and installation of telecommunications and distributing systems) are mainly the concern of Italcable and SIRTI. STET also is active in publishing and communications through its subsidiary SEAT. STET employs about 123,000 people, has a capital of about 4,000 billion lire, and its 1989 turnover was 21,977 billion lire.

STM (Syarikat Telekom Malaysia Berhad). The majority government-owned enterprise incorporated in accordance with the Companies Act of Malaysia, responsible for operating the telecommunications business in Malaysia according to the Telecommunications Services Act of 1985. Now generally referred to as Telekom Malaysia.

Strowger switch. An electromechanical switch based on a stepping relay patented by Strowger in 1891. It was one of the leading technological changes that enabled automatic (as distinct from operator-assisted) telephone service.

subscriber bond. Some form of subscriber financing of telephone company long-term debt. For example, a telecommunications company bond purchased in some countries by a customer as condition to obtain a new telephone connection or resulting in faster connection, and which may be paid back through credits to future telephone bills or sometimes resold in a secondary market. Subscriber bonds played a major role in Japan's developing both telecommunications and the bond market after World War II.

subscriber financing. Any mechanism whereby subscribers contribute an important part of the capital required by the telecommunications operating company for investment. Mandatory subscriber financing sometimes takes the form of obligatory purchase of bonds issued by the operating company, or of shares in the company's stock, as a condition to obtain a new connection. See also **subscriber bond**.

subscriber line charge (SLC). In the U.S., a fixed monthly surcharge to recover a portion of subscriber access costs. The federal SLC is determined by the FCC and recovers a portion of the non-traffic-sensitive access costs assigned to the interstate jurisdiction. The balance of these costs not recovered through the SLC is recovered through the carrier common line charge.

SUBTEL (Subsecretaría de Telecomunicaciones). A department within the Chilean Ministry of Transport and Telecommunications which is responsible for technical regulation, overseeing the operation of all telecommunications networks and services, and granting licenses and franchises.

supplier credit. Financing for the purchase of goods, offered by the supplier of the goods. Usually comprises commercial bank loans and, where available, export development loans, government grants, and other concessional financing organized by the supplier.

surety bond. A three-part guarantee instrument which protects a person, corporation, or other legal entity in case of default in payment of a given obligation, improper performance of a contract, loss due to dishonesty, etc. The three parts are (a) the person, corporation, or legal entity on whose behalf the bond is issued; (b) the person, corporation, or legal entity in whose favor the bond is issued; and (3) the company which issues the guarantee.

swap. A commercial arrangement whereby two companies lend to each other on different terms, e.g., in different currencies, or one at a fixed rate and the other at a floating rate.

SWIFT (Society for Worldwide Interbank Financial Telecommunications). SWIFT operates a computerized telecommunications network to provide automated international message-processing and transmission services between financial institutions. Owned by the international banking community and operational since 1977, it connected in early 1989 more than 2,900 destinations in 60 countries. The network is controlled from two operating centers, in the United States and the Netherlands. The society's headquarters are in Belgium.

Syncordia. The Atlanta-based network management subsidiary of British Telecom, established in September 1991 to offer end-to-end outsourced global network services to large multinational corporations, that is, the provision of end-to-end telecommunications facilities and the management of all of the corporation's telecommunications needs, including equipment, circuits, and staff. Such outsourcing saves multinational corporations from having to negotiate with telephone companies and dealing with different technical, quality-of-service, and cost factors in different countries.

System X. A medium-capacity digital switching system developed jointly by BT, GEC Telecommunications, and Plessey for use in the U.K. public network as a local, trunk, or international exchange.

T-1. A digital transmission system operating at a rate of 1.544 Megabits per second (Mbps) with a standard multiplexing format (equivalent to 24 voice grade circuits).

TACS (Total Access Communication System). A United Kingdom-developed public cellular land mobile system operating in the 900 MHz frequency range, designed to permit automatic exchange of traffic with the public-switched telephone network. It features high voice quality, high reliability, low blocking, and relatively low cost, and can be used for both voice and data transmission.

tariff. The schedule of rates and regulations governing the provision of telecommunications services by a particular carrier.

TAS (Telecommunications Authority of Singapore). The telecommunications regulatory body in Singapore.

TCI (Telecommunications Inc.). The largest owner and operator of cable television systems in the U.S. TCI and its subsidiaries provide cable television services to over 13 million subscribers in 48 states as well as in Washington DC, Puerto Rico, and the United Kingdom. In 1992, the Denver-based TCI had assets of US$13.2 billion and operating revenues of US$3.6 billion. In October 1993, it announced a merger with Bell Atlantic.

TCNZ (Telecommunications Corporation of New Zealand). The largest telecommunications operating company of New Zealand. It provides a variety of telecommunications services, including data and voice communications, telegram, telex, facsimile, videotex/teletex, TV, electronic mail/message service. Along with New Zealand Post and Post Office Bank, TCNZ was one of the three corporations created by the splitting of the functional activities of New Zealand Post Office. TCNZ was privatized in 1990 to a consortium consisting of Fay Richwhite and Freightways of New Zealand, Bell Atlantic, and Ameritech.

TDMA (time division multiple access). A radio scheme in which many signals share a single common transmission frequency band by allocating use of the transmission paths to each signal at discrete instants.

Techint (Compagnia Technica Internazionale). Argentina's largest conglomerate with investments in the industrial, engineering, construction, oil and gas, commercial and financial, transport, electrical energy, and telecommunications sectors. Techint's 1991 income was US$1.9 billion. It is the Argentinean partner of Telefónica de España in Telefónica de Argentina, one of the two regional telephone companies in Argentina.

TELCEL (TELCEL Celular S.A.). A private consortium led by BellSouth of the U.S. with minority Venezuelan private interests, it has a nationwide concession to provide cellular voice and data transmission services in Argentina.

telebanking. A service which allows clients to carry out banking transactions from their home or business over a communication network, such as videotex.

TELEBRÁS (Telecomunicaçoes Brasileiras S.A.). The state-owned holding company of the Brazilian telecommunications system, which owns the 28 operating companies providing public telecommunications services within each state as well as Embratel, the international and interstate long-distance operator.

TELECOM (Empresa Nacional de Telecomunicaciones). The state enterprise in Colombia that operates most domestic long-distance, all international services, and local service in some towns and rural areas.

Telecom Argentina. The northern regional telecommunications company in Argentina owned by a consortium including France Télécom and STET of Italy. It was established in 1990 with the privatization of ENTel. Telecom Argentina was given an exclusive mandate for seven years with possible extension for three years. Before privatization, Telecom Argentina was provisionally called Telco Norte.

Telecom Asia. A joint venture between Charoen Pokphand (85%), a private Thai conglomerate, and NYNEX (15%), a U.S. RBOC, to install 2 million telephone lines in Bangkok. In October 1993, Telecom Asia announced that it would raise US$400 million through a partial public flotation of its shares.

Telecom Australia. Australia's government-owned domestic terrestrial telecommunications carrier which was merged with OTC Limited (Australia's international carrier) under the 1991 Telecommunications Bill.

Telecom Canada. See Stentor.

Telefónica de Argentina. The southern regional telecommunications company in Argentina, owned by a consortium that includes Telefónica de España; it was established in 1991 with the privatization of ENTel, the state-owned national telephone company. Telefónica de Argentina was given a seven-year exclusive mandate to operate domestic telecommunications services in its territory with possible extension for three years. Before privatization it was provisionally called Telco Sur.

Telefónica de España S.A.. The monopoly provider of domestic and international telecommunications services in Spain. The government of Spain owns, directly or indirectly through other state-owned institutions, about 34.9% of the outstanding shares of Telefónica. It exercises control over Telefónica through this shareholding and through the legal regulatory structure within which the company operates. Telefónica directly or indirectly owns 43.6% of Compañía de Teléfonos de Chile (CTC), 20% of ENTEL Chile, 8.04% of Telefónica de Argentina, 16% of the consortium which owns 40% of CANTV in Venezuela, and 79% of Telefónica Larga Distancia de Puerto Rico.

Teleglobe Canada, Inc.. An international telecommunications carrier and the sole authorized operator of international telecommunications facilities linking Canada with all countries other than the United States (guaranteed until at least 1997). The corporation owns a global network which uses fiber-optic and coaxial submarine cables as well as communication satellites to link Canada with 230 countries and major territories. It employs 1,000 individuals and has more than 11,000 cable and satellite circuits in service in various parts of the world. Teleglobe Canada, Inc. is wholly owned by Teleglobe, Inc., which is in turn owned by National Telesystem Ltd. (20%), Bell Canada Enterprises (BCE, 20%), Caisse de Dépôt et Placement du Québec (15%), Ontario Municipal Employees Retirement Society (10%), and Rogers Communications Inc. (5%). The balance of shares is held by the general public.

TELEINTAR. The monopoly international voice carrier of Argentina, a jointly owned subsidiary of Telefónica de Argentina and TELECOM, the two private monopoly regional telephone operating companies. These three companies, as well as a jointly owned subsidiary that provides competitive services, were created with the privatization of ENTel, the Argentine state telecommunications monopoly, in 1991.

Telekom Malaysia. See STM.

TELEKOM 2000. DBP Telekom's strategic infrastructure modernization plan to increase the number of main lines in the eastern states of Germany (the former German Democratic Republic) from 2.4 million in 1991 to 9 million by 1997. The estimated total investment is DM 60 billion.

telematics. The provision of computer-based services to the public over telecommunications networks.

telematic service. Any telecommunications service other than ordinary telephone and telegraph services available to the public and generally requiring the user to interact with a computer-based system. Examples are teletex, videotex, facsimile, and messaging. See **telematics**.

telepoint service. A terrestrial mobile telephone service in which public base stations serve as intermediary points between the public-switched telephone network (PSTN) and portable personal telephone sets, situated in a radius of about 100 meters. See also **CT2**.

teleport. A facility giving access to a satellite network or other long-haul telecommunications network. Though usually connected to a building or real estate complex offering shared tenant services (such as a free enterprise zone or industrial park), a teleport sometimes also services the greater regional community beyond the tenants of the individual development.

teletex. A sophisticated update of the international telex service introduced in many countries in the mid–1980s. Teletex reproduces upper and lowercase characters so the output resembles a facsimile copy of a well-typed letter. Transmission speed is many times faster than telex. Teletex transmission is memory-to-memory between intelligent devices similar to word processors. Teletex systems provide gateways for interconnection with the older and slower telex systems.

telex. A public-switched telecommunications service providing for two-way, nonsimultaneous, written-word communications between subscribers using teletypewriter terminals.

Telex-Chile. A private operating company that provides domestic and international data, telex, and leased-lines services throughout Chile, and more recently through its subsidiary Chilesat, also domestic and international voice carriage in competition with the dominant operator ENTEL and with VTR. Originally Telex-Chile was the telex service of the government's post and telegraph administration, restructured as a commercial, state-owned company and sold to Chilean investors.

Telia AB (formerly Swedish Telecom or Televerket). The major telecommunications operator and the largest investor in Sweden and, since July 1, 1993, a fully state-owned limited liability company. Telia AB provides telephone network services as its main business; other services include data communications, leased circuits, mobile cellular telephony, paging, directories, cable TV, alarm services, customer financing, and consultancy. It is an important manufacturer and provider of telecommunications terminals and PABXs in Sweden. It joined with Ericsson to develop AXE, digital exchanges used both in the fixed and mobile networks. Fifty percent of its exchanges are digital; this will rise to 100 percent by the year 2000. Telia AB formed an alliance called Unisource with PTT Telecom Netherlands and Swiss PTT Telecom. Telia AB also operates in the neighboring Baltic countries. In 1992 it had 39,000 employees and a turnover of SKr 35,000 million (US$ 5,000 million).

TELMEX (Teléfonos de Mexico S.A. de C.V.). The privately owned telecommunications carrier of Mexico.

Telstra. The Australian government-owned provider of domestic and international telecommunications services. Known as AOTC until 1993, Telstra is a result of the merger in 1991 of Australia's domestic telecommunications company, Telecom Australia, and Australia's international telecommunications services provider, OTC Ltd. Until 1991 Telecom Australia and OTC Ltd. had exclusive mandates in the domestic and international services, respectively.

Telus. Holding company of AGT Ltd., a telephone company throughout the province of Alberta, Canada, except for the city of Edmonton, AGT Ldt., Canada's third largest telecommunications carrier, was privatized in 1990 and is a member of the Stentor consortium.

terms of trade. The ratio of the index of export prices to the index of import prices. When export prices rise faster than import prices, a country experiences an improvement in its terms of trade.

Time Telecommunications Berhad. Malaysian telecommunications company which is part of the Renong Group, and which has and operates a fiber-optic cable alongside Malaysia's new North-South Expressway.

TLD (Telefónica Larga Distancia de Puerto Rico Inc.). The international telecommunications service provider in Puerto Rico, which is 79% owned (through a holding company) by Telefónica de España, the Spanish monopoly telecommunications services provider, and 19% by the Puerto Rico Telephone Company, the monopoly local exchange carrier. TLD is authorized to provide international telephone, television, and business services.

toll network. See **long-distance.**

toll office (U.S.). A long-distance switching center.

tort law. Civil liability with respect to harms.

TOT (Telephone Organization of Thailand). The state-owned monopoly provider of domestic telephone services, operating under the Telephone Organization of Thailand Act of 1954. Also provides cellular mobile and digital paging services as well as international services to neighboring countries. See also CAT.

traffic-sensitive costs. Costs which vary as a function of traffic volumes. They include investment and operating costs (including depreciation and return on investment) associated with telephone company facilities, and vary in aggregate quantity with the volume of calls (and other measures of traffic) handled by the telephone system. Also included are the costs associated with common switching facilities in the local central office (end office), interoffice trunks (which connect several end offices either directly or via an intermediate switching point), and intermediate or tandem switching systems used to route calls.

transfer price. The price charged for goods and services when a unit, subsidiary, or affiliate of a company supplies those goods and services to another unit, subsidiary, or affiliate of the same company. Such prices are of concern to fiscal authorities in the countries where such a company operates because prices can be set artificially by the company in order to minimize its overall taxes.

transparency. In a technical sense, the property of a digital transmission channel, telecommunications circuit, or connection that permits any digital signal to be conveyed without change to the value or order of any signal elements. In the context of trade, transparency refers to openness in decisionmaking, to rendering intelligible and accessible the laws, policies, rules, and regulations that govern trade, applied not only to the formulation for prior notification and consultation but also to their implementation through existing regulatory authority.

Treaty of Rome. Treaty establishing the European Economic Community, signed in 1957 in Rome by the representatives of the six initial member states.

TRI (Technology Resource Industries Berhad). A Malaysian holding company, which provides mobile cellular services (E-TACS 900) through its Celcom subsidiary. TRI has obtained an international gateway license.

trunk. A circuit between two telephone exchanges or switching centers, or from an exchange to a customer's switchboard. A circuit capable of being switched at both ends and provided with the necessary terminating and signaling equipment. Called *toll* in the U.S.

trunked radio system. A method of operation in which a number of radio frequency channel pairs are assigned to mobile and base stations in the system for use as a trunk group.

TT&T (Thai Telephone & Telecommunications). A joint venture between Loxley Bangkok, Jasmine International, and NTT to install 1 million telephone lines in the provincial areas outside of Bangkok.

Type I. Class of Japanese telecommunications operators and service providers that own their facilities.

Type II. Class of Japanese telecommunications operators and service providers that lease facilities from Type I carriers to provide service to the public.

type approval. Approval of a specific manufacturer and type of equipment. Some regulatory bodies and telephone companies require that telecommunications equipment meet specific technical performance criteria. Once these criteria have been met and demonstrated, type approval is granted for its general use in their jurisdiction.

UMC (Ukrainian Mobile Communications). A joint venture of PTT Telecom Netherlands, Deutsche Bundespost Telekom, Telecom Denmark, and the Ukrainian government to build and operate a mobile telecommunications network in the 21 largest cities of the Ukraine.

unbundled tariffs. Tariffs in which each component of a communications service or product (called a basic service element by the FCC in its Computer II decision) is priced separately, so that customers may select only those components needed and be charged accordingly.

UNDP (United Nations Development Program). A branch of the UN that finances technical assistance and related investments for economic and social development. For example, many successful national and regional telecommunications training centers have been established and initially operated in developing countries using UNDP funds administered by the ITU.

Unisource. A joint venture among PTT Telecom Netherlands, Telia AB of Sweden, and the Swiss PTT to provide outsourcing for large multinational corporations, i.e. to manage customers' private networks, including virtual private networks for voice and data as well as packet-switched data and value added networks.

Unitel Communications Incorporated. A Canadian telecommunications operator formerly known as CNCP Telecommunications, owned by Canadian

Pacific Limited (48%), Rogers Communications (32%), and AT&T (20%). As a result of CRTC's Decision 92-12 in June 1992, Unitel has been permitted to offer public long-distance telecommunications services in competition with the Stentor companies, the established Canadian regional long-distance carriers. Unitel previously had been able to offer data, telex, and other private voice services.

universal personal telecommunications (UPT). A service that enables access to telecommunications services by allowing personal mobility. UPT enables each user to participate in a user-defined set of subscribed services as well as to initiate and receive calls on the basis of a unique, personal, network-independent UPT number. It can be used across multiple networks at any fixed, movable, or mobile terminal regardless of geographical location. The only limitations are those resulting from terminal and network technical capabilities or restrictions imposed by the network provider.

universal service. The concept that every individual within a country should have basic telephone service available at an affordable price. The concept varies, among countries, from having a telephone in every home and business in the wealthier countries to most inhabitants' being within a certain distance or time away from a public telephone in developing countries.

usage-sensitive pricing (tariffs). A rate or price for telephone service based on the rate of utilization rather than a flat (fixed) periodic fee; often used in respect to some local services and called local measured service (LMS).

US West Inc.. One of the seven U.S. regional Bell operating companies (RBOCs) created by the AT&T divestiture in 1984. As of the end of 1991, US West's largest subsidiary, US West Communications, provided telecommunications services to more than 25 million residential and business customers in the 14 western and midwestern states of Arizona, Colorado, Idaho, Iowa, Minnesota, Montana, Nebraska, New Mexico, North Dakota, Oregon, South Dakota, Utah, Washington, and Wyoming. Additionally, a subsidiary serves more than 293,000 cellular telephone and 210,000 paging customers. US West has foreign joint ventures in cellular telephone packet data, cable TV, and telephone systems.

UTEL (Ukrainian Telecom). A joint venture of PTT Telecom Netherlands, Deutsche Bundespost Telekom, AT&T, and the Ukrainian government to establish, modernize, and operate the Ukraine's international telecommunications services as well as to install and manage a long-haul trunk network.

VAN (value added network). Communications network or system that is enhanced or has value added through data processing. A value added network

744

service provider will lease basic transmission channels from a common carrier, add intelligence, and then resell specialized services that are not available from the original carrier—such as computer-controlled switching, temporary data storage, error detection and correction, protocol conversion, electronic mail service, and videotex. See also **VAS**.

VAS (value added service). Telecommunications service which, in the course of the transmission of information between users, modifies the form of content of the information or defers its delivery. Value added services may be offered either within the network, using enhanced facilities of the network provider, or outside the network, by means of terminal equipment (e.g., the host computer of an independent service provider) connected to the network. The distinction between value added service and enhanced service is essentially geographic. *Value added service* is the prevalent term used in Europe, whereas *enhanced service* is commonly used in North America.

vertical integration. The undertaking by a single firm of successive stages in the process of production of a particular good or service.

VHF (very high frequency). The range of radio frequencies extending from 30 to 300 MHz.

videoconferencing. A two-way telecommunications service that allows live video images and speech of participants in a conference to be transmitted between two or more locations. Videoconferencing services generally require the digital transmission rate of T-1 (1.544 Mbps) or higher.

videotex. A generic term describing an interactive telecommunications system which conveys information by manipulating symbols, particularly text, for display on a video screen. These services provide data storage, retrieval, and processing. They combine customer premises query devices such as a typewriter keyboard or Touch-Tone pad, and a video display, such as a home TV set, that are linked by the public telephone network to a computerized data bank or other information source.

Vodafone. An operator of cellular radio, trunked private mobile radio, packet radio, and radio paging networks in the U.K. Vodafone is also involved in cellular operations in many other countries, including France, Sweden, India, and Australia, as well as Hong Kong.

voice mail. Message and storage service; the telephone equivalent of electronic mail.

VPN (virtual private network). A private network in which public-switched facilities are configured to provide a business with capabilities similar to those of a dedicated private network at a lower cost than would be entailed by leasing private lines. The circuits that are allocated dynamically to form a virtual private network are called virtual leased lines, virtual private lines, or virtual dedicated lines.

VSAT (very small aperture terminal). A class of very small aperture, intelligent satellite earth stations suitable for easy on-premise installation, usually operating in conjunction with a large-size hub earth station and capable of supporting a wide range of two-way, integrated telecommunications and information services, also sometimes known as micro/mini earth station, personal earth station, customer premise earth station, on-premise terminal, etc. VSAT earth stations have a typical antenna size of 1.8 meters to 0.8 meters. Able to transmit or receive in Ku-band, the VSAT is used for one- or two-way transmission of audio, video, or data signals. The small size of a VSAT makes it convenient for customer on-premise use. VSATs often are used to bypass the local telephone company.

VSNL (Videsh Sanchar Nigam Ltd.). An 85 percent state-owned corporation that provides international telecommunications services on an exclusive basis in India. VSNL is due to be partially floated on international markets in 1994.

VTR (Chile). A private consortium of Chilean and foreign investors that owns CNT (see above) and several specialized telecommunications operating companies in Chile. Originally VTR was a private company, partly owned by RCA, which provided international telex service in a few large cities in competition with the state telegraph monopoly (see Telex-Chile) and other foreign-owned private international telex operators. VTR provides international services in competition with ENTEL, Chilesat, and others.

WARC '92 (1992 World Administrative Radio Conference). An intergovernmental conference held under the auspices of the ITU in February 1992 in Torremolinos, Spain to achieve worldwide agreement on frequency allocations and other compatibility questions for all classes of radio communications and broadcasting.

WATS (wide-area telephone service). A nationwide long-distance telephone service in North America, in which users contract for high-volume circuit usage rather than paying for each call individually.

WATTC-88 (World Administrative Telegraph and Telephone Conference 1988). An intergovernmental conference held under the auspices of the ITU in December 1988 in Melbourne, Australia, to draft new international telecommunications regulations which took effect on July 1, 1990, and which provide the basic norms and administrative mechanisms for the existing and future international telecommunications network and services.

Westel. A joint venture between the U.S. regional Bell operating company (RBOC) US West and Hungarian Telecommunications Company (HTC) to provide NMT-450 cellular mobile services in Budapest.

WIK (Wissenschaftliches Institut für Kommunikationsdienste GmbH). A research institute located in Bad Honnef, Germany, associated with the enterprises of the Deutsche Bundespost and whose mission is to conduct research on economic and social issues in the areas of telecommunications, posts, and postal banking. The institute is funded primarily by the German government and the three enterprises of the Deutsche Bundespost (DBP Telekom, DBP Postdienst, DBP Postbank.)

whipsawing (U.S.). In an environment in which a carrier from one country negotiates and interconnects with several carriers in another country, the ability of the single carrier to play one of the other country's carriers against the other(s) in order to enhance its position. Whipsawing is used to increase an accounting rate by promising or threatening to increase or decrease return flow traffic.

white paper. A detailed policy statement published by the U.K. government which usually precedes legislation. For example, in March 1991 the Secretary of State for Trade and Industry presented to Parliament a white paper entitled *Competition and Choice: Telecommunications Policy for the 1990s.* It effectively ended the government's duopoly policy which had been in place since 1980.

World Partners. An international alliance formed in 1993 by some of the world's largest telecommunications corporations. Initiated by AT&T (which remains the lead member), it will cater to the full range of telecommunications needs of multinational corporations. Members include KDD (Japan's main international telecommunications carrier), Singapore Telecom, Telstra of Australia, and Korea Telecom.

Contributors

ROBERT R. BRUCE is a partner in the London office of the law firm of Debevoise & Plimpton. Earlier he had been General Counsel of the U.S. Federal Communications Commission and Director of Communications Planning for the Public Broadcasting Service. Mr. Bruce has a JD degree from Harvard Law School and an MPA from Harvard University. He has written numerous articles on communications law and policy, and he coauthored *From Telecommunications to Electronic Services* (1986) and *The Telecom Mosaic* (1988).

CARLOS CASASÚS is Chief Executive Officer of the Mexico City water authority. Before that he worked for sixteen years in TELMEX, was its Chief Financial Officer at the time of privatization, and represented TELMEX in the drafting of the new Mexican telecommunications regulations and the company's license. Mr. Casasús has a degree in business administration from Universidad Iberoamericana and an MBA from Harvard University. He teaches business policy at the Instituto Tecnológico Autónomo de México.

JOHN J. COLLINGS is a partner in the London office of Coopers & Lybrand. He has led telecommunications restructuring and regulatory projects in sixteen countries in Europe, Latin America, and Asia. In 1986–87 he was the Commercial Regulation Adviser in British Telecom, responsible for corporate pricing policies, interconnection policies, and regulatory analysis. His early career was in university teaching and as a government economic adviser. He holds DPhil and BA degrees from the University of Sussex.

PETER F. COWHEY is Professor at the University of California at San Diego in the Department of Political Science and the Graduate School of International Relations and Pacific Studies. His main interest is in regulation and competition in international telecommunications. Mr. Cowhey coauthored *When Countries Talk: International Trade in Telecommunications Services; Changing Networks: Mexico's Options for Telecommunications Reform;* and *Managing the World's Economy: The Consequences of International Corporate Alliances.*

JEFFREY P. CUNARD is a partner in the Washington, DC, office of the law firm of Debevoise & Plimpton. He has degrees in English and political science from the University of California at Los Angeles and a JD from the Yale Law School. Mr. Cunard has written various articles on communications law and intellectual property, and is a coauthor of *From Telecommunications to Electronic Services* (1986) and *The Telecom Mosaic* (1988).

HUNTER DONALDSON is General Manager of the New Zealand Ministry of Commerce's Communications Division, which is responsible for advising the government on all aspects of broadcasting policy and for managing the radio spectrum. Previously he was General Manager of the Competition Policy and Business Law Division, Assistant Secretary for Business Competition and Corporate Affairs, and Trade Commissioner and First Secretary (Commercial) in Tokyo. Mr. Donaldson has a BCom in economics and business management.

HENRY ERGAS is a Counsellor for Structural Policy in the Economics Department of the Organization for Economic Cooperation and Development. In various positions at the OECD he has been responsible for studies on telecommunications policy, structural adjustment, and various aspects of international trade. Mr. Ergas has also been a professor in the Faculty of Economics and Commerce of Monash University, Melbourne. He studied economics at the Universities of Queensland, Sussex, and Oxford.

DOMINIQUE GARNIER is head of the international relations division of the Forecast and Studies Department of the Directorate for General Regulation in the French Ministry of Posts and Telecommunications. His division deals essentially with all bilateral relations with countries outside of the European Community as well as with issues related to the International Telecommunications Union. He has a Licence-ès-Sciences in mathematics and an engineering degree from the École Nationale Supérieur des Postes et Télécommunications.

FRANÇOIS J. GROSSAS is a Senior Investment Officer in the Capital Markets Department of the International Finance Corporation in Washington, DC. Earlier, he was responsible for IFC business development in telecommunications, computers, and electronics. Earlier, Mr. Grossas was Vice President for Latin American Trade Finance at the Chase Manhattan Bank of New York. He graduated in economics and political science from the Institut d'Études Politiques of Paris, and has an MBA from the University of Michigan.

CHRISTOPHER M. HARLAND is Principal in Morgan Stanley's Corporate Finance Department, with responsibility for telecommunications. Previously he was in charge of Morgan Stanley's high technology effort in the eastern United States and had been a lending officer with the Chase Manhattan Bank. Mr. Harland graduated from Harvard College, attended Oxford University, and received an MBA from the Harvard Business School.

KRISZTINA HELLER is special adviser to the Senior Executive Vice President of the Hungarian Telecommunications Company. Previously she was involved in preparing the new Hungarian telecommunications legislation and regulation at the Hungarian Ministry of Transport, Communications and Watermanagement. Ms. Heller had been Deputy Director of the Research Institute of the Hungarian PTT. She has a PhD from the Hungarian National Academy and degrees from the University of Economics in Budapest.

ERIC HURET is Deputy Director at the French Ministry of Posts and Telecommunications, in charge of the economic and strategic supervision of France Télécom. From 1980 to 1991 he worked for France Télécom, where he was involved in the launching of France's videotex service before becoming the Marketing Director, Business Customers. Earlier Mr. Huret was an adviser to various ministers and Administrator of the Institut National de Statistiques et d'Études Économiques. He is an engineering graduate of the École Polytechnique.

SYED HUSSEIN MOHAMED is Executive Director and Chief Operating Officer of Telekom Malaysia Berhad. He had joined the government's Telecommunications Department, then moved to the private sector, and later became deeply involved in the privatization of telecommunications that led to restructuring and partially privatizing telecommunications operations. He has a BSc (Eng) from the University of London as well as MSc and PhD degrees in statistics and quality control engineering.

MICHAEL J. HUTCHINSON is Deputy Secretary (Communications) in Australia's Department of Transport and Communications, with responsibility for communications policy and operational matters. Earlier, he led the privatization of AUSSAT, advised on the merger of Telecom Australia and OTC, and helped develop new government policies on telecommunications and corporatization of state enterprises. Mr. Hutchinson holds a BSc in civil engineering from the University of Newcastle upon Tyne, United Kingdom.

LOTHAR A. KNEIFEL is an associate in the Washington, DC, office of Debevoise & Plimpton. He is a member of the Bar Association of the District of Columbia and the German American Law Association, and he practices primarily in the area of communications law. Mr. Kneifel has a BS in English and political science from the University of Maryland and a JD from Georgetown University Law Center.

BRUCE LAIDLAW is an independent consultant specializing in telecommunications policy and management. He has advised on sector restructuring and privatization in over a dozen countries worldwide, and is an influential commentator on the British government's privatization program. Mr. Laidlaw was for twelve years an economic adviser in the U.K. civil service, where he played an active part in the telecommunications liberalization and the privatization of British Telecom. Mr. Laidlaw holds a MSc degree in economics from the London School of Economics.

DEAN LEWIS is an Investment Officer at the International Finance Corporation in Washington, DC. For ten years he had been involved in corporatization and privatization policy and transactions in New Zealand and Eastern Europe, including management positions in a merchant bank and adviser to the Minister of Finance during the early development of privatization of New Zealand's state enterprises.

HECTOR A. MAIRAL is a partner in the Buenos Aires law firm of Marval, O'Farrell & Mairal. He was counsel for the Argentine government in the privatization of ENTel and the state gas company. Mr. Mairal is a frequent guest speaker at local and international law conferences. His published books include *Control Judicial de la Administracion Publica*. Mr. Mairal has a doctorate in law from Universidad Nacional de Buenos Aires, where he has been Professor of Administrative Law since 1965.

DONALD MASON is with the U.K. Office of Fair Trading. Until recently he was Head of the Private Networks and International Section of OFTEL. In this capacity he was involved with the development of telecommunications regulatory policy both in the United Kingdom and the European Community and had frequent contact with countries all over the world interested in the U.K. experience. He has a degree in physics and a doctorate in history.

FRANCESCO MASSARI is Director of Corporate International Marketing of STET, Italy, where he is responsible for international projects in Europe, the newly industrialized countries, and the developing countries of Africa, Asia, and Latin America. He is also a member of the board of Consultel, STET's consulting company for telecommunications and electronics. Mr. Massari has degrees from the University of Rome and the Bocconi University in Milan.

JOSÉ RICARDO MELO is Professor of Telecommunications Systems at Universidad de Chile. He has been an adviser to the Chilean telecommunications ministry since 1982 as well as a consultant to Chilean telecommunications companies and to the telecommunications administrations of Ecuador, Venezuela, and Poland. Mr. Melo has an electrical engineering degree from Universidad de Chile and did graduate studies in economics at Universidad Catolica de Chile and in telecommunications in Germany and Japan.

NICHOLAS P. MILLER is a partner in the Washington, DC, law firm of Miller & Holbrooke. Earlier he was an adviser to the White House staff and the Office of Telecommunications Policy as well as communications counsel to the Senate Commerce Committee. Mr. Miller has written articles on the legal, policy, and regulatory aspects of domestic and international telecommunications and cable television. He has a JD degree from the University of Washington.

JÜRGEN MÜLLER is Affiliate Professor of the Berlin Program of Stanford University and Visiting Research Professor of Industrial Organization at INSEAD, Fontainebleau. He has been involved in industrial economics and competition policy studies as well as teaching in universities and research institutions in Canada, France, Germany, and the United Kingdom. Mr. Muller's publications include *Concentration in West Germany* (1974), *Governmental Regulation* (1979), *Lessons from Deregulation* (1984), and *European Telecommunications Organizations* (1989).

KARL-HEINZ NEUMANN is Director of the Wissenschaftliches Institut für Kommunikationsdienste, the German telecommunications research institute, and a member of the Posts and Telecommunications Minister's advisory council on regulation and competition. Mr. Neumann participated in several committees that helped restructure posts and telecommunications in Germany in 1985–89. He has a PhD in economics from the University of Bonn and has written extensively on telecommunications policy, economics, and pricing theory.

TIMOTHY E. NULTY is the principal telecommunications economist at the International Finance Corporation in Washington, DC. Before that he was a senior telecommunications economist at the World Bank and chief economist of the House

Energy and Commerce Committee of the U.S. Congress and the U.S. Senate Commerce Committee. Earlier Mr. Nulty worked in East Africa and Pakistan, taught economics at Durham and Oxford Universities, and was chief economist of the United Auto Workers. He has a PhD in economics from Cambridge University.

EMILIA NYEVRIKEL is with the Department of Strategic Planning of the Hungarian Telecommunications Company (HTC), and previously was with HTC's research institute. She has been involved in telecommunications regulatory reform and institutional development in Hungary, demand studies, and comparative analysis of telecommunications infrastructures in Eastern Europe. Ms. Nyevrikel has a PhD from the University of Budapest.

JUDITH D. O'NEILL is the international telecommunications partner of the Washington, DC, law firm of Steptoe & Johnson. She has represented public and private interests in international transactions in Mexico, Venezuela, Argentina, Chile, Poland, Czechoslovakia, and other countries. Ms. O'Neill founded and is president of the Telecommunications Section of the InterAmerican Bar Association. She has BA and MA degrees from the American University and Universidad de Madrid, and a JD from the University of Baltimore.

JOSEPH E. PILCHER is Regional Director of New Business (West) for Cable & Wireless plc, with responsibility for business development in the Americas. Previously, Mr. Pilcher was General Manager for Corporate Business Development and Manager of Strategic Studies. He is a chartered engineer with an honors degree in electronic engineering design and production.

AILEEN A. PISCIOTTA is International Telecommunications Counsel for the law firm of Latham & Watkins in Washington, DC. Earlier positions include Special Assistant to the FCC's Common Carrier Bureau Chief, Assistant Director for Economic Policy of the Alaska Governor's Office of Telecommunications, and public utility specialist at the U.S. Department of Justice. Mrs. Pisciotta has BA and MA degrees from the University of Pennsylvania and a JD from the Georgetown University Law Center.

PETER R. SCHERER is Division Chief in the World Bank for Energy and Industry in the East Asia and Pacific Region. In his previous position, Mr. Scherer managed the World Bank's technical assistance to the Argentine government in privatizing the state telecommunications, petroleum, gas, and railways enterprises. Earlier he was in private industry and academia in the United

States, Europe, and Latin America. Mr. Scherer has degrees in economics from the J. W. Goethe University in Frankfurt and the Wharton School of the University of Pennsylvania.

THOMAS SCHNÖRING is Deputy Director of the Wissenschaftliches Institute für Kommunikationsdienste, the German telecommunications research institute, and head of the Department of Market Structure and Technology. His research focuses on innovation, market structure, economic development, and regional policy questions in telecommunications and on assessment of information and telecommunications technologies. Mr. Schnöring holds a PhD in economics from the University of Kiel.

RICHARD J. SCHULTZ is Professor of Political Science and former Director of the Centre for the Study of Regulated Industries at McGill University in Montreal. He has been a member of a government advisory group on the Canada–U.S. Free Trade and GATT Uruguay Round negotiations. Mr. Schultz has published extensively, most recently on lessons from Canada on privatization, deregulation, and the changing role of the state. He has an MA in economics from Manchester University and a PhD from York University, Toronto.

PETER A. STERN is Director, Government & International Affairs, at Teleglobe, Inc. in Montreal, with responsibility for policy analysis on international and domestic regulatory and commercial issues. Mr. Stern is Canada's representative on the Commonwealth Telecommunications Council. Earlier experience includes engineering research in Germany and France. Mr. Stern coedited *Restructuring and Managing the Telecommunications Sector* (1989). He has a BSc in electrical engineering from the University of Toronto, a PhD from the Université de Paris, and an MA in economics from Concordia University, Montreal.

DAVID N. TOWNSEND is Vice President (Research) of Economics and Technology, Inc., a Boston consulting firm. He has conducted analyses on behalf of government agencies and private interests of several countries, in the areas of telephone network costs and market structure, regulation and development initiatives, tariff policies, and carrier operating performance. He has been Lecturer in Communication at Boston University. Mr. Townsend holds a Master of Public Policy from Harvard University.

HYDE TUCKER was President and Chief Executive Officer of Bell Atlantic International, Inc. Prior to that he was Vice President, Operations, and Chief

Operating Officer of the C&P Telephone Company, serving nine million customers in the mid-Atlantic United States. Earlier experience includes positions with AT&T and four years with the U.S. Air Force. Mr. Tucker holds a BS in electrical engineering from Virginia Polytechnical Institute and attended management programs at the Universities of Virginia and Illinois.

HERBERT UNGERER is head of the Regulatory Analysis and Sector Studies Division of the Telecommunications Policy Directorate in the EC Commission. In this position he was responsible for drafting the EC Commission's Green Papers on developing the common European market for telecommunications services and equipment (1987) and on satellite communications, as well as for developing the EC Commission's policies on ISDN, digital mobile communications, and other telecommunications issues.

DAN VALLIMARESCU is in the International Emerging Markets group of Merrill Lynch in New York. He was with the International Securities Division of the International Finance Corporation in Washington, DC. He has helped structure, underwrite, and place international equity offerings, primarily for Latin American companies. Mr. Vallimarescu was a Vice President with the Bank of Boston, where he worked for almost ten years in commercial and investment banking positions in Boston, Madrid, London, and Paris. He holds a BA from Harvard College and an MBA from INSEAD.

GERARD J. VAN VELZEN is Executive Vice President and member of the management board of PTT Telecom Netherlands. He is also a director in several subsidiary companies that provide value added services, and had been deputy senior director responsible for the introduction of a new market orientation of PTT Telecom. Earlier experience included microwave and satellite communications projects as well as developing mobile telephone and radiopaging in the Benelux countries.

PAUL WATERSCHOOT is with the EC Commission in Brussels, where he has held several positions at the level of director. He was responsible for promoting competition in electricity and other industries, monitoring state subsidies to the shipbuilding, paper, and pulp industries, and undertaking policy work on tourism and the social sectors. As a Brookings Institution fellow, Mr. Waterschoot worked on regulation of the U.S. posts, telecommunications, and electricity distribution.

DESMOND WATKINS was Citibank's Managing Director of Equity Invest- ments in charge of restructuring of government debt and investments in the private sector. Earlier he was Director of Shell International Petroleum Company and regional coordinator for the Western hemisphere and Africa, with responsibility for some fifty countries. Mr. Watkins is Visiting Professor of International Manage- ment at the European School of Management. He graduated in law from Keble College Oxford, where he is a Fellow.

VERNON WATSON was Chairman of Sri Lanka Telecom, the company that took over operations from the Department of Telecommunications, where he had held senior management positions. Mr. Watson also was head of the Telecommu- nications Division of the Malawi PTT, and later became its Postmaster General. He has a science degree from the University of Ceylon and a degree in electrical engineering from the University of London.

BJÖRN WELLENIUS is principal telecommunications specialist with the World Bank in Washington, DC, for which he has worked in some forty countries worldwide on telecommunications sector and project analysis, policy reform, and restructuring. He was Professor of Telecommunications Systems at Universidad de Chile in Santiago. Mr. Wellenius is coauthor of *Telecommunications and Economic Development* (1983), *Restructuring and Managing the Telecommunications Sector* (1989), and *Developing the Electronics Industry* (1993). He has a PhD from the University of Essex, England, and an electrical engineering degree from Univer- sidad de Chile.

GW01191153

Who's Who in the World

Biographical Titles Currently Published by Marquis Who's Who

Who's Who in America
Who's Who in America derivatives:
  Geographic/Professional Index
  Supplement to Who's Who in America
  Who's Who in America Classroom Project Book
Who Was Who in America
  Historical Volume (1607-1896)
  Volume I (1897-1942)
  Volume II (1943-1950)
  Volume III (1951-1960)
  Volume IV (1961-1968)
  Volume V (1969-1973)
  Volume VI (1974-1976)
  Volume VII (1977-1981)
  Volume VIII (1982-1985)
  Index Volume (1607-1985)
Who's Who in the World
Who's Who in the East
Who's Who in the Midwest
Who's Who in the South and Southwest
Who's Who in the West
Who's Who in American Law
Who's Who of American Women
Who's Who of Emerging Leaders in America
Who's Who in Entertainment
Who's Who in Finance and Industry
Index to Who's Who Books
Directory of Medical Specialists
Supplement to Directory of Medical Specialists

Who's Who
in the World®

9th edition
1989-1990

MARQUIS

Who'sWho

Macmillan Directory Division
3002 Glenview Road
Wilmette, Illinois 60091 U.S.A.

James J. Pfister—President
Paul E. Rose—Executive Vice President
Timothy J. Sullivan—Vice President, Finance
A. Robert Weicherding—Vice President, Publisher
Sandra S. Barnes—Group Vice President, Product Management
Jill E. Lazar—Product Manager

Library of Congress Catalog Card Number 79–139215
International Standard Book Number 0–8379–1109–5
Product Code Number 030508

Distributed in Asia by
United Publishers Services Ltd.
Kenkyu-Sha Bldg.
9, Kanda Surugadai 2-Chome
Chiyoda-ku, Tokyo, Japan

Manufactured in the United States of America

Table of Contents

Preface

Biographical information on important individuals from virtually every nation is presented in the ninth edition of *Who's Who in the World*. With approximately 29,500 sketches, the volume addresses an increasing need for coverage of internationally noteworthy persons. The updated criteria for selection assure timeliness and broad scope in the many areas of endeavor included.

The book contains comprehensive coverage in both the variety of areas of reference interest and in the number of persons within each field. Incumbency in rapidly changing governmental positions, especially among key national leaders, was revised until the book went to press to provide the most up-to-date information available. The standard for religion contains leaders for denominations throughout the world. Coverage of business leaders is broad in its many positions and worldwide scope. Careful research has assured global inclusion of key scholars, scientists, and educators. Similarly, the criteria for inclusion for medicine, publishing and broadcasting, international associations, performing arts, and many other areas cover every country.

Selection of a name for inclusion in *Who's Who in the World* is based on reference value. Some individuals become eligible for listing because of position, while others have distinguished themselves through notable achievements in their fields. Many of the listees qualify by virtue of both position and occupational attainments.

In the editorial evaluation that resulted in the ultimate selection of the names in this directory, an individual's desire to be listed was not sufficient reason for inclusion; rather, it was the person's achievement that ruled. Similarly, wealth or social position was not a criterion; only occupational stature or achievement influenced selection.

In most cases, biographees have furnished their own data, thus assuring a high degree of accuracy. In some cases where individuals of great reference interest failed to supply information, Marquis staff members compiled the data through careful, independent research. Sketches compiled in this manner are denoted by an asterisk. As in previous editions, biographees were given the opportunity to review prepublication proofs of their sketches to make sure they were correct.

In an effort to make this reference volume as useful as possible, researchers have attempted to standardize the English spellings and alphabetizing of names originating in non-Roman alphabets. Arabic names, for example, have a variety of spellings when transposed to English. However, spelling is always based on the practice of each biographee, whether or not it is compatible with general rules. Some biographees use a western form of Arabic word order, while others prefer the Arabic word sequence. Alphabetizing of Arabic names is described under Alphabetical Practices (page xiv).

Similarly, Chinese names generally have no comma between family and given names, but some biographees have chosen to add the comma. In each case, punctuation follows the preference of the biographee. Where more than one spelling or word order of a name is frequently encountered—in the press, for example—the sketch has been entered under the form preferred by the biographee, with cross references under alternate forms.

In assembling this comprehensive world reference source, Marquis Who's Who editors and researchers have exercised diligent care in the preparation of each biographical sketch. Despite all precautions, however, errors occasionally occur. Users of this directory are invited to draw the attention of the publisher to such errors so that corrections can be made in a subsequent edition.

The ninth edition of *Who's Who in the World* continues the tradition of excellence established in 1899 with the publication of the first edition of *Who's Who in America*. The essence of that tradition is the continuing effort at Marquis Who's Who to produce reference works that are responsive to the needs of their users.

Standards of Admission

The foremost consideration in determining possible biographees for *Who's Who in the World* is the extent of an individual's reference value, as determined by either of two factors: (1) the position of responsibility held, or (2) the level of achievement attained by the individual.

Admission based on the factor of position includes the following examples:

Heads of state and other key government officials

High-ranking military officers

Chief justices of the highest national courts

Principal officers of selected international business organizations and corporations

Chief executive officers of major universities and colleges

Selected members of national academies of science and academies in the humanities

Heads of international and national health organizations

Directors of major national cultural, educational, and scientific organizations, such as museums, opera companies, libraries, and research institutes

Admission for individual achievement is based on objective qualitative criteria. To be selected, a person must have attained significant achievement, and may be widely recognized in some field of endeavor for noteworthy accomplishment.

Key to Information

[1] CARLSSON, MATS, [2] banker; [3] b. Uppsala, Sweden, Aug. 22, 1919; [4] s. Lars Odvar and Ingrid (Lindblad) C.; [5] m. Sigrid Søderstrom, Oct. 10, 1947; [6] children: Eric, Gunnar. [7] Grad. Umeå U., 1939. [8] Chartered Accountant. [9] Supervising acct. Svenskabanken, Stockholm, 1948-59, asst. v.p. 1959-61, v.p., 1961-72, pres., chief exec. officer, 1972-81, chmn. bd, 1981—, chmn. exec. com., 1987—; dir. Staatsbank, Zürich, Switzerland, Bekaert-Belgium, Brussels, Barrère et Cie., Paris; adj. prof. Stockholms Universitet, 1975—. [10] Author: Studies in World Monetary Balance, 1982, Common Market Strategies for the Nineties, 1988. [11] Mem. Riksdag, 1965-75; mem. Mayor's Com. Environ. Control, Stockholm, 1977—, chmn., 1980-81, bd. dirs. Stockholm Trade Fair. [12] Served with Swedish Army, 1939-45. [13] Decorated Great Cross of Merit. [14] Mem. Swedish Bankers Assn. [15] Christian Democrat. [16] Protestant. [17] Club: City. [18] Lodge: Rotary (Stockholm). [19] Avocations: reading, opera, photography. [20] Home: Strandvægen 85, 115 27 Stockholm, Sweden also Sønderborg, Denmark [21] Office: Svenskabanken, Blasieholmstorg 15, 103 28 Stockholm, Sweden

KEY

[1]	Name
[2]	Occupation
[3]	Vital statistics
[4]	Parents
[5]	Marriage
[6]	Children
[7]	Education
[8]	Professional certifications
[9]	Career
[10]	Writings and creative works
[11]	Civic and political activities
[12]	Military
[13]	Awards and fellowships
[14]	Professional and association memberships
[15]	Political affiliation
[16]	Religion
[17]	Clubs
[18]	Lodges
[19]	Avocations
[20]	Home address
[21]	Office address

Table of Abbreviations

The following abbreviations and symbols are frequently used in this book.

*An asterisk following a sketch indicates that it was researched by the Marquis Who's Who editorial staff and has not been verified by the biographee.

AA, A.A. Associate in Arts
AAAL American Academy of Arts and Letters
AAAS American Association for the Advancement of Science
AAHPER Alliance for Health, Physical Education and Recreation
AAU Amateur Athletic Union
AAUP American Association of University Professors
AAUW American Association of University Women
AB, A.B. Arts, Bachelor of
AB Alberta
ABA American Bar Association
ABC American Broadcasting Company
AC Air Corps
acad. academy, academic
acct. accountant
acctg. accounting
ACDA Arms Control and Disarmament Agency
ACLU American Civil Liberties Union
ACP American College of Physicians
ACS American College of Surgeons
ADA American Dental Association
a.d.c. aide-de-camp
adj. adjunct, adjutant
adj. gen. adjutant general
adm. admiral
adminstr. administrator
adminstrn. administration
adminstrv. administrative
ADP Automatic Data Processing
adv. advocate, advisory
advt. advertising
AE, A.E. Agricultural Engineer
A.E. and P. Ambassador Extraordinary and Plenipotentiary
AEC Atomic Energy Commission
aero. aeronautical, aeronautic
aerodyn. aerodynamic
AFB Air Force Base
AFL–CIO American Federation of Labor and Congress of Industrial Organizations
AFTRA American Federation of TV and Radio Artists
agr. agriculture
agrl. agricultural
agt. agent
AGVA American Guild of Variety Artists
agy. agency
A&I Agricultural and Industrial
AIA American Institute of Architects
AIAA American Institute of Aeronautics and Astronautics
AID Agency for International Development
AIEE American Institute of Electrical Engineers
AIM American Institute of Management
AIME American Institute of Mining, Metallurgy, and Petroleum Engineers
AK Alaska
AL Alabama
ALA American Library Association
Ala. Alabama
alt. alternate
Alta. Alberta
A&M Agricultural and Mechanical
AM, A.M. Arts, Master of
Am. American, America

AMA American Medical Association
A.M.E. African Methodist Episcopal
Amtrak National Railroad Passenger Corporation
AMVETS American Veterans of World War II, Korea, Vietnam
anat. anatomical
ann. annual
ANTA American National Theatre and Academy
anthrop. anthropological
AP Associated Press
APO Army Post Office
apptd. appointed
Apr. April
apt. apartment
AR Arkansas
ARC American Red Cross
archeol. archeological
archtl. architectural
Ariz. Arizona
Ark. Arkansas
ArtsD, ArtsD. Arts, Doctor of
arty. artillery
AS American Samoa
AS Associate in Science
ASCAP American Society of Composers, Authors and Publishers
ASCE American Society of Civil Engineers
ASHRAE American Society of Heating, Refrigeration, and Air Conditioning Engineers
ASME American Society of Mechanical Engineers
assn. association
assoc. associate
asst. assistant
ASTM American Society for Testing and Materials
astron. astronomical
astrophys. astrophysical
ATSC Air Technical Service Command
AT&T American Telephone & Telegraph Company
atty. attorney
Aug. August
AUS Army of the United States
aux. auxiliary
Ave. Avenue
AVMA American Veterinary Medical Association
AZ Arizona

B. Bachelor
b. born
BA, B.A. Bachelor of Arts
BAgr, B.Agr. Bachelor of Agriculture
Balt. Baltimore
Bapt. Baptist
BArch, B.Arch. Bachelor of Architecture
BAS, B.A.S. Bachelor of Agricultural Science
BBA, B.B.A. Bachelor of Business Administration
BBC British Broadcasting Corporation
BC, B.C. British Columbia
BCE, B.C.E. Bachelor of Civil Engineering
BChir, B.Chir. Bachelor of Surgery
BCL, B.C.L. Bachelor of Civil Law
BCS, B.C.S. Bachelor of Commercial Science

BD, B.D. Bachelor of Divinity
bd. board
BE, B.E. Bachelor of Education
BEE, B.E.E. Bachelor of Electrical Engineering
BFA, B.F.A. Bachelor of Fine Arts
bibl. biblical
bibliog. bibliographical
biog. biographical
biol. biological
BJ, B.J. Bachelor of Journalism
Bklyn. Brooklyn
BL, B.L. Bachelor of Letters
bldg. building
BLS, B.L.S. Bachelor of Library Science
Blvd. Boulevard
bn. battalion
B.&O.R.R. Baltimore & Ohio Railroad
bot. botanical
BPE, B.P.E. Bachelor of Physical Education
BPhil, B.Phil. Bachelor of Philosophy
br. branch
BRE, B.R.E. Bachelor of Religious Education
brig. gen. brigadier general
Brit. British, Brittanica
Bros. Brothers
BS, B.S. Bachelor of Science
BSA, B.S.A. Bachelor of Agricultural Science
BSD, B.S.D. Bachelor of Didactic Science
BST, B.S.T. Bachelor of Sacred Theology
BTh, B.Th. Bachelor of Theology
bull. bulletin
bur. bureau
bus. business
B.W.I. British West Indies

CA California
CAA Civil Aeronautics Administration
CAB Civil Aeronautics Board
Calif. California
C.Am. Central America
Can. Canada, Canadian
CAP Civil Air Patrol
capt. captain
CARE Cooperative American Relief Everywhere
Cath. Catholic
cav. cavalry
CBC Canadian Broadcasting Company
CBI China, Burma, India Theatre of Operations
CBS Columbia Broadcasting System
CCC Commodity Credit Corporation
CCNY City College of New York
CCU Cardiac Care Unit
CD Civil Defense
CE, C.E. Corps of Engineers, Civil Engineer
cen. central
CENTO Central Treaty Organization
CERN European Organization of Nuclear Research
cert. certificate, certification, certified
CETA Comprehensive Employment Training Act
CFL Canadian Football League
ch. church
ChD, Ch.D. Doctor of Chemistry
chem. chemical
ChemE, Chem.E. Chemical Engineer

Chgo. Chicago
chirurg. chirurgical
chmn. chairman
chpt. chapter
CIA Central Intelligence Agency
CIC Counter Intelligence Corps
Cin. Cincinnati
cir. circuit
Cleve. Cleveland
climatol. climatological
clin. clinical
clk. clerk
C.L.U. Chartered Life Underwriter
CM, C.M. Master in Surgery
CM Northern Mariana Islands
C.&N.W.Ry. Chicago & North Western
   Railway
CO Colorado
Co. Company
COF Catholic Order of Foresters
C. of C. Chamber of Commerce
col. colonel
coll. college
Colo. Colorado
com. committee
comd. commanded
comdg. commanding
comdr. commander
comdt. commandant
commd. commissioned
comml. commercial
commn. commission
commr. commissioner
condr. conductor
Conf. Conference
Congl. Congregational, Congressional
Conglist. Congregationalist
Conn. Connecticut
cons. consultant, consulting
consol. consolidated
constl. constitutional
constn. constitution
constrn. construction
contbd. contributed
contbg. contributing
contbn. contribution
contbr. contributor
Conv. Convention
coop. cooperative
CORDS Civil Operations and
   Revolutionary Development Support
CORE Congress of Racial Equality
corp. corporation, corporate
corr. correspondent, corresponding,
   correspondence
C.&O.Ry. Chesapeake & Ohio Railway
CPA, C.P.A. Certified Public Accountant
C.P.C.U. Chartered Property and
   Casualty Underwriter
CPH, C.P.H. Certificate of Public Health
cpl. corporal
C.P.R. Cardio-Pulmonary Resuscitation
C.P.Ry. Canadian Pacific Railway
C.S. Christian Science
CSB, C.S.B. Bachelor of Christian Science
C.S.C. Civil Service Commission
CSD, C.S.D. Doctor of Christian Science
CT Connecticut
ct. court
ctr. center
CWS Chemical Warfare Service
C.Z. Canal Zone

D. Doctor
d. daughter
DAgr, D.Agr. Doctor of Agriculture

DAR Daughters of the American
   Revolution
dau. daughter
DAV Disabled American Veterans
DC, D.C. District of Columbia
DCL, D.C.L. Doctor of Civil Law
DCS, D.C.S. Doctor of Commercial Science
DD, D.D. Doctor of Divinity
DDS, D.D.S. Doctor of Dental Surgery
DE Delaware
Dec. December
dec. deceased
def. defense
Del. Delaware
del. delegate, delegation
Dem. Democrat, Democratic
DEng, D.Eng. Doctor of Engineering
denom. denomination, denominational
dep. deputy
dept. department
dermatol. dermatological
desc. descendant
devel. development, developmental
DFA, D.F.A. Doctor of Fine Arts
D.F.C. Distinguished Flying Cross
DHL, D.H.L. Doctor of Hebrew Literature
dir. director
dist. district
distbg. distributing
distbn. distribution
distbr. distributor
disting. distinguished
div. division, divinity, divorce
DLitt, D.Litt. Doctor of Literature
DMD, D.M.D. Doctor of Medical Dentistry
DMS, D.M.S. Doctor of Medical Science
DO, D.O. Doctor of Osteopathy
DPH, D.P.H. Diploma in Public Health
DPhil, D.Phil. Doctor of Philosophy
D.R. Daughters of the Revolution
Dr. Drive, Doctor
DRE, D.R.E. Doctor of Religious Education
DrPH, Dr.P.H. Doctor of Public Health,
   Doctor of Public Hygiene
D.S.C. Distinguished Service Cross
DSc, D.Sc. Doctor of Science
D.S.M. Distinguished Service Medal
DST, D.S.T. Doctor of Sacred Theology
DTM, D.T.M. Doctor of Tropical Medicine
DVM, D.V.M. Doctor of Veterinary
   Medicine
DVS, D.V.S. Doctor of Veterinary Surgery

E. East
ea. eastern
E. and P. Extraordinary and Plenipotentiary
Eccles. Ecclesiastical
ecol. ecological
econ. economic
ECOSOC Economic and Social Council
   (of the UN)
ED, E.D. Doctor of Engineering
ed. educated
EdB, Ed.B. Bachelor of Education
EdD, Ed.D. Doctor of Education
edit. edition
EdM, Ed.M. Master of Education
edn. education
ednl. educational
EDP Electronic Data Processing
EdS, Ed.S. Specialist in Education
EE, E.E. Electrical Engineer
E.E. and M.P. Envoy Extraordinary and
   Minister Plenipotentiary
EEC European Economic Community
EEG Electroencephalogram

EEO Equal Employment Opportunity
EEOC Equal Employment Opportunity
   Commission
E.Ger. German Democratic Republic
EKG Electrocardiogram
elec. electrical
electrochem. electrochemical
electrophys. electrophysical
elem. elementary
EM, E.M. Engineer of Mines
ency. encyclopedia
Eng. England
engr. engineer
engring. engineering
entomol. entomological
environ. environmental
EPA Environmental Protection Agency
epidemiol. epidemiological
Episc. Episcopalian
ERA Equal Rights Amendment
ERDA Energy Research and
   Development Administration
ESEA Elementary and Secondary
   Education Act
ESL English as Second Language
ESSA Environmental Science Services
   Administration
ethnol. ethnological
ETO European Theatre of Operations
Evang. Evangelical
exam. examination, examining
exec. executive
exhbn. exhibition
expdn. expedition
expn. exposition
expt. experiment
exptl. experimental

F.A. Field Artillery
FAA Federal Aviation Administration
FAO Food and Agriculture Organization
   (of the UN)
FBI Federal Bureau of Investigation
FCA Farm Credit Administration
FCC Federal Communications
   Commission
FCDA Federal Civil Defense
   Administration
FDA Food and Drug Administration
FDIA Federal Deposit Insurance
   Administration
FDIC Federal Deposit Insurance
   Corporation
FE, F.E. Forest Engineer
FEA Federal Energy Administration
Feb. February
fed. federal
fedn. federation
FERC Federal Energy Regulatory
   Commission
fgn. foreign
FHA Federal Housing Administration
fin. financial, finance
FL Florida
Fla. Florida
FMC Federal Maritime Commission
FOA Foreign Operations Administration
found. foundation
FPC Federal Power Commission
FPO Fleet Post Office
frat. fraternity
FRS Federal Reserve System
FSA Federal Security Agency
Ft. Fort
FTC Federal Trade Commission

G-1 (or other number) Division of
   General Staff

GA, Ga. Georgia
GAO General Accounting Office
gastroent. gastroenterological
GATT General Agreement of Tariff and
  Trades
gen. general
geneal. genealogical
geod. geodetic
geog. geographic, geographical
geol. geological
geophys. geophysical
gerontol. gerontological
G.H.Q. General Headquarters
G.N. Ry. Great Northern Railway
gov. governor
govt. government
govtl. governmental
GPO Government Printing Office
grad. graduate, graduated
GSA General Services Administration
Gt. Great
GU Guam
gynecol. gynecological

hdqrs. headquarters
HEW Department of Health, Education
  and Welfare
HHD, H.H.D. Doctor of Humanities
HHFA Housing and Home Finance
  Agency
HHS Department of Health and Human
  Services
HI Hawaii
hist. historical, historic
HM, H.M. Master of Humanics
homeo. homeopathic
hon. honorary, honorable
Ho. of Dels. House of Delegates
Ho. of Reps. House of Representatives
hort. horticultural
hosp. hospital
HUD Department of Housing and
  Urban Development
Hwy. Highway
hydrog. hydrographic

IA Iowa
IAEA International Atomic Energy
  Agency
IBM International Business Machines
  Corporation
IBRD International Bank for
  Reconstruction and Development
ICA International Cooperation
  Administration
ICC Interstate Commerce Commission
ICU Intensive Care Unit
ID Idaho
IEEE Institute of Electrical and
  Electronics Engineers
IFC International Finance Corporation
IGY International Geophysical Year
IL Illinois
Ill. Illinois
illus. illustrated
ILO International Labor Organization
IMF International Monetary Fund
IN Indiana
Inc. Incorporated
Ind. Indiana
ind. independent
Indpls. Indianapolis
indsl. industrial
inf. infantry
info. information
ins. insurance
insp. inspector
insp. gen. inspector general

inst. institute
instl. institutional
instn. institution
instr. instructor
instrn. instruction
intern. international
intro. introduction
IRE Institute of Radio Engineers
IRS Internal Revenue Service
ITT International Telephone &
  Telegraph Corporation

JAG Judge Advocate General
JAGC Judge Advocate General Corps
Jan. January
Jaycees Junior Chamber of Commerce
JB, J.B. Jurum Baccalaureus
JCB, J.C.B. Juris Canoni Baccalaureus
JCD, J.C.D. Juris Canonici Doctor,
  Juris Civilis Doctor
JCL, J.C.L. Juris Canonici Licentiatus
JD, J.D. Juris Doctor
jg. junior grade
jour. journal
jr. junior
JSD, J.S.D. Juris Scientiae Doctor
JUD, J.U.D. Juris Utriusque Doctor
jud. judicial

Kans. Kansas
K.C. Knights of Columbus
K.P. Knights of Pythias
KS Kansas
K.T. Knight Templar
KY, Ky. Kentucky

LA, La. Louisiana
lab. laboratory
lang. language
laryngol. laryngological
LB Labrador
lectr. lecturer
legis. legislation, legislative
LHD, L.H.D. Doctor of Humane Letters
L.I. Long Island
lic. licensed, license
L.I.R.R. Long Island Railroad
lit. literary, literature
LittB, Litt.B. Bachelor of Letters
LittD, Litt.D. Doctor of Letters
LLB, LL.B. Bachelor of Laws
LLD, LL.D. Doctor of Laws
LLM, LL.M. Master of Laws
Ln. Lane
L.&N.R.R. Louisville & Nashville Railroad
LS, L.S. Library Science (in degree)
lt. lieutenant
Ltd. Limited
Luth. Lutheran
LWV League of Women Voters

M. Master
m. married
MA, M.A. Master of Arts
MA Massachusetts
mag. magazine
MAgr, M.Agr. Master of Agriculture
maj. major
Man. Manitoba
Mar. March
MArch, M.Arch. Master in Architecture
Mass. Massachusetts
math. mathematics, mathematical
MATS Military Air Transport Service
MB, M.B. Bachelor of Medicine
MB Manitoba

MBA, M.B.A. Master of Business
  Administration
MBS Mutual Broadcasting System
M.C. Medical Corps
MCE, M.C.E. Master of Civil Engineering
mcht. merchant
mcpl. municipal
MCS, M.C.S. Master of Commercial Science
MD, M.D. Doctor of Medicine
MD, Md. Maryland
MDip, M.Dip. Master in Diplomacy
mdse. merchandise
MDV, M.D.V. Doctor of Veterinary Medicine
ME, M.E. Mechanical Engineer
ME Maine
M.E.Ch. Methodist Episcopal Church
mech. mechanical
MEd, M.Ed. Master of Education
med. medical
MEE, M.E.E. Master of Electrical
  Engineering
mem. member
meml. memorial
merc. mercantile
met. metropolitan
metall. metallurgical
MetE, Met.E. Metallurgical Engineer
meteorol. meteorological
Meth. Methodist
Mex. Mexico
MF, M.F. Master of Forestry
MFA, M.F.A. Master of Fine Arts
mfg. manufacturing
mfr. manufacturer
mgmt. management
mgr. manager
MHA, M.H.A. Master of Hospital
  Administration
M.I. Military Intelligence
MI Michigan
Mich. Michigan
micros. microscopic, microscopical
mid. middle
mil. military
Milw. Milwaukee
mineral. mineralogical
Minn. Minnesota
Miss. Mississippi
MIT Massachusetts Institute of
  Technology
mktg. marketing
ML, M.L. Master of Laws
MLA Modern Language Association
M.L.D. Magister Legnum Diplomatic
MLitt, M.Litt. Master of Literature
MLS, M.L.S. Master of Library Science
MME, M.M.E. Master of Mechanical
  Engineering
MN Minnesota
mng. managing
MO, Mo. Missouri
moblzn. mobilization
Mont. Montana
M.P. Member of Parliament
MPE, M.P.E. Master of Physical Education
MPH, M.P.H. Master of Public Health
MPhil, M.Phil. Master of Philosophy
MPL, M.P.L. Master of Patent Law
Mpls. Minneapolis
MRE, M.R.E. Master of Religious Education
MS, M.S. Master of Science
MS, Ms. Mississippi
MSc, M.Sc. Master of Science
MSF, M.S.F. Master of Science of Forestry
MST, M.S.T. Master of Sacred Theology
MSW, M.S.W. Master of Social Work

MT Montana
Mt. Mount
MTO Mediterranean Theatre of
  Operations
mus. museum, musical
MusB, Mus.B. Bachelor of Music
MusD, Mus.D. Doctor of Music
MusM, Mus.M. Master of Music
mut. mutual
mycol. mycological

N. North
NAACP National Association for the
  Advancement of Colored People
NACA National Advisory Committee for
  Aeronautics
NAD National Academy of Design
N.Am. North America
NAM National Association of Manufacturers
NAPA National Association of
  Performing Artists
NAREB National Association of Real
  Estate Boards
NARS National Archives and Record
  Service
NASA National Aeronautics and Space
  Administration
nat. national
NATO North Atlantic Treaty Organization
NATOUSA North African Theatre of
  Operations
nav. navigation
NB, N.B. New Brunswick
NBC National Broadcasting Company
NC, N.C. North Carolina
NCCJ National Conference of Christians
  and Jews
ND, N.D. North Dakota
NDEA National Defense Education Act
NE Nebraska
NE Northeast
NEA National Education Association
Nebr. Nebraska
NEH National Endowment for Humanities
neurol. neurological
Nev. Nevada
NF Newfoundland
NFL National Football League
Nfld. Newfoundland
NG National Guard
NH, N.H. New Hampshire
NHL National Hockey League
NIH National Institutes of Health
NIMH National Institute of Mental Health
NJ, N.J. New Jersey
NLRB National Labor Relations Board
NM New Mexico
N. Mex. New Mexico
No. Northern
NOAA National Oceanographic and
  Atmospheric Administration
NORAD North America Air Defense
Nov. November
NOW National Organization for Women
N.P.Ry. Northern Pacific Railway
nr. near
NRC National Research Council
NS, N.S. Nova Scotia
NSC National Security Council
NSF National Science Foundation
N.T. New Testament
NT Northwest Territories
numis. numismatic
NV Nevada
NW Northwest
N.W.T. Northwest Territories
NY, N.Y. New York
N.Y.C. New York City

NYU New York University
N.Z. New Zealand

OAS Organization of American States
ob-gyn obstetrics-gynecology
obs. observatory
obstet. obstetrical
Oct. October
OD, O.D. Doctor of Optometry
OECD Organization of European
  Cooperation and Development
OEEC Organization of European
  Economic Cooperation
OEO Office of Economic Opportunity
ofcl. official
OH Ohio
OK Oklahoma
Okla. Oklahoma
ON Ontario
Ont. Ontario
ophthal. ophthalmological
ops. operations
OR Oregon
orch. orchestra
Oreg. Oregon
orgn. organization
ornithol. ornithological
OSHA Occupational Safety and Health
  Administration
OSRD Office of Scientific Research and
  Development
OSS Office of Strategic Services
osteo. osteopathic
otol. otological
otolaryn. otolaryngological

PA, Pa. Pennsylvania
P.A. Professional Association
paleontol. paleontological
path. pathological
P.C. Professional Corporation
PE Prince Edward Island
P.E.I. Prince Edward Island (text only)
PEN Poets, Playwrights, Editors, Essayists
  and Novelists (international association)
penol. penological
P.E.O. women's organization (full name
  not disclosed)
pfc. private first class
PHA Public Housing Administration
pharm. pharmaceutical
PharmD, Pharm.D. Doctor of Pharmacy
PharmM, Pharm.M. Master of Pharmacy
PhB, Ph.B. Bachelor of Philosophy
PhD, Ph.D. Doctor of Philosophy
PhM, Ph.M. Master of Philosophy
Phila. Philadelphia
philharm. philharmonic
philol. philological
philos. philosophical
photog. photographic
phys. physical
physiol. physiological
Pitts. Pittsburgh
Pkwy. Parkway
Pl. Place
P.&L.E.R.R. Pittsburgh & Lake Erie
  Railroad
P.O. Post Office
PO Box Post Office Box
polit. political
poly. polytechnic, polytechnical
PQ Province of Quebec
PR, P.R. Puerto Rico
prep. preparatory
pres. president
Presbyn. Presbyterian
presdl. presidential

prin. principal
proc. proceedings
prod. produced (play production)
prodn. production
prof. professor
profl. professional
prog. progressive
propr. proprietor
pros. atty. prosecuting attorney
pro tem pro tempore
PSRO Professional Services Review
  Organization
psychiat. psychiatric
psychol. psychological
PTA Parent–Teachers Association
ptnr. partner
PTO Pacific Theatre of Operations,
  Parent Teacher Organization
pub. publisher, publishing, published
pub. public
publ. publication
pvt. private

quar. quarterly
qm. quartermaster
Q.M.C. Quartermaster Corps
Que. Quebec

radiol. radiological
RAF Royal Air Force
RCA Radio Corporation of America
RCAF Royal Canadian Air Force
RD Rural Delivery
Rd. Road
REA Rural Electrification Administration
rec. recording
ref. reformed
regt. regiment
regtl. regimental
rehab. rehabilitation
Rep. Republican
rep. representative
Res. Reserve
ret. retired
rev. review, revised
RFC Reconstruction Finance
  Corporation
RFD Rural Free Delivery
rhinol. rhinological
RI, R.I. Rhode Island
RN, R.N. Registered Nurse
roentgenol. roentgenological
ROTC Reserve Officers Training Corps
R.R. Railroad
Ry. Railway

S. South
s. son
SAC Strategic Air Command
SALT Strategic Arms Limitation Talks
S.Am. South America
san. sanitary
SAR Sons of the American Revolution
Sask. Saskatchewan
savs. savings
SB, S.B. Bachelor of Science
SBA Small Business Administration
SC, S.C. South Carolina
SCAP Supreme Command Allies Pacific
ScB, Sc.B. Bachelor of Science
SCD, S.C.D. Doctor of Commercial Science
ScD, Sc.D. Doctor of Science
sch. school
sci. science, scientific
SCLC Southern Christian Leadership
  Conference
SCV Sons of Confederate Veterans
SD, S.D. South Dakota

SE Southeast
SEATO Southeast Asia Treaty Organization
SEC Securities and Exchange Commission
sec. secretary
sect. section
seismol. seismological
sem. seminary
Sept. September
s.g. senior grade
sgt. sergeant
SHAEF Supreme Headquarters Allied Expeditionary Forces
SHAPE Supreme Headquarters Allied Powers in Europe
S.I. Staten Island
S.J. Society of Jesus (Jesuit)
SJD Scientiae Juridicae Doctor
SK Saskatchewan
SM, S.M. Master of Science
So. Southern
soc. society
sociol. sociological
S.P. Co. Southern Pacific Company
spl. special
splty. specialty
Sq. Square
S.R. Sons of the Revolution
sr. senior
SS Steamship
SSS Selective Service System
St. Saint, Street
sta. station
stats. statistics
statis. statistical
STB, S.T.B. Bachelor of Sacred Theology
stblzn. stabilization
STD, STD Doctor of Sacred Theology
subs. subsidiary
SUNY State University of New York
supr. supervisor
supt. superintendent
surg. surgical
SW Southwest

TAPPI Technical Association of the Pulp and Paper Industry
Tb Tuberculosis
tchr. teacher
tech. technical, technology
technol. technological
Tel.&Tel. Telephone & Telegraph
temp. temporary
Tenn. Tennessee
Ter. Territory
Terr. Terrace
Tex. Texas
ThD, Th.D. Doctor of Theology
theol. theological
ThM, Th.M. Master of Theology
TN Tennessee
tng. training
topog. topographical
trans. transaction, transferred
transl. translation, translated
transp. transportation
treas. treasurer
TT Trust Territory
TV television
TVA Tennessee Valley Authority
twp. township
TX Texas
typog. typographical

U. University
UAW United Auto Workers

UCLA University of California at Los Angeles
UDC United Daughters of the Confederacy
U.K. United Kingdom
UN United Nations
UNESCO United Nations Educational, Scientific and Cultural Organization
UNICEF United Nations International Children's Emergency Fund
univ. university
UNRRA United Nations Relief and Rehabilitation Administration
UPI United Press International
U.P.R.R. United Pacific Railroad
urol. urological
U.S. United States
U.S.A. United States of America
USAAF United States Army Air Force
USAF United States Air Force
USAFR United States Air Force Reserve
USAR United States Army Reserve
USCG United States Coast Guard
USCGR United States Coast Guard Reserve
USES United States Employment Service
USIA United States Information Agency
USMC United States Marine Corps
USMCR United States Marine Corps Reserve
USN United States Navy
USNG United States National Guard
USNR United States Naval Reserve
USO United Service Organizations
USPHS United States Public Health Service
USS United States Ship
USSR Union of the Soviet Socialist Republics
USV United States Volunteers
UT Utah

VA Veterans' Administration
VA, Va. Virginia
vet. veteran, veterinary
VFW Veterans of Foreign Wars
VI, V.I. Virgin Islands
vice pres. vice president
vis. visiting
VISTA Volunteers in Service to America
VITA Volunteers in Technical Service
vocat. vocational
vol. volunteer, volume
v.p. vice president
vs. versus
VT, Vt. Vermont

W. West
WA Washington (state)
WAC Women's Army Corps
Wash. Washington (state)
WAVES Women's Reserve, US Naval Reserve
WCTU Women's Christian Temperance Union
we. western
W.Ger. Germany, Federal Republic of
WHO World Health Organization
WI Wisconsin
W.I. West Indies
Wis. Wisconsin
WSB Wage Stabilization Board
WV West Virginia
W.Va. West Virginia
WY Wyoming
Wyo. Wyoming

YK Yukon Territory

YMCA Young Men's Christian Association
YMHA Young Men's Hebrew Association
YM & YWHA Young Men's and Young Women's Hebrew Association
yr. year
YT, Y.T. Yukon Territory
YWCA Young Women's Christian Association

zool. zoological

Alphabetical Practices

Names are arranged alphabetically according to the surnames, and under identical surnames according to the first given name. If both surname and first given name are identical, names are arranged alphabetically according to the second given name. Where full names are identical, they are arranged in order of age—with the elder listed first.

Surnames beginning with De, Des, Du, however capitalized or spaced, are recorded with the prefix preceding the surname and arranged alphabetically under the letter D.

Surnames beginning with Mac and Mc are arranged alphabetically under M.

Surnames beginning with Saint or St. appear after names that begin Sains, and are arranged according to the second part of the name, e.g. St. Clair before Saint Dennis.

Surnames beginning with Van, Von or von are arranged alphabetically under letter V.

Compound hyphenated surnames are arranged according to the first member of the compound. Compound unhyphenated surnames are treated as hyphenated names.

Many hyphenated Arabic names begin Al–, El–, or al–. These names are alphabetized according to each biographee's designation of last name. Thus, Al–Bahar, Mohammed may be listed either under Al– or under Bahar, depending on the preference of the listee.

Parentheses used in connection with a name indicate which part of the full name is usually deleted in common usage. Hence Abbott, W(illiam) Lewis indicates that the usual form of the given name is W. Lewis. In such a case, the parentheses are ignored in alphabetizing. However, if the name is recorded Abbott, (William) Lewis, signifying that the entire name William is not commonly used, the alphabetizing would be arranged as though the name were Abbott, Lewis.

Who'sWho in the World

AAKESSON, LARS-OLOF (OLLE AAKESSON), electrical engineer; b. Viker, Oerebro, Sweden, May 7, 1948; s. Åke Edvin and Inga Elisabet (Norling) Johansson; m. Gudrun Birgitta Ahlström, May 15, 1976; children: Martin, Maria. Degree in Elec. Engring., Rudbecksskolan, örebro, Sweden, 1973. Customer service rep. Gylling, Stockholm, 1974-76; component engr. Asea, Västerås, Sweden, 1976-84; quality mgr. Asea Drives, Västerås, 1984—. Mem. Aeroplane Owners and Pilot Assn. Sweden (sec. 1983). Home: Sveavägen 10, Västerås Sweden 72460 Office: ABB Drives AB, Västerås Sweden 72175

AAKVAAG, TORVILD, petroleum company executive; b. Baerum, Norway, Jan. 18, 1927; s. Torvild and Dagny (Rivertz) A.; m. Dagen Dahl, 1952. Attache Norwegian Ministry Fgn. Affairs, 1951-56; joined legal dept. Norsk Hydro, 1956, head legal dept., 1967-70, gen. mgr. Petroleum Div., 1970-75, exec. v.p., 1975-77, dep. pres., 1977-84, pres., 1984—. Office: Norsk Hydro, PO Box 2594, Solli, Oslo Norway *

AALSETH, JACK ELDON, marketing executive; b. Clark, S.D., Nov. 25, 1932; s. Norman Oliver and Margaret Ella (Blackman) A.; m. Lois M. Gutherie, Oct. 15, 1952 (div. July 1978); m. Marie A. Young, June 26, 1984. BS in Physics, San Diego State U., 1958. Engr. Gen. Dynamics, San Diego, 1956-58, Lockheed Missile and Space, Sunnyvale, Calif., 1958-62; mgr., engr., cons. services officer United Testing Labs., Los Angeles, 1962-63; pres. PRC Tech. Applications, Los Angeles, 1963-70; pvt. practice fin., mgmt., tech. cons. San Diego, 1971-75; pres., chief exec. officer Evaluation Research Corp., Vienna, Va., 1976-85; chmn., chief exec. officer ERC Internat., Vienna, 1985—; bd. dirs. ESI Industries, Dallas, Washington Technology; bd. dirs., past pres. Profl. Services Council, Washington. Bd. dirs. USO-Washington, 1983—. Served to staff sgt. USMC, 1950-54. Club: City Club of Washington. Office: ERC International 3211 Jermantown Rd PO Box 10107 Fairfax VA 22030

AAMOTH, GERALD (JERRY) RODERICK, mechanical and design engineer; b. Bismarck, N.D., Nov. 8, 1935; s. Milton R. and Alma B. (Sayler) A.; grad. Stockton Jr. Coll., 1953; student Stockton Coll., 1953-55, DeVry Tech. Inst., 1965; cert. West Valley Jr. Coll., 1964; m. Wanda Jean Chandler, July 10, 1957; children—Gregory Roderick, Norman Tracy, Eric Jeffery, Jason Edward. Engr. drafting specialist Lockheed Missile & Space Co., Sunnyvale, Calif., 1960-63, 65-67; chief draftsman, asso. engr. Electronics Assos., Inc., Palo Alto, Calif., 1967-69; account exec. Mgmt. Recruiters, San Jose, Calif., 1969-70; sr. designer Kaiser Aerospace & Electronics, Palo Alto, 1970-71, Video Logic Corp., Sunnyvale, 1973-74; sr. elec. designer Omron Systems, Sunnyvale, 1971-73; sr. mech. design engr. Novus div. Nat. Semiconductor, Sunnyvale, 1974-76, Atari Inc., Sunnyvale, 1976-79; pres. Outhouse Enterprises, Fremont, Calif., 1970—; sr. mech. design engr. United Energy Corp., Foster City, Calif., 1984-85; sr. designer Aydin (West), Radar & E.W. Div., San Jose, Calif., 1987—; dir. mech. design, sr. partner Design Four, Inc., Campbell, Calif., 1980-81; sr. mech. engr. corp. staff USI: Internat., Brisbane, Calif., 1983. Head coach Fremont Football League, also bd. dirs., div. coordinator, coaches selection com.; trainer Woodbadge and Acorn, Boy Scouts Am., past mem. youth and adult leadership corps. Mem. Am. Soc. Metals, Soc. Plastic Engrs., Soc. Mfg. Engrs., Internat. Electronics Packaging Soc., Am. Radio Council, Profl. and Tech. Cons. Assn., C. of C. Democrat. Patentee electromech. mechanisms. Home and Office: 47625 Wabana Common Fremont CA 94539

AARON, BERTRAM DONALD, corporation executive; b. Newport News, Va., Jan. 10, 1922; s. Harry and Lillian (Blackman) A.; B.S. in Elec. Engring., Va. Poly. Inst., 1943; children—Harry, Cynthia, Jill; m. Judith Goldstein, Dec. 28, 1985. Aero. research scientist Nat. Adv. Com. for Aeros., Langley AFB, Va., 1946-50; pres. Aaron Investors, Inc., 1948-80; elec. engr. Signal Corps Supply Agy., Phila., 1950-53; propr. Bertram D. Aaron and Co., Los Angeles, 1953-58, pres., Plainview, N.Y., 1958—; pres. Microwave Instrumentation Labs., 1959-80, HAL Antenna Products, Inc., Aaron Tech. Market, Inc. Served to capt., Signal Corps, U.S. Army, 1943-46. Registered profl. engr., N.Y., Pa., Va. Mem. IEEE (various offices), Electronic Reps. Assn. (pres., chmn. bd.), Assn. of Old Crows. Jewish. Author: Hydrogen Thyratron Circuitry Considerations, 1953; Surveillance Under Low Light Level Conditions, 1971; editor Procs. of Integration Com. on Hydrogen Thyratrons, 1951-53; patentee antenna. Home: 65 Cedarfield Rd Laurel Hollow NY 11791 Office: BD Aaron Co Inc 88 Sunnyside Blvd Suite 203 Plainview NY 11803

AARON, CHLOE WELLINGHAM, television executive; b. Santa Monica, Calif., Oct. 9, 1938; d. John Rufus and Grace (Lloyd) Wellingham; m. David Laurence Aaron, Aug. 11, 1962; 1 child, Timothy Wellingham. BA, Occidental Coll., 1961; MA, George Washington U., 1966; HHD, Occidental Coll., 1987. Freelance journalist 1965-70; dir. pub. media program Nat. Endowment for Arts, Washington, 1970-76; sr. v.p. programming Pub. Broadcasting Service, Washington, 1976-81; pres. Chloe Aaron Assocs., 1981—; dir. cultural and children's programs KQED-TV, San Francisco, 1987—. Producer: TV film The Soldier's Tale, PBS (Emmy award 1984), 1984. Mem. trustee com. on film Mus. Modern Art, N.Y.C.; mem. bd. pub. devel. Corp. of N.Y.C., Ctr. Visual History, Nancy Hanks Ctr., Am. Jazz Orchestra. Recipient Alumni Seal award Occidental Coll., 1983. Office: 500 8th St San Francisco CA 94103

AARON, MERIK ROY, educator, financial executive; b. N.Y.C., May 22, 1947; s. Harry and Gertrude S. (Scherl) A.; m. Karen M. Snyder, 1984; 1 child, Stacey Lynn. BA, L.I. U., 1969, MA, 1971; profl. diploma Hofstra U., 1975; EdD, Nova U., 1982. Dist. sci. supr. Carle Place (N.Y.) Pub. Schs., 1969-80; dist. sci. supr. Lawrence (N.Y.) Pub. Schs., 1980-84; adminstr. Bellmore-Merrick Cen. High Sch. Dist., Merrick, N.Y., 1984-86. dir. curriculum, Bellmore-Merrick Cen. High Sch. Dist., 1986—; pres. G.N.S. Investment Fund, N.Y.C., 1971—; v.p. Mervic Enterprises, Smithtown, N.Y., 1980— ; adj. prof. Nassau Community Coll., 1975—, Syracuse (N.Y.) U., 1974-80. Trustee, Carle Place Bd. Edn., 1981-86 . Recipient Outstanding Contributions to Edn., Nassau County, 1981, Outstanding Sci. Supr., State N.Y., 1986; named Educator of Yr., Carle Place Pub. Schs., 1975, 77. Mem. Nat. Assn. Investment Clubs, Nat. Sci. Tchrs. Assn., Nat. Sci. Suprs. Assn. (exec. bd. 1983—, pres. 1986-87), N.Y. State Sci. Suprs. Assn. (pres. 1982-83), N.Y. Acad. Scis., Nassau County Sci. Suprs. Assn. (pres. 1979), Am. Assn. Sex Educators, Counselors and Therapists (cert.), Phi Delta Kappa. Republican. Club: Civic. Lodges: Kiwanis (pres. Westbury, N.Y. club 1982-83), (Merrick club), Masons, Shriners. Home: 544 Green Pl Woodmere NY 11598

AARTS, CHRISTIANUS JOSEPHUS MARIA, educational administrator.; b. Eindhoven, Netherlands, Jan. 29, 1919; s. Johannes and Everdina Hendrika Maria (Eskes) A.; M. Physics and M. Math., U. Utrecht (Netherlands), 1948, D.Sc., 1952; m. Imelda Elisabeth Maria Hennekam, July 20, 1943. Dir., Hennekam, Roosendaal, Netherlands, 1943-53; mng. dir. phys. labs. U. Utrecht, 1952-58; founder, dir. Faculty of Sci., U. Nijmegen (Netherlands), 1957-86, adv. univ. bd., 1985—; sec., treas. Netherlands Found. for Furthering Heating and Ventilation Research and Devel., 1954-75; bd. dirs. Nat. Inst. High Energy Physics of Netherlands, 1970-86; mem. sect. computer sci. Academic Council Netherlands, 1970-83; mem. adv. com. to minister edn. and research on financing structures for research and devel., 1983-86. Recipient Pro Mundi Beneficio medal Brazilian Acad. Human Scis., 1975, medal of Merit Queen Juliana of The Netherlands, 1977; decorated officer Order of Orange Nassau, 1982. Fellow Brit. Computer Soc.; mem. phys. socs. Utrecht, Netherlands, Italy, European, Am. phys. socs., Am. Assn. Physics Tchrs., Acoustical Soc. Am., Optical Soc. Am., Health Physics Soc. (U.S.), Am. Geophys. Union, AAAS, ASTM, Soc. Indsl. and Applied Math. (U.S.), Internat. Airline Passengers Assn., European Soc. Assn. Execs., Am. Soc. Info. Sci., Assn. Computing Machinery (U.S.), N.Y. Acad. Scis., Netherlands Soc. Informatics, SHARE European Assn. (pres. 1972-77, dir. 1967-86), Utrecht Soc. Arts and Scis., Brit. Soc. History Sci., Assn. Univ. Govs. in Netherlands (founding mem.). Roman Catholic. Clubs: Royal Automobile of Netherlands; Flying Dutchman. Author: Investigation of an Arc-Discharge, 1952; The Nijmegen Laboratory for High Magnetic Fields, 1979; Research at the Nijmegen High Field Magnet Laboratory, 1981. Home: Van Randwijckweg 22, 6573 EJ Beek bij, Nijmegen The Netherlands Office: PO Box 9102, 6500 HC, Nijmegen The Netherlands

ABAD, LEOPOLDO ANTONIO, JR., glass company executive; b. Manila, Philippines, Jan. 8, 1928; s. Leopoldo F. and Asuncion (Sandoval) A.; m. Amanda Maneclang, Mar. 20, 1957; children—Leopoldo III, Rosemarie, Natalia, Jose. B.S.E.E., U. Philippines, 1950. Registered profl. elec. engr., electronics and communications engr. X-ray engr. Gen. Electric Co., Manila, Philippines, 1950-51; sales engr. Femec, Inc., Manila, 1958-65; asst. v.p. Republic Glass Corp., Manila, 1966-79; exec. asst. Dole Philippines, Manila, 1966-73; v.p. Republic Glass Corp., Manila, 1980-88 . Chmn., Constrn. Materials Industry Sector, Ministry of Trade and Industry, 1982-86; dir. Bur. of Import Services, Dept. Trade & Industry, 1988—; dir. Orient Overseas, Manila. Served to col. Philippine Air Force, 1951-58. Hon. Consul Gen., Peoples Republic of Bangladesh, 1973. Mem. Philippine Chamber of Industries (bd. dirs. 1975-78), Asean Fedn. Glass Mfrs. (sec.-gen. 1977-79), Consol. Automobile Parts Producers Assn. (dir. 1980-88), Inst. Elec. Engrs., Electronics and Communications Engrs. Soc., Architects Ctr., Res. Officers Legion of the Philippines (pres. chpt. 1985-88). Roman Catholic. Home: 785 Noli St, Malate, Manila 2801, Philippines Office: Republic Glass Corp, Salcedo Village, Tordesillas & Gallardo Sts, Makati, Metro Manila 3117, Philippines

ABAD, RAINERIO SION, gynecologist; b. Manila, Dec. 30, 1936; s. Moises Buenaflor and Fidela Colendrino (Sion) A.; m. Mary Rose Bayot Delgado, June 12, 1963; children: Jaime, Maria Victoria. MD, U. Philippines, Manila, 1960. Resident in ob/gyn Philippine Gen. Hosp., Manila, 1960-65; sr. cancer research surgeon Roswell Park Meml. Inst., Buffalo, 1965-68; practice medicine specializing in ob/gyn Manila, 1968—; prof. ob/gyn U. Philippines, 1974—, U. East, Ramon Magsaysay Meml. Med. Ctr., Quezon City, 1980—; chief gyn. oncology St. Luke's Med. Ctr., Quezon City, 1986—; hosp. dir. Dr. Jesus Delgado Meml. Hosp., Quezon City, 1981—. Editor-in-chief Philippine Jour. OB/Gyn, 1988; designer logos various assns. Vol. cons. Philippine Cancer Soc., 1979—. Fellow Philippine Soc. Oncologists, Soc. Gynecologic Oncologists Philippines (dir. 1986—), Philippine Coll. Surgeons; mem. Makati Mem. Soc. (pres. 1979-80), Philippine Bd. Ob/Gyn (sec. 1979-80), Philippine Obstet. and Gynecol. Soc. (pres 1986) Roswell Park Surg. Soc. Roman Catholic.

ABADIE, JEAN M., mathematician, educator, researcher; b. Mirande, Gers, France, Oct. 19, 1919; s. Maurice C. and Persephone (Theophanides) A.; m. Julia Lalayannis, Aug. 24, 1961; 1 child, Alexandre J. Baccalaureat, Lycee Henry IV, Paris, 1942; Licence, U. Lyon, France, 1947, D.E.A., 1948; Agregation (Math.), U. Paris, 1950. Statistician, Water and Forestry Research Ctr., Nancy, France, 1950-55; head math. group Electricité de France, Paris, 1955-63, sci. adviser, 1963-79; prof. Statis. Inst., U. Paris, 1959-69, prof. U. Paris VI, 1979— , research dir. U. Paris-Dauphine, 1969—; vis. prof. Case Western Res. U., U. Calif.-Berkeley, Stanford U., U. Chgo. French rep. to spl. com. on systems sci. NATO, Brussels, 1978-83. Editor: Nonlinear Programming, 1967; Integer and Nonlinear Programming, 1970; editor-in-chief RAIRO-Ops. Research Jour., 1970—; assoc. editor various jours.; contbr. articles to sci. jours. and internat. meetings. Inventor GRG Method of Optimization. Mem. Math. Programming Soc. (chmn. 1980-83), Inst. Mgmt. Sci. (mem. council 1968-70, 80-82), Internat. Statis. Inst., Societe Mathematique de France, Am. Math. Soc., Assn. for Computing Machinery. Home: 29 Blvd Edgar Quinet, 75014 Paris France Office: U Paris VI, Informatics Dept, 4 Place Jussieu, Paris 75005 France

ABADIR, BASSEM BOTROS, equipment dealership executive, construction equipment consultant; b. Assiut, Egypt, Oct. 9, 1945; s. Botros Abadir and Katherine Malek; m. Samira Fahim, Feb. 28, 1975; 1 child, George. BS in Mining Engring., Assiut U., 1966; diploma in Mgmt., Am. U., Cairo, 1979, MA in Mgmt., 1982. Vocat. tng. specialist Egypt Ministry Industry, Quena, 1966-68; service, parts mgr. IDP, Cairo, 1974-83; chief exec. officer, ptnr. Constrn. Services Ctr., Cairo, 1983—; constrn. equipment cons., 1978—. Author: (in Arabic) A Dealer in Egypt, 1987; contbr. articles on bus. to profl. jours. Served to capt. C.E. Egyptian Army, 1968-74. Mem. Syndicate Engrs., Soc. Mining Engrs. Mem. National Democratic Party. Presbyterian. Home and Office: 5 Anga Hanen St Shoubra, Cairo Egypt

ABAGNALE, FRANK WILLIAM, JR., security company executive, lecturer; b. Bronx, N.Y., Apr. 27, 1948; s. Frank William and Paulette Noel (Anton) A.; m. Kelly Anne Welbes, Nov. 6, 1976; children—Scott, Chris, Sean. Student pub. schs., Houston. Pres., chief exec. officer Abagnale & Assocs., Houston, 1976—; also pub. speaker. Author: Catch Me If You Can, 1980; Green Book, 1982. Mem. Nat. Speakers Assn., Internat. Platform Assn. Republican. Roman Catholic. Home: PO Box 701290 Tulsa OK 74170

ABAJIAN, HENRY KRIKOR, mechanical engineer; b. Aintab, Turkey, Dec. 8, 1909; s. Hagop H. and Vartouhi (Haleblian) A.; came to U.S., 1923, naturalized, 1933; M.E., Rensselaer Poly. Inst., 1933; m. Gladys Lucy Mahseregian, Jan. 12, 1942; 1 dau., Carol. Design engr. Wallace & Tiernan Co., Am. La France Foamite Corp., Heald Machine Co., 1933-40; design specialist Consol. Vultee Aircraft Corp., 1940-46; project engr. Willys Overland Motors, Gen. Tire & Rubber Co., Marquardt Aircraft, Hycon Mfg. Co., 1946-51; v.p., dir., dir. engring. Resdel Industries, 1951-54, pres., chmn. bd., chief exec. officer, from 1954, chmn. bd., 1981; chmn. bd., chief exec. officer Resdel Engring. Corp., 1965—, Mfrs. Assistance Corp., 1970-81, Fanon/Courier Corp., 1971-81, Resdel Internat., 1972-81. Registered profl. engr., Calif. Mem. U.S. Power Squadron, Sigma Xi. Congregationalist (chmn.). Club: Masons. Home: 2052 Midlothian Dr Altadena CA 91001 Office: 300 E Live Oak Ave Arcadia CA 91006

ABAKANOWICZ, MAGDALENA, artist, sculptor; b. Falenty, Warsaw, Poland, June 20, 1930; d. Konstanty and Helena (Domaszowska) A.; m. Jan Kosmowski, Sept. 22, 1956. Grad., Warsaw Acad. Fine Arts, 1954; Dr.H.C. (hon.), Royal Coll. Art, London, 1974. Works include: monumental space forms of woven fibres, cycles of figurative sculptures of burlap, wood, metals, stone and clay drawings, paintings with collage and gouache; relief woven composition for North Brabant Provincial Bldg.; Netherlands; head dept. weaving Acad. Fine Art, Poznan, Poland, 1965, prof., 1979. Exhibited in one-woman shows at Kunsthaus Zurich, 1968; Nationalmuseum Stockholm, 1970; Pasadena (Calif.) Art Mus., 1971; Dusseldorf Kunsthalle, 1972; Whitechapel Art Gallery, London, 1975; Nat. Gallery of Victoria, Melbourne, 1976; Muzeum Sztuki, Lodz, 1978; Musee d'art Modern de la Ville de Paris, 1982; Mus. of Contemporary Art, Chgo., 1982; Musee d'Art Contemporain, Montreal, 1983; Portland Art Mus. (Oreg.), 1984; Dallas Mus. Fine Arts, 1984, Xavier Fourcade Gallery, N.Y.C., 1985; exhibited in group shows Internat. Biennale de Tapisserie, Lausanne, 1962-79; Internat. Biennale of Art, Sao Paulo, 1965, 79; Venice Biennale, 1968, 80; ROSC, Dublin, 1980; Nat. Gallery, Berlin, 1983; ARS '83, Helsinki, 1983; Mus. Moderner Kuns Vienne, 1984, Nürnberg Triennale of Drawing, 1985, Sydney Biennale of Art, 1986; represented in collections Muzeum Sztuki Lodz (Poland); Mus. Modern Art, N.Y.C.; Mus. Modern Art, Kyoto, Japan; Stedelijk Mus., Amsterdam; Australian Nat. Collection, Canberra; Centre Georges Pompidou, Paris; Mus. Contemporary Art, Chgo.; Nat. Mus., Stockholm, Met. Mus., N.Y.C., also others. Recipient prize 1st class Minister of Culture, Poland, 1965; Gold medal VIII Biennale of Art, Sao Paulo, 1965; Polish State prize Polish Govt., 1972; Gottfried Von Herder prize Stiftung F.V.S. Hamburg, Vienna, 1979; Alfred Jurzykowski prize, 1982. Mem. Polish Assn. Authors. Address: Al Stanow Zjednoczonych 16/53, 03-947 Warsaw Poland

ABAL KHAIL, MUHAMMAD-ALI, finance minister Saudi Arabia; b. Bureuda, Saudi Arabia, 1935; B.Sc., Cairo U., 1956; 4 children. With Ministry of Communications, Saudi Arabia, dep. minister fin. and nat. economy, 1964, vice minister, 1970, minister of state for fin. and nat. economy and mem. Council Ministers, 1971, minister of fin. and nat. economy, 1975—; chmn. bd. dirs. Saudi Internat. Bank, London, Pub. Investment Fund, Inst. Pub. Adminstrn., Pension & Retirement Fund, Saudi Fund for Devel.; dir. Supreme Consultative Council of Petroleum and Minerals, Royal Commn. for Indsl. Estates in Jubail and Yanbo, Saudi Arabian Airlines Corp., Council of Labour Power. Recipient Niger medal leader statues, Pakistan Crescent medal, Neilain medal 1st class, Order de Merite du Grand, Isabel La Catolka - Grau-Cruz, Order of Mahabotra Obrandana, medaille du Mérite, Meddaile Nationale Leonard Rang Commandeur, Grand Cross medal, others. Address: Ministry of Fin and Nat Economy, Riyadh Saudi Arabia *

ABARICIO, LIBERATION MORENO, pediatrician; b. Davao City, Philippines, Nov. 22, 1947; parents Emilio Libres and Pilarita (Moreno) A. AB, Ateneo de Davao, Davao City, 1969; MD, Cebu Inst. Medicine, 1972. Diplomate Philippine Pediatric Soc. (sec., treas. 1978-81). Intern Brokenshire Meml. Hosp., Davao City, 1972-73, resident, 1973-76, jr. cons. pediatrics, 1977-78, cons., 1979-85; cons. San Pedro Hosp., Davao Med. Ctr., Davao City, 1985—; asst. prof. pediatrics Davao Med. Sch. Found., Davao City, 1985—; physician Stanfilco Co., Davao City, 1986—. Contbr. articles to profl. jours. Fellow Philippines Gen. Hosp., Manila, 1981-82. Fellow Philippines Coll. Chest Physicians; mem. Davao Med. Soc. Office: Clinica Anda, Anda St Davao del Sur, Davao City Philippines

ABASHIDZE, IRAKLIY VISSARIONOVICH, Soviet government official, poet; b. Khoni, Georgia, USSR, 1909. Grad., State U. Georgia. Mem. Communist Party Soviet Union, 1939—; mng. editor various periodicals, 1930-53; 1st sec. Writer's Union, Georgian Soviet Socialist Republic, 1953-64, chair, 1964-67; mem. Cen. Com. Georgian Communist Party, Tbilisi, 1954-71, 81—, candidate mem., 1971-81; mem. Georgian Acad. Scis., 1960—, v.p., 1970-76; dep. to, chair Supreme Soviet Georgian Soviet Socialist Republic, 1971—. Author: Verse, 1932, New Verse, 1938, Colours, 1962, Palestine, Palestine, 1966, I am the Earth, 1965, Rapprochement, 1966. Decorated Order of Lenin (twice). Office: Georgian Communist Party, Tbilisi USSR *

ABBADIE, DOMINIQUE, dermatologist, phlebotomist, allergist; b. Hasparren, France, Feb. 20, 1947; s. François and Therese (Bordarampe) A.; m. Patricia Huet, July 20, 1973; children: Frederic, Benedicte, Fabrice. MD, U. Bordeaux, 1975. Cert. dermatology, pediatrics, sports medicine, allergology. Intern various hosps., Bordeaux, 1975-79; cons. Hosp. Langon (France), 1979—; cons. Hosp. Pellegrin, Bordeaux, 1979, psychiat. Hosp., Cadillac, 1981. Contbr. articles to med. jours. Mem. Club de Photobiologie, Soc. de Dermatologie, Soc. de Phlebect OMie Ambulatoire. Roman Catholic. Home: 59-61 cours du 14 juillet, 33210 Langon Gironde France

ABBADO, CLAUDIO, conductor; b. Milan, Italy, June 26, 1933; s. Michelangelo A. Grad. as pianist, Giuseppe Verdi Conservatory, Milan, 1955; student conducting, Hans Swarowsky, Vienna Acad. Music. Conducting debut with Orch. Filarmonica, Trieste, 1958, operatic conducting debut, 1959; U.S. conducting debut with N.Y. Philharm. Orch., 1963; debut Salzburg Festival, 1965; music dir. La Scala, Milan, 1968-86, Vienna State Opera, 1986—; conducted Don Carlo, Met. Opera Co., N.Y.C., 1968; permanent condr. Vienna Philharm. Orch., 1971—; prin. condr. London Symphony Orch., 1979, music dir., 1983-88; prin. guest condr. Chgo. Symphony Orch., 1982-85; condr. major orchs., opera cos. in U.S., Europe, Japan, China, including Berlin, Salzburg, Edinburgh Festival, Berlin Deutsche Oper; numerous tours with orchs.; founder, musical dir. European Youth Orch., 1978—; founder Mahler Orch., Vienna, 1986; condr. New Yrs.'s Concert Vienna Philharm., 1988—. Recipient Koussevitzky conducting prize 1958, Mitropoulos prize 1963, Diapason award, several Grand Prix du Disque, Orphee D'Or, Deutscher Schallplatten Preis, Edison prize, Grammy award, Mozart medal Mozart Gemeinde, Vienna 1973, Golden Nicolai medal Vienna Philharm. Orch., 1980, Standard Opera award, Covent Garden, London, 1983, Gran' Croce award for Carmen, La Scala, 1984, Gold medal Internat. Mahler Soc., 1985, others; decorated French Legion D'Honneur, 1986. Office: care Columbia Artists Mgmt Inc 165 W 57th St New York NY 10019

ABBASI, TARIQ AFZAL, psychiatrist, educator; b. Hyderabad, India, Aug. 13, 1946; came to U.S., 1976, naturalized, 1983; s. Shujaat Ali and Salma Khatoon (Siddiqui) A.; m. Kashifa Khatoon, Nov. 10, 1972; children—Sameena, Omar, Osman. B.S., Madrasa-I-Aliya, Hyderabad, 1964; M.B.B.S., Osmania Med. Coll., Hyderabad, 1970; Diploma in Psychol. Medicine, St. John's Hosp., U. Sheffield (Eng.), 1976. Diplomate Am. Bd. Psychiatry and Neurology; diplomate in psychiatry Royal Coll. Physicians of Eng. Sr. house officer St. John's Hosp., Lincoln, Eng., 1972-73, registrar, 1973-76; resident in psychiatry Rutgers Med. Sch., Piscataway, N.J., 1976-79, chief resident, 1979, dir. adult in-patient services Community Mental Health Ctr., Rutgers Med. Sch., also asst. prof. psychiatry, 1979-82; staff psychiatrist Northville Regional Psychiat. Hosp. (Mich.), 1982-83, sect. dir., 1983—; cons. psychiatrist Rahway State Prison (N.J.), 1979-82; clin. instr. psychiatry Wayne State U. Med. Sch., Detroit. Mem. Am. Psychiat. Assn., Mich. Psychiat. Soc. Office: Northville Regional Psychiat Hosp 41001 Seven Mile Rd Northville MI 48167 also: Personal Dynamics Ctr 22646 Michigan Ave Dearborn MI 48124

ABBE, COLMAN, investment banker; b. N.Y.C., Sept. 24, 1932; s. Leo Theodore and Beatrice (Shiff) A.; m. Nancy Adele Hyams, June 23, 1963; children—Elizabeth, Leo, Richard. B.S. in Acctg., Bucknell U., 1953; M.B.A., NYU, 1962. C.P.A., N.Y. Ptnr. Belsky & Abbe C.P.A.s, N.Y.C., 1960-70; stockbroker Loeb Rhoades, N.Y.C., 1971-72; pres. Sagittarius Fund, N.Y.C., 1973, OCG Technology Inc., N.Y.C., Profl. Mediquip Inc., Scarsdale, N.Y., Abbe & Co. Inc., 1984-85; mng. dir. corp. fin. Evans & Co. Inc., N.Y.C., 1985-87; mng. dir. corp. fin. Reich & Co., Inc., 1987—. Trustee Heart Research Found., N.Y.C., 1982—, pres. 1986. Mem. N.Y. State Soc. C.P.A.s, Am. Inst. C.P.A.s. Democrat. Jewish. Office: Reich & Co Inc 50 Broadway New York NY 10008

ABBES, MICHEL-JOSÉ, surgeon; b. Beziers, France, June 29, 1932; s. Marcel Abbes and Claudine Berger; m. Paschetta Janine Abbes, Aug. 7,

1954; children: Veronique, Sophie. MD, U. Toulouse, France, 1957. Extern Toulouse Hosp., 1952; intern M.C.E. (France) Hosp., 1956; chief of staff, surgeon Cancer Ctr., Nice, France, 1975; dir. enseignement Faculté de Médecine de Nice, France, 1975—. Author, 2 books; contbr. over 350 articles to profl. jours. Recipient laureat de la Faculté de Medecine de Toulouse Prix de Thèse, 1957. Mem. Internat. Coll. of Surgeons. Roman Catholic. Office: Ctr A LaCassagne, 36 Voie Romaine, 06054 Nice France

ABBOTT, BENJAMIN EDWARD, JR., corporate executive; b. Washington, Dec. 7, 1928; s. Benjamin Edward and Agnes (Campbell) A.; B. Indls. Engring., U. Fla., 1953; m. Ellianna Gray, May 22, 1955; children—Celeni, Dawn, Mark, Scott. Indsl. engr. E.I. DuPont de Nemours & Co., Martinsville, Va., 1951, Allis Chalmers, Milw., 1953, Pensacola Naval Air Sta., Fla. 1955-61; mem. exec. staff Dr. Wernher von Braun, Marshall Space Flight Center, NASA, Huntsville, Ala., 1960-68; v.p., dir. Investors Corp. of Am., Birmingham, Ala., 1968-75, Internat. Resorts, Inc., 1970-75; pres. Profl. Realty Services Inc., Birmingham, 1977-78, Energy Systems Engrs., Inc., Birmingham, 1978-82, Income Diversification Cons., 1982-84, Abbott Supply Co., 1984-86, Abbott & Assocs., 1986—; dir. Pacific Am. Corp., San Francisco, Life Ins. Co. of Am., Birmingham, 1966-75. Served to lt. (j.g.) USNR, 1953-55. Registered profl. engr., Ala. Mem. Nat. Soc. Profl. Engrs., Pi Kappa Phi. Home: Rt 2 Box 116-B Alpine AL 35014

ABBOTT, CHARLES FAVOUR, JR., lawyer; b. Sedro-Woolley, Wash., Oct. 12, 1937; s. Charles Favour and Violette Doris (Boulter) A.; m. Oranee Harward Sept. 19, 1958; children: Patricia, Stephen, Nelson, Cynthia, Lisa, Alyson. BA in Econs., U. Wash., 1959, JD, 1962. Bar: Calif. 1962, Utah 1981. Law clk. Judge M. Oliver Koelsch, U.S. Ct. Appeals (9th cir.), San Francisco, 1963; assoc. Jones, Hatfield & Abbott, Escondido, Calif., 1964; sole practice, Escondido, 1964-77; of counsel Meuller & Abbott, Escondido, 1977—; ptnr. Abbott, Thorn & Hill, Provo, Utah, 1981-83; sole practice, Provo, Utah, 1983—. Mem. Utah Bar Assn., Calif. Bar Assn., Assn. Trial Lawyers Am. Mem. Ch. of Jesus Christ of Latter Day Saints. Editorial bd. Wash. Law Rev. and State Bar Assn. Jour., 1961-62; author: How to Do Your Own Legal Work, 1976, 2d edit., 1981, How to Win in Small Claims Court, 1981, How to be Free of Debt in 24 Hours, 1981, How to Hire the Best Lawyer at the Lowest Fee, 1981, The Lawyers' Inside Method of Making Money, 1979, The Millionaire Mindset, 1987; contbr. articles to profl. jours. Home: 3737 Foothill Dr Provo UT 84604

ABBOTT, DAVID HENRY, manufacturing company executive; b. Milton, Ky., July 6, 1936; s. Carl and Rachael (Miles) A.; m. Joan Shefchik, Aug. 14, 1976; children—Kristine, Gina, Beth, Linsey. B.S., U. Ky., 1960, M.B.A., 1961. With Ford Motor Co., Louisville, Mpls. and Dearborn, Mich., 1961-69; div. controller J I Case Co., Racine, Wis., 1970-73, gen. mgr. service parts supply, 1973-75, v.p., 1975-81, v.p. and gen. mgr. constrn. equipment, 1975-77; v.p., gen. mgr. Drott div. J I Case Co., Wausau, Wis., 1977-79, exec. v.p. worldwide constrn. equipment, 1979-81; pres., chief operating officer Portec, Inc., Oak Brook, Ill., 1981-87, also dir.; pres., chief exec. officer, dir. E.D. Etnyre & Co., Oregon, Ill., 1988—; dir. Oak Brook Bank, 1982-88. Served with U.S. Army, 1958. Mem. Constrn. Industry Mfrs. Assn. (bd. dirs. 1979-81, 82—), Am. Rd. & Transpn. Builders Assn. (dir. 1988—). Republican. Home: 2690 W Pines Rd Oregon IL 61061 Office: ED Etnyre & Co 1333 S Daysville Rd Oregon IL 61061-9705

ABBOTT, EDWARD LEROY, finance executive; b. Dayton, Ohio, Dec. 18, 1930; s. Roy Edward and Mildred Eileen (Filler) A.; m. Elizabeth Joan Grahame, June 8, 1957; children: Jay Edward, Julie Beth. A.B., Wittenberg U., 1952; postgrad., Ohio State U., 1952-53. With Northwestern Mut. Life Ins. Co., 1956-73; regional mgr. Northwestern Mut. Life Ins. Co., Washington, 1970-73; v.p. real estate Acacia Mut. Life Ins. Co., Washington, 1973-74; fin. v.p. Acacia Mut. Life Ins. Co., 1974-76, fin. v.p., treas., 1976-78, exec. v.p., 1978-83; dir., fin. v.p., treas. Acacia Nat. Life Ins. Co., 1974-82; trustee Westport Co., 1981-87, exec. v.p., 1983-87; pres., chief exec. officer Capital-Union Savs., Baton Rouge, 1987—, also chmn. bd.; chmn. bd. Acacia Fund Corp., 1975-79, Acacia Investment Mgmt. Co., 1975-79; vice chmn., dir. CenTrust Savs. Bank, 1983-87. Mem. Friends of Kennedy Center; vice chmn. United Way Miami, 1986. Served with U.S. Army, 1954-55. Mem. Mortgage Bankers Assn. Am., Washington Bd. Trade, Mortgage Bankers Assn. Met. D.C., Am. Council Life Ins., Internat. Platform Assn., Alpha Tau Omega. Republican. Clubs: Ocean Reef; City, Camelot, Country La. (Baton Rouge). Home: 7958 Wrenwood Blvd Baton Rouge LA 70809 Office: Capital-Union Savs 339 Florida St Baton Rouge LA 70801

ABBOTT, FRANCES ELIZABETH DOWDLE, journalist, civic worker; b. Rome, Ga., Mar. 21, 1924; d. John Wesley and Lucille Elizabeth (Field) Dowdle; student Draughon's Bus. Coll., Columbia, S.C.; m. Jackson Miles Abbott, May 15, 1948; children—Medora Frances, David Field, Elizabeth Stockton, Robert Jackson. Feature writer, Mt. Vernon corr. Alexandria Gazette, Va., 1967-75; librarian, research assoc. Gadsby's Tavern Mus., Alexandria, 1977—. Chmn. ann. George Washington Birthnight Ball, Mt. Vernon, 1974-82; sec. 250th Washington Birthday Celebration Commn., 1979-82; chmn. publicity Waynewood Woman's Club, Waynewood Citizens Assn.; treas. Mt. Vernon Citizens Assn., 1967-82; dist. chmn. Mt. Vernon March of Dimes, 1960-62; sec. Waynewood Sch. P.T.A., 1962-64; tchr. 1st aid Girl Scouts U.S.A., 1964-65; den mother Cub Scouts, 1966; registrar DAR, 1968-77; chmn. publicity Mt. Vernon Women's Republican Club, 1955. Named Mrs. Waynewood by Community Vote, 1969. Mem. Audubon Naturalist Soc., Nat. Trust Historic Preservation. Episcopalian. Home: 8501 Doter Dr Alexandria VA 22308 Office: 135 N Royal St Alexandria VA 22314

ABBOTT, MAX WENDEN, psychologist, administrator; b. Featherston, New Zealand, June 7, 1951; s. Harold C. and Marjory I. (Wenden) A. BA, BSc, Victoria U., Wellington, New Zealand, 1973; tchr.'s diploma with distinction, Christchurch (New Zealand) Tchr.'s Coll., 1974; MA, U. Canterbury, 1977, PhD, 1979, diploma in clin. psychology, 1980. Research asst. U. Canterbury, Christchurch, 1976-78; head counselling service Lincoln U. Coll., New Zealand, 1979-81; clin., community psychologist North Canterbury Hosp. Bd., Christchurch, 1979-81; dir. Mental Health Found. New Zealand, Auckland, 1981—; hon. cons. New Zealand Phobic Trust, 1984—; organizer various nat. seminars and confs. in mental health field; cons. to numerous TV dramas and documentaries on mental health, govt. depts. and agys. Founding editor Mental Health News mag., 1982, Jour. Community Mental Health in New Zealand, 1984; contbr. over 70 articles, reports to profl. jours. Active Victim's Task Force; founding trustee New Zealand AIDS Found., Positive Parenting Inc.; chairperson Nat. Nonviolence Campaign; v.p. World Fedn. for Mental Health. Mem. New Zealand Psychol. Soc. (chair com./applied social div. 1985-86), Internat. Council Psychologists, Am. Psychol. Assn. (coordinator Pacific div. 27 1983—), Social Monitoring Group (New Zealand planning council), New Zealand Pub. Health Assn., Health Promotion Forum of New Zealand, Internat. Acad. Law and Mental Health. Home: 111 Vermont St, Ponsonby Auckland 1, New Zealand Office: Mental Health Found New Zealand, 272 Parnell Rd, Auckland New Zealand

ABBOTT, MURIEL MACPHERSON, psychometrician; b. Montclair, N.J.; d. Graham and Muriel Margaret (Burleigh) Macpherson; B.A., Brown U.; M.A., Newark State Coll., 1961; Ph.D. (NDEA fellow), Columbia U., 1968; m. Charles F. Abbott (div.). Adj. prof. Tchrs. Coll., Columbia U., 1965-75; asst. dir. spl. projects Harcourt Brace Jovanovich Inc. (Psychol. Corp.), N.Y.C., 1965-76, asst. dir. profl. exams., 1976-78; dir. test devel. N.Y.C. Bd. Edn., 1978—; summer fellow in measurement Ednl. Testing Service, 1963. Mem. bd. mgrs. Vanderbilt YMCA, N.Y.C., 1977—, named Woman of Yr., 1982. Mem. Am. Psychol. Assn., Am. Ednl. Research Assn., Internat. Reading Assn., Nat. Council Measurement in Edn., Nat. Assn. Test Dirs., Brown U. Alumni Assn., Columbia U. Alumni Assn., Sigma Xi. Clubs: Brown U., New Eng. Soc. Contbr. articles to profl. jours. Home: 249 E 48th New York NY 10017 Office: 110 Livingston Brooklyn NY 11201

ABBOTT, ROBERT EARL, JR., city official; b. Dallas, Aug. 17, 1935; s. Robert Earl and Jane Ann (Hines) A.; BS, Hardin Simmons U., 1960; m. Gail Evans; 1 son, Mark Arthur. M in Urban and Regional Planning, Va. Poly. Inst. and State U., 1970; D in Pub. Adminstrn., NYU, 1979. City planner City of Richmond (Va.), 1969-71; dir. mayors' council N. Hudson Council Mayors, Hudson County, N.J., 1971-73; exec. dir. Regional Planning Commn., Thomas Jefferson Planning Dist. Commn., Charlottesville, Va., 1973-78; cons., pres. and cheif exec. officer Dallas-Ft. Worth Rail Planning Assn., 1986-87; cons. City of Charlottesville (Va.), 1979-80; sr. transp. planner City of Ft. Worth, 1981-87; transp. planner, engr., DeShazo, Starek and Tang, Ft. Worth, 1987-88; sales cons. EMNET, Carollton, Tex., 1988—; lectr. U. Va., U.S. Army Transp. Sch., Fed. Exec. Inst., Va. Commonwealth U., Va. Poly. Inst. and State U., North Tex. State U., Tex. A&M U., U. Tex.-Arlington. Served with AUS, 1960-62, 63-67. Mem. Am. Inst. Cert. Planners, Inst. Transp. Engrs., Am. Planning Assn., Tau Sigma Delta. Methodist. Lodges: Rotary, Masons. Home: 4525 Mockinbird Ln Dallas TX 75205 Office: EMNET 3033 Kellway Dr Carrollton TX 75006

ABBOTT, WOODROW ACTON, air force officer; b. Eubank, Ky., Dec. 16, 1919; s. William Thomas and Susie Ellen (Gastineau) A.; m. Lois Marie Scobee, May 17, 1944; children: Woodrow Acton II, Celesta Ann, Teletha Gay. Student, Butler U., 1939-43; B.S., U. Md., 1955, postgrad., 1956; M.B.A., Golden State U., 1982, Ph.D, 1984. Commd. 2d lt. USAAF, 1943; advanced through grades to brig. gen. USAF, 1969; B-17 pilot ETO, 1944-45; assigned Far East Air Force, 1950-52; with SAC, 1956-71; comdr. 92d Wing, 1966-67, 93d Wing, 1968-69, 307th Strategic Wing and 4258th Strategic Wing, Thailand, 1969-70, 42d Air Div., 1970-71; insp. gen. SAC, 1971-73; dir. intelligence J-2, also insp. gen. U.S., Readiness Command, MacDill AFB, Fla., 1973-87; pres. Nutech Fluidics, Modesto, Calif., 1987—. Decorated D.S.M. with oak leaf cluster, Legion of Merit with 2 oak leaf clusters, D.F.C., Meritorious Service medal, Air medal with 6 oak leaf clusters, Air Force Commendation medal with 2 oak leaf clusters, Army Commendation medal, Purple Heart; Supreme Command Forward badge 1st class Thailand). Mem. Delta Sigma Pi. Clubs: Tampa (Fla.); Yacht and Country, Merced Golf and Country, Merced Racquet. Home: 2930 Sunnyfield Dr Merced CA 95340

ABBRUZZESE, ALBERT VINCENT, JR., investment executive, educator; b. Boston, May 14, 1950; s. Albert Vincent Sr. and Angelina (Guerrerio) A. BS, Boston Coll., 1972; postgrad., N.Y. Inst. Fin., 1977. Account executive Prudential-Bache Securities, New Orleans, 1976-77; investment exec. Shearson Am. Express, New Orleans, 1977-82; portfolio mgr. E.F. Hutton, Inc., New Orleans, 1982-87; v.p. investments Prudential-Bache Securities, New Orleans, 1987-88, Dean Witter Reynolds, New Orleans, 1988—; adj. prof. fin. Tulane U., New Orleans, 1980—. Bd. dirs. ACLU, New Orleans, 1985—, Mental Health Assn. of Greater New Orleans, 1985—, Mental Health Assn. in La., 1985—; pres. Park Timbers Homeowners Assn., New Orleans, 1984-86. Mem. Internat. Assn. Fin. Planners (assoc.). Democrat. Roman Catholic. Home: #1 Yellowstone Dr New Orleans LA 70131 Office: Dean Witter Reynolds 639 Loyola Suite 200 New Orleans LA 70113

ABBRUZZESE, CARLO ENRICO, physician, writer; b. Rome, Italy, May 28, 1923; s. Aurelio and Maria (Sbriccoli) A.; Liceo-Ginnasio Dante Alighieri, Roma, 1935-43; Facoltà di Medicina e Chirurgia, Università di Roma, 1943-49; m. Jovanka N. Vasin, Feb. 14, 1976; children by previous marriage—Marco A., Carlo M., Eric L., Christopher E. Came to U.S., 1951, naturalized, 1959. Resident in tropical subtropical diseases U. Rome, 1950-51; intern Woman's and Highland Park Gen. hosps., Detroit, 1951-53; resident in family practice Saratoga Gen. Hosp., Detroit, Columbus Hosp., Newark, 1953-57; gen. practice occupational and sport medicine, Rome, 1949-51, Oakland, Calif., 1958-75, Santa Ana, Calif., 1975-84; dir. emergency and outpatients depts. Drs. Hosp. of Santa Ana (Calif.), 1975-77. Founder, leader polit. youth movements, Rome, 1943-47. Co-founder, nat. chmn. divorce reforms orgns., 1975; UN rep. on domestic human rights, 1977. Decorated Commendatore di Merito, 1950. Fulbright fellow, 1951-53. Fellow Am. Acad. Family Physicians; mem. Am. Acad. Gen. Practice, Ordine dei Medici di Roma Società Italiana di Chirurgia, Am. Coll. Emergency Physicians, Union Am. Physicians. Author: Storia della Psicologia, 1949; L'ascoltazione stetoscopica, 1955, 56, 83, 86; Esercitazioni di diagnostica ascoltatoria, 1983, 86; founder, pub., editor-in-chief ESDNA, Rome, 1983, ESDI, Rome, 1986; pub. Med. Newsletter, 1987. Contbr. articles to profl. jours. Office: 316 N Bristol St Santa Ana CA 92703

ABDALLAH, AHMED, president of Federal Islamic Republic of the Comoros; b. 1919. Former businessman; rep. Comoros Islands in French Senate, 1959-72; pres. Govt. Council, 1972-73, of Govt., 1973-75; leader Union democratique des Comoros, 1974, Parti pour l'Independence et l'Unité des Comoros, 1974-75; head of state, 1975, pres. Comoros, 1975; overthrown in coup, 1975; pres. Fed. Islamic Republic of Comoros, 1978—, pres. politicomilitary directory, minister of justice and civil service, 1978—. Address: Office of President, Moroni Comoros *

ABDELHAK, SAMI, shipping company and marketing executive; b. Alexandria, Egypt, May 19, 1947; arrived in Kuwait, 1969; s. Sami Hassan Abdelhak and Aziza Farahat Sobhi; m. Najwa Suleiman Kleibo. BA, Am. Univ., Cairo, 1969. Asst. gen. mgr. Aratrans, Kuwait, 1970-72; sr. cargo sales rep. Kuwait Airways, 1972-74; traffic mgr. Yusuf Ahmad Al Ghanim, Kuwait, 1974-82; mktg. dir. Al Ghanim and Al Qutub, Kuwait, 1982—. Mem. Inst. Phys. Distbn. Mgmt., U.S. Arab C. of C. Home: #3 Area 4 House 23, Kuwait, Bayan Kuwait Office: Al Ghanim & Al Qutub, Kuwait Kuwait

ABDELKADER, MOSTAFA AHMAD, independent researcher; b. Cairo, Egypt, May 15, 1923; s. Ahmad Abdelkader Adaroas and Moneera Ayoub Sharaara. B.E.E., U. Cairo, 1946; postgrad. Swiss Fed. Inst. Tech., Zurich, 1946-50. Ind. researcher, author research papers on geocosmos, electron dynamics, electric circuits and filters, artificial satellite orbits, algebraic equations, spl. functions and polynomials, finite series, exact solutions of nonlinear differential equations. Contbr. research papers to math., sci. and engring. jours. Recipient state prize in engring. scis. Council Sci. Research, Cairo, 1965; Decoration of Sci. and Tech., pres. of Egypt, 1967. Mem. Am. Math. Soc., Soc. Indsl. and Applied Math. Moslem. Home: 25 Sh Champollion, Alexandria Egypt

ABDEL-KHALIK, AHMED RASHAD, business educator; b. Meet-Ghamer, Egypt, May 30, 1940; came to U.S., 1964, naturalized, 1975; s. Mohamed Ahmed and Gamilah El-Morsey (Abdel-bary) Abdel-K.; m. Maria Eugenia, June 30, 1973; children: Jasmine, Catherine, Justin Christopher. BCom hon., Cairo U., 1961; MBA, Ind. U., 1965, AM, 1966; PhD, U. Ill.-Urbana, 1972. Asst. prof. bus. Columbia U., N.Y.C., 1972-74, assoc. prof., 1974-75; assoc. prof. bus. adminstrn. Duke U., Durham, N.C., 1975-77; W.J. Matherly prof. acctg. U. Fla., Gainesville, 1977-80, grad. research prof., 1977-83, 84—, dir. Acctg. Research Ctr., 1977-83, 84—; Weldon Powell prof. U. Ill.-Champaign, 1983-84; vis. Winspear Found. prof. U. Alta., 1982-83. Author, editor several books; contbr. articles to acad. and profl. jours.; founding editor: Jour. Accounting Literature, 1980—. Ernst & Ernst fellow, 1971-72. Mem. Am. Acctg. Assn. (doctoral fellow 1971-72, dir. research 1980-82, editor Acctg. Rev.), Am. Econ. Assn., Fin. Execs. Inst., Am. Fin. Assn., Can. Acad. Acctg. Assn., Beta Alpha Psi, Beta Gamma Sigma. Home: 121 SW 84th Terr Gainesville FL 32607 Office: Fisher Sch Acctg U Fla Gainesville FL 32611

ABDEL MEGUID, AHMED ESMAT, Egyptian minister foreign affairs; b. Alexandria, Egypt, Mar. 22, 1923; m. Eglal Abou-Hamda, 1950; 3 sons. Licence en Droit, Alexandria U., 1944; diploma of Higher Studies in Pub. Law, Paris U., 1947, diploma of Higher Studies in Econs., 1948, diploma of Comparative Law Inst., 1949, diploma of Polit. Sci. Inst., 1949, Ph.D. in Internat. Law, 1951; postgrad. Acad. Internat. Law, The Hague, summer 1949, Inst. Advanced Legal Studies, London U., 1951-52. Atty. legal dept. Egyptian Govt., 1944-45; attache and 3d sec. Embassy of Egypt, London; polit. adviser Anglo Egyptian Agreement, 1954-56; head U.K. desk, Ministry Fgn. Affairs, Cairo, Egypt, 1954-57, dept. dir. legal dept., 1961-63; counsellor Permanent Mission of Egypt to European Office of UN, Geneva, 1957-61; minister plenipotentiary at Egyptian Embassy, Paris, 1963-67; chef de cabinet of Under-sec. of State for Fgn. Affairs, Cairo, 1968; sec.-gen. high interministerial com. of cultural relations and tech. assitance of Arab Republic Egypt, 1969; head of cultural and tech. assistance dept. Ministry of Fgn. Affairs, Cairo, 1968-69; head State Info. Service, ofcl. spokesman of Egyptian Govt. with rank of dep. minister, 1969; ambassador of Egypt to France, 1970; minister of State for Cabinet Affairs, 1970-72; ambassador permanent rep. of Arab Republic of Egypt to UN, 1972-83, minister fgn. affairs, Cairo, 1984—, dep. prime minister, 1985—; external examiner internat. law Faculty of Law, Cairo U. and Alexandria U., 1962-63; charge de cours on diplomacy Faculty of Econs. and Polit. Sci., Cairo, U., 1962; mem. internat. rivers com., ILA; head numerous ministerial coms.; lectr. in field; mem., rep., head various delegations to confs., councils. Contbr. articles to profl. jours. Pres. Egyptian com. for Tut-Ankh-Amon Exhbn. Le Petit-Palais, Paris, 1966; presided over dedication of Sackler Wing housing Egyptian Temple of Dendur at Met. Mus. Art, N.Y.C., 1978. Decorated Grand Croix Govt. of France, 1st Class Arab Republic of Egypt, Govt. of Yugoslavia, Ordre de Merite Govt. of France; Presdl. fellow Aspen Inst. for Humanistic Studies. Mem. Egyptian UN Assn., French-Egyptian Friendship Soc., Egyptian Bar Assn., Internat. Law Assn., Egyptian Soc. Internat. Law (past bd. dirs.). Office: Ministry Fgn Affairs, Cairo Egypt

ABDEL-RAHMAN, AISHA (BINT EL-SHATI), author, educator. Student Cairo U. Asst. lectr. Cairo U., 1939—; lit. critic Al Ahram, 1942—; insp. in Arabic langs. and lit. Ministry of Edn., 1942—; lectr. Arabic Ain Shams U., 1950-57, asst. prof., 1957-62, prof. Arabic lit. Univ. Coll. for Women, 1962—, also chmn. Author: Rissalet el Ghofram by Abul Ala'a, 1950; New Values in Arabic Literature, 1961; The Koran: Literary Interpretation, 1962; Ibn Seeda's Arabic Dictionary, 1962; Contemporary Arab Women Poets, 1963; 6 books on illustrious women of Islam; 2 novels; 4 vols. of short shories. Recipient State prize, 1936; award for Textual Studies Acad. Arabic Lang., 1952. Mem. Higher Council of Arts and Letters. Address: 13 Agam St, Heliopolis, Cairo Egypt *

ABDOUN, AMIN MAGZOUB, diplomat, import-export company owner; b. Berber, Sudan, Aug. 22, 1930; s. Magzoub Abdoun and Khadija Moharam; m. Raga Abdoun; children: Hind, Hala. BA, Khartoum U., Sudan, 1954. Sudan ambassador to India, 1968-70, Cen. African Republic, 1970-72, United Arab Emerates, 1972-73, Czechoslovakia, 1973-74; owner, operator agrl. import business Amin Enterprises Ltd, Khartoum, Sudan and Cairo, Egypt, 1974—; rep. of Sudan UN, N.Y.C., 1986—. Moslem. Office: Sudan Mission UN 210 E 49th St New York NY 10017

ABDUL-GHANI, ABDUL-AZIZ, prime minister of Yemen Arab Republic; b. Haifan, Yemen Arab Republic, July 4, 1939; s. Abdulghani Saleh and Tohfa Moqbel; m. Aceya Hamza, 1966; children: Muhammed, Hanan, Omar, Usama, Walid, Bassam. BS in Econs., U. Colo., 1962, MA in Econs., 1964, PhD (hon.), 1978. Tchr. English, Social Studies, Commerce Belquis Coll., Aden, 1964-67; chmn. tech. office Bd. Planning, 1969-71; chmn. Yemen Oil Co., 1971; gov. Cen. Bank Yemen, 1971-75; lectr. polit. sci. Faculty of Law Sana'a U., Yemen Arab Republic, 1972-74; minister of health Yemen Arab Republic, 1967-68, minister of economy, 1968-69, 70-71, prime minister, 1975-80, 83—, v.p., 1980-83. Mem: Yemen Econ. Soc. Office: Office of Prime Minister, PO Box 2661, Sana'a Yemen Arab Republic *

ABDUL HALIM MU'ADZAM SHAH, IBNI AL-MARHUM SULTAN BADLISHAH, sultan of Kedah; b. Alor Star, Kedah, Malaysia, Nov. 28, 1927; s. Sultan Badlishah of Kadeh; m. Tunku Hajjah Bahiyah, Mar. 1956; 3 children. Grad., Sultan Abdul Hamid Coll., Alor, 1949; diploma social sci. and pub. adminstrn., Oxford (Eng.) U., 1955; D. Polit. Sci. (hon.), Thammasat U., Bangkok, Thailand. With Dist. Office, then Treasury Alor State, 1955—; raja muda of Kedah 1949-57, regent, 1957-58, sultan, 1958—; dep. king, then king Conf. of Rulers, 1965-75; col.-in-chief Royal Malay Rgt., 1975. Decorated D.K., 1964, D.K.M., 1971, D.M.N., 1959, D.U.K., 1958, S.P.M.K., 1964, D.K., 1969, D.K. (Pehang), 1970, 1st class Order Rising Sun (Japan), 1970, Bitang Maha Putera, Klas Satu (Indonesia), 1970, hon. mnight grad cross Order Bath (U.K.), 1972, assoc. knight Order St. John, 1972, Order Ramnata (Thailand), 1973. Office: care Press Attache Malaysian Embassy 2401 Massachusetts Ave NW Washington DC 20008 *

ABDULLAH, ABDULLAH, government administrator; b. Peshawar, Pakistan, Jan. 16, 1941; s. Mohammad Amir Alam. BA with honors, Peshawar U., MA in English. Sec. Bd. of Revenue, NWFP Peshawar, Pakistan; polit. agt. Malakand, Pakistan; registrar Coops., NWFP Peshawar, Pakistan; polit. agt. South Waziristan, Pakistan; first. sec. Pakistan Mission, Jedda, Saudi Arabia; commr. Afghan Refugees, Peshawar, Pakistan; dep. sec. Establishment div., Islamabad, Pakistan; dir. Pakistan Acad. for Rural Devel., Peshawar, Pakistan. Home: Peshawar Pakistan Office: Pakistan Acad for Rural Devel, Peshawar Pakistan

ABDULLAH BIN MOHD SALLEH, TAN SRI, oil company executive; b. Melaka, Malaysia, June 24, 1926; d. Mohd Salleh Bin Jaudin and Sokyah Binti Hassan; m. Mahani Binte Abdul Razak, Aug. 23, 1957; children—Abu Hanifah, Azmi, Azleen Azaidah. B.A. with honors, U. Malaya, 1955; LL.D., Nat. U. Malaysia, 1980. With Malaysian fgn. service, 1955-71; sec.-gen. Ministry of Agr. and Fisheries, 1972, Pub. Service Dept., 1974; chief sec. Govt. Malaysia, Kuala Lumpur, 1976-78; chmn., chief exec. officer Petronas, Kuala Lumpur, 1979-83, pres., 1984—; chmn. Malaysia LNG Sdn Bhd, Bintulu, Sarawak, 1979—, Asean Bintulu Fertilizer Sdn Bhd, Bintulu, 1979—; dep. chmn. Petronas-Carigali Sdn Bhd, Kuala Lumpur, 1979—. Pres. Fedn. Family Planning Assns. Malaysia. Recipient Panglima Mangku Negara award Govt. of Malaysia, 1977; Barjah Mulia Seri Melaka award, 1974; Govt. of Melaka, 1974; Dato Paduka Mahkota Trengganu award Govt. of Trengganu, 1981. Islamic. Club: Subang Nat. Golf (v.p. Kuala Lumpur). Office: Petronas, PO Box 12444, Kuala Lumpur Malaysia *

ABDULLAH IBN ABDUL-AZIZ, PRINCE, crown prince of Saudi Arabia, politician, army officer; b. 1924; s. King Abdulazziz ibn Saud (dec.); ed. in religion, chivalry and politics. Comdr., Nat. Guard, Saudi Arabia, 1962—; sec. dep. prime minister, 1975-82; crown prince, dep. prime minister, 1982—. Address: Office of Deputy Prime Minister, Jeddah Saudi Arabia *

ABDURRAHMAN, MURTALA BAMDELE, pediatrician, medical professor, consultant; b. Offa, Kwara, Nigeria, Aug. 30, 1940; s. Afolabi and Sifawu Apeke (Gbadamasi) A.; m. Maryam A. Banjo, Nov. 29, 1969; children: Olukemi, Olayinka, Mariam, Kabir, Zainab. MB,BS, U. Ibadan, Nigeria, 1967. Diplomate Am. Bd. Pediatrics. Clin. asst. The Hosp. for Sick Children, Toronto, Can., 1973; cons. pediatrician Greater Niagara Gen. Hosp., Niagara Falls, Can., 1973-74; lectr. Ahmadu Bello U., Zaria, Nigeria, 1974-76, sr. lectr., 1976-79, reader, 1979-81, prof., 1981-85; prof. King Saud U., Riyadh, Saudi Arabia, 1985—; cons. pediatrician various hosps. in Can., Nigeria and Saudi Arabia, 1973—; asst. dean, dept. head Ahmadu Bello U., 1976-82. Cons. editor Nigerian Jour. Pediatrics; asst. editor West African Med. Jour.; contbr. articles to profl. jours. Served to capt. Nigerian Armed Forces, M.C. Fellow Internat. Soc. Nephrology, Royal Coll. Can. (Pediatrics); mem. Internat. Pediatric Nephrology Assn. Moslem. Club: Kaduna. Office: Dept of Pediatrics, PO Box 2925, Riyadh 11461, Saudi Arabia

ABE, KOBO, author; b. Tokyo, Japan, Mar. 7, 1924; grad. Tokyo U.; L.H.D., Columbia U., 1975. Recipient 25th Akutagawa prize, 1951, Post-war Lit. prize, 1950, Kishida prize for drama, 1958, Yomiuri Lit. prize, 1962, 75, Tanizaki prize for drama, 1967. Mem. Am. Acad. Arts and Scis. (fgn. hon.). Author: The Road Sign at the End of the Road, 1948; The Red Cocoon, 1950; The Crimes of S. Karma, 1951; Hunger Union, 1954; The Uniform, 1955; Hunt for a Slave, 1955; Animals are Forwarding to their Natives, 1957; The Fourth Unglacial Period, 1959; Here is a Ghost, 1959; Eyes of Stone, 1960; The Woman in the Dunes, 1962; The Face of Another, 1964; You are Guilty Too, 1965; Buyo Enomoto, 1965; Friends, 1967; The Ruined Map, 1967; The Man Who Became a Stick, 1969; Inter Ice Age Four, 1970; Premeditated Act of Uncertain Consequences, 1971; Guidebook, 1971; The Box Man, 1973; Love's Spectacles are Colored Glass, 1973; Green Stocking, 1974; Wee, 1975; Secret Rendez-vous, 1977; Kozo wa Shinda, 1979; Ark Sakuramaru, 1984. Address: 1-22-10 Wakaba Cho, Chofu City, Tokyo Japan

ABE, SHINTARO, Japanese politician; b. Apr. 29, 1924; Mem. Japanese Ho. of Reps., 1958—; pvt. sec. to Prime Minister Nobusuke Kishi, 1957-58; former dep. sec.-gen. Liberal Democratic Party, former v.p. diet policy com., chmn. diet policy com., 1976-77, chmn. policy affairs research council, 1979-81, chmn. exec. council, now sec. gen.; minister of Agr. and Forestry, 1974-76; chief cabinet sec., 1977-78; minister of Internat. Trade and Industry, 1981-82; minister of Fgn. Affairs, 1982-86; former polit. reporter Mainichi newspaper. Office: care Liberal Democratic Party, 1-11-23 Nagata-cho, Chiyoda-ku Tokyo 100, Japan *

ABEDI, JAFAR MEHDI, airline industry executive; b. Juanpour, India, Jan. 16, 1946; parents: Ali Mazhar and Kaniz (Fatima) A.; m. Sajeda Abedi, 1971. Student, Islamia Coll., Karachi, Pakistan; B of Commerce, Karachi U., 1965; diploma of bus. adminstrn., Tokyo U., 1973. From traffic asst. to sta. mgr. Pakistan Internat. Airlines, Karachi, Kuwait, London, Dubai, 1963-75; area sales mgr. United Arab Emirates, Gulf area, Iran and Pakistan Sabena Belgian Airlines, Dubai, United Arab Emirates, 1975—. Home: PO Box 8581, Dubai United Arab Emirates Office: Emirates Express Travel, & Cargo, PO Box 5476, Sharjah United Arab Emirates

ABEDI, SYED MASSOUD ALY-KHAN, investment company executive; b. Hyder Abad, India, June 12, 1929; s. Syed Sulaiman Ali and Karim-Un-Nissa (Ameer) A.; m. Syeda Mazhar Jehan, Apr. 7, 1956; children—Syed Mustapha Kemal, S. Murtuza Shezad Kemal, Syeda Mariam Jehan. B.A. in Econs., Madras U., India, 1947; B.Sc. in Physics, Istanbul U., Turkey, 1949, M.B.A., 1950; B.A.(Hons.), Trinity Coll., Dublin, 1953, D.Polit. Sci., 1955. Asst. comml. supt. P.I.D.C., shipyard, Karachi, Pakistan, 1955-56; exec. Burmah-Shell, Karachi, 1956-57; additional rehab. settlement commr. Pakistan Govt., Sukkur, 1958-60; dep. sec. Atomic Energy Commn. Pakistan Govt., Karachi, 1960-62; various sales promotion positions Pakistan Internat. Air Lines, Karachi, 1962-66; dir. Joyhurst Ltd., London, 1966-81, S.M. Meer, Ltd., Karachi, 1966-81; v.p. Yosriah Hilmi Establishment, Jeddah, Saudi Arabia, 1982; info. mgr. Albaraka Investment & Devel. Co., Jeddah, 1982—; freelance journalist, writing articles, commentary and several books under pseudonyms. Pakistan del. Econ. Commn. For Asia and Far East, Karachi, 1963, Internat. Sci. Conf., Dacca, Pakistan, 1961, various meetings and confs. of IAEA, IATA. Recipient Gold medal A.B.I. of U.S.A., 1988; fellow Internat. Biog. Ctr. (Cambridge U.), Am. Biog. Inst. Avocations: cricket, polo, tennis, hockey, reading. Office: Albaraka Investment & Devel Co, PO Box 6854, Jeddah 21452, Saudi Arabia

ABEL, ALLAN BERNARD, management consultant; b. Williams, Calif., Dec. 22, 1924; s. Allen and Consuelo (Benham) A.; student U. Calif., Berkeley, 1943-50, Golden Gate Coll., 1947, Instituto Cultural Mexicano-Americano, Guadalajara, Mexico, 1961; m. Maria Socorro; children—Allan Bernard, Allen Raymond, Sonya. Practice in Reno, 1954-69, Las Vegas, 1969—; investment adviser, tax cons., rare coinbroker, 1963-67; asso., bus. cons. Bus. Consultants, Inc., bus. and mgmt. cons. in 11 Western states and Mexico, 1967—; pres. SUMCO, Inc.; officer, dir. Centro de Vivienda para Retirados, S.A., Abel de Mexico., S.A.; sec.-treas. Magic Valley Enterprises, Inc.; sec.-treas. Central Devel. Co., Las Vegas, also dir.; sec. Gastrox Constrn. Co., Las Vegas. Agt., Nev. Gaming Control Bd., Nev. Gaming Commn., 1956; dir. So. Nev. conf. Pop Warner Jr. Football, 1st v.p., 1981—; mem. nat. com. Young Democrats Clubs Am., 1955-57, bd. dirs., 1957-59; mem. exec. bd. Clark County Dem. Central Com., 1970—; mem. Nev. State Dem. State Central Com., 1970—, vice chmn., 1957-58; gen. mgr. retirement housing project, Mexico, 1965-67; pres. chpt. 15 Mother Earth News; state chmn. com. select del. Humphrey; chmn. Lucy Branch Kidney Fund; counselor Family Abuse Center; pres. Flame Soccer Club; dir. Las. Las Vegas Under 23 Select Soccer Team; Lic. pub. accountant, Nev. Mem. Nat. Soc. Pub. Accountants, U. Calif. Alumni Assn. (life), Inst. Indsl. Relations Alumni Assn., Internat. Platform Assn., Am. Numis. Assn. Democrat. Spaceite. Clubs: Calif. 23 (Berkeley); Tower and Flame, Daily Californian, Am. Soc. Jalisco. Pub.: Nev. Report. Research on problems of aged living in fgn. country, 1963-64. Home: 900 Antonio Dr Las Vegas NV 89107 Office: 3540 W Sahara Suite 298 Las Vegas NV 89104

ABEL, GENE PAUL, educational business officer; b. Allentown, Pa., Feb. 5, 1941; s. Paul John and Lorraine Charlotte (Hoffner) A.; m. Lucy Diane Brinker, Oct. 15, 1960 (div. June 1977); children: Robert, Paul, Jonathan; m. Carol Lynne Kallenbach, Dec. 11, 1977. BS in Fin. and Econs., Pa. State U., 1963; MBA in Mgmt., Lehigh U., 1964; grad. internat. relations, Army War Coll., 1985. Fin. analyst, space div. Gen. Electric Co., King of Prussia, Pa., 1968-69; bus. mgr. Dept. Biology U. Pa., Phila., 1969-72; dir. communications and materials mgmt. Hahnemann U., Phila., 1972-81; data processing project mgr. U.S. Army Fin. Ctr., Ft. Harrison, Ind., 1981-83; dir. facilities mgmt. Mchts. Nat. Bank, Allentown, 1983-84; chief fin. and bus. officer Reading (Pa.) Area Community Coll., 1984-86; bus. mgr., treas. Cen. Bucks Sch. Dist., Doylestown, Pa., 1986—. Contbr. articles to profl. jours. Mem. Adminstrv. Assembly, U. Pa., chmn. 1971-72; active Pa. Rep. campaigns, Valley Forge, 1974, 76; chmn. Cub Scout pack King of Prussia, 1970, 71. Served as col. USAR. Named Disting. Mil. Grad., Pa. State U.; recipient Commendation and Meritorious Service medals, U.S. Army. Mem. Nat. Assn. College and Univ. Bus. Officers. Republican. Lutheran. Lodge: Masons. Office: Cen Bucks Sch Dist Adminstrn Ctr 315 W State St Doylestown PA 18901

ABEL, ROBERT, JR., ophthalmologist; b. Phila., Nov. 21, 1943; s. Robert and Ruth (Rovner) A.; m. Rosita Michael, June 16, 1984; children: Ari Daniel, Lauren, Adam. BA, Wesleyan U., Middletown, Conn., 1965; MD, Jefferson Med. Coll., Phila., 1969. Diplomate Am. Bd. Ophthalmology. Resident Mount Sinai Hosp., N.Y.C., 1970-73; fellow U. Fla., Gainesville, 1973-74; pres. Del. Ophthalmology Cons., P.A., Wilmington, 1974—; chmn. dept. ophthalmology The Med. Ctr. Del., Wilmington, 1982—; pres. East Coast Eye assocs.; dir. Med. Eye Bank Del., Wilmington, 1982—; cons. E.I. DuPont DeNemours & Co., Wilmington; clin. assoc. prof. Thomas Jefferson U., Phila., 1984—. Mem. editorial bd. Del. Med. Jour., Jour. Ocular Surgery; contbr. articles to profl. jours.; patentee articial cornea. Bd. dirs. Del. Polit. Action Com., Wilmington, 1980-85; advisor State Dept. Social Services; chmn. bd. Wesleyan Schs. Com. Recipient William H. Hoppin award N.Y. Acad. Medicine, 1973. Fellow ACS (bd. councilors 1975-84), Am. Acad. Ophthalmology (Honor award 1984), Am. Coll. Clin. Pharmacy; mem. Del. Acad. Ophthalmology (past pres.), Del. Med. Soc., County Med. Soc., Mensa. Jewish. Lodge: Oddfellows. Home and Office: 1100 N Grant Ave Wilmington DE 19805

ABELA, GEORGE SAMIH, medical educator, internist, cardiologist; b. Tripoli, Lebanon, Jan. 1, 1950; came to U.S., 1976; s. Anthony George and Maro (Kozma) A.; m. Sonia Zablit, May 14, 1977; children—Oliver George, Andrew John, Scott Anthony. B.Sc. in Chemistry and Biology, Am. U. of Beirut, 1971, M.Sc. in Pharmacology, 1974, M.D., 1976. Diplomate Am. Bd. Internal Medicine, Am. Bd. Cardiology. Intern in pathology Emory U., Atlanta, 1976-77, resident in medicine, 1977-80; fellow in cardiology U. Fla., Gainesville, 1980-83, asst. prof. medicine and cardiology, 1983-87, assoc. prof., 1987—. Research fellow Am. Heart Assn., 1982-83; Merck fellow Am. Coll. Cardiology, 1982-83; recipient New Investigator Research award NIH, 1983-86, Research Career Devel. award NIH, 1986-91. Fellow Am. Soc. for Lasers in Medicine, Am. Coll. Cardiology (assoc.), Am. Soc. Laser Medicine and Surgery (chmn. Standards of Tng. and Practice com. 1987-88); mem. Am. Heart Assn., ACP.

ABELAR, INA MAE, equipment technician; b. Jay Em, Wyo., July 18, 1926; d. Merritt Lyle and Leeta May (Worthen) Cameron; B.A., Calif. State Poly. U., 1978; m. Michael Sandoval Abelar, Nov. 17, 1951 (div. 1966); children—Debora Jean, Michelle Elaine, Randolph Lee. Lumber estimator Keith Brown Bldg. Supply, Salem, Oreg., 1946-48; with Whiting-Mead Bldg. Supply, Vernon, Calif., 1949-51, Trojan Lumber Co., Burbank, Calif., 1952-55; bookkeeper Jerry Kalior Bookkeeping Systems, North Hollywood, Calif., 1959-66; with Calif. State Poly. U., Pomona, 1967—, supervising equip. technician II dept. physics, 1979-88, mem. campus staff council, 1970-88, chmn., 1977-78. Recipient outstanding staff award Calif. State Poly U., 1983-84, Disting. Staff Emeritus, 1988. Deaconess, Upland Christian Ch., 1978-81; mem. chancellery choir Bethany Bapt. Ch., 1984—. Mem. Mu Phi Epsilon. (chpt. pres. 1983-86). Democrat. Home: 1833 Benedict Way Pomona CA 91767 Office: 3801 W Temple St Rm 8-238 Pomona CA 91768

ABELE, HOMER E., judge; b. Wellston, Ohio, Nov. 21, 1916; s. Oscar and Margaret (Burke) A.; m. Addie Riggs, 1938; children: Terrell Ann, Peter Burke, Andy. LL.B., Ohio State U., 1953, J.D., 1970. Bar: Ohio 1954, U.S. Supreme Ct. 1954. Mem. CCC, 1935-36; with Anchor Hocking Glass Corp., Lancaster, Ohio; then Austin Powder Co., McArthur, Ohio, to 1941; patrolman Ohio State Hwy. Patrol, Van Wert, 1941-43, 46; solicitor McArthur; Vinton County rep. Ohio Gen. Assembly, 1949-52; asst. to campaign mgr. Sen. Robert A. Taft, Republican Nat. Conv., Chgo., 1952; legis. counsel Spl. Transp. Com., 1953-57; del. Rep. Nat. Conv., San Francisco, 1956; Rep. nominee for Congress, 10th Ohio Dist., 1958; mem. 88th Congress from 10th Dist. Ohio; judge 4th Dist. Ohio Ct. Appeals, 1967-77, presiding judge, 1977-78, 83, 84; chief justice Ct. Appeals Ohio, 1978; Past state dept. judge adv. Am. Legion Ohio; chmn. ct. sect. Am. Legion Buckeye Boy's State, 1969-79, pres., 1981, 82. Program chmn. McArthur Devel. Assn.; Vinton County trustee Southeastern Ohio Regional Council. Served with USAAF, 1943-46. Mem. Am. Legion (exec. officer to past state comdr.), Ohio, Vinton County bar assns., Ohio Bar Found. Clubs: McArthur Lions (past pres.), Soc. South Pole (life). Home: McArthur OH 45651 Office: 4th Appellate Dist McArthur OH 45651

ABELL, ALICE VIRGINIA SIMS (MRS. NORMAN ABELL), civic worker; b. Elizabethtown, Ky., June 29, 1902; d. Francis Leroy and Antoinette (Freeman) Sims; student N.Y. Sch. Design, Otis Art Inst., Cal. Sch. Fine Arts; student U. Ariz., 1921-22; m. Norman Abell, Mar. 19, 1927; children: Norman, Virginia Frances (Mrs. James Langdon Blake), Arlene Alice (Mrs. Francis Bruce Robertson). Pres., Abell Enterprises, Long Beach, Calif., 1954—. Gray Lady ARC, Long Beach, 1942-45; chmn. arts and crafts, 1945; mem. Pan Hellenic Bd., Long Beach, 1961; vol. Meml. Hosp. Aux., Long Beach, 1960—, occupational therapy chmn., 1960-62; organizer minimal universal lang. project, 1958; mem. Regional Arts Council; charter mem. research council Scripps U. Clinic. Recipient first prize Santa Ana (Calif.) Art Exhibit, 1941. Mem. DAR, Art Mus. Assn., Los Angeles World Affairs Council, Civic Light Opera Assn., Fine Arts Affiliates of Long Beach State U., Smithsonian Assocs., Town Hall of Calif., Gamma Phi Beta. Episcopalian. Home: 4022 Pacific Ave Long Beach CA 90807

ABELOV, STEPHEN LAWRENCE, clothing company executive; b. N.Y.C., Apr. 1, 1923; s. Saul S. and Ethel (Esterman) A.; B.S., NYU, 1945, M.B.A., 1950; m. Phyllis S. Lichtenson, Nov. 18, 1945; children—Patricia C. (Mrs. Marvin Demoff), Gary M. Asst. div. mgr. Nat. Silver Co., N.Y., 1945; sales rep. Angelica Uniform Co., N.Y., 1945-50; asst. sales mgr., 1950-56, western regional mgr., Los Angeles, 1956-66, v.p. Angelica Uniform Co. of Calif., 1958-66, nat. v.p. sales, 1966-72, v.p. Angelica Corp. 1968—group v.p. mktg., 1972-80, exec. v.p., chief mktg. officer Angelica Uniform Group, 1980—; vis. lectr. mktg. NYU Grad. Sch. Bus. Adminstrn. Vice comdr. Am. Legion; mem. vocational adv. bd. VA.; adv. bd. Woodcraft Rangers; bd. dirs. Univ. Temple. Served with USAF, 1942-44. Mem. Am. Assn. Contamination Control (dir.), Am. Soc. for Advancement Mgmt. (chpt. pres.), Am. Mktg. Assn., Health Industries Assn. Am. (dir.), Inst. Environ. Scis., various trade assns., St. Louis Council on World Affairs, Sales Execs. Club (bd. dirs.), NYU Alumni Assn., Phi Epsilon Pi (treas.). Mem. B'nai B'rith (past pres.). Clubs: Men's (exec. v.p.); Town Hall, NYU, Aqua Sierra Sportsmen, Clayton. Contbr. articles to profl. jours. Home: 9821 Log Cabin Ct Ladue MO 63124 Office: Angelica Corp 10176 Corporate Square Dr Saint Louis MO 63132

ABELS, HERBERT, mathematics educator; b. Aachen, Fed. Republic Germany, May 4, 1941. D in Math., U. Würzburg, Fed. Republic Germany, 1965, habilitation, 1971. Asst. U. Bochum, Fed. Republic Germany, 1965-71; research fellow U. Calif., Berkeley, 1966-67; prof. U. Bielefeld, Fed. Republic Germany, 1972—; vis. prof. Cornell U., 1987-88. Office: U Bielefeld Fakultat Math, Postfach 8640, 48 Bielefeld Federal Republic of Germany

ABELSHAUSER, WERNER LUDWIG, educator; b. Wiesloch, Baden, Germany, Nov. 24, 1944; s. Franz Josef and Gertrud (Mangold) A.; m. Petra-Monika Jander, Jan. 11, 1974; 1 child, Hans. Diploma Volkswirt, U. Mannheim, 1970; PhD, U. Bochum, 1973, D Phil habil., 1980, prof., 1983. Asst. U. Munich, 1970; asst. U. Bochum, 1970-80, privatdozent, 1980-83, prof., 1983—; bd. dirs. Inst. for Labor Movement Studies, 1985—. Author: Wirtschaftsgeschichte der BRD, 1983, der Ruhrkohlenbergbau seit 1945, 1984, die Weimarer Republik als Wohlfahrtsstaat, 1987. Fellow St.Antony's Coll., Oxford, European U. Inst., Florence, U. Mo. at St. Louis, U. N.S.W., Sydney. Office: U Bochum, PO Box 102148, Bochum D4630, Federal Republic of Germany

ABERCONWAY, CHARLES MELVILLE MCLAREN, business executive; b. Apr. 16, 1913; s. 2d Baron and Christabel Aberconway; m. Deidre Knewstub, 1941 (div. 1949); 3. children; m. Ann Lindsay Bullard, 1949; 1 son. Student Eton Coll.; New Coll., Oxford. Barrister, Middle Temple, 1937; chmn. John Brown & Co. Ltd., 1953-78, pres., 1978—; chmn. English China Clays Ltd., 1963—; dep. chmn. Westland Aircraft Ltd., 1979-84, Sun Alliance, London Ins. Co., 1976-85; dir. Nat. Westminster Bank Ltd. Pres. Royal Hort. Soc., 1961—; commr. gen. Internat. Garden Festival, Liverpool, Eng., 1984. Served with Brit. Army, 1939-45. *

ÅBERG-WISTEDT, ANNA KRYSTYNA, psychiatrist; b. Vilno, Poland, Mar. 22, 1943; arrived in Sweden, 1967; d. Jerzy and Irena Stalewski; m. Börje Wistedt, Nov. 18, 1979; children: Monica, John, Oscar. MD, U. Gdansk, Poland, 1967, Karolinska Inst., Stockholm, 1970. Cert. physician Swedish Med. Bd., 1970; cert. specialist in psychiatry Swedish Med. Bd., 1973. Resident in internal medicine Hudiksvall Hosp., Sweden, 1968; resident in surgery Lindesberg Hosp., Sweden, 1969; resident in neurology Stockholm Hosp., 1971; resident in psychiatry Danderyd Hosp., Sweden, 1971-73, cons. unit psychiatry, 1973-87, chief psychiatrist, 1987—. Contbr. articles to profl. jours. Mem. Swedish Med. Assn., Swedish Psychiat. Assn., Scandinavian Soc. for Psychopharmacology, Internat. Com. for Prevention and Treatment of Depression. Office: Danderyd Hosp Psychiat Unit, S-182 88 Danderyd Sweden

ABERNATHY, DAVID MYLES, producer; b. Connelly Springs, N.C., June 27, 1933; s. James William and Lorena Mae (Alexander) A.; m. Kathryn Lynn Fordham, Oct. 16, 1971; children: Marc Alexander, Chadwick Myles. AB, High Point Coll., 1955; MDiv, Emory U., 1962; STM, Union Theol. Sem. N.Y., 1964; LittD, Rust Coll., 1974; LHD, Tex. Wesleyan U., 1980. Ordained to ministry United Meth. Ch., 1960. With Don Lee Network, Los Angeles, 1955-56; tutor asst., tutor Union Theol. Sem. N.Y., 1963-65; mem. adj. faculty Emory U., 1965-72; producer The Protestant Hour, Atlanta, 1959—, chmn., 1987—; exec. dir. joint communications com. United Meth. Ch., Atlanta, 1974—; lectr. Emory U., U. Md., Meth. Coll., Lon Morris Coll., Pfeiffer Coll., Columbia Sem., Interdenominational Theol. Ctr., Atlanta U.; churchman in residence Candler Sch. Theology, 1985; mem. adv. bd. Protestant Radio and TV Ctr. Author: Hello Japan:, 1957, A Child's Guidebook to Rome, 1964, (with Wayne Knipe) Ideas, Inventions and Patents, 1973, (with Norman Perrin) Understanding the Teaching of Jesus, 1983; editor SEJ United Meth., 1976—. Served to capt. USAF, 1956-59. Recipient Clifford B. Scott award Sigma Phi Epsilon, 1953, C. L. Amos medal High Point Coll., 1955, Gold Mike award Far East Network, 1959, Gold medal Internat. Film and TV Festival, 1983, Bronze medal Internat. Film and TV Festival of N.Y., 1984, Angel award Religion in Media, 1984, 85, 86, 87; Peabody award, 1984; TV, Radio and Film Commn. Ralph W. Sockman fellow, 1964-65. Mem. Nat. Acad. TV Arts and Scis., Broadcast Pioneers (life), Am. Film Inst., Speech Communication Assn., Internat. Communication Assn., Internat. Assn. Bus. Communicators, Internat. Platform Assn., Soc. Bibl. Lit., Am. Acad. Religion, ASCAP, Nat. Acad. Recording Arts and Scis., Pub. Relations Soc. Am., Am. Acad. Polit. and Social Sci., Authors League Am., Religious Pub. Relations Council, Sigma Phi Epsilon, Kappa Chi. Democrat. Home: 935 Bream Ct NE Marietta GA 30068 Office: 159 Ralph McGill Blvd NE Suite 304 Atlanta GA 30365

ABGRALL, JEAN-MARIE, psychiatrist; b. Toulon, France, Apr. 12, 1950; s. Bernard and Aline (Poivey) A.; 1 child, Gaelle. MD, Faculte, Marseille, France, 1975, diploma in forensic psychiatry, 1982; DLaws, Faculte, Aix-en-Provence, France, 1983. Cons. French Red Cross, Toulon, 1968-75; mem. Internat. Council Addiction, Geneva, 1975-78; expert Aix-en-Provence Law Ct., 1979—. Author: Utilisation of Seaweeds, 1975, Psychopathology of Diving, 1977, Murder and Love, 1978, Responsibility of the Psychologist, 1983. Served to capt. French Navy, 1975-77. Mem. Internat. Soc. Med. Law, Internat. Acad. Legal Medicine, Internat. Soc. Criminology, French Soc. Legal Medicine and Criminology. Roman Catholic. Lodge: Gypsies. Home: Jaques Brel St, 83500 La Seyne Sur Mer France Office: Law Court, Blvd de Strasbourg, 83000 Toulon France

ABHAU, WILLIAM CONRAD, operations analyst, retired naval officer; b. Baltimore County, Md., Apr. 5, 1912; s. William Conrad and Gertrude (Lewis); m. Harriet Elliot Sanders, Oct. 17, 1942; children: Elliot, Marcy. B.S., U.S. Naval Acad., 1935; M.S., Naval Postgrad. Sch., 1956; grad., Naval War Coll., 1957. Commd. USN, advanced through grades to rear adm., 1964; gunnery officer USS New Jersey, World War II; asso. with Navy Research and Devel. effort, 1945-70, with specialization in weapon control systems, evaluation of weapons systems effectiveness, anti-submarine warfare devices; comdr. U.S.S. E. A. Greene, 1947-48, Escort Squadron 16, 1953-54, U.S.S. Waccamaw, 1957-58, U.S.S. Helena, 1961-62, Cruiser-Destroyer Flotilla Four, 1965, Manned Spacecraft Recovery Force, Atlantic, 1966-67, Anti-Submarine Warfare Systems Project, Washington, 1967-70; ret. Anti-Submarine Warfare Systems Project, 1970; with Inst. for Def. Analyses, 1970—. Author mil. studies. Decorated Legion of Merit, Bronze Star medal. Mem. Ops. Research Soc. Am. Clubs: Annapolis Yacht; Army and Navy (Washington). Home: 201 Scott Circle Annapolis MD 21401 Office: 1801 N Beauregard St Alexandria VA 22311

ABI-ALI, RICKY SALIM, aerospace corporation executive; b. Dakar, Senegal, Sept. 14, 1940; s. Salim Salman and Zahia (Khazzou) A.; m. Elizabeth Winter; 1 child, Richard. BS in Aeros., Calif. Poly. State U., San Luis Obispo, 1962; BA in Mgmt., Addis Ababa U., Ethiopia, 1976. Sr. systems engr. Middle East Airlines, Beirut, 1962-69; mgr. engring. Ethiopian Airlines, Addis Ababa, 1970-76; regional dir. Sundstrand Aerospace Corp., Dubai, United Arab Emirates, 1977—. Office: Sundstrand Aerospace, PO Box 3880, Dubai United Arab Emirates

ABILDGAARD, ULRICH CHRISTIAN, physician, internal medicine professor; b. Oslo, Sept. 4, 1933; s. Olaf Theodor and Henny Mossen (Smith) A.; m. Aina Uri, June 20, 1956 (dec. Mar. 1977); children: Monica, Andreas. MD, U. Oslo, 1961, PhD, 1969. Intern then resident Ulleval Hosp., Oslo, 1961-63, lectr. in medicine, 1968-70; resident Aker Hosp., Oslo, 1970-75, cons. hematoloty, 1977-86, acting head med. dept., 1986—; leader Norway Soc. Hematology, 1980-82. Leader Norway div. Internat. Physicians for Prevention of Nuclear War, 1983-84. Contbr. sci. papers on thrombosis research and treatment to profl. jours. Mem. Internat. Soc. of Thrombosis and Hemostasis (sr. adviser). Office: Aker Hosp, 0514 Oslo Norway

ABI-SAMRA, RAYMOND WADIH, civil engineer; b. Beirut, Nov. 12, 1944; s. Wadih Chacker Abi-Samra and Justine Hazzan; m. Matar Aziz Jeanne D'Arc, June 12, 1971; children—Gabrielle, Patricia. B.E., Am. U. Beirut, 1968; PhD, Kennedy-Western U., Calif., 1987. Site engr. Engring. Office, Beirut, 1968-75, Solico, Al-Kah I Saudi Arabia, 1975-77; resident engr. C.E.C., Tabuk, Saudi Arabia, 1978-79, Dar-al-Handasah, Kuwait, 1979-80, A.C.E., Algeria, 1980-81; chief resident engr. Tukan & Ptnrs., Abu-Dhabi, United Arab Emirates, 1982-87; area mgr. Arthur Erickson Architects Ltd., Abu-Dhabi, 1987—. Mem. Lebanese Order of Engrs. Christian Maronite. Home: Yarzeh St, Baabda Lebanon Office: PO Box 2131, Abu-Dhabi United Arab Emirates

ABLON, ARNOLD NORMAN, accountant; b. Ft. Worth, July 12, 1921; s. Esir R. and Hazel (Dreeben) A.; B.S., La. State U., 1941; M.B.A., Northwestern U., 1942; m. Carol Sarbin, July 25, 1962; children—Jan Ellen, Elizabeth Jane, William Neal, Robert Jack. Lectr. acctg. So. Meth. U., 1946-47; auditor Levine's Dept. Stores, 1947-49; acct. Peat, Marwick, Mitchell & Co., 1946-47; sr. partner Arnold N. Ablon and Co., C.P.A.s; owner ANA Properties, Dallas; pres., dir. Ablon Enterprises, Inc.; dir. 1st Continental Enterprises, Inc., Hunsaker Truck Lease, Inc. Bd. trustees St. Mark's Sch. of Tex., Lamplighter Sch., mem. exec. com.; past trustee Spl. Care Sch., Greenhill Sch., June Shelton Sch.; co-chmn. Parents Annual Fund Georgetown U., past v.p. Temple Emanuel; past vice chmn. Greenhill Sch.; mem. Parents Council, Georgetown U. Served to capt. AUS, 1942-45. Mem. Am. Inst. C.P.A.s, Tex. Soc. C.P.A.s, Nat. Assn. Cost Accts. Mason (Shriner). Clubs: Columbian, Dallas, City (Dallas). Home: 9129 Clearlake Dallas TX 75225 Office: Republic Bank Bldg Dallas TX 75201

ABLON, BENJAMIN MANUEL, accountant; b. Dallas, Feb. 12, 1929; s. Esir R. and Hazel (Dreeben) A.; B.B.A., So. Meth. U., 1948; M.B.A., Northwestern, 1949; LL.B., Harvard, 1956; m. Renee Angrist, Jan. 6, 1962 (div. Oct. 1969); 1 son, Edward Lawrence. Lic. real estate broker. Admitted to Tex. bar, 1956, D.C. bar, 1957; with tax rulings div. IRS, Washington, 1956-60; asso. law firm, N.Y.C., 1960-62; accountant, tax mgr. Price Waterhouse & Co., N.Y.C., 1963-68; accountant, partner Arnold N. Ablon & Co., C.P.A.'s, Dallas, 1968—. Served to lt. USAF, 1951-53. Mem. Am. Inst. C.P.A.'s, Tex. Soc. C.P.A.'s, State Bar Tex., Am. Assn. Attys.-C.P.A.'s, Dallas Estate Planning Council, Beta Gamma Sigma. Contbr. articles to profl. jours. Office: Republic Nat Bank Bldg Dallas TX 75201

ABOU GHAZALA, MOHAMMAD ABDEL-HALIM, Egyptian minister of defense and military production; b. Delengat Behera, Egypt, Jan. 1, 1930; grad. Mil. Acad., 1949; B.Commerce, Cairo U.; married; 5 children. Commd. lt., Egyptian Army, 1949, advanced through grades to lt. gen., 1980; comdr. div. arty., 1967-71; comdr. army arty., 1973-74; chief of staff arty. corps, 1974-76; mil. attaché, Washington, 1976-79; dir. mil. intelligence and reconnaissance dept., 1979-80; chief of staff Egyptian Armed Forces, 1980-81; minister of def. and mil. prodn. and comdr.-in-chief of Egyptian Armed Forces, 1981—;dep. prime minister, 1982—. Author 17 books on mil. affairs. Decorated Star of Honor Order, Mil. Order of Republic. Office: Ministry of Def Mil Prodn, Cairo Egypt *

ABOU HASHISH, MOHAMED ALI GOMAA, shipping company executive; b. Port Said, Egypt, June 26, 1961; s. Ali Gomaa and Nabila Mahmoud (Nawar) Abou H.; m. Inaam Bahgat Hassanien; 1 child, Hussein. BA, Cairo U., 1982; postgrad. in bus. mgmt., Alexander Hamilton Inst., N.Y.C., 1987. Acct. Internat. Shipping Enterprise, Port Said, 1980; with operation dept. Uiterwick Corp., Tampa, Fla., 1981; acct. Egyptian Internat. Shipping Co., Cairo, 1982-83, asst. line mgr., 1983-84, line mgr., 1985—; asst. gen. mgr. Internat. Shipping Enterprise, 1986-88; gen. mgr. Intertours, Cairo, 1988—. El Wafd. Moslem. Clubs: Gezira Sporting (Cairo), Alexandria Sporting. Office: Egyptian Internat Shipping Co, 48 El Giza St Orman Tower 110, Giza Egypt

ABRAGAM, ANATOLE, physicist; b. Griva-Semagallen, USSR, Dec. 15, 1914; s. Simon and Anna (Maimin) A.; m. Suzanne Lequesme, 1944. Student, Lycee Jeanson, Sorbonne, Oxford U. Research assoc. Centre Nat. de la Recherche Scientifique, 1946; joined French Atomic Energy Commn., 1947, physicist, later sr. physicist, 1947-55, head magnetic resonance lab.,, 1955-58, head solid state physics and nuclear physics dept.,, 1959-65, dir. physics, 1965-70, dir. research, 1971-80; prof. nuclear magnetism Coll. de France, 1960—. Author: Discovery of Anomalous Hyperfine Structure in Solids, 1950; Dynamic Polarization in Solids, 1957, The Principles of Nuclear Magnetism, 1961, Nuclear Anti-ferromagnetism, 1969; (with B. Bleaney) Electron Paramagnetic Resonance of Transition Elements, 1970, Nuclear Pseudomagnetism, 1971, Nuclear Ferromagnetism, 1973; (with M. Goldman) Nuclear Magnetism: Order and Disorder, 1982. Decorated Grand Officier Ordre Nat. du Merite; Officier Legion d'honeur; recipient Holweck prize London Phys. Soc., 1958, Grand Prix Cognac-Jay Acad. Scis., 1970, Lorentz medal, 1982. Fellow Am. Acad. Arts and Scis. (hon.); mem. French Phys. Soc. (pres. 1967), Acad. Scis., U.S. Nat. Acad. Soc., Pontifical Acad. Scis. Office: Commissariat a l'Energie Atomique, PO Box 2, 91190 Gif-sur-Yvette France

ABRAHAM, CARL JOEL, safety engineer, consultant, inventor; b. N.Y.C., Dec. 31, 1937; s. Sol and Mildred (Siegal) A.; B.S., Hofstra U., 1959, postgrad., 1972, J.D., 1978; postgrad. U. Oreg., 1959-60, U. N.C., 1961-63; M.S., U. Pacific, 1961; Ph.D., Clayton U., 1975; m. Sharon Abraham; children—Carl Joel, Elizabeth Jean, Carrie Anne, Scott Ross. Research engr. Aerojet Gen. Corp., Sacramento, 1961; research engr. and chemist, 1963-65; materials specialist, corporate research lab. J.P. Stevens & Co., Inc., Garfield, N.J., 1966-67; dir. research and devel. Mansol Ceramics Co., Belleville, N.J., 1967-69; v.p., tech. dir. Polyphase Chem. Service, Inc., West Hempstead, N.Y., 1968-70; chmn. bd. Inter-City Testing & Cons. Corp., Mineola, N.Y. and Plantation, Fla., 1971—; chmn. bd. Athletics Safety Products Inc., 1984—; pres. Carmal Ltd.; sec., treas. Jesse H. Bidanset and Assocs., Inc.; prof. chemistry Nassau Community Coll., Garden City, N.Y., 1973-75, adj. faculty physics Empire State Coll., Old Westbury, N.Y., 1975-78; adj. faculty engring. Hofstra U., 1974-79; adj. prof. continuing edn. programs. Recipient Civilian award for Outstanding Police Assistance, Police Dept. County of

Nassau, 1974. Cert. chemistry, math. and biology tchr. U. State N.Y.; certified in food tech. and processing N.Y.C. Dept. Health; licensed profl. engr. Fellow Royal Soc. Chemistry (chartered, cert. profl. chemist); mem. Am. Inst. Chemists (cert. profl. chem. engr., profl. chemist), Am. Chem. Soc., AAAS, Am. Inst. Chem. Engrs. (fellow, cert. in chem. engring.), Am. Acad. Law and Medicine, Soc. Automotive Engrs., Am. Inst. Chem. Engrs., Am. Soc. Safety Engrs., Soc. Plastics Engrs., Systems Safety Soc. (chpt. sec.), ASTM, Alpha Chi Sigma. Club: Elks. Contbr. articles to profl. jours. Patentee high temperature carbonaceous and siliceous materials, sports safety equipment, storage battery having a protective shield, copyright registration on battery warnings. Home: 3 Baker Hill Rd Great Neck NY 11023 Office: 167 Willis Ave Mineola NY 11501 also: 8225 NW 13th St Plantation FL 33522

ABRAHAM, CLAUDE, transportation company executive; b. Pont St. Vincent, France, Apr. 4, 1931; m. Nicole Franck; children: Helene, Anne, Pierre. Student, Ecole Poly., Paris, Ecole Nat. des Ponts et Chaussees, Paris; MS in Civil Engring., Northwestern U. Civil engr. Dept. Pub. Works, Versailles, France, 1962-68; dir. Air Transport CAA, Paris, 1975-76; gen. dir. Dept. Civil Aviation, France, 1976-82; chmn. Compagnie Gen. Maritime, Paris, 1982—. Author: Microeconomics, 1970. Office: Compagnie Generale Maritime, 102 Quartier Boieldieu Cedex 18, 92085 Paris France also: Compagnie Generale Maritime, Tour Winter TH U R, Cedex 18 France

ABRAHAM, GEORGE, research physicist, engineer; b. N.Y.C., July 15, 1918; s. Herbert and Dorothy (Jacoby) A.; m. Hilda Mary Wenz, Aug. 26, 1944; children: Edward H., Dorothy J., Anne H., Alice J. Sc.B., Brown U., 1940; S.M., Harvard U., 1942; Ph.D., U. Md., 1972; postgrad., MIT, George Washington U. Registered profl. engr., D.C. Chmn. bd., pres. bd. Intercollegiate Broadcasting System, N.Y., 1941—; radio engr. RCA, Camden, N.J., 1941; with Naval Research Lab., Washington, 1942—; head sci. edn., head exptl. devices and microelectronics sects. Naval Research Lab., 1945-69, head systems applications Office of Dir. Research, 1969-75, research physicist Office Research and Tech. Applications, cons., 1975—; lectr. U. Md., 1945-52, George Washington U., 1952-67, Am. U., 1979; indsl. cons.; mem. D.C. Bd. Registration Profl. Engrs. Contbr. chpts. to books, articles to profl. jours. Chmn. bd. Canterbury Sch., Accokeek, Md.; mem. schs. and scholarships com. Harvard U.; active PTA, Boy Scouts Am. Served to capt. USNR, World War II. Recipient Group Achievement award Fleet Ballistic Missile Program U.S. Navy, 1963, Edison award Naval Research Lab., 1971, Navy Research Publ. award, 1974, 84, Patent awards, 1959-75, D.C. Sci. citation, 1982, Govt. Microcircuit Applications Conf. Founders award, 1986, Outstanding Service award Soc. Profl. Engrs., 1986, D.C. Council Engring. and Archtl. Soc. Nat. Capital Engr. of Yr. award, 1987. Fellow IEEE (Harry Diamond award 1981, Centennial award 1984), Washington Acad. Scis. (pres. 1974-75), N.Y. Acad. Scis., AAAS; Mem. Am. Phys. Soc., Am. Assn. Physics Tchrs., Am. Soc. Naval Engrs., Washington Soc. Engrs. (pres. 1974, award 1981), Philos. Soc. Washington, AAUP, Sierra Club, Sigma Xi, Sigma Pi Sigma, Tau Beta Pi, Sigma Tau, Eta Kappa Nu, Iota Beta Sigma. Clubs: Cosmos (Washington), Harvard (Washington); Appalachian Mountain (Boston); Sierra (San Francisco). Home: 3107 Westover Dr SE Washington DC 20020 Office: Naval Research Lab Washington DC 20375

ABRAHAMS, IVOR, sculptor; b. Wigan, Lancashire, Eng., Jan. 10, 1935; s. Harry and Racheal (Kalisky) A.; m. Victoria Taylor /9div. 1974); 1 child, Saul; m. Evelyne Horvais; 1 child, Etienne. Grad. with honors, St. Martin's Sch. Art, London, 1959. Lectr. Coventry Coll. Art, Warwickshire, Eng., 1965-68; vis. lectr. Royal Coll. Art, London, 1970-80, Slade Sch. Fine Art, London, 1982—. Works represented in permanent collections at Aberbeen Art Gallery and Mus., Arnolfini Gallery, Bristol, Eng., Arts Council Great Britain, Biblioteque Nat., Paris, Bradford (Eng.) Art Gallery and Mus., Brit. Council, London, Buymans Mus., Rotterdam, Netherlands, City Mus. and Art Gallery, Portsmouth, Eng., Denver Mus., Ft. Lauderdale (Fla.) Mus., Liverpool U., Met. Mus., N.Y.C., Middlesbrough (Eng.) Art Gallery, Mpls. Art Inst., Moore Coll., Phila., Mus. Modern Art, N.Y.C., Nat. Gallery Australia, Canberra, Norton Coll. Art, Miami, Fla., Rice U., Houston, Stoke City (Eng.) Art Gallery, Strassburg (France) Mus., Tate Gallery, London, Vassar Coll. Art Gallery, Poughkeepsie, N.Y., Victoria and Albert Mus., London, Walker Art Gallery, Liverpool, Eng., Wedgewood Mus., Barlaston, Stoke-on-Trent, Eng., Wilhelm Lembruck Mus., Duisburg, Fed. Republic Germany, Williams Coll. Mus. Art, Williamstown, Va.; subject numerous books, articles. Jewish. Clubs: Colony Room, Chelsea Arts (London). Home: Flat A Oxford Gardens, London W10 5UN, England Studio: 1 Fawe St, London E14, England

ABRAM, JOHN CHARLES, energy consultant; b. Des Moines, Sept. 1, 1920; s. John C. and Mary (Jones) A.; m. Dorothy Jean Buettner, Dec. 28, 1946; children: James Morgan, Susan Diane. AA, Glendale Coll., 1940; BS in Engring., UCLA, 1949; postgrad., U. Calif., Berkeley, 1949. With Pacific Lighting Service Co., 1959-69, v.p., 1969-71; with So. Calif. Gas Co., Los Angeles, 1951-57, 71-85, v.p., 1972-74, sr. v.p., 1974-81, vice chmn., 1980-81, chmn. bd., chief exec. officer, 1981-85; chief exec. officer AEA Internat. Ltd., Los Angeles, 1985—. Vice chmn. Calif. Mus. Sci. and Industry Found., Los Angeles, 1985-86; vice chmn. Econ. Devel. Corp. Los Angeles County, 1984-85, Cen. City Assn., 1983-85. Mem. Internat. Gas Union, Internat. Energy Economists, The Atlantic Council, U.S.-Japan Energy Conf., Pacific Coast Gas Assn. (bd. dirs. 1973-82, chmn. 1980-81), Am. Gas Assn. (bd. dirs. 1981-85, Disting. Service award 1984), Gas Research Inst. (bd. dirs. 1980-87, chmn. 1981-83), UCLA Alumni Assn., U. Calif. at Berkeley Alumni Assn., Australian Gas Assn., Japan Am. Soc., Asia Soc., Japanese Am. Cultural and Community Ctr. Republican. Congregationalist. Clubs: The Los Angeles, Calif. (Los Angeles); Oakmont Country (Glendale, Calif.). Office: AEA Internat Ltd 810 S Flower St Los Angeles CA 90017

ABRAMOVITZ, ANITA ZELTNER BROOKS (MRS. MAX ABRAMOVITZ), author; b. L.I., N.Y., Jan. 7, 1914; d. Charles Frederick and Amelia (Koch) Zeltner; B.A., Sarah Lawrence Coll., 1934; m. Thomas Vail Brooks, Sept. 25, 1937 (div. July 1957); children—Antoinette Brooks-Floyd, Cora Vail Brooks, Henry Stanford Brooks II; m. Max Abramovitz, Feb. 29, 1964. Editorial asst. New Yorker mag., N.Y.C., 1943-46; editor alumni mag. Sarah Lawrence Coll., 1947-48, asst. to prof. history, 1958-60, asst. in writing to lectr. courses, 1960-62; tchr. remedial reading, 1950; asst. to dir. Sarah Lawrence Paris Summer Sch., 1963. Democratic Party Insp. 18th Dist. Hastings-on-Hudson, N.Y., 1958-61; founding mem. Village League, 1950. Author series Picture Aids to World Geography; Picture Book of Fisheries, 1961; Picture Book of Tea and Coffee, 1962; Picture Book of Grains, 1963; Picture Book of Salt, 1964; Picture Book of Oil, 1965; Picture Book of Timber, 1966; A Small Bird Sang, 1967; Winifred, 1970; Picture Book of Metals, 1972; People and Spaces: A View of History Through Architecture, 1979; also articles and children's stories. Home: Honey Hollow Rd Box 206 Pound Ridge NY 10676

ABRAMOW-NEWERLY, JAROSLAW, playwright; b. Warsaw, Poland, May 17, 1933; s. Igor and Barbara (Abramow) Newerly; children—Magdalena, Barbara, Maria. MA, Warsaw U., 1955. Editor-in-chief Od Nowa, 1956; editor drama dept. Polish Radio, 1960-66; lit. adviser Teatr Ludowy, Warsaw, 1970-72; playwright, 1954—. Dramas include Remanent, 1962, Aniol na dworcu, 1965, Derby w palacu, 1966, Ucieczka z wielkich bulwarow, 1969, Wyciag do nieba, 1971, Klik-klak, 1972, Darz Bor, 1974, Skok przez siebie, 1977, Dno nieba, 1977, Kto mi spiewat serenade, 1980, Maestro, 1982; collection of plays: Dramaty, 1975. Recipient Pietak Literary award, 1965, Koscielski Literary award, 1967. Mem. Polish Writers Union, Internat. PEN Club, Internat. Theatre Inst. (chmn. drama sect. Polish centre, bd. dirs. internat. com. drama authors). Address: Dabrówski 13, 03-909 Warsaw Poland

ABRAMS, JEROME, accountant; b. N.Y.C., Aug. 15, 1926; s. Harold and Nettie (Zilewitz) A.; m. Joan Alice Stillman, Sept. 30, 1956; children—Roy, Lori, Margie. BS magna cum laude, CCNY, 1946, MBA, 1947. CPA, N.Y. Fellow in econs. CCNY, 1946-47; security analyst Value Line Investment Survey, 1946-47; staff acct. Simonoff, Peyser & Citrin, N.Y.C., 1947-53; pvt. practice pub. acctg., N.Y.C., 1954—; treas., dir. Advanced Ctr. for Psychotherapy, Inc., N.Y.C., 1968-75, Advanced Inst. for Analytic Psychotherapy, 1968-86; mem. nat. and state coms. on application of statistical sampling methods to auditing, 1954, 55; trustee numerous pension and profit sharing plans; cons. to numerous TV comml. production cos. . Contbr. articles to profl. jours. Recipient Tremaine award CCNY, 1945, Ward medal in econs., 1946. Mem. N.Y. Soc. C.P.A.s, Am. Inst. C.P.A.s, Phi Beta Kappa, Beta Gamma Sigma. Democrat. Jewish. Home and Office: 29 Sugar Maple Dr Roslyn NY 11576

ABRAMS, JULIUS, construction executive; b. Butrimantzi, Lithuania, Oct. 27, 1902; brought to U.S., 1903; s. Harry Isaac and Etta (Ginsberg) A.; B.C.E., Northeastern U., 1925, D.Eng. (hon.), 1973; m. Eva Hodess, June 2, 1926; children—Fay Rosalind Abrams Wilgoren, Benjamin Emanuel, Phillip. Civil and constrn. engr. Gleason Engring. Corp., Wellesley, Mass., 1932-36; chief engr. B.A. Gardett Corp., 1936-40; civil engr., supt. J. Slotnik Co., Boston, 1940-43; engr. Joseph Bennett Co., Boston, 1943-45; pres. Poley-Abrams Corp., Brookline, Mass., 1945—; pres. J. Abrams Constrn. Co. Inc., 1975—, chmn. bd., 1978—. Dir., past pres. Asso. Gen. Contractors of Mass. Past chmn. Greater Boston Hillel Com., mem., chmn. bd. of examiners Brookline Bldg. Dept.; mem. designer selection bd. Commonwealth of Mass., 1972-76, cons. to spl. commn. on state and county bldgs., 1979; chmn. adv. com. Northeastern U. Hillel; bd. advs. U. Indsl. Mgmt.; mem. corp. Northeastern U., Lesley Coll. Named Outstanding Civil Engr. Alumnus, Northeastern U., 1981; registered profl. engr., Mass. Fellow Am. Inst. Constructors; mem. Nat. Soc. Profl. Engrs., Am. Arbitration Assn., Am. Soc. Engring. Edn., Am. Council Constrn. Edn., Assn. Engrs. and Architects Israel (speaker 4th World Congress, Israel 1976), Alpha Epsilon Pi. Republican. Clubs: Masons, B'nai B'rith (past pres. Architects-Engrs. lodge). Home: 210 Nahanton St Newton MA 02159 Office: 850 Boylston St Brookline MA 02167

ABRAMS, RICHARD BRILL, lawyer; b. Mpls., Nov. 2, 1931; s. Joseph E. and Nettie (Brill) A.; m. Myrna Carole Noodleman, Dec. 5, 1965; children—Jennifer, Adam. B.B.A., U. Minn., 1958, B.S.L., 1958, J.D., 1958. Bar: Minn. 1958, U.S. Ct. Appeals (8th cir.) 1981, U.S. Dist. Ct. Minn. 1981, Wis. 1983. Sole practice Mpls., 1958-64; pres. Abrams & Spector, P.A., Mpls., 1964—; ad hoc instr. labor edn. U. Minn. Bd. dirs. Mpls. United Way; bd. dirs., v.p. Courage Ctr., 1977-83, 85-86; mem pain com. Nat. Acad. Sci., Nat. Inst. Medicine, 1986. Served with U.S. Army, 1955-57. Recipient Disting. and Devoted Service award Human Rights Com., Mpls. Central Labor Union Council, 1975; Meritorious Service award Minn. Rehab. Assn., 1978; Disting. Service award Courage Ctr., 1983. Mem. ABA, Minn. State Bar Assn., Wis. State Bar Assn., Assn. Trial Lawyers Am., Minn. Trial Lawyers Assn., Nat. Acad. Scis. (pain com.), Nat. Inst. Medicine. Office: Abrams & Spector PA 6800 France Ave S Suite 435 Minneapolis MN 55435

ABRIKOSOV, ALEKSEY ALEKSEYEVICH, physicist; b. Moscow, June 25, 1928; s. Aleksey Ivanovich and Fanny Davidovna (Vulf) A.; m. Svetlana Yuriyevna Bun-kova, 1977; 3 children. Degree, Moscow U., 1948; DS in Physics and Math., Inst. Physics, Moscow, 1955; DS (hon.), Lausanne U., 1975. Postgrad. research assoc., research worker Inst. Phys. Problems U.S.S.R. Acad. Scis., 1948-65, head dept. Inst. Theoretical Physics, 1965—; research assoc., asst. prof., prof. Moscow U., 1951-68; prof. Gorky U., 1971-72; prof. Moscow Phys. Engring. Inst., 1974-75; head chair Theoretical physics Moscow Inst. Steel and Alloys, 1976—. Author: Quantum Field Theory Methods in Statistical Physics, 1962; Introduction to the Theory of Normal Metals, 1972; Fundamentals of Metal Theory, 1987; contbr. articles to profl. jours. Recipient Lenin prize, 1966; Fritz London award, 1972; State prize USSR, 1982. Mem. U.S.S.R. Acad. Scis. Office: Landau Inst Theoretical Physics, 2 Kozygin St, 117334 Moscow USSR

ABSHIRE, DAVID MANKER, diplomat, research executive; b. Chattanooga, Apr. 11, 1926; s. James Ernest and Phyllis (Patten) A.; m. Carolyn Lamar Sample, Sept. 7, 1957; children: Lupton Patten, Anna Lamar, Mary Lee Sample, Phyllis Anderson, Carolyn. Student, U. Chattanooga, 1945; B.S., U.S. Mil. Acad., 1951; Ph.D., Georgetown U., 1959. Mem. minority staff U.S. Ho. Reps., 1958-60; dir. spl. projects Am. Enterprise Inst., Washington, 1961-62; exec. dir. Center Strategic and Internat. Studies, Georgetown U., 1962-70, chmn., 1973-82, pres., 1982-83, 88—, chancellor, 1987-88, pres., 1988—; ambassador, U.S. permanent rep. North Atlantic Council, 1983-87; spl. counsellor to pres. North Atlantic Council, White House, 1987; asst. sec. state for congl. relations, 1970-73; presdl. appointee Congl. Commn. on Orgn. of Govt. for Conduct of Fgn. Policy, 1973-75; chmn. U.S. Bd. for Internat. Broadcasting, 1974-77; mem. exec. panel to Chief of Naval Ops., Washington, dir. nat. security group Transition Office of Pres.-Elect Reagan, 1980-81; dir. Procter and Gamble, Ogden Corp; mem. adv. bd. BP Am. Author: (with others) Detente, 1965, Vietnam Legacy, 1976, The South Rejects a Prophet: The Life of Senator D.M. Key, 1967, International Broadcasting: A New Dimension of Western Diplomacy, 1976, Foreign Policy Makers: President vs. Congress, 1979; editor: National Security, 1963, Portuguese Africa, 1969, Research Resources for the Seventies, 1971, The Growing Power of Congress, 1981; co-editor: Washington Quar., 1977-83. Mem. adv. bd. Naval War Coll., 1975-79; vice-chmn. bd. Youth for Understanding, 1979-80; trustee Baylor Sch., 1980—; mem. Pres.'s Fgn. Intelligence Adv. Bd., 1981-83; bd. dirs. Spaak Found. (Brussels), Atlantic Council of U.S. Served with AUS, 1945-46; to 1st lt. 1951-56; capt. Res. ret. Decorated Bronze Star medal with oak leaf cluster, with V for Valor, V commendation ribbon with metal pendant, Order of Crown, Commandeur de L'Ordre de Leopold (Belgium); recipient John Carroll award, Dept. Def. medal for Disting. Pub. Service, 1988. Mem. Council Fgn. Relations, Am. Acad. Polit. and Social Scis., Internat. Inst. Strategic Studies, Gold Key Soc., Phi Alpha Theta. Republican. Episcopalian. Clubs: International, Alfalfa (Washington), Metropolitan (Washington). Home: 311 S St Asaph St Alexandria VA 22314 Office: Ctr Strategic & Internat Studies Suite 1014 1800 K St NW Washington DC 20006

ABT, SYLVIA HEDY, dentist; b. Chgo., Oct. 7, 1957; d. Wendel Peter and Hedi Lucie (Wieder) A. Student, Loyola U., Chgo., 1975-77; cert. dental hygiene, Loyola U., Maywood, Ill., 1979, DDS, 1983. Registered dental hygienist. Dental asst. Office Dr. Baran and Dr. O'Neill, DDS, Chgo., 1977-78; dental hygienist Drs. Spiro, Sudakoff, Kadens, Weidman, DDS, Skokie, Ill., 1979-83, Dr. Laudando, DiFranco, Rosemont, Ill., 1980-83; gen. practice dentistry Chgo., 1983—. Vol. Community Health Rotations, VA Hosps., grammar schs., convalescent ctrs., mental health ctrs., Maywood, Ill. and Chgo., 1978-82. Recipient 1st Place award St. Apollonia Art Show, Loyola U., 1982. Mem. ADA, Ill. State Dental Soc., Chgo. Dental Soc., Loyola Dental Alumni Assn. (golf outing registration chair 1987, awards in golf and tennis 1987), Psi Omega (historian, editor). Office: 6509 W Higgins Chicago IL 60656

ABUBAKAR, S. BELLO, banker; b. Talata Mafara, Sokoto, Nigeria, Jan. 17, 1949; s. Alhaji and Habibatu (Maigida) A.; m. Rakiya Johnson, Apr. 8, 1977; children: Habibatu, Munir, A'ishatu. BS in Econs., A.B. U., Zaria, Kaduna, Nigeria, 1973; MS in Mgmt., A.D. Little Man Edn. Inst., Cambridge, Mass., 1980. Investment exec. II New Nigeria Devel. Co., Kaduna, 1974-76, investment exec. I, 1976, sr. investment exec., 1977, prin. investment exec., 1980-81; asst. gen. mgr. Nigerian Indsl. Devel. Bank, Lagos, Nigeria, 1981—; bd. dirs. First Aluminum of Nigeria, Lagos, Sheraton Hotel, Abuja, Nigeria, Kaduna Furniture Co. Ltd.; cons. in field. Moslem. Clubs: Ikoyi, Lagos Lawn, Tennis (Lagos). Office: Nigerian Indsl Devel Bank, 63/71 Broad St, PO Box 2357, Lagos Nigeria

ABU-GHAZALEH, TALAL TAWFIQ, accountant; b. Jaffa, Palestine, Apr. 21, 1938; s. Tawfiq Salem; m. Nuha Salameh, Oct. 4, 1963; children: Luay, Qusay, May, Jumana. BS in Bus. Administrn., American U., Beirut, Lebanon, 1960; D. of Human Letters (hon.), Canisius Coll., 1988. Licensed auditor and cons. in individual Arab countries. Dep. mng. ptnr. Saba and Co., Kuwait, 1960-72; chmn. Price Waterhouse Abu-Ghazaheh and Co., Kuwait, 1974-79, Tala Abu-Ghazaleh Internat., Kuwait, 1972—. Author: The Abu-Ghazaleh English/Arabic Dictionary of Accountancy, 1978. Recipient Decoration Independence, Jordan, 1976, Chevalier de la Legion D'Honneur, France, 1985, Decoration Republic, Tunisia, 1985. Mem. Arab Soc. Certified Accts. (pres. 1983), Arab Soc. Protection Indsl. Property (pres. 1987), Assn. Licinsed Accts. Individual Arab Countries, Union Arab Banks, Internat. Fiscal Assn., Am. Mgmt. Assn., Tax Inst. Am. Clubs: Maxim's Bus. (France), Internat. (Washington). Office: Talal Abu-Ghazaleh Internat, PO Box 4628 Safat, Kuwait-Safat Kuwait 13047

ABU HASSAN OMAR, government official; b. Bukit Belimbing, Kuala Selangor, Malaysia, Sept. 15, 1940; m. Wan Noor Daud; 5 children. Student, U. Hull, Eng., 1960-63, 71-73. Asst. dir. officer, then dist. officer, asst. sec., dep. state sec. and dep. sec.-gen. Land and Fed. Devel. Govt. of Malaysia, 1964-78, M.P., 1978—, parliamentary sec. Ministry of Commerce and Industry, 1978-80, dep. minister of def., 1980-81, dep. minister of transport, 1981-84, minister of welfare services, 1984-86, minister of fed. territory, 1986-87, miniser of fgn. affairs, 1987—; mem. United Malay Nat. Orgn. Info. Bur. Com., 1974, mem. Supreme Council, 1978—, chmn. Welfare and Labour Bur., State of Selangor, head Kuala Selangor div., 1978—, head Pekan br., 1978—. Chmn. Drug Abuse Sub-com., Kelang High Sch. Old Boys Soc., Selangor's Children Multi-purpose Coop.; advisor State of Selangor Volleyball Soc.; dep. pres. Amateur Boxing Soc. Malaysia, 1982-83. Office: Ministry of Fgn Affairs, Kuala Lumpur Malaysia *

ABU-LISAN, MUSTAFA ABDELRAUF, clinical chemist, consultant; b. Jaffa, Israel, Mar. 31, 1947; came to Kuwait, 1982; s. Abdelrauf Ahmad and Naziha Tawfiq (Chebaro) Abu-L.; m. Selma Bent Youssef Bassoum, Aug. 7, 1981; children: Omar, Rami. BS in Arts and Scis., Lebanon, 1973; MS in Human Scis., Eng., 1976, PhD, 1978. Sr. lectr. Higher Inst. Tech., Malta, Libya, 1977-79; cons. biochemist St. Luke's Hosp., Malta, 1979-82; head emergency labs. Ministry Pub. Health, Malta, 1979-82; assoc. prof. Faculty of Medicine, Malta, 1979-82; cons. clin. biochemistry Sabah Hosp. Ministry Pub. Health, Kuwait, 1982-83, cons. clin. biochemistry, chmn. dept. clin. labs. Amiri Hosp., 1983—, chancellor, 1985—; dir. clin. labs. Amiri Health Region, Kuwait, 1985—; dir. edn. Higher Inst. Tech., Malta, 1977-79; dir. AIDS tng. WHO Collaboration Ctr., Kuwait, 1986—; dir. clin. chemistry Ministry Pub. Health, Kuwait, 1983—; cons. Kuwait Med. Ctr., 1986—. Author: Applied Lab Technology, 1979, Coronary Heart Disease, 1985; editor: Clinical Laboratory Services, 1987. Vice-pres. MAltese-Arab Friendship Soc., 1980, Union Arab Students, U.K., 1975. Recipient Internat. Fellowship award Am. Assn. Clin. Chemistry, 1986, Faithful Reader award Jour. Modern Medicine, Paris, 1986, Clin. Chemist Recognition award Am. Assn. Clin. Chemistry, 1988. Fellow Royal Soc. Medicine, Royal Soc. Health, Royal Microscopical Soc., Nat. Acad. Clin. Biochemistry, Assn. Clin. Scientists; mem. Arab Fedn. Clin. Chemistry (gen. sec. 1988). Sunni Muslim. Clubs: Clin. Biochemistry (Kuwait) (pres. 1983-85), Clubmans (London). Home and Office: PO Box 24570, Safat 13106, Kuwait

ABURUKUN, JABER SHAKEEB, librarian, lecturer, researcher; b. Usifiya, Israel, May 6, 1950; s. Shakeeb Hussien and Fatma Hamra Aburukun. BA, Haifa U., 1971, MA, 1979; postgrad., Century U., Los Angeles. Tchr. high schs., Tamra, Israel, 1973-74, Usifiya, 1974-84; librarian Pub. Library, Usifiya, 1975—; lectr. Adminstrv. and Communal Council, Usifiya, 1977—; dir. edn. Cultural Dept., Isfiya, 1987—; librarian, cons. Israel Dept. Edn., 1982-84. Contbr. articles on Druze culture to profl. publs.; mem. Druze Jewish Pub. Council, Israel. Home: 7-3, Usifiya 30090, Israel Office: Pub Library 77, Usifiya 30090, Israel

ABUSHADI, MOHAMED MAHMOUD, banker; b. Fayoum, Aug. 15, 1913; s. Mahmoud and Seddika (Hashad) Abushadi; m. Colleen Althea Bennet, 1947; 4 children. Student Cairo U., Chartered Inst. Patent Agents, Am. U., Washington. Controller-gen. Ins. dept. Ministry of Fin., 1949-52; dir. gen. Govt. Ins. and Provident Funds, 1953; chmn., mng. dir. Devel. and Pupular Housing Co., 1954-55; sub.-gov. Nat. Bank of Egypt, 1955-60, mng. dir., 1960-67, chmn., mng. dir., 1967-70; chmn. Union de Banques Arabes et Francaises (UBAF), Paris, 1970-87, UBAF Bank Ltd., London, 1971—; chmn. Social Ins. Orgn., 1956-57; chmn., mng. dir. Cairo Ins. Co., 1956-57; mng. dir. Cairo Bank, 1956-57. Author: The Art of Central Banking and its Application in Egypt, 1962; Central Banking in Egypt, 1952; Will New York attract Arab Capital?, 1974; The Experience of the Arab-French Banks, 1974; Oil Funds: The Search for Supplementary Recycling Mechanisms, 1975; The Role of Finance in Promoting Arab European Business Cooperation, 1976. Decorated commabdeur de la Légion d'Honneur. Mem. Internat. Bankers Assn. (pres. 1976—). Office: Union de Banques Arabes et Francaises, 190 ave Charles de Gaullle, 92200 Neuilly sur Seine France

ACCARDO, SALVATORE FRANCIS, investment company executive; b. Newark, Dec. 30, 1937; s. Settimo and Teresa (Mineo) A. B.E.E., Cornell U., 1961; M.B.A. with distinction, NYU, 1963. Bus. planner, market researcher Gen. Electric Co., N.Y.C., 1963-67; v.p. research William D. Witter, Inc., N.Y.C., 1969-76, Drexel Burnham Lambert Group, N.Y.C., 1976-77, Kidder, Peabody & Co., N.Y.C., 1977-79, Shearson Loeb Rhoades, Inc., N.Y.C., 1979-80; v.p. investment banking Shearson-Am. Express, Inc., N.Y.C., 1981-83; v.p. venture capital investments Mfrs. Hanover Investment Corp., N.Y.C., 1983-86, sr. v.p. venture capital group, 1986-87; sr. v.p. venture capital group Mitchell Hutchins Instl. Investors, Paine Webber, N.Y.C., 1988—. Bd. dirs. N.Y. Harp Ensemble; vol. N.Y. Philharm. Served with USAF, 1968. Named Instl. Investor All-Star Analyst, 1975-76, 78. Mem. N.Y. Elec. and Electronics Analysts Group, N.Y. Soc. Security Analysts. Clubs: University, Metropoliton Opera, Lenox, Surf of Quogue. Home: 400 Central Park W Apt 15C New York NY 10025 Office: Mitchell Hutchins 600 Fifth Ave New York NY 10020

ACETO, VINCENT JOHN, librarian, educator; b. Schenectady, N.Y., Feb. 5, 1932; s. Henry and Gilda (Maietta) A.; m. Jean Louise Rasey, Aug. 27, 1955 (div. 1974); children—David, Paul, Andrew. A.B., SUNY, 1953, M.A., 1953, M.L.S., 1959; postgrad. Case Western Res. U., 1959, 62, 65-66. Tchr., Scotia (N.Y.)-Glenville Central Schs., 1956-57; high sch. librarian Burnt Hills (N.Y.)-Ballston Lake Central Schs., 1957-59; library dir. Town Ballston Pub. Library, Burnt Hills, 1958-60; Fulbright lectr. U. Dacca, East Pakistan, 1964-65; asst. prof. Sch. Library Sci., SUNY, Albany, 1959-62, assoc. prof. library sci., 1963-69, prof., 1969—, assoc. dean, 1987—. Joint editor: Film Lit. Index; contbr. articles to profl. jours. Pres., Filmdex Part II, Inc., 1973—; library cons. various pub. schs.: dir. U.S. Office Edn. insts. and traineeships; bd. dirs. Freedom Forum, Schenectady, 1970-78, chmn., 1976-78. Served with AUS, 1954-56. Mem. Am. Library Assn., Pakistan Library Assn., East Pakistan Library Assn., N.Y. Library Assn., Hudson-Mohawk Library Assn. (v.p. 1964-66), NEA, Am. Soc. Indexers, Am. Soc. Info. Scis., Soc. Cinema Studies, Film Library Info. Council, Idaka Forum, Kappa Phi Kappa, Phi Delta Kappa. Democrat. Unitarian. Home: 950 Madison Ave Albany NY 12208 Office: SUNY Sch Info and Library Sci Albany NY 12222

ACEVEDO PERALTA, RICARDO DE JESUS, government official; b. San Salvador, El Slavador, Apr. 14, 1941; s. Ricardo Acevedo and Hortencia Peralta; m. Sonia Escalante (div.); children: Ricardo, Lucia; m. Nuria Leticia Sabater ; children: Nuria, Beatriz. LLD, U. Madrid, 1964. Dir.-pres. Anti-Drug Nat. Commn., San Salvador, 1956-67; dir. Sugarcane Growers Assn., San Salvador, 1968-70, Cotton Growers Assn., San Salvador, 1972-73; commr. San Salvador City Council, 1982-84; under sec. Ministry Fgn. Affairs, San Salvador, 1984-86, sec., 1986—; pres. Internat. Boundary Commn., 1984—, Internat. Refugees Commn., 1984—. Sec. Christian Dem. Internat. Directorate, El Salvador, 1984; under v.p. ODCA Cen. Am., Venezuela, 1985; judge-arbitrator Internat. Ct. Arbitration, The Hague, Netherlands. Recipient Morazan decoration (Honduras); Libertador decoration (Venezuela); Orden de Mayo (Argentina); Merito Civil decoration (Republic Korea); Estrella Brillante decoration (Republic China); La Pinta award Nat. Sch. Chemistry, Spain, 1986. Mem. Nat. Lawyers Assn. Christian Democrat. Home: Pasaje 1 N 109, Colonia San Benito, San Salvador El Salvador Office: Ministerio Relaciones Exteriores, San Salvador El Salvador

ACHEBE, CHINUA, humanist, educator; b. Ogidi, Nigeria, Nov. 16, 1930; s. Isaiah Okafo and Janet N. (Iloegbunam) A.; student Univ. Coll., Ibadan, Nigeria, 1948-52; B.A., U. London, 1953; D.Litt. (hon.), Dartmouth Coll., 1972, U. Southampton (Eng.), 1975, U. Ife (Nigeria), 1978; D.Univ., Stirling U., U.K., 1975, U. Nigeria, Nsukka, 1981, U. Kent, Canterbury, Eng., 1982, Mt. Allison U., Sackville, Can., 1984, U. Guelph, Can., 1984, Franklin Pierce Coll., N.H., 1985; LL.D., U. P.E.I. (Can.), 1976; D.H.L., U. Mass., 1977; m. Christie Chinwe Okoli, Sept. 10, 1961; children: Chinelo, Ikechukwu, Chidi, Nwando. Producer, controller, dir. Nigerian Broadcasting Co., Lagos, 1954-66; sr. research fellow in English, U. Nigeria, 1967-72, prof., head dept. English, 1976-81, emeritus prof., 1985—; vis. prof. English, U. Mass., Amherst, 1972-75, 88, U. Conn., Storrs, 1975-76, Afro-African Studies, U. Mass., Amherst, 1987-88; pro-chancellor Anambra State U. of Tech., Enugu, Nigeria, 1986—; Regents' lectr. UCLA, 1984; dir. Heinemann Ednl. Books (Nigeria) Ltd., Nwamife Pubs. Mem. council Lagos U., 1966; mem. E. Central State Library Bd., 1971-72, Anambra State Arts Council, 1977-79.

Recipient Lit. award New Statesman, 1965; Commonwealth Poetry prize, 1973; Rockefeller fellow, 1960-61; UNESCO fellow, 1963. Fellow MLA (hon.), Royal Soc. Lit. (London); mem. Am. Acad. and Inst. Arts and Letters (hon.). Author: (novels) Things Fall Apart, 1958, No Longer at Ease, 1960, Arrow of God, 1964, A Man of the People, 1966, Anthills of the Savannah, 1988; (poetry) Christmas in Biafra, 1975; (short stories) Girls at War, 1972; (essays) Morning Yet on Creation Day, 1975, The Flute, 1978, The Drum, 1978, The Trouble with Nigeria, 1983. Office: Univ Nigeria Dept English, PO Box 53, Nsukka Anambra State, Nigeria

ACHESON, RICHARD MORRIN, chemistry educator; b. Eng., Feb. 9, 1925; s. Richard William and Amy Florence (Marlow) A.; m. Margarita Schlittler, Mar. 28, 1953; children—Corina Ursula, Marita Barbara, Michael Peter. B.A. with 1st class honors, U. Oxford, 1946, Eng., B.Sc., 1947, D.Phil., M.A., 1948. Postdoctoral fellow U. Chgo., 1949-50; lectr. Magdalen Coll., Oxford, 1953-62, The Queen's Coll., Oxford, 1953-58, fellow, 1958-86; lectr. Oxford U., 1953-86, emeritus fellow, 1986—. Author: Introduction to the Chemistry of Heterocyclic Compounds, (3d edit. 1976); The Acridines (2d edit. 1973). Author numerous papers, reviews. Patentee in field. Trustee A.C. Irvine Travel Fund, Oxford, 1961-87. Recipient H.A. Iddles prize U. N.H., 1966-67. Mem. Am. Chem. Soc., Royal Soc. Chemistry, Midland Assn. Mountaineers. Club: Alpine (Can.). Office: The Queen's College, Oxford 0X1 4AW, England

ACHILLES, CHARLES ALBERT, association executive; b. Berwyn, Ill., Sept. 29, 1946; s. Charles Laddie and Mildred Antonette (Volmut) A.; B.S. in Chemistry, No. Ill. U., 1968; M.B.A., Loyola U., Chgo., 1972; m. Sharon Lee Lullo, May 23, 1970 (div.); children—Amber Lee, Brylan Charles. Tchr., Woodridge (Ill.) Sch. System, 1968-69, asst. prin., 1969-72; dir. membership services Inst. Real Estate Mgmt., Chgo., 1972-76, staff v.p. membership services and communications, 1976-81, staff v.p. legis. and spl. services, 1981—. Active Community Affairs Com., 1977-79; pres. Oakwood Community Assn., 1978, bd. dirs., 1979; bd. dirs. Oakwood Homeowners Assn., 1979, v.p., 1981, pres., 1982-83; active Community Party of Westmont, 1978, 80, 82 Mem. Am. Mktg. Assn., Am. Soc. Assn. Execs., Community Assns. Inst., Am. Statis. Assn., Nat. Housing Conf. (dir.), Nat. Inst. Bldg. Scis., Assn. MBA Execs., Cavaliers, Phi Eta Sigma. Congregationalist. Clubs: 71; Downtown; Capitol Hill. Home: 17 W 521 Portsmouth Dr Westmont IL 60559 Office: Inst Real Estate Mgmt 430 N Michigan Ave Chicago IL 60611

ACHTERMAN, JAMES WILLIAM, management consultant; b. Cin., May 27, 1945; s. Hubert Lewis and Alberta (Moore) A.; B.B.A., U. Cin., 1968; m. Janet C. Gibbs; children—Nicole Lee, Jeffrey Scott. Mgmt. analyst City of Cin., 1968-70; budget dir. Hamilton County Ohio, Cin., 1970-72, asst. county adminstr., 1972-74; controller Cin. Public Schs., 1974-76; mng. cons. Ernst & Whinney, Cin., 1976-82; Peat, Marwick, Main & Co., 1982—. Ptnrs. in charge mgmt. cons., Columbus. Chmn. found. com. United Negro Coll. Fund, 1979-81, also recipient Disting. Leadership award, 1982; councilman City of Wyoming, Ohio, 1979-84; chmn. adv. com. on state acctg. policy State of Ohio. Mem. Ohio-Ky.-Ind. Regional Council Govts. (trustee 1971-74, 81-84), Assn. Govt. Accts., Mcpl. Finance Officers Assn., Ohio Mcpl. Finance Officers Assn. Office: Peat Marwick Main and Co 2 Nationwide Plaza Columbus OH 43215

ACHTON, LEIF, consul general, architect; b. Naestved, Denmark, Feb. 4, 1929; s. Karl and Edith (Achton) Kristensen; m. Birthe Pahl, Oct. 16, 1949; children—Pia Marian, Gitte Karin, Kim. Sec. direction M.A. Pedersen, Horsens, Denmark, 1953-55; sales mgr. J. Nielsen Kirsch, Copenhagen, 1955-57, Thunbo & Co., Kolding, Denmark, 1957-62; owner, dir. Leac Holding ApS, Copenhagen, 1962—; owner, mgr. Axeltorvets Bistro, Taastrup, Denmark, 1977—; archtl. cons. Leac products, Taastrup, 1962—; consul gen. State Guinee, Copenhagen, 1976—, consul gen. Denmark, Sweden, Norway. Chmn. City Council, Taastrup, 1974, chmn. environ. com., 1974. Served with Danish Navy, 1949. Decorated Medal of Def., Polish Cross 1st class, Medal of War 1st class, pistol marksmanship medal U.S. Navy, World War II Star, Royal Danish Homeguard 25 Yr. medal. Conservative Party. Lutheran. Avocation: Sailing. Home: Vestskovgaarden, DK 2630 Taastrup Denmark Office: Leac Holding ApS, Holmearksvej 6, DK 2630 Taastrup Denmark

ACKER, C. EDWARD, airline executive; b. 1929. B.A. in Econs. and Psychology, So. Meth. U., 1950. Pres., chief operating officer Braniff Airways Inc., 1965-75; pres. Transway Internat. Corp., 1975-76, Gulf United Corp., 1976-77; chmn., chief exec. officer Air Fla., 1977-81; chmn., chief exec. officer Pan Am. World Airways, Inc., N.Y.C., 1981—, pres., chief operating officer, 1982—, also dir.; chmn., chief executive officer Pam Am Corp. Office: Pan Am Corp Pan Am Bldg 200 Park Ave 46th Floor New York NY 10166 *

ACKERMAN, FREDA STERN, brokerage house executive; b. N.Y.C.. BA in Polit. Sci., CUNY, 1968; grad. Advanced Mgmt. Program, Harvard U., 1986. Analyst mcpl. bond research Dun & Bradstreet Inc., N.Y.C., 1968-71, sr. analyst mcpl. bond research, 1971-73; asst. v.p. analyst mcpl. bond research Moody's Investors Service Inc., N.Y.C., 1973-75, v.p. assoc. dir., 1975-79, sr. v.p., dir. mcpl. bond dept., 1979-81, exec. v.p., dir. mcpl. bond dept., 1981—. Mem. Mcpl. Forum of N.Y. (past pres.), Soc. Mcpl. Analysts, Fin. Women's Assn., Women's Econ. Roundtable, Mcpl. Analysts Group N.Y., Govt. Fin. Officers Assn., Women's Bond Club. Democrat. Office: Moody's Investors Service 99 Church St New York NY 10007

ACKERSON, CHARLES STANLEY, clergyman, social worker; b. St. Louis, June 19, 1935; s. Charles Albert and Glenda Mae (Brown) A.; m. Carol Jean Stehlick, Aug. 18, 1957; children—Debra Lynn, Charles Mark, Heather Sue. A.B., William Jewell Coll., 1957; M.Div., Colgate Rochester Div. Sch., 1961. Ordained to ministry Baptist Ch., 1961. Pastor, Glens Falls (N.Y.) Friends Meeting, 1961-65; assoc. pastor Delmar Bapt. Ch., St. Louis, 1965-68; resource dir. Block Partnership, St. Louis, 1968-71; group home dir. North Side YMCA, St. Louis, 1971-72; group home supr. St. Louis Juvenile Ct., 1973-74; program dir. Youth Opportunities Unltd., casework supr. St. Louis County Juvenile Ct., 1974-83; youth services specialist St. Louis County Dept. Human Resources, 1985—; instr. adminstrn. of justice Mo. Bapt. Coll., St. Louis, 1980—; mem. ordination council area V, Great Rivers region Am. Bapt. Chs. U.S.A., 1982-84; chmn. youth focus group Interfaith Partnership Met. St. Louis, 1985—, St. Louis Area Youth Services Network, 1987—. Chmn. group home com. Mo. Council on Criminal Justice, 1973-75; chmn. cts. and instns. subcom. Juvenile Delinquency Task Force for Gov. Mo. Action Plan for Pub. Safety, 1976. Mem. Nat. Council Juvenile and Family Ct. Judges, Mo. Juvenile Justice Assn. (v.p., chmn. tng. com.), Cairn Terrier Assn. Am., Three Rivers Kennel Club of Mo. (pres.), Mo. Conservation Fedn., Nat. Rifle Assn., Nat. Muzzle Loading Rifle Assn., Trappers of Starved Rock, Lambda Chi Alpha. Democrat. Baptist. Home: 1221 Havenhurst St Manchester MO 63011

ACKLEN, GERALD GILL, journalist; b. Portland, Oreg., Dec. 9, 1907; s. Gerald Jasper and Josephine (Gill) A.; m. Ruth Dinges, Sept. 7, 1940; children: Ruthann Acklen de la Vega, Linda Jo Acklen Chieffo, Gerald Craig, Daniel William. BS, U. Oreg., 1942. Tchr. schs., 1935-39; sch. prin., Madras, 1940-42, Grants Pass, Oreg., 1942-45; life ins. underwriter Mut. of N.Y., Grants Pass, 1945-69; wire editor Daily Courier, Grants Pass, 1950-61, sports and city editor, 1961-63, regional editor, sports, 1963-65, sports, 1963-77, hist. editor, 1977—; news corr. for AP, also for UPI, 1950-76, Oreg. Jour., 1942-82, Oreg. Sports, 1950-76; publicity dir. So. Oreg. Horse Racing Assn., 1978-81. Pres., Josephine County Diabetes Assn., 1976-79, program chmn., 1979—; bd. dirs. Oreg. affiliate Am. Diabetes Assn., 1981-1 bd. dirs. Josephine County Community Concert Assn., 1946-68, pres., 1961-64; scoutmaster Boy Scouts Am., Grants Pass, 1942-45, mem. troop com., 1945-48; mem. ofcl. bd. Methodist Ch., 1959-65, 70-82, head usher, 1949-87; mem. Grants Pass Centennial Commn., 1983-85. Lodge: Masons. Home: 1250 Oak View Dr Grants Pass OR 97527

ACKROYD, PETER, writer; b. London, Oct. 5, 1949. Grad. with honors, Clare Coll., Cambridge, Eng., 1971. Literary editor The Spectator mag., London, 1973-77, mng. editor, 1977-81; free-lance writer London, 1987—; chief book reviewer The Times, London, 1986—. Author: (poetry) London Lickpenny, 1973, Country Life, 1978, The Diversions of Purley, 1987; (literary criticism) Notes for a New Culture, 1976; (sociological study) Dressing Up, 1979; Ezra Pound and His World, 1980, The Great Fire of London, 1982, The Last Testament of Oscar Wilde, 1983, T.S. Eliot, 1984, Hawksmoor, 1985, Chatterton, 1987. Mellow fellow Yale U., 1971-73; recipient Somerset Maugham prize, 1984, Whitbread prize for best biography, 1984-85, Guardian Fiction award, 1985, Whitbread prize for best novel, 1986. Fellow Royal Soc. Lit. Office: care Anthony Sheil, 43 Doughty St, London WL1N 2LF, England

ACLAND, ANTONY, British diplomat; b. Mar. 12, 1930; s. P.B.E. Acland; m. Clare Anne Verdon, 1956 (dec. 1984); 3 children; m. Jennifer McGougan, 1987. Ed. Eton Coll., Christ Church, Oxford. Joined diplomatic service, 1953; at Middle East Centre for Arab Studies 1954; served in Dubai, 1955, Kuwait, 1956; Fgn. Office, 1958-62; asst. pvt. sec. to Sec. of State, 1959-62; mem. U.K. Mission to UN, 1962-66; head of Chancery, U.K. Mission, Geneva, 1966-68; F.C.O., 1968—, head Arabian Dept., 1970-72; prin. pvt. sec. to Fgn. and Commonwealth Sec., 1972-75; ambassador to Luxembourg, 1975-77, to Spain, 1977-79; dep. Under-Sec. of State, FCO, 1980-82, permanent under-sec. of State, head Diplomatic Service, 1982-86, ambassador to U.S., 1986—. Address: care Fgn & Commonwealth Office, London SW1 England Other: 3100 Massachusetts Ave NW Washington DC 20008

ACOSTA, FRANK XAVIER, psychologist, educator; b. Los Angeles, Apr. 2, 1945; s. Gilbert Lascaurine and Virginia (Posada) A.; m. Mary Ann Gonzales, June 30, 1979; children: Robert Xavier, Jeanette Marie. B.S. in Psychology magna cum laude, Loyola U., Los Angeles, 1968; M.A., UCLA, 1970, Ph.D. in Clin. Psychology, 1974. Lic. psychologist, Calif. Research asst. Neuropsychiat. Inst., UCLA, 1968-71, vis. assoc. prof., 1984-85; clin. psychology intern VA Outpatient Clinic, Los Angeles, 1971-72, Los Angeles Psychiat. Service, 1972-73, Long Beach VA Hosp., Calif., 1973-74; clin. psychologist Los Angeles County/U. So. Calif. Med. Ctr., Los Angeles, 1974—, dir. Spanish-Speaking Clinic, Adult Psychiat. Clinic, 1975—; assoc. dir. clin. psychol. internship tng. program, 1986—; asst. prof. psychiatry Sch. Medicine, U. So. Calif., Los Angeles, 1974-80, assoc. prof. clin. psychiatry, 1980-84, assoc. prof., 1984—; cons. Spanish Speaking Mental Health Research Ctr., Los Angeles, 1974-88 ; cons., reviewer NIMH, 1977—. Author: (with J. Yamamoto and L. Evans) Effective Psychotherapy for Low-Income and Minority Patients, 1982 (Behavioral Sci. Book Club selection 1983). Mem. editorial bd. Hispanic Jour. Behavioral Scis., 1981-85 . Contbr. chpts. to books, articles to profl. jours. Mem. psychol. rev. panel Med. Serviecs Div. and Occupational Health and Safety Div. Personnel Dept. City of Los Angeles, 1986—; cons. Nat. Coalition Hispanic Mental Health and Human Services Orgns., Washington, 1976—; chair Nat. Research Council, Evaluation Panel Psychology, Ford Found. Doctoral Fellowships Minorities Program, Washington, 1986-88. Research grantee Social Sci. Research Council, Los Angeles, 1976, NIMH, 1977—; Ford Found. postdoctoral minorities fellow NRC, 1984; recipient faculty research prize, dept. psychiatry U. So. Calif. Sch. Medicine, 1977. Fellow Am. Psychol. Assn. (accreditation com. 1977-80); mem. Western Psychol. Assn., Interam. Soc. Psychology, AAAS. Democrat. Roman Catholic. Home: 2405 Paloma Pasadena CA 91104 Office: Dept Psychiatry and Behavioral Scis U So Calif Sch Medicine 1937 Hospital Pl Los Angeles CA 90033

ACOSTA, URSULA, psychologist; b. Hannover, Ger., Jan. 14, 1933; came to U.S., 1954, naturalized, 1958; d. Johannes Karl and Irma (Ulrich) Schmidt; B.A., U. P.R., 1971, M.E., 1973; Ph.D. in Psychology, Gutenberg U., Mainz, W. Ger., 1979; m. Sebastian Acosta-Ronda, June 12, 1954; children—Johann, Dennis, Peter. Various occupations, 1954-66; instr., asst. prof., assoc. prof. psychology U. P.R., Mayaguez, 1973—. Chairperson appeal bd. SSS. Mem. LWV (unit chair 1977-78, 86-88), Am. Psychol. Assn., Psychol. Assn. PR. (chair ethics com. 1979-81). Active Puerto Rican Statehood Movement, founder PRP. Republican. Co-author: Familias de Cabo Rojo (History prize Ateneo Puertorriqueno de New York 1983); author: Quien era Cofresi?, 1984, Cabo Rojo: Notas para su historia, 1985, New Voices of the Old: FIve Centuries of Puerto Rican Cultural History, 1987; contbr. articles to various jours. and newspapers. Office: U PR Mayaguez PR 00709

ACOYMO, AUGUSTO VILLANUEVA, accountant, management consultant, educator; b. Manila, Oct. 28, 1928; s. Teofilo Dayte and Carmen Sempio (Villanueva) A.; m. Luz Ibanez Gamir, Feb. 25, 1956; children: Jose Maria, Ramon Maria, Maria Alexandra. BS in Commerce, Far Eastern U., 1949; MBA, NYU, 1954. CPA, cert. mgmt. acct. (CMA). Staff auditor McArdle & McArdle, N.Y.C., 1954-56; prof. Far Eastern U., Philippine Women's U., Manila, 1956-59; v.p. fin. REHCO Electronics Corp., San Juan, Manila, 1959-63; fin. cons. Manila Textile Mills, 1963-64; fin. mgr. Roche Pharms., Makati, Manila, 1964-66; sr. ptnr. Carlos J. Valdes & Co. CPAs, Makati, 1966—; dean of commerce Ctr. Escolar U., Manila, 1981-84; prof. Grad. Sch. Bus. Ateneo U., Makati, 1974—, De La Salle U., Manila, chmn. dept. bus. mgmt. St. Scholastica's Coll., Manila, 1976—; cons. U. Philippines Inst. for Small Scale Industries, Quezon City, Philippines, 1978-82; ,lectr. Philippine Exec. Acad. U. Philippines, Manila, 1975—. Contbr. articles on acctg. to profl. jours. Senator, Jaycees Internat., Manila. senator Manila Jaycee Senate, 1984. Served to 1st lt. Philippine Army Res. Mem. Philippine Assn. Mgmt. Accts. (pres. 1982 83), Philippine Inst. Mgmt. Acctg. (pres. 1976—), Philippine Inst. CPA's (bd. dirs. 1975, Outstanding CPA in profl. devel. 1981, 85, 86). Roman Catholic. Clubs: Metropolitan, Exec. Suite (Makati), Toastmasters (pres. 1986, area gov. 19876), Manila Overseas Press. Lodge: Lions. Office: Carlos J Valdes & Co CPAs, 108 Aquirre St CHVC Bldg, Makati, Manila Philippines

ACTON, EDWARD DAVID JOSEPH, historian, educator; b. Harare, Zimbabwe, Feb. 4, 1949; s. John and Daphne (Strutt) A.; m. Stella Conroy, Apr. 8, 1972; children: Helen Marie, Natalie Elizabeth. BA in History with honors, U. York, Eng., 1971; PhD in History, U. Cambridge, Eng., 1975. Grad. trainee Bank of Eng., 1975-76; lectr. U. Liverpool, Eng., 1976-86, sr. lectr., 1976—. Author: Alexander Herzen, 1979, Russia: The Present and the Past, 1986; contbr. articles to profl. jours. Research grantee Brit. Acad., 1983, 86, Brit. Council, 1983, Leverhulme Trust, 1987. Fellow Royal Hist. Soc.; mem. Hist. Assn. (pres. Liverpool and dist. br. 1984-87). Roman Catholic. Home: 49 Ballantrae Rd, Liverpool L18 6JG, England Office: U Liverpool Dept History, 8 Abercromby Sq, Liverpool L69 3BX, England

ACTON, PETER NEVILLE, editor; b. Manchester, Eng., Oct. 15, 1952; s. James Bernard and Berylle Silvine (Bibb) A.; m. Lesley Angela Wingfield, Aug. 5, 1978; children: Thomas James, Stephen Mark. BA in Geography with honors, London U., 1974; MS, Birmingham U., Eng., 1976. Asst. editor Univ. Tutorial Press, London, 1974-75; traffic engr. Sir Alexander Gibb & Ptnrs., London, 1976-77; mktg. officer Dunlop Ltd., Birmingham, 1977-78; transport corr. Bus. Press Internat., London, 1978-80; editor Transport mag., Colchester, 1980-82; editor Surveyor mag. Bus. Press Internat., London, 1982-84, editor Motor Transport mag., 1984—; proprietor, ptnr. AM Pubs., 1988; specialist Internat. Transport Pub. Co., 1988; owner of distributions bus., 1988. Editor: The British Isles, 1975. Mem. Chartered Inst. Transport (council 1987), Inst. Logistics Distbn. Mgmt. (assoc.), Honorable Worshipful Co. of Carmen. Anglican. Home: 50 Meadow Walk, Walton-on-the-Hill, Tadworth, Surrey KT20 7UG, England

ACUDA, STANLEY WILSON, psychiatrist; b. Kampala, Uganda, Apr. 28, 1942; s. Okello Erieza and Aboce Eseza; m. Violet Nabukenya; children: Caroline, Charles. MBChB, Makerere U., Kampala, 1970. Med. officer Ministry of Health, Uganda, 1970-72; registrar psychiatry Maudsley Atid Bethlem Royal Hosp., London, 1972-75; lectr. U. Nairobi, Kenya, 1976-78, sr. lectr., 1978-80, assoc. prof. psychiatry, 1980-85, prof., 1985—, chmn. dept. psychiatry, 1980—; mem. experts adv. panel WHO, 1975—; organizer various nat. and internat. confs., 1985-87. Contbr. 56 articles to profl. jours. Recipient Research award UN Fund for Drug Abuse Control, 1984; WHO research grantee, 1983, 86. Fellow Royal Coll. Psychiatrists; mem. World Psychiat. Assn., African Psychiat. Assn. (sec. gen. 1986—). Club: United Kenya (Nairobi). Office: U Nairobi Kenyatta Nat Hosp, PO Box 30588, Nairobi Kenya

ACUFF, THOMAS ALDRICH, corporate executive; b. Bklyn., July 26, 1936; s. Fieldon Harpe and Doris (Gray) A.; children: Mark Thomas, Elizabeth Guilliams; m. Vernonica Yvette Packham. BS in Indsl. Engring., Iowa State U., 1961; postgrad., U. Louisville, 1970. Advanced mfg. engr. Gen. Electric Co., Louisville, 1961-66; indsl. engring. mgr. Allis Chalmers Corp., Louisville, 1966-68, supt. mfg., 1968-71; gen. mgr. Famco-Asia, Allis Chalmers Corp., Singapore, 1971-75; mfg. dir. internat. Allis Chalmers Corp., Louisville, 1975-78; regional dir. Far East and Pacific, Allis Chalmers Corp., Singapore, 1978-80; dir. advanced ops. ITT Europe, Brussels, 1980-84, dir. bus. ops., 1984-88; v.p. Andlinger & Co. Inc., Brussels, 1988—; bd. dirs. Famco-Asia, Singapore, Japan Air Filter, Tokyo, AAF Famco B.V., The Netherlands. Contbr. articles to profl. jours. Chmn. Am. Cancer Soc., Louisville, 1971. Served to lt. comdr. USNR, 1954-57. Mem. Inst. Indsl. Engrs. (sr., bd. dirs. 1970), Am. Bus. Council (Singapore), Am. Mgmt. Assn. (div. council), Armed Forces Communications and Electronics Assn. (bd. dirs., pres. 1987). Club: Tanglin (Singapore), Am. (Singapore). Office: Andlinger & Co Inc, 475 Ave Louise Bte 10, B1050 Brussels Belgium

ADA, JOSEPH F., territorial governor. Elected gov. of Guam, 1986. Republican. Office: Office of the Gov Territory of Guam Agana GU 96910 *

ADACHI, ATHAN KEN, civil engineer; b. Honolulu, July 18, 1951; s. Kenneth Korji and Dorothy Takako (Fujioka) A.; m. Maude Miyo Migita, May 10, 1980. BS, U. Hawaii, 1974. Registered profl. engr., Hawaii. Project engr. Avanti Constrn. Co., Honolulu, 1974-77; engr. cons. Unemori Engring. Co., Wailuku, Hawaii, 1977-79; civil engr. IV, County of Maui, Wailuku, 1979-85; design engr. State of Hawaii, Kahului, 1985-86, asst. dist. engr., 1986—. Vol. Maui Young Dem. Com.; bd. dirs. Maui Assn. for Retarded Citizens, 1984; coordinator Blood Bank of Hawaii, Maui United Way. Mem. NSPE. Buddhist. Club: Toastmasters. Home: 102 Kawalea Pl Kula HI 96790 Office: Hawaii State Dept Transp Hwys 650 Palapala Dr Kahului HI 96732

ADACHI, SUEO, trading company executive; b. Tokyo, Aug. 24, 1926; s. Tadashi and Kohko Adachi; m. Yoko Kabashima, Oct. 6, 1960; children: Akiko Sugiyama, Sachiko. BA, Keio U., Tokyo, 1947. Gen. mgr. plant export dept. Marubeni Corp., Tokyo, 1971-78, gen. mgr. machinery IV div., 1979-83, mng. dir., gen. mgr. plant div., 1983-85; pres., chief exec. officer Marubeni Am. Corp., N.Y.C., 1985-87, chmn., chief exec. officer, 1987—. Mem. Japanese C. of C. (bd. dirs. N.Y. chpt. 1985—). Clubs: The Nippon (bd. dirs.), Met. (N.Y.C.); Scarsdale (N.Y.) Golf. Office: Marubeni Am Corp 200 Park Ave New York NY 10016

ADACHI, TAKASHI, educator; b. Osaka, Japan, Apr. 9, 1919; m. Kazuko Uesugi, May 26, 1949; children: Kei, Akira. BArch, Kyoto U., Japan, 1941, D of Engring., 1957. Registered architect. Assoc. prof. Osaka U., 1951-59, prof., 1959-83, prof. emeritus, 1983—; prof. Setsunan U., Osaka, 1983—; chmn. planning com. Expo '90, Osaka, 1986—; chief cons. Gen. Urban Planning City of Osaka, 1976—. Co-editor: History of Public Housing, 1975 (Mainichi Newspaper Pub. award 1962). Served to 1st lt. Japanese Army, 1942-45, World War II China. Mem. Archtl. Assn. Japan (v.p. 1962—), Japan Architects Assn. (v.p. 1964—). Home: 1-11-23 Sonehigashi, 561 Toyonaka, Osaka Japan Office: Setsunan U, 17-8, Ikeda Naka, 572 Neyagawa, Osaka Japan

ADAIKAN, GANESAN PERIANNAN, pharmacologist, scientist; b. Kuala Lumpur, Selangor, Malaysia, Feb. 20, 1944; arrived in Singapore, 1973; s. Periannan and Alagammai Adaikan; m. Selvamani Arumugam, May 17, 1970; children: Kala, Kalpana, Sangeetha, Siva Sanjeevkumar. M in Biology, Inst. Biology, London, 1976; MSc, U. Singapore, 1979; PhD, Nat. Univ. Singapore, 1985. Research asst. Makerere U., Kampala, Uganda, 1971-73; research asst. U. Singapore, 1973-79, research fellow, 1980-82; clin. biochemist Nat. Univ. Singapore, 1982-85, clin. scientist, 1986—. Contbr. 119 articles to sci. jours, 1972—; cons. editor: Drugs of Today, 1984, Drugs of the Future, 1984—, Asia Pacific Journal of Pharmacology, 1986—. Fellow Inst. Biology, London, 1987—; recipient Jean-Francois Ginestie award The Internat. Soc., Prague, Czechoslovakia, 1986; co-recipient Surg Soc. Research award, 1973. Mem. Singapore Planned Parenthood Fedn., Obstet. and Gynecol. Soc. Singapore (Benjamin H. Sheare Meml. Lecture award 1987). Hindu. Home: 109 Jalan Hitam Manis, Singapore 1027, Singapore Office: Nat Univ Singapore, Nat Univ Hosp, Dept Ob-Gyn, Lower Kent Ridge Rd, Singapore 0511, Singapore

ADAIR, IAN HUGH, author, entertainer; b. Kilmarnock, Scotland, Dec. 20, 1940; s. John and Isabel (Henderson) A.; student Scottish schs.; m. Marilyn Rendall Peckitt, Jan. 24, 1986. Ptnr., gen. mgr. Supreme Magic Co. Ltd., 1965—; TV presenter, entertainer and broadcaster, 1966-74; magical inventor, adv., 1975—; profl. children's entertainer, 1976—; author over 150 books on novelty subjects, 1959—, also 5 vol. ency. on specialized magic for magicians; columnist The Magigram. Mem. Inner Magic Circle London (Gold Star 1976), Assn. Wizards South (hon. v.p. 1970), India Magic Circle (hon. mem.), Internat. Brotherhood Magicians (territorial rep. 1977-84), Round Table Orgn. (chmn. 1980). Inventor magical items to trade. Address: Mystique, 8, Fordlands Crescent, Raleigh, Bideford, EX39 3NN Devon England

ADAM, EVELYN THERESA, educator; b. Lanark, Ont., Can., Apr. 9, 1929; d. Ewart Francis and Anna Irene (Dowdall) A. R.N., Hotel Dieu Hosp., Kingston, Ont., 1950; B.Nursing, U. Montreal, 1966; M.Nursing, UCLA, 1971. Gen. duty nurse Deep River Hosp., Ont., 1951-52, Sunnybrook Hosp., Toronto, Ont., 1952-54; gen. duty and head nurse Montreal Neurol. Inst., 1954-61; gen. duty nurse Hopital Cantonal, Lausanne, Switzerland, 1961, Hopital Ste-Justine, Montreal, 1962-63; clin. instr. Montreal Rehab. Inst., 1963-64; lectr. U. Montreal Faculty of Nursing, 1966-69, asst. prof., 1971-77, assoc. prof., 1977-83, prof., 1983—, faculty sec. 1982—; lectr., cons. in field. Author: Etre Infirmiere, 1979, To be a Nurse, 1980, translations of books. Contbr. articles to profl. jours. Mem. Order of Nurses of Que. Avocations: swimming; cooking; theatre. Office: Faculty of Nursing, U Montreal, PO Box 6128, Sta A, Montreal, PQ Canada H3C 3J7

ADAM, HERIBERT ANTON, professor; b. Offenbach, Hessen, Germany, July 1, 1936; s. Ernst and Maria (Kleinmann) A.; m. Kogila Moodley, June 28, 1968; children: Kanya, Maya. Diploma in sociology, U. Frankfurt, Fed. Republic Germany, 1961, PhD, 1965; Habilitation, U. Giessen, Fed. Republic Germany, 1972. Research assoc., lectr. Inst. Social Research U. Frankfurt, 1961-65; research fellow U. Calif., Berkeley, 1966; sr. lectr. U. Natal, Durban, Republic of South Africa, 1967; assoc. prof. Simon Fraser U., Vancouver, B.C., Can., 1968; chmn. dept. sociology Simon Fraser U., Vancouver, 1970-72, prof., 1972—, research prof., 1982. Author: Modernizing Racial Domination, 1971, South Africa Without Apartheid, 1986; co-author: Ethnic Power Mobilized, 1979. Bd. dirs. Inst. Race Relations, Johannesburg, Republic South Africa, 1983. Mem. Can. African Studies Assn., Internat. Sociol. Assn. (mem. research com. ethnicity, pres. 1986—). Office: Simon Fraser U, Vancouver, BC Canada V5A 1S6

ADAMANY, DAVID WALTER, university president; b. Janesville, Wis., Sept. 23, 1936; s. Walter Joseph and Dora Marie (Mutter) A. AB, Harvard U., 1958, JD, 1961; MS, U. Wis., 1963, PhD in Polit. Sci., 1967; LLD (hon.), Adrian Coll., 1984; AAS (hon.), Schoolcraft Coll., 1986. Bar: Wis. 1961. Spl. asst. to atty. gen. State of Wis., Madison, 1961-63, exec. pardon counsel, 1963; commr. Wis. Public Service Commn., 1963-65; instr. polit. sci. Wis. State U., Whitewater, 1965-67; asst. prof., then assoc. prof. Wesleyan U., Middletown, Conn., 1967-72; dean coll. Wesleyan U., 1969-71; assoc. prof., then prof. polit. sci. U. Wis., Madison, 1972-77; sec. of revenue State of Wis., 1974-76; v.p. acad. affairs, prof. Calif. State U., Long Beach, 1977-80, U. Md., College Park, 1980-82; prof. law and polit. sci. Wayne State U., Detroit, 1982—, pres., 1982—; chmn. Wis. Council Criminal Justice, 1973-75, Wis. Elections Bd., 1976-77, sec. Wis. Dept. Revenue; advisor to Gov. Patrick J. Lucey, State of Wis., 1972. Author: Financing Politics, 1969, Campaign Finance in America, 1972, Borzoi Reader in American Politics, 1972; co-author: American Government: Democracy and Liberty in Balance, 1975, Political Money, 1975; editorial bd.: Social Sci. Quarterly, 1973—, State and Local Govt. Rev, 1974-80; contbr. articles to profl. jours. Mem. exec. com. Detroit Med. Ctr., Met. Ctr. High Tech.; chmn. Mich. Bicentennial of Constn. Commn., 1986—; bd. dirs. Detroit Econ. Growth Corp., Detroit Inst. Arts Founders Soc., Detroit Symphony Orch., Mich. Cancer Found., New Detroit, United Found., Gov.'s Commn. on Jobs and Econ. Devel. Mem. Pres.' Council United State Colls. and Univs. (chmn.), Am. Polit. Sci. Assn., ACLU, Wis. Bar Assn. Democrat. Office: Wayne State U Office of Pres Detroit MI 48202 *

ADAMCZAK, EUGENIUSZ, Publisher; b. Leszno, Poland, Aug. 30, 1935; s. Wladyslaw and Helena (Tomaszewska) A.; m. Teresa Jedrasiak, Nov. 18, 1958 (div. Oct 1965); m. Krystyna Marte, Dec. 22, 1966 (div. June 1972); children: Arkadiusz, Joanna; m. Miroslawa Reichel, Feb. 7, 1981; 1 child, Magdalena. M Natural Sci., U. Wroclaw, Poland, 1958. Dir. Ossolineum, Wroclaw, 1969—, editor yearbook, 1976, mem. sci. council of library, 1984—; chmn. Panorama Raclawicka council, Wroclaw, 1986—; mem. philol. commn. Polish Acad. Sci., Wroclaw, 1986—; mem. sci. council Inst. Lit. Research, Warsaw, Poland, 1987—. Head editor ann. Wroclaw calendar, 1971-76; mem. staff Ze Skarbca Kultury, 1977—. Mem. head council Polish Students Assn., Warsaw, 1959-64, pres. local council Wroclaw, 1961-63; mem. hdqrs. Univ. Sports Assn. Poland, Warsaw, 1960-62. Decorated knight of Polonia Restituta Order, 1977, commandery of Polonia Restituta Order, 1985; recipient Golden Cross of Merit People's State Council, 1970, award Minister of Culture and Art, 1972, medal Com. Nat. Edn./Minister of Edn., 1980, Golden Medal of Merit, 1987. Mem. Polish Pubs. Assn. (officer 1976—, v.p. 1979-80). Mem. United Workers Party. Home: Agrestowa 41, 53-006 Wroclaw Poland Office: Ossolineum Pub House, Rynek 9, 50-106 Wroclaw Poland

ADAMS, ALFRED HUGH, college president; b. Punta Gorda, Fla., Mar. 8, 1928; s. Alfred and Irene (Gatewood) A.; m. Joyce Morgan, Nov. 10, 1954; children: Joy, Al, Paul. A.A., U. Fla., 1948; B.S., Fla. State U., 1950, M.S., 1956, Ed.D., 1962; L.H.D., Fla. Atlantic U., 1972. Asst. coach varsity football Fla. State U., 1955-58, asst. dir. housing, instr. edn., 1958-62, asst. dean men, asst. prof. edn., 1962-64; supt. pub. instrn. Charlotte County, Fla., 1965-68; pres. Broward Community Coll., Ft. Lauderdale, Fla., 1968—; bd. dirs. Am. Council on Edn.; vis. lectr. in higher edn. Inst. Higher Edn., U. Fla.; also mem. com. on internat. edn. relations com. on mil-higher edn. relations; mem. adv. com. Inst. Internat. Edn.; dir. Sun Bank/South Fla., N.A.; Vice chmn. Gov. Fla. Commn. Quality Edn., 1968-70; mem. Gov.'s Adv. Com. Edn., 1966-70; mem. regional council Southeastern Edn. Corp., 1966-69; mem. commn. adminstrv. affairs Am. Council on Edn., 1973; pres. Pub. Instns. Higher Learning in So. States, 1975; mem. adv. com. Joint Council on Econ. Edn.; chmn. AACJC Internat./Intercultural Consortium, S.E. Fla. Ednl. Consortium; chmn. council pres. Fla. Community Colls.; Trustee South Fla. Edn. Center, Pub. Service TV. Mem. editorial bd., Soc. for Coll. and Univ. Planning. Pres. United Way, 1973; bd. dirs. local chpt. ARC, 1971; bd. dirs. local State U. Sports Hall of Fame.; bd. dirs. Opera Guild, Ft. Lauderdale, pres., 1983-85; bd. dirs. Coll. Consortium Internat. Studies; exec. dir. Performing Arts Ctr. Authority, Ft. Lauderdale. Served to comdr. USNR, 1945-46, 52-55. Decorated knight Internat. Constantinian Order, 1971; recipient Liberty Bell award, 1975, Patriot award Freedoms Found., Disting. Alumnus award Fla. State U., A. Hugh Adams Coll. Gold Key. cert. of recognition Fla. Ho. of Reps., Disting Omicron Delta Kappa Alumnus of Yr., 1987; named Patriot Fla. Bicentennial Commn. Mem. Fla. Tchr. Edn. Adv. Council, Fla. Edn. Council Ethics Com. Sch. Adminstrs., Am. Assn. Sch. Adminstrs., Ft. Lauderdale C. of C. (v.p.), Profl. Practices Commn., Fla. Assn. Colls. and Univs. (pres. 1975), Naval Res. Assn., Res. Officers Assn., U.S. Naval Inst. (life), Broward Minutemen (pres.), Fla. Inter-agy. Law Enforcement Planning Council, Omicron Delta Kappa, Phi Theta Kappa. Methodist. Clubs: Gulfstream Sailing, Fort Lauderdale; Tower (gov. 1985-86). Lodge: Kiwanis. Home: 105 N Victoria Park Rd Fort Lauderdale FL 33301

ADAMS, BROCK, U.S. senator; b. Atlanta, Jan. 13, 1927; s. Charles Leslie and Vera Eleanor (Beemer) A.; m. Mary Elizabeth Scott, Aug. 16, 1952; children: Scott Leslie, Lewis Dean, Katherine Elizabeth, Aleen Mundy. BA in Econs. summa cum laude, U. Wash., 1944; LLB, Harvard U., 1952. Bar: Wash. 1952, D.C. Ptnr. LeSourd, Patten and Adams (formerly Little, LeSourd, Patten and Adams), Seattle, 1952-61; U.S. atty. U.S. Dist. Ct. (we. dist.) Wash., Seattle, 1961-64; mem. 89th-94th Congresses from 7th Wash. dist., 1965-77, mem. sci. and astronautics com., interstate and fgn. commerce com., chmn. budget com.; U.S. Sec. Transp. Washington, 1977-79; ptnr. Garvey, Schubert, Adams and Barer, 1979-86; U.S. Senator from Wash. 1987—; instr. Am. Inst. Banking, 1954-60. Chmn. Western Wash. dist. Kennedy for Pres. campaign, 1960; former pres. Neighborhood House, Seattle; exec. dir. Wash. dist. Carter for Pres. campaign ; past trustee Civic Unity Commn., Seattle. Served with USN, 1944-46. Recipient Disting. Service award Seattle Jr. C. of C., 1960. Mem. ABA, Fed. Bar Assn., Wash. Bar Assn., Seattle-King County Bar Assn., Puget Sound Assn. (pres. 1962-63), U. Wash. Alumni Assn. (past trustee), Phi Beta Kappa. Democrat. Episcopalian. Office: US Senate 513 Hart Senate Office Bldg Washington DC 20510 •

ADAMS, BRUCE, ornithologist; b. N.Y.C., Oct. 16, 1936; s. Clyde and Evelyn Murray (Queen) A.; student U. Vt., 1957-60. Computer operator McGraw-Hill, Inc., Hightstown, N.J., 1970—. Served with Army N.G., 1960-66, USAF Res., 1977—. Mem. Am. Ornithologists Union, Brit. Ornithologists Union, Wilson, Cooper ornithol. socs., Eastern, Northeastern bird banding assns., Am. Liszt Soc. Episcopalian. Club: Explorer's. Contbr. articles and papers to ornithological jours.; inventer bird trap, 1959; developer techniques trapping and banding birds for sci. research. Home: 271 Edgerstoune Rd Princeton NJ 08540

ADAMS, CHARLES ARTHUR, municipal financial analyst; b. Caldwell, Idaho, July 25, 1933; s. John Woodrow and Eileen (Vail) A.; B.A., Coll. Idaho, 1962; m. Susan Rae Donovan, Jan. 30, 1960; children—Michael C., Teresa M. Sales mgr. Hoppins Ins. Agy., Nampa, Idaho, 1961-63; auditor Indsl. Indemnity Ins. Co., Boise, Idaho, 1964-65, Argonaut Ins. Co., Portland, 1966-67; br. mgr. Am. Mut. Ins. Co., Portland, 1968-70; underwriting mgr. Alaska Pacific Assurance Co., Juneau, 1970-73; pres. A.I.M. Ins. Inc., Anchorage, 1973-78, pres. parent co. A.I.M. Corp., 1977-78, also sr. v.p. A.I.M. Internat., Tokyo, 1975-78; fin. officer City of Petersburg (Alaska), 1978, City of Homer (Alaska), 1979; fin. analyst Municipality of Anchorage, 1980—; community adv. bd. KSKA, 1983— . Vol. in corrections, State of Alaska, 1981; mem. central com. Libertarian Party of Alaska, 1981-84, vice chmn., 1985—, chmn., Anchorage, 1982-83. Served with AUS, USARSF 1952-76. Mem. Resource Devel. Council Alaska, Homebuilders Alaska (dir. 1974-78), Homeowners Warranty Council Alaska (v.p. 1977), Porsche Club Am., Airborne Assn., VFW,, Am. Legion, Spl. Forces Decade Assn., Alaska Council Sports Car Clubs (dir. 1976-78), Alaska World Affairs Council (chmn. fin. and devel. com. 1983-84, dir. 1984—, univ. and coll. liaison com. 1985—). Clubs: Toastmasters (named Summit Club Speaker of Yr. 1969), Wednesday Club, Captain Cook Athletic. Lodge: KC. Author: fin. procedures and master policy to insure constrn. of Alaska pipeline. Home: 3258 Montpelier Ct Anchorage AK 99503 Office: Pouch 6-650 Anchorage AK 99502

ADAMS, CHARLES FRANCIS, advertising and real estate executive; b. Detroit, Sept. 26, 1927; s. James R. and Bertha C. (DeChant) A.; m. Helen R. Harrell, Nov. 12, 1949; children: Charles Francis, Amy Ann, James Randolph, Patricia Duncan. BA, U. Mich., 1948; postgrad., U. Calif., Berkeley, 1949. With D'Arcy-MacManus & Masius, Inc., San Francisco, 1947-80, exec. v.p., dir., 1970-76, pres., chief operating officer, 1976-80; pres. Adams Enterprises, 1971—; exec. v.p., dir. Washington Office, Am. Assn. Advt. Agys., 1980-84; chmn., chief exec. officer Wajim Corp., Detroit; past mem. steering com. Nat. Advt. Rev. Bd.; mem. mktg. com. U.S. Info. Agy.; pres. Internat. Visitors Ctr. of the Bay Area, 1988—. Author: Common Sense in Advertising, 1965, Heroes of the Golden Gate, 1987. Past chmn. exec. com. Oakland U. Mem. Am. Assn. Advt. Agys. (dir., mem. govt. relations com.), Advt. Fedn. Am. (past dir.), Nat. Outdoor Advt. Bur. (past chmn.), Theta Chi, Alpha Delta Sigma (hon.). Republican. Roman Catholic. Clubs: Bloomfield Hills Country; Carmel Valley Ranch (Calif.); Nat. Golf Links Am. (Southampton, L.I.); Olympic, The Family (San Francisco). Home: 2240 Hyde St San Francisco CA 94109 also: 25450 Loma Robles Carmel CA 93923 Office: 10 W Long Lake Rd Bloomfield Hills MI 48013

ADAMS, DAYTON WARREN, JR., developer company executive; b. Denison, Tex., June 10, 1941; s. Dayton Warren and Amelia Francis (Roots) A; m. Shelley Annette West, Oct. 10, 1968. BA, Tex. Tech U., 1965; M Fgn. Trade, Am. Grad. Sch. Internat. Mgmt., 1967. Auditor Ernst and Ernst, Phoenix, 1965-66, Touche, Ross, Baily and Smart, Phoenix, 1966-67; with internat. mgmt. dept. Am. Internat. Groups, N.Y.C., Milan, Italy and London, 1967-71; assoc. v.p. Coldwell Banker & Co., Phoenix, 1972-84; gen. ptnr. The WESTCOR Co., Phoenix, 1984—; bd. dirs. Compas, Phoenix., YMCA, Phoenix, 1980-86; trustee Claremont Sch. Theology, Calif. Named one of Country's Top 20 in Sales, Coldwell Banker & Co., 1968, 69. Mem. Sigma Chi. Republican. Club: Phoenix Country. Office: The Westcor Co 11411 N Tatum Blvd Phoenix AZ 85028

ADAMS, FRANCIS DONALD (FRANK), electronics engineer, naval reserve engineering officer; b. Pottsville, Pa., Sept. 23, 1943; s. Matthew and Frances Catherine (Guetling) A.; m. Jacqueline Irene Chapman, May 12, 1967; children: Donald Wayne, James Douglas, Deborah Marie. BSEE, U. Miami, 1974; MSEE, U. Central Fla., 1980, postgrad., 1984—. Cert. master instr. USAF. Electronics technician, instr. USAF Crypto Tech. Sch., Lackland AFB, Tex., 1966-70; airborne radar technician Homestead AFB, Fla., 1971-74; electronics engr. Naval Tng. Systems Ctr., Orlando, Fla., 1974—, acquisition dir., project engr., 1974-81, electronics engr., software engr., computer resources cons., 1981—; commd. ensign USNR, 1979, advanced through grades to lt. commdr., 1987; foster parent, 1986—; mem. Seminole County Local Sch. Adv. Com., 1982-83; sec. Cen. Fla. Foster Parents Assn., 1987-88. Mem. Winter Springs Civic Assn. Served with USAF, 1961-70, USAFR, 1971-79, USNR, 1979—. Decorated Army Commendation Medal; Fla. Engring. Soc. scholar, 1973-74, Navy Long Term Tng. scholar, 1977-78, 84-85. Mem. U.S. Naval Inst., Winter Springs C. of C., VFW, Sigma Xi, Tau Beta Pi, Eta Kappa Nu, Sigma Pi Sigma. Baptist. Home: 502 Murphy Rd Winter Springs FL 32708 Office: Naval Training Systems Ctr Code 251 Orlando FL 32813

ADAMS, GRAHAM, architect, consultant; b. Newcastle, Eng., July 10, 1925; emigrated to Can., 1925; s. John George and Gwendolyn (Wood) A.; m. Marjory Anne Cassells, Oct. 6, 1950; children: Jeffrey John, Martha Elaine, Karen Elizabeth, Sara Dianne. BArch, U. Toronto, 1952. With Province of Ont., Can., 1955-83, head extension and field services community planning br. Ministry Mcpl. Affairs, 1966-70, dir. uniform bldg. standards br. Ministry Consumer and Comml. Relations, 1970-75, dir. bldg. code br., 1976-83; prin. Graham Adams Consulting Services, Inc., Toronto, Ont., 1984—; mem. nat. bldg. and fire code adv. coms.; lectr., author on bldg. codes. Elder Leaside Presbyn. Ch., Toronto, 1968; bd. dirs. E.H. Johnson Meml. Trust Fund, 1984. Fellow Royal Can. Inst. Architects; mem. Ont. Assn. Architects, Can. Inst. Planners., Royal Can. Mil. Inst. (curling exec. 1983—), Delta Tau Delta (alumni v.p. 1984—, v.p. house corp. 1987—). Avocations: golf, gardening, winter sports. Office: Graham Adams Cons Services Inc, 110 Eglinton Ave E, Suite 701, Toronto, ON Canada M4P 2Y9

ADAMS, HAROLD GENE, judge; b. Muskogee, Okla., July 1, 1926; s. William Clyde and Daisy (McAlister) A.; m. Carole Jean Harbuck, Feb. 10, 1962 (div.); 1 child, Patrick Andrew; Melissa Ann Graves, Dec. 22, 1986. B.S., Okla. State U., 1950; J.D., So. Meth. U., 1960, M.L.A., 1974; grad. Air War Coll., 1975. Bar: Tex. 1960, U.S. Dist. Ct. (no. dist.) Tex. 1962, U.S. Supreme Ct. 1968, U.S. Ct. Appeals (5th cir.) 1971, Okla. 1974. Regional mgr. Am. Arbitration Assn., 1957-60; asst. dist. atty., chief prosecutor Dallas County Criminal Ct., Dallas, 1961-62; Harold G. Adams, Inc., P.C., 1962-77; spl. asst. to Gov., dep. dir. Okla. Crime Commn., 1974; mil. judge, state of Tex., 1975; U.S. adminstrv. law judge, Santa Ana, Calif., 1977-79; U.S. adminstrv. law judge in charge Office of Hearings and Appeals, New Orleans, 1979-82; regional chief adminstrv. law judge Region VI, Office of Hearings and Appeals, Social Security Adminstrn., HHS, Dallas, 1982-85, hearing office, chief adminstrv. law judge, North Dallas, 1985—; instr. real estate law and oil and gas law Dallas County Community Coll.; instr. contracts and probate So. Meth. U. Dist. Served with USN, 1944-46; to lt. col. USAFR (ret.); with Tex. Air N.G., 1946-78. Decorated Air Force Res. medal World War II Victory medal, Combat Aircrew Wings, Am. Campaign medal; recipient Tex. Faithful Service medal. Mem. ABA, Dallas Bar Assn., Conf. Adminstrv. Law Judges, Fed. Adminstrv. Law Judges Conf. Methodist. Clubs: Tex. Game Fishing, Sonova Beach Rod and Reel, Sail Fish and Tarpon of Mex. Lodges: Masons, Shriners, Jesters. Grand champion Internat. Bill Fish Tournament, Alcapulco, Mex., 2 times. Office: 10830 N Central Expressway Suite 252 Dallas TX 75231

ADAMS, HENRY HITCH, retired educator, author; b. Ann Arbor, Mich., Mar. 26, 1917; s. Henry Foster and Susan (Hitch) A.; A.B., U. Mich., 1939; M.A., Columbia U., 1940, Ph.D., 1942; m. Catherine Abigail Sanders, Aug. 22, 1943; children—Catherine (Mrs. James F. Hartmann, Jr.), Henry Arthur Sanders. Instr. English, Cornell U., Ithaca, N.Y., 1945-51; asst. prof. English and history U.S. Naval Acad., Annapolis, 1951-58, assoc. prof., 1958-63, prof., 1963-68; prof., head dept. English, Ill. State U., Normal, 1968-73. Served to lt. USNR, 1943-45; PTO; capt. Res. ret. Mem. MLA, Am. Hist. Assn., Coll. English Assn. (pres. 1967-69), Nat. Council Tchrs. English, Assn. Depts. English, Acad. Sr. Profls. Eckerd Coll. (charter), Ret. Officers Assn. Clubs: Annapolis Yacht; Kiwanis; American (London). Author: English Domestic or Homiletic Tragedy, 1575-1642, 1943; (with Baxter Hathaway) Dramatic Essays of the Neoclassic Age, 1950; (with E.B. Potter) U.S. and World Sea Power, 1955; (with E.B. Potter) Sea Power, 1960; 1942: The Year that Doomed the Axis, 1967; Years of Deadly Peril, 1969; Years of Expectation, 1973; Years to Victory, 1973; Harry Hopkins: A Biography, 1977; Italy at War, 1982; Witness to Power: The Life of Fleet Admiral William D. Leahy, 1985. Home: 1986 Carolina Circle NE Saint Petersburg FL 33703

ADAMS, JACK EARL, economist, educator; b. Gorman, Tex.; B.S., Tex. Tech. U., 1963, M.A. in Econs., 1968; Ph.D. in Econs., Okla. State U., 1975. m. Ingrid, Apr. 2, 1959; children—Lance, Melissa. Asst. prof. econs. Southwestern Okla. State U., Weatherford, 1972-75; asso. prof. econs., dir. bus. and econ. research Coll. of Bus., Southeastern La. U., Hammond, 1975-76; asso. prof. econs. U. Ark. at Little Rock, 1976-80, prof., 1980—. Served with USAF, 1956-59. Recipient Prof. of Distinction award Grad. Bus. Assn. U. Ark., 1982. Mem. Am. Arbitration Assn. (labor panel), Am. Econ. Assn., Southwest Soc. of Econs., Midsouth Acad. of Economists, Southwestern Econs. Assn., Greater Little Rock C. of C. (econ. devel. council), Omicron Delta Epsilon, Beta Gamma Sigma, Alpha Kappa Psi. Author: The Potential Impact of Negotiable Order of Withdrawal Accounts on the Banking Industry in Ark., 1979; co-author: An Attitudinal Profile of Bank Executives and Consumers of Bank Services in the State of Ark., 1982; contbr. numerous articles on econs. to profl. jours. Home: 1810 Hillsborough Little Rock AR 72212 Office: Coll Bus Adminstrn U Ark at Little Rock AR 72204

ADAMS, JO-ANN MARIE, realtor associate; b. Los Angeles, May 27, 1949; d. Joseph John and Georgia S. (Wein) A.; A.A., Pasadena City Coll., 1968; B.A., Pomona Coll., 1970; M.A., Calif. State U., Los Angeles, 1971; M.B.A., Pacific Luth. U., 1983. Secondary tchr. South Pasadena (Calif.) Unified Schs., 1970-71; appraiser Riverside County (Calif.) Assessor's Office, 1972-74; systems and procedures analyst Riverside County Data Processing Dept., 1974-76, supervising systems analyst, 1976-79; systems analyst computer Boeing Computer Services Co., Seattle, 1979-81; sr. systems analyst Thurston County Central Services, Olympia, Wash., 1981-83, data processing systems mgr., 1983-84; data processing systems engr. IBM Corp., 1984-87; instr. Riverside City Coll., 1977-79. Chairperson legis. task force Riverside/San Bernardino chpt. NOW, 1975-76, chpt. co-chairperson, 1978; mem. ethics com. Calif. NOW Inc., 1978; alt. del. Calif Democratic Caucus, 1978. Mem. Nat. Abortion Rights Action League, Nat. Assn. Female Execs., Assn. Systems Mgrs., Nat. Assn. Computing Machinery, Pomona Coll. Alumni Assn. Home: 1031 Maunaihi Pl #502 Honolulu HI 96822 Office: Dower Honolulu HI 96822

ADAMS, JOHN ARTHUR, soil science educator; b. Yarrawonga, Victoria, Australia, Dec. 11, 1944; s. Arthur Francis Reginald and Margaret June (Radcliffe) A.; m. Bridget Mary Corry, Aug. 21, 1971; children: Martin, Catherine, Thomas. BSc with honors, U. Canterbury, New Zealand, 1967, PhD, 1970. Postdoctoral fellow U. Rhodesia, Zimbabwe, 1970-71; scientist New Zealand Soil Bur., Taita, New Zealand, 1971-76; asst. prof. Lincoln Univ. Coll., Canterbury, 1976-77, assoc. prof., 1978—; cons. UN Fgn. Agrl. Orgn., Chile, 1978. Contbr. 40 papers to profl. jours. Recipient Travelling fellowship Royal Soc., London, 1984. Mem. New Zealand Inst. Chemistry, New Zealand Soil Sci. Soc. Anglican.

ADAMS, JOHN CARTER, JR., insurance executive; b. Williston, Fla., June 13, 1936; s. John Carter and Katharine Anna (Beall) A.; B.S. in Bus. Adminstrn., U. Fla., 1958; m. Leila Nora Johnson, Nov. 28, 1958; children—Julia Katharine, Ruth Anne. Agt., Pan Am. Ins. Co. 1958-59; acct. exec. Guy B. Odum & Co., Inc. 1959-63, v.p. 1963-66, exec. v.p. 1966-71, pres. 1971-76; pres. Jay Adams & Assocs., Inc. Daytona Beach, Fla., 1976-85, pres. Hilb Rogal & Hamilton Co., Daytona Beach, 1986—, mem. exec. com., 1988—, also bd. dirs.; pres. Futures, Inc., 1987-88; chmn. bd. Am. Pioneer Savs. Bank, Orlando, Fla., 1983-86; dir. Consolidated-Tomoka Land Co. Bd. visitors Embry-Riddle Aero. U., Daytona Beach, 1967-69, trustee, 1969—, mem. exec. com., 1972—, vice chmn. bd., 1981—, chmn. exec. com., 1983—, devel. council chmn. fund drive Hunt Meml. Library Embry-Riddle Aero U., 1985; campaign chmn. Easter Seal Soc. 1969, trustee 1970-73, pres. 1972-73; bd. dirs. YMCA, Daytona Beach 1968-76, 78-81, treas. 1970, v.p. 1971-82, pres., 1983; dir. Futures, Inc., 1985, pres. 1987, Nat. Intercollegiate Sports Festival, 1985-87; gen. campaign chmn. United Way of Volusia County, Fla. 1977, pres. 1979, dir. 1976-82, trustee, 1985—; chmn. Civic League of Halifax Area, 1983-84, exec. com., 1977—, vice chmn., 1981-82; mem. Tourist Devel. Council Volusia County, 1983-85, Halifax Advt. Authority, 1985; bd. dirs. Volusia County Bus. Devel. Council, 1984—; bd. dirs. Daytona Beach Community Found., 1984-87. Served with USNR 1953-61. Recipient Disting. Service award Bd. visitors Embry-Riddle Aero. U. 1975; CHIEF award (Champion Higher Ind. Edn. in Fla.), Ind. Colls. and Univs. of Fla., 1973. Mem. Daytona Beach C. of C. (bd. govs. 1968-70, v.p. bus. and govt. 1970, pres. 1975, gen. campaign chmn. devel. fund drive 1984, Louis Fuchs Man of Yr. award, 1985), Volusia County Insurors Assn., Fla. Assn. Ins. Agts. (bd. dirs. 1978-81), Nat. Assn. Casualty & Surety Agts. Democrat. Episcopalian. Home: 3 Riverside Circle Ormond Beach FL 32074 Office: 121 N Ridgewood Ave Daytona Beach FL 32014

ADAMS, JOHN FRANCIS, JR., real estate executive; b. Hartford, Conn., Nov. 10, 1936; s. John Francis and Ruth Jane (Craddock) A.; m. Vera Ann Raczkowski, Nov. 26, 1960; children—John Francis III, Kristina Marie. BA, Trinity Coll., 1959. Ins. salesman J. F. Adams Agy., New Britain, Conn., 1960-61, real estate appraiser, 1960-63; ptnr. J.F. Adams Assocs., New Britain, 1964-73; founder, ptnr. J. F. Adams Realtors, New Britain, 1965-73; pres. J. F. Adams Assocs. & Realtors, New Britain, 1973—; dir. CT SREA Ednl. Found., 1987—; chmn. Realtors Com. for Multiple Listing Service, New Britain, 1962; charter pres. Multiple Listing Service Greater New Britain, Inc., 1963. Bd. dirs. YMCA, Berlin, Conn., 1982; corporator, New Britain, Berlin, Kensington YMCA, 1975—. Served with Army N.G., 1959-60. Recipient Officer Candidate Sch. Leadership award Assn. U.S. Army, 1964. Mem. Greater New Britain Bd. Realtors (pres. 1969, dir. 1970-71, Realtor of Yr. 1976), Conn. Assn. Realtors, Nat. Assn. Realtors, Soc. Real Estate Appraisers (sr. real estate analyst), Soc. Real Estate Appraisers (New Eng. vice gov. 1974-75), Soc. Real Estate Appraisers (Conn. chpt.) pres. 1973-74, M.A.I., Am. Inst. Real Estate Appraisers, Am. Inst. Real Estate Appraisers (Conn. chpt.) pres. 1981. Republican. Roman Catholic. Clubs: Shuttle Meadow Country, Kensington; Berlin Strollers Rugby (pres. 1978-79) Berlin, Conn. Lodge: Elks. Home: 125 Crater Ln Kensington CT 06037 Office: John F Adams Assocs & Realtors 19 Bassett St New Britain CT 06051

ADAMS, JOHN MARSHALL, lawyer; b. Columbus, Ohio, Dec. 6, 1930; s. H.F. and Ada Margaret (Gregg) A.; m. Janet Hawk, June 28, 1952; children: John Marshall, Susan Lynn, William Alfred. B.A., Ohio State U., 1952; J.D. summa cum laude, 1954. Bar: Ohio 1954. Mem. Cowan & Adams, Columbus, 1954-55; asst. city atty. City of Columbus, 1955-56; mem. Knepper, White, Richards & Miller, 1956-63; practiced in Columbus, 1963-74; partner Porter, Wright, Morris & Arthur, Columbus, 1975—; dir. Ohio Bar Liability Ins. Co.; Trustee Ohio Legal Center Inst., 1976-81, Ohio Lawpac, 1980—. Fellow Am. Coll. Trial Lawyers, Am. Bar Found., Ohio Bar Found. (trustee 1975-84); mem. ABA, Ohio Bar Assn. (exec. com. 1975-80, pres. 1978-79), Columbus Bar Assn. (gov. 1970-76 pres. 1974-75), Lawyers Club (pres. 1968-69), Order of Coif, Delta Upsilon, Phi Delta Phi. Republican. Clubs: Masons, Athletic, Scioto Country. Home: 1717 Arlingate Dr N Columbus OH 43220 Office: 41 S High St Columbus OH 43215

ADAMS, J(OHN) ROBERT, air force officer; b. Provo, Utah, Mar. 7, 1948; s. John Hortt and Betty Lou Jean (Ellis) A.; m. Mary Lucinda Allen, Nov. 26, 1969; children—Jennifer, John Dareld, Matthew Robert, Emily, Samuel David, Rebecca, Joseph. B.S. in Acctg., Brigham Young U., 1972; M.S. in Systems mgmt., U. So. Calif., 1982. Commd. 2d lt. U.S. Air Force, 1972, advanced through grades to lt. col., 1984; with research and devel. program evaluation dept. systems command, Wright-Patterson AFB, Ohio, 1972-75; chief mgmt. and budget USAF Europe, Hahn AB, Fed. Republic Germany, 1975-78; chief budget Tactical Air Command, George AFB, Calif., 1978-80; chief cost and mgmt. analysis SAC, Malmstrom AFB, Mont., 1980-82; chief budget Pacific Air Force, Osan AB, Korea, 1983; exec. officer Hdqrs SAC, Offutt AFB, Nebr., 1984-86; chief comptroller's plans office Air Force Accounts and Fin. Ctr., Lowry AFB, Colo., 1986—. Scouting coordinator Boy Scouts Am., Omaha, 1984—; lay minister Ch. of Jesus Christ of Latterday Saints, various locations, 1967—. Recipient Eagle Scout award Boy Scouts Am., 1963, awards from U.S. Air Force. Mem. Air Force Assn. (life), Am. Soc. Mil. Comptrollers (founder chpt.). Home: 14733 E Evans Pl Aurora CO 80014

ADAMS, JOSEPH PETER, retired lawyer, consultant; b. Seattle, Nov. 15, 1907; s. Joseph and Selma Margaret (Peterson) A.; m. Margaret Bare Adams, Jan. 13, 1940; 1 dau., Janis Margaret. A.B., U. Wash., 1928, J.D., 1932; grad. naval aviator, U.S. Naval Air Sta., Pensacola, Fla., 1930. Bar: Wash. 1932, D.C. 1953. Practiced Seattle, 1932-40; dir. aeros. State of Wash., 1946-49; mem. CAB, 1951-56, vice chmn., 1955-56; aviation cons. Senate Commerce Com.; Mem. NACA, 1952-56; exec. dir., gen. counsel Assn. Local Transport Airlines, Washington, 1957-73; fed. affairs counsel Assn. Local Transport Airlines, 1973-80. Charter mem. Nat. Capital Democratic Club; trustee U.S. Naval Aviation Mus. Found., Pensacola. Served as capt. USMCR, 1929-40; released from World War II as col. Res. aviation, 1946; promoted to brig. gen. 1959. Decorated Combat Legion of Merit. Mem. USMC Res. Officers Assn. (life), Marine Corps League, Nat. Aero. Assn. (Elder Statesman of Aviation 1984), Legion of Honor of Order of DeMolay, Sigma Alpha Epsilon, Phi Delta Phi. Democrat. Clubs: Cosmos, Aero (pres. 1962) Army-Navy (Washington) National Aviation (award for achievement 1970); Wings (N.Y.C.); Executive, Pensacola Country (Fla.). Home: 1004 Harbourview Circle Pensacola FL 32507

ADAMS, MIKE See GEERTS, LEO

ADAMS, NORMAN JOSEPH, economist, corporate mergers broker; b. Los Angeles, Feb. 21, 1930; s. Joseph O'Neil and Florence Mary (Michalek) A.; B.S., U. So. Calif., 1951; diploma Oxford U., 1953; postgrad. Harvard U., 1956; Ph.D., U. Karachi (Pakistan), 1958; m. Julia Jewell, Oct. 16, 1960; children—Darlene, Janet. Pres., Adams & Co., mergers and aquisitions, Los Angeles.

ADAMS, PETER JOHN, educator; b. Melbourne, Victoria, Australia, Feb. 15, 1948; s. Malcolm Elliston and Marjorie Gordon (Douglas) A.; m. Janet Bronwyn Griffiths, Jan. 16, 1970 (div. 1979). Tchr. English Salisbury East High Sch., South Australia, 1977-81, Meningie Area Sch., South Australia, 1982-85, Banksia Park High Sch., South Australia, 1986—. Co-author: A Single Impulse: Developing Responses to Literature, 1984; contbr. articles to profl. jours. Mem. South Australian English Tchrs. Assn. Anglican. Home: PO Box 65, Magill South Australia 5072, Australia

ADAMS, RICHARD GEORGE, writer; b. Newbury, Berkshire, Eng., May 9, 1920; s. Evelyn George Beadon and Lilian Rosa (Button); m. Elizabeth Acland, Sept. 26, 1949; children: Juliet Vera Lucy, Rosamond Beatrice Elizabeth. M.A., Oxford U., 1948. Author: Watership Down, Shardik, The Plague Dogs, The Girl in a Swing, Maia, The Unbroken Web, Nature Through the Seasons, Nature Day and Night, Voyage Through the Antarctic, A Nature Diary, The Ship's Cat, The Tyger Voyage, The Bureaucats, The Legend of Te Tuna, Traveller. Served with Brit. Army, 1940-46. Recipient Carnegie medal, 1972, Guardian award for children's lit., 1972. Fellow Royal Soc. Lit., Royal Soc. Arts; mem. Royal Soc. for Prevention of Cruelty to Animals (former pres.). Mem. Ch. of Eng. Club: Marylebone Cricket. Address: 26 Church St, Whitchurch Hampshire, England

ADAMS, THOMAS LAWRENCE, lawyer; b. Jersey City, Apr. 14, 1948; s. Lawrence Ignatius and Dorothy Tekla (Halgas) A.; m. Elizabeth Anne Russell, June 14, 1969 (div. 1981); children: Thomas, Katherine; m. Deanna Louise Mollo, July 30, 1983; stepchildren: Kathy, Kerry. BS, N.J. Inst. of Tech., 1969; JD, Seton Hall U., 1975. Bar: N.J. 1975, N.Y. 1976, U.S. Dist. Ct. N.J. 1975, U.S. Patent Office 1975. Systems engr. Grumman Aerospace, Bethpage, N.Y., 1969-71; sr. engr. Weston Instruments, Newark, 1971-74; with patent staff RCA Corp., Princeton, N.J., 1974-75; corp. atty. Otis Elevator, N.Y.C., 1975-77; ptnr. Goebel & Adams, Morristown, N.J., 1978-80, Behr & Adams, Morristown & Edison, N.J., 1981—. Author, editor: B & A Newsletter, 1984. Councilman Twp. Council, Livingston, N.J., 1985-89, dep. mayor, 1987; commr. Environ. Commn., Livingston, 1984-87; mem. Bd. Edn. Long Range Planning Com., Livingston, 1978; sec. Livingston Rep. Club, 1984. N.J. State scholar, 1965. Mem. N.J. Patent Law Assn., Morris County Bar Assn., West Essex C. of C. (rep.), Trial Attys. of N.J., Am. Arbitration Assn. (arbitrator), Seton Hall Law Rev., Tau Beta Pi, Eta Kappa Nu. Roman Catholic. Lodges: K.C. (Grand Knight 1980), Rotary.

ADAMS, THOMAS WALTON, probation agent; b. Midland, Mich., Apr. 15, 1947; s. Lawrence Walton and Elizabeth (Miller) A.; m. Karen Lynn Perry. BS with honors, Mich. State U., 1973, MS, 1987. Probation agt. 75th Dist. Ct., Midland, 1973—. Mem. Midland County Alcohol Services Bd., 1975-78, Midland-Gladwin County Community Mental Health Bd., 1978-87, chmn. 1980-82; mem. adv. Mt. Pleasant Regional Ctr. for Devel. Disabilities, 1988—. Named One of Outstanding Young Men Am., 1982; recipient Liberty Bell award, Midland Bar Assn., 1983. Mem. Am. Correctional Assn., Alpha Phi Sigma. Home: 5823 Leeway Dr Midland MI 48640 Office: Adult Probation Courthouse Midland MI 48640

ADAMS, WESTON, diplomat, lawyer; b. Columbia, S.C., Sept. 16, 1938; s. Robert and Helen Hayes (Calhoun) A.; m. Elizabeth Nicholson Nelson, Mar. 2, 1962; children—Robert VI, Weston III, Daniel Wallace, Julian Calhoun II. A.B. in History, U. S.C., 1960, LL.B., 1962. Bar: S.C. 1962. Research dir. S.C. Republican Orgn., Columbia, 1966-67; trust officer S.C. Nat. Bank, Columbia, 1967-70; assoc. counsel Select Com. on Crime, U.S. Ho. of Reps., Washington, 1970-71; sole practice Columbia, 1971-84, 86—; ambassador to Malawi U.S. Dept. of State, Lilongwe, 1984-86. Mem. S.C. House of Reps., 1972-74; presdl. elector U.S. Electoral Coll., S.C., 1980; del. Rep. Nat. Conv., Kansas City, Mo., 1976, alt. del., Detroit, 1980; mem. U.S. presdl. del. to inauguration of Pres. of Dominican Republic, 1982; mem. UNESCO, 1982-84. Served to capt. USAF, 1963-66. Recipient Order of Palmetto, Gov. S.C., 1974. Mem. S.C. Bar, Richland County Bar Assn., U. S.C. Alumni Assn., S.C. Hist. Soc., U. South Carolina Hist. Soc., S.C. Geneal. Soc., S.C. Soc. of Cincinati, Magna Charta Barons (Somerset chpt.), St. Andrews Soc., Huguenot Soc. of S.C., Soc. Lower Richland, St. David's Soc., Jamestowne Soc., Welcome Soc. Pa. Episcopalian. Club: Palmetto Columbia). Home: 303 Saluda Ave Columbia SC 29205 Office: 1527 Blanding St PO Box 291 Columbia SC 29202

ADAMS, WILLIAM ALAN, trade association executive; b. Chicago Heights, Ill., Feb. 13, 1943; s. Clark and Janet (McAllister) A. B.S., Fla. So. Coll., 1965; M.S., U. Ill., 1966, C.P.A., Ill., 1966, cert. in Mgmt. Acct., 1978. Staff auditor Peat, Marwick, Mitchell & Co., Chgo., 1966; staff auditor Arthur Andersen & Co., Washington, 1968-69; div. controller Cousins Properties, Inc., Washington, 1970-76; asst. controller Booz, Allen & Hamilton, Inc., Bethesda, Md., 1977-78; v.p. Tobacco Inst., Washington, 1978—; co-founder, dir. Chelsea Systems, Inc., McLean, Va., 1980-85. Mem. fin. com. Am. Chamber Orch., Washington, 1984-85. Served to 1st lt. U.S. Army, 1966-68. Mem. Am. Inst. C.P.A.s, D.C. Soc. C.P.A.s, Omicron Delta Kappa. Republican. Methodist. Clubs: Metropolitan, Capitol Hill, Potomac (pres. 1982-83), Decade Soc. Home: 2127 N St NW Washington DC 20037 Office: The Tobacco Inst 1875 Eye St NW Washington DC 20006

ADAMS, WILLIAM MANSFIELD, educator; b. Kissimmee, Fla., Feb. 19, 1932; s. Shirah Devoy and Olive (Goding) A.; m. Roberta Kay Blackwell, July 23, 1955; children: William Mansfield, Johnathan Blackwell, Christopher Daniel; m. Naoko Nakashizuka, 1976; children: Henele Iitaka, Alden Fernald. A.B. (Univ. scholar), U. Chgo., 1951; B.A., U. Calif., 1953; M.S. (Gulf scholar), St. Louis U., 1955, Ph.D., 1957; M.B.A., Santa Clara U., 1964; postgrad., M.I.T., 1967-70. Instrument man Shell Oil Co., Merced, Calif., 1953; geophys. trainee Stanolind Oil Co., New Orleans, 1953, Western Geophys. Co., Rankin, Tex., 1954; tech. officer Govt. Can., Ottawa, 1956; chief seismologist Geotech Corp., Laramie, Wyo., 1957-59; program tech. dir. U. Calif., Livermore, 1959-62; pres. Planetary Scis., Inc., Santa Clara, Calif., 1962-64; prof. geophysics U. Hawaii, Honolulu, 1964—; exchange prof. Ind. U., Bloomington, 1975-76; UNESCO expert seismology Internat. Inst. Seismology and Earthquake Engring., Bldg. Research Inst., Tokyo, 1971-72; vis. fellow Co-op. Inst. Research in Environ. Scis., U. Colo., Boulder, 1970-71; research oceanographer Atlantic Marine and Environ. Lab., NOAA, Miami, Fla., 1979-80; cons. Del E. Webb, Kahuku Point, Oahu, Hawaii, 1969, Oceanic Properties, Lanai City, Lanai, Hawaii, 1969, C. Brewer Co., Punaluu, Hawaii, 1970, 74, Desert Research Inst. U. Nev., 1983. Contbr. numerous articles to profl. jours. Fulbright grantee, 1956-57; NATO grantee Internat. Inst. Geothermal Research, Pisa, Italy, 1973. Mem. Am. Geophys. Union, Geol. Soc. Am., Seismol. Soc. Am. (editor Bull 1962-65), Acoustical Soc. Am., Soc. Exploration Geophysicists, AAUP, European Assn. Exploration Geophysicists, European Geophysical Soc., Tsunami Soc. (founder, hon. member), Fulbright Alumni Assn., Assn. Geoscientists for Internat. Devel., Sigma Xi. Office: U Hawaii Dept Geophysics 2525 Correa Rd Honolulu HI 96822

ADAMSON, GEOFFREY DAVID, reproductive endocrinologist, surgeon; b. Ottawa, Ont., Can., Sept. 16, 1946; came to U.S., 1978, naturalized, 1986; s. Geoffrey Peter Adamson and Anne Marian Allan; m. Rosemary C. Oddie, Apr. 28, 1973; children: Stephanie, Rebecca, Eric. BSc with honors, Trinity Coll., Toronto, Can., 1969; MD, U. Toronto, 1973. Diplomate Am. Bd. Ob-Gyn; cert. Bd. Reproductive Endocrinology. Resident in ob-gyn Toronto Gen. Hosp., 1973-77, fellow in ob-gyn, 1977-78; fellow reproductive endocrinology Stanford (Calif.) U. Med. Ctr., 1978-80; practice medicine specializing in infertility Los Gatos, Calif., 1980-84, San Jose, Calif., 1984—; dir. Fertility and Reproductive Health Inst. No. Calif., 1988—; clin. asst. prof. Stanford (Calif.) U. Sch. Medicine, 1980—. Mem. editorial adv. bd. Can. Doctor mag., 1977-83; contbg. editor In Fertility Today; contbr. articles to sci. jours. Ontario Ministry of Health fellow, 1977-78. Fellow ACS, Royal Coll. Surgeons Can., Am. Coll. Ob-Gyns.; mem. AAAS, AMA, Soc. Reproductive Endocrinologists (charter), Soc. Reproductive Surgeons (charter), Fallopius Soc. (charter), Pacific Coast Fertility Soc., Am. Assn. Gynecol. Laparoscopists, Gynecologic Laser Soc., N.Y. Acad. Scis., Shufelt Gynecologic Soc.,Peninsula Gynecol. Soc., Calif. Med. Assn., San Mateo County Med. Assn., Santa Clara County Med. Assn., No. Calif. Resolve (bd. dirs.), Am. Fedn. Clin. Research, Can. Assn. Internes and Residents (hon. life, pres. 1977-79, bd. dirs. 1974-79, rep. AMA resident physician sect. 1978-79, rep. Can. Med. Protective Assn. 1975-78, rep. Can. Med. Assn. 1975-78, Disting. Service award 1980), Profl. Assn. Internes and Residents Ont. (bd. dirs. 1973-74, v.p. 1974-75, pres. 1975-76), Royal Coll. Physician and Surgeons Can. (com. examinations 1977-80), Ont. Med. Assn. (sec. internes and residents sect. 1973-74). Home: 16520 S Kennedy Rd Los Gatos CA 95032 Office: 540 University Ave #200 Palo Alto CA 94301

ADAMSON, ROBIN, French language educator; b. Ayr, Queensland, Australia, Mar. 30, 1938; arrived in Scotland, 1967; d.Reginald Thomas and Nellie Hawthorn (Jolly) Andison; m. Iain Thomas Adamson, Aug. 26, 1967; 1 child, Margaret. BA, U. Queensland, Brisbane, 1959, diploma in edn., 1960; PhB, U. St. Andrews, Scotland, U.K., 1973; PhD, U. Edinburgh, Scotland, U.K., 1984. Prin. tchr. French Ayr State High Sch., 1960-62; sr. tutor in French U. Western Australia, Perth, 1965-67; lectr. in French U. Dundee, Scotland, 1968-88; dir. lang. unit U. Dundee, 1988—. Author: (with others) En Fin de Compte, 1986; editor, contbg. author: Le Francais en Faculté, 1980, 2d rev. edit., 1986. Mem. Scottish Univs. French Lang. Research Assn. (sec. research project 1980—, assn. treas. 1986-87, pres. 1987—), Dundee Assn. Univ. Women (com. mem. 1980-83). Office: U Dundee, Dundee DD1 4HN, Scotland

ADDAD, MOSHE DAVID, criminology educator; b. Beja, Tunisia, May 20, 1939; s. Eugene and Suzanne (Bellity) Addad; m. Naomi Rossel, June 2, 1968; children: Efrat, Hanan, Avishai, Tsurit, Nirit. BA, Tel Aviv U., 1968, MA magna cum laude, 1974; PhD summa cum laude, Sorbonne U., Paris, 1976. Prin. Agrl. High Sch. Yeshiva, Kfar Aroe, Israel, 1970-73; asst. lectr. inst. criminology Tel Aviv U., 1972-74; lectr. psychology Regional Coll. Menashe, Hadera, Israel, 1976-78; lectr. criminology Bar Ilan U., Ramat Gan, Israel, 1976-78, sr. lectr., 1979-82, prof., 1982—, chmn. dept. criminology, 1982-86. Author: Being Delinquent: Psychoanalytic Views on Delinquency; co-author: Irresponsabilite Penale des Handicapes Mentaux, 1978, Criminology, 1986, Criminology: Theories and Research, 1987; contbr. articles to profl. jours. Served with Israeli mil., 1958-61. Mem. Logotherapy Assn., Psychopathology Crime Orgn. Jewish. Home: Ahane #4, Hadera Israel Office: Bar Ilan U, Dept of Criminology, Ramat Gan Israel

ADDIS, RICHARD BARTON, lawyer; b. Columbus, Ohio, Apr. 9, 1929; s. Wilbur Jennings and Leila Olive (Grant) A.; m. Marguerite C. Christjohn, Feb. 9, 1957; children—Jacqueline Carol, Barton David. B.A., Ohio State U., 1954, J.D., 1955. Bar: Ohio 1956, U.S. Dist. Ct. (no. dist.) Ohio 1957, N.Mex. 1963, U.S. Dist. Ct. N.Mex. 1963. Sole practice, Canton, Ohio, 1956-63, Albuquerque, 1963—, admitted to practice before Pueblo Ct., Laguna Pueblo, N.Mex., 1986—. Served with USMC, 1946-48, 50-52. Mem. Ohio Bar Assn., N.Mex. Bar Assn., Am. Arbitration Assn. (arbitrator 1968—), Soc. Mining Engrs. Address: 5111 San Mateo Blvd NE Albuquerque NM 87109

ADDIS, SARA ALLEN, franchise executive; b. El Paso, Tex., May 15, 1930; d. Waldo Rufus and Cordelia Dean (Kerr) Allen; m. Bobby Joe Addis, June 5, 1949; children—Craig Dell, Alan Blake, Neil Clark, Sara Kathleen. Sec. to adminstr. Southwestern Gen. Hosp., El Paso, 1948-49; sec. to dir. of personnel U. Tex., El Paso, 1964-65; pres., founder Sara Care Franchise Corp., El Paso, 1978—. Named Small Bus. Person of Yr., Small Bus. Adminstrn., 1986, 87. Mem. Internat. Franchise Assn., Nat. Fedn. Ind. Businesses, Presidents Assn. Am. Mgmt. Assn., El Paso Better Bus. Bur., El Paso C. of C., Assn. Pioneer Women. (Entrepreneur of Yr.), Bus. and Profl. Women El Paso (Small Bus. Person of Yr. 1983, 85, 86, 87), Exec. Forum, Profl. Women's Network U. Tex. El Paso. Republican. Club: Lower Valley Women's. Lodge: Order Eastern Star. Avocations: oil painting; music; travel. Home: 8417 Parkland St El Paso TX 79925 Office: Sara Care Franchise Corp 1200 Golden Key Circle Suite 368 El Paso TX 79925

ADDISON, EDWARD L., utility holding company executive; b. 1930; married. B.E.E., U. S.C., 1950. Pres., chief exec. officer So. Co. Services, Inc., Atlanta, 1983—, chmn. exec. com., also bd. dirs.; dir., chmn. exec. com. So. Co. Services Inc. subs. So. Co., Birmingham, Ala.; bd. dirs. Ala. Power Co., Ga. Power Co., Gulf Power Co., Miss. Power Co., So. Electric Internat. Inc., So. Investments Group, So. Electric Generating Co., SW Forest Industries. Served with U.S. Army, 1951-53. Office: So Co Services Inc 64 Perimeter Ctr E Atlanta GA 30346 *

ADDY, DOUGLAS PETER, pediatrician, consultant; b. Barnsley, Eng., May 6, 1939; s. Edmund and Ivy Irene Pauline (Mollard) A.; m. K. Jennifer Wood, Mar. 27, 1965; children: Richard, Catherine, Christopher. MBChB, U. Leeds, Eng., 1962. Various tng. posts Leeds Hosps., 1962-68; registrar pediatrics Royal Postgrad. Med. Sch., London, 1968-70; sr. registrar pediatrics Alder Hey Childrens Hosp., Liverpool, Eng., 1970-72; resident pediatric neurology Johns Hopkins U. Hosp., Balt., 1973-74; cons. pediatrician Dudley Rd. Hosp., Birmingham, Eng., 1972—; regional advisor pediatrics U. Birmingham, 1980—; examiner U. Birmingham, 1980—. Contbr. articles to profl. jours. Chmn. child health servces com. West Midlands Regional Health Authority, Eng., 1986—; editorial bd. Archives Disease in Childhood. Fellow Royal Coll. Physicians London (examiner); mem. Brit. Pediatric Assn. (council mem. 1979-82, 84-85), Brit. Med. Assn., Brit. Pedatric Neurology Assn. Methodist. Club: Moseley Golf (Birmingham). Home: 15 Dyott Rd, Birmingham B13 9QZ, England Office: Dudley Rd Hosp, Birmingham B18 7QH, England

ADEDEJI, ADEBAYO, economist, under-secretary-general and executive secretary United Nations Economic Commission for Africa; b. Ijebu-Ode, Ogun, Nigeria, Dec. 21, 1930; came to Ethiopia, 1975; s. L.S. and Adeola Olufowobi A.; m. Aderinola Ogun, Aug. 11, 1957; children—Adedoyin, Adekunle, Adeleke, Adeniyi, Adeola, Adeyinka, Adepoju. Diploma in Local Govt. Adminstrn., Univ. Coll., U. Ibadan, 1953-54; B.Sc. in Econs., Leicester U. Coll., 1958; M.P.A., Harvard U., 1961; Ph.D. in Econs., U. London, 1967; Litt.D. (hon.), Ahmadu Bello U., 1976; LL.D. (hon.), U. Dalhousie, 1984; LL.D. (hon.), U. Zambia, 1984; LL.D. (hon.), U. Calabers, 1987. Sr. asst. sec. for revenue Nigerian Civil Service, 1958-63; dep. dir. Inst. Adminstrn., U. Ife, 1963-67; dir. Inst. Adminstrn., prof. pub. adminstrn., 1967-75; fed. commr. Ministry for Econ. Devel. in Reconstrn. Nigeria, 1971-75; under-sec.-gen., exec. sec. UN Econ. Commn. for Africa, Addis Ababa, Ethiopia, 1975—; mem. Ad Hoc Com. of Experts of Fins. of UN and its Specialized Agys., 1965; mem. Expert Com. on Restructuring Econ. and Social Sectors of UN System, 1975; chmn. senate UN Inst. for Namibia, 1975—; trustee dept. econs. U. Boston, 1978—. Author books, the most recent being: Africa, the Third World and the Search for a New Economic Order, 1976; Africa: The Crisis of Development and the Challenge of a New Economic Order, 1977; The Political Class, the Higher Civil Service and the Challenge of Nation Building, 1981; the Deepening International Economic Crisis and its Implications for Africa, 1982; editor: Indigenization of African Economics, 1981; Economic Crisis in Africa: African Perspectives on Development Problems and Potentials, 1985. Chmn. Western Nigerian Govt. Broadcasting Corp., 1966-67; mem. Nigerian Nat. Manpower Bd., 1968-71; chmn. Directorate of Nat. Youth Service Corps of Nigeria. Decorated grand officer Order of Mono (Togo); comdr. Order of Merit of Islamic Republic Mauritania; grand comdr. Order of Disting. Service First Class (Zambia); Grand Comdr. Order of the Lion (Senegal), 1987; recipient Gold Mercury Internat. award, 1982. Fellow Nigerian Inst. Mgmt. (dir. 1968-75); mem. Nigerian Econ. Soc. (pres. 1971-72), Royal Commonwealth Soc., African Assn. for Pub. Adminstrn. and Mgmt. (v.p. 1971-74). Office: Asiwaju Ct, GRA Erunwon Rd PO Box 203, Ijebu ode Nigeria

ADELI, HOJJAT, civil engineer, educator; b. Langrood, Iran, June 3, 1950; came to U.S., 1974; s. Jafar and Mokarram (Soofi) A.; m. Nahid Dadmehr, Feb., 1979; children—Amir, Anahita. MS in Civil Engring., U. Teheran, Iran, 1973; Ph.D. in Civil Engring., Stanford U., 1976. Asst. prof. Northwestern U., Evanston, Ill., 1977; asst. prof. U. Teheran, 1978-81, assoc. prof., 1981-82; assoc. prof. U. Utah, Salt Lake City, 1982-83; assoc. prof. Ohio State U., Columbus, 1983-88, prof., 1988—; cons. Atomic Orgn. of Iran, Teheran, 1978-79, Iran Ministry of Housing, Teheran, 1979-82. Co-author: Expert Systems for Structural Design-A New Generation, 1988; author: Computer-Aided Design of Steel Structures, 1989, Interactive Microcomputer-Aided Structural Steel Design, 1988; editor: Expert Systems in Construction and Structural Engineering, 1988, Microcomputer Knowledge-Based Expert Systems in Civil Engineering, 1988, Parallel and Distributed Processing in Structural Engineering, 1988, Knowledge Engineering Vol. 1 and 2, 1989; contbr. more than 20 articles to profl. jours.; editor-in-chief Internat. Jour. Microcomputers in Civil Engring; editor-at-large Computer Sci. Applications, Marcel Dekker. Recipient First Degree Medal of Knowledge, Iran Ministry of Higher Edn., 1973. Mem. ASCE, IEEE, Earthquake Engring. Research Inst. Home: 1131 Fifth Ave Worthington OH 43210

ADELMAN, MICHAEL SCHWARTZ, lawyer; b. Cambridge, Mass., June 6, 1940; s. Benjamin Taft and Sally Frances (Schwartz) A.; m. Amy Kay, June 15, 1962; children: Robert, Jonathon. Student Boston U., 1958-59; BA with honors in English, U. Mich., 1962, JD cum laude. Bar: Mich. 1968, Miss. 1974. Assoc. Zwerdling, Miller, Klimist & Maurer, Detroit, 1968-69; ptnr. Philo, Maki, Ravitz, Glotta, Adelman, Cockrel & Robb, Detroit, 1969-70; ptnr. Glotta, Adelman & Dinges, Detroit, 1970-74; ptnr. Andalman, Adelman, & Steiner P.A., Hattiesburg, Miss., 1974—; sec., bd. dirs. SE Miss. Legal Services, Hattiesburg. Contbr. short stories: The Deputy, The Detention Center to New Renaissance. Treas., Hattiesburg Area Equal Rights Council; chairperson Hattiesburg Biracial Adv. Com., 1988-89. Recipient Ralph T. Abernathy award Jackson County (Miss.) SCLC, 1978. Mem. ABA, South Central Miss. Bar Assn.

ADELMAN, RAPHAEL MARTIN, physician; b. Plainfield, N.J., May 4, 1915; s. Samuel and Betty (Taich) A.; m. Charlotte M. Koepke, Aug. 25, 1945 (dec. July, 1985); children—Karen Rae, Robert John. DDS, U. Pa., 1939; MSc, Northwestern U., 1940; BM, Chgo. Med. Sch., 1943, MD, 1944. Intern Norwegian-Am. Hosp., Chgo., 1943-44; assoc. in surgery Chgo. Med. Sch., 1945-50; assoc. in plastic surgery Dr. A.M. Brown, Chgo., 1946-50; gen. practice medicine Wauconda, Ill., 1950—; chief of staff St. Therese Hosp., 1963—, chief exec. com., 1965, asst. adminstr., med. dir., 1965—; v.p. med. affairs St. Therese Hosp. and Med. Ctr., 1966-85; dir. St. Therese Hosp., 1974—, dir. med. edn.; chief sect. ear, nose, throat Victory Meml. Hosp., Waukegan, Ill., 1963, 65-66; clin. asst. prof. family medicine U. Health Scis.-Chgo. Med. Sch., 1979—; med. dir. Am. Hosp. Supply Corp.; cons. physician Coll. Lake County Health Services Trust; physian cons. utilization rev. Region V HEW, 1973-75, cons. quality and standards, 1975; physician cons. Lake County Bd. Health, 1974-76; cons. continuing med. edn. Downey VA Hosp., 1974-76; authorized agt. Lake County Dept. Pub. Health, 1974-76; sr. examiner FAA, 1973—; mem. Am. Bd. Quality Assurance and Utilization Rev. Physicians, 1978—; mem. ancillary services rev. Crescent Counties for Med. Care, 1979—. Mem. exec. com. Lake County chpt. Am. Cancer Soc., 1963—; pres. Wauconda High Sch. Bd. Edn., 1954-60; mem. Wauconda Grade Sch. Bd. Edn., 1952-60; chmn. health and safety N.W. Dist., North Suburban council Boy Scouts Am., 1964-65, vice chmn. N.W. dist. North Shore council, 1967, 75, mem. exec. com. Northeastern Ill. council; mem. Lake County Health Services Com., 1969—; mem. profl. adv. com. United Community Services Planning Div., 1969—; mem. exec. com., exec. bd. Evanston-North Shore Area Council, 1969; mem. mgmt. com. Lake County Mental Health Clinic, 1967-69; mem. budget and fin. com., 1968-69, group chmn. Regional Conf. on Health Care Costs, Health,-Edn. and Welfare, Cleve., 1968; del. Hosp. Planning Council Chgo., 1967-69; chmn. subcom. Ill. Hosp. Licensing Bd. Com., 1969; pres. 1968-69 class U. Ala. Health Service Adminstrs. Devel. Program; chmn. Lake County Health Services Planning Council, Inc.; mem. regional com. Hosp. Admission Surveillance Program, State of Ill., 1972-77; mem. Lake County Drug Commn., 1972-73; mem. Lake County Bd. Health, 1973-77; chmn. orgn. and search com. for exec. dir. Lake County Health Dept.; mem. com. on search for dean Univ. Health Scis-Chgo. Med. Sch., 1975; mem. Lake County Coroner's Adv. Commn., 1977; mem. adv. council health edn. programs Coll. Lake County, 1970-77; bd. dirs. Blumberg Blood Bank, St. Therese Nurse Scholarship Fund, 1962, Lake County Health Planning Council, 1969-72. Fellow Am. Pub. Health Assn. (life mem., community health edn. accreditation panel 1975-76), AAAS, Chgo. Inst. Medicine, Royal Soc. Health, Am. Acad. Med. Adminstrs., Soc. Acad. Achievement (life), Am. Coll. Hosp. Adminstrs.; mem. Am. Acad. Family Practice, Ill. Acad. Family Practice (state del. 1960-63, dir.), Lake County Acad. Family Practice (past pres.), AMA, ADA, Assn. Mil. Surgeons U.S. (life), Ill. Hosp. Assn., Ill. Soc. Med. Research, Ill. Med. Soc. (com. physician-hosp. relationship 1974-75), Am. Acad. Dental Radiology, Ill. Pub. Health Anns. (exec. council 1976-78), Assn. Hosp. Med. Assn., Ill. Found. Med. Care, Am. Coll. Preventive Medicine, Am. Soc. Law and Medicine, Chgo. and Acad. Legal Medicine, Ill. Hosp. Attys., Am. Legion (life), Sigma Xi, Alpha Omega, Phi Lambda Kappa. Home: 1600 Wedgewood Dr Gurnee IL 60031

ADELMAN, STEVEN HERBERT, lawyer; b. Chgo., Dec. 21, 1945; s. Irving and Sylvia (Cohen) A.; m. Pamela Bernice Kozoll, June 30, 1968; children—David, Robert. B.S., U. Wis.-Madison, 1967; J.D., DePaul U., 1970. Bar: Ill. 1970, U.S. Dist. Ct. (no. dist.) Ill. 1970, U.S. Ct. Appeals (7th cir.) 1975. Ptnr. Keck, Mahin & Cate, Chgo., 1970—. Contbr. chpts. to books, articles to profl. jours. Bd. dirs. Bur. Jewish Employment Problems, Chgo., 1983—; employment relations com. Chgo. Assn. Commerce and Industry, 1982—. Mem. Chgo. Bar Assn. (vice chmn. labor and employment law com. 1987-88), ABA (Silver Key award 1969), Ill. State Bar Assn., Chgo. Council Lawyers, Decalogue Soc. Club: River (Chgo.). Office: Keck Mahin & Cate 8300 Sears Tower 233 S Wacker Dr Chicago IL 60606

ADELMAN, WILLIAM JOHN, educator; b. Chgo., July 26, 1932; s. William Sidney and Annie Teresa (Goan) A.; m. Nora Jill Walters, June 26, 1952; children: Michelle, Marguerite, Marc, Michael, Jessica. Student, Lafayette Coll., 1952; BA, Elmhurst Coll., 1956; MA, U. Chgo., 1964. Tchr. Whitecross Sch., Hereford, Eng., 1956-57, Jefferson Sch., Berwyn, Ill., 1957-60, Morton High Sch., Berwyn, 1960-66; mem. faculty dept. labor and indsl. relations U. Ill., Chgo., 1966—; prof. U. Ill., 1978—; coordinator Chgo. Labor Edn. Program, 1981-87. Author: Touring Pullman, 1972, Haymarket Revisited, 1976, Pilsen and the West Side, 1981; writer: film Packingtown U.S.A., 1968; narrator: Palace Cars and Paradise: Pullman's Model Town, 1983. Bd. dirs. Chgo. Regional Blood Program, 1977-80; mem. Ill. State Employment Security Adv. Bd., 1974-75; Democratic candidate U.S. Ho. of Reps. from 14th dist. Ill., 1970; organizer Haymarket Centennial Events, 1986. Ill. Humanities Council grantee, 1977; German Marshall Fund U.S. grantee, 1977. Mem. Ill. Labor History (founding mem., v.p.), Am. Fedn. Tchrs. Unitarian. Home: 613 S Highland Ave Oak Park IL 60304 Office: Box 4348 U Ill Chicago IL 60680

ADELSBERG, HARVEY, hospital administrator; b. Bronx, N.Y., Aug. 5, 1931; s. Joseph and Becky (Rindner) A.; B.A., N.Y.U., 1953, M.P.A., 1960, postgrad., 1960-65; m. Miriam Levine, June 20, 1964; children—Jonathan, Risa, Seth. Adminstrv. resident Beth David Hosp., N.Y.C., 1953 54; adminstrv. asst. Mel. Jewish Geriatric Center, Bklyn., 1954-58; asst. dir. Kingsbrook Jewish Med. Center, Bklyn., 1958-61; asst. dir. Hosp. for Joint Diseases, N.Y.C., 1961-64; exec. dir. Theresa Grotta Center for Restorative Services, Caldwell, N.J., 1964-70; asst. dir. Mt. Sinai Hosp., N.Y.C., 1970-72; cons. med. care and services to aged Fedn. Jewish Philanthropies, N.Y.C., 1972-74; exec. dir. Daus. of Miriam Center for Aged, Clifton, N.J., 1974-76, exec. v.p., 1977—; adj. asst. prof. health care adminstrn., Bernard M. Baruch Coll., Mt. Sinai Sch. Medicine, CUNY, 1973—; mem. adv. com. Rutgers U., 1969—; mem. N.J. Licensing Bd. for Nursing Home Adminstrs., 1969—, vice chmn., 1969-77; mem. Adv. Council on Aging, Livington, N.J., 1977—. Trustee Hosp. and Council Met. N.J., 1967-70, Health and Hosp. Council So. N.Y., 1972-74, N.J. Assn. Non-Profit Homes for Aging, 1976—, Jewish Community Housing Corp., Paterson, N.J., 1975—; v.p. Solomon Schechter Day Sch. of Essex and Union, 1980—; trustee Synagogue of Suburban Torah Center, Livingston, 1978—; bd. govs. Greater N.Y. Hosp. Assn., 1972-74; v.p. Temple Beth Shalom, Livingston, 1970-71, 73, trustee, 1968-70, 75—; mem. governing com. Camp Ramah, Wingdale, N.Y., 1979—. Fellow Am. Coll. Hosp. Adminstrs., Am. Coll. Nursing Home Adminstrs., Am. Geriatric Soc., Am. Pub. Health Assn.; mem. Am., N.J. hosp. assns., Hosp. Exec. Club. Mem. B'nai B'rith (v.p. 1960-64). Home: 27 Tuxedo Dr Livingston NJ 07039 Office: 155 Hazel St Clifton NJ 07015

ADELSON, ALEXANDER M., physicist; b. Williamport, Pa., Oct. 14, 1934; s. Harold J. and Idele H. (Hanshaft) A.; m. Marjorie Meyers, Apr. 24, 1960; children—Amy Louise, Jennifer Lee, Nina Gwen. B.S., Muhlenberg Coll., 1956; postgrad. Brooks Inst., 1957. Research scientist K&E, Hoboken, N.J., 1957-59; optical engr. Razdow Labs., Orange, N.J., 1959-65; chief engr. Microspace, Inc., Englewood, N.J., 1965-66; v.p. engring. Hall-Barkan-Opticon, Tuchahoe, N.Y., 1966-67; pres., chmn. bd. Wild Rover Corp., Northvale, N.J., 1967-74; pres. RTS Research Lab, Inc., N.Y., 1974—; chmn. bd. Target Transp. Corp., 1974—; chief technical cons. Symbol Techs. Co., Bohemia, N.Y., 1977—; bd. dirs. QVS, Inc., Dimensional Communications, Inc., Alpine Sci., Inc., Tensiodyne Corp., Nocopi Internat. Inc. Patentee in elec. switch field, optics and computer mechanisms; monolithic touch operated keyboard, switches, laser bar code scanning equipment (51 patents and trade marks). Active Big Bros. Am. Co-winner gold medal Nat. Retailers Am., 1983. Mem. Am. Optical Soc., N.Y. Acad. Scis. Home: Mountainside Trail Peekskill NY 10566 Office: PO Box 564 Watch Hill Rd Crugers NY 10521

ADELZADEH, SEYED MOHAMMAD, import company executive, researcher; b. Haftkal, Khouzestan, Iran, Dec. 20, 1959; s. Seyed Jafar Adelzadeh and Fatemeh (Nahid) Ale Ali. BA in Journalism, Coll. Mass Communication, Tehran, Iran, 1973; BA in Film Studies, Stockholm U., 1984, postgrad., 1987—. Prin. Kam Import, Flen, Sweden, 1987—. Home: Smedshagsv 18 BV, 162 41 Stockholm Vullingby, Sweden Office: Kam-Import, PO Box 162, 64200 Flen Sweden

ADERTON, JANE REYNOLDS, lawyer; b. Riverside, Calif., Dec. 22, 1913; d. Charles Low and Verna Mae (Marshall) Reynolds; m. Robert Granville Johnson (div. 1959); children: Marshall Fallon, Jeannette Townsend; m. Thomas Radcliffe Aderton, Oct. 18, 1964. BS in Merchandising, U. So. Calif., 1935; JD, Southwestern U., Los Angeles, 1965. Bar: Calif.

1968. Sole practice Beverly Hills, Calif., 1968-79; jud. sec. Dist. Ct. Appeals, Los Angeles, 1960-65; sole practice Riverside, 1979—; assoc. Wyman, Bautzer, Rothman & Kuchel, 1970-79; del. Calif. Bar Conf., 1976, 77, 78. Mem. Founders' Club, Riverside Community Hosp., 1980—; mem. women's aux. Salvation Army, 1981-83, pres., adv. bd., 1983, sec., 1985-87; mem. World Affairs Council Inland So. Calif., 1981—, Affiliates U. Calif., Riverside, 1984—, Mus. Photography, 1985—; v.p., pres.-elect Art Alliance of the Riverside Art Mus., 1984-85, pres. 1985-86, mem., 1982—; mem. Riverside Hospice, 1983—, Riverside Opera Guild; bd. dirs. Friends of Mission Inn, 1986—, sec., 1987—; bd. dirs. San Gorgonio Girl Scout Council, 1987—. Mem. ABA, Calif. Bar Assn., Riverside Bar Assn., Beverly Hills Bar Assn. (bd. govs. 1976-79, chmn. probate and trust com. 1975-77, chmn. del. to Calif. bar conf. 1978), Calif. Mus. Photography, Phi Alpha Delta, Pi Beta Phi (pres. Riverside alumni club 1981-83, 88-89). Clubs: Victoria Country (Riverside); Newport Harbor Yacht (Newport Beach, Calif.). Lodge: Soroptimist Internat. Home: 5190 Stonewood Dr Riverside CA 92506 Office: Riverside CA

ADEYEMI, GREGORY OTUNOLA AJIBOYE, pharmacist; b. Oro, Kwara, Irepodun, Nigeria, Apr. 26, 1950; s. Ajiboye Gbadamosi and Folasayo Ajike (Ajiboye) A.; m. Esther Olubunmi Omotosho, Apr. 2, 1977; 1 child, Oluremi Folasayo. BS in Pharmacy with honors, Ahmadu Bello U., Zaria, Nigeria, 1975; MS in Pharmacy, U. Bradford, Eng., 1979; Doctorate, Kenton U., Singapore, 1987. Intern pharmacist Lagos (Nigeria) State Ministry Health, 1975-76; pharmacist Nat. Youth Service Corps, Anambra, Nigeria, 1976-77; mktg. pharmacist May & Baker Nigeria Ltd., Lagos, 1977-80, Kakaki Chemists Ltd., Lagos, 1980—; chmn. Kakaki Plastics Ltd., Lagos, 1984; bd. dirs. Sayotek Nigeria Ltd., Lagos, Kakaki Ltd., Lagos. Mem. Pharm. Soc. Nigeria. Democrat. Roman Catholic. Club: Ikoyi 1938 (Lagos). Lodge: Rotary (internat. chmn. Akoka, Lagos). Home: 84 Odunfa St, Ebute-Metta, Lagos Lagos Nigeria Office: Kakaki Chemist Ltd, 91A Lagos St, Ebute-Metta, Lagos Lagos Nigeria

ADHIN, HERMAN SOOKDEW, Suriname minister of development, educator; b. Ornamibo Dist., Surinam, July 27, 1933; s. Ram and Dowlatia A.; B.Sc. in Rds., Traffic and Civil Engring., U. Delft (Netherlands), 1958, M.Sc. in Rds. (hons.), Traffic and Civil Engring., 1959, D.Tech. Scis. (hons.), 1963; Ph.D. (hon.), Internat. Univ. Found., 1985; student in math. U. Leiden (Netherlands), 1955-57; student in economy U. Rotterdam (Netherlands), 1958; student in law U. Utrecht (Netherlands), 1958; m. Soebhagi Doerga, Apr. 12, 1960; children—Lalita, Ravi. With Suriname Ministry Public Works, Paramaribo, 1959—, head dept. phys. and urban planning, 1964-70, acting dir. of ministry, 1970—, v.p. bd. dirs. Govtl. Nat. Telephone and Telegraph Co., 1973-80, minister of devel., 1980—; mng. dir. Bur. Multipurpose Corantijn Project; lectr., acting dean Faculty Engring., U. Suriname, Paramaribo, 1977—; adv. on hydraulics, irrigation to Suriname Govt.; bd. dirs. Ministry Public Works; mem. Suriname Adv. Bd. Cultural Affairs, 1960-64, acting pres., 1964-66, pres. bd., 1966-68, 70—; mem. Nat. Bd. for Boundaries of Suriname, 1970—; sec. Suriname, Nat. Com., Internat. Commn. on Irrigation and Drainage, 1964—; mem., chmn. various govt. commns., including mem., sec., acting chmn. Coordination Commn. on Cables for Utilities, 1960-65, chmn. commn., 1965—. Rep. Suriname various occasions, including at UN Conf. on Sci. and Tech., Vienna, Austria, 1979. Mem. council Cultural Centre of Suriname, Paramaribo, 1961—, acting chmn. council, 1966—; mem. council Sanatan Dharm Maha Sabha, Surinamese Hindu orgn., 1967-70, acting pres. High-council, 1970—; mem. Hindu-Moslim Nat. Com., 1969—, acting pres. com., 1970; acting chmn. Nat. Found. Hindostani Immigration, 1969—, chmn. bd. found., 1974—. Recipient Suriname Bauxite Maatschappij, award, 1950, AMS, 1953; Nat. distinction in behalf of Independency of Suriname, 1975 Bronze medal Dr. Albert Einstein Internat. Acad., 1986. Mem. Royal Soc. Dutch Acad. Engrs., Suriname Soc. Acad. Engrs. (co-founder 1959, sec. and acting chmn. 1960-67, hon. mem. 1967—), Soc. Sci. Workers, Suriname Red Cross Soc., Suriname History Soc. (council 1967—), Union Lectrs. and Higher Tchrs., Union Higher Govt. Ofcls. Co-author: Ency. of Suriname, 1977; contbr. articles, chpts. to books, newspapers, mags.; author publs. for radio, TV. Home: 15 Herman Snostraat, Paramaribo Suriname Office: 167 Coppenamestraat, Paramaribo Suriname

ADHVARYU, JAYKRISHNA HARGOVINDDAS, librarian; b. Chhalala, India, Jan. 9, 1932; s. Hargovinddas Garbaddas and Jayaben (Hargovinddas) A.; m. Sudhaben, Jan. 25, 1953; children: Beena, Janak, Devi, Damini. BA, Gujarat U., 1964, B in Library Sci., 1965; MA, Saurashtra U., 1972; postgrad., Gujarat U. Clk. Gujarat U., Ahmedabad, India, 1951, sr. clk. to tech. asst., 1965-67; asst. librarian and head Saurashtra U. Library, Rajkot, India, 1967-73, Bhavnagar, India, 1973-79; asst. librarian and head Bhavnagar U. Library, 1979—, co-coordinator dept. library and info. sci., 1982—; lectr. in field. Contbr. articles to profl. jours. Mem. Indian Library Assn., Gujarat Pustakalaya Mandal. Home: Plot #1 Shreeji Park, Anantwadi, Bhavnagar 364002, India Office: Bhavnagar U Library, Waghawadi Rd, Gujarat 3640002, India

ADISESHIAH, MALCOLM SATHIANATHAN, educational administrator; b. Madras, Tamilnadu, India, Apr. 18, 1910; s. Paul Veranaci and Nassamma A.; m. Dec. 26, 1952; 2 children. Ed. Voorhees Sch. and Coll., Vellore, India, Loyola Coll., Madras, London Sch. Econs., U. London, Kings Coll., Cambridge U. (Eng.); hon. degrees. From lectr. to prof. econs. U. Calcutta (India), U. Madras, 1931-46; dir. UNESCO, Paris, from 1946, asst. dir. gen., dep. dir. gen., to 1970; dir. Madras Inst. Devel. Studies, from 1971, now chmn; vice chancellor Madras U., 1975-78. Author numerous books, the most recent being: Literacy Discussion, 1976; Towards a Functional Learning Society, 1976; Backdrop to Learning Society, 1980; Adult Education Faces Inequalities, 1981; Mid Year Review of the Economy 1987—; Mid Year Assessment of the VI Plan, 1983; Seventh Plan Perspectives, 1985; The Why, What and Whither of the Public Sector Enterprises, 1985; Shaping the National Events—The Economy as Seen in Parliamentary Statements, 1985; Comments on the Black Money, 1986. Mem. Parliament Rajya Sabha, 1978—; v.p. Tamil Nadu Bd. Continuing Edn. (India), Tamil Nadu State Council for Sci. and Tech. Decorated Padma Bhushan (India). Mem. Indian Econ. Assn., Internat. Council for Adult Edn., Indian Adult Edn. Assn., Internat. Inst. for Ednl. Planning. Office: Madras Inst Devel Studies, 79 II Main Rd, Madras 600020 Gandhinager, Adyar, India

ADJAMAH, KOKOUVI MICHEL, physician; b. Lome, Togo, West Africa, Jan. 21, 1942; s. Carl Yao and Antoinette Afi (Tourné) A.; m. Francoise Legendre, July 30, 1975; children: Isabelle, Celine. MS, U. Paris, 1970, MD, 1973, MPH, 1974, M of Human Ecology, 1975, M of Clin. Toxicology-Pharmacology, 1976. Pub. health physician Dreux, France, 1973-74; gen. practice medicine, homeopathy, acupuncture, holistic medicine Vernouillet, France, 1976; expert in human ecology Paris, 1976, cons. clin. pharmacology, 1977—. Author: Onchocerchosis in West Africa, 1973; contbr. aritcles to profl. jours. Mem. Fellow Rabelais Med. Brotherhood; mem. French Com. for Med. Lexicon, Soc. Functional Medicine, French Soc. Pharmacology-Toxicology (assoc.) Social Medicine Club, Human Rights Assn. Quaker. Home: 25 rue de Chailloy, Garnay Vernouillet, 28500 Eure et Loire France Office: 5 Ter rue Louis Jouvet, Vernouillet, 28500 Eure et Loire France

ADKIN, NEIL, classicist, educator; b. Hull, Eng., July 4, 1954; came to U.S., 1986; s. Gordon William and Marion (Buttle) A. MA, Oxford U., 1980; PhD, U. Glasgow, 1982. Mem. editorial staff Thesaurus Linguae Latinae Bavarian Acad. Scis., Munich, 1976-79; lectr. medieval Latin Liverpool (Eng.) U., 1981-82, univ. research fellow, 1982-86; asst. prof. classics U. Nebr., Lincoln, 1986—; asst. editor ARCA classical and medieval texts, papers and monographs, 1983—; exchange fellow Acad. Scis. German Dem. Republic, East Berlin, 1984. Contbr. articles to profl. publs. Hertford and De Paravicini scholar, Ireland and Craven scholar, 1973. Anglican. Home: 1741 K St Lincoln NE 68508 Office: U Nebr Lincoln NE 68588-0337

ADKINS, BARBARA L., mediator; b. Sugarland, Tex., Oct. 26, 1946; d. Thomas H. and Patricia M. Adkins. M.B.A., U. Dallas, 1982. With Pier 1 Imports, 1967-83, dir. European fin., 1973-76, mgr. mdse. stats., 1977, asst. to exec. v.p., 1977-78, merchandising systems analyst, 1979, real estate property mgr., 1980, real estate mgr. eastern U.S., 1981-83; v.p. Bright Banc, Tex., 1984-88; pres. Adkins and Assocs., 1988—. Mem. Irving Tex. Women's C. of C., Sigma Iota Epsilon.

ADKINS, LESLEY, archaeologist; b. East Sussex, Eng., Apr. 6, 1955; m. Roy Adkins, Aug. 12, 1978. BA with honors in Archaeology and Ancient History, Latin, U. Bristol, Eng., 1976; M in Philosophy, U. Surrey, Guildford, Eng., 1982. Archaeol. asst. Milton Keynes (Eng.) Devel. Corp., 1976; field officer Surrey Archaeol. Soc., London, 1977-83; sr. archaeologist Mus. of London, 1983-87; archaeol. cons. Somerset, Eng., 1987—; bd. dirs., council mem. Surrey Archaeol. Soc., Guildford, 1983-87; extra-mural U. London, 1982-83; adult edn. lectr. London Borough of Croydon, London, 1983-84. Author: A Thesaurus of British Arhchaeology, 1982, Under the Sludge - Beddington Roman Villa, 1986. Mem. Inst. Field Archaeologists, Royal Archaeol. Inst., Soc. for Promotion of Roman Studies. Home and Office: Longstone Lodge, Aller, Langport, Somerset TA10 0QT, England

ADKINS, ROY ARTHUR, archaeologist; b. Berkshire, Eng., Aug. 21, 1951; s. Frederick Arthur Charles and Ivy May (Clarke) A.; m. Lesley Smith, Aug. 12, 1978. BA with honors in Archaeology, Univ. Coll., Cardiff,, 1974. Asst. archaeologist Milton Keynes (Eng.) Devel. Corp., 1974-78; field officer Surrey Archeol. Soc., London, 1978-83; sr. archaeologist Mus. London, 1983-87, archaeol. cons., 1987—; extra-mural lectr. U. London, 1982-83. Author: Neolithic Stone and Flint Axes from the River Thames, 1978, A Thesaurus of British Archaeology, 1982, Under the Sludge-Beddington Roman Villa, 1986; contbr. articles to profl. jours. Mem. Inst. Field Archaeologists, Royal Archaeol. Inst., Prehistoric Soc. Home and Office: Longstone Lodge, Aller, Langport, Somerset TA10 OGT, England

ADLER, ERWIN ELLERY, lawyer; b. Flint, Mich., July 22, 1941; s. Ben and Helen M. (Schwartz) A.; m. Stephanie Ruskin, June 8, 1967; children—Lauren, Michael, Jonathan. B.A., U. Mich., 1963, LL.M., 1967; J.D., Harvard U., 1966. Bar: Mich. 1966, Calif. 1967. Assoc. Pillsbury, Madison & Sutro, San Francisco, 1967-73; assoc. Lawler, Felix & Hall, Los Angeles, 1973-76, ptnr., 1977-82; ptnr. Rogers & Wells, Los Angeles, 1982-84, Richards, Watson & Gershon, Los Angeles, 1984—. Bd. dirs. Hollywood Civic Opera Assn., 1975-76, Children's Scholarships Inc., 1979-80. Mem. ABA (vice chmn. appellate advocacy com. 1982-87), Calif. Bar Assn., Phi Beta Kappa, Phi Kappa Phi. Jewish. Office: Richards Watson & Gershon 333 S Hope St 38th Floor Los Angeles CA 90071

ADLER, FREDA SCHAFFER (MRS. G. O. W. MUELLER), criminologist, educator; b. Phila., Nov. 21, 1934; d. David and Lucia G. (de Wolfson) Schaffer; children by previous marriage: Mark, Jill, Nancy. B.A., U. Pa., 1956, M.A., 1968, Ph.D. (fellow), 1971. Instr. dept. psychiatry Temple U., Phila., 1971; research coordinator Addiction Scis. Center, 1971-72; research dir. sect. on drug and alcohol abuse Med. Coll. Pa., 1972-74, asst. prof. psychiatry, 1972-74; asso. prof. criminal justice Rutgers U., Newark, 1974-79; prof. Rutgers U., 1979-82, disting. prof., 1982—, acting dean grad. sch. criminal justice, 1986-87; cons. on female criminality UN, 1975—; vis. fellow Yale U., 1976; cons. to Nat. Commn. on Marijuana and Drug Abuse, 1972-73, N.Y. U. Sch. Law, 1972-74; mem. faculty Nat. Jud. Coll., U. Nev., 1973—, Nat. Coll. Criminal Def. Lawyers and Public Defenders U. Houston, 1975; Mem. adv. com. Gen. Fedn. Women's Clubs, 1975-77; UN rep. Internat. Prisoner Aid Assn., 1973-75, Internat. Soc. Social Def.; sec. bd. dirs. Inst. for Continuous Study of Man, 1974-77, v.p., 1977—; UN rep. Internat. Assn. Social Def. Author: Sisters in Crime, 1975, The Incidence of Female Criminality in the Contemporary World, 1981, Nations Not Obsessed with Crime, 1983; co-author: A Systems Approach to Drug Treatment, 1975, Medical Lollypop, Junkie Insuline, or What?, 1974, The Criminology of Deviant Women, 1978, Outlaws of the Ocean, 1985; contbr. numerous articles on criminology and psychiatry to profl. jours.; editor Advances in Criminological Theory, 1987—; editorial bd.: Criminology, 1971-73, Jour. Criminal Law and Criminology, 1982—; co-editor: Politics, Crime and the International Scene, 1972, Revue Internationale de Droit Penal, 1974, Advances in Criminological Theory, 1987; assoc. editor: LAE Jour., 1977-85; cons. editor: Jour. Criminal Law and Criminology. Recipient (with G.O.W. Mueller) Beccaria medal in Gold Deutsche Kriminologische Gesellschaft, 1979. Mem. Am. Soc. Criminology (Herbert Bloch award 1972), Am. Sociol. Assn., Internat. Assn. Penal Law, U. Pa. Alumnae Assn (dir. 1974-77), Chi Omega (award 1956). Home: 30 Waterside Plaza Apt 37J New York NY 10010 Office: Rutgers U Sch Criminal Justice 15 Washington St Newark NJ 10010

ADLER, JOYCE SPARER, literary critic, educator; b. N.Y.C., Dec. 2, 1915; d. Louis and Lillian (Solomon) Lifshutz; m. Irving Adler, Sept. 16, 1968; children: Ellen, Laura. B.A. cum laude, Bklyn. Coll., City U. N.Y., 1935, M.A., 1951. Tchr. English public high schs., N.Y.C., 1940-54, acting chmn. dept. English, 1950-52; editor Blood, Jour. Hematology, N.Y.C., 1954-55; tchr. English to fgn. dels. to UN, N.Y.C., 1956-63; tchr. English, Ramaz High Sch., N.Y.C., 1960-63; founding mem. U. Guyana, Georgetown, 1963-68, prof. lit., 1963-68, editor univ. newsletter, 1964-68. Author: (books) Attitudes Towards Race in Guyanese Literature, 1967, Language and Man, 1970; War in Melville's Imagination, 1981, (play) Melville, Billy and Mars, 1987; contbr. critical essays to anthologies, PMLA and lit. jours.; contbr. articles on Wilson Harris, 1967-86. U.S. and Commonwealth Countries; occasional mem. coll. faculties, 1981—; lectr. in field, China, Japan, India, Australia, Singapore, N.Z. invited main speaker Internat. Conf. on Commonwealth Lit., Liège, Belgium, 1974, Nat. Conf. African and Caribbean Lit., U. Mo., 1973, ann. Melville Soc. Meeting, 1978, Bennington Coll. Conf. on Am. Indian, 1977. Recipient Nat. Second prize English Jour., 1953. Mem. MLA, Internat. Assn. Commonwealth Lit. and Lang. Studies, Vt. Acad. Arts and Scis. (trustee 1981—, sec. 1981—), Melville Soc. (program chmn. 1985, organizer conf. Women in Melville's Art, Chgo. 1985, conf. Melville's Response to the Modern World, Nantucket, Mass. 1986, pres. 1988). Author (play) Melville, Billy, and Mars, 1987; freelance writer song lyrics, short stories, plays, 1956-63; articles referee PMLA. Home and Office: North Bennington VT 05257

ADLER, LAUREL ANN, educational administrator, consultant; b. Cleve., Sept. 6, 1948; d. Clarence Linsley and Margaret Ann (Roberts) Wheeler; m. Thomas Jay Johnson, June 6, 1981; children—David, Anthony, Jennifer. B.A., U. Calif.-Irvine, 1968; M.A., Calif. State U.-Los Angeles, 1972; Ed.D., U. La Verne, 1980. Audlt Edn. adminstr. Hacienda La Puente Unified Sch. Dist., 1972-79; dir. career and vocat. edn. El Monte Union High Sch. Dist., 1979-83; dir. East San Gabriel Valley Regional Occupational Ctr., West Covina, Calif., 1984—; instr. Calif. State U.-Los Angeles, 1979-81; cons. Trust Ty. Pacific Islands, 1979—. Active El Monte Coordinating Council. Recipient Nat. Vol. Action award 1974; Calif. Consortium Ind. Study Recognition award of Outstanding Ednl. Program, 1983, Calif. Sch. Adminstrs. award, 1981; named Citizen of Yr., La Puente C. of C., 1977, Outstanding Vocat. Educator, Hoffman Ednl. Systems, 1983. Mem. Assn. Calif. Sch. Adminstrs., Internat. Reading Assn., Assn. Supervision and Curriculum Devel., Calif. Consortium Ind. Study, Phi Delta Kappa. Club: Soroptimist. Author: A Self Evaluation Model for Micronesian Education Programs, 1980, Poor Readers, What Do They Really See on the Page?, 1987; pub. Essential English for Micronesians, Beginning, 1980; Essential English for Micronesians, 1980; Reading Exercises for Micronesians, 1980; contbr. articles to profl. jours. Home: 3366 Garden Terr Hacienda Heights CA 91745 Office: East San Gabriel Valley Regional Occupational Ctr 1024 W Workman West Covina CA 91790

ADLER, LEONORE LOEB, psychologist; b. Karlsruhe, W. Ger., May 2, 1921; d. Leo and Elsie (Laemle) Loeb; m. Helmut E. Adler, May 22, 1943; children—Barry Peter, Beverly Sharmaine, Evelyn Renée. B.A. cum laude, Queens Coll., CUNY, 1968; Ph.D., Adelphi U., 1972. Research asst. Am. Mus. Natural History, N.Y.C., 1956-84; adj. asst. prof. psychology Coll. S.I., CUNY, 1974-80; research assoc. Mystic Marinelife Aquarium (Conn.), 1976-85; assoc. prof. dept. psychology, dir. Inst. for Cross-Cultural and Cross-Ethnic Studies, Molloy Coll., Rockville Centre, N.Y., 1980—; chmn. internat. and nat. confs. Author book chpts.; translator: This is the Dachshund, 1966, 2d rev. edit., 1975; mem. editorial bd Internat. Jour. of Group Tensions, 1985—; co-editor: Comparative Psychology at Issue, 1973, Language, Sex and Gender: Does "la Différence" Make a Difference, 1979; editor: Issues in Cross-Cultural Research, 1977; Cross-Cultural Research at Issue, 1982; contbr. articles and chpts. to handbooks, profl. jours. and encys. Mem. to gov.'s com. on women N.Y. State Women's Com., 1977. Recipient Disting. Contbr. of Decade award, Internat. Orgn. Study Group Tensions, 1981. Fellow N.Y. Acad. Scis.; mem. Am. Psychol. Assn. (network of reps. of com. on women in psychology 1982-87), Eastern Psychol. Assn. (bd. dirs. 1985-86, 87—), N.Y. State Psychol. Assn. (pres. div. social psychology 1978-79, 80-82, 84-85; pres. div. acad. psychology 1982-83, 88—; mem. council reps. 1981-84, 86-87; chmn. com. women's issues 1982-84, plaque for outstanding achievement from women's com. 1984, medallion from social div. 1984, Kurt Lewin award 1985), Internat. Assn. Cross-Cultural Psychology, Soc. Cross-Cultural Research, Internat. Orgn. Study Group Tensions (mng. editor Internat. Jour. Group Tensions, 1978-84, assoc. editor 1984-85, mem. editorial bd. 1985—), Animal Behavior Soc., Internat. Soc. Comparative Psychology, Assn. Women in Sci., Soc. Advancement Social Psychology, Internat. Council Psychologists (treas. 1983-85), Cheiron, the Internat. Soc. for History of Behavioral and Social Scis., Queens County Psychol. Assn. (pres.-elect 1985-87, pres. 1987-88), Psi Chi (faculty adviser Molloy Coll., 1980—), Alpha Sigma Lambda, Zeta Epsilon Gamma. Jewish. Home: 162-14 86th Ave Jamaica NY 11432 Office: Molloy Coll Inst Cross Cultural and Cross Ethnic Studies 1000 Hempstead Ave Rockville Centre NY 11570

ADLER, MILTON LEON, psychologist; b. Bronx, N.Y., June 11, 1926; s. Siegmund and Josephine (Eppsteiner) A.; B.S., Rutgers U., 1951; M.S., City U. N.Y., 1952; postgrad. N.Y. U., 1952-53; Ph.D., U. Ill., 1963; m. Margrit Klein, Mar. 5, 1948; children—Sandra Ellen, Mark Lawrence. Psychiat. case worker N.J. Neuropsychiat. Inst., Blauenberg, 1953; clin. psychology intern, staff psychologist Manteno (Ill.) State Hosp., 1953-57; regional psychologist Ill. Inst. Juvenile Research, Champaign, 1957-66; sr. psychologist, clin. supr., subregion dir. Herman M. Adler Children's Center, Champaign, 1966-74; cons. psychologist Frederic Chusid and Co., Chgo., 1963-64; lectr. psychology Ill. State U., Normal, 1974-75; instr. psychology Parkland Coll., Champaign, Ill., 1979-80; pvt. practice clin. counseling, cons. psychology, Urbana, Ill., 1965—; mem. staff Cole Hosp., 1985-88; med. cons. Ill. Dept. Rehab. Services and Disability Determination Services, 1986—; presenter growth in groups seminars and workshops on personal growth and interpersonal relationships, Stress Mgmt. Services. Served with USAAF, 1944-47. Registered psychologist, Ill. Fellow Am. Group Psychotherapy Assn. (mem. fellowship com. 1982—, dir. 1974-76, instr. tng. inst., mem. inst. com.); mem. Internat. Group Psychotherapy Assn., Ill. Assn. Maternal and Child Health (dir. bd. dirs. 1975-83, v.p. 1980-81, pres-elect 1981-82 pres. 1982-83, workshop, seminar presenter), Champaign-Urbana State Employees Assn. (past v.p., pres.), Ill. Group Psychotherapy Soc. (workshop presenter, council rep., awards of distinction 1977, 83, v.p., pres.-elect 1980-81, pres. 1982), Am. Psychol. Assn. (divs. psychotherapy, ind. practice, cons., community, humanistic and family psychology), Nat. Assn. Sch. Psychologists, Am. Assn. for Counseling and Devel., Am. Assn. Mental Health Counselors, Ill. Psychol. Assn. (clin. sect.), Ill. Acad. Criminology, Ill. Assn. for Counseling and Devel., Ill. Assn. Mental Health Counselors, Nat. Assn. Disability Examiners, Am. Acad. Psychotherapists, Saab Club Am., N. Am. Hunting Club, Phi Delta Kappa. Democrat. Unitarian-Universalist. Contbr. workshops/seminars for community groups on anxiety, risk-taking/and interpersonal relationships, and personal growth, workshops on group psychotherapy to profl. insts. Home: 1507 W University Ave Champaign IL 61821 Office: 404 W Green St Urbana IL 61801

ADLER, NORMAN ABNER, lawyer, former broadcasting and advertising executive; b. N.Y.C., Oct. 8, 1909; s. Isaac Julius and Anna (Bluestein) A.; m. Leona Kleban, June 28, 1934; children—John Robert, Louise Rachel. B.A., NYU, 1930; J.D., Yale, 1933. Bar: N.Y. bar 1933. Asso. mem. firm Rosenberg, Goldmark & Colin, N.Y.C., 1933-38; spl. asst. to U.S. atty. gen., anti-trust div. Dept. Justice, 1938-45; asst. gen. atty. RCA, 1945-48; gen. atty. Columbia Records, 1948-55; v.p. charge Columbia Record Club, 1955-60; exec. v.p. Columbia Records (div. CBS), 1960-66; v.p., gen. mgr. CBS Ednl. Services Div., 1966-67; v.p., gen. exec. CBS, Inc., 1967-71; chmn. exec. com. Wunderman Ricotta & Kline, 1971-74. Mng. editor Yale Law Jour., 1932-33. Recipient Cullen prize for excellence in legal scholarship Yale, 1931. Mem. Fed. Bar Assn., Assn. Bar City N.Y., Order of Coif, Phi Beta Kappa Assos., Phi Beta Kappa. Home: 2214 Caminito Castillo La Jolla CA 92037

ADLER, SEYMOUR JACK, social services administrator; b. Chgo., Oct. 22, 1930; s. Michael L. and Sarah (Pasnick) A.; B.S., Northwestern U., 1952; M.A., U. Chgo., 1958; m. Barbara Fingold, Mar. 24, 1958; children—Susan Lynn, Karen Sandra, Michelle Lauren. Caseworker, Cook County Dept. Pub. Aid, Chgo., 1955; juvenile officer Cook County Sheriff's Office, 1955-56; U.S. probation-parole officer U.S. Dist. Ct., Chgo., 1958-68; exec. dir. Youth Guidance, Chgo., 1968-73; dir. court services Juvenile Ct. Cook County, Chgo., 1973-75; exec. dir. Methodist Youth Services, Chgo., 1975-85; program mgr. Dept. Social Services, Kenosha, Wis., 1985—; mem. Ill. Law Enforcement Commn., 1969-72; instr. corrections program Chgo. State U., 1972-75; instr. Harper Coll., 1977, St. Joseph's Coll., 1978; case developer Nat. Ctr. on Instns. and Alternatives, 1985-86. Bd. dirs. Child Care Assn. Ill., 1979-84. Served to 1st lt. USMCR, 1952-55. Recipient Morris J. Wexler award Ill. Acad. Criminology, 1975, Meritorious Service award Chgo. City Colls., 1968. Mem. Ill. Acad. Criminology (pres. 1972), Nat. Assn. Social Workers (del. Assembly 1977, 79, 81, 84, 87, chmn. Chgo. dist. 1978-80, chmn. group for action planning childrens services 1980-84, Disting. Service award Criminal Justice Council 1978), Ill. Probation, Parole and Correctional Assn., Internat. Half-way House Assn. (Ill. dir.), Alpha Kappa Delta, Tau Delta Phi. Contbr. articles to profl. jours. Home: 232 Grandview Ln Twin Lakes WI 53181 Office: Kenosha Dept Social Services 714 52d St Kenosha WI 53140

ADLER-KARLSSON, GUNNAR, philosopher, social scientist; b. Karlshamn, Sweden, Mar. 6, 1933; arrived in Italy, 1968; s. Herbert and Elsa (Andersson) A.; m. Marianne Ehrnford, Dec. 27, 1960. Student, Harvard U., 1960-61, U. Calif., Berkeley, 1961-62; D of Law, Stockholm U., 1962, PhD in Econs., 1968. Prof. Roskilde U. Ctr., Denmark, 1974—; exec. dir. Capri Inst. for Internat. Social Philosophy, Italy, 1979—. Author books in field; contbr. articles to profl. jours. Home: Via Donna Olimpia 20, I-00152 Rome Italy Office: Inst Internat Social Philosophy, CP 79, I-80071 Anacapri Italy

ADMANI, HAJI ABDUL KARIM, physician, educator; b. Palitana, Gujarat, India, Sept. 19, 1934; came to Eng., 1962; s. Haji Abdul Razzak and Hajiani Rahimabai (Akbani) A.; m. Seema Robson, Mar. 23, 1968; children—Nadim, Nilofer. B.Sc. with 1st class honors, Gujarat U., Ahmedabad India, 1955; M.B.B.S., Dow Med. Coll., Karachi U., Pakistan, 1962; DTM&H, London U., 1963. Jr. house physician in gen. medicine Jinnah Post Grad. Med. Ctr., Karachi, 1961-62, sr. house physician, 1962; house physician in gen. medicine Ashington Gen. Hosp., Eng., 1963; sr. house officer in neurology Newcastle Gen. Hosp., Sunderland Gen. Hosp., 1963-64; sr. house officer, registrar in gen. medicine Newcastle Gen. Hosp., Newcastle-upon-Tyne, Eng., 1964-66; registrar physician Darlington Group Hosps., Newcastle Regional Bd., Eng., 1966-67; registrar physician St. Catherine's Hosp., Birkhead, Eng., 1967-68, gen. med. registrar, 1969; sr. registrar in neurology Civil Hosp., Karachi, 1969; sr. registrar dept. medicine for elderly No. Gen. Hosp. and Nether Edge Hosp., Sheffield, Eng., 1970-71; clin. tutor dept. medicine for elderly Sheffield U., 1970-71; cons. physician with spl. interest in elderly dept. medicine and rehab. Sheffield Area Health Authority, 1971—; hon. clin. lectr. in acad. div. medicine Sheffield Med. Sch., 1972—; chmn. Stinrole Ltd., Sheffield, Sunningdale Yorkshire Ltd., Sheffield; mem. Cen. Com. Hosp. Med. Services in U.K., 1979-85; researcher in field. Editor: Guidance to the National Health Dervice for Overseas Doctors, 1982. Justice of Peace, City of Sheffield, 1974—; county med. officer Brit. Red Cross Soc. for South Yorkshire, 1974-82, pres., 1982—; mem. Profl. Adv. Com. of Deputising Services, Sheffield, 1976—; mem. Sheffield Area Health Authority, 1977-82; chmn. Sheffield Campaign Against Rickets and Osteo-Malacia and Asian Health Care, 1981—; chmn. adv. council BBC Radio Sheffield, 1982-85; vice chmn. Sheffield Com. Racial Equality, 1979-87; chmn. post-grad. tng. and sponsorship tng. program for overseads doctors in U.K., 1986— . Recipient Adamjee Silver Jubilee Gold medal Pres. Zia of Pakistan, 1984; decorated officer Brit. Empire, 1987. Mem. Overseas Doctors Assn. U.K. (fellow, chmn. postgrad. tng. com. 1976-82, chmn. welfare, info. and adv. service 1976-82, chmn. 1981-87, pres. 1987—), Royal Coll. Physicians (fellow), Royal Soc. Medicine (fellow), Brit. Med. Assn. (fellow), Sheffield Stroke Club (pres. 1977—), Pakistan Med. Soc. (v.p.1971—). Anglo-Asian Soc., Conf. Pakistani Orgns. in U.K. (chmn. 1978—), Nat. Orgn. Afro-Asian Carribean People in U.K. (sr. vice chmn. 1976—), Gen. Med. Council. Islam. Clubs: Liberal (London); European Movement and the Union of European Federalists. Lodges: Rotary; Stafford Lodge. Avocations: cricket; table tennis; snooker; chess; golf. Home: 1 Derriman Glen, Sheffield, South Yorksire S11 9LQ, England Office: Northern Gen Hosp, Herries Rd, Sheffield, South Yorkshire S5 7AU, England

ADNYANA, I. GUSTI NGURAH PUTU, pathology educator, university rector; b. Penebel, Bali, Indonesia, Dec. 25, 1928; s. Putera I. Gusti Ngurah and Made Anakagung; m. Apr. 5, 1957; children: Agung, Mahayasa, Dharmawan, Rika, Alit, Aryanai. MD, U. Airlangga, Surabaya, 1960. Resident in pathology U. Calif., San Francisco, 1960-63; head dept. pathology Med. Faculty Udayana U., Denpasar, Bali, 1963—, dean Med. Faculty, 1968-75, dir. planning bd., 1975-78, dir. devel. planning bd., 1978-83, rector of Univ., 1986—; acting rector Marhaen U., Denpasar, 1964-68; dir. Social Found., Denpasar, 1978—. Mem. Golongan Darya, Denpasar, 1967—, Majelis Permusyawaratan Rakyat, Jakarta, 1987—. Mem. Indonesian Med. Assn., Indonesian Assn. Pathologists (chmn. Bali br. 1972). Office: U Udayana, Panglima Besar Sudirman, Denpasar Bali Indonesia

ADOLPHI, RONALD LEE, government official; b. Bremerton, Wash., Aug. 8, 1946; s. Robert L. and Margaret May (Hitland) A.; m. Sherry Lee Klepach, Oct. 5, 1968 (div. Jan. 1974), Celia Louise Fields, May 10, 1975; children: Christina, Lani. BA in Bus. Adminstrn., U. Wash., 1968; M.S. in Ednl. Adminstrn., Butler U., 1974; M.B.A., Syracuse U., 1976; grad. Indsl. Coll. of Armed Forces, 1984; PhD in Mgmt. Calif. Coast U., 1986. Cert. cost analyst. Br. chief, capt. U.S. Army Fin. Sch., Indpls., 1972-73; fin. analyst Continental Steel Corp., Kokomo, Ind., 1973-74; fin. services officer Hdqrs. U.S. Army Pacific, Honolulu, 1974; fiscal specialist Office of Comptroller of Army, Washington, 1974-76; internat. economist Office Sec. of Def., Washington, 1976-82, asst. dir. for overseas banking, 1982-86, asst. dir. policy analysis and spl. studies, 1987-88, asst. dir. policy analysis and disbursing systems, 1988—; dir. Fin. Ctr. Fed. Credit Union., Indpls, 1972-74. Editorial bd. Armed Forces Comptroller Jour., 1979-83. Contbr. articles to profl. publs. Treas. St. John's Luth. Ch., Alexandria, 1978-80, fin. sec., 1980-81, v.p. 1982-84, pres. 1984-86, comptroller, 1987—; Chmn. publs., 1987—, Nat. Luth. Assn. Scouters, pres. 1980-82, regional v.p., 1983-84, sec., 1984-86; newsletter editor Capital Luth. Assn. Scouters, 1983—, pres., 1977-80; chmn. protestant com. on scouting Nat. Capital Area council Boy Scouts Am., chmn. 1984—, nat. mem. at large, 1980—. Served to capt. U.S. Army, Vietnam, Fed. Republic Germany, col. Res. Decorated Bronze Star with oak leaf cluster, Meritorious Service medal, Air medal, others; recipient Encased George Washington Honor medal Freedoms Found. at Valley Forge, 1964, Silver Beaver award Boy Scouts Am., 1979, Lamb award Luth. Council in USA, 1981, U.S. Treasury Dept. award for excellence in cash mgmt., 1985. Mem. Assn. Syracuse Army Comptrollers (1st v.p. 1978-83), Res. Officers Assn., Am. Econ. Assn., Am. Mgmt. Assn., Sr. Execs. Assn., Am. Soc. Mil. Comptrollers (chmn. nat. research com. 1987—), Assn. Govt. Accts., Fed. Exec. Inst. Alumni Assn., Fin. Corps Assn., Phi Theta Kappa, Beta Gamma Sigma. Republican. Avocations: travel, scouting and church activities.

ADOMAKOH, ALBERT, banker; b. Apr. 8, 1924. Student Downing Coll., Cambridge; postgrad. London Sch. Econs., 1961-62. Sec., Bank of Ghana, 1957-62; mng. dir., chmn. Nat. Investment Bank, 1962-65; gov. Bank of Ghana, 1965-68; commr. (minister) for Agr., 1968-69; asst. dir.-gen. FAO, 1969-70; vice chmn. Soc. Internat. pour les Investissements et le Developpement en Afrique S.A., 1978-80; dir. investments Africa and Middle East IFC, 1970-72; devel. and fin. cons., 1972—; chmn. Ghana Consol. Diamonds Ltd., 1973-79; dir. C.F.A.O. (Ghana) Ltd. Author: The History of Currency and Banking in West African Countries, 1962. Office: PO Box 4104, Accra Ghana *

ADORNO, MARSHALL SEBASTIAN, accountant; b. Floridia, Italy, May 28, 1910; s. Joseph and Josephine (Cornelio) A. (parents Am. citizens); m. Monica Serra, Oct. 30, 1977. Grad., Bentley Sch. Acctg. and Fin., 1930. CPA, Conn. Auditor State of Conn., Hartford, 1931-34; various positions Torrington (Conn.) Nat. Bank, 1934-41; instr. bus. Torrington Secreterial Sch., 1934-36; former controller, sales mgr. Sweeco Wiring, Inc., Winsted, Conn.; pvt. practice acctg. Torrington, 1942—; co-founder, pres., treas. Just-Write Systems, Inc., Torrington, 1980—; selected to participate in people-to-people travel program to Europe, 1978. Author numerous articles on acctg. and bus. related topics. Charter mem. Republican Presdl. Task Force. Mem. Am. Inst. CPA's, Am. Inst. Mgmt. Club: Elks. Office: 1144 E Main St Torrington CT 06790

ADRIANI, JOHN, physician, emeritus educator; b. Bridgeport, Conn., Dec. 2, 1907; s. Nicola and Lucia (Caseria) A.; m. Eleanor Anderson, Dec. 1936 (div. Feb. 1947); 1 child, John Nicholas; m. Irene Miller, Sept. 7, 1953. A.B., Columbia U., 1930, M.D., 1934. Diplomate Am. Bd. Anesthesiology, (dir. 1960-72, chmn. exams. com. 1963-, pres. 1967-68). Intern surgery French Hosp., N.Y.C., 1934-36; resident anesthesiology Bellevue Hosp., N.Y.C., 1936-37; fellow N.Y.U., 1937-39, instr. anesthesiology dept. surgery, 1939-41; asst., then asso. clin. prof. surgery La. State U. Sch. Medicine, 1941-54, clin. prof. surgery and pharmacology, 1954; asst. prof., later asso. prof. anesthesiology Loyola Sch. Dentistry, New Orleans, 1945-56; prof. gen. anesthesiology Loyola Sch. Dentistry, 1956-71; prof. surgery Tulane U., 1947-75, emeritus, 1975—; prof. anesthesiology La. State Med. Center, 1975—; dir. dept. anesthesiology Charity Hosp., 1941-75, emeritus dir., 1975 ; dir. dept. inhalation therapy, 1941-69, dir. blood plasma bank, 1944-70, asst. dir., 1960-64; clin. prof. oral surgery Sch. Dentistry, La. State U., 1971—; assoc. dir. Charity Hosp., 1966-76, center chmn. regional med. program, 1967-70; cons. anesthesiologist Flint-Goodridge, VA, USPHS, Ochsner Found. hosps., Hotel Dieu, New Orleans; cons. anesthesiology, pharmacology and medico-legal problems La. Health and Human Resources Adminstrn., 1975-82; cons. to Touro Infirmary, New Orleans; mem. adv. com. div. investigational drugs FDA, 1963-65, 72—, chmn. adv. com. on anesthetic and respiratory drugs, 1968-70, mem. adv. panel topical analgesics over-the-counter drugs, 1972-78, mem. adv. panel oral cavity preparations, 1974-80, cons. consumer protection div., 1980—; cons. FTC; mem. founders group expansion program Holy Cross Coll., 1963; mem. revision com., chmn. com. on anesthesia, subcom. on scope U.S. Pharmacopoeia, 1960-70; mem. U.S. Pharmacopeal Conv., 1970—, Nat. Formulary Admissions Com., 1970—. Author: Pharmacology of Anesthetic Drugs, rev. edit, 1970, Chemistry of Anesthesia, 1946, Techniques and Procedures of Anesthesia, 3d edit., 1964, Nerve Blocks, 1954, Selection of Anesthesia, 1955, General Anesthesiology For Students and Practitioners of Dentistry, 1958, The Recovery Room, 1958, Chemistry and Physics of Anesthesia, 1962, Appraisal-Current Concepts Anesthesiology (Mosby), Vol. 1, 1961, Vol. 2, 1964, Vol. 3, 1966, Vol. 4, 1969, Revision of Labat's Region Anesthesia, 1967, edit. 4, 1985, also numerous scientific and med. papers.; Editor: American Lecture Series in Anesthesiology; cons. editor: The Resident G. P. Survey Anesthesiology; editor: Anesthesiology, 1958-67; cons. editor: Dorland's Illustrated Med. Dictionary, 1969—, Internat. Corr. Soc. Anesthesiology. Bd. dirs. Cancer Soc., New Orleans; mem. Met. Action Com. of New Orleans, Public Affairs Research Council, Bur. of Govtl. Research of La., Italian-Am. Culture Center, Piazza Italiana, New Orleans.; trustee, mem. acad. bd. St. George's U. Med. Ctr., Granada, W.I.; life v.p. Civil Service League La. Named hon. col. staff Gov. La., 1965; hon. dep. atty. gen. State of La., 1980; hon. dep. Sheriff La Fourche Parish, 1980; recipient Disting. Service award Am. Soc. Anesthesiologists, 1949, Disting. Service award Internat. Anesthesiology Research Soc., 1957; Guedel medal for anesthesiology, 1959; Gold medal Assn. Alumni Coll. Physicians and Surgeons, Columbia, 1967; silver medal for achievements in medicine Columbia U. Sch. Medicine; Ralph M. Waters award internat. achievements in anesthesiology, 1968; decorated knight comdr. Order of Merit, Italy, 1969; named Nat. Italian Am. of Year, 1969; recipient Hon. Alumnus award Tulane Sch. Medicine, 12, Cert. of Honor Library of Congress, 1973; Monte M. Lemann award Civil Service League La., 1975; named hon. senator La. Legislature, 1975, hon. atty. gen. State of La., 1980; recipient William McQuiston award Ill. Soc. Anesthesiology, 1982, NYU Med. Coll. Alumni award, 1982; Disting. Service award So. Med. Assn., 1986. Fellow Am. Soc. Clin. Pharm. and Chemotherapy, Am. Soc. Clin. Pharmacology and Therapeutics, Am. Coll. Anesthesiologists (gov. 1944-50, 56-60); mem. Am. Heart Assn., Assn. Colonic Surgeons, AAAS, Soc. Exptl. Biology and Medicine, So. Soc. Clinical Research, Internat. Anesthesia Research Soc., NRC, Columbia U. Alumni Assn., Am. Hosp. Assn., Assn. Univ. Anesthesiologists (pres. 1955), Assn. Univ. Anesthesiology Departmental Chmn., AMA (mem. council on drugs 1964-72, vice chmn. 1967, chmn. 1967-71), 50 Yr. Club AMA, La. Med. Soc. (50 yr. pin and cert.), Internat. Soc. Comprehensive Medicine, Am. Soc. Anesthesiologists, La. Soc. Anesthesiologists (pres. 1950), New Orleans Soc. Anesthesiology (hon. mem. 1982), So. Soc. Anesthesiologists (pres. 1952-53, cert. of recognition 1975), Acad. Anesthesiology (pres. 1985-86, exec. com., citation of merit 1982), Cuban Soc. Anesthesiologists (hon.), Venezuelan Soc. Anesthesiologists (hon.), So. Med. Assn., Southeastern Surg. Congress, Am. Soc. Regional Anesthesia (hon.), History of Anesthesiology Soc. (hon.), Am. Soc. Regional Anesthesia (Gaston Labat award 1980), History of Medicine Club, Am. Coll. Angiology, Am. Surg. Assn., Mexican Soc. Anesthesiology (hon. pres. 1954), La. Thoracic Soc., Yucatan Soc. Anesthesiology (hon. pres. 1966), Philippines Acad. Anesthesiology, Alton Ochsner Med. Found. Soc. (advisor), John Jay Assocs. Columbia Coll., Samuel Bard Assocs. of Columbia U. Coll. Physicians and Surgeons, Civil Service League La. (dir.), Assn. Wild-life and Fisheries of La., Sigma Xi, Alpha Omega Alpha. Clubs: Thoracophilis Horse Shoe, Century (Phys. and Surg.), Columbia U. Alumni New Orleans; 1834, Emeritus (Tulane U.). Home: 67 N Park Pl New Orleans LA 70124 Office: Charity Hospital New Orleans LA 70140 *Died June 14, 1988.*

ADUBIFA, OLUDOTUN AKINYINKA, research institute executive; b. Oshu, Oyo, Nigeria, June 17, 1940; s. Emmanuel Fakoya and Comfort Bolaji (Osinbajo) A.; m. Ayodeji Oluremi Adamolekun, Feb. 1968; children: Omotola, Omololu, Olubukayome. BS in Chem. Engring., U. Calif., Berkeley, 1964; MS in Chem. Engring., U. Pa., 1966; PhD in Chem. Engring., NYU, 1970. Petroleum engr. Shell Oil Co. B.P., Lagos, Nigeria, 1970-72; lectr. U. Lagos, 1972-73; cons. Nigerian Inst. for Social and Econ. Research, Ibadan, 1973-78, chief cons., dir. dept. bus. and projects cons., 1978-84, acting dir.-gen., 1984-86, cons. dir., 1987—; program advisor UN, N.Y.C., 1986-87; mem. gas pricing com. OPEC, Vienna, Austria, 1975-78; cons. Econ. Commn. for Africa, Addis Ababa, Ethiopia, 1980-82, African Regulatory Ctr. for Tech., Dakar, Senegal, 1983-87, UN Financing System for Sci. and Tech., N.Y.C., 1984-87, Internat. Devel. Research Ctr., Ottawa, Can., 1984-87; chmn. Nat. Adv. Com. on Stats., Nigeria, 1985-86. Contbr. research reports and papers in field. Mem. Joint Planning Bd., Nigeria, 1985-86. Fellow Nigerian Soc. Chem. Engrs. (nat. sec. 1973-76). Methodist. Club: Coconut Country (Lagos) (chmn. 1974-76). Office: Nigerian Inst Social/Econ Research, 11 Kofo Abayomi Rd, Victoria Island, Lagos Nigeria

ADULAVIDHAYA, KAMPHOL, agricultural economist, university administrator; b. Muang, Nakhon Si Thammarat, Thailand, Dec. 26, 1935; s. Yuan and Daeng Adulavidhaya; m. Patcharaprapa Paeratakul, Jan. 6, 1982; children: Pacharaphol, Pichamonch. BS in Agriculture with honors, Kasetsart U., Bangkok, 1959; MS in Agrl. Econs., Oreg. State U., 1962; PhD in Agrl. Econs., Purdue U., 1970. Lectr. dept. agrl. econs. Faculty Econs. and Bus. Adminstrn. Kasetsart U., 1962-63, asst. prof., 1973-79, assoc. prof., 1979—, head dept., 1974-79; dir. Research and Devel. Inst., 1979-86, vice-rector for research and devel. planning, 1986%; cons. Dept. Fisheries, Bangkok, USAID Thailand, Nat. Econ. and Social Devel. Bd.; advisor to Ministry of Agriculture and Coops., Thailand, 1979-80, Ministry of Sci., Tech., Energy, Thailand, 1984-85; chmn. Com. on Research Promotion in Pvt. Univs., Thailand, 1986—; mem. Con. on Thailand Agrl. and Coops. Devel. Planning, 1986—. Author: (textbook) Principle of Agricultural Production Economics, 1981; editor: (textbook) Improving Farm Management Teaching in Asia, 1980. Agrl. Devel. Council fellow, 1960-62, 66-69; research scholar Stanford U., 1973; sr. fellow Food Inst. East-West Ctr., Hawaii, 1974; recipient Outstanding Research award Kasetsart U., 1983. Mem. Agrl. Econs. Assn., Agrl. Econs. soc. of Thailand (pres. 1984—), Internat. Fedn. Agrl. Research Systems for Devel. (sec. Asia chpt. 1985—), Nat. Research Com. in Agriculture and Biology. Office: Kasetsart U, Phaholyothin Rd, 10900 Bangkok Thailand

ADVANI, CHANDERBAN GHANSHAMDAS (G. A. CHANDRU), merchant; b. Hyderabad, India, July 23, 1924; s. Ghanshamdas Gobindux and Rukibai Advant; m. Devi K. Jagtiani, Nov. 30, 1958; children: Meera, Nalin. BA, Sind U., 1947. Mgr. V.H. Advani & Co., Karachi, 1941-48, French Drug Co., Karachi, 1941-48, Paragon Products Co., Karachi, 1941-48; pres. Nephew's Internat. Comml. Corp., Karachi, 1949-51; mgr. Indo French Traders, Pondichary, India, 1951-52, Ms. L. Mohnani, 1953-59; pres. G.A. Chandru, Shokai, Yokohama, Japan, 1959—, Nephew's Internat., Inc., Yokohama, 1985—; cons. in field. Recipient medal Mayor of Bombay, letter of Appreciation Mayor of Yokohama. Mem. Indian Mchts. Assn. (hon. past pres.), Indian C. of C. Japan (hon. joint sec.), Propeller Club U.S.-Yokohama-Tokyo (past bd. govs.), Fgn. Corrs., Yokohama Fgn. Trade Inst., Yokohama Bombay Sister-City Assn. (vice chmn.), Yokohama C. of C. and Industry (dir. internat. div.). Lodges: Masons, Shriners. Home: 502 NewPort Bldg 25-6, Yamashita-cho, Naka-ku, Yokohama 231, Japan

ADVINCULA, MARIETTA MAGSAYSAY, college dean, real estate broker; b. Manila, May 4, 1939; came to U.S., 1961, naturalized, 1978; d. Gregorio and Rosalia (Peralta) Magsaysay; m. Ronaldo C. Advincula, Dec. 4, 1965 (dec.); children: Monica Rose, Ronna Marisse, Melanie Rhoda. BS in Home Econs., U. Philippines, 1959; MS, U. Kans., 1965; cert. in hosp. adminstrn. U. Ill., 1980-81. Dietetic intern Philippine Gen. Hosp., Manila, 1960, U. Minn. Hosp., Mpls., 1962; reviewer/lectr. Bd. Exam. for Dietitians, Philippines, 1967-71; nutritionist YWCA, Philippines, 1971; tng. specialist applied nutrition program in Philippines, UNICEF, 1970-71, instr. food and nutrition Coll. Home Econs., U. Philippines, 1965-71; supr. menu selection West Suburban Hosp., Oak Park, Ill., 1971-72; clin. dietitian/teaching dietitian Weiss Meml. Hosp., Chgo., 1972-73, chief therapeutic dietitian, 1973-76; devel. specialist Malcolm X Coll., City Colls. of Chgo., 1976-78; reviewer/lectr. Northside Traineeship Council/U. Ill., 1974-81; clin. asst. prof. U. Ill. Sch. Associated Med. Scis., Med. Dietetics Curriculum, 1975-79; asst. dir. dept. dietetics U. Ill. Hosp., Chgo., 1976-79; asst. prof. dept. nutrition and med. dietetics U. Ill. Coll. Associated Health Professions, Chgo., 1979-81; asst. dean adult continuing edn. dept. Truman Coll., City Colls. Chgo., 1981—, dir. vol. services office, 1987—; cons. food service and nutrition education Intervention, 1979-80; cons., instr. inquiry edn. Augustana Hosp. Sch. Nursing, 1980; preceptor Am. Dietetic Assn. Traineeship, Weiss Hosp., 1973-76, Hosp. and Ednl. Food Service Suprs., 1973-76, Am. Dietetic Assn., U. Ill. Hosp., 1976-77; assoc. Nat. Inst. Edn. Inquiry, 1976-78; coordinator staff devel., continuing edn. seminars Weiss Hosp., 1973-76, U. Ill. Hosp., 1976-79; coordinator interviewing, counseling and med. recording skills workshop Am. Dietetic Assn., 1979-81; lectr. dept. nutrition and med. dietetics Coll. Associated Health Profs., U. Ill., 1979-80; cons. nutrition program Mayor's Office Sr. Citizen and the Handicapped, Chgo. City Wide Coll., 1981, Nutrition Edn. Tng. Program, Ctr. Urban Program, Bd. Edn., Chgo., 1981; founding pres. Lakambini (Filipino) Performing Arts, 1975—; pres.-elect Networking Together, Inc., 1987-88; bd. dirs. Midwest Women's Ctr.; mem. adv. bd. Alderman Schiller's Social Service Com. Author videotape program: Sociocultural Aspect of Food Behavior Slide, 1981; chmn. revision com. Manual of Clinical Dietetics, 1981; author: Nutrition of Children, Mothers, and the Aged, 1973. Editor: The Home Economist, 1968-70. Contbr. articles to profl. jours. Mem. Arts and Humanities Task Force; organizer, liaison Filipino Community of OLM Parish, 1979-85; chmn. Ill. Minority Women's Caucus, 1986-88; bd. mem. Mother's Club, Our Lady of Mercy Sch., 1980-82; treas. Eugene Civic Neighborhood Assn., 1982-83, v.p., 1981-82; mem. sch. bd. Our Lady of Mercy Sch., 1982-85, pres., 1983-85; mem. Archdiocesan Pastoral Council, 1984—; chmn. Task Force on Consolidation and Expansion, 1986; mem. adv. bd. Assn. Chinese from Indochina., exec. bd. Filipino Am. Council of Chgo., U. Philippines scholar, 1955-59; named Most Outstanding New Citizen, Nutrition Care Adminstrn., Met. Chgo. Citizenship Council, 1979, Most Active Sponsor, 1987-88; recipient Certs. of Recognition, Filipino Spiritual Community Action, Philippines Week, 1983, Truman Coll. Student Govt., 1984-86; named Most Outstanding Filipino in the Midwest in the Field of Edn., Cavite Assn. Am., 1987; recipient Disting. Women's award Women's Network to Re-elect Mayor Harold Washington, Outstanding award in Field of Edn. Networking Together, Inc., 1987. Mem. Am. Assn. Philippines Dietitians (chmn. 1985-87), Am. Dietetic Assn., Ill. Adult and Continuing Educators, Ill. Dietetic Assn., Soc. Nutrition Edn., Women in Mgmt., Chgo. Nutrition Assn., Food and Instn. Systems Mgmt. Edn. Council, Filipino Am. Women's Network, Philippine Educators Assn., Chgo. Dietetic Assn., Ill. Consultation Ethnicity in., Womens' Coalition on Ethnicity, Nutrition Today, Ill. Council Women's Programs, Am. Assn. Diabetes Educators, Nat. Assn. Female Execs., Cons. Dietitians in Health Care Facilities, Asian/Pacific Womens' Network, Northside Realty Bd., Minority Women's Caucus, Phi Kappa Phi. Roman Catholic. Avocations: sewing, gardening, cooking, reading, swimming. Home: 5021 N Monticello Chicago IL 60625 Office: Truman Coll 1145 W Wilson St Chicago IL 60640

ADYASA, SILVERIUS JOHANES BAMBANG, physician; b. Purworejo, Jawa Tengah, Indonesia, July 2, 1938; s. Jusup and Mari Mulyati; married; children: Stanislaus, Ignatius, Katarina, Fransiskus Xaverius. MD, Gajah Mada U., Yogyakarta, Indonesia, 1968. Diplomate Indonesian Bd. Medicine. Chief health office, dir. pub. hosp. Govt. Indonesia, Soe, 1969-71; chief Tb erradication programme Govt. Indonesia, Kupang, 1971-73; dr. Govt. Indonesia Mil. Hosp., Kupang, 1973-76, Purwokerto, 1976-77; chief internal, psychiatry dept. Mil. Hosp., Purwokerto, 1982-87, comdr. health detasement, 1987—; chief Govt. Indonesia Mil. Hosp., Tegal, 1977-82, supr. active case funding Tb control, 1979-80; comdr. health security Health and Mil. Resort Command, Dili, Indonesia, 1978-79. Served as mayor Dept. Health Govt. Indonesia, 1969—. Named Seroja, Nusa Tenggara Timur, 1979. Mem. Persatuan Karya Dharma Kesehatan Indonesia Subwilayah Purwokerto (chief 1987—), Persatuan Renang Seluruh Indonesia Cabang Banyumas (health sect. 1985—), Indonesian Med. Assn. in Banyumas (med. law sect. 1985—). Home: Jalan Beringin Blok D1 234/235, Purwokerto Jawa-Tengah 53146, Indonesia

AEGIDIUS, CARL CHRISTIAN, business machinery company executive; b. Copenhagen, Jan. 1, 1944; s. Holger and Ingeborg (Aegidius) Poulsen; m. Janne Ulrich. MS in Econs. and Ops. Research, U. Copenhagen, 1968. Various positions IBM Denmark, Copenhagen, 1969—; mgr. bus. devel. European hdqrs. IBM Corp., Paris, 1980-81; dir. adminstrn. IBM Denmark, Paris, 1981-83; dir. mktg. IBM Denmark, Copenhagen, 1984—. Author: Patient-strommens effektivisering, 1967. Mem. Personal Computer Soc. Denmark (bd. dirs. 1985-87). Office: IBM, Nymollevej 91, 2800 Lyngby Denmark

AEH, RICHARD KENT, telecommunications executive, organization effectiveness consultant; b. Jackson, Ohio, Aug. 3, 1939; s. Richard Clayton and Julia (Bryan) A.; m. Sandra Leigh Magruder, June 28, 1969; children: Jennifer Kristin, Allison Leslie, Meridith Courtney. B.S. in Bus. Adminstrn., Ohio State U., 1966. Dist. mgr. info. mgmt. AT&T Communications, Cin., 1966—; chair adv. council minority programs U. Cin., 1987—; mem. adv. council Miami U. Sch. Applied Sci., Oxford, Ohio, 1982-85. Vol. mgmt. cons. Community Chest, Cin., 1979—; trustee Housing for Older Ams., 1984-87, Better Housing League, Cin., 1982-83, Lower River Nursing Assn., Cin., 1980-83; mem. Citizens Adv. Com. on Cable TV, Cin., 1979. Served with U.S. Army, 1959-62. Recipient Community Service award Community Chest and United Appeal, 1985. Mem. Assn. for Systems Mgmt. (chpt. v.p. 1984-85, chpt. pres. 1985—, mem. internat. pub. policy com. 1985—). Republican. Episcopalian. Avocations: running, camping. Home: 7059 Royalgreen Dr Cincinnati OH 45244 Office: AT&T Communications 221 E 4th St Atrium II Cincinnati OH 45202

AFANASIYEV, GEORGIY DMITRIYEVICH, geologist; b. Novorossiysk, USSR, Mar. 17, 1906. Student Leningrad State U. Research worker Inst. Petrology, 1930; sr. sci. assoc. Inst. Geol. Scis. U.S.S.R. Acad. Scis., 1937-56, head dept. gen. petrography Inst. Geology of Ore deposits, Petrography, Mineralogy and Geochemistry, 1950, sr. sci. assoc., 1956—, sci. sec. dept. geol. and geog. scis., 1948-53, dep. chief sci. sec., 1958-78, asst. to chief editor procs. Geol. Series, 1954-59, chief editor, 1969-76; v.p. Com. for Absolute Dating of Geol. Formations, 1962-63, pres., 1963—; pres. Petrographic com., 1962—. Decorated Order of Lenin, Order of Red Banner of Labour, Badge of Honour, Order of Patriotic War. Communist. Office: USSR Acad of Sci, 14 Leninsky Prospekt, Moscow USSR *

AFANASIYEV, SERGEY ALEKSANDROVICH, Soviet government official; b. Novorossiysk, Krasnodar Territory, Aug. 30, 1918. Ed. Bauman Tech. Inst., Moscow. Engr., Ministry of Armaments, 1941-46, dep. head, 1946-53; head Technol. Bd., USSR Ministry of Def. Industries, 1953-57; dep. chmn. Leningrad Council of Nat. Economy, 1958-61, chmn. R.S.F.S.R., dep. chmn. Council of Ministers, 1961-65; USSR Minister of Gen. Machine Bldg., 1965-87; mem. Cen. State com. CPSU, 1961—; dep. to USSR Supreme Soviet, 1962—. Recipient USSR State prize, Order of Lenin (4), others. Address: USSR Supreme Soviet, Moscow USSR *

AFEISUME, IRIABEKHAI SAMUEL, civil engineer; b. Otuo, Nigeria, June 6, 1954; s. Dickson Afeisume and Bamidele (Ayeni) Okugbe; m. Ohita Blessing, July 21, 1984; children: Ohiogbauan, Ehihumeme. BSc in Civil Engring., U. Lagos, Nigeria, 1977; MSc in Water Resources, U. Newcastle Upon Tyne, Eng., 1981. Engr. Nat. Youth Service Corp., Ibadan, Nigeria, 1977-78; engr. grade II Bendel State Water Bd., Benin City, Nigeria, 1978-79, engr. grade I, 1979-81, sr. engr., 1981-83, area mgr., 1983-86; chief engr. Bendel State Pub. Utilities Bd., Benin City, Nigeria, 1987-88, dep. gen. mgr., 1988—. Contbr. articles on engring. to profl. jours. Mem. Nigerian Soc. Engrs. (protocol officer 1979-80), Instn. Water and Environ. Mgmt., Instn. Civil Engrs., Council Registered Engrs Nigeria, Engring Council U.K. Home: 264 Upper Mission Rd, PO Box 1945, Benin City Nigeria Office: Bendel State Pub Utilities Bd, Sapele Rd, Benin City PMB 1146, Nigeria

AFFAN, ALI OSMAN, agricultural company executive, agricultural development consultant; b. Medani, Gezira, Sudan, Jan. 1, 1934; s. Osman Affan Mohamed and Fatma Ahmed Dawood; m. Afaf Ahmed Abdel Ber, July 23, 1963; children—Mayada, Amjad, Ashraf, Howayda. Diploma in Gen. Agr., U. Khartoum, Sudan, 1957, M.Sc. in Agrl. Engring., 1960. Mng. dir. Affan Agrl. Co., Khartoum, 1960-69, 1973-79, 1981-87; state minister agr., natural resources (Sudan), 1987—; dep. mng. dir. and chief engr. Girba Agrl. Project, Sudan, 1969-71; gen. mgr. Nat. Agr. Orgn., Khartoum, 1972-73; farm power expert FAO, UN, Tripoli, Libya, 1979-81; cons. Arab Sugar Fed., Khartoum, 1978—, Gulf Group, Geneve, Switzerland, 1983-84, Harrington Mfg. Co., Lewiston, N.C., 1975-76; mem. Tech. com. for cotton mechanization, Rahad, Sudan, 1978-79; dir. feasibility study on farm mechanization in the Gezira, 1976. Mem. The First Nat. Econ. Conf., Khartoum, 1981; mem. high polit. council UMMA Nat. Party, Khartoum, 1985. Fellow The Econ. Devel. Inst. of the World Bank in Agro Indsl. Projects; mem. Sudanese Soc. Agrl. Engrs., Sudan-U.S. Bus. Council. Moslem. Avocation: photography. Office: Affan Agrl Co, PO Box 1719, Khartoum Sudan

AFFATATO, JOSEPH FRANK, marketing executive; b. Bklyn., June 26, 1952; s. Joseph and Anna (Russo) A.; m. Linda Marie Borodich, Nov. 4, 1972. Student NYU Sch. Engring., 1969, Poly. Inst. Bklyn., 1970-72, Columbia U., 1973-74. Engr., IBM Corp., N.Y.C., 1973-76; regional tech. mgr. Memorex Corp., Santa Clara, Calif., 1976-79; OEM system mgr. Hazeltine Corp., Commack, N.Y., 1980-82; mktg. support mgr. Corvus Systems, San Jose, Calif., 1982-83; mktg. mgr. Gen. Optronics, Edison, N.J., 1983-85; v.p. Data Retention Labs., N.Y.C., 1979-80; pres. Synergetic Systems, S.I., 1982-88; v.p., sr. cons. Integrated Optical Systems, Alexandria, Va., 1984-87. Mem. Republican Presdl. Task Force, Washington, 1984-86, Republican Senatorial Club, Nat. Senatorial Congl. Com., 1985-86. ROTC scholar, 1970; U.S. Naval Res. Officers Assn. scholar, 1970; NYU Sch. Engring. grantee, 1969. Mem. N.Y. Acad. Sci., Am. Phys. Soc., Optical Soc. Am., AAAS. Roman Catholic. Lodge: Lions. Home: 630 Ramona Ave Staten Island NY 10309 Office: PO Box 1235 GPO Staten Island NY 10301

AFFATICATI, GIUSEPPE EUGENIO, telecommunications, instrumentation engineer; b. Cortemaggiore, Piacenza, Italy, July 25, 1932; s. Paolo Giovanni and Maria Anna (Sozzi) A.; Perito Industriale, Istituto Tecnico G Marconi, Piacenza, 1955. With AGIP, 1958—, instrumentation project engr. engring. dept., Gela, Italy, 1961-79, telecommunications, instrumentation project engr. Milan, Italy, 1979—; cons. engring. Served to lt., arty. Italian Army, 1956-57. Roman Catholic. Home: 7 Via Manfredi, Picenza 29100 Italy Office: AGIP Name Ltd, Milanofiori C2, Assago 20090, Italy

AFNAN, ALI-MOHAMMAD MASOUD, obstetrician, gynecologist; b. Gondar, Ethiopia, Sept. 24, 1957; arrived in Eng., 1959; s. Abbas and Shomais (Alai) A. Grad., Bishop's Stortford Coll., Eng., 1975; MB, BS, U. London, 1980. Sr. house officer dept. ob-gyn Hammersmith Hosp., London, 1981-83, research fellow, 1983-85; registar dept. ob-gyn Royal Free Hosp., London, 1985-88; sr. registrar dept. ob-gyn St. Helier Hosp., Carshalton Surrey, 1988—. Contbr. articles to profl. jours. Dir. Patient Adv. Bd., London, 1987—, London Med., 1988. Mem. Royal Coll. Ob-Gyn. Mem. Bahai Faith. Office: St Helier Hosp, Carshalton Surrey England

AFRAH, HUSSEIN KULMIE, first deputy prime minister of Somalia, army officer; b. Margeh, 1920; ed. Italian Secondary Sch., Mogadishu, Italian Officers Acad., Rome. Shopkeeper, until 1943; joined Police Force, 1945; instr. and translator Police Tng. Sch. Mogadishu; a.d.c. to former Pres. Osman, 1960; mem. Supreme Revolutionary Council, 1970-76, v.p., 1973-76, chmn. econ. com., 1973, sec. of state for interior, 1970-74; dep. head of state and mem. polit. bur. Somali Socialist Revolutionary Party, 1976—, presdl. adviser on govt. affairs, 1980-84; exec. inspector for econ. affairs, 1988—. Address: Somali Socialist Revolutionary, Party Hdqrs, Mogadishu Somalia *

AFRIDI, MOHAMMAD ALAM KHAN, physician, educator, hospital administrator; b. Peshawar, Pakistan, July 9, 1930; s. Ghufran Khan Afridi and Khewagara Ghufran; m. Aisha Alam Afridi; children: Shamim Alam, Salma Alam, Saima Alam, Arif Alam, Nasim Alam. MBBS, K.E. Med. Coll., Lahore, Pakistan, 1952; DLO, London U., 1957; FRCS, Edinburgh Royal Coll. Surgeons, Scotland, 1964. House surgeon Mayo Hosp., Lahare, 1953, Whipps Cross Hosp., London, 1957; registrar, sr. registrar, cons. various hosps. UK, 1964; assoc. prof. Khyber Med. Coll., Peshawar, Pakistan, 1966; adminstr. Khyber Hosp., Peshawar, 1988; vis. surgeon Khyber Hosp., 1966—. Author: Diseases of Ear, Nose & Throat, 1984, Management of F.B. in Larynx & Tracheo-Bronchial-Tree in Children, Ca. Upper Alimentary Tract in Adolescence & its Relation to Nutrition; co-author and author of prof. jours. Home: 37 Jamaluddin Afghani Rd, Univ Town, Peshawar Pakistan

AFSHAR, AMIR ASLAN, former Iranian government official; b. Tehran, Iran, Nov. 21, 1922; s. Amir Massoud and Amir Banou A.; D.Polit.Sci., U. Vienna, 1943; H.H.D., U. Utah, 1971; m. Camilla Saed, Feb. 19, 1950; children—Fatima, Mohammad. Joined Iranian Fgn. Service, 1948; service in Netherlands; civil aide to Shah, 1957-79; dep. of Parliament, 1956-60; ambassador to Austria; chmn. bd. govs. Internat. Atomic Energy Agy., Vienna, 1967-69; ambassador to U.S., 1969-73, to Mex., 1970-73, to Fed. Republic Ger., 1973-77; grand master of ceremonies of The Shah, 1977-79; del. UN gen assemblies, 1957, 58, 60, head 15 other Iranian dels. to internat. meetings. Decorated Order Homayoun 1st and 2d class, Order Taj 3d, 4th and 5th class, medal of Farhang 2d class, Medal of Pas 1st class, Commemorative medal, Coronation medal, 2500 Ann. Founding Persian Empire medal, Fifty Years Pahlavi Dynasty medal; also 20 fgn. 1st class decorations; Eisenhower exchange fellow, U.S., 1955-56. Author: (in German) The Possibilities of the Development and Expansion of the Iranian Economy; (in Farsi) The Fall of the Third Reich, Iran's Participation in International Organization, God Created the World, The Dutch Built Holland; (in English) Report on America; German Law and Constitution of the Third Reich; also studies in German on German law. Home: 38 Promenade des Anglais, F-0600 Nice France

AF TROLLE, ULF, industrialist, educator, researcher; b. Burlöf, Sweden, Aug. 18, 1919; m. Gunilla Elisabet Hörstadius, 1956; children—Cecilia Elisabet, Nils Rikard; m. Marika Elisabeth af Trolle, Nov. 2, 1977; 1 dau., Kristina Marika. Ekon lic, Stockholm Grad. Sch. Bus. and Econs., 1947; Dr. Econs (hon.) Handelshögskolan, Gothenbürg, Sweden, 1965, Chulalongkorn U., Thailand, 1973. Prof., dean Handelshö gskolan; Gothenburg, 1951-68; dir. various internat. industries, 1945—. Author numerous books including Strategy for New Welfare Efficient Directorship, Torsten Kreuger-Director (A study in moral and law), Industrial Diseses, medicine and cure Part 1 Individual Disease, Part 2 General Diseases, 1945—. Mem. various govtl. coms., 1949—. Decorated Knight of North Star, Comdr. of Wasa (Sweden); Commdr. Lion of Finland; Kings' Gold medal, 1980; recipient John Hanson award for excellence in Pub. service Am. Swedish Cultural Found., 1977. Avocations: gardening; literature. Home: La Vulpillie, 13 100 Le Tholonet France

AFZALI, MANSOUR, mechanical engineering head; b. Masjed-Soleiman, Iran, Dec. 1, 1949; arrived in France, 1973; s. Rajab and Narques Arti A.; m. Dominique Jeanne Louise Vedrines, Sept. 7, 1988; children: Nassime, Darius. MME, U. Tehran, 1973, I.S.M.C.M., Paris, 1975; DEng, U. Paris IV, 1977. Postdoctoral student Northwestern U., Evanston, Ill., 1977-78; asst. prof. U. of Tech. (Arya-Mehr), Isfahan, Iran, 1978-79; assoc. prof., v.p. U. of Tech. (Arya-Mahr), Isfahan, Iran, 1979-80; research engr. CETIM (French Tech. Ctr. Mech. Industry, Senlis, France, 1980-84, head of software devel. group, 1984—. Contbr. articles to profl. jours. Mem. ASME, Societé Francaise Mécanicienne (Paris), Soc. Indsl. and Applied Math. Office: CETIM, 52 Ave Felix Louat, Senlis 60300, France

AGADI, VENKAPPA M., finance executive; b. Lakshmeshwar, Karnataka, India, Apr. 1, 1932; s. Marthandappa B. and Ratnamma Agadi; m. T.N. Kamala, Mar. 5, 1961; children: Harshavardhan, Ravindra. B of Law, Bombay (India) U., 1955, M of Commerce, 1957. Chief acct. Bharitya Vidya Bhavan, Bombay, 1955-60; chief acct., sec. Carrier Corp., Bombay, 1960-61; fin. acct. Pfizer, Bombay, 1961-66; fin. acct. Warner-Hindustan Ltd., Bombay, 1966-68, chief acct., 1969-71, dep. fin. controller, 1971, fin. controller, 1972-74, dir. fin., 1974-78, v.p. fin., 1978—; dir. fin. India region Warner-Lambert, Bombay, 1978-82; bd. dirs. Parke-Davis Ltd., Bombay. Announcer Sch. Broadcasting, 1960-61. Mem. Am. Mgmt. Assn. N.Y., Orgn. Pharm. Producers India (vice chmn. pricing com. 1977—, mem. adminstrn. com. 1984—). Clubs: Bombay Presidency Golf, Otters (Bombay). Lodge: Rotary (pres. Bombay North club 1985-86, dist. sec. 1986-87, dist. chmn. internat. trade and profl. relations com. 1987-88, dist. chmn. constn. and bye-laws com. 1987-88). Home: 201 Moraba Mansion, 405 Linking Rd Khar, Bombay 400052, India

AGA KHAN, HIS HIGHNESS PRINCE KARIM, IV, religious leader, Imam of Ismaili Muslims; b. Geneva, Dec. 13, 1936; s. Prince Aly Salomon and Princess Joan Aly Khan; m. Sarah Frances Croker Poole , 1969; children—Zahra, Rahim, Hussein. Student Le Rosey, Switzerland; B.A. with honors, Harvard U.; LL.D. (hon.), Peshawar U., 1967, U. Sind, 1970, McGill U., 1983. Became Aga Khan on death of grandfather Sir Sultan Mohamed Shah, Aga Khan III, 1957; granted title of His Highness by Queen Elizabeth II, 1957, His Royal Highness by the Shah of Iran, 1959; founder chancellor Aga Khan U., Karachi, Pakistan, 1983—; head Aga Khan Found., Switzerland, 1967—, Aga Khan Fund for Econ. Develop., Geneva, 1984—, Aga Khan Award for Arch., 1976—, Inst. Islamic Studies, 1977—; Decorated comdr. Ordre du Merite Mauritanien, 1960; grand croix Order Nat. de la Cote d'Ivoire, 1965; Ordre Nat. de la Haute-Volta, 1965; Ordre Nat. Malgache, 1966; Ordre du Croissant Vert des Comores, 1966; grand cordon Ordre du Taj Iran, 1967; Nishan-i-Imtiaz, Pakistan, 1970; cavaliere di Gran Croce (Italy), 1977; Nishan-e-Pakistan, 1983, Grand Gordon of Quissam-al Arch Morocco, 1986; recipient Thomas Jefferson award in arch. U. Va., 1984, honor award AIA, 1984. Clubs: Royal Yacht Squadron, Costa Smeralda Yacht (founder, pres.). Avocations: leading owner and breeder of race horses in France, U.K., Ireland; tennis, skiing, yachting. Address: Aiglemont, 60270 Gouviex France

AGA KHAN, SADRUDDIN (PRINCE), former UN official, writer; b. Paris, Jan. 17, 1933; s. Sultan Mohammed and Andree Josephine (Carron) Aga Khan; B.A., Harvard U., 1954; m. Nina Sheila Dyer, 1957; m. Catherine Sursock. Cons. for Afro-Asian projects UNESCO, 1958, spl. cons. to dir.-gen., 1961; head mission, adv. UN High Commn. Refugees, 1959-60; exec. sec. Internat. Action Com. Preservation Nubian Monuments, 1961; UN dep. high commnr. for refugees, 1962-65, high commr., 1965-77; cons. to sec.-gen. UN, 1978; chmn., founding mem. Ind. Com. on Internat. Humanitarian Issues, 1983—. Decorated Papal Order St. Sylvester (Vatican); Order Star Nile (Sudan); Order Homayoun 1st class (Iran); comdr.'s cross with star Order Merit (Poland); comdr. Legion of Honor (France); recipient UN Human Rights award, 1978; Dag Hammarskjö ld medal German UN Assn., 1979; co-recipient Olympia prize Alexander Onassis Found., 1982. Mem. Harvard Islamic Assn. (founder 1951, sec. 1952), Council Islamic Affairs (pres. 1960), Inst. Differing Civilizations, Groupe de Bellerive (a founder 1977, pres. 1977), World Wildlife Fund, Consortium Costa Smeralda (chmn.). Author: International Protection of Refugees, 1976; pub. Paris Rev. Home: Château de Bellerive, 1245 Collogne-Bellerive, Geneva Switzerland *

AGARWAL, ASHOK KUMAR, chemical engineer, researcher; b. Firozabad, India, Aug. 14, 1950; came to U.S., 1975, naturalized, 1983; s. Satyanarain and Shakuntla Devi (Garg) A.; m. Neena Garg, Dec. 28, 1981. B.Tech. in Chem. Engring., Indian Inst. of Tech., Kanpur, 1971, M. Tech. in Chem. Engring., 1974; Ph.D. in Chem. Engring., W.Va. U., 1978. Project engr. Indian Cons. Bur., New Delhi, 1974; research assoc. W.Va. U., Morgantown, 1978; sr. research chem. engr. Monsanto Research Corp., Miamisburg, Ohio, 1978-84; contract mgr. Monsanto Co., Dayton, Ohio, 1984-85; project supr., Monsanto Agrl. Co., Dayton, 1985—. Contbr. articles to sci. jours. Recipient Gold Medal Agarwal Inter Coll., 1966, Shalimar Gold medal Indian Pulp and Paper Tech. Assn., 1974. Mem. Am. Inst. Chem. Engrs. (profl. devel. recognition cert.). Mem. editorial bd. Energy Progress jour., 1981—. Office: Monsanto Agrl Co 1515 Nicholas Rd Dayton OH 45418

AGARWAL, MANJUL KUMAR, health care and research adminstr.; b. Najibabad, India, Mar. 12, 1942; s. Ram Rakshpal and Shakuntala (Gupta) A.; B.Sc., U. Allahabad, 1959, M.Sc., 1962; M.D., U. Paris, 1980; Ph.D., Bryn Mawr Coll., 1967; Sci. asst. CSIR, India, 1962; teaching and research asst. Bryn Mawr Coll., 1963-67; postdoctoral fellow U. N.Y., Buffalo, 1968, Columbia U., 1969; research asso. U. Sheffield (Eng.), 1970; sr. investigator Centre National Recherche Scientifique, Paris, 1970—, dir. Lab. Physio-Hormono-Recepterology, 1979—; organizer internat. workshops. Nato fellow, 1987-88; USPHS grantee, 1967-69. Mem. N.Y. Acad. Scis., AAAS, Endocrine Soc., Biochem. Soc., Immunology Soc., Sigma Xi. Editor: Multiple Molecular Forms of Steroid Hormone Receptors, 1977; Proteases and Hormones, 1979; Antihormones, 1979; Bacterial Endotoxins and Host Response, 1980; Streptozotocin: Fundamentals and Therapy, 1981; Hormone Antagonists, 1982; Principles of Recepterology, 1983; Immunopharmacology of Endotoxicosis, 1984; Adrenal Steroid Antagonism, 1984; Receptor Mediated Antisteroid Action, 1987; contbr. over 100 articles to profl. jours. Office: U Paris VI CNRS, 15 rue de l'Ecole de Medecine, 75270 Paris 06 France

AGBETTOR, EMMANUEL OFOE, engineer; b. Ghana, Nov. 5, 1927; s. Isaac Tetteh and Agnes Doe (Bannerman) A.; m. Hilda Alba Pratt, 1960 (dec.); m. 2d Doris Ocansey, 1970; children—Eva, Vincent, Eunice, Isaac, Emmanuel, Deborah, Michella. Student U. Coll. Gold Coast, Accra, Ghana, 1948-50; B.S. in Engring., U. London, 1953; postgrad. Manchester U. (Eng.), 1953-54, Tech. U. Copenhagen, 1954-55. With Shell Co. of West Africa, Accra, Lagos, Kano, Freetown, 1956-67; chief engr. Shell Ghana Ltd., 1965-67; mng. dir. ACME Engring. & Constrn. Co., road contractors, Accra, 1967-71; chief cons. Engring. & Indsl. Cons., Accra, 1972—; chmn. Acme Fin. & Investment Trust Ltd., Accra; dir. Ballast Nedam (Ghana) Ltd., Ghana Internat. Devel. Co., Eurometal Works Ltd., Ada Rural Bank, Paramount Ins. Co.; chmn. tech. com. investigation into Electricity Corp. of Ghana, 1980, coordinator for early implementation tech. com. report, 1981. Candidate for Nat. Assembly Ghana, 1969; bd. dirs. Ada Secondary Sch. (Ghana), 1973-79, Ghana Investment Centre, 1985—; chmn. Ada Citizens Congress, 1980—, mem. nat. energy bd., 1985—. Danish Govt. fellow, 1954-55. Fellow Ghana Inst. Engrs.; mem. Brit. Instn. Elec. Engrs., Brit. Inst. Mech. Engrs., Boston Soc. Civil Engrs., AFIT Nationwide Bldg. Soc. Presbyterian. Clubs: Achimota Golf, Accra-Tema Yacht. Lodges: Academic, Unity, Research (Accra); Ada (primus). Office: Acme Fin & Investment Trust Ltd, Investment House, PO Box 2547, Accra Ghana

AGER, ERIC EDUARD, solicitor; b. Kristianstad, Sweden, Sept. 9, 1940; s. A. Bertil and Kerstin H. (Persson) A.; m. Dagmar Fornander, Sept. 18, 1965 (div. 1984); children: Helena, Henrik. LLB, Stockholm U., 1966. Ct. clk. City Ct., Skovde, 1966-68; solicitor/assoc. Advokatfirman Lagerlof, Stockholm, 1968-75, ptnr., 1975-82; solicitor/ptnr. Advokatfirman Cederquist, Stockholm, 1982—; mng. dir. Westinghouse Energy Systems Inc. (USA) Filial; chmn., dir. J I Case Sweden AB, AB Starla-Werken, Backstroms Repro AB, Yashica Svenska AB, Grey Svenska AB, Spektrum-Butikerna AB, Stockholms Stads Brandförsäkringskontor, Scholl (Sverige) AB, Riksbilar AB-Avis Licensee, Okobank Sverige, Tenneco Transicol AB; Mem. econ. adv. bd. to catholic bishop of Sweden. Mem. Swedish Bar Assn., ABA, Club: Rotary (treas. 1976—) (Stockholm, Sweden), Drottningholm Golf. Home: Moravagen 16, S-16142 Bromma Stockholm 42, Sweden Office: Advokatfirman Cederquist, Sveavagen 17, S111 57 Stockholm Sweden

AGGARWAL, ANAND BHUSHAN, publishing executive; b. Lahore, Pakistan, Aug. 2, 1946; s. Pitambar Lal and Lajwanti (Bansal) A.; m. Purnima Bhartia, Feb. 11, 1973; children: Shuchi, Pooja, Garima. BA, Hansraj Coll., Delhi, India, 1965; LLb, U. Delhi, 1967. Ptnr. Pitambar Pub. Co., New Delhi, 1964-72, Bharat Enterprises, Delhi, 1972-82; dir. Plyush Printers Pub. Ltd., New Delhi, 1982; ptnr. Computel Systems and Services, New Delhi, 1982-84; dir. Reliant Microsystems Ltd., New Delhi, 1984—. Contbr. articles to profl. jours. V.p Rajasthan Club, Delhi, 1981. Recipient award for excellence in Printing Indian Govt., 1982. Mem. Indian Reading Assn., Fedn. Indian Pubs. Home: 5 W Patel Nagar, New Delhi 110005, India Office: Pitambar Pub Co, 888 E Park Rd, New Delhi 110005, India

AGGARWAL, OM PARKASH, manufacturing executive; b. Amritsar, India, Mar. 2, 1940; s. Banwari Lal and Kailash Wati (Janki) A.; m. Prabha Aggarwal, Feb. 13, 1966; children: Lalit, Anita. BSc in Mech Engring. with honors, Panjab Engring. Coll., 1963. Indsl. engr. Hindustan Motors, Calcutta, India, 1963-74; mgr. indsl. engring. Goodyear India Ltd., Delhi, 1974-80, mgr. quality assurance, 1980—; advisor Govt. of India, 1977-79. Mem. Inst. Indian Engrs., Indsl. Engrs. Home: House 95, Sector 7A, Faridabad 121006, India Office: Goodyear India Ltd, Mathura Rd, Ballabgarh 121 004, India

AGGEBO, SOREN ANKER, industry federation executive; b. Aarhus, Denmark, Oct. 18, 1928; s. Anker Jens and Esther (Jorgensen) A.; divorced; 1 child, Louise. Student econs., U. Aarhus, 1953. Asst. prof. Sch. Bus. U. Aarhus, 1953-57; various mgmt. positions Danish mfg. cos., 1957-64; dep. dir. Fedn. Danish Industry, Copenhagen, 1964—; examiner Sch. Bus. Adminstrn. U. Copenhagen, 1959—; chmn. Danish Productivity Council, Copenhagen, 1974—. Author several books on mgmt. in Danish corps. Decorated Knight of Dannebrog Queen of Denmark, 1976. Office: Fedn Danish Industry, 18 HC Andersens Blvd, DK-1596 Copenhagen Denmark

AGGERYD, THORSTEN U., dental association administrator; b. Solleftea, Sweden, Feb. 27, 1921; s. David Ji and Hilma S. (Sands) A.; m. Margareta Tandefelt, Oct. 11, 1921 (dec. 1973); children: Marianne, Barbro, Ulf; m. Kari Jansen, May 10, 1931; children: Otto, Anne, Marte. DDS, Royal Dental Soc., Stockholm, Sweden, 1945. Chmn. bd. Praktikertjanst AB, Group Practice, Stockholm, 1966-87, Nordbanken, City Region, Stockholm, Sweden, 1986—, Swecare Found., Stockholm, 1984—; bd. dirs. Swedish Ball-Bearing Competition, Am. Coll. Dentists; cons. in field. Recipient Gold medal Children's Day Orgn., Silver medal City of Paris, Gold medal City of Paris; named Internat. Dentist of Yr. 1985. Mem. Swedish Dental Assn. (pres. 1964-72), Internat. Dental Fedn. (London pres. 1981-83), Fedn. Dentistry Internat. (pres. European region 1971-81); hon. mem. Am. Dental Assn., Danish Dental Assn., Finnish Dental Assn., French Dental Assn., German Dental Assn., Norwegian Dental Assn., Brazilian Dental Assn., Chilean Dental Assn., Acad. Estomatologia Peru, Acad. Dentistry Internat., Knight of Royal Order Wasa. Office: Praktikertjanst Inc, PO Box 1304, 111 83 Stockholm Sweden

AGHA, BABAR, pharmaceutical company executive; b. Multan, Punjab, Pakistan, Dec. 4, 1954; parents Agha Fakhar Hussain and Ifzal Begum; m. Bia Babar Agha, Dec. 29, 1983; 1 child, Taimur. BA, Govt. Coll., Lahore, Pakistan, 1974; LLB, Panjab U., Lahore. Bar: Lahore, 1982. Gen. mgr. Apparel Internat., Karachi, Pakistan, 1977-80; exec. dir. Whitewear Industries Ltd., Lahore, 1980-83; dir. Fafco Ltd., Lahore, 1983-85; exec. dir. Highnoon Labs Ltd., Lahore, 1985—; bd. dirs. Whitewear Industries Ltd., Lahore, Fafco Ltd., Lahore, Atlantic Trading Ltd.; cons. Fast Food Developers Assn., Lahore, 1982—. Mem. Local Council Gulberg, Lahore, 1984. Mem. Liberty Market Traders Assn., Amusement Machine Assn. Pakistan (pres. 1984-85), Lahore High Court Bar Assn. Club: Gymkhana. Home: 7-A C/3 Gulberg III, Lahore-11 Punjab, Pakistan Office: High Noon Labs Ltd, PO Box 3318, Gulberg, Lahore-11 Punjab, Pakistan

AGHA, JALAL, filmmaker, actor; b. Bombay, July 11, 1945; s. Agha Jan Baig and Masoom A.; m. Valerie Agha (div. July, 1972); children: Saleem-Christopher, Vanessa Ann. Diploma in Cinema, Film and TV Inst. of India, Pune, 1966. Sr. ptnr. Maja Mediums, Bombay, 1968-82, Jalal Agha Films, Bombay, 1983; proprietor Vanessa Visions, India. Author: (screenplay) Nirvana, 1975, producer, dir., choreographer, 1982. Spl. Exec. Magistrate City of Bombay, 1977. Recipient Spl. Recommendation Tashkent Film Festival, 1968, Hon. Mention Nat. awards, 1969, Best Actor award Utter Pradesh Film Journalist Assn., 1970, Best Supporting Actor Andhra Pradesh Film Journalist Assn., 1972. Mem. Indian Motion Picture Producers Assn., Indian Documentary Producers Assn., Cine Artists Assn., A.I.A.F.A. Home and Office: 303 Sea Nymph, A B Nair Rd Juhu, Bombay 400 049, India

AGNELLI, GIOVANNI, automotive executive; b. Torino, Italy, Mar. 12, 1921; s. Edoardo and Princess Virginia Bourbon (del Monte) A.; Dr. Laws, U. Torino; m. Princess Marella Caracciolo di Castagneto; children: Edoardo, Margherita. With Fiat Co., 1943—, vice chmn. bd., 1945-66, chmn., 1966—; chmn. Istituto Finanziario Industriale, IFI Internat.; dir. Credito Italiano Mediobanca, Eurafrance, Paris, SKF Goteborg (Sweden); mem. internat. adv. com. Chase Manhattan Bank, N.Y.C., Atlantic adv. council United Technologies Corp., adv. bd. Petrofina. Chmn. Agnelli Found.; mem. exec. com. Trilateral Commn., Paris; mem. Groupe des Présidents des Grandes Entreprises Européennes, Brussels; adv. bd. Bilderberg Meetings, The Hague; vice chmn. Internat. Indsl. Conf. San Francisco; corresponding mem. Moral and Polit. Sci. Acad. Inst. de France. Served with Italian Army, 1941-43. Decorated Cross Mil. Valour. Mem. Italian Stock Cos. Assn. (dir.), Torino Indsl. Assn. (dir.), Italian Mfrs. Assn. (dir., mem. exec. bd.), Internat. Indsl. Conf. San Francisco, Atlantic Inst. Internat. Affairs (gov.), Turin Indsl. Assn., Italian Stock Cos. Assn., Assn. Monetary Union Europe (vice chmn.). Address: Fiat SpA, corso Marconi 10, 10125 Torino Italy

AGNELLI, UMBERTO, automobile manufacturing company executive; b. Lausanne, Switzerland, Nov. 1, 1934; s. Edoardo and Virginia Bourbon del Monte Agnelli; m. Allegra Caracciolo, 1974; three children. Student U. Turin. Pres. Federazione Nazionale Calcio, 1959; pres., mng. dir. Società Assucuratrice Industriale, 1962-71; pres., chmn. Fiat-France, 1965-80; pres. Piaggio & Co., 1965—; mng. dir. Fiat SpA, 1970-76, v.p., 1976-79, 80—, v.p., mng. dir., 1979-80; pres. Fiat Auto SpA, 1980; pres. TEXSID, 1978-80; dir. RIV-SKF, 1962-79; dir. Banco di Roma; v.p., mng. dir. IRI, 1981; v.p., mem. bd. dirs. Fondazione Agnelli; pres. CCMC; mem. Senate (CD), 1976-79; mem. European Adv. Council to ATT. Contbr. articles to profl. publs. Mem. Confederazione Generale dell'Industria Italiana, Chambre Syndicale des Constructeurs d'Automobiles, Allianz Versicherungs AG (adv. com.), Am. Communities Assn., European Communities Assn. Office: Fiat SpA, Corso Marconi 10, Turin Italy

AGNES, BIAGIO, journalist, radio/TV executive; b. Severino/Avellino, Italy, July 25, 1928. Editor various newspapers until 1956; with RAI, 1957—, editor Giornale Radio, editor-in-chief, Rome, vice dir. and co-dir. Telegiornale, dir. gen., Rome, 1982—. Office: RAI-Radiotelevisione Italiana, Via Mazzini 14, I-00195 Rome Italy *

AGNEW, RUDOLPH ION JOSEPH, mining company executive; b. Mar. 12, 1934; s. Rudolph John and Pamela Geraldine (Campbell) A.; m. Whitney Warren, 1980. Ed. pub. schs., Eng. With Consolidated Gold Fields, 1957—; chief exec. officer Amey Roadstone Corp., 1974 78, chmn., 1974-77; group chief exec. Consolidated Gold Fields, London, 1978—, chmn., 1983—. Fellow Game Conservancy. Served with His Majesty's 8th Royal Irish Hussars, 1953-57. Office: Consolidated Gold Fields, 49 Moorgate, London England EC2R 6BQ also: Gold Fields Am 230 Park Ave New York NY 10169 *

AGO, ROBERTO, judge, educator; b. Vigevano, Pavia, Italy, May 26, 1907; s. Pietro and Maria (Marini) A.; LL.D., U. Naples (Italy); Dr. (hon.), Geneva, Nancy, France, Nice, France, Paris, Toulouse, France; m. Luciana Cova, 1936; 5 children. Lectr. internat. law U. Cagliari (Italy), 1930-33, U. Messina (Italy), 1933-34; prof. internat. law U. Catania (Italy), 1934, U. Genoa (Italy), 1935, Milan (Italy) U., 1938, Rome U., from 1956; pres. Italian Soc. Internat. Orgns.; Italian del. ILO Conf., from 1945, to UNESCO, 1949-50, Law of Sea Conf., 1958-60, Vienna Conf. on Diplomatic Relations, 1961; pres. Vienna Conf. Law of Treaties, 1968-69; mem. Com. for drafting European Constn., 1952; chmn. governing bd. ILO, 1954-55, 67-68; mem., former pres. Internat. Law Com. UN, 1957-79; mem. Permanent Ct. Arbitration, from 1957; hon. pres. World Fedn. UN Assns.; judge ad hoc Internat. Ct. Justice, 1959-60, judge, 1979—; pres. curatorium Hague Acad. Internat. Law, Arbitration Tribunal France-Germany, France-U.S.; mem. and pres. numerous other internat. tribunals and conciliation coms. Decorated grand croix Order of Merit (Italy); Order of Merit (W. Ger.); officier Legion d'honneur (France); comdr. Order Brit. Empire. Mem. Inst. de Droit International (v.p.), Accademia Nacionale dei Lincei, Am. Acad. Polit. and Social Scis., Inst. Hellenique Droit International, Societe Royale de Belgique, Indian Soc. Internat. Law (hon.), Am. Soc. Internat. Law (hon.). Author: Teoria del diritto internazionale privato, 1934; Il requisito dell'effettivita dell'occupazione in diritto internazionale, 1934; Règles générales des conflits de lois, 1936; La responsabilité indireötta in diritto internazionale, 1936; Lezioni di diritto internazionale privato, 1939; Le delit international, 1939; Lezioni di diritto internazionale, 1943; Scienza giuridica e diritto internazionale, 1950; Diritto positivo e diritto internazionale, 1956; International Organisations and their Functions in the Field of Internal Activities of States, 1957; Positive Law and International Law, 1957; Il Trattato istitutivo dell'Euratom, 1961; The State and International Organisation, 1963; La responsabilité internationale des Etats, 1963; La qualité de l'Etat pour agir en matière de protection diplomatique des sociétés, 1964; La Nazioni Unite per il diritto internazionale, 1965; La cooperation internationale dans le domaine du droit international public, 1966; La codification du droit international et les problèmes de sa réalisation, 1968; Sur la protection diplomatique des personnes morales, 1969; La fase conclusiva dell'opera di codificazione del diritto internazionale, 1969; Premier, deuxieme, troisieme, quatrieme, cinquieme, sixieme, septieme et huiteme rapport a la C.D.I. sur la responsabilite des Etats, 1969-79; Nazioni Unite: venticinque anni dopo, 1970; Droit des traités a la lumière de la Convention de Vienne, 1971; Caratteri generali della communità internazionale e del suo diritto, 1974-75; Eccezioni non esclusivamente preliminari, 1975; Il pluralismo della communità internazionale alle sue origini, 1977; Pluralism and the Origins of International Community, 1978; The First Internat. Communities in the Mediterranean World, 1982; Studi sulla responsabilità internazionale, 1979-1986; Le droit international dans la conception de Grotius, 1983; Positivism (International Law), 1984; I quaranta anni delle Nazioni Unite, 1986; individual and dissenting opinions in cases before the I.c.y., 1980, 82, 86. Office: care Internat Ct Justice, Peace Palace, 2517 KJ Hague The Netherlands

AGOSTI, GIACOMO FEDERICO MARIA, art historian; b. Milan, Italy, Dec. 19, 1962; s. Gianfranco and Anna Maria (Pallini) Agosti. Master's degree, U. Pisa, Italy, 1985; cert., Scuola Normale Superiore, Pisa, Italy, 1985. Researcher Biennale di Venezia, Venice, Italy, 1986; cultural cons. Comune di Bergado, Bergamo, Italy, 1986-87; lectr. in field. Contbr. articles to profl. jours. Roman Catholic. Office: Scuola Normale Superiore, Pzza dei Cavalieri, 56100 Pisa Tuscany, Italy

AGRAWAL, HARISH CHANDRA, neurobiologist, researcher, educator; b. Allahabad, Uttar Pradesh, India; came to U.S., 1970, naturalized, 1982; s. Shambhu and Rajmani Devi A.; m. Daya Kumari Bhushan, Feb. 6, 1960; children—Sanjay, Sanjeev. B.Sc., Allahabad U., 1957, M.Sc., 1959, Ph.D., 1964. Med. research assoc. Thudichum Psychiat. Lab., Galesburg, Ill., 1964-68; lectr. dept. biochemistry Charing Cross Hosp., London, 1968-70; prof. pediatrics Washington U. Sch. Medicine, St. Louis, 1970—, prof. neurology, 1979—; mem. neurology study sect. NIH, 1979-82. Author: Handbook of Neurochemistry, 1969, Developmental Neurobiology, 1970, Biochemistry of Developing Brain, 1971, Membranes and Receptors, 1974, Proteins of the Nervous System, 1980, Biochemistry of Brain, 1980, Handbook of Neurochemistry, 1984; edit. bd. Neurochem. Research, Critical Revs. in Neurobiology. Jr. research fellow Council Sci. and Indsl. Research, New Delhi, 1960-62, sr. research fellow, 1963-64; Research Career Devel. award Nat. Inst. Neurol. and Communicative Disorders, 1974-79. Mem. Internat. Soc. Neurochemistry, Internat. Brain Research Orgn., Am. Soc. Neurochemistry, Am. Soc. Biol. Chemists, Am. Soc. Physiologists. Soc. for Neurosci. Mem. Internat. Soc. Neurochemistry, Internat. Brain Research Orgn., Am. Soc. Neurochemistry, Am. Soc. Biol. Chemists, Am. Soc. Physiologists., Soc. for Neurosci. Home: 18 Chafford Woods Saint Louis MO

63144 Office: Washington U Dept Pediatrics 400 S Kingshighway Blvd Saint Louis MO 63110

AGRAWAL, SURENDRA PRASAD, information scientist, director documentation center; b. Gowan, Budaun, India, May 23, 1929; s. Janki Prasad and Kamla Devi. BA, Agra U., India, 1952; cert. library sci., Aligarh Muslim U., 1952, MA Prev., 1954; postgrad. in French, Sch. Fgn. Langs., Govt. of India, New Delhi, 1966-68. Sci. tchr. Dist. Bd., Higher Secondary Sch., Gabhana, Aligarh, 1951-52; hon. lectr. in library sci. Aligarh Muslim U., 1952-54; librarian Cen. Secretariat Library, 1954-57, 60-64, 68-70; librarian, Hindi Library Dept. Edn., Ministry of Human Resources Devel., New Delhi, 1957-60; with Indian Nat. Commn. for Cooperation with UNESCO, New Delhi, 1964-68; documentation officer, UNESCO div. Dept. Edn. Ministry of Human Resource Devel., 1970-72; dep. dir. documentation Indian Council Social Sci.Research, New Delhi, 1972-77, div. head, 1977-79; dir. Nat. Social Sci. Documentation Ctr., New Delhi, 1979-88; exec. dir. Shri Ramayan Vidyspeeth, New Delhi, 1972-80; pres. Shiksha Sansthan, New Delhi, 1972—. Author: (with Md Zubair) Pustak Sankhya Praveshikya, 1954, Education for International Understanding, 1964, (with A.Biswas) Indian Educational Documents since Independence, 1971, (with J.C. Aggarwal) Children's Literature in Hindi since Independence, 1972, Mohandas Karamchand Gandhi: A Bibliography, 1974, (with J.C. Aggarwal) Role of UNESCO in Education, 1981, (with A.Biswas) Development of Edcation in India, 1986, Social Science Information and Dcumentation, 1986, Library and Information Services in India, 1987, (with J.C. Aggarwal) Our Survival, Nehru on Social Issues, Unesco and Social Sciences, 1988; gen. editor Indian Education Index, 1947-78; assoc. editor Senani, 1940-47; editor Current Administration Literature, 1960-64, INC Current Awareness Service, 1970-72, INC Newsletter, 1970-72, Shree Hari Katha, 1975—; mem. editorial bd. Indian Council Social Sci. Research Newsletter, 1977—, Indian Library Assn. Bull., 1981-83; contbr. articles to profl. jours. Mem. Ramayan Sammalen (bd. dirs.), Indian Inst. Edn., Indian Standards Instn. (documentation and info., library sci. com.), Indian Council World Affairs (library com.), Indian Assn. Spl. Libraries and Info. Ctr., Soc. Info. Sci., Govt. India Libraries Assn., Inst. Peace Research and Action, New Delhi, Info. Ctr. Devel. Policy Modelling, Pune, IFIA Round Table on Research in Reading, Bratislava (exec. com.), Asia Pacific Info. Network in Social Scis., Bangkok (vice-chmn.). Home: B12/223, Lodi Colony, New Delhi 110 003, India Office: Indian Assn Social Sci Instns, care Inst Applied Manpower, New Delhi 110 002, India

AGRELL, JEFFREY, musician; b. Mpls., Feb. 25, 1948; s. Robert Leonard and Isabel (Lewis) A.; m. Donna Hyry, July 22, 1972 (div. June 1978); m. Martha Hablitzel, Nov. 10, 1979. BA, St. Olaf Coll., Northfield, Minn., 1970; MMus, U. Wis., 1973; postgrad., Inst. de Hautes Etudes Musicales, Montreux, Switzerland, 1975. Prin. horn Lucerne Symphony, Switzerland, 1975—; composer, arranger works for brass, jazz guitar, songwriter, lyricist. Performances on Swiss TV; horn editor Brass Bulletin mag., 1976—. Served with U.S. Army Bands, 1970-73. Mem. Internat. Horn Soc. (life) (dir. composition 1984—, contbg. editor Horn Call mag. 1980—), Swiss Composer's Soc., Boston Computer Soc. Home: Gibraltarstrasse 1, CH-6003 Lucerne Switzerland

ÅGREN, HANS ERIK, psychiatrist, educator; b. Gavle, Sweden, Apr. 1, 1945; s. Klas Julius Seved and Sonja Maria (Engstrom)Å.; m. Keiko Funa, July 10, 1976; children— Nina, Nils. B.A., Uppsala U., Sweden, 1969, M.D., 1971, M.D., Ph.D., 1981. Clin. resident dept. psychiatry Univ. Hosp., Uppsala, 1973-79, sr. registrar, 1979-83, assoc. prof. psychiatry, 1983—; Fogarty vis. fellow Nat. Inst. Mental Health, Bethesda, Md., 1984-85; postdoctoral fellow Swedish Med. Research Council, 1982-85, research fellow, 1988—. Recipient Hwasser prize Uppsala Med. Soc., 1982. Mem. Scandinavian Soc. Biol. Psychiatry, European Coll. of Neuropsycho-Pharmacology, Scandinavian Soc. Psychopharmacology, Internat. Assn. Study of Time, Internat. Assn. Study of Asian Medicine, Swedish Psychiatric Assn. Avocations: East Asian medical history; traveling. Home: Ralsvagen 27, S-756 53 Uppsala 52 Sweden Office: University Hosp, Dept Psychiatry, S751 Uppsala 85 Sweden

AGRESTI, MIRIAM MONELL, psychologist; b. N.Y.C., Mar. 23, 1926; d. James McCloud and Marion Henrietta (Zippel) Monell; B.S., Queens Coll., 1947; M.A. in Sci. Edn., Columbia U., 1949; Ph.D. in Clin. Psychology, Yeshiva U., 1976; postgrad. Ackerman Inst. Family Therapy, 1977-81, L.I. Jewish Hosp. Human Sexuality Center; children—Robert, Carol. Psychology intern Creedmoor Psychiat. Center, Queens, N.Y., 1963-64, family therapist, 1964-69; psychologist Northeast Nassau Psychiat. Center, Kings Park, N.Y., 1969-72; adminstrv. dir. Friendship House Day Hosp., Glen Cove, N.Y., 1972-74; psychologist and team leader Central Islip (N.Y.) Psychiat. Center, 1974-75; tchr., coordinator family therapy program Pilgrim Psychiat. Center, West Brentwood, N.Y., 1976-80; pvt. practice psychotherapy, 1977—; co-dir. L.I. Family Inst., 1976-79; cons. family therapy Cath. Charities, 1979, St. Vincent's Hall, 1979, Nassau County Mental Health Assn., 1980; adj. faculty Sch. Edn., C.W. Post Coll., L.I. U., 1972, CUNY, 1978-80, St. John's U., 1983, Hofstra U., 1985—. Exec. dir. movie/videotape Beware the Gaps in Medical Care for Older People (1st prize Am. Film Festival). Lic. psychologist, N.Y. Diplomate Am. Bd. Family Psychology (pres. 1984 85). Fellow Am. Orthopsychiat. Assn., Internat. Council Sex Edn. and Parenthood of Am. U.; mem. Am. Psychol. Assn., N.Y. State Psychol. Assn., Nassau County Psychol. Assn., Suffolk County Psychol. Assn., Am. Assn. for Marriage and Family Therapy (pres. L.I. chpt. 1981-83, approved supr.), Am. Orthopsychiat. Assn., Pi Lambda Theta. Unitarian. Address: 11 Wren Dr Woodbury NY 11797

AGUADO-JOU, RAMON, former United Nations officer; b. Barcelona, Spain, Sept. 5, 1920; s. Luis Aguado Petri and Carmen Jou; m. Helena de Aguado-Jou, Jan. 25, 1946; children—Maria del Carmen, Maria Luisa, Ramon, Alfonso. Chem. Engr., Indsl. Sch., Tarrasa, Spain, 1941; Indsl. Engr., Escuela Superior Ingenieros Industriales, Barcelona, 1947; Ph.D., Universidad Central, Madrid, 1963. Chief prodn. Fosforera Espanola, Madrid, 1948-49; gen. mgr. Fosforera Marroqui, Tetuan, Morocco, 1950-56; mission chief ILO/UN, Central Am., 1961-68, project mgr., Santiago, Chile, 1968-73; br. head Internat. Devel. Orgn., UN, Vienna, 1973-80, ret., 1980; sr. adviser UN Internat. Devel. Orgn./UN Devel. Program, Brasilia, Brazil, 1975-76, prin. cons., Vienna, also N.Y.C., 1981-82; mgmt. cons. E.A. Assocs., San Sebastian, Spain, 1956-60; cons. on several UN missions, Dominican Republic, Ecuador, Zaire, others. Author: Musica en el Trabajo, 1957; also many articles and studies on mgmt. and productivity. Decorated Cruz Caballero Cisneros (Spain). Mem. Colegio Oficial de Ingenieros Industriales (mem. bd. 1950-60). Roman Catholic. Home: Bori y Fontesta 16 3-2, 08021 Barcelona Spain Office: UNIDO, Vienna Internat Ctr, PO Box 3000, 1400 Vienna Austria

AGUAYO, MIGUEL MANCERA, banker; b. Mexico City, Dec. 18, 1932; s. Rafael and Luisa (Aguayo) Mancera; m. Sonia Corcuera, July 18, 1959; children: Miguel, Carlos, Alvaro, Jaime, Gonzalo. Officer Banco de Comercio, Mexico City, 1953-56; economist Govt. of Mex., Mexico City, 1957-58; economist Banco de Mex., Mexico City, 1958-62, adminstr. Fomex div., 1962-67, mgr. internat. affairs, 1967-71, dep. dir., 1971-73, gen. dep. dir., 1973-82, dir. gen., 1982—. Home: Salvador Novo No 94, 04000 Mexico City Mexico Office: Bank of Mexico, Apdo 98 dis, Avada 5e Mayo 2, 06059 Mexico City Mexico

AGUILUZ, ANTONIO J. I., industrial engineer, consultant; b. Mexico City, Dec. 9, 1955; s. Cuauhtemoc and Margarita (Aceves) A. BS, Universidad Iberoamericana, 1979; MS, N.C. State U., 1982. Cert. engr. Mktg. researcher Grupo Cydsa, Mexico City, 1978; project engr. Pepsi-Cola Mexicana, Mexico City, 1983-85; planning engr. Novaquim, Mexico City, 1985-86; planned services engr. Mobil Oil de Mexico S.A. de C.V., Mexico City, 1986—; cons. Aceves, Ornelas, Quevedo y Asociados, Mexico City, 1978—, Feed Flavors Mexicana, Mexico City, 1979—. Co-author project of Diammonium Phosphate plant in Mex., 1979; author: Analysis of Materials Handling and Plant Layout Improvements for A Mexican Automobile Manufacturer, 1981. Vice pres. Grad. Students Assn. N.C. State U., 1980-81; sec. Assn. Latin Am. Students N.C. State U., 1980-81. Scholar Consejo Nacional de Ciencia y Tecnologia, Raleigh, 1980-81. Mem. N.C. State U. Alumni Assn., Universidad Iberoamericana Alumni Assn., Am. Inst. Ind. Engrs. Roman Catholic. Avocations: reading, concerts, theater, chess. Home: Apartado Postal 12-608, Col Narvarte 03020, Mexico City Mexico Office: Mobil Oil de Mexico SA de CV, Mier y Pesado 210, Col del Valle, 03100 Mexico City Mexico

AGUINSKY, RICARDO DANIEL, electronic engineer; b. Buenos Aires, Dec. 26, 1958; s. Elias Lorenzo and Rosa Isabel (Grille) A. Electronics Engr., Univ. Tech. Nacional, Avellaneda, 1984. Serial prodn. technician Norman S.A., Buenos Aires, 1978-80; electronics lab. technician Univ. Technologica Nacional, Avellaneda, 1980-84; engring. sub mgr. Northern Telecom, Buenos Aires, 1983-86; design engr. No. Telecom, Santa Clara, Calif., 1986—. Instr. digital technics Univ. Tech. Nacional, Avellaneda, 1985. Contbr. articles to Revista Telegrafica Electronica, No. Telecom, Am. Nat. Standard Telecommunications. Avocations: travel, camping, windsurfing. Office: 1559 Ellis Ave Milpitas CA 95035

AGUIRRE BIANCHI, RENATO, surgeon; b. Santiago, Chile, Nov. 10, 1943; s. Renato and Lina (Bianchi) Aguirre; m. Sara Aguirre, Nov. 30, 1968; children: Renato, Paula. Bachiller, Internado Nacional Barros Arana, 1960; MD, U. Chile, 1969. Surg. resident Hosp. Salvador, Santiago, 1970-72; chief surgery Hosp. Juan Noe, Arica, Chile, 1973-83, Clinica Mutual, Arica, 1983-86; dir. Clinica Lautaro, Arica, 1982—. Contbr. articles to profl. jours. Recipient David Benavente award Sociedad de Cirujanos de Chile, 1976, Juan Gandulfo award, 1978. Fellow A.C.S., Internat. Cardiovascular Soc., Sociedad de Cirujanos de Chile; mem. Sociedad Medica del Norte (Chile) (founder), N.Y. Acad. Sci., Sociedad Chilena de Cirugia Toraxica y Vascular (founder), Colegio Brasileiro de Cirurgioes (corr.). Club: Arica's Yacht. Office: Clinica Lautaro, Lautaro 487, Arica Chile

AGUIRRE-MILLING, HOMERO, university administrator; b. Nuevo Laredo, Tamaulipas, Mex., July 26, 1951; s. Homero and Elisa-Maria (Milling) A.; m. Maria-Estela Herrera, Aug. 22, 1975; children: Maria-Estela, Homero, Berta-Elisa. BBA, U. Tamaulpas, Nuevo Laredo, 1972; MBA, Tex. A&I U., Laredo, 1977. Pvt. practice bus. cons. Nuevo Laredo, 1972—; dean adminstrv. affairs U. Tamaulipas, 1975-76, dean acad. affairs, 1976-81, pres., 1981-85, pres. sch. bus., 1985—; cons. Com. Para el Desarrollo de Nuevo Laredo A.C., 1986-87. Coordinator spl. com. Com. Para el Desarrollo Indsl. de Nuevo Laredo, 1987; with campaign aux. Partido Revolucionario Instl., Nuevo Laredo, 1986. Recipient spl. award Consejo Internat. de la Buena Vecindad AC, 1987, Camara Jr. de Nuevo Laredo AC, 1981. Mem. Colegio Nacional de Licenciados en Adminstrn. AC (pres. 1979-81, diploma 1984). Baptist. Office: U Autonoma de Tamaulipas, Facultad de Comercio y Adminstrn, Colonia Infonavit, Nuevo Laredo Mexico

AGURCIA EWING, JUAN, businessman, former ambassador; b. Tegucigalpa D.C., Honduras, June 11, 1921; m. Lisette Fasquelle de Agurcia; children—Juan, Ricardo Antonio, Jose Maria, Jorge Arturo. Ed., U. Calif.-Berkeley and Tulane U., 1939-41; bus. adminstrn. degree. Acctg. asst. Rosario Mining Co., N.Y. and Honduras, 1942-45; acctg. mgr. Tex. Petroleum Co., Honduras, 1945-48; adminstr. Hotel Prado, Tegucigalpa, 1949-51; mgr. Constructora Hondureña, S.A., 1951-57; exec. sec. to Pres. of Honduras, 1957-63; mgr. I. Agurcia E. y Hnos, 1963-81; rep. Union Oil Co. Honduras, Calif., 1964-81; mgr., dir. Hoteles de Honduras, S.A. de C.V., 1968-70, pres., 1970-73, dir., 1972-79; pres. Tabacalera Nacional, S.A., 1970-72, dir., 1972-79; comptroller Inversiones Atlantida, S.A., 1975-81; pres. Inversiones Patria, S.A. de C.V., 1975-81; co-founder, pres. Aseguradora Hondureña, S.A., 1954, v.p., 1954-59, exec. dir., sec. adminstrv. council, 1961-81; former ambassador of Honduras to U.S. Washington, until 1987; ind. businessman 1987—. Mem. Nat. Assn. Industry (bd. dirs. 1972-74, pres. 1974-75, bd. dirs., advisor 1974-79), Honduran Council Pvt. Enterprise (bd. dirs. 1974-75, advisor 1979-81). Office: Embassy of Republic of Honduras 4301 Connecticut Ave NW Washington DC 20008

AGURELL, STIG LENNART, pharmacist, research administrator; b. Hogsby, Smaland, Sweden, Oct. 16, 1932; s. Claes L. and Astrid E. (Carlsson) A.; m. A. Birgitta E. Nilsson, June 27, 1957; children—Eva, Lena. Ph.D., Purdue U., 1962; Lic. pharmacist Royal Pharm. Inst.-Stockholm, 1963, Dr.pharm., 1966, D.Sc. h.c., Purdue U., 1985. Asst. prof. Purdue U., West Lafayette, Ind., 1962; from research asst. to asst. prof. Royal Pharm. Inst., Stockholm, 1959-60, 62-69; head drug research and info. Central Mil. Pharmacy, Stockholm, 1969-71, head, 1971-73; asst. dir. research Astra Lakemedel AB, Sodertalje, Sweden, 1974-76, dir. research, 1976-84, pres., 1984—. Author: Cannabinoids, 1984; contbr. articles to profl. jours. Served with Swedish Army, 1953-54. Named Disting. Alumnus, Purdue U., 1983. Mem. Am. Coll. Neuropsychopharmacology, Swedish Acad. Pharm. Scis. (dir. 1973-81), Scheele Award Com. Address: Astra Alab AB, S151 Sodertalje 85 Sweden

AGUZZI-BARBAGLI, DANILO LORENZO, language educator; b. Arezzo, Italy, Aug. 1, 1924; came to U.S., 1950; s. Guglielmo and Marianna (Barbagli) Aguzzi-B. Dottore in Lettere, U. Florence (Italy), 1949; Ph.D., Columbia U., 1959. Instr., asst. U. Chgo., 1959-64; assoc. prof. Tulane U., New Orleans, 1964-71; prof. U. B.C., Vancouver, 1971—; Mem. Fulbright-Hayes final scholarship com., 1970—; adviser on scholarship application Can. Council, 1972-73. Author: Critical Edition of Della Poetica of Francesco Patrizi, 3 vols, 1969, 70, 71, 72, Critical Edition of Francesco Patrizi's Lettere ed opuscoli inediti, 1975; contbr. articles in field to profl. jours. Newberry Library fellow Chgo., 1974; Folger Shakespeare Library fellow Washington, 1975. Fellow Am. Philos. Soc.; mem. Newberry Library Assn., Dante Soc. Am., Italian Honor Soc. (regional rep.), Accademia Petrarca, Medieval Soc. Am., Renaissance Soc. Am., Modern Lang. Assn., AAUP, Am. Assn. Tchrs. Italian. Office: Univ of British Columbia, Vancouver, BC Canada V6T 1W5

AHEER, NASIM AHMAD, government official; b. Khushab, Punjab, Pakistan, Oct. 18, 1936. Chmn. town com., Jauharabad, Pakistan, 1966-72; mem. Dist. of Council Sargodha, Pakistan, 1966-72, Nat. Assembly, Pakistan, 1977, 85; minister edn. Pakistan, 1986-87; formerly with Ministries of Health, Special Edn., Culture, Tourism and Social Welfare and Cmmunications, Pakistan; minister interior Pakistan, 1987—; mem. Pakistan del. to 38th UN Gen. Assembly, 1975. •

AHLBERG, GORAN LARS, publishing executive; b. Stockholm, Mr. 24, 1942; s. Fritiof and Marta (Jonsson) A.; m. Dec. 27, 1967 (div. Apr. 1982); children: Ann-Sofi, Christine; m. Kerstin Ahlberg, May 23, 1987. M.B.A., Stockholm Sch. Econs., 1963, Ph.D., 1968; vis. scholar Grad. Sch. Bus., Stanford U., 1969. Lectr., Swedish Inst. Mgmt., Stockholm, 1966-71; asst. controller Esselte, Stockholm, 1972-74, controller Esselte Studium, 1974-77, mktg. exec., 1977-79; pres. Esselte Forlag, Stockholm, 1979—. Bd. dirs. Book of the Month Club Stockholm, 1979—, Mediplast AB, 1982-87. Mem. Swedish Publishers Assn. (dir. 1980-87). Home: Kapellvagen 22, S13146 Nacka Sweden Office: Esselte Forlag AB, Tryckerigatan 2, S10312 Stockholm Sweden

AHLEFELDT-LAURVIG, COUNT JORGEN WILLIAM, museum curator, farmer; b. Skamstrup, Denmark, Nov. 29, 1924; s. Kai Frederik Sophus and Astrid Ingeborg (Holm) Ahlefeldt-Laurvig; m. Birgit Moller, 1966; 1 child, Christian Benedict. M.A., Mich. State U., 1948. Estate owner, Fogedbygard by Nnestved, 1954-63, Eriksholm, Vippenaod, 1959—; mus. keeper Kobenhavns Bymus, Copenhagen, 1963—; chamberlain to H.M. The Queen of Denmark; dir. various banks and trading cos. Author books on ceramic subjects. Contbr. articles to profl. jours. Mem. Danish Arms and Amour Soc. (pres. 1966—). Address: Eriksholm, DK-4390 Vipperod Denmark

AHLERS, MANFRED HERMANN, educator; b. Lüneburg, Germany, Aug. 26, 1934; arrived in Argentina, 1968; s. Arnold and Dorothea (Wolffram) A.; m. Teresa Pascual, Dec. 29, 1977; children: Christian, Mora. Diploma in Physics, U. Göttingen, Fed. Republic Germany, 1961, Dr. Rer. Nat., 1965. Investigator Mellon Inst., Pitts., 1965-68; investigator, educator Centro Atomico Bariloche Inst. Balseiro, Argentina, 1968—; researcher Max Planck Inst., Düsseldorf, Fed. Republic Germany, 1974-76; vis. prof. U. Leuven (Belgium), 1986, U. Mallorca (Spain), 1987; jefe div. metales, Centro Atomico, 1985. Contbr. articles to profl. jours.; patentee in field. Home and Office: Centro Atomico, 8400 San Carlos de Bariloche, Rio Negro Argentina

AHLGREN, MILDRED CARLSON (MRS. OSCAR ALEXANDER AHLGREN), club woman, lecturer, writer, public relations consultant; b. Chgo.; d. August John and Hilda Sophia (Peterson) Carlson; student Columbia Coll., U. Chgo.; m. Oscar Alexander Ahlgren, June 6, 1923; 1 dau., Adrienne Haeuser. Spl. corr. Hammond (Ind.) Times 1935-52. Pres. Ind. Fedn. Women's Club, 1941-44; dean of dirs., mem. exec. com. Gen. Fedn. Women's Clubs, 1943-44, rec. sec., 1944-47, 2d v.p., 1947-50, 1st v.p., 1950-52, pres., 1952-54; nat. sponsoring com. Allied Youth; nat. adv. com., public relations panel Savs. Bonds, U.S. Treasury; mem. Planning Commn. Ind. State, 1941-43, Personnel Bd., 1943-46; chmn. women's div. Ind. War Fin. Com., 1940-46; chmn. women's com. Ind. War History Commn., 1945-48; mem. Ind. com. George Foster Peabody radio awards; mem. Gov's. Com. of Children and Youth. Chmn. Women's Nat. Com. Savs. Bonds; mem. nat. planning com. White House Conf. on Edn., 1953-54; asst. to dir. U.S. Savs. Bonds Div., Treas. Dept., 1955-57; public relations cons.; observer food gift program FAO Austria, 1953; ruling elder Nat. Presbyn. Ch. Trustee, Ind. State Employes Retirement Fund, 1949-52, Ind. State Tchrs. Colls., 1952-58; bd. dirs. Ind. Inst. Psychiat. Research: trustee Radio Liberty Com.; v.p. All Am. Conf. Nat. co-chmn. Women for Nixon and Lodge, 1960. Recipient Royal Order of Vasa (Sweden), 1954; George Washington medal Freedoms Found., 1954, 70; Hoosier Halo, Hammond Newspaper Guild, 1953; numerous other honors and awards; named Ind. Woman of Yr., Theta Sigma Phi, 1952. Mem. Nat. Fedn. Press Women, Nat. League Am. Penwomen, Bus. and Profl. Women's Am. Legion Aux., Am. Women in Radio and Television, Women in Communications, Scandinavian Found. (hon.), LWV, PEO, Alpha Delta Pi, Phi Beta, Beta Gamma Epsilon. Republican. Presbyterian. Clubs: San Antonio Breakfast; Chautauqua (N.Y.) Woman's; Ind. Harbor (Ind.) Women's (hon.); Ind. Women's Press; Whiting (Ind.) Woman's (hon. life, dir.); Nat. Press (Washington); Lake Hills Country; Am. Newspaper Women's (Washington); Washington. Research on status of women, S.Am., 1950, W.I. and Alaska, 1953, Russia, 1956, 71. Home: Dupont East 1545 18th St NW Washington DC 20036 Office: 1734 N St NW Washington DC 20036

AHLSTEN, STIG AKE GUSTAF, dental surgeon; b. Linkoping, Sweden, Feb. 15, 1913; s. Nils and Hulda (Lundh) A.; m. Ann-Mari Helsinger, Aug. 16, 1941; children—Anders, Gustaf, Olof, Gunnar, Karin. Dental Surgeon, Dental Sch. Stockholm, 1935, Master Examination, 1939. Cert. oral surgery, oral prosthetics, Sweden. Asst. prof. Dental Sch., Stockholm, 1935-39, assoc. prof., 1939-43; cons. dental surgeon St. Gorans Hosp., Stockholm, 1936-46; dental adminstr. Pub. Dental Service, Uppsala, 1943-79; chief dental surgeon, head oral surgery dept. Univ. Hosp., Uppsala, 1944-79; rep. dental surgeon Dental Care Ins., Uppsala, 1973—; master in odontology for med. students Faculty of Medicine, Uppsala U., 1949-80. Editor Jour. Odontological Soc., 1939-56; author 2 books and numerous papers in dentistry. Recipient Medal of Merit, Swedish Red Cross, 1940; decorated Cross of Liberty, Order Finland, 1942; knight comdr. Swedish North Star Order, 1973. Mem. Swedish Dental Fedn. (exec. mem. pub. co. 1982—), Swedish Oral Surgery Assn., Uppsala Med. Soc., Odontological Soc. Stockholm (hon.), Swedish Soc. Dental Adminstrs (hon.). Home: Borgvagen 1, S 75236 Uppsala 36 Sweden Office: Swedish Dental Fedn, Nybrogatan 53, S102 Stockholm 48 Sweden

AHLUVALIA, JASJIT T., management consultant; b. Ajmer, India, Nov. 17, 1938; came to U.S., 1973, naturalized, 1979; s. Tara and Beyant Kaur (Ahluwalia) Singh; m. Jyoti Balbirsingh Ahluwalia, Jan. 19, 1969; children: Taruna, Vineeta. Grad. Brit. Inst. Mgmt., London, 1966; D.S.M., Jamnalal Bajaj Inst. Mgmt. Studies, U. Bombay, 1972; B.S. in Ops. Mgmt., SUNY, Albany, 1977; M.S. in Computer Sci., Fairleigh Dickinson U., 1978. Cert. systems profl. Materials asst. Kaiser Engrs., Jamshedpur, India, 1956-58; adminstr. New Activity Sch., Bombay, 1958-59; chief of cardex Brown & Root, Inc., Bombay, 1959-61; sr. systems analyst Union Carbide India Ltd., Bombay, 1961-73; v.p. mgmt. info. systems Indsl. Acoustics Co., Inc., Bronx, N.Y., 1973—; pres. Data Processing Solutions, Inc., Westwood, N.J. Mem. Assn. Computing Machinery, Computer and Automated Systems Assn. SME, Assn. Systems Mgmt. (cert. systems profl.), Data Processing Mgmt. Assn.

AHMAD, IFTIKHAR, medical educator; b. Jullundher, Pakistan, Mar. 26, 1930; s. Niaz Ud Din and Sakina (Begum) A.; m. Zahida Iftikhar; 4 children. Intermediate Diploma, Govt. Coll., Lahore, Pakistan, 1947; B of Surgery, King Edward Med. Coll., Lahore, 1952. Asst. prof. medicine Nishter Med. Coll., Multan, Pakistan, 1958-65, prof. medicine, 1969-71; prof. medicine Dow Med. Coll., Karachi, Pakistan, 1965-68; med. supt. Nishter Hosp., Multan, 1971; prof. medicine King Edward Med. Coll., Lahore, 1971-77; sec. health Govt. of the Punjab, Lahore, 1977-78; prin., prof. medicine Allama Iqbal Med. Coll., Lahore, 1978-86; spl. duty officer Gen. Admin. and Info. Dept./Health Services Govt. Punjab, Lahore, 1982; prof. medicine, prin. King Edward Med. Coll., Lahore, 1986—. Author, presenter numerous papers in field. Recipient several acad. honors in hygiene and medicine upon graduation from King Edward Med. Coll. Fellow Brit. Royal Coll. Physicians, Pakistan Acad. Med. Scis., Pakistan Coll. Physicians and Surgeons. Home: 319 Rivaz Gardens, Lahore Pakistan Office: Pakistan Med Assn, Garden Rd, PO Box 7287, Karachi 3, Pakistan

AHMAD, JAMAL, endocrinology educator; b. Sultanpur, India, July 31, 1951; s. Fariyad and Kulsoom Khan; m. Shabnam Khan, Dec. 30, 1983; 1 child, Farah. BSc with hons., Aligarh Muslim U., India, 1973, MBBS, 1977, MD in Gen. Medicine, 1983; DM in Endocrinology, Postgrad. Inst. Med. Edn. and Research, Chandigarh, India, 1986. Intern Aligarh Muslim U., 1978-79, housemanship, 1979, clin. registrar, 1980-83, lectr. in medicine, 1983-84, 1987—; sr. resident P.G.I.M.E.R., 1985-86. Contbr. 45 articles to profl. jours. Fellow Am. Coll. Cardiology and Chest Physicians; life mem. Endocrine Soc. India. Home: A-8 Med Coll Campus, Aligarh 202 001, India Office: Aligarh Muslim U J N Med Coll, Dept Medicine, Aligarh 202 001, India

AHMAD, MASRUR, oil company executive; b. Delhi, India, Dec. 12, 1931; s. Munzir and Begum Sarwar A.; children: Maruf, Sadia Muzaffar. BS in Mechanical Engring., U. Lahore, Pakistan, 1951; diploma in mechanical engring. with honors, Loughborough Coll. Tech., Eng., 1954. From engr. field, maintenance, progress and planning to chief Pakistan Petroleum Ltd., Karachi, 1954-66, mgr. ops., 1966-70, tech. mgr., 1970-72, gen. mgr., 1972—; bd. dirs. Pakistan Petroleum Ltd., Karachi. Gov. Nat. Mgmt. Found., Lahore, 1985; bd. dirs. Petroleum Inst. Pakistan, Karachi, 1972. Home: 52/2 Khayaban-E-Shamsheer DHA, Karachi Pakistan Office: Pakistan Petroleum Ltd, 4th Floor PIDC House, Dr Ziauddin Ahmed Rd, Karachi Pakistan

AHMAD, MOHAMMAD, librarian; b. Sirsi, India, Jan. 1, 1939; s. Aijaz Husain and Nihal Fatma; m. Jamal Fatma, Mar. 6, 1970; children: Aijaz Basheer, Sameena Jamal, Ali Sameer. BA, Delhi U., 1965; BLS, Aligarh U., India, 1966. Librarian Indian Council for Africa, New Delhi, 1961-66, United Services Inst., New Delhi, 1967-68; acting dir. Nat. Archives, Lusaka, Zambia, 1968-71, Nat. Library Service, Gaborone, Botswana, 1971-84; mng. dir. Jamal Trading Co. Ltd., Gaborone, Botswana, 1984—, Nata Timber Industries Ltd., Gaborone, 1985—, Jamco Iron & Steel Industries, Gaborone, 1987—. Mem. Botswana Library Assn. Clubs: Notswane (Gaborone); Sun Friend (Gaborone). Home: House 2855 Church Rd, PO Box 493, Gaborone Botswana Office: Jamal Trading Co Ltd, Moapaqe Rd, Gaborone Botswana

AHMAD, NASEER, physician; b. Sulehriankalan, East Punjab, India, Jan. 4, 1937; s. Chaudry Fagir Mohammad and Begum Bibi; m. Riffat Naseer, Apr. 10, 1964; children: Mobashshar, Taugir, Asna. LSMF, Punjab Med. Sch., 1958; MBBS, King Edward Med. Coll., 1976. House physician Bahawal (East Punjab) Victoria Hosp., 1958; practice medicine specializing in gen. practice. Nominated for membership Punjab Assembly, Nat. Assembly., Pakistan Nat. Alliance. Muslim. Office: Naseer Hosp, Tobatek-sing, Punjab Pakistan

AHMAD RITHAUDEEN BIN ISMAIL, Malaysian government official; b. Jan. 24, 1932; LL.B., Nottingham (Eng.) U., 1951; m. Tengku Nor Aini; 5 children. Called to English bar, 1956, Malaysian bar, 1965; magistrate, Ipoh, Malaysia, 1956-58; pres. Session's Ct., 1958-60; dep. public prosecutor and fed. counsel, Kuala Lumpur, 1960-62; state legal adv., sr. fed. counsel, Kota Bharu, Kelantan, 1962-65; practiced law, Kuala Lumpur and Kota Bharu,

1965-70; M.P. for Kota Bharu Hilir, 1969—; dep. minister of def., 1970-73; minister with spl. functions, 1973-74; minister of info., 1974, 1986—, former minister with spl. functions for fgn. affairs; minister of fgn. affairs, 1975-81, 84-86; minister of trade and industry, 1981-84; now minister of def.; mem. council of advisers to Sultan of Kelantan; chmn. Kota Bharu div. and mem. supreme council United Malays Nat. Orgn. Recipient Darjah Paduka Mahkota Kelantan, SPMP (Perlis), SSAP (Pahang), Grand Cross 2d class Order Merit (Fed. Republic Germany), Merit awards Saudi Arabia, Republic Korea. Office: Ministry of Defense, 50602 Kuala Lumpur Malaysia *

AHMAD SHAH IBNI AL-MARHUM SULTAN ABU BAKAR, Sultan of Pahang, Malaysia; b. Pekah, Malaya, Oct. 24, 1930; s. Sultan Abu Bakar; student public adminstrn., Worcester Coll., Oxford (Eng.) U., 1950-53; grad. Royal Mil. Acad., Sandhurst, Eng.; m. Tengku, 1954; 7 children. Tengku Mahkota of Pahang, from 1944; trainee in local govt. Urban Dist. Council, Sidmouth, Devon, Eng., 1950-53; adminstrv. officer Pahang State Secretariat; regent of Pahang, 1964, 65, 69; sultan of Pahang, 1974—; elected Timbalon Yang di-Pertuan Agong, 1975; elected 7th Yangdi Pertuan, 1979; supreme head State of Malaysia, 1979-84. Address: care Malaysian Embassy 2401 Massachusetts Ave NW Washington DC 20008 *

AHMED, AYAZ AHMED, municipal services administrator; b. Cherat, NWFP, Pakistan, July 30, 1934; s. Mohammad Sarwar Khan and Nur Fatima; m. Misbah Ayaz; children: Aliya, Faisal, Ayesha, Umar. BS in Civil Engring., Mil. Coll. Engring., Risalpur, Pakistan, 1960. Registered profl. engr. Cmdr. MES Pakistan Air Force, Rawalpindi-Peshawar, 1973-77; cmdr. engring. group Pakistan Army, Karakrum Highway, 1977-78; cmmdr. engring. group Pakistan Army, Rawalpindi, 1981-82; chief engr. Pakistan Navy, Karachi, 1979-81; mng. dir. Airports Devel. Agy., Karachi, 1982-85, Water & Sanitation Agy., Lahore, Pakistan, 1985—. Recipient Republic medal Pakistan Army, 1956, Sitra-Harb Pakistan Army, 1965, Sitra-Imtiaz Pakistan Army, 1986. Fellow Inst. Engrs. Pakistan; mem. Pakistan Soc. for Pub. Health Engrs. Pakistan, ASCE, Am. Water Works Assn. Islam. Club: Officers (Rawalpindi). Home: House 55 St 3 CMA Colony, Abid Majid Rd, Lahore Cantt Pakistan

AHMED, KHALIL, scientist, educator; b. Lahore, Pakistan, Nov. 30, 1934; came to U.S., 1960, naturalized, 1965; s. Abdul and Ghulam (Sughra) Haq; m. Ritva Helena Veikkamo, June 27, 1969; children: Karim, Rehana. B.S. with honors, Panjab U., Pakistan, 1954, M.S. with honors, 1955; Ph.D., McGill U., Montreal, Can., 1960. Research asso. Wistar Inst., Phila., 1960-63; asst. prof. metabolic research Chgo. Med. Sch., 1963-67; mem. sr. staff Nat. Cancer Inst., Balt., 1967-71; research biochemist, chief toxicology research lab. VA Med. Center, Mpls., 1971—; asso. prof. lab. medicine and pathology U. Minn., Mpls., 1973-77; prof. U. Minn., 1977—; research career scientist VA Med. Research Service, 1978—; mem. pathology study sect. NIH, 1978-81; vis. scientist Lab. of Physiology, Helsinki, Finland, 1962; vis. lectr. Chgo. Med. Sch., 1968-69; mem. pharmacology study sect. NIH, 1988—. Contbr. articles to profl. jours.; bd. consultants: Jour. Urology, 1981—. Named outstanding citizen Met. Chgo. Citizenship Council, 1966. Mem. Am. Soc. Pharm. and Exptl. Therapeutics, AAAS, Am. Soc. Biol. Chemists, Am. Soc. Cell Biology, Am. Soc. Biochemistry and Molecular Biology, Sigma Xi. Office: Mpls VA Med Ctr (151) One Veterans Dr Minneapolis MN 55417

AHMED, MOUDUD, government official, lawyer; b. 1940; m. Hasna Jasimuddin; 2 children. MA in Polit. Sci., Dhaka (Bangladesh) U.; Barrister-at-law, Lincoln's Inn, Eng. Student's leader Dhaka U., 1955-60, Eng., 1971; sec.-gen. Com. for Civil Liberties and Legal Aid, Dhaka, 1974; advisor to pres. Govt. of Bangladesh, 1977-78, minister for telecommunications, 1977-79, dep. prime minister and minister for power and water resources, 1979-80, dep. leader of parliament, 1979-80, minister for communications, 1985-86, minister for industries, 1986—, dep. prime minister, 1986-88, prime minister, 1988—. Contbr. articles to polit. jours. South Asian Inst. of Heidelberg U. fellow, Harvard U. Ctr. for Internat. Affairs fellow. Office: Office of Prime Minister, Dhaka Bangladesh *

AHMED CHAUHDRI, NAZEER, import/export company executive; b. Multan, Pakistan, Apr. 10, 1947; s. Mian Muhammad Boota and Karam Bibi Chauhdri; m. Azra Ahmed, Dec. 10, 1976. BS, U. Punjab, Lahore, Pakistan, 1969. Quality controller CTM Ismail Abad, Multan, 1970-74; prodn. mgr. Galway Textile, Galway, Ireland, 1974-80; chief exec. Top Trend Ltd., Dublin, Ireland, 1980-85; mng. dir. Nazka Ltd., Dublin, 1985—. Mem. Soc. Dyeres and Cohourist. Moslem. Home: 65-B, Gulgasht, Multan Pakistan Office: Nazka Ltd, 1A-2A Bath Rd, Balbriggan, Dublin Ireland

AHN, YOUNGOK, chemical engineer; b. Seoul, Korea, Dec. 29, 1932; s. Kukhyung Ahn and Chunghyun Kim; m. Chunghee, Aug. 16, 1958; children—Hyunsuk, Hyunjin, Hyunduk. Student Seoul Nat. U., 1952-55; B.S., U. Calif.-Berkeley, 1958; M.S., Iowa State U., 1960, Ph.D., 1966. Devel. engr. Union Carbide Corp., Tonawanda, N.Y., 1960-63; research engr. E.I. DuPont de Nemours & Co., Inc., Wilmington, Del., 1965-69; founding mem. Korea Inst. Sci. and Tech., 1969, head polymer lab., 1969-70, also dir. chemistry and chem. engring., 1971-78; exec. cons. for market devel. Korea Pacific Chems. Co. (Dow joint venture), 1977; exec. dir. Cheil Synthetic Textiles Co. of Samsung Group, 1978-82, also sr. advisor to chmn. Samsung Group; pres. Korea Tech. Advancement Corp., Seoul, 1982-87; pres. Olin Far East Ltd. div. Olin Corp., Seoul, 1988—. Decorated Nat. Civil Merit medal, Nat. medal Republic Korea. Mem. Chem. Engring. Inst. (bd. dirs. 1969—), Chem. Soc. (bd. dirs. 1969—), Sigma Xi, Phi Lambda Upsilon. Office: Olin Corp, 80-6 Soosong-Dong, Suktan Bldg, Chongro-ku, Seoul Republic of Korea

AHNERT, FRANK, geomorphologist; b. Wittgensdorf, Ger., Dec. 12, 1927. Dr.phil., U. Heidelberg, 1953. Postdoctoral research fellow U.S. NRC, 1954-56; from asst. prof. to prof. geography U. Md., 1956-74; prof. phys. geography Tech. U. Aachen, 1974—, dir. dept., 1974—; mem. Internat. Geog. Union Commn. on Measurement, Theory and Application in Geomorphology. Editor: Geomorphological Models--Theoretical and Empirical Aspects, 1987; co-editor: Earth Surface Processes and Landforms, 1982—, Catena, 1972—; also articles in field. Grantee German and U.S. research founds. Mem. Deutsche Quartärvereinigung, Deutscher Arbeitskreis Geomorphologie, Inst. Brit. Geographers, Brit. Geomorphological Research Group. Home: Moreller Weg 18, D-5100 Aachen Federal Republic of Germany Office: Geog Inst Tech Univ, Aachen Templergraben 55, D-5100 Aachen Federal Republic of Germany

AHO, JOHN KARE, communications executive; b. Froson, Jamtland, Sweden, June 24, 1936; came to U.S., 1947; s. John Isa and Anna (Anderson) A.; m. Charlotte Gutkais. BS, N.Y.U., 1958; MS, Boston (Mass.) U., 1971. Communications cons. ITT Fed. Labs., Nutley, N.J., 1963; engring. mgr. ITT Fed. Labs., Frankfurt, Fed. Republic Germany, 1964-68; regional v.p. ITT, Teheran, Iran and Istanbul, Turkey, 1973-85; dir. Ea. Europe ITT, Brussels, Belgium, 1985-86; gen. mgr. Europe Internat. Standard Engring. Inc., Heidelberg, Fed. Republic Germany, 1968-73; gen. mgr. Ea. Europe Alcatel, Brussels, 1987—; bd. dirs. Standard Elec. Telecommunications. Served to capt. Signal Corps., U.S. Army, 1958-63. Mem. IEEE. Office: Alcatel NV, Ave Louise 480, B-1050 Brussels Belgium

AHRENS, GILBERT POMEROY, banker; b. Hartford, Conn., June 24, 1938; s. Bernhard John August and Mary Weston (Bissell) A.; m. Christine von der Schulenburg, Dec. 30, 1961; children—Gilbert von der Schulenburg, Margot Hatheway. B.S. in Econs., U. Pa., 1962. Security analyst Phoenix Ins. Co., Hartford, 1962-67; asst. investment officer First Bank and Trust, Springfield, Mass., 1967-69; trust officer Hartford Nat. Bank and Trust Co., 1969-74; v.p. Conn. Nat. Bank, Hartford, 1974—; dir. Brookside Drive Co., Suffield, Conn. Treas. Wildwood Property Owners Assn. Tolland (Mass.), 1982—; bd. dirs. YMCA Camp Jewel, Colebrook, Conn., 1979—, Am. Baptist Chs. of Conn., 1978—; mem. Hist. Dist. commn., Suffield (Conn.), 1980—; pres. John Bissell 1628 Assn., Windsor, Conn., 1968—. Fellow Fin. Analysts Fedn.; mem. Hartford Soc. Fin. Analysts. Republican. Club: Suffield Country. Lodge: Rotary (treas. 1985). Avocations: tennis; fishing; photography; travel; jazz music. Home: 391 S Main St Suffield CT 06078 Office: Conn Nat Bank 777 Main St Hartford CT 06115

AHRENS, WILLIAM HENRY, architect; b. N.Y.C., May 12, 1925; s. John Karl and Sophie (Hashage) A.; m. Joyce Nolan, Mar. 27, 1951. Student, R.I. Sch. Design, 1946; A.B. in Architecture, Princeton U., 1950, M.F.A., 1953; postgrad., Tehran U., 1960. Chief architect Litchfield, Whiting, Bowne, Iran, 1958-61, Rome, 1961-64; dir. internat. ops. Whiting Assos., Rome, 1964-67; architect William H. Ahrens, AIA, Rome, Italy. Prin. archtl. works include ITT Sheraton Hotel, Tunisia, 1971, 83, Aerhotel, Dakar, Senegal, Salalah Hotel, Sultanate of Oman, Esso hotels, Bordeaux, France, Bologna, Italy, Marriott Hotel, Tehran, Iran, Faberge Plant, Italy, Quisisana Hotel, Capri. Served with USAAF, World War II, PTO. Recipient Book award AIA, 1953, Pub. Service award Tehran Lions Club, 1961. Mem. AIA, N.Y. State Assn. Architects. Clubs: Princeton (N.Y.C.); American (Rome), Circolo del Golf (Rome). Home: 3 Piazza Remuria, Rome Italy 00153

AHUJA, OM PARKASH, mathematician, educator; b. Chowdhary Station, Bhawalpur State India (now Pakistan), Apr. 18, 1942; s. Nounit Ram and Narain Devi A.; m. Kirti Juneja, Oct. 11, 1972; children—Chhavi, Charu, Yachna, Namrata. B.Sc. in Math. with honors, U. Delhi, 1964, M.Sc. in Math., 1966; M.A. in Econs., Panjab U., Chandigarh, India, 1975; B.Ed. in Sci. and Maths., Rajasthan U., India, 1976; Ph.D. in Math., U. Khartoum, Sudan, 1981. Lectr. math. Dayanand Anglo Vedic Coll., Abohar, affiliated Panjab U., Chandigarh, India, 1967-69, 70-76, U. Addis Ababa, Ethiopia, 1976-78; lectr. math. U. Khartoum, 1978-84, chmn. exams. Sch. Math. Scis., 1983-84; sr. lectr. math. U. Papua New Guinea, Nat. Capital Dist., 1984-86, assoc. prof., head dept. math., 1987—; Univ. Grants Commn. fellow U. Bombay and Tata Inst. Fundamental Research, 1969-70; vis. scholar U. Mich., Ann Arbor, 1982, SUNY-Albany, 1982; speaker U. Bombay, 1970, U. Madras, 1981, U. New Orleans, 1982, Bowling Green State U., 1982, U. South Fla., Tampa, 1982, Indian Math. Soc. Conf., 1985, Math. Edn. Conf., U. Tech., Lae, Papua New Guinea, 1985, Indian Math. Soc. Conf., 1986, 87. Author: (with P.K. Jain) A textbook Functional Analysis. Reviewer Math. Revs., 1983—. Contbr. articles on geometric functions theory to profl. jours. of U.S., Japan, India, Korea, Romania, Italy, Czechoslovakia, Malayasia, New Zealand, also others. Mem. Am. Math. Soc., Indian Math. Soc. (life), Indian Sci. Congress (life), Allahabad Math. Soc. (life.), All India Sci. Tchrs. Assn. (v.p. Panjab br. 1976), Ramanujan Math. Soc. (pres. Abohar chpt. 1970-76). Home: House 2123, Dr Mukherji Nagar, New Delhi 110009, India Office: Nat Capital Dist Dept Math, U Papua New Guinea, Box 320, Waigani Papua New Guinea

AHWIRENG-OBENG, FREDERICK, economics educator, consultant; b. Accra, Ghana, May 28, 1944; s. James Asare Obeng and Elizabeth (Akorley) Aryee; m. Frederica Ampofo-Anti; children: Sharon, Shirley, Sara-Ann. BSc in Agrl. Econs. with honors, U. Ghana, 1972; PhD in Econs., U. Leeds, Eng., 1981. Project officer Agrl. Devel. Bank, Ghana, 1972-75; regional bus. promotion rep. Ghanaian Enterprises Devel. Commn., 1975-77; lectr. in econs. U. Ife, Nigeria, 1982-83; sr. lectr. econs. U. Transkei, Cape Province, Republic South Africa, 1983-87; dep. dir. Inst. Devel. Research, U. Bophuthatswana, Republic South Africa, 1987—. Contbr. articles to profl. jours. Mem. Econ. Soc. South Africa, Devel. Soc. South Africa, Econ. Soc. Ghana, Ghana Soc. Agrl. Economists. Office: U Bophutswana Inst Devel, Research, PB 2046, Mafikeng 8670, Republic of South Africa

AIDA, ICHIRO, production management educator; b. Shinjuku-Ku, Tokyo, May 2, 1932; s. Haruo and Tome (Kawahara) A.; m. Keiko Suzuki, Apr. 1, 1964; children—Masashi, Miwako, Satoshi. B.A., Sch. Commerce, Meiji U., Tokyo, 1955; M.A., Grad. Sch., Meiji U., 1957. From asst. to prof. prodn. mgmt. Sch. Commerce, Meiji U., Tokyo, 1957—. Mem. Japan Soc. Study Bus. Adminstrn., Japan Indsl. Mgmt. Assn. Buddhist. Office: Sch Commerce Meiji Univ, 1 Chome Kanda-Surugadai, Chiyo da-Ku, 101 Tokyo Japan

AIDINOFF, M(ERTON) BERNARD, lawyer; b. Newport, R.I., Feb. 2, 1929; s. Simon and Esther (Miller) A.; m. Celia Spiro, May 30, 1956 (dec. June 28, 1984); children: Seth G., Gail M. B.A., U. Mich., 1950; LL.B., Harvard U., 1953. Bar: D.C. 1953, N.Y. 1954. Law clk. to Judge Learned Hand, U.S. Ct. of Appeals, N.Y.C., 1955-56; with firm Sullivan & Cromwell, N.Y.C., 1956-63; partner Sullivan & Cromwell, 1963-; dir. Am. Internat. Group Inc., Gibbs & Cox, Inc., Goody Products, Inc.; adv. com. to IRS commr., 1979-80, 85-86. Editor-in-chief: The Tax Lawyer, 1974-77. Trustee Spence Sch., 1971-79; adv. com. Gibbs Bros. Fedn.; vis. com. Harvard U. Law Sch., 1976-82 Served as 1st lt. JAGC AUS, 1953-55. Mem. ABA (vice chmn. sect. taxation 1977-77, chmn.-elect 1981-82, chmn. 1982-83, chmn. commn. on taxpayer compliance 1983-88), N.Y. State Bar Assn., Assn. Bar City N.Y. (exec. com. 1974-78, chmn. exec. com. 1977-78, v.p. 1978-79, chmn. taxation com. 1979-81), Am. Law Inst. (cons. fed. income tax project 1974—), Council Fgn. Relations, Confrerie des Chevaliers du Tastevin, Commanderie de Bordeaux, St Luke's Chamber Ensemble, Inc. (chmn. bd. dirs. 1987—), East Hampton Hist. Soc. (trustee 1983—), Phi Beta Kappa. Clubs: Metropolitan (Washington), India House. Home: 1120 Fifth Ave New York NY 10128 Office: Sullivan & Cromwell 125 Broad St New York NY 10004

AIGINGER, KARL, economist, educator; b. Vienna, Austria, Oct. 23, 1948; s. Josef and Hilda (Hanusch) A.; m. Elsa Mayer, Apr. 26, 1975; children: Thomas, Philipp. MA, U. Vienna, 1970, D of Econs., 1974, grad., 1984. Economist Austrian Inst. Econ. Research, Vienna, 1970-84, co-dir., 1984—; prof. econs. U. Vienna, 1985—; mng. editor Empirica (Austrian Jour. for Econ. Research), Vienna, 1975. Author: Investment Behavior, 1981, Applied Decison Theory, 1987; co-author: Small Business in Austria, 1984; editor: World Economic Development, 1986. Mem. Verein f. Socialpolitik, Nationalökonomische Gesellschaft. Roman Catholic. Office: Austrian Inst Econ Research, Arsenal Obj20, 1103 Vienna Austria

AIGRAIN, PIERRE RAOUL, scientific consultant, advisor; b. Poitiers, France, Sept. 28, 1924; s. Marius and Germaine (Ligault) A.; m. Francine Bogard, Feb. 12, 1947; children— Philippe, Yves, Jacques. Student French Naval Acad., 1942-44; D.Sc., Carnegie Inst. Tech., 1948; Dr. Scis., U. Paris, 1950; D.Sc. (hon.), U. Thessaloniki (Greece), 1979, Carnegie Mellon U., 1981. Prof., U. Lille, France, 1952-54, U. Paris, 1958-73; sci. dir. Def. Research Agy., Paris, 1961-65; dir. higher edn. Ministry Edn., Paris, 1965-68; gen. del. research and devel. French Govt., 1965-73; gen. tech. mgr. Thomson, Paris, 1974-78; minister research French Govt., Paris, 1978-81; sci. adviser to pres. Thomson group. Co-author: Les Semiconductors, 1954, Electronic Processes in Solids, 1959; author: Simples Propos d'un homone de Science, 1983. Served to capt. French Navy, 1942-52. Recipient Tate award Am. Phys. Soc., 1982; Prix du Rayonneaent Français, 1985. Mem. French Phys. Soc. (pres. 1985, Ancel medal, 1954, Robin prize 1974). Avocations: mountian climbing. Home: 56 rue de Boulaoinvilliers, 75016 Paris France Office: SICS, 186 rue du faubourg St Honoré, 75008 Paris France

AIKMAN, ALBERT EDWARD, lawyer; b. Norman, Okla., Mar. 11, 1922; s. Albert Edwin and Thelma Annette (Brooke) A.; m. Shirley Barnes, June 24, 1944; children—Anita Gayle, Priscilla June, Rebecca Brooke. B.S., Tex. A&M U., 1947; J.D. cum laude, So. Meth. U., 1948, LL.M., 1954. Bar: Tex. 1948, U.S. Supreme Ct. 1955. Staff atty. Phillips Petroleum Co., Amarillo, Tex., 1948-49; sole practice, Amarillo, 1949-53; tax counsel Magnolia Petroleum Co., Dallas, 1953-56; ptnr. Locke, Purnell, Boren, Laney & Neely, Dallas, 1956-71; sole practice, Dallas, 1972-81; sec., counsel Pickens Energy Corp., Dallas, 1981—. Served with inf. U.S. Army, 1943-45. Mem. ABA, Tex. Bar Assn., Dallas Bar Assn. Methodist. Contbr. articles in field to profl. jours.

AILLON, JULIO GARRET, vice president Bolivia; b. Sucre, Bolivia, May 22, 1925; m. Maria Luisa Kent; children—Julio, Juan. Dr. Jurisprudence and Politics, Universidad Mayor de San Francisco Xavier de Chuquisaca; postgrad. in Brazil and France. Mem. Nat. Revolutionary Movement; senator of Republic of Bolivia from State of Oruro, 1964-69, senator from State of Chuquisaca, 1979-80, pres. Nat. Senate, 1982, 83, 84, 85; pres. Nat. Congress of Bolivia, 1985—; rector Universidad Tecnica de Oruro, 1964-69; prof. sociology Faculty of Law; ambassador to Soviet Union 1969-73; chancellor of Republic of Bolivia, 1979-80, v.p., 1985—. Office: Office of Vice Pres, La Paz Bolivia *

AILLONI-CHARAS, DAN, business executive; b. Ploiesti, Rumania, May 22, 1930; came to U.S., 1950, naturalized, 1960; s. Max and Felicia (Lupescu) Charas; m. Miriam C. Taytelbaum, Oct 8, 1957; children—Ethan Benjamin, Orrin, Adam. A.B. with honors, U. Calif., Berkeley, 1952, M.A., 1953; M.A. Coro Found. fellow, 1953; Ph.D. (Univ. honors scholar), N.Y.U., 1968. Project dir. Marplan div. Communications Affiliates, Inc., N.Y.C., 1958-60; supr. advt. studies NBC, N.Y.C., 1960-62; dir. consumer and communications research Forbes Research, Inc., N.Y.C., 1962; mgr. market research Chesebrough-Pond's, Inc., N.Y.C., 1963-64; new products mgr. Chesebrough-Pond's, Inc., 1964-68, mgr. internat. mktg. services dept., 1968-69; pres. Stratmar Systems, Inc., Port Chester, N.Y., 1969—; asst., then prof. mktg. Pace U., 1963-85. Author: Promotion: A Guide to Effective Promotional Planning, Stategies and Execution, 1984; editor: Mktg. Rev, 1960-63, Proc. 1st Ann. Conf. on Research Design, 1964, New Directions in Research Design, 2d Conf, 1965, Planning, 1968-71; Bd. editors: Jour. Consumer Marketing, 1982—. Trustee Inst. Advanced Mktg. Studies, 1965-66, Philharmonic Symphony of Westchester, 1977-80; bd. dirs. Young Men's Bd. Trade, 1960-63, state dir. 1962-63; state dirs. N.Y. State Jr. C. of C., 1962;; bd. advisers Ad Expo, 1978. Mem. Am. Mktg. Assn. (pres. N.Y. chpt. 1965-66, nat. v.p. 1970-71), Promotion Mktg. Assn. Am. (dir. 1978—, chmn. edn. com. 1979-81, 85—, chmn. premium show com. 1982—, exec. com. 1986-87, chmn. nat. conf. 1988), N.Am. Soc. Corp. Planning (dir. 1970-72), Inst. of Dirs., AAUP, Sigma Delta Chi, Phi Sigma Alpha. Clubs: Canadian, Met. Home: Woodland Dr Rye Brook NY 10573 Office: Stratmar Bldg 109 Willett Ave Port Chester NY 10573

AILSLIEGER, ROSS EDWARD, aviation engineer; b. Hays, Kans., Sept. 24, 1937; s. Herbert George and Mary May (Pizinger) A.; m. Sharon Marie Shue, June 12, 1965; children—Paul Edward, Kristafer Ross, Alex Mathew. A.B. in Psychology, Ft. Hays State U., 1964, M.S. in Exptl. Psychology, 1965. Cert. flight instr., FAA. Human factors engr. N.Am. Rockwell, Los Angeles, 1966-68; human factors and maintainability lead engr. Spartan Missile program McDonnell-Douglas Astronautics Co., Huntington Beach, Calif., 1968-76; sr. human factors engr. AH-64 attack helicopter program Hughes Helicopters, Culver City, Calif., 1976-77; supr. human factors engring., and flight simulation Boeing Mil. Airplane Co., Wichita, Kans., 1977—; cons. aircraft cockpit design requirements, Wichita, Kans., 1977—; mgr. crew systems tech., 1986—. Served with U.S. Army, 1955-59. Mem. Tri-Service Aircrew Sta. Standardization Panel. Republican. Lutheran. Patentee in field. Home: 303 Wheatland Pl Wichita KS 67235 Office: Boeing Mil Airplane Co PO Box 7730 Wichita KS 67277

AINE, VELI VALO, corporate executive; b. Tornio, Finland, Feb. 17, 1919; s. Eelis Iikka and Elsa Elina (Kantola) A.; grad. Comml. Coll. Businessmen Finland, Helsinki, 1941; m. Eila Rantanen, June 23, 1942; children: Kristiina, Heli, Ulla, Sakari. Mng. dir. Aine Oy, Tornio, Kemi, Rovaniemi, Oulu, Finland, 1945-76, Alpa Oy, Tornio, Kemi, 1945-76, Tornion Seurahuone Oy, Tornio, 1970-76; chmn. bd. Aine Oy, Tornio, Kemi, Oulu, Rovaniemi, Raahe, Kuusamo, 1976—. Founder Mus. for Pictorial Art, Found. Pictorial Art of Aine. Served with Finnish Armed Forces, World War II. Decorated Cross of Liberty 4th class with sword, 4th class with oak leaf, 3rd class with sword, 3rd class with oak leaf, comdr. Cross of Lion of Finland, knight comdr. Mil. and Hosp. Order of St. Lazarus, knight Companion of Merit, Merit Cross; named Councillor of Commerce, 1969, Chevalier Order Arts and Letters France. Mem. Cultural Founds. of Finland, Lappland, Hotel Assn. Finland, N. Finnish Fair, Central, Lapland chambers commerce, Central Assn. Automobiles Finland. Conservative. Evangelical Lutheran. Lodges: Rotary, Masons. Home: 1 Uusikatu, Tornio 95400, Finland Office: 4 Itäranta, Tornio 95400, Finland

AINSWORTH, THOMAS HARGRAVES, JR., physician, medical administrator, author; b. Schenectady, June 16, 1920; s. Thomas Hargraves and Flora Cameron (MacCracken) A.; m. Shirley Ann Sanford, Dec. 23, 1950; children—Ann Louise McFarland, Thomas Hargraves III. B.S., Pa. State U., State Coll., 1941; M.D., Temple U., 1944; postgrad. exec. program in health services mgmt. Harvard Bus. Sch., 1977. Diplomate Am. Bd. Surgery. Intern Bryn Mawr Hosp., Pa., 1944-45, mem. staff, 1951-70, chief gen. surgery, 1964-70; resident in surgery Bellevue Med. Ctr., N.Y.C., 1948-51; practice medicine specializing in surgery, Bryn Mawr, 1951-70; assoc. dir. Am. Hosp. Assn., Chgo., 1970-74; med. dir. Ill. Masonic Hosp., Chgo., 1974-79; chmn. bd. Hale, Inc., Carmel, Calif., 1979—; asst. prof. surgery and anatomy Temple U., Phila., 1964-70; prof. clin. surgery U. Ill., Chgo., 1974-79, prof. health care services Sch. Pub. Health, 1975-79; cons. Ainsworth Assocs., Chgo., Phila., Carmel Valley, 1974—. Author: Quality Assurance: Medical Care in Hospitals, 1972; Quality Assurance in Long Term Care, 1976; Live or Die, 1983; Health Promotion in the Workplace, 1984. Editor Hosp. Med. Staff, 1972-74. Patentee Ainsworth (hip) Nail, 1967. Elder Presbyn. Ch. in U.S.A., Bryn Mawr, 1960—. Served to capt. USMC, 1946-48. Recipient Award of Honor, Am. Hosp. Assn., 1969. Fellow ACS (com. on cancer 1970-79); mem. Coll. Physicians Phila., Am. Coll. Preventive Medicine, Acad. Surgery Phila., Inst. Medicine of Chgo., Am. Acad. Med. Dirs., Carmel Valley Garden Assn. (pres. 1982-83), Internat. Wine and Food Soc. (Monteray Peninsula br. pres. 1988). Republican. Club: Phila. Country. Home: PO Box 1201 Carmel Valley CA 93924 Office: Hale Inc PO Box 223580 Carmel CA 93922

AIRD, JOHN BLACK, lawyer, university officer, former lieutenant governor; b. Toronto, Ont. Can., May 5, 1923; s. Hugh Reston and May (Black) A.; m. Lucile Jane Housser, July 27, 1944; children: Lucille Elizabeth Aird Menear, Jane Victoria Aird Blackmore, Hugh Housser, Katherine Aird Porter. BA, U. Toronto, 1946; postgrad., Osgoode Hall Law Sch., 1949; LLD (hon.), Wilfrid Laurier U., 1975, Royal Mil. Coll. Can, 1980, U. Western Ont., 1983, Lakehead U., 1984, U. Toronto, 1984; DSL, Wycliffe Coll., 1985. Bar: Ont., 1949. Assoc. Wilton and Edison, 1949-53; ptnr. Edison, Aird and Berlis, 1953-74, Aird, Zimmerman, and Berlis, 1974-78, Aird and Berlis, Toronto, 1978—; lt. gov. Ont., 1980-85; chancellor U. Toronto, 1986—; Gov. (ex officio) Upper Can. Coll., 1986—; Gillette lectr. U. Western Ont., 1984; chmn. Can. sect. Can.-U.S. Permanent Joint Bd. Def., 1971-79; chmn. Inst. Research on Pub. Policy, 1974-80; mem. Senate of Can., 1964-74. Hon. counsel St. Paul's Anglican Ch., Toronto; hon. chmn. United Way of Greater Toronto, Variety Village, Can. Liver Found.; dep. chmn. Duke of Edinburgh's Award in Can., Can.-China Trade Council. Served as lt. Royal Can. Navy, 1942-45, capt. Can. Forces Res., 1981. Decorated officer Order Can., First recipient of the Order of Ont., award of Merit-City of Toronto, Officer of the Order of Red Cross, 35th Humanitarian award Beth Shalom Brotherhood, Silver Acorn Boy Scouts of Can., Human Relations award Can. Council of Christians and Jews, Great Lakes Man of Yr., Knight of Justice of the Most Venerable Order of the Hosp. of St. John of Jerusalem; named Queen's Counsel, 1960; Paul Harris award Rotary Found.; Promise Hope award Can. Children's Found. Mem. Naval Officers Assn. Can. (hon. pres.), Alpha Delta Phi. Anglican. Clubs: York, Toronto, Toronto Golf, Granite, Royal Can. Yacht, Royal and Ancient Golf Club of St. Andrews; The Mid Ocean (Bermuda). Office: Aird and Berlis, 145 King St W 15th Floor, Toronto, ON Canada M5H 2J3 also: University of Toronto, Toronto, ON Canada M5S 1A1

AITCHISON, BEATRICE, transportation economist; b. Portland, Oreg., July 18, 1908; d. Clyde Bruce and Bertha (Williams) Aitchison; AB, Goucher Coll., 1928, ScD (hon.), 1979; AM, Johns Hopkins, 1931; PhD in Math., 1933; MA with honors in Econs., U. Oreg., 1937. Asso. prof. math. U. Richmond, 1933-34; lectr. statistics Am. U., 1934-44; instr. econs. U. Oreg., 1939-41; jr. statistician advancing to sr. statistician ICC, 1938-48, prin. transport economist, 1948-51; dir. transport econs. div. Office Transp., Dept. Commerce, 1951-53; dir. transp. research Post Office Dept., Washington, 1953-58, dir. transp. research and statistics, 1958-67, dir. transp. rates and econs., 1967-71; transp. cons., 1971—. Cons. Traffic Analysis and Forecasting Office Def. Transp., 1942-45; cons. mil. traffic. service U.S. Dept. Def., 1950-53. Recipient Alumnae Achievement citation Goucher Coll., 1954; First Ann. Fed. Woman's award, 1961, Career Service award Nat. Civil Service League, 1970. Fellow Am. Statis. Assn., AAAS; mem. Am. Econ. Assn., Am. Soc. Trans and Logistics, Phi Beta Kappa, Sigma Xi, Pi Lambda Theta, Phi Delta Gamma. Episcopalian. Contbr. to numerous govt. publs. Home and Office: 3001 Veazy Terr NW Apt 534 Washington DC 20008-5402

AITCHISON, THOMAS MORTON, information scientist; b. Glasgow, Scotland, July 31, 1923; s. James and Helen Murdoch (Meikle) A.; m. Jean Binns, Feb. 4, 1961; children: James Douglas, Margaret Hilary. BS, U. St.

Andrews, Scotland, 1944. Tech. exptl. officer Admiralty Signal and Radar Establishment, Haslemere, Eng., 1944-47; librarian Courtaulds Ltd., Braintree, Eng., 1948-55; divisional librarian Brit. Aircraft Corp., Stevenage, Eng., 1955-64; tech. officer Nat. Electronics Research Council, London, 1964-66; dep. dir. INSPEC, Instn. Elec. Engrs., Hitchin, Eng., 1967-79, dir., 1980—; hon. research fellow U. Coll., London, 1970—; bd. dirs. Peter Peregrinus Ltd., London. Contbr. articles to profl. jours. Decorated officer Order Brit. Empire. Fellow Inst. Info. Scientists (hon., pres. 1987—); mem. Am. Soc. for Info. Sci., Library Assn. (assoc.). Methodist. Home: 12 Sollershott W, Letchworth Herts SG6 3PX, England Office: Instn Elec Engrs, Nightingale Rd, Hitchin Herts SG5 1RJ, England

AITKEN, RONALD WILLIAM, accountant; b. Murree, India, Sept. 20, 1933; s. William Henry and Mary Dorothea (Davidson) A.; m. Frances Barbara Farmer, Nov. 3, 1962; children—Fiona, Sarah, Lucinda, Alexandra, Penelope, Georgiana. Higher Edn. cert., Cheltenham Coll., 1951. Ptnr., Binder Hamlyn, London, 1960-80; chmn. Ronnie Aitken & Assocs., London, 1980—; chmn. Bentleys of Piccadilly PLC, Ecobric Holdings PLC, Sherwood Oil PLC, Stanley Gibbons Holdings PLC, Ford Sellar Morris Properties PLC, Good News Christian Holdings Ltd.; dir. Belvoir Petroleum Corp., Chrles Letts (Holdings) Ltd., N. Brown Investments PLC, Welsh Mineral Resources Lts., others. Mem. CBI Fin. and Econ. Policy Com., London, 1977-80. Served to 2d lt. Royal Arty. 1957-59. Clubs: Brooks, Berkshire (London). Home: 212 Ashley Gardens, London SW1, England Office: Ronnieaitken & Assocs, 52 Grosvenor Gardens, London SW1, England

AITKIN, DONALD ALEXANDER, professor, administrator; b. Sydney, Australia, Apr. 8, 1937; s. Alexander George and Edna Irene (Taylor) A.; m. Janice Aitkin, Dec. 20, 1958 (div.); children: Susan Jill, Lesley Jennifer, Gabrielle Vanessa, Alexander Lewis; m. Susan Tracy Elderton, May 20, 1977; 1 child, Max. BA with honors, U. New Eng., Armidale, Australia, 1959, MA, 1961; PhD, Australia Nat. U., Canberra, 1964. Research fellow Australia Nat. U., 1965-68, sr. research fellow, 1968-71; found. prof. politics Macquarie U., Sydney, Australia, 1971-79; prof. pol. sci., head of dept. Research Sch. Soc. Scis. Australia Nat. U., 1980-88; chmn. Australian Research Council, 1988—; Mem. Australian Sci. and Technol. Council, Canberra, Nat. Research Fellowship Adv. Com., 1986—, Australian Research Grants Com., Canberra, 1984—, chmn. 1986-88. Author: The Colonel, 1969, Stability and Change in Australian Politics, 1977, 2d edit., 1982; co-author Australian Political Institutions, 1980, 2d edit., 1982, 3d edit., 1985. Fellow Acad. Social Scis. in Australia; mem. Australasian Polit. Studies Assn. (pres. 1979, treas. 1981-88). Office: Australian Research Council, GPO Box 9880, 2601 Canberra ACT Australia

AITZETMÜLLER, KURT, chemist, research administrator; b. Austria, Nov. 3, 1938. PhD, U. Vienna, 1966. Research assoc. Argonne (Ill.) Nat. Lab., 1966-68; scientist Unilever Research, Hamburg, Fed. Republic Germany, 1969-84; dir. Inst. for Chemistry and Physics, Fed. Ctr. for Lipid Research, Münster, Fed. Republic Germany, 1986-88, head of ctr., 1988—. Office: Fed Ctr for Lipid Research, Piusallee 68-76, D-4400 Münster Federal Republic of Germany

AIZU, IZUMI, communications executive; b. Sendai, Miyagi, Japan, May 26, 1952; s. Shin Aizu and Kaoru Kawanishi; m. Mamiko Tamura, Apr. 23, 1973; children: Hatsuho, Miho, Naho, Sachiho. Grad. high sch., Kamakura/Kanagawa, Japan. Printing operator Nippon Print Ctr., Tokyo, 1972-73, printing salesman, 1973-75; printing salesman Hokkai Sangyo Co., Tokyo, 1975-76; salesman Obun Intereurope Ltd., Tokyo, 1976-80, mgr. sales, 1980-82, creative dir., 1982-85; dir. communicaitions High Tech. Communications, Tokyo, 1983-85; pvt. practice communication cons. Tokyo, 1985-87; v.p. Inst. Networking Design, Tokyo, 1987-88, prin., 1988—. Author/editor: (book) My First Apple, 1984; author: (books) Reports on US PC Network, 1985, Personal Computer Network Revolution, 1986; translator: (book) Complete Guide to Software Users Manual, 1985, Odyssey, 1988. Mem. Computer Press Assn. (rep.), Electronic Networking Assn. (David E. Rodale award for contributions to global community 1988), Tech. Communication Soc. (pres.). Home: 1-28-15 Kakinokizaka, Meguro, Tokyo 152, Japan Office: Inst Networking Design, 2-17-12-502 Higashi, Shibuya, Tokyo 150, Japan

AJAYI, OLADEJO OYELEKE, statistician; b. Ekusa, Oyo, Nigeria, Apr. 21, 1942; s. Michael Soladoye and Emily (Subuola) A.; m. Oyeyemi Adunni, Aug. 14, 1971; children—Omotayo, Omotope, Omotola, Omotunde. B.Sc. with honors in Statistics, U. Ibadan, Nigeria, 1966; M.A. in Statistics, U. Mich., 1970. Statistician, Fed. Office of Statistics, Lagos, Nigeria, 1966-70, statistician Grade I, 1970-72, sr. statistician, 1972-75, prin. statistician, 1975-76, asst. chief statistician, 1976-78, asst. dir., 1978-84, dir., 1984—; assoc. researcher Nigeria Inst. Econ. & Social Research, Ibadan, 1982-85; part-time lectr. dept. stats. U. Ibadan, 1986; cons., participant UN/Econ. Comm. for Africa, Addis Ababa, Ethiopia, 1981; participant UNESCO Expert Group, Paris, 1978; UNESCO cons., 1985. Fed. Govt. Nigeria Scholar, 1963; Inst. for Social Research, U. Mich., fellow, 1969. Fellow Inst. Statisticians; mem. Nigeria Statis. Assn. (governing council), Am. Statis. Assn., Internat. Statis. Inst., Internat. Assn. Survey Statisticians (v.p., council), Nigerian Inst. Mgmt. (assoc.), Internat. Assn. Ofcl. Stats. (vice pres. 1987—). Home: Falomo PO Box 52724, Ikoyi Lagos Nigeria Office: Fed Office Statis 10 Okotie-Eboh St PMB 12528 Lagos, Nigeria

AKAHOSHI, KENJI, manufacturing executive; b. Ohita, Japan, Mar. 9, 1937; s. Masaru and Chika A.; m. Takako Hori, Nov. 6, 1963; children: Kayoko, Makiko, Akiko. LLB, Chuo U., Tokyo, 1960. Mgr. Akahoshi Mfg. Co., Ltd., Ichihara, Japan, 1961, dir., 1962-70, pres., 1970—. Inventor heat exchanger cell (Gov. prize 1979). Mem. Japan Light Metal Welding and Constrn. Assn. (bd. dirs. 1983), Ichihara C. of C. and Industry (assemblyman 1973). Clubs: Mobara Country; Hamano Golf (Ichihara). Lodge: Rotary. Office: Akahoshi Mfg Co Ltd, 5-4 Yawata, Kaigan-Dori, Ichihara-City Chiba 290, Japan

AKAIKE, HIROTUGU, statistician; b. Fujinomiya, Shizuoka, Japan, Nov. 5, 1927; s. Takeharu and Ume (Fukasawa) A.; m. Miyoko Sano (div.); 1 child, Yumi; m. 2d, Ayako Nakajima, Jan. 1, 1957 (dec. 1983); children—Chie, Maki; m. 3d, Mitsuko Nakatani, Nov. 12, 1984. B.S., U. Tokyo, 1952, D.S., 1961. Researcher Inst. Statis. Math., Tokyo, 1952-62, head 2d sect. 1st div., 1962-73, dir. 5th div., 1973-85, prof., head dept. prediction and control, 1985-86, dir. gen., 1986—. Author: Statistical Analysis and Control (in Japanese), 1972; editor: Annals of the Inst. of Statis. Math., 1988; assoc. editor: Jour. Time Series Analysis, 1980—, Jour. Bus. and Econ. Stats., 1982—; contbr. articles to profl. lit.; introduced info. criterion for statis. model selection, 1971. Recipient Ishikawa prize Ishikawa Prize Com., 1972; Okochi prize Okochi Meml. Found., 1980. Fellow Am. Statis. Assn., Inst. Math. Stats., IEEE, Royal Statis. Soc. (hon.); mem. Internat. Statis. Inst. (v.p. 1981-83). Home: Toride 1-7-14-204, 302 Toride-shi Japan Office: The Inst Statistical Math, 4-6-7 Minami-Azabu, Minato-ku, Tokyo 106 Japan

AKASAKI, TOSHIRO, machinery manufacturing executive; b. Tokyo, Sept. 14, 1925; s. Toshifumi and Ine (Kawanabe) A.; BS in Engring., Keio U., Tokyo, 1948; m. Yoshiko, Mar. 23, 1954; children: Shoko, Sayuri. Engr., Ministry Internat. Trade and Industry, Tokyo, 1948-50; asst. comml. sec. Japanese embassy, Ottawa, Ont., Can., 1950-53; dir. Japan Trade Center, Cairo, 1953-58; mgr. research sect. JETRO, Tokyo, 1958-60; mgr. plastic sect. Marubeni Co. Ltd., 1960-61; v.p. Sekisui Plastic Corp., Hazelton, Pa., 1962-67; pres. Danfoss Japan Mfg. Co., Tokyo, 1968-72, Toyo Carrier Engring. Co., Tokyo, 1972-78; v.p. Nordson Corp., Amherst, Ohio, 1978-87, cons., advisor, 1987—; pres., chmn. bd. Nordson K.K., Tokyo, 1978—. Home: 5-2-18-1403 Mita, Minato-ku, 108 Tokyo Japan Office: Nordson KK, 3-32-36 Higashi-Shinagawa, 140 Shinagawa-ku Tokyo Japan also: Nordson Corp 28601 Clemens Rd Westlake OH 44145

AKASHI, YASUSHI, government official; b. Akita, Japan, Jan. 19, 1931; parents: Morinosuke and Aya (Saito) A.; m. Itsuko Akashi Kobayashi; children: Nobuko, Hiroshi. BA, U. Tokyo; MA, U. Va.; postgrad., Columbia U. Polit. affairs officer UN, N.Y.C., 1957-74, Japanese mission, 1974-79, undersec. gen. pub. info., 1979-87, undersec. gen. disarmament affairs, 1987—; bd. dirs. Internat. Peace Acad., N.Y.C., Better World Soc., Washington; advisor UN Assn. Japan. Author: From the Windows of the United Nations, The Lights and Shadows of the United Nations. Home: 40 Hampton Rd Scarsdale NY 10583 Office: care United Nations Office of the Under-Sec-Gen Rm S-3161 New York NY 10017

AKBAR, HUZOOR, pharmacologist, educator, researcher; b. Karachi, Pakistan, Dec. 2, 1948; came to U.S., 1977, naturalized, 1986; s. Hasan and Taeed Fatima (Rehbar) A.; m. Ildiko St. George, Apr. 9, 1977; children: Vazeer Daniel, Imran Shaan, Jason Adam. B.S. with honors, Karachi U., Pakistan, 1971; M.S., 1972; Ph.D., Australian Nat. U., Canberra, 1978. Research assoc. in pathology Vanderbilt U., Nashville, 1977-78; in medicine Boston U., 1978-79; in pharmacology Ohio State, Columbus, 1979-81; asst. prof. pharmacology and biomed. sci. Ohio U., Athens, 1981-87, assoc. prof., 1987—. Contbr. articles on pharmacology to profl. jours.; editor Biochemica, 1970; weekly columnist Mashriq and Hurriat newspapers, 1969-71. Grantee Am. Heart Assn., 1982—, Am. Osteo. Assn., 1984—, Am. Health Assistance Found., 1988. Mem. Am. Physiol. Soc., Internat. Soc. on Thrombosis and Haemostatis, Am. Soc. for Pharmacology and Exptl. Therapeutics. Home: 24 Ball Dr Wonderhills Athens OH 45701 Office: Irvine Hall Ohio Univ Athens OH 45701

AKCA, SAKIR, dental educator; b. Antalya, Turkey, Oct. 29, 1933; s. Arif and Hatice A.; m. Belkis Akca; children: Selmin, Ayca. DDS, Gazi U., Besevler, Ankara, Turkey, 1957, PhD, 1968. Assoc. prof. Gazi U., 1975-80, prof., 1980-83, rector, 1983—. Author: Agiz Dis Hastaliklari ve Cene Cerrahisinde Semptomdan Teshise; contbr. more than 50 articles to profl. jours. Mem. Turkish Assn. Maxillofacial Surgeons, Fedn. Dentaire Internat. Home: Buklum Sr, Kavaklidere, Ankara Turkey Office: Gazi Universitesi, Besevler, Ankara Turkey

AKE, SIMEON, Ivory Coast minister of foreign affairs, lawyer; b. Birgenville, Jan. 4, 1932; m. Aune Maud Bonful, 1958; 5 children. Student Univs. Dakar and Grenoble. Chief of cabinet to Minister Pub. Service, Ivory Coast, 1959-61; 1st counsellor Ivory Coast Mission to UN, 1961-63; dir. protocol Ministry Fgn. Affairs, 1963-64; ambassador to U.K., Sweden, Denmark and Norway, 1964-66; permanent rep. of Ivory Coast to UN, 1966-77; minister fgn. affairs, 1977—; mem. guiding com. Parti democratique de la Cote d'Ivoire, 1975—. Decorated comdr. Nat. Order Republic Ivory Coast; officer Légion d'Honneur. Address: Ministere des, Affaires Etrangéres, Abidjan Ivory Coast *

AKERMAN, ALF KNUT LENNART, banker; b. Lund, Sweden, Feb. 24, 1923; s. Ake Ernst and Hildur Elin (Sonesson) A.; m. Gun Widding, Mar. 17, 1953; children: Bertil, Ake, Alexandra, Alf. MS in Chem. Engring., Royal Tech. U., Sweden, 1949; BS in Econs., Stockholm Sch. Econs., 1954; postgrad. MIT, 1954-55; hon. DEng., Chalmers U. Tech., Gothenburg, Sweden. With Reymersholms Gamla Industri AB, Helsingborg, Sweden, 1949-55, head research and devel. dept., 1956-58; head tech. and devel. dept. AB Marabou, Sundbyberg, Sweden, 1959-61, ep. mng. dir., 1961-67; chief exec. officer, pres. Skandinaviska Banken, Stockholm, 1968-71, Skandinaviska Enskilda Banken, Gothenburg, 1972-84; chmn. Swedish BP AB, Victor Hasselblad AB; bd. dirs. Perstorp AB, Trygg-Hansa Ins., BASF Svenska AB, AB ABV, Databolin AB, Safe Offshore AB, Scandinavian Heart Ctr. AB, SSPA Maritime Consulting AB, STUF-Eng. Research Council of the Swedish Nat. Bd. for Tech. Devel., BioVäst Found. for Biotech.; bd. dirs. AB SKF, Forbo SA, Zörich, Volvo Fin. SA, Geneva, Gadelius AB, Nordstjernan AB, Johnson Line AB, KabiVitrum AB, Mölnlycke AB. Mem. Royal Swedish Acad. Scis., Fedn. Swedish Industries, Swedish Nat. Com. for Pure and Applied Chem. Decorated Knight Comdr. of the Order of the Seraphim, 1988; recipient Govern medal, 12th Dim., 1988. Home: Box 76, 43041 Kullavik Sweden Office: Ostra Hamngatan 18, S405 Gothenburg 04 Sweden

AKERS, JOHN FELLOWS, information processing company executive; b. Boston, Dec. 28, 1934; s. Kenneth Fellows and Mary Joan (Reed) A.; m. Susan Davis, Apr. 16, 1960; children: Scott, Pamela, Anne. B.S., Yale U., 1956. With IBM Corp., Armonk, N.Y., 1960—, v.p., asst. group exec., 1976-78, v.p., group exec., 1978-82, sr. v.p., group exec., 1982-83, pres., dir., 1983—, chief exec. officer, 1985—, chmn., 1986—; dir. N.Y. Times Co. Mem. adv. bd. Yale Sch. Orgn. and Mgmt.; co-chmn. Bus. Roundtable; trustee Met. Mus. Art, Calif. Inst. Tech.; bd. govs. United Way Am. Served to lt. USNR, 1956-60. Office: IBM Corp Old Orchard Rd Armonk NY 10504 *

AKERT, KONRAD HANS, neuroscientist, physiology, educator; b. Zürich, Switzerland, May 21, 1919; married; 4 children. MD, U. Zürich, 1949; MD (hon.), U. Geneva, 1976; D (hon.), U. Fribourg, Switzerland, 1987. Asst. Dept. Physiology U. Zürich, 1946-51, prof. neurobiology, dir. Brain Research Inst., 1961—, dean Med. Sch., 1974-76, dir. Physiology Inst., 1979-84, bd. dirs. Brain Research Inst., 1979-84, rector, 1984—; research fellow Swiss Acad. Med. Scis. Johns Hopkins U., Balt., 1951-52, instr. physiology, 1952-53; asst. prof. U. Wis., Madison, 1953-55, assoc. prof., 1955-60, prof. anatomy and physiology, 1960-61; vis. prof. psychology Stanford U., Palo Alto, Calif., 1958; distng. lectr. Japanese Soc. for Advancement of Scis., 1980. Founder, editor-in-chief Jour. Brain Research, 1966-76; contbr. more than 330 articles to sci. jours. Recipient Robert Bing prize Swiss Acad. Med. Scis., 1960, Otto Naegeli prize, 1969; hon. research prof. Inst. Biophysics of the Academia Sinica Peking, Republic of China, 1980. Mem. European Brain and Behaviour Soc. (co-founder, co-founder European Tng. Programme Winter Sch.), European Neurosci. Assn. (co-founder), others. Office: Univ Zurich, Ramistr 71, 8006, Zurich & Winterthurerstr 190, 8057 Zurich Switzerland

AKHTAR, ABDUL HAFEEZ, Pakistan government official, educator; b. Faisalabad, Punjab, Pakistan, May 1, 1940; s. Haji Abdul Rahman; m. Kalsoom Akhtar, Mar. 28, 1966; children—Tahira, Khalid, Shaista, Saima, Masud. B.A., Punjab U., Lahore, 1959; diploma in L.S., Karachi U., 1963; M.A. in L.S., Ind. U., 1965. Lectr., librarian Inst. of Edn. and Research Punjab U., Lahore, 1965-68, lectr. Library Sch., 1968-71; dep. dir. libraries Ministry of Edn., Govt. Pakistan, Karachi, 1971-73, registrar of copyrights, 1973-76, dir. libraries, Islamabad, 1974—, sec. Tech. Working Group on Pub. Libraries, 1983-84. Author: Reader in Library Cataloging, 1972; dir. Pakistan National Bibliography, 1972; Analytical Catalog of Books on Quaid-i-Azam, 1978, Analytical Catalog of Books on Allama Iqbal, 1978; Catalog of Books on Seeratun Nabi, 1979. Mem. Pakistan Library Assn. (asst. sec. 1967, pres. 1984—). Islam. Office: Dept Libraries, Ministry of Edn, Islamabad Pakistan

AKHTAR, SHAMIM, obestetrician, gynecologist; b. Hyderabad, Deccan, India; s. Syed Zahid and Wazir (Fatima) Hussain; m. Akhter Ahmed, Nov. 28, 1958; children: Yasmeen, Zarina, Mona, Erum. MBBS, Dow Med. Coll., Karachi, Pakistan, 1957; Lic. in Midwifery, D of Ob/Gyn, Trinity Coll., Dublin, Ireland, 1960. House surgeon dept. gen. surgery Civil Hosp. Karachi, 1957-58; intern gen. medicine Evang. Deaconess, Cleve., 1959; resident gen. medicine High View Hosp., Cleve., 1959-60; house officer Banbury (Eng.) Hosp., 1961-62; resident med. officer Lady Duffrin Hosp., Karachi, 1962; cons. obstetrician Mohammadi Hosp., Karachi, 1962-64; med. supt. ob/gyn, originator nurse tng. program Akram Khatoon All Pakistan Women's Assn. Hosp., Karachi, 1964-73; owner, med. supt. Specialist's Clinic, Karachi, 1973—; cons. in field. Mem. Royal Coll. Ob/Gyn, Pakistan Med. Assn. (life).

AKIMOTO, EIICHI, economics educator; b. Tokyo, Mar. 12, 1943; s. Shoichi and Yachiyo (Noguchi) A.; m. Natsuko Nakahara; children: Yuki, Mari. BA, U. Tokyo, 1966, MA, 1968. Lectr. dept. econs. Kantogakuin U., Yokohama, Japan, 1972-75, assoc. prof., 1975-79; assoc. prof. Chiba (Japan) U., 1979-87, prof., 1987—. Author: (with others) State and Economy, 1982; contbr. articles to profl. jours. Grantee Am. Council Lerned Socs., 1977, Japan-U.S. Ednl. Commn., 1984. Mem. Hist. Sci. Soc. of Japan, Socio-Econ. History Soc., Orgn. Am. Historians, Japanese Assn. for Am. Studies (councillor 1985—), Agrarian History Soc. (mem. planning com. 1985—). Office: Chiba U Dept Econs, 1-33 Yayoi-cho, Chiba-shi 260, Japan

AKIN, CAVIT, biotechnologist, research scientist; b. Nigde, Turkey, Feb. 28, 1931; came to U.S., 1957; s. Ahmet and Fatma Kenan (Yuceeren) A.; m. Ingeborg Katharina Tange, Feb. 24, 1978; children—Deniz Leyla, Suzan Sema, Tulin Selma, Aylin Neva. M.S.Chem.E., U. Ankara, 1954; M.S. in Food Tech., U. Ill., 1959, Ph.D., 1961; postdoctoral U. Mass., 1962. Research scientist Sugar Research Inst., Turkey, 1956-57; sr. bioengr. Falstaff Research Lab., St. Louis, 1962-67; sr. research engr. Am. Oil Co., Whiting, Ind., 1967-70; sr. research engr. Standard Oil Co., Naperville, Ill., 1971-73, research assoc., supr. biotech. research, 1979-87; research supr. Amoco Chems., Naperville, Ill., 1973-77; mgr. foods exploratory research Amoco Foods, Naperville, 1978-79; assoc. dir. biotech. research Inst. Gas Tech., Chgo., 1987—. Served to lt. Signal Corps, Turkish Armed Forces, 1955-56. Fulbright scholar U. Ill., 1957-61. Mem. Am. Chem. Soc., Am. Soc. Microbiology, Soc. Indsl. Microbiologists, Inst. Food Technologists, AAAS. Moslem. Patentee in field; contbr. articles to profl. jours. Home: 1462 Inverrary Dr Naperville IL 60540 Office: Inst Gas Tech Chicago IL 60616

AKIN, RALPH HARDIE, JR., oil company executive; b. Decatur, Ill., Oct. 18, 1938; s. Ralph Hardie and Darla (Sutterfield) A.; m. Joan Clements, Dec. 30, 1960 (div. 1972); children—Laura Elizabeth, Michael Hardie; m. Elaine Fleming, June 28, 1974; children—Jennifer Aimee, Julie Alicia. B.S., Centenary Coll., 1960; M.S., U. Tulsa, 1966. Computer opr. Western Geophys. Co., Shreveport, La., 1960-62, geologist Apache Corp., Tulsa and Houston, 1963-67; geologist, exploration mgr. Ada Exco, Houston, 1967-70; v.p. T.C. Bartling and Assocs., Houston, 1971-76; pres. Akin Energy Corp., Houston, 1977—. Mem. Am. Assn. Petroleum Geologists, Am. Assn. Petroleum Landmen, Houston Geol. Soc. Republican. Methodist. Home: 11611 Windy Ln Houston TX 77024 Office: Akin Energy Corp Americana Bldg Room 1417 Houston TX 77002

AKINKUGBE, OLADIPO OLUJIMI, cardiologist, educator; b. Ondo, Nigeria, July 17, 1933; s. David A. and Grace (Talabi) A.; m. Folasade Modupeore Dina, May 8, 1965; children—Olumide, Olukayode. M.B., B.S., London U., 1958, M.D., 1968; D.T.M., Liverpool U. (Eng.), 1960; D.Phil., Oxford U. (Eng.), 1964; D.Sc. (hon.), U. Ilorin (Nigeria), 1982. House physician Kings Coll. Hosp., London, 1959; clin. asst. med. unit London Hosp., 1960; from lectr. to prof. medicine U. Ibadan (Nigeria), 1964, 66, 68, head medicine, dean med. sch., 1972, 70-74; prin., vice chancellor U. Ilorin, 1975-78; vice chancellor Ahmadu Bello U., Zaria, Nigeria, 1978-79; vis. prof. medicine, fellow Balliol Coll., Oxford U. (Eng.), 1981-82, Harvard Med. Sch., Boston, 1974-75; pro-chancellor U. Port Harcourt, 1986—. Author: High Blood Pressure in the African, 1972; Priorities in National Health Planning, 1974; Cardiovascular Disease in Africa, 1976; Clin. Medicine in the Tropics Series, 1987; contbr. articles to profl. jours. Com. mem. Univ. Grants Commn., 1973; chmn. Joint Admission and Matric Bd. (Nigeria), 1977; chmn. planning com. Ondo State U. (Nigeria), 1981, Fed. Capital U. at Abuja, 1983. Decorated comdr. Order of the Niger, Fed. Republic Nigeria; officier de l'Ordre Nat. de la Republique de Cote d'Ivoire. Fellow Royal Coll. Physicians Edinburgh, West African Coll. Physicians, Nigerian Acad. Sci.; mem. Ciba Found. (sci. adv. council), Internat. Soc. Hypertension (council 1982—), Med. Research Soc. Gt. Britain. Office: Univ of Ibadan, Dept of Medicine, Ibadan Nigeria

AKINRELE, MARSHALL OLATUNDE, manufacturing executive, management consultant; b. Ondo, Nigeria, Dec. 8, 1936; s. Jacob Fadase and Victoria Olasimpo (Akinkugbe) A.; m. Dora Modupe Dale, Oct. 3, 1963; children: Adewale, Oladapo, Abiodun, Ajoke, Olusola, Oluyemisi. BA, Trinity Coll., Cambridge, Eng., 1959, MA, 1963. Mech. engr. West Nigeria Devel. Corp., Ibadan, Nigeria, 1961-63; asst. factory mgr. Galvanising Industry Ltd., Lagos, Nigeria, 1963-65; ops. engr. Brit. Petroleum Ltd., Lagos, 1965-70; lectr., cons., dir. Nigerian Inst. Mgmt., Lagos, 1970-75; chmn., chief exec. Mgmt. Systems Ltd., Lagos, 1975—; chmn., mng. dir. Gen. Appliances Co. Ltd., Lagos, 1976—; mem. engring. faculty, bd. dirs. Lagos U., 1978-79; bd. dirs. Nigeria Securities and Exchange Commn., Lagos, 1979-83. Co-author: Curriculum for Mangement Training and Development, 1973, Readings in Production Management, 1987; patentee in field. Named Hon. Chief, Ondo Town Chieftaincy Instn., 1979, Ota Town Chieftaincy Instn., 1987. Fellow Nigerian Inst. Mgmt.; mem. Brit. Instn. Mech. Engrs., Internat. Cons. Found. (exec. bd. 1979-83), Nigerian Soc. Engrs., Inst. Mgmt. Cons. of Nigeria (pres. 1982), Mfrs. Assn. Nigeria (chmn. automotive sector 1985—). Home: 10 Alli Balogun Ave, Industrial Estate, Ikeja, Lagos Nigeria Office: Gacol Nigeria Ltd, 46 Allen Ave, PO Box 9678, Ikeja, Lagos Nigeria

AKINS, GEORGE CHARLES, accountant; b. Willits, Calif., Feb. 22, 1917; s. Guy Brookins and Eugenie (Swan) A.; A.A., Sacramento City Coll., 1941; m. Jane Babcock, Mar. 27, 1945. Accountant, auditor Calif. Bd. Equalization, Dept. Finance, Sacramento, 1940-44; controller-treas. DeVons Jewelers, Sacramento, 1944-73, v.p., controller, 1973-80, v.p., chief fin. officer, dir., 1980-84; individual accounting and tax practice, Sacramento, 1944—. Accountant, cons. Mercy Children's Hosp. Guild, Sacramento, 1957-77. Served with USAAF, 1942. Mem. Soc. Calif. Pioneers, Nat. Soc. Pub. Accountants, U.S. Navy League, Calif. Hist. Soc., English Speaking Union, Drake Navigators Guild, Internat. Platform Assn., Mendocino County Hist. Soc., Sacramento County Hist. Soc. Republican. Roman Catholic. Clubs: Commonwealth of Calif., Comstock. Contbg. author: Portfolio of Accounting Systems for Small and Medium-Sized Business, 1968, rev., 1977. Home and Office: 96 S Humboldt St Willits CA 95490

AKIYAMA, HARUHIKO, service executive; b. Tokyo, Japan, Sept. 7, 1933; s. Keishiro and Hide A.; m. Shizue, Oct. 21, 1933, children: Kazuko, Yukihiko. MS in Econs., Musashi U., 1976. Pres. Hotel Nikko de Paris, Paris, 1976-80; pres. Internat. Food Co. Ltd, Tokyo, 1981-84; exec. v.p. Hotel Nikko Fukuoka, Fukuoka, Japan, 1984—. Home: 3-14-2-708 Higashiizumi, 201 Komae Tokyo Japan Office: Hotel Nikko Fukuoka, 8-24 Tenyamachi Hakata, 812 Fukuoka Japan

AKIYAMA, MASAYUKI, educator; b. Kaminokawa, Tochigi, Japan, Feb. 5, 1930; s. Tokumatsu and Masa A.; BA, Nihon U., 1952; postgrad. U. Oreg., 1964-65; m. Sakiko Higashijima, Mar. 10, 1958; children: Risa, Yuka, Mika. Instr., Jr. Coll., Nihon U., 1956-63, instr. Coll. Humanities and Sci., 1963-66, asst. prof., 1966-74, prof. English and comparative lit., 1974—, dean acad. affairs Coll. Internat. Relations, 1979-85, vice dean, 1987—; senator Nihon U., 1987—; vis. prof. U. Ill., 1975-76. Dir., Mishima Assn. Fgn. City Affiliation. Nihon U. grantee, 1980. Mem. Am. Lit. Soc. Japan, English Lit. Soc. Japan, Japanese Comparative Lit. Assn., Am. Comparative Lit. Assn., MLA, Henry James Soc. Author: American Way of Life, 1963, Henry James: His World, His Thought, His Art, 1981; East-West editorial bd. Comparative Lit. Studies, 1980—; contbr. articles to profl. jours. Home: 1-3-1 Kataseyama, Fujisawa, Kanagawa 251, Japan Office: 2-31-145, Bunkyo-cho, Mishima Shizouka 411, Japan

AKIYAMA, SATOSHI, architect; b. Fukuoka, Fukuoka, Japan, Jan. 13, 1940; s. Takeshi and Yaeko Akiyama; m. Miwako Suzuki, Feb. 6, 1977; children: Yukiko, Taishi. BArch, Nihon U., Tokyo, 1963. Registered architect, Japan. Devel. engr. Nittoboseki Co., Ltd., Tokyo, 1963-65; architect Sugi Architects & Engrs., Inc., Tokyo, 1965-67; pres. Akiyama Architects & Engrs., Inc., Tokyo, 1967—, Tokyo Living Co., Ltd., Tokyo, 1977—. Mem. Japan Inst. Architects. Office: Tokyo Living Co, 1-33-7 Chuo, Nakano-ku, 164 Tokyo Japan

AKKARI, SAMIR, contracting company executive, business and management consultant; b. Broummana, Lebanon, Aug. 3, 1939; s. Akl and Alice (Mizher) A.; m. Juliette Pira, Sept. 22, 1969; 1 child, Lara. B.A., Am. U. Beirut, 1961, M.A., 1974. Sr. indsl. tng. specialist Aramco, Dhahran, Saudi Arabia, 1962-69; developer curriculum air cadet program Saudia, Jeddah, Saudi Arabia, 1970-74, mgmt. cons., 1975-78; gen. mgr. adminstrn. and ops. Sapdco, Jeddah, 1978-83; dep. gen. mgr. Almajd Alsaudi, Jeddah, 1983-84, v.p., 1984—; bd. dirs. Cable and Wireless Saudi Arabia Ltd. Greek Orthodox. Avocations: swimming; tennis; golf; horse back riding. Office: PO Box 11794, Jeddah 21463, Saudi Arabia

AKYÜZ, RINT, trading company executive, consultant; b. Ankara, Turkey, Jan. 3, 1949; s. Kenan and Emel (Iliris) A.; m. Ayfer Caycizade, June 1, 1978; 1 child, Iren Akyuz. BSc, Middle East Tech.U., Ankara, Turkey, 1971. Asst. Teknim Co. Ltd., Ankara, 1971-75, mgr. export, 1975-80, v.p., 1980-82; v.p. Karat Corp., Istanbul, Turkey, 1982-83; pres. Karat Corp., Istanbul, 1983-85; cons. Diler Corp., Istanbul, 1985-86, Cukurova Corp., Istanbul, 1985-86; chmn. Rotel Corp., Istanbul, 1985—; cons. Cukurova Fgn. Trade Copr., Istanbul, 1985-86, Diler Fgn. Trade Corp., Istanbul, 1985-

86; bd. dirs. Rom Gida Corp. Contbr. articles to profl. jours. Mem. Clothing Mgrs. Assn., Union Chambers, Chamber of Industry (pres. 1975-82). Moslem. Clubs: Büyük Kulüp, Bizim Tepe (Istanbul). Home: Cemil Topuzlu cad 143-6, 81060 Istanbul Turkey Office: Rotel Corp, Nisantasi Ihlamur Yolu 27, 80200 Istanbul Turkey

ALADJEM, SILVIO, obstetrician, gynecologist, educator; b. Bucharest, Romania, June 16, 1928; came to U.S., 1964, naturalized, 1969; s. Nahman and Lea (Campus) A. M.D. summa cum laude, U. Uruguay, 1961. Diplomate: Am. Bd. Obstetrics and Gynecology; cert. subsplty. in maternal-fetal medicine. Intern Uruguay Pub. Health Service, Montevideo, 1961-62; resident in obstetrics and gynecology U. Uruguay, 1962-63, Cleve. Met. Gen. Hosp., 1964-67; fellow in obstetrics and gynecology Western Res. U., 1967, asst. prof., attending obstetrician and gynecologist, 1969-74; instr. Med. Coll. Ga., 1967-68, asst. prof., 1968-69; assoc. prof. U. Ill., Chgo., 1975-76; prof. U. Ill., 1976-78, head div. perinatal medicine, 1976-78; prof., chmn. dept. obstetrics and gynecology Stritch Sch. Medicine, Loyola U., Chgo., 1978-84; dir. perinatal ctr. Bronson Hosp., Kalamazoo, 1984—; practice medicine specializing in obstetrics and gynecology; cons. Nat. Found. March of Dimes, Cleve., Chgo. Author: Risks in the Practice of Modern Obstetrics, 1972, 75, (with Audrey Brown) Clinical Perinatology, 1975, 79, Perinatal Intensive Care, 1976, Obstetrical Practice, 1980; contbr. (with Audrey Brown) articles to med. jours. Mem. Am. Coll. Obstetricians and Gynecologists (E. McDowell award 1967), Am. Fertility Soc. (C. Hartman award 1968), Soc. Gynecologic Investigation, Am. Soc. Anatomists, N.Y. Acad. Scis., Chgo. Gynecol. Soc., Chgo. Med. Soc., AMA, Mich. Med. Assn., Perinatal Group of Ill. (pres. 1976), Am. Assn. Maternal Neonatal Health (pres. 1978—). Office: Bronson Hosp 252 E Lovell Kalamazoo MI 49007

AL ADSANI, AHMAD MOHAMMED SALEH, engineer; b. Kuwait, Oct. 17, 1942; s. Mohammed Saleh Al Adsani and Husa Al Duwairi; m. Maryam Siliman Al-Luhaib; children: Mohammed, Naser, Riyad, Salah. BSME, U. Tex., 1966; MS in Engring., U. Glasgow, Scotland, 1970; Dip. B.A., U. Kuwait, 1974. Power engr. Ministry of Electricity and Water, Kuwait, 1966-68, project engr., 1969-73, dir. water resources, 1974-76, asst. undersec., 1977-78; vice chmn. Oman Cement Co., Muscat, Oman, 1978-80; ptnr., dir. Ctr. Engring. Discipline, Kuwait, 1980—; bd. dirs. Shuaiba (Kuwait) Paper Products Co. Fellow Brit. Inst. Mgmt.; mem. ASME, Nat. Water Supply Improvement Assn., Kuwait Soc. Engrs., Am. Mgmt. Assn., Am. Inst. Chem. Engrs., Nat. Soc. Profl. Engrs. Club: Kadisia Sports (Kuwait). Home: PO Box 39333, 73054 Nuzha Kuwait

ALAINI, MOHSIN AHMED, ambassador; b. Sana'a, Yemen, Oct. 20, 1932; s. Ahmed Hasan and Saadia A.; m. Aziza Bolohom Saleh, July 25, 1962; four children. Ed., U. Paris-Sorbonne; Law Degree, U. Cairo, 1959. Minister fgn. affairs Yemen Arab Republic, 1962, 65, 70-72, 74, 85, prime minister, 1967, 70, 71-74, 86-87, permanent rep. to UN, 1962-64, 65, 68, 80; A.E. and P. Yemen Arab Republic, U.S., 1962, 65-67, 84—, USSR, 1968-69, France, 1971, U.K., 1973-74, Fed. Republic Germany, 1981-84; gen. sec. Tchrs. Trade Union Aden; mem. exec. bd. Aden Trade Union Congress; rep. Aden Trade Union Congress in Internat. Confedn. Arab Trade Unions, Cairo. Author: Battles and Conspiracy Against Yemen, 1957. Mem. Free Yemeni Movement. Office: Embassy of Yemen Arab Republic 600 New Hampshire Ave NW Suite 860 Washington DC 20037

ALAM, A. Z. M. SHAMSUL, architect, engineer; b. Calcutta, West Bengal, India, Feb. 3, 1940; came to Pakistan/Bangladesh, 1947; s. Mohammad Abdul Khaleque and Begum Khodeza Khatoon; m. Meherun Nessa Alam, Feb. 16, 1961; children—Fatema, Ayesha, Ameena, Ahmad Mustafa. B.S. in Civil Engring., Dacca U., Bangladesh, 1960; B. Arch., Bangladesh U. of Engring. and Tech., Dhaka, 1966. Jr. engr. Parsons Corp., Dacca, 1960-62; engr. grade II Assoc. Cons. Engring., Dacca, 1962-64; jr. architect Vastukalabid & A.A.E., Dacca, 1964-66; cons. architect and engr. The Cons. Collaborative, Dacca, 1966-70; cons. architect Jabber & Assocs., Dacca, 1970-75, Alam & Assocs., Dacca, Abu Dhabi, United Arab Emirates, 1975—; pres. Alam & Assocs., Abu Dhabi, 1975—, Dhaka, 1966—; chmn. Alam Bros. Ltd., Dhaka, 1980—; pres. Gunga Din, Inc., St. Paul, Minn., 1985—. Fellow Inst. Engrs.; mem. Inst. Architects (life), AIA (profl. affiliate 1984—). Club: Bangledesh Assn. (pres. 1980-82). Lodge: Lions (sec. 1973-75). Avocations: gardening; music. Office: Alam & Assocs, PO Box 3294, Abu Dhabi United Arab Emirates

AL-AMRI, SAAD SAEED, civil engineer; b. Altalha, Saudi Arabia, Dec. 22, 1953; children: Reem, Badr. BCE, U. Petroleum and Minerals, Dhahran, Saudi Arabia. Civil engr. Dar Alriyadh Cons., Riyadh, Saudi Arabia, 1980-82; resident mgr. Dar Alriyadh Cons., Manila, 1982-84; dep. mgr., chief engring. preace shield project Dar Al Riyadh Cons., Riyadh, Saudi Arabia, 1984—. Mem. Soc. Am. Mil. Engrs. Home and Office: Dar Al Riyadh Cons, PO Box 5364, Riyadh 11422, Saudi Arabia

ALANIS, JOAN MARTI, co-prince of Andorra. Episcopal bishop Urgel, Andorra; then co-prince. Office: Office of Co-Prince, Andorra La Vella Andorra *

ALAOUI, MOULAY AHMED, government official; b. Fez, Morocco, 1919. Student, U. France, Paris, U. France, Montpellier. Head Dept. Info. and Tourism, Morocco, 1960, 63; with Dept. Fine Arts and Dept. Handicrafts, Morocco, 1961, 64; minister Industry and Mines, Morocco, 1966-67; with Ministry Econ. and Handicrafts, Morocco, 1967; head Ministry Tourism and Handicrafts, Morocco, 1968; minister of State in charge of nat. promotion and handicrafts Morocco, 1969-71, minister of State, 1983—. Address: Ministry of State, Rabat Morocco *

ALAPOUR, ADEL, nuclear engineer; b. Tehran, Iran, June 17, 1948; came to U.S., 1974; s. Mostafa and Mehry (Latifi) A.; m. Cynthia Ann Jackson, Feb. 20, 1980; children—Kavon A., Vida N. B.S.M.E., Arya-Mehr U. Tech.-Iran, 1970; M.S.N.E., Ga. Inst. Tech., 1975, Ph.D., 1980. Operation coordinator Iran Electric Power Generation & Transmission Co., Tehran, 1970-72, plant analyst, 1972-74; grad. research asst. dept. nuclear engring. Ga. Inst. Tech., Atlanta, 1974-78; nuclear engr. Brookhaven Nat. Lab., Upton, N.Y., 1978-80, So. Co. Services Inc., Birmingham, Ala., 1980-81, sr. engr., 1981—. Mem. Am. Nuclear Soc. (Birmingham sect. chmn. 1982-83, dir. 1983-86), N.Y. Acad. Scis., So. Co. Services Leadership Devel. Assn., Sigma Xi. Research on steady state and time dependent analysis of nuclear reactor systems. Home: 5193 Selkirk Circle Birmingham AL 35243 Office: So Co Services Inc PO Box 2625 Birmingham AL 35202

ALAQUIL, FAYSAL IBRAHIM, trading company executive; b. Taiff, Saudi Arabia, Sept. 15, 1954; s. Ibrahim and J. (Alfadl) A.; m. D. Gardey, Sept. 11, 1983; children: Sultan, Khaled, Abdulaziz. BBA, Coll. Notre Dame, Calif., 1979, MBA, 1982. V.p. AlBayda Trading, Jeddah, Saudi Arabia, 1979-80, dep. pres., 1980; mng. dir. Alsharkiah Devel. Co., Athens, 1980-81; project dir. Alsharkiah Devel. Co., Ridyah, Saudi Arabia, 1980-81; pres. ALBAYDA, 1981; asst. dir. Alsulaiman Enterprises, San Francisco, 1981-82; dep. chmn. African Arabian Islamic Bank, San Francisco, 1982-83; cons. INCOPA, Geneva, 1983-84; dep. project dir. Youssef I. Elakiel Trading Establishment, Riyadh, 1984—, ALBAYDA Trading Co., also v.p. Recipient achievement award Youssef I. Elakeel Trading Establishment, 1984. Mem. Saudi Arabia C. of C. Muslim. Home: PO Box 42614, 11551 Ridayh Saudi Arabia Office: AlBayda Trading Co, PO Box 42614, 11551 Riyadh Saudi Arabia

AL-ARASHI, ABDUL KARIM, vice president of Yemen Arab Republic. Formerly minister for local govt., minister treasur; speaker Constituent People's Assembly, 1978—; chmn. Provisional Presdl. Council, 1978; v.p. Yemen Arab Republic, 1978—. Address: Office of Vice Pres, Sanaa Yemen Arab Republic *

ALARCON, OSCAR V., publisher; b. Puebla, Puebla, Mex., Mar. 18, 1942; s. Gabriel and Herminia (Velazquez) A.; m. Diana Zamacona, July 22, 1970; children: Diana, Monica, Lucia, Oscar. Licenciado in Bus. Administrn., Inst. Tech. Mex., 1967; Licenciado in Journalism, U. Columbia, 1969; PhD. in Journalism, U. Md., 1975. Subdir. El Heraldo of Mex., Mexico City, 1965-86; counselor DESC, Mexico City, 1976—; dir. Interamerican Soc. of Prensa, Mex., 1978-87, El Heraldo of Mex., Mexico City, 1986-87; editor La Assn. de Edit de Periodicos Diarios de la Republica Mex., Mex., 1987—. Author: The Earthquake That Shook Mexico City. Roman Catholic. Club: Raqueta Bosques. Office: El Heraldo de Mexico, Carmona y Valle 150, Mexico City Mexico 06720

AL-ASHTAL, ABDALLA SALEH, ambassador; b. Addis Ababa, Ethiopia, Oct. 5, 1940; children—Lamees, Azal. B.B.A., Am. U. Beirut, 1966; M.A., NYU, 1973. Asst. dir. Yemeni Bank, Sanaa, Yemen Arab Rep., 1967-68; mem. supreme peoples council Hadramout province People's Democratic Republic Yemen, 1967-68, mem. gen. command nat. liberation front, 1968-70, polit. adviser permanent mission to UN, 1970-72, sr. counsellor permanent mission, 1972-73, non-resident ambassador to Mex., 1975-79, Can., 1974—, Brazil, 1984, Argentina, 1988; permanent rep. to UN, 1973—. Office: Perm Mission of Dem Yemen to UN 413 E 51st St New York NY 10022

ALATAS, ALI, Indonesian government official; b. Jakarta, Indonesia, Nov. 4, 1932; s. Abdullah A.; m. Yunisa Alatas, 1956; 3 daughters. Ed., Acad. Fgn. Affairs, Sch. Law U. Indonesia. Sec. to v.p. Indonesia, Jakarta, 1978-82; permanant rep. to UN N.Y.C., 1976-78, 82-84, 85-87; minister fgn. affairs Indonesia, Jakarta, 1988—. Office: Ministry Fgn Affairs, Jakarta Indonesia *

AL-ATHEL, HUSSEIN ABDULRAHMAN, service executive; b. Riyadh, Saudi Arabia, Dec. 16, 1944; s. Abdulrahman Saleh Al-Athel and Luluwah (Hussein) Al-Assaf; m. Nora Mansour Al-Assaf; children: Fahad, Fahada, Fadwa May, Abdulrahman, Luluwah. Diploma in statistics, Internat. Stats. Ctr., Beirut, 1965; MB in Bus. Adminstrn.magna cum laude, Seattle U., 1976, MBA, 1977. Dep. dir. stats. Ministry of Interior, Riyadh, Saudi Arabia, 1968-73, dir. budgeting, 1978-81; comptroller GAMA Services Ltd., Riyadh, 1981-82, v.p., 1982-84, exec. v.p., 1984-87, chief exec. officer, 1987—; bd. dirs. Saudi Arabian Computer Mgmt. Cons., Riyadh. Mem. Am. Coll. Healthcare Execs., Alpha Sigma Nu, Beta Gamma Sigma. Muslim. Home: Al-Worood Quarter, South of Prince Abdullah, Bin Abdulaziz Rd, PO Box 41726, Riyadh Saudi Arabia 11531 Office: GAMA Services Ltd, PO Box 41726, Al-Nassim, Riyadh Saudi Arabia 11531

AL-ATTAS, SYED MUHAMMAD AL-NAQUIB, philosopher, educator; b. Bogor, Java, Indonesia, Sept. 5, 1931; s. Syed Ali and Sharifah Raguan (Al-Aydrus) Al-A.; student Royal Mil. Acad., Sandhurst, Eng., 1953-55, U. Malaya, 1957-59; M.A., McGill U., 1962; Ph.D., London U., 1965; m. Latifah (Moira Maureen O'Shay) Oct. 9, 1961; children— Sharifah Faizah, Syed Ali Tawfik, Sharifah Shifa, Syed Haydar. Lectr., then sr. lectr./reader classical Malay Islamic lit. U. Malaya, 1964-69, dean faculty arts, 1969-70; prof. Malay lang. and lit., formerly dean faculty arts, founder, Inst. Malay Lang., Lit. and Culture, Nat. U. Malaysia, 1970—; state guest scholar Institut Vostokovedenia, Moscow, 1970; vis. scholar, vis. prof. Temple U., Phila., 1976-77; disting. prof., Tun Abdul Razak chair S.E. Asian studies, disting. prof. Islamic studies Ohio U., 1981-82; prof. Islamic thought and civilization, Internat. Islamic U., Kuala Lumpur, 1987; dir., 1988; lectr. throughout world on Islam in S.E. Asia; created Arabic calligraphic panel for Tropen Mus., Amsterdam, 1954; discovered, established true and correct date of Trengganu inscription, 1971; del. numerous internat. philos. congresses; prin. cons. World of Islam Festival, speaker Internat. Islamic Conf., London, 1976; UNESCO expert on Islamic history and civilization. Served with Malay Inf., 1950-56. Recipient Iqbal Centenary Commemorative medal Pres. Pakistan, 1979. Can. Council fellow, 1960-62; Commonwealth fellow, 1963; Brit. Council and Asia Found. grantee, 1963-64; Asia Found. grantee, 1971. Fellow Imperial Iranian Acad. Philosophy; mem. Am. Philos. Assn., Société Thomiste Internationale. Islam. Author: RANGKAIAN Rubaiyat, 1959; Some Aspects of Sufism as Understood and Practiced Among the Malays, 1963; Raniri and the Wujudiyyah of 17th Century Acheh, 1966; The Origin of the Malay Shair, 1968; Preliminary Statement on a General Theory of the Islamization of the Malay-Indonesian Archipelago, 1969; The Mysticism of Hamzah Fansuri, 1970; Concluding Postscript to the Origin of the Malay Shair, 1970; The Correct Date of the Trengganu Inscription, 1971; Islam dalam Sejarah dan Kebudayaan Melayu, 1971; Buku Panduan Jabatan Bahasa dan Kesusasteraan Melayu, 1972; Comments on the Reexamination of al-Raniri's Hujjatu'l-Siddiq: A Refutation, 1975; Islam: The Concept of Religion and the Foundation of Ethics and Morality, 1976; Islam: Faham Agama dan Asas Akhlak, 1977; Islam and Secularism, 1978; Risalah Untuk Kuam Muslimin, 1978; The Concept of Education in Islam, 1980; Islam dan Sekularisme, 1981; Konsep Pendidikan dalam Islam, 1984; Islam, Secularism and the Philosophy of the Future, 1985; A Commentary on the Hujjat-al-Siddig of Nural-Din al-Raniri, 1986; The Oldest Malay Manuscript: A 16th Century Translation of the Aqaid of al-Nasafi, 1987, others; editor Aims and Objectives of Islamic Education, 1979. Contbr. to Ency. of Islam, also numerous articles to publs. Home: 11 14-47A Petaling Jaya, Selangor Malaysia Office: Internat Islamic U, Kuala Lumpur Malaysia

AL-AZMEH, AZIZ, professor; b. Damascus, Syria, July 23, 1947; s. Malak and Salma (Nabulsi) Al-A.; m. Kasturi Sen; 1 child, Omar. License-ès-lettres, Beirut Arab U., 1971; MA, Eberhard-Karls U., Tübingen, 1973; D. of Philosophy, U. Oxford, 1978. Lectr. U. Kuwait, 1981-83; fellow dept. Arabic and Islamic studies U. Exeter, Eng., 1983-84, Sharjah prof. Islamic studies, 1985—; cons. project for translation of Arabic lits. UNESCO, ALESCO, UNITAR; bd. dirs. Arts Worldwide, London. Author: Ibn Khaldun in Modern Scholarship, 1981, Ibn Khaldun: An Essay in Reinterpretation, 1982, Historical Writing and Historical Culture (in Arabic), 1983, Arabic Thought and Islamic Societies, 1986, The Politics and History of Heritage (in Arabic), 1987; gen. editor Arabic and Islamic Studies; editor Studies in Arab Thought and Culture; editorial bd. Review of Middle East Studies. Chmn. Arab Orgn. for Human Rights, London, 1986. Fellow British Soc. for Middle East Studies, Arab Social History Group. Office: U Exeter, Prince of Wales Rd, Exeter EA4 4QJ, England

ALBACH, RICHARD ALLEN, microbiology educator; b. Chgo., Mar. 31, 1930; s. Maurice and Martha (Silverman) A.; m. Janice Elaine Boewe, Jan. 23, 1962; children—Michael, Karren, Kimala, David, Brian, Julie, Barry. B.S., U. Ill., 1956, M.S., 1958; Ph.D., Northwestern U., 1963. Asst. prof. U. Health Scis., Chgo. Med. Sch., 1968-69, North Chicago, Ill., assoc. prof., 1969-73, prof., 1973—, vice chmn., 1975-82, acting chmn., 1982—; editorial cons. Yearbook Med. Pubs., Chgo., 1975-81. Contbr. articles to profl. jours. Served with U.S. Army, 1953-55, NIH grantee, 1965-78; LAbbott Found. fellow, 1961; Trustees Research award Chgo. Med. Sch., 1968; Teaching Prof. of the Yr., 1976, 78, 82. Fellow Am. Acad. Microbiology; mem. Am. Soc. Microbiology, Soc. Protozoologists (exec. com. 1984—), Am. Soc. Parasitologists, Ill. Soc. Microbiology (membership chmn. 1969-70) Research in biology of parasitic protozoa. Address: Univ Health Sci Chicago Med Sch 3333 Green Bay Rd North Chicago IL 60064

ALBAN, ROGER CHARLES, construction equipment distribution executive; b. Columbus, Ohio, Aug. 3, 1948; s. Charles Ellis and Alice Jacqueline (Hosfeld) A.; student pub. schs.; m. 2d Rebecca Lynn Gallicchio, Aug. 12, 1978; children—: Roger Charles II, Charles Michael; 1 dau. by previous marriage, Allison Ann. With Alban Equipment Co., Columbus, 1963—, sales mgr., 1972-75, gen. mgr., 1975-85, treas., 1978-85, v.p., 1980-85, pres. 1985—. Mem. Grandview Heights Bd. Edn., Columbus, 1978-85, pres., 1979, v.p., 1982, legis. liaison, 1978-79, 83-84; elected Grandview Heights City Council, 1986; mem. Met. Ednl. Council, Columbus Area Leadership Program, 1982-83. Mem. Assoc. Equipment Distbrs. (lt. dir. region 6 1980, 85, 86, 88, chmn. light equipment dist. com. 1985, chmn. sales and mktg. com. 1987), Ohio Sch. Bds. Assn. (mem. all cen. region bd. 1984), Bldg. Industry Assn. Cen. Ohio, Internat. Platform Assn., Am. Rental Assn., Builders Exchange Cen. Ohio (trustee 1987—), Am. Mgmt. Assn., Nat. Right To Work Com., Nat. Fedn. Ind. Bus., Ohio Equipment Distbrs. Assn. (dir. 1982, 84—, pres. 1983), Roundtable, Am. Mensa Ltd. (chpt. exec. com. 1979-80). Roman Catholic. Clubs: Rotary, Downtown Columbus. Home: 1430 Cambridge Blvd Columbus OH 43212-3207 Office: 1825 McKinley Ave Columbus OH 43222

ALBARET, JEAN-CLAUDE, stomatologist; b. Courbevoie, France, Feb. 6, 1934; s. Paul Marie Joseph and Marie Louise (Tardieu) A.; m. Raymonde Jeandrieu, Dec. 29, 1968; children: Elisabeth, Pierre-Antoine, Hélène. MD, U. Paris, 1959. Practice medicine specializing in stomatology Paris, 1959—; cons. various hosps. Paris, 1964—. Patentee in field. Served with med. corp French Army, 1961-62. Office: Alphonse XIII N 6, 75016 Paris France

ALBEDA, WILLEM FREDERICK, scientific council executive; b. Rotterdam, The Netherlands, June 13, 1925; s. Frederik and Jansje (deVries) A.; m. Van de Wilde, Oct. 2, 1952; children: Erik, Peter, Hein, Louens. Doctoral, Rotterdam Sch. Econs., 1950; PhD, Free U., Amsterdam, The Netherlands, 1957. Advisor Bldg., Amsterdam, 1951-60; with Philips Corp., Eidhoven, The Netherlands, 1960-61; sec. Christian Fedn. T.U., Utrecht, The Netherlands, 1961-66; prof. Erasmus U., Rotterdam, 1966-67; minister social affairs Govt. of Netherlands, The Hague, 1977-81, pres. Sci. Council for Govt. Policy, 1985—; dean, founder faculty econs. State U., Maastricht, The Netherlands, 1981-85; mem. supervisory bd. KOK publs., Kampen, The Netherlands, 1981—, A.B.N. Bank, Amsterdam, 1982—, KLM Airlines, 1983—; pres. Com. for Advice and Arbitration for Govt. and Civil Servants. Author numerous books and articles on various econ., social and polit. subjects. Pres. Ecumenical Devel. Coop. Soc., World Council of Chs. Decorated Knight Order Dutch Lion, commd. Order of Orange Nassau; fellow Vanier Inst. of Family, Ottawa, 1981-82. Mem. Orgn. Economists (bd. dirs., pres. 1983-87), Am. Acad. Artitration (corr.). Mem. Christian Democrat Party. Mem. Reformed Ch. Home: Al Jacobslaan 32, 2314 EN Leiden The Netherlands Office: WRR Plein 1813 No 2, 2514JN The Hague The Netherlands

ALBEE, EDWARD FRANKLIN, author, playwright; b. Mar. 12, 1928; s. Reed A. and Frances (Cotter) Albee. Student, Trinity Coll., Hartford, Conn., 1946-47. Messenger Western Union, 1955-58. Plays written include The Zoo Story, 1958, The Death of Bessie Smith, 1959, The Sandbox, 1959, The American Dream, 1960, Who's Afraid of Virginia Woolf?, 1961-62, The Ballad of the Sad Cafe (adaption of Carson McCullers' novella), 1963, Tiny Alice, 1964, Malcolm, 1966, A Delicate Balance, 1966 (Pulitzer Prize winner 1967), Everything in the Garden, 1968, Box, Quotations from Chariman Mao, 1970, All Over, 1971, Seascape, 1975 (Pulitzer prize 1975), Counting the Ways, 1976, Listening, 1977, The Man Who Had Three Arms, 1983, The Lady from DuBuque, 1978-79; adaptation of Lolita (Nabokov), 1980, Finding the Sun, 1982, Walking, 1984, Marriage 1986-87; dir. plays, including Seascape, Coconut Grove Playhouse, Miami, 1986; lecturer, Brandeis U., Johns Hopkins U., Webster U., others; scholar in residence, disting. adj. prof. drama, Northeastern State Coll., Tahlequah, Okla. Com. chmn. Brandeis U. Creative Arts Awards, 1983, 84; pres. Edward F. Albee Found. Recipient Pulitzer prize, 1967, 75; Gold medal in Drama Am. Acad. and Inst. Arts and Letters, 1980; inducted Theater Hall of Fame, 1985. Mem. Nat. Inst. Arts and Letters. Home: Old Montauk Hwy Montauk NY 11954 *

ALBERDING, CHARLES HOWARD, petroleum and hotel executive; b. Clayville, N.Y., Mar. 5, 1901; s. Charles and Doris (Roberts) A.; m. Bethine Wolverton, May 2, 1930; children: Beth Ann, Mary Katherine, Melissa Linda. EE, Cornell U., 1923. Lab. asst., draftsman, operator Producers & Refiners Corp., Parco, Wyo., 1923-25; engr., cracking plant supt. Imperial Refineries, Ardmore, Okla., Eldorado, Ark., 1925-27; head fgn. operating dept. Universal Oil Products Co., London, Eng., Ploesti, Roumania, Rangoon, Burma, Venice, Italy, 1927-33; head operating, service depts., Chgo. hdqrs. Universal Oil Products Co., 1933-42; pres., dir. Paradise Inn, Inc., Jokake Inn, Inc., Vinoy Park Hotel Co., Holiday Hotel Corp., Alsonett Hotels, Sabine Irrigation Co., Sabine Canal Co., Tides Hotel Corp., Harmony Oil Corp., London Square Corp., Petroleum Spltys., Lincoln Lodge Corp., Peabody Hotel Corp., Memphis, Hermitage Hotel Co., Nashville, Royal Palms Inn, Inc., Torrey Pines Inn, La Jolla, Calif., Charleston First Corp.; petroleum cons., dollar-per-yr. man WPB, 1942-43; dist. dir. petroleum refining Petroleum Adminstrn. for War, 1943-45. Presdl. councilor Cornell U.; bd. govs. Endowment Found., Heritage Trust. Mem. Scorpion. Republican. Congregationalist. Clubs: Valley (Phoenix); Kenilworth (Chgo.), Cornell (Chgo.); Sunset Country (St. Petersburg, Fla.), Bath (St. Petersburg, Fla.); Tides Country (pres., dir.), Rolling Greens Golf (pres., dir.), Sunrise Golf (Sarasota, Fla.) (pres., dir.). Home: 99 Tudor Pl Kenilworth IL 60043 Office: 9 E Huron Chicago IL 60611

ALBERGA, ALTA WHEAT, artist; b. Ala.; d. James Richard and Leila Savannah (Sullivan) Wheat; B.A., M.A., Wichita State U., 1954; B.F.A., Washington U., St. Louis, 1961; M.F.A., U. Ill., 1964; m. Alvyn Clyde Alberga, Dec. 3, 1930. Mem. faculty Wichita (Kans.) State U., 1955-56, Webster Coll., St. Louis, 1962, Presbyn. Coll., Clinton, S.C., 1969-74; pvt. art tchr., Greenville, S.C., 1974—; substitute tchr. Greenville County Schs.; tchr. painting Tempo Gallery Sch., Greenville, 1974—, Greenville County Mus. Sch., 1975—, Tryon (N.C.) Fine Arts Ctr., 1986; one-woman shows: Greenville County Mus., 1979, Greenville Artists Guild Gallery, 1979, 83, Wichita State U., 1954, St. Louis Artists Guild, 1956, N.C. State U., 1965, Met. Arts Council, Greenville, 1980, 83; group shows include: Pickens County Mus., 1979, Inter/Art 81, Washington 1981, Greenville Artists Guild, 1982, Art/7, Washington, 1983; represented in pvt. collections; bd. dirs. Greenville Artists Guild, 1977-79, pres., 1985; bd. dirs. Guild Gallery, 1978, Guild Greenville Symphony, 1982-83. Recipient Richard K. Weil award St. Louis Mus., 1957; Purchase prize S.C. Arts Commn., 1972; Merritt award Greenville Mus., 1986, Pickens County Mus., 1987, 88. Mem. Artists Equity (pres. St. Louis chpt. 1962), Internat. Platform Assn. (life), Art Students League, Guild Greenville Artists (pres. 1984-85), S.C. Artists Guild, Southeastern Council Printmakers, Greenville Symphony Guild, Kappa Pi, Kappa Delta Pi. Democrat. Home: 11 Overton Dr Greenville SC 29609

ALBERIGI, ALESSANDRO, electronics engineer; b. Reggio Emilia, Italy, June 15, 1927; s. Max and Maria (Peviani) A.; Laurea in Physics, U. Rome, 1948. Mem. faculty U. Modena, prof. electronics, 1967—; past chmn. bd. Italsiel S.p.A.; past vice chmn. bd., chief exec. officer Finsiel S.p.A.; chmn. bd. Finsiel IRI Group, 1987—. Fellow IEEE; mem. Am. Phys. Soc., Italian Phys. Soc., Italian Elec. Soc. Author papers in field. Office: Finsiel SpA, Via Isonzo 21/b, 00198 Rome Italy

ALBERT, JEAN-PAUL, physician; b. Freyming, Moselle, France, Nov. 7, 1946; s. Jean-Pierre and Anne-Marie (Mayer) A.; m. Linda Elharrar, July 3, 1969; children: Jean-David, Hélène, Sarah. MD, U. Strasbourg, France, 1972, also cert. work and sports medicine, tropical diseases. Médicin des mines Soc. de Secours Miniere, Merlebach, France, 1972-75; médecin liberal, Illkirch, France, 1975—. Office: 1 Rue des Lilas, 67400 Illkirch France

ALBERT, MAURICE GABRIEL, radiologist; b. Bannalec, France, Dec. 9, 1939; s. Gabriel Gustav and Eugenie (Daniel) A.; m. Elisabeth Baron, Nov. 28, 1941; children: Marie-Agnes, Gabriel, Helene, Anne, Cecile, Thibault. Intern Hosp. of Nantes, France, 1961, asst. lectr., 1967, sr. hosp. lectr., faculty of medicine, 1967-68; practice medicine specializing in pediatrics, Nantes, 1968-71; radiologist Ctr. de Radiodiagnostic—Exploration Cardio-Vasculaire, Nantes, 1971—. Mem. French Soc. Radiology. Roman Catholic. Club: Lagourmette (Nantes). Home: Gresset No 9, Nantes France 44000 Office: Ctr de Radiodiagnostic, 27 D Feuillet, Nantes France 44000

ALBERT, VASHER JEORGE, banker; b. Prague, Czechoslovakia, Sept. 3, 1926; came to England, 1970; s. Wenzel and Maria (Zeithammer) A.; m. Zaria Iva Albert, Sept. 20, 1950; children— Zaria Natalie, Edith Jeanny, Albert Frank David. Diploma, Sorbonne U., Paris, 1946; BSc, Air Force Staff Coll., Koeniggraetz, 1954; MSc, Czech Tech. U., Prague, 1958; diploma Charles U., Prague, 1962. Registered fin. planning cons. Inst. Sales and Mktg. Mgmt. Eng.; registered mktg. services cons. Officer, fighter pilot Air Force Czechoslovakia, 1946-56; dir. transport and engring. dept. Nat. Tech. Mus., Prague, 1956-59; head Pan African div. Ministry Fgn. Affairs, Prague, 1959-61; head chancery, chargé d'affaires Czechoslovak embassy, Rabat, Morocco, Nairobi, Kenya, 1961-70; area dir. Lloyds Bank Internat. Group, London, 1970-80; chmn. Dalebond Fin. Internat. Ltd., London, 1980—; vis. prof. Czech Tech. U., 1956-59; attaché, cons. Giles & Overbury, Stock-exchange, London, 1980-86; chmn. Bridgecrown Ltd., London, 1980—; dir. Euro-African Advisors Ltd., London, 1983—, Prudentfine, Ltd., London, Freeman and Liveryman, London; assoc., cons. Grosz Cons., Lyon, France, 1980—. Author: Senegal, Gambia, 1967; Somalia, Djibouti, 1970; Transport History Outline, 1958; contbr. articles to profl. jours. Hon. treas., Anglo-Ivory Coast Soc., London, 1972—. Fellow Inst. of Instl. Adminstrv. Accts., London, Inst. Dirs. London, Inst. Sales and Mktg. Mgmt.; mem. Westminster C. of C., Stock exchange London, Lloyds of London (underwriting mem.), London Chamber Commerce and Industry, Royal African Soc. London. Clubs: Royal Auto, May Fair, Kelvin, Carnavon, Premier, Lions Internat. (past pres. London Host Club). Home: Norman Lodge, 53 Higher Dr, Banstead Surrey GB-SM7 IPW England Office: Dalebond Finance Internat Ltd, Diana House, 33 Chiswell St, London EC1Y 4SE, England

ALBERTI, DUCCIO NERI, manufacturing company executive; b. Nerviano, Italy, Oct. 11, 1952; arrived in The Netherlands, 1985; s. Francesco Nicolo and Carla Maria (Fumagalli) A.; m. Daria Beatrice Langosco, Aug. 7, 1978; children: Nicolò, Micaela. Diploma in Chem. Engring., Fed. Inst. Tech., Zurich, 1975. Mktg. specialist DuPont de Nemours, Geneva and Paris, 1978-80; mktg. rep. Paris, 1981-83; automotive mktg. specialist Gen. Electric Plastics, Paris, 1983-84; automotive field mgr. Bergen Op Zoom, The Netherlands, 1985-86; product mgr. 1987—. Served with Italian mil. Corps Engrs., 1976-78. Mem. Soc. Automotive Engrs., Soc. Ingenieurs Automobile. Home: 12 Bis Rye Des Marroniers, 75016 Paris France Office: Gen Electric Plastics, PO Box 117, 4600 AC Bergen Op Zoom The Netherlands

ALBION, MARK STEVEN, business economics and marketing educator, consultant; b. Boston, Apr. 3, 1951; s. Donald Leo Albion and Leni Cohen Joyce; m. Johanna Lee Hughson, May 31, 1981. A.B., Harvard U., 1973, A.M., 1977, Ph.D., 1981. Cert. real estate broker. Various mktg. positions J.E.M. Assocs., Inc., Coral Gables, Fla., 1971-81; research asst./assoc. Mktg. Sci. Inst., Cambridge, Mass., 1978—; head bus. econs. tutor Harvard U., Cambridge, 1978-81, instr., 1978-81, asst. prof. bus., 1982—; cons. Atlanta, 1981-82; dir. Multigroup Health Plan, Wellesley, Mass., 1982—, Leni's Inc., Watertown, Mass., 1980—, Mars Stores Inc., New Bedford, Mass., 1984—; cons. various cos., 1981—. Author: The Advertising Controversy, 1981; Advertising's Hidden Effects, 1983; Decision Making with the Personal Computer, 1988. Contbr. articles to profl. jours. and newspapers including N.Y. Times, Washington Post. Author first computer caseseries Harvard Bus. Sch. Fund raiser St. Mark's Sch., Southboro, Mass., 1982—, class agt., 1969-73. Harvard Bus. Sch. fellow, 1980; recipient Outstanding Teaching award Harvard-Danforth Ctr., 1980; Procter & Gamble research award, 1985. Mem. Am. Mktg. Assn. (Outstanding Dissertation award, 1981). Club: Hasty Pudding (Cambridge, Mass.). Home: 6 Longfellow Rd Wellesley Hills MA 02181 Office: Harvard U Bus Sch Fowler 25 Boston MA 02163

ALBOR, LARRY JOHN, marketing professional; b. Chgo., Jan. 15, 1948; s. Enedino John and Mary Eve (Kaminski) A. BA, Quincy Coll., 1971; MA, St. Louis U., 1974. Sales rep. Garner Soc. St. Louis, 1976-78; coordinator Inroads/Chgo., 1978-80; acct. exec. Ill. Bell, Chgo., 1980-83, mgr. mktg., 1983-87; adminstr. market research Contel Service Corp., St. Louis, 1987—. Pres. Buena Park Neighbors Assn., 1985-87; bd. dirs. Uptown Chgo. Commn., 1987. Grad. fellow St. Louis U., 1971-75, Fulbright-Hays fellow, 1976. Mem. Am. Mgmt. Assn., Chgo. Computer Soc. Republican. Roman Catholic. Club: Kiwanis. Office: Contel Service Corp 600 Mason Ridge Ctr Dr Saint Louis MO 63141

ALBRECHT, JAN, neurochemist, educator; b. Warsaw, Poland, June 22, 1944; s. Stanislaw and Kamilla (Flisowska) A.; m. Jolanta Karasiewicz, May 31, 1983; 1 child, Grzegorz. MS, U. Warsaw, 1966; PhD, U. Leiden, 1970; postgrad., Polish Acad. Sci., 1980. Research asst. U. Leiden, The Netherlands, 1966-70; research assoc. Med. Research Ctr. Polish Acad. Sci., Warsaw, 1970-80, asst. prof., 1980-84, assoc. prof. in neurochemistry, 1984—; research fellow Mayo Med. Sch., Rochester, Minn., 1976-78; research mgr. Unilever Research Lab., Vlaardingen, The Netherlands, 1982-83; lectr. Med. Ctr. Postgrad. Studies, Warsaw, 1986—. Contbr. articles to profl. publs., chpts. to books. Recipient Sci. Sec.'s award Polish Acad. Sci., 1977, 79. Mem. Internat. Soc. Neuropathology, Assn. Polish Neuropathology (sec. 1984-87), Polish Biochem. Soc. (v.p. Warsaw chpt. 1986—), European Soc. Neurochemistry, Mayo Alumni Assn. Home: Lasek Brzozowy 7 m 10, 02-792 Warsaw Poland Office: Med Research Ctr, Polish Acad Sci, Dworkowa St 3, 02-792 Warsaw Poland

ALBRIGHT, DOROTHY JANE, sales and marketing executive; b. Charlotte, N.C., Sept. 16, 1945; d. George Franklin and Dorothy (Severs) A. Student Queens Coll., Charlotte, N.C., 1963-66. Mgr. sales and mktg. J.M. Garner Devel., Atlanta, 1978-82; account exec. sales and mktg. Bryant Lithographing, Atlanta, 1982-83; sr. account mgr. sales and mktg. COMPACK-Comprehensive Packaging, Atlanta, 1983-85; sales and mktg. mgr. Brock, Green & Assocs., Atlanta, 1985-86; owner Albright and Assocs. Mktg. Services, Atlanta, 1986—. Bd. dirs. High Mus. Art, Atlanta, 1981-85. Mem. Am. Mktg. Assn. (bd. dirs. Atlanta chpt. 1983-84, sec. 1984-85, v.p. 1986-88, pres-elect 1988—). Republican. Episcopalian. Office: Albright & Assocs 2796 Alpine Rd NE Atlanta GA 30305

ALBRIGHT, JAMES CURTICE, physicist; b. Madison, Wis., Sept. 8, 1929; s. Penrose Strong and Mary (Lucas) A.; B.S., Wichita U., 1950; M.S., U. Okla., 1952, Ph.D., 1956; m. Velma Lee Pliley, June 3, 1951; children—James Pliley, Kristine, Tamera, Gayle. With Conoco Inc., 1955—, sect. supr., 1971-74, research asso., Ponca City, Okla., 1974-82, sr. research assoc., 1982—. Pres. Ponca Playhouse, Ponca City, 1961-62; chmn. Ponca City Republican Com., 1965-66; pres. Kay County Assn. Children with Learing Disabilities, 1978-79; vice chmn. zone 12 Camp Fire Inc., 1976-80, pres. Ponca Area council, 1979-80; mem. United Way Bd., Ponca City, 1980-81; bd. dirs. North Burma Christian Mission, 1982—. Recipient Ernest Thompson Seaton award Camp Fire Inc., 1978, Wakan award, 1979, Luther Halsey Gulick award, 1980. Mem. Soc. Petroleum Engrs., Soc. Profl. Well Log Analysts, Sigma Xi. Club: Rotary (Paul Harris fellow 1988). Contbr. in field. Home: 131 Elmwood Ave Ponca City OK 74601 Office: PO Box 1267 Ponca City OK 74603

ALBRITTON, WILLIAM HAROLD, III, lawyer; b. Andalusia, Ala., Dec. 19, 1936; s. Robert Bynum and Carrie (Veal) A.; m. Jane Rollins Howard, June 2, 1958; children: William Harold IV, Benjamin Howard, Thomas Bynum. A.B., U. Ala., 1959, LL.B., 1960. Bar: Ala. 1960. Assoc. firm Albrittons & Rankin, Andalusia, 1962-66, partner, 1966-76; partner firm Albrittons & Givhan, Andalusia, 1976-86, Albrittons, Givhan & Clifton, Andalusia, 1986—; dir. TV Cable Co., Andalusia, Comml. Bank Andalusia. Bd. dirs. Ala. Law Sch. Found., Ala. Law Inst.; mem. exec. com. Ala. Republican Party, 1967-78; chmn. Covington County Rep. Party, 1967-87; trustee, elder 1st Presbyn. Ch., Andalusia. Served to capt. AUS, 1960-62. Fellow Am. Coll. Trial Lawyers; mem. ABA, Covington County Bar Assn. (pres. 1973), Ala. State Bar (commr. 1981—, disciplinary commn. 1981-84, v.p. 1985-86), Andalusia C. of C. (pres. 1967-68), Nat. Assn. R.R. Trial Counsel, Am. Judicature Soc., Ala. Def. Lawyers Assn. (pres. 1976-77), Internat. Assn. Def. Counsel, Trial Attys. Am., Assn. Ins. Attys., Phi Beta Kappa, Phi Delta Phi, Omicron Delta Kappa, Alpha Tau Omega. Clubs: Rotary (pres. 1979), Andalusia Country (pres. 1977), Bluewater Bay Sailing. Home: 730 Albritton Rd Andalusia AL 36420 Office: 109 Opp Ave Andalusia AL 36420

ALBRITTON, WILLIAM HOYLE, training and consulting executive, lectr., writer; b. Cleveland, Tenn., May 29, 1942; s. Hoyle Franklin and Marie Arlene (Mount) A.; m. June Ellington, June 20, 1964; children: Elizabeth Anne, William Hoyle. BA, Tenn. Wesleyan Coll., 1964; postgrad. in bus. adminstrn. U. Chgo., 1974-75. Assoc. Lendman Assocs., Los Angeles, 1969-70, dir. West Coast ops., 1970-71; ter. mgr. Baxter-Travenol, Deerfield, Ill., 1971-72, field sales trainer, 1972, sales edn. mgr., 1973; nat. sales recruiter The Kendall Co. div. Colgate-Palmolive, Boston, 1973-75, tng. and devel. mgr., 1975-76, dir. compensation, 1976-77, dir. staffing and mgmt. devel., 1978-81; pres. Tng. Concepts, Inc., Boston, 1981-86, chmn. bd. dirs., chief exec. officer 1986—. Team capt. Jordan Hosp. Spl. Funds. Plymouth, Mass., 1978-82; mem. personnel bd. Town of Duxbury, Mass., 1980—, chmn., 1984—. Author: Managing Yourself and Others, Internal Consulting for Results, Results-Oriented Selling, Results-Oriented Management, Presenting Technical Information. Vestryman, lay reader Episc. ch. Served as officer USNR, 1966-69. Mem. Am. Soc. Tng. and Devel., Internat. Platform Assn., Am. Mgmt. Assn. (Pres. Assn.), Greater Boston C. of C., Instrnl. Systems Assn. Democrat. Clubs: Exec., Algonquin, Duxbury Yacht. Lodge: Rotary (v.p. 1978-79, pres. 1979-80). Home: 781 West St Duxbury MA 02332 Office: 140 Wood Rd Braintree MA 02184

ALBUQUERQUE, PEDRO ALCEBÍADES DE, construction company executive; b. Varginha, Brazil, Mar. 21, 1941; s. Pedro Álvaro Rodrigues de Albuquerque and Marieta Pizzo Rodrigues de Albuquerque (Pizzo); m. Fernanda Lenisa Amata; 1 child, Irma Lenisa. Electr. and Mech. Engr., Escola Engenharia U. Fed., Belo Horizonte, 1964. Line engr. Volkswagen, São Bernardo, São Paulo, Brazil, 1965; chief engr. Companhia Vale do Rio Doce, Itabira-Minas Gerais, Brazil, 1966-69; div. mgr. Companhia Vale do Rio Doce, Itabira-Minas Gerais, 1970-72; gen. supt. Mendes Jr., Belo Horizonte MG, Brazil, 1973-78; exec. dir. Mendes Jr., Belo Horizonte MG, 1979-86, gen. dir., 1987—; pres., cons. Mendes/ENSA/Paranapanema, Goiânia, Goiás, 1985-86, Consortium Mendes/Paranapanema, Belém, Pará, 1985-86; supt. dir. Mentech, Rio de Janeiro, 1983-87; sr. v.p. Mendes Jr. Internat., Cayman Islands, 1983—; supt. dir. Mendes Jr. Motores, Belo Horizonte, 1987—. Mem. ASME, Soc. Automotive Engrs., Am. Mgmt. Assn. Clukbs: Iate Tênis, Pampulha Iate (Belo Horizonte). Lodge: Rotary. Office: Construtora Mendes Jr SA, Av Prof Mário Werneck 1685, 30430 Belo Horizonte MG Brazil

ALBY, JAMES FRANCIS PAUL, priest, educator; b. Milw., July 16, 1936; s. Francis Joseph and Sarah Sophie (Hansen) A.; B.A., Gallaudet U., 1963, M.S. in Edn., 1964; M.Div., Va. Theol. Sem., 1971; m. Jan Lorraine Peplinski, Aug. 2, 1980; 1 child. Ordained priest Episcopal Ch., 1971; priest to the deaf St. James Mission of the Deaf, Milw., 1971-76; priest assoc. St. Peter's Ch., West Allis, Wis., 1972-83; asst. to rector: Ministry of the Deaf, St. James Parish, Milw., 1983—; tchr. high sch. hearing impaired Milw. Pub. Schs., 1972—; priest assoc. Holy House of Our Lady of Walsingham, Norfolk, Eng., 1984—; instr. interpreting for deaf U. Wis., Milw., 1975-77; sr. high sch. boys dorm supr.-counselor St. John's Sch. for the Deaf, St. Francis, Wis., 1971-72; tchr. lang. of signs Milw. Area Tech. Coll., 1974-75; mem. adv. com. continuing edn. deaf adults, Milw., 1976-84, mem. adv. com. on edn. hearing impaired Milw. Pub. Schs., 1977—; mem. sect. 504 com. Southeastern Wis. Disabilities Coalition, 1979-81, mem. adult edn. adv. com. Milw. Hearing Soc., 1976-83. Contbr. articles to profl. jours. Mem. Nashotah House Sem. Alumni Assn. (assoc.), Nat. Fraternal Soc. Deaf, Nat. Assn. of Deaf, Wis. Assn. Deaf, Danish Brotherhood in Am., Greater Milw. Lions Club (charter pres.), Lioness (liaison 1980-84), Gallaudet U. Alumni Assn., Alpha Sigma Pi. Avocations: collecting Danish blue plates and firematic collectibles. Office: St James Episcopal Ch 833 W Wisconsin Ave Milwaukee WI 53233

ALBY, PIERRE ANDRÉ ALEC, mining engineer; b. Paris, Nov. 23, 1921; s. Henry Georges and Yvonne Lilian Nicoletis A.; grad. engr. Ecole Poly. Paris, 1940-42, Ecole des Mines de Paris, 1942-45; m. Marine Yvonne Marie Thérèse Amet, July 2, 1948; children— Sabine, Veronique, Eric Thierry Benedicte Nathalie Sandrine. Govt. mining engr. Bethune, 1945-49; gen. staff of Def., Paris, 1949-53; asst. sec. Interministerial Com. of European Econ. Affairs, 1953-57; gov., dir. of mines, Paris, 1957-64; asst. gen. mgr. Gaz de France, Paris, 1964-69, gen. mgr., 1969-79, pres., 1979-86, hon. pres. 1986—; pres. Entreprise de Recherches et d'Activités l'étrolières, 1980-82. Mem. Gen. Council of Mines, France, 1974-87, v.p., 1982-87; pres. Internat. Group Liquefied Natural Gas Importers, 1987—. Decorated comdr. Legion of Honour, comdr. Order of Merit (France); comdr. Order of Merit (Italy); comdr. St. Charles (Monaco). Club: Union Interalliée Paris. Home: 8 rue Guy de Maupassant, 75116 Paris France Office: 62 rue de Courcelles, 75008 Paris France

ALCAMO, FRANK PAUL, retired educator; b. South Fork, Pa., May 25, 1920; s. Carmelo and Antonia (Trifiro) A.; student Johnstown Coll., 1938-39; B.S., Indiana U. Pa., 1942; M.Ed., Pa. State U., 1954; m. Josephine Giusto, June 22, 1944; 1 dau., Antoinette. Math. and sci. tchr. Wilmore (Pa.) High Sch., 1942-54, Beaverdale (Pa.)-Wilmore High Sch., 1954-56; math. tchr. South Fork (Pa.)-Croyle High Sch., 1956-61, Triangle Area High Sch., Sidman, Pa., 1961-62; asst. prin. Windber (Pa.) Area High Sch., 1962-63, prin., 1963-81. Author: The Windber Story, 1983, The South Fork Story, 1987. Treas., Windber Summer Playground Assn., 1963; chmn. Windber Police Civil Service Commn., 1964-81. Bd. dirs., pres. Mid-State Auto Club of Johnstown, 1965—; bd. dirs. Windber Indsl. Devel. Assn., Cambria County Hist. Soc., 1988—; founder, v.p. CBW Schs. Fed. Credit Union, 1956—; v.p. Windber Public Library, 1976-81; bd. dirs. Windber Recreation Assn., treas., 1974-80; bd. dirs., v.p. Johnstown Flood Mus., 1985—. Served to lt. (j.g.) USNR, 1944-46. Named to Windber Hall of Fame, 1984. Mem. Pa. Edn. Assn. (local br. com. 1966-70, dept. adminstrn. pres. 1971-75, pres. Windber 1965-66), Somerset County Secondary Prins. Assn. (pres. 1965-66), NEA (life), Nat., Pa. assns. secondary sch. prins., PIAA (dist. treas. 1970—), Greater Johnstown Assn. Sch. Retirees (pres. 1983-85, 88—), Am. Assn. Retired Persons Tax Counselors for Elderly, Sons of Italy, Pa. Assn. Sch. Retirees, Phi Delta Kappa, Sigma Tau Gamma. Democrat. Roman Catholic. Club: Rotary (dir. Windber 1964-69, pres. 1968-69). Home: 603 Harshberger St Johnstown PA 15905

ALCANTARA, AVELINA GILBUENA GUEVARA, surgeon; b. Manila, Aug. 22, 1913, d. Juan Amandi Gilbuena and Simona Ponce Guevara; m. Bienvenido G. Alcantara, Jan 8, 1944 (dec. 1977); children: Angelita, Josefina, Enrique, Virgilio, Benjamin. MD in Surgery, U. Santo Tomas, 1941. Intern Med. Services div. Bur. of Prisons, Muntinlupa, Metro Manila, 1942-45; sr. bacteriologist Med. Services div. Bur. of Prisons, Muntinlupa, Manila, 1945-47, radiologist, 1947-53, physician, bacteriologist, 1953-55, med. officer, resident, 1955-58, med. specialist, 1958-59, supr. resident, physician, 1959-71, chief NBP Hosp. IV, 1971-76, med. advisor, 1976-80, coordinator prison hosps. and med. coordinator, 1980-82; retired 1983; supt. Correctiona Inst. for Women, Mandaluyong, 1971-72; sec., chmn. Rizal Med. Care Council, 1972-87. Pres., vol. Puericulture and Family Planning Ctr., Muntinlupa, 1960—; pres. different apostolate prison Cath. orgns.; charter mem. Girl Scouts Phillipines; in service Eye Bank and Kidney Found of Phillipines. Served with Phillipine Guerilla Mil., 1943-45. Named Outstanding Correctional Officer Pres. Ferdinand Marcos, 1975; recipient Gold Service award Phillipines Nat. Red Cross. Home: Katihan Jose Rizal St, Muntinlupa Philippines Office: Rizal Med Care Council, Rizal Provincial Health Services, Pasig Philippines

ALCARAZ LOZANO, FEDERICO NESTOR, engineering company executive, educator; b. Mexico, D.F., Mex., Apr. 19, 1931; s. Federico Alcaraz Tornel and Maria Elena (Alcaraz) Lozano; m. Graciela Minor De Alcaraz, Oct. 11, 1958; children: Lourdes, Ana Laura, Lorena, Luisa. CE, Univ. Nacional Autonoma de Mex., 1957; postgrad., Sociedad Mexicana de Ingenieria De Costos, 1979. Cert. civil engr., Mex. Ops. mgr. Recursos Hidraulicos, Mexico City, 1956-60; constrn. mgr. Constructora Morelos S.A., Mexico City, 1960-70; engring. mgr. Sacmag De Mex. S.A., 1970-73, gen. mgr., 1973-78; gen. mgr. Grupo Ingenieria Integral S.A., Mexico City, 1978—; prof. Univ. Autonoma de Mex., 1958-61, 68—; lectr. in field. Author: (with C. Chavarri, J. Cabezut) Pavements, 1972, Formwork Design, 1985, Creativeness for Engineers, 1988; contbr. articles to profl. jours.; patentee in field. Recipient diplomas from several univs. and orgns. Fellow Constrn. Specifications Inst.; mem. Colegio De Ingenieros Civiles De Mex. (econ. dir. 1978, info. dir. 1982), Am. Concrete Inst. (347 com., formwork for concrete), Sociedad Exalumnos Facultad De Ingenieria, Sociedad Mexicana De Ingenieria De Costos. Roman Catholic. Club: France (Mexico D.F.).

AL-CHALABI, FADHIL JAFAR, international petroleum organization executive; b. Baghdad, Iraq, Sept. 27, 1929; s. Jafar Mohammed and Fatima Al-C.; m. Abla Bahjat Salih, May 25, 1956; children—Talik Fadhil Jafar, Aysar Fadhil Jafar, Jafar Fadhil Jafar, Dounia. B.A. in Law, Baghdad U., 1951; postgrad. diploma in econs. U. Poitiers, France, 1956, 58; Doctorat d'Etat in Econ. Scis., U. Paris, 1962. Dir.-gen. oil affairs Iraqi Ministry of Oil, Baghdad, 1968-73, permanent undersec., 1973-76; asst. sec. gen. OAPEC, Kuwait, Kuwait, 1976-78; dep. sec. gen. OPEC, Vienna, Austria, 1978—, acting for sec. gen., 1983—; speaker in field. Author: OPEC and the International Oil Industry: A Changing Structure, 1980; numerous articles. Decorated officer Order of the Liberator (Venezuela). Mem. North-South Roundtable Islamabad (Pakistan), Soc. Internat. Devel. (Rome), Oxford Energy Policy Club (Eng.), Arab Thought Forum (Jordan), Economists Assn. Iraq. Moslem. Avocations: music; reading. Office: OPEC, Obere Donaustrasse 93, 1020 Vienna Austria

AL-CHALABI, ISSAM ABDULRAHEEM, oil minister Iraq; b. Baghdad, Iraq, 1942; s. Abdul Raheem; married; four children. BS in Mech. Engring., University Coll., London, 1965. Pres. State Orgn. Oil Projects, Baghdad, 1975-81; v.p. Iraq Nat. Oil Co., Baghdad, 1981-83; undersec. Iraq Ministry Oil, Baghdad, 1983—. Office: Ministry Oil, Mansour, PO Box 6178, Baghdad Iraq

ALDEN, INGEMAR BENGT, pharmaceutical executive; b. Stockholm, Feb. 23, 1943; s. Bengt Erik and Agnes (Eriksson) A.; m. Estelle Cuni Skrabanek, June 18, 1977; children—Lars, Sonja, Ingela. M.Social and Bus. Sci., Stockholm U., 1969. Field supr. Astra Lakemedel Sweden, Sodertalje, 1970-71, nat. sales mgr., 1971-72, mgr. mktg. and sales, 1973-74; internat. mktg. mgr. Astra Pharms., Sodertalje, 1975-76; dir. pharm. div. Astra Ltd., Watford, Eng., 1977-78; mng. dir. Merck Sharp & Dohme, Sweden, 1979—; bd. mem. Assn. Fgn. Pharm. Cos., Kronans Droghandel AB, Biodistra AB; chmn. Alliaxen AB, Stockholm; ptnr. Midway Internat. Co. Club: SVD Executive.

ALDERMAN, MICHAEL HARRIS, public health educator; b. New Haven, Mar. 26, 1936; s. Julius and Anna (Vener) A.; m. Betsy Feinstein, July 28, 1968; children—John F., Peter B. B.A. magna cum laude, Harvard U., 1958; M.D., Yale U., 1962. Intern Bronx Mcpl. Hosp. Ctr., N.Y., 1962-64; resident N.Y. Hosp.-Cornell Med. Ctr., N.Y.C., 1966-68; vis. prof. U. West Indies, Kingston, Jamaica, 1968-70; attending physician N.Y. Hosp., N.Y.C., 1982—; prof. pub. health Cornell U. Med. Coll., N.Y.C., 1980-84; prof. medicine Cornell U. Med. Coll., 1982-84; prof., chmn. dept. epidemiology and social medicine Albert Einstein Coll. Medicine, N.Y.C., 1984—; program dir. Robert Wood Johnson Found., Princeton, N.J., 1979-81; med. cons. UN, N.Y.C., 1981; chmn. African Med. Research Found., 1981—; mem. Com. on Pub. Health and Preventive Medicine; chmn. com. on pub. health & preventive medicine Nat. Bd. Med. Examiners, 1988. Contbr. articles to med. jours. Mem. Council Fgn. Relations, N.Y.C., U.S. Civil Rights Commn., Albany, N.Y., 1972-76; U.S. Delegation to USSR, Moscow, 1979; trustee Sharon (Conn.) Hosp., Wallenberg Found., N.Y. Served to lt. cmdr. USPHS, 1964-66. Glorney Raisbeck fellow N.Y. Acad. medicine, 1967-68; WHO travelling fellow, 1973, 77. Fellow Am. Soc. Clin. Nutrition, Am. Fedn. Clin. Research, Royal Soc. Medicine, Am. Heart Assn., Council on Epidemiology, ACP; mem. Nat. Council Internat. Health (bd. govs.), Am. Soc. Hypertension (pub. affairs com.), Explorers. Democrat. Jewish. Clubs: Century Assn., Harvard (N.Y.C.). Home: 1261 Madison Ave New York NY 10028 Office: Albert Einstein Coll Medicine 1300 Morris Park Ave Bronx NY 10461

AL-DHAHIR, MOHAMMAD WASSIL, mathematician; b. Mosul, Iraq, July 1, 1924; s. Ahamed and Khadeja (Hassoon) A.; m. Adela Mohammad, July 14, 1956; children: Nedhal, Basila, Wafa, Naofal. MA, Columbia U., 1952; PhD, U. Mich., 1955. Lectr. in math. Baghdad (Iraq) U., 1954-56, asst. prof., 1956-63; postdoctoral fellow Nat. Research Council Can., Toronto, Ont., 1960-61; prof. Baghdad (Iraq) U., 1963-69, asst. to the pres., 1962-64, dean Coll. Scis., 1964-69; prof. math. Kuwait U., 1969—, dean. Coll. Scis., 1977-82; cons. UNESCO, Kuwait, 1966-72, Kuwait Found. for Advancement of Scis., 1978—. Contbr. articles to profl. jours., chpts. to books. Mem. Am. Math. Soc. Office: Kuwait U, Dept Math, PO Box 5969, Kuwait Kuwait 13060

ALDISS, BRIAN WILSON, author; b. Dereham, Norfolk, Eng., Aug. 18, 1925; s. Stanley and Elizabeth May (Wilson) A.; student Framlingham Coll., 1936-39, W. Buckland Sch., 1939-43; children: (by previous marriage) Clive, Wendy; m. 2d, Margaret Manson, Dec. 11, 1965; children: Timothy, Charlotte. Bookseller, 1947-56; lit. editor Oxford Mail, 1958-69; author, critic, 1970—. Served with Brit. Army, 1943-47. Mem. Brit. Sci. Fiction Assn. (past pres.), Soc. Authors (chmn. 1977—), Arts Council (lit. panel 1978-80), European Sci. Fiction Com. (joint pres. 1976-80), World Sci. Fiction (pres. 1982-84), Soc. Anglo-Chinese Understanding (v.p.). Recipient Hugo award for Hothouse, 1962, Trillion Year Spree, 1987; Nebula award for The Saliva Tree, 1965; Ditmar award for World's Best Contemporary Sci. Fiction Writer, 1969; Brit. Sci. Fiction Assn. award for Moment of Eclipse, 1972; Jules Verne award for Non-Stop, 1977; First James Blish award for excellence in criticism, 1977; Pilgrim award, 1978; First IAFA award for Disting. Scholarship, 1986; Eaton award, 1988. Author: Brightfount Diaries, 1955; Starship, 1958; No Time Like Tomorrow, 1959; Galaxies Like Grains of Sand, 1960; Bow Down to Nul, 1960; The Primal Urge, 1961; The Male Response, 1961; Long Afternoon of Earth, 1962; Starswarm, 1964; Dark Light Years, 1964; Greybeard, 1965; Earthworks, 1966; Who Can Replace A Man?, 1965; Cryptozoic!, 1968; Report on Probability A, 1969; Barefoot in the Head, 1970; Neanderthal Planet, 1970; The Hand-Reared Boy, 1970; A Soldier Erect, 1971; Moment of Eclipse, 1972; Frankenstein Unbound, 1973; The Eighty-Minute Hour, 1974; The Malacia Tapestry, 1976; Last Orders, 1977; Brothers of the Head, 1977; A Rude Awakening, 1978; Enemies of the System, 1978; The World and Nearer Ones, 1979; Pile, 1979; New Arrivals, Old Encounters, 1979; Moreau's Other Island, 1980; Life in the West, 1980; Foreign Bodies, 1981; Helliconia Spring (Brit. Sci. Fiction award, John W. Campbell meml. award), 1982; Helliconia Summer, 1983; Seasons in Flight, 1984; Helliconia Winter, 1985 (British Sci. Fiction Assn. award); (non-fiction) Cities & Stones: A Traveller's Jugoslavia, 1964; The Shape of Further Things, 1970; Billion Year Spree: The History of Science Fiction, 1973; Hell's Cartographers, 1975; Science Fiction Art, 1975; This World and Nearer Ones, 1979; Science Fiction Quiz Book, 1983; The Pale Shadow of Science, 1985; ... And the Lurid Glare of the Comet, 1986, Trillion Year Spree, 1986, Ruins, 1987, World Omnibus of Science Fiction, 1987, (stage review) Science Fiction Blues, 1987; Best SF Stories of Brian Aldiss, 1988; Forgotten Life, 1988; Science Fiction Blues: The Story of the Show, 1988. Co-editor: Nebula Award Stores II, 1967; All About Venus, 1968; Best SF, 1967-76; Decades SF, 1975-77; SF Master Series, 1976-78. Home: Woodlands Foxcombe Rd, Boars Hill, OX1 5DL Oxford England

AL-DOURI, IZZAT IBRAHIM, statesman; b. Al-Dour, Iraq, July 1, 1942; s. Ibrahim Khalil Al-D.; children: Hawazen, Ahmed, Ibrahim, Ablah, Fatima, Aliaa, Hamraa, Ali. Grad. secondary sch., Baghdad, Iraq. Editor Voice of the Peasant, Baghdad, 1968; chmn. Supreme Com. People's Work, Baghdad, 1968-70; minister Ministry Agrarian Reform, Iraq, 1970-72, Ministry Agri. and Agrarian Reform, Iraq, 1972-74, Ministry of Interior, Iraq, 1974-79; vice chmn. Revolutionary Command Council, Iraq, 1979—; v.p. Supreme Agrl. Council, Iraq, 1970-76, pres. 1976-79; pres. Supervisory Bd. Nat. Assembly Elections, Iraq, 1980—. Mem. Nat. Leadership of Arba Baath Socialist Party, Iraq, 1977—, Regional Leadership Arab Baath Socialist Party, 1979, dep. sec., 1979—. Muslim. Office: Revolutionary Command Council, Baghdad Iraq

ALDRED, KENNETH JOHN, international organization executive; b. Bristol, Eng., Sept. 11, 1937; s. John Arthur and Edith Lorna (Williams) A.; m. Judith Barbara Buckley, Apr. 22, 1961; children—Alison Jane, Alexandra Zoe. Grad., Kingswood Grammar Sch., Bristol, Eng. Coordinator, Fanfare for Europe (Brit. Govt.), 1972; dir. publicity European Movement (Brit. Council), London, 1972-73; dir. orgn. and publicity English Speaking Union, London, 1974-81; dir. regional info. Brit. Atlantic Com., 1981-83; sec. gen. Peace Through NATO, London, 1983—. Nat. v.p. Brit. Jr. Chambers, 1970-72, pub. relations dir., 1972-74; bd. dirs. City Westminster C. of C., 1979-85, Hanover Band, 1983-86; vice chmn., 1986—; mem. council London Tourist Bd., 1981-85; exec. sec. for U.K., Com. for Community Democracies, 1982-87, chmn., 1988—, also asst. sec. internat. council; chmn. Westminster Welcome 84, 1983—. Mem. European Mgmt. Assn. (chmn. 1977-80), Royal United Services Inst., Royal Inst. Internat. Affairs, Internat. Inst. Strategic Studies. Mem. Ch. of England. Clubs: E.S.U. (mgmt. com.) (London), Europe House. Editor, mng. editor: Concord-Jour. of English Speaking Union, 1979-81; editor: British Atlantic CTTEE News, 1982-83; Peace Through NATO News, 1983—. Home: 27 Rowden Rd, Chippenham, Wiltshire England Office: Peace through NATO, Oldebourne House, 46-47 Chancery Ln, London WC2A 1JB, England

ALDRICH, DAVID LAWRENCE, public relations executive; b. Lakehurst Naval Air Sta., N.J., Feb. 21, 1948; s. Clarence Edward and Sarah Stiles (Andrews) A.; m. Benita Susan Massler, Mar. 17, 1974. B.A. in Communications, Calif. State U.-Dominguez Hills, 1976. Pub. info. technician City of Carson (Calif.), 1973-77; pub. relations dir./adminstrv. asst. Calif. Fed. Savs., Los Angeles, 1977-78; v.p., group supr. Hill & Knowlton, Los

Angeles, 1978-81; v.p., mgr. Ayer Pub. Relations western div. N.W. Ayer, Los Angeles, 1981-84; pres. Aldrich and Assocs. Inc., Los Angeles, 1984—. Bd. dirs. Harbor-SE region United Way, chmn. public infos. mktg.; chmn., mktg. adv. com. Drum Corps Internat. Served with USAF, 1968-72. Democrat. Club: Los Angeles Athletic. Home: 550 Orange Ave #125 Long Beach CA 90802 Office: Aldrich and Assocs 110 Pine Ave #510 Long Beach CA 90807

ALDRICH, FRANK NATHAN, banker; b. Jackson, Mich., June 8, 1923; s. Frank Nathan and Marion (Butterfield) A.; m. Edna Dora DeJan, Nov. 21, 1956; children: Marion Dolores, Clinton Pershing. Student, U. Md., summer 1943; A.B. in Govt, Dartmouth Coll., 1948; postgrad., Harvard U., summer 1948. Sub-mgr. First Nat. Bank of Boston, Havana, Cuba, 1949-60, Rio de Janeiro, Brazil, 1961-62; sub-mgr. Rio de Janeiro, Sao Paulo, Brazil, 1963-64; mgr. Rio de Janeiro, 1965, exec. mgr., 1966; v.p. Latin Am.-Asia-Africa-Middle East div., Boston, 1970-73; sr. v.p. Latin Am. div., Boston, 1973—; pres., dir. Caribbean Am. Service Investment & Finance Co., Georgetown, Cayman Island; exec. v.p., dir. Boston Overseas Financial Corp., Boston; chmn. bd. Bank of Boston Trust Co. (Bahamas) Ltd., Nassau; dir. Corporacion Financiera Boston, La Paz, Bolivia, Banco de Boston Dominicano S.A., Santo Domingo, Dominican Republic, Corporacion Internacional de Boston S.A., San Jose, Costa Rica, Sociedad Anonima Servicios e Inversiones, Buenos Aires, Boston S.A. Administracao e Empreendimentos, Sao Paulo, Brazil, Arrendadora Industrial Venezolana C.A., Caracas, Venezuela, Boston Internat. Fin. Corp., Curacao, Netherlands Antilles, Bank of Boston Internat., N.Y.C., Los Angeles and Miami., Banco Latinoamericano de Exportaciones, Panama City. Trustee Latin Am. Scholarship Program Am. Univs., Cambridge, Mass. Served with USAAF, 1943-46. Decorated Air medal with 4 oak leaf clusters, D.F.C. U.S.; Medalha Marechal Candido Mariano da Silva Rondon (Brazil); Ordem Nacional do Cruzeiro do Sul (Brazil). Fellow Brit. Interplanetary Soc.; mem. Air Force Assn., Res. Officers Assn., Confederate Air Force, Inst. Nav., Royal Astron. Soc. Canada, Md. Hist. Soc., Am. C. of C. Rio de Janeiro, Am. C. of C. Sao Paulo, Sphinx Soc., Vets. of the Battle of the Bulge, Beta Theta Pi. Clubs: Harvard (Boston), Dartmouth College, Yale (N.Y.C.), American (Miami, Fla.), Wellesley (Mass.) Country, Wellesley Coll. Lodges: Masons, Shriners. Home: 3 Indian Spring Rd Dover MA 02030 Office: 100 Federal St Boston MA 02106

ALDRICH, FREDERIC DELONG, historian, educator; b. Port Huron, Mich., Nov. 2, 1899; s. Horace Nathan and Helen Grace (Champlain) A.; m. Dorothy May Lindquist, June 19, 1937; children: Frederic DeLong, John L., William J., Andrew L. AB, Willamette U., 1921; postgrad. U. Oreg., summer 1923; MA, Western Res. U., 1931, EdD, 1953. Tchr. history and English, coach Cleve. Sr. High Sch., 1921-40, 47-53; lectr. Western Res. U. Grad. Sch., Cleve., 1953-56; prof. edn., head edn. dept. Alderson-Broaddus Coll., Philippi, W.Va., 1956-57; dir. audio-visual center, chmn. edn. dept. Chatham Coll., Pitts., 1957-61; lectr. U. Vt., Burlington, 1962—; edn. specialist Vt. State Dept. Edn., 1966; cons. Gifted Children's Workshop, Kent State U., 1954; lectr. Pa. State U., 1958. Author: A Brief Outline of Church History, 1927, rev., 1977, The School Library in Ohio, 1959, History of Calvary Episcopal Church, Underhill, Vermont, 1978. Mem. Cuyahoga County Republican Exec. Com., 1934-38; chmn. finances Richmond (Vt.) Town Rep. Com., 1963-65, town chmn., 1965—; member Chittenden County Rep. Committee, 1965—; del. Vt. Rep. Conv., 1964, 66, Rep. Platform Conv., 1968—, Oreg. Rep. Nat. Conv., Cleve., 1924; justice of peace, mem. Bd. Civil Authority, Richmond, 1983—. Served to lt. col. AUS, 1941-46. Mem. Am. Hist. Assn., Orgn. Am. Historians, Medieval Acad. Am., North Central, Middle States Assns. Colls. and Secondary schs., Pitts. C. of C. (colls. and univs. com. 1957-61), Burlington-Lake Champlain C. of C. (legis. affairs and edn. coms. 1962—), Delta Theta Phi, Phi Delta Kappa. Episcopalian. Club: Barbour Country (Philippi, W.Va.); Univ. (Cleve.). Address: RD 1 Box 293 Richmond VT 05477

ALDRICH, MICHAEL RAY, organization executive; b. Vermillion, S.D., Feb. 7, 1942; s. Ray J. and Lucile W. (Hamm) A.; A.B., Princeton, 1964; M.A., U. S.D., 1965; Ph.D., SUNY, 1970; m. Michelle Cauble, Dec. 26, 1977. Fulbright tutor Govt. Arts and Commerce Coll., Indore, Madhya Pradesh, India, 1965-66; founder Lemar Internat., 1966-71; mem. faculty Sch. Critical Studies, Calif. Inst. Arts, Valencia, 1970-72; workshop leader Esalen Inst., San Francisco, 1972; co-founder, co-dir. AMORPHIA, Inc., The Cannabis Coop., non-profit nat. marijuana research and reform group, Mill Valley, Calif., 1969-74; curator Fitz Hugh Ludlow Meml. Library, San Francisco, 1974—. Freelance writer, photographer, lectr., cons. on drug research, and sociolegal reform specializing in drug laws and history to various colls., drug confs., publishers, service groups; cons. Commn. of Inquiry into Non-Med. Use of Drugs, Ottawa, Ont., 1973; research aide, select com. on control marijuana Calif. Senate, 1974. Bd. dirs. Ethno-Pharmacology Soc., 1976-83. Calif. Marijuana Initiative, 1971-74; mem. nat. adv. bd. Nat. Orgn. for Reform of Marijuana Laws, 1976—; asst. dir. Nat. Inst. on Drug Abuse AIDS Project Menu Youth Environment Study, San Francisco, 1987-88. Author: The Dope Chronicles 1850-1950, 1979, Coricancha, The Golden Enclosure, 1983; co-author: High Times Ency. of Recreational Drugs, 1978, Fiscal Costs of California Marijuana Law Enforcement, 1986; editor: Marijuana Review, 1968-74, Ludlow Library Newsletter, 1974—; contbg. author Cocaine Handbook, 1981, 2d edit., 1987; mem. editorial rev. bd. Jour. Psychoactive Drugs, 1981—, marijuana theme issue editor, 1987, 88; research photographer Life mag., 1984; contbg. editor High Times, 1979-85; contbr. articles to profl. publs. Office: PO Box 640346 San Francisco CA 94164-0346

ALDRIDGE, DONALD O'NEAL, air force officer; b. Solo, Mo., July 22, 1932. B.A. in History, U. Nebr.-Omaha, 1974; postgrad. Creighton U., 1975. Commd. 2d lt. U.S. Air Force, 1958, advanced through grades to lt. gen., 1978; asst. dir. plans U.S. Air Force, Washington, 1978-79; spl. asst. to dir. Joint Chiefs of Staff, Washington, 1979-80; dep. dir. Def. Mapping Agy., Washington, 1980-81; dep. U.S. rep. NATO Mil. Com., Brussels, Belgium, 1981-83; rep. Joint Chiefs of Staff, Geneva, Switzerland, 1983-86; commr. 1st Strat. Aerospace div. Vandenberg AFB, Calif., 1986-88; vice-CINC STrategic Air Command, Offutt AFB, Nebr., 1988—. Office: Office of Vice CINC Hdqrs SAC Offutt AFB NE 68113

ALDRIDGE, RONALD GORDON, social worker, army officer; b. Toronto, Ont., Can., Sept. 16, 1943; s. Gordon James and Gladys Parker (Chapman) A.; came to U.S., 1950, naturalized, 1955; B.A., Mich. State U., 1965, M.S.W., 1967, Ph.D., 1980; m. Cheryl Lee Holmes, Mar. 19, 1966; children—Danielle Marie, Michelle Lee. Social worker Lansing (Mich.) Family Service Agy., 1967-68; commd. 2d lt., U.S. Army, 1968, advanced through grades to lt. col., 1983; social worker Correctional Tng. Facility, Ft. Riley, Kans., 1968-69; div. social worker 3d Inf. Div., Germany, 1969-73; chief social work service DeWitt Army Hosp., Ft. Belvoir, Va., 1973-77; emergency service social worker Woodburne Center for Community Mental Health, Annandale, Va., 1973-77; dir. Family Problem Center, Dumfries, Va., 1976-77; social worker Mich. Family Inst., Lansing, 1977-80; dir. mental hygiene U.S. Disciplinary Barracks, Ft. Leavenworth, Kans., 1980-83; chief social work service William Beaumont Army Med. Center, El Paso, Tex., 1983-88; exec. dir. Dallas Child Guidance Clinics, 1988—; adj. assoc. prof. dept. social work N.Mex. State U., 1984—; field agy. liaison U. Tex.-El Paso, U. Tex.-Arlington, U. Tex.-Austin, N.Mex. State U. Schs. Social Work; clin. instr. Coll. Osteo. Medicine, Mich. State U., 1979-80; instr. couples communication U. Minn. Assoc. editor Corrective and Social Psychiatry, Jour. Behavior Tech. Methods and Therapy. Mem. exec. bd. Chief Okemos council Boy Scouts Am., 1978-81, v.p. Yucca council, 1985-88, mem. nat. com. Nat. Eagle Scout Assn., 1977-86; bd. dirs. Planned Parenthood, El Paso; pres. bd. dirs. Mental Health Assn., El Paso; chmn. regional alcoholism adv. com. Council Govts.; mem. statewide adv. council Tex. Commn. on Alcohol and Drug Abuse, Health Planning Adv. Com., West Tex. Council Govts.; M.S.S.W. adv. com. U. Tex., Austin, U. Tex., El Paso; social work adv. bd. N.Mex. State U.; mem. adv. com. Mesilla Valley Hosp., Las Cruces. Decorated Army Commendation medal with oakleaf cluster, Meritorious Service medal with oakleaf cluster; recipient Disting. Service award Nat. Eagle Scout Assn.; award Kans. Correctional Assn., Outstanding Leadership award El Paso Mental Health Assn. (past pres.), Conquistador award, highest award city of El Paso, Adm. of El Paso Navy, highest award County of El Paso. Mem. Am. Assn. Sex Educators, Counselors and Therapists, Acad. Cert. Social Workers, Assn. Mil. Social Workers, Nat. Assn. Social Workers (unit past pres. El Paso, Tex. state v.p.), Am. Corrections Assn., Assn. Mental Health Profls. in Corrections (nat. v.p.), chair Mayor's com. on gang intervention), Tex. Correctional Assn., Acad. Criminal Justice Scis., Southwestern Assn. Criminal Justice Educators, Assn. Sex Therapists and Counselors, Kans. Correctional Assn. (past pres.), Phi Alpha, Alpha Phi Omega, Phi Kappa Phi. Office: Dallas Child Guidance Clinics 2101 Welborn Dallas TX 75219

ALEBUA, EZEKIEL, prime minister of the Solomon Islands; b. Avu Avu, Guadalcanal, Solomon Islands, 1947; married; 4 children. Student, U. South Pacific, Suva, Fuji, 1974. With Solomon Islands Govt. Service, 1966-80; former minister for fgn. affairs and internat. trade Solomon Islands, now prime minister. Address: Office of Prime Minister, Honiara Solomon Islands *

ALEKSANDROV, ANATOLIY PETROVICH, physicist; b. Tarashcha, Kiev Region, Ukraine, Feb. 13, 1903. Student Kiev U., 1925-30, Leningrad. Phys.-Tech. Inst., 1930-46, Corr. mem. USSR Acad. Scis., 1943-53, mem., 1953—, pres., 1976—; dir. Inst. Physical Problems, USSR Acad. Scis., 1946-54; dir. Kurchatov Inst. Atomic Energy, 1960—, pres., 1975-86. Patentee anti-mine defense for ships during World War II, 1941-45. Mem. Communist Party Soviet Union, 1962—, mem. central com., 1966—, dep. to Supreme Soviet, 1960-66, from 1976. Recipient USSR State prize, 1942, 49, 51, 53, Lenin prize, 1959, Order of Lenin (9), Hero of Socialist Labour (3), Gold Star of Friendship Between Peoples, 1983, others. Address: IV Kurchatov Atomic Energy Inst, Ul Kurchatova 46, Moscow USSR also: USSR Acad of Scis, Leninsky Prospekt 14, Moscow USSR *

ALEKSANDROWICZ, DARIUSZ LEOPOLD, philosopher; b. Wroclaw, Poland, Oct. 30, 1949; s. Zygmunt and Maria Magdalena (Dluzniewska) A.; m. Izabela Kiszczynska, Oct. 13, 1973; children: Paula, Lech, Ewa. MA in German Philology, U. Wroclaw, 1972, MA in Philosophy, 1974, PhD, 1976, D. habil. Philosophy, 1982. Jr. asst. U. Wroclaw, 1972-74, asst. lectr., 1974-76, tutor, 1976-83, asst. prof. philosophy, 1983—, chmn., 1977-81; mem. senate U. Wroclaw, 1983-84, dean faculty, 1984-87; research fellow East Lorand U., Budapest, Hungary, 1979, U. Mannheim, Fed. Republic Germany, 1982-84. Author: (books) Knowledge and Criticism, 1979 (ministry of higher edn. award 1980), Philosophical Foundations in Lukacs Theory of Knowledge, 1983 (Rectors award 1984); contbr. numerous articles to profl. jours. Mem. Polish Philos. Soc., Polish Sociol. Soc., Wroclaw Sci. Soc. Roman Catholic. Home: Odkrywcow 13, 53-212 Wroclaw Poland Office: U Wroclaw Dept History of Philosophy, Szewska 36, 50-139 Wroclaw Poland

ALESANA, TOFILAU ETI, Prime Minister of Western Samoa, politician; b. Vaitogi, A.S., June 4, 1924; s. James Enoka and Vaoita Aiono Malaitai; m. Pitolua Toomata; 14 children. Educated Poyer Sch., A.S., Maluafou Sch., Western Samoa. Br. mgr. I.H. Carruthers Ltd., 1949-57; entered politics, 1957; minister of health, 1959-61; mem. Western Samoa Pub. Service Commn., 1961-64; pres. Faasaleleaga Wharf Com., 1964-67; M.P., 1967-73, 76—; appointed dep. prime minister, minister of fin., now leader of Human Rights Protection Party; appointed prime minister, 1982-86, 88—, minister of fin., 1982-86, now also atty. gen., minister of broadcasting, fgn. affairs, justice, labor, police and prisons. Served to cpl. Samoa Local Def. Force, 1941-45. Chmn. Congl. Christian Ch. Samoa. *

ALESCHUS, JUSTINE LAWRENCE, land broker; b. New Brunswick, N.J., Aug. 13, 1925; d. Walter and Mildred Lawrence; student Rutgers U.; m. John Aleschus, Jan. 23, 1949; children—Verdene Jan, Janine Kimberley, Joanna Lauren. Dept. sec. Am. Baptist Home Mission Soc., N.Y.C., 1947-49; claims examiner Republic Ins. Co., Dallas, 1950-52; broker Damon Homes, L.I., 1960-72; exclusive broker estate of Kenneth H. Leeds, L.I., 1980—; pres. Justine Aleschus Real Estate. Past-pres. Nassau-Suffolk Council of Hosp. Aux., 1981-82; hon. mem. aux. of St. John's Episcopal Hosp., Smithtown, N.Y., also past pres., mem. hosp. adv. bd.; pres. L.I. Coalition for Sensible Growth, Inc.; mem. Smithtown Industry Adv. Bd.; exec. bd. dirs. Suffolk County council Boy Scouts Am.; mem. adv. bd. Suffolk County council Girl Scouts U.S. Mem. Suffolk County Real Estate Bd. (pres.), L.I. Mid-Suffolk Businessmen's Assn., Eastern L.I. Execs. (sponsor-trustee), Smithtown Bus. and Profl. Women's Network, L.I. Assn., JEI Com., Hauppauge Indsl. Assn. Advancement Commerce & Industry. Republican. Lutheran. Club: Sky Island (gov.). Office: 300 Hawkins Ave Lake Ronkonkoma NY 11779

ALESIA, JAMES H(ENRY), judge; b. Chgo., July 16, 1934; m. Kathryn P. Gibbons, July 8, 1961; children—Brian J., Daniel J. B.S. Loyola U., 1956; LL.B., IIT/Chgo.-Kent Coll. Law, 1960; grad. Nat. Jud. Coll., U. Nev.-Reno, 1976. Bar: Ill. 1960, Minn. 1970. Police officer City of Chgo., 1957-60; with Law Office Anthony Scariano, Chicago Heights, Ill., 1960-61; assoc. Pretzel & Stouffer, Chgo., 1961-63; asst. gen. counsel Chgo. & North Western Transp. Co., Chgo., 1963-70; assoc. Rerat Law Firm, Mpls., 1970-71; asst. U.S. atty. No. dist. Ill., Chgo., 1971-73, trial counsel Chessie System, Chgo., 1973; U.S. adminstrv. law judge, 1973-82; ptnr. Reuben & Proctor (firm merged with Isham, Lincoln & Beale), Chgo., 1982-87; judge U.S. Dist. (no. Ill.), 1987—; faculty Nat. Jud. Coll., U. Nev.-Reno, 1979-80. Mem. ABA, Ill. Bar Assn. (assembly 1978-84), Fed. Bar Assn., Justinian Soc. Lawyers, Celtic Legal Soc. Republican. Roman Catholic. Office: US Dist Ct 219 S Dearborn St Chicago IL 60604

ALEVRAS, YANNIS, Greek government official; b. Messini, Greece, 1912. Formerly with Bank of Greece; M.P. Greece, 1963; speaker Greek Parliament (Vauli), 1981—; founder, mem. Panhellenic Socialist Movement. Address: Greek Parliament (Vauli), Office Pres, Athens Greece *

ALEXANDER, SIR ALEX SANDOR, food company executive; b. Nov. 21, 1916; m. Margaret Irma Alexander, 1946; 4 children. Grad., Charles U. Founder Westwick Frosted Products (merged with Ross Group 1954); dir. The Ross Group, 1954-69, chmn. Ross Frozen Foods Div., 1954-61, chmn. Poultry Div., 1961-68, mng. dir., chief exec. officer, 1967-69, chmn., 1969—; chmn. Imperial Foods Ltd., 1969-79; chmn. Imperial Group Ltd. (formerly Imperial Tobacco Group), 1986—, also bd. dirs.; chmn., chief exec. officer J. Lyons & Co., London, 1979—; bd. dirs. Marchwiel, Inchcape Ins. Holdings, Ltd., Allied Lyons Ltd., London Wall Holdings, Tate & Lyle, Unigate Cos.; pres. Brit. Food Export Council, 1973-76; mem. Eastern Gas Bd., 1963-72, Agrl. Econ. Devel. Com., 1974-78. Mem. ct. U. East Anglia, 1961; trustee, vice chair Glyndebourne Arts Trust, 1975—; chmn. Appeals Com. of the Brit. Red Cross, Norfolk, Eng., 1958-74; trustee Charities Aid Found., 1979-86; High Sheriff of Norfolk, 1976-77; chmn. Theatre Royal Trust, Norwich County, 1969-84. Fellow Royal Soc. Arts, Inst. Mgmt., Inst. Grocery Distbn.; mem. Royal Coll. Physicians. Home: Westwick Hall, Westwick, Norwich England NR10 5BW Office: J Lyons & Co Ltd, Cadby Hall, London England W14 OPA also: Almed House, 156 St John St, London EC1P 1AR, England *

ALEXANDER, CARL ALBERT, ceramic engineer; b. Chillicothe, Ohio, Nov. 22, 1928; s. Carl B. and Helen E. A.; m. Dolores J Herstenstein, Sept. 4, 1954; children—Carla C., David A. B.S., Ohio U., 1953, M.S., 1956; Ph.D., Ohio State U., 1961. Mem. staff Battelle Columbus Labs., 1956—, research leader, 1974—, mgr. physico-chem. systems, 1976—; mem. faculty Ohio State U., 1963—, prof. ceramic and nuclear engring., 1977—; sr. research leader, chmn. tech. council of Biol. and Chem. Scis. Directorate, 1987—, chief scientist, 1987; prof. materials sci. and engring, 1988—. Author. Served to lt. (j.g.) USNR, 1951-54. Recipient Merit award NASA, 1971, IR-100 award, 1987, R&D-100 award, 1988; citations Dept. Energy, citations AEC, citations ERDA. Mem. Am. Soc. Mass Spectrometry, Keramos, Sigma Xi. Home: 4249 Haughn Rd Grove City OH 43123 Office: 505 King Ave Columbus OH 43201

ALEXANDER, CHARLES CALVERT, advertising executive; b. St. Louis, Jan. 7, 1937; s. Eben Roy and Mary Louise (Webb) A.; B.S. in Econs., Coll. Holy Cross, 1958; m. Diana S. Hunter, June 28, 1960; children—Michael S., Scott D., Richard A. Tech. writer truck div. Gen. Motors, Pontiac, Mich., 1962-63, supr. service tng., 1963-69; Detroit mgr. Ziff-Davis Mag. Network, 1969-78, nat. automotive mgr., 1978-80, dir. advt., N.Y.C., 1980-85; eastern advt. dir. Petersen Pub. Co., mktg. dir. Petersen Mag. Network. Served with USMCR, 1954-58, U.S. Army, 1958-62. Decorated various medals. Mem. Adcraft, N.Y. Advt. Club, Los Angeles Advt. Club, Sons of Danger (founder), Aircraft Owners and Pilots Assn., Am. Motorcyclist Assn. Clubs: Press, Fairlane (Detroit); Thimble Island Sail, Manhattan Yacht. Home: 34 School St Rehoboth MA 02769 Office: 437 Madison Ave New York NY 10022

ALEXANDER, CHERYL LEE, executive search and consulting firm executive; b. Mpls., Feb. 22, 1946; d. Wallace Einar and Dorothy Florence (Abrahamson) Arneson; m. Douglas Joel Hawkinson, Mar. 5, 1966; children: Tamara Lee, Alexander Lowell. Student, Gustavus Adolphus Coll., 1964-66, Nan Yang U., Singapore, 1971; BA summa cum laude, U. Minn., 1972. Personnel recruiter Nat. Recruiters, Mpls., 1972; pres. Alexander Recruiters, Mpls., 1973-79, Alexander Cos., (formerly Alexander Recruiters), Mpls., 1979—; former dir. Micro Application Systems, Inc., Proto Circuits, Inc.; lectr. numerous univs.; faculty, adv. Master Class, Inc. Author: Up The Typewriter, 1977; Transition Management, 1980; subject of interviews by profl. jours, TV and radio. Advisor Hennepin County Pvt. Industry Council, Mpls., 1981-83; mem. St. Paul Set-Aside Adv. Com., 1981-82, Mpls. Tech. Enterprise Ctr., 1984—; participant White House Conf. on Small Bus., 1980; judge Internat. Sci. and Engring. Fair, 1980; bd. dirs. Children's Communication Exchange, 1981-82. Mem. Soc. Women Engrs. (founder, bd. dirs., sec.), Assn. Women in Computing (founder, bd. dirs., v.p. 1978-79), Nat. Assn. Women Bus. Owners (founder, bd. dirs. v.p., nat. sec. 1978-81). Avocations: tennis, public speaking, seminar leader, skiing, sailing. Office: Alexander Cos 3205 Casco Circle Wayzata MN 55391

ALEXANDER, DAVID CLEON, III, lawyer; b. New Orleans, July 13, 1941; s. David Cleon Alexander Jr. and Joyce (Bragg) Crane. BBA, U. Ga., 1963; MBA, Ga. State U., 1969; JD, U. Va., 1973; LLM in Taxation, NYU, 1976. Bar: N.Y. 1974, U.S. Tax Ct. 1974, Ariz. 1975. Assoc. White & Case, N.Y.C., 1973-75, Murphy & Posner, Phoenix, 1975-78; ptnr. Lewis & Roca, Phoenix, 1978—. Served to 1st lt. U.S. Army, 1962-64. Fellow Ariz. Bar Found; mem. ABA, Ariz. Bar Assn. (lectr., cert. specialist in taxation), Sports Car Club Am., Phi Kappa Phi, Beta Gamma Sigma. Republican. Episcopalian. Home: 8520 N 52d St Paradise Valley AZ 85253 Office: Lewis & Roca 100 W Washington Suite 1800 Phoenix AZ 85003

ALEXANDER, DIETRICH BIEMANN, JR., building components manufacturing and construction company executive; b. Greenwood, S.C., Aug. 28, 1902; s. Dietrich Biemann and Lillian (Malone) A.; B.C.E., The Citadel, 1922; LL.B., Woodrow Wilson Coll. Law, 1938; postgrad. Babson Inst., summers 1940-41; m. Merridy Wefing, Mar. 3, 1930; children—Dietrich Biemann III, Merridy Wefing (Mrs. Alexander Lloyd), Stanton Malone. Tchr., coach Thomas Indsl. Inst., De Funiak Springs, Fla., 1922-23; with Atlantic Steel Co., Atlanta, 1923-45, asst. sec.-treas. 1925-45; admitted to Ga. State bar, 1938; partner Mitchell & Alexander Lumber Co., Daytona Beach, Fla., 1945-49; chmn. bd., chief exec. officer Prefab Bldg. Components, Holly Hill, Fla., 1969—; pres. Alexander Constrn. Co., Holly Hill, 1969—; pres. Daytona Beach Builders Exchange, 1962. Mem. Daytona Beach Zoning Bd., 1947-50; mem. Recreation and Parks Adv. Council, Region IV, State of Fla., 1972—; pres. Daytona Community Chest, 1948; chmn. camping com. Central Fla. council Boy Scouts Am., 1956-62; bd. visitors Embry-Riddle U., 1971—. Mem. Fla. Bldg. Material Dealers Assn. (pres. 1958-59), Daytona Beach C. of C. (v.p. 1953, dir. 1952-55), Daytona Beach Mchts. Assn. (dir. 1947-51), U.S. Navy League. Episcopalian (sr. warden 1962, vestryman 1954-62). Clubs: Kiwanis (pres. Daytona Beach, 1949), Piedmont Driving (hon. life mem.) (Atlanta); University of Volusia County (dir. 1963-68, pres. 1966), Halifax River Yacht, Daytona Beach Quarterback. Home: The Pendleton Club 1224 S Peninsula Dr Daytona Beach FL 32018 Office: 336 11th St Holly Hill FL 32017

ALEXANDER, FRANZ C., agricultural organization administrator; b. Kingston, Jamaica, Nov. 2, 1928; s. Selwyn Augustus and Rosina Grace (Murray) A.; m. Barbara Elaine Walsh (div.); 1 child, Sean Andrew; m. Barbara Elaine Evans, Feb. 8, 1965; step-children: Marcia Elaine Bullock, Jennifer Ann Tomlinson. BS in Veterinary Med., Cambridge U., 1956; MS, U. Minn., 1967. Veterinary officer Jamaican Ministry of Agr., Kingston, 1956-67, sr. veterinary officer, 1967-74, dep. dir. veterinary services, 1974-78, dir. veterinary services, 1978-80; animal health specialist Inter-Am. Inst. for Coop. on Agr., Georgetown, Guyana, 1980-87; rep. Inter-Am. Inst. for Coop. on Agr., Castries, St. Lucia, 1987—; animal health specialist Caribbean area, 1980-87, dir. Guyana, 1983-87. Decorated Order of Distinction Govt. of Jamaica, 1976. Mem. Royal Coll. Veterinary Sci., Jamaica Veterinary Assn. (life), Caribbean Veterinary Assn., Jamaica Cricket Assn. (exec. com. 1960-80), Phi Zeta Kappa. Roman Catholic. Club: Kingston Cricket (v.p. 1978-80). Office: Inter-Am Inst for Coop on Agr, Choc Bay, Castries Saint Lucia

ALEXANDER, HAROLD CAMPBELL, insurance consultant; b. Houston, Dec. 11, 1920; s. Henry Campbell and Essie Mae (Gilbert) A.; m. Dorothy Emma Schraub, Aug. 21, 1925; children: Linda Carol, Beverly Lynn Whitworth, Daniel James Alexander, William Campbell. BS, Miss. State U., 1938-42; postgrad., South Tex. Sch. Law, 1954-56, Harvard U., 1943, Navy Fin. and Supply Sch., 1942-43. Asst. div. credit mgr. Continental Emsco Co., Houston, 1953-56; gen. agt. and mgr. United Founders Life Ins. Co., 1956-69; mgr. Holt & Bridges Ins., Houston, 1960-69; owner, pres. Holt & Alexander Ins. Agy., Inc., Houston, 1969-85; ins. cons. Lawrence Ilfrey & Co., Houston, 1985—. Mem. Houston Adv. Council Bd., 1985; bd. dirs. 500 Club Ltd., Houston, 1984—. Served as lt. commdr. USN, 1942-46, 1950-52. Mem. Profl. Ins. Agts. Tex. (state bd. dirs. 1973-74), Soc. Cert. Ins. Counselors. Republican. Presbyterian. Club: Pine Forest Country, Club of Houston. Home: 8727 Manhattan Houston TX 77096 Office: Lawrence Ilfrey & Co 5200 San Felipe Houston TX 77056

ALEXANDER, JAMES EDWIN, business executive; b. Indianola, Iowa, Feb. 16, 1930; s. James Eugene and Lillian Esther (Gamble) A.; B.A., U. Pacific, 1959; S.T.B., Boston U., 1962; M.A., Claremont Grad. Sch., 1965; Ph.D., Vanderbilt U., 1972, postgrad. in Law, 1976; m. Joan Frances Harris, June 28, 1952 (div. 1981); children—James Michael, Michele Alene, Marsha Ann; m. 2d, Wanda Draper, Jan. 17, 1982. Chief engr. Radio Sta. KJOY, Stockton, Calif., 1955-59; instr. broadcasting U. Pacific, 1956-59, lectr. Bible, 1963-65; owner, operator Stockton Teletronics, 1956-59; studio engr. Radio Sta. WHDH, Boston, 1960; teaching fellow Boston U., Coll. Bus. Adminstrn., 1960-62; ordained to ministry Methodist Ch., 1960; pastor Gleasondale (Mass.) Meth. Ch., 1960-62; asso. pastor Central Meth. Ch., Stockton, 1962-65, Claremont (Calif.) Meth. Ch., 1966-67; dir. printed resources Meth. Bd. Edn., United Meth. Ch., Nashville, 1967-70, asst. gen. sec., 1970-75, exec. dir. communications, 1976-78; exec. dir. The Other Sch. System, Inc., 1978—; pres. Music City Thirty, Inc., 1979-83, TV 52 Broadcasting, 1980-83, Macedon Prodn. Co., Inc., 1981—; acting dean Sch. Mgmt. and Bus. Scis., Oklahoma City U., 1982-83; pres. Nat. Land Mgmt., Inc., 1983-84; investment broker A.G. Edwards, 1984-87; assoc. v.p., Prudential-Bache Securities, 1987—; dir. Pub. Service Satellite Corp., Am. TV and Satellite Corp., Bus. Ware, Inc., Child Care Systems, Inc., Frontier Community Communications, Inc., Omni Family Productions, Inc. Mem. Calif. Gov.'s Council on Aging, 1964-65, panel disting. scholars New Media Bible, 1975—; mem. exec. bd. Christian Youth Publs., 1967-75; mem. adv. com. Nat. Orgns. Corp. for Public Broadcasting, 1974—; mem. Lake Placid Winter Olympics Com., 1977-80; mem. adv. com. Edn. Futures Internat.; bd. dirs. Urban League, 1982— (life mem.). Served with USN, 1947-55. Decorated Letter of Commendation; recipient Walker awards for excellence in classical studies U. Pacific, 1956, 57, 58, citation Senate and Assembly State of Calif. for TV series, 1965; Jacob Sleeper fellow Boston U., 1965. Mem. Am. Acad. Religion, Am. Mgmt. Assn., Nat. Assn. Ednl. Broadcasters, Soc. Bibl. Lit., Religious Pub. Relations Council, Soc. for Antiquity and Christianity. Author: Abstracts from Federal Communications Law, 1958; Audiovisual Facilities for Churchmen, 1970; Ethical Factors in Management Decision, 1972; Mass Media Models of Education, 1975; Emerging Developments in Educational Television, 1976; Footprints in Space: Religious Applications of Communications Satellites, 1977; Investing Made Simple, 1986; writer weekly newspsper column; contbr. articles to religious publs. Exec. producer The Other School System, 1978. Home: 600 NE 16th St Oklahoma City OK 73104 Office: PO Box 60773 Oklahoma City OK 73146

ALEXANDER, MARY E., lawyer; b. Chgo., Nov. 16, 1947; d. Theron and Marie (Bailey) A.; m. Lyman Saunders Faulkner, Jr., Dec. 1, 1984; 1 child, Michelle. BA, U. Iowa, 1969; MPH, U. Calif.-Berkeley, 1975; JD, U. Santa Clara, 1982. Bar: Calif. 1982. Researcher, U. Cin., 1969-74; dept. dir., sr. environ. health scientist Stanford Research Inst., Menlo Park, Calif., 1975-80; cons. Alexander Assocs., Ambler, Pa., 1980-82; assoc. Caputo, Liccardo Rossi Sturges & McNeil, San Jose, Calif., 1982-84; assoc. Cartwright, Slobodin, Bokelman, et al, San Francisco, 1984-88, ptnr., 1988—. Com. mem. Cancer Soc., San Jose, 1983. Nat. Inst. Occupational Safety and Health scholar U. Calif.-Berkeley, 1975. Democrat. Home: 967 Clinton Rd Los Altos CA 94022 Office: Cartwright Slobodin Bokelman et al 101 California 26th Floor San Francisco CA 94111

ALEXANDER, MARY LOUISE, biology educator; b. Ennis, Tex., Jan. 15, 1926; d. Emmett F. and Florence (Hill) Alexander; B.A., U. Tex., 1947, M.A., 1949, Ph.D., 1951. Instr., research asst. Genetics Found., U. Tex., 1944-51; postdoctoral fellow biology div. AEC, Oak Ridge, 1951-52; postdoctoral research fellow U. Tex., 1952-55; research asso. U. Tex.-M.D. Anderson Hosp. and Tumor Inst., Houston, 1956-58, asst. biologist, 1959-62; research scientist Genetics Found. U. Tex., Austin, 1962-67; research cons. Brookhaven Nat. Lab., Upton, N.Y., 1955; research participant Oak Ridge Inst. Nuclear Studies, 1951-77; asso. prof. biology S.W. Tex. State U., San Marcos, 1966-69, prof., 1970—. Nat. Cancer Inst. fellow Inst. Animal Genetics, Edinburgh, Scotland, 1960-61. Mem. Genetics Soc. Am., Radiation Research Soc., Am. Soc. Human Genetics, Sigma Xi, Gamma Phi Beta, Phi Sigma, Alpha Epsilon Delta. Home: Hunter's Glen Route 2 Box 119 San Marcos TX 78666

ALEXANDER, RICHARD, lawyer; b. Cleve., Sept. 26, 1944; m. Nancy L. Biebel, Mar. 16, 1968; children—Marshall, Meredith. B.A., Ohio Wesleyan U., 1966; J.D. (Nat. Honor scholar), U. Chgo., 1969. Bar: Mich. 1969, U.S. Dist. Ct. (ea. and we. dists.) Mich. 1970, U.S. Dist. Ct. (so. dist.) Ind. 1970, Calif. 1971, U.S. Dist. Ct. (no. dist.) Calif. 1971, U.S. Ct. Appeals (9th cir.) 1971, U.S. Dist. Ct. (cen. dist.) Calif. 1972, U.S. Dist. Ct. (ea. dist.) Calif. 1973, U.S. Dist. Ct. D.C. 1980. Diplomate Nat. Bd. Trial Advocacy, 1980. Asst. prof. Grad. Sch. Bus., Mich. State U., 1969-71; assoc. Belli, Ashe, Ellison, Choulos & Lieff, San Francisco, 1971-72, Lieff, Alexander, Wilcox & Hill, San Francisco, 1972-74, Boccardo, Lull, Niland & Bell, San Francisco and San Jose, Calif., 1974-80; ptnr. Boccardo Law Firm, San Jose, 1980-87; Alexander & Bohn, San Jose, 1987—; mem. Santa Clara County Criminal Justice Adv. Bd., 1978-82, chmn., 1978-80; mem. Santa Clara County Jail Over-crowding Task Force, 1978-81; mem. Santa Clara County Pub. Defender Charter Amendment Task Force, 1980; judge pro tem Santa Clara County Superior Ct., 1976-83, 85-86 arbitrator, 1976—; co-chmn. Superior Ct. Arbitration Adminstrn. Com., 1979—; spl. master State Bar Calif., 1980—, lectr. continuing edn., 1975, 78, 81, 82, 83, 84, 85, 86, bd. govs. 1985—, mem. com. profl. ethics, 1977-80; speaker legal seminars. Contbr. articles to profl. jours. Mem. Palo Alto (Calif.) Unified Sch. Dist. Task Force on Spl. Edn., 1975-79; vice chmn. sch. improvement program Palo Alto Unified Sch. Dist., 1977-78, mem. found. exploration com., 1984; mem. Santa Clara County Data Confidentiality Commn., 1976-78, chmn., 1977-78; mem. Santa Clara County Democratic Central Com., 1978-80; bd. dirs. Japanese Am. Environ. Conf., 1979-81. Recipient Santa Clara County Youth Commn. medal, 1980; commendation for disting. service Mayor San Jose, 1982; Roscoe Pound fellow; named one of Outstanding Young Men of Am. Mem. San Francisco Bar Assn., Santa Clara County Bar Assn. (pres. 1984), Calif. Attys. for Criminal Justice (founding; treas. 1972-74, gov. 1972-75), Calif. Trial Lawyers Assn. (recognized trial lawyer 1980-86), State Bar Calif. (bd. govs., 1985—, v.p. 1987—), Assn. Trial Lawyers Am., Sierra Club, NAACP, Stanford Alumni Assn., Alexander Graham Bell Assn. for Deaf, Nat. Trust Hist. Preservation, San Jose Mus. San Jose Symphony. Clubs: U. Chgo. Alumni, San Jose Athletic. Office: Alexander & Bohn 55 South Market St Suite 1080 San Jose CA 95113

ALEXANDER, ROBERT JACKSON, economist, educator; b. Canton, Ohio, Nov. 26, 1918; s. Ralph S. and Ruth (Jackson) A.; m. Joan O. Powell, Mar. 26, 1949; children: Anthony, Margaret. B.A., Columbia U., 1940; M.A., Columnbia U., 1941; Ph.D., Columbia U., 1950. Asst. economist Bd. Econ. Warfare, 1942, Office Inter-Am. Affairs, 1945-46; mem. faculty Rutgers U., 1947—, prof. econs., 1961—; mem. Pres.-elect Kennedy's Latin Am. Task Force, 1960-61. Author: (28 books) books including Juan Domingo Peron: A History, 1979, Romulo Betancourt and the Transformation of Venezuela, 1982, Bolivia: Past, Present and Future of its Politics, 1982, Biographical Dictionary of Latin American and Caribbean Politics, 1988. Mem. nat. bd. League Indsl. Democracy, 1955—; mem. nat. exec. com. Socialist Party-Social Dem. Fedn., 1957-66. Served with USAAF, 1942-45. Decorated officer Order Condor of the Andes Bolivia. Mem. Am. Econ. Assn., Latin Am. Studies Assn., Middle Atlantic Council Latin Am. Studies (v.p. 1986-87, pres. 1987—), Council Fgn. Relations, Internam. Assn. Democracy and Freedom (chmn. N.Am. com. 1970—), Phi Gamma Delta. Home: 944 River Rd Piscataway NJ 08854 Office: Rutgers U New Brunswick NJ 08903

ALEXANDER, ROBERT WILLIAM, radiologist; b. Reading, Pa., May 30, 1924; s. Robert Mackey and Jessie Forbes (Smith) A.; m. Nancy Ann Wetty, June 19, 1964; children—William, Heather. Student Swarthmore Coll., 1942-44; M.D., Jefferson Med. Coll., 1948. Diplomate Am. Bd. Radiology. Intern, Phila. Gen. Hosp., 1948-49, resident in radiology, 1950-52; radiologist San Antonio Med. and Surg. Clinic, 1954, Hamburg, Pa. Hosp., 1965—; practice medicine specializing in radiology, Reading, 1955—; cons. VA Hosp., Lebanon, Pa. Contbr. articles to profl. jours. Bd. dirs. Vis. Nurses Assn. Reading, 1959—, pres., 1984—; bd. dirs. Reading chpt. Am. Lung Assn., 1960—; chmn. profl. div. United Fund Reading, 1968; bd. dirs. Reading chpt. ARC, 1970-76, 78-84; pres. Berks County Tb Soc., 1970—, Levi Mengel Fund of Reading Mus. and Art Gallery; mem. Wyomissing Bd. of Health, 1984—. Served with U.S. Army, 1952-54. Nat. Cancer Assn. fellow, 1952-53. Fellow Am. Coll. Radiology; mem. Berks County Med. Soc. (pres. 1964), Pa. Med. Soc. (chmn. council govt. relations 1977-79), AMA (del. 1974—, pres. 1985-86), Pa. Radiology Soc., N.Am. Radiology Soc., Phila., Radiology Soc., Blockly Radiology Soc., Reading-Berks C. of C. (dir. 1966-73). Republican. Lutheran. Clubs: Kiwanis (pres. Reading 1966), Berkshire Country (dir. 1964-69, life). Home: 1417 Old Mill Rd Wyomissing PA 19610 Office: 544 Elm St Reading PA 19601 Other: 260 State St Hamburg PA 19526

ALEXANDER, SAMUEL ALLEN, JR., electronics company executive; b. Washington, Oct. 9, 1938; s. Samuel Allen and Mary Pearl (Last) A.; B.S. and B.A., Tufts U., 1962; postgrad. in biochemistry George Washington U., 1963; m. Susan Karinch, Aug. 25, 1973; children—Carolyn, Samuel Allen, Emily, Jonathan, David, Susan M. Investment banker, registered rep. Ferris & Co., Washington, 1966-69; pres. Command Fin., Washington, 1969-72, Potomac Fed. Corp., Washington, 1973-75; v.p. adminstrn. and ops. officer Potter Instrument Co., Gonic, N.H., 1975-78, pres., chief exec. officer, 1978-83; pres. successor firm Precision Magnetics and Ceramics, 1984-86; chmn. bd., chief exec. officer ETI Techs., 1986—; participant investment banking seminar Wharton Sch. Bus., U. Pa., 1968-69. Mem. Delta Tau Delta. Roman Catholic. Clubs: Chevy Chase (Md.); Army Navy (Washington); Lake Sunapee Yacht (Sunapee, N.H.).

ALEXANDERSSON, EIRIKUR, municipal government official; b. Grindavik, Iceland, June 13, 1936; s. Alexander Georg and Margret (Eiriksdottir) Sigurdsson; m. Hildur Gudrun Juliusdottir, Oct. 2, 1960; children—Almar, Leifur. Grad. Comml. Sch. Iceland, Reykjavik, 1954. Retail dealer Eikabud, Grindavik, 1956-68; banker Landsbanki Islands, Sudurnes, Iceland, 1968-70; mayor City of Grindavik, 1971-83; mng. dir. Fedn. Sudurnes Municipalities, 1983—, chmn., 1972-73, 80-81; chmn. Fedn. Municipalities Reykjanes Region, Gardabae, Iceland, 1974-78, Sudurnes Incinerat Authority, 1980-81, Sudurnes Regional Heating, Njardvik, Iceland, 1981-84. Contbr. articles to profl. jours. Councillor Town of Grindavik, 1962-70; vice congressman Congress of Iceland, Reykjavik, 1978-79. Independence Party. Lutheran. Lodges: Lions Internat., Odd Fellows. Home: Greniteig 34, Keflavik Iceland 230 Office: Fedn Sudurnes Municipalities, Vesturbraut 10a, Keflavik 230, Iceland

ALEXANDRE, GÉRARD-EUGENE, orthopedic surgeon, medical school administrator; b. Paris, Jan. 13, 1930; s. André-Maurice and Marcelle (Blum) A.; m. Liliane Martha Pierre, June 13, 1956; children—Fabienne-Jacqueline, Dominique Liliane. M.D., U. Paris, 1963. Intern Hosp. of Paris, 1961-66, head surgical orthopedic clinic, 1966-69; cons. surgeon Nat. Inst. Disabled, Ministery of War Veterans, 1963-74; asst. dept. child surgery St. Vincent-de-Paul Hosp., Paris, 1967; asst. dept. orthopedic surgery Hosp. Cochin, Paris, 1969-82; orthopedic surgeon Clinique de Marly, Marly le Roi, France, 1969—, dir. massage, physiotherapy and chiropody sch., 1963—. Contbr. articles to profl. jours. Mem. Conseil Supérieur Professions Paramédicales, Health Ministry, 1973-81, 86—. Mem. Nat. Orgn. Dirs. Physiotherapy Schs. (sec. gen. 1969—), French Soc. Surgical Orthopedy, Nat. Coll. Orthopedic Surgeons, French Assn. Artificial Limb Supply, Hand Study Group, West Orthopedic Soc. Lodge: Rotary. Avocations: skiing; windsurfing. Home: 59 Ave de Briens, Villennes Sur Seine 78670, France Office: Clinique de Marly, Chemin du Clos Courche, Marly Le Roi 78160, France

ALEXANDRE, PIERRE, hematologist, educator; b. Nancy, France, Nov. 4, 1926; s. Lucien and Lucie (Gentilini) A.; m. Inge Scherer, Aug. 27, 1960. MD, Faculté Medecin Nancy, 1964. Hosp. assistant hematologist Nancy, 1964-74; prof. hematology Ctr. Regionale Transfus Sanguine, Nancy, 1974-85; lab. dir., chief of staff Ctr. Regional de Transfusions Sanguine, Nancy, 1985—. Served to capt. French Army. Mem. Cercle Clin. France-Allemagne (pres. 1972—), Assn. Française des Hemophiles, Soc. Française de Transfusion. Roman Catholic. Lodge: Lions. Home: 9 Rue des Glacis, Nancy 54000, France Office: Centre Regional de Transfusion, 9-11 Rue Lionnois, Nancy 54000, France

ALEXANDRU, CAMPEANU, physician; b. Pascani, Iasi, Romania, Mar. 29, 1936; s. Constantin and Vasilicia (Stratulat) C.; m. Ana Varvara Iov Campeanu, Jan. 5, 1947; children: Andreea Ileana, Nicora Alexandru. MD, U. Sch. Medicine, Bucharest, Romania, 1960, D.Med. Sci., 1973. Resident Caritas, Colentina and other univ. hosps., Bucharest, 1960-62; gen. practice medicine Baicoi, Romania, 1963; asst. prof. Med. Clinic U. Caritas Hosp., 1964-73, sr. physician internal medicine, 1974-87, prof. Med. Clinic, 1974—, dep. coronary care unit, 1979-87, chief internal medicine service, 1987; mem. Com. Cardiology, Bucharest, 1980—. Author: Internal Medicine, 1979, Up-to-Date Internal Medicine, 1981, Cardiology, 1988; contbr. articles to med. jours. Mem. Polit. Com. Med. Sch., Bucharest, 1980—. Mem. Romanian Soc. Internal Medicine, Romanian Soc. Cardiology, Balkanic Med. Union. Romanian Communist. Home: Lunca Bradului Nr 2 Bloc H5, scara I ap 5, 74624 Bucharest Romania Office: Med Clinic U Caritas Hosp, 29 Traian St, 74122 Bucharest Romania

ALEXIOU, MARINA S., business management company executive; b. N.Y.C., Feb. 12, 1940; d. Stanley and Mary S. (Couloumbi) A. Cert. in bus. mgmt. U. N.C., 1959; student bus. mgmt. Ctr. for Degree Studies, Scranton, Pa. Legal sec. Jordan, Wright, Henson & Nichols, attys., Greensboro, N.C., 1959-60; with North Am. Philips Co., 1961— (company mergered with Consol. Electronics 1969 then became North Am. Philips Corp.), adminstrv. asst. to pres. and dir., 1965-69, adminstrv. asst. to chmn., chief exec. officer, pres. and dir., 1969-77, adminstrv. asst to chmn., chief exec. officer and dir., 1978-80, adminstrv. asst. to chmn. and dir., chmn. governing com. U.S. Philips Trust, 1981-84, adminstrv. asst. to dir., chmn. governing com. U.S. Philips Trust, 1985-86, mgr. corp. purchasing, 1985—. Mem. U.S. Senatorial Bus. Adv. Bd. and Steering Com., Washington; adv. bd. Am. Security Council, Washington. Asst. chmn. fund raising Am. Cancer Soc., 1978—, mem. exec. com., 1985—. Dep. chmn. exec. Republican Com. of Bronxville (N.Y.), 1980—; mem. Rep. Presdl. Task Force, Washington, Rep. Senatorial Inner Circle. Mem. Nat. Assn. Exec. Sec., Nat. Assn. Female Execs., Am. Soc. Profl. and Exec. Women, Internat. Platform Assn., UN We Believe (exec. planning com.), Smithsonian Nat. Assocs., N.Y. Philharm. Soc. Republican. Greek Orthodox. Lodge: Toastmasters (charter). Home: Northgate Alger Ct Bronxville NY 10708 Office: N Am Philips Corp 100 E 42nd St New York NY 10017

ALEXIS, JODY RAE, real estate broker; b. Langdon, N.D., Mar. 2, 1940; d. Raymond and Ada (Widwick) Armstrong; student Stephens Coll., 1959-61; BA, U. Nebr., 1963; MA, U. Colo., 1968; JD, U. Denver, 1971; div.; 1 son, Clark Kendall. Bar: Colo. 1971. Asst. dir. USO, Colorado Springs, Colo., 1964-65; asst. to dir. adminstrn. Aircraft Mechanics, Inc., Colorado Springs, 1965-67; pub. relations dir. Red Ram of Am. Corp., Colorado Springs, 1967-70, The Woodmar Corp., 1971; exec. dir. Rocky Mountain Land Devel. Assn., Denver, 1970-74; pres. Alexis & Assocs., Denver, 1974—; sole practice, Denver, 1974—; broker assoc. Van Schaack Fine Homes; dir. Colo. Mgmt. Rocky Mountain Log Homes Inc., Designs Internat. Bd. dirs. Colo. Convs.and Reservations, 1974—; chmn. Denver Art Mus.; mem. Denver Ctr. for Performing Arts, Jr. Symphony Guild, Denver Ctr. Alliance, Hope for the Children. Republican. Roman Catholic. Home: 202 Adams St Denver CO 80206

AL-FADHLI, SALEH NASSER, transportation company executive; b. Abyan, Democratic Yemen, Jan. 15, 1954; s. Nasser Abdulla Bin Hussein and Alam (Bint Fadhel) A.; m. Nabila Ahmed, Aug. 8, 1981; children: Khulood, Badr, Mohammad. BS in Fluid Mechanics, Manchester U., Eng., 1980. Engr. Arabian Bulk Trade, Al-Khobar, Saudi Arabia, 1981-82; dep. project mgr. Arabian Bulk Trade, Al-Khobar, 5, 1982-83; project mgr. Arabian Bulk Trade, Jeddah, Saudi Arabia, 1983-85, Agri Bulk Trade, Jeddah, Saudi Arabia, 1985-86; tech. mgr. Saudi Bulk Transport, Jeddah, Saudi Arabia, 1986—. Prince of Sultanate of Al-Fadhli, Democratic Yemen, 1954-67. Moslem. Home: PO Box 19627, Jeddah 21445, Saudi Arabia

ALFADL, MOHAMED ABDULKADER, sales executive; b. Jeddah, Saudi Arabia, Dec. 20, 1955; s. Abdulkader Mohamed and Nahida (Halabi) A.; m. Haya; children: Lana, Abdulkader, Nahida. BS in Bus. Econ., U. Calif. Pres. Rabya Landscaping Ltd., Jeddah, 1974—, Alpha Trading and Shipping Agy., Jeddah, 1977—, Arabian Trading and Indsl. Services Ltd., Jeddah, 1982—, Aldewan Fast Food Co. Ltd., Jeddah, 1983—. Office: Alfadl Group of Cos, Al Hamra - Mustashpa Alwilada St, Jeddah 21411, Saudi Arabia

ALFALAHI, HUSSAIN ALI, linguist, educator; b. Baghdad, Iraq, Mar. 27, 1949; s. Ali Jassim Alfalahi and Hasna Faraj Alamri; m. Emira Ahmed, Feb. 21, 1971; children: Ansam, Ula, Jasmine. BA in English, U. Baghdad, 1970; MA in English, U. S.C., 1977, PhD, 1981. English instr. Ministry Edn., Alanbar, Iraq, 1970-76; asst. prof. Inst. Pub. Adminstrn., Riyadh, Saudi Arabia, 1981—, ednl. cons., 1981—. Translator: Management Information Systems: A User Perspective, 1988. Moslem. Home and Office: Inst Pub Adminstrn, PO Box 205, Riyadh 11141, Saudi Arabia

ALFANDARI, JEAN-PIERRE, cardiologist; b. Tours, France, Mar. 19, 1934; m. Marie-Jose Rouch, July 19, 1963; children: Christophe, Marie-Laurence, Paule, Bruno, Henri. MD, U. Paris, 1963. Intern Hosp. Broussais, Paris, 1962, Hosp. Bicetre, Paris, 1963, Hosp. Pitie, Paris, 1963, Geneva Hosp., 1964, Hosp. Cochin, Paris, 1965, Hosp. Laennec, Paris, 1966; clin. chief Hosp. Beaujon, Paris, 1966-67; practice medicine specializing in cardiac surgery Tours, 1967—; pres. Union Indre et Loire, Tours, 1984. Served to lt. French Army, 1960-62. Mem. Pvt. Hosps. Fedn. France (pres. 1980-82, exec. mem. 1982—), Pvt. Hosps. Centre (pres. 1976-80), CNPF (permanent assembly 1984—), St. Galien Soc. Tours (chmn. 1974—), Pvt. Hosp. (HP) SA, Tours (chmn. 1985—), Holding H Plus, Tours (chmn. 1986—). Roman Catholic. Clubs: Golf (Tours) (exec. com.); Cercle Interallie Union (Paris). Office: Saint Gatien SA, Place de la Cathedrale, 37000 Tours France

ALFANGE, DEAN, lawyer; b. Constantinople, Dec. 2, 1900; came to U.S., 1901; m. Thalia Perry, Aug. 11, 1929; children—Whitman, Dean. A.B., Hamilton Coll., 1922; LL.B., Columbia U., 1925. Bar: N.Y. U.S. Supreme Ct. 1925. Since practiced in N.Y.C.; Chmn. N.Y.C. Appeals Bd. 6, Enemy Alien Hearing Bd. So. Dist. N.Y.; mem. N.Y. State Bd. Inquiry in Longshore Industry; founder Legion for Am. Unity, 1940; mem. exec. com. Citizens for Victory; dir. Better Understanding Found. for Religious and Racial Tolerance, Greek War Relief Assn.; nat. chmn. Emergency Com. to Save Jewish People of Europe; chmn. N.Y. State Quarter Horse Racing Commn., 1971—, Am. Christian Palestine Com. of Greater N.Y.; Chmn. Fgn. Lang. Speakers Bur. Dem. Presdl. Campaign Com., 1940; Dem. candidate for Congress 17th N.Y. Dist., 1941; nominated for gov. N.Y., Am. Labor Party, 1942; chmn. Liberal and Labor Com. which founded Liberal party State of N.Y., 1944, Israel Anniversary Celebration Com., 1949. Author: My Creed This Week mag. and Reader's Digest The Horse Racing Industry, 1976. Trustee Fashion Inst. Tech., N.Y., United Greek Orthodox Charities, Archdiocesan Greek Cathedral of Holy Trinity, N.Y.; pres. LaGuardia Meml. Settlement House. Recipient Freedom Found. Award, 1960; Theodore Roosevelt Meml. award for non-fiction book The Supreme Court and the National Will, 1937; Donor scholarship endowments Hamilton Coll. to promote democratic govt. and religious understanding; elected to Settlement House Hall of Fame, 1986. Mem. Nat. Inst. Social Scis., Am. Acad. Polit. and Social Sci., UN Assn. (dir.), NAACP, Am., N.Y. bar assns., Am. Legion, Nat. Inst. Social Scis., Am. Hellenic Congress (nat. chmn.), Order of Ahepa (past nat. pres.), Am. Quarter Horse Assn. (racing com.), Grand St. Boys Assn., United Hunts Assn., Phi Beta Kappa, Pi Delta Epsilon, Delta Sigma Rho. Clubs: Mason, Elk, Turf and Field, Economic of N.Y, Circus Saints and Sinners; Governor's (N.Y.) (exec. com.). Home: 65 Central Park W New York NY 10023 Office: 9 E 40th St New York NY 10016

ALFARO, FELIX BENJAMIN, physician; b. Managua, Nicaragua, Oct. 22, 1939; came to U.S., 1945, naturalized, 1962; s. Agustin Jose and Amanda Julieta (Barillas) A.; student (State scholar) U. San Francisco, 1958-59, 61-62; M.D., Creighton U., 1967; m. Carmen Heide Meyer, Aug. 14, 1965; children—Felix Benjamin, Mark. Clk., Pacific Gas & Electric Co., San Francisco, 1960-61; intern St. Mary's Hosp., San Francisco, 1967; resident Scenic Gen. Hosp., Modesto, Calif., 1970; practice family medicine, Watsonville, Calif., 1971—; active staff Watsonville Community Hosp., 1971—. Served to capt., M.C., U.S. Army, 1968-69. Lic. physician, Nebr., La., Calif. Diplomate Am. Bd. Family Practice. Fellow Am. Acad. Family Practice; mem. AMA, Calif. Med. Assn., Santa Cruz County Med. Soc., 38th Parrallel Med. Soc. of Korea, Nat Rifle Assn., VFW. Republican. Roman Catholic. Office: 30 Brennan St Watsonville CA 95016

ALFARO-SEQUEIRA, JOSÉ LUIS, civil engineer, educator; b. Tegucigalpa, Honduras, Jan. 5, 1945; s. Jose Luis and Pastora (Sequeira) A.; m. Dora Adriana Flores, Dec. 6, 1962; children: Nalda, Kathia, Victor, José. CE, Nat. U., 1971; grad. in computer sci. U. Denver, 1977. Project engr. SANAA/IDB, Tegucigalpa, 1973-74, water project chief designer, 1974-75, project chief engr., 1977-78, data processing chmn. 1978-81, comml. data program chmn., 1981-82; exec. sec. Coll. of Engring. of Honduras, Tegucigalpa, 1982-83; prof. UNAH, Tegucigalpa, 1979—; chmn. Ctr. of Informatics of Sec. Pub. Works and Transport, 1984-87; projects control cons. IDB Project, 1987—. Co-author manual short course water projects design. Mem. Colegio de Ingenieros Civiles, Asociación Interamericana de Ingenieros Sanitarios. Roman Catholic. Home: Loarque No 7409, Tegucigalpa Honduras Office: Colegio de Ingenieros Civiles, Colonia Florencia Nor, Tegucigalpa Honduras

ALFONSIN, RAUL RICARDO, president of Argentina, lawyer; b. Chascomus, Argentina, Mar. 13, 1927; m. Maria Lorenza Barrenchea, 1950; 6 children. Law degree Universidad Nacional de la Plata, 1950; LLD (hon.) U. N.Mex., 1985. Dep., Provincial Assembly Buenos Aires, 1950, 58-62, mem. Chamber of Deps., 1963-66, 73-76; pres. Argentina, 1983—. Mem. La Union Civica Radical (pres. 1983—); co-founder Provincial Assembly for Human Rights. Author: La Question Argentina; El Radicalismo; Ahora, Mi Propuesta. Roman Catholic. Office: Casa Rosada, Oficina del Presidente, Buenos Aires Argentina *

ALFONSO, ANTONIO ESCOLAR, surgeon; b. Manila, Philippines, Nov. 25, 1943; came to U.S., 1968, naturalized, 1978; s. Ricardo Lagdameo and Marita (Escolar) Alfonso; m. Teresita Nazereno, Apr. 25, 1970; children: Margaretta, Roberto. A.B. cum laude, Ateneo U., 1963; M.D. cum laude, U. Philippines, 1968. Diplomate: Am. Bd. Surgery. Intern U. Philippines-Philippine Gen. Hosp., 1968; instr. surgery Temple U., Phila., 1968-72; sr. fellow surg. oncology Meml. Sloan-Kettering Cancer Ctr., N.Y.C., 1972-74; dir. head and neck surgery service SUNY Downstate Med. Ctr., Bklyn., 1974—, assoc. dir. div. surg. oncology, 1974—, asst. prof. surgery, 1974-77, assoc. prof., 1977-82, prof., 1982—, vice-chmn. dept. surgery, 1988—; chmn. dept. surgery Bklyn. Hosp., 1982-88; chmn. Dept. Surgery L.I. Coll. Hosp., 1988—; vice chmn. Dept. Surgery SUNY Downstate Med. Ctr., 1988—; cons. head and neck surgery Bklyn. VA Hosp., 1974—. Author: Principles of Surgery Oncology; contbr. articles in med. to profl. jours., chpts. to med. books. Recipient research essay prize N.Y. Colon and Rectal Surg. Soc., 1973; grantee Am. Cancer Soc., 1978. Mem. Assn. Acad. Surgeons, Am. Soc. Clin. Oncology, Am. Assn. Cancer Edn., Soc. Head and Neck Surgeons, ACS (bd. govs. Bklyn.-L.I. chpt.), N.Y. Surg. Soc., Bklyn. Surg. Soc. (pres. 1986-87), N.Y. Cancer Soc. (v.p. 1986-87, pres. elect 1987-88, pres. 1988—), Soc. Surg. Oncology, N.Y. Head and Neck Soc., N.Y. Soc. Colon and Rectal Surgeons, Phi Kappa Phi. Roman Catholic. Home: 50 Olive St Forest Hills NY 11375 Office: The LI Coll Hosp Dept Surgery Brooklyn NY 11201

ALFORD, NEILL HERBERT, JR., legal educator; b. Greenville, S.C., July 13, 1919; s. Neill Herbert and Elizabeth (Robertson) A.; m. Elizabeth Talbot Smith, June 26, 1943; children: Neill Herbert III, Margaret Dudley, Eli Thomas Stackhouse. B.A., The Citadel-Mil. Coll. S.C., 1940; LL.B., U. Va., 1947; J.S.D., Yale U., 1966. Bar: Va. 1954. Mem. faculty law U. Va. Law Sch., Charlottesville, 1947-61, 62-74; Doherty Found. prof. U. Va. Law Sch., 1966-74, spl. cons. to pres. univ., legal adviser to rector and bd. dirs., 1972-74; Joseph Henry Lumpkin prof., dean Law Sch. U. Ga., Athens, 1974-76; Percy Brown Jr. prof. law U. Va., 1976—; state reporter Supreme Ct. Va., 1977-84; prof. chair internat. law Naval War Coll., 1961-62, cons., 1962-68; Spl. counsel Va. Code Commn., 1954-57; dir. Va. Bankers Assn. Trust Sch., 1958-61; summer tchr. George Washington U., U. N.C.; chmn. bd. dirs. U. Va. Press., 1970-74, 87—. Author: Cases and Materials on Decedents Estates and Trusts, 7th edit, 1988, Modern Economic Warfare: Law and the Naval Participant, 1967; Contbr. articles to profl. jours. Comdr. civil affairs group U.S. Army Res., 1947-66. Served to lt. col. AUS, 1941-46, ETO. Decorated Bronze Star, Combat Inf. badge.; Sterling fellow Yale U., 1950-51, Ford fellow U. Wis., 1958, Thomas Jefferson fellow U. Va., 1988. Mem. Selden Soc., Am. Soc. Legal History, Am. Judicature Soc., Am. Soc. Internat. Law, Am. Law Inst., Am. Coll. Probate Counsel, Va. State Bar, Va., Am. bar assns., Order of Coif, Phi Alpha Delta, Omicron Delta Kappa. Club: Colonnade (Charlottesville). Home: 1868 Field Rd Charlottesville VA 22901 Office: Law Sch U Va Charlottesville VA 22901

ALFRED, KARL SVERRE, orthopedic surgeon; b. Stavanger, Norway, July 10, 1917; s. Aldred Bjarne Abrahamsen Floen and Thora Garpestad; m. Amalia Leona Bombach, July 26, 1951; children—Patricia (Mrs. Dennis Alleman) Richard Lincoln, Peter Karl. Student, U. Va., 1935-38; M.D., L.I. Coll. Medicine, 1942. Intern Mountainside Hosp., Montclair, N.J., 1942-43; resident orthopedics Univ. Hosps., Cleve., 1947-50; practice medicine specializing in orthopedic surgery Cleve., 1950—; chief orthopedic surgery St. Vincent Charity Hosp., Cleve., 1955-81, chief orthopedic surgery emeritus, 1981—, chief of staff, 1971-75; assoc. staff Euclid Gen. Hosp., Cleve., mem. cons. staff; courtesy staff Univ., St. Luke's hosps., Cleve., Geauga Community Hosp., Chardon, O.; orthopedic cons. Norfolk & Western R.R.; affiliate tchr. orthopedics Bunts Edn. Inst., Cleve. Contbr. articles to profl. jours. Trustee, St. Vincent Charity Hosp., Cleve. Served with M.C., USNR, 1942-47. Episcopalian. Lodges: Masons, Rotary. Home: 20 Brandywood Dr Pepper Pike OH 44124 Office: 2475 E 22d St Cleveland OH 44115

ALFVÉN, HANNES OLOF GOSTA, physicist; b. May 30, 1908; Ph.D., U. Uppsala, 1934. Prof. theory of electricity Royal Inst. Tech., Stockholm, 1940-45, prof. electronics, 1945-63, prof. plasma physics, 1963-73; prof. dept. applied physics and info. sci. U. Calif.-San Diego, from 1967; mem. Swedish Sci. Adv. Council, 1963-67; past mem. Swedish AEC; past gov. Swedish Def. Research Inst., Swedish Atomic Energy Co.; past sci. adv. Swedish Govt.; pres. Pugwash Confs. on Sci. and World Affairs, 1970-75; mem. panel on comets and asteroids NASA. Recipient Nobel prize for physics, 1970; Lomonsov gold medal USSR Acad. Scis., 1971; Franklin medal, 1971, Bowie Gold medal Am. Geophysical Union, 1987. Fellow Royal Soc. (Eng.); mem. Swedish Acad. Scis., Akademia NAUK (USSR), Nat. Acad. Scis. (fgn. assoc.), others. Author: Cosmical Electrodynamics, 1950; On the Origin of the Solar System, 1954; Cosmical Electrodynamics: Fundamental Principles, 1963; Worlds-Antiworlds, 1966; The Tale of the Big Computer, 1968; Atom, Man and the Universe, 1969; Living on the Third Planet, 1972; Evolution of the Solar System, 1976; Cosmic Plasma, 1981. Office: Univ Calif Dept Elec Engring & Computer Scis La Jolla CA 92093 also: Dept Plasma Physics, Royal Inst of Tech, S-100-44 Stockholm 70, Sweden *

ALGABID, HAMID, prime minister of Niger. Past Minister of State for Planning, Commerce and Transp.; past Minister del. for Fin.; Prime Minister of Niger, 1983—. Address: Office du Premier Ministre, Niamey Niger *

ALGAZI, JACQUES E, psychiatrist; b. Paris, Sept. 25, 1934; s. Leon Jeuda and Tatiana (Kaganoff) A.; m. Liliane Claude Morain, June 28, 1976; children: Nathalie, Beatrice. PCB, Faculty Scis., Paris, 1953; degree in medicine, Faculty Paris, 1963; degree in homeopathy, Centre D'etudes Ecole, Franc d'Homeopathie, Paris, 1981. Cert. psychiatrist, 1975. Gen. practice medicine Massy, France, 1964-82; practice pscyhosomatic medicine Paris, 1967-75; charge de cours homeopathy Centre d'Études, Paris, 1982; practice medicine specializing in psychiatry Paris, 1982—; v.p. Homeopathy Specialist Soc., France, 1986, Groupement Homeopathique d'Etudes Psychopathologiques, France, 1982; gen sec., prof. Centre d'Etudes, paris, 1987—. Served to maj. French Med. Corps., 1963-64, Algeria. Recipient Medaille du Maintien de l'ordre en Algerie et au Sahara, 1963-64. Office: 45 Av de Villeirs, 75017 Paris France

AL-GIZAWI, AHMED MOHAMMAD, marketing and sales manager, consultant; b. Mahallah, Al-Delta, Egypt, Nov. 6, 1955; s. Mohammad Awad Al-Gizawi; m. Osman Hanna Mohammed, Mar. 21, 1983; children: Riham, Mohammad, Mouamen. B of Commerce and Bus. Adminstrn., 1977, diploma computer sci. and infos., 1981. Sales rep. Al-Kateb Al-Massry, Cairo, 1978-82; sales exec. Riyadh Bus. Machines Ctr., Riyadh, Saudi Arabia, 1982-83; sales mgr. Pan Arab Computer Center, Al-Khobar, Saudi Arabia, 1983-87; mktg. mgr. Al-Khaleej Computer & Electronic System, Al-Khobar, Saudi Arabia, 1987-88, Nat. COmputer Systems Co., Riyadh, 1988—. Office: NATCOM, PO Box 7902, Riyadh 11472, Saudi Arabia

AL-HAFEEZ, HUMZA, police officer; b. N.Y.C., Feb. 28, 1931; s. Asa Mose and Rose Mae (Danielson) Weir; m. Clarissa Ramona Mitchell, Mar. 1, 1980; children: Rasul, Roland, Habib, Wardi, John, Larry, Don, Mariama, Jacqueline, Nia. Student, Food Trades Vocat. Sch., 1947-48. Patrolman N.Y.C. Police Dept., from 1959; now owner, dir. Al-Hafeez Security and Investigations Service Inc., Bklyn.; chmn. CLAR-MAR-WARDI, Inc., 549 Nostrand Ave. Assocs., Inc.; founder Nat. Soc. Afro-Am. Policemen Inc.; also past pres.; cons. community relations to chief insp. N.Y.C. Police Dept., to; U.S. Dept. Justice; investigator of corruption among N.Y.C. police officers Knapp Commn.; undercover narcotic officer, investigator Manhattan office Dist. Atty.; investigator Office of 1st Dep. Policy Commr.; undercover investigator U.S. Dept. Justice.; insp. N.Y. State Athletic Commn.; Lectr. Princeton U., Mich. State U., N.Y. State U., Pace Coll., Bklyn. Coll., U. Chgo., NYU, Satellite Acad., N.Y.C., Kinlock Mission for Blind, City N.Y. Police Acad., Nassau Community Coll.; others. Appeared on radio and TV.; Editor-in-chief: Your Muhammad Speaks newspaper; author The Slanderer, 1987. Mem. pastoral bd. Interfaith Hosp. Recipient Father of Yr. award Kinlock Freedom Found. for the Blind, 1973; Community Service award United Council of Chs., 1975; named Person of Yr. Nat. Assn. Black Policemen, 1982. Mem. Internat. Platform Assn. Mem. Nation of Islam; minister Muhammad's Temple of Islam, Bklyn. Home: 361 Clinton Ave 12C Brooklyn NY 11238 Office: 549 Nostrand Ave Brooklyn NY 11216

AL-HAMMAMI, RAFIK ISMAIL, marketing company executive; b. Damascus, Syria, May 31, 1947; s. Ismail Abdullah and Shahira Ahmed (Al-Sawwaf) Al-H.; m. Rana Yousef Eche, Oct. 19, 1979; children: Ismail, Omar. BS, U. Tex., 1973; MS, U. Dallas, 1975. Mgmt. cons. Applied Mgmt. Inst., Irving, Tex., 1975-77; with constrn. co., Damascus, 1978-82; mng. dir. Emerson Systems Ltd., Nicosia, Cyprus, 1982—. Home: 7 Yiannis Taliotis St, Nicosia 141 Cyprus Office: Emerson Systems Ltd, 304 Alpha House, 50 Makarios III Ave, Nicosia 136 Cyprus

AL-HASSAN, SALEH ABDULAH, electric corporation executive; b. Al-Hariq, Riyadh, Saudi Arabia, Aug. 15, 1957; s. Abdulah Abdulaziz and Shama (Abdulrahman) Al-Sinedi; m. Huda Abdulmohsen Al-Jamaz; children: Ashwaq, Aila. B in Gen. Electricity, Royal Tech. Inst., Ireland, 1980. Project mgr. Electricity Corp., Riyadh, 1977—, also bd. dirs. Home: Swedy PO Box 40963, Riyadh RUH 11511, Saudi Arabia Office: Electricity Corp, Omar Ben Alktab St PO Box 1185, Riyadh Saudi Arabia

AL-HAZZANI, KHALED A., school administrator; b. Saudi Arabia, 1952; s. Abdullah A. and Muneera Al-Hazzani; m. Manal A. Al-Tuwaijri, 1975; children: Bandar, Bader, Mohammed, Yazeed. BA, King Saud U., Saudi Arabia, 1975; MA, U. Ind., 1979, postgrad. Asst. King Saud U., Riyadh, Saudi Arabia, 1975-76, lectr. English, 1979-86; gen. mgr. Saudi Acad., Riyadh, 1986—; adj. lang. instr. Am. Lang. Acad., Riyadh, 1986—. Co-author: Arab Student Guide to English, 1986. Mem. Modern Lang. Assn., Tchrs. of English to Speakers of Other Langs. Home and Office: Saudi Acad, Box 16765, Riyadh Saudi Arabia

AL-HMOUD, HAZIM MANSOUR, civil engineer; b. Aidon, Irbid, Jordan, Jan. 25, 1950; s. Mansour Mohamed Al-Hmoud and Ayshah (Mohamed) Kassab; m. Wafa Khalil Marii, Dec. 5, 1974; children—Linda, Hussam, Laura, Shatha. B.Sc. in Civil Engring., Basrah U., 1972. Designer engr. Dammam Municipality, Saudi Arabia, 1972-75, mgr. dept. roads, 1975-76; contracting mgr. Hmoud Aljalhami Est., Dammam, 1976-82; gen. mgr. Fahad Muhawes Constrn. Est, Dammam, 1982—. Mem. Assn. Engrs. Avocations: music; playing cards. Home: PO Box 145, Dammam 31411, Saudi Arabia Office: Fahad Muhawes Constrn Est, PO Box 2945, Dammam 31461, Saudi Arabia

ALHONIEMI, PIRKKO KAARINA, literature educator; b. Turku, Finland, Mar. 16, 1935; d. Aarne Johannes and Hildur Josefina (Tähtinen) Salokas; m. Alho Esa Vesa Alhoniemi, Sept. 13, 1958; Leena Maaria, Esa Juhana. Degree, U. Turku, Finland, 1957, PhD, 1969. Asst. prof. Finnish lit. U. Turku, 1959-74, assoc. prof. Finnish lit., 1974—; docent Finnish lit. Åbo Akademi, 1971—. Author: Isänmaan Korkeat Veisut, 1969, Idylli Särkyy, 1972. Recipient Kalevala prize, 1966. Fellow Assn. Lit. Scholars, Finnish Lit. Soc., Kalevala Soc. (award 1966), Porthan Soc.; mem. Assn. Lit. Critics. Home: Ratialank 18 as 5, 20840 Turku Finland Office: Turun yliopisto, Henrikink 2/Juslenia, 20500 Turku Finland

ALI, AHMAD MOHAMED, banker; b. Medina City, Saudi Arabia, 1932; married; 4 children. B.A., Cairo U., 1957; M.A., U. Mich., 1962; D.P.A., SUNY-Albany, 1967. Dir., Sci. and Islamic Inst., Aden, 1958-59; dep. rector King Abdul Aziz U., 1967-72; dep. Ministry Edn. for Tech. Affairs Saudi Arabia, 1972-75; pres. Islamic Devel. Bank, Jeddah, 1975—; mem. adminstrv. bd. Saudi Credit Bank. Bd. dirs. council King Abdul Aziz U., Jeddah, King Saud U., Riyadh, Oil and Mineral U., Dhahran, Islami U., Medina, Imam Mohamed Ben Saud U., Riyadh. Contbr. articles to profl. jours. Avocations: cycling; walking. Office: Islamic Devel Bank, PO Box 5955, Jeddah 21432 Saudi Arabia *

ALI, SAIBOU, president of Niger. Pres. Supreme Mil. Council, Niamey, Niger, 1987—, also minister of def., 1987—. Office: Office of President, Niamey Niger *

ALIA, RAMIZ, government official; b. Shköder, 1925. Served in 2d World War, 1939-45, mem. polit. shock 7th brigade, polit. leader 2d Div., fought in Kosova, Metohia and Sandjak, Yogoslavia; polit. commissar 5th Div.; 1st sec. Central Com. Communist Youth, 1955; minister of edn.; mem. Central Com. Communist Party, from 1st Congress, mem. Politburo and sec. Central Com., from 4th Congress; first sec. gen. Central Com., 1985—; vice chmn. gen. council Democratic Front Albania; dep. from 2d Legislature to People's Assembly; chmn. Presidium of People's Assembly (head of state) People's Socialist Republic of Albania, 1982—. Address: Office of Pres, Tirana Albania *

ALIG, FRANK DOUGLAS STALNAKER, construction company executive; b. Indpls., Oct. 10, 1921; s. Clarence Schirmer and Marjory (Stalnaker) A.; m. Ann Bobbs, Oct. 22, 1949; children—Douglas, Helen, Barbara. Student U. Mich., 1939-41; BS, Purdue U., 1948. Registered profl. engr., Ind. Project engr. Ind. State Hwy. Commn., Indpls., 1948; pres. Alig-Stark Constrn. Co., Inc., 1949-57, Frank S. Alig, Inc., 1957—; chmn. bd. Concrete Structures Corp., Indpls.; v.p., dir. Bo-Wit Products Corp., Edinburg, Ind.; pres. dir. Home Stove Realty Co.; pres. dir. Home Land Investment Co., Inc. Served with AUS, 1943-46. Mem. U.S. Soc. Profl. Engrs., Ind. Soc. Profl. Engrs., Indpls. C. of C. Republican. Presbyterian. Clubs: Woodstock, Dramatic, Lambs (Indpls.). Home: 8080 N Pennsylvania St Indianapolis IN 46240 Office: 8080 N Pennsylvania St Indianapolis IN 46240

ALIJANI, BOHLOUL, geography professor; b. Tabriz, Iran, Aug. 24, 1946; s. Nasrollah Alijani and Khanom Moameni; children: Vajiheh, Taha, Saideh; m. Robab Alijani, July 10, 1972. BA in Geography, Tchrs. Tng. U., Tehran, Iran, 1973; MA, Mich. State U., 1979, PhD, 1981. Tchr. elem. sch. Ministry of Edn., Demavand, Iran, 1968-71; tchr. secondary sch. Ministry of Edn., Firoozkoh, Iran, 1971-76, 81-83; tchng. assistantship Mich. State U., E. Lansing, 1978-81; asst. prof., chmn. geography dept. Tchrs. Tng Coll., Yzad, Iran, 1983—; v.p. Tchrs. Tng. U., Yzad, 1983-85. Mem. bd. editors Geog. Research mag., 1987—. Mem. Iranian Geographers. Office: Geography Dept, Tchrs Training Coll Yzad, Azadshahr, Yzad Iran

ALIMUDDIN, MOHAMMAD, ophthalmologist; b. Ranisagar, India, Apr. 1, 1917; s. Raza Hussain and Gulshan A.; m. Khair-Un-Nisa, July 26, 1935; children: Sabra, M. Salahuddin Hajra, Nazra, Shakira, Babur Z. Din. MBBS, P.W. Med. Coll., Patna, India, 1942; DO, Inst. Ophthalmology, London, 1960. Eye housesurgeon Prince of Wales Med. Coll., Patna, 1942, resident eye surgeon, 1943; commd. Indian Army, 1943, advanced through grades to brig. gen., 1971; specialist in eye diseases Indian and Pakistan Army, 1945-74; instr. ophthalmology Armed Forces Med. Coll., Rawalpindi, Pakistan, 1956-74; ret. 1974; practice medicine specializing in ophthalmology Raza Eye Clinic, Rawalpindi, Pakistan, 1974—. Contbr. articles to profl. jours. Recipient Tamgha-i-Imtiaz award Govt. Pakistan, 1964. Fellow Coll. of Physicians and Surgeons. Muslim. Home: 123-A Market Rd, Rawalpindi, Punjab Pakistan Office: Raza Eye Clinic, 123-B Market Rd, Rawalpindi, Punjab Pakistan

AL-IRYANI, ABDUL KARIM, minister foreign affairs of Yemen Arab Republic; b. Iryan, Yemen, Feb. 20, 1935; s. Qadi Ali al-Iryani; m. Feb. 1969; children—Rasha, Rabab. Student U. Tex., U. Ga.; Ph.D. in Biochem. Genetics, Yale U. Dir., Wadi Zeid Agrl. Project, 1968-69; head Central Planning Orgn., 1972-74, 74-77; minister of devel. Govt. Yeman Arab Republic, Sana'a, 1974-77, minister edn., 1976-79, minister agr., 1979-80, prime minister, 1980-83, minister fgn. affairs and dep. prime minister, 1984—; pres. Sana's U., 1976-79. Office: Ministry Fgn Affairs, Sana'a Yemen Arab Republic

ALIVISATOS, SPYRIDON G. A., physician, physiology educator; b. Cephalonia, Greece, Oct. 20, 1918; came to U.S., 1952, naturalized, 1959; s. Maria (Kassapoglu) A.; m. Athanasia Malavazos; children—Maria-Regina, Armand-Paul; m. 2d, Maria Pavlopoulou. M.D., U. Athens, 1946; M.Sc., U. McGill, Montreal, P.Q., Can., 1949, Ph.D. in Biochemistry, 1951. Merck postdoctoral fellow NYU, N.Y.C., 1952-53; Damon-Runyon Meml. Fellow Rockefeller U., N.Y.C., 1953-55; chief dept. biochem. research Mt. Sinai Med. Research Found. and Hosp., Chgo., 1955-62; prof., chmn. dept. biochemistry Athens Med. Sch., 1967; prof., chmn. dept. biochemistry Chgo. Med. Sch., 1968-74; prof., chmn. dept. biochemistry U. Athens Med. Sch., Dept. Physiology, 1974-86. Contbr. numerous articles to profl. jours. Served with Greek Army, 1941-42. Recipient Bd. Trustees Research award, 1959, Morris Parker award, 1971, Empirikos Found. award, 1986. Grantee Nat. Def. Bd. Can., 1948-51, AEC, NSF, NIH, Cancer Soc.; fellow Nat. Research Council Can., Damon Runyon Meml. Fund. Mem. AAAS, AAUP, Am. Soc. Biol. Chemistry, Am. Chem. Soc., Am. Neurochemistry, Am. Soc. Pharm. and Exptl. Therapeutics, Assn. Am. Med. Colls., Athens Med. Soc., Biochemistry Soc. (London), Can. Biochemistry Soc., Greek Chem. Soc., Can. Soc. Microbiologists, Can. Physiol. Soc., Greek Physiol. Soc., Greek Biochemistry Soc., Internat. Histamine Club, Internat. Soc. Neurochemistry, Internat. Soc. Biochem. Pharm. Home: 31 Sporadon St, 113 61 Athens Greece Office: Univ Athens Med Sch, Dept Physiology, 609 Athens Greece

ALIYEV, GEIDAR ALI RZA OGLY, Soviet government official; b. Baku, Azerbaidzhan, May 10, 1923. Ed. Azerbaidzhan State U. Ofl. of security forces and mem. Council of Ministers of Nakhichevan Autonomous Republic, 1941-49; leading ofcl. of Ministry of Internal Affairs and Com. of State Security (KGB) of Azerbaidzhan S.S.R., dep. chmn. 1964-67, chmn. with rank of maj.-gen. 1967-69; cand. mem. Central Com. of Communist Party of Azerbaidzhan (CPA), 1966-69, mem. Cen. Com., 1969—, mem. Bur., 1969—, 1st sec. Central Com., 1969-82; mem. Communist Party of Soviet Union, 1945—, mem. Central Com., 1971—, cand. mem. Politburo of Central Com. 1976-82, mem., 1982-87; dep. to USSR Supreme Soviet, 1970-74; vice chmn. Soviet of the Union, 1974; 1st dep. chmn. USSR Council of Ministers, 1982-87, chmn. bur. social devel. until 1987. Recipient Order of Lenin (2), and others. Address: Moscow USSR *

AL JARWAN, SAEED OBEID, association executive; b. Sharjah, United Arab Emirates, Oct. 10, 1955. BSc in Gen. Adminstrn. and Mktg., Ariz. U., 1979. Dir. gen. Sharjah C. of C. & Industry, 1979—. Mem. Gulf Mktg. Assn. Home: PO Box 580, Sharjah UAE Office: Sharjah C of C & Industry, PO Box 580, Sharjah United Arab Emirates

AL-JUBEIHI, HUSSEIN EID, chemical company executive; b. Tabuk, Saudi Arabia, 1940. BS in Chem. Engring., Cairo (Egypt) U., 1965. Various supervisory positions in processing and prodn. Petrochem. Industries, Kuwait, 1966-79; supt. ammonia Saudi Arabian Fertilizer Co., Dammam, 1979-80; mgr. ops. Saudi Arabian Fertilizer Co., Sammam, 1980-82, mgr. works, 1982, mgr. corp. affairs, 1982-83, asst. gen. mgr., 1983-84, gen. mgr., 1984—, also bd. dirs.; bd. dirs. Nat. Chem. Fertilizer Co., Jubail, Saudi Arabia. Mem. Am. Inst. Chem. Engrs., Arab Fedn. Chem. Fertilizer Producers (bd. dirs., chmn. tech. com.), Internat. Fertilizer Assn. (council). Home and Office: Saudi Arabian Fertilizer Co, Khobar Dammam Hwy, PO Box 553, Dammam 31421, Saudi Arabia

AL-KAWARI, HAMAD ABDELAZIZ, ambassador; b. Doha, Qatar, May 18, 1948; s. Abdelaziz and Aminah Al-K.; m. Zainab Albadrawy; children: Eman, Tamin, Omran. BA in Arabic and Islamic Studies, Cairo U., Egypt, 1970; diploma in oriental studies, Jesuit U., Lebanon, 1977; postgrad., Sorbonne U., Paris, N.Y.C., 1986—. Dir. schs. Ministry of Edn., Doha, 1970-71; 1st sec. Embassy of Quatar, Beirut, 1972-74; A.E. and P. State of Qatar, Damascus, Syria, 1974-78, Paris, 1979-84; non-resident ambassador State of Qatar, Switzerland and Italy, 1979-84; rep. UNESCO State of Qatar, Spain, Greece and France, 1979-83; ambassador Ministry of Fgn. Affairs, Doha, 1979; permanent rep. Qatar UN, N.Y.C., 1984—. Recipient Syrian Badge of Honor, 1979, French Badge of Honor, 1981, Spanish Badge of Honor, 1982, French Legion of Honor, 1984. Office: Mission of Qatar to UN 747 3rd Ave 22nd Floor New York NY 10017

AL-KHALIFA, SHEIKH HAMAD IBN ISA (SHEIKH HAMAD BIN ISA AL-KHALIFA), crown prince of Bahrain; b. Bahrain, Jan. 28, 1950; ed. Cambridge U.; student Mons Officer Cadet Sch., Aldershot Eng., U.S. Army Command and Gen. Staff Coll., Ft. Leavenworth, Kans.; m. Sheikha Sabeeka bint Ibrahim, 1968; 3 children. Formed Bahrain Def. Force, 1968, comdr.-in-chief, head def. dept., 1968—, raised Def. Air Wing, 1978; mem. State Adminstrv. Council, 1970-71; minister of def., from 1971; dep. pres. Family Council Al-Khalifa, 1974—; created Hist. Documents Center, 1976. Founder-mem., pres. Bahrain High Council Youth and Sports, 1975—; initiated Al-Areen Wildlife Parks Rev., 1976; founder Sulman Falcon Centre, 1977, Amiri Stud Bahrain, 1977; founder, pres. Bahrain Equestrian and Horse Racing Assn., 1977—. Decorated 1st class Order Star Joradan, 1967; 1st class Order Arafa Dain (Iraq), 1968; 1st class Order Nat. Def. Kuwait, 1970; 1st class Order Al-Muhammedi (Morocco), 1970; 1st class Order An-Nahatha (Jordan), 1972; 1st class Order Giladst Gumhooreeya (Egypt), 1974; 1st class Order Taj (Iran), 1973; 1st class Order King Abdul-Aziz (Saudi Arabia), 1976; 1st class Order Republic Indonesia, 1977; 1st class Order Republic Mauritania, 1969; 1st class Order El-Fateh Al-Adheem (Libya), 1979; hon. knight comdr. Order St. Micheal and St. George (U.K.), 1979; hon. mem. Helicopter Gt. Brit. Address: Office Heir Apparent, Ct of His Highness Amir, Rifa's Palace, Manama Bahrain *

AL-KHALIFA, SHEIKH ISA IBN SALMAN (SHEIKH ISA BIN SALMAN AL-KHALIFA), amir of Bahrain; b. July 3, 1933; s. Sheikh Sulman Ibn Hamad Al-Khalifa. Appointed heir apparent, 1958; ruler of Bahrain, 1961—, amir, 1971—. Decorated knight comdr. St. Michael and St. George (Eng.); knight comdr. Order of Garter (Eng.). Muslim. Office: Office of Ruler, Amir, Rifa'a Palace, Manama Bahrain *

AL-KHALIFA, SHEIKH KHALIFA IBN SALMAN (SHEIKH KHALIFA BIN SALMAN AL-KHALIFA), prime minister Bahrain; b. Bahrain, 1935; married. Pres. Edn. Council, from 1957; head of fin., 1960; dir. fin. and pres. Electricity Bd 1961; pres. Adminstrn. Council, Bahrain, 1966-70, State Council, 1970-73; prime minister of Bahrain, 1973—; chmn. Bahrain Monetary Agy. Address: Office Prime Minister, PO Box 1000, Manama Bahrain *

AL-KHALIFA, SHEIKH MUHAMMAD IBN KHALIFA (SHEIKH MUHAMMAD BIN KHALIFA BIN HAMID AL-KHALIFA), Bahrain minister of interior; b. 1937; s. Khalifa Bin Hamed Bin Issa Al-Khalifa; grad. Royal Mil. Acad., Sandhurst, Eng.; married, 1959; children—Fawaz, Tallal, Lamia, Amani. Police insp. Public Security Dept., Bahrain, from 1959; dir. immigration and passports Govt. of Bahrain, from 1966; dep. dir. gen. Public Security Dept., 1970-73; minister of interior, 1973—. Address: Ministry of Interior, PO Box 13, Manama Bahrain

AL-KHARAFI, JASSIM MOHAMED, Kuwaiti minister of finance and economy; b. Kuwait, Dec. 8, 1940; s. Mohamad Abdulmohsin Al-Kharafi and Ghanemah Boodai; m. Sabeeka Saad Al-Jasser; children—Abdulmohsin, Loay, Iyad, Anwar, Talal, Ghalya. Student Victorian Coll., Egypt, diploma in bus. adminstrn. Manchester Coll., Eng. Mem. Kuwait Nat. Assembly, 1975-79, 81—, mem. fin. and econ. com., 1975-79, chmn. fin. and econ. com., 1981-85; minister fin. and economy, 1985—; mng. dir. Mohamed Al-Kharafi Ind. and Est., 1961-85; mng. dir. Kuwait Hotel Co., 1962-75; chmn. Kuwait Internat. Hotel Co., 1972-73; vice chmn. Morroc-Kuwait Hotels Co., 1972-78; bd. dirs. Sudan-Kuwait Hotels Co., 1972-78, United Contracting Co., 1972-85, United Fisheries, 1972-76, Al-Ahleia Ins. Co., 1965-76; mng. dir. Aluminium Industries Co., 1967-85. Home: PO Box 886, Safat Kuwait Office: Ministry of Fin, PO Box 9, Safat Kuwait *

AL KUHAIMI, SOLAIMAN ABDUL AZIZ, family business owner; b. Beirut, 1960; s. H.E. Abdul Aziz Al-K. BBA, George Washington U., 1981. Apprentice Al Kuhaimi Holding Co., Ltd., Riyadh, Saudi Arabia, 1981-83, mng. dir., chief exec. officer, 1983—. Office: PO Box 86994, Riyadh Saudi Arabia

ALLAIN, YVES, radiotherapist; b. Carhaix, Finistère, France, Mar. 14, 1927; s. Yves and Perrine (Le Bloas) A.; m. Annie Derché, Dec. 5, 1940; 1 child, Louis. Doctorat, Ecole du Service de Santé et Faculté de Medecine, Lyon, 1953. Asst. Hôpitaux Des Armées, Paris, 1958-63; electroradiologiste Hôpitaux Militaires, Paris; chef de service de radiologie Hôpital Begin, 1963-68; chef de service de radiotherapie Cen. Anticancereux, Rennes, France, 1968-70; chef de service de radiologie Hopital N.D. de Bon Secours, Paris, 1970-72; chef de service de radiotherapie Hopital Des Peupliers, Paris, 1972-75, Cen. Anticancereux, Angers, France, 1976—. Named Chevalier de l'ordre, Nat. Du Mérite, 1967. Mem. Fedn. des Cens. Anticancereux Français (urology group pres. 1985). Roman Catholic. Home: 5 rue du Quinconce, 49100 Angers France Office: Cen Paul Papin, 2 rue Moll, 49036 Angers France

ALLAIRE, PAUL ARTHUR, office equipment company executive; b. Worcester, Mass., July 21, 1938; s. Arthur E. Allaire and Elodie (LePrade) Murphy; m. Kathleen Buckley, Jan. 26, 1963; children—Brian, Christiana. B.S.E.E., Worcester Poly. Inst., 1960; M.S.I.A., Carnegie-Mellon U., 1966. Fin. analyst Xerox Corp., Rochester, N.Y., 1966-70; dir. fin. analysis Rank Xerox Ltd., London, 1970-73; dir. internat. ops. fin. Xerox Corp., Stamford, Conn., 1973-75; chief staff officer Rank Xerox Ltd., London, 1975-79, mng. dir., 1979-83; sr. v.p., chief staff officer Xerox Corp., Stamford, 1983-86, pres., 1986—, also bd. dirs.; mem. investment policy adv. com. U.S. Trade Rep.; dir. Rank Xerox Ltd., Crum & Forster, Morristown, N.J. Patron, Am. European Community Assn., London, 1982; bd. dirs. Nat. Planning Assn., Washington, 1986, chmn. Com. on New Am. Realities, 1986; bd. dirs. Waveny Care Ctr., New Canaan, Conn., 1984; bus. adv. council Grad. Sch. Indsl. Adminstrn. Carnegie Mellon U., also univ. trustee; trustee Worchester Poly. Inst. Mem. Tau Beta Pi, Eta Kappa Nu. Democrat. Office: Xerox Corp PO Box 1600 Stamford CT 06904 *

ALLAN, PAUL STUART, animator; b. Adelaide, Australia, Jan. 15, 1962; s. James Alfred and Avis Ann (Lean) A. Animator trainee Reynolds Film Prodns., Auckland, New Zealand, 1983-84; writer, animator Fungus Film Prodns., Auckland, 1984—. Writer, animator: (cartoon films) One Summery Springs Autumn, 1983, The Chocolate Monster, 1986; (animated film, series) Starship Gizzmo, 1985-87.

ALLANA, GHULAM ALI, university chancellor; b. Thatta, Pakistan, Mar. 15, 1930; s. Ghulam and Karama Sain Allana; m. Sher Bano, Jan. 22, 1958; 7 children. BA with honors, U. Sind, Jamshoro, Pakistan, 1953, MA, 1955, PhD, 1971; MA, U. London, 1963. Lectr. City Coll. Hyderabad, Pakistan, 1954-58; lectr. Sindhi U. Sind, Jamshoro, 1958-70, asst. dir. Inst. Sindhology, 1963-70, 71-77, assoc. prof., 1970-76, prof., 1976-77, prof. in charge, 1977-83, dean Faculty of Arts, 1981; vice-chancellor Allama Iqbal Open U., Islamabad, Pakistan, 1983—. Author numerous books; contbr. articles to profl. jours.; editor monthly "Mehran", monthly mag. "Roshni"; co-editor Jour. in English-Sindhological Studies, Jour. in English-Sindhi Adab; editor-in-chief Pakistan Jour. Distance Edn. Mem. His Highness' Fed. Council for Pakistan, Karachi. Recipient SIGA Lit. Award 1979, Writers' Guild Award 1980, 84. Mem. Distance Edn. Council Asia (chmn. 1985—), Inst. Sindhology, Pakistan Mus. Assn., Pakistan Presdl. Archives Com. Home: House #21, Street 61 F-8/4, Islamabad Pakistan Office: Allama Iqbal Open Univ, Sector H-8, Islamabad Pakistan

ALLART, JEAN CLAUDE, dermatologist; b. Lievin, France, Feb. 26, 1944; s. Adolphe and Carmen (Mollet) A.; m. Michele DuPont, June 26, 1965; children: Laurence, Catherine. B.E.P.C., Lycee A. Chateler, France, 1958; BAC I, Lycee A. Chateler, 1960, BAC II, 1961. Externe U. Hosp. Lille, 1961, attache cons., 1970; chief service Med. Clinic, Bruay, 1981; cons. Sainte Anne Clinic, Bethune, 1972, Bois-Bernard Clinic, Lens, France, 1974. Author: Arterial Legs Ulcers, 1969; contbr. articles to profl. jours. Served to capt. French Army, 1970-71. Mem. Soc. Francaise Dermotologie, Soc. Belge Dermatologie, Soc. Internat. Dermatology Tropicale, Acad. Am. Dermatology, Fedn. Francaise de Dermatology (treas.). Roman Catholic. Home: 12 Rue Lamendin, 62700 Bruay La Buissiere France Office: Cabinet Medical, 10 Rue Arthur Lamendin, 62700 Bruay En Artois France

ALLDREDGE, ROBERT LOUIS, manufacturing company executive; b. Johnston City, Ill., Feb. 11, 1922; s. Samuel and Mary Elizabeth (Kreie) A.; B.S. in Chem. Engring., U. Denver, 1942; m. Shirley Alice Harrod, Dec. 15, 1944; children—Alice Louise, Mark Harrod. Research assoc. E.I. DuPont de Nemours & Co., Eastern Lab., Gibbstown, N.J., 1942-44; enging. research assoc. Manhattan Project, Los Alamos (N.Mex.) Sci. Lab., 1944-46; chem. engr. Denver Research Inst., U. Denver, 1946-50; pres. Alldredge & McCabe, Denver, 1950-81, exec., 1981—; pres. Serpentix Conveyor Corp., Denver, 1969—, Serpentix, Inc., Denver, 1969—; dir. Beryl Ores Co., Broomfield, Colo. Served with C.E., U.S. Army, 1944-46. Mem. Nat. Soc. profl. Engrs. (founding mem. Colo. div.), U. Denver Alumni Assn. (dir. 1965-72), Am. Chem. Soc., Profl. Engrs. Colo., AAAS, Sigma Alpha Epsilon. Methodist. Contbr. articles to profl. jours. Home: 130 Pearl St 1108 Denver CO 80203 Office: Alldredge & McCabe 9085 Marshall Ct Westminster CO 80030

ALLDRIDGE, PETER WILLIAM, law educator; b. Birmingham, Eng., Oct. 24, 1956; s. Sidney Ernest and Margaret Mary (Chaffer) A. LLB, U. London, 1978; LLM, U. Wales, Cardiff, 1985. Tutorial fellow law U. Wales, 1979-80, lectr. law, 1980—. Contbr. articles to profl. jours. Mem. Assn. Internat. De Droit Penal, Radical Alternatives to Prison, Soc. Pub. Tchrs. Law. Labour Party. Home: 18 Rhymney St, Cardiff CF2 4DF, Wales Office: U Wales Faculty Law, PO Box 78, Cardiff CF1 1XL, Wales

ALLEGRA, MARISA IDA CALZOLARI, psychiatrist; b. Verbania, Torino, Italy; came to U.S., 1956, naturalized, 1962; d. Amilcare and Paola Bice (Alberizzi) Calzolari; MD summa cum laude, Bologna U., 1949; postgrad. Brown U., 1976; children: Ludwig Armand, David Paul, Christopher John. Pediatric and gen. practice medicine, Bologna, Italy, 1949-53; permanent staff physician Ospedale Maggiore, Bologna, 1953-56; resident in psychiatry Brown U., Providence, 1973-76; fellow in child psychiatry Bradley Hosp., Providence, 1976; practice medicine specializing in psychiatry, Providence, 1976— ; cons. Family Service, 1976-80. Pres. R.I. Civic Choral and Orch., 1974-76, bd. dirs., hon. pres., life mem.; bd. dirs. R.I. Philharm. Orch.; active R.I. Sch. Design. Diplomate Am. Bd. Psychiatry and Neurology. Mem. AMA. Am. Psychiat. Assn., R.I. Med. Assn., Providence Med. Assn., N.Y. Acad. Scis., Butler Hosp. Staff Assn., Am. Med. Womens Assn., Providence Preservation Soc., Newport Preservation Soc. Clubs: Conamicut Yacht (Jamestown, R.I.); University, Faculty, Brown (Providence). Home: 220 Blackstone Blvd Providence RI 02906 also: 150 Bradley Pl Palm Beach FL 33480

ALLEGRO, JOHN MARCO, author, playwright; b. London, Feb. 17, 1923; s. John Marco and Mable Jessie (Perry) A.; M.A. in Oriental Studies (David Bles Hebrew prize 1950), U. Manchester, 1953; m. Joan Ruby Lawrence, June 17, 1948; children—Judith Anne, John Mark. Lectr., Oriental and O.T. studies U. Manchester, 1954-70; 1st Brit. rep. Internat. Dead Sea Scrolls editing team, 1953—; adv. Jordian Govt. on Dead Sea Scrolls, 1961—; trustee, adv., hon. sec. Dead Sea Scrolls Fund, 1962-70; author: Dead Sea Scrolls, 1956; People of the Dead Sea Scrolls, 1958; Treasure of the Copper Scroll, 1960; Shapira Affair, 1965; Discoveries in the Judean Desert, vol. V, 1968; Sacred Mushroom and The Cross, 1970; End of a Road, 1970; Chosen People, 1971; Lost Gods, 1977; Dead Sea Scrolls and the Christian Myth, 1979; All Manner of Men, 1982; Physician, Heal Thyself, 1985. Served with Brit. Navy, 1941-46. Recipient Leverhulme Research award, 1958. Life mem. Soc. O.T. Study; mem. Explorers Club. Address: 18 Wellbank, Sandbach, Crewe, Cheshire CW11 0EP, England *

ALLEHOFF, WOLFGANG HEINRICH, psychologist; b. Bad Wimpfen, Fed. Republic Germany, Aug. 17, 1949; s. Theodor Friedrich and Eva Katharina (Schmidt) A.; m. Karin Czauderna. Diploma in Psychology, U. Heidelberg, Fed. Republic Germany, 1977, Dr. Phil., 1984. Researcher U. Stockholm, 1973-75; cons. U. Heidelberg, 1976, Prognos, Basel, Switzerland, 1977; research exec. Compagnon, Stuttgart, Federal Republic Germany, 1978-79; Central Inst. Mental Health, Mannheim, Fed. Republic Germany, 1980-86; head psychology dept. Inst. für Demoskopie Allensbach, Fed. Republic Germany, 1987—. Author psychol. interest test; contbr. articles to profl. jours. Home: Kronengasse, D-7107 Bad Wimpfen Federal Republic of Germany Office: Inst für Demoskopie, D-7753 Allensbach Federal Republic of Germany

ALLEN, BELLE, management consulting firm executive, communications company executive; b. Chgo.; d. Isaac and Clara (Friedman) A. Ed., U. Chgo. Cons., v.p., treas., dir. William Karp Cons. Co. Inc., Chgo., 1961-79, chmn. bd., pres., treas., 1979—; pres. Belle Allen Communications, Chgo., 1961—; v.p., treas., bd. dirs. Cultural Arts Survey Inc., Chgo., 1965-79; cons., bd. dirs. Am. Diversified Research Corp., Chgo., 1967-70; v.p., sec., bd. dirs. Mgmt. Performance Systems Inc., 1976-77; cons. City Club Chgo., 1962-65, Ill. Commn. on Tech. Progress, 1965-67; mem. Ill. Gov.'s Grievance Panel for State Employees, 1979—; mem. grievance panel Ill. Dept. Transp., 1985—; mem. adv. governing bd. Ill. Coalition on Employment of Women, 1980—; spl. program advisor President's Project Partnership, 1980—; mem. consumer adv. council FRS, 1979—. Editor, contbr.: Operations Research and the Management of Mental Health Systems, 1968; editor, contbr. articles to profl. jours. Mem. campaign staff Adlai E. Stevenson II, 1952, 56, John F. Kennedy, 1960; founding mem. women's bd. United Cerebral Palsy Assn., Chgo., 1954, bd. dirs., 1954-58; pres. Democratic Fedn. Ill., 1958-61; pres. conf. staff Eleanor Roosevelt, 1960; mem. Welfare Pub. Relations Forum, 1960-61; bd. dirs., mem. exec. com., chmn. pub. relations com. Regional Ballet Ensemble, Chgo., 1961-63; bd. dirs. Soc. Chgo. Strings, 1963-64; mem. Ind. Dem. Coalition, 1968-69; bd. dirs. Citizens for Polit. Change, 1969; campaign mgr. aldermanic election 42d ward Chgo. City Council, 1969. Recipient Outstanding Service award United Cerebral Palsy Assn., Chgo., 1954, 55, Chgo. Lighthouse for Blind, 1986; Spl. Communications award The White House, 1961; cert. of appreciation Ill. Dept. Human Rights, 1985, Internat. Assn. Ofcl. Human Rights Agys., 1985; selected as reference source Am. Bicentennial Research Inst. Library Human Resources, 1973; named Hon. Citizen, City of Alexandria, Va., 1985. Mem. Affirmative Action Assn. (bd. dirs. 1981—, chmn. mem. and program coms. 1981—, pres. 1983—), Fashion Group (bd. dirs. 1981-83, chmn. Retrospective View of An Historical Decade 1960-70, editor The Bull. 1981), Indsl. Relations Research Assn. (bd. dirs., chmn. personnel placement com. 1960-61), AAAS, NOW, Sarah Siddons Soc., Soc. Personnel Adminstrs., Women's Equity Action League, Nat. Assn. Inter-Group Relations Ofcls. (nat. conf. program 1959), Publicity Club Chgo. (chmn. inter-city relations com. 1960-61, disting. service award 1968), Ill. C. of C. (community relations com., alt. mem. labor relations com. 1971-74), Chgo. C. of C. and Industry (merit employment com. 1961-63). Club: Chgo. Press (chmn. women's activities 1969-71). Office: 111 E Chestnut St Chicago IL 60611

ALLEN, BERTHA LEE, social worker, family counselor; b. Bexley, Miss., Mar. 28, 1908; d. Charles H. and Winnie (McLeod) A. Student, Maryville Coll., 1928-29; BA, Miss. U. for Women, 1932; postgrad., U. Ala., 1936, La. State U., 1937, Miss. State U., 1939, U. Miss., 1940; MSW, Tulane U., 1949. Cert. tchr. life, Miss., social worker, La., Ala., Miss., first aid instr.; diplomate clin. social work. Tchr. high sch. English and Latin, Rocky Creek and Lucedale, Miss., 1932-33, Agricola, Miss., 1933-36, Tchula, Miss., 1936-44; child welfare worker Miss. Dept. Public Welfare, Jackson, Columbus, Pascagoula, 1944-48; caseworker Columbia (Miss.) Tng. Sch., 1949-50; case work supr., chief social worker Osawatomie (Kans.) State Hosp., 1950-51; dir. casework Miss. Children's Home Soc., Jackson, 1952-54; casework supr. Child and Family Service, Mobile, Ala., 1954-58; supr. casework practice Family Counseling Ctr., Mobile, 1958-65; caseworker ARC Disaster Services, Hurricane Betsy, New Orleans, 1965, Family Service Soc., New Orleans, 1965-66, Jewish Family and Children's Service, New Orleans, 1966-71, Willow Wood, New Orleans Home for Jewish Aged, 1971-73; pvt. practice individual, marital and family counseling, New Orleans, Mobile, Lucedale, 1969—; cons. Wilmer Hall, Protestant Children's Home, YWCA, Mobile, 1954-65, Providence Nursing Home, New Orleans, 1972-77, Willow Wood, New Orleans Home for Jewish Aged, 1974-75. Bd. dirs. Mulherin Home for Spastic Children, Mobile, 1958-59; charter mem., sec. Miss. Mental Health Assn., 1953-54; mem. casework com. Mobile Council Social Agys., 1954-58, mem. inter-agy. planning com., 1958-62, mem. in-service tng. com., 1963-65; mem. program com. Southeastern Inst., Family Service Assn. Am., 1960; mem. planning com. Mobile County Mental Health Assn., 1964-65; sec. Assn. Maternity and Adoption Agys., New Orleans, 1969-70. Nat. Assn. Social Workers (diplomate), Acad. Cert. Social Workers, La. Soc. Clin. Social Work, Internat. Platform Assn., Oakliegh Garden Soc., Eta Sigma Phi. Presbyterian. Home and Office: Route 9 Box 796 Lucedale MS 39452 Other: 1050B Palmetto St Mobile AL 36604

ALLEN, BONNIE LYNN, pension actuary; b. Los Angeles, Oct. 2, 1957; d. David and Lucille M. (Scott) A. B.A. summa cum laude, UCLA, 1979. Math. tutor, Los Angeles, 1971—; reader math. dept. UCLA, 1977-79; pension actuary Martin E. Segal Co., Los Angeles, 1980—. Author short stories and poetry. Active mentor program UCLA Alumni Assn., 1978-79. Mem. Math. Assn. Am., Am. Math. Soc., Acad. Sci. Fiction, Fantasy and Horror Films, UCLA Alumni Assn. (life), Los Angeles Actuarial Club, Phi Beta Kappa. Office: Martin E Segal Co 500 S Virgil Ave Los Angeles CA 90020

ALLEN, CLAXTON EDMONDS, III, investment banker; b. N.Y.C., Aug. 27, 1944; s. C. Edmonds and Helen (McCreery) A. A.B., Washington and Lee U., 1964, J.D., 1967. Bar: N.Y. 1969. Assoc. Simpson Thacher & Bartlett, N.Y.C. 1967-70; assoc. gen. counsel Gen. Electric Credit Corp., 1970-71; investment banker Merrill Lynch, Pierce, Fenner & Smith, Inc., N.Y.C., 1971-72; pres. Gloucester Internat. Ltd., N.Y.C., 1972—, Comanche Exploration Corp., 1981-86, Compass Internat. Corp., 1982—, Horizon Coal Corp., Mineral Res. Corp., 1982-85, Compass Coal Corp., 1986—. Clubs: Players, Canadian, Met. Home: 405 E 54th St New York NY 10022

ALLEN, DAVID JAMES, lawyer; b. East Chicago, Ind., May 3, 1935; s. David F. and Emma (Soderstrom) A. B.S., Ind. U., 1957, M.A., 1959, J.D., 1965. Bar: Ind. 1965, U.S. Dist. Ct. (so. dist.) Ind. 1965, U.S. Ct. Appeals 1965, U.S. Tax Ct. 1965, U.S. Ct. Mil. Appeals 1966, U.S. Supreme Ct. 1968, U.S. Ct. Appeals 1983. Ptnr. Hagemier, Allen and Smith, Indpls., 1975—; adminstrv. asst. Gov. of Ind., 1961-65, 65-69; mem. Spl. Commn. on Ind. Exec. Reorgn., 1967-69; mem. Ind. Utility Regulatory Commn., 1970-75; mem. Ind. Law Enforcement Acad. Bd. and Adv. Council, 1968-85; mem. Ind. State Police Bd., 1968—; mem. Ind. Commn. on Recodification and Revision of Ind. Adminstrv. Adjudication Act, 1985-87; nat. judge advocate Acacia Fraternity, 1980-86; chief counsel Ind. Ho. of Reps., 1975-76; spl. counsel Ind. Senate Majority, 1977-78; legis. counsel Ind. Ho. of Reps., Ind. Senate minority parties, 1979—; adj. prof. pub. law Ind. U., Bloomington, 1976—. Author: New Governor In Indiana: Transition of Executive Power, 1965. Mem. ABA, Ind. State Bar Assn. (mem. adminstrv. law com. 1968-77, chmn. adminstrv. law com., 1973-76, mem. law sch. liaison com. 1977-78, criminal justice law exec. com., 1966-72), Am. Soc. Pub. Adminstrn. Office: 819 Circle Tower Bldg Indianapolis IN 46204

ALLEN, GEOFFREY, polymer scientist; b. Clay Cross, Eng., Oct. 29, 1928; s. John James and Marjorie (McKinnel) A.; B.Sc., U. Leeds (Eng.), 1949, Ph.D., 1952, MS (hon.), U. Manchester; m. Valerie Frances Duckworth, Sept. 20, 1973; 1 dau., Naomi Frances. Postdoctoral fellow NRC Can., 1952-54; lectr. U. Manchester (Eng.), 1955-65, prof. chem. physics, 1965-75; prof. chem. tech. Imperial Coll., U. London, 1975-76; chmn. Sci. Research Council, Swindon, Wilshire, Eng., 1977-81; head research Unilever, London, 1981—; vis. fellow, Robinson Coll., Cambridge, 1980—. Knighted 1979. Fellow Royal Soc.; mem. Chem. Soc., Inst. Physics, Inst. Rubber and Plastics. Club: Athenaeum. Contbr. articles on polymer sci. to profl. jours. Home: 16 Burghley Rd, Wimbledon SW19 5BH, England Office: co Royal Soc, 6 Carlton House Terr, London SW1Y 5AG, England *

ALLEN, GERALD CAMPBELL FORREST, management consulting company executive; b. Boston, Nov. 1, 1923; s. Charles Francis and Sarah Ann (Campbell) A.; m. Anne Elisabeth Conrad, May 23, 1944; children—Katherine Sarah Anne, Ethan William John Campbell, Elisabeth Amy Martha Joan. Student Harvard U., 1945-49, U. Chgo., 1950-52. Ordained to Ministry Unitarian Ch., 1978. Ency. editor Consol. Book Pub., Chgo., 1952-54; advt. exec. Chgo. Tribune, 1954-59; pres. Gerald Allen Co., Chgo., 1960-66; v.p. Klau-Van Pietersom-Dunlap, Inc., Milw., 1967-71; v.p., dir. Unidex Pub. Co. Inc., Milw., 1971-80; chmn., chief exec. officer Allen Mgmt. Group, Inc., Milw., 1980—; pres. Psychologists in Advt., Chgo., 1965; instr. mktg. U. Wis., 1967-68; v.p., dir. Benchmark Mfg. Co., Inc., Milw. Mem. Ad Hoc Low Income Energy Task Force, State of Wis.; mem. Energy Crisis Planning Com., City of Wis. Served with Royal Arty., 1944-45, ETO. Fellow Royal Hort. Soc.; mem. Am. Mktg. Assn., Am. Statis. Assn., AAAS, Am. Econ. Assn. Republican. Clubs: Harvard of Wis., Harvard of Chgo. Home: 712 Knapp Milwaukee WI 53202 Office: Allen Mgmt Group Inc 700 Knapp Milwaukee WI 53202

ALLEN, HENRY JOSEPH, management consultant; b. Passaic, N.J., Sept. 6, 1931; s. Edward J. and Mary B. Allen; ed. Fairleigh Dickinson U., 1952, Am. Grad. U., 1975—; M.B.A., Met. Collegiate Inst., 1986; m. Clare B. Reardon, Jan. 21, 1956; children—Patricia Ann, Mark Terrence. Service engr. Curtiss-Wright Corp., Woodridge, N.J., 1952-56, customer service rep. 1956-60, mil. salesman, 1960-64, sr. sales engr., 1964-66, mgr. mktg., 1966-77, dir. mil.-govt. mktg., 1977-79; corp. dir. mktg. and bus. devel. Advanced Technology, Inc., McLean, Va., 1979-80; prin. Challenger Assocs., Elmwood Park, N.J., 1980—. Bd. dirs. First Am. Fin. Corp., Providence. Served with U.S. Army, 1952-55. Mem. Tech. Mktg. Soc. Am., Assn. U.S. Army, U.S. Naval Inst., Am. Mktg. Assn., Soc. Automotive Engrs., Am. Soc. Profl. Cons., Remotely Piloted Vehicle Assn., Am. Def. Preparedness Assn. Republican. Roman Catholic. Home: 21 Roosevelt Ave Elmwood Park NJ 07407 also: 18 Dresser St Newport RI 02840 Office: Challenger Assocs 21 Roosevelt Ave Elmwood Park NJ 07407

ALLEN, HERBERT, steel company executive; b. Ratcliff, Tex., May 2, 1907; s. Jasper and Leona (Matthews) A.; m. Helen Daniels, Aug. 28, 1937; children: David Daniels (dec.), Anne (Mrs. Jonathan Taft Symonds), Michael Herbert. B.S. in Mech. Engring., Rice U., 1929. Registered profl. engr., Tex. Engaged in research 1929-31; with Cameron Iron Works, Inc. (and predecessor), Houston, 1931—; v.p. engring. and mfg. Cameron Iron Works, Inc. (and predecessor), 1942-50, v.p., gen. mgr., 1950-66, pres., 1966-73, chmn. bd., 1973-77, also dir.; dir. Tex. Commerce Bank. Bd. govs. Rice U., Houston, 1949-64, trustee, 1964-76, chmn., 1972-76. Named Inventor of Year Houston Patent Attys. Assn., 1977; recipient Gold medal for distinguished service Assn. Rice Alumni, 1975. Hon. mem. ASME (Petroleum Div. award 1977); mem. Nat. Acad. Engring., Am. Inst. Mining, Metall. and Petroleum Engrs., Am. Petroleum Inst., Tex. Soc. Profl. Engrs. (named Engr. of Year 1961), Houston C. of C. (bd. dirs. 1952-54, v.p. 1954-55, dir.-at-large 1962), Houston Engring. and Sci. Soc., Tau Beta Pi. Episcopalian. Clubs: River Oaks Country, Petroleum, Ramada, Houston, Bayou (Houston); Metropolitan (N.Y.C.). Home: 3207 Groveland Ln Houston TX 77019 Office: PO Box 943 Houston TX 77001

ALLEN, HERBERT JOSEPH, hospital social work administrator; b. Jersey City, May 19, 1922; s. Benjamin James and Jeanetta Gladys (Casey) A.; m. Gwen Cann, July 26, 1949 (div.); 1 child, Deborah Allen Kane. B.S. in Edn., U. Cin., 1946; M.S. in Social Work, Case Western Res. U., 1948. Lic. ind. social worker. Dir. social work dept. Barney Children's Med. Center, Dayton, Ohio, 1967; supr. Family and Children's Service, Dayton, 1968; dir. social work dept. Good Samaritan Hosp., Dayton, 1968; field service asso. prof., dir. social work dept. Cin. Gen. Hosp.-U. Cin. Med. Center, 1970—; adj. asst. prof. Thomas More Coll., Ft. Mitchell, Ky., 1978; field service asso. prof. Coll. Community Services, U. Cin., 1979; adj. assoc. prof., dir. dept. social work U. Cin. Pres., Central Community Health Bd. Catchment Area 11, 1976, Mt. Auburn Health Center, 1977; lectr. Am. Hosp. Assn., Soc. for Dirs. Hosp. Social Work Depts. Pres. Cin. chpt. Nat. Friends of Amistad, 1976—. Served with U.S. Army, 1942-46. Named Cin. Social Worker of Year, Social Service Assn. Greater Cin., 1952, Nat. Assn. Black Social Workers, 1973; Recipient award Pride mag., Cin., 1979, Key to City of Cincinnati, 1987, Ida M. Cannon award Soc. Hosp. Social Work Dirs. Am. Hosp. Assn., 1987. Mem. Nat. Assn. Social Workers (cert.), Ohio Hosp. Soc. Workers (pres. 1982), Nat. Soc. Hosp. Social Work Dirs. (pres. 1983), Soc. Dirs. Hosp. Social Work Depts., Am. Hosp. Assn. (dir. 1975-77, v.p. personal membership com. 1984-85), Soc. Hosp. Social Work Dirs. (pres.-elect 1982), Ohio Hosp. Assn. (pres. 1982-83), NAACP, Kappa Alpha Psi (Community Service award Cin. chpg. 1985, 87). Democrat. Roman Catholic. Home: 144 Dorsey St Cincinnati OH 45210 Office: Univ Hosp U Cin Med Center 234 Goodman St ML 743 Cincinnati OH 45267

ALLEN, HOWARD PFEIFFER, electric utility executive; b. Upland, Calif., Oct. 7, 1925; s. Howard Clinton and Emma Maud (Pfeiffer) A.; m. Dixie Mae Illa, May 14, 1948; 1 child, Alisa Cary. AA, Chaffey Jr. Coll., 1946; BA in Econs. cum laude, Pomona Coll., 1948; JD, Stanford U., 1951; LLD (hon.), Pepperdine U. Bar: Calif. 1952, U.S. Supreme Ct. Asst. prof. law, asst. dean Law Sch., Stanford (Calif.) U., 1951-54; with So. Calif. Edison Co., Rosemead, Calif., 1954—, v.p., 1962-71, sr. v.p., 1971-73, exec. v.p., 1973-80, pres., 1980-84, chmn., chief exec. officer, 1984-88; chmn. bd., chief exec. officer SCEcorp, 1988—; mem. exec. com. The Bus. Council; trustee, sr. mem., mem. nominating com. The Conf. Bd.; bd. overseers Rand/UCLA Ctr. for Study Soviet Internat. Behavior; bd. dirs., mem. exec. com. Calif. Econ. Devel. Corp.; bd. dirs. CalFed., Inc., Calif. Fed. Savs. and Loan, PS Group, Inc., Computer Scis. Corp., MCA, Inc., Northrop Corp., Trust Co. of West, Edison Electric Inst. Trustee Com. for Econ. Devel.; trustee, mem. exec. com. Los Angeles Mus. Art, Pomona Coll.; bd. dirs. LAOC Amateur Athletic Found., Los Angeles County Fair Assn.; nat. bd. dirs. NCCJ; mem. comdr. council The Salvation Army. Recipient award of merit for outstanding community service Los Angeles Jr. C. of C., 1982, Whitney M. Young Jr. award Los Angeles Urban League, 1985, Carrie Chapman Catt award LWV, 1985, Human Relations award Am. Jewish Com., 1986, Am. Spirit award Council Energy Resource Tribes, 1987, Spl. Award for Improvement of Sci. Edn. Calif. State Dept. of Edn., 1988, Brotherhood award NCCJ, 1988. Mem. ABA, Am. Judicature Soc., Pacific Coast Elec. Assn. (pres. 1984-85, bd. dirs.), Inst. for Resource Mgmt. (chmn. bd.), Assn. Edison Illuminating Cos. (bd. dirs.), Electric Power Research Inst., Calif. C. of C. (bd. dirs.), The Bus. Roundtable (policy com.), Calif. C. of C. (bd. dirs.). Clubs: Los Angeles Country, Calif. (Los Angeles); Pacific-Union, Bohemian (San Francisco); La Quinta (Calif.) Hotel Golf, Prof. Golf Assn. West Golf, Mission Hills Country, 100 (mem. exec. com.). Office: So Calif Edison Co 2244 Walnut Grove Ave Rosemead CA 91770

ALLEN, JEFFREY MICHAEL, lawyer; b. Chgo., Dec. 13, 1948; s. Albert A. and Miriam (Feldman) A.; m. Anne Marie Guaraglia, Aug. 9, 1975; children: Jason M., Sara M. BA in Polit. Sci. with great distinction, U. Calif., Berkeley, 1970, JD, 1973. Bar: Calif. 1973, U.S. Dist. Ct. (no. and so. dists.) Calif. 1973, U.S. Ct. Appeals (9th cir.) 1973, U.S. Dist. Ct. (ea. dist.) Calif. 1974, U.S. Dist. Ct. (cen. dist.) Calif. 1977, U.S. Dist. Ct. (so. dist.) N.Y., U.S. Supreme Ct.; lic. real estate broker. Ptnr. Graves, Allen, Cornelius & Celestre and predecessor firms Graves & Allen and Graves & Mallory, Oakland, Calif., 1973—; teaching asst. dept. polit. sci. U. Calif., Berkeley, 1970-73; lectr. St. Mary's Coll., Moraga, Calif., 1976—; prin. M.C. Techs., Inc., Microtech. Cons., Inc.; bd. dirs. Family Services of the East Bay, 1987—; mem. panel arbitrators Ala. County Superior Ct. Project editor U. Calif. Law Rev., 1971-73; contbr. articles to profl. jours. Treas. Hillcrest Elem. Sch. PTA, 1984-86, pres., 1986-88; pres. PTA unit, 1985-88; mem. GATE adv. com., strategic planning com. on fin. and budget, instructional strategy counsel Oakland Unified Sch. Dist., 1986—; mem. Oakland Met. Forum, 1987—, Oakland Strategic Plannig Com., 1988—; mem. adv. com. St. Mary's Coll. Paralegal Program; bd. dirs. Montera Sports Complex, 1988—; mem. Oakland Met. Forum, Oakland Strategic Planning Com., adv. coms. Oakland Unified Sch. Dist.; bd. dirs. Jack London Youth Soccer League, 1988—; commr. Bay Oaks Youth Soccer, 1988—; active YMCA Indian Guides, Indian Princesses, Cub Scouts. Mem. ABA (chmn. real property com. gen. practice sect. 1987-88, chmn. subcom. on use of computers in real estate transactions), Calif. Bar Assn., Alameda County Bar Assn. (vice chmn. com. on continuing edn.), Calif. Trial Lawyers Assn., Am. Trial Lawyers Assn., Am. Arbitration Assn. (panel), Calif. Scholarship Fedn. (life), Calif. Youth Soccer Assn. (cert. coach), U.S. Soccer Fedn. (lic. referee), Phi Beta Kappa. Club: Commonwealth (San Francisco). Lodge: Rotary (chmn. youth service com. Oakland club 1986-87, chmn. long range planning com. 1987—, dist. youth services com. 1987—). Office: Graves Allen Cornelius & Celestre 2101 Webster St Suite 1600 Oakland CA 94612

ALLEN, JESSIE LEE, nurse; b. Clarke County, Miss., Mar. 8, 1925; d. Roosevelt and Margie (Collins) Harper; G.E.D., Emily Griffith Opportunity Sch., Denver, 1963; A.A.S. in Mental Retardation Tech., Angelina Jr. Coll., 1972; L.P.N., Meridian Jr. Coll., 1976; m. Lawrence Allen, Oct. 26, 1974; 1 son, Renard Williams. Attendant, then head attendant and relief attendant supr. Ridge State Home and Tng. Sch., Denver, 1962-66; attendant, then attendant supr. I Tex. Research Inst. of Mental Scis., Houston, 1968-70; therapist asst. Lufkin (Tex.) State Sch., 1970-72; nurse Watkins Meml. Hosp., Quitman, Miss., 1976-77, staff nurse, 1981-88, ret., 1988 ; nurse Archusa Convalescent Center, 1977—. Mem. Nat. Fedn. L.P.N.'s. Baptist. Home: Rt 3 Box 176 Vossburg MS 39366

ALLEN, JOHN LOGAN, geographer; b. Laramie, Wyo., Dec. 27, 1941; s. John Milton and Nancy Elizabeth (Logan) A.; m. Anne Evelyn Gilroy, Aug. 9, 1964; children: Traci Kathleen, Jennifer Lynne. B.A. (Gen. Motors Corp. scholar 1959-63), U. Wyo., 1963, M.A., 1964; Ph.D. (univ. grad. fellow 1964-67), Clark U., Worcester, Mass., 1969; Ph.D. NSF postdoctoral fellow, 1970-71. Mem. faculty U. Conn., Storrs, 1967—; prof. geography U. Conn., 1979—, head dept., 1976—; cons. in field. Author: Passage Through the Garden: Lewis and Clark and the Geographical Lore of the American Northwest, 1975; editor: Environment 82/83, Environment 83/84, Environment 84/85, Evironment 85/86, Environment 87/88; project dir., gen. editor North American Exploration: A Comprehensive History; contbr. articles to profl. jours., chpts. to books. Pres. Mansfield (Conn.) Middle Sch. Assn., 1979-80; mem. Mansfield Conservation Commn.; vice chmn. Mansfield Zoning Bd. Appeals; mem. Mansfield Planning and Zoning Commn. Recipient Meritorious Achievement award Lewis and Clark Trail Heritage Found., 1976, Excellence in Teaching award U. Conn. Alumni Assn., 1987. Fellow Am. Geog. Assn., Royal Geog. Soc.; mem. Assn. Am. Geographers, Western History Assn., Soc. Historians Early Am. Republic, Soc. History Discovery, AAAS, Phi Beta Kappa, Phi Kappa Phi, Omicron Delta Kappa. Democrat. Congregationalist. Clubs: Elks, Masons. Home: 21 Thomas Dr Storrs CT 06268 Office: U Conn U-148 Storrs CT 06268

ALLEN, JOHN THOMAS, JR., lawyer; b. St. Petersburg, Fla., Aug. 23, 1935; s. John Thomas and Mary Lita (Shields) A.; m. Joyce Ann Lindsey, June 16, 1958 (div. 1985); children—John Thomas, III, Linda Joyce, Catherine Lee (1968-87). BS in Bus. Adminstrn. with honors, U. Fla., 1958; JD, Stetson U., 1961. Bar: Fla. 1961, U.S. Dist. Ct. (mid. dist.) Fla. 1962, U.S. Ct. Appeals (5th cir.) 1963, U.S. Supreme Ct. 1970. Assoc. Mann, Harrison, Mann & Rowe and successor Greene, Mann, Rowe, Stanton, Mastry & Burton, St. Petersburg, 1961-67, ptnr., 1967-74; sole practice, St. Petersburg, 1974; counsel Pinellas County Legis. Del., 1974; counsel for Pinellas County as spl. counsel on water matters, 1975—. Mem. Com. of 100, St. Petersburg, 1975—. Mem. ABA, Fla. Bar Assn., St. Petersburg Bar Assn., St. Petersburg C. of C., Beta Gamma Sigma. Democrat. Methodist. Club: Lions (St. Petersburg). Office: 4508 Central Ave Saint Petersburg FL 33711

ALLEN, JOHN TREVETT, JR., lawyer; b. Ill., Apr. 9, 1939; s. John Trevett and Elinor Rose (Hatfield) A.; m. Marguerite DeHuszar, Jan 18, 1969; children: John Trevett, Samuel DeHuszar. AB in English with highest honors and Spanish cum laude, Williams Coll., 1961; LLB, Harvard U., 1964; postgrad., Central U. Ecuador, Quito, 1964-65. Bar: Ill. 1964, U.S. Dist. Ct. (no. dist.) Ill. 1964, U.S. Dist. Ct. (ea. dist.) Ill. 1965, U.S. Ct. Appeals (7th cir.) 1967, U.S. Supreme Ct. 1970. Assoc. Goodrich, Dalton, Little & Riquelme, Mexico City, 1962, Graham, James & Rolph, San Francisco, 1963; assoc. MacLeish, Spray, Price & Underwood, Chgo., 1963-71, ptnr., 1973-80; gen. atty. U.S. Gypsum Co., Chgo., 1971-73; ptnr. McBride, Baker & Coles, Chgo., 1980-86, Burditt, Bowles & Radzius, Ltd., Chgo., 1988—. Contbr. articles to profl. jours. Alderman City of Evanston, 1977-81; governing mem. Orchestral Assn. Chgo., 1980—; pres. Internat. Bus. Council MidAm., 1982-84, also mem. bd. dirs.; trustee Library Internat. Relations, 1983—, pres. 1986—; vice chmn. Ill. Export Council, 1983—; counsel and dir. Ill. 4-H Found. Fulbright scholar, 1964-65. Mem. ABA, Ill. Bar Assn., Chgo. Bar Assn. (past chmn. internat. and fgn. law com., founder and past chmn. agri-bus. law com.), Vermilion County Bar Assn., Legal Club Chgo., Law Club Chgo., Phi Beta Kappa (Chgo. area assn.). Republican. Presbyterian. Club: Union League (Chgo.). Office: Burditt Bowles & Radzins 333 W Wacker Dr Suite 1900 Chicago IL 60606

ALLEN, J(OSEPH) GARROTT, surgeon, educator; b. Elkins, W.Va., June 5, 1912; s. James Edward and Susan H. (Garrott) A.; m. Dorothy O. Travis, July 15, 1940 (div. 1968); children: Barry Worth, Edward Henry, Nannette (Mrs. Antonio Alarcón), Lester Travis, Joseph Garrott; m. Kathryn L. Shipley, Dec. 27, 1968; children: Robert Kelman, Grant Frederick, Susan. Student, Davis and Elkins Coll., 1930-32; AB, Washington U., St. Louis, 1934; MD, Harvard, 1938. Diplomate: Am. Bd. Surgery (mem. bd. 1958-64). Intern Billings Hosp., U. Chgo., 1939; asst. resident surgery U. Chgo., 1940-44, instr. surgery, 1943-47, asst. prof., 1947-48, asso. prof., 1948-51, prof., 1951-59; research asso. metall. labs. Manhattan Project, 1944-46; group leader Argonne Nat. Lab., 1946-59; prof. Stanford, 1959-77, active emeritus, 1977—; exec. dept. surgery, 1959-61; Mem. surgery study sect. USPHS, 1955-59. Author: (with others) Surgery-Principles and Practice, 1957, 4th edit., 1970, Shock and Transfusion, Therapy, 1959, The Epidemiology of Hepatitis, 1972, also sci. papers.; Editor: (with others) Peptic Ulcer, 1959; co-editor: (with others) Family Health Ency, 1970; chief editor: (with others) Archives of Surgery, 1960-70; mem. editorial bd.: (with others) Lab World, 1978. Trustee Am. Youth Found., 1954-67; Mem. NRC, 1950-54; Mem. standards com. Am. Assn. Blood Banks, 1958. Recipient prize for protamine sulfate/heparin work Chgo. Surg. Soc., 1940; John J. Abel prize for research irradiation injury Am. Assn. Pharmacology and Exptl. Therapeutics, 1948; Ednl. award Am. Assn. Blood Banks, 1954; Gold medal for original research Ill. Med. Soc., 1948, 52; Samuel D. Gross award Pa. Acad. Surgery, 1955; First Merit award Chgo. Tech. Securities Council, 1955; First John Elliott award Am. Assn. Blood Banks, 1956; citation Washington Alumni Assn., 1960; Ford Found. grant, 1986-87. Fellow AAAS; Mem. Soc. Exptl. Biology and Medicine, Am. Physiol. Soc., A.C.S. (chmn. com.

blood and allied problems), Internat. Surg. Group (founder), AMA (Gold medal for original research 1948), Am. Surg. Assn., Soc. Clin. Surgery (sec. 1958-60), S.F. Surg. Soc., Soc. Univ. Surgeons, Am. Cancer Soc. (chmn. com. cancer therapy), Western, Pacific Coast surg. assns., Surg. Infection Soc. (founder mem. 1980), Halsted Soc., Alpha Omega Alpha. Home and Office: 583 Salvatierra Stanford CA 94305

ALLEN, LEWIS, JR., oil and gas operator, rancher; b. Hallettsville, Tex., Oct. 16, 1925; s. Lewis and Elma (Appelt) A.; B.A., U. Tex., 1949. Landman Deep Rock Oil Co., Tex. and La., 1950-54; ind. trader oil and gas properties, 1954—; rancher, South Central Tex., 1954—. Mem. Am. Assn. Petroleum Landmen, Tex. Ind. Producers and Royalty Owners Assn. (past dir., mem. state petroleum issues com.), Tex. SW cattle raisers assns., Ind. Cattlemen's Assn., Chi Phi. Methodist. Club: Petroleum (Houston). Home and Office: PO Box 124 Hallettsville TX 77964

ALLEN, MICHAEL WAKEFIELD, educational psychologist; b. Hampton, Iowa, June 6, 1946; s. Eugene Richard and Wilma Mary (Wakefield) A.; B.A., Cornell Coll., 1968; M.A., Ohio State U., 1969, Ph.D., 1971; m. Mary Ann Hoel, Oct. 23, 1976; children: Christopher Wakefield, Emily Elizabeth. Dir. research and devel. in computer assisted instrn. Ohio State U., 1970-73; sr. cons. advanced ednl. systems Control Data Corp., Mpls., 1974-78, prin. cons., 1979-80, exec. dir. advanced ednl. systems research and devel., 1980-87; pres., chief exec. officer, Authorware, Inc., 1985—; mem. faculty dept. curriculum and instructional systems U. Minn., 1981-86. Recipient Software Design first place award, Comdex, Singapore, 1987. Mem. Assn. for Devel. of Computer-Based Instructional Systems (pres. 1980-83), Am. Ednl. Research Assn., Am. Assn. Artificial Intelligence, Assn. for Intelligence Stimulation and Behavior Modeling, Assn. Devel. Computer-Based Instructional System. Methodist. Founding editor Jour. Computer Based Instrn., 1975-79, mem. editorial rev. bd., 1980-86, editor emeritus, 1986—. Home: 8400 Normandale Lake Blvd Suite 430 Bloomington MN 55437 Office: 8621 Pine Hill Rd Bloomington MN 55438

ALLEN, PAULINE VIRGINIA, accountant; b. Guntown, Miss., Feb. 7, 1909; d. Henry James and Madia Jane (Kennedy) A.; student Southwestern U., Memphis, 1927-29, 32-33, U. Miss., 1933-34; A.B., Duke U., 1935. Math. tchr. high sch., Pleasant Grove, Miss., 1936-37; clk. ins. agy., Tunica, Miss., 1940-48; bookkeeper, Tunica, 1952-56; accountant Tunica County Hosp., 1956—. Mem. Hosp. Fin. Mgrs. Assn. Democrat. Methodist. Club: Order Eastern Star. Home: Box 96 Tunica MS 38676

ALLEN, PETER MARTIN, geology educator; b. Chgo., Sept. 18, 1947; s. Simon and Marian (McCarthy) A.; m. Margaret Grinnan, May 19, 1979; children—Sarah, Maggie, Annabel. B.A., Denison U., 1970; M.S., Baylor U., 1972; Ph.D., Southern Meth. U., 1977. Environmental planner, geologist Dept. Urban Planning, Dallas, 1972-78; asst. prof. geology Baylor U., Waco, Tex., 1978-86, assoc. prof., 1986—; cons. in field. Contbr. numerous articles to profl. jours. Bd. dirs. Waco Symphony Orchestra, 1984-85; mem. Waco Planning Commn., 1986—. Recipient Biennial Urban Design award Dept. Housing and Urban Devel., 1975; Planning award Am. Inst. Planners, 1976. Fellow Inst. Study Earth and Man; mem. Geol. Soc. Am., Am. Planning Assn., Am. Water Resource Assn., Assn. Engring. Geologists (past chmn. Tex. sect.), Am. Inst. Profl. Geologists. Episcopalian. Club: Ridgewood Country (Waco). Home: 2611 Lake Air St Waco TX 76710 Office: Baylor U Dept Geology Waco TX 76798

ALLEN, RANDY LEE, management consulting executive; b. Ithaca, N.Y., June 24, 1946; d. Richard Hallstead and Mary Elizabeth (Howe) Hallstead Baker; m. John James Meehan, Apr. 24, 1983 (div. Aug. 1987); 1 child, Scott Hallstead. BA in Physics, Cornell U., 1968; postgrad. Syracuse U., 1968, Seattle U., 1973-74. Cert. mgmt. cons., cert. systems profl. Programmer, IBM, Endicott, N.Y., 1968-69; product and industry mgr. Boeing Computer Service, Seattle, 1969-74; dir. mktg. Androcor subs. Boeing Computer, Calumet City, Ill., 1974-76; ptnr. Touche Ross & Co., Newark, 1976—; trustee N.J. Inst. Tech., Newark, 1984-87, bd. of overseers N.J. Inst. Tech., 1988—. mem. adv. bd. computer info. scis. dept. Author: OCR-A Cost/ Benefit Guide; Pos Trends in the '80's; Bottom Line Issues in Retailing; Pos Current Trends and Beyond, 1987; also articles. Regional fund raiser Cornell U., 1983-84, 87-88; chmn. long range plan United Meth. Ch. Bishop Janes, Basking Ridge, N.J., 1983. Recipient Acad. Women Achievers award YWCA, 1984. Mem. Inst. Mgmt. Cons. (nominating com.), Am. Mgmt. Assn., Am. Arbitration Assn., Exec. Women N.J. (pres. 1979-81, dir. 1981-85). Clubs: Cornell; Basking Ridge Golf. Avocations: skiing, tennis, stamp collecting, symphony, art, swimming, boating, reading. Office: Touche Ross & Co One Gateway Ctr Newark NJ 07102

ALLEN, RICHARD VINCENT, international business consultant; b. Collingswood, N.J., Jan. 1, 1936; s. Charles Carroll and Magdalen (Buchman) A.; m. Patricia Ann Mason, Dec. 28,1957; children: Michael, Kristin, Mark, Karen, Kathryn, Kevin, Kimberly. B.A., U. Notre Dame, 1957, M.A., 1958; postgrad., U. Munich, W. Ger., 1958-61; hon. doctorate, Hanover Coll., Korea U. Instr. U. Md. Overseas Div., 1959-61; asst. prof. polit. sci. Ga. Inst. Tech., 1961-62; sr. staff mem. Center for Strategic and Internat. Studies, Georgetown U., 1962-66, Hoover Instn. on War, Revolution and Peace, Stanford U., 1966-69, Nat. Security Council, White House, 1969; dep. asst. to Pres. U.S., White House, 1971-72; pres. Potomac Internat. Corp., Washington, 1972-80; sr. fgn. policy and nat. security adv. to Pres. Ronald Reagan, 1978-80; asst. for nat. security affairs Pres. U.S., White House, 1981-82; pres. Richard V. Allen Co., Washington, 1982—; disting. fellow and chmn. Asian Studies Ctr. Heritage Found., 1982—; sr. counselor for fgn. policy and nat. security Republican Nat. Com., 1982—; sr. fellow Hoover Instn., 1983—; vice chmn. Internat. Democratic Union, 1983—; chmn. German-Am. Tricentennial Found., 1983—. Author: Peace or Peaceful Coexistence, 1966, (with others) Communism and Democracy: Theory and Action, 1967; editor: (with David M. Abshire) National Security: Political, Military and Economic Strategies in the Decade Ahead, 1963, Yearbook on International Communist Affairs, 1969. Chmn. com. on intelligence Republican Nat. Com., 1977-80; trustee St. Francis Prep. Sch., Spring Grove, Pa. Named Patriot of Yr. SAR, 1981; H.B. Earhart fellow Relm Found., 1958-61; decorated Order of Diplomatic Merit Republic of Korea, 1982, Knight Comdr.'s Cross Fed. Republic of Germany, 1983, Badge and Star of Order of Merit Fed. Republic of Germany, 1983, Order of Brilliant Star, Republic of China, 1986, Sovereign Mil. Order of Knights of Malta, 1987. Mem. Am. Polit. Sci. Assn., Intercollegiate Studies Inst. (trustee), Com. on Present Danger (dir.). Clubs: Univ., Fed. City, 1925 F St. Capital Hill, Tournament Players at Avenel (Washington); Farmington Country (Charlottesville, Va.). Office: 905 16th St NW Washington DC 20006

ALLEN, ROBERT EUGENE, communications company executive; b. Joplin, Mo., Jan. 25, 1935; s. Walter Clark and Frances (Patton) A.; m. Elizabeth Terese Pfeffer, Aug. 4, 1956; children: Jay Robert, Daniel Scott, Katherine Louise, Ann Elizabeth, Amy Susan. B.A., Wabash Coll., 1957, LL.D (hon.), 1984; postgrad., Harvard Bus. Sch., 1965. With Ind. Bell Telephone Co. Inc., Indpls., 1957-74, traffic student, 1957-61; dist. traffic supr. Ind. Bell Telephone Co. Inc., Bloomington, 1961-62, dist. comml. mgr., 1962-66; div. comml. mgr. Ind. Bell Telephone Co. Inc., Bloomington, Indpls., 1966-68, asst. to operations v.p., 1968, gen. comml. mgr., 1968-72, v.p., sec., treas., 1972-74; v.p., gen. mgr. Bell Telephone Co. of Pa., Phila., 1974-76; v.p., chief operating officer, dir. Ill. Bell Telephone Co., Phila., 1976-78; v.p. AT&T, Basking Ridge, N.J., 1978-81; pres., chmn. bd. C&P Telephone Cos., Washington, 1981-83, exec. v.p. corp. adminstrn. and fin., 1983-84; chmn., chief exec. officer AT&T Info. Systems, Morristown, N.J., 1985; pres., chief operating officer AT&T, N.Y.C., 1986-88, chmn., chief exec. officer, 1988—; dir. Bristol Myers Co., Mfrs. Hanover Trust, Mfrs. Hanover Corp., Shell Oil Co., Bus. Council N.Y. State Inc., Ing. C. Olivetti & c.S.p.A., Am. Telephone & Telegraph Co., AT&T Labs., Inc.; chmn. AT&T Techs. Trustee Wabash Coll., Columbia U.; mem. leadership com. for Lincoln Ctr. Consol. Corp. Fund; bd. dirs. Japan Soc. Mem. Nat. Assn. Wabash Men. Presbyterian. Clubs: Short Hills, Baltusrol Golf, Burning Tree, Congressional Country; Bay Head Yacht; Country of Fla. Home: 60 Stewart Rd Short Hills NJ 07078 Office: AT&T 550 Madison Ave New York NY 10022

ALLEN, ROBERT EUGENE BARTON, lawyer; b. Bloomington, Ind., Mar. 16, 1940; s. Robert Eugene Barton and Berth R. A.; m. Cecelia Ward Dooley, Sept. 23, 1960; children—Victoria, Elizabeth, Robert; m. Judith Elaine Hecht, May 27, 1979. B.S., Columbia U., 1962; LL.B., Harvard U., 1965. Bar: Ariz. 1965, U.S. Dist. Ct. Ariz. 1965, U.S. Tax Ct., 1965, U.S. Supreme Ct. 1970, U.S. Ct. Customs and Patent Appeals 1971, U.S. Dist. Ct. D.C. 1972, U.S. Ct. Appeals (9th cir.) 1974, U.S. Ct. Appeals (10th and D.C. cirs.) 1984, Ptnr., dir. Streich, Lang, Weeks and Cardon, Phoenix, 1965-83; ptnr., dir. Brown & Bain, Phoenix, Palo Alto (Calif.), 1983—. Nat. pres. Young Democrat Clubs Am., 1971-73; mem. exec. com. Dem. Nat. Com., 1972-73; mem. Ariz. Gov.'s Kitchen Cabinet working on wide range of state projects; bd. dirs. Phoenix Baptist Hosp. and Health Systems, Phoenix and Valley of the Sun Conv. and Visitors Bur., United Cerebral Palsy Ariz., 1984—, Planned Parenthood of Cen. and No. Ariz., 1984—; mem. Ariz. Aviation Futures Task Force; chmn. Ariz. Airport Devel. Criteria. Subcom.; mem. Apache Junction Airport Rev. Com., former mem Vestry and Sunday Sch. Tchr. Trinity Episcopal Cathedral; Am. rep. exec. bd. Atlantic Alliance of Young Polit. Leaders, 1973-77, 1977-80; trustee Am. Counsel of Young Polit. Leaders, 1971-76, 1981-85, mem. Am. delegations to Germany, 1971, 72, 76, 79, USSR, 1971, 76, 88, France, 1974, 79, Belgium, 1974, 77, Can., 1974, Eng., 1975, 79, Norway, 1975, Denmark, 1976, Yugoslavia and Hungary, 1985; Am.observer European Parliamentary elections, Eng., France, Germany, Belgium, 1979. Mem. ABA, Ariz. Bar Assn., Maricopa County Bar Assn., N. Mex. State Bar, D.C. Bar Assn., Am. Judicature Soc., Fed. Bar Assn., Am. Arbitration Assn., Phi Beta Kappa. Democrat. Episcopalian (lay reader). Club: Harvard (Phoenix). Contbr. articles on comml. litigation to profl. jours.

ALLEN, RONALD W., airline company executive; b. 1941; married. B.S.I.E., Ga. Inst. Tech. With Delta Air Lines, Inc., Atlanta, 1963—, asst. v.p. adminstrn., 1967-69, v.p. adminstrn., 1969-70, sr. v.p. personnel, 1970-79, sr. v.p. adminstrv. personnel, 1979-83, pres., chief operating officer, from 1983, chmn., chief exec. officer, 1987—, also dir. Office: Delta Air Lines Inc Hartsfield Atlanta Internat Airport Atlanta GA 30320 *

ALLÉN, STURE, academic administrator, linguistics educator; b. Göteborg, Sweden, Dec. 31, 1928; s. Bror G. and Hanna (Johanson) A.; m. Solveig Janson, June 5, 1954; children: Karin, Eivor, Ingemar. BA, U. Göteborg, 1954, lic. philosophy, 1961, PhD, 1965; PhD (hon.), Åbo (Finland) U., 1988. Asst. prof. Scandinavian langs. U. Göteborg, 1965-70, prof. computational linguistics, 1979—, pro-rector, 1980-86, founder dept. computational linguistics, 1972, founder Swedish Lang. Bank, 1975; assoc. prof. computational linguistics Human Research Council, 1970-72, prof., 1972-79; permanent sec. Swedish Acad., Stockholm, 1986—. Author: Graphemic Analysis 1-2, 1965, (with others) Frequency Dictionary of Present-Day Swedish 1-4, 1970-80, (with others) Swedish Dictionary, 1986; editor: Text Processing, 1979—. Bd. dirs. Nobel Found., Stockholm, 1987—. Served with Swedish Royal Coast Artillery, 1948-49. Recipient Henrik Ahrenberg prize U. Göteborg, 1966, Lang. Cultivation prize, Swedish Acad., 1979, Erik Wellander prize Swedish Lang. Com., 1980, Golden Ladder award Studema, 1987, H.M. King's medal King Charles XVI Gustavus, 1987. Mem. Soc. Linguistica Europeae, Nordic Assn. Linguists, Assn. for Literary and Linguistic Computing (bd. dirs. 1977—), Swedish Lang. Com. (vice chmn. 1979—), Philo. Soc. Göteborg, Royal Soc. Arts and Scis., Royal Acad. Letters, History and Antiquities, Swedish Acad. Lutheran. Office: Swedish Acad, Källärgrand 4, S-111 29 Stockholm Sweden

ALLEN, TERRIL DIENER, author; b. Douglas, Okla., Aug. 13, 1908; d. David M. and Clara (Cline) Diener; A.B., Phillips U., 1929; M.A., B.D. cum laude, Yale U. Div. Sch., 1935; postgrad. U. Okla., 1940, Columbia U., 1941-42, N.Y. U., 1958-59, Stanford U., 1968, U. Calif. at Santa Cruz, 1968; student U. Calif. at Los Angeles, 1965; m. Don Bala Allen, 1941 (dec.). Student work dir. med. schs. Chgo., 1929-32; editor Young People's Materials, Presbyn. Ch., Phila., 1936-39; established, dir. written arts dept. Inst. Am. Indian Arts, Santa Fe, 1963-68; dir. communications project elementary and secondary schs. Bur. Indian Affairs, 1968—; asso. staff specialist Indian affairs, lectr. Coll. V, U. Calif. at Santa Cruz, 1969-74; prof. Chapman Coll., 1975—; free-lance author, 1940—; contract author motion pictures, filmstrips Family Films, Hollywood, Calif., after 1960; free lance creative writing cons. elem. and secondary schs. Recipient Distinguished Alumnus award Phillips U., 1970. Mem. Authors League, Contemporary Authors, Western Writers Am. Presbyterian. Author: (with Don Bala Allen) Doctor in Buckskin, 1951; Troubled Border, 1954; Ambush at Buffalo Wallow, 1956; Prisoners of the Polar Ice, 1961; Tall As Great Standing Rock, 1963; Navahos Have Five Fingers; Vol. 68 Civilization of the American Indians Series, 1963, 2d edit., 1981; Doctor, Lawyer, Merchant, Chief, 1965; Miss Alice and the Cunning Comanche, 1959; And Now Tomorrow, 1952; (with Emerson Blackhorse Mitchell) Miracle Hill, 1967; Not Ordered By Man, 1967; Writing to Create Ourselves, 1969, rev. edit., 1983; editor: Arrow I, 1969, Arrow II, 1970, Arrow III, 1971, Arrow IV, 1972, Arrow V, 1973; Arrow VI, 1974; The Whispering Wind, Anthology of American Indian Poetry, 1972; Arrows Four, 1974; (with Gloria D. Autry) The Color-Coded Allergy Cookbook, 1984. Home: PO Box 2775 Carmel-by-the-Sea CA 93921

ALLEN, TERRY WAYNE, hospital administrator, accountant; b. Frankfort, Ind., Jan. 23, 1949; s. Billie Calvin and Marilyn Jane (Allen) Shires; m. Cheryl Elaine Utter, Dec. 16, 1972; 1 child, Heather. Student, U. Ky., 1970; BS in Bus., Ind. U., Indpls., 1977; MBA, Ball State U., 1988. CPA, Ind. Staff acct. Cleon Point & Assocs., Kokomo, Ind., 1977-78; acct. S.P.E.D.Y.-O.I.C./O.D.C., Kokomo, 1978; asst. comptroller Kolux div. Gen. Indicator Corp., Kokomo, 1978-79; staff acct. Bergstrom & Bergstrom Pub. Accts., Kokomo, 1979-82; dir. fiscal services Duke's Meml. Hosp., Peru, Ind., 1982-87; v.p. mgmt. info. systems Howard Community Hosp., Kokomo, 1987—; cons. Kokomo Creative Arts Council, 1978; cons. tax and fin., Kokomo, 1982-87. Served to 1st lt., U.S. Army, 1968-71. Mem. Am. Inst. CPA's, Ind. CPA Soc., Healthcare Fin. Mgmt. Assn., Nat. Fedn. Intersholastic Ofcls. Assn., Howard County Vietnam Vets., Ind. U. Alumni Assn. Methodist. Club: Ind. U. Varsity (Bloomington). Lodge: Elks. Home: 1903 Olds Ct Kokomo IN 46902 Office: Howard Community Hosp 3500 S LaFountain St Kokomo IN 46902

ALLERBRAND, TOM ALLAN, controller; b. Stockholm, Sweden, Dec. 19, 1941; s. Carl Allan amd Margit Allerbrand; m. Ingrid Falkenberg, June 15, 1969; children: Tove, Martin, Ylva. Grad. bldg. engr., Stockholm Tech. Inst., 1962; BS, Stockholm U., 1968. Cons. Bohlin & Strömberg, Stockholm, 1969-71, Öhrlings revisionbyrå, Stockholm, 1972-75; mgr. result reporting group Sandvik AB, Sandviken, Sweden, 1976-82, ASEA AB, Västerås, Sweden, 1983; chief controller Asea Brown Boveri Generation AB, Västerås, Sweden, 1984—. Editor: Controller's Manual, 1986, Finance in Focus, 1987. Bd. dirs. Västerås City Bus Co., 1986—. Mem. Mekanförbundet (com. 1983), Sveriges Industriförbund (com. 1979). Home: Sikgatan 9, 723 48 Västerås Sweden Office: ABB Generation AB, 721 76 Västerås Sweden

ALLEY, JAMES WILLIAM, physician, educator; b. Follansbee, W.Va., Mar. 13, 1929; s. John Joseph and Mary Edith (Allison) A.; m. Jean Marie Kinney, Nov. 15, 1958; children: Curtis, John, Mark. A.A., Roberts Wesleyan Coll., 1949; A.B. cum laude, U. Buffalo, 1955; M.D., State U. N.Y., 1959; M.P.H., Harvard U., 1962; D.Sc. (hon.), Marquette U., 1969. Intern Rochester (N.Y.) Gen. Hosp., 1959-60; gen. practice medicine Lodi, Ohio, 1961; missionary United Methodist Ch., Bolivia, 1964-68, 69-72; internat. resident Johns Hopkins U. Sch. Hygiene, 1968-69; dir. div. public health Ga. Dept. Human Resources, Atlanta, 1972—; asso. prof. dept. internat. health Johns Hopkins U. Sch. Hygiene, 1969-72; prof. community health U. San Simon, Cochabamba, Bolivia, 1967-72; clin. prof. dept. preventive medicine Emory U. Sch. Medicine, 1978—; clin. prof. dept. community medicine Mercer Sch. Medicine, 1983, Morehouse Sch. Medicine, 1984—. Assoc. editor: A Companion to the Life Sciences. Mem. Bishop's Cabinet, United Meth. Ch. in, Bolivia, 1969-72; mem. Gov. Carter's Council on Family Planning, Atlanta, 1973-75, Gov. Busbee's Council on Developmental Disabilities, 1977—; bd. dirs. Ga. div. Am. Cancer Soc., 1978—; bd. dirs. WHO W.Am. Ctr. Perinatal Care and Health Service Research; mem. med. adv. com. Butler St. YMCA, 1981—; trustee United Meth. Ch., Atlanta. Served with U.S. Army, 1950-52. Named Roberts Wesleyan Coll. Alumnus of Year, 1982; WHO fellow Inst. Nutrition, Guatemala, 1962; recipient Disting. Provider award Ga. Assn. Primary Health Care. Mem. Am., Pub. Health Assn., Ga. Pub. Health Assn. (pres. 1985-86), Assn. State and Territorial Health Ofcls., Utah Acad. Preventive Medicine (hon.), Phi Beta Kappa. Democrat. Club: Rotary. Home: 5098 Timber Ridge Ct Stone Mountain GA 30087 Office: 878 Peachtree St NE Atlanta GA 30309

ALLEY, REWI, writer, poet. Author: (books) There Is a Way, 1952, The People Have Strength, 1954, Human China, 1957, Our Seven- Their Five, 1963, A Highway and an Old Chinese doctor, 1973, Prisoners, 1973, The Rebels, 1973, Travels in China, 1973; (autobiography) At 90: Memoirs of My China Years, 1986; (poetry) Gung Ho, 1948, Leaves from a Shandan Notebook, 1950; (anthology) Light and Shadow Along a Great Road, 1984; translator ancient Chinese poets Li Bai, Du Fu and Bai Juyi; contbr. articles on travel in China. Mem. Chinese PEN. Address: care Chinese PEN Ctr, Beijing People's Republic of China *

ALLHOFF, PETER GINO, epidemiologist; b. Lendringsen, W.Ger., Feb. 12, 1953; s. Wilhelm and Ada (Tavella) A.; m. Beate Rennen, Aug. 21, 1980. Diploma, U. Cologne, 1977. Researcher dept. psychology U. Cologne, 1977-80, researcher Polyclinic, 1980-81; prin. investigator, Central Inst., Cologne, 1981—; cons. Ministry Edn., Luxembourg, 1978-82, Dornier Systems Inc., Friedrichshafen, 1980—, Health Econ., Basel, 1983—; dir. Working Group Health Research Cologne, 1982—. Contbr. articles to profl. jours. Fellow Royal Statis. Soc.; mem. Internat. Soc. Clin. Biostats., Am. Statis. Assn., Am. Heart Assn., German Soc. Social Medicine. Home: Imbach 27, D-5090 Leverkusen 3 Federal Republic of Germany

ALLIN, LAWRENCE CARROLL, historian, educator; b. Independence, Mo., July 17, 1932; s. John Marshall and Josephine Vivian (Luther) A.; m. Roswitha Bresinsky, July 17, 1988; children by previous marriage—L. Kirk, L. Kyle, L. Kevin, Lisa. A.B., Coll. of Pacific, 1954; M.A., Syracuse U., 1967; Diplomate, Frank C. Munson Inst., 1971; Ph.D., U. Maine, 1976. Tchr., Cucamonga (Calif.) Jr. High Sch., 1958-69; instr. history U. Maine, Orono, 1970-79; dist. historian Omaha Dist., U.S. Army C.E., 1979-82; Maine historian U. Maine, Orono, 1982—; vis. prof. history Bangor Theol. Sem., 1983-87; columnist Naval Inst. Proceedings, 1987. Author: U.S. Naval Institute: Intellectual Forum of the New Navy, 1917; America's Maritime Legacy, 1979; Searsport Master Builders, 1980; Maine in Print, 1983; A Maine Maritime Miscellany, 1984; Little Long and Mud Ponds: An Environmental History, 1986; Ships, Seafaring and Society, 1987, New Dimensions in Maritime History, 1987; contbr. articles to profl. jours. Bd. overseers Marine Maritime Mus., 1971—. Served with USN, 1955-57. Fulbright-Hays fellow Brown U., Am. U., Beirut, 1967; grantee Price Found., 1964, 69, U. Maine, 1976, 79, NEH, 1977. Mem. Soc. Am. Mil. Engrs., U.S. Naval Inst., Orgn. Am. Historians, Phi Alpha Theta. Club: University. Home: 24 Kineo St Bangor ME 04401 Office: U Maine 115 A Stevens Hall Orono ME 04469

ALLISON, HOWARD MERVYN, lawyer; b. Akron, Ohio, June 27, 1943; s. Jack William and Sara (Goldstein) A.; m. Sandra Leslie, Aug. 26, 1965 (dec.); 1 son, Scott. B.A. in Edn., U. Akron, 1966, J.D., 1969. Bar: Ohio 1969, U.S. Dist. (no. dist.) Ohio 1970, U.S. Ct. Appeals (6th cir.) 1971. Claims adjustor CNA Ins. Co., 1965-71; assoc. Parker & Parker, 1969-71; ptnr. Allison & Miller, 1971-79; sole practice, Akron, 1979—. Chmn. ACLU, 1976, counsel Akron area, 1969—. Mem. Akron Bar Assn., Portage County Bar Assn., Stark County Bar Assn., Ohio Bar Assn., ABA.

ALLISON, JANE SHAWVER, medical school administrator, management consultant; b. San Angelo, Tex., Dec. 29, 1938; d. Floyd McKinzie and Bertha J. (Hicks) Shawver; m. Cecil Wayne Allison, June 22, 1957; children: Jana Lea, David Wayne, Don McKinzie. Student U. Denver, 1954, Northwestern U., 1955, Tex. Tech. U., 1956-57, Midwestern U., Wichita Falls, Tex., 1958. Continuity writer, Sta. KFDX-TV, Wichita Falls, Tex., 1957-58; sec. Wichita Falls Symphony, Tex., 1968-70; adminstrv. asst. Coll. of Bus. Tex. Tech U., Lubbock, 1971-74, coordinator programs dept. family medicine Health Sch. Ctr., 1974-77, adminstr. dept. family medicine, 1978-87, clin. adminstrv. dir. dept. family medicine, 1987—; cons. Family Practice Residency, Amarillo, Tex., 1984, Temple, Tex., 1984-85. Bd. dirs. Lubbock Symphony Orch., Inc., 1976—, mem. nominating com., 1986, exec. com., 1987-88, v.p. 1988—; bd. dirs. Helen A. Hodges Charitable Trust, Lubbock, 1983—; mem. Tex. Tech U. Coll. Bus. Adminstrn. Lubbock Council, 1988—. Recipient Superior Achievement award Tex. Tech U. Health Scis. Ctr., 1987, HSC award of Excellence Tex. Tech. U. Health Scis. Ctr., 1987; honoree 75th Birthday Celebration, Caprock Council Girl Scouts USA. Mem. Med. Group Mgmt. Assn., Acad. Practice Assembly, Assn. Family Practice Adminstrs. (bd. dirs. 1985, 87, 88, charter pres. 1984, chmn. steering com. 1983). Mem. Disciples of Christ. Club: Soroptimist Internat. (pres. 1986-87, regional parlimentarian, 1986-88, regional laws and resolutions chmn. 1988-90.). Office: Tex Tech U Health Sci Ctr Dept Family Medicine Lubbock TX 79430

ALLISON, LAIRD BURL, business educator; b. St. Marys, W.Va., Nov. 7, 1917; s. Joseph Alexander and Opal Marie (Robinson) A.; m. Katherine Louise Hunt, Nov. 25, 1943 (div. 1947); 1 child, William Lee; m. Genevieve Nora Elmore, Feb. 1, 1957. BS in Personnel and Indsl. Relations magna cum laude, U. So. Calif., 1956; MBA, UCLA, 1958. Chief petty officer USN, 1936-51, PTO; asst. prof. to prof. mgmt. Calif. State U., Los Angeles, 1956-83; asst. dean Calif. State U. Sch. Bus. and Econs., Los Angeles, 1971-72, assoc. dean, 1973-83, emeritus prof. mgmt., 1983—; vis. asst. prof. mgmt. Calif. State U., Fullerton, 1970. Co-authored the Bachelors degree program in mgmt. sci. at Calif. State U., 1963. Mem. U.S. Naval Inst. Ford Found. fellow, 1960. Mem. Acad. Mgmt., Inst. Mgmt. Sci., Western Econs. Assn. Internat., World Future Soc., Am. Acad. Polit. Social Sci., Calif. State U. Assn. Emeriti Profs., Emeriti Assn. of Calif. State U. (v.p. programs 1986-87, v.p. administrn. 1987-88, pres. 1988—), Am. Assn. Individual Investors, Am. Assn. Retired Persons, Alpha Kappa Psi. Club: Retired Pub. Employees Assn. of Calif. (sec. Calif. State U. Los Angeles 1984-88). Home: 1615 S El Molino Alhambra CA 91801 Office: Calif State U Dept of Mgmt 5151 State University Dr Los Angeles CA 90032

ALLISON, MARVIN LAWRENCE (LARRY), journalist; b. Phoenix, Aug. 8, 1934; s. George Lewis and Dorothy (Kinsella) A.; m. Patricia Ann Kiley, Apr. 2, 1954; 1 child, Marvin Lawrence. Student, Sorbonne, Paris, 1952-53, Long Beach State Coll., 1953-54. Reporter Downey (Calif.) Live Wire, 1955-57; copy editor Stars & Stripes newspaper, Darmstadt, Fed. Republic Germany, 1962, Press Telegram (formerly Ind. Press-Telegram), Long Beach, Calif., 1957-62; reporter Press Telegram (formerly Ind. Press-Telegram), 1963-66; copy editor Press Telegram (formerly Ind. Press-Telegram), Long Beach, 1966-68, mng. editor, 1969-76, editor, 1978—; asst. to pub. Lexington (Ky.) Herald-Leader, 1976-77; assoc. editor Detroit Free Press, 1977-78. Nieman fellow Harvard U., 1968-69. Mem. AP Mng. Editors Assn. (pres. 1981), Sigma Delta Chi. Club: Harvard (Los Angeles). Office: Ind Press-Telegram 604 Pine Ave Long Beach CA 90844

ALLISON, RICHARD CLARK, judge; b. N.Y.C., July 10, 1924; s. Albert Fay and Anice (Clark) A.; m. Anne Elizabeth Johnston, Oct. 28, 1950; children: Anne Sidney, William Scott, Richard Clark. B.A., U. Va., 1944, LL.B., 1948. Bar: N.Y. 1948. Practiced in N.Y.C., 1948-52, 54-55, 55—; partner firm Reid & Priest, 1961-87; mem. Iran-U.S. Claims Tribunal, The Hague, 1988—; with USNR, 1952-54. Served to ensign USNR, 1942-46. Mem. ABA (chmn. com. Latin Am. Law 1964-68, chmn. Internat. Law Sect. 1977, chmn. Nat. Inst. on Doing Bus. in Far East 1972, chmn internat. legal exchange program 1981-85), Internat. Bar Assn. (chmn. 1986 Conf., ethics com. 1986—), Société Internationale des Avocats, Inter-Am. Bar Assn., Am. Fgn. Law Assn., Am. Arbitration Assn. (nat. panel), Southwestern Legal Found. (adv. bd.), Am. Soc. Internat. Law, Council on Fgn. Relations, Am. Bar Found., Assn. of Bar of City of N.Y. (internat. law com.), Raven Soc., SAR, St. Andrew's Soc. N.Y., Phi Beta Kappa, Omicron Delta Kappa, Pi Kappa Alpha, Phi Delta Phi. Congregationalist. Clubs: Union League, Manhasset Bay Yacht. Office: Park Weg 13, 2585 JH, The Hague The Netherlands

ALLISON, ROY WILLIAM, science education educator, consultant; b. Lock Haven, Pa., Jan. 2, 1925; s. Rictor Roy and Margaret Ellen (Reich) A.; m. Zana Louise Cramer, Feb. 26, 1955; 1 son, Roy William. Student, Bucknell U., 1946-50; B.S., Shippensburg State Coll., 1952; M.Ed., Pa. State U., 1957, D.Ed., 1966. Math.-sci. tchr. Marple-Newtown Sch., Newtown Square, Pa., 1952-56, head secondary sci. dept., 1956-59, elem. sci. cons., 1959-68; asst. prof. Pa. State U., Middletown, Pa., 1968-70; Fulbright lectr. Republic of South Korea, Seoul, 1970-71; assoc. prof. sci. edn. Pa. State U.,

Middletown, 1971-87, prof. emeritus, 1987—; cons. sci. edn., 1987—. Author: (with Plank and Webb) Energy, Pennsylvania's Energy Curriculum for the Middle Grades, 1977; Investigative Science in Elementary Education, 1980; Pennsylvania's Energy Curriculum for the Primary Grades, 1980; Science Unlimited, 1984. Explorer advisor Boy Scouts Am., Broomall, Pa., 1954-62, com. chmn., Harrisburg, Pa., 1974-78, scoutmaster, 1975-77. Served with USAAF, 1943-46. Recipient Plaques, Seoul Jr. Tchrs. Coll., Korea, 1971, Inchon Jr. Tchrs. Coll., Inchon, Korea, 1971; citation for Disting. Contbns. to Advancement of Edn., Pa. Dept. Edn., 1984. Mem. Nat. Assn. for Research in Sci. Teaching, Sch. Sci. and Math. Assn., Nat. Sci. Tchrs. Assn. (life, Disting. Service to Sci. Edn. 1985), Pa. Sci. Tchrs. Assn. (life, bd. dirs. 1972-80, v.p. 1976, pres. 1976-77, meritorious service award 1976, distinguished service award 1980, fellow, 1986), Delaware County Sci. Tchrs. Assn. (pres. 1954-55), Phi Sigma Pi, Kappa Delta Pi, Phi Delta Kappa. Club: Lions (Broomall, Pa.) (tail twister 1953-54). Lodge: Masons. Home and Office: Allison & Assocs 504 Redwood St Harrisburg PA 17109

ALLMAN, MARGO HUTZ, sculptor, painter; b. N.Y.C., Feb. 23, 1933; d. Werner H. and Avis (Newcomb) Hutz; student Smith Coll., 1950-51, Moore Coll. Art, 1952-54, Hans Hofmann Sch. Art, 1953, U. Del., 1967-70; m. William B. Allman, Feb. 19, 1954; children—Avis Louise, David Drue. One-person shows include: Wallingford (Pa.) Art Center, 1964, Windham Coll., 1974, Bloomsburg State Coll., 1976, 77, Moore Coll. Art, 1979, Marian Locks Gallery, Phila., 1984; group shows include: Phila. Art Alliance, 1954, Del. Art Museum, Wilmington, 1958 (Ann. Show Drawing prize), 65, 67, Print Club, Phila., 1959, U. Del., 1977, Del. State Arts Council, Wilmington, 1981, C. Grimaldis Gallery, Balt., 1983, Art in Form Gallery, Karlsruhe, W.Ger., Contemporary Women Artists of Phila., 1986-87; represented in permanent collections, including: Del. Mus., Phila. Mus.; works include: Ferro Cement Sculpture, Tidewater Pub. Co., Centerville, Md., 1975, Crocheted Sculpture of Herculon, Hercules Inc., Wilmington, 1975. Bd. dirs. Robert Small Dance Co., N.Y.C., 1979-80. Recipient Mildred Boericke prize Print Club, Phila., 1958, Landscape prize Wilmington Trust Bank, 1969. Mem. Moore Coll. Art Alumnae Assn., Del. Center Contemporary Arts, Del. Art Mus. Unitarian. Home: 202 E State Rd West Grove PA 19390

ALLMON, MICHAEL BRYAN, accountant; b. Oceanside, Calif., July 14, 1951; s. William Bryan and Cecelia Audrey (Wright) A.; m. Monika Ann Arth, Sept. 15, 1979. BBA, U. Tex., 1975; MBT U. So. Calif. CPA, Calif. Staff acct. Alexander Grant & Co., Los Angeles, 1976-77; acct. Laventhol & Horwath, CPA's, Los Angeles, 1977-85; dir. tax, fin. planning services Zusman, Cameron and Allmon, CPA's, 1985—; chief exec. officer, dir. Essential Profl. Services, Inc., 1985-86. Mem. Am. Inst. CPA's (fed. tax div.), Calif. Soc. CPA's (fin. planning com.), Internat. Assn. for Fin. Planning, Acctg. Circle U. So. Calif., Am. Assn. Profl. Fin. Planners (Los Angeles chpt. pres.). Clubs: Walnut Track (pres. team) (Los Angeles), Manhattan Country (Manhattan Beach, Calif.).

ALLOCCA, JOHN ANTHONY, medical research scientist; b. Bklyn., Aug. 27, 1948; s. Frank and Dorothy (Aulicino) A.; children—Jennifer, Jerry. A.A.S., SUNY-Farmingdale, 1972; B.A., SUNY-Old Westbury, 1975; M.S., Poly. Inst. N.Y., 1979; D.Sc., Pacific Western U., 1981. Adminstr. Hofstra U., 1967-71; psychotherapist Creedmore State Hosp., 1975-76; biomed. engr. Doll Research Inc., 1971-77; research scientist Albert Einstein Coll. Medicine, 1977-78; research cons. L.I. Coll. Hosp., 1979-80; research scientist, tech. dir. pulmonary labs. Mt. Sinai Med. Center, 1980-82; research scientist Langer Biomech. Group, Inc., 1983-85; pres., research scientist, pres. Andromeda Research, Inc., 1985—. Author: Electrical/Electronic Safety, 1982; Electronic Instrumentation, 1983; Transducer Theory and Applications, 1983; Medical Instrumentation for the Health Care Professional, 1984; Physiology and Nutrition, 1986. Mem. IEEE, Assn. Advancement Med. Instrumentation, AAAS, Am. Assn. Physicists in Medicine, N.Y. Acad. Scis. Alumni Assn. Mt. Sinai Med. Ctr. Home: 3 West Harbour Dr Bayville NY 11709 Office: Andromeda Research Inc, 188 W Main St Oyster Bay NY 11721

ALLOTT, MIRIAM, literature educator; b. London, June 16, 1920; d. Labib and Ada Violet (Rennie) Farris; widowed. MA, U. Liverpool, Eng., 1946, PhD, 1949. Andrew Cecil Bradley prof. modern English lit. U. Liverpool, 1974-82, hon. fellow, 1986—; prof. English U. London, 1982-85, prof. emeritus, 1985—; organiser Matthew Arnold Centennial Conf., Liverpool, 1988. Author: Novelists on the Novel, 1959; Co-author: (with Kenneth Allott) The Art of Graham Greene, 1951; editor several books of poetry; contbr. articles to profl. jours. Mem. English Assn. (mem. exec. com. 1981—, chmn. membership com. 1984—). Home: 21 Mersey Ave, Liverpool, Merseyside L19 3QU, England

ALLOUBA, NAELA HASSAN, international trading distribution company executive; b. Cairo, Aug. 5, 1928; d. Hassan Aly Allouba And Esmat Fahmy; m. Adel Allouba, Aug. 30, 1944; children: Samiha, Esmat, Samia. BA, Cairo U., 1970. Freelance writer Al-Ahram, Al-Akhbar, Al-Goumhouria, Cairo, 1944—, Rose-El-Youssef, El Mussawar Mags., Cairo, 1944—; prin. Nahal Trading, Cairo, 1971—. Contbr. articles to profl. jours. Founder, pres. Guiza Mother Child Welfare Assn., 1961—; bd. dirs. Egyptian UN Assn., Cairo, 1971—, Hoda Shaarawi Assn., 1942—; active Heliopolis Services Dist. Devel. Soc., Cairo, 1981—. Recipient Golden medal of Excellence Pres. Arab Republic Egypt, Medal Appreciation Cairo govt., Guiza govt. 1972; named Ideal Mother Arab Republic Egypt 1958. Mem. Egyptian Businessmen Assn. (pres. export com. 1981—, bd. dirs. 1979—), Egypt U.S. Bus. Council (pres. export com. 1981—, bd. dirs. 1975—). Moslem. Clubs: Automobile, Gezira, Maadi Sporting. Office: Nahal Trading, 16 Sherif Pasha Street, Cairo Arab Republic of Egypt

ALLOWAY, ANNE MAUREEN SCHUBERT, industrial waste administrator; b. Martinez, Calif., Oct. 19, 1954; d. James Benjamin and Mariel Ann (Phillips) Schubert; m. William Glenn Alloway, Apr. 27, 1974; children: Joseph Benjamin, Odinn Glenn, Aaron Dean. AS in Life Sci., Allan Hancock Coll., 1982, AA in Liberal Arts, 1982. Cert. indsl. waste insp., 1984. Indsl. waste insp. City of Santa Maria, Calif., 1982-86; mgr. indsl. pretreatment program, collection systems Simi Valley (Calif.) County Sanitation Dist., 1986—; sect. chmn. Tri-Counties Pub. Edn. Mem. State Pub. Edn. Com., Ventura county Hazardous Waste Mgmt.(adv. com. bd. supr), Tri Counties Voluntary Cert. Com (sec. chmn.), State Voluntary Cert. Com., Tri Counties Pub. Edn. (sec. chmn.), Calif. Water Pollution Control Assn. indsl./hazardous waste com., pub. edn. com.), Water Pollution Control Fedn., Ventura County Hazardous Waste Mgmt. (adv. com.). Recipient Merit award Industrial Waste Inspection Tech., 1986. Republican. Roman Catholic. Club: Coast and Valley Health. Lodge: Keepers of the Flame. Avocations: painting, writing, sports, reading. Home: 1753 Cochran #G Simi Valley CA 93065 Office: Simi Valley County Sanitation Dist 500 W Los Angeles Ave Simi Valley CA 93065

ALLPORT, WILLIAM WILKENS, lawyer; b. Cleve., May 31, 1944; s. H. Burnham and Vernes Sophia (Wilkens) A.; m. Roberta Charlotte Warfield, Dec. 17, 1966; children—Christine Anne, Laura Warfield. A.B., Gettysburg Coll., 1966; J.D., Case Western Res. U., 1969. Bar: Ohio 1969, U.S. Ct. Appeals (6th cir.) 1971, U.S. Supreme Ct. 1973, U.S. Ct. Appeals (8th cir.) 1976, U.S. Ct. Appeals (7th cir.) 1978, U.S. Ct. Appeals (1st cir.) 1980, N.Y. 1981, U.S. Ct. Appeals (5th, 3d, 4th cirs.) 1981, U.S. Ct. Appeals (11th cir.) 1982, U.S. Ct. Appeals (2d cir.) 1983. Assoc. Baker & Hostetler, Cleve., 1969-75; chief labor counsel Leaseway Transp. Corp., Cleve., 1975-84, v.p. labor, 1984—. Ward chmn. Rep. Com.; trustee Soap Box Derby Assn.; explorer advisor Boy Scouts Am.; mem. Citizens League of Greater Cleve.; bd. govs. Case Western Res. Law Sch., 1983—, trustee Jr. Achievement of Greater Cleve., N.E. Ohio Soap Box Derby Assn. Mem. ABA, Ohio Bar Assn., N.Y. state Bar Assn., Cleve. Bar Assn., Internat. Law Soc., Case Western Res. Law Sch. Alumni Assn. (pres. 1985—), Eagle Scout Assn., Phi Delta Phi, Theta Chi, Pi Lambda Sigma. Editor: Case Western Res. U. Law Rev., 1968-69. Republican. Presbyterian (elder). Club: Smoker's (pres. 1969-73). Avocations: sailing, motorcycling. Home: 3337 Thomson Circle Rocky River OH 44116 Office: Leaseway Transp Corp 3700 Park East Blvd Cleveland OH 44122

ALLRED, EVAN LEIGH, chemistry educator; b. Deseret, Utah, May 22, 1929; s. Leigh Richmond and Louise (Cowley) A.; m. Barbara Klea Hawkins, Apr. 21, 1955; children—Kevin Michael, Richard Paul, Steven Leigh and Craig Lynn (twins). B.S., Brigham Young U., 1951, M.S., 1956; Ph.D., UCLA, 1959. Research chemist Phillips Petroleum Co., Bartlesville, Okla., 1951-54; instr. chemistry U. Wash., 1960-61; sr. research chemist Rohm & Haas Co., Phila., 1961-63; asst. prof. chemistry U. Utah, 1963-67, asso. prof., 1967-70, prof., 1970—. David P. Gardner faculty fellow, 1976; NSF postdoctoral fellow, 1959-60. Mem. Am. Chem. Soc., Sigma Xi, Phi Kappa Phi. Mem. Ch. of Jesus Christ of Latter Day Saints. Home: 4195 S 2700 E Salt Lake City UT 84124

ALLWOOD, MICHAEL JOHN, clinical physiologist; b. Stoke-on-Tent, Staffs, Eng., July 31, 1925; s. Edgar Henry and Florance (Nicholson) A.; m. Rosemary Marguerite Harrison, July 15, 1950 (dec. 1983); 5 children. M.B., B.S., U. London, 1950, Ph.D., 1959; M.D., 1970. Diplomate Eng. Bd. Med. Examiners. Researcher, Nat. Inst. Med. Research, London, 1951-53, Inst. Aviation Medicine, Farnborough, 1963-67; lectr. U. London, 1953-63; cons. Walsgrave Gen. Hosp., Coventry, 1967—; hon. lectr. U. Birmingham, 1967-76. Contbr. articles to profl. jours. Served to surg. capt. Eng. Naval Res. 1949-82. Decorated Vol. Res. decoration with clasp. Mem. Interallied Confedn. Med. Res. Officers (U.K. rep. 1974, pres. 1980-82, cons. 1984), Midland Naval Officers Assn. (chmn. 1983), Res. Forces Assn. (council 1977-83), Sea Cadet Assn. (pres. Midland area 1988—) Mem. Ch. of Eng. Club: Naval. Home: Ridge Barn, Harbury Ln Ufton, Leamington Spa CV33 9PE, England Office: Walsgrave Gen Hosp, Coventry CV2 2DX, England

ALMADA, IGNACIO LORENZO, government official; b. Navojoa, Mex., July 3, 1949; s. Rafael J. and Lydia (Bay) A.; m. Ana Luisa Perez Gautrin, Aug. 6, 1988. BS, U. Sonora, 1972; MD, U. Nat. Autonoma, 1978; MPH, Harvard U., 1981; postgrad., Coll. Mex., 1986. Asst. prof. Sch. Medicine, UNAM, Mexico City, 1977-87; gen. dir. Ctr. for Study of Politics, Econs. and Social Sci. Partido Revolucionario Inst., Hermosillo, Mex., 1987—; analyst, office of the pres. of the Republic of Mex., 1981, staff mem., 1982; staff mem., advisor dir. gen. Econ. and Social Policy SPP, Mexico City, 1983-87; advisor to subsec. Health Planning, Mexico City, 1985; project asst. Ctr. for Study of Demographics, Mexico City, 1985-86; project coordinator Ctr. Interdisciplinary Research, Mexico City, 1986-87; cons. Pan-Am. Health Orgn., Washington, 1983. Editor: Mortality in Mexico 1922-75, 82; contbr. articles to profl. jours. Mem. Am. Pub. Health Assn., Mex. Soc. Salud Publica. Roman Catholic. Home: PO Box 1614, 83000 Hermosillo Mexico Office: Partido Revolucionario Inst, Estadio 4, 83000 Hermosillo Mexico

AL-MAHMOUD, AHMED ABDULLA ZAID, ambassador; b. Doha, Qatar, Nov. 23, 1953; m. Na'ima Abdulrahman; children: Abdulaziz, Yasmen, Jawhara, Ghada. BA in Arabic Lit. and Islamic Studies, Cairo U., Egypt, 1976; MA in Econs., Cen. Mich. U., 1981. Various posts Ministry of Fgn. Affairs, Doha, 1976-84; ambassador extraordinary and plenipotentiary State of Qatar to the Sultanate of Oman, 1984-86; ambassador extraordinary and plenipotentiary of the State of Qatar to U.S., 1987-88, to Venezuela, 1988—; rep. of Ministry of Fgn. Affairs at Qatari Com. for Edn., Culture and Sci., Ministry of Fgn. Affairs to Arab Council for Econ. and Social Affairs, Tunisia, rep. of the state of Qatar to the Conf. of experts Com. on discussions with U.S., European Econ. Community, and Japan; mem. Qatari del. to 4th Gulf Coop. Council Summit, Doha, 1983, 6th Summit, Muscat, 1985; participant in Conf. of Ministers of Fgn. Affairs for Non-aligned Countries held in Cuba; head. of Qatar del. to Conf. on the Evaluation of the UN Tech. Assistance to Countries of the Arabian Gulf. Office: Embassy of Qatar 600 New Hampshire Ave NW Suite 1180 Washington DC 20037

AL-MAKTUM, SHEIKH HAMDAN IBN RASHID (SHEIKH HAMDAN IBN RASHID AL-MAKTUM), United Arab Emirates minister finance and industry; b. 1945; s. Sheikh Rashid al-Maktum. Dep. prime minister Govt. of United Arab Emirates, Abu Dhabi, 1971-73, minister of fin. and industry, 1973—; pres. Dubai Mcpl. Council; mem. gov. bd. Rashid Port, Dubal, 1973—; rep. at IMF, OPEC. Office: Ministry Fin and Industry, Abu Dhabi United Arab Emirates *

AL-MAKTUM, SHEIKH MAKTUM IBN RASHID (SHEIKH MAKTUM BIN RASHID AL-MAKTUM), United Arab Emirates deputy prime minister; b. 1943; s. Sheikh Rashid al-Maktum; m. 1971. Dep. ruler Dubai, United Arab Emirates; now dep. prime minister United Arab Emirates, Abu Dhabi. Office: Office of Prime Minister, Abu Dhabi United Arab Emirates *

AL-MAKTUM, SHEIKH MUHAMMAD IBN RASHID (SHEIKH MUHAMMAD IBN RASHID AL-MAKTUM), United Arab Emirates minister of defense; b. 1946; s. Sheikh Rashid al-Maktum; student Mons Officer Cadet Tng. Coll., U.K. Dir. Police and Public Security City of Dubai (United Arab Emirates); now minister of def. Govt. of United Arab Emirates, Dubai. Office: Ministry of Defense, Abu Dhabi United Arab Emirates *

AL-MAKTUM, SHEIKH RASHID IBN SAID (SHEIKH RASHID BIN SAID AL-MAKTUM), ruler of Dubai, vice president and prime minister United Arab Emirates; b. 1914; s. Sheikh Said bin Maktum; married; 5 children; ed. privately. Ruler of Dubai, 1958—; v.p. United Arab Emirates, 1971—, prime minister, 1979—. Address: Royal Palace, Abu Dhabi United Arab Emirates *

AL MALKI, FAHD ABDULLA, military officer; b. Doha, Qatar, Oct. 20, 1956; s. Abdullah Jassim and Mariam (Hassan) A.; m. Amal Rashid; children: Abdullah, Rashid, Dana. BSc, Qatar U., 1982. Tchr. Ministry Edn., Doha, 1974-78, Royal Army Ednl. Corp., U.K., 1982-83; commanding officer Qatar Armed Forces Interpreting Unit, Doha, 1986; second-in-command Qatar Armed Forces Edn. Ctr., Doha, 1978—. Author: Military Abbreviation and Vocabulary English/Arabic, 1985, Essential Gulf Arabic, 1987. Home: PO Box 1983, Doha Qatar Office: Qatar Armed Forces Hdqrs, PO Box 37, Doha Qatar

ALMANSA PASTOR, ANGEL F., chest physician; b. Malaga, Idem, Spain, Sept. 12, 1934; s. Salvador Almansa de Cara and Paula Pastor Roda; m. Isabel Mendez Peña, May 16, 1970; children: Maria Isabel, Angel, Paloma. Student Agustinos Coll., Malaga, 1943-47, Salesianos Coll., 1948-51; U. Grad., F. Medicine, Granada, 1957, Specialist Thoracic Surgeon, 1965, Specialist Pneumologie, 1980, Specialist Cardiologie, 1980. Diplomate Spain Bd. Med. Examiners. Asst. Hosp. Princesa, Madrid, 1958-59, Spezial-lungenklinik Hemer, Westfalhem, Fed. Republic Germany, 1969-76, U. Chirurg Klinik, Dusserdorf, 1961-65; chief pneumology Hosp. Civil Provincial, Malaga, 1966-75; med. dir. Hosp. Torax, Malaga, 1975—; prof. pneumologie Diputacion Provincial, Malaga, 1966, Valencia, 1965. Patentee blood circulation activator. Contbr. articles to profl. jours. Served with Spain Mil. Service, 1956-57. Pre-Univ. Grad. with honors, U. Granada, 1952; Med. Grad. with honors, F. Medicine, 1957. Fellow Am. Coll. Chest Physicians; mem. Coll. Internat. Angyologiae, Soc. Spain Patology A. Respiratorio, Soc. Spain Cardiologia, Soc. Andaluza Cardiologia, Soc. Spain Geriatria, Assn. Med. Naturistas. Roman Catholic. Club: Mediterraneo. Avocations: tennis; golfing. Office: San Lorenzo 2, Malaga 29001, Spain

AL-MANSOUR, KHALID ABDULLAH, lawyer, banker; b. Pitts., Jan. 29, 1936; s. George Jamil and Arma (Jackson) Warden. B.A., Howard U., 1958; J.D., U. Calif., Berkeley, 1962. Bar: Calif. 1962. Sr. ptnr., co-founder firm Al-Talal, Al-Waleed and Al-Mansour, San Francisco, N.Y.C., Africa, Saudi Arabia and Qatar, 1964—; dir. Al-Bakah Corp., Kapital Bank, Zurich, TranSyt Internat. Ltd., J.B. Broadcasting Corp., African ArabianIslamic Bank Ltd., Nassau, Bahamas. Mem. ABA, African Am. Assn., Internat. Bar Assn., Phi Beta Kappa. Islamic. Author: Legal and Business Aspects of Conducting Business in the Middle East, 1976; Islamic Economics, 1982. Office: African Arabian Islamic Bank Ltd 601 California St Suite 300 San Francisco CA 94108

AL-MAWLAWI, ABDULWAHED ABDULLAH, trading and contracting company executive; b. Doha, Qatar, Feb. 14, 1950; s. Abdullah Hassan and Mariam Mahmood (Abdulaziz) A.; m. Pamela Hutchinson, Jan. 1, 1986. BA, Hope Coll., Holland, Mich., 1976; MA, Western Mich. U., 1981. Dir. internat. affairs Ministry Pub. Health, Doha, 1977-83, dir. planning, 1977-83; dep. gen. mgr. The Comml. Bank Qatar, Doha, 1983-86; dir. Dubai (United Arab Emirates) Office Mannai Corp., 1986—; del. UN, Geneva and Middle East, 1977-83. Speaker in field. Sec. gen. Qatar Red Crescent Soc., Doha, 1978-81; exec. bd. dirs. Gulf Council Health Ministers, 1977-83; bd. dirs. Hamad Gen. Hosp., Doha, 1979-81. Home: PO Box 11665, Dubai United Arab Emirates

ALMEIDA, EDUARDO, social psychologist; b. Torreon, Coahuila, Mexico, Oct. 6, 1937; s. Ernesto Pablo and Maria Concepcion (Acosta) A.; B.A. in Psychology, Nat. U. Mexico, Mexico City, 1969, M.A. in Psychology, 1970; Ph.D. in Psychology (OAS fellow), Cornell U., 1976; postdoctoral studies, France, 1981, 85, Hungary, 1985, Israel, 1985, India, 1986; m. Maria Eugenia Sanchez, July 31, 1977; 1 son, Eduardo Jose. Tchr. elem., secondary and prep. schs., Monterrey, Puebla and Mexico City, Mexico, 1958-68; chmn. dept. philosophy U. La Salle, Mexico City, 1969-70; teaching asst. fellow Cornell U., 1973-74; vis. prof. psychology and Chicano studies U. Calif., Riverside, 1974-75; dir. eco-psychology dept. Nat. Inst. Behavioral Scis., Mexico City, 1976-80; co-dir. Research Center, PRADE, Asociación Civil, San Miguel Tzinacapan, Puebla, 1980—, also mem. PRADE interdisciplinary team, facilitator, resource person, State Puebla, 1977—; researcher dept. psychology Nat. U. Mexico, 1979—; mem. sci. com. XXIII Internat. Congress of Psychology, Acapulco, Mexico, 1984; cons. in field. Recipient Wilhelm Wundt medal XXIId Internat. Congress Psychology, Leipzig, E. Ger., 1980; Found. Child Devel. grantee, 1975. Mem. Sociedad Mexicana de Psicologia, Asociación Latinoamericana de Psicologia Social, Asociación Mexicana de Psicologia Social, Psychometric Soc., Mexican Network Participatory Research, N.Y. Acad. Scis. Roman Catholic. Research on effects of parental participation in tchr. tng., 1975-76, on polit. attitudes of Mexico City residents, 1979, on psychol. factors affecting women's roles and status, 1979-81, on human devel. in rural setting, 1981—, rural participatory devel. project, 1982—. Home: 157-402-D Tennis, Mexico City 04220 Mexico Office: 6 Apartado Postal, Cuetzalan, 73560 Puebla Mexico

ALMEIDA, JOSÉ AGUSTÍN, Romance languages educator; b. Waco, Tex., Aug. 28, 1933; s. Jesse M. and Teodora (Mancillas) A.; m. Maritza Barros, Sept. 5, 1964; 1 son, José Rodolfo. B.A., Baylor U., 1961; M.A., U. Mo., 1964, Ph.D., 1967. Teaching asst. U. Mo., Columbia, 1961-66; instr. Baylor U., Waco, 1962-63; asst. prof. dept. Romance langs. U. N.C., Greensboro, 1966-77, assoc. prof., 1977—, chmn. Latin Am. studies, 1979-81; vis. prof. Elmira (N.Y.) Coll., summer 1967; asst. prof. Inst. in Middle Am., summer 1968, 69; asst. prof., Cali, Colombia, summer 1973; assoc. prof. U. N.C.-Greensboro-Guilford Coll. Study Abroad Program, Madrid, Spain, 1980; cons. verbal-active teaching method Hampton Inst., 1976, 77, U. N.C.-Charlotte, 1984, lectr. First Internat. Conf. of Picaresque Lit., Madrid, 1976, 6th Conf. Internat. Assn. Hispanists, 1977, First Internat. Conf. on Lope de Vega, 1980. Author: (with Stephen C. Mohler and Robert R. Stinson) Descubrir y crear, 1976, 3d edit., 1986; La critica literaria de Fernando de Herrera, 1976. Active Common Cause, ACLU. Served with USAF, 1953-57. Nat. Endowment for Humanities fellow, 1970. Mem. MLA, S. Atlantic MLA, Am. Assn. Tchrs. Spanish and Portuguese, Internat. Assn. Hispanists, Cervantes Soc. Am., Sigma Delta Pi, Democrat. Roman Catholic. Home: 1410 Valleymede Rd Greensboro NC 27410

ALMOND, THOMAS CLIVE, ambassador; b. Preston, Eng., Nov. 30, 1939; s. Thomas and Eveline (Moss) A.; m. Auriol Elizabeth, Sept. 4, 1965. Ed. pub. schs., Bristol, Eng. In fgn. office Accra, Ghana, 1967-70, Paris, 1971-75, London, 1975-77, Brussels, 1978-79, Jakarta, 1980-83; Brit. ambassador to Rep. of Congo Brazzaville, 1983-88. Office: care Fgn and Commonwealth Office, King Charles St, London SW1A 2AH, England

AL-MUALLA, SHEIKH RASHID BIN AHMAD (SHEIKH RASHID IBN AHMAD AL-MUALLA), ruler of United Arab Emirates; b. 1930. Dep. ruler Umm Al-Qaiwain, ruler, 1981—; chmn. Umm Al-Qaiwain Municipality, 1967; constituted the Emirate's first mcpl. council, 1975. Address: Ruler's Palace, Umm Al-Qaiwain United Arab Emirates *

ALMUBARAK, TALEB, airline executive; b. Kuwait, Mar. 13, 1954; arrived in United Arab Emirates, 1979.; s. Salem Mohammad and Sakina (Alsaffar) A.; married, 1954; children: Ali, Mohammad, Shaima. BC, Kuwait U., 1977. Clk. Ministry of Pub. Health, Kuwait, 1973-78; with Kuwait Airways 1978—; mgr. United Arab Emirates, 1985—. Islam. Clubs: Marina, Hiltonia. Home: 302/1 Nawala Rd, Nawala Sri Lanka Office: Ceylinco House, 69 Janadhipathi Mawatha, Colombo 1, Sri Lanka

AL-MUSTADI, IBRAHIM YOUSIF, oil company executive, electrical engineer; b. Rabiq, Saudi Arabia, 1949; s. Yousif Al-Mustadi and Ganimah (Ghanam) Al-Harbi; m. Rawiyeh Mohamad; children: Wijdan, Mohammad, Amjad, Fatimah. BEE, King Fahd U. Petroleum & Minerals, Dhahran, Saudi Arabia, 1975. Chief elec. maintenance Arabian Oil Co., Ltd., Al-Khafji, Saudi Arabia, 1975-76, asst. supr., 1977-78, supr. elec. maintenance, 1979-80, supr. div. research, maintenance, 1980-81, asst. supt. onshore facilities maintenance, 1981, supt. onshore facilities maintenance, 1981-82, supt. A, facilities maintenance, 1982-83, mgr. project and engrng. office, 1984-85, mgr. A, project and engrng. office, 1985—. office: Arabian Oil Co Ltd, 31971 Al-Khafji PO Box 256, Al-Khafji 31971, Saudi Arabia

ALMY, EARLE VAUGHN (BUDDY), JR., real estate executive; b. Fort Worth, July 29, 1930; s. Earle Vaughn and Minnye Ruth (Rounsaville) A.; m. Gorden Yetive McGowan, July 31, 1964 (div. 1967). B.S. in Animal Husbandry, Tex. Tech. U., 1952; postgrad., Am. Inst. Banking, 1956-62, grad. Realtors Inst. Cert. Real Estate Brokerage Mgr.; Accredited Land Cons. Credit analyst First Nat. Bank, Fort Worth, 1956-62; dir. finance and poultry feed sales Burrus Feed Mills, Saginaw, Tex., 1963-69; pres., mgr. Almy and Co., Hurst, Tex., 1970-79, Granbury, Tex., 1979—; v.p., dir. Northeast Tarrant County Bd., Hurst, 1972-74; pres. Almy and Co. Realtors, Weatherford, Tex., 1973-78. Mem. Fort Worth Farm and Ranch Club; head usher Acton United Meth. Ch., Served with USAF, 1952-56. Sears Roebuck scholar, 1951. Mem. Nat. Assn. Realtors, Tex. Assn. Realtors, Granbury Bd. Realtors, Realtors Mktg. Inst., Nat. Realtors Land Inst., Tex. Realtors Land Inst., Nat. Assn. Real Estate Appraisers (cert. real estate appraiser). Republican. Clubs: Pecan Plantation Country. Avocations: golf; hunting; fishing; boating; swimming. Home: Rt 2 Box 65-1 PO Box 129 Granbury TX 76048

AL-NAHAYAN, SHEIKH HAMDAN IBN MUHAMMAD (SHEIKH HAMDAN IBN MUHAMMAD AL-NAHAYAN), United Arab Emirates deputy prime minister; b. 1930; s. Sheikh Muhammad Bin Khalifa al-Nahayan. Represented ruler Govt. Abu Dhabi, United Arab Emirates, Das Island, 1957-66, minister public works, 1971, head dept. works Abu Dhabi Exec. Council, 1973-77, dep. prime minister, 1977—; chmn. Fed. Comml. Bank, Abu Dhabi. Office: Office of Deputy Prime Minister, Abu Dhabi United Arab Emirates *

AL-NAHAYAN, SHEIKH ZAYID IBN SULTAN (SHEIKH ZAYED BIN SULTAN AL-NAHAYAN), president of United Arab Emirates, ruler of Abu Dhabi; b. Abu Dhabi, Trucial States, 1918; s. Khalifa Bin Zayid Al-Nahayan; married. Gov. Eastern Province, 1946-66; ruler of Abu Dhabi, 1966—; pres. Fedn. Arabian Emirates, 1969-71, United Arab Emirates, 1971—. Decorated knight comdr. Hon. Order of Garter (U.K.). Address: Amiri Palace, Abu Dhabi United Arab Emirates *

AL-NASER, MOHAMMED HAMAD, library administrator; b. Doha, Qatar, Arabia, Nov. 3, 1952; s. Hamad Abdulla Al-N. B.A. in Library Sci., Cairo U., Egypt, 1974. Dir. Qatar Nat. Library, Doha, 1974—; mem. adminstrv. council Edn. Mag., 1980—; mem. adminstrv. council humanity documents and studies ctr., U. Qatar, 1982—; v.p. Council Qatari Documents, 1983—; participant in internat. profl. confs.; vis. scholar Oxford U., Eng., Library of Congress, Washington; arranger internat. book exhibits. Mem. Qatar Nat. Commn. Edn., Culture and Sci. Home: PO Box 205, Doha Qatar Office: National Library, PO Box 205, Doha Qatar

ALOIA, ROLAND CRAIG, research scientist; b. Newark, Dec. 21, 1943; s. Roland S. and Edna M. (Mahan) A.; m. Kathyrn A. Platt, June 15, 1974. BS, St. Mary's Coll., 1965; PhD, U. Calif., Riverside, 1970. Postdoctoral fellow City of Hope, Duarte, Calif., 1971-75; research biologist U. Calif., Riverside, 1975-76; asst. prof. biology Loma Linda (Calif.) U., 1976-79, assoc. prof., 1979—; chemist Vets. Hosp., Loma Linda, 1979—.

Editor: Membrane Fluidity in Biology vols. 1-4, 1983, 85; sr. editor: (series) Advances in Membrane Fluidity vols. 1-5. Pres. Riverside chpt. Calif. Heart Assn., 1979-80, 1984-86, bd. dirs., exec. com. mem., 1973-86. Calif. Heart Assn. fellow, 1971-73. Mem. Am. Chem. Soc., N.Y. Acad. Scis., Soc. Cell Biology, Sigma Xi. Address: Jerry Pettis Vets Hosp Anesthesiology Service Loma Linda CA 92357 Office: Loma Linda U Med Ctr Dept Anesthesiology Loma Linda CA 92354

ALOJIPAN, ROBERT PETER, plastic surgeon; b. Pandan, Antique, Philippines, Apr. 19, 1951; s. Francisco Alojipan and Teodora (Dioso) A.; m. Eleonor Garcia, Jan. 15, 1983; 1 child, Melissa Daian. BS in Psychology, U. Santo Tomas, Manila, 1969, BS in Pre-med., 1971, MD, 1975. Diplomate Philippine Bd. Surgery. Intern Makati (Manila) Med. Ctr., 1975-76, resident in surgery, 1977-84, chief pres., 1982, chief med. officer outpatient dept. charity, 1983—. Founder, pres. Urihing Tubo (The Youth), Pandan, 1977; founder, chmn. Pagtatap (Care), Manila, 1986, The Mangyan (Drs. of the People), Manila, 1986. Fellow Philippine Coll. Surgeons; mem. Philippine Med. Assn., Makati Med. Soc., Philippine Soc. Cosmetic Surgery (cert.). Home: Pandan, Antique 217, Philippines Office: Makati Med Ctr, 2 Amorsolo St Legaspi Village, Makati Metro Manila 1200, Philippines

ALONEFTIS, ANDREAS, Cypriot government official; b. Nicosia, Cyprus, Aug. 24, 1945. BA, Sch. Accountancy and Bus. Studies, Glasgow, Scotland, 1973; MBA, So. Meth. U., 1978. Acct. Cyprus Devel. Bank, Nicosia, 1966-72, chief acct., 1972-76, mgr. fin., 1976-78, sr. mgr. investments, 1978-82; gen. mgr., chief operating officer Cyprus Investment and Securities Corp., Nicosia, 1982-88; minister of def. Republic of Cyprus, 1988—; exec. dir. Cosmopolitan Properties, Nicosia, 1978-88, Corotsos Textiles, Limassol, Cyprus, 1978-85; sec. Cyprus Stock Exchange Interim Com., 1980-82. Contbr. articles to profl. jours. Served to 2d lt. Army of Cyprus, 1964-66. Fulbright Found. grantee, 1977-78; So. Meth. U. fellow, 1977-78. Fellow Assn. Internat. Accts. Greek Orthodox. Lodge: Rotary (asst. sec. Nicosia club 1986-88). Home: 10 Kastellowzo St, Nicosia 123, Cyprus Office: Ministry of Def, Nicosia Cyprus

ALONSO, AGUSTIN, economics educator; b. Madrid, Nov. 8, 1941; s. Agustin Alonso and Rafaela Rodriguez. Lic. in Theology, Lateran U., Rome, 1967; Lic. in Econs., U. Complutense, Madrid, 1972, postgrad., 1988. Ordained priest Order of Saint Augustine Roman Cath. Ch., 1966. Asst. dir. Col. Mayor Escorial, El Escorial, Spain, 1967-71, Col. Mayor Elias Ahuja, Madrid, 1971-74; vice-rector Royal U. Coll. Maria Cristina, El Escorial, Spain, 1980-82, prof. econs. and stats., 1979—, prof. computers, 1980—, chmn. econs. dept., 1985—; assoc. pastor Roman Cath. Ch., La Jolla, USA, 1975-79, El Escorial, 1979—, London, 1981, 84, 85. Contbr. articles on theology, econs. and stats. Mem. Internat. Statis. Inst., Am. Econ. Assn., Am. Statis. Assn., Econometric Soc., N.Y. Acad. Scis. Home: Paseo de los Alamillos 1, San Lorenzo del Escorial, 28200 Madrid Spain Office: Real C Univ Maria Cristina, San Lorenzo del Escorial, 28200 Madrid Spain

ALONSO, ALICIA, ballerina; b. Havana, Cuba, Dec. 21, 1921; d. Antonio Martinez-Arrenondo and Ernestina del Hoyo; D.Arts (hon.), U. Havana, 1963; m. Pedro Simon, Aug. 6, 1975; 1 dau. by previous marriage, Laura Alonso. Prima ballerina Am. Ballet Theatre, 1940-41, 43-48, 50-55, 58-59, Ballet Russe de Monte Carlo, 1955-59; prima ballerina assuluta, artistic dir. Ballet Nacional de Cuba, 1948—; guest artist Paris Opera, Bolshoi Theatre of Moscow, Kirov of Leningrad, others; v.p. of jury internat. ballet competitions, Moscow, Varna, Tokyo; mem. adv. council Ministerio de Cultura, Cuba. Recipient annual award Dance Mag., U.S., 1958, Grand Prix de la Ville de Paris, 1966, 70, Orden del Trabajo, Republica Democratica de Vietnam, 1964, Orden Ana Betancourt, Cuba, 1974, Orden Felix Varela, Cuba, 1981. Choreographer established works including: Giselle, Swan Lake, Fille Mal Gardee, Sleeping Beauty, Grand Pas de Quatre, Copelia, original works: Ensayo Sinfonico, Lydia, El Pillete, El Circo, Mision Korad, others. Office: Ballet Nacional de Cuba, Calzada 510, Vedado, Havana 4 Cuba *

ALONSO, ANTONIO ENRIQUE, lawyer; b. Habana, Cuba, Aug. 31, 1924; came to U.S. 1959; s. Enrique and Inocencia (Avila) A.; m. Daisy Ojeda, July 20, 1949; children: Margarita, Antonio, Enrique, Jorge. JD, U. Habana, Cuba, 1946; PhD, U. Habana, 1952; student, U. Fla., 1974-76. Bar: Fla. 1976. Pub. defendant High Ct. Las Villas, Cuba, 1946-49; atty. Provincial Gov., Cuba, 1950-52; under sec. Treasury, Cuba, 1952-54; mem. House of Reps. Congress of Cuba, 1954-58; sole practice Miami, 1976—. Author: (with others) History of the Communist Party of Cuba, 1970; Violation of Human Rights in Cuba, 1962; contbr. articles to profl. jours. Mem. ABA, Fla. Bar Assn., Inter-Am. Bar Assn., Hispanic Nat. Bar Assn. Republican. Roman Catholic. Home: 11125 SW 128th Ct Miami FL 33186 Office: 1699 Coral Way Suite 315 Miami FL 33145

ALONSO GARCIA, MANUEL JOSE, university administrator; b. Santa Lucia, Spain, Mar. 31, 1939; s. Francisco Alonso and Corine Garcia. MA in Theology, Pontifical U. Comillas-Spain, 1963; MA in English Philology, U. Granada-Spain, 1972, MA in Spanish Philology, 1973; MA in Philosophy, U. S. Tommaso, Rome, 1973, U. Valencia-Spain, 1974; PhD, U. Granada, 1977. Asst. prof. U. Granada, 1974-76; vis. prof. Tchrs. Tng. Sch., 1978-84, prof., 1985-86, full prof., 1987—; dir. First Meeting of Mediterranean Artists and Writers, Melilla, 1987, Seminar on Spanish-Barber Cultures 1981, 83, 87, First Hispanic African Congress on Mediterranean Cultures, 1984, The Mediterranean and the Canaries, 1984; staff Fourth Internat. Congress on Galdos-Las Palmas, 1985. Author: On the Spanish Review Cruz y Raya, 1977, Liturgy and Song, 1977; contbr. articles to profl. jours. Ministry of Edn. grantee, 1974-76; Fulbright scholar, 1977; Brit. Council scholar, 1978, grantee, 1985; recipient Extraordinary Prize of Doctorate, U. Granada, 1979. Mem. Assn. Spanish Catholic Laymen (founder), Gen. Soc. Spanish Authors, Internat. Assn. Hispanic-African Studies (pres.). Roman Catholic. Office: Internat Assn H-A Studies, Lopez Moreno 4, 29801 Melilla Spain

ALONZO, RONALD THOMAS, manufacturing executive; b. Mexico City, June 12, 1942; came to U.S., 1958; s. Rosendo and Alice Jane (Ratcliff) A.; m. Denise Angèle Rufin, Feb. 10, 1968; children: Rodrigo, Micaela. BA in Polit. Sci., Tulane U., 1965. Adminstrv. asst. Humble Oil & Refinery Co., New Orleans, 1965-67; advt. and sales promotion mgr. internat. div. Whirlpool Corp., Benton Harbor, Mich., 1968-72; regional mgr. Europe and Latin Am. internat. div. Whirlpool Corp., Benton Harbor, 1972-78; internat. sales mgr. Kohler (Wis.) Co., 1978-83; internat. v.p. Vollrath Co., Sheboygan, Wis., 1983-84; v.p., chief mktg. and internat. officer Jet Spray Corp., Norwood, Mass., 1984—. Mem. Nat. Assn. Food Equipment Mfrs. (vice. chmn. internat. com., steering com. mem. 1987—), Nat. Council U.S. China Trade, Internat. Bus. Ctr., Internat. Food Mfrs. Assn., Am. Mktg. Assn., Nat. Assn. Food Mfrs. (vice chmn. internat. com. and mem. of steering com. 1987—), U.S. Arab C. of C. Avocations: gastronomy, oenology, photography. Home: 45 Alexander Way PO Box 2452 Duxbury MA 02331 Office: Jet Spray Corp 825 University Ave Norwood MA 02062

ALPA, GUIDO PETER, lawyer, educator; b. Ovada, Alessandria, Italy, Nov. 26, 1947; s. Carlo and Domenica (Cavanna) A. Bachelor's degree, Coll. Andrea D'Oria, Genoa, Italy, 1966; Law degree, U. Genoa, 1970. Legal asst. Genoa, 1973-79, sole practice law, 1980—; regional lawyer Ct. Cassazione Rome, 1984—; asst. prof. U. Genoa Sch. Law, 1971-75, assoc. prof., 1975-80, prof., 1980—, dir. Inst. Pvt. Law, 1981—; vis. prof. law U. Oreg. Editor Directory of Info. Jurisprudence Civic Com. Padua and Rome; author Products Liability, 1975, Consumer Protection, 1977, Definition of "Tort", 1979, Interpretation of Contract, 1984. Mem. Ctr. for Law and Soc. (asst. pres.), Young Assn. Lawyers (pres.), Law and Informatics Assn. (pres. 1985-86), European Consumer Affairs Assn. Office: Via SS Giacomo e Filippo 15, 16122 Genoa Italy

ALPAN, HASAN SADRETTIN, mining engineer; b. Aksehir, Turkey, June 22, 1924; s. Bahri and Mebrure A.; B.S. with honors, Birmingham (Eng.) U., 1948, Ph.D., 1951; m. Annie Mary Heal, Nov. 5, 1952; 1 child, Kenan. Asso. prof. Tech. U., Istanbul, Turkey, 1954; chief engr. Mineral Research and Exploration Inst. Turkey, Ankara, 1951-55, dir. exploration dept., 1955-58, dep. gen. dir., 1958-60, gen. dir., 1960-78; interregional adviser Div. Natural Resources and Energy, UN, N.Y.C., 1979—; chmn. bd. trustees Middle East Tech. U., Ankara, 1960-70; mem. AEC, Turkey, 1960-75; part time lectr. Istanbul Tech. U., Istanbul U., Ankara U., Trabzon Tech. U., Ege-Izmir U., Hacettepe U., Middle East Tech. U., 1955-79. Served as res. officer Turkish Armed Forces, 1951-52. Recipient Victor prize, 1950. Mem. Chamber of Engrs. Ankara-Turkey, Geol. Soc. Ankara-Turkey, Internat. World Mining Congress (organizing com.). Moslem. Contbr. papers on mining prodn. and mineral resources to publs. Home: 166 E 34th St Apt 12-D New York NY 10016 Office: UN DTCD-DNRE Room DC1-838 New York NY 10017

ALPERIN, GOLDIE GREEN, consulting librarian, lawyer; b. Des Moines, Aug. 16, 1905; d. Morris and Bessie (Miliwer) Green; LL.B., Drake U., 1927; m. Moses Alperin, Dec. 25, 1930 (dec. 1950); children—Herschel Burton, Judith Miriam. Admitted to Iowa bar, 1927, U.S. Supreme Ct. bar, 1959; practice in Des Moines, 1927-30; law librarian Chgo. Bar. Assn., 1951-63; dir. Def. Information Office, Chgo., 1963-65; librarian book selections Northwestern U. Law Sch. Library, 1966-72; ret., 1972. Named one of 20 rep. U.S. women lawyers of various phases practice Women's Adjustment Bd., London, Eng., 1957; One of Outstanding Women of Am. Bicentennial, Austin (Tex.) Bicentennial Com., 1976; cert. religious sch. tchr. Bd. Jewish Edn., Chgo., 1951. Mem. Am. (sec. 1960-65), Chgo. (past exec. bd., editor 1958-59) assns. law libraries, Nat. Assn. Women Lawyers (regional) dir. 1960-64). Jewish religion. Asst. editor Women Lawyers Jour., 1961-67, exec. bd., 1961-67. Home: 3100 Lake Shore Dr #1512 Chicago IL 60657

ALPERIN, IRWIN EPHRAIM, clothing company executive; b. Scranton, Pa., Apr. 29, 1925; s. Louis I. and Bessie (Wickner) A.; m. Francine Leah Friedman, Dec. 5, 1948; children: Barbara Joy, Jane Leslie. BS in Indsl. Engring., Lehigh U., 1947; cert. mech. engring. Pa. State U., 1945. Mgmt. trainee Mayflower Mfg. Co., Scranton, Pa., 1947-49, sec., 1952-79, pres., 1980—; with Triple A Trouser Mfg. Co., Inc., Scranton, 1952, v.p., treas., 1958-79, pres., 1980—; with Gold Star Mfg. Co., Inc., Scranton, 1956, pres., 1956—; sec. Astro Warehousing, Inc., Scranton, 1962—; sec.-treas. Bondeal, Inc., Scranton, 1978—; vice chmn. Montage Inc., 1979—; sec. Alperin, Inc., 1982—; bd. dirs. Sacquoit Industries Inc., Scranton. Bd. dirs. Econ. Devel. Council N.E. Pa., Avoca, 1974—, v.p., 1978-83; bd. dirs. ARC, Scranton, 1968—; bd. dirs. Jewish Home Eastern Pa., Scranton, 1970—, treas., 1981—; bd. dirs. Jewish Community Ctr., Scranton, 1971-86, Pa. United Way, Harrisburg, Pa., 1973-78, Scranton Mental Health-Mental Retardation Ctr., 1975-78; pres. Planning Council Social Services Lackawanna County, 1972-74, now life mem.; pres. Jewish Family Service of Lackawanna County, 1967-70, now life bd. mem.; v.p. United Way Lackawanna County, 1974-78, exec. com., 1978-86; pres. Alperin Found., Scranton, 1962—; treas. Scranton-Lackawanna Jewish Fedn., 1973-75, life mem. bd. dirs.; trustee Amos Lodge Found., 1982—, Found. Jewish Elderly, 1984—, v.p. 1985—; trustee Pocono Northeast Devel. Fund, 1983-86, sec. 1986—. Temple Hesed pres., 1969-71, life mem., bd. dirs., Scranton, Pa.; mem. Lackawanna County Library Bd., 1983-85; treas. Community Arts Project, Lackawanna County, 1987—. Served with C.E., AUS, 1944-46. Recipient Americanism award, 1982; named Man of Year, Jewish Community Ctr., 1973, Disting. Pennsylvanian, Phila. C. of C., 1982. Mem. Am. Inst. Indsl. Engrs. (sr.). Club: Glen Oak Country (Clarks Summit, Pa.). Lodges: Masons, Shriners, Elks, B'nai B'rith (trustee; Man of Yr. 1982). Home: 600 Colfax Ave Scranton PA 18510 Office: Penn and Vine Sts PO Box 470 Scranton PA 18503

ALPERIN, RICHARD MARTIN, clinical social worker, psychoanalyst; b. Mt. Vernon, N.Y., Oct. 16, 1946; s. Israel and Sara Alperin; m. Linda Lande, Feb. 27, 1972; children: Heather, Nicole, Alexander, Scott. BBA, Western Mich. U., 1968; MSW, Fordham U., 1974; DSW, Columbia U., 1982; postdoctoral diploma in psychotherapy and psychoanalysis G. Dernier Inst. Advanced Psychol. Studies, Adelphi U., 1988. Cert. social worker, N.Y., cert. Acad. Cert. Social Workers; diplomate Am. Bd. Clin. Social Work. Cons., Mt. Vernon Youth Bd., 1972-75; adj. faculty Marymount Manhattan Coll., N.Y.C., 1974-76; psychotherapist Riverdale Mental Health Clinic, N.Y.C., 1974-77; psychol. counselor, psychotherapist Ctr. Counseling and Psychol. Services, Ramapo Coll., N.J., 1976-81, also adj. faculty Ramapo Coll., 1977—, moderator evening forums, 1978, 80; counselor, psychotherapist Ctr. Counseling and Psychol. Services, SUNY, Purchase, 1981-82, part-time, 1984-85, acting dir., 1982-84; clin. cons. Westside Ctr. for Family Services, N.Y.C., 1985-87; guest lectr. Cabrini Med. Ctr., 1979; pvt. practice psychotherapy and psychoanalysis, Riverdale, N.Y., 1977—, Teaneck, N.J., 1980—, N.Y.C., 1984—; field instr. Columbia U. Sch. Social Work, 1983-85; adj. asst. prof. Fordham U. Sch. Social Service, 1985—. Contbr. articles to profl. jours. Nat. Jewish Welfare Bd. fellow Fordham U., 1974. Mem. Nat. Assn. Social Workers, Met. Coll. Mental Health Assn., Soc. Clin. Social Work Psychotherapists, Adelphi Soc. Psychoanalysis and Psychotherapy, Am. Group Psychotherapy Assn., Inc., Eastern Group Psychotherapy Soc. Research on psychotherapy, suicide and provision of preventative services.

ALPERIN, STANLEY I., publisher, writer, editor, consultant; b. Boston, Jan. 3, 1931; s. Herman and Esther (Gorovitz) A.; m. Sondra Price, Sept. 8, 1957; children: Lisa Alperin Rose, Marlene Alperin Hochman, Hillary Price. Editor U.S. Directory Service, Miami, Fla., 1966—. Author: Careers in the Health Care Field, Careers in Nursing; editor, researcher numerous medical directories. Home: 7960 SW 89th Terr Miami FL 33156 Office: US Directory Service Publishers 655 NW 128 St Miami FL 33168

ALPERT, WARREN, corporate executive; b. Chelsea, Dec. 2, 1920; s. Goodman and Tena (Horowitz) A. B.S. Boston U, 1942; M.B.A., Harvard U., 1947. Mgmt. trainee Standard Oil Co. of Calif., 1947-48; financial specialist The Calif. Oil Co., 1948-52; pres. Warren Petroleum Co., 1952-54; now chmn. bd.; founder, pres., chmn. bd. Warren Equities, Inc., from 1954; pres., chmn. Ritz Tower Hotel; chmn. bd. Kenyon Oil Co., Inc., Mid-Valley Petroleum Corp., Puritan Oil Co., Inc., Drake Petroleum Co., Inc.; Mem. of U.S. Com. for UN, 1958; exec. com. Small Bus. Adminstrn., 1958; adminstr. for adminstrn. U.S. AID, 1962; Former trustee, mem. exec. com. Boston U.; trustee Emerson Coll.; former v.p. Petroleum Marketing Edn. Found.; bd. dirs. Assocs. of Harvard Bus. Sch.; mem. com. for resource and devel. Harvard Med. Sch. Served with Signal Intelligence AUS, 1943-45. Andrew Wellington Cordier fellow Sch. Internat. Affairs, Columbia U. Mem. Am. Petroleum Industry 25 Year Club, Young Presidents Orgn. (past dir.), Am. Petroleum Inst. (dir. mktg. div.). Clubs: Harvard Business School (exec. com., dir., bd. govs., pres. 1960-61), Harvard, Met (N.Y.C.); Harvard (Boston); Friars, Marco Polo, Metropolitan. Home: 465 Park Ave New York NY 10022 Office: Waren Equities Inc 10 E 53rd St New York NY 10022

AL-QASIMI, SHEIKH SAQR IBN MUHAMMAD (SHEIKH SAQR BIN MUHAMMAD AL-QASIMI), ruler of Ras al-Khaimah, United Arab Emirates; b. 1920; married. Ruler of Ras al-Khaimah, United Arab Emirates, 1948—; mem. Supreme Council of United Arab Emirates, 1948—. Office: Ruler's Palace, Ras al-Khaimah, Abu Dhabi United Arab Emirates *

AL-QASSIMI, SHEIKH SULTAN BIN MOHAMMED (SHEIKH SULTAN BIN MUHAMMAD AL-QASIMI), ruler of Sharjah, United Arab Emirates; b. 1939; s. Shaikh Mohammed Bin Bin Saqur Al-Qasimi; ScB in Agr. Cairo (Egypt) U.; PhD Exeter U., London; married; 6 children. Tchr., Sharjah Tech. Tng. Sch.; minister of edn. United Arab Emirates, 1971-72, ruler of Sharjah, 1972—; mem. Supreme Ct. of Rulers, 1972—. Office: Ruler's Palace, Sharjah United Arab Emirates

AL-RASHID, SAMI ABDUL-HAMID, real estate developer; b. Kofranjah, Ajloun, Jordan, Apr. 20, 1940; s. Abdulhamid and Hanieh Al-Rashid; m. Maias Al-Ghoul, Dec. 29, 1966; children: Hanin, Sama, Reem. BCE, Alexandria (Egypt) U., 1963; degree in constrn. mgmt., Am. U. Beirut, Lebanon, 1975; degree in decision making analysis, Harvard U., 1987; grad. exec. program in ops. mgmt., MIT, 1987. Supervisory engr. Ministry of Communications, Riyadh, Saudi Arabia, 1963-66; mgr. projects Housing Corp., Amman, Jordan, 1968-75; dir. Material Research Ctr. Royal Sci. Soc., Amman, 1975; mgr. tech. Ranco Contracting Co., Amman, 1975-79; dir. gen. Amman Devel. Corp., 1979—. Contbr. articles to profl. publs. Served with Royal Jordanian Air Force, 1966-68. Mem. Engring. Soc., Concrete Soc., Road Soc. Moslem. Club: Automobile (Amman). Home: PO Box 17041, Amman Jordan Office: Amman Devel Corp, Shabsough St, PO Box 926621, Amman Jordan

AL-SABAH, ALI AL-KHALIFA AL-ATHBI, minister of oil of Kuwait; b. Kuwait, Oct. 22, 1945; married; 4 children. Cert. Victoria Coll., Cairo, Egypt; B.Sc., San Francisco State U., 1968; M.Sc. in Econs., London U. Head econ. dept. Ministry of Fin. and Oil, Kuwait, 1968-73, asst. under-sec., 1973-75; undersec. Ministry of Fin., Kuwait, 1975-78; minister of oil, 1978—, minister of fin., from 1983-85, minister of oil and industry, 1985-86; chmn. Kuwait Petroleum Corp., 1980—; chmn. Council of Ministers of OPEC, 1978. Office: Ministry of Oil, Kuwait City Kuwait

AL-SABAH, SHEIKH JABIR AL-AHMAD AL-JABIR (SHEIKH JABIR AL-AHMAD AL-JABIR AL-SABAH), amir of Kuwait; b. Kuwait City, Kuwait, June 29, 1926; s. His Highness Sheikh Ahmad Al-Jabir Al-Sabah; Student Al-Mubarakiyyah Sch.; married. Gov. of Ahmadi and oil areas, Kuwait, 1949-59; pres. Dept. Fin. and Economy, Kuwait, 1959—, minister of fin. and economy, 1962-63, minister of fin. and industry, 1963-65, minister of fin. and industry and minister of commerce, from 1965, prime minister, 1965-77, crown prince, 1966-78, amir of Kuwait, 1977—; chmn. Supreme Def. Council, Kuwait, Supreme Petroleum Council. Chmn. bd. dirs. Kuwait Fund for Arab Econ. Devel., Kuwait Found. for Sci. Advancement; chmn. Supreme Com. for Master Plan and Maj. Projects, Kuwait. Home: Amir Royal Palace, Kuwait City State of Kuwait Office: care Press Attache Embassy of State of Kuwait 2940 Tilden St NW Washington DC 20008 *

AL-SABAH, SHEIKH SABAH AL-AHMAD AL-JABIR, minister foreign affairs Kuwait; b. 1929; s. Sheikh Ahmad Al-Jaber Al-Sabah; ed. Mubarakiyyah Nat. Sch., Kuwait; married. Mem. Supreme Com. Kuwait, 1955-62; minister of public info. and guidance and social affairs, 1962-63; minister fgn. affairs, 1963—; acting minister fin. and oil, 1965-67; acting minister of info., 1971-75, 78, minister of interior, 1978; dep. prime minister, 1978—. Address: Ministry of Foreign Affairs, Kuwait City Kuwait *

AL-SABAH, SHEIKH SA'D AL-ABDALLAH AL-SALIM (SHEIKH SAAD AL-ABDALLAH AL-SALIM AL-SABAH), crown prince of Kuwait and prime minister; b. 1924; pvt. edn. Kuwait; married. With police dept., 1945-53; trained at Met. Police Coll., Hendon, U.K., 1953-54; dep. head Kuwait Met. Police, 1954-59; dep. pres. Police and Public Security Dept., 1959-61; minister of interior, 1961-65; minister of interior and def., 1965-78; head Ministerial Com. on Labor Problems, 1975-78; crown prince, 1978—; prime minister of Kuwait, 1978—. Address: Office of Prime Minister, Kuwait City Kuwait *

AL-SABAH, SALIM AL-SABAH AL-SALIM, government official; b. Kuwait, June 18, 1937; s. Sabah Al-Salem A.; married; 4 children. Student, Gray's Inn, London, Oxford U. Dir. legal polit. depts. ministry of fgn. affairs Govt. of Kuwait, 1962, ambassador to Eng., 1965-70, non-resident ambassador to Denmark, Sweden and Norway, 1968-70, ambassador to U.S., 1971-75, non-resident to Can. and Venezuela, 1971, minister social affairs and labour, 1975-78, minister of def., 1978-88, minister of interior, 1988—. Office: Ministry of Interior, Kuwait City Kuwait *

AL-SABAH, SAUD NASIR, foreign diplomat, barrister; b. Kuwait, Oct. 3, 1944; s. Nasir Saud and Sabikah Abdullah Al-Sabah; m. Awatif Sabah Al-Salem, 1962; children—Fawaz, Marahib, Nawaf, Nayirah, Sabah. Barrister-at-law, Gray's Inn, Eng., 1968. With legal dept. Fgn. Ministry, State of Kuwait, 1969—; mem. Seabed com. UN Conf. on Law of Sea, 1969-73; ambassador to Great Britain, Norway, Sweden and Denmark, 1975-80, U.S., Can. and Venezuela, 1981—. Office: Embassy of Kuwait 2940 Tilden St NW Washington DC 20008

AL-SAID, FAHAD IBN MAHMOUD (FAHAD BIN MAHMOUD AL-SAID), Omani deputy premier for legal affairs; b. 1944; ed. U. Cairo; diploma in diplomatic studies, Paris; student Acad. Arts in The Hague (Netherlands). Dir. Ministry of Fgn. Affairs, Govt. of Oman, 1971, minister of state, 1971-72, minister info. and culture, 1972-80, dep. premier for legal affairs, 1980—. Office: Ministry of Legal Affairs, Bait Al Falaj, PO Box 113, Muscat Oman *

AL-SAID, FAHR IBN TAIMUR (FAHR BIN TAIMUR AL-SAID), deputy premier for security and defense of Sultanate of Oman; b. 1928; grad. Mil. Acad. Dehra Dun, 1940. With Sayyed Tariq al Said, Beirut, 1966-70; liaison officer Dept. of Def., Govt. of Oman, 1970-74, dep. minister of interior, from 1974, then minister youth affairs; now dep. premier for security and def.; represented Royal Family on fgn. missions. Office: Ministry of Defense, Bait al Falaj, PO Box 113, Muscat Oman *

AL-SAIGH, NASSIR MOHAMMAD, academic administrator; b. Riyadh, Saudi Arabia, Oct. 10, 1942; s. Mohammad Hussein and Noura A. Al-Saigh. BA in Commerce, King Saud U., Riyadh, 1969; MBA, U. Ind., 1974; D in Bus. Adminstrn., U. Ky., 1979. Asst. prof. bus. adminstrn. King Saud U., 1979—, chmn. dept. bus. adminstrn., 1980-83; dir. gen. Arab Org. Adminstrv. Scis., Amman, Jordan, 1983—. Editor: Administrative Reform in the Arab World: Readings, 1986, Public Administration and Administrative Reform in the Arab World, 1986; editor-in-chief Arab. Jour. Adminstrn., 1984—. Mem. Internat. Inst. Adminstrv. Scis. (exec. council), Internat. Assn. Schs. and Insts. of Adminstrn. (v.p.), Internat. Network Informatics/Internat. Labor Orgn. (cons. com.), Am. Mgmt. Assn., Am. Inst. Decision Scis., Internat. Inst. Mktg. Office: Arab Orgn Adminstrv Scis, PO Box 17159, Amman Jordan

AL SALAMI, MOHAMED ABDULLAH SULTAN, government official; b. Dibba, United Arab Emirates, Dec. 25, 1960; s. Abdullah Sultan A. BS in Polit. Sci., Pub. Adminstrn., Ind. State U., 1984. Dir. Dept. Industry and Economy, Fujairah, United Arab Emirates, 1984-86; chmn. Dept. Civil Aviation, Fujairah, United Arab Emirates, 1986—; dir. Fujairah Seaport, 1984, Fujairah Aviation Ctr., 1986, Ins. Co., Fujairah, 1984. Mem. Fed. Nat. Council, Abu Dhabi, United Arab Emirates, 1987. Mem. Internat. Civil Airports Assn. Club: Dibba Sports (United Arab Emirates). Office: Fujairah Internat Airport, PO Box 977, Fujairah United Arab Emirates

AL-SARI, AHMAD MOHAMMAD, data processing exec.; b. Al-Mukalla, South Yemen, Feb. 22, 1947; s. Mohammad Salem and Fatima Daoud (Al-Jilani) Al-S.; student U. Petroleum and Minerals, Dhahran, Saudi Arabia, 1965-67; B.Sc. in Chem. Engring., U. Tex., Austin, 1970. Lab. asst. Center Hwy. Research, Austin, 1969-70; programmer/analyst Data Processing Center, U. Petroleum and Minerals, 1970-76, dir. data processing center, 1976-80; chmn. Al-Khaleej Computers & Electronic Systems, Al-Khobar, Saudi Arabia, 1980—; dir. Internat. Systems Engring. Co.; co-founder Al-Falak Electronic Equipment and Supplies Co., United Computer Services Co., United Systems Engring. Co.; cons. various Saudi Arabian ministries; chmn. 1st Nat. Computer Conf., 1974. Mem. Assn. Computing Machinery U.S. (asso.), Saudi Computer Soc. (founding mem.). Editor Procs. Symposium on Arabic Code Standards, Saudi Arabian Standards Orgn., 1981, The DPC Bull., 1972-76. Office: PO Box 16091, Riyadh 11464, Saudi Arabia

AL-SHAKAR, KARIM EBRAHIM, ambassador; b. Manama, Bahrain, Dec. 23, 1945; s. Ebrahim and Radieh Al-Shakar; m. Fatima Mansoori, Nov. 25, 1951; children: Areije, Elham, Hessa. BA, Delhi U., India, 1970. Attaché Ministry Fgn. Affairs, Bahrain, 1970, third sec., 1971; mem. Permanent Mission State of Bahrain to UN, 1972-76; second sec. Ministry Fgn. Affairs, Bahrain, 1972, first sec., 1974, chief sect. Fgn. Affairs Internat. Orgn., 1977-82, sr. first sec., 1978, counsellor, 1981; rep. Bahrain ILO Governing Body, 1982-84; A.E. and P. to UN Bahrain, Geneva, 1982-87; consul gen. to Switzerland Bahrain, 1982-87, ambassador UNIDO, 1986—; A.E. and P. to Fed. Republic Germany, 1984-87; A.E. and P. (non-resident) to Austria, 1987; headed Bahrain delegation to UN Conf. on Trade and Devel., Belgrade, 1983, Seventh Session UNCTAD, Geneva, 1987, Second Conf. to Combat Racism and Racial Discrimination, 1983; chmn. Spl. Com. Preferences UNCTAD, 1986, Group 77, Geneva, 1986. Office: Permanent Mission State of Bahrain to UN 2 UN Plaza 25th Floor New York NY 10017

AL SHAMALI, MAJED ABDULLAH, banker; b. Jeddah, Saudi Arabia, Dec. 23, 1961; s. Abdullah M. and Ngaht M. (Imam) Al S.; m. Hanan M. Serafi, Jan. 16, 1985; 1 child, Mohammad. Student, Hawthorne Coll., 1983, Ministry Edn., Jeddah, 1984. Acct. Aramco, Dahran, Saudi Arabia, 1978-80; ops. supr. Avco Dallah, Riyadh, Jeddah, 1980-83; mgr. pub. relations Alshamali for Trading Est, Jeddah, 21414 (1984); mgr. ops. Saudi Operation & Maintenance Co., Riyadh, 1985; system liberian Nat. Comml. Bank,

Jeddah, 1985—. Mem. Alexander Hamilton Inst. Home: PO Box 13710, 21414 Jeddah Saudi Arabia

AL-SHARA, FAROUK (FAROUK AL- SHARA), foreign minister Syria; b. Daraa, Syria, Jan. 17, 1938; s. Hussein and Farha (Hariri) Al-Shara; m. Anal Marouf, Sept. 29, 1964; children—Mudar, Nuwaar. B.A. in English Lit., Damascus U., 1963; student internat. law London U., 1971-72. Regional mgr. Syria Air, London, 1968-72, comml. dir., Damascus, 1972-76; Syrian ambassador to Italy, Rome, 1976-80; minister of state for fgn. affairs, Damascus, 1980-84, fgn. minister, 1984—. Mem. central com. Baath Arab Socialist Com., Damascus, 1985. Avocations: reading; art; literature; chess. Office: Ministry Fgn Affairs, Damascus Syria *

AL-SHARHAN, YACOUB SALEH, investment banker; b. Kuwait, Kuwait, May 22, 1959. BBA, Kuwait U., 1981. With prodn. dept. Kuwait Ins. Co., 1981-83; investor Pub. Instn. for Social Security, Kuwait, 1983; credit and adminstrn. mgr. Arab Trust Co. KSC, Kuwait, 1984—; mng. dir. Burgan Internat. Ins. Office, Kuwait, 1984—; bd. dirs. Elec. Projects Co., Kuwait, Arab Agrl. Co., Kuwait. Home: Tower 6, Al-Tameer Complex, Gulf St, Kuwait Kuwait Office: Arab Trust Co KSC 7 Fl PO 5365, IBK Bldg Joint Banking Ctr, Safat 13054 Kuwait Kuwait

AL-SINAN, TAYSEER ABDULALI, infosystems specialist; b. Qatif, Saudi Arabia, Sept. 2, 1951; s. Abdulali Mohammed Al-Sinan and Zahra (Mansoor) Al-Jishi; m. Huda Al-Shaikh Mansoor, Apr. 6, 1984; children: Nesreen, Ghadeer. BA social science with honors, Miami-Dade Community Coll., 1981. Computer operational specialist KEMYA Petrochem. Co., Houston, 1982-83; computer operational supr. Arabian Bechtel Co., Jubail, Saudi Arabia, 1984-86; with King Fahd U., Dhahran, Saudi Arabia, 1971-79, 87—, lead computer operator, 1978-79, systems analyst, 1987; systems analyst econs. and indsl. research King Fahd U., 1987—. Office: King Fahd U, PO Box 1905, 31261 Dhahran Saudi Arabia

ALSOBROOK, HENRY BERNIS, JR., lawyer; b. New Orleans, Nov. 9, 1930; s. Henry Bernis and Ethel (Smith) A.; m. Eugenie Loie Wilson, June 6, 1956; children—Eugenie Wilson, John Gleason, Emily Woodward. B.A., Tulane U., 1952, J.D., 1957. Bar: La. 1957. Since practiced in New Orleans; sr. partner firm Adams & Reese; past mem. faculty Tulane U. Law Sch.; bd. dirs. Def. Research Inst., 1978-81, 85-88, chmn. med.-legal com., 1967-72; lectr. in field. Author articles in field; mem. editorial bds. legal jours. Chmn. dean's council Tulane U., 1983-88; elder St. Charles Ave. Presbyn. Ch., New Orleans; first pres. Les Compagnons du Barreau de La Louisiane, 1985—; treas., bd. dirs. La. State Mus.; bd. dirs. New Orleans Philharm. Symphony Soc. Served with USNR, 1953. Fellow Am. Bar Found., Am. Coll. Trial Lawyers; mem. ABA (past chmn. standing com. commerce, ho. of dels. 1984—), La. Bar Assn. (pres. 1982-83), New Orleans Bar Assn., Internat. Assn. Def. Counsel (exec. com. 1982-88, pres. 1986-87), Fedn. Ins. Counsel, New Orleans Assn. Def. Counsel, La. Assn. Def. Counsel (gov. 1965), La. Law Inst. (council 1984—), Soc. Med. Assn. Counsel (charter), Soc. Hosp. Attys. (charter), AMA (hon.). Clubs: New Orleans Country, La, Avoca Duck, Lakeshore, Pickwick. Office: Adams & Reese 4500 One Shell Sq New Orleans LA 70139

AL-SOLAIM, SOLIMAN ABDUL-AZIZ, Saudi Arabian minister of commerce; B.Com. in Polit. Sci., U. Cairo, 1962; M.A. in Internat. Relations, U. So. Calif., 1966; Ph.D. in Internat. Relations, Sch. Advanced Internat. Student, Johns Hopkins U., 1970; married; 4 children. Prof. polit. sci. U. Riyadh, 1971-74; dep. minister of commerce, 1974-75, minister of commerce, 1975—; chmn. bd. Grain Silos and Flour Mills Orgn., Saudi Arabian Standards and Specifications Orgn. Office: Ministry of Commerce, Riyadh Saudi Arabia *

ALSTON, RICHARD JOHN WILLIAM, choreographer; b. Stoughton, Sussex, Eng., Oct. 30, 1948; s. Gordon Walter and Margaret Isabel (Whitworth) A. Ed. Eton Coll., Windsor, Berkshire, Eng., 1965, Croydon Coll. Art, London, 1966, London Sch. Contemporary Dance, 1971. Choreographer, London Contemporary Dance Theatre, 1970-72; founder, dir. Strider Dance Co., London, 1972-75; choreographer, U.S., 1975-77; freelance choreographer, educator, 1977-80; resident choreographer Ballet Rambert (now Rambert Dance Theatre), London, 1980-86, artistic dir., 1986—; choreograph ballets, latest including The Kingdom of Pagodas Royal Danish Ballet, 1983, Midsummer, Royal Ballet London, 1983, Chicago Brass, 1983, Voices and Light Footsteps, 1984, Dangerous Liaisons, 1985, Java, 1985, Zansa, 1986, Dutiful Ducks, 1987, Pulcinella, 1987, Strong Language, 1987. Office: Ballet Rambert, 94 Chiswick High Rd, London W4 1SH, England *

ALSUHAIMI, AZIZ MOHAMED, architect; b. Bahrain, Manama, Bahrain, Mar. 21, 1949; s. Mohammed Saleh and Mounira (Alshebel) A.; m. Fawzia Abdulaziz, Feb. 22, 1978; children: Andel, Nijla. B.S., U. Oreg., 1974, B. Arch., 1974. Architect A&R Saleh, Dammam, Saudi Arabia, 1974-76, project mgr., 1976-79; mng. prin. Alsuhaimi Design, Dammam, 1979—; exec. v.p. Alsuhaimi Co., Dammam, 1982—; mgr. dir. Alsuhaimi Hortiplan, 1984—. Dir. Saudi Arabian Pakaging Co., Ltd., 1985—, Dhahran Expo Co., 1986—, Saudi Ceramics Co., 1988—. Contbr. articles to mags. and newspapers; co-author books. Mem. Saudi Engring. Body. Avocations: sports; art work; carpet making. Office: Alsuhaimi Design Office, PO Box 161, Dammam 31411, Saudi Arabia

AL-SUWAIDI, SALEM MOHAMMED, management professional; b. Dareen, Ea. Province, Saudi Arabia, Jan. 15, 1956; s. Mohammed Salem Al-Suwaidi and Sarah (Rashid) Al-Sopai; m. May Sayegh Al-Suwaidi, Feb. 14, 1983; children: Nadia and Sarah (twins). BS in Bus., William Carey Coll., Hattiesburg, Miss., 1984; MBA, Century U., Beverly Hills, Calif., 1986. V.p. comml. M.S. Al-Suwaidi Orgn., Rahima, Saudi Arabia, 1984—. Author: Joint-venture in Saudi Arabia, 1986. Recipient Mgmt. Challenge cert. Bensen and Hedges Co. and Ashridge Coll. of London, Bahrain, 1985. Home and Office: Al-Suwaidi Orgn, PO Box 12, Rahima 31941, Saudi Arabia

ALTENBURGER, OTTO ANDREAS, management educator; b. Vienna, Austria, Oct. 29, 1951; s. Otto Leopold and Gertraud Eva M. (Hofer) A.; m. Veronika Maria Weber, June 26, 1981; children: Angelika Johanna, Dorothea Christine. MBA, Vienna U. Econs. and Bus. Adminstrn., 1975, Dr. rer. soc. econs., 1979; postgrad., Miami U., Oxford, Ohio, 1976. CPA, Austria. Research and teaching asst. Vienna U. Econs. and Bus. Adminstrn., 1974-79, 81—; auditor Alpen-Treuhand Co., Vienna, 1979-81; lectr. Vienna Bd. Trade, 1975-78, Vienna Chamber Accts., 1976—, St. Gall (Switzerland) Grad. Sch. Econs., Law, Bus. and Pub. Adminstrn., 1982—. Author: Elements of a Theory of Production of Services, 1980 (Cardinal Innitzer Encouragement award 1981); contbr. articles to jours. and books. Served to 1st lt. Austrian armed forces. Mem. Austrian Soc. Ins. Sci., Austrian Soc. Ops. Research, Austrian Chamber Accts. Roman Catholic. Home: Hauptstrasse 70, A-3420 Kritzendorf Austria Office: Vienna U Econs and Bus Adminstrn, Augasse 2-6, A-1090 Vienna Austria

ALTER, GERALD L., business executive; b. Rensselaer, Ind., Aug. 24, 1910; s. Leslie and Lettie (Willis) A.; m. Margaret A. Davis, Sept. 15, 1939; children: Judith Ann (dec.), John Edward. Student Bus. Coll., 1927-28. Clk. and office mgr., 1929-35; bldg. contractor, 1936-45; real estate broker and ins. agt., 1946—; pres. Alter Realty & Ins., Leads, Inc., investments, Alter Ins. Agy., Inc., REMCO Real Estate Mgmt. Co., Alter Devel. Co.; pres. Developers & Builders. Planning commr. City of Torrance, 1966-83, chmn. Torrance Planning Commn. 1982-83; water commr. City of Torrance, 1984—, chmn. 1987-88; former bd. dirs. Harbor Area United Way. Mem. Torrance-Lomita-Carson Bd. Realtors (pres. 1978, v.p. 1980-81), Calif. Assn. Realtors (dir. 1978-81), Nat. Assn. Realtors, Torrance C. of C. (past dir.), Am. Legion. Republican. Clubs: OX-5 (pioneer airman). Lodge: Rotary. Home: 1337 Engracia Ave Torrance CA 90501 Office: 2305 Torrance Blvd Torrance CA 90501

ALTERMATT, URS J., history educator; b. Biberist, Switzerland, July 18, 1942; s. Urs Joseph and Margrit (Heri) A.; m. Martha Verena Joller; children: Bernhard, Christopher, Monika. PhD, U. Berne, Switzerland, 1970. Sr. lectr. U. Berne, Switzerland, 1973-80; vis. lectr. U. Fribourg, Switzerland, 1973, dep. prof., 1978-79, prof. Swiss history, 1980; research fellow dept. polit. sci. Stanford U., Palo Alto, Calif., 1976, Ctr. European Studies Harvard U., Cambridge, Mass., 1976-77; vis. prof. dept. religious studies U. Berne, 1987, U. Lucerne, 1988; chmn. dept. history U. Fribourg, 1981-84, dean faculty of arts, 1985-86. Contbr. articles to profl. jours; chief editor Swiss Cultural Mag. Swiss Revue of History of the Church, 1986—. Pres. Govt. Commn. for 7th Centennial of Switzerland, 1987-88. Mem. Allgemeine Geschichtsforschende Gesellschaft der Schweiz, Schweizerische Vereinigung fur Kirchengeschichte, Schweizerische Vereinigung fur Politische Wissenschaft. Office: Univ of Fribourg, Misericorde, CH 1700 Fribourg Switzerland

ALTEROVITZ, SAMUEL ADAR, physicist; b. Bucharest, Roumania, Aug. 25, 1939; came to U.S., 1981; s. Nathan and Bracha (Schiller) A.; m. Dalia Grinberg, Oct. 6, 1970; children—Gil, Ron. M.Sc., Hebrew U., Jerusalem, 1964; Ph.D., Tel Aviv U., 1971. Sr. research assoc. NASA, Cleve., 1976-78, research physicist, 1983-85, sr. research scientist, 1985—; sr. lectr. Tel Aviv U., 1978-81, assoc. prof., 1982-83; sr. scientist U. Nebr., Lincoln, 1981-82. Contbr. chpts. to books, articles to profl. jours. Recipient Young Scientist award Bath Sheva de Rotschild Fund, Tel-Aviv, 1974. Mem. Am. Phys. Soc. Jewish. Home: 19219 Story Rd Rocky River OH 44116

AL-THANI, SHEIKH ABDUL AZIZ BIN KHALIFA (SHEIKH ABDUL AZIZ BIN KHALIFA AL THANI), Qatar government official; b. Doha, Qatar, Dec. 12, 1948; s. Sheikh Khalifa ibn Hamad al-T.; married; 4 children. BS in Polit. Sci. and Econs., 1972; M.S., No. Ind. U., 1974. Dep. Minister fin. and petroleum Government of Qatar, 1972, minister fin. and petroleum, 1972—; chmn. investment bd., 1972—; chmn. Qatar Nat. Bank, 1972—; chmn. Qatar Gen. Petroleum Corp., 1973—; gov. IMF, 1972—, World Bank, 1972—; chmn. OPEC, 1976; sr. mem. Qatar Investment Bd.; rep. at numerous internat. confs. Office: Ministry Finance and Petroleum, PO Box 413, Doha Qatar

AL-THANI, SHEIKH HAMAD BIN KHALIFA (SHEIKH HAMAD BIN KHALIFA AL THANI), Qatar government official; b. 1949; s. Shaikh Khalifa Bin Hamad al-Thani; ed. Royal Mil. Coll., Sandhurst, U.K.; married; 3 children. Commdr. in chief Security Forces Govt. Qatar, Doha, after 1972; heir apparent, 1977, prime minister, from 1977, minister of def., 1977—. Office: Ministry of Defense, Doha Qatar *

AL-THANI, SHEIKH HAMAD BIN SUHAM, Qatar government official; b. 1940. Minister fgn. affairs Govt. of Qatar, Doha, from 1972, 87—. Office: Ministry of Fgn Affairs, Doha Qatar *

AL-THANI, SHEIKH KHALID BIN HAMAD (SHEIKH KHALID BIN HAMAD AL THANI), government official Qatar; minister of interior Doha, Qatar. Office: Ministry of Interior, Doha Qatar *

AL-THANI, SHEIKH KHALIFA BIN HAMAD (SHEIKH KHALIFA BIN HAMAD AL THANI), Amir and prime minister of Qatar; b. Rayyan, 1932; s. Shaikh Hamad Bin Abdullah Bin Qassim Al-Thani; married. Ed. Royal Mil. Coll., Sandhurst, U.K. Appt. heir apparent of Qatar, 1948; began service as chief security forces petroleum project, Qator, then chief of civil cts., minister of edn., 1960-70; dep. ruler of Qatar, 1960-72, minister of fin., 1960; chmn. Watar and Dubai Currency Bd., 1966; an organizer Gulf Nine-State Fed. Union, 1968, provisional chmn., 1968; prime minister of Qatar, 1970-72, minister of fin. and petroleum, 1970-72, fgn. affairs, 1971-72; chmn. Bd. Reserves Investment of State of Qatar, 1972; amir State of Qatar, 1972—; now also prime minister. Address: Office of Amir, Doha Qatar *

AL-THANI, SHEIKH NASIR BIN KHALID (SHEIKH NASIR BIN KHALID AL THANI), Qatari minister economy and commerce, businessman; b. 1915; married. Businessman in Doha; agt. for Mercedes Benz; with Nat. Qatar Cinema Corp.; minister economy and commerce, 1970—. Pres., Qatar Israel Boycott Com. Address: Ministry Economy and Commerce, PO Box 1968, Doha Qatar *

ALTHAUS, DAVID STEVEN, research company executive; b. Massilon, Ohio, Dec. 25, 1945; s. James Horace and Mary Jane (Horan) A.; m. Joan Elizabeth Wrenn, Aug. 4, 1973; children: D. Steven Jr., Matthew, Beth Anne. BA, Miami U., Oxford, Ohio, 1967; cert., Def. Lang. Inst., Monterey, Calif., 1969; MBA, Miami U., Oxford, Ohio, 1976. CPA; Cert. profl. in human resources. Internal auditor Harris Corp., Cleve., 1976-77; sr. staff acct. Harris Corp., Rochester, N.Y., 1977-78; acctg. supr. Imperial Group Ltd., Wilson, N.C., 1978-80; dir. planning Am. Mortgage Ins. Cos., Raleigh, N.C., 1980-83; asst. v.p., budget mgr. Gen. Electric Mortgage Ins. Cos., Raleigh, 1983-84; controller Chem. Industry Inst. Toxicology, Research Triangle Park, N.C., 1984—. Served as capt. USMC, 1968-74, Vietnam. Decorated Cross of Galantry, Rep. of Vietnam, Da Nang, 1970. Mem. Nat. Assn. Accts., Am. Soc. for Personnel Adminstrn., Am. Compensation Assn., Controller's Council, Bus. Planning Bd., Am. Inst. CPA's, U.S. Naval Inst. Methodist. Office: Chem Industry Inst Toxicology PO Box 12137 Research Triangle Park NC 27709

ALTIER, WILLIAM JOHN, management consultant; b. Drexel Hill, Pa., July 22, 1935; s. William John and Gertrude (Soule) A.; BA, Lafayette Coll., 1958; MBA, Pa. State U., 1962; m. Mileen Rishel Bower, June 21, 1958; children—William Clark, Dwight Douglas. Assoc., Kepner-Tregoe Inc., Princeton, N.J., 1964-68; gen. mgr. div. Princeton Research Press, 1970-75, sr. assoc., 1975-76; assoc. Applied Synergetics Ctr., Waltham, Mass., 1968-69; dir. mktg. Comstock & Wescott Inc., Cambridge, Mass., 1969-70; pres. Princeton Assocs. Inc., Buckingham, Pa., 1976—; grad. asst. Dale Carnegie Courses; lectr. Assn. for Media-Based Continuing Edn. for Engrs.; guest lectr. Grad. Sch. Mgmt., New Sch. for Social Research, bd. dirs. Inst. Mgmt. Cons. Co-chmn. indsl. div. United Community Fund, Carlisle, Pa., 1963; elder Doylestown Presbyn. Ch.; exec. v.p. Bucks County br. ARC, also mem. planning com. Southeastern Pa. chpt.; vol. worker civic orgns. Cert. mgmt. cons. Mem. Acad. Mgmt., Am. Chem. Soc., Am. Vacuum Soc., Armed Forces Communications and Electronics Assn., Am. Mgmt. Assn., Product Devel. and Mgmt. Assn. (v.p.), Indsl. Mgmt. Club, Inst. Mgmt. Cons., Am. Arbitration Assn. (panel arbitrators), U. So. Calif. Ctr. for Futures Research, Assn. Mng. Cons. (trustee), Mensa, Kappa Sigma Alumni Corp. (chpt. pres.). Clubs: Exchange (bd. control 1960-64) (Carlisle); 1000. Research and devel. fundamental analytical thinking processes relative to change; patentee, author articles in field. Home: RD 4 Doylestown PA 18901 Office: PO Box 820 Buckingham PA 18912

ALTING, LEO LARSEN, manufacturing engineer, educator; b. Aalborg, Denmark, Apr. 15, 1939; s. Edvard and Caroline Marie (Larsen) A.; M.Sc. in Mech. Engring., Tech. U. Denmark, 1965, Ph.D., 1969; m. Greta Jakobsen, Nov. 6, 1965; children—Rasmus, Caroline. Postdoctoral research fellow U. Denver, 1970-71; head lab. process and prodn. engring. Tech. U. Denmark, 1971—, prof. mfg. engring., 1976—; div. dir. Inst. Product Devel.; dir. AGA Inc., Industriharderiet A/S, CIM Cons. ApS, Surfcoat Aps; co-dir. mfg. consortium Brigham Young U. Served in Danish Army, 1965-67. Recipient Prof. Wilkens award, 1967, SKF Indsl. award, 1974; registered profl. engr. Mem. Danish Acad. Sci., Soc. Mfg. Engrs. (Internat. Edn. award 1988), Am. Soc. Engring. Edn., Danish Metall. Soc., Danish Engring. Soc., Danish Welding Soc., Sci. Research Council, Inst. Mfg. Engring. Tech. U. Denmark (chmn.). Author: Manufacturing Engineering Processes, 1974, English edit. (Marcel Dekker), 1981; Tool and Die Design, 1975; also articles. Home: 60 Harreshojvej, DK 3080 Tikob Denmark Office: AMT Tech Univ, Bldg 425, DK 2800 Lyngby Denmark

ALTING VON GEUSAU, FRANS A. M., law educator, institute director, consultant; b. de Bilt, Netherlands, June 26, 1933; s. George M.M. and Laura G.M. (Westerwoudt) A. von G.; m. Anne Marie J.F. Houben, Sept. 3, 1960; children—Carolijn, Alexander, Michiel, Marie-Pauline, Jeroen, Christiaan. Dr. Law, Leiden U., 1958, LL.D., 1962; diploma College of Europe, Bruges, Belgium, 1959. Research asst. U. Calif.-Berkeley, 1959-60; lectr. Catholic U., Tilburg, Netherlands, 1960-62, 64-65, prof. law, 1965—; dir. Dutch Peace Corps, Ministry Fgn. Affairs, The Hague, 1963; dir. John F. Kennedy Inst., Tilburg, 1967-87; vis. prof. MIT, 1971-72, U. Mich., 1977; mem. Dutch del. to UN Gen. Assembly, 1973, 75; chmn. Adv. Commn. on Disarmament and Security, 1976-84; spl. prof. post-war western cooperation U. Leiden, 1985—; cons. to Netherlands Govt. Author: European Perspectives on World Order, 1975; The Security of Western Europe, 1985; editor; Uncertain Detente, 1979; Allies in a Turbulent World, 1982, also 15 other books, also articles. Dir. pilgrimage Sovereign Mil. Order of Malta, Utrecht, (Rome), 1981—; mem. Jerusalem Com., 1979—; v.p. European Cultural Found., Amsterdam/Brussels, 1984—. Resident fellow Rockefeller Found., Villa Serbelloni, Bellagio, 1973; visitor Wilson Ctr., Washington, 1982; decorated Knight, Order of Netherlands Lion; named Guardian of Jerusalem. Mem. Internat. Polit. Sci. Assn., Internat. Inst. for Strategic Studies, Netherlands Internat. Law Assn., Netherlands Assn. for European Law, European Inst. for Security Matters. Christian Democrat. Roman Catholic. Club: Haagsche Societeit. Home: George Perklaan 10, 5061 VP Oisterwijk The Netherlands Office: John F Kennedy Inst, Hogeschoollaan 225, 5037 GC Tilburg The Netherlands

ALTMAN, LOUIS, lawyer, author, educator; b. N.Y.C., Aug. 6, 1933; s. Benjamin and Jean (Zimmerman) A.; m. Sally J. Schlesinger, Dec. 26, 1955 (dec.); 1 child, Cynthia; m. Eleanor H. Silver, Oct. 30, 1966; 1 child, Robert. A.B., Cornell U., 1955; LL.B., Harvard U., 1958. Bar: N.Y. 1959, Conn. 1970, Ill. 1973. Assoc. Amster & Levy, N.Y.C., 1958-60; patent atty. Sperry Rand, N.Y.C., 1960-63; chief patent csl. Gen. Time Corp., N.Y.C., 1963-67; ptnr. Altman & Reens, Stamford, Conn., 1967-72; chief patent csl. Baxter-Travenol Labs., Deerfield, Ill., 1972-76; assoc. prof. John Marshall Law Sch., 1976-79, adj. prof., 1979—; of counsel Gerlach, O'Brien & Kleinke, Chgo., 1981-83; ptnr. Laff, Whitesel, Conte & Saret, Chgo., 1983—. Author: Callmann on Unfair Competition, Trademarks & Monopolies, 4th edit., 1981; editor Business Competition Law Adviser, 1983, Construction Law, 1986. Contbr. articles to legal jours. Home: 3005 Manor Dr Northbrook IL 60062 Office: Laff Whitesel et al 401 N Michigan Ave Suite 2000 Chicago IL 60611

ALTMAN, SHELDON, veterinarian; b. Denver, May 15, 1937; s. Sam Bernard and Bessie (Radetsky) A.; B.S. in Biol. Sci., Colo. State U., 1959, D.V.M., 1961; m. Arlene Barbara Heller, Aug. 23, 1959; children—Susan Wendy, Howard William, Eden Debra. With Newmark Animal Hosp., 1961-62, Lockhart Animal Hosp., 1964; founder, operator Universal City Pet Clinic, North Hollywood, Calif, 1965-70, merged with M.S. Animal Hosps., Inc., Burbank, 1970—, v.p., 1970—; dir. vet. research and cons. acupuncture research project, pain control unit UCLA, 1975-80; hon. prof. Chinese Medicine U. Oriental Studies, Sch. Chinese Medicine, Los Angeles; mem. faculty Internat. Vet. Acupuncture Soc. Ctr. for Chinese Medicine. Author: An Introduction to Acupuncture for Animals; mem. editorial adv. bd. Calif. Veterinarian, Internat. Jour. Chinese Medicine; contbr. articles on vet. acupuncture to vet. jours. Bd. dirs. Emek Hebrew Acad. Served with AUS, 1962-64. Mem. AVMA (conv. speaker 1982), So. Calif., Calif. (co-chmn. com. on alternative therapies) vet. med. assns., Am. Animal Hosp. Assn., Am. Veterinarians for Israel (chpt. pres. 1972-73), Assn. Orthodox Jewish Scientists, Internat. Vet. Acupuncture Soc. (dir.), Center for Chinese Medicine, Acad. Vet. Cardiology, Internat. Congress Chinese Medicine, Acupuncture Research Inst., Colo. State U. Alumni Assn., Nat. Assn. Vet. Acupuncture (dir. research), Phi Kappa Phi, Phi Zeta, Beta Beta Beta. Jewish (pres. congregation 70-71, dir. 1964—). Home: 5647 Wilkinson Ave North Hollywood CA 91607 Office: 2723 W Olive St Burbank CA 91505

ALTMAN, WILLIAM KEAN, lawyer; b. San Antonio, Feb. 18, 1944; s. Marion K. and Ruth (Nunnelee) A.; m. Doris E. Johnson, May 29, 1964; children: Brian, Brad, Blake. BBA, Tex. A&M U., 1965, MBA, 1967; JD, U. Tex., 1979. Bar: Tex., U.S. Dist. ct. (no. and ea. dists.) Tex., U.S. Ct. Appeals (5th and 11th cirs.), U.S. Supreme Ct. Prin., owner William K. Altman P.C., Wichita Falls, Tex., 1970—. Mem. ABA, Tex. Bar Assn., Assn. Trial Lawyers Am. (bd. of govs. 1980-83, active coms. and sects.), Tex. Trial Lawyers Assn. (assoc. bd. dirs. 1977-78, bd. dirs. 1978—, active various coms. and sect.). Democrat. Baptist. Office: PO Box 500 Wichita Falls TX 76307-0500

ALTOBELLO, MILDRED FRANCES, realtor; b. West Palm Beach, Fla., Mar. 3, 1953; d. Francis Anthony and Ethel Hamner (Martin) A. BA, U. Ala., 1975; MBA, Samford U., 1977. Ter. mgr. Burroughs Corp., Miami, Fla., 1978-80; mgmt. trainee Coral Gables Fed. Savs. and Loan (Fla.), 1981; realtor-assoc. Keyes Co., Coral Gables, 1981-88; mem. Keyes Million Dollar Sales Club, Keyes Inner Circle, 1986; active Coral Gables Bd. of Realtors (realtor-lawyer com., communications com. 1985—, realtors polit. action com. 1987—), Civic Opera of Palm Beaches, 1969—; chmn. liturgical com. U. of Ala., Tuscaloosa, 1973. Mem. Soc. Profl. Journalists, Women in Communications, Inc., Sunset Jaycees, Coral Gables C. of C. Democrat. Roman Catholic.

ALTON, ANN LESLIE, lawyer; b. Pipestone, Minn., Sept. 10, 1945; d. Howard Robert, Jr. and Camilla Ann (DeMong) Alton; m. Gerald Russell Freeman Sr.; children: Matthew Alton (dec.), Brady Michael Alton. BA Smith Coll., 1967; JD U. Minn., 1970. Bar: Minn. 1970, U.S. Dist. Ct. Minn. 1972, U.S. Supreme Ct. 1981. Asst. county atty., Hennepin County, Mpls., 1970—, felony prosecutor, criminal div., 1970-75, acting chief citizen protection div., 1975-76, chief citizen protection/econ. crime div., 1976-79, chief econ. crime unit, 1979-85, sr. atty. civil div. handling labor and employment, 1985—; instr. Hamline U. Law Sch., St. Paul, 1973-76; adj. prof. law William Mitchell Coll. Law, St. Paul, 1977—; adj. prof. U. Minn. Law Sch., 1978-82; lectr. in field, 1970—; bd. dirs. Pan-O-Gold Realty Co., Alton Realty Co. Vice chmn. bd. dirs. Minn. Program on Victims of Sexual Assault, 1974-76; bd. dirs. Physician's Health Plan, Health Maintenance Orgn., 1976-80, exec. com. 1977-80; mem. legal drug abuse subcom. Gov. Minn. Adv. Com. Drug Abuse, 1972-74; bd. visitors U. Minn. Law Sch., 1979-85; mem. child abuse project coordinating com. Hennepin County Med. Soc., 1982-83, chmn. corp., labor, ins. subcom. 1982. Mem. ABA (criminal law, labor and employment law, civil litigation sects., chmn. criminal law com.), Minn. Bar Assn., Hennepin County Bar Assn. (ethics com. 1973-76, criminal law com. 1973—, vice chmn. 1979-80, unauthorized practice law com. 1977-78, individual rights and responsibilities com. 1977-78, labor and employment law com. 1985—), Nat. Dist. Attys. Assn., Minn. County Attys. Assn., Minn. Trial Lawyers Assn., Am. Judicature Soc., Minn. Women Lawyers, U. Minn. Law Sch. Alumni Assn. (dir. 1979-85). Author articles, pamphlet, manual. Home: 2105 Xanthus Ln Plymouth MN 55447 Office: 2000 Hennepin County Govt Center Minneapolis MN 55487

ALTURA, BURTON MYRON, physiologist, educator; b. N.Y.C., Apr. 9, 1936; s. Barney and Frances (Dorfman) A.; m. Bella Tabak, Dec. 27, 1961; 1 dau., Rachel Allison. B.A., Hofstra U., 1957; M.S., N.Y. U., 1961, Ph.D. (USPHS fellow), 1964. Teaching fellow in biology N.Y. U., 1957-58, 1960-61; instr. exptl. anesthesiology Sch. Medicine, 1964-65, asst. prof., 1965-66; asst. prof. physiology and anesthesiology Albert Einstein Coll. Medicine, N.Y.C., 1967-70; assoc. prof. Albert Einstein Coll. Medicine, 1970-74, vis. prof., 1974-76; prof. physiology SUNY Health Sci Ctr. at Bklyn., Bklyn., 1974—; research fellow Bronx Mcpl. Hosp. Center, 1967-76; mem. spl. study sect. on toxicology Nat. Inst. Environ. Health Scis., 1977-78; mem. Alcohol Biomed. Research Rev. Com., Nat. Inst. Alcohol Abuse and Alcoholism, 1978-83; adj. prof. biology Queens Coll., CUNY, 1983-84; cons. NSF, Nat. Heart, Lung and Blood Inst., CUNY, Miles Inst., Nat. Inst. Drug Abuse, Merck, Sharpe and Dohne, Millipore Corp., Internat. Ctr. Disabled, Upjohn Co., Bayer AG, Ciba-Geigy, Zyma SA., Parke, Davis & Co.; hon. pres. Internat. Symposium on Interactions of Magnesium and Potassium on Cardiac and Vascular Muscle, Montbazon, France, 1984; organizer, condr. symposia; judge Am. Inst. Sci. and Tech., 1984, 85, 86, 88, Jr. Acad. N.Y. Acad. of Scis., 1987; mem. adv. council Nat. Found. for Addictive Drugs, 1986—. Author: Microcirculation, 3 vols., 1977-80, Vascular Endothelium and Basement Membranes, 1980, Pathophysiology of the Reticuloendothelial System, 1981, Ionic Regulation of the Microcirculation, 1982; Handbook of Shock and Trauma, Vol. 1: Basic Science, 1983, Cardiovascular Actions of Anesthetic Agents and Drugs Used in Anesthesia, 1986, Magnesium in Biochemical Processes and Medicine, 1987; editor-in-chief: Physiology and Patho-physiology Series, 1976-81, Microcirculation, 1980-84, Magnesium: Exptl. and Clin. Research, 1981—, Microcirculation, Endothelium and Lymphatics, 1984—; mem. editorial bd.: Jour. Circulatory Shock, 1973-85, Advances in Microcirculation, 1976—, Jour. Cardiovascular Pharmacology, 1977-84, Prostaglandins and Medicine, 1978—, Substance and Alcohol Actions/Misuse, 1979-84, Alcoholism: Clin. and Exptl. Research, 1982—; assoc. editor: Jour. of Artery, 1974—; asso. editor: Microvascular Research, 1978-85, Agents and Actions, 1981—, Biogenic Amines, 1985—, Jour. Am.

Coll. Nutrition, 1982—; contbr. over 500 articles to profl. jours. Recipient Research Career Devel. award USPHS, 1968-72; Silver Medal, Mayor of Paris for furthering French-U.S.A. Sci. Relations, 1984; Medaille Vermeille, French Acad. Medicine, 1984; travel awards NIH, 1968; travel awards Am. Soc. Pharm. and Exptl. Therapeutics, 1969; NIH grantee, 1968—; NIMH grantee, 1974-78; Nat. Inst. Drug Abuse grantee, 1979-83. Fellow Am. Heart Assn. (mem. council on stroke 1973—, council basic sci. 1969—, council on thrombosis 1971—, council on circulation 1978—, council on high blood pressure 1978—, cardiovascular A study sect. 1978-81), Am. Coll. Nutrition, Am. Physiol. Soc. (mem. circulation group 1971—, pub. info. com. 1980-84); mem. Microcirculatory Soc. (past mem. exec. council, mem. nominating com. 1973-74), mem. Soc. Exptl. Biology and Medicine (editorial bd. 1976-83), AAUP, Am. Assn. for Clin. Chemistry, Am. Pub. Health Assn., Am. Chem. Soc. (div. medicinal chemistry), Am. Soc. Pharm. and Exptl. Therapeutics, Endocrine Soc., Harvey Soc., Am. Coll. Toxicology, Research Soc. on Alcoholism, Am. Thoracic Soc., Soc. for Neurosci., Shock Soc. (founder), Am. Fedn. Clin. Research, AAAS, European Conf. Microcirculation, Internat. Anesthesia Research Soc., Fedn. Am. Soc. Exptl. Biology (pub. info. com. 1981-86), Am. Inst. Nutrition, Am. Assn. Pathologists, Internat. Soc. Thrombosis and Haemostasis, Internat. Soc. Biomed. Research on Alcoholism (founding mem.), Internat. Soc. Biorheology, Soc. Environ. Geochemistry and Health, Soc. Neurosci., Reticuloendothelial Soc., Soc. of Parenteral and Enteral Nutrition, Soc. Scholarly Pub., Gerontol. Soc., Internat. Platform Assn., Am. Inst. Biol. Sci., Assn. Gnotobiotics, Am. Microscopical Soc., Am. Soc. Zoologists, Am. Soc. Cell Biology, Am. Soc. Bone and Mineral Research, Am. Soc. Magnesium Research (founder, pres., exec. dir. 1984—), N.Y. Acad. Scis., Am. Public Health Assn., N.Y. Heart Assn., Council Biology Editors, Soc. for Scholarly Pub., Internat. Anesthesia Soc., Internat. Soc. for Hypertension, Am. Soc. Hypertension (founding mem.), Am. Assn. Clin. Chemistry, Am. Med. Writers Assn., Sigma Xi. Office: 450 Clarkson Ave Brooklyn NY 11203

ALUKAL, VARGHESE GEORGE, metallurgical engineer; b. Chengal, India, Jan. 3, 1945; came to U.S., 1967; s. Kunjipaulo and Elizabeth Lizy (Alapat) A.; m. Lyla Chandy, July 11, 1976. B in Tech., Indian Inst. Tech., Madras, 1965; MS, Marquette U., 1969; postgrad., Cornell U., 1969-72; postgrad. in mgmt., Northwestern U., 1988—. Cert. quality engr. Sci. pool officer Nat. Metall. Labs., Jamshedpur, India, 1973-74; metall. engr. Internat. Harvester Corp., Melrose Park, Ill., 1975; quality control mgr. Charles E. Larson & Sons, Chgo., 1976-85, tech. dir., 1985—, also bd. dirs.; lectr. metallurgy Calicut (India) Univ., 1965-67; adj. faculty mem. Triton Coll., River Grove, Ill., 1984-85; instr. Affiliated Ednl. Cons., Harwood Heights, ill., 1985—; cons. metallurgy, 1984—; quality cons., 1981—. Counselor Crossroads Student Ctr. U. Chgo., 1981—. Mem. ASTM, Am. Soc. Metals, Am. Soc. for Non-Destructive Testing, Am. Soc. Quality Control (assoc. dir. Chgo. chpt. 1983—), Mensa. Roman Catholic. Club: Toastmasters (adminstrv. v.p. Park Ridge chpt. 1986-87). Home: 1801 S Courtland Ave Park Ridge IL 60068 Office: Charles E Larson & Sons 2645 N Keeler Ave Chicago IL 60639

ALVA CASTRO, LUIS JUAN, government official; b. Trujillo, Peru; m. Julia Elisa Parodi; children: Julia Elisa, Ana Luisa. Ed. Universidad Nacional de Trujillo, also in Peru fgn. countries. Councellor, exec. for several enterprises; exec. dir. Corporacion de Desarrollo Economico y Social de la Libertad (Corlib); pres. nat. commn. planning of Partido Aprista Peruano, sec. gen. of No. dist. Command Orgn., mem. polit. commn.; dir. various pub. cos. in field of econs.; nat. sec. for electoral technique; prime minister, Peru, 1985-87, minister of economy and fin., 1985-87, second v.p., 1985—. Author: Deuda Externa, un reto para los latinoamericanos; Endeudamiento Externo en el Peru; Con Todos los Peruanos; El Fondo de la Crisis o la Crisis del Fondo; El Futuro Comienza Hoy. Decorated Medalla Gran Kwanghwa (South Korea); La Orden El Sol del Peru; Collar de la Gran Cruz de la Orden Libertador (Argentina). Office: Office of Second Vice Pres, Lima Peru *

ALVAR, MANUEL EZQUERRA, Spanish educator, lexicographer; b. Saragossa, Spain, Sept. 3, 1950; s. Manuel Lòpez Alvar and Elena Marcial Ezquerra; m. Aurora Dominguez Mirõ; children: Aurora, Manuel. D in Spanish Philology with honors, Autonomous U. Madrid, 1974; D in Linguistics, U. Paris, 1976. Asst. tchr. Autonomous U. Madrid, 1975-77; prof. U. La Laguna, Tenerife, Spain, 1977, U. Màlaga, Spain, 1977-79, 1980—; dir. publs. service U. Malaga, Spain, 1977-79, dir. dept. Spanish lang., 1980—; prof. U. Alicante, Spain, 1980; dir. Lexicographical Ctr. Vox (Celex) Publs. Biblograf-Anaya, Màlaga and Barcelona, 1987—; vis. prof. U. Louvain, Belgium, 1985-86, U. Wis., Madison, 1978, 79, 81, U. La Havana, Cuba, 1985, U. Bergamo, Italy, 1987; lectr. internat. univs. Author: Proyecto de Lexicografía Española, 1976; co-author, reviser dictionaries; contbr. to profl. jours. Mem. European Assn. Profs. of Spanish (gen. sec. 1984-87), Assn. Linguistics and Philology Latin Am., Real Academia Española (corr. mem.). Office: U Malaga Campus, Univ de Teatinos, 29071 Malaga Spain

ALVAREZ, LUIS W., physicist; b. San Francisco, June 13, 1911; s. Walter C. and Harriet S. (Smyth) A.; m. Geraldine Smithwick, 1936; children: Walter, Jean; m. Janet L. Landis, 1958; children: Donald and Helen. B.S., U. Chgo., 1932, M.S., 1934, Ph.D., 1936, Sc.D., 1967; Sc.D., Carnegie-Mellon U., 1968, Kenyon Coll., 1969, Notre Dame U., 1976, Ain Shams U., Cairo, 1979, Pa. Coll. Optometry, 1982. Research asso., instr., asst. prof., asso. prof. U. Calif., 1936-45, prof. physics, 1945-78, prof. emeritus, 1978-88; asso. dir. Lawrence Radiation Lab., 1954-59, 75-78; radar research and devel. Mass. Inst. Tech., 1940-43, Los Alamos, 1944-45. Recipient Collier Trophy, 1946; Medal for Merit, 1948; John Scott medal, 1953; Einstein medal, 1961; Nat. Medal of Sci., 1964; Michelson award, 1965; Nobel prize in physics, 1968; Wright prize, 1981; Rockwell medal, 1986; Enrico Fermi award U.S. Energy Dept., 1987; named Calif. Scientist of Year, 1960; named to Nat. Inventors Hall of Fame, 1978. Fellow Am. Phys. Soc. (pres. 1969); mem. Nat. Acad. Scis., Nat. Acad. Engring., Am. Philos. Soc., Am. Acad. Arts and Scis., Phi Beta Kappa, Sigma Xi; asso. mem. Institut D'Egypte. Office: Univ of Calif Dept of Physics Berkeley CA 94720 *Died Aug. 31, 1988.*

ALVAREZ DEL BLANCO, ROBERTO MARCOS, consulting company executive; b. Bolivar, Argentina, Jan. 5, 1949; s. Isidoro Alvarez and Elsa (Eugenia) del Blanco; m. Maria Amelia Salerno, Mar. 26, 1976. BA, U. Buenos Aires, Argentina, 1974; MBA, ESADE, Barcelona, Spain, 1977; D in Econs., U. Barcelona, 1978; post doctoral fellow Bus. Adminstrn., U. Calif., Berkeley, 1979. Internat. mktg. dir. Rovema Packaging Machinery S.A., Barcelona, 1979-81; mng. dir. Sodastream España, S.A., Barcelona, 1981-84; mktg. dir. Oficina Olimpica Barcelona'92, Barcelona, 1984-86; prof. mktg. E.S.A.D.E., Barcelona, 1984—; exec. pres. Eventos Globales, S.A., Barcelona, 1986—. Co-author: Management de la Publicadad: Perspectivas Practicas, 1983, Management Estrategico del Mercads, 1987; contbr. articles to profl. jours. Scholarship Spanish Ministry of Edn., 1976. Mem. Am. Mktg. Assn., European Mktg. Acad., Strategic Mgmt. Soc., European Found. for Mgmt. Devel. Roman Catholic. Lodge: Rotary (Internat. fellow 1978, Paul Harris fellow, 1987). Home: Freixa 38 2, 08021 Barcelona Spain Office: Eventos Globales SA, Calabria 267, Barcelona Spain

ALVAREZ GARDEAZABAL, GUSTAVO, writer; b. Tuluá, Valle, Colombia, Oct. 31, 1945. Letras, U. del Valle, Cali, Colombia, 1970. Author: La Tara Del Papa, 1971, Condores NoEntierran Todos Los Dias, 1972, Dabeiba, 1972, La Boba Y El Buda, 1973, El Bazar De Los Idiotas, 1974, El Titiritero, 1977. Los Mios, 1981, Pepe Botellas, 1985, El Divino, 1986, El Ultimo Gamonal, 1987, Cuentos Del Parque Boyaca, 1979. Alderman, Mcpl. Council of Cali, 1978-82, Tuluá, 1984-86; dep. State Duma, Cali, 1982-84; maj. Tuluá, 1988—. Guggenheim fellow, 1984-85. Mem. Am. Orchid Soc. Home: Aptdo 400, Tulua Colombia

ALVERNAZ, RODRIGO, fraternal society insurance company executive; b. Faial, Azores, Dec. 28, 1936; came to U.S., 1954; ; s. Frank P. and Ana (Leal) A.; m. Jean Bettencourt, May 31, 1958; children: Roderick, Mario, Anina, Gina. Gen. edn., Liceu Passos Manuel, Lisbon, Portugal, 1954; BA in Acctg., Heald Coll., 1958; cert. bus. mgmt., Calif. State U., Hayward, 1980. Acct. United Nat. Life Ins. Soc., Oakland, Calif., 1958-62, asst. sec., agy. supr., 1962-64, asst. sec., treas., 1964-81, asst. v.p., 1970-81, sec., treas., 1981-83, v.p., sec., 1983—; sec. Luso-Am. Fraternal Fedn. div. United Nat. Life, Oakland, 1981—; v.p. Luso-Am. Edn. Found., 1979—. Pres. League Portugese Fraternal Socs. of Calif., 1986; co-chmn. Portugese-Ams. for Statue of Liberty, 1985-86. Recipient Commendation Order of Merit, Portugal, 1987. Mem. No. Calif. Life Ins. Assn., No. Calif. Policyowners' Service Assn. Republican. Roman Catholic. Lodge: Lions (local pres. 1980-81, local treas. 1981-86).

ALVES, CARLOS PEREIRA, surgeon, consultant; b. Oporto, Portugal, Jan. 2, 1942; s. Camilo Alves Pais and Julia Augusta Pereira; m. Zuilda Maria Pereira Alves, Dec. 10, 1982. M.D., Oporto U. 1966. Cons. in gen. surgery Hosp. Civis, Lisbon, Portugal, 1976, in vascular surgery, 1983; fgn. clin. asst. St. Thomas Hosp., London, 1977—, Hopital St. Joseph, Paris, 1979—, Hosp. Salpetriere, Paris, 1981; med. advisor Wellcome Found., Lisbon, 1972—. Contbr. articles to profl. jours. Sec. Gen. Assembly Portuguese Med. Order, 1985; Served with Portuguese Med. Corps, 1968-71. Mem. European Soc. Cardiovascular Surgery, Internat. Union Angiology, Royal Soc. Medicine (fgn.), Portuguese Coll. Surgeons, Soc. Portuguesa Cirurgia Cardiotoracica e Vascular, Soc. Portuguesa de Cirurgia, Soc. Portuguesa Gastroenterologia. Roman Catholic. Club: Gremio Literario. Avocations: sports; tennis; squash; wine collecting. Home: R Rodrigues Sampaio, 96-2 E, 1100 Lisbon Portugal Office: Med Office, R Garret 74 S/L, 1200 Lisbon Portugal

ALVES, JOAQUIM PAREDES, hotel executive; b. Mealhada, Aveiro, Portugal, Dec. 9, 1922; s. Adelino Rodrigues Paredes and Madalena Rosário Alves; m. Gilda Nunes de Abreu, Nov. 19, 1947; children: Luis Miguel, Joana, João. Degree in hotel adminstrn., Cornell U., 1962; student, Inst. Estudios Turisticos, Madrid, 1963. Chief acct. Hotel Avenida, Coimbra, Portugal, 1939-46; gen. mgr Palacio Hotel & Casino, Espinho, Portugal, 1946-50, Hotel Astória, Monfortinho, Portugal, 1950-55, Hotel Embaixador, Lisbon, Portugal, 1955-57; mgr., owner Hotel Eduardo VII, Lisbon, 1957—, Curitiba, Brazil, 1975—; mgr., owner Hotel Continental, Luanda, Angola, 1958—, Hotel turismo, Abrantes, Portugal, 1981—; pres. Best Western Hotels, Portugal, 1986—, Fed. Fortuguesa Skäl Clubs, 1970-72; v.p. Skäl Club Lisbon, 1966-70. Author: Modern Systems of Accounts for Hotels, 1969; editor: Who's Who in Tourism and Hotels in Portugal, 1984; contbr. articles to profl. jours. V.p. Assn. Intercontinental Estudos Turisticos Culturais, Lisbon, 1977-80. Recipient Merit Order of Tourism award Portuguese Govt., 1982. Mem. Portuguese Hotels Dirs. Assn., Internat. Hotels Assn., Portuguese Hotels Assn., Portuguese Travel Agts. Assn., Portuguese Golf Fedn. (treas. 1982-86), ASTA. Roman Catholic. Clubs: Golf (Estoril and Cascais, Portugal), Grémio Literário (Lisbon). Home: Rua D Afonso Henriques, 1590, 2765 Estoril Portugal Office: Eduardo VII Hotels, 5 Ave Fontes P de Melo, 1000 Lisbon Portugal

ALVIAL, GABRIEL, physicist, educator; b. Santiago, Chile, Nov. 8, 1922; s. Francisco and Esther (Caceres) A.; Faculty of Philosophy and Edn., U. Chile, 1946, degree tchr. of math. and physics summa cum laude, 1947, fac. of physics and math. scis. Prof. Extraordinario de Rayos Cosmicos summa cum laude, 1963; m. Elba Luz Collao, Sept. 17, 1948; 1 dau., Francisca Alejandra. Faculty of Philosophy and Edn., prof. phys. chemistry dept. physics U. Chile, 1952-53, chmn., founder Cosmic Ray Center, 1952-58, head dept., 1952-56, mem. faculty phys. and math. scis., head Cosmic Ray Center, 1958-86, prof. physics, 1963-83; mem. faculty basic scis., dept. physics U. Metropolitana Edn. Scis., 1986—; coordinator OAS Multinat. Project of Physics in Chile, 1968-77; pres. Chilean Nuclear Commn., 1971-72. Recipient Al Mejor Estudiante de Fisica, U. Chile, 1946; La Stella della Solidarieta of Italy, 1955; medaglia U. Pisa (Italy), 1955; Guggenheim Found. fellow, 1959; medalla Rectoral, U. Chile, 1977; médaille Société d'Encouragement aux Progrès, 1980. Mem. Academico de Numero of Acad. Sci. of Inst. Chile, Latin Am. Council Cosmic Rays (v.p. 1970-77, pres. 1977-82), World Acad. Art and Sci. Geneva (fellow), N.Y. Acad. Sci. (hon. life). Contbr. articles to profl. jours. Home: 6689 Ave Echenique, Santiago Chile Office: Cosmic Ray Lab, 1314 Santiago Chile

ALVINE, ROBERT, manufacturing company executive; b. Newark, Aug. 25, 1938; s. James C. and Marie Alvine; m. Diane C. Marzulli, May 6, 1961; children: Robert James, Laurie Anne. BS, Rutgers U., 1960; postgrad., Syracuse U., 1968-69, Harvard U., 1972. With Celanese Corp., 1960-77; bus. mgr. Celanese Plastics Co., Newark, 1969-72; dir. mktg. and ops. Celanese Piping Systems and Fabricated Products Co., Hilliard, Ohio, 1972-75; v.p. comml. Celanese Polymer Spltys. Co., Louisville, 1975-77, Uniroyal Inc., 1977-87; dir. strategy planning and bus. devel. Uniroyal-Chem., Naugatuck, Conn., 1977; v.p. corp. planning and devel. Uniroyal Inc., Middlebury, Conn., 1978-79; v.p., gen. mgr. Uniroyal Tire Co., 1979-80; pres. Uniroyal Merchandising Co., 1979-82, Uniroyal Devel. Co., 1980-82; sr. v.p. mergers and acquisitions Uniroyal Inc., 1980-82; group v.p. Engineered Products, Worldwide, 1983-87; pres. Uniroyal Plastics & Power Transmission Cos., 1983-87; also corp. sr. officer responsible for mergers and acquisitions Uniroyal, Inc., 1982-87; and sr. corp. officer and major prin. in mgmt. leverage buy-out of Uniroyal, Inc. 1985; founder, chief exec. officer, chmn. bd. dirs. i-Ten Cap. Corp., i-Ten Capital Corp., founder Aim Capital Group, Woodbridge, Conn., 1987; vice-chmn. Charter Power Systems, Meeting House, Pa., 1988—; prin. Charter House Internat., N.Y.C., 1988—, Uniroyal Holdings, Waterbury, Conn., 1985—; bd. dirs. Wedge Computer, Boston, 1987—. Served with AUS, 1962-68. Honor grad. Southeastern Signal Sch.; named Ky. Col., 1976. Mem. Nat. Assoc. Corp. Dirs., Pres.'s Assn., Am. Inst. Mgmt., Nat. Planning Inst., Assn. for Corp. Growth, N.Am. Planning Soc., Nat. Assn. Corp. Growth, Rubber Mfrs. Assn., Newcomen Soc. Am., Soc. Plastics Industry, Soc. Plastics Engrs. (past dir.), Mfg. Chemists Assn., Nat. Paint and Coatings Assn., Council of Americas. Mem. Ch. of Christ. Clubs: Oaklane Country, Renaissance. Home: 55 N Racebrook Rd Woodbridge CT 06525 Office: i-Ten Mgmt Corp Woodbridge CT 06525

ALWAYE, MOHIADDIN MACKAR, writer; b. Alwaye, Kerala, India, June 1, 1925; s. Mackar Maulavi Aricodath; m. Amina Beevi, Aug. 18, 1957; children: Muneera, Jamal. Studies with Bakiatal Salihat, Madras, India, 1947-49; MA, Al-Azhar U., Cairo, 1953; PhD, Al-Azhar U., Cario, 1971. Prof. Rawdatal Ulum-Ferok, Kerala, India, 1949-50; radio announcer Arabic Unit All India Radio, Delhi, India, 1955-63; prof. Al-Azhar U., Cairo, 1964-72; editor Voice of India Mag. Indian Embassy, Cario, 1972-77; prof Medina U., Medina, Saudi Arabia, 1977-85; Islamic editor Qatar Daily, Al-Khaleej, Alyom, Doha, Qatar, 1985—. Author: Essence of Islam, Contemporary Indian Literature, Code of Preachers, Islamic Call and Its Spread in India, others; contbr. articles to jours. Mem. Islamic Literature Soc., Ernakulam Islamic Soc. (pres. 1987—). Home: Veliyathunad, Alwaye Kerala India Office: Al-Sharq Newspaper, PO Box 3488, Doha Qatar

ALZAIBAG, MUAYED ABDULLAH, cardiologist, consultant; b. Baghdad, Iraq, Nov. 27, 1951; (parents Saudi Arabian citizens); s. Abdullah Abdulaziz and Majida Abdulraouf (Alferra) A.; m. Ayesha Gaynor Kay Parsons, Oct. 3, 1981. MB ChB, Cairo U., 1975. Resident King Abdulaziz U. Hosp., Riyadh, Saudi Arabia, 1976-77, U. Hosp. Wales, Cardiff, 1977-78, Royal Gwent Hosp., Newport, U.K., 1978-80; fellow in cardiology Armed Forces Hosp., Riyadh, Saudi Arabia, 1980-82; fellow in invasive cardiology Loma Linda (Calif.) U., 1982-83; cons. cardiologist and head adult cardiology div. Armed Forces Hosp., Riyadh, Saudi Arabia, 1983—. Fellow Am. Coll. Cardiology, Royal Coll. Physicians of Edinburgh. Office: Armed Forces Hosp, C157 PO Box 7897, Riyadh 11159, Saudi Arabia

AL-ZAMIL, FAISAL SALEH, retail stores executive; b. Alkhobar, Saudi Arabia, Feb. 6, 1955; s. Saleh Abdulaziz Al-Zamil and Taibah (Abhullah) Al-Omran; m. Fawzia Al-Mousa, May 5, 1961; 1 child, Abdullah Ibn Faisal. BS, U. Bridgeport, 1977; MBA, U. Petroleum and Minerals, Dhahran, Saudi Arabia, 1979. Gen. mgr. Zamil Internat., Aklhobar, 1981-85; pres. Al-Zamil Stores, Aklhobar, 1985—. Office: Al-Zamil Stores Corp, PO Box 217, Alkhobar 31952, Saudi Arabia

AMADIO, BARI ANN, metal fabrication executive; b. Phila., Mar. 26, 1949; d. Fred Deutscher and Celena (Lusky) Garber; m. Peter Colby Amadio, June 24, 1973; children: P. Grant, Jamie Blair. BA in Psychology, U. Miami, 1970; diploma in Nursing, Thomas Jefferson U., 1973, Johnston-Willis Sch. Nursing, 1974; BS in Nursing, Northeastern U., 1977; MS in Nursing, Boston U., 1978; JD, U. Bridgeport, 1983. Faculty Johnston-Willis Sch. Nursing, Richmond, Va., 1974-75; staff, charge nurse Mass. Gen. Hosp., Boston, 1975-78; faculty New England Deaconess, Boston, 1978-80, Lankenau Hosp. Sch. of Nursing, Phila., 1980-81; pres. Original Metals, Inc., Phila., 1985—, also bd. dirs.; owner Silver Carousel Antiques, Rochester, Minn. Treas. Women's Assn. Minn. Orch., Rochester, 1986-87, pres., 1987—, newsnotes editor, 1985-87; mem. mayor's coms. All. Am. City Award Com., Rochester, 1984—, Mayor's coms. Entertainment League, Rochester, 1987—; bd. dirs. Rochester Civic League, 1988—. Mem. Am. Soc. Law and Medicine, Zumbro Valley Med. Soc. Aux. (Rochester) (fin. chmn. 1986—, treas. 1988—), Nat. Assn. Female Execs., Nat. Assn. Food Equipment Manufacturers, Friends of Mayowood, Phi Alpha Delta, Sigma Theta Tau. Home: 816 9th Ave SW Rochester MN 55902

AMADO, JORGE, author; b. Bahia, Brazil, Aug. 10, 1912; s. João Amado Faria and Eulalia Leal Amado; lawyer, U. de Brazil, 1935; m. Zelia Gattai, July 14, 1945; children: João Jorge, Paloma. Deputado nacional, 1946-48. Author: Pais do carnaval, 1931; Cacau, 1933; Suor, 1934; Jubiaba, 1935; Mar Morto, 1936; Capitaes da Areia, 1937; ABC de Castro Alves, 1941; Terras do Sem Fim, 1943; São Jorge dos Ilheus, 1944; Bahia de Todos os Santos, 1945; Seara Vermelha, 1946; O Amor do Soldado, 1947; Os subterraneos da liberdade, 1954; Gabriela, Cravo e Canela, 1958; Os velhos marinheiros, 1961; Os pastores da noite, 1964; Doña Flor e seus dois maridos, 1966; Tenda dos milagres, 1969. Tereza Batista Cansada de Guerra, 1972; O Gato Malhadoea Andorinha Sinha, 1976, Tietado Agieste, 1977, Farda Fardao Camisola de Dormir, 1979, A Bolaeo Goleiro, 1984, Tocaia Grandei, 1984; editor Para Todos (cultural periodical), Rio de Janeiro, 1956-59. Recipient Calouste Gulbenkian prize Acad. du Monde Latin, 1971; Stalin Internat. Peace Prize, 1951. Mem. Brazilian Assn. Writers, Brazilian Acad. Letters. Address: Rua Alagoinhas 33, Rio Vermelho-Salvador, Bahia Brazil *

AMADORI CESAR, GUNDELACH, information services company executive; b. Santiago, Chile, Dec. 21, 1956; s. Enrique M. Amadori and Ludmila C. Gundelach; m. Elena Barriga, Dec. 14, 1984; 1 child, Elena Amadori. Diploma in civil and indsl. engring., Catholic U. of Chile, Santiago, 1982. Systems analyst AFP Summa SA, Santiago, 1982-83, chief ops. dept., 1984; project mgr. Sigma SA, Santiago, 1985—. Home: La Es Puela 12540, STGO-10, Santiago Chile Office: Sigma Servicios Informaticos, Huerfanos 863 PO 10, Santiago Chile

AMAN, MOHAMMED MOHAMMED, university dean, library and information science educator; b. Cairo, Jan. 3, 1940; came to U.S., 1963, naturalized, 1975; s. Mohammed Aman and Fathia Ali (al-Maghrabi) Mohammed; m. Mary Jo Parker, Sept. 15, 1972; 1 son, David. B.A., Cairo U., 1961; M.S., Columbia U., 1965; Ph.D., U. Pitts., 1968. Librarian Egyptian Nat. Library, 1961-63, Duquesne U., Pitts., 1966-68; asst. prof. library sci. Pratt Inst., N.Y.C., 1968-69; asst. prof., then assoc. prof. St. John's U., Jamaica, N.Y., 1969-73; prof., dir. div. library and info. sci. St. John's U., 1973-76; prof. library sci., dean Palmer Grad. Library Sch., C.W. Post Center, L.I. U., 1976-79; prof., dean Sch. Library and Info. Sci., U. Wis., Milw., 1979—; cons. for UNESCO, AID and; UNIDO. Author: Librarianship and the Third World, 1976, Cataloging and Classifications of Non-Western Library Material: Issues, Trends and Practices, 1980, Arab Serials and Periodicals: A Subject Bibliography, 1979, On Line Access to Databases (Arabic), 1983, Developing Computer-Based Library Systems (Arabic), 1984, Information Services (Arabic), 1985. Bd. dirs. Awiscon African Relief Effort, Wis. Black Historical Soc./Mus. Mem. ALA (chmn. internat. relations roundtable 1976-77, chmn. internat. relations com. 1984-86), Am. Soc. for Info. Sci. (chmn. spl. interest group in internat. info. issues, internat. relations com.), Am.-Arab Affairs Council (Wis. chpt.), Egyptian-Am. Scholars Assn., Assn. for Library and Info. Sci. Edn. (chmn. internat. relations com. 1983-85), Wis. Library Assn. (chmn. library careers com. 1981-1982) Library Services and Constrn. Act (adv. com. 1986—). Democrat. Moslem. Office: Sch Library and Info Sci Univ Wis Milwaukee WI 53201

AMANO, JUN, surgeon, educator; b. Tokushima, Japan, Sept. 24, 1948; s. Tamotsu and Toyoko A.; M.D., Shinshu U., 1975; Ph.D., Juntendo U., 1980; m. Mieko Takei, July 1986. Resident surg. dept. Juntendo U. Hosp., Tokyo, 1975, mem. staff dept. cardio-thoracic surgery, 1980-83; research fellow Harvard U. Med. Sch., 1983-85; clin. asst. dept. thoracic and cardiovascular surgery Tokyo Med. and Dental U., 1985—. Mem. Internat. Soc. Heart Research, Japanese Assn. Gen. Surgeons, Japanese Assn. Thoracic Surgeons, Japanese Soc. Cardiovascular Surgeons, Japanese Circulation Soc., Japanese Assn. Pediatric Surgeons, Japanese Coll. Angiology. Office: 1-5-45, Yusima, Bunkyo, 113 Tokyo Japan

AMANO, YOSHIFUMI, technical company executive; b. Japan, Nov. 29, 1941; s. Bunzo and Kishiko (Shimizu) A.; m. Naoe Hirosawa, Apr. 28, 1971 (div.); children—Shiho, Yukari; m. Kumi Sekiguchi, Dec. 30, 1985; 1 child, Yoshitaka. M.S. in Electronics, Keio U., Japan, 1967; M.S. in Mgmt., MIT, 1976; Ph.D., Keio U., Japan, 1985. Dep. gen. mgr. Sony Corp., Tokyo, 1976-84; pres., chmn. Dixy Corp., Yokohama, Japan, 1984—. Patentee new plasma display panel. Fellow Soc. Info. Display; mem. Inst. TV Engrs. Japan. Roman Catholic. Avocation: sailing. Home: 19-14 Komachi 2-chome, 248 Kamakura-shi Japan Office: Dixy Corp, 5-5 Katsuradai 1-chome, 227 Midori-ku, Yokohama Japan

AMARAL, MARY ELLEN, lawyer; b. Kenosha, Wis., Aug. 5, 1946; s. Nestor Johnson and Mary Louise (Parker) Thompson; m. Donald Earl Mielke, Apr. 27, 1968 (div. Jan. 1978); m. Charles Patrick Amaral, Aug. 31, 1980; children—Maura Patricia, Brian Patrick. B.A. in Journalism, U. Mich., 1968; postgrad. Temple U., 1968-69; M.S. in Mgmt., Pace U., 1979; J.D., U. Denver, 1973. Bar: Colo. 1974. With Mountain Bell, Denver, 1970-76; with regulatory matters AT&T, N.Y.C., 1976-79, regulatory matters dist. mgr., 1981-83, regional atty. govt. relations, Denver, 1983-87; assoc. Davis, Graham & Stubbs, Denver, 1987—; Senate banking-internat. fin. minority staff mem. Conf. Bd. Congl. Asst., Washington, 1980. Mem. Gotham Bus and Profl. Women (legis. chmn. 1978-80, Outstanding Profl. Woman of Yr. 1982), ABA, Denver Bar Assn., Colo. Bar Assn., Colo. Women's Bar Assn., Alliance Profl. Women. Lodge: Zonta (N.Y. chpt. pres. 1983, Denver chpt. chmn. internat. and community relations com. 1984-86, 2d v.p. membership com. 1986-87). Home: 1725 Fillmore Ct Louisville CO 80027 Office: Davis Graham & Stubbs 370 17th St Suite 4700 Denver CO 80201-0185

AMARULLAH, MUNAWAR, utility company executive, economist; b. Ujungpandang, Indonesia, Sept. 6, 1939; s. Daeng Mamaro Amarullah and Ummi (Salmah) Daeng Bau; m. Ida Zuraida Thaha Karim, Dec. 8, 1963; children: Suhrawardi, Fifie, Nurul, Yayuk. Insinyur, Inst. Tech., Bandung, Indonesia, 1962; MA in Econs., U. Houston, 1981, PhD in Econs., 1983. Registered profl. engr., Indonesia; cert. in mgmt., econs., computer sci. Br. mgr. Indonesia State Electricity Corp., Ujungpandang, Surabaya, 1962-70; with planning div. Indonesia State Electricity Corp., Jakarta, 1970-77, with mgmt. div., 1977-79, sr. staff, 1983—; sr. staff Nat. Planning Bd., Jakarta, 1983—; head faculty U. Mercu Buana, Jakarta, Indonesia, 1987—; lectr. to various univs., 1962—; cons. on pub. utilities, energy and pricing, 1962—; speaker on energy and pub. utilities to various seminars and confs., Indonesia, U.S., and other ASEAN countries, 1974—. Mem. Energy Economists, IEEE. Home: PLN 9 jl, Tebet Barat Dalam X, Jakarta Selatan Indonesia Office: State Electricity Corp jl, Sunan Ngampel Kebayoran, Jakarta Indonesia

AMATANGELO, NICHOLAS S., financial printing company executive; b. Monessen, Pa., Feb. 12, 1935; s. Sylvester and Lucy Amatangelo; m. Kathleen Driscoll, May 3, 1964; children: Amy Kathleen, Holly Megan. BA, Duquesne U., 1957; MBA, U. Pitts., 1958. Indsl. engr. U.S. Steel Co., Pitts., 1959-61; indsl. engr. mgr. Anaconda Co., N.Y.C., 1961-63; product mktg. mgr., Xerox Corp., N.Y.C., 1965-68; dir. mktg. Macmillan Co., N.Y.C., 1968-70; dir. product planning Philco-Ford Corp., Phila., 1970-72; pres. Bowne of San Francisco, Inc., 1972-79; pres. Bowne of Houston, Inc., 1979-86, Bowne of Chgo., Inc., 1982—, Bowne of Detroit, Inc., 1987—; instr. U. Pitts., 1959-61; asst. prof. Westchester Community Coll., N.Y.C., 1961-64, 70-72. Contbr. articles in field to profl. jours. Bd. dirs. San Francisco Boys Club, 1974-79, Boys Towns Italy, 1973-79, Alley Theatre, Houston, 1982-86; mem. pres. council Houston Grand Opera, 1980-86. Served with U.S. Army, 1958-59, 61-62. Mem. Printing Industries Am. (bd. dirs.), Am. Soc. Corp. Secs., Am. Mgmt. Assn.-Pres. Assn., Am. Inst. Indsl. Engrs., Am. Soc. Tng. and Devel. Clubs: Forest, Houston, University (Houston); Executive, Economics (Chgo., Detroit); Olympic (San Francisco). Lodge: Kiwanis. Office: Bowne of Chgo 325 W Ohio St Chicago IL 60610

AMATO, GUILANO, Italian government official; b. May 13, 1938; married; 2 children. LLB, U. Pisa, Italy, 1960; M in Comparative Constitutional Law, Columbia U., 1963. Asst. prof. Italian and comparative constitutional law U. Rome, 1964-69, prof., 1975—; prof. constitutional law U. Perugia, Italy, 1970-74; prof. law U. Florence, Italy, 1974-75; head legis. office Ministry Budget and Econ. Programming, Rome, 1967-68, 73-74; M.P. Italy, Rome, 1983—, under sec. state, 1983, v.p. cabinet ministers treasury, dep. premier, 1987-88, minister of treasury, 1987—. Home: Via A Nibby 3, I-00161 Rome Italy Office: U Rome, Rome Italy *

AMAYA, NAOHIRO, government official; b. Fukui Prefecture, Japan, 1925. Grad., U. Tokyo, 1948. With Ministry of Commerce and Industry (now Ministry of Internat. Trade and Industry), 1948, dir.-gen. Internat. Econ. Affairs Dept. and Internat. Trade Bur., then councillor internat. trade and industry, then dir.-gen. Basic Industries Bur. and dir.-gen. Agy. of Natural Resources and Energy; vice-minister for internat. affairs 1979-81, spl. adviser to minister and adv. Japan Indsl. Policy Research Inst., 1981-84; pres. Japan Econ. Found., 1984; exec. adviser Dentsu Inc., 1987; exec. dir. Dentsu Inst. for Human Studies, 1987—. Office: Dentsu Inc, 11-10 Tsukiji 1-chome, Chuo-ku, Tokyo 104 Japan *

AMAZIGO, JOHN CHUKWUEMEKA, mathematics educator; b. Onitsha, Anambra, Nigeria, Aug. 6, 1939; s. Johnson Ezigbo and Grace Nneabuka (Omaliko) A.; m. Oleatha Ann Craig, Nov. 26, 1965 (div. June 1981); children—John C. Jr., Eric I., Joy I.; m. Uchechukwu Veronica Onubogu, Oct. 1, 1981. B.S., Rensselaer Poly. Inst., 1964; S.M., Harvard U., 1965, Ph.D., 1968. Tutor, Govt. Coll., Ibadan, Nigeria, 1961; research fellow Harvard U., Cambridge, Mass., 1967-68; asst. prof. Rensselaer Poly. Inst., Troy, N.Y., 1968-72, assoc. prof., 1972-78, prof. math., 1978-80; prof. math. U. Nigeria, Nsukka, 1978—, head dept. math., 1978-81, assoc. dean faculty phys. scis., 1980-81, dean, 1981-83; mem. governing council Anambra State U. of Tech. and Inst. of Mgmt. and Tech., 1986—. Author: (with others) Advanced Calculus, English and Spanish edits., 1980 (Book Club selection 1980), Solution Manual Advanced Calculus, 1981; also articles. Research grantee NSF, 1968-78, U.S. Army Research Office, 1977-80; scholar Rensselaer Poly. Inst., 1961-64; grad. fellow Harvard U., 1964-66. Fellow Nigerian Acad. Sci.; mem. Nigerian Math. Soc. (mem. council 1981-83), Soc. for Indsl. and Applied Math., ASME, N.Y. Acad. Sci., Sigma Xi. Club: Lawn Tennis (capt. 1983—) (Nsukka). Avocations: lawn tennis, reading. Office: Math Dept Univ of Nigeria, Nsukka Nigeria

AMBLAT, JOAO, diversified company executive; b. Tangier, Morocco, Apr. 19, 1941; s. Joao Dos Santos Amblat and Maria del Pilar Arquimbau-Romero; m. Nicole Roulet, July 1, 1966; children: Jean-Pascal, Jean Philippe, Sonia. Brevet Enseignment Comml., Coll. Des Orangers, Rabat, Morocco, 1960; Inst. Control de Gestion, Inst. Français des Gestion, Paris, 1974. CPA. Prof. Nat. Edn., Le Blanc, France, 1960-65; controller Air France, Paris, 1965-70; exec. Rhone Poulenc, Paris, 1970—; asst. to chmn. Rhone Poulenc Textile, Paris, 1978-82; dir. control Rhone Poulenc Chems. div., Paris., 1982-85; dir. strategy & control Rhone Poulenc Media, Paris, 1985-87; bd. dirs. Rhone Poulenc Systems, Paris, 1985-87; gen. mgr. Rhone Poulenc Pyral, 1988—. Served to sgt., arty., 1964-65. Home: Allee du Roussillon, Velizy France Office: Rhone Poulenc Group, 25 Quai Paul Doumer, 92000 Paris Courbevoie France

AMBLER, DAVID SAMUEL, account manager; b. Danbury, Conn., Apr. 24, 1954; s. DeAlton St.John (dec.) and Barbara Jane (Blodgett) A.; m. Beverly Lynn Dunn, May 29, 1976; children: Nicole Marie, Jennifer Rebekah, Peter James. BA in Religion and Bus. Adminstrn., Lebanon Valley Coll., Annville, Pa., 1976; postgrad., U. New Haven, Conn., 1983-84; student, Phila. Coll. Textiles and Sci., 1987-88. Lic. realtor N.J. Mgr. Jack's Religious Gift Shop, Salisbury, Md., 1976-78, The Living Word, Danbury, 1978; controller Conn. Appliance Distbrs., Danbury, 1978-82; sr. credit rep. Union Carbide Corp., Danbury, 1982-85; mgr. fin. services accounts Union Carbide Corp., Chgo., 1985-86, Moorestown, N.J., 1986—; fin. analyst Waste Site Rev. Bd. Union Carbide Corp., 1987-88; fin. analyst Waste Site Inspection Consortium, 1987-88. Treas. Bible Study Fellowship, Ridgefield, Conn., 1983-85, Cornerstone Evangelical Free Ch. Washington Twp., 1987-88, Indian Princesses Cree Tribe, 1987-88; asst. treas. Grace Community Ch., Brookfield, Conn., 1984-85; trustee Glen Ellyn (Ill.) Bible Ch., 1986; com. mem. Washington Twp. Young Life, 1988. Republican. Fundamental Evang. Christian. Home: 804 Richmond Dr Washington Twp Sicklerville NJ 08081 Office: Union Carbide Corp 308 Harper Dr Moorestown NJ 08057

AMBORSKI, KRZYSZTOF SLAWOMIR, control systems educator, researcher control systems and systems simulation; b. Lublin, Poland, Aug. 14, 1941; s. Jan and Krystyna (Chwastniewska) A.; m. Joanna Malgorzata Koziol, June 17, 1965; children—Jan, Adam. M.S., Warsaw Tech. U., 1964, D.Sc., 1972; M.A., Warsaw U., 1971. Asst. Warsaw Tech. U., 1964-66, sr. asst., 1966-72, asst. prof., 1973—; ofcl. expert in electronics and computer systems, 1987—; dep. editor-in-chief Przeglad Elektrotechniczny, Warsaw, 1974-78. Author: Exercises in Control Systems (ministry award 1972), 1971, Control Theory in Exercises (ministry award 1979), 1978, Control Theory-A Programmed Approach, 1987; also articles. Treas. Warsaw Sailing Assn., 1970-76; active Polish Youth Hostel Assn., 1965—. Mem. Am. Math. Soc., Polish Soc. Theoretical and Applied Electrotechnics, Assn. Polish Elec. Engrs., Polish Yachting Assn. (sec. capts. commn. 1978-80, pres. Disciplinary Attys. 1987—). Roman Catholic. Clubs: Acad. Sailing (officer 1960-63), Yacht of Warsaw Tech. U. (officer 1968—). Avocations: sailing, ocean-going yacht master 1977—; skiing. Home: Madalinskiego 4A M5, 02 513 Warsaw Poland Office: Warsaw Tech Univ, Koszykowa 75, 00-662 Warsaw Poland

AMBROSETTI, ALFREDO, mgmt. cons.; b. Varese, Italy, June 25, 1931; s. Antonio and Jolanda (DeMattei) A.; grad. in econs. U. Cattolica, Milan, 1955; postgrad. in mgmt. various Am. univs.; m. Maria Conte, July 29, 1970; children—Chiara, Antonio. Mgr. EDP and orgn. dept. Edison Co., Milan, 1957-65; pres. Studio Ambrosetti, Milan, 1965—; dir. Marzotto Textile Group, Safilo Corp., Bulgheroni-Lindt, Sic-Mazzucchelli, Internat. Studies and Services, Perform, Phonema, Proper Ratio, PAR, SA-Mark Synopsis, Tecnos, Ambrosetti Cons. Group, London, Ambrosettie Europe-London, Ambrosetti Iberica-Madrid and Bilbao, Ambrosetti Internat. London, Ambrosetti Italia, Barry Ambrosetti & Assoc., Los Angeles. Strategic Mgmt. Soc. Served wotj artu. Italian Army, 1955-57. Club: Freccia Alata. Lodge: Rotary. Contbr. articles to profl. jous. Home: 134 Via Ciro Menotti, Varese 21100 Italy Office: Via degli Omenoni, 2 Milan 20121 Italy

AMBUHL, FRANK JERROLD, psychotherapist; b. Toronto, Ont., Can., Apr. 27, 1925 (parents U.S. citizens); s. Frank Frederick and Martha Lillian (Sasser) A.; m. Susan Tandy Durrett, Sept. 20, 1960; children: Elizabeth, Dan, Frank, Donald, Robert, Susanne, Tandy, Martha, Paul. BA in Sci., U. Toronto, 1952; MBA, Harvard U., 1954; MDiv, Ch. Div. Sch., Berkeley, Calif., 1968; DMin, Austin Presbyn. Sem., 1981. Lic. profl. counselor, Tex.; ordained priest Episcopal Ch., 1968. Vice pres. ops. Adminstrn. Services Internat., Monaco, 1959-63; assoc. rector St. Paul's Ch., Lubbock, Tex., 1968-70; priest-in-charge St. Stephen's Ch., Sweetwater, Tex., 1970-72, Holy Cross Episc. Ch., San Antonio, 1972-82; pvt. practice psychotherapy, San Antonio, 1980—; dir. counseling St. Mark's Episc. Ch., San Antonio, 1982—. Author: Enjoying Being Together, 1985; also newspaper articles, 1970—. Fellow Am. Assn. Pastoral Counselors; mem. Internat. Transactional Analysis Assn. (clin.), Am. Assn. Marriage and Family Therapists (clin.), Am. Assn. Sex Educators, Counselors, and Therapists. Republican. Club: Torch (San Antonio). Lodge: Masons. Avocations: photography, making reproductions of flintlock rifles and pistols, fishing, hunting, swimming. Home: 342 Maplewood San Antonio TX 78216 Office: 3030 Nacogdoches Suite 208 San Antonio TX 78217

AMBYJÖRNSSON, RONNY, humanities educator; b. Göteborg, Sweden, Mar. 21, 1936; s. Evert Ambyjornsson and Alice Andersson; m. Gunila Falklind (div. 1972); 1 child, Ola; m. Lilian Levin, Mar. 14, 1973; children: Fanny, Siri, Nadja, Liv. PhD, U. Göteborg, 1974. Lectr. U. Göteborg, 1965-70; asst. prof. U. Umeå, Sweden, 1970-81, prof., 1981—, also head dept. history of ideas and sci.; mem. Swedish Fund for Research in Humanities and Social Scis. Author books on history of ideas, children's books, dramatical works. Recipient Swedish Acad. award, 1978, many others for sci. works. Home: Naset 2107, 910 31 Tavelsjo Sweden Office: U Umea, 901 82 Umea Sweden

AMELING, ELLY, soprano; b. Rotterdam, Netherlands, Feb. 8, 1938; d. Dirk and Aleida (Zikking) A.; m. Arnold W. Belder, Nov. 6, 1964. Student, Conservatory of Music, The Hague, Netherlands; hon. degree, U.B.C., Vancouver, Can., Westminster Choir Coll., Princeton, N.J. Debut, Victoria Hall, Geneva, Switzerlands; numerous solo recitals, also with orchs. throughout world, rec. artist, Philips, CBS, Decca London, EMI Angel, RCA, Odeon, Harmonia Mundi, Peters Internat. and, Vanguard records. Decorated Order Oranje Nassau Netherlands; recipient preis der Deutschen Schallplattenkritic; Grand prix du Disque. Office: care Sheldon Soffer Mgmt 130 W 56th St New York NY 10019 *

AMEN, IRVING, artist; b. N.Y.C., July 25, 1918; s. Benjamin and Bessie (Glusack) A.; m. Dora Beck, May 21, 1941. Student, Pratt Inst., N.Y.C., 1933-35, Art Students League, N.Y.C., 1946-48, Academie de la Grande Chaumiere, Paris, France, 1949-50. Tchr. Pratt Inst., 1957, 58, U. Notre Dame, 1962. One man shows, N.Y.C., San Francisco, Denver, Washington, Louisville, Detroit, Albuquerque, Cleve., Phila., Memphis, Salt Lake City, numerous other cities in, U.S., also in, Jerusalem, Israel, rep. permanent collections, Met. Mus. Art, Mus. Modern Art, Library of Congress, Smithsonian Instn., Bibliotheque Nationale, Paris, Bibliotheque Royale, Brussels, Belgium, Bezalel Nat. Mus., Jerusalem, Victoria and Albert Mus., London, Eng., Albertina Mus., Vienna, Austria, Stadtische Mus., Wilberfeld, Germany, N.Y. Pub. Library, Phila. Mus. Art, Boston Mus. Fine Art, Balt. Mus. Art, Cambridge (Mass.) Pub. Library, Cin. Mus. Art, de Cordova and Dana Mus., Lincoln, Mass., numerous others; designer peace medal to commemorate end of Vietnam War, illus., Gilgamesh for Ltd. Edits. Club; designer stained glass windows depicting 12 Tribes of, Israel, Agudas Achim Synagogue, Columbus, Ohio. Served with USAAF, 1942-45. Mem. Artists Equity (dir.), Soc. Am. Graphic Artists (dir.), Internat. Inst. Arts and Letters, Internat. Soc. Wood Engravers, Am. Color Print Soc., Audubon Artists, Boston Printmakers, L'Accademia Fiorentina delle arti del disegno Florence (hon.). Address: 90 SW 12th Terr Boca Raton FL 33486

AMEN, ROBERT ANTHONY, investor and corporate relations consultant; b. N.Y.C., June 7, 1937; s. Louis Joseph and Angela Amen; children—Brian, Allison. Vice pres. mktg. and communications Combustion Engring., Inc., Stamford, Conn., 1969-75; v.p. corp. relations Gulf and Western Inc., N.Y.C., 1975-77, Norton Simon Inc., N.Y.C., 1977-78; mng. dir. D.F. King & Co., Inc., N.Y.C., 1978-80; pres. Robert Amen & Assocs., Inc., Greenwich, Conn., 1980—. Mem. Nat. Investor Relations Inst. (chmn., chief exec. officer), N.Y. Soc. Security Analysts. Home: 337 North St Greenwich CT 06830 Office: Robert Amen & Assocs Inc Melrose Sq Greenwich CT 06830

AMENTA, PETER SEBASTIAN, anatomist, researcher; b. Cromwell, Conn., Mar. 26, 1927; s. Peter and Mary (DeMauro) A.; m. Rose Phyllis Russo, June 20, 1953; children: Mary Vincenza, Rosemarie. Student, Conn. Wesleyan U., 1947-49; B.S., Fairfield U., 1952; M.S., Marquette U., 1954; Ph.D., U. Chgo., 1958. Undergrad. asst. Fairfield U., 1949-52; grad. asst. Marquette U., 1952-54, U. Chgo., 1955-58; instr., ind. investigator Marine Biol. Lab., Woods Hole, Mass., summer 1956; instr. anatomy Hahnemann Med. Coll., 1958-60, asst. prof. anatomy, 1960-63, asso. prof., 1963-71, prof., 1971—, acting chmn. dept., 1973-75, chmn. dept., 1975—; head microscopic anatomy, 1968-75, treas., exec. faculty, 1970-73, dir. div. electron microscopy, 1970-75; vis. prof. cytology Cambridge U., 1962, Rome U., 1966, 76, Estacao Agronomica National, Oeiras, Portugal, 1970, Edinburg (Scotland) U., 1972, Catholic U., Rome, 1984, U. Ark., 1980, U. Padoua, Italy, 1987; instr. Trenton Diocese High Sch. Religion, 1967-72; lectr. N.J. Right to Life Com., 1969-73, Am. Cancer Soc., 1969—; Continuing Edn. Program, Roxborough Hosp., Phila., 1970; pres. Humanity Gifts Registry, U. Pa., 1976-81. Author: Histology and Embryology Review, 1977, 2d edit., 1983, Review of Medical Histology, 1977, Histology, 4th edit., 1989, Histology and Human Microanatomy, 5th edit., 1987. Twp. chmn. Burlington County Juvenile Conf. Com., 1967-70; mem. Trenton Diocesan Pastoral Council, 1968-73, vice-chmn., 1970-72; dir. St. Joan of Arc Choir; mem. S. Jersey String Band. Served with AUS, 1946-47. Named Man of Year, Fairfield U., 1962; Distinguished Alumnus, Am. Jesuit U., 1967. Fellow AAAS; mem. Am. Assn. Anatomists, Assn. Anatomy Chairmen, Albertus Magnus Guild of Catholic Scientists, AMA, N.Y. Acad. Scis., Am. Inst. Biol. Scis., Tissue Culture Assn., Am. Soc. Photobiology, Internat. Congress Photobiology, Am. Soc. Zoologists, N.Y Acad. Sci., Hahnemann Alumni Assn. (hon.), Sigma Xi, Phi Sigma. Office: Hahnemann U Dept Anatomy MS #408 Broad and Vine Philadelphia PA 19102

AMER, MAGID HASHIM, physician; b. Cario, June 5, 1941; came to U.S. 1968; s. Hashim and Zeinab (Iskander) A.; m. Sabah El Sayed Shehata, Mar. 12, 1973; children—Sophi, Mona, Hoda. M.B.B.Ch., Cairo U. Med. Sch., 1963. Rotating intern Cairo U. Hosp., 1964-65; resident internal medicine Worcester City Hosp., Mass., 1971-73, Lemuel Shattuck Hosp., Boston, 1973-74; fellow med. oncology Wayne State U., Detroit, 1974-76, asst. prof., 1977-78; cons. oncologist King Faisal Specialist Hosp., Riyadh, Saudi Arabia, 1978-84, head div. med. Oncology, 1984—, chmn. med. ethics com., 1986—. Contbr. articles to profl. jours. Fellow Royal Coll. Physicians Can., ACP, Royal Coll. Surgeons Edinburgh; mem. Am. Soc. Clin. Oncology, Am. Assn. Cancer Research, AAAS. Muslim. Address: King Faisal Specialist Hosp, PO Box 3354, Riyadh 11211, Saudi Arabia

AMES, JOHN LEWIS, lawyer; b. Norfolk, Va., July 15, 1912; s. Harry Lee and Catherine I. (Betty) A.; m. Margaret Kilbon, Apr. 8, 1939; children—Margaret Lee, John Lewis. A.B., Randolph-Macon Coll., 1933; LL.B., U. Richmond (Va.), 1937; postgrad. NYU Law Sch., 1939-40. Bar: Va. 1936, N.Y. 1940. Mem. tax div. Home Life Ins. Co., N.Y.C., 1937-38; trial atty. Tanner, Sillocks & Friend, N.Y.C., 1938-41; house counsel Ruthrauff & Ryan, Inc., N.Y.C., 1941-42, house counsel and asst. to pres., 1945-48, sec., counsel, 1948-50, v.p., sec., 1950-55, v.p., sec., treas., 1955-57, also dir.; v.p., sec. Erwin, Wassey, Ruthrauff & Ryan, Inc., 1957-59; asst. dir. bus. affairs CBS TV Network, Inc., N.Y.C., 1959-62; v.p., sec., treas. Kudner Agy., Inc., 1962-65, also dir.; sr. v.p. adminstrn. and fin. West, Weir & Bartel, Inc., N.Y.C., 1966, exec. v.p., dir., until 1968; v.p., sec. Lennen & Newell, Inc., 1968-73; v.p. bus. and legal affairs Dancer-Fitzgerald-Sample, Inc., 1973-83, legal cons. Saatchi & Saatchi DFS Inc., 1983—; dir. Carroll Products, Inc.; spl. agt. FBI, Washington and N.Y.C., 1942-45; spl. dep. atty. gen. N.Y. State, 1946-48; mem. Nassau County N.Y. Crime Commn., 1973-83. Trustee, Randolph-Macon Coll., 1955-85, trustee emeritus, 1985—. Mem. Massapequa Bd. Edn., 1952-79, pres., 1957-78; past pres. Nassau-Suffolk Sch. Bds. Assn. Past chmn. trustees Am. Assn. Advt. Agencies Group Ins. Mem. N.Y. County Lawyers Assn., Am. Arbitration Assn. (mem. nat. panel), Soc. Former Spl. Agts. FBI (past nat. sec.), Alumni Soc. Randolph-Macon Coll. (past pres.), Phi Kappa Sigma, Omicron Delta Kappa, Tau Kappa Alpha. Methodist. Club: Indian Creek Yacht and Country (Kilmarnock, Va.). Home: PO Box 727 White Stone VA 22578 Office: 375 Hudson St New York NY 10014-0036

AMES, SANDRA PATIENCE, sales office executive; b. Quincy, Calif., May 23, 1947; d. Bruce Ray Richards and Margaret Elizabeth (Steiner) Richards Johnson; m. Martin P.M. Bettenhausen, Dec. 10, 1965 (div. 1972); m. Thomas William Ames, Nov. 28, 1975. Student Yuba City Jr. Coll., 1965-66. Sales corr. Nat. Can Corp. (now known as Am. Nat. Can Co.), Seattle, 1974-76, Lehigh Valley, Pa., 1976-79, nat. account sales corr., Chgo., 1979-81, dist. sales office mgr., 1981-82, sales analyst I, Oakbrook, Ill., 1982-84, regional sales office mgr., 1984-86; mgr. regional sales office, Oakbrook, 1987—. Mem. Nat. Assn. Female Execs. Republican. Office: Am Nat Can Corp 915 Harger Rd Oak Brook IL 60521

AMEZCUA, CHARLIE ANTHONY, counselor, educator; b. Los Angeles, Sept. 1, 1928; s. Carlos and Inez (Nunez) A.; B.A., UCLA, 1958; M.S., Calif. State U., Los Angeles, 1961; m. Kathleen Joyce Greene, Mar. 7, 1964; children—Colleen Alvita, Charles Anthony. Student psychologist Rancho Los Amigos Hosp., Downey, Calif., 1959-60; instr. in psychology East Los Angeles Coll., 1962-72, asst. prof. counseling, 1972-74, assoc. prof. counseling, 1974—, prof. psychology, 1980—, spl. edn. counselor, 1981—, coordinator vet. affairs, 1972—; personnel asst. Los Angeles City Sch. Dist., 1963-64; counselor Youth Tng. and Employment Project, Los Angeles, 1965-66, counseling supr., 1966, project dir., 1966-67; counseling psychologist VA, Los Angeles, 1967-70; dir. Head Start, Los Angeles County Econ. and Youth Opportunities Agy., 1970-71; bd. dirs. Tng. and Research Found., Child and Family Resources Centers; lectr. counselor edn. Calif. State U., Los Angeles; guest lectr. John F. Kennedy U., 1987—. Mem. Calif. Gov.'s Adv. Com. on Children and Youth, 1966-67; judge blue ribbon panel Nat. Acad. TV Arts and Scis., 1966-76. Served with USN, 1948-52; Korea; cert. community coll. counselor, supr.-adminstrn., jr. coll. teaching in psychology. Mem. Am. Psychol. Assn., Calif. State Psychol. Assn., Assn. Chicano Educators, Calif. Assn. Post-Secondary Educators of the Disabled, Nat. Assn. Vets. Program Adminstrs., Western Psychol. Assn. Democrat. Home: 8348 Fable Ave Canoga Park CA 91304 Office: East Los Angeles Coll 1301 Brooklyn Ave Monterey Park CA 91754

AMIR-MOEZ, ALI REZA, mathematician, educator; b. Teheran, Iran, Apr. 7, 1919; s. Mohammad and Fatema (Gorgestani) A.-M.; B.A., U. Teheran, 1942; M.A., U. Calif. at Los Angeles, 1951, Ph.D., 1955. Came to U.S., 1947, naturalized, 1961. Instr. math. Teheran Tech. Coll., 1942-46; asst. prof. math. U. Idaho, 1955-56, Queens Coll., N.Y.C., 1956-60, Purdue U., 1960-61; asso. prof. U. Fla., Gainesville, 1961-63; prof. math. Clarkson Coll., Potsdam, N.Y., 1963-65, Tex. Tech U., Lubbock, 1965—. Author: Elements of Linear Space, 1961; (play) Kaleeheh & Demneh, 1962; Three Persian Tales, 1961, Matrix Techniques Trigonometry and Analytic Geometry, 1964; Mathematics and String Figures, 1966; Classes Residues et Figures ovec Ficelle, 1968; Extreme Properties of Linear Transformations and Geometry in Unitary Spaces, 1971; Elements of Multilinear Algebra, 1971; Linear Algebra of the Plane, 1973; contbr. articles to math. jours. on proper and singular values of linear operators and matrices. Served to 2d lt. Persian Army, 1936-38. Decorated Honor emblem Persian Royal Ct., medal Pro Mundi Beneficio Academia Brasileira de Ciencias Humanas. Mem. Am. Math. Soc., Math. Assn. Am., Sigma Xi, Pi Mu Epsilon. Office: Tex Tech U Dept Math Lubbock TX 79409

AMIS, KINGSLEY, novelist; b. Apr. 16, 1922; s. William Robert and Rosa A.; m. Hilary Ann Bardwell (div. 1965); 3 children; m. Elizabeth Jane Howard, 1965 (div. 1983). Ed., City of London Sch., St. John's, Oxford. Lectr. English U. Coll., Swansea, 1949-61; vis. fellow creative writing Princeton, 1958-59; fellow in English Peterhouse, Cambridge U., Eng., 1961-63. Author: verse A Frame of Mind, 1953, Lucky Jim, 1954; filmed, 1957, That Uncertain Feeling, 1955; filmed as Only Two Can Play, 1961; verse A Case of Samples, 1956, I Like it Here, 1958, Take a Girl Like You, 1960; non-fiction New Maps of Hell, 1960, My Enemy's Enemy, 1962, One Fat Englishman, 1963, The James Bond Dossier, 1965, (with Robert Conquest) The Egyptologists, 1965, The Anti-Death League, 1966, A Look Round the Estate; verse, 1967, I Want It Now, 1968, The Green Man, 1969; What Became of Jane Austen, 1970, Girl, 20, 1971, On Drink, 1972, The Riverside Villas Murder, 1973, Ending Up, 1974, Rudyard Kipling and his World, 1975, The Alteration, 1976, Jake's Thing, 1978, Collected Poems, 1979, Russian Hide-and-Seek, 1980, Stanley and the Women, 1984, The Old Devils, 1986 (Booker prize), Difficulties With Girls, 1988; collected Short Stories, 1980; editor: The New Oxford Book of Light Verse, 1978, The Faber Popular Reciter, 1978, The Golden Age of Science Fiction, 1981, Amis Anthology, 1988; contbr. to pubs. Served with Army, 1942-45. Office: care of Jonathan Clowes & Co, 22 Prince Albert Rd, London NW1 7ST, England

AMISSAH, JOHN KODWO, archbishop; b. Elmina, Ghana, Nov. 27, 1922; s. John Bentil and Mary Efua (Busumafi) A. JCD, Pontifical Urban U., Rome, 1954; DD honoris causa, LLD honoris causa, U. Cape Coast, Ghana, 1972. Asst. priest Sekondi (Ghana) Parish, 1950; tchr. St. Teresa's Minor Sem., Amisano, Elmina, Ghana, 1950-51, sr. Latin master, lectr. in canon law, 1954-57; aux. bishop Archdiocese of Cape Coast, 1957-59, archbishop, 1959—. Author: Fante Funeral Eulogy. Mem. Council of State, Accra, Ghana, 1969-72, Ghana Edn., Service Council, Accra, 1973-77. Recipient Grand medal Govt. of Ghana, 1975. Mem. Canon Law Soc. Am. Address: care Archbishop's House, PO Box 112, 52A/2 Elmina Rd, Cape Coast Central, Ghana

AMLADI, PRASAD GANESH, management consulting executive, health care consultant, researcher; b. Mudhol, India, Sept. 12, 1941; came to U.S., 1967, naturalized, 1968; s. Ganesh L. and Sundari G. Amladi; m. Chitra G. Panje, Dec. 20, 1970; children—Amita, Amol. B.Tech. with honors, Indian Inst. Tech., Bombay, 1963; M.S., Stanford U., 1968; M.B.A. with high distinction U. Mich., 1975. Sr. research engr. Ford Motor Co., Dearborn, Mich., 1968-75; mgr. strategic planning Mich. Consol. Gas Co., Detroit, 1975-78; mgr. planning services The Resources Group, Bloomfield Hills, Mich., 1978-80; project mgr., sr. cons. Mediflex Systems Corp., Bloomfield Hills, 1980-85; mgr. strategic planning services Mersco Corp., Bloomfield Hills, 1985-86, mgr. corp. planning and research Diversified Techs., Inc., New Hudson, Mich., 1986—. Author numerous research papers. Recipient Kodama Meml. Gold medal, 1957; India Merit scholar Govt. of India, 1959-63, K.C. Mahindra scholar, 1967, R.D. Sethna Grad. scholar, 1968. Mem. Inst. Indsl. Engrs. (sr.), N.Am. Soc. Corp. Planning, Economic Club Detroit, Beta Gamma Sigma. Office: Blue Cross & Blue Shield of Mich 600 E Lafayette Detroit MI 48226

AMMAR, RAYMOND GEORGE, physicist, educator; b. Kingston, Jamaica, July 15, 1932; came to U.S., 1961, naturalized, 1965; s. Elias George and Nellie (Khaleel) A.; m. Carroll Ikerd, June 17, 1961; children—Elizabeth, Robert, David. A.B., Harvard U., 1953; PhD., U. Chgo., 1959. Research assoc. Enrico Fermi Inst., U. Chgo., 1959-60; asst. prof. physics Northwestern U., Evanston, Ill., 1960-64; assoc. prof. Northwestern U., 1964-69; prof. physics U. Kans., Lawrence, 1969—; (on sabbatical leave Fermilab and Deutsches Elektronen Synchrotron, 1984-85); cons. Argonne (Ill.) Nat. Lab., 1965-69, vis. scientist, 1971-72; vis. scientist Fermilab, Batavia, Ill., summers 1976-81, Deutsches Elektronen Synchrotron, Hamburg, Fed. Republic Germany, summers 1982-87; project dir. NSF grant for research in high energy physics, 1962—. Contbr. articles to sci. jours. Fellow Am. Phys. Soc.; mem. AAUP. Home: 1651 Hillcrest Rd Lawrence KS 66044 Office: U Kans Dept Physics Lawrence KS 66045

AMMARI, NABIH AYOUB, high technology executive, consultant; b. Amman, Jordan, Dec. 18, 1933; s. Ayoub Awad and Hana (Nimer) A.; m. Mary Dalia Mazelis, Mar. 23, 1967; children—Moneef Juri, Anna Raja'a. B.A., Oklahoma City U., 1958, B.S., 1960; M.S., East Tex. State U., 1974, Ed.D., 1976. Analytical chemist Okla. State Bd. Agr., Oklahoma City, 1957-60; research chemist C.P. Hall Co. Ill., Chgo., 1960-65, Darling & Co., Chgo., 1965-70, Anderson-Clayton Co., Sherman, Tex., 1970-72; gen. mgr. The Perkin-Elmer Corp., Norwalk, Conn., 1977—, gen. mgr. Middle East affairs, 1977-87, cons., 1987—. Recipient Pres. award The Perkin-Elmer Corp., Norwalk, 1981, 85. Mem. Am. Chem. Soc. Mem. Eastern Orthodox Ch. Home and Office: PO Box 5329, Amman Jordan

AMNUAY VIRAVAN, bank executive; b. 1932. B. Commerce, Chulalongkorn U., Thailand, 1952; MBA, U. Mich., 1954, MA in Econs., 1957, PhD in Bus. Adminstrn., 1958. Econ. advisor to Prime Minister of Thailand; dir.-gen. Customs Dept.; permanent sec. fin. Govt. of Thailand, minister fin.; chmn. exec. bd. Bangkok Bank Ltd., 1984—; chmn. Saha-Union Group; bd. dirs. Asian Pacific Banking Council; gov. Asian Inst. Mgmt. Mem. Asian Bankers Assn. (chmn.). Office: Bangkok Bank Ltd, POB 95, 333 Silom Rd, Bangkok 10500, Thailand *

AMOLOCHITIS, GEORGE, sales executive; b. Athens, Greece, Feb. 6, 1951; s. Emmanuel and Dimitra (Paraskevopoulou) A.; m. Marguerite Gabrielian, Sept. 27, 1979; children: Emmanouil, Natalia. M of Chemistry, U. Athens, 1981, M of Computer Sci., 1985. Tech. chemist BASF A.G., Ludwigshafen, 1978; wine chemist Schaan Vinimex, 1981-82; product specialist Bacacos S.A., Athens, 1983-85; sales support exec. Hewlett-Packard S.A., Athens, 1985—. Mem. Assn. Greek Chemists, Greek Stats. Inst., Hellenic Assn. Ops. Research. Office: Hewlett-Packard SA, Rue Du Bois Du Lan 7, PO Box 364, Geneva Switzerland

AMOS, CHARLES CLINTON, insurance company executive; b. Tucson, Sept. 3, 1940; s. Charles Cliff and Lucille Elizabeth (Pierce) A.; m. Joan Marie LaBelle, Feb.2, 1962; 1 child, Jonathan Ashley. Student, N.Mex. Mil. Inst., 1955-58, Boston U., 1969-70. CPCU. Salesman and field sales mgr. Employers Ins. Co. of Wausau, Pitts. and Belmont, Mass., 1965-69; pres., chief exec. officer Henry J. LeBianc Ins. Agy., Inc., Fitchburg, Mass., 1969-

74, Aanco Underwriters, Inc., St. Petersburg, Fla., 1972—, Aanco Ins. Services, Inc., Culver City, Calif., 1983-87; pres., chief exec. officer Pass-A-Grille Fishery, Inc., St. Petersburg, Fla., 1981—, Countryside Insurors, Inc., St. Petersburg, 1983-85; pres. Latat Devel. Corp., 1985—, Lanax Constrn., Inc., 1985—, Gulfport Mini-storage Inc., 1986—; chmn. Flagship Mortgage Corp., Culver City, 1985-87; sec. treas. Blue Marlin Inc., Clearwater, Fla., 1982-85, Cruising World Inc., St. Petersburg, 1983-85; v.p., treas. Ins. Premium Acceptance Corp. Active Pinellas Assn. Retarded Children, Pinellas County Com. of 100, Fla. Gulf Coast Symphony; commr., chmn. Pinellas County Housing Authority, 1975-79. Served with security agy. U.S. Army, 1960-63. Named Agt. of Yr, Travelers Ins. Co., 1981, Nat. Sales Leader, Aetna Life Ins. Co., 1978; recipient other sales awards. Mem. Soc. CPCU's, Ind. Agts. Assn., Sales and Mktg. Execs., Kappa Alpha, Hon. Order Ky. Cols. Democrat. Baptist. Lodge: Rotary. Home: 300 Rafael Blvd NE Saint Petersburg FL 33704 Office: Aanco Undewriters Inc 10033 9th St N Saint Petersburg FL 33702

AMOS, FRANCIS JOHN CLARKE, academic administrator; b. London, Sept. 10, 1924; s. Frank and Alice Mary (Clarke) A.; m. Geraldine Mercy Sutton; children: Zephyr Lucie, Gideon John. Diploma in architecture, London Poly., 1951; diploma in town planning, Sch. Planning, London, 1952; BSc, London Sch. Econs., 1955. Architect Harlow New Town Devel. Corp., Essex, Eng., 1951; urban planner London County Council, 1952-53; regional planning officer Ministry Housing and Local Govt., London, 1957-59, 61-62; gen. tech. adviser Govt. Ethiopia, 1959-61; city planning officer Liverpool City Council, Merseyside, 1962-73; chief. exec. Birmingham City Council, West Midlands, 1973-77; sr. fellow U. Birmingham, West Midlands, 1977—; cons. various internat. banks and govts., 1977—; commr. London and Metropolitan Govt. Staff Commn., 1983-86; asst. commr. Local Govt. Boundary Commn., 1987—. Mem. Exec. Com. Action Resource Ctr., 1976-86, Nuffield Inquiry into Town and Country Planning, 1984-87; trustee Community Projects Found., 1978—. Served to capt. Indian Army, 1942-47. Named Comdr. British Empire, Her Majesty the Queen. Mem. Royal Inst. British Architects, Royal Town Planning Inst. (pres. 1971-72, hon. sec. 1979—). Home: 20 Westfield Rd, Edgbaston, Birmingham B15 3QG, England Office: ILGS, U Birmingham, JG Smith Bldg, PO Box 363, Birmingham B15 2TT, England

AMOS, JOAN MARIE, insurance agency executive; b. Leominster, Mass., Nov. 22, 1935; d. Louis Adelard and Cecelia Irene (Lamoreux) LaBelle; m. Charles Clinton Amos, Feb. 2, 1962; 1 child, Jonathan Ashley. Cert. in Acctg., LaSalle U., Chgo., 1968; charter property and casualty underwriting courses Boston U., 1968-69. Sec., treas. Henry Leblanc Inc., Fitchburg, Mass., 1969-74, Marsolais Ins. Agy., Ayer, Mass., 1970-74, Aanco Underwriters, Inc., St. Petersburg, Fla., 1973—, Countryside Insurors, Inc., Tarpon Springs, Fla., 1982-85; pres. Ins. Premium Acceptance Corp., St. Petersburg, 1986—; pres. Gulfport Mini-Warehouse, Inc., Fla., 1986—. owner, operator Jomar Charter & Properties, St. Petersburg, 1973—. Bd. dirs. Fla. Orch., St. Petersburg, 1981-83, bd. govs., 1984-87; fund raising chmn. Pinellas Assn. for Retarded Children, St. Petersburg, 1982; life mem. Arthritis Found., Family Services. Am. Nat. Novice Ladies Figure Skating Champion, Roller Skating Rink Operators Assn. Am., 1953. Mem. Nat. Assn. Ins. Women, Ins. Women of St. Petersburg, Nat. Assn. Ins. Agts., Am. Cancer Soc. (life), Arthritis Found. (Sword of Hope chpt.), Nat. Notary Assn., Nat. Assn. Female Execs. Roman Catholic. Clubs: Cross of Lorraine Soc., Infinity, Boley's Angels. Home: 300 Rafael Blvd NE Saint Petersburg FL 33704 Office: Aanco Underwriters Inc 10033 9th St Saint Petersburg FL 33716

AMOSSY, RUTH, French literature educator; b. Arad, Romania, July 25, 1946; d. Leopold and Regina (Schreiber) Brenes; m. David Amossy, Dec. 29, 1965 (div. Dec. 1976); 1 child, Yossi. PhD, U. Paris VIII, 1976. Asst. dept. French lit. Tel Aviv U., 1968-78, asst. prof., 1978-85, assoc. prof., 1985—. Author: Les Jeux de L'Allusion Litteraire dans un beau Tenebreux de J. Gracq, 1980, Parcours Symboliques chez J. Gracq, 1982, Les Discours du Cliche, 1982; editor: (in Hebrew) Anthology of Dada and Surrealism. Home: Arazi 15, Tel Aviv 69693, Israel Office: Tel Aviv U French Dept, Ramat Aviv, Tel Aviv 69978, Israel

AMPOLA, MASSIMO FILIPPO, sociologist; b. Pontremoli, Toscana, Italy, Oct. 19, 1944; s. Renato Fortunato and Maria Luisa (Zanoboli) A.; m. Giuliana Marisol Buchignani, Apr. 8, 1972; children—Massimiliano, Matteo. Ph.D., U. Italy, 1971. Asst. prof. U. Camerino, 1971-80; expert judge Minor's Ct., Florence, Italy, 1976-80; prof. sociology Naval Acad., Leghorn, 1980-83; expert judge Ct. Appeal, Florence, 1980—; prof. med. sociology U. Sch. for Hygienics, Pisa, Italy, 1981—, also dir.; prof. methodology of social research U. Pisa, 1980—. Author: Research and Social Activity, 1974; Vital, Secular and Religious Worlds, 1983. Editor review Nuova Linea (New Line), 1970—. Research Nat. Research Com., Rome, 1971-74; research dir. Internat. Aid Activities, 1972-77; councillor Cristian Assns. Italian Works, 1969; pres. E.N.A.I.P., Leghorn, 1980—, Ctr. Social Research A. Grandi, 1978—; mem. Sci. Com. Old Age Movement of Cristian Democratic Party, Rome, 1980—. Mem. Nat. Order Journalists, Internat. Conf. Sociology Religion, Council Social Service Sch U. Pisa; fellow Italian Sociol. Assn. (fellow Sci. Com. sect.). Avocations: collecting pipes; microcomputer applications. Home: Di Franco St 9, 57100 Leghorn Italy Office: Inst Sociology, Serafini St 3, 56100 Pisa Italy

AMSEL, BRAM JULES, cardiologist; b. Amsterdam, Netherlands, Mar. 3, 1949; s. Naftali Hersch and Ruth Henriette (Simons) A.; m. Judith Grunblatt; 1 child, Alon. SB in Applied Math., Brown U., 1971; MD, U. Amsterdam, 1977, cert. in cardiology, 1983. Cardiologist-in-charge Univ. Hosp., Antwerp, Belgium, 1984—. Served with med. corps Army of Netherlands, 1977-78. Office: Univ Hosp of Antwerp, Wilrijkstraat 10, Edegem B-2520, Belgium

AMSELLE, JEAN-LOUP GASTON, anthropologist; b. Marseille, France, July 2, 1942; s. Jacques Nathan and Perle Georgette (Cahen) A.; m. Marie Sylvie Courtade, Sept. 2, 1968; 1 child, Simon. D of Sociology, The Sorbonne, Paris, 1972. Sociologist Office Overseas Sci. and Tech. Research, Paris, 1970-76; anthropologist Inst. for Advanced Studies in Social Scis., Paris, 1976—. Author: Les Négociants de La Savane, 1977; editor: Les Migrations Africaines, 1976, Le Sauvage á La Mode, 1979, Au Coeur de l'Ethnie, 1985, Cahiers d'Etudes Africaines, Paris, 1987—. Office: Sch for Higher Study Social Scis, 54 Blvd Raspail, 75006 Paris France

AN, ZHIMIN, archaeologist; b. Yantai, Shandong, China, Apr. 5, 1924; s. Shiwen and Ziping (Ji) A.; m. Yuzhu Zhang, July 19, 1944; children: Jiaqi, Jiayao, Jiaao, Jiayuan. BA, Chinese U., Beijing, 1948; MA, Peking U., Beijing, 1952. Asst. Yenching Inst., Beijing, 1948-50; asst. Inst. Archaeology, Beijing, 1950-52, assrt researcher, 1953-56, assoc. research fellow, 1956-79, research fellow, 1979—, dep. dir., 1982-85; mem. Nat. Commn. on Ancient Monuments and Antiquities, 1983—. Author: Bibliography of Chinese Prearchaeology, 1951, Miao Ti Kow and San Li Chao, 1959, Essays on the Neolithic Age of China, 1982, Recent Archaeological Discoveries in the People's Republic of China, 1984. Dep. 7th People's Congress Beijing, 1977-82. Mem. Chinese Soc. Archaeology (permanent mem. council 1979—), Chinese Soc. History, Chinese Soc. Ancient Ceramics (vice chmn. 1981—), German Archaeol. Inst. (corr.), Internat. Union Prehistoric Protohistoric (permanent mem. council 1987—). Home: 712 21st Apt, Fuxingmenwai Dajie, Beijing 100045, People's Republic China Office: Inst Archaelogy, 27 Wangfujing Dajie, Beijing 100710, People's Republic China

ANAGNOST, MARIA ATHENA, surgeon; b. Chgo., Oct. 21, 1943; d. Themis John and Catherine (Cook) A.; B.A., Northwestern U., 1965; M.D., U. Ill., 1973. Resident in surgery U. Chgo. Hosps. and Clinics, 1973-74; gen. surgery resident Michael Reese Med. Center, Chgo., 1975-79, chief resident, 1979-80; practice medicine specializing in surgery; surg. staff Oak Park (Ill.) Hosp., Westlake Community Hosp., Melrose Park, Ill., Gottlieb Meml. Hosp., Melrose Park, St. Anne's Hosp., Chgo., St. Anne's Hosp. West, Northlake, Ill. (past sec. treas.), Good Samaritan Hosp., Downers Grove, Ill., Ravenswood Hosp., Chgo.; chmn. dept. surgery Loretto Hosp., Chgo. Diplomate Nat. Bd. Med. Examiners, 1974; cert. Am. Bd. Surgery. Recipient Physicians' Recognition award AMA. Fellow ACS, Internat. Coll. Surgeons (vice-regent); mem. AMA, Ill. Med. Soc., Chgo. Med. Soc., Am. Soc. Abdominal Surgeons, Hellenic Med. Soc., U. Ill. alumni Assn., Northwestern U. Alumni Assn. Contbr. articles to profl. jours. Office: 1545 Clinton Pl River Forest IL 60305 also: 3825 Highland Ave Downers Grove IL 60515 also: 11 S LaSalle St Chicago IL 60603

ANAGNOSTOPOULOS, CONSTANTINE EMMANUEL, venture capitalist, former company executive; b. Athens, Greece, Nov. 1, 1922; came to U.S., 1946; s. Emmanuel Constantine A. and Helen (Michaelides) Kefalas; m. Maria Tsagarakis, July 10, 1949; 1 son, Paul Constantine. Sc.B. in Chemistry, Brown U., 1949; M.S. in Chemistry, Harvard U., 1950, Ph.D. in Chemistry, 1952; postgrad. in bus. adminstrn., Columbia U., 1964. Dir. research and devel. organic div. Monsanto Co., St. Louis, 1962-67, research scientist, 1952-61, bus. dir., 1967-71, gen. mgr. New Enterprise div., 1971-75, gen. mgr. rubber chem. div., 1975-80; v.p. mng. dir. Monsanto Europe-Africa, Brussels, 1980-82; corp. v.p., vice chmn. corp. devel. and growth com. Monsanto Co., St. Louis, 1982-85; cons. 1986-87; mng. gen. ptnr. Gateway Venture Ptnrs., L.P., St. Louis, 1987—; chmn. bd. Monsanto Europe S.A., Brussels, 1980-82, Kinetek Corp.; dir. Advent Capital Ltd., London, U.S.A., Advent Internat. Corp., Genzyme Corp., Aspect Systems, Laser Diode Products, Inc.; mem. com. on patent system Nat. Acad. Engring., 1971; mem. nat. inventors council Dept. Commerce, 1964-72. Patentee in organic and polymer chemistry, 1953-67; contbr. articles to profl. jours. Bd. dirs. Am. C. of C., Brussels, 1981-82; mem. European Govt. Bus. Council, Strasbourgh, France, 1981-82; pres. United Fund Belgium, 1982; mem. presdl. com. prizes for innovation, Washington, 1972, U.S.-USSR Trade and Econ. Council, 1980-82; chmn. bd. St. Louis Tech. Ctr. Served to capt. Brit. Army, 1944-46. Recipient chemistry prize Brown U., 1949, teaching award Harvard U., 1950, 51, 52, St. Louis Tech. award Regional Comml. and Growth Assn., 1987. Mem. Research Soc. Am., Indsl. Research Inst., Comml. Devel. Assn., Am. Chem. Soc., St. Louis Art Mus. Republican. Episcopalian. Club: Bellerive Country (St. Louis). Home: 13003 Starbuck Rd Saint Louis MO 63141 Office: Gateway Venture Ptnrs 8000 Maryland Ave Suite 1190 Saint Louis MO 63105

ANAGNOSTOPOULOS, STAVROS ARISTIDOU, earthquake engineer, educator; b. Megalo Horio, Evrytania, Greece, Jan. 8, 1946; came to U.S., 1968; s. Aristides A. and Agapi (Katsiyanni) A.; m. Panagiota Papacosta, Aug. 31, 1975; children—Aristides, Haralampos, Demetrios. Diploma Nat. Tech. U. Athens, 1968; M.S., MIT, 1970, Sc.D., 1972. Research assoc. MIT, Cambridge, 1975-76; research engr. Shell Devel., Houston, 1976-81, sr. research engr., 1981; dir. Inst. Engring. Seismology and Earthquake Engring., Thessaloniki, Greece, 1981-86; prof. dept civi. engring. U. Patras, Greece, 1986—. Contbr. articles to profl. jours. Greek state fellow, Athens, 1964-68; doctoral fellow Greek Ministry Coordination, Athens, 1969-72. Mem. ASCE, Seismol. Soc. Am., Earthquake Engring. Research Inst. Office: U Patras, Detp Civil Engring, 26110 Patras Greece

ANAND, PRADEEP, manufacturing company executive; b. Amritsar, Punjab, India, Jan. 15, 1955; s. Chaman Lal and Sheila (Asha) A.; m. Neelam Anand, July 24, 1984; 1 child, Aditi. B of Commerce, Punjab U., India, 1975; PMD, Harvard U., 1984. Adminstrv. officer Toshiba Anand Batteries Ltd., Cochin, India, 1975-77, vice chmn., joint mng. dir., 1986—; dir.-in-charge Punjab Anand Batteries Ltd, Chandigarh, India, 1977-78, mng. dir., 1978-86. Mem. telephone adv. com. Ministry of Communications, Govt. of India, Cochin, 1987—. Mem. Soc. for Advancement of Electro-Chem. Sci. and Tech. (v.p. 1984-85). Home: Anand House, Srikandeth Ln, Cochin Kerala 682 016, India Office: Toshiba Anand Batteries Ltd, Anand House, Mahatma Gandhi Rd, Cochin Kerala 682 011, India

ANAND, SURESH CHANDRA, physician; b. Mathura, India, Sept. 13, 1931; s. Satchit and Sumaran (Bai) A.; came to U.S., 1957, naturalized, 1971; M.B., B.S., King George's Coll., U. Lucknow (India), 1954; M.S., U. Colo., 1962; m. Wiltrud, Jan. 29, 1966; children—Miriam, Michael. Fellow pulmonary diseases Nat. Jewish Hosp., Denver, 1957-58, resident in chest medicine, 1958-59, chief resident allergy-asthma, 1960-62; intern Mt. Sinai Hosp., Toronto, Ont., Can., 1962-63, resident in medicine, 1963-64, chief resident, 1964-65, demonstrator clin. technique, 1963-64, U. Toronto fellow in medicine, 1964-65; research assoc. asthma-allergy Nat. Jewish Hosp., Denver, 1967-69; clin. instr. medicine U. Colo., 1967-69; pres. Allergy Assocs. & Lab., Ltd., Phoenix, 1974—; mem. staff Phoenix Bapt. Hosp., chmn. med .records com., 1987; mem. staff St. Joseph's Hosp., St. Luke's Hosp., Humana Hosp., Phoenix Bapt., John C. Lincoln, Maryvale Meml., Good Samaritan, Phoenix Children's Hosp., Tempe St. Luke, Desert Samaritan, Mesa Luth., Scottsdale Meml. Mem. Camelback Hosp. Mental Health Center Citizens Adv. Bd., Scottsdale, Ariz., 1974-80; mem. council Phoenix Symphony; mem. Ariz. Opera Co. Diplomate Am. Bd. Allergy and Immunology. Fellow ACP, Am. Coll. Chest Physicians (crit. care com.), Am. Acad. Allergy, Am. Coll. Cert. Allergists, Am. Assn. Clin. Immunology and Allergy; mem. AAAS, AMA, Ariz. Med. Assn., Maricopa County Med. Soc., West Coast Soc. Allergy and Immunology, Ariz. Soc. Allergists, Greater Phoenix Allergy Soc. (v.p. 1984-86, pres. 1986—), AAAS, Phoenix Zoo, N.Y. Acad. Scis., World Med. Assn., Internat. Assn. Asthmology, Assn. Care of Asthma, Ariz. Thoracic Soc., Nat. Geog. Soc., Ariz. Hist. Soc., Smithsonian Instn., Phoenix Art Mus., Nat. Audobon Soc. Clubs: Village Tennis, Ariz. Lodge: Sertoma Internat. Contbr. articles in field to profl. jours. Office: 2200 W Bethany Home Rd Phoenix AZ 85015 Other: 1006 E Guadalupe Rd Tempe AZ 85283

ANAND, YOGINDRA NATH, civil engineer; b. Peshawar, India, Dec. 5, 1939; came to Can., 1965, came to U.S., 1967; s. Amar Nath and Prakash (Chaddah) A.; m. Helga Tieves, Jan. 9, 1971 (div. 1980); children: Lara, Martin; m. Pancharathna Anand, Sept. 25, 1980. MSCE, Wayne State U., 1968; D in Engring., U. Detroit, 1972. Registered profl. engr., Mich. Apprentice Stein, Chattertee and Polk, New Delhi, 1959-62; structural designer R. Reiser Co., New Delhi, 1962-65, Arthur G. McKee Co., Toronto, Ont., Can., 1965, Stelco, Hamilton, Ont., 1966; sr. project engr. Harley Ellington Co., Detroit, 1968-71; staff civil engr. Detroit Edison Co., 1972—; adj. prof. structural design Lawrence Inst. Tech., 1974-84. Editor: Seismic Experience Data, Nuclear and Other Plants, 1985, Structural Design Cementitions, Products and Case Histories, 1985; author: several software programs. Mem. ASCE (pres. southeastern br. 1986-87), Am. Soc. Engrs. from India (pres. 1984-85), Am. Concrete Inst., Engg Soc. of Detroit. Home: 308 Longford Dr Rochester Hills MI 48309 Office: Detroit Edison Co 2000 2d Ave Detroit MI 48226

ANAST, NICK JAMES, lawyer; b. Gary, Ind., Apr. 20, 1947; s. James Terry and Kiki (Pappas) A.; m. Linda K. Skirvin, Oct. 28, 1972; children: Jason, Nicole. AB, Ind. U., 1969, JD, 1972. Bar: Ind. 1972, U.S. Dist. Ct. (no. and so. dists.) Ind. 1972, U.S Ct. Appeals (7th cir.) 1975, U.S. Supreme Ct. 1976. Ptnr. Pappas, Tokarski & Anast, Gary, 1972-74; ptnr. Tokarski & Anast, Gary, 1974-85, Schererville, Ind., 1985—; dep. pros. atty. Lake County Prosecutors Office, Crown Point, Ind., 1973-74; pub. defender Lake County Superior Ct., Gary, 1974-78; atty. Town of Schererville, 1982, 88, Lowell, 1983, City of Lake Station, Ind., 1978. Pres. St. John (Ind.) Twp. Young Dems., 1980. Recipient Service to Youth award YMCA, 1980, Outstanding Service award Schererville Soccer Club, 1985. Fellow Ind. Bar Found.; mem. ABA, Ind. Bar Assn., Lake County Bar Assn. (bd. dirs.) 1983-85, Outstanding Service award 1985). Democrat. Greek Orthodox. Lodge: Lions (pres. Schererville chpt. 1985-86). Office: Tokarski & Anast 7803 W 75th Ave Suite 1 Schererville IN 46375

ANASTACIO, ROBERTO VALERO, cardiologist; b. Manila, Apr. 26, 1940; s. Arsenio Austria and Josefa (Valero) A.; m. Sonia Martinez, Sept. 12, 1965; children: Ramon, Teresa, Rolando, Melissa. AA, U. Santo Tomas, Philippines, 1958, MD, 1964. Diplomate Philippine Coll. Cardiology. Intern U. Santo Tomas, 1963-64, resident in internal medicine, 1964-68, instr. internal medicine, 1968-70; research assoc. cardiology U. Chgo. Hosps. and Clinics, 1970-72; assoc. prof. cardiology U. Santo Tomas, 1972—, head residency program dept. medicine, 1980—, head non-invasive cardiac lab. Heart Ctr., 1983-86. Contbr. articles to profl. jours. Named Outstanding Tomasian in Sci., U. Santo Tomas, 1981. Fellow Philippine Heart Assn., Philippine Coll. Internal Medicne. Roman Catholic. Club: Quezon City. Lodge: Rotary. Home: Avalon Condominium, San Juan Metro Manila, Philippines Office: U Santo Tomas Hosp, Espana Manila, Philippines

ANBAR, MICHAEL, biophysics educator; b. Danzig, Danzig, June 27, 1927; came to U.S., 1967, naturalized, 1973; s. Joshua and Chava A.; m. Ada Komet, Aug. 11, 1953; children: Ran D., Ariel D. M.Sc., Hebrew U., Jerusalem, 1950, Ph.D., 1953. Instr. chemistry U. Chgo., 1953-55; sr. scientist Weizmann Inst. Sci., 1955-67; prof. Frienberg Grad. Sch., Rehovoth, Israel, 1960-67; sr. research asso. Ames Research Center, 1967-68; dir. phys. sci. SRI Internat., Menlo Park, Calif., 1968-72; dir. mass spectrometry research ctr. SRI Internat., 1972-77; prof. biophysical sci., chmn. dept. Sch. Medicine, SUNY, Buffalo, 1977—, exec. dir. Health Instrument and Device Inst., 1983-85; assoc. dean applied research Sch. Medicine, SUNY, 1983-85. Author: The Hydrated Electron, 1970, The Machine of the Bedside—Strategies for Using Technology in Patient Care, 1984, Clinical Biophysics, 1985, Computers in Medicine, 1986; editor-in-chief Health Care Instrumentation; Contbr. articles to profl. jours. Served with Israeli Air Force, 1947-49. Grantee in field. Mem. Assn. Am. Med. Colls., N.Y. Acad. Sci., Am. Chem. Soc., Biophys. Soc., Am. Inst. Ultrasound in Medicine, Am. Assn. Clin. Chemistry, Internat. Assn. Dental Research, Radiation Research Soc., Am. Assn. Dental Research, Am. Assn. Mass Spectrometry, Assn. Advancement of Med. Instrumentation, IEEE, AAAS, Am. Acad. Thermology. Office: SUNY 118 Cary Hall Buffalo NY 14214

ANCELL, ROBERT M., publisher; b. Phoenix, Oct. 16, 1942; s. Robert M. and Alice (Lovett) A.; m. Janet C. Neuber, Dec. 21, 1966 (div. 1984); children: Kevin, Kristin; m. Christine Marie Miller, Mar. 30, 1985. BA, U. N.Mex., 1971. Announcer KDEF Radio, Albuquerque, 1966-67; reporter Sta. KOB TV, Albuquerque, 1967-72; sr. sales representative Xerox Corp., Albuquerque, 1972-78; gen. sales mgr. Sta. KRDO-TV, Colorado Springs, Colo., 1978-79; publisher Titsch Pub., Denver, 1979-82; publ. dir. Denver Bus. Mag., 1982-83; advt. mgr. U.S. Naval Res. (recalled to active duty), New Orleans, 1984-85; publisher Endless Vacation Pubs., Indpls., 1985—; cons. Media Masters, Denver, 1983-84. Contbr. articles to mags., profl. jours., newspapers, 1960—. Served to lt. comdr. USNR, 1980. Recipient First Place award N.Mex. Broadcasters, 1970; First Place award UPI, 1970, Pres. Club award Xerox Corp., 1973, 75-76. Mem. Reserve Officers Assn. of U.S. (tng. officer 1980-81, Cert. of Appreciation 1981), U.S. Naval. Inst., Air Force Assn., Manuscript Soc. Republican. Presbyterian. Avocations: private pilot, bicycling, bridge, writing, photography. Office: Endless Vacation Pubs One RCI Plaza 3502 Woodview Indianapolis IN 46268

ANCES, I. G(EORGE), obstetrician/gynecologist, educator; b. Balt., July 3, 1935; s. Harry and Fanny A.; m. Marlene Roth, Oct. 23, 1966; 1 son, Beau Mark. B.S., U. Md., 1956, M.D., 1959. Diplomate: Am. Bd. Obstetrics and Gynecology. Intern Ohio State U. Hosp., 1959-60; resident in obstetrics and gynecology Univ. Hosp., Balt., 1960-61, 63-65; mem. faculty U. Md. Med. Sch., Balt., 1966—; prof. obstetrics and gynecology U. Md. Med. Sch., 1975-83, dir. labs. obstetrics and gynecol. research and clin. labs., 1967-83, dir. div. adolescent obstetrics and gynecology and family planning, 1981-83;; prof. ob-gyn. Rutgers U. Sch. Medicine,, Camden,, N.J.,, 1983—,; chmn. dept., 1983—. Contbr. chpts. to books, articles to profl. jours. Capt. sustaining fund drive Balt. Symphony Orch., Opera Co. Phila.; med. adv. com. Fire Dept. Balt. City. Served with USAF, 1961-63. Fellow Am. Coll. Obstetrics and Gynecology; mem. Endocrine Soc., Soc. Gynecol. Investigation, Soc. Study Reprodn. (charter), Internat. Soc. Research in Biology Reprodn. (charter), Md. Obstetrics and Gynecol. Soc. (sec. 1978-81, dir. 1979—), Med. and Chirurgical Soc. Md., Soc. Adolescent Medicine, Douglas Obstet. and Gynecol. Soc. (pres. 1984—), N.J. State Med. Soc. (chmn. neonatal coop. so. Jersey 1986—), English Speaking Union, Cooper Found., N.J. Conservation Council, Sigma Xi. Clubs: Maryland, Towson Golf and Country. Home: 1 Lane of Acres Haddonfield NJ 08033 Office: Rutgers U Sch Medicine Dept Obstetrics and Gynecology 300 Cooper Plaza Camden NJ 08103

ANCETTI, CARLO GUIDO, construction company executive; b. Udine, Italy, Oct. 7, 1933; s. Carlo C. and Laura Maria Luisa (Bozzola) A.; m. Nicoletta M. Menzaghi, Oct. 7, 1961; children: Barbara, Giancarlo, Claudio. Degree in Geometry, Antonio Zanon U., Udine, Italy, 1953. Job site supr. Italscavi Udine, San Quirino, Italy, 1953-54; mgr. rock drilling and blasting Italscavi Udine, Val Frera, Italy, 1954-55; mgr. job site Italscavi Udine, Val di Non, Italy, 1956-57; mgr. excavation Farsura Milano, Pertusillo, Italy, 1958; mgr. project research Farsura Milano, Milan, 1958-59; mgr. sales Acesa Milano, Milan, 1959-66; chmn. Anbel SpA, Milan, 1966—; pres. Tamrock Italiana SpA, San Donato Milanes, Italy, 1971—. Named Cavaliere di Santo Sepolcro di Gerusalemme, 1988. Mem. Fogolar Furlan Assn. Roman Catholic. Club: Malaspina Sporting (Milan, San Felice). Office: Tamrock Italiana SpA, Via A Grandi 18, 20097 San Donato Milanese Italy

ANDERBERG, ROY ANTHONY, journalist; b. Camden, N.J., Mar. 30, 1921; s. Arthur R. and Mary V. (McHugh) A.; m. Louise M. Brooks, Feb. 5, 1953; children: Roy, Mary. AA, Diablo Valley Coll., 1975. Enlisted USN, 1942, commd. officer, 1960, ret., 1970; waterfront columnist Pacific Daily News, Agana, Guam, 1966-67; pub. relations officer Naval Forces, Mariana Islands, 1967; travel editor Contra Costa (Calif.) Times, 1968-69; entertainment and restaurant editor Concord (Calif.) Transcript, 1971-75; entertainment editor Contra Costa Advertiser, 1975-76; free-lance non-fiction journalist, 1976—. Mem. U.S. Power Squadron, DAV, Ret. Officers Assn., Am. Legion, VFW, U.S. Submarine Vets. World War II Assn. Democrat. Clubs: Martinez Yacht. Home: 2720 Lyon Circle Concord CA 94518 Office: Box 52 Concord CA 94522

ANDERLE, RICHARD JOHN, mathematician, engineer; b. N.Y.C., Oct. 8, 1926; s. Joseph and Jennie Helen (Styskal) A.; B.A., Bklyn. Coll., 1948; D.Sc. (hon.), Ohio State U., 1981; m. Fay A. Leitch, June 12, 1960 (dec.). Mathematician, Exterior Ballistics br. Naval Surface Weapons Center, Dahlgren, Va., 1948-59, head Exterior Ballistics Br., 1959-60, head Astronautics and Geodesy div., 1960-81, research asso. dept. strategic systems, 1981-85; sr. systems engr. Space Systems div. Gen. Electric Co., King of Prussia, Pa., 1985—; lectr. Am. U., 1964-65; corr. astronomer (hon.) Royal Obs. Belgium, 1984. Treas., Christ Luth. Ch., Fredericksburg, Va., 1963-64, councilman, 1963-65, fin. sec., 1976-85. Recipient Superior Civilian Service award USN, 1960, John A. Dahlgren award Naval Surface Weapons Center, 1977. Fellow Am. Geophys. Union (pres. Geodesy sect. 1980-82); mem. AAAS, IEEE, AIAA, N.Y. Acad. Sci., Internat. Assn. Geodesy (sec. space techniques sect. 1979-83, pres. sect. 1983-87), Inst. Navigation, Am. Soc. Photogrammetry, Am. Congress on Surveying and Mapping. Lutheran. Contbr. articles, chpts. to profl. publs., procs., 1960—. Home: 1257 Muhlenberg Dr Wayne PA 19087 Office: Space Systems Div Gen Electric PO Box 8555 Philadelphia PA 19101

ANDERS, PRZEMYSLAW TOMASZ, lawyer, economist; b. Lodz, Poland, Jan. 10, 1941; s. Brunon and Janina (Ziemek) A.; m. Maria Kurzepa, Dec. 26, 1967; 1 son, Maciej Anders. B.A. in Economy, A. Mickiewicz, 1964, M.A. in Law, 1963; postgrad. Acad. Econs., 1964, Warsaw Univ., 1965. Legal advisor Morska Agencja w Gdyni, Poland, 1964-71; dir. maritime dept. Ministry Fgn. Trade and Shipping, Warsaw, 1971-80; permanent rep. to I.M.O. counsellor, head Polish shipping mission Polish Embassy in London, 1980-84; legal advisor, solicitor Morska Agencja w Gdyni, 1985—; sec. diplomatic conf. fishing and conservation living resources, Gdansk, 1973; bd. dirs. Am.-Polish Fisheries Bd., N.Y., 1975—; v.p. N.E. Atlantic Fishery Commn., London, 1980-81; chmn. staff pension com. Internat. Maritime Orgn., London, 1983—. Author numerous books and articles. Del. Poland UN Law of Sea Conf., Geneva, N.Y., 1976-80, Internat. Maritime Satellite Orgn., London, 1980-84, Internat. Oil Pollution Compensation Fund, London, 1980—, London Dumping Conv. Consultative Meetings, London, 1980—, N.E. Atlantic Fisheries Commn., London, 1980—. Recipient Disting. Seafarer award Minister of Shipping, Poland, 1974; Officer, Dom Henry, The Navigator award Pres. Portugal, 1975. Mem. Polish Bar Assn., Polish Maritime Law Assn. Avocations: gardening, tennis. Home: K Sosnickiego St 3, Gdansk-Oliwa 80-307, Poland Office: Morska Agencja w Gdyni, Pulaskiego 8, Gdynia 81-963, Poland

ANDERSEN, CHRISTOPHER PETER, editor, author; b. Pensacola, Fla., May 26, 1949; s. Edward Francis and Jeanette (Peterson) A.; B.A. in Polit. Sci., U. Calif.-Berkeley, 1971; m. Valerie Jean Hess, Feb. 3, 1972; 1 dau., Katharine. San Francisco corr. Time mag., 1969-70, contbg. editor, N.Y.C., 1971-72, contbg. editor, Montreal, Que., Can., 1972-74; assoc. editor People mag., N.Y.C., 1974-80, sr. editor, 1980-86. Club: Players. Author: The Name Game, 1977; A Star, Is A Star, Is A Star!, 1980; The Book of People, 1981;

Father, The Figure and the Force, 1983; Success Over Sixty, 1984; The New Book of People, 1986; The Baby Boomer's Name Game, 1987; The Po-Po Principle, 1987; The Serpent's Tooth, 1987, Young Kate, 1988; contbr. articles to various publs. including N.Y. Times, Good Housekeeping, Reader's Digest, Parade, Life. Home: 200 E 66th St New York NY 10021

ANDERSEN, DANA KIMBALL, surgeon, educator; b. Utica, N.Y., Mar. 6, 1946; s. Cyril C. and Elizabeth (Kimball) A.; m. Ronnie Ann Rosenthal, Oct. 22, 1983. A.B., Duke U., 1968, M.D., 1972. Diplomate Am. Bd. Internal Medicine, Am. Bd. Surgery. Intern, resident internal medicine Duke U. Med. Ctr., Durham, N.C., 1972-73, resident gen. surgery, 1974, 76-79, instr. surgery, 1979-80; asst. prof. medicine and surgery SUNY-Downstate Med. Ctr., Bklyn., 1980-85, assoc. prof., 1985—; clin. assoc. NIH, Balt., 1974-76; asst. in internal medicine Johns Hopkins U., Balt., 1974-76; cons. surgery VA Med. Ctr., Bklyn., 1982—; dir. surg. research lab. SUNY Health Scis. Ctr., 1982-86, dir. surg. residency program, 1986—. Contbr. articles to profl. jours., chpts. to books. Served to lt. comdr. USPHS, 1974-76. NIH grantee, 1983—; Am. Surg. Assn. Found. fellow, 1982-84. Fellow ACS; mem. Assn. for Acad. Surgery, Am. Gastroenterol. Assn., Soc. for Surgery of Alimentary Tract, Soc. Univ. Surgeons, Am. Assn. Endocrine Surgeons, Surg. Biology Club I, Sigma Xi, Alpha Omega Alpha. Episcopalian. Avocations: photography; sailing. Office: SUNY Health Scis Ctr Box 40 450 Clarkson Ave Brooklyn NY 11203

ANDERSEN, ERNEST CHRISTOPHER, lawyer; b. Minden, Nebr., Sept. 10, 1909; s. Dines Peter and Marie (Jensen) A.; m. Audrey Etta Robertson, Sept. 10, 1954; 1 dau., Elaine Carolyn Andersen Smith; 1 stepson, Albert Henry Whitaker. J.D., U. Denver, 1952, B.S. in Bus. Adminstrn., 1956. Bar: Colo. 1954, U.S. Supreme Ct. 1960. With U.S. Treasury Dept., Denver, 1935-39; accountant, Denver, 1939-41; with Civilian Prodn. Adminstrn., Denver, 1946-49; dep. state auditor Colo., 1949-51; with U.S. Commerce Dept., Denver, 1951-52; mgmt. cons., Denver, 1953-54; sole practice law, Denver, 1955-56, 69-75; asst. dir. GAO, Los Angeles, 1957-58, Denver, 1959, Washington, 1960-69, cons., 1969-75; sole practice law, Cedaredge, Colo., 1975-86; owner Cedar Crest Farm, 1983—, Stand Sure Press (later Christopher Pub. Co.), 1977—; mem. faculty U. Denver, 1948-56; mcpl. judge Cedaredge, 1977-86; exec. in residence Tulane U., spring 1973. Bd. dirs. Delta Montrose Electric Assn., 1976-84, Colo.-Ute Electric Assn., 1980-84. Served to lt. col. U.S. Army, 1941-46. Recipient Meritorious Service award GAO, 1968. Republican. Presbyterian. Clubs: Masons, Shriners. Home: 1856 Road 2375 Cedaredge CO 81413 Office: PO Box 747 Cedaredge CO 30747

ANDERSEN, K(ENT) TUCKER, investment executive; b. Manchester Conn., June 5, 1942; s. Alfred Hans and Dorothy Emily (Ray) A.; m. Karen Ann Kirchofer, Oct. 11, 1963; children: Heather Michele, Kristen Eileen. Student, Phillips Exeter Acad., N.H., 1957-59; BA, Wesleyan U., 1963. Chartered fin. analyst. Actuarial student Travelers Ins. Co., Hartford, Conn., 1963-66; security analyst Smith Barney & Co., N.Y.C., 1968-69; ptnr. Rudman Assocs., N.Y.C., 1969-72; ptnr. Cumberland Assocs., N.Y.C., 1972—, mng. ptnr., 1982—. Bd. dirs. Cato Inst., Washington, 1987—; trustee YWCA of Montclair, North Essex, N.J., 1980—, 1st United Meth. Ch. of Montclair, 1976—; admission rep. for N.J. area Phillips Exeter Acad., N.H., 1983—. Served with USPHS, 1966-68. Recipient Distinguished Alumni award Wesleyan U., 1988. Mem. Soc. Actuaries, N.Y. Soc. Security Analysts, Inst. Chartered Fin. Analysts, Polit. Club for Growth (mem. exec. com. 1984—), Kappa Nu Kappa (pres. 1963). Republican. Avocation: marathons. Office: Cumberland Assocs 1114 Ave of Americas New York NY 10036

ANDERSEN, MARIANNE SINGER, clinical psychologist; b. Baden nr. Vienna, Austria, June 18, 1930; came to U.S., 1940, naturalized, 1946; d. Richard L. and Jolanthe (Garda) Singer; 1 son, Richard Esten. BA, CUNY, 1950, MA, 1974; PhD, Fla. Inst. Tech., 1980. Book editor specializing in psychology and psychiatry various pub. firms including W.W. Norton Co., Sterling Pub. Co., E.P. Dutton Co., N.Y.C., 1950-71; research assoc. Inst. for Research in Hypnosis, N.Y.C., 1974-76, fellow in clin. hypnosis, 1976, dir. seminars, 1978-82, dir. edn., 1982—; psychotherapist specializing in hypnotherapy Morton Prince Ctr. for Hypnotherapy, 1976—, dir. weight control clinic, 1980—, dir. clin. services, 1981-82; dir. adminstrn. Internat. Grad. U., N.Y.C., 1974-77; pvt. practice psychotherapy, 1977—; adminstrv. coordinator Internat. Grad. Sch. Behavior Sci., Fla. Inst. Tech., 1978; co-dir. The Melbourne Group, 1983—; lectr. hypnosis and hypnotherapy to mental and phys. health profls., 1977—. Author: (with Louis Savary) Passages: A Guide for Pilgrims of the Mind, 1972; research on treatment obesity with hypnotherapy. Mem. Soc. for Clin. and Exptl. Hypnosis, Internat. Soc. for Clin. and Exptl. Hypnosis, Am. Psychol. Assn., Am. Soc. Bariatric Physicians (affiliate), N.Y. Acad. Scis.

ANDERSEN, MOGENS, painter, author; b. Copenhagen, Aug. 8, 1916; s. Einar F. T. and Erna Ingeborg (Andersen) A.; m. Inger Therkildsen, Nov. 28, 1947; children: Christian, Benedicte. Student P. Rostrup Boyesen, Copenhagen. Tchr. art, Copenhagen, 1952-59; mem. art faculty Academie de la Grande Chaumiere, Paris, 1963, Royal Acad. Fine Arts, Copenhagen, 1970-72; pres. Danish State Art Found., Copenhagen, 1977-80. Author: Moderne Fransk Kunst, 1948; Omkring Kilderne, 1967; Nødigt, Men Dog Gerne, 1976; Ungdoms Rejsen, 1979; Uset, 1986. Mem. Council Danish Radio and TV, 1968-74. Decorated knight Legion d'honneur, officier Art et Lettres (France), knight of Dannebrog (Denmark); recipient Eckersberg medal Royal Acad. Fire Arts, 1949, Thorvalden medal, 1984.

ANDERSEN, PAUL KENT, linguist, educator; b. Omaha, July 10, 1948; s. Milton Huxley and Vera Faye (Krick) A.; m. Gun Lisbet Gustafsson, July 31, 1981. B.S., U. Colo., 1972; Ph.D., U. Freiburg, W. Ger., 1980; Habilitation, U. Bielefeld, Fed. Republic Germany, 1988. Asst. prof. dept. linguistics U. Bielefeld, 1980-88, prof., 1988—; lectr. U. Munster, Fed. Republic Germany, 1981-86 , numerous other univs. throughout the world. Author: Word Order Typology and Comparative Constructions, 1982, Minor Rock Edicts of Aśoka (critical edition, 1987, textual criticism, 1988), Studien zur Anwendung funktionaler Theorien auf die Syntax älterer Sprachen des indischen Kulturbereiches, 1987. Contbr. articles to scholarly publs. Mem. Am. Oriental Soc., Linguistic Soc. Am. Office: LiLi Fakultat der Universitat, D4800 Bielefeld Federal Republic of Germany

ANDERSEN, RICHARD ESTEN, lawyer; b. N.Y.C., Oct. 26, 1957; s. Arnold and Marianne (Singer) A.; m. Patricia Anne Woods, May 9, 1987. BA, Columbia U., 1978, JD, 1981. Bar: N.Y. 1982, U.S. Tax Ct. 1982. Assoc. Walter, Conston Alexander & Green, P.C., N.Y.C., 1981-88, Milbank, Tweed, Hadley & McCloy, N.Y.C., 1988—; atty. Vol. Lawyers for Arts, N.Y.C., 1985—. John Jay scholar, Columbia U., N.Y.C., 1974. Mem. ABA, N.Y. State Bar Assn. Office: Milbank Tweed Hadley & McCloy 1 Chase Manhattan Plaza New York NY 10005

ANDERSEN, TORBEN MAGNUS, economist, educator; b. Brønderslev, Denmark, Sept. 27, 1956; s. Magnus and Kirsten (Olesen) A.; m. Anne Mahler, Aug. 18, 1983; children: Jacob, Simon. MS, U. London, 1981; lic. econs., U. Aarhus, Denmark, 1984; PhD, Ctr. Operational Researcha and Econometrics, Belgium, 1986. Fellow Danish Social Sci. Research Council, Denmark, 1981-83; asst. prof. econs. U. Aarhus, 1983-84, assoc. prof., 1984-86, research prof., 1986—. Contbr. articles to profl. jours. Home: Aungingvej 43, 8344 Morke Denmark Office: U Aarhus, Universitetsparken, 8000 Aarhus Denmark

ANDERSON, BARRY STANLEY, health care executive; b. Atlanta, Sept. 6, 1942; s. Rex and Virginia A.; m. Katherine Krupp, Dec. 26, 1966 (div. 1973); 1 child, Jon Robert; m. Patricia Ann O'Neil, May 25, 1974; children: Russell Barry, Robert Bruce. AA, Foothill Coll., 1968; BA, San Francisco State U., 1976; MBA, U. N.D., 1984. V.p. Ventilation Assocs., Inc., Houston, 1971-74; program dir. Inst. Med. Studies, Berkeley, Calif., 1976-78; program dir. Sch. Respiratory Care, St. Alexius Med. Ctr., Bismarck, N.D., 1978-84, health care cons., dir. edn., 1984-87; mgr. respiratory care ops. Cardio Pulmonary Mgmt. Services, 1988—; chmn. bd. dirs., pres. Creative Mktg., Inc., Bismarck, Sacramento, 1982—; v.p. Baby Products Ltd., 1987—; asst. prof. U. of Mary, 1982-85. Author: (with D. Quesinberry) Blood Gas Interpretations, 1974; mem. editorial adv. bd. Respiratory Mgmt.; contbr. articles to profl. jours. Nominee Am. Coll. Healthcare Execs. Mem. Am. Mktg. Assn., Am. Mgmt. Assn., Am. Hosp. Assn., Acad. for Health Services Mktg., Assn. MBA Execs., Ctr. for Entrepreneurial Mgmt., U. N.D. Alumni Assn. Lodge: Elks. Avocations: computer programming, writing, reading, lecturing, sailing. Office: Yolo Gen Hosp 170 W Beamer St Woodland CA 95695

ANDERSON, BRADFORD WILLIAM, food company sales executive; b. Redlands, Calif., Feb. 17, 1956; s. B.W. and Helen Louise (Wisel) A.; m. Diane Elizabeth Hutt, Aug. 22, 1981. BS in Mgmt., U. Redlands, 1978; MBA in Mktg. Mgmt., Calif. State U., 1982. Cert. instr. in bus. edn., Calif. Store mgr. Fringer's Market, Redlands, Calif., 1978-80; ter. mgr. Carnation Co., Fullerton, Calif., 1980-82, sr. ter. mgr., trainer, 1982-84, dist. sales coordinator, 1984-85; nat. mgr. sales planning Carnation Co., Los Angeles, 1985—, implementation coordinator, 1984; instr. Chaffey Coll., Alta Loma, Calif., 1984-87. Active Muckenthaler Cultural Ctr, and Theater, Friends of Santa Ana Zoo, Diamond Bar Improvement Assn., Diamond Bar Ranch Festival. Named one of Outstanding Young Men in Am., Jaycees, 1984; recipient P. Pat Patterson Meml. Award, Santa Fe Fed. Savs., 1978; Harris Meml. scholar Harris Dept. Stores, 1978. Mem. Food Industry Sales Club, Alumni Assn. San Bernardino, Calif., Young Alumni Com. U. Redlands, Alpha Gamma Nu. Republican. Methodist. Home: 24442 Rosegate Pl Diamond Bar CA 91765 Office: Carnation Co 5045 Wilshire Blvd Los Angeles CA 90036

ANDERSON, BRUCE MORGAN, computer scientist; b. Battle Creek, Mich., Oct. 8, 1941; s. James Albert and Beverly Jane (Morgan) A.; B.S. in Elec. Engring., Northwestern U., 1964; M.S. in Elec. Engring., Purdue U., 1966; Ph.D. in Elec. Engring. (NASA fellow), Northwestern U., 1973; m. Jeannie Marie Hignight, May 24, 1975; children—Ronald, Michael, Valerie, John, Carolyn. Research engr. Zenith Radio Corp., Chgo., 1965-66; asso. engr. Ill. Inst. Tech. Research Inst., Chgo., 1966-68; sr. electronics engr. Rockwell Internat., Downers Grove, Ill., 1973-75; computer scientist Argonne (Ill.) Nat. Lab., 1975-77; mem. group tech. staff Tex. Instruments, Dallas, 1977-88, sr. scientist BBN Labs., 1988— ; lectr. computer sci. U. Tex.-Arlington and Dallas; adj. prof. computer sci. N. Tex. State U.; vis. indsl. prof. So. Meth. U.; computer systems cons. Info. Internat., Culver City, Calif., HCM Graphic Systems, Gt. Neck, N.Y.; computer cons. depts. geography, transp., econs., sociology and computer sci. Northwestern U., also instr. computer sci.; expert witness for firm Burleson, Pate and Gibson. Mem. IEEE Computer Soc. (chmn. Dallas 1984-85), Am. Assn. Artificial Intelligence, Assn. Computing Machinery (publs. chmn. 1986 fall joint computer conf. IEEE and Assn. Computing Machinery), Sigma Xi, Eta Kappa Nu, Theta Delta Chi. Contbr. articles to tech. jours. Club: Toastmasters Internat. Home: 94-491 Alamea Place Mililani HI 96789 Office: BBN Labs 61496 10 Moulton St Cambridge MA 02238

ANDERSON, CARL DAVID, scientist; b. N.Y.C., Sept. 3, 1905; s. Carl David and Emma Adolfina (Ajaxson) A.; m. Lorraine Elvira Bergman; children—Marshall David, David Andrew. B.S., Calif. Inst. of Tech., 1927, Ph.D. magna cum laude, 1930; hon. Sc.D., Colgate U., 1937, Gustavus Adolphus Coll., 1963; LL.D. (hon.), Temple U., 1948. Coffin research fellow Calif. Inst. Tech., 1927-28, teaching fellow in physics, 1928-30, research fellow in physics, 1930-33, asst. prof. physics, 1933-37, asso. prof., 1937-39, prof., 1939-76, prof. emeritus, 1976—, chmn. div. physics, math. and astronomy, 1962-70. Awarded gold medal Am. Inst. of City of N.Y., 1935; Nobel prize in physics, 1936; Elliott Cresson medal of the Franklin Inst., 1937; John Ericsson medal Am. Soc. Swedish Engrs., 1960. Mem. Am. Phys. Soc., Am. Philos. Soc., Nat. Acad. Scis., Sigma Xi, Tau Beta Pi. Address: Dept Physics Calif Inst of Tech Pasadena CA 91109 *

ANDERSON, CAROL HOUREN, real estate broker; b. Dallas, Nov. 12; d. C.C. and Adelaide (Graham) Randle; children—Jay R., Laura M. B.B.A., So. Meth. U., 1959, postgrad., 1975-76. Vice pres. Cromwell Corp., Dallas, 1971-75; pres. Balanced Investment Securities Corp., Dallas, 1973-75; real estate broker, Dallas, 1965—. Mem. tax adv. com. City of Dallas, 1981—; mem. women's bd. Dallas Civic Opera, 1979—; bd. dirs. Dallas Ballet, 1978—, pres. women's com., 1984-85, exec. com., 1984—; pres. Bentwood Republican Womans Club, Dallas, 1981; bd. dirs. Dallas County Council Rep. Women, 1982; Bd. dirs., pres. women's com. Creative Learning Ctr., 1987-88; chmn. Dallas Opera Opening Night, fa.. 1988; bd. dirs. N.D. Shared Ministries, 1987-88; del. state and nat. women's convs. Rep. Party, numerous yrs. including 1984; charter mem. Republican Forum, Dallas. Mem. Nat. Assn. Realtors, Tex. Assn. Realtors, Dallas Bd. Realtors Nat. Assn. Security Dealers, Press Club, AAUW, Northwood Inst. Womens Bd. Episcopalian. Clubs: Altrusa, Bentree Country, Dallas Charity Guild, others.

ANDERSON, CHARLES DAVID BEAUMONT, research psychologist; b. Dunfermline, Scotland, Oct. 31, 1952; s. Hector MacDonald and Catherine (Pratt) A. MA with honors, St. Andrew's U., 1975; MEd with distinction, Edinburgh U., 1984. Tchr., researcher Fife Regional Council Ednl. Psychology, Scotland, 1978-85; research assoc. dept. edn. U. Edinburgh, 1985-87, lectr., 1987—. Author, editor: Counselling in Aids and HIV, 1989; contbr. articles to profl. jours. Tng. officer Scottish Aids Monitor, Edinburg, 1987; mem. numerous social work coms. on drug and HIV problems. Mem. Brit. Psychol. Soc. Home: 68 Montpelier Park, Edinburgh EH 10, Scotland Office: U Edinburgh, Dept Edn, 10 Buccleuch Pl, Edinburgh EH8 9JT, Scotland

ANDERSON, CHARLES ROSS, civil engineer, surveying and cartography executive; b. N.Y.C., Oct. 4, 1937; s. Biard Eclare and Melva (Smith) A.; m. Susan Breinholt, Aug. 29, 1961; children: Loralee, Brian, Craig, Thomas, David. BSCE, U. Utah, 1961; MBA, Harvard U., 1963. Registered profl. engr.; cert. land surveyor. Owner, operator AAA Engring. and Drafting, Inc., Salt Lake City, 1960—. Mayoral appointee Housing Devel. com., Salt Lake City, 1981-86; bd. dirs., cons. Met. Water Dist., Salt Lake City, 1985—; bd. dirs., v.p., sec. bd. dirs. Utah Mus. Natural History, Salt Lake City, 1980—; asst. dist. commr. Sunrise Dist. Boy Scouts Am., Salt Lake City, 1985-86; fund raising coordinator architects and engrs. United Fund; mem. Sunstone Nat. Adv. Bd., 1980—; bd. dirs. Provo River Water Users Assn., 1986—. Fellow Am. Gen. Contractors, Salt Lake City, 1960; recipient Hamilton Watch award, 1961. Mem. ASCE, Am. Congress on Surveying and Mapping, Harvard U. Bus. Sch. Club (pres. 1970-72), Pres. Club U. Utah, Pi Kappa Alpha (internat. pres. 1972-74, trustee endowment fund 1974-80, Oustanding Alumnus 1967, 72), Phi Eta Sigma, Chi Epsilon, Tau Beta Pi. Clubs: The Country, Bonneville Knife and Fork (Salt Lake City). Lodge: Rotary (chmn. election com. 1980— Salt Lake City chpt.). Home: 2689 Comanche Dr Salt Lake City UT 84108 Office: AAA Engring & Drafting Inc 1865 S Main St Salt Lake City UT 84115

ANDERSON, DAVID DANIEL, writer, educator, editor; b. Lorain, Ohio, June 8, 1924; s. David and Nora Marie (Foster) A.; m. Patricia Ann Rittenhour, Feb. 1, 1953. B.S., Bowling Green State U., 1951, M.A., 1952; Ph.D., Mich. State U., 1960; D. Litt., Wittenberg U., 1986. From instr. to prof. dept. am. thought and lang. Mich. State U., East Lansing, 1957—; lectr. Am. Mus., Bath, Eng., 1980; editor U. Coll. Quar., 1971-80; Fulbright prof. U. Karachi, Pakistan, 1963-64; Am. del. to Internat. Fedn. Modern Langs. and Lit., 1969-84, Internat. Congress Orientalists, 1971-79. Author: Sherwood Anderson, 1968 (Book Manuscript award 1961), Louis Bromfield, 1964, Critical Studies in American Literature, 1964, Sherwood Anderson's Winesburg, Ohio, 1967, Brand Whitlock, 1968, Abraham Lincoln, 1970, Suggestions for the Instructor, 1971, Robert Ingersoll, 1972, Woodrow Wilson, 1978, Ignatius Donnelly, 1980, William Jennings Bryan, 1981; editor: The Black Experience, 1969, The Literary Works of Abraham Lincoln, 1970, Sunshine and Smoke: American Writers and the American Environment, 1971, (with others) The Dark and Tangled Path, 1971, MidAmerica I, 1974, II, 1975, III, 1976, IV, 1977, V, 1978, VI, 1979, VII, 1980, VIII, 1981, IX, 1982, X, 1983, XI, 1984, XII, 1985, XIII, 1986, XIV, 1987, Sherwood Anderson: Dimensions of his Literary Art, 1976, Sherwood Anderson: The Writer at His Craft, 1979, Critical Essays on Sherwood Anderson, 1981, Michigan: A State Anthology, 1983; editor Midwestern Miscellany, 1974—; also numerous articles, essays, short stories, poems. Served with USN, 1942-45; with AUS, 1952-53. Decorated Silver Star, Purple Heart; recipient Disting. Alumnus award Bowling Green State U., 1976, Disting. Faculty award Mich. State U., 1974, Mich. Assn. Governing Bds., 1988. Mem. AAUP, MLA, Popular Culture Assn., Soc. Study Midwestern Lit. (founder, exec. sec., Disting. Service award 1982), Assn. Gen. and Liberal Edn. Am. Assn. Advancement Humanities. Club: University. Home: 6555 Lansdown Dr Dimondale MI 48821 Office: Mich State U Dept Am Thought and Lang East Lansing MI 48824

ANDERSON, DEBORAH GAIL COOK, educator; b. San Antonio, Dec. 26, 1956; d. Clarence Edward and Dorothy Mae (Colvin) Cook; m. Dwight Edward Anderson, June 22, 1980 (div. Sept. 1981). BS, Tex. Woman's U., 1979; postgrad. U. Houston, 1982—. Spl. edn. tchr. Ashford Elem., Sch., Houston Ind. Sch. Dist., 1979-80, resource tchr., 1981—, sec. hospitality com., 1982—; substitute tchr. Marshall Elem. Sch., Detroit, 1980-81; spl. edn. pvt. tutor, Houston, 1982—; tutor Denton Assn. Student Helpers (Tex.), 1977; vol. behavior technician North Tex. State U. Ctr. Behavioral Studies, Denton, 1976-77; vol. Spl. Olympics, Denton, 1978, Lowry Hall, Denton, 1978. Mem. Young Women's Aux., Mt. Calvery Bapt. Ch., Denton, 1977-79, pres., 1978-79, mem. usher bd., 1977-79, youth worker, 1978-79; youth worker, Sunday sch. tchr., mem. outreach com., Christian debutante com. Liberty Bapt. Ch.; named Outstanding Young Educator Ashford Elem. Sch., 1985, Teacher of Yr. Ashford Elem. Sch., 1987; mem. Houston Council Edn., 1981—. Mem. Council Exceptional Children, Assn. Childhood Edn. Internat., NEA, NAACP (named most prominent black woman Tex. Woman's U. chpt. 1979), Nat. Assn. Black Social Workers, Tex. State Tchrs. Assn., Houston Tchrs. Assn., Mortar Bd., Sarah Circle, Alpha Chi, Delta Sigma Theta. Democrat. Home: 2020 Bentworth St Apt 414 Houston TX 77077 Office: Ashford Elem Sch 1815 Shannon Valley Houston TX 77077

ANDERSON, DONALD MORGAN, entomologist; b. Washington, Dec. 27, 1930; s. John Kenneth and Alice Cornelia (Morgan) A. B.A., Miami U., Oxford, Ohio, 1953; Ph.D., Cornell U.l, 1958. Grad. teaching asst. Cornell U., 1954-57; asst. prof. sci. SUNY-Buffalo, 1959-60, research fellow, 1960; research entomologist Dept. Agrl., Washington, 1960—; research assoc. Buffalo Mus. Sci., 1972—, Smithsonian Instn., 1978—. Contbr. articles to profl. jours., chpts to books. Sigma Xi grantee, 1959. Mem. Entomol. Soc. Washington (corr sec. 1963-65, pres. 1985), Entomol. Soc. Am., Soc. Systematic Zoology, Coleopterists Soc., Am. Inst. Biol. Scis., St. Andrews Soc. Washington, Clan Anderson Soc. (editor 1979-84, treas. 1985—), Sigma Xi, Phi Kappa Phi. Home: 1900 Lyttonsville Rd #804 Silver Spring MD 20910 Office: Systematic Entomology Lab Dept Agr Nat Mus Natural History Washington DC 20560

ANDERSON, DORRINE ANN PETERSEN (MRS. HAROLD EDWARD ANDERSON), librarian; b. Ishpeming, Mich., Feb. 24, 1923; d. Herbert Nathaniel and Dorothy (Eman) Petersen; B.S. with distinction, No. Mich. U., 1944; postgrad. Northwestern U., summer 1945, U. Wash., summer 1967, U. Mich. Extension, 1958-65; M.S. in L.S., Western Mich. U., 1970; m. Harold Edward Anderson, Aug. 23, 1947; children—Brian Peter, Kent Harold, Bruce Herbert, David (dec.), Timothy Jon. Tchr. English jr. high sch., Eaton Rapids, Mich., 1944-45; tchr. English, speech Arlington Heights (Ill.) High Sch., 1945-48; tchr. English high sch., Nahma, Mich., 1948-49, 54-61, Gladstone, Mich., 1961-62; librarian Gladstone Sch. and Pub. Library, 1962-70; dir. media services Gladstone Area Pub. Schs., 1971-87, Bicentennial coordinator, 1975-76, ret., 1987; mem. planning com. Upper Peninsula Region Library Cooperation, 1982—; rep.-at-large Mich. Citizens for Libraries. Acting dir. Mid-Peninsula Library Fedn., 1965-66; chmn. Region 21 Media Advisory Council, 1972-85; chmn. adv. com. Regional Ednl. Materials Center 21, 1973-85; regional del. Mich. White House Conf. on Libraries and Info. Services, 1979. Pres., Delta County League Woman Voters, 1970-72; mem. human resources subcom. Upper Peninsula Com. for Area Progress, 1964—; mem. com. for library devel. Upper Peninsula, chmn. Delta County Library Bd., 1967-76; mem. region 17, Polit. Action Team, 1968-70, Upper Peninsula Region of Library Cooperation Council, 1983-85, 86—; history chmn. Gladstone City Centennial Com., 1982-87 . County del. Delta County Democratic Com., 1968; trustee Library of Mich., 1984—; bd. dirs. Library of Mich. Found., 1985—. Named Tchr. of Year, Region 17 (Mich.), 1969. Mem. NEA, Mich. Edn. Assn. (pres. region 17 council 1967-68, chmn. Upper Peninsula dels. to rep. assembly 1966-68), ALA, Mich. Library Assn., Internat. Reading Assn., Mich. Assn. Media in Edn. (state Library Week chmn. 1973-74; recipient leadership award 1977, Spl. Services award 1987), Mich. Assn. Sch. Library Suprs., Upper Peninsula Reading Conf. (program chmn. Leadership award planning com. 1981), AAUW, Assn. Ednl. Communications and Tech., Kappa Delta Pi, Phi Epsilon, Beta Phi Mu, Delta Kappa Gamma (recipient citation for seminars in mgmt. for women 1977, v.p., program chmn. Beta Sigma chpt. 1980-82). Home: 1723 Montana Ave Gladstone MI 49837

ANDERSON, DOUGLAS SCRANTON HESLEY, investment banker; b. Springfield, Mass., Aug. 23, 1929; s. Lloyd Douglas Hesley and Alice Scranton (Eastman) Anderson. grad. Deerfield Acad., 1947; A.B., Harvard U., 1951; cert. investment banking Northwestern U., 1959; m. Elizabeth Bartram Radley, Sept. 20, 1969; 1 dau., Katherine Scranton. Gen. partner The Anderson Co., Greenwich, Conn., 1953—, MAH Co., Greenwich, 1979—; investment banker Lehman Bros., Salomon Bros. & Hutzler, Legg & Co. and Sterling, Grace & Co., Inc., N.Y.C., 1960-81. Pres., Pecksland Rd. Assn., 1977-78; bd. dirs. Indian Harbor Assn., 1979—, treas., 1986— ; rep. Greenwich Town Meeting, 1979—, legis. com., 1979—, vice chmn., 1986-87, chmn., 1988—, founder, mem. spl. cost containment com., 1984-86, sec., 1986; assoc. Rep. town com., 1984-87, mem., 1988—; trustee Round Hill Community Ch., Greenwich, 1980-85, treas., 1982-85 ; sec. Greenwich Selectman's Utility Watch Com., 1982—. Served to lt. USNR, 1951-53. Mem. Assn. Former Intelligence Officers, Conn. Police Chiefs Assn., Soc. Colonial Wars (council 1984—, gov. 1988—), Mayflower Descs., Order Founders and Patriots, Soc. Cincinnati. Clubs: Round Hill, Fox, Harvard Varsity, Harvard of Boston; Army and Navy (Washington); West Palm Beach Fishing; Edgartown (Mass.) Yacht, Chappaquiddick Beach. Home: 39 Vista Dr Greenwich CT 06830-7128

ANDERSON, EDGAR, history educator; b. Tukums, Latvia, June 17, 1920; s. Voldemar and Emilija Alma (Kaneps) A.; Historian, U. Riga (Latvia), 1939-44; postgrad. U. Wurzburg (Germany), 1946-49, U. Leiden (Netherlands), 1948; Ph.D. in History, U. Chgo., 1956; m. Ligita Apinis, June 19, 1958; children: Raymond Edgar, Philip Rudolf. Came to U.S., 1949, naturalized, 1956. Lectr. U. Extension Wurzburg, 1945-49; asst. dept. mgr. Sharp & Dohme, 1950-52; instr. Lake Forest (Ill.) Coll., 1953-57; prof. history San Jose State U., 1957—; guest prof. Australian Nat. U., U. Melbourne, U. Adelaide, U. Sydney, U. Göttingen, U. Bonn, U. Münster, U. Kiel, U. Erlangen, U. Riga, U. West Indies, U. Toronto; lectr., Europe, 1949, 50, 56, 57, 67, 71, 73, 75, 77, 79, 81, 83, 84, 85, 86, W.I., S.Am., 1957, 59, 60, 74, 76, 78, 80, 82, 85, Can., 1972, 74, 75, 78, 84, 85, Australia, N.Z., 1967, Soviet Union, 1977, 79, Israel, 1983, Vatican, 1986; gen. chmn. 2d Internat. Conf. Baltic Studies; leader hist., archaeol. expdn., Trinidad, Tobago, 1960, co-leader, 1979; disting. prof. Livingston U., 1969. Named Outstanding Educator in Am., 1972, Outstanding Prof., San Jose State U., 1974-75, Pres.'s scholar, 1981. Mem. Am. Hist. Assn., AAUP, Am. Assn. Slavic Studies, Soc. Advancement Scandinavian Study, Assn. for Advancement of Baltic Studies (pres. 1972-73), Am. Acad. Polit. Sci., Inst. Caribbean Studies, Baltisches Forschungsinstitut (Germany), Phi Kappa Phi (Disting. Acad. Achievements award 1978), Tau Kappa Epsilon. Author: Western World, Western Horizon, 1949; Cross-Road Country Latvia, 1953; History of Latvia; 1914-20, 1967; Tobago, 1962; Die militarische Situation der Baltischen Staaten, 1969; The Ancient Couronians in Africa, 1970; The Ancient Couronians in America and the Colonization of Tobago, 1971; World Communism, 1971; Baltic History, 1974; Guide to the Diplomatic Archives of Western Europe, 1975; The Baltic States in Peace and War, 1978; The United States and the Soviet Union in the 1980s, 1981; History of Latvia, 1920-1940, 2 vols., 1982-84; The Armed Forces of Latvia and Their Historical Background, 1983; others; editor-in-chief Latvian Ency., 1979—; contbr. numerous articles to profl. jours., chpts. to books, also Ency. Brit., Harvard Ency. Am. Ethnic Groups. Hist. research in U.S., Eng., France, Germany, Holland, W.I., Italy, Vatican, Spain, Pacific, USSR, Scandinavian and Baltic states. Home: 2571 Booksin Ave San Jose CA 95125

ANDERSON, ERROL, government official; b. Highgate, St. Mary, Jamaica, Feb. 1, 1940; s. Noel and Geraldine (Johnson) A.; m. Dec. 13, 1969; children: Eroleen, Erica. B in Econs., Univ. Coll. of the West Indies. Asst. Island supr. Bustamente Indsl. Trade Union, Jamaica, 1969-70; worker del. Internat. Labour Orgn. Conv., Geneva, 1969-70; then co-chmn. Joint Indsl. Council, Kingston, Jamaica; minister of youth and community devel. Govt.

of Jamaica, 1980-83, minister of the pub. service, 1984-86, minister of nat. security, 1986—; dep. chmn. Jamaica Labour Party. Mem. Disciples of Christ Ch. Club: Kingston Cricket. Office: 12 Ocean Boulevard, Kingston Mall Jamaica *

ANDERSON, FLEMMING GOTTHELF, humanities educator; b. Fraugde, Denmark, Sept. 20, 1950; s. Lars Viggo and Tove (Gotthelf) A.; m. Anne Schmidt, Apr. 13, 1984; children: Else Marie, Kristian. Grad., Odense (Denmark) U., 1977, D in Philosophy, 1985. Research fellow Odense U., 1979-85, adj. prof., 1986-87, sr. lectr., 1987—, bd. dirs. Medieval Ctr. Danish Research Council for Humanities fellow, Copenhagen, 1983, 84, 85, Inst. for Advanced Studies in Humanities fellow, Edinburgh, Scotland, 1985. Mem. SIEF Kommission Volksdichtung, Kommission Lied, Musik und Tanzforschung. Home: Bredbjergvej 62, 5462 Morud Denmark Office: Odense U, Campusvej 55, 5230 Odense Denmark

ANDERSON, FRANCES SWEM, nuclear medical technologist; b. Grand Rapids, Mich., Nov. 27, 1913; d. Frank Oscar and Carrie (Strang) Swem; student Muskegon Sch. Bus., 1959-60; cert. Muskegon Community Coll., 1964; m. Clarence A.F. Anderson, Apr. 9, 1934; children—Robert Curtis, Clarelyn Christine (Mrs. Roger L. Schmelling), Stanley Herbert. X-ray file clk., film librarian Hackley Hosp., Muskegon, Mich., 1957-59; student refresher course in nuclear med. tech. Chgo. Soc. Nuclear Med. Techs., 1966; radioisotope technologist and sec. Hackley Hosp., 1959-65; nuclear med. technologist Butler Meml. Hosp., Muskegon Heights, Mich., 1966-70, Mercy Hosp., Muskegon, 1970-79; ret., 1979. Mem. Muskegon Civic A Capella choir, 1932-39; mem. Mother-Tch. Singers, PTA, Muskegon, 1941-48, treas. 1944-48; with Muskegon Civic Opera Assn., 1950-51, office vol. Alive '88 Crusade, mem. com. for 60th High Sch. class reunion. Soc. Nuclear Medicine Cert. nuclear medicine technologist Soc. Nuclear Medicine. Mem. Am. Registry Radiologic Technologists. Mem. Forest Park Covenant Ch. (mem. choir 1953-79, 83—, choir sec. 1963-69, Sunday sch. tchr. 1954-75, supt. Sunday sch. 1975-78, treas. Sunday sch. 1981-86, chmn. master planning council, coordinator centennial com. to 1981, ch. sec. 1982-84, 87); co-chmn. Jackson Hill Old Timers Reunion, 1982, 83, 85; mem. Muskegon Body Building Assn. Health and Wellness Ctr. (permanent, member of month Mar., 1985). Home: 5757 E Sternberg Rd Fruitport MI 49415

ANDERSON, G. NORMAN, foreign service officer; b. Lewes, Del., Mar. 26, 1932; m. Mary Bonnie Churchill; 3 children. BA, Columbia Coll., 1954; MIA, Sch. Internat. Studies, 1960. Personnel officer Fgn. Service, 1960-62; Arabic lang. tng. Fgn. Service Inst., Beirut, 1963-66; polit. officer Beirut, 1963-66; Russian lang. tng. U.S. Army Inst. for Advanced Russian Studies, Garmisch, Fed. Republic Germany, 1966-67; asst. adminstrv. officer Moscow, 1967-68, polit. officer, 1968-69; Soviet desk officer Dept. State, 1969-71, Egyptian desk officer, 1971-74; polit. counselor Rabat, Morocco, 1974-78; spl. asst. to Sr. Advisor to Pres. and Sec. of State on Mid. East and Soviet Affairs, 1978-79; dep. chief U.S. Mission, Sofia, Bulgaria, 1982-86, Tunis, Tunisia, 1986—; now ambassador to Sudan. Served to lt. USN, 1954-58. Office: Embassy of Sudan care State Dept 2201 C St NW Washington DC 20520 *

ANDERSON, GERALDINE LOUISE, laboratory scientist; b. Mpls., July 7, 1941; d. George M. and Viola Julia-Mary (Abel) Havrilla; m. Henry Clifford Anderson, May 21, 1966; children—Bruce Henry, Julie Lynne. BS, U. Minn., 1963. Med. technologist Swedish Hosp., Mpls., 1963-68; hematology supr. Glenwood Hills Hosp. lab., Golden Valley, Minn., 1968-70; assoc. scientist dept. pediatrics U. Minn. Hosps., Mpls., 1970-74; instr. health occupations and med. lab. asst. Suburban Hennepin County Area Vocat. Tech. Ctr., Brooklyn Park, Minn., 1974-81, St. Paul Tech. Vocat. Inst., 1978—; research med. technologist Miller Hosp., St. Paul, 1975-78; research assoc. Children's and United Hosps., St. Paul, 1979-88; mem. health occupations adv. com. Hennepin Tech. Ctrs., 1975—, chairperson, 1978-79; mem. hematology slide edn. rev. bd. Am. Soc. Hematology, 1976—. Contbr. articles to profl. jours. Mem. Med. Lab. Tech. Polit. Action Com., 1978—; resource person lab. careers Robbinsdale Sch. Dist., Minn., 1970-79; del. Crest View Home Assn., 1981—; mem. sci. and math. subcom. Minn. High Tech. Council. Recipient service awards and honors Omicron Sigma. Mem. Minn. Soc. Med. Tech. (sec. 1969-71), Am. Soc. Profl. and Exec. Women, Am. Soc. Med. Tech. (del. to ann. meetings 1972—, chmn. hematology sci. assembly 1977-79, nomination com. 1979-81, bd. dirs. 1985-88), Twin City Hosp. Assn. (speakers bur. 1968-70), Assn. Women in Sci., World Future Soc., AAAS, AAUW, Minn. Med. Tech. Alumni, Am. Soc. Hematology, Soc. Analytical Cytology, Nat. Assn. Female Execs., Sigma Delta Epsilon (corr. sec. Xi chpt. 1980-82, pres. 1982-84), Alpha Mu Tau. Lutheran. Office: United Hosps Inc 333 Smith Ave N Saint Paul MN 55102

ANDERSON, J. TRENT, lawyer; b. Indpls., July 22, 1939; s. Robert C. and Charlotte M. (Pfeifer) A.; m. Judith J. Zimmerman, Sept. 8, 1962; children: Evan M., Molly K. BS, Purdue U., 1961; LLB, U. Va., 1964. Bar: Ill. 1965, Ind. 1965. Teaching asst. U. Cal. Law Sch., Berkeley, 1964-65; assoc. Mayer, Brown & Platt, Chgo., 1965-72, ptnr., 1972—; instr. Loyola U. Law Sch., Chgo., 1985. Mem. ABA, Ill. Assn. Hosp. Attys., Law Club. Clubs: Union League (Chgo.), Mich. Shores (Wilmette, Ill.). Home: 2312 Lincolnwood Dr Evanston IL 60201 Office: Mayer Brown & Platt 190 S LaSalle St Chicago IL 60603

ANDERSON, JACK JOE, communications executive; b. Lipan, Tex., Oct. 22, 1928; s. William Amon and Tommie Lucille (Roberts) A.; B.A., San Jose State U., 1965, M.A., 1967; postgrad. in bus. adminstrn. Pepperdine U., Los Angeles; m. Maria I. Kamantauskas, Mar. 13, 1976; children—Mark, Douglas, Craig. Asst. mgr. edn. systems Lockheed Missiles & Space Co., Sunnyvale, Calif., 1966-69; v.p. Learning Achievement Corp., San Jose, Calif., 1969-74; mgr. instrnl. systems Ford Aerospace & Communications Corp., Pasadena, Calif., 1974-83; pres. Anderson & Assocs., Alta Loma, Calif., 1983—; cons. tng. programs and systems, 1969-74. Served with USAF, 1946-66. Decorated 2 Air Force commendation medals; recipient nat. award for tng. program design Indsl. TV Assn., 1974. Mem. Am. Mgmt. Assn., Am. Soc. Tng. and Devel. Contbr. tech. and gen. instrnl. materials in field. Office: Anderson & Assocs 9155 Carrari Ct Alta Loma CA 91701

ANDERSON, JANICE LINN, real estate broker; b. Paris, Tenn., Sept. 2, 1943; d. Orel Vernon and Rosie Elizabeth (Brockwell) L.; m. David James Anderson, June 11, 1965 (div. Oct. 1973). Entertainer, recording artist 4-Sons Record Co., Paris, Tenn., 1958-73; med. transcriptionist The Paris Clinic, 1965-73; computer operator, asst. to v.p. Medicare Adminstrn./Equitable, Nashville, 1973-74; property mgmt. asst. Dobson & Johnson, Inc., Nashville, 1974-76; dir. leasing and mgmt. Fortune-Nashville Co., 1976-78; real estate brokerage asst. J.G. Martin, Jr./Caudill Properties, Inc., Nashville, 1978—; pvt. practice resume preparation, Nashville, 1982—. Active Girl Scouts U.S., Paris, 1967-69; mem. ARC, Nashville, 1978, Am. Inst. for Cancer Research, Washington, D.C., 1985, Christian Appalachian Project, Lancaster, Ky., 1986. Mem. Nat. Assn. Female Execs., Bus. and Profl. Womens Club (Pres. 1965-73), Profl. Musicians Union, Womens Missionary Union (bd. dirs. Paris chpt. 1970-71), Internat. Platform Assn., Realtors' Secs. Assn., Am. Biographical Inst., Inc. Baptist. Home: 812 Elissa Dr Nashville TN 37217 Office: J G Martin Jr/Caudill Properties Inc American Trust Bldg 15th Fl Nashville TN 37201

ANDERSON, JERRY ALLEN, operations analysis manager; b. Ashland, Wis., Feb. 10, 1947; s. Elmer and Thelma Louise (Fallis) A.; m. Anne Marie Brown, June 7, 1975; 1 child, Kristen Marie. BBA, Temple U., 1969, MBA, 1975. Sr. investment officer Girard Bank, Phila., 1970-80; sr. investment analyst Sanford C. Bernstein, N.Y.C., 1980-83; dir. planning Sperry New Holland (Pa.), Inc., 1983-85, mgr. ops. analysis, 1985—; cons. in fin.; instr. Temple U. Sch. Bus., 1976-79, Sch. Bus. and Govt. Services, 1979-80. Recipient Cert. of Recognition, Am. Mktg. Assn., 1968, 69, Outstanding Performance award Ford New Holland, 1987. Fellow Fin. Analysts Fedn.; mem. Fin. Analysts of Phila., N.Y. Soc. Security Analysts, Model A Ford Club Am., Beta Gamma Sigma, Theta Chi. Avocations: Model A restoration, numismatics, fishing, scuba diving, hunting. Home: 544 Norwyck Dr King of Prussia PA 19406 Office: Ford New Holland Inc 500 Diller Ave New Holland PA 17557

ANDERSON, JOHN MACKENZIE, lawyer; b. Newark, Ohio, Dec. 1, 1938; s. Samuel Albert Jr. and Margaret Lillian (MacKenzie) A.; m. Jane Venable Shelton, Aug. 17, 1963; children—Graham, Gregory, Jonathan. A.B. with high honors, Kenyon Coll., 1960; LL.B., Yale U., 1963. Bar: Ohio 1963, Ky., 1985, Pa. 1988. Assoc., Peck, Shaffer & Williams, Cin., 1963-70, ptnr., 1970—, also chmn. adminstrv. com.; lectr. Practising Law Inst., 1975-77. Chmn. Am. Scotch Highland Breeders Assn., 1985-87; trustee Seven Hills Schs., 1976-81; del. Democratic Nat. Conv., 1976; trustee Ohio Nut Growers Assn., 1979-87. Mem. Am. Bar Assn., Ky. Bar Assn., No. Ky. Bar Assn., Ohio State Bar Assn., Pa. Bar Assn., Cin. Bar Assn., Assn. of Bar of City of N.Y. Democrat. Episcopalian. Clubs: Cincinnati, Bankers; Yale (N.Y.). Author: Next of Kin, 1980; The Kincade Chronicles, 1986; contbr. articles to profl. jours. Home: 2717 Johnstone Pl Cincinnati OH 45206 Office: 2200 1st Nat Bank Center Cincinnati OH 45202

ANDERSON, JOSEPH NORMAN, executive consultant, former food company executive, former college president; b. Mpls., May 12, 1926; s. Joseph E. and Helen (Larson) A.; m. Ruth E. Anderson, Sept. 6, 1952; children: Peter, Timothy, Paul, Matthew, Robin, Kathryn, Charles. B.B.A. with distinction, U. Minn., 1947. With Sears, Roebuck & Co., 1947-49, Gamble-Skogmo, Inc., 1950-64; v.p. finance, dir. Nat. Bellas Hess, Inc., 1964-67, pres., chief exec. officer, dir., 1967-69, chmn. bd., pres., chief exec. officer, 1969-75; pres. Jamestown (N.D.) Coll., 1975-83, Dakota Bake-n-Serv, Inc., 1979-86; exec. cons. Gladstone, Mo., 1986—; Pres. Merchants Research Council, 1961-62. Served with AUS, 1953-55. Mem. Phi Beta Kappa, Beta Gamma Sigma. Republican. Presbyn.

ANDERSON, KARL RICHARD, aerospace engineer, consultant; b. Vinita, Okla., Sept. 27, 1917; s. Axel Richard and Hildred Audrey (Marshall) A.; B.S., Calif. Western U., 1964, M.A., 1966; Ph.D., U.S. Internat. U., 1970; m. Jane Shigeko Hiratsuka, June 20, 1953; 1 son, Karl Richard. Engr. personnel subsystems Atlas Missile Program, Gen. Dynamics, San Diego, 1960-63; design engr. Solar div. Internat. Harvester, San Diego, 1964-66, sr. design engr., 1967-69, project engr., 1970-74, product safety specialist, 1975-78; aerospace engring. cons., 1979-86; cons. engring., 1979—; lectr. Am. Indian Sci. and Engring. Soc. Served to maj. USAF, 1936-60. Recipient Spl. Commendation San Diego County Bd. Supervisors, 1985, Spl. Commendation San Diego City Council, 1985. Registered profl. engr., Calif. Republican. Episcopalian. Home: 5886 Scripps St San Diego CA 92122

ANDERSON, KENNETH NORMAN, editor, author; b. Omaha, July 10, 1921; s. Duncan McDonald and Letitia Jane (Steed) A.; m. Lois Elaine Harmon, Jan. 12, 1945; children—Eric Stephen, Randi Laine, Jani Jill, Douglas Duncan. Student, U. Omaha, 1939-41, Oreg. State Coll., 1943-44, Stanford U., 1944-45, Northwestern U. Coll. Medicine, 1945-46, U. Chgo., 1958-60. With U.S. Army Fin. Office, Nebr. and Mont., 1941-42; engring. aid U.S. Army C.E., Omaha, 1946; radio news editor Sta. KOIL, Omaha, 1946-47; bur. mgr. Internat. News Service, Omaha, 1947-56, Kansas City, Mo., 1947-56; spl. features editor Better Homes and Garden mag., 1956-57; assoc. editor Popular Mechanics mag., 1957-59; editor Today's Health mag., pub. by AMA, Chgo., 195-65, Holt, Rinehart & Winston, N.Y.C., 1965-70; exec. dir. Coffee Info. Inst., N.Y.C., 1970-81; pres. Pubs. Editorial Services, Inc., Katonah, N.Y., 1981—, The Editorial Guild, Inc., Katonah, N.Y., 1981—; lectr. mag. writing New Sch. Social Research, 1959, NYU, 1960, Omaha U., 1961, Rensselaer Poly. Inst., 1964; cons. med. editor Ferguson Pub. Co., 1971-76. Author: (with others) Lawyers' Medical Cyclopedia, 1962, The Family Physician, 1963, Today's Health Guide, 1965, Pictorial Medical Guide, 1967, Field and Stream Guide to Physical Fitness, 1969, New Concise Family Medical and Health Guide, 1971, Complete Illustrated Book of Better Health, 1973, The New Complete Medical and Health Ency., 4 vols., 1977, The Sterno Guide to the Outdoors, 1977, Eagle Claw Fish Cookbook, 1978, Guide to Weight Control and Fitness, 1978, Newsweek Ency. of Family Health, 1980, Urdang Dictionary of Current Medical Terms, 1981, Pocket Guide to Coffee and Teas, 1982, Bantam Medical Dictionary, 1982, Mosby's Medical and Nursing Dictionary, 1982, Longman's Dictionary of Psychology and Psychiatry, 1983; editor: Hudson Health Newsletter, 1982—, Orphan Drugs, 1983, Gourmet Guide to Fish and Shellfish, 1984, Prentice-Hall Dictionary of Nutrition and Health, 1984, U.S. Military Operations, 1945-84, 1984, Mosby's Medical Encyclopedia, 1985, The Language of Sex, 1986, Industrial Medicine Desk Reference, 1986, New Pediatric Guide to Drugs & Vitamins, 1987, Symptoms after 40, 1987, Signet/Mosby Medical Encyclopedia, 1987, Consumer Guide Illustrated Medical Dictionary, 1988; contbr. Grolier, Funk & Wagnalls Encys.; adv. editor Nutrition Today, 1965-75. Home: 23 McQueen St Katonah NY 10536 Office: PO Box 247 Katonah NY 10536

ANDERSON, KENNETH OSCAR, film company executive; b. Rembrandt, Ia., Dec. 23, 1917; s. Oscar Frank and Ethel Mae (Anderson) A.; student Wheaton Coll., 1936-37, 45-51, Northwestern U., 1947-48; m. Doris Ilene Jones, Nov. 16, 1938; children—Naomi (Mrs. Larry Clark), Margaret (Mrs. T. Landon Mauzy), Donn, Lane, Max, Ken D., Melody. Editor, Campus Life Mag., Wheaton, Ill., 1945-51; with Gospel Films, Muskegon, Mich., 1949-61, exec. producer, 1949-61; pres. Ken Anderson Films, Winona Lake, Ind., 1963—; dir. Master Investments Corp., Warsaw, Ind.; dir. Internat. Films, London, 1969-72, Reach & Teach, London; vis. instr. Haggai Inst., Singapore, 1974—; vis. lectr. St. Xavier's Coll., Bombay, 1979. Mem. pres.'s com. Grace Coll., Winona Lake, 1972—; adv. com. League for the Handicapped, Walworth, Wis., 1965—; bd. dirs. Youth Haven Ranch, Rives Junction, Mich., Crusade Evangelism, London, Ont., Can. Named Evang. Press Assn. Writer of Year, 1962; Nat. Evang. Film Found. award as Dir. of Year, 1970. Mem. Gidions Internat. Presbyterian (elder 1963—). Author: Himalyan Heartbeat, 1966; Stains on Glass Windows, 1969; Adjustable Halo, 1969; Satan's Angels, 1975, Contemporary Concordance, 1988; (with Tony Mockus) I'm Learning from Protestants How to be a Better Catholic, 1975; producer, dir. film of book Pilgrim's Progress, 1977, film Christiana, 1978, Some Through the Fire (Uganda), 1980, Hudson Taylor, 1981; dir. Mud, Sweat and Cheers, 1984; Fanny Crosby, 1984. Home: 720 N Lake St Warsaw IN 46580 Office: PO Box 618 Winona Lake IN 46590

ANDERSON, LEIF GUNNAR, chemical oceanography educator; b. Trollhättan, Sweden, May 25, 1951; s. Gunnar and Sigrid Margareta (Andersson) A.; m. Marie Kathy Svensson. Masters degree, U. Goteborg (Sweden), 1975, Doctoral degree, 1981, docent, 1985. Postdoctoral Swedish Natural Sci. Research Council to Can., 1982-83; research asst. U. Göteborg, 1981-82, 83-87; asst. prof. U. Gäteborg, 1987. Contbr. articles to profl. jours. Natural Sci. Research Council grantee, 1982-87, YMER-80 Bd. grantee, 1984-87. Mem. Swedish Environ. Protection Bd. (marine com.), Nat. Council of Oceanography. Office: Dept of Analytical and Marine Chem, CTH/GU, S-41296 Goteborg Sweden

ANDERSON, LINDSAY GORDON, film and theater director; b. Bangalore, India, Apr. 17, 1923; s. Alexander Vass and Estelle Bell (Gasson) A.; ed. Cheltenham Coll., Wadham Coll., Oxford. Dir. films: (documentary) Meet the Pioneers, 1948; (theatrical) This Sporting Life, The White Bus, If . . . , O Lucky Man!, In Celebration, Britannia Hospital, If You Were There ..., The Whales of August; dir. theatrical prodns.: In Celebration, Home, The Changing Room, Life Class; dir. for TV: The Old Crowd, 1979, Sister Ruth, 1988; dir. Hamlet, Royal Theatre, Stratford, 1981, The Cherry Orchard, 1983, The Playboy of The Western World, 1984, In Celebration, 1984, Holiday, 1986. Recipient Acad. award for Thursday's Children, 1953; Venice Grand prix for Every Day Except Christmas, 1957; Grand prix Cannes Internat. Film Festival for If . . ., 1969. Author: Making a Film, 1952; About John Ford, 1981; co-founder, editor Sequence, 1947-51. Office: Rep Maggie Parker, A1 Prker Ltd, 55 Park Ln, London WI 01-499 4232, England

ANDERSON, LLOYD LEE, animal science educator; b. Nevada, Iowa, Nov. 18, 1933; s. Clarence and Carrie G. (Sampson) A.; m. JaNelle R. Sanny, June 15, 1970; children—Marc C., James R. Student, Simpson Coll., 1951-52, Iowa State U., 1952-53; B.S. in Animal Husbandry, Iowa State U., 1957, Ph.D. in Animal Reproduction, 1961. NIH postdoctoral fellow Iowa State U., Ames, 1961-62, asst. prof., 1961-65, assoc. prof., 1965-71, prof. animal sci., 1971—; Lalor Found. fellow Station de Recherches de Physiologie Animale, Institut National de Recherche Agronomique, Jouy-en-Josas, France, 1963-64; researcher physiology of reproduction; mem. reproductive biology study sect., NIH, 1984-88, Nat. Insts. of Health Reviewers Reserve (NRR), 1988-92; mem. peer rev. panel animal health spl. research grants on beef cattle and dairy cattle reproductive diseases U.S. Dept. Agriculture, 1986—. Editorial bd. Biology Reproduction, 1968-70, 86—, Jour. Animal Sci., 1982—, Animal Reproduction Sci., 1978—, Inst. for Sci. Info. Atlas of Sci., 1987—; contbr. articles to profl. jours. Served with U.S. Army, 1953-55. USDA grantee, 1978—; recipient Animal Physiology and Endocrinology award Am. Soc. of Animal Sci., 1988. Fellow Am. Soc. Animal Sci. (hon.); mem. Endocrine Soc., Am. Physiol. Soc., Am. Assn. Anatomists, Soc. for Study of Reproduction, Soc. for Experimental Biology and Medicine (council 1980-83), Brit. Soc. for the Study Fertility, AAAS, Sigma Xi, Gamma Sigma Delta. Methodist. Home: 1703 Maxwell Ave Ames IA 50010 Office: Iowa State U Dept Animal Sci 11 Kildee Hall Ames IA 50011

ANDERSON, MARILYN NELLE, educator; b. Las Animas, Colo., May 5, 1942; d. Mason Hadley Moore and Alice Carrie (Dwyer) Coates; m. George Robert Anderson, Sept. 4, 1974; children: Lisa Lynn, Edward Alan, Justin Patrick. BEd magna cum laude, Adams State Coll., 1962, postgrad., 1965; MEd, Ariz. State U., 1967; postgrad., Idaho State U., 1971, 86. Cert. elem. tchr., K-12 sch. counselor. Tchr. Wendell (Idaho) Sch. Dist. 232, 1962-66, Union-Endicott (N.Y.) Sch. Dist., 1967-68; counselor, librarian West Yuma (Colo.) Sch. Dist., 1968-69; elem. sch. counselor Am. Falls (Idaho) Sch. Dist. 381, 1969-73; project dir. Gooding County (Idaho) Sr. Citizens Orgn., 1974-75; tchr. Castleford (Idaho) Sch. Dist. 417, 1982—; mem. Castleford Schs. Merit Pay Devel. program, 1983-84, Accreditation Evaluation com., 1984-85, Math. Curriculum Devel. com., 1985-86. Leader Brownie Scouts, Endicott, 1967-68; chmn. fundraising com. Am. Falls Kindergarten, 1971-73; leader Gooding County 4-H Council, Wendell, 1983—. Recipient Leader's award Nat. 4-H Conservation Natural Resources Program, 1984. Mem. NEA, Idaho Edn. Assn., Idaho Council Internat. Reading Assn., Magic Valley Reading Assn., Internat. Platform Assn., Castleford Parent-Tchr. Youth Orgn., Castleford Tchr.'s Orgn. (sec.-treas. 1984-86). Republican. Baptist. Home: Rt 1 PO Box 293 Wendell ID 83355 Office: Castleford Schs Castleford ID 83355

ANDERSON, MARION CORNELIUS, medical educator; b. Concordia, Kans., Oct. 9, 1926; s. Cornelius Oscar and Mildred Marian (Watson) A.; m. Sonia Blue Bennett, Jan. 30, 1949; children: Dudley Scott, James Christopher, Julia, Laura Gail. Student, U. Kans., 1946-49; B.S., Northwestern U., 1950, M.D., 1953, M.S., 1960. Diplomate: Am. Bd. Surgery. Intern Passavant Meml. Hosp., Chgo., 1953-54; resident in surgery Passavant Meml. Hosp., 1954-55, Kanavel fellow in surgery, 1956-57; resident in surgery VA Research Hosp., Chgo., 1955-56; assoc. in surgery Cook County Hosp., Chgo., 1957-59; clin. asst. dept. surgery Northwestern U. Med. Sch., 1958, instr., 1958-59, assoc., 1960-62, asst. prof., 1962-64, asso. prof., 1964-68; prof., chmn. dept. surgery Med. Coll. Ohio, Toledo, 1969-72; pres. Med. Coll. Ohio, 1972-77; vice chmn. dept. surgery Med. U. S.C., 1977, chmn. dept. surgery, 1978; cons. Stedmans Med. Dictionary, 1970. Editorial bd.: Am. Jour. Surgery, Am. Surgeon; Contbr. articles to profl. jours. Served with USNR, 1944-46. ACS. Kemper research scholar, 1960. Mem. AAAS, Am. Assn. Med. Writers, Am. Assn. for Surgery of Trauma, A.C.S. (gov. 1984-87), Am. Gastroent. Assn., AMA., Am., Central, Western surg. assns., Cleve., Midwest, Pan-Pacific, Toledo (pres. 1970-71) surg. socs., So. Surg. Assn., Assn. Am. Med. Colls., Detroit Gastroent. Soc., Internat. Soc. Surgery, Nat. Soc. Med. Research, N.Y. Acad. Sci., Northwestern U. Med. Sch. Alumni Assn. (pres. 1965-66, Service award 1968), Pancreas Club (sec. 1968-69), Soc. Clin. Surgery, Soc. for Surgery Alimentary Tract (v.p. 1983), Soc. Surg. Chairmen, Southeastern Surg. Congress, Soc. Univ. Surgeons, Surg. Biology Club III, S.C. Med. Assn., Charleston County Med. Soc., Sigma Xi, Alpha Omega Alpha, Phi Chi. Club: Charleston Country. Home: 1580 Fairway Dr Charleston SC 29412

ANDERSON, MARY CROW (MRS. JAMES ROBERT DICKIE ANDERSON), educator; b. Sumter, S.C., July 21, 1922; d. Orin Faison and Innis (Cuttino) Crow; student Winthrop Coll., 1938-39; m. James Robert Dickie Anderson, July 5, 1942; children: James Orin, Barbara Innis, Richard Cothonneau. A.B. magna cum laude, U. S.C., 1942, M.Ed., 1952, Ph.D., 1966; postdoctoral study Exeter Coll., Oxford U., 1971; Tchr. high sch., Bamberg, S.C., 1942, Dentsville, S.C., 1950-51, Columbia, S.C., 1951-56, 60-71; prin. Heathwood Hall Episcopal Sch., Columbia, 1956-60; tchr. English and humanities Dreher High Sch., Columbia, 1960-71, chmn. English dept., 1967-69; asst. prof. U. S.C., Columbia, 1971-75, assoc. prof., 1975-87, prof. emerita, 1987—; mem. faculty senate, 1973-76, 79-82. Author: The Huguenot in the South Carolina Novel; Drama in the English Department. Mem. creative writing, sch. participation coms. S.C. Tricentennial Commn.; chmn. Trinity Cathedral Hosp. Visitation Ministry, 1981-84; lic. layreader diocese of Upper S. Carolina Episcopal Ch., 1981—. Mem. Société de l'Histoire Protestantisme français, South Caroliniana Soc. (exec. council 1979-83, v.p. 1983-86), S.C. Hist. Soc., Robert Burns Soc., Nat. S.C. (pres. 1967-68) councils tchrs. English, MLA, South Atlantic Modern Lang. Assn., DAR (chpt. 1st vice regent 1960-62), Daus. Holy Cross (chmn. chpt. 1953, co-chmn. chpt. 1967-68, chmn. chpt. 1983), Huguenot Soc., Columbia Music Festival Assn., Columbia Stage Soc., Workshop Theatre, Columbia Historic Found., Columbia Art Assn., English-Speaking Union (bd. dirs. Columbia br. 1971-73), Phi Beta Kappa (v.p. Alpha of S.C. chpt. 1976-77, pres. 1977-78, exec. com. 1983-85), Delta Kappa Gamma (v.p. Alpha Eta of S.C. 1976-78, pres. 1978-80), Alpha Psi Omega, Chi Omega. Home: 727 Abelia Rd Columbia SC 29205

ANDERSON, MARY LOU, educator; b. Mt. Pleasant, Iowa, Aug. 29, 1949; d. Carl Marion and Hazel Lucile (Mitchell) A. B.S. in Edn., Northeast Mo. State U., 1971, M.S. in Elem. Guidance, 1974. Lic. elem. tchr., Mo. Elem. tchr. Waynesville pub. schs., Mo., 1971-73, Hannibal pub. schs., Mo., 1973-79, Bel Ridge Elem. Sch., St. Louis, 1979-86; counselor Bel Ridge Elem. Sch., 1986-87; counselor Lincoln Elem. Sch., 1987—; ERA cons. ERAmerica, Washington, 1980-81, NEA, Washington, 1980-82; state conf. workshop leader NEA, 1979-83; co-founder, chmn. Mo. NEA Women's Caucus, 1975-78. Pres. Mo. ERA Coalition, 1980-82; pres. Polit. Action Com. St. Louis Women's Polit. Caucus, 1984-85, endorsement com. chair, 1987; campaign worker Mo. Democratic Orgn., 1982—. Mem. NEA (LEAST discipline cons. 1981—, Lorna Bottger Polit. Action award 1982), St. Louis Suburban Tchrs. Assn. (bd. dirs. 1983-87), Normandy Tchrs. Assn. (chmn. instrn. and profl. devel. com., mem. negotians com. 1985—), St. Louis Internat. Reading Assn., Mo. Sch. Counselors Assn., St. Louis Suburban Counselors Assn., NOW, ACLU, Phi Delta Kappa. Mem. United Ch. of Christ. Avocations: playing piano; aerobics; reading; plays and movies. Home: 4497 Pershing St Apt 107 Saint Louis MO 63108 Office: Bel Ridge Elem Sch 8930 Boston Ave Saint Louis MO 63121

ANDERSON, MICHAEL ROBERT, marketing representative; b. Mpls., Nov. 3, 1953; s. Arthur Robert Anderson and Patricia Roberta Carlson; m. Rebecca Ellan Pierce, June 6, 1981; children: Jenna Courtney, Evan Brendan. BSEE, U. Minn., 1976; MS in Systems Mgmt., U. So. Calif., 1981. Microelectronics engr. Hughes Aircraft Co., Fullerton, Calif., 1977; mktg. rep. Hewlett Packard, Orange County, Calif., 1977-81; regional mgr. Group III Elec., Orange County, 1981-85; mktg. rep. Lisp Machines Inc., Los Angeles, 1985-87, SUN Microsystems, Inc., Orange, Calif., 1987—. Big Brother, Big Bros. Inc., Orange, Calif., 1979-81. Fellow mem. AAAS, Am. Assn. Artificial Intelligence, Planetary Soc. Home: 28152 Bedford Dr Laguna Niguel CA 92677 Office: Sun Microsystems 765 City Dr Suite 100 Orange CA 92677

ANDERSON, NILS, JR., business executive; b. Plainfield, N.J., Jan. 28, 1914; s. Nils and Marguerite (Stephens) A.; m. Jean Derby Ferris, July 30, 1938; children: Nils III (dec.), Derby Ferris, Stephens Massie, Ward Reynolds. B.A., Williams Coll., 1937. With Koppers Co., summers 1933-37, Bakelite Corp., 1937-41; With War Prodn. Bd., 1941-45, chief adhesives sect., chief plastics br., 1945-50; v.p. chem. div. Borden Co., 1950—; pres. Debevoise-Anderson Co. Inc., also bd. dirs.; bd. dirs. Sturm, Ruger Inc. Trustee, pres. U.S. Naval War Coll. Found. Mem. Def. Orientation Conf. Assn. (v.p.), Soc. Colonial Wars, Soc. War 1812, Pilgrims Soc., Alpha Delta Phi. Clubs: Links (N.Y.C.), University (N.Y.C.); Country (Fairfield); Pequot Yacht (Southport). also: 1456 NE Ocean Blvd Stuart FL 34996

ANDERSON, OLIVER DUNCAN, consulting statistician, educator; b. Bournemouth, Eng., July 31, 1940; s. Edward William and Mary Barbara (Weller) A.; m. Luisa Ros-Montfort, Aug. 28, 1967; children: Edward, John. BA in Engring., Caius Coll., Cambridge U., 1962, MA, 1966, PhD, 1985; BS in Natural Scis., U. London, 1966, BS with 1st class honours in Math., 1973, BS with 1st class honours in Econs., 1977; MS in Stats., U.

Birmingham, 1968; MS in Math., U. Nottingham, 1974. Engr. Mott, Hay & Anderson, London, 1962; schoolmaster Lancing Coll., Sussex, 1963-64; lectr. Southampton Coll. Tech., Hampshire, 1965-66; sr. lectr. Rugby Coll. Engring. Tech., Warwickshire, 1968-73; course dir. Civil Service Coll., London, 1974-76; tech. dir. Statis. Applications Ltd., Nottingham, 1977-79; chmn. Oliver Anderson Cons., Nottingham, 1980-85; prof. mgmt. sci. Pa. State U., 1986-87; prof. stats.Temple U., Phila., 1987—; lectr.; vis. prof. various univs.; organizer internat. confs.; chmn. internat. confs. Author: Time Series Analysis and Forecasting: The Box-Jenkins Approach, 1975; contbr. tech., ednl. and sci. articles to jours. and encys.; editor: Forecasting 1979, Time Series, 1980, Analysing Time Series, 1980, Forecasting Public Utilities, 1980, Time Series Analysis, 1981, Time Series Analysis: Theory and Practice 1, 1982, Applied Time Series Analysis, 1982, Time Series Analysis: Theory and Practice 2, 1982, Time Series Analysis: Theory and Practice 3, 1983, Time Series Analysis: Theory and Practice 4, 1983, Time Series Analysis: Theory and Practice 5, 1984, Time Series Analysis: Theory and Practice 6, 1985, Time Series Analysis: Theory and Practice 7, 1985, Time Series Analysis: Theory and Practice 8, 1986, TSA&F News, 1979-86, TSA&F Flyer, 1980-86; acting editor: Statistician, 1975-77; mng. editor: Jour. of Time Series Analysis, 1980-82; assoc. editor: internat. jours. State scholar, 1959-62; State Studentship, 1967; Royal Soc. vis. fellow, 1980. Fellow Royal Statis. Soc., Inst. Math. and Its Applications, Inst. of Statisticians (mem. council 1976-79, 79-82), Brit. Inst. Mgmt., Inst. Tng. and Devel., Am. Statis. Assn.; mem. Operational Research Soc. Am., Brit. Computer Soc., Inst. Word Processing, Math. Assn., Soc. Indsl. and Applied Math., Nat. Council Tchrs. Math. (U.S.), Econometric Soc., Inst. Math. Stats., Royal Inst. Navigation, Royal Econ. Soc., Statis. Soc. Can., Statis. Soc. Australia, Internat. Inst. Forecasters, Inst. Mgmt. Scis., SE Asian Math. Soc. (corr.), Internat. Statis. Inst., Time Series Analysis and Forecasting Soc. (bd. dirs. 1981-86, chmn. 1982-86). Anglican. Office: Temple U Stats Dept 338 Speakman Hall Philadelphia PA 19122

ANDERSON, PAUL NATHANIEL, physician; b. Omaha, May 30, 1937; s. Nels Paul E. and Doris Marie (Chesnut) A.; BA, U. Colo., 1959, MD, 1963; m. Dee Ann Hipps, June 27, 1965; children:Mary Kathleen, Anne Christen. Intern Johns Hopkins Hosp., 1963-64, resident in internal medicine, 1964-65; research asso., staff assoc. NIH, Bethesda, Md., 1965-70; fellow in oncology Johns Hopkins Hosp., 1970-72, asst. prof. medicine, oncology Johns Hopkins U. Sch. Medicine, 1972-76; attending physician Balt. City Hosps., Johns Hopkins Hosp., 1972-76; dir. dept. med. oncology Penrose Cancer Hosp., Colorado Springs, Colo., 1976-86; clin. asst. prof. dept. medicine U. Colo. Sch. Medicine, 1976—; dir. Penrose Cancer Hosp., 1979-86; founding dir. Cancer Ctr. of Colorado Springs, 1986; med. dir. So. Colo. Cancer Program, 1979-86; mem., chmn. treatment com. Colo. Cancer Control and Research Panel, 1980-83; prin. investigator Cancer Info. Service of Colo., 1981-86. Mem. Colo. Gov.'s Rocky Flats Employee Health Assessment Group, 1983-84; mem. Gov.'s Breast Cancer Control Commn. Colo., 1984—; pres., founder Oncology Mgmt. Network, Inc., 1985—; founder, bd. dirs. Timberline Med. Assocs., 1986—; founder So. Colo. AIDS project 1986—; mem. adv. bd. Colo. State Bd. Health Tumor Registry, 1984—; chmn., bd. dirs. Preferred Physicians, Inc.; bd. dirs. Share Devel. Co. of Colo., Share Health Plan of Colo., Preferred Health Plan, Inc. Served with USPHS, 1965-70. Diplomate Am. Bd. Internal Medicine. Mem. Am. Soc. Clin. Oncology, Am. Assn. Cancer Research, Am. Assn. Cancer Insts. (liaison mem. bd. trustees 1980—), Am. Acad. Med. Dirs., Nat. Cancer Inst. (com. for community hosp. oncology program evaluation 1982—), Assn. Community Cancer Centers (chmn. membership com. 1980—, chmn. clin. research com. 1983-85, sec. 1983-84, pres.-elect 1984-85, pres. 1986-87, trustee 1981—), AAAS, N.Y. Acad. Scis., Johns Hopkins Med. Soc., AMA, Colo. Med. Soc., Am. Mgmt. Assn., Am. Assn. Profl. Cons., El Paso County Med. Soc., Coalition for Cancer, Alpha Omega Alpha. Contbr. articles to med. jours. Office: Cancer Ctr Colorado Springs 320 E Fontanero St Suite 100 Colorado Springs CO 80907 Address: 32 Sanford Rd Colorado Springs CO 80906

ANDERSON, PHILIP WARREN, physicist; b. Indpls., Dec. 13, 1923; s. Harry W. and Elsie (Osborne) A.; m. Joyce Gothwaite, July 31, 1947; 1 dau., Susan Osborne. B.S., Harvard U., 1943, M.A., 1947, Ph.D., 1949; D.Sc. (hon.), U. Ill., 1979. Mem. staff Naval Research Lab., 1943-45; mem. tech. staff Bell Telephone Labs., Murray Hill, N.J., 1949-84; chmn. theoretical physics dept. Bell Telephone Labs., 1959-60, asst. dir. phys. research lab., 1974-76, cons. dir., 1976-84; Fulbright lectr. U. Tokyo, 1953-54; Loeb lectr. Harvard U., 1964; prof. theoretical physics Cambridge (Eng.) U., 1967-75; prof. physics Princeton U., 1975—; Overseas fellow Churchill Coll., Cambridge U., 1961-62; fellow Jesus Coll., 1969-75, hon. fellow, 1978—; Bethe lectr., 1984. Author: Concepts in Solids, 1963, Basic Notions of Condensed Matter Physics, 1984. Recipient Oliver E. Buckley prize Am. Physical Soc., 1964; Dannie Heinemann prize Göttingen (Ger.) Acad. Scis., 1975; Nobel prize in physics, 1977; Guthrie medal Inst. of Physics, 1978; Nat. Medal Sci., 1982. Fellow Am. Phys. Soc., Am. Acad. Arts and Scis., AAAS; mem. Nat. Acad. Scis., Royal Soc. (fgn.), Phys. Soc. Japan, European Phys. Soc., Accademia Lincei. Office: Princeton Univ Dept of Physics Princeton NJ 08544

ANDERSON, RAYMOND QUINTUS, diversified company executive; b. Jamestown, N.Y., Nov. 27, 1930; s. Paul N. and Cecille (Ogren) A.; m. Sondra Rumsey, June 5, 1954; children: Heidi, Kristin, Gerrit, Mitchell, Tracy, Brooks. Grad., Phillips Acad., Andover, Mass., 1949; BS in Engring., Princeton U., 1953; postgrad., Grad. Sch. Indsl. Mgmt., MIT. With Dahlstrom Corp., Jamestown, 1957-76, exec. v.p., 1965, pres., 1968-76; founder, pres. Aarque Steel Corp., Jamestown, 1976-78, Aarque Mgmt. Corp., Jamestown, 1978—; founder, chmn. Aarque Cos., Jamestown, 1980—; bd. dirs. Chase Lincoln 1st Bank, N.A., Bus. Council N.Y. State, Inc.; chmn. Aarque Office Systems, Inc., Aarque Holdings Ltd., Cold Metal Products Co., Inc., Aarque Steel Group, Kardex Systems, Inc.; trustee Northwestern Mut. Life Ins. Co. Patentee in field. Chmn. Jamestown United Fund drive, 1964, 74. Served with USNR, 1954-57. Mem. Mfrs. Assn. Jamestown Area (pres. 1967-68), Empire State C. of C. (pres. 1974-76), Tau Beta Pi. Republican. Episcopalian. Clubs: Moon Brook Country (Jamestown); Sportsmen's (Chautauqua, N.Y.); Union League Met. (N.Y.C.). Office: The Aarque Cos 111 W 2d St Jamestown NY 14701

ANDERSON, REX HERBERT, insurance company executive; b. Rockford, Ill., Jan. 18, 1920; s. Herbert E. and Ethel V. (Helin) A.; m. Martha Jean Baker, Sept. 11, 1943; 1 child, Rex Herbert. A.B., Beloit Coll., 1941. Group field rep. Wash. Nat. Ins. Co., 1951-52, advt. and sales promotion, 1946-50; supr. Great West Life Assurance Co., 1950-52; br. office supr. Great West Life Assurance Co., St. Louis, 1952-53; dir. accident and sickness sales N.Y. Life Ins. Co., 1953-55, dir. sales promotion, 1955-56, asst. v.p. charge sales devel., 1956-57; v.p. mktg. Life Ins. Co. N.Am., Phila., 1957-62; charge individual sales and agy. ops. Life Ins. Co. N.Am., 1962-64, exec. officer charge individual life and health lines, life reins. dept., 1964-72, sr. v.p., 1970-79, in charge internat. life ins. ops., 1972-79; chmn. bd. Hawkeye Nat. Life Ins. Co., Des Moines, 1982-85; vice chmn. bd. Interam. Life, Athens, Greece, 1971-79, dir., 1982-87; pres., dir. Interam. Fin. Services Corp., USA, 1987—; pres., dir. Interam. Holdings Inc. USA, United Nat. Life Corp. USA; bd. dirs. Inter Trust Ins. Co., Athens, 1974-87, INA Security Corp., 1965-79, GAN Anglo-Am. Ins. Co., N.Y.C., 1981-85, IMMOTEL S.A., France, Interhellenic Pub. Co. USA; Am. rep. Groupe des Assurances Nationales, Paris, 1979-85. Trustee Phila. Coll. Art, 1966-75, Westminster Theol. Sem., Phila., 1985—. Served with USAAF, 1942-46. Mem. Life Ins. Agy. Mgmt. Assn., Tau Kappa Epsilon, Delta Sigma Rho. Republican. Presbyterian. Home: 1210 Pine Wood Rd Villanova PA 19085 Office: PO Box 431 Villanova PA 19085

ANDERSON, RICHARD ERNEST, energy and chemical research and development company executive, rancher; b. North Little Rock, Ark., Mar. 8, 1926; s. Victor Ernest and Lillian Josephine (Griffin) A.; m. Mary Ann Fitch, July 18, 1953; children: Vicki Lynn, Lucia Anita. B.S.C.E., U. Ark., 1949; M.S.E., U. Mich., 1959; Registered profl. engr., Mich., Va., Tex., Mont. Commd. ensign U.S. Navy, 1952, advanced through grades to capt., 1968; ret., 1974; v.p. Ocean Resources, Inc., Houston, 1974-77; mgr. maintenance and ops. Holmes & Narver, Inc., Orange, Calif., 1977-78; pres. No. Resources, Inc., Billings, Mont., 1978-81; v.p. Holmes & Narver, Inc., Orange, Calif., 1981-82; owner, operator Anderson Ranches, registered Arabian horses and comml. Murray Grey cows, Pony, Mont., 1982—; pres., dir. Carbon Resources Inc., Bozeman, Mont., 1983—. Trustee Lake Barcroft-Virginia Watershed Improvement Dist., 1973-74; pres. Lake Barcroft-Virginia Recreation Center, Inc., 1972-73. Served with USAAF, 1944-45. Decorated Silver Star, Legion of Merit with Combat V (2), Navy Marine Corps medal, Bronze Star with Combat V, Meritorious Service medal, Purple Heart; Anderson Peninsula in Antarctica named in his honor. Mem. ASCE, Soc. Am. Mil. Engrs. (Morrell medal 1965). Republican. Methodist. Clubs: Billings Petroleum, Elks. Home: PO Box 266 Pony MT 59747 Office: Carbon Resources Inc 305 W Mercury St Butte MT 59701

ANDERSON, ROBERT, manufacturing company executive; b. Columbus, Nebr., Nov. 2, 1920; s. Robert and Lillian (Devlin) A.; m. Constance Dahlun Severy, Oct. 2, 1942 (div.); children: Robert, Kathleen D.; m. Diane Clark Lowe, Nov. 2, 1973. BS in Mech. Engring, Colo. State U., 1943, LLD, 1966; M Automotive Engring., Chrysler Inst. Engring., 1948; DHL (hon.), U. Neb., 1985; JD (hon.), Pepperdine U., 1986; D of Engring. (hon.), Milw. Sch. Engring., 1987. With Chrysler Corp., 1946-68, v.p. corp., gen. mgr. Chrysler-Plymouth div., 1965-67; with Rockwell International Corp., 1968—, pres. comml. products group, 1968-69, v.p. corp., 1968-69, exec. v.p., 1969-70, pres., chief operating officer, 1970-74, pres., 1974-79, chief exec. officer, 1974—, chmn., 1979-88, dir., 1968—, chmn. exec. com., 1988—; dir. Security Pacific Corp. and subs. Security Pacific Nat. Bank, Los Angeles, Hosp. Corp. Am. Trustee Calif. Inst. Tech., bd. of overseers Exec. Council Fgn. Diplomats; chmn. bus.-higher edn. forum Am. Council on Edn., 1982-84; chmn. Western Hwy. Inst., 1983-84. Served to capt. F.A. AUS, 1943-46. Named Exec. of Yr. Nat. Mgmt. Assn., 1980. Mem. Soc. Automotive Engrs., Phi Kappa Phi, Tau Beta Pi, Sigma Nu. Clubs: Rolling Rock (Ligonier, Pa.), Laurel Valley Golf (Ligonier, Pa.); Fox Chapel (Pa.) Golf, Vintage Country, Desert Horizons (Calif.), Country; Duquesne (Pitts.); Los Angeles Country. Office: Rockwell Internat Corp 600 Grant St Pittsburgh PA 15219

ANDERSON, ROBERT CLETUS, educator, consultant; b. Birmingham, Ala., July 18, 1921; s. Allie Cletus and Dana (Hilliard) A.; m. Evalee R. Pilgrim, 1977; children by previous marriage: Margaret Campbell, William Robert. B.S., Auburn U., 1942; M.A., U. N.C., 1947; Ph.D., N.Y. U., 1950. Research asst. Inst. Research in Social Sci., U. N.C., 1946-47; asst. to dean Sch. Edn., N.Y. U., 1948-50; dean Grad. Sch., Memphis State U., 1950-53; exec. assoc. So. Regional Edn. Bd., 1953-55, assoc. dir., 1955-57, dir., 1957-61; exec. v.p. Auburn U., 1961-65; v.p. research U. Ga., Athens, 1965-84; prof. sociology U. Ga., 1965—, Univ. prof., 1984—, spl. asst. to pres., 1984-86; pres. U. Ga. Research Found., 1978-84; prof. emeritus, v.p. research emeritus 1987—; dir. So. Regional Project on Ednl. TV, So. Regional Edn. Bd., 1952, So. Regional Conf. on Edn. Beyond the High Sch., 1957; mem. Surgeon Gen.'s cons. group on Med. Edn., 1958-59, W.K. Kellogg Found. Ednl. Adv. Com., 1960-64, Joint Council on Ednl. Telecommunications, 1961-70, v.p., 1965-67; mem. council for research policy and adminstrn. Nat. Assn. State Univs. and Land-Grant Colls., 1965—, chmn., 1965-67; mem. exec. com. Nat. Conf. Advancement Research, 1981-85; mem. Nat. Council Univ. Research Administrs., 1965—, mem. exec. com., 1982-85, editor newsletter, 1985; dir. Nat. Conf. Future Univ. Research, 1984-85, prof., 1984—; mem. Nat. Inst. Higher Edn., 1986-87. Mem. editorial bd. Soc. Research Adminstrs., 1981-84. Served from 2d lt. to capt. AUS, 1942-46, ETO. Decorated Purple Heart. Fellow Nat. Acad. Univ. Research Adminstrn (charter, pres. 1985-86); mem. AAAS, N.Y. Acad. Scis., Am. Council on Edn. (council on fed. relations 1963-67), Am. Assn. Higher Edn., Phi Kappa Phi, Alpha Tau Omega, Alpha Kappa Delta, Kappa Delta Pi, Omicron Delta Kappa, Phi Delta Kappa, Phi Eta Sigma, Pi Gamma Mu. Home: 110 Holmes Ct Athens GA 30606 *Died Aug. 28, 1987.*

ANDERSON, ROBERT GEOFFREY WILLIAM, museum director; b. London, May 2, 1944; s. Herbert Patrick and Kathleen Diana (Burns) A.; m. Margaret Elizabeth Callis Lea, Mar. 31, 1973; children: William Thomas Edmund, Edward Tobias Gilbert. BA (converted to MA 1972), U. Oxford, Eng., 1967, BSc, 1968, D Philosophy, 1972. Asst. keeper Royal Scottish Mus., Edinburgh, Scotland, 1970-75, dir., 1984-85; asst. keeper Sci. Mus., London, 1975-80, keeper, 1980-84; dir. Nat. Mus. Scotland, Edinburgh, 1985—. Author: The Playfair Collection, 1978, (catalogue) Science in India, 1982, Science, Medicine and Dissent, 1987; editor: The Early Years of the Edinburgh Medical School, 1976. Recipient Dexter award Am. Chem. Soc., 1986. Fellow Royal Soc. Chemistry, Soc. Antiquaries London, Soc. Antiquaries Scotland; mem. Internat. Union of History and Philosophy of Sci. (pres. sci. instrument commn. 1982—), Brit. Soc. History of Sci. (pres. 1988—). Club: Athenaeum (London). Home: 11 Dryden Pl, Edinburgh EH9 1RP, Scotland Office: Nat Mus of Scotland, Royal Mus of Scotland, Chambers St, Edinburgh EH1 1JF, Scotland

ANDERSON, ROBERT HENRY, pathology educator; b. Wellington, Salop, Eng., Apr. 4, 1942; s. Henry and Doris Amy (Callear) A.; m. Christine Ibbotson, July 9, 1966; children—Elizabeth Jane, John Robert. B.Sc., U. Manchester, 1963, M.B.Ch.B., 1966, M.D., 1970; F.R.C.Path., Royal Coll. Pathologists, London, 1987. Lectr., U. Manchester (Eng.), 1967-72; MRC travelling fellow U. Amsterdam, 1973; sr. lectr. Cardiothoracic Inst., London, 1974-77, reader, 1977-80, prof., 1980—; hon. cons. Brompton Hosp., London, 1974—; hon. prof. Hosp. For Sick Children, London, 1982—; hon. clin. prof. U. N.C., Chapell Hill, 1984—; hon. sr. lectr. U. Liverpool, 1973—; editor Internat. Jour. Cardiology, Amsterdam, 1983—; hon. vis. prof. U. Pitts., 1984—. Author: Cardiac Anatomy, 1980; Pathology of Congenital Heart Disease, 1981; Pathology of Conduction System, 1983, Paediatric Cardiology (2 vols.), 1987; contbr. articles to profl. jours. Recipient Excerpta Medica award Excerpta Medica, Amsterdam, 1977; Thomas Lewis lectr. and medal Brit. Cardiac Soc., 1978; Brit. Heart Found. prize for cardiovascular research, 1984. Mem. Brit. Cardiac Soc., Anat. Soc. U.K., Royal Soc. Medicine U.K., Pathol. Soc. U.K. Socialist. Club: Roehampton. Home: 60 Earlsfield Rd, Wandsworth, London SW18 3DN, England Office: Cardiothoracic Inst, Pediatric Dept, Fulham Rd, London SW3 6HP, England

ANDERSON, RONALD HOWARD, consumer packaged goods company marketing executive; b. Worcester, Mass., Aug. 12, 1935; s. Carl Howard and Evelyn (Johnson) A.; BA, Middlebury Coll., 1959; MBA (Scott Paper Co. fellow), Mich. State U., 1967; MDP, Harvard U., 1972; m. Jo Ann Witmer, Aug. 22, 1959; children: David Gordon, Carol Lynn. Mktg. mgr. Scott Paper Co., Phila., 1959-67, sales and mktg. positions, product mgr. Gen. Foods Corp., White Plains, N.Y., 1967-72; group product mgr. Am. Can Co., Greenwich, Conn., 1972-74; v.p. sales and mktg. Cadbury Schweppes, Stamford, Conn., 1974-76, Tetley Inc., Shelton, Conn., 1976-85; sr. v.p. mktg. Penn Mut. Life Ins. Co., Phila., 1985-86; gen. mgr. Chock Full O' Nuts Corp., 1986—; instr. in mktg. Pace U. Officer N.Y. State Republican Com., 1967—; bd. dirs. Bedford (N.Y.) Presbyterian Ch., 1974-78, Bedford Assn., 1975-80; trustee Low-Heywood Sch., Stamford, Conn. Served with U.S. Army, 1953-55. Mem. Am. Mgmt. Assn., Assn. Nat. Advertisers, Nat. Coffee Assn. (chmn. pub. relations com.), Nat. Tea Assn. (chmn. pub. relations com.). Republican. Clubs: Princeton (N.Y.); Bedford Golf and Tennis. Office: 370 Lexington Ave New York NY 10017

ANDERSON, ROYAL J., advertising agency executive; b. Portland, Oreg., Sept. 12, 1914; s. John Alfred and Martha Marie (Jacobsen) A.; B.A., Albany Coll., 1939; postgrad. U. Oreg., summers 1939-41, Oreg. Inst. Tech., 1940-41; m. Leticia G. Anderson; children: Michael, Johnny, Dora Kay, Mark Roy, Stan Ray, Ruth Gay, Janelle A., Jennifer T., Joseph, Daisy, Dina; 1 adopted dau., Muoi-Muoi. Corp. cons. Dupont Corp., Beverly Hills, Calif., 1967-68; editor-pub. Nev. State Democrat, Carson City, Nev. State Pub. Observer, Nev. State Congl. Assn., Carson City, 1962-78; pres. Allied-Western Produce Co., Yuma, Ariz., Nev. Dem. Corp., 1966-78; pres. Western Restaurant Corp., 1978-81, Nev. State Sage Co., 1979—, Midway Advt. Co., Environ. Research Corp., 1983—, Mid-City Advt. Agy., 1983—, Nat. Newspaper Found., 1969, 71-76, The Gt. North Banks Seafood Co., 1984—, Food Services Corp., 1985—, Sterling Cruise Lines, 1986—, No-Tow Mfg. Inc.; chmn. bd. Press/Register Daily Newspapers, Foster Mortgage Co., 1983—. Bishop, Ch. of Palms, Mexico. Dep. registrar voters, Washoe County, Nev., 1966. Recipient Heroism award for rescue, 1933. Research fellow, Alaska, 1936. Mem. Am. Hort. Soc., Sparks (pres. 1970-81), Nev. chambers commerce, C. of C. of U.S., Chatso Farm Assn. (pres. 1962-88), Smithsonian Assos., N.Am. C. of C. Execs., Nat. Geog. Soc., Am. Newspaper Alliance (v.p. 1976), Club: Millionare. Lodges: Kiwanis, Elks, Lions. Designer prefabricated milk carton container, 1933, well water locating under-stream device, 1938. Home: PO Box 4349 North Las Vegas NV 89030 Home: 5600 E Sundance Ave Las Vegas NV 89116

ANDERSON, WILLIAM HENRY, psychiatrist, educator; b. Phila., Nov. 10, 1940; s. William Henry Schoen and Elizabeth Winifred (Laverty) A.; m. Catherine Sacchetti, Oct. 7, 1967; 1 dau., Jennifer Ann Gist. B.S., MIT, 1962; M.A., U. Pa., 1967; M.D., Thomas Jefferson U., 1967; M.P.H., Harvard U., 1977. Diplomate: Am. Bd. Psychiatry and Neurology. Intern. Pa. Hosp., Phila., 1967-68; resident in psychiatry Mass. Gen. Hosp., Boston, 1968-71, assoc. psychiatrist dept. psychiatry, 1976—, dir. postgrad. edn., 1976-81; instr. psychiatry Harvard U., Boston, 1973-75, asst. prof., 1975-81, asst. clin. prof., 1981-82, lectr., 1982—; chief psychiatry St. Elizabeths Hosp., Boston, 1981—; asst. attending psychiatrist Mclean Hosp., Belmont, Mass.; Cons. Scientists' Inst. Pub. Info. Contbg. editor: The New Physician, 1977-79; editorial bd. Topics in Geriatrics, 1981-87, Jour. Geriatric Psychiatry and Neurology. Served to lt. comdr., M.C. USNR, 1971-73. Fellow Am. Psychiat. Assn.; mem. AAAS, Am. Acad. Clin. Psychiatrists, Internat. Soc. Polit. Psychology, Com. on Fgn. Relations (Boston com.), Med. Assn. P.R. (hon.), Mass. Med. Soc., Am. Coll. Emergency Physicians, Soc. Ethnobiology, U.S. Naval Inst., Am. Pub. Health Assn., Boston Athenaeum, Handel and Hayden Soc., Sigma Xi. Club: Harvard (Boston).

ANDERSON, WILLIAM HENRY, JR., clergyman, sociologist; b. Dover, N.J., Sept. 21, 1921; s. William Henry and Gaynell J. A.; B.A., Wheaton Coll., 1943; Th.M., Pitts. Sem., 1949; Ph.D., NYU, 1960; m. Lucile Whieldon Thomas, June 11, 1948; children—William W., Nadyne G., Anders C. Ordained to ministry United Presbyn. Ch., 1949; pastor, Ohio, N.Y. and Pa., 1949-64; prof. sociology Va. Union U., 1964-74; cons. sociology, Richmond, Va., 1974—. Mem. Richmond Democratic Com., 1971-88. Served to lt. col., USAFR, 1942-77. Fellow AAAS, Am. Anthrop. Assn., Am. Sociol. Assn.; mem. Archeol. Soc. Va., Phi Delta Kappa. Home and Office: Box 885 Mathews VA 23109

ANDERSSON, ALF LENNART, psychologist, researcher; b. Karlskrona, Blekinge, Sweden, Nov. 10, 1935; s. Ernst L. and Viola M. (Eriksson) A.; m. Mai-Lise G. Sandberg, Aug. 1, 1969; children: Emma, Klara. PhD, Lund U., Sweden, 1970. Cert. psychologist. Instr. psychology Lund U., Sweden, 1960-69; research assoc. dept. psychology Lund U., 1969-71, prof. psychology, 1971-76, sr. lectr. researcher applied psychology, 1976—; vis. prof. psychology CUNY, 1973. Editorial bd., Psychological Research Bulletin, Lund U., 1971-87; contbr. articles to profl. jours. and books. Mem. Internat. Soc. Study Behavioral Devel. Home: Arkeologvägen 82, S-222 54 Lund Sweden Office: Lund U Dept Applied Psychology, Paradisgatan 5, S-223 50 Lund Sweden

ANDERSSON, HANS JAN-ERIK, microcomputer company executive; b. Norrkoping, Sweden, May 27, 1940; s. Erik Hugo and Anna Ingegardlinnea A.; student Valdemarsvik, 1952; m. Gorel Ann-Sofi Albinsson, May 30, 1970 (div.); 1 child. Mng. dir., owner H.A. Data i LinkÖping, Atvidaberg, Sweden, 1961—. Home: Egendomen Bredal, S597 00 Atvidaberg Sweden Office: Bielkegatan 4, S581 02 Linkoping Sweden

ANDERSSON, STEN, Swedish minister for foreign affairs; b. Stockholm, Apr. 20, 1923; m. Britta A.; 5 children. Ed., U. Stockholm. Tchr., courier Worker's Ednl. Assn., from 1944; sec. Internat. Youth Campaign, from 1944; mem. Stockholm City Council, mem. city exec., fin. and real estate com., 1951-62; dist. rep. Stockholm br. Social Democratic Party, Sweden, from 1953, sec. Stockholm br., 1958-62, nat. party sec., 1963-82, chmn. Stockholm br., from 1975; mem. Swedish Parliament, 1966—; minister of health and social affairs, Sweden, 1982-85, minister for fgn. affairs, 1985—. Chmn. club br. Social Democratic Youth League, 1982-85, chmn. dist. internat. com., The Olof Palme Meml. Fund for Internat. Understanding and Common Security, 1986—, Peace Forum of Swediah Labour Movement, 1986—. Address: Ministry Fgn Affairs, Stockholm Sweden

ANDO, HIRONOBU, medical educator, cardiologist; b. Kobe, Japan, Nov. 23, 1940; s. Masanobu and Chieko (Masai) A.; m. Mariko Fujiwara, Nov. 17, 1968; children—Aiko, Yasuhiro, Kenji. B.S., Himeji Inst. Tech., 1962; M.D., Kobe Med. Coll., 1966, Ph.D., 1971. Diplomate Am. Bd. Internal Medicine (Cardiovascular Disease). Intern, Kobe Univ. Hosp. (Japan), 1966-67, instr. medicine, 1971-72; med. resident U. Miss. Med. Ctr., Jackson, 1972-74, fellow in cardiology, 1974-76; asst. prof. Hyogo Coll. Medicine, Nishinomiya, Japan, 1976—; med. cons. Japan Life Ins. Co., Osaka, 1981—, Idemitsu Oil Co., Himeji, 1977—; chief medicine Takatsuki (Japan) Red Cross Hosp., 1986—. Fellow Am. Coll. Cardiology, Am. Heart Assn.; mem. Japanese Soc. Internal Medicine, Japanese Circulation Soc., Japan Clin. Cardiology Ednl. Soc. (trustee 1983). Buddhist. Author: Electrocardiographic Manual, 1979; Radionucleid Scanning, 1981; Cardiology-Programmed Learning, 1983; Cardiology Review Book, 1985; Patient Management in Cardiology, 1985, Textbook of Advanced Clinical Cardiology, 1986. Home: 1 45 Tomoyma cho, Nishinomiya, Hyogo 663, Japan Office: Takatsuki Red Cross Hosp, 1-1 Buno Takatsuki, Osaka 569, Japan

ANDO, KUNIO, optical company executive; b. Tokyo, Jan. 15, 1935; s. Bunji and Ume (Yamashita) A.; m. Yasuko Honda, Apr. 14, 1971; children: Keiko, Yoshiaki. B in Engring., U. Chiba, Japan, 1959. Engr. Fuji Photo Optical Co., Omiya, Saitama, 1959-71, design sect. mgr., 1971-80, mgr. optical instrument dept., 1980-87, dir., 1987—. Inventor motor driven camera, image stabilized optical system. Mem. Inst. TV Engrs. Japan, Soc. Photographic Sci. and Tech. Japan, Japan Soc. Applied Physics (optics div.). Home: Kamiochiai 324-4-4-838, 338 Yono, Saitama Japan Office: Fuji Photo Optical Co, Uetakemachil-324, 330 Omiya, Saitama Japan

ANDO, MIKIO, metal processing executive; b. Tsuyama, Okayama, Japam, Oct. 16, 1947; s. Koshi and Tamako Ando; m. Mikiko Hozumi, Oct. 12, 1974; children: Kentaro, Maya. BA in Law, Kobe (Japan) U., 1970; PG diploma in econs., U. East Anglia, Norwich, Eng., 1981. Staff mem. tng. sect. Sumitomo Metals, Kainan, Japan, 1970-76; staff mem. internat. fin. sect. Sumitomo Metals, Tokyo, 1976-79; asst. mgr. personnel devel. and edn. dept. Sumitomo Metals, Osaka, Japan, 1981-84, mgr., 1984—; bd. dirs. Sumikin Intercom, Inc., Osaka. Office: Sumikin-Intercom, 5-15 Kitahama, Higashi-Ku, Osaka Japan

ANDO, TSUYOSHI, mathematician, university professor; b. Sapporo, Hokkaido, Japan, Feb. 1, 1932; s. Jyusuke and Kou (Hara) A.; m. Yoshie Matsumura, May 17, 1961; children: Yukako, Naohiko. BS, Hokkaido (Japan) U., 1953, MS, 1955, DSc, 1958. Instr. Research Inst. Applied Electricity, Hokkaido U., 1958-64, assoc. prof., 1964-69, prof., 1969—. Assoc. editor Jour. Operator Theory, 1981, Linear Algebra & its Applications, 1982. Mem. Math. Soc. Japan, Am. Math. Soc., Soc. Indsl. and Applied Math. Office: Hokkaido U, Kitaku Kita 12 Nishi 6, 060 Sapporo Japan

ANDOLSHEK, RICHARD ANDERS, retail executive; b. Crosby, Minn., Mar. 13, 1952; s. Albin Henery and Alice Louise (Arvidson) A.; student U. Minn., 1970-73; children—Kimberly, Albin, Daren. Owner, operator Crosslake IGA Grocery Store (Minn.), 1973—, Dick's Package Liquor Store, Crosslake, 1973—, Andy's Restaurant, Crosslake, 1973—; v.p. Country Printing Enterprises Inc., Pequot Lakes, Minn., 1977-80, LAR, Inc., night club and restaurant, Crosslake, 1977-82; pres. Jonable Inc., chain restaurant, Crosslake, 1979-86, Richard-Curtis, Inc., Pequot Lakes, 1980-85, Brann and Assos., Inc., Brainerd, Minn., 1981-82, Chadco of Duluth, Inc., 1982-84, No. Food King, 1982—, R-C Mktg. & Leasing, Inc., 1982—, Regent Enterprises, Inc., 1987—; chmn. bd. Sport Shacks, Inc., 1982-87, Lakes Broadcasting Corp., Inc., 1984-85, Andolshek Properties, Inc., Fabel Constrn., Inc., Lakes Leasing, Inc.; bd. dirs. Beverage Retailers Ins. Co., Risk Retention Group, Consortium Lic. Beverage Assns. Mem. Crosslake Planning and Zoning Commn., 1973-74, Region 5 Devel. Commn., 1975-77; mem. Minn. Outdoor Recreation Commn., 1978; mem. Ind. Sch. Dist. 186 Bd. Edn., Pequot Lakes, Minn., 1975—, chmn., 1977. Named Minn. Liquor Retailer of Yr., Midwest Beverage Jour., 1977. Mem. Minn. Food Retailers, Minn. Liquor Retailers (pres. 1978-80), Midwestern States Fedn. Beverage Licensees (adv. bd.), Nat. License Beverage Assn. (pres., sec., bd. dirs.), Crosslake C. of C., Nat. Fedn. Small Bus. Club: North Oaks (Minn.) Country. Lodge: Elks. Office: 3450 N Lexington Ave Suite 100 Saint Paul MN 55127

ANDON, JERAR, consulting engineer; b. Milford, Mass., Feb. 8, 1921; s. Karnig and Zumrout (Khacharian) Andonian; m. Nancy Jane Simons, Aug. 29, 1953. B.M.E., Gen. Motors Inst., 1951; M.S.M.E., Stanford U., 1968. Registered profl. engr., Calif., Mich. Sr. research engr. Gen. Motors Corp., Warren, Mich., 1951-63, Santa Barbara, Calif., 1965-69; mech. engr. U.S. Naval Civil Engring. Lab., Port. Hueneme, Calif., 1964-65; cons. engr. various mfg. and legal firms, 1969—; vis. lectr. U. Calif.-Santa Barbara, 1981—. Patentee in field. Served with U.S. Army, 1942-45. Decorated Bronze Star medal. Mem. Soc. Automotive Engrs. (Horning Meml. award 1963), ASME, Instn. Mech. Engrs., Tau Beta Pi. Democrat. Unitarian. Address: 98 Loma Media Rd Santa Barbara CA 93103

ANDRE, BABETTE YVONNE, flight instructor, media consultant, publisher, pilot; b. San Francisco, Jan. 26, 1942; d. Leo Fred and Dorothy (Fisher) Andre. B.A. in Polit. Sci., U. Calif.-Berkeley, 1963; postgrad. San Francisco State Coll., 1966, U. Colo., Denver, 1970. Cert. tchr., Calif., Hawaii, N.Y.; cert. flight and ground instr., FAA. Peace Corps vol., Bafoussam, Cameroun, Africa, 1963-65; French tchr. Punahou Acad., Honolulu, 1966-68; pub. info. officer Commn. Community Relations City and County of Denver, 1970-71, info. writer, 1973-78; traffic reporter Sta. KOA-AM, Denver, 1978, Sta. KHOW Sky Spy, 1982; mem. faculty dept. aerospace sci. Met. State Coll., Denver, 1975-80; pub. Wings West Mag.; gold seal flight instr.; pub. relations/advt. cons. Active various social agys. and programs, including Head Start. Contbr. articles to Colo. Bus., Rocky Mountain News. Author and photographer various informational city publs. Accident prevention counselor FAA, 1982—. Mem. Colo. Flight Instrs. Assn., Aircraft Owners and Pilots Assn., CAP, Colo. Pilots Assn., 99's, Alpha Eta Rho. Clubs: PC Flyers, Denver Press. Home: 89 Sherman St Denver CO 80203 Office: Wings West Mag Jeffco Air Bldg B8 Jefferson County Airport Broomfield CO 80020

ANDRE, CARL, sculptor; b. Quincy, Mass., Sept. 16, 1935; s. George Hans and Margaret (Johnson). Represented in public collections, Tate Gallery, London, Mus. Modern Art, N.Y.C., Rose Art Mus., Brandeis U., Columbus (Ohio) Gallery Fine Arts, Walker Art Center, Mpls., Milw. Art Center, La Jolla (Calif.) Mus. Contemporary Art, Dayton (Ohio) Art Inst., Albright-Knox Art Gallery, Buffalo, Monchengladbach Mus., Germany, Wallraf-Richartz Mus., Cologne, Haus Lange Mus., Krefeld, Germany, Kunstmus. Basel, Switzerland, Hessisches Landesmus., Darmstadt, Germany, Stedelijk Mus., Amsterdam, Van Abbe Mus., Eindhoven, Netherlands, Art Soc. Ghent, Belgium, Art Inst. Chgo., Los Angeles County Mus. Art, Musée Nat. d'Art Moderne, Paris, Carnegie Inst Mus. Art, Pitts., Musèo de Arte Moderno, Bogota, Colombia, Seattle Art Mus., High Mus. Art, Atlanta, Ohio State U. Gallery Fine Art, Bayerischen Staatsgemäldesammlungen, Munich, Kröller-Müller Mus., Otterlo, Netherlands, Detroit Inst. Arts, Guggenheim Mus., N.Y.C., City of Hartford, Conn., Mus. Boymans-van Beuningen, Rotterdam, Netherlands. Address: PO Box 1001 Cooper Sta New York NY 10276 also: care Paula Cooper 155 Wooster St New York NY 10012 also: Konrad Fischer, Platanenstr 7, Dusseldorf Federal Republic of Germany

ANDREAE, CLEMENS-AUGUST, economist, educator; b. Graz, Steiermark, Austria, Mar. 5, 1929; s. Wilhelm and Illa (Lackmann) A.; m. Ilse Konrad, Feb. 13, 1962; children: Maximilian, Maria-Theresia. Dr. rerum politicarum, Philipps-U. Marburg, Fed. Republic Germany, 1950; Dr. philosophiae honoris causa, Ukrainische Freie U., Munich, 1982. Asst. prof. U. Cologne, Fed. Republic Germany, 1950-58; assoc. prof. U. Innsbruck, Austria, 1958-62, prof., 1962—. Contbr. articles to profl. publs. Recipient Ehrenzeichen Govt. Austria, 1971, Bundesverdienstkreuz Govt. Fed. Republic Germany; named Commendatore, Govt. Italy. Mem. Peoples Party. Roman Catholic. Lodge: Rotary (pres. Innsbruck club 1973-75). Home: Anton Rauch Strasse 13C, A-6020 Innsbruck Austria Office: U Innsbruck, Herzog Friedrich Strasse 3, A-6020 Innsbruck Austria

ANDRÉANI, JACQUES, diplomat; b. Paris, Nov. 22, 1929; s. Paul and Suzanne (Hugon) A.; m. Huguette De Fonclare (div. 1981); children: Gilles, Olivia; m. Donatella Monterisi; children: Marie-Emmanuelle, Fabrice. Diploma, Inst. d'Etude Politiques, Paris, 1969, Ecole Nationale d'Administration, Paris, 1953. 2d sec. French Embassy, Washington, 1955-60; 1st sec. Moscow, 1961-64; chief Bur. Soviet Affairs Ministry Fgn. Affairs, Paris, 1964-67, chief Bur. East European and Soviet Affairs, 1967-70, dir. for Europe, 1975-79, dir. polit. affairs, 1981-84; asst. govt. rep. NATO, Brussels, 1970-72; chief French del. Conf. on Security and Corp. in Europe, Helsinki and Geneva, 1972-75; ambassador to Egypt, Cairo, 1979-81, Italy, Rome, 1984—. Naemd Comdr., French Nat. Order Merit, 1987, Chevalier, French Legion Honor. Home and Office: 67 Piazza Fornese, 00186 Rome Italy

ANDREAS, DWAYNE ORVILLE, corporation executive; b. Worthington, Minn., Mar. 4, 1918; s. Reuben P. and Lydia (Stoltz) A.; m. Bertha Benedict, 1938 (div.); 1 dau., Sandra Ann Andreas McMurtie; m. Dorothy Inez Snyder, Dec. 21, 1947; children: Terry Andreas. Student, Wheaton (Ill.) Coll., 1935-36; hon. degree, Barry U. Vice pres., dir. Honeymead Products Co., Cedar Rapids, Iowa, 1936-46; chmn. bd., chief exec. officer Honeymead Products Co. (now Nat. City Bancorp.), Mankato, Minn., 1952-72; v.p. Cargill, Inc., Mpls., 1946-52; exec. v.p. Farmers Union Grain Terminal Assn., St. Paul, 1960-66; chmn. bd., chief exec. officer Archer-Daniels-Midland Co., Decatur, Ill., 1970—, also mem. exec. com., dir.; pres. Seaview Hotel Corp., 1958—; dir. Salomon, Inc., Lone Star Industries, Inc., Greenwich, Conn.; mem. Pres.'s Gen. Adv. Commn. on Fgn. Assistance Programs, 1965-68, Pres.'s Adv. Council on Mgmt. Improvement, 1969-73; chmn. Pres.'s Task Force on Internat. Pvt. Enterprise. Pres. Andreas Found.; trustee U.S. Naval Acad. Found., Freedom from Hunger Found.; nat. bd. dirs. Boys' Club Am.; chmn. U.S.-USSR Trade and Econ. Council; chmn. Exec. Council on Fgn. Diplomats; trustee Hoover Inst. on War, Revolution and Peace, Woodrow Wilson Internat. Ctr. for Scholars; mem. Trilateral Commn.; chmn. Found. for Commemoration of the U.S. Constitution, 1986. Mem. Fgn. Policy Assn. N.Y. (dir.). Clubs: Union League (Chgo.); Indian Creek Country (Miami Beach, Fla.); Mpls., Minikahda (Mpls.); Blind Brook Country (Purchase, N.Y.); Economic of N.Y. (chmn.), Links, Knickerbocker, Friars (N.Y.C.). Office: Archer-Daniels-Midland Co 4666 Faries Pkwy Box 1470 Decatur IL 62525

ANDREAS, GLENN ALLEN, JR., agricultural company executive; b. Cedar Rapids, Iowa, June 22, 1943; s. Glenn Allen and Vera Irene (Yates) A.; m. Toni Kay Hibma, June 19, 1964; children: Bronwyn Denise, Glenn Allen III, Shannon Tori. BA, Valparaiso U., 1965, JD, 1968. Bar: Colo. 1969. Atty. U.S. Treas. Dept., Denver, 1969-73; atty. Archer Daniels Midland Co., Decatur, Ill., 1973-75, asst. treas., 1975-86, treas., 1986—; bd. dirs. Nat. City Bancorp., Mpls. Chmn. Ill. Job Tng. Coordinating Council, Springfield, 1985; vice chmn. Ill. Devel. Fin. Authority, Chgo., 1974; mem. Gov.'s Econ. Adv. Group, Chgo., 1985. Mem. ABA, Colo. State Bar Assn., Decatur Bar Assn. Democrat. Clubs: Country of Decatur, Decatur. Home: 2 Parsons Ln Decatur IL 62526 Office: Archer-Daniels Midland Co PO Box 1470 4666 Faries Pkwy Decatur IL 62525

ANDREASON, GEORGE EDWARD, univ. adminstr.; b. Seattle, July 4, 1932; s. Alfred M. Andreason and Alberta (Brewer) Andreason Thompson; B.S. in Bus. Adminstrn., Tex. Wesleyan U., Ft. Worth, 1960; M.P.A. (Ford. Found. scholar), Ind. U., 1966; Ph.D., Clayton U., St. Louis, 1979; m. Carolyn A. McKown, June 30, 1973; 1 son, Paul Edward. Program analyst U.S. Army, Washington, 1963-64; asst. chief mgmt. analysis div. FAA, Ft. Worth, 1964-67, chief mgmt. analysis div., Oklahoma City, 1968-70, exec. officer, 1970-71; mgmt. cons. Dept. Transpo., 1966-67; asst. dir. IRS, Denver, 1971-72, asst. regional commr. adminstrn., Dallas, 1972-74, dist. dir., Denver, 1974, asst. dir. dir., St. Louis, 1974-76; dir. adminstrv. services McLennan Community Coll., Waco, Tex., 1976-77; v.p. bus. and adminstrn. U. Mary Hardin-Baylor, Belton, Tex., 1977-80, exec. v.p., 1980—; partner McGregor Assos., bus. and mgmt. cons., McGregor, Tex. Served with USN, 1951-55. Recipient Career Edn. award FAA and Nat. Inst. Public Affairs, 1965. Fellow Nat. Inst. Public Affairs; mem. Am. Soc. Public Adminstrn., Personnel and Mgmt. Assn., Nat. Coll. and Univ. Bus. Officers, So. Assn. Coll. and Univ. Bus. Officers, Belton C. of C. Baptist. Clubs: Rotary (Belton); Masons (master McGregor 1977, Tex. dist. dep. grand master 1980) (McGregor and Ft. Worth). Home: PO Box 181 McGregor TX 76657 Office: U Mary Hardin-Baylor MHB Station Belton TX 76513

ANDREI, STEFAN, Romanian government official, former minister of foreign affairs; b. Podari, Dolj County, Romania, Mar. 29, 1931; grad. Inst. Civil Engrs., 1956; married, 1 son. Mem. Union of Communist Youth, 1949-54, joined student movement, 1951, mem. Bur. Central Com., 1962-65; mem. exec. com. Union of Student Assns., 1958-62; mem. Romanian Communist Party, 1954—; alt. mem., central com., 1969-72, mem., 1972—; 1st dep. head internat. sect. central com. 1965-73, sec. central com., 1972-78, 85—, alt. mem. exec. polit. com., 1974—, minister of fgn. affairs Socialist Republic of Romania, to 1975; sec. Party Econ. Affairs, 1975—; mem. Grand Nat. Assembly, 1975—; del. numerous internat. confs. and congresses. Recipient Orders and Medals, Socialist Republic of Romania. Mem. Nat. Council Front of Socialist Democracy and Unity. Author studies and articles on internat. workers' movement and internat. politics. Address: Cen Committee Romanian, Communist Party, Bucharest Romania *

ANDREJKO, DENNIS ANDREW, architect, educator; b. Wyandotte, Mich., Apr. 30, 1952; s. H. Andrew and Bridget Ann (Jenca) A.; m. Mary Ellen Krolczyk, June 1986; children—Erik, Bryan, Jynelle. B.Arch. cum laude, Ariz. State U., 1975; M.Arch. in Advanced Studies, MIT, 1977. Lic. architect, N.Y., Calif., Ariz. Designer, David Wright Assocs., The Sea Ranch, Calif., 1977-78; prin. SeaGroup Solar Environ. Architecture, Nevada City, Calif., 1979-81; prin. Andrejko & Assocs., Williamsville, N.Y., 1981—; asst. prof. Ariz. State U., Tempe, 1981-82; assoc. prof. dept. architecture SUNY-Buffalo, 1982—, dir. summer program, 1983, 84, 85, 87, 88. Author (with others): Solar 4: Architektur Und Energie, 1980, Passive Solar Architecture: Logic and Beauty, 1982 (Book of Mo. award McGraw Hill, Library of Urban Affairs 1983);Out of the Cold: Emerging Architectural Ideas, 1988; co-editor Nat Passive Solar Conf. Proceedings, 1983, 87, ASES Annual Conf. Proceedings, 1987; co-author, curator Aesthetics for the Cold: Emerging Architectural Ideas, 1983; assoc. editor of architecture Passive Solar Jour., 1985-87, Solar Energy Jour., 1987—. Exhibitor Amerika Haus, Berlin in 12 major West German cities, 1980-84. Invited exhibitor Passive Solar Forum, Tokyo, 1987. Mem. AIA (design award 1974), Am. Solar Energy Soc. (dir. passive systems div., chmn. passive architecture and constrn. div. 1985, gen. chmn. Nat. Passive Solar Conf. 1984, tech. program chmn. Nat. Passive Solar Conf. 1981), Nat. Council Archtl. Registration Bds. Democrat. Roman Catholic. Home: 203 Delamere Rd Williamsville NY 14221 Office: SUNY Sch Architecture-Environ Design Buffalo Hayes Hall Buffalo NY 14214

ANDREOFF, CHRISTOPHER ANDON, lawyer; b. Detroit, July 15, 1947; s. Andon Anastas and Mildred Dimitry (Kolinoff) A.; m. Nancy Anne Krochmal, Jan. 12, 1980; children: Alison Brianne, Lauren Kathleen. BA, Wayne State U., 1969; postgrad. in law Washington U., St. Louis, 1969-70; JD, U. Detroit, 1972. Bar: Mich. 1972, U.S. Dist. Ct. (ea. dist.) Mich. 1972, U.S. Ct. Appeals (6th cir.) 1974, Fla. 1978, U.S. Supreme Ct. 1980. Legal intern Wayne County Prosecutor's Office, Detroit, 1970-72; law clk. Wayne County Cir. Ct., Detroit, 1972-73; asst. U.S. atty. U.S. Dept. Justice, Detroit, 1973-80, asst. chief Criminal Div., U.S. Atty.'s Office, 1977-80, spl. atty. Organized Crime and Racketeering sect. U.S. Dept. Justice, 1980-84, dep. chief Detroit Organized Crime Strike Force, 1982-85, mem. narcotics adv. com. U.S. Dept. Justice, 1979-80; ptnr. Evans & Luptak, Detroit, 1985—; lectr. U.S. Atty. Gen. Advocacy Inst., 1984. Recipient numerous spl. commendations FBI, U.S. Drug Enforcement Adminstrn., U.S. Dept. Justice, U.S. Atty. Gen. Mem. ABA, Fed. Bar Assn. (speaker criminal law sect. Detroit 1983—), Mich. Bar Assn., Fla. Bar Assn., Detroit Bar Assn. Greek Orthodox. Home: 4661 Rivers Edge Dr Troy MI 48098 Office: Evans & Luptak 2500 Buhl Bldg Detroit MI 48226

ANDREONI, GIOVANNI, writer, educator; b. Grosseto, Italy, Aug. 9, 1935; arrived in Australia, 1964; s. Guglielmo and Maria (Bertocci) A.; m. Helen Cook, 1968; children: Marco, Francesca. PhD, Pisa (Italy) U., 1962. Vis. lectr. U. Western Australia, Perth, 1964-65, lectr., 1966-67; assoc. prof. U. Auckland, New Zealand, 1968-73; head Italian sch. U. New Eng., Armidale, Australia, 1974—; vis. prof. U. Venice, 1984, U. Pisa, 1984-85, U. Wollongong, Australia, 1986. Author: (short story collections) Sedici Notti d'Insonnia, 1962, La Lingua degl'Italiani d'Australia e Alcuni Racconti, 1978, (novels) Martin Pescatore, 1967, Cenere, 1982; editor: Multicultural Australia: The Italian Experience, 1985—, textbooks and anthologies; contbr. poetry, short stories, revs. to numerous lit. mags. Trustee of crown, Mus. New Eng., Armidale, Australia, 1987—. Mem. Italian Orgns. Western Australia (sec. cen. com. 1967), Dante Alighieri Soc. New Zealand (pres. 1970-73), La Presenza Italiana-Australia (pres. 1982—). Office: U New Eng, Dept Modern Lang, Armidale Australia

ANDREONI, RUBENS, mechanical engineer; b. São Paulo, Brazil, Jan. 30, 1944; s. Alphio and Alba Maria (Siqueira) A.; m. Lilian Cury, Jan. 31, 1969; 1 child, Luciana. Degree in Mech. Engring., U. São Paulo, 1967; degree in bus. adminstrn., U. Mackenzie, São Paulo, 1976. Mgr. prodn. Sul Americana de Engenharia S.A., São Paulo, 1967-68; indsl. adviser S.A. Phillips do Brasil, Guarulhos, 1969-72; responsible engr. Lutz Ferrando S.A., São Paulo, 1969-74; tech. adviser Coop. Agrícola de Cotia, São Paulo, 1973-76, head exec. engring., 1976—; indsl. dir. Indústria de Oleos Paranaense S.A., Ibiporã, Paraná, Brazil, 1976-84; cosn. Giusti Ltd., São Paulo, 1968-83. Recipient Disting. Citizen award City of São Paulo, 1971. Mem. Inst. Engring., Engring. and Architecture Regulatory Council, Bus. Adminstrn. Regulatory Council. Roman Catholic. Clubs: Country Club Castelo, Coop. (São Paulo). Lodge: Rosacruz. Home: Rua Jesuino Arruda, #187 Apt 111, Sao Paulo 04532, Brazil Office: Coop Agricola de Cotia Coop Cen, Avenida Jaguare 1487, Sao Paulo 05346, Brazil

ANDREOPOULOS, SPYROS GEORGE, writer; b. Athens, Greece, Feb. 12, 1929; s. George S. and Anne Levas) A.; came to U.S., 1953, naturalized, 1962; A.B., Wichita State U., 1957; m. Christiane Loesch Loriaux, June 6, 1958; 1 dau., Sophie. Pub. info. specialist USIA, Salonica, Greece, 1951-53; asst. editorial page editor Wichita (Kans.) Beacon, 1955-59; asst. dir. info. services, editor The Menninger Quar., The Menninger Found., Topeka, 1959-63; info. officer Stanford U. Med. Ctr., 1963-83, dir. communications and editor Stanford Medicine, 1983—; editor Sun Valley Forum on Nat. Health, Inc. (Idaho), 1972-83, 85—. Served with Royal Hellenic Air Force, 1949-50. Mem. AAAS, Assn. Am. Med. Colls., Nat. Assn. Sci. Writers, Am. Med. Writers Assn., Am. Hosp. Assn., Am. Soc. Hosp. Pub. Relations, Council for Advancement Edn. Co-author, editor: Medical Cure and Medical Care, 1972; Primary Care: Where Medicine Fails, 1974; National Health Insurance: Can We Learn from Canada? 1975; Heart Beat, 1978, Health Care for an Aging Society, 1988. Contbr. articles to profl. jours. Home: 1012 Vernier Pl Stanford CA 94305

ANDREOSATOS, ANASTASIOS, mechanical and design engineer; b. Athens, Greece, Aug. 16, 1952; came to U.S., 1969, naturalized, 1974; s. Eleftherios and Theodora (Adam) A.; ed. in archtl. engring., Franklin Inst., 1973, in mfg. engring., Northeastern U., 1974, in Biomed. Engring., 1975; m. Cynthia Jameson, Jan. 25, 1976; children—Alexis, Apollene. Biomed. engr. B-D Life Support Systems, Sharon, Mass., 1973-77; project engr. Rockwell Internat., Hopedale, Mass., 1977-78; design engr. Alpine Am., Natick, Mass., 1978-79; project engr. Inforex, Burlington, Mass., 1979-80; biomed. design engr. Intermedics-INFUSAID Inc., Norwood, Mass., 1980—. Home: 3 School St Natick MA 01760 Office: Shiley-INFUSAID div Pfizer Pharms 1400 Providence Hwy Norwood MA 02062

ANDREOTTI, GIULIO, Italian minister of foreign affairs; b. Jan. 14, 1919; m. Livia Danese, 1945; 4 children. Grad. U. Rome, 1945; Hon. causa, Sorbonne U., Paris, Loyola U., Chgo., Copernicus U., Torun, Poland, Notre Dame U., South Bend, Ind., U. La Plata, Argentina, U. Salamanca, Spain, St. John's U., N.Y. Pres., Fedn. Cath. Univs. in Italy, 1942-45; dep. to Constituent Assembly, 1945, to Parliament, 1946—; under-sec., 1947-53; minister for interior, 1954; minister of fin., 1955-58, minister of treasury, 1958-59, minister of def., 1959-66, 74-76, minister of industry and commerce, 1966-68; pres. orgn. com. Rome olympics, 1960; chmn. Christian Dem. Parliamentary Group in Chamber of Deputies, 1968-72, chmn. fgn. affairs commn., 1973-74, 79-83; prime minister of Italy, 1972-73, 76-79; minister of balance for econ. planning and spl. econ. interventions in South, 1973-74; minister of fgn. affairs, 1983—; mem. European Parliament; pres. European Popular Party, until 1985; active Interparliamentary Union, chmn. polit. affairs and disarmament com., 1981-85; chmn. Christian Dem. Party Directorate. Author: biography of De Gasperi, 1964; La Sciarada di Papa Mastai, 1967; Ore 13: Il Ministro deve Morire, 1975; Visti da Vicino, Vols I-III (3d vol. received Premio Bancarella 1985); De Gasperi, 1987; Onorevolestia Zitto, 1987. Editor: Concretezza, 1954-76. Office: Ministry of Fgn Affairs, Piazzale della Farnesina 1, 00194 Rome Italy

ANDRES, FREDERICK WILLIAM, lawyer; b. Alexandria, Egypt, Sept. 21, 1906; s. Frederick Henry Augustus and Laura Edith (Bezell) A.; m. Katherine Pratt Weeks, Sept. 9, 1931; children: Katherine Weeks Andres Moore, Anita Andres Rogerson, William McKenzie. A.B., Dartmouth Coll., 1929, A.M. (hon.), 1963, LL.D. (hon.), 1979; LL.B., Harvard U., 1932; LL.D. (hon.), Colby Coll., 1977. Bar: Mass. bar 1932. Since practiced in Boston; mem. firm Sherburne, Powers & Needham, 1940-83, of counsel, 1983—; bd. dirs. George B.H. Macomber Co.; clk., bd. dirs. Hamilton Constrn. Corp., Investors Bank & Trust Co.; trustee Boston Broadcasters Liquidating Trust, Charlesbank Homes, Boston, 1981—. Author: (with others) The College on the Hill-A Dartmouth Chronicle, 1964. Regional chmn. Dartmouth Capital Fund campaign, 1958-61; sec.-chmn. Dartmouth class 1929, 1929-63; trustee Dartmouth Coll., 1963-77, chmn. bd. trustees, 1972-77; pres. Dartmouth Alumni Assn., Boston, 1950; chmn. Dartmouth Athletic Council, 1956-61; regional chmn. United Negro Coll. Fund, 1960; mem. Brookline (Mass.) Town Meeting, 1947-53, Brookline Personnel Bd., 1957-66; bd. dirs. Brookline Citizens Com., 1948-57; trustee Phillips Exeter Acad., 1962-72, 77-81, pres. bd., 1965-72; trustee Champlain Coll., 1966-70, Bennington Coll., 1956-63; trustee Beaver Country Day Sch., Chestnut Hill, Mass., 1947-64, pres., 1949-64; trustee Elizabeth Carleton House, Boston, 1954-72, pres., 1957-66; mem. corp. New Eng. Deaconess Hosp., 1963-82; bd. dirs. Grenville Clark Fund at Dartmouth Coll., Inc., 1973—; mem. corp. Mass. Gen. Hosp., 1982—. Recipient Alumni award Dartmouth Coll., 1963, Disting. Friend Edn. award Council Advancement and Support Edn., 1982. Mem. Am. Bar Assn., Boston Bar Assn. (council 1966-68), Mass. Bar Assn., Dartmouth Alumni Assn. Boston (pres. 1950), Phi Gamma Delta, Casque and Gauntlet Sr. Soc., Gen. Alumni Assn. Phillips Exeter Acad. (pres. 1962-63), Nisi Prius Club. Republican. Episcopalian (vestry 1957-60). Clubs: The Country (Brookline); Harvard (Boston), Union (Boston). Home: 106 Laurel Rd Chestnut Hill Brookline MA 02167 Office: 1 Beacon St Boston MA 02108

ANDRESEN, MALCOLM, lawyer; b. Medford, Wis., July 26, 1917; s. Thomas Whelen and Ethel (Malkson) A.; m. Ann Kimball, Oct. 17, 1942; children—Anthony M., Susan A. Bridges, Abbott K.; m. Barbara Brown, May 23, 1971; m. Nigi Sato, Dec. 12, 1979. B.A., U. Wis., 1940, LL.B., 1941. Bar: Wis. 1941, N.Y. 1946, U.S. Supreme Ct. 1958. Acct., J.D. Miller & Co., N.Y.C., 1946-47; jr. tax acct. Peat Marwick Mitchell & Co., N.Y.C., 1947-48; assoc. Davis Wagner Hallett & Russell, N.Y.C., 1948-52; tax counsel, then sr. tax counsel, then sr. govt. relations adviser Mobil Oil Corp., N.Y.C., 1952-70; dir. tax legal affairs Nat. Fgn. Trade Council, N.Y.C., 1970-73; of counsel Delson & Gordon, N.Y.C., 1973-77, Whitman & Ransom, N.Y.C., 1977-86; sole practice, 1986—. Trustee, treas. Cathedral Ch. of St. John the Divine, N.Y.C., 1977-84. Served to capt. USMCR, 1942-46. Decorated Bronze Star medal. Mem. Assn. of Bar of City of N.Y., Internat. Fiscal Assn. (council U.S.A. br.), Tax Mgmt., Inc. (adv. bd.). Democrat. Episcopalian. Club: Univ. (N.Y.C.). Home: 2 Lincoln Sq Apt 24-D New York NY 10023 Office: 600 3d Ave New York NY 10016

ANDRETTI, MARIO (GABRIEL), professional race car driver; b. Montona, Italy, Feb. 28, 1940; came to U.S., 1955, naturalized, 1964; s. Alvise and Rina (Benvegnu) A.; m. DeeAnn Beverly Hoch, Nov. 25, 1961; children: Michael Mario, Jeffrey Lewis, Barbra Dee. Foreman Retter Line, Inc., Easton, Pa., 1959-61; with Delwick Co., Easton, 1961; foreman Motovator, Springfield, N.J., 1961-64; profl. race car driver Dean Van Lines, Long Beach, Calif., 1964-67, Overseas Nat. Airways, 1968, STP Corp., Des Plaines, Ill., 1969-71, Vel's Parnelli Jones, Torrance, Calif., 1972-76, John Player Team Lotus, Norwich, Eng., 1968-68, 70, 76-80, Ferrari, 1971-72, Penske Racing, Reading, Pa., 1976-80, Patrick Racing, 1981-82, Alfa Romeo, 1981, Newman/Haas Racing, 1983—; pres. M.A. 500 Inc., Nazareth, 1968—. Named Indianapolis 500 Rookie of Yr., 1965, U. S. Auto Club Dirt Track champion, 1974, Internat. Race of Champions titlist, 1979, Driver of Yr., 1976, 78, 84. Mem. U.S. Auto Club, Fedn. Inter. L'automobile. Roman Catholic.

ANDREWS, BARBARA PARKER, librarian; b. Nantucket, Mass., Mar. 18, 1918; d. James S. and Elizabeth H. (Parker) A.; B.S., Simmons Coll., 1944. Cataloguer, U. Cin. Library, 1944-46; with descriptive cataloguing div. Library of Congress, Washington, 1946-65, adminstrv. asst., 1950-63, research asst., 1963-65; librarian Nantucket Atheneum, 1965—. Mem. ALA, Nantucket Hist. Assn., Maria Mitchell Assn. Home: 1 E York St Nantucket MA 02554 Office: Nantucket Atheneum India St Nantucket MA 02554

ANDREWS, BILLY FRANKLIN, pediatrician; b. Alamance County, N.C., Sept. 22, 1932; s. Dean Franklin and Arlee (Byers) A.; B.S. cum laude, Wake Forest U., 1953; M.D. (Lederle fellow, USPHS fellow), Duke U., 1957; m. Faye Rich, Dec. 25, 1953; children—Ann Elizabeth, Billy Franklin, David Ashley. Intern, Fort Benning (Ga.) Hosp., 1957-58; resident in pediatrics Walter Reed Gen. Hosp., Washington, 1958-60; resident in basic sci. and metabolism Walter Reed Inst. Research, 1960-61; asst. prof. pediatrics U. Louisville Sch. Medicine, 1964-66, dir. newborn services, 1964-76, co-dir. genetic counseling unit, 1965-68, asso. prof., 1966-68, prof. pediatrics, 1968—, chmn. dept., 1969—, dir. neonatology, nurses, regional tng. programs, 1966—, dir. Comprehensive Health Care Center for High Risk Infants and Children, 1968—, co-dir. health profls. spl. project grant for preceptorship tng., 1974, dir. community tng. in pediatrics, 1975, pilot project in community pediatrics, 1976; chief of staff children's div. Norton-Children's Hosp., 1969; cons. in field, 1966—; Jour. Pediatrics Found. lectr., 1972; participant Oslerfest, Oxford, Eng., 1984; 1st Munster paediatric lectr., Cork, Ireland, 1984; Louisville Pediatric Soc. lectr., 1986; spl. guest South African Perinatal Assn., 1985, Brit. Pediatric Assn., 1985; chmn. newborn session XVIII Internat. Congress Pediatrics, Honolulu, 1986. Pres., Kornhauser Library, Health Sci. Center, 1981-82; Wyeth vis. prof. Golden Jubilee Meeting, Sydney, Australia, 1988. Served to maj. M.C., U.S. Army, 1957-64. Named Outstanding Clin. Prof., U. Louisville Sch. Medicine, 1965; recipient Helen B. Fraser award, Norton-Children's Hosp. award, 1978; Disting. Alumni Service citation Wake Forest U., 1983; award of recognition XVII Internat. Congress Pediatrics Organizing Com., Manila, 1983; award for service to children and dedication to edn. osteo. pediatricians, 1984; diplomate Am. Bd. Pediatrics. Fellow Am. Acad. Pediatrics, ACP, N.Y. Acad. Scis., Royal Soc. Medicine (London), founding mem. So. Soc. for Pediatric Research, Southeastern Perinatal Soc., Nat. Assn. Childrens Hosps. and Related Instns., Nat. Perinatal Soc.; mem. AAAS, Ky. Med. Assn. (Faculty Sci. Achievement award 1971, del. 1981-82), AMA, Jefferson County Med. Assn., Ky. Pediatric Soc., Louisville Pediatric Soc., Am. Soc. Law and Medicine, Am. Pediatric Soc., Soc. for Pediatric Research, Am. Osler Soc. (bd. govs. 1977), Tex. Pediatrics Soc. (hon.), Assn. Med. Sch. Pediatric Dept. Chairmen, Hastings Inst. Soc., Ethics and Life Scis., Irish-Am. Paediatric Soc., Nat. Hist. Soc., Ky. Ob-Gyn Soc., U. Louisville Sch. Medicine Alumni Assn. (bd. govs. 1972), Alpha Omega Alpha. Editor: Children's Bill of Rights, 1968, Small-for-Date Infants, 1970, The Newborn, Pediatric Clinics of North America, 1977; editor: Aphorisms, Tributes and Tenets of Billy F. Andrews: In Walls, M.E., 1986; contbr. articles, abstracts to profl. jours. Mem. United Ch. of Christ. Office: Univ Louisville Sch Med Health Scis Ctr, Dept Pediatrics Louisville KY 40232

ANDREWS, CLARENCE ADELBERT, historian, educator, writer, publisher; b. Waterloo, Iowa, Oct. 24, 1912; s. Harry Leon and June Jennie (Jones) A.; m. Ollie Mae Easley, June 12, 1937; children: Linda Andrews Thompson, Terry Andrews Lasansky, Steven Randall. B.A., U. Iowa, 1954, M.A., 1960, Ph.D., 1963. Mem. War Price and Rationing Bd., Sheldon, Iowa, 1941-42; exec. sec. Sheldon C. of C., 1941-42; owner House of Andrews, Sheldon, 1942-49; asst. prof. Colo. State U., Ft. Collins, 1960-61; from instr. to assoc. prof. English and journalism U. Iowa, 1961-69; vis. prof. journalism, 1976-82; prof. lang. and lit. Mich. Tech. U., Houghton, 1971-75; also dir. tech. and sci. communications; adj. prof. Am. thought and lang. Mich. State U., East Lansing, 1975—; pub. Midwest Heritage Pub. Co., 1979—; vis. prof. Naval Ordnance Test Sta., China Lake, Calif., 1959; cons. Measurement Research Center, 1960; Mem. Mich. Council Humanities, 1974-76. Author: Technical and Scientific Writing, 1964, Writing, 1972, A Literary History of Iowa, 1972, Technical and Business Writing, 1974,

Growing Up In Iowa, 1978, A Bibliography of Chicago Literature, 1978, The American Dream in the Heartland, 1982, Chicago in Story, 1983; Editor: Personnel Adminstr, 1960-61, Christmas in Iowa, 1979, Growing Up in the Middle West, 1981, Christmas in the Midwest, 1985. Bd. dirs. N.W. Iowa Def. Bonds Sales, 1942. Served with USAAF, 1944-46. Recipient Mid-Am. Award, 1982; Grantee NDEA, 1968; Grantee NSF, 1964,'66; Grantee Ednl. Profl. Devel. Act, 1969; Grantee Mich. Tech. U., 1973. Mem. Soc. Study Midwest Lit., Iowa State Hist. Soc., Phi Beta Kappa, Kappa Tau Alpha. Address: 108 Pearl St Iowa City IA 52245

ANDREWS, DAVID CHARLES, energy consultant, computer consultant, management consultant; b. London, Mar. 10, 1950; s. Alan Charles and Maisie Joy (Brien) A.; m. Janet Alison Hooker; children: Joseph James, Annabel Jane. BS in Engring. with honors, U. Cardiff, 1973. Engr. Mouchel & Ptnrs., Bath, Eng., 1974-78; researcher Open Univ., Milton Keynes, Eng., 1978-82; area mgr. Ellis Tylin, London, 1982-84, Apllied Energy Systems, Watford, Eng., 1984-86; mgr. sales and mktg. KFS (CHP Conversions) Ltd., Llantrisant, Eng., 1986—; prin. David Andrews Assocs., Bath, 1988—. Author: The IRG Solution, 1984, The Hidden Manager, 1985; inventor info. routing group concept. Mem. Assn. Ind. Electricity Producers (founder, officer).

ANDREWS, EDWIN EVERTS, prosthodontist, forensic odontologist; b. Syracuse, N.Y., July 30, 1934; s. George Bouton and Marie (Buggeln) A.; B.S., Syracuse U., 1956; D.M.D., Fairleigh Dickinson U., 1963; M.Ed., Central State U., 1976; m. Patricia Ann McCarthy, Nov. 27, 1963; 1 son, Mark Robert. Intern Upstate Med. Center, Syracuse, 1963-64; resident in prosthetics N.Y. U., 1964-66; practice prosthetics, Syracuse, 1966-72; chief maxillofacial prosthetics State Univ. Hosp. Upstate Med. Center, Syracuse, 1967-72; asst. prof. maxillofacial prosthodontist U. Mo. Sch. Dentistry, Kansas City, 1972-73; asso. prof., chmn. maxillofacial prosthetics U. Okla. Coll. Dentistry, Oklahoma City, 1973-77; pvt. practice prosthodontics and maxillofacial prosthetics, Oklahoma City, 1977-85; attending maxillofacial prosthetics Okla. Meml. Hosp., Children's Meml. Hosp, 1973-85, Presbytn. Hosp., 1976-85, Health Scis. Center, Oklahoma City. Cons. VA Hosp, Oklahoma City, Muskogee, Okla., 1973-76, Okla. Office of Chief Med. Examiner, 1974-81, FAA, 1974-86; courtesy staff Mercy Health Ctr., 1982-85, O'Donoghue Rehab. Inst., 1982-87. Served USAF, 1956-58; lt. col. USAR Dental Corps. Diplomate Am. Bd. Prosthodontics, Am. Bd. Forensic Odontology. Fellow Am. Coll. Prosthodontists, Am. Acad. Forensic Scis., Am. Acad. Maxillofacial Prosthetics (bd. dirs. 1983-86), Acad. Internat. Dental Studies, Midwest Acad. Prosthodontics (councillor 1984-87); mem. ADA, Am. Prosthodontic Soc. (chmn. nomenclature com. 1983-85), Am. Soc. Forensic Odontology (bd. govs. 1983—), Fedn. Prosthodontic Orgns., Internat. Reference Orgn. in Forensic Medicine and Scis., Am. Bd. Forensic Odontology (bd. dirs. 1984-86), Brit. Acad. Forensic Scis., Ark. State Dental Assn. Home: 108 Ravens Roost Rogers AR 72756-9178

ANDREWS, HARVEY WELLINGTON, med. co. exec.; b. Stowe Twp., Pa., Sept. 9, 1928; s. Robert W. and Theresa R. (Reis) A.; B.B.A. cum laude, U. Pitts., 1952; M.B.A., Harvard, 1957; m. Jane Garland, Aug. 9, 1969; children—Marcia Lynne, Glynis Suzanne, Elizabeth Jane. With Gen. Electric Co., Syracuse, N.Y., 1952-55, Scovill Mfg. Co., Waterbury, Conn., 1957; comptroller Alcon Labs., Inc., Ft. Worth, 1958-61, comptroller, treas., 1961-65, v.p. finance, 1964-68; founder, pres. Medimation, Inc., Ft. Worth, 1968—; bd. dirs. Hearing Health Group, Inc., Med. Scis. Computor Corp., 1st Clin. Labs., Senca Inc. Real Estate Devels., 1988—, Tex. Commerce Bank, Fort Worth, 1969-78; pres., chmn. bd. Dalworth Med. Labs. Bd. dirs., mem. exec. com. Fort Worth Opera Assn. Served with AUS, 1946-48. Mem. Am. Acad. Polit. and Social Scis., A.A.A.S., Ft. Worth C. of C., Soc. Advancement Mgmt. Order Artus, Scabbard and Blade, Golden Eagle Assn., Sigma Alpha Epsilon. Lutheran. Mason (32 deg.). Clubs: Rotary, Met. Knife and Fork, Tex. Christian U. Pres.'s Round Table Assn., Colonial Country, Century II. Home: PO Box 1786 Fort Worth TX 76101 Office: 2912 W Sixth St Fort Worth TX 76107

ANDREWS, JOHN FRANK, educational administrator, editor; b. Carlsbad, N.Mex., Nov. 2, 1942; s. Frank Randolph and Mary Lucille (Wimberley) A.; m. Vicky Roberta Anderson, Aug. 20, 1966 (div. 1983); children: Eric John, Lisa Gail. AB, Princeton U., 1965; MAT, Harvard U., 1966; PhD, Vanderbilt U., 1971. Instr. English U. Tenn., Nashville, 1969-70; asst. prof. Fla. State U., Tallahassee, 1970-74, dir. grad. studies in English, 1973-74; dir. acad. programs Folger Shakespeare Library, Washington, 1974-84; chmn. Folger Inst. Renaissance and 18th Century Studies Washington, 1974-84; exec. editor Folger Books, Washington, 1974-84; dep. dir. div. edn. programs NEH, Washington, 1984-88; editor-in-chief The Guild Shakespeare, 1988—; cons. Time-Life TV, WNET/Thirteen, Corp. for Pub. Broadcasting, Pub. Broadcasting Service, Exxon Corp., others; chmn. Nat. Adv. Panel for The Shakespeare Plays, 1979-85; core adviser The Shakespeare Hour, 1985-86; mem. adv. bds. Inst. Humanistic Studies SUNY-Albany, Newberry Library Ctr. Renaissance Studies, Theatre for a New Audience, Shakespeare Theater at the Folger, and others; cons. Shakespeare: The Globe and the World, touring exhbn., 1978-81, Nat. Pub. Radio, 1978-81, Doubleday, 1982-83; adminstr. program grants NEH, Andrew W. Mellon Found., Exxon Found., Met. Life, Surdna Found., others. Asst. editor: Shakespeare Studies, 1972-74; editor: Shakespeare Quar., 1974-85; editor-in-chief, contbr.: William Shakespeare: His World, His Work, His Influence, 1985; contbr. numerous articles to scholarly jours. Recipient Research awards Folger Shakespeare Library, Fla. State U. Mem. AAUP (sec. chpt. 1972-74), Modern Lang. Assn., Milton Soc. Am., Nat. Council of Tchrs. of English, Renaissance Soc. Am. (mem. council 1975-84), Internat. Shakespeare Conf., Shakespeare Assn. Am. (trustee 1979-82), The Lit. Soc. Club: Cosmos. Home and Office: 2032 Belmont Rd NW 605 Washington DC 20009

ANDREWS, JOHN HAMILTON, architect; b. Oct. 29, 1933; s. K. A.; m. Rosemary Randall, 1958; children: John, Lee, Craig, James. BArch, U. Sydney, 1956, MArch, Harvard U., 1958. Pvt. practice architecture, Toronto, Ont., Can., 1962, Sydney, Australia, 1970—; mem. faculty U. Toronto Sch. Architecture, 1962-67, chmn., prof., 1967-69; mem. Visual Arts Bd. Australia Council, 1977-80, chmn. architecture and design com., 1980—; juror Australian Archives Nat. Headquarters Bldg., 1979, Parliament House Competition, 1979-80. Works include: Scarborough Coll., Toronto, Harvard U. Grad. Sch. Design, Cameron Offices, Canberra, American Express Tower, Sydney, Intelsat Headquarters Bldg., Washington, Merlin Hotel site project, Perth, West Australia; author: Architecture: A Performing Art, 1982. Recipient Centennial medal Can., 1967; Massey medal Can., 1967; Arnold Brunner award U.S. Acad. Arts and Letters, 1971; Advance Australia award, 1982. Fellow Royal Archtl. Inst. Can., Royal Australian Inst. Architects (Gold medal 1980), AIA (Honor award 1973). Office: John Andrews Internat Pty Ltd, 1017 Barrenjoey Rd, Palm Beach NSW 2108, Australia *

ANDREWS, JULIE, actress, singer; b. Walton-on-Thames, Eng., Oct. 1, 1935; d. Edward C. and Barbara Wells; m. Tony Walton, May 10, 1959 (div.); 1 dau., Emma; m. Blake Edwards, 1969. Studied with pvt. tutors, studied voice with Mme. Stiles-Allen. Debut as singer, Hippodrome, London, 1947; appeared in pantomime Cinderella, London, 1953; appeared: Broadway prodn. The Boy Friend, N.Y.C., 1954, My Fair Lady, 1956-60 (N.Y. Drama Critics award 1956), Camelot, 1960-62; films include Mary Poppins, 1964 (Acad. award for best actress 1964), The Americanization of Emily, 1964, Torn Curtain, 1966, The Sound of Music, 1966, Hawaii, 1966, Thoroughly Modern Millie, 1967, Star!, 1968, Darling Lili, 1970, The Tamarind Seed, 1973, 10, 1979, Little Miss Marker, 1980, S.O.B, 1981, Victor/Victoria, 1982, The Man Who Loved Women, 1983, That's Life!, 1986, Duet For One, 1986; TV debut in High Tor, 1956; star TV series The Julie Andrews Hour, 1972-73; also spls.; Author: (as Julie Edwards): Mandy, 1971, The Last of the Really Great Whangdoodles, 1974. Recipient Golden Globe award Hollywood Fgn. Press Assn., 1964, 65; named World Film Favorite (female), 1967. Office: care Greengage Prodns 11777 San Vicente Blvd #501 Los Angeles CA 90049 also: Hanson & Schwam 9200 Sunset Blvd Los Angeles CA 90069

ANDREWS, MARK EDWIN, III, oil and gas exploration company executive; b. Houston, June 1, 1950; s. Mark Edwin and Lavone (Dickensheets) A.; m. Elizabeth Quay, June 28, 1975 children: Elizabeth Quay, Mark Edwin IV. BA, Harvard U., 1972, MBA, 1975. V.p. corp. fin. Rotan Mosle Inc., N.Y.C., 1975-80; pres., chmn. bd. Am. Exploration Co., N.Y.C., 1980—; bd. dirs. IVAX Corp., Miami, Fla. Mem. Rockefeller U. Council, N.Y.C. Episcopalian. Clubs: River, Links, Knickerbocker (N.Y.C.); Fishers' Island (N.Y.); Houston Country, Houston, Bayou (Houston). Home: 812 Park Ave New York NY 10021 Office: Am Exploration Co 885 3d Ave New York NY 10022

ANDREWS, MICHAEL CURTIS, public relations specialist; b. Columbus, Ohio, Oct. 22, 1949; s. Michael Frank and Helen W. (Baker) A.; m. Dorothy Ann Andrews; 1 child, Michael George. Student U. Hawaii, 1967; B.S. in Radio and TV, Syracuse U., 1971. Dir. prodn. WHEN Radio, Syracuse, N.Y., 1972-74; dir. programming WRGI Radio, Naples, Fla., 1974-75; asst. gen. mgr. Sterling Communications, Naples, Fla., 1976-76; program dir. WFBL Radio, Syracuse, N.Y., 1976-77; dir. comml. prodn. and promotion WFLA AM & FM, Tampa, 1977-81; dir. pub. relations The Shrine of N.Am. and Shriners Hosps., Internat. Shrine Headquarters, Tampa, 1981—. Mem. exec. com. Univ. Tampa Bd. Counselors, 1983—; chmn. pub. affairs com. ARC, Tampa, 1987—; Hall of Fame Bowl com., 1986. Mem. Tampa C. of C. (chmn. internal promotions council 1983), Pub. Relations Soc. Am. (bd. dirs.), Internat. Assn. Bus. Communicators, Am. Soc. Hosp. Mktg. and Pub. Relations (mem. Tampa area council), Sigma Phi Epsilon. Clubs: Masons, Shriners. Office: 2900 Rocky Point Dr Tampa FL 33607

ANDREWS, RICHARD JOHN, educator; b. Braintree, Essex, Eng., Apr. 1, 1953; s. John William and Sylvia (Thacker) A.; m. Dorothy Fordyce Beardshaw, Aug. 2, 1979; children: David Eric, Zoe Virginia. MA, Oxford (Eng.) U., 1974. Tchr. in English Cedars Upper Sch., Leighton Buzzard, Bedfordshire, Eng., 1977-79, George Green's Sch., London, 1979-81, Joseph Rowntree Sch., York, Eng., 1981-83; head of English Island Sch., Hong Kong, 1983-87; edn. lectr. U. Hull, Eng., 1987—. Author: Words 1-3, 1983, From Rough to Best, 1982, Into Poetry, 1984, Poetry Horizons, 1987. Recipient Urban Council Poetry prize, 1984, Double Distinction award and David Forsyth prize U. Leeds, 1977; Samuel Courtauld scholar, 1971, Baring Open scholar, 1971. Office: U Hull Sch Edn, Cottingham Rd, Hull HU6 7RX, England

ANDREWS, SUSAN LYNN, insurance agent, marketing specialist; b. Los Angeles, Feb. 1, 1962; d. John Morton Machunka-Andrews and Charmaine Mary (Wells) Andrews Gordon. Student U. Colo., Boulder, 1980-83. Dir. Gordon Gen. Ins., Los Angeles, 1978-84; mortgage specialist Am. Internat. Group, Los Angeles and N.Y.C., 1984-86; U.S. agt. confidential program Bayly Martin and Fay, Los Angeles, 1986-87; sr. account exec., Safeguard Health Enterprises, Inc., Anaheim (Calif.) and Los Angeles, 1986—; pres., Infinity Ins. Agy., Beverly Hills, Calif., 1987—. Vol. City of West Hollywood City Hall, Calif., 1986; mem. Lupus Found., Los Angeles, Multiple Schlerosis Soc. of Los Angeles, AIDS Project, Los Angeles. Mem. Am. Mgmt. Assn., Hispanic Acad. of Media Arts and Scis., Calif. Assn. of Affiliated Agys., Am. Film Inst., Women in Mgmt. (bd. dirs. Los Angeles chpt.), Art Deco Soc. Los Angeles, Nat. Assn. Female Execs., Amnesty Internat., Los Angeles Jr. C. of C., Kappa Kappa Gamma. Avocations: tennis; nordic skiing; travel; art deco; theatre. Mailing Address: PO Box 10986 Beverly Hills CA 92013-3986

ANDREWS, WILLIAM COOKE, physician; b. Norfolk, Va., June 7, 1924; s. Charles James and Jean Curry (Cooke) A.; m. Elizabeth Wight Kyle, Nov. 10, 1951; children—Elizabeth Randolph, William Cooke, Susan Carrington. A.A., Princeton U., 1946; M.D., Johns Hopkins U., 1947. Diplomate Am. Bd. Obstetrics and Gynecology. Intern N.Y. Hosp., 1947, resident in obstetrics and gynecology, 1948-50, 52-53; practice medicine specializing in obstetrics and gynecology Norfolk, Va., 1953—; asst. in obstetrics and gynecology Cornell U. Med. Sch., 1948-50, 52-53; mem. attending staff Med. Ctr. Hosp.; prof. obstetrics and gynecology Eastern Va. Med. Sch., Norfolk, 1975—; pres. faculty senate Eastern Va. Med. Sch., 1976-77; mem. Fertility and Maternal Health Drug Adv. Com., FDA, 1979-83, chmn., 1982-83, cons., 1983—. Contbr. articles in field to profl. jours. Chmn. Bicentennial Commn., City of Norfolk, 1969-71; commr. Community Facilities Commn., 1971-73, chmn., 1973—; bd. dirs. Va. League for Planned Parenthood, 1966-68; pres. Norfolk chpt. Planned Parenthood, 1966-68. Served with M.C. USN, 1950-52. Named Hon. Officer of the Most Excellent Order of the Brit. Empire Queen Elizabeth II, 1967. Fellow Am. Coll. Obstetricians and Gynecologists (vice-chmn. dist. IV 1985—), Am. Assn. Obstetricians and Gynecologists; mem. Am. Fertility Soc. (dir. 1970-73, pres. 1977), Med. Soc. Va., Norfolk Acad. Medicine, Va., Tidewater obstet. and gynecol. socs., Continental Gynecol. Soc., So. Med. Assn., AMA, South Atlantic Assn. Obstetricians and Gynecologists, Norfolk C. of C. (chmn. armed forces com. 1966-68, v.p. 1968-69, pres. 1970), Internat. Fedn. Fertility Socs. (asst. treas. 1974-80, pres. 1983-86, chmn. sci. program com. 1986—), Navy League U.S. (pres. Hampton Roads council 1968-70, nat. dir. 1970-74), English Speaking Union U.S. (pres. Norfolk-Portsmouth br. 1964-66), Planned Parenthood Fedn. Am. (cons. nat. med. com. 1975-85, chmn. 1981-83). Presbyterian. Club: Norfolk Yacht and Country (commodore 1966). Home: 929 Graydon Ave Norfolk VA 23507 Office: 903 Medical Tower Norfolk VA 23507

ANDREWS, WILLIAM HENRY, clergyman, school psychologist; b. Decatur, Ga., May 4, 1929; s. John Edward and Semite Rebecca (Hall) A. B.S., U. Ga., 1953, M.Ed., 1969, Ed.S., 1972; A.B., Ga. State U., 1963; M.S. in Edn., Baylor U., 1968; B.D., So. Baptist Sem., 1956, M.Div., 1969; Th.M., Luther Rice Sem., 1971, Th.D., 1973, D.Ministry, 1982. Ordained to ministry Bapt. Ch., 1956. Pastor 1st Bapt. Ch., Danielsville, Ga., 1956-61, County Line Bapt. Ch., Douglasville, Ga., 1962-67, 71-75, New Ga. Bapt. Ch., Dallas, 1968-71, 1st Bapt. Ch., Damascus, Ga., 1984—; evangelist Bill Andrews Assocs., Blakely, Ga., 1976-84; sch. psychologist Early County Bd. Edn., Blakely, 1977-85; moderator Tallapoos Bapt. Assn., Dallas, 1969-71. Mem. Am. Assn. Pastoral Counselors, So. Bapt. Religious Edn. Soc. Republican. Lodge: Masons (sr. deacon 1959-60). Avocations: hunting; fishing; stamp collecting. Home: 617 Meadowbrook Dr PO Box 227 Blakely GA 31723 Office: First Bapt Ch of Damascus PO Box 227 Blakely GA 31723

ANDRIATSIAFAJATO, APOLINAIRE, diplomat; b. Beloha, Androy, Democratic Madagascar, July 23, 1929; s. Célestin Rainialohotsy and Marguerite Rakala; m. Rosette Raziairinela, Aug. 4, 1951; children: suzy, Dolorés, Anick, Patrick. Supérieure, Le Myre de Vilers, Democratic Madagascar, 1947; formation, Institut Hautes Etudes Outre-Mer (IHEOM), Paris, 1963; adminstr. civil (hon.), IHEOM, Paris, 1963. Commis des services civils Adminstrn. Gen., Tuléar, Democratic Madagascar, 1952-53; contrôleur du Travail Direction Gen. du Travail, Tuléar, 1954-58; attaché de cabinet Ministère de l'Edn. Nat., Tananarive, Democratic Madagascar, 1958-59, chef de cabinet, 1959-60; conseiller technique Ministère de l'Intérieur, Tananarive, 1960, 73-75; conseiller politique Pres. de la République, Tananarive, 1964-68; ambassadeur Ministère Affaires Etrangères, Port Louis, Ile Mauriee, 1968-72; conseiller gen. Directoire Militaire, Tananarive, 1975; ambassadeur Ministère Affaires Etrangères, Tokyo, 1975-82, Rome, 1984—; Publ. dir. La République, 1959-60, Madagascar-Indépendant, 1959-60. Nat. sec. Parti Social Démocrate, Democratic Madagascar, 1958-60, bur. exécutif, 1964-68. Decorated officier de Lère classe Croix de la R.F.A. (Fed. Republic Germany); officier Mérite Civique Français (France); officier Etoile Royale des Comores (Grande Comore); grand officier Ordre Nat. (Democratic Madagascar). Mem. Ville de Quatre Bornes (citoyen d'honneur), Acad. Scis. Culture Tiberne (hon.), Acad. Tour. Euro-Afro-Asie (hon.), Barbarano Romano (citoyen d'honneur). Roman Catholic. Office: Ambassade de Madagascar, Via Riccardo Zandonai 84/A, 00194 Rome Italy

ANDRISANI, PAUL J., business educator, personnel consultant; b. Wilmington, Del., Oct. 19, 1946; s. Paul and Mary (Tavani) A.; B.S., U. Del., 1968, M.B.A., 1970; Ph.D., Ohio State U., 1973, postgrad., 1973-74; m. Barbra Lee Frank, Nov. 23, 1968; children—Nathan, Damian, Danielle. Sr. research assoc. Center for Human Resource Research, Ohio State U., Columbus, 1973-74, vis. research assoc., 1979; asst. prof. Sch. Bus., Temple U., Phila., 1974-76, assoc. prof., 1977-83, prof., 1983—, dir. Bur. Econ. Research, 1977-78, dir. Ctr. for Labor and Human Resource Studies, 1985—; pres. St. Anthony's Edn. Fund, 1986-88; pres. Paul J. Andrisani Personnel Cons. Services, Wilmington, Del., 1977—, St. Anthony's Edn. Fund, 1986-88; cons. Price Waterhouse, U.S. EEOC, Acme Markets, CBS, City of Tucson, Chevron, La. Power and Light, La. Land and Exploration, PanAm, Smith Kline, Carpenter Tech., The Aerospace Corp. of Am., Dynalectron Corp., Lukens Steel, Traveler's Ins., Suffolk County Police Dept., Internat. Communications Agy., N.Y. Times, U.S. Steel, Lukens Steel, Travelers Ins. Cos., Readers Digest, K-Mart, Ins. of N.Am., City of Tucson, Suffolk County Police Dept., Russell Sage Found., Del. Econ. Forecasting Adv. Com., New Orleans Public Service Inc., CBS, Del. Disability and Pension Rev., Rockwell Internat., ARCO, Nationwide Ins., ICI Ams., DuPont, GTE, Inco, govt. agys., others; lectr. Internat. Communications Agy., Japan and Portugal, Brandeis U., Pa. State U., Columbia U., William and Mary Coll., U. So. Calif., Nat. Employment Law Inst., San Francisco and Washington; pres. St. Anthony's Edn. Fund, 1985-88. Salzburg fellow; Roosevelt Youth Policy fellow. Served to capt. U.S. Army, 1972-73. Grantee, U.S. Dept. Labor, 1974-77, Nat. Commn. for Employment Policy, 1979-83, Adminstrn. on Aging, 1981-82, U.S. Dept. Army, 1986. Mem. Am. Econs. Assn., Indsl. Relations Research Assn., Am. Sociol. Assn., Am. Acad. Polit. and Social Sci., Gerontol. Soc. Am. Author: Work Attitudes and Labor Market Experience, 1978; editorial bd. Jour. Econs. and Bus., 1979-83; contbr. over 40 articles to profl. jours. Office: Temple U Sch Bus Philadelphia PA 19122

ANDROSCH, HANNES, banker, former vice-chancellor of Austria; b. Vienna, Apr. 18, 1938; s. Hans and Julie (Saller) A.; diploma U. Econs., Vienna, 1959, D. Econs., 1969; m. Brigitte Schärf, 1964; children: Claudia, Natascha. Asst. auditor Austrian Ministry of Fin., 1956-66; sec. econ. affairs sect. Socialist Parliamentary Party, 1963-66; chartered acct., tax cons., 1966-70; M.P., 1967-81, minister of fin., 1970-81, vice-chancellor Austria, 1976-81; vice-chmn. Socialist Parliamentary Party, from 1974; mem. Nat. Council, from 1967; chmn., gen. mgr. Creditanstalt-Bankverein, Vienna, 1981—; chmn. supervisory bd. Oesterreichische Kontrollbank Aktiengesellschaft, Semperit Aktiengesellschaft, Steyr-Daimler-Puch Aktiengesellschaft, Stölzle-Oberglas Aktiengesellschaft, Treibacher Chemische Werke Aktiengesellschaft; vice-chmn. supervisory bd. Chemiefaser Lenzing Aktiengesellschaft; mem. supervisory bd. AVA-Bank Gesellschaft mbH, Bank für Kärnten Aktiengesellschaft, Bank für Oberösterreich und Salzburg, Bank für Tirol und Vorarlberg Aktiengesellschaft, European Banks' Internat. Co. S.A. Decorated grand cross 1st class Order of Merit, grand cross Order No. Star (Austria); decoration of honor Province of Tyrol; recipient Grand Gold medal of Honeur. Mem. Austrian Bankers Assn. (pres.). Office: Creditanstalt-Bankveren, Schottengasse 6, A-1011 Vienna Austria *

ANDRUS, CECIL DALE, governor of Idaho; b. Hood River, Oreg., Aug. 25, 1931; s. Hal Stephen and Dorothy (Johnson) A.; m. Carol Mae May, Aug. 27, 1949; children: Tana Lee, Tracy Sue, Kelly Kay. Student, Oreg. State U., 1948-49; LLD (hon.), Gonzaga U., U. Idaho, U. N.Mex. State gen. mgr. Paul Revere Life Ins. Co., 1969-70; gov. State of Idaho, 1971-77, 87—; sec. of interior 1977-81; dir. Albertson's, Inc., 1985-87; Mem. Idaho Senate, 1961-66, 69-70; Mem. exec. com. Nat. Gov.'s Conf., 1971-72, chmn., 1976; chmn. Fedn. Rocky Mountain States, 1971-72. Chmn. bd. trustees Coll. of Idaho, 1985—; bd. dirs. Sch. Forestry, Duke U. Served with USN, 1951-55. Recipient Disting. Citizen award Oreg. State U., 1980, Collier County Conservancy medal, 1979; named Conservationist of Yr., Nat. Wildlife Fedn., 1980, Idaho Wildlife Fedn., 1972, Man of Yr., VFW, 1959. Mem. V.F.W., Idaho Taxpayers Assn. (dir. 1964-66). Democrat. Home: 1805 N 21st Boise ID 83702 Office: Office of Gov State Capitol 2d Floor Boise ID 83720 *

ANDRUS, MIRIAM JAY WURTS, civic worker; b. N.Y.C., Nov. 26, 1909; d. Pierre Jay and Edith Maud (Benedict) Wurts; m. E. Cowles Andrus, June 10, 1933 (dec. 1978). AB, Vassar Coll., 1931; postgrad. Columbia U., 1932-33; M.A., Johns Hopkins U., 1934. Mem. Woman Power Com., War Mobilization Com., 1943; chmn. Balt. com. Council of the Living Theatre, 1952-55; pres. women's assn. Brown Meml. Presbyn. Ch., 1957-59, ruling elder, 1957-59; mem. Women's Nat. Planning com. for Japan Internat. Christian U., Tokyo, 1970—; bd. dirs., exec. com., Ctr. Stage, Balt., 1980—; mem. Commn. on U.S. Cen. Am. Relations Internat. Ctr. for Devel. Policy, 1982—, others; chmn. Associated Orgns. for Internat. Peace; founder Md. Assn. World Federalists; del. World Congress, Luxembourg. Author: (textbook) American Intervention in Russia 1919-21. Democrat. Clubs: Hamilton St., Guilford Garden. Avocations: photography; music; gardening. Home: 209 E Highfield Rd Baltimore MD 21218

ANDUJAR, RAFAEL, sales executive; b. Melilla, Spain, Dec. 20, 1946; s. Antonio and Ines (Vilches) A.; m. Montserrat Murcia; children: Emmanuel, Valerie, Delphine, Xavier. MBA in Fin., N.W. London, 1985; PhD Internat. Commerce, U. London, 1985; MBA in Sales Mktg., CESEM, Barcelona, Spain, 1986, MBA in Sales and Mktg., 1986. Salesman RUMASA, Madrid, 1970-72, sales mgr., 1972-76; area rep. C.R. Bard, Inc.-USCI Int. Div., Billerica, Mass., 1977-80, mng. dir., 1981-88; v.p., mng. dir. for South Europe C.R. Bard, Inc., 1988—; gen. mgr. Bard de España, S.A., Barcelona, gen. mgr. Bard Belgium N.V., Louvin, Belgium; exec. v.p. BARD Italia S.R.L., Rome. Office: Bard de España SA, USCI Int Div, Avda Diagonal 429, Barcelona 08036, Spain

ANFINSEN, CHRISTIAN BOEHMER, biochemist; b. Monessen, Pa., Mar. 26, 1916; s. Christian Boehmer and Sophie (Rasmussen) A.; m. Florence Bernice Kenenger, Nov. 29, 1941 (div. 1978); children: Carol Bernice, Margot Sophie, Christian Boehmer; m. Libby Shulman Ely, 1979. B.A., Swarthmore Coll., 1937, D.Sc., 1965; M.S., U. Pa., 1939; Ph.D., Harvard, 1943; D.Sc. (hon.), Georgetown U., 1967, N.Y. Med. Coll., 1969, Gustavus Adolphus Coll., 1975, Brandeis U., 1977, Providence Coll., 1978, M.D. (hon.), U. Naples Med. Sch., 1980, Adelphi U., 1987. asst. prof. biol. chemistry, Harvard Med. Sch., 1948-50, prof. biochemistry, 1962-63; chief lab. cellular physiology and metabolism Nat. Heart Inst., Bethesda, Md., 1950-62; chief lab. chem. biology Nat. Inst. Arthritis and Metabolic Diseases, Bethesda, 1963-82; prof. biology Johns Hopkins U., Balt., 1982—; vis. prof. Weizmann Inst. Sci., Rehovot, Israel, 1981-82, bd. govs. 1962. Author: The Molecular Basis of Evolution, 1959; contbr. articles to profl. jours. Am. Scandinavian fellow Carlsberg Lab., Copenhagen 1939; sr. cancer research fellow Nobel Inst., Stockholm, 1947; Markle scholar 1948; Guggenheim fellow Weizmann Inst., 1958; recipient Rockefeller Pub. Service award, 1954-55, Nobel prize in chemistry, 1972. Mem. Am. Soc. Biol. Chemists (pres. 1971-72), Am. Acad. Arts and Scis., Nat. Acad. Scis., Washington Acad. Scis., Am. Philos. Soc., Fedn. Am. Scientists (treas. 1958-59, vice chmn. 1959-60, 73-76), Pontifical Acad. Sci. Home: 4 Tanner Ct Baltimore MD 21208 Office: Johns Hopkins U Dept Biology 34th & Charles St Baltimore MD 21218

ANG, MANUEL MEDRANO, communications executive; b. Manila, Dec. 14, 1954; s. Chai Ang and Natividad (Barut) Medrano. Cert., Slim's Fashion Sch., Manila, 1969-70; postgrad., Alexander Hamilton Inst., N.Y., 1980. Exec. sec. Am. Oriental Enterprises, Manila, 1972-74, Orient Express Placement Philippines, Manila, 1975-76; exec. sec./head communications sec. F.E. Zuellig (M), Inc., Manila, 1976-82; exec. sec. Daniel Internat. (SA) Ltd., Alkhobar, Saudi Arabia, 1982-83, dep. personnel mgr., 1983-86; adminstrv. mgr. Sandstill Factory, Alkhobar, 1986—. Mem. Communications Operators Assn. Philippines (named Model Operator, 1981). Office: Sandstill Factory, PO Box 1884, 31952 Alkhobar Saudi Arabia

ANG, SAM, marketing executive; b. Singapore, Jan. 5, 1957; s. Hock Hoe and Cheng Lian (Uam) A. BS in Pharmacy, Nat. U. Singapore, 1984. Mgr. mktg. Nicholas Kiwi/Sara Lee USA, Singapore, 1985-87, Sterling Drug Co., Singapore, 1987—; cons. health foods Nature's Way, Singapore, 1986-87. Officer Boys Brigade, Singapore, 1980. Served to lt. inf. Singapore Army, 1975-78. Fellow Nutritional Foods Assn. Australia; mem. Pharm. Soc. Singapore (social chmn. 1980-81). Home: Blk 122 Bukit Batok Cen, 06-409, 0314 Singapore Singapore

ANGEL, DENNIS, lawyer; b. Bklyn., Feb. 14, 1947; s. Morris and Rosalyn (Sobiloff) A.; m. Linda Marlene Lobel, May 15, 1977; children: Stephanie Lee, Ilana Nicole, Michele Bari. Cert. pratique de langue francaise ler Degre U. Rouen (France), 1967, diplome d'etudes françaises (2e Degre), 1967; BA, St. Lawrence U., 1968; J.D., Washington and Lee U., 1972. Bar: N.Y. 1972, U.S. Dist. Ct. (so. dist.) N.Y. 1977. Assoc. Johnson & Tannenbaum, N.Y.C., 1972-77; sole practice, N.Y.C., 1978—. Contbr. articles to profl. jours. Served with USAR, 1969-75. Mem. ABA (subcommittee chman. 1977-82), N.Y. State Bar Assn., Bar Assn. City N.Y., Lawyers Alliance for Nuclear Arms Control, Phi Alpha Delta. Home: 8 High Point Ln Scarsdale NY 10583 Office: 33 Lynwood Rd Scarsdale NY 10583

ANGEL, STEVEN MICHAEL, lawyer; b. Frederick, Md., Sept. 19, 1950; s. Charles Robert and Laura Emily (Holland) A.; m. Joan Comproni, Dec. 7, 1972 (div. May 1975); m. Constance McCarthy, Apr. 24, 1981; children—Michael Sean, James Curtis. B.S., U. Md., 1972; J.D., Oklahoma City U., 1976; LL.M., George Washington U., 1979. Bar: Okla. 1976, Tex. 1981, D.C., 1986, U.S. Dist. Ct. Md. 1977, U.S. Dist. Ct. (no. dist.) Tex. 1979, U.S. Dist. Ct. (we. dist.) Okla. 1981, U.S. Dist. Ct. (we. dist.) Tex 1981, U.S. Ct. Claims 1981, U.S. Ct. Appeals (5th, 10th, and 11th cirs.) 1981, U.S. Ct. Appeals (D.C. cir.) 1983, U.S. Supreme Ct. 1984, D.C. 1986. Field atty. NLRB, Balt., 1976-79; supervising trial atty. Fed. Labor Relations Authority, Dallas, 1979-80; mem. Hughes & Nelson, Oklahoma City and San Antonio, 1980—. Articles editor Oklahoma City U. Law Rev., 1976, 77. Contbr. articles to profl. jours. Recipient cert. Spl. Confidence in Labor, Law Tex. Bd. Legal Specialization, 1982; various awards Oklahoma City U., 1975, 76; Spl. Achievement cert. Fed. Labor Relations Authority, 1980. Mem. ABA, Assn. Trial Lawyers Am., Okla. Bar Assn., Okla. Trial Lawyers Assn., State Bar Tex., Tex. Trial Lawyers Assn., Phi Delta Phi. Democrat. Baptist. Home: 4506 Karen Dr Edmond OK 73034 Office: Hughes & Nelson 5801 N Broadway Extension Suite 302 Oklahoma City OK 73118 also: 6243 I-10 Suite 290 San Antonio TX 78201

ANGELES, MANUEL VALLO, dentist; b. St. Barbara, Philippines, June 3, 1947; s. Felipe C. and Juanita (Vallo) A.; m. Marlye De Guzman, Mar. 14, 1973; children: Emmanuel, Marnie Matthews, Minelli. Degree in Liberal Arts and Sci., Univ. of East, Manila, 1965; DMD, Manila Cen. U., 1970. Practice dentistry Quezon City, Philippines, 1971—. Patentee Hexagauze for Dental Hemmorhage, 1976. Coordinator Namfrel free election movement. Mem. Philippine Dental Assn. (chmn. various coms., bd. trustees, presdl. citation 1987, leadership award 1985), San Juan Dental Soc. (pres. 1984-85), Fedn. Dentaire Internat., Manila Dental Soc. Roman Catholic. Lodge: Rotary (numerous offices 1983—, civic involvement award, 1985, dynamic leadership award, 1986). Home: 8 Amsterdam St, Capitol Park Homes, Quezon City Philippines Office: PPSTA Bldg, 251 Banawe, Quezon City 3008, Philippines

ANGELI, PIERRE L., government commissioner; b. St. André de Cotone, Corse, France, Aug. 7, 1921; s. Philippe F. and Felicia (Ferrandi) A.; m. Ariane Schmidt; children: Dovimia, David. Diploma, Nat. Sch. Oriental Lang., Paris, 1942, Nat. Sch. France Overseas, Paris, 1942; lic. Faculty of Letters, U. Paris, 1942, D in Law, 1946; diploma, Sch. Nat. Adminstrn., 1952. Adminstr. for French territories Senegal, 1949; other govt. positions France, 1950-59; chief of mission to cabinet Gen. De Gaulle Paris, 1959-65; dir. cabinet Minister Overseas Territories, Paris, 1965-68; gov. French Polynesia Papeete, Tahiti, 1969-73; state councillor Paris, 1974-85; high commr. French Republic in French Polynesia, Tahiti. Office: Office High Commr, Papeete Tahiti, French Polynesia

ANGELO, GAYLE-JEAN, mathematics and physical science educator; b. Winchester, Mass., Nov. 27, 1951; d. John William and Josephine Marie (Tavano) A.; B.A. in Physics with honor, Northeastern U., 1975, M.Ed. in Curriculum and Instrn. of Sci. and Math., 1978; M.S. in Applied Statis., Columbia U., 1984, postgrad., 1984—. Clin. chemist Boston Med. Lab., Inc., 1971-73; exptl. physicist Northeastern U., 1975-76; tchr. natural scis., head sci. dept. Girls Cath. High Sch., Malden, Mass., 1977-78; research and teaching asst. Columbia U., N.Y.C., 1978-80, research assoc., 1982-83; research scientist Air Force Rocket Propulsion Lab., Edwards AFB, Calif., 1980-82; research and devel. analyst, engr. Varian-Extrion Div., Gloucester, Mass., 1984-86; instr. math. Golden Gate U., Cerro Coso Community Coll., 1981-82, Columbia U., N.Y.C., 1982-83; instr. chemistry North Shore Community Coll., 1985-86; instr. math., physics Imperial Valley Coll., Imperial, Calif., 1986—. Served with USAF, 1980-82; mem. Air N.G., 1982-85. Decorated Air Force Commendation; cert. secondary tchr., Mass.; cert. community coll. tchr., Calif. Mem. Am. Assn. Physics Tchrs., Am. Phys. Soc., Mathematical Assn. of Am., Nat. Council Tchrs. Math., Nat. Sci. Tchrs. Assn., Soc. Coll. Sci. Tchrs., Mensa, Sigma Xi, Phi Delta Kappa, Sigma Pi Sigma. Sigma Delta Epsilon, Kappa Delta Pi.

ANGELOPOULOS, ANGELOS GEORGE, economist, airline executive; b. Athens, Greece, Aug. 29, 1952; s. George and Angeliki A.; m. Victoria Kitsara; children: Roee, Lilika, Dionee. BA in Econs., U. Athens, 1976; MA in Econs., Columbia U., 1977, M Philosophy in Econs., 1979. Gen. mgr. Angelopoulos Bros. Co., Patras, Greece, 1979-81; advisor to Minister fin. Ministry of Fin., Athens, 1982-84; fin. and fiscal counselor Greek Delegation OECD, Paris, 1984-86; chief fin. officer, fin. dir. Olympic Airways, Athens, 1986—. Fulbright fellow, 1976-78, Pres.'s fellow Columbia U., 1979. Office: Olympic Airways, 98-100 Syngkou Ave, 117.41, Athens Greece

ANGENIEUX, BERNARD EDOUARD, optical company executive; b. Paris, July 2, 1937; s. Pierre A.; m. Monique Laffitte, Oct. 11, 1962; children: Florence, Brigitte. Licence es sci., U. Sorbonne, Paris, 1959; MBA, U. Chgo., 1960. Trainee Eastman Kodak Co., Rochester, N.Y., 1963-66; sales mgr. Angenieux, St. Heand, France, 1966, dir. gen., 1980; pres. Opticam, Geneva, Switzerland, 1969—. Office: Opticam, 4 Pedro Meylan, 1208 Geneva Switzerland

ANGENIOL, BERNARD, mathematician, artificial intelligence engineer; b. St. Etienne, Loire, France, Aug. 25, 1951; s. Andre and Lea (Deleage) A.; m. Nicole Portat, Oct. 6, 1973; children—Sandrine, Bruno, Christelle. Agregation de Math., U. Paris, 1973, Doctorat d'Etat de Math., 1980, Habilitation, 1985; postgrad., Ecole Normale Superieure, Paris, 1974. Researcher, CNRS, Paris, 1974-85; engr. Thomson-CSF, Paris, 1985—; assoc. prof. Purdue U., Lafayette, Ind., 1984. Author: Schema de Chow, 1981; Classes Caracteristiques, 1985. Served with French Army, 1978-79. Mem. Societe Mathematique de France, Am. Math. Soc. Roman Catholic. Avocations: piano; tennis; football. Home: Zallee Baudelaire, 80 Ave Larroumes, 94240 L Hay les Roses France Office: Thomson-CSF, 1 Rue des Mathurins, 92222 Bagneux Cedex France

ANGERER, PAUL, musician, educator, composer, conductor; b. Vienna, Austria, May 16, 1927; s. Otto and Elisabeth (Denk) A.; m. Anita Rosser; children: Pierre, Ursula, Veronica, Christoph. Student, Hochschule Musik Acad. and Vienna Conservatory, 1940-47. Viola player Tonhalle Zurich Orch. de la Suisse Romande, Zurich, 1948-53; viola soloist Vienna Symphony Orch., 1953-57; chef Wiener Kammer Orch., 1956-63; conductor, dir. opera Bonn, Ulm and Salzburg Theaters, Fed. Republic Germany, 1964-72; leader, conductor S.W. German Orch., 1971-81; prof. Hochschule Musik Acad., 1982—; leader, violinist Concilium Musicum, Vienna, 1982—; permanent guest conductor Orch. Hayn, Bolzano, Italy, 1960—; artistic dir. Hellbrunner Spiele, 1970-71. Compositions include Concert pour la Jeunesse, 1956, Die Passkontrolle (TV opera), 1958, Konzerte fur Klavier, 1962, fur Viola, 1962, Cogitatio fur 9 Instruments, 1964, Inklination der Ariadne des Monteverdi (orch. and balllet), 1967, Hotel Comedie (musical), 1970, Altoposaune, 1977, Exercitium Canonicum for 2 viols, 1980, Harfe, 1981, stage music for various theatres, film, TV; recordings include Mozart and Beethoven piano concertos, Schubert Overtures, Weihnachtslieder, Strauss Waltzes, Barockmusik, Konzerte fur Oboe und Posaune. Recipient Osterreich Staatspreis, 1956, 1st prize Salzburg Opera Competition, 1959, Kulturpreis der Stadt Wien, 1983, Nö-Kulturpreis, 1987. Home and Office: Esteplatz 3/26, A-1030 Vienna Austria other: Unternalb 21, A-2070 Retz Austria

ANGLEMIRE, KENNETH NORTON, retired publishing company executive, writer, environmentalist; b. Chgo.; s. Fred Rutherford and Isabel (Alguire) A.; m. Anne Hayes. (dec.); m. Geraldine Payne. Student, Northwestern U.; B.S., U. Ill., Urbana; LL.B., J.D., Chgo.-Kent Coll. Law, Ill. Inst. Tech. Bar: Ill. bar. Pvt. practice of law to 1936; atty. Chgo. Title and Trust Co., 1936-42; chief acct., office mgr. Graphic Arts Displays, Inc., Chgo., 1942-50; comptroller Marshall Industries, Chgo., 1950-53, Marquis-Who's Who, Inc., Chgo., 1953-59; v.p. Marquis-Who's Who, Inc., 1958-59, exec. v.p., chief ops. officer, 1959-69, chmn. bd., pub., 1969-70; pres., dir. A.N. Marquis Co., Inc., Chgo., 1964-69; Mem. Ill. State Scholarship Commn., 1966-69; charter mem. Bus. Adv. Council, Chgo. Urban League; hon. mem. staff N.Mex. Atty. Gen., 1971-74; mem. Adult Edn. Council Greater Chgo., bd. dirs., 1968-70. Writer articles on music, natural history and conservation, mountain adventure. Mem. Ill. Audubon Soc. (v.p. fin., dir. 1961-65), Greater North Michigan Ave. Assn. (dir. 1966-70), Dickens Fellowship, Santa Fe Opera Guild, Internat. Alban Berg Soc., Sangre de Cristo Audubon Soc. N.Mex. (founder, pres. 1972-73, dir. 1972-75), Friends of Santa Fe (N.Mex.) Public Library, Historic Santa Fe Found., Wilderness Study Com. N.Mex., Santa Fe Concert Assn., ACLU, Bus. Execs. Move for Peace in Viet Nam, Ridges Sanctuary, Bailey's Harbor, Wis., Armory for the Arts, Santa Fe., Pi Kappa Alpha, Delta Theta Phi, Sierra Club (founder, chmn. Great Lakes chpt. 1959-61, 64-66, exec. com. 1959-69). Club: N.Mex. Mountain.

ANGUIANO, RAUL, painter; b. Guadalajara, Jalisco, Mexico, Feb. 16, 1915; s. Jose Anguiano and Abigail V. de A.; 3 children from previous marriage; m. Brigita Anderson, 1977. Studies with Jose Vizcarra and Ixca Farias, Art Students League, N.Y.C., 1941. Founder, mem. Taller de Grafica Popular; guest tchr., lectr. invited to exhibit works U. West Indies, Kingston, 1970. One-man shows include Mex., Paris, 1962, 65, 67, San Francisco, 1953-65, Havana, 1956, Chile, 1960, Moscow, 1962, Rome, 1965-67, Miami, 1965, San Antonio, 1966, Quito, 1971, Mexico City, 1972, Palm Springs, Calif., 1974; exhibited in group shows in London, Warsaw, Tokyo, Berlin, Prague, Peking, Lille, France, Los Angeles, Lugano, others; works include murals for Hormona Labs., Onyx-Mex. industries and Nat. Mus. Anthropology, Mexico City, mural at Olympia Hotel, Kingston, Jamaica; retrospective exhbn. Salon de la Plastica Mexicana, Mex., 1969. Decorated by Italian Govt., 1977; recipient numerous prizes in field. Office: Anaxagoras 1326, Colonia Narvarte, Mexico 13 Mexico

ANGUIZOLA, GUSTAVO ANTONIO, historian, educator, writer, consultant; b. Chiriqui, Panamá, Feb. 29, 1928; came to U.S., 1944, naturalized, 1961; s. Antonio Anguizola Palma and Melida Guerra Gómez children: Phillip Anthony, Jerome James. B.A., Evansville Coll., 1948; M.A., Ind. U., 1951, Ph.D., 1954; Cert., Am. Sch. Classics, Athens, Greece, 1964, Stanford U., 1975. Sr. chem. tester Allby Corp., Gary, Ind., 1956-59; dept. chmn. Morris Coll., Sumter, S.C., 1959-62; spl. asst. Panam. Games Mayor of Chgo., 1959; vis. prof. SUNY, Geneseo, summers 1961, 62; chmn. dept. Elizabeth City State Coll., N.C., 1962-63; asst. prof. Purdue U., Lafayette, Hammond, Ind., 1963-66; asst. prof. history U.Tex., Arlington, 1966-82, research prof., 1982—; chmn. midwest Collegiate Council UN, N.Y.C., 1962-76; cons. N.C. Bd. Edn., Raleigh, 1962-63, Hispanic Am. Hist. Rev., Austin, 1970-72, Gov. of Tex., Austin, 1980-82, Inter-Am. Security Council, Washington, 1977—; chmn. bd. The Freedom Fedn., Washington, 1982—; mem. Minorities Commn. of Tex. Author: Isthmian Political Instability: 1821-76, 1977, 78; Life of Philippe Bunau-Varilla, 1980; Violation of Human Rights in Panama, 1980; The Taft Convention; Research Sites Panama and Canal Zone, 1986; also articles. Precinct chmn. Republican Party Tex., 1979—, election judge, 1985—; mem. Nat. Com. Rep. Party, Washington, 1982—; del. State Rep. Convention, Tex., 1978—; cons. Heritage Found., Washington, 1980—, Freedon Fedn. Recipient Hays-Mundt Award U.S. Dept. State, 1953, Fulbright-Hays award, 1964, Andrew Mellon award, 1982; NEH grantee Stanford U., 1975, U. Chg., 1985—; named Alumnus of Yr., Evansville U., 1984. Mem. Am. Hist. Assn., AAUP (region sec. 1982—), Tex. State Tchrs. Assn., Conf. on Latin Am. History, Pacific Coast Council Latin Am. Studies, Nat. Soc. Sci. Assn. Roman Catholic. Clubs: Dallas Men's; Arlington Rep., Hispanic Assembly of Tex. (chmn. Metroplex area 1980—). Office: Univ Texas Box 194489 Arlington TX 76019

ANGULO, CHARLES BONIN, foreign service officer; b. N.Y.C., Aug. 6, 1943; s. Manuel R. and Carolyn C. (Bonin) A.; m. Penelope Snare, June 28, 1986. B.A., U. Va., 1966; cert., U. Madrid, 1966; J.D., Tulane U., 1969. Bar: Va. 1969. Assoc., Michael & Dent, Charlottesville, Va., 1969-73; assoc. editor The Michie Publishing Co., Charlottesville, 1973; fgn. service officer U.S. Dept. State, Washington, 1973-75, Am. Embassy, Brussels, 1976-78, Legal Advisor's Office, Dept. State, Washington, 1978-81, Am. Embassy, Santo Domingo, 1981-85; exec. dir. office of insp. gen. Dept. State, Washington, 1985-86, asst. chief protocol for U.S. Dept. State, Washington, 1986-88; Am. consulate gen. Jeddah, Saudi Arabia, 1988—. Mem. Council Fgn. Relations. Home: 200 N Pickett St Apt #107 Alexandria VA 22304

ANGULO, MANUEL RAFAEL, lawyer; b. N.Y.C., Sept. 5, 1917; s. Charles and Ysabel (Piedra) A.; m. Carolyn Louise Bonin, Nov. 6, 1937; children: Charles B., M. Ralph; m. Diana Hutchins Rockwell, June 12, 1970. BA, Yale U., 1939; LLB, Harvard U., 1942; postgrad., Columbia U., 1952. Bar: N.Y. 1947, Pa. 1987. Assoc. Davis, Polk, Wardwell, Sunderland & Kiendl, 1942-48; attaché, econ. analyst Am. embassy, Santo Domingo, 1943-44; attaché embassy Lisbon, Portugal, 1944-46; with OSS, London, 1944; gen. solicitor Creole Petroleum Corp., Caracas, Venezuela, 1948-54; ptnr. Escritorio J.M. Travieso Paul, Caracas, 1954-61, Curtis, Mallet-Prevost, Colt & Mosle, N.Y.C., 1961—; lectr. Law Sch. U. Va., 1963-71, U. Villanova (Pa.), 1986—. Contbr. profl. jours. Mem. council Boy Scouts Am., Venezuela, 1955-59; pres. N. Am. Assn. Venezuela, 1957-59. Mem. ABA, N.Y. State Bar Assn., N.Y.C. Bar Assn., Internat. Bar Assn., Inter Am. Bar Assn., N.Y. County Lawyers Assn., Am. Fgn. Law Assn., Pan Am. Soc. U.S., Sigma Xi. Clubs: Yale, Union League, Broad St. Met. (Washington); Farmington Country (Charlottesville, Va.); Merion Cricket (Haverford, Pa.); Gulph Mills Golf (King of Prussia, Pa.). Office: 101 Park Ave New York NY 10178

ANGUS, MICHAEL RICHARDSON, chemical company executive; b. Ashford, Eng., May 5, 1930; s. William R. Angus and Doris Margaret Breach; m. Eileen Elliott, 1952; 3 children. Grad., Bristol (Eng.) U. Joined Unilever PLC, 1954, sales dir. Lever Bros. U.K., 1967-70, Co-ordinator toilet preparation products, 1970-76, Co-ordinator chemicals, 1976-80, regional dir. N.Am., 1979-84; chmn., chief exec. officer Unilever U.S., Inc., N.Y.C., 1980-84; vice chair Unilever PLC, London, 1984-86, chmn., 1986—; mktg. dir. Thibaud Gibbs, Paris, 1962-65; mng. dir. Research Bur., 1965-67. Bd. govs. Ashridge Mgmt. Coll., 1974—. Served with Royal Air Force, 1951-54. Mem. Netherlands-Brit. C. of C. (joint chair 1984—). Office: Unilever PLC, PO Box 68, Unilever House, London EC4P 4BQ, England *

ANKERSMIT, FRANKLIN RUDOLF, historian, educator; b. Diepenveen, The Netherlands, Mar. 20, 1945; s. Rudolf and Catherina Maria (Dekker) A. Litt. Doctorandus, Groningen U., The Netherlands, 1973, Phil. Doctorandus, 1977, Litt. Doctor, 1981. Asst. prof. dept. history Groningen U., 1974-82, lectr. intellectual history, philosophy of history, 1982—. Author: Narrative Logic, 1983, Denken Over Geschiedenis, 1984, The Historian's Language is an Object, 1988; editor: Knowing and Telling History, 1986. Mem. Koninklijke Nederlandse Acad. van Wetenschappen, Prins Bernhard Fonds (sci. dept.), Maatschappij voor Letterkunde. Home: Oosterweg 65, 9751 PC Haren Groningen, The Netherlands Office: Groningen U, Grote Rozenstraat 38, 9712 TJ Groningen The Netherlands

ANLIKER, RUDOLF, trade association executive, chemist; b. Burgdorf, Bern, Switzerland, July 25, 1926; s. Hector and Luisa (Pervangher) A.; m. Elisabeth Anliker-Weber, Oct. 17, 1953; children—Christine, Barbara, Susanne. Dipl. Ing. Chem., Swiss Inst. Tech., Zurich, 1950, Dr. sc. tech., 1953. Postdoctoral fellow Rice Inst., Houston, 1953-54; research group leader Swiss Inst. Tech., Zurich, 1955-57; head agrochemical research CIBA AG, Basel, Switzerland, 1958-61; dep. dir. research CIBA-Geigy AG, Basel, 1961-77; exec. sec. ETAD, Basel, 1977—. Patentee fluorescent whitening agts.; editor (with G. Muller) Fluorescent Whitening Agents, 1975; contbr. articles to profl. jours. Pres., City Council, Binningen, 1966; pres. Christian Democratic Party, 1960-67. Mem. Am. Chem. Soc., Swiss Chem. Soc., German Chem. Soc., Internat. Acad. Environ. Safety, Soc. Ecotoxicology and Environ. Safety. Roman Catholic. Office: ETAD, Clarastrasse 4, Head Office, CH-4005 Basel 5 Switzerland

ANNAN, LORD (NOEL GILROY), educator, writer; b. London, Dec. 25, 1916; s. James and Fannie (Quinn) A.; student Stowe Sch., Buckingham, 1930-35; B.A., King's Coll., Cambridge U., 1938, M.A., 1943; m. Gabriele Ullstein, June 30, 1950; children: Lucy, Juliet. With Brit. Army, 1939-46, ended mil. career as lt. col. polit. div. Control Commn. Germany, 1946; fellow Kings Coll., Cambridge, 1946, asst. tutor, 1947, provost, 1956-66; provost Univ. Coll., London, 1966-78; vice chancellor U. London, 1978-81; univ. lectr. politics Cambridge U., 1948-66; mem. Public Schs. Commn. Trustee, Churchill Coll., Cambridge; chmn. acad. planning bd. U. Essex; mem. arts com. Gulbenkian Found., 1957-64; chmn. Dept. Com. on Teaching Russian in Schs., 1960; chmn. Com. on Future of Broadcasting, 1974-77; mem. acad. planning bd. U. East Anglia, Brunel U. trustee Brit. Mus., 1963-80; chmn. bd. trustees Nat. Gallery, 1980—; bd. dirs. Royal Opera House, Covent Garden, 1967-78; bd. govs. Stowe Sch., 1945-66, Queen Mary Coll., London, 1959-60. Decorated Order Brit. Empire. Mem. Am. Acad. Arts and Scis. (fgn. hon. mem.). Author: Leslie Stephen, 1951, 2d edit., 1984; The Intellectual Aristocracy, 1956; The Curious Strength of Positivism in English Political Thought, 1959; Kipling's Place in the History of Ideas, 1964; Roxburgh of Stowe, 1965; A Man I Loved, 1974; Report of the Annan Enquiry on the Disturbances in the University of Essex, 1974; Annan Report on the Future of Broadcasting, 1977. Address: 16 St John's Wood Rd, London NW8 8RE, England Office: Nat Gallery, Trafalgar Sq, London WC2 England

ANNE, PRINCESS (ELIZABETH ALICE LOUISE) (MRS. MARK PHILLIPS), HER ROYAL HIGHNESS, b. Aug. 15, 1940; d. Queen Elizabeth II and Prince Philip, Duke of Edinburgh; m. Capt. Mark Anthony Peter Phillips, Nov. 14, 1973; children: Peter Mark Andrew, Zara Anne Elizabeth. Student Benenden Sch., Kent, Eng. Col. in chief, 14th/20th King's Hussars, Worcestershire and Sherwood Foresters Regt., 8th Canadian Hussars, Royal Corps of Signals, The Canadian Armed Forces Communications and Electronics Br., The Royal Australian Corps of Signals, Royal N.Z. Corps of Signals, Royal N.Z. Nursing Corps, The Grey and Simcoe Foresters Militia; chief comdt. W.R.N.S., pres. Benevolent Trust; hon. air commodore RAF Lyneham; pres. Brit. Acad. Film and TV Arts, Hunters Improvement and Light Horse Breeding Soc., Save the Children Fund, Windsor Horse Trails, The Royal Sch. for Daugs. of Officers of Royal Navy and Royal Marines; patron numerous Brit. and worldwide orgns.; ofcl. visits throughout the world as rep. of the Crown; comdt. in chief St. John Ambulance and Nursing Cadets, Women's Transport Service; freeman City of London, Fishmongers Co., Middle Warden Farriers Co.; hon. liverman Carmen's Co., Farriers Co.; hon. freeman Farmers Co., Loriners Co., Yoeman Saddlers Co.; chancellor U. London, 1981—; participant in numerous equestrian competitions including Montreal Olympics, 1976, Horse of the Year Show, Wembley and Badminton Horse Trials. Recipient Raleigh Trophy, 1971; Silver medal Individual European Three Day event, 1975; named Sportswoman of the Yr. Sports Writers Assn., Daily Express, World of Sport, BBC Sports Personality, 1971. Mem. RNVR Officers Assn., Brit. Equine Veterinary Assn. (hon.), Internat. Equestrian Fedn. (pres. 1986—). Clubs: Royal Yacht Squadron, Royal Thames Yacht, Minchinhampton Golf, others. *

ANNETT, JOHN, psychology educator; b. Gillingham, Eng., July 11, 1930; s. Frederick Annett and Irene Laura Simmons; m. Marian Elsie Drabble, Apr. 9, 1956; children: Lucy, James. BA, Oxford (Eng.) U., 1953, MA, 1957, D.Phil., 1959. Psychologist Burden Mental Research Dept., Bristol, Eng., 1953-56; researcher Oxford U., 1953-60; sr. researcher Sheffield (Eng.) U., 1960-63; lectr. psychology Aberdeen (Scotland) U., 1963-65; sr. lectr. Hull U., East Yorkshire, Eng., 1965-68, reader, 1968-72; prof. Open U., Milton Keynes, Eng., 1972-74, Warwick U., Coventry, Eng., 1974—. Author: Feedback and Human Behaviour, 1969; editor Introduction to Psychology, 1974. Recipient G. H. Miles prize Nat. Inst. Indsl. Psychology, 1968. Fellow Brit. Psychol. Soc., Ergonomics Soc.; mem. Motor Skills Research Exchange (chmn. 1981—). Office: U Warwick Psychology Dept, Coventry CV4 7AL, England

ANNIGONI, PIETRO, painter; b. Milan, Italy, June 7, 1910; attended Accademia di Belle Arti, Florence, Italy; m. Anna Maggini, 1937 (dec. 1968); m. 2d, Rosella Segreto, 1976; 2 children. Exhbns. include: Florence, 1932, Milan, 1936, Wildenstein's, London, 1950, Paris, London, 1954, N.Y.C., 1957, Bklyn. Museum, 1969, Calif. Palace of Legion of Honor, San Francisco, 1969, Galleria Levi, Milan, 1971; works include: Portraits of The Duchess of Devonshire, Miss Margaret Rawlings, Lord and Lady Howard de Walden, Dame Margot Fonteyn, Deposition of Christ with Dominican Saints 1936-40, Say You This is Man?, 1953, Way to the Sermon on the Mount, 1954, Portrait of H.M. Queen Elizabeth II, 1955, Portrait of H.R.H. Princess Margaret, 1958, Life, 1961, Portrait of President Kennedy, 1961, fresco Crucifix in S. Martino Castagno, Florence, Portrait of Pope John XXIII, altarpiece Ch. of Claretian Fathers, Hayes, Middlesex, The Immaculate Heart of Mary, 1962, Portrait of H.M. Queen Elizabeth, the Queen Mother, 1963, St. Joseph altarpiece Ch. of S. Lorenzo, Florence, 1964, Resurrection fresco in Ch. of S. Michele, Ponte Buggianese (Montecatini), 1967, Apocalypse fresco, 1973, The Last Supper, 1975, St. Benedict altarpiece Ch. of Montecassino, 1975, Portraits of Shah of Iran and Queen Farah Diba, 1968, second portrait of H.M. Queen Elizabeth II, 1970, Il Misericordioso for Venerabile Arciconfraternita della Misericordia, Florence, 1970, Portrait of H.R.H. the Duchess of Kent, 1971, The Gold Age frescos Sala Pontormo, 1972-73, Portrait of H.R.H. Prince Henrik of Denmark, 1977, Portrait of H.M. Queen Margrethe II of Denmark, 1978, Abraham and Moses, Apotheosis of St. Benedict fresco Ch. of Montecassino, 1978, Facts of St. Benedict's Life fresco on dome, 1979, Facts of St. Anthony's Life fresco in Basilica del Santo, Padua, 1982-83, Last Supper Fresco in Basilica del Santo Padva, 1984, The Prodigal Son, 1987, St. Anthony Preaching Fresco in Basilica del Santo Padva, 1985. Mem. Accademia di S. Luca, Arti del Disegno. Author: An Artist's life.

ANNO, JAMES NELSON, scientist, educator; b. Niles, Ohio, Feb. 6, 1934; s. James Nelson and Opal Mae (Gentry) A.; m. Janet Winkel, June 12, 1955; children—James David, Sara Jennifer, Jefferson Nelson. B.S., Ohio State U., 1955, M.S., 1961, Ph.D., 1965. Technician Battelle Meml. Inst., Columbus, Ohio, 1953-55; supr. research reactor Battelle Meml. Inst., 1955-60, asst. chief applied nuclear physics div., 1960-65, chief lubrication mechanics div., 1967-70; assoc. prof. nuclear engring. U. Cin., 1970-73, prof., 1973—; pres. Research Dynamics, Inc., 1977—. Author: Encyclopedia of Draw Poker, 1973, (with J.A. Walowit) Modern Development in Lubrication Mechanics, 1975, Wave Mechanics for Engineers, 1976, Mechanics of Liquid Jets, 1977, Notes on Radiation Effects on Materials, 1984; contbr. articles to profl. jours. Recipient Civic award Columbus Jr. C. of C., 1961; honored by Saturday Evening Post, 1961. Mem. Am. Phys. Soc., AAAS, Phi Beta Kappa. Lodge: Masons. Home: 6405 Clough Pike Apt 3 Cincinnati OH 45244 Office: U Cin 509 Old Chemistry Bldg Cincinnati OH 45221

ANNUNZIATA, NORBERTO LEANDRO, manufacturing company executive; b. Cassino, Italy, Apr. 11, 1933; s. Giovanni and Livia (Cavanna) A.; m. Annamaria Angelini, Apr. 25, 1963; children: Marco, Andrea. M of Mech. Engring., U. Rome, 1958. Project engr. Montecatini SPA, Milan, 1960-64; prodn. mgr. Rockwell Rimoldi SPA, Milan, 1964-75; plant mgr. M. Maraldi SPA, Forli, Italy, 1975-77; gen. mgr. La Faenza (Italy) SPA, 1977-80; cons. engr. Soc. Orgn. Aziendale, Bologna, Italy, 1980-82; mng. dir. Inudtria Elettromeccanica Complessi Automaci SPA, Faenza, 1982—. Served as sgt. Italian Army, 1958-60. Mem. Coll. Engrs. Lodge: Rotary. Office: IEMCA SPA, Via Emilia Ponente 6, Faenza 48018, Italy

ANSARI, MEGILL SHAKIR, company owner; b. Tuskegee, Ala., May 11, 1957; s. John Thomas and Ethel Mae (Mims) P.; married, 1975. Student Vocat. Nursing, So. Vocat. Coll., 1975-76, Tuskegee Inst., 1977-79, Troy State U. (Ala.), 1981, Federated Tax Service, Chgo., 1983-85, N.Am. Sch. Animal Sci., 1982-83, Atlanta Sch. Med. Assts., 1984, Internat. Corr. Schs., 1984-85. Songwriter, Tuskegee, 1980-83; home care nurse, Tuskegee, 1982; author, songwriter Sweet Musicman Products, Tuskegee, 1981-83; music reporter Troy State U. newspaper, 1982; editor Sweet Musicman Songwriters, Tuskegee, 1981-83; assoc. Songwriter with Talent Inc., 1986; sec. Air Force R.O.T.C., 1982—. Author: (books of poems) Loneliness is my Only Friend, 1983, Barroom, 1983, It Is I, 1984, A Boy Without a Home, 1986, Blue Space of Love, 1987, Confine Love, (novel) The First Time, 1984, others. Scoutmaster Tuskegee Housing Dept., 1980-83; sustaining mem. Rep. Nat. Com., 1984. Recipient Silver Poet award World of Poetry, 1986, Golden Poet award World of Poetry, 1987. Mem. Am. Film Inst., Nat. Writer's Union, C. of C. U.S., Internat. Platform Assn., The Nat. Com. Home: Rural Rt 3 Box 1045 Tuskegee AL 36083

ANSARI, RASHID LATIF, recording industry executive; b. Azamgarh, India, July 2, 1931; s. Abdul Wali and Khadijat-Ul-Kubra (Shah) A.; married (div. Mar. 1975); m. Neelam Rosie Latif, Aug. 31, 1975; children: Sabina, Natasha. Degree in Inter. Sci., D.J. Sci. Coll., Karachi, Pakistan, 1948; degree in Mech. Engring., 1954. Asst. engr., factory mgr., mng. dir. EMI, Ltd., Karachi, 1954-71; officer on spl. duty EMI, Ltd., London, 1971-72; mng. dir. Thailand, Ltd., Bangkok, 1972-74; mng. dir. Shalimar

Recording Co., Ltd., Islamabad, Pakistan, 1974-78, exec. vice-chmn., 1978—; chmn. bd. dirs. Mehran Internat., Ltd., Karachi, Pakistan Indsl. Promoters, Ltd., Lahore, Pakistan, Pure Foods, Ltd. Author: Music, Law and You, 1978. Mem. Army Gen. Hdqrs. Music Com. Clubs: Sind (Karachi), Karachi Boat. Home: G-1 .The Marine Blessings, Karachi Pakistan Office: Mehran Internat Ltd, Polkà Annex, Hotel Metropole, Karachi 75520, Pakistan

ANSELMO, ROMUALDO SANTA ANA, physician; b. Obando, Philippines, Feb. 7, 1932; s. Manuel Bernardo and Santiaga (Santa Ana) A.; m. Ermelinda Mercado, June 21, 1962; children: Melissa Anne, Rodney Emmanuel, Derrick Paul, Carlo, Rosa Ma Teresita. AA, U. Santo Tomas, Manila, 1951, MD, 1957. Diplomate Philippine Bd. Psychiatry, Philippine Bd. Military Medicine. Resident Harper Hosp., Wayne State U., Detroit, 1959-61; psychiatric resident various hosps. including McGill U. and Dalhousie U., Detroit, Montreal, Halifax, Can., 1961-65; dir. children's unit Nova Scotia Hosp., Dartmouth, Can., 1965-66; chief mental health clinic Philippines Mental Health Assn., Quezon City, 1969-72; chief rehabilitation ctr. Philippine Mental Health Assn., Quezon City, 1970-77; chief section psychiatry, faculty of medicine and surgery U. Santo Tomas, Manila, 1970-80; chmn. dept. psychiatry Philippines Muslim Christian Coll. of Medicine Found., Antipolo, 1981—, chmn. dean's council, 1982-87, exec. asst. to dean, 1983-85, assoc. dean, 1985-87, dean, 1987—; cons. psychiatrist Good Shephard Convent Sch. for Girls, Manila, 1968-73, child care insts. Ministry of Social Services, Manila, 1968-80; lectr. Inst. Maternal and Child Health, Quezon City, 1970-76, Coll. Nursing U. Santo Tomas, Manila, 1971-78, bur. research and tng. Ministry Social Services, Manila, 1969-76; chmn. admissions commn. medicine and surgery U. Santo Tomas, Manila, 1973-79. Chmn. commn. on psychiatric rehabilitation Philippine Found. for Rehabilitation of the Disabled, Manila, 1974. Fellow Philippine Psychiatric Assn. (bd. dirs. 1987—), Philippine Assn. Military Surgeons (bd. dirs. 1986, 87, chmn. scientific com.); mem. Philippine Bd. Psychiatry (gov.-sec. examiner 1973-88, gov.-sec. 1988—), Philippine Mental Health Assn. (bd. dirs. 1986-87, v.p. 1988), Manila Med. Soc. (treas. 1984,85, interim v.p. 1988), Philippine Soc. Psychiatry and Neurology (pres. 1969, 70, fellow), Collegio Medico Farmaceutico de Filipinas (bd. dirs. 1984-85), World Psychiatric Assn. (resident liaison officer to the Western Pacific Region WHO 1980-88), Internat. Assn. Child Psychiatry and Allied Professions. Mem. Corazon Aquino's Coalition Party. Roman Catholic. Clubs: Quezon City Sports and Country, Makati Exec. Ctr., Nayong Kalikasan. Home: 53 Santiago St, SFDM, Quezon City Philippines Office: Santo Tomas U Hosp, Espana, Manila Philippines

ANTES, HORST, painter, sculptor; b. Heppenheim a.d.B., Germany, Oct. 28, 1936; s. Valentin and Erika Antes; m. Dorothea Grossman, 1961; 2 children. student Heppenherm Coll., 1948-52; prof. State Acad. Fine Arts, Karsruhe, W. Ger., 1957-59, Karlsrhe, Berlin, 1984—. One man shows: Troisieme Biennale de Paris, Mus. Ulm, Stadtische Galerie Munich, 1964, Gallery Stangl Munich, 1965, 68, 72, 75, Gallery Defet, Nürnberg, 1966, 72, Gimpel and Hanover Gallery, Zurich and London, 1967, 70, 73, 76, 80, Lefebre Gallery, N.Y.C., 1967, 69, 72, 74, 76, 78, 80, 82, 84, 86, 23d Biennale Venice, 1966, 10th Biennale Sao Paulo, 1969, Staatliche Kunsthalle Baden-Baden, Kunsthalle Bern, Kunsthalle Bremen, Frankfurter Kunstverein, 1971-72, Badischer Kunstverein Karlsruhe, 1978, Galerie Gunzenhauser, Munich, 1979, 83, 86, 87, Galerie Brusberg, Hanover and Berlin, 1979, 82, 83, 88, Bruhl, Schloss Augustenburg, 1980, Galerie Valentien, Stuttgart, 1966, 70, 81 Nishimura Gallery, Tokyo, 1981, 84, Galerie der Spiegel, Köln, 1982, 84, 87, Kunsthalle Bremen, 1983, Städel Frankfurt Sprengel Mus. Hannover, Wilhelm-Hack Mus., Ludwigshafen, 1983, Gallery Krohn, Badenweiler, 1984, Gallery Neumann, Düsseldorf, 1985, 88, Nationalgalerie, Berlin, 1985; group shows include: Pitts. Internat. Exhbn., 1961, 64, 70, 77; Dokumenta, Kassel, 1964, 68, 77; Europalia, Brussels, 1977; Im Namen des Volkes, Duisburg, Remscheid, Vienna, Sculptrues Europeenes, Brussels, 1979; Skulptur im 20. jahrhundert, Basel Wenkenpark, 1980, Biennale Middelheim, Antwerp., Nat. Mus. Seoul, Goethe Inst., London, 1983, Intergrafik, DDR Berlin 1987, Internat. Art Show for End of World Hunger, Minn., 1987; Kolner Stadt-museum, Koln, 1988, Lepold-Hoesch Mus., Duren, 1988, dokumenta Found., Berlin, 1988, Badischer Kunstverein, Karlsruhe, 1988. Recipient UNESCO prize Biennale, Venice, 1933; Villa Romana prize, Florence, 1962; Villa Massimo prize, Rome, 1963. Address: Hohenbergstrasse 11, 7500 Karlsruhe-41 Federal Republic of Germany

ANTHONY, DAVID VINCENT, lawyer; b. Erie, Pa., June 15, 1929; s. Frederick Peter and Marion Esther (Scharrer) A.; m. Rose Marie Mulvaney, Nov. 29, 1958; children—Joseph, Mary Catherine, Paul. B.A., Villanova U., 1951; J.D., Georgetown U., 1956, LL.M., 1960. Bar: D.C. 1956, U.S. Claims Ct. 1982, U.S. Ct. Appeals (D.C. cir.) 1956, U.S. Ct. Appeals 1982, U.S. Supreme Ct. 1963. Trial atty. civil div. U.S. Dept. Justice, Washington, 1956-63; ptnr. Sellers, Conner & Cuneo, Washington, 1963-74; ptnr. Pettit & Martin, Washington, 1974—; lectr. fed procurement, Fed. Pubs. Inc.; provider procurement courses NASA, Dept. of Navy; bd. advisors Bur. Nat. Affairs, Fed. Contracts Reports. Served to lt. USN, 1947-66. Mem. ABA, Fed. Bar Assn., Bar Assn. D.C., Assn. Trial Lawyers Am., Am. Judicature Soc., Nat. Security Industry Assn., Nat. Contract Mgmt. Assn. Republican. Roman Catholic. Clubs: Univ. (Washington), Belle Haven Country. Contbr. numerous articles on govt. contracts, claims, and litigation to profl. jours. Office: Pettit & Martin 1800 Massachusetts Ave NW Washington DC 20036

ANTHONY, HARRY ANTONIADES, city planner, architect, educator; b. Skyros, Greece, July 28, 1922; came to U.S., 1951, naturalized, 1954; s. Anthony G. and Maria G. (Ftoulis) Antoniades; m. Anne C. Skoufis, Sept. 23, 1950; children: Mary Anne Anthony Smith, Kathryn Harriet. B.Arch., Nat. Tech. U., Athens, Greece, 1945; student, Ecole Nat. Supérieure des Beaux Arts, Paris, France, 1945-46; M.City Planning, U. Paris, 1947; Docteur d'Université, Sorbonne, Paris, 1949; Ph.D. in Arch. and Urban Planning, Columbia, 1955. Architect-planner with Constantinos A. Doxiadis, Athens, 1943-45, LeCorbusier, Paris, 1946-47, ECA, Paris, 1949-51; city planner with Maurice E.H. Rotival, N.Y.C., 1951-52; chief planner Brown & Blauvelt, N.Y.C., 1952-54; city planner Skidmore, Owings & Merrill, N.Y.C., 1954-56; prin. planning cons. Brown Engrs. Internat., N.Y.C., 1956-60; prin. Brown & Anthony City Planners, Inc., N.Y.C., 1960-69; v.p. Doxiadis Assocs., Inc., Washington, 1971-72; Mem. faculty Columbia, 1953-72, prof. urban planning, 1963-72, dir. grad. div. urban planning Grad. Sch. Architecture and Planning, 1962-65; prof. urban planning Calif. State Poly. U., Pomona, 1972-83, prof. emeritus urban and regional planning, 1983—; chmn. dept. Calif. State Poly. U., 1972-76; vis. prof. urban design Tulane U., 1967-68; vis. lectr. U. Calif. at Berkeley, Stanford U., Dartmouth, San Diego State U., CUNY, U. Okla., Ohio U., Auburn U., Salk Inst. Biol. Studies, U.S. Internat. U.; vis. prof. urban studies and planning U. Calif., San Diego, 1980-82; scholar-in-residence U. B.C., Vancouver, 1978; planning, zoning, urban renewal and urban design cons. to several cities, U.S. and abroad; also cons. to UN, Am. Med. Bldg. Guild, corps. and pvt. firms, to govts. and univs.; planning commr., Leonia, N.J., 1958-64. Author, co-author, contbr.: Four Great Makers of Modern Architecture: Gropius, Le Corbusier, Mies Van Der Rohe, Wright, Dictionary of American History, The Challenge of Squatter Settlements—With Special Reference to the Cities of Latin America, La Défense à Paris et le Quartier d'Affaires de Vancouver: Une Comparaison Urbaine, New Orleans Air Rights Study, Woodstock Growth Plan and Land Use Controls, others; several master plans, city and regional planning reports, urban design plans and programs, environ. impact reports, zoning ordinances, educational videocassettes on urban planning subjects.; Contbr. articles to profl. jours., mags., newspapers. Recipient Premier Grand Prix Internat. Exhbn. Housing and City Planning, Paris, 1947; William Kinne Fellows travelling fellow in planning N.Am., 1956; research award Urban Center of Columbia U., 1969; named Outstanding Prof. Calif. State Poly. U., 1975. Mem. AIA (Arnold W. Brunner scholar 1958), Am. Inst. Cert. Planners, Am. Planning Assn. (Disting. Service award 1984), Order of Am. Hellenic Ednl. Progressive Assn., Land Econs. Soc. of Lambda Alpha. Home: 7665 Caminito Avola La Jolla CA 92037 Office: Dept Urban and Regional Planning Sch Environmental Design Calif State Poly Univ Pomona CA 91768

ANTHONY, ROBERT ARMSTRONG, lawyer, educator; b. Washington, Dec. 28, 1931; s. Emile Peter and Martha Graham A.; m. Ruth Grace Barrons, Feb. 7, 1959 (div.); 1 child, Graham Barrons; m. Joan Patricia Caton, Jan 3, 1980; 1 child, Peter Christopher. B.A., Yale U., 1953; B.A. in Jurisprudence (Rhodes scholar), Oxford U., 1955; J.D., Stanford U., 1957. Bar: Calif. 1957, N.Y. 1971, D.C. 1972. Assoc. Pillsbury, Madison & Sutro, San Francisco, 1957-62, Kelso, Cotton & Ernst, San Francisco, 1962-64; asso. prof. law Cornell U. Law Sch., 1964-68, prof., 1968-75, dir. internat. legal studies, 1964-74; chief counsel, later dir. Office Fgn. Direct Investments, Dept. Commerce, 1972-73; cons. Adminstrv. Conf. U.S., Washington, 1968-71; chmn. Adminstrv. Conf. U.S., 1974-79; ptnr. McKenna, Conner & Cuneo, Washington, 1979-82; sole practice Washington, 1982-83; prof. law George Mason U., Arlington, Va., 1983—; lectr. Acad. Am. and Internat. Law, Southwestern Legal Found., Dallas, summers 1967-72. Contbr. articles to profl. jours. Active Pres.'s Inflation Program Regulatory Council, 1978-79; mem. Fairfax County (Va.) Rep. Com., 1984-86; mem. chmn. panel U.S. Dept. Edn. Appeal Bd., 1981-83; cons., chmn. pubs. adv. bd. Internat. Law Inst., 1984—; bd. dirs. Marin Shakespeare Festival, San Rafael Calif., 1961-64, Nat. Ctr. for Adminstrv. Justice, 1974-79; commr. Sausalito (Calif.) City Planning Commn., 1962-64. Mem. Am. Bar Assn. (mem. council, sec. sect. adminstrv. law and regulatory practice 1988—), DC Bar Assn., Calif. Bar Assn., San Francisco Bar Assn., Assn. Am. Rhodes Scholars, Am. Soc. Internat. Law, Am. Law Inst., Stanford Law Soc. of Washington (pres. 1982). Club: Cosmos. Home: 2011 Lorraine Ave McLean VA 22101 Office: George Mason U Sch Law 3401 N Fairfax Dr Arlington VA 22201

ANTHONY, WENCESLAUS MELCHOIR, academic administrator; b. Vailankanni, Tamil Nadu, India, Sept. 28, 1957; s. Amala Vailankanni and Gracy (Martin) A.; m. Susan Cherian, Oct. 15, 1983; 1 child, Sneha Gracy. B of Communications with honors, St. Xaviers Coll., Calcutta, India, 1979; MBA, Loyola Inst., Madras, India, 1982; degree in data processing, Nat. Inst. for Info. and Tech., New Delhi, India, 1983. Sales exec. Godrej & Boyce Co., Ltd., Madras, 1982-83, Hindustan Computers, Ltd., Madras, 1983-84; dep. dir. bus. adminstrn. Loyola Inst., 1984—; ptnr. Tamilnadu Mercantile Corp., Madras, 1984—, Inter Continental Clothing Co., 1984—. Mem. bd. studies Madras Productivity Council, 1986-87. Mem. All India Cath. U. Fedn. (pres. 1979). Home: 11 7th Cross St W, 600 030 Shenoy Nagar India Office: Loyola Inst Bus Adminstrn, 600 034 Madras India

ANTHONY, YANCEY LAMAR, clergyman; b. Cordova, Ala., Feb. 13, 1922; s. Clifford Elmo and Tula (Barton) A.; m. Betty Pratt. B.A., Samford U., 1944; B.Th., So. Baptist Theol. Sem., 1947; Dr. è s scis., Paris; D.Th., Pioneer Theol. Sem., Rockford, Ill., Vanderbilt U., 1956, Galileo U., Italy; D.Ph., Accademia Universitaria Internazionale, Rome, 1957; D.D., Ministerial Tng. Coll., Sheffield, Eng., 1973; Ph.D. in History, Gt. China World U., Hong Kong. Ordained to ministry Baptist Ch., 1942; pastor Valley Grove Bapt. Ch., Tuscumbia, Ala., 1942-44, Walnut Grove Bapt. Ch., Lodiburg, Ky., 1945-47, First Bapt. Ch., Fort Walton Beach, Fla., 1947-53, Harsh Chapel Bapt. Ch., Nashville, 1953-56, Central Bapt. Ch., Fort Walton Beach, 1957-67; ambassador to all the Americas, Republik Danizig in Exile, N.Y.C., 1973—; moderator Okaloosa County Bapt. Assn., 1949-50; pres. Fort Walton Beach Ministerial Assn., 1952-55; mem. exec. bd. Fla. Bapt. Conv., 1948-56. Pres. Okaloosa County Better Govt. League, 1950-52; mem. Fla. Bd. Social Welfare, 1959-68, chmn., 1960-64; dir. Ch. Missions Fund Bapt. Found., 1947—; dir. Ch. Devel. Found. Fla., 1962—; lt. col. and a.d.c. Gov. Ala.; a.d.c. Gov. Miss., 1976. Decorated Knights of Malta, 1973, knight Ordre dela Courtoisie Francais; Ordine Internazionale della Legion d'Onore de l'Immacolata (Italy); Gold medal of Labour (Netherlands), 1975; grand officier Ordre du Merite Africain; d'Honneur de l'Institut des Relations Diplomatiques, Brussels; Lit. award Belgian High Fidelity Inst., 1976; Legion of Honor, Chapel of Four Chaplains, Phila., 1981; numerous others; hon. academician W.A. Mozart (Germany), French Acad. Golden Letters. Fellow Brit. Inst. Adv. Cons.'s; mem. Accademia Delle Scienze di Roma (life), Inst. Diplomatic Relations Brussels (hon.), Royal Acad. Golden Letters (hon.), Accademia Gentium Populorum Progressie, Accademia Gentium Pro Pace, Nobility Acad. of Kaspis, Nat. Soc. Univ. Profs. (pres. 1981), Albert Schweitzer Soc. (pres. 1982-85). Democrat. Lodge: Masons. Club: Mt. Kenya Safari (exec. com.). Home: 1913 Stanford Rd Jacksonville FL 32207

ANTHONY-PEREZ, BOBBIE MURPHY, psychology educator, researcher, consultant; b. Macon, Ga., Nov. 15, 1923; d. Solomon Richard and Maude Alice (Lockett) Cotton; m. William Anthony, Aug. 22, 1959 (dec.); 1 dau., Freida; m. Andrew Silviano Perez, June 20, 1979. B.S., DePaul U., 1953, M.S., 1954; M.S., U. Ill., 1959; Ph.D., U. Chgo., 1967; M.A., DePaul, 1975. Tchr. Chgo. Pub. Schs., 1954-68; math. cons. U. Chgo., 1965; prof. Chgo. State U., 1968—; psychol. cons. Chgo. Pub. Schs., 1971-72; ednl. cons. Urban Affairs Inst., Howard U., Washington, 1978; coordinator Higher Edn. Careers Counseling Campus Ministry, Ingleside Whitfield Parish, 1978-84. Vice-pres. Community Affairs Chatham Bus. Assn., 1981-85, asst. sec., 1985-86, sec., 1986-87, directory com., 1987; bus. relations chmn. Chatham Avalon Park Community Council; bd. dirs. United Meth. Found. at U. Chgo., 1980-84, Community Mental Health Council, Inc., 1979-83; pub. info. chairperson Chatham Avalon Unit Am. Cancer Soc., 1977-88. NSF fellow, 1957, 1958-59; recipient numerous awards religious, civic and ednl. instns. and assns. Mem. Am. Psychol. Assn., Internat. Assn. Applied Psychology, Internat. Assn. Cross-Cultural Psychology, Internat. Assn. Ednl. and Vocat. Guidance, Assn. Black Psychologists, Chgo. Psychol. Assn., Nat. Council Tchrs. Math., Am. Ednl. Research Assn., Midwest Ednl. Research Assn., Am. Soc. Clin. Hypnosis, Midwestern Psychol. Assn. Methodist. Contbr. numerous articles to profl. jours. Office: Chicago State University Dept Psychology 9500 S Stewart Ave Chicago IL 60628

ANTICH, CARLOS, oil company executive; b. Rio Cuarto, Cordoba, Argentina, Apr. 2, 1923; s. Santiago and Amélia Antonia (Herrera) A.; m. Maria Carmen Tecera; children: Ana Maria Antich Nóbrega, Maria Ines Antich Monteiro de Barros. Degree in Chemistry, Mackenzie Coll., São Paulo, Brazil. Plant mgr. Molinos Rio de la Plata, Santa Fé, Argentina, 1951-60; gen. mgr. Moinhos Rio Grandenses, Porto Alegre, Brazil, 1961-65; gen. mgr. Soc. Algodoeira do Nordeste Brasileiro, São Paulo, 1965-68, pres., 1968—; pres. Moinho Fluminense/Indústrias Gerais, Rio de Janeiro; bd. counselors Moinho Santista/Indústrias Gerais, São Paulo; bd. dirs. Tintas Coral Ltd., São Paulo. Founder Brazil-Argentine Cultural Inst. Recipient Order of Rio Branco, Govt. of Brazil, 1986. Mem. São Paulo Indsl. Ctr. (bd. dirs.), Brazilian Provision Industry Assn. (bd. dirs.), Brazilian Bus. Assn. (bd. dirs.), Internat. Trade Assn. (bd. dirs.),Brazilian-Argentine Assn. for Integration, Brazilian-Am. Bus. Council, Brazilian-Argentine Bus. Council, Argentine-Brazilian Bus. Council, Am. C. of C. for Brazil, Argentine C. of C. for São Paulo. Roman Catholic. Clubs: Harmonia, São Paulo Country. Home: Wilton Paes de Almeida 25, São Paulo 05678, Brazil Office: Sociedade Algodoeira do, Nordeste Brasileiro, Avenida Maria Coelho Aguilar 215, Sao Paulo 05804, Brazil

ANTIP, FELICIA RENE, journalist, writer; b. Focsani, Romania, Jan. 29, 1927; d. Moise Solomon and Clara (Revici) Becher; m. Constantin Antip, 1953; children: Igor, Florin. Instr. philosophy U. Iassy, Romania, 1952; sr. editor fgn. news Agerpres (Romanian press agy.), Bucharest, Romania, 1950-63; editor Am. dept. Lumea Mag., Bucharest, 1963-72; editor fgn. news Tribuna României, 1972-86; reviewer fgn. books România Literarǎ, Bucharest, 1972—; translator Drew Pearson The Senator, 1968, Sun Tzi, The Art of War, 1976, Marshall Kilduff and Ron Javers, The Suicide Cult, 1981, many others. Mem. Romanian Journalists' Assn. Home: Str Londra 33, Bucharest Romania

ANTLE, CHARLES EDWARD, mathematics educator; b. East View, Ky., Nov. 11, 1930; s. Bayard Pierpoint and Mary Elizabeth (Blaydes) A.; m. Elna Thomas Hall, Nov. 25, 1953; children—James, Rebecca, Susan Hall, Mark Edward. A.A., Lindsey Wilson Coll., 1950; B.S., Eastern Ky. State U., 1954, M.A., 1955; postgrad., U. Ky., 1954-55; Ph.D. (NDEA fellow), Okla. State U., 1962. Sr. aerophysics engr. Gen. Dynamics Corp., Fort Worth, 1955-57; mem. faculty U. Mo., Rolla, 1957-60, 62-68; prof. math. U. Mo., 1966-68; asso. prof. statistics Pa. State U., University Park, 1968-70; prof. Pa. State U., 1970—. Contbr. articles to profl. jours. Served with AUS, 1951-53. Decorated Bronze Star medal. Mem. Am. Statis. Assn., Royal Statis. Soc., Inst. Math. Statistics. Home: 2302 W Branch Rd State College PA 16801 Office: Pa State U Dept Statistics University Park PA 16802

ANTON, BRUCE NORMAN, textile company executive; b. N.Y.C., Dec. 27, 1951; s. Harvey and Betty L. (Weintraub) A.; m. Laurie Sue Weinberger, Mar. 7, 1981; children: Jamie Nicole, Ashley Blair, Emily Britt. BS in Textile Engring., Phila. Coll. Textile & Sci., 1973; MBA, Fairleigh Dickinson U., 1978. Salesman, Robison-Anton Textile Co., Fairview, N.J., 1973-79, v.p., 1979—; pres. Arrow Spinning Co., Inc., 1985—. Mem. Am. Assn. Textile Tech. Office: Robison Anton Textile Co 175 Bergen Blvd Fairview NJ 07022

ANTON, HARVEY, textile co. exec.; b. N.Y.C., Nov. 10, 1923; s. Abraham J. and Byrdie (Casin) A.; student Western State Coll. Colo., 1941, Savage Sch. Edn., 1941-42; B.S., N.Y. U., 1949; m. Betty L. Weintraub, Dec. 18, 1949; children—Bruce Norman, Lynne Beth. Pres., Anton Yarn Corp. (merged with Robison Textile Co. to form Robison-Anton Textile Co. 1959), N.Y.C., 1949-50, pres., 1973—; v.p. Arrow Spinning, Susquehanna, Pa.; adv. bd. 1st Jersey Nat. Bank. Trustee, Emerson Jewish Center, 1958-59, Erza Charitable Found.; pres. Anton Found. Served to 1st lt. AUS, 1943-46. Clubs: Masons, KP; Leonia Tennis; N.Y. Univ. Letter (N.Y.C.). Home: 41 Longview Dr Emerson NJ 07630 Office: Robison Anton Textile Co 175 Bergen Blvd Fairview NJ 07022

ANTON, NICHOLAS GUY, consulting physicist, engineer; b. Trieste, Austria, Dec. 14, 1906; came to U.S., 1926, naturalized, 1943; s. Joseph and Ann (Mandle) A.; m. Bernice Irene Skripsky, June 19, 1932; children—Joan Carol Anton Pearlman, Linda Elaine Anton Kincaid, Nancy Helen Anton Bobrow. Grad., Tech. Inst. Leonardo da Vinci, 1926; student, Columbia U., 1926-28. Various engring. positions Duovac Radio Tube Corp., Bklyn., 1928-31; pres., chmn. bd. Electronic Labs., Inc., Bklyn., 1931-32; founder, gen partner in charge mfg., factory engring. Amperex Electronics Products, 1932-48; pres., dir. research, devel., engring. Anton Electronic Labs., Bklyn., 1948-61; chmn. bd. Anton Imco Corp., 1959-61; founder, pres., dir. research, devel. EON Corp., Bklyn., 1961-78; cons., lectr. N.Y.C., 1978-79; pres., chmn. Dosimeter Corp., 1963-75; lectr. L.I. U., 1969-78; indsl. tech. cons. AEC for UN Internat. Conf. on Peaceful Uses of Atomic Energy, Geneva, 1955; Mem. Pres.'s Conf. on Indsl. Safety, 1967—, Albert Gallatin Assos.-N.Y. U., 1951-54; Centennary com. Poly. Inst. Bklyn., 1963-64, U.S. Nat. UN Day Com., 1972-74, 76. Contbr. numerous articles, papers to profl. lit. Recipient cert. of appreciation Office of Pres. Fellow IEEE, Am. Phys. Soc., N.Y. Acad. Scis., N.Y. Acad. Medicine (asso.), AAAS, Am. Philos. Soc.; mem. ASME, Am. Math. Soc., Am. Soc. for Nondestructive Testing, Electronic Industries Assn. (past chmn. various coms.), Am. Standard Assn. Jewish. Clubs: Unity, Engineers. Home: 2501 Antigua Terr A3 Coconut Creek FL 33066

ANTONACCI, ANTHONY EUGENE, food corporation engineer; b. Sept. 21, 1949; s. Salvatore Natali and Odile Estella (Stanton) A.; m. Sherry Lee Kessler, Mar. 6, 1971; children—Don Warren, Lance Anthony. Student U.S. Air Force Acad., 1968-69; Assocs. in Sci., Forest Park Coll., St. Louis, 1971. Lic. stationary engr. Asst. supr. data processing ops. 1st Nat. Bank, St. Louis, 1969-71; engr. Installation and Service Engring. (Mech. and Nuclear) div. Gen. Electric Corp., St. Louis, 1971-76; engr. Anheuser-Busch Corp., St. Louis, 1976—; software author. Trustee, treas. Antonette Hills Trusteeship, Affton, Mo., 1976-80. Recipient Spl. Performance awards Gen. Electric Co., 1972, 74. Mem. Brewers and Maltsters Local 6 (del. 1982, 83), Nat. Aerospace Edn. Council, Apple Programmers and Developers Assn. Republican. Roman Catholic. Avocations: classic auto restoration, music (trumpet). Home: 8971 Antonette Hills Saint Louis MO 63123

ANTONACCI, LORI (LORETTA MARIE), marketing executive, consultant; b. Riverton, Ill., Mar. 31, 1947; d. Antonio and Gena Marie A. B.A., Bradley U., 1969. Broadcast copywriter Sta. WIRL-TV, Peoria, Ill., 1969; communications specialist Walgreen Co., Chgo., 1970-72; creative supr. Nat. Assn. Realtors, Chgo., 1973; creative dir., producer Steve Sohmer, Inc., N.Y.C., 1974-77; owner, exec. producer Antonacci Prodns., N.Y.C., 1977-79; promotion specialist Ziff-Davis Publs., 1979-80; promotion mgr. Psychology Today, 1980-81; pres. Antonacci & Assocs., N.Y.C., 1982—; adj. prof. Gallatin Div. NYU, 1986—. Bd. dirs. Artists Talk on Art, Inc., Artists Community Fed. Credit Union; founder Artists Talk on Art Panel series, 1974. Recipient Golden Eagle award CINE, 1976; award U.S. Indsl. Film Festival, 1977; CEBA award, 1979; Bronze medal Internat. Film and TV Festival N.Y., 1979. Mem. Advt. Women N.Y. (profl. devel. com. 1983-85, program com. 1986—, chmn. speakers bur. 1988—), Women in Communications, Media Marketers, Assn. Am. Women in Radio and TV. Address: 15 E 10th St New York NY 10003

ANTONELLI, FERDINANDO GIUSEPPE CARDINAL, Italian ecclesistic; b. Subbiano, Italy, July 14, 1896. Joined Order of Friars Minor, Roman Catholic Ch., 1914, ordained priest, 1922; tchr. ch. history Antonianum, 1928-32, instr. Christian archeology, 1932-65, rector magnificus, 1937-43, 53-59; definator gen. Friars Minor, 1939-45; various offices Roman Curia, sec. Congregation of Rites, 1965-69, Congregation for Causes of Saints, 1969-73; consecrated titular archbishop of Idicra, 1966; elevated to Sacred Coll. of Cardinals, 1973. Address: Vatican City Vatican *

ANTONELLI, LUIZ KUSTER, psychology educator; b. Sao Francisco de Assis, Brazil, Feb. 27, 1918; s. Pedro B. and Almerinda (Kuster) A.; student State Tchrs. Coll., Cruz Alta, Brazil, 1935-37, U. Chile, 1947-48; B.A., U. Rio Grande de Sul, 1949; postgrad. U. Denver, 1951-52; M.A., Columbia U., 1953, Ed.D., 1961; postgrad. Inst. Practicing Psychotherapists, N.Y.C., 1962-64, Postgrad. Center for Mental Health, N.Y.C., 1964-68. Came to U.S., 1958. Pres. State Tchrs. Coll., Cachoeira do Sul, Brazil, 1943-50; supt. State of Rio Grande do Sul, Brazil, 1953-54; prof. psychology Inst. Edn., Porto Alegre, Brazil, 1953-54; dean of students Aero. Inst. Tech., San Jose dos Campos, Sao Paulo, Brazil, 1955; dir. Inter-Am. Center, Pan Am. Union, Venezuela, 1956-58; counselor Bklyn. Coll., 1961; dir. div. gen. edn. Voorhees Tech. Inst., N.Y.C., 1961-66; staff mem. Met. Center for Mental Health, N.Y.C., 1963-64; mem. staff Postgrad. Center for Mental Health, 1964-68, staff, 1968-69; assoc. prof. Queen's Coll., City U. N.Y., 1966—, dir. counseling and guidance center, 1969-72, dir. master tng. program for urban sch. counselors, 1969-72, dir. peer counseling tng. program, 1976-78, coordinator, supr. Family Counseling Program, 1980—; vis. prof. U. Brasilia (Brazil), 1981. Hon. chmn. Campaign Against Juvenile Delinquency, Venezuela. Served with Brazilian Army, 1938. Mem. Am. Psychol. Assn., Am. Anthrop. Assn., AAAS, NEA, Am. Ednl. Research Assn., AAUP, Am. Coll. Personnel Assn., Am. Personnel and Guidance Assn., Kappa Delta Pi, Phi Delta Kappa. Address: PO Box 64 Ansonia Sta New York NY 10023-5302

ANTONINI, JOSEPH E., apparel company executive. Grad., W.Va. U. With K Mart Corp., Troy, Mich., 1964—, pres., dir., K Mart Apparel Corp., North Bergen, N.J., 1984-86, chief operating officer, 1986-87, pres., 1986—, chmn., chief exec. officer, 1987—, pres., 1988—. Office: K-Mart Corp 3100 W Big Beaver Rd Troy MI 48084 Other Office Adr: K Mart Apparel Corp 7373 Westside Ave N North Bergen NJ 07047 *

ANTONINI, MASSIMILIANO ALBERTO ALESSANDRO, museum administrator; b. Rome, Italy, Apr. 28, 1929; s. Camillo Filippo Alessandro and Evelyn (Bendit) A.; comml. diploma Institut Minerva, Zurich, 1948; m. Elvira von Ostheim, Feb. 25, 1965 (div. Jan. 1984); 1 dau., Gwendolyn. Asst., Swiss Inst. for Art Research, Zurich, 1953-63; adminstr. collection of photographs Swiss Nat. Mus., Zurich, 1963—. Mem. Zurich Art Soc., Soc. of Antiquarians, Soc. of Swiss Nat. Mus., Soc. of Swiss Inst. of Art Research, Soc. History of Art in Switzerland, Art Historians Soc., Swiss Numismatic Soc., Amis suisses de la Cé ramique. Clubs: Assn. Internationale des Anciens Roseens, Swiss Automobile Club, Acad. Ice-Hockey Club. Home: 23 Langwattstrasse, Zollikerberg by, CH-8125 Zurich Switzerland Office: 2 Museumstrasse, CH-8006 Zurich Switzerland

ANTONIO, DOUGLAS JOHN, lawyer; b. N.Y.C., Sept. 14, 1955; s. John and Joan (Deitz) A.; m. Sarah Kathrine Nadelhoffer, Aug. 31, 1986. BS, BA, U. Md., 1977, JD, 1980, MBA, 1981; LLM in Taxation, Georgetown U., 1983. Bar: Md. 1980, D.C. 1981, Mo. 1983, U.S. Tax Ct. 1983, U.S. Supreme Ct. 1983, U.S. Ct. Claims 1983. Atty.-advisor U.S. Labor Dept., Washington, 1980-83; atty. Thompson & Mitchell, St. Louis, 1983-84; assoc. Blumenfeld, Sandweiss, Marx, Tureen, Ponfil & Kaskowitz, St. Louis, 1984-86; assoc. Sugar, Friedberg and Felsenthal, Chgo., 1986-88, ptnr., 1988—. Contbr. articles to profl. jours. Home: 555 W Madison St Tower #1 Apt 4010 Chicago IL 60606 Office: Sugar Friedberg and Felsenthal 30 N LaSalle St Suite 2600 Chicago IL 60602

ANTONIO, LUIS REYES, architect; b. Manila, Feb. 11, 1947; s. Pablo S. and Marina (Reyes) A. Student, De La Salle Coll., Manila, 1966; BS in Architecture, U. Santo Tomas, Manila, 1971. Pres. Paradise Rattan, Pasay, Philippines, 1976—, Paradiso Couture, Manila, 1980—. Columnist The Philippine Star, 1987; editorial cons. Lifestyle Asia mag., 1987. Mem. Philippine Inst. Architects, Philippine Inst. of Interior Designers, United Architects Assn. Club: Alabang Country, Valle Cerde Country, Chaine de Roitisseurs, Cheese and Wine, Manila Polo. Lodge: Rotary. Home: 8 Sampaguita St Valle Verde 2, Pasig Philippines Office: Paradiso Couture, Trend Bldg, Ground Floor, San Agustin and Sedeno Sts, Makati Philippines

ANTONIONI, MICHELANGELO, film director; b. Ferrara, Italy, Sept. 29, 1912; s. Carlo and Elisabetta Antonioni; m. Letizia Balboni, 1942 (div.); m. Enrica Fico, 1986. Grad., U. Bologna, Italy. Film critic Corriere Padano, L'Italia Libera. Directed films Gente del Po, 1943-47, Amorosa Menzogna, 1949, (documentaries) Sette Canne un Vestito, La Villa dei Mostri, Superstizione, 1949, Cronaca di un Amore, 1950, La Signora Senza Camelie, 1952, I Vinti, 1952, Amore in Città, 1953, Le Amiche, 1955, Il Grido, 1957, L'Avventura, 1959 (Cannes Critics' Award 1960), La Notte, 1961 (Silver Bear Berlin Film Festival 1961), L'Eclisse, 1962, Il Deserto Rosso (The Red Desert), 1964 (Golden Lion 25th Venice Film Festival 1964), Blow Up, 1966 (Golden Palm Cannes Festival 1967, Best Director Nat. Soc. Film Critics), Zabriskie Point, 1970, Chung Kuo-China, 1972, The Passenger, 1974, Il Mistero di Oberwald, 1979, Identificazione di una Donna, 1982 (Grand Prix Cannes 1982). Recipient City of Munich Prize, 1968. Office: Via Vencenzo Tiberio 18, 00191 Rome Italy *

ANTRIM, MINNIE FAYE, residential care facility administrator; b. Rochester, Tex., June 30, 1916; d. Charles C. Montandon and Myrtle Caldona (Brown) Montandon Taylor; m. Cecil C. Antrim, Jan. 1, 1938; children—Linda Faye Antrim Hathway, Cecil C. Student Central State Tchrs. Coll., Edmond, Okla., 1937. Asst. purchasing agt. Scenic Gen. Hosp., Modesto, Calif., 1955-68, Health Dept., Probation Dept., Stanislaus, Calif., 1955-68; owner, adminstr. Sierra Villa Retirement Home, Fresno, Calif., 1968-77, Mansion Home, Fresno, 1977—. Mem. Am. Coll. Health Care Adminstrs., Calif Bus. and Profl Club. Methodist. Club: Garden. Avocation: glee clubs. Home: 6070 E Townsend Fresno CA 93727

ANUAR, HEDWIG ELIZABETH, librarian; b. Johore Bahru, Malaysia, Nov. 19, 1928; d. Percival Frank and Agnes Beatrice (Danker) Aroozoo; children: Azmi Anuar, Shirin Aroozoo. BA with honors in English Lit., U. Malaya, Singapore, 1951; postgrad. Northwestern Poly. Sch. Librarianship, London, 1955-57. Library asst. U. Malaya Library, Singapore, 1952-59; asst. librarian U. Malaya in Kuala Lumpur Library, 1959-62, dir., 1960-61; asst. dir. Nat. Library of Singapore, 1962-64, dir., 1965—; dir. Nat. Archives and Records Centre, Singapore, 1969-78; cons. pub. library devel. for Malaysia, 1968. Author: Blueprint for Pub. Library Development in Malaysia, 1968; Issues in South East Asian Librarianship, 1985. Contbr. articles to profl. pubs. Hon. sec. Nat. Book Devel. Council Singapore, 1969-80, vice chmn., 1980, chmn., 1980—. Overseas fellow Inter-Univ. Council for Commonwealth Univs. Overseas, London, 1955-57; recipient Pub. Adminstrn. Gold medal Singapore Govt., 1969. Fellow Library Assn. Britain (hon.); mem. Library Assn. of Singapore (hon. life), Persatuan Perpustakaan Malaysia (hon. life mem.), Congress of Southeast Asian Librarians, Internat. Assn. Orientalist Librarians. Office: Nat Library, Stamford Rd, 0617 Singapore Singapore

ANWAR, CHOUDRY MUHAMMAD, pediatrician, educator; b. Kohat, Pakistan, Oct. 14, 1938; s. Khair-Ud-Din Choudhry and Hasmat Begum; m. Razia Sultana, Sept. 11, 1969; chidren: Kamila, Siama, Vaqas, Hina. BS, B of Medicine, Khyber Med. Coll., 1960. House surgeon Lady Reading Hosp., Peshawar, Pakistan, 1960, house physician, 1961; gen. duty Dr. various army units, 1961-64; with Armed Forces Med. Coll. and Mil. Hosp., Rawalpindi, Pakistan, 1964-65; physician various army hosps., Pakistan, 1965-70; clin. asst. Western and Ea. Gen. Hosps., Edinburgh, Scotland, 1970-72; physician East Fortune Hosp., Haddington, Scotland, 1972; cons. physician, vis. instr. Armed Forces Med. Coll., various army hosps., Pakistan, 1972-77; clin. asst. pediatrics Ea. Gen. Hosp., Edinburgh, 1977-78, Hosp. Sick Children, Edinburgh, 1977-78; pediatrician Royal Victoria Hosp., Kerkardy, Scotland, 1977-78; clin. asst. Queen Elizabeth Hosp. for Sick Children, London, 1977-78; asst. prof. pediatrics Army Med. Coll., Rawalpindi, Pakistan, 1978-80; sr. instr. Armed Forces Med. Coll., Rawalpindi, 1978—; assoc. prof. Army Med. Coll., Rawalpindi, Pakistan, 1980-83, prof., head dept., 1984—; cons. pediatrician, head dept. Mil. Hosp., Rawalpindi, 1978—; advisor pediatrics Pakistan Armed Forces, Rawalpindi, 1978—; chmn. 8th Biennial Internat. Pediatrics Conf., Rawalpindi/Islamabad, 1986. Contbr. articles scholarly jours. Served to brigadier with Army Med. Corps of Pakistan. Recipient Tamgha-i-Jhang Ministry Def., 1965, 71, Tamgha-i-Sad Saala Jashan-i-Willadat-i-Quaid-i-Azam Hijri Tamgha, 1981. Mem. Pakistan Pediatrics Assn. (pres. 1984—), Pakistan Med. and Dental Council, Pakistan Med. Assn. (life). Muslim. Club: Rawalpindi. Home: 107 B Rumi Rd, Rawalpindi Cantonment Pakistan Office: Mil Hosp, Pediatrics Dept, Rawalpindi Pakistan

ANYAMANI, SUTIN, wire and cable manufacturing executive; b. Thailand, Mar. 5, 1939; s. Oonla and Kong A.; m. Kanista A., May 16, 1966; children—Nathapol, Ronnawat, Vathanai. B.S. in Elec. Engring., Chulalongkorn U., Bangkok, Thailand, 1961, M.S. in Elec. Engring., 1966; postgrad. in mgmt. Harvard U., 1978. Elec. power distbn.-design engr. Met. Electricity Authority, Bangkok, 1961-65; elec. insp. O.I.C.C. Thailand, Bangkok, 1965-66; with Pacific Electric Co., Bangkok, 1966-67; asst. v.p. Phelps Dodge Thailand Ltd., Bangkok, 1967—; v.p. PD-Siam Rod Co., Ltd., Bangkok, 1983—; tech. dir. PDTL Trading Co. Ltd., Bangkok, 1981—; mem. authors' com. Thailand indsl. standard for copper insulated wire and cable, 1975. Mem. Engring. Inst. Thailand (bd. dirs. elec. div. 1978-83, cons. 1984—), Wire Assn. Internat., Am. Mgmt. Assn. Home: 43 Mitraparb Village, Sukhumvit 77, Prakanong 10250, Thailand Office: Phelps Dodge Thailand Ltd, 220 Sukhumvit Rd SOI 113, Bangkok 10270, Thailand

ANYANWU, TIMOTHY UWADIEGWU, marketing executive; b. Nguru Mbaise, Owerri, Nigeria, Apr. 6, 1949; s. Donatus Anyanwu and Anna Ego (Nkemakolam) Onyenwere; diploma in accountancy Nigerian Inst. Mgmt., 1973, diploma in mktg., 1976, diploma in commerce, 1978; B.Sc. with honors in Mgmt. Studies, U. Sokoto, Nigeria, 1985; m. Obioma Nnennaya Anyanwu, Apr. 18, 1976; children—Adaku Chikodinaka, Nwakaego Nneka, Chinaemerem Nkechi, Chijioke Uwadiegwu, Chidinma Ugochi. Sec., Need Consultancy Ltd. Lagos, 1974; accounts rep., coop. officer Nics Ltd., Lagos, Owerri, 1976; mktg. mgr./export mgr. Tee-Jee Internat., Lagos, 1977; mng. dir. Fertimike Constrn. & Supply Co., Ltd., Lagos, Owerri, 1979; chmn., mng. dir. Anyanwu Enterprises (Nigeria) Ltd., Lagos, Owerri. Nat. dir. publicity Ukandu/Ezindu Social Club Nigeria, 1980—; youth leader Nigerian Peoples Party, Ward 15, Imo State, 1980—; sec. Imo Bros. Coop. Soc. Ltd, 1988—; coordinator Owerri pre-group Amnesty Internat., 1988—. Served to capt. Biafran Army, 1967-70. Mem. Nigerian Inst. Mgmt. (assoc.), Chartered Inst. Sales Mgmt. and Mktg. (assoc.), Inst. Commerce (assoc.), Nat. Assn. Imo State Students Unisokoto (pres. 1983-84), Sokoto U. Mgmt. Students Assn. (fin. sec. 1983-84). Roman Catholic. Clubs: Pyrates Social, Cultural, Mbaise, Neighborhood Social. Author: Modern Commerce and Business Studies for Schools and Colleges, 1980; Objective Questions on Modern Commerce for Schools and Colleges, 1981; Mortgage Banking in a Developing Economy, 1985; Merchant Banking and the Growth of Nigeria's Foreign Trade, 1986, Commercial Banking in Nigeria, 1987. Home: Amaohuru Nguru, Nkwogwu Mbaise, Owerri Nigeria Office: Plot 203A, No 9, Ohaozara, Aladinma Housing Estate, Owerri Nigeria

ANYOG, MARIO JIMENEZ, surgeon; b. Caoayan, Ilocos Sur, Philippines, July 4, 1953; s. Guillermo Cabaldon Anyog and Luciana Reyes Jimenez; m. Thelma Santa Cruz Eddun, Sept. 7, 1985; 1 child, Philip Omar. BS, U. Santo Tomas, Manila, 1972, MD, 1976; Diploma in Gen. Surgery, V. Luna Gen. Hosp., 1983. Diplomate Philippine Bd. Surgery. Resident in surgery Manila Drs. Hosp., 1978-79, V. Luna Gen. Hosp., Quezon City, 1979-83; acting surgeon Maj. Ferdinand E. Marcos Veterans Regional Hosp., Neuva Vizcaya, 1983-84; med. officer Ministry of Health, Sultanate of Oman, Philippines, 1984—; vis. cons. Holy Rosary Gen. Hosp., Manila, 1983-84. Recipient Topnotcher award Philippine Med. Bd., 1977, Hermogener Santos award U. Santos Tomas Med. Alumni Assn., 1978. Mem. U. Santos Tomas Med. Alumni Assn., Philippine Med. Assn.; fellow Philippine Bd. Surgery. Roman Catholic. Home: 414 C Concha St, Tondo Manila 2807, Philippines Office: Ministry of Health, PO Box 32503, IBRA Sultanate of Oman Philippines

ANZ, REG DEAN, architect; b. Clifton, Tex., Jan. 21, 1942; s. Edward Walter and Elizabeth Helen (Holman) A.; student U. Tex., Arlington, 1960-62, BS in Archtl. Studies, Austin, 1965; m. Patrice Ann Niehaus, Jan. 9, 1977; children: Adrian Van, Marisa Santana. Project architect Envirodynamics Inc., Dallas, 1971-72, Dahl/Braden/Jones/Chapman, Dallas, 1973-74, Dan Dworsky, Beverly Hills, Calif., 1974; assoc. Martin Stern, Jr., Beverly Hills, 1975-79, Maxwell Starkman, Beverly Hills, 1979-83; pvt. practice cons., 1983-84; cons. Lee & Sakahara, Costa Mesa, Calif., 1985; with Jones Cons. Mgmt., Beverly Hills, Calif., 1986—. Lic. architect, Tex., Calif. Mem. AIA (corp.), Constrn. Specifications Inst., Am. Arbitration Assn., Nat. Council Archtl. Registration Bds. (cert.). Supervising architect M.G.M. Grand Hotel, Reno, 1977-78; project architect Sahara Hotel & Casino, Las Vegas and Atlantic City, 1978-79; project dir. Sheraton Grande Hotel, Los Angeles, 1979-83; project mgr. UCLA Med. Ctr., 1986—. Office: 1008 5th St Santa Monica CA 90403

AOKI, JUNJIRO, chemical engineer; b. Japan, Feb. 17, 1910; s. Ihei and Sada (Nohara) A.; B.Eng., Waseda U., 1934; m. Sumie Takanoha, Dec. 3, 1939; children—Hajime, Minoru, Arata. Head research tech. research and devel. dept. Fujikura Rubber Works Co., Tokyo, 1934-64; head staff KPE Co., Tokyo, 1965-75; dir. Chubu Kogyo Co., Nagoya, Japan, 1965-77; chem. engr. Aoki Chem. Lab., Tokyo, 1965—; adviser Nitto Shoji, Fujikagaku Shi, Takada Co., Mikasa Communication Parts Co., Japan Univac Supply Co., Courier Internat. Corp.; Nippon Sheet Glass Co., Nippon Steel Co. Served with Japanese Army, 1944-45. Mem. Adhesion Soc. Japan, Japanese Assn. Leather Tech., Japan Soc. Colour Material, Soc. Rubber Industry Japan, Soc. Powder Tech. Japan, Soc. Surface Sci. Japan. Club: Tokyo Chofu Lions. Research on polyamid and polyurethane artificial leather, coupling agts. application in inorganic and organic composites, magnetic tapes and desk, tonner and carrier. Home and Office: 4 20 8 Higashi Nogawa, Komae City, Tokyo 201 Japan

AONA, GRETCHEN MANN, artist, photographer; b. Omaha, June 25, 1933; d. Albert Paul and Gladys Louise (Mann) Andersen; AB, San Jose State U., 1951, MA in Art, 1966; m. Daniel Kaleikoa Aona, Jr., June 16, 1979. Textbook illustrator math. and stats. dept. Stanford U., 1960-63; sci. illustrator Melabs, Mountain View, Calif., 1967; instr. art, crafts, and photography Kapiolani Community Coll., Honolulu, 1967-88, chmn. humanities dept., 1978-79; one-woman shows in photography include: Fantasy Images, Queen Emma Gallery, Honolulu, 1977, Foyer Gallery, Leeward Community Coll., Honolulu, 1980; group exhbns. include: Photo '70, '71, '72, Sixty Yrs. World in Color, Hague, Netherlands, 1973, Honolulu, Art Hawaii One, Honolulu Acad. Art, 1974, 75, Gt. Hawaiian Open Art Exhbn., 1981, Artists of Hawaii, Honolulu Acad. Arts, 1981, Honolulu Printmakers 55th Ann. Exhbn., 1983, 60th Ann. Exhbn., 1988, Windward Artists Easter Art Show, 1984, 85, 88, Hawaii Watercolor Soc. Exhibit, 1985, 86, Image 13 Hawaii, 1987; invitational exhbns. include Koa Gallery, Kapiolani Community Coll., 1987, Florals and Nature Scenes, Ho'omaluhia Botanical Garden, 1987, Aloha Ho'omaluhia, 1988. Represented by South Shore Gallery, Honolulu. Recipient Purchase award Honolulu Acad. Art, 1981, Hawaii State Found. Culture and Arts, 1987 (2). Mem. Hawaii Watercolor Soc., Pacific Handcrafters Guild. Democrat. Roman Catholic. Author: Creative Exploration in Crafts, 1976. Home: 45-453 B Mokulele Dr Kaneohe HI 96744

AOYAMA, HIROYUKI, structural engineering educator; b. Shinjuku, Tokyo, Japan, July 14, 1932; s. Hidesaburo and Sadako (Nishimura) A.; m. Kikuko Sugiura, Apr. 16, 1960; children: Masako Aoyama Kaburaki, Nobuyuki. B in Engring., U. Tokyo, 1955, M in Engring., 1957, DEng., 1960. Registered first class architect. Lectr. U. Tokyo, 1960-64, assoc. prof., 1964-78, prof., 1978—; vis. researcher, U. Ill., Urbana, 1961-63, vis. prof., 1971-72; vis. prof. U. Canterbury, Christchurch, N.Z., 1980-81. Fellow Am. Concrete Inst.; mem. Archtl. Inst. Japan (award 1976), Japan Concrete Inst. (award 1975), Japan Soc. Civil Engrs., ASCE. Home: 4-2-13 Takadanobaba, Shinjuku-ku, Tokyo 169, Japan Office: U Tokyo Dept Architecture, 7-3-1 Hongo, Bunkyo-ku, Tokyo 113, Japan

APA, ALBERT ALEX, association executive; b. Chgo., June 5, 1921; s. Michael and Rose (Tenuta) A.; student schools Chgo.; 1 child, Candice Sue Apa Kvitek; m. Diane L. Gooch, June 4, 1988. Supr. Stewart Warner Corp., 1939-42; sgt. Chgo. Police Dept., 1947-79; exec. dir. Ill. Local Govtl. Law Enforcement Officers Tng. Bd., Springfield, 1979—; chmn. Police of Ill., 1975-78. Pres., Chgo. Police Pension Protective Assn., 1967-78, trustee, 1978-79; mem. Gov.'s Arson Adv. Bd.; mem. adv. bd. Fed. Law Enforcement Tng. Ctr. Served with U.S. Army, 1942-46. Decorated Bronze Star with 3 oak leaf clusters, Purple Heart. Named Man of Year, Chgo. Patrolmen's Assn., 1973; recipient achievement award Ill. Fraternal Order of Police, 1978, Ill. Sheriff's Assn., 1980. Mem. Ill. Police Assn., Internat. Assn. Chiefs of Police, Nat. Assn. State Dirs. of Law Enforcement Tng. (pres.), Nat. Sheriff's Assn. (standards, ethics, edn. and tng. com), Am. Soc. Tng. and Devel. Roman Catholic. Clubs: Fraternal Order of Police, Exchange of Springfield. Author: Handbook on Pensions, 1964; contbr. legis. articles to Ill. Police Jour. Office: 524 S 2d St Suite 400 Springfield IL 62706

APELO, RUBEN ALMEDA, gynecologist, educator; b. Laguna, Philippines, May 16, 1917; s. Dominador and Josefa (Almeda) A.; m. Irma Reyes; children: Ruben Jr., Emaline, Alma, Bella. MD, U. Philippines, 1941. Resident in gynecol. Philippine Gen. Hosp., Manila, 1941; instr. Coll. Medicine U. Philippines, Manila, 1950-54, asst. prof., 1954-74, prof. ob.-gyn., 1974-82; med. specialist Dept. Health Jose Fabella Meml. Hosp., Manila, 1953-87; dir. Comprehensive Family Planning Ctr., Manila, 1970-88, Collaborative Ctr. Clinic Research U. Philippines-Philippine Gen. Hosp., Manila, 1976-82; commr. Commn. Population, 1987; pres. Found. Philippine Family Planning Inc., Manila, 1977-79; cons. Dept. Health, 1988; mem. steering com. on oral contraceptives WHO, 1977-80, mem. steering com. on sterilization, 1977-79, mem. adv. group to program research devel. and tng. in human reproduction, 1982-85. Contbr. articles to profl. jours. Chmn. Southeast Asia and Oceania Regional Council, 1970-78. Fellow Philippine Coll. Surgeons (regent 1961-64), Philippine Ob.-Gyn. Soc. (pres. 1961); mem. Philippine Med. Assn., Am. Fertility Soc., Soc. Advancement Contraceptives, Family Planning Assn. Philippines (pres. 1966-71), Philippine Assn. Study Sterilization (pres. 1975-80), U. Philippines Med. Alumni Soc. (pres. 1970-71). Roman Catholic. Club: Wack-wack Golf and Country. Home: 136 West Ave, Quezon City Philippines Office: Jose Fabella Meml Hosp, Lope de Vega St Santa Cruz, Manila Philippines 711-76-86

APONTE MARTINEZ, LUIS CARDINAL, archbishop; b. Lajas, P.R., Aug. 4, 1922; s. Santiago E. Aponte and Rosa Martinez. Student, San Ildefonso Sem., San Juan, P.R., 1944, St. John's Sem., Boston, 1950; LL.D. (hon.), Fordham U., 1965. Ordained priest Roman Cath. Ch., 1950; asst. in Patillas, P.R.; pastor in Maricao, P.R., Sta. Isabel, P.R., 1953-55; sec. to bishop of Ponce, P.R., 1955-57; pastor in Aibonito, P.R., 1957-60; aux. bishop of Ponce, 1960-63, bishop, 1963-64; archbishop of San Juan, 1964—; elevated to cardinal 1973; Chancellor Cath. U. P.R., Ponce, 1963—; pres. Puerto Rican Episcopal Conf. Served as chaplain P.R. N.G., 1957-60. Club: Lion. Address: Calle San Jorge 201 Santurce PR 00912 *

APPEL, ANDRÉ, historian; b. Oudtshoorn, Cape, Republic of South Africa, Nov. 5, 1942; s. Marthinus Johannes and Isabella Margaretha (Olivier) A.; m. Margaretha Elizabeth Fourie, June 22, 1968; children: Lise, Maryke, Anneri, André Martinus. BA, U. Stellenbosch, 1962, MA, 1966; PhD, U. Port Elizabeth, 1980. Lectr. history U. Stellenbosch, Republic of South Africa, 1965; tchr. high sch. Tulbagh, Republic of South Africa, 1967-69; tchr. Outeniqua High Sch., George, Republic of South Africa, 1970; tchr. high sch. Heidelberg, Cape, Republic of South Africa, 1971; sr. lectr. history U. Port Elizabeth, Republic of South Africa, 1972—. Author: The Dutch Reformed Congregation Oudtshoorn, 1853-1978, 1979, The District of Oudtshoorn Up to the 1880's: A Socio-Economic Study, 1988, Die Oosterlig 1937-1948: A Press Historical Study, 1985; contbr. articles to profl. jours. Recipient South African Tchr.'s Union and U. Stellenbosch Gold Medal, 1966. Mem. South African Hist. Soc. Progressive Fed. Party. Mem. Dutch Reformed Ch. Home: 24 Kuruman Kloof, Summerstrand, Port Elizabeth 6001, Republic of South Africa Office: Univ of Port Elizabeth, PO Box 1600, Port Elizabeth 6000, Republic of South Africa

APPEL, KAREL CHRISTIAN, artist, illustrator; b. Amsterdam, The Netherlands, Apr. 25, 1921; s. Jan and Johanna (Chevallier) A. Ed., Royal Acad. Art, Amsterdam. Numerous one-man shows, most recent being Palais des Beaux-Arts, Brussels, 1983, Gimpel Fits Gallery, London, 1983, St. Mary's Gallery, N.Y.C., 1984, Annina Nosri Gallery, N.Y.C., 1984, Gimpel & Weitzenhoffer Gallery, N.Y.C., 1984; exhibited in numerous group shows; represented in permanent collections Tate Gallery, London, Mus. Modern Art, N.Y.C., Stedelijk Mus., Amsterdam, Mus. Fine Arts, Boston, also others. Recipient Guggenheim Nat. prize, Netherlands, 1951, UNESCO prize Venice Biennials, 1953, Lissone prize, Italy, 1958, Sal Paulo exhbn. acquisition prize, 1959, Graphique Internat. prize, Ljubljana, Yugoslavia, 1959, Guggenheim Internat. prize, 1961. Office: care Stephen Gill Gallery 122 E 57th St New York NY 10022 also: care Galarie Statler, 51 rue de Seine, Paris France *

APPEL, NORMAN, ophthalmologist, educator, real estate company executive, importing company executive; b. N.Y.C., Dec. 4, 1945; s. Robert M. and Anne K. (Kleiner) A.; m. Rena Lee Moskovits, Sept. 2, 1973; m. Sheila Gail Popkin Wasserman, Aug. 16, 1984; children: Steven Mordechai, Ronit Danielle, James Moshe. B.A., U. Louisville, 1966, M.D., 1970; postgrad., Harvard U., 1974. Diplomate: Am. Bd. Ophthalmology. Intern Maimonides Med. Ctr., Bklyn., 1970-71; resident in ophthalmology Strong Meml. Hosp. of U. Rochester, N.Y., 1973-76; fellow The Edward S. Harkness Eye Inst., Columbia-Presbyn. Med. Ctr., N.Y.C., 1976; practice medicine specializing in orbit, lacrimal and oculoplastic surgery and oncology N.Y.C., 1977-86; sr. clin. asst. ophthalmologist Mt. Sinai Hosp., 1977-86; asst. attending ophthalmologist Beth Israel Med. Ctr., 1977-85; assoc. attending ophthalmologist St. Clare's Hosp., 1977-86; asst. attending surgeon ophthalmology N.Y. Infirmary Beekman Downtown Hosp., 1977-84; attending ophthalmologist Bronx VA Hosp., 1977-86; asst. attending ophthalmologist Montefiore Hosp. and Med. Ctr., 1979-86, Cabrini Med. Ctr., 1982-86, Westchester County Med. Ctr., 1983-86, St. Vincent's Hosp. and Med. Ctr. of N.Y., 1983-86; founder, dir. Orbit Clinic Mt. Sinai Hosp., 1977-78, Orbit and Oculoplastic Surgery Clinic Beth Israel Med. Ctr., 1977-79, St. Clare's Hosp., 1977-86, Bronx Va Hosp., 1977-86, North Central Bronx Hosp., 1980-86, Orbit Clinic N.Y. Infirmary Beekman Downtown Hosp., 1977-84; physician in charge orbit, lacrimal and oculoplastic surgery service Brookdale Hosp. Med. Ctr., 1982-84; founder, dir. Orbit, Lacrimal and Oculoplastic Surgery Clinic, 1982-84; dir. Orbit, Lacrimal and Oculoplastic Service Interfaith Med. Ctr., 1982-86; owner, dir. Appel Enterprises, Englewood, N.J., 1986—, Appel Importers, Englewood, 1986—; cons. Cabrini Med. Ctr., Jewish Hosp. and Med. Ctr. of Bklyn.; faculty Mt. Sinai Sch. Medicine, Albert Einstein Coll. Medicine; cons. in field. Contbr. articles to med. jours. and books. Served with USAF, 1971-73, Vietnam. N.Y. State Regents scholar, 1963. Fellow ACS, Am. Acad. Ophthalmology and Otolaryngology; mem. Bklyn. Ophthalmol. Soc., N.Y. State Med. Soc., N.Y. County Med. Soc., Phi Delta Epsilon. Office: 120 S Woodland St Englewood NJ 07631

APPLE, DAINA DRAVNIEKS, management, administrative systems designer; b. Kuldiga, Latvia, USSR, July 6, 1944; came to U.S., 1951; d. Albins Dravnieks and Alina A. (Bergs) Zelmenis; divorced; 1 child, Almira Moronne; m. Martin A. Apple, Sept. 2, 1986. BS, U. Calif., Berkeley, 1977, MA, 1980. Economist U.S. Forest Service, Berkeley, 1974-84; mgmt. analyst U.S. Forest Service, San Francisco, 1984—. Author: Public Involvement In the Forest Service-Methodologies, 1977, Public Involvement-Selected Abstracts for Natural Resources, 1979, The Management of Policy and Direction in the Forest Service, 1982, An Analysis of the Forest Service Civil Rights Program, 1984, Organization Design-Abstracts for Natural Resources Users, 1985. Mem. AAUW, Am. Forestry Assn., Sigma Xi, Phi Beta Kappa (nat. sec. 1985—, pres. No. Calif. chpt. 1982-84, 1st v.p. 1981), Phi Beta Kappa Assocs. Club: Commonwealth of Calif. (100 Leaders of Tomorrow). Home: PO Box 26155 San Francisco CA 94126 Office: US Forest Service Planning and Budgeting Office 630 Sansome St San Francisco CA 94111

APPLE, MARTIN ALLEN, high technology company executive; b. Duluth, Minn., Sept. 17, 1938; children—Deborah Dawn, Pamela Ruth, Nathan, Rebeccah Lynn; m. Daina Draunicks, Sept. 1986. A.B., A.L.A., U. Minn., 1959, M.Sci., 1962; Ph.D., U. Calif., 1968. Pres., Internat. Plant Research Inst., San Carlos, Calif., 1978-81; with EAN-Tech., Inc., Daly City, Calif., 1982-84, chmn. bd., 1983-84; with Adytum Internat., Mountain View, Calif., 1982—, chief exec. officer, 1983—; cons. MIT, Stanford U., U. Calif., 1981-83; adj. prof. computers in medicine U. Calif. San Francisco, 1982-84. Author: (with F. Myers) Review Medical Pharmacology, 1976; (with M. Fink) Immune RNA in Neoplasia, 1976; (with F. Becker et al) Cancer: A Comprehensive Treatise, 1977; (with M. Keenberg et al) Investing in Biotechnology, 1981; (with F. Ahmad et al) From Genes to Proteins: Horizons in Biotechnology, 1983. Mem. Calif. Council Indsl. Innovation, 1982. Mem. Assn. Venture Founders Internat. (bd. govs. 1982-83), East-West Center Assn. (bd. trustees, vice chmn. 1983-85), Profl. Software Programmers Assn., Phi Beta Kappa (Disting. Service award 1984, 85). Home: PO Box 391043 Mountain View CA 94039 Office: PO Box 2629 San Francisco CA 94126

APPLEGATE, EDNA (KAY), civic worker; b. Las Vegas, N.Mex., May 15, 1919; d. George Washington and Dora Maude (Bearce) Howell; m. George Edward Applegate, Nov. 30, 1945 (dec. 1980); 1 child, Nancy Kay. R.N., Hotel Dieu Sch. Nursing, 1942; B.S., Columbia U., 1956, M.S., 1963. Sch. nurse tchr. Garden City Pub. Sch., N.Y., 1960-73; pub. health nurse Nassau County Dept. Health, Garden City, 1953-60. Author: Breakfast Book, 1976; Little Book of Baby Foods, 1979. Bd. dirs. Maternal and Child Health Ctr., Santa Fe, 1978-80, Myasthenia Gravis Found. N.Mex. chpt., 1986—, LWV, Santa Fe, 1974-80, Vol. Involvement Service, Santa Fe, 1977-83, Santa Fe Opera Guild, 1981-82, Santa Fe Cancer Soc., 1983-84; mem. steering com. March of Dimes Birth Defects Found., Santa Fe, 1979-85, vol. coordinator N.Mex. chpt., 1985-86; mem. adv. bd. women's unit Charter Sunrise Hosp., Albuquerque, 1985—; mem. fin. com. St. John's Coll., Santa Fe, 1978-83, mem. fine arts com., 1979-83; co-founder The Gilbert & Sullivan Soc., Santa Fe, 1984; charter mem. Compadres del Palacio, 1986; chmn. N.Mex. com. to restore the Montezuma (N.Mex.) Hotel, 1986—. Served as 2d lt. Army Nurse Corp, 1942-44. Fellow Am. Sch. Health Assn., Royal Soc. Health; mem. N.Y. Mental Health Assn. Democrat. Mailing Address: PO Box 2688 Santa Fe NM 87504

APPLEY, MORTIMER HERBERT, psychologist, university president emeritus; b. N.Y.C., Nov. 21, 1921; s. Benjamin and Minnie (Albert) A.; m. Dee Gordon, June 5, 1942 (div. Oct. 1969); children: Richard Gordon, John Benton; m. Mariann B. Hundahl, Jan. 10, 1971; stepchildren: Scott, Eric, Heidi Hundahl. B.S., CCNY, 1942; M.A., U. Denver, 1946; Ph.D., U. Mich., 1950; D.Sc. (hon.), York U., 1975; D.H.L. (hon.), Northeastern U., 1983; Litt.D. (hon.), Am. Internat. Coll., 1984; LL.D. (hon.), Clark U., 1984. Instr. U. Denver, 1945-47; instr. U. Mich., 1947-49; asst. prof. Wesleyan U., Middletown, Conn., 1949-52; prof., chmn. psychology Conn. Coll., New London, 1952-60, So. Ill. U., Carbondale, 1960-62, York U., Toronto, Ont., Can., 1962-67; dean faculty grad. studies York U., 1965-68; prof., chmn. psychology U. Mass., Amherst, 1967-69; dean Grad. Sch., 1969-74, asso. provost, 1973-74; pres. Clark U., Worcester, Mass., 1974-84; vis. scholar psychology Harvard U., 1984-88; exec. dir., commn. on the Future ofthe Univ. U. Mass., Boston, 1988—; cons. NSF, NIMH, NRC of Can., Can. Council, VA., AAAS, MacArthur Found. Author: (with C.N. Cofer) Motivation: Theory and Research, 1964, (with R. Trumbull) Psychological Stress, 1967, (with J. Rickwood) Psychology in Canada, 1967, (with R. Trumbull) Dynamics of Stress, 1986, (with L. Lasagna) Who are the Elderly, 1986; editor: Adaption Level Theory: A Symposium, 1971, Motivation and Emotion, 1976-88; assoc. editor Psychol. Abstracts, 1961-62; editor, contbr. Internat. Ency. Neurology, Psychology, Psychoanalysis and Psychiatry, Ency. Brit.; contbr. articles to profl. jours. Served with USAAF, 1942-45. NSF Sci. Faculty fellow, 1959-60; Fulbright fellow Germany, 1973-74; recipient Townsend Harris medal CCNY, 1986. Fellow Am. (past chmn. edn. and tng. bd.), Canadian psychol. assns.); mem. Conn. Psychol. Assn. (past pres.), New Eng. Psychol Assn. (past pres.), Sigma Xi, Psi Chi, Phi Sigma. Democrat. Unitarian (chmn. bd. mgrs. congregation). Clubs: St. Botolph, Worcester Econ. (pres. 1980-81); University (N.Y.C.). Home: 18

Robinson St Cambridge MA 02138 Office: Univ Mass Pres Office 250 Stuart St Boston MA 02116

APTER, MICHAEL JOHN, psychologist, educator; b. Stockton-on-Tees, Durham, Eng., June 17, 1939; s. Kenneth Carl and Vera Blanche (Apter) Smith; m. Claude Annik Deburaux (div. June 1977), June 29, 1964; 1 child, Carolyn Sophie; m. Ivy Williams, June 21, 1977; children: Sarah Jane, Samantha Isobel. BS with honors, Bristol (Eng.) U., 1960, PhD, 1964. Research asst. Princeton (N.J.) U., 1960-61; research fellow King's Coll., U. London, 1963-64; head dept. research Teaching Programmes Ltd., Bristol, 1964-67; lectr. psychology U. Coll. Cardiff, Wales, 1967-73, sr. lectr., 1973-84, reader in psychology, 1984—; mem. psychologist's panel Civil Service Selection Bd., London, 1974-76; owner Alexandra Park Residential Home, Penarth, Wales, 1979-84; mem. Avebury Com., 1983-84; vis. prof. Purdue U., West Lafayette, Ind., 1988—. Author: Cybernetics and Development, 1966, Computer Simulation of Behavior, 1970, Experience of Motivation, 1982; author, editor 5 books. Disting. vis. scholar Social Scis. and Humanities Research Council Can., 1985; life fellow the Netherlands Inst. Advanced Studies. Fellow Brit. Psychol. Soc., Cybernetics Soc. Eng.; mem. Internat. Council Psychologists, Psychology and Psychotherapy Assn. U.K. Office: U Coll Cardiff, PO Box 78, Cardiff CF1 1XL, Wales

APTIDON, HASSAN GOULED (HASSAN GOULED APTIDON), president Republic of Djibouti; b. Djibouti, Djibouti, 1916; m. Asha Bogore. Contractor; senator, Paris, 1952-58; del. Chamber of Deps., Assembly of Ters., Paris, 1958; minister of edn., Djibouti; mem. Territorial Assembly, Djibouti, 1967-77; leader Issas Dem. Union, until 1977; now leader African People's League for Independence, also mem. Djibouti Nat. Assembly; pres. Council of Govt., 1970, Republic of Djibouti, 1977—. Moslem. Office: Office of the Pres, Djibouti Republic of Djibouti

APTOWITZER, WILLI ZEEV, insurance executive; b. Austria, Apr. 13, 1918; s. Adolph George Moses Aaron and Regina Ryfka (Weber-Cirer) A.; m. Margit Manzi Stern, Sept. 22, 1944. Student Handelsakademie and Hochschule für Welthandel, 1938, Chartered Inst. Ins., London, 1941-44. Co-founder NIO Group cos., 1949, mng. dir. Nat. Ins. Office Ltd., 1955-67, chmn. group, 1967—; mem. Lloyd's Underwriters, London, 1976—; dir. Haifa Econ. Corp., Sci. Based Industry Corp., Haifa, Hassneh (U.K.) Ltd., London, Israel Reins. Co. Ltd., mem. Israel Ins. Council, 1979-82, Internat. Union Marine Ins., 1984—, mem. Cargo Loss Prevention Com., 1984—. Chmn., Aptowitzer Found. for Haifa; founding trustee Haifa Found.; trustee, bd. govs. Haifa U.; trustee, bd. dirs. Tel Aviv Mus.; founding mem., now chmn. Gan Hayeled; bd. dirs. Israel-Am. Cultural Found. Served to lt. col. Res. Israel Def. Forces, 1948—. Hon. citizen City of Haifa, 1988—, recipient diploma of honor Internat. Inst. Community Service; Cert. of Merit DIB, London. Mem. Chamber Commerce and Industry, various bi-country leagues, Maccabi Sports Assn. (past dep. chmn.). Internat. Ins. Soc. (bd. dirs. 1983—). Clubs: Masons, Rotary (past pres. Carmel, cert. of merit 1980). Home: 154 Sd Aba Khoushi Hod Hacarmel, Haifa Israel Office: PO Box 20, Haifa 34980, Israel

AQUAISUA, NYONG ARCHIBONG, business executive, retired Nigerian diplomat; b. Obong Itam, Nigeria; s. Akpan and Affiong (Eton) A.; m. Geraldine Okon, Jan. 2, 1973; children—Akon, Affiong, Aquaisua, Inyang, Effiong, Emem-Obong. B.A. with honors, U. Leicester-Eng., 1961; Diploma in Edn., Edinburgh U., 1955; cert. in pub. adminstrn. Pitts. U., 1978. Sch. master Macgregor Coll., Afikpo, Nigeria, 1955-57; adminstrv. officer Govt. Eastern Nigeria, Enugu, 1961-70; permanent sec. Govt. of Cross River, State of Nigeria, 1971-85; chief exec. Leap Year Enterprises, Calabar, 1985—; chmn. governing council Rubber Research Inst. of Nigeria, Benin City, 1988—. Author: The Politics of Foreign Aid, 1961, Progress in Industry, 1964. Mem. revs. com. Local Govt. System in Nigeria, 1984. Presbyterian. Avocations: reading; travel. Address: PO Box 1214, Unit C, Second Ave, State Housing Estate, Calabar, Cross River State Nigeria

AQUARONE, EUGENIO, biochemist, educator; b. Genova, Italy, May 16, 1927; came to Brazil, 1928; s. Alfredo and Domenica (Molteni) A.; m. Saveria Rosa Annunciata Borrelli, Oct. 7, 1953; children—Alfredo, Francisco, Paulo de Tarso, Maria Eugenia; m. Maria Alice de Oliveira, July 23, 1975; 1 son, Eugenio. Biochem. pharmacist Faculdade Ciencias Farmaceuticas, U. Sao Paulo, 1948, Dr., Escola Politecnica, 1955. Technician, Pirelli, Sao Paulo, 1945; tech. dir. Laboratorio Veiga, S.A., Sao Paulo, 1948-50; dir. sci. documentation Lab. Fontoura Wieth, Sao Paulo, 1950; sci. asst. dir. Laboratorio Andromaco S.A., Sao Paulo, 1951-55; asst. prof. U. Sao Paulo, 1954-67, vice dean faculty pharm. sci., 1974-78, prof. indsl. fermentation, 1968—. Author: (with others) Biotechnology Colection vols. I, II, III, V, 1975-83. Patentee in field. Contbr. articles to and sci. profl. jours. Mem. Sociedade de Farmacia e Quimica de Sao Paulo (pres. 1968-70), Accademia Economico-Agraria dei Georgofili (Florence). Roman Catholic. Home: Apt 94, Rua Senador Cesar Lacerda Vergueiro 531, 05435 Sao Paulo Brazil Office: Faculdade Ciencias Farmaceuticas USP, Caixa Postal 37.086, Cep 01051 Sao Paulo Brazil

AQUINO, CORAZON COJUANGCO, president of Republic of Philippines; b. Manila, Philippines, Jan. 25, 1933; d. Joee Conjuangco, Sr. and Demetria Sumulone; m. Benigno S. Aquino, Jr., Oct. 11, 1954 (dec. 1983); children—Maria Elene, Aurora Corazon, Benigno III, Victoria Elisa, Kristina Bernadette. B.A., Coll. Mt. St. Vincent, N.Y., 1953, D.H.L., 1984; postgrad. Coll. of Law, Far Eastern U., Philippines; H.H.D., Stonehill Coll. Pres., Republic of Philippines, 1986—. Mem. United Nationalist Dem. Orgn., 1985—. Office: Office of Pres, Manila Philippines *

ARABIA, PAUL, lawyer; b. Pittsburg, Kans., Mar. 28, 1938; s. John K. and Melva (Jones) A. B.A., Kans. State Coll.; J.D., Washburn U. Bar: Kans. 1966, U.S. Dist. Ct. Kans. 1966, U.S. Ct. Appeals (10th cir.) 1968. Ptnr., Fettis & Arabia, Wichita, 1968-74, Arabia & Wells, Wichita, 1974-78; sole practice, Wichita, 1978—. with "Peoples Lawyer" Sta. KAKE-TV. Mem. Kans. Bar Assn., Wichita Bar Assn. General practice, Contracts commercial. Office: 200 E First Suite 200 Wichita KS 67202

ARAD, MOSHE, ambassador; b. Romania, Aug. 15, 1934; arrived in Israel, 1950; m. Rivka Weisman, Sept. 21, 1965; children: Michael, Odelia. BS in Polit. Sci. and Internat. Relations, Hebrew U., Jerusalem, 1959, LLB, 1962. Asst. in Dept. for Internat. Cooperation Ministry of Fgn. Affairs, Jerusalem, 1962-64; exec. asst., ministry spokesman Minister of Justice, Jerusalem, 1964-68; 1st sec. for press, then counselor Israeli Embassy, London, 1968-72; dep. consul-gen. Israeli Embassy, N.Y.C., 1972-73; minister-counselor for information Israeli Embassy, Washington, 1973-76; head office of dir.-gen. Ministry of Fgn. Affairs, Jerusalem, 1976-77, asst. dir.-gen. for information, 1977-80, inspector-gen. for diplomatic services, 1981-83; ambassador to Mexico Ministry of Fgn. Affairs, 1983-87, ambassador to U.S., 1987—. Office: Embassy of Israel 3514 International Dr NW Washington DC 20008

ARAGON, GLORIA TAMAYO, physician, obstetrics and gynecology educator; b. Manila, Nov. 30, 1918; d. Ponciano Cabrera and Maria Antonia (Tamayo) A. MD magna cum laude, U. Philippines, 1940. Research assoc. Coll. Medicine U. Philippines, Manila, 1940-47, from instr. obstetrics to assoc. prof., 1947-65, prof. ob-gyn., 1965-83, chmn. dept. ob-gyn., 1967-72, dean Coll. Medicine, 1979-83, bd. regents, 1983-86, prof. emeritus, 1984—; dir. Philippines Gen. Hosp., 1979-83. Sr. author: Guides to Physiologic and Pathologic Obstetrics, 1967, rev. edit., 1972, also numerous ob-gyn. research reports; sr. editor: Training Manual for Surgical Sterilization, 1975, Field Manual for Surgical Sterilization, 1976. Bd. dirs. Commn. on Population Republic Philippines, 1973—, Commn. on Women Republic Philippines, 1975—; pres. U. Philippines Med. Found., 1980—. Fellow Philippines Ob-Gyn. Soc. (pres. 1962-63), Philippines Coll. Surgeons, Am. Coll. Surgeons, Ob-Gyn, Internat. Acad. Reproductive Medicine (hon.), Nat. Research Council Philippines. Roman Catholic. Home: 25 Hidalgo, San Lorencos Village Philippines

ARAI, KIYOMARU, maritime and foreign commerce consultant; b. Toyko, June 2, 1918; s. Kiyoshi and Tokuko Arai; m. Sumiko Arai, Feb. 20, 1947 (dec. 1970); children: Chieko, Masao; m. Tomoko Arai, Feb. 2, 1972. BA, Tokyo U. Fgn. Affairs, 1941. Mgr., research commr. Nippon Yusen Kaisha, Ltd., Tokyo, 1941-74; dir., rep. Port San Diego, 1974-86; cons. in internat. transp. and commerce Yokohama, Japan, 1987—. Co-author: Containerization, 1973. Mem. World Trade Ctr. Club Japan. Home and Office: 971 Harajuku Totsuka, 245 Yokohama Japan

ARAIZA, FRANCISCO (JOSÉ FRANCISCO ARAIZA ANDRADE), opera singer; b. Mexico City, Oct. 4, 1950; s. José and Guadalupe (Andrade) A.; m. Vivian Jaffray, Sept. 30, 1977; children: José Riccardo, Maria del Carmen Cecilia. Grad. in Bus. Adminstrn., U. Mexico City, 1972; grad., Nat. Sch. Music, Mexico City, 1974, Nat. Conservatory, Mexico City, 1974, Musikhochschule, Munich, 1975. Tenor roles include performances in opera houses in Karlsruhe, Fed. Republic of Germany, 1975-77, Zurich, Munich, Vienna, Salzburg Festival, Rome, Bayreuth Festival, Hamburg, Berlin, Milau, London, Chgo., San Francisco, N.Y.C., Tokyo, Mexico City, 1977; numerous recordings include works by Mozart, Mahler, Schubert, Haydn and others; also six solo albums of opera arias. Recipient Prphee d'Or, 1984, Deutscher Schallplattenpreis, 1984. Address: care Rita Schutz, Artists Mgmt, Rutistrasse 52, CH-8044 Zurich-Gockhausen Switzerland

ARAKAWA, KASUMI, physician, educator; b. Toyohashi, Japan, Feb. 19, 1926; came to U.S., 1954, naturalized, 1963; s. Masumi and Fayuko (Hattori) A.; m. Juen Hope Takahara, Aug. 27, 1956; children—Jane Riet, Kenneth Luke, Amy Kathryn. M.D., Tokyo Med. Coll., 1953; Ph.D., Showa U. Sch. Med., Tokyo, 1984. Diplomate: Am. Bd. Anesthesiology. Intern Iowa Meth. Hosp., Des Moines, 1954-56; resident U. Kans. Med. Center, Kansas City, 1956-58; practice medicine specializing in anesthesiology Kansas City, 1958—; instr. anesthesiology U. Kans. Med Center, Kansas City, 1961-64; asst. prof. U. Kans. Med Center, 1964-71, asso. prof., 1971-77, prof., 1977—, chmn. dept. anesthesiology, 1977—; clin. asso. prof. U. Mo.-Kans. City Sch. Dentistry, 1973—; dir. Kansas City Health Care, Inc. Fulbright scholar, 1954. Recipient Outstanding Faculty award Student AMA, 1970. Fellow Am. Coll. Anesthesiology; mem. Asso. Univ. Anesthetists, Acad. Anesthesiology (pres. 1986-87), Japan-Am. Soc. Midwest (v.p. 1965, 71). Home: 7917 El Monte St Shawnee Mission KS 66208 Office: Univ Med Ctr 39 Rainbow St Kansas City KS 66103

ARAKI, YOSHIRO, banker; b. Aichi Prefecture, Japan, July 9, 1921; s. Danzo and Mitsuyo A.; m. Kimiko, Dec. 17, 1952; children—Akiko, Masao. Ed. Faculty of Law, Kyoto Imperial U. (Japan), 1944. Chief mgr. The Fuji Bank, Ltd., Hiroshima, Japan, 1968-70, dir. and chief mgr. bus. devel. div., Tokyo, 1970-73, mng. dir., 1973-75, dep. pres., 1975-81, pres., 1981—; v.p. Japanese Com. for Econ. Devel., 1982—. Mem. Fedn. Bankers Assn. Japan (dir. 1981—, chmn. 1982-83, 86—), Japan Fedn. Econ. Orgns. (exec. mem. bd. from 1982). Office: The Fuji Bank Ltd, 1-5-5 Otemachi 1 Chome, Chioda-ku, Tokyo 100 Japan *

ARAMBURU, JUAN CARLOS CARDINAL, archbishop of Buenos Aires; b. Reduccion, Argentina, Feb. 11, 1912; Ordained priest Roman Catholic Ch., 1934; ordained titular bishop of Plataea and aux. of Tucuman, Argentina, 1946, bishop, 1953, 1st archbishop, 1957; titular archbishop of Torri di Bizacena and coadjutor archbishop of Buenos Aires, 1967, archbishop of Buenos Aires, 1975, elevated to cardinal, 1976; titular ch., St. John the Baptist of Florentines; ordinary for Eastern Rite Catholics in Brazil without ordinaries of their own rites. Mem. of Congregations: Oriental Chs., Cath. Edn. Office: Arzobispado, Suipacha 1034, 1008 Buenos Aires Argentina *

ARANDA, MIGUEL ANGEL, surgeon, educator; b. Chihuahua, Mexico, Nov. 25, 1939; s. Miguel Aranda-Lezama and Rebeca Gomez-Ibarra; student St. Michael's Coll., Sante Fe, N.Mex., 1956;student English Lang. Inst., Ann Arbor, Mich., 1957; M.D. with honors, U. Chihuahua, 1964; postgrad. in aviation medicine. m. Bertha Lucia Vargas, Oct. 31, 1964; children: Berta Miriam Irais, Rebeca Cristina Isabel, Miguel Angel, Jorge Xavier, Alejandro Manuel. Intern Sanatorio Moderno, Chihuahua, 1963-64; trained in legal medicine, Mexico City, 1971, aerospace medicine, 1972; prof. legal medicine Sch. Law, U. Chihuahua, 1965—; sec. transp. and communication, Mexico City, 1972; prof. legal medicine Med. Sch., 1972-77, assoc. prof. surgery, 1968-77; head teaching dept. Univ. Hosp., 1974-77, jr. surgeon men's surgery service, 1972-77; asst. prof. clin. gastroenterology, 1974-76, asst. prof. clin. path. neurology, 1974-75; vis. prof. U. Ill. Med. Center, Chgo., 1975; prof. legal medicine, Sch. Law Inst. Tech., Monterry, 1983-84; prof. of psychology, anatomy and human physiology, 1972—; dean (dir.) Clinic Sanatorio Mederno, Chihuahua City; prof. criminalistics, U. Chihuahua, 1988—; mem. forensic toxicology Miguel Aranda U. conf. First. Nat. Congress on Forensic Med. Crim. and Criminalís, Villahermosa, Mex., 1987. Served with Instituto Regional, 1948-56. Fellow Internat. Coll. Surgeons, Internat. Assn. Coroners and Med. Examiners; mem. Asociación de Médicos Egresados de la Universidad Autónoma de Chihuahua, Asociación Mexicana de Cirugía General, Colegio Nacional de' Medicina Psicosomática, Asociación Mexicana de Medicina de Aviación y del Espacio, Sociedad de Cirugía del Hospital Juárez, Sociedad Chihuahuense de Med. Foren. Criminología y Criminalística (founder), Vocal de Asociac., Mex. de Soe. de Med. For., Criminol. y Criminalos, Internat. Assn. of Coroners and Med. Exam., N.Y. Acad. Scis., Soc. Cirog. Hosp. Juárez, Assn. Mex. de Cirugia Oral. Roman Catholic. Club: Country of Chihuahua. Author of handbook of legal medicine; contbr. arti.cles to profl. jours. Home: 1400 26th St, Santa Rita Mexico Office: 510 Bolivar St, Chihuahua Mexico

ARANGO, JORGE SANIN, architect; b. Bogota, Colombia, Nov. 29, 1916; s. Fernando Arango and Maria Sanin A.; m. Elizabeth Leighton, 1944; 1 child, Pedro; m. Judith Brooks Wolpert, Dec. 14, 1951; children: Richard, Virginia; m. Penelope Corey, Aug. 18, 1976. Student, Universidad Catolica de Chile Sch. Architecture, 1935-42, Harvard Grad. Sch. Design, 1942-43. Head archtl. firm Arango & Murtra, Bogota, 1946-59; prof. architecture and urban design Nat. U., Bogota, 1945-47; vis. prof. Sch. Architecture U. Calif., Berkeley, 1956, 58; Pub. bldgs. dir. Colombia, 1948-49; pres. Colombian Soc. Architects, 1946-51, Colegio Engrs. and Architects of Colombia, 1955. Co-author basic plan for devel. Bogota, 1948; Author: (with C. Martinez) Architecture in Colombia, 1951, The Urbanization of the Earth, 1970; mem. Bd. Contbrs. Miami Herald. Recipient Excellence in Design awards Miami and Fla. chpts. AIA, 1967. Mem. AIA. Home: 6740 N Kendall Dr D103 Miami FL 33156

ARANT, EUGENE WESLEY, lawyer; b. North Powder, Oreg., Dec. 21, 1920; s. Ernest Elbert and Wanda (Haller) A.; m. Juanita Clark Flowers, Mar. 15, 1953; children: Thomas W., Kenneth E., Richard W. B.S. in Elec. Engring, Oreg. State U., 1943; J.D.,, U. So. Calif., 1949. Bar: Calif. 1950. Mem. engring. faculty U. So. Calif., 1947-51; practiced in Los Angeles, 1950-51; patent atty. Hughes Aircraft Co., Culver City, Calif., 1953-56; pvt. practice Los Angeles, 1957—. Author articles. Mem. La Mirada (Calif.) City Council, 1958-60; trustee Beverly Hills Presbyn. Ch., 1976-78. Served with AUS, 1943-46, 51-53. Mem. Am. Bar Assn., Am. Intellectual Property Law Assn., Los Angeles County Bar Assn., State Bar Calif., Los Angeles Patent Law Assn. (chmn. legis. com. 1981-82), Ala. State Bar. Democrat. Lodges: Century City Rotary. Home: 1248 Woodland Dr Santa Paula CA 93060 Office: Arant Kleinberg & Lerner 2049 Century Park E Los Angeles CA 90067

ARANYOS, ALEXANDER SANDOR, international operations executive; b. Zilina, Czechoslovakia; s. Ludwig and Ethel (Wilhelm) A.; m. Gertrude Reisman, Aug. 22, 1937; children: Alexander Paul, Vivian Jane. Degree Comml. Engring. cum laude, Grad. Sch. Commerce U. Prague, 1931. Adminstrv. asst. to pres. and export mgr. Coburg Mining & Foundry Co., Bratislava, Czechoslovakia, 1940-41; mgr. import div. Gen. Motors Distbrs., Republic of Panama, 1940-41; mgr. Latin Am. div. Van Raalte Co., N.Y.C., 1941-53; with Fruehauf Corp., Detroit, 1953—; v.p. internat. ops. Fruehauf Corp., 1956—, dir., 1973—; pres., dir. Fruehauf Internat. Ltd., 1957, chmn., dir., 1976-82, hon. chmn., 1982—; mem. adminstrv. council Viaturas PNV-Freuhauf S.A., Sao Paulo, Brazil; assoc. dir. Fruehauf Trailers (Australasia) Pty. Ltd.; bd. dirs. Fruehauf Finance Corp. (Pty.) Ltd., Melbourne, Australia, Fruehauf France, S.A., RIS-ORANGIS, France, Fruehauf de Mexico, S.A., Çoacalco, Nippon Fruehauf Co., Ltd., Tokyo, Henred-Fruehauf Trailers (Pty.) Ltd., Johannesburg, S. Africa, Fruehauf S.A., Madrid, Spain. Mem. regional export expansion council U.S. Dept. Commerce, 1970-73. Decorated French Legion of Honor. Mem. Research Inst. Am., AIM, Detroit Bd. Commerce, Internat. Execs. Assn. N.Y., World Trade Club Detroit, Am. Australian Assn. N.Y., C. of C. U.S. (internat. com.). Clubs: Rotary (N.Y.C.), Rockefeller Center Luncheon (N.Y.C.). Home: 2 Bridle Ln Sands Point NY 11050

ARAPOV, BORIS ALEKSANDROVICH, composer, educator; b. St. Petersburg, Russia, Sept. 12, 1905; s. Alexander Borisovich and Eliszbeta Ivanovna (Merz) A.; m. Tatiana Pavlovna Todorova, Dec. 2, 1933; children: Margarita, Tatiana. Student, conservatoire, Leningrad, 1923-30. Dozent Conservatoir, Leningrad, 1930-40, prof., 1940—; head dept. instrumentiae Conservatoire, Leningrad, 1951-74, compositons dept, 1974. Author: Analysis of Musical Form, 1956 rev. edit. 1982; contbr. articles to profl. jours.; composer 62 musical works, 1928-84. Recipient Order of Red Banner, 1953, People Artist of the Russian Fed. award Verhovnogo Sovietra of Russian Fedn, 1976, Order Lenin's award Verchovnogo Sovieta USSR, 1986. Mem. Union Soviet Composers (sec. 1977). Address: Prospekt Y Gagarina 35, kv 65, Leningrad 196135, USSR Office: Conservatoire, Teatralnaja Pl 3, Leningrad USSR

ARASKOG, RAND VINCENT, telecommunications and electronics company executive; b. Fergus Falls, Minn., Oct. 30, 1931; s. Randolph Victor and Hilfred Mathilda A.; m. Jessie Marie Gustafson, July 29, 1956. B.S.M.E., U.S. Mil. Acad., 1953; postgrad., Harvard U., 1953-54. Spl. asst. to dir. Dept. Def., Washington, 1954-59; dir. mktg. aero. div. Honeywell, Inc., Mpls., 1960-66; former v.p. ITT Corp.; group exec. ITT Aerospace, Electronics, Components and Energy Group, Nutley, N.J., 1971-76; pres. ITT Corp., N.Y.C., 1979-85, chief exec. officer, 1979—, chmn. bd., chmn. exec. and policy coms., 1980—; dir. ITT Corp., Hartford Ins., Dayton-Hudson Corp.; chmn. Nat. Security Telecommunications Adv. Com., from 1983. Served with U.S. Army, 1954-56. Mem. Aerospace Industries Assn. (bd. govs.), Air Force Assn. (mem. exec. council). Episcopalian. Office: ITT Corp 320 Park Ave New York NY 10022 *

ARAÚJO, JOSÉ EMILIO GONCALVES, soil scientist; b. Rio de Janeiro, Sept. 8, 1922; d. Antonio Araújo Ferná ndez and Emerenciana Goncalves; m. Laurinda Lopez, 1946; three children. Ed. Universidade Rural do Brasil, Universidade Federal Rural do Sul, Pelotas, Cornell U. Acting prof. Coll. Agr., Universidade Federal de Pelotas, 1946-48, prof., 1948-65; prof. Escola Agrotécnica Visconde de Graca, Pelotas, 1952-60; natural resources expert Inter-Am. Inst. Agrl. Scis., OAS, 1965, dir.-gen., 1970—; dir. Inter-Am. Program for Rural Devel. and Agrarian Reform of Secretariat of OAS, 1965-70; chief soils sect. Instituto Agronomico do Sul, 1947-50, dir., 1952-53, mem. permanent tech. council on soils, 1958-61. Author papers and books in field. Decorated officer Order Agrl. Merit, 1970, comdr., 1973, Order Isabel la Catolica (Spain). Mem. Brazilian Soc. for Soil Sci., Brazilian Geol. Soc., Brazilian Soc. for Advancement of Sci., Am. Soc. Agronomy, Latin-Am. Soc. Soil Sci., Internat. Soil Sci. Assn. Office: Inter-Am Inst for Coop on Agr, 2200 Coronado, Apart Post 55, San José Costa Rica *

ARBASINO, ALBERTO, writer; b. Voghera, Italy, Jan. 22, 1930; s. Edoardo and Gina (Manusardi) A. LLD, U. Milan, 1955. Mem. Italian Parliament Chamber of Deps., 1983-87. Author: Fratelli d'Italia, L'Anonimo Lombardo, Super-Eliogabalo, La Bella di Lodi; also essays; contbr. articles to profl. jours.; columnist La Repubblica, Italy. Home: Via E Gianturco 4, 00196 Rome Italy

ARBEL, BENJAMIN E., historian, educator; b. Petach-Tikva, Israel, June 23, 1945; s. Joseph and Alisa (Thorz) Ambach. BA cum laude, Tel-Aviv U., 1971; PhD, Hebrew U., Jerusalem, 1982. Lectr. history Tel-Aviv U., 1983—; adminstr. dept. history Tel-Aviv U., 1987—. Contbr. articles to profl. jours.; mem. editorial panel The Mediterranean Hist. Rev., 1986—. Served with Israeli Army, 1963-66. Mem. Soc. for Study of Crusades and the Latin East, Isreal Hist. Soc., Soc. for Study of the Later Middle Ages and the Renaissance. Office: U Tel-Aviv, Dept History, Tel-Aviv 69978, Israel

ARBER, WERNER, microbiologist; b. Gränichen, Switzerland, Jan. 3, 1929; married; 2 children. Ed., Aargau (Switzerland) Gymnasium, Eidgenössische Technische Hochschule, Zurich. Asst. Lab. Biophysics, U. Geneva, 1953-58, docent, then extraordinary prof. molecular genetics, 1962-70; research assoc. dept. microbiology U. So. Calif., 1958-59; vis. investigator dept. molecular biology U. Calif., Berkeley, 1970-71; prof. microbiology U. Basel (Switzerland), 1971. Co-recipient Nobel prize for physiology or medicine, 1978. Mem. Nat. Acad. Scis. (fgn. assoc.). Office: Biozentrum der Universitat, U Basel, 70 Klingelbergstrasse, CH-4056 Basel Switzerland

ARBMAN, STAFFAN OLOF, forest products company executive; b. Sundsvall, Sweden, Apr. 2, 1929; s. Olof Johannes and Hanna Maria (Andersson) A.; m. Kerstin Maria Lundback, June 5, 1954; children—Mats Olof, Elisabeth Kerstin, Helena Cecilia. Student Comml. Univs., Stockholm, 1950-52. Asst. mgr. Pilgrimstad AB (Sweden), 1952-56, Marma-Langror AB, Soderhamn, Sweden, 1956-61; sales mgr. Uddeholms AB (Sweden), 1961-66; mng. dir. Jon Jonsson AB, Ljusdal, Sweden, 1966-70; dir. timber div. Stora Kopparberg, Falun, Sweden, 1970-80; mng. dir. Assi Timber Co., Stockholm, 1980-88. Contbr. articles on forest products to profl. jours. Served with Swedish Army, 1948-49. Lutheran. Home: Skiftesvagen 11, S-18338 Taby Sweden Office: AB Statens Skogsindustrier Assi, Sveavagen 59, S-10522 Stockholm Sweden

ARCARO, HAROLD CONRAD, JR., lawyer; b. Providence, Aug. 9, 1935; s. Harold Conrad and Ines (Cicerchia) A.; divorced; children—Harold Conrad III, Meredith, James E., John T., Elizabeth T. A.B., Brown U., 1956; J.D., U. Va., 1959; LL.M. in Taxation, Boston U., 1963. Bar: R.I. 1959, U.S. Tax Ct. 1962, U.S. Dist. Ct. R.I. 1961, U.S. Ct. Appeals (1st cir.), U.S. Claims Ct. 1981, U.S. Supreme Ct. 1981. Assoc. Arcaro, Belilove & Kolodney, Providence, 1959-61; trial atty. Office of Regional Counsel, IRS, Boston, 1961-65; ptnr. Salter, McGowan, Arcaro & Swartz, 1965-81; propr. Law Offices of Harold C. Arcaro, Jr., Providence, 1981-85; ptnr. Arcaro & Reilly, 1985—; adj. prof. Bryant Coll. Grad. Tax Program, 1978—. Past pres. R.I. Civic Chorale, Arts R.I.; mem. corp. R.I. Hosp., Butler Hosp., Women and Infants Hosp., Bradley Hosp, Blue Cross Assn. R.I.; mem. R.I. Senate, 1967-72; fed. bar examiner, U.S. Dist. Ct.; mem. R.I. Commn. on Criminal Justice, 1978-85. Mem. ABA (civil and criminal penalties com. sect. of taxation, white collar crime com. criminal justice sect, litigation sect.), R.I. Bar Assn. (IRS regional liaison mem. 1974-82, sect. taxation, fed. bench bar com.), Nat. Assn. Criminal Def. Lawyers. Democrat. Roman Catholic. Clubs: Aurora Civic Assn. (Providence); Dunes, Point Judith Country (Narragansett, R.I.). Office: Arcaro & Reilly Suite 1040 Fleet National Bank Bldg Providence RI 02903

ARCE-CACHO, ERIC AMAURY, engineer, consultant; b. Morovis, P.R., Sept. 24, 1940; s. Eduardo and Celia Arce-Cacho; m. Carmen Ruth Gonaalez, Nov. 19, 1960; children—Eric Edmaury, Ruth Dagmar. Student, Coll. Engring., Myz, P.R., 1960, U.S. Air Force Adminstrn. Sch., 1963; M.A. in Econs., InterAm. U., Bay, P.R., 1972; M.A., Ch. of God Sch. of Theology, 1985. Registered profl. engr., P.R. Intercept control tech. Dept. Defense, San Juan, P.R., 1963-77; safety engring. cons., Bay, 1978-80; ; cons., researcher Energy Saving Equipment Inc., Bay, 1980—; dir. World Vocat. Sch. Missioneries, San Juan; dir., founder Internat. Recreational Areas, World Christian Embassies, 1986. Author: (poems) Soledad, 1979. Editor articles. Mem. Am. Soc. Safety Engrs., Am. Biog. Inst. Research Assn. (dep. gov.), Internat. Platform Assn. Clubs: Community (Fort Buchanan, P.R.), Gulf Course. Avocations: paso fino horse riding. Home: C-17 Forest Hills Bay PR 00619

ARCHER, CARL MARION, oil and gas company executive; b. Spearman, Tex., Dec. 16, 1920; s. Robert Barton and Gertrude Lucille (Sheets) A.; student U. Tex., Austin, 1937-39; m. Peggy Garrett, Aug. 22, 1939; children—Mary Frances, Carla Lee. Pres., Anchor Oil Co., Spearman, 1959—, Carl M. Archer Farms, Spearman, 1960—; gen. mgr. Speartex Grain Co., Spearman, 1967—, Speartex Oil & Gas Co., 1974—. Chmn. County Democratic Com., 1969—. Mem. Tex. Grain Dealers Assn., Tex. Grain and Feed Assn., Ind. Royalty Owners and Producers Assn., Nat. Grain Dealers Assn., Am. Petroleum Landmen Assn., Nat., Tex. Bankers Assn. Mem. Ch. of Christ. Clubs: Perryton, Borger Country, Amarillo. Home: 304 S Endicott Spearman TX 79081 Office: 405 Collard St Spearman TX 79081

ARCHER, JAMES HOWARD, architect; b. Nairobi, Kenya, Mar. 30, 1937; s. Howard Dennis and Kathleen Aida (Newton-Moss) A.; m. Linda Hamilton Werner, Dec. 18, 1987; children: Mathew Francis, Alison Jean, Hugh James. Diploma in architecture, Sch. Architecture, Oxford, Eng., 1960. Registered architect, Kenya, Tanzania, Eng. Ptnr. Cobb Archer & Ptnrs., Kampala, Uganda, 1963-72, Watkins Gray Woodgate Internat., Manchester, Eng., 1973-75; lectr. U. Nairobi, 1975-76, sr. lectr., 1976-81; founding ptnr. Planning Systems Services, Nairobi, 1978—; sr. ptnr. Planning Systems Services, Tanzania, 1979—, Conservation Planning, Dar Es Salaam, 1980—, Interplan Partnership, Kampala, 1981—; dir. Planning Mgmt. Ltd., Nairobi, 1986—; hon. sec. East African Inst. Architects, Nairobi, 1961-63, examiner, 1976-80; chmn. Com. Revision Bldg. Regulations, Kampala, 1972. Prin. works include: detailed design of Dubai Internat. Airport Arrivals Bldg., 1986, Fedha Towers, Nairobi, 1985. Mem. Royal Inst. British Architects, Archtl. Assn. Kenya, Uganda Soc. Architects. Club: Aero of East Africa (Nairobi). Office: Planning Mgmt Ltd, PO Box 57009, Nairobi Kenya

ARCHER, JEFFREY HOWARD, author, politician; b. Apr. 15, 1940; s. William and Lola (Cook) A.; m. Mary Weeden, 1966; 2 sons. Student Wellington Sch., Brasenose Coll., Oxford. Mem. GLC for Havering, 1966-70; M.P. for Louth (Conservative), 1969-74; dep. chmn. Conservative Party, 1985—. Mem. exec. Brit. Theatre Mus. Author: Not a Penny More, Not a Penny Less, 1975; Shall We Tell the President?, 1977; Kane and Abel, 1979; A Quiver Full of Arrows, 1980; The Prodigal Daughter, 1982; First Among Equals, 1984; A Matter of Honor, 1986. Avocations: theatre; cinema; cricket.

ARCHER, JOHN SKIDMORE, civil engineer; b. Phila., Nov. 10, 1923; s. John Blazer and Hattie Leo (Skidmore) A.; B.S. in Civil Engring., W.Va. U., 1944; M.S. in Civil Engring., M.I.T., 1948, Sc.D., 1950; m. Juanita Hadaway, Sept. 21, 1985; children from previous marriage: John Beatty, Evelyn Eleanor Archer Mayfield, Nathan Charles, Philip James, Rosemary Rene Archer Farley; stepchildren: Brenda Gayle Krieter, Lynn Denise Martin, Dana Risé Shebeck, Randy Lee Echols. Bridge draftsman B.& O. R.R., 1944-46; bridge designer State Road Commn. W.Va., 1946-47; research asso. M.I.T., Cambridge, 1950-51, asst. prof. civil engring. dept., 1951-55; project structures engr. Gen. Dynamics Corp., Ft. Worth, 1955-60; lectr. dept. civil engring. So. Meth. U., Dallas, 1955-60; mgr. dynamics dept. TRW/S&TG, Redondo Beach, Calif., 1960-65, asst. mgr. mech. engring. lab., 1966-75, sr. tech. staff, mech. systems ops., 1976-85, sr. tech. staff, controls and mech. systems ops., 1986— engring. and test div., TRW/S&TG; lectr. dept. civil engring. U. So. Calif., Los Angeles, 1960-63; lectr. structural dynamics and analysis UCLA, 1961-63, 65, 66; guest lectr. U. Wis., 1968, Cornell U., 1968; guest participant Joint U.S.-Japanese Symposium on Matrix Structural Analysis, Tokyo, 1969; speaker. Registered profl. engr., Tex., Calif. Mem. ASCE (com. exptl. analysis 1956-59, chmn. com. electronic computation 1961-64), AIAA, Sigma Xi, Tau Beta Pi, Phi Kappa Alpha. Mormon. Club: King Harbor Yacht. Contbr. articles on finite-element structural analysis, advanced composite materials applications, precision spacecraft antenna reflectors and space station solar dynamic power to engring. jours.; patentee in field. Home: 30827 Rue Valois Rancho Palos Verdes CA 90274 Office: TRW/S&TG R4/1190 One Space Park Redondo Beach CA 90278

ARCHER, RICHARD EARL, product designer and alternative energy design cons.; b. Springfield, Ill., Aug. 24, 1945; s. Earl Wiley and Era Marie (Fentress) A.; m. Elizabeth Lou Lutz, Aug. 9, 1969; children—Jeremy Richard, William Earl. B.A. in Design, So. Ill. U., Carbondale, 1970; M.S., Gov.'s State U., 1979. Instr. design So. Ill. U., 1971-79, coordinator design program, 1979-80, asst. prof. comprehensive planning and design, 1980—; dir. Applied Alternatives. Mem. Nat. Alcohol Fuels Commn., 1980; chmn. Carbondale Energy Futures Task Force, 1980-81; mem. Ill. Legislature Alternative Energy Commn., 1981-83; mem. adv. panel US. Congl. Office Tech. Assessment, 1982. Editor: Ill. Solar Resource Adv. Council Grants Newsletter, 1979-81; contbr. articles to profl. jours.; originator great cardboard boat regatta. Recipient Outstanding Tchr. Year award Coll. Human Resources, So. Ill. U., 1979; U.S. Dept. Energy grantee, 1979-81; U.S. Dept. Labor grantee, 1978-79; Ill. Dept. Energy grantee, 1980-81; named Outstanding Tchr. of Yr., Sch. Art, 1985. Mem. Solar Lobby (dir. 1978-80). Home: RR 1 Box 667 DeSoto IL 62924 Office: So Ill U Design Program Bldg 0720 Carbondale IL 62901

ARCHER, STEWART HENRY, geophysicist; b. Burton-Upon-Trent, Eng., Aug. 3, 1949; s. Samuel James and Edith Rose (Salt) A.; m. Susan McLean Smith, June 2, 1973; children: Simon Christopher, Thomas David, Rosemary Jenifer. BS, U. Birmingham, Eng., 1970; MS, U. Durham, Eng., 1971; PhD, DIC, Imperial Coll., London, 1976. Research geophysicist Geophys. Service Internat., Bedford, Eng., 1975—. Designer computer programs for modeling geologic structures from seismic data. Mem. Soc. Exploration Geophysicists, European Assn. Exploration Geophysicists. Office: Geophys Service Internat, Manton Ln, Bedford MK41 7PA, England

ARCHES, JOSEFINA OCBINA, pediatrician; b. Roxas City, Capiz, Philippines, June 12, 1944; d. Jose Arcenas and Cinderella Olivera (Ocbina) A. BA, U. Santo Tomas, Manila, 1964; BS, U. of East, Manila, 1966; MD, U. of East, Quezon City, Philippines, 1971. Diplomate Philippine Bd. Pediatrics. Intern U. the East Ramon Magsaysay Meml. Med. Ctr., Quezon City, 1970-71; resident in pediatrics Children's Med. Ctr., Quezon City, 1972-76; pvt. practice pediatrics Quezon City, 1976-79, 86—; cons. pediatrician Emmanuel Hosp., Roxas City, Philippines, 1977-78; resident in pediatric cardiology Philippine Heart Ctr. for Asia, Quezon City, 1979-80; sr. registrar II in pediatrics Plateau State Health Services Mgmt. Bd., Vom Christian Hosp., Nigeria, 1981-85. Mem. Philippine Med. Assn., Philippine Pediatric Soc., Inc., Quezon City Med. Soc. Roman Catholic. Home and Office: 8-A Marikit St, W Triangle Homes Diliman, 1104 Quezon City Metro Manila, Philippines

ARCHIBALD, MICHAEL MONTBATTON, banker; b. St. Georges, Grenada, July 13, 1947; s. Fisher Jellico and Evadne (Gordon) A.; m. Terese Nicole Sylvester; children: Shaka Leon, Reina Nkeisha. Grad. high sch., Grenada; cert. banking, Stonier Sch.-Rutgers U., 1984. From teller to officer-in-charge Can. Imperial Bank Commerce, Sauteurs, Grenada, 1967-73; internat. auditor Can. Imperial Bank Commerce, Toronto, Ont., 1973-85; acct. Can. Imperial Bank Commerce, St. Georges, 1984-85; mgr. Can. Imperial Bank Commerce, Grenville, Grenada, 1979-85, Grenada Devel. Bank, St. Georges, 1979-80; gen. mgr. Nat. Comml. Bank, St. Georges, 1980—; chmn. Grenada Mktg. and Nat. Importing Bd., 1985—. Mem. Grenada Nat. Econ. Council, 1986—; bd. dirs. Nat. Devel. Found., East Caribbean Orgn. Devel. Founds. Mem. Caribbean Assn. Industry and Commerce (bd. dirs. 1987—), Grenada C. of Industry and C. (bd. dirs. 1985—). Methodist. Lodge: Rotary (treas. Grenada). Office: Nat Comml Bank Grenada Ltd, Hillsborough and Halifax Sts, PO Box 57, Saint Georges Grenada

ARCHIBALD, RUSSELL DEAN, management consultant; b. Independence, Mo., Jan. 10, 1924; s. David Myron and Henrietta McKinley (Roberts) A.; B.S., U. Mo., 1948; M.S. in Mech. Engring., U. Tex., 1956; m. Marion Alice Eobets, May 25, 1946; children: Donna, Barbara, Robert, Mark. Mech. engr. Creole Petroleum Corp., Venezuela, 1948-51; sr. engr. Aerojet Gen. Corp., 1959-60; dept. mgr. Hughes Aircraft Co., Los Angeles, 1961-62, Hughes Dynamics, 1963-64; pres. CPM Systems, Inc., Los Angeles, 1964-65, v.p. CPM Systems, div. Informatics, Inc., Los Angeles, 1965-67; assoc. Booz Allen & Hamilton, Los Angeles, 1967-69; v.p., gen. mgr. Symcon Marine Corp., Long Beach, Calif., 1969-70; asst. dir. Office of pres., IT&T, N.Y.C., 1970-75; dir., spl. projects Société Anonyme DBA (Bendix), Paris, 1975-76; v.p. internat. planning Bendix Corp., Southfield, Mich., 1977-82; pres. Archibald Assocs., Los Angeles; v.p. Growth Mgmt. Ctr., Palos Verdes, Calif.; prin. Tech-Mark Cons. Group, Westlake Village, Calif.; bd. dirs. Essex Specialty Products, Inc.Served with USAAF, 1943-46, USAF, 1951-58. Mem. Project Mgmt. Inst. (past v.p.), Internat. Project Mgmt. Assn., The Planning Forum. Episcopalian. Author: (with R.L. Villoria) Network Based Management Systems, 1967; Managing High Technology Programs and Projects, 1976. Address: 343 Medio Dr Los Angeles CA 90049

ARDEN, JOHN, playwright; b. Barnsley, Eng., Oct. 26, 1930; s. Charles Alwyn and Anne Elizabeth (Layland) A.; m. Margaretta Ruth D'Arcy, 1957; 4 children. Student Sedbergh Sch., King's Coll., Cambridge, Edinburgh Coll. Art. Fellow in playwriting Bristol U., 1959-60; vis. lectr. politics and drama NYU, 1967; Regent's lectr. U. Calif.-Davis, 1973; writer in residence U. New England, Australia, 1975; co-founder Corrandulla Arts Club, 1971, Galway Theatre Workshop, 1975. Plays: All Fall Down, 1955, The Life of Man, 1956, The Waters of Babylon, 1957, Live Like Pigs, 1958, Sergeant Musgrave's Dance, 1959, Soldier, Soldier, 1960, The Business of Good Government, 1960, (with Margaretta d'Arcy) The Happy Haven, 1960, Wet Fish, 1962, The Workhouse Donkey, 1963, Ironhand, 1963, (the following plays all with Margaretta D'Arcy) Ars Longa Vita Brevis, 1964, Armstrong's Last Goodnight, 1964, Left Handed Liberty 1965, Friday's Hiding, 1966, The Royal Pardon, 1966, Muggins is a Martyr, 1968, The Hero Rises Up, 1968, The Ballygombeen Bequest, 1972, The Island of the Mighty, 1972, Keep These People Moving, 1972, The Non-Stop Connolly Show, 1975, Pearl, 1977, Vandaleur's Folly, 1978, The Little Grey Home in the West, 1978, The Making of Muswell Hill, 1979, The Manchester Enthusiasts, 1984; TV documentary (with Margaretta d'Arcy): Profile of Sean O'Casey, 1973; essays: To Present the Pretence, 1977; novel: Silence Among the Weapons, 1982. Office: care Margaret Ramsay Ltd, 14A Goodwin's Ct, London WC2 England *

ARDITTI, FRED D., economist, educator; b. N.Y.C., Jan. 30, 1939; s. David A. and Marie (Ben Nathan) A.; m. Margaret Monroe, Jan. 1981; children: Elizabeth Marie, Anne Sarah, David Frederick. B.S. in Elec. Engring, M.I.T., 1960, M.S. in Indsl. Mgmt, 1962, Ph.D. in Econs, 1966. Economist Rand Corp., Santa Monica, Calif., 1965-67; lectr., asst. prof. fin. U. Calif., Berkeley, 1967-71; from assoc. prof. to prof. fin. U. Fla., Gainesville, 1971-77; Walter J. Matherly chair fin. and econs. U. Fla., 1974-80, chmn. dept. econs., 1977-80; v.p. research, chief economist Chgo. Merc. Exchange, 1980-82; pres. GNP Fin. Inc., 1982-86, GNP Commodities Inc., 1984-86, Drexel, Burnham, Lambert Quantitative Asset Mgmt. Group, Chgo., 1986—; vis. prof. Hebrew U., 1973, U. Toronto, 1976-77, U. Chgo., 1981-83. Contbr. articles to profl. jours., chpts. to books. NSF fellow; Ford Found. research grantee; NDEA fellow; other fellowships. Mem. Am. Econs. Assn., Am. Fin. Assn. Jewish. Office: Drexel Burnham Lambert Inc Quantitative Asset Mgmt Group 1 S Wacker Dr Suite 1580 Chicago IL 60606

ARDUINI, FRANCA, government official; b. Rimini, Italy, Aug. 19, 1943; d. Corrado and Augusta (Lugli) A. BA, Urbino U., Italy, 1967. Librarian Florence Nat. Library, Italy, 1971-86; dir. library Bologna U. Library, Italy, 1986—. Contbr. articles to profl. jours. Mem. Italian Libraries Assn. Office: Univ Library, Zamboni 35, 40126 Bologna Italy

AREKAPUDI, VIJAYALAKSHMI, obstetrician-gynecologist; b. Davajigudem, Andhra Pradesh, India, Sept. 28, 1948; came to U.S., 1974; parents: Subba Rao and Ramatulasamma (Ravi) Gondi; m. Bapu P. Arekapudi, May 5, 1974; children: Smitha, Swathi. MBBS, Guntur Med. Coll., Andhra Pradesh, India, 1970; DGO, Coll. Physicians and Surgeons Bombay, 1973. Intern Ill. Masonic Med. Ctr., Chgo., 1975-76, resident in ob-gyn, 1976-79, jr. attending staff, 1979-82, assoc. attending staff, 1982-84, attending physician, 1985—; practice medicine specializing in ob-gyn Lake Shore Med. Assocs., Ltd., Chgo., 1979—, sec., treas., 1981—. Fellow Am. Coll. Obstetricians-Gynecologists. Democrat. Hindu. Office: Lake Shore Med Assocs Ltd 2734 N Lincoln Ave Chicago IL 60614

ARENA, ALAN JOSEPH, manufacturing executive; b. Chgo., June 23, 1950; s. Joseph James and Madelyn Adele (Castrovillari) A.; m. Mary Ann Guglielmo, Nov. 26, 1972 (dec.); 1 child, Monica Kristen. BS in Mech. and Aerospace Engring., Ill. Inst. Tech., 1972; MME, Calif. State U., Los Angeles, 1984. Research and devel. engr. Fiat-Allis CMI, Deerfield, Ill., 1973-80; sr. project engr. Signet Sci. Co., El Monte, Calif., 1980-83; project mgr. def. electronics ops. Autonetics Strategic Systems div. Rockwell Internat., Anaheim, Calif., 1983-87; dir. engring. Ride and Show Engring., Inc., San Dimas, Calif., 1987—; Instr. Calif. Poly. Inst., Pomona, 1983—. Patentee in field. Roman Catholic. Home: 12515 Sterling Pl Chino CA 91710 Office: Ride and Show Engring Inc 276 E Arrow Hwy San Dimas CA 91773

ARENDALL, CHARLES BAKER, JR., lawyer; b. Portsmouth, Va., Feb. 13, 1915; s. Charles B. and Kate (Peacock) A.; m. Nan Eager Boone, Oct. 26, 1944; children—Nan Boone McGinley, Lawrence Barclay Manley, Kathryn Baker Weller, Elizabeth Charles Tilney. A.B., U. Richmond, 1935; LL.B. cum laude, Harvard, 1938. Bar: Ala. bar 1938. Asso. firm Smith & Johnston, Mobile, 1938-41; mem. firm Hand, Arendall, Bedsole, Greaves & Johnston (and predecessor), Mobile, 1941—; Adv. bd. Cumberland Law Sch., Samford U. Trustee Mobile Coll. Fellow Am. Coll. Trial Lawyers; mem. Internat., Am., Ala., Inter-Am., Mobile bar assns., Am. Judicature Soc., Assn. Bar City N.Y., Internat. Assn. Ins. Counsel, Am. Law Inst., Assn. Railroad Trial Counsel, Omicron Delta Kappa, Pi Delta Epsilon, Alpha Psi Omega, Kappa Sigma. Baptist. Clubs: Athelstan, Lakewood, Country. Office: First Nat Bank Bldg Mobile AL 36601

ARENDS, TULIO, federal official; b. Coro, Venezuela, Nov. 11, 1918; s. Juan de Dios and Dalinda (Wever) A.; m. Trina Rodriguez. MD, U. Cen. Venezuela, Caracas, 1946; degree in hematology, Duke U., 1950-53. Pres. sci. commn. faculty of medicine U. Cen. Venezuela, 1976-78; mem. superior council U. Simón Bolívar, Caracas, 1978-79; dean U. Nat. Experimental Francisco de Miranda, Coro, Venezuela, 1978-82; prof. faculty Simón Bolívar U. Cambridge, Eng., 1979-80; advisor sci. and tech. commn. Chamber of Deps., Caracas, 1982—; pres. Consejo Nacional de Investigaciones Cientificas y Tecnologicas, Caracas, 1985—; researcher Venezuelan Inst. Sci. Investigation, Caracas, 1958—. Recipient Nat. prize José María Vargas, 1956. Mem. Internat. Soc. Hematology (coordinator hematologist exchange program 1976-78, mem. expert panel 1974—, 2d prize sci. exhbn. 1956), Internat. Assn. Human Biologists, Internat. Soc. Blood Transfusion, German Soc. Hematology, Venezuelan Soc. Hematology. Office: CONICIT, Ave Prin Coritjos de Lourdes, 1071 Caracas Venezuela

ARENOWITZ, ALBERT HAROLD, psychiatrist; b. N.Y.C., Jan. 12, 1925; s. Louis Isaac and Lena Helen (Skovron) A.; m. Betty Jane Wiener, Oct. 11, 1953; children: Frederick Stuart, Diane Helen. BA with honors, U. Wis., 1948; MD, U. Va., 1951. Diplomate Am. Bd. Psychiatry, Am. Bd. Child Psychiatry. Intern Kings County Gen. Hosp., Bklyn., 1951-52; resident in psychiatry Bronx (N.Y.) VA Hosp., 1952-55; postdoctoral fellow Youth Guidance Ctr., Worcester, Mass., 1955-57; dir. Ctr. for Child Guidance, Phila., 1962-65, Hahnemann Med. Service Eastern State Sch. and Hosp., Trevose, Pa., 1965-68; dir., tng. dir. Child and Adolescent Psychiat. Clinic, Phila. Gen. Hosp., 1965-67; asst. clin. prof. psychiatry Jefferson Med. Coll., Phila., 1974-76; exec. dir. Child Guidance and Mental Health Clinics, Media, Pa., 1967-74, Intercommunity Child Guidance Ctr., Whittier, Calif., 1976—; clin. asst. prof. child psychiatry Hahnemann Med. Coll., Phila., 1966-74; asst. clin. prof. psychiatry U. Wis., Madison, 1960-62, clin. asst. prof. psychiatry, behavioral scis., and family medicine U. So. Calif., Los Angeles, 1976—; mem. med. staff Presbyn. Intercommunity Hosp., Whittier, 1976—. Pres. Whittier Area Coordinating Council, 1978-80. Served with USAF, 1943-45. Fellow Am. Psychiat. Assn., Am. Acad. Child Psychiatry; mem. AMA, AAAS, Los Angeles County Med. Assn., So. Calif. Psychiat. Soc., So. Calif. Soc. Child Psychiatry, Phila. Soc. Adolescent Psychiatry (pres. 1967-68). Office: Intercommunity Child Guidance Ctr 8106 S Broadway Whittier CA 90606

AREVALO ALBUREZ, RAUL HORACIO, pharmaceutical company executive; b. San Martin Jilotepeque, Chimaltenango, Guatemala, June 22, 1949; s. Jose Venancio and Marta Elena (Alburez) Arevalo; m. Ana Maria Rabe, May 19, 1973; children: Ana del Pilar, Marta Lucia, Fabiola Alejandra. MD, U. San Carlos, Guatemala City, 1973; degree in internal medicine, Mt. Sinai Hosp., Miami, Fla., 1977; degree in tech. immunology, Pharmacia Aktienbolaget, Uppsala, Sweden, 1978; degree in bus. mgmt., Inst. Centroamericano Administración Empresas, San Jose, Costa Rica, 1985; grad. mgmt. devel. program, Pharma Ausbildung, Egerkingen, Switzerland, 1987. Medical diplomate Programa de Alta Gerencia. Intern Herrera-Llerandi Hosp., Guatemala City, 1971-73; resident Guatemalan Heart League, Guatemala City, 1974; med. cons. Ames div. Miles Labs., San Jose, 1977; med. dir. Knoll Centroamericana, S.A., Guatemala City, 1978, Central Am. Sci. Office, S-W, Guatemala City and Panama City, 1979-80; country mgr. Sandoz, S.A., Guatemala City, 1981-82; dir. tng. and devel. Sandoz Latinoamericana, S.A., Panama City, 1983-87; mktg. mgr. Sandoz Peru, Lima, Peru, 1988—. Editor: Hyperlipidemias in Guatemala, 1974; author: (manual) Basic Supervisory Skills, 1985; editor videotapes on pharm. tng.; contbr. articles to profl. publs. Mem. Am. Soc. Tng. and Devel., Am. Mgmt. Assn., Guatemalan Mgmt. Assn., Guatemalan Med. Coll., Aircraft Owners and Pilots Assn., Jaycees. Roman Catholic. Club: Flying Physicians. Home: 18 Avenida 0-14, Vista Hermosa II, Guatemala City Guatemala Office: Sandoz Peru, Paseo de la Republica, 3755, San Isidro 27, Lima Peru

ARGENTIERI, FEDERIGO, political scientist, researcher; b. Rome, Aug. 24, 1953; s. Benedetto and Elena (Federzoni) A.; m. Irene Gironi Carnevale, Sept. 4, 1981; 1 child, Giulia. Grad. Polit. Sci., U. Rome, 1985. Dep. head internat dept. Italian Communist Youth Fedn., Rome, 1977-79; sec., mem. bur. World Fedn. Dem. Youth, Budapest, Hungary, 1979-82; coordinator, researcher Gramsci Research Inst. Ctr. for Studies on Socialist Countries, Rome, 1983-87; researcher Centro Studi Di Politica Internazionale, Rome, 1987—; mem. sci. bd. Gramsci Inst., Rome, 1983—. Co-author: L'Ottobre Ungherese, 1986, La Rivoluzione Ungherese, Imre Nagy, la Sinistra, 1988; contbr. periodicals, jours. Mem. Italian Communist Party. Home: Via Leone IV 38, I-00192 Rome Italy Office: Centro Studi Di Politica, Internazionale, Via Della Vite 13, I-00187 Rome Italy

ARGUE, JOHN CLIFFORD, lawyer; b. Glendale, Calif., Jan. 25, 1932; s. J. Clifford and Catherine Emily (Clements) A.; m. Leah Elizabeth Moore, June 29, 1963; children: Elizabeth Anne, John Michael. AB in Commerce and Fin., Occidental Coll., 1953, LLD (hon.), 1987; LLB, U. So. Calif., 1956. Bar: Calif. 1957. Since practiced in Los Angeles; mem. firm Argue & Argue, 1958-59, Flint & MacKay, 1960-72, Argue, Pearson, Harbison & Myers, 1972—; bd. dirs. Cal Fed Inc., Calif. Fed. Savs. and Loan Assn. LAACO, Ltd., Trust Services Am., Inc., Avery Internat.; adv. bd. Automobile Club So. Calif., 1983-88. Pres. So. Calif. Com. Olympic Games, 1972—; founding-chmn. Los Angeles Olympic Organizing Com., 1978-79; bd. dirs. Amateur Athletic Found. Los Angeles; trustee, vice chmn. Pomona Coll., U. So. Calif., UCLA Med. Scis., Mus. Sci. and Industry; chmn. bd. Greater Los Angeles affiliate Am. Heart Assn., 1982, chmn. adv. bd. 1985—; chmn. Verdugo Hills Hosp., chmn., 1979, chmn. adv. bd., 1983—; bd. govs. Alumni Occidental Coll., 1962-64; pres. Town Hall Calif., 1985, U. So. Calif. Assocs.; chmn. PGA Championship, 1983, La. Sports Council, 1986—; vice chmn., sec. Los Angeles 2000 Com.; bd. dirs. Boy Scouts Am. Served with U.S. Army, 1956-58. Mem. Los Angeles Bar Assn., State Bar Calif., Nat. Club Assn. (dir.) So. Calif. Golf Assn. (pres. 1979), Calif. Golf Assn. (v.p. 1979), Los Angeles Area C. of C. (dir., vice chmn.), Cen. City Assn. (bd. dirs.), Phi Delta Phi, Alpha Tau Omega. Clubs: Chancery (pres. 1985-6), California (pres. 1983-84), Los Angeles Athletic, Riviera Country, Oakmont Country (pres. 1972), Los Angeles Country (Los Angeles); Flint Canyon Tennis (La Canada, Calif.). Lodge: Rotary (Los Angeles). Home: 1314 Descanso Dr La Canada CA 91011 Office: 801 S Flower St Suite 5000 Los Angeles CA 90017

ARIARAJAH, WESLEY SEEVARATNAM, clergyman, church administrator; b. Jaffna, Sri Lanka, Dec. 2, 1941; s. Ponniah David and Grace Annalukshimi (Sinnappu) S.; m. Christine Shyamala Chinniah, Dec. 7, 1953; children: Sudharshini, Niroshini, Anushini. BSc, Madras Christian Coll., India, 1963; BD, United Theol. Coll., Bangalore, India, 1966; ThM, Princeton (N.J.) Seminary, 1972; M. Phil., U. London, 1974, PhD, 1987. Ordained to ministry Methodist Ch. Minister Meth. Ch. of Sri Lanka, Jaffna, 1966-68; lectr. Theol. Coll. Lanka, Pilimatalawa, Sri Lanka, 1969-71; chmn. North and East Dist. Meth. Ch., Jaffna, 1974-81; program staff WCC program on Dialogue with People of Living Faiths, Geneva, 1981-83; dir. World Council Chs. program on Dialogue with People of Living Faiths, Geneva, 1983—. Author: Dialogue, 1980, The Bible and People of Other Faiths, 1986; contbr. articles to profl. jours. Home: Avenue des Amazones 16, 1224 Chene Bougeries, Geneva Switzerland Office: World Council Chs Dialogue, 150 Rte de Ferney, CH1211 Geneva 20 Switzerland

ARIAS, JULIO ERNESTO, insurance company executive; b. Panama City, Panama, May 9, 1945; s. Juan Bautista and Elvira (Zubieta) A.; m. Dilia Raquel de la Guardia, Aug. 15, 1965; children: Giselle Marie, Marissa Raquel, Julio Ernesto. BBA, Nichols Coll., Dudley, Mass., 1964. Cert. ins. underwriter. Asst. mgr. Compania Gen. de Seguros, S.A., Panama City, 1965-70; pres., chief exec. officer Internat. Fin. Corp., S.A., Panama City, 1970-78, Estacion Pasadena, S.A./Transportes Especiales, S.A., Panama City, 1978-84; sec., chief exec. officer Compania Universal de Seguros, S.A., Panama City, 1984—; sec. Grupo Clayco, Panama City, 1980—; bd. dirs. Seven Eleven, S.A., Panama City. Mem. Assn. Panameña de Aseguradores. Roman Catholic. Lodge: Rotary. Home: Ave 4 B Sur, Box 7385, 05 Panama City Panama Office: Compania Universal de Seguros SA, Calle 50 #60 Box 1840, 9A Panama City Panama

ARIAS, MARGOT FONTEYN DE (MARGOT FONTEYN), prima ballerina; b. Reigate, Eng., May 18, 1919; Litt.D. honoris causa, Leeds U.; Mus.D. honoris causa, U. London; Mus. D., Oxford, 1959, U. Manchester, 1966; LL.D., Cambridge, 1962, Edinburgh, 1963; hon. doctorate Durham U., 1982; m. Roberto E. Arias, 1955. Decorated comdr. Order Brit. Empire, 1951, dame comdr., 1956; Order Finnish Lion, 1960; Order Estacio de Sa (Guanabara State, Brazil), 1973; Benjamin Franklin medal Royal Soc. Arts, London, 1974; recipient Anglo-German Shakespeare prize, 1977. Pres., Royal Acad. Dancing, 1954—; appeared in film I am a Dancer, 1972; narrator BBC-TV series The Magic of Dance, 1979; Chancellor Durham U., 1982—. Author: Margot Fonteyn (autobiography), 1975; A Dancer's World, 1978; The Magic of Dance, 1980. Address: Royal Opera House, Covent Garden, London WC2, England *

ARIAS SANCHEZ, OSCAR, president of Costa Rica; b. Sept. 13, 1941; m. Margarita Penon; children: Silvia Eugenia, Oscar Felipe. Licenciatura en Ambas, U. Costa Rica, 1967; M. in Polit. Sci., U. Essex, London, 1967. Prof., U. Costa Rica, 1969-72; mem. econ. council Pres. of Republic of Costa Rica, 1970-72, minister Nat. Planning and Polit. Econs., Costa Rica, 1972-77, mem. Legis. Assembly, 1978-82, pres. Republic of Costa Rica, 1986—; internat. sec. Nat. Liberation Party, 1975, gen. sec., 1979—; v.p. bd. dirs. Cen. Bank of Costa Rica, 1970-72, dir., 1972-77; bd. dirs. Tech. Inst., Costa Rica, 1974-77; mem. Nat. Council Univ. Rectors, 1974-77; bd. dirs. Internat. U. Exchange Fund, Switzerland, 1976; participant numerous profl. confs. and seminars throughout the world. Author: Grupos De Presion En Costa Rica, 1970; Quien Gobierna En Costa Rica, 1976; Democracia, Independencia y Sociedad Latino-americana, 1977; Los Caminos Para El Desarollo De Costa Rica, 1977; Nuevos Rumbos Para El Desarrollo Costarricense, 1980. Contbr. chpts. to books, articles in govt. and politics to profl. jours. and mags. Recipient Nobel Peace prize, 1987. Office: Oficina del Presidente, San Jose Costa Rica *

ARIENZO, MARIANO CARLO, organization administrator; b. Napoli, Italy, Jan. 10, 1920; s. Gabriele M. Arienzo and Nunzi (Carla) Carlone; m. Tosca Mafalda Sponticcia. B in Civil Engring., U. Naples, 1943; MS in Radar Electronics, Inst. of Telecommunications, Rome, 1953. Registered profl. engr., Italy. Officer Italian Army, Rome, 1940-57, NATO Shape, Paris, 1957-62; bd. dirs. Gen. Telephone and Electronics, Geneva, 1962-69, Selenia Internat. Mktg., Rome, 1969-84; sec. gen. Iranian-Italian C. of C., Rome, 1985—. Author: Radiopropagation, 1959, Iran, 1986. Decorated Bronze Medal, Yugoslavia. Christian Democrat. Roman Catholic. Clubs: Freccia Alata (Rome), Canoa (Castel Gandolfo). Office: Italian-Iranian C of C, 169 B Corso Trieste, 00198 Rome Italy

ARIFIN, HOUTMAN ZAINAL, banker; b. Kediri, Indonesia, July 27, 1950; s. Mohammad Zainal and Siti Fatimah Arifin; m. Srie Rezeki; children: Eva Maulini, Bram Zulvi, Evi Muwage. MA, U. Beverly Hills (Calif.), 1987. Several clerical positions Citibank NA, Jakarta, Indonesia, 1970-74, ops. officer, 1975-84, resident auditor, 1984-87, v.p., 1987—; bd. dirs. Bank Angkasa Putra; instr. Banking U. Perbanas, Jakarta, 1985—; sr. cons. P.T. Indoconsult, 1988—. Club: ISCI. Home: 33 Jalan Ulujami, Gung H Buang, Jakarta 12250, Indonesia Office: Citibank, 70-A Jalan Jend. Sudirman Kavash, Jakarta 12930, Indonesia

ARIKAWA, HIROO, industrial company executive; b. Tokyo, Nov. 27, 1926; s. Goroosaku and Ishi (Kawashima) A.; m. Mitsuko Kimura, Nov. 13, 1955; children: Kayoko, Kimiko. Grad., Japan Mil. Acad., 1945. Mgr. Tokiwa Trading Co., Tokyo, 1948-58; pres., chief exec. officer S.O.C. Corp. (formerly San-O Indsl. Co., Ltd.), Tokyo, 1958—, Nagano (Japan) S.O.C. Corp., 1967—, San-O Indsl. Corp., N.Y.C., 1970—, Brasan-O Electronica Ltda., Sao Paulo, Brazil, 1973—; mem. indsl. adv. conf. Underwriters Labs, Inc., Chgo., 1973—; mem. Patent Commn.for Small to Medium Sized Enterprises, Japan Inst. Invention and Innovation, Tokyo, 1986—; dir. Japan Inst. Invention and Innovation, Tokyo, 1988—. Co-author: Electrical Fuses, 1987; patentee elec. fuse, other numerous patents in Japan and U.S. Trustee Den-En-Chofu Futaba Sch., Tokyo, 1986—. Served with Japanese Army, 1944-45. Recipient Dark Blue Ribbon Prime Minister's Office, 1982-87, Encouragement prize Chmn. Patent Attys. Assn., 1985, Dir. Gen. Japanese Patent Office, 1986. Lodge: Rotary. Office: SOC Corp 43 Mori Bldg, 3-13-16 Mita, Minato-ku, Tokyo 108, Japan

ARIMOTO, MASAO, exports/imports company executive; b. Kobe, Hyogo, Japan, Dec. 1, 1947; s. Shohei and Teruko (Ohtani) A.; m. Takako Ohnishi; children: Yuki, Manna, Masatora. BA, Kwansei Gakuin U., Nishinomiya, Japan, 1970; postgrad., U. Kans., 1971. Dir. Pacific Co., Kobe, Japan, 1980-82, pres., 1982—; councillor Kwansei Gakuin U., 1982—. Club: Kobe (Japan). Home: 3-13 Atagoyama, 662 Nishinomiya City Japan Office: The Pacific Co, 1-6 8-chome Goko-dori, Chuo-ku, Kobe 651, Japan

ARIS, THEODOOR WILLEBRORD, transport company executive; b. Noordgouwe, Zeeland, The Netherlands, Apr. 16, 1940; s. Hendrik and Alida Sophie (Kraal) A.; m. Elisabeth van Duinhouen, July 13, 1965. BBA in Mktg. and Mgmt., Lyceum Bus., Amsterdam, The Netherlands, 1963. Mgmt. trainee Muller Internat., Spain, 1965-66; pres. Transport Mgmt. TMI BV, Schiphol-Zuid, The Netherlands; chmn. RoadAir, The Netherlands, 1966—. Served to lt. col. Acting Res Royal Dutch Army, 1964—. Recipient Silver Shoe Mgr. of Yr. award, 1986, Mgr. of Yr. award, The Netherlands, 1986. Lodge: Kiwanis (Rotterdam, The Netherlands). Office: Transport Mgmt Internat TMI BV, Snipweg 1, 1118 ZH Schipol Ctr, Schipol-Zuid The Netherlands

ARKIL, NIELS, construction company executive; b. Copenhagen, June 8, 1939; s. Ove and Ellen (Hessellund) A.; m. Lisbeth Sorenson, May 27, 1981; children: Vibeke Florin, Jesper, Jens, Helene. M, Tech. U., Copenhagen, 1966. Tech. mgr. N.S. Høm, House Constructors, Copenhagen, 1968-70; staff engr. Ove Arkil A/S, Contractors, Haderslev, Denmark, 1970-73; direction mem. SAW Asphalts and Contractors, Schleswig/Schlei, Fed. Republic Germany, 1974-84; mng. dir. SAW Asphalts and Contractors, Schleswig and Schlei, Fed. Republic Germany, 1984—, Ove Arkil A/S, Contractors, Haderslev, 1974—; hon. vice consul for France Haderslev, 1976—; vice-chmn. Eccolet A/S Shoe Factory, Bredebro, Denmark; bd. dirs. Dieselgarden A/S, Haderslev; bd. reps. PRIVATbanken, Copenhagen, 1982—; chmn. local council Kreditforeningen Danmark, Copenhagen, 1983—. Recipient Ordre Nat. du Mérite, Pres. of France, 1987. Mem. Danish Contractors' Assn. (bd. dirs.). Lodge: Rotary. Home: Tjørnebakken 17, Haderslev DK-6100, Denmark Office: Ove Arkil A/S, Åstrupvej 19, Haderslev DK-6100, Denmark

ARKILIC, GALIP MEHMET, civil engineer, educator; b. Sivas, Turkey, Mar. 10, 1920; came to U.S., 1943, naturalized, 1960; s. Sabir Mehmet and Zahra Fatima (Hocazade) A.; m. Ann A. Bryan, Mar. 31, 1956; children—Victor, Dennis, Layla, Errol. B.M.E., Cornell U., 1946; M.S., Ill. Inst. Tech., 1948; Ph.D., Northwestern U., 1954. Mech. engr. Miehle Printing Press and Mfg. Co., Chgo., 1948-49, analyst, 1954-56; research and devel. engr. Mech. and Chem. Industries, Turkey, 1949-52; asst. prof. Pa. State U., University Park, 1956-58; assoc. prof. dept. civil engring. George Washington U., Washington, 1958-63, prof. applied sci., 1963—, chmn. dept. engring. mechanics, 1966-69, asst. dean, 1969-74. Contbr. articles to sci. jours. Vice pres. Courtland Civic Assn., Arlington, Va., 1965-66; pres. Am. Turkish Assn., Washington, 1967-71. Served to 2d lt. Turkish Army, 1939-41. Recipient Disting. Leadership award Am. Turkish Assn., 1972; Recognition of Service award Sch. Engring. and Applied Sci., George Washington U., 1976; Air Force Office of Sci. Research grantee, 1963-69. Mem. ASME, AAUP, Am. Acad. Mechanics, Math. Assn. of Am., Sigma Xi. Club: George Washington U. (Washington). Home: 8403 Camden St Alexandria VA 22308 Office: George Washington U Washington DC 20052

ARKIN, JOSEPH, mathematician; b. Bklyn., May 25, 1923; s. Ben and Helen (Heller) A.; m. Judith H. Lobel, Aug. 28, 1954; children—Helen, Aviva, Jessica, Sarah. Ph.D. (hon.), Brantridge Sch. (Eng.), 1967. Vis. lectr. Orange Community Coll., Middletown, N.Y., 1962-67; lectr. Nanuet Pub. Schs., Rockland County, N.Y., 1962-67; Researcher various profs., 1965—; math. reviewer Am. Math. Soc., R.I., 1976—; contbr. articles to profl. jours. Active, Mus. Village, Monroe, N.Y., 1978. Served with U.S. Army, 1942-43. Mem. N.Y. Acad. Scis., Internat. Congress Math (Can.), AAAS, Fibonacci Assn. (charter mem.), Math. Assn. Am., Am. Math. Soc., Can. Math. Soc., Calcutta Math Soc., Soc. Indsl. and Applied math., Am. Legion, DAV Club: NCO (West Point). Home: 197 Old Nyack Turnpike Spring Valley NY 10977 Office: U S Mil Acad Dept Math West Point NY 10996

ARKIN, RONALD CRAIG, computer science educator, administrator, researcher; b. N.Y.C., Sept. 1, 1949; s. Herbert and Irene Mary (McQuaig) A.; m. Michaelle Halfacre, June 5, 1974; children—Matthew Daniel, Rebekah Leah, Sarah Elizabeth, Hannah Priscilla. B.S., U. Mich., 1971; M.S., Stevens Inst. Tech., 1977; PhD, U. Mass., 1987. Lab. technician, chemist Verona Dyestuffs, Bayonne, N.J., 1974-75; devel. chemist Napp Chem. Co., Lodi, N.J., 1975-77; assoc. prof. computer sci., chmn. dept. Hawthorne Coll., Antrim, N.H., 1977-85, mem. engring. adv. bd., 1984-85; research asst. robotics dept. computer and info. sci. U. Mass.-Amherst, 1985-87; asst. prof. sch. info. and computer sci. Ga. Inst. Tech., Atlanta, 1987—. Textbook referee Addison-Wesley, 1982-83. Co-author software; Statistical Sampling for Auditors, 1984; numerous tech. pubs.. Mem. IEEE Computer Soc. Assn. Computing Machinery, Am. Assn. Artificial Intelligence, Digital Equipment Computer Users Soc., Soc. Photo-Optical Instrumentation Engrs. Home: 339 Cove Island Way Marietta GA 30067 Office: Ga Inst Tech Sch Info and Computer Sci Atlanta GA 30332

ARKING, LUCILLE MUSSER, nurse epidemiologist; b. Centre County, Pa., Jan. 26, 1936; d. Boyd Albert and Marion Anna (Merryman) Musser; m. Robert Arking, May 8, 1959; children—Henry David, Jonathan Jacob. R.N., Episcopal Sch. Nursing, 1958; BS in Nursing, U. Pa., 1968; MS in Nursing, Wayne State U., 1986. Psychiat. research nurse Boston City Hosp., 1958; hosp. supr. Phila. Psychiat. Ctr., 1959-61; pub. health nurse Community Nursing Service, Phila., 1961-64; dir. nursing Green Acres Nursing Ctr., Phila., 1966-67; head nurse U. Va., Charlottesville, 1967-68; asst. dir. nursing U. Ky., Lexington, 1968-70; asst. dir. nursing edn. Rio Hondo Hosp., Downey, Calif., 1973-75; dir. nursing Bellwood Hosp., Bellflower, Calif., 1974-75; nurse epidemiologist Henry Ford Hosp., Detroit, 1975-84, dir. hosp. epidemiology, 1984—; instr. Santa Ana Coll., 1971-73; lectr. drug abuse Fountain Valley, Calif., 1970-75. Co-founder Parents and Friends Learning Disabilities Orgn., 1968-70; den leader Cub Scouts, Fountain Valley, Calif. 1968-75; bd. dirs. Wellness Networks, Detroit, 1982-86. Women's Club of Centre County scholar, 1954-58; grantee Community Nursing Service Ednl., 1963-64; USPHS nursing trainee, 1965; mem. Mich. Gov. AIDS task force, 1985-86, Mich. Med. Soc. AIDS task force, 1986. Mem. Am. Nurse's Assn., Mich. Nurse's Assn. (AIDS task force 1987—), Am. Pub. Health Assn. (mem. epidemiology sect. 1975—), Assn. Practitioners of Infection Control, Mich. Infection Control Soc., Nat. League of Nursing. Contbr. articles to profl. jours. Home: 4705 Stoddard Troy MI 48098 Office: Henry Ford Hosp Dept Epidemiology 2799 W Grand Blvd Detroit MI 48202

ARKLES, BARRY CHARLES, chemical and steel company executive; b. Phila., Feb. 1, 1949; s. Sydney J. and Beatrice M. Arkles; B.A., Temple U., 1969, Ph.D., 1975; m. Linda Laffey, Aug. 14, 1967; children—Elise, Amanda, Jeffrey. Mgr. tech. devel. Liquid Nitrogen Processing Engring. Plastic Co., Malvern, Pa., 1970-76; pres. Petrarch Systems Inc., Bristol, Pa., 1975—, M. Arkles & Son Steel Inc., Bensalem, Pa., 1976—. Recipient Indsl. Research 100 award, 1984. Mem. Am. Chem. Soc. (Leo Friend award 1983), Soc. Mfg. Engrs., Soc. Plastic Engrs., Am. Inst. Chem. Engrs., Soc. Biomaterials. Contbr. articles to profl. publs.; patentee polymers, composites, immobilized cell organelles, silanes, med. devices. Home: 1542 Cooper Dr Ambler PA 19002 Office: 600 Center Ave Bensalem PA 19020

ARLANT, PEDRO ALBERTO, neurosurgeon; b. Caçador, Brazil, Oct. 8, 1945; s. Pedro and Irma (Fleck) A.; m. Veralucia Pugliese, June 28, 1971 (div. June 1984); children: Alessandro, Pedro Jr. Student, Colegio Estadual do Parana, Curitiba, Brazil, 1958-64; MD, U. Parana, Curitiba, 1970. Diplomate Am. Bd. Neurol. Surgery. Surg. intern U. Conn. Hosp., Farmington, 1971-72; chief resident in neurosurgery U. Utah Med. Ctr., Salt Lake City, 1972-76; fellow in neurology U. London Inst. Neurology, 1973; supr. neurosurgeon U. São Paulo Med. Sch., Brazil, 1977-82; chief neurosurgery Sirio-Libanes Hosp., São Paulo, 1982—; staff neurosurgeon Albert Einstein Hosp., Sao Paulo, 1978—; founder, v.p. Brazilian Dislexia Assn., São Paulo, 1984-86. Contbr. articles to profl. jours. Recipient Physician's Recognition award AMA, 1978, Annual award Brazilian Acad. Neurology, 1980. Fellow ACS, Internat. Coll. Surgeons; mem. Am. Assn. Neurol. Surgery, Congress Neurol. Surgeons, N.Y. Acad. Scis. Lodge: Rotary. Office: Rua Itapeva 490 conj 105, 01332 Sao Paulo Brazil

ARLE, HENRIK, airline executive; b. Helsinki, Finland, Mar. 7, 1948; s. Alec and Christina (Lundstrom) A.; m. Andrea Standertskjold, Dec. 30, 1971; children: Henrika, Fred. LLB, Helsinki U., 1971. Lawyer Hertzberg & Orndahl, Helsinki, 1971-74; broker Bensow OY, Helsinki, 1975-78; gen. counsel Finnair OY, Helsinki, 1979-84, v.p. fin., 1984—; bd. dirs. Finnair OY, 1988—; bd. dirs. Nordic Hotel, Helsinki; auditor Sampo Ins. Co., Turku, Finland. Home: Degero gard, 00840 Helsinki Finland Office: Finnair OY, PO Box 6, 00251 Helsinki Finland

ARLEN, MICHAEL J., writer; b. London, Eng., Dec. 9, 1930; s. Michael and Atlanta (Mercati) A.; m. Ann Warner, 1957 (div. 1971); children—Jennifer, Caroline, Elizabeth, Sally; m. Alice Albright Hoge, 1972; stepchildren—Alicia, James Patrick, Robert Hoge. Grad., St. Paul's Sch., Concord, N.H., 1948, Harvard U., 1952; LLD (hon.), Colby Coll., 1984. Reporter Life mag., 1952-56; contbr., TV critic The New Yorker mag., 1957—; juror Columbia U.-Dupont awards for broadcast journalism, 1969-72, 78-80; faculty Bread Loaf Writers Conf., 1980. Author: Living-Room War, 1969, Exiles, 1970, An American Verdict, 1973, Passage to Ararat, 1975, The View from Highway 1, 1976, Thirty Seconds, 1980, The Camera Age, 1981, Say Goodbye to Sam, 1984. Recipient award for television criticism Screen Dirs. Guild, 1968; Nat. Book award for contemporary affairs, 1976; Le Prix Brémond, 1976. Mem. Authors Guild (exec. council). Clubs: Harvard, Century Assn. (N.Y.C.). Office: care The New Yorker 25 W 43d St New York NY 10036

ARLINGHAUS, EDWARD JAMES, health administration educator; b. Cin., Jan. 6, 1925; s. Edward A. and Irene (Custer) A.; B.B.A., U. Cin., 1948, Ph.D., 1981; M.B.A., Xavier U., 1958, M.Ed., 1971, M.S., 1973; m. Ilse Denninger, Aug. 10, 1974; 1 dau., Toni Gail. Dir. personnel tng. Mabley & Carew Co., Cin., 1948-51; sales researcher John Shillito Co., Cin., 1951-53; personnel devel. specialist Gen. Elec. Co., Cin., 1953-57; dir. personnel, pub. relations and security Jewish Hosp. of Cin., 1957-66; dir. grad. program in hosp. and health adminstrn. Xavier U., Cin., 1966—; mem. health care sect. Cath. Conf. Ohio; sec. bd. trustees Providence Hosp., 1968-77, St. Francis Hosp., 1968-75, St. Mary's Hosp., 1968-72 (all Cin.); trustee Epp Meml. Hosp., 1983—, Otterbeni Homes, 1981—; chmn. health manpower com. CORVA, Cin., 1970-75; mem. Ohio Bd. Examiners Nursing Home Adminstrs., 1974-76. Served with AUS, 1943-45; col. Res. (ret.). Fellow Royal Soc. Health; Am. Coll. Healthcare Execs., Am. Acad. Med. Adminstrs.; mem. Assn. Mental Health Adminstrs., Cath. Hosp. Assn., Am. Public Health Assn., Scarbard and Blade, Phi Delta Kappa. Home: 8060 Indian Hill Rd Cincinnati OH 45243 Office: Xavier University Cincinnati OH 45207

ARLOOK, THEODORE DAVID, dermatologist; b. Boston, Mar. 12, 1910; s. Louis and Rebecca (Sakansky) A.; BS, U. Ind. Sch. Medicine, 1932, M.D., 1934; postgrad. dermatology U. So. Calif., 1946-47. Intern, Luth. Meml. Hosp., Chgo., 1934-35; resident in dermatology Indpls. Gen. Hosp., 1947-49; practice medicine specializing in dermatology, Elkhart, Ind., 1950—; mem. staff Elkhart Gen. Hosp.; assoc. mem. dermatology dept. Wishard Meml. Hosp., Indpls, 1950-86, Regenstrief Hosp., Indpls., 1987—. Pres., Temple Israel, Elkhart, 1963-64; pres. B'nai B'rith, 1955. Served to capt. M.C. AUS, 1941-46; PTO. Diplomate Am. Bd. Dermatology. Mem. AMA, Ind. State Med. Assn., Am. Acad. Dermatology, Elkhart County Med. Soc. (pres. 1967), Noah Worcester Dermatol. Soc. Contbr. articles to med. jours. Office: 912 W Franklin St Elkhart IN 46516

ARLOTT, (LESLIE THOMAS) JOHN, writer, broadcaster; b. Basingstoke, Eng., Feb. 25, 1914; s. William John and Nellie Jenvey (Clarke) A.; m. Dawn Rees (dissolved); 1 child, Timothy Mark John; m. Valerie France (dec.); 1 child, Robert Francis John; m. Beryl Patricia Hoare. MA (hon.), Southampton U.; D (hon.), Open U. Named to Order Brit. Empire. Liberal. Anglican. Club: Marylebone Cricket. Office: care The Guardian, 119 Farringdon Rd, London EC1R 3ER, England

ARLT, WOLFGANG, chemical engineer; b. Bochum, Fed. Republic Germany, 1952; s. Heinz and Luzie (Karbaum) Posywio; m. Ute Arlt, May 23, 1978; children: Bastian, Tobias. Diploma, U. Dortmund, 1976, D in Chem. Engring., 1981. Researcher Bayer Co., Leverkusen, Fed. Republic Germany, 1981-87, prodn. engr., 1987—. Author: DECHEMA Chemistry, 1979; patentee in field. Office: Bayer Co, 4150 Uerdingen Federal Republic of Germany

ARMACOST, SAMUEL HENRY, bank executive; b. Newport News, Va., Mar. 29, 1939; s. George Henry and Verda Gae (Hayden) A.; m. Mary Jane Levan, June 16, 1962; children: Susan Lovell, Mary Elizabeth. BA, Denison U., 1961; MBA, Stanford U., 1964. With Bank of Am. NT & SA, San Francisco, 1961-81, v.p. mgr. London br., 1972-74, sr. v.p., mgr. San Francisco, 1975-77; exec. v.p. Europe, Middle East and Africa div. Bank of Am. NT & SA, London, 1977-79; exec. v.p., cashier Bank of Am. NT & SA, San Francisco, 1979-81; pres., chief exec. officer Bank of Am. and Bank Am. Corp., San Francisco, 1981-86; chmn., chief exec. officer Bank of Am., San Francisco, 1986-87; mng. ptnr. Merrill Lynch and Co., San Francisco, from 1987; now mng. dir. Merrill Lynch Capital Markets, San Francisco, 1988; chmn. Bank Am. Internat. Ltd., London, Banco Comercial para America, Madrid; dir. Banco Intercontinental Espanol, Madrid, Bank Am. Internat. S.A., Luxembourg, Bank Am. N.Y., Fin. Group Kuwait, Banca d'America d'Italia, Milan, Societe Financiere puor le Pays d'Outre Mer, Geneva. Mem. Bankers Assn. for Fgn. Trade (dir.). Republican. Presbyterian. Clubs: Bohemian, Pacific Union, San Francisco Golf; Augusta (Ga.) Nat. Golf. Office: Merrill Lynch Capital Markets 101 California St Suite 1420 San Francisco CA 94111 *

ARMAGOST, ELSA GAFVERT, computer industry communications consultant; b. Duluth, Minn., Jan. 26, 1917; d. Axel Justus and Martina Emelia (Magnuson) Gafvert; m. Byron William Armagost, Dec. 8, 1945; children: David Byron, Laura Martina. Grad. with honors, Duluth Jr. Coll., 1936; BJ, U. Minn., 1938, postgrad. in pub. relations, bus. mgmt. and computer tech., 1965-81; PhD in Computer Communication Cons. Sci. (hon.), Internat. U. Found. Freelance editor, Duluth, 1939-42; procedure editor and analyst U.S. Steel, Duluth, 1942-45; fashion advt. staff Dayton Co., Mpls., 1945-48; systems applications and documentation mgr. Control Data Corp., Mpls., 1969-74, promotion specialist, mktg. editor, 1974-76, corp. staff coordinator info. on edn., 1976-78; instr. communications, publ. specialist, 1978-79, communication cons. peripheral products group, 1979-83; industry communications cons., 1983—; mem. steering com. U.S. Senatorial Bus. Adv. Bd., 1962-68; mem. U.S. Congrl. Adv. Bd., 1958-62; mem. North Cen. Deming Mgmt. Forum. V.p. Sewickley (Pa.) Valley Hosp. Aux., Sewickley Valley Mental Health Council; dir. publicity Sacred Arts Expo, World Affairs Council radio program, Pitts., 1962-68. Recipient Medal of Merit Rep. Presdl. Task Force. Mem. AAUW (1st v.p. Caracas, Venezuela), Women in Communication (dir. job mart), Am. Security Council (mem. adv. bd.), Internat. Platform Assn., Friends of Mpls. Inst. Art., Walker Art Inst., LWV (bd. dirs. Pitts. chpt.), Minn. Alumni Assn., Am. Swedish Inst., Phi Beta Music Soc. (co-chair), Pi Epsilon (leadership award 1988). Club: Toastmasters (Communications award 1984). Home and Office: 9500 Collegeview Rd Bloomington MN 55437

ARMANI, GIORGIO, fashion designer; b. Piacenza, Emilia Romagna, Italy, July 11, 1934. Student, U. Bologna, Italy. Asst. menswear buyer, fashion coordinator La Rinascente, Milan, 1957-64; designer Cerutti Co., Milan; freelance designer Milan, 1975; founder Giorgio Armani Corp., Milan. Served with Italian Army, 1953-54. Recipient Neiman Marcus award, 1979; named Most Influential Designer Outside Am. Council of Fashion Designer of Am., 1983; Cutty Sark award, 1980, 81; Nanstyle award for best designer in the world, 1982. Office: Giorgio Armani Corp 815 Madison Ave New York NY 10021 Office: Via Borgonuovo 21, 20122 Milano Italy *

ARMOUR, ALLAN A., film company executive; b. Bklyn., Apr. 25, 1933; s. Arthur Harris and Gertrude (Kornblue) A.; student New Inst. Film and Television, 1952, N.Y. U. Film Inst., 1956, Sch. Bus., 1956-60; m. Susan Lois Newman, June 25, 1967; children—Steven Douglas, David Newman. Asst. film editor Bray Studios, N.Y.C., 1951-53, asst. to film producer, 1955-57; TV film producer Milton Wynne Advt. Agy., Babylon, N.Y., 1957-59; owner, co-founder Cine Magnetics, Inc., N.Y.C., 1961—, also dir.; pres. Projection Systems, Internat., N.Y.C., 1964—. Trustee, Lenox Sch., N.Y.C.; co-chmn., E. 79th St. Block Assn., Coalition to Save City and Suburban Homes. Served with Signal Corps, AUS, 1953-55. Mem. Nat. Audio Visual Assn. (cons.), Soc. Motion Picture Engrs. Contbr. numerous articles on audio visuals to various publs. Home: 501 E 79th St New York NY 10021 Office: 219 E 44th St New York NY 10017

ARMOUR, JAMES LOTT, lawyer; b. Jackson, Tenn., May 19, 1938; s. Quintin and Francis (Breeden) A.; m. Nancy Stokes Johnson, Mar. 17, 1962; 1 son, John Lawson. B.A., Vanderbilt U., 1961, LL.B., 1964; LL.M., So. Meth. U., 1967. Bar: Tenn. 1964, Tex. 1965, U.S. Supreme Ct. 1967, N.Y. 1969, Okla. 1972. Assoc. firm Turner & Rodgers, Dallas, 1965-67; internat. atty. Mobil Corp., N.Y.C., 1967-71, Phillips Petroleum Co., Bartlesville, Okla., 1971-74; asst. gen. counsel Conoco, Inc., Stamford, Conn., 1974-83; ptnr. firm Locke Purnell Rain Harrell, Dallas, 1984—. Mem. adv. council internat. oil and gas SW Legal Fedn. Mem. Assn. of Bar of City of N.Y., ABA, State Bar Tex., Dallas Bar Assn., Phi Delta Phi. Episcopalian. Clubs: Petroleum (Dallas); Field (New Canaan, Conn.). Home: 4541 Belfort Pl Dallas TX 75205 Office: Locke Purnell Rain Harrell 3600 Tower 2 First Republic Bank Ctr Dallas TX 75201

ARMOUR, RICHARD (WILLARD), writer, educator; b. San Pedro, Calif., July 15, 1906; s. Harry Willard and Sue (Wheelock) A.; m. Kathleen Fauntleroy Stevens, Dec. 25, 1932; children—Geoffrey Stevens, Karin Elizabeth. A.B., Pomona Coll., 1927, Litt.D., 1972; A.M., Harvard U., 1928, Ph.D., 1933; Litt.D., Coll. of Ozarks, 1944; L.H.D., Whittier Coll., 1968, So. Calif. Coll. Optometry, 1972; LL.D., Coll. Idaho, 1969, Claremont Men's Coll., 1974. Instr. in English U. Tex., 1928-29, Northwestern U., 1930-31; Dexter Scholar (research fellow) from Harvard at John Forster Library, Victoria and Albert Museum, London, 1931; prof. English, head div. of modern langs. Coll. of the Ozarks, 1932-33; Am. lectr. U. Freiburg, Germany, 1933-34; asst. prof., asso. prof. and prof. English Wells Coll., 1934-45; prof. English Scripps Coll. and Claremont Grad. Sch., 1945-63; dean of faculty Scripps Coll., 1961-63, Balch lectr. in English lit., 1963-66, dean and prof. emeritus, 1966—; Chancellor's lectr. Calif. State U. and Colls., 1964-68; writer-in-residence U. Redlands, 1974, Stanford U., 1965; vis. prof. Whittier Coll., 1975; served as Am. specialist abroad for U.S. State Dept., 1964, 66, 67, 68, 70; Fund Advancement Edn.; faculty fellow, 1953-54; Carnegie vis. prof. English U. Hawaii, 1957; leader of European tours, summers, 1926-31. Author: of numerous books, including Barry Cornwall, 1935, (with Raymond F. Howes) Coleridge the Talker, 1940, Yours for the Asking, 1942, Golf Bawls, 1946, Writing Light Verse, 1947, For Partly Proud Parents, 1950, It All Started with Columbus, 1953, Light Armour, 1954, It All Started with Europa, 1955, It All Started with Eve, 1956, Twisted Tales from Shakespeare, 1957, Nights with Armour, 1958, It All Started with Marx, 1958, Drug Store Days, 1959, The Classics Reclassified, 1960, Golf Is a Four-Letter Word, 1962, Armour's Almanac, 1962, The Medical Muse, or What to Do Until the Patient Comes, 1963, Through Darkest Adolescence, 1963, Our Presidents, 1964, The Year Santa Went Modern, 1964, American Lit Relit, 1964, An Armoury of Light Verse, 1964, The Adventures of Egbert the Easter Egg, 1965, Going Around in Academic Circles, 1965, Animals on the Ceiling, 1966, Punctured Poems, 1966, It All Started with Hippocrates, 1966, It All Started with Stones and Clubs, 1967, A Dozen Dinosaurs, 1967, Odd Old Mammals, 1968, My Life with Women, 1968, English Lit Relit, 1969, On Your Marks: A Package of Punctuation, 1969, A Diabolical Dictionary of Education, 1969, All Sizes and Shapes of Monkeys and Apes, 1970, A Short History of Sex, 1970, Who's in Holes?, 1971, Writing Light Verse and Prose Humor, 1971, All in Sport, 1972, Out of My Mind, 1972, The Strange Dreams of Rover Jones, 1973, It All Started with Freshman English, 1973, Going Like Sixty: A Lighthearted Look at the Later Years, 1974, Sea Full of Whales, 1974, The Academic Bestiary, 1974, The Spouse in the House, 1975, The Happy Bookers: A History of Librarians and Their World, 1976, It All Would Have Startled Columbus, 1976, It All Started with Nudes: An Artful History of Art, 1977, Strange Monsters of the Sea, 1979, Insects All Around Us, 1981; Anyone for Insomnia?, 1982; Educated Guesses, 1983; Have You Ever Wished You Were Something Else?, 1983; mem. editorial bd.: The Writer; contbr. regular feature to Quote, The Weekly Digest; contbr. articles and poems to nat. mags. Trustee Claremont Men's Coll., Claremont McKenna Coll., 1968—. Served as 2d lt. inf. Res. Corps U.S. Army, 1927-37; active duty in Antiaircraft Arty. 1942-46; lt. col., detailed to War Dept. Gen. Staff (mem.) 1944-46; col. U.S. Army Res. Decorated Legion of Merit with oak leaf cluster. Mem. Modern Lang. Assn. Am., Am. Assn. Univ. Profs., Calif. Writers Guild, P.E.N., Phi Beta Kappa. Conglist. Home: 894 W Harrison Ave Claremont CA 91711

ARMOUR, ROGER HANIF, consultant surgeon; b. Murree, Punjab, Pakistan, Aug. 19, 1934; s. Aziz and Edith Florence (Raymond) Ahmed; m. Gillian Margaret Evans, Dec. 5, 1957; children—Jasmin, Sara, Steven. M.B.B.S., King Edward Med. Coll., Pakistan, 1956; Ch.M., U. Liverpool, 1965; M.R.C.P., Royal Coll. Physicians, 1968. Neurosurg. sr. registrar, Walton Hosp., Liverpool, Eng., 1964; cardiothoracic surg. registrar Broadgreen Hosp., Liverpool, 1965; sr. surg. registrar D.L. Northern Hosp., Liverpool, 1967-69; cons. surgeon Liverpool Region, 1969-72, Lister Hosp., Stevenage, Eng., 1972—. Contbr. articles to profl. jours. Recipient Hamilton Bailey Travellin prize, Internat. Coll. Surgeons, 1973; Nathaniel Bishop Harman award, Brit. Med. Assn., 1979. Fellow Royal Soc. Tropical Medicine and Hygiene, Internat. Coll. Surgeons, Royal Coll. Surgeons; mem. Vascular Surg. Soc. G.B. and Ireland, Soc. Brit. Neurol. Surgeons (assoc.). Home: 88 Wymondley Rd, Mitchin SG4 9PX, England Office: Lister Hosp, Coreys Mill Ln, Stevenage SG1 4AB, England

ARMSTRONG, CURTIS EDWARD, music publishing executive; b. Martins Ferry, Ohio, Sept. 8, 1946; s. Ralph Edward and Eileen Virginia (Brown) A.; student West Liberty (W.Va.) State Tchrs. Coll., 1964-66, Franklin U., 1970-71. Employment mgr. Grossman & Sons, Inc., Columbus, Ohio, 1976-77; state coordinator handicapped services safety and hygiene div. Indsl. Commn. Ohio, Columbus, 1977-79, dir. public relations rehab. div., 1979-81, acting dir. rehab. div., 1981-82; mktg. rep. P.M. Computer Services, 1982-86 ; owner/operator Mobile Music Servie "One of a Kind", 1984—; pres. Jackson, Armstrong, Sargus Music Pub. Co., 1988—; record producer Capt. Woodwin Records, 1988—. pres. dir. Time, Inc., Columbus, 1979-82 ; adviser Ohio Gov.'s Com. for Employment Handicapped, Nat. Center Research in Vocat. Edn., Ohio State U., rep. President's Com. on Employment Handicapped, Washington, 1977-78; pres., co-founder Handi-Capable, Inc., 1980-83 ; pres. Central Ohio Employability Awareness Council, 1976-78. Mem. Nat. Assn. Accts., Am. Soc. Personnel Adminstrn., Press Club of Ohio. Rec. artist Gateway Records, 1962-70. Home and Office: 5452 Carbondale Dr Columbus OH 43232

ARMSTRONG, EDWIN RICHARD, lawyer, publisher, editor; b. Chgo., Sept. 25, 1921; s. Robert S. and Ella (Bremer) A.; m. Catherine Claire Graeber, June 29, 1957; children—Catherine Jane, Diane Claire, Douglas Edwin, Gregory Charles. B.A., Knox Coll., 1942; J.D., Northwestern U., 1948. Bar: Ill. 1949, U.S. Dist. Ct. (no. dist.) Ill. 1949, U.S. Ct. Appeals (7th cir.) 1949, U.S. Supreme Ct. 1961. Ptnr. Reimers & Armstrong, 1949-55; assoc. Friedman & Friedman, 1957-62; ptnr. Friedman, Armstrong & Donnelly, 1962-78, Armstrong & Donnelly, Chgo., 1978—; lectr. Ill. Inst. Continuing Legal Edn., 1979—. Mem. Oak Park (Ill.) Elem. Sch. Bd. 1963-69, pres. 1964-67; mem. exec. bd. Thatcher Woods Area council Boy Scouts Am. 1978—, pres., 1983-84. Served to maj. USMCR 1942-46. Mem. Ill. Bar Assn., Chgo. Bar Assn., West Suburban Bar Assn. Club: Oak Park. Home: 637 N Euclid St Oak Park IL 60302 Office: 77 W Washington St Suite 1717 Chicago IL 60602

ARMSTRONG, JACK GILLILAND, lawyer; b. Pitts., Aug. 10, 1929; s. Hugh Collins and Mary Elizabeth (Gilliland) A.; m. Ellen Lee Gliem, June 10, 1951; children—Thomas G., Elizabeth Armstrong Pride. A.B., U. Mich., 1951, J.D., 1956. Bar: Pa. 1956, Mich. 1956, U.S. Supreme Ct. 1968, Fla. 1981. Assoc. Buchanan, Ingersoll, Rodewald, Kyle & Buerger, Pitts., 1956-65; ptnr. Buchanan Ingersoll P.C., 1965—; dir. Standard Steel Splty. Co., Beaver Falls, Pa.; lectr. profl. assns. Trustee Union Dale Cemetery, 1972—; elder Southminster Presbyterian Ch. Served to lt. U.S. Army, 1951-53. Mem. ABA (sects. taxation, real property, probate and trust law), Pa. Bar Assn. (real property, probate and trust law sect., mem. council 1981-84, treas. 1985, vice chmn. probate div. 1986-88, tax law sect. 1986—, chmn. probate div. 1988—), State Bar Mich. (probate and trust law sect., taxation sect.), Fla. Bar (real property, probate and trust law sect., tax sect.), Allegheny County Bar Assn. (taxation, probate and trust law), Estate Planning Council Pitts., Am. Coll. Probate Counsel, Am. Coll. Tax Counsel, U. Mich. Alumni Assn. (disting. alumni service award 1981), Am. Arbitration Assn. (nat. panel 1965—), Order of Coif, Phi Alpha Delta, Sigma Nu. Republican. Clubs: Duquesne, University (pres. 1988—), Chartiers Country, St. Clair Country, Pine Tree Golf. Lodges: Masons, Shriners, Royal Order Jesters. Asst. editor Mich. Law Rev., 1955-56. Home: 1500 Cochran Rd Apt 1010 Pittsburgh PA 15243 Office: 600 Grant St 57th Floor Pittsburgh PA 15219

ARMSTRONG, JANE BOTSFORD, sculptor; b. Buffalo; d. Samuel Booth and Edith (Pursel) Botsford; m. Robert Thexton Armstrong, July 3, 1960. Student, Middlebury Coll., 1939-40, Pratt Inst., 1940-41, Art Students' League, 1962-64. One-man shows Frank Rehn Gallery, N.Y.C., 1971, 73, 75, 77, Columbus (Ohio) Gallery Fine Arts, 1972, Columbia (S.C.) Mus. Art, 1975, New Britain (Conn.) Mus. Am. Art, 1972, Johnson Gallery, Middlebury Coll., 1973, Mary Duke Biddle Gallery for Blind N.C. Mus. Art, 1974, J.B. Speed Art Mus., Louisville, 1975, Buffalo State U., 1975, Marjorie Parr Gallery, London, 1976, Ark. Art Center, 1977, Dallas Mus. Fine Art, 1978, Wichita (Kans.) Art Mus., 1978, 82, Wadsworth Atheneum, 1979, Harmon Gallery, 1979, 81, Washington County (Md.) Mus. Fine Arts, Hagerstown, 1979, Chautauqua (N.Y.) Nat. Exhbn. Am. Art, 1980, Southeastern Center Contemporary Art, Winston-Salem, N.C., 1980, Rollins Coll., Winter Park, Fla., 1981, The Sculpture Center, N.Y.C., 1981, Sid Deutsch Gallery, N.Y.C., 1983, Boca Raton Mus. (Fla.), 1983, Burchfield Ctr., Buffalo, 1985, Glass Art Gallery, Toronto, 1985, Schiller-Wapner Galleries, N.Y.C., 1987, St. Gaudens Gallery, St. Gaudens Nat. Hist. Site, 1988; exhibited in USIA group exhbn., Europe, 1975-76, Artists of Am., Denver, 1981, 82, 83, 84, 85, 86, 87; represented in numerous acad., indsl., pub. and pvt. collections. Recipient Pauline Law prize Allied Artists Am., 1969, 70, Gold medal, 1976, Ralph Fabri medal honor, 1978, Chaim Gross Found. award, 1980; cert. merit NAD, 1973; Council Am. Artists' Socs. prize Nat. Sculpture Soc., 1973; Porton award, 1981. Fellow Nat. Sculpture Soc. (Bronze medal 1976, Tallix Foundry award 1985, Percival Dietsch prize 1986); Mem. Nat. Arts Club (gold medal for sculpture 1968, 69, 71, best in show 1973, Edith W. Macguire award 1975, Plaque Honor 1977, Alexander Saltzman award 1983), Audubon Artists (medal of honor 1972), Sculptors Guild, Allied Artists Am., Nat. Assn. Women Artists (Charles N. Whinston Meml. prize 1973, Anonymous Mem. award. 1975, 77, Mrs. C. D. Murphy Meml. prize 1979, Elizabeth S. Blake prize 1980, Amelia Peabody award 1986), Knickerbocker Artists (Elliot Liskin award 1979, Knickerbocker award 1982, Marian Weisberg award 1985, Gold medal for disting. achievement in sculpture 1986), Catharine Lorillard Wolfe Art Club (Liskin award 1981, Anna Hyatt Huntington award 1982). Home and Studio: Dorset Hill Rd Rural Rt Box 684 East Dorset VT 05253

ARMSTRONG, JOHN KREMER, lawyer; b. Washington, Apr. 15, 1934; s. Stuart Morton and Marion Louise (Kreutzer) A.; m. A.M.E. (Mieke) van Haersma Buma, Apr. 1963; children: Marca Carine van Heloma, Jeb Stuart. BA with honors, Haverford Coll., 1956; postgrad. U. Delhi, 1956-57; LL.B., Yale U., 1960. Bar: N.Y. 1961. Assoc. Davies, Hardy and Schenck, N.Y.C., 1960-68; ptnr. Davies, Hardy, Ives and Lawther, N.Y.C., 1968-72, Armstrong and Ulrich, N.Y.C., 1973-81, Cole and Deitz, N.Y.C., 1981-85, Carter, Ledyard & Milburn, 1985—; dir., sec. Kinney Shoes Can. Inc., 1973—; lectr. Longwwod Garden Fellows Program, 1987—. Trustee Bklyn. Bot. Garden, chmn. bd., 1982—; bd. regents L.I. Coll. Hosp., 1968-72, asst. sec., 1973—; fellow Rotary found. 1956-57; mem. N.Y. State Rep. Fin. Com., 1988—. Mem. ABA, N.Y. State Bar Assn. (co-chmn. com. health law 1987—), Assn. of Bar of City of N.Y., Phi Beta Kappa. Episcopalian. Republican. Clubs: Bronxville (N.Y.) Field, Church, The Pilgrims, Downtown Assn. Home: 14 Carlton Rd Bronxville NY 10708 Office: Carter Ledyard & Milburn 2 Wall St New York NY 10005

ARMSTRONG, JOSEPH EDGAR WILLIAM, transportation executive, computer professional; b. Kottayam, Kerala, India, Aug. 4, 1956; s. John and Margaret (Saywell) A. B of Commerce, U. Delhi, 1977. Cert. systems analyst. Resident rep. Globe Express Travels, New Delhi, 1977-79; traffic asst. Indian Airlines, New Delhi, 1979-81; passenger services, sta. ops. officer Lufthansa German Airlines, New Delhi, 1981—. Mem. Old Columbans Assn. (exec. com. 1978-79). Roman Catholic. Club: Arsenal Youth Football (sec. 1974-79). Home: 380 Double Storey, New Rajinder Nagar, 110 060 New Delhi India Office: Lufthansa German Airlines, Indira Gandhi Internat Airport, New Delhi India

ARMSTRONG, NAOMI YOUNG, real estate executive; b. Dermott, Ark., Oct. 17, 1918; d. Allen Wesley and Sarah Elizabeth (Fluker) Young; B.S., Northwestern U., 1961; L.H.D. (hon.), U. Libre, Karachi, Pakistan, 1974; Ph.D. (hon.), World U., Tucson, 1979; D.LiH. (hon.), Universal Orthodox Coll., Iperu-Remo, Ogun State, Nigeria, 1980; Litt.D. (hon.) World Acad. Arts and Culture, Taipei, Taiwan, 1981; m. Joe Leslie Armstrong, July 17, 1938; 1 dau., Betty-Jo Armstrong Dunbar. Actress, Skyloft Players, also Center Aisle Players, Chgo., 1945-59; silk dress operator Rue-Ann Originals, Chgo., 1947-55; clk. Bur. Pub. Debt, 1955-56, IRS, 1956-59; caseworker Cook County Dept. Pub. Aid, Chgo., 1961-62; tchr. Chgo. pub. schs., 1962-83, creative writing instr., 1975-77, instr. Social Center, 1965-67; dramatic instr. Crerar Meml. Presbyn. Ch., Chgo., 1972; real estate salesman Century 21 Maner, 1978—; pres., dir., founder Chrysopoets, Inc., 1987. Mem. exec. bd., membership chmn. Northwestern U. Young Alumni Council, 1971-72; trustee World U., 1973-74. Recipient Hon. Gold diploma, spl. award 3d World Congress Poets, 1976, Silver cup and Silver medallion 9th World Congress Poets, 1986 merit award for oil painting Internat. Platform Assn., 1988; named Internat. Woman of 1975, United Poets Laureate Internat. others; lic. real estate salesman. Mem. United Poets Laureate Internat. (exec. bd.), Internat. Platform Assn. (life; bd. govs.; 3d Preview winner 1976), World Poets Resource Center, Poetry Soc. London, Centro Studi e Scambi Internat., Intercontinental Biog. Assn. (life), World Poetry Soc. (life), Internat. Poets Acad. (Internat. Eminent Poet 1987), NAACP (life, chpt. chmn. edn. com. 1983), Sigma Gamma Rho. Author: A Child's Easter, 1971; Expression I, 1973; Expression III, 1976; Naomi's Two Line Sillies (A Guide for Living) Expression IV, 1985. Address: 9257 S Burnside Ave Chicago IL 60619

ARMSTRONG, NEIL A., computer systems company executive, former astronaut; b. Wapakoneta, Ohio, Aug. 5, 1930; s. Stephen Armstrong; m. Janet Shearon; children: Eric, Mark. B.S. In Aero. Engring, Purdue U., 1955; M.S. in Aero. Engring, U. So. Calif. With Lewis Flight Propulsion Lab., NACA, 1955; then aero. research pilot for NACA (later NASA, High Speed Flight Sta.), Edwards, Calif.; astronaut Manned Spacecraft Center, NASA, Houston, 1962-70; command pilot Gemini 8; comdr. Apollo 11; dep. asso. adminstr. for aeros. Office Advanced Research and Tech., Hdqrs. NASA, Washington, 1970-71; prof. aerospace engring. U. Cin., 1971-79; chmn. bd. Cardwell Internat., Ltd., 1980-82; chmn. CTA, Inc., 1982—; dir. Cin. Gas & Electric Co., Eaton Corp., Taft Broadcasting Co., Cin. Milacron, UAL Inc., USX Inc. Mem. Pres.'s Commn. on Space Shuttle, 1986, Nat. Commn. on Space, 1985-86. Served as naval aviator USN, 1949-52, Korea. Recipient numerous awards, including Octave Chanute award Inst. Aero. Scis., 1962, Presdl. Medal for Freedom, 1969, Exceptional Service medal NASA, Hubbard Gold medal Nat. Geog. Soc., 1970, Kitty Hawk Meml. award, 1969, Pere Marquette medal, 1969, Arthur S. Fleming award, 1970, Congl. Space Medal of Honor, Explorers Club medal. Fellow AIAA (hon., Astronautics award 1966), Internat. Astronautical Fedn. (hon.), Soc. Exptl. Test Pilots; mem. Nat. Acad. Engring.

ARMSTRONG, ORVILLE A., lawyer; b. Austin, Tex., Jan. 21, 1929; s. Orville Alexander and Velma Lucille (Reed) A.; m. Mary Dean Macfarlane; children. B.B.A., U. Tex., Austin, 1953; LL.B., U. So. Calif., 1956. Bar: Calif., 1957, U.S. Ct. Appeals (9th cir.) 1958, U.S. Supreme Ct. 1980. Ptnr., Gray, Binkley & Pfaelzer, 1956-61, Pfaelzer, Robertson, Armstrong & Woodard, Los Angeles, 1961-66, Armstrong & Lloyd, Los Angeles, 1966-74, Macdonald, Halsted & Laybourne, Los Angeles, 1975-88, Baker & McKenzie, 1988—; lectr. Calif. Continuing Edn. of Bar. Served with USAF, 1946-49. Fellow Am. Coll. Trial Lawyers; mem. State Bar Calif. (gov. 1983-87, pres. 1986-87), ABA, Los Angeles County Bar Assn. (trustee 1971-72), Am. Judicature Soc., Chancery Club (pres. 1988), Assn. Bus. Trial Lawyers, Am. Arbitration Assn. Democrat. Baptist. Clubs: Calif. (Oakmont). Home: 2385 Coniston Pl San Marino CA 91108 Office: 725 S Figueroa St 36th Floor Los Angeles CA 90017

ARMSTRONG, RICHARD BURKE, television director; b. Bklyn., May 12, 1924; s. John Andrew and Christine (Dougherty) A.; m. Carolyn Millett Jones, Oct. 2, 1954; children—Robert James, Jennifer Marlowe, Christina Louise. Student, U. Scranton, 1942-43; B.A., Catholic U. Am., 1950, postgrad., 1952. Stage mgr. Sta WMAL-TV, Washington, 1953-54; dir. Sta WMAL-TV, 1954-62, ABC-TV News Bur., Washington, 1962—. Actor, Players Inc., Washington, 1952-53. Served with U.S. Army, 1943-46. Office: 1717 De Sales St Washington DC 20036

ARMSTRONG, ROBERT BRADLEY, manufacturer; b. Mpls., Dec. 25, 1929; s. Harry George and Mary Evelyn (Sutherl) A.; m. Lucille Dolores Miller, Mar. 12, 1960; children—Mary Gregg, Brad Lee. B.Mech. Engring., Gen. Motors Inst., 1959. With Gen. Motors Corp., Detroit and Flint, Mich., 1958-69; v.p., gen. mgr. Simplicity Engring. Co., Durand, Mich., 1969-71; exec. v.p. Cardinal of Adrian, Dryden, Mich., 1971-72; sr. v.p. Champion Home Builders Co., Dryden, 1972-75; founder, pres. Bending Spltys., Inc. (spl. machinery), Madison Heights, Mich., 1976—, Bold Corp. (automotive parts mfg.), Madison Heights, Mich., 1986—, Tri-Power Engring., Madison Heights, Mich., Bd. dirs. Blue Shield of Mich. Served with USAF, 1950-54. Recipient 10 Year key for outstanding job performance Gen. Motors Inst., 1958. Club: Lion. Home: 2624 Hounds Chase Troy MI 48098 Office: 580 Ajax Dr Madison Heights MI 48071

ARMSTRONG, THOMAS NEWTON, III, museum director; b. Portsmouth, Va., July 30, 1932; s. Thomas Newton, Jr. and Mary Saunders (Tabb) A.; m. Virginia Whitney Brewster, May 18, 1963; children—Thomas Newton IV, Whitney, Eliot, Amory. Student, Cornell U., 1950-54, Art Students League, summer 1953, Inst. Fine Arts, NYU, 1965-67. Personnel coordinator, asst. to chmn. bd. Stone & Webster, Inc., N.Y.C., 1957-65; curator, assoc. dir. Colonial Williamsburg-Abby Aldrich Rockefeller Folk Art Collection, Williamsburg, Va., 1967-71; dir. Pa. Acad. Fine Arts, Phila., 1971-73; assoc. dir. Whitney Mus. Am. Art, N.Y.C., 1973-74; dir. Whitney Mus. Am. Art, 1974—; assoc. Gannett Ctr. for Media Studies, Columbia U.; mem. selection com. Luce Scholars Program, Henry Luce Found., Inc.; mem. U.S. Internat. Council, cons. Ctr. for U.S.-China Arts Exchange; fellow R.I. Sch. Design. Trustee Am. Fedn. Arts, Internat. Exhbns. Found.; mem. N.Y. adv. com. Archives of Am. Art; mem. adv. council dept. art, history and archaeology Columbia U.; mem. Senate Spl. Com. on the Culture Industry, N.Y. State; bd. dirs. Herbert F. Johnson Mus. Art, Cornell U.; mem. creative arts award com. Brandeis U. Office: Whitney Mus Am Art 945 Madison Ave New York NY 10021

ARMSTRONG, WALTER PRESTON, JR., lawyer; b. Memphis, Oct. 4, 1916; s. Walter Preston and Irma Lewis (Waddell) A.; m. Alice Kavanaugh McKee, Nov. 3, 1949; children: Alice Kavanaugh, Walter Preston III. Grad., Choate Sch., Wallingford, Conn., 1934; A.B., Harvard U., 1938, J.D., 1941; D.C.L. (hon.), Southwestern at Memphis, 1961. Bar: Tenn. 1940. Practiced in Memphis, 1941—; assoc. firm Armstrong, Allen, Prewitt, Gentry, Johnston & Holmes (and predecessor firms), 1941-48; of counsel Armstrong, Allen, Braden, Goodman, McBride & Prewitt (and predecessor firms), 1986—; Commr. for Promotion of Uniformity of Legislation in U.S. for Tenn., 1947-67. Author law rev. articles. Pres. bd. edn. Memphis City Schs., 1956-61; mem. Tenn. Higher Edn. Commn., 1967-84, chmn., 1974-75; mem. Tenn. Hist. Commn., 1969-80, hon. French consul, 1978-88 . Served from pvt. to maj. AUS, 1941-46. Fellow Am. Bar Found. (sec. 1960-62), Tenn. Bar Found. (chmn. 1983-84), Am. Coll. Trial Lawyers; mem. ABA (ho. of dels. 1952-75), Tenn. Bar Assn. (pres. 1972-73), Memphis and Shelby County Bar Assn., Inter-Am. Bar Assn., Internat. Bar Assn., Fed. Bar Assn., Assn. Bar City N.Y., Am. Law Inst., Nat. Conf. Commrs. on Uniform State Laws (pres. 1961-63), Harvard Law School Assn. (sec. 1957-58), Order of Coif, Scribes (pres. 1960-61), Phi Delta Phi, Omicron Delta Kappa. Home: 1530 Carr Ave Memphis TN 38104 Office: 1900 One Commerce Sq Memphis TN 38103

ARMSTRONG, WILLIAM L., senator; b. Fremont, Nebr., Mar. 16, 1937; s. William L. and Dorothy (Steen) A.; m. Ellen M. Eaton, July 15, 1962; children: Anne Elizabeth, William. Student, Tulane U., 1954-55, U. Minn., 1956. Pres. Sta. KPV1-TV, Pocatello, Idaho; mem. 93d-95th Congresses from 5th Dist. Colo.; mem. U.S. Senate from Colo., 1979—, chmn. Republican Policy Com., 1984—. mem. Colo. Senate, 1965-72, majority leader, 1969-72; mem. Colo. Ho. of Reps., 1963-64. Served with U.S. Army N.G., 1957-63. Mem. AP Broadcasters Assn. (dir. 1971-72, v.p. 1972). Office: 528 Hart Senate Office Bldg Washington DC 20510

ARN, KENNETH DALE, city official, physician; b. Dayton, Ohio, July 19, 1921; s. Elmer R. and Minna Marie (Wannagat) A.; m. Vivien Rose Fontini, Sept. 24, 1966; children—Christine H. Hulme, Laura P. Hafstad, Kevin D., Kimmel R. B.A., Miami U., Oxford, Ohio, 1943; M.D., U. Mich., 1946. Intern Miami Valley Hosp., Dayton, Ohio, 1947-48; resident in pathology U. Mich., 1948-49, fellow in renal research, 1949-50; fellow in internal medicine Cleve. Clinic, 1950-52; practice medicine specializing in internal medicine, pub. health and vocat. rehab. Dayton, 1952—; commr. of health City of Oakwood, Ohio, 1953—; assoc. clin. prof. medicine Wright State U., 1975—; mem. staffs Kettering Med. Ctr., Dayton, Miami Valley Hosp.; adj. assoc. prof. edn. Wright State U.; field med. cons. Bur. Vocat. Rehab., 1958—, Bur. Services to Blind, 1975—; med. dir. Ohio Rehab. Services Commn., 1979-87; mem. Pres.'s Com. on Employment of Handicapped, 1971—; chmn. med. adv. com. Goodwill Industries, 1960-75, chmn. bd. trustees 1985-87; mem., chmn. lay adv. com. vocat. edn. Dayton Pub. Schs., 1973-82; exec. com. Gov.'s Com. on Employment Handicapped; bd. dirs. Vis. Nurses Assn. Greater Dayton; chmn. profl. adv. com. Combined Gen. Health Dist. Montgomery County. Named City of Dayton's Outstanding Young Man, Jr. C. of C., 1957; 1 of 5 Outstanding Young Men of State, Ohio Jr. C. of C., 1958; Physician of Yr., Pres.'s Com. on Employment of Handicapped, 1971; Bishop's medal for meritorious service Miami U., 1972. Mem. AMA, Ohio Med. Assn., Montgomery County Med. Soc. (chmn. com. on diabetic detection 1955-65, chmn. polio com. 1954-58), Nat. Rehab. Assn., Am. Diabetes Assn., Am. Profl. Practice Assn., Am. Heart Assn., Am. Pub. Health Assn., Ohio Pub. Health Assn., Aerospace Med. Assn., Fraternal Order Police, Nu Sigma Nu, Sigma Chi. Lutheran. Club: Dayton Country. Lodges: Kiwanis, Royal Order Jesters, Masons (past potentate), Shriners, K.T. Home: 167 Lookout Dr Dayton OH 45409 Office: 55 Park Ave Dayton OH 45419

ARNAUD, CLAUDE DONALD, JR., physician, educator; b. Hackensack, N.J., Dec. 4, 1929; s. Claude Donald and Alice Marie (Minnet) A.; children: Claude Michael, Ellen Marie. B.A., Columbia Coll., 1951; M.D., N.Y. Med. Coll., 1955. Intern St. Luke's Hosp., N.Y.C.; also resident; resident, endocrine fellow Milwaukee County Hosp.; fellow U. Wis.; instr. biochemistry U. Pa., 1959-66; cons. dept. endocrine research Mayo Clinic, Rochester, Minn., 1967-77; head mineral research unit Mayo Clinic, 1972-74, head endocrine research unit, mineral research lab., 1974-77, assoc. prof. medicine Grad. Sch. Medicine, 1970-74, prof., 1974-77; prof. medicine and physiology U. Calif., San Francisco, 1977—; chief endocrine unit San Francisco VA Med. Ctr., 1977—. Contbr. numerous articles to profl. jours. Served with M.C. U.S. Navy, 1957-59. NIH grantee, 1968—. Mem. Am. Fedn. Clin. Research, Am. Soc. Biol. Chemists, Am. Soc. Clin. Investigation, Am. Physiol. Soc., Assn. Am. Physicians, Endocrine Soc., Western Assn. Physicians, AAAS., Am. Soc. Bone Mineral Research (past pres.), Nat. Research Council, Nat. Acad. Sci. (com. on diet, health and chronic disease 1985—), NIH (musculoskeletal study sect. 1985—).

ARNAULT, BERNARD JEAN, trade company executive; b. Roubaix, France, Mar. 5, 1949; s. Jean and Marie Jo (Savinel) A.; diploma Ecole Polytechnique Paris, 1971; m. Anne Dewavrin, May 21, 1973; children—Delphine, Antoine. With Ferret Savinel S.A., Roubaix, 1972—, gen. mgr., 1976—, pres., 1983—; pres. Financiere Agache, Christian Dior, Boussac St. Freres-Belle Jardiniere. Recipient Chevalier Order Nat. Merit. Club: Polo Interallie. Avocations: tennis, piano. Home: 23 ave Emile, Deschanel, Paris 7e France Office: Financiere Agache, 11 rue Francois Ier, 75008 Paris France

ARNBERG, ROBERT LEWIS, mathematician; b. San Francisco, Mar. 19, 1945; s. Wilbur H. and Elverne Evelyn (Lewis) A.; m. Judith Davis Urey, June 18, 1967 (div. 1977); 1 son, Christopher John. Student, U. Oreg., 1972-75, MA, 1969; AB, U. Calif.-Berkeley, 1967. Ops. research systems analyst Hdqrs. Dept. of Army, Washington, 1969-72; sr. programmer Cons. & Designers, Beltsville, Md., 1975; cons., tchr., writer Cons. & Designers, Washington, Md., 1976-78; programmer analyst Data Transformation Corp., Washington, Md., 1978; mathematician, programmer, analyst Nat. Econ. Research Assocs., Washington, Md., 1978-80; research fellow Logistics Mgmt. Inst., Washington, Md., 1980-88, cons., 1988—; book reviewer Am. Assn. Advancement Sci., 1977—; instr. George Washington U., 1978; cons. Dept. Army, 1972; adj. asst. prof. U. Md., College Park, Md., 1988—. Author: AAM User's Guide, 1984, F16 FIMS User's Guide, 1982, Integrated Requirements and Inventory System User's Guide and Reference Manuals, 1988, Petroleum Quality Information System User's Guide and Performance Manual, 1988, Federal Energy Usage System User's Guide, 1988; others. Campaign worker Eugene McCarthy campaign 1976. Served to capt. U.S. Army, 1969-72. Mem. AAAS, Am. Math. Soc., Math. Assn. Am., Soc. for Indsl. and Applied Math., Internat. Congress of Mathematicians, N.Y. Acad. Scis., Washington Ethical Soc., Chi Psi. Home: 4107 W St NW Apt 202 Washington DC 20007 Office: Logistics Mgmt Inst 6400 Goldsboro Rd Bethesda MD 20817-5886

ARNDT, CYNTHIA, educator; b. N.Y.C., Sept. 27, 1947; d. Charles Joseph and Pura Maria (Rios) A.; B.A., Hunter Coll., 1971, M.A., 1975; profl. diploma in adminstrn. Fordham U., 1981. Adminstrv. asst. to asst. registrar Hunter Coll., N.Y.C., 1968-69; cataloguer asst. Finch Coll. Library, N.Y.C., 1974; tchr. N.Y. Bd. Edn., N.Y.C., 1974-82; bilingual coordinator Jr. High Sch. 143, 1982—. Mem. Am. Artist Soc., Center Inter-Am. Relations, Hispanic Am. Hist. Soc., Nat. Council Social Studies, N.Y. Assn. Curriculum Devel., Puerto Rican Edn. Assn., Assn. Curriculum Devel., Nat. Travel Club, Kappa Delta Pi, Phi Delta Kappa. Democrat. Roman Catholic. Reviewer Booklist, 1981. Home: 50 W 97th St New York NY 10025

ARNDT, DIANNE JOY, artist, photographer; b. Springfield, Mass., Dec. 20, 1939; d. Samuel Vincent and Carrie Lillian Annino; student Art Students League, 1965-71; B.F.A. with honors in Painting, Pratt Inst., 1974; student journalism, Columbia U., 1979-80, 86; MFA, Hunter Coll., 1981; m. Joseph Vincent Bower, June 16, 1979; 1 dau. by previous marriage—Christabelle Nita Arndt. Photojournalist, photo cons. to mags. and bus., N.Y.C., 1978—; artist, filmmaker, 1962—; recent exhbns. include: Pyramid Arts Ctr., Rochester, N.Y., 1986, Food Stamp Gallery, N.Y.C., 1988, ABC No Rio, 1986, Storefront for Art and Architecture, N.Y.C., 1986, Post Machina Group, Bologna, Italy, 1986, Postaes, Brazil, 1987, Am. Cultural Ctr., U.S., New Delhi and Bombay, 1987, Bathurst Arms Installation, Eng., 1987, Cuando, N.Y.C., 1987, Camden Arts, London, 1987, Nat. Inst. of Archtl. Edn., 1988, Phillip Morris Traveling Photo Exhibit, 1988, Centennial Library Gallery, Isca Graphics, Edmonton, Alta., Can., 1988. Recipient Exptl. Writing award Columbia U., 1967, 1st prize in show Springfield (Mass.) Mus. Fine Art, 1967. Mem. AIA (art and architecture com.), Am. Soc. Mag. Photographers, Artists Talk on Art (bd. dirs., exec. dir.), Profl. Women Photographers, West Side Arts Coalition, The Nat. Mus. of Women in the Arts, Found. for Community of Artists.

ARNELL, RICHARD ANTHONY, radiologist, nuclear medicine physician; b. Chgo., Aug. 21, 1938; s. Tony Frank and Mary Martha (Oberman) Yaki; B.A. (Younker Achievement scholar), Grinnell Coll., 1960; M.D., U. Iowa, 1964; m. Paula Ann Youngberg, June 28, 1964; children—Carla Ann, Paula Marie, Paul Anthony. Intern, Mercy and St. Luke's hosps., Cedar Rapids, Iowa, 1964-65; resident in radiology and nuclear medicine U. Iowa Hosps., 1965-68; practice medicine specializing in radiology and nuclear medicine, Moline, Ill., 1968—; mem. Moline Radiology Assos., 1968—, v.p., 1970-78, sec., 1978—, trustee pension and profit plan, 1979—; mem. staff Luth. Hosp., Moline, dir. continuing med. edn. program for physicians, 1979-83, bd. dirs., 1977-83; mem. staff Moline Pub. Hosp., Hammond-Henry Dist. Ill., Geneseo, Ill.; trustee Midstate Found. for Med. Care, 1975-79, exec. com., 1976-79; v.p. Quad City HMO Health Plan, 1979; clin. lectr. U. Iowa, 1980—. Supt. Sunday Ch. Sch. St. John's Luth. Ch., Rock Island, Ill., 1974-79, mem. ch. cabinet, 1975-76; del. Chs. United of Scott and Rock Island counties, Ill., 1977; mem. nat. exec. com. Augustana Coll., Rock Island, Ill., 1977-81; assoc. chmn. profl. div. United Way, 1985; bd. dirs. Luth. Hosp. Found., 1981-84, pres., 1982-84; bd. dirs. Quad Cities Health Care Resources, Inc., 1984—; chmn. Luth. Health Care Found., 1984—. Recipient David Theophillus trophy for outstanding athlete Grinnell Coll., 1960; diplomate Am. Bd. Radiology, Am. Bd. Nuclear Medicine. Mem. Am. Coll. Radiology, Ill. Radiol. Soc., Am. Coll. Nuclear Medicine, Soc. Nuclear Medicine, AMA, Ill. (ho. of dels. 1974-79), Rock Island County (exec. com. 1974-79, peer-rev. com. 1975-79), Iowa-Ill. Central (pres.-elect 1977, pres. 1978) med. socs., Central Ill. Med. Assn. (v.p. 1977, pres. 1978), Ind. Physicians Assn. Western Ill. (dir. 1984-86, v.p. 1985, pres. 1986), World Med. Assn., Tri-City Med. Jour. Club (sec.-treas. 1972-77), Am. Coll. Med. Imaging. Club: Short Hills Country. Home: 3904 7th Ave Rock Island IL 61201 Office: 1505 7th St Moline IL 61265

ARNELL, WALTER JAMES WILLIAM, engineering educator, consultant; b. Farnborough, Eng., Jan. 9, 1924; came to U.S., 1953, naturalized, 1960; s. James Albert and Daisy (Payne) A.; m. Patricia Catherine Cannon, Nov. 12, 1955; children—Sean Paul, Victoria Clare, Sarah Michele Arnell. Aero. Engr., Royal Aircraft Establishment, 1946; BSc, U. London, 1953, PhD, 1967; MA, Occidental Coll., Los Angeles, 1956; MS, U. So. Calif., 1958. Lectr. Poly. and Northampton Coll. Advance Tech., London, 1948-53; instr. U. So. Calif., Los Angeles, 1954-59; asst. prof. mech. engring. Calif. State U., Long Beach, 1959-62, assoc. prof., 1962-66, prof., 1966-71, chmn. dept. mech. engring., 1964-65, acting chmn. div. engring., 1964-66, dean engring., 1967-69, researcher Ctr. Engring. Research; affiliate faculty dept. ocean engring. U. Hawaii, 1970-74; adj. prof. systems and insdl. engring. U. Ariz., 1981—; pres. Lenra Assocs. Ltd., 1973—; chmn., project mgr. Hawaii Environ. Simulation Lab., 1971-72. Contbr. articles to profl. jours. Trustee, Rehab. Hosp. of the Pacific, 1975-79. Mem. Royal Aero. Soc., AIAA, IEEE Systems Man and Cybernetics Soc., AAUP, Am. Psychol. Assn., Soc. Engring., Psychology, Human Factors Soc., Ergonomics Soc., Psi Chi, Alpha Pi Mu, Tau Beta Pi, Phi Kappa Phi, Pi Tau Sigma. Home: 4491 E Fort Lowell Tucson AZ 85712

ARNETT, FOSTER DEAVER, lawyer; b. Knoxville, Tenn., Nov. 28, 1920; s. Foster Greenwood and Edna (Deaver) A.; m. Jean Medlin, Mar. 3, 1951; children: Melissa Lee Arnett Campbell, Foster Deaver. BA, U. Tenn., 1946; LLB, U. Va., 1948. Bar: Va. 1948, Tenn. 1948, U.S. Dist. Ct. (ea. dist.) Tenn. 1949, U.S. Ct. Appeals (6th cir.) 1954, U.S. Supreme Ct. 1958. Practice law Knoxville, 1948—; partner Arnett, Draper & Hagood (and predecessors), 1954—; mem. Nat. Conf. Commrs. on Uniform State Laws, 1980-83; life mem. U.S. Ct. Appeals (6th cir.) Conf. Contbr. articles to profl. jours. Pres. Knox Children's Found., 1959-61, 75-76, East Tenn. Hearing and Speech Center, 1963-65, Knoxville Teen Ctr., 1969-71, Knoxville News-Sentinel Charities, 1985—; v.p. Ft. Loudon Assn., 1972-75; del. Republican Nat. Conv., 1964; bd. dirs., exec. com. Tenn. Mil. Inst., 1973-75; nat. chmn. appeals U. Va. Law Sch. Found., 1986-88; active ARC, Am. Cancer Soc., United Fund. Served with AUS, 1942-46, PTO; to lt. col. USAR, ret. Decorated Silver Star, Bronze Star, Purple Heart. Fellow Am. Coll. Trial Lawyers, Internat. Acad. Trial Lawyers (dean 1988-89, bd. dirs., trustee Found.), Internat. Soc. Barristers, Am. Bar Found. (life), Tenn. Bar Found.

(charter) Am. Bd. Trial Advocates (pres. Tenn. chpt. 1985-86); mem. Southeastern Legal Found. (legal adv. bd.), ABA (unauthorized practice of law com. and assn. communications com., aviation and space law com., state cert. of legal specialists com.), Tenn. Bar Assn. (pres. 1968-69), Knoxville Bar Assn. (pres. 1959-60), Internat. Assn. Def. Counsel (sec.-treas. 1981-84), S.E. Def. Counsel Assn. (v.p. 1966), Assn. Trial Lawyers Am., Am. Acad. Hosp. Attys. of Am. Hosp. Assn. (charter), Fedn. Ins. and Corp. Counsel, Am. Bd. Trial Advs. (adv., pres. Tenn. chpt.), Def. Research Inst. (charter), Product Liability Adv. Council Inc. (sustaining, U. Tenn. Devel. Council), U. Tenn. Nat. Alumni Assn. (pres. 1961-62, chmn. nat. ann. giving program 1961-63), SAR, Scribes, Scabbard and Blade, Scarrabbean, Torchbearer, Phi Gamma Delta, Phi Delta Phi (hon.), Omicron Delta Kappa (hon.). Republican. Presbyterian. Clubs: Civitan (Knoxville); Farmington Country (Charlottesville, Va.); Cherokee Country, LeConte, U. Tenn. Faculty (hon.), Men's Cotillion (dir. 1960-61, 63-64, 66-68, trustee 1962—); Appalachian (pres. 1974-76). Home: 4636 Alta Vista Way SW Knoxville TN 37919 Office: Arnett Draper & Hagood 2300 Plaza Tower Knoxville TN 37929-2300

ARNETT, JAMES EDWARD, educator; b. Gullett, Ky., Oct. 3, 1912; s. Haden and Josephine (Risner) A.; A.B., San Jose State Coll., 1947, M.A., 1955; Ed.S., Stanford, 1959; m. Helen Mae Vallish, Mar. 23, 1943. Tchr., prin. pub. schs., Salyersville, Ky., 1930-41; tchr., adminstr. pub. schs., Salinas, Calif., 1947-52; owner-mgr. Arnett Apts., Salinas, 1950-53; tchr., Innes High Sch., Akron, Ohio, 1953-73; owner-mgr. Arnett Apts., Akron, 1953-72; dir. Educator & Exec. Co., 1962-73, Educator and Exec. Insurers, 1957-76, Educator and Exec. Life Ins. Co., 1962-76, Great Am. of Dallas Fire and Casualty Co., 1974-76, Great Am. of Dallas Ins. Co., 1974-76, J.C. Penney Casualty Ins. Co., 1976; cons., 1976-77. Mem. county, state central coms. Democratic party, 1952. Served with AUS, 1942-45. Mem. NEA (life mem.; del. conv. 1957-65), Ohio (del. convs. 1957-73), Akron (1st v.p. 1964-65, parliamentarian 1965-72), edn. assns., San Jose State Coll., Stanford alumni assns., Phi Delta Kappa. Home: 691 Payne Ave Akron OH 44302-1347 Office: 800 Brooksedge Blvd Westerville OH 43081

ARNETZ, BENGT BIRGER LENNART, physician, researcher; b. Stockholm, Dec. 3, 1954; came to U.S., 1986; s. Allan Gustav and Solveig Olivia (Kallkvist) A.; m. Judith Ellen Cohen, Aug. 25, 1979; children: Lisa Faye Julia, Erik, Benjamin Daniel. BS, Karolinska Inst., Stockholm, 1976, MD, 1981, PhD in Psychophysiology, 1983; MPH, Harvard U., 1987, MSc in Epidemiology, 1988. Fellow Dag Hammarskiolds Coll., Washington, 1976-77; research asst. dept physiology Karolinska Inst., Stockholm, 1977-80, stresslab., 1978-81; research assoc. dept. psychiatry Yale U., New Haven, 1980; research physician Nat. Inst. Psychosoc. Fcts. and Health, Stockholm, 1981—; gen. practice Physicians Services, Stockholm, 1979—; with stress mgmt. ctr., Complehealth, Stockholm, 1980—; tchr. occupational health, Health Resurces, Woburn, Mass., 1986—; mem. com. Local Theoretic Research Council, Stockholm, 1985-87. Mem. Stockholm Med. Assn. (bd. dirs. 1983-86), Am. Geriatrics Soc., Internat. Soc. Psychoneuroendocrinology, Brit. Geriatric Soc., Swedish Soc. Medicine, Swedish Geriatric Soc., Swedish Acad. Youth Assn. (chmn. 1981-82), Stockholm Med. Student Assn. (chmn., sec. 1978-80), Am. Pub. Health Assn., Am. Assn. Occupational Medicine. Lutheran. Home: 110 Chestnut St Bound Brook NJ 08805 Office: Exxon Biomed Scis Inc Occupat Health & Epidemiology Div Mettlers Rd CN 2350 East Millstone NJ 08875-2350

ARNITZ, LOUIS, travel company executive; b. Frankfurt, Fed. Republic Germany, Mar. 20, 1956. Grad. high sch., Frankfurt. Mng. dir. Fao Travel Gesellschaft mit beschrankter Haftung, Frankfurt, 1976—; bd. dirs. World Intravel Mag., Frankfurt, 1985—; pres. FAO Travel of N.Am., Inc. Author: Travel the World, 1984. Mem. Deutscher Reiseburo Verband, Am. Soc. Travel Agents. Jewish. Home: 46 Eysseneckstrasse, 6000 Frankfurt 1 Federal Republic of Germany Office: Fao Travel GMBH, Glauburgstrasse 95, 6000 Frankfurt 1 Federal Republic of Germany

ARNOLD, DARYL, diplomat; b. Santa Monica, Calif., Nov. 12, 1924; 3 children. Student, U. So. Calif., 1942-44, Midshipman Sch., 1945. With Family Farming, West Los Angeles, Calif., 1946-51; owner Cee Dee Ranch Co., Ventura, Calif., 1951-59; ptnr., mgr. Ocean View Farms, Ventura, 1960-69; div. mgr. Freshpiet Foods, Ventura, 1969-70; pres. Free Mktg. Council, Los Angeles, 1970-71; pres., chief exec. officer Western Growers Assn., Irvine, Calif., 1971-87; ambassador to Singapore, Washington, 1987—; mem. U.S. Agrl. Tech. Adv. Com., Washington, 1973, Calif. Lt. Gov.'s Econ. Devel. Com., Sacramento, Bd. for Internat. Food and Agrl. Devl., 1982-83. Mem. Ventura County Grand Jury, 1983, Pres. Commn. of Conduct of U.S.-Japan Relations, 1983-84. Office: US Ambassador to Singapore care US Dept of State Washington DC 20520 *

ARNOLD, DAVID PAUL, sales professional; b. Pitts., May 11, 1942; s. Arthur and Elizabeth (Novak) A.; m. Patricia Arda Graham, Sept. 3, 1966; children: Nichelle, Bret, Janelle. BA in Bus., Ohio No. U., 1964; grad., Ohio State Inst. Fin., 1971. Sales engr. Reliance Electric, various cities, 1964-70; sales dir. Columbia Nat., Columbus, Ohio, 1970-73; owner Mint Lake Valley Lumber, Ashtabula, Ohio, 1973-76; v.p. sales Preformed Line Products, Cleve., 1976—. Founder, BOGSAT. Named to Hon. Order Ky. Cols. Mem. Am. Mgmt. Assn. Republican. Methodist. Home: 2221 Gageville Rd Ashtabula OH 44004 Office: Preformed Line Products 660 Beta Dr Mayfield Village OH 44143

ARNOLD, GARY STEPHEN, real estate developer; b. 1954; m. June Elizabeth Borg, Sept. 1, 1979. Attended Ga. Inst. Tech.; BA, Georgetown U., 1976; pres. Monarch Holding Co. Office: Monarch Holding Co 2839 Paces Ferry Rd Suite 1020 Atlanta GA 30339

ARNOLD, GLEN ELDRED, management consultant; b. Shreveport, La., Nov. 4, 1931; s. Eulice Eldred and Myrtle Elizabeth (Comalander) A.; student La. Tech. U., 1949-52; B.S. in Acctg., Centenary Coll., La., 1960; postgrad. So. Meth. U., 1970; m. Delores Nickels, Aug. 15, 1952 (div. 1984); children—David Bruce, James Rendall. Plant acct. Ark. La. Gas Co., Shreveport, La., 1955-56, jr. engr. trainee, 1956-57, asst. supr. gen. accounting dept., 1957-59; traveling auditor So. Union Gas Co., Dallas, 1960-62, methods engr., 1962-63, data systems analyst, 1963-65, compensation mgr., 1965-69; corp. dir. personnel Great Southwest Corp. and subs.'s Six Flags, Inc. and GSC Devel. Corp., Arlington, Tex., 1969-72; sr. prin. with Hay Assocs., mgmt. cons.'s, Dallas, 1972—; instr. Eastfield Jr. Coll., Dallas, 1973-76. Served to sgt. U.S. Army, 1953-54. Mem. Am. Soc. Personnel Adminstrn., Dallas Personnel Assn., Am. Mgmt. Assn. (guest lectr. 1966—), Kappa Alpha, Omicron Delta Kappa, Pi Kappa Delta. Republican. Baptist. Office: The Hay Group Four Forest Plaza Suite 500 12222 Merit Dr Dallas TX 75251

ARNOLD, HARRY LOREN, JR., dermatologist, editor, author; b. Owosso, Mich., Aug. 7, 1912; s. Harry L. and Meda (Sheldon) A.; m. Blanche G. Wetherald, 1934 (div. 1941); children—Sara Joan, Charles R.; m. Jeanne M. Prevost, July 11, 1942 (dec. Jan. 1983); children: Harry Loren III, John P., Susan M.; m. Jeanne S. Herman, Dec. 16, 1983. A.B. cum laude, U. Mich., 1932, M.D. cum laude, 1935; M.S., 1939. Diplomate: Am. Bd. Dermatology (mem. bd. 1966-76, pres. 1972-73). Intern U. Mich. Hosp., 1935-36, resident, 1936-37, instr. dermatology, 1937-39; chief dermatology Straub Clinic, Honolulu, 1939-69; clin. prof. medicine U. Hawaii.; clin. prof. dermatology U. Calif., San Francisco; pres. Straub Med. Research Inst., 1961-63; Frederick G. Novy, Jr. vis. scholar in dermatology U. Calif. Med. Sch., Davis, 1975; cons. emeritus U.S. Army Health Services Command, 1980. Author: Modern Concepts of Leprosy, 1953, Raibyo Gentaiteki Gainen, 1956, (with P. Fasal) Leprosy, 1973, (with R.B. Odom and W.D. James) Andrews' Diseases of the Skin, 8th edit, 1988; also numerous articles, editorials, columns, and chpts. in textbooks.; editor Hawaii Med. Jour, 1941-83, founding editor, 1983—; editor Straub Clinic Procs., 1941-77, editor emeritus, 1978—; editor The Schoch Letter, 1975—, Internat. Jour. Dermatology, 1978—; corr. editor: Internat. Jour. of Leprosy, 1950-84; editorial bd. Cutis, 1965—, Group Practice, 1966-74, Jour. Internat. Med. Research, 1972—, Archives Dermatology, 1973-83, Jour. AMA, 1973-74. Named Practitioner of Yr. Dermatol. Found., 1983, Janssen Master in Dermatology, 1987. Fellow ACP, AAAS, Royal Soc. Medicine; mem. Hawaii Med. Assn. (past pres.), Honolulu County Med. Assn. (past pres.), Hawaiian Acad. Sci. (past pres.), Am. Acad. Dermatology (hon.; pres. 1975-76), Internat. Soc. Tropical Dermatology (past v.p.), Internat. Leprosy Assn., Hawaii Dermatol. Soc. (hon. 1986), Pacific Dermatol. Assn. (hon. mem., pres. 1968), AMA (past del., sect. chmn., del. sect. dermatology), Am. Dermatol. Assn. (bd. dirs. 1969-70, pres. 1971), Sociedad Argentina de Leprologia (corr.), Sociedad Cubana de Dermatología y Sifilografía (corr.), Asociacion Argentina de Dermatologia (corr.), Sociedad Venezolana de Dermatologia, Venereologia y Leprologia (corr.), Sociedad Mexicana de Dermatologia (hon.), Sociedad Brasileira de Dermatologia (hon.), S. African Dermatol. Assn. (hon.), N.Y. Dermatol. Assn. (hon.), Swedish Dermatol. Soc. (corr.), Honolulu chpt. Internat. Wine and Food Soc. (pres. 1977), Social Sci. Assn. Honolulu (pres. 1984, hon. mem.), Sigma Xi, Kappa Beta Phi, Alpha Omega Alpha, Nu Sigma Nu, Phi Kappa Psi, Zeta Psi. Home: 250 Laurel St Apt 301 San Francisco CA 94118 Office: 450 Sutter Suite 1432 San Francisco CA 94108

ARNOLD, HUGH JAMES, management educator; b. Lethbridge, Alta., Can., Nov. 9, 1949; s. Hugh Alexander and Islay May (Brown) A.; m. Clara Jean Fergusson, Sept. 2, 1978; children: Jennifer Lee, Christine Marie. BA, U. Alta., Edmonton, 1970; MA, Oxford (Eng.) U., 1972, Yale U., 1974; PhD, Yale U., 1976. Asst. prof. mgmt. U. Toronto, Ont., 1976-81, assoc. prof., 1981-85, prof., 1985—, assoc. dean, 1985-87, assoc. dean Sch. Grad. Studies, 1987-88; prof. bus. strategy Magna Internat, 1988—; cons. Canadian GE, Harley-Davidson Motorcycles, Honeywell, Met. Toronto Police, IBM Can. Author: Managing Individual and Group Behavior in Organizations, 1983, Organizational Behavior, 1986; mem. editorial bd. Acad. of Mgmt. Jour., 1983-85. Treas. York Mills Valley Assn., Toronto, 1986—. Mem. Can. Inst. Advanced Research, Acad. Mgmt., Am. Psychol. Assn., Adminstrv. Scis. Can. Club: Granite, Devil's Glen (Glen Huron, Ont.). Home: 31 Donino Ave, Toronto, ON Canada M4N 2W6 Office: U Toronto Faculty of Mgmt, 246 Bloor St W, Toronto, ON Canada M5S 1V4

ARNOLD, KARL WERNER, lawyer; b. Luzern, Switzerland, June 29, 1940; s. Emil Hans and Emilie (Steinmann) A.; m. Martina Vonwyl, Aug. 23, 1974; children: Dominik, Christof, Philipp. Grad., U. Fribourg (Switzerland), 1964, D.iur., 1969; Diplôme de Droit Comparé, U. Luxembourg, 1967. Asst., Law Sch. U. Fribourg, 1965; clk. Dist. Ct., Kriens-Luzern, Switzerland, 1966; trainee Ruegg Law Firm, Luzern, 1967; sec. Dist. Ct., Kriens-Luzern, 1968; assoc. Pestalozzi & Gmuer, Zurich, Switzerland, 1969-73, ptnr., 1974—. Author: Verwaltungs und Regierungstatigkeit durch eidgenossische Kommissionen, 1969; contbr.: International Handbook on Comparative Business Law, 1979; Legal Aspects of Doing Business in Western Europe, 1983; A World Guide to Exchange Control Regulations, 1985; Survey of the International Sale of Goods, 1986. Mem. Verein Zurcherischer Rechtsanwalte, Schweizerischer Juristenverein, Internat. Bar Assn., ABA, N.Y.C. Bar Assn. Club: Zofingia (Fribourg). Home: Bellevueweg 5, 6300 Zug Switzerland Office: Pestalozzi Gmur & Heiz, Lowenstrasse 1, 8001 Zurich Switzerland

ARNOLD, KENNETH JAMES, lawyer, publishing company executive; b. Brighton, Colo., Sept. 10, 1927; s. Kenneth Wilburt and Frances Irene (Lloyd) A. Student, U. Paris, 1950-51, U. Rabat, Morocco, 1951-52; A.B., U. Calif., Berkeley, 1949; M.A., U. Calif., 1950; J.D., U. Calif., Hastings Coll. Law, San Francisco, 1958. Bar: Calif. 1959. Sole practice San Francisco, 1959-60, 63—; sole practice Sacramento, 1960-62; owner Law Book Service Co., San Francisco, 1969—; research atty. Calif. Supreme Ct., Sacramento, 1960-62, Calif. Ct. Appeal 1st Appellate Dist., San Francisco, 1958-60; asst. sr. editor-in-chief Matthew Bender & Co., San Francisco, 1963-81, staff author, 1981-87, sr. staff author, 1987—; lectr. in field, 1972-81; cons. to Calif. State Jud. Council, 1970—, Calif. Ctr. Jud. Edn. and Research, 1974—, Calif. Coll. Trial Judges, 1975, McGeorge Coll. Law, U. Pacific, 1975-80; mem. Calif. Legal Forms Com., 1971-73. Author: California Courts and Judges Handbook, 1968, 5th revised edit., 1988; California Justice Court Manual, 1971 supplement; (with others) California Points and Authorities, 23 vols., 1964—, California Forms of Pleadings and Practice, 55 vols., 1966—, California Legal Forms, 25 vols., 1967-69; Commencing Civil Actions in California, 1975, and supplements; (with others) California Family Law Practice, 6 vols., 1977-78, California Civil Actions, 5 vols., 1982—; other manuals and handbooks; feature writer Barclays Law Monthly, 1979-82; editor Vector Mag., 1965-67. Bd. dirs. Soc. for Individual Rights, 1965-67, PRIDE Found., San Francisco, 1974-77. Served with AUS, 1952-55, Korea. Mem. State Bar Calif., Hastings Alumni Assn., San Francisco Gem and Mineral Soc., Am. Legion. Home: 369 Harvard St San Francisco CA 94134 Office: 2101 Webster St Oakland CA 94612

ARNOLD, LYNN ELLIS, metallurgical engineer; b. Nov. 17, 1934; s. Leslie Lee and Emma R. (Betscher) A. Metall. Engr., U. Cin., 1957; M.S. in Mech. Engring., U. Ill., 1959. Registered profl. engr., Ohio. Grad. asst. U. Ill., Urbana, 1957-59; with Xtek, Inc., Cin., 1959—, mgr. tech. services, 1984-86, research engr., 1986—. Author articles in field. Served with USAF, 1958-59. Fellow AAAS, Am. Soc. Metals (past pres. Cin. chpt., past mem. tech. div. bd., Wm. H. Eisenman Meml. award 1979); mem. NSPE (past chmn. indsl. div., past v.p.), Ohio Soc. Profl. Engrs. (past pres. Cin. chpt., Young Engr. award 1965), ASME (past pres. Cin. sect., past pres. Ohio council), Soc. Mfg. Engrs. (past pres. Cin. chpt.), Cin. Tech. and Sci. Socs. Council (past pres., Community Service award 1979), Engring. Soc. Cin. (past pres.), Soc. Advancement of Mgmt. (pres. Cin. chpt.), Cin. Mgmt. Assn. (past pres.), Cin. Editors Assn. (past pres.), Tool Steel Mgmt. Club (past pres.), U. Cin. Engring. Alumni Assn. (past pres., Disting. Alumnus award 1979), SAR (past pres. Cin. chpt.), Audubon Soc. Ohio (past pres., chmn. fin. com., bd. dirs.), Ohio Audubon Council (past pres.), Am. Gear Mfg. Assn. (chmn. metallurgy and materials com.), AIME-ISS (co-chmn. roll Tech. com.), Ctr. for Mfg. Tech. (bd. dirs.), Ohio Geneal. Soc. (corr. sec. Hamilton County chpt.), Tau Beta Pi, Alpha Sigma Mu, Alpha Phi Omega, Pi Delta Epsilon, Alpha Chi Sigma. Republican. Methodist. Home: 6538 Kugler Mill Rd Cincinnati OH 45236 Office: 11451 Reading Rd Cincinnati OH 45241

ARNOLD, MARY ANN, mathematical statistician; b. Louisville, Dec. 8, 1938; d. Stanley A. Gatewood and Mary Elizabeth (Church) G.; m. Gabriel Thomas Arnold, July 2, 1960; 1 child, Gabriel Thomas II. AB, Spalding Coll., 1960. Math. statistician Bur. of Census, Jeffersonville, Ind., 1967—. Mem. Am. Statis. Assn., Internat. Assn. of Survey Statisticians, Am. Soc. Quality Control. Roman Catholic. Avocation: walking, aerobics. Home: 104 Tanglewood Trail Louisville KY 40223-2816 Office: Bur of Census 1201 E 10th St Jeffersonville IN 47132

ARNOLD, PHILIP MILLS, retired oil company executive; b. Springfield, Mo., Feb. 9, 1911; s. Anthony L. and Mary Genevieve (Hodnett) A. B.S., Washington U., 1932, Chem. E., 1941, Sc.D. hon., 1983. Chem. engr. research div. Philips Petroleum Co., 1937-45, asst. mgr. chem. engring. div., 1946-48, asst. mgr. chem. dept., 1948-50, mgr. research and devel. dept., 1950-64, v.p. research and devel., 1964-76; Exec. com. div. chemistry and chem. tech. NRC, 1961-65; mem. U.S. nat. com. Internat. Union Pure and Applied Chemistry, 1961-75, chmn., 1964-68, mem. bur., 1969-75; dir. Coordinating Research Council, 1964, pres., 1969-71; pres. Indsl. Research Inst., 1964-65, bd. dirs., 1958-61; mem. Com. on Scholarly Communication with People's Republic of China. Mem. World Petroleum Congresses (permanent council 1965-71), AAAS, Dirs. Indsl. Research, Nat. Acad. Engring., Sigma Chi, Tau Beta Pi, Alpha Chi Sigma. Republican. Home: Box 1457 Bartlesville OK 74005

ARNOLD, SHEILA, state legislator; b. N.Y.C., Jan. 15, 1929; d. Michael and Eileen (Lynch) Keddy; coll. courses; m. George Longan Arnold, Nov. 12, 1960; 1 son, Peter; 1 son by previous marriage, Michael C. Young; stepchildren—Drew, George Longan, Joe. Mem. Wyo. Ho. of Reps., 1978—, mem. com. on appropriations, com. on rules and procedures; dir. First Interstate Bank of Laramie. Former mem., sec. Wyo. Land Use Adv. Coms.; past pres. Dem. Women's Club, Laramie; past vice-chmn. Albany County Dem. Cen. Com.; past mem. Dem. State Com.; mem. Nat. Conf. State Legislatures Com. on Fiscal Affairs and Oversight. Recipient Spl. Recognition award from Developmentally Disabled Citizens of Wyo., 1985. Mem. Laramie Area C. of C. (pres. 1982; Top Hand award 1977), LWV, Internat. Platform Assn. Clubs: Faculty Women's (past pres.), Zonta, Laramie Women's, Cowboy Joe. Office: Capitol Bldg Cheyenne WY 82002

ARNOLD, THOMAS BURTON, physician; b. Mpls., May 29, 1929; s. Duma Carroll and Ann (Whelan) A.; m. Janet Onstad, June 16, 1957 (div. 1977); children: Pamela, Thomas, Virginia Ann. BA, Dartmouth Coll., 1951; MD, U. Pa., 1955. Diplomate Am. Bd. Internal Medicine. Rotating intern U. Chgo. Clinics, 1955-56; fellow in internal medicine Mayo Found., Rochester, Minn., 1960-63; practice medicine specializing in internal medicine, Mpls., 1963-77, Edina, Minn., 1977—; mem. staffs Abbott Hosp., Northwestern Hosp., Fairview Hosp., Southdale Hosp.; regional med. dir. Standard Oil Co. Ind., Chgo., 1966—; sr. aviation med. examiner FAA, 1963—; asst. prof. medicine U. Minn., Mpls., 1970—. Served to capt. USAF, 1956-59. Fellow ACP; mem. AMA, Minn. Med. Assn., Hennepin County Med. Soc. Republican. Avocation: gardening. Office: Thomas Arnold & Assocs 681 Southdale Med Bldg 6545 France Ave S Edina MN 55435

ARNOLD, WILLIAM EDWIN, manufacturing executive; b. Charleston, S.C., Aug. 13, 1938; s. Edwin Gustaf and Sara Louise (Hitchcock) A.; B.A., Yale U., 1960. Pres., Dixon & Rippel, Inc., Saugerties, N.Y., 1965-70; v.p. Taj Enterprises Ltd., 1965-67, Bellern Research Corp., pres. Dixon & Rippel div., Saugerties, 1970-75; v.p. H & G Industries, Inc., pres. Indsl. Brush Div., Belleville, N.J., 1975-82; pres. World Brushworks, Inc., 1982-84; v.p., chief fin. officer Optimax III, Inc., N.Y.C., 1983-84; mng. dir. Brush Trading, Ltd., 1983-88; pres. Chestnut Holdings Ltd., 1985—; mng. dir. Cassi Properties, 1984—; pres. Swan Holding Ltd., 1985-88; bd. dirs. ARCS, 1986—; served to 1st lt. U.S. Army, 1961-63. Mem. Internat. Platform Assn., Res. Officers Assn. Home: 19 Chestnut St Rhinebeck NY 12572 Office: PO Box 341 Rhinebeck NY 12572

ARNS, PAULO EVARISTO CARDINAL, cardinal, archbishop; b. Criciuma, Brazil, Sept. 14, 1921; s. Gabriel and Helena (Steiner) A.; ed. U. Parana, Sorbonne, 1952; LL.D. (hon.), U. Notre Dame (Ind.), 1977, Siena Coll., Albany, N.Y., 1981; Fordham U., N.Y.C., 1981, Seton Hall U., South Orange, N.J., 1982. Ordained priest Roman Catholic Ch.; prof. patrology and didatics Cath. U. Petropolis; pastor, 1956-66; aux. bishop of São Paulo, 1966-70, archbishop, 1970—; created cardinal of São Paulo, 1973; chancellor Pontifical Cath. U., São Paulo, 1970—; mem. Vatican Sacred Congregation Sacrements and Divine Worship. Recipient Hansen medal for def. of human rights in Latin Am., U.N., 1985. Author 39 books. Office: Caina Postal 30-405, São Paulo Brazil *

ARNSDORF, MORTON FRANK, cardiologist, educator; b. Chgo., Aug. 7, 1940; s. Selmar N. and Irmgard C. (Steinmann) A.; m. Mary Hunter Tower, Dec. 26, 1963 (div. 1982); m. Rosemary Crowley, Dec. 27, 1986. B.A. magna cum laude, Harvard U., 1962; M.D., Columbia U., 1966. Diplomate Am. Bd. Internal Medicine. House staff officer U. Chgo., 1966-69; fellow cardiology Columbia-Presbyn. Med. Ctr., N.Y.C., 1969-71; asst. prof. medicine U. Chgo., 1973-79, assoc. prof., 1979-83, prof., 1983—, chief sect. cardiology, 1981—; mem. pharmacology study sect. NIH, 1981-84. Contbr. articles to profl. jours. Served to maj. USAF, 1971-73. Recipient Research Career Devel. award NIH, 1976-81; research grantee Chgo. Heart Assn., 1976-78, NIH, 1977—. Fellow ACP, Am. Coll. Cardiology, Am. Coll. Physicians; mem. Am. Heart Assn. (dir. 1981-83, chmn. exec. com. basic sci. council 1981-83, steering com. 1983-86), Chgo. Heart Assn. (v.p. 1986, pres.-elect 1987—, bd. govs., chmn. research council), AMA, Am. Fedn. Clin. Research, Assn. Univ. Cardiologists, Cen. Soc. Clin. Research (chmn. cardiovascular council 1986-87), Chgo. Med. Soc., Ill. Med. Soc., Cardiac Electrophysiology Soc. (sec.-treas. 1984-86, pres. 1986—). Club: Quadrangle. Office: Chief Sect Cardiology Univ Chgo Hosps and Clinics Box 423 5841 S Maryland Chicago IL 60637

ARNST, ALBERT, editor, forester; b. Portland, Oreg., July 9, 1909; s. David and Alwina (Lorenz) A.; B.S. in Forestry, Oreg. State U., 1931; m. Della Coleen Irwin, May 1, 1939; children—Audrey Karen, Robert Craig, Rosemary. Forester, Forest Service, U.S. Dept. Agr., Portland, Oreg., 1931-35, Medford, Oreg., 1935-36, Lakeview, Oreg., 1937, public info. officer, Washington, 1962-75, with Soil Conservation Service, Dayton, Spokane and Sedro-Woolley, (all in Wash.), 1937-45, Corvallis and Portland, Oreg., 1941-43; sales rep Skagit Steel & Iron Works, Sedro-Woolley, 1945-46; public info. rep. Weyerhaeuer Co., Tacoma, 1946-52; editor Timberman mag., Portland, 1952-53; editor Miller Freeman Publs., Portland, 1954-62; mng. editor Western Conservation Jour., Portland, 1975-82. Fellow Soc. Am. Foresters (53-yr. mem.); mem. Soil Conservation Soc. Am., Oreg. Logging Conf. (hon. life), Internat. Assn. Bus. Communicators (Rodney Adair Meml. award 1978, pres. 1962, 71, 79, named Communicator of Yr. 1966 nat. Pres.'s award 1983). Democrat. Clubs: Foggy Bottom (pres. 1971) (Washington). Lodge: Lions, Hoo-Hoo. Contbr. articles on forestry to profl. jours. Address: 2430 NE Stanton Portland OR 97212

ARNTHORSSON, VALUR, cooperative society executive; b. Eskifjordur, Iceland, Mar. 1, 1935; s. Arnthor Jensen and Gudny Petursdottir; Bus. Dipl., Coop Sch. Iceland, Reykjavik, 1953; student lang., bus. and ins., London 1955-56; student Swedish Coop. Sch., Saltsjöbaden, 1965; m. Sigridur Olafsdottir, July 16, 1955; children: Brynja Dis, Olafur, Arna Gudny, Olof Sigridur, Arnbjorg Hlif. Ins. clk. Samvinn Coop. Ins. Co., Reykjavik, Iceland, 1953-58, mgr. reins. dept., 1958-64, dir. underwriting dept., 1964-65; asst. to dir. gen. KEA, The Coop. Soc. Eyjafjordur (Iceland), 1965-70, dep. dir., 1970-71, dir. gen., 1971—, also chmn. bd. dirs. various subs. cos.; vice chmn. bd. Samvinn Group of Ins. Cos., 1977—, Esso Oil Co. Iceland, 1978-87, chmn. bd. dirs., 1987—; chmn. bd. dirs. Fedn. of Iceland Coop. Socs., 1978—, sec., 1975-78. Mem. Town Council Akureyri (Iceland), 1970-78, chmn., 1974-78, mem. Danish Consul, 1987—; chmn. bd. dirs. Laxarvirkjun Elec. Power Works, Akureyri, 1970-83; alt. mem. bd. dirs. Nat. Power Co. Iceland, 1983—. Decorated knight Cross of Icelandic Falk Order. Mem. Soc. Coop. Soc. Dirs., Icelandic Mgmt. Soc. Lutheran. Lodges: Rotary, Masons (Akureyri). Home: Byggdavegur 118, 600 Akureyri Iceland Office: Hafnarstraeti 91-95, 600 Akureyri Iceland

ARNTSEN, ARNT PETER, engineer; b. Hvaler, Norway, Oct. 23, 1921; s. Arnt Peter and Helene Oleane (Helgesen) A.; m. Margot Petra Nilsen, Oct. 24, 1953; children—Tom David, Carol Ann, John Frederick. Engr., Westinghouse Research Center, Pitts., 1962-64; sr. engring. scientist RCA Corp., Burlington, Mass., 1964—. Registered prof. engr., Mass. Mem. IEEE, Nat. Soc. Profl. Engrs., Sigma Xi. Patentee in field. Home: 9 Lincoln Ave Manchester MA 01944 Office: Rts 3 and 62 Burlington MA 01803

ARNTZEN, HELMUT, language educator; b. Duisburg, North Rhine-Westphalia, Fed. Republic of Germany, Jan. 10, 1931; s. Otto and Elisabeth Gertrude (Kröck) A.; m. Regina Gabriele Martha Pienkny, Mar. 23, 1965; 1 child, Viola. PhD, U. Cologne, Fed. Republic of Germany, 1957, diploma in library scis., 1958. Sci. asst. Free U. Berlin, 1959-67, lectr., 1967-68; prof. German lang. and lit., dir. Inst. German Lang. and Lit. Westphalian Wilhelms-U. Münster, Fed. Republic of Germany, 1968—, dean Sch. German Lang. and Lit., 1976-77; lectr. Sch. Theology, Berlin, 1961-62; vis. prof. Ain Shams U., Cairo and Heliopolis, Egypt, 1982; Max Kade Disting. vis. prof. U. Kans., Lawrence, 1987. Author 10 books; editor 4 books; contbr. articles to profl. jours. Recipient Robert Musil medal City of Klagenfurt, Austria, 1983. Mem. Internat. Union German Lang. and Lit., Internat. PEN. Club: Ambassador (Münster). Home: Am Schlosspark 21, D 4403 Senden Federal Republic of Germany Office: Westphalian Wilhelms-U Munster, Domplatz 20-22, D 4400 Munster Federal Republic of Germany

ARON, ROBERTO, lawyer, writer; b. Mendoza, Argentina, Nov. 1, 1915; s. David and Catalina (Trostanetzky) A.; m. Catalina Berstein, May 1, 1940 (dec. Oct. 1965); children: Jaim, Sylvia, Daniel; m. Eva Coriat, Dec. 14, 1968; stepchildren: Sonia, Aileen (twins). BA in Law, U. Chile, 1943; LLM in Internat. Law, N.Y.U., 1977, LLM in Corp. Law, 1979; postgrad., Harvard U., 1981. Bar: Israel 1960. Sr. ptnr. Aron and Cia, Santiago, Chile, 1943-57, Aron, Tamir and Aron, Tel Aviv, 1960—; tchr. N.Y.U., 1983, Tel Aviv U., Israel, 1985; gov. bd. Tel Aviv U., 1982; mem. directory Otzar Itiashvut Hayeudim Bank, Tel Aviv, 1972—; cons. Taurel and Cia, Caracas, Venezuela, 1976—; mem. Israeli delegation to UN, 1975. Co-author: How to Prepare Witnesses for Trial, 1985, Trial Communications Skills, 1986. Mem. Nat. Inst. Trial Advocacy, Advocates Assn., Assn. Trial Lawyers Am. Jewish. Home: 985 Fifth Ave Apt 12A New York City NY 10021 also: Maale Habanim 17-Ramat Gan, Tel Aviv 65215, Israel Office: Arón Tamir and Arón, 1 Melchet St, Tel Aviv 65215, Israel

ARONOW, EDWARD, psychologist, educator; b. N.Y.C., Dec. 22, 1945; s. Hyman and Gertrude (Bakst) A.; B.A. in Psychology, Queens Coll., CUNY, 1967; M.A. in Psychology, Fordham U., 1969, Ph.D. in Clin. Psychology, 1973; m. Audrey Susan Gimpelson, Dec. 25, 1967; children—David, Rebecca. Psychology trainee VA, N.Y.C., 1968-72; assoc. prof. psychology Montclair (N.J.) State Coll., 1972—; sr. clin. psychologist St. Vincent's Hosp., N.Y.C., 1972-79; clin. psychologist, Montclair, N.J., 1974—. Mem. Am. Psychol. Assn., Eastern Psychol. Assn., N.J. Psychol. Assn., Soc. Personality Assessment, Sigma Xi. Author: Rorschach Content Interpretation, 1976; A Rorschach Introduction: Content and Perceptual Approaches, 1982. Home and Office: 59 Gordonhurst Ave Upper Montclair NJ 07043

ARONSON, EDGAR DAVID, brokerage company executive; b. N.Y.C., June 17, 1934; s. Aaron Solomon and Ida Claire (Minevitch) A.; m. Nancy Carol Pforzheimer, Dec. 23, 1956; children: Edgar David, Alison C., Edith S., Peter Borrah. A.B., Harvard U., 1956, M.B.A., 1962. Successively trainee, asst. cashier, v.p. 1st Nat. Bank of Chgo., 1962-67; v.p. Republic Nat. Bank of N.Y., 1968; trainee Salomon Bros., N.Y.C., 1968-69; ltd. partner Salomon Bros., 1970, v.p., 1971-72, gen. partner, 1972-79; mng. dir. Salomon Bros. Internat. Ltd., London, 1971-76; chmn. bd. Dillon, Read Internat., 1979-81; pres. EDACO, Inc., 1981—; dir. Salomon Bros. Asia, Hong Kong, 1975-79, Merrie-Go-Round, Inc., Dallas, APL N.V., Curacao, Petrogas Ltd., Hong Kong, Burnwood Corp., N.Y.C., Calif. Energy Co., San Francisco, Everett & Co., London. Author: (with others) New Old World, 1962, Response to Change, 1963. Trustee Lesley Coll., Cambridge, Mass., 1981-84. Served to 1st lt. USMCR, 1956-60. Mem. Marine Corps Res. Officers Assn., 1st Marine Div. Assn., The Cruising Assn. (U.K.), Mensa. Clubs: N.Y. Yacht, Bass Harbor Yacht, Harvard, Down Town Assn. (N.Y.C.); Annabel's (London). Office: 770 Lexington Ave 11th Floor New York NY 10021

ARONSON, MARITA HALLGERD ANNA, psychologist; b. Ljungby, Sweden, May 10, 1939; d. Eric M.L. and Daga G.V. Bauner; m. Nils Aronson; children: David, Johanna, Eric. Grad. in Philosophy, U. Göteborg, Sweden, 1962, postgrad. in Philosophy, 1972, D in Philosophy, 1983. Lic. Psychologist. Educator U. of Göteborg, 1963-72; psychologist Pediatric dept. East Hosp., Göteborg, 1972—; psychologist Dept. for Handicapped Children East Hosp., 1973-78. Author: Children of Alcoholic Mothers, 1983. Active in the Commune of Mölndal, 1985—. Folkpartiet.

ARONSON, MARK BERNE, lawyer; b. Pitts., Aug. 24, 1941; s. Richard J. and Jean (DeRoy) A.; m. Ellen Jane Askin, July 20, 1970; children: Robert M., Andrew A., Michael D. BS in Econs., U. Pa., 1962; JD, U. Pitts., 1965. Bar: Pa. 1965, U.S. Dist. Ct. (we. dist.) Pa. 1965, U.S. Ct. Appeals (3d cir.) 1968, U.S. Ct. Claims 1978, U.S. Supreme Ct. 1966; lic. real estate broker, 1972. Sole practice, Pitts., 1965-66, 83—; sr. ptnr. Behrend & Aronson, Pitts., 1967-80, Behrend, Aronson & Morrow, Pitts., 1980-83. Past pres. Community Day Sch., Pitts., Rodef Shalom Jr. Congregation; past trustee Rodef Shalom Congregation, Pitts., 1979-87, trustee Pitts. Child Guidance Found., 1987—; mem., Pitts. Council on Edn. (head budget review com. 1987), 1986—. Mem. Am. Trial Lawyers Assn. (sustaining mem., prior Pa. rep. to exchange com.), Pa. Trial Lawyers Assn. (Pres.'s Club), Allegheny County Bar Assn., N.Y. State Trial Lawyers Assn., Pa. Bar Assn., Am. Arbitration Assn. (mem. Nat. Panel Arbitrators). Republican. Jewish. Clubs: Concordia, Rivers. Lodge: Masons (master). Office: 429 4th Ave Suite 707 Pittsburgh PA 15219

ARONSON, MIRIAM KLAUSNER, gerontologist, consultant, researcher, educator; b. N.Y.C., July 12, 1940; d. Joseph and Martha (Sklower) Klausner; children: Eric, Andrew, Elliott. AB, Barnard Coll., 1961; MEd, Columbia U., 1970, EdD, 1980. Cons., researcher geriatric facilities N.Y, N.J., 1969-75; dir. geriatric program Soundview-Throgs Neck Community Mental Health Ctr., Bronx, N.Y., 1975-78; chief services to elderly Bronx-Lebanon Hosp. Community Mental Health Ctr., Bronx, 1978-79; dir. longterm care Gerontol Ctr. Albert Einstein Coll. Medicine, Bronx, 1979—; asst. prof. neurology and psychiatry, 1980-85, assoc. prof. 1985—, prin. investigator senile dementias, risks and course, 1984—. Author, dir.: film series Teaching Series on Alzheimers Disease, 1980; author (with R. Bennett and B. Gurland) The Acting Out Elderly, 1983; editor, contbr. Understanding Alzheimers Disease, 1988. Mem. Hillsdale (N.J.) Bd. Health, 1975-82, pres. 1977-81; mem. planning and policy com. Outreach Health Service Program, Bergen County, N.J., 1976. N.Y. State Regents scholar, 1957-61; adminstrn. Aging grantee, 1968-70, 74-75; Nat. Council Community Mental Health Ctrs. Best Outreach Program award, 1976; Alzheimers Disease Soc. Greater N.Y. award, 1982. Fellow Gerontol. Soc. Am. (dir. task force on long term care 1981-85), Am. Orthopsychiat. Soc. (program com. 1985-88, co-chair study group on aging 1988—, N.Y.C. mayor's alzheimers disease adv. com.); mem. Am. Geriatrics Soc., Nat. Alzheimers Disease and Related Disorders Assn. (dir. edn. and pub. awareness com. 1979-84, cons. 1985—, Founders award 1987), Western Gerontol. Soc. (bd. dirs. 1983-85). Home: 305 Ell Rd Hillsdale NJ 07642 Office: Albert Einstein Coll Medicine Resnick Gerontology Ctr 1300 Morris Park Ave Bronx NY 10461

ARONSON, PETER DAMIEN, chemical company executive; b. Middlesbrough, Yorkshire, England, Mar. 2, 1943; s. Eric Reinhold and Teresa (Carolan) A.; m. Maureen Hunter; children: Helen Ruth, Mark Geoffrey, Clare Teresa. BSc with honors, U. Durham, Newcastle Upon Tyne, Eng., 1964. Dynamics engr. Hawker Siddeley Dynamics Ltd., London, 1964-65; sr. tech. officer Tioxide Internat. Ltd., Stockton on Tees, Eng., 1965-74; tech. service mgr. Titanio SA, Madrid, 1974-78; regional export mgr. Tioxide Group PLC, London, 1978-83, mktg. research mgr., 1983-86, sales mgr. Europe, 1986-87, sales ops. mgr., 1987—. Contbr. articles to profl. jours. Mem. Royal Soc. Chemistry. Roman Catholic. Office: Tioxide Group PLC, Tioxide House 137-143 Hammersmith Rd, London W14 OQL, England

ARONSSON, GUNNAR TORBJÖRN, psychologist, researcher; b. Nössemark, Sweden, Nov. 22, 1943; s. Oskar Teodor and Ottelia Josefina (Otter) A. MA in Psychology, U. Stockholm, 1970, MS in Psychology, 1974, PhD in Psychology, 1985. Lic. psychologist, Sweden. Research asst. U. Stockholm, 1974-77, project leader, 1977-83, acting prof. social psychology, 1985-87, assoc. prof. psychology, 1987—; research psychologist Nat. Inst. Occupational Health, Solna, Sweden, 1983—; cons. Ericsson Telephone Co., Stockholm, 1982. Author, editor: Occupational Skill, 1983, Occupational Stress, 1987; editor Critical Psychology jour., 1984. Mem. Internat. Assn. Applied Psychology, Psychologists Against Nuclear Weapons. Home: Sankt Paulsgatan 23, S-11648 Stockholm Sweden Office: Nat Inst, Ekelundsv 16, S-17184 Solna Sweden

ARORA, PRINCE KUMAR, immunologist; b. New Delhi, India, Nov. 15, 1947; came to U.S., 1972, naturalized, 1981; s. Manohar Lal Narayana and Khem (Kumari) A.; BS with honors, Panjab U., 1970, MS with honors, 1973; PhD in Microbiology, Mich. State U., 1978; m. Kit-ying Barbara Chin, 1982; children: Hans Chin A., Naveen Chin A. Grad. research asst. Mich. State U., 1976-78; John E. Fogarty internat. vis. fellow lab. immuno-diagnosis Nat. Cancer Inst., NIH, 1978-79, John E. Fogarty internat. vis. fellow immunology br., 1979-82, staff fellow Lab. Molecular Genetics, Nat. Inst. Child Health and Human Devel., 1982-83, staff fellow Lab. Devel. and Molecular Immunity, Nat. Inst. Child Health and Human Devel., 1983-87; sr. scientist lab. neurosci. NIH, Bethesda, Md., 1987—. Recipient Gold medal Panjab U., 1971, Internat. Travel awards, 1983, 88; Merit scholar, 1967-72. Mem. Am. Soc. Microbiology, N.Y. Acad. Scis., Am. Assn. Immunologists, Sigma Xi. Contbr. articles to profl. jours. Home: 10108 Ashburton Ln Bethesda MD 20817 Office: NIH Lab Neurosci Bldg 8 Room 111 NIDDK Bethesda MD 20892

ARRABAL, FERNANDO, writer; b. Melilla, Spain, Aug. 11, 1932; m. Luce Moreau; 2 children. Author: (novels): Baal Babylone, 1959, The Burial of Sardine, 1952, Fetes et Rites de la Confusion, 1965, La Torre Herida por el Rayo (Prix Nadal 1983); (poetry): Pierre de la folie, 1963, 100 Sonnets, 1966; numerous plays include: The Architect and the Emperor of Assyria, And They Put Handcuffs on the Flowers, Garden of Delights, The Automobile Graveyard, Guernica, The Grand Ceremonial; (essays): The Panic, The New York of Arrabal, Letter to General Franco, Fischer, 1973; writer and dir. films: Viva la Muerte, J'irai comme un cheval fou, L'arbre de Guernica, Odyssey of the Pacific. Recipient Grand Prix du Theatre, 1967, Grand Prix Humour Noir, 1968, Prix de l'Humour noir, 1969. Founder Panique movement with Topor, Jodorowsky and others; polit. prisoner, Spain, 1967.

ARRAU, CLAUDIO, concert pianist; b. Chillan, Chile, Feb. 6, 1903; married; children: Carmen, Mario (dec.), Christopher. Endowed as child prodigy by Chilean Govt. to study at, Stern Conservatory, Berlin, with Martin Krause, 1912-18. Made debut, Berlin, 1915, London debut, 1920, toured, Germany, Europe, S.Am., 1st U.S. tour, 1923-24; returned permanently, 1941, toured, USSR, 1929, 30, 68, Australia, 1947, 57, 62, 68, 70, 74, South Africa, 1949, 52, 56, Japan, 1965, 68, 72, 79, 82, 84, 87, Israel, 1950, 52, 58, 60, 64, 67, 71, 72; presented 32 Beethoven piano sonatas in, N.Y., 1953, 62; toured world many times.; Recorded: major piano works of Debussy, Beethoven, Brahms, Chopin, Liszt, Schumann, Schubert, Mozart. Decorated chevalier Order Arts and Letters, comdr. Legion of Honor (France); Deutsches Verdienst Kreuz Ger.; recipient Liszt prize, 1913, 14; Ibach prize, 1917; Grand Internat. prize at Geneva, 1927; Internat UNESCO Music prize, 1983; streets name in his honor in Santiago and Chillan. Office: care Internat Creative Mgmt Artists 40 W 57th St New York NY 10019 *

ARRIGHI DE CASANOVA, JEAN-FRANCOIS, oil company executive; b. Nimes, Gard, France, Oct. 31, 1949; s. Jean and Francoise (Decarpentry) A.; m. Florence Motte, June 30, 1984; 1 child, Antoine. M in Law, Faculte De Droit, Montpellier, France, 1971; BBA, Inst. Adminstrn. and Enterprise, Montpellier, France, 1972; MBA, INSEAD, Fontainbleau, France, 1979. Asst. comml. attaché French Embassy, Tokyo, 1973-76; comml. attaché French Consulate Gen., San Juan, P.R., 1976-78; internat. lawyer Total Compagnie Francaise des Petroles, Paris, 1979-83; adminstr., fin. mgr. Total Mineraria S.p.A., Rome, 1983—, fin. mgr. Africa/Mediterranean area, 1988—; gen. mgr. Compagnia Ricerche Minerarie S.p.A., Rome, 1984—; bd. dirs. Francarep Italia S.p.A., Rome, 1987—. Home: 91 Rue De La Republique, 92150 Suresnes France Office: Total Compagnie Française, des Petroles, Cedex 47, 92069 Paris France

ARRIGONI, ENRICO LAMBERTO, consulting company executive; b. Parma, Italy, July 11, 1937; s. Alessandro and Maria Paola (Cusani) A.; m. Antonia Gabellini, June 25, 1977; children—Francesco A., Alessandra A. Degree in Geology, U. Parma, 1962; merit diploma Superior Sch. Hydrocarbons, Milan, Italy, 1963; M.S.C.E., Colo. State U., 1968. Asst. prof. U. Parma, 1964-65; research asst. Colo. State U., Ft. Collins, 1966-68; soil engr. Chen & Assocs., Denver, 1968-70; sr. engr. Geotecna Progetti Spa., Milan, 1970-77; project mgr. Ecosol Spa., Mialn, 1977-78; supr. Aquater Spa., Milan, 1978-83; tech. mgr. Rocksoil Srl., Milan, 1983—. Contbr. articles to profl. jours. Mem. ASCE, Associaz. Geotecnica Ital., Internat. Soc. Rock Mechanics, Internat. Soc. Soil Mechanics and Found. Engring., Soc. Italian Gallerie, Assn. Mine Subalpina; assoc. mem. Sigma Xi. Home: Viale Legioni Romane 44, 20147 Milan Italy Office: Rocksoil Srl, Piazza San Marco 1, 20121 Milan Italy

ARRIGONI, GIAMPIERA, classicist, educator; b. Villa d'Almè, Bergamo, Italy, Jan. 28, 1944; s. Vincenzo and Maria Esther (Carminati) A. Laurea, Univ. Statale, Milan, Italy, 1967; postgrad., U. Bonn, Fed. Republic Germany, 1967, école Pratique U. Paris, 1975-76. Asst. prof. Latin literature Univ. Statale, Milan, 1967-82, assoc. prof. classical philology, Latin grammar, 1982-87, assoc. prof. History Religions of the Classical World, 1987—. Author: Il de oratore e l'Orator nella Tradizione del codice Trivulziano 723, Milano Varese, 1969, Camilla Amazzone e Sacerdotessa di Diana, 1982, Le Donne in Grecia, 1985; bibliographer (book by Arnaldo Momigliano) Filippo il Macedone, 1987. Premix Cesare Manaresi, Elia Lattes, 1967. Home: Via Petrarca 22, 20123 Milan Italy Office: Univ Statale Milan, Via Festa del Perdono 7, 20122 Milan Italy

ARRIGONI, GIANNI ALBERTO, consulting engineer, engineering geologist; b. Bergamo, Italy, Dec. 28, 1939; s. Luigi and Margherita (Bertaina) A.; m. Gabriella Balzarotti, Sept. 15, 1966. Dr. (Hon.) Geology, State U., Italy, 1962; D in Engring., Turin Poly. U., Italy, 1965. Research fellow C.N.R. Mining Inst., Turin, Italy, 1963-65; site engr. Codelfa S.P.A., Milan, Italy, 1966-67; tunnel mgr., Turangi, New Zealand, 1967-69; project mgr., Sydney, Australia, 1970-75, asst. gen. mgr., Codelfa-Cogefar group, Turangi, 1976-80; cons. engr. Englaw Ltd., Lugano and Turangi, 1980—; cons. profl. engr. in contractual claims and arbitration fields. Fellow Inst. Engrs. Australia, Chartered Inst. Arbitrators London; mem. Inst. Engrs. Italy, Inst. Mining and Metallurgy London, Chartered Inst. Arbitrators. Roman Catholic. Club: Turangi Golf. Avocations: photography, travel, skiing, mountaineering, golf. Home: 245 Taupehi Rd, PO Box 195, Turangi 3371, New Zealand Office: Englaw Ltd v Cattori 3, PO Box 249, CH-6902 Lugano Switzerland

ARRILLAGA, JOSEFINA, lawyer, banker; b. Bilbao, Spain, Feb. 5, 1933; d. Pedro and Mercedes (Lansorena) Arrillaga. Baccalaureate, Colegio Immaculada Concepcion, Madrid, Spain, 1950; Law Degree, Madrid, U., 1955, doctoral studies, 1955-57; Doctorate, Munich U., 1971. Atty., Madrid Legal Office, 1959-66; atty. dept. fgn. commerce Dresdner Bank A.G., Munich, 1974-75, legal advisor credit dept. Madrid br., 1979-81, head legal dept., 1981—; asst. mgr. dept. fgn. banking Banco Urquijo, Madrid, 1974-75, head internat. legal dept., 1975-77; co-rep. Banco Urquijo and Banco de Quilnes, Frankfurt/Main, 1978-79; asst. lectr. dept. procedural law Madrid U., 1955-57. Mem. Internat. Bar Assn., Madrid Bar Assn., Internat. Union Lawyer (mem. permanent commn.), Spanish Nat. Found. Lyrical Arts (founding mem.), Spanish Assn. Friends of the Opera. Clubs: Club XXI, Ateneo, Club Liberal (Madrid). Author: The Responsibility of the Manufacturer, 1981. Home: Marceliano Santamaria 9, Madrid 16 Spain Office: Banco Exterior de Espana, Carrera de San Jeronimo, Madrid 16, Spain

ARRINDELL, CLEMENT ATHELSTON, governor general St. Christopher and Nevis; b. Basseterre, West Indies, Apr. 19, 1931. Student St. Kitts Grammar Sch.; called to bar, Lincoln's Inn, 1958, also postgrad. Practice as barrister and solicitor, 1959-66; acting magistrate, 1964-66, magistrate, 1966-71, chief magistrate, 1972-78; judge WI Assoc. States Supreme Ct., 1978-81; gov. St. Kitts-Nevis, 1981-83; gov. gen. St. Christopher and Nevis, 1983—. Recipient Knight Grand Cross of the Most Disting. Order of St. Michael and St. George, Knight Grand Cross of the Royal Victorian Order. Address: Government House, Basseterre Saint Kitts, West Indies

ARRON, HENCK ALPHONSUS EUGENE, Suriname government official; b. Paramaribo, Apr. 25, 1936; m. Antoinette Leeuwin. Student internat. banking, Amsterdam, 1959. Dep. mgr., head fgn. affairs dept. Hakrinbank, Suriname, 1960-63; mem. bd. mgmt. Volkscredietbank, Suriname, 1963-73, 80—; mem. Parliament of Suriname, 1963—; prime minister, minister gen. and fgn. affairs, minister fin. Republic Suriname, 1973-77, prime minister, minister gen. and fgn. affairs, 1977-80; v.p. Suriname, 1988—. Address: Office VP, Paramaribo Suriname *

ARROW, KENNETH JOSEPH, economist, educator; b. N.Y.C., Aug. 23, 1921; s. Harry I. and Lillian (Greenberg) A.; m. Selma Schweitzer, Aug. 31, 1947; children: David Michael, Andrew. B.S. in Social Sci., CCNY, 1940; M.A., Columbia U., 1941, Ph.D., 1951, D.Sc., 1973; LL.D. (hon.), U. Chgo., 1967, City U. N.Y., 1972, Hebrew U. Jerusalem, 1975, U. Pa., 1976; D.Social and Econ. Scis. (hon.), U. Vienna, Austria, 1971; D.Social Scis. (hon.), Yale, 1974; Doctor (hon.), Université René Descartes, Paris, 1974, U. Aix-Marseille III, 1985; Dr.Pol., U. Helsinki, 1976; M.A. (hon.), Harvard U., 1968; D.Litt., Cambridge U., 1985. Research assoc. Cowles Commn. for Research in Econs., 1947-49; asst. prof. econs. U. Chgo., 1948-49; acting asst. prof. econs. and stats. Stanford, 1949-50, assoc. prof., 1950-53, prof. econs., statistics and ops. research, 1953-68; prof. econs. Harvard, 1968-74, James Bryant Conant univ. prof., 1974-79; exec. head dept. econs. Stanford U., 1954-56, acting exec. head dept., 1962-63, Joan Kenney prof. econs. and prof. ops. research, 1979—; economist Council Econ. Advisers, U.S. Govt., 1962; cons. RAND Corp. Author: Social Choice and Individual Values, 1951, Essays in the Theory of Risk Bearing, 1971, The Limits of Organization, 1974, Collected Papers, Vols. I-VI, 1983-85; co-author: Mathematical Studies in Inventory and Production, 1958, Studies in Linear and Nonlinear Programming, 1958, Time Series Analysis of Inter-industry Demands, 1959, Public Investment, The Rate of Return and Optimal Fiscal Policy, 1971, General Competitive Analysis, 1971, Studies in Resource Allocation Processes, 1977, Social Choice and Multicriterion Decision Making, 1985. Served as capt. AUS, 1942-46. Social Sci. Research fellow, 1952; fellow Center for Advanced Study in the Behavioral Scis., 1956-57; fellow Churchill Coll., Cambridge, Eng., 1963-64, 70, 73, 86; Guggenheim fellow, 1972-73; Recipient John Bates Clark medal Am. Econ. Assn., 1957; Alfred Nobel Meml. prize in econ. scis., 1972, von Neumann prize, 1986. Fellow Am. Acad. Arts and Scis. (v.p. 1979-81), Econometric Soc. (v.p. 1955, pres. 1956), Am. Statis. Assn., Inst. Math. Stats., Am. Econ. Assn. (mem. exec. com. 1967-69, pres. 1973), AAAS (chmn. sect K 1983), Internat. Soc. for Inventory Research (pres. 1983—); mem. Internat. Econs. Assn. (pres. 1983-86), Nat. Acad. Scis., Am. Philos. Soc., Inst. Mgmt. Scis. (pres. 1963, chmn. council 1964), Finnish Acad. Scis. (fgn. hon.), Brit. Acad. (corr.), Western Econ. Assn. (pres. 1980-81). Office: Stanford Univ Dept of Economics Stanford CA 94305

ARROYO, EDUARDO CABRAL, JR., stockbroker, real estate developer, corporate planner; b. Manila, Aug. 18, 1938; s. Eduardo Evangelista and Mary (Cabral) A.; m. Mercedes Marina Valderrama, July 6, 1969; children—Sergio, Katharine, Ava Marie Consuelo. Degree in Liberal Arts, U. Santo Tomas, Philippines, 1960, B.S. in Commerce, 1961; postgrad. Commerciaux, Geneva, Switzerland, 1963-64, Ateneo Grad. Sch. Bus., 1967. Asst. trust officer Far East Bank & Trust Corp., Philippines, 1964-70; trust officer Consol. Bank & Trust Corp., Philippines, 1970-74; v.p. corp. planning Valderrama Mgmt. Corp., Philippines, 1975—; exec. v.p. Valderrama Arroyo Securities Corp., Philippines, 1976—; pres., chief operating officer Equitiworld Stockbrokers Inc., 1987—; dir., chmn. bd. Preferred Properties, Inc., Philippines, Supreme Commodities Inc.; dir., pres. Atkins Fairchild Internat. Corp., U.S.A., dir. several other corps. Founder, trustee Found. for Ednl. Evolution and Devel., Inc., Philippines, 1979—; mem. Nat. Movement for Free Elections, Philippines, 1983—. Mem. Makati Stock Exchange Philippine Wood Producers Assn. (bd. dirs. 1976—), Jaycees Internat. (senate). Lodge: Manila Rotary. Avocations: tennis; horseback riding; golf; concerts. Office: 107 Esteban St, Legaspi Village, Makati, Metro Manila Philippines

ARSENAULT, ALFRED JUDE, retired publishing company executive; b. N.Y.C., Sept. 15, 1929; s. George S. and Mary (Roach) A.; B.A., St. John's U., 1960; m. Arlene Jeanne Semon, Aug. 20, 1955; children—James J., Jeanne M., Thomas J., Jane R., Nancy J., Patricia J., Barbara J. Sales rep. Met. Sunday Newspapers, Inc., N.Y.C., 1956-58; sales mgr. Med. Econs., Inc., Oradell, N.J., 1958-64; asst. to pub. Med. World News, N.Y.C., 1965; v.p., dir. advt. Med. World News, N.Y.C. 1966-69; pres. Insight Pub. Co., Inc., 1969-85; now cons. in field. Served with USN, 1950-54. Clubs: Wheatly Hills Golf; Cornell of N.Y. Home: 47 Orchard Dr East Williston NY 11596

ARSHAD, WAHEED UDDIN, mechanical engineering company executive, consultant; b. Ferozpur, India, Mar. 21, 1926; s. Alauddin and Zeb A.; widowed; 1 child, Tanveer. BA, U. Punjab, Lahore, India, 1944, BE, 1947. Commd. Pakistan Army, 1948, advanced through grades to maj. gen.; dep. prin., tech. exec. Ordnance Factories, Pakistan, 1963-68, dir. new projects, 1968-69, prin. tech. exec., 1969-71, dir. indsl., 1973-75, chmn., 1975-77; chief instr. Coll. Elec. and Mech. Engring. Pakistani Army, 1971-72; dir. munition prodn. Ministry of Def., Pakistan, 1972-73, officer spl. duty, 1977-86; ret. Pakistan Army, 1980; cons. in field. Served to maj.-gen., Pakistan Army, 1948-80. Recipient Tamga-E-Intaz award Govt. Pakistan, 1970. Fellow Inst. Mech. Engrs. Eng., Pakistan Inst. Engrs., Engring. Council; mem. Services Club. Club: Rawalpindi. Home: 20-I Tipu Sultan Rd, Multan Cantt Pakistan

ARSHT, ADRIENNE, banker, lawyer; b. Wilmington, Del., Feb. 4, 1942; d. S. Samuel and Roxana (Cannon) A.; m. Myer Feldman, Sept. 28, 1980. B.A., Mt. Holyoke Coll. (Mass.), 1963; J.D., Villanova U., 1966. Bar: Del. 1966. Assoc., Morris, Nichols, Arsht & Tunnell, Wilmington, 1966-69; dir. govt. affairs Trans World Airlines, N.Y.C., 1969-79; atty. Bregman, Abell, Kay & Simon, Washington, 1979-85; chmn. bd. Totalbank Corp. Fla., 1986—. Chmn. bd. dirs. Kennedy Ctr. Prodns. Inc., Washington, 1981—; trustee Mt. Vernon Coll., Washington, 1983-84, Am. Ballet Theatre, N.Y.C., 1984—. Mem. Com. of 200, Women's Forum, Del. Bar Assn. Office: 1250 Connecticut Ave NW Washington DC 20036

ARSLAN, ORHAN ENAYET OMAR, anatomist, veterinary scientist; b. Kirkuk, Iraq, May 15, 1951; came to U.S., 1981; s. Enayet Omar and Zubeydeh (Ahmed) A. BVMS, DVM, U. Baghdad (Iraq), 1973; PhD, Hacettepe U., Ankara, Turkey, 1979. Postdoctoral fellow Med. Sch., 1981-83; postgrad. asst. anatomist Hacettepe U., Ankara, Turkey, 1975-79, instr., 1979-81; asst. prof. Nat. Coll. Chiropractic, Lombard, Ill., 1983-86, dept. biol. chemistry and structure U. Health Scis. Chgo. Med. Sch., North Chicago, Ill., 1986—. Mem. AVMA, Found. for Advancement Edn. in Scis., N.Y. Acad. Scis., Am. Assn. Anatomists, Internat. Soc. Drs. Sci., Internat. Platform Assn. Home: 1115 Lorraine Rd Apt 139 Wheaton IL 60187 Office: Univ Health Scis Chgo Med Sch 3333 Green Bay Rd North Chicago IL 60064

ARSLANOV, MARAT MIRSAEVICH, mathematics educator; b. Kazan, USSR, Feb. 7, 1944; s. Mirsa Shagivalievich and Fatima (Galimovna) A.; m. Farida Abusarovna Chairetdinova, May 21, 1966; children: Asat, Kamil. Grad., Kazan State U., USSR, 1966. Asst. prof. Kazan State U., 1969-75, assoc. prof., 1975—. Author: Recursively Enumerable Sets and Degrees of Unsolvability, 1986. Mem. Am. Math. Soc., Assn. Symbolic Logic. Home: 13 Karbishevstr Apt 109, 420087 Kazan USSR Office: Kazan State U, 18 Leninstr, 420008 Kazan USSR

ARTAZ, JEANNINE FORD, radio and television personality, fashion designer; b. San Antonio, May 22, 1929; d. Grady Carlton and Volahelen (Latham) Ford; m. Ches T. Von Baronofjski-Childres, Sept. 9, 1946 (dec. May 1964); children—Ginger Dona Watts, Honey Dawn Johnson, Carlton Ford Childres-Artaz, Grady Baron Childres-Artaz; m. Souvenir James Artaz, Jan. 24, 1968; stepchildren—Soundra Lee Crabtree, Bob Gene, Cheri Ann Bleyeu, Danny Joe, Bonnie Lynn Harris, Marlene Denise Halstad. Illustration degree Paris Art Inst., 1946; B.A., Tex. Christian U., 1949; student radio engring. Colo. State U., 1972-74; B.A. in Comml. Art, Art Inst. Chgo., 1949; student Coco Chanel's Studios, Paris, 1947-48. Designer, Originals by Jeannine, San Antonio, also Denver and Glenwood Springs, Colo., 1942—; disc jockey, announcer Stas. WOAI and KTSA, San Antonio, 1944-50; air personality Stas. KOA/KBTV and KIMN, Denver, 1951-68; women's program dir., announcer Radio Sta. KGLN, Glenwood Springs, Colo., 1970-82; dir. Tails Ranch, Garfield County Humane Assn., Glenwood Springs, 1982—; weather watcher Sta. KCNC-TV, Denver, 1982—; host talk show Everybody's Talkin' Sta. KDNK-Radio, Carbondale, Colo., 1986—; also mem. bd. dirs. humane assn., 1982—; tchr. radio/TV, J.F. Modeling Agy., Denver, 1956-60; owner, operator Just Me Designs, Aspen, Colo., 1987—. Author, editor: (children's plays) Play Time, 1976 (Illustrating award 1976). Designer Gidetts household appliance covers (Am. Design award 1980). Leader, 4-H Club, Glenwood Springs, 1972-83; active Valley View Hosp. Aux., 1966—; chmn. Am. Hosp. Aux., Denver, 1963-64; mem. Glenwood Springs Parks and Recreation Commn., 1973—; counselor Children Against Drugs, Glenwood Springs, 1982—; advisor Parent Adv. Bd., Glenwood Springs, 1970-83. Named Vol. of Yr., Garfield Sch. Dist., Glenwood Springs, 1973; Woman Broadcaster of Yr., Am. Broadcasting System, N.Y.C., 1956, 58; recipient award for multiple sclerosis work Borden Co., 1980; Ford Found. grantee, 1984. Mem. Colo. Women Broadcasters Assn. (Colo. Woman Broadcaster of Yr. 1956, 58), Airplane Pilots and Owners Assn., Am. Weather Observers Assn., Am. Designers Inc. (Coty award 1959), Am. Design Assn. (sec. Denver 1955-57), Am. Humane Assn. (founding mem., local dir. 1982—). Avocations: flying, needlework, gardening, reading, drawing. Home: 509 W 12th St Glenwood Springs CO 81601

ARTHUR, WILLIAM SEYMOUR, school administrator; b. St. Philip, Barbados, Mar. 26, 1909; s. Robert Massiah and Mary (Pounder) A.; tchrs. diploma Rawle Inst., Codrington Coll.; m. Enid Clotilde Odle, Dec. 10, 1936 (dec. July 1979); children—Ivan, Monica, Orma, Howard, Marion, Ingrid, Wilmore. Asst. tchr. Buxton Boys Sch., 1927-32, headmaster, 1938-69; asst. tchr. Montgomery Boys Sch., 1932-37; adminstr. Industry High Sch., St. Philip, Barbados, 1969—; founder, dir. Caribbean Pen Pal Assos. Justice of peace. Recipient Silver medals religious poetry contests, 1976. Mem. Barbados Tchrs. Union, Barbados Mus. Moravian. Author: Whispers of the Dawn, 1941; Morning Glory, 1944; No Idle Winds, 1955; editor Cosmos mag., Jour. Pen Pal Assos. Home: Arthur Seat, Saint Thomas Barbados Office: Industry High School, Heddings, Saint Philip Barbados

ARTIGOU, JEAN-MARIE, orthopedist; b. Angers, France, June 9, 1940; s. Maurice and Jeanine (Daval) A.; m. Anne Villeminot, Aug. 1, 1967; children: Xavier, Laurent, Fabien. MD, U. Paris, 1966. Cert. orthopaedic surgeon. Extern Paris Hosp., 1962-67, intern, 1968-72, asst. to clin. chief, 1972-74; pvt. practice medicine specializing in orthopaedic surgery Melun, France, 1974—. Contbr. articles to med. jours. Gen. sec. Syndicat des Medecins de Seine et Marne, Melun, 1977-83; mem. Ordre des Medecins, Melun, 1982—. Mem. Societe Française de Chirurgie Orthopedique et Traumatologique (gen. sec.), Assn. des Orthopedistes de Langue Française (adviser). Home: 10 Quai Lallia, Le Mée sur Seine France 77350 Office: Clinique les Fontaines, 54 Bd Aristide Briand, Melun France 77000

ARTIGUES, JEAN MARIE, ophthalmologist; b. Narbon, France, Aug. 22, 1934; s. Francois and Genevieve (Caillassou) A.; m. Daniele Richard, June 11, 1957 (div. 1965); 1 child, Philppe; m. Chantal Tondreau, Nov. 9, 1967; 1 child, Alexandre. MD, U. Paris, 1961. Externe various hosps., Paris, 1955-61; interne in ophthalmology Hopital des 15/20, Paris, 1959-63; practice medicine specializing in ophthalmology Bayonne, France, 1963—. Served to lt. M.C. French Army, 1961-63. Mem. Societe Francaise Ophthalmologie, Societe Francaise Photocoagulation. Club: Vet. Car (St. Jean de Luz, France). Home: Pessenia, 64200 Arcangues France Office: Centre Medico Chirurgical, Ophthalmologie, 3 place du Reduit, 64100 Bayonne France

ARTIS, EDWARD ALLEN, mortgage and financing consultant, educator, television producer; b. Highland Park, Ill., July 9, 1945; s. Edgar and Lenore (Healy) A.; student U. Calif., Berkeley, 1966-68, Glendale Community Coll., 1974; LL.D. (hon.), U. Saigon, 1972. Dist. mgr. Jr. Achievement So. Calif., N. Hollywood, 1973-75; realtor asso. Stevenson, Dilbeck Inc. Realtors, Glendale, Calif., 1975-78; asst. treas. Advance Mortgage Corp., Van Nuys, Calif., 1976-78; exec. v.p., prin. Classic Fin. Corp., Panorama City, Calif., 1978-79; prin., chief exec. officer Ed Artis & Assos., mortgage brokerage, real estate devel., syndications, Glendale, 1979—; fin. cons. Western Fin. Diversified Ltd., Encino, Calif., 1981—; prof. real estate fin. Los Angeles City Coll., 1980—; exec. producer tv series Fun in the Sun, 1986; pres. Viking Performance Cars of P.R., Inc., 1987—. Bd. dirs. Nat. Research Found. on Aging, 1975-80; lifetime benefactor John F. Kennedy Spt. Warfare Mus., Ft. Bragg, N.C. Served as Spl. Forces Green Beret, U.S. Army, 1963-73. Decorated Silver Star (3), D.F.C., Bronze Star (3), Purple Heart (3); recipient Distinguished Service award City of Concord, Calif., 1972; named an Outstanding Young Man, Calif. Jaycees, 1971, Calif. Humanitarian of Yr., 1973. Mem. Calif. Jaycees (spl. presdl. asst. on child abuse 1974-76, pres. internat. USA Mexico Border Fedn. 1974), Glendale C. of C., Calif. Assn. Realtors, Nat. Assn. Realtors, Calif. Mortgage Bankers Assn., Assn. Profl. Mortgage Women, Glendale Bd. Realtors, Glendale Days of Verdugos Assn., Am. Fedn. Tchrs. Republican. Address: 24343 Vanowen St West Hills CA 91307-2848

ARTUSHENIA, MARILYN JOANNE, internist; b. Glen Ridge, N.J., Feb. 16, 1950; d. Gregory and Julia (Markewicz) A.; A.B., Boston U., 1970; M.D., Hahnemann Med. Coll., 1974. Intern, Mount Sinai Hosp., N.Y.C., 1974-75, resident medicine, 1975-77; fellow nephrology Bronx (N.Y.) VA Hosp., also Mt. Sinai Hosp., 1977-79; research fellow endocrinology Bronx VA Hosp., 1979-80, research cons. endocrinology, 1980—; asst. attending physician in medicine and psychiatry Elmhurst Gen. Hosp., N.Y., 1980-85; attending staff St. Joseph's Hosp., 1982—; instr. medicine Mt. Sinai Hosp., 1980—; instr. advanced cardiac life support and cardiopulmonary resuscitation Am. Heart Assn., 1980—; practice medicine specializing in internal medicine and nephrology, Torrington, Conn. Mem. A.C.P., AAAS, AMA, N.Y. Acad. Scis., Queens County Med. Soc., Internat. Platform Assn., Phi Beta Kappa, Alpha Omega Alpha. Home and Office: 732 Weigold Rd Torrington CT 06790

ARTZY, RAFAEL, mathematics professor; b. Königsberg, Fed. Republic Germany, July 23, 1912; arrived in Israel, 1933; s. Eduard and Ida (Freundenheim) Deutschländer; m. Elly Iwiansky, Oct. 12, 1933; children: Ehud, Michal, Barak. MA, Hebrew U., Jerusalem, 1934; PhD, Hebrew U., 1945. Tchr., prin. various high schs., Israel, 1935-51; prof. Technion, Haifa, Israel, 1951-60, U. N.C., Chapel Hill, 1960-61, Rutgers U., New Brunswick, N.J., 1961-65, SUNY, Buffalo, 1961-67, Temple U., Phila., 1967-73, U. Haifa, Israel, 1973—. Author: Linear Geometry, 1965; contbr. numerous articles to internat. prof. jours. Mem. Israel Math. Union (pres. 1984-86), Am. Math. Soc. Jewish. Home: 36 Hazvi Ave, Haifa 34355, Israel Office: U Haifa, Math Dept, Haifa 31999, Israel

ARUN, KODUVAUR CHANDRASEKHAR, corporate affairs counselor; b. Vellore, India, June 20, 1927; s. K.V. Chandrasekhar and K.V. Chellammal; B.S. with honours, Annamalai U., 1948, M.S., 1949, D in Communication (hon.), World U. Roundtable, Benson, Ariz.; m. Indira Sundar, June 19, 1958; children—Mahalakshmi, Saraswathy, Chandrasekhar, Wigneswaran, Janaki. Editor, fgn. corr. Reuters, Press Trust India, 1948-53; fedn. editor Singapore Standard, 1953-57; mng. editor Tamil Nesan, Kuala Lumpur, 1957-61; guest editor Courier-Mail, Brisbane, Australia, 1960; head external publicity/publs. divs., sr. liaison officer Ministry Info., Malaysia, 1961-66; head publs. and info. div. Rubber Research Inst. Malaysia, 1966-71; asst. exec. dir. info., edn. and communication Internat. Planned Parenthood Fedn., S.E. Asia and Oceania region, 1971-74; sr. mng. dir., chief cons. Preedisco (Sdn) Berhad, Kuala Lumpur, 1974—; tech. exec. Malaysian Rubber Producers' Council, 1971-85; tech. exec. Nat. Smallholders' Assn., Malaysia, 1985—; group co. sec. Syarikat Perniagaan Pehebun-Pehebun Kecil (M) Berhad; exec. dir. Pk Komoditi SDN Berhad; lectr., cons. in field. Recipient Ahli Mangku Negara, 1969; Malaysia Bronze medal, 1963; Pahang Silver Jubilee medal, 1954. Fellow Malaysia Inst. Public Relations, Brit. Inst. Mgmt.; Public Relations Soc. Am., Internat. Pub. Relations Assn., Malaysian Sci. Assn., Malaysian Inst. Physics, CAM Soc. (London). Hindu. Club: Royal Selangor (Kuala Lumpur). Home: Flat K2-1, Happy Apts Jalan 17/13, Petaling Jaya, 46400 Selangor Malaysia Office: Wisma Getah Asli I 1st Floor, No 148 Jalan Ampung, 50450 Kuala Lumpur Malaysia

ARUNDEL, IAN BRESSON, art dealer; b. Mitchell, S.D., Feb. 22, 1914; s. Charles Henry and Mary Porter (Bresson) A.; student U. Mich., 1934-37; m. Millie Lewis Waugh, Nov. 8, 1952; children—Ann Waugh, Colin Waugh. Restorer paintings and art objects, Detroit, 1937-43; dealer antique art, conservator, Los Angeles, 1945-52; art dealer, appraiser, Los Angeles, 1952—; expert primitive tribal art, appraiser U.S. govt.; exhibited tribal art in group shows at Santa Barbara (Calif.) Mus. Art, Los Angeles County Mus. Art, Miami U., Pomona Coll., U. Calif. at Fullerton, Otis Art Inst. Served with AUS, 1943-45. Fellow Am. Inst. for Conservation Historic and Artistic Works; mem. Smithsonian Instn., Brit. Mus. Soc., Archives Am. Art, Mus. Alliance Los Angeles County Mus., Victorian Soc. Office: 7152 SE 13th Ave Portland OR 97202

ARUNDELL, VICTOR CHARLES, accountant, business consultant; b. Greenwich, London, Eng., July 15, 1931; s. William Hewitt and Constance (Hook) A.; m. Margaret Howe, June 6, 1961 (dec.); children—Deborah, Caroline, Sally, Jill, Zoe. Student Roan, Greenwich, 1942-47. Mgr. Fluor Ltd., London, 1964-67; controller Chgo. Pneumatic Tool Co., N.Y.C., 1967-72; group controller, dir. Siebe PLC, Windsor, Eng., 1972-78; group coordinator Parinter, S.A., Paris, 1978-84; dir. Comasec Ltd., Durban, South Africa, 1980-84; mng. dir. Dipco Ltd., Slough, Eng., 1979-85 ; gen. mgr. Arundell Internat. Cons., London, 1978—; chmn. Apsleybrook Ltd., London, 1983—; chmn. Pinkcast Ltd, London, 1985— . Leader opposition Fulham Borough Council, London, 1960-63; chmn. Barons Ct. Young Conservatives, London, 1959-63. Served with RAF, 1954-56. Fellow Inst. Chartered Acct. Eng. and Wales, Inst. of Dirs., London. Conservative. Anglican. Club: Wimereux Golf (France). Home and Office: 164 Ealing Rd, Brentford, Middlesex TW8 9PX, England

ARUNRUGSTICHAI, NARONG-RIT, company executive, ceramic consultant; b. Bangkok, Apr. 2, 1948; s. C. H. and Ngo (Teo) Mah; m. Sew Ching Chok, Aug. 1, 1972; children: Sunh, Wynn. Diploma, Assumption Comml. Coll., Bangkok, 1968. Export officer Eiho Trading Co. Ltd., Nagoya, Japan; project mgr. S.P. Ceramic Co. Ltd., Bangkok, 1970-72; sales mgr. Thai Mosaic Industry Co. Ltd, Bangkok, 1972-73; mng. dir. Eastern Chinaware Co. Ltd., Bangkok, 1973-76; mng. ptnr. Pacific Impex (Thailand) Ltd., Bangkok, 1974—; mng. dir. Thai Orient Express Travel Services Co. Ltd., Bangkok, 1986-87; chmn. bd. Mend-A-Bath (Thailand) Ltd., Bangkok, 1987—; sec. gen. Ceramic Industry Club of Thailand, Bangkok, 1979-80, 81-84, Ceramic Industry Club of Asean, 1984-86. Office: Pacific Impex (Thailand) Ltd, 27 Soi Pradit Suriwongse Rd, BKK-10500 Bangkok Thailand

ARVANITAKIS, CONSTANTINE S., gastroenterologist; b. Thessaloniki, Greece, Nov. 9, 1939; s. Spyros and Terpsithea A.; m. Sanda Nousia, June 3, 1967; 1 child, Marianna. Diploma, Anatolia Coll, 1958; MD, U. Thessaloniki, 1965, postgrad., 1976. Diplomate Am. Bd. Internal Medicine, Am. Bd. Gastroenterology. House physician Nat. Health Service, Eng., 1967-70; resident, fellow U. Wis., Madison, 1970-73; asst. prof. medicine U. Kans., Kansas City, 1973-77, assoc. prof., 1977-79; assoc. prof. medicine U. Thessaloniki, 1979—; dir. gastrointestinal unit, first dept. medicine U. Thessaloniki, AHEPA Gen. Hosp., 1980—. Author: Drug Treatment of Gastrointestinal Disease, 1970; mem. editorial bd. Hellenic Jour. Gastrointerology, 1987, Helleniki Iatriki, 1985. NIH grantee, Bethesda, Md., 1978. Fellow ACP; mem. Am. Gastroent. Assn., Hellenic Soc. Gastroenterology (bd. dirs. 1987-88), Cen. Soc. Clin. Research, Am. Physiol. Assn., Internat. Assn. Pancreatologists., Gastroent. Research Group, Am. Pancreatic Assn. Christian Orthodox. Home: 50 Sofouli St, 54655 Thessaloniki Greece Office: U Thessaloniki, AHEPA Gen Hosp, Thessaloniki Greece

ARVAY, NANCY JOAN, insurance company executive; b. Pitts., Aug. 27, 1952; d. William John and Cornelia (Prince) A. BA in History, Duke U., 1974; postgrad., Columbia U., 1974-75. Polit. and internat. communications specialist U.S. Senate Fgn. Relations Com., Washington, 1975-77; broadcast media relations rep. Am. Petroleum Inst., Washington, 1977-79; broadcast media relations rep. Chevron U.S.A., San Francisco, 1979-82, coordinator electronic news media relations, 1982-85; sr. media relations rep. Chevron Corp., San Francisco, 1985-87; dir. pub. relations Fireman's Fund Corp., Novato, Calif., 1987—; lectr. Dept. Interior-Park Service, Beckley, W.Va., 1983; chmn. pub. relations Internat. Oil Spill Conf., Washington, 1984-85. Author, coordinator: Research Studies in Business and the Media, 1980-83; contbg. author This Is Public Relations, 1985. Founding mem. San Francisco chpt. Overseas Edn. Group; mem. pub. relations com. World Affairs Council San Francisco. Mem. Pub. Relations Soc., Radio/TV News Dirs. Assn. (assoc.), San Francisco Women in Bus. Office: Firemen's Fund Corp 777 Marin Dr Novato CA 94998

ARVESCHOUG, NILS WEYER, sales manager, air force officer; b. Oslo, Norway, Feb. 19, 1924; s. Cato Anker and Anna Leth (Herlofsen) A.; divorced; children—Jan, Anne; m. 2d, Hjordis Iveland, July 29, 1983. Student Royal Norwegian Air Force Flying Sch., Muskoka, Can., 1944, Staff Coll., Oslo, 1951-52, NATO Def. Coll., Rome, 1970-71. col. Royal Norwegian Air Force, 1963, advanced through grades to maj. gen. 1971; served as squadron commdr., Gardermoen, North Oslo, 1953-56, group commdr., Orland, West Trondheim, 1956-58, chief ops. div. Oslo, 1958-63, chief ops. staff, Bodo, 1963-68, sta. commdr. Orland Air Sta., 1969-71, air commdr., Bodo, 1971-75, gen. insp. 1975-78; mgr. Buskerud Central Hosp., Drammen, Norway, 1979-88. Decorated comdr. Order St. Olav, 1976, comdr. Legion of Merit, 1977. Mem. Royal Air Force Assn. (pres. Norwegian br. 1976-79), Royal Norwegian Sailing Assn. Club: Rotary (v.p. 1973-74) (Bodo, Oslo). Home: Lauritz Sands v 15, 1343 Eiksmarka Norway Office: Buskerud Central Hospital, 3004 Drammen Norway

ARVIN, CHARLES STANFORD, librarian; b. Loogootee, Ind., Apr. 17, 1931; s. Leland Stanford and Mary Hope (Armstrong) A.; A.B., Wayne State U., 1953, postgrad., 1956-57; M.A. in Library Sci., U. Mich. 1960. Asst. divisional Librarian U. Mich. Natural Sci. Library, 1960-62; head reference Genesee County Library, Flint, Mich., 1962-67, 77-83, head central services, 1967-77, head acquisitions, 1983—. Served with AUS, 1953-56. Mem. ALA, Mich. Library Assn., Mich., Ind., Genesee County hist. socs., ACLU. Club: Flint Library. Editor: Flint Geneal. Quar., 1981—. Home: 702 W Oliver St Owosso MI 48867 Office: 4195 W Pasadena St Flint MI 48504

ARVYSTAS, MICHAEL GECIAUSKAS, orthodontist, educator, sculptor; b. Vilnius, Lithuania, Dec. 18, 1942; came to U.S., 1949; naturalized, 1961; s. Mykolas and Antanina (Kleiza) A.; m. Jane Grannis, 1969 (div. 1978). B.A., Colgate U., 1965, D.M.D., Tufts U., 1969; cert. Columbia U., 1973. Diplomate Am. Bd. Orthondontics. Chief orthodontic sect. Morrisania City Hosp., Bronx, N.Y., 1973-76; dir. orthodontics ctr. for cranio facial disorders and cleft palate ctr. Montefiore Hosp. and Med. Ctr., Bronx, 1973—; chief orthodontic sect. N. Central Bronx Hosp., 1976-83; clin. prof. N.J. Dental Sch., Newark, 1974—, dir., lectr. undergrad. and postgrad. dental students, 1974—; lectr. in field. Contbr. numerous articles to profl. jours., also chpts. to books. Served to capt. Dental Corps, USAF, 1969-71. Mem. ADA, First Dist. Dental Soc. N.Y.C., Am. Assn. Orthodontists, Northeastern Soc. Orthodontists, N.Y. Acad. Dentistry, Tufts U. Dental Alumni Assn., Orthondontic Alumni Soc. Columbia U., Colgate U. Alumni Assn., Sigma Xi. Office: 24 Washington Sq N New York NY 10011

ARZT, LEE ROBERT, lawyer; b. Yonkers, N.Y., Sept. 23, 1948; s. Arthur A. and Marion (Bernstein) A.; m. Mary Wilson, Aug. 14, 1970; 1 child, Sarah Elizabeth. B.A., Hofstra U., 1970; J.D., Coll. William and Mary, 1973. Bar: Va. 1973, U.S. Dist. Ct. (ea. dist.) Va. 1973, U.S. Ct. Appeals (4th cir.) 1974, U.S. Supreme Ct. 1977. Assoc. Horwitz, Baer, Neblett, and successor firm, Richmond, Va., 1973-76; mng. ptnr. Arzt, Monahan, Sager, and predecessor firms, Richmond, 1977-80; sole practice, Richmond, 1981—; instr. J. Sargeant Reynolds Community Coll., Richmond, 1976-77. V.p. land trustee, chmn. various coms., bd. dirs. Congregation Or Ami, Richmond, 1974—; 3d ward chmn., Richmond City Dem. Com.; del. 3d Congl. Dist. and Va. Democratic Convs., Richmond, 1984; bd. dirs. Beth Sholom Home, Richmond, 1974-81. N.Y. State Regents scholar Hofstra U., 1966-70. Mem. ABA, Va. Bar Assn., Bar Assn. Richmond, Bar Assn. Henrico County. Democrat. Jewish. Office: 5001 W Broad St Richmond VA 23230

ASAD, GHAZI ANWAR, architect, consultant; b. Batala, Punjab, India, Aug. 15, 1922; came to Can., 1964, naturalized, 1971; s. Abdul Karim and Nawab Begum (Khan) Rana; m. Amir Akhtar Khera, Dec. 4, 1947; children—Shahzadi Urfana, Shaheen Anjum, Iftikhar Akmal, Gul-e-Zarin. Diploma in Civil Engring., Govt. Sch. Engring., Punjab, 1948; Diploma Architecture, Sch. Architecture, Karachi, Pakistan, 1959; B.Arch., U. Man., Winnipeg, Can., 1966. Supr. civil engring. Pub. Works Dept., Punjab, 1947-53; asst. engr. Karachi Devel. Authority, 1954-64; grad. architect Page & Steele Architects, Toronto, Ont., Can., 1965; project architect Govan, Kaminkar Langley, Keenleyside, Melick, Devonshire, Wilson, Toronto, 1966-68; prin. G.A. Asad Architect, Toronto, 1968—; chmn. ACI Cons., Ltd., Toronto, 1973-75, pres. ACI Cons. Inc., 1977—. Active in pub. relations Art Club, Karachi, 1954-64; active in policy Liberal Party York Scarborough, Toronto, 1980; sec., bd. dirs. Central Haj Orgn. Can., Toronto, 1978; pres. York Condo Corp., 1985-87; trustee Pakistan Can. Community Ctr., Toronto, 1986—. Served with Royal Indian Navy, 1939-46. Recipient Single Family Dwelling Design Award First prize Central Mortgage Housing Corp., 1969. Mem. Ont. Assn. Architects, Royal Archtl. Inst. Can., Royal Inst. Brit. Architects, Inst. Architects Pakistan, Fedn. Architects and Engrs. (Pakistan), Project Mgmt. Inst. (U.S.). Lodge: Lions. Avocations: painting; sculpturing. Home: 56 Village Greenway, Willowdale, ON Canada M2J 1K8

ASADA, TOSHI, seismologist; b. Tokyo, Dec. 15, 1919; s. Shunsuke and Sumi (Asakura) A.; B.S., U. Tokyo, 1944, D.Sc., 1958; m. Teruko Uchida, Nov. 29, 1955; children—Takashi, Satoshi, Yuko. Research asst. U. Tokyo, 1944-55, mem. faculty, 1955—, prof. seismology, 1966-80, prof. emeritus, 1980—; prof. geophysics Inst. Research and Devel., Tokai U., 1980—; chmn. geodetic council Ministry Edn., Sci. and Culture; chmn. coordinating com. for earthquake prediction Geog. Survey Inst.; chmn. earthquake assessment com. Japan Meteorol. Agy. Sr. fellow Carnegie Instn., Washington, 1960-61. Mem. Seismol. Soc. Japan, Am. Geophys. Union. Author papers on microearthquakes, explosion seismology, ocean bottom seismometers. Home: 3-13-12 Shimo-ochiai, Shinjuku-ku, Tokyo 161, Japan Office: Inst Research and Devel Tokai U, 1117 Kitakaname, Hira, tsuka-shi, 259-12 Kanagawa-ken Japan

ASADI, REZA DAN, language educator; b. Gonabad, Iran, Oct. 14, 1948; s. Gholamreza Asadi and Fatemeh Nouri. M of Polit. Sci., M of Linguistics, M of English, EdD. Faculty, head sci. dept. Razi U., Kermanshah, Iran, 1975-76; instr. ESL Western Mich. U., Kalamazoo, 1981-83, coordinator acad. skills, 1982-83; asst. prof. Inst. Pub. Adminstrn., Riyadh, Saudi Arabia, 1983—; cons., curriculum designer, developer Inst. Pub. Adminstrn., Riyadh, 1987—. Author: Ebglish for the Computer Science Instructor, 1988; contbr. articles to profl. jours. Research grantee Western Mich. U., 1981, U.S. Dept. Edn., 1983. Office: Inst Pub Adminstrn, Farazdaq St, Riyadh 11141, Saudi Arabia

ASAJI, SHOICI, building maintenance company group owner; b. Tokyo, Feb. 25, 1938; s. Shotaro and Shizue Asaji; m. Takako Asaji; children: Shogo, Satoko. BA, Keio (Tokyo) U., 1960. Pres. Nihon Bldg. Service Co. Ltd., Tokyo, 1975—, chmn., 1986—; pres. Osaka (Japan) Bldg. Service Co. Ltd., 1983—, Sapporo Bldg. Service Co. Ltd., Hokkaido, 1974—, Kanagawa Bldg. Service Co. Ltd., Yokohama, 1972—, Ishikawa Bldg. Service Co. Ltd., Kanazawa, 1973—, Nihon Hotel Service Co. Ltd., Tokyo, 1970—, Nagisa Beach Hotel, 1971—, Interior Green Co. Ltd., Tokyo, 1985—. Mem. Cen. Minimum Wage Council Ministry of Labor, Tokyo, 1986, Tokyo Met. Council Employment Security, Tokyo, 1983; councillor The Japan Opera Foundation, Tokyo, 1986; bd. dirs. Community Chest of Tokyo, 1970. Mem. Japan Bldg. Maintenance Assn. (bd. dirs. 1977-85, advisor Tokyo chpt. 1985—, Meritorious Service award 1987), Japan Assn. Corp. Execs., Marunouchi Police Security and Guard Service Council (chmn. 1978—), Japan Hotel Assn. (bd. dirs. 1971—), Tokyo C. of C. and Industry (councillor 1982—), Japan Jr. Chamber (exec. v.p. 1976), Tokyo Jr. Chamber (pres. 1975). Lodge: Rotary. Office: Nihon Bldg Service Co Ltd, Marunouchi 3-3-1, Chiyada-ku, Tokyo 100, Japan

ASAJIMA, YOSHIO, manufacturing executive; b. Kyoto, Japan, Mar. 10, 1933; s. Chouzo and Sai (Sato) A.; m. Junko Hosoda, Nov. 9, 1959. Grad. in chem. engring., Nat. Kyoto Kogeiseni U., 1958. Mgr. mktg. and sales Horiba Instrument Co., Ltd., Japan, 1958-63; mgr. mktg. and sales Kyoto Electronics Mfg., Co., Ltd., Japan, 1963-78, dir. mktg., 1978—; dir. Japan Analytical Instruments Mfrs. Assn., Tokyo, 1978-86. Home: 3 51 201 Shiroyamacho, Ikeda 563 Osaka Japan Office: Kyoto Electronics Mfg Co Ltd, 4 9 Yonbancho Chiyoda-ku, Tokyo 102, Japan

ASAMOAH, OBED YAO, government official Ghana; b. Likpe Bala, Ghana, Feb. 6, 1936; s. William Kofi and Monica Akosua A.; m. Yvonne Marguerite Asamoah, Feb. 1, 1964; children: Yolanda Afua, Keli Komla, Senanu Yao. Grad. U. London, 1956, LLB with honors, 1960; LLM, Columbia U., 1963, JD, 1967. Bar: Middle Temple 1960, Ghana 1960. Practiced law, Ghana, 1960-61, 65—; research asst. Carnegie Endowment for Internat. Peace, N.Y.C., 1964, 65; asst. dir. Dag Hammarskjold Seminar in Internat. Law, The Hague, 1964, 65; lectr. law, U. Ghana, Legon, 1965-69; chmn. bd. Ghana Films Industries, Inc., Ghana Bauxite Co.; mem. Constituent Asembly, M.P. 1969-72; gen.-sec. United Nat. Conv., 1979, All Peoples Party, 1981; sec. fgn. affairs Govt. Ghana, 1982—. Author: The Legal Significance of the Declarations of the General Assembly of the United Nations; contbr. articles to law jours. Mem. Ghana Bar Assn. Presbyterian. Avocations: reading, farming. Home: PO Box 14581, Accra Ghana Office: Ministry of Fgn Affairs, Accra Ghana

ASCANI, PAOLO, foundation administrator; b. Rome, May 2, 1957; came to U.S., 1982; s. Mario Ascani and Marisa Scarpellini. B.S. in Fgn. Service, Georgetown U., 1984; M.A. in Internat. Affairs, George Washington U., 1986. Prodn. mgr. Pont-Royal Film TV, Rome, 1980-81; bus. mgr. Valmaris, Rome, 1981—; hist. researcher Mcpl. Govt., San Miniato, Pisa, Italy, 1984-85; researcher World Peace Through Law Ctr., Washington, 1984-86; asst. country rep. Cath. Relief Services, Tunisia, 1987—; asst. dir. Internat. Cooperation, Centro Italiano di Solidarietá , Rome; research asst. Italian dept. Georgetown U., 1982-84; art cons., Rome, Milan and Washington. Recipient Silver Eagle award Rome C. of C., 1986, Internat. Cultural Diploma of Honor, Disting. Leadership award. Mem. Acad. Polit. Sci. N.Y., Am. Polit. Sci. Assn. Roman Catholic. Lodge: Lions. Avocations: photography; art collecting; poetry. Home: 1280 21st St NW Apt 705 Washington DC 20036

ASCHER, AMALIE ADLER, author, journalist, columnist; b. Balt.; d. Charles and Alene (Steiger) Adler; B.A., Goucher Coll., 1949; m. Eduard Ascher, May 18, 1954; children—Kenneth Charles Weinberg, Cynthia Cecille. Garden columnist Balt. Sun, Los Angeles Times and Washington Post Wire Services, 1976—, feature writer, 1968—, contbr. Sunday Sun mag., 1968—; hostess, writer The Flower Show, Md. Center for Public Broadcasting, 1973—; lectr. numerous states and fgn. countries, 1965—; columnist Los Angeles Times-Washington Post Wire Service. Recipient Quill and Trowel award Garden Writers Assn. Am., 1980; Cert. of Merit for hort. lit. Nat. Council State Garden Clubs, Inc., 1975, named Flower Arranger of Year, 1973; Garden Writers award Bedding Plants, Inc., 1984, 88. Mem. Garden Writers Assn. Am. (dir. 1975-76), Indoor Gardening Nat. Council State Garden Clubs, Inc. (dir., chmn. 1977-79), Authors Guild, Authors League, Am. Hort. Soc. Republican. Jewish. Author: The Complete Flower Arranger, 1974. Contbr. numerous articles to various mags. and newspapers. Home and Office: 610 W 40th St Baltimore MD 21211

ASCHER, JAMES JOHN, pharmaceutical executive; b. Kansas City, Mo., Oct. 2, 1928; s. Bordner Fredrick and Helen (Barron) A.; student Bergen Jr. Coll., 1947-48, U. Kans., 1946-47, 49-51; m. Mary Ellen Robitsch, Feb. 27, 1954; children—Jill Denise, James John, Christopher Bordner. Rep., B.F. Ascher & Co., Inc., Memphis, 1954-55, asst. to pres., Kansas City, Mo., 1956-57, v.p., 1958-64, pres., 1965—. Bd. dirs. Childrens Cardiac Center, 1964-70, pres., 1968-70; mem. central governing bd. Children's Mercy Hosp., 1968-80; bd. dirs. Jr. Achievement of Middle Am., 1970—, pres., 1973-76, chmn., 1979-81; edn. chmn. Young Pres.'s Orgn. 6th Internat. Univ. for Pres., Athens, 1975. Served to 1st. lt. inf., U.S. Army, 1951-53; Korea. Decorated Bronze Star, Combat Infantryman's Badge. Mem. Pharm. Mfrs. Assn., Drug, Chem. and Allied Trades Assn., World Bus. Council, Proprietary Assn., Chief Execs. Orgn., Midwest Pharm. Advt. Club, Sales and Advt. Execs. Club, Am. Mgmt. Assn. (pres.'s assn.), Kansas City C. of C., Am. Legion, VFW, Delta Chi. Clubs: Lotos, N.Y. Athletic; Kansas City; Mercury; Indian Hills Country (Prairie Village, Kans.); Rotary. Home: 6706 Glenwood Shawnee Mission KS 66204 Office: 15501 W 109th St Lenexa KS 66219

ASCHER, RICHARD ALAN, lawyer; b. Hartford, Conn., June 3, 1945; s. Richard Oscar and Bernice (Spiegel) A.; m. Barbara Haberman, May 22, 1967; children—Jonathan Colin, Andrew David. B.A., SUNY-Buffalo, 1967, J.D., 1970. Staff atty. Legal Aid Soc., Queens, N.Y., 1970-73; ptnr. Ascher & Goldstein, Queens, N.Y., 1973-83, Ascher & Novitt, Queens, 1983—; counsel Assemblyman L. Stavisky, Albany, N.Y., 1974-75, Assemblyman I. Lafayette, Albany, 1976—; counsel, bd. dirs. Jackson Heights Community Devel. Corp., Queens, 1980-82. Pres., Queens Ind. Democrats, 1976; mem. lawyers com. Hart presdl. campaign, 1984; chmn. Com. to Make Watergate Perfectly Clear, Queens, 1973-74. Mem. Queens County Bar Assn., Criminal Courts Bar Assn. Jewish. Club: JFK Democratic (Jackson Heights) (exec. bd. 1981-82 and 87). Office: Ascher & Novitt 125-10 Queens Blvd Kew Gardens NY 11415

ASCHER-NASH, FRANZI, writer; b. Vienna, Austria, Nov. 28, 1910; came to U.S., 1938, naturalized, 1944; d. Luise Frankl and Leo Ascher; grad. cum laude, Humanistisches Maedchengymnasium, Vienna, 1928; student Vienna Acad. Music, 1929-31; m. Edgar R. Nash, Nov. 21, 1959. Free-lance short story writer, Vienna, 1934-38; after arrival in U.S., lectr. women's clubs under auspices of N.Y. Herald Tribune; music reviewer Neue Volkszeitung weekly, N.Y.C.; monthly light essay Austro-Am. Tribune; writer radio playlets German-Am. Writers Assn.; host short German lang. radio programs Sta. WBNX; tchr. New Sch. Social Research, N.Y.C.: writer annotations for classical records; host radio program The Story of the Art Song, Sta. WFUV-FM; appearances on Spoken Words Program Sta. WNYC; lectr. on the art song; lectr. music CUNY, York (Pa.) Coll., others; contbr. essays and poems to German-Am. Studies mag., Lyrik und Prosa mag., Lyrica Germanica mag., Inspiré, Swiss mag., Schatzkammer; author: (novella) Das Zwoelftonwunder, 1952; (novella) Confession in the Twilight (1st prize The Villager mag.), 1948; (books) Bilderbuch aus der Fremde, 1948, Gedichte eines Lebens, 1976, others; also poetry anthologies pub. in U.S., India, Germany and Austria. Founder Leo Ascher Award program Millersville U. Recipient citation Soc. German-Am. Studies, 1973. Mem. Assn. German Lang. Authors in Am., Soc. German-Am. Studies, Literarische Union (W. Ger.), Tagore Inst. of Creative Writing (India). Club: B'nai B'rith. Home: 118 N George St Millersville PA 17551

ASCHINGER, ERHARD FRIEDRICH IGNAZ, small business owner; b. Vienna, Austria, Aug. 6, 1934; s. Adolf and Maria (Anton) A.; m. Ilse Maria (Hofmann) Sept. 9, 1961; children: Barbara, Robert. Student, Vienna Acad. Music, 1952-58, Tech. U., Vienna, 1952-60. Free-lance designer, cons. Vienna, 1958—; dir. Recording Studio for Ancient Music, Vienna, 1964-70; tech. dir. Transaudio Ltd., Vienna, London, 1964—; chief engr. Filteron, Inc., Vienna, Dallas, 1970-75; mgr. owner Novatronic GmbH, Vienna, 1970—; cons. Austrian Acad. Scis., 1975—. Contbr. articles to profl. jours. Inventor and patentee in field. Mem. AES Audio Engring. Soc. (treas. 1974-78, sec. 1978-82, vice chmn. 1982-84). Roman Catholic. Office: Novatronic E Aschinger GmbH, Goergengasse 27/5, A-1190 Vienna Austria

ASEER, GHULAM NABI, business executive; b. Sohawa, Punjab, Pakistan, Feb. 2, 1940; s. Dhanpat Rai and Kaniz Fatima A.; children from previous marriage: Tabassam, Shabana. MS, Punjab U., 1963; Shorthand degree, Danton Shorthand Sch., Delhi, India, 1959. Civilian clk. Army Sch. of Adminstrn., Kuldana-Murre Hills, 1958-59; stenographer Mangla Dam Project, Wapda, Mangla, 1960-62; asst. devel. officer Ideal Life Ins. Co., Karachi, 1963-64; prodn. officer Adamjee Ins. Co., Ltd., Lahore, 1965-66; proprietor Aseer Sohawy Corp., Lahore, Pakistan, 1968—. Muslim League. Clubs: Am. Library, Brit. Library. Avocation: reading. Office: Aseer Sohway Corp, GPO Box 1752, Lahore Punjab 5400, Pakistan

ASFAW, TESFAYE, trade company executive; b. Addis Ababa, Ethiopia, May 9, 1947; s. Asfaw Bante and Bizunesh Haile; m. Almaz Tsegaye, Nov. 5, 1983; children: Daniel, Dawit. B.B.A., H.S.I. U., 1970; M.B.A., Northeastern U., 1974. With aviation mktg. dept. Shell Ethiopia Ltd., Addis Ababa, 1970-71; adminstrv. asst., dep. gen. mgr. Ethiopian Domestic Distbn. Corp., 1975-77; gen. mgr. Ethiopian Import Export Corp., 1977—. Mem. Assn. State Trading Orgns. (2nd vice chmn. 1984—), Avocations: coin collecting; stamp collecting; music; reading. Home: Addis Ababa 6646, Ethiopia Office: Ethiopian Import Export Corp, Addis Ababa 2313, Ethiopia

ASGHAR, ALI ABBAS, civil engineer; b. Buland Shahr, India, Jan. 4, 1934; s. Asghar and Kaneez (Fatima) Husain; m. Naseem Kausar; children: Huma Ali, Saima Ali, Faisal Ali, Imran Ali. BSc in Engring., Punjab Coll. Engring. and Tech., Pakistan, 1955; MA Sc in Engring., U. Toronto, Can., 1965. Registered profl. and structural engr., Pakistan. Asst. engr. Warsak Dam, H.G. Acres & Co. Cons. Engrs., 1956-57; asst. design engr. Punjab Irrigation Dept., Lahore, Pakistan, 1957-63; sr. structural engr. Alex Tobias & Assocs., Toronto, 1964-65; chief design engr. Cons. Assocs. Ltd., Lahore, 1966-67, William Perry Assocs. Architects, Lahore, 1967-68; chief design, ptnr. Internat. Cons. Consortium, Lahore, 1968-72; prin., dir. Republic Engring. Corp. Ltd., Lahore, 1972—; with overseas tng. Ove Arup & Ptnrs., London, 1971, Cohen Barrato Merchartas, Chgo., 1971-72; ptnr. Pioneer Cons., Lahore, 1976—; bd. dirs. Republic Devel. Ltd., Lahore, PAAF Assocs. Ltd., Lahore. Designer, cons. Alhamra Arts Ctr, Lahore, other bldgs. in Lahore. Governing mem. Anjumani Mohammadi, Lahore, 1980—; mem. Anjuman Wazifa Sadaat, Lahore, 1980—. Mem. Instn. Civil Engrs. Clubs: Lahore Gymkhana, Punjab (Lahore). Home: 124 Ahmad Block, Lahore 16 Pakistan Office: Republic Engring Corp, 7-D Kashmir Egerton Rd, Lahore Pakistan

ASGRIMSSON, HALLDOR, minister of fisheries of Iceland; b. Iceland, 1947; m. Sigurjona Sigurdardottir; 3 daus. Grad. Coop. Comml. Coll., 1965; post-grad. comml. colls. in Bergen and Copenhagen, 1971-73. Chartered acct., Iceland, 1970. Lectr. auditing and acctg. U. Iceland, 1973-75; M.P. representing Eastern parts of Iceland, 1974-78, 79—; minister of fisheries, 1983—; chmn. bd. dirs. Cen. Bank of Iceland, 1981-83; Icelandic mem. Nordic Council, 1977-78, 79-83, chmn. del., 1982-83. Address: Ministry of Fisheries, Reykjavik Iceland *

ASH, MAJOR MCKINLEY, JR., dentist, educator; b. Bellaire, Mich., Apr. 7, 1921; s. Major McKinley Sr. and Helen Marguerite (Early) A.; m. Fayola Foltz, Sept. 2, 1947; children: George McKinley, Carolyn Marguerite, Jeffrey LeRoy, Thomas Edward. BS, Mich. State U., 1947; DDS, Emory U., 1951; MS, U. Mich., 1954; Doctoris Medicine Honoris Causa, U. Bern, 1975. Instr. sch. dentistry Emory U., Atlanta, 1952-53; instr. U. Mich., Ann Arbor, 1953-56, asst. prof., 1956-59, assoc. prof., 1959-62, prof., 1962—, chmn. dept. occlusion, sch. dentistry, 1962-87, dir. stomatognathic physiology lab., sch. dentistry, 1969-87, dir. TMJ/oral facial pain clinic, sch. dentistry, 1983-87, Marcus L. Ward prof. dentistry, 1984—; pres. Basic Sci. Bd., State of Mich., 1962-74; cons. over the counter drugs FDA, Washington, 1985—. Author, co-author 30 textbooks, 1958—; editor 4 books; contbr. 160 articles to profl. jours. Served to tech. sgt. Signal Corps, U.S. Army, 1942-45, ETO. Nat. Inst. Dental Research grantee, 1962-85. Fellow Am. Coll. Dentists, Internat. Coll. Dentists, European Soc. Craniomandibular Disorders; mem. N.Y. Acad. Scis., AAAS, Am. Dental Assn. (cons. council on dental therapeutics 1982—), Washtenaw Dist. Dental Soc. (pres. 1963-64), Phi Kappa Phi. Presbyterian. Home: 1206 Snyder Ann Arbor MI 48103 Office: U of Mich Sch of Dentistry Ann Arbor MI 48109

ASH, MARY ELLEN (MRS. JAMES THEODORE ASH), lawyer; b. Wichita, Kans., Oct. 3, 1908; d. Loyd Inman and Nora (Martin) Aldrich; Brown's Bus. Coll., 1925, Western Ill. U., 1926-27; LL.B., Columbus U., 1940; m. James Theodore Ash, Oct. 4, 1941 (dec. June 1969); 1 dau., Mary Jo (Mrs. E.O. Farley). Admitted to U.S. Dist. Court, U.S. Ct. of Appeals, 1941, Ill. bar, 1949; adjudicator Social Security Bd., Washington, 1940-41, Chgo., 1942-43; pvt. law practice, Mendota, Ill., 1956—. Mem. Ill. Bar Assn., Sigma Delta Kappa. Club: Mendota Woman's. Home and Office: 909 21st St Mendota IL 61342

ASH, PHILIP, psychologist; b. N.Y.C., Feb. 2, 1917; s. Samuel Kieval and Estella (Feldstein) A.; m. Ruth Clyde, Sept. 16, 1945 (div. Dec. 1972); children—Peter, Sharon; m. Judith Nelson Cates, June 6, 1973; 1 son, Nelson E. B.S. in Psychology, City U. N.Y., 1938; M.A. in Personnel Adminstrn, Am. U., 1949; Ph.D. in Psychology, Pa. State U., 1949. Diplomate: Indsl. Psychlogy Am. Bd. Profl. Psychology. Analyst to unit chief occupational research Dept. Labor, 1940-47; research fellow Pa. State U., 1947-49, asso. prof., 1949-52; asst. to v.p. indsl. relatons Inland Steel, 1952-68; prof. psychology U. Ill., Chgo., 1968-80; prof. emeritus U. Ill., 1980—; dir. research John E. Reid Assocs., Chgo., 1969-87; v.p. research Reid Psychol. Systems, 1985-87; cons. London House, Inc., Park Ridge, Ill., 1987—; dir. Ash, Blackstone & Cates, Blacksburg, Va., 1973—. Author: Guide for Selection and Placement of Employees, 2d edit. 1977, also articles; Editor: Forensic Psychology and Disability Evaluation, 1972. Mem. public adv. com. Chgo. Commn. Human Relations, 1957-80; retirement com. Chgo. Commn. Sr. Citizens, 1960-80; chmn. Ill. Psychologist Examining Com., 1963-72. Fellow Am. Psychol. Assn. (pres. div. indsl. psychology 1968-69), AAAS; mem. Ill. Psychol. Assn. (pres. 1963-64), Chgo. Psychol. Assn., Midwest Psychol. Assn., Am. Personnel and Guidance Assn., Am. Psychology-Law Soc., Indsl. Relations Research Assn., Internat. Assn. Applied Psychology, Internat. Gerontol. Assn., Phi Beta Kappa, Sigma Xi, Psi Chi. Home: 817 Hutcheson Dr Blacksburg VA 24060

ASHBACH, DAVID LAURENCE, internist, nephrologist; b. Chgo., Nov. 17, 1942; s. Sol Henry and Lila Mae A.; A.B., Knox Coll., 1964; M.S., Case Western Reserve U., 1969, M.D., 1970; m. Arlene Rosenthal Nov. 28, 1963; children—Barbara, Deborah, Robert. Intern, Presbyterian-St. Luke's Hosp., Chgo., 1970-71, resident, 1971-73, fellow in nephrology, 1973-75; practice medicine specializing in nephrology, Hammond, Ind., 1975—; mem. staffs St. Margaret's Hosp., Hammond, Ind., Presbyterian-St. Luke's Hosp., Chgo., Meth. Hosp., Gary, Ind., St. Anthony's Hosp., Crown Point, Ind.; asst. clin. prof. medicine Ind. U.; asst. prof. health sci. Purdue U. Diplomate Am. Bd. Internal Medicine. Mem. A.C.P., Am. Internat. socs. nephrology. Jewish. Home: 20457 Ithaca St Olympia Fields IL 60461 Office: 5500 Hohman Ave Hammond IN 46320

ASHBERY, JOHN LAWRENCE, English educator, poet, playwright; b. Rochester, N.Y., July 28, 1927; s. Chester Frederick and Helen (Lawrence) A. Grad., Deerfield Acad., 1945; B.A., Harvard U., 1949; M.A., Columbia U., 1951; postgrad., NYU, 1957-58; D.Litt. hon., Southampton Coll. of L.I.U., 1979. Copywriter Oxford U. Press, N.Y.C., 1951-54; copywriter McGraw Hill Book Co., N.Y.C., 1954-55; art critic European edit. N.Y. Herald Tribune, Paris, 1960-65; Paris corr. Art News, 1964-65; exec. editor Art News, N.Y.C., 1966-72; prof. English Bklyn. Coll., 1974—, Disting. prof., 1980—; editor quar. rev. Art and Lit., Paris, 1963-66; art critic Art Internat., Lugano, Switzerland, 1961-64; editor Locus Solus, Lans-en-Vercors, France, 1960-62; poetry editor Partisan Rev., 1976-80; art critic New York Mag., 1978-80, Newsweek, 1980-85. Author: (poems) Turandot and Other Poems, 1953, Some Trees, 1956, 70, 78, The Poems, 1960, The Tennis Court Oath, 1962, Rivers and Mountains, 1966, 77, Selected Poems, 1967, Three Madrigals, 1968, Sunrise in Suburbia, 1968, Fragment, 1969, The Double Dream of Spring, 1970, 76, The New Spirit, 1970, Three Poems, 1972, 77, The Vermont Notebook, 1975, Self-Portrait in a Convex Mirror, 1975, 76, 77, Houseboat Days, 1977, As We Know, 1979, Shadow Train, 1981, 82, A Wave, 1984, Selected Poems, 1985, 86, April Galleons, 1987; (plays) The Heroes, 1952, The Compromise, 1956, The Philosopher, 1963; author: (novel) (with James Schuyler) A Nest of Ninnies, 1969, 76; works represented in numerous anthologies; also author numerous articles art criticism, translations; contbr. verse to lit. periodicals; verse set to music. Recipient Yale Series of Younger Poets prize, 1956; Harriet Monroe Poetry award Poetry Mag., 1963, 75; Union League Civic and Arts Found. prize, 1966; Nat. Inst. Arts and Letters award, 1969; Shelley award Poetry Soc. Am., 1973; guest of honor Poetry Day Modern Poetry Assn., 1973; Frank O'Hara prize Modern Poetry Assn., 1974; Pulitzer prize, 1976; Nat. Book award, 1976; Nat. Book Critics Circle award Harvard U., 1976; poetry award English-Speaking Union, 1979; Mayor's award N.Y.C., 1983; Charles Flint Kellogg award Bard Coll., 1983; Jerome J. Shestack poetry award Am. Poetry Rev., 1984, Bollingen prize in poetry Yale U. Library, 1985, Lenore Marshall poetry prize the Nation, 1985, Common Wealth award in lit. Modern Lang. Assn., 1986; named Phi Beta Kappa Poet Harvard U., 1979, Literary Lion, N.Y. Pub. Library, 1984, Poet of Yr. Pasadena City Coll., 1984; Fulbright scholar U. Montpellier, France, 1955-56; Fulbright scholar Paris, France, 1956-57; Poets' Found. grantee, 1960, 64; Ingram Merrill Found. grantee, 1962, 72; Guggenheim fellow, 1967, 73; Rockefeller Found. grantee, 1979-80; Wallace Stevens Fellow Yale U., 1985; McArthur Found. Fellow, 1985-90. Fellow Acad. Am. Poets ; Mem. Am. Acad. and Inst. Arts and Letters, Am. Acad. Arts and Scis. Address: care Georges Borchardt Inc 136 E 57th St New York NY 10022 *

ASHBY, JOHN EDMUND, JR., marketing executive; b. Dallas, Mar. 5, 1936; s. John Edmund and Lillian Eloise (Cox) A.; B.B.A., U. Tex., 1957; m. Martha DeLarios; children—Vicki, Dana, Suzanne, Shelley, Elizabeth. Salesman, IBM, Corpus Christi, Tex., 1959-64, sales mgr., 1964-67; regional mgr. Recognition Equipment Inc., Dallas, 1967-69, v.p., 1969-81; v.p. Teknekron Fin. Systems, Dallas, 1981-83, exec. v.p. TRW Fin. Systems (formerly Teknekron Fin. Systems), 1983—. Served with USMC, 1957-59. Recipient Sales award Sales and Mktg. Execs. Assn., 1961, IBM, 1964. Mem. Sales and Mktg. Execs. Assn., Beta Theta Pi. Presbyterian. Home: 3429 Cornell Dallas TX 75205 Office: TRW Fin Systems 3100 Monticello Suite 612 Dallas TX 75205

ASHBY, WILLARD EDWIN, optometrist; b. Pittsburg, Tex., Jan. 18, 1946; s. Oran Donnaly and Eva Istaline (Bunn) A. B.S., Southern Coll. Optometry, 1969, O.D., 1969. Diplomate Am. Bd. Optometry. Staff doctor So. Coll. Optometry, Memphis, Tenn., 1969; practice optometry Longview, Tex., 1970; chief optometry U.S. Air Force bases at McConnell, Kans., Eielson AFB, Alaska, Davis-Montran, Ariz., 1971-80; chief optometry, area eye care coordinator USPHS Indian Health Service, Red Lake, Minn., 1980-88, Bemidji area, Minn., Wis., Mich., 1988—; chmn. Indian Health Service Profl. Splty. Group for Devel. Eye Care Resource and Patient Mgmt. System, 1985—. Author: Indian Health Service Eye Care Manual. Contbr. articles to Jour. of Safari Club Internat., 1975-76, The Longbow, Western Bowhunter. Served as comdr. USPHS, 1971—. Mem. Commissioned Officers Assn. USPHS, Commissioned Officers Optometric Soc., Nat. Rifle Assn. (life), Armed Forces Optometric Soc. Sigma Alpha Sigma. Baptist. Club: N. Am. Hunting. Avocations: bow hunting (only person to have taken a white rhino with bow and arrow, Oct. 1984); competitive rifleman; hunter. Researcher arrow, broadhead performance. Home: Rural Route 1 Box 139A Puposky MN 56667 Office: 203 Federal Bldg Bemidji MN 56601

ASHCROFT, JOHN, governor of Missouri; b. Chgo.; married; children—Martha, Jay, Andrew. Grad. cum laude, Yale U., 1964; J.D., U. Chgo., 1967. Bar: Mo., U.S. Supreme Ct. Assoc. prof. S.W. Mo. State U., Springfield, 5 yrs; practice law Springfield, Mo., until 1973; state auditor State of Mo., 1973-75, asst. atty. gen., 1975-77, atty. gen., 1977-84, gov., 1985—. Gospel singer: records include In the Spirit of Life and Liberty; Author: (with wife) College Law for Business, 7th, 8th, 9th edits., It's the Law, 1979. Mem. Am. Bar Assn. (ho. of dels.), Mo. Bar Assn., Cole County Bar Assn., Nat. Assn. Attys. Gen. (past pres., chmn. budget com., mem. exec. com.). Republican. Mem. Assembly of God Ch. Office: State Capitol Office of Governor Room 216 PO Box 720 Jefferson City MO 65102 *

ASHCROFT, PEGGY (DAME EDITH MARGARET EMILY HUTCHINSON), actress; b. Dec. 22, 1907; d. William Worsley and Violet Maud (Bernheim) A.; m. Rupert Hart-Davis, 1929 (dissolved); m. Theodore Komisarjevsky, 1934 (dissolved); m. Jeremy Hutchinson, 1940 (dissolved 1966); two children. Ed. Croydon and Central Sch. of Speech Tng., Albert Hall, London; D.Litt. (hon.), Oxford U., 1961, Leicester U., 1964; D.Lit. (hon.), London U., 1965, Cambridge U., 1972. Debuted at Birmingham Repertory Theatre, 1926; mem. Royal Shakespeare Co., Stratford and London, 1960-64, dir., 1968—. Appeared in theatrical prodns. including, The Seagull, 1964, Days in the Trees, 1966, Ghosts, 1967, Delicate Balance, 1968, Landscape, 1969, Katherine of Aragon in Henry VIII, The Plebeians, 1970, The Lovers of Viorne (Evening Standard Best Actress award 1972), 1971, Lloyd George Knew My Father, 1972, Old Times, 1972, John Gabriel Borkman, 1975, Happy Days, 1975, Old World, 1976, Watch on the Rhine, 1980, Family Voices, 1981, All's Well That Ends Well, 1981; in films including The Wandering Jew, Thirty-Nine Steps, The Nun's Story, Sunday Bloody Sunday, Three into Two Won't Go, Passage to India (Acad. award 1984); TV appearances include Cream in My Coffee, Caught on a Train, 1980, The Jewel in the Crown, 1984. Recipient King's Gold medal Norway. Address: Manor Lodge, Frognal Lane, London NW3 England *

ASHDOWN, MARIE MATRANGA (MRS. CECIL SPANTON ASHDOWN, JR.), writer, lecturer; b. Mobile, Ala.; d. Dominic and Ave (Mallon) Matranga; m. Cecil Spanton Ashdown Jr., Feb. 8, 1958; children: Cecil Spanton III, Charles Coster; children by previous marriage: John Stephen Gartman, Vivian Marie Gartman. Student Maryville Coll. Sacred Heart, Springhill Coll.Feature artist, women's program dir. daily program Sta. WALA, also WALA-TV, Mobile, 1953-58; v.p., dir. Met. Opera Guild, N.Y.C., 1970-78; opera instr. in-service program Met. Opera Guild, N.Y.C., 1970-80, Marymont Coll., N.Y.C., 1979-85; exec. dir. Musicians Emergency Fund Inc., N.Y.C., 1985—; cons. No. Ill. U. Coll. of Visual and Performing Arts, 1985—; lectr. in field. Author: Opera Collectables, 1979, contbr. articles to profl. jours. Recipient Extraordinary Service award March of Dimes, 1958, Medal of Appreciation award Harvard Bus. Sch. Club N.Y.C., 1974, Cert. Appreciation, Kiwanis Internat., 1975, Arts Excellence award N.J. State Opera, 1986. Mem. Successful Meetings Directory, Nat. Inst. Social Scis., Com. for U.S.-China Relations. Avocations: collecting art, antique ceramics and porcelains, bookbinding. Home: 25 Sutton Pl S New York NY 10022 Office: Musicians Emergency Fund Inc 16 E 64th St New York NY 10021

ASHE, BERNARD FLEMMING, lawyer; b. Balt., Mar. 8, 1936; s. Victor Joseph Ashe and Frances Cecelia (Johnson) Flemming; m. Grace Nannette Pegram, Mar. 23, 1963; children: Walter Joseph, David Bernard. BA, Howard U., 1956, JD, 1961. Bar: Va. 1961, D.C. 1963, Mich. 1964, N.Y. 1971. Tchr., Balt. Pub. Schs., 1956-58; atty. NLRB, Washington, 1961-63; asst. gen. counsel Internat. Union United Auto Workers, Detroit, 1963-71; gen. counsel N.Y. State United Tchrs., Albany, 1971—; mem. adj. faculty Cornell Sch. Indsl. and Labor Relations, Albany div., 1981, 87. Bd. dirs. Urban League Albany, 1979-85, 1st v.p., 1981-85; trustee N.Y. State Client Security Fund, 1981—. Fellow Am. Bar Found.; mem. ABA (chmn. sect. labor and employment law sect. 1982-83, consortium on legal services and the public 1979-84, commn. on public understanding of law 1987—, Ho. of Dels.), Nat. Bar Assn., Am. Arbitration Assn. (dir. 1982—), Assn. of Bar of City of N.Y., N.Y. State Bar Assn., Nat. Lawyers Club, Albany County Bar Assn. Contbr. articles on labor and constl. law to profl. jours. Office: NY State United Tchrs 159 Wolf Rd Box 15-008 Albany NY 12212

ASHE, OLIVER RICHARD, government official; b. Washington, Nov. 25, 1933; s. Paul Joseph and Mary (Tomardy) A.; B.S., Georgetown U., 1955; M.B.A., Hofstra U., 1971; postgrad. Pace U., 1972—; m. Helen Marie Curtin, Feb. 15, 1958; children—Mary, Pauline, Margaret, Kathleen, Oliver, Cecilia, Caroline. Regional personnel rep. Marriott Corp., N.Y.C., 1965-68; personnel specialist Navy Resale System Office, N.Y.C., 1968-70, head, career mgmt., 1970-74, dep. dir., indsl. relations, 1974-76; dir. civilian personnel programs, spl. asst. to asst. sec. navy, manpower, res. affairs and logistics U.S. Dept. Def., Washington, 1976-81; asst. for adminstrn. Office Under Sec. of Navy, 1981—. Served to capt. U.S. Army, 1955-65. Recipient Sustained Superior Accomplishment award U.S. Govt., 1976, 78, 79, Outstanding Fed. Exec. award, 1983, 84, 85, Outstanding Sr. Exec. Service Performance awards, 1982, 83, 84, 85, 86. Author book chpt. Home: 10600 Vale Rd Oakton VA 22124

ASHERY, ALY MAHMOUD, journalist; b. Cairo, July 4, 1938; s. Aly and Sayyeda (Mousa) Ashery; m. Rawhia Naguib, May 5, 1958; children: Nahed, Nagwa, Nahla. BA in Social Scis., Am. U., Cairo, 1961; PhD in Pub. Adminstrn., Kennedy-Western U., Los Angeles, 1986. Photog. editor AP, Cairo, 1960-66, news editor, 1966-71; reporter AP, Beirut, Nicosia, Cyprus, 1971-80; correspondent AP, Manama, Bahrain, 1980-85, bur. chief, 1985—; econs. editor Sketch mag., Beirut, 1972-74; mng. editor The Arab Economist, Beirut, 1974-75. Author: A False Eden, 1978, An Egyptian Story, 1980, Armageddon, A Search for God, 1981. Mem. Soc. Profl. Journalists. Moslem. Office: AP, PO Box 11022, Rd 1701, Manama Bahrain

ASHIHARA, YOSHINOBU, architect, educator; b. Tokyo, July 7, 1918; s. Nobuyuki and Kikuko (Fujita) A.; m. Hatsuko Takahashi, Dec. 24, 1944; children—Yukiko, Taro. B.Arch., U. Tokyo, 1942; D.Engring. in Architecture, 1962; M.Arch., Harvard U., 1953. Prin. Yoshinobu Ashihara Architect & Assocs., Tokyo, 1955—; prof. architecture U. Tokyo, 1970-79, Musashino Art U., Tokyo, 1979—; archtl. councillor Nat. Diet Library, Tokyo. Designer numerous bldgs., including: Chuo-Koron Bldg. (Archtl. Inst. Japan award 1960), Komazawa Olympic Gymnasium, (Archtl. Inst. Japan Spl. award 1965), Japanese Pavilion, Exo'67 (Ministry of Edn. award of Arts 1968). Mem. adv. com. on grant aid Ministry Fgn. Affairs, Tokyo; mem. council Nat. Mus. Modern Arts, Tokyo. Decorated Order Commendatore (Italy); recipient Golden Triangle award Nat. Soc. Interior Designers, 1970. Fellow Am. Inst. Architects (hon.), Royal Australian Inst. Architects (hon.); mem. Archtl. Inst. Japan (pres. 1985-86). Lodge: Rotary.

ASHIKAWA, SATORU, architecture educator; b. Inamuragasaki, Japan, Jan. 1, 1945; s. Monjiro and Tokiko (Sakama) A.; m. Noriko Kohda, Nov. 15, 1975; 1 child, Tomoko. BA, Yokohama Nat. U., Japan, 1968, MA, 1970; MA, Tokyo U., 1972, PhD, 1980. Registered architect. Asst. U. Tokyo, 1975-80; lectr. architecture Shouwa Women's U., Tokyo, 1980-81, assoc. prof., 1981-84, prof., 1984—; dir. Ashikawa Archtl. Design Office, Tokyo, 1979—. Co-author: Dwelling Group, Vol. 1, 1973, Vol. 2, 1976, Vol. 3, 1978; co-translator: Fabrige Wohnfibel, 1980. Mem. Archtl. Inst. Japan (archtl. planning com. 1982-85), Assn. Agrl. Experience (spl. com. 1980—). Home: 1-11-1-1-504 Aobadai, Midoriku 227, Japan Office: Shouwa Womens U, 1-7 Taishido, Setagayaku, Tokyo 154, Japan

ASHJIAN, MESROB, clergyman; b. Beirut, Lebanon, Jan. 3, 1941; s. Nerces and Martha (Kassabian) A. Student, Armenian Theol. Sem., Antelias, Lebanon, 1957-61, Ecumenical Inst., Bossey, Switzerland, 1962-63; B.A., Princeton Theol. Sem., 1964, postgrad., 1970-74. Ordained priest Armenian Apostolic Ch., 1961; mem. faculty Armenian Theol. Sem., Antelias, Lebanon, 1961-62, 64, 65, 66-70; vice dean Armenian Theol. Sem., 1964-65, dean, 1966-70; instr. Karen Jeppe Coll., Aleppo, Syria, 1965-66; preacher St. Gregory Ch., Aleppo, Syria, 1965-66; prelate Diocese of Armenians in Iran and India, Isfahan, Iran, 1974-77; consecrated bishop 1977, consecrated archbishop, 1983; prelate Armenian Apostolic Ch. of Am., Eastern States and Can., N.Y.C., 1978—. Editor: Hask monthly, 1966-70, Deghegadou, 1976-77, The Holy Week in the Armenian Church Tradition, 1978, Unpublished Papers and Works of Mesrob Taliatine, 1979. Decorated grand protector Order Hospitallers St. George of Carinthea. Mem. World Council Chs. Clubs: Princeton (N.Y.C.), Icomos, The Asia Soc. Office: 138 E 39th St New York NY 10016

ASHKENAZY, VLADIMIR DAVIDOVICH, concert pianist; b. Gorky, USSR, July 6, 1937; s. David and Evstolia (Plotnova) A.; m. Thorunn Johannsdottir, Feb. 25, 1961; children—Vladimir Stefan, Nadia Liza, Dimitri Thor, Sonia Edda, Alexandra Inga. Student, Cen. Music Sch., Moscow, Moscow Conservatory; studies with, Sumbatyan, Lev Oborin. condr., music dir. Royal Philharm. Orch., London, 1987—; prin. guest condr. Cleve. Orch., 1987—. London debut, London Symphony Orch. under George Hurst, later solo recital, Festival Hall, 1963, recs., concerts throughout world. Recipient 2d prize Internat. Chopin Competition, Warsaw, 1955, Gold medal Queen Elizabeth Internat. Piano Competition, Brussels, 1956, Grammy awards 1973, 78, 81, 85, 87; co-recipient Tchaikovsky Piano Competition award, Moscow, 1962. Home: Sonnenhof 4, CH-6004 Lucerne Switzerland

ASHKIN, RONALD EVAN, chemical executive; b. New Rochelle, N.Y., Apr. 5, 1957; s. Abraham and Arleen (Wollins) A.; m. Rajasperi Maliapen, Nov. 25, 1984. AB, Harvard U., 1977; MBA, U. Pa., 1982. V.p. Continental Chem. Corp., Terre Haute, Ind., 1978-83, pres., 1983-86; pres. New Concepts Inc., Terre Haute, 1987—; bd. dirs. A & C Distbg. Co., New Concepts, Inc., Terre Haute. Moderator TV show, Terre Haute, Ind., 1985-86. Mem. Terre Haute sch. adv. com., 1984-86; bd. dirs. Glenn Civic Ctr., Terre Haute, 1985-86. Recipient group study exchange grant Rotary Found., Sri Lanka and India, 1985-86; scholarship Harvard U., 1973-76. Mem. Leadership Terre Haute Alumni Assn. (chmn. 1986), Am. Prodn. and Inventory Control Soc. (local v.p. 1982-84, 86, local pres. 1985), Phi Beta Kappa. Jewish. Club: Country of Terre Haute. Lodge: Toastmasters (local v.p. 1981-82. Home: Rural Rt 23 Box 388 Terre Haute IN 47802 Office: New Concepts Inc 1330 Beech St Terre Haute IN 47804

ASHLEMAN, IVAN RENO, II, health care executive, lawyer, mortgage banker; b. Kansas City, Mo., June 9, 1940; s. Ivan Reno and Ellen Lorraine (Fisher) A.; m. Susan Haase, July 25, 1986; children—Brian Eugene, Michael Scott. B.S., U. Nebr., 1963, J.D., 1963. Bar: Nev. 1963, U.S. Dist. Ct. Nebr. 1963, U.S. Dist. Ct. Nev. 1964, U.S. Tax Ct. 1975, U.S. Ct. Appeals (9th cir.) 1968, U.S. Supreme Ct. 1975. Sole practice, Las Vegas and Reno, Nev., 1966-69; ptnr. Davis, Cowell & Bowe, San Francisco and Las Vegas, 1969-80, Ashleman & Clontz, Las Vegas, 1982-83, Raggio, Ashleman, Wooster, Clontz & Lindell, Las Vegas and Reno, 1981, Ashleman, Evans, and Kelly, 1987—; Clark County dep. dist. atty., Las Vegas, 1964-66; exec. v.p., dir. Equivest Mortgage Co., Inc., Reno, Las Vegas, 1981—; pres. Ins. Services, Inc., 1983—; bd. dirs., pres. Geriatric Health Resources, Inc., Consol. Hospitality Services, Inc.; sec.-treas., bd. dirs. Sierra Health Care Mgmt. Assocs., Inc.; exec. mem. Gov. Bryan's Fin. Com., 1980. Contbr. articles to profl. jours. Trustee Nev. Bd. Museums and History, Carson City; exec. bd. dirs., treas. Nathan Adelson Hospice, Las Vegas, 1981—; pres. Young Dems. of Las Vegas, 1970; bd. dirs. Sparks Family Hosp., 1980-83, Spring Valley Community Hosp. Mem. Assn. Trial Lawyers Assn. Am., Am. Judicature Soc., ABA, Nev. Bar Assn., Nebr. Bar Assn., Washoe County Bar Assn., Clark County Bar Assn., Nev. Homebuilders, So. Nev. Arbitration Assn., Indsl. Relations Reps. Assn., Am. Acad. Med. Adminstrs., Reno C. of C. Episcopalian. Clubs: Las Vegas Country, Hualapai (Las Vegas); Virginia, Press (Reno). Home: 235 Country Club Reno NV 89509 Office: 350 S Center St Suites 542-544 Reno NV 89501

ASHLER, PHILIP FREDERIC, international trade and development advisor; b. N.Y.C., Oct. 15, 1914; s. Philip and Charlotte (Barth) A.; m. Jane Porter, Mar. 4, 1942 (dec. 1968); children: Philip Frederic, Robert Porter, Richard Harrison; m. Elise Barrett Duvall, June 21, 1969; stepchildren: Richard Edward Duvall, Jeffries Harding Duvall. B.B.A. cum laude, St. Johns Coll., 1935; M.B.A., Harvard U., 1937; grad., Indsl. Coll. Armed Forces, 1956; Sc.D., Fla. Inst. Tech., 1969; LL.D. (hon.), U. West Fla., 1969. Enlisted USMCR, 1932; commd. ensign USN, 1938, advanced through grades to rear adm., 1959; served in Normandy, So. France, Iwo Jima, Korea; dir. Office Small Bus. Dept. Def., Washington, 1948-51; mem. joint staff Joint Chiefs Staff, 1957-59; ret. 1959; dir. devel. Pensacola Jr. Coll., 1960-68; vice chancellor adminstrn. State Univ. System Fla., 1968-70, exec. vice chancellor, 1970-75; treas., ins. commr., fire marshal State of Fla., 1975-76, sec. of commerce, 1977-79; pres. Philip F. Ashler & Assos., Tallahassee, 1979—; chmn. bd. Cambridge Community Care, Inc., Tallahassee, 1981-86, Mfrs. Internat. Trade Corp., Tampa, Fla.; dir. Fidelity Guaranty Life Ins. Co., Balt., 1977-85, U.S. Fidelity & Guaranty Co., 1977-85, 1st Fla. Bank N.A., Tallahassee; sec., dir. Fringe Benefits Mgmt. Co., Tallahassee, 1987—; mem. Fla. Edn. Council, 1967-68; commr. from Fla. Edn. Commn. States, 1967-68; mem. U.S. Dept. Commerce Dist. Export Council, 1978—; mem. legis. adv. council So. Regional Edn. Bd., 1966-68; mem. Fla. Bd. Ind. Colls. and Univs., 1971-75, mem. adv. council for mil. edn., 1980-85; chmn. Fla. Civil Def. Adv. Council, 1966-69; mem. Fla. Council Internat. Devel., 1973—, vice chmn., 1979-80, chmn., 1980-82; mem. Select Council on Post High Sch. Edn., 1967-68; chmn. Fla. Med. Liability Ins. Commn., 1975-76, Fla. Task Force on Auto and Workers Compensation, 1975-76; mem. Yugoslavia Adv. Council, 1976—, InterAm. Congress on Psychology, Bogota, Colombia, 1974, NATO Advanced Sci. Inst., W.Ger., 1973; guest lectr. U. Belgrade, Yugoslavia, 1973; adviser econ. devel. to gov. Fla., 1977-78; mission leader Japan/S.E. U.S. Assn., Tokyo, 1977; trustee Fla. Council on Econ. Edn., 1979-81; mem. services policy adv. com. Office of U.S. Trade Rep., Exec. Office of Pres., Washington, 1980-85; mem. Republic of China/U.S.A. Econ. Council, 1979—; dir. Fringe Benefits Mgmt. Co., Tallahassee, Reflectone Inc., Tampa. Mem. Fla. Ho. of Reps., 1963-68; chmn. bd. dirs. Fla. Heart Assn., 1969-71; bd. dirs., treas. Internat. Cardiology Found.; bd. dirs. Tallahassee Meml. Hosp., Easter Seal Soc., 1963-68; bd. dirs., exec. com. Am. Heart Assn., 1971-77, Internat. Cardiology Fedn., Geneva, Switzerland, 1975-77; founding chmn. Tallahassee Symphony Orch., 1981-82; trustee So. Ctr. Internat. Studies, Atlanta, 1988—; mem. adv. bd. Fla./China Inst., Miami, Fla./Japan Inst., Tampa, Fla./Brazil Inst. Decorated Bronze Star with Combat V, Korean Presdl. citation; recipient Internat. Distinguished Service award Kiwanis Internat., 1965; Distinguished Service award Am. Heart Assn., 1965, 71; Distinguished Achievement award, 1975; Legislative award St. Petersburg Times, 1967. Mem. Fla. Med. Malpractice Joint Underwriting Assn. (chmn. bd. govs. 1975-76), Nat. Assn. Ins. Commrs. (vice chmn. exec. com. 1976), Internat. C. of C. (U.S. council 1979—), U.S. S.E./Japan Assn. (chmn. 1981-83), S.E. U.S./Korea Econ. Cooperation Council (vice-chmn.), Kappa Delta, Fla. Council 100. Democrat. Episcopalian (lic. lay eucharistic minister). Clubs: Capital City Tiger Bay (Tallahassee) (chmn. bd. dirs.); Curzon House (London); Fla. Econs. (chmn. 1987—). Lodge: Masons (32 degree), Shriners, Rotary. Home: 2115 E Randolph Circle Tallahassee FL 32312 also: 11 Riad Sultan Kasbah, Tangier Morocco Office: Reflectone Inc 407 E Sixth Ave Tallahassee FL 32303

ASHLOCK, JAMES ALLEN, minister; b. Flint, Mich., Aug. 10, 1955; s. James Andrew and Lowanda June (Proctor) A.; m. Mary Beth Wood, Aug. 20, 1977; children—Sarah Elizabeth, Jason Ashlock. B.S., Freed-Hardeman Coll. Ordained minister Church of Christ, 1977. Minister, Church of Christ, Bay, Ark., 1977-87, Collinsville, Ill., 1987-88, minister Main St. Ch. of Christ, Walnut Ridge, Ark., 1988—; tchr. Ch. of Christ Coll., Paragould, Arks., 1984; radio and TV speaker Northeast Ark.; lectr. in field. Author publs. in field; editor weekly religious jours. Dir. Craighead Country Youth Orgn. Named Outstanding Young Men Am., 1981, 83, 86; recipient Cert. Appreciation Freed-Hardeman Coll., 1977, Outstanding Service award, 1977; Appreciation award Soc. Disting. High Sch. Students, 1985, 86. Mem. Crowleys Ridge Acad. (plaque 1983), Am. Philatelic Soc. Republican. Avocations: stamp collecting; hiking; swimming; fishing. Home: 123 Fontaine Walnut Ridge AR 72476

ASHTON, BETSY FINLEY, broadcast journalist, author, lecturer; b. Wilkes-Barre, Pa., May 13, 1944; d. Charles Leonard Hancock Jones and Margaretta Betty (Hart) Jones Layton; m. Arthur Benner Ashton, Nov. 5, 1966 (div. 1972); m. Robert Clarke Freed, May 18, 1974 (div. 1981); m. Jacob B. Underhill III, Oct. 17, 1987. BA, Am. U., 1966, postgrad. in fine arts, 1969-71; student in painting Corcoran Sch. Art, 1968. Tchr. art Fairfax County (Va.) Pub. Schs., 1967-70; reporter, anchor Sta. WWDC, Washington, 1972-73, Sta. WMAL-AM-FM, Washington, 1973-75; corr. Sta. WTTG-TV, Washington, 1975-76, Sta. WJLA-TV, Washington, 1976-82; consumer corr. CBS News and Sta. WCBS-TV, N.Y.C., 1982-86; sr. corr. Today's Bus., 1986-87; personal fin. contbr. CBS Morning Program, 1987, Lifetime Cable TV, 1988—; bd. dirs. Lowell E. Mellett Fund for a Free and Responsible Press, Washington, 1979-82; courtroom artist numerous trials, Washington, 1978-81. Reporter TV news report Caffeine, 1981 (AAUW award 1982); reporter spot news 6 P.M. News, 1979 (Emmy award); author: Betsy Ashton's Guide to Living on Your Own, 1988. Concert master of ceremonies Beethoven Soc., Washington, 1979-82. Recipient Laurel award Columbia Journalism Rev., 1984, Outstanding Alumna award Am. U., 1985, Outstanding Media award Am. U., 1986, Best Consumer Journalism citation Nat. Press Club, 1983. Mem. Sigma Delta Chi (pres. Washington chpt. 1980-81), Alpha Chi Omega (v.p. chpt. 1964-66). Methodist. Club: The Liberty (N.Y.C.). Avocations: painting, drawing, skiing, golf.

ASHTON, CHRYSTAL HEATHER, pharmacology educator; b. Dehra Dun, India, July 11, 1929; arrived on Eng., 1935; d. Harry George and Chrystal Tempé (Parsons) Champion; m. John Ashton, Nov. 11, 1951 (dec. 1986); children: John, Caroline, James, Andrew. BA in Phsyiology, Oxford U., Eng., 1951, MA, BM, BCh, 1954, DM, 1961. Cert. med. diplomate, univ. educator. House physician, surgeon Middlesex Hosp., London, 1954-57, research scholar, 1957-59; lectr. pharmacology Middlesex Hosp. Med. Sch., London, 1961-64, U. Newcastle-upon-Tyne, Eng., 1965-74; sr. lectr. U. Newcastle-upon-Tyne, 1974-86; cons. in clin. pharmacology U. Area Health Authority, Newcastle upon Tyne, 1975—, reader in clin. psychopharmacology, 1986—. Co-author: Smoking Psychology and Pharmacology, 1982; author: Brain Systems, Disorders and Psychotropic Drugs, 1987; contbr. numerous articles to profl. jours. Grantee Tobacco Research Council, 1968-80, Med. Research Council, 1973-76, 81-84, Wellcome Found., 1986—, Wolfson Found., 1987—. Mem. Royal Coll. Physicians (life), Royal Soc. Med., Brit. Pharm. Soc., Brit. Assn. for Psychopharm., and others. Office: Univ Newcastle upon Tyne, Dept Pharmacology, Framlington Pl, Newcastle upon Tyne NE2 4HH, England

ASHTON, DAVID JOHN, business and finance educator; b. Somerville, Mass., June 29, 1921; s. Albert Carter and E. Edna (Spry) A.; m. Grace Christine Higgins, June 21, 1943; children: Leslie Jean, Jeffrey Carter, John Mark. B.S., Tufts Coll., 1942; M.B.A., Boston U., 1950; M.A., Fletcher Sch. Law and Diplomacy, 1952, Ph.D., 1959. Instr., asst. prof. Coll. Bus. Adminstrn. Boston U., 1947-59, assoc. prof., 1959-61, prof., 1961-87, prof. emeritus, 1987—; editor Boston U. Bus. Review, 1958-59; chmn. Internat. Bus. Curriculum, 1958-64; chmn. dept. Internat. Bus., 1964-68, 74-79, internat. curriculum coordinator, 1968-87, chmn. dept. fin. and econs., 1979-82; acting chmn. acctg., 1983-85; mng. dir. Boston U., Brussels, Belgium, 1972-74, 77-78; vis. lectr. U. Libre de Bruxelles, 1972-74, Luxembourg Econ. Inst., 1982; econ. cons. U.S. Naval War Coll., 1963-64, vis. lectr., 1964-65; v.p., dir., mem. exec. com. Internat. Bus. Center of New Eng., Inc., 1975-87; econ. and fin. cons. U.S. Dept. Commerce, U.S. Dept. Treasury, Fed. Res. Bank of Boston, Ednl. Testing Service, Internat. Exec. Service Corps, New Eng. Econ. Research Found., New Eng. Regional Commn., Saudi Iron and Steel Corp. Author: New England Manfacturers and European Investments, 1963, The International Component in England's Economic Base, 1968, New England's Exports of Manufactures, 1975, Business Services and New England's Export Base, 1978, also numerous articles in field.; Editorial bd.: The International Executive. Mem. Arlington (Mass.) Bd. Pub. Edn., 1955-58, chmn. bd., 1957-58; mem. Planning Bd., Arlington, 1959-62; mem. Tufts Alumni Council, 1959—, mem. exec. com., 1959-62; mem. exec. bd. Fletcher Sch. Alumni Assn., 1958-65; mem. Mass. Gov.'s Adv. Council on Internat. Trade, 1964, Winchester (Mass.) Town Meeting, 1964-70, 76; vice chmn. Town Govt. Study Commn., 1968-70; mem. Town Mgr. Selection Com., 1975; Bd. dirs. Found. for Advancement of Edn. in Internat. Bus., 1962-85, Income Fund Boston. Served to lt. USNR, 1942-45. Decorated chevalier Order of Leopold II Belgium; recipient George L. Plimpton Alumni award Tilton Sch., 1976. Mem. Am. Econ. Assn., Nat. Planning Assn., Am. Acad. Polit. and Social Sci., Acad. Internat. Bus., Am. Arbitration Assn., Delta Tau Delta, Beta Gamma Sigma, Alpha Kappa Psi. Home: 22 Myrtle St Winchester MA 01890 Office: Boston U 704 Commonwealth Ave Boston MA 02215

ASHTON, DAVID NORMAN, sociologist, educator; b. Cottingham, Yorkshire, Eng., Apr. 25, 1942; s. Charles Stanley and Sylvia (Tate) A.; m. Gillian Diane Hytch, July 30, 1966 (div. May 1980); children: Wendy Elizabeth, Heidi Suzanne; m. Maureen Valerie Sangster, Jan. 10, 1981; 1 child, Kate Louise. BA in Sociology, U. Leicester, Eng., 1964. Personnel officer Tube Investments Ltd., Nottingham, Eng., 1964-65; asst. lectr. dept. sociology U. Reading, Berkshire, Eng., 1965-66; lectr. dept. sociology U. Leicester, 1966-80, sr. lectr., 1980—; mem. com. Econ. and Social Research Council, London, 1984-87; acad. cons. Vocat. Edn. and Tng. Group of Manpower Services, 1986—. Author: Young Workers, 1976, Unemployment Under Capitalism, 1986, also research monographs. Mem. Brit. Sociol. Assn. Home: 40 Briar Walk, Oadby, Leicester LE2 5UF, England Office: U Leicester Dept Sociology, University Rd, Leicester LE2 7RH, England

ASHTON, DEBORAH PATRICIA, psychologist; b. Chgo., Dec. 5, 1950; d. Charles Joseph and Ruby (Hooks) A. B.A., Clarke Coll., 1972; Ph.D., Harvard U., 1978. Cons., Am. Inst. Research, Cambridge, Mass., 1975; research asst. Harvard U., 1976-78, postdoctoral clin. fellow in psychology, faculty of medicine, 1978-79; clin. psychology intern VA Hosp., Bedford, Mass., 1977-78; sr. civil service examiner dept. personnel adminstrn. Commonwealth of Mass., Boston, 1978-79, chief of test devel. and validation, 1979-82; clin. psychologist Second Wind Boston, 1980-81; lectr. Assumption Coll., Worcester, Mass.; asst. prof. Calif. Sch. Profl. Psychology, Berkeley, 1982—; test and measurement specialist Office Personnel, City of Oakland, 1983—; clin. psychologist Vols. in Corrections, Inc., bd. dirs., 1977-78, supr., 1976-78, vol. tchr., 1975; pvt. practice psychology, Berkeley, 1982—; mem. Trans-Africa; presenter Internat. Congress Psychology, 1988. Contbr. articles to profl. jours. Pullman scholar, 1968-72; scholar Catholic Negro Scholarship Fund, 1968-74; Harvard Tng. Tchrs. of Tchrs. fellow, 1972-73; fellow Nat. Fellowship Fund, 1973-78; named Outstanding Young Woman Am. 1983. Mem. Am. Psychol. Assn., AAAS, Phi Delta Kappa. Roman Catholic. Office: 1417 Clay St 1st Floor Oakland CA 94610

ASHTON, ROBERT, historian, educator; b. Chester, England, July 21, 1924; s. Joseph and Edith Frances (Davies) A.; m. Margaret Alice Sedgwick, Aug. 30, 1946; children: Rosalind Helen Fisher, Celia Elizabeth Ahlquist. BA with first class honors, U. London, 1949; PhD, London Sch. Econs., 1953. Asst. lectr. econ. history U. Nottingham, Eng., 1952-54, lectr. econ. history, 1956-61, sr. lectr., 1961-63; prof. English history U. East Anglia, Norwich, Eng., 1963—, dean sch. English studies, 1964-67; vis. assoc. prof. U. Calif., Berkeley, 1962-63; vis. fellow All Souls Coll., Oxford, Eng., 1973-74, 87. Author, editor: The Crown and the Money Market, 1960, James by his Contemporaries, 1969; author: The English Civil War, 1978, The City and The Court 1603-43, 1979, Reformation and Revolution 1558-1660, 1984. Served with RAF, 1943-46, ETO, Egypt. Fellow Royal Hist. Soc. (v.p. 1983-86). Home: The Manor House, Brundall, Norwich NR13 5JY, England Office: U East Anglia, Norwich England

ASHTON, THOMAS WALSH, investment banker; b. Rochester, N.Y., May 11, 1929; s. Charles Edward and Marie Margaret (Walsh) A.; B.S., U.S. Mil. Acad., 1952; M.B.A., Harvard U., 1957; m. Frances E. Hickey, May 16, 1953; children—Lucy M. Van Atta, Mary B. Ashton Anders, Monica H., William T. Assoc. corp. fin. Eastman Dillon Union Securities, N.Y.C., 1957-61, gen. partner, 1967-69; asst. v.p. Harris Upham & Co., N.Y.C., 1961-67; v.p. duPont Glore Forgan, Inc., N.Y.C., 1971-73; sr. v.p. ABD Securities Corp., N.Y.C., 1973-75; fin. cons. Am. Cancer Soc. of N.Y.C., East West Group Inc.; chmn. Peninsular Investments, Treasure Island, Fla., 1977—; cons. Dept. Commerce, 1971. Chmn. parents's council Smith Coll., 1974-76. Served with AUS, 1946-48, 52-55. Mem. Soc. Harvard Engrs. and Scientists (gov. 1974-75), West Point Soc. N.Y. (dir. 1971-75). Republican. Clubs: Army and Navy (Washington); Seminole Lake Country (Seminole, Fla.). Office: 153d Ave Madeira Beach FL 33708

ASHWORTH, JOHN CHARLES, chemical engineer, consultant; b. Makahu, Taranaki, New Zealand, Sept. 15, 1949; arrived in Eng., 1974; s. Charles Edward Ashworth and Pearl Winifred (Greenhill) Searle; m. Maureen Ann Jennings. BE in Chem. Engring., U. Canterbury, Christchurch, New Zealand, 1969, PhD in Chem. Engring., 1977. Research fellow U. Birmingham, Eng., 1974-82; prin. cons., mng. dir. Drying Research Ltd., Kenilworth, Eng., 1982—; mem. Internat. Adv. Com. for Drying Symposiums, Montreal, Can., 1980-84; chmn., organizer 3d Internat. Drying Symposium, Birmingham, 1982. Editor: Proceedings Third International Drying Symposium, 1982. Scientific Approach to Solution of Solids Drying Problems, 1982; contbr. articles to profl. jours. Mem. Instn. Chem. Engrs. (chmn. solids drying group 1980-82), Am. Inst. Chem. Engrs., Instn. Prof. Engrs. New Zealand, Paper Industry Tech. Assn.

ASHWORTH, WILLIS LOUIS, finance company executive; b. Birmingham, Ala., Aug. 30, 1939; s. Willis Louis and Glenda (Collins) A.; m. Margaret Rodgers As (div.); children—Philip Rodgers, Margaret Collins. B.S., Am. U., 1966. fin. cons., market timerAm. Security Fin. Services, Inc. Mem. Internat. Game Fishing Assn., Mercedes Benz Motor Club. Avocations: deep sea fishing; travel; hunting. Home: 11820 Stuart Mill Rd Oakton VA 22124

ASIJA, S(ATYA) PAL, patent lawyer, engineer; b. Leiah, India, Apr. 26, 1942; came to U.S., 1967, naturalized, 1972; s. Chander Bhanu and Radha Bai (Chugh) P.; m. Madeline Rich Magill, June 1, 1974 (dec. June 1982). Grad. IERE (Lond), Southampton, Eng., 1964; postgrad. diploma U. Wales, Cardiff, 1967; M.B.A., U. Dayton, 1970; J.D., No. Ky. State U., 1974. Bar: U.S. Patent Office 1974, U.S. Supreme Ct. 1978, Conn. 1983, U.S. Ct. Appeals (fed. cir.) 1984. Supr. electronics AEC Radiation Lab. U. Notre Dame, Ind., 1967-68; research & devel. systems engr. NCR, Dayton, Ohio, 1968-71; systems analyst Police Dept., Dayton, 1971-73; exec. dir. MINCIS, State of Minn., St. Paul, 1974-76; systems engr. Sperry Univac, Eagan, Minn., 1977-80; sr. mem. tech. staff ITT, Shelton, Conn., 1980-84 ; cons., avionics engr. Sikorsky Aircraft, Div. United Technologies Corp., Stratford, Conn., 1985-88; pvt. practice law, Ansonia, Conn., 1988—; advisor Computer Users Legal Reporter, Westport, Conn., 1984—, Yale Sci. Park Legal Clinic, New Haven, 1984—. Author: 4 books, Software Patents, 1983. Editor newsletter Chasette, 1972; contbr. articles to profl. jours.; patentee in field. Inventor Swiftanswer, 1977 (3d pl. award 1977), Magicfold, 1976 (2d pl. award 1976). Candidate for Minn. Ho. of Reps., 1976; capt. CAP, 1979-80. Mem. Toastmasters Internat. (able toastmaster 1972, pres. 1972), Minn. Computer Soc. (pres. 1977), IEEE (sr.), Am. Arbitration Assn. (panelist 1972—), Internat. Bar Assn., ABA, Republican. Mormon. Home: 7 Woonsocket Ave Shelton CT 06484

ASIKAINEN, AIMO OLAVI, software company executive; b. Parikkala, Finland, Feb. 3, 1945; m. Aili Marda Tervonen, Dec. 31, 1967; children: Riku Petteri, Liisi Johanna. Operator Kansallis-Osake-Pankki, Helsinki, Finland, 1968-69; programmator Ovako Steel, Imatra, Finalnd, 1969-71; analyst Medica, Helsinki, 1971-73; system mgr. SISU-Auto, Helsinki, 1973-76; mng. dir. Tietolinkki OY, Helsinki, 1976-87, Tietolinkki, Helsinki, 1976—. Home: Elontie 21 G, 00660 Helsinki Finland Office: Tietolinkki OY, Sulkapolku 3, 00370 Helsinki Finland

ASIMOV, ISAAC, biochemist, author; b. Petrovichi, Russia, Jan. 2, 1920; came to U.S., 1923; s. Judah and Anna Rachel (Berman) A.; m. Gertrude Blugerman, 1942 (div. 1973); children: David, Robyn Joan; m. Janet Jeppson, 1973. BS, Columbia U., 1939, MA, 1941, PhD, 1948; holder 14 hon. degrees. Faculty Boston U. Sch. Medicine, 1949—, asso. prof. biochemistry, 1955-79, prof., 1979—. Author: Pebble in the Sky, 1950, I, Robot, 1950, The Stars, Like the Dust, 1951, Foundation, 1951, Foundation and Empire, 1952, Currents of Space, 1952, Second Foundation, 1953, Caves of Steel, 1954, End of Eternity, 1955, Races and People, 1955, The Naked Sun, 1957; textbook Biochemistry and Human Metabolism, rev. edit, 1957; World of Carbon, 1958, World of Nitrogen, 1958, Nine Tomorrows, 1959, The Words of Science, 1959, Realm of Numbers, 1959, The Living River, 1960, Kingdom of the Sun, 1960, Realm of Measure, 1960, Wellsprings of Life, 1960, Words from Myths, 1961, Realm of Algebra, 1961, Life and Energy, 1962, Words in Genesis, 1962, Fact and Fancy, 1962, Words on the Map, 1962, Search for the Elements, 1962, Words from the Exodus, 1963, The Human Body, 1963, The Genetic Code, 1963, Intelligent Man's Guide to Science, 1960, View from a Height, 1963, Kite that Won the Revolution, 1963, Human Brain, 1964, A Short History of Biology, 1964, Quick and Easy Math, 1964, Adding a Dimension, 1964, A Short History of Chemistry, 1865, The Greeks, 1965, Of Time and Space and Other Things, 1965, The New Intelligent Man's Guide to Science, 1965, An Easy Introduction to the Slide Rule, 1965, Fantastic Voyage, 1966, The Noble Gases, 1966, The Neutrino, 1966, The Roman Republic, 1967, Understanding Physics, 1966, Is Anyone There?, 1967, To the Ends of the Universe, 1967, Mars, 1967, Egyptians, 1967, Asimov's Mysteries, 1968, Science, Numbers and I, 1968, Stars, 1968, Galaxies, 1968, A Whiff of Death, 1968, Near East, 1968, Asimov's Guide to the Bible, vol. 1, 1968, vol. 2, 1969, The Dark Ages, 1968, Words from History, 1968, Photosynthesis, 1969, The Shaping of England, 1969, Twentieth Century Discovery, 1969, Nightfall and Other Stories, 1969, Opus 100, 1969, ABC's of Space, 1969, Great Ideas of Science, 1969, Solar System and Back, 1970, Asimov's Guide to Shakespeare (2 vols.), 1970, Constantinople, 1970, ABC's of the Ocean, 1970, Light, 1970, The Stars in Their Courses, 1971, Where Do We Go from Here?, 1971, What Makes the Sun Shine?, 1971, The Sensuous Dirty Old Man, 1971, The Best New Thing, 1971, Isaac Asimov's Treasury of Humor, 1971, The Hugo Winners, Vol. 2, 1971, The Land of Canaan, 1971, ABC's of the Earth, 1971, The Left Hand of the Electron, 1972, The Gods Themselves, 1972, Asimov's Guide to Science, 1972, More Words of Science, 1972, ABC's of Ecology, 1972, The Early Asimov, 1972, The Shaping of France, 1972, The Story of Ruth, 1972, Asimov's Annotated Don Juan, 1972, The Shaping of North America, 1973, Today and Tomorrow and, 1973, Jupiter, the Largest Planet, 1973, Please Explain, 1973, How Did We Find Out About Numbers, 1973, How Did We Find Out About Dinosaurs, 1973, The Tragedy of the Moon, 1973, Asimov on Astronomy, 1974, The Birth of the United States, 1974, Before the Golden Age, 1974, Our World in Space, 1974, How Did We Find Out About Germs, 1974, Asimov's Annotated Paradise Lost, 1974, Tales of the Black Widowers, 1974, Earth: Our Crowded Spaceship, 1974, Asimov on Chemistry, 1974, How Did We Find Out About Vitamins, 1974, Of Matters Great and Small, 1975, The Solar System, 1975, Our Federal Union, 1975, How Did We Find Out about Comets, 1975, Science Past—Science Future, 1975, Buy Jupiter and Other Stories, 1975, Eyes on the Universe, 1975, Lecherous Limericks, 1975, Heavenly Host, 1975, The Ends of the Earth, 1975, How Did We Find Out About Energy, 1975, Asimov on Physics, 1976, Murder at the ABA, 1976, How Did We Find Out About Atoms, 1976, The Planet That Wasn't, 1976, The Bicentennial Man and Other Stories, 1976, More Lecherous Limericks, 1976, More Tales of the Black Widowers, 1976, Alpha Centauri, The Nearest Star, 1976, How Did We Find Out About Nuclear Power, 1976, Familiar Poems Annotated, 1977, The Collapsing Universe, 1977, Asimov on Numbers, 1977, How Did We Find Out About Outer Space, 1977, Still More Lecherous Limericks, 1977, Hugo Winners, Vol. II, 1977, The Beginning and the End, 1977, Mars, The Red Planet, 1977, The Golden Door, 1977, The Key Word and Other Mysteries, 1977, Asimov's Sherlockian Limericks, 1977, One Hundred Great Science Fiction Short Short Stories, 1978, Quasar, Quasar, Burning Bright, 1978, How Did We Find Out About Earthquakes, 1978, Animals of the Bible, 1978, Life and Time, 1978, Limericks: Too Gross, 1978, How Did We Find Out About Black Holes?, 1978, Saturn and Beyond, 1979, In Memory Yet Green, 1979, Opus 200, 1979, Extraterrestrial Civilizations, 1979, How Did We Find Out About Our Human Roots?, 1979, The Road to Infinity, 1979, A Choice of Catastrophes, 1979, Isaac Asimov's Book of Facts, 1979, The Science Fictional Solar System, 1979, The Thirteen Crimes of Science Fiction, 1979, How Did We Find Out About Antarctica?, 1979, Casebook of the Black Widowers, 1980, How Did We Find Out About Oil?, 1980, In Joy Still Felt, 1980, Microcosmic Tales, 1980, Who Dun It?, 1980, Seven Deadly Sins of Science Fiction, 1980, The Annotated Gulliver's Travels, 1980, How Did We Find Out About Coal, 1980, In the Beginning, 1981, Asimov on Science Fiction, 1981, Venus: Near Neighbor of the Sun, 1981, How Did We Find Out About Solar Power?, 1981, How Did We Find Out About Volcanoes?, 1981, Views of the Universe, 1981, The Sun Shines Bright, 1981, Change, 1981, A Glossary of Limericks, 1982, How Did We Find Out About Life in the Deep Sea, 1982, The Complete Robot, 1982, Laughing Space, 1982, Exploring the Earth and the Cosmos, 1982, How Did We Find Out About the Beginning of Life, 1982, Foundations Edge, 1982, How Did We Find Out About the Universe, 1982, Counting the Eons, 1983, The Winds of Change and other Stories, 1983, The Roving Mind, 1983, The Measure of the Universe, 1983, The Union Club Mysteries, 1983, Norby, the Mixed-Up Robot, 1983, How Did We Find Out About Genes, 1983, The Robots of Dawn, 1983, others. X Stands for Unknown, 1984, Norby's Other Secret, 1984, How Did We Find Out About Computers, 1984, Opus 3000, 1984, Banquet of the Black Widowers, 1984, Limericks for Children, 1984, Asimov's New Guide to Science, 1984, How Did We Find Out About Robots, 1984, Asimov's Guide to Halley's Comet, 1985, Exploding Suns, 1985, Norby and the Lost Princess, 1985, How Did We Find Out About the Atmosphere, 1985, The Edge of Tomorrow, 1985, The Subatomic Monster, 1985, The Disappearing Man and Other Stories, 1985, Robots and Empire, 1985, Norby and The Invaders, 1985, How Did We Find Out About DNA?, 1985, The Alternate Asimovs, 1986, The Dangers of Intelligence, 1986, How Did We Find Out About the Speed of Light, 1986, Best Science Fiction of Isaac Asimov, 1986, Best Mysteries of Isaac Asimov, 1986, Foundation and Earth, 1986, Robot Dreams, 1986, Norby and the Queen's Necklace, 1986, Far as Human Eye Could See, 1987, How Did We Find Out About Blood, 1987, Past, Present and Future, 1987, How Did We Find Out About Sunshine?, 1987, How to Enjoy Writing, 1987, Norby Finds a Villain, 1987, Fantastic Voyage II, 1987, How did We Find Out About the Brain?, 1987, Did Comets Kill the Dinosaurs?, 1987, Beginnings, 1987, Asimov's Annotated Gilbert and Sullivan, 1988, How did We Find Out About Superconductivity?, 1988, Other Worlds of Isaac Asimov, 1988, Relativity of Wrong, 1988, Prelude to Foundation, 1988. Served as cpl. U.S. Army, 1945-46. Recipient James T. Grady award Am. Chem. Soc., 1965, AAAS-Westinghouse Sci. Writing award, 1967. Democrat. Home and Office: 10 W 66th St New York NY 10023

ASKARI, HASAN, investment banker; b. Calcutta, India, June 29, 1945; s. Syed Mohammed and Kishwar Jahan (Mirza) A.; m. Nasreen Hassam Ismail, Oct. 24, 1976; children: Syed Iman Hashim, Sehr Kishwar. BA with honors, Oxford U., 1975, MA, 1980. Mgr. S.G. Warburg & Co. Ltd., London, 1975-80; dir. Chase Manhattan Asia Ltd., Hong Kong, 1980-84; mng. dir. Chase Manhattan Asia Ltd., Tokyo, 1985-86; sr. mng. dir. Chase Investment Bank, Tokyo and N.Y.C., 1986—; bd. dirs. Chase A.M.P. Capital Markets Ltd., Sydney, Chase Manhattan Trust Banking, Tokyo, Chase Japan Leasing Ltd., Tokyo. Mem. Am. Japan Soc., Royal Soc. for Asian Affairs, Royal Asiatic Soc. London, Oxford U. Union. Islam. Club: The Oriental (London). Office: Chase Investment Bank, 1-2-1 Marunouchi, Chiyoda-ku, Tokyo 100, Japan

ASKEDAL, JOHN OLE, language professional; b. Øyestad, Arendal, Norway, July 30, 1942; s. Ole Emil and Signe (Engeset) A.; m. Anne Martha Aarsaether Heli, Jan. 8, 1971; children: Johanne, Anne Cathrine, Maria. Candidate Philosophy, U. Oslo, Norway, 1969. Lectr. U. Trondheim, Norway, 1970-75; assoc. prof. U. Oslo, Norway, 1975-84, prof., 1985—. Author: Neutrum Plural mit persönlichem Bezug im Deutschen, 1973, Innføring i tysk grammatikk, 1976; co-editor: Festschrift für Laurits Saltveit, 1983, Gedenkschrift für Ingerid Dal, 1988; contbr. articles to profl. jours. Home: Nordbergvn 61, N-0875 Oslo 8, Norway Office: U Oslo, PB 1004 Blindern, N-0315 Oslo 3, Norway

ASKIN, LEON, director, actor, producer, writer; b. Vienna, Austria, Sept. 18, 1907; came to U.S., 1940, naturalized, 1943; s. Samuel and Malvine (Susman) Aschkenasy; m. Annelies Ehrlich, Apr. 12, 1955; 1 child, Irene Hartzell. Grad., New Sch. for Dramatic Arts (now Reinhardt Seminar), Vienna, 1927; postgrad., Columbia U., 1951. Actor Dumont Playhouse, Dusseldorf, Fed. Republic of Germany, 1927-33; dir. cabaret, writer, actor Paris, 1933-35; dir. 1st Legion, Linz, Austria, 1935; artistic dir. lit. and polit. cabaret ABC, Vienna, 1935-38; scriptwriter films Paris, 1938-40; artistic dir. Washington Civic Theatre, 1940-42; tchr. modern play analysis Am. Theater Wing, 1946-47; dir. Dramatic Workshop, N.Y.C., 1947-48; hon. life dir., chmn. various coms. Actors Equity Library Community Theatre, 1947-52; founder Actors Equity Community Theatre, 1948; lectr. theater UCLA, U. So. Calif., Riverside, 1988, The Denver Ctr. for Performing Arts Conservatory, 1985; lectr., mem. panel polit. discussions on cabaret in Austria and on Piscator U. So. Calif., UCLA, 1987-88. Dir. Troilus and Cressida (Most Outstanding Prodn. 1941), The Applecart, American Way; staged: Faust for Goethe Festival, 1948-49; dir., actor: (broadway play) The Merchant of Venice, 1952; appeared in motion pictures including The Robe, 1953, One, Two, Three, 1962, Do Not Disturb, 1966, Guns for San Sebastian, 1967, Hammersmith is Out, Going Ape, 1980, Horror Star, 1981, Airplane II, 1982; starring roles in films including First Strike, 1984, Savage Island, 1984, Summer Jobs, 1984, Stiffs, 1985, Deshima, 1986; starred as Gen. Burkhalter in TV series Hogan's Heroes, 1966-71, Martin Luther and Karl Marx in TV series Meeting of Minds; dir.: (plays) St. Joan (George Bernard Shaw), 1954, Julius Caesar (Shakespeare), 1964, The Egg (Felicien Marceau), 1975, Fever in the Brain (Marvin Aron), 1980; co-starred with Jack Lemmon in Idiots Delight; played Othello on stage in Berlin and Hamburg, Fed. Republic of Germany, 1957 (acclaimed as greatest German Othello of 20th Century); contbr. articles to Los Angeles Times, Der Morgen, Vienna, Die Furche, Vienna, also essays to U. Hamburg Arbeitastelle fur Exilliteratur. Served with U.S. Army, 1942-46; editor-in-chief The Orientation Digest Air Tech. Service Command (15 citations). Recipient Medal of honor City of Vienna, 1983, Austrian Cross of Honor for outstanding services in scis. and the arts, 1988. Mem. Actors Equity (dir. West Coast adv. com. 1952-55), Screen Actors Guild (dir. 1973), AFTRA, Am. Film Inst., Acad. Motion Picture Arts and Scis. (mem. com. for selecting best fgn. lang. film), Acad. TV Arts and Scis., ANTA (nat. bd.), Am. Nat. Theatre and Acad. West (chmn. bd. 1976-78, pres. 1979-82, pres. emeritus 1983—, organized and presented Nat. Artist award to Fred Astaire, Henry Fonda, Bob Hope, Jimmy Stewart and Roger Stevens), Equity Library (hon. lifetime bd. dirs.).

ASKINS, ARTHUR JAMES, service executive, accountant; b. Phila., Dec. 12, 1944; s. William J. and Rita M. (O'Brian) A.; m. Nancy E. Paulsen, Apr. 28, 1979. BS, LaSalle U., 1967; MA, Rider Coll., 1971. CPA, Pa., N.J. Tchr. Cardinal Dougherty High Sch., Phila., 1967-70; pvt. practice acctg., 1967—; staff acct. Gross Master & Co., Jenkintown, Pa., 1970-74; asst. controller Hankin Trustee, Willow Grove, Pa., 1974-79; mgr. internal audit Resorts Internat. Hotel Casino, Atlantic City, N.J., 1979-87, dir. revenue acctg., 1987—. Recipient cert. of Commendation Twp. of Abington (Pa.), 1967, Disting. Service award Community Accts., Phila., 1982, Superstar award Resorts Internat. Casino-Hotel, 1982, Brotherhood award NCCJ, Atlantic City, 1983, Mgmt. award Resorts Internat. Casino Hotel, 1986, 1st Mgrs. award Resort Internat. Casino-Hotel, 1986, Outstanding Vol. Service award Big Bros./Big Sisters, 1987. Mem. Nat. Assn. Accts. (nat. bd. dirs. 1983-85), pres. South Jersey Shore chpt. 1979-81, Community Affairs award Suburban Northeast Phila. 1978), Inst. Internal Auditors (bd. dirs. 1984—), Am. Inst. CPA's, N.J. Soc. CPA's, Pa. Inst. CPA's, Greater Mainland C. of C. (audit com. 1979—). Republican. Roman Catholic. Home: PO Box 398 Somers Point NJ 08244 Office: Resort Internat Hotel Casino North Carolina & Boardwalk Atlantic City NJ 08401

ASLAM, MOHAMMAD, textile company executive; b. Sialkot, Pakistan, Mar. 23, 1936; s. Fazal and Fatima Bibi Ellahi; A.G. Inst. Tech. (Australian Govt. Colombo Plan fellow), Gordon Inst. Tech., Geelong, Victoria, Australia, 1962; L.T.I., Textile Inst., Manchester, Eng., 1963, C Tex A.T.I., 1986; P.M.D., Harvard U., Boston, 1974; m. Zahida Iqbal, Nov. 21, 1966; children—Imran, Rizwan, Adnan, Rehan, Bilal. In charge prodn. Harnai Woollen Mills Ltd. (Pakistan), 1960-66, mills mgr., 1968-70; mills mgr. Qaidabad Woollen Mills Ltd. (Pakistan), 1966-68; prodn. mgr. Lawrencepur Woollen & Textile Millls Ltd., Dawoodpur, Pakistan, 1970-77, dep. gen. mgr. ops., 1977-81, dep. gen. mgr., 1981-84, gen. mgr., 1984—. Named Best Student, Gordon Inst. Tech., 1959. Mem. Textile Inst. (exec. mem. Pakistan sect.), Mgmt. Assn. Pakistan. Moslem. Clubs: Woollen (sec. Harnai 1964-66, pres. 1968-70; pres. Qaidabad 1966-68), Officers (pres. 1977-80) (Dawoodpur). Home: 188 St 10, Cavalry Ground Extension, Lahore 54810, Pakistan Office: Lawrencepur Woollen, & Textile Mills Ltd, 35-A Empress Rd, Lahore Pakistan

ASLAM, MOHAMMAD, microbiologist; b. Sargodha, Punjab, Pakistan, Jan. 5, 1959; s. Mohammad Boota and Barakat Bibi; m. Shamim Shinah, July 20, 1984; children: Misbah, Umair. BSc, Punjab U., 1977, MSc, 1983. Registered med. practitioner, Punjab. Cons. Med. Ctr., Sarhodha, 1983—. Muslim. Club: Ambala Muslim. Home: Block 17 HN 4 S54, Sargodha 961, Punjab Pakistan Office: Medicine House, Sargodha Pakistan

ASLAM, MUHAMMAD, engineering consultant; b. R. Prapat, North Sumatra, Indonesia, Dec. 20, 1951; s. Chandra Syahbudin and Aisah A.; m. Ely Aslam; children: Muhammad Haadi Suarna, Karina Anggiany Aslam, Muhammad Ihsan Sutrisna. Engring. diploma, Inst. Teknologi Bandung, Indonesia, 1976. Asst. project mgr. PT. Widya Pertiwi Engring., Jakarta, Indonesia, 1974-76, supr., 1976, project vice mgr., 1976-78; resident engr. PT. Widya Pertiwi Engring., Medan, Indonesia, 1978-80, br. mgr., 1980—. Mem. Nat. Assn. Indonesian Cons. in North Sumatra (treas. 1982-85, 1988—), Union Bandung Inst. Tech. Alumni (sec. North Sumatra br. 1985-88), Indonesians Engrs. Assn. (chief of sport sect. 1985-88, treas. 1988—), North Sumatra Chamber Commerce and Industry (chief dept. gen. energy 1987—), Indonesian Geotech. Engr. Assn. in North Sumatera (treas. 1987—), Indonesian Assn. Hydraulic Engrs. (sec. Medan br. 1987—). Club: Medan Raya. Lodge: Lions (dir. Medan 1986-87). Home: JL Sei Mencirim #28A, Medan Indonesia Office: PT Widya Pertiwi Engring, JL Sriwijaya #60, Medan 20153, Indonesia

ASMUSSEN, INGER MARIE, physician; b. Frederikssund, Denmark, May 5, 1945; d. Ingrid and Nis Asmussen; M.D., U. Copenhagen, 1971; postgrad. Hammersmith, London, 1975-77, 79, 83, 84, 85. Staff depts. internat. medicine and cardiology Univ. Hosp., Copenhagen, 1971-77, 80-86; research faculty U. Copenhagen, 1977-80; vis. prof. U.S., Can., U.K., Fed. Republic Germany, The Netherlands, Sweden, Japan, Denmark; physician dept. cardiovascular lab. B, Rigshospitalet, Copenhagen, 1981-85; lectr. in field; mem. planning group for multicenter study of atherosclerosis, WHO. Author: The Human Umbilical Vasculature; contbr. articles to profl. jours. Avocations: painting, drawing. Home: Falkoner Alle 53 Apt 616, DK 2000 Frederiksberg Copenhagen, Denmark Office: U Copenhagen Dept Cardiology, Frederiksberg Hosp, Copenhagen Denmark

ASMUSSEN, JES, JR., electrical engineering educator, researcher, consultant; b. Milw., June 12, 1938; s. Jes and Anita (Weltzien) A.; m. Judith Adele Knopp, June 18, 1960 (div. 1980); children—Kirsten, Jes III, Stig; m. Colleen Cooper, Jan 4, 1987. B.S.E.E., U. Wis., 1960, M.S.E.E., 1964, Ph.D. in Elec. Engring., 1967. Design and devel engr. Louis Allis Co., Milw., 1960-62; asst. prof. elec. engring. Mich. State U., East Lansing, 1967-71, assoc. prof., 1971-75, prof., 1975—, acting assoc dir. div. engring. research, 1983-84; U.S./France coop. researcher U. Paris/CNRS, Orsay, France, 1986—; cons. Kimberly Clark Corp, Lear Siegler Corp., NASA, Lewis Research Ctr., S.D. Warren/Scott Paper Co., 1971—. Contbr. articles to profl. jours. Patentee in field. Grantee NSF, Dept. Energy, NASA, Def. Advanced Research Projects Agy., 1971—; recipient Disting. Faculty award Mich. State U., 1988. Mem. IEEE, AIAA, AAAS, Sigma Xi. Home: 4138 Luff Ct Okemos MI 48864

ASNONG, EDDY LÉON JUSTIN, food products executive; b. Ixelles, Belgium, Feb. 19, 1950; s. Armand Fernand and Marie Brigitte (Visart De Bocarme) A.; m. Ghislaine Straet, July 8, 1972; children: Valérie, Virginie. Salesman various food cos., Belgium, 1969-76; sales mgr. Suzy Internat. div. Borden Food Co., Benelux, Belgium, 1976-79, comml. dir., 1979-86; sales mgr. Del Monte Belgium, 1986, Nabisco Brands, Brussels, 1986—. Served as sgt. Belgium Army, 1967-68. Office: Nabisco Brands, Chaussée de la Hulpe, 181 Hi 6, Brussels Belgium B1170

ASO, YUTAKA, cement company executive; b. Fukuoka, Japan, Aug. 28, 1946; s. Takakichi and Kazuko (Yoshida) A.; m. Kazuko Takemi, Oct. 10, 1973; children: Iwao, Takeshi. BA, Keio U., Tokyo, 1969; postgrad., New Coll., Oxford, Eng., 1969-72. Salesman J. Osawa & Co. Ltd., Tokyo, 1973-76; auditor Aso Cement Co. Ltd., Iizuka, Japan, 1976-77, exec. dir., 1977-79, pres., 1979—. Mem. Japan Fedn. Employers, Cement Assn. Japan (vice chmn.), Kyusyu Rugby Assn. (vice chmn.). Liberal Democrat. Roman Catholic. Club: Aso Iizuka. Home: 214 Kayanomori, Iizuka Fukuoka Japan 820 Office: Aso Cement Co Ltd, 3-25-24, Hakataku Fukuoka Japan 812

ASPIOTOU, KOULA, shipping company executive; b. Athens, Greece, July 19, 1946; d. John Aspiotis and Ana (Beni-Psalti) Seimenis; m. Nikitas Harhalakis, Mar. 1, 1981; children: Mando, Eriana. Diploma, Athens U., 1968. Jr. clk. Nat. Bank Greece, Athens, 1965-69; asst. to prof. constl. law Athens U., 1969; asst. v.p., sr. credit officer Bank of Am., Athens, 1969-85; mng. dir. Seastar Navigation Co. Ltd., Piraeus, Greece, 1985—; bd. dirs. Seastar Navigation Ltd., London, Seastar Chartering Ltd., Piraeus. Home: 1 Kithiron St, 145 62 Athens Greece Office: Seastar Group of Cos, 27/31 Hatzikiriakou St, 185 38 Piraeus Greece

ASPLUND, AKE GUSTAV, manufacturing executive; b. Helsingborg, Sweden, Sept. 23, 1917; s. Per Gustav and Anna Venhilda (Andersson) A. m. Annie Maria Nilsson, Apr. 30, 1949; children—Ingrid, Dag, Bo. Attended schs. Helsingborg. Clk. Swedish Ry., Perstorp, 1935-41, sta. master dep., Paarp, Grevie, 1942-55; dir. AB Cernelle, Engelholm, 1955-60, chmn. bd., 1960—; dir. devel. and research Cernitin S.A., Lugano, Switzerland, 1971—; auditor MHF Helsingborg, 1970-85, Helsingborgs Ungdomsrad, 1973—. Sec. Swedish Frisksport, Helsingborg, 1933-45; mgr. Unddomsberedskapen, Malmohus, Malmo, 1941-45. Mem. Swedish Mfrs. Assn., Swedish Frisksportforbundet. Moderate. Lutheran. Research on biology and chemistry of pollen. Home: Drottninggatan 127c, S 25233 Helsingborg Sweden Office: AB Cernelle, Vegeholm 6250, S 26200 Engelholm Sweden

ASSAD, HAFIZ, president of Syria; b. Kerdaha, Syria, 1928; ed. Mil. Coll., Aviation Coll., grad., 1955; hon. doctorate Damascus U.; married; 4 sons, 1 dau. Commd. officer Syrian Army, advanced through ranks to gen., 1964; comdr.-in-chief Air Force, 1966-70; minister def., 1966-70; instigated coup d'etat, 1970; mem. Ba'ath (Arab Socialist Renaissance) Party, 1946—, sec., 1970—; prime minister Syria, 1970-71; pres. Syrian Arab Republic, 1971—; mem. Pres.'s Council, Fedn. Arab Republics, 1971—; pres. Syrian Nat. Progressive Front, 1972—; comdr.-in-chief Armed Forces, 1973—. Decorated Grand Cordon de l'Ordre Nat. du Cedre (Lebanon), other Syrian and fgn. decorations. Address: Office of the Pres, Damascus Syria *

ASSADOURIAN, ROBERT HENRI, surgeon; b. Cannes, France, Dec. 10, 1933; s. Sarkis and Emma (Hovsepian) A.; m. Yvonne-Marie Voirin; children: Sylvie, Michel. MD, Faculty Medicine Marseilles, France, 1965. Intern Marxeille Hosp., 1959; practice medicine specializing in surgery Marseilles, 1962—; prof. surgery La Timone Hosp, 1974-79, Med. Coll. Marseilles, 1974—, Michel Levy, 1979-86, Hotel-Dieu, 1986—. Contbr. articles to profl. jours. Mem. Union des Medicine de France (pres. 1981-82). Office: Hotel Dieu, Service Chirurgie, 6 Place Daviel, 13224 Marseille France

ASSAEL, MICHAEL, lawyer, accountant; b. N.Y.C., July 20, 1949; s. Albert and Helen (Hope) A.; m. Eiko Sato. B.A., George Washington U., 1971; M.B.A., Columbia U. Grad. Sch. Bus., 1973; J.D., St. John's Law Sch., 1977. Bar: N.Y. 1978, U.S. Dist. Ct. (so. and ea. dists.) N.Y. 1980, U.S. Supreme Ct. 1982; CPA, N.Y. Tax sr. Price Waterhouse & Co., N.Y.C. and Tokyo, 1977-78; pvt. practice law, N.Y.C., 1978—; pvt. practice acctg., N.Y.C., 1978—. Author: Money Smarts, 1982. Pres. bd. dirs. 200 Block East 74th Street Assn., 1982; bd. dirs. 200 E 74 Owners Corp., 1981—, treas., 1983-84, pres., 1984-85; mem. Yorkville Civic Council, tenant adv. com. Lenox Hill Neighborhood Assn., 1981-82. Recipient N.Y. Habitat/Citibank mgmt. achievement award, 1985. Mem. ABA, N.Y. State Bar Assn., N.Y. County Lawyers Assn., Am. Inst. CPA's, Am. Assn. Atty. CPA's, Inc., Nat. Assn. Accts., N.Y. State Soc. CPA's, Aircraft Owners and Pilots Assn. Clubs: N.Y. Road Runners, Columbia Bus. Sch. (N.Y.).

ASSEO, ROGER ROBERT, manufacturing company executive; b. Istanbul, Turkey, May 14, 1931; s. Robert Niso and Baronne de Verdor Nadine (Pantelides) A.; m. Jenny Michioff, Aug. 11, 1960; 1 child, Robert Roger. Grad. high sch., Istanbul. Mgr. various import-export and fgn. agencies, Istanbul, 1952-56; dir. Pvt. Bank, Rio de Janeiro, 1956-58; fin. dir. Pharm./Cosmetic Plant, Istanbul, 1960-63, mng. dir., 1963-76; exec. bd., controller Tekyar Holding Co., Istanbul, 1977-87, exec. bd., mng. dir. seafood op. co., 1980-88; adminstrv./sales mgr. Marshall Paints, Istanbul, 1981—. Contbr. articles to profl. jours. Pres. Religious/Social Community, Istanbul. 1980—. Served to lt. Turkish Air Force, 1952-53. Fellow Assn. of Protection of People in Need; mem. Istanbul Chamber of Industry (bd. dirs. 1970-76). Clubs: fencing, horse riding. Lodge: Masons (treas.). Home: Liman Sokak No 32, Yesilkoy, Istanbul Turkey

ASSERAF, ISAAC, physician; b. Settat, Morocco, Apr. 30, 1947; came to France, 1964; s. Charles and Sol (Benlolo) A.; m. Pedouth Cohen, Jan 29, 1975; children: Emmanuelle, Michael, Judith. MD, U. Toulouse, France, 1976. Intern Belison Hosp., Israel, 1975-76; pres. of med. orgn. to Israel's aid, Toulouse, 1978, Maguen David Adam, Toulouse, 1978; mem. regional com. Foods Social Juif Unifié, Toulouse, 1985, dir. nat. com. Paris, 1985, v.p., 1980, consul rep. Institusions Juives de France, 1980, Jewish Community Radio, Toulouse, 1982. Mem. Regional Order of Medicine. Club: Occitan. Home: 12 Ave de l'Urss, 31400 Toulouse France

ASSION, PETER, European ethnology educator; b. Walldürn, Baden, Fed. Republic Germany, Aug. 5, 1941; s. Adolf and Johanna (Bausback) A. PhD, U. Heidelberg, Fed. Republic Germany, 1969. Habilitation, U. Heidelberg, 1975. Leader Landesstelle f. Volkskunde, Freiburg, Fed. Republic Germany, 1969-80; prof. ethnology U. Marburg, Fed. Republic Germany, 1980—. Author: Mirakel d.Hl. Katharina, 1969, Altdeutsche Fachlit., 1973, Bauen und Wohnen im dt. Südwesten, 1984, Von Hessen in die Neue Welt, 1987. Roman Catholic. Home: Ringstr 40, D-6968 Walldürn Baden, Federal Republic of Germany Office: U Marburg Inst European, Ethnologie, Bahnhofstrasse 5a, D-3550 Marburg Hessen, Federal Republic of Germany

ASSMANN, JAN, Egyptologist; b. Langelsheim, Fed. Republic Germany, July 7, 1938; s. Hans and Charlotte (Böning) A.; m. Aleida B. Bornkamm, Aug. 7, 1968; children: Vincent, David, Marlene, Valerie, Corinna. PhD, U. Heidelberg, Fed. Republic Germany, 1965. Habilitation, U. Heidelberg, 1971. Lectr. U. Heidelberg, 1971-76, prof., 1976—. Author: Liturg. Lieder a.d. Sonnengott, 1969, Das Grab des Basa, 1973, Ägyptische Hymen und Gebete, 1975, Ägypten--Theologie und Frömmigkeit, 1984, plus six monographs, five editorships. Recipient travel grant Deutsches Archäol. Inst., 1966-67; fellow Wissenschaftskolleg zu Berlin. Mem. Akad. der Wissenschaften, Deutsches Archäol. Inst., Inst. Historische Anthropologie, Egypt Exploration Soc. Home: Im Neulich 5, D-6900 Heidelberg Federal Republic of Germany Office: Inst Egyptology, Marstallhof 4, D-6900 Heidelberg Federal Republic of Germany

ASSOUSA, GEORGE ELIAS, physicist, corporate executive; b. Jerusalem, Mar. 15, 1936; emigrated to U.S., 1953, naturalized, 1965; s. Elias Theodore and Virginia George (Saboura) A.; divorced; children: Mark Andrew, Virginia Noel. B.A., Earlham Coll., 1957; postgrad. (Rockefeller Bros. fellow), Union Theol. Sem., 1957-58; M.A., Columbia U., 1960; Ph.D. (Nuclear Sci. fellow, Grad. fellow), Fla. State U., 1968. Mem. faculty Earlham Coll., Richmond, Ind., 1960-63; research asst., instr. nuclear physics Fla. State U., Tallahassee, 1963-68; fellow Carnegie Instn. of Washington, 1968-70, research prof., mem. sci. staff, 1970-80, sr. fellow, 1980-81; chief sci. and tech. advisor Coats Viyella, PLC, London, 1988—; chmn. Coats Viyella Technologies, Ltd., London, 1988—; sci. and ednl. affairs v.p. Ideas, Inc., Washington, 1974-75; cons. Princeton U. Obs., 1971-72; cons. on Mid-East sci. Nat. Acad. Scis., 1975; advisor sci. and tech. policy to Crown Prince Hassan of Jordan, 1976-78; cons. N.J. Marine Scis. Consortium, 1980-87; Presdl. fellow, fellow program in sci., tech. and humanism Aspen Inst. for Humanistic Studies, 1978-80. Contbr.: articles in field to Phys. Rev. Cofounder, pres. Found. for Arab-Israeli Reconciliation, Washington, 1974-77, co-chmn. bd., 1977-78; founder, dir. Salzburg Internat. Affairs Seminar, 1979—; dir.-gen. Trust for Internat. Devel. and Edn., London, 1980—; pres. Partnership for Internat. Devel., Inc., Washington, 1981-86; vice chmn. Internat. Scholars for Environ. Studies Inc., 1987—; pres. Gryphon Tech. Investors, 1987-88. Mem. Internat. Astron. Union, Am. Astron. Soc., AAUP, Am. Phys. Soc., Council Fgn. Relations, Royal Inst. Internat. Affairs (assoc.), Sigma Xi. Clubs: Cosmos (Washington); Athenaeum (London). Office: Coats Viyella PLC, 28 Savile Rd, London W1X 2DD, England

ASTALDI, ALBERTO, pharmaceutical executive, educator; b. Pavia, Italy, Dec. 25, 1944; s. Giovannia and Stefana (Gaggero) A.; m. Gilia Ricotti, July 27, 1970. MD, U. Pavia, 1970; PhD, U. Amsterdam, The Netherlands, 1980. Asst. Mcpl. Hosp., Voghera, Italy, 1970-72; asst. prof. Gaslini Inst. for Sick Children, Genoa, Italy, 1972-74; mem. staff Lab. Exptl. Clin. Immunology U., Amsterdam, The Netherlands, 1974-81; dir. clin. research and devel. Smith, Kline and French, Milan, 1981-83, med. dir., 1983-86, operating dir., 1986—. Contbr. numerous articles to profl. jours. Recipient Cavaliere award Pres. of Italy, 1985. Mem. Am. Assn. Immunologists, Brit. Soc. Immunology. Home: Cascina Spessa 35, 27051 Cava Manara Italy Office: Smith Kline and French SPA, Viale Ortles 12, 20139 Milan Italy

ASTNER, GUNNAR LARS, atomic physicist, researcher; b. Stockholm, Aug. 8, 1939; s. Einar and Maria (Soderlund) A.; m. Ulrika Ocklind, May 8, 1965 (div. 1972); 1 child, Karin Maria. D Tech. in Physics Engring., Royal Inst. Tech., Stockholm, 1972. Research asst. Royal Inst. Tech., 1962-65; fellow CERN (European Orgn. for Nuclear Research), Geneva, 1965-70; research asst. Research Inst. Physics, Stockholm, 1970-75, sr. researcher, 1975—. Contbr. articles to profl. jours. Humboldt scholar Goethe U., 1980-81. Mem. Swedish Phys. Soc. Home: Vattingsv 4, 18132 Lidingi Sweden Office: Research Inst Physics, Frescativ 24, 10405 Stockholm Sweden

ASTON, SHERRELL JERONE, plastic surgeon; b. Nansemono County, Va., July 14, 1942; s. Walter Mathew, Jr. and Mary Louise (Bracy) A.; B.A., U. Va., 1964, M.D., 1968; m. Michelle Sykes, Nov. 24, 1967; children—Walter Mathew III, Sherrell Jerone, Bradford Sykes. Intern, UCLA, 1968-69, resident, chief resident in surgery, 1969-73; Halsted fellow Johns Hopkins Hosp., 1971; resident, chief resident in plastic surgery NYU, 1973-75; chief plastic surgery service Manhattan VA Hosp., 1975-79; assoc. prof. plastic surgery NYU Med. Center, 1977—; attending surgeon Inst. Reconstructive Plastic Surgery, NYU Med. Center; attending surgeon Manhattan Eye, Ear and Throat Hosp., Bellevue Hosp. Diplomate Am. Bd. Surgery, Am. Bd. Plastic Surgery. Fellow ACS, N.Y. Acad. Medicine, Am. Soc. Plastic and Reconstructive Surgery; mem. N.Y. State, N.Y. County med. socs., Soc. Academic Surgeons, Pan Am. Med. Assn., Brazilian Plastic Surgery Soc., Am. Soc. for Aesthetic Plastic Surgery, Am. Assn. for Accreditation Ambulatory Plastic Surgery Facilities (founding mem., dir. 1980—), Am. Assn. Plastic Surgeons. Author numerous surg. publs. Home: 765 Park Ave New York NY 10021 Office: 728 Park Ave New York NY 10021

ASUBEIE, ABDULAZIZ MOHAMED, civil engineer; b. Qasseem, Saudi Arabia, 1945; s. Mohamed Abdullah Asubeie; 4 children. BSCE, Seattle U., 1974. Dir. Ministry of Def., Riyadh, Saudi Arabia, 1974-80; pres. Asubeie Cons. Engrs., Riyadh, 1980—; bd. dirs. Asubeie Poultry Farms, Durma, Saudi Arabia, Asubeie Poultry Feed Mills, Durma, Saleh M. Asubeie Bros. and Co., Riyadh; active in real estate, agrobusiness, construction and maintenance. Mem. ASTM, Am. Water Works Assn., Conf. Bd. N.Y., British Standard Inst. Home and Office: King Fahd St, PO Box 55001, Riyadh 11534, Saudi Arabia

ATACK, STEVEN, executive search consultant; b. Mirfield, Eng., Jan. 19, 1953; s. Albert and Evelyn (Parr) A. Student, Eastbourne Coll. Edn., Eng., 1971-73. Nat. chmn. The Brit. Young Liberal Movement, London, 1975-77; borough councillor Eastbourne Borough Council, 1978-83; cons. The Electronic Recruitment Co. Ltd., Sussex, 1983-85, The Davis Co. Ltd., London, 1985-86; chief executive The Berkeley Consultancy, London, 1986—. Candidate Liberal party Henley-upon-Thames, 1979, Bath, 1981, 82. Home: 33 Cleveland Sq, London W2, England

ATAIE, ATA JENNATI, oil products marketing executive; b. Mashad, Iran, Mar. 15, 1934; s. Hamid Jennati and Mohtaram (Momeni) A.; came to U.S., 1957, naturalized, 1969; B.S. in Agr., Fresno (Calif.) State U., 1964; B.A. in Econs., San Francisco State U., 1966; m. Judith Garrett Bush, Oct. 7, 1961; children—Ata Jennati, Andrew J. Mktg. exec. Shell Oil Co., Oakland, Calif., 1966-75; pres. A.J. Ataie & Cos., Concord, Calif., 1975—; Am. Value Inc., 1976—. Served as 2d lt. Iranian Army, 1953. Mem. Nat. Petroleum Retailers Assn. Democrat.

ATANASIÚ, ANDRÉS HOMERO, writer, educator; b. Ensenada, Argentina, Jan. 11, 1926; s. Felipe and Próspera (D'Antoni) A.; m. Maria Elena Santos, Jan. 11, 1955. Student, Nat. Coll. U. La Plata, 1940-45, LittD, 1959. Prof. art history Nat. Coll. La Plata (Argentina), 1961, prof. contemporary lit., 1961-62, prof. universal lit., 1962-63; prof. Castilian Indsl. Coll., Ensenada, 1960—; prof. Spanish Lit. Sch. #1, Ensenada, 1961-64; collaborator daily La Nación, Buenos Aires, El Dia, La Plata, Revista de Educación de La Provincia de Buenos Aires; essayist, commentator, lectr. in field. Author: The Return and Other Stories, 1962, (novels) Sandro or Solitude, 1963, The Remains of the Shipwreck, 1971, La Luna en Menguante, 1974 (Nat. Fund of the Arts prize), El Hombre Que Escuchaba Mozart, 1982 (first prize Biennial Novel Competition Argentina Union Carbide). Recipient award Argentine Writers Soc., 1961, 64, Nat. Fund Arts, 1961, 70, 74, Writers Council Buenos Aires, 1964, Lit. award Municipality of La Plata, 1962, Provincial award lit. Province Buenos Aires, 1970, Hon. mention Bd. of Culture of Municipality of La Plata, 1972. Mem. Argentine Writers Soc. (library commn.), Com. Argentino de la Soc. Internat. Studies Homéricos. Home: Casilla de Correo #545, Buenos Aires Argentina

ATIENZA, ALICIA MARILINA SALVO, physician; b. Manila, Aug. 3, 1939; d. Mariano Estrada and Flaviana (Atienza) Salvo; m. Fidelino Hizon Atienza, Oct. 24, 1964; children: Arminda, Aileen, Alma Soledad, Adriane Antonio. MD, Manila Cen. U., 1965; MPA, Philippine Women's U., Manila, 1980. Adj. resident in internal medicine San Lazaro Hosp., Manila, 1969, resident in infectious and communicable diseases, 1969-73, clinic physician, 1973-75, sr. resident, 1975-82; mem. faculty, lectr. De Ocampo Meml. Coll., Manila, 1980-82; bd. reviewer Systec Rev. Ctr., Manila, 1982; sr. med. officer Kano (Nigeria) Infectious Disease Hosp., 1982-86; chief clinics, personnel mgr. Arguelles Med. Ctr., Manila, 1986—; bd. dirs. Computer Research Devel., Manila, 1986—. Mem. Philippine Med. Assn., Manila Med. Soc., Philippine Soc. of Microbiology and Infectious Diseases, Nigerian Med. Assn. Roman Catholic. Home: 2435 Opalo St San Andres, Manila 1009, The Philippines Office: Arguelles Med Ctr Inc, 1271-1277 Zobel Roxas, Manila The Philippines 586113

ATINC, ETHEM, export company executive; b. Ankara, Turkey, May 12, 1948; s. Hikmet Yasar and Latife (Demir) A.; m. Ayfer Tanyeri, Dec. 7, 1973; 1 dau., Funja. B.S. in Regional Geography, Faculty of Geography, Ankara, 1972; M.B.A., Middle East Tech. U., 1976. Dir., owner Emsel Dis Ticaret Co. Ltd., Export-Import, Ankara, 1971—. Served to lt. gen. Turkish Army, 1975. Recipient Awards of Export Turkish Indsl. Chamber, 1981, Awards of High Tax Payer (ranked 223 in Ankara) Ministry of Fin., 1983. Mem. Exporters Com. Mersin, Olive Oil Exporters Com. of Izmir, C. of C. Ankara. Lodge: Masons. Home: Enis Behic Koryürek, Sok 26/7 Cankaya, Ankara Turkey Office: Emsel Dis Ticaret Co Ltd Export-Import, Bulbuldere Cad 38, Ankara Turkey

ATIYAH, MICHAEL FRANCIS, mathematician; b. London, Eng., Apr. 22, 1929; s. Edward Selim and Jean (Levens) A.; B.A., Trinity Coll., Cambridge, 1952, Ph.D., 1955; D.Sc. (hon.), Warwick and Bonn, 1968, U. Durham, 1977, U. Dublin, U. Chgo., Cambridge U., others; m. Lily J. Brown, July 30, 1955; children—John, David, Robin. Fellow, Trinity Coll., Cambridge, 1954-58, hon. fellow, 1976; univ. lectr., fellow Pembroke Coll., Cambridge, 1958-61, hon. fellow, 1983; Commonwealth Fund fellow Princeton, 1955-56, prof. Inst. for Advanced Study, 1969-72; reader Oxford U., 1961-63, Savilian prof. geometry, 1963-69, Royal Soc. research prof., fellow St. Catherine's Coll., 1973—. Knighted 1983; recipient Fields medal Internat. Congress Mathematicians, Moscow, 1966; De Morgan medal London Math. Soc., 1980; Feltrinelli prize Accademia Nazionale dei Lincei, 1982; King Faisal Found. Internat. Prize for Sci., Saudi Arabia, 1987. Fellow Royal Soc. (Royal medal 1969); mem. Internat. Math. Union (exec. com. 1966-74) Math. Assn. (pres. 1981), London Math. Soc. (pres. 1975-77), Nat. Acad. Scis. U.S.A. (fgn.), Leopoldina Acad. (fgn.), Am. Acad. Arts and Scis. (fgn.), Swedish Royal Acad. (fgn.), Academie des Sciences (fgn.), Royal Irish Acad. (fgn.). Author: K-Theory, 1966; Commutative Algebra, 1969. Contbr. articles to math. jours. Address: Math Inst, 24-29 St Giles, Oxford OX1 3EB, England also: care Royal Soc, 6 Carlton House Terr, London SW1Y 5AG, London *

ATKIN, LOUIS PHILLIP, business executive, screenwriter, media producer; b. Rochester, N.Y., Apr. 18, 1951; s. Morris and Etta (Korpeck) A.; m. Jodi Rosenshein. M.A., George Washington U., 1973; student Am. Coll. Paris, 1970-71; M.A., U. So. Calif., 1977. Asst. editor Alan Landsburg Prodns., Los Angeles, 1977-78; v.p. L. Atkins Sons, Rochester, 1978—; pres. Day for Night Prodns., Rochester, 1985—. Producer (with others), Jewish Community Fedn., documentary, 1982, Flights of Fancy, 1980; producer stage play Paradoxical Effects, 1987; writer, producer (play aired on Cable TV): Paradoxical Effects; writer, dir. Ceremony of Carols, 1974; scriptwriter, photographer, Posters of the First World War, 1983, exhibitor of posters, 1983. Interviewer, Holocaust Com., Rochester, 1984; mem. Rochester Mus. and Sci. Ctr., 1985—, GEVA Angels Repertory Contributors, 1985, Landmark Hist. Soc., Rochester, 1985, Nat. Trust for Hist. Preservation. NEH grantee, 1979, LIFT grantee N.Y. State Council Arts, 1987. Mem. Dramatists Guild (assoc.), Internat. Soc. Dramatists, AAAS, George Eastman House, Friends of Photography, U. So. Calif. Cinema Alumni Assn., Nat. Assn. Watch and Clock Collectors. Avocations: collecting World War I posters; photography; writing.

ATKINS, CHARLES GILMORE, medical school administrator; b. Stambaugh, Mich., July 4, 1939; s. Howard B. and Bernice M. (Gilmore) A.; m. Kay Roberta Bueschen, Dec. 28, 1958 (div. 1983); children—Robert Howard, Karla Marie, James Charles. B.A., Albion Coll., 1961; postgrad. Med. Sch., U. Mich., 1960-62; M.S., Eastern Mich. U., 1963; Ph.D., N.C. State U., 1969. Instr. Coe Coll., 1963-66; lectr. genetics Cornell Coll., Mt. Vernon, Iowa, 1964-65; NIH predoctoral genetics trainee N.C. State U., Raleigh, 1966-69; asst. prof. microbiology Ohio U., Athens, 1969-74, assoc. prof., 1974—, dir. Appalachian life sci. coll. tng. program, 1972-74, dir. willed body program, 1976-77, assoc. dean for basic scis., 1976—, del. to state-level Ohio faculty senate, 1970-73; cons. in field. Elder 1st Presbyn. Ch., Athens, 1977—; scoutmaster Boy Scouts Am., 1972-82, dist. and council commr., 1979-86. Served to lt. col. USAR, 1981—. Dist. Award of Merit, Boy Scouts Am., 1976; Silver Wreath award, Nat. Eagle Scout Assn., 1981; Alfred E. Noyes scholar, 1957-60. Mem. Genetics Soc. Am., AAAS, Assn. Am. Med. Colls., Am. Soc. Microbiology, Ohio Acad. Sci., Nat. Eagle Scout Assn., Order of the Arrow, Sigma Xi. Lodge: Rotary. Contbr. articles to profl. jours. Home: 4914 Fox Lake Rd Athens OH 45701 Office: Ohio Univ 226 Irvine Hall Athens OH 45701

ATKINS, JOSEPH P., otorhinolaryngologist, head, neck and facial plastic surgeon; b. Red Lion, Pa., May 1, 1940; s. Joseph Preston and Genevieve (Knaus) Atkins; m. Maureen Anne Mahony, Aug. 7, 1965; children—Joseph, Timothy, Elizabeth, Kathleen. Student St. Josephs Coll., Phila., 1958-59; B.S. cum laude, Mt. St. Mary's Coll., 1962; M.D., U. Pa., 1966. Diplomate Am. Bd. Otolaryngology. Intern, Pa. Hosp., Phila., 1966-67; resident in otolaryngology, Johns Hopkins Hosp., Balt., 1967-72, fellow in laryngology and otology Med. Sch., Balt., 1967-72; asst. chief dept. otolaryngology Nat. Naval Med. Ctr., Bethesda, Md., 1972-74; chief dept. otorinolaryngology and human communication Pa. Hosp., Phila., 1974—; asst. clin. prof. otorhinolaryngology and human communication U. Pa. Med. Sch., Phila., 1974—; cons. Nat. Inst. Allergy and Infectious Diseases, 1972-74; dir. Pa. Ctr. for Voice, 1979—; mem. staff U. Pa. Hosp., Childrens Hosp. Phila., Northeastern Hosp.; cons. VA Hosp. Mem. parents bd. St. Aloysius Acad., 1976-83, chmn., 1979-81; mem. adv. bd., 1979-83; bd. dirs. Am. Cancer Soc., 1982—(vol. achievement award, 1987); trustee Acad. Notre Dame de Namur, 1988—. Lt. comdr. M.C., USNR, 1972-74. Fellow I.C.S., Am. Acad. Otolaryngology-Head and Neck Surgery (honor award 1983), Am. Acad. Facial Plastic and Reconstructive Surgery, Am. Soc. Head and Neck Surgery, Soc. Head and Neck Surgeons, ACS; mem. Coll. Physicians, Phila. Laryngol. Soc. (officer 1985—), Phila. Soc. Facial Plastic and Reconstructive Surgery, Pa. Acad. Ophthalmology and Otolaryngology, Centurion Club Deafness Research Fund, AMA, Pa. Med. Soc., Phila. County Med. Soc., Am. Council Otolaryngology, Phila. Broncoscopic Club, Phi Rho Sigma. Republican. Roman Catholic. Lodge: K.C. Clubs: Aronimink Golf, Lake Naomi Timber Trails. Avocations: Photography; skiing; golf. Home: 1718 Weedon Rd Wayne PA 19087

ATKINSON, ALAN, materials scientist; b. Dewsbury, Yorkshire, Eng., Oct. 4, 1944; s. Norman and Marion Smith (Firn) A.; m. Rita Jain, Apr. 20, 1979; children: Stephen, Rahul, Sophie Radha. BAwith honors, Selwyn Coll., Cambridge, Eng., 1967; MA, U. Cambridge, 1970, PhD in Physics, 1971. Research fellow dept. ceramics Leeds U., Eng., 1970-75; with Harwell Lab., Didcot, Oxfordshire, Eng., 1975—, research scientist materials devel. div., 1975-77, sr. sci. officer, 1977-83, prin. sci. officer, 1983—, project coordinating officer, 1986, leader applied chemistry group, 1988. Contbr. articles to profl. jours. Recipient Carl Wagner prize Max Planck Soc., Fed. Republic of Germany, 1983. Mem. Inst. Physics. Office: Harwell Laboratory, Materials Devel Div, Didcot OX110RA, England

ATKINSON, HAROLD WITHERSPOON, utilities consultant, real estate broker; b. Lake City, S.C., June 12, 1914; s. Leland G. and Kathleen (Dunlap) A.; B.S. in Elec. Engring., Duke, 1934; M.S. in Engring., Harvard U., 1935; m. Pickett Rancke, Oct. 6, 1946; children—Henry Leland, Harold Witherspoon. Various positions in sales, engring. Cambridge Electric Light Co. (Mass.), 1935-39, 46-73, asst. mgr. power sales dept., 1946-49, gen. mgr., 1957-73, dir., 1959-84, exec. v.p., 1972-73; mgr. Pee Dee Electric Membership Corp., Wadesboro, N.C., 1939-46; gen. mgr. Cambridge Steam Corp., 1951-73, v.p., 1959-73, dir. 1955-84. Chmn., Cambridge Traffic Bd., 1962-73; pres. Cambridge Center Adult Edn., 1962-64; v.p. Cambridge Mental Health Assn.; chmn. allocations com. Greater Boston United Community Services, 1971-72; chmn. Cambridge Commn. Services, 1955-56; adv. bd. Cambridge Council Boy Scouts Am.; mem. corp., chmn. camping com. Cambridge YMCA, 1964-71; chmn. Cambridge chpt. ARC, 1969-71; trustee of trust funds Town of Harrisville, N.H., 1976-83; treas. North Myrtle Beach Citizens Assn., 1982-84. Served from pvt. to capt. AUS, 1942-45. Registered profl. engr., Mass. Mem. IEEE (sr.), Mass. Soc. Profl. Engrs., Elec. Inst. (pres. 1971), Harvard Engring. Soc., Cambridge C. of C. (pres. 1957-58). Newcomen Soc. N.Am., Phi Beta Kappa, Tau Beta Pi, Pi Mu Epsilon. Clubs: Cambridge Boat (treas. 1962-65), Cambridge (pres. 1972-73); Carolina Golf; Bay Tree Golf; Plantation; Civitan (pres. Wadesboro 1940-41); Rotary (v.p.) (North Myrtle Beach, S.C.). Home: 705 Holloway Circle N North Myrtle Beach SC 29582 Office: PO Box 533 North Myrtle Beach SC 29597

ATKINSON, HARRY HINDMARSH, physicist; b. Wellington, New Zealand, Aug. 5, 1929; s. Harry Temple and Constance Hindmarsh (Shields) A.; m. Anne Judith Barrett, 1958; children: John Benedict, Harry David, Katherine Hindmarsh. BS, Canterbury (New Zealand) U., 1952; MS in Physics with hons., Cornell U., 1952; PhD, Cambridge U., 1959. Asst. lectr. physics Canterbury U., New Zealand, 1952-53; research asst. Cornell U., Ithaca, N.Y., 1954-55; sr. research fellow Atomic Energy Research Establishment, Harwell, Eng., 1958-61; head Gen. Physics Group, Rutherford (Eng.) Lab., 1961-69; staff chief sci. advisor Govt. U.K., London, 1969-72; head of Astronomy, Space and Radio div. U.K. Sci. Research Council, London, 1972-78, under sec., dir. Astronomy, Space, and Nuclear Physics, 1979-83, under sec., dir. sci., 1983—; vice-chmn. of council European Space Agy., 1981-84, chmn. council, 1984-87; U.K. del. to council European Synchrotron Radiation Facility, 1986—. Fellow Royal Astronomical Soc.; mem. Anglo-Australian Telescope Bd. (U.K. del.), Anglo-Dutch Astronomy Com. (chmn.), European Incoherent Scattering Sci. Assn. (del. council), Inst. Laue Langevin (chmn. 1984, 87). Club: The Atheneum (London). Office: Sci and Engring Research Council, North Star Ave, Swindon SN2 1ET, England

ATKINSON, MARK ARTHUR LEONARD, biochemist; b. London, Eng., Feb. 21, 1952; s. John Leonard and Gwenda Mary (Loveday) A.; m. Lynn Dickerson Morrow, June 13, 1984; children: Jeremy David, Joshua Aubrey. B.A., Oxford U., 1974, M.A., 1978, D.Phil., 1979. Postdoctoral fellow Yale U., New Haven, 1979-82; vis. assoc. Nat. Heart, Lung, and Blood Inst., NIH, Bethesda, Md., 1982-87; assoc. prof. biochemistry U. Tex. Health Scis. Ctr., Tyler, 1987—. Contbr. articles to profl. jours. Erin research scholar Linacre Coll., Oxford U., Eng., 1977; James Hudson Brown and Alexander B. Coxe fellow Yale U., 1981. Mem. AAAS, Biophys. Soc., Am. Soc. Cell Biology, Am. Soc. Biol. Chemists, Club: Leander (Henley, Eng.). Home: 1702 Old Oak Dr Tyler TX 75703 Office: U Tex Health Ctr Dept Biochemistry PO Box 2003 Tyler TX 75710

ATKINSON, PAUL PHILLIP, art dealer; b. Chgo., Nov. 28, 1924; s. Roy Richard and Violet Henrietta (Robellaz) A.; m. Nancy James, May 13, 1950; 1 child, Katherine Jane. Student, Northwestern U., Evanston, Ill., 1948, U. Chgo., 1948-50; UN exchange student, France, 1948. Travel writer Chgo. Tribune, 1948-49; market researcher Chgo. Am., 1950-53; art dealer James-Atkinson Ltd., Houston, 1953—; U.S. rep. English painting Newman & Cooling Ltd., Eng., 1970—. Contbr. articles to newspapers. Served with U.S. Army, 1943-46, ETO. Decorated Croix de Guerre avec Palme, Silver Battle Star. Republican. Presbyterian. Club: Winter (Lake Forest, Ill.). Avocations: painting, drawing. Home: 1601 S Shepherd #105 Houston TX 77109

ATKINSON, RICHARD CHATHAM, educator, experimental psychologist, university chancellor; b. Oak Park, Ill., Mar. 19, 1929; s. Herbert and Margaret (Feuerbach) A.; m. Rita Loyd, Aug. 20, 1952; 1 dau., Lynn Loyd. Ph.B., U. Chgo., 1948; Ph.D., Ind. U., 1955. Lectr. applied math. and stats. Stanford (Calif.) U., 1956-57, assoc. prof. psychology, 1961-64, prof. psychology, 1964-80; asst. prof. psychology UCLA, 1957-61; dep. dir. NSF, 1975-76, acting dir., 1976-77; dir., 1977-80; chancellor U. Calif., San Diego, 1980—; Mem. Pres.'s Com. Nat. Medal Sci. Author: (with Atkinson, Smith and Hilgard) Introduction to Psychology, 9th edit, 1987, Computer Assisted Instruction, 1969, An Introduction to Mathematical Learning Theory, 1965, Studies in Mathematical Psychology, 1964, Contemporary Developments in Mathematical Psychology, 1974, Mind and Behavior, 1980, Stevens' Hanbook of Experimental Psychology, 1988. Served with AUS, 1954-56. Guggenheim fellow, 1967; fellow Ctr. for Advanced Study in Behavioral Scis., 1963; recipient Distinguished Research award Social Sci. Research Council, 1962. Fellow Am. Acad. Arts and Scis., Am. Psychol. Assn. (pres. exptl. div. 1974-75, Disting. Sci. Contbn. award 1977, Thorndike award 1980), AAAS (chmn. psychology sect. 1975-76, pres.-elect 1988); mem. Soc. Exptl. Psychologists, Nat. Acad. Scis. (council 1982-85), Am. Philos. Soc., Nat. Acad. Edn., Inst. of Medicine, Psychonomic Soc. (chmn. 1973-74), Western Psychol. Assn. (pres. 1975-76), Psychometric Soc., Cognitive Sci. Soc., Sigma Xi. Clubs: Cosmos (Washington); Explorers (N.Y.C.). Home: 9630 La Jolla Farms Rd La Jolla CA 92037 Office: Univ Calif San Diego Office the Chancellor La Jolla CA 92093

ATKINSON, RUPERT LEIGH, neurosurgeon; b. Dec. 12, 1938; s. J.A.L. Atkinson. m. Sallyanne Kerr; 5 children. Ed. St. Joseph's Coll., Brisbane, Australia, 1948-54, Downlands Coll., Toowoomba, Australia, 1955-56; M.B., B.S., U. Queensland, Australia, 1962. Neurosurg. registrar Mater Pub. Hosp., 1965-66; sr. registrar dept. surg. neurology U. Edinburgh, 1967-69; neurosurgeon, Princess Alexandra Hosp., 1974—, Mater Pub. Hosp., 1970—, Greenslopew Repatriation Hosp., Brisbane, 1971—, Ipswich Gen. Hosp., 1971—. Bd. dirs. Australian Brain Found.; state exec. Liberal Party of Australia, 1975-85, v.p., 1980; mem. Neurolog. Bd., 1985—. Kellogg travelling fellow U.S.A., 1982. Mem. Australasian Coll. Surgeons (chmn. state com. 1984-86, co-opted council mem. 1986, mem. ct. examiners 1987, mem. bd. neurosurgery 1987—). Clubs: Queensland Golf; Indooroopilly Golf. Address: 3 Castile St, Indooroopilly Queensland 4068, Australia

ATKINSON, SALLY ANN, graphologist; b. Lafayette, Ind., June 19, 1932; d. Myrl Herbert and Merta Marie (Lawler) Bolds; student Purdue U., 1949-52, Rutgers U., 1963; diploma Internat. Graphoanalysis Soc., 1973, Master in Graphoanalysis, 1974; proficiency degree World Assn. Document Examiners, 1974; 1 son, William Gregory Wnuck. Engring. aide Boeing Airplane Co., Seattle, 1954-56; engring. graphanalyst Allison div. Gen. Motors Corp., Indpls., 1956-57; freelance artist, N.J., 1958-64; jr. microbiologist Johnson & Johnson Research Corp., Brunswick, N.J., 1960-62; tchr. art Jamesburg (N.J.) Pub. Schs., 1962-64, Wallenpaupack (Pa.) Pub. Schs., 1964-65; freelance artist, tchr., Seattle, Whidbey Island, Wash., 1965-72; pres. Handwriting, Inc., Seattle, 1975-80; asst. to dir. U. Puget Sound, Seattle, 1978-79; profl. handwriting analyst, 1979—; cons. to software designer, 1987—; instr. Seattle Central Community Coll., S. Seattle Community Coll., Bellevue (Wash.) Community Coll., 1980—; exec. sec., dir. product devel. Computerized Handwriting Analysis Services, Inc., Seattle, 1981—. Area rep. Wash. Arts Commn., 1969. Wash. State Arts Commn. grantee, 1968. Mem. South Whidbey Arts Assn. (pres., founder 1966-69), Am. Mgmt. Assn., World Assn. Document Examiners, Internat. Graphoanalysis Soc., Internat. Platform Assn., Wash. State Geneal. Soc. Aide in jury selection by handwriting analysis; in graphology: increased known, graphically definable traits from 150 to 300 and developed geometric configuration formulas for each; discovered 4th graphically definable zone. Address: 10523 24th Ave NE Seattle WA 98125

ATKINSON, SALLYANNE, Australian municipal official; b. Sydney, Australia, July 23, 1942; d. C. T. and Ruth Margaret (Helmore) Kerr; m. Rupert Leigh Atkinson, May 1, 1964; children—Nicola, Eloise, Damien, Genevieve, Stephanie. Student Royal Naval sch., Colombo, Ceylon, St. Hilda's Sch.; B.A. in History and Polit. Sci., U. Queensland, Australia, 1966. Formerly cadet journalist Brisbane Telegraph, Australia, then journalist Sydney Telegraph, Brisbane Courier-Mail; free-lance journalist, U.K., Australia, 1966-74; research asst. to D.J. Killen, Former Australian minister for def., 1975-78; alderman City of Brisbane, 1979-82; leader of council opposition, 1983-85; lord mayor City of Brisbane, 1985—. Leader Brisbane's bid to host the 1992 Olympic Games; chmn. com. to organize the Brisbane Olympics; councillor Australian Inst. of Urban Studies. Author: Around Brisbane, 1978, rev. edit. Sallyanne Atkinson's Brisbane Guide, 1985. Recipient Internat. Visitor's award. Fellow Australian Mktg. Inst., Australian Inst. Mgmt.; mem. Pub. Relations Inst. Australia (hon. life mem.), Australian Commonwealth Games Assn. (v.p.). Avocations: tennis, theatre. Office: Brisbane City Council, 69 Ann St, Brisbane Queensland 4000, Australia

ATKINSON, SHERIDAN EARLE, lawyer, financial and management consultant; b. Oakland, Calif., Feb. 14, 1945; s. Arthur Sheridan and Esther Louise (Johnson) A.; m. Margie Ann Lehtin, Aug. 13, 1966. 1 son, Ian Sheridan. B.S., U. Calif.-Berkeley, 1966, M.B.A., 1971; J.D., U. San Francisco, 1969. Bar: Calif. 1970. Prin. Atkinson & Assocs., fin. and mgmt. cons., corp. and bus. valuations, San Francisco, 1968—; assoc. Charles O. Morgan, Jr., San Francisco, 1972-76; sole practice, San Francisco Bar Area, 1976—. Served with USAR, 1970-76. Mem. Calif. Bar Assn., ABA. Republican. Office: The Watergate 1327A Solano Ave Albany CA 94706

ATKINSON, WILLIAM JAMES, JR., internist; b. Mobile, Ala., July 4, 1917; s. William J. and Gertrude (Smith) A.; m. Glenda E. Street, Oct. 29, 1949; children—Glenda Street, Regina Creswell, William James. B.A., Amherst Coll., 1939; M.D., U. Pa., 1943; M.S. in Internal Medicine, St. Louis U., 1949. Intern, Phila. Gen. Hosp., 1943-44; resident in medicine St. Louis City Hosp., 1946-48; resident in cardiology St. Louis U., 1948-49; practice medicine specializing in internal medicine and cardiology, Mobile, Ala., 1949—; mem. staff U. South Ala. Med. Ctr. Hosp., Mobile Infirmary, Providence Hosp.; chmn. bd. Diagnostic and Med. Clinic P.A., 1973—; clin. assoc. prof. medicine U. Ala., 1964—; clin. assoc. prof. medicine U. South Ala., 1973—. Served as capt. M.C., AUS, 1944-46. Decorated Bronze Star. Diplomate Am. Bd. Internat. Medicine, Am. Bd. Cardiovascular Disease. Fellow ACP, Am. Coll. Cardiology, Am. Coll. Chest Physicians; mem. Am. Heart Assn., Ala. Heart Assn. (chmn. bd. 1956), AMA, Am. Soc. Clin. Pharmacology and Therapeutics, Mobile C. of C. Republican. Episcopalian. Clubs: Rotary, Mobile Country, Mobile Yacht. Home: 3965 Byronell Ct Mobile AL 36609 Office: 1217 Government St Mobile AL 36604

ATKYNS, ROBERT LEE, marketing communication specialist; b. Boston, Jan. 20, 1948; s. Glenn C. and Syme M. (Vataja) A.; B.A., Rutgers U., 1971; M.A., U. Conn., 1974; Ph.D., Temple U., 1986. Grad. asst. communication div. U. Conn., Storrs, 1971-73; communications researcher drug abuse info. research project, 1971-74; instr. U. Conn., Hartford, 1973-74; health care analyst The Phila. Health Plan, 1974-76, asst. dir. research and evaluation, 1976-78, dir. research and evaluation, 1978-80; mktg. scientist mktg. research and forecasting div. AT&T Long Lines, Bedminster, N.J., 1980-82, mktg. research staff mgr. AT&T Gen. Depts., Basking Ridge, N.J., 1982-83, mktg. staff mgr. AT&T Communications, Basking Ridge, N.J., 1984-85, advt. staff mgr., 1985—; cons. Chmn., Cheltenham Twp. Drug, Alcohol and Mental Health Com. Recipient Community Service award Cheltenham Twp., AT&T Eagle award. Mem. Internat. Communication Assn., Am. Assn. Pub. Opinion Research, AAAS, Am. Mktg. Assn., Am. Pub. Health Assn., Am. Acad. Polit. and Social Sci. Contbr. to profl. jours. and confs. Home: Box 39 RD 2 Frenchtown NJ 08825 Office: AT&T Hdqrs 295 N Maple Ave Basking Ridge NJ 08720

ATLAN, PAUL, gynocologist; b. Algiers, Algeria, France, June 13, 1942; s. Gabriel Nathan and Rosine (Chemaoun) A.; m. Liliane Haddad, Dec. 26, 1968; children: Sophie, Catherine. MD, U. Paris, 1969, degree gynecology, 1973. Resident Psychiatric Hosp., Epinay, 1971-74; planning ctr. dir. Fontenay Sous Bois (France), 1973—; gynecology St. Anne Psychiatric Hosp., 1980—; cons. RTL radio station, Paris, 1979-86; attaché First Paris Hosp., 1980—; dir. Internat. Conf. on Jewish Ethics and New Med. Procreation, conf. on Laws and Ethics for New Med. Procreations in French Nat. Assembly. Mem. French Psychosomatic Gynocological Soc. Office: 105 Rue de la Convention, 75015 Paris France

ATLURI, SATYA N(ADHAM), aerospace and mechanical engineer, educator; b. Gudivada, Andhra, India, Oct. 7, 1945; came to U.S., 1966, naturalized, 1976; s. Tirupati Rao and Tulasi (Devi) A.; m. Revati Adusumilli, May 17,, 1972; children: Neelima, Niroupa. B.E., Andhra U., Vizag, 1964; M.E., Indian Inst. Sci., Bangalore, India, 1966; Sc.D., MIT, 1969. Researcher MIT, Cambridge, Mass., 1966-71; asst. prof. U. Wash., Seattle, 1971-74; assoc. prof. engring. sci. and mech. Ga. Inst. Tech., Atlanta, 1974-77, prof., 1977-79, Regents' prof. mechanics, 1979—, dir. Ctr. for Advancement Computational Mechanics, 1980—; co-chmn. Internat. Conf. on Computational Mechanics, Tokyo, Japan, 1986; chmn. series of biennial Internat. Conf. on Computational Engring. Sci., 1988—; gen. lectr. and invited keynote speaker over 100 internat. tech. confs.; adv. prof. Southwestern Jiaotong U., Emei, Sichuan, Peoples Republic China, 1988. Contbr. over 300 articles to profl. jours.; author 16 books, including Computational Methods in the Mechanics of Solids and Structures, 1984; editor: books including Hybrid and Mixed Finite Element Methods, 1983; Computational Methods in the Mechanics of Fracture, 1985, Handbook of Finite Elements, 1986, Dynamic Fracture Mechanics, 1986, Computational Mechanics '86, 1986, Large-Space-Structures: Dynamics and Control, 1987, Computational Mechanics '88, 1988; editor-in-chief Internat. Jour. Computational Mechanics; mem. editorial bd. Computers and Structures, Engring. Fracture Mechanics, Internat. Jour. Plasticity, Internat. Jour. for Numerical Methods in Engring., also others. Grantee NSF, 1975—, USAF Office Sci. Research, 1973—, Office Naval Research, 1978—, Air Force Rocket Propulsion Lab., 1976-79, NASA, 1980—, NRC, 1978-80, Dept. Transp., 1987—; recipient V.K. Murti Gold medal Andhra U., India, 1964, Roll of Honors award Indian Inst. Sci., 1966, Disting. Prof. award for 1986 Ga. Inst. Tech., Outstanding Faculty Research award Ga. Inst. Tech., 1986, Structures, Structural Dynamics and Materials award, 1988, Survey Paper Citation, 1988, Monie Ferst Meml. award for Sustained Research, Sigma Xi, 1988; fellow Japan Soc. for Promotion Sci., 1987—; named Southwest Mechanics lectr., 1987, Midwestern Mechanics lectr., 1988. Fellow Am. Acad. Mechanics, ASME (chmn. com. computing in applied mechanics 1983-85, assoc. editor Applied Mech. Revs.); mem. AIAA (assoc. editor AIAA Jour. 1983—), ASCE (assoc. editor Jour. Engring. Mechanics 1982-84, Aerospace Structures and Materials award 1986), Internat. Assn. for Computational Mechanics (founding mem.). Home: 871 Springdale Rd Atlanta GA 30306 Office: Ctr for Advancement Computational Mechanics Sch Civil Engring Ga Tech Atlanta GA 30332

ATMOSOEDARYO, SOEKIMAN, forestry educator; b. Solo, Java, Indonesia, June 2, 1923; m. Napsijah, Sept. 10, 1950; children—Gatot Harmanto, Harmastini, Tri Juwono, Endang Wahjuningsih, Ratna Daruki. B.C., Acad. Land Survey, Jogya, Indonesia, 1950; cert. Internat. Inst. Aerial Survey and Earth Sci., Delft, Netherlands, 1953; forest engr. Faculty Forestry, Bogor, 1972. Dir., Inst. Aerial Survey, Jakarta, 1957-65; dir. Forestry Planning div., Bogor, 1966-71; pres., dir. Forest State Enterprise, Jakarta, 1972-80; lectr. Forest Faculty, Institut Pertanian Bogor, 1958-71; prof. Forest Faculty, Samarinda, 1979—. Mem. editorial bd. Forestry jour., 1954. Chmn., Forestry Alumni, Bogor, 1979; chmn. Ret. forester Orgn., Jakarta, 1984. Recipient medals Independence War, 1958, National Devel., 1976; fellow Internat. Inst. Aerial Survey and Earth Sci., Netherlands, 1976. Mem. Internat. Council Research on AGro Forestry (trustee 1982—), Indonesian Sawmilleres Assn. (chmn. 1985). Mem. panel group forestry community FAO, Rome, 1976-80. Avocations: photography. also: Centre, PO Box 3 JKWB, Jakarta Indonesia

ATRAN, SCOTT, anthropologist, philosopher, historian; b. N.Y.C., Feb. 6, 1952; arrived in France, 1974; s. Leonard and Hazel Dawn (Balkin) A.; children: Tatiana, Laura. BA, Columbia Coll., 1972; MA, Johns Hopkins U., 1973; MPh, Columbia U., 1975, PhD, 1984. Charge de conference Coll. Internat. de Philosophie, Paris, 1983-84; charge de cours École des Hautes Etudes en Sciences Sociales, Paris, 1984-85; charge de recherche Centre Nat. de la Recherche Scientifique, Paris, 1986; coordinator program in animal and human communication Royaumont Ctr., Paris, 1974-76; vis. lectr. Cambridge U., 1983. Author: Fondements de L'Histoire Naturelle, 1986; contbr. articles to profl. jours. Asst. to Dr. Margaret Mead Am. Mus. Natural History, N.Y., 1969-74. Fellow Thyssen Found., 1986, SSRC-MacArthur Fellow, 1987, Truman Ctr.; Scholar's award Nat. Sci. Found., 1985; Fyssen fellow. Mem. Am. Anthrop. Assn., Assn. Francaise de Anthropologues, Mid. East Inst. Office: Mus Nat D'Histoire Naturelle, 57 rue Cuvier, 75005 Paris France

ATREYA, SUSHIL KUMAR, science educator, researcher; b. Ajmer, India, Apr. 15, 1946; came to U.S., 1966, naturalized, 1975; s. Harvansh Lal and Kailash Vati (Sharma) A.; m. Evelyn M. Bruckner, Dec. 31, 1970; 1 dau., Chloé E. Sc.B., U. Rajasthan, India, 1963, M.Sc., 1965; M.S., Yale U., 1968; Ph.D., U. Mich., 1973. Research assoc. physics U. Pitts., 1973-74; asst. to assoc. research scientist Space Physics Research Lab., U. Mich., Ann Arbor, 1974-78, asst. prof., 1978-81, assoc. prof. atmospheric sci., 1981-87, prof. atmospheric and space scis., 1987—; prof. associé U. Paris, 1984-85; mem. sci. teams Voyager, Galileo, Space Lab I and Comet Rendezvous Asteroid Flyby Projects; prin. guest investigator Copernicus Orbiting Astron. Observatory; guest investigator Internat. Ultraviolet Explorer Satellite; mem. sci. working groups NASA and Jet Propulsion Lab. Recipient NASA award for exceptional sci. contbns. Voyager Project, 1981, Group Achievement award for Voyager Ultraviolet Spectrometer Investigations, 1981, 86. Author: Atmospheres and Ionospheres of the Outer Planets and their Satellites, 1986; contbr. numerous articles to books and profl. jours. Mem. Internat. Assn. Meteorology and Atmospheric Physics (pres. commn. planetary atmospheres and their evolution), Am. Geophys. Union, AAAS, Internat. Astron. Union, Am. Astron. Soc. Office: U Mich Dept Atmospheric Oceanic & Space Sci Space Research Bldg 2 455 Hayward Ann Arbor MI 48109

ATSUJI, MASAHIKO, mathematics educator; b. Kobe, Japan, Jan. 25, 1922; s. Katsumi and Masue (Nagatomo) A.; m. Hideko Handa, Apr. 20, 1964. B.S., Hokkaido Imperial U., 1944; D.Sc. Tokyo Kyoiku U., 1970. Lectr., Kanazawa U., Japan, 1952-53, asst. prof., 1953-61; prof. mathematics Senshu U., Tokyo, 1961-65, Josai U., Sakado, Japan, 1965—. Reviewer, Zentralblatt für Mathematik, 1962-83; editor Symposium Gen. Topology, 1983—. Mem. Math. Soc. Japan (councilor 1983-84), Am. Math. Soc. Avocation: classical music. Office: Josai U, Keyaki-dai 1-1 Sakado, Saitama 350-02, Japan

ATTAL, GENE (FRED EUGENE), hospital executive; b. Austin, Tex., Oct. 6, 1947; s. Sam Arthur and Olga (Johns) A.; B.J. with spl. honors (NDEA fellow in langs. 1968-69), U. Tex., 1970; M.S. (Internat. fellow 1972), Columbia U., 1972; m. Marsha Ablah, July 26, 1970; children—Christopher, Allison, Anne. Public relations exec. Westinghouse Electric Corp., 1972-75; dir. public relations and devel. Seton Med. Center, Austin, 1975—; exec. dir. The Seton Fund; mem. faculty U. Tex. Recipient Telstar Excellence in Communication award, annually 1978-81, Arthur W. Page award U. Tex., 1986. Mem. Am. Soc. Hosp. Public Relations (regional dir.), Tex. Soc. Hosp. Public Relations (pres. 1981). Greek Orthodox. Club: Lost Creek Country. Home: 1201 Constant Springs Dr Austin TX 78746 Office: 1201 W 38th St Austin TX 78705

ATTALLAH, NAIM IBRAHIM, publisher, financial consultant; b. Haifa, Palestine, May 1, 1931; came to Eng., 1949; s. Irahim and Genevieve (Geadah) A.; m. Maria Nykolyn, Jan. 5, 1957; 1 son, Ramsay. Ed. Battersea Poly., London, 1950. Fgn. exchange dealer Credit Foncier d'Algerie et de Tunisie, London, 1957-59; bank mgr. Intra Bank, London, 1960-66; chmn.

Namara Group of Cos., London, 1966—; fin. dir. and joint mng. dir. Asprey & Co. PLC, London, 1973—. Author: Women, 1987; editor: The Last Corner of Arabia, 1976; contbr. book revs. to newspapers, periodicals. Office: Namara Ltd, 51 Beak St, London WL England

ATTALLI, GEORGET YVES, physician, health information consultant; b. Constantine, Algeria, June 22, 1943; s. David and Simone (Guedj) A.; m. Marie-Agnes Leveque, April 11, 1970 (div. Feb. 1983); children: Gaelle, Estelle; m. Yvette Charveys, Dec. 17, 1983; children: Sarah, Alexis. Degree in engring., Ecole Des Mines, Saint-Etienne, 1966; D in Math., Faculte Des Scis., Lyon, France, 1969; D in Medicine, Faculte De Medecine, Lyon, France, 1975. Asst. Faculte Cath. Des Scis., Lyon, 1966-70, Faculte Des Scis., Lyon, 1969-76; research physiologist Comex, Marsielle, 1975; regional dir. Labs. Dausse, Lyon, 1975-78; med. relation dir. Labs Resins-Iscovesco, Paris, 1978-79; sci. dir. Medee-Informatics, Lyon, 1979—; cons. Cabinet Attalli, Lyon, 1980—. Creator of software. Served with French Army, 1970-71. Laureat de la Fondation De la Vocation , 1968. Mem. CORPS (pres. 1978-83), AGCS (pres. 1978-83), CIRCE (pres. 1982). Home and Office: 47 Rue Pierre Bonnaudson, 69003 Lyon France Office: 7 Rue du Professeur Florence, 69003 Lyon France

ATTARDO, LEWIS CHARLES, research administrator, consultant; b. Wilkes Barre, Pa., Dec. 3, 1950; s. Charles J. and Gertrude (Volpe) A.; children: Aimee, Jessica, Jill, L. Antonio. AS, Luzerne Community Coll., 1970; BA in Econs., Bloomsburg U., 1972. Appraiser SBA, Wilkes-Barre, Pa., 1972-73; comml. indsl. relocation specialist Redevel. Authority, City of Wilkes-Barre, 1973-75; dir. relocation Redevel. Authority, City of Lock Haven, Pa., 1975-78; coordinator community devel. Redevel. Authority, Dauphin County, Steelton, Pa., 1978-84; pres., chief exec. officer Attardo Enterprises, Harrisburg, Pa., 1976—; dir. Advanced Tech. Ctr., Pa. State U. at Harrisburg, Middleton, Pa., 1984—; evaluator, panelist Commonwealth of Pa., 1987—; bd. dirs. Control Techtronics, Inc., Harrisburg, State U.-Harrisburg Small Bus. Devel. Ctr., WITF/TV Netsource; mem. tech. adv. council Pa. State U.-York, 1985—; v.p., bd. dirs., charter mem. Venture Investment Forum of Cen. Pa., Inc., 1986—, Mfg. Tech. Ctr. S. Cen. Pa., Inc., 1988—. Mem. Eastern Econ. Assn. (charter), Smithsonian (charter) Nat. Geog. Soc. (sec., bd. dirs.), Cen. Pa. Internat. Bus. Assn. (sec., bd. dirs. 1986—), AAAS (votingsec.), Wilson Ctr. Assocs. Roman Catholic. Office: Pa State U Advanced Tech Ctr of Central and Northern Pa Inc Middletown PA 17057 also: Attardo Enterprises PO Box 6186 Harrisburg PA 17112 also: Attardo Assocs 5508 Lily Pl Holiday FL 34691

ATTAS, HAYDAR ABU BAKR AL-, president of Peoples Democratic Republic of Yemen; b. al-Haraida, People's Democratic Republic of Yemen, 1939. B.Sc. in Electronics, Cairo, 1966. Head, Pub. Works Dept., Fifth Province; minister works, 1969-75; minister communications, 1975-79; mem. Central Com., 1975; minister constrn., 1979-85; chmn. Council Ministries, 1985-86, pres., 1986—. Office: Chmn Supreme People's Council, Presidium, Khormaksar, Aden People's Democratic Republic of Yemen *

ATTENBOROUGH, SIR RICHARD (SAMUEL ATTENBOROUGH), actor, producer, director; b. Aug. 29, 1923; s. Frederick L. A.; m. Sheila Beryl Grant Sim. Student (Leverhulme scholar, Bancroft medal), Royal Acad. Dramatic Art. chm. Capital Radio, London, Royal Acad. Dramatic Arts, Film Inst., Channel Four TV, British Screen Adv. Council; pro-chancellor Sussex U. Theatrical appearances include Ah Wilderness, 1941, Awake and Sing, 1942, The Little Foxes, 1942, Brighton Rock, 1943, The Way Back (Home of the Brave), 1949, To Dorothy, a Son, 1950, Sweet Madness, 1952, The Mouse Trap, 1952-54, Double Image, 1956-57, The Rape of the Belt, 1957-58; motion picture appearances include Journey Together, 1943, A Matter of Life and Death, 1946, School for Secrets, 1946, The Man Within, 1947, Dancing with Crime, 1947, London Belongs to Me, 1948, The Guinea Pig, 1949, The Lost People, 1950, Boys in Brown, 1950, Morning Departure, 1950, Hell is Sold Out, 1951, The Magic Box, 1951, The Gift Horse, 1952, Father's Doing Fine, 1953, Eight O'Clock Walk, 1954, The Ship that Died of Shame, 1954, Private's Progress, 1955, The Baby and the Battleship, 1956, Brothers in Law, 1956, The Scamp, 1958, Dunkirk, 1958, The Man Upstairs, 1958, Danger Within, 1958, I'm All Right Jack, 1958, Sea of Sand, 1958, Jetstorm, 1959, SOS Pacific, 1959, The Angry Silence (co-producer), 1959, The League of Gentlemen (also co-producer), 1959, Only Two Can Play, 1962, The Dock Brief, 1962, All Night Long, 1962, The Great Escape, 1963, Seance on a Wet Afternoon (also producer), 1964, The Flight of the Phoenix, 1965, The Sand Pebbles, 1966, Doctor Doolittle, 1967, The Bliss of Mrs. Blossom, 1968, The Last Grenade, 1968, David Copperfield, 1969, The Magic Christian, 1970, A Severed Head, 1970, Loot, 1971, 10 Rillington Place, 1971, Conduct Unbecoming, 1975, Rosebud, 1975, Brannigan, 1975, And Then There Were None, 1975, The Chess Players, 1977, The Human Factor, 1979; producer Whistle Down the Wind, 1961, The L-Shaped Room, 1962; dir. films Oh! What a Lovely War, 1968, Young Winston, 1971-72, A Bridge Too Far, 1975, Magic, 1978, A Chorus Line, 1985; producer, dir. Gandhi, 1980-81, Cry Freedom, 1986; co-founder Beaver Films. Decorated comdr. Order Brit. Empire, 1967; Knighted, 1976; recipient Best Actor award Brit. Film Acad., 1964; six Golden Globe awards.; Acad. awards best dir., best film 1983. Mem. Brit. Acad. Film and TV Arts v.p., UN award 1977, nominated for best dir. 1969, 77, best dir. award 1982). Clubs: Garrick, Beefstake, Green Room. Address: care Martin Baum Creative Artists Agy 1888 Century Park E Suite 1400 Los Angeles CA 90067 also: Old Friars, Richmond Green, Surrey England *

ATTRA, HARVEY DAVID, petroleum company executive; b. Houston, Feb. 21, 1931; s. John E. and Helen (Faraha) A.; B.S., U. Tex., 1954; m. Aleeta D. Broderick, May 21, 1954; children—John Kevin, Broderick Cory. Prodn. engr. Humble Oil Co., 1954-56, computing coordinator, 1959-62, dist. chief engr., 1965-67, div. chief, reservoir engr., 1967-69; Western Hemisphere adviser gas coordination dept. Standard Oil Co. (N.Y.), N.Y.C., 1969—; mgr. marine planning Exxon Corp., 1972-73, prodn. adviser, 1974-75, prodn. mgr. Esso Middle East, 1976-80; gen. mgr. Abu Dhabi Petroleum Co., United Arab Emirates, 1982-85; pres. Esso Egypt, Esso Suez Inc., 1985—. Bd. govs. Weston Field Club; mem. Rep. Town Com; pres. Am. C. of C. in Egypt, 1987—. Registered profl. engr., Tex. Mem. AIME (Rossiter W. Raymond award 1963), Am. Petroleum Inst., Weston Boosters, Am. C. of C. in Egypt (pres.). Episcopalian (sr. warden, vestryman). Home: 17 Lords Hwy Weston CT 06883

ATTWOOD, PETER ROBERT, industrial engineer, educator, consultant; b. Corsham, Wiltshire, Eng., Mar. 15, 1928; s. Robert Attwood and Alice Lilian (Ware) Greenwood; m. Sheila Mary Martin, Oct. 17, 1951; children: Nigel, Stephen. BS, U. Wales, Aberystwyth, 1951; MS, Durham U., Newcastle-upon-Tyne, Eng., 1953; PhD, Edinburgh (Scotland) U., 1960; MS, U. Mich., 1962. Registered indsl. engr., U.S.A, U.K., The Netherlands. Lectr. engring. Aberdeen (Scotland) U., 1953-55, Edinburgh U., 1955-60; sales engr. Caltex Oil Co., Nairobi, Kenya, 1960-64; cons. Moore Mgmt. Assocs., London, 1964-67; expert UN Internat. Labour Office/UN Indsl. Devel. Orgn., Vienna and Geneva, 1967-70; indsl. engr. U.A.C. Lagos, Nigeria, 1970-73; prof. U. Benin, Benin City, Nigeria, 1973-76, Eindhoven (The Netherlands) U. Tech., 1976—; freelance tng. advisor, tech. translator. Author: Simplified Management, 1965, Planning Distribution, 1971, (handbook) DARSIRI Value Analysis, 1968 (ILO award 1969), (manual) Production Control, 1973; editor: Quantitative Methods of Management, 1984, Space in Architecture, 1986, Optical Fiber Communication, 1988. Bd. govs. Internat. Sch., Bombay, 1968-70; chmn. bd. govs. Internat. Sch., Eindhoven, 1978—; mem. council Eindhoven U., 1983-87; churchwarden Anglican Ch., Eindhoven, 1978—. Served to lt. RAF, 1946-48. Mem. Operational Soc., Inst. Indsl. Engrs., Inst. Mgmt. and Work Study, Brit. Legion (pres. Eindhoven br. 1984—). Mem. Liberal Party. Lodge: Masons. Home: De Greide 71, 5622 NE Eindhoven The Netherlands Office: Eindhoven U Tech, PO Box 513, 5600 MD Eindhoven The Netherlands

ATWATER, HORACE BREWSTER, JR., food company executive; b. Mpls., Apr. 19, 1931; s. Horace Brewster and Eleanor (Cook) A.; m. Martha Joan Clark, May 8, 1955; children—Elizabeth C., Mary M., John C., Joan P. A.B., Princeton U., 1952; M.B.A., Stanford U., 1954. Divisional v.p., dir. mktg. Gen. Mills. Inc., Mpls., 1958-65, mktg. v.p., 1965-70, exec. v.p., 1970-76, chief operating officer, 1976-81, pres., 1977-82, chief exec. officer, 1981—, chmn. bd., 1982—, also dir.; dir. Northwestern Nat. Life Ins. Co., Honeywell Inc., N.W. Bancorp. Trustee Princeton U., MacAlester Coll., Walker Art Ctr.; mem. adv. council Stanford U. Grad. Sch. Bus. Served to lt. USNR, 1955-58. Club: Woodhill Country (Wayzata, Minn.). Office: Gen Mills Inc 1 General Mills Blvd Minneapolis MN 55426 *

ATWELL, HERBERT, minister of national security; b. July 20, 1937; Separated; 3 children. Student, Richmond St. Boys E.C. Sch.; Cmbridge Sch. Cert., Queen's Royal Coll. 1st chmn. Orgn. Nat. Reconstrn., Trinidad and Tobago, Nat. Alliance for Reconstrn.; minister of nat. security Trinidad and Tobago, 1988—. Anglican. Office: Ministry Nat Security, Port of Spain Trinidad and Tobago *

ATWOOD, MARY SANFORD, author; b. Mt. Pleasant, Mich., Jan. 27, 1935; d. Burton Jay and Lillian Belle (Sampson) Sanford; B.S., U. Miami, 1957; m. John C. Atwood, III, Mar. 23, 1957. Author: A Taste of India, 1969. Mem. San Francisco/N. Peninsula Opera Action, Hillsborough-Burlingame Newcomers, Suicide Prevention and Crisis Center, DeYoung Art Mus., Internat. Hospitality Center, Peninsula Symphony, San Francisco Art Mus., World Affairs Council, Mills Hosp. Assos. Mem. AAUW, Suicide Prevention Aux. Republican. Club: St. Francis Yacht. Address: 40 Knightwood Ln Hillsborough CA 94010

ATWOOD, RAYMOND PERCIVAL, JR., lawyer; b. Ossining, N.Y., June 25, 1952; s. Raymond Percival and Berniece Lucille (Beach) A.; m. Theresa Carol Goeken, Aug. 13, 1977; children—Shannon, Heather, Sarah, Raymond III, Jennifer. B.S. cum laude, U. Nebr., 1972, J.D., 1974; cert. Trial Advocacy, Hastings Coll. Law, U. Calif.-San Francisco, 1978, Advanced Trial Advocacy, Harvard U. Law Sch., 1988. Bar: Nebr. 1975, Mo. 1978, U.S. Dist. Ct. Nebr. 1975, U.S. Ct. Appeals (8th cir.) 1979, U.S. Bankruptcy Ct. 1975. Agy. legal counsel Nebr. Workmen's Compensation Ct., Lincoln, 1975-77; staff counsel Hartford Ins. Co., Kansas City, Mo., 1977-78; ptnr. McCord, Janssen & Atwood, Lincoln, 1978-80, Healey, Wieland, Kluender, Atwood Jacobs & Geier, Lincoln, 1980—; educator Lincoln Sch. Commerce, Nebr., 1978-81; dir. legal studies Lincoln Sch. Commerce, Nebr., 1979-81; educator U. Nebr. Coll. Law, Lincoln, 1982—; legal seminar lectr., 1976-86. Contbr. articles to profl. jours. Organizer United Way, Lincoln, 1975-77; campaign chmn. Larson for Legislature, Lincoln, 1984. Mem. ABA (com. workmen's compensation), Nebr. Order Barristers, Nebr. Trial Lawyers Assn., Am. Trial Lawyers Assn. (sustaining), Nebr. State Bar (com. workman's compensation), Delta Theta Phi. Methodist. Club: Lincoln U. Office: Healey Brown Wieland Kluender Atwood & Jacobs 1141 H St PO Box 83104 Lincoln NE 68501

AU, BAK LING, publisher; b. Hong Kong, May 13, 1928; m. Lam Man Ling, Sept. 15, 1962; children—Alex, Anita, Allen, Augustus, Angela. Self-taught. Founder, owner, chmn., chief exec. officer Ling Kee Group of Cos., Hong Kong, Taipei, Singapore, London, N.Y.C., 1949—, Ling Kee Internat. Group of Cos., 1981—, Bak Ling Group of Cos., Hong Kong, 1970—, Unicorn Group of Cos., Hong Kong, Singapore, N.Y.C., 1982—. Pres., Hong Kong Fedn. of Youth Group, 1977—; dir. Tung Wah Group of Hosps., 1965-66. Charter fellow Coll. of Preceptors, Eng., 1984. Mem. Hong Kong Ednl. Pubrs. Assn. (council mem., founder, pres. 1975-79, 83-85), Hong Kong Booksellers and Stationers Assn. (chmn. 1960). Clubs: Rotary, Oriental Ceramics, Royal Commonwealth Soc. Address: Bak Ling Ent Ltd, Yau Yue Bldg 11th Floor, 127-131 Des Voeux Rd C, Hong Kong Hong Kong

AU, KA LEUNG, hematologist; b. Hong Kong, Feb. 11, 1953; s. Chun Kwai and Wing Chi (Chan) A. MBBS, U. Hong Kong, 1976. Pathologist Govt. Hong Kong, 1977-82, sr. pathologist, 1984-85; cons. hematologist Princess Margaret Hosp., 1985—; hon. registrar St. Bartholomew's Hosp., London, 1983-84; mem. Govt. Hosp. Blood Banks Com., Hong Kong, 1987—. Fellow Royal Coll. Pathologists Australasia; mem. Royal Coll. Pathologists Eng., Hong Kong Soc. Pathology, Hong Kong Soc. Hematology (hon. sec. 1985-87). Office: Princess Margaret Hosp, Clin Pathology Unit, Hong Kong Hong Kong

AUBERT, PIERRE, former Swiss government official, lawyer; b. La Chaux-de-Fonds, Switzerland, Mar. 3, 1927; s. Alfred and Henriette (Erni) A.; ed. U. Neuchatel; m. Anne-Lise Borel, 1953; 2 children. Mem. Local Assembly, La Chaux-de-Fonds, 1960-68, pres., 1967-68; mem. Legis. Assembly Canton of Neuchatel, 1961-75, pres., 1969-70; Labor mem. Council of States of Fed. Assembly, 1971-77; mem. Fed. Council, Berne, from 1978, head dept. fed. fgn. affairs, 1978-87, v.p., 1982-83, 87, pres., 1983-84, 87; mem. Parliamentary Assembly of Council of Europe. Office: Office of President, Palais Federal, 3003 Bern Switzerland

AUBURN, MARK STUART, educator, administrator; b. Cin., Dec. 9, 1945; s. Norman Paul and Kathleen (Montgomery) A.; m. Sandra Korman, Jan. 25, 1969; children—David Andrew, Benjamin Max Joseph. B.S. in Math., B.A. in English, U. Akron, 1967; A.M. in English, U. Chgo., 1968, Ph.D., 1971. Mem. faculty Ohio State U., 1971-83, assoc. prof. English, 1977-83, asst. vice provost, sec. Coll. Arts and Scis., 1980-82, assoc. vice provost, 1982-83; dean Coll. Arts and Scis., prof. English, Ark. State U., 1983-85; v.p. for planning and mgmt. support U. Ark. System, 1985-88; vice chancellor acad. affairs Ind. U.-Purdue U., Ft. Wayne, Ind., 1988—; prof. English, adj. prof. English, U. Ark., Fayetteville, 1986—; cons. various univs., founds.; bd. dirs. Ark. Endowment for Humanities, pres. 1987—. Trustee, First Unitarian Ch. Columbus, 1976-79, pres., 1977-78, moderator, 1979-80. Grantee Am. Philos. Soc., 1972, Ohio State U., 1972, 73, 75, 76, 78, 80, NEH, 1984. Mem. Am. Soc. 18th Century Studies, MLA, AAUP, Coll. English Assn. Ohio (exec. com. 1979), Am. Soc. Theater Research, Midwest MLA, SW MLA, Lambda Chi Alpha, Phi Kappa Phi, Phi Delta Kappa, Omicron Delta Kappa. Author: Sheridan's Comedies, 1977; (with others) Drama Through Performance, 1977. Editor: Marriage a la Mode, 1981; editorial bd. Theatre Assn., Theatre Jour., South Atlantic Rev., Restoration and 18th Century Theatre Research. Home: 2101 E Coliseum Blvd Fort Wayne IN 46805-1499 Office: Indiana U-Purdue U Fort Wayne IN 46805

AUCHINCLOSS, LOUIS STANTON, writer; b. Lawrence, N.Y., Sept. 27, 1917; s. Joseph Howland and Priscilla (Stanton) A.; m. Adele Lawrence, Sept. 1957; children: John, Blake, Andrew. Student, Yale U., 1939; LL.B., U. Va., 1941; Litt.D., N.Y. U., 1974, Pace U., 1979, U. of the South, 1986. Bar: N.Y. bar 1941. Asso. firm Sullivan & Cromwell, 1941-51; asso. Hawkins, Delafield & Wood, N.Y.C., 1954-58; partner Hawkins, Delafield & Wood, 1958-86. Author: The Indifferent Children, 1947, The Injustice Collectors, 1950, Sybil, 1952, A Law for the Lion, 1953, The Romantic Egoists, 1954, The Great World and Timothy Colt, 1956, Venus in Sparta, 1958, Pursuit of the Prodigal, 1959, The House of Five Talents, 1960, Reflections of a Jacobite, 1961, Portrait in Brownstone, 1962, Powers of Attorney, 1963, The Rector of Justin, 1964, Pioneers and Caretakers, 1965, The Embezzler, 1966, Tales of Manhattan, 1967, A World of Profit, 1968, Motiveless Malignity, 1969, Second Chance, 1970, Edith Wharton, 1971, I Came As a Thief, Richelieu, 1972, The Partners, A Writer's Capital, 1974, Reading Henry James, 1975, The Winthrop Covenant, 1976, The Dark Lady, 1977, The Country Cousin, 1978, Persons of Consequence, 1979, Life, Law and Letters, 1979, The House of the Prophet, 1980, The Cat and the King, 1981, Watchfires, 1982, Exit Lady Masham, 1983, The Book Class, 1984, Honorable Men, 1985, Diary of a Yuppie, 1986, Skinny Island, 1987, The Golden Calves, 1988. Trustee Josiah Macy, Jr. Found.; pres. Mus. City of N.Y. Served as lt. USNR, 1941-45. Mem. Nat. Inst. Arts and Letters, Assn. Bar City N.Y. Episcopalian. Club: Century Assn. Home: 1111 Park Ave New York NY 10028 Office: 67 Wall St New York NY 10005

AUDERSKA, HALINA, playwright; b. Warsaw, Poland, July 3, 1904; s. Roman and Helena Auderski. MA in Philosophie, Warsaw U., 1931. Tchr. secondary sch. Warsaw, 1923-39; tchr. underground activities Polish Underground, 1939-44; mil. press. corr. Warsaw uprising 1944; head pub. house Trzaska Evert i Michalski, Warsaw, 1946-50. Author: (book) Poczwarki Wielkiej Parady, 1935; (novels) Children Cannot Wait, 1946, Jablko Granatu, 1971, Ptasi Gosciniec, 1973, Babie Lato, 1974, Miecz Syreny, 1980, Zwyczajnie Cztowiek, 1980, Smok w Herbie, 1983, Zabic Strach, 1985, ; (short stories) Szmaragdowe Oczy, 1977, Bratek, 1977, Kon, 1985; (plays) Zbiegowie 1952, Rzeczpospolita Zaplaci, 1954, Zaczarowana Zatoka, 1959, Sciezka Przez Pole, 1960, Spotkanie w Ciemnosciach, 1961; numerous others; editor: Dictionary of Polish Language 11 vols., 1950-69, Concise Dictionary of Polish Language, 1969-70. Mem. Polish Parliament, 1980—, sec. Dialog, Warsaw, 1956-59. Served with Polish Home Army, 1940-44. Decorated Cross Valour (2), Cross Merit with Swords, Cross Warsaw Uprising, Order Banner of Labour, Cross Order Polonia Restituta; recipient Prime Minister prize, 1975, City of Warsaw prize, 1977, Culture prize, 1977, Prime Nat. prize, 1984, Homo Varsoviensis, 1986. Mem. Writer's Assn. (hon. pres. 1980—), Internat. Theatre Inst., Soc. Authors, SEC, PEN. Roman Catholic. Address: ul Kopernika 11 m 11, 00-359 Warsaw Poland

AUDETT, THEOPHILUS BERNARD, lawyer; b. Giltedge, Mont., Feb. 12, 1905; s. Joseph Abraham and Katherine Amanda (Johnson) A.; m. Beverly Corinne Lowery, Sept. 21, 1939 (dec.); m. Barbara M. Terini, Nov. 6, 1976 (div. Mar. 1978); 1 dau., Katherine Ann Audett MacCluer. J.D., U. Wash., 1926. Bar: Wash. 1926, Calif. 1964. With U.S. Customs Service, 1930-63, asst. dep. commr., hdqrs., Washington, 1951-63; of counsel Stein, Shostak, Shostak & O'Hara, Los Angeles, 1965—; customs expert with U.S. del. GATT, Geneva, 1956, 61; U.S. rep. on panel of experts on antidumping and countervailing duties GATT, Geneva, 1959, 60; chmn. Interdepartmental Com. for Study Antidumping Legis., Washington, 1962. Served to capt. U.S. Army, 1942-45. Recipient Exceptional Service award Dept. Treasury, 1963. Mem. ABA, Calif. State Bar, Am. Judicature Soc., Assn. Customs Bar. Republican. Club: Los Angeles Athletic. Home: 348 S Orange Grove Blvd Pasadena CA 91105 Office: 3580 Wilshire Blvd Los Angeles CA 90010

AUERBACH, FRANK, artist; b. Berlin, Apr. 29, 1931; s. Max and Charlotte A.; m. Julia Wolstenholme, 1958; 1 child. Student St. Martin's Sch. Art, London, Royal Coll. Art. One man shows: Beaux-Arts Gallery, London, 1956, 59, 61, 62, 63, Marlborough Fine Art, London, 1965, 67, 71, 74, 83, 87, Marlborough Gallery Inc., N.Y.C., 1969, Villiers Art Gallery, Sydney, 1972, U. Essex, Colchester, 1973, Galleria Bergamini, Milan, 1973, Marlborough, Zurich, 1976, Retrospective Exhbn., Arts Council, Hayward Gallery, London, Fruit Market Gallery, Edinburgh, 1978, Bernard Jacobson, N.Y.C., 1979, Marlborough Gallery, N.Y.C., 1982, Brit. Pavilion Venice Biennale, 1986 (joint winner Golden Lion), Kunstverein, Hamburg, 1986, Folkwang Mus., Essen, 1987, Centro De Arte Reina Sofia, Madrid, 1987; group shows include: Tooths Gallery, London, 1958, 71, N.Y. Found., Rome, 1958, Carnegie Internat. Exhbn., Pitts., 1958, 61, Dunn Internat. Exhbn., London, 1963, Gulbenkian Exhbn., London, 1964, Marlborough Graphics, London, 1966-71, Peter Stuyvesant Found. Collection, London, 1967, Graphics Triennial, Bienne 1970, Palazzo dell'Accad. and Palazzo Reale, Genoa, 1972, Marlborough-Godard, Toronto, 1973; Los Angeles County Mus., 1975, European Painting in the Seventies, U.S.A. 1976, New Spirit in Painting, London, 1981, Westkunst, Cologne, 1981, Eight Figurative Painters, Yale Ctr. for Brit. Art, Santa Barbara Mus., 1981-82, Venice Biennale, 1982, Mus. Modern Art, N.Y., 1984, Tate Gallery, London, 1984; works in pub. collections in U.K., Australia, Brazil, U.S.A., Mexico, Israel. Recipient Silver medal for painting Royal Coll. Art. Office: Marlborough Fine Art Gallery, 6 Albemarle St, London W1X 3HF, England

AUERBACH, JOSEPH, business educator, lawyer; b. Franklin, N.H., Dec. 3, 1916; s. Jacob and Besse Mae (Reamer) A.; m. Judith Evans, Nov. 10, 1941; children: Jonathan L., Hope B. Pym. A.B., Harvard U., 1938, LL.B., 1941. Bar: N.H. 1941, Mass. 1952, U.S. Ct. Appeals (1st, 2d, 3d, 5th, 7th and D.C. cirs.), U.S. Supreme Ct. 1948. Atty. SEC, Washington and Phila., 1941-43, prin. atty., 1946-49; fgn. service staff officer U.S. Dept. State, Dusseldorf, W. Ger., 1950-52; ptnr. Sullivan & Worcester, Boston, 1952-82, counsel, 1982—; lectr. Boston U. Law Sch., 1975-76; lectr. Harvard Bus. Sch., Boston, 1980-82, prof., 1982-83, Class of 1957 prof., 1983-87, prof. emeritus, 1987—; bd. dirs. Nat. Benefit Life Ins. Co., N.Y.C., Valcom Inc., Omaha, J.L. Auerbach & Co., The Netherlands, Auerbach, Christenson, Taguiri, Inc., Boston. Author: (with S.L. Hayes, III) Investment Banking and Diligence, 1986, also papers and articles in field. Mem. editorial bd., Harvard Bus. Rev. Bd. dirs. Friends of Boston U. Libraries; mem. exec. com. Eastern br. Shakespere Globe Ctr. (N.A.), N.Y.C., 1983—; trustee Mass. Eye and Ear Infirmary, Boston, 1981—, chmn. devel. com., 1985—; trustee Old Colony Charitable Found., 1976—; mem. adv. bd. Am. Repertory Theatre, Cambridge, Mass., 1985—, also chmn. endowment com. Served with AUS, 1943-46. Decorated Army Commendation medal. Mem. ABA, Mass. Bar Assn. Clubs: Federal, Harvard of N.Y.C., Sky, Grolier, Shop, Harvard Mus. Assn., Sesquincentennial Harvard Musical Assn. (chmn.). Home: 23 Lime St Boston MA 02108 Office: Sullivan & Worcester One Post Office Sq Boston MA 02109 also: 1 Post Office Sq Boston MA 02109

AUERBACH, MARSHALL JAY, lawyer; b. Chgo., Sept. 5, 1932; s. Samuel M. and Sadie (Miller) A.; m. Carole Landsberg, July 3, 1960; children—Keith Alan, Michael Ward. Student, U. Ill.; J.D., John Marshall Law Sch., 1955. Bar: Ill. 1955. Sole practice Evanston, Ill., 1955-72; ptnr. in charge matrimonial law sect. Jenner & Block, Chgo., 1972-80; mem. firm Marshall J. Auerbach & Assocs., Ltd., Chgo., 1980—; mem. faculty Ill. Inst. Continuing Legal Edn. Author Illinois Marriage and Dissolution of Marriage Act, enacted into law, 1977; Historical and Practice Notes to Illinois Marriage and Dissolution of Marriage Act, 1980—; contbr. chpts. to Family Law, Vol. 2. Fellow Am. Acad. Matrimonial Lawyers; mem. Ill. State Bar Assn. (chmn. family law sect. 1971-72), ABA (vice-chmn. family law sect. com. for liaison with tax sect. 1974-76). Home: 2314 Orrington Ave Evanston IL 60201 Office: 180 N LaSalle St Chicago IL 60601

AUFRAY, JEAN-CLAUDE, psychiatrist; b. Le Mans, Sarthe, France, Dec. 10, 1944; s. Georges Alfred and Germaine (Ferrand) A.; m. Brigitte Maria Meyer, Aug. 1, 1978; children: Antoine, Celine. Dr. in Medecine, U. Rennes, France, 1967; and U. Nat. de Ivory Coast, Abidjan, 1969; grad. in psychiatry, U. Montpellier, France, 1977. Asst. attaché in psychiatry service Univ. Hosp., Montpellier, 1977-81; practice medicine specializing in psychiatry and psychoanalysis Montpellier, 1978—; chief cons. Reception Ctr. for Drug Addicts, Montpellier, 1978—. Office: 50 Ave Prof Grasset, 34000 Montpellier France

AUGER, JOHN BRIAN, dust and fume control company executive; b. Birmingham, Eng., Dec. 3, 1933; s. Charles and Margaret Ivy (Allcott) A.; m. Beatrice Mabel Watts, Mar. 29, 1958; children—Timothy John, Richard Peter, Christopher Brian. Cert. Mech. Engring., Coll. Tech.; Cert. Indsl. Mgmt., Coll. Advanced Tech., 1963. Apprentice, Belliss & Morcom Ltd., Birmingham, 1949-57; lectr. Edn. Com., Birmingham, 1957-61; sales engr. Metco Ltd., Dce Ltd., Birmingham, 1961-72; project engr. Lucas Girling Ltd., Birmingham, 1972-74; dir. J.B.Auger (Midlands) Ltd., Bromsgrove, Eng., 1974—; cons. Lucas Griling Ltd., 1985—. Patentee flexible bodied cyclonic filters. Served with Royal Engrs., 1955-57. Fellow Inst. of Plant Engrs.; mem. Bur. Engr. Surveyors (dir. 1982—). Club: Bromsgrove Operatic Soc. Avocations: Music; singing. Home: Timberhonger Ct, Timberhonger Ln, North Bromsgrove England

AUGER, PIERRE MICHEL, physics educator, researcher; b. Neuilly, Hauts de Seine, France, Mar. 8, 1953; s. Gaetan Bertrand and Claude Christiane (Botte) A.; m. Martine Forest, Sept. 28, 1985; 1 child, Juliette. Physics Maitrise, U. Paris VI, 1976, Thèse 3éme cycle, 1979; PhD Thése d'Etat, U. Angers, France, 1982. Tchr. Lycée Pasteur, Hénin-Beaumont, France, 1982-86, Lycée Diderot, Paris, 1986-87; prof. faculté pharmacie U. Dijon, France, 1987—; researcher Inst. Nat. Santé et de la Recherche Médicale, U141, Paris, 1984-87. Contbr. articles in systems sci. and theoretical biology to profl. jours. Mem. Soc. Gen. Systems Research (pres. French div. 1986-87), Soc. Française Biologie Théorique (conseil admninstrn. 1986-87), Assn. Française Cybernétique. Served with sci. branch French military, 1979-80. Home: 20 rue Nicolas Berthot, 21000 Dijon France Office: Laboratoire Biophysique, Fac Pharmacie, 7 Bd Jeanne d'Arc, 21000 Dijon France

AUGHUET, MICHEL, rubber company executive; b. Tubize, Belgium, July 21, 1944; s. Hubert and Lucie (Moustin) A.; m. Michele Jadot, Aug. 10, 1967; children: Cedric, Damien. Student, I.R.A.M., Mons, Belgium, 1966. Mgr. project Gen. Contracting Firm-Moustin, Tubize, 1967-73; gen. mgr. Constrn. Co. Jardimme Braine, L'Alleud, Belgium, 1973-78; mgr. div. Constrn. Mat. Div. Carlisle Europe, Brussels, 1978-82; dir. div. Constrn. Mat. Div. Carlisle Syntec Systems, Brussels, 1982-85; mgr. br. Internat. Ops. Brussels Ctr. Carlisle Syntec Systems, 1985—. Author: (study report) Prefabrication Systems in Europe, 1966. Served with Army, 1966-67. Home: Bois No 7, 1360 Tubize Brabant, Belgium

AUGIER, SERGE JEAN, physician; b. Tarascon, France, July 14, 1927; s. Jean-Marie and Germaine (Colinmaire) A.; m. Germaine Soumille, June 21, 1961; children: Hervé, Agnès, Michel, Bernard. MD, Faculty of Medicine, Montpellier, France, 1961. Intern CHPM, Avignon, France, 1958-61; research in parasychology Carpentras, France, 1961—. Orthodox Catholic. Office: 75 Ave Nortre-Dame de Santé, 84 200 Carpentras France

AUGSTEIN, RUDOLF, publisher; b. Nov. 5, 1923. D.H.C., Bath U., 1983, U. Wuppertal, 1987. Publisher, Der Spiegel (weekley), Hamburg, 1947—; under arrest (for alleged polit. offence), 1962-63. Author: Spiegelunge 1964; Konrad Adenauer, 1964; Preussens Friedrich und die Deutschen, 1968, Jesus Menschensohn, 1972. Served to lt. German Army, World War II. Elected Bundestag, 1972, resigned, 1973. Mem. German PEN. Office: Der Spiegel, Ost-West-Strasse, D-2000 Hamburg 11 Federal Republic of Germany

AUGUIS, LOURDES DEGRACIA, pediatrician; b. Tacloban, Leyte, Philippines, Feb. 7, 1940; d. Ireno Tanudra and Angela Novales (Guisumbing) De Gracia; m. Mateo Buaya Auguis, June 18, 1970; children: Adora, Benjamin. MD, Southwestern U., Cebu City, Philippines, 1964. Diplomate Am. Bd. Pediatrics. Rotating intern St. John's Episcopal Hosp., Bklyn., 1965-66; pediatric resident King County Hosp. State U., Bklyn., 1966-68; fellow ambulatory pediatrics Kings County Hosp., Bklyn., 1968-69; practice medicine specializing in pediatrics General Santos City, Philippines; med. dir. Auguis Clinic, General Santos City. Mem. Philippine Pediatric Soc., Philippine Med. Women's Assn. (pres. 1985-87), Philippine Cancer Soc. (pres. 1985—), General Santos City Med. Soc. (pres. 1987—). Office: Auguis Clinic, 32 N Osmena Ave, General Santos City 9701, Philippines

AUGUSTE LE BRETON, (MONTFORT), author; b. Lesneven (Finistere) France, Feb. 18, 1913; s. Eugene and Rosalie (Gorel) M.; m. Marguerite Lecacheur, Aug. 14, 1965; 1 child, Maryvonne. Served with French Forces, 1940-44. Decorated Croix de Guerre with stars au titre de la Resistance. Mem. Société des Auteurs, Compositeurs, Editeurs de Musique, Société Auteurs, Compositeurs, Dramatiques. Club: Grande Loge Maconique de France. Author: Rififi, 1954; Les Hauts Murs, 1955; La Loi des Rues, 1956; Razzia sur la Chnouf, 1958; Le Rouge est mis, 1957; Rififi in New York, 1961; le clan des Siciliens, 1965; Les Pegriots, 1969; (poems) Du Vent, 1970; malfrats and Co., 1971; Les Bourlinguers, 1972; Rouges Étaient les Emeraudes, 1974; Monsieur Rififi (biography), 1976; Aventures sous les Tropiques, 1974; La mome Piaf, 1980; Série Rififi, 12 vols., Fortif's, 1982; 2 sous D'Amour (biography), 1986; others. Address: 12 rue Pasteur, 78110 Le Vesinet France

AUGUSTINE, JEROME SAMUEL, investment adviser; b. Racine, Wis., May 7, 1928; s. Lester Samuel and Pearl (Hilker) A.; A.B. cum laude, Harvard U., 1950, M.B.A., 1952; m. Camilla Sewell, Feb. 7, 1953; children—Theodore Samuel Purnell, Julia Sewell Augustine Marshall, Elizabeth Stroebel. Cons., Scudder, Stevens & Clark, Boston, 1952-56; founder, treas., dir. Vencap, Inc., Boston, 1956-58; treas., dir. Consumer Products, Inc., Boston, 1956-58; founder, treas., dir. Microsonics, Inc, Hingham, Mass., 1956-58; treas., dir. Capitol Mgmt. Corp., Boston, 1956-58; cons. Kidder, Peabody & Co., Boston, 1958-64; pres. Cosmos Ann. Corp., N.Y.C. 1964-66; founder, pres. dir. Cosmos Securities Corp., 1965-70, Cosmos (Bahamian) Ltd., Nassau, 1964-70, Augustine Fin. Co., Bridgeport, Conn., 1966—; first v.p. Van Alstyne, Noel & Co., N.Y.C., 1973-74; v.p. Wright Investors' Service, Bridgeport, 1974-87, sr. v.p., 1987—. Trustee, Low-Heywood Sch. Named to Washington Hall of Fame, 1986. Mem. Boston Fin. Research Assos. (gov. 1960-64, v.p. 1963-64), New Eng. Amateur Rowing Assn. (past pres.). Episcopalian. Clubs: Union Boat, Harvard (Boston); Harvard (N.Y.C.); Noroton (Conn.) Yacht; Ox Ridge Hunt (Darien, Conn.); Royal Ascot (Berkshire, U.K.) Polo. Home: 155 Long Neck Point Rd Darien CT 06820 Office: Park City Plaza Bridgeport CT 06604

AUGUSTINE, NORMAN RALPH, industrial executive; b. Denver, July 27, 1935; s. Ralph Harvey and Freda Irene (Immenga) A.; m. Margareta Engman, Jan. 20, 1962; children: Gregory Eugen, René Irene. B.S.E. magna cum laude, Princeton U., 1957, M.S.E., 1959. Research asst. Princeton U., 1957-58; program mgr., chief engr. Douglas Aircraft Co., Inc., Santa Monica, Calif., 1958-65; asst. dir. def. research and engring. U.S. Govt., Office of Sec. Def., Washington, 1965-70; v.p. advanced systems Missiles and Space Co., LTV Aerospace Corp., Dallas, 1970-73; asst. sec. army The Pentagon, Washington, 1973-75; undersec. army The Pentagon, 1975-77; v.p. ops. Martin Marietta Aerospace Corp., Bethesda, Md., 1977-82; pres. Martin Marietta Denver Aerospace Co., 1982-85, pres., chief operating officer, 1986-87, vice chmn., chief exec. officer, 1987—, also bd. dirs., chmn., chief exec. officer, 1988—; bd. dirs. Internat. Laser Systems, Inc., Orlando, Fla., Colo. Nat. Bank; mem. of corp. C.S. Draper Lab.; cons. Office of Sec. Def., 1971—, Exec. Office of Pres., 1971-73, Dept. Army, Dept. Air Force, Dept. Navy, Dept. Energy, Dept. Transp., mem. USAF Sci. Adv. Bd.; chmn. Def. Sci. Bd.; mem. NATO Group Experts on Air Def., 1966-70, NASA Research and Tech. Adv. Council, 1973-75; chmn. Space Systems and Tech. Adv. Bd., 1985—; chmn. adv. bd. dept. aeromech. engring. Princeton U., 1975-83; chmn. bd. visitors procurement and acquisition program Am. U., 1977-82; bd. advisors Center for Advancement of Procurement, Fla. State U.; chmn. adv. council, MIT Lincoln Lab. Author: Augustine's Laws; Mem. adv. bd.; Jour. of Def. Research, 1970—; asso. editor: Def. System Mgmt. Rev, 1977-82; editorial bd.: Astronautics & Aeros; contr. articles to profl. jours. Trustee Johns Hopkins U.; fund raiser YMCA, Arlington, Tex., 1971-72; chmn. nat. program evaluation com., council v.p. Boy Scouts Am.; mem. Immanuel Presbyterian Ch., McLean, Va. Recipient Meritorious Service medal Dept. Def., 1970, Disting. Civilian Service medal Dept. Def., 1975, others. Fellow Am. Astron. Soc., AIAA (hon., v.p. public policy 1978-82, dir. 1978-85 , 1983-84); mem. IEEE (sr.), Am. Helicopter Soc. (dir. 1974-75), Nat. Acad. Engring., Internat. Acad. Astronautics, Assn. U.S. Army (pres. 1980-84), Phi Beta Kappa, Sigma Xi, Tau Beta Pi. Office: Martin Marietta Corp 6801 Rockledge Dr Bethesda MD 20817

AUJLA, GURNAM SINGH, electronics engineer; b. Bohan, India, Oct. 15, 1960; s. Sucha Singh and Swarn Kaur; m. Crewal Grewal, June 30, 1984; 1 child, Amandeep. BSc with honors, Trent Poly., Eng., 1983. Test engr. Gen. Electric Co., Wembley, Eng., 1984; engr. design/devel. Gen. Electric Co., Wembley, 1984-85, Birmingham Sound Reproduction, Strourbridge, Eng., 1985-88, Eddy Stone Radio GEC Marconi, Birmingham, Eng., 1988—. Mem. Instn. Elec. Engrs., Sikh Soc. (treas. Nottingham, Eng.). Home: 48 St Philips Ave, Bradmore, Wolverhampton West Midlands England WV3 7ED Office: Eddy Stone Radio GEC Marconi, West Heath Birmingham England B31 3PP

AULD, SAMUEL HAYWARD, JR., aircraft and electronics company executive; b. Pasadena, Calif., Sept. 16, 1925; s. Samuel Hayward and Wilda (Jackson) A.; m. Evelyn Lorraine Maydeck, June 15, 1952; children—John, James, Kathleen. BSEE Calif. Poly. State U., San Luis Obispo, 1955. Elec. engr. Lear, Inc., 1956-62; gen. mgr. Avionics div. Lear Jet Corp., Wichita, Kans., 1962-65, v.p. 1965-67; v.p. Static Power div., Newport Beach, Calif., 1967-72, pres., chief operating officer Static Power Inc., 1972-76; pres., chief exec. officer Lear Avia Corp., Reno, 1976-86, also dir.; vice chmn., dir. Lear Fan Ltd., London; with Bruce Industries, Inc., Dayton, Nev., 1988—. Patentee in field. Served to capt. USAF, 1943-48. Republican. Home: 1324 Dartmouth Dr Reno NV 89509

AULIN, ARVID YRJÖ, mathematician; b. Oulu, Finland, Aug. 7, 1929; s. K. Arvi E. and Jenny (Päkkilä) A.;m. Pirkko Anneli Aulin-Ahmavaara, May 26, 1970. MA, U. Helsinki, Finland, 1950, PhD, 1954. Research fellow Nordic Inst. for Theoretical Atom Physics, Copenhagen, 1957-59; researcher Atomic Energy Commn., Helsinki, 1960-61; lectr. theoretical physics U. Helsinki, 1962-63, acting prof. philosophy, 1968-70; prof. theoretical physics U. Turku, Finland, 1963-67; research prof. Acad. Finland, Helsinki, 1971-74; prof. math. and methodology U. Tampere, Finland, 1974—; cons. The Finnish State Broadcasting Co. Helsinki, 1968-70. Author: Information, 1969, 2d. edit., 1970, 3d edit., 1975, Cybernetic Methodology, 1969, 2d. edit., 1970, The Cybernetic Laws of Social Progress, 1982, Essays on This Time, 1987; also numerous papers; essayist Kanava mag., Helsinki, 1982—. Fellow Finnish Acad. Sci. and Letters. Home: Oulunkylantori 2 C 16, 00640 Helsinki Finland Office: U Tampere, Box 607, 33101 Tampere Finland

AULT, THOMAS JEFFERSON, III, manufacturing company executive, manufacturing consultant; b. Portland, Ind., June 23, 1911; s. Ross Earl and Olga (Sattler) A.; Asso. in Sci., Cumnock Coll., 1932; B.A. in Econs., UCLA, 1934; student Los Angeles Stock Exchange Inst., 1930-32; cert. Am. Mgmt. Assn. m. Mary C. Carr, June 30, 1938; 1 child, Brian Carr. Mgmt. trainee, buyer, Borg-Warner Corp., Chgo., 1935-41, asst. purchasing agt., 1941-51, dir. purchasing, 1951-53, v.p. and asst. gen. mgr. Detroit Gear Div., 1953-54, pres., 1954-56; gen. mgr. Long mfg. div., Detroit, 1956-58; pres., chief exec. officer Saco-Lowell Shops, Boston, 1958-60, also dir.; pres., gen. mgr. The Budd Co., Detroit, 1960-64, dir. automotive div. Can., Mexico, Argentina, 1960-64; v.p. McCord Corp., Detroit, 1965-68, dir. 1965-70; pres., chief exec. officer Avis Indsl. Corp., Madison Heights, Mich., 1968-70, also dir.; pres., gen. mgr. Flyer Industries Ltd., Winnipeg, Man., Can., 1970-73, chmn. bd., 1972-76, chief exec. officer, 1970-76; chmn. bd., chief exec. officer Saunders Aircraft Corp. Ltd., Gimi, Man., Can., 1972-73; chmn. bd., dir Austinite Corp., Southfield, Mich., 1972-76; chmn. bd., chief exec. officer Superior Kendrick Bearings, Inc., Detroit, 1974-76, also dir.; chief exec. officer Washington Heat Transfer, Inc., Polo, Ill., 1976-79, also dir.; pres. v.p. Duffy Tool and Stamping Corp., Muncie, 1979—, also sr. exec. in residence lectr. and exec. in residence Ball State U. Coll. Bus., Muncie, Ind., 1980-87; pres. The T.J. Ault Co., 1987—; cons. to mgmt. Arthur D. Little Consulting, Inc., 1959—. Bd. dirs. United Found. of Southeastern Mich., 1961-64, ARC, Detroit, 1961-64, dir. Jr. Achievement of Southeastern Mich. 1960-63, Employers Assn. of Detroit, 1955-58, Boston Mus. Sci., 1958-60, Mass. Meml. Hosp., 1958-60; chmn., Muncie Ind. Transit System, 1983-87 . Served to capt. U.S. Army, 1941-45. Recipient Purchasing Progress award Purchasing News, 1953, Outstanding Service award Jr. Achievement of Detroit, 1963, S.A.M. award, 1982; named to Automotive Hall of Fame, Coll. Bus. Prof. of Yr. Ball State Univ., 1983, All Univ. We-ness award Student Leadership Devel. Bd. Ball State Univ., 1984. Mem. President's Profl. Assn. Engring. Soc. Detroit, NAM, Mich. Mfrs. Assn., Soc. for Advancement Mgmt., Nat. Safety Council, Acad. of Mgmt., Am. Inst. Mgmt., Nat. Assoc. Purchasing Mgmt., Am Textile Machinery Assn., Automotive Parts Mfg. Assn., Farm Equipment Assn., Am. Ordinance Assn., Am. Soc. for Metals, Soc. Mfg. Engrs. (robotics internat.), Am. Prodn. and Inventory Control Soc., Am. Soc. Quality Control, U.S. C. of C., Air Conditioning and Refrigeration Inst., Econ. Club of Detroit (dir. 1961-64), Ind. Soc., Am. Security Council, Sigma Nu, Sigma Iota Epsilon, Delta Sigma Pi, Beta Gamma Sigma. Clubs: Elks, Masons, Shriners, Country of Detroit, University; La Coquille (Palm Beach); Delaware Country, Muncie (Muncie); Columbia (Indpls.), Rotary (Muncie). Contbr. articles on material control, long range planning and mgmt. to indsl. publs. Home: 4501 N Wheeling St Apt 3-102 Muncie IN 47304 Office: Ball State Univ Dept Mgmt Sci Coll Bus Muncie IN 47306

AUNGST, JOHN WAYNE, JR., historian, preservationist; b. Landisville, Pa., Apr. 26, 1920; s. John Wayne and Adeline D. (Kauffman) A.; m. Margaret C. Wagner, 1941; 1 child, Dora Jo Aungst Bentos. A.B., Dickinson Coll., 1948; postgrad. Dickinson Sch. Law, 1948-50. Law clk. Alspach & Wenger, Lancaster, Pa., 1951-53 with U.S. Post Office, Landisville, 1954-72; trustee Wm. Klein Trust, Elizabethtown, Pa., 1972-84; adminstr. Lancaster County Hist. Soc., Pa., 1973-87, dir. emeritus, 1987—; founder, dir. Hist. Preservation Trust Lancaster County, 1966-88, now hon. dir., 1988—, pres., 1973-77; dir. James Buchanan Found., Lancaster, 1976-87, hon. dir., 1988—. Ed. Hand Med. Heritage Found., 1982-87, hon. dir., 1988—; mem. Lancaster County Land Use Adv. Com., 1976—, Lancaster County Records Retention Com., 1978—, Mus. Council Lancaster County, 1983—. Sustaining mem. Republican Nat. Com., 1972—; charter mem. Rep. Presdl. Task Force, 1982—. Served to 1st lt. U.S. Army, 1941-46; PTO. Mem. Am. Assn. State and Local History, Nat. Trust Hist. Preservation, Mid-Atlantic Regional Archives Conf., Soc. Archtl. Historians, Newcomen Soc. N.Am., Decorative Arts Trust, Library Co. Phila., Pa. German Soc., Phila. Mus. Art, Victorian Soc. Am., Winterthur Guild, Friends of Am. Philos. Soc., Cliosophic Soc. Lancaster, Bowden's Chapl Soc., Donegal Soc., Elizabethtown Hist. Soc., Ephrata Cloister Assocs., Fulton Opera House Found., Heritage Ctr. Lancaster County, Hist. Soc. Cocalico Valley, Lancaster Pirates, Landis Valley Mus. Assocs., Manheim Hist. Soc., Mount Joy Area Hist. Soc., Sigma Alpha Epsilon. Clubs: Hamilton (Lancaster); Capitol Hill (Washington); Classic Car of America, Lincoln Owners, Lincoln Zephyr Owners, Rolls-Royce Owners. Lodge: Rotary (Lancaster). Deceased Apr. 15, 1988. Home: 226 Main St Box 34 Landisville PA 17538 Office: 230 N President Ave Lancaster PA 17603

AURIACH, ALBERT NOEL HENRI, physician, educator; b. St. Féliu, Pyrénées-Orientales, France, Dec. 25, 1923; s. Vincent Justin and Marguerite Elisa (Baux) A.; m. Blanche Lucienne Soupa, Oct. 10, 1950; children: Jean, René, Christian. MD, U. Toulouse, France, 1951; specialist degree in phys. medicine and rehab., Nat. Council Medicine, Paris 1973. Various positions pub. and pvt. hosps., France, 1948-52; head dept. bone and lung Tb Nat. Social Security Office, Les Escaldes, France, 1952-57; dir. rehab. ctr. infantile paralysis Nat. Social Security Office, Lamalou, France, 1952-84; tchr. phys. medicine Univ. Hosp., Montpellier, France, 1975-87, cons. physiology, 1971—, tchr. physiotherapy, 1962—. Co-author: L'Enfant Paralysé, 1985; contbr. articles to profl. jours. Pres. Municipal Nat. Gen. Confederation Managerial Staff Médecins Spécialistes Salariés Rééducation Fonctionnelle, d'Honneur Lamalou Handisport; mem. Conseil Surveillance Crédit Mut. Served as officer in French health med. corps, 1943-45. Recipient Gold medal Montpellier, 1984, Paul Harris fellow Rotary, 1977. Mem. St. Francaise Médecine Physique, St. d'Appareillage (Cerebral Palsy Com.1969-87), Rehab. Talks Soc. (pres. 1971-82), Assn. Multinat. Polio-Plus (v.p. 1987-88). Roman Catholic. Lodge: Rotary (pres. Lamalou 1976-77, dist. gov. 1984-85). Home and Office: Chemin Mas d'Anglade, 66330 Cabestany France

AURIN, ROBERT JAMES, advertising agency executive; b. St. Louis, Feb. 13, 1943; s. George Henry and Elizabeth Anastasia (Krauska) A.; m. Mary L. Martin, Mar. 1981. B.J., U. Mo., 1965. Copywriter Leo Burnett Co., Chgo., 1971-72, Young & Rubicam, Inc., Chgo., 1972-73; from copywriter to v.p., creative dir. Foote, Cone & Belding, Inc., 1973-79; exec. v.p., dir. creative services Grey-North Inc., Chgo., 1979-82; pres. Robert Aurin Assocs., Chgo., 1982—; co-owner ROMAR Mgmt. Co., Chgo., 1984—. Served to lt. USN, 1965-74, Vietnam. Mem. Chgo. Council Fgn. Relations., Art Inst. Chgo.

AUSBURN, FLOYD BONNESS, instructional technology educator, consultant; b. Tulsa, Jan. 21, 1940; s. Bonness D. and Alee (Mercer) A.; m. Lynna Joyce Burt, July 30, 1966. BA in Edn., Northeastern Okla. State U. 1970, MEd, 1973; PhD, U. Okla., 1975. Advt. producer, photographer Huddleston Assocs., Tulsa, 1965-70; tchr. Muskogee pub. schs., Okla., 1970-72, dir. media services Coll. Arts and Scis., U. Okla., Norman, 1975-76; sr. lectr. ednl. tech. Faculty Edn., Monash U., Melbourne, Australia, 1976—. Vis. research fellow, resaerch fellow, Papua New Guinea U. Tech., Lae, 1980; cons., lectr. ednl. tech. program UNESCO, Melbourne, 1981-83; vis. specialist in ednl. resource mgmt. Colombo Plan Staff Coll., Singapore, 1983; vis. communications specialist Australian Devel. Assistance Bur., Bangladesh, 1985; cons., lectr. instructional tech. RECSAM, Penang, Malaysia, 1986; vis. lectr., 1988. Author: Instructional Development Skills for Teaching, 1985; contbr. articles to profl. jours. Grantee USAF, 1977-79, Monash U., 1980, Nat Centre for Research and Devel. Australia, 1983-84. Mem. Assn. Ednl. Communications and Tech. Australian Soc. Ednl. Tech. (exec. council 1977-84). Avocations: photography; fishing; diving; sailing. Office: Monash Univ, Faculty Edn, 3168 Clayton Victoria Australia

AUSNEHMER, JOHN EDWARD, lawyer; b. Youngstown, Ohio, June 26, 1954; s. John Louis and Patricia Jean (Liguore) A.; m. Margaret Mary Kane, Oct. 17, 1981; 1 child, Jill Ellen. BS, Ohio State U., 1976; JD, U. Dayton, 1980. Bar: Ohio 1980, U.S. Dist. Ct. (no. dist.) Ohio 1981, U.S. Supreme Ct. 1984, U.S. Ct. Appeals (6th cir.) 1984. Law clk. Ohio Atty. Gen., Columbus, 1978, Green, Schiavoni, Murphy, Haines & Sgambati Co. L.P.A., 1978; assoc. Dickson Law Office, Petersburg, Ohio, 1979-85; sole practice, Youngstown, Ohio, 1984—; asst. prosecuting atty. Mahoning County, Ohio, 1986—. Mem. Am. Trial Lawyers Assn., Ohio Acad. Trial Lawyers, ABA, Ohio State Bar Assn., Nat. Assn. Criminal Def. Lawyers, Mahoning County Bar Assn., Columbiana County Bar Assn., Phi Alpha Delta. Democrat. Roman Catholic. Club: Mahoning Valley Soccer (pres. 1982-84). Home: 51 South Shore Dr Youngstown OH 44512 Office: 14 Boardman-Poland Rd Youngstown OH 44512-4601

AUSSEIL, JEAN, government official; b. Vincennes, France, Apr. 30, 1925; s. Jean Achille Ausseil and Francine Bonnet; m. Catherine Hine, Aug. 19, 1940; children: Sarah, David. Student, Ecole France D'Outre Mer, Paris, 1946-48. Counsellor technique Cabinet du Premier Minister, Paris, 1968-69; consul gen. Ministry Fgn. Affairs, Tanger Maroc, France, 1969-75; French ambassador to Montevideo, Uruguay, 1975-78, Addis Abeba, Ethiopia, 1978-80; dir. African affairs Paris, 1981-85; minister of state Principality of Monaco, 1985—. Home and Office: Place de la Visitation 98000, Monaco

AUSTEN, W(ILLIAM) GERALD, surgeon, educator; b. Akron, Ohio, Jan. 20, 1930; s. Karl A. and Bertl (Jehle) A.; m. Patricia Ramsdell, Jan. 28, 1961; children: Karl Ramsdell, William Gerald, Jr., Christopher Marshall, Elizabeth Patricia. B.S., MIT, 1951; M.D., Harvard U., 1955; H.H.D. (hon.), U. Akron, 1980; D.Sc. (hon.), U. Athens, Greece, 1981, U. Mass. 1985. Intern, then resident surgery Mass. Gen. Hosp., Boston, 1955-61, chief of surgery, 1969—; Edward D. Churchill prof. surgery Harvard Med. Sch., 1974; mem. surgery tng. com. NIH, 1965-68, mem. surgery study sect., 1968-72; mem. heart and lung program project com. Nat. Heart and Lung Inst., Bethesda, Md., 1973-76; mem. Inst. Medicine of Nat. Acad. Scis., 1975—; regent Am. Coll. Surgeons, 1982—. Contbr. articles to med. jours. Mem. corp. MIT, 1972—, life mem., 1982. Served as surgeon USPHS, 1961-62. Bd. dirs. Whitehead Inst. Biomed. Research, 1982—. Markle scholar, 1963-68. Fellow Royal Coll. Surgeons (hon.), Am. Acad. Arts and Scis.; mem. Assn. Acad. Surgery (pres. 1970), Soc. Univ. Surgeons (sec. 1967-70, pres. 1972-73), Am. Surg. Assn. (sec. 1979-84, pres. 1985-86), Am. Heart Assn. (pres. 1977-78), Mass. Heart Assn. (pres. 1972-74), New Eng. Cardiovascular Soc. (pres. 1972-73), Am. Bd. Surgery (bd. dirs. 1969-74), Am. Assn. Thoracic Surgery (v.p. 1987—), Am. Bd. Thoracic Surgery (bd. dirs. 1984—). Home: 163 Wellesley St Weston MA 02193 Office: Mass Gen Hosp Chief Surgical Services Boston MA 02114

AUSTEN, WILLIAM JOHN, oil company executive; b. Dalhousie, Himalayas, India, Apr. 23, 1920; s. Frederick Henry and Lillie (Adams) A.; m. Anneliese Barbara Romers, July 11, 1964. Student, SE Essex Coll., Eng., 1938-41; grad. MechE, SW Essex Coll., Walthamstown, Eng., 1948. Trainee Ford Motor Co., Dagenham Essex, Eng., 1938-42; engr. Burmah Shell, India and Pakistan, 1948-64; prop. and methods advisor Burmah Ea., Chittagong, East Pakistan, 1965-68; mgr. job evaluation Burmah Oil Trading, London, 1969-70; personnel and adminstrn. mgr. Burmah Castrol Europe, Hamburg, Fed. Republic Germany, 1971-76; tng. advisor Burmah Oil Deutschland, Hamburg, 1977—. Served with mil., U.K., 1943-47. Mem. Brit. Inst. Mgmt., Royal Overseas League. Baptist. Club: The Brit. (Hamburg). Office: The Burmah Oil Deutschland, Esplanade 39, 2000 Hamburg 36, Federal Republic of Germany

AUSTIN, EILEEN KAY, educator; b. Chgo., Mar. 6, 1947; d. Richard James and Alice Antoinette (Holefelder) Austin; B.S.N., Spalding Coll., 1968; M.Ed., U. Fla., 1971, Ed.D., 1976. Nursing instr. Edison Community Coll., Ft. Myers, Fla., 1971-74; assoc. coordinator Interinstl. Registered Nurse Program, Jacksonville, Fla., 1974-75; dir. nursing edn. U. No. Fla., Jacksonville 1975-80; adj. instr. div. continuing edn. U. Fla., Gainesville, 1980—; pres. Eileen K. Austin, Inc., Jacksonville, 1980—; adj. prof. Central Mich. U., Offcampus Grad. program, 1981—. Bd. dirs. Oak Psychiat. Center, Jacksonville, 1977-85; treas. N.E. Fla. Nurses Council for Continuing Edn. 1981-83. Mem. Fla. League for Nursing (chmn. public affairs and legis. com. 1981-83), Fla. Nurses Assn., Dist. Nurses Assn. (2d v.p. 1978-79, dir. 1979-80), Nurse Cons. (assoc., membership com.), Phi Kappa Phi, Phi Delta Kappa, Phi Lambda Theta, Kappa Delta Pi. Democrat. Roman Catholic. Author: Guidelines for the Development of Continuing Education Offerings for Nurses, 1981; A Report of the 1982 Nursing Survey on the Impact of Rules and Regulations and Continuing Education; mem. editorial rev. bd. Fla. Nursing and Health Care. Office: PO Box 168 Crystal Beach FL 34681

AUSTIN, ROBERT EUGENE, JR., lawyer; b. Jacksonville, Fla., Oct. 10, 1937; s. Robert Eugene and Leta Fitch A.; div. Feb. 86; children: Robert Eugene, George Harry Talley. B.A., Davidson Coll., 1959; J.D., U. Fla., 1964. Bar: Fla. 1965, D.C. 1983, U.S. Supreme Ct. 1970; cert. in civil trial law Nat. Bd. Trial Advocacy, Fla. Bar. Legal asst. Fla. Ho. Reps., 1965; assoc. firm Jones & Sims, Pensacola, Fla., 1965-66; ptnr. firm Warren, Warren & Austin, Leesburg, Fla., 1966-68, McLin, Burnsed, Austin & Cyrus, Leesburg, 1968-77, Austin & Burleigh, Leesburg, 1977-81; sole practice Leesburg, 1981-83, Leesburg and Orlando, Fla., 1984-86; ptnr. firm Austin & Lockett P.A., 1983-84; ptnr. Austin, Lawrence & Landis, Leesburg and Orlando, 1986—; state atty., 1972; mem. Jud. Nominating Commn. and Grievance Com. 5th Dist. Fla.; gov. Fla. Bar, 1983—. Chmn. Lake Dist. Boy Scouts Am.; asst. dean Leesburg Deanery, Diocese of Central Fla.; trustee Fla. House, Washington, U. Fla. Law Center, 1983—. Served to capt. U.S. Army, 1959-62. Mem. Acad. Fla. Trial Lawyers, Am. Arbitration Assn., ABA, Am. Judicature Soc., Am. Law Inst., Assn. Trial Lawyers Am., Nat. Inst. Trial Advocacy, Def. Research Inst., Fed. Bar Assn., Lake County Bar Assn., Roscoe Pound Am. Trial Found., Kappa Alpha, Phi Delta Phi. Democrat. Episcopalian. Clubs: Timuquana Country (Jacksonville, Fla.); University (Orlando, Fla.). Home: 6300 N Silver Lake Dr Leesburg FL 32788 Office: Austin Lawrence & Landis 1321 W Citizens Blvd Leesburg FL 32748

AUTEN, DAVID CHARLES, lawyer; b. Phila., Apr. 4, 1938; s. Charles Raymond and Emily Lillian (Dickel) A.; m. Suzanne Crozier Plowman, Feb. 1, 1969; children: Anne Crozier, Meredith Smedley. B.A., U. Pa., 1960, J.D., 1963. Bar: Pa. 1963. Mng. ptnr. firm Reed Smith Shaw & McClay (and predecessor), Phila., 1963—. Author articles in field. Vice pres. Northeast Community Mental Health Center, 1971-72; vice chmn. alumni ann. giving U. Pa., 1975-77, 81-82, chmn. alumni ann. giving, 1982-84, trustee, 1977-80, 83—; pres. Gen. Alumni Soc., 1977-80; chmn. Benjamin Franklin Assocs., 1977-85; 82; trustee Springside Sch., 1985-88, v.p. 1987-88; pres. of Coll., 1975-77; v.p. Assn. Republicans for Educated Action, 1971-79; bd. mgrs. Presbyn.-U. Pa. Med. Center, 1980—; vice chmn., 1983-85; bd. mgrs. Phila. City Inst., 1981—, Kearsley Home, 1974—; bd. mgrs. St. Peter's Sch., 1975—, pres., 1978-79. Mem. ABA, Pa. Bar Assn. (vice chmn. real property sect. 1985-87, chmn. 1987), Phila. Bar Assn. (vice chmn. young lawyers sect. 1971-72), Juristic Soc. (pres.), Interfrat. Alumni Council U. Pa. (pres. 1970-74), Phi Beta Kappa, Theta Xi (pres. 1974-76, chmn. found. 1977-86). Episcopalian (vestryman). Clubs: Rittenhouse (pres.), Union League (bd. dirs.), Fourth St., Philadelphia, Philadelphia Cricket. Home: 120 Delancey St Philadelphia PA 19106 Office: Reed Smith Shaw & McClay 1600 Ave of the Arts Bldg Philadelphia PA 19107

AUTERINEN, OLLI, retired church official; b. Helsinki, Finland, Sept. 13, 1921; s. Lauri Hendell and Mathilde Louise (Donner) A.; B. Forestry, U. Helsinki, 1949; m. Victoria Schauman, Oct. 27, 1960; son Lassi Johan. Sec., Student Christian Movement Finland, 1948-49, 50-51; forest officer State Forest Adminstrn., also tchr. State Forest Inst., 1949-50, 54-56; research asst. U. Helsinki, 1951-54; worker Finnish Seamen's Mission, Hamburg, W. Ger., 1956-60; youth sec. Diocese Helsinki, Lutheran Ch. Finland, 1961-63, gen. sec. council on youthwork Luth. Ch. Finland, 1963-74, dir. Conf. Center, 1974-84; 1st pres. Biel Youth Orgns. Finland, 1962-64. Chmn. youth com. Finnish Red Cross, 1962-69. Served as officer Finnish Army, 1940-44. Decorated Knight of Finnish White Rose 1st class, Cross of Freedom 4th class with swords; recipient Finnish Red Cross medal, 1967; Boy Scouts silver medal, 1967. Mem. Assn. Foresters Finland, Finnish-Am. Soc., Finnish-W. German Soc. Liberal. Club: Helsinki-Hietalahti Lions (past pres.). Home: Professorintie 4A6, SF 00330 Helsinki 33 Finland

AUVENSHINE, ANNA LEE BANKS, educator; b. Waco, Tex., Nov. 27, 1938; d. D.C. and Lois Elmore Banks; B.A., Baylor U., 1959, M.A., 1968, Ed.D., 1978; postgrad. Colo. State U., 1970-71, U. No. Colo., 1972; m. William Robert Auvenshine, Dec. 21, 1963; children—Karen Lynn, William Lee. Tchr. math. and English, Lake Air Jr. High Sch., Waco Ind. Sch. Dist., 1959-63, Ranger (Tex.) Ind. Sch., Ranger High Sch., 1964, Canyon (Tex.) Ind. Sch. Dist., Canyon Jr. High Sch., 1964-66; instr. English, Baylor U., 1963; instr. math. Canyon Ind. Sch. Dist., Canyon High Sch., 1968-70; tchr. math. and English, St. Vrain Sch., Loveland (Colo.) High Sch., 1970-71; tchr. English and reading Thompson Sch. Dist., Loveland (Colo.) High Sch., 1971-72; instr. reading program dir. Ranger Jr. Coll., 1972-84, chmn. humanities div., 1978-82; tchr. math. Hillsboro High Sch., 1984-85, adminstr. Hillsboro Ind. Sch. Dist., 1985—. Trustee, Ranger (Tex.) Ind. Sch.

Dist., 1979-84, v.p. bd. trustees, 1980-82, pres., 1982-84; community chmn., publicity chmn., troop leader Ranger Girl Scout Assn., 1974-77; sec. Eastland County Heart Assn., 1975-77; ch. sch. supt. First United Meth. Ch., Ranger, 1979-81, organist, 1974-77, mem. adminstrv. bd., 1979-84. Mem. Internat. Reading Assn., Assn. Supervision and Curriculum Devel., Western Coll. Reading Assn., Tex. Assn. Sch. Adminstrs., Tex. Assn. Gifted and Talented, Tex. Jr. Coll. Tchrs. Assn. (cert. of appreciation 1979, mem. profl. devel. com. 1974-79, vice chmn. 1976-77, mem. resolutions com. 1979-80), Ranger PTA (parliamentarian 1978-79), Ranger Jr. Coll. Faculty Orgn. (pres. 1980-81), Baylor Alumni Assn. (life), Delta Kappa Gamma (pres. Beta Upsilon chpt. 1978-80, pres. Gamma Delta chpt. 1986—, achievement award 1980). Methodist. Clubs: 1947 (pres. 1977-78) (Ranger); Baylor Bear (Waco). Home: 412 Corsicana St Hillsboro TX 76645 Office: Hillsboro Ind Sch Dist Box 459 Hillsboro TX 76645

AUWAERTER, ALBRECHT, marketing specialist; b. Balzers, Liechtenstein, Feb. 24, 1951; s. Max and Hildegard (Reinoehl) A.; m. Cheryl Anne Plant, June 18, 1983; children: Markus, Monika. Cert. Communication and Electronics Tech., Gewerbeschule, Buchs, Switzerland, 1974; MBA, Imede U., Lausanne, Switzerland, 1982. Apprentice Balzers (Liechtenstein) AG, 1970-74, trainee, 1974; supr. research and devel. Balzers Union AG, 1975-76; sales engr. Balzers, Hudson, N.H., 1976-77, product mgr., 1977-81; mktg. specialist Balzers AG, Liechtenstein, 1983—; cons. Lausanne, 1982, Balzers Union AG, Liechtenstein, 1983. Pres. youth group Gesicht, Balzers, 1972, 73. Mem. Velbag, Imede Alumni Assn. Club: Interferencia. Home: Schwefelstrasse 37, FL 9490 Vaduz Liechtenstein Office: Balzers AG, FL 9496 Balzers Liechtenstein

AUXIETRE, CAMILLE-GEORGES, internist; b. Chatelus-Malvaleix, Creuse, France, Apr. 2, 1922; s. Charles Georges and Germaine (Passelat) A.; m. Nicole Maître. MD, U. Paris, 1951. Created two dispensaries Chad, 1951-52; practice medicine specializing in digestive system, Vichy, France, 1953-83; cons. Internat. Enterprises Indsl. Soc., Paris, 1984—. Author: Hypoglycémie Spontanée Chez l'Adulte, 1968; editor: Maloine Paris. Decorated Legion of Honor, Gommandeur, Croix de Guerre with palm. Mem. Soc. d' Entraide de la Legion d' Honneur. Roman Catholic. Home and Office: 6 Rue Max Durand Fardel, 03200 Vichy France

AVALLONE, RICCARDO, classicist, educator; b. Salerno, Italy, May 9, 1915; s. Alberto and Carmela (Siano) A.; laureate in lettere, U. Naples, 1938; m. Elvira Quercia, Nov. 19, 1955; children—Carmela, Margherita, Paola, Isabella. Lectr. Latin lang. U. Naples, 1938-44; founder, editor Antiquitas, 1946; lectr. Roman history and early Christian lit., vice dir. U. Salerno, 1944-45, prof. Latin lang. and lit., 1944—; lectr. Classical philology U. Rome, 1955—; hon. pres. Teatina Acad. Sci.; mem. senate Internat. Burkhardt Acad., Acad. Internat. di Propaganda Culturale; cons. U. Toronto (Can.); discoverer Med. Sch. of Salerno, also Masuccio birthplace, Salerno. Recipient Internat. award Internat. Inst. Arts and Letters, 1965; Europe prize, 1970; candidate for Nobel prize, 1973. Mem. Acad. Tiberina, Acad. 500 (Trophy award 1973). Author numerous works, including Catullo e i suoi modelli romani, 1944; Mecenate, 1963; Sorrento patria del Tasso, 1980; Nuovi scritti latini, 1980. Home: 122 Via Roma, Salerno Italy Office: U degli Studi, Salerno Italy

AVALOS, JUAN CARLOS, petrochemical company executive; b. Hdedo, Argentina, Feb. 17, 1954; s. Carlos Antonio and Celia Irma (Mancini) A.; m. Silvia Cristina Cambiasso, Feb. 24, 1979; children: Barbara Silvia, Guillermo Carlos, Federico Tomas. Student, U. Buenos Aires, 1975-80. Sr. buyer Ceramica San Lorenzo, Buenos Aires, 1973-75; sr. buyer Celulosa Argentina, Buenos Aires, 1976-77, planning engr., 1977-78; planning engr. Polisur Project, Buenos Aires, 1978-82; mgr. purchasing Polisur/Ipako, Buenos Aires, 1982—; cons. Tequim, Buenos Aires, 1985-87. Mem. Am. Purchasing Soc., Nat. Assn. Purchasing Mgmt., Inst. Desarrollo Empres. Argentina. Club: Jose Jurado Golf (Benos Aires). Home: El Ceibo 638, 1706 Haedo Argentina

AVELINE, MARK OXENFORD, psychotherapist, author; b. Henfield, Sussex, Eng., July 23, 1941; s. John Oxenford and Elnora Rosemary (Fieldhart) A.; m. Anna Jennet Dudley Page, Sept. 10, 1966; children: Robin John, James Austin. MBBS, U. London, 1965, DPM, 1969. Sr. house officer, registrar in psychiatry Guy's Hosp., London, 1967-70; sr. registrar in psychiatry Royal Edinburgh (Scotland) Hosp., 1970-74; clin. tutor U. Edinburgh, 1971-74; cons. psychiatry and psychotherapy, dir. Nottingham (Eng.) Psychotherapy Unit, St. Ann's Hosp., 1974—; clin. tchr. U. Nottingham, 1974—; cons. advisor Nottinghamshire Marriage and Guidance Council, 1976—, Nottinghamshire Constabulary, 1981—; advisor in psychotherapy Trent Regional Health Authority, East Midlands, Eng., 1979—; vis. prof. U. Auckland, New Zealand, 1980; dir. course on contemporary Brit. psychotherapy UCLA and U. Cambridge, Eng., 1982-83; chmn. Trent Regional Com. in Mental Illness, 1984—; chmn. tng. com. South-Trent Tng. in Dynamic Psychotherapy,. Author, editor: Group Therapy in Britain, 1988; contbr. articles to profl. jours. and chpts. to books. Nuffield Found. travelling scholar, Delhi, India, 1964. Mem. Royal Coll. Psychiatrists (psychotherapy sect., hon. sec. 1980-84, mem. ct. electors 1984—, M.R.C. psychiat. examiner 1985—, fellow 1983), Internat. Fedn. for Med. Psychotherapy (bd. dirs. 1985—, Mental Health Found. (mem. research com. 1986—). Office: Nottingham Psychotherapy Unit, St Ann's Hosp Porchester Rd, Nottingham NG3 6LF, England

AVERBOOK, BERYL DAVID, physician; b. Superior, Wis., Aug. 17, 1920; s. Abraham B. and Clara (Zeichig) A.; student Superior State Tchrs. Coll., 1938-39; B.S., U. Wis., 1942, M.D., 1945; postgrad. U. Colo., 1948-50; m. Gloria Sloane, Apr. 2, 1955; children—Bruce Jeffrey, Allan Wayne. Intern Akron (Ohio) City Hosp., 1945-46; resident VA Hosp., Denver, 1948-50, Rochester (N.Y.) Gen. Hosp., 1950-51, VA Hosp., Los Angeles, 1951-54; practice medicine specializing in gen. surgery, Torrance, Calif., 1948—; instr. surgery U. Calif. at Los Angeles-Harbor Gen. Hosp., 1954-58; practice tumor and vascular surgery, Torrance, 1961—; asst. prof. surgery U. Calif. Med. Center, Los Angeles, 1958-61, asst. clin. prof. surgery, 1961-64; chief surg. services Los Angeles County Harbor Gen. Hosp., Torrance, 1954-61. Served to capt. M.C., AUS; Res. Diplomate Am. Bd. Surgery. Fellow A.C.S.; mem. Am. Los Angeles County med. assns., N.Y. Acad. Scis., Los Angeles Acad. Medicine, Am. Geriatric Soc., Am. Assn. Med. Colls., Soc. Head and Neck Surgeons, Soc. Clin. Vascular Surgeons, Long Beach Surg. Soc. Contbr. articles to profl. jours. Home: 6519 Springpark Ave Los Angeles CA 90056 Office: 3640 W Lomita Blvd Torrance CA 90505

AVERSA, DOLORES SEJDA, educational administrator; b. Phila., Mar. 26, 1932; d. Martin Benjamin and Mary Elizabeth (Esposito) Sejda; B.A., Chestnut Hill Coll., 1953; m. Zefferino A. Aversa, May 3, 1958; children—Dolores Elizabeth, Jeffrey Martin, Linda Maria. Owner, Personal Rep. and Public Relations, Phila., 1965-68; ednl. cons. Franklin Sch. Sci. and Arts, Phila., 1968-72; pres., owner, dir. Martin Sch. of Bus., Inc., Phila., 1972—; mem. ednl. planning com. Ravenhill Acad., Phila., 1975-76. Active Phila. Mus. of Art, Phila. Drama Guild. Mem. Nat. Bus. Edn. Assn., Pa. Bus. Edn. Assn., Am. Bus. Law Assn., Pa. Sch. Counselors Assn., Am.-Italy Soc., Phila. Hist. Soc., World Affairs Council Phila., Hist. Soc. Pa. Mem. ASTA (sch. div.). Roman Catholic. Home: 2111 Locust St Philadelphia PA 19103 Office: 2417 Welsh Rd Philadelphia PA 19114

AVERY, HENRY, business development service executive; b. Boston, Oct. 6, 1919; m. Mary Ruth Halverson. SB in Chem. Engring., MIT, 1941. Bus. devel. engr. G.L. Cabot Co., Boston, 1946-51; gen. mgr., plasticizer Coal Chems., Indsl. Chems. divs. Pitts. Coke and Chem. Co., 1951-60; exec. v.p. Pitts. Chem. Co., 1960-66, also bd. dirs.; group v.p. adminstrn. and devel. USS Chem., 1966-68, v.p. plastics, 1968-76, v.p. planning and devel., 1976-79, v.p. planning, devel. and adminstrn., 1979; v.p. Koch Devel. Co., 1979-81, Koch Venture Capital, 1979-81; pres. Avery Bus. Devel. Services, Waltham, Mass., 1981—; Lectr. seminar Strategic Planning, UN Econ. Commn., Poland, 1979, Strategy Planning, Japan, 1979; civilian aide to Sec. of Army for Western Pa., 1978-86; regional advisor SBA. Editor ordnance sect. U.S. Army Mil. Ency. for 15th Army Group; editor sch. text book Organization and Functions of the Army Ordnance Department, Business Planning. Mem. Regional Export Expansion Council, U.S. Dept. Commerce; mem. steering com. Nat. Service Corps.; United Mental Health Services of Allegheny County; chmn. MIT Ednl. Council for Western Pa., Am. Wind Symphony (past v.p.), NCCJ; past elder and deacon Mt. Lebanon Presbyn. Ch. Mem. MIT Alumni Assn. (past regional v.p., bd. dirs.), Am. Def. Preparedness Assn. (past pres. Pitts. chpt., nat. vice chmn., exec. com.), Mil. Order of World Wars (commdr. 1976), Res. Officer Assn., Mayflower Descs., SAR, Greater Pitts. C. of C. (hon. life, past pres., chmn. bd. dirs.). Clubs: Duquesne, University, Tchrs. Coll. Press, Chemists, Sawgrass, MIT Faculty. Home and Office: 2506 Saint Michel Ct Ponte Vedra Beach FL 32082

AVERY, WILLIAM HERBERT, lawyer; b. Jacksonville, Fla., July 16, 1905; s. William Herbert and Annelyle (Graves) A.; m. Eugenie Petrequin, Oct. 6, 1934; children: Nancy (Mrs. H. Paul Pressler), Cameron Scott, Richard Manchester. B.S. high honors, Princeton U., 1927; J.D., Harvard U., 1930. Bar: bar 1930. Practiced in Chgo. with Cutting, Moore & Sidley (and successor firms); former partner, now counsel Sidley & Austin, 1944—; lectr. Nat. Trust Sch., 1947-64; dir. Carson, Pirie, Scott and Co., Chgo. Title and Trust Co., Equitable Life Assurance Soc. of U.S.; Mem. adv. council Ill. Dept. Public Welfare, 1948-52; pres. Kenilworth Sch. Bd., 1950-53; mem. citizens' bd. U. Chgo., Northwestern U. Assos. Past chmn. Legal Aid Bur. Chgo., Nat. Legal Aid and Defender Assn., YMCA; past pres. United Charities; trustee Council Legal Edn. for Profl. Responsibility, Sunday Evening Club, Presbyn. Home, Evanston, Ravinia Festival. Mem. Ill. Bar Assn., Chgo. Bar Assn., Internat. Bar Assn., Am. Law Inst., Chgo. Estate Planning Council. Presbyterian (elder). Clubs: Commercial (Chgo.) (past pres.), Commonwealth (Chgo.) (past pres.), Economic (Chgo.) (past pres.), Harvard Law (Chgo.) (past pres.), Law (Chgo.), Legal (Chgo.), Princeton (Chgo.) (past pres.), Tax (Chgo.) (past pres.), Mid-Day (Chgo.), University (Chgo.); Indian Hill (Winnetka, Ill). Home: 99 Indian Hill Rd Winnetka IL 60093 Office: Sidley and Austin One First Nat Plaza Chicago IL 60603

AVIDOM, MENAHEM, composer; b. Stanislau, Austria, Jan. 6, 1908; s. Isaac Izidore and Helen (Mahler) Kalkstein; m. Suzanne Ividom, Jan. 31, 1935; children: Danielle, Miriam. BA in Arts and Scis., Am. U. Beirut, 1928; student, Conservatory of Music, Paris, 1928-31. Tchr. music govt. insts. Egypt, 1932-35; lectr. Conservatory of Music, Tel Aviv, 1935-45; sec. gen. Israel Philharmonic Orch., Tel Aviv, 1945-52; dir. arts dept. Govt. of Israel, Jerusalem, 1952-55; dir. gen.copyright soc. Assn. Composers and Authors, Tel Aviv, 1955-80. Composer 10 symphonies, 7 operas, 3 string-quartets, 3 concertors, chamber, instrumental and choral music. Israel State Prize Laureate Govt. of Israel, 1961; recipient Israel Philharm. Prize, 1953, various municipality prizes, 1947-58. Mem. Internat. Inst. Arts and Letters (life), Assn. Composers and Authors (dir. for life), Israel Composers League (pres. 1958-72, hon. pres. 1982—). Home: 30 Samadar St, Ramat-Gan 52596, Israel Office: ACUM House, Rothschild Blvd 118, Tel-Aviv Israel

AVILA, JESUS, biochemist; b. Madrid, Dec. 25, 1945; s. Honorio and Felisa (De Grado) A.; m. Nieves Villanueva, 1980; 1 child, Marina. M in Chemistry, Complutense Madrid, 1967, PhD in Biochemistry, 1971. Fellow C.S.I.C., Madrid, 1968-71; postdoctoral fellow NIH, Bethesda, Md., 1972-75; mem. staff Centro de Biologia Molecular, Madrid, 1976-85; dir. Centro de Biologia Molecular, 1986—. Contbr. sci. articles to profl. publs. Mem. Internat. Union Biol. Scientists (pres. Spanish com. 1985), Am. Soc. Cell Biology. Home: 205 Principe de Vergara, 28002 Madrid Spain Office: Centro de Biologia Molecular, Universidad Autonoma F Ciencias, 28049 Cantoblanco Madrid, Spain

AVINERI, SHLOMO, Israeli political science educator; b. Bielsko, Poland, Aug. 20, 1933; came to Israel, 1939; s. Michael and Erna (Groner) A.; m. Dvora Nadler, 1957; 1 child, Maayan. M.A., Hebrew U., Jerusalem, 1960; Ph.D., London Sch. of Econs., 1961. Prof. polit. sci. Hebrew U., 1971—, dir. Eshkol Research Inst., 1971-74, dean faculty of social scis., 1974-76; dir.-gen. Ministry Fgn. Affairs, 1976-77; vis. prof. Yale U., 1966-67, Wesleyan U., Middletown, Conn., 1971-72, Research Sch. Social Scis., Australian Nat. U., 1972, Cornell U., 1973, U. Calif., 1979; fellow Wilson Ctr., Washington, 1983-84. Brit. Council scholar, 1961; recipient Maphtali prize for study of Hegel, 1977, Present Tense award for study of Zionism, 1982. Author: The Social and Political Thought of Karl Marx, 1968; Karl Marx on Colonialism and Modernization, 1968; Isreal and the Palestinians, 1971; Marx' Socialism, 1972; Hegel's Theory of the Modern State, 1973; Varieties of Marxism, 1977; The Making of Modern Zionism, 1982; Moses Hess: Prophet of Communism and Zionism, 1985. Office: Dept Polit Sci, Hebrew Univ, Jerusalem 91905, Israel Address: 50 Harlap Street, Jerusalem Israel

AVIS, PAUL DAVID LOUP, clergyman, theologian; b. Essex, Eng., July 21, 1947; s. Peter George Hobden and Diana Joan (Loup) A.; m. Susan Janet Haywood, July 11, 1970; children: Edward, Jonathan, Daniel. Student, London Bible Coll., 1967-70; BD with honors, U. London, 1970, PhD, 1976; postgrad., Wescott House Cambridge U., 1973-75. Ordained to ministry Anglican Ch., 1975. Asst. curate South Molton Group Parishes, Devon, Eng., 1975-80; vicar Stoke Canon, Devon, 1980—; cons. editor Marshall Pickering Pubs., Basingstoke, Eng., 1980—. Author: The Church in the Theology of the Reformers, 1982, Ecumenical Theology-- Truth Beyond Words, 1986, Foundations of Modern Historical Thought, 1986, The Methods of Modern Theology, 1986, Gore: Construction and Conflict, 1988; editor: Contemporary Christian Studies, History of Christian Theology, 1986—, Threshold of Theology, 1988; contbr. articles to profl.jours. Mem. Soc. for Study Theology. Office: Stoke Canon Vicarage, Exeter EX5 4AS, England

AVNER, YEHUDA, ambassador; b. Manchester, Eng., Dec. 30, 1928; m. Miriam Cailingold; 4 children. Student, London Sch. Journalism, 1950-52. Editor publs. Jewish Agy., Jerusalem, 1956-64; ministry fgn. affairs, editor polit. publs., asst. to Prime Minister Levi Eshkol, 1964-67; counsul Israel, N.Y., 1967-68; first sec., counsellor, Embassy of Israel, Washington, 1968-72; ministry Jerusalem, asst. to Prime Minister Golda Meir, 1972-74; seconded from Fgn. Ministry to Prime Minister's Bur., adviser to Prime Minister Yitzhak Rabin, 1974-77; adviser to Prime Minister Menachem Begin, 1977-83; ambassador of Israel to Ct. St. James, London, 1983—. Author: The Young Inheritors A Portrait of Israeli Youth, 1983. Office: Embassy of Israel, 2 Palace Green, Kesington, London W8 4QB, England

AVRIGIAN, HARRY CASPAR, industrial management executive; b. Phila., Nov. 23, 1921; s. Harry Toros and Nevart Avrigian; m. Bernice Bess, May 15, 1943; children: Barry, Brian, Diane. Diploma in indsl. moblzn., U.S. Staff Coll., 1961; diploma city and county planning and plan implementation, U. Mo., 1976. Machinist Nat. Def. Tng. Inst., Phila., 1938-40, Baldwin Locomotive Works, Eddystone, Pa., 1940-41; armament machinist Empire Ordnance Co., Phila., 1941-42, indsl. mgmt. cons., 1948-69; with Western States Exploration, Inc., Salt Lake City, 1972-80, chief exec. officer, chmn. bd., 1975-79; chief exec. officer, chmn. bd. Am. Fuel and Power Corp., Panama City, Fla., 1980—; cons. UN Habitat and Human Settlement Found., Nairobi, Kenya; active SCORE program SBA, 1970-72. Served with U.S. Army, 1942-45. Mem. U.S. Indsl. Council, Am. Chem. Soc., Am. Soc. Metals, Soc. Automotive Engrs. Episcopalian. Home: 147 Miramar Dr Mexico Beach FL 32410 Office: Am Fuel and Power Corp 2930 Hwy 231 Box 15189 Panama City FL 32406

AVRIL, PROSPER, government official. Pres. Haiti, Port-Au-Prince, 1988—. Office: Office of Pres, Port-Au-Prince Haiti *

AWAKESSIEN, HERBERT SIMON, oil company executive; b. Ikot Obio Asanga, Nigeria, July 27, 1957; s. Simon and Mayen (Ebong Umoh) A.; m. Eno S. Offiong, Oct. 4, 1981; 1 child, Ekemini H. B.Sc. with honors in mgmt. U. Nigeria, 1978; MBA in Mgmt., U. Pt. Harcourt, Nigeria, 1986. Asst. editor Newbreed Orgns., Lagos, 1979; pub. relations officer Ogun State Housing Corp., Abeokuta, Nigeria, 1978-79; corp. planning officer Nigerian Nat. Petroleum Corp., Lagos, 1979—; assoc. cons. Amhurst Investments, Ltd., Lagos, 1980—; exec. dir. Universal Communications, Ltd., Lagos, 1982—. Contbr. articles to profl. jours. Editor Bus. Adminstr., 1977-78. Gen. sec. Petroleum and Natural Gas Sr. Staff Assn. Nigeria, 1981-84. Recipient Disting. Service award U. Nigeria, 1978, State award Nat. Youth Service Corps, 1979; named Best Young Nigerian Mgr., Nigerian Inst. Mgmt., 1984. Fellow Salzburg sem.; mem. Nigerian Inst. Mgmt., Brit. Inst. Mgmt., Am. Mgmt. Assn., Strategic Mgmt. Assn., Nigerian Inst. Indsl. Mgmt. (assoc.), Internat. Assn. of Students in Econs. and Mgmt., Strategic Planning Soc., Inst. Sci. Bus. Lutheran, Assn. MBA Students (pres. 1984-86). Clubs: Jaycees, Internat. Airline Passengers Assn. Avocations: reading; writing; tennis; social work. Office: Nigerian Nat Petroleum Corp, Falomo Office Complex, Ikoyi, PMB 12701, Lagos Nigeria

AWALT, MARILENE KAY, educational administrator; b. Mineral Wells, Tex., Mar. 20, 1942; d. Pat O. T. and Mary Lee (Curry) Morse; m. H. Mike Awalt, Aug. 25, 1962; children—Stacy (dec.), Bradley. B.S., Tex. Wesleyan Coll., 1966; M.S. in Edn., Baylor U., 1972; Ph.D., George Peabody Coll., Vanderbilt U., 1988. Cert. tchr., prin., supr. Elem. tchr. San Antonio Pub. Schs., 1966, LaVega Pub. Schs., Waco, Tex., 1966-68; with reading clinic Baylor U., Waco, 1969-70; tchr. reading Franklin Spl. Schs. (Tenn.), 1970-71, first grade tchr., 1971-80, asst. prin., 1980-84, prin., 1984—. Mem. adv. council for tchr. cert. and edn. Tenn. State Sch. Bd., 1977-86; adminstr. career level III State of Tenn., 1987—. Tenn. spl. scholar, 1983-84. Mem. Middle Tenn. Council Internat. Reading Assn., Internat. Reading Assn., Assn. Supervision and Curriculum Devel., Tenn. Assn. Supervision and Curriculum Devel.(pres. 1986-87), Delta Kappa Gamma (pres. Rho chpt.). Baptist. Co-author Religious Christian Day Sch. Curriculum, 1978; author: Study Book for 6-8 Year Olds, 1980; chmn. for revision elem. cert. State of Tenn. Office: Franklin Elem Sch Cannon St Franklin TN 37064

AWASTHI, RAJENDRA KUMAR, political science; b. Kanpur, India, Feb. 9, 1940; s. Baboo Ram Shastri and Champa Devi Awasthi; m. Tejeshwari Dwivedi, Feb. 21, 1958; children: Pushpa, Indira, Rakesh. BA, U. Agra, India, 1959, MA, 1961; PhD, Kashi Vidyapith, Varanasi, India, 1985. Investigator Khadi and V.I. Commn., New Delhi, India, 1962-65; area organizer Khadi and V.I. Bd., Lucknow, India, 1965; asst. lectr. Regional Planning Inst., Varansai, India, 1965-70; lectr. Regional Planning Inst., Varanasi, India, 1970-72; research assoc. Gandhian Inst. Studies, Varanasi, 1972-87, research fellow, 1988—. Co-author: Gramdan and People, 1969, State Politics in India, 1986; author: Urban Development and Metropolitics in India, 1985, Governing Urban India, 1988. Mem. Indian Inst. Pub. Adminstrn., Indian Polit. Sci. Assn. Hindu. Home and Office: Gandhian Inst Studies, PO Box 1116 Rajghat, Varanasi 221 001, India

AWIRA, TIWAU, government minister; b. Nikunau, Kirabati, Jan. 20, 1941; s. Taboia and Teabike (Karuang) A.; m. Taara Ngaebi, June 19, 1965; children: Ribanataake, Etita. Diploma in Bus. Studies, U. South Pacific Fiji Sch. Sec. Thrift and Credit Soc., Fiji, 1968-69; treas. Trade Union, Fiji, 1971-72; acct. Gilbert and Ellice Islands Devel. Authority, 1974-78; minister Ministry of Fin., Kiribati, 1978-83, Ministry of Pub. Works, Kirabati, 1983—, Ministry of Home Affairs, Kirabati. Mem. Kirabati Parliamentary Assn., Royal Commonwealth Soc.

AWOONOR, KOFI NYIDEVU, educator, diplomat; b. Mar. 13, 1935; s. Kowiwo and Atsu A.; ed. U. Ghana, Univ. Coll. London, SUNY; Ph.D., married; 4 children. Research fellow Inst. African Studies; mng. dir. Film Corp.; asst. prof. comparative lit. program, prof., chmn. SUNY, Stony Brook; now chmn. dept. English, U. Cape Coast, Ghana, also dean Faculty Arts; sec.-gen. Action Congress Party, Ghana; ambassador to Brazil, 1984—; vis. prof. U. Tex., Austin, New Sch. Social Research, N.Y.C.; adj. prof. U. Fla., Gainesville; detained in Ghana for allegedly harbouring leader of coup, 1975, on trial, 1976, sentenced 1 year imprisonment, 1976, pardoned, 1976. Longmans fellow; Fairfield fellow; recipient Gurrey prize for poetry, 1979, Nat. Book Council award for poetry, 1979. Author: (poetry) Rediscovery, 1964; Messages, 1970; Night of My Blood, 1971; House by the Sea, 1978; (prose) This Earth My Brother, 1971; Guardians of the Sacred Word, 1973; Ride Me Memory, 1973; Breast of the Earth, 1974; Where Is the Mississippi Panorama, 1974; Fire in the Valley: Folktales of the Ewes, 1980; (novel) Alien corn, 1974; (poems) Until the Morning After, The Ghana Revolution. Address: Ghana Embassy, Q 110 Conj 8, Casa 2, 70466 Brasilia Brazil Address: Univ of Cape Coast, Cape Coast Ghana *

AX, EMANUEL, pianist; b. Lvov, Poland, June 8, 1949; s. Joachim and Hellen (Kurtz) A.; m. Yoko Nozaki, Nov. 23, 1974; 2 children. Student of Mieczyslaw Munz, Juilliard Sch. Music.; BA, Columbia U. Appeared as soloist Chgo., Los Angeles, Phila., Rochester, Seattle, St. Louis and London, Philharm. orchs., N.Y. Philharm., Israle Philharm., Pitts. Symphony; recitalist (with Yo-Yo Ma) Avery Fisher Hall, Carnegie Hall, N.Y.C., festival at Tanglewood, Hollywood Bowl and Ravinia; toured extensively in C.Am. and S.Am., performed in joint recital (with violinist Nathan Milstein), extensive tours, Europe, Japan; with major orchs.; also recs. Winner Arthur Rubinstein Internat. Competition 1974, Avery Fisher prize 1979; recipient Young Concert Artist's Michaels award 1975; 4 Grammy awards. Office: care ICM Artists Ltd 30 W 57th St New York NY 10019 *

AXELROD, BARRY LEON, real estate financier; b. N.Y.C., Apr. 25, 1947; s. John and Frances Virginia (Cohen) A.; m. Holly Beth Golding, July 19, 1970; children—Rebecca Elyse, Jessica Gayle. B.A., No. Mich. U., 1969; M.A., Northeastern Ill. U., 1970. Producer, dir. New Trier Twp. Instructional TV, Winnetka, Ill., 1969-71; mortgage analyst Heitman Mortgage Co., Chgo., 1971-74; loan officer B.B. Cohen & Co., Chgo., 1974-75; asst. v.p. Banco Mortgage Co., Chgo., 1975-79; v.p. Cohen Fin. Corp., Chgo., 1979-83; pres. Golding Axelrod & Co., Chgo., 1983-86; Axelrod & Co., Park Ridge, Ill., 1983. Sportcaster, football, basketball and hockey, high sch. and colls. Chgo. area, 1981—. Bd. dirs. Young Men's Jewish Council, Chgo., 1972-79, v.p. 1979; mem. Jr. Real Estate Bd. Chgo., pres. 1978. Mem. Internat. Council Shopping Ctrs., Assn. Ind. Real Estate Brokers, Aircraft Owners and Pilots Assn., No. Mich. U. Alumni Assn. (co-chmn. Chgo. chpt.), Pal-Waukee Airport Assn. (co-founder, bd. dirs.). Office: Axelrod & Co 1300 Higgins Rd Park Ridge IL 60068

AXELROD, HERBERT RICHARD, publishing executive; b. Bayonne, N.J., June 7, 1927; s. Aaron and Edith (Gurwitz) A. BS, NYU, 1949, MS, 1950, PhD, 1960; DSC (hon.), U. Guelph, Can., 1978. Cert. fisheries scientist. Pres. TFH Publs., Neptune, N.J., 1952—. Author more than 100 books dealing with fishes and music, 650 articles dealing with fishes. Served to lt. U.S. Army, 1944-47, 50-52, Korea. Mem. Am. String Tchrs. Assn. (six Man of Yr. awards). Office: TFH Publs PO Box 427 Neptune NJ 07753

AXELROD, JULIUS, biochemist, pharmacologist; b. N.Y.C., May 30, 1912; s. Isadore and Molly (Leichtling) A.; m. Sally Taub, Aug. 30, 1938; children: Paul Mark, Alfred Nathan. B.S., CCNY, 1933; M.A., NYU, 1941, D.Sc. (hon.), 1971; D.Sc. (hon.), Hahneman U., 1987; Ph.D., George Washington U., 1955, LL.D. (hon.), 1971; D.Sc. (hon.), U. Chgo., 1965, Med. Coll. Wis., 1971, U. Pa., 1986; LL.D., Coll. City N.Y., 1972; Dr.h.c., U. Panama, 1972, Ripon Coll, 1984, Tel Aviv U., 1984; Sc.D., Med. Coll. Pa., 1974; Dr. honoris causa, U. Paris (Sud), 1982. Chemist Lab. Indsl. Hygiene, 1935-46; research asso. 3d N.Y. U. research div. Goldwater Meml. Hosp., 1946-49; asso. chemist sect. chem. pharmacology Nat. Heart Inst., NIH, 1949-50, chemist, 1950-53, sr. chemist, 1953-55; acting chief sect. pharmacology Lab. Clin. Sci. NIMH, 1955, chief sect. pharmacology, 1955-84; guest worker Lab. Cell Biology NIMH, 1984—; Otto Loewi meml. lectr. N.Y. U., 1963; Karl E. Paschkis meml. lectr. Phila. Endocine Soc., 1966; NIH lectr., 1967; Nathanson meml. lectr. U. So. Calif., 1968; James Parkinson lectr. Columbia U., 1971; Wartenberg lectr. Am. Acad. Neurology, 1971; Arnold D. Welch lectr. Yale U., 1971; Harold Carpenter Hodge distinguished lectr. toxicology U. Rochester, 1971; Bennett lectr. Am. Neurol. Assn., 1971; Harvey lectr., 1971; Mayer lectr. Mass. Inst. Tech., 1971; distinguished prof. sci. George Washington U., 1972; Salmon lectr. N.Y. Acad. Medicine, 1972; Eli Lilly lectr., 1972; Mike Hogg lectr. U. Tex., 1972; Fred Schueler lectr. Tulane U., 1972; numerous other hon. lectures; vis. scholar Herbert Lehman Coll. City U. N.Y., 1973; professorial lectr. George Washington U., 1959—; panelist U.S. Bd. Civil Service Examiners, 1958-67; mem. research adv. com. United Cerebral Palsy Assn., 1966-69; mem. psychopharmacology study sect. NIMH, 1970-74; mem. Internat. Brain Research Orgn.; mem. research adv. com. Nat. Found.; vis. com. Brookhaven Nat. Lab., 1972-76; bd. overseers Jackson Lab., 1974. Mem. editorial bd. Jour. Pharmacology and Exptl. Therapeutics, 1956-72, Jour. Medicinal Chemistry, 1962-67, Circulation Research, 1963-71, Currents in Modern Biology, 1966-72; mem. editorial adv. bd. Communication in Behavioral Biology, 1967-73, Jour. Neurobiology, 1968-77, Jour. Neurochemistry, 1969-77, Jour. Neurovisceral Relation, 1969, Rassegna di Neurologia Vegetativa, 1969—, Internat. Jour. Psychobiology, 1970-75; hon. cons. editor Life Scis, 1961-69; co-author: The Pineal, 1968; contbr. papers in biochem. actions and metabolism of drugs, hormones, action of pineal gland, enzymes, neurohormone transmission to profl. jours. Recipient Meritorious Research award Assn.

Research Nervous and Mental Diseases, 1965; Gairdner award distinguished research, 1967; Nobel prize in med. physiology, 1970; Alumni Distinguished Achievement award George Washington U., 1968; Superior Service award HEW, 1968; Distinguished Service award, 1970; Claude Bernard professorship and medal U. Montreal, 1969; Distinguished Service award Modern Medicine mag., 1970; Albert Einstein award Yeshiva U., 1971; medal Rudolf Virchow Med. Soc., 1971; Myrtle Wreath award Hadassah, 1972; Leibniz medal Acad. Sci. East Germany, 1984; Salmon medal N.Y. Acad. Medicine. Fellow Am. Acad. Arts and Scis., Am. Soc. Neuropsychopharmacology; mem. German Pharmacol. Soc. (corr.), Am. Chem. Soc., Am. Soc. Pharmacology and Exptl. Therapeutics (Torald Sollmann award 1973), AAAS, Nat. Acad. Scis., Am. Neurol. Assn. (hon.), Royal Soc. London (fgn.), Inst. Medicine (sr.), Deutshe Academie Naturfoucher (East Germany) Sigma Xi, Am. Psychopathol. Assn. (hon.). Home: 10401 Grosvenor Pl Rockville MD 20852 Office: NIH Dept of Health Edn & Welfare Bldg 10 Room 2D47 Bethesda MD 20014

AXELROD, LEONARD, management consultant; b. Boston, Oct. 27, 1950; s. Morris and Doris S. Axelrod. BA, Ind. U., 1972; MPA, U. So. Calif., 1974; JD, Hamline U., 1982. Asst. dir. Ind. Jud. Ctr. Ind. U. Sch. Law, Indpls., 1974-76; cons. Booz, Allen & Hamilton, Washington, 1976-77; staff assoc. Nat. Ctr. State Cts., St. Paul, 1977-82; ptnr. Ct. Mgmt. Cons., Mpls., 1982-87, prin., 1987—; ptnr. Friedman, Farrar & Axelrod, Mpls., 1984-86; cons. Ctr. Jury Studies, Vienna, Va., 1979-82, Calif. Atty. Gen., 1972-73, Control Data Bus. Advisers, Mpls., 1982—; prin. Ct. Mgmt. Concepts, Mpls.,1987—; mem. presdl. search com. Hamline U., 1980-81. Author: North Dakota Bench Book, 1982; contbr. articles to profl. jours.; assoc. editor Law Rev. Digest, 1982. Mem. exec. bd. Am. Jewish Com., Mpls.-St. Paul, 1980; reporter Minn. Citizen Conf. on Cts., 1980. Samuel Miller scholar, 1981. Mem. ABA, Am. Soc. Pub. Adminstrn., So. Calif. Soc. Public Adminstrn., Am. Judicature Soc., Booz, Allen & Hamilton Alumni (pres. Minn. 1980), Brandeis Soc. (exec. dir. Mpls. 1980), U. So. Calif. Midwest Alumni (exec. bd. Chgo. 1974), Phi Alpha Alpha. Republican. Jewish. Home: 2051 Loop Sta Minneapolis MN 55402 Office: Court Mgmt Cons 11868 Airmail Ctr Saint Paul MN 55111

AXELROD, NORMAN N(ATHAN), opticist, physicist; b. N.Y.C., Aug. 26, 1934; s. Louis E. and Sadie (Katz) A.; A.B., Cornell U., 1954; Ph.D., U. Rochester, 1959; m. Victoria Ann Grant; children—Lauren Grant, Brian George. Aerospace scientist NASA, Goddard Space Flight Center, Washington, 1959-60; research fellow U. London, 1960-61; asst. prof. U. Del., 1961-65; mem. tech. staff Bell Labs., Murray Hill, N.J., 1965-72; prin. Axelrod Assocs., 1972—; dir. World Resources Devel. Co.; mem. adv. bd. Del. Dept. Edn., 1963-64; cons. Met. Mus. Art, N.Y.C., 1969-72; participant vis. scientist program Am. Inst. Physics, 1963-64; adviser to White House, 1969-70; cons. French Ministry Nat. Def. and War, 1971, C.R. Bard, Compuscan, CPC, Gen. Electric Co., IBM, ITT, Konishiroku, Johnson & Johnson, Perkin-Elmer, Sharp, Proctor & Gamble, RCA, Teradyne, Timken Co., Wall St. Jour. Fellow AAAS; mem. Am. Phys. Soc., Am. Optical Soc., IEEE, Machine Vision Assn. (cert. mfg. engr.), Del., N.Y. acads. sci., Electrochem. Soc., Sigma Xi, Sigma Pi Sigma, Pi Mu Epsilon. Editor: Optical Properties of Dielectric Films, 1968; book reviewer, cons. John Wiley & Sons, 1965-68, Rheinhold-Van Nostrand, 1968-70, Pergamon Press, 1969-70; contbr. articles to profl. jours. Patentee in field. Office: 445 E 86th St New York NY 10028 also: 56 W 45th St New York NY 10036

AXELSON, JOSEPH ALLEN, professional athletics executive; b. Peoria, Dec. 25, 1927; s. Joseph Victor A. and Florence (Ealen) Massey; m. Malcolm Rae Smith, Oct. 7, 1950; children: David Allen, Mark Stephen, Linda Rae. B.S., Northwestern U., 1949. Sports info. dir. Ga. So. Coll., Statesboro, 1957-60, Nat. Assn. Intercollegiate Athletics, Kansas City, Mo., 1961-62; tournament dir. Bowling Proprs. Assn. Am., Park Ridge, Ill., 1963-64; asst. exec. sec. Nat. Assn. Intercollegiate Athletics, Kansas City, Mo., 1964-68; exec. v.p., gen. mgr. Cin. Royals Profl. Basketball Team, Cin., 1969-72; mgr. Cin. Gardens, 1970-72; pres., gen. mgr. Kansas City Kings Profl. Basketball Team, Kansas City, Mo., 1972-79, 82-85; pres., gen. mgr. Sacramento Kings Profl. Basketball Team, 1985-88, exec. v.p., 1988—; pres. Arco Arena, Sacramento, 1985-88; exec. v.p. Sacramento Sports Assn., Arco Sports Complex, 1988—; v.p. ops. NBA, N.Y.C., 1979-82, chmn. competition and rules com., 1975-79; trustee Naismith Basketball Hall of Fame. Served to capt. Signal Corps. AUS, 1949-54. Named Nat. Basketball Exec. of Yr. The Sporting News, St. Louis, 1973; recipient Annual Dirs. award Downtown, Inc., Kansas City, Mo., 1979, Nat. Assn. Intercollegiate Athletics Frank Cramer nat. service award, 1983. Mem. Am. Philatelic Soc., Phi Kappa Psi. Republican. Presbyterian. Home: 2950 Pasatiempo Pl Sacramento CA 95833 also: 230 B Ave Coronado CA 92118 Office: Sacramento Kings 1515 Sports Dr Sacramento CA 95834

AXER, ERWIN, producer, educator; b. Vienna, Austria, 1917; arrived in Poland, 1920; s. Maurycy and Fryderyka (Schuster) A.; children: Jerzy, Andrzej. Diploma, States Theatrical Inst., Warsaw, 1939. Producer Teatr Kameralny, Todz, 1946-49; dir., producer Teatr Wspolczesny, Warsaw, 1946-81; prof. Theatre Acad., Warsaw, 1946-81. Contbr. essays and short stories to mags. Decorated Kainz medal, Vienna. Address: Ul Odynca 27 m II, 02-606 Warsaw Poland

AXFORD, ROY ARTHUR, nuclear engineering educator; b. Detroit, Aug. 26, 1928; s. Morgan and Charlotte (Donaldson) A.; m. Anne-Sofie Langfeldt Rasmussen, Apr. 1, 1954; children: Roy Arthur, Elizabeth Carole, Trevor Craig, Charles. B.A., Williams Coll., 1952; B.S., Mass. Inst. Tech., 1952, M.S., 1955, Sc.D., 1958. Supr. theoretical physics group Atomics Internat., Canoga Park, Calif., 1958-60; asso. prof. nuclear engring. Tex. A&M, 1960-62, prof., 1962-63; asso. prof. nuclear engring. Northwestern U., 1963-66; asso. prof. U. Ill. at Urbana, 1966-68, prof., 1968—; cons. Los Alamos Nat. Lab., 1963—. Vice-chmn. Mass. Inst. Tech. Alumni Fund Drive, 1970-72, chmn., 1973-75; sustaining fellow MIT, 1984. Recipient cert. of recognition for excellence in undergrad. teaching U. Ill., 1979, 81; Everitt award for teaching excellence, 1985. Mem. Am. Nuclear Soc., ASME, AIAA, SAR (sec.-treas. Piankeshaw chpt. 1975-81, v.p. chpt. 1982-83, pres. chpt. 1984-86), Sigma Xi., Phi Kappa Phi, Tau Beta Pi. Home: 2017 S Cottage Grove Urbana IL 61801

AYA, RODERICK HONEYMAN, tax consultant; b. Portland, Oreg., Sept. 17, 1916; s. Alfred Anthony and Grace Myrtle (Honeyman) A.; student U. Oreg., 1935-36, Internat. Accts. Soc., 1937-39, LaSalle Extension U., 1940-42, Walton Sch. Commerce, 1942, U. Calif. Extension, 1945; m. Helen Marjorie Riddle, June 16, 1945 (dec. Dec. 1983); children: Roderick Riddle, Deborah Germaine Aya Reynolds, Ronald Honeyman; m. Kathryn Rehnstrom Chatalas, June 22, 1986; stepchildren: John Todd, Paul Seth, Elizabeth Kate. Chief statistician Hotel Employers Assn., San Francisco, 1939-42; acct. Pacific Tel. & Tel. Co., San Francisco, 1942-52, spl. acct., 1952-63; tax acct., 1963-65; spl. acct. AT&T, N.Y.C., 1965-68, mgr. tax studies, 1968-73, div. mgr. tax research and planning, 1973-80; public acct., San Francisco, 1940—; music tchr., 1959—; v.p., treas., dir. Snell Research Assos., Inc., 1974-79; guest lectr. on taxes Westchester County Adult Edn. Program. Committeeman, Marin County council Boy Scouts Am., 1959-60, com. chmn., 1959-61; mem. Marin County Sheriffs' Reserve, 1963-65; law enforcement liaison com. on Juvenile Control; sec. Am. Nat. Standards Inst. Com. on Protective Headgear, 1967-80. Vice pres., treas., bd. dirs. Snell Meml. Found., 1957-80; trustee Snell Meml. Found. (U.K.), Ltd., 1972-88; mem. chmn.'s com. U.S. Senatorial Bus. Adv. Bd.; mem. Republican Presdl. Task Force; dir., past pres. Stuart Highlanders Pipe Band of San Francisco. Recipient Wisdom award of honor Wisdom Soc., 1970; Pres.'s Medal of Merit, 1981. Mem. ASTM, Nat. Soc. Pub. Accts., St. Andrews Soc., Telephone Pioneers Am., Soc. for Ethnomusicology (contbr. to jour.), U.S. Naval Inst., Phi Chi, Sigma Nu. Clubs: Corinthian Yacht (Tiburon, Calif.); Astoria Golf & Country; Sports Car of Am. (San Francisco region treas. 1957-58, dir. 1957-59); U.S. Yacht Racing Union. Author: The Legacy of Pete Snell, 1965; Determination of Corporate Earnings and Profits for Federal Income Tax Purposes, 2 vols., 1966. Home: PO Box 668 Seaside OR 97138

AYAD, JOSEPH MAGDY, psychologist; b. Cairo, Egypt, May 21, 1926; s. Fahim Gayed and Victoria Gabour (El-Masri) A.; came to U.S., 1949, naturalized, 1961; B.A. in Social Scis., Am. U., Cairo, 1946; M.A. in Clin. Psychology (Univ. scholar), Stanford U., 1952; Ph.D. in Clin. Psychology (Univ. scholar), U. Denver, 1956; m. Widad Fareed Bishai, May 29, 1954; children—Fareed Merritt, Victor Maher, Michael Joseph, Mona Elaine. Lectr., Fitzsimmons Army Hosp., Denver, 1953-54; staff psychologist Cons. Psychol. Services, Denver, 1954-55; psychologist, Denver, 1956-57, High Plains Neurol. Center, Amarillo, Tex., 1957—. Pres. JMA Cattle Co., Amarillo, 1973—; v.p., treas. Filigon Inc., Amarillo, 1962-75, pres., 1976—; cons. psychologist Tex. Dept. Pub. Welfare. Mem. profl. adv. bd. Amarillo Mental Health Assn., 1968-69. Mem. Amarillo Child Welfare Bd., 1961-63; area chmn. U. Denver Fund Raising Campaign, 1963; mem. profl. adv. bd. St. Paul's Meth. Ch. Sch. for Children with Learning Disabilities, Amarillo, 1969-70. Recipient Grad. Sr. award in Philosophy Am. U. at Cairo, 1946. Mem. Am. Psychol. Assn., Internat. Assn. Applied Psychology, Am. Assn. Marriage and Family Counselors, Am. Nat. Cattlemen's Assn., Potter-Randall County (Tex.) Psychol. Soc. (pres. 1974). Presbyn. Club: Amarillo Country. Contbr. articles to profl. jours. Home: 4239 Erik St Amarillo TX 79106 Office: 2301 W 7th St Amarillo TX 79106

AYBAR, JOSE IGNACIO, steel company executive; b. La Felguera, Spain, May 26, 1947; s. Manuel and Maria Pilar (Martin) A.; m. Trinidad-Gonzalez Aybar, June 28, 1975; children: Jose Ignacio, Marta. Pr. Bachelor, St. Peter's Coll., 1962; Sup. Bachelor, St. Thomas Coll., 1964; student, Oviedo U., Spain, 1965; Dr. Engring., Oviedo U., 1980. With Ensidesa, Gijon, Spain, 1975-77; B.O.F.'s asst. Ensidesa, Gijon, 1977-80, steel plant metallurgist, 1980-83, metal mgr., 1983—; cons. Aenor, Madrid, 1980—. Mem. Superior Council Sci. Research.

AYENI, PETER MODUPE, journalist, Nigerian government official; b. Evbiamen, Bendel, Nigeria, Dec. 8, 1925; s. Ayeni Okpeku Uanreroro and Aleke Azegberemi Esechie; student United Coll. Warri, Nigeria, 1943-46; diploma in audio-visual communication Ind. U., 1961; m. Flora Oseken Ohenrein, Dec. 29, 1956; children: Imonitie, Okpeifo, Airaoa, Eromose, Uenesen, Ehimiaghe, Egbeziemi, Obokhai. Asst. editor So. Nigeria Defender, Ibadan, 1949-53; publicity officer Nigerian govt., Ibadan, 1954-61; editor Western News, Western State, Ibadan, 1962-63; sr. info. officer Midwest, Benin, Nigeria, 1963-65; pub. relations adviser to mil. gov. of Bendel State, Benin, 1966-69; prin. info. officer Ministry of Info., Benin, 1969-73; chief info. officer Bendel State (Nigeria), Benin, 1974-84; apptd. permanent sec. Bendel Pub. service Bds., 1983; pres. Customary Ct. of Justice, 1984—. chmn. bd. govs. Evbiamen Girls Grammar Sch., 1986. UNESCO fellow, East Africa, 1962. Honored with traditional beads by Oba of Benin, Omo N'Oba Erediauwa, 1979. Mem. Nigerian Inst. Pub. Relations (asso.), Nigerian Inst. Journalism, Nigerian Union Journalists (pres. 1970-72), Irish Soc. Arts (cert. in bookkeeping), London C. of C. (cert. in English). Anglican Clubs: Press, Masons. Author: (pamphlet) 100 Nigerian Sayings, 1966; Festivals of Bendel State, 1975; (with Ojé Ojéhomon) Midwest At A Glance, 1971; Folklore of Nigeria, 1978. Home: No 2, 2d West Circular, Benin City Nigeria Office: Sabongidda Dist Customary Ct, Ora, Owan Local Govt Area, PO Box 1431, Benin City Bendel State, Nigeria

AYER, SIR ALFRED JULES, philosopher, educator, writer; b. Oct. 29, 1910; s. Jules Louis Cyprien A.; m. Grace Isabel Renee Lees, 1932; 2 children; m. Alberta Constance Chapman (Dee Wells), 1960 (div. 1983); 1 child; m. Vanessa Mary Addison Lawson Salmon. Scholar, Eton Coll.; scholar with honors 1st class in Lit. Hum., Christ Church Oxford, 1932, M.A., 1936; Dr. hon., U. Brussels, 1962; D.Litt. hon., East Anglia, 1972, U. Trent, London U., Durham U.; DHL hon., Bard Coll., 1983. Lectr. in philosophy Christ Church, 1932-35, research student, 1935-44; fellow Wadham Coll., Oxford, Eng., 1944-46, hon. fellow, 1957, dean, 1945-46; Grote prof. philosophy of mind and logic U. London, 1946-59, dean arts faculty, 1950-52; Wykeham prof. logic U. Oxford, 1959-78; fellow New Coll., U. Oxford, 1959-78, hon. fellow, 1980; fellow Wolfson Coll., 1978-83; hon. fellow Coll. U. London, 1979; vis. prof. NYU, 1948-49, CCNY, 1961-62, Surrey U., 1978, Bard Coll, 1986—; Montgomery fellow Dartmouth Coll., 1982-83. Editor: The Humanist Outlook, 1968; author: Metaphysics and Common Sense, 1969, Russell and Moore: The Analytical Heritage, 1971, Probability and Evidence, 1972, Russell, 1972, Bertrand Russell as a Philosopher, 1973 (Brit. Acad. lectr.), The Central Questions of Philosophy, 1974, Part of My Life, 1977, Perception and Identity, 1979 (Festschrift reply to critics), Hume, 1980, Philosophy in the Twentieth Century, 1982, Freedom and Morality, 1984, More of My Life, 1984, Wittgenstein, 1985, Voltaire, 1986, Thomas Paine, 1988; contbr. articles to profl. jours.; lectr.: William James, Harvard U., 1970, John Dewey, Columbia U., 1970, Gifford, St. Andrews, 1972-73; author: Language, Truth and Logic, 1936, 1946, The Foundations of Empirical Knowledge, 1940, Thinking and Meaning, 1947 (Inagural lectr.); editor: (with Raymond Winch) British Empirical Philosophers, 1952; author: Philosophical Essays, 1954, The Problem of Knowledge, 1956; editor: Logical Positivism, 1959; author: Privacy, 1960 (Brit. Acad. lectr.), The Concept of a Person and Other Essays, 1963, Man As a Subject for Science, 1964 (Auguste Comte lectr.), The Origins of Pragmatism, 1968. Mem. Central Advisory Council for Edn., 1963-66; pres. ind. Adoption Soc., 1965—. Served in Welsh Guards, 1940-45; served to capt. Welsh Guards, 1940-45, Attache at HM Embassy, Paris 1945. Decorated Chevalier de la Legion d'Honneur, 1977; decorated Order of Cyril and Methodius, 1st class Bulgaria, 1977. Mem. Humanist Assn. (pres.), Modern Lang. Assn., Internat. Inst. Philosophy (chmn. Booker Prize Com. 1978), Am. Acad. Arts and Scis. (hon.), Royal Danish Acad. Scis. and Letters (fgn. mem.). Office: 51 York St, London W1H 1PU, England also: British Acad, 20-21 Cornwall Terrace, London NW1 4QP, England

AYERS, HARRY BRANDT, editor, publisher, columnist; b. Anniston, Ala., Apr. 8, 1935; b. Harry Mell and Edel Olga (Ytterboe) A.; m. Josephine Ehringhaus, Dec. 10, 1961; 1 dau., Margaret. B.A. in History, U. Ala.-Tuscaloosa, 1959. Polit. writer The Raleigh Times (N.C.), 1959-61; Washington corr. Bascom Timmons Bur., Washington, 1961-63; mng. editor The Anniston Star (Ala.), 1963-69, editor, pub., 1969—; dir. Nat. News Council, N.Y.C., 1981-84. Trustee, Talladega Coll. (Ala.), 1972—, 20th Century Fund, 1985—, Ctr. for Excellence in Govt., 1985—; bd. dirs. So. Ctr. for Internat. Studies, Atlanta, 1979—, Bd. Fgn. Scholarships, Washington, 1981-84; mem. Council Fgn. Relations, N.Y.C., 1983—. Named Disting. Journalism Grad., U. Ala., 1967; recipient Human Relations award Am. Jewish Com., 1977; Green Eyeshade award Sigma Delta Chi, 1985. Fellow Nieman Found. Harvard U., 1968; trustee Am. Com., Internat. Press Inst., London, 1985—; mem. Ala. Press Journalism Found. (founding pres. 1969), Am. Soc. Newspaper Editors, So. Newspaper Pubs. Assn. (dir. 1981-84). Democrat. Episcopalian. Clubs: Metropolitan (Washington), Relay House (Birmingham, Ala.). Mem. adv. bd. Inside Story, Pub. Broadcasting System, N.Y.C., 1981-85; co-editor: You Can't Eat Magnolias, 1972; co-author: A Bicentennial Portrait of the American People, 1975, U.S. News Books, 1976, 1977 Inaugural Book President Carter, 1977, Dixie Dateline, 1983; frequent contbr. to "International Herald-Tribune". Home: 1 Booger Hollow Anniston AL 36201 Office: Anniston Star 216 W 10th St Anniston AL 36201

AYILIATH CHANDROTH, KUTTY KRISHNAN, economics educator; b. Cannanore, India, June 10, 1950; s. Kandoth kunhi Krishnan and Ayiliath Chadroth Devaki Amma; m. Kallorath Suchetha Kumari, Dec. 21, 1981; children: Keerthi, Sudev, Divya. BA, U. Calicut, 1972, MA, 1974; PhD, U. Mysore, 1987. Research fellow Inst. Social and Econ. Change, Bangalore, India, 1975-78; lectr. P.D. Lions Coll., Bombay, 1980; economist City and Indsl. Devel. Corp. Maharashtra, Bombay, 1981-83; lectr. U. Calicut, India, 1984—. Contbr. articles to profl. jours. Mem. Indian Econ. Soc., Indian Soc. Agrl. Econs. Home: Madathil House, Chala West Cannonore, Kerala 670007, India Office: U Calicut, Aranattukara, PO Trichur, Kerala 680618, India

AYISI, ERIC OKYERE, social anthropologist, educator; b. Mampong Akwapin, Ghana, Sept. 22, 1926; citizen of U.K.; came to U.S., 1974; s. Kofi and Mercy (Adebra) A.; B.Sc. in Sociol. and Anthropology, U. London, 1961, B.A. in Subs. Econs., 1960, Ph.D. in Social Change, 1965; m. Dorothy Evelyn Nayler, July 31, 1957; children—Kathleen Judith, Ruth Margaret Doddrell. Headmaster, Meth. Elem. Sch., Ghana, 1940-43; preacher Meth. Catechist, Ghana, 1943-45, Lagos, Nigeria, 1945-50; mem. faculty U. Ghana, 1965-74; Fulbright prof., curriculum cons. Ramapo, Mahwah, N.J., also Bloomfield (N.J.) Coll., 1972-73; disting. Fulbright lectr. humanities Dillard U., New Orleans, 1973-74; prof. religion and philosophy Fisk U., Nashville, 1973-74; vis. prof. Hampton (Va.) Inst. 1974-78; lectr. Christopher Newport Coll., Newport News, Va., 1979-81; vis. assoc. prof. anthropology Coll. William and Mary, Williamsburg, Va., 1980—, also asst. to provost; guest lectr. various colls., univs. Commr. of inquiry Nat. Liberation Council, Govt. Ghana, 1966-68; mem. nat. adv. com. Workers Brigade Ghana, 1966-72; mem. Ghana Meth. Conf., 1965—. NEH fellow, summer 1980. Mem. Ghana Sociol. Assn., Brit. Sociol. Assn., Internat. African Inst., U.K. African Studies Assn., Royal Anthrop. Inst., Internat. Polit. Sci. Assn., Current Anthropology (assoc.), Am. Acad. Polit. and Social Sci., Polit. Platform Assn. Author: An Introduction to the Study of African Culture, 3d edit., 1980; The Political Institutions of Akwapims, 1972; Kinship and Local Community of the Akwapims, 1972; also articles; research in African politics, Caribbean Basin. Home: Brookside Haven 1 Sparrow Ct Williamsburg VA 23185 Office: Anthropology Dept Coll William and Mary Williamsburg VA 23185

AYLMER, GERALD EDWARD, historian, educator; b. near Ludlow, Shropshire, Eng., Apr. 30, 1926; s. Edward and Gladwys Phoebe (Evans) A.; m. Ursula Adelaide Nixon, Aug. 6, 1955; children: Thomas Bartholomew, Emma Clare. BA in Modern History with honors, U. Oxford, 1950, DPhil, 1955. Asst. lectr. dept. history U. Manchester, Eng., 1954-57, lectr., 1957-62; prof. head dept. history U. York, Eng., 1963-78; master St. Peter's Coll. U. Oxford, Eng., 1978—; vis. mem. Inst. Advanced Study, Princeton U., N.J., 1975. Author: The King' Servants, 1961, 2d edit., 1974, The Struggle for the Constitution, 1963, 2d edit., 1975, A Short History of 17th Century England, 1963, 2d edit. 1975, The State's Servants, 1973; contbr. articles to profl. jours. Served with Royal Navy, 1944-47. Fellow Brit. Acad.; mem. Royal Hist. Soc. (pres. 1984-88). Home: Canal House, St Peter's Coll, Oxford OX1 2DL, England Office: St Peter's Coll, Oxford OX1 2DL, England

AYLOUSH, CYNTHIA MARIE, personnel director, corporate treasurer; b. Jackson, Mich., July 2, 1950; d. Leonard Edward and Violet Caroline (Kroeger) Ullrich; m. Abbott Selim Ayloush, June 21, 1980; children: Sasha Christine, Nadia Marie. AA, Fullerton Coll., 1970; diploma in fashion mdse., Brooks Coll., 1975; BS, Pepperdine U., 1980. Receptionist, Hydraflow, Commerce, Calif., 1968-74, personnel mgr., Cerritos, Calif., 1979—, treas., 1979—, corp. sec., 1985—; with sales dept. Robinson's, Cerritos, Calif., 1974-75, dept. mgr., 1975-79. Mem. Am. Soc. Personnel Adminstrs., Personnel Indsl. Relations Assn., Merchants and Mfrs. Assn., Cerritos C. of C. (dir. 1983—). Republican. Roman Catholic. Clubs: Soroptimist (sec. 1979—), Century, Pepperdine Univ. Office: Hydraflow 13259 E 166th St Cerritos CA 90701

AYLWARD, JAMES FREDRIC, marketing professional; b. Toronto, Ont., Can., Jan. 23, 1951; s. James Marsh and Shirley Jane (Chaytor) A. Diploma in Bus., Ryerson Poly. Inst. U., Toronto, 1972; BBA, Ryerson Poly. U., Toronto, 1975; MBA, U. Western Ont., London, 1977. Adminstrn. mgr. Bank Montreal, Toronto, 1972-74, account mgr., 1974-75; mgr. logistics BF Goodrich Can., Inc., Kitchener, Ont., 1977-81, dir. mktg., 1979-82; v.p. mktg. Epton Industries, Inc., Kitchener, 1983—; adj. lectr. Wilfrid Laurier U., Waterloo, Ont., 1982. Mem. Can. Inst. Mines, Western Bus. Sch. Club (pres. 1985-86). Home: 75 John St E, Waterloo, ON Canada N2J 1G2 Office: Epton Industries Inc, 521 King St W, Kitchener, ON Canada C5N 2G1

AYOUB, MAHMOUD AMIN, industrial engineering educator; b. Cairo, Jan. 1, 1942; s. Amin E. and Fardous (Said) A.; m. Amira Deif, Jan. 26, 1967; children—Shahinaz, Nader. B.S., Cairo U., 1964; M.S., Tex. Tech. U., 1969, Ph.D., 1971. Asst. prof. indsl. engring. N.C. State U.-Raleigh, 1971-73, assoc. prof., 1973-79, prof., 1979—; cons. govt. and industry. Contbr. over 200 articles to profl. jours. Named Outstanding Tchr., N.C. State U., 1987, Outstanding Faculty, 1985. Mem. Human Factors Soc., Ergonomics Research Soc., Inst. Indsl. Engrs. (Phil Carrol award 1980, Dr. David Baker disting. research award 1987, fellow 1988). Muslim. Office: NC State U Dept Indsl Engring PO Box 7906 Raleigh NC 27695

AYRES, JONATHAN GEOFFREY, respiratory physician; b. Potters Barr, Hertfordshire, Eng., Feb. 14, 1950. BSc, London U., 1971; MBBS, Guys Hosp., 1974; MD, U. London, 1984. Tng. Guys Hosp., Brompton Hosp., East Birmingham Hosp.; respiratory physician dept. chest medicine East Birmingham Hosp, Birmingham, West Midlands, Eng. Contbr. papers to profl. publs. Mem. Brit. Thoracic Soc. (sec. epidemiology sect.), Royal Coll. Physicians, Internat. Epidemological Assn., The Brit. Soc. Allergy and Clin. Immunology, Am. Thoracic. Office: East Birmingham Hosp, Dept Respiratory Medicine, Bordesley Green E, Birmingham B9 England

AYTON, PETER JOHN, psychologist, lecturer; b. Bristol, Eng., May 22, 1956; s. Robert and Dorothy (Gillibrand) A. BS in Psychology with honors, N.E. London Poly., 1977; postgrad., U. London, 1977-80; PhD in Psychology, Univ. Coll., London, 1988. Tutor, lectr. Royal Free Hosp., Cen. Sch. Speech and Drama, Middlesex Poly. U., The Am. Coll. London, London, 1980-83; research assoc. decision analysis group City of London Poly., 1983-85, lectr. psychology dept., 1985-86, sr. lectr., 1986—; cons. Sound Thinking Ltd., London, 1986-87. Editor, contbr.: Judgmental Forecasting, 1987; contbr. articles to profl. jours. Club: Lancaster (London) Palace Football. Office: City London Poly Psychology Dept, Old Castle St, London E1 7NT, England

AZAD, ASHFAQUE, construction equipment company executive; b. Calcutta, India, Jan. 1, 1944; s. Khawja Mohd and Begum Dolly Azad; m. Wasima Khan, Jan. 1, 1970; children: Ayla, Anika. Cert. in mech. engring., Coll. Tech., Lincoln, Eng., 1966. Engr. sales and service Greaves Cotton & Co., Ltd., Dacca, Bangladesh, 1966-68; br. mgr. Paktrack, Bangladesh, 1968-72; asst. sales mgr. Mohamed Abdulrahman Al-Bahar, Dubai, United Arab Emirates, 1972-73; br. and sales mgr. Doha, Qatar, 1973-75, Abu Dhabi, United Arab Emirates, 1975-76, Dubai and Sharjah, United Arab Emirates, 1977-85; area mgr. United Arab Emirates, 1985—. Mem. Am. Soc. Mech. Engrs. Offfice: MAR Al-Bahar, PO Box 6038, Sharjah United Arab Emirates

AZAD, KHALIL ASHRAF, marketing professional; b. Patna, Bihar, India, Mar. 16, 1939; s. Nasimuddin and Sabra (Khatoon) A.; m. Ishrat Jamal, Jan. 29, 1968; children: Itrat, Wequas. BSc, Aligarm Muslim U., India, 1959. Correspondent sales Walmore Electronics Ltd., London, 1965-72; engr. internal sales Impectron Ltd., London, 1972-77; sr. sales engr. Impectron Ltd., London and Horsham, Eng., 1977-83; mgr. sales and mktg. Impectron Ltd., Horsham, 1983—; dir. Bishopcross Ltd., Horsham, 1986—, Barlec Richfield Ltd., Horsham 1986—. Office: Impectron Ltd, Foundry Ln, Horsham England RH13 5PX

AZAM, MOHD ZAKI, banker, economic administrator; b. Rawalpindi, Pakistan, Dec. 30, 1931; s. S. Sharafat Hussain and Bibi Tasliman; m. Nasera Begum, July 30, 1954; children—Naqi, Nadra T., Shafi, Shahida J.T. B.A. in Econs. with distinction, Patna U., 1951; M.A. in Econs., Dacca U., 1953; diploma in econs. Oxford U., 1958. With civil service, Govt. Pakistan, 1954-67; fin. advisor, dep. sec. Econ. Ministry, 1967-86; dir. irrigation and rural devel. dept., 1986, sr. project economist, mgr., dep. dir. Asian Devel. Bank, Manila, 1987, dir. agr. 1987—. Contbr. numerous articles to profl. jours. Active numerous charitable orgns. in Pakistan, Bangladesh, Philippines. Recipient Likas Yaman award for services to Philippine environment and ecology. Avocations: bridge; swimming, chess. Home: House No 1 Street No 34, Sector F-8/1, Islamabad Pakistan

AZCONA HOYO, JOSÉ SIMON, president of Republic of Honduras; b. La Ceiba, Atlantida, Honduras, Jan. 26, 1927; s. José Simón Azcona Velez and Carmen Hoyo Pérez; m. Miriam Bocock Selva; children: Miriam Elizabeth, José Simón, Javier Enrique. Degree in Civil Engring., Universidad Nacional Autónoma de Honduras, Tegucigalpa, 1963. Photogrammetrist, draftsman Instuto Geográfico Nacional, Tegucigalpa; head design sect., 1961-63; rd. bldg. supr. Dirección Central Gaminos, 1964; distbn. asst. div. del norts Empresa Nacional de Energía Eléctrica, San Pedro Sula, Cortés, 1964-66; design engr., factory bldg. engr. Industria Aceitera Hondueña, San Lorenzo, Valle, 1966-67; urbanization and housing bldg. project supr. El Sauce, La Ceiba, 1967-68; head tech. dept. Federación Hondurena de Cooperativas de Vivienda Limitada, Tegucigalpa, 1969-72, gen. mgr., 1973-82; minister of communications, pub. works and transp., Republic of

Honduras, Tegucigalpa, 1982-83; pres. Republic of Honduras, 1986—. Mem. Liberal Party Action Front, Tegucigalpa, 1962, 63, 64; candidate for congress, Francisco Morazám, 1963; coordinator Liberal Party Engrs. Ridista Faction, 1973-74, orgn. and publicity sec. of central directory, 1975-76; polit. tng. sec. Liberal Party Exec. Central Council, 1977-78, orgn. and publicity sec., 1979-80; pres. exec. council Liberal Party, 1983; mem. congress for Francisco Morazán, 1982-85. Office: Office of Pres, Tegucigalpa Honduras *

AZEREDO PERDIGÃO, MARIA MADALENA BAGÃO DA SILVA BISCAIA, foundation director; b. Figueira da Foz, Coimbra, Portugal, Apr. 28, 1923; d. Severo da Silva Biscaia and Lidia Maria Bagão da Silva Biscaia; m. Joã o José Lopes Farinha, Sept. 17, 1944 (dec. Oct. 19, 1957); m. 2d Jose de Azeredo Perdigão, Nov. 6, 1960; 1 son, Pedro Paulo Biscaia de Azeredo Perdigão. License in Math., U. Coimbra (Portugal), 1944; superior course of piano Nat. Conservatory, Lisbon, Portugal, 1948. Tchr. math., high schs., Coimbra, 1944-47; pianist, lectr., Coimbra and Lisbon, 1948-54; lectr. Portuguese Nat. Radio, Coimbra, 1954-57; head, music dept. Calouste Gulbenkian, Lisbon, 1958-74; dir. Cabinet for Artistic Edn., Ministry of Edn., Lisbon, 1978-84; dir. artistic creation and animation dept. Modern Art Ctr. Calouste Gulbenkian Found., 1984—; pres. Internat. Music Festival, Ministry of Culture, Lisbon, 1983. Pres., bd. dirs. Portuguese sect. Internat. Soc. Music Edn., 1977. Recipient Commendam of Santiago da Espada Pres. Republic of Portugal, 1963, Commendam of Infante, 1983; Commendam d'Honneur France, 1981; Commendam of Afonso X oSábio Spain, 1975; various other awards from Italy, 1970, Germany, 1974, Brazil, 1973. Roman Catholic. Author: (with others) Sistema de ensino em Portugal, 1981. Contbr. articles to profl. publs., Bull. of Portuguese sect. Internat. Soc. Music Edn. Home: R Marquês da Fronteira 8-2, 1000 Lisbon Portugal Office: Calouste Gulberkian Found, 1093 Lisbon Codex Portugal

AZFAR, KAMAL UDDIN, lawyer, politician, author; b. Mogulserai, India, Mar. 1, 1938; s. Muhammad and Zubaida (Ishaq) A.; m. Naheed Kamal, March 25, 1967; children: Omar Najmuddin, Sarah Fatima, Fariduddin Mohammad. BA with honors, Govt. Coll., Lahore, Punjab Pakistan, 1957; MA, Balliol Coll., Oxford U., Eng., 1960. Barrister-at-law InnerTemple, London, 1963; advocate High Ct. Sind, Karachi, 1963—, Supreme Ct. Pakistan, Islamabad, 1968—. Research asst. Prof. Gunnar Myrdal, Stockholm, 1960-63; practice law Karachi, Pakistan, 1963—; TV compere Pakistan TV, Karachi, 1968-70; standing counsel Orr Dignam & Co., Karachi, 1988—. Author: Chinese Synthesis, 1975, Pakistan Odyssey, 1976, Pakistan: Political and Constitutional Dilemmas, 1987. Minister Fin., Planning and Devel., Sind, 1972-73; leader devel. del. to People's Republic China, 1974; mem. Senate of Pakistan, 1975-77; sec. cen. com. Nat. Peoples Party, 1986—, del. internat. conf. ruling parties of Iran and Romania, 1975; personal rep. of prime minister to meeting of heads of govt. Club of Rome, Austria, 1975; rep. Pakistan at Harvard Internat. Seminar, 1969. Mem. High Ct. Bar Assn. Sind, Convocation of Oxford U. Moslem. Clubs: Oxford/Cambridge (London); Sind (Karachi). Home: 31 F Kahkashan, Clifton, Karachi Pakistan Office: Kashif Ctr 8th Fl, Sharea Faisal, Karachi Pakistan

AZIZ, TARIQ MIKHAYL, minister of foreign affairs of Iraq; b. Mosul, Iraq, 1936. Student Coll. of Arts, Baghdad U. Mem. of staff Al'Jumhuriyah, 1958; chief editor Al'Jamahiir, 1963; with Baath press, Syria; chief editor Al-Thawra Pub. House; mem. Revolutionary Command Council Gen. Affairs Bur., 1972; res. mem. Arab Baath Socialist Party Leadership, 1974-77; elected mem. Baath Regional Leadership, 1977; dep. prime minister, 1981—; minister of fgn. affairs, 1983—. Address: Ministry of Fgn Affairs, Baghdad Iraq *

AZIZ, UNGKU ABDUL, university adminstrator; b. London, Jan. 28, 1922; m. Sharifah Azah Bt Syed Muhd Alsagof; 1 dau., Zeti Akhtar. Diploma in Arts, Class II, Raffles Coll., Singapore, 1947; B.A. with honors, U. Malaya, Singapore, 1951; D. Econs., Waseda U., Tokyo, 1964, D. Jw, 1982. Lectr. econs. U. Malaya, Singapore, after 1952, head dept. econs. faculty arts, Kuala Lumpur, after 1961, dean faculty econs. and adminstrn., after 1965, vice chancellor, royal prof. econs., 1968—; mem. UN Univ. Council, 1980-86; mem. internat. adv. council U. Coll. at Buckingham (Eng.), 1976—; mem. Sci. Comm. Internat. Council Research in Coop. Devel.; mem. joint adv. com. FAO/UNESCO/ILO; mem. adv. group Research Register Studies on Coops. in Developing Countries and Selected Biography; mem. editorial adv. bd. Asia Pacific Community, 1978—; chmn. Malaysian Exams. Council, 1980-86; chmn. Malaysian Nat. Council, Assn. Southeast Asian Instns. Higher Learning, 1978—; mem. Malaysian Rubber Research and Devel. Bd., 1970—; pres. Nat. Coop. Movement Malaysia, 1971—; dir. Malaysian Coop. Bank, 1983-84; mem. Commn. Joint UNESCO-IAU Research Programme in Higher Edn.; mem. supervisory council Majlis Penyeliaan Bernama, 1983-86. Editor, chmn. editorial bd. Kajian Ekonomi Malaysia. Bd. dirs. Armed Forces Defence Coll., 1983-86. Recipient Malaysian award Tun Abdul Razak Founds. awards, 1978; award Japan Found., 1981; World Acad. Arts and Sci. fellow, 1965. Mem. Internat. Assn. Agrl. Econs., Econ. Assn. Malaysia. Home: No 12 Lonong 16/9A, Petaling Jaya, Selangor Malaysia Office: Univ of Malaya, Office of the Vice Chancellor, Kuala Lumpur 22-11 Malaysia *

AZIZ-BEYLI, AHMED BEHZAT, architect, government official; b. Nicosia, Cyprus, Aug. 27, 1935; s. Ahmed and Fatima (Muftu Zyaeddin) A.B.; m. Sözen Ertugrul; children: Fatima, Zehra. BA, Istanbul U., Turkey, 1958, BA in Arch., 1959, MSc in Arch, 1959; diploma in town planning, U. Coll., London, 1965; Cert. Archtl. Conservation, York U., Eng., 1976; postgrad., Docsiadis, Athens, 1971, York U., 1976, Bassel U., Switzerland, 1979. Chartered architect, cons. town planner. Architect Alister MacDonald & Ptnrs., London, 1960-62; site architect H. Loeberman Architects, Nurenberg, Fed. Republic Germany, 1962-63, Howard V. Lobb Co. BB & Ptnrs. Architects, London, 1963-65; architect, town planner London Borough of Haringay, 1965-68, London Borough of Hillingdon, 1968-71; dep. mayor Nicosia Municipality, Cyprus, 1976-81; ptnr. E. Reshad & Assocs., Nicosia, 1971-74; dep. v.p., liaison officer with UN and Red Cross Nicosia, 1974-75, part-time dep. v.p., liaison with UN and Red Cross, 1975—; bd. dirs. Beyli & Assocs. Architects and Town Planners, Nicosia, 1975—; dep. dir. Red Crescent Internat., Nicosia, 1974—; council mem. Evbaf-Turkish Turst, Nicosia, 1981—; cons. Turkish Bank Ltd., Nicosia, 1975—. Author: Town Planning, 1965 (honors 1966). Served to lt. Cyprus Mil., 1971-73. Mem. Royal Inst. Brit. Architects, Royal Inst. Town Planning, Turkish Architects Assn. (25 yr. award), Cyprus Architect Council. Club: Tennis (Cyprus); Tennis (Istanbul). Lodge: Rotary (chmn. Kyninia). Home: 40 Miujti Ziyai Eff St, Nicosia Cyprus Office: Red Crescent, Nicosia Cyprus

AZKOUL, KARIM, retired diplomat, philosophy educator, researcher; b. Rashaya, Lebanon, July 15, 1915; s. Nageeb Azkoul and Latifeh Assaly; m. Eva Corey, Sept. 3, 1948; children—Jihad, Randa. Ed., Inst. Oriental Studies, Jesuit U., Beirut, 1933-34, La Sorbonne, Paris, 1936-37, Inst. for Foreigners, Berlin U., 1934, U. Berlin, 1934-35, U. Bonn. 1935-36; Ph.D., U. Munich, 1938. Tchr. philosophy, history, Arabic Lit., French Lit., French, Arabic transl. College de la Sagasse, 1932-33, 1938-39, College des Dames de Nazareth, 1933-34, College Makassad, 1939-49, College Universel of Aley, 1940-41, 1945-46; prof. philosophy and Humanities Beirut U. Coll., 1968-72; prof. philosophy Lebanesee U., 1970-72; head of Office of Lebanese Dels. to UN in N.Y.C., 1947-49; charge d'Affaires of Lebanese Permanent Mission to U.N. in N.Y.C., 1950-54; dir. Dept. Internat. Affairs and Confs. and Treaties in Ministry of Fgn. Affairs, Beirut, 1954-57; chief permanent rep of Lebanon to UN in N.Y.C., 1957-59; consul-gen. to Australia and N.Z., 1959-61; ambassador to Ghana, Guinea, Mali, 1961-64, Iran, Afghanistan, 1965-66; vice chmn. Human Rights Com., 1958, Com. for Freedom of Info. and Press, 1957. Author: Reason in Islam, 1946; Al-Hurriyat, 1956; numerous other publs.; editor-in-chief Arabic Ency., Joy of Knowledge, 1981. Decorated Order of Cedar (Lebanon); Order of Holy Sepulchre (Jerusalem); Order of St. Marc (Egypt); Order of Brilliant Star (Republic of China); Order of So. Cross (Brazil); Order of St. Peter and Paul (Damascus). Home: 6 Rue Rene Blanc, 74100 Annamasse France

AZLAN MUHIBBUDDIN SHAH YUSSUFF IZZUDDIN SULTAN SHAH IBNI AL-MARHUM, His Royal Highness Sultan of Perak, deputy Head of State; b. Batu Gajah, Perak, Malaysia, Apr. 15, 1928; s. Sultan Yussuff Izzuddin Shah; m. Tuanku Bainum binti Hohd, 1955; children: Raja Nazrin, Raja Azureen, Raja Ashman, Raja Eleen, Raja Yong Sofia. Student, Malay Coll., Nottingham U. and Lincoln Inn.; DLitt (hon.), U. Malaya, 1979, U. Sains Malaysia, 1980. Bar: Eng. 1954. Asst. sec. state Perak, 1954-55, magistrate, 1955-56, session camp resident, 1957-59, fed. counsel and Dy pub. prosecutory, 1959, state legal advisor, 1959-62; registrar high ct. Kuala Lumpur, Malaysia, 1962-63; chief registrar Fed. Ct., Kuala Lumpur, 1963-65, high ct. judge, 1965, fed. judge, 1973, chief justice, 1979; Lord Pres. 1982, 34th Sultan of Perak, 1985—. Author: The Role of Constitutional Rulers. Co-chancellor U. Sains Malaysia, 1971; chmn. Higher Edn. Adv. Council, 1974; v.p. Olympic Council, Malayisa. Decorated PMN, 1979, SSM, 1983. Mem. Internat. Hockey Fedn., Malaysian Hockey Fedn. (pres.). Office: care Malaysian Embassy 2401 Massachusetts Ave NW Washington DC 20008 also: Istana Iskandarish, 33000 Kuala Kangsar, Perak Malaysia *

AZNAVOUR, CHARLES (VARENAGH AZNAVOURIAN), singer, actor; b. May 22, 1924. Ed., Ecole Centrale de T.S.F., Centre de Spectacle, Paris. With Jean Dasté Co., 1941. Pierre Roche in Les facheux and Arlequin, 1944. Performed numerous song recitals in Europe and U.S.A., Films include: La Tets Contre les Murs, 1959; Ne Tirez pas sur le Pianiste, 1960; Un Taxi pour Trobrouk, Le Testament d' Orphée, Le Diable et les dix Commandments, Houte-Infidélité, 1964; La Métamorphose des Cloportes, 1965; Paris au mois d'Aout, 1966; Le Facteur s' en Va-t-en Guerre, 1966; Le Diable par le Queue, 1968; Candy, 1969; Les Intrus, 1973; Sky Riders, 1976; Fodies Gourgeoises, 1976; Dix Petits Négres, 1976; the Twist, 1976; The Tin Drum, 1979. Composer, singer numerous songs. Composer operetta: Monsiuer Carnaval, 1965. Decorated chevalier des Arts et des Lettres. Address: 4 ave du Lieutel, Galluis, 78490 Montfort l'Amaury France *

AZUMA, TAKAMITSU, architect, educator; b. Osaka, Japan, Sept. 20, 1933; s. Yoshimatsu and Yoshiko (Ikeda) A.; m. Setsuko Nakaoka, Mar. 17, 1957; 1 dau., Rie. B.Arch., Osaka U., 1957, D.Arch., 1985. Designer, Ministry of Postal Services, Osaka, 1957-60; chief designer Junzo Sakakura Architect & Assocs., Osaka, 1960-63; chief designer Junzo Sakakura Architect and Assocs., Tokyo, 1963-67; prin. Takamitsu Azuma Architect & Assocs., Tokyo, 1967-85; instr. Tokyo U. Art and Design, 1976-78, Tokyo Denki U., 1980-82, Tokyo U., 1983-85; instr. Osaka U., 1981-85, prof., 1985—; instr. Osaka Art U., 1985—; architecht Azuma Architects & Assocs., 1985—. Recipient 1st prize Kinki Br., Japan Inst. Architects Competition, 1957. Mem. Archtl. Inst. Japan, Japan Architects Assn. Author: Reevaluation of the Residence, 1971; On the Japanese Architectural Space, 1981; Takamitsu Azuma-Contemporary Japanese Architects Series, 1982; Philosophy of Living in the City, 1983; Device from Architecture, 1986; Space Analysis of Urban Residence, 1986; 100 Chpt. for Children's Place, 1987; White Book about Tower House, 1987. Home: 3-39-4 Jingumae, Shibuya-ku, Tokyo 150 Japan Office: Azuma Architects & Assocs, 3-6-1 Minami-Aoyama Minato-ku, Tokyo 107, Japan

AZZATO, JUDITH ANNE, social worker; b. Floral Park, N.Y., Dec. 23, 1946; d. John August and Eleanor (Buckley) Rissmeyer; BA, Queens Coll., Flushing, N.Y., 1967; MSW, Fordham U., 1971; m. Michael J. Azzato, Jr., Aug. 19, 1967 (div. Aug. 1974). Caseworker, community organizer Suffolk County Dept. Social Services, Bay Shore, N.Y., 1967-73; lectr. Cornell U. Coll. Human Ecology, Ithaca, N.Y., 1974; social worker Northport-East Northport (N.Y.) Community Council, 1974-75; project dir. YMCA Outreach Project, Bay Shore, 1976-77; therapist Luth. Community Services, 1978-79; social worker L.I. Devel. Ctr., Melville, N.Y., 1978—. Bd. dirs. Econ. Opportunity Council of Suffolk, Inc., Patchogue, N.Y., 1974-77; mem. 2d Congl. Dist. Com. on Youth, 1976; bd. dirs. Suffolk County Youth Bd., 1974-75; mem. Suffolk County Conf. Juvenile and Criminal Justice, Inc., 1976-80; founding mem. Day Care Council of Suffolk, 1971-74, N.Y. State Assn. Child Day Care Councils, Inc., 1972-74; fundraiser Women's Polit. Caucus, 1973; mem. Youth Services Coordinating Council of Suffolk, 1975-77; chair ELAN N.Y. state Legislation Com., 1987-88. Qualified cert. social worker N.Y.; recipient award Suffolk County Community Service, 1977; N.Y. State-Suffolk County Dept. Social Services scholar, 1969-71. Mem. Nat. Assn. Social Workers (del. 1977, 79, 81, 84, treas. Suffolk div. 1978-81, sec. Suffolk div. 1988—, editor newsletter 1971-75, 88—, sec. N.Y. State council 1973-75, legis. com. 1987—), Clin. Register Social Workers (diplomate 1978, 82, 85, 87), Queens Coll. Alumni Orgn., Alpha Sigma Alpha. Contbg. author: First Directory of Child Day Care Centers in Suffolk County, 1972; founding social worker Victims Info. Bur. of Suffolk, Inc., 1975-76.

AZZI, WALID CHAHINE, publishing company executive; b. Rmeyleh, Lebanon, Nov. 22, 1936; s. Chahine Joseph and Madeleine (Dauo) A.; m. Yolla Harb, Feb 24, 1968; children: Ghada, Reem, Chahine. BS, Boston U., 1958; MS in Communications, Harvard U., 1963. Mgr. econ. research Intra Bank, Beirut, 1964-69; gen. mgr. Al Hayat Group of Publs., Beirut, 1969-73, Dar An-Nahar Press Services, Media Press, Coop. de Presse, Beirut, 1973-76; founder, gen. mgr. Tamam Sal, Beirut, 1976-86; pres. Better Baby Products, Beirut, 1979—, Multi Media Group Holding, Paris, 1986—; gen. mgr. Media Mgmt., Beirut, 1986; pub. Arab Ad Mag., Paris and London, 1986—. Author: Struggle Over the Holy Land, 1963. Mem. Internat. Advt. Assn. (pres. Lebanon chpt.), Pan Arab Media Assn. (treas.), Alpha Epsilon Rho. Roman Catholic. Club: Internat. Press Inst. Lodge: Lions. Home: 14 Rue de Sablons, 75015 Paris France Office: Multi Media Group, 36 Rue Washington, 75008 Paris France

BA, BOUBAKAR, mathematics educator; b. Diapaga, Burkina-Faso, Dec. 29, 1935; s. Daifour and Maimouna (Cisse) B.; m. Alice Claude Romain, July 29, 1961; children: Ismael, Myriam, Safiatou, Laurent. Agrege de Math., Ecole Normal Superieure, Paris, 1958; Doctorat d'Etat, U. Paris, 1965. Maitre de conférences U. Rennes, France, 1964-65, U. Dakar, Senegal, 1965-68; prof. U. Madagascar, Tananerive, 1968-71; recteur U. Niamey, Niger, 1971-79; prof. math. U. Abidjan, Ivory Coast, 1979—. Contbr. articles to prof. jours. Recipient award Minister of Edn. (France), 1973. Mem. Societe Mathematique de France, Am. Math. Soc., Societe Mathematique de Cote d'Ivoire, Union Mathematique Africaine. Office: U Abidjan, Faculty of Scis, Dept Math, 22 BP 582 Abidjan 22 Ivory Coast

BABA, HISAO, anthropologist, anatomist; b. Tokyo, Jan. 3, 1945; s. Masaji and Nobuko (Yabe) B.; m. Misako Tomisawa, Oct. 25, 1972; children: Sayaka, Hatami, Okie. Grad., U. Tokyo, 1968, MS, 1970, MD, 1983. Research assoc. U. Chiba, Japan, 1971-73; research assoc. Dokkyo U. Sch. Medicine, Tochigi, Japan, 1973-78, sr. lectr., 1978-88, assoc. prof., 1988; curator Nat. Sci. Mus., Tokyo, 1988—. Author: Minatogawa Man, 1982, Akashi innominate, 1982. Mem. Anthrop. Soc. Nippon, Japan Assn. Anatomy, Am. Assn. Phys. Anthropology. Home: Iriya 5-1891-21, Zama 228, Japan Office: Nat Sci Mus, Hyakunincho Shinjuku, Tokyo 160, Japan

BABAEV, A. G., science foundation administrator; b. Mary, USSR, May 10, 1929; s. Geldy and Ogulbek B.; m. Dunyagozel Palvanova, 1951; children: Sapar, Aina, Tylla, Sona, Guljan, Nabat, Bakhar, Merdan. Postgrad., Turkmen State U., Ashkhabad, USSR, 1949-52. Head dept. geography Turkmen State U., Ashkhabad, 1952-59; dir. desert inst. Turkmen Acad. Scis., Ashkhabad, 1959—, pres., 1975-86; chmn. Scientific Council for Desert Problems, 1967—. Editor-in-chief jour. Problems of Desert Development, Ashkhabad, 1967—; author 8 monographs; contbr. more than 200 articles to profl. jours. Chmn. Turkmen Geog. Soc., Turkmen, Ashkhabad; dep. The Supreme Soviet of the USSR, Moscow; mem. com. Soviet Scientists for Peace Against Nuclear War. Recipient Sign of Honour award, 1976, Heroic Labour medal, 1970, USSR State Prize Winner Sco. and Tech., 1981, Medal Academician Vavilov, 1976. Mem. Turkmen Soc. Chinese Soviet Friendship (chmn.), UNEPCOM, Turkmen Geog. Soc,. Communist. Home: 8 Kurban Durdy St, 744 Ashkhabad USSR Office: Turkmen SSR Acad of Scis, 15 Gogol St, Ashkhabad USSR

BABANGIDA, IBRAHIM, Nigerian head of state; b. Minna, Niger State, Aug. 1941; s. Muhammadu and Aishatu B.; m. Hajiya Mariya King; three children. Grad. Govt. Coll., Bida, Nigeria, 1962; postgrad. Nigerian Mil. Tng. Coll., 1963, Indian Mil. Acad., 1964, Royal Armoured Ctr., Eng., 1966-67, U.S. Army Armour Sch., 1972, Command and Staff Coll., 1977, Nigerian Inst. Policy and Strategic Studies, 1979-80. Commd. Nigerian Army, 1963, advanced through grades to lt. col., 1974; Comdg. officer Nigerian Civil War, 1968-70; co. comdr., instr., Nigerian Def. Acad., 1970-72, regimental comdr., 1973-75, comdr. Armoured Corps, 1975-81, dir. Army Staff Duties and Plans, 1981-83, chief Army Staff, mem. Supreme Mil. Council, 1984-85; pres., comdr.-in-chief Armed Forces, Nigeria, 1985—. Office: Office of Head of State, Lagos Nigeria *

BABAR, RAZA ALI, industrial engineer, utility consultant, management educator; b. Shujabad, Punjab, Pakistan, May 29, 1947; came to U.S., 1972; s. Syed Mohammad Ali Shah and Syeda Hafeeza (Gilani) Bukhari; m. Sufia K. Durrett, July 23, 1974 (div. 1983); children: Azra Yasmeen, Imran Ali, Amenah Andaleep; m. Syeda Afshan Gilani, Aug. 23, 1983; children: Abdullah Ali, Hammad Ali, Omaima Ali. Student Government Coll., Lahore, Pakistan; BS in Mining Engring., U. Engring. and Tech., Lahore, 1969; MS in Indsl. Engring., Wayne State U., 1978; postgrad Detroit Coll. Law, 1982, U. Mich., 1977-84. Engr., planner Bukhari Elec. Concern, Multan, Pakistan, 1969-70; mgr. mining operations Felezzate Yazd Co., Iran, 1970-72; salesman Great Books, Inc., Chgo., 1972-73; field underwriter N.Y. Life Insurance Co., 1972-73; indsl. engr. Ellis/Naeyaert Assocs., Inc., Warren, Mich., 1973-74; grad. asst. dept. indsl. engring. and ops. research Wayne State U., Detroit, 1974-75; prin. engr., work leader project services div. Generation Constrn. Dept., Detroit Edison Co., 1975-79; tech. advisor Ministry of Prodn., Govt. Pakistan, Islamabad, 1979-80; chmn. dept. bus. adminstrn. Zakariya U., Multan, Pakistan, 1980-82; prin. engr. project controls Enrico Fermi 2 Detroit Edison Co., 1981-82, supr. Fermi 2 rate case task force, 1982-84, spl. projects engr. planning, 1984—; mgr. econ. support service Syndeco, Inc., 1985—; vis. prof. grad. Sch. Bus. Adminstrn., Wayne State U., 1987—. Author research papers, presentations to Am. Assn. of Cost Engrs., Am. Power Conf., Internat. Assn. of Energy, Power and Environ. Systems. Founder Fedn. Engring. Assns. Pakistan, 1969; pres. acad. staff assn., mem. chancellor's com. Zakariya U., Pakistan, 1980-81; pres. Pakistan Cultural Group, Detroit, 1975-76; bd. dirs. Detroit Islamic Library, 1976-77; mem. Econ. Outlook Conf., U. Mich., Ann Arbor, 1977-84, Rep. Presdl. Task Force, Rep. Nat. Com. Recipient Pride of Performance medal Engring. U., Pakistan, 1967; Acad. Merit scholar Detroit Coll. Law, 1982. Mem. Am. Mgmt. Assn., Am. Mgmt. Assn. Internat., Econ. Club Detroit, Am. Inst. Indsl. Engrs., Am. Assn. Cost Engrs., Engring. Soc. Detroit, ESD Profl. Activities Council, Pakistan Engring. Congress, Pakistan Inst. Mining Engrs., ABA (student chpt.), Am. Assn. of MBA Execs., Assn. Muslims Scientists and Engrs., Assn. Muslim Social Scientists, Internat. Platform Assn., Islamic Soc. N.Am., Am. Moslem Soc., Islamic Cultural Inst., Tanzeen e Islami Pakistan and N.Am. Avocations: reading, writing, photography, sports, travel. Home: 15672 Golfview Dr Dr Riverview MI 48192 Office: 2000 Second Ave Detroit MI 48226

BABAYANS, EMIL, financial planner; b. Tehran, Iran, Nov. 9, 1951; came to U.S., 1969; s. Hacob and Jenik (Khatchatourian) B.; m. Annie Ashjian. B.S., U. So. Calif., 1974, M.S., 1976; m. Annie Ashjian. Cert. fin. planner. Pres. Babtech Internat., Inc., Sherman Oaks, Calif., 1975-85; sr. ptnr. Emil Babayans & Assocs., Woodland Hills, Calif., 1985—. Mem. Am. Mgmt. Assn., Nat. Assn. Life Underwriters, Inst. Cert. Fin. Planners, Internat. Assn. Fin. Planners. Armenian Orthodox. Office: 21041 Burbank Blvd Suite 200 Woodland Hills CA 91367

BABBITT, DONALD PATRICK, radiologist; b. Oshkosh, Wis., Aug. 24, 1922; s. James Sylvester and Loretta Gertrude (Sensenbrenner) B.; m. Elizabeth May Gerhard, Apr. 28, 1945 (dec. Nov. 1971); children—Patrick, Ann, James; m. Jill Ann Sieg, Jan. 29, 1975 (div. Apr. 1984); m. Katherine J. Zehren, Dec. 12, 1987. Student, U. Wis., River Falls, 1939-42; M.D., Med. Coll. Wis., 1946. Diplomate Am. Bd. Radiology. Intern Meth. Hosp., Indpls., 1946-47; resident Milw. Hosp. and Milw. Ch. Hosp., 1949-52; practice medicine specializing in radiology Milw.; mem. staff Milw. Children's Hosp., 1952—, chief radiology, 1964-82; mem. staff Milw. County Gen. Hosp., 1964—; cons. St. Mary's Hosp., Milw., 1968-76, attending staff, 1982—; instr. radiology Med. Coll., Wis., 1958; assoc. prof. radiology Med. Coll., 1964-70, clin. prof. pediatrics, 1979—; assoc. clin. prof. radiology U. Wis. Center Health Scis., Madison, 1968-70, clin. prof., 1970—. Active Boy Scouts Am. (century mem.). Served to capt. M.C., AUS, 1947-49. Named Tchr. of Yr. Milw. Children's Hosp. Dept. Pediatrics, 1980. Fellow Am. Coll. Radiology (medallion in nuclear medicine 1959), Am. Acad. Pediatrics; mem. Am. Roentgen Ray Soc., European Soc. Pediatric Radiology, Soc. Pediatric Radiology, Radiol. Soc. N.Am., Wis. Radiol. Soc. (pres. 1976), Wis. State Med. Soc., Milw. Surg. Soc. (pres. 1978), Milw. Roentgen Ray Soc. (pres. 1975-77), Milwaukee County Med. Soc. (pres. 1974), Milw. Acad. Medicine, Milw. Pediatric Soc., AMA Med. Coll. Wis. Alumni Assn., Alpha Omega Alpha, Phi Chi. Roman Catholic. Club: Flying Physicians. Lodge: Rotary (Milw.). Home: 2701 E Beverly Rd Milwaukee WI 53211

BABCOCK, CATHERINE EVANS, artist, educator; b. Rydal, Pa., Feb. 23, 1924; d. William Wayne and Marion Catherine (Watters) Babcock; diploma Sarah Lawrence Coll., 1942; BFA, Tyler Sch. Fine Arts, Temple U., 1944, MFA, 1948; m. Douglas Paul Torre, May 28, 1977; 2 stepchildren. Tchr., Rudolf Steiner Sch., 1949; tchr. jr. high sch., Stratford, Conn., 1959-63; tchr. elem. art Locust Valley Primary and Elem. Schs., 1963-68; instr. Darien Community Ctr., 1975-81; art tchr. Rowayton (Conn.) Arts Ctr., 1979—, also bd. mem., rec. sec. Portrait painter; artist to the Sea Services (USCG and USN); illustrator; Cutaneous Cryosurgery (Douglas Torre), 1978, rev., 1979, Undertow (Finn Havrevold), 1968; designer, painter mural for Babcock Surg. Wards. Temple U., Hosp., Phila., 1944; designer display Cryosurgery of Skin Cancer, Dallas, 1979; exhbns. include: internat. miniature shows, Fine Arts Club, Washington, 1984; participant various art shows permanent collection U.S. Navy. Recipient awards including 6 awards, Am. Acad. Dermatology Art Shows, 2 awards Darien Art Shows, gold award, Dallas, 1979; certs. of appreciation USCG, 1971, 82, Naval Sta. of N.Y., 1981. Fellow Internat. Biog. Assn. of Cambridge (Eng.); mem. Met. Portrait Soc., Conn. Pastel Soc., Pastel Soc. Am. (cert. of merit), USCG Art Program (offcl. artist), Navy Art Coop. and Liaison Com., Salmagundi Club. Congregationalist. Illustrator: Atheneum, 1968 (library award). Home and Office: 122 Rowayton Ave Rowayton CT 06853

BABCOCK, JANICE BEATRICE, health system specialist; b. Milw., June 2, 1942; d. Delbert Martin and Constance Josephine (Dworschack) B. BS in Med. Tech., Marquette U., 1964; MA in Healthcare Mgmt. and Supervision, Cen. Mich. U., 1975, postgrad. in Edn. in Health Care, 1975—. Registered med. technologist and microbiologist., clin. lab. scientist, Wis.; cert. bioanalytical lab. mgr. Intern St. Luke's Hosp., Milw., 1963-64; microbiologist St. Michael's Hosp., Milw., 1964-65; supr. clin. lab. service VA Regional Office, Milw., 1965-66; hosp. epidemiologist VA Ctr., Milw., 1966-74; supr. anaerobic microbiology and research lab. VA Ctr., Wood, Wis., 1974-78, adminstrv. officer, chief med. tech., 1978-83, quality assurance coordinator, 1983-86, asst. to chief of staff profl. services, 1986—; research assoc. dept. surgery Med. Coll. Wis.; tchr. in field Marquette U., U. Wis., Med. Coll. Wis.; lectr., cons. in field. Contbr. numerous articles to profl. jours. Recipient Wood VA Fed. Woman's award, 1975, Profl. Achievement award Lab. World jour., 1981, Disting. Alumni award Cen. Mich. U., 1986. Fellow Royal Soc. Health, Am. Acad. Med. Adminstrs. (Wis. state dir. 1986—); mem. Inernat. Acad. Healthcare Mgmt., Am. Soc. Microbiology, Am. Coll. Healthcare Execs., Am. Soc. Med. Tech. (Nat. Sci. Creativity award 1974, Nat. Microbiology Sci. (Achievement award 1978, Mem. of Yr. award 1979, Profl. Achievement Lectureship award 1981, French Lectureship award 1983), Assn. Practitioners in Infection Control, Fed. Execs. Assn., Wis. Hosp. Assn., AAUW, Nat. Geog. Soc., Marquette U. Alumni Assn. (Merit award 1979, Profl. Achievement award 1987), Internat. Acad. Healthcare Mgmt., Assn. Marquette U. Women (bd. dirs. 1987-91, v.p. 1988-89), Alpha Mu Tau (pres. 1984-85), Alpha Delta Theta, Sigma Iota Epislon, Alpha Delta Pi (Alumni Honor award 1979). Club: Holiday Camera. Home: 6839 Blanchard St Wauwatosa WI 53213 Office: VA Med Center 5000 W National Ave Milwaukee WI 53295

BABCOCK, WILLIS, mechanical engineer; b. Waukesha, Wis., May 31, 1922; s. Barney and Helen (Reuter) B.; student Northland Coll., 1941-42, M.I.T., 1945-48, Cornell U., 1948; M.S.M.E., Century U., 1982; m. Elizabeth Anne Zimmerman, Sept. 26, 1947; children—Rudolph, Kathryn, Willis W., Gregory, Janet, Deborah. Chief engr. Domestic Engine and Pump Co., Shippensburg, Pa., 1948-53; chief engr. research and devel. Aurora Pump Co. (Ill.), 1953-59; v.p. engring., exec. v.p., gen. mgr. Carver Pump Co., Muscatine, Iowa, 1959-63, cons., 1963-64; chief engr. Mission Valve & Pump Co., Houston, 1964-66; dir. research and devel. Mech. Equipment Co., New Orleans, 1966-68; program mgr. Battelle N.W. Labs., Richland, Wash., 1968-71; sr. project engr. Emco Wheaton Inc., Conneaut, Ohio, 1971-72; chief engr. Sta-Rite Industries, Inc., Delavan, Wis., 1972-77; mgr. engring. Wayne Home Equipment Co., Ft. Wayne, Ind., 1977-80; with Rockwell Internat., Richland, Wash., 1980—. Served with AUS, 1942-45. Mem. ASME, Nat.

Soc. Profl. Engrs. Baptist. Home and Offfice: 3937 Austin St West Richland WA 99352

BABER, WILBUR H., JR., lawyer; b. Shelby, N.C., Dec. 18, 1926; s. Wilbur H. and Martha Corinne (Allen) B.; B.A., Emory U., 1949; postgrad. U. N.C., 1949-50, U. Houston, 1951-52; J.D., Loyola U., New Orleans, 1965. Bar: La. 1965, Tex. 1966. Sole practice, Hallettsville, Tex., 1966—. Served with U.S. Army. Mem. ABA, La. Bar Assn., Tex. Bar Assn., La. Engring. Soc., Tex. Surveyors Assn. Methodist. Lodge: Rotary. Office: PO Box 294 Hallettsville TX 77964

BACARISSE, SALVADOR, Spanish and American literaure educator; b. Madrid, Aug. 17, 1923; s. Salvador and Pilar (Cuadrado) B.; m. Hélène Nolle, Dec. 1946 (div.); m. Barbara Willis, 1958 (dec. 1970); children: Benjamin, Claire; m. Pamela Phillips, June 1970 (div. Jul. 1988); m. Jennifer McGregor, Sept. 1988. BA, U. London, 1958, MA, 1960. Lectr. modern Spanish, Spanish and Am. lit., lang. U. Bristol, Eng., 1960-64, U. St. Andrews, Scotland, 1964—. Gen. editor Forum for Modern Langs. Studies, 1972-84; contbr. articles to profl. jours. Mem. Assn. Hispanists. Home: 21 Eglinton Crescent, Edinburgh EH12 5BY, Scotland Office: U St Andrews, Saint Andrews KY16 9AL, Scotland

BACCINI, LAURANCE ELLIS, lawyer; b. Darby, Pa., Nov. 16, 1945; BS, Drexel U., 1968; JD, Villanova U., 1971. Bar: Pa. 1971, U.S. Dist. Ct. (ea. dist.) Pa. 1973, U.S. Ct. Appeals (3d cir.) 1979. Law clk. to chief judge U.S. Dist. Ct. (ea. dist.) Pa., 1971-73; assoc. Schnader, Harrison, Segal & Lewis, Phila., 1973-78, ptnr., 1979—; speaker, faculty mem. on labor law Practising Law Inst., N.Y.C.; trustee Phila. Bar Found., 1986—. Author: NLRA Supervisor's Handbook; assoc. editor Villanova Law Rev. Mem. Phila. Bar Assn. (bd. govs. 1978—, chmn. 1982, vice chancellor 1986, chancellor-elect 1987, chancellor 1988, commn. on jud. selection, retention and evaluation 1978-79), Pa. Bar Assn. (ho. of dels. 1983—), ABA (former chair, and dir. young lawyers div. 1981-82, mem. exec. council Sect. Labor and Employment Law 1981-82, exec. council 1980-81, chancellor-elect 1987, chancellor, 1988, chair long-range planning com., young lawyers div.'s Fed. practice com., fed. jucicial standards com., judicial conf. for 3d cir., house of dels. 1988—). Office: 1600 Market St Suite 3600 Philadelphia PA 19103

BACCOUCHE, HEDI, prime minister of Tunisia; b. Hanman-Sousse, Tunisia, Jan. 15, 1930; Married; 2 children. BA, Sorbonne; grad. in internat. relations, Inst. of Polit. Studies, Paris. V.p. Fed. of destourian students France and Europe, 1954-59; dep. dir. party in charge of youth and orientation, 1961-63; gov. Bizert, Sfax and Gabes, Tunisia, 1963-70; pres.-dir. gen. Social Security Nat. Bank, Tunisia, 1971, Nat. Office of Fishing, Tunisia, 1973; in charge of mission of prime minister Tunisia, 1978079; Tunisian ambassador Berne and Vatican, 1979-81, Alger, 1982-84; mem. polit. bur. PSD, Tunisia, 1987; prime minister Tunis, Tunisia, 1987—. Office: Office of Prime Minister, Tunis Tunisia *

BACH, STEVE CRAWFORD, lawyer; b. Jackson, Ky., Jan. 31, 1921; s. Bruce Grannis and Evelyn (Crawford) B.; m. Rosemary Husted, Sept. 6, 1947; children—John Crittenden, Greta Christine. A.B., Ind. U., 1943, J.D., 1948; postgrad. Eastern studies, U. Mich., 1944, Nat. Trial Judges Coll., 1966; U. Minn. Juvenile Inst., 1967. Bar: Ky. 1948, Ind. 1948. Atty. Bach & Bach, Jackson, Ky., 1948-51; investigator U.S. CSC, Indpls., 1951-54; sole practice Mt. Vernon, Ind., 1954-65, 83—; judge 11th Jud. Circuit, Mt. Vernon, 1965-82; pres. Internat. Inst. for Youth, Inc., Mt. Vernon, 1985—; spl. overseas rep. Nat. Council Juvenile and Family Ct. Judges, bd. trustees, 1978—; moderator Ind. Conf. Crime and Delinquency, Indpls., 1968; tchr. seminar on juvenile delinquency, Ind. Trial Judges Assn., 1969, del. Internat. Youth Magistrates Conf., Geneva, 1970, Oxford, Eng., 1974, Can., 1977; faculty adviser Criminal Law Inst., Nat. Trial Judges Coll., 1973; treas. Ind. Council Juvenile Ct. Judges, 1975, v.p., 1976, pres., 1978-79, mem. juvenile study com., 1976; bd. dirs. Jud. Conf., Ind. Jud. Ctr.; faculty adviser Nat. Jud. Coll., 1978; mem. faculty Seminar for Inst. for New Judges, State of Ind., 1979. Pres. Greater Mt. Vernon Assn., 1958-59; bd. dirs. Regional Mental Health Planning Commn., Criminal Justice Planning Commn. 8th Region Ind., Evansville, Ind.; mem. Juvenile Justice div. Ind. Jud. Study Commn.; mem. Ind. Gov.'s Juvenile Justice Delinquency Prevention Adv. Bd., 1976-78, community adv. council Ind. U. Sch. Medicine, 1986—. Served with intelligence Signal Corps, AUS, 1943-46. Mem. Nat. Council Juvenile Ct. Judges, Am. Legion, Ind. Soc. Chgo., Ind. Bar Assn. (del.), Ind. Judges Assn. (bd. mgrs. 1966-71), Sigma Delta Kappa, Delta Tau Delta. Democrat. Methodist. Lodges: Masons, Shriners, Kiwanis, Elks. Home: 512 Walnut St Mount Vernon IN 47620 Office: 203 E 4th St Mount Vernon IN 47620

BACHE, CARL, language educator; b. Kotagiri, Nilgiris, India, Aug. 9, 1953; s. Ib Fenger and Elise (Thorsell) B.; m. Hanne Lisbeth Holst Pedersen, Dec. 21, 1973; children: Nicolai, Stefan. Student, Odense (Denmark) U., 1977, PhD, 1980, 85. Lectr. English dept. Odense U., 1977, research fellow English dept., 1978-83, prof. English dept., 1984—; research fellow U. Sussex, England, 1983-84. Author: The Order of Premodifying Adjectives in Present-Day English, 1978, Verbal Aspect, 1985; contbr. numerous articles on linguistics to profl. jours. Office: Odense U, English Dept, Campusvej 55, 5230 Odense Denmark

BACHELERIE, ROBERT, homeopathic physician, educator; b. Arlanc, Puy de Dome, France, Dec. 15, 1937; s. Félix and Antonia (Vye) B.; m. Christiane Stroheker, May 30, 1964; children: Sophie, Caroline. D in Medicine, U. Clermont-Ferrand, France, 1966. Intern, then resident Hosp. Aurillac, France, 1963-65; prof., école d'homéopathie U. Clermont-Ferrand, 1970-86, chargé de cours d'homéopathie à la faculté de pharmacie, 1981—. Author: Homeorep, 1983, Introduction à l'Homéopathie Pure, 1987. Mem. Assn. Hahnemannienne du Ctr. (pres.), Office de Documentation Homéopathique (pres., founder), Club Informatique et Homéopathie. Home and Office: 6 Rue Blatin, 63000 Clermont-Ferrand France

BACHER, ROSALIE WRIDE, educational administrator; b. Los Angeles, May 25, 1925; d. Homer M. and Reine (Rogers) Wride; AB, Occidental Coll., 1947, MA, 1949; m. Archie O. Bacher, Jr., Mar. 30, 1963. Tchr., English, Latin, history David Starr Jordan High Sch., Long Beach, Calif., 1949-55, counselor, 1955-65, Lakewood (Calif.) Sr. High Sch., 1965-66; research asst., counselor Poly. High Sch., Long Beach, 1966-67; counselor, office occupational preparation, vocational guidance sect. Long Beach Unified School Dist., Long Beach, 1967-68; vice prin. Washington Jr. High Sch., Long Beach, 1968-70; asst. prin. Lakewood Sr. High Sch., Long Beach, spring 1970; vice prin. Jefferson Jr. High Sch., Long Beach, 1970-81, Marshall Jr. High Sch., Long Beach, 1981-87; vice prin. Lindbergh Jr. High Sch., Long Beach, 1987—; counselor Millikan High Sch., 1988—, Hill Jr. High Sch., 1988—; chmn. vocat. guidance steering com. Long Beach Unified Sch. Dist., 1963—. Mem. Internat. Platform Assn., AAUW, Long Beach Personnel and Guidance Assn. (dir. 1958-60), Long Beach Sch. Counselors Assn. (sec. high sch. segment 1963-64), Phi Beta Kappa, Delta Kappa Gamma (pres. Delta Psi chpt., area dir.; Calif. profl. affairs com. chmn. 1972-74), Phi Delta Gamma (pres. chpt. 1977-78, 87—, nat. chmn. bylaws com. 1980-81, Nat. Conv. Com. 1987-88), Pi Lambda Theta (pres. chpt. 1974-76, v.p. So. Calif. council 1974-76), Phi Delta Kappa (sec. Long Beach chpt. 1977-80, pres. 1988—). Home: 265 Rocky Point Rd Palos Verdes Estates CA 90274 also: 17721 Misty Lane Huntington Beach CA 92649 Office: Hill Jr High Sch 1100 Iroquois Ave Long Beach CA 90815

BACHMAN, GEORGE, educator; b. N.Y.C., Jan. 17, 1933; s. Frederick Joseph and Ruth (Benson) B.; m. Joan Caggiano. B.E.E., N.Y. U., 1950, M.S., 1952, Ph.D. in Math, 1956. Asst. prof. math. Rutgers U., New Brunswick, N.J., 1957-60; mem. faculty Bklyn. Poly. Inst., 1960—, asso. prof., 1962-66, prof., 1966—. Author: (with L. Narici and E. Beckenstein) Functional Analysis and Valuation Theory, 1971, (with L. Narici) Functional Analysis, 1966, Elements of Abstract Harmonic Analysis, 1964, Introduction to p-adic Numbers and Valuation Theory, 1964; Contbr. articles to profl. jours. Recipient Disting. Teaching award Bklyn. Poly. Inst., 1974, Disting. Research award Sigma Xi, 1982; NSF grantee, 1968—. Mem. Am., Indian math. socs., Math. Assn. Am., Canadian Math. Congress, Societe Mathematique de France. Home: 27 Summit Rd Riverside CT 06878 Office: 333 Jay St Brooklyn NY 11201

BACHMANN, HELGI, banker; b. Reykjavik, Iceland, Feb. 22, 1930; s. Hallgrimur and Gudrun B.; m. Erla Haraldsdottir, July 14, 1951; children: Edda, Sjöfn, Hrönn, Sif; m. Kristin Sveinsdottir, Feb. 20, 1987. Grad. in econs., U. Iceland, 1955. Exec. dir. Nat. Bank Iceland, Reykjavik. Mem. I.O.O.F. Lodge: Internat. Order of Odd Fellows. Home: Granaskjol 20, Reykjavik Iceland Office: Landsbanki Islands, Laugaveg 7, 101 Reykjavik Iceland

BACHMANN, (KURT) MANFRED, folklorist, general director, educator; b. Oberwartha, Dresden, Germany, May 17, 1928. Ed. Technische Hochschule, Dresden, E.Ger., 1947-50, Karl-Marx-U., Leipzig, E.Ger., 1950-51; Dr.paed. Tech. U. Dresden, 1957, Dr.phil. h.c. Tech. U. Dresden, 1986. Wissenschaftliche Aspirantur, 1953-57; dir. Haus der Volkskunst Schneeberg, 1956-58; dir. Mus. fur Volkskunst Dresden, 1957-68; Gen. dir. Staatliche Kunstsammlungen Dresden, 1968—; hon. prof. Hochschule fur Bildende Kunste, Dresden, 1973—. Author many books on folklore and cultural history, including: Berchtesgadener Volkskunst, 1985; Deutsches Spielzeug, 1965; Das grosse Puppenbuch, 1971; Die Dresdner Gemaldegalerie, 1978; Holz spielzeug aus dem Erzgebirge, 1984. Mem. Union Internationale de la Marionette, Internat. Council Mus. Office: Staatliche Kunstsammlungen, Dresden, Pf 450, 8012 Dresden German Democratic Republic

BACHMANN, MEINOLF CHRISTOPH, psychologist; b. Gütersloh, Fed. Republic Germany, Jan. 28, 1952; s. Bruno and Anna (Kaupenjohann) B.; m. Ulrike Fuchs, Apr. 25, 1980; children: Matthias, Annemarie. Indsl. Economist Grad., Coll. Industrial Econs., Bielefeld, 1974; Diploma Psychology, U. Bielefeld, 1980. Group therapist, leading psychologist Clinic for Addicts, Fredeburg, 1980-81, Bernhard-Salzmann-Klinik, Gutersloh, 1982—; lectr. in field. Contbr. articles on therapy for addiction and eating disorders to profl. jours. Home: Fliederweg 13, D-4830 Gutersloh Federal Republic of Germany Office: Bernhard Salzmann Klinik, Im Füchtei 150, D-4830 Gütersloh Federal Republic of Germany

BACHMANN, WILLIAM VINCENT, combustion engine consultant, inventor; b. Bozen, S. Tyrol, Italy, Apr. 8, 1913; s. Johann and Franziska (Demetz) B.; student engring. Koenigliche Staatsgewerbeschule, 1929-30, pvt. study art and graphics, 1931-34; m. Diane Thomson, Jan. 3, 1977; children by former marriages—George, Francisca, Vincent. With Massey Ferguson Co., Toronto, Ont., Can., 1953-56; with Dilworth Ewbanks, cons. Can. Air Research Project, Toronto, 1956-58; body A engr. Chrysler Corp., Highland Park, Mich., 1958-70; test engr. cons. Volkswagen Mfg. Corp. Am., Warren, Mich., 1977-78; pres. Bachmann Fire Ring Engine Research Co., St. Clair Shores, Mich., 1979—; pres. ALBA Eagle Co., 1988—. Holder 15 U.S., numerous fgn. patents in field. Mem. Soc. Automotive Engrs., Engring. Soc. Detroit, The Inventors' Assn. of Met. Detroit. Address: 22517 Ten Mile Rd Saint Clair Shores MI 48080

BACHNER, JOHN PHILIP, business consultant; b. Boston, Nov. 8, 1944; s. Barnard and Bertha (Bellar) B.; AB, Harvard, 1966; m. Marcia L. Davis, Aug. 7, 1966; children—Barnard David, Lissa Suzanne. Screenplay writer Screen Presentations, Inc., film prodn. co. Washington, 1967-68; account exec. Hoffman Assocs., Inc., Silver Spring, Md., 1968-71; pres. Bachner Communications, Inc., communications-mktg. co., Silver Spring, 1971—; pres. Bachner Mgmt. Systems, multiple assn. mgmt. co. Silver Spring, 1973—; exec. v.p. Cons. Engrs. Council of Met. Washington, Silver Spring, 1971—, Property Mgmt. Assn. Met. Washington, Silver Spring, 1973—, Washington Area Council Engring. Labs., Silver Spring, 1975—, Property Mgmt. Assn. Am., Silver Spring, 1979—; exec. v.p. ASFE/The Assn. of Engring. Firms Practicing in the Geosciences, Assn. Soil Found. Engrs., Silver Spring, 1973—; chmn. bd. Constrn. Industry Tech., Inc., Silver Spring, 1973—. Exec. dir. Spruce Knob Assn., Silver Spring, 1975—; pres. Most for the Lease, 1982—; v.p. Bachner Real Estate, 1985—; exec. v.p. Mid-Atlantic Council of Shopping Ctr. Mgrs., 1986—. Author: Marketing and Promotion for Design Professionals, 1977; writer 25 motion pictures; contbr. numerous articles to profl. publs., popular mags. Home: 9206 Sterling Montaque Dr Great Falls VA 22066

BACHSTEIN, HARRY SAMUEL, lawyer, educator; b. Oakland, Calif., Aug. 6, 1943; s. Elizabeth (Rodenhouse) B.; m. Kathy Ann Hill; children—Harry S. III, David Jason, Shane Thomas, Jacob William, Jesse Remington. BS in Bus. Adminstrn., No. Ariz. U., 1966; JD with honors, U. Ariz., 1969. Bar: Ariz. 1969, U.S. Supreme Ct. 1973, U.S. Ct. Customs and Patent Appeals, U.S. Dist. Ct. Ariz., U.S. Ct. Appeals (9th cir.), U.S. Bankruptcy Ct. Spl. investigator ethics com. Pinal County Bar Assn., 1971; juvenile ct. referee Ariz. Superior Ct., 1972-76, mem. Superior Ct. Med. Liability Rev. Panel, 1981, Domestic Relations Rules com., 1988; lawyer arbitrator Better Bus. Tucson. Mem. Devel. Authority for Tucson's Expansion, 1970-76; mem. U.S. Presdl. Task Force, 1981—; faculty Pima Coll., 1982-83. Mem. State Bar of Ariz. (sec., exec. council young lawyers' sect. 1972-73), ABA (Ariz. rep. com. on div. law and procedures 1976), Pima County Bar Assn. (grievance com. 1978-86, spl. investigator for ethics com. 1971), Profl. Assn. of Diving Instrs., Profl. Diving Instrs. Corp. (cert. open water scuba instr. 1980), Delta Chi (sec., pledgemaster 1961-65). Clubs: Optimist Internat. (state gov. Ariz. 1976, lt. gov. 1972-73, pres. 1971-72, Outstanding Gov. and Disting. Gov. 1976), Mason. Editor: Ariz. Law Rev., 1967-69. Avocations: hunting, deep sea diving. Office: PO Box 43188 Tucson AZ 85733-3188

BACIU, CLEMENT, orthopedic surgeon; b. Bucharest, Rumania, Sept. 2, 1922; s. Stan Clement and Maria (Georgescu) B.; M.D.D., Faculty Human Medicine, Bucarest, 1948; grad. Acad. Phys. Edn., Bucarest, 1947; children: Radu Valeriu, Mihnea Clement. Orthopedic surgeon, then 1st orthopedic surgeon Orthopedic Clinic, Brincovenesc Hosp., Bucharest, 1959-68; orthopedic surgeon Gastartz Unfallkrankenhaus XX, Vienna, Austria, 1967; prof.'s asst. Acad. Phys. Edn., 1964-73; 1st surgeon Queen Elizabeth Hosp., Aden, South Yemen, 1968-69; chief orthopedic dept. Colentina Hosp., Bucharest, 1970—. Decorated Ordin Merit Munca Sanitara, Bucharest, 1972; recipient Evidentiat Munca Medico Sanitara, 1958, 77; diploma Internat. Red Cross, Geneva, 1969. Mem. Soc. Belge d'Orthopaedie (hon.), Soc. Française d'Orthopaedie, Össtereichische Gesellschaft Unfall-Chirurgie, West-Deutsche Gesellschaft Ortopaedie. Author: The Knee, 1963; Heine-Medin Disease, 1955; Treatise for Orthopaedic Surgery, 1956; Osteo-articular Traumatology, 1967; Functional Anatomy of Locomotor System, 3d edit., 1977; Semeiology of Locomotor System, 1975; Surgery and Prosthesis of the Locomotor System, 1986; History of Orthopedics and Tranmatology in Rumania, 1988. Home: 2b Ronda, 73 221 Bucharest Romania Office: 22 Stefan cel Mare, 72 202 Bucharest Romania

BACK, GEORGE LEONARD, television program syndicator; b. Bronx, N.Y., Nov. 20, 1939; s. Aaron and Anna (Herman) B.; B.B.A., Hofstra Coll., 1962; M. Media Ecology, N.Y. U., 1974, Ph.D. in Media Ecology, 1979; m. Patricia Davis, Aug. 30, 1980; children—Alexandra Davis, Lauren Anne, Roxanne Eva. Mgmt. trainee CBS/Columbia Group, N.Y.C., 1966, Chgo., 1967; div. mgr. ABC Films, Chgo., 1969, Los Angeles, to 1970; v.p., gen. mgr. mktg. Group W Prodns., N.Y.C., 1970-77; chief operating officer Hughes TV Network, N.Y.C., 1977-79; exec. dir. Nat. Assn. TV Program Execs., 1979-82; prin. George Back & Assocs., N.Y.C., 1979—; pres. All Am. TV, 1982—, chmn. bd. dirs. 1985. Mem. adv. bd. Babies Heart Fund, 1987. Served to capt., inf., U.S. Army, 1962-66. Mem. World Future Soc. Jewish. Contbr. articles to TV jours. Office: All American Television 304 E 45th St 2d Floor New York NY 10017

BACK, ROBERT WYATT, investment executive; b. Omaha, Dec. 22, 1936; s. Albert Edward and Edith (Elliott) B.; m. Linaya Gail Hahn, Aug. 30, 1964; children—Christopher Frederick, Gregory Franklin. B.A., Trinity Coll., 1958; M.A., Yale U., 1960; postgrad. Northwestern U., 1958, London U., 1959-60, Harvard U., 1960-61. Head trader and security analyst Lincoln Nat. Life Ins. Co., Fort Wayne, Ind., 1964-69; sr. investment analyst Allstate Ins. Co., Northbrook, Ill., 1969-72; chmn. Consumer Analyst Group, Chgo., 1972-74; investment adv. acct. mgr. Brown Bros. Harriman & Co., Chgo., 1972-74; asst. v.p., investment analyst Harris Trust & Savs. Bank, 1974-82; v.p., instl. equity analyst Prescott Ball & Turben, 1982-83; v.p., sr. investment analyst Blunt, Ellis & Loewi, Inc., 1983-84; v.p. instl. equity sales Rodman & Renshaw, Inc., 1984-87; v.p. instnl. research ins. Legg, Mason, Wood & Walker, Inc., 1987—; instr. Purdue U., Indiana U., DePaul Univ., Mich. Tech. Univ. Contbr. numerous articles to profl. jours. Corp. mem. Scholarships for Ill. Residents, Inc., 1969—; mem. planning com. Fin. Analysts Fedn. Conv., 1984—; pres. Buffalo Grove (Ill.) Police Pension Fund, 1973—; del. Assn. Yale Alumni, 1983-85. Served to capt. USAF, 1958-64. Mem. Ill. Police Pension Fund Assn. (investment, edn. coms.). Clubs: Yale Chgo. (bd. dirs. 1983-85, chmn. grad. and profl. programs 1983—), Yale N.Y., Harvard Chgo., Harvard Grad. Soc. Home: 942 Twisted Oak Ln Buffalo Grove IL 60090 Office: Rodman & Renshaw Inc 120 S LaSalle St Chicago IL 60090

BACKENROTH, GUNNEL ANNE MAJ, psychologist, researcher; b. Grums, Värmland, Sweden, June 12, 1951; parents: K. Hugo and Maj E.I.S. (Joelsson) B. BA, Göteborgs U., Gothenberg, Sweden, 1974; MA, Umeå U., Sweden, 1976; PhD, Stockholm U., 1983. Lic. psychologist, Sweden. Child psychologist Barn-och ungdomspsykiatrisk Kliniken, Lidköping, Sweden, 1973-76; researcher, program leader Dept. Psychology U. Stockholm, 1976-79, 1981—; psychologist, program leader Parental Assn. for Cooperation, Stockholm, 1980; lectr. various univs.; cons. Stockholms läns Landsting, 1985—. Contbr. numerous articles to profl., acad. jours. Lecture award Singapore Assn. for the Deaf, 1984. Mem. Swedish Assn. for Psychologists (sci. adv. council), Internat. Assn. Human Relations Lab. Tng. (hon., life), Univ. Assn. Stockholm, Assn. for Female Researchers, Scandinavian Assn. for Research of the Deafs Mental Health, Internat. Round Table for the Advancement of Counseling. Home: Skidbacken 4, S-17245 Sundbyberg Sweden Office: U Stockholm, Dept Psychology, S-10691 Stockholm Sweden

BACKENSTOSS, HENRY BRIGHTBILL, electrical engineer, consultant; b. Washington, Sept. 28, 1912; s. Ross Elwood and Susan Catherine (Brightbill) B.; m. Violet Pentleton, Jan. 23, 1942 (div. 1952); m. Bernadette Humbert, Sept. 24, 1954; 1 child, Martine Susan. B.S., M.S. in Elec. Engring., MIT, 1935. Registered profl. engr., Pa., Mass., Conn. Project mgr. Jackson & Moreland, Engrs., Boston, 1945-59; prof. power tech. Am. U. Beirut (Lebanon), 1959-61; spl. cons. Gen. Pub. Utilities Corp., N.Y.C., 1961-62; v.p. Jackson & Moreland Internat., Beirut, 1962-68; sr. cons. Gen. Pub. Utilities Service Corp., Reading, Pa., 1970-77; cons. Devel. Analysis Assocs., Cambridge, Mass., 1977-82; Govt. Saudi Arabia, 1962-69; panelist fuel crisis and power industry IEEE Tech. Conf., 1973. Contbr. articles to profl. publs. Bd. dirs. Reading Symphony Orch. (Pa.), 1975-86, Berks County Conservancy (Pa.), 1984—, Reading Mus. Found., 1986—, pres., 1988—. Mem. IEEE (life sr., power system engring. com. 1952—, system econs. subcom. 1952-76), Nat. Soc. Profl. Engrs., Pa. Soc. Profl. Engrs., Sigma Xi (assoc.), Tau Beta Pi. Congregationalist. Home: 408 S Tulpehocken Rd Reading PA 19601

BÄCKER, LASZLO, metallurgist; b. Debrecen, Hungary, Apr. 12, 1931; immigrated to France, 1957, naturalized, 1967; s. Joseph and Maria (Vilaghy) B.; grad. chemiste, U. Debrecen, 1953; D.Sc., U. Paris, 1964; m. Elisabeth Bali, May 18, 1957 (div. 1982); children—Sophie, Christine; m. Odile DuFour, Oct. 25, 1986. Engr., Csepel Steelworks, Hungary, 1953-56; research engr. Pompey Steelworks, France, 1957-66; chief metallurgy and quality Soc. des Aciers Fins de L'est, Hagondange, 1966-86; tech. mgr. Gen. Steel France, Metz, 1987—; cons. Vsines Gerlach, France, Aforsa, Spain, 1987—. Recipient Charles H. Herty, Jr. award AIME, 1970, Robert Woolston Hunt award, 1972, Charles Hatchett award Inst. of Metals, CBBM, 1988. Mem. French Soc. Metallurgy. Roman Catholic. Author numerous papers in field. Home: 30 rue Chaziere les Hetres, No 1, 69004 Lyon France Office: Gen Steel France, 57000 Metz France

BACKES, LUTZ (BUBEC), cartoonist, sculptor; b. Mannheim, Ger., July 16, 1938; s. Ernst M. and Emma A. (Paulus) B.; m. Karin Bubeck, Dec. 6, 1974. Cartoonist, Kicker, Nuremberg, W. Ger., 1961—, editorial cartoonist, 1968—; collaborated with Rothco Cartoons, Inc., Yonkers, N.Y., 1968—; exhbns. include: Nuremberg, 1967, Bonn, 1971, 82, World exhbn., Montreal, 1976, Antwerpen, 1977, Istanbul, 1977, Skopje, 1978, Cologne, 1982, Tokyo, 1984, Zürich, 1984, N.Y.C., 1985. Recipient numerous awards including Italian Minister of Cultural Affairs award, 1975, 81, Turkish Press Office award, 1977, World exhbn. award, Montreal, 1976, 79. Mem. German Assn. Journalists. Author: Auf's Maul Geaugt, 1968; Kopfjagd, 1969; Die Pracht Am, Rhein, 1972; Showt Her, wir Sind's, 1974; Bubec Cartoons, 1977, 79; Personiflage, 1982. Office: 7 Hofer Weg, D-8671 Tauperlitz Federal Republic of Germany

BACKIS, ROBERT JOSEPH, social worker; b. Sept. 3, 1949; m. Pamela Backis, 1985; 1 child, Alexandra; 1 stepchild, Kimberly. BA in Sociology, Loyola U., Chgo., 1971, M of Clin. Social Work, 1987; postgrad., Mid-Am. Inst. Cath. Charities, Chgo., 1972-73; MDiv, U. St. Mary of the Lake, Mundelein, Ill., 1973. Assoc. pastor St. Charles Lwanga Ch., Chgo., 1975-80, pastor, 1980-82; adminstr. St. Charles Lwanga Lifeline Ctr., Chgo., 1975-80; program dir. Proyecto Libre Ada S. McKinley Community Services, Chgo., 1982-83; chaplain, dir. dept. pastoral care Mercy Hosp. and Med. Ctr., Chgo., 1983-85; social worker II Ill. Dept. Children and Family Services, Chgo., 1985-88, supr., 1988—; social worker Martha Washington Hosp., Chgo., 1986—. Recipient Coordinating Bd. award Assn. Chgo. Priests, 1981, Community Recognition award Robert Taylor Home Local Adv. Council, 1981. Mem. Nat. Assn. Social Workers, Nat. Assn. Cath. Chaplains, Corps Resigned priests in U.S. Home: 7022 N Sheridan Rd Chicago IL 60626

BACON, BARBARA MCNUTT, social worker; b. London, Nov. 6, 1946; came to U.S., 1952; d. Peter Joseph and Margaret (Strong) O'Reilly; m. Michael McNutt, Nov. 15, 1969 (div. 1977); m. John Lockhart Bacon, Apr. 29, 1978; children: Patricia, Ann Catherine. B.A., Ursuline Coll. for Women, 1968; postgrad. Harvard U., 1968-69; M. Edn., U. Ill., 1971; M.S.W., U. Iowa, 1981. Psychometrist, Child Devel. Lab., Mass. Gen. Hosp. and Harvard Med. Sch., Boston, 1968-69; research assoc. Inst. Child Behavior and Devel., U. Ill., Champaign, 1969-78; clin. social worker Family and Children's Services, Davenport, Iowa, 1979-83; psychologist Gt. River Mental Health Ctr., Muscatine, Iowa, 1978-79; behavioral sci. coordinator family practice residency program Mercy-St Luke's Hosp., Davenport, Iowa, 1979-82; family therapist Family Counseling Service, Albuquerque, 1984—; pvt. practice Profl. Counseling Assocs., 1984-86; clin. dir. adolescent psychiatric program Charter Hosp. Albuquerque, 1987—; cons. CIBA-Geigy Corp., Summit, N.J., 1975-77, Council for Children at Risk, Rock Island, Ill., 1981-83. Mem. Nat. Assn. Social Workers, Phi Beta Kappa. Republican. Episcopalian. Office: Charter Hosp Albuquerque 5901 Zuni SE Albuquerque NM 87108

BACON, DOUGLAS EUGENE, petroleum geologist, rancher; b. Boone, Iowa, June 11, 1925; s. Raymond H. and Lola M. (Adams) B.; m. Emily Jane Coghlan, Oct. 15, 1949; children—S. Douglas, Robert M., Barbara S. Bacon McKeithen. B.S., U. Ark., 1948, M.S., 1949. Cert. geologist. Geologist, Atlantic Refining Co., Wichita, Kans., 1949-52, dist. geologist, Bismarck, N.D., 1952-55, asst. to chief geologist, Dallas, 1955-56, dist. geologist, Houston, 1956-60; pvt. practice cons. geologist, Houston, 1969-70; ptnr. Bock & Bacon Oil Co., Houston, 1970—. Contbr. publs. in field. Chmn. phys. com. YMCA, Houston, 1967-69, bd. dirs., 1967-75. Mem. Am. Assn. Petroleum Geologists (dist. rep.), Soc. Ind. Profl. Earth Scientists (chpt. v.p., bd. dirs., nat. treas.), Houston Geol. Soc., Am. Inst. Profl. Geologists, Am. Geol. Inst. Methodist. Clubs: Meadowbrook Civic, Lions. Home: PO Box 128 Utopia TX 78884 Office: Bock & Bacon Oil Co 3110 Southwest Freeway Suite 234 Houston TX 77098

BACON, FRANCIS, painter; b. Dublin, Ireland, 1909. Self-taught painter. First one-man shows: London, 1949, N.Y.C., 1953; exhbns. include: Venice Biennale (Italy), 1954, Brussels Internat. Exhbn., 1958, travelling exhbns. Mannheim, Turin, Zurich, Amsterdam, 1962, Hamburg, Stockhol, Dublin, 1965, New London Gallery, 1963, Solomon Guggenheim Mus., N.Y.C., 1963, Galerie Maeght, Paris, 1966, Marlborough New London Gallery, 1967, Marlborough-Gerson Gallery, N.Y.C., 1968, Grand Palais, Paris, 1971, Kunsthalle, Dusseldorf, Germany, 1972, Met. Mus. Art, N.Y.C., 1975, Musée Cantini, Marseilles, France, 1976, Museo de Arte Moderna, Mexico, 1976, Galerie Claude Bernard, Paris, 1977, Museo Contemporáneo, Caracas, Venezuela, 1977, Nat. Mus. Mos Art, Tokyo, 1983, Galerie Beyeler, Basle, 1987—, Hirshorn Mus., Washington, 1988—; retrospective exhbns.: Tate Gallery, London, 1962, 85, Guggenheim Mus., N.Y.C., 1963, Kunstverein, Hamburg, 1965, Paris, 1971, Nat. Mus. Modern Art, Tokyo, 1983; works include: triptychs: Three Studies for Figures at the Base of a Crucifixion, 1944, Crucifixion, 1965, Sweeney Agonistes, 1967, Triptych, 1970, 72, 73, 76,

86-86, 87; single oil paintings: Man with Dog, 1953, Study After Velazquez's Portrait of Pope Innocent X, 1953, Two Figures, 1953, Study for a Portrait of Van Gogh, 1957, Crucifixion, 1965, Portrait of Isabel Rawsthorne Standing in a Street in Soho, 1967, Landscape, 1978, Jet of Water, 1979, Triptych inspired by the Oresteia of Aeschylus, 1981, Study of the Human Body. 1982. Recipient Rubens prize City of Siegen, 1967, award Carnegie Inst., Pitts., 1967. Address: care Marlborough Fine Art, 6 Albemarle St, London W1X 4BY England

BACON, J. RAYMOND, management professional; b. Chgo., Aug. 11, 1906; s. Elmer Winfield and Alma C. (Romburg) B.; diploma in commerce Northwestern U., 1943; M.A., Western U., 1950; Ph.D. in Bus. Adminstrn. (hon.), Colo. State Christian Coll., 1972; m. Florence I. Burdine, Nov. 5, 1927 (dec. Nov. 1960); 1 dau., Grace Florence (Mrs. John W. Bacher); m. 2d, Margaret Austin, Nov. 30, 1963. Asst. mgr. King Woodworking Co., Chgo., 1926-34; dept. head Montgomery Ward & Co., Chgo. and Albany, N.Y., 1935-40; v.p., gen. mgr. O. D. Jennings & Co., Chgo., 1940-48; exec. v.p. Rockola Mfg. Co., Chgo., 1948-54; pres., treas., dir. F. H. Noble & Co., Chgo., 1954-67; pres., dir. F. H. Noble & Co. (Can.) Ltd., 1956-67; mng. dir. F. H. Noble & Co. (Ireland), Belfast, No. Ireland, 1963-67; pres., dir. Draftette Co., Hemet, Calif., 1967-86. Mem. Am. Mgmt. Assn., Soc. for Advancement Mgmt., A.I.M. (asso.), YMCA, Art Inst. Chgo. (life), Hemet C. of C., Calif. Mfrs. Assn. Presbyn. Kiwanian (past pres.). Home: PO Box 895 Hemet CA 92343

BACON, LEONARD ANTHONY, accounting educator; b. Santa Fe, June 10, 1931; s. Manuel R. and Maria (Chavez) Baca; m. Patricia Balzaretti; children—Bernadine M., Jerry A., Tiffany A. B.E., U. Nebr.-Omaha, 1965; M.B.A., U. of the Americas, Mexico City, 1969; Ph.D., U. Miss., 1971. CPA; cert. mgmt. acct., internal auditor. Commd. 2d lt. U.S. Army, 1951, advanced through grades to maj., 1964, served fin. and acctg. officer mainly Korea, Vietnam; ret., 1966; asst. prof. Delta State U., Cleveland, Miss., 1971-76; assoc. prof. West Tex. State U., Canyon, 1976-79; prof. acctg. Calif. State U., Bakersfield, 1979—; cons. Kershen Co. (now Atlantic Richfield Oil Co.), Canyon, 1979-80. Contbr. articles to profl. jours. U.S., Mex., Can., papers to profl. confs. Leader Delta area Boy Scouts Am., Cleveland, 1971-76; dir. United Campus Ministry, Canyon, 1976-79; minister Kern Youth Facility, Bakersfield, 1983—. Paratrooper Brazilian Army, 1955. Mem. Am. Acctg. Assn., Am. Inst. CPA's, Am. Assn. Spanish Speaking CPA's, Nat. Assn. Accts. (pres. Bakersfield chpt. 1981-82, Most Valuable Mem. award 1981), Am. Mgmt. Assn., Inst. Mgmt. Acctg., Calif. Faculty Assn., Acad. Internat. Bus., Inst. Internal Auditors, Inst. Cost Analysts, Alpha Kappa Psi (Dedicated Service award 1979). Clubs: Jockey (Rio de Janeiro). Lodges: Lions (v.p. Cleveland 1971-73), Kiwanis (v.p. 1974-79, A Whale of a Guy award, Cleveland 1975). Office: Calif State Univ Bakersfield 9001 Stockdale Hwy Bakersfield CA 93309

BACQUE, HARVEY G., fraternal organization administrator; b. Rayne, La., Oct. 12, 1943; s. Edward F. and Eurav Voiselle (Simon) B.; B.S. in Bus. Communication and Journalism, U. Southwestern La., Lafayette, 1968; m. Mary Canavan, Oct. 9, 1970. Program cons. service dept. Knights of Columbus Supreme Council, New Haven, 1968-73, asst. dir. dept., 1973-77, dir., frat. services, 1977-88, sr. v.p. frat services, 1988—, editor Program Supplement, 1970-85, Squires Newsletter, 1973-77; grand knight, dep. grand knight, program dir., recorder, pub. relations chmn. Council 4683, K.C., Lafayette; named Knight of Yr., 1966; 4th degree 1968. Mem. Goodspeed Opera House Found.; inpatient vol. Conn. Hospice, Branford, 1983—; vol. The Nat. Ctr., Washington; bd. dirs. New Haven Vol. Action Ctr. Vol. Named hon. La. col. Ho. of Reps. La. House of Reps scholarship. Mem. Am. Mgmt. Assn., Tenn. Squires, Assn. Voluntary Action Scholars, Nat. Operation Care and Share (White House exec. com.), New Eng. Frat. Congress (pres. 1986-87), Am. Family Soc. (nat. adv. council). Home: 816 Townsend Ave New Haven CT 06512 Office: 1 Columbus Plaza New Haven CT 06507

BACQUIER, GABRIEL, opera singer; b. Beziers, France, May 17, 1924; s. Augustin and Fernande (Severa) B.; student Paris Conservatoire; m. Simone Teisseire, 1943; m. 2d, Mauricette Benard, 1958; 2 sons. Debut at Theatre Royal de la Monnaie, Brussels, 1953, as Figaro in Il Barbiere di Siviglia, at Opera Comique, Paris, 1956, Paris Opera Tosca, 1960, at Carnegie Hall, 1960, Met. Opera, N.Y.C., 1961; appears regularly at Vienna State Opera, Covent Garden, La Scala, Opera de Paris and other leading opera houses; repertoire includes Otello, Don Giovanni, Pelleas et Melisande, Damnation de Faust, Tosca, Falstaff. Decorated Prix nat. du disque français, 1964; chevalier de la Legion d'honneur; chevalier de l'ordre nationale du Merite; officier des Arts et des Lettres. Address: 141 rue de Rome, 75017 Paris France *

BADDELEY, ALAN DAVID, psychologist; b. Leeds, Eng., Mar. 23, 1934; s. Donald and Nellie (Hansen) Baddeley; m. Hilary Ann White; children: Roland, Gavin, Barty. BA in Psychology with honors, U. Coll., London, 1956; MA in Psychology, Princeton U., 1957; PhD, Cambridge (Eng.) U., 1963. Scientist Med. Research Council Applied Psychology Unit, Cambridge, 1958-67, dir., 1974—; lectr. then reader in psychology U. Sussex, Eng., 1967-72; prof. dept. psychology U. Stirling, Scotland, 1972-74. Author: The Psychology of Memory, 1976, Your Memory: A User's Guide, 1982, Working Memory, 1986. Mem. Brit. Psychological Soc., Exptl. Psychology Soc., Psychonomic Soc., European Soc. for Cognitive Psychology, Amnesia Assn. Office: Med Research Appleid Psychology Unit, 15 Chaucer Rd, Cambridge CB2 2EF, England

BADDILEY, JAMES, biochemist; b. Manchester, Eng., May 15, 1918; s. James and Ivy Logan (Cato) B.; B.Sc. with 1st class honors, U. Manchester, 1941, M.Sc., 1942, Ph.D., 1944, D.Sc., 1954; D.Sc. (hon.), Heriot-Watt U., Bath U.; ScD, U. Cambridge, 1986; m. Hazel Mary Townsend, Sept. 20, 1944; 1 son, Christopher James. Sir Clement Royds Meml. scholar U. Manchester, 1942, Beyer fellow, 1943-44; Imperial Chem. Industries fellow U. Cambridge, 1945-49; fellow Swedish Med. Research Council, Stockholm, 1947-49; staff dept. biochemistry Lister Inst. Preventive Medicine, London, 1949-54; Rockefeller travelling fellow Harvard U. Med. Sch., 1954; prof. organic chemistry U. Newcastle upon Tyne (formerly U. Durham), 1955-77, prof. chem. microbiology, 1977-83; dir. microbiology chemistry research lab., head Sch. Chemistry, 1968-78; Sci. and Engring. Research Council sr. fellow U. Cambridge, 1981-84. Mem. adv. bd. Brit. Nat. Com. for Biochemistry, 1961-66; mem. Govt. Grant Bd. Royal Soc., 1962-66, council, 1977-79, also mem. coms.; mem. Sci. and Engring. Research Council, 1979-81; Karl Folkers lectr. U. Ill., 1962. Created knight, 1977; recipient Meldola medal Royal Inst. Chemistry, 1947; fellow Pembroke Coll., Cambridge U. Fellow Royal Soc., 1961 (Leeuwenhoek lectr. 1967, Davy medal 1974), Royal Soc. Edinburgh, Royal Soc. Chemistry (past mem. council, Corday-Morgan medal and prize 1952, Tilden lectr. 1959, Pedler lectr. 1978); mem. Biochem. Soc. (com. 1964), Soc. Gen. Microbiology (council 1973-75), Am. Soc. Biol. Chemists (hon.). Research, numerous publs. on nucleosides, penicillin, pyridoxal phosphate, active methionine, biosynthesis, nucleotide coenzymes, carbohydrates, bacterial cell walls, microbiology. Office: Univ Cambridge, Dept Biochemistry, Tennis Court Rd, Cambridge CB2 1QW, England Other: care Royal Soc, 6 Carlton House Terrace, London SW1Y 5AG England

BADDOUR, ANNE BRIDGE, aviatrix; b. Royal Oak, Mich.; d. William George and Esther Rose (Pfiester) Bridge; m. Raymond F. Baddour, Sept. 25, 1954; children—Cynthia Anne, Frederick Raymond, Jean Bridge. Student Detroit Bus. Sch., 1948-50. Stewardess, Eastern Airlines, Boston, 1952-54; instr. aeros. Powers Sch., Boston, 1958; co pilot, flight attendant Raytheon Co., Bedford, Mass., 1958-63; flight dispatcher, ferry Pilot Comerford Flight Sch., Bedford, 1974-76; adminstrv. asst., ferry pilot, Jenney Beachcraft, Bedford, 1976; mgr., pilot Baltimore Airways, Inc., Bedford, 1976-77; pilot, flight facility M.I.T. Lincoln Lab. Flight Test Facility, Lexington, Mass., 1977—; aviation cons., corp. pilot Energy Resources, Inc., Cambridge, Mass., 1974-84. Bd. dirs. Cambridge Opera, 1977-79; mem. campaign council Mus. Transp., Boston; mem. council assos. French Library in Boston; commr. Commonwealth of Mass., Mass. Aero. Commn., 1979-83; chmn. regional adv. council FAA, 1984-88. Winner trophy Phila. Transcontinental Air Race, 1954, New Eng. Air Race, 1957. World Class speed records Boston to Goose Bay, Labrador, 1985, Boston to Reykjavik, Iceland, 1985, Portland, Me. to Goose Bay, 1985, Portland to Reykjavik, 1985, Goose Bay to Reykjavik, 1985. Mem. Fedn. Aeronautique International, Nat. Aero. Assn., Ninety-Nines (winner New Eng. Safety Trophy 1986), Aero Club New England (v.p., dir.), Aircraft Owners Pilots Assn., Nat. Pilots Assn., U.S. Sea Plane Pilots Assn., Assn. Women Transcontinental Air Race, Republican. Episcopalian. Clubs: Bostonian Soc., English Speaking Union, Friends of Switzerland, French Center Library, Belmont Hill, Aero of New Eng. (dir. 1978—), St. Botolph. Home: 96 Fletcher Rd Belmont MA 02178 Office: Draper Flight Test Facility Lincoln Lab MIT PO Box 98 Concord MA 01742

BADEER, HENRY SARKIS, physician, educator; b. Mersine, Turkey, Jan. 31, 1915; came to U.S., 1965, naturalized, 1971; s. Sarkis and Persape Hagop (Koundakjian) B.; m. Mariam Mihran Kassarjian, July 12, 1948; children: Gilbert H., Daniel H. M.D., Am. U., Beirut, Lebanon, 1938. Gen. practice medicine Beirut, 1940-51; asst. instr. Am. U. Sch. Medicine, Beirut, 1938-45; adj. prof. Am. U. Sch. Medicine, 1945-51, asso. prof., 1951-62, prof. physiology, 1962-65, acting chmn. dept., 1951-56, chmn., 1956-65; research fellow Harvard U. Med. Sch., Boston, 1948-49; prof. physiology Creighton U. Med. Sch., Omaha, 1967—; acting chmn. dept. Creighton U. Med. Sch., 1971-72; vis. prof. U. Iowa, Iowa City, 1957-58, Downstate Med. Center, Bklyn., 1965-67; mem. med. com. Azounieh Sanatorium, Beirut, 1961-65; mem. research com. Nebr. Heart Assn., 1967-70, 85-88. Author textbook; contbr. chpts. to books, articles to profl. jours. Recipient Golden Apple award Students of AMA, 1975; Rockefeller fellow., 1948-49; grantee med. research com. Am. U. Beirut, 1956-65. Mem. AAAS, Internat. Soc. Heart Research, Am. Physiol. Soc., Alpha Omega Alpha. Home: 2808 S 99th Ave Omaha NE 68124 Office: Creighton U Med Sch 2500 Calif St Omaha NE 68178-0224

BADEN, MICHAEL M., pathologist, educator; b. N.Y.C., July 27, 1934; s. Harry and Fannie (Linn) B.; m. Judianne Densen-Gerber, June 14, 1958; children—Trissa, Judson, Lindsey, Sarah. B.S., CCNY, 1955; M.D., NYU, 1959. Diplomate Am. Bd. Pathology. Intern, first med. div. Bellevue Hosp., N.Y.C., 1959-60, resident, 1960-61, resident in pathology, 1961-63, chief resident in pathology, 1963-64, fellow in pathology, 1964-65; practice medicine specializing in pathology N.Y.C.; asst. med. examiner City of N.Y., 1961-65, jr. med. examiner, 1965-66, assoc. med. examiner, 1966-70, dep. chief med. examiner, 1970-78, 79-81, 83-86, chief med. examiner, 1978-79; dep. chief med. examiner, dir. labs. Suffolk County, N.Y., 1981-83; instr. in pathology NYU, N.Y.C., 1964-65, asst. prof. pathology, 1966-70, assoc. prof. forensic medicine, 1970—; dir. forensic scis. unit N.Y. State Police, 1986—; adj. prof. law N.Y. Law Sch., N.Y.C., 1975—; vis. prof. pathology Albert Einstein Sch. Medicine, 1975—; lectr. pathology Coll. Physicians and Surgeons, Columbia U., N.Y.C., 1975—; asst. vis. pathologist Bellevue Hosp., N.Y.C., 1965—; lectr. Drug Enforcement Adminstrn., Dept. Justice, 1973—; vis. lectr. Fairleigh Dickinson Dentistry, 1968-70; spl. forensic pathology cons. N.Y. State Organized Crime Task Force, 1971-75; chmn. forensic pathology panel U.S. Ho. of Reps. select coms. on assassinations of Pres. John F. Kennedy and Dr. Martin Luther King, Jr., 1977-79; mem. med. adv. bd. Andrew Menchell Infant Survival Found., 1969-74; mem. cert. bd. Addiction Services Agy., N.Y.C., 1966-69; preceptor health research tng. program N.Y.C. Dept. Health, 1968-79; v.p. Council for Interdisciplinary Communication in Medicine, 1967-69; forensic pathology cons. N.Y. State Police, 1985—. Author: Alcohol, Other Drugs and Violent Death, 1978. Contbr. articles on forensic medicine to profl. jours. Mem. editorial bd. Am. Jour. Drug and Alcohol Abuse, 1973—, Internat. Microfilm Jour. Legal Medicine, 1969-73, Contemporary Drug Problems, 1971. Mem. N.Y. adv. bd. Odyssey House, Inc., 1966-76; bd. dirs. N.Y. Council on Alcoholism, sec., 1969-79; bd. dirs. Belco Scholarship Found., Inc., 1971—. Recipient Great Tchr. award NYU, 1980. Fellow Coll. Am. Pathologists (chmn. toxicology subcom. 1972-74), Am. Soc. Clin. Pathologists (mem. drug abuse task force 1973—), Am. Acad. Forensic Scis. (program chmn. 1971-72, sec. sect. pathology and biology 1970-71, exec. com. 1971-74, v.p. 1982-83); mem. Med. Soc. County N.Y. (mem. pub. health com. 1966-76), Soc. Med. Jurisprudence (corr. sec. 1971-78, v.p. 1979-81, pres. 1981-85, chmn. bd. 1985—), Nat. Assn. Med. Examiners, N.Y. Path. Soc., N.Y. State Med. Soc., AMA, Internat. Royal Coll. Health. Office: 142 East End Ave New York NY 10028

BÁDENAS DE LA PEÑA, PEDRO, Greek philology researcher, educator; b. Madrid, Jan. 8, 1947; s. Pedro and Manuela (de la Peña) Bádenas; m. Mercedes Arias, July 6, 1971; children: Maria, Pedro. BA in Philosophy and Letters, U. Madrid, 1969, PhD, 1974; D. of Edn. (hon.), Open U., Madrid, 1979. Asst. prof. U. Complutense, Madrid, 1969-72; assoc. prof. Open U., Madrid, 1973-79; research prof. Council for Scientific Research, Madrid, 1979—; Scientific cons. Nat. Evaluating Agy., Madrid, 1986—. Author: The Structure of Platonic Dialogue, 1984, Menander's Theater, 1986, (with others) Greek-Spanish Dictionary I-II, 1980-86; translator of the Cavafy and Seferis' poetry; chief editor, founder: Erytheia Jour. on Byzantine and Modern Greek Studies, 1980—; also 9 other books; contbr. articles to profl. jours. Fellow Hispanic-Greek Soc. (co-founder, dir. sci. programs 1985—, sec.-gen. 1979—), Spanish Soc. Classical Studies, Spanish Soc. Linguistics, Profl. Assn. Research Workers (mem. exec. com. 1984—); mem. World Fedn. Scientific Workers. Office: Council Sci Research, Duque de Medinaceli 6, Madrid 28014, Spain

BADER, FRANZ, retired gallery administrator; b. Vienna, Austria, Sept. 19, 1903; s. David and Elsa (Steindler) B.; educated Vienna; D.F.A. (hon.), George Washington U., 1984; L.H.D. (hon.), Corcoran Sch. Art, 1984; m. Antonia Blaustein, Dec. 2, 1928; m. 2d, Virginia Forman, July 31, 1971. Owner, Wallishausser Book Shop, Vienna, until 1939; v.p., gen. mgr. Whyte Gallery, Washington, 1939-53; pres. Franz Bader Gallery, specializing in contemporary art, Washington, 1953-85; photographer, exhibited Corcoran Gallery Art, Washington, 1973, Nat. Acad. Scis., Washington, 1975; one-man shows Phillips Collection, Washington, 1977, Am. U., Washington, 1981, Cheekwood, Nashville, 1980; represented in collections Air and Space Mus., Washington, U.S. Ct. Gen. Sessions, Washington, Phillips Collection, Washington, also pvt. collections. Decorated Goldene Ehrenzeichen fuer Verdianste (Austria); Verdienstkreuz Erster Klasse (Germany); recipient (Washington) Mayor's Art award, 1981. Home: 2242 48th St NW Washington DC 20007

BADER, RICHARD EUGENE, performing arts executive, theatre owner and producer, city planner, real estate developer. s. Benjamin and Beatrice A. B. Grad. in econs., Hobart Coll.; M.C.P.A. in City Planning, Yale U. Sch. Architecture. Jr. planner Candub, Fleissig & Assocs., Newark, 1960-61; asst. planner Raymond & May Assocs. for N.Y.C. Community Renewal Program, 1961-63; dir. sch. planning N.Y.C. Planning Commn., 1963-66; exec. dir. United Parents Assn., N.Y.C., 1966-67; asst. to commr. N.Y.C. Dept. Pub. Works, 1967-68; asst. adminstr. N.Y.C. Parks, Recreation and Cultural Affairs Adminstrn., 1968-72, dep. adminstr., 1972-74; curator for met. N.Y.C., N.Y. State Mus., Albany, 1974-76; cons. N.Y. State Mus., N.Y. State Bicentennial Commn., N.Y. City Cultural Affairs Commn., Westchester County Dept. Parks and Recreation, 1976-77; exec. dir. Am. Shakespeare Theatre, Conn. Ctr. for Performing Arts, Stratford, 1977-81; pres. Wilbur Theatre Operating Corp., Boston, 1981—; cons., Palace Theatre Redevel. Project, El Paso, Tex., Pvt. Industry Council, Phila., State Theatre Rehab. Project, Easton, Pa., preservation evaluation Boyd Theatre, Phila., 1984—; lectr. Sch. Law Rutgers U., New Sch., Columbia U., Sch. Drama Yale U., MIT; juror Yale U. Sch. Architecture. Mem. Com. for Harvard Theatre Collection; founder League of Boston Theatres; bd. dirs. Fine Arts Fedn. of N.Y. Recipient Parks Council award, 1973. Mem. Am. Planning Assn., Am. Assn. Museums, Internat. Council Museums, Friends of Cast Iron Architecture, Spanish Inst., Adirondack Council, Adirondack Conservancy. Clubs: St. Botolph (Boston); Yale; Met. Opera (N.Y.C). Home: 47 E 64th St New York NY 10021 Office: 246 Tremont St Boston MA 02116

BADER, TALAT ABDELAZIZ, civil engineer, research institute executive; b. Al-Khalil, Saudi Arabia, Mar. 24, 1948; s. Abdel Aziz Abdul Haleem Bader; m. Hannan Abdul Jawad Al-Mohtaseb; children: Omar, Sara, Majed, Salma. BS, King Faud U. of Petroleum and Minerals, Dhahran, Saudi Arabia, 1972; MS, Purdue U., 1975; PhD, Northwestern U., 1980. Engring. grad. asst. King Faud U. of Petroleum and Minerals, 1972-73, asst. prof. civil engring., 1979—, coordinator div. geology, minerals, 1984-85, mgr. div., 1985—. Mem. ASCE. Address: King Faud U Petroleum/Minerals, Research Inst Div Geology/Minerals, Box 1803, Dhahran 31261, Saudi Arabia

BADETTI, ROLANDO EMILIO, health science facility administrator; b. Istanbul, Turkey, Mar. 25, 1947; s. Umberto and Iole (Bianchi) B.; m. Emanuela Ponte, Oct. 29, 1973; children: Barbara, Fabiana. PhD in Pharmacy, U. Padua, Italy, 1971. Mfg. supr. Gruppo Lepetit, El Tadida, Morocco, 1971-76, plant mgr., 1977-79; quality assurance mgr. Gruppo Lepetit, Milan, 1980-81, material mgr., 1982-83; tech. dir. Lirca Synthelabo, Milan, 1983—. Office: Lirca Synthelabo Spa, Via Rivoltana 35, 20090 Limito Italy

BADGLEY, JOHN ROY, architect; b. Huntington, W. Va., July 10, 1922; s. Roy Joseph and Fannie Myrtle (Limbaugh) B.; AB, Occidental Coll., 1943; MArch, Harvard, 1949; postgrad., Centro Internazionale, Vincenza, Italy, 1959; m. Janice Atwell, July 10, 1975; 1 son, Adam; children by previous marriage: Dan, Lisa, Holly, Marcus, Michael. Prin. architect own firm, San Luis Obispo, Calif., 1952-65; chief architect, also planner Crocker Land Co., San Francisco, 1965-80; v.p. Cushman & Wakefield Inc., San Francisco, 1980-84; pvt. practice architecture, San Rafael, Calif., 1984—; tchr. Calif. State U. at San Luis Obispo, 1952-65. Served with USCGR, 1942-46. Mem. AIA, Am. Arbitration Assn. Oceanic Soc. (trustee). Clubs: Golden Gate Wine Soc. Home and Office: 1356 Idylberry Rd San Rafael CA 94903

BADRI, BABIKER ALI, clinical psychologist; b. Omdurman, Khartoum, Sudan, Aug. 31, 1939; s. Ali Babiker Badri and Nafisa Bashier Amer; m. Nafisa Yousif, Sept. 21, 1967; children: Aliya, Dina, Areej. BA, Am. U., Beirut, 1962, postgrad., 1964; postgrad., Tavistock Cen. for Projective Techniques, London, 1972-73; PhD, North East London Poly., 1977. Lectr. Prison Officer's Coll., Khartoum, Sudan, 1963-65, Police Acad., Buri, Sudan, 1966-68, Jr. Nursing Coll., Omdurman, 1967-70, Sr. Nursing Coll., Khartoum, 1969-71; tchr. lang. fluency for mentally handicapped children Brian Didsbury Cen., Eastham, London, 1974; asst. prof. psychology Riyad U., Saudi Arabia, 1977-82, head dept. psychology, 1981-82, mem. bd. dirs. Ednl. Research Cen., Coll. Edn., 1978-80; assoc. prof., mem. acad. bd. Ahfad U. for Women, Omdurman, 1982—, asst. dean, 1982-86, dep. dean, 1986-87; assoc. prof. King Saud U., Saudi Arabia, 1987—; co dir. linkage project Iowa State U. and Ahfad U., 1984-87; psychologist juvenile sect. Prison Dept., Sudan, 1962-64, sr. psychologist, 1964-67, sr. psychologist adult criminal sect., 1967-68; clin. psychologist Kober Mental Hosp., Khartoum, 1970-71, Psychiatry Clinic Ministry of Health, Sudan, 1970-71, (trainee) St. Olave Mental Hosp., London, 1977; mem. Sudan delegation to UN Conf. on Juvenile Delinquency, Damascus, Syria, 1964; mem. prepartory com., sec. translation com. 1st Symposium on Psychology and Islam, Riyad U., 1978. Contbr. articles to profl. jours. and books. Mem. Sudanese Psychol. Soc. (founding 1964-71), Am. U. Beirut Grads. Assn.-Sudan Br. (fin. sec. 1963-71), Brit. Psychol. Soc. Clubs: Blue Nile Sailing, Sudanese-Am. Friendship Soc. (Khartoum). Office: Ahfad U for Women, PO Box 167, Omdurman Sudan

BADSTUEBNER, HANS ALEXANDER, electric company executive; b. Berlin, Feb. 26, 1916; came to U.S. 1960; s. Alexander and Emilie (Luechters) B.; grad. E.E., Berlin, 1938, Ph.D.; 1972; m. Vera Ott, Jan. 9, 1939; 1 son, Stefan. Asst. to gen. mgr. research, devel. depts. Telefunken G.M.B.H., Leubus and Berlin, 1942-45; cons. efficiency engring., Berlin, 1945-52; owner Elba Electric Co., Burnaby, B.C., Can., 1952-60; v.p. prodn. engring. R.M. Hadley Co., Inc., Los Angeles, 1960-64; sr. v.p. engring. Baum Electric Co., Inc., Garden Grove, Calif., 1964—; owner Hansera Co., Fullerton, Calif., 1969—; cons. Foster-Mathews Electric Co., 1981—. Mem. Soc. Plastic Engrs., Am. Mensa Selection Agy., Triple Nine Soc., Cincinnatus High IQ Soc., Minerva High IQ Soc. Lodges: Masons, Shriners. Inventor in various fields. Home: 1312 Norman Pl Fullerton CA 92631 Office: 114 S Lemon Ave Fullerton CA 92632

BADURA, BERNHARD, sociology educator; b. Oppeln, Oberschlesien, Federal Republic of Germany, Feb. 12, 1943; s. Alois and Ursula (Pischel) B.; m. Christine Ehrenberg, 1971 (div.); children: Isabelle, Benjamin; m. Petra May, 1984; 1 child, Raphael. Student, Univs. of Devel. Study, Tübingen, Freigburg, Konstanz, 1964-68, 68-75. With U. Konstanz, 1970-75, prof. social policy, 1975-81; prof. social policy U. Oldenburg, 1981-86; prof. sociology Tech. U. Berlin, 1986—; temporary advisor health promotion program office for Europe WHO, Copenhagen, 1985. Author: Leben mit dem Herzinfarkt, 1987; editor Zeitschfift für Soziologie, 1986; mem. edit. bd. Health Promotion, 1986; expert Social Sci. and Medicine Pub., 1984. Office: Technische U Berlin, Dovestrasse 1-5, 1000 Berlin 10 Federal Republic of Germany

BAEHR, MELANY ERNA, psychologist; b. Kimberley, Republic South Africa, Oct. 25, 1920; came to U.S., 1948, naturalized, 1953; d. Ernest Horace and Hester Cecilia (Van Niekerk) White; m. George Otto Baehr, Sept. 9, 1949; children: Alexandra Elaine, Karen Estelle. BS, U. Witwatersrand, Johannesburg, S. Africa, 1940, BEd, 1941, MS, 1946, PhD, 1950; postgrad U. Chgo., 1948-49. Cert. psychologist, Ill. Research officer South African Council for Sci. and Indsl. Research, 1946-49; project dir. Human Resources Ctr., U. Chgo., 1950-53, research assoc., 1955-57, cons., 1957-62, div. dir., 1962-70, sr. research psychologist, 1970-78, assoc. dir. research, 1979-82, assoc. prof. social sci. div., 1970-85; dir. human resources research and programs Office Continuing Edn., 1982-85, psychol. research cons., 1986—; sr. research cons. London House, Inc., 1984—; adj. prof. DePaul U., 1985—. Author psychol. tests and measurement instruments; contbr. articles to profl. jours., chpts. to textbooks. Served with South African Air Force, 1939-45. Fellow Am. Psychol. Assn.; mem. Ill. Psychol. Assn. (past pres. indsl. sect.), Sigma Xi, Psi Chi. Episcopalian. Home: 5555 S Everett Ave Chicago IL 60637 Office: 1550 Northwest Hwy Park Ridge IL 60068

BAEHR, RUDOLF, philologist; b. Bamberg, Fed. Republic of Germany, Jan. 6, 1922; s. Georg and Barbara (Goertler) B.; m. Gabriele Seemeier, June 30, 1950; children: Christoph, Susanne. Abitur, Humanistisches Gymnasium, Bamberg, Fed. Republic of Germany, 1940; PhD, Univ., Munich, 1952, pvt. docent, 1954; PhD (hon.), Univ., Reims, France, 1973. Asst. prof. Univ., Munich, 1952-63; prof. Univ., Salzburg, Austria, 1964—. Author: Spanische Verslehre, 1962 (Gebhardt award 1963), Französische Verslehre, 1970; editor: Romanische Übungstexte, 1969—; contbr. articles to profl. jours. Decorated Grosses Silbernes Ehrenzeichen (Austria); Officier Légion d'Honneur (France); Officier Palmes académiques (France); Österreichisches Ehrenkreuz für Wissenschaft und Kunst I. Klasse (Austria); recipient Festschrift Internat. colleagues Göppingen, 1981, Internat. colleagues Tübingen, 1987. Mem. Deutsche Dante-Gesellschaft, Internat. Arthurian Soc., Österreichische Akademie der Wissenschaften. Roman Catholic. Office: Institut für Romanistik, Akademiestrasse 24, A-5020 Salzburg Austria

BAEHR, THEODORE, communications executive; b. May 31, 1946; student in French lit. U. Bordeaux and Toulouse (France), 1967; student English lit. Cambridge (Eng.) U., 1967; student German lit. U. Munich (W. Ger.), 1968; B.A. in Comparative Lit. with high distinction (Rufus Choate scholar), Dartmouth Coll., 1969; J.D., N.Y.U., 1972; postgrad. Inst. Theology, Cathedral St. John the Divine, N.Y.C., 1978—; m. Liliana Milani, 1975; children—Theodore Peirce, James Stuart Castiglioni, Robert Gallatin. Research engr. Precision Sci. Co., Chgo., 1964-65; legal cons. firm Dandeub, Fleissig & Assocs., N.Y.C., 1970-71; law student asst. U.S. Atty.'s Office, So. Dist. N.Y., 1971-72; pres. Agape Prodns., N.Y.C., 1972-79, chmn. bd., 1979-82; exec. dir. Good News Communications, Inc., N.Y.C., 1978-80, chmn. bd., 1980—; pres. Episcopal Radio-TV Found., Inc., Atlanta, 1981-82, Trinity Concepts, 1982; cons. media; dir. TV Center, CUNY at Bklyn. Coll., 1979-80; AT&T, Cocoa, Fla., 1979-80, Episc. Communicators, 1981-84; exec. producer Ch.'s Presence at World's Fair, Knoxville, Tenn., 1982; dir. Am. Theater Actors. Vice pres. Ctr. for TV in Humanities, 1982; bd. dirs. Christian Conciliation Service, Dorsey Theatre SUP, Inc., Coalition on Revival, Habitat for Humanity. Mem. Soc. Motion Picture and TV Engrs., Nat. Religious Broadcasters (dir., sec. TV com.), Bishop in Ind. Christian Chs. Internat. Episcopalian. Clubs: Seawanhaka Corinthian Yacht, Cathedral St. John the Divine Layman's, Brotherhood of St. Andrew (v.p. 1984—). Editor, Commentator, NYU Law Sch. newspaper, 1969-72, Contemporary Drug Problems, 1971-72, Atlanta Area Christian News; creator, coordinator

Communicate Workshops, 1979; creator, writer, editor Episc. Ch. Video Resource Guide and Episcopal Video/TV Newsletter, 1979; producer, dir., writer various TV and radio programs including Movieguide, Joy of Music, Perspectives, PBS, 1981-82, Religionwise on WGST, CBS, 1981—(Religion in Media award), Searching, 1978-80, others; editor, writer various books, including TV and Reality, Asking the Right Question, Tangled Christian Communications, Getting the Word Out, Movie and Video Guide for Christian Families (Religion in Media award, Wilbur award); dir. Runaways (Chgo. Intercom Gold Plaque and Religion in Media award), producer In Their Own Words, Was It Love (Religion in Media award).

BAEHREL, PETER WILLIAM, manufacturing company executive; b. Jamaica, N.Y., July 15, 1940; s. William Julius and Frances Elizabeth (Gingell) B.; student U. Fla., 1958-60; m. Judith Geuder, June 20, 1970; children—Michael Christian, Suzanne Michelle. Office mgr. Mehron Inc., N.Y.C., 1960-64; supr. facilities AMF Inc., White Plains, N.Y., 1965-73, mgr. facilities and equipment, purchasing agt., 1974-77, mgr. adminstrv. services and purchasing agt., 1978-81; dir. adminstrv. Services Carter-Wallace, Inc., N.Y.C., 1981—. Served with Army N.G., 1961-68. Mem. Soc. Food Service Mgmt., Purchasing Assn. Seven Counties, Nat. Fire Protection Assn., Employee Relocation Council, Adminstrv. Mgmt. Soc. Club: Rotary. Home: 21 Lark Ln Croton-on-Hudson NY 10520 Office: Carter Wallace Inc 767 Fifth Ave New York NY 10153

BAEK, SE-MIN, plastic surgeon; b. Busan, Republic Korea, Apr. 13, 1943; s. Young-Woo and In-Soon (Yoo) B.; m. Boyung Hah, Apr. 30, 1968; children: Siunna, William, Shivonne. MD, Seoul Nat. U., 1967. Diplomate Am. Bd. Plastic Surgery, Am. Bd. Surgery. Intern Sisters of Charity Hosp., Buffalo, 1968-69; resident in plastic surgery Mt. Sinai Hosp., N.Y.C., 1970-75, St. Louis U., 1975-77; prof., chmn. dept. plastic surgery Kyung Hee U., Seoul, 1982-83; chief plastic surgery Bronx (N.Y.) VA Hosp., 1977-82; prof., dir. Inst. Plastic Surgery Korea U., Seoul, 1983-88; chmn. dept. plastic surgery Injae U., Seoul, 1988—, dir. Plastic Facial Deformity Ctr., 1988—; acting chief plastic surgery Mt. Sinai Hosp., 1980-82; dir. plastic surgery Mt. Sinai Sch. Medicine, 1980-82. Contbr. articles to profl. jours. Fellow ACS; mem. Am. Soc. Plastic and Reconstructive Surgery (1st prize Ednl. Found. 1982), Soc. Head and Neck Surgeons, Am. Soc. Maxillofacial Surgeons, Am. Soc. Head and Neck Surgery, Am. Soc. Aesthetic Surgery, Am. Assn. Hand Surgery, N.Y. Acad. Scis. Home: Chung Ryang, PO Box 256, Dongdaemun-ku, Seoul Korea

BAENA SOARES, JOAO CLEMENTE, professional society administrator; b. Belem do Para, Brazil, May 14, 1931; m. Glaucia de Lima; 3 children. Office: care Orgn of Am States 17th St & Constitution Ave NW Washington DC 20006

BAENDER, MARGARET WOODRUFF, free-lance writer; b. Salt Lake City, Apr. 1, 1921; d. Russell Kimball and Margaret Angline (McIntyre) Woodruff; m. Phillip Albers Baender, Aug. 17, 1946 (dec.); children: Kristine Lynn, Charlene Anne, Michael Phillip, Russell Richard. B.A., U. Utah, 1944. In clerical, personnel work various firms, San Francisco Bay area, 1970-75; reporter, columnist Valley Pioneer, Danville, Calif., 1975-77; editor Diablo (Calif.) Inferno, 1971-76; author Shifting Sands, 1981, Tail Waggings of Maggie, 1982. Fellow Internat. Biog. Assn.; mem. Nat. Writers Club, AAUW, Soc. Children's Book Writers, Internat. Women's Writers Guild, Alpha Delta Pi. Republican. Episcopalian.

BAER, JOHN METZ, entrepreneur; b. Md., June 30, 1908; s. Adam Daniel and Leah Bertie (Metz) B.; BS, Goshen Coll., 1932; m. Joan Cushwa, Oct. 16, 1974; children—John Metz, Deborah Ann. Owner, pres. Baer Foods Inc., Hagerstown, Md.; pres. Profl. Arts Assocs. Inc., Greencastle (Pa.) Ice and Cold Storage Inc., Baer Packing Corp., Greencastle; Nat. Frozen Foods Assn. ofcl. rep. to 1st Internat. Foods Conf., Paris, 1950; participant numerous internat. food confs. Pres., Washington County Hosp., Hagerstown, 1958-60, Washington County Bd. Edn., 1962-68; bd. dirs. Am. Heart Assn. of Md., Hagerstown Jr. Coll.; chmn. Hagerstown Parking Authority. Mem. Produce Mktg. Assn. (past pres.). Republican. Methodist. Clubs: Fountainhead Country, Assembly of Hagerstown. Lodge: Rotary. Home: 745 Briarcliff Dr Hagerstown MD 21740 Office: 5 Public Sq Hagerstown MD 21740

BAER, JOHN RICHARD FREDERICK, lawyer; b. Melrose Park, Ill., Jan. 9, 1941; s. John Richard and Zena Edith (Ostreyko) B.; m. Linda Gail Chapman, Aug. 31, 1963; children—Brett Scott, Deborah Jill. B.A., U. Ill.-Champaign, 1963, J.D., 1966. Bar: Ill. 1966, U.S. Dist. Ct. (no. dist.) Ill. 1967, U.S. Ct. Appeals (7th cir.) 1969, U.S. Ct. Appeals (D.C. cir.) 1975, U.S. Ct. Appeals (9th cir.) 1979, U.S. Supreme Ct. 1975. Assoc. Keck, Mahin & Cate, Chgo., 1966-73, ptnr., 1974—; instr. Advanced Mgmt. Inst., Lake Forest Coll., 1975-76; speaker various legal seminars, 1975, 76, 77, 80, 81; mem. adv. com. legal asst. program. Nat. Coll. Edn., 1980-83, chmn., 1982-83. Mem. Plan Commn., Village of Deerfield (Ill.), 1976-79, chmn., 1978-79, mem. Home Rule Study Commn., 1974-75, mem. home rule implementation com., 1975-76. Mem. Ill. State Bar Assn. (competition dir region 8 Nat. Moot Ct. Competition 1974, co-chmn. nat. moot competition 1976, profl. ethics com. 1977-84, chmn. 1982-83, spl. com. on individual lawyer advt. 1981-83, profl. responsibility com. 1983-84), ABA, Fed. Bar Assn., Am. Judicature Soc., Nat. Lawyer's Club. Clubs: River (Chgo.). Editorial bd. U. Ill. Law Forum, 1964-65, asst. editor, 1965-66; contbg. editor: Commercial Liability Risk Management and Insurance, 1978. Office: 8300 Sears Tower 233 S Wacker Dr Chicago IL 60606

BAER, LUKE, lawyer; b. Portage La Prarie, Man., Can., Aug. 7, 1950; came to U.S., 1951; s. Allan and Edna (Brubacher) B.; m. Leslie Ann Swazee, Sept. 11, 1982; children: Jessica Ann, Edward Allan. Student, U. Wis., Whitewater, 1971-73; BA in German, History, U. Wis., 1974; student, Rheinische Fredrich Willhems U., Bonn, Fed. Republic of Germany, 1973-74; JD, William Mitchell Coll. Law, 1978. Bar: Minn. 1979, Nev. 1985, U.S. Dist. Ct. Nev. 1985, Minn. 1979, U.S. Ct. Appeals (9th cir.) 1984. Law clk. to chief judge U.S. Dist. Ct., St. Paul, 1979-81; assoc. Dorsey & Whitney, Mpls., 1981-86; v.p., gen. counsel Porsche Cars N.Am., Inc., Reno, 1986—. Del. U.S.-China Joint Session on Trade, Investment and Econ. Law; U.S. Chmn. Joint Session in Trade, Investment and Econ. Law. Recipient West Pub. Book award, 1976, 1977, Am. Jurisprudence Book award, 1977, , Hornhood award, 1977; CJS scholar, 1977, Space Ctr. Acad. scholar, 1977, 3M Acad. scholar, 1978. Mem. ABA, Internat. Platform Assn., Minn. Bar Assn., Nev. Bar Assn., Hennepin County Bar Assn., Nat. Order Barristers (Excellence in Appellate Adv. award). Republican. Office: Porsche Cars N Am Inc 200 S Virginia St Reno NV 89501

BAER, RICHARD MYRON, college administrator; b. Chgo., May 26, 1928; s. Ernest Conroy and Elma Harriet (Billquist) B.; m. Carol Louise Moyer, Aug. 31, 1956; children: Dana. David, Caron, John. BS in Edn., No. Ill. State Tech. Coll., 1954; MS in Bus. Adminstrn., No. Ill. U., 1962, Cert. of Advanced Standing in Bus. Mgmt., 1967. Dist. field engr. Barber-Coleman Co., Rockford, Ill., 1957-62; coordinator, cen. stores No. Ill. U., DeKalb, 1962-67; dean, bus. services Rock Valley Coll., Rockford, 1967-73; bus. mgr. Rockford Coll., 1973-81; v.p. fin., adminstrv. services Met. Com. Coll., Omaha, 1981—. Served as sgt. U.S. Army, 1952-53, Korea. Mem. Nat. Assn. Coll. and Univ. Bus. Officers, Assn. Sch. Bus. Officials, Nebr. Community Coll. Bus. Officers (chmn. 1983-84), Sigma Iota Epsilon. Lodge: Rotary. Office: Met Tech Community Coll PO Box 3777 Omaha NE 68118

BAER, ROGER, psychiatrist; b. Strasbourg, France, Mar. 3, 1937; s. Marcel Baer and Marthe Reins; m. Lucie Maire, Sept 9, 1972; children: Antoine, Vincent. MD, U. Strasbourg, 1967. Intern Hosp. de Strasbourg, 1961-67, chef de clin. faculty, resident, 1967-69; chief of psychiatric services Ctr. Hospitalier de Thionville, France, 1969—. Contbr. articles on psychopharmocology, dream psychology. Home: 5 Rue d'Orly, 57157 Metz France Office: Ctr Hospitalier, Thionville France

BAER, RUDOLF LEWIS, physician, educator; b. Strasbourg, France, July 22, 1910; came to U.S., 1934, naturalized, 1940; s. Ludwig and Clara (Mainzer) B.; m. Louise Jeanne Grumbach, Nov. 6, 1941; children: John Reckford, Andrew Rudolph. M.D., U. Basel, Switzerland, 1934; postgrad. dermatology, N.Y. Postgrad. Med. Sch., 1937-39; M.D. (hon.), U. Munich, Germany, 1981. Diplomate: Am. Bd. Dermatology (mem. 1964-72, pres. 1967-70). Intern Beth Israel Hosp., N.Y.C., 1934-35; resident dermatology Montefiore Hosp., N.Y.C., 1936-37; faculty Columbia Sch. Medicine, 1939-48; dir. dept. dermatology Univ. Hosp., 1961-81; faculty N.Y.U. Sch. Medicine, 1948—, prof. dermatology, 1961—, chmn. dept. dermatology, 1961-81, George Miller MacKee prof., 1961-81; dir. dept. dermatology Bellevue Hosp. Center, 1961-81; sr. cons. VA Hosp., N.Y.C.; cons. Goldwater Meml. Hosp., N.Y.C., Elizabeth A. Horton Meml. Hosp., Middletown, N.J., Hackensack (N.J.) Hosp.; surgeon gen. U.S. Army, FDA; mem. Internat. Com. Dermatology, 1967-82, pres., 1972-77; mem. com. on revision U.S. Pharmacopeia, 1970-75; mem. commn. cutaneous diseases Armed Forces Epidemiologic Bd., 1967-72. Editor: Office Immunology, 1947, Atopic Dermatitis, 1955, Year Book Dermatology, 1955-65; also past mem. numerous editorial bds.; Author over 300 articles. Chmn. bd. Dermatology Found., 1974-77; bd. dirs. Rudolf L. Baer Found. for Skin Diseases, 1975—. Dohi lectr. and recipient Dohi medal Japanese Dermatol. Soc., 1965; Von Zumbusch lectr. Munich, 1967, Hellerstrom lectr. Stockholm, 1970, O'Leary lectr. Mayo Clinic, Rochester, Minn., 1971, Robinson lectr. U. Md., 1972, Barrett Kennedy lectr., 1973, Louis A. Duhring lectr., 1974, Samuel M. Bluefarb lectr., 1975, Frederick J. Novy Jr. vis. scholar, 1978, Morris Samitz lectr., 1979, Ruben Nomland-Robert Carney lectr., 1979, Barrett Kennedy meml. lectr., 1980, A. Harvey Neidorff lectr., 1985, Ferdinand von Hebra meml. lectr., 1988; recipient von Hebra medal U. Vienna, 1988. Fellow N.Y. Acad. Medicine (chmn. sect. dermatology 1963-64), Am. Acad. Dermatology (pres. 1974-75, Dome lectr. 1976, Gold medal 1978, hon. mem. 1980), Am. Acad. Allergy, Am. Coll. Allergists; mem. AMA (chmn. sect. dermatology 1965-66), Am. Dermatol. Assn. (pres. 1977, hon. mem. 1980), Soc. Investigative Dermatology (pres. 1963-64, Stephen Rothman medal 1973, hon. mem. 1980), Bronx Dermatol. Soc. (pres. 1952), N.Y. Dermatol. Soc. (pres. 1982-83), N.Y. Allergy Soc., N.Y. Acad. Scis., N.Y. County and State Med. Soc., Internat. League Dermatol. Socs. (pres. 1972-77, Alfred Marchionini Gold medal 1977); hon. mem. Argentinian, Austrian, Brit., Brazilian, Danish, Finnish, German, Iranian, Israeli, Italian, Japanese, Mexican, Polish, Swedish, Yugoslav, Venezuelan dermatol. socs., Brazilian Nat. Acad. Medicine; corr. mem. Pacific, Cuban, French, dermatol. socs., French Allergy Soc. Home: 1185 Park Ave New York NY 10128 Office: 530 1st Ave New York NY 10016

BAER-KAUPERT, FRIEDRICH-WILHELM, political scientist, educator; b. Berlin, Oct. 1, 1930; s. Ernst Fritz and Hedda (Kaupert) Baer; m. Barbara Haver; children: Martin, Susanne, Friederike, Ulrich, Britt, Anjoushka; student U. Göttingen, U. Berlin, 1952, U. Saarbrücken, 1953-58; Dr. Roman and Common Law, U. Saarbrücken, 1967. Asst. prof. European law, U. Saarbrücken; prof. public law and polit. sci. U. Berlin, 1974—; bd. dirs. several insts. and research ctrs. Contbr. numerous articles on law and problems of security policy to books and jours. Home: 8 Giesebrechtstrasse, D-1000 Berlin 12 Federal Republic of Germany Office: 206 Kurfürstendamm, D-1000 Berlin 15 Federal Republic of Germany

BAERLECKEN, MARTA, literature educator; b. Dusseldorf, Germany, Mar. 3, 1909; d. Albert and Elizabeth (Heubler) Hechtle; Dr. phil., univs. Bonn, Berlin, Cologne, 1937; m. Wilhelm Baerlecken; children—Stefan, Michael. Univ. lectr., developer Dutch studies programs U. Cologne, 1937-61, U. Aix la Chapelle, 1966-74, U. Berlin, 1975-77, public schs. North Rhine, 1971-74. Pres., German Dutch Assn. Germany, 1953-63; bd. dirs. German group Internat. Fedn. Univ. Women, 1952-58; bd. dirs. found. Europe German sect., 1985—; mem. 8th Commn. Status of Women, UN, 1954. Mem. Internat. Assn. Dutch Studies, Internat. Assn. German Studies, Steuben Schurtz Assn., German-Dutch Assn. Roman Catholic Author: Walter v.d. Vogelweide, 1937; The Flemish Literature, 1942; Modern Literature in the Netherlands, 1968; Lyric Poetry of the Netherlands, 1974. Home: 117a Rheinallee, 4000 Dusseldorf Federal Republic of Germany

BAERTSCHI, PIERRE, architect; b. Geneva, Jan. 2, 1950; s. Frederic and Paulette (Varin) B. BArch, Geneva U., 1975. Asst. master Secondary Tech. Sch., Geneva, 1975-77; chief service monuments and sites Pub. Works of Canton, Geneva, 1977—; mem. Nat. Com. for Landscape and Environ. Preservation, Bern, Switzerland, 1987—. Author: Carouge, 1975, Hermance, 1985; editor Heimatschuz/Sauvegarde, 1977—. Pres. Carouge City Council, 1984. Mem. Nat. Congress Conservators (pres. 1985-87), Swiss Soc. Engrs. and Architects. Mem. Social Dem. Party. Roman Catholic. Club: New Helvetic Soc. (Geneva) (pres. 1982-86). Home: 58 rue Ancienne, 1227 Carouge Switzerland Office: Pub Works of Canton Geneva, 5 rue David Dufour, 1205 Geneva Switzerland

BAERWALD, JOHN EDWARD, civil and traffic engineer, former educator, consultant; b. Milw., Nov. 2, 1925; s. Albert J. and Margaret M. (Brandt) B.; m. Elaine S. Eichstaedt, Apr. 3, 1948 (dec.); children: Thomas J., James K., Barbara Baerwald Bowman; m. Donna D. Granger, May 24, 1975. BS in Civil Engring., Purdue U., 1949, MS in Civil Engring., 1950, PhD in Civil Engring., 1956. Registered profl. engr., Calif., Ill., Ind. Research asst. Purdue U., 1949-50, research assoc., instr. hwy. engring., 1950-52, research engr., instr. hwy. engring., 1952-55; asst. prof. traffic engring. U. Ill., Urbana, Champaign, 1955-57; assoc. prof. traffic engring. U. Ill., Urbana, 1957-60, prof. traffic engring., 1960-69, prof. transp. and traffic engring., 1969-83, prof. emeritus, 1983—, univ. traffic engr., 1957-63, dir. Hwy. Traffic Safety Ctr., 1961-83; pres. John E. Baerwald P.C., Santa Fe, 1983—, prof. emeritus, 1983—; staff assoc. Police Tng. Inst., 1969—; cons. traffic engr., 1952—; chmn. Champaign Parking and Traffic Commn., Ill., 1960-69; liaison mem. staff subcom. Ill. Gov.'s Ofcl. Traffic Safety Coordination Com., 1962-69, mem. subcom. hwy. safety program deficiencies, 1970-72; mem. Champaign-Urbana Urbanized Area Transp. Study, 1963-83, tech. adviser to policy com., 1963-75, chmn. policy com., 1977-83; mem. Ill. Sec. State Adv. Com. Vehicle Registration and Titling Matters, 1973-74; trustee Champaign-Urbana Mass Transit Dist., 1973-83, chmn., 1975-83; mem. tech. adv. com. Ill. Transp. Study Commn., 1977-81. Served with AUS, 1943-46. Recipient Pub. Service award Ill. Sec. State, 1976, past. pres. award Ill. Sec. Inst. of Transp. Engrs., 1983. Fellow ASCE, Inst. Transp. Engrs. (internat. pres. 1970, dir. 1964-65, 67-71, internat. council 1977-83, dir. Ill. sect. 1963-64, other offices and coms., exec. com. expert witness council 1986—, Past Pres.' award 1953, Theodore M. Matson Meml. award 1988); mem. Nat. Safety Council (dir. 1975-80, other offices and coms.), Am. Rd. and Transp. Builders Assn. (safety and environ. com. 1975-78, mem. transp. safety adv. council 1976-83, pres. edn. div. 1979, dir. 1979-83, mem. exec. com. 1979-80), Transp. Research Bd. (div. B council 1974-83, other offices and coms.), Pan Am. Hwy. Congress (best tech. paper award 1963, 67), Sigma Xi, Chi Epsilon. Lutheran. Lodges: Lions, Masons.

BAFILE, CORRADO CARDINAL, b. L'Aquila, Italy, July, 1903; s. Vincenzo and Maddalena (Tedeschini) B.; LL.D., U. Rome, 1926, D.C.L., Lateran U., Rome, 1939. Ordained priest, Roman Catholic Ch., 1936, consecrated bishop, 1960; elevated to cardinal, 1976; officer Sec. of State, Vatican, 1939-58; privy chamberlain of the Pope, 1958-60; apostolic nuncio, Germany, 1960-75; prefect Sacred Congregation for the Causes of Saints, 1976-80; cardinal Roman Curia, Rome, 1976—. Home: 10 Via P Pancrazio Pfeiffer, 00193 Rome Italy

BAGAZA, JEAN-BAPTISTE, former president of Burundi; b. Murambi, Aug. 29, 1946; ed. Ecoles des Cadets, Brussels, Belgian Mil. Sch., Arlon. Former asst. to Gen. Ndabe meye; lt.-col., chief of staff Armed Forces; led coup to overthrow Pres. Micombero, 1976; chmn. Supreme Revolutionary Com., pres. Republic of Burundi, 1976-87, minister of def., 1977; attained rank of col., 1977. Chmn. Comité de l'Unité pour la Progrés National, 1979—. Address: Office of Pres, Bujumbura Burundi *

BAGBY, WESLEY ST. JOHN, financial consultant; b. Los Angeles, Mar. 22, 1910; s. Wesley Abner and Ethel (Allan) B.; A.B., UCLA, 1932, M.B.A., 1949; m. Evelyn Alice Hall, June 30, 1934; children—Linda Alice (Mrs. James M. McCue), Bonnie Ann (Mrs. Richard Payne). Instr., UCLA, 1932-34; clk. Pacific Mut. Life Ins. Co., Los Angeles, 1927-34, supr., 1934-42, mgr. underwriting dept., 1946-49, mgr. underwriting and issue depts., 1949-51, asst. treas., 1951-53, asst. v.p., 1953-54, comptroller, 1954-63, v.p., controller, 1963-70, v.p., treas., 1970-72; account exec. Pacific Equity Sales Co., Newport Beach, Calif., 1972-73; salesman Wick Realty, Inc., Lahaina, Hawaii, 1973-77; broker Jack Huddleston, Inc., Realtors, Lahaina, 1977-85, Maui Realty Co. Inc., Lahaina, 1985—; v.p. Art Industries, Inc., Los Angeles, 1952-63. Bd. dirs. Honokeana Cove Apt. Owners Assn., Hawaii, 1968-79, pres., 1972-73; bd. dirs. Mahina Surf Apt. Owners Assn., 1974—, pres., 1975-76; bd. dirs. Calif. div. Am. Cancer Soc., 1959-73, Maui United Way, 1973—; bd. dirs. Alaeloa Homeowners, 1972—, pres., 1981; bd. dirs. Honokowai-Napili-Kapalua Taxpayers Assn., 1976-81, pres., 1979-80. Served to comdr. USNR, 1942-46. Fellow Life Office Mgmt. Assn. (dir. 1966—, exec. com., chmn. bd. 1970—); mem. Am. Cancer Soc., Fin. Execs. Inst. (dir. 1966-70), Navy League (dir. Maui chpt.), Res. Officers Assn., Am. Mgmt. Assn., Med. Research Assn. Calif. (dir. 1967—, treas. 1969—), Health Care Systems Adminstrs. (treas. Los Angeles 1970-72), Maui Whalewatchers (v.p. 1979-80), Lahaina Restoration Found., Phi Beta Kappa, Beta Gamma Sigma, Alpha Kappa Psi, Alpha Gamma Omega. Republican. Presbyterian. Clubs: Lahaina Yacht (bd. trustees 1986—), Kapalua Golf (Lahaina). Lodge: Rotary. Home: 20 Alaeloa 25 Lahaina HI 96761 Office: PO Box 5 Lahaina HI 96761

BAGBY, WILLIAM RARDIN, lawyer; b. Grayson, Ky., Feb. 19, 1910; s. John Albert and Nano A. (Rardin) B.; m. Mary Carpenter, Sept. 3, 1939; 1 child, John Robert; m. Elizabeth Hinkel, Nov. 22, 1975. AB, Cornell U., 1933; JD, U. Mich., 1936; postgrad., Northwestern U., Evanston, Ill., 1946-47. Bar: Ky. 1937, Ohio 1952, U.S. Tax Ct. 1948, U.S. Supreme Ct. 1950, U.S. Ct. Appeals (6th cir.) 1952. Sole practice, Grayson, 1937-43; atty., judge City of Grayson, 1939-43; counsel Treasury Dept., Chgo., Cleve. and Cin., 1946-54; sole practice Lexington, Ky., 1954—; prof. U. Ky., 1956-57; gen. counsel Headley-Whitney Mus., 1974-84; mem. Bd. of Adjustment, Lexington-Urban County City Govt., 1965—, chmn. 1981—. Trustee Bagby Found. Musical Arts, N.Y.C., 1963-74; trustee, gen. counsel McDowell Cancer Found., 1979—, pres. 1988—. Served to lt. USN, 1943-46. Mem. ABA, Am. Judicature Soc., Ky. Bar Assn. (hon. life), Fayette County Bar Assn. Democrat. Episcopalian. Clubs: Spindletop, Keeneland, Lexington, Iroquois Hunt, U. Ky. Faculty. Lodge: Rotary Home: 228 Market St Lexington KY 40508 Office: 1107 1st Nat Bank Bldg Lexington KY 40507

BAGDAN, GLORIA, interior designer; b. Bronx, N.Y., May 24, 1929; d. Max and Molly (Trufelman) Green; student CCNY, 1947-49, Inst. Interior Design, 1964, Wharton Sch., 1977; m. Kenneth Bagdan, Nov. 25, 1948 (dec. 1974); children—Meryl Bagdan Robins, Scott, Stacy. Founder, 1st pres. Bronx Mcpl. Hosp. Aux., 1955-60; interior designer, Scarsdale, N.Y., 1964—; v.p., treas. Gold Medal Farms, Bronx, 1974-79. Active in fundraising Grasslands Hosp. Heart Assn.; cons. Mental Health Assn., 1967—; bd. dirs. 20 Sutton Pl. S., N.Y.C.; mem. Republican Senatorial Inner Circle, Washington. Mem. Internat. Platform Assn., Mcpl. Art Soc. N.Y., Nat. Trust Hist. Preservation, U.S. Congl. Adv. Bd. Clubs: Atrium (N.Y.C.); Internat. Beaux Arts. Home: 20 Sutton Place S New York NY 10022

BAGGE, CARL ELMER, association executive, lawyer; b. Chgo., Jan. 12, 1927; s. Hjalmar and Adele (Elmquist) B.; m. Margaret Evelyn Carlson, June 27, 1953; children: Carol Eileen, Charles Edward, Barbara Ann, Beverly Jean. B.A. summa cum laude, Augustana Coll., 1949; postgrad., Uppsala (Sweden) U., 1947, U. So. Calif., 1956; J.D., Northwestern U., 1952; LL.D. (hon.), Alderson Broaddus Coll., 1980. Bar: Ill. 1951, D.C. 1982. Practiced in Chgo., 1951-52; atty. A., T. & S.F. Ry., Chgo., 1952-62; asst. gen. atty. A., T. & S.F. Ry., 1962-63, spl. asst. exec. dept., 1963-64, gen. atty., 1964-65; commr. FPC, Washington, 1965-70; vice chmn. FPC, 1966-67; pres., chief exec. officer, dir. Nat. Coal Assn., Washington, 1971—; dir. Bituminous Coal Research, Inc., 1971—, Coal Exporters Assn., 1975—; Mem. gen. tech. adv. com. to Energy Research and Devel. Adminstrn.; mem. nat. adv. com. Project Independence; mem. nat. coal adv. com. Fed. Energy Adminstrn.; mem. coal adv. com. to sec. Interior; vice chmn. Internat. Coal Research Commn., 1974; bd. dirs. U.S. nat. com. World Energy Conf. Contbr. articles to legal and bus. publs.; contbr. to: The Supreme Court, 1961. Bd. dirs. Nat. Energy Found.; Mem. commn. ch. and econ. life Nat. Council Chs. Christ.; Mem. Deerfield Zoning Bd. Appeals, 1955-58, Deerfield Plan Commn., 1958-62; Bd. dirs. Augustana Coll., Bituminous Coal Research; trustee Luth. Student Found. Met. Chgo. Served to ensign USNR, 1945-46. Mem. Nat. Assn. R.R. and Pub. Utility Commrs. (exec. com.), Am., Ill., Chgo. bar assns., ICC Practitioners Assn., Legal Club Chgo., Econ. Club Chgo., Assn. Western Ry. Counsel, Lexington Group Ry. Historians, Ill. Jr. C. of C., Am. Scandinavian Found., Ill. Hist. Soc., Ry. Systems and Mgmt. Assn., Phi Beta Kappa, Phi Alpha Delta, Pi Kappa Delta. Republican. Lutheran. Clubs: Capitol Hill (Washington), Nat. Press (Washington), University (Washington), Congressional Country (Washington). Home: 10019 Kendale Rd Potomac MD 20854 Office: 1130 17th St NW Washington DC 20036

BAGGIO, SEBASTIANO CARDINAL, church official; b. Rosà, Italy, May 16, 1913; s. Giovanni Battista and Pierina B.; ed. Seminario Vescovile di Vicenza, Pontificia Universita Gregoriana, Pontificia Accademia Ecclesiastica and Scuola di Paleografia e Biblioteconomia in Vaticano. Ordained priest Roman Catholic Ch., 1935; sec. Nunciatures in El Salvador, Bolivia, Venezuela, 1938-46; with sec. state, 1946-48; chargé d'Affaires, Colombia, 1948-50; Sacra Congregazione Concistoriale, 1950-53; titular archbishop of Ephesus, 1953—; apostolic nuncio, Chile, 1953-59; Apostolic del., Can., 1959-64; Apostolic Nuncio, Brazil, 1964-69; elevated to Cardinal, 1969; archbishop of Cagliari, 1969; head Sacred Congregation for Bishops of Roman Cath. Ch.; pres. Pontifical Commn. for Latin Am., 1973, for Vatican City's State, 1984-85; chamberlain Roman Ch., 1985; cardinal patron Sovereign Mil. Order of Malta. Decorated orders from Bolivia, Brazil, Chile, Colombia, Ecuador, Venezuela, Portugal; knight of Malta. Address: Piazza della Citta Leonina 9, 00193 Rome Italy *

BAGGS, WILBUR JAMES, gynecologist; b. Balt., Nov. 10, 1919; s. Wilbur James and Evelyn Thistle (McCoy) B.; B.A., U. Richmond, 1940; M.D., Med. Coll. Va., 1943; m. Jessie Joyner, Nov. 17, 1980; children by previous marriage—Beverly Lynn, Barbara Denise. Intern, Charity Hosp. La., New Orleans, 1944; resident Norfolk (Va.) Gen. Hosp., 1946-47, Charity Hosp. La., 1947-50; practice medicine specializing in gynecology, New Orleans, 1950, Newport News, Va., 1951—. Served with USN, 1944-46. Diplomate Am. Bd. Ob-Gyn. Fellow A.C.S.; mem. Am. Acad. Thermology, Soc. Study Breast Disease, Med. Soc. Va., Newport News Med. Soc. (pres. 1968). Episcopalian. Club: James River Country (Newport News). Office: 328 Main St Newport News VA 23601

BAGINSKI, GERARD HENRY, physicist, engineering analyst; b. Bialystok, Poland, Aug. 4, 1951; came to U.S., 1964; s. Julian L. and Henrietta (Kmiecik) B.; m. Yvonne Teresa Ziminski, Apr. 16, 1983; 1 child, Catherine. BS, Gannon U., 1973; MA, Kent State U., 1974, PhD, 1980. Subject matter specialist Kentron Internat., Inc., Dallas, 1979-80; physicist Sargent & Lundy Engrs., Chgo., 1980—. Contbr. articles to profl. jours. Mem. Sigma Pi Sigma. Republican. Roman Catholic. Home: 31499 Marlo #12F Madison Heights MI 48071 Office: Sargent & Lundy Engrs 55 E Monroe St Chicago IL 60603

BAGLEY, BRIAN G., physicist; b. Racine, Wis., Nov. 20, 1934; s. Wesley John and Ethel (Rasmussen) B.; BS, U. Wis., 1958, MS, 1959; AM, Harvard U., 1964, PhD, 1968; m. Dorothy Elizabeth Olson, Nov. 20, 1959; children: Brian John, James David, Kristin Marie, Metall. engr. U. Wis., Madison, 1959-60; mem. tech. staff Bell Telephone Labs., Inc., Murray Hill, N.J., 1967-83, Bell Communications Research Inc., Red Bank, N.J., 1984—. Served to 1st lt. AUS, 1960-61. Mem. Am. Phys. Soc., Materials Research Soc. Home: 467 Ridge Rd Watchung NJ 07060 Office: Bell Communications Research Inc Room 3X-257 331 Newman Springs Rd Red Bank NJ 07701

BAGLEY, COLLEEN, marketing executive; b. Mountain Home, Ark., Feb. 18, 1954; d. Roy Louis and Dorothy (Fry) B.; m. William A. Haskin, June 28, 1986. BA cum laude, U. South Fla., 1975. Lic. radio broadcaster, FCC 3d class. TV and radio producer Sta. WUSF-TV-FM, Tampa, Fla., 1974-76; TV announcer Sta. WFLA-TV, Tampa, 1974-76, news reporter, 1976-77, news producer, 1977-79; sr. producer Sta. KSTP-TV, Mpls., 1979-80; exec. producer Sta. WPVI-TV, Phila., 1980-82; dir. mktg. Grand Traverse Resort, Traverse City, Mich., 1982—; cons., bd. dirs. Enough Seminars, Phila., 1981-82. Contbg. author Strategic Hotel/Motel Marketing (Am. Hotel and Motel Assn. award), 1985. Mem. Traverse City Ski Council, 1983—, local host com. Nat. Govs.' Assn., 1986-87; chmn. N.Am. Vasa Cross Country Ski Race Mktg. Com., 1987—. Mem. Traverse City Ad Club (awards for advt. excellence 1984-87), Traverse City C. of C. (air service transp. com. 1984-87), Grand Traverse Conv. and Visitors Bur. (mktg. com. 1984—), N.Am. Vasa

Cross Country Ski Race Mktg. (chmn. 1987-88), No. Mich. Golf Council (exec. bd. 1986, 88). Republican. Avocations: private pilot, aerobics, weightlifting, yoga, scuba diving. Home: 3471 Blackwood St Traverse City MI 49684 Office: Grand Traverse Resort 6300 US 31 N Grand Traverse Village MI 49610-0404

BAGLEY, JAMES EDWARD, hospital administrator; b. Waterloo, Iowa, Sept. 21, 1930; s. William Franklin and Margaret Cecilia (Craig) B.; m. Kathie Rebecca Smith, Nov. 30, 1968; children: Cheryl, Debra, Kathleen, Vicki, Sharri, Lauri. Diploma, Albia Community Coll., 1948; B.A. in Pub. Adminstrn., Upper Iowa U., 1975; M. Hosp. Adminstrn., U. Minn., 1977. Sr. patrolman State of Iowa, Iowa Falls, 1956-63; adminstr. Ellsworth Hosp., Iowa Falls, 1963-68; pres. Greene County Med. Ctr., Jefferson, Iowa, 1968-83; sr. exec. v.p., bd. dirs. Phoenix Bapt. Hosp., 1983—. Pres. Greene County Arts Council, Jefferson, 1980; bd. dirs. Greenwood Homes, Inc., Jefferson, 1981; del. Republican County Conv., Greene County, Iowa, 1982. Served with USN, 1948-52. Named Boss of Yr., Jefferson Jaycees, 1978. Fellow Am. Acad. Med. Adminstrs. (chmn. 1983—, Med. Adminstr. Yr. 1977, Regional Dir. of Yr. 1980), Am. Coll. Health Care Adminstrs. (cert.), Royal Soc. Health; mem. Am. Soc. Hosp. Personnel Adminstrs., Iowa Hosp. Assn. (chmn. 1982-83, Seaman Meml. award 1980). Republican. Methodist. Lodges: Lions, Elks. Home: 15012 N 46th St Phoenix AZ 85032 Office: Phoenix Bapt Hosp and Med Ctr 6025 N 20th Ave Phoenix AZ 85015

BAGOLOR, DIONITO SORIANO, physician; b. Calape, Bohol, The Philippines, July 31, 1947; s. Juan Baquial and Patricia (Soriano) B.; m. Candelaria Calibu Diu, July 8, 1972; children: Charlotte, Mitzi Patricia, Kent Dioneth. BS in Pre-medicine, Cebu Inst. Tech., Cebu City, The Philippines, 1967; MD, Southwestern U., Cebu City, 1972. Resident physician Surigad (Philippines) Med. Ctr., 1972-74, St. Vincent Ferrer Clinic, Calape, 1974-78, Loon (Bohol) Emergency Hosp., 1978-79; pediatrician Bagolor Med. and Diagnostic Clinic, Calape, 1979—. Mem. exec. com. People's Econ. Council, Calape, 1987; treas. Barrangay Council, Besamparados, Calape, 1987. Mem. Philippine Med. Assn., Bohol Med. Assn. Clubs: Calape Tennis (pres. 1986-87), Atong Bulangan (Calape) (pres. 1987). Lodge: KC. Home: Desamparados, Calape Bohol, Philippines

BAGOTT, JOHN See WATSON, SIR FRANCIS

BAHALIM, ABDUL LATIF, international business executive; b. Gangapur, Rajistan, India, Aug. 10, 1940; s. Abdul Rahim and Habib un Nisa (Merchant) Bahalim; m. Shaukat Jahan Esmail, Mar. 4, 1970; children—Naz, Tariq, Saba, Hina; m. Hajira Abdullah, Sept. 9, 1960 (div. 1970); 1 child, Khalid. Student pub. schs; B.A., Karachi U., Pakistan, 1962, LL.B., 1962. Cons. dir. Manpower Services, London, Eng., 1962-78; mng. dir. Senatewise, Ltd., London, 1978—, Senatewise Internat., Ltd., London, 1982—, Saudi Express Ltd., London, 1983—, Visa Express, Ltd., 1984—; cons. Brown and Root, Al-Khobar, Saudi Arabia, 1979-84, British Steel, London, Eng., 1983—, IBM-SBM, Jeddah Saudi Arabia, 1984—, Rolls-Royce, Coventry, United Kingdom, 1984—. Nat. sec. United Kingdom Anglo-Asian Conservative Soc. 32 Smith Square, London, 1978-79, Orgn. British Muslims, London, 1979—. Mem. Inst. Dirs. Advocations; cricket; swimming. Home: 5 Calbourne Rd, London SW12 8LW, England Office: Saudi Express Ltd, 16 The Blvd, London SW17 7BW, England

BAHARLOU, HOUSHANG, cinematographer; b. Sari, Iran, Dec. 14, 1936; arrived in France, 1980; Diploma, Centro Sperimentale di Cinematografia, Rome, 1963. Free-lance cameraman Tehran, Iran, 1964-70; free-lance dir. photography Iran and France, 1970—; prof. Sch. Cinema and TV, Tehran, 1968-73; mem. directorial com. Tehran Internat. Film Festival, 1974-78; bd. dirs. New Film Group, Tehran, 1973-79. Home and Office: 85 blvd Pasteur, 75015 Paris France

BAHARY, WILLIAM SHAUL, chemist, researcher; b. Kermanshah, Iran, Jan. 20, 1936; came to U.S., 1951, naturalized, 1956; s. Shaul S. and Victoria (Menashi) B.; m. Susan C. Kurshan, Nov. 23, 1979. BA, Harvard U., 1957; MA, Columbia U., 1958, PhD, 1961. Sr. research chemist Tex.-U.S. Chem. Co., Parsippany, N.J., 1961-68; vis. asst. prof. Fairleigh Dickinson U., Teaneck, N.J., 1968-73; adj. asst. prof. Stevens Inst. Tech., Hoboken, N.J., 1973-79; supervising engr. Duracell, Inc., Tarrytown, N.Y., 1979—; treas. Bahary & Co., Pearl River, N.Y., 1960—. Contbr. articles to profl. jours. Patentee in field. Mem. Am. Chem. Soc., AAAS, Hudson-Bergen Chem. Soc. (div. program dir. 1975-79). Club: Harvard (N.Y.). Home: 325 E 79th St New York NY 10021

BAHLS, GENE CHARLES, agricultural products company executive; b. Danville, Ill., June 9, 1929; s. Martin Joseph and Renetta Fredrica (Rook) B.; m. Marilyn Bernice Lane, June 9, 1951; children: Steven Charles (dec.), Sara Lynn Bahls Durre, David Lane. BMechE, Purdue U., 1951; postgrad., Miami (Ohio) U., 1958-59, Western Mich. U., 1965-66. Indsl. engr. Gardner Board & Carton Co., Middletown, Ohio, 1951-60; mgr. insdl. engring. Brown Paper Co., Kalamazoo, 1960-70; dir. engring. Armour Pharm. Co., Kankakee, Ill., 1970-76; dir. engring. Corn Processing div. Am. Maize Products Co., Hammond, Ind., 1976-80, v.p. ops., 1980-86, sr. v.p. mfg., 1986—; v.p. ops. sub. Am. Fructose Corp., Hammond, 1980—. Bd. dirs. Kankakee Symphony Assn., 1986—. Served with U.S. Army, 1954-56. Mem. Corn Refiners Assn. (bd. dirs.), Whiting, Ind. C. of C. Republican. Lutheran. Home: 2 Bristol Green Bourbonnais IL 60914 Office: Am Maize Products Co 1100 Indianapolis Blvd Hammond IN 46320

BAHNER, THOMAS MAXFIELD, lawyer; b. Little Rock, 1933; B.S., Carson-Newman Coll., 1954; B.D., So. Baptist Theol. Sem., 1957; J.D., U. Va., 1960. Admitted to practice Tenn. 1960, Va. 1960, U.S. Dist. Ct. (ea. dist.) Tenn. 1961, U.S. Supreme Ct. 1970, U.S. Ct. Appeals (6th cir.) 1970, U.S. Ct. Appeals (8th cir.) 1972, U.S. Ct. Appeals (4th cir.) 1975. Assoc. Kefauver, Duggan and McDonald, Chattanooga, 1960-62; ptnr. Duggan, McDonald and Bahner, Chattanooga, 1962-64, Chambliss, Bahner, Crutchfield, Gaston and Irvine, Chattanooga, 1964—; mem. adv. commn. civil rules Tenn. Supreme Ct., chmn., 1982—, mem. bd. profl. responsibility, 1982-85, chmn. fin. com., 1984-85. Sr. contbg. editor: Evidence in America, the Federal Rules in the United States, 1987. Life fellow Am. Bar Found.; founding fellow Tenn. Bar Found.; mem. Am. Coll. of Trial Lawyers, Am. Bd. Trial Advocates, Chattanooga Bar Assn. (pres. 1969-70), Tenn. Bar Assn. (lectr. 1965, bd. govs. 1975-82, pres. 1980-81), Conf. So. Bar (pres., chmn. 1980-81), ABA (Tenn. del. 1984—), Va. State Bar, Chattanooga Trial Lawyers Assn., Tenn. Def. Lawyers Assn., Am. Judicature Soc., Estate Planning Council (bd. dirs. 1971-72), Delta Theta Phi. Baptist (deacon, former chmn., chmn. pulpit com.). Clubs: Mountain City, Walden, Signal Mountain Golf and Country. Lodge: Rotary. Home: 718 Parsons Ln Signal Mountain TN 37377 Office: Chambliss Bahner Crutchfield Gaston & Irvine 1000 Tallan Bldg Two Union Sq Chattanooga TN 37402

BAHNINI, M'HAMED, government official; b. Fez, Morocco, 1914. Grad., Lycée Gouraud (now Lycée Hassan II), Rabat, Morocco. Sec. Royal Palace, Morocco; magistrate Haut Tribunal Chéien, Morocco; instr. Collège Impérial, Morocco; pvt. tutor Royal Family, Morocco; dir. Imperial Cabinet, Morocco, 1950-51; del. judge Meknès, Morocco, 1951; exiled 1952-54; sec.-gen. of cabinet Morocco, 1955-72, minister of justice, 1958-65, minister adminstrv. affairs, 1965-70, minister nat. defense, 1970-71, minister justice, sec.-gen. govt., 1971-72, dep. prime minister, 1972, minister of state for culture, 1972-81, minister of state without portfolio, 1981—. Address: care Ministry of State, Royal Palace, Rabat Morocco *

BAHRI, AHMED MALEK, international organization executive; b. Souk Naaman, Constantine, Algeria, July 15, 1938; arrived in Ethiopia, 1977; s. Hammana Othman and Fatima Bahri; m. Fatima Benabbou, 1967; children: Ibtisam, Tarub. Degree in Stats. and Econs., Ecole Statistique, Paris, 1965; diplome études sujérieures, U. Algiers, 1967. Cert. adminstr. Chief advisor, dir. Statis. Office, Algiers, Algeria, 1965-73; dir. higher edn. and research planning Ministry Higher Edn. and Sci. Research, Algiers, 1973-75; dir. human resources planning Ministry Planning, Algiers, 1975-76; chief population div. UN, Addis Ababa, Ethiopia, 1977—; cons. in field. Co-author: Africa in the 21st Century, 1987; co-editor: Population in African Development, 1974. Zellidja Found. grantee, Paris, 1958. Mem. Internat. Statis. Inst., Internat. Union for Sci. Study of Population, Assn. Maghrebine Etude Population. Home and Office: Box 3005, Addis Ababa Ethiopia

BAI, XIQING, pathologist; b. Shen Yang, People's Republic of China, Oct. 2, 1904; s. Wen-Lin and Hua (Cheng) B.; m. Jiang Yi., July 1, 1935; children: Jie, Yan, Shi. MD, Mukden Med. Coll., Shen Yang, 1930. Asst. pathologist Mukden Med. Coll., Shen Yang, 1930-32, prof. pathology, 1943-45; lectr. pathology Peking Union Med. Coll., People's Republic of China, 1936-42; v.p. Shen Yang Med. Coll., 1946-54, Chinese Acad. Med. Scis., Beijing, 1954-79; scientific vis. dept. pathology Glasgow, Scotland, U. Leads (Eng.) U., 1933-35. Chief editor Pathology, 1987. Scientific advisor Ministry of Pub. Health, Beijing, 1954-83. Mem. Chinese Med. Assn. (pres. 1980-84, hon. pres. 1985—), Chinese Assn. Pathology, Internat. Acad. Pathology, Chinese Assn. Sci. & Tech. Home: 304 3d Gate, Bldg 24 Wu Xi De, Beijing Peoples Republic China Office: Chinese Med Assn, 42 Dongsi Xidaji, Beijing Peoples Republic of China

BAIER, AUGUSTO CARLOS, plant researcher; b. Bagé, Rio Grande do Sul, Brazil, May 10, 1941; s. Karl Fabian and Johanna (Bossard) B.; m. Selma Mielke; children: Luciane Mielke, Auro Augusto. Bel. Agronomy, E.A Eliseu Maciel, Pelotas, Brazil, 1968; D in Agr., Tech. U., Munich, 1972. Wheat breeder EMBRAPA/CNPT, Passo Fundo, Brazil, 1972-77; triticale breeder EMBRAPA/CNPT, Passo Fundo, 1977—, coordinator nat. triticale research program, 1981—, lupin breeder, 1982—; lectr. U. Passo Fundo, 1981—; coordinator, organizer Nat. Wheat Research Ctr., Brazil, 1974. Author: As Lavouras de Inverno, 1988; contbr. articles to profl. jours. Recipient Medalha Hermes award Minstro do Exército, Bagé, 1960. Mem. Am. Soc. Agronomy, Soc. Brasileira P/Prog.da Ciência, Soc. Brasileira de Genética. Lutheran. Club: Passo Fundo (pres. 1982-83), Loj. Luz do Planalto (ven. master 1986-87). Lodge: Rotary. Home: R Independencia 2245, 99025 Passo Fundo RS Brazil Office: Nat Wheat Research Ctr, Cx Postal 569, 99001 Passo Fundo RS Brazil

BAIG, ZAMMURAD, physician; b. Jhelum, Punjab, Pakistan, Dec. 12, 1942; s. Brig Beg Abbas and Resham Begum; m. Saeeda Begum; children: Nargis, Amer, Faisal. FSc., Emerson Coll. Multan, Punjab, 1961; MBBS, U. London, Diploma in Tropical Medicine and Hygiene, 1970. Sr. house officer Nishstar Hosp. Multan, Punjab, 1966-67; med. officer Prime Glass Works, Jhelum, 1967-69; sr. officer St. Mary's Hosp., Newport, Isle of Wight, Eng., 1969-70; sr. house officer Old Ch. Hosp., Ramford, Eng., 1970; pathologist Pakistan Army, Kharian, Punjab, 1970-72; practice medicine specializing in family medicine Jhelum Hosp., 1972—; cons. med. specialist Pak Family Hosp., Jhelum, 1985—. Sr. v.p. Pakistan People's Party, Jhelum, 1977, ret., 1977. Served to capt. Pakastani Army, 1970-72. Decorated War medal. Mem. Pakastani Med. Assn. (gen. sec. 1978-80), Pakistan Tuberculosis Assn. (life), Nat. Geographic Soc. (life). Home: River Rd, Jhelum Pakistan Office: Pak Family Hosp, Old GT Rd, Jhelum Pakistan

BAILEY, AMOS PURNELL, clergyman, journalist; b. Grotons, Va., May 2, 1918; s. Louis William and Evelyn (Charnock) B.; m. Ruth Martin Hill, Aug. 22, 1942; children: Eleanor Carol (Mrs. Thomas T. Harriman), Anne Ruth (Mrs. Peter S. Page), Joyce Elizabeth (Mrs. David L. Richardson II), Jeanne Purnell (Mrs. James M. Allen). BA, Randolph-Macon Coll., 1942, DD, 1956; BD, Duke U., 1948; ThM, Union Theol. Sem., 1957. Ordained to ministry United Meth. Ch., 1942; pastor Emporia, Va., 1938, Beulah UMC Ch., Richmond, Va., 1938-43; pastor New Kent circuit, 1943-44, Norfolk, 1948-50, Newport News, Va., 1950-54; pastor Centenary Ch., Richmond, 1954-61; supt. Richmond dist. United Meth. Ch., 1961-67; sr. minister Reveille Ch., Richmond, 1967-70; assoc. gen. sec., div. chaplains Bd. Higher Edn. and Ministry United Meth. Ch., Washington, 1970-79; v.p. Nat. Meth. Found., 1979-82; interim minister Herndon Ch., 1985-86; pres. Nat. Temple Ministries, Inc., 1981—; pres. S.E.J. and S.C.U. Communications, 1968-76; dir. Reeves-Parvin Co., 1978-85; v.p. Va. Conf. Bd. Missions, 1955-61, Meth. Commn. Town and Country Work, 1956-67; mem. Meth. Commn. on Higher Edn., 1960-70, Meth. Interbd. Council, 1960-70; del. Southeastern Jurisdictional Conf., 1964, 68, Gen. Conf., 1964, 66, 68, 70, World Meth. Conf., London, 1966, Denver, 1970, Dublin, 1976; exec. com., Congress, 1987-88; fin. com. Nat. Ch. Growth Research Ctr., 1986—; frequent chaplain U.S. Senate, U.S. Ho. of Reps., Va. Gen. Assembly; mem. council, exec. com., pres. communications com. Southeastern Jurisdiction, 1968-76; pres. Joint Communications Com., 1968-76; vice chmn. Ministry to Service Personnel in East Asia, 1972-79; mem. Commn. on Interpretation, Va. Conf.; participant Ednl. Study Mission to Eng., 1988. Writer: syndicated column Daily Bread, syndicated radio devotional, 1945-69; condr.: weekly radio counseling program The Night Pastor, 1955-69, Sunshine and Shadows, 1967-70; Contbr. articles to profl. publs. Mem. exec. com. Va. Conf. Bd. Edn., 1968-72; mem. World Meth. Council.; Mem. Va. Commn. Aging; pres. adv. bd. Richmond Welfare Dept., 1956-68; group chmn. industry div. Richmond United Givers Fund, 1961; mem. Va. Conf. Bd. Ministry, Richmond Pub. Assistance Com., Richmond Council on Alcoholism; chmn. chaplains adv. council VA, Washington; bd. mgrs. Richmond YMCA, 1961-69; Bd. dirs. Va. Meth. Advisers; trustee Randolph-Macon Coll., 1960-82, trustee emeritus, 1986; bd. visitors Duke Div. Sch., 1964-70; trustee So. Sem., 1961-76. Served with Chaplains Corps AUS, 1945-47. Mem. Meth. Hist. Soc., Duke Div. Alumni Assn. (pres.). Club: Kiwanis. Home: 7815 Falstaff Rd McLean VA 22102 Office: 1835 N Nash St Arlington VA 22209

BAILEY, CARL FRANKLIN, telecommunications company executive; b. Birmingham, Ala., Sept. 17, 1930; married. B.B.A., Auburn U., 1952. Asst. v.p. (Ala. area) So. Bell Telephone & Telegraph Co., before 1968; exec. asst. fed. dept. AT&T, 1968-71; with South Central Bell Telephone Co., Birmingham, Ala., 1968—, asst. v.p. Ala. area, 1968-71, asst. to pres., 1971-72, gen. mgr. ops., 1972-76, v.p. customer facility services, 1976-77, v.p. La. area, 1977-80, exec. v.p. corp. affairs, from 1980, now pres., chief exec. officer, dir. Served to 1st lt. U.S. Army, 1952-55. Office: South Central Bell Telephone Co PO Box 771 Birmingham AL 35201 *

BAILEY, CECIL CABANISS, lawyer; b. LaGrange, Ga., Oct. 29, 1901; s. Daniel B. and Maude (Layfield) B.; m. Augusta Mann, Feb. 15, 1923; children: Dorothy Bailey McGehee, Marilyn Evans-Jones, William C. Student, Young Harris Coll., 1922, U. Ga., 1923; LL.B., Stetson U., 1927, LL.D. (hon.), 1978. Bar: Fla. 1927. High sch. prin. Byromville, Ga. and Madison, Fla., 1923-24; assoc. Scarlett, Jordan, Futch & Fielding, DeLand, 1927-29; clk. Judge's Ct. Volusia (Fla.) County, 1929-30; assoc. Rogers & Towers, Jacksonville, 1930-37; sr. partner Rogers, Towers, Bailey, Jones & Gay, 1937—; sr. v.p., gen. counsel Gulf Life Ins. Co.; sr. dir. Cain & Bultman, Inc. Bd. overseers Stetson U. Coll. Law, St. Petersburg, Fla.; trustee Charles A. Dana Law Center Found., Hope Haven Hosp.; past pres. and trustee Jacksonville Public Library System; mem. Fla. Game and Fresh Water Fish Commn. Mem. ABA, Fla. Bar Assn., Jacksonville Bar Assn. (pres. 1946), Am. Judicature Soc., Newcomen Soc., Phi Alpha Delta. Methodist. Clubs: Civitan, San Jose Country, Univ., River. Home: 6000 San Jose Blvd Unit 5-A Jacksonville FL 32217 Office: 1300 Gulf Life Dr Jacksonville FL 32207

BAILEY, CECIL DEWITT, aerospace engineer, educator; b. Zama, Miss., Oct. 25, 1921; s. James Dewitt and Matha Eugenia (Roberts) B.; m. Myrtis Irene Taylor, Sept. 8, 1942; children: Marilyn, Beverly. B.S., Miss. State U., 1951; M.S., Purdue U., 1954, Ph.D., 1962. Commd. 2d lt. U.S. Air Force, 1944, advanced through grades to lt. col., 1965; pilot 1944-56, sr. pilot, 1956-60, command pilot, 1960-67, ret., 1967; asst. prof. Air Force Inst. Tech., 1954-58, assoc. prof., 1965-67; assoc. prof. aero. and astronautical engring. Ohio State U., Columbus, 1967-69; prof. Ohio State U., 1970—; dir. USAF-Am. Soc. Engring. Edn. summer faculty research program Wright-Patterson AFB, Ohio, 1976-78. Contbr. numerous articles to profl. jours. Mem. Soc. Exptl. Stress Analysis, Am. Soc. Engring. Edn., Am. Acad. Mechanics, Soc. Natural Philosophy, Air Force Assn., Sigma Xi, Sigma Gamma Tau. Club: USAF Officers. Home: 4176 Ashmore Rd Columbus OH 43220

BAILEY, CHARLES-JAMES NICE, linguistics educator; b. Middlesborough, Ky., May 2, 1926; s. Charles Wise and Mary Elizabeth (Nice) B. A.B., Harvard Coll., 1950, M.Th., 1955; D.Min., Vanderbilt U., 1963; A.M., U. Chgo., 1967, Ph.D., 1969. Mem. faculty dept. linguistics U. Hawaii, Manoa, 1968-71, Georgetown U., 1971-73, U. Mich., Ann Arbor, 1973; mem. tech. faculty U. Berlin, 1974—, prof., 1974—. Fellow Netherlands Inst. Advanced Study; mem. European Acad. Arts, Scis. and Humanities (corr.), Linguistic Soc. Am., Internat. Phonetic Assn., Soc. Linguistica Europaea, Am. Dialect Soc., Am. Hort. Soc. Home: Orchid Land Dr PO Box 1042 Keaau HI 96749 Office: Tech Univ Berlin, Ernst Reuter Pl 7 (815), D 1000 Berlin Federal Republic of Germany

BAILEY, DANA KAVANAGH, radiophysicist, botanist; b. Clarendon Hills, Ill., Nov. 22, 1916; s. Dana Clark and Dorothy (Kavanagh) B. B.S. with highest distinction, U. Ariz., 1937; postgrad., Harvard U., 1940; B.A. (Rhodes scholar) Queen's Coll., Oxford U., 1940, M.A., 1943, D.Sc., 1967. Astronomer expdn. to Peru for Hayden Planetarium, N.Y.C., 1937; physicist Antarctic expdn. U.S. Antarctic Service, 1940-41; project engr. Project RAND Douglas Aircraft Co., Santa Monica, Calif., 1946-48; physicist Nat. Bur. Standards, Washington, 1948-55; physicist, cons. Nat. Bur. Standards, Boulder, Colo., 1959-66; radiophysicist, research botanist Space Environment Lab., Environ. Research Labs., Nat. Oceanic and Atmospheric Adminstrn., Boulder, 1966-76; sci. dir. Page Communications Engrs., Inc., Washington, 1955-59; U.S. Exchange rep. Brit. Antarctic Survey Falkland Islands and Antarctica, 1967-68; research assoc. in physics Rhodes U., Grahamstown, Republic South Africa, 1970-71; assoc. in gymnosperms U. Colo. Mus., 1972—; internat. chmn. study group internat. radio consultative com. Internat. Telecommunication Union, Geneva, 1956-78. Contbr. articles to profl. jours. Served to maj., Signal Corps AUS, 1941-46. Decorated Legion of Merit; recipient Arthur S. Flemming govt. award Washington Jr. C. of C., 1951; Silver medal Dept. Commerce, 1952; Gold medal, 1956. Fellow AAAS, Am. Phys. Soc., Am. Geog. Soc., Royal Astron. Soc., Royal Geog. Soc.; mem. Sci. Research Soc. Am. (pres. Boulder br. 1967-68), Am. Geophys. Union, Am. Astron. Soc., Geog. Soc. Lima (hon.), Phi Beta Kappa, Sigma Xi. Clubs: Cosmos (Washington); Explorers (N.Y.C.). Home: 1441 Bluebell Ave Boulder CO 80302 Office: Univ Colo Museum Boulder CO 80309

BAILEY, DANNY GALE, college counselor, educator; b. Paintsville, Ky., Feb. 7, 1947; s. Andrew Lowell and Lorraine (Ferguson) B. BS U. Ky., 1968, MS 1971; MA Morehead State U., 1983, M. Higher Edn., 1983. Tchr. agr. and forestry Johnson County Bd. Edn., Paintsville, 1969; extension agt. Cooperative Extension Service, Paintsville, 1969-70; tchr. agriculture and horticulture Franklin County Bd. Edn., Frankfort, Ky., 1970-73; coordinator spl. services, asst. prof. Ashland Community Coll., Ky., 1973-79, counselor, assoc. prof., 1979-86, prof., 1986—; mem. grad. curriculum com. Morehead State U., 1982—, coll. commn. vis. com. So. Assn. Colls. Schs., 1981—. Chmn. Ashland Area Consumer Fair, 1975-77, Boyd County Community Chest 1977-78; trustee GED Found. for Adult Edn., Ky., treas., 1986-87, vice chmn. 1987—; mem. com. Bluegrass State Games, 1986—. Served to maj. U.S. Army Res., 1969—. Recipient Outstanding Young Educator award Frankfort Jaycees, 1973, Maj. Gen. Benjamin J. Butler Community Relations award U.S. Army Res., 1979, Disting. Alumnus award U. Ky. Coll. Agr., 1981. Mem. Ea. Ky. Assn. Counseling and Devel. (pres. 1981-82, 85-86), Ky. Assn. Counseling and Devel. (bd. dirs. 1981-82, 85-86) Ky. Assn. Res. Officers Am. (v.p. chpt. 1985-86), Alpha Zeta, Phi Delta Kappa, Coll. Personnel Assn. Ky. Democrat. Baptist. Avocations: running; reading; basketball; travel. Home: 2427 Boone St A Ashland KY 41101-4407 Office: Ashland Community Coll 1400 College Dr Ashland KY 41101

BAILEY, DAVID ROYSTON, photographer; b. London, Jan. 2, 1938; s. William Herbert and Gladys (Green) B.; m. Catherine Dyer, Aug. 14, 1986; children: Paloma Lola, Fenton Fox. Photographer Vogue mag./Conde Nast, London, 1959—. Dir. TV commls., documentaries. Served with RAF. Fellow Royal Photographic Soc., Soc. Indsl. Artists and Designers. Address: care R Montgomery and Ptnrs, 5-6 Portland Mews, D'Arblay St, London W1, England Office: Camera Eye Ltd, 24-26 Brownlow Mews, London OC1N 2LA, England

BAILEY, FREDERICK EUGENE, JR., polymer scientist; b. Bklyn., Oct. 8, 1927; s. Frederick Eugene and Florence (Berkeley) B.; m. Mary Catherine Lowder, May 7, 1979. B.A., Amherst Coll., 1948; M.S., Yale U., 1950, Ph.D., 1952. Sr. chemist Union Carbide Research Devel., 1952-59, group leader, 1959-62, asst. dir., 1962-69; mgr. mktg. research Union Carbide, N.Y.C., 1969-71; sr. research scientist Union Carbide Research Devel., South Charleston, W.Va., 1971—; adj. prof. chemistry Marshall U., Huntington, W.Va., 1975—; adj. prof. chem. engring. W.Va. Coll. Grad. Studies, 1981—; adj. prof. chemistry dept. U. Charleston, Morris Harvey Coll., 1962-63, 65; mem. grad. faculty W.Va. U., 1959-61; chmn. Gordon Research Conf. on Polymers, Calif. chmn., 1972, N.H. chmn., 1984; mem. Gordon Research Conf. Council. Author: Poly(ethylene Oxide), 1976; editor: Initiation of Polymerization, 1983; (with K.N. Edwards) Urethane Chemistry and Applications, 1981; (with A. Eisenberg) Interactions in Macromolecules, 1986; patentee in field. Am. InsAddison Brown scholar Amherst Coll., 1948; Forrest Jewett Moore fellow, 1949. Fellow AAAS, Am. Inst. Chemists (cert. chemist, Chem. Pioneer award 1987), N.Y. Acad. Scis.; mem. Am. Chem. Soc. (chmn. divisional officer caucus 1980-85, chmn. div. polymer chemistry 1976, councilor div. 1978—, com. sci. 1978, 82-83, gen. sec. Macromolecular secretariat 1978, sec. divisional activities com. 1986, com. on coms. 1987—). Republican. Episcopalian. Club: Tennis (Charleston, W.Va.). Home: 848 Beaumont Rd Charleston WV 25314 Office: Union Carbide Corp Tech Center South Charleston WV 25303

BAILEY, JAMES LOVELL, conservationist, former state official; b. Portland, Tenn., Dec. 18, 1907; s. James Johnson and Annie May (Lovell) B.; m. Fairrelle Brown, June 1, 1940 (dec. Dec. 1976); 1 child, Annie Elizabeth Genung; m. Hester W. Brown, Apr. 29, 1979; 3 stepchildren. Student, Bowling Green U., 1925, Mid. Tenn. State Tchrs. Coll., 1926-29, Western Ky. State Coll., 1929-30, George Washington U., 1931-33, U. Tenn., 1938-41. With U.S. Bur. of Census, 1930-32, U.S. Dept. of Agr., 1933-37; with Tenn. Dept. Conservation, Nashville 1937-76, dir. ednl. service, 1957-76; organized 1st soil conservation dist. in Tenn., 1940; mem. Tenn. Conservation Commn., 1978-85, sec., 1980—. Author: Our Land and Our Living, 1940; assoc. editor: Tenn. Conservationist, 1959-72, editor-in-chief, 1972-76, editor emeritus, 1976—. Pres. Davidson County (Tenn.) chpt. Muscular Dystrophy Assn., 1957; mem. garden com. Tenn. Bot. Gardens and Fine Arts Ctr., Nashville, 1969—; mem. Vol. State Coll. Adv. and Devel. Council, 1976—; charter mem., bd. dirs. Tenn. Environ. Council, 1970-77, life mem., 1977—; bd. dirs. Tenn. Beautiful, 1972; trustee West Coast Christian Corp. Served with USNR, 1942-45. Recipient Cartter Patten award Tenn. Conservation League, 1963, Key Man award Conservation Edn. Assn., 1967, Gov.'s Conservationist of Yr. award, 1971, silver seal Nat. Council State Garden Clubs, 1973, Forestry Recognition award Soc. Am. Foresters, 1976, cert. of appreciation Nat. Resources Socs. Tenn., 1982, citation Hort. Soc. Davidson County, 1983, Spl. Conservation Achievement award Woodmen of World, 1987; honored for exemplay career in conservation edn. Tenn. Gen Assembly, 1988, others. Fellow Soil Conservation Soc. Am. (pres. Tenn. council chpts. 1961, regional rep., conservation history com., meritorious service award 1985); mem. Mid. Tenn. Conservancy Council, East Tenn. Edn. Assn., Nat. Assn. Conservation Edn. and Publicity (life, pres. 1949), Conservation Edn. Assn. (life), Highland Rim (bd. dirs.) Hist. Soc., Dickson County Hist. Soc., Nat. Wildlife Fedn., Tenn. Assn. Preservation Antiquities, Nat. Trust for Hist. Preservation, Nat. Resources Def. Council, Nature Conservancy, Bowen Campbell House Assn. (life, v.p.), Common Cause, Tenn. Fedn. Garden Clubs Inc. (life). Mem. Ch. of Christ. Club: Nashville Torch (pres. 1963-64). Home: 384 Hwy 47 S White Bluff TN 37187

BAILEY, KEITH ANTHONY, tool company executive; b. Birmingham, Eng., Dec. 2, 1934; s. William and Ethel Rose (Liggins) B.; m. Sylvia Beatrice Garland, Apr., 13, 1957; children: Russell, Julia. Higher nat. cert. in mech. engring., Aston Tech. Coll., Birmingham, 1956; BSc in Indsl. Adminstrn., Aston U., Birmingham, 1960. Quality mgr. Morris Comml. Cars Ltd., Birmingham, 1960-66, works mgr., 1966-68; ops. control man Brit. Leyland, Birmingham, 1968-75; dir. supply Austin/Morris, Birmingham, 1975-76; mng. dir. Alfred Herbert Ltd, Birmingham, 1976-80, WCI Machine Tool Group Ltd., Birmingham, 1980-86, BSA Tools Ltd., Birmingham, 1986—. Served to cpl. RAF, 1957-59. Fellow Brit. Prodn. and Inventory Control Soc.; mem. Brit. Inst. Mgmt., Inst. Mech. Engrs., Machine Tool Trade Assn. (v.p., 1986—), Advanced Mfg. Tech. Research Inst. (dep. chmn. 1986—). Club: Naval and Mil. (London). Lodge: Prometheus Warwickshire Ins. Masters. Home: The Pines, Streetly Crescent, West Midlands B74 4PX, England Office: BSA Tools Ltd, Kitts Green, Birmingham BEE OLE, England

BAILEY, MILTON, chemist; b. N.Y.C., May 20, 1917; s. Abraham and Lillian (Ruderman) Bialek; B.B.A., CCNY, 1940, M.S., 1949; cert. Pratt Inst., 1951; postgrad. Bklyn. Coll., 1958-61; m. Lucille Rubin, Jan. 9, 1954; 1 son, Joseph Adam. Editor newspaper and ednl. materials Adj. gen.'s office Dept. Army, 1941-43; feature editor S. Pacific Daily News, 1945-46; chem. supt. Ruderman Inc., N.Y.C., 1946-52; leather chemist U.S. Naval Supply Research and Devel. Facility, 1952-67; phys. sci. adminstr. USN Clothing and Textile Research Unit, Natick, Mass., 1967—. Lectr. CCNY, 1951-52, N.Y.C. Community Coll., 1953-61. Arbitrator, Am. Arbitration Assn., 1973; sec. Am. Leather Chemists Assn.-ASTM, 1960-64; chmn. subcom. safety shoe com. Am. Nat. Standards Inst., 1973. Served with AUS, 1943-46. Recipient commendation Undersec. Navy, 1964; Presdl. citation for accomplishment in field, 1980. Mem. Soc. Fed. Labor Relations Profls., Am. Leather Chemists Assn., ASTM (chmn. safety and traction for footwear com. 1978-81, chmn. Footwear leather subcom. 1982), Boston Orgn. Devel. Network, Am. Legion, Internat. Assn. Quality Circles (chmn. Navy Clothing and Textile Research Facility steering com. 1982), N.Y. Acad. Sci. Club: Toastmasters (area gov. Bklyn. 1963). Patentee in field. Home: 18 Bayfield Rd Wayland MA 01778 Office: 21 Strathmore Rd Natick MA 01760

BAILEY, PATRICIA SUSAN, physician; b. N.Y.C., Dec. 18, 1943; d. Joel and Ethel (Miller) Salzburg; B.S. magna cum laude, Central Mich. U., 1970, M.A., 1972; M.D., Mich. State U., 1977 . Clin. instr. Mich. State U. Coll. Human Medicine, 1976-77; resident Los Angeles County-Harbor Gen. Hosp., UCLA Med. Center, Torrance, 1977-78; partner, physician in emergency medicine Kaiser-Permanente Hosp., Harbor City, Calif., 1978—; instr. Am. Heart Assn.; clin. instr. U. So. Calif. Coll. Medicine. Trustee, Delta Coll., 1972-74. Mem. Am. Coll. Emergency Medicine, Am. Physicians for Human Rights, Am. Physicians for Social Responsibility, Gay Acad. Union, So. Calif. Women for Understanding, NOW. Jewish. Author: (novel) The Summer of the Flea, 1980; contbr. to Echoes from the Heart (poetry anthology), 1982; contbr. articles to various publs. Office: Kaiser Permanente Hosp 1050 W Pacific Coast Hwy Harbor City CA 90710

BAILEY, RAY VERNON, lawyer, patent atty., property mgr.; b. Royal, Iowa, Dec. 14, 1913; s. George Lewis and Marie (Albers) B.; B.A. cum laude, State U. Iowa, 1935, J.D. cum laude, 1937; m. Velda Maxine Sheldon, June 18, 1938; children—Theron Sheldon, George Bryan. Admitted to Iowa bar, 1937, Ill. bar, 1938; research patent counsel U.S. Gypsum Co., Chgo., 1937-39; asso. Home State Bank, Royal, 1940; partner Dick, Bailey & Fletcher, also Dick and Bailey, Des Moines, 1941-42; investigator U.S. Civil Service Commn., 1942-43; patent adviser Rock Island (Ill.) Arsenal, 1943-45; property mgmt., legal and patent work, Clarion, Iowa, 1945-74, Millers Bay, Milford, Iowa, 1974—; participant World Peace Through Law Ctr. Confs., Madrid 1979, Sao Paulo, Brazil 1981, Cairo 1983, Berlin 1985, Seoul, Korea, 1987 (mem. panel on real estate law), People to People's 6th Worldwide Conf., Aalborg, Denmark 1984. Dir., past pres. Okoboji Protective Assn.; owner Century Farm. Past mem. Iowa Ho. Reps., past mem. ethics com., departmental rules review com., banking laws revision com. Mem. exec. bd. Prairie Gold council Boy Scouts Am.; mem. Iowa Bd. Regents, 1969-81, past chmn. banking com.; mem. Iowa Coll. Aid Commn., 1971-81; past bd. dirs. Iowa Student Loan Liquidity Corp., also past chmn. bylaws com. past mem. alumni council U. Iowa; past chmn. public affairs com. Wright County Extension Council, past pres. Clarion Devel. Commn.; past mem. State of Iowa Com. on Mental Hygiene; mem. People to People Higher Edn. Adminstrs. Del. to People's Republic of China, 1978; mem. planning and goals com. World Peace Through Law Center, Nat. Com. Iowa Endowment 2000 campaign; past bd. dirs. Iowans for Tax Relief; past bd. dirs. U. Iowa Research Found.; Mem. Iowa Campaign Fin. Disclosure Commn.; sponsor U. Iowa Coll. of Law Faculty Library Lounge. Recipient Silver Beaver award Boy Scouts Am. Mem. ABA (patent legis. com.), Iowa (past mem. com. on patent, trademark and copyright law), Wright County, Dickinson County bar assns., State U. Iowa Alumni Assn. (past pres. Clarion chpt.), Iowa Patent Law Assn. (bd. dirs.), Dickinson County Taxpayers Assn. (bd. dirs.) , U. Iowa Parents Assn. (past pres.), Dickinson County Corn Growers Assn. (bd. dirs.), Northwest Iowa/Southwest Minn. U.S. Hwy. 71 Assn. (rep. City of Wahpeton). Club: U. Iowa Pres.'s. Lodge: Iowa State U. Order of the Knoll, Lions. Author papers in field. Address: Millers Bay RR 2 Box 190 Milford IA 51351

BAILEY, RICHARD BRIGGS, investment company executive; b. Weston, Mass., Sept. 14, 1926; s. George William and Alice Gertrude (Cooper) B.; m. Rebecca C. Bradford, June 20, 1950 (div. Dec. 1974); children—Ann, Elizabeth, Richard, Rebecca; m. Anne D. Prescott, Dec. 14, 1974 (div. 1980); m. Anita S. Lawrence, Sept. 12, 1980; 1 dau., Alexandra. B.A., Harvard, 1948, M.A., 1951; postgrad., Grad. Sch. Bus. Adminstrn., 1966. Prodn. engr. C. Brewer & Co., Honolulu, 1951-53; prodn. engr. Raytheon Co., Waltham, Mass., 1953-54; security analyst Keystone Custodian Funds, Boston, 1955-59; industry specialist Mass. Investors Trust, 1959-69; now mng. trustee; mng. partner Mass. Fin. Services, Co., Boston, 1969—; pres. Mass. Fin. Services, Co., 1978-82; chmn., dir. Mass. Fin. Services Co., 1982—; dir. Cambridge Trust Co., Lombard Odier Internat. Portfolio Mgmt. Ltd., London., Sun Life Assurance Co. Can. (U.S.); Chmn. Finance Com., Lincoln, Mass., 1966-68. Trustee Plimoth Plantation, Inc., Plymouth, Mass., Phillips Exeter Acad., Exeter, N.H., 1978-82; mem. adv. bd. Coll. Mental Health Center of Boston. Served to 2d lt., Signal Corps AUS, 1944-46. Decorated Letter of Commendation. Mem. Boston Security Analysts Soc. Republican. Episcopalian. Clubs: Knickerbocker (N.Y.C.), Harvard of N.Y. (N.Y.C.); Somerset (Boston); Eastern Yacht (Marblehead); Coral Beach and Tennis (Bermuda). Home: 63 Atlantic Ave Boston MA 02110 Office: 200 Berkeley St Boston MA 02116

BAILEY, RUTH HILL (MRS. A. PURNELL BAILEY), foundation executive; b. Roanoke, Va., Sept. 17, 1916; d. Henry Palmer and Carolyn Ruffin (Andrews) Hill, m. Amos Purnell Bailey, Aug. 22, 1942; children: Eleanor Carol Bailey Harriman, Anne Ruth Bailey Page, Joyce Elizabeth Bailey Richardson, Jeanne Purnell Bailey Allen. AA Va. Intermont Coll., 1936; student Hollins Coll., 1936-38; BS in Edn., Longwood Coll., Farmville, Va., 1939; postgrad. Ecumenical Inst., Jerusalem, 1979. High sch. tchr. in Va., 1939-48; tour dir. to Europe and Mid. East, 1963-73; participant ednl. study mission to Eng., 1988; syndicated columnist family newspaper, 1954-70; exec. sec. Nat. Meth. Found., Arlington, Va., 1979-82; pres. Va. Conf. Bishop Cabinet Wives, United Meth. Ch., 1963-64; pres. Richmond (Va.) Ministers Wives, 1965-66; chmn. bd. missions Trinity United Meth. Ch., McLean, Va., 1975-79, adminstrv. bd., 1971-79; life mem. United Meth. Women. Div. sec. United Givers Fund, 1964-65; sec. bd. dirs. N.T.M., Inc., 1981—. Recipient Staff award Bd. Higher Edn. and Ministry, United Meth. Ch., 1976, Chaplain Ministry award, 1981. Clubs: Country of Va., Jefferson Woman's. Home: 7815 Falstaff Rd McLean VA 22102 Office: PO Box 5646 Washington DC 20016-0146

BAILEY, WILLIAM O., insurance company executive; b. Syracuse, N.Y., July 1, 1926; s. William E. and Kate (Oliver) B.; m. Carole Watts Parsons, 1979; children: George, Janet, Thomas, Carolyn. A.B. in Econs., Dartmouth Coll., 1947; M.B.A. in Ins., Wharton Sch., U. Pa., 1949. Asst. sec. Nat. Bur. Casualty Underwriters, 1952-54; with Aetna Life & Casualty Co., Hartford, Conn., 1954—, sr. v.p. casualty and surety div., 1968-72, exec. v.p., dir., 1972-76, pres., from 1976, now vice chmn., dir. Corporator, mem. ins. com. Hartford Hosp.; trustee Hartford Rehab. Ctr.; bd. corporators Hartford Sem. Found.; bd. dirs. St. Francis Hosp. Served with USNR, World War II. Mem. Oil Ins. Assn. (past pres.), Soc. C.P.C.U. Office: Aetna Casualty & Surety Co 151 Farmington Ave Hartford CT 06156 *

BAILEY, WILLOUGHBY JAMES, banker; b. Murrumbeena, Victoria, Australia, Mar. 29, 1933; s. William Henry and Alice May (Willoughby) B.; m. Dorothy Jean Miles, Apr., 1956; children—Alison, Robyn, Merryn. Chief mgr. internat. Australia and New Zealand Banking Group Ltd., London, 1977-80, asst. gen. mgr. br. banking, Victoria, 1980-82, gen. mgr. mgmt. services, 1982-83, chief gen. mgr., 1983-84, dir., 1984—, chief exec. officer, group mng. dir., 1984—, dir. ANZ Banking Group (New Zealand) Ltd., Wellington, ANZ Merchant Bank Ltd., London, ANZ Capital Markets Corp. Ltd., Victoria, Dalgety Farmers Ltd., Victoria, Esanda Fin. Corp., Greater Pacific Life Assurance Co. Ltd., Australian Cap. Territory; chmn. ANZ Holdings (New Zealand) Ltd., Wellington, ANZ Holdings U.K. plc., London, ANZ Savs. Bank Ltd., Victoria, ANZ Executors and Trustees, Victoria; dep. chmn. Grindlays Bank plc, London. Mem. Bus. Council Australia, Econ. Planning Adv. Council; hon. treas. Baker Med. Research Found., New South Wales, Queen Elizabeth II Silver Jubilee Trust for Young Australians, Victoria, Baker Med. Research Found., Victoria; mem. governing bd. U. Melbourne Grad. Sch. Mgmt. Found., Victoria; dir. Australian Opera, New South Wales, The Ctr. for Ind. Studies, New South Wales. Fellow Australian Mktg. Inst., Australian Inst. Mgmt., Inst. Dirs.; mem. Australian Bankers Assn., Australian Inst. Bankers (assoc.). Clubs: Anthenaeum, Australian (Melbourne). Avocations: classical music, farming, reading. Office: Australia and New Zealand, Banking Group Ltd, 55 Collins St, Melbourne Victoria 3000, Australia

BAILEY-WHICHARD, SANDRA ANITA, insurance company executive; b. Los Angeles, May 13, 1949; d. Ernest and Mattie Mae (Nash) Bailey. Student, UCLA, 1967-68, Calif. State U.-Los Angeles, 1977-78; BS in Mgmt., Pepperdine U., 1987. Actuarial clk. Transamerica Occidental Life Ins. Co., Los Angeles, 1968-72, supr., 1972-75, asst. mgr., 1975-79, dept. mgr., 1979-83, asst. sec., 1981-83, asst. v.p., 1983-84, 2d v.p., 1984—, instr., 1980—. Vol. Am. Cancer Soc. Fellow Life Mgmt. Inst. of Life Office Mgmt. Assn. Office: Transamerica Occidental Life Ins Co 1150 S Olive St Los Angeles CA 90015

BAILIE, ROBIN JOHN, solicitor; b. Mar. 6, 1937; m. Margaret Boggs, 1961; 1 son, 3 daus. Ed. Queen's U. Belfast. Solicitor, Supreme Ct. Judicature No. Ireland, 1971—; M.P. No. Ireland, 1969-72; minister commerce No. Ireland, 1971-72; bd. dirs. Good Yr. Gt. Britain Ltd., N.W. Exploration plc; chmn. bd. Fine Wine Wholesalers plc, Jones Engring. Services Ltd. Mem. Privy Council. also: S Tuhurloe Close, London SW7, England

BAILLIE, IAIN CAMERON, lawyer; b. Kenmore, Perthshire, Scotland, July 14, 1931; came to U.S. 1960; s. David B. and Agnes (Thomson) B.; m. Joan Mary Christine Miller, Apr. 4, 1959; 1 child, Gordon Cameron. B.Sc., Glasgow U., 1953; J.D., Fordham U., 1965. Bar: N.Y. 1966, U.S. Supreme Ct. 1970, U.K. Patent Office 1961, U.S. Patent Office, 1967, European Patent Office 1978. Patent agt. Monsanto Chem. Ltd., Fulmer, Eng., 1955-59, Potter & Clarkson, London, 1959-60; internat. patent atty. Am. Cyanamid, Stamford, Conn., 1960-61; assoc., later ptnr. Ladas Parry et al, N.Y.C., 1961-76; sr. European ptnr. Ladas & Parry, London, 1976—; lectr. in field. Contbr. articles to profl. jours. Fellow Chartered Inst. Patent Agts.; mem. ABA, Am. Intellectual Property Law Assn., Inst. Trademark Agts., Brit. Am. C. of C. Republican. Presbyterian. Club: Caledonian. Home: 20 Chester St, London SW1X 7BL, England Office: Ladas and Parry, 52 High Holborn, London WC1V 6RR, England

BAILLIE, MYRA ATKINS, public relations company executive; b. Phila., May 22; d. Robert and Lillian Atkins; m. Hugh Scott Baillie, Feb. 20, 1943; 1 child, Mark Mead. Student U. Miami (Fla.), 1940, Columbia Tchrs. Coll., 1939, Calif. Inst. Tech., 1942. Tng. dir. Broadway Dept. Store, Pasadena, Calif., 1941-43; asst. buyer ready-to-wear, floor mgr. G.C. Willis Dept. Store, Champaign, Ill., 1944-45; personnel interviewer Helen Edwards Agency, Los Angeles, 1945; teen promotion dir., fashion coordinator Hale Bros. Stores Calif., San Francisco, 1946-48; buyer Bloomingdales, N.Y.C., 1949-51; resident dir. Field Coordinators, merchandising and mktg. service, N.Y.C., 1967; pres. Myra A. Baillie Cons., pub. relations, mktg. and fund raising, San Francisco, 1968—; cons. in field. Actress, Pasadena Playhouse, 1941-43; mem. San Francisco Mayor's Com. Wine and Flower Festival, 1975-76, San Francisco, Mayor's Litter Com., 1977-78; mem. central com. San Francisco Republican Party, 1963—; mem. nat. com. Women's Crusade for Common Sense Economy, 1978—; mem. San Francisco Conv. Bur., 1974—; mem. devel. com. United Cerebral Palsy Assn. of San Francisco; bd. dirs., pres. Light House for Blind Aux.; 1st v.p. St. Luke's Hosp. Aux.; bd. dirs. Bay Area Benefit Concerts, Presbyn. Hosp. Aux., Stanford Children's Hosp. Aux., Mission Hospice of San Mateo County Aux., The Annex, Mills Meml. Hosp. League (also organizer), San Francisco Ambassadors (also founder), Am. Cancer Soc., Chinese Culture Found.; mem. resource devel. com. United Cerebral Palsy Assn. San Francisco; bd. dirs. ways and means com. St. Francis Meml. Hosp. Aux. Mem. English Speaking Union, Internat. Platform Assn., Am. Soc. Interior Designers, Calif. Press Women (pres. no. dist., State Woman of Wchievement award 1988-89), Pacific Mus. Soc., Alta Bates Hosp. Aux., Am. Women in Radio and TV, Fine Arts Mus. Soc., Mus. Modern Art, San Francisco Symphony Assn., San Francisco Ballet Assn., Meeting Planners Internat. Clubs: San Francisco Bay Area Publicity (dir. 1975—), Peninsula Press (chmn. 1977—), Commonwealth of Calif., San Francisco Garden (chmn. fundraising), Alliance Française, St. Francis Ch. Episcopal Women's Guild (past pres.). Home: 100 Saint Elmo Way San Francisco CA 94127

BAILY, ALFRED EWING, environmental engineer; b. Carmichaels, Pa., Jan. 20, 1925; s. Richard L. and Alta (Hebel) B.; student Waynesburg (Pa.) Coll., 1943, Bethany (W.Va.) Coll., 1943-44; B.S. in Physics, Duke U., 1945, B.S. cum laude in Civil Engring., 1949; m. Hannah Jane Drake, Sept. 1, 1946; children—Judith Ann, Frank Henry, Louise Jane, Nancy Lee. With Chester Engrs., Coraopolis, Pa., 1949—, partner, 1965, dir. municipal services, 1974, pres., dir., 1977—. Mem. Scott Twp. Planning Commn., 1963-64. Served from ensign to lt., USNR, 1943-46, 52-53. Registered profl. engr., D.C., Del., Pa., W.Va., Ky., N.Y., Md., Va., Fla.; diplomate Am. Acad. Environ. Engrs.; certified Nat. Council Engring. Examiners. Fellow ASCE; mem. Nat. Soc. Profl. Engrs., Water Pollution Control Fedn., Am. Water Works Assn., Assn. Iron and Steel Engrs., Tau Beta Pi. Presbyterian (elder). Office: PO Box 9356 Pittsburgh PA 15225

BAIM, DEAN VERNON, economist, educator; b. Rockville Centre, N.Y., Dec. 3, 1949; s. Vernon Blyman and Lillian Bernice (Cornwell) B. BA in Econs. and Polit. Sci. with high honors, U. Calif., Santa Barbara, 1972; MA in Econs., UCLA, 1976, postgrad., 1983, PhD, 1988. Cert. community coll. instr., Calif.; cert. elem. and secondary tchr., Calif. Adj. prof. econs. Pepperdine U., Malibu, Calif., 1977-83, instr., 1983-84, asst. prof., 1984-88, assoc. prof., 1988—; dir. spl. projects Pacific Acad. for Advanced Studies, Los Angeles, 1979-86; cons. Internat. Assn. Auditorium Mgrs., Chgo., 1986-87; instr. Acad. Econ. Edn., Richmond, Va., 1985—; mem. adv. bd. Ctr. Econ. Research and Edn., Northridge, Calif., 1984-85. Editor: Contemporary Econ. Issues, 1982-87, econs. edn. newsletter, 1982—. Named Outstanding Prof. of Yr., Soc. Advancement Mgmt., Pepperdine U. chpt., 1984, Outstanding Young Man of Am., 1986. Mem. Western Econ. Assn., Assn. Pvt. Enterprise Educators, Omicron Delta Epsilon (co-founder, treas. Pi chpt. 1970-71; pres. 1971-72). Home: 21315 Bellini Dr Topanga CA 90290 Office: Pepperdine U Dept Bus Adminstrn Malibu CA 90265

BAIN, WILLIAM JAMES, JR., architect; b. Seattle, June 26, 1930; s. William James and Mildred Worline (Clark) B.; m. Nancy Sanford Hill, Sept. 21, 1957; children: David Hunter, Stephen Fraser (dec.), Mark Sanford, John Worthington. B.Arch., Cornell U., 1953. Partner NBBJ Group (formerly Naramore, Bain, Brady & Johanson), Seattle; juror, lectr. U. Wash., Seattle, Wash. State U.; bd. dirs. Pacific N.W. Bank. Prin. works include various research insts., mcpl. bldgs., office bldgs., hotels, retail and research facilities. Bd. dirs. Arboretum Found., 1971-74, Downtown Seattle Assn., 1980—; bd. dirs. Seattle Symphony Orch., 1974-87, pres., 1977-79; mem. affiliate program steering com. Coll. Architecture and Urban Planning, U. Wash., 1969-71. Served with C.E., U.S. Army, 1953-55. Recipient cert. of achievement Port of Whittier, Alaska, 1955, Disting. Alumnus award Lakeside Sch., 1985. Fellow AIA (pres. Seattle chpt. 1969, chmn. N.W. Regional Student-Profl. Fund 1971, pres. Wash. State council 1974), N.W. Regional Archtl. Found. (pres. 1975); mem. Seattle C. of C. (dir. 1980-83), Nat. Assn. Indsl. and Office Parks, Urban Land Inst., Nat. Assn. Corp. Real Estate Execs., Downtown Seattle Assn. (dir. 1980—, exec. com. 1983—, treas. 1988—), Northwest Forum, Am. Arbitration Assn. (comml. panel 1975—), L'Ogive Soc., Lambda Alpha, Phi Delta Theta. Episcopalian. Clubs: Rainier, Wash. Athletic, Tennis (Seattle); University, Columbia Tower (founding bd. dirs.). Home: 1631 Rambling Ln Bellevue WA 98004 Office: NBBJ Group 111 S Jackson St Seattle WA 98104

BAINBRIDGE, BERYL, author; b. Nov. 21, 1934; d. Richard and Winifred (Baines) Bainbridge; m. Austin Davies, 1954 (div.); 3 children. Student Merchant Taylor's Sch., Liverpool, Arts Ednl. Schs., Tring. Appeared in plays: Tiptoe Through the Tulips, 1976, The Warriors Return, 1977, It's a Lovely Day Tomorrow, 1977, Journal of Bridget Hitler, 1981, Somewhere More Central (TV), 1981; author books: A Weekend with Claude, 1967, Another Part of the Wood, 1968, Harriet Said ..., 1972, The Dressmaker, 1973, The Bottle Factory Outing (Guardian Fiction award), 1974, Sweet William, 1975, A Quiet Life, 1976, Injury Time (Whitbread award), 1977, Young Adolf, 1978, Winter Garden, 1980, Watson's Apology, 1984, Mum and Mrs. Armitage, 1985, Forever England, 1986; (tv series) Filthy Lucre, 1986. *

BAINBRIDGE, JOHN SEAMAN, law school administrator; b. N.Y.C., Nov. 1, 1915; s. William Seaman and June Ellen (Wheeler) B.; m. Katharine Barker Garrett, Feb. 3, 1943 (div. July 24, 1968); 1 son, John Seaman; m. 2d, Elizabeth Kung-Ji Liu, May 13, 1978. B.S., Harvard U., 1938; LL.B., J.D., Columbia U., 1941. Bar: N.Y. 1941, Md. 1946, U.S. Dist. Ct. Md. 1946, U.S. Supreme Ct. 1946, U.S. Dist. Ct. (so. dist.) N.Y. 1948. Gen. practice law, Md. and N.Y., 1945-56; asst. dean Columbia U. Law Sch., 1956-65, assoc. dir. Internat. Fellows Program, 1960-62, asst. to pres. Columbia U., 1965-66; dir. Project on Staffing of African Instns. of Legal Edn. and Research, 1962-72; assoc. dir. Ctr. for Adminstrn. of Justice, Wayne State U., Detroit, 1972-74; dir. planning Sch. Law, Pace U., Westchester County, N.Y., 1974-76; assoc. dean, dean, prof. law No. Ill. U. Coll. Law, Glen Ellyn, 1976-81; vis. prof., assoc. dean Del. Law Sch., Wilmington, 1981-82; dean, prof. law Touro Coll. Sch. Law, Huntington, N.Y., 1982-85; cons. Edward John Noble Found., 1959-61, Inst. Internat. Edn., 1962-67; mem. adv. com. Peace Corps Lawyers Project, 1963; founder, dir. African Law Assn. in Am., Inc., 1965-72. Served to lt. comdr. USNR, 1940-46. Mem. ABA, Sons of Revolution, S.R. Presbyterian. Club: Harvard (N.Y.C.). Author: The Study and Teaching of Law in Africa, 1972. Home: 17 Ringfield Chadds Ford PA 19317

BAINBRIDGE, ROLAND AYLWIN, sales and marketing executive; b. London, Mar. 29, 1946; s. Oliver George and Muriel F.L.A. (Whitcher) B.; m. Avril Anne Bainbridge, Oct. 9, 1971; children: Jenny, Natalie, Isabel. Cert. in engring., Derby Tech. Coll., 1969. Engring. apprentice aero dengine div. Rolls-Royce, Derby, 1965-70, systems analyst data processing, 1970-72; sales exec. Burroughs Machines, Nottingham, Eng., 1972-80; sales and mktg. mgr. Counting House Computer Systems, Bury St. Edmunds, 1980-85; sales mgr. Norsk Data, Ltd., Newbury, Eng., 1985-88, br. mgr. southwest region, 1988—. Office: Norsk Data Ltd, Benham Valence, Newbury RG16 8LU, England

BAINBRIDGE, RUSSELL BENJAMIN, JR., oil and gas property management executive, consultant; b. Chgo., Feb. 24, 1945; s. Russell Benjamin, Sr. and Mary (Hudson) B.; m. Nancy H. Ferguson, Nov. 13, 1982. PhB, Duquesne U., 1968; MS in Geology, Iowa State U., 1976; MBA in Fin., DePaul U., 1980. Instr., Iowa State U., Ames, 1975-76; banking assoc. Continental Ill. Bank, Chgo., 1976-81; v.p. Penn Square Bank, Oklahoma City, 1981-82; sr. v.p. Union Bank and Trust, Oklahoma City, 1982-85; pres., chief exec. officer Magnolia Investors, Ltd., Oklahoma City, 1988—, also dir. Mem. governing bd. Okla. Mus. of Art Assocs., Oklahoma City, 1984—; pres. affiliate bd. Omniplex Assocs.. Mem. AAAS, Am. Assn. Petroleum Geologists, Internat. Platform Assn., N.Y. Acad. Sci. Office: Trust Co of Okla 123 NW 8th Oklahoma City OK 73102

BAINS, LEE EDMUNDSON, lawyer, state official; b. Birmingham, Ala., June 18, 1912; s. Herman Lipsey and Myrtle (Edmundson) B.; m. Ruel Eneida Burton, Jan. 1, 1938; children: Sandra Anita (Mrs. Henry Barnard Hardegree), Myrtle Lee, Lee Edmundson. Student, Birmingham So. Coll., 1930-31; B.S., U. Ala., 1934, J.D., 1936. Bar: Ala. 1936, U.S. Supreme Ct 1936; diplomate: Nat. Coll. Advocacy. Practiced in Bessemer, 1936—, city atty., 1950-58; instr. Birmingham Sch. Law, 1937-41; faculty Nat. War Coll., 1960; atty. for Ala. Power Co., South Central Bell Telephone Co., Phillips Petroleum Co., AmSouth Bank; apptd. by gov. as spl. asst. atty. gen. State of Ala., 1980—. Contbr. article to profl. jour.; Author: Basic Legal Skills, 1976. Pres. Bessemer Bd. Edn., 1955-58, Bessemer YMCA, 1961; Mem. Nat. Naval Res. Policy Bd., 1952-53; advisor Bd. Family Ct., Jefferson County, 1966—; chmn. finance com. Nat. Vets. Day for Birmingham, 1973; Alternate del. Democratic Nat. Conv., 1941; tchr. Men's Bible class First United Meth. Ch., 1966—. Served to rear adm. USNR, 1941-46, ETO, PTO; rear adm. Res. Fellow Am. Coll. Trial Lawyers; mem. Am., Ala. assns. trial lawyers, ABA (vice chmn. environ. law sect. 1979—), Ala. Bar Assn. (chmn. unauthorized practice com. 1977-79, mem. mil. law com.), Bessemer Bar Assn. (pres. 1983-84), Birmingham Bar Assn., Res. Officers Assn., Naval Res. Assn., Soc. Colonial Wars (state gov. 1972-73, corr. sec. 1976—), SAR (pres. Ala.), Phi Gamma Delta, Beta Gamma Sigma. Clubs: Kiwanian; Birmingham Ski (Birmingham), Downtown (Birmingham), The Club (Birmingham). Home: 621 Melody Ln Bessemer AL 35020 Office: 1813 3d Ave Bessemer AL 35020

BAINTON, DONALD J., diversified manufacturing company executive; b. N.Y.C., May 3, 1931; s. William Lewis and Mildred J. (Dunne) B.; m. Aileen M. Demoulins, July 10, 1954; children—Kathryn C., Stephen L., Elizabeth A., William D. B.A., Columbia U., 1952; postgrad., Advanced Mgmt. Program, Rutgers U., 1960. With The Continental Group, Inc., 1954-83, gen. mgr. prodn. planning, 1967-68; gen. mgr. mfg. The Continental Group, Inc. (Eastern div.), 1968-73; gen. mgr. (Pacific div.), 1973-74, (Eastern div.), 1974-75; v.p., gen. mgr. ops. U.S. Metal, 1975-76; exec. v.p., gen. mgr. CCC-USA, 1976-78, corp. exec. v.p., pres. diversified ops., 1978-79; pres. Continental Can Co., 1979-81; pres. Continental Packaging, 1981-83, exec. v.p., operating officer parent co., 1979-83; chmn., chief exec. officer, dir. Viatech Inc., Syosset, N.Y., 1983—; dir. Cablec Inc., Appollo Industries, Dixie Metal Box Ltd. Gen. Pub. Utilities, Dixie Union. Bd. dirs. Columbia Coll. Served with USN, 1952-54, Korea. Mem. Nat. Center for Resource Recovery (dir.), Inst. Applied Econs. (dir.), Columbia U. Alumni Assn. Republican. Roman Catholic. Clubs: Milbrook Country (Greenwich, Conn.); Winged Foot (Mamaroneck, N.Y.); Chemical, Madison Sq. Garden (N.Y.C.). Office: Viatech Inc 1 Aerial Way Syosset NY 11791

BAIR, WILLIAM J., radiation biologist; b. Jackson, Mich., July 14, 1924; s. William J. and Mona J. (Gamble) B.; m. Barbara Joan Sites, Feb. 16, 1952; children: William J., Michael Braden, Andrew Emil. B.A. in chemistry, Ohio Wesleyan U., 1949; Ph.D. in Radiation Biology, U. Rochester, 1954. NRC-AEC fellow U. Rochester, 1949-50, research asso. radiation biology, 1950-54; biol. scientist Hanford Labs. of Gen. Electric Co., Richland, Wash., 1954-56, mgr. inhalation toxicology sect., biology dept., 1956-65; mgr. inhalation toxicology sect., biology dept. Battelle Meml. Inst., 1965-68; mgr. biology dept. Pacific Northwest Labs., Richland, Wash., 1968-74, dir. life scis. program, 1973-75, mgr. biomed. and environ. research program, 1975-76, mgr. environ. health and safety research program, 1976-86, mgr. life scis. ctr., 1986—; lectr. radiation biology Joint Ctr. Grad. Study, Richland, 1955—; cons. to adv. com. on reactor safeguards Nuclear Regulatory Commn., 1971—; mem. several coms. on plutonium toxicology; mem. subcom. inhalation hazards, com. pathologic effects atomic radiation Nat. Acad. Sci., 1957-64; mem. ad hoc com. on hot particles of subcom. biol. effects of ionizing radiation Nat. Acad. Scis.-NRC, 1974-76, vice chmn. Com. on Biol. Effects of Ionizing Radiation IV Alpha Radiation, 1985—; chmn. task force on biol. effects of inhaled particles Internat. Commn. on Radiol. Protection, 1970-79, mem. com. 2 on permissible dose for internal radiation, 1973—; chmn. Task Group on Respiratory Tract Models, 1984—; chmn. Hanford Symposium Inhaled Radioactive Particles and Gases, 1964; co-chmn. Hanford Symposium Biol. Implications of Transuranium Elements, 1971; chmn. Life Scis. Symposium on Radiation Protection: A Look to the Future, 1986; chmn. Am. Inst. Biol. Scis.-AEC-Energy Research and Devel. Adminstrn. Transuranium Tech. Group, 1972-75; mem. Nat. Council on Radiation Protection and Measurements, 1974—, bd. dirs., 1976-82, mem. com. of radionuclides on maximum permissible concentrations for occupational and non-occupational exposure, 1970-77, mem. com. basic radiation protection criteria, 1975—, chmn. ad hoc com. on hot particles, 1974, chmn. ad hoc com. internal emitter activities, 1976-77, mem. com. 57 on internal emitter standards, 1977—; U.S. participant and rep. numerous internat. confs., invited lectr. Japan AEC, Nat. Radiol. Health Inst., Chiba, 1969, South African Assn. Physicists in Medicine and Biology, Pretoria, 1980, North China Inst. Radiation Protection, 1984; mem. rev. com. Argonne Univs. Assn., 1977-80; chmn. Marshall Islands radiol. adv. group Dept. Energy, 1978-81; mem. staff Pres.'s Commn. on Accident at Three Mile Island, 1979-80; mem. regional steering com. on health effects from eruption of Mt. St. Helens, 1980-84; chmn. Dept. Energy task group on health and environ. consequences of Soviet nuclear accident, 1986-87; mem. U.S. delegation in meetings with USSR on Chernobyl accident Internat. Atomic Energy Agy. Author 200 books, articles, reports, chpts. in books.; lectr. Japan AEC. Recipient E.O. Lawrence Meml. award, 1970; cert. of appreciation AEC, 1975; Alumni Disting. Achievement citation Ohio Wesleyan U., 1986. Fellow AAAS, Health Physics Soc. (dir. 1970-73, 83-86, pres.-elect 1983-84, pres. 1984-85); mem. Radiation Research Soc., N.Y. Acad. Sci., Soc. Exptl. Biology and Medicine (vice chmn. N.W. sect. 1967-70, 74-75), Reticuloendothelial Soc., Soc. Occupational and Environ. Health, Sci. Soc. Pres. (council 1984-85), Sigma Xi. Club: Kiwanis (dir.). Home: 102 Somerset St Richland WA 99352 Office: Battelle Pacific Northwest Labs PO Box 999 Richland WA 99352

BAIRD, HAYNES WALLACE, pathologist; b. St. Louis, Jan. 28, 1943; s. Harry Haynes and Mary Cornelia (Wallace) B.; BA, U. N.C., 1965, MD, 1969; m. Phyllis Jean Tipton, June 26, 1965; children—Teresa Lee, Christopher Wallace, Kelly Wallace. Intern, N.C. Meml. Hosp., Chapel Hill, 1969-70, resident in pathology, 1970-72, chief resident in pathology, 1972-73; asso. pathologist Moses H. Cone Meml. Hosp., Greensboro, N.C., 1973—; practice medicine, specializing in pathology Greensboro, 1973—; clin. asst. prof. U. N.C., Chapel Hill, 1978—; clin. lectr. chemistry U. N.C., Greensboro, 1973—. Mem. adminstrv. bd. West Market St. United Meth. Ch., 1985-88; bd. dirs. Greensboro unit Am. Cancer Soc., 1980-81. Diplomate Am. Bd. Pathology. Fellow Coll. Am. Pathologists (ho. of dels. 1983-85); mem. AMA, So. Med. Assn., Am. Assn. for Clin. Chemistry, Am. Soc. Cytology, Am. Soc. Clin. Pathologists, Internat. Acad. Pathology, N.C. Med. Soc., Guilford County Med. Soc., N.C. Soc. Pathologists (sec.-treas. 1977-79), Greensboro Acad. Medicine. Methodist. Home: 2805 New Hanover Dr Greensboro NC 27408 Office: 1200 N Elm St Greensboro NC 27401

BAIRD, JOHN ABSALOM, JR., college official; b. Honolulu, Sept. 13, 1918; s. John Absalom and Helen (Bates) B.; A.B., Princeton U., 1940; postgrad. Johns Hopkins U., 1941; m. Virginia Walton, Mar 8, 1941 (dec. 1983); children—Suzanne W. Baird Perot, Linda W., Barbara Baird Rogers; m. 2d, Clare A. Emmons, May 12, 1984. Asst. supt. Charles S. Walton Co., 1942-47, asst. sec. and dir., 1947-52, v.p., 1952-72; asst. pres. Eastern Baptist Theol. Sem., Phila., Eastern Coll., St. Davids, Pa., 1952-61, v.p., 1961—. Bd. corporators, bd. dirs. Presbyn. Ministers Fund Ins. Co., Phila. Main Line dist. chmn. Valley Forge council Boy Scouts Am., 1952-54, dist. commr., 1954-56; vice chmn. Main Line br. YMCA Greater Phila., 1947-63; trustee, v.p. Pa. Lupus Found.; v.p. Pa. chpt. Lupus Found. Am.; trustee Vol. Services for Blind, Phila., 1971-85; mem. adv. bd. Phila. Home for Incurables; chmn. bd. trustees Shipley School, Bryn Mawr, Pa., 1972-78; trustee 4th Bapt. Mission Found., 1976-80, Ludington Library, Bryn Mawr; v.p., dir. Am. Sunday Sch. Union (Phila.) 1957-69; dir. Watchman Examiner Corp. (N.Y.C.), 1958-70; dir. Pa. United Theol. Sem. Found. (Pitts), Am. Ednl. and Hist. Film Center (St. Davids). Recipient Freedom Founds. Honor medal, 1973. Mem. Am. Bapt. Pub. Relations Assn., Am. Alumni Council, Am. Coll. Pub. Relations Assn., U.S. Naval Inst., U.S. Naval Found., Loyal Legion, Soc. of Cincinnati (pres. Del. 1972-75, sec. gen. 1977-83), Colonial Soc. Pa., Soc. Colonial Wars, Order Fgn. Wars, S.R., Am. Assn. Sem. Staff Officers (pres. 1966-68), Pa. Acad. Fine Arts, Am. Rose Soc., Am. Philatelic Soc., English-Speaking Union, Hist. Soc. Pa., Nat. Hist. Soc., Newcomen Soc. N.Am., Geneal. Soc. Pa. Republican. Baptist. Clubs: Princeton, Franklin Inn, Penn, Athenaeum (Phila.); Merion Cricket (Haverford, Pa.); Army-Navy (Washington). Author: A Leap of Faith; the Whole Gospel for the Whole World; All Things Are Thine; Profile of a Hero; The Shining Fire; Horn of Plenty; Great House; contbr. articles to profl. jours. Home: 108 Sunset Ln Haverford PA 19041 Office: Ea Bapt Theol Sem City Line and Lancaster Ave Philadelphia PA 19151

BAIRD, PATRICIA MARIE, university educator, researcher; b. Rothesay, Scotland, May 10, 1941; d. Cornelius and Mary (Taggart) Shields; m. Daniel Lone Baird, July 3, 1965; children: Maureen Ann, Helen Marie, Paul Daniel, Katherine Frances. BA with joint honors, U. Strathclyde, Glasgow, Scotland, 1979. Tax officer Inspector of Taxes, Glasgow, London, 1961-66; librarian Strathclyde Regional Council, Glasgow, 1979; tutor, librarian Clydebank (Scotland) Tech. Coll., 1979-81; lectr. pub. U. Strathclyde, 1981—; dir, cons. Glasgow Herald Index Project, 1984-88; coordinator Glasgow Online. Editor: Glasgow Herald Index, 1986, Expert Systems For Decision Making, 1987; contbr. articles to profl. jours. Mem. Library Assn. (assoc.), Inst. Info. Scientists, Library Assn. Tech. Group. Mem. Labour Party. Roman Catholic. Office: U Strathclyde, Dept Info Sci, 26 Richmond St, Glasgow G1 1XH, Scotland

BAIRD, ROGER NEALE, surgeon; b. Edinburgh, Scotland, Dec. 24, 1941; s. John Allan and Margaret Edith (Shand) B.; m. Affra Mary Varcoe-Cocks, Oct. 12, 1968; children: Susan Catherine, Richard Douglas. BSc with honors, Edinburgh U., 1963, M of Surgery, 1966, ChM, 1977. House surgeon Royal Infirmary, Edinburgh, 1966-67, research scholar dept. clin. surgery, 1967-69, registrar, 1969-72; lectr. surgery Bristol (Eng.) U., 1973-77, sr. lectr., 1977-81, Long Fox lectr., 1981; cons. surgeon Royal Infirmary, Bristol, 1981—. Author books on vascular surgery; contbr. articles to med. jours. Fulbright scholar Harvard U. Med. Sch., Boston, 1975-76. Fellow Royal Coll. Surgeons (Eng.) (examiner 1981-86, Hunterian prof. 1980, Kinmonth lectr. 1984), Royal Coll. Surgeons (Edinburgh) (Learmonth lectr. 1980); mem. Vascular Surg. Soc. Gt. Britain and Ireland, Assn. Surgeons Gt. Britain and Ireland (hon. treas. 1985—), Internat. Cardiovascular Soc. (Brit. nat. del.). Club: Army and Navy (London). Home: 23 Old Sneed Park, Bristol BS9 1RG, England Office: Royal Infirmary, Bristol BS2 8HW, England

BAISE, WALKER NATHAN, loss prevention executive; b. Tampa, Fla., Apr. 11, 1931; s. Walker Nathan Baise and Lucille (Fountain) Baise Smith; m. Sandra Louise Rogers, Mar. 26, 1983. B.S. in Geology, U. Fla., 1957; postgrad. Calif. State U.-Fullerton, 1963-64. Geophysicist Continental Oil Co., Ponca City, Okla., 1957-63; engr. Rockwell Internat., Fullerton, Calif., 1963-69; cons. Marsh & McLennan, N.Y.C., 1970-83; pres. Loss Prevention Services, El Paso, 1983—; fin. officer energy and environ. com. N.Y. Bd. Trade, N.Y.C., 1976-77. Served with U.S. Army, 1951-54, Korea. Mem. Soc. Exploration Geophysicists, Am. Geol. Soc., El Paso Indsl. Safety Council, El Paso County Hist. Soc. Republican. Lodge: Elks.

BAJENESCU, TITUS-MARIUS I., telematics and reliability consulting engineer; b. Cimpina, Rumania, Apr. 2, 1933; s. Ion T. and Lelia Constanta (Petrescu) B.; M.S., Inst. Tech., Bucharest, Rumania, 1956; Quality and reliability assurance engr., Berne, 1974; m. Andrea-Ana Bogdan, Sept. 26, 1961; 1 dau., Christine-Susanne. Research engr. Electronics Research Inst., Bucharest, 1956-61; with Inst. Power Engring., Rumanian Acad. Scis., 1961-68; head cybernetics div. Mktg. Research Inst., 1968-69; devel. and project engr. Brown Boveri Ltd., Switzerland, 1969-74; quality and reliability assurance engr. Hasler Ltd., Berne, Switzerland, 1974-80; telematics and reliability cons. engr., Lutry, 1980—; tchr. and cons. Mem. IEEE (sr.), Swiss Tech. Assn. (expert), Reg. A, Electronics Group Switzerland. Author: The Tape Recorder, 1959; Introduction to Reliability in Modern Electronics, 1978; Electronics and Reliability, 1979; Reliability of Active Electronic Components, 1980; Reliability of Passive Electronic Components, 1981; Reliability Problems of Electronic Components, 1985, Quo Vadis LANs, 1987; also numerous articles in telematics, electronics, office automation, telecommunications, Local Area Networds, Wide Area Networks, automation, econometry, reliability, quality and reliability assurance and control. Home: 13 Chemin de Riant-Coin, CH-1093 Lutry Switzerland

BA JIN (LI YAOTANG), author; b. Chengdu, Sichuan, China, 1904; m. Xiao Shan, 1944 (dec. 1972). Ed. Fgn. Lang. Sch., Chengdu, also ed. Paris, France. Author, 1972—; editor Ban Yue, Chengdu, People's Republic of China, 1928; chief editor Shanghai Cultural Life Pub. House, from 1935; then with China Literary Work Soc.; co-editor Shouting Weekly and Bonfire Weekly, from 1937; chief editor Renmin Wenxue (People's Literature), 1957-58; chief editor Shanghai Wenxue (Shanghai Literature), from 1961; branded as a counterrevolutionary and purged, 1968-77; vice chmn. China Fedn. Literary and Art Circles, 1978—. Publs. include: Miewang (Extinction), Fuchou (Revenge), Guangming (Brightness), Dianyi (Electric Chair), 1928; Sigu De Taiyang (The Dead Sun), 1930; Xin Sheng (new Life), Jia (The Family), 1931; Aiqing De Sanbuqu (Trilogy of Love), Yu (Rain), 1932, Wu (Fog), 1933, Dian (Lightning), 1933; Hai De Meng (Dream of the Sea), 1932; Xu (Snow), 1933; History of the Nihilist Movement, 1936; Chun (Spring), 1937; Qiu (Autumn), 1940; Huo (Fire: a trilogy), 1938-43; Fathers and Sons (translated from Turgenev), Virgin Lands; Qi Yuan (The Garden of Rest), 1944; Han Ye (Cold Nights), 1945; Festival Day of Warsaw, 1950; Living Among Heroes, 1953; Three Comrades, 1962. Mem. Nat. People's Congress (standing com.), Chinese Writers' Assn. (former 1st vice chmn., now chmn.), Assn. Literary Workers (standing com.), Govt. Adminstrv. Council (cultural and ednl. commn.). Address: care China PEN, Shatan Beijie 2, Beijing People's Republic of China *

BAJOHR, STEFAN PAUL, historian, political consultant; b. Bad Harzburg, Niedersachsen, W.Ger., Oct. 4, 1950; s. Frank-Christian and Christa B. Magister Artium, U., Marburg, 1977, Ph.D., 1978. Journalist Niedersaechsisches Tageblatt, Winsen/L and Luneburg, W.Ger., 1969-71; lectr., research assoc. Philipps U., Marburg (W.Ger.), 1979-80; acad. adviser Office of Fed. Chancellor, Bonn, W.Ger., 1980-82; head of sect. Ministry of Labor, Health and Social Affairs, Dusseldorf, 1982, personal cons. to Minister, 1982-85; personal sec. chmn. Social Democratic Group in the Parliament of Northrhine-Westphalia, 1985—; Author: Die Haelfte der Fabrik, 1979; Vom bitteren Los der kleinen Leute, 1984; author articles and revs. Friedrich-Ebert-Stiftung scholar, 1975-78. Mem. Gewerkschaft Öffentlicher Dienst, Transport und Verkehr. Mem. Social Democratic Party. Home: Buergerstr 10, 4000 Dusseldorf 1 Federal Republic of Germany Office: SPD-Fraktion, Platz des Landtages, 4000 Dusseldorf 1 Federal Republic of Germany

BAKER, ALTON WESLEY, educator, corporate administrator; b. Chickasha, Okla., May 28, 1912; s. Charles Wesley and Frances Cornelia (Hennington) B.; m. Mary Elizabeth Dill, June 4, 1938; children: Don Wesley, Viki Joan. B.B.A., U. Tex., 1936; A.M., George Washington U., 1947; Ph.D., Ohio State U., 1952; degree, Cambridge U. Asso. prof. Ohio State U., 1947-54; prof., chmn. dept. mgmt. So. Meth. U., 1954—; prof. Southwestern Legal Found. U. Tex.; prof. Southwestern Grad. Sch. Banking; div. head Fairchild Corp.; chmn. bd. Dill Mfg. Corp.; dir. research Ohio State U. Research Found., U.S. and Orient; Chmn. bd. regional postmaster selection U.S. Post Office Service, 1969—; cons. to postmaster gen., 1968—; cons. to industry in, U.S. and S.Am.; cons. S.W. Legal Found., S.W. Grad. Sch. Banking; prof. Air U.; dir. research intelligence SAC, USAF, Far East. Author: numerous publs. including Supervisor and His Job, 3d ed, 1978, internat. edit., 1979, Management: Small Manufacturing Plants, 1955. Chmn. bd. dirs. So. Meth. U. Retirement System, Inc. Mem. Acad. Mgmt. Clubs: Country (Dallas), Rotary (Dallas). Home: 6211 W Northwest Hwy Unit 1400 Preston Towers Dallas TX 75225

BAKER, ANITA DIANE, lawyer; b. Atlanta, Sept. 4, 1955; d. Byron Garnett and Anita (Swanson) B. BA summa cum laude, Oglethorpe U., 1977; JD with distinction, Emory U., 1980. Bar: Ga. 1980. Assoc. Hansell & Post, Atlanta, 1980—. Mem. ABA (com. on savs. and loan instns.), Atlanta Bar Assn., Ga. Bar Assn., Atlanta Hist. Soc., Order of Coif, Phi Alpha Delta, Phi Alpha Theta, Alpha Chi, Omicron Delta Kappa. Office: Hansell & Post 56 Perimeter Ctr E Suite 500 Atlanta GA 30346

BAKER, BARTON, lawyer, lecturer; b. Webster, N.Y., Jan. 9, 1901; s. Charles John and Emma (Martin) B.; m. Bernice Maude Dennis, June 6, 1925; 1 dau., Betty Baker Trost. LL.B., Cornell U., 1922; D.C.L. cum laude, Chgo. Law Sch., 1926, Ph.D., 1928. Bar: N.Y. 1923, U.S. Sup. Ct. 1926. Asst. law librarian Cornell U., 1921-22; asst. Rochester (N.Y.) Legal Aid Soc., 1921; atty. MacFarlane & Harris, 1922-26; atty. Baker & Carver, Baker & Weldgen; now gen. counsel Auditing Bur. Rochester; columnist Damascus News, 1982. Bd. dirs. Internat. Bell Orch., 1952—; formerly council chief N.Y. and N.J. Boy Scouts Am. Lone Scout Div.; founder Barton Baker Youth Edn. Center, Monroe County Fair Park, 1973; trustee Minett Fund; past pres. Rochester Internat. Friendship Council, Inc.; mem. adv. bd. Salvation Army. Recipient Monroe County Citizens Civic Com. Achievement citation, 1977; achievement award Internat. Assn. Fairs and Expns., Reagan Republican Task Force Citation, 1985; Order of Lincoln. Methodist. Clubs: Shrine Lunch (past pres.), Masons (past master), Cornell (past pres.). Contbr. articles to profl. jours.; former assoc. editor Cornell Law Rev.; former editor Reveille, Universal Scout, Universal Tribune. Avocation: stamp collecting. Home: 100 Brookwood Rd Rochester NY 14610 Office: 1030 Times Square Bldg Rochester NY 14614

BAKER, BERNARD ROBERT, state district court judge; b. Chgo., Apr. 5, 1937; s. Bernard F. and Pearl L. (Beesley) B.; m. Caroline Spanier, Mar. 22, 1958; children—Susan Caroline, Deborah Ann, Pamela Ruth. B.S.B.A., Northwestern U., 1958; J.D., Ind. U., 1964. Bar: Colo. 1968, Ind. 1964, U.S. Supreme Ct. 1969, U.S. Ct. Mil. Appeals 1965, U.S. Dist. Ct. Colo. 1968, Ind. 1964; ins. counselor Equitable Life Ins., N.Y.C., 1958-60; acct. Chevrolet div. Gen. Motors Corp., Indpls., 1960-61; claims investigator, supr. Allstate Ins. Co., Indpls., 1961-64; assoc. firm Agee & Fann, Colorado Springs, Colo., 1968; dep., chief dep. dist. atty. Office Dist. Atty., State of Colo., 1968-75; dist. ct. judge 4th Jud. Dist., State of Colo., Colorado Springs, 1976—; guest prof. Nat. Jud. Coll., Reno, Nev., 1982. Pres., Citizens Lobby for Sensible Growth, 1974; bd. dirs. Salvation Army, 1973-78, Mental Retardation Found., 1972-76. Served to capt. JAG Corps, U.S. Army, 1965-67. Decorated Army Commendation medal; recipient Presdl. citation Colo. Health Dept., 1975. Mem. ABA, Colo. Bar Assn., El Paso County Bar Assn., Am. Judicature Soc. Democrat. Methodist. Club: Moose. Contbg. editor, bd. editors Colo. Environ. Law Handbook, 1971-72. Address: El Paso County Courthouse 20 E Vermijo St Colorado Springs CO 80903

BAKER, BRUCE EDWARD, orthopaedic surgeon; b. Oswego, N.Y., Mar. 22, 1937; s. Elbert J. and Reatha (Hartranft) B.; m. Patricia Therese Gormel, Aug. 19, 1961; children—Brett, Clayton, Sean, Reatha. B.S.M.E., Syracuse U., 1959, M.D., SUNY-Syracuse, 1965. Intern, State U. Iowa, Iowa City, 1965-66, asst. resident, 1966-67; resident orthopaedics SUNY-Upstate Med. Ctr., Syracuse, 1969-72, NIH orthopaedic research fellow, 1972-73, asst. prof. orthopaedic surgery, 1973-79, assoc. prof., 1979-86, prof., 1986— , dir. univ. sports medicine service div. dept. orthopaedic surgery 1980—; team physician, dir. sports medicine athletic dept., Syracuse U., 1973—, orthoapedic cons. Student Health Ctr., 1973—; staff SUNY Hosp., Syracuse, 1973—, Syracuse VA Hosp., 1973—, A.C. Silverman Pub. Health Hosp., 1973-77, Crouse-Irving Meml. Hosp., 1973—; cons. in field. Contbr. numerous articles to profl. jours. Served to capt. USAF, 1967-69. Syracuse U. scholar, 1955; N.Y. State Regents scholar, 1955-59; recipient AMA Physicians Recognition award, 1978; Bronze medal award Am. Roentgen Ray Soc., 1980; Gold medal award Sound Slide Prodn. Conditioning, 1977; USPHS grantee, 1973-74; Hendricks Research fund grantee, 1973-75; NIH grantee, 1974-76, 76-77. Fellow ACS, Am. Acad. Orthopaedic Surgeons; mem. AMA, Med. Soc. State N.Y., Onondaga County Med. Soc., Orthopaedic Research Soc., Am. Coll. Sports Medicine, Am. Orthopaedic Soc. for Sports Medicine, N.Y. Soc. Orthopaedic Surgeons, Royal Soc. Medicine, Internat. Arthroscopy Assn., Arthroscopy Assn. N.Am., Bioelec. Repair and Growth Soc. Office: Dept Orthopedics 550 Harrison Ctr Syracuse NY 13202

BAKER, CHARLES DUANE, educator; b. Newburyport, Mass., June 21, 1928; s. Charles Duane and Eleanor (Little) B.; m. Alice Elizabeth Ghormley, 1955; children: Charles D., Jonathan G., Alexander K. A.B., Harvard, 1951, M.B.A., 1955. With Westinghouse Electric Corp., Elmira, N.Y., 1955-57; with Westinghouse Electric Corp., Jersey City, 1957-61; v.p., treas. United Research, Inc., Cambridge, Mass., 1961-65; various positions through chmn., chief exec. Harbridge House, Inc., Boston, 1965-69, 72-83; prof. bus. adminstrn. Northeastern U., Boston, 1985—; dep. under sec. U.S. Dept. Transp., Washington, 1969-70, asst. sec. policy and internat. affairs, 1970-71; under sec. U.S. Dept. of HHS, Washington, 1984-85; presiding dir. Millipore Corp. Author various studies dealing with mgmt. transp., health care, pub. policy. Mem. vis. com. Harvard U., bd. dirs. Bus. Sch. Assocs.; bd. dirs. Family Counseling and Guidance Ctrs. Served to lt. (j.g.) USNR, 1946-48, 51-53. Recipient Award for Outstanding Achievement U.S. Govt., 1971. Mem. Pi Eta. Republican. Congregationalist. Clubs: Essex County; Harvard, Comml., Clover (Boston); E. India (London); Metropolitan (Washington). Home: 115 Marmion Way Rockport MA 01966 also: 255 Beacon St Boston MA 02116 Office: Hayden Hall Northeastern U 360 Huntington Ave Boston MA 02115

BAKER, CLARENCE ALBERT, SR., structural steel constrn. co. exec.; b. Kansas City, Kans., July 2, 1919; s. Earl Retting and Nancy Jefferson (Price) B.; student Kans. U., 1939-40, Finley Engring. Coll., 1937-39, Ohio State U., 1967, 69; m. Marjorie Ellen Yoakum, Mar. 19, 1959 (dec. Feb. 1981); children—Clarence Albert, Jorgeann Baker Hiebert; stepchildren—Robert Beale, Barbara Anne Stegner (Mrs. Robert T. Kenney II); m. 2d, Katherine V. Cochran, Nov. 6, 1982. With Kansas City (Kans.) Structural Steel Co., 1937-84, shop supt., 1959-68, v.p., plant mgr., 1968-73, v.p. plant ops., 1973-76, v.p. engring., 1976—, dir., 1969—. Curriculum adv. Kansas City (Mo.) Met. Jr. Coll., 1971-72, Kansas City Vocat. Tech. Sch., 1973—. Committeeman, Republican Party, 1970-72; chmn. City of Mission (Kans.) Rep. Party, 1970-72; councilman. City of Merriam (Kans.), 1957-59. Adv. bd. Wentworth Mil. Acad.; bd. dirs. Kansas City Jr. Achievement. Served with USNR, 1944-46. Mem. Am. Welding Soc. (pres. 1970-71, chmn. 1970, code com.), ASTM, Kans. Engring. Soc., Kans. City C. of C. Lodge: Masons. Home: 6635 Milhaven Dr Mission KS 66202 Office: 21st and Metropolitan Sts Kansas City KS 66106

BAKER, CLIFFORD HOWARD, marketing professional; b. Paoli, Ind., Oct. 14, 1932; s. James A. and Alice (Limeberry) B.; B.S., U.S. Mil. Acad., 1956; M.S., Purdue U., 1965; Ph.D., N.C. State U., 1972; m. Joan B. Meyer, Feb. 4, 1958; children—Steven Conrad, Bradford Nelson, Paul Milton, Jeffrey Todd, Douglas Ross, Matthew Kent. Indsl. mktg. exec. Tex. Instruments, Dallas, 1959-61; market research exec. Gen. Motors Corp., Kokomo, Ind., 1961-65; supr. market analysis Corning Glass Works, Raleigh, N.C., 1965-70; pres. Market Research and Statistics Co., 1970-71, Indsl. Edn. Inst., Mailmax, Raleigh and Columbia, S.C., Village Printer, Raleigh; v.p. Su Casa Mexican Restaurants, Raleigh, Quinn Mfg., Chapel Hill, N.C. Served with AUS, 1956-59. Recipient Nat. Def. Service medal West Point, 1956. Mem. IEEE, Assn. Grads. West Point, Alpha Kappa Psi (hon.), Delta Mu Delta (hon.). Mem. Ch. of Christ. Republican. Home: 4816 Deerwood Dr Raleigh NC 27612 Office: 4505 Creedmoor Rd Raleigh NC 27612

BAKER, EDWARD GEORGE, retired mechanical engineer; b. Freeport, N.Y., Oct. 20, 1908; s. Edward George and Mary (Dunham) B.; m. Mary Louise Freer, Feb. 7, 1931; children—Edward Clark, Marna Larson, Ellen Freer (Mrs. George W. Lewis), John Durrin, Bruce Robert. B.A., Columbia Coll., 1930, M.A., 1931, Ed.D., 1938. Assoc. prof. math. Newark Coll. Engring., N.J., 1930-42; mem. tech. staff Am. Bur. Shipping, N.Y.C., 1942-73. Author: First Course in Mathematics, 1942. Contbr. articles on marine engring. to profl. jours. Pres. Nutley (N.J.) Symphony Soc., 1939-41; chmn. zoning bd. of adjustment, Pine Knoll Shores, N.C., 1979-84. Recipient Order of Long Leaf Pine award State of N.C., 1982. Mem. Am. Math. Soc., ASME, Soc. Naval Architects and Marine Engrs., N.Y. Acad. Sci., Phi Beta Kappa. Republican. Episcopalian. Home: 106 Carob Ct Pine Knoll Shores Route 3 Morehead City NC 28557

BAKER, FRANCIS EUSTACE, government official; b. Apr. 19, 1933; s. Stephen and Jessica Wilhelmina Baker; m. Constance Anne Shilling, 1959; 3 children. MA, U. Oxford. RN Nat. Service, 1955-57; administrv. officer HMOCS, 1957, Solomon Islands, 1958-63; in farming 1963-67; administrv. officer Condominium of New Hebrides, 1967-79; chief sec. to Falkland Islands Govt., 1979-83; gov., comdr.-in-chief St. Helena and Dependencies, 1984—. Decorated CBE, 1984, OBE, 1979; recipient Silver Jubilee medal, 1977. Office: Plantation House Saint Helena also: Dark Orchard, Primrose Ln, Bredgar, near Sittingbourne, Kent ME9 8EH, England *

BAKER, GEOFFREY HEWETT, zoologist, research scientist; b. Adelaide, Australia, Sept. 25, 1949; s. Rex Hewett and Marjorie Jean (Carr) B.; m. Mary Frances Shannon, Dec. 29, 1980. BS with honors, U. Adelaide, 1972, PhD, 1977. Tutor in ecology Field Studies Council of Great Britain, Pembroke, Wales, 1976-78; postdoctoral research fellow U. Coll., Dublin, Ireland, 1978-80; prin. research scientist Entomology div. CSIRO Australia, Lisbon (Portugal) and Adelaide, 1980—. Contbr. sci. papers relating to ecology and biol. control of introduced pests to profl. jours. Recipient Commonwealth Postgrad award Australian Govt., Adelaide, 1972-76; postdoctoral research fellow Sci. and Engring. Irish Govt., Dublin, 1978-80; research grantee South Australian Barley Industry, Adelaide, 1985-88. Mem. British Ecol. Soc., Australian Entomol. Soc. Club: Mt. Lofty Golf (South Australia). Home: 8 The Crescent Crafers, 5152 Adelaide Australia Office: CSIRO Div of Entomology, PO Box 2 Glen Osmond, 5064 Adelaide Australia

BAKER, GORDON NEWTON, library media specialist; b. Atlanta, June 30, 1954; s. Howard Franklin and Mary Ina (Newton) B. A.A., Clayton Jr. Coll., 1973; B.S. in Edn., Valdosta State Coll., 1975; M.L.S., Atlanta U., 1978, specialist in library service diploma, 1981. Tchr., librarian Griffin-Spalding Schs., Griffin, Ga., 1975-76; tchr. Clayton County Schs., Jonesboro, Ga., 1976-77; pub. services librarian Clayton Jr. Coll., Morrow, Ga., 1979—; library/media specialist Clayton County Schs., Jonesboro, 1977—; library cons. Meadow Creek Acad., McDonough, Ga., 1982; pub. services librarian, Clayton State Coll., Morrow, Ga., 1986—; 6th dist. chmn. Ga. Library/Media Dept., Decatur, 1979, treas., 1980-82, pres., 1982-83, exec. sec., 1983—; mem. Area IV media com. Ga. Dept. Edn., 1983. Co-author: Study Guide for TCT for Media Specialists, 1983. Vice pres. Kilpatrick P.T.A., Jonesboro, Ga., 1979-80. Mem. ALA, Am. Assn. Sch. Librarians, Ga. Library Media Dept. (conf. coordinator 1980, 86, William E. Patterson service award 1986), Ga. Library Assn., Clayton County Library/Media Assn. (treas. 1978-79, pres. 1979-81), Clayton County English Lang. Arts Council (pres. 1979-80), Ga. Council Media Orgns. (steering com. joint conf. com. 1988), Beta Phi Mu (mem. nat. exec. council), Sigma Alpha Chi. Republican. Methodist. Home: 3087 Drexel Ln Jonesboro GA 30236 Office: Edwin S Kemp Elem Sch 10990 Folsom Rd Hampton GA 30228

BAKER, HAROLD CECIL, architect, consultant; b. Wheeling, W.Va., June 23, 1954; s. Harold Cecil Jr. and Virginia Ann (Gonot) B.; m. Amy Jean Taylor, Aug. 23, 1975; children: Nathan Taylor, Kyle Thomas. BS in Architecture, Ohio State U., 1978, MArch, 1980. Registered profl. architect, Fla., Ga., Ind., Md., Mich., Mo., N.C., Ohio, Okla., Penn., R.I., S.C., Tenn., Tex., Va. Project architect William Gilfillen Architects, Columbus, Ohio, 1977-79; v.p. Solar Design Group, Columbus, 1979-84; v.p. retail architecture Nexus Am., Columbus, 1984-86; prin. Harold C. Baker, AIA, Inc., Columbus, 1986—. Author: Town Franklin Design Guidelines, 1978. Solar Energy grantee Dept. Housing and Urban Devel., Dublin, Ohio, 1978, Silver award Inst. Bus. Designers, Nexus Corp. Hdqrs., 1985, Excellence award Columbus Inst. Bus. Designers, 1985. Mem. AIA (environ. awareness com. Columbus chpt. 1983—, critic liaison high sch. design competition 1983-84, co-chmn. hon. award com. 1983-84, chmn. 1984-85), Architects Soc. Ohio. Republican. Roman Catholic. Office: Harold C Baker AIA Inc 673 High St Suite 204 Worthington OH 43085

BAKER, IAN HELSTRIP, university official; b. Johannesburg, South Africa, Nov. 26, 1927; s. Henry Hubert and Mary Clare B.; m. Susan Anne Lock, June 23, 1956; children—Edward Ian (dec.), Robert William, Joanna Susan. Ed., St. Peter's Sch., York, St. Edmund Hall, Oxford. Commd. lt. Royal Arty., 1948, transfered to Royal Tank Regt., 1955, advanced through grades to maj. gen., 1978; comdg. officer 1st Royal Tank Regt., 1967-70; comdr. 7th Armored Brigade, 1972-74; brig. gen. staff hdqrs. U.K. Land Forces, 1975-77, asst. chief gen. staff, 1978-80, gen. officer comdg. N.E. dist., 1980-82; sec., head adminstrn. Univ. Coll. London, 1982—. Mem. Order of Brit. Empire (Decorated comdr. 1977). Club: Athenaeum (London). Address: Owen's Farm Hook, Hampshire England

BAKER, IRA LEE, journalist, former educator; b. Fairwood, Va., Sept. 5, 1915; s. Joseph Franklin and Celia (Blackburn) B.; BA, Wake Forest Coll., 1936; MA, Columbia U., 1952; postgrad. U. Ill., U. Wis., U. Tenn., Syracuse U.; MSc in Journalism, U. Ill., 1963. Instr. English, N.C. State Coll., Raleigh, 1946-50, asst. extension editor State Coll. Extension Service and mng. editor Extension Farm-News, 1950-51; head journalism dept. Furman U., Greenville, S.C., 1951-65; assoc. prof. journalism and English, High Point (N.C.) Coll., 1965-68; prof. journalism East Carolina U., Greenville, 1968-80, prof. emeritus, 1983—, columnist, mem. editorial staff Communication: Journalism Education Today, 1977—; corr. Religion News Service, 1953—; prof. Wingate Coll., 1980-83; permanent advisor S.C. Collegiate Press Assn. Publicity chmn. Wake County council N.C. Symphony Orch., 1947-51; active Raleigh Music Club, Raleigh Little Theatre, 1946-51, Greenville Little Theater, 1951—; mem. alumni council Wake Forest Coll., 1964, Rowan County Bd. Social Services, 1987; relationships chmn. Pitt County council Boy Scouts Am., 1975; del. S.C. Republican Conv., 1958; chmn. bd. deacons 1st Baptist Ch., China Grove, N.C., 1982-84; historian Rowan County Bapt. Assn., N.C., 1984-85, 87. Served with USAAF, 1942-44. Recipient Scholastic Pioneer award Nat. Scholastic Press Assn., 1970; named Distinguished Newspaper Adviser, Nat. Council Coll. Publs. Advisers, 1973. Mem. Am. Assn. Coll. and Univ. Profs. (v.p. Furman U. chpt.), Am. Assn. Tchrs. Religious Journalism, Assn. Ednl. Journalism (state dir.), S.C. Press Assn., Nat. Council Coll. Publs. Advisers (membership chmn. dist. III 1967-68), Pub. Relations Soc. Am. (asso.), S.C. Assn. Coll. Publs. Advisers (pres. 1957—), South Atlantic Modern Lang. Assn., Pitt County (N.C.) Hist. Soc., (publicity chmn.) SAR, Sigma Delta Chi, Tau Kappa Epsilon, Alpha Phi Gamma (nat. pres. 1968-70). Lodge: Rotary (China Grove) (dir. 1981-82, editor Rotary Log). Co-author: Modern Journalism, 1961, A History of China Grove, 1988; mem. adv. bd. Student Writer; chmn. adv. bd. Cerebral Palsy News of S.C.; mem. bd. editors Scholastic Mag.; mem. book reviewing staff Greensboro News, 1960, Richmond News Leader, 1975; editor The Collegiate Journalist; contbr. book revs. to Raleigh News and Observer, 1968—, Richmond (Va.) News Leader, 1974—, also articles to Ency. So. Bapts., 1958. Lodge: Rotary (editor 1981—). Home: 106 Stevens St China Grove NC 28023

BAKER, JAMES ADDISON, III, former secretary of treasury; b. Houston, Apr. 28, 1930; s. James A. and Bonner (Means) B.; m. Susan Garrett, Aug. 6, 1973; 8 children. B.A., Princeton U., 1952; LL.B., U. Tex., 1957. Bar: Tex. 1957. Mem. firm Andrews, Kurth, Campbell & Jones, Houston, 1957-81; undersec. Dept. Commerce, Washington, 1975-76; deputy chmn. del. ops. Pres. Ford Com., Washington, 1976; campaign chmn. George Bush, 1979-80; sr. adviser Reagan-Bush Com., 1980-81; mem. Reagan Transition Team, Washington, 1980-81; chief of staff White House, Washington, 1981-85; sec. Dept. Treasury, 1985-88.; campaign chmn. George Bush's Presidential campaign, 1988. Trustee Woodrow Wilson Internat. Center for Scholars, Smithsonian Inst., 1977—. Served with USMC, 1952-54. Mem. ABA, State Bar Tex., Houston Bar Assn.; mem. Am. Judicature Soc.; Mem. Phi Delta Phi. Office: Dept Treasury Office of the Sec 15th & Pennsylvania Ave NW Washington DC 20220 *

BAKER, JAMES EDWARD SPROUL, lawyer; b. Evanston, Ill., May 23, 1912; s. John Clark and Hester (Sproul) B.; m. Eleanor Lee Dodgson, Oct. 2, 1937 (dec. Sept. 1972); children: John Lee, Edward Graham. A.B., Northwestern U., 1933, J.D., 1936. Bar: Ill. 1936, U.S. Supreme Ct. 1957. Practice in Chgo., 1936—; assoc. Sidley & Austin, and predecessors, 1936-48, ptnr., 1948-81; of counsel Sidley & Austin, 1981—; lectr. Northwestern U. Law Sch., 1951-52; Nat. chmn. Stanford U. Parents Com., 1970-75; mem. vis. com. Stanford Law Sch., 1976-79, 82-84, Northwestern U. Law Sch., 1980—, DePaul U. Law Sch., 1982-87. Served to comdr. USNR, 1941-46. Fellow Am. Coll. Trial Lawyers (regent 1974-81, sec. 1977-79, pres. 1979-80); mem. ABA, Bar Assn. 7th Fed. Circuit, Ill. State Bar Assn., Chgo. Bar Assn., Soc. Trial Lawyers Ill., Northwestern U. Law Alumni Assn. (past pres.), Order of Coif, Phi Lambda Upsilon, Sigma Nu. Republican. Methodist. Clubs: John Evans (Northwestern U.) (chmn. 1982-85); University (Chgo.); John Henry Wigmore (past pres.); Midday (Chgo.), Legal (Chgo.), Law (Chgo.) (pres. 1983-85); Westmoreland Country (Wilmette, Ill.). Home: 1300 N Lake Shore Dr Chicago IL 60610 Office: 1 First Nat Plaza Chicago IL 60603

BAKER, JANET ABBOTT, mezzo-soprano; b. Aug. 21, 1933; d. Robert Abbott and May (Pollard) B.; m. James Keith Shelley, 1957. Student, Coll. for Girls, York, Eng., Wintringham, Grimsby, Eng.; D.Mus. (hon.), Birmingham U., Leicester, Eng., 1973, London U., 1974, Oxford U., 1975, Hull U., 1975, U. Leeds, 1980; LL.D. (hon.), U. Aberdeen, 1980. Concert artist; co-dir.: Kings Lynn Festival. Fellow St. Anne's Coll., Oxford (Eng.) U., 1975; Decorated dame Brit. Empire; recipient Daily Mail Kathleen Ferrier award, 1956; Queen's prize Royal Coll. Music, 1959; Shakespeare prize Hamburg, 1971; Sonning prize Copenhagen, 1979. Fellow Royal Soc. Arts; mem. Munster Trust. Home: 450 Edgware Rd, London W2 England Office: care Shaw Concepts Inc 1995 Broadway New York NY 10023 also: care Ibbs and Tillett Ltd, 450-452 Edgware Rd, London W2 1EG, England *

BAKER, JOSEPHINE L. REDENIUS (MRS. MILTON G. BAKER), minister, civic leader, retired U.S. Army officer, former public relations company executive; b. Oceanville, N.J., Aug. 31, 1920; d. Jacob and Josephine (Palmer) Redenius; student Columbia U., 1948-49, L.I. U., 1957-58, George Washington U., 1947-48; M.A. in Journalism, Am. U., 1963; L.H.D., Temple U., 1964; M.A. in Religious Studies, St. Charles Sem., 1981; M.Div., Eastern Baptist Theol. Sem., 1984; postgrad., 1987—. Ordained Deacon Episcopal Ch. Enlisted as pvt. WAAC, 1943, advanced through grades to lt. col. U.S. Army, 1963, to col. Pa. N.G., 1967; intelligence officer atomic installations throughout U.S. and Can., 1943-53; asst. in Office Chief of Staff, Army Forces Far East, Japan, 1954-56; public info. officer Office Chief of Info., Washington, 1958-61; chief Women's Army Corps Recruiting, U.S. Army, 1962-66; info. liaison officer U.S. Army, 1966-67, ret., 1967; dir. pub. relations and devel. Valley Forge Mil. Acad. and Jr. Coll., Wayne, Pa., 1967-71, dir., 1970-79; pres. Potential Inc., Ardmore, Pa., 1979-83, Intercounty Trading Co., Inc., Surfside, Fla., 1976-80; deacon All Souls' Episcopal Ch., Miami Beach, Fla. Bd. dirs. Valley Forge Freedom Valley dist. Girl Scouts Am., Republican Women of Pa., Opera Guild of Miami; pres. bd. dirs. St. Cornelius the Centurian Found., 1976—; v.p. Episcopal Ch. Women, Diocese of Pa., 1984-86. Decorated Legion of Merit, Pa. Meritorious Service medal; U.S. Army Commendation medal with oak leaf cluster. Recipient Order Golden Sword Valley Forge Mil. Acad., 1986; named Disting. Alumnus Am. U., 1969; Doctor Ministry fellow Eastern Baptist Theol. Sem., 1985-87. Mem. Pub. Relations Soc. Am., Am. Personnel and Guidance Assn., Am. Coll. Personnel Assn., Nat. Vocat. Guidance Assn., Am. Sch. Counselors Assn., Pa. Med. Missionary Soc. (dir. 1983—), Am. Legion Aux., Ret. Officers Assn., Assn. U.S. Army (Anthony J. Drexel Biddle medal 1968), Army-Navy Union, Assn. Measurement and Evaluation in Guidance, Am. Legion, La Boutique Des Hult Chapeaux et Quarante Femmes, Emergency Aid of Pa., Women in Communications, Soc. of St. Francis, Mil. Order World Wars, Miami Heart Inst. Aux. Episcopalian. Clubs: Surf, Bald Peak Colony (N.H.), Miami Beach (fla.) Women's, St. David's Golf; Acorn. Lodge: Soroptimists. also: 9 Island Ave Belle Isle Miami Beach FL 33139

BAKER, KENNETH (WILFRED), secretary of state for education and science; b. England, Nov. 3, 1934; s. W. M. and Mrs. (Harries) B.; m. Mary Elizabeth Gray-Muir; 1 son, 2 daus. Grad., St. Paul's Sch., 1955, Magdalen Coll., Oxford, 1958. Lt. in gunners Royal Artillery, North Africa, 1953-55; artillery instr. to Libyan Army Oxford, 1955-58; mem. Twickenham Borough Council, 1960-62; mem. for Acton Parliament, London, 1968, mem. for St. Marylebone, 1970, mem. for Mole Valley, 1983; minister at Civil Service Dept. 1972-74, Parliamentary Pvt. Sec. to Mr. Edward Heath (then Leader of the Opposition), 1974-75, Minister of State for Industry and Info. Tech., 1981-84; Minister for Local Govt. Dept. of the Environment, 1984-85; Sec. of State for the Environment 1985, Sec. of State for Edn. and Sci., 1986—; mem. of Pub. Accounts Com., 1969-70, Exec. of the 1922 Com. (of Conservative Backbenchers); chmn. of Hansard Soc., 1978-81, Conservative Parliamentary Industry Com.; sec.-gen. UN Conf. of Parliamentarians on World Population and Devel., 1978. Author: I Have No Gun But I Can Spit, 1980, London Lines, 1982. Clubs: Athenaeum, Carlton. Office: House of Commons, London SW1 England *

BAKER, KERRY ALLEN, proprietary drug company executive; b. Selmer, Tenn., Sept. 21, 1949; s. Austin Clark and Betty Ann (Brooks) B.; m. Ellen Fleming. BIE, Ga. Inst. Tech., 1971; MBA, Ga. State U., 1973; JD, Memphis State U., 1987. With dept. law State of Ga., 1971-73; div. engr. N.W. Ga. div. Gold Kist Inc.,Ellijay, Ga., 1977-80; sr. mfg. engr. Plough, Inc., Memphis, 1980-82, mgr. indsl. engring., 1983-86; supr. mfg. engring., 1986—. Served to capt. U.S. Army, 1973-77. Decorated Order of St. Barbara. Mem. Am. Inst. Indsl. Engrs., Am. Mgmt. Assn., Soc. Advancement Mgmt., Am. Inst. Plant Engrs., Soc. Am. Mil. Engrs., Scabbard and Blade, Sigma Phi Epsilon, Pi Delta Epsilon, Alpha Phi Omega, Phi Delta Phi. Baptist. Lodge: Masons. Home: 3548 Evening Light Dr Bartlett TN 38135 Office: Plough Inc 3030 Jackson Ave Box 377 Memphis TN 38151

BAKER, LAWRENCE COLBY, JR., insurance company executive; b. Carleton, Mich., Oct. 6, 1935; s. Lawrence Colby and Margaret Ellen (Close) B.; m. Ida Wasil, June 26, 1960. B.A., U. Mich., 1957. Underwriter SAFECO, Panorama City, Calif., 1960-61; dist. mgr. Travelers Ins. Co., Los Angeles, 1961-71; chief dep. commr. Calif. Dept. Ins., Los Angeles, 1971-75; pres. Argonaut Ins. Co., Menlo Park, Calif., 1975-85; v.p., gen. mgr. Inter-ins. Exchange of Automobile Club of So. Calif., Los Angeles, 1985—; dir. Auto Club of So. Calif. Mgmt. Services Co.; trustee Am. Inst. Property and Liability Underwriters and Ins. Inst. Am.; past chmn. bd. dirs. Calif. Workers Compensation. Served to lt. (j.g.) USN, 1957-60. Mem. Calif. Ins. Guarantee Assn. (past chmn.), Nat. Assn. Ind. Insurors (past gov.), Ins. Ednl. Assn. (past chmn.), Assn. Calif. Ins. Cos. (past treas.). Office: 2601 S Figueroa St Los Angeles CA 90007

BAKER, LILLIAN, author, historian, artist, lecturer; b. Yonkers, N.Y., Dec. 12, 1921; student El Camino (Calif.) Coll., 1952, UCLA, 1968, 77; m. Roscoe A. Baker; children: Wanda Georgia, George Riley. Continuity writer Sta. WINS, N.Y.C., 1945-46; columnist, freelance writer, reviewer Gardena (Calif.) Valley News, 1964-76; freelance writer, editor, 1971—; lectr. in field.; founder/editor Internat. Club for Collectors of Hatpins and Hatpin Holders, monthly newsletter Points, ann. Pictorial Jour., 1977—, conv. and seminar coordinator, 1979—; co-founder Ams. for Hist. Accuracy, 1972, Com. for Equality for All Draftees, 1973; chair S. Bay primary campaign S.I. Hayakawa, for U.S. Senator from Calif., 1976; witness U.S. Commn. Wartime Relocation, 1981, U.S. Senate Judiciary Com., 1983, U.S. Ho. Reps. Judiciary Com., 1986. Recipient award Freedoms Found., 1971; Ann. award Conf. Calif. Hist. Socs., 1983; monetary award Hoover Instn. Stanford (Calif.) U., 1985; recipient award Pro-Am. Orgn., 1987. Mem. Nat. League Am. Pen Women, Nat. Writers Club, Soc. Jewelry Historians USA, (charter), Art Students League N.Y. (life), Nat. Historic Soc. (founding), Nat. Trust Historic Preservation (founding), other orgns. Author: Collector's Encyclopedia of Hatpins and Hatpin Holders, 1976, second edit. 1988, 100 Years of Collectible Jewelry 1850-1950, 1978, rev. edit., 1988, Jewelry: Art Nouveau and Art Deco, 1980, rev. edit. 1985, 87, The Concentration Camp Conspiracy: A Second Pearl Harbor, 1981 (Scholarship Category award of Merit, Conf. of Calif. Hist. Socs. 1983), Hatpins and Hatpin Holders: An Illustrated Value Guide, 1983, rev. edit. 1988, Creative and Collectible Miniatures, 1984, Fifty Years of Collectible Fashion Jewelry: 1925-1975, 1986, 2d edit., 1987, Dishonoring America: The Collective Guilt of American Japanese, 1988; also articles; author poetry; editor: Insider; contbg. author Vol. VII Time-Life Encyclopedia of Collectibles, 1979; numerous radio and TV appearances. Home and Office: 15237 Chanera Ave Gardena CA 90249

BAKER, LOUIS COOMBS WELLER, chemistry educator, researcher; b. N.Y.C., Nov. 24, 1921; s. F(rancis) Godfrey and Marion Georgina (Weller) B.; m. Violet Eva Simmons, June 28, 1964; children—William W.S., Godfrey A.S. A.B., Columbia Univ., 1943; M.S., U. Pa., 1947, Ph.D., 1950; LHD honoris causa Georgetown U., 1988. Asst. instr. chemistry Towne Sci. Sch. U. Pa., Phila., 1943-50, instr. chemistry The College, U. Pa., 1945-50, assoc. in chemistry The Johnson Found., U. Pa., Phila., 1950-51; instr. Martin Coll. and Rittenhouse Coll., Phila., 1945-48; asst. prof. to assoc. prof., head inorganic div. Boston U., 1951-62; prof. chemistry Georgetown U., Washington, 1962—, chmn. dept., 1962-84; co-project dir. OPRD high thermal efficiency engine project, N.Y.C. and Boundbrook, N.J., 1943-45; chmn. Internat. Symposium on Heteropoly Electrolytes, Am. Chem. Soc., 1956; chmn. Nat. Acad. Sci. Com. on Recommendations to U.S. Army for Basic Sci. Research, 1974-78; plenary lectr. Internat. Conf. Coordination Chemistry, Moscow, 1973; sci. mem. com. on accrediation Coll. and Univs. Middle States Assn. Coll. and Secondary Schs.; sci. mem. vis. com. Ferdowsi Univ., Mashhad, Iran, 1974-75; speaker Gordon Research Confs., 1956, 1967; cons. in field. Contbr. articles on inorganic chemistry to profl. jours. Co-inventor High Thermal Efficiency Internal Combustion Engine, 1943-45. Guggenheim fellow, 1961—; recipient Tchugaev medal USSR Acad. Scis., 1973; Vicennial Gold medal Georgetown U., 1983, Pres.'s medal Disting. Service, 1984; grantee NSF, NIH, numerous others. Fellow Washington Acad. Scis.; mem. Am. Chem. Soc. (chmn. com. rev. inorganic papers 1957-59, councilor, bd. mgrs.), Sigma XI (past pres. Georgetown chpt.). Quaker. Club: Cosmos (Washington). Office: Georgetown U Dept of Chemistry Washington DC 20057

BAKER, RICHARD BROWN, art collector; b. Providence, Nov. 5, 1912; s. Harvey Almy and Marion North (Brown) B.; B.A., Yale, 1935; student Students Internat. Union, Geneva, 1932; B.A. (Rhodes scholar), Christ Ch. Oxford U., 1943, M.A., 1943; D.F.A. (hon.), R.I. Sch. Design, 1978. Reporter, edit. librarian Providence Jour., 1938-40; attache Am. embassy, Madrid, 1940; editorial asst. FCC, Washington, 1941; asso. social sci. analyst Western European sect. div. spl. info. Library of Congress, 1941-43; research analyst Western European sect. research and analysis br. OSS, Washington, London, Paris, 1943-45; research analyst Office Intelligence Research, Dept. State, 1945-47; fgn. affairs officer CIA, 1947-48; nongovt. observer Internat. League Rights of Man UN, 1954-56; mem. museum com. R.I. Sch. Design, 1966-75, mem. fine arts com. of mus., 1976—; mem. com. on art gallery Univ. Council, Yale, 1962-66, 71-76; mem. governing bd. Yale U. Art Gallery, 1974—, mem. exec. com., 1978—; mem. drawings com. Whitney Mus. Am. Art, 1976—; collection of contemporary art has been basis for exhibits at R.I. Sch. Design Mus., Providence, 1959, 64, 73, 85, Drew U., Madison, N.J., 1960, 62, Walker Art Center, Mpls., 1961, Wellesley (Mass.) Coll. exhibit, 1963, Yale, New Haven, 1963, 75, Larry Aldrich Museum, Ridgefield, Conn., 1965, Oakland U., Rochester, Mich., 1967, 74, 79, U. South Fla., Tampa, 1967, 69, Selected Works World Art, Mexico City, 1968, U. Notre Dame, South Bend, Ind., 1969, San Francisco Mus. Art, 1973, U. Pa., Phila., 1973, Stamford (Conn.) Mus., 1978, Squibb Gallery, Princeton, N.J., 1979, Katonah (N.Y.) Gallery, 1980, San Diego Mus., 1985, Portland Mus. Art, 1985; mem. N.Y.C. Art Commn., 1977-80. Fellow Morgan Library; mem. Met. Mus. (life), Art Students League (life), Am. Fedn. Arts, Archives of Am. Art, Friends Am. Arts at Yale, Mus. Modern Art, Mus. Art R.I. Sch. Design, Whitney Circle, Guggenheim Mus. (asso.), Yale Library Assn., Friend of Columbia Libraries, Phi Beta Kappa. Clubs: Hope (Providence); University (Washington); Grolier, Century, Yale (N.Y.C.); Elizabethan (New Haven). Author: The Year of the Buzz Bomb: A Journal of London, 1944, 1952; Stairways to Another Stage: Verse, 1952. Home: 1185 Park Ave New York NY 10128

BAKER, RICHARD SOUTHWORTH, lawyer; b. Lansing, Mich., Dec. 18, 1929; s. Paul Julius and Florence (Schmid) B.; m. Marina Joy Vidoli, July 24, 1965; children: Garrick Richard, Lydia Joy. Student, DePauw U., 1947-49; A.B. cum laude, Harvard, 1951; J.D., U. Mich., 1954. Bar: Ohio 1957, U.S. Dist. Ct. (no. dist.) Ohio 1958, U.S. Tax Ct. 1960, U.S. Supreme Ct. 1971, U.S. Ct. Appeals (6th cir.) 1972. Since practiced in Toledo; mem. firm Fuller & Henry, and predecessors, 1956—; Chmn. nat. com. region IV Mich. Law Sch. Fund, 1967-69, mem.-at-large, 1970-85. Bd. dirs. Asso. Harvard Alumni, 1970-73; mem. Epworth Assembly, Ludington, Mich.. Served with AUS, 1954-56. Fellow Am. Coll. Trial Lawyers; mem. ABA, Ohio Bar Assn., Toledo Bar Assn., Lawyer-Pilots Bar Assn., Phi Delta Theta, Phi Delta Phi. Clubs: Toledo, Harvard (pres. 1968-77), Inverness, Brandywine Country (all Toledo); Lincoln Hills Golf (Ludington, Mich.). Home: 2819 Falmouth Rd Toledo OH 43615 Office: Fuller & Henry One Seagate PO Box 2088 Toledo OH 43603

BAKER, RONALD PHILLIP, service company executive; b. Kansas City, Mo., Feb. 15, 1942; s. Harry and Ruth Sarah (Bornstein) B.; m. Marilyn Gitterman, Dec. 27, 1964; children: Kevin, Corey. Student, U. Okla., 1960-63; BA in Sociology and Govt., U. Mo., Kansas City, 1965, postgrad., 1965. Acct. rep. Am. House and Window Cleaning Co., Kansas City, 1965-69; dist. ops. mgr. Am. Bldg. Services, Kansas City, 1969-72; pres. BG Maintenance Mgmt., Kansas City, 1972-86; chmn. bd. dirs. BGM Industries, Kansas City, 1987—. V.p. Jewish Community Ctr., Kansas City, 1985, 86, 87; pres. Jewish Vocat. Services, Kansas City, 1979, 80, 81; bd. dirs. Beth Shalom Synagogue, Kansas City, 1985-88, Jewish Welfare Bd., 1986, 88; co-chmn. Jewish Fedn. Greater Kansas City, 1986. Mem. Bldg. Service Contractors Assn. Internat. (bd. dirs., chmn. seminars 1981, 85, speaker conv., pres. club 1981-87, mem. edn. com. 1981-87, info. cen. com. 1985, 86, 87, chmn. annual conv. 1988, exec. com. 1988), Bldg. Owners and Mgrs. Assn. Kansas City, Jewish Fedn. Kansas City (v.p. 1986, 87, Young Leadership award 1981), Menninger Found. (pres. club Topeka 1986, 87), Sigma Alpha Mu, Delta Sigma Pi.. Republican. Club: Meadowbrook Country. Office: BGM Industries 1225 E 18th St Kansas City MO 64108

BAKER, SAUL PHILLIP, geriatrician, cardiologist, internist; b. Cleve., Dec. 7, 1924; s. Barnet and Florence (Kleinman) B. B.S. in Physics, Case Inst. Tech., 1945; postgrad., Western Res. U., 1946-47; M.Sc. in Physiology, Ohio State U., 1949, M.D., 1953, Ph.D. in Physiology, 1957; J.D., Case Western Res. U., 1981. Intern Cleve. Met. Gen. Hosp., 1953-54; sr. asst. surgeon Gerontology Br. Nat. Heart Inst, NIH, now Gerontology Research Ctr., Nat. Inst. Aging, 1954-56; asst. vis. staff physician dept. medicine Balt. City Hosps. (now Francis Scott Key Hosp.) and Johns Hopkins Hosp., 1954-56; sr. asst. resident in internal medicine U. Chgo. Hosps., 1956-57; asst. prof. internal medicine Chgo. Med. Sch., 1957-62; assoc. prof. internal medicine Cook County Hosp. Grad. Sch. Medicine, Chgo., 1958-62; assoc. attending physician Cook County Hosp., 1957-62; practice medicine specializing in geriatrics, cardiology, internal medicine Cleve., 1962-70, 72—; head dept. geriatrics St. Vincent Charity Hosp., Cleve., 1964-67; cons. internal medicine and cardiology Bur. Disability Determination, Old-Age and Survivors Ins., Social Security Adminstrn., 1963—; cons. internal medicine City of Cleve., 1964—; medicare med. cons. Gen. Am. Life Ins. Co., St. Louis, 1970-71; cons. internal medicine and cardiology Ohio Bur. Worker's Compensation, 1964—; cons. cardiovascular disease FAA, 1973—; cons. internal medicine and cardiology State of Ohio, 1974—. Contbr. articles to profl. and sci. jours. Mem. sci. council Northeastern Ohio affiliate Am. Heart Assn.; former mem. adv. com. Sr. Adult div. Jewish Community Ctr. Cleve.; mem. vis. com. bd. overseers Case Inst. Tech.; former mem. com. older people Fedn. Community Planning Cleve. Fellow Am. Coll. Cardiology, AAAS, Gerontol. Soc. Am. (former Ohio regent), Am. Geriatrics Soc., Cleve. Med. Library Assn. (life); mem. Am. Physiol. Soc., AMA, Ohio Med. Assn., N.Y. Acad. Scis., Chgo. Soc. Internal Medicine, Am. Fedn. Clin. Research, Soc. Exptl. Biology and Medicine, Am. Diabetes Assn., Diabetes Assn. Greater Cleve. (profl. sect.), Am. Heart Assn. (fellow council arteriosclerosis), Nat. Assn. Disability Examiners, Nat. Rehab. Assn., Am. Pub. Health Assn., Assn. Am. Med. Colls., Acad. Medicine Cleve., Internat. Soc. Cardiology (council epidemiology and prevention), Am. Soc. Law and Medicine, Sigma Xi, Phi Delta Epsilon, Sigma Alpha Mu (past pres. Cleve. alumni club). Club: Cleve. Clinical (past sec.). Lodges: Masons (32 degree), Shriners. Office: 6803 Mayfield Rd PO Box 24246 Cleveland OH 44124

BAKER, SHIRLEY HODNETT, marketing professional; b. Halifax, Va., Aug. 11, 1951; d. Charlie Thompson and Earlene (Dance) Hodnett; m. Robert H. Baker. Student Cen. Va. Community Coll., 1974-76. Sec. Lynchburg (Va.) Coll., 1969-72; sec. Leggett Dept. Store, Lynchburg, 1972-75, sales mgr., 1975-76; co-owner Decorating Den, Lynchburg, 1976-81; adminstrv. asst. TV Bur. Advt., Atlanta, 1981-82, mktg./sales exec., Dallas, 1982-84; mktg. dir. N.Y. Market Radio Broadcasters Assn., N.Y.C., 1985-87; v.p. sales and mktg. Radio Advt. Bur., N.Y.C., 1987—. Bd. dirs. Mother's Day Council, Father's Day Council. Mem. Am. Women in Radio and TV, Nat. Assn. Female Execs. Baptist. Home: 57 Warren St New York NY 10007 Office: Radio Advt Bur 304 Park Ave S New York NY 10010

BAKER, VERNA TOMLINSON (MRS. EARL M. BAKER), writer, former librarian; b. Phila., Apr. 14, 1915; d. Joseph Ullman and Mabel (Dolton) Tomlinson; student (scholar) Temple U., 1937-39, Phila. Coll. Bible, 1959-62; B.S., Bryan Coll., 1963; M.A., George Peabody Coll., 1964; M.A., Chgo. Grad. Sch. Theology, 1970; m. Earl M. Baker, Dec. 31, 1938 (dec. Nov. 1958); children—Earl M. III, B. Kimball. Asst. to expediter Brit. Admiralty Del., Naval Aviation Supply Depot, Phila., 1944-45; sec., manuscript reader Westminster Press, Phila., 1947-53; librarian Ben Lippen Sch., Asheville, N.C., 1953-58; gen. library work Nashville Pub. Library, 1963-64; with The King's Coll., Briarcliff Manor, N.Y., 1964-85, reader services librarian, 1967-85. Mem. N.Y., Westchester library assns. Christian Librarians fellow, 1965—. Author: Here in the Spring, 1968; editor: Poems Revisited, 1976; contbr. poems to anthologies, various mags.

BAKER, WALTER LOUIS, engineering company executive; b. Earlton, N.Y., Aug. 7, 1924; s. Alberti and Louise (Schmidt) B.; m. Janet Katherine Sprague, Sept. 7, 1944 (dec.); children: Walter Kent (dec.), Lawrence Albert, Linda Louise, Louis Milton; m. Marion M. King, July 1, 1976 (dec.); stepchildren: Vinton P. King, John S. King; m. Shirley E. Lindsay, Mar. 30, 1985; stepchildren: Thomas M. Lindsay, Christopher J. Lindsay, Margaret S. Lindsay, Janet Lindsay Keeble, William D. Lindsay. B.E.E. (N.Y. State scholar, Coll. scholar), Clarkson Coll., 1944; M.S., Pa. State U., 1954. Registered profl. engr., Pa. Tech. supr. Tenn. Eastman Corp., 1944-45; sr. engr. Philco Corp., 1945-49; research asso. Pa. State U., State Coll., from 1949, prof., sr. mem. grad. faculty, 1965-82, now prof. emeritus engring., mem. grad. faculty; pres. Baker Engring. Co., Portsmouth, R.I., 1981—; cons. Spartan Electric Corp., 1960-61, U.S. Marine Corps, 1965, John I. Thompson & Co., 1952-68, HRB-Singer Co., 1958-67, Vitro Corp., 1981, Woods Hole Oceanography Inst., 1981-83, Dynamic Systems, Inc., 1980-84. Co-author: Acoustic Performance Handbook, 1974; contbr. articles to profl. jours. Recipient U.S. Navy Meritorious Public Service citation. Mem. IEEE (sr., chmn., sec.-treas. Central Pa. sect.), Acoustical Soc. Am., N.Y. Acad. Scis., Sigma Xi. Republican. Methodist. Lodges: Elks, Lions. Address: Baker Engring Co 22 Oliver Hazard Perry Rd Portsmouth RI 02871

BAKER, WILLIAM ALLISON, architect; b. Wheatland, Wyo., May 24, 1944; s. Wallace Allison and Ruth (Hill) B.; m. Constance Henriette Francisca de Vos, Dec. 27, 1970; children: Garrett, Eileen, Jesse, Hillary. B.C.E. with hons., U. Wyo., 1967; M.Arch., Princeton U., 1973. Registered profl. engr., Wyo.; registered architect, Wyo., S.D., Colo. Architect Banner Assocs., Inc., Laramie, Wyo., 1973-77, head archtl. dept., 1985—; asst. prof. dept. civil & archtl. engring. U. Wyo., 1977-79; ptnr. Malone, Baker & Assocs., Sheridan, Wyo., 1980-84; v.p. Wyo. Bd. Architects, 1984-85, pres. 1986—. Mem. Laramie Code appeals Bd., 1978-79. Served as 1st lt. U.S. Army, 1967-70, Vietnam. Recipient award of merit Soc. Mil. Engrs., 1968, teaching award, Amoco Corp., 1979. Mem. AIA, Nat. Trust Historic Preservation, Wyo. Hist. Soc., U. Wyo. Alumni Assn. Princeton Grad. Alumni, Sigma Tau, Phi Epsilon Phi, Phi Kappa Phi, Omicron Delta Kappa. Office: Banner Assocs Inc 620 Plaza Ct Laramie WY 82070

BAKER, WILLIAM HERBERT, insurance company executive; b. Buffalo, Oct. 23, 1932; s. Guy Andrew and Ella Mae (Beeler) B.; BS in Econs., Purdue U., 1954; postgrad. Ball State U., 1956-58, Rider Coll., 1980—; children—Scott Andrew, Karen Lynn. Prodn. supr., safety dir., labor relations supr. Gen. Motors Corp., Muncie, Ind., New Brunswick, N.J., Anderson, Ind., 1956-69; dir. personnel mgmt. N.J. Hosp. Assn., Princeton, 1969-75, v.p., 1975-81; sr. v.p. Middle Atlantic Shared Services Corp., 1982-86; v.p. Ctr. for Health Affairs Ins. Services, Inc., 1986—; mem. faculty hosp. seminars. Former mem., v.p. Montgomery Twp. Bd. Edn., pres., 1977-80; mem. Hightstown YMCA; former bd. dirs. Am. Heart Assn. N.J. affiliate; officer, former bd. dirs. Princeton Area United Fund; bd. dirs. Hightstown (N.J.) YMCA, 1988—. Served with CIC, AUS, 1954-56. Mem. Am. Mgmt. Assn., Am. Hosp. Assn., Am. Soc. Hosp. Personnel Adminstrn. Lutheran. Home: 95 Meadow Dr Hightstown NJ 08520 Office: 760 Alexander Rd CN-1 Princeton NJ 08540

BAKER, WINTHROP PATTERSON, JR., broadcasting executive; b. N.Y.C., July 12, 1931; s. Winthrop Patterson and Josie Lou (Kendrick) B.; m. Elizabeth Muriel Allegret, July 30, 1955; children: Winthrop Patterson III, John Adams, Michael Kendrick. Student, Vanderbilt U., 1952; BS in Bus. Adminstrn., La. State U., 1953. Dir. Sta. WJMR-TV, New Orleans, 1954-55; producer, dir. Sta. WBRZ-TV, Baton Rouge, 1955-56; program dir. Sta. KLFY-TV, Lafayette, La., 1956-57, Sta. WMBD-TV, Peoria, Ill., 1957-60; asst. program mgr. Sta. WBZ-TV, Boston, 1960-61; program mgr. Sta. WJZ-TV, Balt., 1962-65, Sta. KYW-TV, Phila., 1965-67; asst. gen. mgr. Sta. KDKA-TV, Pitts., 1967; gen. mgr. Sta. WBZ-TV, Boston, 1968-73; v.p. Sta. WBZ-TV, 1970-73; pres. Westinghouse Broadcasting Co., N.Y.C., 1973-79; corp. v.p., dir. Westinghouse Broadcasting Co., 1974-79; dir. TV Advt. Reps., N.Y.C., 1969-79; pres. P.M. Mag. Inc. subs. Westinghouse Broadcasting Co., 1978-79; pres. Gen. Electric Broadcasting and Cablevision Co., Fairfield, Conn., 1981-82; pres., dir., gen. mgr. Sta. WNEV-TV, Boston, 1982-84; pres. Target Video Inc., Wilton, 1984—; gen. ptnr. William Street Ptnrs., Westport, Conn., 1984—. Mem. Boston Youth Activities Commn., Boston, 1970-71; adv. com. U.S. Youth Games, 1971; mem. Gov.'s Commn. on Ednl.

Reorgn., 1972-73; bd. dirs., vice-chmn. Boston Community Media Com., 1970-73; bd. dirs. Intercom, Boston, 1970-73, Consumer-care Council, 1970-71; mem. adv. bd. broadcasting and communications curriculum U. Pa. Wharton Sch. Bus., 1978-79, Mercer (N.J.) Community Coll., 1978-79. Mem. Am. Advt. Fedn. (dir. 1974-79), Nat. Assn. TV Program Execs., New Eng. Broadcast Assn., Mass. Broadcasters Assn. (v.p. dir. 1970-71), Mass. Audubon Soc., De Cordova Mus., Phi Kappa Phi, Mu Sigma Rho, Phi Eta Sigma, Pi Tau Pi, Beta Gamma Sigma.

BAKER-LIEVANOS, NINA GILLSON, jewelry store executive; b. Boston, Dec. 19, 1950; d. Rev. John Robert and Patricia (Gillson) Baker; m. Jorge Alberto Lievanos, June 6, 1981; children: Jeremy John Baker, Wendy Mara Baker, Raoul Salvador Baker-Lievanos. Student Mills Coll., 1969-70; grad. course in diamond grading Gemology Inst. Am., 1983; student in diamondtology designation Diamond Council Am., 1986—. Artist, tchr., Claremont, Calif., 1973-78; escrow officer Bank of Am., Claremont, 1978-81; retail salesman William Pitt Jewelers, Puente Hills, Montclair, Calif., 1981-83, asst. mgr., Montclair, 1983, mgr., 1983—, corp. sales trainer, 1988—. Artist tapestry hanging Laguna Beach Mus. Art, 1974. Recipient Cert. Merit Art Bank Am., 1968, High Sales award William Pitt Jewelers, 1983, 84, Key award Am. Biographical Inst. for Mgmt. Achievement, 1987. Mem. Nat. Assn. Female Execs., Internat. Platform Assn., C. of C., Compassion Internat. Roman Catholic. Republican. Avocations: tapestry weaving, creative writing. Office: William Pitt Jewelers 158 Towne Ctr Santa Maria CA 93454

BAKES, PHILIP JOHN, JR., lawyer, airline executive; b. Little Rock, Mar. 6, 1946; s. Philip John and Theresa B.; m. Priscilla C. Smith, June 19, 1977; children: Tia, Justin. B.A. magna cum laude, Loyola U., Chgo., 1968, J.D. magna cum laude (Sheldon fellow), Harvard U., 1971. Bar: Ill. 1971, D.C. 1975. Assoc. firm Devoe, Shadur & Krupp, Chgo., 1972-73; asst. spl. prosecutor Watergate Spl. Prosecution Force, Washington, 1973-74, asst. chief counsel Senate Subcom. on Adminstrv. Practice and Procedures, Washington, 1974-77; spl. counsel Senate Antitrust Subcom., Washington, 1977; gen. counsel CAB, Washington, 1977-79; dep. campaign mgr. Kennedy for Pres., 1979-80; sr. v.p. Tex. Air Corp., Houston, 1980-82; exec. v.p., chief operating officer Continental Air Lines, Houston, 1982-84, pres., 1984-86, now pres., chief operating officer; pres., chief exec. officer Eastern Air Lines Inc., Miami, Fla., 1986—; mem. adv. com. govtl. relations Am. Enterprise Inst. Mem. D.C. Bar Assn., Ill. Bar Assn. Office: Eastern Airlines Inc Miami Internat Airport Miami FL 33148

BAKHIREV, VYACHESLAV VASILIYEVICH, Soviet government official, engineer; b. Sept. 17, 1916, Dudorovo village, Ivanovo Region. Grad. Moscow State U., 1941. Engr., head dept., head constrn. bur., chief constructor, chief engr. of plant, 1941-60, then dir. mech. and machine bldg. factory Vladimir Oblast, 1960-65; joined Communist Party Soviet Union, 1951—; dep. to USSR Supreme Soviet, 1962—; first dep. minister def. and industry, 1965-68; minister machine bldg., 1968-87. Mem. cen. com. Communist Party Soviet Union, 1971—. Recipient Lenin prize; Order of Lenin (three times), Hero of Socialist Labour, 1976, Badge of Honour, others. Office: Communist Party Soviet Union, Staraya Pl 4, Moscow USSR *

BAKHUIZEN, WILLEM ANTHONIE HENDRIK JOHANNES, civil engineer; b. Vlaardingen, Netherlands, Apr. 25, 1945; came to Sweden, 1969; s. Martinus and Johanna K. (van Leeuwen) B.; m. Anita S.G. Lofman, Sept. 5, 1970; 1 child, Mattias H. B.Sc., HTS-Inst. of Advanced Tech., Utrecht, Netherlands, 1967. Cert. cons. civil engr. Area mgr. Far East Viak Cons., Gothenburg, Sweden, 1969-83; mgr. offshore Benima Engring., Gothenburg, 1983-87; pres. Hasselblad Engring. AB, Gothenburg, 1987—; survey cons. Ingenieros Consultadores Associados/Tunel S.A., Mexico City, 1973; cons. Food and Agr. Orgn. for Remote Sensing Project Mekong Delta-Ho Chi Minh City, 1987; chief surveyor Swedish Internat. Devel. Authority, Bai Bang, Vietnam, 1975-77. Active Nat. Swedish Devel. Authority, Stockholm, 1979. Fellow Remote Sensing Soc., Am. Soc. Photogrammetry; mem. Civil Engrs. Assn. Sweden, Chartered Land Surveyor Sweden.

BAKKENKIST, SIEBRAND CORNELIS, business executive; b. Amsterdam, Sept. 23, 1914; m. Elisabeth Wegenaar; 2 children. Degree, U. Amsterdam. Founder, gen. mgr. Bakkenkist, Spits & Co., 1942-64; chmn. VMF-STORK, Amsterdam, until 1985; now chmn. emeritus VMF-STORK; former pres. Verband von Nederlandsche Ondernemingen. Mem. Order Orange-Nassau. Office: VMF-STORK, Vlaardingenlaan 11, PO Box 9251, 1017 Amsterdam The Netherlands *

BAKR, ABDULLAH, university administrator; b. Taif, Saudi Arabia, Jan 1, 1938; s. Abdullah Mohammed and Aisha Mohammedhassan (Maghraby) B.; B.Petroleum Engring., U. Tex., 1963; M.B.A., Stanford U., 1967; D.B.A., U. So. Calif., 1970; m. Fakhriah Salah Ramadhan, Aug. 8, 1965; children—Osama, Maha, Wael, Zahia, Abdullah, Hani, Ahmed. Owner bus., Taif, Saudi Arabia, 1953-58; petroleum engr. ARAMCO, Dhahran, 1963-64; asst. dean Coll. Petroleum and Minerals, Dhahran, 1964-66, dean, 1970-74; exec. asst. to gov. of PETROMIN, Riyadh, 1966-70; pres. King Fahd U. Petroleum and Minerals, Dhahran, Saudi Arabia, 1974—, UPM Found.; bd. dirs. Riyadh U., King Abdul Aziz U., Imam Mohammad Ibn Saud U., Islamic U., King Faisal U., King Saud U.; bd. regents Qatar U.; trustee Bahrain Univ. Coll.; vice chmn. UN Univ Council; cons. in field. Bd. dirs. various charity orgns. Mem. Arab Univ. Pres. Assn., Internat. Assn. Sci. and Tech. for Devel., Am. Mgmt. Assns., Am. Mgmt. Assn. Engrs., UN Inst. Tng. and Research, Internat. Social Prospects Acad. Moslem. Home and Office: King Fahd U of Petroleum and Minerals, Dhahran 31261, Saudi Arabia

BAKSAY, LASZLO ANDREW, physicist, educator; b. Budapest, Hungary, July 22, 1945; came to U.S., 1978, naturalized, 1981; s. Laszlo and Jolan (Bethlen) B.; m. Marika Gallo, July 16, 1983. Dipl. Phys., RWTH Aachen, 1972, Dr. rer. nat., 1978, Sport-Staatsexamen, 1979. Chercheur visiteur CERN, Geneva, 1972-75; research assoc. RWTH, Aachen, Fed. Republic Germany, 1975-78; vis. scientist Stanford U. Calif., 1978-82; asst. prof. physics Northeastern U., Boston, 1978-83; staff scientist Lawrence Berkeley Lab., Calif., 1982-83; assoc. prof. physics U. Dallas, Irving, Tex., 1983-85; assoc. prof. physics Union Coll., Schenectady, 1985—; guest scientist Brookhaven Nat. Lab., 1985—; textbook cons. to several pubs., 1980-82. Contbr. articles to profl. publs. Henkel scholar, 1967-72; Thyssen scholar, 1968-72; research scholar Fed. Republic Germany, 1972-74; Fulbright scholar, 1988. Mem. Am. Phys. Soc., Deutsche Physikalische Gesellschaft, European Phys. Soc., N.Y. Acad. Scis.

BAL, JEAN-PIERRE, automotive company executive; b. Wilryk, Antwerp, Belgium, Aug. 8, 1958; s. Louis Charles and Micheline (Janssens) B.; m. Marie-Noelle Waterkeym, Oct. 25, 1980; children: Jean-Michel, Anthony, Nicolas. Cert. in sci., Georgetown U., 1976; BBA, European U., Antwerp, Belgium, 1981, MBA, 1986. Internal auditor Royal Packaging Van Leer, Amsterdam, Holland, 1981-83; European audit supr. Wickes Europe, Inc., London, 1983-85; asst. dir. Commodore Computer Co., Brussels, 1985-86; sales mgr. D'Ieteren S.Am., Brussels, 1986—; adj. assoc. prof. European U., Antwerp, 1985—. Authors: American Automotive Industry: Prospects for the 80's, 1981; contbr. articles to Belgian Bus. mag. Mem. Am. Mgmt. Assn., Belgian Mktg. and Mgmt. Assn. Home: 7 de Fienneslaan, 2520 Edegem Belgium Office: D'Ieteren SA, 50 Rue du Mail, 1050 Brussels Belgium

BALADI, ROLAND, artist; b. Cairo, July 12, 1942; s. Albert and Laura Elena (Ventura) B.; grad. in plastic arts and audio-visual communications Folkwanghochschule fü r Gestaltung, Germany, 1970; m. Catherine Chatiliez, 1972 (div. 1980); 1 child, Antonin. Art dir. SNIP, advt. agy., Paris, 1970-71; founder Internat. Selected Ideas and Systems, Paris, 1971-74; prof. U. Nancy (France), 1974-76, U. Bourges, 1984, UCLA, summer 1978; insp. French Nat. Bd. Architecture and Plastic Arts, 1974—; exhibited Mus. Modern Art, Paris, 1971, Annick Le Moine Art Gallery, Paris, 1974, La Defense Art Gallery, Paris, 1976, Pompidou-Beaubourg Center, Paris, 1977, Mus. Modern Art, N.Y.C., 1978, Galleria del Naviglio, Milan, 1979, O.K. Harris Gallery, N.Y.C., 1981, 83, 85, O.K. Harris West, Scottsdale, Ariz., 1982, Sculpture Tricentennial, Phila., 1982, Taft Mus., Cin., 1983, O.K. Harris Artists, Palm Beach; prin. works include Electricity Festival, itinerant exhbn. for French Nat. Electricity Corp., 1971, Ephemeral Graffiti Wall, 1973, Kinoplan at French Indsl. Exhbn. China, Peking, 1974, Solar Low Relief, 1975, Les Halles, 1978, The Marble Cadillac Project, 1986; researcher artistic application sci. and tech.; patentee artistic applications of computer scis. Fellow M.I.T. Center for Advanced Visual Studies. Home: 13 rue St Sauveur, 75002 Paris France other: 301 W Broadway New York NY 10013 also: OK Harris Gallery 383 W Broadway New York NY 10012

BALAGUER, JOAQUIN, president Dominican Republic; b. Villa Bisono, Dominican Republic, Sept. 1, 1907; s. Joaquin Balaguer Lespier and Carmen Celia Ricardo Vda Balaguer. Ed., U. Santo Domingo, also U. Paris, Sorbonne. Served in Madrid, 1932-35; undersec. fgn. affairs, Domincan Republic, 1936-40, minister to Colombia, 1940-46, alt. rep. to UN, 1947; minister fgn. affairs, 1954-55, minister edn. and arts, 1955-57, v.p. Dominican Republic, 1957-60, pres., 1960, 66-78, 1986—; vol. exile in U.S., 1962-65. Founder, Reformist Party, 1962, leader, 1962-85, leader Reformist Social Christian Party, (formerly Revolutionary Social Christian Party, merged with Reformist Party), after 1985. Address: Office of Pres, Santo Domingo Dominican Republic *

BALAKRISHNAN, KUNNATH VEETTIL, company executive; electrical engineer; b. Cochin, Kerala, India, Sept. 30, 1947; s. Achuthamenon Karumathil Vadakkath and Janakiamma; m. Ambikadevi Parameswaran Nair, Sept. 4, 1974; 1 child, Reshmy. B.S.E.E., NSS Coll. Engring.-India, 1969. Jr. elec. engr. Cochin Shipyard, Ltd., Kerala, India, 1971-74, asst. exec. elec. engr., 1974-77, exec. elec. engr., 1977-82, sr. elec. engr., 1982-86, dep. mgr., 1986—. Mem. Instn. of Engrs. India, Indian Inst. Plant Engrs., Soc. of Power Engrs. India, Y's Men Internat. Home: VIII/1741, AM Cross Rd, Cochin, Kerala 682 002, India Office: Cochin Shipyard Ltd, M G Road, Cochin, Kerala 682015, India

BALANIS, GEORGE NICK, electrical engineer; b. Athens, Greece, Oct. 7, 1944; came to U.S., 1963, naturalized, 1977; s. Nicholas G. and Mary (Traganoudaki) B.; m. Toula Koutis, Nov. 15, 1971; children—Nikolas, Thalassa. BS with honors, Calif. Inst. Tech., 1967, MS, 1968, PhD, 1972; MBA, UCLA, 1987. Research asst. Calif. Inst. Tech., Pasadena, 1968-71; staff scientist Applied Theory, Inc., Los Angeles, 1971-77, Arete Assocs., 1977-80; sr. engr. Garrett Airesearch, Torrance, Calif., 1980—. Contbr. articles to profl. jours. Mem. IEEE, ASME, Soc. Indsl. and Applied Math., Am. Math. Soc., Am. Acad. Mechanics, Tau Beta Pi, Sigma Chi. Greek Orthodox. Home: 2702 11th St Santa Monica CA 90405

BALARAC, NORBERT RENE FELIX, endocrinologist, diabetologist; b. Rieumes, Haute-Garonne, France, Mar. 9, 1946; s. Pierre Francois and Josephine Suzanne (Pezet) B.; m. Marie Laurence Lamarque, 1966 (div. 1976); 1 child, Loic-Olivier; m. Bridgitte Claude Cauvin, Sept. 30, 1976; children: Olivia, Guillaume. Laureat de la faculte, Prix Cabane de Discipline Medicale, Toulouse, France, 1970; MD, Faculty Medicine, Montpellier, France, 1973. Mem. staff various pvt. labs., Toulouse, 1967-68, Montpellier, 1972-73; cons. endocrinology, diabetology Inst. Arnault Tzanck, St.-Laurent-du-Var, France, 1974—; tchr. med. statistics Lab. Pharmacology, Nice, France, 1982—. Contbr. articles to profl. jours.; patentee insulin regulating device. Served with French Navy, 1973-74. Mem. French Lang. Assn. and European Assn. for the Study Diabetes and Metabolic Diseases, French Soc. for the Study Fertility, French Soc. Endocrinology. Roman Catholic. Office: Inst Arnault Tzanck Ave, Maurice Donat, 06700 Saint-Laurent-du-Var France

BALASKO, YVES, economics educator; b. Paris, Aug. 9, 1945; arrived in Switzerland, 1982; s. Arpad Andre and Genevieve (Tanguy) B.; m. Marie-Noelle Lecoeur, Sept. 23, 1965 (div. 1979); children: Anne, Marc, Evelyne; m. Martine Orelio; 1 child, Gregoire. Agregation de math. (cert. France), Ecole Normale Superieure, Paris, 1964; DSc (France), U. Paris IX, 1976. Research assoc. CNRS, Paris, 1968-71; economist Electricite de France, Paris, 1971-77; prof. math. U. Paris, 1977—; prof. math. econs. U. Geneva, 1982—. Author: Foundations of the Theory of General Equilibrium, 1988. Fellow Econometric Soc. Home: 6 Chemin de Beausoleil, 1206 Geneva Switzerland Office: U Geneva, 2 Rue Dancet, 1211 Geneva Switzerland

BALASUBRAMANIAM, KUNJITHAPATHAM, physician; b. Kuala Lumpur, Malaysia, Sept. 28, 1939; s. Balasubramaniam and Kunjamma Mahalingham; m. Sudha Natarajan Kunjithapatham; children: Geetha, Balasubramaniam. MBBS, U. Bombay, India, 1967. Govt. India Scholar, U. Bombay, 1967. Life mem. Malayan Med. Assn., Automobile Assn. Malaysia, Geetha Asharam Malaysia, Brahmin Samaj, Pure Life Soc. Puchong K.L. Malaysia. Club: Raintree (life). Office: Klinik Templer, 46 Jalan Midah Besar, Taman Midah, 56000 Kuala Lumpur Malaysia

BALAZS, BILL ANTAL (BELA), mechanical engineer; b. Miercurea-Ciuc, Romania, June 13, 1933; s. Andras and Emilia (Sallo) B.; came to U.S., 1957, naturalized, 1962; B.S., U. Budapest (Hungary), 1955; diploma tool die engring. Acme Tech. Inst., Cleve., 1963; A.P.M., John Carroll U., 1976; m. Vivienne Miskey, Apr. 1, 1960; 1 dau., Corrinne. Instr. tool die engring., machine design, indsl. electronics, Acme Tech. Inst., 1960-65; design engr., heating, ventilating, Morrison Product Inc., Cleve., 1963-65; project engr. Reuter-Stokes, Inc., Cleve., 1965-70, engring. project mgr., 1970-73, engring. mgr., chief engr., 1973—. Pres., Transylvania Hungarian League, 1960—. Registered profl. engr., U.S.A., Can.; cert. cost engring. engr., mfg. mgmt. engr., plant engring. engr. Mem. Am. Inst. Indsl. Engrs., Instrument Soc. Am., Soc. Mfg. Engrs., ASME, Am. Nuclear Soc., Nat., Ohio socs. profl. engrs. Designer nuclear radiation detectors and multi-sensor environ. radiation monitoring systems. Home: 7500 Woodlake Dr Walton Hills OH 44146 Office: 8499 Darrow Rd Twinsburg OH 44087

BALBIR, NALINI, Indic studies researcher; b. Neuilly, France, May 27, 1955; parents: Jagbans Kishore and Nicole (De Tugny) B. Agrégation de Grammaire, France, 1977; PhD in Indology, U. Paris III, 1980, DLitt in Indology, 1986. Tchr. secondary sch. France, 1977-79; attaché de recherche Ctr. Nat. Recherche Sci., France, 1980-84; chargé de recherche Ctr. Nat. Recherche Sci., Paris, 1984—; specialist in Indic Studies: Jainism, Middle Indo-Aryan langs. Author: Dānāstakakathā; co-editor (with G. Pinault) Bulletin d'Etudies Indiennes, 1983— (award). Mem. Conseil Asiatique, French Assn. for Sanskrit Studies (sec. 1986—, treas. 1982-86). Office: Institut de Civilisation Indienne, 22 Av Pdt Wilson, 75116 Paris France

BALDASSARRINI, MARIO, construction company executive; b. Bologna, Italy, Nov. 9, 1920; m. Maria Eugenia Martini, May 1947 (dec. July 1976); children: Ruggero, Annalisa; m. Hedy Hochstrasser, Sept. 1983. BSc, Pisa (Italy) U., 1946. Site office engr. Lodigiana S.p.A., Italy, 1947-50, site agt., 1950-56, also bd. dirs.; site agt. Impresit Kariba, Rhodesia, 1956-60; project mgr. Impregilo S.p.A., Ghana, 1960-64; overseas mgr. Impregilo S.p.A., Milan, Italy, 1965-68, gen. mgr., 1969-87; mem. exec. com. Impregilo S.p.A., Milan, 1987—, also bd. dirs.; gen. mgr. Tarbela joint venture Pakistan and Indus River Contractors, Pakistan, 1968—; gen. mgr. Lar Dam joint venture Pakistan and Indus River Contractors, Iran, 1974—. Named to Order Grande Ufficiale Office della Repubblica Italiana, 1981. Mem. ASCE, Collegio Ingegneri Toscana. Home: Via A D'Aosta 5, 20129 Milan Italy Office: Impregilo SpA, Via S Sofia 37, 20122 Milan Italy

BALDAUF, RICHARD BIRGE, JR., educator, researcher; b. Hartford, Conn., May 27, 1943; s. Richard Birge and Isabel Margaret (Warley) B.; m. Christina Limbunis Bison, Dec. 14, 1968; 1 child, Pamela Sandra. BA, Dickinson Coll., 1965; MEd, U. Hawaii, 1970, PhD, 1975; grad. diploma lang. studies, Western Australian C.A.E., Perth, 1984. Tchr. English Peace Corps, Sabah, Malaysia, 1966-68; child care worker Salvation Army, Honolulu, 1969-71; research asst. Edn. Research and Devel. Ctr., Honolulu, 1970-72; supr. ednl. testing Dept. Edn., Pago Pago, Am. Samoa, 1972-75; lectr., sr. lectr., then assoc. prof. Faculty of Edn., James Cook U., Townsville, Queensland, Australia, 1975-85; profl. assoc. East-West Ctr., Honolulu, 1980-81; dept. head Lang. and Arts Studies in Edn. James Cook U., Townsville, Queensland, Australia, 1986-88; cons. Micronesian Title I Program, Saipan, Mariana Islands, 1977-79. Editor: book Language Planning and Education, 1988; Kabar Seberang Jour., 1983, 84; contbr. chpts. to books, articles to profl. jours. Mem. Oak Valley Bush Fire Brigade. Mem. Am. Ednl. Research Assn., Internat. Assn. Cross-Cultural Psychology (regional rep. 1983-84), Tchrs. of English to Speakers of Other Langs., Applied Linguistics Assn. Australia (info. officer 1985—), Pi Lambda Theta. Office: James Cook U, Dept Lang Art Studies Edn, Townsville Queensland 4811, Australia

BALDERSTONE, JAMES SCHOFIELD, finance company executive; b. Melbourne, Australia, May 2, 1921; s. J.S. Balderstone; m. Mary Tyree, 1946; 4 children. Grad., Scotch Coll., Melbourne. Gen. mgr., dir. for Australia Thomas Borthwick and Sons, 1953-67; chmn. Squatting Investment Co., 1966-73; mng. dir. Stanbroke Pastoral Co. Ltd., 1964-81, chmn. bd., 1982—; dir. Comml. Bank Australia (later became Westpac Banking Corp.), 1970-82; chmn. The Broken Hill Proprietary Co., Ltd., Melbourne, 1984—; bd. dirs. Chase-AMP Bank; chmn. Commonwealth Govt. Policy Discussion Group on Agr., 1981-82. Mem. Victoria Inst. Pub. Affairs (pres. 1981-84), Australian Mut. Provident Soc. (bd. dirs. Victoria br. 1962—, chmn. 1984—). Home: 115 Mont Albert Rd, Canterbury 3126, Australia Office: Broken Hill Proprietary Co Ltd, 140 William St, Melbourne 3000, Australia *

BALDO, I CATARINA, journalist; b. Södertälje, Sweden, Jan. 22, 1953; d. Sigurd and Inger (Grebell) Brinkberg; m. José Martinez Cheriguià, Dec. 31, 1969 (div. 1974); m. Diego Baldo, July 14, 1974; 1 child, Sakarias. Grad., Sch. of Journalism, Stockholm, 1979. Reporter Radio Stockholm, 1980, Expressen, Stockholm, 1981-82; reporter, editor Svenska Dagbladet, Stockholm, 1982—; free-lance reporter Swedish Radio, Stockholm, 1986—. Mem. Swedish Journalists Assn. Home: Lägatan 13, 18500 Vaxholm Sweden Office: Svenska Dagbladet, S-10517 Stockholm Sweden

BALDOCK, RICHARD STEPHEN, educational administrator; b. London, Nov. 19, 1944; s. John Allan and Marjorie Procter (Taylor) B.; m. Janet Elizabeth Cottrell, July 5, 1969; children: Sarah Ruth, Andrew James, Emma Stephanie, Rachel Elizabeth. BA, U. Cambridge, Eng., 1967, MA, 1970. Asst. master St. Paul's Sch., London, 1970-77, housemaster, 1977-84, 1977-84, surmaster, 1984—. Mem. Soc. for Promotion Hellenic Studies, Tyndale Fellowship for Bibl. Research. Club: Marylebone Cricket. Home and Office: St Paul's Sch, Lonsdale Rd Barnes, London SW13 9JT, England

BALDON, CLEO, interior designer; b. Leavenworth, Wash., June 1, 1927; d. Ernest Elsworth and Esther Jane (Hannan) Chute; m. Lewis Smith Baldon, Nov. 20, 1948 (div. July 1961); 1 child, Dirk; m. Ib Jørgen Melchior, Jan. 18, 1964; 1 stepson, Leif Melchior. BS, Woodbury Coll., 1948. Ptnr. Interior Designs Ltd., Los Angeles, 1948-50; freelance illustrator Los Angeles, 1952-54; prin. Cleo Baldon & Assocs., Los Angeles and Venice, Calif., 1954—; ptnr. Galper/Baldon Assocs., Venice, 1970—. Author: Steps and Stairways, an Illustrated Survey; contbr. articles to profl. jours.; patentee in field. Recipient City Beautification awards Los Angeles 1974-77, 80, 83, 85-87, Beverly Hills 1982, Calif. Landscape Contractors, 1975, 79, Pacifica award Resources Council, Calif., 1979. Home: 8228 Marmont Ln Los Angeles CA 90069 Office: Galder/Baldon Assocs 723 Ocean Front Walk Venice CA 90291

BALDWIN, ANDREW LEWIS, management consultant; b. Birmingham, Eng., May 15, 1934; s. Horace Leonard and Alice (Hearnshaw) B.; m. Margaret Peggy Peasley, Dec. 14, 1957; children—Jocelyn, Jeremy, Timothy. Diplomas in Agr., Harper Adams Coll. and Royal Agrl. Soc., Eng., 1958; diploma in Mktg., Inst. Mktg., Eng., 1970. Dist. agr. officer HM Overseas Civil Service, Tanzania, 1958-62; mgmt. trainee food processing and distbn., Eng., 1962-63; cons., indsl. engr. estates mgmt., Eng., 1963-64; mktg. staff Massey Ferguson, Eng., 1964-66; mgmt. cons. B.S.E., Ltd., Guyana, S.Am., 1966-70; mgmt. cons., mktg. Consultancy and Fin. Services, London, 1970-71; dir. Price Waterhouse Assocs., Hong Kong, 1972-76; dir. Africa and Middle East ops. PA Cons. Services, Ltd., London, 1976-84; dir. internat. ops Inbucon Mgmt. Cons. Ltd., Reliance Cons. Group Internat., Inc., London and N.Y.C.; cons. to banks, corps., govts., internat. aid agencies, 1984-87, ptnr. Price Waterhouse Africa, 1987—, dir. Price Waterhouse Assocs., Kenya, 1987—. Contbr. articles profl. jours. Silver medallist Harper Adams Coll., 1958. Fellow Chartered Inst. Mgmt. Accts., Chartered Assn. Cert. Accts., Instn. Agrl. Engrs., Inst. Mgmt. Cons., Inst. Dirs.; mem. Chartered Inst. Arbitrators (assoc.), Royal Agrl. Soc. Eng. (bd. govs.). Club: Sudan (Khartoum). Home: Muthega, Nairobi Kenya

BALDWIN, BRUCE WAYNE, paper company executive; b. Toronto, Ont., Can., June 29, 1953; s. Hector Carl and Edna (Burton) B.; m. Brenda Susan Marshall. V.p. Baldwin Paper Co., Ltd., Woodbridge, Ont., 1976-85, pres., 1985—; pres. The Sheeting Edge Co., Ltd., Woodbridge, Ont., 1987—. Advisor Indsl. Devel. Bd. Mem. Vaughan C. of C., Can. Pulp and Paper Assn., Can. Paper Box Mfrs. Assn., TAPPI, Bd. Trade. Office: Baldwin Paper Co Ltd, 101 Hanlan Rd, Woodbridge, ON Canada L4L 3P5

BALDWIN, JANICE MURPHY, lawyer; b. Bridgeport, Conn., July 16, 1926; d. William Henry and Josephine Gertrude (McKenna) Murphy; m. Robert Edward Baldwin, July 31, 1954; children: Jean Margaret, Robert William, Richard Edward, Nancy Josephine. AB, U. Conn., 1948; MA, Mt. Holyoke Coll., 1950; postgrad. U. Manchester, Eng., 1950-51; MA, Fletcher Sch., Tufts U., 1952; JD, U. Wis., 1971. Bar: Wis. 1971, U.S. Dist. Ct. (we. dist.) Wis. 1971. Staff atty. Legis. Council, State of Wis., Madison, 1971-74, 75-78, sr. staff atty., 1979—; atty. adviser HUD, Washington, 1974-75, 78-79. Mem. Dane County Bar Assn. (legis. com. 1980-81), Wis. Bar Assn. (pres. govt. lawyers div. 1985-87, bd. govs. 1985—, treas. 1987—), Wis. Women's Network, AAUW, NOW, LWV, Legal Assn. for Women, Wis. Women's Polit. Caucus, U. Wis. Univ. League, Older Women's League (health, legis., marital property, state and local taxation coms.). Home: 125 Nautilus Dr Madison WI 53705 Office: Legis Council Room 147N State Capitol Bldg Madison WI 53702

BALEELA, MOUSTAFA, architect and urban planner; b. Saudi Arabia, 1941. D of Urban Planning, U. Rome, 1969; PhD in Architecture, U. Pa., 1975. Teaching asst. King Saud U., Riyadh, Saudi Arabia, 1869-71; dep. chmn. dept. architecture King Saud U., 1975-80, asst., assoc. prof. archtl. design, 1975-80; pres. Environ. Design & Cons. Ctr., Riyadh, 1976—; condr. seminar in field; lectr. in field. Works include King Saud U. Housing, Mecca Master Planning, Medina-Yanbu Desalination Plant and Housing, Gen. Assembly Hall, Emirate Bldg., Police Hdqtrs. and Municipality Bldgs; contbr. articles to profl. jours. Govt. rep. Saudi Govt. Centre, 1975; bd. dirs. Real Estate Devel. Fund, 1975, Montazah Tabarka and Societe Touristique Tunisie-Golfe, Tunis; mem. steering coms. for bldg. King Saud U., Ministry of Higher Edn., Ministry of Interior and several other pub. bldgs.; regional rep. UNESCO Council on Tall Bldgs., Bethlehem, Pa.; arbitrator Gulf States and Saudi Arabia pvt./pub. disputes. Mem. Nat. Inst. Arch. Rome, Internat. Assn. Housing Sci. Moslem. Home and Office: PO Box 51087, Riyadh Saudi Arabia 11543

BALEKJIAN, WAHE HAGOP, legal educator; b. Cairo, Oct. 2, 1924; s. Hagop and Zaruhi (Yergatian) B.; m., Nov. 20, 1971. Student in Edn., Am. U., Cairo, 1949-50; diploma in Musical Composition, Conducting, Piano Teaching, Vienna Acad. Music, 1953; Dr. rer. pol., U. Vienna, 1958, Dr. jur., 1961; Ph.D. in Internat. Law, U. Manchester (Eng.), 1965. Univ. lectr. U. Vienna, 1957-73; head dept. European studies Nat. Inst. Higher Edn., Limerick, Ireland, 1973-76; head dept. European law, U. Glasgow, Scotland, 1976—, also sr. lectr., later reader, 1986—; vis. asst. prof. internat. law U. Salzburg, Austria, 1974-81, titular univ. prof., 1981—; titular prof. European Faculty Land Use and Devel., Strasbourg, France, 1982—; reporter Calouste Gulbenkian Found., Lisbon, Portugal, 1960; participant experts' conf. Internat. Progress Orgn., Vienna, 1982; cons. in field. Author: Legal Aspects of Foreign Investment in the European Economic Community, 1967 (prize of European Communities 1967); book on relations between non-recognized states (in German), 1971. Calouste Gulbenkian Found. grantee, 1959. Mem. Am. Soc. Internat. Law, Am. Polit. Sci. Assn., Royal Inst. Internat. Affairs (assoc.), Brit. Inst. Internat. and Comparative Law, German Soc. Internat. Law. Office: The Univ, Dept European Law, Glasgow G12 8QQ, Scotland

BALES, DOROTHY JOHNSON, violinist, educator; b. Ketchikan, Alaska, Aug. 31, 1927; d. Harry and Lillian Mae (Pierce) Johnson; B.A., U. Oreg., 1948; B.Mus. with honors, New Eng. Conservatory, 1949; M.Mus., Boston U., 1950; postgrad. Marlboro Sch. Music, Acad. Internat. d'Ete; pupil of Ivan Galamian, Gabriel Bouillon, Henryk Szeryng; m. Robert Fred Bales,

Sept. 14, 1951. Instr. violin New Eng. Conservatory, 1949-50, 85—; tchr. violin Longy Sch. Music, Cambridge, Mass., 1950-58; violin and chamber music tchr., orch. dir. Winsor Sch., Boston, 1950-55; lectr. music Emmanuel Coll., Boston, 1961-69, 1974-78, asst. prof., 1969-74; lectr. Northeastern U., Boston, 1975-78, 82-83 ; vis. asso. prof. U. Mass., Amherst, 1978, bd. dirs. Kodaly Ctr. of Am., 1988—; solo concert tours throughout U.S., 1964-68; concerts in Paris 1952, Salzburg, 1952, 56, 64, 72, Vienna, 1964, 72, Geneva, 1964, Saarbruken, Konstanz, 1984; contractor-concertmaster, 1962—; concertmaster Ch. of the Advent, Boston, 1964-83. Asso. artist tchr. N.J. String tchrs. Summer Conf., 1980-83; founder, music dir. Chamber Music Soc. Cape Ann, 1960-62; bd. dirs., Young Audiences, 1986—; workshop leader, cons. in field. Bd. dirs. Choral Art Soc., Scituate, Mass., 1978-87; concert master Marlborough Symphony, 1985—. Grantee Ella Lyman Cabot Trust, 1956; winner N.W. Dist. Young Artists award Fedn. Music Clubs, 1939, Mus. Guild Boston Debut award, 1948, Mem. Am. String Tchrs. Assn. (pres. Mass. chpt. 1974-84, chmn. nat. solo competition, 1981), Music Educators Nat. Conf., Am. Fedn. Musicians, Music Tchrs., Sierra Club, Audubon Soc., Nature Conservancy, World Wildlife Fedn. Episcopalian. Author articles in field. Recs.: Twentieth Century Folk Songs for Violin, 1984. Home: 61 Scotch Pine Rd Weston MA 02193

BALES, KEITH STUART, marketing executive; b. London, Feb. 13, 1946; s. Leslie and Ruby Joan (Somes) B.; m. Carolyn Newfield, 1972 (div. 1983); children: Emma Mary, Nicholas Leslie Charles, Jonathan Stuart; m. Geraldine Mary Papworth, Jan. 17, 1987. BA, U. Western Australia; M. Inst.M., AIA; postgrad., F. Inst.D. Promotions mgr. Sun-times Broadcaster, Perth, Australia; broacaster TVW Channel 7, Perth; promotions mgr. News Internat., London; chmn. bd. Westwood Pl. Mgmt. Ltd.; v.p. The Walt Disney Co., 1972-88; chief exec. Mktg. and Mgmt. Group Internat., Keith Bales Assocs.; bd. dirs. Skybird Ltd., Celebrity Group, Zodiac Toys Hook Rise Surbitor. Mem. Mktg. Panel Gt. Ormond St. Hosp. Wishing Well Appeal. Mem. Inst. Dirs., Inst. Advt., Inst. Mktg. Conservative. Mem. Ch. of England. Clubs: Belfry, Annables, RAC, Tramps. Home: Regency House, Westwood Place, Westwood Ln, Normandy, Guildford Surrey, England

BALESCU, RADU CONSTANTIN, educator; b. Bucarest, Romania, July 18, 1932; s. Constantin C. and Gabriela (Opreanu) B.; Ph.D. in Scis., U. Brussels, 1958. Mem. faculty U. Libre, Brussels, 1960—, prof. theoretical physics, 1964—; mem. Euratom Liaison Group Thermonuclear Fusion, 1968—, chmn. ad-hoc com. inertial confinement fusion, 1977-78. Recipient Prix Francqui, Belgium, 1970. Mem. Belgian Acad. Scis. (de Donder prize 1961). Author: Statistical Mechanics of Charged Particles, 1963; Equilibrium and nonequilibrium Statistical Mechanics, 1975. Office: Faculty Scis, CP 231 Campus Plaine, U Libre, 1050 Brussels Belgium

BALFOUR, HENRY HALLOWELL, JR., medical educator, researcher, physician; b. Jersey City, Feb. 9, 1940; s. Henry Hallowell and Dorothy Kathryn (Dietze) B.; m. Carol Lenore Pries, Sept. 23, 1967; children: Henry Hallowell III, Anne Lenore, Caroline Dorothy. BA, Princeton U., 1962; MD, Columbia U., 1966. Diplomate Am. Bd. Pediatrics. Attending pediatrician Wright-Patterson AFB, Ohio, 1968-70; asst. prof. U. Minn., Mpls., 1972-75, assoc. prof., 1975-79, prof. lab. medicine, pathology and pediatrics, 1979—, dir. div. clin. microbiology, 1974—; prin. investigator NIH grants, 1976—; NIH Nat. AIDS Clin. Trials Unit, 1987—. Author: (with Ralph C. Heussner) Herpes Diseases and Your Health, 1984; contbr. numerous sci. articles to profl. jours. Mem. Am. Soc. Microbiology, Soc. Exptl. Biology and Medicine, Soc. Pediatric Research, Am. Pediatric Soc., Infectious Disease Soc. Am., Cen. Soc. Clin. Research. Presbyterian. Home: 6820 Harold Ave N Minneapolis MN 55427 Office: U Minn Health Sci Ctr Box 437 420 Delaware St SE Minneapolis MN 55455

BALGOWAN, WILLIAM LESLIE, Mining and Metals company executive, civil engineer; b. Condobolin, Australia, June 23, 1941; s. William Michael and Elsie May (Grayden) B.; m. Janette Mary Cording, Jan. 6, 1967; children—Sarah Louise, Nicholas Alfred, Matthew James. B.Engrng. with honors, U. Sydney, Australia, 1964; M.S., U. Calgary, Alta., Can., 1970; Fellowship Diploma Mgmt., Royal Melbourne Inst. Tech., Australia, 1976. Engr., Commonwealth of Australia, Canberra, 1965-68; research asst. U. Calgary, 1968-70; project engr. Bougainville Copper, CRA Group, Papua, New Guinea, 1970-73, Conzinc Riotinto Australia, Melbourne, 1973-83; dir., mgr. Hardys Pty. Ltd., Wagga Wagga, Australia, 1983-85; dir., mgr. Wagga Wagga Holdings, 1983-85; dir., treas. Regional Apprentice Scheme, Wagga, 1984-85; alt. dir. Australian Assoc. Smelters, Pty. Ltd., dir. 1985-86, Broken Hill Assoc. Smelters Proprietary Ltd., dir. 1985-87, Pirie Alloys Pty. Ltd., 1985—; alt. dir., dir. Australian Mining, & Smelting Ltd., 1985-86; alt. dir. Australian Refined Alloys Pty. Ltd., 1985—, Electrolytic Refining and Smelting Co. Australia Ltd., 1985-86; dir. Thai Ping Metal Indsl Co. Ltd., Taiwan, Republic China, 1987—. Pres., Rosanna Golf Links Pub. Sch. Council, Melbourne, 1979-80. Research grantee U. Calgary, 1968 70, Nat. Research Council, Ottawa, Ont., Can., 1970. Assoc. fellow Australian Inst. Mgmt.; mem. Co. Dirs. Assn. Australia, Econ. Soc. Australia, Instn. Engrs. Australia, Australasian Inst. Mining and Metallurgy, Eastern Riverina Forestry Industry Council (dep. chmn. 1984-85), Radiata Pine Assn. Australia (com. mem. 1983-85), So. Tablelands Br. Forest Products Assn. (chmn. 1984-85), Australian Soc. Corp. Treasurers. Clubs: Royal Automobile, Heidelberg Golf (Melbourne). Lodge: Lions. Avocations: jogging; squash; golf; reading; chess. Home: 145 Bonds Rd, Lower Plenty 3093, Australia Office: Australian Assoc Smelters, 21 Fl Qantas Ho/114 William, Melbourne 3000, Australia

BALI, DOMKAT YAH, minister of defense, Nigeria, military officer; b. Langtang, Plateau, Nigeria, Feb. 27, 1940; s. Hassan Bali Tabut and Mela Yinkat Mwang; married; children—Nanna, Ponfa Yakubu. Student Royal Mil. Acad. Sandhurst, Camberley, Eng., 1962-63, Staff Coll., Camberley, 1972, Royal Coll. Def. Studies, London, 1980; cert. pub. adminstrn. Centre for Mgmt. Studies, Cambridge, Eng., 1982. Commd. 2d lt. Nigerian Army, 1963, advanced through grades to maj. gen., 1978; troop comdr. 1 Field Arty. Bartery, Kaduna, Nigeria, 1964; bty. capt. 2 Field Arty. Bty., Abeokuta, 1965-66; bartery comdr., Ibadan, 1966-67; comdr. 1 Regit., Enugu Sector, 1967-70; comdr. Arty. Corps, 1970-71; comdr. 1 Inf. Div., 1978, 4 Inf. Div., 1978-79; comdt. Staff Coll., 1981-83; dir. Army Tng. and Ops., 1983—; minister of def. Nigeria, Lagos, 1984—. Author poetry book: War Cries, 1984. Decorated Forces Service Star, Republican medal, Def. Service medal, officr Order of Fed. Republic. Club: Ikoyi (Lagos). Avocations: golf; reading; chess. Office: Ministry Def, Tafawa Balewa Sq, Lagos Nigeria *

BALILES, GERALD L., governor of Virginia; b. Stuart, Va., July 8, 1940. BA, Wesleyan U., 1963; JD, U. Va., 1967. Bar: Va. 1967, U.S. Supreme Ct. 1971. Asst. atty. gen. of Va., 1967-72, dep. atty. gen., 1972-75, atty. gen., 1982-86; gov., Va., 1986—; mem. Va. Ho. of Dels., 1976-82, mem. appropriations com., 1978-82, com. corp. ins. and banking, 1976-82, com. conservation and natural resources, 1979-82; formerly ptnr. Lacy and Baliles, Richmond; chmn. Joint House-Senate Ins. Study Com., 1977-79; Legal Drafting Sub-Com., State Water Study Commn., 1977—; vice chmn. Joint House-Senate Com. on Nuclear Power Generation Facilities, 1977-79. Mem. Richmond Bar Assn., Va. Bar Assn. (exec. com. 1979), ABA (environ. quality com., natural resources law sect. 1973—, environ. control com., corp., banking and bus. law sect. 1974—), Va. State Bar (chmn. environ. quality com. 1975-77). Office: Office of Gov Capitol Bldg 3d Fl Richmond VA 23219 *

BALIN, DONNA FAYE, geologist; b. Hampton, Va., July 5, 1956; d. Henry and Fayrene (Timm) B. BS summa cum laude, U. Tex. at Austin, 1978. Exploration geologist Houston Oil and Minerals Corp., 1978-80; geologist U.S. Geol. Survey, Menlo Park, Calif., 1980-81, Amoco Oil Co., Denver, summer 1983; Amoco found. fellow U. Ariz., Tucson, 1982-83; NSF grad. fellow U. Cambridge, Eng., 1983—. Free-lance interviewer BBC-Radio; contbr. articles to profl. publs. Active Sierra Club, Servas. Getty Oil Co. scholar, 1977-78, Grad. Tuition scholar U. Ariz., 1982-83; recipient Overseas Research Student award U. of Cambridge, England, 1983-86Cambridge Chancellor's Bursary award, 1983-84. Fellow Geol. Soc. London, Cambridge Philos. Soc.; mem. Am. Assn. Petroleum Geologists, Phi Beta Kappa, Phi Kappa Phi. Avocations: running, athletics, camping. Home: 127 Claywell San Antonio TX 78209

BALKA, SIGMUND RONELL, lawyer; b. Phila., Aug. 1, 1935; s. I. Edwin and Jane (Chernicoff) B.; m. Elinor Bernstein, May 29, 1966. A.B., Williams Coll., 1956; J.D., Harvard U., 1959. Bar: Pa. 1961, D.C. 1961, N.Y. 1970, U.S. Supreme Ct. 1966, other fed. cts. Sr. atty. Lilco, Mineola, N.Y., 1969-70; v.p., gen. counsel Brown Boveri Corp., North Brunswick, N.J., 1970-75; asst. gen. counsel Power Authority State N.Y., N.Y.C., 1975-80; gen. counsel Krasdale Foods, Inc., N.Y.C. 1980—. bd. dirs. Am. Corp. Counsel Assn., Met. N.Y. chpt., 1986—; pres. Graphic Arts Council N.Y., 1980—; chmn. Hunts Point Environ. Protection Council, N.Y.C., 1980—; mem. N.Y.C. Community Bd. 6-Queens and chmn. law com., 1980—; chmn. Soc. for a Better Bronx, 1985—; bd. dirs. Bronx Arts Council, 1981—, Greater N.Y. Met. Food Council, 1986—, Jewish Repertory Theatre, 1987—; mem. Borough Pres.'s Task Force on Hunts Point, 1987—. Mem. Assn. of Bar of City of N.Y., ABA (co-chmn. corp. law dept. pro bono project 1986—), Fed. Bar Assn. Office: Krasdale Foods Inc 400 Food Center Dr New York NY 10474

BALL, CHESTER EDWIN, editor, consultant, business owner; b. Seth, W.Va., Aug. 19, 1921; s. Roman Harry and Hattie (White) B.; A.B., Marshall U., 1942; M.A., Ohio State U., 1947; m. Betty June Hively, Dec. 29, 1945; children—Beth Elaine (Mrs. John Michael Watkins), Harry Stuart, Chester Edwin. Stringer, Charleston (W.Va.) Daily Mail, 1936-40; reporter, copy editor Huntington (W.Va.) Pub. Co., 1945, 47-48; assoc. pub. Wolf Pub. Co., Cin., 1953-55; instr. journalism Marshall Coll., Huntington, W.Va., 1947-51; asst. prof. journalism Ohio State U., Columbus, 1951-56, publs. editor Engrng. Expt. Sta., 1956-63; tech. editor, dir. reprographics Ohio State U. Research Found., Columbus, 1963-81, editorial cons. Ohio State U. Ednl. Resources Info. Ctr., 1981—, dept. family medicine, 1983—. Mem. Hilliard (Ohio) Charter Commn., 1958-63, vice-chmn., 1958, sec., 1960-61, 62-63; treas. Hilliard chpt. Am. Field Service, 1974-76, pres., 1976-77; mem. Scioto Darby Bd. Edn., Hilliard, 1962-78; bd. dirs. Franklin County Epilepsy Assn., 1976-82, treas., 1978-80, pres., 1980-81. Served with AUS, 1942-45; col. Res. (ret.). Decorated Silver Star, Bronze Star medal with one oak leaf cluster, Purple Heart with two oak leaf clusters. Mem. In-Plant Printing Mgmt. Assn. (pres. 1971, cert. graphics communication mgr.), Res. Officers Assn. (sec.-treas., pres. Huntington, W.Va. 1948-50), U.S. Army 5th Div. Soc. (pres. 1984-85, editor 1985—), Columbus Zoo Docent Assn. (parliamentarian 1985). Republican. Methodist (mem. bd. ushers 1956—). Club: Hilliard Kiwanis (pres. 1983-84). Home: 6174 Sunny Vale Dr Columbus OH 43228

BALL, EDWARD STEPHEN, accountant; b. Walsall, Staffordshire, Eng., Jan. 17, 1940; s. Harry and Florence Miriam (Smart) B.; m. Ann Margaret Mary Hart, Oct. 20, 1962; children: Katharine Mary, Alison Margaret. Assoc. degree, East Anglia Inst. Taxation. Ptnr. Scrutton Goodchild & Sanderson, Ipswich, Suffolk, Eng., 1972—. Freeman City of London, 1979. Fellow Inst. Chartered Accts. Eng. Wales (East Anglia dist. pres. 1983-84), mem. Inst. Taxation (assoc.). Club: Worshipful Co. Chartered Accts. (London). Home: 14 Vere Gardens, Henley Rd, Ipswich IP1 4NZ, England Office: Scrutton Goodchild & Sanderson, Museum St, Ipswich IP1 1HE, England

BALL, IVAN CHARLES, financial consultant; b. Salisbury, Wilts, England, Jan. 28, 1929; s. Victor and Julie (Pitman) Dorouthy; m. Lillian Georgina Fussell, Mar. 24, 1951; children: Lynn, Christine Khin Madment, Stephan Ivan. Mortgage broker Ball Pitman & Co., 1960-61; bd. dirs. Charles Ivor & Assocs. Europe Ltd., 1964—, Charles Ivor & Assocs. Intercontinental Ltd., 1965—; dir. Dream Homes Ltd., 1964; mng. dir. Charles Ivor & Assocs. Ltd., London, 1964. Lodge: Masons. Home: 35 Sparrow Farm Rd, Stoneleigh, Epsom Surrey, England

BALL, JOHN DUDLEY, JR., writer; b. Schenectady, July 8, 1911; s. John Dudley and Alena (Wiles) B.; m. Patricia Hamilton, Aug. 22, 1942; 1 son, John David. B.A., Carroll Coll., Waukesha, Wis., 1934, L.H.D., 1978. Mem. editorial staff Fortune mag., 1937-40; asst. curator Hayden Planetarium, N.Y.C., 1940-41; with Columbia Rec. Corp., 1945-47; music editor Bklyn. Eagle, 1946-51; columnist N.Y. World Telegram, 1951-52; dir. pub. relations Inst. Aero. Scis., 1958-61; editor-in-chief DMS, Inc., 1961-62; author 1963—. Author: Records for Pleasure, 1947, Operation Springboard, 1958, Spacemaster I, 1960, Edwards: USAF Flight Test Center, 1962, Judo Boy, 1964 (Jr. Lit. Guild selection), In the Heat of the Night, 1965 (Edgar award, Critics award, London, Acad. award Best Picture of Yr. 1968), Arctic Showdown, 1966, Rescue Mission, 1966, The Cool Cottontail, 1966 (Mystery Guild selection), Dragon Hotel, 1968, Miss 1000 Spring Blossoms, 1968 (Readers Digest Condensed Book Club selection), Johnny Get Your Gun, 1969, Last Plane Out, 1969, The First Team, 1971, Five Pieces of Jade, 1972 (Detective Book Club selection), The Fourteenth Point, 1973, Mark One-The Dummy, 1974 (Detective Book Club selection), The Winds of Mitamura, 1975, The Eyes of Buddha, 1976, Phase Three Alert, 1977 (Mil. Book Club selection), Police Chief, 1977 (Detective Book Club selection), The Killing in the Market, 1978, The Murder Children, 1979, Then Came Violence, 1980, Trouble for Tallon, 1981, Ananda, 1982, Chief Tallon and the S.O.R., 1984, Singapore, 1986, The Kiwi Target, 1988, The Van, 1989; editor: Cop Cade, 1978, The Mystery Story, 1976. Served with Air Transport Command, 1942-45. Mem. Mystery Writers Am., PEN, Baker St. Irregulars, All Am. Karate Fedn., Japanese-Am. Citizens League, Calif. Aikido Assn. (black belt), Ox-5 Club, Mensa, Civil Air Patrol (lt. col.). Lutheran. Address: 16401 Otsego St Encino CA 91436

BALL, WILLIAM PAUL, physicist, engineer; b. San Diego, Nov. 16, 1913; s. John and Mary (Kajla) B.; m. Edith Lucile March, June 28, 1941 (dec. 1976); children: Lura Irene Ball Raplee, Roy Ernest. AB, UCLA, 1940; PhD, U. Calif., Berkeley, 1952. Registered profl. engr. Calif. Projectionist, sound technician studios and theatres in Los Angeles, 1932-41; tchr. high sch. Montebello, Calif., 1941-42; instr. math. and physics Santa Ana (Calif.) Army Air Base, 1942-43; physicist U. Calif. Radiation Lab., Berkeley and Livermore, 1943-58; mem. tech. staff Ramo-Wooldridge Corp., Los Angeles, 1958-59; sr. scientist Hughes Aircraft Co., Culver City, Calif., 1959-64; sr. staff engr. TRW-Def. Systems Group, Redondo Beach, Calif., 1964-83, Hughes Aircraft Co., 1983-86; cons. Redondo Beach, 1986—. Contbr. articles to profl. jours.; patentee in field. Bd. dirs. So. Dist. Los Angeles chpt. ARC, 1979-86. Recipient Manhattan Project award for contbn. to 1st atomic bomb, 1945. Mem. Am. Phys. Soc., Am. Nuclear Soc., AAAS, AIAA, N.Y. Acad. Scis., Torrance (Calif.) Area C. of C. (bd. dirs. 1978-84), Sigma Xi. Home and Office: 209 Via El Toro Redondo Beach CA 90277

BALLANTINE, MORLEY COWLES (MRS. ARTHUR ATWOOD BALLANTINE), newspaper publisher; b. Des Moines, May 21, 1925; d. John and Elizabeth (Bates) Cowles; m. Arthur Atwood Ballantine, July 26, 1947 (dec. 1975); children—Richard, Elizabeth Ballantine Leavitt, William, Helen Ballantine Healy. A.B., Ft. Lewis Coll., 1975; L.H.D. (hon.), Simpson Coll., Indianola, Iowa, 1980. Pub. Durango (Colo.) Herald, 1952—, editor, pub., 1975-83, editor, chmn. bd., 1983—; dir. 1st Nat. Bank, Durango, 1976—, Des Moines Register & Tribune, 1977-85, Cowles Media Co., 1982-86. Mem. Colo. Land Use Commn., 1975-81, Supreme Ct. Nominating Commn., 1984—; pres. S.W. Colo. Mental Health Center, 1964-65; bd. dirs. Colo. Nat. Hist. Preservation Act, 1968-78; trustee Choate/Rosemary Hall, Wallingford, Conn., 1973-81, Simpson Coll., Indianola, Iowa, 1981—, U. Denver, 1984—, Fountain Valley Sch., Colorado Springs, 1976—; pres. Four Corners Opera Assn., 1983-86, mem. bd. govs. Mill Reef, Antigua, West Indies. Recipient 1st place award for editorial writing Nat. Fedn. Press Women, 1955, Outstanding Alumna award Rosemary Hall, Greenwich, Conn., 1969, Outstanding Journalism award U. Colo. Sch. Journalism, 1967, Distinguished Service award Ft. Lewis Coll., Durango, 1970; named to Colo. Community Journalism Hall of Fame, 1987. Mem. Nat. Soc. Colonial Dames, Colo. Press Assn. (bd. dirs. 1978-79), Colo. AP Assn. (chmn. 1966-67), Federated Women's Club Durango. Episcopalian. Club: Mill Reef (Antigua, W.I.) (bd. govs. 1985—). Address: care Herald PO Drawer A Durango CO 81302

BALLARD, LOWELL DOUGLAS, mechanical engineer; b. Seiling, Okla., June 27, 1933; s. Auty Wayne and Mabel (Henderson) Haynes; B.S., U. Md., 1962. Mech. engr. Rabinow Inc., Rockville, Md., 1962; mech. engr. Nat. Bur. Standards, 1962-82; export licensing officer Dept. Commerce, Washington, 1981—; panel mem. Nat. Elec. Code, 1975 edit.; chmn. Joint Bd. on Sci. and Engring. Edn., 1981-82. Vice pres. South Townhouse Assn., 1974-77, pres., 1978. Served with USAF, 1954-58. Fellow Washington Acad. Sci.; sr. mem. IEEE; mem. Am. Def. Preparedness Assn., Philos. Soc. Washington, Optical Soc. Am. Presbyterian. Club: Toastmasters (area gov. 1981-82). Home: 7823 Mineral Springs Dr Gaithersburg MD 20877 Office: Dept Commerce Washington DC 20230

BALLARDIE, QUINTIN, musician. Mem. London Piano Quartet; prin. viola London Philharmonic Orch.; founder, dir., prin. viola English Chamber Orch., London, 1960—. Decorated Order of Brit. Empire. Fellow Royal Acad. Music.

BALLENBERGER, WOLFGANG, advertising and publishing executive, graphologist; b. Stuttgart, Baden-Württemberg, Federal Republic of Germany, Dec. 9, 1925; s. Theodor and Friedel (Fenchel) B. Grad. high sch., Zeppelin-Gymnasium, Stuttgart. Cert. in accountancy. Apprentice Thebal-Verlag, Stuttgart, 1945-47; producer Thebal-Werbung, Stuttgart, 1948-63, confidential clk., 1963-78; owner Thebal-Werbung-Verlag, Stuttgart, 1978—. Mem. Werbefachverband Südwest e.V. Stuttgart, Industrie und Handelskammer Stuttgart. Mem. Evangelisch Ch. Home: Leonorenstrasse 21, Stuttgart 70, D-7000 Baden Württemberg Federal Republic of Germany Office: Thebal-Werbung, Alexanderstr 32, D-7000 Stuttgart Federal Republic of Germany

BALLESTEROS, FRANCO JORGE, entrepreneur; b. Mexico City, Dec. 18, 1946; s. Crescencio and Josefina (Franco) B.; m. Ileana Zavala, Apr. 22, 1972; children: Jorge Eduardo, Ileana Paola, Cecilia Yvette, Sandra Claudia. C.E., Universidad Iberoamericana, 1964-68; M.S., Stanford U., 1969, Universidad Iberoamericana, 1968. Pres. Grupo Mexicano de Desarrollo, S.A. de C.V., Mexico City, 1975—; chmn. bd. Aeroenvios Corp.; vice chmn. Industrias Synkro S.A.; dir. Derivados Macroquimicos, S.A., Compania Mexicana de Aviación, S.A., Kimberly Clark de Mexico S.A., Sistemas Mexicanos de Datos, S.A., Desc, Sociedad de Fomento Industrial, S.A. de C.V., Matacapan Tabacos, S.A., Labor Tecnica y De Ventas Ltv., Cannon Mills Inc., Calzado Puma, Grupo Prolar, Fondo Reto Inc., Industrias Synkro, S.A., Nalcomex, S.A., Segugos America. Pres. constrn. com. Universidad Iberoamericana, Mexico City, 1981—, v.p. econ. patronage, 1975—, mem. senate, 1975-80; prof. adminstrn. of engring. firms. U. Nacional Automoma, 1975-79. Mem. Stanford Alumni Assn., Colegio de Ingenieros Civiles. Clubs: Club de Banqueros, Club de Industriales, University, Club Raqueta Bosques, Club de Tenis Lomas, Club de Golf Chapultepec, Club la Sierra. Office: Grupo Mexicano de Desarrollo, Carretera Mexico-Toluca 4000, 05000 Cuajimalpa Mexico

BALLESTEROS, SEVERIANO, professional golfer; b. Pedrena, Spain, Apr. 9, 1957; s. Baldomero and Carmen (Sota) B. Chmn. Fairway, S.A., Madrid, 1981; main victories include: Under 25 Nat. Championship, Vizcaya Open, 1974; Under 25 Nat. Championship, 1975; Profl. Championship Catalonia, Profl. Championship Tenerife, Dutch Open, Lancome Trophy, Donald Swaelens Meml., World Cup, 1976; French Open, Braun Internat., UniRoyal Internat., Swiss Open, Japanese Open, Dunlop-Phoenix (Japan), Otago Charity (N.Z.), World Cup, 1977; Kenia Open, Under 25 Nat. Open Championship, Greensboro Open, Martini Internat., German Open, Scandinavian Open, Swiss Open, 1978; Lada English Golf Classic, Brit. Open, El Prat Open (Spain), 1979; Masters, 1980,83; Madrid Open, Martini Internat., Dutch Open, 1980; Scandinavian Open, Spanish Open, Suntory World Match Play, Australian P.G.A. Championship, Dunlop-Phoenix, 1981; San Remo Masters, Madrid Open, French Open, Suntory World Match Play, 1982; Masters, Brit. P.G.A., M.H.T. Westchester Classic (U.S.A.), Irish Open, Lancome Trophy, Sun City Challenge, 1983; British Open, 1979, 84, 88; USF & G Classic, World Match Play Championship, 1985; Dunhill Brit. Masters, Carrolls Irish Open, Johnnie Walker Montecarlo Open, Peugeot French Open, KLM Dutch Open, Lancome Trophy, 1986; Suze Open, APG Larios, Ryder Cup winning team, 1987. Roman Catholic. Office: care, R Joseph Collet, Fairway SA, C/Ruiz Zorrilla 16-20, 39009 Santander Spain

BALLESTRERO, ANASTASIO ALBERTO, archbishop; b. Genoa, Italy, Oct. 3, 1913; Professed in Order of Discalced Carmelites, 1929; ordained priest Roman Catholic Ch., 1936; provincial, 1948-54; superior gen., 1955-67, of Carmelites; ordained archbishop of Bari, Italy, 1974; archbishop of Turin, Italy, 1977—; cardinal, 1979; titular ch. S. Maria sopra Minerva; pres. Italian Episcopal Conf., 1979-86. Mem. Consiglio per gli Affari Pubblici della Chiesa. Mem. Congregation Religious and Secular Insts., S. Congregazione per i Vescovi. Author of many books. Office: Via Arcivescovado 12, Turin 10121 Italy

BALLIN, WILLIAM CHRISTOPHER, shipping, finance and energy company executive, advisor; b. Ft. Wayne, Ind., May 3, 1927; s. Christopher Theodore and Katherine (Nolles) B.; m. Dolores Mary Jack, June 18, 1948; children: Stuart, Kirk, Scott, Elizabeth. BA, U. Toledo, 1950; postgrad., Colo. Coll., Am. U., U. Lausanne, Switzerland. Pub. affairs coordinator Marathon Oil Co., Findlay, Ohio, 1954-61; Washington rep. Marathon Oil Co., 1961-63; European mgr. govt. relations Marathon Internat. Oil Co., Geneva, 1963-69; v.p. Crosby Kelly Fin. Relations, N.Y.C., 1969-70; exec. v.p. Am. Export Lines, Inc., N.Y.C., 1970-77; U.S. and Mid East adv. bd. Overland Trust Bank, Lugano, Zurich and Geneva, Switzerland, N.Y.C., 1978—; dir. Contship Holdings, B.M.V., Transimex S.A., Asfimar S.A., Shipping & Fin. Ltd., Valley Trading & Transport Ltd., Columbus Fund. Mem. Pres.'s Delegation to Algeria, 1987. Mem. Am. Near East Refugee Aid, Mid. East Inst. Home: 200 E 66th St New York NY 10021 Office: Overland Trust Bank, 3 Rue Du Mont Blanc, Geneva Switzerland 1211

BALLINGALL, PATRICK CHANDLER GORDON, solicitor; b. Devonport, Eng., Dec. 5, 1926; s. David Charles Gordon and Rosa Beatrice (Chandler) B.; m. Mary Hamilton Mackie, Dec. 10, 1951; children: Anne Helen Ballingall Lever, James Gordon Mackie. MA, Cambridge (Eng.) U., 1950. Ptnr. Barwell, Blakiston & Ballingall, Seaford, Eng., 1958—. Chmn. Lewes Constituency Conservative Assn., Eng., 1978-81, East Sussex European Constituency Council, Eng., 1984—. Named to the Order of the British Empire, 1984. Mem. Sussex Law Soc. (pres. 1974-75). Home: 4 Chyngton Gardens, Seaford BN25 3 RP, England Office: Barwell Blakiston & Ballingall, 10 Sutton Park Rd, Seaford BN25 1RB, England

BALLON, ROBERT JEAN, economics educator; b. Laeken, Belgium, Apr. 28, 1919; s. Joseph and Emma (Roeykens) B.; B.A., U. Louvain (Belgium), 1941, M.A., 1948; M.A., Catholic U. Am., 1957. Asst. prof. Sophia U., Tokyo, 1957-63, prof., 1963—, dir. fin., 1958-70, chmn. Socio-Economic Inst., 1970-81, dir. Internat. Mgmt. Devel. Seminars, 1981—. Mem. Indsl. Relations Research Assn., Japan Indsl. Relations Research Assn., Japan Mgmt. Research Assn., Japan Soc. London. Author, editor: Doing Business in Japan, 1967; Joint Ventures in Japan, 1967; The Japanese Employee, 1969; Japan's Market and Foreign Business, 1971; Foreign Investment and Japan, 1972; Marketing in Japan, 1973; author: Financial Reporting in Japan, 1976; Consideration on Japanese-like Business, 1978; Salaries in Japan: The System, 1982; Industrial Relations in Japan, 1983; Non-Western Work Organization, 1983; Recruiting Japanese Managers, 1984; The Business Contract in Japan, 1985; Labor-Management Relations in Japan, 1986; Financial Behavior of Japanese Corporations, 1988. Roman Catholic. Home: SJ House, 7 Kioicho Chiyoda-ku, Tokyo 102, Japan Office: Sophia U IMDS, 4 Yonbancho Chiyoda-ku, Tokyo 102, Japan

BALLY, PETER, hotel executive; b. Linz, Austria; Sept. 30, 1937; s. Peter and Anne Marie (von Pirquet) B.; m. Paloma Magaz Carrillo de Albornoz, Mar. 21, 1963; children: Hubert, Blanca, Cristina. Student, Gourdonstoun Sch., Scotland, 1954-57, Cambridge U., Eng., 1956. Asst. mgr. Palace Hotel, Madrid, 1961-62; Hotel Ritz, Madrid, 1962-63; reception mgr. Dochester Hotel, London, 1964-65; mng. dir. Park Hotel Vitznau, Switzerland, 1968—; pres. Tourist Bd. Vitznau, 1973—, Central Swiss Fin. Bd. Tourime, 1977—; trustee Ecole Hotelière Lausanne, 1974-87. Served to capt., inf., 1968. Mem. Central Swiss Hotel Assn. (pres. 1974-81), Relais et Chateaux Switzerland (pres. 1978-87). Roman Catholic. Lodge: Rotary. Home and Office: Park Hotel Vitznau, CH 6354 Vitznau Switzerland

BALME, LOUIS, research institute adminstrator, educator; b. Grenoble, France, Aug. 23, 1951; s. André Joseph Marcel and Marie Louise Andrée

(Meunier) B.; m. Evelyne Germaine Couer, Apr. 7, 1973; children: David, Julien, Matthieu. Master, Institut d'Etudes Politiques, Grenoble, 1972; PhD in Electronics, Institut Nat. Polytechnique, Grenoble, 1976. Ednl. adminstr. Ecole Normale Instituteurs, Grenoble, 1968-72; prof. Institut Nat. Polytechnique, Grenoble, 1972—, dir. indsl. liaison program; pres., founder SYMAG Computers, Grenoble, 1979-84; sci. cons. Internat. Bur. for Informatics UNESCO subs., Rome, 1981-86. Contbr. articles to sci. publs. Roman Catholic. Club: Informatique Française (Paris) (pres. synergie commn. 1983—). Home: 21 rue de Stalingrad, 38100 Grenoble France Office: Institut Nat Polytechnique, 46 Ave Felix Viallet, 38031 Grenoble France

BALSBORG, KAJ, management consultant; b. Copenhagen, Oct. 4, 1937; s. Adolf Peter Oersted and Elna Emilie Ravnsborg (Hansen) B.; m. Kirsten Nygaard Thestrup, July 23, 1977. MS in Engring., Tech. U., Denmark, 1964. Lic. engr. Engr. Scandinavian Airlines, Copenhagen, 1964-75, sta. mgr., 1976-77; exec. v.p. ISS-Internat. Service System A/S, Copenhagen, 1977-80; dir., chief exec. officer Viggo Bendz A/S, Copenhagen, 1981; pres., chief exec. officer Nissan Motor Denmark A/S, Kvistgaard, 1981-84; owner, mgr. K. Balsborg Cons. Aps., Copenhagen, 1981—; bd. dirs. Venture Gruppen Danmark II A/S; chmn. bd. Jensen Auto A/S, Vinther & Larsen A/S, Sulik Ventiler A/S, Viggo Bendz A/S; examiner Copenhagen Sch. Econs. and Bus. Adminstrn., 1974—. Inventor firing mechanism for semi-automatic arm. Home: Erantisvej 12, 2300 Copenhagen Denmark Office: Stamholmen 155, 2650 Hvidovre Denmark

BALSLEY, HOWARD LLOYD, educator; b. Chgo., Dec. 3, 1913; s. Elmer Lloyd and Katherine (McGlashing) B.; m. Irol Verneth Whitmore, Aug. 24, 1947. A.B., Ind. U., 1946, M.A., 1947, Ph.D., 1950; postgrad., Johns Hopkins U., 1947-48, U. Chgo., summer 1948. Asst. prof. econs. U. Utah, Salt Lake City, 1949-50; assoc. prof. econs., dir. Sch. Bus., Russell Sage Coll., Troy, N.Y., 1950-52; asso. prof. econs. Washington and Lee U., Lexington, Va., 1952-54; prof. bus. stats., head dept. bus. and econ. research La. Tech. U., Ruston, 1954-65; prof. bus. adminstrn. and stats. Tex. Tech U., Lubbock, 1965-75; head dept. econs. and fin., prof. econs. and stats. U. Ark., Little Rock, 1975-80; adj. prof. econs. and stats. Hardin-Simmons U., Abilene, Tex., 1980-81. Author: (with James Gemmell) Principles of Economics, 1953, Readings in Economic Doctrines, vols. 1 and 2, 1961, Introduction to Statistical Method, 1964, Quantitative Research Methods for Business and Economics, 1970, (with Vernon Clover) Business Research, 1974, 2d edit., 1979, 3d edit., 1984, 4th edit., 1988, Basic Statistics for Business and Economics, 1978. Served with USAAF, 1943-46. Mem. So. Econ. Assn., S.W. Fedn. Adminstrv. Disciplines, Am. Inst. Decision Scis. Home: 6501 15th Ave W Bradenton FL 34209

BALSLEY, IROL WHITMORE, emeritus management educator; b. Venus, Nebr., Aug. 22, 1912; d. Sylvanus Bertrand and Nanna (Carson) Whitmore; m. Howard Lloyd Balsley, Aug. 24, 1947. B.A., Nebr. State Coll., Wayne, 1933; M.S., U. Tenn., 1940; Ed.D., Ind. U., 1952. Tchr. high schs. Osmond and Walthill, Nebr., 1934-37; asst. prof. Ind. U., 1942-49; lectr. U. Utah, 1949-50, Russell Sage Coll., 1953-54; prof. office adminstrn. La. Tech. U., 1954-65, also head dept. office adminstrn., 1963-65; prof. bus. edn. Tex. Tech. U., 1965-72, prof. edn., 1972-75; prof. adminstrv. services U. Ark., Little Rock, 1975-80; prof. emeritus U. Ark., 1980—; adj. prof. Hardin-Simmons U., Abilene, Tex., 1980-81; coordinator USAF clk.-typist tng. program Pa. State U., 1951, instr., head office tng. sect. TVA, 1941-42; editorial asst. South-Western Pub. Co., 1940-41. Author: (with Wanous) Shorthand Transcription Studies, 1968; (with Robinson) Integrated Secretarial Studies, 1963; (with Wood and Whitmore) Homestyle Baking, 1973; Century 21 Shorthand, Vol. I, 1974, (with Robert Hoskinson) Vol. II, 1974; Self-Paced Learning Activities for Century 21 Shorthand, Vol. I, 1977; High Speed Dictation, 1980, Where On Earth?, 1986. Mem. Nat. Bus. Edn. Assn. (past pres. research found.), Adminstrv. Mgmt. Soc., Nat. Collegiate Assn. Secs. (co-founder, past pres., nat. exec. sec. 1976-81), Pi Lambda Theta, Delta Pi Epsilon (past nat. sec.), Beta Gamma Sigma, Phi Delta Kappa, Pi Omega Pi, Sigma Tau Delta, Alpha Psi Omega, Delta Kappa Gamma. Home: 6501 15th Ave W Bradenton FL 34209

BALTAKE, JOE, film critic; b. Camden, N.J., Sept. 16, 1945; s. Joseph John and Rose Clara (Bearint) B.; m. Susan Shapiro Hale. B.A., Rutgers U., 1967. Film critic Gannett Newspapers (suburban), 1967-69, Phila. Daily News, 1969-86; movie editor Inside Phila., 1986—; film critic The Sacramento Bee, 1987—; leader criticism workshop Phila. Writer's Conf., 1977-79. Contbg. editor: Screen World, 1973—; author: The Films of Jack Lemmon, 1977, updated, 1986; contbr. articles to Films in Rev., 1969—, broadcast criticism for Prism Cable TV, 1985. Recipient Motion Picture Preview Group award for criticism, 1986, citation Phila. Mag., 1985. Office: The Sacramento Bee 2100 Q St Sacramento CA 95852

BALTENSWEILER, ARMIN O., business executive; b. Mollis, Glarus, Switzerland, Apr. 20, 1920; s. Otto and Bertha (Roth) B.; m. Ruth Frei; children: Urs, Claudia, Roger. MS, Zurich (Switzerland) Inst. Tech., 1946. Commd. 2d lt. Swiss Air Force, 1940, advanced through grades to capt., resigned, 1952; research engr. Swiss Fed. Aircraft Factory, Emmen, 1947-48; chief engr. Swissair Co. Ltd., Zurich, 1948-56, v.p. planning, 1956-60, dep. pres., 1960-72, pres., 1972-82, chmn. bd., 1982—; chmn. bd. Sulzer Bros. Ltd., Zurich, 1982—; bd. dirs. Nestlé SA, Vevey, Switzerland, Crédit Suisse, Zurich. Fellow Inst. Aero. Scis. Lodge: Rotary. Home: 61 Sonnhalde, 8704 Herrliberg, Zurich Switzerland

BALTIMORE, DAVID, microbiologist, educator; b. N.Y.C., Mar. 7, 1938; s. Richard I. and Gertrude (Lipschitz) B.; m. Alice S. Huang, Oct. 5, 1968; 1 dau., Teak. BA with high honors in Chemistry, Swarthmore Coll., 1960; postgrad., MIT, 1960-61; PhD, Rockefeller U., 1964. Research assoc. Salk Inst. Biol. Studies, La Jolla, Calif., 1965-68; assoc. prof. microbiology MIT, Cambridge, 1968-72, prof. biology, 1972—, Am. Cancer Soc. prof. microbiology, 1973-83, dir. Whitehead Inst. Biomed. Research, 1982—. Mem. editorial bd.: Jour. Molecular Biology, 1971-73, Jour. Virology, 1969—, Sci., 1986—. Bd. govs. Weizmann Inst. Sci., Israel; bd. dirs. Life Sci. Research Found.; co-chmn. Commn. on a Nat. Strategy of AIDS; bd. mgrs. Swarthmore; ad hoc program adv. com. on complex genome, NIH. Recipient Gustav Stern award in virology, 1970; Warren Triennial prize Mass. Gen. Hosp., 1971; Eli Lilly and Co. award in microbiology and immunology, 1971; U.S. Steel Found. award in molecular biology, 1974; Gairdner Found. ann. award, 1974; Nobel prize in physiology or medicine, 1975. Fellow AAAS, Am. Med. Writers Assn. (hon.); mem. Nat. Acad. Scis., Am. Acad. Arts and Scis., Inst. Med. of the NAS, Pontifical Acad. Scis., Royal Soc. (Eng.) (fgn.). Home: 26 Reservoir St Cambridge MA 02138 Office: Whitehead Inst Biomed Research 9 Cambridge Ctr Cambridge MA 02142

BALY, SLAHEDDINE, minister of state for justice of Tunisia; b. Tunis, Tunisia, July 29, 1926; Married; 3 children. Grad., law schs., France and Tunisia. Treas. inspector Tunisia, 1949-54, magistrate, 1954-57; state prosecutor Mil. Ct. of Justice, Tunisia, 1957-66; chief of staff Sec. of State of Def., Tunisia, 1966-71; sec. gen. of ministry of def. Tunisia, 1971; permanent sec. Nat. Def. Council, Tunisia, 1971; minister of justice Tunisia, 1973, minister of nat. def. (now minister of state for nat. def.), 1980; treas. of Constitutional Dem. Rally, 1988—. Sec.-Gen. Tunisian Olympic Com., 1960-86, pres. 1986—. Recipient several nat. and fgn. medals. Office: Office of Ministry of Justice, Tunis Tunisia *

BALZAC, AUDREY FLOBELLE ADRIAN, psychologist; b. N.Y.C., May 5, 1928; d. Allen Isaac and Mildred Florence (Brown) Adrian; m. Ralph P. Balzac, Jr., May 3, 1961; children: Stephen Rafael, Elena Adrian, Rebecca Lisa. BA in Psychology with honors, Hunter Coll., 1951; MS with honors, Purdue U., 1952; ABD, Columbia U., 1963. Intern in psychology Howard Rusk Inst., NYU and Bellevue Hosp., N.Y.C., 1956-57; clin. psychologist Westchester Community Mental Health Bd., and Children's Ct., White Plains, N.Y., 1957-63; psychol. cons. div. Vocat. Rehab., N.Y.C., 1957—; pvt. practice, 1963—; research psychologist Psychiat. Inst., Columbia Presbyn. Med. Ctr., N.Y.C., 1955-57; cons. Pound Ridge Elem. Sch., 1975-76. Chairwoman Community Relations bd. Pound Ridge Jewish Community Ctr., 1975-79, treas., 1978-79; mem. Westchester Women's Adv. Bd., 1986-87; candidate Bedford Cen. Sch. Bd., 1987, 88. Fellow Rusk Inst., 1956-57; research grantee Columbia U., 1960—. Fellow AAUW; mem. Am. Psychol. Assn., Eastern Psychol. Assn., N.Y. Soc. Clin. Psychologists, Soc. Psychol. Study of Social Issues, Am. Sociol. Assn., Sigma Xi, Psi Chi (treas. 1951-52). Jewish. Home: Route 4 Box 267 Pound Ridge NY 10576

BAM, FOSTER, lawyer; b. Bridgeport, Conn., Jan. 11, 1927; s. Frederick and Alma (Foster) B.; children: Sylvia Carol, Sheila Catherine, Eric Foster. Grad., Loomis Sch., 1944; A.B., LL.B., Yale, 1950. Bar: N.Y. 1954, Conn. Mem. faculty acctg. Yale, 1952-53; with firm Spence & Hotchkiss, N.Y.C., 1954-55; asst. U.S. dist. atty. So. Dist. N.Y., 1955-58; partner firm Feldman, Kramer, Bam Nessen, N.Y.C., 1958-67; now partner Cummings & Lockwood.; Bd. dirs. Interstate Bakeries Corp., Cities Service Co., Evergreen Fund, Evergreen Total Return Fund, Chartwell Group Ltd., Evergreen Valve Timing Fund, Evergreen Ltd. Market Fund, Am. Mus. of Fly Fishing. Trustee Phoenix Sci. Ctr., Am. Mus. Fly Fishing. Recipient Johny Foyle Meml. award, 1969. Mem. ABA, Conn. Bar Assn., Greenwich Bar Assn., Oceanic Soc. (chmn. bd. trustees), N.Y. County Lawyers Assn., N.Y. State Dist. Attys. Assn., Exptl. Aircraft Assn., Phi Beta Kappa. Home: 51 Londonderry Dr Greenwich CT 06830 Office: Cummings & Lockwood 2 Greenwich Plaza Greenwich CT 06830

BAMBRICK, SUSAN CAROLINE, economist, educator; b. Brisbane, Queensland, Australia, Oct. 20, 1941; d. Harold Wilson and Viola (Dent) Russell; m. Rayno Hugh Bambrick; 2 sons, 1 daughter. BS in Econs. with honors, U. Queensland, 1964; PhD, Australian Nat. U., 1970. Sr. tutor econs. Australia Nat. U., Canberra, 1969-71; lectr. econs. Australian Nat. U., Canberra, 1972-79; sr. lectr. Australia Nat. U., Canberra, 1980—, dean of students, 1984-86, master Univ. House, 1987—; dir., lectr. Australian Min. Found., 1976—; Fulbright scholar-in-residence Pa. State U., 1982; dir. studies Australia Pub. Service Bd., Canberra, 1982. Author: Australian Minerals and Energy Policy, 1979. Vice-chmn. bd. Canberra Grammar Sch., 1982—. Fellow Australian Inst. Energy (fed. pres. 1981). Office: Univ House, Australian Nat U, GPO Box 1535, Canberra ACT Australia 2601

BAMFORD, DAVID ELLERY, lawyer; b. New Salem, Pa., Sept. 5, 1921; s. George Kyle and Hazel (Reid) B.; m. Theodora Mary Kenny, Jan. 7, 1949; children: Mary Ann, David Reid, James Douglas. LLB with honors, George Washington U., 1949. Bar: D.C. 1949, Ill. 1960. Assoc. Law Offices C.S. Rhyne, Washington, 1949-51; counsel Gen. Electric Co., N.Y.C., 1951-66; v.p., gen. counsel Gen. Electric Credit Corp., Stamford, Conn., 1966-76; corp. counsel Gen. Electric Co., Fairfield, Conn., 1976—. Served to sgt. U.S. Army, 1942-46, CBI. Mem. Ill. State Bar Assn., D.C. Bar Assn., Order of Coif. Presbyterian. Home: 1 Wedgewood Rd Westport CT 06880 Office: Gen Electric Co 3135 Easton Turnpike Fairfield CT 06431

BANACH, ART JOHN, graphic artist.; b. Chgo., May 22, 1931; s. Vincent and Anna (Zajac) B.; grad. Art. Inst. of Chgo., 1955; pupil painting studies Mrs. Melin, Chgo.; m. Loretta A. Nolan, Oct. 15, 1966; children: Heather Anne, Lynnea Joan. Owner, dir. Art J. Banach Studios, 1949—, cartoon syndicate for newspapers, house organs and advt. functions, 1954—, owned and operated advt. agy., 1954-56, feature news and picture syndicate, distbn. U.S. and fgn. countries. Dir. Speculators S Fund. Recipient award 1st Easter Seal contest Ill. Assn. Crippled, Inc., 1949. Chgo. Pub. Sch. Art Soc. Scholar. Mem. Artist's Guild Chgo., Am Mgmt. Assn., Chgo. Assn. of Commerce and Industry, Chgo. Federated Advt. Club, Am. Mktg. Assn., Internat. Platform Assn., Chgo. Advt. Club, Chgo. Soc. Communicating Arts. Clubs: Columbia Yacht, Advt. Execs.; Art Directors (Chgo.). Home: 1076 Leahy Circle E Des Plaines IL 60016

BANAL, VICENTE HERALDO, physician; b. Daet, Philippines, Apr. 5, 1938; s. Santiago dela Torre and Sixta (Heraldo) B.; m. Leonida Castro Arenas, Jan. 25, 1964; children: Vanessa, Violeta, Jose Vernon, Jose Vaughn. AA, UST, Manila, 1958, MD, 1961-62. Intern Vet's. Meml. Hosp., Quezon City, Philippines, 1961-62; resident Philippine Iron Mines Hosp., Norte, Philippines, 1962-64; Rural Health Unit Philippines Dept. Health, San Vicente, 1965-67; physician Pargum, Gumaus, Philippines, 1964-65; practice medicine Daet, 1966—. Lt. Gov. Luzon Dist., 1977-78; chmn. Provincial Health Coordinating Council, Daet, 1986-88, Provincial Affairs Adv. Council Office of Provincial Gov. Com. Health and Sanitation, Daet, 1987, Citizens Com. on INP Performance, Daet, 1987, Provincial Food and Agrl. Council, Daet, 1987. Mem. Camarines Norte Med. Soc. (sec.-treas. 1964-72, v.p. 1972-73, pres. 1986-88), Coconut Fedn. (local v.p. 1979-85, sec.-treas. 1985—, sec.-treas. Camarines Norte chpt. 1980-86, pres. 1985-88), Philippines Med. Assn. (named outstanding physician 1970). Lodge: Lions (bd. dirs. 1987-88, 1st v.p. 1988-89). Home: 1309 Dasmarinas St, Daet, Camarines Norte Philippines 4600 Office: President Cocofed Camarines, Norte Chpt, UCPB Bldg Daet, Camarines Norte Philippines Other: Potica Arenas, Corner Felipe II and Vinzons Ave, Daet, Camarines Norte Philippines

BANANA, CANAAN SODINDO, former president of Zimbabwe; b. Esiphezini, Essexvale dist., Zimbabwe, Mar. 5, 1936; m. Janet Mbuyazwe, Sept., 1961; children: Michael, Nathan, Martin, Nobuhle. Trained as sch. tchr., Tegwani Tng. Inst., 1958; student of theology, Epworth Theol. Coll., Zimbabwe, 1960-62; dip., Kasai Indsl. Ctr., Japan, 1970; M.T.S., Wesley Theol. Sem., Washington, 1975; BA (hons.) in Theology, U. S.Africa, 1980; LLD (hon.), Am. U., Washington, 1981, U. Zimbabwe, 1983. ordained to ministry Meth. Ch., 1966. Mgr. Meth. Sch., Wankie and Plumtree areas, Zimbabwe, 1963-66; prin. Matjinge Boarding Sch., 1965; vis. chaplain Tegwani High Sch., 1965-75; founding mem., 1st v.p. African Nat. Council, 1971; jailed as polit. prisoner in Zimbabwe several times 1975-79, pres. of Zimbabwe, 1980-88; chancellor U. Zimbabwe, 1983—; chmn. Nat. Council rep. in N. Am. and the UN, 1973-75; founder mem. and publicity sec. People's Movement, 1976; regional co-ordinator Zimbabwe African Nat. Union, North and South provinces, 1979-80; pres., chmn. Bulawayo Council of Chs., 1969-71; mem. adv. com. World Council Chs., 1970—; chaplain Am. U., Wahington, 1973-75. Author four tracts on politics and religion, Gospel According to the Ghetto, Woman of my Imagination, Theology of Promise; contbr. articles to mags. and jours. Office: World Council of Churches, 150 route de Ferney, PO Box 66, 1211 Geneva 20 Switzerland *

BANASIK, ROBERT CASMER, nursing home administrator, educator; b. Detroit, Dec. 8, 1942; s. Casmer John and Lucille Nathalie (Siperek) B.; BS in Mech. Engring., Wayne State U., 1965; MS in Indsl. Engring., Tex. Tech. Coll., 1967; MBA, Ohio State U., 1973, PhD, 1974; m. Jacqueline Mae Miller, Aug. 28, 1965; (div. 1985); children: Robert John, Marcus Alan, Jason Andrew; m. Barbara Jean Willows, Oct. 12, 1985. Mgmt. systems engr. Riverside Methodist Hosp., Columbus, Ohio, 1970, 71; owner, mgmt. systems cons. Banasik Assoc., Columbus, 1972—; dir. mgmt. systems engring. Grant Hosp., Columbus, 1973-78; owner, mgr. RMJ Investment Enterprises, Columbus, 1975-85; pres. Omnilife Systems, Inc., Columbus, 1979—, RMJ Mgmt., Inc., 1983-85. Bryant Health Ctr., Inc., Ironton, Ohio, 1983—, Equity Mgmt., 1985—; owner Omnivend, 1985—; adminstr. Patterson Health Ctr., Columbus, 1980—, Parkview Health Ctr., Inc., Volga, S.D, 1986—, Hamilton (Ohio) Health Ctr., Inc., 1986—, Shelby Manor Health Ctr., Inc., Shelbyville, Ky., 1986—, Samaritan Care Ctr., Inc., Medina, Ohio, 1988—; asst. prof. Capital U. Grad. Sch. Adminstrn., Columbus, 1973-79, assoc. prof., 1979—; dir. Asset Data Systems, Columbus. Pres. bd. dirs. United Cerebral Palsy Franklin County, 1979-80; mem. founding bd. Support Resources, Inc., 1978-85; bd. dirs. Transp. Resources, Inc., 1979-80, Dennison Health Systems, 1988—; pres., bd. dirs. Ohio Acad. Nursing Homes, Columbus, 1986—. Registered profl. engr., Ohio; lic. nursing home adminstr., Ohio. Mem. Am. Hosp. Assn., NSPE (dir. Franklin County chpt. 1976-77), Ohio Soc. Profl. Engrs., Am. Inst. Decision Scis., Am. Coll. Health Care Adminstrs., Sigma Xi, Beta Gamma Sigma, Alpha Pi Mu, Phi Kappa Phi, Alpha Kappa Psi. Republican. Lutheran. Editor: Topics in Hospital Material Management, 1978-84; contbr. articles to profl. jours. Office: 1207 N High St Suite 300 Columbus OH 43201

BANCHERI, LOUIS PETER, JR., retired educator; b. Flushing, N.Y., July 17, 1928; s. Louis Peter and Frances Nela (Mascali) B.; BS, Georgetown U., 1949; MA, Hofstra U., 1950, MS, 1957; m. Patricia Marie Hynes, July 9, 1955; children: Susan E., James L., Robert W., Kathryn J. Engring. asst. Sperry Corp., 1953-54, tchr. biology Sewanhaka High Sch., Floral Park, N.Y., 1954-57; chmn. sci. dept. H. Frank Carey Jr.-Sr. High Sch., Franklin Square, N.Y., 1957-75, Sewanhaka High Sch., Floral Park, N.Y., 1975-85; tng. specialist Hanover Indsl. Machine Co., Pa. for Peoples Rep. China, 1988; sales cons., trainer and rep., 1984—; tng. specialist Hanover Industrial MAchine Co., Pa. for Peoples Republic of China, 1988; adj. prof. Molloy Coll., Rockville Centre, N.Y., 1967-68; assoc. prof. Energy Inst. Math. and Sci. Tchrs., C.W. Post Coll., 1981; cons. Diocese of Rockville Centre, 1965-67, Rand McNally Pub. Co., 1971, Seaford Pub. Schs., 1968. Served with U.S. Army, 1950-52, Korea. Mem. citizens adv. com. South Huntington Pub. Schs., 1960-61. Bd. dirs. Netherwood Civic Assn., 1957-60. Recipient William Gaston Educator of Year award Georgetown U., 1974. NSF fellow, 1966-73, NSF/Leadership Devel. Inst., U. Md., 1973-74, Dept. Energy Inst., 1977, 79, 80, others. Fellow Sci. Tchrs. Assn. N.Y. State; mem. AAAS (life), Nat. Sci. Tchrs. Assn. (life), Nat., N.Y. State, Nassau County (pres. 1968) sci. suprs. assns., Phi Delta Kappa (pres. L.I. chpt. 1974-75). Author: (with M. Stock) Investigations in Modern Biology, 1971, 77; Reading Embracing All Disciplines-Science, 1970; co-author: Regents Review Series—Biology, 1982, 83; contbg. author Laboratory Exercises in Marine Sciences, 1969; Energy, Its Alternate Forms, 1977; contbg. editor Concepts in Modern Biology (D. Kraus), 1970, 75; contbr. articles to profl. jours. Home: 18 Glendale Dr Melville NY 11747-1235 also: 36 Bon Pinck Way Springs East Hampton NY 11937

BANCROFT, JAMES RAMSEY, business executive, lawyer; b. Ponca City, Okla., Nov. 13, 1919; s. Charles Ramsey and Maude (Viersen) B.; m. Jane Marguerite Oberfell, May 28, 1944; children: John Ramsey, Paul Marshall, Sara Jane Bancroft Clair. A.B., U. Calif., Berkeley, 1940, M.B.A., 1941; J.D., Hastings Coll. Law, 1949. Bar: Calif. 1950; C.P.A., Calif. With McLaren, Goode, West & Co., C.P.A.s, San Francisco, 1946-50; partner firm Bancroft, Avery & McAlister, San Francisco, 1950-86, of counsel, 1986—; owner, mgr. Bancroft Vineyards, 1982—; pres. Madison Properties, Inc., San Francisco, 1967—, Adams Properties, Inc., 1969-79, Adams-Western Inc., 1969-78; chmn. bd. UNC Resources, 1978-82, dir., 1984-85; chmn. bd. United Nuclear Corp., Falls Church, Va., 1972-82, Madison Capital Inc., San Francisco, 1986—, Adams Investment Advisors, Inc., San Francisco, 1984—, Adams Capital Mgmt. Co., San Francisco, 1987—; bd. dirs. The Canadian Ins. Co. of Calif., Costa Mesa, 1986—. Former pres. Suisun Conservation Fund; former dir. Suisun Resource Conservation Dist.; trustee Dean Witter Found.; pres. Harvey L. Sorensen Found.; bd. dirs. Calif. Urology Found., San Francisco Found. for Research and Edn. Orthopedic Surgery, Pacific Vascular Found. Served to lt. USNR, 1942-46. Mem. ABA, Order of Coif, Phi Beta Kappa. Clubs: Bohemian, Pacific-Union, Olympic (San Francisco). Office: 601 Montgomery St Suite 800 San Francisco CA 94111

BANCROFT, MARGARET ARMSTRONG, lawyer; b. Mpls., May 9, 1938; d. Wallace David and Mary Elizabeth (Garland) Armstrong; m. Alexander Clerihew Bancroft, Mar. 14, 1964; 1 child, Elizabeth. BA magna cum laude, Radcliffe Coll., 1960; JD cum laude, NYU, 1969. Bar: N.Y. 1971. Reporter Mpls. Star and Tribune, 1960-61, UPI, N.Y. and N.J., 1961-66; assoc. Donovan Leisure Newton & Irvine, Paris, France, 1969-71, N.Y.C., 1971-78, ptnr., 1978-84; ptnr. Finley, Kumble, Wagner, Heine, Underberg, Manley, Myerson & Casey, N.Y.C., 1984-88, Dechert, Price & Rhoads, N.Y.C., 1988—; adj. prof. law NYU. Bd. dirs., exec. com. Vis. Nurse Service N.Y. Mem. ABA (mem. subcom. tender offers and proxy contests), Assn. Bar City N.Y., N.Y. County Lawyers Assn. (com. on securities and exchanges), N.Y. State Bar Assn. (exec. com. banking, bus. law and corps. sect., com. securities regulation). Democrat. Office: Dechert Price & Rhoads 477 Madison Ave New York NY 10022

BANCROFT, PAUL, III, investment company executive; b. N.Y.C., Feb. 27, 1930; s. Paul and Rita (Manning) B.; B.A., Yale U., 1951; postgrad. Georgetown Fgn. Service Inst., 1952; m. Monica M. Devine, Jan. 2, 1977; children by previous marriage—Bradford, Kimberly, Stephen, Gregory. Account exec. Merrill Lynch Pierce Fenner & Smith, N.Y.C., 1956-57; asso. corporate finance dept. F. Eberstadt & Co., N.Y.C., 1957-62; partner Draper, Gaither & Anderson, Palo Alto, Calif., 1962-67; with Bessemer Securities Corp., 1967—; v.p. Venture Capital Investments, 1967-74, sr. v.p. securities investments, 1974-76, pres., chief exec. officer, dir., 1976-87; cons. Bessemer Securities Corp., 1988—; dir. Am. Standard, Inc., Measurex Corp., Albany Internat., Inc., Watts Industries, Inc., Scudder Devel. Fund, Scudder Capital Growth Fund, Scudder Internat. Fund, Scudder Global Fund, Scudder Equity Income Fund, Scudder New Asia Fund, Maxim Integrated Products; ind. venture capitalist, 1988—; founder, past pres. and chmn. Nat. Venture Capital Assn.; trustee Carnegie Mellon U. Served to 1st lt. USAF, 1952-56. Clubs: River, Yale (N.Y.C.); Pacific Union, Bohemian (San Francisco). Home: 238 Newtown Turnpike Redding CT 06896 Office: 1212 Ave of Americas Suite 1802 New York NY 10036

BANDA, ARPAD FREDERIC, finance and economics educator; b. N.Y.C., June 16, 1928; s. John and Terecia (Varga) B.; BS in Social Scis., City Coll. N.Y., 1950; MBA, N.Y. U., 1956, PhD, 1964, CFA, 1977. Instr. econs. Milw.-Downer Coll., 1959-61, Upsala Coll., 1961-62; asst. prof. econs., fin. U. Hartford (Conn.), 1963-66, asso. prof., 1966-68, chmn. dept., 1966-67; assoc. prof. fin. U. Akron (O.), 1968-71, prof., 1971—, head dept., 1970-73, 77-78; pres. C.P. Banda & Co. Inc., registered investment advisors, 1981—, Banda Fin. Services Inc., Buda Pub. Co. Inc., Hungarian Found. Inc. Chief elder Free Hungarian Reformed Ch. Diocese; v.p. Lorantffy Care Ctr., Inc.; trustee Gaspar Karoli Theol. Sem.; bd. dirs. Am. Hungarian Fedn., 1977-79, 83—. Mem. Fin. Mgmt. Assn. (coordinating editor jour. 1970-75), Am. Fin. Assn. (Ohio chpt. pres. 1972-73), Ea. Fin. Assn. (bd. dirs. 1975-78). Home: 2299 Winter Pkwy Apt 295 Cuyahoga Falls OH 44221 Office: 302 E Buchtel Ave Akron OH 44325

BANDA, NGWAZI (HASTINGS) KAMUZU, president Malawi; b. Kasungu Dist., Nyasaland (now Malawi), 1906; ed. Livingstonia Mission Ch. of Scotland, later night sch., Johannesburg; grad. (scholar) Wilberforce Inst., Xenia, Ohio, 1928; student U. Ind., 1928; PhB, U. Chgo., 1931; MD, Meharry Med. Coll., 1937; student univs. Glasgow and Edinburgh; student tropical medicine, U. Liverpool. Practice medicine, Liverpool, also North Shields, Eng., 1942-44, Mission for Colored Seamen, 1944-45, Kilburn Dist. of London, 1945-53, Gold Coast (became independent nation of Ghana 1957), 1953-58; leader opposition to fedn. Rhodesia and Nyasaland, 1949-53; assisted establishment Nyasaland African Congress, 1950, elected pres.-gen., 1958; imprisoned for polit. activities, 1959-60; apptd. minister natural resources and local govt. Malawi, 1961, prime minister, 1963-66, pres., 1966-71, life pres., 1971—, now also minister of agr., external affairs, justice, works and supplies. Chancellor, U. Malawi, 1965—. Address: Office of Pres, State House, Lilongwe Malawi also: U Malawi, PO Box 278, Zomba Malawi *

BANDEIAN, JOHN JACOB, physician, surgeon; b. Gurin, Armenia, Mar. 15, 1912; s. John and Flora (Gureghian) B.; B.S., Harvard U., 1935; M.D., Tufts U., 1941; m. Alice M. Kechijian, Apr. 4, 1952; children—Natalie, John Jacob, Stephen H. Intern, Med. Center Jersey City, 1941-42, Mass. Meml. Hosp., 1942; resident in diseases of chest Trudeau San., Saranac Lake, N.Y., 1943, in oncol. surgery, Pondville State Hosp., Walpole, Mass., 1943-45; fellow gynecology Mass. Gen. Hosp., Boston, 1945-46; surg. resident Beverly (Mass.) Hosp., 1946-48; practice surgery, Holyoke, Mass., 1948—; pres. John J. Bandeian M.D. Assocs., Inc. Vestryman, St. Paul's Ch. Diplomate Am. Bd. Surgery. Fellow ACS; mem. AMA, Mass. Med. Soc. (councilor), Hampden Dist. Med. Soc. (pres. 1971-72), New Eng. Cancer Soc., Holyoke C. of C. Republican. Home: 1265 Northampton St Holyoke MA 01040 Office: 210 Pine St Holyoke MA 01040

BANDER, THOMAS SAMUEL, dentist; b. Grand Rapids, Mich., Mar. 3, 1924; s. Samuel and Jennie (David) B.; m. DoLores Abraham, Sept. 7, 1947; children: Samuel T., Jacquelyn Marie. AS, Grand Rapids Jr. Coll., 1944; DDS, U. Mich., 1948. Pvt. practice dentistry Grand Rapids, Mich., 1948—. Pres. St. Nicholas Orthodox Ch., Grand Rapids, 1965. Served with U.S. Army, 1941-44, to capt. USAF, 1955-57. Fellow Am. Coll. Dentists, Internat. Coll. of Dentists, Acad. Gen. Dentists, ADA, Acad. Operative Dentistry; mem. West Mich. Dental Soc. (pres. 1978), Mich. Dental Assn. (chmn. sci. program 1977-78), Kent County Dental Soc. (pres. 1965), Chgo. Dental Soc. Republican. Eastern Orthodox. Clubs: Cascade Hills Country (Grand Rapids). Home: 616 Manhattan Rd SE Grand Rapids MI 49506-2025 Office: 2426 Burton St SE Grand Rapids MI 49506

BANDLER, RICHARD, advertising executive; b. N.Y.C., July 12, 1917; s. Maurice and Edna (Lee) B.; m. Eleanor Slater Trenholm, Jan. 7, 1966; children—Judith Finch, Patricia Hornblower, Elise, Tatiana. Dir. purchasing B. T. Babbitt Co., N.Y.C., 1939-42; nat. sales mgr. Reuben H. Donnelley Corp., N.Y.C., 1946-49; founder, pres. Richard Bandler Co. Inc., directory advt., N.Y.C., 1949-87. Served with U.S. Army, 1942-45. Decorated Purple Heart with three battle stars. Mem. Masters of Foxhounds Assn., Greenville County (S.C.) Hounds (founding master) Am., Graphical Assn. , ABI Research Assn. (dep. gov.-elect) Roman Catholic. Clubs: Union League, Metropolitan. Home: Rt 2 Box 322 Tryon NC 28782

BANDOW, DOUGLAS LEIGHTON, editor, columnist, policy consultant; b. Washington, Apr. 15, 1957; s. Donald E. and Donna J. (Losh) B. A.A., Okaloosa-Walton Jr. Coll., Niceville, Fla., 1974; B.S. in Econs., Fla. State U., 1976; J.D., Stanford U., 1979. Bar: Calif. 1979 D.C. 1984. Sr. policy analyst Reagan for Pres. Com., Los Angeles, 1979-80, Arlington, Va., 1980; sr. policy analyst Office of Pres. Elect, Washington, 1980-81; spl. asst. to the Pres. for policy devel. White House, Washington, 1981-82; editor Inquiry Mag., Washington, 1982-84; sr. fellow Cato Inst., Washington, 1984—; nat. columnist Copley News Service, San Diego, 1983—; editor U.S. Aid to Developing World, 1985. contbg. editor Reason mag. 1983—. Author: Unquestioned Allegiance, 1986, Beyond Good Intentions: A Biblical View of Politics, 1988; editor: Protecting the Environment, 1986; contbr. articles to periodicals. Recipient Freedom Leadership award Freedoms Found., Valley Forge, Pa., 1977; recipient cert. for polit. and journalistic activities Freedoms Found., Valley Forge, Pa., 1979; named Man of Yr. N.Y. State Coll. Reps., 1982; recipient Nat. Young Am. award Boy Scouts Am., 1977. Mem. Calif. Bar Assn., ABA, D.C. Bar Assn., Washington Ind. Writers. Home: 8478 Magic Tree Ct Springfield VA 22153 Office: Cato Inst 224 2d St SE Washington DC 20003

BANDURSKI, BRUCE LORD, ecologist and environmental scientist; b. Waterbury, Conn., June 28, 1940; s. Stanley Alexander Bandurski and Virginia Ann (VanRensselaer) Bandurski Hinckley. B.S. with honors, Mich. State U., 1962; postgrad. George Washington U., 1964-65, U.S. Dept. Agr. Grad. Sch., 1965-66. Park ranger Nat. Park Service, 1962-63; sci. reference analyst USPHS, Washington, 1963-65; intelligence ops. specialist U.S. Army, Washington, 1965-66; analyst planner U.S. Dept. Interior, Washington, 1966-74, coordinator, br. chief, 1974-84, on detail as ecologist, ecomgmt. advisor Internat. Joint Commn. U.S. and Can., 1983-85, ecomgmt. advisor, ecologist, 1985—; mem. faculty U.S. Dept. Agr. Grad. Sch., 1968—; guest lectr. No. Va. Community Coll., U. Wis., Bucknell U., Am. U., U. Pitts.; mem. subcom. Fed. Interagy. Com. on Edn., 1967—; watch dir., dep. and acting mission dir. U.S. Man-in-Sea program, St. John, V.I., 1970; chmn. Conservation Roundtable of Washington, 1970-71; chmn. com. on definitions, spl. com. on environ. protection U.S. nat. com. World Energy Conf., Washington, 1981—; initiator, dir. Binat. Workshop on Transboundary Monitoring, 1984, mem. exec. com. Great Lakes Sci. Adv. Bd., 1986—. Writer planning and recreation impact mgmt. series, 1967-73; author U.S. Bur. Land Mgmt. Environ. Mgmt. Procedures 1976-84 (Achievement award 1978, 79, 84), steering group on marine environ. monitoring, Commn. on Engring. and TEch. Studies, Nat. Research Council, 1986-87. Mem. Ecol. Soc. Am. (charter Met. Washington chpt.), Internat. Assn. for Ecology, Am. Soc. Naturalists, The Wildlife Soc., Am. Soc. Mammalogists, Fed. Profl. Assn., Wash. Soc. Engrs., Outdor Ethics Guild, Nature Conservancy, Maine Coast Heritage Trust, Alpha Zeta, Beta Beta Beta. Current work: Complementarities between holism and reductionism as they pertain to governance of man/environs relations. Subspecialty: Transdisciplinary ecomanagement. Home: Bandura/Point of Maine/Starboard Bucks Harbor ME 04618

BANDY, MARLIN ROBERT, clinical sexologist; b. Lancaster, Pa., Feb. 26, 1946; s. Ervin Marlin Bandy and Doris May Hilliar; married, Feb. 19, 1966; 1 child, Theresa Ann. BS in Nursing Edn., NYU, 1971; MPHEd, Tulane U., 1977; PhD in Pub. Health, Rosevelt U., 1984; Dr. Sexology, Am. Coll. Sexologists, San Francisco, 1986; Dr. Gen. Medicine, Nat. U., Mexico, 1988. Paramedic instr. City of Los Angeles, 1978-81; community services health edn. specialist Santa Monica (Calif.) Coll., 1981-82; pres. Los Angeles Free Clinic, 1982-84; exec. dir. Med. Edn. Services (formerly Med. Ednl. Devel. Assocs.), Los Angeles, 1984—, pres., 1980—; health edn. cons. Med. Edn. Services, Los Angeles, 1980-85. Author: Bilingual Education, 1982; contbr. articles to profl. jours. Bd. dirs. Santa Monica CPR Group, 1986, Aid for AIDS, Los Angeles, 1986, Emergency Disaster Group, Los Angeles, 1986; outstanding program dir. Paramedic Tng. Red Cross Emergency Hosp., Tijuana, 1988. Named Tchr. of Yr., Assn. Supervision and Curriculum Devel., 1980. Mem. Am. Heart Assn. (Outstanding CPR Trainer 1985), Am. Assn. Physician Assts., Soc. Emergency Medicine Tchrs., Calif. Health Educators Assn. (Outstanding Health Educator 1984), Am. Assn. Trauma Specialists. Office: Med Edn Service 1705 Pico Blvd Suite 169 Santa Monica CA 90405

BANE, BERNARD MAURICE, publishing company executive; b. Salem, Mass., Nov. 23, 1924; s. Julius and Rhoda (Trop) B. Student Northeastern U., 1946-48, law sch., 1948-49. Various sales and merchandising positions, 1949-55; with The Ivy League Enterprise, Boston, 1955-65; with BMB Pub. Co., Boston, 1965—, pub., 1970—. Author, pub.: The Bane in Kennedy's Existence, 1967, Is President John F. Kennedy Alive... and Well?, 1973, 12th edit., 1987, On the Impact of Morality in Our Times, 1985, Vatican "One": The Fault Line of Vatican II, 1986. Chmn. local Miss Am. Pageant, 1961. Mem. Am. Soc. Notaries. Home: 854 Massachusetts Ave Cambridge MA 02139 Office: PO Box 1622 Boston MA 02105

BANERJEE, NITAIDAS, engineer; b. Suri, West Bengal, India, May 9, 1936; arrived in Fed. Republic Germany, 1962; s. Ramkanai and Hemlata (Mukherjee) B.; m. Gertrud Schmitt, July 22, 1966. Grad., Staatliche Ingenieur Sch., Frankfurt, 1967. Registered profl. engr., Fed. Republic Germany. Planning engr. Farbwerke-Hoechst GmbH, Frankfurt, 1970-72; project and sales engr. Devilbiss GmbH, Dietzenbach, Fed. Republic Germany, 1972-81; process and cons. engr. automotives Herberts GmbH, Wuppertal, Fed. Republic Germany, 1981—. Clubs: Managers. Home: Schdeidtstrasse 112, 5600 Wuppertal 21 Federal Republic of Germany Office: Herberts GmbH, Christbusch 25, 5600 Wuppertal 2 Federal Republic of Germany

BANERJEE, SAMARENDRANATH, orthopaedic surgeon; b. Calcutta, India, July 12, 1932; s. Haridhone and Nihar Bala (Mukherjee) B.; m. Hima Ganguly, Mar. 1977; 1 child, Rabindranath. M.B. B.S., R.G. Kar Med. Coll., Calcutta, 1957; postgrad., U. Edinburgh, 1965-66. Intern R.G. Kar Med. Coll., Calcutta, 1956-58; resident in surgery Bklyn. Jewish Hosp. Med. Ctr., 1958-60, Brookdale Med. Ctr., Bklyn., 1960-61, Jersey City Med. Ctr., 1961-63; research fellow Hosp. for Sick Children, U. Toronto, Ont., Can., 1968-69; practice medicine specializing in orthopedics Sault Ste. Marie, Ont.; past pres. med. staff, chmn. exec. com. Gen. Hosp., Sault Ste. Marie, Ont., chief dept. surgery, mem. adv. com., 1980—; cons. orthopaedic surgeon Gen. Hosp. Plummer Meml. Hosp., Crippled Children Ctr., Ministry Nat. Health and Welfare, Dept. Vets. Adminstrn; civilian orthopaedic surgeon to 44th Div. Armed Forces Base Hosp., Kaduna, Nigeria, 1969. Trustee, Gen. Hosp., Sault Ste. Marie, 1975-76. Miss Betsy Burton Meml. fellow N.Y. U. Med. Ctr., 1963-64. Fellow Royal Coll. Surgeons Can., ACS, Royal Coll. Surgeons Edinburgh; mem. Can. Orthopaedic Assn., N.Y. Acad. Sci., Ont. Orthopaedic Assn., Can. Med. Assn., Am. Fracture Assn. Home: 50 Alworth Pl, Sault Sainte Marie, ON Canada P6B 5W5 Office: 125-955 Queen St E, Sault Sainte Marie, ON Canada P6A 2C3

BANERJI, DEBABAR, community physician, educator; b. Delhi, India, Aug. 10, 1930; s. Bhubaneshwar and Pratibha (Ganguli) B.; m. Shibani Ray, June 26, 1966; children: Disha, Anisha, Ipsita. MBBS, Med. Coll., Calcutta, 1953; MA in Anthropology, Cornell U., 1963. Med. officer Indian Trade Agy., Gartok, Western Tibet, 1956-57; demostrator physiology All India Inst. Med. Scis., New Delhi, India, 1957-58; med. officer Himachal Pradesh Adminstrn., India, 1958-59; sociologist Nat. Tuberculosis Inst., Bangalore, India, 1959-64; from asst. to assoc. prof. Nat. Inst. Health Adminstrn. and Edn., New Delhi, 1964-71; from assoc. to prof. Jawaharlal Nehru U. Ctr. Social Medicine and Community Health, New Delhi, 1971—; cons. in field. Author: Family Planning in India, 1971, Poverty, Class & Health Culture, 1982, The Making of the Health Services of a Country, 1985, Health and Family Planning Services in India, 1985, Social Science and Health Service Development in India, 1987; contbr. articles to profl. jours. Home: 24 Dakshinapuram, New Campus JNU, II0067 New Delhi India Office: Jawaharlal Nehru U, Block III, Old Campus JNU, II0067 New Delhi India

BANFIELD, STEPHEN DAVID, musicologist, musician; b. Dulwich, London, July 15, 1951; s. Dennis Ronald and Joan Mary Kathleen (Hadlow) B. BA with 1st class honors, Clare Coll., Cambridge U., Eng., 1972; PhD, St. John's Coll.. Oxford U., Eng., 1980; postgrad., Harvard U., 1975-76. Tutor music faculty Oxford (Eng.) U., 1976-78; prof. Guildhall Sch. Music and Drama, London, 1977-78, Royal Acad. Music, London, 1977-78; lectr. music U. Keele, Staffs, Eng., 1978-88, sr. lectr. music, head music dept., 1988—; council mem. English Song Award, London, 1986—; Brit. area rep. Sonneck Soc., 1986—. Author: Sensibility and English Song, 1985. Recipient Young Composers' award So. Ind. TV, Southampton, 1969, Carlsburg Student Lit. award, London, 1974; Knox fellow Harvard U., 1975-76. Fellow Royal Coll. Organists (Limpus prize 1968, Read prize 1969); mem. Royal Mus. Assn., Brit. Music. Soc., Sonneck Soc., Viola da Gamba Soc., Nat. Early Music Assn. (council mem. 1986—, dir. Sneyd Consort). Office: U Keele, Dept Music, Keele ST5 5BG, England

BÅNG, KARL-LENNART OSKAR, civil engineer; b. Sweden, Feb. 16, 1941; married. BCE, Royal Inst. Tech., Stockholm, 1964; MS in Civil Engring., Ohio State U., 1967; PhD in Civil Engring., Lund U., 1975. Traffic engr. Stockholm City Municipality Services Dept., 1964-66, chief traffic signal sect., 1967-69; traffic engr. V.B.B. Cons. Engrs., Malmö, Sweden, 1969-73, chief traffic sect., 1974-75; mng. dir. Swedish Transport Research Commn., Stockholm, 1975—; sr. lectr. traffic engring. Univ. Coll., London, 1985-86, Inst. Tech., Bandung, Indonesia, 1985-86; sr. lectr. De Leuw Cather Internat., Ltd., 1987; research asst. Transp. Research Ctr. Ohio State U. and Sweden-Am. Found., 1966-67. Contbr. numerous articles to profl. jours. Fulbright travel grantee, 1966-67; recipient Logistics prize Swedish Jour. Transp. and Materials Handling, Past Pres. award IIE, 1970. Mem. Internat. Inst. Transp. Engrs., Swedish Soc. Civil Engrs., Swedish Soc. Traffic Engrs., Swedish Soc. Transp. Engrs. Office: Transporation Research Commn, Grev Turegat 12A, Stockholm Sweden

BANGERTER, HANS ERNST, sport association executive; b. Studen/Bienne, Switzerland, June 10, 1924; s. Gottfried and Lina (Rihs) B.; m. Hedy Tanner, May 15, 1948; children—Annelies, Therese, Daniel. Diploma, Tech. Coll., Bienne, 1943. Sec., Swiss Sch. for Sports and Gymnastics, Macolin/Berne, 1946-53; asst. sec. Federation Internationale de Football Association, Zurich, 1953-59; gen. sec. Union des Associations Europeenes de Football, Berne, 1950—. Decorated officer Order of Leopold (Belgium). Club: Golf and Panathlon. Home: 25 Hubelgasse, 3065 Bolligen Switzerland Office: Union des Assns Européennes, de Football, Jupiterstrasse 33, PO Box 16, 3000 Berne Switzerland

BANGERTER, NORMAN HOWARD, governor of Utah, building contractor; b. Granger, Utah, Jan. 4, 1933; s. William Howard and Isabelle (Bawden) B.; m. Colleen Monson, Aug. 18, 1953; children: Garrett, Ann, Jordan, Blair, Alayne, Adam, Erdman (foster son). Student, U. Utah, 1956-57, Brigham Young U., 1951-55. Vice-pres. B and H Real Estate Co., West Valley City, Utah, 1970—; sec. Dixie-Six Land Devel., West Valley City, Utah, 1980—; pres. Bangerter and Hendrickson Co., West Valley City, Utah, 1970—, NHB Construction Co., West Valley City, Utah, 1983—; gov. Utah 1985—. Mem. Utah Ho. of Reps., 1974-85, speaker, 1981-84, majority leader, 1977-78; chmn. task force for alternative forms of govt. West Valley City, 1982. Recipient Outstanding Legislator award VFW, 1981; recipient Disting. Service award Home Bldg. Industry; named Outstanding Businessman West Valley C. of C. Mormon. Office: Office of Gov 210 State Capital Salt Lake City UT 84114 *

BANIAK, SHEILA MARY, accountant; b. Chgo., Feb. 26, 1953; d. DeLoy N. and Ann (Pasko) Slade; m. Mark A. Baniak, Oct. 7, 1972; 1 child, Heather Ann. Assocs. in Acctg., Oakton Community Coll., 1986; student, Roosevelt U., 1986—. Owner, mgr. Baniak and Assocs., Park Ridge, Ill., 1984—; acct. Otto & Snyder, Park Ridge, 1984-87; spl. projects coordinator, supplemental instr. Oakton Community Coll., Des Plaines, Ill., 1986—; acctg. computer instr. Oakton Community Coll., Des Plaines, 1987—; Adv. mem. acctg. Oakton Community Coll., Des Plaines, 1986—; cons., mem. Edn. Found. Oakton Community Coll., 1986—; instr. Ray Coll. Design, 1988. Author: A Small Business Collection Cycle Primer For Accountants, 1985. Ill. CPA Soc. scholar, 1984, Roosevelt U. scholar, 1986, Nat. Assn. Accts. scholar, 1985. Mem. Nat. Assn. Accts. (dir. community responsibility suburban Chgo. chpt. 1986—, speaker 1988, dir. profl. devel. seminars 1988—), Nat. Assn. Tax Practitioners. Home and Office: 1704 S Clifton Ave Park Ridge IL 60068

BANIC, IVO DRAGO, electronic company executive; b. Ljubljana, Yugoslavia, Slovenia, Slovenian, Oct. 26, 1932; s. Drago Ivan and Livija Gisela Julija (Feher) B.; m. Ivana Wilma Klemencic, Oct. 1, 1960; children—Helena, Gregor. BS, Faculty Electronics, Ljubljana, 1960, PhD, 1986; MS, Faculty Econs., Ljubljana, 1980. Asst. mgr. internat. div. ISKRA, Ljubljana, Yugoslavia, 1964-67, dep. dir. internat., 1976-78, mng. dir. mktg., 1978-82, mng. dir. microelec. div., 1982-85, exec. v.p., 1985-87; sr. researcher, Inst. Econ. Research, Ljubljana, 1987—; mng. dir. ISKRA Electronic, Stuttgart, 1968-72, PERLES, Pieterlen, CH. 1972-75. Roman Catholic. Office: Inst Econ Research, Kardeljeva ploscad 17, 61000 Ljubljana Yugoslavia

BANIK, SAMBHU NATH, psychologist; b. Joypara, India, Nov. 7, 1935; s. PadmaL. and Kadambini B.; B.Sc., Calcutta U., 1956, M.Sc., 1958; Ph.D., Bristol U., 1964; m. Promila Roy, Nov. 16, 1968; children—Sharmila, Kakali. Staff psychologist Des Moines Child Guidance Center, 1965; sr. psychologist, dir. internship tng. Univ. Hosp. Saskatoon, Sask., Can., 1965-69; dir. psychol. services, 1969-71; asst. chief mental health services Glenn Dale Hosp. and D.C. Village, 1971-81; chief South Community Mental Health Center, Washington, 1981—, chief child and youth services, 1984-88, clin. adminstr. NE/SE Family Ctr., Washington, 1988—; asst. prof. U. Sask., 1965-71; vis. prof. Bowie State Coll. (Md.), 1972-81. Mem. nat. adv. council drug abuse, 1987—; mem. advisory bd. ARC, Washington, 1987—; founder, pres. Prabashi, Inc., 1974-78; v.p. India Cultural Coordinating Com., 1979-80; pres. Assn. Indians in Am., 1980-84 (community services award, 1987); sec. gen. Asian Pacific Am. Cultural Heritage Council, 1981-82; treas. Asian Pacific Am. Heritage Council, 1982-84; mem. spl. com. 3d Conv. Asian Indians in N.Am., 1984, chmn. Indian Am. Forum Polit. Edn., 1986-88. Recipient DHS Humanitarian award U.S. Govt., 1986, Citizen award Mayor of Balt. Mem. Am. Psychol. Assn., Am. Group Psychotherapy Assn., D.C. Psychol. Assn., Internat. Acad. Forensic Psychology, Nat. Health Services Providers in Psychology. Contbr. articles to profl. jours. Home: 8606 Bradmoor Dr Bethesda MD 20817 Office: 1905 E St SE Washington DC 20003

BANISTER, HALCYONE JUDITH, silver specialist, writer; b. London, May 8, 1925; d. Charles John an May (Fowler) B. BA in English with honors, King's Coll., London, 1946. Asst. info. officer London Press Exchange, 1946-48; asst. editor Argentor, London, 1946, Watchmaker, Jeweller & Silversmith, London, 1948-60; pub. relations officer Smiths Industries, London, 1961-63; free-lance writer, cons. Surbiton, Surrey, Eng., 1963—; curator The James Walker Silver Mus., London, 1963-84. Author: Old English Silver, 1964, English Silver, 1965, Country Life Pocket Book of Silver, 1982; editor The Silver Society, 1961-87, The Goldsmiths's Rev., 1985-86, Conservative Party Right Ahead mag., 1958-60. Fellow Gemmological Assn. G.B. Anglican. Home: 20 Marlborough Gardens, Lovelace Rd, Surbiton, Surrey KT6 6NF, England

BANK, CHARLES NICKY, financial services company executive; b. Chgo., Sept. 29, 1943; s. Julius Charles and Sylvia (Kaplan) B.; m. Charlotte A. Hurt, Nov. 2, 1974; children—Bradley Tod, Martin Lee, Ryan Clayton, Darren Daniel. Student, Lincoln Jr. Coll., 1963-65. Clk. E.F. Hutton & Co., Inc., Chgo., 1966-69, account exec., 1969-73, br. mgr., 1973-85; nat. sales mgr. E.F. Hutton & Co., Inc., 1983—, sr. v.p. commodities, 1985—; dir. Hutton Internat. Ltd., E.F. Hutton Commodity Res. Fund. Ltd.; dir., v.p. E.F. Hutton Commodity Mgmt., Hutton Commodity Ptnrs., E.F. Hutton Futures Fund; mem. Mid Am. Commodity Exchange, Chgo., bd. dirs., 1981-83; mem. coms. Chgo. Bd. Trade; mem. Chgo. Bd. Trade Exchange, Chgo. Mercantile Exchange. Home: 1665 Duffy Ln Bannockburn IL 60015 Office: Prudential Bache Secutities 1900 E Golf Rd Schaumburg IL 60173

BANK, JAN THEODOR MARIA, historian, educator; b. Amsterdam, The Netherlands, May 10, 1940; s. Jan A. and Antonia H.M. (Boezeman) B.; m. Nevenka Nesic, Dec. 23, 1969; 1 child, Ivan. PhD, U. Amsterdam, 1983. Newspaper journalist de Volkskrant, Amsterdam, The Netherlands, 1965-75; staff mem. history dept., State U., Utrecht, The Netherlands, 1975-83, lectr. modern history, 1983-88; prof. history Erasmus U., Rotterdam, The Netherlands, 1985-88; prof. Dutch history Leiden U., The Netherlands, 1988—; mem. adv. bd. de Volkskrant, Amsterdam, 1980—; v.p. The Netherlands Film Mus., Amsterdam, 1985—. Author numerous books on Indonesian Revolution and Dutch polit. history; editor TV programs on Dutch history, 1987—. Recipient Van Blankenstein award Leiden U., 1970, Nieuwenhuys award Assn. Sci. Filmmakers, 1986. Mem. Internat. Orgn. Mass Media and History. Office: Leiden Univ, PO Box 9515, 2300 RA Leiden The Netherlands

BANK, WILLIAM JULIUS, manufacturing company executive; b. N.Y.C., Dec. 17, 1913; s. Hyman and Mollie (Berg) B.; m. Esther Sawney Kaplan, Aug. 24, 1935; children: Barrie Alan, Michael Stephan, Marshall Peter. Student, U. Va., 1945, U. La., 1946, Purdue U., 1948. Foreman Simon Ackerman, 1929-36; mgr. Eagle Clothes, 1936-41; field insp. Phila. Q.M. Depot, 1941-42; plant mgr. Stuart Keith Mfg. Co., 1942-47; asst. v.p. Blue Ridge Mfrs., Inc., 1947-49, v.p. mfg., 1949-58, v.p. research and devel., 1958-59, asst. to pres., 1960, exec. v.p., 1961-68; exec. v.p. Imperial Shirt Co., 1961-68; ptnr. Jonbil Inc., 1966-67, exec. v.p., 1967-68, pres., 1968-70, owner, 1970—, chmn., chief exec. officer, 1984—; pres. Blue Jeans Mfg. Co., Inc., 1968—. Chmn. Employment Physically Handicapped, Lynchburg, Va., 1958; pres. Apparel Research Found. Mem. Am. Mgmt. Assn., Am. Soc. Personnel Mgmt., Soc. Advancement Mgmt., Am. Apparel Mfrs. Assn. (bd. dirs., mktg. com.), Nat. Acad. Scis. (adv. com. on textiles and apparel research), Inter Am. Commn. Textile Square Club (exec. com.). Lodges: Masons, Shriners. Home: 60 Ward Dr New Rochelle NY 10804 Office: Jonbil Inc 350 Fifth Ave New York NY 10001

BANKA, MUHAMMAD RAMZAN, financial administrator, consultant; b. Bhagiari, Pakistan, 1943; s. M. Sardar Din and Sardaran Banka; m. Rafia Banka, Dec. 15, 1964; 1 child, Zakia Nazila; m. Saida Banka, Nov. 15, 1979; 1 child, Muhammad Saeed. B Commerce, U. Karachi, Pakistan, 1967. Jr. acct. Gen. Tyre & Rubber Co. Pakistan Ltd., Karachi, 1963-76; asst. mgr. fin. Fed. Chem. & Ceramics Corp., Karachi, 1976-77; cost acct. Tanzania Shoe Co., Ltd., Dares-Salaam, 1978-79; chief acct. United Refrigeration Industries, Karachi, 1980-81, Morogoro (Tanzania) Shoe Co., Ltd., 1982-83; sr. mgr. fin. Sind Engring. (PVT) Ltd., Karachi, 1984—; mgmt. cons. Fellow Inst. Cost and Mgmt. Accts. Pakistan. Home: 12/60-4 Model Colony, Karachi 27, Pakistan Office: Sind Engring (PVT) Ltd, PO Box 5262, Karachi Pakistan

BANKS, J(OSEPH) EUGENE, investment economist; b. Kirksville, Mo., Jan. 26, 1908; s. Charles and Etta May (Dille) B.; m. Ruth Henckler, Oct. 1, 1932; m. Barbara H. Vietor, Apr. 21, 1956; 1 foster dau., Diana V. Mundy. B.S., Washington U., 1930. Investment analyst Boatmen's Nat. Bank, St. Louis, 1930-31; mgr. pvt. investment funds St. Louis, 1932-37; market analyst Merrill Lynch, Pierce, Fenner & Beane, N.Y.C., 1938-42; investment economist Brown Bros. Harriman & Co., N.Y.C., 1942, 45-80; asst. mgr. Brown Bros. Harriman & Co., 1950-57, mgr., 1957-61, ptnr., 1962—, head instnl. div., 1950-77; now semi-ret. Author: Guides to Stock Market Policy, 1949, Institutional Investment Guides, 1955, Guides to Growth Stock Investing, 1959; also articles in field. Bd. dirs. St. Margaret's House, N.Y.C. Served to lt. comdr. USCGR, 1942-45. Mem. Mil. Order World Wars, Navy League, Pilgrims, Theta Xi. Episcopalian. Club: Downtown Assn. (N.Y.C.). Home: 880 Fifth Ave New York NY 10021 also: Long Beach Rd Saint James NY 11780 Office: 59 Wall St New York NY 10005

BANKS, LISA JEAN, government official; b. Chelsea, Mass., Dec. 19, 1956; d. Bruce H. and Jean P. (Como) Banks. B.S. in Bus. Adminstrn., Northeastern U., 1979. Coop trainee IRS, Boston, 1975-79, revenue officer, Reno, 1979-81, spl. agt., Houston, 1981-84, Anchorage, 1984—, fed. womens program mgr., 1980-81. Recipient Superior Performance award IRS, 1981. Mem. Nat. Assn. Treasury Agts., Nat. Assn. Female Execs. Democrat. Roman Catholic Office: PO Box 1500 Anchorage AK 99510

BANKS, RUSSELL, chemical company executive; b. N.Y.C., Aug. 2, 1919; s. Thomas and Fay (Cowen) B.; m. Janice Reed, July 19, 1949; 1 son, Gordon L. B.B.A., CCNY, 1936-40; J.D., N.Y. Law Sch., 1960. Bar: N.Y. 1961. Sr. acct. Selverne, Davis Co., N.Y.C., 1940-45; pvt. practice as C.P.A. N.Y.C., 1945-61; exec. v.p. Met. Telecommunications Corp., Plainview, N.Y., 1961-62; pres., chief exec. officer Grow Group, Inc. (formerly Grow Chem. Corp.), N.Y.C., 1962—; also dir. Grow Group, Inc. (formerly Grow Chem. Corp.); dir. Bainco Corp., Fenimore Fund; mem. regional adv. bd. Chem. Bank. Editor: Managing the Small Company. Chmn. Liberty Cup Races; bd. dirs. N.Y.C. Harbor Festival Found. Recipient award of achievement Sch. of Bus. Alumni Soc. of CCNY, 1977; Winthrop-Sears medal Chem. Industry Assn., 1980. Mem. Nat. Paint and Coatings Assn. (pres., bd. dirs., mem. exec. com.), Am. Mgmt. Assn. (gen. mgmt. planning council 1966—, also trustee), Conf. Bd. (regional council), Solvent Abuse Found. for Edn. (bd. dirs.). Clubs: Metropolitan (N.Y.C.); Annabel's (London). Home: 1000 Park Ave New York NY 10028 Office: Grow Group Inc 200 Park Ave New York NY 10166

BANKSTON, WILLIAM MARCUS, lawyer; b. San Angelo, Tex., Feb. 16, 1946; s. Wyatt Lester and Mary Alice (Powell) B.; m. Janna Coe Herridge, Aug. 15, 1965 (div.); children—Darla Kae, Kendra Lynne; m. Judith Ann Railsback, Nov. 20, 1981. B.A., Tex. Tech U., 1968, B.S., 1968; J.D., U. Tex., 1971. Bar: Alaska 1971, Tex. 1971, U.S. Tax Ct. 1983, U.S. Ct. Claims 1984, U.S. Supreme Ct. 1986. Assoc. Croft & Bailey, Anchorage, 1971-73; ptnr. Croft, Bailey, Guetschow & Bankston, 1973-74; instr. Anchorage Community Coll., 1972-74; ptnr. Greene & Bankston, Anchorage, 1974-76, Bankston, McCollum & Fossey, 1976—. Mem. ABA, Alaska Bar Assn., State Bar Tex. Methodist. Office: Bankston McCollum & Fossey PC 550 W 7th Suite 1800 Anchorage AK 99501

BANNISTER, SIR ROGER GILBERT, neurologist, college administrator; b. London, Mar. 23, 1929; s. Ralph and Alice B.; m. Moyre Elver Jacobson; 4 children. Student Univ. Coll. Sch., Exeter Coll. B.A. with honors in Physiology, Merton Coll., Oxford, 1950; M.Sc., St. Mary's Hosp., 1952; M.R.C.S., C.R.C.P., B.M., B.Ch., Oxford U., 1954, D.M., 1983; LL.D. (hon.), U. Liverpool, 1972; D.Litt. (hon.), U. Sheffield, 1978; numerous other hon. degrees. Cons., neurologist Nat. Hosp. for Nervous Disease, London and hon. cons. neurologist, St. Mary's Hosp., London; v.p. St. Mary's Hosp. Med. Sch., 1985—; master Pembroke Coll., Oxford, 1985—; hon. cons. neurologist, Oxford Regional and Dist. Health Authority. Author: First Four Minutes, 1955; editor: Brain's Clinical Neurology; Autonomic Failure, 1988; contbr. numerous articles to med. jours. Brit. Mile Champion, 1951, 53, 54; world record one mile, 1st mile run in under 4 minutes, 1954; recipient Hans-Heinrich Siegbert prize, 1977. Club: Oxford U. Athletic (pres. 1948). Address: Pembroke Coll, Oxford England

BANNY, JEAN KONAN, Ivory Coast minister of defense and marine; b. Divo, Ivory Coast, July 14, 1929; B.Law. Minister of def. of Ivory Coast, 1981—. Decorated comdr. de l'ordre du Merite Sportif (Ivory Coast); chevalier de l'ordre du Merite Sportif (France); grand officier de la Legion de'Honneur. Office: Ministry of Def, Abidjan Ivory Coast *

BAÑOS, JOSE LUIS, banker, lawyer, sugar planter; b. New Orleans, Aug. 25, 1918; s. Jose Rodrigo and Julia Sussmann (del Olmo) B.; m. Catherine Dunbar, Mar. 29, 1927; children—Catherine, Julia, Margot, J. Luis, George. B.B.A., Tulane U., 1939, LL.B., 1946. Bar: La. 1946, U.S. Supreme Ct. 1970. With Whitney Nat. Bank of New Orleans, 1946—, v.p., 1960-83; of counsel Jones Walker Waechter Poitevent Carrere & Denegre, 1984-88; past lectr. Sch. Banking of South, Baton Rouge, Midwest Sch. Banking, Madison, Wis., Emory U., Atlanta. Past pres. pres.'s council St. Mary's Dominican Coll., New Orleans; bd. dirs., past pres. World Trade Ctr. New Orleans; bd. dirs.

Online Resource Exchange, Inc., New Orleans Symphony; chmn., bd. dirs. White-Lafourche, Inc.; vice chmn. devel. com. Tulane U. Served to lt. comdr. USNR 1941-46; PTO, ETO. Decorated knight comdr. Isabel La Catolica (Spain); knight Grand Cross, Bacula de la Paz (Vatican), knight grand cross Mil. and Hospitaller Order of St. Lazarus of Jerusalem (Malta); knight Sovereign order of St. John of Jerusalem knight comdr. with star. Equestrian Order of the Holy Sepulchre (Rome). Mem. ABA, La. Bar Assn., La. Bankers Assn., New Orleans C. of C. (past sec.-treas. exec. com.), Phi Delta Theta. Roman Catholic. Clubs: Boston, Southern Yacht, Pickwick, New Orleans Country, Bayou Country, Plimsoll, Lake Shore, Army Navy (Washington). Home: 9 Richmond Pl New Orleans LA 70115 Office: Pan Am Life Ctr 601 Poydras New Orleans LA 70130

BANOVIC, ZLATKO JOSIP, electronic company executive; b. Virovitica, Slavonia, Yugoslavia, Mar. 10, 1951; s. Zvonko and Nada (Petraš) B.; m. Venuška Novoselnik, Apr. 30, 1977; children: Hrvoje, Ana. Diploma in electrotechnics engring., Electrotehnic Acad., Zagreb, 1974. Prof. Electrotechnic Medium Sch., Zagreb, 1974-76; maintenance engr. Televizia-Video Maintenance Dept., Zagreb, 1976-77, 78, sr. maintenance engr., 1978, sr. systems engr., 1979; head engr. Automatic Measurement Equipment, Zagreb, 1977-78; chief engr. Televizia-Video Maintenance Dept., Zagreb, 1980; owner Video Electronic Lab., Zagreb, 1986—; expert for electronics Republic Ct. of Croatia, Zagreb, 1986; video cons., projector various pvt. recording studios. Author: (sports competition videos) Central Video Masters, 1980-84. Recipient Achievement award AMPEX European Tng. Cen., 1980-85. Mem. United Engrs. Soc. Yugoslavia, United Republic Experts Ct. Croatia. Office: Video Electronic Lab Ltd, K Zahradnika 25, 41000 Zagreb, Croatia Yugoslavia

BANSE, TIMOTHY PAUL, consultant, author; b. Clinton, Iowa, Oct. 12, 1951; s. Robert Louis and Helen Leone B.; B.A. in Journalism, U. Iowa, 1981; children—Christopher Patrick, Jessica Marie. Pres., Banse and Kelso Assocs., Iowa City, 1979—; author articles in mags. including Mechanix Illustrated, Timex/Sinclair User, Personal Computer World (U.K.), MicroComputing, Boating, Pick-Up, Van; contbg. editor Motor Boating and Sailing; monthly columnist Tim Banse's Engine Room. Served with M.I., Spl. Forces, U.S. Army, 1969-72. Recipient Wilbur Petersen award U. Iowa Sch. Journalism, 1975, James W. Blackburn award, 1975. Mem. Am. Defense Preparedness Assn., Washington Ind. Writers Group, Writers Guild Am., Author's Guild, Authors League Am. Author: Home Applications and Games for Atari Computer, The Atari Book of Secrets. Home: 3512 N 2d St Clinton IA 52732 Office: PO Box 5535 Coralville IA 52241

BANTA, HENRY DAVID, physician, educator; b. Electra, Tex., Mar. 3, 1938; arrived in The Netherlands, 1985; s. Henry Eugene and Hazel (Rippy) B.; divorced; children: Elizabeth Christian, Barbara Shawn, Michael David, Heather Alexandra. Student, Duke U., 1956-59, MD, 1963; MPH, Harvard U., 1968, MS, 1969. Diplomate Am. Bd. Preventive Medicine. Intern King County Hosp., Seattle, 1963-64; resident U. Wash. Hosps., Seattle, 1964-65, Health Services Adminstrn. Harvard Sch. Pub. Health, 1968-69; from asst. to assoc. prof. med. tech. Mt. Sinai Sch. Medicine, N.Y.C., 1969-75; from researcher to asst. dir. office tech. assessment U.S. Congress, Washington, 1975-83; dep. dir. Pan Am. Health Orgn., Washington, 1983-85; prof. health econs. U. Limburg, Maastricht, The Netherlands, 1987—; cons. WHO, Hague, The Netherlands and Copenhagen, 1985—, European Commn., Brussels, 1986—, World Bank, Washington, 1987—, Netherlands Ministry Health, Hague, 1987—, Nordic Council, Stockholm, 1987. Author: (with others) Toward Rational Technology in Medicine, 1981, Anticipating and Assessing Health Care Technology, 1987; contbr. articles to profl. jours. Served to lt. comdr. USPHS, 1965-67. Milbank Fund fellow, 1970-73, Robert Wood Johnson Health Policy fellow, 1974, Ctr. Advanced Study Behavioral Sci. fellow, 1986. Fellow Am. Pub. Health Assn.; mem. Internat. Soc. Tech. Assessment in Health Care (bd. dirs. 1985—), Assn. Tchrs. Preventive Medicine (bd. dirs. 1984-87). Office: Health Council, PO Box 90517, 2909 LM Hague The Netherlands

BANTON, MICHAEL PARKER, educator; b. Birmingham, Eng., Sept. 8, 1926; s. Francis Clive and Kathleen Blanche (Parkes) B.; m. Rut Marianne Jacobson, July 23, 1952; children: Sven Christopher, Ragnhild Cecilia, Lars Nicholas, Dagmar Hulda. BSc, London Sch. of Econs., 1950; PhD, U. Edinburgh, 1954, DSc, 1964. Lectr. in social anthropolgy U. Edinburgh, Scotland, 1954-62, reader in social anthropology, 1962-65; prof. sociology U. Bristol, Eng., 1965—, pro vice chancellor, 1985-88. Justice of the Peace, Bristol, 1966—; mem. Royal Commn. on Criminal Procedure, 1978-81, Royal Commn. on Bermuda, 1978, UN com. on Elimination of Racial Discrimination, 1986—. Served with Royal Naval Res., 1944-47. Mem. Royal Anthrop. Inst. (pres. 1987—). Office: U Bristol, 12 Woodland Rd, Bristol BS8 1UQ, England

BAPTIE, CHARLES, photographer, printer, publisher; b. Munhall, Pa., Mar. 13, 1914; s. Charles and Constance B.; m. Joan Pratt, Jan. 1, 1970; 1 son by previous marriage, Ronald. Photographer, Trans World Airways, Pitts., 1933-34, Capital Airlines, Washington, 1935-45; freelance photographer, Annandale, Va., 1945—; illustrator numerous books; owner, operator Charles Baptie Studios, Annandale, 1945—; cons. graphic arts. Mem. Photog. Soc. Am. (asso.), Nat. Press Club, Nat. Photographers Assn. Author: (with Ollie Atkins) Camera on Assignment, 1958; (with Hope Ridings Miller) Great Houses of Washington, D.C., 1970; (with Jack Lloyd) How to Play Baseball; (with Margaret MacBeth Seiler) Mid the Hills of Pennsylvania, 1980; The Steel Valley, 1982; Capital Airlines a Nostalgic Flight into the Past, 1984; picture editor 16-vol. United States History, 1963—; photo illustrator Guest House of the Presidents (Eleanor Lee Templeman), 1980. Office: 4124 Village Ct Annandale VA 22003

BAPTIST, JEREMY EDUARD, allergist; b. Chgo., Mar. 22, 1940; s. Arthur Henry and Margaret Jane (Beck) B.; m. Sylvia Evelyn Bonin, July 21, 1962; children—Sarah, Margaret, Catherine. B.S. in Physics, U. Chgo., 1960, Ph.D. in Biophysics (USPHS predoctoral fellow), 1966; M.D., U. Mo., Kansas City, 1978. Asst. prof. radiation biophysics U. Kans., 1966-73; claims authorizer Social Security Adminstrn., 1974-75; intern in medicine Northwestern U., 1978-79; allergist Speer Allergy Clinic, Shawnee Mission, Kans., 1979—, v.p., 1985—. Co-author: Handbook of Clinical Allergy, 1982; contbr. to Britannica Yearbook of Science and the Future, 1973, 74; mem. editorial bd. Topics in Allergy and Clinical Immunology, 1982-83. Appointed mem. Ethnic Enrichment Commn. of Kansas City, Mo., 1988—. Brown-Hazen grantee, 1970. Fellow Am. Assn. Clin. Immunology and Allergy; mem. So. Med. Assn., AMA, Am. Coll. Allergists, Kans. Med. Soc., Johnson County Med. Soc., AAAS, N.Y. Acad. Scis., Internat. Corr. Soc. Allergists (asst. editor Allergy Letters 1984-85, assoc. editor 1985—), Internat. Assn. Aerobiology, Sigma Xi. Mem. Reorganized Ch. of Jesus Christ of Latter-day Saints. Lodge: Vasa (chmn., pres. Kansas City club 1986—). Home: 3501 W 92d St Leawood KS 66206 Office: 5811 Outlook Dr Shawnee Mission KS 66202

BAPTISTA, WILSON, JR., textile company executive; b. Belo Horizonte, Minas Gerais, Brazil, June 21, 1945; s. Wilson and Hortensia (Teixeira de Lima) B.; m. Ana Maria Lopes Nunes, Feb. 8, 1971; children: Manuel and Pedro (twins). Degree in Bus. Adminstrn., Pontificia U. Catolica, Minas Gerais, 1979, degree in econs., 1979. Cert. bus. adminstr. Computer programmer various cos., Belo Horizonte, 1969-72; systems analyst Grupo Banco Co. Industries M.G., Belo Horizonte, 1972-74, Engedata S.A., Belo Horizonte, 1974-75; EDP mgr., cons. RR Projetos and Consultoria, Belo Horizonte, 1975-78; EDP mgr., project cons. Leme Engenharia, Belo Horizonte, 1979-82; planning asst., chief exec. officer Companhia Indsl. Belo Horizonte, 1982—; cons. in field, 1974—; tech. coordinator info. program Postgrad. Studies Ctr., Faculty Adminstrn. Champagnat, Belo Horizonte, 1983. Author: An Introduction to Cobol, 1972. Mem. Soc. Brazilian Planners (bd. dirs.), Assn. Brazilian Adminstrs. Roman Catholic. Club: Mineiro dos Cacadores. Home: Rua Pium i 312 #303, 30 310 Belo Horizonte Brazil Office: Companhia Indsl Belo Horizonte, Rua Senhora Conceicao 780, 31 150 Belo Horizonte Brazil

BAR, CHRISTIAN FRIEDRICH-WILHELM VON, legal educator; b. Hannover, Fed. Republic Germany, May 5, 1952; s. Otto Ludwig and Elisabeth (Reichardt) von Bar; m. Ingard von Prittwitz und Gaffron, June 5, 1981; children: Moritz, Philipp, Ludwig, Cecilie. Dr. jur., U. Göttingen (W.Ger.), 1976, Dr. Jur. habil., 1979. Privat dozent U. Göttingen, 1979-81; prof. law U. Osnabrück, Fed. Republic Germany, 1981—, dir. Inst. European Law, 1985, Inst. Pvt. Internat. Law, 1988, dean, 1988; research fellow Churchill Coll., Cambridge, Eng., 1981-82; vis. fellow Waseda U., Tokyo, 1985; invited prof. Aix-en-Provence, 1986. Author: Territorialità t des Warenzeichens, 1977; Verkehrspflichten, 1980 (trans. into Japanese 1981); co-author: Richterliche Rechtspolitik im Haftungsrecht, 1981; author: Internationales Eherecht, 1983, Internationales Privatrecht I, 1987; contbr. to Internat. Ency. Comparative Law, also articles in German, Italian, Austrian and Japanese legal jours. Ehrenitter des Johanniterordens. Mem. Deutsche Zivilrechtslehrervereinigung, Société de législation comparée, Deutsche Gesellschaft für Rehtsvergleichung, Deutscher Rat für IPR, Deutsche Gesellschaft für Volkerrecht, others. Club: Corps Bremensia (Gottingen). Home: Rolandstrasse 15, D-4500 Osnabruck Federal Republic of Germany Office: Inst für Internat, Privatrecht und Rechtsvergleich, Postfach 44-69, D-4500 Osnabrück Federal Republic of Germany

BARABE, TIMOTHY CRAIG, chemical company executive; b. Hyannis, Mass., Mar. 15, 1953; s. Eugene George Barabe and Myrtle Elizabeth (Poole) Still; m. Anne Jeannette Labbe, June 12, 1976; children: Gregory, Deborah. BBA, U. Mass., 1975; MBA, U. Chgo., 1977. Mgr. trainee Olin Corp., Stamford, Conn., 1977-78; fin. analyst Olin Corp., New Haven, 1978-80, mgr. internat. fin., 1980-82; bus. analyst CIBA-GEIGY, Hawthorne, N.Y., 1982-84; controller CIBA-GEIGY, Basel, Switzerland, 1984-87; mgr. reporting and analysis CIBA-GEIGY, Basel, 1987-88, dir. corp. fin., 1988—. Treas. Internat. Sch. Basel, 1986-87, now chmn. 1988. Office: CIBA-GEIGY Corp 444 Saw Mill River Rd Ardsley NY 10502

BARAC, BOSKO A., neurologist, educator; b. Zagreb, Yugoslavia, Sept. 11, 1930; s. Antun Mate and Nevenka Mihovil Barac; m. Dragica R. Sokacic, Sept. 21, 1963; children: Iva, Ana, Mirna. MD, U. Zagreb, 1956, Dr. Med. Sc., 1965. Neuropsychiatrist Hosp. Dr. M. Stojanovič, Zagreb, 1959-62; clin. asst. dept. neurology Med. Faculty U. Zagreb, 1965-68, asst. prof. neurology, 1968-75, assoc. prof., 1975-77, prof., 1977—, founder, 1st head neurol. intensive care unit, 1970-79, chief neurology, 1979-87; organizer symposia on cerebrovascular disease, 1971, 74, 79, 85; sec.-gen. Internat. Neuropsychiat. Symposia, Pula, Yugoslavia, 1985—; v.p. Assembly for Sci. Work Croatia, Zagreb, 1982, pres., 1985-87. Author: Neurology, 1978, 79; pres. editorial bd. Neurologija; contbr. over 200 articles to profl. jours. Dep. Parliament Croatia, 1978-82. Fellow Intensive Care Soc. of the Brit. Med. Assn.; mem. Assn. Neurology and Psychiatry Yugoslavia (sec.-gen. 1965-68, trustee 1974—, pres. 1979—), Soc. E.E.G. and Clin. Neurophysiology Croatia (pres. 1972-81), Med. Acad. Zagreb, N.Y. Acad. Scis., Am. Acad. Neurology (hon. corr.), Am. Neurol. Assn., World Fedn. Neurology (Yugoslav del. 1984—), Brit. Med. Assn. Office: U Zagreb Clin Ctr, Dept Neurology, 12 Kispaticeva, 41000 Zagreb Yugoslavia

BARAKAT, GHALEB ZAKI, diplomat; b. Jaffa, Palestine, Sept. 20, 1927; s. Zaki and Fatmeh B.; m. Jalia al Imam, May 4, 1959; children: Sireen, Salwa, Zaki. BBA honours, American U., Beirut, Lebanon, 1949. Tchr. Nat. Coll., Tripoli, Lebanon, 1949-50; tchr., asst. to prin. Tchrs. Coll., Triploi, Libya, 1950-52; with Jordan Civil Service, 1952; chief clk., press attache Jordan Tourist Dept., Jerusalem, 1952-54; tourist, press attache Royal Jordan Embassy, Rome, 1954-60; dir. gen. Jordan Tourism Authority, Amman, 1960-72; dir. ALTA/The Royal Jordanian Airline, 1963-74; undersec. Ministry of Tourism and Antiquities, 1967-72; lectr. econs. and commerce U. Jordan, Amman, 1967-79; minister transport and tourism 1972, minister of tourism and antiquities, 1972-79; chmn. Jordan Hotels and Resthouses Corp., 1973-79; spl. envoy World Tourism Orgn., 1980; ambassador Permanent Rep. of Jordan to the UN, Geneva, 1980-85; mem. UN Commn. Human Rights, Geneva, 1980-85; asst. dir.-gen. Internat. Labour Orgn., Geneva, Arab region, 1986—. Contbr. articles and booklets on tourism to profl. jours. Recipient Chevalier de la Couronne, Belgium, 1958, Istiqlal decoration, Jordan, 1959, 61, Kawkab decoration, 1964. Mem. Arab Tourist Union (pres. 1964, 70). Clubs: Royal Automobile (dir. 1966-75), SKal (hon. pres. 1975-85). Home: PO Box 9064, Amman Jordan Office: Internat Labour Orgn, PO Box 500, 1211 Geneva 22, Switzerland

BAR-AM, MICHA, photographer; b. Berlin, Aug. 26, 1930; came to Israel; m. Orna Zmirin, 1961; children—Barak, Nimrod. Educated Israeli pub. schs., until age 14. Locksmith, mounted guard, youth instr. Kibbutz Gesher-Haziv, Western Galilee, Israel, 1949-57; photojournalist Bamahane mag., Israel, 1957-66; free-lance photojournalist, Israeli newspapers, 1966-67; photo-corr. N.Y. Times, Middle East, 1968—; assoc. mem. Magnum Photos, Paris and N.Y.C., 1968—; adviser photography Mus. Art, Tel Aviv, from 1977; one-man shows: Journalists House, Tel Aviv, 1958, 60, 62, Israel Mus., Jerusalem, 1974, The Little Gallery, Jerusalem, 1974, Neikrug Gallery, N.Y.C., 1978, Mus. of Jewish Diaspora, Tel Aviv, 1979, 80, White Gallery, Tel Aviv, 1981, G. Ray Hawkins Gallery, Los Angeles, 1981, Internat. Ctr. Photography, N.Y.C., 1982, Judah L. Magnes Mus., Berkeley, Calif., 1983; group shows include: Tel Aviv Mus., 1967, 78, Jewish Mus., N.Y.C. (also on tour U.S. and Can.), 1968, Israel Mus., Jerusalem (travelled to Jewish Mus., N.Y.C., then tour U.S.), 1973, White Gallery, 1981, Gallery Photog. Arts, North Olmstead, Ohio, 1982; represented in permanent collections: Israel Mus., Tel Aviv Mus., Mus. of Jewish Diaspora, Bibliotheque Nationale, Paris, Photographers' Gallery, London, Internat. Ctr. Photography, N.Y.C.; photographer books: Across Sinai, 1957; Castle of Shells and Sand, 1958; (text by Moshe Brilliant) Portrait of Israel, 1970; The Israel Air Force, 1971; Bat-Chen: The Story of the Women's Corps of the Israeli Army, 1971; (text by Arnold Sherman) When God Judged: A Yom Kippur War Battle Report, 1973; (text by Tammar Avidar-Ettinger) On Beauties, Men, and All the Rest, 1976; Israel: Face of a People, 1978; (text by Burton Bernstein) Sinai: The Great and Terrible Wilderness, 1979; (text by Michael Snunit) Yoram and the Puppy, 1981; photographer, author book: The Jordan, 1981; editor (with Cornell Capa): Jerusalem: City of Mankind, 1974; photo editor: I.D.F. at Eighteen, 1966. Active Haganah, 1945-48; served with Palmach unit Israeli Inf., 1948-49. Office: PO Box 923, Ramat Gan 52109, Israel *

BARANY, JAMES WALTER, industrial engineering educator; b. South Bend, Ind., Aug. 24, 1930; s. Emery Peter and Rose Anne (Kovacsics) B.; m. Judith Ann Flanigan, Aug. 6, 1960 (div. 1982); 1 child, Cynthia. BS in Indsl. Engring., Notre Dame U., 1953; MS in Indsl. Engring., Purdue U., 1958, PhD, 1961. Prodn. worker Studebaker-Packard Corp., 1949-52; prodn. liaison engr. Bendix Aviation Corp., 1955-56; mem. faculty Sch. Indsl. Engring. Purdue U., West Lafayette, Ind., 1958—, now prof., assoc. head indsl. engring. Sch. Indsl. Engring.; cons. Taiwan Productivity Ctr., Western Electric, Gleason Gear Works, Am. Oil Co., Timken Co. Served with U.S. Army, 1954-55. Recipient best counselor award Purdue U., 1978, best engring. tchr. award, 1983, 88; NSF and Easter Seal Found. research grantee, 1961, 63, 64, 65. Mem. Inst. Indsl. Engring. (Fellows award 1982), Am. Soc. Engring. Edn., Methods Time Measurement Research Assn., Human Factors Soc., Order of Engr., Sigma Xi, Alpha Pi Mu, Tau Beta Pi. Home: 101 Andrew Pl Apt 201 West Lafayette IN 47906 Office: Purdue U Dept Indsl Engring West Lafayette IN 47907

BARBACHANO, FERNANDO G.R., banker; b. Merida, Yucatan, Mexico, Apr. 24, 1926; s. Fernando P. and Carmen (G.R.) B.; student Harvard U., U. Yucatan; m. Maruja G. Herrero, Dec. 11, 1947; children—Fernando, Maruja, Carmen, Cristina, Isabel, Juan. Founder, present chmn. constrn. co., food packing co., land-marine transp. co., airline co., also chain of hotels; founder 2 schs. tourism; developer Cozumel Island, Mexican Caribbean for tourists. chmn. bd. bank. Hon. consul of Guatemala in Merida, Mexico. Chmn. bd. dirs. Maya Found. Mem. Nat. Hotel Assn. (dir.), Nat. Travel Agts. Assn. (dir.), Merida C. of C. (dir.), Chamber Public Transport, Chamber Constrn., Chamber Tourism, Chamber Air Transport, Bankers Club, Internat. Assn. Travel Agts., Am. Soc. Travel Agts., Am. Hotel Mgmt. Assn., AMAV, AMH, COTAL, ICA. Club: Country. Home: 495 Montejo Ave, Merida Yucatan, Mexico Office: 472 60th St, Merida Yucatan, Mexico

BARBANNEAU, JEAN-LUC, publishing executive; b. Algiers, Algeria, Sept. 18, 1949; arrived in Eng., 1969; MA, U. Sorbonne, Paris, 1970. Editor Harrap Ltd., London, 1978-79, mng. editor, 1979, editorial dir., 1979—; bd. dirs. Impact Books, London. Office: Harrap Ltd, 19-23 Ludgate Hill, EC4M 7PD London England

BARBARA, AGATHA, former president Republic of Malta; b. Zabbar, Malta, Mar. 11, 1923; d. Joseph and Antonia (Agius) B.; ed. Govt. Grammar Sch., Valletta; Ph.D. h.c., Beijing U. Tchr., Edn. Dept., Valletta, Malta, 1942-47; mem. exec. com. Malta Labour Party, 1947—, also chmn. women's sect., chmn. exec. com.; mem. Maltese Ho. of Reps., 1947—; minister of Edn., 1955-58, 71-74; minister of Labor, Culture and Welfare, 1974-81; intermittantly dep. prime minister; pres. Republic of Malta, 1982-87. Mem. Air Raid Precautions, Supr. Victory Kitchens Cen. Ammunition Depot, World War II; gen. mgr. Freedom Press. Decorated Stara Planina 1st degree (Bulgaria), Order of Nat. Flag 1st class (Dem. People's Republic Korea), Hishan-e-Pakistan 1st degree; recipient Keys and Freedom of Cities of Lahore (Pakistan), Buenos Aires, Lima (Peru), San José (Costa Rica), Bogota (Colombia), Aden (People's Repubic of Yemen), Montevideo (Uruguay); hon. academician Accademia Universale Alessandro Magno, Prato, Italy. Mem. Bus. and Profl. Women U.K., St. John Alliance U.K., Internat. Social Democratic Women, Women's Internat. Democratic Fedn., Maltese Settlers Club (hon. pres.). Office: Kenn Taghna, Wied Il-Ghajn Street, Zabbar Malta

BARBE, WALTER BURKE, education educator; b. Miami, Fla., Oct. 30, 1926; s. Victor Elza and Edith (Burris) B.; m. Marilyn E. Wood, Feb. 7, 1967; 1 son, Frederick Walter. B.S., Northwestern U., 1949, M.A., 1950, Ph.D., 1953. Tchr. Dade County Bd. Pub. Instrn., 1947; asst. Psycho-Ednl. Clinic, Northwestern U., 1949-50; instr. psychology, dir. reading clinic Baylor U., 1950; asst. prof. elementary edn. Kent State U., 1952-53, prof., head spl. edn. dept., 1960-64; adj. prof. U. Pitts., 1964-72, Ohio State U., 1972—; editor Highlights for Children, 1964—, dir., 1965—; prof. edn., dir. Jr. League Reading Center, U. Chattanooga, 1953-59; dir. Zaner-Bloser, 1972—; bd. dirs. internat. council Improvement of Reading Inst., 1954-55. Author: Reading Clinic Directory, 1955, (with Ralph Roberts) Teenage Tales, 1957, (with Dorothy Hinman) We Build Our Words, 1957, Educators Guide to Personalized Reading, 1961, Helping Children Read Better, 1970; sr. author: (with Paul Witty) Creative Growth with Handwriting Series, 1975, Personalized Reading Instruction: New Techniques that Increase Reading Skill and Comprehension, 1975, (with Jerry Abbott) Barbe Reading Skills Check Lists, 1975, (with Swassing and Milone) Teaching through Modality Strengths: Concepts and Practices, 1979; sr. editor: (with Joseph Renzulli) Psychology and Education of the Gifted: Readings, 3d edit, 1980, Basic Skills in Kindergarten, 1980, Resource Book for Kindergarten Teachers, 1980; editor: Teaching of Reading; Selections, 1965, (with Edward Frierson) Educating Children with Learning Disabilities, 1967, Compass Points in Literature, Searchlights in Literature, 1969, Helping Children with Special Needs Series, 1974; author: (with Francis, Braun) Spelling: Basic Skills for Effective Communication, 1982, (with Lucas, Wasylyk) Basic Skills for Effective Communication, 1984, (with others) Handwriting: Basic Skills and Application Series, 1984, Growing Up Learning, 1985, (with Francis, Gentry, San Jose) Spelling Connections: Words Into Language, 1988. Served with AUS, 1944-46. Fellow Am. Psychol. Assn.; mem. Nat. Assn. Gifted Children (pres. 1958). Democrat. Presbyterian. Home: Box 229 RD 1 Beach Lake PA 18405 Office: Highlights for Children Honesdale PA 18431

BARBEE, STEVEN GEORGE, engineer; b. Hastings, Nebr., Feb. 2, 1953; s. James Max and Betty Lavonne (Gustafson) B.; m. Deborah Kay Hultman, June 7, 1975; children—Paul Steven, David Lyle. A.B. summa cum laude in Physics and Math., Doane Coll., 1974; M.S. in Plasma Physics, Columbia U., 1976. Devel. engr. IBM Corp., East Fishkill, N.Y., 1978—. Contbr. articles to profl. jours. Patentee in field. Author jour. IBM Tech. Disclosure Bull. 1979. Mem. Am. Phys. Soc., Am. Vacuum Soc., Electrochem. Soc., N.Y. Acad. Scis. Republican. Episcopalian.

BARBER, ANTHONY PERRINOTT LYSBERG (BARON BARBER), banker; b. July 4, 1920; s. John Barber; m. Jean Patricia, 1950 (dec.); 2 children. MA, Oriel Coll., Oxford U. Barrister at law, Inner Temple, 1948, Doncaster, 1951-64; Altrincham and Sale, 1965-74; sec. to Under Sec. of State for Air, 1952-55; asst. whip, 1955-57; a Lord commr. of the Treasury, 1957-58; sec. to the Prime Minister, 1958-59; econ. sec. to Treasury, 1959-62; fin. sec. to Treasury, 1962-63; minister of Health, mem. of the Cabinet, 1963-64; chancellor of Duchy of Lancaster, 1970; Chancellor of the Exchequer, 1970-74; chmn. Standard Chartered Bank plc, London, 1974-87; govt. dir. Brit. Petroleum, 1979—. Chmn. Conservative Party Orgn., 1967-70; chmn. council Westminster Med. Sch., 1975; mem. Falkland Islands Inquiry, 1982. Office: Standard Chartered Bank plc, 38 Bishopsgate, London EC2N 4DF, England

BARBER, EUGENE JOHN, chemist; b. Kit Carson, Colo., Jan. 8, 1918; s. Emery Eugene and Addie Margaret (Craft) B.; m. Doris Margaret Pfeifer, Oct. 7, 1945; children—Gail Margaret, Thomas Allan, Daniel John, James Wallace. B.S., U. Nev., 1940; Ph.D., U. Wash., 1949. Research chemist SAM Labs. Columbia U., N.Y.C., 1942-45; research fellow U. Wash., Seattle, 1945-48; chemist Nuclear Div. Union Carbide Corp., Oak Ridge, 1948-77, sr. research sci., 1977-84; sr. research sci. Martin Marietta Energy Systems, Oak Ridge, 1984-85; cons. MMES, Oak Ridge, 1984—, corp. fellow, 1986—. Contbr. articles to profl. jours.; patentee in field. Patron Community Children's Theater, Kingston, Tenn., 1984. Mem. Am. Chem. Soc. (local sect. chmn., 1963-64), AAAS, Gideons Internat., Phi Beta Kappa, Sigma Xi, Phi Kappa Phi, Phi Lambda Upsilon. Republican. Presbyterian. Lodge: Lions (Kingston). Home: 122 Westcliff Dr PO Box 476 Kingston TN 37763

BARBER, FRANK DAVID, lawyer; b. Hot Springs, Ark., Apr. 2, 1929; s. Frank David and Mary Margaret (Venus) B.; m. Sarah Frances McMullan, Dec. 23, 1953 (div. 1967); children—Amanda, Frank David, Melanie, Annabel, John Paul; m. Mary Jane Burch, Dec. 28, 1974; children—Mary Jane Burch, William Cameron. Student U. Miss., 1947-48, postgrad., 1954-55; B.A., U. So. Miss., 1954; J.D., George Washington U., 1957. Bar: Miss. 1958, D.C. 1958, U.S. Dist. Ct. D.C. (D.C. Circuit), 1958, U.S. Supreme Ct. 1978, U.S. Ct. Appeals (5th, 11th cirs.) 1981. Atty. Gen. Legis. Investigating Com., Jackson, Miss., 1958-59; mem. Miss. State Senate, Jackson, 1960-64; exec. asst. to gov. of Miss., Jackson, 1964-68; atty. Miss. Agr. and Indsl. Bd., Jackson, 1968-72; legis. asst. U.S. Sen. James O. Eastland, Washington, 1972-78; sole practice, Jackson, 1978—. Author: The Pursuit of Excellence: Summary of Administration of Governor Paul B. Johnson, 1968. Del. Dem. Nat. Conv., Los Angeles, 1960, Atlanta, 1988. Served with U.S. Army, 1948-49, 50-52. Recipient Project Cairo award Am. Assn. States and Local History, 1967. Mem. ABA, Miss. State Bar Assn., Fed. Bar Assn., Miss. Hist. Soc., Hinds County Bar Assn., Omicron Delta Kappa, Phi Alpha Delta, Sigma Nu, Pi Kappa Delta, Alpha Gamma Rho. Roman Catholic. Clubs: University, Capital City Petroleum (Jackson); Nat. Capital Democratic (Washington). Lodges: Masons, Royal Arch., Scottish Rite, York Rite. Home: 4061 Roxbury Rd Jackson MS 39211 Office: 316 Heritage Bldg Congress at Capitol St Jackson MS 39201

BARBERA, AUGUSTO ANTONIO, public law educator, member of parliament; b. Aidone, Italy, June 25, 1938; s. Giovanni and Alessandra (Locatelli) B.; m. Maria Montemagno, Dec. 16, 1970; children: Alessandro, Teresa. Degree, U. of Catania Laurea, Giurisprudenz, Italy, 1960; postgrad., U. Heidelberg, Fed. Republic Germany. Prof. various colls., Catania, Ferrara, Bologna; prof. pub. law U. Bologna, Italy; M.P. Govt. of Italy. Contbr. articles to profl. jours. Communist. Roman Catholic. Home: 29 IV Raibolini, 40069 Bologna Italy Office: 33 Zamboni St, 40126 Bologna Italy

BARBIER, ANDRE ALBERT, surgeon; b. Dijon, France, Jan. 10, 1929; s. Henri and Lucienne (Mias) B.; m. Nicole Renee Philippe, July 12, 1958; children—Helene, Isabelle, Anne. Baccalaureat, Lycee Carnot, Dijon, 1948; Certificat Physique Chimbie Biologie Faculte Scis., Dijon, 1949; Doctorat Medicine, Faculte Medicine, Paris, 1955; Chirurgien des Hopital Val De Grace, 1964. Chirugien militaire Hopitaux Militaire, Alger-Toulouse, 1956-65; with Centre Experimentation du Pacifique, Tahiti, 1965-67; surgeon Hopital Lyautey, Strasbourg, France, 1968, Hopital Averoes, Casablanca, Moroco, 1968-70, Hopital Grall, Saigon, Vietnam, 1970-74, Liberal Clinique, Fontenay Aux Roses, France, 1976—. Served to col. Armed Forces, 1956-75. Decorated Croix De Guerre, Croix De La Valeur Militaire, Chevalier Ordre Du Merite, Chevalier Legion Honneur. Fellow Assn. Francaise De Chirurgie, Internat. Coll. Surgeons; mem. Societe Internationale de Chirurgie. Roman Catholic. Avocations: Tennis. Home: 18 Allee Fleurie, 92260 Fontenay Aux Roses France Office: Clinique Chirurgicale, 40r D Estienne D'Orves, 92260 Fontenay Aux Roses France

BARBIERI, MARGARET ELIZABETH, ballet dancer; b. Durban, South Africa, Mar. 2, 1947; came to Eng., 1963, naturalized, 1964; d. Ettore and Lea (Donati) B.; student ballet Iris Manning and Brownie Sutton, Durban, 1952-63; student Royal Ballet Sr. Sch., London, 1963-65. Mem. Royal Ballet, London, from 1965, prin. dancer, 1970-75, sr. prin. dancer, from 1975, appeared in Giselle, Sleeping Beauty, Swan Lake, Romeo and Juliet, Papillon, Taming of the Shrew, Lady and the Fool, Coppelia, Checkmate, Invitation, Lilac Garden, others; guest appearances in Germany, Norway, Czechoslovakia, Zimbabwe, South Africa, U.S.; TV appearances, including master class with Markova on Giselle, Sylphides, Swan Lake and Nutcracker, 1979, Coppelia, 1980. Roman Catholic. Travelled with Royal Ballet to France, Italy, Germany, Switzerland, Spain, Portugal, Holland, Finland, Norway, Egypt, Israel, Greece, Australia, N.Z., Far East, N. and S. Am.; numerous TV appearances. Office: Royal Ballet, London England

BARBIN, RYTHER LYNN, lawyer; b. Port Arthur, Tex., July 15, 1943; s. L.B. and Edna Mae (Ryther) B.; m. Marla Egbert Sankey, Dec. 24, 1987; 1 child, Jordan Ross. BBA, Tex. Tech U., 1966; JD, Baylor U., 1968. Bar: Tex. 1968, Hawaii, 1976, U.S. Dist. Ct. Hawaii, 1976; lic. realtor, Hawaii. Law clk. U.S. Dept. Justice, Washington, 1967; officer trust dept. Bank of Am., San Francisco, 1968-71; officer Investors Bank & Trust Co., Boston, 1972-74; sole practice, Wailuku, Hawaii, 1974-82, 84—; ptnr. Barbin & Ball, Wailuku, 1982-84; arbitrator Hi Supreme Ct. Bd. dirs. Maui United Way, 1980-88, v.p., 1987-88; mem. sch. bd. Maui Dist. Sch., 1980-84; state del., dist. council Hawaii Dems., Wailuku, 1978-84; Field Rep. for U.S. senator Daniel K. Inouye; campaign mgr. Dem. Presdl. Campaigns Maui County, 1983; vice-chmn. Maui County Dem. Party, 1986-87; bd. dirs. Maui Humane Soc., Maui Kokua Service. Recipient cert. of appreciation Gov. State of Hawaii, 1981. Mem. ABA, Hawaii Bar Assn. (bd. dirs.), Maui Bar Assn. (pres. 1984-86), Upcountry Jaycees Makawao (officer 1979-83). Episcopalian. Lodge: Rotary (pres. Wailuku club 1986-87). Home: 57 Lino Pl Pukalani HI 96788 Office: 61 N Church St Wailuku HI 96793

BARBOSA, LUIZ ZITTO, airline company executive; b. Porto Alegre, Rio Grande do Sul, Brazil, Sept. 23, 1935; s. Assis and Pedrolina (Zitto) B.; m. Vera Hedi Lorenz, Apr. 22, 1961; children: Tania Barbosa Reis, Ricardo Lorenz, Claudio Lorenz. Degree in econs., D. Pedro U., São Paulo, Brazil, 1972; degree in acctg., Fac. Tabajara, São Paulo, 1985. Mgr. cost. div. VARIG Airlines, São Paulo, 1963-70, mgr. cost and stats. dept., 1970-75, asst. to dir. acctg., 1975-84, acctg. directorate gen. supt., 1984—; adminstrv. council mem. Group Tropical Hotels, São Paulo, 1983-86; del., route coordinator IATA Cost Com., 1987. Treas. Luth. Ch. Brazil, São Paulo, 1986—, mem. council, 1985-86. Recipient Santos Dumont medal Aero. Ministry of Brazil, São Paulo, 1984. Fellow Regional Econ. Council, Regional Acctg. Council. Home: R Bela Vista 326 Apt 61, 04709 Sao Paulo Brazil Office: VARIG Airlines Acctg Dir, Pr Linneu Gomes-, Congonhas Airport, 04628 Sao Paulo Brazil

BARBOUR, JAMES KEITH, chemical packaging and distribution company executive; b. N.Y.C., Jan. 30, 1948; s. James Morse and Rita Elizabeth (Edwards) B.; B.A., Vanderbilt U., 1969; M.B.A. with distinction, Adelphi U., 1973; m. Carole Barbour, June 25, 1982; children: Scott Ryan, Allison Cori, Daniel Adam. With N.Y. Telephone Co., N.Y.C., 1970-76; with AT&T, Morristown, N.J., 1977-78; v.p. mktg. and adminstrn., v.p. ops. Chas. Schaefer Sons, Inc. (name now Schaefer Salt & Chem.), Elizabeth, N.J., 1978-82, v.p., 1982-83, exec. v.p., 1983-87, chief operating officer, 1982-87, pres., prin., 1987—; pres., prin. Klein Sales Corp., Woodbridge, N.J., 1982—; prin., pres. Apocalypse Inc., 1983—; cons. in field communications, strategic planning, reorgn., and negotiations. Mem. Republican Congl. Com.; water safety instr. ARC. Mem. Am. Mktg. Assn., Nat. Assn. Chem. Distbrs., Sales Assocs. Chem. Industry, Nat. Pilots Assn., Am. Mgmt. Assn., Aircraft Owners and Pilots Assn., U.S. Judo Assn. Clubs: Scarsdale (N.Y.) Golf; Fairmount Country; Rainbow Springs Golf and Country; Beacon Hill Country (corp. mem.); Atlantic Highlands Yacht, N.J. Chemist. Home: 933 W Front St Red Bank NJ 07701-5615 Office: PO Box 236 Elizabeth NJ 07207

BARCA, GEORGE GINO, winery executive; b. Sacramento, Jan. 28, 1937; s. Joseph and Annie (Muschetto) B.; m. Maria Sclafani, Nov. 19, 1960; children—Anna, Joseph, Gina and Nina (twins). A.A., Grant Jr. Coll.; student LaSalle U., 1963. With AeroJet Gen. Corp., Sacramento, 1958-65, United Vintners, Inc., San Francisco, 1960-73; pres., gen. mgr. Barcamerica Corp., Sacramento, 1963—; pres., gen. mgr. Barca Wine Cellars, Calif. Wine Cellars, Inc., Calif. Grape Growers, Inc., Calif. Vintage Wines, Inc., Am. Vintners, Inc.; cons. in field. Named Best Producer of Sales, United Vintners, Inc. Mem. Calif. Farm Bur., Met. C. of C., Better Bus. Bur., Roman Catholic. Club: KC. Developer wine trademarks.

BARCHAS, JACK DAVID, psychiatrist, educator; b. Los Angeles, Nov. 2, 1935; s. Samuel Isaac and Cecile Margaret (Pasarow) B.; m. Patricia Ruth Corbitt, Feb. 9, 1957; 1 son, Isaac Doherty. B.A., Pomona Coll., 1956; M.D., Yale U., 1961. Intern Pritzker Sch. Medicine, U. Chgo., 1961-62; postdoctoral fellow in biochemistry and pharmacology NIH, 1962-64; resident in psychiatry Stanford Med. Sch., 1964-67, instr., 1966-67, asst. prof., 1967-71, assoc. prof., 1971-76, prof., 1976—, Nancy Friend Pritzker prof. psychiatry and behavioral scis., 1976—; dir. Nancy Pritzker Lab. of Behavioral Neurochemistry, 1976—. Editor; author: Serotonin and Behavior, 1973, Neuroregulators and Psychiatric Disorders, 1977, Psychopharmacology from Theory to Practice, 1977, Catecholamines - Basic and Clinical Frontiers, 1979, Isoquinolines and Beta-Carbolines, 1981, Research on Mental Illness and Addictive Disorders: Progress and Prospects, 1984, Neuropeptides in Neurology and Psychiatry, 1986, In Situ Hybridization in Neurobiology, 1987, Perspectives in Psychopharmacology, 1988, Biological Rhythms and Mental Illness, 1988; contbr. articles to profl. jours. Served with USPHS, 1962-64. Recipient Psychopharmacology award Am. Psychol. Assn., 1970, Research Scientist award NIMH, 1980—. Fellow Am. Psychiat. Assn., Am. Coll. Neuropsychopharmacology; mem. Soc. Neurosci., Am. Coll. Neuropsychopharmacology (Daniel Efron award 1978), Am. Soc. Pharmacology and Exptl. Therapeutics, Am. Physiol. Soc., Am. Soc. Neurochemistry, Am. Chem. Soc., Am. Psychosomatic Soc., Psychiat. Research Soc., Soc. Biol. Psychiatry (A.E. Bennett award 1968), Am. Psychopathol. Assn., Inst. Medicine Nat. Acad. Scis. (chmn. bd. Mental Health and Behavioral Medicine). Office: Dept Psychiatry Stanford Med Sch 300 Pasteur Dr Stanford CA 94305

BARCHOFF, HERBERT, business executive; b. N.Y.C., Apr. 3, 1915; s. Abraham and Mollie (Berkowitz) B.; B.S., N.Y. U., 1935, J.D. (Eliot Shepard scholar), 1938; m. Lilyan Blum; 1 child, Jared Blum. Vice pres. Eastern Brass & Copper Co. (name now Eastern Rolling Mills, Inc.), 1938-45, exec. v.p., sec., 1945-54, pres., 1954—, chmn. bd., 1978-84; pres. Tubotron, Inc., 1959; cons. Copper Recovery Corp., 1942; guest lectr. Columbia U., Farleigh Dickinson Coll., Pace Coll.; seminar leader conf., program Alliance for Progress, Bogotá, Colombia. Mem. Pres.'s Council Econ. Advs., 1952; mem. exec. com. Action Com. for Internat. Devel.; mem. industry adv. com. NPA, 1951-53; survey small plants NATO area Europe, Mut. Security Agy., 1952; mem. citizens adv. com. on fgn. trade Senate Banking and Currency Com.; nat. adv. SBA; dir. mgmt. decision lab. NYU Grad. Sch. Bus., 1986—; mem. bd. govs. Joint Def. Appeal, 1956; mem. adv. com. to small bus. Nat. Dem. Com., 1956; dir. United Cerebral Palsy, 1959; nat. commr. Anti-Defamation League, 1968—, assoc. chmn. N.Y. appeal, 1971—; chmn. mgmt. of smaller cos. Am. Mgmt. Assn.; mem. Canadian Am. Nuclear Proliferation Conf., 1967, Am. Assembly Arden House Conf.-Uses of Sea, 1968; vice chmn., then chmn. Com. Release Stockpile Copper, 1973-74; pres. Am. Copper Council, 1975-79, chmn. bd., 1979-84; dir. Bronx River Restoration Project, 1980—; pres. 50 Sutton Pl. South Owners, Inc., 1981—; mem. restoration coordinating com. Statue of Liberty/Ellis Island Found., 1983—. Decorated Knight of Malta. Mem. Nat. Assn. Ind. Bus. (pres.), Copper and Brass Warehouse Assn. (treas., dir. 1951-54, v.p. 1954, pres. 1955), Young Presidents Orgn. (vice chmn. N.Y. chpt. 1959, dir. 1961, dir. Met. Pres.'s Orgn. 1973—), Conf. to Plan Strategy for Peace, Def. Orientation Conf. Assn., Am. Assembly Arms Control, Am. Baseball Acad. (exec. bd. dirs.), Nat. Planning Assn. (nat. council), Knights of Malta, Theta Sigma Lambda. Club: Copper (dir.). Author, pub. monthly copper letter Sticking My Neck Out; editor: N.Y. U. Law Quar. Rev. Contbr. articles to trade publs. Home: 50 Sutton Pl S New York NY 10022

BARCLAY, BRUCE STUART, corporate professional; b. Tauranga, New Zealand, Apr. 20, 1959; s. Ian Robin Garden and Patricia Stuart (Melville) B. B in Mgmt. Studies, U. Waikato, Hamilton, New Zealand, 1981. Acct. programmer NCR Ltd., Auckland, New Zealand, 1981-84; mktg. rep. Meta Machines Ltd., Oxford, Eng., 1985-87; bd. dirs. Innovative Techs., London, 1987—, also bd. dirs. Conservative. Presbyterian. Home: 82 Kings Rd, Richmond, London TW10 6EE, England

BARCLAY, JAMES EDWARD, footwear company executive; b. Camden, N.Y., Mar. 12, 1941; s. John A. and Hazel I. (Leavenworth) B.; m. Jane Alice Chariton, Dec. 26, 1964; children: Sean, Kimberly, Adam. AAS, Morrisville Tech. Coll., 1961; BS, U. Ga., 1965. Sales rep. Gen. Foods, Atlanta, 1966-67; tech. sales rep. R.T. Vanderbilt Co., Inc., N.Y.C., 1967-69; dist. sales mgr. Beech Nut Foods, N.Y.C., 1969-70, div. sales mgr., 1970-72; nat. sales mgr. B.C. Recreational Industries, Braintree, Mass., 1972-79; v.p. sales and mktg. Reebok Internat., Ltd., Hingham, Mass., 1979-82; exec. v.p. Reebok Internat., Ltd., Avon, Mass., 1982-86; pres. footwear div. Reebok Internat., Ltd., Canton, Mass., 1986-87, exec. v.p., 1987—. Bd. dirs. Two/Ten Charity Trust, Watertown, Mass., 1986—. Office: Reebok Internat Ltd 150 Royal St Canton MA 02021

BARCO, VIRGILIO, president of Colombia; b. Cucuta, Colombia, Sept. 17, 1921; s. Jorge Enrique Barco and Julieta Vargas Duran; m. Carolina de Barco; children: Carolina, Julia, Diana, Virgilio. Student Nat. U., Bogota, Colombia; BCE, MIT, 1943, postgrad., 1951-54; MS in Social Scis., Boston U., 1952. Sec. pub. works and pub. fin. Norte de Santander, 1943-45; sec. gen., acting minister of communications, Republic of Colombia, 1945-46, mem. Ho. of Reps., 1949-51, senator, 1958-66, Minister of Pub. Works, 1958-61, ambassador to U.K., 1961-62, Minister of Agr., 1963-64, acting Minister of Fin., 1964, mayor of Bogota, 1966-69, senator, fgn. relations com., fgn. affairs nat. adv. bd., 1974-78, ambassador to U.S., 1977-80, pres. Republic of Colombia, 1986—; cons. and lectr. in govt., econs. and politics. Colombian rep. to numerous internat. confs. and seminars including World Bank, IMF, UN, others. Decorated for profl. and govtl. service in numerous countries including Gran Cruz de la Orden de Boyaca, de San Carlos, del Merito Militar Jose Maria Cordoba, al Merito Julio Garavito, Colombia, numerous others. Mem. Colombian Soc. Economists (pres. 1960), Colombian Soc. Civil Engrs. (honor roll), Chi Epsilon, Pi Gamma Mu. Mem. Colombian Liberal Party. Address: Office of Pres, Bogota Colombia *

BARDA, JEAN FRANCIS, electronic engineer, corporate executive; b. Gargilesse, France, June 26, 1940; s. Ernest and Clothilde (Darmon) B.; m. Monique Marie Vianey, July 28, 1980; children: Nathalie, Xavier, Louis. Diploma in math., St. Louis and Paris, 1959; diploma in engring., Ecole Nationale de l'Aviation Civile, Paris-Orly, 1963. Registered electronic engr. Sect. mgr. Service Technique de la Navigation Aérienne Civil Aviation, Paris, 1965-70; tech. mgr. Utilisations Nouvelles de L'informatique et de la Television Sarl, Paris, 1970-83, Ateliers Techniques de Gargilesse Sarl, 1983-85; gen. mgr. Logiciel, Materiel et Applications de la Videographie Sarl (AVELEM) SA, Gargilesse, 1985—; tchr. math., Paris, 1967-70, electronics, Chambre de Commerce, Chateauroux, France, 1982-85; lectr. in parapsy studies Sirius Assn., Paris. Patentee in field. Recipient 1st prize Conseil Gen. Indre, 1983. Mem. Soc. Motion Picture and TV Engrs. Home and Office: La Billardiere, 36190 Gargilesse France

BARDARO, CARLO, mathematics educator; b. Foligno, Perugia, Italy, Dec. 4, 1954; s. Telesforo and Silvana (Ascani) B.; m. Luciana Mengaroni, June 26, 1982. Gad. in math., U. Perugia, Italy, 1981. Researcher U. Perugia, 1981—; assoc. prof. U. Rome, 1988—. Office: U Perugia, Dept Math, Via Pascoli, 06100 Perugia Italy also: U Rome, Dept M M Math, via Scarpa 10, Rome Italy

BARDEEN, JOHN, physicist, emeritus educator; b. Madison, Wis., May 23, 1908; s. Charles Russell and Althea (Harmer) B.; m. Jane Maxwell, July 18, 1938; children—James Maxwell, William Allen, Elizabeth Ann Bardeen Greytak. B.S., U. Wis., 1928, M.S., 1929; Ph.D., Princeton U., 1936. Geophysicist Gulf Research & Devel. Corp., Pitts., 1930-33; mem. Soc. Fellows Harvard, 1935-38; asst. prof. physics U. Minn., 1938-41; with Naval Ordnance Lab., Washington, 1941-45; research physicist Bell Telephone Labs., Murray Hill, N.J., 1945-51; prof. physics, elec. engring. U. Ill., 1951-75, emeritus, 1975—; mem. Pres.'s Sci. Adv. Com., 1959-62. Recipient Ballantine medal Franklin Inst., 1952; John Scott medal Phila., 1955; Fritz London award, 1962; Vincent Bendix award, 1964; Nat. Medal Sci., 1966; Morley award, 1968; medal of honor IEEE, 1971; Franklin medal, 1975; co-recipient Nobel prizes in physics, 1956, 72; Presdl. medal of Freedom, 1977; Lomonosov medal Soviet Acad. Scis., 1987. Fellow Am. Phys. Soc. (Buckley prize 1954, pres. 1968-69); mem. Am. Acad. Arts and Sci., IEEE (hon.), Am. Philos. Soc., Royal Soc. Gt. Britain (fgn. mem.), Acad. Sci. USSR (fgn. mem.), Indian Nat. Sci. Acad. (fgn.), Japan Acad. (hon.), Pakistan Acad. Sci. (fgn.), Austrian Acad. Sci. (corr.), Hungarian Acad. Sci. (fgn.). Office: Dept Physics Univ of Ill Urbana IL 61801

BARDEN, KENNETH EUGENE, lawyer, educator; b. Espanola, N.Mex., Nov. 21, 1955; s. Lloyd C. and Beverly A. (Coverdale) B.; m. Janice Reece, 1986. B.A. cum laude, Ind. Central U., 1977; J.D., Ind. U., 1977; cert. Harvard U. Law Sch., 1983. Bar: Ind. 1981, U.S. Dist. Ct. (so. dist.) Ind. 1981, U.S. Tax Ct. 1983, U.S. Ct. Mil. Appeals 1983, U.S. Ct. Appeals (7th cir.) 1983, U.S. Ct. Internat. Trade 1983. Law clk. Marion County Prosecutor's Office, Ind., 1976-78, Krieg Devault Alexander & Capehart, Indpls., 1978-79; bailiff Marion County Mcpl. Ct. 7, 1979-81, commr.-judge pro tem, 1981; pub. defender criminal div. 1, Marion County Superior Ct., 1981; asst. to U.S. magistrate, U.S. Dist. Ct. (so. dist.) Ind. Indpls., 1982-84; city atty. City of Richmond, Ind., 1984—; corp. counsel Richmond Power and Light Co., 1984—; pres. City of Richmond Bd. Pub. Works and Safety, 1988—; adj. prof. law Ind. Central U., Indpls., 1983. Nat. v.p. Coll. Democrats of Am., 1979-82; ward chmn. Marion County Dem. Party, 1977-81; precinct committeeman Wayne County Dem. Party, 1985—, treas. 2d dist. 1986— ; del. to NATO European Youth Leadership Conf., 1980; co-founder Hubert H. Humphrey Tng. Inst. for Campaign Politics, 1980; treas. Perry Twp. Dem. Club, 1980-83; alt. del. Dem. Nat. Conv., 1980; del. White House Forum on Domestic and Econ. Policy, 1975; del. Youth Conf. on Nat. Security and the Atlantic Alliance, Mt. Vernon Coll., Washington, 1976, Am. Council Young Polit. Leaders Fgn. Policy Conf., 1987; mem. U.S. Youth Council under Pres. Carter, 1980; mem. Ind. Gov.'s Community Corrections Com., 1973-75; mem. adv. council Friends of the Battered, 1985—; mem. personnel policies forum Bur. Nat. Affairs, 1985—; mem. Dem. Leadership Council, 1987—; mem. Am. Council of Young Polit. Leaders, 1986—. Recipient Youth In Govt. award, Optimist Club, 1972; named one of Outstanding Young Men of Am., 1986. Mem. ABA (com. on industry regulation, Young lawyers div. labor law com., lawyers and arts com., chmn. town hall com. 1987—, vice-chmn. citizinship edn. com. 1987—), Fed. Bar Assn., Ind. State Bar Assn., Indpls. Bar Assn., Wayne County Bar Assn., Ind. Council on World Affairs, Fed. Energy Bar Assn., Phi Alpha Delta, Epsilon Sigma Alpha, Alpha Phi Omega. Methodist. Clubs: Athenaeum (Indpls.): World Trade of Ind., Kiwanis. Home: 426 S 23d St Richmond IN 47374 Office: 50 N 5th St Richmond IN 47374

BARDEN, MICHAEL JOHN, writer; b. Dromore, Northern Ireland, Sept. 20, 1944; s. Laurence Aloysius and Alice (Dobbin) B.; m. Irene Buchanan, Oct. 31, 1970 (div. Dec. 1984); children: Scott Buchanan, Peter Oliver. Student, St. Colman's Coll., Newry, Northern Ireland, 1956-63, Queen's U., Belfast, Northern Ireland, 1963-66. Computer programmer Internat. Computer Ltd., London, 1967-69, advt. copywriter, 1969-73; press and publicity officer Cen. Electricity Generating Bd., London, 1973-74; dep. editor Power News, London, 1974-78; account dir. John Fowler & Ptnrs. Ltd., London, 1978-79; creative dir. Nationwide Advt. Services, London, 1979-80; account dir. Woods Barden Assocs. Ltd., Colchester, Essex, Eng., 1982-86; freelance writer London, Colchester, Eng., 1980-82, 86—. Author: Royal Mail Special Stamps 1984, 1984 (Design and Art Dirs. Gold award 1985), Royal Mail Special Stamps 1985, 1985, Royal Mail Spl. Stamps 1986, 1986. Home: 79 Hillview Close, Rowhedge CO5 7HS, England

BARDIE, FELIX ROBERT, pediatrician, consultant; b. Mostaganem, Algeria, Sept. 5, 1940; s. Henri Michel and Catherine (Darius) B.; m. Lina Mariette Mery, Aug. 5, 1967; children: Jean-Pierre, Veronique. MD, Medicine U., 1971. Cert. pediatrician, France. Extern Univ. Hosp., Montpellier, France, 1964-67; resident Univ. Hosp., Tours, France, 1967-72; asst. prof. Univ. Hosp., Tours, 1972-74; sr. research fellow UCLA and Cedars Sinai Hosp., 1972-73; practice medicine specializing in pediatrics Aix, France, 1974—; cons., attending physician Univ. Hosp., Marsielle, France, 1987—. Ciba-Geigy scholar, 1969; fellow Fulbright Found., 1972-73, French Fgn. Minister, 1972-73. Mem. French Pediatric Soc. Club: Anglo-Am. Group of Provence. Home and Office: 18 Blvd Republique, 13100 Aix en Provence France

BARDIS, PANOS DEMETRIOS, sociologist, editor, author, poet, educator; b. Lefcohorion, Arcadia, Greece, Sept. 24, 1924; came to U.S., 1948; s. Demetrios George and Kali (Christopoulos) B.; m. Donna Jean Decker, Dec. 26, 1964; children: Byron Galen, Jason Dante. Student, Panteios Supreme Sch., Athens, Greece, 1945-47; B.A. magna cum laude, Bethany (W.Va.) Coll., 1950; M.A., Notre Dame U., 1953; Ph.D., Purdue U., 1955. Mem. faculty Albion Coll., 1955-59; mem. faculty U. Toledo, 1959—, prof. sociology, 1963—; sec.-treas. World Student Relief, Athens, 1946-48; mem. adv. bd. New World Communications, 1980—; U.S. rep. Internat. Congress Social Scis., Spain, 1965, 66, 71, Italy, 1969; participant World Congress Sociology, France, 1966, Italy, 1969, Bulgaria, 70, Can., 1974, Sweden, 1978; Inst. Internat. de Sociologie, Italy, 1969, Venezuela, 1972, Algeria, 1974, Portugal, 1980; Inst. Sociology of Religion, Italy, 1969, Internat. Sci. Congress, Greece, 1973, 77, Internat. Conf. Unity Scis., annually, 1976-88, Internat. Conf. Sociology of Religion, France, 1977, Lausanne, Switzerland, 1981, London, 1983, Louvain, Belgium, 1985, Inst. Internat. Conf. on Love and Attraction, Swansea, Wales, 1977, Internat. Seminar on Philosophy and Religion, P.R., 1978, 79, Acapulco, Mex., 1980, 81, Athens, Greece, 1985, Inst. Internat. Conf. World Peace, Taipei, Taiwan, 1980, Geneva, 1985, Internat. Seminar Marxist Theory, 1981, World Peace Acad. Conf., 1979-88, numerous others; deliverer keynote address Internat. Conf. Peace and Apartheid, Johannesburg, 1986; lectr., Japan, Korea, Taiwan, 1980, 87; chmn. crime reduction com. Commn. Community Devel., Toledo, 1967-68; trustee Marriage Mus., N.Y.C.; mem. acad. adv. bd. Georgetown U. Inst., 1981—. Author: (novel) Ivan and Artemis, 1957, (books) The Family in Changing Civilizations, 1967, 69, Encyclopedia of Campus Unrest, 1971, The Future of the Greek Language in the United States, 1975, Studies in Marriage and the Family, 1975, 76, History of the Family, 1975, The Family in Asia, 1978, History of Thanatology, 1981, Poetry Americas, 1982, Atlas of Human Reproductive Anatomy, 1983, Evolution of the Family in the West, 1983, Global Marriage and Family Customs, 1983 Nine Oriental Muses, 1983, Dictionary of Quotations in Sociology, 1985; A Cosmic Whirl of Melodies (poems by Bardis; articles by others), 1986, Marriage and Family: Continuity, Change and Adjustment, 1988, The Monocritics, 1987; editor: Social Sci., 1959—, book rev. editor, 1963—; assoc. editor: Indian Social. Bull, 1965-71, Indian Psychol. Bull, 1965—, Revista del Instituto de Ciencias Sociales, Spain, 1965—, Internat. Jour. Sociology of Family, 1970—, Internat. Jour. Contemporary Sociology, 1971—, Jour. Polit. and Mil. Sociology, 1972—, Jour. Marriage and the Family, 1975-78, Ocarina, 1987—; book rev. editor Internat. Rev. History and Polit. Sci, India, 1966—; asst. Am. editor: book rev. editor Indian Jour. Social Research, 1965—; adv. editor: book rev. editor S.African Jour. Sociology, 1971—, Synthesis: The Interdisciplinary Jour. Sociology, 1973-74; Am. editor: book rev. editor Sociology Internat, India, 1967—; mem. editorial bd.: book rev. editor Darshana Internat, India, 1965—; Jour. Edn, India, 1965—, Sociologia Religiosa, Italy, 1966—; co-editor: Internat. Rev. Sociology, 1970-72, Internat. Rev. Modern Sociology, 1972—; editorial cons.: Soc. and Culture, 1972—, Coll. Jour. Edn, 1973—; adv. editor: Sociol. Inquiry, 1981—, Jour. Sociol. Studies, 1979—; editorial adv.: Am. Biog. Inst, 1980—; assoc. editor, book rev. editor: Sociol. Perspectives, 1981—; editor, book rev. editor Internat. Social Sci. Rev.; editor-in-chief, book rev. editor Internat. Jour. World Peace; contbr. poems, articles to profl. jours.; composer 21 songs for mandolin. Bd. advisors Internat. Middle E. Alliance. Recipient Couphos prize Anglo-Am.-Hellenic Bur. Edn., 1949, award for outstanding achievement in edn. Bethany Coll., 1975, Outstanding Teaching award Toledo Uetry prizes and awards. Fellow Am. Sociol. Assn. (membership com. 1966-71), AAAS, Internat. Inst. Arts and Letters (life), Inst. Internat. de Sociologie (chmn. membership com. 1970— , coordinator for U.S.A. 1974—), World Acad. Scholars, Intercontinental Biog. Assn., Internat. Poets Acad.; mem. AAUP, Nat. Council Family Relations, Ohio Council Family Relations, Global Congress World Religions, Internat. Sociol. Assn. (research coms. on social change 1972—, sociology of edn. 1972—, family sociology 1974—), Profs. World Peace Acad. (a founder), Conf. Internationale de Sociologie de la Religion, N. Central Sociol. Assn., Inst. Mediterranean Affairs (adv. council 1968—), Internat. Personnel Research (hon. adviser 1971—), Internat. Sci. Commn. on Family, Am. Soc. Neo-Hellenic Studies (bd. advisers 1969—), Group for Study Sociolinguistics, N.Y. Acad. Scis., Nat. Acad. Econs. and Polit. Sci. (dir. 1959—), Nat. Writers Club, Nat. Assn. Standard Med. Vocabulary (cons. 1963—), Inst. Study Plural Socs. (hon. asso.), Internat. Assn. Family Sociology, Modern Greek Soc., Nat. Soc. Lit. and Arts, Ohio Soc. Poets, Nat. Soc. Published Poets, World Poetry Soc. Intercontinental, Sigma Xi, Alpha Kappa Delta, Pi Gamma Mu (ann. regional, nat., internat. confs. 1959—), Phi Kappa Phi, Kappa Delta Pi., numerous others. Home: 2533 Orkney St Ottawa Hills Toledo OH 43606 Office: U Toledo Bancroft St Toledo OH 43606

BARDOT, BRIGITTE, actress; b. Paris, Sept. 28, 1934; d. Louis and Ann Marie Bardot; m. Roger Vadim, Dec. 12, 1952 (div.); m. Jacques Charries, June 19, 1959 (div.); 1 child, Nicholas; m. Gunther Sachs, July 14, 1966 (div.). Ed. Paris Conservatory. Films include: Act of Love, 1954, Doctor at Sea, 1955, The Light Across the Street, 1955, Helen of Troy, 1955, And God Created Woman, 1956, Heaven Fell That Night, 1957, Une Parisienne, 1957, En Cas de Malheur, 1957, Please Mr. Balzac, 1957, The Devil is a Woman, 1958, Mam'zelle Pigalle, 1958, Babette Goes to War, 1959, Please Not Now, 1961, The Truth, 1961, Vie Privee, 1961, Love on a Pillow, 1962; Contempt, 1964, Dear Brigitte, 1965, Viva Maria, 1965, Musculin Feminin, 1967, Two Weeks in September, 1967, Shalako, 1968, The Novices; 1970, The Legend of Frenchy King, 1972, Don Juan, 1973, L'Histoire Tres Bonne et Tres Joyeuse de Colinot Trousse-Chemise, 1973. Decorated d'Honneur, 1985. Address: La Madrague, 83990 Saint-Tropez France Address: 65 Blvd Lannes, 75116 Paris France *

BAREISS, LYLE EUGENE, aerospace engineer; b. Rawlins, Wyo., Nov. 4, 1945; s. Godfrey Matthew and Vera Edith Bareiss; m. Barbara Nadine. B.S. in Mech. and Aerospace Engring., Wyo. U., 1969; postgrad. in indsl. mgmt. Colo. State U., 1970. Skylab systems engr. Martin Marietta Aerospace Co., Denver, 1969-73, sr. staff engr. shuttle/spacelab contamination, 1974-79, mgr. tech. unit, contamination and laser effects, from 1980, dep. mgr. materials engring., 1984-85, dep. mgr. systems engring. specialties sect., 1985-87, mgr. defensive shields demonstration program, 1987—; chmn. Air Force strategic tech. planning panel on survivability/contamination, 1986. Recipient NASA Skylab Achievement award, 1974; NASA New Tech. awards, 1977, 82, 85; Martin Marietta author, performance awardee, 1974, 75, 79, 82, 84, Tech. Achievement award, 1987; named Prin. Investigator of Yr. Ind. Research and Devel., 1987. Mem. AIAA (Nat. Thermophysics Com.), Soc. For Advancement of Materials and Processes Engring., Sigma Tau, Omicron Delta Kappa, Sigma Alpha Epsilon. Presbyterian. Lodge: Odd Fellows (Rawlins, Wyo.). Contbr. articles to profl. jours.; architect computer model simulating spacecraft contamination to evaluate US satellite systems; basic research of effects of laser irradiation and other hostile threats on satellite/booster systems and materials oxidation/glow of satellites in low earth orbit. Home: 8031 E Phillips Circle Englewood CO 80112 Office: PO Box 179 Denver CO 80201

BARENBOIM, DANIEL, conductor, pianist; b. Buenos Aires, Argentina, Nov. 15, 1942; s. Enrique and Aida (Schuster) B.; m. Jacqueline DuPre, June 15, 1967. Student, Mozarteum, Salzburg, Austria, Accademia Chigiana, Siena, Italy; grad., Santa Cecilia Acad., Rome, 1956. Debut with Israel Philharm. Orch., 1953, Royal Philharm. Orch., Eng., 1953, debut as pianist, Carnegie Hall, N.Y.C., 1957, Berlin Philharm. Orch., 1963, N.Y. Philharm. Orch., 1964, 1st U.S. solo recital, N.Y.C., 1958, as pianist performed in N.Am., South Am., Europe, Soviet Union, Australia, New Zealand, Near East; conductor, 1962—, conducted English Chamber Orch., London Symphony Orch., Israel Philharm. Orch., N.Y. Philharm. Orch., Phila. Symphony, Boston Symphony, Chicago Symphony Orch., others; musical dir., Orchestre de Paris, 1975—, artistic adviser, Israel Festival, 1971-74, over 100 recordings as pianist and conductor. Recipient Beethoven medal, 1958; Harriet Cohen Paderewski Centenary prize, 1963, Legion of Honor,

France, 1987. Office: Orchestre de Paris, 252 Rue Faubourg St Honore, F-75008 Paris France also: care Israel Philharm Orch, Tel Aviv Israel *

BARETSKI, CHARLES ALLAN, political scientist, librarian, educator, historian; b. Mt. Carmel, Pa., Nov. 21, 1918; s. Charles Stanley and Mary Ann (Gorzelnik) B.; B.A. cum laude (scholar), Rutgers U., 1945; B.S. in L.S. (Edna Sanderson fellow), Columbia, 1946, M.S. in L.S. (Newark Pub. library scholar), 1951, Inst. Bibliog. Orgn. of Knowledge U. Chgo., 1960; diplomas in archival adminstrn. Am. U., 1951, 55; M.A. in Polit. Sci. (research fellow), U. Notre Dame, 1957, Ph.D., 1958; M.A. in Govt. and Internat. Relations, N.Y. U., 1965, Ph.D. in Politics, 1969, university scholar NYU, 1970; m. Gladys Edith von Nyitrai Yartin, Aug. 19, 1950. Research intern Am. State Dept. Archives, Nat. Archives, 1951; from reference librarian to sr. librarian Newark Pub. Library, 1938-54, librarian Van Buren br., 1954-56, br. dir., 1957-88, dir. fgn. lang. book collection, 1954-88; nat. archivist, historian Am. Council Polish Cultural Clubs, 1954—; cons. doctoral candidates in grad. studies, 1957—; chief judge award com. Joseph Conrad Lit. Contest, 1968; mem. faculty Univ. Coll., Rutgers U., Newark, 1965-66; coordinator Slavic-Am. hist. studies Sr. Citizens' Inst., Essex County Coll., Newark, 1977-78; dir. Baretski Tutorial Service, 1935-68; founder, dir. Ethnic Research Archives, 1971—, dir. Research Library; pres. Asso. Community Councils Newark, 1969-88; pres. Ironbound (Newark) Community Council, 1961-88; lectr., cons. Am. Ethnic Polit. History, 1968—; cons. Doctoral Candidates, U. Notre Dame, 1957—, genealogical research, 1987—; mem. adv. council North Essex Ednl. Center, Essex County Coll., Belleville, N.J., 1973-88; treas., chmn. N.J. Coalition for Safe Communities, Anti-Crime N.J. Statewide Fedn., 1978-80; Republican Clean Govt. candidate for U.S. Congress, 10th Dist. N.J., 1962; N.J. chmn. Polish-Am. Citizens Goldwater, 1964; N.J. liaison dir. Polish Am. Rep. Nat. Council, 1971-88; research dir., pub. relations dir. Polish-Am. Rep. Club N.J. Founder, dir. Inst. Polish Culture, Seton Hall U., South Orange, N.J., 1953-88; nat. gen. sec. Am. Polish Civil War Centennial com. 1961-65; founder, dir., librarian Ctr. Advancement Slavic Studies, 1970—; chmn. internat. com. 300th Ann. of Founding of Newark, 1965-66; founder, pres. Ind. Polish-Am. Voters of N.J., 1953—; state del. Polish Hungarian World Fedn., 1977-83; founder, pres. Newark Pub. Library Employees Union Local 2298, Am. Fedn. State, County and Municipal Employees, AFL-CIO, 1971-77, del. internat. convs., 1974, 76, 78, 80, 82, trustee N.J. Pub. Employers Council 52, No. N.J. Pub. Employee Unions, 1978-84; mem. exec. bd. Newark Labor Coalition, 1972-77; bd. dirs. N.J. chpt. Confedn. Am. Ethnic Groups; organizer, cons. Newark Ironbound Sr. Citizen's Multi-Purpose Ctr. Satellite Library, 1986-88; resource scholar N.J. Gov.'s Commn. on Eastern European and Captive Nation History, 1985—; historian Newark Multi-Ethnic Council, 1986-88; active numerous other civic orgns. Recipient Presdl. Leadership and Distinguished Service award Am. Fedn. State, County and Municipal Employees, 1972, Service awards Newark Pub. Library, 1972, 74, 76, 85, Nat. Am. Heritage award J.F. Kennedy Library for Minorities, 1972, Outstanding State Labor Leader award N.J. Pub. Employees, AFL-CIO, 1978; Disting. Educator Am. award, 1979; New Internat. award Polish Govt. in exile, London, 30 years Profl. Service award Newark's Ironbound Community, 1984, Sixty Yr's Dedicated Vol. Turoring award, 1987; Named for the outstanding contbns. to the geater. Newark community and devoted services to the growth of the Newark Pub. Library system. numerous others; decorated Knight's cross Polonia Restituta. Mem. Polish-Am. Unity League, Polish-Am. Hist. Assn. (asst. editor monthly Bull. 1959-61, nat. editor-in-chief 1961-65) , Writers Soc. N.J. (exec. dir. 1947-56), Am. Polit. Sci. Assn., Am. Soc. Internat. Law, Am. Sociol. Assn., Soc. Historians Am. Fgn. Relations, Am. Hist. Assn., N.Y. Library Club, Polish-Hungarian World Fedn., Immigration HistoryJ., Middle States councils social studies, Am. Council Polish Cultural Clubs, Newark Pub. Library Guild (founder, pres. 1970), Library Pub. Relations Council, ALA, N.J. Library Assn., Essex County Librarians Assn. Roman Catholic. Clubs: Polish U. (Newark). Author: Our Quarter Century: History of the American Council of Polish Cultural Clubs 1948-1973, 1973, Fond Memories of Ann Street School: 1920's to 1950's, 1986; co-author: The Polish University Club of New Jersey; A Concise History: 1928-88, 1988; author taped narrative The Legend of America's Santa Claus, 1987; editor: Higher Horizons Ednl. Program N.Y.C., 1961; editor and pub. Ironbound (N.J.) Counselor, Newark, 1965. Contbr. articles to numerous profl. jours., also chpts. to books. Research on contbns. Polish and other immigrants to Am. culture and history. Club: N.J.; Historian (pres. 1980-88); Polish Art of Newark. Home and Office: 2426 West Tremont Ct Richmond VA 23225

BARFIELD, BOURDON REA, investor; b. Amarillo, Tex., Oct. 28, 1926; s. Bourdon Ivy and Oliver Rea (Eakle) B.; BBA, U. Tex., 1951; m. Carolyn Grissom, Jan. 4, 1951; children: Deyanne, Amanda, Bourdon Ivy, John Callaway. Vice pres. Barfield Corp., Amarillo, 1951-57, pres. 1957—; pres. Guaranty Mortgage Corp., 1979—; dir. Mr. Burger Inc. Pres. Penbrooke Corp., Amarillo, 1969—. Mem. Durett Scholarship Com. Amarillo Pub. Schs., 1951—; area chmn. Crusade for Freedom, 1957; pres. Amarillo Symphony Orch., 1959-61; chmn. Citizens' Action Program, Amarillo, 1961-63; v.p. U. Tex. Dads' Assn., 1975—; mem. exec. com. Panhandle Plains Historical Soc., 1984, Llano Cemetery Bd, 1984; co-chmn. Amarillo Centennial Com., 1987. Mem. dist. Democratic Congl. Campaign Com., 1962-65, chmn., 1969; bd. dirs. Dallas Civic Opera, 1962, St. Andrew's Day Sch., Amarillo, 1962, Family Service Inc., Amarillo, 1969, Amarillo Art Ctr., 1972—; chmn. bd. dirs. Amarillo Pub. Library, 1963; exec. com. Panhandle Plains Mus., 1984—; co-chmn. Amarillo Centennial, 1987. Recipient Young Man of Yr. award Jr. C. of C., 1960, Man of Yr. award Amarillo Globe-News, 1988, First Citizen of the 2nd Century City of Amarillo, Amarillo C. of C., 1987, award of Honor Downtown Amarillo Unltd. for Redevel. Work., 1966. Mem. Amarillo C. of C. (pres. 1961), U.S. C. of C. (dir. Civic Devel. Com. 1960), Jovian, 49ers, Vagabond Club. Beta Theta Pi. Episcopalian (lay reader, vestryman 1958-61). Clubs: Masons (32 deg.), Rotary, Amarillo Country, Palo Duro. Home: 3201 Ong St Amarillo TX 79109 Office: 1620 Tyler St Amarillo TX 79105

BARG, M MICHAEL ABRAHAM, historian, researcher; b. Satanov, Ukrain, USSR, May 1, 1915; s. Abraham Moshe and Rosa Nathan (Diamond) B.; m. Anna Israel Goder, Sept. 10, 1958; 1 child, Alexander. Grad. cum laude, State U. Kharkov, USSR, 1941; postgrad., Inst. World History, Moscow, 1943-47, DSc, 1958. Lectr. Inst. Fgn. Langs., Moscow, 1948-49; lectr. State Pedagogical Inst., Moscow, 1950-56, prof., 1960-68; asst. prof. gen. history City Pedagogical Inst., Moscow, 1956-60; sr. researcher Inst. History, Moscow Acad. Scis., Moscow, 1968—. Author: (monographs) English Feudalism XI-XIII, 1962, Lower Orders in English Revolution, 1967 (Volgin prize), Categories of Historical Science, 1984, Rise of Historicism, 1987, Shakespeare and History, 1976, 2nd edition, 1979, 6 others; contbr. over 250 articles to sci. jours. Served as lt. Russian Army, 1939-40. Recipient Presidium award Moscow Acad. Sci., 1979. Mem. Hist. Soc. Hungary (hon.). Office: USSR Acad Scis Inst History, Dm Ulyanova 19, Moscow USSR

BARGATZKY, THOMAS, anthropology educator; b. Brannenburg, Fed. Republic Germany, Sept. 13, 1946; s. Eugen Bargatzky and Thilde (Huber) Bargatzky Engelhardt; m. Eva Hupfer, 1982. PhD, U. Hamburg, Fed. Republic Germany, 1977; PhD in Habilitation, U. Munich, Fed. Republic Germany, 1988. Asst. lectr. U. Munich, Fed. Republic Germany, 1979-80, lectr. dept. anthropology, 1981—; scholar Deutsche Forschungsgemeinschaft, 1980-81, 85. Author: Die Rolle des Fremden beim Kulturwandel, 1978, Ethnologie, 1985, Kulturokologie, 1986. Served alt. mil. service Old Folks' Home, Fed. Republic Germany, 1967-69. Mem. German Ethnological Soc., Polynesian Soc., Inst. Encyc. Uram. Home: Meister Mathis Weg 3, 8000 Munich 21 Federal Republic of Germany Office: Inst Volkerkunde, Ludwigstrasse 27, 8000 Munich 22 Federal Republic of Germany

BARGEON, HERBERT ALEXANDER, JR., writer; b. Fayetteville, N.C., May 23, 1934; s. Newett Drew Jr. and Emeline (Burkett) Edwards; BS in Bus. Adminstrn., U. Va., 1956; LLB, U. Fla., 1968; m. Gail Freer, Mar. 14, 1963; 1 child, Violet Gail. Bar: Fla., D.C. Pres., chmn. bd. Royal Poinciana Playhouse, Palm Beach, Fla., 1973-81. Served to 2d lt. AUS, 1957. Mem. Am. Bar Assn. Republican. Presbyterian. Home: Barker's Creek Rural Route 2 Box 145AA Whittier NC 28789

BARGER, JAMES DANIEL, physician; b. Bismarck, N.C., May 17, 1917; s. Michael Thomas and Mayte (Donohue) B.; m. Susie Belle Helm, 1945 (dec. 1951); m. Josephine Steiner, 1952 (dec. 1971); m. Jane Ray Regan, Apr. 21, 1980; children: James Daniel, Mary Susan, Michael Thomas, Mary Elizabeth. Student, St. Mary's Coll., Winona, Minn., 1934-35; A.B., U. N.D., 1939, B.S., 1939; M.D., U. Pa., 1941; M.S. in Pathology, U. Minn., 1949. Diplomate: Am. Bd. Pathology; registered quality engr., Calif. Intern. Milw. County Hosp., Wauwatosa, Wis., 1941-42; fellow in pathology Mayo Found., Rochester, Minn., 1941-49; pathologist Pima County Hosp., Tucson, 1949-50, Maricopa County Hosp., Phoenix, 1950-51; chmn. dept. pathology Good Samaritan Hosp., 1951-63; assoc. pathologist Sunrise Hosp., Las Vegas, Nev., 1964-69, chief pathology dept., 1969-81, sr. pathologist, 1981—; emeritus clin. prof. pathology U. Nev. Sch. Medicine, 1988—; former med. dir. S.W. Blood Bank, Blood Services, Ariz., Blood Services Nev.; treas. Commn. for Lab. Assessment, 1988. Served to maj. AUS, 1942-46. Recipient Sioux award U. N.D. Alumni Assn., 1975; recipient disting. physician award NSMA, 1983; ASCP-CAP Disting. Service award, 1985. Mem. AAAS, Am. Assn. Pathologists, Am. Assn. Clin. Chemists, Am. Assn. History Medicine, Coll. Am. Pathologists (gov. 1966-72, sec.-treas. 1971-79, v.p. 1979-81, pres. 1980-81, Pathologist of Yr. 1977), Nev. Soc. Pathologists, Am. Assn. Blood Banks, Am. Soc. Quality Control, Am. Mgmt. Assn., Soc. Advancement Mgmt., Am. Soc. Clin. Pathologists, Am. Cancer Soc. (nat. dir. 1974-80), European Acad. Sci., Arts and Letters (corr.), Sigma Xi. Lodge: Knights of St. Lazarus (comdr. 1983). Home: 1307 Canosa Ave Las Vegas NV 89104 Office: Humana Sunrise Hosp PO Box 14157 Las Vegas NV 89114

BARHAM, DEREK KEITH, mining automation company executive; b. London, Apr. 20, 1939; s. Arthur Ernest and Florence Grace (Emberson) B.; m. Mary Evelyn Askew; children: Nicholas Francis, Christopher Gerard, Stephen Matthew. B in Mining Engring. with honors, U. Birmingham, Eng., 1960. Chartered engr., cert. colliery mgr. With underground mine mgmt. Nat. Coal Bd., Midlands, Eng., 1963-69; research mgr. Mining Research and Devel. Establishment, Midlands, Eng., 1969-82; divisional head automation and mechanization Mining Research and Devel. Establishment, Burton-on-Trent, Eng., 1982-86, nat. research mgr. automation and advanced mining, 1986-87; owner, prin. cons. Advanced Mining Automation and Robotics Cons., Leicester, Eng., 1987—. Contbr. articles to profl. jours; patentee mine automation field. Fellow Inst. Mining Engrs. Office: Advanced Mining Automation, and Robotic Cons, 1 Zion Hill, Leicester LE6 4JP, England

BARIDON, PHILIP CLARKE, criminologist, policy analyst, consultant; b. Washington, Aug. 1, 1946; s. R. Clarke and Juanita (Ayers) B.; m. Andrea Paulette Blauser, June 16, 1975. B.A., Bucknell U., 1968; M.A., SUNY-Albany, 1971, Ph.D., 1975. Police officer Met. Police D.C., 1968-72; asst. prof. Am. U., Washington, 1972-74, mem. adj. faculty, 1974-76; research assoc. Mid-Atlantic Research Inst., Bethesda, Md., 1974-75; prin. cons. P.R.C., McLean, Va. and San Francisco, 1975-78; chief program evaluation br., forensic programs St. Elizabeth's Hosp., Washington, 1978-84; sr. policy analyst criminal div. U.S. Dept. Justice, Washington, 1984—. Author: Addiction, Crime and Social Policy, 1976; contbr. articles to profl. jours. N.Y. State fellow, 1970-71; Ford Found. fellow, 1971-72; Nat. Inst. Justice grantee, 1980. Mem. Am. Soc. Criminology, Nat. Council on Crime and Delinquency, Am. Acad. Polit. and Social Sci. Buddhist. Home: 4160 S 36th St Arlington VA 22206

BARIFF, MARTIN LOUIS, information systems educator, consultant; b. Chgo., Jan. 26, 1944; s. George and Mae (Goldberg) B. BS in Acctg., U. Ill., 1966, MA in Acctg., 1967, PhD in Acctg., 1973. CPA, Chgo. Asst. prof. acctg. and decision scis. Wharton Sch., Phila., 1973-78; vis. asst. prof. acctg. U. Chgo., 1978-79; assoc. prof. acctg. and mgmt. info. decision systems Case Western Res. U., Cleve., 1979-83; Coleman-Fannie May Candies Found. assoc. prof. info. resources mgmt., dir. Ctr. for Research on the Impacts of Info. Systems, Ill. Inst. Tech., Chgo., 1983—; cons. in field, N.Y.C., Phila., Washington, 1976—; exec. v.p. EDP Auditors Found., 1979-80; program chmn. Internat. Conf. Info. Systems, Phila., 1980. Contbr. articles to profl. jours. Bd. dirs. Community Accts. Inc. of Phila., 1974-75. Mem. Am. Inst. CPA's, Am. Acctg. Assn. (chmn. acctg., behavior and orgns. sect. 1987-88), Assn. Computing Machinery (sec. 1981-85), Soc. Info. Mgmt. (treas. Chgo. chpt. 1988—), Inst. Mgmt. Sci. Jewish. Office: Ill Inst Tech 10 W 31st St Chicago IL 60616

BARISAS, BERNARD GEORGE, JR., chemistry educator, immunology researcher; b. Shreveport, La., July 16, 1945; s. Bernard George and Edith (Bailey) B.; m. Judith Kathleen O'Rear, May 19, 1973 (div. Sept. 1978); m. Deborah Anne Roess, Aug. 6, 1981. BA, U. Kans., 1965; BA, Oxford (Eng.) U., 1967, MA, 1983; MPhil., Yale U., 1969, PhD, 1971. NIH postdoctoral trainee Yale U., New Haven, 1971-72, research assoc., 1972; NIH postdoctoral fellow U. Colo., Boulder, 1973-75; asst. prof. biochemistry St. Louis U., 1975-80, assoc. prof., 1980-81; assoc. prof. chemistry and microbiology Colo. State U., Ft. Collins, 1981-87, prof., 1987—. Contbr. articles to tech. jours. Sec. Mo. Rhodes Scholarship Selection Com., 1976-81, mem. Colo. Selection Com., 1982-86. Rhodes scholar, 1965; Woodrow Wilson fellow, 1965, Fulbright sr. fellow, 1986; recipient Research Career Devel. award NIH, 1978. Mem. Am. Soc. Biol. Chemists, Am. Assn. Immunologists, Biophys. Soc., Am. Chem. Soc., AAAS, N.Y. Acad. Scis., Soc. Applied Spectroscopy, Phi Beta Kappa, Sigma Xi, Omicron Delta Kappa, Pi Mu Epsilon, Phi Lambda Upsilon, Delta Phi Alpha. Episcopalian. Clubs: Am. Alpine (N.Y.C.); Colo. Mountain (Denver); St. Louis Mountain (pres. 1976-77). Home: 1701 Glenwood Dr Fort Collins CO 80526 Office: Colorado State U Dept Chemistry Fort Collins CO 80523

BARKENSTRAND, KENT LENNART, pharmaceutical company executive; b. Malmoe, Sweden, Mar. 17, 1943; s. Knut and Gurli Bengtsson; m. Maj Ingegard Lundquist, June 4, 1966; 2 children. BSc in Bus. Adminstrn. and Econs., U. Lund, 1985. Auditor Kristerssons Revisionsbyro, Malmoe, 1965-67; controller EUROC, Malmoe, 1967-69; fin. mgr. Spriella-Masterland Garments, Malmoe, 1969-74, Ferring AB Pharms., Malmoe, 1974—; local mem. bd. PK-Banken, Malmoe, 1985—; dir. FAB Med. Ltd., London; mem. exec. bd. The Hypothalamus Group, 1987—. Home: Malusgatan 1, 21232 Malmoe Sweden Office: Ferring AB, Box 30561, 20062 Malmoe Sweden

BARKER, C(LARENCE) AUSTIN, finance executive, economist; b. Centralia, Wash., Dec. 2, 1911; s. Clarence G. and Susan (McElroy) B.; m. Mary Ellen Brown, Mar. 29, 1941; children: Beverly Jean, Stephen Warner. AB, Stanford U., 1934; postgrad. Columbia U. Grad. Sch. Bus., 1935-36; MBA, NYU, 1939. Acct., regulatory analyst Public Service Electric & Gas Co. of N.J., Newark, 1936-44; sr. economist charge fin. and econ. research Cleve. Electric Illuminating Co., 1944-59, sec. to fin. com. bd. dirs., 1954-59; dir. research Hornblower, Weeks Noyes & Trask Inc. (name changed to Loeb, Rhoades, Hornblower & Co.), N.Y.C., 1959-65, gen. partner, 1962-71, public utility cons., 1965-78, v.p., cons. economist 1972-78, fin. cons., 1978-79; pres. Barker Cons., Inc., 1979—; fin. cons. Noyes Partners, Inc., 1980—; dir. Western Mining & Exploration Co., Inc., 1977—, v.p., 1983—; lectr. corp. fin. and investment analysis Case-Western Res. U. Grad. div., 1955-59; lectr. public utility seminars Irving Trust Co., 1959-76; prepared testimony on stock splits SEC. Bd. dirs. Rye Conservation Soc., 1965-80, pres., 1965-68; mem. nat. adv. council Stanford Alumni, 1952-57; trustee Mt. Gulian Soc., 1972—; founder, sponsor Nat. Tax Limitation Com., 1976-85, mem. fed. amendment drafting com., 1978-82. Chartered fin. analyst. Mem. Nat. Economists Club (charter mem.), Acad. Polit. Sci. (life), Com. for Monetary Research and Edn. (life). Nat. Assn. Bus. Economists (charter mem.), N.Y. Soc. Security Analysts (pres. Westchester chpt. 1988—), Descs. Colonial Govs., Founders and Patriots (treas. 1965-68, councillor 1970-81, dep. gov. 1981-88, historian gen. 1983-84, dep. genealogist 1988—), Rye Hist. Soc. Republican. Episcopalian. Clubs: Stanford (N.Y.C.); Rowfant (Cleve.). Assoc. editor Financial Analysts Jour., 1969-70. Contbr. articles to profl. jours. Home and Office: 2 Hickory Dr Rye NY 10580

BARKER, CLYDE FREDERICK, surgeon, educator; b. Salt Lake City, Aug. 16, 1932; s. Frederick George and Jennetta Elizabeth (Stephens) B.; m. Dorothy Joan Bieler, Aug. 11, 1956; children—Frederick George II, John Randolph, William Stephens, Elizabeth Dell. BA, Cornell U., 1954, MD, 1958. Diplomate Am. Bd. Surgery. Intern Hosp. U. Pa., Phila., 1958-59, resident in surgery, 1959-64, fellow in vascular surgery, 1964-65; fellow in med. genetics U. Pa. Sch. Medicine, Phila., 1965-66, assoc. in surgery, 1964-68, assoc. in med. genetics, 1966-72; attending surgeon Hosp. U. Pa., Phila., 1966—; chief div. transplantation U. Pa. Sch. Medicine, Phila., 1968—, asst. prof. surgery, 1968-69, assoc. prof. surgery, 1969-73, prof. surgery, 1973—, J. William White prof. surg. research, 1978-82, chief div. vascular surgery, 1982—, Guthrie prof. surgery, 1982—, John Rhea Barton prof. surgery, 1983—, chmn. dept. surgery, 1983—; chief surgery Hosp. U. Pa., Phila., 1983—; dir. Harrison Dept. Surgery research U. Pa., Phila., 1983—; mem. immunobiology study sect. NIH; chmn. clin. practices U. Pa., 1987-89. Mem. editorial bd. Jour. Transplantation, 1977—, Jour. Surg. Research, 1979—, Jour. Diabetes, 1981—, Archives of Surgery, 1987— ; contbr. articles to profl. jours. and textbooks. Markle Found. Scholar, 1968-74; NIH grantee, 1974—. Fellow ACS (com. Forum on Fundamental Surg. Problems 1983-88, vice chmn. 1987-88), Coll. Physicians Phila.; mem. Soc. Univ. Surgeons, Am. Surg. Assn., Soc. Clin. Surgery (chmn. membership 1984-85), Halsted Soc. (chmn. membership 1984-85, v.p. 1985-86, pres. 1986-87), Surg. Biology Club II, Soc. Vascular Surgery, Internat. Cardiovascular Soc., Internat. Surg. Group (treas. 1988—), Transplantation Soc. (councilman 1978-84), Am. Soc. Transplant Surgeons (chmn. membership 1980-81, treas. 1988—), Assn. Acad. Surgery, Am. Diabetes Assn., Am. Soc. Artifcial Internal Organs, AMA, Am. Fedn. Clin. Research, Phila. Acad. Surgery (program chmn. 1984-86, v.p. 1986-88, pres. 1988-89), Greater Del. Valley Soc. Transplant Surgeons (pres. 1978-80), Juvenile Diabetes Found. Clubs: Merion Cricket, Phila. Home: 3 Coopertown Rd Haverford PA 19041 Office: Hosp U Pa Dept Surgery 3400 Spruce St Philadelphia PA 19104

BARKER, HAROLD GRANT, surgeon; b. Salt Lake City, June 10, 1917; s. Frederick George and Jennetta (Stephens) B.; m. Kathleen Butler, July 29, 1949; children: Janet Stephens, Douglas Reid. A.B., U. Utah, 1939, post-grad., 1939-41; M.D., U. Pa., 1943. Diplomate Am. Bd. Surgery. Intern. Hosp. U. Pa., 1943-44, asst. resident in surgery, 1947-51, sr. resident in surgery, 1951-52, asst. attending surgeon, 1952-53; also asst. instr., research fellow U. Pa., 1946-51, instr., research fellow, 1951-52, assoc. in surgery, 1952-53; asst. prof. surgery Columbia U., 1953-57, assoc. prof., 1957-68, prof., 1968-82, prof. emeritus, 1982—; asst. attending surgeon Presbyn. Hosp., 1953-57, asso. attending surgeon, 1957-69, attending surgeon, 1969—, dir. med. affairs, 1974-82; practice medicine specializing in surgery, Phila., 1952-53, N.Y.C., 1953—. Contbr. articles med. jours. Served from 1st lt. to capt., M.C. AUS, 1944-46, ETO. Fellow ACS; mem. Soc. U. Surgeons, N.Y. Surg. Soc., Am. Physiol. Soc., Soc. Exptl. Biology and Medicine, AMA, Halsted Soc., N.Y. State (chmn. surg. sect. 1961-62), N.Y. County med. socs., Am. Surg. Assn., N.Y. Gastroent. Assn., Société Internationale de Chirurgie, Soc. Surgery Alimentary Tract, Allen O. Whipple Surg. Soc., Am. Assn. History Medicine, Collegium Internationale Chirurgiae Digestivae. Republican. Presbyn. Clubs: Century Assn; Manursing Island (Rye, N.Y.); Am. Yacht. Home: 1 Forest Ave Rye NY 10580 Office: 161 Ft Washington Ave New York NY 10032

BARKER, KEITH RENE, investment banker; b. Elkhart, Ind., July 28, 1928; s. Clifford C. and Edith (Hausmna) B.; A.B., Wabash Coll, 1950; M.B.A., Ind. U., 1952; children by previous marriage—Bruce C., Lynn K.; m. Elizabeth S. Arrington, Nov. 24, 1965; 1 dau., Jennifer Scott. Sales rep. Fulton, Reid & Co., Inc., Ft. Wayne, Ind., 1951-55, office, 1955-59, asst. v.p., 1960, v.p., 1960, dir., 1961, asst. sales mgr., 1963, sales mgr., 1964, dir. Ind. ops.; sr. v.p. Fulton, Reid & Co., 1966-75; pres., chief exec. officer Fulton, Reid & Staples, Inc., 1975-77; ptnr. William C. Roney & Co., 1977-79; exec. com. Cascade Industries, Inc.; assoc. A.G. Edwards & Sons, Inc., 1984—; dir. Fulton, Reid & Staples, Inc., Craft House Corp., Nobility Homes, Inc. Pres. Historic Ft. Wayne, Inc.; cons. to Mus. Historic Ft. Wayne; nominee, trustee Ohio Hist. Soc.; mem. Smithsonian Assocs.; bd. dirs. Ft. Wayne YMCA, 1963-64. Served to lt. USNR, 1952-55. Recipient Achievement certificate Inst. Investment Banking, U. Pa., 1959. Mem. Ft. Wayne Hist. Soc. (v.p.), Alliance Française, VFW (past comdr.), Co. Mil. Historians, Cleve. Grays, Am. Soc. Arms Collectors, 1st Cleve. Cavalry Assn., Nat. Assn. Securities Dealers (bus. conduct com.), Phi Beta Kappa. Episcopalian. Mason. Clubs: Beaver Creek Hunt, Cleve. Athletic, Rockwell Spring Trout. Home: 351 Cranston Dr Berea OH 44017 Office: 1965 E 6th St Cleveland OH 44114

BARKER, LLYLE JAMES, JR., former army officer, journalism educator, public relations executive; b. Columbus, Ohio, July 28, 1932; s. Llyle James and Mabel Lucile (Johnson) B.; B.S., Ohio State U., 1954; postgrad. U. Wis., 1961; M.S. in Mass Communication, Shippensburg State Coll., 1975; m. Maxine Ruth Metcalf, Jan. 15, 1956; children—Llyle J., Daryl Alan Commd. officer U.S. Army, advanced through grades to maj. gen.; served in Korea, Vietnam, Thailand and W.Ger.; pub. affairs officer, Hawaii, 1957-59, NORAD, 1961-63, Dept. Army, 1966-69, 7th Army, 1969-71, Joint Casualty Resolution Ctr., 1974, European Command, 1975-77, U.S. Army Europe, 1979-80; dep. chief info. Dept. Army, 1980-81, chief pub. affairs, 1981-84; prof. Sch. Journalism, Ohio State U., Columbus, 1984—; assoc. Gannett Ctr. Media Studies, Columbia U. Decorated D.S.M., Legion of Merit, others. Mem. World Future Soc. Pub. Relations Soc. Am., Assn. Edn. in Journalism and Mass Communications, Internat. Assn. Bus. Communicators. Contbr. articles to mil. and journalism jours. Home: 152 Caren Ave Worthington OH 43085 Office: Ohio State U Sch Journalism 242 W 18th Ave Columbus OH 43210

BARKER, MICHAEL DAVID, design engineer; b. Hertford, England, Sept. 29, 1926; s. Noel Ernest and Mary (Detrolio) B.; m. Irene Mabel Marsh, Sept. 12, 1959 (dec.). Student corr. coll., Cambridge (Eng.) U., 1948. Engring. apprentice D. Wickham & Co. Ltd., Ware, Hertfordshire, Eng., 1943-45, 48-51, draughtsman, 1951-61, design engr., 1961—. Patentee 5 indsl. pumps, 2 braking devices. Served to cpl. Royal Signal Corps, 1945-48, MTO. Decorated Palestine Service medal with clasp. Home: Woodlands Hunsdonbury, Hunsdon near Ware, Hertfordshire SG12 8PW, England Office: D Wickham & Co Ltd, Crane Mead near Ware, Hertfordshire SG12 9QA, England

BARKER, NANCY L., college official; b. Owosso, Mich., Jan. 22, 1936; d. Cecil L. and Mary Elizabeth (Stuart) Lepard; m. J. Daniel Cline, June 6, 1956 (div. 1971); m. R. William Barker, Nov. 18, 1972; children—Mary Georgia, Mark Lepard, Richard Earl, Daniel Packard, Melissa Bess, John Charles, Helen Grace, Wiley David, James Glenn. B.Sc., U. Mich., Ann Arbor, 1957. Spl. edn. instr. Univ. Hosp., U. Mich., Ann Arbor, 1958-61; vice pres. Med. Educator, Chgo., 1967-69; asst. to chmn., dir. careers for women Northwood Inst., Midland, Mich., 1970—, chmn. dept. fashion mktg. and merchandising, 1972-77; v.p. Northwood Inst., 1978—; cons. and lectr. in field. Author: Wendy Well Series, children's books, 1970—. Contbr. chpts. to books, articles to profl. jours. Advisor, Mich. Child Study Assn., 1972—; chmn. Matrix: Midland Festival, 1978; bd. dirs. Nat. Council of Women, 1971—, pres., 1983-85, chmn. centennial com., 1988; bd. dirs. Concerned Citizens for the Arts, Mich. Recipient Honor award Ukrainian Nat. Women's League, 1983; Disting. Woman award Northwood Inst., 1970; Outstanding Young Woman, Jr. C. of C., 1974; nominee Mich. Women's Hall of Fame, 1984, 85. Mem. The Fashion Group, Nat. Home Fashions League (pres. Mich. chpt. 1974-77), Mich. Women's Studies Assn. (founding mem.), Midland Art Council (pres. 2 terms, 25th anniversary award), Internat. Women's Forum, Women's Forum of Mich., Phi Beta Kappa, Phi Kappa Phi, Alpha Lambda Delta, Phi Lambda Theta, Phi Gamma Nu, Delta Delta Delta. Republican. Episcopalian. Clubs: Contemporary Review, Midland County Lawyer's Wives (Midland); Zonta. Home: 209 Revere Midland MI 48640 Office: Northwood Inst Midland MI 48640

BARKER, PHILIP GEORGE, computer science educator, researcher, author, chemist; b. Pontypool, Wales, Apr. 21, 1944; s. Joshua and Ada Maud (Bruntly) B.; m. Jennifer Wright, Oct. 5, 1970 (div. 1983). B.Sc. in Chemistry, U. Wales, 1965, Ph.D., 1968. Chartered Engr.,registered chemist, U.K. SRC research fellow U. Wales, Swansea, 1968-70; computer cons. BHC Chems., Port Talbot, Wales, 1970-71; lectr. computer sci. Teesside Poly., Middlesbrough, Eng., 1971-73, prin. lectr. computer sci., 1979-87, reader applied computing and info. technology, 1987— ; lectr. computing U. Durham (Eng.), 1973-79; dir. Programming Language One Ltd., Milton Keynes, Eng., 1976-82, Interactive Systems Research Group, Middlesbrough, Eng., 1978—. Author: Computers in Analytical Chemistry, 1983 (Russian edit. 1987), Introducing Computer Assisted Learning, 1985, Author Languages for CAL, 1987; editorial bds. Engineering Applications of Artificial Intelligence, 1987; contbr. numerous tech. articles to profl. publs. Recipient Ayling prize Univ. Coll. Swansea, 1965. Fellow Brit. Computer

Soc. (sec. 1976-79), Royal Soc. Chemistry; mem. Assn. Computing Machinery, IEEE, Long Distance Walkers Assn. Clubs: Stockton Rambling, IVC. Home: 35 Stokesley Rd, Marton, Middlesbrough, County Cleveland TS7 8DT, England Office: Teesside Poly, Sch Info Engring, Borough Rd, Middlesbrough County Cleveland TS1 3BA, England

BARKER, ROBERT RANKIN, business executive; b. Brookline, Mass., July 12, 1915; s. James Madison and Margaret (Rankin) B.; A.B. magna cum laude, Harvard U., 1936; m. Elizabeth VanDyke Shelly, Mar. 7, 1942; children—James Robertson, Ann Shelly, William Benjamin, Margaret Welch. With investment and credit analysis, investment adv. depts. J. P. Morgan & Co., 1936-49; with Wm. A.M. Burden & Co., N.Y.C., 1949-78, gen. partner, 1954-78; gen. partner Barker, Lee & Co., 1973—. Spl. asst. to asst. sec. commerce for air U.S. Dept. Commerce, 1942-43. Past chmn. adv. com. endowment mgmt. Ford Found. Past trustee Am. Geog. Soc., New Canaan Country Sch. (pres.), Am. Farm Sch. Thessaloniki, Greece, Silvermine Guild Artists, New Canaan Library, Mus. Modern Art, Hudson Inst.; trustee Am. Mus. Natural History, J.M.R. Barker Found., Florence V. Burden Found.; bd. overseers Harvard U. (pres.). Served as officer USNR, 1943-46. Mem. Council Fgn. Relations, N.Y. Soc. Security Analysts, Phi Beta Kappa. Clubs: Anglers, Univ., Harvard, Brook, Century (N.Y.C.). Home: 809 Oenoke Ridge New Canaan CT 06840 Office: 630 Fifth Ave New York NY 10111

BARKER, ROBERT WILLIAM, television personality; b. Darrington, Wash., Dec. 12; s. Byron John and Matilda Kent (Tarleton) B.; m. Dorothy Jo Gideon, Jan. 12, 1945 (dec. Oct. 1981). BA in Econs. summa cum laude, Drury Coll., 1947. Master of ceremonies: Truth or Consequences, Hollywood, Calif., 1957-75, Price is Right, 1972—, Miss Universe Beauty Pageant, 1966-87, Miss U.S.A. Beauty Pageant, 1966-87, Pillsbury Bake-Off, 1969-85, Bob Barker Fun and Games Show, 1978—; host: Rose Parade, CBS, 1969—. Served to lt. (j.g.) USNR, 1943-45. Recipient Emmy award for Best Daytime TV Host, 1981-82, 82-83, 86-87, 87-88. Mem. AGVA, AFTRA, Screen Actors Guild. Office: care Goodson-Todman Prodns 6430 Sunset Blvd Hollywood CA 90028

BARKER, SAMUEL BOOTH, former university dean, physiology and biology educator; b. Montclair, N.J., Mar. 3, 1912; s. Harry and Marion (Booth) B.; m. Justine Rogers, July 31, 1934. Sc.D (hon.), U. Vt., 1984, B.S. cum laude, 1932; student, Yale U., 1932-34; Ph.D., Cornell U., 1936, Ph.D. (medicine fellow), 1941; Sc.D. (hon.), U. Ala., 1979. Mem. faculty U. Tenn. Coll. Medicine, 1941-44; asst. prof. State U. Iowa Coll. Medicine, 1944-46, asso. prof. physiology, 1946-52; prof. pharmacology U. Ala. in Birmingham, 1952-62, prof. physiology-biophysics, 1965—, prof. biology, 1970—, disting. prof., 1976—; dir. grad. studies, assoc. dean Med. Coll. and Sch. Dentistry, 1965-70; dean Grad. Sch., 1970-78, dean emeritus, 1978—; prof. pharmacology Coll. Medicine, U. Vt., 1962-65; Cons. NIH, NSF, 1944-84. Author: (with J.H.U. Brown) Basic Endocrinology, 2d edit, 1966. Krichesky fellow, 1951; recipient Career Research award USPHS, 1962-65. Fellow AAAS, Am. Inst. Chemists; mem. Am. Physiol. Soc., Soc. Exptl. Biology and Medicine, Harvey Soc., AAUP (pres. Iowa chpt. 1950), Ala. Acad. Scis. (pres. 1959-60, chmn. bd. trustees 1972—), Am. Fedn. Clin. Research, Endocrine Soc., Am. Chem. Soc. (chmn. Ala. sect. 1957-58), Biochem. Soc. London, N.Y. Acad. Scis., Am. Thyroid Assn. (pres. 1970-71), Phi Beta Kappa, Sigma Xi, Phi Kappa Phi. Home: 1812 Woodcrest Rd Birmingham AL 35209 Office: University Station Birmingham AL 35294

BARKIN, BEN, public relations consultant; b. Milw., June 4, 1915; s. Adolph and Rose Dora (Schumann) B.; m. Shirley Hinda Axel, Oct. 19, 1941; 1 child, Coleman. Student pub. schs. Nat. field dir. Jr. B'nai B'rith, 1937-41; cons. war finance dept. U.S. Treasury Dept., 1941-45; pub. relations cons. Ben Barkin & Asso., 1945-52; chmn. Barkin, Herman, Solochek & Paulsen, Inc. (and predecessor firm), Milw., N.Y.C.; pub. relations counsel Barkin, Herman, Solochek & Paulsen, Inc. (and predecessor firm), 1952—; partner Milw. Brewers Baseball Club, Inc., 1970—. Bd. dirs., v.p., mem. exec. com. Mt. Sinai Med. Center, also chmn. corp. program; pres. Mt. Sinai Med. Center Found.; chmn. bd. trustees Athletes for Youth, Inc.; corp. mem. Milw. Children's Hosp., Columbia Hosp., United Way; mem. mgmt. adv. com. Milw. Urban League, We-Milwaukeeans, Greater Milw. Com.; mem. civil rights exec. com. Anti-Defamation League; mem. Wis. exec. com. United Negro Coll. Fund, 1981. Named man yr. Milw., 1945; recipient Knight of Bohemia award Milw. Press Club, 1978, Headliner award Milw. Press Club, 1983; Disting. Service award Sales and Mktg. Execs. Milw., 1986; Benefactor of Yr. award Wis. United Negro Coll. Fund, 1986; Lamplighter award Greater Milw. Conv. and Visitors Bur., 1986; Father of Yr. award Children's Outing Assn., 1986; Community Service award Am. Legion, 1987; Charles E. Zehner, Jr. Innovation award Assn. Model Railroad Clubs, 1987; Vol. Ctr. Greater Milw., Inc. award, 1987, Community Service award St. Francis Children's Ctr., 1987. Mem. Pub. Relations Soc. Am. (Paul Lund award 1978), NCCJ., B'nai B'rith (nat. chmn. youth commn. 1966-68). Home: 1610 N Prospect Ave Milwaukee WI 53202 Office: Barkin Herman Solochek & Paulsen Inc 606 E Wisconsin Ave Milwaukee WI 53202

BARKLEY, HENRY BROCK, JR., research and development executive; b. Raleigh, N.C., Apr. 5, 1927; s. Henry Brock and Thelma Maurine (Dutt) B.; m. Edith Sumner Stowe, June 24, 1950; children—Margaret Susan, Henry Brock III, Jane Stowe. Student U. N.C., 1944-45; B.S., U.S. Naval Acad., 1949; B.S. in E.E., U.S. Naval Postgrad. Sch., 1954, M.S. in E.E., 1955. Supr. space power sect. Bendix, Ann Arbor, Mich., 1962-63; chief reactor div. Lewis Research Center, NASA, Sandusky, Ohio, 1963-73; asst. gen. mgr., dir. power reactors EG&G Idaho, Inc., Idaho Falls, 1973-81; mgr. internat. bus. Babcock & Wilcox Co., Lynchburg, Va., 1981-83, mgr. 205 plant project services, 1983-87, mgr. space power and propulsion, 1987—; dir. Devel. Workshop, Inc., Idaho Falls., 1977-81; IEEE disting. lectr. in S.Am. and C.Am., 1984. Bd. dirs. Sandusky (Ohio) Concert Assn., 1965-73; chmn. Huron (Ohio) sch. levy campaigns, 1970. Served to lt. comdr. USN, 1949-61. Mem. Am. Nuclear Soc., IEEE, Am. Guild Organists. Presbyterian. Home: 1216 Norvell House Ct Lynchburg VA 24503 Office: PO Box 10935 Lynchburg VA 24506

BARKLEY, MARILYN JANE, accountant; b. Yakima, Wash., July 9, 1934; d. Philip and Pauline Marie (Coulter) Barkley; m. Frederick Paul Fazi, Nov. 26, 1968 (div. July 1970). Cert. Lawton Sch., 1953. Office nurse W.A. Blampin, M.D., Los Angeles, 1953-55; jr. acct. Markson Bros., Los Angeles, 1955-57; office mgr. Deaf Smith Research Labs., Hereford, Tex., 1958-59; acct. Roy M. Guest, P.A., Dallas, 1960-68; comptroller, gen. mgr. Restaurant Chablis, Dallas, 1970-78; acct. Tannebaum, Bindler & Co., P.C., CPAs, Dallas, 1978—. Mem. Internat. Platform Assn., Humane Soc. U.S. Presbyterian. Office: Tannebaum Bindler & Co PC CPAs 2323 Bryan Suite 700 Dallas TX 75201

BARKLEY, THIERRY VINCENT, lawyer; b. Paris, Mar. 21, 1955; s. Jacques and Michéline Marié (Rossi) B.; came to U.S., 1967, naturalized, 1974; m. Mary Ellen Gamble, June 18, 1983; children: Richard A., Robert V., Marriah E. B.A. in Polit. Sci., UCLA, 1976; J.D., Calif. Western Sch. Law, San Diego, 1979. Bar: Nev. 1980, U.S. Dist. Ct. Nev. 1982, U.S. Supreme Ct. 1986. Intern, Calif. Ct. Appeals 4th Circuit, San Diego, 1978-79; law clk. Nev. Dist. Ct., 7th Jud. Dist., Ely, 1979-81; assoc. firm C.E. Horton, Ely, 1982-83; asst. city atty. Ely, 1982-83; assoc. firm Barker, Gillock & Perry, Reno, 1983-87, Perry, Hebert & Spann, 1987—. Assoc. editor Internat. Law Jour., 1979. Mem. Internat. Moot Ct. Team, 1978; recipient Dean's award Calif. Western Sch. Law, 1979. Mem. ABA, Nev. Bar Assn., Washoe Bar Assn., U.S. Jaycees (past pres. White Pine, Nev.). Republican. Roman Catholic. Lodge: Elks (past treas. Ely club). Office: Perry Hebert & Spann 620 Humboldt St Reno NV 89509

BARLETTA, GIUSEPPE ANTONIO, cardiologist; b. Novara, Italy, Mar. 28, 1954; s. Francesco and Eleonora (Benevento) B.; m. Laura Ferrini, Mar. 7, 1981; 1 child, Tommaso. BS, U. Florence, 1978. Research fellow cardiology unit U. Florence, Italy, 1980-82; cons. cardiologist Florence Hosp., 1981—, asst. chief physician, 1988—. Co-author book on semeiotics; contbr. articles to profl. jours. Grantee Nat. Com. Research. Mem. European Heart Soc., Italian Soc. Cardiology, Italian Group Haemodynamic Studies. Home: Via Medaglie D'Oro N 43, 50047 Prato Florence Italy Office: Viale Morgagni, Cardiology Unit, 50134 Florence Italy

BARLOW, AUGUST RALPH, JR., clergyman; b. Sewickley, Pa., Oct. 9, 1934; s. August Ralph and Kathryn Viola (Adams) B.; B.A., Haverford Coll., 1956; B.D., Yale U., 1959, S.T.M., 1964; m. Elizabeth Evone Anderson, Aug. 27, 1960; children—Paul Martin, Andrew Ralph, Ann Kathryn. Ordained to ministry, 1959; pastor Fox Chapel Methodist Ch., Pitts., 1959-60, Butler St. Meth. Ch., Pitts., 1961-62, Lawrenceville Community Ch., Pitts., 1962-63; intern Cleve. Inner City Protestant Parish, 1960-61; teaching minister Beneficent Congl. Ch., Providence, 1964-70, pastor, 1970—; bd. govs. Beneficent House; bd. dirs. Pastoral Counseling Center Greater Providence, 1973—, v.p., 1984-86; bd. dirs. Steere House, Providence, 1980-86, pres., 1983-86; bd. dirs. Home Health Services of R.I., 1986—; research fellow Yale U. Div. Sch., 1979; chmn. ch. in soc. com., 1985-86; mem. R.I. Conf., United Ch. of Christ, 1964—, mem. com. on ministry, 1981-83; mem. urban div. R.I. Council Chs., 1979-82. Mem. adv. council Providence Public Library, 1968-71; bd. dirs. Mouthpiece Coffee House, Providence, 1969-75, pres., 1974-75. Mem. Dodeka, Providence Intown Chs. Assn., Ministers Assn. R.I. Conf. United Ch. of Christ., Phi Beta Kappa. Democrat. Clubs: Rotary (trustee Rotary Charities Found. 1977-82), Beneficent Order of Spike. Contbr. articles to Christian Century, editorials, commentaries to Providence Jour.-Bull., Religious Broadcasting Sta. WEAN. Home: 95 Cole Ave Providence RI 02906 Office: 300 Weybosset St Providence RI 02903

BARLOW, COLIN HASTINGS, agricultural economist; b. Banstead, Surrey, England, Nov. 28, 1932; s. Harold Monteagle and Janet Hastings (Eastwood) B.; m. Ruth Elizabeth Manly, Dec. 27, 1959; children: Patrick, Caroline, Yvonne, Oliver, Nicholas. BSc in Agr., London U., England, 1954; MS in Agr. Econs., Cornell U., 1956; PhD in Agr. Econs., Aberdeen U., Scotland, 1963. Asst. mgr. Thriplow Farms Ltd., Cambridge, England, 1957-59; asst. lectr. Aberdeen U., 1960-63; head economist Rubber Research Inst., Malaysia, 1963-69; various positions to sr. fellow Australian Nat. U., Canberra, 1969—; Vis. fellow Internat. Rice Research Inst., Los Banos, Philippines, 1977, 84; mem. Malaysian Rubber Task Force, Kuala Lumpur, 1983, Malaysian Oil Palm adv. Com. 1984—, Internat. Rubber Study Group, London, 1985—. Author: Natural Rubber Industry, 1978, Philippine Rice Farming, 1983, North Sumatran Economy, 1988; contbr. articles to profl. jours. Decorated Mem. of Brit. Empire, Brit. Crown, 1967; recipient of numerous grants for research projects, Australia, SE Asia, 1970—. Mem. Internat. Assn. Agrl. Economists, European Assn. Agrl. Economists, Australian Agrl. Econ. Soc., Asian Studies Assn. Australia, Australian Inst. Sci. Office: Australian Nat U, Econs Pacific Studies, ACT GPO Box 4, Canberra 2601, Australia

BARLOW, F(RANK) JOHN, mechanical contracting company executive; b. Milw., July 12, 1914; s. Ernest A. and Alice E. (Norton) B.; m. Dorothy M. Marx, Oct. 13, 1935; children—Joyce D., Bonnie M., Joan C., Grace M., Jacqueline S., Wendy J., Terri L., Alice M. B.S. in Mech. Engring., U. Wis., 1937. Engr. Buffalo Forge Co., 1937-40; sales engr. Buffalo Forge Co., Chgo., 1940-42; plant engr. A.O. Smith Corp., Milw., 1942-44; chief mech. engr. Western Condensing Co., Appleton, Wis., 1944-46, profl. mgr., 1946-53; owner Azco, Inc., Appleton, Wis., 1953—, pres., 1959-80, chmn. bd., 1959—; chmn. bd., pres. Azco Group Ltd., 1982—; pres. Sanco, Ltd., Appleton, 1959—, Bardwin Barlow Corp., Appleton, 1965—, The Downey Co., Milw.; pres. Ave. Dept. Inc., Appleton, Inc.; treas. Winagamie Corp., 1965—; dir. First Nat. Bank Appleton; dir., mem. exec. com. AIR Wis., 1965—; chmn. bd. dirs. Transpace Carriers, Inc., 1986—;. County chmn. March of Dimes, 1957—, state co-chmn., 1958; industry chmn. com. fund dir., 1968-69; bd. dirs. Nat. Cert. Pipe Welding Bur., Community Found., 1986—; trustee Azco Employees Profit Sharing Trust; pres. Appleton Devel. Council, 1983—. Recipient Industry award Wis. Soc. Profl. Engrs., 1967. Mem. Mech. Contractors Assn. Am. (nat. dir., pres. 1974-75, disting. service award 1982), Mech. Contractors Assn. Wis. (pres.), Wis. Soc. Profl. Engrs. (chpt. pres. 1968—), Am. Soc. Heating, Refrigerations and Airconditioning Engrs., Appleton C. of C., ASCE, Flying Engrs., Nat. Soc. Profl. Engrs., C.A.P. Clubs: Butte Des Morts Golf (dir., pres. 1961, 62). Lodges: Masons, Shriners, Rotary, Elks (past exalted ruler). Home: 178 River Dr Appleton WI 54911 Office: PO Box 567 Appleton WI 54912

BARLOW, HORACE BASIL, physiologist; b. Chesham Bois, Eng., Dec. 8, 1921; s. James Alan and Emma Nora Barlow; m. Miranda Weston-Smith, June 28, 1980; 1 child, Oscar Hugh; children by previous marriage: Rebecca Nora, Natasha Helen, Naomi Jane, Emily Anne. BA, Cambridge (Eng.) U., 1943; MD, Harvard U., 1946; MBB, Univ. Coll. Hosp. of London, 1947. Fellow Trinity Coll., 1950-54; demonstrator, asst. dir. research physiology lab. King's Coll., 1954-63; Royal Soc. research prof. Cambridge U., 1973-87; prof. physiol. optics U. Calif., Berkeley, 1963-73. Editor Jour. of Physiology, 1972-77; contbr. articles to profl. jours. Mem. Physiol. Soc., Exptl. Psychology Soc., Brain Research Assn. Home: 9 Selwyn Gardens, Cambridge CB3 9AX, England Office: U Cambridge Physiol Lab, Downing St, Cambridge CB2 3EG, England

BARLOW, JOHN BRERETON, cardiologist; b. Cape Town, Republic S. Africa, Sept. 10, 1924; s. Lancelot White and Madeline (Dicks) B.; m. Shelagh Maud Cox, Dec. 10, 1949; Richard John, Clifford William. MB BCh, U. Witwatersrand, Johannesburg, 1951; MD, U. Witwatersrand, 1967. Intern Baragwanath Hosp., Johannesburg, 1952; med. registrar Royal Post Grad. Med. Sch., London, 1955-57; adhominem prof. cardiology U. Witwatersrand, Johannesburg, 1971-80; cardiology prof. U. Witwatersrand, 1980—; physician-in-charge Johannesburg Hosp., 1963—, chief physician, 1980—; cons. U. Witwatersrand U., 1960—, S. African Airways, 1975—; dir. Cardiovascular Research Fund, U. Witwatersrand, 1964—; internal med. examiner, S. African Coll. Med., 1967—. Author: Perspectives on the Mitral Valve, 1987; contbr. chpts. to textbook; contbr. articles to numerous profl. jours. Served with the S. African army, 1942-45. Stella and Paul Lowenstein Research grantee, 1964, Wellcome Found grantee, 1964; Recipient Seymour Lectureship medal, 1984; André Allard medal Internat. Acad. Aviation and Space Medicine, 1987. Fellow Am. Heart Assn., Royal Coll. of Physicians, Royal Soc. Med., Royal Soc. of South Africa; mem. Am. Heart Journal (internat. editorial bd. 1977-81, St. Cyres lectr. 1987), British Cardiac Soc., Cardiovascular Ultrasonagraphy(internat. editorial bd. 1981—), Brit. Med. Assn., South African Med. Assn., South African Cardiac Soc. Club: Johannesburg Country. Home: 48 Rutland Rd Parkwood, 2193 Johannesburg Republic of South Africa Office: U Witwatersrand, Dept Med, 2193 Johannesburg Republic of South Africa

BARNA, JOSEPH, architect; b. Toronto, Ont., Can., Mar. 30, 1930; s. Joseph and Franciska (Zachar) B.; m. Maria Terezia Szakonyi, Oct. 5, 1957; children—Maria-Melinda, Joseph-Richard, Emese-Clara. Diploma in Architecture, Tech. U. Budapest, Hungary, 1955. Asst. architect XXI. Troszt Co., Budapest, 1955-56; Flood-Reconstrn. Co., Mohach, Hungary, 1956; archtl. cons. A.M. Lount and Assocs., Toronto, 1957-65; archtl. designer Meridian Group, Toronto, 1966-67; chief architect Peel Elder Group, Toronto-Brampton, 1968-80; sole proprietor Joseph Barna Architect, Toronto, 1980—; advisor cons. engring. firm, Toronto, 1957-66; apt. bldg. designer Meridian-Belmont Group, Toronto, 1966-67; research bldgs. cons. Peel Village Devel., Brampton, 1968-80; cons. St. Raphael's Nursing Homes, Toronto, 1981—; archtl. advisor bridges, bldg. design Dept. of Hwy., 1957-65, Peel Cheshire Home for Handicapped, Streetville, Ont., 1973-74, Community Recreation Ctrs., Toronto, 1970-76. Prin. works include Graydon Hall Community, Forest Hill Community, Peel Village Community. U. Budapest scholar, 1950-55. Mem. Ont. Assn. Architects, Royal Archtl. Inst. Can., Can.-Hungarian Assn. Avocations: chess; painting; gardening; travel; designed and built own architect's house. Home: 78 Olsen Dr, Don Mills, ON Canada M3A 3J3 Office: 1020 McNicoll Ave, Scarborough, ON Canada M1W 2J6

BARNABY, CHARLES FRANK, writer; b. Andover, Eng., Sept. 27, 1927; s. Charles Hector and Lilian (Sainsubry) B.; m. Wendy Elizabeth Field, Dec. 19, 1972; children: Sophie Elizabeth, Benjamin Frank. BSc, U. London, 1948, MSc, 1951, PhD, 1960; D (hon.), Free U., Amsterdam, 1981. Scientist Atomic Weapons Research Establishment, Aldermaston, Eng., 1957; physicist U. Coll., London, 1957-67; exec. sec. Pugwash Confs. on Sci. and World Affairs, London, 1967-70; dir. Stockholm Internat. Peace Research Inst., 1971-81; chmn. Just Def., 1986—; co-chmn. World Disarmament Campaign, 1986—. Author: Prospects for Peace, 1984; The Automated Battlefield, 1986; Star Wars Brought Down to Earth, 1986. Home: Brandreth Station Rd, Chilbolton, Stockbridge O2O 6AW, England

BARNARD, CHRISTIAAN NEETHLING, surgeon; b. Beaufort, West, C.P., South Africa, Nov. 8, 1922; s. Adam Hendrik and Maria Eliabeth (Swardt) B.; M.B.,Ch.B., U. Cape Town (South Africa), 1946, M.D., M.Med., 1953, also hon. doctorate; M.S., Ph.D., U. Minn., 1958; hon. doctorate of medicine Pahlavi U., Shiraz, Iran; D.Sc. (hon.), Gama Filho U., Brazil, Collegii Spei, Holland, Mich., Fla. So. Coll.; m. Aletta Gertruida Louw, Nov. 6, 1948 (div.); children: Deirdre Jeanne, Andre Hendrik; m. 2d, Barbara Maria Zoellner, Feb. 14, 1970 (div. 1982). Dir. surg. research U. Cape Town, 1958—, assoc. prof., 1962-72, prof. dept. surgery, 1972-83, prof. emeritus, 1983—; sr. cardiothoracic surgeon Groote Schuur Hosp., Cape Town, 1968-83, head cardiothoracic surg. unit, 1961—; scientist in residence Okla. Heart Ctr., Bapt. Med. Ctr., Pklahoma City, 1985—. Recipient Dag Hammarskjold Peace prize, Dag Hammarskjold Internat. prize; diploma of honor Internat. Fedn. Arts, Letters and Scis., France; Knights of Humanity award, Italy; La Madonnina Internat. prize for Sci.; diploma Internat. Cardiol. Symposium, Naples; Honor award World Assn. Mil. Surgeons; Gold medal Med. Assn. South Africa; Christo Veryers award South African Acad. Arts and Sci.; Gold medal Cape Town Chris Barnard Fund; medal South African Cape Provincial Council, Nat. Fedn. Blood Donors, Lyons (France) Adminstrn. Hosp.; Honor award N.Y. Cardiol. Soc.; plaque and medal Stritch Award; Blignault medal South African Med. Jour., 1975; medal Bombay Med. Research Center; cert. of honor Eugen Moog Found. Ger. and US.; medallion from Pope Paul VI; Kennedy Found. award; public tribute City of N.Y.; plaque Govt. Que.; cert. of recognition Prime Minister Can.; hon. citizen Cahtillon-les-Dombes (France), Carpineta, Rome, Birmingham (Ala.), Riberao Proto (Brazil), New Orleans, Winnipeg (Man., Can.), State of Guanabara (Brazil); Gold medal U. Pretoria; Silver medal Am. Coll. Cardiology, Coll. Surgeons Ireland; medal Sydney U. Med. Soc., Albert Einstein Coll. Medicine, Lombardi Med. Acad., Milan, Italy, Pasteur Inst.; Internat. award St. Boniface Gen. Hosp. Research Found., Winnipeg, 1977; Hendrik Verwoerd medal (South Africa); Order of Republic Andres Bello (Venezuela); Silver Cross (Dominican Republic); Order of Sun, Order Hipolito Unanue (Peru); cross of Nat. Cedar Decoration (Lebanon); Blue Cross award (Spain); grand cordon Order of Al-Kawkab Al-Urduni (Jordan); grand ufficiale Order of Merit (Italy); comdr. Order of Phoenix (Greece); Order of Brilliant Star (Republic of China); Cecil Adams bursary and Dazian Found. scholar, 1956; Ernest Oppenheimer Meml. Trust grantee, 1960. Hon. fellow ACS, Am. Coll. Cardiology, N.Y. Cardiol. Soc.; mem. South African Med. Assn., Soc. Thoracic Surgeons, South Africa Soc. Physicians, Surgeons and Gynecologists (founder mem.); hon. mem. Société de Medicine (Paris), Pan Am. Med. Assn., Montreal Clin. Soc., Venezuelan Soc. Cardiology, Brazilian Coll. Surgeons, Cardiology Soc. Dominican Republic. Club: Lions (hon.). Author: (with V. Schrire) Surgery of Common Congenital Cardiac Malformations, 1968; (with C. B. Pepper) One Life, 1970; Heart Attack: All You Have to Know About It, 1971; (with S. Stander) (novel) The Unwanted, 1974; South Africa - Sharp Dissection, 1977; (with S. Stander) (novel) In the Night Season, 1977; Best Medicine, 1979; Good Life, Good Death, 1980; (with Peter Evans) Christian Barnard's Program for Living with Arthritis, 1984. Research, numerous publs. on congenital intestinal atresia; introduction of open heart surgery to South Africa; developed new design artificial heart valves; performed world's 1st human heart transplant operation, Dec. 3, 1967, world's first double-heart transplant operation, Nov. 25, 1974. also: PO Box 988, 8000 Cape Town Republic of South Africa *

BARNARD, DONALD ROY, entomologist; b. Santa Ana, Calif., June 7, 1946; s. Alan Whittaker and Ethel Mae (Kennedy) B.; m. Priscilla Margaret Grier, Aug. 12, 1967; children—Jennifer Erin, David Michael. B.S. in Zoology, Calif. State U., 1969, M.A. in Biology, 1972; Ph.D. in Entomology, U. Calif.-Riverside, 1977. Postdoctoral fellow Colo. State U., Ft. Collins, 1977-79; research entomologist agrl. research service USDA, Poteau, Okla., 1979-85, supervisory research entomologist, 1985-88; research leader agrl. research service USDA, Gainesville, Fla., 1988—; cons. WHO/FAO, 1980—, Bay Region Agrl. Devel. Project, AID, Somali Democratic Republic/U.S.A., 1981—, Dept. Def., 1985—, Dept. Agr., Republic S. Africa, 1988—. Contbr. chpts. to books, articles to profl. jours; mem. Jour. of Med. Entomology editorial bd., Bull. of the Soc. Vector Ecologists editorial bd. Mem. Entomol. Soc. Am., Entomol. Soc. Can., Ecol. Soc. Am.

BARNARD, EUGENE GEORGE, oil company executive; b. London, Aug. 9, 1919; s. Dudley James and Violet Eugenie (Beasley) B.; m. Joan Maud Harvey; 1 child, Victoria Gillian. B. in Commerce, London U., 1948. Cert. acct. Mgr. fin. div. Iraq Petroleum Co., Ltd. and Assoc. Cos., London, 1948-72; fin. head Maplin Devel. Authority, London, 1973; pres. Viking Jersey Equipment Ltd., Brussels, 1974-77; exec. dir. Oil Exploration Holdings, Edinburgh, 1977-79, London and Scottish Marine Oil Co., London, 1979-84; v.p., dir. Belden & Blake Internat., Ltd., Hamilton, Bermuda, 1986—. Served with the British Navy, 1940-46. Anglican. Club: E. India. Office: Belden & Blake Internat, 30 Cedar Ave, Hamilton Bermuda

BARNARD, KATHLEEN RAINWATER, educator; b. Wayne City, Ill., Dec. 28, 1927; d. Roy and Nina (Edmison) Rainwater; BS, So. Ill. U., 1949, MS, 1953; postgrad. Ind. U., 1953; PhD, U. Tex., 1959; m. Donald L. Barnard, Aug. 17, 1947 (div. Mar. 1973); children: Kimberly, Jill. Tchr. pub. high sch., Wayne City, Ill., 1946-51; faculty asst., lectr. Vocat. Tech. Inst., So. Ill. U., Carbondale, 1951-53; lectr. bus. edn. Northwestern U., Chgo., 1953-55; chmn. dept. bus. adminstrn. San Antonio Coll., 1955-60; chmn. dept. bus. edn. DePaul U., Chgo., 1960-62; chmn. dept. bus. Loop Coll. (now Harold Washington Coll.), City Colls. Chgo., 1962-67, prof., 1968—, exec. sec., bd. dirs. credit union, 1975-78; cons., evaluator Ill. Program for Gifted Children, State Demonstrator Center, Oak Park (Ill.) Pub. Schs.; cons. First Nat. Bank Chgo., 1974; ednl. cons. Ency. Brit., 1969. Cons. edn. and tng. div. Continental Ill. Nat. Bank & Trust Co., Chgo., 1967, Victor Corp., 1965—; cons. IBM, Inc., summer 1968. Mem. North Central Bus. Edn. Assn., Nat. Bus. Edn. Assn., Chgo. Assn. Commerce and Industry, Delta Kappa Gamma, Pi Omega Pi, Alpha Delta Pi (sponsor), Sigma Phi (sponsor), Delta Pi Epsilon (pres. Alpha Theta chpt. 1958). Contbg. author: College Typewriting, 1960; Business Correspondence, 1962. Home: 920 Courtland Ave Park Ridge IL 60068 Office: 30 E Lake St Chicago IL 60601

BARNARD, ROLLIN DWIGHT, financial executive, retired; b. Denver, Apr. 14, 1922; s. George Cooper and Emma (Riggs) B.; m. Patricia Reynolds Bierkamp, Sept. 15, 1943; children: Michael Dana, Rebecca Susan (Mrs. Paul C. Wulfestieg), Laurie Beth (Mrs. Kenneth J. Kostelecky). B.A., Pomona Coll., 1943. Clk. Morey Merc. Co., Denver, 1937-40; ptnr George C. Barnard & Co. (gen. real estate and ins.), Denver, 1946-47; v.p. Foster & Barnard, Inc., 1947-53; instr. Denver U., 1949-53; dir. real estate U.S. P.O. Dept., Washington, 1953-55; dep. asst. postmaster gen., bur. facilities U.S. P.O. Dept., 1955-59, asst. postmaster gen., 1959-61; pres., dir. Midland Fed. Savs. & Loan Assn., Denver, 1962-84; vice chmn. Bank Western Fed. Savs. Bank, 1984—; vice chmn. Western Capital Investment Corp., 1985—, pres., 1985-87; dir. Verex Assurance Inc., 1983-86. Pres. Denver Area council Boy Scouts Am., 1970-71, mem. exec. bd., 1962-73; adv. bd. Denver Area council Boy Scouts Am, 1973—; chmn. Planning and Zoning Commn. Greenwood Village, Colo., 1969-73; mem. Greenwood Village City Council, 1975-77; mem. nat. council Pomona Coll., 1963—; bd. dirs. Downtown Denver Improvement Assn., pres., 1965; bd. dirs. Bethesda Found., Inc., 1973-82; bd. dirs. Children's Hosp., 1979-84, treas., 1983-84; bd. dirs., Rocky Mountain Child Health Services, Inc., 1982—; trustee Mile High United Fund, 1969-72, Denver Symphony Assn., 1973-74; mem. bd. Colo. Council Econ. Edn., 1971-80, chmn., 1971-76; trustee, v.p., treas. Morris Animal Found., 1969-81, pres., chmn., 1974-78, trustee emeritus, 1981—. Served to capt. AUS, World War II. Nominated One of Ten Outstanding Young Men in Am. U.S. Jaycees, 1955, 57; recipient Distinguished Service award Postmaster Gen. U.S., 1960; Silver Beaver award Boy Scouts Am., 1969; Outstanding Citizen of Year Sertoma, 1982; Colo. Citizen of Year Colo. Assn. Realtors, 1982. Mem. Denver C. of C. (pres. 1966-67), U.S. League Savs. Instns. (bd. dirs. 1972-77, vice chmn. 1979-80, chmn. 1980-81, mem. nat. legis. com., exec. com. 1974-77), Savs. League Colo. (exec. com. 1969-73, pres. 1971-72), Colo. Assn. Commerce and Industry (dir. 1971-76), Fellowship Christian Athletes (Denver area dir. 1963-76), Western Stock Show Assn. (dir. 1971—, exec. com. 1982—, 1st v.p. 1985—), Nu Alpha Phi. Republican. Presbyn. Clubs: 26 (Denver) (pres. 1970), Rotary (Denver) (dir. 1979-81, 2d v.p. 1980); Mountain and Plains Appaloosa Horse (pres. 1970-71), Roundup

Riders of the Rockies (dir. 1979—, treas. 1980-87, v.p. 1987—). Home: 3151 East Long Rd Littleton CO 80121

BARNARD, THOMAS ELLIOT, electrical engineer; b. Oklahoma City, Dec. 5, 1941; s. Thomas Elvis and Verdun V. (Johnson) B. Sc.B. in Applied Math., Brown U., 1963, M.S. in Engring., 1986, postgrad. elec. engring., Catholic U., 1986—. Mem. tech. staff Tex. Instruments, Dallas, 1964-69, Washington, 1969-79; sr. staff engr. Gould Ocean Systems Div., Glen Burnie, Md., 1979—. Contbr. articles to profl. jours. Mem. IEEE, Am. Geophys. Union, AAAS. Republican. Club: Whitehurst Garden (Severna Park, Md.) (v.p. 1982-83, treas. 1983-84, pres. 1984-85).

BARNES, CANDACE RAY, retail company executive; b. Kodiak, Alaska, Oct. 23, 1952; d. Marion Carlyle Welch and Virginia (Caldwell) Steineker; m. William L. Barnes, Oct. 8, 1972 (div. July 1979); children—Chadwick W., Kelly C. Student U. Louisville. with Casual Corner, 1972, J. Riggings, Mentor, Ohio, 1972-76; nat. supr. Dan Howard Industries, Chgo., 1979-87; midwest regional mgr. Mondi Internat., Northbrook, Ill., 1987, gen. mgr. Spiegler's Dept. Store 1987—. Avocations: tennis, baseball; needlepoint.

BARNES, DALPHNA RUTH, nurse, poet; b. Lamesa, Tex., May 11, 1933; d. Raymond Vernon and Hazel Blanche (Lemons) Boatright; m. Alvin Burwell Barnes, Jan. 18, 1958; children: David Lynn, Jeanne Michele Barnes O'Neal. AA in Nursing, Texarkana Coll., 1966; BA in Psychology, U. Houston, 1974. intensive care nurse Hermann Hosp., Houston, 1968-69; office nurse, therapist, 1969; from staff nurse to infection control nurse Parkway Hosp., Houston, 1970-77; infection control, employee health coordinator Houston N.W. Med. Ctr., 1977-86, patient advocate, 1986—; adv. bd. Houston Hospice, 1980-82, bd. dirs., 1982-84; meml. chmn. North Harris unit Am. Cancer Soc., 1979, v.p., 1980-81, founder, facilitator Cancer Interaction Group, 1978—, cons. death and dying, dialogue facilitator coach, Tex. div., 1985—; trainer, dialogue facilitator Tex. div. Am. Cancer Soc., 1986—. Contbr. poetry Am. Jour. of Nursing and Sun. Served with USN, 1957-58. Recipient Sword of Hope award North Harris chpt. Am. Cancer Soc., 1980, 81, 82, 83. Mem. Assn. Practitioners Infection Control (pres. Houston chpt. 1980-81), Tex. Soc. Infection Control Practitioners (William L. Benson Meml. award 1980), Am. Soc. Profl. and Exec. Women, Poets Northwest (hospitality chmn. 1988), Tex. Poetry Soc., Tex. Soc. Patient Reps., Poets N.W., Poetry Soc. Tex. Club: Toastmasters (pres. Frankly Speaking Chpt. 1986, edn. v.p. 1987, adminstrv. v.p. 1988—). Home: 20319 Belleau Wood Dr Humble TX 77338 Office: 710 FM 1960 West Houston TX 77090

BARNES, HARRY G., JR., ambassador; b. St. Paul, June 5, 1926; s. Harry George and Bertha Pauline (Blaul) B.; m. Elizabeth Ann Sibley; children: Pauline, Adrienne, Douglas, Sibley. BA summa cum laude, Amherst Coll., 1949, LLD (hon.), 1984; MA in History, Columbia U., 1968; PhD in Engring. (hon.), Stevens Inst., 1985. With fgn. service U.S. Dept. State, 1951—; vice-consul Bombay, India, 1951-53; vice consul, 2d sec. Prague, Czechoslovakia, 1953-55, Moscow, 1957-59; polit. officer Office of Soviet affairs, Dept. State, Washington, 1959-62; dep. chief mission Kathmandu, Nepal, 1963-67; dep. chief of mission Bucharest, Romania, 1968-71; chief jr. officer program Dept. State, Washington, 1971-72, dep. exec. sec., 1972-74; ambassador to Romania Bucharest, 1974-77; dir. gen. fgn. service, dir. personnel Dept. State, Washington, 1977-81; ambassador to India, New Delhi, 1981-85, Chile, Santiago, 1985—. Served with U.S. Army, 1944-46. Recipient Pres. Meritorious Service award, 1983, 87. Presbyterian. Home and Office: American Embassy Ambassador to Chile APO Miami FL 34033

BARNES, JOHN GILBERT PRESSLIE, computer language designer; b. London, Aug. 19, 1937; s. Gilbert Arthur and Edith Helen (Presslie) B.; m. Barbara Winifred Juffkins, Sept. 8, 1962; children: Janet Elizabeth, Helen Jane. BA in Math., Cambridge U., 1961, MA, 1964. Mathematician Imperial Chem. Industries, Reading, Eng., 1961-68, sect. mgr., 1969-75; cons. Imperial Chem. Industries, Slough, Eng., 1975-78; vis. fellow U. Edinburgh (Scotland), 1968-69; dir. lang. research S P L Internat., Abingdon, Eng., 1978-84; tech. dir. Systems Designers, Camberley, Eng., 1984-85; mng. dir. Alsys Ltd., Henley, Eng., 1985—; cons. Dept. Industry, London, 1976-78; indsl. fellow Wolfson Coll., Oxford, Eng., 1979-81; vis. prof. Imperial Coll., London, 1982-84; chmn. ADA Lang. UK Ltd.; mem. bd. Ada, Washington, 1986-87. Author: RTL/2 Design and Philosophy, 1976, Programming in ADA, 1982; editor: ADA in Use, 1985; contbr. articles to software to profl. publs. Fellow Brit. Computer Soc. Home: 11 Albert Rd, Caversham, Reading RG4 7AN, England Office: Alsys Ltd, Newtown Rd, Henley on Thames RG9 1EN, England

BARNES, MARSHALL HAYES, II, personnel relations executive; b. Canton, Ohio, May 15, 1937; s. Frederick Dancy and Mary Anna (Burns) B.; m. Mary Elizabeth Watkins, Mar. 23, 1958; children: Marshall H. III, Mitchell L. BSBA, Ohio State U., Columbus, 1985. Budget analyst Columbia Gas of Ohio, Inc., Columbus, 1966-68, supr. reports unit, 1968-72, EEO coordinator, 1972-77, dir. personnel relations, 1977—. Bd. dirs. Met. YMCA, Columbus, 1983—, No. Cen. Mental Health Ctr., 1988—; mem. Columbus Area Civil Rights Council, 1973-76, employment task force Council on Ethics and Economics, 1988—. Mem. Adminstrv. Mgmt. Soc. (chpt. pres. 1984-85, asst. area dir. 1985-88, merit award 1985, internat. membership com. 1987-88, internat. chpt. programming resources com. 1988—), Acad. Cert. Adminstrv. Mgrs., Columbus Bar Assn. (fee arbitration com. 1984—profl. ethics and grievance com.), Ohio State U. Alumni Assn., Ohio State U. Pacesetters, Midwest Coll. Placement Assn. (treas. 1983-84), Am. Assn. Blacks in Energy, Am. Gas Assn. (chmn. community affairs com. 1987-88), Columbus Spokesman Grad. Club. Mem. Worldwide Ch. God. Club: Ohio State U. Faculty. Lodge: Civitan. Office: Columbia Gas Distbn Companies 200 Civic Center Dr Columbus OH 43216-0117

BARNES, MICHAEL DENNIS, coal mining company executive; b. San Antonio, Tex., Jan. 26, 1948; s. William David and Mildred Boatner (Crosley) B.; B.S. in Mech. Engring., Mont. State U., 1972; A. in Mechanics and Welding, No. Mont. Coll., 1969; m. Carol Ann Faller, June 17, 1972; children—Shaina, Ian, Rachel. Mechanic, partsman, engr. Long Constrn. Co., Colstrip, Mont., 1972-77; master mechanic Arch Minerals Corp., Hanna, Wyo., 1977-78; dragline erection engr., constrn. supt. N.Am. Coal Co., Bismarck, N.D., 1978-80, shop ops. mgr., 1981-83, maintenance mgr., 1984-88, shop supr., 1988—. Den leader, com. chmn. Big Sky council Boy Scouts Am., 1972-77; vol. fireman City of Colstrip, 1973-77; squad leader Mercer County Ambulance Services, 1983—; religious edn. instr. 1983-88. Mem. Assn. Emergency Care Technicians, Nat. Registry Emergency Med. Technicians. Mem. Ch. Word of Faith. Home: 1201 Sunrise Dr Hazen ND 58545 Office: North American Coal Co 2200 Schaffer Dr Bismarck ND 58501

BARNES, PER, marketing executive; b. Oslo, Norway, Jan. 5, 1943; s. Einar and May (Quist) B.; diploma Mktg. Sch. Oslo, 1967, Oslo Inst. Bus. Econs., 1968, Inst. Mktg., Oslo, 1970; m. Veslemöy Didriksen, Sept. 27, 1967; children: Erik, Hanne. Chief account exec. Kverneland Advt. Agy., Oslo, 1968-70; creative dir. Ogilvy and Mather, Oslo, 1971-77, mng. dir., 1978-81, 82—; creative dir. Scandinavia, Ogilvy and Mather, Inc., San Francisco, 1981-82; founder Scandinavian Am. Mktg. Inc., San Francisco, 1982; bd. dirs. Norwegian Bus. Forum, Best Selection, Inc. Recipient numerous awards for advt. including award Cannes Comml. Film Festival, 1978, Clio awards, N.Y.C., 1980, 81. Mem. Norwegian Am. C. of C. (chmn. No. Calif. chpt. 1983-87). Home: 350 Karen Way Tiburon CA 94920

BARNES, PHILIPPA KAY, educator; b. Abingdon, Oxfordshire, Eng., Feb. 10, 1956; d. Robert Sandford and Julia Frances Marriot (Grant) B. Cert. of Edn., Froebel Inst. U. London, 1977. Tchr. St. Michael's Sch., Woking, Surrey, Eng., 1978, Norland Pl. Sch., London, 1979, Hampshire Sch., London, 1979, Faringdon (Eng.) Sch., 1979-80, North Hinksey Primary Sch., Oxford, Eng., 1981, West Hanney Village Sch., Wantage, Eng., 1981, Thameside Sch., Abingdon, 1982, Hawtreys Malborough, Wiltshire, Eng., 1982-83; tchr. math. and French Edgeborough Farnham, Surrey, 1983-85; tchr. Surrey County Council, Banstead, Eng., 1985-87, Newlands Sch., Seaford, Eng., 1987—. Mem. Assn. Christian Tchrs., Nat. Union Tchrs., London U. Gilbert and Sullivan Soc., Oxford U. Gilbert and Sullivan Soc., Abingdon Sch. Choral Soc., Marlborough Choral Soc., Farnham and Bourne choral Soc., Michaelis Guild. Home: 46 Alterton Close, Goldsworth Park, Woking Surrey GU21 3ED, England

BARNES, ROBERT ALLAN, motor carrier executive; b. Cleve., May 3, 1927; s. Ernest Winfred and Ethel (Lanham) B.; m. Betty Ammerman, June 24, 1950; children—Paul R., Carolyn Barnes Hughes. B.S., Miami U.-Ohio, 1950; M.A. Columbia U., 1952; Ph.D., Ohio State U., 1963. Dir., dept. music N.C. State U., Raleigh, 1950-62; asst. to pres. Ohio State U., Columbus, 1962-65, dean Newark campus, 1965-79; pres. Central Ohio Tech. Coll., Newark, 1971-79, B & L Motor Freight, Newark, 1979-82, United Carriers Corp., Newark, Ohio, 1982—; dir. First Fed. Savs. & Loan, Newark, United Carriers Corp. Author: Fundamentals of Music, 1964; contbr. articles to profl. jours. Bd. dirs. United Way, Newark, Ohio, 1968, YMCA, 1972; pres. Weathervane Summer Playhouse, 1977. Served with USN, 1945-46. Paul Harris fellow, 1983. Mem. Interstate Carriers Conf. (bd. dirs.), Ohio Trucking Assn. (bd. dirs.), Am. Trucking Assn., Newark C. of C. (pres.). Republican. Methodist. Club: Moundbuilders Country. Lodge: Rotary (past pres. Newark club). Office: United Carriers Corp 140 Everett Ave PO Box 4070 Newark OH 43055

BARNES, ROBERT VERTREESE, JR., masonry contractor executive; b. Dallas, Oct. 7, 1946; s. Robert Vertreese and Doris Corinne (Haffen) B.; m. Deborah Dee Brown, May 31, 1968; children: Robert V. III, John David, Leslie Shannon. BS in Indsl. Tech., E. Tex. State U., 1976. Salesman Sears, Roebuck and Co., Dallas, 1965-66, dept. mgr., 1967-69; estimator Dee Brown Masonry, Inc., Dallas, 1970-75, contract adminstr., 1976-77; v.p. Cardinal Masonry Co., Houston, 1978-79; v.p. Dee Brown Masonry, Inc., Houston, 1980-85, exec. v.p., 1985—; exec. v.p. Dee Brown, Inc., 1985—; v.p. Shiloh Investment Co.; trustee, chmn. bricklayers health and welfare Bricklayer's Pension Fund, 1983-85. Pres. Katy Youth Soccer Assn., 1980-81; mgr. Solor "74" Soccer Club, 1986-88; dir. Whiterock Ch.'s Athletic Assn., 1972-77; bishop warden St. Cuthbert's Episcopal Ch.; bd. dirs. St. John's Episcopal Sch., 1987—, sch. fin. com., health, safety and ins. com., bldg. facility com. Mem. Mason Contractors Assn. Am. (contract research com. 1982-83, chmn. labor com.), Associated Gen. Contractors of Dallas (subcontractor relations com. 1988—), Assn. Masonry Contractors Tex. (pres. 1983, sec./treas. 1981-82), Assn. Masonry Contractors Houston (pres. 1982-83, v.p. 1981), Am. Subcontractor Assn. (v.p. 1982-83, bd. dirs. Houston 1982-85, also mem. nat. coms.), Dallas Exec. Assn., Houston C. of C., N.W. Houston C. of C., Delta Sigma Pi. Republican. Clubs: Pine Forest Country (Houston); Dallas Athletic, Country. Office: PO Box 28335 Dallas TX 75228

BARNES, THOMAS JOSEPH, United Nations official; b. St. Paul, June 18, 1930; s. Ralph Weikert and Helen (O'Connor) B.; m. Mai Tang; children: Ann, Kim, Kevin; children by previous marriage: Christopher, Ross, Karen, Shannon. B.A., U. Minn., 1950, M.A., 1951. With fgn. service 1957-80; vice consul Saigon, Vietnam, 1958-60; prin. officer Am. consulate, Hue, Viet Nam, 1960-61; polit. officer Bangkok, Thailand, 1962-64, Vientiane, Laos, 1964-67; province sr. adviser Binh Long, Vietnam, 1967-68; country officer for Laos State Dept., 1968-70; prin. officer Am. Consulate, Udorn, Thailand, 1970-71; asso. dir. AID, Nhatrang, Vietnam, 1971-72; consul gen. Tangier, Morocco, 1972-73, Can Tho, Vietnam, 1973; polit. counselor Bangkok, 1973-75; sr. staff mem. for East Asia Nat. Security Council, 1975-76; student Sr. Seminar in Fgn. Policy, State Dept., 1976-77; regional refugee coordinator Bangkok, 1977-78; diplomat-in-residence U. Hawaii, 1978-79; dir. Interagy. Working Group on Kampuchea, Dept. State, Washington, 1979-80; with UN High Commn. for Refugees, 1980—; dep. rep. UN High Commn. for Refugees, Somalia, 1980-81; chief Southwest Asia sect. UN High Commn. for Refugees, Geneva, 1982-86; head supplies and food aid service UN High Commn. for Refugees, 1986-87, head orgn. and mgmt., 1987—. Author: (monograph) Of All the 36 Alternatives; Indochinese Resettlement In America, 1977. Served to capt. AUS, 1951-56. Recipient Award for Valor, Meritorious Honor award State Dept., Superior Honor awards State Dept, AID. Home: 6 Chemin De La Pie, 1292 Chambesy Switzerland Office: UN High Commn for Refugees, Case Postale 2500, 1211 Geneva 2 Depot, Switzerland

BARNESS, AMNON SHEMAYA, finance executive; b. Israel, Oct. 16, 1924; s. Nahum and Lea (Muhlmann) B.; m. Caren Heller, 1978; children: Rena Barness Lahav, Dalia Barness Kempler, Danny, Jordan. B.A., Am. U. Cairo, 1947; M.A., Syracuse U., 1950; Ph.D. (hon.), Stonehill Coll., 1974. Pres. Trans-Internat. Mgmt. Corp., 1976—; founder, pres., chmn. bd. Daylin Inc. (now subs. W.R. Grace Co.); chmn. bd. Handy Dan Home Improvement Centers, Inc. (now subs. W.R. Grace Co.), Commerce, Calif., 1972—; gen. partner Adam Assocs., Beverly Hills, Calif., 1965—; sr. partner Adam Fin. Corp., 1966—; chmn. exec. com., dir. PharmaControl Corp. (OTC), Englewood Cliffs, N.J., 1982—; dir. IFEX, Inc. (OTC), 1983—, Serpro S.A., Unico Mortgage Bank, Tel Aviv, Israel, Bourguet de Clausade Traders, Paris, JOBA B.V., Amsterdam. Founder, chmn. Fund Higher Edn.; founder, pres. Fund for Job Corp. Grads., 1965; pres. Lyndon Johnson Youth Opportunity Campaign Council, 1965; Gen. chmn. Israel Bond campaign; pres. Job Corp Grad. Found., 1966—, Juvenile Opportunities Endeavor Found., 1974—; v.p. Brandeis Inst., 1964-70; bd. dirs. Temple Sinai, Los Angeles, 1968-72; bd. govs. Weizman Inst. Sci., 1970—; Andean Pact countries rep. Mecaform, Paris, Am. Med. Internat., 1977-82; founder, bd. dirs. European Found. for Scis., Arts, and Culture, 1982—. Decorated knight comdr. merit Equestrian Order, Holy Sepulcher of Jerusalem, Israel Prime Minister's medal, others; honored Inst. Pasteur-Weizmann, Paris, 1985. Address: 1500 Broadway Suite 808 New York NY 10036

BARNESS, LEWIS ABRAHAM, physician; b. Atlantic City, N.J., July 31, 1921; s. Joseph and Mary (Silverstein) B.; m. Elaine Berger, June 14, 1953 (dec. Jan. 1985); children: Carol, Laura, Joseph; m. Enid May Fischer Gilbert, July 5, 1987; stepchildren: Mary, Elizabeth, Jennifer, Rebecca. A.B., Harvard U., 1941, M.D., 1944; M.A. (hon.), U. Pa., 1971. Intern Phila. Gen. Hosp., 1944-45; resident Children's Med. Center, Boston, 1947-50; asst. chief, then chief dept. pediatrics Phila. Gen. Hosp., 1951-72; vis. physician U. Pa. Hosp., 1952-57, acting chief, then chief, 1957-72; mem. faculty U. Pa. Sch. Medicine, 1951-72, prof. pediatrics, 1964-72; prof. pediatrics, chmn. dept. U. So. Fla. Med. Sch., Tampa, 1972—; vis. prof. Univ. Wis., 1987-88. Author: Pediatric Physical Diagnosis Yearbook, edits. 1-5, 1957—; editor: Advances in Pediatrics, 1976—; asst. editor Pediatric Gastroenterology and Nutrition, 1981—; editorial bd. Cons., 1960-84, Pediatrics, 1978-83, Core Jour. Pediatrics, 1980—, Contemporary Pediatrics, 1984—, Jour. Clin. Medicine and Nutrition, 1985—, Nutrition Rev., 1985-87. Served to capt. AUS, 1945-46. Recipient Lindback Teaching award U. Pa., 1963; Borden award nutrition, 1972; Noer Disting. Prof. award, 1980, Joseph B. Goldberger award in clin. nutrition, 1984. Mem. Am. Pediatric Soc. (recorder-editor 1964-75, pres. 1985-86), Soc. Pediatric Research, Am. Acad. Pediatrics (chmn. com. on nutrition 1974-81), Am. Coll. Nutrition, Am. Inst. Nutrition, AAAS, Sigma Xi, Alpha Omega Alpha. Home: 548 W Davis Blvd Tampa FL 33606

BARNETT, BENJAMIN LEWIS, JR., physician, educator; b. Woodruff, S.C., July 22, 1926; s. Benjamin Lewis and Mattie Bernice (Skinner) B.; m. Annalyne Louise Hall, Oct. 25, 1958; children: Benjamin Lewis III, Jane Kristen. B.S., Furman U., 1946, LL.D., 1978; M.D., Med. U. S.C., 1949. Diplomate Am. Bd. Family Practice (mem. exam. bd. 1975-81, dir. 1976-81, exec. com. 1979-81, pres. 1980-81). Intern Protestant Episcopal Hosp., Phila., 1949-50; pvt. practice gen. medicine Woodruff, 1950-70; assoc. prof. family practice Med. U. S.C., Charleston, 1970-74; prof. family practice Med. U. S.C., 1974-77, asst. dir. family practice residency program, 1970-75, chief undergrad. curriculum, 1970-77; vice chmn. dept. family practice 1973-77, asst. dean for student affairs, 1975-77; mem. clin. staff Med. U. Hosp., Charleston County Hosp., 1970-77; Walter M. Seward prof., chmn. dept. family medicine U. Va. Med. Sch., 1977—, baccalaureate, 1986; family medicine physician-in-chief U. Va. Med. Center Hosp., 1977—; chief of staff Woodruff Hosp., 1966-69; vis. lectr. numerous med. schs.; Stoneburner lectr. Med. Coll. Va., 1975; Daniel Drake lectr. U. Cin., 1976; Robert P. Walton lectr. Med. U. S.C., 1978; Goodlark prof. U. Tenn., 1979; vis. scholar U. Mich. Med. Sch., 1984; vis. prof. Med. Coll. of Ga., 1982, Case Western Res. Sch. Medicine, 1984; Mack Lipkin Vis. Prof. U. Oreg., 1987; 7th Leland Blanchard meml. lectr. Soc. Tchrs. Family Medicine ann. meeting, Nashville, 1985; Health officer, Town of Woodruff, 1950-54. Editor: S.C. Family Physician, 1973-74; contbr. articles to med. jours. and chpts. to textbooks. Mem. Spartanburg County Bd. Edn., 1968-70, sec., 1969-70; trustee Bethea Bapt. Home for Aged, Darlington, S.C., 1972-73. Served with USNR, 1954-56. Named Citizen of Year Woodmen of World, 1968; recipient Golden Apple award for clin. teaching Student AMA, 1973; Thomas W. Johnson award Am. Acad. Family Physicians, 1976. Mem. AMA (mem. residency rev. com. for family practice 1974-79), Va., Albemarle County med. socs., Soc. Tchrs. Family Medicine (v.p. 1974, sec.-treas. 1975, dir. 1981-85, cert. of excellence 1983), Am. Acad. Family Physicians, S.C. Acad. Family Physicians (v.p. 1973, pres. 1975-76), Spartanburg County Med. Soc. (v.p. 1968), Am. Philatelic Soc., Am. Manuscript Soc., Council Acad. Socs., Furman U. Alumni Assn. (dir. 1972-77), Alpha Omega Alpha (faculty councilor), Alpha Kappa Kappa (pres. 1948), Kappa Alpha (v.p. 1944). Baptist (deacon, chmn. bd.). Club: Masons (32 degree). Home: 2406 Northfields Rd Charlottesville VA 22901

BARNETT, BERNARD HARRY, lawyer; b. Helena, Ark., July 13, 1916; s. Harry and Rebecca (Grossman) B.; BA U. Mich., 1934-36; J.D., Vanderbilt U., 1940; m. Marian Spiesberger, Apr. 9, 1949; 1 son, Charles Dawson. Bar: Ky. 1940, D.C. Practiced in Louisville, 1940-42; assoc. firm Woodward, Dawson, Hobson & Fulton, 1946-48; partner firm Bulitt, Dawson & Tarrant, 1948-52, firm Greenbaum, Barnett, Wood & Doll, 1952-70, firm Barnett & McConnell, 1972, firm Barnett, Greenebaum, Martin & McConnell, 1972-74, firm Barnett, Alagia, Greenebaum, Miller & Senn, 1974-75; sr. ptnr. Barnett & Alagia, 1975-87; bd. dirs. Fuqua Industries, Inc., Hasbro, Inc., Advanced World Techs. Inc., U.S. Container Corp.; mem. adv. group Joint Com. on Internal Revenue Taxation, U.S. Congress, 1953-55, Com. on Ways and Means, U.S. Ho. of Reps., 1956-58. Chmn., Louisville Fund, 1952-53; mem. Louisville and Jefferson County Republican Exec. Com., 1954-60; chmn. Ky. Rep. Fin. Com., 1955-60; nat. exec. com., nat. campaign cabinet United Jewish Appeal, 1959-71, nat. chmn., 1967-71, campaign chmn., Louisville, 1968-69; trustee Spalding Coll., Louisville, 1975-82, Benjamin N. Cardozo Sch. Law, 1979-84, Ford's Theatre, 1981-87; bd. dirs. Norton Gallery and Sch. Art, 1980-87. Served as lt. USNR, 1942-45. Mem. ABA, D.C. Bar, Louisville Bar Assn., Ky. Bar Assn., Fellows of Am. Bar Found. Deceased, Dec. 10, 1987. Office: Barnett & Alagia 250 S County Rd Palm Beach FL 33480 also: 1000 Thomas Jefferson St NW Suite 600 Washington DC 20007

BARNETT, CHARLES RADCLIFFE, film writer, producer, director, health physicist; b. N.Y.C., Feb. 23, 1934; s. Carlyle Reginald and Anne Nathalie (Mooney) B.; m. Noel Ray Phillips, Feb. 3, 1963 (div. 1963). B.A., Columbia Coll., 1956; Ph.D., Union Grad. Sch., Cin., 1980. Cert. profl. geologist. Health physicist U. Calif., Los Alamos, N.Mex., 1962-69, writer, producer, dir., 1975—, head motion picture prodn., 1977—; pvt. practice geol. cons., Woodstock, N.Y., 1971-73; dir., v.p. Anthrop. Film Found., Santa Fe, 1978—; dir. audio-visuals Albuquerque Mus. Maya Project, 1983-87; Writer, producer, dir. more than 60 documentary films, 1975—(90 awards); editorial bd.Explorers Jour., 1988—; contbr. Smithsonian mag., various jours. Mem. N.Mex. Arts Commn. Media Panel, 1978, chmn., 1979, 80. Served with U.S. Army, 1956-58, W.Ger. Recipient film awards, France, Belgium, Italy, Yugoslavia, Germany, Gt. Brit., Czechoslovakia, Poland, Egypt, Brazil, 1978—, 18 CINE Golden Eagle awards, Council on Internat. Non-theatrical Events, 1978—. Mem. Univ. Film Assn., Am. Film Inst., Rio Grande Producers Assn., Ind. Video and Filmmakers, Am. Inst. Profl. Geologists, Edouard Manet Soc. (Paris, regional v.p. 1967—), Explorers Club of N.Y. Roman Catholic. Club: Quien Sabe. Home: 331 Calle Loma Norte Santa Fe NM 87501 Office: Univ Calif Los Alamos Nat Lab Motion Picture/Video Prodn Unit Mail Stop D-415 Los Alamos NM 87545

BARNETT, CRAWFORD FANNIN, JR., physician; b. Atlanta, May 11, 1938; s. Crawford Fannin and Penelope Hollinshead (Brown) B.; student Taft Sch., 1953-56, U. Minn., 1957; A.B. magna cum laude, Yale U., 1960; postgrad. (Davison scholar) Oxford (Eng.) U., 1963; M.D. (Trent scholar), Duke, 1964; m. Elizabeth McCarthy Hale, June 6, 1964; children: Crawford Fannin III, Robert Hale. Intern internal medicine Duke U. Med. Center, Durham, N.C., 1964-65, resident, 1965; resident internal medicine Wilmington (Del.) Med. Center, 1965-66; dir. Tenn. Heart Disease Control Program, Nashville, 1966-68; practice medicine specializing in internal medicine, Atlanta, 1968—; mem. staff Crawford Long, Northside, Grady Meml., West Paces Ferry, hosps. (all Atlanta); mem. teaching staff Vanderbilt Med. Center, Nashville, 1966-68, Crawford Long Meml. Hosp., 1969—; clin. instr. internal medicine, dept. medicine Emory U. Med. Sch., Atlanta, 1969—. Bd. govs. Doctors Meml. Hosp., 1971-80; bd. dirs. Atlanta Speech Sch., 1976-80, Historic Oakland Cemetery, 1976-86, So. Turf Nurseries, 1977—, Tech Industries, 1978—. Served as surgeon USPHS, 1966-68. Fellow Am. Geog. Soc.; mem. Am. Fedn. Clin. Research, Council Clin. Cardiology, Am., Ga., Atlanta med. assns., Am., Ga. heart assns., Am., Ga. socs. internal medicine, Am. Assn. History Medicine, Ga., Atlanta (dir. 1976-84), hist. socs., Ga., Nat. Trust for Historic Preservation, Internat. Hippocratic Found. Soc. (Greece), Faculty of History of Medicine and Pharmacy Worshipful Soc. Apothecaries of London, Atlanta Com. on Fgn. Relations (chmn. exec. com.), So. Council Internat. and Public Affairs, Newcomen Soc., Atlanta Clin. Soc., Victorian Soc. Am. (bd. advisers Atlanta chpt. 1971-86), Mensa, Gridiron, Phi Beta Kappa. Episcopalian. Clubs: Piedmont Driving, Yale (dir. 1970-74), Nine O'Clocks (Atlanta); Pan Am. Doctors (Hidalgo, Mex.). Contbr. articles to profl. publs. Home: 2739 Ramsgate Ct NW Atlanta GA 30305-2830 Office: 3250 Howell Mill Rd NW Atlanta GA 30327

BARNETT, DAVID RICHARD, illustrator, designer; b. Leicester, England, Sept. 18, 1931; s. Thomas Samuel and Annie (Needham) B.; m. Jean Winifred Gatton, March 23, 1957; children: Robert, Christine, Edward. Student, Coll. of Art, Eng., 1947-49. Apprentice to Frank Gayton, Leicester; designer, visualiser Advt., Ltd., Leicester, 1950-1977; free-lance illustrator Leicester, 1977—. Illustrator: Wild White Stallion, 1977, My First Prayer Book, 1977. Recipient award Design Council, London, 1987. Mem. Nat. Graph. Assn. Anglican. Clubs: Granville Tennis, Oadby. Home and Office: 41 Hidcote Rd, Oadby Leicester LE2 5PG, England

BARNETT, JONATHAN, architect, city planner; b. Boston, Jan. 6, 1937; s. David and Josephine (Wolff) B.; m. Nory Miller, Mar. 19, 1983. B.A. magna cum laude, Yale U., 1958, M. Arch., 1963; M.A. Mellon fellow, U. Cambridge, Eng., 1960. Designer Haines, Lundberg & Waehler, Archts., N.Y.C., 1963, 64; assoc. editor Archtl. Record, N.Y.C., 1964-67; planning cons. N.Y.C.; New City Exhbn. at Mus. Modern Art, 1966, 67; prin. urban designer N.Y.C. Planning Dept., 1967-68, dir. urban design group, 1969-71; prof., dir. grad. program in urban design CCNY, 1971—; cons. AIA, South St. Seaport Mus., Nat. Park Service, Louisville, Kansas City, Cleve., Charleston, S.C., Norfolk, Va., Pitts., Salt Lake City, N.Y., others, 1971—; bd. dirs. N.Y. Landmarks Conservancy. Author: Urban Design as Public Policy, 1974, (with John C. Portman, Jr.) The Architect as Developer, 1976, Introduction to Urban Design, 1982, The Elusive City, 1986; editor: Perspecta 8, 1962; contbr.: New Zoning, 1970, Collaborations: Artists and Architects, 1981; editorial cons.: Archtl. Record, 1968—; contbr. articles to profl. jours. Mem. adv. bd. Environment and Behavior, 1968-78; mem. adv. bd. Urban Design Internat., 1977—, Process: Architecture, 1977—. Fellow AIA; mem. Am. Inst. Certified Planners, Archtl. League N.Y. (v.p. 1968-70, dir. 1975—, pres. 1977-81), Mcpl. Art Soc. (dir. 1970-78, 81—), Berzelius Soc. Unitarian. Clubs: Yale, Century Assn. (N.Y.C.); Elizabethan of Yale. Home: 30 Park Ave New York NY 10016 Office: Sch Architecture City Coll New York NY 10031

BARNETT, MARGARET EDWINA, nephrologist, researcher; b. Ft. Benning, Ga., July 28, 1949; d. Eddie Lee and Margaret Thomas (Herndon) Barnett. B.S. magna cum laude with distinction in Zoology, Ohio State U., 1969; M.D., Johns Hopkins U., 1973; Ph.D. in Anatomy, Case Western Res. U., 1984. Intern, Greater Balt. Med. Center, Towson, Md., 1973-74; med. resident Cleve. Clinic Ednl. Found., 1974-75, Univ. Hosps. Cleve., 1975-76; nephrology fellow, 1976-78, med. teaching fellow, 1978-84; nephrology rounding physician Community Dialysis Ctr., Cleve. and Mentor, Ohio, 1978-83; research assoc. Case Western Res. U., Cleve., 1978-79, 83-84; physician emergency medicine Huron Regional Urgent Care Ctrs., Inc., Cleve., 1983-84; preceptor renal correlation conf., Case Western Res. Sch. Medicine, 1980-81, lectr. anatomy and histology 1979-83; asst. prof. medicine/nephrology Milton S. Hershey Med. Ctr. Pa. State Univ., Hershey, 1984-87; practice medicine specializing in nephrology Arnett Clinic, Lafayette, Ind., 1987—. Scholar Gen. Motors, Leo Yassinoff, Alpha Epsilon

Delta, Beanie Drake, Am. Heart Assn., 1977; recipient NIH-Nat. Research Service award, 1979-82; Ohio div. Am. Heart Assn. grantee, 1980-81; Ohio Kidney Found. grantee, 1977-78; Pres.'s Scholarship award, 1967-69; AMA Physician Recognition award, 1984-87. Mem. John Hopkins Med. and Surg. Soc., AMA (physician research evaluation panel 1981-83), Internat. Soc. of Nephrology, Nat. Kidney Found., World Tae Kwon Do Fedn., Seoul, Korea, MENSA, Am. Film Inst., Phi Beta Kappa, Alpha Epsilon Delta, Alpha Kappa Alpha. Democrat.

BARNETT, MARILYN, advertising agency executive; b. Detroit, June 10, 1934; d. Henry and Kate (Boesky) Schiff; B.A., Wayne State U., 1953; children: Rhona, Ken. Supr. broadcast prodn. Northgate Advt. Agy., Detroit, 1968-73; founder, part-owner, pres. Mars Advt. Co., Southfield, Mich., 1973—. Named Advt. Woman of Yr., Women's Club of Detroit, 1986, Outstanding Woman in Agy Mgmt., Am. Women in Radio and TV, Inc., 1987, Outstanding Woman in Broadcast, 1980. Mem. AFTRA (dir. 1959-67), Screen Actors Guild, Adcraft, Women's Adcraft. Creator, producer radio and TV programs, 1956-58; nat. spokesperson on TV, 1960-70. Club: Economic (Ad Woman of Yr. 1986). Office: 24209 Northwestern Hwy Southfield MI 48075 also: Mars Advt Co 7720 Sunset Blvd Los Angeles CA 90046

BARNEVIK, PERCY NILS, electrical company executive; b. Simrishamn, Sweden, Feb. 13, 1941; s. Einar and Anna Barnevik; m. Aina Orvarsson, 1963; 3 children. MBA, Gothenburg Sch. Econs., Sweden, 1964; postgrad., Stanford U., 1965-66. With The Johnson Group, Sweden, 1966-69; with Sandvik AB, Sandviken, Sweden, 1969-80, group controller, 1969-75; pres. U.S. affiliate 1975-79, exec. v.p., 1979-80; pres., chief exec. officer ASEA, 1980-87; chmn. Sandvik AB, 1983—; pres., chief exec. officer Asea Brown Boveri Ltd., 1988—. Office: ABB Asea Brown Boveri Ltd, PO Box 8131, CH-8050 Zurich Switzerland also: Sandvik AB, S-81181 Sandviken Sweden

BARNEY, DUANE LOWELL, scientist, consultant; b. Topeka, Kans., Aug. 3, 1928; s. James Earl and Irene (Franz) B.; m. Virginia Beulah Eddy, June 30, 1950; children—Linda Elizabeth, Mary Virginia. B.S. in Chemistry with honors, Kans. State U., 1950; M.A., Johns Hopkins U., 1951, Ph.D., 1953. Research chemist Gen. Electric Co., N.Y., 1953-66, mgr. battery tech. lab., battery bus. sect., 1966-68, mgr. engring., 1968-72, mgr. battery bus. sect., 1972-74, gen. mgr. home laundry engring. dept., Ky., 1974-78; assoc. dir. chem. tech. div. Argonne Nat. Lab., Ill., 1978-84, sr. engr., 1978. DuPont fellow, 1952-53. Fellow Am. Inst. of Chemist; mem. Am. Chem. Soc., Electrochem. Soc., AAAS, Phi Kappa Phi, Sigma Xi. Presbyterian. Contbr. articles in field.

BARNHARD, SHERWOOD ARTHUR, printing company executive; b. Newark, Mar. 14, 1921; s. Charles L. and Blanche (Tarnow) B.; m. Esther Lasky, Feb. 21, 1946; children—Ronald Harris, Paul Ira. BS, Franklin and Marshall Coll., 1942. With Lasky Co., Millburn, N.J., 1946—, exec. v.p., 1956-61, pres., 1961-86, chmn., 1986—; pres. N.J. Web and Sheetfed Color Lithographers; sec., v.p. Daus. of Israel Geriatric Ctr., West Orange; N.J.; past trustee Temple Sharey Tefilo-Israel, South Orange, N.J.; bd. overseers N.Y.C. Ctr. Graphic Arts Mgmt. and Tech. Mem. Printing Industries N.J. (past pres.), Assn. Graphic Arts (past pres., past bd. dirs.), Met. Lithographers Assn. (past pres., mem. labor com.), Mktg. Communications Execs., Advt. Club N.Y., Zeta Beta Tau. Clubs: Crestmont Golf and Country (West Orange); Maplewood (N.J.) Country; Del-Aire Country (Delray Beach, Fla.).

BARNHART, WILLIAM RUPP, clergyman, educator; b. Saegerstown, Pa., Feb. 7, 1903; s. John L. and Emma A. (Rupp) B.; m. Eleanor Welch Lyles, Sept. 1, 1927 (dec. July 1981); children: Eleanor Hoyle, Joanne Sanford. A.B., Johns Hopkins U., 1923; A.M., Columbia U., 1924; student, Union Theol. Sem., 1923-25, 1926-27; D.D., Pacific U., 1938. Student asst. Madison Ave. Presbyn. Ch., N.Y.C., 1926-27; prof. philosophy and religion Pacific U., Oreg., 1927-30; head dept. religion Hood Coll., Frederick, Md., 1930-47; head dept. religion and philosophy Hood Coll., 1947-58; minister Circular Congregational Ch., Charleston, S.C., 1958-68; minister emeritus Circular Congl. Ch., 1968—; exec. sec. Fedn. of Chs., Washington, 1940-41; ordained to ministry Congl. Ch., 1930; mem. Potomoc Synod of Evang. and Ref. Ch., 1930-58; past mem. Edn. and Research of Fed. Council of Churches of Christ in Am.; mem. Inter-Faith com. on Religious Life in Nation's Capital, 1940-42; lectr. religious emphasis weeks at various univs. and colls.; weekly religious broadcaster, 1958-80; mem. Md.-Del. Council Chs., 1942-58, Univ. Christian Mission Team sent out by Fed. Council Chs. of Christ, 1946-49, preaching mission teams; lectr. ministerial confs. Contbr. articles to religious jours. Bd. dirs. Community Chest, Washington, 1940-42; trustee S.C. State Coll., 1972—. Mem. Am. Philos. Assn., Nat. Assn. Bibl. Instrs., Charleston Ministerial Assn. (pres. 1964). Clubs: University (Balt.); Interchurch (Washington) (pres. 1948-49); Rotary (Charleston, S.C.), Charleston Country (Charleston, S.C.). Home: 16 Broughton Rd Charleston SC 29407

BARNS, WILLIAM DERRICK, historian, emeritus educator; b. Fayette County, Pa., Apr. 3, 1917; s. William Post and Lida (Williams) B.; m. Doretha Mae Clayton, Sept. 3, 1947. A.B., Pa. State U., 1939, M.A., 1940; Ph.D., W.Va. U., 1947. Instr. history Pa. State U., 1939-40, vis. prof., 1949; mem. faculty W.Va. U., Morgantown, 1940—; prof. history W.Va. U., 1977-85, prof. emeritus, 1985—; vis. prof. Marshall U., Huntington, W.Va., 1951, McMaster U., Hamilton, Ont., Can., 1957, 59, 61. Author: The Granger and Populist Movements in West Virginia, 1873-1914, 1947, Highlights in West Virginia's Agricultural History, 1863-1963, 1963, The West Virginia State Grange: The First Century, 1873-1973, 1973; also articles. Field agt. Am. Friends Service Com., 1944-46; co-founder, dir. W.Va. Civil Liberties Union, 1970-79, v.p., 1979-81. Mem. Am. Hist. Assn., Orgn. Am. Historians, Agrl. History Soc., AAUP (co-founder W.Va. conf. 1961, dir. 1961-71), W.Va. Hist. Assn. Coll. and Univ. Tchrs. (co-founder 1959, pres. 1962-63, archivist, adv. 1973—), English Speaking Union, Phi Kappa Phi, Phi Alpha Theta, Pi Gamma Mu, Alpha Tau Omega. Libertarian. Mem. Soc. of Friends. Office: W Va U Dept History Morgantown WV 26506

BARNUM, OTIS RAY, physician, consultant; b. Guymon, Okla., Apr. 16, 1951; s. Phillip R. Barnum and Jewel M. (Gross) Darnell; m. Cindy Marie Von Bargen, Nov. 25, 1983; children—Keely Lauren, Aaron Rider. B.S., U. Okla., 1973; D.O., Kansas City Coll. Osteopathic Medicine, 1977. Resident in internal medicine Tulane Sch. Medicine, New Orleans, 1977-80; chief resident USPHS Hosp., New Orleans, 1980; gen. practice medicine, Guymon, 1981—; dir. intensive care unit Meml. Hosp., Guymon, 1982—, dir. cardiac rehab., 1982—, dir. med. edn., 1982—; med. advisor Tex. County Heart Assn., Okla., 1983—. Profl. del. Hosp. Planning Com., Guymon, 1983-85. Served to lt. comdr. USPHS, 1977-80. Mem. AMA, So. Med. Assn., Nat. Am. Osteopathic Assn., Okla. Osteopathic Assn. (v.p. northwest dist. 1983), Am. Diabetes Assn. Republican. Methodist. Avocation: photography. Home: 406 William Ave Natchitoches LA 71457 Office: Meml Specialty Clinic 215 Highway 1 South Natchitoches LA 71457

BARNUM, WILLIAM DOUGLAS, communications company executive; b. Denton, Tex., July 28, 1946; s. Billie Douglas and Leticia Christina (Cox) B.; BSBA with distinction in Econs., Georgetown U., 1967; MBA, Fairleigh Dickinson U., 1985; m. Mary Ann Mook, Aug. 10, 1968. Acct., RCA Corp., Cherry Hill, N.J., 1967-68, Andros Island, Bahamas, 1968-70, budget and cost analyst, Cherry Hill, 1970, adminstr. telephone systems, 1970-73; mgr. project adminstrn. White Sands Radar Project, Holloman AFB, N.Mex., 1973-74; coordinator profit center acctg., N.Y.C , 1974-76, adminstr. globcom systems, N.Y.C., 1976-77, mgr. spl. project and accounts-payable, N.Y.C., 1978-79, mgr. fin., 1979-81, mgr. gateway ops., dir. field support services, 1982-88; mgr. network services MCI Internat., 1988—. Mem. Republican Presdl. Task Force. Mem. Am. Def. Preparedness Assn., Am. Security Council, NRA (life), Knifemakers Guild (hon.) Am. Knife Throwers Alliance (hon.), Mensa, Delta Phi Epsilon, Delta Mu Delta. Presbyterian. Author: Kroodley Made Knife Catalog, 1977. Home: PO Box 893 Polo NJ 07931 Office: MCI Internat 201 Centennial Ave Piscataway NJ 08854

BARNUM, WILLIAM MILO, architect; b. N.Y.C., June 17, 1927; s. Phelps and Catharine (Davis) B.; student Phillips Andover Acad., 1942-45; B.A., Yale, 1950; M.Arch., U. Pa., 1952; m. Katharine Miller, Aug. 10, 1971; children—Anne Lyttleton, Catharine Hollerith, William Milo, Nathaniel Phelps, Caleb Townsend. Archtl. asst. job capt. Eggers & Higgins, 1952-54; job capt. W. Stuart Thompson & Phelps Barnum, architects, 1954-58, jr. partner, 1958-60; sr. partner Phelps Barnum & Son, N.Y.C., 1960-68; pres. William Milo Barnum Assos., Inc., N.Y.C., 1968—. Chmn. Archtl. Rev. Bd., Greenwich. Mem. selectmen's com. High Sch. Property, Greenwich, Conn., 1964—; bd. dirs. Community Chest, Greenwich, 1964—. Mem. alumni council Phillips Acad., Andover, Mass., 1965-68; v.p. bd. trustees Putnam Indian Field Sch.; bd. dirs. Episcopal Ch. at Yale, bd. dirs. bldg. fund. Served with USNR, 1945-46. Mem. Concrete Industry Bd. (dir.), AIA (N.Y. chpt. office practices com.), Met. Builders Assn., (liaison com.), Andover Alumni Assn. N.Y.C. (pres. 1964-65), Hist. Soc. Greenwich (v.p.). Clubs: Yale (council 1958-79, pres. 1970-72) (N.Y.C.); Field (gov. 1965-66) (Greenwich, Conn.). Prin. works include Westminster Sch. Chapel, 1961, Westminster Sch. Acad. Center, 1964, Howmet Office Bldg., Greenwich, Conn., Mfrs. Hanover Bank, Bklyn., Pickwick Plaza, Greenwich, R.T. Vanderbilt Corp. Hdqrs., Norwalk, Conn., Union Trust Sq., Greenwich, Gen. Host Corp. Hdqrs., Stamford, Conn., Gateway Center, Greenwich, The Boatyard Condominium, City Island, N.Y., Gorham Island Office Bldg. Clubs: Indian Harbor Yacht, Acoaxet, Hollenbeck, Spindle Rock, Yale, Field. Office: 115 E Putnam Ave Greenwich CT 06830

BARON, FREDERICK DAVID, lawyer; b. New Haven, Dec. 2, 1947; s. Charles Bates and Betty (Leventhal) B.; m. Kathryn Green Lazarus, Apr. 4, 1982; children—Andrew K. Lazarus, Peter D. Lazarus, Charles B. B.A., Amherst Coll., 1969; J.D., Stanford U., 1974. Bar: Calif. 1974, D.C. 1975, U.S. Supreme Ct. 1978, U.S. Dist. Ct. D.C. 1979, U.S. Ct. Appeals (D.C. cir.) 1979, U.S. Dist. Ct. (no. dist.) Calif. 1982, U.S. Ct. Appeals (9th cir.) 1982. Counsel select com. on intelligence U.S. Senate, Washington, 1975-76; spl. asst. to U.S. atty. gen., Washington, 1977-79; asst. U.S. atty. for D.C., 1980-82; atty. Clark, Baron & Korda, San Jose, Calif., 1982-83; ptnr. Cooley, Godward, Castro, Huddleson & Tatum, San Francisco, 1983—; lectr. U.S. Info. Service, 1979-80; pres. bd. trustees Keys Sch., Palo Alto, Calif., 1983-87; bd. dirs. Retail Resources Inc., 1987-88. Co-author, editor U.S. Senate Select Com. on Intelligence Reports, 1975-76; also articles. Issues dir. election com. U.S. Senator Alan Cranston, 1974, Gov. Edmund G. Brown Jr., 1976; mem. transition team Pres. Carter, 1976-77. Mem. ABA, Calif. Bar Assn., San Francisco Bar Assn., D.C. Bar Assn., Palo Alto Bar Assn., Santa Clara County Bar Assn., D.C. Bar (chmn. criminal justice legis. com. 1981). Club: University. Office: Cooley Godward Castro Huddleson & Tatum 5 Palo Alto Sq Suite 400 Palo Alto CA 94306

BARON, JEREMY HUGH, gastroenterologist; b. London, Apr. 25, 1931; s. Edward and Lillian Hannah (Silman) B.; m. Wendy Dimson, Sept. 8, 1960; children: Richard, Susannah. BA, Queen's Coll., Oxford, Eng., 1951, BM, BCh, 1954, MA, 1955, DM, 1964. Successively house physician, registrar, research scholar, lectr., sr. registrar Middlesex Hosp. and Med. Sch., London, 1954-67; successively med. research counsel, Eli Lilly Fgn. Ednl. Traveling fellow, fellow in gastroenterology, Mt. Sinai Hosp., N.Y.C., 1961-62; cons. physician Prince of Wales' and St. Anne's Hosps., London, 1968-71, St. Charles' Hosp., London, 1971—, St. Mary's Hosp., London, 1988—; sr. lectr. cons. depts. surgery and medicine Royal Postgrad. Med. Sch. and Hammersmith Hosp., London, 1968—; sub-dean St. Mary's Hosp. Med. Sch., London, 1982-87. Author: Clinical Tests of Gastric Secretion, 1978, U.S. edit., 1979; editor: History of British Society of Gastroenterology 1937-87, 1987; co-editor: Foregut, 1981, USSR edit., 1985, 88, Mex. edit., 1986, Theoretical Surgery periodical, 1986—. Former mem. Paddington and North Kensington Dist. Health Authority, London, 1981-86; chmn. beautification com. St. Charles Hosp., 1983—. Served as capt. Royal Army M.C., 1956-58. Recipient Gold medal Soc. Argentina Gastroenterologia, 1973, Koster prize Danish Gastroenterologists, 1981, Siurala prize Finnish Gastroenterologists, 1988. Fellow Royal Coll. Physicians, Royal Coll. Surgeons; mem. Soc. Nat. Francaise Gastroenterologie (hon.), Med. Research Soc., Surgical Research Soc., Brit. Med. Assn., Brit. Soc. Gastroenterology (pres. 1988-89), European Gastro Club, Royal Soc. Medicine (former v.p. soc., past pres. clin. sect., now sr. hon. editor), Soc. Authors (chmn. med. writers' group 1985-87). Office: Royal Med Sch, Hammersmith Hosp, Du Cane Rd, London W12 OHS, England

BARON, LINDA ANN, cosmetic co. exec.; b. Flushing, N.Y., Nov. 9, 1943; d. Leonard Michael Baron and Margaret Mary Cotone. Grad. Gardner Sch. Bus., 1968; student George Washington U., 1970. Adminstrv. asst. U.S. Underseas Cable Corp., Washington, 1968-69; analyst programmer Friden div. Singer Co., Washington, 1969, programming mgr., 1970, systems sales exec., 1971; acct. exec. Clinique Labs., Inc., Washington and Balt., 1972, regional mktg. mgr. Md. and Va. markets, 1973-75, regional mktg. dir. Washington and Mid-Atlantic states, 1976-81, regional v.p. Southeast, 1981-86; v.p. South and Mid-Atlantic, Lancome Inc., 1986—; instr. merchandising, 1976—. Vol., ARC Walter Reed and Bethesda Naval Hosp., Washington, 1969-71. Mem. Washington Fashion Group, Nat. Assn. for Female Execs., U.S. Dressage Fedn., Potomac Valley Dressage Assn., Am. Horse Show Assn. Roman Catholic. Home: 9110 Town Gate Ln Bethesda MD 20817

BARON, SALO W., historian, educator; b. Tarnow, Austria, May 26, 1895; came to U.S., 1926; s. Elias and Minna (Wittmayer) B.; m. Jeannette G. Meisel, June 12, 1934; children: Shoshana Baron Tancer, Tobey Baron Gitelle. Ph.D., U. Vienna, 1917, Polit. Sc.D., 1922, Jur.D., 1923; Rabbi, Jewish Theol. Sem., Vienna, 1920; D.H.L., Hebrew Union Coll., Cin., 1944, Spertus Coll., Chgo., 1975, Jewish Theol. Sem. Am., 1983; LL.D., Dropsie U., 1962; Litt.D., Rutgers U., 1963, Columbia U., 1964; golden doctorate Vienna, 1969; Ph.D., U. Tel-Aviv, 1970, Hebrew U., Jerusalem, 1975; L.H.D., Yeshiva U., 1975, Bard Coll., 1979, SUNY-Stony Brook, 1985, Hobart Coll., 1986. Lectr. history Juedisches Paedagogium, Vienna, 1919-25; vis. lectr. Jewish Inst. Religion, N.Y.C., 1926; prof. history, acting librarian Jewish Inst. Religion, 1927-30, dir. dept. advanced studies, 1928-30; prof. Jewish history, lit. and instns. Columbia, 1930-63, prof. emeritus, 1963—; dir. Columbia (Center of Israel and Jewish Studies), 1950-68, dir. emeritus, 1968—; Rauschenbusch lectr. Colgate-Rochester Div. Sch., 1944; vis. prof. history Jewish Theol. Sem., 1954-71, Hebrew U., Jerusalem, 1958, Rutgers U., 1964-69; vis. prof. dept. religious studies Brown U., 1966-68; Pres. Conf. Jewish Social Studies, 1941-55, 59-68, hon. pres., 1955-59, 68—; pres. Jewish Cultural Reconstrn., Inc., 1947-80; chmn. commn. survey Nat. Jewish Welfare Bd., 1947-49; chmn. library information Am. Jewish Com.; mem. citizens fed. com. edn. U.S. Dept. Edn., 1947-52; chmn. cultural adv. com. Conf. Jewish Material Claims against Germany, 1953-55; corr. mem. internat. com. for sci. history mankind UNESCO, 1953—. Author: Die Judenfrage auf dem Wiener Kongress, 1920, Die Politische Theorie Ferdinand Lassalle's, 1923, Azariah de Rossi's Attitude to Life, 1927, The Israelitic Population under the Kings (Hebrew), 1933, A Social and Religious History of the Jews, 3 vols, 1937, rev. edit. vols. I-XVIII, 1952-83, Bibliography of Jewish Social Studies, 1938-39, 1941, The Jewish Community, 3 vols, 1942, Modern Nationalism and Religion, 1947, The Jews of the United States, 1790-1840, (with Joseph L. Blau), (3 vols.), 1963, The Russian Jew under Tsars and Soviets, 1964, rev. edit., 1976, paperback edit., 1987, History and Jewish Historians, 1964, Ancient and Medieval Jewish History: Essays, 1972, Steeled by Adversity: Essays and Addresses on American Jewish Life, 1971, The Contemporary Relevance of History, 1986; Editor: Jewish Studies in Memory of G.A. Kohut, 1935, Jewish Social Studies, quar, 1939—, Essays on Maimonides, 1941, (with George S. Wise) Violence and Defense in the Jewish Experience, 1977, (with Isaac E. Barzilay) Jubilee Vol. of American Academy for Jewish Research, 2 vols, 1980; Contbr. articles to various publs. Trustee Jewish Inst. Religion, 1937-55; pres. acad. council Hebrew U., 1940-50; bd. govs. U. Tel-Aviv, 1968—, U. Haifa, 1971—. Decorated knight Order of Merit Republic of Italy, 1972; Akiba award Am. Jewish Com., 1987; Salo Wittmayer Baron professorship in Jewish history, culture and society named in his honor Columbia U., 1979; hon. fellow Oxford Ctr. for Postgrad. Hebrew Studies, 1983, Mus. for Jewish Diaspora, Tel Aviv, 1984. Fellow Am. Acad. Jewish Research (pres. 1940-43, 58-63, 67, 69-79, hon. pres. 1980—), Am. Acad. Arts and Scis.; mem. Am. Jewish Hist. Soc. (pres. 1953-55), Am. Hist. Assn., Soc. Bibl. Lit. Home: Honey Hill Rd RD 1 Box 473 Canaan CT 06018 Office: 420 W 118th St New York NY 10027

BARON-COHEN, SIMON, psychologist, researcher; b. London, Aug. 15, 1958; s. Vivian and Judith (Greenblatt) B. MA in Human Scis., U. Oxford, Eng., 1981; PhD in Psychology, U. Coll., London, 1985; M of Philosophy in Psychology, Inst. Psychiatry, London, 1987. Lic. clin. psychologist. Tchr. Family Tree Autistic Unit, London, 1981-82; researcher MRC Cognitive Devel. Unit, London, 1982-85; staff psychologist Inst. Psychiatry, London, 1985-87; lectr. psychology U. Coll. London and St. Mary's Hosp. Med. Sch., London, 1987-88; lectr. devel. psychology Inst. Psychiatry, London, 1988—. Reviewer Jour. Autism and Devel. Disorders, 1987, Jour. Child Psychology and Psychiatry, 1988, Brit Jour. Devel. Psychology, 1988, Psychol. Med., 1988; contbr. articles to profl. jours. Mem. British Psychol. Soc., Assn. Child Psychology and Psychiatry (research award 1986-87), Nat. Autistic Soc. (editor jour. 1985—).

BARONE, DONALD ANTHONY, neurologist, educator; b. Bklyn., Dec. 18, 1948; s. John Dominick and Nancy Anne (Salzano) B.; m. Kathleen Ann Kelley, May 22, 1976; children—Steven, Matthew, Daniel. A.B., Rutgers U., 1970; D.O., Phila. Coll. Osteo. Medicine, 1974. Diplomate Am. Bd. Psychiatry and Neurology. Intern Kennedy Meml. Hosp., Stratford, N.J., 1974-75; resident in neurology U. Vt. Med. Ctr., Burlington, 1975-78; fellow in neuromuscular diseases Columbia-Presbyn. Med. Ctr., N.Y.C., 1978-79; practice medicine specializing in neurology, Camden and Stratford, N.J., 1979—; clin. asst. prof. U. Medicine and Dentistry of N.J. Sch. Osteo. Medicine, Camden, 1979-88, clin. assoc. prof., 1988—; sect. head neurology Kennedy Meml. Hosp., Stratford, 1979—, dir. Muscular Dystrophy Assn. Clinic, 1984—; cons. Nat. Bd. Examiners for Osteo. Physicians and Surgeons, 1980—; med. adv. bd. Garden State chpt. Myasthenia Gravis Found.; profl. adv. com. Greater Delaware Valley chpt. Multiple Sclerosis Soc.; adv. com., Del. Valley Transplant Assn., 1987—; examiner Am. Bd. Psychiatry and Neurology, 1981—. Contbr. articles to med. jours. Recipient Golden Apple award for teaching N.J. Sch. Ostoepathic Med., 1987, 88, Excellence in Teaching award U. Medicine and Dentistry of N.J. Found., 1980. Mem. Am. Acad. Neurology, Am. Assn. Electromyography and Electrodiagnosis, Am. Osteo. Assn., N.J. Assn. Osteo. Physicians and Surgeons, Camden County Assn. Osteo. Physicians and Surgeons, Sigma Sigma Phi. Roman Catholic. Office: Voorhees Profl Bldg Suite 101 102 White Horse Rd PO Box 330 Voorhees NJ 08043

BARONE, ROSE MARIE PACE, writer, former educator; b. Buffalo, Apr. 26, 1920; d. Dominic and Jennie (Zagara) Pace; B.A., U. Buffalo, 1943; M.S., U. So. Cal., 1950; cert. advanced study Fairfield (Conn.) U., 1963; m. John Barone, Aug. 23, 1947. Tchr., Angola High Sch. (N.Y.), 1943-46, Puente High Sch. (Calif.), 1946-47, Jefferson High Sch., Lafayette, Ind., 1947-50; dir. Warren Inst., Bridgeport, Conn., 1951-53; instr. U. Bridgeport, 1953-54; tchr. bus. subjects Bassick High Sch., Bridgeport, 1954-74, Harding High Sch., Bridgeport, 1974-80; instr. Fairfield U., 1969 freelance writer, 1980—; chair State Poetry Festival, 1987; founder Pet Rescue. Pace-Barone Minority scholar Fairfield U.; recipient Playwriting prize Conn. Federated Women's Clubs, 1955, 1st prize for poetry, 1985, Federated Women Conn. State Short Story award, 1987, 88; Auerbach Found. scholarship, 1956; Citizen award Bridgeport Dental Assn., 1982; State/Town Hero award, 1986; also craft and flower awards. Mem. NEA, AARP (v.p. 1987-88, pres. 1988—), Owl (sec. 1987—), AAUW (treas. 1957-58), Nat. League Am. Pen Women (Bridgeport historian 1966-84, state historian 1983—, treas. br. 1985—, State pres. 1986—, Nat. Historian award 1976, 88), UN Assn. U.S.A. (pres. Bridgeport, 1964-66, 68-70, chmn. area UN Days, 1960—, pres. Conn. 1971—, state chmn. UNICEF to 1984, area UNICEF Ctr., 1984—, state historian 1984—), Conn. Bus. Tchrs., Bridgeport Edn. Assn. (sec. 1966-68), Fairfield Philatelic Soc. (sec. 1971-78, founder advisor Philatelic Jrs. 1972-80), Pi Omega Pi. Clubs: Fairfield University Women's (founder, pres. 1950, 74—, v.p. 1973-74) Southport Woman's (garden dept. sec. 1981-85, chmn. 1985-87) (Fairfield). Home: 1283 Round Hill Rd Fairfield CT 06430

BAROSS, ZSUZSA, social scientist; b. Leva, Hungary, July 5, 1943; arrived in Can., 1968, The Netherlands, 1975; BA, U. B.C., Can., 1973; MA, U. London, 1975; PhD, U. Amsterdam, 1987. Research fellow Rijks U. Utrecht, The Netherlands, 1976-77, Cath. U., Nijmegen, The Netherlands, 1978-79; dir. research Ctr. for Human Settlements U.N., Bandung, Indonesia, 1979-81; asst. prof. social scis. Inst. Med. Psychology, Utrecht, The Netherlands, 1981—. Cons. editor Maieutics (Internat. Jour. Social Theory); guest editor Theoretical Medicine, Internat. Jour. for Philosophy Medicine; contbr. articles to sci. jours. Fulbright Found. sr. research sholar U. Ala., 1985. Fellow Ctr. Theory in Humanities and Social Scis.; mem. Can. Sociol. Assn., Vereniging Antropologie en Sociologie.

BAROUDY, BAHIGE MOURAD, biochemist, researcher; b. Beirut, Lebanon, July 1, 1950; came to U.S., 1973; s. Mourad Bahige and Ludmila Adelheid (Obermuller-Haddad) B. B.S., Am. U. of Beirut, 1972; Ph.D., Georgetown U., 1978. Teaching asst. Wesleyan U., Middletown, Conn., 1973-74; research asst. Georgetown U., Washington, D.C., 1974-78, fellow, 1982, research assoc. prof., 1985—; vis. fellow scientist NIH, Bethesda, Md., 1979-81, vis. assoc. scientist, 1982-85. Contbr. articles to profl. jours., chpts. to books. Mem. Am. Soc. Biochemistry and Molecular Biology, Am. Soc. for Microbiology, Am. Soc. for Virology, Sigma Xi (award for outstanding publ. Georgetown U. chpt. 1977). Lutheran. Avocations: fencing; viola. Office: Georgetown U Dept Microbiology Div Virology and Immunology 5640 Fishers Ln Rockville MD 20852

BARQUÍN, RAMÓN CARLOS, computer company executive; b. Havana, Cuba, Aug. 8, 1942; s. Ramón María and Hilda Graciela (Cantero) B.; m. Jean C. Campbell, Sept. 3, 1977; children—Nicolas Philip, Elisa Leslie; 1 son by previous marriage, Ramón Carlos III. B.S., U. P.R., 1965, B.S. in Elec. Engring., 1966, M.S., 1969; E.E., M.I.T., 1972, Ph.D., 1974. Systems engr. IBM Co., San Juan, P.R., 1966-69; mktg. rep. P.R. and V.I., 1969-70; research assoc. project MAC, M.I.T., Cambridge, 1971-72; mgr. plans and controls staff IBM Americas/Far East Corp., Tarrytown, N.Y., 1974-77, mgr. external programs staff, 1977-79; mgr. external affairs IBM World Trade Asia Corp., Hong Kong, 1979-83; mgr. pub. affairs programs IBM Co., Washington, 1983—; program chmn. Hong Kong Computer Conf., 1983; stats. dir. Internat. Judo Fedn., 1969—. Author: The Transfer of Computer Technology: A Framework for Policy in the Latin American Nations, 1975; The Statistics of Judo, 1975; Towards the Information Society, 1984, New Ethics for the Computer Age? (with A. Parrent, et al.); cons. editor (with G. Mead): Bioscience and Medical Research, 1980-83; adv. editor Communicaciones e Informática, 1980-84. Trustee Am. Mil. Acad. P.R., 1965—; mem. edn. council M.I.T.; bd. dirs. Atlantic Coll., 1985—. CISR research fellow, 1976-79; M.I.T. seed fund grantee, 1972-73; IBM resident study grantee, 1970-74; NEH grantee, 1978. Mem. IEEE Computer Soc. (area chmn. internat. chpts. 1977-83, Centennial medal), IEEE (Centennial medal 1984), Sigma Xi, Tau Beta Pi. Clubs: Seven Bridge Field, Aberdeen Boat, Washington Squash and Nautilus, Island Squash Racquet, Kenwood Country, American. Office: IBM 1801 K St NW Suite 1200 Washington DC 20006

BARR, JAMES, educator; b. Mar. 20, 1924; s. Allan B.; student Daniel Stewart's Coll., Edinburgh, Scotland; M.A., Edinburgh U., 1948, B.D., 1951; M.A., Oxford (Eng.) U., 1976 D.D., 1981; D.D. (hon.), Knox Coll., Toronto, Ont., Can., 1964, U. Dubuque, 1974, U. St. Andrews, 1974, U. Edinburgh, 1983, U. South Africa, 1986; M.A. (hon.), U. Manchester, 1969; m. Jane J. S. Hepburn, 1950; 3 children. Minister of Ch. of Scotland, Tiberias, Israel, 1951-53; prof. N.T. lit. and exegesis Presbyn. Coll., Montreal, Que., Can., 1953-55; prof. Old Testament lit. and theology Edinburgh U., 1955-61, Princeton Theol. Sem., 1961-65; prof. Semitic langs. and lits. Manchester (Eng.) U., 1965-76; Oriel prof. interpretation Holy Scripture, and fellow Oriel Coll., Oxford U., 1976-78, hon. fellow, 1980; Regius prof. Hebrew, Oxford U. and student Christ Ch., 1978—; vis. prof. Hebrew U., Jerusalem, 1973, U. Chgo., 1975, 81, Strasbourg U., 1975-76, Brown U., Providence, R.I., 1985, U. Otago, New Zealand, 1986, U. South Africa, 1986, Vanderbilt U., 1987—; lectr. Princeton U., 1962-63, Union Theol. Sem., 1963; Currie lectr. Austin Theol. Sem., 1964; Guggenheim Meml. fellow for study Biblical semantics, 1965; Cadbury lectr. Birmingham U., 1969; Croall lectr. Edinburgh U., 1970; Grinfield lectr. on Septuagint, Oxford U., 1974-78; Firth lectr. Nottingham U., 1978; Schweich lectr., Brit. Acad., 1986. Served as pilot RNVR (Fleet Air Arm), 1942-45. Fellow Brit. Acad., RAS, SOAS (hon.; mem. governing body 1980-85); mem. Soc. O.T. Studies (pres.1973), Brit. Assn. Jewish Studies (pres. 1978), Göttingen Acad. Scis. (corr.), Soc. Bib. Lit. U.S.A. (hon.), Norwegian Acad. Sci. and Letters. Publs.: The Semantics of Biblical Language, 1961; Biblical Words for Time, 1962; Old and New in Interpretation, 1966; Comparative Philology and the Text of the Old Testament, 1968; The Bible in the Modern World, 1973; Fundamentalism, 1977;

The Typology of Literalism, 1979; Explorations in Theology 7: The Scope and Authority of the Bible, 1980; Holy Scripture: Canon, Authority, Criticism, 1983; Escaping from Fundamentalism, 1984; contbr. articles to profl. jours.; editor Jour. Semitic Studies, 1965-76, Oxford Hebrew Dictionary, 1974-80. Office: Christ Ch Oxford, Oriental Inst, Oxford England

BARR, JAMES HOUSTON, III, lawyer; b. Louisville, Nov. 2, 1941; s. James Houston Jr. and Elizabeth Hamilton (Pope) B.; m. Sara Jane Todd, Apr. 16, 1970; 1 child, Lynn Jamison. Student U. Va., 1960-63, U. Tenn., 1963-64; B.S.L., J.D., U. Louisville, 1966. Bar: Ky. 1966, U.S. Ct. Appeals (6th cir.) 1969, U.S. Supreme Ct. 1971, U.S. Ct. Mil. Appeals 1978. Law clk., Ky. Ct. Appeals, Frankfort, 1966-67; asst. atty. gen. Ky., Frankfort, 1967-71, 1979-82; asst. U.S. atty. U.S. Dept. Justice, Louisville, 1971-79, 1983—; 1st asst. U.S. Atty., 1978-79; asst. dist. counsel U.S. Army C.E., Louisville, 1982-83. Served to lt. comdr. USNR, 1967-81, to lt. col. USAR, 1981—. Mem. Fed. Bar Assn. (pres. Louisville chpt. 1975-76, Younger Fed. Lawyer award 1975), Ky. Bar Assn., Louisville Bar Assn., Soc. Colonial Wars, SAR, Soc. Ky. Pioneers, Delta Upsilon. Republican. Episcopalian. Clubs: Pendennis, Louisville Boat, Filson (Louisville). Home: 100 Westwind Rd Louisville KY 40207 Office: US Atty 211 US Courthouse Louisville KY 40202

BARR, JOSEPH WALKER, corporate director; b. Vincennes, Ind., Jan. 17, 1918; s. Oscar Lynn and Stella Florence (Walker) B.; m. Beth Williston, Sept. 3, 1939; children—Bonnie (Mrs. Michael Gilliom), Cherry, Joseph Williston, Elizabeth Eugenia (Mrs. Andrew LoSasso), Lynn Hamilton (Mrs. Keith Fineberg). A.B., DePauw U., 1939; M.A., Harvard, 1941; LL.D., Vincennes U., 1966, DePauw U., 1967. Partner J&J Co., 1976—; mem. 86th Congress, 11th Ind. Dist.; asst. to sec. of treasury 1961-64; chmn. FDIC, 1964-65; under sec. of treasury 1965-68, sec. of treasury, 1968-69; pres. Am. Security & Trust Co., Washington, 1969-72; chmn. bd. Am. Security & Trust Co., 1972-74; bd. dirs. Manor Care, Jiffy Lube. Bd. dirs. Student Loan Marketing Assn.; bd. regents Georgetown U. Served to lt. comdr. USN, 1942-45. Decorated Bronze Star. Mem. Phi Beta Kappa. Democrat. Home: Houyhnhnm Farm Hume VA 22639 Office: 2111 Jefferson Davis Hwy Suite 422 N Arlington VA 22202

BARR, TERENCE DAVID, clergyman; b. Bristol, Eng., July 17, 1945; s. Reginald William and Doris Lilian (Hand) B.; married, 1969; children: Paul, John, Simon, Ruth, Hannah. Diploma in Mgmt. Studies, Bristol Poly., 1971; MS in Bus. Adminstrn., Bath (Eng.) U., 1980. Ordained Ch. of Eng., 1974. Exec. officer Brit. Civil Service, London and Bristol, 1963-69; higher exec. officer Post Office Corp., Bristol, 1969-76; warden, youth chaplain Legge House Youth Ctr., Swindon, Eng., 1976-79; vicar of Locklease Parish Ch. of St. Mary Magdalane with St. Francis, Bristol, 1979—; vicar St. Andrew's and Bishop's Indsl. Chaplain, Avonmouth, Bristol, 1988—. Mem. governing body Romney Avenue Infant and Jr. Schs., Filton Avenue Jr. Sch., Lockleaze Comprehensive Sch.; chmn. Lockleaze Youth Club, Scout Assn., Bristol, 1980—, Bristol Scout group, 1980—. Fellow Brit. Inst. Mgmt. Mem. Conservative Party. Club: Redwood Lodge Country (Bristol). Lodge: Ind. Order Forresters. Office: St Andrew's Vicarage, St Andrew's Rd, Avonmouth Bristol BS11 9ES, England

BARRACK, WILLIAM SAMPLE, JR., petroleum company executive; b. Pitts., July 26, 1929; s. William Sample and Edna Mae (Henderson) B. B.S., U. Pitts., 1950; postgrad., Dartmouth Coll. With Texaco, Inc., N.Y., 1953—; mktg. mgr. Northeast Texaco, Inc., 1953-62; dist. mgr. Texaco, Inc., Portland, Maine, 1962-63, Portland, 1963-65; asst. mgr. distbn. and devel. Texaco, Inc., N.Y., 1965-66, asst. mgr. mktg. research and project devel., 1966-67; asst. div. mgr. Texaco, Inc., Norfolk, Va., 1967-68; area dir. Texaco, Inc., Brussels, Belgium, 1968-70; gen. mgr. Texaco, Inc., N.Y., 1970; asst. to chmn. bd. Texaco, Inc., N.Y.C., 1971; v.p. internat. Europe Texaco, Inc., 1971-76, v.p. producing Eastern hemisphere, 1976-77; v.p. personnel and corp. services Texaco, Inc., White Plains, N.Y., 1977-80; chmn., chief exec. officer Texaco Ltd., London, Eng., 1980-83; sr. v.p. Texaco Inc., White Plains, N.Y., 1983—; pres. Texaco Oil Trading & Supply Co., White Plains, N.Y., 1983-84; dir. Caltex Petroleum Corp.; Mem. Naval War Coll. Found., Newport, R.I. Trustee Manhattanville Coll.; bd. dirs. Texaco Philanthropic Found., Mary Rose Soc. Served as comdr. USNR, 1951-53. Mem. Fgn. Policy Assn. N.Y. (gov.). Clubs: Ida Lewis Yacht; North Sea Yacht (Belgium); Woodway Country, Ox Ridge Hunt; Clambake (Newport, R.I.); Australian (Sidney, Australia). Office: Texaco Inc 2000 Westchester Ave White Plains NY 10650

BARRAGAN, LUIS, architect; b. Guadalajara, Jalisco, Mex., 1902. Hon. doctorate, Autonomous U. Guadalajara, 1984. Practice architecture Mexico City, 1936—; owner real estate properties Avenida San Jerónimo, Mexico City, Pedregal de San Angel; developer Jardines del Pedregal de San Angel S.A. Prin. works include apt. bldgs., Cuauhtémoc, Mexico City, gardens and ornamental work Jardines del Pedregal de San Angel S.A., Mexico City, convent and chapel, Tlalpan, urban devels., Manzanillo zone, Mex., gardens and ornamental works Jardines del Bosque, Guadalajara, gardens Pierre Marquez Hotel, Acapulco, Mex., symbol for Satellite City, Mexico, ornamental works and landscape architecture Las Arboledas S.A., State of Mexico, residential zone Lomas Verdes, State of Mexico, residences and horse stables Los Clubes, Gilardi's House, Mexico City, Gárate's House; exhbns. include Mus. Modern Art, N.Y.C., 1976, Museo Rufino Tamayo, Mex., 1985, various others; subject of numerous articles and books. Recipient Art Nat. prize Mex., Pres. Luis Echeverría Alvarez, 1976, Pritzker prize, 1980, Jalisco Architecture award State of Jalisco Coll. Architects, 1985, Jalisco Prize for Plastic Arts, 1985. Fellow AIA (hon.); mem. Mex. Acad. Architects, N.Y. Acad. Arts and Lit., World Acad. Architecture. Address: Gen Francisco Ramirez #12, Col Daniel Garza, 11830 Mexico City Mexico

BARRATT, ERIC GEORGE, accountant; b. Stokenchurch, England, Apr. 15, 1938; s. Frank Ronald and Winifred Mary (Hayward) B. Chartered acct. Ptnr. Tansley Witt & Co., London, 1966-79, Arthur Andersen & Co., London, 1979-82, MacIntyre Hudson, London, 1982—; dir. Automotive Products P.L.C., Leamington, 1977-86, Montague Boston Investment Trust P.L.C., London, 1982-85, Milton Keynes Devel. Corp., 1980-85. Chmn. Stokenchurch Parish Council, 1975-86; vice-chmn. Buckinghamshire County Council, Aylesbury, 1981-85; dir. Commn. for New Towns, 1986—; treas. Oriel Coll., Oxford, 1986. Fellow Inst. Chartered Accts. Conservative. Anglican. Clubs: Atheneaum, Carlton, City of London (London). Home: Stockfield, Stokenchurch HP14 3SX, England Office: MacIntyre Hudson, 28 Ely Place, London EC1N 6RL, England

BARRE, RAYMOND, former prime minister of France; Saint-Denis, Réunion, b. Apr. 12, 1924; s. Rene and Charlotte (Deramond) B.; student Faculté de Droit, Paris, Inst. d'Etudes Politiques, Paris; m. Eva Hegedus, Nov. 19, 1954; children: Olivier, Nicolas. Prof., Inst. des Hautes Etudes, Tunis, 1951-54; prof. Faculté de Droit et de Scis. Economiques, Caen, 1954-63, mem., 1962; prof. Inst. d'Etudes Politiques, Paris, 1961—; dir. du Cabinet to Minister of Industry, 1959-62; mem. experts com. studying financing of investments in France, 1963-64; mem. commn. Gen. Economic and Financing of 5th Plan and other govt. coms.; v.p. Commn. of European Communities, 1967-72; mem. Gen. Council Banque de France, 1973; minister fgn. trade, 1976, economy and fin., 1976-78, prime minister, 1978-81, M.P. from Rhone dist., Nat. Assembly, 1978—; prof. U. Paris, Pantheon-Sorbonne. Author: Economie Politique, 1956. Office: 4-6 Ave Emile-Acollas, 75007 Paris France *

BARREAU, HERVE ALBERT, philosopher; b. Le Mans, France, Apr. 27, 1929; s. Rene Albert and Simone (Lemire) B.; m. Marianne Horstel, Dec. 28, 1965. Lic. in philosophy, Le Saulchoir, Paris, 1953, U. Strasbourg, France, 1957; agregation philosophie, U. Paris, 1959. Prof. enseignement secondaire Oran, Lille, France, 1959-62; asst. enseignement superieur Strasbourg, 1962-66; charge de recherche Centre National de la Recherche Scientifique, Paris, 1966-81; maitre de recherche Strasbourg, 1981-85, dir. research, 1985—, mem. elu, 1971-80; sec. scientifique de la sect. 65 1975-80; dir. de l'ER 265 Strasbourg, 1983—. Author: Aristote et l'analyse du savoir, 1972; editor: L'Explication dans les sciences de la vie, 1983, Le Meme et l'Autre, 1986, Théories biologiques Ethique et Expérimentation en Médecine, 1988. Sec. Congres du peuple europeen, Paris and Rome, 1958. Served with French Army, 1951-52. Fellow Soc. Francaise d'Histoire des Scis. (v.p. 1984-88). Office: U Louis Pasteur, 3 rue de l'Universite, Strasbourg France

BARREN, BRUCE WILLARD, merchant banker; b. Olean, N.Y., Jan. 28, 1942; s. James Lee and Marion Frances (Willard) B.; m. Roseanne Hundley, Apr. 17, 1976; children: James Lee, Christina Roseanne. BS, Babson Coll., 1962; MS, Bucknell U., 1963; grad. cert., Harvard U., 1967, Cambridge U., England, 1968. CPA, Pa., FCA, England. Sr. cons. Price Waterhouse, N.Y., 1963-67; v.p. Walston & Co., Inc., N.Y., 1967-70; sr. v.p. Delafield Childs, Inc., N.Y., 1970-71; chmn. The EMCO/Hanover Group, Los Angeles, 1971—; vice-chmn. Four Winds Enterprises Inc., San Diego 1985-87; bd. dirs. various U.S. and internat. cos.; exec. mng. and gen. ptnr. Emco/Barren Fund 1988—. Recipient Disting. Service awards Calif. State Senate and State Assembly, Counties of Los Angeles, Orange, Calif., San Diego, City of Los Angeles; U.S. Senate. Roman Catholic. Home: 1153 Chantilly Rd Los Angeles CA 90077 Office: EMCO Fin Ltd 11611 San Vicente Blvd Los Angeles CA 90049 also: 1932 Rittenhouse Sq Philadelphia PA 19103

BARRERA, RUBEN RIVERA, banker, scholar; b. Nogales, Sonora, Mex., Mar. 24, 1939; s. Raymundo Barrera and Ofelia Rivera; C.P.A., Tech. de Monterrey, 1955-61; M.S., Inst. Poly. Nacional, 1965, D.Sc., 1967; m. Blanca Rosa Morales del Rio, Sept. 12, 1964; children—Maria Luisa Ofelia, Blanca Maria, Ruben Raymundo Esteban. With Banco Nacional de Mex., 1962—, chief fin. and market stock analysis, then pub.-sub-dir., 1972, dir., 1977—. Mem. Colegio Mex. Contadores Publicos, Nat. Assn. Accountants, Inst. Mex. Ejecutivos de Finanzas.*Soc. Mex. Geografia y Estadistica. Roman Catholic. Home: Albatroces 182, Col Lomas de las Aguilas, 01730 Mexico City Mexico Office: I LA Catolica, #39-30 Piso Centro, 06000 Mexico City Mexico

BARRETT, BERNARD MORRIS, JR., plastic and reconstructive surgeon; b. Pensacola, Fla., May 3, 1944; s. Bernard Morris and Blanche (Lischkoff) B.; B.S., Tulane U., 1965; M.D., U. Miami, 1969; m. Julia Mae Prokop, Nov. 26, 1972; children—Beverly Frances, Julie Blaine, Audrey Blake, Bernard Joseph. Surg. intern Meth. Hosp. and Ben Taub Hosp., Houston, 1969-70; resident in gen. surgery Baylor Coll. Medicine, Houston, 1970-71, UCLA, 1971-73; resident in plastic surgery U. Miami Affiliated Hosps., Fla., 1973-75, chief resident in plastic surgery, 1975; fellow in plastic surgery Clinica Ivo Pitanguy, Rio de Janeiro, Brazil, 1973; instr. surgery Baylor Coll. Medicine, 1970-71, clin. instr. plastic surgery, 1977-80, clin. asst. prof., 1980—; instr. surg. emergencies Los Angeles County Paramedics, 1972-73; plastic surgery coordinator for jr. med. students Sch. Medicine U. Miami, 1975; practice medicine specalizing in plastic and reconstructive surgery, Houston, 1976—; pres., chmn. bd. dirs. Plastic and Reconstructive Surgeons, P.A., Houston, 1978—; chmn. Tex. Inst. Plastic Surgery, Houston; attending physician Jr. League Clinic, Tex. Children's Hosp., Houston, 1977—; active staff St. Luke's Hosp., Houston, Meth. Hosp., Houston; clin. assoc. in plastic surgery U. Tex. Med. Sch., Houston, 1976—; instr. surg. emergencies Harris County Community Coll.; dir. Am. Physicians Ins. Exchange, Austin, API Life Ins. Co., Austin, Tex. Am. Bank/Southwest; chief of staff, chief plastic surgery Travis Centre Hosp., Houston, 1985—; cons. physician Houston Oilers, 1978—; attending physician Ontario Motor Speedway, Calif., 1972-73. Bd. dirs. Plastic Surgery Ednl. Found., Chgo. Served to lt. comdr., M.C., USNR, 1969-74. Surg. exchange scholar to Royal Coll. Surgeons, London, 1968; hon. dep. sheriff Harris County, Tex. (Houston); diplomate Am. Bd. Plastic Surgery. Fellow ACS; mem. Am. Soc. Plastic and Reconstructive Surgeons, Royal Soc. Medicine, Michael E. DeBakey Internat. Cardiovascular Surg. Soc., Am. Soc. for Aesthetic Plastic Surgery, Denton A. Cooley Cardiovascular Surg. Soc., Tex. Med. Assn., Tex. Soc. Plastic Surgery, Harris County Med. Assn., Lipoplasty Soc. N.Am., Houston Soc. Plastic Surgery, D. Ralph Millard Plastic Surg. Soc. (v.p. 1977-79, sec., treas. 1975-77, historian 1980—), U. Miami Sch. Medicine Nat. Alumni Assn. (bd. dirs. 1975-77), Alpha Kappa Kappa (pres., 1968-69). Clubs: University, Houstonian, Briar (Houston); Royal Biscayne Racquet; Commodore (Key Biscayne, Fla.). Author: Patient Care in Plastic Surgery, 1982; Manuel de Ciudados en Cirugia Plastica, 1985. Contbr. articles to med. publs., presentations to profl. confs.; inventor Barrett sterling surgigrip. Office: 6655 Travis St Suite 950 Houston TX 77030

BARRETT, CHARLES MARION, insurance company executive, physician; b. Cin., Mar. 10, 1913; s. Charles Francis and May (Ryan) B.; m. May Belle Finn, Apr. 27, 1942; children: Angela, Charles, John, Michael, Marian, William. AB, Xavier U., 1934, LLD (hon.), 1974; MD, U. Cin., 1938. Assoc. med. dir. Western & So. Life Ins. Co., Cin., 1942, med. dir., 1951-73, exec. v.p., 1965-73, pres., 1973-84, chmn., 1984—, also bd. dirs.; prof. depts. surgery and radiology U. Cin. Coll. Medicine, after 1957, prof. emeritus, 1974—; chmn. Columbus Mut. Life Ins. Co., 1982—. Bd. dirs. Our Lady of Mercy Hosp., Bethesda Hosp. and Deaconess Assn.; bd. trustees U. Cin., chmn. emeritus, 1987—; chmn. Cin. Bus. Com., 1986-87. Recipient Taft medal U. Cin., 1973, spl. award Ohio Radiol. Soc., 1974, Daniel Drake award, 1985; named Great Living Cincinnatian, 1987. Fellow Am. Coll. Radiology; mem. AMA, Life Ins. Assn. Am., Greater Cin. C. of C. (chmn. 1985-86), Great Living Cincinnatian. Office: Western & So Life Ins Co 400 Broadway Cincinnati OH 45202

BARRETT, ETIENNE MARK CHRISTOPHER, entrepreneur; b. Reading, Berkshire, Eng., Feb. 26, 1954; s. Etienne Rodney William and Margaret (Green) B.; m. Sarah Claudia Fenton, Feb. 3, 1979; children: William and Thomas. BSc with honors, Southampton U., 1977. Planning engr. Mears Constrn. Ltd., London, 1977-78; engr. Mears Constrn. Ltd., Liverpool, Eng., 1978-79; sect. engr. Edmund Nuttall Ltd., Dover, Eng., 1979-80; contracts mgr. Barrett Estate Services Ltd., Reading, 1980-87; also bd. dirs.; bd. dirs. Francis Bros. Builders Ltd., Reading, Chiltern Queen's Ltd., Reading, C. and R.B. Constrn. (So.) Ltd., Reading. Chmn. Burghfield Village Residents Assn., 1986—. Mem. Instn. Civil Engrs. (assoc.). Club: Southampton Univ. Office: Barrett Estate Services, 11 Armour Rd, Reading Berkshire England RG3 6EX

BARRETT, EVELYN CAROL, educator; b. Ocean Springs, Miss., Feb. 6, 1928; d. Charles Edward and Irene Effie (Hopkins) Engbarth; diploma with honors Jr. Coll., Perkinston, Miss., 1945; B.S. in Commerce with high honors, Miss. So. Coll. (now U. So. Miss.), 1947; M.B.A. in Acctg., La. State U., 1950; also numerous continuing edn. courses, 1950-82; m. Arthur James Barrett, June 10, 1951; children—George Stanley, Ruth Anne, James Sidney, Carolyn Jean. Bookkeeper-sec. Non-Commn. Officers Club, Kessler AFB, Miss., summer 1947; asst., secretarial practice office and div. research, instr. in typing Coll. Commerce, La. State U., 1947-50; instr. Miss. So. Coll., summer 1950; clk.-stenographer dept. physics U. Ill., Urbana, 1951-52; instr. in shorthand Ill. Comml. Coll., 1951-52; tchr. Milford (N.H.) High Sch., 1957-58; tchr. bus. edn. Merrimack (N.H.) High Sch., 1958—, head dept. bus. edn., 1971-81; instr. auditing Rivier Coll., 1982; registered rep. R. Danais Investment Co., Manchester, N.H.; account exec. John, Edward & Co., Lebanon, N.H.; beauty cons. Mary Kay Cosmetics, Merrimack; tutor in shorthand, acctg.; cons. acctg. systems. Grad. asst. La. State U., 1947-50. Active Girl Scouts U.S.A., including Cadette leader, 1959-63, sr. troop leader Swiftwater council, 1970-72, adult vol. trainer, 1964-66, troop program cons., 1963-64. Mem. N.H. Bus. Educators Assn. (v.p. 1964-65, pres. 1965-67, rep. to N.H. Vocat. Assn. 1986-87 (sec. 1967-68, treas. 1973-75, historian 1986-87), N.H. Supervisory Union 27 (sec.-treas. 1961-62), NEA, N.H. Edn. Assn., Merrimack Tchrs. Assn. (Disting. Educator award 1980, Excellence in Edn. award 1985, sec. 1984-85), New Eng. Bus. Educators Assn., Am. Vocat. Assn., N.H. Assn. Computer Edn. Statewide, Eastern Bus. Edn. Assn., Nat. Bus. Edn. Assn., AAUW, Delta Zeta, Phi Theta Kappa, Pi Omega Pi, Delta Pi Epsilon, Alpha Delta Kappa (historian N.E. region 1981-83, v.p. N.H. Alpha chpt. 1978-79, pres. N.H. Alpha chpt. 1979-82, N.H. State sgt.-at-arms 1982-84, N.H. State treas. 1984-88, State membership chmn. 1988-90., chpt. award of appreciation 1980), Delta Sigma Epsilon (chpt. corr. sec.). Roman Catholic. Clubs: Gen. Electric Women's, Manchester Coll. Women's, Our Lady of Mercy Ch. Guild (treas. 1968-70).d (treas. 1968-70).

BARRETT, JAMES EDWARD, JR., management consultant; b. Lowell, Mass., Dec. 9, 1929; s. James E. and Margaret A. (Holland) B.; A.B., Harvard U., 1951; postgrad. Air Command and Staff Coll., 1953; m. Dorothy G. Walle; children—James Edward III, Dorothy Anne, William H., M. Stephen. Asst. prof. Harvard U., 1955-58; systems analyst, mgr. Raytheon Co., 1958-62; mktg. mgr. Kepner-Tregoe, Inc., Princeton, N.J., 1962-65; mgr., dir. K-T Europe, 1966-67; pres. AAI, 1967-68; pres. Cresheim Co., Inc., Phila., 1968—, chmn. Cresheim, Ltd. (U.K.), 1979—, Cresheim do Brasil, Sao Paulo, 1980—. bd. dirs. Swansea Press, Inc. 1986—. Pres., Wyndmoor (Pa.) Community Assn., 1977-79. Served to capt. USAF, 1951-55. Mem. Am. Assn. Small Research Cos. (pres. Phila. chpt. 1977-80), Inst. Mgmt. Cons. (v.p. chpt. 1977-81, nat. dir. 1981-87, nat. v.p. 1983-86). Clubs: Harvard (N.Y.C., Phila.). Author: Managing Your Distributors; contbr. numerous articles to profl. jours. Home: 8315 Flourtown Ave Wyndmoor PA 19118 Office: Cresheim Co Inc Box 27785 803 E Willow Grove Ave Philadelphia PA 19118

BARRETT, MARTYN DAVID, psychologist, lecturer; b. London, June 18, 1951; s. William Henry and Miriam (Baskind) B.; m. Annette Jennifer Krysler, Aug. 4, 1974; children: Adam Bruno, Alexander Hector. BA, U. Cambridge, 1973, MA, 1977; PhD, U. Sussex, 1979. Tchr. London Borough Brent Dept. Edn., 1973-74; lectr. psychology Roehampton Inst., London, 1978-85, sr. lectr. psychology, 1985-87; hon. research fellow U. London, 1984—, lectr. in psychology, 1988—; editor revs. First Lang., London, 1987—. Editor: Children's Single-Word Speech, 1985; (with others) The Development of Word Meaning, 1986, Jour. Language and Cognition in Early Social Interaction, 1986; contbr. articles to profl. jours. Econ. and Social Research Council U.K. Grantee, 1984-87. Fellow Brit. Psychol. Soc. (assoc., treas. devel. psychology sect. 1984-87); mem. Internat. Assn. Study Child Lang. Office: Royal Holloway & Bedford New Coll, Dept Psychology, Egham Hill, Egham Surrey TW20 0EX, England

BARRETT, TOM HANS, rubber company executive; b. Topeka, Aug. 13, 1930; s. William V. and Myrtle B.; m. Marilyn Dunn, July 22, 1956; children—Susan and Sara (twins), Jennifer. Grad. Chem. Engr., Kans. State U., 1953; grad., Sloan Sch. Mgmt. MIT, 1969. With Goodyear Tire & Rubber Co., various locations, 1953—; pres., chief operating officer Goodyear Tire & Rubber Co., Akron, Ohio, 1982—, also dir.; dir. A.O. Smith Corp., Rubbermaid Corp. Served with U.S. Army, 1953-55. Decorated officer with crown Order Merite Civil et Militaire, Luxembourg, 1976; recipient Sigma Phi Epsilon citation, 1979. Home: 2135 Stockbridge Rd Akron OH 44313 Office: Goodyear Tire & Rubber Co 1144 E Market St Akron OH 44316 *

BARRIER, GENEVIEVE PAULE LOUISE, anesthesiologist; b. May 22, 1933; d. Rémi and Marie Thérèse (Giraud) B. MD, U. Paris, 1960. Specialist anesthesia; diplomate French bd. Anesthesiology. Anesthesiologist Hosp. Notre-Dame-de-Bon-Secours, Paris, 1961-72; prof. Hosp. Cochin-Port-Royal, 1977-83; chief dept. anesthesiology, chmn. Hosp. Necker-Engants MaLades, Paris, 1983—; also dir. Samu de Paris, 1984—. Author: L'Accouchement Avec ou sans Douleur?, 1977, Petit Guide de La Medecine Auotidienne, 1977; contbr. articles to profl. jours. Mem. Soc. French Anesthesiology (mem. bd.), Union European Medicine Specialists (pres.-elect 1986), European Acad. Anaesthesiology (Sen. 1986—), Am. Soc. Anesthesiologists. Roman Catholic. Office: Hosp Necker-Enfants Malades, 149 Rue de Sevres, 75015 Paris France

BARRIONUEVO PEÑA, JOSÉ, former minister of the interior, Spain; b. Berja, Spain, Mar., 1942; married; 3 children. Degree in journalism and law. Sole practice law, Guipuzcoa and Madrid; dep. head Factory Inspectorate, Madrid; sub. dir. gen. for labour planning; lectr. labour law, U. Madrid; city councillor, Madrid, 1979; appointed 3d dep. mayor and councillor for security and mcpl. police; 2d dep. mayor, 1981; minister of the interior Govt. of Spain, until 1988. Address: Amador de los Rios 7, Gabinete Tecnico del Ministro, del Interior, Madrid 4, Spain *

BARRON, BRYTON, writer, lecturer; b. Doon, Iowa, Dec. 6, 1898; s. Hiram H. and Emma J. Barron (grandparents); A.B., Sioux Falls Coll., 1922; B.Litt. (Rhodes scholar at Pembroke Coll. 1920-23), Oxford (Eng.) U., 1923, diploma in econ. and polit. sci., 1922; m. Ella Rosalie Lillibridge, Dec. 31, 1922 (dec. Jan. 24, 1983); children: Bebe, Roger L.; m. Louisa H. Stanton, Dec. 20, 1983. Editorial writer Daily Argus-Leader, Sioux Falls, S.D., 1923-25; div. chief, bur. edn., editor monthly mag. for tchrs., author lang. manual, Philippines, 1925-28; asst. editor Dept. State, Washington, 1929, chief pub. sect., 1929-40, asst. chief div. research and publs., 1940-44, chief of treaty staff, adv. on treaty affairs, 1944-50, research historian, 1950-56; pub. Crestwood Books, 1962-66, sr. editor, 1966-72; lectr. on fgn. affairs throughout the U.S., 1956—. Founder, treas., gen. mgr. Dept. State Fed. Credit Union, 1935-42; founder, pres. Dept. State Recreation Assn., 1935. Active conservative causes; charter mem. Reagan Presdl. Task Force, 1988, Rep. Senatorial Inner Circle, 1987. Recipient award Am. Acad. Public Affairs Los Angeles, 1964, Liberty award Congress Freedom, 1959; award Young Ams. Against Communism, 1964; Disting. Alumnus award Sioux Falls Coll., 1972. Mem. Acad. Model Aeros. (nat. sec. 1952, Superior Service award 1979), Fla. Modelers Assn. (sec.-treas. 1969-74), Gold Coast Free Flighters (sec. 1976-82). Author: Inside the State Department, 1956; The Untouchable State Department, 1962, rev. as State Department: Blunders or Treason?, 1965; co-author: Dream Becomes a Nightmare: The UN Today, 1964; The Inhumanity of Urban Renewal, 1965; compiler: Trouble Abroad: An Independent Survey of World Affairs, 1965; Heaven on Earth for 60 Years: The Lifelong Romance of Ella Lillibridge and Bryton Barron-Their Adventures, their Writings, their Revelations of Washington Political Intrigues, 1983; editor newsletter for sr. citizens, 1983-85; contbr. articles to mags. and newspapers; co-author (with wife) series of lang. textbooks; played leading role in release of secret Yalta Papers. Barron papers in Library U. Oreg. Address: 5300 W 16th Ave Hialeah FL 33012

BARRON, CHARLES ELLIOTT, electronics executive; b. Midland, Tex., Feb. 17, 1928; s. Thomas Paul and Hollie Belle (Pickerill) B.; m. Sarah Alice Crawford, July 18, 1950; children: Thomas, Sarah, Robert. BSEE, Vanderbilt U., 1949; BD, Southwestern Bapt. Theol. Sem., 1958. Geophysicist Shell Oil Co., various locations, 1949-54, Tex. Pacific Coal and Oil Co., Ft. Worth, 1954-59; engrng. mgr. then gen. mgr. Gen. Electric Co., Utica, Syracuse and Binghamton, N.Y., 1959-87; pres. ops. Eaton Corp., Melville, N.Y., 1987—. Bd. dirs. Roberson Ctr., Binghamton, N.Y., 1981-84; chmn. major firms drive Broome County (N.Y.) United Way, 1981-83; mem. engrng. adv. bd. Syracuse U., 1986—; mem. engrng. sch. council SUNY Binghamton, 1982-83. Mem. Nat. Security Indsl. Assn. (Comcac com. 1986—), L.I. Assn. (bd. dirs. 1988—). Republican. Baptist. Office: AIL Div Commack Rd Deer Park NY 11729

BARRON, PAUL DOUGLAS, film producer; b. Toronto, Ont., Can., Dec. 26, 1949; arrived in Australia, 1972; s. Alex E. and Nina M. (Burrows) B.; m. Marina Medigovich, Nov. 3, 1984; children: Aleksia Helen, Nikolas Stefan, Kristian James. BA with honors, Queens U., Ont., 1972. Community arts officer Fed. Pub. Service, Canberra, Australian Capital Territories, 1973-75; dir. Frevideo, Fremantle, Western Australia, 1975-76, Film and TV Inst. of Western Australia, Fremantle, 1976-81; mng. dir. Barron Films Ltd., Perth, Western Australia, 1981—. Producer: (feature films) Shame, Windrider; (mini-series) A Waltz Through the Hills; (documentary) First Impressions; (telefeature) Tudawali; co-producer: (feature) Where the Outback Ends; exec. producer: (featues) I Own the Racecourse, Fran, Long Time No See, Ronnie, River of Giants, Anyone Can Be A Genius, Reflections of Myself; (TV series) Falcon Island; co-producer, exec. producer: (feature) Bush Christmas; producer, exec. producer: (TV series) Kicking Around. Mem. Screen Producers Assn. Australia. Office: Barron Films Ltd, 3 Ventnor Ave, West Perth 6005, Australia

BARRON, WILLIAM RAYMOND JOHNSTON, educator; b. Ballyclare, No. Ireland, Great Britain, Dec. 14, 1926; s. William Rea and Elizabeth Jane (McMinn) B. MA, St. Andrews U., Scotland, 1948; student, Yale U., 1950-51; PhB, St. Andrews, Scotland, 1951; postgrad., Strasbourg U., 1951-52; PhD, St. Andrews U., Scotland, 1959. Asst. lectr. U. Aberdeen, Scotland, 1952-57; lectr. U. Manchester, Eng., 1957-68, sr. lectr., 1970—; prof. Pahlavi U., Shiraz, Iran, 1968-70; dir. Eugene Vinaver Trust, Great Britain, 1986—. Author: "Trawthe" and Treason, 1980, English Medieval Romance, 1987; editor, translator Sir Gawain and the Green Knight, 1974, (with .C. Weinberg Layamon's Arthur: the Arthurian section of Layamon's Brut, 1988; editor Poetry of Robert Henryson, 1981; contbr. articles to profl. jours. Served to sgt. Territorial Army, 1944-50. Carnegie Trust for Scotland research scholar, 1948-50; Rotary Internat. fellow, 1950-51, 1951-52. Mem.

Internat. Arthurian Soc. (pres. British br. 1983-86). Office: U Manchester, Oxford Rd, Manchester M13 9PL, England

BARROSO, MARIA ALICE GIUDICE, librarian, writer; b. Rio de Janeiro, Brazil, Nov. 6, 1926; d. Oscar Barroso Soares and Aurora (Giudice) Barroso. Degree in English Literature, Sch. English Culture, Rio de Janiero, 1949. Librarian Guanabara State, Rio de Janeiro, 1955-72; chief Music Library, Rio de Janeiro, 1965-70; gen. dir. Nat. Book Inst., Brasilia, Brazil, 1970-74; editor Exped Edit., Rio de Janeiro, 1974-79, Livro Técn.e Cientifico Edit., Rio de Janeiro, 1979-82; dir. asst. Brazil Nat. Library, Rio de Janeiro, 1982-84, gen. dir., 1984—; cons. in field. Author: A Name to Kill, 1967 (Walmap award), Who Killed Pacific, 1969, The Globe of Death, 1974, The Indoomed Horse, 1988. Recipient Ednl. medal Ministry of Edn., 1970, Rio Branco Medal Ministry of Fgn. Affairs, 1971. Mem. Nat. Library Friends Assn., Pen Club. Home: R Nascimento Silva 183-C-02, Rio de Janeiro Brazil Office: Biblioteca Nacional, (Nat Library), Av Rio Branco 219-39, 20042 Rio de Janeiro Brazil

BARROW, GEOFFREY WALLIS STEUART, Scottish history educator; b. Leeds, Eng., Nov. 28, 1924; s. Charles Embleton and Marjorie (Steuart) B.; m. Heather Elizabeth Agnes Lownie, July 6, 1951; children: Julia Steuart, Andrew Charles Steuart. MA, U. St. Andrews, Scotland, 1948, D.Litt, 1971; B.Litt, U. Oxford, Eng., 1950; D.Litt (hon.), Glasgow U., Scotland, 1988. Lectr. U. London, 1950-61, U. Newcastle upon Tyne, Eng., 1961-74, U. St. Andrews, Scotland, 1974-79; Sir William Fraser prof. Scottish history and palaeography U. Edinburgh, Scotland, 1979—; mem. Royal Commn. on Hist. Manuscripts, 1984—. Author: Feudal Britain, 1956, rev. edit., 1971, Robert Bruce, 1965, 3d edit., 1988, Kingdom of the Scots, 1973, Kingship and Unity, 1981; editor: Acts of Malcolm IV, 1960, Acts of William I, 1971. Served to sub-lt. Royal Navy, 1943-46, CBI. Recipient Alexander prize Royal Hist. Soc., 1952, Agnes Mure Mackenzie award Saltire Soc., 1965, book award Scottish Arts Council, 1981. Fellow Brit. Acad. (councillor 1982-84), Royal Soc. Edinburgh. Mem. Scottish Episcopal Ch. Office: U Edinburgh Dept Scottish Hist, 17 Buccleuch Pl, Edinburgh EH8 9LN, Scotland

BARROW, GEORGE TERRELL, lawyer; b. Wichita Falls, Tex., July 23, 1909; s. George W. and Jena (Magee) B.; m. Margaret Forrest, Nov. 5, 1954; children: David G., Blake W. J.D., U. Tex., 1932. Bar: Tex. 1932. Since practiced in Housto; of counsel Able & Able; adj. prof., vis. prof. South Tex. Coll. Law, Houston, 1985-87; mem. Bd. Law Examiners Tex., 1964-80, chmn., 1975-80. Bd. dirs. Houston Pub. Library, 1974-76; trustee Retina Research Found. Served to lt. comdr. USNR, 1942-46. Life fellow Am., Tex. bar founds., Houston Bar Found., Am. Coll. Probate Counsel, ABA (ho. of dels. 1972-76); mem. Nat. Conf. Bar Examiners (bd. mgrs. 1973-80, chmn. 1979-80), Houston Bar Assn. (pres. 1963-64), State Bar Tex. (dir. 1959-62, State Bar Bd. cert. estate planning and probate law, also oil, gas and mineral law), Coll. State Bar Tex., Am. Judicature Soc., Am. Arbitration Assn., Tex. Soc. SAR, Sons Republic of Tex., Jamestowne Soc. (San Antonio chpt.), Magna Charta Barons (Somerset chpt.), English Speaking Union (pres. Houston br. 1970-72), Navy League U.S., Am. Vets. World War II, Korea and Vietnam, Houston Mus. Natural Sci., Houston Mus. Fine Arts, Zool. Soc. Houston, Inst. Internat. Edn., Friends Houston Pub. Library, Houston Symphony Soc., Army-Navy Assn. Houston, Harris County Heritage Soc., Big Bros. Houston (pres. 1959), Friends Fondren Library Rice U., U. Houston Libraries, Alpha Tau Omega. Democrat. Methodist. Clubs: Forum, Petroleum (pres. 1969-70), Reading for Pleasure (Houston); Inns of Court, Forest; Columbia Lakes Country (Brazoria County, Tex.); Warwick, Brazos River, The 100. Lodge: Kiwanis. Home: 6151 Bordley Dr Houston TX 77057 Office: Two Houston Center Suite 3450 909 Fannin St Houston TX 77010

BARROW, MARTIN GILBERT, holding company executive; b. Lancaster, Eng., Mar. 10, 1944; s. George Erskine and Margaret Armine (Macinnes) B.; m. Noriko Koike, Nov. 25, 1969; children: Lawrence John William, Edward Michael. Student, Harrow Sch., 1957-61. Dir. Jardine, Matheson & Co., Ltd., 1980-82; pres. Olayan Saudi Holding Co., Saudi Arabia, 1982-83; regional mng. dir. Jardine, Matheson & Co., Ltd., Hong Kong, 1983, mng. dir., 1984; dep. chmn. Jardine, Matheson Holdings, Ltd. and Jardine Pacific Bd., Hong Kong, 1987—; chmn. Jardine Matheson Ltd., Peoples Republic of China, 1983—, Lombard Alliance Ins. Co. Ltd., 1985—; bd. dirs. Gammon Ltd., Hong Kong, Zung Fu Co. Ltd. Bd. dirs. Aviation Adv. Bd., Hong Kong, Community Chest of Hong Kong; chmn. The Sailors' Home & Missions to Seamen, Hong Kong Tourist Assn.; trustee China Fleet Club. Decorated Officer of Most Excellent Order of Brit. Empire, 1979. Office: Jardine Matheson Holdings Ltd, 48th Connaught Centre, 1 Connaught Pl, Hong Kong Hong Kong

BARROW, THOMAS DAVIES, former oil and mining company executive; b. San Antonio, Dec. 27, 1924; s. Leonidas Theodore and Laura Editha (Thomson) B.; m. Janice Meredith Hood, Sept. 16, 1950; children—Theodore Hood, Kenneth Thomson, Barbara Loyd, Elizabeth Ann. B.S., U. Tex., 1945, M.A., 1948; Ph.D., Stanford U., 1953; grad. advanced mgmt. program, Harvard U., 1963. With Humble Oil & Refining Co., 1951-72; regional exploration mgr. Humble Oil & Refining Co., New Orleans, 1962-64, sr. v.p., 1967-70, pres., 1970-72, also dir.; exec. v.p. Esso Exploration, Inc., 1964-65; sr. v.p. Exxon Corp., N.Y.C., 1972-78, also dir.; chmn., chief exec. officer Kennecott Corp., Stamford, Conn., 1978-81; vice chmn. Standard Oil Co., 1981-85; investment cons. Houston, 1985—; mem. commn. on natural resources NRC, 1973-78, commn. on phys. sci., math. and natural resources, 1984-87, bd. on earth scis., 1982-84; dir. Tex. Commerce Bankshares, McDermott Internat. Inc., Am. Gen. Corp., GeoQuest Internat., Inc., Cameron Iron Works; trustee Woods Hole Oceanographic Instn., 20th Century Fund-Task Force on U.S. Energy Policy. Pres. Houston Grand Opera, 1985-87, chmn., 1987—; trustee Am. Mus. Natural History, Stanford U. 1980—, Baylor Coll. Medicine, Tex. Med. Ctr., 1983—, Geol. Soc. Am. Found., 1982-87. Served to ensign USNR, 1943-46. Recipient Disting. Achievement award Offshore Tech. Conf., 1973, Disting. Engring. Grad. award U. Tex., 1970, Disting. Alumnus, 1982, Disting. Geology Grad., 1985; named Chief Exec. of Yr. in Mining Industry, Fin. World, 1979. Fellow N.Y. Acad. Scis.; mem. Nat. Acad. Engring., Am. Mining Congress (bd. dirs. 1979-85, vice chmn. 1983-85), Am. Assn. Petroleum Geologists, Geol. Soc. Am., Internat. Copper Research Assn. (bd. dirs. 1979-85), Nat. Ocean Industry Assn. (bd. dirs. 1982-85), AAAS, Am. Soc. Oceanography (pres. 1970-71), Am. Geophys. Union, Am. Petroleum Inst., Am. Geog. Soc., Sigma Xi, Tau Beta Pi, Sigma Gamma Epsilon, Phi Eta Sigma, Alpha Tau Omega. Episcopalian. Clubs: Houston Country, Clove Valley, Petroleum, River Oaks Country, Ramada.

BARRY, DESMOND THOMAS, JR., lawyer; b. N.Y.C., Mar. 26, 1945; s. Desmond Thomas and Kathryn (O'Connor) B.; m. Patricia Mellicker, Aug. 28, 1971; children—Kathryn, Desmond Todd. A.B., Princeton U., 1967; J.D., Fordham U., 1973. Bar: N.Y. 1974, U.S. Dist. Ct. (so. and ea. dist.) N.Y. 1974, U.S. Ct. Appeals (2d cir.) 1974, U.S. Ct. Appeals (9th cir.) 1980, U.S. Ct. Appeals (5th cir.) 1983, U.S. Ct. Appeals (3d cir.) 1984, U.S. Supreme Ct. 1985. Assoc. firm Condon & Forsyth, N.Y.C., 1973-79, ptnr., 1979—. Trustee Canterbury Sch., New Milford, Conn., 1970-80. Served to capt. USMC, 1967-70, Vietnam. Decorated Navy Commendation medal with combat V; Combat Action medal, 1969, Vietnamese Cross of Gallantry, 1969. Mem. Assn. Bar City N.Y., ABA, N.Y. State Bar Assn., Internat. Assn. Ins. Counsel. Republican. Roman Catholic. Club: Winged Foot Golf (Mamaroneck, N.Y.). Home: 5 Point O'Woods St Darien CT 06820 Office: Condon & Forsyth 1251 Ave of Americas New York NY 10020

BARRY, DONALD LEE, investment broker; b. Ft. Gordon, Ga., Sept. 1, 1953; s. C. Donald and Della (Newman) B.; m. Peggy Summerfield, Aug. 8, 1980 (div. June 1983). Student, Wichita State U., 1974-1981. Lic. stocks and commodity trader, life ins. agt. Instr. Cyr's Driving Sch., Wichita, Kans., 1974-78, v.p., 1978-81; investment broker A.G. Edwards & Sons, Wichita, 1981-85, v.p. investments, 1985—. Bd. dirs. Wichita Pub. Library, 1980, treas. 1981-83; bd. dirs. Interfaith Ministries Exec. Com., Wichita, 1983—; co-chmn. fin. com. to elect. Margalee Wright, Wichita, 1984. Served as cpl. USMC, 1972-74. Recipient Pres.' Council award Oppenheimer Mgmt. Co., 1983, AG Edwards & Sons, 1986, 87. Mem. Am. Mensa Ltd., Internat. Assn. for Fin. Planners. Republican. Episcopalian. Club: Wichita. Home: 1303 Farmstead Wichita KS 67208 Office: AG Edwards & Sons 250 N Water Wichita KS 67202

BARRY, HERBERT, III, psychologist; b. N.Y.C., June 2, 1930; s. Herbert and Lucy Manning (Brown) B. B.A., Harvard U., 1952; M.S., Yale U., 1953, Ph.D., 1957. USPHS-NIMH postdoctoral research fellow Yale U., 1957-59, asst. prof. psychology, 1960-61; asst. prof. psychology U. Conn., Storrs, 1961-63; research assoc. prof. pharmacology, Sch. Pharmacy U. Pitts., 1963-70, prof., Sch. Pharmacy, 1970-87, prof. physiology and pharmacology, Sch. Dental Medicine, 1987—; mem. alcohol research rev. com. Nat. Inst. Alcohol Abuse and Alcoholism, 1972-76; mem. sociobehav. subcom., AIDS research rev. com. Nat. Inst. Drug Abuse, 1988—. Author: (with H. Wallgren) Actions of Alcohol, 1970; editor: (with A. Schlegel) Cross-Cultural Samples and Codes, 1980, (with A. Yacobi) Experimental and Clinical Toxicokinetics, 1984; field editor Psychopharmacology, 1974—; Contbr. articles to profl. jours. Recipient NIMH Research Scientist Devel. award, 1967-77. Fellow Am. Psychol. Assn. (council reps. 1975-76, pres. div. psychopharmacology 1980-81), Acad. Pharm. Sci. (chmn. sect. pharmacodynamics and drug disposition 1984-85), Am. Assn. Pharm. Scientists, AAAS, Am. Anthrop. Assn.; mem. Am. Soc. Pharm. Exptl. Therapeutics, Psychonomic Soc., Am. Coll. Neuropsychopharmacology, Phi Beta Kappa, Sigma Xi. Home: 552 N Neville St Apt 83 Pittsburgh PA 15213 Office: Univ Pittsburgh 615-1 Salk Hall Pittsburgh PA 15261

BARRY, JERARD MICHAEL, principal research scientist, educator; b. Sydney, Australia, Aug. 24, 1942; s. James and Alma Beatrice (Hunt) B.; m. Enda Jacqueline Barry; 1 child, Tara Dale. BSc, U. New South Wales, 1966; MSc, Sydney U., 1975; PhD, Wollongong U., 1982; BA, U. New South Wales, 1982. Tchr. New South Wales Dept. Edn., 1962-66; research scientist Australian Atomic Energy Commn., Sydney, 1967-72, sr. research scientist, 1975-84, prin. research scientist, 1984—; vis. prof. U. Tenn., Knoxville, 1986; vis. scientist Oak Ridge Nat. Lab., Tenn., 1986. Author monograph Introduction to Pascal, 1984; contbr. nuclear sci. and engring. articles to profl. jours. Organizer, lectr. Summer Sch. on Sci. for high sch. students, Sydney, 1972-82. Mem. Soc. Indsl. and Applied Math., Australian Math. Soc. (com. computational math. group 1987), Lucas Height Sci. Soc. (treas. 1978-81, Sci. medal 1983). Roman Catholic. Home: 7 Geelong Rd, Engadine New South Wales 2233, Australia Office: Australian Atomic Energy Commn, Pvt Mail Bag 1, Menai New South Wales 2234, Australia

BARRY, JOHN KEVIN, lawyer; b. Akron, Ohio, Mar. 23, 1925; s. John Henry and Mary Ellen (O'Hara) B.; m. Ann L. Trainer, June 14, 1952 (div. 1958); children: Mona A., Barry de Sayve; m. Barbara Ann Lacek, Dec. 15, 1973; children: J. Kevin, Nicholas A.; Liza M. A.B., Princeton U., 1947; J.D., Northwestern U., 1951. Bar: Ohio 1951, Pa. 1963. Assoc. Brouse, McDowell Inc., Akron, 1951-54; trial atty. IRS, Washington, 1954-57; atty., mem. legal adv. staff U.S. Treasury Dept., Washington, 1957-60, mem. office of tax legis. counsel, 1960-62; assoc. Reed Smith Shaw & McClay, Pitts., 1962-66, ptnr., 1966-86, inactive ptnr., 1987—. Bd. dirs. Pitts. Symphony Soc., 1981—; trustee Sewickley (Pa.) Acad., 1982—. Served with USN, 1943-46. Mem. ABA, Fed. Bar Assn., Pa. Bar Assn., Am. Coll. Tax Counsel, Am. Arbitration Assn., Northwestern U. Sch. Law Alumni Assn. (regional v.p. 1979-87). Republican. Roman Catholic. Clubs: Allegheny Country (Sewickley Heights, Pa.); Duquesne, Harvard-Yale-Princeton (Pitts.); Columbia Country (Chevy Chase, Md.); Portage Country (Akron); Princeton (N.Y.C.). Home: Scaife Rd Sewickley PA 15143 Office: Reed Smith Shaw & McClay Mellon Sq 435 6th Ave Pittsburgh PA 15219

BARRY, JOHN PATRICK, occupational health engineer; b. Bangor, Maine, July 12, 1947; s. John Thomas and Patricia Josephine (Byrnes) B.; m. Jean Marie Devos, Apr. 7, 1984; children: Patricia Rose, John Louis, James Edward. B.A. in Zoology, U. Maine, 1969; M.Sc. in Pub. Health, U. Mass., 1971; Sc.D. in Acoustics (Rotary Found. fellow 1972-73, USPHS fellow 1973-76), U. Pitts., 1976. USPHS trainee U. Mass., 1969-71; health engr. Southeastern region Mass. Dept. Pub. Health, 1971-72; research fellow in occupational hygiene U. Manchester (Eng.), 1972-73; research asst. dept. otolaryngology Eye and Ear Hosp., Pitts., 1974-76; regional health engr. (specialist in noise control and hearing conservation) Phila. regional office Dept. Labor OSHA, 1976—; adj. prof. environ. studies Drexel U. Mem. Phila. div. Am. Cancer Soc. Registered sanitarian, Va., Mass.; cert. occupational hygienist, U.K. Mem. Acoustical Soc. Am. (past pres. Delaware Valley chpt.), Am. Inst. Physics, Audio Engring. Soc., Am. Conf. Govtl. Indsl. Hygienists (dir.), Brit. Inst. Occupational Hygiene, Am. Pub. Health Assn., Phila. Orch. Assn., Phila. Mus. Art, Sigma Xi. Roman Catholic. Club: Rotary (Phila.). Home: 4 McPherson St Philadelphia PA 19119 Office: Dept Labor Occupational Safety and Health Adminstrn 3535 Market St Philadelphia PA 19104

BARRY, MARION SHEPILOV, JR., mayor of Washington; b. Itta Bena, Miss., Mar. 6, 1936; s. Marion S. and Mattie Barry; m. Effi Barry, 1978; 1 son, Marion Christoper. B.S. in Chemistry, LeMoyne Coll., 1958; M.S., Fisk U., 1960; postgrad., U. Kans., 1960-61, U. Tenn., 1961-64. Dir. ops. Pride, Inc., Washington, from 1967; co-founder, chmn., dir. Pride Econ. Enterprises, Inc., Washington, 1968; mem. Washington Sch. Bd., 1971-74; mem. city council Washington, 1974-78; mayor 1979—. First nat. chmn. Student Nonviolent Coordinating Com.; mem. 3d World Coalition Against the War. Office: Office of the Mayor District Bldg 14th and E Sts Washington DC 20004 *

BARRY, PETER, former Irish minister for foreign affairs; b. Cork, Ireland, 1928; s. Anthony and Rita B.; m. Margaret O'Mullane, 1958; 6 children. chmn. of tea firm; mem. Dáil, 1969—; past chmn. Oireachtas com. Fine Gael Party; former lord mayor Cork, past chmn. Cork and Kerry Regional Devel. Bd.; Fine Gael spokesman on Labour, and the Pub. Service, 1972-73; minister for transport and power Govt. of Ireland, 1973-76, minister for edn., 1976-77; Fine Gael spokesman on econ. affairs and pub. services, 1977-81; minister for environment Govt. of Ireland, 1981-82, minister for fgn. affairs, 1982-87; party spokesman on Fgn. Affairs, 1987—. Office: Former Ministry for Fgn Affairs, Dublin Ireland

BARSALONA, FRANK, theatrical agent; b. S.I., N.Y., Mar. 31, 1938; s. Peter and Mary (Rotunno) B.; m. June Harris, Sept. 1, 1966; 1 dau., Nicole. Student, Wagner Coll., S.I., 1955-58, Herbert Berghof Sch., N.Y.C., 1959-60. Agt. Gen. Artists Corp., N.Y.C., 1960-64; founder, since pres. Premier Talent Agy., N.Y.C., 1964—; co-founder, pres. Phila. Fury, 1977-80; lectr., moderator music industry; co-owner WKSS Radio, Hartford, Conn., WMYF/WERZ-FM, Exeter, N.H. Bd. govs. T.J. Martell Leukemia Fund; bd. dirs. Rock & Roll Hall of Fame Mus. Recipient numerous awards Billboard Publs., cover subject spl. issue, 1984; named to Performance Mag. Hall of Fame, 1988. Office: Premier Talent Agy 3 E 54th St New York NY 10022

BARSAMIAN, J(OHN) ALBERT, lawyer, lecturer educator, criminologist, arbitrator; b. Troy, N.Y., May 1, 1934; s. John and Virginia (Tachdjian) B.; m. Alice Missirlian, Apr. 21, 1963; children—Bonnie, Tamara. B.S. in Psychology, Union Coll., 1956; LL.B., Albany Law Sch., 1959; J.D., Union U., 1968. Bar: N.Y. 1961, U.S. Dist. Ct. (no. dist.) N.Y. 1961, U.S. Supreme Ct. 1967; fire tng. cert. N.Y. State Exec. Dept. Sole practice, Troy, 1961—; founder, chmn. dept. police sci. Hudson Valley Community Coll., 1961-69; dir. criminal sci. Russell Sage Coll., 1070-88 , assoc. prof. criminal sci., 1977-82, prof., 1982-87, Emeritus prof., 1987—; faculty Nelson A. Rockefeller Coll. Pub. Affairs and Policy, 1986—, Cornell U. Sch. Labor Relations, 1986; spl. counsel Office of Police Chief, Cohoes, N.Y. 1986— ; counsel North Greenbush Police Assn., 1985—, Office of Police Chief, Syracuse, N.Y., 1986—, Fire Dept. Union, Albany, N.Y., 1986; police and media cons.; public sector and negligence arbitrator; gen. counsel Internat. Narcotic Enforcement Officers Assn., 1982-83, Troy Uniformed Firefighters Assn. 1977—; spl. investigator Rensselaer County Dist. Atty., 1959-61. Mem. Union Coll. Alumni Council, 1981-86; mem. parish council St. Peter Armenian Ch., Watervliet, N.Y. 1979-83, chmn., 1981-83, vice chmn., 1984; evaluator N.Y. State Edn. Dept. Office of Non-Collegiate Programs, 1985—; hon. dep. sheriff St. Mary Parish (La.). Decorated chevalier, knight comdr. Sovereign Order Cyprus; recipient Police Sci. Students' award Hudson Valley Community Coll., 1968; award for meritorious service to law enforcement Law Enforcement Officers Soc. N.Y., 1969, Archbishop's cert. merit Armenian Ch. Am., 1973; Union Coll. Tarzian scholar, 1952-56, Porter scholar, 1954-56; Albany Law Sch. Saxton scholar, 1956-59; Lawyers Coop. Pub. Co. prize in criminal law, 1957. Mem. ABA (com. on police selection and tng. 1967-69), Rensselaer County Bar Assn., Acad. Criminal Justice Scis., N.Y. State Bar Assn. (chmn. com. on police criminal justice sect. 1970-72, trial lawyers sect com. continuing legal edn. 1977—), Assn. Trial Lawyers Am., N.Y. State Trial Lawyers Assn., Am. Correctional Assn., Am. Arbitration Assn., N.Y. State Chiefs of Police Assn., Internat. Assn. Chiefs of Police, Northeastern Chiefs of Police Conf., Am. Assn. Fed. Investigators, N.Y. State Tng. Dirs. Assn., Union Coll. Alumni Assn. (Silver medal 1956), Les Amis d'Escoffier Soc., Northeastern Assn. Criminal Justice Educators, Masonic Vet. Assn. Troy (life), N.Y. Vet. Police Assn. (life, hon. counsel), Phi Delta Theta, Psi Chi, Alpha Phi Sigma. Clubs: Mason (32 degree), Rose Croix (most wise master Delta chpt. 1986), Royal Order Jesters, Shriners, Albany Country. Contbr. articles to legal jours. Home: 5 Sage Hill Ln Albany NY 12204 Office: 21 2d St Troy NY 12180

BARSAN, ROBERT BLAKE, dentist; b. Akron, Ohio, Apr. 7, 1948; s. Emil O. and Letitia (Dobrin) B.; m. Cheryl Lee Adams, Dec. 16, 1972; children: Erin Lee, Kathleen Letitia. BS, U. Cin., 1970; DDS, Ohio State U., 1974. Resident U. Chgo., 1976; gen. practice dentistry Cuyahoga Falls, Ohio, 1976—. Contbr. editor Modern Dental Mag., 1984—. Fellow Acad. Gen. Dentistry; mem. Am. Dental Assn. (chmn. CPR 1984—), Am. Endodontic Soc., Akron Gnathological Soc. (pres. 1986). Home: 3084 Silver Lake Blvd Silver Lake OH 44224 Office: 330 Stow Ave Cuyahoga Falls OH 44221

BARSI, LOUIS MICHAEL, university administrator research assistant, educational consultant; b. Port Reading, N.J., Aug. 26, 1941; s. Louis Joseph and Mary Alice B. BA, U. Okla., 1963; MA, Central Mich. U., 1966; MA, U. No. Iowa, 1971; EdS, U. Wis., Stout, 1978. Tchr. Searing Sch., N.Y.C., 1963-64; East Cath. High Sch., Detroit, 1964-65; instr. history, polit. sci., Muskegon (Mich.) Community Coll., 1966-68; dean of students Mount St. Clare Coll., Clinton, Iowa, 1969-76, chmn. social sci. div., 1975-76, athletic dir., 1970-76; coordinator fin. aids U. Wis., Waukesha, 1977-80, adminstr. honors program, 1978-80; asst. campus dir., dean of student affairs Pa. State U., DuBois, 1980-87; research asst. George Mason U., Fairfax, Va., 1987-88; program assoc. acad. programs Am. Assn. State Colls. and Univs., 1988—; group leader Student Personnel Conf., U. No. Iowa; speaker on student leadership tng. to various high schs., colls. and confs., 1980-87—. Contbr. articles to profl. jours. Bd. dirs. HANDS, Clinton, Iowa, 1970-71; mem. personnel com. Du Bois YMCA, 1982-84; bd. dirs., mem. budget and fin. com. DuBois United Way, 1983-87, chmn. long-range planning com., 1984-86, co-chmn. edn. div. 1985 campaign, sec., 1985-87, v.p. and chmn. campaign com., 1986, pres., 1987; adv. Explorer Post, Boy Scouts Am., 1981-83, mem. exec. com. Bucktail council, 1982-87, dir. career services, 1984-87; mem. planning com. Tom Mix Festival, 1983-87. Teaching assistant Central Mich. U., 1965-66; research assistant U. No. Iowa, 1968-69, George Mason U.; assistantship U. Wis., Stout, 1976-77; recipient Disting Service award for developing career awareness program Boy Scouts Am., 1985, Nat. Quality Dist. award Bucktail Council, BSA, 1987. Mem. Pa. Personnel and Guidance Assn., Am. (task force on consultation teams), Pa. coll. personnel assns., Nat. Assn. Student Personnel Adminstrs., Eastern Assn. Coll. Deans, DuBois C. of C. (dir. 1981-84, chmn. govtl. affairs com. 1981-83), Pa. State U. DuBois Campus Alumni Soc. (bd. dirs. 1980-87, bd. dirs. DuBois Ednl. Found. 1987—), DuBois Area Hist. Soc. (co-founder), Phi Delta Kappa, Phi Alpha Theta. Club: DuBois Rotary (dir. 1982-87, v.p. 1983, pres.-elect 1984, pres. 1985-86). Home: 4701 Connecticut Ave NW Suite 405 Washington DC 20008 Office: 1 Dupont Circle Suite 700 Washington DC 20036

BARSKY, BRIAN ANDREW, computer scientist, educator; b. Montreal, Que., Can., Sept. 17, 1954; s. Arthur Harold and Audrey Barbara (Epstein) B. D.C.S., McGill U., 1973, B.Sc., 1976; M.S., Cornell U., 1978; Ph.D., U. Utah, 1981. Vis. researcher Sentralinstitutt, Oslo, 1979; instr. U. Calif., Santa Cruz, 1982—; assoc. prof. computer sci., U. Calif.-Berkeley, 1981—; adj. assoc. prof. U. Waterloo (Ont., Can.), 1982—; vis. researcher Ecole Nationale Supérieure des Télé communications, Paris, 1985—. Contbr. articles to profl. jours. U. Utah fellow; Natural Scis. and Engring. Research Council scholar; U. Calif. Berkeley Regents Jr. Faculty fellow; NSF grantee, 1982—; Presdl. Young investigator awardee, 1985; IBM Young Faculty awardee, 1985. Mem. Spl. Interest Group on Graphics (chmn. tech. program 1985), Assn. Computing Machinery, Nat. Computer Graphics Assn., IEEE Computer Soc., Can. Man-Computer Communications Soc., Soc. Indsl. and Applied Math. Office: Computer Sci Div U Calif Berkeley CA 94720

BARSUK, SIDNEY ALAN, hospital fund raising executive; b. Batavia, N.Y., June 22, 1941; s. Max and Nellie (Greenberg) B.; m. Maxene Frances Soloway, Aug. 19, 1967; children: Peter Scott, Jeffrey Howard. BS, Rochester Inst. Tech., 1969, MBA, 1971. Acting devel. dir. Rochester (N.Y.) Inst. Tech., 1969-72, spl. asst. to v.p., 1971-72; dir. devel. Upper Iowa Coll., Fayette, 1972-73; regional devel. officer Northwood Inst., Midland, Mich., 1973-75; asst. v.p. devel. Jackson Park Hosp., Chgo., 1975-80, v.p. resource devel., 1980—. Chmn. Citizens Referendum Com., Homewood, Ill., 1980; mem. Homewood Sch. Dist. 153 Bd., 1980—, chmn. property and fin. com., 1982—; chmn. South Shore Revitalization Ctr., Chgo., 1980; vice-chmn. Rosenblum Boys Club, Chgo., 1980-84, chmn., 1984—; mem. Homewood Cultural Arts Com., 1986—; bd. dirs. South Shore YMCA, 1984—. Named Outstanding Young Person, Chgo.-Southend Jaycees, Chgo., 1977. Mem. Nat. Soc. Fund Raising Execs. (dir., mem. exec. com. 1977-82), Nat. Assn. Hosp. Devel. (legislative chmn. 1983—), South Shore C. of C. (pres. 1978-79), Cosmopolitan C. of C. (vice chmn. 1986—). Republican. Jewish. Home: 18612 Carpenter St Homewood IL 60430

BART, HARM, mathematician, educator; b. Enkhuizen, North-Holland, The Netherlands, Aug. 5, 1942; s. Pieter and Jantje (Stoter) B.; m. Margaretha Doef, July 6, 1967; children: Jannette Alida, Helena Johanna, Femke Margaretha. Doctorandus, Free U., Amsterdam, 1969; Dr., Free U., 1973. Mem. staff Free U., 1973-77, sr. sci. staff mem., 1977-84; prof. mathematics Tech. U., Eindhoven, The Netherlands, 1982-85, Erasmus U., Rotterdam, The Netherlands, 1984—; dir. Erasmus U. Econometric Inst., Rotterdam, 1986—. Author: Meromorphic Operator Valued Functions, 1973, Minimal Factorization of Matrix and Operator Functions, 1979; editor: Operator Theory and Systems (Proceedings), 1986; contbr. articles in field. Grantee Netherlands Orgn. Advancement of Pure Research, U. Maryland 1975-76. Mem. Wiskundig Genootschap, Am. Math. Soc. Office: Econometric Inst Erasmus U, P O 1738, 3000 DR Rotterdam The Netherlands

BART, ISTVAN, publisher, writer, translator; b. Budapest, Hungary, June 1, 1944; s. Ede Bart and Ilona Gombas; m. Kinga Klaudy, 1973; children: Daniel, Istvan Laszlo. MA in English and Hungarian Philology, U. Budapest, 1963-68. Editor Europa Publishers, Budapest, 1972-84; dir., gen. mgr. Corvina Pub. House, Budapest, 1984—; cons. editor Valosag-Social Sci. Monthly, Budapest, 1977—; gen. sec. Hungarian Pen Ctr., 1982—. Author: The Unfortunate Crown Prince, 1984; contbr. articles to profl. jours. Mem. Hungarian Writers' Union. Office: Corvina Pubs, Vorosmarty-ter 1, Budapest V Hungary 1051 Office: Corvina Pubs, 1 Vorosmarty Ter, Budapest Hungary

BART, LIONEL, composer, lyricist; b. Aug. 1, 1930. Prin. works include: lyrics for Lock Up Your Daughters, 1959, music and lyrics for Fings Ain't Wot They Used t'be, 1959, music, lyrics and book for Oliver!, 1960, film, 1968, music, lyrics and direction of Blitz!, 1962, music and lyrics of Maggie May, 1964; film scores include: Serious Charge, In the Nick, Heart of a Man, Let's Get Married, Light Up the Sky, The Tommy Steele Story, The Duke Wore Jeans, Tommy the Toreador, Sparrers Can't Sing, From Russia with Love, Man in the Middle; many hit songs. Recipient Ivor Novello award, 1957, 59, 60; Variety Club Silver Heart for Show Bus. Personality of the Yr., Broadway, U.S.A., 1960; Antoinette Perry award (Tony) for Oliver!, 1962; Gold disc award for soundtrack of Oliver!, 1969; Ivor Novello Jimmy Kennedy award, 1985. Office: care Patricia McNaughton, 200 Fulham Rd, London SW10 9PN, England *

BARTA, FRANK RUDOLPH, SR., psychiatrist, neurologist; b. Omaha, Nov. 3, 1913; s. Rudolph J. and Anna (Smejkal) B.; m. Mildred K. Ware, Aug. 12, 1939; children—Frank Rudolph, Nancy and Carol (twins), Richard, Matthew, Michael. A.B., Creighton U., 1935; M.D., Johns Hopkins, 1939. Diplomate Am. Bd. Psychiatry and Neurology. Intern

Harper Hosp., Detroit, 1939-40; asst. psychiatry Yale Sch. Medicine, 1942-43; resident neurology U. Chgo. Clinics, 1942-43; pvt. practice psychiatry and neurology 1946—; instr. psychiatry and neurology Creighton U. Sch. Medicine, 1946-49, dir. dept., 1949-56, prof. psychiatry and neurology, 1956-70, prof. emeritus, 1970—; clin. prof. psychiatry Chgo. Med. Sch., 1970-74; attending psychiatrist St. Joseph's Hosp., St. Catherine's Hosp., 1949-67; cons. in psychiatry A.R.C., VA Hosp., Cath. Charities, SAC, 1949-67; med. dir. Mental Health Center LaSalle County, Ottawa, Ill., 1968-73; clin. dir. Tideland Mental Health Center, Washington, N.C., 1973-75; psychiatrist Gulfport div. VA Center, 1975-85. Author: The Moral Theory of Behavior—A New Answer to the Enigma of Mental Illness, 1952; Contbr. articles med. jours. Chmn. personnel bd., City of Omaha, 1959-67. Dir. mental hygiene unit U.S. Army, 1943-46, Fort Bliss, Tex. Fellow ACP (life), Am. Geriatrics Soc., Am. Psychiat. Assn. (life); mem. Ill. Psychiat. Soc., Nat. Acad. Religion and Mental Health (charter, life mem.), So. Med. Assn. Roman Catholic. Home: Great Oaks 6904 Shore Dr Ocean Springs MS 39564

BAR-TAL, DANIEL, psychology educator; b. Stalinabad, USSR, Jan. 31, 1946; arrived in Israel, 1957; s. Yaakov and Sofia (Balter) B.; m. Yaffa Zygiel, Aug. 12, 1970; children: Shai, Daphne. BA, Tel-Aviv U., Israel, 1970; MS, PhD, U. Pitts., 1973. Research assoc. U. Pitts., 1974-75; sr. lectr. Tel-Aviv U., Israel, 1979-83, lectr., 1975-79; vis. assoc. prof. Vanderbuilt U., Nashville, 1981-82; fellows prof. Tel-Aviv U., Isreal, 1983—; vis. prof. Brandeis U., Waltham, Mass., 1987—; cons. Ministry Edn., Israel, 1977—. Author: Prosocial Behavior, 1976; co-editor: Social Psychology of Education, 1978, Social Psychology of Knowledge, 1988; editor: Annals of Psychology and Counseling jour., 1977—. Mem. Nat. Bd. Israel Consumers Council, Internat. Soc. Polit. Psychology, Soc. Experimental Social Psychology, Soc. Psychological Study Social Issues, Am. Ednl. Research Assn. Jewish. Office: Tel-Aviv Univ, Sch Edn, Tel-Aviv 69978, Israel

BARTEE, THOMAS CRESON, computer scientist, educator; b. Moberly, Mo., Dec. 18, 1926; s. Thomas Monroe and Verna Miller (Tippett) B.; m. Mildred Higdon, Sept. 5, 1953; 1 child, Thomas Quentin. B.A., Westminster Coll., 1949. Mem. staff computer research M.I.T.-Lincoln Lab., Lexington, Mass., 1955-63; Gordon MacKay lectr. in computer engring. Harvard U., Cambridge, Mass., 1963-69; dir. electronic design center Harvard U., 1969-72, Gordon MacKay prof. computer engring., 1970—; cons. Nat. Acad. Scis., IDA, IBM, Honeywell, Raytheon; IEEE disting. computer sci. lectr., 1972-74. Author: Digital Computer Fundamentals, 6th edit, 1985, Basic Computer Programming, 1981, 2d edit., 1985, Introduction to Computer Science, 1972, Data Communications, Networks and Systems, 1985, Digital Communications, 1986, Expert Systems in AI, 1987 (with G. Birkhoff) Modern Applied Algebra, 1971; editor IEEE-IRE Computer Jour, 1963-66. Recipient Disting. contbn. in computer sci. award Westminster Coll., 1980. Mem. IEEE (chmn. N.E. computer group 1973-74), Am. Math. Soc. Office: Aiken Computation Lab Harvard Univ Cambridge MA 02138

BARTEK, FREDERIC JOHN, corporate bond trader; b. Pitts., July 2, 1947; s. Elmer and Victoria (Mroz) B.; m. Ann C. Draper. BA in Econs., Columbia Coll., 1969; MBA, Harvard U., 1976. Corp. bond trader Goldman Sachs & Co., N.Y.C., 1976-79, Morgan Stanley & Co., 1979-86; sr. v.p. Dillon Read & Co., 1986—. Served to capt. USAF, 1969-74. Republican. Roman Catholic. Home: 24 Monroe Pl Apt 2A Brooklyn NY 11201 Office: Dillon Read & Co 535 Madison Ave New York NY 10022

BARTEK, GORDON LUKE, radiologist; b. Valpraiso, Nebr., Dec. 27, 1925; s. Luke Victor and Sylvia (Buner) B.; m. Ruth Evelyn Rowley, Sept. 10, 1949; children—John, David, James. B.Sc., U. Nebr., 1948, M.D., 1949. Diplomate Am. Bd. Radiology. Intern Bishop Clarksen Hosp., Omaha, 1949-50; resident in medicine Henry Ford Hosp., Detroit, 1952-53, resident in radiology, 1953-56; staff radiologist Ferguson Hosp., Grand Rapids, Mich., 1956-76, Holland City Hosp., Mich., 1956-76, Logan Hosp., Utah, 1976-78, St. Lawrence Hosp., Lansing, Mich., 1978—; dir. Accord Ins. Co., Cayman Islands, 1983—. Served to lt. USN, 1949-52. Fellow Am. Coll. Radiology; mem. Mich. Radiology Practice Assn. (bd. dirs. 1984—, chmn. western Mich. sect. 1970-71), Am. Coll. Radiology (councilor 1972-76). Republican. Roman Catholic. Club: Manhattan Tennis (pres.). Avocations: flying; photography; skiing; snorkeling. Home: 1350 Briarcliff Dr SE Grand Rapids MI 49506-9737

BARTELL, GERALD AARON, corporate executive; b. Chgo., May 20, 1914; s. Benjamin and Lena (Tartakowsky) Beznor; m. Joyce Jaeger, Nov. 2, 1941; children: Jeffrey, Denis, Laura, Jane, Thad and Thomas, (twins). Ph.B., U. Wis., 1937, M.A., 1939, postgrad. Law Sch., 1939-40. Radio actor, dir., producer 1932-37; faculty dept. radio edn. U. Wis., 1937-47, asso. prof., 1946; founder Bartell Broadcasting Corp., Milw., 1947; pres. Bartell Broadcasting Corp., 1947-66; pres., pub. Macfadden Publs. Inc., N.Y.C., 1960-61; pres., pub., chmn. Macfadden-Bartell Corp., N.Y.C., 1962-65; chmn. Bartell Media Corp., N.Y.C., 1965-69; pres. Emerald Realty Co., Milw., 1965—, Theater Classic Recitals, Ltd., 1976—; co-founder, chmn. Telstar Corp., Los Angeles, 1981—; pres. Telstar Satellite Corp. Am., 1986—; founder, pres., chmn. Am. Med. Bldgs., Inc., Milw., 1964-74; founder former pres. Netherlands Antilles Broadcasting Corp., Curacao and Aruba, Tele Haiti, Port-au-Prince; bd. dirs. CEL Communications, Inc., N.Y.C.; past bd. dirs. Capital Indemnity Corp., Madison, Milw. Equity Fund, Inc., Continental Mortgage Ins., Inc., Madison. Producer, performer children's radio programs, records, TV movies. Chmn., Wis. Found. for Arts, 1974—; former bd. dirs. Am. Council Arts, N.Y.C.; founding chmn. Wis. Arts Bd., 1973. Served to lt. (j.g.) USNR, 1942-45. Rockefeller fellow NBC, N.Y.C. and Chgo., 1938. Mem. Phi Kappa Phi. Unitarian. Home: 64 Oak Creek Trail Madison WI 53717 Office: 6441 Enterprise Ln Madison WI 53719 also: 1900 Ave of Stars Los Angeles CA 90067

BARTELS, GEORGE THOMAS, physician, obesity researcher; b. Wilmington, Del., Jan. 14, 1954; s. George William and Helen Anna (MacFarland) B.; m. Susan Elizabeth Haney, July 27, 1979; children—Elizabeth, Laura Paige, Jillian. A.B. in Psychology, U. N.C., 1975; M.D., Duke U., 1978. Diplomate Am. Bd. Bariatric Medicine. Intern Tallahassee Regional Med. Ctr., 1979, resident, 1979-80; med. dir. Bartels Clinic, Garner, N.C., 1981-86 clin. preceptor sch. medicine E. Carolina U., 1986—; mem. staff Wake Med. Ctr., Raleigh, N.C., Raleigh Community Hosp. Mem. AMA (Physician's Recognition award 1983, 86), Am. Soc. Bariatric Physicians, N.C. Med. Soc., Wake County Med. Soc., Am. Acad. Family Physicians, Phi Beta Kappa, Alpha Epsilon Delta. Presbyterian. Office: Bartels Clinic 1201 Aversboro Rd Garner NC 27529

BARTELSKI, LESLAW M., writer; b. Warsaw, Poland, Sept. 8, 1920; s. Zygmunt and Zofia (Ulanowska) B.; m. Maria Zembrzuska, June 29, 1947; children: Agnieszka Baranowska, Jan. ML, U. Warsaw, 1948. Author: (novels) People From Beyond the River, 1951, A Twice Seen Landscape, 1958, Golden Mahmudia, 1962, Dialogue With A Shadow, 1968, Blood-stained Wings (3 vols.), 1975; (poetry) Against Annihilation, 1948; (prose) Genealogy of the Survivors, 1963, The Rider of Madara, 1963, Mokotow 1944, 1971, The Independent Song, 1988. Dep. pres. Warsaw Town Council, 1973, Maine Council, 1980; mem. ZBOWID (Union of Combatants), 1979. Named to Order Banner of Labour II Class, 1987; recipient Cross of Valour, 1944, Warsaw's Rising Cross, 1981, Cross of Home Army, 1967, Commander Cross of Polonia Resituta, 1980, State Lit. prize, 1951, Warsaw prize, 1969, Minister of Defense prize, 1969, Pietrzaks prize, 1969, 85, Minister Culture prize, 1977. Mem. Internat. Korczaks Soc. Home and Office: Fr Joliot Curie 17 F 1, 02-646 Warsaw Poland

BARTER, ROBERT HENRY, physician, emeritus educator; b. Harvard, Ill., Mar. 15, 1913; s. Francis Albert and Lula Mae (Rowbottom) B.; m. Joanne Rae Blied, Dec. 29, 1948; children: Robert Raymond, James Francis, Mary Joanne. B.S., U. Wis., 1937, M.D., 1940. Intern Cleve. City Hosp., 1940-41; resident Chgo. Lying-In Hosp., 1941-42, Wis. Gen. Hosp., Madison, 1946-48; chief med. officer obstetrics and gynecology Galinger Municipal Hosp., Washington, 1948-50; faculty George Washington U. Sch. Medicine, 1950—, prof., 1958-83, prof. emeritus, 1983—, chmn. dept. obstetrics and gynecology, 1958-67; cons. emeritus surgeon gen. USAF; sr. cons. emeritus Walter Reed Army Med. Center. Served to maj., M.C. AUS, 1942-46. Mem. Am. Gynecol. and Obstet. Soc., Am. Assn. Obstetricians and Gynecologists, A.C.S., Am. Coll. Obstetricians and Gynecologists, Soc. Gynecol. Surgeons, N.Am. Ob-Gyn Soc., So. Gynecol. and Obstet. Soc., Gynecol. Vis. Soc. Gt. Brit. and Ireland (hon.), AMA, Sigma Xi, Alpha Omega Alpha, Nu Sigma Nu, Kappa Sigma. Clubs: Burning Tree, Congressional Country; Hole in the Wall Golf (Naples, Fla.), Port Royal (Naples, Fla.); Rehoboth Beach (Del.) Country. Home: 6406 Goldleaf Dr Bethesda MD 20817 Office: 2141 K St NW Washington DC 20037

BARTH, ERNEST, chemical company executive; b. Vienna, Austria, Feb. 17, 1926; s. Jacob and Regina (Hecht) B.; m. Rita Spiegel, Dec. 30, 1951; 1 dau., Karen Nina. Pres., Continental Fertilizer Corp., N.Y.C., also v.p. Continental Ore Corp., 1953-72; pres. Agrico Internat., Inc., Tulsa and N.Y.C., 1972-73; pres. Beker Internat. Corp., Greenwich, Conn., also sr. v.p. Beker Industries, 1973-75; v.p. Philipp Bros./Engelhard Minerals & Chem. Corp., N.Y.C., 1975-77; sr. v.p. Beker Industries Corp., Greenwich, 1977-79; pres., dir. Superfos Am., Inc., Greenwich, 1979-85, chmn. bd., chief exec. officer, 1985-86; pres. Superfos Investments Ltd., Greenwich, 1985-86 ; dir. Mineral GMBH, Hamburg, Germany, Minex Corp. subs., Greenwich, 1978—; dir. affiliated cos.; cons. Chemie Linz AG of Austria, Balfour Maclaine Internat. Group—Wall St. Plaza. Mem. White House Food for Peace Council, 1962; co-chmn. U.S. Indsl. Mission to Korea, 1962. Clubs: Board Room (N.Y.C.); Burning Tree Country, Belle Haven (Greenwich, Conn.); Landmark (Stamford, Conn.); Longboat Key (Sarasota, Fla.). Home: 25 Lindsay Dr Greenwich CT 06830 Office: 35 Mason St Greenwich CT 06830

BARTH, JOHN SIMMONS, writer, educator; b. Cambridge, Md., May 27, 1930; s. John Jacob and Georgia (Simmons) B.; m. Harriette Anne Strickland, Jan. 11, 1950; children: Christine Anne, John Strickland, Daniel Stephen; m. Shelly I. Rosenberg, Dec. 27, 1970. B.A., Johns Hopkins U., 1951, M.A., 1952. From instr. to assoc. prof. English Pa. State U., 1953-65; prof. English SUNY, Buffalo, 1965-73; prof. English and creative writing Johns Hopkins U., 1973—. Author: The Floating Opera, 1956, The End of the Road, 1958, The Sot-Weed Factor, 1960, Giles Goat-Boy, 1966, Lost in the Funhouse, 1968, Chimera, 1972 (Recipient Nat. Book award in fiction 1973), Letters, 1979, Sabbatical: A Romance, 1982; The Friday Book, 1984, The Tidewater Tales: A Novel, 1987. Office: Johns Hopkins U Writing Seminars Baltimore MD 21218

BARTH, RICHARD, lawyer; b. N.Y.C., May 23, 1931; s. Alexander Haddon and Georgina (Grant) B.; m. Mary Elizabeth McAnaney, June 13, 1959; children: Leanore, Jennifer, Richard, Michele, Alexander. Grad., Hill Sch.; A.B. cum laude, Wesleyan U., Middletown, Conn., 1952; LL.B., Columbia, 1955; student, N.Y.U. Grad. Sch. Law, 1959-62. Bar: N.Y. 1958, N.J. 1966. Asso. firm Burke & Burke, 1957-65; gen. counsel, sec., mem. mgmt. com. CIBA, 1965-70; v.p., gen. counsel, mem. mng. com., dir. CIBA-GEIGY Corp., Ardsley, N.Y., from 1971, now pres., chief exec. officer, dir.; dir. Radio Shack Corp., 1964-65. Author articles. Mem. substandard housing bd., Summit, N.J., 1968-70. Served with AUS, 1955-57. Mem. Am., N.Y., N.J. bar assns., Phi Delta Phi, Psi Upsilon. Home: 431 Grace Church St Rye NY 10580 Office: CIBA-GEIGY Corp 444 Saw Mill River Rd Ardsley NY 10502 *

BARTHELMAS, NED KELTON, investment banker; b. Circleville, Ohio, Oct. 22, 1927; s. Arthur and Mary Bernice (Riffel) B.; m. Marjorie Jane Livezey, May 23, 1953; children: Brooke Ann, Richard Thomas. B.S. in Bus. Adminstrn., Ohio State U., 1950. Stockbroker Ohio Co., Columbus, 1953-58; pres. First Columbus Corp., 1958—; pres., dir. Ohio Fin. Corp., Columbus, 1960—; trustee, chmn. Am. Guardian Fin., Republic Fin.; dir. Nat. Foods, Liebert Corp., Midwest Capital Corp., Lancaster Colony Corp., Capital Equity Corp., Franklin Nat. Corp., Midwest Nat. Corp., 1st Columbus Realty Corp., Court Realty Co., all Columbus. Served with Adj. Gen.'s Dept. AUS, 1945-47. Mem. Nat. Assn. Securities Dealers (past vice chmn. dist. bd. govs.), Investment Bankers Assn. Am. (exec. com. 1973), Investment Dealers Ohio (sec., treas. 1956-72, pres. 1973), Nat. Stock Traders Assn., Young Pres.'s Orgn. (pres. 1971), Nat. Investment Bankers (pres. 1973), Columbus Jr. C. of C. (pres. 1956), Ohio Jr. C. of C. (trustee 1957-58), Columbus Area C. of C. (dir. 1956, named an Outstanding Young Man of Columbus 1962), Newcomen Soc., Phi Delta Theta. Clubs: Kiwanis, Execs., Stock and Bond, Columbus, Scioto Country (Columbus); Crystal Downs Country (Frankfort, Mich.). Home: 1000 Urlin Ave Columbus OH 43212 Summer Home: 6498 Bixler Rd Beulah MI 49617

BARTHLOME, RANDIE LEE, law enforcement administrator, consultant; b. Laramie, Wyo., May 4, 1948; d. Ralph Randall and Wilma Lee (Hawk) Benintendi; m. Edward Earl Barthlome, May 5, 1973; children—Sherri Lanee, Lori Lynn, Thomas Arthur, Greg Edward. Student Community Coll. of Denver, 1971-72, Idaho State U. Law Enforcement Acad., 1972-73, Idaho Peace Officer Acad., 1973, Idaho State U., 1977, Duke U., 1985. Advanced law enforcement cert.; cert. law enforcement instr. Advt., pub. relations dir. Consumer Enterprises, Denver, 1969-72; tutor Idaho State U., Pocatello, 1972; officer Blackfoot Police Dept. (Idaho), 1972-73; sec. Idaho Peace Officer Acad., Pocatello, 1973-74; crime prevention officer Pocatello Police Dept., 1974-80, dir., 1980-85; pres. SYNTAX, 1985—; pvt. practice cons., 1983—; circuit rider city mgr. Towns of Fowler, Orduay, and Sugar City, Colo., 1987—. Author weekly newspaper column: Police Watch, 1974-85, also articles. Adv. bd. Salvation Army, Pocatello, 1982-85; com. chmn. Mayor's Com. for Handicapped, Pocatello, 1982—; pres. Pocatello Community Services Council, 1975-76; founder Women's Advocates for Battered Women, Pocatello, 1976—. Named Citizen of Yr., Idaho Pros. Attys. Assn., 1982, Idaho Outstanding Supr., Manpower Consortium, 1981, Disting. Young Woman, Pocatello Jay-C-Ettes, 1979; recipient Nat. Award of Merit, Nat. Crime Prevention Coalition, 1981. Mem. Idaho Crime Prevention Assn. (founding, pres. 1981-82), Idaho Peace Officers Assn., Am. Soc. Tng. and Devel., Internat. City Mgmt. Assn., Idaho Press Club, Am. Bus. Women's Assn., Idaho Assn. for Affirmative Action, Am. Mktg. Assn., Centennial C. of C., Denver C. of C. Baptist. Lodge: Zonta. Home: 1170 E Phillips Dr Littleton CO 80122 Office: Syntax 13111 E Briarwood Ave Suite 250 Englewood CO 80112

BARTHOFER, ALFRED, language educator; b. Graz, Steiermark, Austria, Feb. 8, 1937; s. Josef and Maria (Dietenberger) B.; m. Renate Ingeborg Stadnikow, July 10, 1967; children: Natalie, Christine. Diploma in edn., Teachers Coll., Linz, Austria, 1957; PhD, U. Vienna, Austria, 1965, magister in philosophy, 1966. Lectr. Inst. Nat. Scis. Appliquées, Lyon, France, 1966-67, Goethe Inst., Lyon, 1966-67; lektor U. Newcastle, Australia, 1967-69, lectr., 1969-74, sr. lectr., 1974-84, assoc. prof., 1985—. Author: contbr. articles to profl. jours. Recipient Grillparzer-Ring Austrian Ministry Edn. and Arts, Vienna, 1985; Fulbright scholar U.S. Govt., 1957-58. Home: 46 Carolyn St, Newcastle New South Wales 2289, Australia Office: U Newcastle, Rankin Dr, Newcastle New South Wales 2308, Australia

BARTHOLOMEW, DAVID JOHN, statistics educator; b. Oakley, Eng., Aug. 6, 1931; s. Albert and Joyce (Payne) B.; m. Marian Elsie Lake, 1955; children: Ruth Elizabeth, Ann Christine. BSc, Univ. Coll., London, 1953; PhD, Univ. Coll., 1955. Scientist Nat. Coal Bd., London, 1955-57; lectr. U. Keele, Eng., 1957-60, U. Coll. Wales, Aberystwyth, Eng., 1960-67; prof. U. Kent, Canterbury, Eng., 1967-73; prof. stats. London Sch. Econs., 1973—; vis. prof. Harvard U., Cambridge, Mass., 1964-65, U. Calif.-Berkley, 1969, U. Melbourne, Australia, 1977, 86; vis. scientist Bell Telephone Labs., Holmdel, N.J., 1973. Author: Stochastic Models for Social Processes, 1967, Statistical Techniques for Manpower Planning, 1979, Mathematical Methods in Social Science, 1982, God of Chance, 1984, and others; contbr. articles to profl. jours. Fellow Royal Statis. Soc. (sec. 1976-82, recipient Guy medal in bronze 1971), Brit Acad., Inst. Math. Stats.; mem. Internat. Statis. Inst., Manpower Soc. (hon. v.p. 1986). Methodist. Office: London Sch Econs, Houghton St, London WC2A 2AE, England

BARTHOLOMEW, DONALD DELKE, inventor, business executive, engineer; b. Atlanta, Aug. 2, 1929; s. Rudolph A. and Rubye C. (Delke) B.; m. Paula Hagood; children: John Marshall, Barbara Ann, Deborah Paige, Sandra Dianne. Student in Physics, Ga. Inst. Tech., 1946-48, 55-58. Owner Happy Cottons and Jalopy Jungle, Atlanta, 1946-48, Beach Hotel Supply, Miami Beach, Fla., 1949-50; engr. Sperry Microwave Electronics, Clearwater, Fla., 1958-61; v.p., owner Draft Pak, Inc., Tampa, Fla., 1961-65, Merit Plastics, Inc., East Canton, Ohio, 1966-79; pres., owner Modern Tech., Inc., Marine City, Mich., 1979—; owner, officer and dir. various internat. mfg. companies, 1981—. Patentee in field. Served as sgt. USAF, 1951-54. Mem. Soc. Automotive Engrs., Soc. Plastics Engrs. (dir. 1982), Soc. Mfg. Engrs., Holiday Isles Jr. C. of C. (founding dir.). Republican.

BARTHOLOMEW, REGINALD, diplomat; b. Portland, Maine, Feb. 17, 1936; m. Rose-Anne Dognin; children: Sylvie, Christian, Damien, Jonathan. B.A., Dartmouth Coll., 1958; M.A., U. Chgo., 1960. Instr. U. Chgo., 1961-64; instr. Wesleyan U., Conn., 1964-68; dep. dir. Policy Planning Staff Dept. State, 1974, dep. dir. Bur. Politico-Mil. Affairs, 1977, dir. Bur. Politico-Mil. Affairs, 1979-81, spl. Cyprus coordinator, 1981-82, spl. negotiator for U.S.-Greek def. and econ. cooperation negotiations, 1982-83, U.S. ambassador to Lebanon, 1983-86; with NSC, 1977-79; U.S. ambassador to Spain Dept. of State, 1987—. Mem. Council on Fgn. Relations (internat. inst. for strategic studies). Office: US Embassy-Spain care US State Dept Washington DC 20520 *

BARTHOLOMEW, TRACY, II, geological economist; b. Pitts., June 17, 1952; s. George Anderson and Nancy Davis (Large) B.; B.A. in Econs., Ohio Wesleyan U., 1975; m. Rebecca Joan Phillips, Apr. 5, 1975. Geol. asst. Huntley & Huntley, Inc., Pitts., 1973-75, exec. asst. to pres., 1975-79, asst. sec., 1976—, v.p. ops., chief operating officer, 1979-83, exec. v.p., 1983—, dir., 1981—, treas., 1983—; v.p. ops., chief operating officer Royalty Oil Co., 1980-84, dir., treas., 1983—; v.p. ops., chief operating officer Indsl. Fuel Cons., 1980-85, exec. v.p., 1985—, dir., treas., 1983—. Deacon 3d Presbyn. Ch., Pitts., 1976-82, 83-86, rec. sec., 1978-82, 83-86; mem. council Twp. of O'Hara, 1982-86; bd. dirs. Allegheny Valley North Council of Govts., 1983-86. Mem. Am. Mgmt. Assn., Soc. Petroleum Engrs., Pitts. Geol. Soc., Engrs. Soc. Western Pa., Pa. Oil, Gas and Minerals Assn., Ohio Oil and Gas Assn., Internat. Oil Scouts Assn., Soc. for Advancement of Mgmt., Am. Assn. Petroleum Landmen, Am. Assn. Petroleum Geologists, Ind. Oil and Gas Assn. W.Va., Internat. Right of Way Assn., Alpha Sigma Phi (dir. Beta Gamma chpt. 1981—, various offices, pres. 1986—); exec. com. Pitts. area 1982—). Republican (dist. chmn. 1972 presdl. election). Clubs: Pitts. Athletic Assn., University, Longue Vue, Laurel River. Home: 537 Guyasuta Rd Pittsburgh PA 15215 Office: 1600 Benedum-Trees Bldg 221 4th Ave Pittsburgh PA 15222

BARTLETT, BOYD C., farm equipment company executive; b. Cameron, Wis., Oct. 21, 1925; s. Roy M. and Verna E. (Boortz) B.; m. Joyce M. Sanborn, Dec. 28, 1946; children: Jeffrey, Gregory, Martha. BS, U. Wis., Superior, 1949. From mktg. trainee to sales br. mgr. Deere & Co., Mpls. and Lansing, Mich., 1952-67; v.p. farm equipment and consumer products mktg. Deere & Co., Moline, Ill., 1972-79, sr. v.p., 1979-83, exec. v.p. ops., 1983-85, pres., chief operating officer, 1985-87, also bd. dirs., ret. Dir. Quad City Devel. Group, Rock Island, Ill., 1979-85; chmn. Luth. Hosp., Moline, 1981-82. Served to lt. USN, 1943-46. Mem. Farm and Indsl. Equipment Inst. (bd. dirs. 1980-87), Farm Found. (bd. dirs. 1976-87). Office: Deere & Co John Deere Rd Moline IL 61265

BARTLETT, CODY BLAKE, lawyer, educator; b. Syracuse, N.Y., Apr. 21, 1939; s. Stanley Jay and Izora Elizabeth (Blake) B.; m. Claudine Germaine Bouthillette, Dec. 27, 1968; 1 child, Cody Blake. A.A.S., Auburn Community Coll., 1960; B.A. with high honors, Mich. State U., 1963; J.D., Harvard U., 1966. Bar: Mich. 1967, N.Y. 1967, U.S. Dist. Ct. (no. dist.) N.Y. 1967, U.S. Dist. Ct. (ea. dist.) Mich. 1967, U.S. Supreme Ct. 1984, U.S. Dist. Ct. (we. dist.) N.Y. 1985. Law clk. Onondaga County Dist. Atty.'s Office, Syracuse, N.Y., 1965; assoc. atty. Touche, Ross, Bailey & Smart, Detroit, 1966; law clk. Onondaga County Family Ct., Syracuse, 1967; assoc. atty. Melvin & Melvin, Syracuse, 1967; budget and accounts officer Appellate Div., 4th Dept., Rochester, N.Y., 1967-69, dep. dir. adminstrn., 1969-72, dir. adminstrn., 1972-80; chief atty. State Commn. on Jud. Conduct, 1980-84; ptnr. Newman, Kehoe, Wunder and Bartlett, Lyons, N.Y., 1984—; spl. adminstr. N.Y. State Dangerous Drug Program, Western N.Y., 1973-75; adj. prof. polit. sci. dept. SUNY-Brockport, 1983-85, Grad. Sch. Pub. Adminstrn., SUNY-Brockport, 1985—; adj. prof. Syracuse U. Coll. Law, 1980-84, Coll. Criminal Justice, Rochester Inst. Tech., 1979-80; grad. asst. polit. sci. dept. Mich. State U., 1962-63. Mem. adv. com. Regional Criminal Justice Edn. and Tng. Ctr., Monroe Community Coll., Rochester, N.Y., 1974-80; div. leader YMCA, Midtown Rochester Membership drive, 1976; mem. East Bloomfield Planning Bd., 1984-87, chmn., 1985-87; trustee Village of East Bloomfield, 1985-87; mem. Zoning Bd. of Appeals, Village of Sodus Point, 1986-87. Recipient Disting. Alumni award Assn. Bds. Trustees of SUNY, 1980. Mem. N.Y. State Bar Assn. (spl. com. on jud. conduct 1984—), Wayne County Bar Assn., Onondaga County Bar Assn. (chmn. Syracuse City Ct. com. 1968-72), Phi Kappa Phi, Pi Sigma Alpha. Club: Sodus Bay Heights Country. Lodge: Lyons. Home: 7094 Overlook Dr Sodus Point NY 14555 Office: Newman Kehoe Wunder & Bartlett 12 William St PO Box 404 Lyons NY 14489

BARTLETT, HALL, motion picture producer, director; b. Kansas City, Mo., Nov. 27, 1929; s. Paul Dana and Alice (Hiestand) B.; m. Lupita Ferrer, Apr. 30, 1977 (div.); children: Cathy Bartlett Lynch, Laurie Bartlett Schrader. BA, Yale U., 1948. Owner, operator Hall Bartlett Prodn., Los Angeles, 1960—; pres. Jonathan Livingston Seagull Mcht. Co.; bd. dirs. Huntington Hartford Theatre, Hollywood, Calif., founder Music Ctr., Los Angeles. Producer, dir. (films) Navajo, 1953, Crazylegs, 1958, Unchained, 1957, All the Young Men, 1961, Durango, 1959, Zero Hour, 1961, The Caretakers, 1963, A Global Affair, 1968, Changes, 1968, Sandpit Generals, 1971, Jonathan Livingston Seagull, 1973, The Children of Sanchez, 1979, Leaving Home, 1985, Catch Me If You Can, 1988, Kiss of Fire, 1988, (TV spl.) The Search of Zubin Mehta, 1975, The Cleo Laine Story, 1978, Comeback, 1983, Love is Forever, 1983; author: The Rest of Our Lives, 1987. Mem. Friends of Library, Los Angeles, Cinema Circulus. Served to lt. USNR, 1949-51. Recipient 11 Acad. award nominations, Film Festival awards from Cannes 1961, 63, Venice 1959, 65, Edinburgh 1952, San Sebastian 1969, Moscow 1971, NCCJ 1955, Fgn. Press awards. Mem. Motion Picture Acad. Arts and Scis., Acad. TV Arts and Scis., Phi Beta Kappa. Republican. Presbyterian. Clubs: Bel-Air Country, Kansas City Country. Home: 861 Stone Canyon Rd Bel Air CA 90077 Office: 9200 Sunset Blvd Suite 908 Los Angeles CA 90069

BARTLETT, SHIRLEY ANNE, accountant; b. Gladwin, Mich., Mar. 28, 1933; d. Dewey J. and Ruth Elizabeth (Wright) Frye; m. Charles Duane Bartlett, Aug. 16, 1952 (div. Sept. 1982); children: Jeanne, Michelle, John, Yvonne. Student, Mich. State U., 1952-53, Rutgers U., 1972-74. Auditor State of Mich., Lansing, 1951-66; cost acct. Templar Co., South River, N.J., 1968-75; staff acct. Franco Mfg. Co., Metuchen, N.J., 1975-78; controller Thomas Creative Apparel, New London, Ohio, 1978-80; mgr. gen. acctg. Ideal Electric Co., Mansfield, Ohio, 1980-85; staff acct. Logangate Homes, Inc., Girard, Ohio, 1985-88; pvt. practice acctg. Youngstown, 1985—; acct. Universal Devel. Enterprises, Liberty Twp., Ohio, 1987—; v.p. Lang Industries, Inc., Youngstown, 1984—. Author: (play) Our Bicentennial-A Celebration, 1976. Soloist various orchestras, Mich., Va.; mem. Human Relations Commn., Franklin Township, 1971-77, Friends of Am. Art; treas. Heritage Found., New Brunswick, N.J., 1973-74, New London Proceeds Corp., 1979-83; commr. Huron Park Commn., Ohio, 1979-83; elected Dem. com. mem., N.J., Ohio, 1970-82. Mem. NOW (treas. Youngstown 1986—), Am. Soc. Women Accts. (bd. dirs. 1986-88, v.p. 1988—), Nat. Assn. Female Execs., Bus. and Profl. Women (v.p. 1980—), Am. Soc. Notaries, Women's Jour. Network, Citizen's League of Greater Youngstown, Internat. Platform Assn., 1988—. Democrat. Unitarian. Club: Franklin JFK (treas. 1970-72, v.p. 1973-78), Chataqua Literary, Scientific Circle (pres. 1979—). Home: 4793 Ardmore Ave Youngstown OH 44505-1101 Office: Bartlett Acctg Services 4795 Ardmore Ave Youngstown OH 44505

BARTLETT, THOMAS EDWARD, research executive; b. Tulsa, Sept. 3, 1920; s. Michael Leo and Elizabeth (Stadden) B.; B.A., U. Okla., 1942; M.S., Columbia U., 1947; postgrad. Purdue U., 1957-59, U. Fla., 1965, Ariz. State U., 1966. Engr., Montgomery Ward & Co., 1947-48; chief indsl. engr. Bank of Am., 1948-50; mem. tech. staff Hughes Research and Devel., 1950-54, Ramo-Wooldridge, 1954; prof. Purdue U., 1955-63; mem. teaching staff Calif. State Poly. Coll., 1964-65; ops. research cons., 1965-67; dir. ops. research Lester Gorstene Assocs., 1967-68; pres., chmn. bd. dirs. Wyvern Research Assos., Inc., Mill Valley, Calif., 1968—; dir., chmn. bd. JEBOR, Inc. Served with CIC, U.S. Army, 1942-46. Registered profl. engr., Calif. Mem. Am. Inst. Indsl. Engrs., Inst. Mgmt. Scis., Ops. Research Soc. Am., Fedn. Am. Scientists, Soc. Indsl. and Applied Math., Scis., AAAS, Am. Soc.

Personnel Adminstrn., Am. Math. Assn., Sigma Xi, Phi Kappa Phi, Phi Kappa Psi. Club: San Francisco Press. Home: 992 Marquette Lane Foster City CA 94404 Office: 335 Beach Rd Burlingame CA 94010

BARTLETTE, DONALD LLOYD, social worker, counselor, educator, consultant, public speaker, lay minister; b. Walhalla, N.D., Dec. 17, 1939; s. Abraham Bruno and Lily Alice (Houle) B.; Ph.B., U. N.D., 1962; M.A., N.D. State U., 1966; Ph.D., C.P.U., 1981; m. Julie Gay Poer, Feb. 1, 1969; children—Lisa Maaca, Joanna Leigh, Andrea Gay, Marisa Anne, Laura Bethany, Sara Elizabeth, Seth VanAdams, Vanessa Joy. Camp worker, program dir. Camp Grassick, N.D., 1957-62; Unit supr., counselor Cambridge State Sch. and Hosp., 1963-64; group worker Children's Village, Fargo, N.D., 1964-65; supr. Meth. Children's Village, Detroit, 1966-68; program dir. Mich. Children's Inst., Ann Arbor, 1968-70; exec., program dir. Madison County (Ind.) Assn. for Retarded, 1970-71; dir. program and social work services Outreach Community Center, Mpls., 1972-73; exec. dir. Minn. Epilepsy League, St. Paul, 1974-75; pvt. cons. in retardation, 1972-75; coordinator spl. services, adviser Human Rights Commn. City of Bloomington (Minn.), 1975-78; assoc. pastor, dir. social services Am. Indian Evang. Ch., Mpls., 1978-79; dir. social services Stark County (Ohio) Bd. Mental Retardation, 1979-80; field work instr. Sch. Social Work, U. Minn., Augsburg Coll., Mpls., 1972-73; off-campus tchr. in retardation and social work Anderson Coll., 1970-71; adj. faculty Univ. Without Walls, U. Minn., 1972-73. Founder Bartlette Scholarship award U. N.D., 1971-75; pres. Nat. Minority Affairs Coalition, 1977-78, sec., 1976-77; mem. Met. Developmental Disabilities Task Force, 1975; chmn. Pub. Info. Coalition Project on Developmental Disabilities, 1974-75; vol. mem. Pres.'s, Minn. Gov.'s coms. on employment handicapped; task force minority affairs Pres.'s Com. Mental Retardation. Bd. dirs. N.W. Hennepin Human Services Council, 1975-76; bd. dirs., chmn. poverty com. Anoka County Assn. for Retarded, 1974-79; bd. dirs. Family and Childrens Services of Greater Mpls., Stark County Mental Health Bd., Citizen Advocacy Program of Stork County; cons. People First of Stark County; adv. Indian children Council for Exceptional Children; patron and com. mem. Lake Center Christian Sch., Hartville, Ohio; trustee Cuyahoga Valley Christian Acad., 1985-86 ; Heritage Christian Sch. patron, 1985—; adv. cons. Christian Berets, Keystone Acad. and Navajo Missions; mem. adv. bd. Mentor, Inc., Ohio; speaker Assn. Christian Schs. Internat.; founder travel ministry, 1974—. Fellow Acad. Ednl. Disciplines; mem. Am. Acad. Mental Retardation, Nat. Assn. Christian Social Workers, Nat. Assn. Retarded Citizens (dir., chmn. com. on poverty and mental retardation 1973-74), Internat. Platform Assn., Assn. Am. Indian Social Workers, Soc. for Protection Unborn through Nutrition (life mem.), Reading Reform Found., Am. Coalition Citizens with Disabilities, Focus on Family, Internat. Inst. for Christian Sch. Tchrs., Christian Home Educators Ohio, Christian Council on Disabilities, Phi Delta Kappa, Kappa Delta Pi. Club: The 700. Author presentation: Macaroni at Midnight; film participant Believing for the Best in You, 1985, A Time for Truth, 1987. Focus of play Macaroni at Midnight, Erie, Pa., 1986. Home: 2602 Ocelot NE North Canton OH 44721

BARTLEY, ROBERT PAUL, state official, consultant; b. Worcester, Mass., Oct. 17, 1926; s. Harry Eugene and Helen (Hamilton) B.; B.S., U.S. Naval Acad., 1952; M.B.A., U.S. Air Force Inst. Tech., 1959; Cert. Energy Mgr.; m. Joan Anne Leahy, 1952; children—Robert, Brian, Maureen, Michael, Bridget, Timothy, Terrence, Patricia. Commd. 2d lt. U.S. Air Force, 1952, advanced through grades to capt., 1972, ret., 1972; mng. dir. Del. Soc. for Prevention of Cruelty to Animals, Newark, 1975; fiscal asst. Pres.'s Office, Del. Tech. and Community Coll., Dover, 1976-77; dir. Del. State Energy Conservation Plan, Office of Mgmt. and Budget and Planning, Dover, 1977-79; asst. dir. Del. Energy Office, Dover, 1979-81, acting dir., 1982, asst. dir. for energy div. facilities mgmt., 1982—; instr. U. Dayton (Ohio), 1959; presenter 2d Mid-Atlantic Energy Conf. Chmn. com. on devel. and enforcement of energy savings in public schs., 1977-78; mem. citizens adv. group on regional transp., Kent County, Del., 1969; mem. tuition guidelines com. Holy Cross Sch., 1971-74. Decorated Air medal. Mem. Del. Assn. Public Adminstrn., Mcpl. Fin. Officers Assn., Del. Assn. Govt. Fin. Officers (treas. 1978-79, sec. 1982-83, exec. com. 1984), Nat. Assn. State Energy Ofcls., Assn. Energy Engrs., U.S. Dept. Energy Commn. Alternative Fin. Roman Catholic. Clubs: Cavaliers of Del., Blue and Gold. Contbr. articles to profl. jours. Home: 3706 Golfview Dr Newark DE 19702 Office: Margaret O'Neill Bldg Dover DE 19901

BARTLEY, WILLIAM WARREN, III, philosopher, biographer; b. Pitts., Oct. 2, 1934; s. William Warren and Elvina (Henry) B. A.B., Harvard U., 1956, A.M., 1958; Ph.D., London (Eng.) Sch. Econs. and Polit. Sci., 1962. Lectr. logic London Sch. Econs., 1960-63; lectr. history of philosophy of sci. Warburg Inst. U. London, 1961-64; vis. assoc. prof. philosophy U. Calif.-Berkeley, 1963-64; assoc. prof. U. Calif.-San Diego, 1964-67, co.-dir. humanities program, 1965-66; S.A. Cook Bye fellow Gonville and Caius Coll., Cambridge U., 1966-67; assoc. prof. philosophy U. Pitts., 1967-69; assoc. prof. U. Pitts. (Population Div.), 1967-69; prof. philosophy and history and philosophy of sci., sr. research assoc., assoc. dir. Philosophy of Sci. Center U. Pitts., 1969-73; prof. philosophy Calif. State U. at Hayward, 1970—, Outstanding prof., 1979—; vis. scholar Hoover Instn. War, Revolution and Peace, Stanford U., 1984, sr. research fellow, 1985—; cons. .mem. Centro Superiore di Logica e Scienza Comparate, Bologna, Italy, 1972—; treas. Struction, Inc., 1978—; dir. N.Y. Tribune, 1981—; fellow Ludwig Boltzmann Research Inst., Vienna, 1986-87; staff philosopher, est, ednl. corp., 1975-78; Neil Arnott lectr. Robert Gordon's Inst. Tech., Aberdeen, Scotland, 1982; seminar leader Austrian Coll., Alpbach, 1961, 65, 75, 80, 82, 85; spl. lectr. Royal Inst. Philosophy, London, 1961, 68, Institut für Wissenschaftstheorie U. Salzburg, Austria, 1962; vis. asso. prof. U. Ill., 1964; spl. lectr. U. Karlsruhe, 1965; adj. prof. philosophy L.I.U., 1966; bd. dirs. Salzburg Seminar in Am. Studies, 1956-58, History and Theory, 1960-65, Centro Superiore di Logicae Scienze Comparate, Bologna, Italy, 1972—, Werner Erhard Charitable Settlement, Jersey, Channel Islands, 1976-81, est, an ednl. co., Ltd., London, 1977-81, Internat. Conf. on Unity of Scis., 1979-84, Inst. on Comparative Polit. and Econ. Systems, Georgetown U., 1980—, Inst. Methodology and Philosophy Sci., Turin, Italy, 1982—, Carl Menger Inst., Vienna, 1984—, Washington Inst. Values in Pub. Policy, 1988—; fellow adj. scholar Inst. Humane Studies, George Mason U., 1986—. Author: The Retreat to Commitment, 1962, 64, 84, Flucht ins Engagement, 1964, 86, Morality and Religion, 1971, Wittgenstein, 1973, 74, 75, 77, 83, 85, 86, Die Notwendigkeit des Engagements, 1974, 77, Wittgenstein e Popper, 1976, Lewis Carroll's Symbolic Logic, 1977, 78, 86, Werner Erhard, 1978, The Philosophy of Karl Popper, 1982, Evolutionary Epistemology, Rationality, and the Sociology of Knowledge, 1987; assoc. editor: History and Theory, 1958-65; editor: Sir. Karl Popper's Postscript, 1982, 83, The Collected Works of F.A. Hayek, 1984—; bd. editors: Soundings, 1967-69, Philos. Forum, 1967—, Critical Rev., 1986—, The Collected Works Karl Popper, 1986—. Contbr. articles profl. jours. Danforth Found. fellow, 1956-61, 66-67; U. Calif. Inst. for Humanities fellow, 1966-67; Am. Council Learned Socs. fellow, 1972-73, 79-80; Am. Philos. Soc. fellow, 1979-80; est Found. fellow, 1982-83; DAAD fellow, 1983; Thyssen Found. fellow, 1984; Earhart Found. fellow, 1984; Morris Found. fellow, 1984; Inst. Humane Studies fellow, 1984—; Wincott Found. fellow, 1984; Adam Smith Inst. fellow, 1984; Parshad award, 1952,; Fulbright award, 1958-60, 83; Dana Reed award, 1956; Bowen prize Harvard, 1958. Mem. Oxford and Cambridge Soc., Signet Soc., Brit. Soc. Philosophy of Sci. (mem. exec. com. 1964), Am. Philos. Assn., AAUP, Phi Beta Kappa. Clubs: Harvard, Commonwealth (San Francisco); Mont Pèlerin Soc. Office: Stanford U Hoover Instn Stanford CA 94305

BARTLING, JUDD QUENTON, research corp. exec.; b. Muncie, Ind., July 24, 1936; s. Hubert George and Hildagarde (Good) B.; m. Madeline Levesque, June 9, 1973; stepchildren—Mary Johnson, Michael Johnson. BA, U. Calif., 1960, PhD, 1969; MS, Purdue U., 1964. Research asst. U. Calif., Riverside, 1965-69; cons. Azak Corp., Chatsworth, Calif., 1969-71, pres., 1971—. Served with U.S. Army, 1960-62. NSF grantee U. Fla., 1969. Research in bus., solid state physics, quantum electronics, electromagnetics and radar. Office: 4644 Whitewood Long Beach CA 90808

BARTOK, LE ANN, painter, sculptor, filmmaker; b. Martins Ferry, Ohio, Aug. 1, 1937; d. Joseph and Margaret (Dvoracek) B.; m. Bernard L. Wilchusky, July 18, 1959 (div. 1987); children—Shari, Mark, Dennis, Jayce. R.N., Mercy Sch. Nursing, 1958; student Carnegie Mus. Art, 1958-59, Carnegie Mellon U., 1968-69. Actress Japanese films, Tokyo, 1960; model, 1960; tchr. Univercitiesertokyo, 1960; artist, Pitts., N.Y.C., 1968—; lectr. Edinboro Coll., Pa., 1977, Carnegie Mus., Pitts., 1969, PNB Bank, Pitts., 1969. Film screenings include Banff Fine Arts Ctr., Alta., Can., Eye Music, San Francisco Millenium, 1978, Monterey Coll., Carnegie Mus., Carnegie-Mellon U., Pitts., 1974-77, Annenberg Internat. Film Festival, Phila., 1978, numerous others throughout U.S., Can., Spain, Italy. Exhibited in group shows at Pa. State U., 1975, 3 Rivers Art Festival, Pitts., 1976-77, Carlow Coll., Pitts., 1975, Carnegie Mus., 1969, Carnegie-Mellon U., 1974, 77, 15th Ann. Avant Garde Art Exhibit, N.Y.C., 1980. Conceptual artist Antiobject Art Issue in Pioneer Book, 1975 (named Pioneer in Field); artist, dir. of conceptual "Skyworks" drops, 1977 (Tallest Piece of Art in World), 1973-77, film Skyworks documentary (Golden Fleece award 1977-78), 1973-77; artist, painter 48 acrylic colleges, 1980-85; artist, filmmaker: An Introduction to American Underground Film, 1975; patentee in field. NEA grantee; painting prize Carnegie Mus. Art Exhbn., 1959, Pitts. Filmmakers, 1977; prodn. cons. short subject A Quarter Till...., 1987; screenwriter The Salvage Merchants, 1988. Mem. Guggenheim Mus. (assoc. com. 1983-85), Am. Film Inst., Ind. Cinema Artists and Producers, N.Y. Filmmakers Co-op, Canyon Cinema Co-op, Am. Soc. for Psychical Research, Am. Mus. Natural History, Japan Soc., Internat. Platform Assn., Met. Mus. Art, Mus. Modern Art. Club: Ikebana Internat. (Tokyo). Avocations: vintage collectibles, swimming, hiking, travel, writing poetry. Studio: 425 W Broadway Apt 6-D New York NY 10012 also: PO Box 378 Laurel Mountain Park Walnut Rd Laughlintown PA 15655

BARTOLETTI, BRUNO, conductor; b. Sesto Fiorentino, Italy, June 10, 1926; m. Rosanna Bartoletti; 2 children. Ed., Conservatory Florence. Operatic debut Teatro Comunale di Firenze, 1953, symphonic debut at Maggio Musicale Fiorentino, 1954; condr. opera houses: Copenhagen, Lisbon, Wiesbaden, Teatro Colon Buenos Aires, San Francisco, N.Y.C., Milan, Rome, Tokyo, Munich, Spoleto; Am. debut with Lyric Opera of Chgo., resident condr., 1956-63, co-artistic dir., 1964-75, prin. condr., artistic dir., 1975—; artistic dir. Teatro Comunale di Firenze, 1987-88. Office: Lyric Opera Chgo care Danny Newman 20 N Wacker Dr Chicago IL 60606 *

BARTOLI, ADOLFO, director of photography; b. Rome, Aug. 12, 1940; s. Cesare and Bernardina (Giorgi) B.; m. Noemi Nicolai, Sept. 6, 1965; 1 child, Tatum. Diploma in english, Queensway Sch., London, 1968. Camera asst.: The Story of Juliane, 1970, The Moses, 1975, Conversation Piece, 1978, L'Innocente, 1980; camera operator: Padre E Figlio, 1982, Tagament, 1983, Zoom on Fellini, 1984, Guts and Glory, 1985; dir. photography: Lone Runner, 1986, Bill and Ted's, 1987, Delta Force Commando, 1987, Sonny Boy, 1987, The Fortunate Pilgrim, 1987. Mem. Assn. Operatori Cinema Italiani, Nat. Geographic Soc., Profl. Assn. Diving Instrs. Home: via Del Monte Di Casa 65, 00138 Rome Italy Office: Tecnovisual SRL, via Della Farnesina 228, Rome Italy

BARTOLOMEI, MARGARET MARY, community education director, nursing consultant; b. Detroit, Nov. 28, 1933; d. Fred and Mary Dolores (Bonaudo) Colombo; m. Peter Bartolomei, Aug. 18, 1956 (div.); children—Frederick, Edward. B.S. in Nursing, Mercy Coll. Detroit, 1955; M.S. in Edn., U. Mich., 1978, Ph.D. in Edn., 1984. R.N., Mich. Mem. faculty Mercy Sch. Nursing, Detroit, 1955-57; charge nurse St. John Hosp., Detroit, 1958-64; mem. faculty St. Joseph Sch. Practical Nursing, Mt. Clemens, Mich., 1967-70; inservice coordinator Harrison Community Hosp., Mt. Clemens, 1970-73; nursing cons. Qualicare Nursing Ctr., Detroit, 1973-85; tchr., coordinator Fraser (Mich.) High Sch., 1973-85; program asst. leadership devel. program in adminstrn. of vocat. tech. edn. U. Mich., 1979-80; cert. instr. Competency Based Edn.; secondary chairperson for health occupations Macomb Occupational Articulation project; mem. task force on health occupations Mich. Vocat.-Tech. Edn. Service. Recipient John Trytten award; named Mich. Vocat. Tchr. of Yr., Mich. Vocat. Tchr. of Excellence. Mem. Am. Vocat. Assn., Am. Vocat. Edn. Personnel Devel. Assn., Council Vocat. Edn., Macomb Oakland Coordinators Assn., Mich. Health Occupations Educators (past pres.), Mich. Occupational Edn. Assn. (sec. 1978-86), Mich. Vocat. Coordinators Assn., Mich. Vocat. Curriculum Leaders, Nat. Assn. Health Occupations Tchrs., Mich. Assn. Adult and Community Edn., Macomb/St. Clair Adult and Community Edn. Assn., Phi Delta Kappa, Iota Lambda Sigma. Democrat. Roman Catholic. Club: Prosperity (pres. women's aux.) (Detroit). Co-author: Tuned-in Teaching, 1977. Home: 19442 Rockport Dr Roseville MI 48066 Office: 33466 Garfield Rd Fraser MI 48026

BARTON, ALEXANDER JAMES, ecologist, educator, naval officer; b. Mt. Pleasant, Pa., May 9, 1924; s. Paul Carnahan and Barbara (Eggers) B.; BS, Franklin and Marshall Coll., 1946; MS, U. Pitts., 1957; m. Arlene Florence Arment, Oct. 6, 1945; children: Sandra, Lynne, Alexander James III. Herpetologist, Highland Park Zool. Gardens, Pitts., 1946-52; instr. biology Stony Brook (N.Y.) Sch., 1952-63, dir. admissions and fin. aid, 1957-63; profl. asst. NSF, Washington, 1963-65, profl. assoc., 1965-70, program dir., 1970-87, sect. head sci. and engring. edn., 1987—; extended mil. furlough serving as capt. U.S. Navy, naval mem. OSD staff revising Res. Officers' Personnel Mgmt. Act, 1981-83; adj. asst. prof. biology C.W. Post Coll., Brookville, N.Y., 1961-63; dir. Savannah (Ga.) Natural History Mus., 1957; chmn. Fed. Interagency subcom. Environ. Edn., 1980-81; chmn. U.S. planning com., mem. U.S. delegation UN Conf. on Environ. Edn., Tbilisi, USSR, 1977; cons. sci. books Doubleday & Co., 1962-64. Scoutmaster Allegheny County council Boy Scouts Am., Pitts., 1947-52, mem. nat. adv. com., 1950-54, mem. exec. council Suffolk County council, 1957-63; mem. Internat. Com. on Endangered Reptiles and Amphibians, 1967-74. Served to capt. USNR, 1943-45, 81-83. Fellow Explorers Club; mem. Acad. Ind. Scholars (charter mem.), Arlington Rose Found. (pres. 1970-71), Potomac Rose Soc. (1st v.p. 1972-73, pres. 1974-75, dir. 1976—, gold medal 1983), Am. Rose Soc. (vice chmn. Colonial dist. 1971-72, chmn. 1985—, cons. rosarian 1970—, chmn. nat. long-range planning com. 1973-75; accredited rose show judge 1970-77, life judge 1978—, gen. chmn. nat. conv. 1981, bd. dirs. 1985—, outstanding dist. judge award 1983, Silver Honor Medal 1984), Assn. Admissions Officers Ind. Secondary Schs. (pres. 1959-62), Am. Inst. Biol. Sci., Ecol. Soc. Am., others. Presbyn. (deacon 1946—, lay preacher 1954-65, tchr. adult bible class 1964-68). Contbr. numerous articles, papers to profl. publs.

BARTON, ANN ELIZABETH, fin. exec.; b. Long Lake, Mich., Sept. 8, 1923; d. John and Inez Mabel (Morse) Seaton; student Mt. San Antonio Coll., 1969-71, Adrian Coll., 1943, Citrus Coll., 1967, Golden Gate U., 1976, Coll. Fin. Planning, 1980-82; m. H. Kenneth Barton, Apr. 3, 1948; children—Michael, John, Nancy. Tax cons., real estate broker, Claremont, Calif., 1967-72, Newport Beach, Calif., 1972-74; v.p., officer Putney, Barton, Assos., Inc., Walnut Creek, Calif., 1975—; bd. dirs., officer Century Fin. Enterprises, Inc., Century Adv. Corp., F.F.A., Inc., SKAIFE & Co. Cert. fin. planner. Mem. Internat. Assn. Fin. Planners, (registered investment advisor), Calif. Soc. Enrolled Agts., Nat. Assn. Enrolled Agts., Nat. Soc. Public Accts., Inst. Cert. Fin. Planners. Office: Putney Barton Assocs Inc 1705 N California Blvd Walnut Creek CA 94596

BARTON, BLAYNEY JONES, investment executive; b. Beaver City, Utah, Oct. 22, 1910; s. Ray Hunter and Emma Jay (Jones) B.; student U. Utah, 1929-30, 33; LL.B., George Washington U., 1938; m. Hazel Lavina Whitaker, July 31, 1937; 1 son, John Whitaker. Admitted to Utah bar, 1938, D.C. bar, 1938, U.S. Supreme Ct. bar, 1964; lawyer Reconstrn. Fin. Corp., Washington, 1938-40; spl. agt. FBI, N.Y., Va., Nebr., Calif., Utah, 1940-44; dir. indsl. and pub. relations Bayer Aspirin, Winthrop-Stearns Pharm. Co., Sterling-Winthrop Research Inst., Rensselaer, N.Y., 1945-51;dir. employee relations M & M Woodworking Co., Portland, Oreg., 1952-53; dir. labor relations Am. Stores Co. (name changed to Acme Markets, Inc.), Phila., 1954-56, v.p. labor relations, 1957-68; pres., chief negotiator, Food Indsutry Council, 1957-68, Meritorious Achievement award for stabilizing labor-mgmt. relations, Phila., 1965, acting dir. fed. labor-mgmt. relations Dept. Labor, Washington, 1968-70; pres. Barton Investment Co., 1971-84. Nat. committeeman Boy Scouts Am., 1950-51, commr. Ft. Orange council, Albany, N.Y., 1948-51; asst. dir. Albany Community Chest. 1949-51; missionary Ch. Jesus Christ Latter-Day Saints, Br. Isles, 1930-33; v.p. YMCA, 1950-51. Mem. Am. Arbitration Assn., Capitol Dist. Personnel Assn. (pres. 1946-51), Albany C. of C. (bd. dirs. 1949-51). Kiwanian (v.p. Albany, N.Y.), Rotarian. Clubs: Pa. Soc., Union League (Phila.). Office: PO Box 99 Berwyn PA 19312

BARTON, CHARLES ANDREWS, JR., clergyman; b. Memphis, Apr. 25, 1916; s. Charles Andrews and Martha Lee (Stewart) B.; BS, Rhodes Coll., Memphis, 1937, DD, 1964; MS, NYU, 1939; MDiv, Union Theol. Sem., 1952; m. Jane Irby Teague, Aug. 19, 1950; children: Martha, Carol, Stewart, Susan. Chief sales engr., wire and cable dept. U.S. Rubber Co., N.Y.C., 1939-47; ordained to ministery United Methodist Ch., 1952; pastor City Island Ch., N.Y.C., 1952-54, Crawford Meml. Ch., N.Y.C., 1954-56, 1st Ch. Jamaica, N.Y.C., 1956-67, Mt. Kisco Ch., N.Y.C., 1967-73; asso. exec. dir. United Meth. City Soc., N.Y.C., 1973-84; ret., 1984; v.p. East Calvary Nursery, 1973-84; pres. bd. missions N.Y. Conf. United Meth. Ch., 1968-72, pres. bd. evangelism, 1962-68; pres., bd. dirs. Bklyn. Deaconess Fund, 1973-78, Five Points Mission, 1973-84; bd. dirs., v.p. N.Y. Deaconess Assn., 1973-84; pres., bd. dirs. Chinese Meth. Community Center, 1977-84, Anchor House, 1973-84, Harlem Interfaith Counseling Service, 1975-84. Sec. ethics com. Mt. Kisco, 1971-74; chmn. Mt. Kisco Narcotics Guidance Council, 1970-73; mem. Mt. Kisco Park Commn., 1970-73; treas. Religious Com. on N.Y.C. Health Crisis, 1982-84, Capitol Area Ministries, Atlanta, 1984—; bd. dirs. Habitat for Humanity, Atlanta, 1984—, Wesley Community Ctrs., Atlanta, 1984—. Served as 1st lt., Signal Corps, U.S. Army, 1942-46. Named Disting. Citizen Mt. Kisco, 1972, Man of Yr., Chinese Meth. Community Center, 1982; Edn. Bldg. at 1st Ch., Jamaica named in his honor, 1982, hall at Wakefield-Grace United Meth. Ch., 1981, swimming pool at Camp Olmsted, Cornwall-on-Hudson, N.Y., 1984. Mem. St. Andrews Soc. (life), Omicron Delta Kappa, Pi Kappa Alpha, Tau Kappa Alpha. Democrat. Lodge: Rotary. Home: 3945 Back Trails Clarkston GA 30021

BARTON, DEREK HAROLD RICHARD, chemist; b. England, Sept. 8, 1918; s. William Thomas and Maude Henrietta (Lukes) B.; B.Sc. with 1st class honours, Imperial Coll., London, 1940, Ph.D. in Organic Chemistry (Hofmann prize), 1942; D.Sc., U. London, 1949; D.Sc. (hon.), U. Montpelier (France), 1962, U. Dublin (Ireland), 1964, U. St. Andrews (Scotland), 1970, Columbia U., 1970, U. Coimbra (Portugal), 1971, Oxford U., 1972, Manchester U., 1972, U. S. Africa, 1973, U. La Laguna, Tenerife, Spain, 1975, U. Western Va., 1975, U. Sydney (Australia), 1976; Dr. (h.c.), U. Valencia, 1979, U. Sheffield, 1979, U. Western Ont., 1979, U. Metz, 1979, Weizmann Inst. Sci., 1979; m. Jeanne Wilkins, Dec. 20, 1944; 1 son, William Godfrey Lukes; m. 2d, Christiane Cosnet, Nov. 5, 1969. Govt. research chemist, 1942-44; research chemist Messrs. Albright & Wilson, Birmingham, 1944-45; asst. lectr., then ICI research fellow Imperial Coll., 1945-49; vis. lectr. Harvard U., 1949-50; reader organic chemistry Birkbeck Coll., London, 1950-53, prof. organic chemistry, 1953-55, fellow 1970-85, emeritus prof., 1978; Regius prof. chemistry Glasgow U., 1955; Max Tishler lectr. Harvard U., 1956; Aub lectr. Med. Sch., 1962; prof. organic chemistry Imperial Coll., 1957-78; dir. Inst. of Chemistry and Natural Substances, Gif-sur-Yvette, France, 1978-85; prof. chemistry Tex. A&M U., College Station, 1985—; Arthur D. Little prof. M.I.T., 1958; Karl Folkers vis. prof. univs. Ill. and Wis., 1959; Falk-Plaut lectr. Columbia U., 1961; Renaud lectr. Mich. State U., 1962; inaugural 3M's lectr. U. Western Ont. (Can.), 1962; 3m's lectr. U. Minn., 1963; Sandin lectr. U. Alta., 1969; Graham Young lectr., Glasgow, 1970; Rose Endowment lectr. Bose Inst., Calcutta, 1972; Sieglitz lectr. U. Chgo., 1974; Bachman lectr. U. Mich., 1975; Woodward lectr. Yale U., 1972; 1st Smissman lectr. U. Kans., 1976; Priestley lectr. Pa. State U., 1977; Cecil H. and Ida Green vis. prof. U. B.C., 1977; Benjamin Rush lectr. U. Pa., 1977; Firth vis. prof. U. Sheffield, 1978-79; Romanes lectr., Edinburgh, 1979; mem. Council Sci. Policy U.K., 1965—. Created knight bachelor, 1972; decorated Order Rising Sun 2d class (Japan), 1972; chevalier Legion of Honor (France), officier, 1986, 1974; knight of Mark Twain, 1975; recipient Nobel prize in chemistry, 1969; Royal medal, 1972; B.C. Law Gold medal Indian Assn. Cultivation Scis., 1972; medal Soc. Cosmetic Chemistry Gt. Britain, 1972; medal Union Sci. Workers Bulgaria, 1978; medal U. Sofia, 1978; medal Acad. Scis. Bulgaria. Fellow Chem. Soc. (1st Corday-Morgan medal 1951, Tilden lectr. 1952, 1st Simonsen meml. lectr. 1958, Hugo Muller lectr. 1963, Pedler lectr. 1967, Robert Robinson lectr. 1970, 1st award natural product chemistry, 1961, Longstaff medal 1972; pres. Perkin div. 1971; nat. pres. 1973), Royal Soc. (Davy medal 1961), Royal Soc. Edinburgh; fgn. fellow Am. Chem. Soc. (Fritzsche medal 1956, 1st Roger Adams medal 1959, 2d Centennial Priestly Chemistry award 1974), Indian Nat. Sci. Acad.; fgn. assoc. Nat. Acad. Scis.; fgn. hon. mem. Am. Acad. Arts and Scis., Pharm. Soc. Japan, Royal Acad. Scis. Spain; hon. fellow Deutsche Akademie der Naturforscher Leopoldina, Indian Chem. Soc.; hon. mem. Soc. Quimica de Mex., Belgium Chem. Soc., Chilean Chem. Soc., Acad. Pharm. Scis. U.S., Danish Acad. Scis. and Letters, Nacional Acad. Exact, Phys. and Natural Scis. Argentina, Hungarian Acad. Scis., Soc. Italiana per il Progresso delle Scienze, Acad. Scis. France; corr. mem. Argentinian Chem. Soc.; fgn. mem. Acad. des Ciencias da Lisboa, Acad. Nazionale dei Lincei; mem. Brit. Assn. Advancement Sci. (pres. Sect. B, 1969), Internat. Union Pure and Applied Chemistry (pres. 1969). Office: Tex A&M Univ Chemistry Dept College Station TX 77843 also: Imperial Coll of Sci & Tech, Prince Consort Rd S Kensington, London SW7, England *

BARTON, JOHN BERNARD ADIE, drama director and dramatic adaptor; b. London, Nov. 26, 1928; s. Sir Harold Montagu and Joyce (Wale) B.; ed. Kings Coll., Cambridge; m. Anne Righter. Asst. dir. Royal Shakespeare Co., London, 1959-64, asso. dir., 1964—, dir., fight dir.; co dir. Royal Shakespeare Co. at Stratford, 1968-74; works include: Othello, 1972, Richard II, 1973, Dr. Faustus, King John, Cymbeline, 1974-75, Much Ado About Nothing, Winter's Tale, Troilus and Cresida, King Lear, 1976, Midsummer Night's Dream, Pillars of the Community, The Way of the World, 1977, The Merchant of Venice, Love's Labours Lost, 1978, The Greeks, 1980, Hamlet, 1980, The Merchant of Venice, Titus Andronicus and Two Gentlemen of Verona, 1981, La Ronde, 1982, Playing Shakespeare for London Weekend TV, 1982, The Vikings, 1983, Life's A Dream, 1983, The Pit, 1984, Dream Play, The Rover, The Mermaid, 1987, The Swan (Royal Shakespeare Co.), 1986, Three Sisters, Barbican, 1988. Author: The Hollow Crown, 1962, 2d edit., 1971; The Wars of the Roses, 1970, The Greeks, 1981, La Ronde, 1981. Office: 14 DeWalden Ct, 85 New Cavendish St, London W1, England

BARTON, LEON SAMUEL CLAY, JR., architect; b. Orangeburg, S.C., Jan. 9, 1906; s. Leon Samuel Clay and Georgia (Hadley) B.; m. Alice Barbara Mosher, Dec. 2, 1941 (dec. Sept. 3, 1971); 1 child, Mary Jane (Mrs. Thomas C. Murray). B.S. in Architecture, Clemson U., 1928; postgrad., NYU, 1932-34, Atelier Morgan, N.Y.C., 1932-35, Inst. Effective Speaking & Human Relations, N.Y.C., 1952, N.Y. Med. Coll., 1966, Columbia U., 1970, Eastern Sch. Real Estate, N.Y.C., 1971; cert., U.S. Civil Def. Preparedness Agy., 1974, Summer Seismic Inst., U. Ill., 1978. Registered architect, Colo., Fla., Md., N.J., N.Y., S.C. certified Nat. Council Archtl. Registration Bds. Designer, draftsman engring. div. E.R. Squibb & Sons, 1928-35, dir. master planning, asst. to chief exec. engr., 1944-47; partner Barton & Pilafian, Architects & Engrs., Teheran, Iran; also cons. to Iranian Govt. Barton & Pilafian, Architects & Engrs., 1935-38; prin. Leon S. Barton, 1939-41; chief architect head archtl. dept. Robert & Co., Inc., Atlanta, 1941-44; naval architect shipbldg. div. Bethlehem Steel Co., 1944; with Vitro Corp. Am., N.Y.C.; chief architect nuclear energy projects U.S. AEC, 1948-54; sr. partner Barton and Pruitt and Assocs. (Architects, Engrs. and Planners), N.Y.C., 1954—; chmn. bd. pres. Walton Resiliant Floors, Inc., N.Y.C., 1968—. Project architect in charge: design Peter Cooper br. Chase Manhattan Bank, Shreve Lamb & Harmon Assocs., N.Y.C., 1947-48; Prin. works include Engring. and Maintenance Facilities Bldg, E.R. Squibb & Sons, New Brunswick, N.J., Vitro Research Lab. Facilities, Silver Spring, Md., Gen. Nuclear Research Lab. Facilities and Radiation Effects Research Lab. Facilities, Lockheed Aircraft Corp., Dawsonville, Ga., U.S. Food and Drug Adminstrn. Research Lab. and Office Facilities, Bklyn.; assoc. architect: (with Gen. Charles B. Ferris, Engrs.) Barnert Meml. Hosp. Center, Paterson, N.J. Recipient First Hon. mention Nat. WGN Broadcasting Theater Competition, 1934; Grand prize Internat. Teheran Stock Exchange (Bourse) Competition, 1935; First Hon. mention Prix de Rome archtl. Competition, 1935; Certificate of Merit for loyal and efficient services during World War II def. projects Robert & Co., Inc., 1944. Mem. AIA (corp. mem., mem. nat. task force for devel. health facilities research 1969-77, mem. publ. com. 1957-58, mem. pub. affairs com. 1967-68, mem. speakers bur. 1967-71, mem. hosp. and health com. 1967—, mem. sch. and coll. archtl. com. 1971-78, mem. urban planning com. 1972-78, mem. LeBrun Scholarship com. 1972-78, mem. criminal justice facilities com. 1974-75, mem. W. Side Hwy. subcom. 1973-75), N.Y. State Assn. Architects (corp. mem., mem. housing and urban devel. planning com. 1971-78, mem. sch. and coll. com. 1971-78, mem. honors and awards com. 1974-75, mem. environmental and community planning com. 1974-78), Am. Arbitration Assn. (nat. panel arbitrators 1970—), Greater N.Y. Hosp. Assn. (engring. adv. com. 1978—).

Episcopalian. Home: PO Box 294 537 North Country Rd Saint James NY 11780 Office: 299 Madison Ave New York NY 10017

BARTON, LEWIS, food manufacturing company executive; b. N.Y.C., Mar. 9, 1940; s. Louis and Mary (Mosca) Bologna; m. Barbara Joan Hummell, Sept. 6, 1964; children—Glenn Scott, Gregory Jon. Student, Adelphi U., 1957-59. Sales rep. Olivetti Corp., N.Y.C., 1962-64, W. Ralston Co., Chgo., 1964-65, Milprint Co., N.Y.C., 1965-66; chmn. bd., pres., founder Sigma Quality Foods Corp., Farmingdale, N.Y., 1966—. Patentee package design construction. Charter contbr. Statue of Liberty-Ellis Island Found., 1983; nat. mem. Smithsonian Assocs. Served with USAF, 1961-62. Named to Pres. Council for Ednl. Distinction, Adelphi U. Mem. Nat. Single Service Food Assn. (charter, chmn. 1977-79, Service award 1982), Internat. Food Service Mfrs. Assn., Am. Mgmt. Assn., Internat. Platform Assn., Italy-Am. C. of C., Dwight D. Eisenhower Soc. (founder). Republican. Clubs: Columbus Citizen's Found., Senator D'Amato's Senate (N.Y.C.), Carlton. Avocations: reading; woodworking; sailing; chess. Home: 45 Sutton Pl S New York NY 10022 Office: Sigma Quality Foods Corp 92 Central Ave Farmingdale NY 11755

BARTON, REX PENRY EDWARD, surgeon, head and neck oncologist, educator; b. Carmarthen, South Wales, U.K., May 3, 1944; s. Edward Cecil and Gwendolen Margaret Gwladys (Thomas) B.; m. Nicola Margaret St. John Allen, July 19, 1969; children—Thomas, Jennifer, Samuel. Student Harrow Sch., Middlesex, Eng., 1957-62; M.B.B.S., Univ. Coll. Hosp., U. London, 1967. House physician and surgeon Univ. Coll. Hosp., London, 1967-68; sr. house officer Hosps. in Bristol and Bath, Eng., 1969-71; registrar and sr. registrar St. Mary's Hop., Royal Marsden Hosp., Royal Postgrad. Med. Sch., London, 1971-79; cons. surgeon otolaryngology/head and neck oncology Leicester Royal Infirmary, Eng., 1979—; hon. adviser otolaryngology to Oxfam and Tear Fund, Oxford and London, 1979—. Contbr. articles to profl. jours. Lectr. in field. Univ. sec. Christian Med. Fellowship, Leicester, 1979—; area rep. Music in Worship, Leicester, 1984—. Fellow Royal Soc. Medicine, Royal Coll. Surgeons of Eng.; mem. Leicester Med. Soc., Christian Med. Fellowship U.K., European Acad. Facial Plastic and Reconstructive Surgery. Avocations: trout fishing; musical composition and arrangement. Home: Southfield, 37 Chapel Ln, Knighton, Leicester LE2 3WF, England Office: Ear Nose and Throat Surgery, Sch Med U Leicester, Leicester LE1 7RH, England

BARTON, WILLIAM ARNOLD, lawyer, educator; b. Morton, Wash., Mar. 15, 1948; s. Marvin Buryl and Jo Ellen (Wilson) B.; m. Almine De Villiers, Dec. 4, 1974; children: Monique, Almine, Brent. BS, Pacific U., 1969; JD, Willamette U., 1972. Bar: Oreg. 1972. Sole practice Newport, Oreg., 1973—; adj. prof. Willamette U. Coll. Law, Salem, Oreg., 1983—; trial judge pro tem all state cts. Author: Recovering for Psychological Injuries, 1985. Brooks scholar, 1971. Fellow Internat. Soc. Barristers, Am. Bd. Trial Advocates; mem. Oreg. State Bar Assn. (v.p. 1986—), Western Trial Lawyers Assn. (pres. 1985), Oreg. Trial Lawyers Assn. (pres. 1983). Home: 2114 NE Crestview Newport OR 97365 Office: 214 SE Coast Hwy Newport OR 97365

BARTRA, ROGER, anthropologist, sociologist; b. Mexico City, Nov. 7, 1942; s. Agusti and Anna (Muria) B.; m. Josefina Alcazar, Oct. 12, 1979; children: Belisa, Ari, Iliana, Bruno. M in Anthropology, Escuela Nat. de Antropologia e Historia, Mex., 1967; D in Sociology, U. Paris, 1974. Museograph Inst. Antropologia, Mex., 1961-62; researcher Inst. del Seguro Social, Mex., 1963-64; prof. U. Estado de Mex., Toluca, Mex., 1964-65; researcher Comision del Rio Balsas, Mex., 1965-67; prof. U. los Andes, Merida, Venezuela, 1967-69, Facultad Latinoamericana de Ciencias Sociales, Mex., 1978-79; Tinker vis. prof. U. Wis., Madison, 1985-86; research fellow U. Calif., San Diego, 1987—; sr. researcher U. Nacional Autonoma de Mex., 1971—. Author: Las Redes Imaginarias del Poder Politico, 1981, La Democracia Ausente, 1986, La Jaula de la Melancolia, 1987. Guggenheim fellow, 1985. Home: Cerro del Dios del Hacha 59, 04310 Mexico City Mexico Office: U Nacional Autonoma de Mexico, Ciudad U, Inst Investig Sociales, 04310 Mexico City Mexico

BARTRAM, RALPH HERBERT, physicist; b. N.Y.C., Aug. 16, 1929; s. Herbert L. and Grace L. Bartram; student Northwestern U., 1948-49; B.A. cum laude, N.Y. U., 1953, M.S., 1956, Ph.D., 1960; m. Ellen Anderson Devlin, Oct. 9, 1953; children—Ellen Ruth, Robert Arthur. Engr., Sylvania Electric Products Inc., Kew Gardens, N.Y., 1953-56; advanced research physicist Gen. Telephone & Electronics Labs., Inc., Bayside, N.Y., 1956-61, cons., 1961—; faculty U. Conn., Storrs, 1961—, prof. physics, 1971—, dept. head, 1986—; research asso. Atomic Energy Research Establishment, Harwell, Eng., 1967-68; vis. prof. U. Oxford, Eng., 1978; cons. U.S. Army, 1966-71, Am. Optical Co., 1966-78, Brookhaven Nat. Lab., 1971—, Timex Corp., 1981-82, Polaroid Corp, 1987—. Served with USN, 1946-48. Research grantee U.S. AEC, 1963-69, U.S. Army Research Office, 1971-78, 82—, NSF, 1974-77, 83—, NATO, 1985—. Fellow Am. Phys. Soc.; mem. Optical Soc. Am., AAAS, AAUP, Conn. Acad. Sci. Engring., Phi Beta Kappa, Sigma Xi, Phi Kappa Phi, Sigma Pi Sigma, Phi Eta Sigma. Contbr. articles on physics to profl. jours.; patentee microwave devices. Home: 36 Ridge Rd Storrs CT 06268 Office: U Conn Dept Physics Storrs CT 06268

BARTSOCAS, CHRISTOS SPYROS, physician, educator; b. Athens, Greece, June 20, 1937; s. Spyros and Dora (Papaioannou) B.; M.D., U. Athens, 1960, D.M.S., 1963; m. Anna N. Petridou, Nov. 10, 1965; children—Spyros Nicholas, Nicholas Alexander. Resident in pediatrics Ag. Sofia Children's Hosp., Athens, 1963-64, attending pediatrician, 1968-73; resident in pediatrics Yale-New Haven (Conn.) Hosp., 1964-66; clin. and research fellow in pediatric endocrinology and metabolism Mass. Gen. Hosp., Boston, 1966-68; teaching asst. Yale U., New Haven, 1964-65, instr., 1965-66; research fellow Harvard U., Cambridge, Mass., 1966-68; assoc. prof. pediatrics Athens U., 1974—; dir. First Pediatric Dept., Athens Children's Hosp. P&A Kyriakou. Served with Hellenic Navy, 1960-63. Fellow Am. Acad. Pediatrics; mem. Soc. Pediatric Research, European Soc. Pediatric Research, European Soc. Human Genetics (dir. 1976), Am. Soc. Human Genetics, Internat. Coll. Pediatrics. Greek Orthodox. Author: Mycenaen Medicine, 1964; Management of Genetic Disorders, 1979; Progress in Dermatoglyphic Research, 1982; Skeletal Dysplasias, 1982; Endocrine Genetics and Genetics of Growth, 1985; contbr. articles in field to profl. jours. Home: 47 Vasilissis Sofias Ave, 10676 Athens Greece Office: P & A Kyriakou Children's Hosp, 11527 Athens Greece

BARTUSSEK, WOLFRAM, software company executive; b. Erfelden, W. Ger., May 5, 1947; s. Hans Erwin and Helmtraud (Wilsch) B.; m. Ulrike Ingeborg Kuehn, June 29, 1973; children—Till, Dennis, Annika. Diplom Informatiker, U. Karlsruhe, 1973. Sci. asst. Technische Hochschule, Darmstadt, 1973-76; research fellow U. N.C., Chappel Hill, 1977; cons. Siemens AG, Muenchen, 1977-80; dir. Prosys GmbH, Darmstadt, 1980—; reviewer Assn. for Computing Machinery, 1983—. Contbr. articles to profl. jours. Mem. Gesellschaft fuer Informatik, Assn. for Computing Machinery. Office: Prosys GmbH Heidelberger, Landstrasse 253, D6100 Darmstadt Eberstadt Federal Republic of Germany

BARUCH, EDUARD, management consultant; b. Bklyn., Dec. 19, 1907; s. Emile and Grace (Willis) B.; m. Dorothy Hurd, Sept. 8, 1934; 1 child, Hurd. Student, Rhenania Coll., Switzerland, 1924-26; A.B., Columbia, 1930; postgrad., Law Sch., 1933. Trust adminstr. spl. loan div. Irving Trust Co., N.Y.C., 1933-39; sales exec. Bankers Life Co., Des Moines, 1939-42; v.p. charge sales James H. Rhodes & Co., 1942-47; nat. sales mgr. vending div. Pepsi Cola Co., 1947-49; v.p. Heli-Coil Corp., Danbury, Conn., 1949-55; exec. v.p. Heli-Coil Corp., 1955-56, pres., 1956-70; corp. cons. 1970—; dir. Barden Corp., N.B.I. Mortgage Co., New Haven, Savs. Bank of Danbury, Lago Mar Pl., Ft. Lauderdale, Fla. Mem. Soc. Automotive Engrs., Psi Upsilon, Phi Delta Phi. Presbyterian. Clubs: Mason, Shriner, Jester, Princeton University, Wings (N.Y.C.); K.T. (Bridgeport, Conn.); Ridgewood Country (Danbury); Coral Ridge, Yacht Tower , Lago Mar Beach and Tennis, Navy League (Fort Lauderdale, Fla.). Home: Candlewood Point 16 Lake Drive New Milford CT 06776 also: Harbor Beach Fort Lauderdale FL 33316 Office: 57 North St Danbury CT 06810

BARYSHNIKOV, MIKHAIL, ballet dancer, ballet company executive; b. Riga, Latvia, Jan. 28, 1948; s. Nicholai and Alexandra (Kisselov) B.; 1 child, Aleksandra. Student, Ballet Sch. of Riga, Kirov Ballet Sch., Leningrad, Russia; DFA (hon.), Yale U., 1979; DHL (hon.), Columbia U., 1985. Mem. Kirov Ballet Co., 1969-74, N.Y.C. Ballet, 1978-79; prin. dancer Am. Ballet Theatre, 1974-78, dir. designee, 1979-80, artistic dir., 1980—. Since 1974 guest artist with leading ballet cos. throughout world including Nat. Ballet of Can., Royal Ballet, Hamburg (Germany) Ballet, Ballet Victoria, Australia, Stuttgart (W.Ger.) Ballet, appeared at, Covent Garden, Spoleto (Italy) Festival; dances premier danseur roles in the traditional repertory; other repertory includes: Le jeune homme et la morte, Vestris, Medea, Push Comes to Shove, Hamlet Connotations, Other Dances, Pas de Duke, Santa Fe Saga, Pique Dame, Four Seasons, Opus 19, Rhapsody Apollo, Configurations, The Wild Boy, The Little Ballet, Follow the Feet, Sinatra Suite, Requiem; ballets staged for the Am. Ballet Theatre include The Nutcracker, 1976, Don Quixote (Kitri's Wedding), 1978, Cinderella, 1983; motion pictures include The Turning Point, 1976, White Nights, 1985, That's Dancing, 1985, Dancers, 1987; numerous TV appearances including Dance in America series, Baryshnikov at the White House, Baryshnikov on Broadway, Baryshnikov in Hollywood, Baryshnikov by Tharp, A Salute to Fred Astaire, A Salute to Gene Kelly. Gold medalist Varna Competition, Bulgaria 1966, First Internat. Ballet Competition, Moscow, USSR 1968; recipient Nijinsky prize at First Internat. Ballet Competition Paris Acad. Dance 1968, Dance mag. award 1968, Liberty award, N.Y.C., 1986. Office: care Am Ballet Theatre 890 Broadway New York NY 10003 also: care Edgar Vincent Assoc 124 E 40th St New York NY 10016 *

BARZUN, JACQUES, author, literary consultant; b. Créteil, France, Nov. 30, 1907; came to U.S., 1920, naturalized, 1933; s. Henri Martin and Anna-Rose B.; m. Mariana Lowell, Aug. 1936 (dec. 1979); children: James Lowell, Roger Martin, Isabel; m. Marguerite Davenport, June 1980. Ed., Lycée Janson de Sailly, Paris; A.B., Columbia U., 1927, M.A., 1928, Ph.D., 1932. Lectr. history Columbia U., 1927, instr., 1929, asst. prof., 1938, asso. prof., 1942, prof., 1945, dean grad. faculties, 1955-58, dean faculties and provost, 1958-67, Univ. prof. emeritus, also spl. adviser on arts, 1967-75; lit. adviser Scribner's, N.Y.C., 1975—. Author: The French Race, 1932, Teacher in America, 1945, Berlioz and the Romantic Century, 1950, 3d edit., 1969, Pleasures of Music, 1951, 2d edit., 1977, God's Country and Mine, 1954, Music in American Life, 1956, Darwin, Marx, Wagner, 1941, The Energies of Art, 1956, Of Human Freedom, 2d edit, 1964, Race: A Study in Superstition, 1937, The Modern Researcher, 1957, 3d edit., 1977, The House of Intellect, 2d edit, 1975, Classic, Romantic and Modern, 1961, Science: The Glorious Entertainment, 1964, The American University, 1968, A Catalogue of Crime, 1971, On Writing, Editing and Publishing, 1971, The Use and Abuse of Art, 1974, Clio and the Doctors, 1974, Simple and Direct, 1975, Critical Questions, 1982, A Stroll With William James, 1983, A Word or Two Before You Go, 1986; Editorial bd.: The American Scholar, 1946-76, Ency. Brit, 1979—; editor: Selected Letters of Lord Byron, 1953, Nouvelles Lettres de Berlioz, 1954, The Selected Writings of John Jay Chapman, 1957, Follett's Modern American Usage, 1966; mem. adv. bd. Univ. Press Am. Trustee N.Y. Soc. Library; bd. dirs. Am. Friends of Cambridge U., Peabody Inst.; adv. council U. Coll. at Buckingham. Decorated Legion of Honor; Extraordinary fellow Churchill Coll., U. Cambridge (Eng.). Fellow Royal Soc. Arts; mem. Am. Hist. Assn., Mass. Hist. Soc. (corr.), Am. Acad. and Inst. Arts and Letters (pres. 1972-75, 77-78), Inst. Arts and Letters, Friends Columbia Libraries, Am. Philos. Soc., Phi Beta Kappa. Clubs: Authors (London), Century (N.Y.C.). Address: Charles Scribner's Sons 115 Fifth Ave New York NY 10003 *

BASDEN, ANDREW, computer science educator; b. Edinburgh, Scotland, July 31, 1948; s. Eric Bernard and Joan Frances (Blacklocks) B.; m. Ruth Carol Angel, Sept. 22, 1973; children: Alastair Graham, Stuart Jeffrey. BSc, Southampton U., Eng., 1969, PhD, 1973. Programmer Warner Lambert, Ltd., Eastleigh, Eng., 1974, U. Southampton, 1974-80; sr. research scientist ICI plc., Runcorn, Eng., 1980-86; sr. research fellow U. Salford, Eng., 1986-87, lectr., 1987—. Mem. Frodsham Parish Council, Cheshire, Eng., 1985-87, Frodsham Evang. Fellowship; Green Party candidate for Parliament, 1987. Home: 24 Penrith Close, Frodsham, Cheshire WA6 7ND, England Office: Univ Salford, The Crescent, Salford England

BASE, ROMULO ALEGARBES, international trading company executive, mining equipment consultant; b. Cebu City, Philippines, Aug. 7, 1947; s. Balmes Cabrera and Efigenia (Alegarbes) B.; m. Agnes Lu Shun, July 8, 1973; children—John Carlo, John Paolo, Anna Katrina. Degree in Mining Engring., Cebu Inst. Tech. Mine supt. Filipinas Carbon and Mining Corp., Toledo City, Cebu, Philippines, 1973-74; sales engr. Atlas Copco Inc., Mandaue City, Cebu, 1974-78; div. mgr. B.B. Fischer & Co. Inc., Metro Manila, 1978-79, regional mgr., Mandaue City, 1979-81; pres., chmn. Mining Indsl. Exponents, Metro Manila, 1981—, Base Mining Corp., Tri-Asia Corp., Arfab, Inc.; pres. Dynatech Internat. Sales; v.p., dir. Coaltech and Mineral Corp. dir. Electrophil, Inc., Metro Manila. Tech. dir. Eaglecom Soc., Inc., Cebu City, 1983-84. Recipient Loyalty medal Jr. Knights Fraternity, 1963; Most Outstanding Sr. award Univ. So. Philippines, 1964. Mem. Philippine Soc. Mining, Metall. and Geol. Engrs. Club: Cebu Eagles. Home: 44 F Gochan St Mabolo, Cebu City Philippines Office: CCH Bldg Suite 209, Alfaro St Salcedo Village Makati Mero, Manila Philippines

BASEL, FRANCES RITA, printing company executive; b. Calumet City, Ill., Mar. 8, 1933; d. Henry Adolph and Genevieve Veronica (Novak) Kaminski; m. Raymond John Basel, Feb. 19, 1955; children—Cynthia, Laura, Mark. Grad. Griffith Sch., Ind., 1950. Sec., Aeroquip/Barco, Barrington, Ill., 1955-62; freelance typist, Barrington, 1962-68; bookkeeper, office mgr. R.A.G. Enterprises, Fox Lake, Ill., 1968-78; corp. officer Classic Printery, Inc., Round Lake, 1978—. Republican. Roman Catholic. Office: Classic Printery Inc 316 Main St Round Lake Park IL 60073

BASELITZ, GEORG, painter, sculptor; b. Deutschbaselitz, Germany, Jan. 23, 1938. Studied painting in East Berlin, 1956-57, Acad. of Arts, West Berlin (w/Hans Trier), 1957-64. One man shows E. Schonebeck, Berlin, 1961, 62, Galerie Werner and Katz, Berlin, 1963, Freie Galerie, Berlin, 1964, Galerie Werner Berlin, 1964, 65, Galerie Fredrich and Dahlem, Munich, Galerie Krohn, Baden Weiler, 1965, Galerie Springer, Berlin, 1966, Galerie Obere Zaune, Zurich, 1967, Galerie Beck Erlangen, 1969, Gelerie Heiner Friedrich, Munich, 1970, K.M. Galerie, Basle, 1970, Galerie Berner, Stuttgart, 1970, Franz Dahlem, Cologne, 1970, Wide White Space Gallery, Antwerp, 1970, Galerie Roth, Heidelberg, 1971, Galerie Borgmann, Cologne, 1971, Galerie Tobies and Silex, Cologne, 1972, Galerie Graphikmeier Karlsruhe, 1972, Kunsthaus Mannheim, 1972, Junsteverein, Hamburg, 1972, Galerie Heiner Friedrich, Munich, 1972, Moderne Kunst, Municy, 1981, Galerie und Edition Annemarie Verna, Zurich, 1981, Galerie Dr. Margaret Biedermann, Munich, 1981, Galerie Michel Werner, Cologne, 1982, Xavier Fourcade Gallery, N.Y.C., 1982, Marion Goodman Gallery, N.Y.C., 1983, Mus. Modern Louis P.S. 1, Art, N.Y.C., 1983, Feedman Gallery, N.Y.C., 1983; exhibited in group shows at Kunsthalle, Baden, W.Ger., 1966, Goethe Instutut, Athens, 1967, Kunsthale, Baden-Baden, 1968, Stadtisches Mus., Wiesbaden, 1969, Von Der Heydt Mus., Wuppertal, W.Ger., 1969, Staditisches Mus., 1970, Schloss Mursbroich, Leverkusen, 1970, Staatsgalerie, Stuttgart, 1971, Royal Acad. Arts, London, Palais des Beaux-Arts, Brussels, both 1981, 4th Biennale, Sydney, 1982, Stedlijk Mus., Amsterdam, 1982, Art Gallery of Ont., 1982, Junsthalle, Basle, 1982, Stadtisches Kunstmus, Bonn, 1982, St. Lois Mus. Art, 1984, P.S. N.Y.C., 1983. Author: Pandemonium: First Manifesto, 1961; Pandemonium: Second Manifesto, 1962; Landschaften, 1972. Villa Romana, Florence scholar, 1965; Kulturpreis in der Deutsche Industrie, 1968. Address: Schless Derneburg, D-3201 Holle bei Hildesheim Federal Republic of Germany also: care Xavier Fourcade 36 E 75th St New York NY 10021

BASHAM, LLOYD MOMAN, manufacturing service company executive; b. Paris, Tex., June 30, 1947; s. Ralph Allen and Faye (Frith) B.; B.B.A., East Tex. State U., 1968, M.B.A., 1970; M.A. in Internat. Corp. Mgmt., U. Tex., Dallas, 1979; m. Donna Jean Walker, Aug. 27, 1965; children—Jason, Adam. Div. cost mgr. Tex. Instruments, Inc., Dallas, 1973-75, corp. fin. analyst, 1975-76, div. controller, 1977-78; subs. corp. controller Ciba Geigy, Richardson, Tex., 1979-80, also dir.; mgmt. cons. Ernst & Whinney, Dallas, 1981; subs. v.p. fin., dir. Pritchard Services, Inc., Dallas, 1982-83; v.p. fin. Cable & Wireless N.Am., Dallas, 1983-87; v.p. ops. Pritronix Inc., 1987—. State adviser U.S. Adv. Bd. Fgn. Policy, Nat. Security and Internal Affairs, Republican Presdl. Task Force. Served with USAF, 1970-73. Mem. Nat. Assn. Wholesalers Distbrs. Fin. Execs. Inst., Nat. Assn. Corp. Treas., Nat. Assn. Corp. Dirs., Am. Mgmt. Assn., Assn. M.B.A. Execs., Nat. Assn. Accts. Republican. Club: Rotary Internat. Home: 330 Marriott St Garland TX 75046

BASHAM, WILLIAM HARRISON, civil engineer; b. Daylight, Tenn., May 25, 1941; s. Flavil L. and Ella Florine (Mitchell) B.; student Calif. State Poly. Coll., 1963; BBA, Nat. U., 1983, MBA in Fin., 1985; m. Marifrances Renfro, Aug. 4, 1973; children—Barbara Lynn, Gregory William, Marty Eileen. Project job leader Calif. Dept. Transp., San Bernardino, 1963-72; project planner CM Engring. Assos., San Bernardino, 1972-77; v.p., office mgr. W.R. Showalter & Assos., San Bernardino, 1977-78; v.p., office mgr. land devel. CM Engring. Assos., San Bernardino and Vista, Calif., 1978—; bd. dirs. CM Engring. Assocs. Active Boy Scouts Am.; trustee Judson Bapt. Ch., San Bernardino, 1974-75; mem. Vista Land Use Circulation Com., 1981-82; bd. dirs. Santa Margarita YMCA, 1985—. Registered profl. engr., Calif., Ariz., Colo., Nev. Mem. Nat. Soc. Profl. Engrs. Calif. Soc. Profl. Engrs. (1st v.p. San Bernardino-Riverside chpt.), ASCE, Am. Public Works Assn., San Bernardino Hist. Soc., Vista C. of C. (econ. devel. com. 1982—, pres. 1988—), Nat. Platform Assn. Republican. Lodge: Rotary (bd. dirs. Vista club 1984—, pres. 1987-88). Home: 831 Williamston #140 Vista CA 92084

BASHIR, NASIR AHMAD, physiologist, educator, researcher; b. Sialkot, Punjab, Pakistan, Jan. 9, 1935; s. B. Ahmad and Rasulbibi (Sivia) B.; m. Lynne Lennox, Sept. 20, 1960 (div. 1973); children: Shaan J., Kirin R.; m. Rubina Bashir Vance, Apr. 26, 1980; children: Zarshi, Wajahat, Shujaat. MSc, U. Punjab, 1956; PhD, Tulane U., 1967; MD, Meharry Med. Coll., 1976. Head biology dept. Talimul Islam Coll., Rabwah, Pakistan, 1956-58; head inst. zoology Otero Jr. Coll., La Junta, Colo., 1961-63; chmn. dept. physiology Loyola U., New Orleans, 1966-68; asst. prof. physiology Meharry Med. Coll., Nashville, 1968-76; head physiology dept. Army Med. Coll., Rawalpindi, Pakistan, 1977-79; prof., head physiology dept. Punjab Med. Coll., Faisalabad, Pakistan, 1979—; cons. physiologist Camaal Lab., Faisalabad, 1985—. Contbr. articles to profl. jours. Pres. Pakistan Assn., New Orleans, 1965-67. Fulbright scholar, 1958; NIH fellow, 1963-66. Ahmadi. Office: Punjab Med Coll, Sargodha Rd, Faisalabad, Punjab Pakistan

BASHLINE, TERRY LEE MORGAN, lawyer; b. Brookville, Pa., Mar. 16, 1953; s. Gearld Kent and Mary Jo (Parks) B.; B.A. cum laude, Clarion State Coll., 1975; J.D. cum laude Duquesne U., 1979; m. Kathleen Ann Foglia, Aug. 11, 1979. Student intern Pa. Gov.'s Office, Pa. Commn. on Status of Women, 1974; law clk. Baskin & Sears, Pitts., 1977-79; assoc. Friedman & Friedman, Pitts., 1979-80, Kyle & Ehrman, Pitts., 1980-82, Hutton, McCrory, Baginski & Bashline, Pitts., 1982-83, Baginski & Bashline, 1983—; counsel Liberty Mut. Ins. Co., 1980—. Mem. Pa. Bar Assn. (mem. workmen's compensation sect.), Clarion State Coll. Alumni Assn., Allegheny County Bar Assn., Pi Kappa Delta, Phi Alpha Delta. Mem. Disciples of Christ. Home: 5210 Glenburn Dr Pittsburgh PA 15236 Office: 2201 Grant Bldg Pittsburgh PA 15219

BASHWINER, STEVEN LACELLE, lawyer; b. Cin., Aug. 3, 1941; s. Carl Thomas and Ruth Marie (Burlis) B.; m. Arden J. Lang, Apr. 24, 1966 (div. 1978); children: Heather, David; m. Donna Lee Gerber, Sept. 13, 1981; children: Margaret, Matthew. AB, Holy Cross Coll., 1963; JD, U. Chgo., 1966. Bar: Ill. 1966, U.S. Dist. Ct. Ill. 1967, U.S. Ct. Appeals (7th cir.) 1968, U.S. Supreme Ct. 1970. Assoc. Kirkland & Ellis, Chgo., 1966-72, ptnr., 1972-76; ptnr. Friedman & Koven, Chgo., 1976-86, Katten Muchin & Zavis, Chgo., 1986—. Served to sgt. USAFR, 1966-72. Mem. ABA, Fed. Bar Assn., Ill. State Bar Assn., Chgo. Bar Assn., Legal Club Chgo., Law Club Chgo. Clubs: Tavern, University (Chgo.). Home: 834 Green Bay Rd Highland Park IL 60035 Office: Katten Muchin & Zavis 525 W Monroe Chicago IL 60606

BASI, MANJEET SINGH, construction company executive; b. Punjab, India, Dec. 13, 1946; s. Sohan Singh and Basant (Kaur) B.; m. Erica Dawn Starin, June 15, 1976; children: Tara, Chand. BME, BMS, Coll. Engring., Bangalore, India, 1970; postgrad. in Civil Engring., Ohio State U., 1873-74. Dir. constrn. Continental Constrn. Ltd., New Delhi, 1975—; exec. dir. in charge overseas project Continental Constrn. Ltd., New Delhi, 1977—; joint mng. dir. Continental Constrn. Ltd., New Delhi, 1982—. Home: C-20 Rajouri Garden, New Delhi 110 027, India Office: Continental Constrn Ltd, 28 Nehru Pl, New Delhi India

BASILE, PAUL LOUIS, JR., lawyer; b. Oakland, Calif., Dec. 27, 1945; s. Paul Louis and Roma Florence (Paris) B.; m. Linda Lou Paige, June 20, 1970; m. 2d Diane Chierichetti, Sept. 2, 1977. B.A., Occidental Coll., 1968; postgrad. U. Wash., 1969; J.D., UCLA, 1971. Bar: Calif. Supreme Ct. 1972, U.S. Dist. Ct. (cen. dist.) Calif. 1972, (no. dist.) 1985, U.S. Supreme Ct. 1977, U.S. Tax Ct. 1977, U.S. Ct. Clms. 1978, U.S. Customs Ct. 1979, U.S. Ct. Customs and Patent Appeals 1979, U.S. Ct. Internat. Trade 1981. Assoc., Parker, Milliken, Kohlmeier, Clark & O'Hara, Los Angeles, 1971-72; corporate counsel TFI Cos., Inc., Irvine, Calif., 1972-73; sole practice, Los Angeles, 1973-80; ptnr., Basile & Siener, Los Angeles, 1980-86; ptnr. Clark & Trevithick, Los Angeles, 1986—; sec. J.W. Brown, Inc., Los Angeles, Calif.; sec. Souriau, Inc., Valencia, Calif.; v.p., sec. Pvt. Fin. Assocs., Los Angeles. Trustee, sec. Nat. Repertory Theatre Found., 1975—, mem. exec. com. 1976—; active Los Angeles Olympic Organizing Com.; dir. March Dimes Birth Defects Found., Los Angeles County, 1982-87, exec. com. 1983-86, sec. 1985-86; dir. Canadian Soc. Los Angeles, 1980-83, sec., 1982-83; dist. fin. chmn. Los Angeles Area council Boy Scouts Am., 1982-83; active numerous other civic orgns. Mem. ABA, Can.-Am. Bar Assn., Los Angeles County Bar Assn., Italian-Am. Lawyers Assn., Asia Pacific Lawyers Assn., Fgn. Trade Assn. So. Calif., Can. Calif. C. of C. (dir. 1980—, 2d v.p. 1983-84, 1st v.p. 1984-85, pres. 1985-87), French-Am. C. of C. (councilor 1979-84, v.p. 1980, 82-84), Los Angeles Area C. of C. (dir. 1980-81), Grand Peoples Co. (bd. dirs., 1985—, chmn. bd. 1986—). Democrat. Baptist. Club: Jonathan. Home: 3937 Beverly Glen Blvd Sherman Oaks CA 91423 Office: Clark & Trevithick 800 Wilshire Blvd 13th Floor Los Angeles CA 90017

BASINGER, RICHARD LEE, lawyer; b. Canton, Ohio, Nov. 24, 1941; s. Eldon R. and Alice M. (Bartholomew) B.; m. Rita Evelyn Gover, May 14, 1965; children: David A., Darron M. BA in Edn., Ariz. State U., 1963; postgrad. Macalester Coll., 1968-69; JD, U. Ariz., 1973. Bar: Ariz. 1973, U.S. Dist. Ct. Ariz. 1973, U.S. Tax Ct. 1977, U.S. Ct. Appeals (6th cir.) 1975, U.S. Ct. Appeals (9th cir.) 1976, U.S. Supreme Ct. 1977. Assoc. law offices, Phoenix, 1973-74; sole practice, Scottsdale, Ariz. 1974-75; mem., pres. Basinger & Assocs., P.C., Scottsdale, 1975-88, dir., pres. Basinger & Morga PC, 1987— . Contbr. articles to profl. jours. Bd. dirs. Masters Trail Ventures, Scottsdale, 1984-85, Here's Life, Ariz., Scottsdale, 1976—; precinct committeeman Republican Party, Phoenix, 1983—. NSF grantee, 1968-69. Mem. ABA, Ariz. Bar Assn., Maricopa County Bar Assn., Ariz. State Horseman's Assn. (bd. dirs. 1984-86, 1st up 1986), Scottsdale Bar Assn. Baptist. Clubs: Western Saddle (Phoenix) (bd. dirs. 1983-86, pres. 1985-86); Scottsdale Saddle, Saguaro Saddle. Office: Basinger & Morga PC 4120 N 70th St Suite 211 Scottsdale AZ 85251

BASKAR, JOHN F(REDERICK), pathobiologist, biomedical researcher; b. Madras, India, July 17, 1936; came to U.S., 1964; s. David V. Dhyriam and Leelavathy Jane Savarus; m. Nirmala Adhilingham, May 3, 1969. BS, U. Madras, 1959; MS, Howard U., 1967; DSc, Johns Hopkins U., 1975. Asst. Madras Secretariat, 1960-64; grad. teaching asst. Howard U., Washington, 1964-67; sr. technician Microbiol. Assocs., Inc., Bethesda, Md., 1967-69; NIH postdoctoral research fellow in reproductive physiology Harvard U. Med. Sch., Boston, 1975-77, research assoc., 1977-78; research assoc. Lineberger Cancer Research Ctr., U. N.C., Chapel Hill, 1978-84, mem., 1984—, research asst. prof. dept. microbiology and immunology, 1984—. Contbr. numerous articles to profl. publs. John Hopkins U. scholar, 1971-75; Nat. Inst. Child Health and Human Devel. grantee, 1980—. Mem. AAAS, Am. Soc. for Microbiology, N.Y. Acad. Scis., Sigma Xi. Biomed. researcher on effect of cytomegalovirus on embryonic devel. Office: U NC Lineberger Cancer Research Ctr Chapel Hill NC 27514

BASOV, NIKOLAI GENNADIEVICH, physicist; b. Usman nr. Voronezh, USSR, Dec. 14, 1922; s. Gennadiy Fedorovich and Zinaida Andreevna (Molchanova) B.; grad. Moscow Mech. Inst., 1950, Cand. Phys. Math. Sci.,

1953, D. Phys. Math. Sci., 1956; LL.D. (hon.), Polish-Mil.-Tech. Acad., 1972, Jena U., 1974, Prague Poly. Inst., 1975, U. Pavia (Italy), 1977, Madrid Poly. U., 1985; m. Ksenia Tikhonovna, July 18, 1950; children—Gennadiy, Dmitriy. With P. N. Lebedev Phys. Inst., USSR Acad. Sci., 1948—, vice dir. for sci. work, 1958-73, head lab. quantum radio physics, 1963—; prof. solid state physics Moscow Inst. Phys. Engrs., 1963—. dir. P.N. Lebedev Phys. Inst., 1973—. Mem. Communist Party, 1951—; dep. USSR Supreme Soviet, 1974—; mem. praesidium Supreme Soviet, 1982—; v.p. exec. council World Fedn. Sci. Workers, 1976—, v.p., 1983—; pres. All-Union Soc. Znanie, 1978—. Decorated Order Lenin (5), hero twice Socialist Labour; recipient Lenin prize, 1959; Nobel prize for fundamental research in quantum electronics resulting in creation of masers and lasers, 1964; Gold medal Czechoslovakian Acad. Scis., 1975; A. Volta's gold medal, 1977; Order of Kirill and Mephodii (Bulgaria), 1981; E. Henkel gold medal German Dem. Republic, 1986; Commodor's cross of Order of Merit, Poland, 1986, Kalinga prize UNESCO, 1986. Fellow Optical Soc. Am., Indian Nat. Sci. Acad.; mem. USSR Acad. Scis. (mem. presidium), Acad. Scis. German Dem. Republic, Polish, Czechoslovakian acads. scis., German Acad. Natural Scis. Leopoldina, Bulgarian Acad. Scis., Royal Sweden Acad. Engring. Scis. Author over 500 works. Research on principle of molecular generator, 1952, realized molecular generator on molecular beam of ammonia, 1955, 3-level system for receiving states with inversal population suggested, 1955, proposed use of semicondrs. for creation lasers, 1958, realized various types of semicondr. lasers with excitation through p-n junctions, electronic and optical pumping, 1960-65, research on obtaining short powerful pulses of coherent light; proposed thermal and chem. methods for laser pumping, 1962, gas dynamic lasers, 1966; research optical data processing, 1965—; proposed, 1961, realized thermonuclear reactions by using powerful lasers, 1968; inventor electron-beam pumped semicondr. laser projection TV, 1968; proposed, 1966, realized eximer lasers, 1970; realized stimulation of chem. reactions by infrared laser radiation, 1970; proposed and realized electroionization laser, 1971. Chief editor Priroda, 1967—, Kvantovaya Elektronika, 1971—. Address: PN Lebedev Phys Inst, 53 Leninsky Prospekt, Moscow USSR

BASRA, DEVINDER SINGH, plastic surgeon; b. Thanabipur, India, Jan. 9, 1942; came to Eng., 1968; s. Bishan Singh and Harnam Kaur Basra; m. Sukhraj Bajwa, 1966 (div. 1970; children—Devina, Sukhdev. M.B.B.S., Med. Sch., (India), 1966; F.R.C.S., Royal Coll. Surgeons (Scotland), 1976; fellow Internat. Acad. Cosmetic Surgery (Switzerland), 1982. House surgeon Govt. Hosp., Amritsar, India, 1966-68; sr. house surgeon accident, orthopedics, plastics and surgery Nat. Health Hosps., Eng., 1968-74; registrar Health Authority, Dundee, Scotland, 1974-75; registrar surgery Noble Hosp., Douglas, Isle of Man, 1976-77; facial aesthetic surgeon, London, 1977—. Author: The Ageing Skin, 1986; also articles; editorial com. Internat. Jour. Aesthetic Surgery, 1981—. Recipient Best Artist prize Col. Brown Sch., India, 1958; Best Artist prize Med. Sch., India, 1964, 65. Fellow Royal Soc. Medicine; mem. Brit. Assn. Cosmetic Surgeons (sec. 1984—), Internat. Soc. Aesthetic Surgery (charter mem. 1981—) Gedn. Europeene des Societes Nat. de Chirurgie Esthetique (v.p. 1987—), Indian Assn. Cosmetic. Surgeons (pres. 1988—). Avocations: photography, interior designing, art, sculptor. Home: 33A Weymouth Mews, London W1 England Office: Clinic for the Medicine, 111 Harley St, London W1N 1DG, England

BASS, CHARLES MORRIS, financial consultant; b. Miami, Fla., Sept. 21, 1949; s. Benjamin and Ellen Lucille (Williams) B; children—Cheryl Ellen, Benjamin Charles. B.A., U. Md., 1972; M.S., Am. Coll., 1982. C.L.U.; chartered fin. cons. Group rep. Monumental Life Ins. Co., 1972-73; agt. Equitable Life Ins. Co., N.Y., 1973-76; ptnr. Bass, Bridge and Assocs., Columbia, Md., 1976-81; pres. Multi-Fin Service, Inc., Balt., 1981-83; gen. mgr. Mfrs. Fin. Group, Denver, 1983-85; ptnr. Regency Econometrics Group, Denver, 1985—; speaker in field. Chmn. United Way Howard County, 1977-78; mem. Econ. Devel. Adv. Council Howard County, 1979-83. Served with USAF, 1968-71. Mem. Million Dollar Round Table, Nat. Assn. Life Underwriters, Am. Soc. C.L.U.s, Gen. Agts. and Mgrs. Assn., Columbia Life Underwriters Assn. (pres. 1982), Estate Planning Council, Howard County C. of C., Howard County Bus. Club, Columbia Bus. Exchange. Methodist. Home and Office: Regency Econometrics PO Box 621519 Littleton CO 80162

BASSAN, NESSIN M., retail executive; b. Panama, Repubic of Panama, Jan. 2, 1950; s. Haim S. and Esther (Mishaan) B.; m. Jinette Tawil, May 21, 1954; children: Deborah, Haim, Marco. A in Bus. Adminstrn., Chamberlayne Jr. Coll., 1970; student, Northeastern U., 1970-72. Sales mgr. INCSA, Panama, 1973-75; v.p., co-owner Tejidos Polipan, Panama, 1975-76; sales mgr. Corp. Montaigne, Colon Free Zone, Republic of Panama, 1976-79; gen. mgr. Euro Am. Ent. Inc., Colon Free Zone, 1979-81, United Garments Inc., Colon Free Zone, 1981-84; pres., co-owner Bronson Internat. SA, Colon Free Zone, 1984—; advisor to stockholders I. New Port, S.A., Colon Free Zone, 1986—. Mem. Colon Free Zone C. of C. (bd. dirs. 1985-87, asst. treas. 1987, El Dios del Sol award 1983, Dir. Recognition diploma 1986, 87), Assn. Numismatica Nacional(bd. dirs. 1986—), Am. Numismatic Assn., Fla. United Numismatic Assn. Club: Las Mananitas Country. Lodge: B'nai B'rith. Home: 57 S Conbominio La Ronda, Panama City Republic of Panama Office: Bronson Internat SA, PO Box 4222, Colon Free Zone Republic of Panama

BASSAN, SURINDER PAL SINGH, engineer; b. Jallandhar, Punjab, India, Dec. 10, 1942; s. Sham Singh and Parmeshri (Saund) B.; m. Rajinder Kaur Bassan, Nov. 11, 1962; children: Raminder, Aminjit, Amandeep. Cert. in edn., London U., 1977. Technologist Plessey, Towcester, Eng., 1977-80; sr. devel. engr. Ferranti, Edinburgh, Eng., 1980-82, G.E.C., Coventry, Eng., 1982-86; product engring. mgr. Walmsley Microsystems Ltd., Birmingham, Eng., 1986—; dir. Bassanics Systems and Software Devels. Ltd., 1988—. Treas. Ramgarhia Bd. Northampton, Eng., 1983—. Fellow Soc. Electronic and Radio Technicians (assoc.). Home: Amandeep House, 206 Hazeldene Rd, Northampton NN2 7NH, England Office: Walmsley Microsystems Ltd, Aston Science Park Love Ln, Birmingham B7 4BJ, England

BASSETT, LELAND KINSEY, communication company executive, educator, author; b. May 27, 1945; s. Wilfred George and Vera Agnes (Scheffel) B.; m. Tina Bassett; children: Joshua Allan, Robert Ian. B.A., Mich. State U., 1968, postgrad., 1969, 70, 76, 84; postgrad. Wayne State U., 1972, 74, 75, 81, U. Mich., 1970, 76, 77, 78. Legis. page Mich. Ho. of Reps., Lansing, 1957-58; owner, prin. Communication Assocs., East Lansing, 1969-72; pres. East Lansing-Meridian Area C. of C., 1968-70; project assoc. Mgmt. Assistance Program Mich. State C. of C., Lansing, 1970-71, dir. communication, 1971-72; legis. analyst Greater Detroit C. of C., 1972, v.p. communication div., 1973-76; prin. Leland K. Bassett & Assocs., Detroit, 1976-86; strategic programs developer pub. affairs Detroit Edison Co., 1977-81, dir. communication analysis and plng., 1981-86; chmn. Bassett and Bassett, Inc., 1986—; vis. lectr. Mich. State U., 1985—. Editor The Detroiter Bus. News, 1974-76; assoc. pub. The Detroiter Mag., 1974-75. Producer, dir., writer (film) Detroit: Our Decisive Moment in History, 1973; creator, producer Alive and Well, 1973, collaborator A Play Half Written: The Energy Adventure (winner numerous awards), 1979, collaborator Radiation ... Naturally (winner numerous awards), 1981. Auctioner WTVS Annual Fund Raising Auction, 1975-76; mem. exec. com. Detroit Bicentennial Commn., 1975-76; area chmn. YMCA Capitol Funds Drive, Lansing, 1969; bd. dirs. Greater Lansing Assn. Retarded Children, 1972; trustee Music Hall Ctr. for Performing Arts, Detroit, 1984—, mem. exec. com., 1986—, chmn. nominating com., 1988—. Recipient Mayor's Citation East Lansing, 1972; named Outstanding Young Man East Lansing-Meridian Area C. of C., 1970. Mem. Greater Detroit C. of C., Mich. State C.of C., Council of Communication Mgmt., Internat. Communication Assn., Mich. Speech Assn., Pub. Relations Soc. Am., Speech Communication Assn., Detroit Artists Market, Founders Soc. Detroit Inst. Arts, Detroit Hist. Soc., Mich. Assn. Retarded Citizens, Mich. State U. Alumni Assn., Nat. Assn. Retarded Persons. Clubs: Press, Renaissance, Economic, Detroit Soc. of Clubs (Detroit). Office: 672 Woodbridge St Detroit MI 48226-4302

BASSETT, MICHAEL EDWARD RAINTON, government official; b. Auckland, New Zealand, Aug. 28, 1938; s. Edward Bassett and Lillias Clare (Brown) B.; m. Judith Ola Petrie, Oct. 17, 1964; children: Emma Louise, Samuel Michael William. BA, U. Auckland, 1958, MA (hons.), 1961; PhD, Duke U., 1963. Lectr. U. Auckland, New Zealand, 1964-72, sr. lectr. history, 1976-78; mem. parliament Govt. of New Zealand, Wellington, 1972-75, 78—, minister of health, 1984-87, minister of internal affairs, 1987—, also minister of arts, civil def. and local govt. Author: 1951 Waterfront Dispute, 1972, Third Labour Government, 1976, Three Party Politics, 1982. City councilor Auckland City Council, 1971-74; regional chmn. New Zealand Labour Party, 1970-73, mem. policy council, 1976-79. James B. Duke fellow, 1961, Am. Studies fellow Am. Council Learned Socs., Smithsonian Inst., 1967. Mem. Commonwealth Parliamentary Assn. (exec. 1980, 83). Home: 17 Stilwell Rd, Auckland 3 New Zealand Office: Govt of New Zealand, Parliament Bldgs, Wellington New Zealand

BASSETT, PAUL MERRITT, educator; b. Lima, Ohio, May 28, 1935; s. Paul Gardner and Ruth Abbott (Wiess) B.; B.A., Olivet Nazarene Coll., 1957; B.D., Duke U. Div. Sch., 1960; postgrad. Ohio State U., 1960-62; Ph.D., Duke U., 1967; m. Pearl Ann Householter, Aug. 8, 1958; children—Emilie Ruth, Paul Stephan, Anita Suzanne. Tchr., Southeastern High Sch., Ross County, Ohio, 1961-62; asso. prof. Greek and history Trevecca Nazarene Coll., Nashville, 1965-66; asst. prof. religious studies W. Va. U., Morgantown, 1966-69; asso. prof. history of Christianity, Nazarene Theol. Sem., Kansas City, Mo., 1969-76, prof., 1976—, dir. Master of Div. program, 1981-86, dir. Mex. Extension program, 1981—; vis. prof. Point Loma Coll., San Diego, 1969-72, Seminario Nazareno Centroamericana, San Jose, Costa Rica, 1972-76; lectr. U. Mo., Kansas City, others. Mem. Oxford Inst. Meth. Theol. Studies, 1982, 87. Rockefeller fellow in religion, 1964-65, Asbury fellow, 1981—; Assn. of Theol. Schs. in U.S. and Can. grantee, 1976-77. Mem. Am. Soc. Ch. History, Am. Hist. Assn., Am. Cath. Hist. Soc., Mediaeval Acad. Am., Acad. Religion, Soc. Bibl. Lit., Wesleyan Theol. Soc. (pres. elect 1980-81, pres. 1981-82), Kansas City Soc. for Theol. Studies (sec.-treas. 1981-86), Acad. of Research Historians in Medieval Spain. Mem. Ch. of the Nazarene. Author: Keep the Wonder, 1979, Exploring Christian Holiness, vol. II; contbr. articles to profl. jours. Home: 9930 Linden Ln Overland Park KS 66207 Office: 1700 E Meyer Blvd Kansas City MO 64131

BASSETT, ROBERT COCHEM, lawyer, publisher; b. Sturgeon Bay, Wis., Mar. 2, 1911; s. Clark Patterson and Lillian Catherine (Cochem) B.; m. Frances E. Whiting, Feb. 28, 1942 (dec. Jan. 1945); m. Mary Catherine Holmes, Mar. 28, 1946; children: Robert Andrew, Jane, Pamela, Karen. BA, U. Wis., 1932; JD, Harvard, 1935. Bar: Wis. bar 1935, U.S. Supreme Ct. bar 1942. Partner Minahan & Bassett, lawyers, Green Bay, Wis., 1935-46; gen. counsel Wis. Daily Newspaper League, 1936-43; spl. counsel Inland Daily Press Assn., Chgo., 1937-43; labor counsel Hearst Corp., 1946-54, also dir., v.p., 1954-56; pub. Milw. Sentinel, 1954-56, Sphere Mag., 1971-73; pres., dir. Haywood Pub. Co. of, Ill., 1961-63; exec. v.p., dir. Haywood Pub. Co., 1961-63; v.p., dir. Haywood Tag Co., 1961-63; pres., dir. Visual Communications, Inc., 1963-65; chmn., pres. Bassett Pub. Co., 1965—; mktg. dir. Grant/Jacoby, Inc., 1968-70; exec. v.p., dir., editorial dir. Omnibus Mag., 1965-67; pub. Boxboard Containers Mag., 1961-63; pres. Vertical Mktg., Inc., 1971-73; v.p. Jos. Schlitz Brewing Co., Milw., 1956-61; Pub. mem. shipbldg. stablzn. com. WPB, 1943-46; shipbldg. commn. Nat. War Labor Bd., 1943; mem. nat. Wage Stblzn. Bd., 1952-53; industry del. Internat. Labor Conf., Switzerland, 1953; mem. Sec. Labor's Mgmt. Adv. Com.; bus. mem. Pay Bd., 1971-72. Author: Wisconsin Laws Affecting Newspapers, 1938, Labor Guide for Italy, 1944; Contbr. articles to profl. jours. Regent U. Wis., 1958-61, regent emeritus, 1973—; trustee Nat. SBA; bd. dirs. Better Bus. Chgo., chmn. pub. relations. Served as lt. comdr. USNR, 1942-46. Mem. U.S. C. of C. (dir.), N.A.M. (dir.), Artus, Phi Kappa Phi, Phi Eta Sigma, Delta Sigma Rho, Delta Upsilon, Sigma Delta Chi. Clubs: Lake Barrington Shores Golf; Racquet (Chgo.), Bob O'Link (Chgo.). Home: 483 Valley View Lake Barrington Shores Barrington IL 60010 Office: 200 James St Barrington IL 60010

BASSING, JENNIFER, public relations and fundraising specialist, writer; b. N.Y.C., July 26, 1944; d. Gregory C. and Violet T. (Fischer) Drobinko; m. Peter J. Bassing, Sept. 14, 1979. B.A., SUNY, 1973; A.A., Foothill Coll., 1968. Dir. pub. relations San Francisco Conservatory Mus., 1975-78; pub. info. officer Peninsula Humane Soc., San Mateo, Calif., 1978-81; animal columnist and feature writer San Mateo Times, 1981-82; dir. devel. Guide Dogs for the Blind, Inc., San Rafael, Calif., 1983—; writer Internat. Eco Features Syndicate, West Hollywood, Calif., 1983—; corr. Israel Today, Los Angeles, 1983—; cons. pub. relations. Mem. Internat. Assn. Bus. Communication, Nat. Soc. Fundraising Execs., Pub. Relations Soc. Am., Am. Jewish Press Assn., Peninsula Press Club (1st place award best new feature release 1979), Calif. Press Women, Dog Writers' Assn. Am. (1st place award 1982, 83). Contbr. articles to periodicals. Office: Guide Dogs for the Blind Inc PO Box 1200 San Rafael CA 94915

BASSIOUNI, M. CHERIF, lawyer, legal educator; b. Cairo, Egypt, Dec. 19, 1937; came to U.S., 1961, naturalized, 1966; s. Ibrahim and Amina (Khatab) B.; m. Nina I. Del Missier. A.B.A., Coll. Holy Family, Cairo, 1955; postgrad., Dijon U. Sch. Law, France, 1955-57, U. Geneva, Switzerland, 1957, U. Cairo, 1958-61; J.D., Ind. U., 1964; LL.M., John Marshall Lawyers Inst., 1966; S.J.D., George Washington U., 1973; D.Law (hon.), U. Torino, Italy, 1981. Bar: Ill. 1967, D.C. 1967. Practiced in Chgo., 1967—; prof. law DePaul U., 1964—; Fulbright-Hays vis. prof. internat. criminal law U. Freiburg, Germany, 1970; vis. prof. law NYU, 1971; guest scholar Woodrow Wilson Internat. Center for Scholars, Washington, 1972; cons. Chgo. Bd. Edn., 1965-69, chmn. advisory bd. law in Am. soc. project, 1973-75; mem. Ill. Com. Law and Justice Edn., 1977-80; lectr. in field; spl. cons. 5th, 6th, 7th and 8th UN Congresses Crime Prevention, 1975, 80, 85; bd. dirs., dean Internat. Inst. Advanced Criminal Scis., Italy, 1976—; bd. dirs., sec.-gen. Internat. Assn. Penal Law, 1974—. Author: Criminal Law and Its Processes, 1969, The Law of Dissent and Riots, 1971; (with V.P. Nanda) International Criminal Law, 2 vols, 1973; (with Eugene Fisher) Storm Over the Arab World, 1972, International Extradition and World Public Order, 1974, International Terrorism and Political Crimes, 1975; editor: Issues in the Mediterranean, 1976, Citizens Arrest: The Law of Arrest, Search and Seizure, 1977, Substantive Criminal Law, 1978; (with V. Savitski) The Criminal Justice System of the USSR, 1979, International Criminal Law: A Draft International Criminal Code, 1980, The Islamic Criminal Justice System, 1982, International Extradition in U.S. Law and Practice, 2 vols., 1983, 2d rev. edit., 1987, Introduction to Islam, 1985 International Crimes: A Digest/Index of Conventions and Relevant Penal Provisions, 2 vols., 1986, International Criminal Law, 3 vols., 1&2, 1986, 3, 1987, A Draft Internat. Criminal Code and Draft Statute for an Internat. Criminal Tribunal, 1987; (with E. Muller-Rappard) European Inter-State Co-operation in Criminal Matters: The Council of Europe' Legal Instruments, 3 vols., 1987; (with E. Amadio) Il Processo Penale Negle Stati Uniti D'America, 1987, Legal Responses to Internat. Terrorism: U.S. Procedural Aspects, 1988; co-editor-in-chief Revue Internat. de Droit Penal, 1973-85; editor The Globe, 1970-77; bd. editors Am. Jour. Comparative Law, 1972—; adv. bd. Jour Internat. Law and Policy. Decorated Order of Merit, Order of Scis. 1st class (Egypt); commendatore Order of Merit, also grande ufficiale (Italy); recipient Outstanding Citizen of Yr., Citizenship Council Met. Chgo., 1967. Mem. Am. Soc. Internat. Law, Am. Bar Assn. (chmn. com. internat. legal edn. 1976-78, vice chmn. com. internat. criminal law), Ill. Bar Assn. (chmn. sect. internat. law 1972-73), Chgo. Bar Assn., Mid Am. Arab. C. of C. (chmn. 1973-74, 76-77, sec., gen. counsel 1970-77, pres. 1978—), Assn. Arab-Am. U. Grads. (bd. dirs. 1967-74, pres. 1969-70), Phi Alpha Delta. Home: 666 N Lake Shore Dr Chicago IL 60611 Office: 25 E Jackson St Chicago IL 60604

BASSIRI, HABIBOLLAH, agricultural machinery executive; b. Tehran, Iran, Oct. 10, 1944; s. Abbas Nikaiin and Zahra Moneh-Motlagh; m. Parirokh Nikaain, Aug. 25, 1972; children: Parisa, Parinaz. BS in Math., Tehran U., 1966. Audit clk. Coopers Lybrand, London, 1970-75; sr. auditor Winney Murray & Co., Tehran, 1975-76; audit mgr. Pars & Co., Tehran, 1976-77; dep. dir. Fideco, Tehran, 1977-78; dep. dir. Ind. Devel. & Ren. Orgn., Tehran, 1979-83, comml. mgr., 1984; fin. mgr. Ministry Commerce, Tehran, 1983-84; mng. dir. Agrl. Machinery Service, Tehran, 1984—. Served to lt. Iranian Army, 1966-68. Fellow Inst. Chartered Accts. in Eng. and Wales. Home: 49 Sh Araghi Sh Kolohdooz, Gholak, Tehran Iran

BASSOT, JACQUES, aesthetic surgeon; b. France, Sept. 5, 1924. Ex chirurgien Des Hopitaux de la Region, Sanitaire De Lille. Mem. De La Societe Francaise De Chirurgie Esthetique (pres.), Internat. Acad. Cosmetic Surgery Internat. Soc. Aesthetic Surgery (exec. bd.), La Fed. Europeene des Soc. Nat. de Chirugie Estetique (pres., fondateur). Home: 54 Ave Lefeure, 94420 Le Plessis Trevise France

BASTEDO, RALPH W(ALTER), political scientist, statistician; b. Port Jefferson, N.Y., Feb. 18, 1953; s. Walter Jr. and Barbara Catherine (Manning) B. BA in Politics with honors, Princeton U., 1975; MA in Polit. Sci. with honors, U. Calif., Berkeley, 1976; PhD in Polit. Psychology with honors, U. Calif., Berkeley and SUNY, Stony Brook, 1983. Pollster, journalist various N.Y. and N.J. newspapers, 1969-74; author, researcher Survey Research Ctr. and dept. polit. sci. U. Calif., Berkeley, 1975-78, lab. behavioral research, social sci. data lab and dept. polit. sci. SUNY, Stony Brook, 1978-83, co-dir. exptl. analysis of polit. concepts project, 1978-83, prof. polit. sci., 1978-80; pollster Gallup Poll, 1984-86, Vanderveer Group, 1986—; prof. Furman U., Greenville, S.C., 1988—; editor Harbour Chronicle newspaper, 1981-82, Wopowog bull., 1980-84. Pollster, campaign adv. L.I. Citizens for Kennedy, 1979-80; speaker Princeton faculty alumni forum on 1980 presdl. election, 1980. N.Y. State Regents scholar, 1971-75; U. Calif., Berkeley scholar, 1975-78; SUNY, Stony Brook scholar, 1980. Mem. Am. Assn. Public Opinion Research, Am. Statis. Assn., Am. Assn. Polit. Cons., Am. Polit. Sci. Assn., Nat. Center Employee Ownership, Stony Brook Polit. Sci. Assn. (pres. 1979-83), Pi Sigma Alpha. Ethical Humanist, Unitarian-Universalist. Author: Electoral Attributes of Party Identification, 1983; Survey of State Legislators, 1985; contbr. articles to profl. jours. Co-author: Paranormal Borderlands of Science, 1981; Consumer Financial Services Monitor, 1985. Home: 76 Deer Run Hendersonville NC 28739

BASTEDO, WAYNE WEBSTER, lawyer; b. Oceanside, N.Y., July 13, 1948; s. Walter Jr. and Barbara Catherine (Manning) B.; m. Bina Shantilal Mistry, Dec. 29, 1978. AB in Polit. Sci. cum laude, Princeton U., 1970; postgrad., NYU, 1977-78; JD, Hofstra U., 1978; LLM, NYU, 1988. Bar: N.Y. 1980. Mgr. adminstrv. Law Jour. Seminars Press, N.Y.C., 1978-79; editor decisions and legal digests N.Y. Law Jour., N.Y.C., 1979-81; sole practice N.Y.C., 1981-82; atty., mem. corp. restructuring staff Western Union Corp., Upper Saddle River, N.J., 1983—; cons. litigation Exxon Corp., N.Y.C., 1982, Western Union Corp., Upper Saddle River, 1983, mem. corp. restructuring staff, 1986-88. Author: A Comparative Study of Soviet and American World Order Models, 1978, Who Has the Edge on Justice? Computer Services Alter Fair Play, 1979; assoc. editor Hofstra U. Law Rev. 1976-77; editor (directory series) Outside Counsel: Inside Director, 1976-81; contbr. articles to profl. jours. Mem. policy com. Roosevelt Island (N.Y.) Residents Assn., 1981-82. Served to lt. USN, 1970-75, Vietnam. N.Y. State Regents scholar, 1966-70, USN Officer Tng. scholar, 1967-70. Mem. ABA, N.Y. County Lawyers Assn. Democrat. Methodist. Home: 370 Park St Apt 203 Hackensack NJ 07601 Office: Western Union Corp Office Gen Counsel 1 Lake St Upper Saddle River NJ 07458

BASTIAN, JAMES HAROLD, air transport company executive, lawyer; b. Hannibal, Mo., Nov. 26, 1927; s. Ira Russell and Opal (Maddox) B.; m. Mary Jean Zugel, Feb. 5, 1955; children: Raphael Maria, Marquette Maria, Bartholomew Barnabas, Boniface Benedict. B.S., U. Mo., 1950; J.D. with honors, George Washington U., 1956. Bar: D.C., Va. 1956, U.S. Supreme Ct. 1960, Md. 1975. Assoc. Adair, Ulmer, Murchison, Kent & Ashby, 1956-61; v.p., sec. Pacific Corp., 1961-74; sec. Air Am., Inc., 1961-74, Air Asia Co. Ltd., 1973-74; ptnr. Howard, Poe & Bastian, 1965-84, Bastian and Bastian, 1984—; sec., dir. Permawick Co., 1974—; v.p., sec., dir. So. Air Transport, Inc., 1974-79, pres., chief exec. officer, 1979-83, chmn. bd., chief exec. officer, 1983—. Served with USNR, 1945-46. Mem. Am., Va., Md., D.C. bar assns., Order of Coif. Clubs: Metropolitan, Army and Navy (Washington), Riviera Country (Miami, Fla.), Brichell, Congressional Country (Bethesda, Md.), Wings (N.Y.C.). Home: 140 Arvida Pkwy Coral Gables FL 33156 also: 3627 Winfield Ln Washington DC 20007 Office: Southern Air Transport Inc Miami Internat Airport PO Box 52-4093 Miami FL 33152

BASTIDE, FRANCOIS-REGIS, ambassador, writer; b. Biarritz, France, July 1, 1926; s. d'Edouard and Suzanne (Canton) B.; m. Monica Sjöholm (div.); children: Anica, Thomas; m. J. Huguenin, Sept. 16, 1966; 1 child, Emmanuelle. Student, Coll. St. Louis-de-Gonzague, Lycée de Bayonne, France. Attaché d'info. Pres. Govt. Militaire de Sarre, France, 1945-47; sec.-gen. Ctr. Culturel Royaumont, France, 1947-50; pensionnaire Maison Descartes, Amsterdam, 1950-53; conseiller littéraire Editions du Seuil, 1953—; producteur d'émissions littéraires et dramatiques l'ORTF, 1949—. Decorated officer legion d'honneur Nat. Order of Merit, Comdr. Arts and Letters. Office: Embassy of France, Technikerstr 2, 1040 Vienna Austria

BASTOKY, BRUCE MICHAEL, human resource executive; b. Cleve., June 15, 1953; s. Irving Benjamin and Esther (Naff) B. Student, Cuyahoga Community Coll., 1971-73, U. Akron, 1984-85. Personnel/tng. adminstr. The May Co., Cleve., 1974-77; cons. Roth Young, Cleve., 1978-80; dir. human resources The Lawson Co., Cuyahoga Falls, Ohio, 1980-86, Cardinal Industries, Columbus, Ohio, 1986—. Author: Supervisor's Guide, 1985, Sixty Minute Mastery, 1987; producer (films/videos) The Visitor, 1984, Deli Heros, 1985. Mem. Youth Motivation Task Force, Akron, Ohio, 1983—; officer Pvt. Industry Council, Akron, 1983—. Recipient Silver Quill for Scriptwriting award Internat. Assn. Bus. Communicators, 1985, Best Film/Video Series award Nat. Assn. Convenience Stores, 1985, Exec. of Yr. award Profl. Secs. Internat., 1987. Mem. Am. Soc. Personnel Adminstrn. (bd. dris. 1985-86), Am. Soc. Tng. and Devel., German Village Soc. Jewish. Home: 602 E Town St #7 Columbus OH 43215 Office: Cardinal Industries Inc 4223 Donlyn Ct Columbus OH 43232

BATAILLARD, VICTOR, editor; b. Zurich, Oct. 4, 1929; s. Louis and Marie (Walker) B.; m. Erna Birrer, Oct. 6, 1956; children: Roger, Pierre, Madeleine. Dr. oec. publ., U. Zurich, 1963. Dir., SIB, Zurich, 1963-76; rector HWV, Zurich, 1969-76; pres. Verlag Organisator AG, Zurich, 1977—, GfP, 1977—, rondom technic, 1982—; Wassex AG, 1985—; Neuland AG, 1988—. Author: Finanzausgleich, 1964, Direktwerbung, 1979, Geschaeftsgruendung, 1988, Pinwandtechnik, 1984 . Pres., Primarschule, Birmensdorf-Zurich, 1970-78, Jugendkommission, Zurich, 1968-76. Mem. Schweiz Buchaendler und Verleger Verband (pres. 1985-86). Club: Lions (pres. 1976-77). Home: Howielstrasse 13, 8903 Birmensdorf, Zurich Switzerland Office: Verlag Organisator AG, Loewenstrasse 16, 8021 Zurich Switzerland

BATAILLE-BENGUIGUI, MARIE CLAIRE, anthropologist; b. Paris, Dec. 6, 1936; d. Louis Bataille and Paulette Beaumont; m. Georges Benguigui; 2 children. D in Ethnology, Paris X-Nanterre U., 1986. Med. lab. technician Paris, 1957-62; adminstr. Les Glénans, Paris, 1963-69; asst. dept. Oceania Musée Nat. d'Histoire Naturelle, 1971-86, supr. Pacific COllections, 1976-86, supr. Ichtyology Lab., 1986—. Contbr. articles to profl. jours. Mem. Nat. Ctr. of Scientific Research (3 research teams), Soc. des Océanistes Musée de l'Homme (asst. gen. sec. 1978-83). Office: Lab d'Ichtyologie, 43 Rue Cuvier, 75005 Paris France

BATAL, ABDULRAHMAN MISBAH, airline ofcl.; b. Haifa, Palestine, Aug. 28, 1931; s. Misbah Husein and Miriam Mahmed (Abbas) B.; student public schs., Haifa; m. Aysha Mohamed Batal, May 15, 1954; children—Iman, Ghassan, Ihsan, Canaan, Razan, Safwan. Sr. health insp. Aramco, Saudi Arabia, 1950-55; civic aviation dep. sta. mgr. Damascus Airport, 1955-62; mgr. for Syria, Pakistan Internat. Airlines, 1962-79, mgr. for Tanzania and Mozambique, Dar es Salaam, from 1979; chmn. Hannibal Tourism and Transport Co. Mem. Syrian Nationalist Social Party, Dharhran, Saudi Arabia, chief militia dept., 1952; founder, chmn. Airlines Workers Union Syria., 1958-71; co-founder Pan Arab Transport Workers Fedn., Port Said, Egypt, 1965. Served to 2d lt. Syrian Armed Forces, 1947-49. Mem. Arab Travel Tourism Agys., Internat. Airline Passengers Assn. Sonni Moslem, Damascus C. of C., Syrian Assn. Tourist and Travel Agents. Clubs: Gliding, Orient (Damascus, Syria). Home: 297G Sa'D Bin, WAQAS St, Mezze, New Damascus Syria Office: Hannibal Tourism and Transport Co, PO Box 4088, Damascus Syria

BATCHA, GEORGE, mechanical and nuclear engineer; b. Marblehead, Ohio, Oct. 24, 1928; s. John and Anna (Groholy) B.; m. Erika Voelker, Jan. 1, 1982; 1 child, Susan Kolodziejczyk. B.A., Bowling Green State U., 1951; M.S. in Engring. Sci., U. Toledo, 1968; certs. numerous U.S. Army tng. schs. Registered profl. engr., Ohio, Mich. With Standard Products Co., Port Clinton, Ohio, 1951, A.O. Smith Co. Landing Gear div., Toledo, Ohio, 1951, army rep. at Glenn L. Martin Co., Balt., 1952-54, Cleve. Pneumatic Tool Co., 1954-55, Hardware Stamping div. Ford Motor Co., Sandusky, Ohio, 1955-59; mech. design and test engr. Missile and Def. Engring. divs. Chrysler Corp., Detroit, 1959-62; mech. and nuclear engr. NASA, Lewis Research Ctr., Plum Brook Sta., Sandusky, 1962-74; mech. and system mgmt. engr. Armament Research and Devel. Command, U.S. Army, Dover, N.J., and Rock Island, Ill., 1974-81, mech. engr. Tank Automotive Command, Warren, Mich., 1981—. Author numerous tech. reports. Served with U.S. Army, 1952-54. Scholar, Bowling Green State U., 1948; recipient Apollo Achievement award NASA, 1969, accomplishment awards, 1981, 82, Cost Reduction awards, 1971, 74, Dept. Army Achievement award Tank Automotive Command, 1985. Mem. Nat. Soc. Profl. Engrs., Order of Engr., Nat. Council Engring. Examiners (cert.), Am. Acad. Environ. Engrs. (diplomate), Soc. Logistics Engrs. (cert. profl. logistician), Assn. U.S. Army, Port Clinton Power Squadron of Ohio. Byzantine Catholic. Current work: Technical assessment and guidance of developmental programs of all elements of integrated logistics support in tank-automotive weapon system and equipment. Subspecialties: Mechanical engineering; Nuclear engineering. Home: 1410 Bishop Rd Grosse Pointe Park MI 48230

BATCHELDER, ANNE STUART, former publisher, political party official; b. Lake Forest, Ill., Jan. 11, 1920; d. Robert Douglas and Harriet (McClure) Stuart; student Lake Forest Coll., 1941-43; m. Clifton Brooks Batchelder, May 26, 1945; children: Edward, Anne Stuart, Mary Clifton, Lucia Brooks. Clubmobile driver ARC, Eng., Belgium, France, Holland and Germany, 1943-45; pub., editor Douglas County Gazette, 1970-75; bd. dirs. Firstier Bank Omaha; dir., treas. U.S. Checkbook Com. Mem. Rep. Cen. Com. Nebr., 1955-62, 70-83, vice chmn. Central Com., 1959-64, chmn., 1975-79, mem. fin. com., 1957-64; chmn. women's sect. Douglas County Rep. Finance Com., 1955, vice chmn. com., 1958-60; v.p. Omaha Woman's Rep. Club, 1957-58, pres., 1959-60; alt. del. Nat. Conv., 1956, 72, del., 1980, 84; mem. Rep. Nat. Com. for Nebr., 1964-70; asst. chmn. Douglas County Rep. Central Com., 1971-74; 1st v.p. Nebr. Fedn. Rep. Women, 1971-72, pres., 1972-74; chmn. Nebr. Rep. Com., 1975-79; chmn. fundraising com. Nat. Fedn. Rep. Women, 1981-85; mem. Nebr. State Bldg. Commn., 1979-83; Rep. candidate for lt. gov., 1974. Sr. v.p. Nebr. Founders Day, 1958; bd. dirs. YWCA, 1983—; past trustee Brownell Hall, Vis. Nurse Assn.; trustee Hastings Coll., Nebr. Meth. Hosp. Found.; past pres. Nebr. chpt. Freedoms Found. at Valley Forge. Elected to Nebr. Rep. Hall of Fame, 1984. Mem. Mayflower Soc., Colonial Dames, P.E.O., Nat. League Pen Women. Presbyterian (elder). Clubs: Omaha Country, Omaha. Home: 6875 State St Omaha NE 68152

BATDORF, SAMUEL B(URBRIDGE), physicist; b. Jung Hsien, China, Mar. 31, 1914; s. Charles William and Nellie (Burbridge) B.; m. Carol Catherine Schweiss, July 19, 1940; children: Samuel Charles, Laura Ann. A.B., U. Calif.-Berkeley, 1934, A.M., 1936, Ph.D., 1938. Asso. prof. physics U. Nev., 1938-43; aero. research scientist Langley Lab., NACA, 1943-51; dir. devel. Westinghouse Elec. Corp., Pitts., 1951-56; tech. dir. weapons systems Lockheed Missile & Space Co., Palo Alto, Calif., 1956-58; mgr. communication satellites Inst. Def. Analysis, Washington, 1958-59; dir. research in physics and electronics Aeronutronic, Newport Beach, Calif., 1959-62; prin. scientist Aerospace Corp., El Segundo, Calif., 1962-77; Sigma Xi lectr. communication satellites; disting. prof. Tsing Hua U., Republic of China, 1969; vis. scholar Va. Poly. Inst. and State U., 1984; adj. prof. engring. and applied sci. UCLA, 1973-86. Contbr. articles to profl. jours. Fellow Am. Phys. Soc., Am. Acad. Mechanics (pres. 1982-83), AIAA ASME (hon. mem., edn., structures, materials and space flight coms.), NSF (solid mechanics com.), Phi Beta Kappa, Phi Kappa Phi. Republican. Presbyterian. Home: 5536 B Via La Mesa Laguna Hills CA 92653 Office: 6531 Boelter Hall UCLA Los Angeles CA 90024

BATE, ROBERT THOMAS, physicist; b. Denver, Apr. 1, 1931; s. Harold Thomas and Eunice (Redmond) B.; m. Helen Marie Giehm, Mar. 17, 1951; children—Donna Bate Kinney, Barbara Bate Wortham, Susan Bate Moore, Richard, Beverly Bate Bates. B.S. in Engring. Physics, U. Colo., 1955; M.S. in Physics, Ohio State U., 1957. Physicist U.S. Bur. Standards, Boulder, Colo., 1955; research asst. Ohio State U., Columbus, 1955-57; physicist Battelle Inst., Columbus, 1957-64, Tex. Instruments, Inc., Dallas, 1964—, br. mgr. central research labs., 1974—, sr. scientist, 1966-74; mem. Solid State scis. com. NRC, 1981-84. Contbr. numerous articles to profl. jours., chpts. to books. Patentee electronic devices. Served with USMCR, 1952-54. Tex. Instruments fellow, 1985—. Fellow Am. Phys. Soc.; mem. IEEE (sr.). Home: 3106 Kristin Ct Garland TX 75042

BATEMAN, DAVID ALFRED, lawyer; b. Pitts., Jan. 28, 1946; s. Alfred V. and Ruth G. (Howe) B.; m. Trudy A. Heath, Mar. 13, 1948; children—Devin C., Mark C. A.B. in Geology, U. Calif.-Riverside, 1966; J.D., U. San Diego, 1969; LL.M., Georgetown U., 1978. Bar: Calif. 1970, U.S. Dist. Ct. (so. dist.) Calif. 1970, U.S. Ct. Mil. Appeals 1972, Wash. 1973, U.S. Dist. Ct. (we. dist.) Wash. 1973, U.S. Supreme Ct. 1974, D.C. 1976, U.S. Dist. Ct. D.C. 1977, U.S. Ct. Claims 1979, U.S. Ct. Appeals (9th cir.) 1981. Assoc. Daubney, Banche, Patterson and Nares, Oceanside, Calif., 1969-72; asst. atty. gen. State of Wash., Olympia, 1977-81; ptnr. Bateman & Woodring, Olympia, 1981-85, Woodring, Bateman & Westbrook, 1985—; instr. Am. Inst. Banking, San Diego, 1972, U. Puget Sound, Olympia campus, spring, 1979. Served to capt. JAGC, USAF, 1972-77; maj. JAGC, USAFR, 1977—. Mem. ABA (internat. law and environ. law sect.), Am. Soc. Internat. Law (environ. law sect.), Wash. State Bar Assn. Roman Catholic. Club: Rotary (past chmn. internat. services com.).

BATEMAN, DOTTYE JANE SPENCER, realtor; b. Athens, Tex.; d. Charles Augustus and Lillie (Freeman) Spencer; student Fed. Inst., 1941-42, So. Meth. U., Dallas Coll., 1956-58; m. George Truitt Bateman, 1947 (div. Apr. 1963); children—Kelly Spencer, Bethena; m. 2d, Joseph E. Lindsley, 1968. Sec. to state senator, Tyler, Tex., 1941-42; sec. to pres. Merc. Nat. Bank, Dallas, State Fair of Tex., Dallas, 1942-48; realtor, broker, Garland, Tex., 1956—; co-ptnr. Play-Shade Co.; appraiser Assoc. Soc. Real Estate Appraiser; auctioneer, 1963—; developer Stonewall Cave, 1964—, Guthrie East Estates. Pres., Central Elementary Sch. PTA, 1955-56, Bussey Jr. High PTA, 1956-57; former Rep. Precinct chair, Garland; mem. Rep. Senatorial Inner Circle, 1986—; den mother Cub Scouts Am., 1957-59; chmn. Decent Lit. Com., 1956-58; chmn. PTA's council, 1958; dir. Dallas Heart Assn., 1960, local chmn., 1955-57, county chmn., 1957-60; spl. dir. Henderson County Red Cross, 1945; local chmn. March of Dimes, 1961-63; mem. Dallas Civic Opera Com., 1963-64; mem. homemaker panel Dallas Times Herald, 1955-74, Nat. Rep. Womne and Regents, 1986—. Named Outstanding Tex. Jaycee-Ette Pres., 1953, hon. Garland Jay-Cee-Ette, 1956, hon. Sheriff, Dallas County, 1963; headliner Press Club Awards dinner, 1963-68. Mem. Garland, Dallas (chmn. reception com., past dir., mem. comml.-investment div., mem. make Am. better com. 1973-78, mem. beautify Tex. council 1977-78, by-laws com. 1977-78) bds. realtors, Auctioneers Assn., Internat. Real Estate Fedn., Soc. Prevention Cruelty to Animals, Dallas Women's (project chmn.). Garland (chmn. spl. services com. 1955-56) chambers commerce, Consejo Internacional De Buena Vecindad, Delphian Study Club, Eruditis Study Club, D.A.R. (Daniel McMahan chpt.). Christian Scientist. Clubs: Garland (past v.p., pres.), Tex. (past treas., ofcl. hostess) Jaycee-Ettes, Garland Fedn. Women's (past pres.), Garland Garden, Trinity Dist. Fedn. Women's (past pres.), Pub. Affairs Luncheon, Dallas Press (dir. 1973-74), chmn. house com. 1973-74, chmn. hdqrs. com. 1973-74). Home: 6313 Lyons Rd Garland TX 75043 Office: 5518 Dyer St #1 Dallas TX 75206

BATES, ALAN (ARTHUR BATES), actor; b. Derbyshire, Eng., Feb. 17, 1934; s. Harold Arthur and Florence Mary (Wheatcroft) B.; m. Victoria Ward, May, 1970; twin sons. Student, Royal Acad. Dramatic Art, London. Appeared in stage prodns. including Hamlet, London, Butley, London and N.Y.C. (Antoinette Perry award for Best Actor 1973), Poor Richard, N.Y.C., Merry Wives of Windsor and Richard III, Stratford, Ont., Taming of the Shrew at Stratford-on-Avon, Eng., 1973, Life Class, 1974, Otherwise Engaged, 1975, The Seagull, 1976, Stage Struck, 1979-80, A Patriot for Me, London and Los Angeles, 1983, One for the Road, Victoria Station, 1984, The Dance of Death, 1985, Yonadab, Nat. Theatre, 1986, Melon, 1987; films include The Fixer (Oscar award nomination), Women in Love, The Three Sisters, A Day in the Death of Joe Egg, The Go-Between, Second Best, Impossible Object, London, Los Angeles, N.Y.C., In Celebration, Royal Flash, An Unmarried Woman, The Shout, The Rose, Very Like a Whale, Nijinsky, Quartet, The Return of the Soldier, 1982, The Wicked Lady, 1983, Duet for One, 1986, A Prayer for the Dying, 1987, We Think the World of You, 1988; television plays include The Collection, 1977, The Mayor of Casterbridge, 1978, Very Like a Whale, The Trespasser, 1981, A Voyage Round my Father, 1982, A Englishman Abroad, 1983, Separate Tables, 1983, Dr. Fischer of Geneva, 1984, One for the Road, 1985, Pack of Lies, 1987; poetry recital (with Patrick Garland) Down Cemetery Road, 1986. Served with RAF. Recipient Clarence Derwent award Royal Acad. Dramatic Art; Antoinette Perry Best Actor award for Butley, 1973; Evening Standard award, 1972. Office: Chatto & Linnit Ltd, Prince of Wales Theatre, Coventry St, London W1V 7FE, England

BATES, BARBARA J. NEUNER, municipal official; b. Mt. Vernon, N.Y., Apr. 8, 1927; d. John Joseph William and Elsie May (Flint) Neuner; B.A., Barnard Coll., 1947; m. Herman Martin Bates, Jr., Mar. 25, 1950; children—Roberta Jean Bates Jamin, Herman Martin III, Jon Neuner. Confidential clk. to supr. town Ossining (N.Y.), 1960-63; pres. BNB Assocs., Briarcliff Manor, N.Y., 1963-83, Upper Nyack Realty Co., Inc., Briarcliff Manor, 1966-71; receiver of taxes Town of Ossining (N.Y.), 1971—. Vice pres. Ossining (N.Y.) Young Republican Club, 1958; pres. Young Womens Rep. Club Westchester County (N.Y.), 1959-61; regional committeewoman N.Y. State Assn. Young Rep. Clubs, 1960-62; mem. Westchester County Rep. Com., 1963—; mem. Ossining Women's Rep. Club, 1960—, pres., 1984-85; mem. Westchester County Women's Rep. Club, 1957—. Mem. Jr. League Westchester-on-Hudson, DAR, N.Y. State Assn. Tax Receivers and Collectors, Receivers of Taxes Assn. of Westchester County, (legis. liaison, v.p., pres. 1984-85), Hackley Sch. Mothers Assn. (pres. 68), R.I. Hist. Soc., Ossining Hist. Soc., Ossining Bus. and Profl. Women's Club, Am. Soc. Notaries, Westchester County Hist. Soc., Briarcliff-Scarborough Hist. Soc. Congregationalist. Home: 78 Holbrook Ln Briarcliff Manor NY 10510 also: 663 Reynolds Rd Chepachet RI 02814

BATES, BONNIE-JO GRIEVE, physician, medical geneticist; b. N.Y.C., Jan. 1, 1949; d. Jesse Terry and Josephine (Stanton) G.; m. 1983. B.S., Cornell U., 1969; M.D., U. Utah, 1973; M.S. in Med. Genetics, U. Wis., 1979. Intern, U. Wis., Madison, 1973-74, resident in pediatrics, 1974-76, Stetler Found. postdoctoral fellow in clin. genetics, 1976-78, NIH postdoctoral fellow in molecular genetics, 1978-79; asst. prof. human genetics and pediatrics Med. Coll. Va., Richmond, 1979-81; regional med. adv., mem. Nat. Ski Patrol Systems, 1976-84. Diplomate Am. Bd. Pediatrics, Am. Bd. Med. Genetics. Fellow Am. Acad. Pediatrics; mem. AMA, Am. Med. Women's Assn., Am. Soc. Human Genetics, Med. Soc. Wis., Am. Inst. Ultrasound in Med., Phi Kappa Phi, Alpha Lambda Delta. Office: Great Lakes Genetics Milwaukee WI 53226

BATES, CHARLES WALTER, human resource executive; b. Detroit, June 28, 1953; s. E. Frederick and Virginia Marion (Nunneley) BA in Psychology and Econs. cum laude, Mich. State U., 1975, M in Labor and Indsl. Relations, 1977; postgrad. DePaul U., 1979-80; JD William Mitchell Coll. Law, 1984. Vista vol., paralegal, Legal Aid Assn. Ventura County, Calif., 1975-76; substitute tchr. social studies and history, Lansing, Holt and Okemos, Mich. pub. sch. systems, 1976-77; job analyst Gen. Mills, Inc., Mpls., 1977-78, plant personnel asst., Chgo., 1978-80, asst. plant personnel mgr. II, Chgo., 1980, personnel mgr. consumer foods and mktg., Mpls., 1981-82; personnel mgr. consumer foods and mktg. divs. Saluto Pizza, Mpls., 1982-84; human resource div. mgr. Western region, Godfather's Pizza, Costa Mesa, Calif., 1984-85; regional mgr. human resources, Bellevue, Washington, 1985—. Candidate lt. gov., 1982, Minn.; asst. scoutmaster Boy Scouts of Am., 1971—. Named Eagle Scout, Boy Scouts Am., 1969; recipient God and Country award Boy Scouts Am., 1967, Scouter's Tng. award Boy Scouts Am., 1979. Mem. Nat. Eagle Scout Assn., Nat. Assn. JD/MBA Profls., Pacific NW Personnel Mgmt. Assn., Indsl. Relations Research Assn., Am. Soc. Personnel Adminstrn., Mich. State U. Alumni Assn., William Mitchell Coll. Law Alumni Assn. Libertarian. Unitarian-Universalist. Home: 232 168th Ave NE Bellevue WA 98008-4522 Office: Godfather's Pizza Inc 11400 SE 6th St Suite 100 Bellevue WA 98004

BATES, HAROLD MARTIN, lawyer; b. Wise County, Va., Mar. 11, 1928; s. William Jennings and Reba (Williams) B.; m. Audrey Rose Doll, Nov. 1, 1952 (div. Mar. 1978); children—Linda, Carl. m. Judith Lee Farmer, June 23, 1978. B.A. in Econs., Coll. William and Mary, 1952; LL.B., Washington and Lee U., 1961. Bar: Va. 1961, Ky. 1961. Spl. agt. FBI, Newark and N.Y.C., 1952-56; tech. sales rep. Hercules Powder Co., Wilmington, Del., 1956-58; practice law, Louisville, 1961-62; sec.-treas., dir., house counsel Life Ins. Co. of Ky., Louisville, 1962-66; practice law, Roanoke, Va., 1966—; sec., dir. James River Limestone Co., Buchanan, Va., 1970—; sec. Eastern Ins. Co., Roanoke, 1984-87. Pres., Skil, Inc., orgn. for rehab. Vietnam vets., Salem, Va., 1972-75. Served to cpl. U.S. Army, 1946-47, PTO. Mem. Va. Bar Assn., Roanoke Bar Assn., William and Mary Alumni Assn. (bd. dirs. 1972-76), Soc. Former Spl. Agts. of FBI (chmn. Blue Ridge chpt. 1971-72). Republican. Home: 2165 Laurel Woods Dr Salem VA 24153 Office: 604 Professional Arts Bldg Roanoke VA 24011

BATES, JAMES EARL, professional college president; b. Ligonier, Pa., Aug. 10, 1923; s. Earl Barrington and Margaret (Kinsey) B.; m. Lauralou Courtney, Apr. 15, 1950; children: Susan Bates Jaren, Sara Bates Hudson, James Barrington, Willa Laurens. D.S.C., Temple U., 1946; D.P.M., Pa. Coll. Podiatric Medicine, 1970; Ed.D. (hon.), Franklin Pierce Coll., 1972. Practice podiatric medicine Phila., 1946-71; asso. prof. roentgenology Temple U., 1948-60; prof., pres. Pa. Coll. Podiatric Medicine, Phila., 1962—; cons. BHRD Region IX, HEW, San Francisco, 1973-74, Region V, Chgo., 1974-75; del. Nat. Commn. on Certifying Health Manpower; mem. health adv. com. HEW, 1972-73; adv. panel for podiatry Inst. Medicine, Nat. Acad. Scis., 1972-74; adv. council for comprehensive health planning Pa. Dept. Health, 1972-75, health manpower task force edn. com., 1976; mem. task force on health manpower distbn. Nat. Health Council, 1973, mem. com. on manpower, 1976-83; mem. Nat. Adv. Council on Health Professions Edn., 1983-87; cons. team So. Regional Ednl. Bd. Feasibility Study for So. Podiatry Sch., 1975-76; mem. Statewide Profl. Standards Rev. Council, 1976-82, Greater Phila. Com. for Med.-Pharm. Scis. Contbr. sci. articles to profl. jours. Trustee First United Meth. Ch. of Germantown, 1965-72, past chmn. fin. com.; v.p. bd. Germantown Businessmen's Assn., Disting. Service award, 1964; chmn. 277th and 278th Ann. Germantown Week, 1958-59; dep. service dir. Phila. CD Council, 1966-73; mem. Health Adv. Commn., Phila., 1976; past pres., bd. mgrs. Germantown YWCA; v.p. Phila. Boosters Assn.; trustee Univ. City Sci. Center, Phila. Served with M.C. AUS, World War II. Recipient citation Pa. Coll. Podiatric Medicine, 1970, citation Gov. Pa., 1973. Fellow Internat. Acad. Preventive Medicine (dir. 1973-78), Royal Soc. Health (Eng.), Am. Coll. Foot Roentgenologists (pres. 1958-59), Coll. Physicians Phila.; mem. Am. Podiatry Assn. (Merit award 1962, gen. chmn. Region Three Ann. Conv. 1975—), Pa. Podiatry Assn. (pres. 1959-60, Man of Yr. award 1961, Spl. citation 1973), Greater Phila. Podiatry Soc. (pres. 1955-56), Fedn. Assns. Schs. of Health Professions (pres. 1975-76), Am. Assn. Colls. Podiatric Medicine (pres. 1969-72), Pi Epsilon Delta, Pi Delta. Republican. Clubs: Sands Country, Downtown, Union League. Office: Pa Coll Podiatric Medicine Race at 8th Sts Philadelphia PA 19107

BATES, LURA WHEELER, trade association executive; b. Inboden, Ark., Aug. 28, 1932; d. Carl Clifton and Hester Ray (Pace) Wheeler; B.S. in Bus. Adminstrn., U. Ark., 1954; m. Allen Carl Bates, Sept. 12, 1954; 1 dau., Carla Allene. Sec.-bookkeeper, then officer mgr. Assoc. Gen. Contractors Miss., Inc., Jackson, 1958-77, dir. adminstrv. services, 1977—, asst. exec. dir., 1980—; adminstr. Miss. Constrn. Found., 1977—; sec. AIA-Assoc. Gen. Contractors Liaisonship Coms., 1977—; sec. Carpenters Joint Apprenticeship Coms., Jackson and Vicksburg, 1977—. Sec., Marshall Elem. Sch. PTA, Jackson, 1962-64, v.p., 1965; sec.-treas. Inter-Club Council Jackson, 1963-64; tchr. adult Sunday sch. dept. Hillcrest Bapt. Ch., Jackson, 1975-82; Bapt. Women dir. WMU First Bapt. Ch., Crystal Springs, Miss., 1987—; mem. exec. com. Jackson Christian Bus. and Profl. Women's Council, 1976-80, sec., 1978-79, pres., 1979-80. Named Outstanding Woman in Constrn. Miss., 1962-63; Outstanding Mem. Nat. Assn. Women in Constrn., various times. Fellow Internat. Platform Assn.; mem. Nat. Assn. Women in Constrn. (chpt. pres. 1963-64, 76-77, nat. v.p. 1965-66, 77-78, nat. dir. Region 5, 1967-68, nat. sec. 1970-71, 71-72, pres. 1980-81, coordinator cert. constrn. assoc. program 1973-78, 83-84 guardian-controller Edn. Found. 1981-82, chmn. nat. bylaws com. 1982-83, 85-88, nat. parliamentarian 1983—), Nat. Assn. Parliamentarians, Delta Delta Delta. Editor NAWIC Image, 1968-69, Procedures Manual, 1965-66, Public Relations Handbook, 1967-68, Profl. Edn. Guide, 1972-73, Guidelines & Procedures Handbook, 1987-88; author digests in field. Home: 272 Lee Ave Crystal Springs MS 39059 Office: 2093 Lakeland Dr Jackson MS 39216

BATES, MALCOLM ROWLAND, company director; b. Portsmouth, Hampshire, Eng., Sept. 23, 1934; s. Rowland and Ivy (Hope) B.; m. Lynda Margaret, June 4, 1960; children—Karen Jane, Diana Margaret, Joanna Catherine. M.Sc., Warwick U., 1974. Mng. dir. within Delta Metal Group, U.K., 1961-67; sr. exec. Indsl. Reorgn. Corp., 1968-69; mng. dir. Spey Investments, Ltd., 1970-72, Wm. Brandts and Sons, Ltd., 1972-75; dep. mng. dir. Gen. Electric Co., Plc, London, 1976—; chmn. Picker Internat. Inc., Cleve., 1981—; dir. A.B. Dick Inc., Chgo., 1980—; pres. G.E.C., Inc., N.Y.C., 1982—. Served with RAF, 1955-57. Fellow Chartered Inst. Secs.; companion Brit. Inst. Mgmt. Home: Mulberry Close, Croft Rd, Goring-On-Thames, Oxon RG8 9ES, England Office: The General Electric Co PLC, 1 Stanhope Gate, London W1A 1EH, England

BATES, NORMAN JAMES, manufacturing engineer, mechanical technologies educator; b. Bay City, Mich., Jan. 28, 1952; s. Norman R. and Theresa Mary (Carbary) B.; m. Barbara Jane Houle, June 4, 1988; 1 child, Matthew James. B.S.E. in Aerospace, U. Mich., 1974. Coordinator numerical control Wilson Machine, Saginaw, Mich., 1978—; instr. mech. techs. Delta Coll., University Center, Mich., 1980—; mgr. numerical control programming Am. Hoist & Derrick, Bay City, 1976-78. Author: SPIDAR (Solar Powered Ion Driven Asteroid Belt Research), 1974; chpt. preface Metalworking, 1982. Sr. mem. Soc. Mfg. Engrs. Roman Catholic. Avocations: botanist; hang gliding; ultralight pilot; cross country skiing. Home: 1620 E North Boutell Road Linwood MI 48634 Office: Wilson Machine Div 400 Florence St Saginaw MI 48602

BATES, RALPH SAMUEL, history educator; b. Oshkosh, Wis., June 19, 1906; s. Samuel and Alice (Burns) B.; m. Susie Mabell Thombs, Aug. 9, 1947; children—Thomas Samuel, James Ralph. AB, U. Rochester, 1927, AM, 1931; AM, Harvard U., 1930, PhD, 1938. Instr. history MIT, Cambridge, 1938-41, 46; instr. bibliography Brown U., Providence, 1946-47; prof. history Findlay Coll., Ohio, 1947-51; from instr. to prof. Bridgewater State Coll. (Mass.), 1952-76, prof. emeritus of history, 1976—. Author: Scientific Societies in the U.S., 1945; contbr. articles to profl. jours. Chmn., Bridgewater Hist. Commn. (Mass.), 1976-84. Served to 1st lt. U.S. Army, 1941-45. Mem. Mass. Archaeol. Soc. (pres. 1971-73, corr. sec., 1976-84, archivist, 1982—), Old Bridgewater (Mass.) Hist. Soc. (pres. 1957-76). Republican. Mem. United Ch. Christ. Home: 42 Leonard St Bridgewater MA 02324

BATES, ROBERT ERNEST, tour company executive; b. Newcastle, New South Wales, Australia, Jan. 12, 1940; arrived in Papua New Guinea, 1964; s. Thomas and Priscilla Bamborough (Locker) B.; m. Pamela Joy Mansfield, Dec. 19, 1981; 1 child, Michael Luke. B in Engring., U. New South Wales, 1964. Engr. Pub. Works Dept., Goroka, Papua New Guinea, 1964-70, Bob Bates Pty., Ltd., Mt. Hagen, Papua New Guinea, 1970-78; mng. dir. Trans Niugini Tours, Mt. Hagen, 1978—.

BATES, SIR DAVID ROBERT, physicist; b. Omagh, No. Ireland, Nov. 18, 1916; s. Walter V. and Mary O. (Shera) B.; m. Barbara B. Morris, 1956; two children. Student, Royal Belfast Acad. Inst.; M.Sc., Queen's U., 1938; student U. Coll., London, 1938-39; D.Sc. (hon.), Ulster U., 1972, Nat. U. Ireland, 1975, U. Dublin, 1979; LL.D. (hon.), U. Glasgow, 1979, U. York, 1983, others. With admiralty Research Lab., Teddington, 1939-42; with mine design dept. H.M.S. Vernon, 1941-45; lectr. in math. Univ. Coll., London, 1945-50, reader in physics, 1951; cons. U.S. Naval Ordnance Test Sta., Inytern, Calif., 1950; prof. applied math. Queen's U., Belfast, 1951-68, prof. theoretical physics, 1968-74, spl. research chmn., 1968-82; Smithsonian Regent's fellow Ctr. for Astrophysics, Cambridge, Mass., 1982-83, research assoc. Harvard U., 1982-83. Recipient Hughes medal Royal Soc., 1970, Gold medal Royal Astronomical Soc., 1977, Chree medal Inst. Physics, 1973, Fleming medal Am. Geophysics Union, 1987. Fellow Royal Soc.; mem. Royal Irish Acad., AAAS (fgn.), Nat. Acad. Scis. U.S. (fgn. assoc.), Royal Acad. Belgium; mem. Brit. Assn. Advancement Sci. (pres. physics section 1977). Address: 1 Newforge Grange, Belfast BT9 5QB, Northern Ireland also: care Royal Society, 6 Carlton House Tce, London SW1Y 5AG, England

BATES-NISBET, (CLARA) ELISABETH, piano educator, poet, lawyer; b. Houston, Dec. 4, 1902; d. William David and Kate Broocks (Arnall) Bates. BA, U. Tex., 1938; MA, U. Houston, 1941; LLB, S. Tex. Sch. Law, 1937. Bar: Tex. 1937. Tchr. pub. schs., Houston, 1923-49; prin. Longfellow Elem. Sch., Houston, 1950-52, Mamie Sue Bastian Elem. Sch., Houston, 1952-60, James Arlie Montgomery Elem. Sch., Houston, 1960-73; tchr. piano, Houston, 1928—. Life mem. chancellor's council U. Tex., Tex. Congress Parents and Tchrs.; established John Pelham Border Meml. Fund, San Jacinto Mus. of History Assn.; founder perpeutally endowed Presdl. scholarship in law, history, govt. or music, U. Tex. at Austin; founder Kate Broocks Bates award for research in Tex. history, Tex. State Hist. Assn. and DAR, also two Kate Harding Bates Parker Award funds, Jr. Historians Orgns. of Tex. Hist. Assn., and Library of DAR; established Emma Broocks Arnall perpetually endowed Geology Scholarship Fund, U. Okla. at Norman; creator perpetual endowment Fine Arts Ctr., U. Tex. at Austin. Recipient Woman of Achievement award to be honored in the Hereditary Register of the U.S. in celebration of the Bicentennial of the Constn. of the U.S., 1987. Mem. Tex. Bar Assn. (50-year mem. award 1987), Houston Bar Assn., Tex. Tchrs. Assn. (life), Tex. Geneal. Soc., Magna Carta Dames (organizing charter mem. E. Tex. Colony, 3d vice regent courier Round Table Tex. div. 1962-66), Tex. Hist. Assn. (patron, life), Colonial Dames XVII Century (registrar Col. John Alston chpt. 1966-68, mem. nat. com. on Am. history 1966-68), Alston-Willems-Boddie-Hillard Soc. N.C., Colonial Order Crown, San Augustine County Hist. Soc. (charter), San Jacinto Descs., Daus. Republic Tex. (organizing charter mem. Ezekial Cullen chpt. 1953, co-founder perpetual endowment found. for Ezekial Cullen chpt., rec. sec. gen. 1963-65, compiler, editor anns. 1963-65, 2d v.p. gen., chmn. orgn. 1965-67, state chmn. Kate Broocks Bates Award com.), Soc. Descs. Charlemagne, DAR (Texas chpt. regent 1966-68, mem. nat. coms.), Soc. Descs. Knights of Most Noble Order of Garter, Daus. Am. Colonists (organizer charter mem. LaSalle chpt.), UDC Jefferson Davis Chpt., Sovereign Colonial Soc. Ams. Royal Descent, Plantagenet Soc., Dames of Ct. of Honor, Daus. of Founders and Patriots of Am., Freedoms. Found. Valley Forge, Internat. Platform Assn., Smithsonian Instn., Bates Family of Old Va. Assn., Jamestowne Soc. (organizing gov. First Tex. Co. 1982), Nat. Soc. Poets, Ex-Students Assn. U. Tex., Delta Kappa Gamma (life, 1st v.p. Eta Delta chpt. 1966-68). Address: 2305 Woodhead St Houston TX 77019

BATEY, PETER WILLIAM JAMES, town, regional planning educator, urban, regional analysis consultant; b. West Hartpool, Eng., Aug. 17, 1948; s. George Thomas and Ruth (Garstang) B.; m. Joyce Dover, Jan. 25, 1975; children: Rachel Alexandra, James Richard. BS, U. Sheffield, Eng., 1969; M of Civic Design, U. Liverpool, Eng., 1971, PhD, 1985. Planning officer Lancashire County Council, Preston, Eng., 1969-73; sr. planning officer Greater Manchester (Eng.) Council, 1973-75; lectr. civic design U. Liverpool, 1975-84, sr. lectr., 1984-87, reader, 1987—; cons. Littlewoods Orgn., Liverpool, 1978—; vis. research scholar geography U. Ill., Urbana, 1981-82. Editor: Town Planning Rev., 1984-87, (book series) London Papers in Regional Science, 1984—; editorial bd. Internat. Regional Sci. Rev., 1986—; contbr. articles to planning and regional sci. jours., chpts. to books. Recipient Silver Jubilee medal Hungarian Econ. Assn./Regional Sci. Assn., 1985; George A. Miller scholar, Fulbright scholar U. Ill., 1981-82. Fellow Royal Statis. Soc., Royal Town Planning Inst. (chmn. edn. bd. 1986-87); mem. Regional Sci. Assn. (sec. Brit. sect. 1975-80, internat. council 1982-85, v.p. 1988), Inst. Brit. Geographers. Anglican. Home: 4 Agnes Rd Blundellsands, Liverpool L23 6ST, England Office: U Liverpool, Civic Design Dept, Abercromby Sq, PO Box 147, Liverpool L69 3BX, England

BATLA, RAYMOND JOHN, JR., lawyer; b. Cameron, Tex., Sept. 1, 1947; s. Raymond John and Della Alvina (Jezek) B.; m. Susan Marie Clark, Oct. 1, 1983; children: Sara, Charles, Michael, Traci. BS with highest honors, U.

Tex., 1970, JD, with honors, 1973. Bar: Tex. 1973, D.C. 1973, U.S. Dist. Ct. D.C. 1974, U.S. Dist. Ct. (so. dist.) Tex. 1982, U.S. Ct. Appeals (D.C. cir.) 1974, U.S. Ct. Appeals (5th cir.) 1982, U.S. Ct. Appeals (10th cir.) 1978, U.S. Supreme Ct. 1977. Structural engr. Tex. Hwy. Dept., Austin, 1970; assoc. Hogan & Hartson, Washington, 1973-82, gen. ptnr., 1983—; dean's adv. bd. com. U. Tex. Law Sch., Austin, 1983—. Author: Petroleum Regulation Handbook, 1980; contbr. articles to profl. jours. Chmn. bd. deacons Meml. Bapt. Ch., Arlington, 1978-80; pres., bd. dirs. Randolph Sq. Condominium Assn., Arlington, 1986-87; pres. bd. dirs., Randolph Square Condominium Assn., Arlington, 1986-87. Mem. ABA (vice chmn. energy com. 1981), Fed. Energy Bar Assn., Fed. Bar. Assn., D.C. Bar Assn., State Bar Tex., U. Tex. Law Sch. Assn. (bd. dirs.), Assn. Energy Engrs., Cogoneration Inst., Order of Coif, Phi Delta Phi, Chi Epsilon, Tau Beta Pi. Episcopalian. Club: City of Wash. (founder), Nat. Lawyers. Home: 12406 Shari Hunt Grove Clifton VA 22024 Office: Hogan & Hartson 555 13th St NW Washington DC 20004

BATMONH, JAMBYN, chairman Council of Ministers of Mongolia; b. Mar. 10, 1926; ed. Mongolian State U., Acad. Social Scis. C.P.S.U. Central Com., USSR. Lectr., Mongolian State U. and Pedagogical Inst., 1951-52; lectr., vice-rector Higher Party Sch. of Mongolian People's Revolutionary Party Central Com., 1952-58; head dept., vice-rector, then rector Higher Sch. Econs., 1962-67; vice-rector, then rector Mongolian State U., 1967-73; head sci. and edn. dept. MPRP Central Com., 1973-74; dep. chmn. Council of Ministers, 1974, chmn., 1974; chmn. Presidium, People's Gt. Hural of Mongolia, 1984—; mem. Central Com., MPRP, 1976—, politburo, 1974—; dep. to People's Gt. Hural. Decorated Order of Suhbaatar. Address: Council of Ministers, Govt Palace, Ulan Bator Mongolia *

BATS, DOMINIQUE, physician; b. Alger, Algerie, Apr. 24, 1948; s. Edouard Auguste and Helene Simone (Galanides) B.; m. Michele Dupont, Apr. 20, 1972; children: Valerie, Anne-Sophie. Student, Stanislas Coll., Nice, France, 1963-67; MD, Medecine Faculty, Amiens, France, 1976. Del. Medecine Students, Amiens, 1968-70; anatomy instr. Medecine Faculty, Amiens, 1970-72, gen. practice medicine, 1976—; organizer post univ. teaching, 1987-88. Roman Catholic. Club: AAC (Amiens). Home and Office: 11 Rue Andre Chenier, 80000 Amiens France

BATT, RONALD ELMER, gynecologist; b. Buffalo, Sept. 24, 1933; s. Elmer Lawrence and Mary Catherine (Roll) B.; student Niagara U., 1951-54; M.D., U. Buffalo, 1958; m. Carol Mary Schaab, Dec. 28, 1957; children—Paula, Douglas, Thomas, Neil, Jennifer, John; m. 2d, Kathleen Over Cansdale, May 19, 1982; stepchildren—William, James, Suzanne, Timothy, John, Mark. Intern, Millard Fillmore Hosp., Buffalo, 1958-59; resident in ob-gyn SUNY, Buffalo, 1959-60, 62-66; research fellow Harvard U. Med. Sch., 1963-64; asst. in surgery Peter Bent Brigham Hosp., Boston, 1963-64; fellow in gynecologic surgery Mayo Clinic, 1965; practice medicine specializing in reproductive surgery, reproductive endocrinology, Buffalo, 1966—; clin. assoc. prof. gynecology SUNY Buffalo, co-founder Ctr. for Advanced Reproductive and Endometriosis Surgery, 1986. Served with M.C., USN, 1960-62. Fellow Royal Coll. Surgeons Can., Am. Coll. Obstetricians and Gynecologists, ACS; mem. Am. Fertility Soc., Soc. Reproductive Surgeons, Soc. Study Reproduction, Am. Assn. History Medicine, Internat. Soc. History Medicine, N.Am. Soc. for Pediatric and Adolescent Gynecology. Coauthor: The Chapel, 1979; Conservative Surgery for Endometriosis in the Infertile Couple, 1982; contbr. chpts. to books, articles to profl. jours. Office: 1000 Youngs Rd Buffalo NY 14221

BATTAGLIA, ADOLFO, Italian government official; b. Viterbo, Italy, Feb. 10, 1930; married; 4 sons. LLD. Vice leader Italian Republican Party, 1970-74; mem. Chamber Deps., 1972—; pres. parliamentary group Italian Republican Party, 1981-87; under sec. Fgn. Affairs Ministry, Rome, 1974-76, 79; minister industry Italy, Rome, 1987—. Contbr. articles to profl. jours. Address: Ministry Industry, Rome Italy *

BATTAGLIA, TIMOTHY JOSEPH, lawyer; b. Belleville, Ill., Mar. 14, 1947; s. Olis Alfred and Ann Agnes (Frey) B.; m. Dorothy Traphagen, Dec. 5, 1970; children—Nicole Ann, Bradley Joseph. BA, Cornell U., 1969, JD, 1972. Bar: 1972. Assoc. Emens, Hurd, Kegler & Ritter, Columbus, Ohio, 1972-76, ptnr., 1976—; lectr. on energy law. Mem. Energy Task Force, Ohio, 1978, Natural Gas Task Force Ohio, 1986—. Mem. Columbus Bar Assn. (profl. ethics and grievance com. 1977-81, energy com. 1979—, chmn. energy com. 1986-88), Ohio State Bar Assn. (vice chmn. natural resources law com. 1982-85, chmn. 1985-87), ABA (natural resources and pub. utility law sects. 1986—) Eastern Mineral Law Found. (trustee 1981—, chmn. ann. inst. program com. 1982-83, chmn. spl. insts. com. 1984-85, exec. com. 1985—, chmn. membership com. 1987—, v.p. 1987-88, pres. 1988—), Ohio Oil and Gas Assn.(chmn. natural gas and crude oil com. 1984-85, co-chmn. legal com. 1986—, trustee 1987—, exec. com. 1987—), Independent Petroleum Assn. Am., Ohio Gas Assn. Republican. Roman Catholic. Clubs: Athletic of Columbus (Ohio); Muirfield Village Golf (Dublin, Ohio), Swiss (Columbus, Ohio). Co-mng. editor Cornell Law Forum, 1971. Office: Capitol Square 65 E State St Columbus OH 43215

BATTAT, EMILE A., management executive; b. Mar. 17, 1938; s. Abe N. and Marguerite (Elias) B.; m. Vivian L. Masri, Apr. 12, 1964; children—Lisa, David. B.S., MIT, 1959, M.S., 1960; M.B.A., Harvard U., 1962. Mktg. analyst Standard Oil Co., N.J., N.Y.C., 1962-65; mgr. corp. diversification Kaiser Aluminum, Oakland, Calif., 1965-69, v.p., dir. Kaiser Internat., Oakland, 1969-78; pres., chief exec. officer, dir. Minemet Inc., N.Y.C., 1978—; bd. dirs. Minemet Belgium, Alatenn Resources, Inc., Ala. Tenn. Pipeline Co., Aleaciones No Ferrosas S.Am., Coalco B.V., CTC-Minemet SA. Mem. Sigma Xi, Pi Tau Sigma, Tau Beta Pi. Club: Hurlingham (London). Avocations: tennis; sailing. Office: Minemet Inc 6 Stamford Forum Stamford CT 06901

BATTEN, JAMES WILLIAM, educator; b. Goldsboro, N.C., Aug. 5, 1919; s. Albert LeMay and Lydia Annie (Davis) B.; A.B., U. N.C., 1940, M.A., 1947, Ed.D., 1960; postgrad. Columbia U., 1942; D.C.A. (hon.), U.Ariz., 1982; m. Sara Magdalene Storey, June 1, 1945. Tchr., Glendale High Sch., Kenly, N.C., 1940-41, Wilmington Jr. Coll., 1946-47; tchr., coach Princeton (N.C.) High Sch., 1947-50; prin. Micro (N.C.) High Sch., 1950-58; teaching fellow, narrator Morehead Planetarium, Chapel Hill, N.C., 1958-60; prof. edn. East Carolina U., Greenville, N.C., 1960—, chmn. dept. secondary edn., 1967-86, also asst. dean Sch. Edn. Active in civic affairs. Served to lt. comdr. USNR, 1941-46. Mem. NEA, N.C. Assn. Educators (chpt. pres. 1961-62), Nat. Sci. Tchrs. Assn., Assn. for Supervision and Curriculum Devel., Phi Delta Kappa (pres. 1961-62), Horace Mann League (pres. 1975-77), Nat. Soc. Study of Edn., Am. Ednl. Research Assn., N.C. Lit. and History Assn., Kappa Delta Pi (counselor 1967-74). Democrat. Baptist (deacon). Lion (pres. 1949-51). Author: Our Neighbors in Space, 1962, rev. edit., 1969; Research as a Tool for Understanding, 1965; Stars, Atoms, and God, 1968; (with J. Sullivan Gibson) Soils, 1970, rev. edit., 1977; Understanding Research, 1970, rev. edit., 1972; Human Perspectives in Educational Research, 1973; Rumblings of a Rolling Stone, 1974; Procedures in Educational Research, 1975, rev. edit., 1978; Developing Competencies in Educational Research, 1981; Research in Education, 1984, rev. edit., 1986, The Batten Clan in Johnston County, N.C., 1987; contbr. numerous articles to profl. jours.

BATTIN, (ROSABELL HARRIET) RAY, neuropsychologist, audiologist; b. Rock Creek, Ohio; d. Harry Walter and Sophia (Boldt) Ray; A.B., U. Denver, 1948; M.S., U. Mich., 1950; Ph.D., U. Fla., 1959; postgrad. U. Miami (Fla.) Sch. of Medicine, 1957, U. Iowa, 1958; m. Tom C. Battin, Aug. 24, 1949. Instr. in speech pathology U. Denver, 1949-50; audiologist Ann Arbor (Mich.) Sch., 1950-51; audiologist Houston (Tex.) Speech and Hearing Center, 1954-56; dir. speech pathology-psychology Hedgecroft Hosp. and Rehab. Center, Houston, 1956-59; audiologist with Drs. Guilford, Wright and Draper, Houston, 1959-63; pvt. practice in psychology, audiology and psycholinguistics, Houston, 1959—; clin. instr. dept. otolaryngology U. Tex. Sch. Medicine, Galveston, 1964-80; dir. of audiology vestibulography and speech pathology lab. Houston Ear Nose and Throat Hosp. Clinic, 1963-73; adj. clin. instr. U. Houston, 1981—; lectr. The First Word program Sta. KUHT-TV, 1959; guest lectr. to various workshops and schs., 1959—; v.p. Behavioral Perceptual Ctr., 1986—. Bd. dirs. Juvenile Ct. Vols., 1980-83, Children's Resource and Info. Ctr., 1981-85, Dyslexic Adult Support Services, 1986—. Lic. psychologist, Tex. Recipient Gold award for Ednl. Exhibit, Am. Acad. Pediatrics, 1969. Fellow Am. Speech and Hearing Assn. (profl. services bd. 1967-70, com. on pvt. practice 1971-74), World Acad. Inc.; mem. Acad. Pvt. Practice in Speech Pathology and Audiology (pres. 1968-70), Am. Psychol. Assn., Tex. Speech and Hearing Assn. (v.p. 1968), Cleft Palate Assn., Tex., Houston psychol. assns., Harris County Biofeedback Soc. (pres. 1984), Acad. of Aphasia, Internat. Assn. of Logopedics and Phoniatrics, Am. Auditory Soc., Orthopsychiat. Assn., Am. Biofeedback Soc., Tex. Biofeedback Soc., Sigma Alpha Eta. Author: (with C. Olaf Haug) Speech and Language Delay, 1964; Vestibulography, 1974; Private Practice: Guidelines for Speech Pathology and Audiology, 1971; editor (with Donna R. Fox) Private Practice in Audiology and Speech and Language Pathology, 1978; contbr. author: Seminars in Speech, Language, Hearing (Northern); Auditory Disorders in School Children (Roeser and Downs); Current Therapy of Communications Disorder (Perkins); editor Jour. Acad. Pvt. Practice in Speech Pathology and Audiology, 1981-84; contbr. articles in field to profl. jours.; author (with Irvin A. Kraft) The Dysynchronous Child (film), 1971; The Battin Clinic Language Learning Screening Test for Preschool Children, 1985., The Battin Scale of Parent's Attitude Toward Family Experience and Need for Child Cochlear Implant Candidates. Home: 3837 Meadow Lake Ln Houston TX 77027 Office: Battin Clinic 3931 Essex Ln Houston TX 77027

BATTISTA, GIAMPIERO, engineering and construction company executive; b. Piacenza, Italy, Feb. 15, 1942; s. Saverio and Santina (Gobbi) B.; m. Anna Monno, Sept. 11, 1971; children—Carlo Alberto, Eleonora, Edoardo, Isadora. Student in econ. scis. U. Parma (Italy), Syrs.; degree in Econ. Scis., Northwest London U.; M.B.A. (hon.), Columbia Pacific U., 1983. Gen. mgr. Agind S.P.A., Piacenza, Italy, 1971-77; pres. Cisic SRL, Piacenza, 1977—, Cisic Ambiente SRL, Piacenza, 1978—, Sais Group, Rome, 1979—; gen. proxy SBS Cons. Co., Munich, FAO expert agro-indsl. problems in Third World. Hon. consul Ecuador, Bologna, Italy, 1974, hon. consul-gen. Ecuador, 1976; mem. council Sovereign Order of New Aragon, 1982, grand commr., 1982; acad. mem. Accademie delle Scienze e delle Arti degli Ardenti di Viterbo; Knight Order of Santi Maurizio e Lazzaro, Knight of Crown of Italy, Knight-High Officer of Crown of Italy. Mem. C. of C. for African Countries in Rome (bd. dirs. 1979—), Centro Azione Latina (bd. dirs. 1982). Home: Via Papa Giovanni XXIII, Quarto Di Gossolengo PC 29020 Italy

BATTISTINI-MOORE, GERMÁN, pathologist; b. Contamana, Peru, Dec. 16, 1916; s. Ulises Cabrera and Consuelo Maldonado (Moore) B.; m. Bargarita Scagnetti Blaser; children: Martha, Ana, Hedy. Bachelor's degree, U. Nacionales San Marcos, Peru, 1943, MB, BChir, 1944; degree in microbiology, Inst. Nacionales Salud, Peru, 1945; degree in clin. pathology, Colegio Médico, Peru, 1977. Asst. in blood vaccination Inst. Salud Pub., Peru, 1945-49, asst. in investigative medicine, 1949-59, chief spl. programs, 1960-61, chief div. diagnostic investigation, 1962-74; chief vaccination investigation Inst. Sanitas Sp., Peru, 1950-86; sci. assessor div. gen. Inst. Nacionales Salud, 1975, dir. coordination, 1975, dir. gen., 1979-85; cons. Inst. Sanitas S.P., Lima, Peru, 1944-88. Recipient Gold medal Municipality of Lima, 1946, Hipolito Unanue Ministry of Edn., 1952. Mem. Soc. Peruana Patologia, Assn. Peruana Microbiologia, Soc. Peruana Immunopatologia and Alergia, Colegio Med. Peru. Lodge: Lions. Home: Genaro Castro Iglesias, 429, Miraflores Peru

BATTLE, ALLEN OVERTON, JR., educator, psychologist; b. Memphis, Nov. 19, 1927; s. Allen Overton and Florence Louise (Castelvecchi) B.; m. Mary Madeline Vroman, June 14, 1952; 1 son, Allen Overton, III. B.S., Siena Coll., 1949; M.A., Cath. U. Am., 1953, Ph.D., 1961; certificate in clin. psychology, U. Tenn. Coll. Medicine, 1953. Diplomate: in clin. psychology Am. Bd. Profl. Psychology, 1971. Instr. dept. psychiatry U. Tenn. Coll. Medicine, 1956-61, asst. prof., 1961-67, asso. prof., 1966-72, prof., 1972—; chief clin. psychologist U. Tenn. Mental Health Center, 1971-78, chief div. clin. psychology, 1974—; vis. lectr. Southwestern U. at Memphis, 1962-84; vis. prof. Rhodes Coll., 1984—. Author: Clinical Psychology for Physical Therapists, 1975, Suicide and Crisis Intervention Training Manuals, 1978, The Psychology of Patient Care: A Humanistic Approach, 1979; contbr. articles to profl. jours. Cons. USPHS, Suicide and Crisis Intervention Service; mem. Mayor's Commn. on Alcohol and Drug Abuse, 1974-77; Bd. dirs. Runaway House, St. Peter's Home for Children, De Neuville Heights Sch. Recipient Disting. Service award Tenn. Dept. Mental Health, 1971. Mem. Am., Tenn. psychol. assns., Am. Anthrop. Assn., N.Y. Acad. Sci., AAAS, Brit. Soc. Projective Techniques, Sigma Xi. Home: 2220 Washington Ave Memphis TN 38104 Office: 66 N Pauline St Memphis TN 38105

BATTLE, JEAN ALLEN, writer, educator; b. Talladega, Ala., June 15, 1914; s. William Raines and Lemerle McLemore (Allen) B.; m. Lucy Troxell, Aug. 25, 1940; 1 dau., Helen Carol Battle Salmon. Student, Birmingham So. Coll., 1932-33; B.S., Middle Tenn. State U., 1937; M.A., U. Ala., 1941; Ed.D., U. Fla., 1952; postgrad., Oxford U., 1980. Dept. chmn., dean students Fla. So. Coll., 1940-55, dean coll., 1956-59; dean Coll. Edn. U. South Fla., Tampa, 1959-71; prof. higher edn. U. South Fla., 1971; guest lectr. Rewley House, Oxford U., 1981; editor, pub. Tenn. Valley News.; Mem. Fla. Tchrs. Edn. Adv. Council, Fla. Continuing Edn. Council; mem. courses study com. Fla. Bd. Edn.; mem. Tampa Bay Com. on Fgn. Affairs; adv. com. Hillsborough County Hosp.; bd. dirs. Fla. Univ. System Honduras Program, World Trade Council, Tampa, Poynter Found., St. Petersburg, Fla., Harold Benjamin Found., U. Md.; bd. dirs., v.p. Southeastern Edn. Lab., Atlanta. Author: Culture and Education for the Contemporary World, 1969, (with others) The New Idea in Education, 1974, Choices for an Intelligent and Humane School and Society, 1981, Education: The Fate of Humanity, 1982, rev., 1983; Contbr. papers to tech. lit. Served to capt. USAAF, 1942-46. Recipient Disting. Service awards Fla. So. Coll., 1952, Disting. Service awards Fla. Citizenship Clearing House, 1957; Outstanding Alumnus award Middle Tenn. State U. Mem. SAR, Fla. Hist. Soc., NEA, Fla. Edn. Assn. (co-chmn. tchr. recruitment com.), Tampa C. of C. (edn. com.), Acad. Polit. Sci., Omicron Delta Kappa, Pi Gamma Mu, Kappa Delta Pi, Phi Delta Kappa, Sigma Alpha Epsilon. Methodist. Club: Carrollwood Village Golf and Tennis. Lodge: Rotary. Home: 11011 Carrollwood Dr Tampa FL 33618 Office: U South Fla Fowler Ave Tampa FL 33620

BATTLE, KATHLEEN DEANNA, soprano; b. Portsmouth, Ohio; d. Grady and Ollie (Layne) B. MusB, U. Cin., MusM, D of Performing Arts (hon.), 1983; D of Performing Arts (hon.), Westminster Choir Coll., Ohio U. Appeared with Met. Opera, San Fransisco Opera, Chgo. Opera, Salzburg Festival, N.Y. Philharm., Boston Symphony, Phila. Orch., Chgo. Symphony, Berlin Philharm., Vienna Staatsoper, Paris Opera, Royal Opera/Covent Garden, others; roles include Semele, Cleopatra in Julius Caesar, Pamina in Magic Flute, Rosina in Barber of Seville, Adina in Elixir of Love, Sophie in Der Rosenkavalier, Zerlina in Don Giovanni, Zdenka in Arabella, Zerbinetta in Ariadne Auf Naxos, Susanna in The Marriage of Figaro. Recipient Grammy awards, 1987, 88. Mem. Delta Omicron. Methodist. Office: care Columbia Artist Mgmt Inc 165 W 57th St New York NY 10019

BATTLE, LUCY TROXELL (MRS. J.A. BATTLE), educator; b. Bridgeport, Ala., June 28, 1916; d. John Price and Emily Florence (Williams) Troxell; student U. Ala., Montevallo, 1934-35; B.S. Fla. So. Coll., 1951; postgrad. U. Fla., 1954, Fla. State U., 1963, Oxford (Eng.) U., 1979, 80, 81; M.A., U. South Fla., 1970; m. Jean Allen Battle, Aug. 25, 1940; 1 dau., Helen Carol. Asst. postmaster, Bridgeport, Ala., 1936-40; asst. dir. personnel office Sebring (Fla.) AFB, 1942-44; tchr. Cleveland Court Sch., Lakeland, Fla., also Forest Hill Sch., Carrollwood Sch., Tampa, Fla., 1949-64; dean of girls Greco Jr. High Sch., Tampa, 1964-68. Bd. dirs. Tampa Oral Sch. for Deaf. Recipient Outstanding Service award Fla. So. Coll. Woman's Club, 1942. Mem. NEA, Am. Childhood Edn. Internat., AAUW, Delta Kappa Gamma, Kappa Delta Pi, Phi Mu. Methodist. Club: Carrollwood Village Golf and Tennis. Author: (with J.A. Battle) The New Idea in Education, 1968. Home and Office: 11011 Carrollwood Dr Tampa FL 33618

BATTLE, TURNER CHARLES, III, educator, executive; b. Oberlin, Ohio, Mar. 13, 1926; s. Turner and Annie (McClellan) B.; student Andrews U., 1944-45; B.A., Oakwood Coll., 1950; postgrad. Wagner Inst. Sci., 1953-54, Cheyney State Coll., 1957-58, Sch. Edn., Temple U., 1959-60, Tchrs. Coll., Columbia U., 1960, NYU, 1970-78 ; M.F.A., Tyler Sch. Art, Temple U., 1958; HHD Wiley Coll, 1986; m. Carmen Helena Gonzalez Castellanos; children—Yvonne Conchita, Carmen Rosario, Anne E. McAndrew, Turner C. IV. Exhibited in group shows eastern U.S., including Bucknell U., Phila. Art Alliance, Newport (R.I.) Art Assn., Phila. Mus. Art, Susquehanna U., Atlantic City Boardwalk Show, shows Greenwich Village, N.Y.C., and many others; represented in pvt. collections throughout U.S., India, Eng., Africa, Japan; instr. art Oakwood Coll., Huntsville, Ala., 1946-50; auditor, acct. Navy Regional Accountants Office, 1950-55; instr. art, Phila., 1955-66; head Sch. Gifted Children, Phila., 1959-66; asst. prof. art Elmira (N.Y.) Coll., 1966-68; asso. prof. art Moore Coll. Art, Phila., 1968-70; vis. asso. prof. N.Y.U., 1970, teaching fellow, 1971-72; vis. asso. prof., also dir. program Westminster Choir Coll., 1971-74; art cons., lectr. pvt. and pub. orgns., 1958—. Exec. dir. Higher Edn. Coalition Southeastern Pa., 1969-71; dir. Open Door Program, LaSalle Coll., 1969-70; edn. cons. community planners group U.S. Office Edn., 1969-70; asst. exec. dir., sec. of corp. United Negro Coll. Fund, N.Y.C., 1974—. Mem. Am. Assn. Higher Edn., Tyler Sch. Temple U. Alumni Assn. (pres. 1965-66), Am. Soc. Assn. Execs., Sierra Club, Am. Mus. Nat. History, Smithsonian Inst., Phi Delta Kappa. Office: 500 E 62d St New York NY 10021

BATTS, WARREN LEIGHTON, diversified industry executive; b. Norfolk, Va., Sept. 4, 1932; s. John Leighton and Allie Belle (Johnson) B.; m. Eloise Pitts, Dec. 24, 1957; 1 dau., Terri Allison. B.E.E., Ga. Inst. Tech., 1961; M.B.A., Harvard U., 1963. With Kendall Co., Charlotte, N.C., 1963-64; exec. v.p. Fashion Devel. Co., Santa Paula, Calif., 1964-66; dir. mfg. Olga Co., Van Nuys, Calif., 1964-66; v.p. Douglas Williams Assocs., N.Y.C., 1966-67; co-founder Triangle Corp., Orangeburg, S.C., 1967; pres., chief exec. officer Triangle Corp., 1967-71; v.p. Mead Corp., Dayton, Ohio, 1971-73; pres. Mead Corp., 1973-80, chief exec. officer, 1978-80; pres., chief operating officer Dart Industries, Inc., Los Angeles, 1980-81, Dart & Kraft, Inc., Northbrook, Ill., 1981-86; chmn., chief exec. officer Premark Internat. Inc., Deerfield, 1986—. Trustee Am. Enterprise Inst., 1980—, Art Inst. Chgo., 1983—, Children's Meml. Hosp., Chgo., 1984—, Chgo. Symphony Orch., 1986—. Office: Premark Internat Inc 1717 Deerfield Ave Deerfield IL 60015

BAUCUS, MAX S., U.S. Senator; b. Helena, Mont., Dec. 11, 1941; s. John and Jean (Sheriff) B.; m. Wanda Minge, Apr. 23, 1983. BA, Stanford U., 1964, LLB, 1967. Bar: D.C. 1969, Mont. 1972. Staff atty. CAB, Washington, 1967-69; lawyer SEC, Washington, 1969-71; legal asst. to chmn. SEC, 1970-71; sole practice Missoula, Mont., 1971-74; mem. Mont. Ho. of Reps., 1973-74; mem. 94th-95th congresses from 1st Dist. Mont., 1975-79, mem. com. appropriations; U.S. senator from Mont. 1979—; acting exec. dir., com. coordinator Mont. Constl. Conv., 1972. Home: Missoula MT 59801 Office: Senate Office Bldg 706 Hart Washington DC 20510 *

BAUD, CLAUDE RENE, cardiologist; b. Thonon les Bains, France, June 18, 1946; s. Marius and Paulette (Glaume) B. Baccalaureat, Inst. St. Joseph, Thonon, 1962; M.D., U. Clermont-Fd., 1970. Intern, U. Clermont-Fd. Hosp. (France), 1970, chef de clinique, 1975, asst. hosp., 1975; adj. prof. medicine Laval U., Quebec, Que., Can., 1978; practice medicine specializing in invasive cardiology, Douai, France, 1979—. Co-author book, 1972. Active Inuit art market. Served to capt. M.C., French Army, 1970. Mem. Can. Soc. Cardiology, N.Y. Acad. Scis., French Soc. Cardiology (assoc.). Roman Catholic. Office: Clinique de Bois-Bernard, 62320 Rouvroy France

BAUDO, SERGE, conductor; b. Marseille, France, July 16, 1927; s. Etienne and Genevieve (Tortelier) B.; student Conservatory of Paris; m. Madelein Reties, June 16, 1947; children—Stephane, Catherine. Music dir. Radio Nice, Fance, 1957-59; condr. Paris Opera Orch., 1962-66; titular condr., interim orch. dir. Paris Orch., 1968-70; music dir. Opera de Lyon, 1969-71; music dir. Orch. of Lyon, 1971—; condr. many internat. orchs. including Tonhalle Orch., Zurich, Orchestre de la Suisse Romande, Berlin Symphony, La Scala, Met. Opera, Dallas Orch., Deutsche Oper Berlin; founder Berlioz Fistival, Lyon, 1979—. Decorated chevalier Ordre National du Merite; officer des Arts et des Lettres; recipient Grand Prix du Disque, 1976. Address: Orch Nat de Lyon, 82 rue de Bonnel, 69003 Lyon France *

BAUDOUIN, HIS MAJESTY (BAUDOUIN ALBERT CHARLES LEOPOLD AXEL MARIE GUSTAVE), I, King of Belgium; b. Brussels, Sept. 7, 1930; s. King Leopold III and Queen Astrid, Princess of Sweden; m. Dona Fabiola Mora y Aragon, Dec. 15, 1960. During invasion of Belgium by Germany, 1940, went to France, later to Spain, returning to Belgium, 1940; was removed to Germany, 1944; liberated after Allied invasion of Normandy; May 1945; lived in Switzerland until Leopold returned to Belgium as king, 1950; Prince Royal, Aug. 1950; held office as Chief of State until accession to throne; became king upon abdication of King Leopold, July 1951. Address: Royal Palace, Brussels Belgium *

BAUDUSCH, RENATE, Germanist; b. Erfurt, Germany, June 4, 1929; d. Arthur and Margarethe (Kahle) Walker; m. Heinz Baudusch, Nov. 26, 1957; 1 child, Sondra. PhD, Humboldt U., Berlin, 1956; DSc, Humboldt U., 1970. Germanist Akademie der Wissenschaften, Berlin, 1956—. Author: Klopstock als Sprachwissenschaftler, 1958, Die nominalen Kategorien in der dänischen Grammatik, 1970, Punkt, Punkt, Komma, Strich, 1984. Mem. Goethe Gesellschaft, Internationale Vereinigung für germanische Sprach- und Literaturwissenschaft. Evangelisch. Home: Moldaustrasse 11, 1136 Berlin German Democratic Republic Office: Akademie der Wissenschaften, Prenzlauer Promenade 149-152, 1100 Berlin German Democratic Republic

BAUER, A(UGUST) ROBERT, JR., surgeon; b. Phila., Dec. 23, 1928; s. A(ugust) Robert and Jessie Martha-Maynard (Monie) B.; B.S., U. Mich., 1949, M.S., 1950, M.D., 1954; M. Med. Sci.-Surgery, Ohio State U., 1960; m. Charmaine Louise Studer, June 28, 1957; children—Robert, John, William, Anne, Charles, James. Intern Walter Reed Army Med. Center, 1954-55; resident in surgery Univ. Hosp., Ohio State U., Columbus, also instr., 1957-61; individual practice medicine, specializing in surgery, Mt. Pleasant, Mich., 1962-74; chief surgery Central Mich. Community Hosp., Mt. Pleasant, 1964-65, vice chief of staff, 1967, chief of staff, 1968; clin. faculty Mich. State Med. Sch., East Lansing, 1974; mem. staff St. Mark's Hosp., Salt Lake City, 1974—; individual practice surgery, Salt Lake City, 1974—; clin. instr. surgery U. Utah, 1975—. Trustee, Rowland Hall, St. Mark's Sch., Salt Lake City, 1978-84; mem. Utah Health Planning Council, 1979-81. Served with M.C., U.S. Army, 1954-57. Diplomate Am. Bd. Surgery. Fellow ACS, Southwestern Surg. Congress; mem. AMA, Salt Lake County Med. Soc., Utah Med. Assn. (various coms.), Utah Soc. Certified Surgeons, Salt Lake Surg. Soc., Royal Soc. Medicine (affiliate), Pan Am. Med. Assn. (affiliate), AAAS (affiliate), Sigma Phi Epsilon, Phi Rho Sigma. Episcopalian. Club: Zollinger. Contbr. articles to profl. publs., researcher surg. immunology. Office: PO Box 17533 Salt Lake City UT 84117

BAUER, EDWARD EWING, management consultant; b. Moline, Ill., Dec. 18, 1917; s. Harry E. and Elma (Ewing) B.; B.S., U. Wis., 1939; M.S., U. Pa., 1945; LL.B., LaSalle U., 1954; m. Margaret Lamont McConnell, May 17, 1941; children—Annette Louise Bauer Tucker, Barbara Ann Bauer Erickson, Cheryl Ewing Bauer Rowder. Application engr. Gen. Electric Co., Pitts., 1939-45, gen. mgr., 1952-59; sales mgr. Food Machinery Corp., Chgo., 1945-50; sales mgr. Heyl & Patterson, Pitts., 1950-52; v.p., gen. mgr. Aerovox Co., New Bedford, Mass., 1959-63; became v.p. mfg. LeTourneau Westinghouse, Peoria, 1963, later v.p. mktg. Constrn. Equipment div. Westinghouse Air Brake Co.; v.p., dir. Wabco Distbg. Co.; group v.p. constrn. and mining equipment A-T-O Inc., Willoughby, Ohio; v.p., gen. mgr. hard rock mining div. Joy Mfg. Co., Denver, 1976-83; mgmt. cons., 1983; dir. Consol. Techs. Registered profl. engr., S.C. Mem. Soc. Automotive Engrs., Am. Mgmt. Assn., Am. Inst. Mining Engrs. Lutheran. Clubs: Columbine Country, Cactus, N.Y. Mining. Home: 4505 S Yosemite Stoney Brook Denver CO 80237

BAUER, FRANCES BRAND, research scientist; b. N.Y.C., July 5, 1923; d. Benjamin and Gussie (Fuchs) Brand; A.B., Bklyn. Coll., 1943; M.S., Brown U., 1945, Ph.D. in Applied Math., 1948; m. Louis Bauer, Oct. 1, 1948 (dec. 1978). Research asso. applied math. Brown U., 1945-48; research asso. aero. engring. structures Poly. Inst. Bklyn., 1949-50; sr. mathematician Reeves Instrument, N.Y.C., 1950-51, 52-61; sr. research scientist elasticity, fluid dynamics and computing Courant Inst. Math. Scis., N.Y. U., 1961—; mathematician Bur. Standards, 1951-52. Recipient Pub. Service award NASA, 1976, certificate recognition, 1977, 80; Rockefeller Found. fellow, 1945. Mem. Math. Soc., Assn. Computing Machinery, Sigma Xi. Democrat. Jewish. Club: Zonta (treas.) (N.Y.C.). Co-author: Supercritical Wing Sections I, 1972, Sections II, 1975, Sections III, 1977, A Computational Method in

Plasma Physics, 1978, Magnetohydrodynamic Equilibrium and Stability of Stellarators, 1984, The BETA Equilibrium, Stability and Transport Codes, 1987. Home: 200 East End Ave New York NY 10128 Office: Courant Inst 251 Mercer St New York NY 10012

BAUER, FRIEDRICH LUDWIG, mathematician, educator; b. Regensburg, Bavaria, Fed. Republic of Germany, June 10, 1924; s. Ludwig and Elisabeth (Scheuermayer) B.; m. Irene Maria Theresia Laimer, June 15, 1949 (dec. Aug. 1973); m. Hildegard Vogg, Mar. 16, 1974; children: Gertrud Josefine, Martin Alston, Margret Elisabeth, Ulrich Alexander, Bernhard Klaus. PhD, U. Munich, 1952, DSc, 1954; DSc (hon.), Grenoble (France) U., 1974. Tchg. asst. Tech. U. Munich, 1952-54, lectr., 1954-58, prof. math., 1963-72, prof. math. and computer sci., 1972—; prof. applied math. Mainz (Fed. Republic of Germany) U., 1958-62; co-dir. Leibniz Computing Ctr., Munich, 1968—. Contbr. articles to profl. jours. Served as 2d lt. German Army, 1943-45. Awarded Bavarian Order of Merit, 1971, Wilhelm Exner medal Republic of Austria, 1978, Fed. Cross of Merits, Fed. Republic of Germany, 1982, Goldener Ehrenring des Deutschen Mus., 1988, IEEE Pioneer award, 1988. Mem. Bavarian Acad. of Sci., Deutsche Akademie der Naturforscher Leopoldina, Bayerischer Maximiliansorden für Wissenschaft. Roman Catholic. Home: Villenstrasse 19, D-8081 Kottgeisering Federal Republic of Germany

BAUER, GASTON EGON, cardiologist; b. Vienna, Austria, May 7, 1923; m. Phyllis Smith, Jan. 7, 1949; children: Christopher, Michael, Timothy. MB, BS, U. Sydney, Australia, 1946. Hon. physician Sydney Hosp., 1956-76; hon. cons. physician Hornsby and Kuringai Hosp., Australia, 1964-81, Manly Dist. Hosp., Australia, 1964-88; hon. physician in cardiology Royal North Shore Hosp., St. Leonard's, Australia, 1976—; warden of clin. sch. Royal North Shore Hosp., Australia, 1979-85. Contbr. articles to profl. jours., chpts. to med. books. Fellow of senate U. Sydney, 1982—. Recipient univ. medal and Arthur E. Mills grad. prize U. Sydney, 1946, Archie Telfer prize Sydney Hospitallers, 1963. Mem. Royal Coll. Physicians (London), Royal Australian Coll. Physicians (councillor 1975-81), Am. Coll. Cardiology; mem. Cardiac Soc. Australia and N.Z., Australian Med. Assn., Royal Soc. Med. London (corr.), Order of Australia. Home: 115 Shirley Rd, 2069 Roseville, New South Wales Australia

BAUER, JEROME LEO, JR., chemical engineer; b. Pitts., Oct. 12, 1938; s. Jerome L. and Anna Mae (Tucker) B.; divorced; children: Lori, Trish, Jeff. BSChemE, U. Dayton, 1960; MSChemE, Pa. State U., 1963; postgrad., Ohio State U., 1969. Registered profl. engr., Ohio. Asst. prof. chem. engring. U. Dayton, Ohio, 1963-67; mgr. advanced composites dept. Ferro Corp., Cleve., 1967-72; engring. material and process specifications mgr. Lockheed Missiles & Space Co., Inc., Sunnyvale, Calif., 1972-74; gen. dynamics design specialist Convair Div., San Diego, 1974-76, project devel. engr., 1976-77; dir. research Furane div. M&T Chems. Inc., Glendale, Calif., 1980-82; mem. tech. staff Jet Propulsion Lab., Calif. Inst. Tech., Pasadena, Calif., 1977-80, 82—. Editor: Materials Sciences for Future, 1986; contbr. articles to profl. jours. Jr. warden St. Luke Episcopal Ch., La Crescenta, Calif., 1980, sr. warden 1981. Mem. Am. Inst. Chem. Engrs. (founder, chmn. Dayton sect. 1964-66, spl. projects chmn. Cleve. sect. 1968-69), Soc. Advancement of Material Process Engring. (membership chmn. no. Calif. sect. 1973-74, sec. San Diego sect. 1974-75, vice chmn. 1975-76, chmn. 1976, chmn. Los Angeles sect. 1977, nat. treas. 1978-82, gen. chmn. 31st internat. symposium exhibition, Las Vegas, Nev., 1986, Meritorious Achievement award 1983, internat. v.p. 1987—), Internat. Electronics Packaging Soc. (pres. Los Angeles chpt. 1982), Phi Lambda Upsilon, Delta Sigma Epsilon. Republican. Home: 1935 E Alpha 205 Glendale CA 91208 Office: Jet Propulsion Lab Calif Inst Tech 4800 Oak Grove Dr Pasadena CA 91109

BAUER, NANCY MCNAMARA, television and radio network executive; b. Madison, Wis., Mar. 17, 1929; d. Richard Hughes and Lucy Jane (Whitaker) Marshall; B.A., U. Wis., 1950, M.S., 1963; m. J.B. McNamara, Dec. 29, 1952 (div. Mar. 1962); children—Margaret Ann, William Patrick; m. 2d, Helmut Robert Bauer, Mar. 4, 1974. Elem. tchr., Madison, 1963-66; specialist ednl. communications U. Wis., Madison, 1966-71, asst. prof., 1971-72; dir. educative services Ednl. Communications Bd., Wis. Ednl. TV and Radio Networks, Madison, 1972—; dir. Central Ednl. Network, 1973-80, 83—, exec. com., 1973-74, chmn. Instructional TV Council, 1977-79; adv. bd. Instructional TV Coop., 1972-75, exec. com., 1976-77; mem. instrnl. radio adv. com. Nat. Public Radio, 1979-82; mem. instructional TV adv. com. Public Broadcasting System, 1978-79, service com., 1980-83; mem ITV Study com. Corp. for Pub. Broadcasting, 1983-85. Ford Found. scholar, 1961-63; recipient Ohio State award, 1975, ABA Gavel award, 1975, Am. Legion Golden Mike award, 1976. Mem. Nat. Assn. Ednl. Broadcasters. Producer, writer numerous instructional series, as nationally distributed Patterns in Arithmetic and Looking Out Is In, TV, 1967, Inquiry: The Justice Thing, radio, 1973. Home: 127 Kensington Dr Madison WI 53704 Office: 3319 W Beltline Hwy Madison WI 53713

BAUER, RANDY MARK, mgmt. tng. firm exec.; b. Cleve., Sept. 2, 1946; s. Ralph I. and Gloria P. Bauer; B.S. summa cum laude, Ohio State U., 1968; M.B.A., Kent State U., 1971; m. Sue Dellva, July 4, 1975; children—Sherri, Kevin. Mgmt. auditor Peat Marwick Mitchell & Co., Cleve., 1971-72; mgmt. devel. specialist GAO, Denver, 1972-80; adj. prof. mgmt. Columbia Coll., Denver, 1979—; pres. Leadership Tng. Assos., Denver, 1979—; condr. exec. devel. workshops U. Colo., Denver, 1979—. Recipient Best in 1976 award GAO. Mem. Am. Soc. for Tng. and Devel., Beta Gamma Sigma. Address: 16275 E Crestline Pl Aurora CO 80015

BAUER, RAYMOND GALE, manufacturers representative; b. Merchantville, N.J., June 19, 1934; s. Robert Irwin and Florence Winifred (Guyer) B.; A.A., Monmouth Coll., West Long Branch, N.J., 1955; B.B.A., U. Miami, 1958; m. Jayne Whitehead, Feb. 15, 1955; 1 dau., Linda Joan. Div. mgr. R.J. Reynolds Tobacco Co., Winston-Salem, N.C., 1959-68; Middle Atlantic mgr. U.S. Envelope Co., Springfield, Mass., 1968-74; div. sales mgr. Eastern Tablet Corp., Albany, N.Y., 1974-75; owner Ray Bauer Assos., mfrs. reps., Haddonfield, N.J., 1975—. Served with USAFR, 1959-64; officer Air Force Aux. Mem. Friends of Haddonfield (N.J.) Library, Haddonfield Civic Assn., Smithsonian Assos., Monmouth Coll., U. Miami alumni assns., Nat. Philatelic Soc., Am. Security Council, Air Force Assn., Am. Conservative Union, Am. Mgmt. Assn., Internat. Platform Assn., Lambda Sigma Tau, Lambda Chi Alpha. Clubs: Republican (Haddonfield), U.S. Senatorial, Arrowhead Racquet, Iron Rock Swim and Country. Home and Office: 132 Maple Ave Haddonfield NJ 08033

BAUGH, JOHN FRANK, wholesale company executive; b. Waco, Tex., Feb. 28, 1916; s. John Frank and Nell (Turner) B.; m. Eula Mae Tharp, Oct. 3, 1936; 1 child, Barbara (Mrs. Robert L. Morrison). Student, U. Houston, 1934-36. With A & P Food Stores, Houston, 1932-46; owner, operator Zero Foods Co., Houston, 1946-69; chmn. bd. Sysco Corp., Houston, 1969-85, sr. chmn. bd., 1986—; adv. dir. 1st City Nat. Bank of Houston; bd. dirs. Bank of Houston. Bd. dirs. Baptist Found. Tex.; founding trustee Houston Bapt. U.; chmn. deacons Bapt. Ch., Houston, 1954-55, chmn. bd. trustees, 1966-86; trustee Baylor U. Clubs: University, Petroleum, Lakeside Country (Houston); Quail Creek Country (San Marcos). Lodge: Rotary. Office: Sysco Corp 1390 Enclave Pkwy Houston TX 77077

BAUGH, L. DARRELL, financial executive; b. Prairie Grove, Ark., Oct. 7, 1930; s. Lacey D. and Mary Grace (Brown) B.; BBA, U. Ark., 1954; MBA, U. Colo., 1960; CLU, Am. Coll., 1967, chartered fin. cons., 1983; m. Wileeta Claire Gray, June 15, 1958; children: Adrienne Leigh Calvo, John Grayson. With Penn Mut. Life Ins. Co., 1961-71, gen. agt., Sacramento, 1968-71; pres. Nat. Estate Planning Inst., Boulder, Colo., 1974—; bd. dirs. Sunshower Acres Ltd; faculty estate planning seminars Colo. State U.; cons. U. Colo. Center for Confs. Mgmt./Tech. Programs, 1975-80; sponsor ednl. programs for profl. estate planners and estate owners. Bd. dirs. Stronghold Youth Found. Served with U.S. Army, 1954-56. Mem. Boulder C. of C., Am. Soc. C.L.U.s, Rocky Mountain C.L.U.s (chmn. grad. studies programs), Boulder County Estate Planning Council (pres. 1972-73), Sacramento Estate Planning Council, Nat. Registry Fin. Planners (interview com.), Am. Soc. Agrl. Cons. (cert.). Contbr. articles to profl. jours. Club: Flatirons Country. Home: 92 Caballo Ct Boulder CO 80303 Office: 75 Manhattan Dr Boulder CO 80303

BAUGHMAN, GEORGE WASHINGTON, III, university official, fin. cons.; b. Pitts., July 7, 1937; s. George W. and Cecile M. (Lytel) B.; m. Sandra Ann Johnson, June 21, 1987; 1 child, Lynn. B.S. in Psychology, Ohio State U., 1959, M.B.A., 1961, postgrad., 1961-63; Pres., Advanced Research Assos., Worthington, Ohio, 1960—; asst. instr. fin. Ohio State U., Columbus, 1961-63, research asso., office of controller, 1964-66, dir. data processing, 1966-68, 70-72, dir. adminstrv. research, 1966-72, asso. to acad. v.p., 1968-70, exec. dir. univ. budget, 1970-72, dir. spl. projects, office of pres., 1972—; chmn. bd. Hosp. Audiences, Inc., 1974-80. Founding bd. dirs. Coll. and U. Machine Records Conf., 1971-73; bd. dirs. Uniplan Environ. Groups, Inc., 1970-73, chmn., 1971-73; chmn. Franklin County (Ohio) Republican Demographics and Voter Analysis Com., 1975-80; bd. dirs. Cedar Hill Assocs., 1980—, Alarm Ctr. Internat., Forerunner Corp. 1984—, Inventors Council Ohio, 1984-86; Home Health Inst., 1984-86; mem. Ohio State Dental Bd., 1980-85; mem. Gov.'s Export Council, 1982-83; mem. Gov.'s Tech. Task Force, 1982-83. Am. Council on Edn. grantee, 1976-77; Nat. Assn. Coll. and Univ. Bus. Officers grantee, 1977-79; NSF grantee, 1980-86; Reisman fellow, 1962. Mem. Assn. Instl. Research, Press Club Ohio, Coll. and Univ. Systems Exchange, AAAS, Phi Alpha Kappa, Delta Tau Delta. Republican. Presbyterian. Author: (with D.H. Baker) Writing to People, 1963; (with R.W. Brady) University Program Budgeting, 1968, Administrative Data Processing, 1975; contbr. articles to profl. publs. Home: 833 Lakeshore Dr Worthington OH 43085 Office: 190 N Oval Mall Columbus OH 43210

BAUGHMAN, R(OBERT) PATRICK, lawyer; b. Zanesville, Ohio, Nov. 18, 1938; s. Robert G. and Kathryn E. B.; m. Joyce Hall, June 17, 1959; 1 dau., Patricia. B.S., Ohio State U., 1960, J.D., 1963. Bar: Ohio 1963. Assoc. firm Sindell & Sindell, Cleve., 1964-71, Jones, Day, Reavis & Pogue, Cleve., 1972-73; asst. atty. gen. State of Ohio, Columbus, 1971-72; pres., prin. firm Baughman & Assocs., Cleve., 1973—. Mem. ABA, Ohio Bar Assn., Cuyahoga County Bar Assn., Nat. Council Self-Insurers, Internat. Assn. Indsl. Accident Bds. and Commns., Internat. Platform Assn. Episcopalian. Club: Columbia Hills Country. Office: 55 Public Sq Cleveland OH 44113

BAULIEU, ETIENNE-EMILE, endocrinologist; b. Strasbourg, France, Dec. 12, 1926; s. Léon Blum and Thérèse (Lion) B.; Dr. Medicine and Phys. Scis., Faculty Medicine and Scis., U. Paris; m. Yolande Compagnon, Oct. 4, 1947; children: Catherine, Laurent, Frédérique. Intern, Hosp. of Paris, 1951; from lectr. to prof. biol. chemistry U. Reims Sch. Medicine, 1958, U. Rouen Sch. Medicine, 1960, Faculty Medicine, U. Paris, 1961; vis. lectr. Columbia U., N.Y.C., 1961-62; sci. dir. Nat. Inst. Health and Med. Research, 1963—; co-founder Internat. Soc. for Research in Biology of Reprodn., 1967, Karolinska Symposia in Reproductive Endocrinology, 1970; chmn. sci. council Fondation pour la Recherche médicale française, 1973-75; chmn. sci. council Inst. Nat. de la Santé et de la Recherche Médicale, 1975-79; chmn. sci. council Centre Internat. de Recherches Médicales de Franceville (Gabon), 1978-85. Decorated chevalier Order of Merit, officer Legion of Honor; recipient Reichstein award Internat. Soc. Endocrinology, 1972, Grand Prix Scientifique, City of Paris, 1973; (with E. Jensen) Roussel prize, 1976, Pincus Meml. award, 1978; 1st European medal English Soc. Endocrinology, 1985. Mem. French Acad. Scis., French Soc. Biochemistry, French Soc. Endocrinology, Royal Soc. Medicine, Endocrine Soc. (U.S.), N.Y. Acad. Scis. Research on secretion, metabolism, physio-pathology and mechanism of action of steroid hormones, and biology of reprodn. Address: Hopital de Bicêtre, 94 Bicêtre France

BAUM, CARL EDWARD, electromagnetic theorist; b. Binghampton, N.Y., Feb. 6, 1940; s. George Theodore and Evelyn Monica (Bliven) B.; B.S. with honors, Calif. Inst. Tech., 1962, M.S., 1963, Ph.D., 1969. Commd. 2d lt. USAF, 1962, advanced through grades to capt., 1967, resigned, 1971, project officer Air Force Weapons Lab., Kirtland AFB, N.Mex., 1963-71, sr. scientist for electromagnetics, 1971—; U.S. del. to gen. assembly Internat. Union Radio Sci., Lima, Peru, 1975, Helsinki, Finland, 1978, Washington, 1981, Florence, Italy, 1984, Tel Aviv, 1987; mem. Commn. B U.S. Nat. Com., 1975—, Commn. E, 1982—. Commendation medal; recipient research and devel. award USAF, 1970, award Honeywell Corp., 1962. Fellow IEEE (Harry Diamond Meml. award, 1987, Richard R. Stoddart award, 1984); mem. Electromagnetics Soc. (pres. 1983-85), Sigma Xi, Tau Beta Pi. Roman Catholic. Author: (with others) Transient Electromagnetic Fields, 1976; Electromagnetic Scattering, 1978; Acoustic, Electromagnetic and Elastic Wave Scattering, 1980, Fast Electrical and Optical Measurements, 1986, EMPI Interaction: Principles, Techniques and Reference Data, 1986; contbr. articles to profl. publs. Home: 5116 Eastern SE Unit D Albuquerque NM 87108 Office: Air Force Weapons Lab Kirtland AFB NM 87117

BAUM, HADASSA, civil engineer, educator; b. Haifa, Israel, Oct. 3, 1952; d. Israel and Mala (Golomb) Pinchouk; m. Aharon H. Baum, Nov. 3, 1975; children: Abraham, Moshe. BSc, Technion, Haifa, 1975; MSc, Technion, 1979, PhD, 1983. Tchr. jr. coll. Haifa, 1973-75; asst. and instr. Technion, Haifa, 1975-83; research assoc. Technion, 1983-84, postdoctoral fellow, 1984-85; postdoctoral fellow MIT, Boston, 1985-86; lectr. Bosmat Coll., Haifa, 1987—, research assoc., 1988—. Contbr. articles to profl. jours. Served with Israeli Army, 1972-73. Recipient B'nai B'rith Gold medal, 1972; M. Golan Meml. prize, Technion, 1982, Lastor Aronborg award, 1984. Office: Technion Israel Inst Tech, Bldg Res Sta, Haifa Israel

BAUM, INGEBORG RUTH, librarian; b. Berlin, Sept. 20; d. Ella Koch; Oberlyceum (scholar), Kassel, Germany, 1926-33; postgrad. Georgetown U., 1963-70; m. Albert Baum, Feb. 16, 1938 (div. 1960); children—Harro Siegward, Helma Sigrun (Mrs. George Meadows). Came to U.S., 1951, naturalized, 1957. Export corr. Bitter-Polar, Germany, 1933-35, Henschel Locs, Germany, 1936; exec. sec. Fieseler Airplane Mfrs., Germany, 1936-38; interpreter, sec. UNRRA, Germany, 1946-48; payroll supr., civilian dept. U.S. Army, Wetzlar PX, Germany, 1948-51; asst. librarian Supreme Council, Ancient and Accepted Scottish Rite, Washington, 1951-70, librarian and museums curator, 1970—; appraiser rare books and documents; v.p. Merical Elec. Contractors, Inc., Forestville, Md., 1974—. Mem. Am. Soc. Appraisers, Calligraphers Guild. Mem. Ch. Jesus Christ of Latter-day Saints. Free-lance contbr. to Pabelverlag, Rastatt, Germany, Harle, Ofcl. Publs., Inc., others. Home: 2480 16th St NW Apt 416 Washington DC 20009 Office: 1733 16th St NW Washington DC 20009

BAUM, KARL, journalist; b. Czechoslovakia, Oct. 6, 1907. Head Exchange Telegraph Fgn. News Service, London, 1939-47; dir. info. dept. European Tracing Office for Missing Persons World Jewish Congress, London, 1945-55; editor News and Feature Service World Jewish Affairs, 1947-60; London bur. corr. various newspapers, Switzerland, Germany and Israel, 1945-65; ind. cons. pub. relations 1960—. Contbr. numerous articles to profl. jours. Mem. Nat. Union Journalists, Inst. Pub. Relations, Fgn. Press Assn., Internat. Council Jews From Czechoslovakia (chmn.). Address: Long Hall, 14 Kidderpore Gardens, London NW3 7SR, England

BAUM, NICHOLAS, advertising executive; b. Bryn Mawr, Pa., Apr. 25, 1947; s. Chester Earle Baum and Kathryn (Valdes) Baum Edwards; m. Anne Jourdan-Barry; children: Alexandra, Olivia, Victoria. Grad., City of London Coll., 1969. Account exec. Ogilvy & Mather, London, 1969-71; account dir. Ogilvy & Mather, Paris, 1972-80, v.p., 1980-85, v.p. Europe, 1985-87; mng. dir. BDDP Internat., Boulogne, France, 1987—. Episcopalian. Clubs: M.C.C. (london); Polo (Paris). Home: 66 R Boursault, 75017 Paris France Office: BDDP Internat, 162-164 rue de Billancourt, 92100 Boulogne France

BAUM, RICHARD THEODORE, engineering company executive; b. N.Y.C., Oct. 3, 1919. BA, Columbia U., 1940, BS, 1941, MS, 1948. Registered profl. engr., Nat. Bureau Engring. Registration, N.Y., 20 other states and D.C. Engr. Electric Boat Co., Groton, Conn., 1941-43; with Jaros, Baum & Bolles, N.Y.C., 1946—, ptnr., 1958-86, ptnr. emeritus, cons. to firm, 1986—; mem. adv. council, faculty of engring. and applied sci. Columbia U., N.Y.C., 1972—. Served to 1st lt. USAAF, 1943-46. Egleston medalist Columbia U., 1985. Fellow Am. Cons. Engrs. Council, ASME, ASHRAE; mem. Nat. Acad. Engring., NSPE, Nat. Soc. Energy Engrs., Nat. Research Council (chmn. bd. bldg. research bd.), Am. Arbitration Assn. (panel of arbitrators 1973—), Council on Tall Bldgs. and Urban Habitat (vice chmn. N.Am., mem. steering group). Club: Univ. (N.Y.C.). Office: 345 Park Ave New York NY 10154

BAUM, SAMUEL SEYMOUR, accountant; b. N.Y.C., Feb. 5, 1921; s. Joseph and Esther (Schuminskey) B.; m. Grace Lament, July 2, 1949; children—Judith Baum Morrow, E. Richard. Student Henderson State Coll., 1943; B.B.A., CCNY, 1950. C.P.A., N.Y., N.J., Pa., Fla., Tex. Mng. ptnr. Lopez, Edwards, Frank & Co., N.Y.C., 1939—; pres. Transtrade USA, Ltd., Rockville Centre, N.Y., 1980—; arbitrator Am. Arbitration Assn. Contbr. articles to various mags. Pres. Temple Emanuel of East Meadow, N.Y., 1973-74, chmn. bd., 1974-75. Mem. Am. Inst. C.P.A.s, N.Y. State Soc. C.P.A.s (pres. Nassau chpt. 1984—, bd. dirs.), Fla. Soc. C.P.A.s, Pa. Inst. C.P.A.s, N.J. Soc. C.P.A.s, Nat. Conf. C.P.A. Practitioners (chpt. pres. 1982-83). Republican. Jewish. Office: Lopez Edwards Frank & Co 70 E Sunrise Hwy Box 547 Valley Stream NY 11582-9990 also: 1 Penn Plaza New York NY 10019-0141

BAUM, WILLIAM CARDINAL, former archbishop; b. Dallas, Nov. 21, 1926; s. Harold E. and Mary Leona (Hayes) W. Student, Kenrick Sem., St. Louis, 1947-51, U. St. Thomas Aquinas, Rome, 1956-58; STD, U. St. Thomas Aquinas, Rome, 1958; STL, Muhlenberg Coll., Allentown, Pa., 1957, DD, 1967; LLD, Georgetown U., St. John's U., Bklyn. Ordained priest Roman Cath. Ch., 1951. Elevated to cardinal Roman Cath. Ch., 1976; assoc. pastor St. Aloysius Parish, St. Therese's Parish and St. Peter's Parish, Kansas City, Mo., 1951-56, 61-64, 67-68; adminstr. St. Cyril's Parish, Sugar Creek, Mo., 1960-61; pastor St. James Parish, Kansas City, 1968-70; chancellor Diocese Kansas City-St. Joseph, 1967-70; bishop of Springfield-Cape Girardeau, Mo., 1970-73; archbishop of Washington, 1973-80; prefect Sacred Congregation for Cath. Edn., Rome, 1980—; instr., then prof. Avila Coll., Kansas City, Mo., 1954-56, 58-63; Hon. chaplain of the Pope, 1961; peritus 2d Vatican Council, 1962-65; hon. prelate of the Pope, 1968; 1st exec. dir. Bishops' Commn. Ecumenical and Inter-religious Affairs, 1964-67; mem. Joint Working Group; reps. Cath. Ch. and World Council Chs., 1965-69; mem. Mixed Commn.; reps. Cath. Ch. and Lutheran World Fedn., 1965-66; mem. Vatican's Congregations Cath. Edn., Doctrine of Faith and Secretariat for Non Christians, Bishop's Welfare Emergency Relief Com. Author: The Teaching of Cardinal Cajetan on the Sacrifice of the Mass, 1958, Considerations Toward the Theology on the Presbyterate, 1961. Trustee, chancellor Cath. U. Am.; chmn. bd. trustees Nat. Shrine Immaculate Conception. Mem. Nat. Conf. Cath. Bishops (adminstrv. com.). Office: Piazza della Citta Leonina 9, 00193 Rome Italy *

BAUMAN, EARL WILLIAM, accountant, government official; b. Arcadia, Nebr., Jan. 30, 1916; s. William A. and Gracia M. (Jones) B.; B.S. with honors, U. Wyo., 1938; postgrad. Northwestern U., 1938-39; m. Margaret E. Blackman, Oct. 21, 1940 (dec. 1984); children—Carol Ann Bauman Ammerman. Earl William Jr. Acct., Haselmire, Cordle & Co., Casper, Wyo., 1939-42; asst. dir. finance VA, Chgo., 1946-49, chief acctg. group VA, Washington, 1949-52, supr. systems acctg. GAO, Washington, 1952-55; supervising auditor GAO, Washington, 1955-58; dir. finance, asst. dir. Directorate Acctg. and Financial Policy, Office Asst. Sec. Def., Washington, 1958-63; tech. asst. to comdr. AF Acctg. and Finance Ctr., Denver, 1963-73; mem. investigations staff Ho. of Reps. Appropriations Com., 1953-54; prof. acctg. Benjamin Franklin U., 1960-63; mem. exec. council Army Finance, 1963-64; dir. Real Estate Investment Corp., 1962-64; sr. ptnr. EMB Enterprises, 1973—; chmn. Acctg. Careers Council Colo., 1969-71. Chmn. Aurora Citizens Adv. Budget Com., 1975-76; chmn. fin. and taxation com. Denver Met. Study, 1976-78. Served with AUS, 1942-46; col. Res., now ret. C.P.A. Mem. Am. Inst. C.P.A.s, Wyo. Assn. C.P.A.s, Fed. Govt. Accts. Assn. (nat. v.p. 1972-73, pres. Denver 1973-74), Army Finance Assn., Am. Soc. Mil. Comptrollers, Denver Am. Soc. Mil. Comptrollers (pres. 1968-69), Citizens Band Radio Assn. (pres. 1963), Nat. Assn. Ret. Fed. Employees (Aurora 1072 pres. 1986-87), Alpha Kappa Psi, Beta Alpha Psi, Phi Kappa Phi. Club: Columbine Sertoma (pres. 1975-76). Avocations: photography, tennis, collector cars. Home: 536 Newark Ct Aurora CO 80010

BAUMAN, JEROME ALAN, lawyer; b. N.Y.C., July 7, 1931; s. Melville J. and Tillie (Cohn) B.; m. Esme Pamela Joseph, July 4, 1966; children—David Meredith, Oren Reid. B.S. in Chemistry, Queens Coll., 1953; LL.B. cum laude, Harvard U., 1958. Bar: N.Y. bar 1959, Fla. bar 1971. Asso. counsel firm Levin, Rosmarin & Schwartz, N.Y.C., 1958-62, Sperry, Weinberg & Cutler, N.Y.C., 1962-64; gen. counsel Inland Credit Corp., N.Y.C., 1964-66; assoc. counsel firm Golenbock & Barell, N.Y.C., 1966-68; assoc. counsel GAC Corp., Allentown, Pa., Miami, Fla., 1968-72; v.p., gen. counsel GAC Properties, Inc., Miami, 1970-72, Gulfstream Land & Devel. Corp., Plantation, Fla., 1972-78; ptnr. Bauman, Wurtenberger & Schottenfeld, 1979—. Pres. Plantation Jewish Congregation, 1975-79; mem. campaign cabinet Fedn. Jewish Philanthropies New York N.L.D., 1963-65. Served with U.S. Army, 1953-55. Mem. N.Y., Fla. bar assns. Home: 440 W Tropical Way Plantation FL 33317 Office: Bauman Wurtenberger & Schottenfeld 8211 W Broward Blvd Plantation FL 33324

BAUMAN, ROBERT PATTEN, diversified company executive; b. Cleve., Mar. 27, 1931; s. John Nevin and Lucille (Patten) B.; m. Patricia H. Jones, June 15, 1961; children: John, Elizabeth. B.A., Ohio Wesleyan U., 1953; M.B.A., Harvard Bus. Sch., 1955. Mktg. adminstrn. Maxwell House div. Gen. Foods, White Plains, N.Y., 1958-65, gen. mgr. Post div., 1967, corp. v.p., 1968, exec. v.p., 1968, pres., dir. internat. ops., 1973; dir. Avco Corp., Greenwich, Conn., 1980-85, vice chmn. bd., 1981-85; vice chmn. Textron Inc., Providence, R.I., 1985-86; chmn. Beecham Group, Brentford, Middlesex, Eng., 1986—; bd. dirs. Capitol Cities/ABC Inc., Union Pacific Corp. Author: Plants as Pets, 1982. Trustee Ohio Wesleyan U.; bd. mgrs. N.Y. Bot. Garden; mem. The Conf. Bd., Council Fgn. Relations. Clubs: Weshannet Golf (Kennebunk, Maine); Blind Brook (Port Chester, N.Y.). Office: Beecham Group, Great West Rd, Brentford Middlesex, England also: Beecham Inc 3 Garret Mountain Plaza West Peterson NJ 07424

BAUMAN, ZYGMUNT, sociologist; b. Poznan, Poland, Nov. 19, 1925; s. Maurice and Sophie (Cohn) B.; m. Janina Gustawa Lewinson, Aug. 18, 1926; children: Anna, Irena, Lydia. BA, U. Warsaw, Poland, 1950, MA, 1954, PhD, 1956, Habilitation, 1960. Lectr., sr. lectr. U. Warsaw, Poland, 1953-64, chmn. gen. sociology dept., 1964-68; prof. sociology U. Tel-Aviv, Israel, 1968-71, U. Leeds, Eng., 1971—; chief editor Studia Sociologizne quar., Warsaw, 1960-68, Studia Sociologicano-Polityczne, Warsaw, 1962-68. Author: Between Class and Elite, 1970, Culture as Praxis, 1972, Hermeneutics and Social Science, 1980, Memories of Class, 1982, Legislators and Interpreters, 1987, Freedom, 1988; contbr. articles to profl. jours. Mem. Brit. Sociol. Assn. Office: Univ of Leeds, Leeds LS2 9JT, England

BAUMANN, EUGENE HEINZ, pilot; b. San Francisco, Sept. 2, 1950; s. Eugene Paul and Liane Helga (Lautenschlager) B.; m. Vicki Suzanne Nolan, Apr. 1, 1986. BS, U. Nev., 1976; cer. Cert. flight engr., flight instr., aircraft dispatcher, airline transport pilot. Pilot Golden Gate Airlines, Monterey, Calif., 1979-81, Swift Aire Lines, San Luis Obispo, Calif., 1979, Commuter Airlines, Binghamton, N.Y., 1981-82; pilot and check airman Empire Airlines, Utica, N.Y., 1982-83; pilot Mid Pacific Airlines, Honolulu, 1983-84, Ryan Internat. Airlines, Wichita, Kans., 1984-85, Am. Airlines, San Francisco, 1985—; U.S. rep. Europa Cup Alpine Ski Circuit, 1974-75. Won U.S. Sr. Nat. Downhill Championships Silver medal Class I, 1977, Sr. Class I Championship Far West Competition, 1981, 1st place Regional Ski Club Championship, 1981, 2d place Nat. Ski Club Championship, 1981, Western States Masters Championship Class II, 1st Downhill, 2d Giant Slalom, 1st Combined, 1987, 1st place Internat. Masters Championship Gian Slalom, Squaw Valley, 1987, Final Standings N.Am. Airlines Ski Fedn. 2d Slalom, 3d Giant Slalom, 3d Overall, 1987, Internat. Airlines Ski Fedn., Söll, Austria 8th Combined, 9th Giant Slalom, 1987, U.S. Masters Nat. Alpine Championships, Class III, Silver medal Giant Slalom, Bronze medal Downhill, Silver medal Combined, 1988, Far West Ski Competition Masters Class 30 Champion and Overall Champion, 1988, Masters Western States Nat. Championships Class III, 1 Gold and 3 Silver medals, 1988, 3d place Internat. Masters Championships Class II Giant Slalom, Sun Valley, Idaho, 1988; named Outstanding Masters Ski Racer of the Yr., Far west Ski Competition, 1988; final standings N.Am. Airline Ski Fedn. 2d place Overall, 2d place Giant Slalom, 2d place Slalom, 1988. Mem. Allied Pilots Assn., Future Aviation Profls. Am., Am. Airlines Ski Team. Republican. Roman Catholic. Home: 3151 Shelter Creek Ln San Bruno CA 94066

BAUMANN, FELIX MARTIN ANDREAS, museum director; b. Zurich, Switzerland, Aug. 17, 1937; s. Rudolph T. and Alice J. (Schenker) B.; grad. U. Bern; m. Marie Louise Bruckner, Sept. 12, 1975; 4 children. Asst. curator, Art Mus. Bern, Switzerland, 1965-71, curator, 1971-76; asst. dir. Mus. of

Fine Art, Zurich, from 1976, now dir. Author: Das Erbario Carrarese, 1974; Pablo Picasso, Leben und Werk, 1976; Wilfrid Moser, 1978. Office: Zurcher Kunstgesellschaft, Mus of Arts, 1 Heimplatz, 8024 Zurich Switzerland

BAUMANN, FRANCOIS, physician; b. Paris, June 19, 1945; s. Jean Pierre and Andrée Piel Andure: m. Annick Boisset, July 7, 1946; children: Anne Sophie, Raphael, Olivier. MD, Faculty of Medicine, Paris, 1972. Physician of liberal medicine Paris, 1972—; tchr. Paris 5 U., 1985—; cons. Cochin Hosp., Paris, 1986—, Mutuelle Gen. Edn. Nat., Paris, 1973—, Bur. Aide Soc. Paris, SNCF, 1974—. Contbr. articles to profl. jours.; author films on medicine. Mem. Soc. Formation Therapeutique du Generaliste (pres. 1978—), Fedn. Francaise Medicine Generale (v.p. 1986—), Conseil Regional Formation Medicale Continue (v.p. 1985), Coll. Francaise Pathologie Vasculaire, Am. Coll. Angiology, Soc. Française Phlebologie, Union Nat. Assn. Formation Med. Continue. Club: CAM. Home: 19 rue Victor Hugo, 92120 Montrouge France Office: Cabinet Med, 10 Ave de la Soeur Rosalie, 75013 Paris France

BAUMBACH, HENRY DALE, psychologist; b. Lodi, Calif., Sept. 13, 1944; s. Henry C. and Loma D. Baumbach; children: Catherine, Pamela, Christopher, Carrie. BA, U. Calif., Riverside, 1969, MA, 1973, PhD, 1975; MA in Sociology, Loma Linda U., 1970; postgrad. in psychology, U. Mo., 1970-71. Lic. psychologist, Am. Bd. Med. Psychotherapists, Calif. From instr. to asst. prof. psychology Loma Linda U., 1971-75; postdoctoral fellow in neurology Stanford U. Sch. Medicine, 1975-78, research assoc., 1978-79; clin. neuropsychologist Idaho Dept. Health and Welfare, 1979-81; staff psychologist Napa (Calif.) State Hosp. 1981-83; instr. psychology Ohlone Coll., Fremont, Calif., part-time 1978; spl. cons. clin. neuropsychology San Joaquin Gen. Hosp., Stockton, Calif., 1982—, Kentfield (Calif.) Med. Hosp., 1985— ; adj. asst. prof. Chapman Coll., 1982-83; adj. prof. U. Pacific, 1983-84; clin. neuropsychology cons. Los Medanos Community Hosp., Pittsburg, Calif., 1982-83; pvt. practice neuropsychology, Stockton, 1982—, Walnut Creek, Calif., 1986—; pres. Sierra Inst. Med. and Neuropsychology Inc., Walnut Creek, 1986—; cons. neuropsychology and behavioral medicine Kentfield Med. Hosp. and Ctr. for Occupational Health, Kentfield, Calif., 1986-87; clin. dir. Pain Mgmt. Ctr., Mt. Diablo Hosp. Med. Ctr., Concord, Calif., 1983—; dir. psychlogy No. Calif. Rehab. Services, Pleasant Hill, 1985-86. Recipient Chancellor's Patent Fund award U. Calif., Riverside, 1974; NSF fellow, 1968. Mem. Am. Psychol. Assn., AAAS, Internat. Assn. Study Pain, Inst. Advancement Health, Calif. Soc. Indusl. Medicine and Surgery, Behavioral Neurology Internat. (charter), Soc. Behavioral Medicine. Democrat. Contbr. sci. articles to profl. jours. Home: PO Box 540 Concord CA 94522 Office: 2522 Grand Canal Blvd Suite 1 Stockton CA 95207

BAUMEISTER, ELEANOR H. (MRS. CARL F. BAUMEISTER), club woman; b. Lake Linden, Mich., Oct. 2, 1909; d. Thomas and Sarah (Madigan) Hoskins; B.; Music Edn., U. Minn., 1930; m. Carl Frederick Baumeister, Apr. 8, 1929; 1 son, Richard. Co-founder, advt. mgr. The Corn Belt Livestock Feeder trade mag., 1948-51. Publicity dir. Patron's Council, Riverside-Brookfield High Sch., 1951-53; pres. MacNeal Meml. Hosp. Women's Auxiliary, 1956, mem. adv. bd., 1957. Bd. dirs. Riverside Pub. Library, 1961-71, pres., 1967-71; dir. Ill. P.E.O. Home, Knoxville, 1956-58, fin. adviser, 1958-63; vice chmn. bd. dirs. Southwest Suburban chpt. Am. Cancer Soc., 1968-69, chmn. bd. dirs. Central Suburban unit, 1969-71, sec.-treas. Central Suburban unit, 1972-84; sect. Dist. 208 Caucus; mem. citizens adv. bd. Morton Coll. Sch. Nursing, 1972—. Mem. Gen. Fedn. Women's Clubs, P.E.O. (pres. Riverside 1955-56, 60-61, Ill. corr. sec., 1956-57, rec. sec. 1957-58). Republican. Presbyterian. Clubs: Chgo. Farmers, Riverside Woman's (pres. 1954-56, chmn. auditing com. 1963). Home: 120 S Delaplaine Rd Riverside IL 60546

BAUMER, BEVERLY BELLE, journalist; b. Hays, Kans., Sept. 23, 1926; d. Charles Arthur and Mayme Mae (Lord) B.; B.S., William Allen White Sch. Journalism, U. Kans., 1948. Summer intern reporter Hutchinson (Kans.) News, 1946-47; continuity writer, women's program dir. Sta. KWBW, Hutchinson, 1948-49; dist. editor Salina (Kans.) Jours., 1950-57; commd. writer State of Kans. Centennial Year, 1961; contbg. author: Ford Times, Kansas City Star, Wichita (Kans.) Eagle, Ojibway Publs., Billboard, Modern Jeweler, Floor Covering Weekly, other bus. mags., 1962-69; owner and mgr. apts., Hutchinson, 1970—; broadcaster Reading Radio Room, Sta. KHCC-FM, Hutchinson, 1982—; info. officer, maj. Kans. Wing Hdqrs. CAP, 1969-72; participant People to People Citizen Ambassador program, People's Republic of China, summer 1988. Mem. Republican Presdl. Task Force. Recipient Human Interest Photo award Nat. Press Women, 1956; News Photo award AP, 1952, 2d place award Kans. Press Women Contest, 1986. Mem. Fellows Menninger Found., Suffolk County Hist. Soc., Nat. Fedn. Press Women, Kans. Press Women (Communications Contest award 1986), Am. Soc. Profl. and Exec. Women, Am. Film Inst., Nat. Soc. Magna Charta Dames, Nat. Soc. Daus. Founders and Patriots Am., Nat. Soc. Daus. Am. Colonists, Kans. Soc. Daus. Am. Colonists (organizing regent Dr. Thomas Lord chpt., state chmn. insignia com.), Nat. Soc. Sons and Daus. Pilgrims (elder Kans. br.), D.A.R., Ben Franklin Soc. (nat. adv. bd.), Daus. Colonial Wars, Order Descs. Colonial Physicians and Chirurgiens, Colonial Dames 17th Century (chaplain, charter mem. Henry Woodhouse chpt.), Plantagenet Soc., Internat. Platform Soc., U. Kans. Alumni Assn., Nat. Geneal. Soc. Author book of poems, 1941; editor: A Simple Bedside Book for People Who Are Kinda, Sorta Interested in Genealogy, 1983. Home and Office: 204 Curtis St Hutchinson KS 67502

BAUMGARDNER, JOHN DWANE, manufacturing company executive; b. Minburn, Iowa, Aug. 21, 1940; s. John Henry and Oda Lee Baumgardner; m. Shirley Ann Hoene, Sept. 4, 1965 (dec. Oct. 1985); children: Kenneth Mark, Sandra Lynn; m. Kathy Lynn Ende, May 2, 1987. BS in Physics, U. Mo., 1963; PhD in Optics, U. Rochester, 1969. Research asst. McDonnell Douglas, St. Louis, 1963-65; mgr. research and devel. Donnelly Corp., Holland, Mich., 1969-75, mgr. advanced devel., 1975-78, v.p. tech., 1978-80, chmn., chief exec. officer, pres., 1980—; bd. dirs. Scanlon Plan Assocs. Bd. dirs. Econ. Alliance for Mich. Mem. Am. Mgmt. Assn. Republican. Club: Econ. Grand Rapids. Office: Donnelly Corp 414 E 40th st Holland MI 49423

BAURS-KREY, DETLEV H. U., international management consultant; b. Berlin, July 13, 1943; U.S., permanent resident U.S., 1975; s. Reinhold W.H. and Ingeborg (Brauer) B-K.; B.B.A., U. Bonn, 1967; LL.M., U. Mainz, 1969; m. Kirsten Christine Geier, 1982. Mktg. trainee Pfizer, Inc., W.Ger., 1970; asst. to gen. mgr. H. Mack Nachf., W.Ger., 1971-74; mktg. mgr. Pfizer Internat., Inc., N.Y.C., 1974; v.p. Panta, Inc., internat. cons., N.Y.C., 1975-78; pres., chief exec. officer Baurs-Krey Assos., Inc., N.Y.C., 1978—; chmn., chief exec. officer Thermascan Inc. (Nasdaq) (formerly BCD Products, Inc.), N.Y.C., 1981—; dir. Baurs-Krey Assos., Inc., Thermascan, Inc., Inter-Hermes Pharma, Inc., Miles USA, Inc.; minister plenipotentiary-at-large Republic of San Marino, 1985—; vis. prof. econs. and tech. transfer U. Francisco Marroquin, Guatemala, 1984; vice chmn. Internat. Symposium on AIDS, Republic of San Marino, 1988; mem. permanent sci. com. Annual San Marino Med. Confs., selection com. Annual San Marino Prize of Medicine. Mem. adv. bd. Am. Health Found., 1983, trustee, 1986; vice chmn., trustee Cultural Ctr., Village of Southampton, 1988. Decorated knight Order of St. Maria in Jerusalem, 1977; comdr. Order of St. Agatha, 1983, knight comdr. cross Order of Merit, 1988 (San Marino). Mem. German-Am. C. of C. (N.Y.), Am. C. of C. in Germany (Frankfurt), Fgn. Friends N.Y., Am. Council on Germany (N.Y.), N.Y. Fgn. Lawyers Assn. Roman Catholic. Clubs: Metropolitan, Rockefeller Ctr., Doubles (N.Y.C.). Lodge: Lions (Wiesbaden, W.Ger.), Teutonic Order (knight comdr.). Office: Thermascan Inc 41 East 42d St New York NY 10017 also: Baurs-Krey Assocs Inc 41 East 42d St New York NY 10017

BAUSINGER, HERMANN WILHELM, ethnologist, educator; b. Aalen, Germany, Sept. 17, 1926; m. Brigitte Schoepel, June 23, 1967; children: Susanne, Dorothea, Dominik, Mirabel. PhD, U. Tubingen, Fed. Republic Germany, 1952, Dr. habil., 1959. Asst. prof. ethnology and folklore U. Tubingen, Fed. Republic Germany, 1952-59, docent, 1959-60, prof., 1960—; dir. Ludwig Uhland Inst. Comparative Culture, Tubingen, 1960—. Contbr. to numerous books and jours.; editor Zeitschr fur Volkskunde, 1967-83, handbook Encyclopaedie des Maerchens, 1975. Home: Moltkestr 77, D7410 Reutlingen Federal Republic of Germany Office: Ludwig Uhland, Inst Schloss, D7400 Tubingen Federal Republic of Germany

BAUSTAD, TERJE, manufacturing executive; b. Stavanger, Rogaland, Norway, Oct. 20, 1957; s. Lars and Gunvor (Pawels) B. Student, St. Svithun Gymnas, 1975-78. Operator Flopetrol Johnston, Stavanger, Norway, 1979-81; supr. Flopetrol Johnston, Alkmaar, The Netherlands, 1981-83; field service supr. Flopetrol Norge A/S, Stavanger, 1983-84, Flopetrol Internat. S.A., Great Yarmouth, Eng., 1984-86; field service mgr. Flopetrol Norge A/S, Stavanger, 1986—. Inventor fluid sampler. Served to corp. Norwegian Army, 1978-79. Mem. Soc. Petroleum Engrs. Office: Flopetrol Norge A/S, Gamle Forusvei 49, Forus 4033, Norway

BAUTISTA, BASILIO NERY, plastic surgeon; b. Labo, Camarines Norte, Philippines, Mar. 2; came to U.S., 1961, naturalized, 1978; s. Basilio Borja and Nazaria Robel (Nery) B.; MD, U. Santo Tomas, Manila, 1960. Intern, Meml. Hosp., Niagara Falls, N.Y., 1961-62; resident Hahnemann Med. Coll. and Hosp., Phila., 1962-63, Malden Hosp., Boston, 1963-65, Roswell Park Meml. Inst., Buffalo, 1965-67, U. Man. Med. Center Winnipeg Gen. Hosp. and Children's Hosp. Winnipeg, 1967-69; teaching and research fellow U. Man., 1969-70; practice medicine specializing in plastic surgery, Dover, Seaford and Lewes, Del., 1972—; founder, dir. Laser & Plastic Surgery Ctr. of So. Del., 1987—; mem. staff Kent Gen. Hosp., Nanticoke Meml. Hosp., Beebe Hosp.; cons. plastic surgeon USAF Base Hosp., Dover; founder, dir. Galeria de Artes Internacionales, Dover, 1976—. Editor Plastikos/Papyrus, 1980—, Tri-State Thomasian, 1987—, Philippine Med. Soc. of Del. News, 1987—; assoc. editor The Philippine Surgeon, 1982—, Am. Coll. Internat. Physicians News, 1983—; fgn. corr. Fil-Am. News, 1968-70. Vice pres. Citizenship Council Man., 1968-70, recipient Community Service award, 1970; pres. Kayumanggi-Philippine Assn. Man., 1968-69. Recipient Robert J. Sims award N.E. Natural Sci. League, 1979; Physician's award AMA, 1973, 76, 79, 81, 82, 83; Outstanding Filipino award Del. Valley Assn. Filipinos, 1978; First Physician-Artist award Assn. Philippine Practicing Physicians in Am., 1983. Fellow Am. Soc. Laser Medicine and Surgery, Internat. Soc. Laser Medicine and Surgery, Am. Coll. Internat. Physicians, Philippine Coll. Surgeons, Internat. Soc. Aesthetic Plastic Surgery; mem. Am. Assn. Hand Surgery, Internat. Acad. Cosmetic Surgery, Internat. Coll. Surgeons (vice-regent 1984-85, regent 1985—), Med. Soc. Del., AMA, Robert Ivy Soc., Kent County Med. Soc., Philippine Assn. Plastic Surgeons in Am. (co-founder, pres., chmn. bd. 1978-80, exec. dir. 1980—), Pan Am. Med. Assn., Am. Cancer Soc. (pres. Kent County chpt. 1982), Philippine Med. Soc. Del. (v.p., 1972-76, pres. 1983-85), Soc. Philippine Surgeons in Am. (gov. 1979-86), Internat. Soc. Burn Injuries, Internat. Assn. Maxillo-facial Surgery, U. Santo Tomas Med. Alumni Assn. Tri-State (v.p. Del. 1982-85, pres. 1985—). Roman Catholic. Contbr. articles to profl. jours. Home: 228 Old Mill Rd Dover DE 19901 Office: 896 S State St Dover DE 19901

BAUTISTA, FLORENTINO AGUINALDO, pediatrician; b. Binakayan, Philippines, July 10, 1928; d. Florentino Sarao and Rosalia Sañez (Aguinaldo) B. BS in Zoology, U. Philippines, Manila, 1948; MD, U. Santo Tomas, Philippines, 1954. Diplomate Philippine Bd. Pediatrics. Intern Lynn (Mass.) Hosp., 1955-56; resident in pediatrics Charles V. Chapin Hosp., R.I., 1956-68, Foxboro (Mass.) State Coll. Med. Ctr., 1958-59; from sr. resident to asst. chief of dept. pediatrics Vets. Meml. Med. Ctr., Quezon City, Philippines, 1960-73; cons. physician in pediatric and adolescent medicine Cavite (Philippines) Med. Ctr., 1973—, Our Savior Hosp., Rosario, Philippines, 1973—. Author: Applied Pediatrics, 1968. Bd. dirs. Pastoral Council Our Lady of Fatima Parish, 1975-79, treas., 1976-79, treas., 1979-85; core leader Aliw Ng Espiritu Santo Prayer Group, Binakayan, 1975—; pres. Yellow Brigade of Kawit, 1986-87; co-chmn. Mcpl. Food and Agrl. Council Kawit, 1987; mem. sem. bd. Diocese of Imus, 1987. Recipient Cert. of Appreciation Binakayan chpt. KC, 1975. Fellow Philippine Pediatric Soc. (Appreciation placque 1978, Appreciation awards 1979-82; mem. Cavite Med. Soc. (treas. 1982-83, Appreciation cert. 1970), Maternal and Child Health Assn. Philippines, Philippine Med. Women's Assn. (v.p. 1976-78), U. Santo Tomas Alumni Assn. (trustee 1982—). Roman Catholic. Clubs: Binakayan Women's (pres. 1979—), Makabayang Kabitenyo, Yellow Brigade Inc., Barangayette. Home: Bautista Compound, Binkayan, Kawit Cavite 2713, Philippines Office: Cavite Med Ctr, Cavite Philippines

BAXANDALL, PETER ROBERT, mathematican, educator; b. Liverpool, Lancashire, U.K., Apr. 28, 1938; s. Harry and Mary Hannah (Hillman) B.; m. Alison Jane Eady Surgey, July 3, 1963; children—John Surgey, James Peter. B.Sc., Manchester U., 1960, Diploma Advanced Studies in Sci., 1964; postgrad., Cambridge U., 1960-62. Lectr. U. Cape Town, South Africa, 1962-64, lectr. U. Keele, Eng., 1965-83; warden, Horwood Hall 1974-83; tchr. Bryanston Sch., Dorset, Eng., 1983—; tutor Open U., Eng., 1970—. Author: (with others) Proof in Mathematics, 1980; Differential Vector Calculus, 1981, Vector Calculus, 1986. Keele U. fellow 1984—. Fellow Inst. Math. and Applications; mem. Am. Math. Soc., Assn. Tchrs. of Math. Avocations: squash; canals. Home: West Court, 4A West Street, Blandford Forum, Dorset DT11 7AJ, England Office: Bryanston Sch, Blandford Forum, Dorset DT11 OPX, England

BAXENDELL, PETER (BRIAN), petroleum executive, director; b. Runcorn, Eng., Feb. 28, 1925; s. Leslie Wilfred Edward and Evelyn Mary (Gaskin) B.; m. Rosemary Lacey, 1949; children: Anne, Gillian, Peter, John. BSc, ARSM, Royal Sch. Mines, London; DSc (hon.), Heriot-Watt U., Queen's U. Belfast, U. London, U. Tech. Loughborough. With Royal Dutch/Shell Group, 1946—, mng. dir. Shell-BP Nigeria, 1969-72, mng. dir. Royal Dutch/Shell Group, London, 1973-85, chmn. Shell U.K., 1974-79; chmn. Shell Transport & Trading Co. PLC, 1979-85, also bd. dirs.; chmn. Shell Can. Ltd., 1980-85; dir. Shell Oil Co., U.S.A., 1982-85, Shell Transport & Trading Co. PLC, 1973—, Hawker Siddeley Group PLC, 1984—, chmn. 1986—; bd. dirs. Sun Life Assurance Co. Can. Decorated comdr. Order Brit. Empire, 1972, Knight bachelor, 1981, Comdr. Order Orange-Nassau, 1985; fellow Imperial Coll. Sci. and Tech. Fellow Inst. Petroleum, Fellowship Engring., Inst. Mining and Metallurgy. Address: Shell Ctr, London SE1 7NA, England Office: Hawker Siddeley Can Inc, 7 King St E, Toronto, ON Canada M5C 1A3

BAXTER, GENE KENNETH, mechanical engineer, company executive; b. Emmett, Idaho, Sept. 4, 1939; s. Glen Wilton and Mable Velhelmina (Casper) B., Sr.; A.A. in Mech. Engring. (scholar), Boise Jr. Coll., 1959; B.S. in Mech. Engring., U. Idaho, 1961; M.S. in Aero. Engring. (NDEA fellow), Syracuse U., 1966, Ph.D. in Mech. Engring., 1971; m. Laraine Marie Mitchell, Jan. 20, 1968; children—Gretchen Lynn, Aaron Gregory. Engr. Pratt & Whitney Aircraft Co., East Hartford, Conn., 1961; teaching and research asst. Syracuse (N.Y.) U., 1962-67; engr. Galson & Galson Cons. Engrs., Syracuse, 1968; sr. mech. engr., staff engr. electronic systems div. Gen. Electric Co., Syracuse, 1968-77, advanced project mgr. mech. design engring. mgr., space div. Daytona Beach, Fla., 1977-82; engring. dept. head Schlumberger Tech. Corp., Rosharon, Tex., 1982-83; mgr. engring., downhole services div. Exploration Logging, Inc. div. Baker Internat. Corp., Sacramento, 1983-85; mgr. handling qualities sect. engring. and tng. simulation systems dept. McDonnell Douglas Helicopter Co., Mesa, Ariz., 1985-87, mgr. projects mgmt., 1987—; dir. mech. projects creating visual simulation and tng. systems, nuclear power controls, shipboard digital control systems; dir. elec./mech. projects creating equipment for measurement, analysis and control of wellhead, formation and drilling parameters for oil well services industry; dir. projects creating hardware systems and software models of flight, control and aircraft subsystem performance characteristics for helicopter simulation and training systems; tchr. refresher course N.Y. State Profl. Engrs., Syracuse, 1975-76. Chmn. fin. and stewardship com. United Ch. of Christ, Liverpool, N.Y., 1974-77, chmn. bd. trustees, 1977; ruling elder Ormond Beach (Fla.) Presbyn. Ch., 1979-82, chmn. stewardship com., 1979-80, pres. corp., 1980-82, chmn. fin. com., 1981-82. Recipient design award Machinery Mag., 1961; Raymond J. Briggs award Idaho Bd. Engring. Examiners, 1961; profl. lic. engr., N.Y. Mem. IEEE (sr.; treas. Daytona sect. 1978-79, chmn. 1979-80), ASME, Am. Helicopter Soc., Research Soc. of Am., Am. Inst. Aeros. and Astronautics, Army Aviation Assn. Am., Phi Kappa Phi, Tau Beta Pi. Speaker numerous profl. confs.; contbr. over 30 research papers in field. Home: 1243 N Norwalk Mesa AZ 85205

BAXTER, HARRY STEVENS, lawyer; b. Ashburn, Ga., Aug. 25, 1915; s. James Hubert and Anna (Stevens) B.; m. Edith Ann Teasley, Apr. 4, 1943; children: Anna Katherine Baxter Worley (dec.), Nancy Julia Baxter Sibley. A.B. summa cum laude, U. Ga., 1936, LL.B. summa cum laude, 1939; postgrad., Yale U., 1939-40. Bar: Ga. 1941. Instr. U. Ga. Law Sch., Athens, 1941; assoc. Smith Kilpatrick Cody Rogers & McClatchey, Atlanta, 1942-51; ptnr. Kilpatrick & Cody, Atlanta, 1951-86, of counsel, 1986—; mem. State Bd. Bar Examiners Ga., 1960-66; chmn. State Bd. Bar Examiners, 1961-66; mem. Ga. Jud Qualifications Commn., 1979-86, chmn., 1984-85. Pres. Atlanta Community Chest, 1963; mem. bd. visitors U. Ga. Law Sch., 1965-68, chmn., 1965-66, chmn. alumni adv. com. on reorgn., 1963-64; chmn. chancellor's alumni adv. com. on selection of pres. U. Ga., 1966-67; gen. co-chmn. Joint Ga. Tech.-Ga. Devel. Fund, 1967; trustee U. Ga. Found., chmn., 1973-76; former William E. Honey Found., St. Joseph's Hosp., Atlanta, 1976-84. Served with AUS, 1942-45. Recipient Disting. Alumnus award U. Ga. Law Sch., 1967. Fellow Am. Bar Found.; mem. Am. Law Inst., ABA, Ga. Bar Assn., Atlanta Bar Assn., Atlanta C. of C. (dir. 1959-62), Atlanta Legal Aid Soc. (pres. 1956-57), Phi Beta Kappa, Phi Beta Kappa Assocs., Phi Kappa Phi, Omicron Delta Kappa, Phi Delta Phi. Clubs: Capital City (pres. 1965-67), Lawyers (pres. 1958-59), Piedmont Driving, Commerce, University Yacht. Home: 3197 Chatham Rd NW Atlanta GA 30305 Office: Equitable Bldg 100 Peachtree St NW Atlanta GA 30043

BAXTER, JOSEPH DIEDRICH, dentist; b. New Albany, Ind., Sept. 11, 1937; s. James William, Jr. and Beatrice (Diedrich) B.; A.B., Ind. U., 1959, D.M.D., U. Louisville, 1969; m. Carroll Jane Bell, Dec. 23, 1972. Practice dentistry, New Albany, 1969—. Bd. dirs. Floyd County (Ind.) Econ. Opportunity Corp., 1971-76. Served with AUS, 1960-61. Mem. Floyd County Dental Soc. (pres. 1972-74), Am. Dental Assn., Phi Gamma Delta. Republican. Methodist. Home: 36 Bellewood Dr New Albany IN 47150 Office: Professional Arts Bldg New Albany IN 47150

BAXTER, NORMAN, helicopter manufacturing company executive; b. Phila., May 21, 1930; s. Nathan and Grace Louise; B.Sc., Neumann Coll., 1982; postgrad. Widener U., Del. Sch. Law; m. Cecile Marion Kattinge, Mar. 16, 1963; children—Frances Marie, Norma Jean, Jamie Lynne. Prodn. planner, mfg. engr. Boeing Helicopters, Phila., 1963-65, sr. systems analyst, 1965-67, adminstrv. asst. to dir., indsl. engr., 1967-70; mgr. mfg. program, 1970-72, mgr. materiel program, 1974-78, traffic mgr., 1979-83, sr. material mgr., 1983—; v.p. Baxter Mgmt. Cons.; mem. freight systems adv. bd. Am. Airlines. Bd. dirs. Aston Town Watch, 1977-80; pres. Village Green Knolls Civic Assn., 1967-69. Served with USAF, 1946-49. Mem. Aerospace Industries Assn. (traffic com.), Boeing Mgmt. Assn. (past pres.), Am. Helicopter Soc., Nat. Def. Transp. Assn. (v.p.), Neumann Coll. Alumni Assn. (exec. bd.).

BAXTER, RICHARD BRIAN, lawyer; b. Detroit, Feb. 22, 1927; s. Charles Lewis and Madelyn (Kilburtus) B.; m. Margaret Elizabeth, May 28, 1949; children—Judith Ann, Janet Carole, Richard Brian, Jr. A.B., U. Mich., 1951, J.D., 1954. Bar: Mich. 1954, U.S. Ct. Appeals (6th cir.) 1960, U.S. Supreme Ct. 1967. Ptnr. Dykema, Gossett, Spencer, Goodnow & Trigg and predecessor, Grand Rapids, 1965—, sr. ptnr., 1979—; mem. faculty, participant continuing legal edn., Advocacy Inst. Served with USAAC, 1944-46. Recipient Exceptional Performance citation Def. Research Inst., 1981. Fellow Mich. Bar Found., Am. Bar Found.; mem. ABA, Mich. Bar Assn., Grand Rapids Bar Assn. (pres. 1977), Mich. Def. Trial Counsel (pres. 1981), Am. Coll. Trial Lawyers, Internat. Acad. Trial Lawyers (dir. 1985—), Internat. Soc. Barristers, Fedn. Ins. Counsel Internat. Assn. Def. Counsel Am. Judicature Soc. Club: Cascade Hills Country (Grand Rapids). Author: Michigan Continuing Legal Education Defenses in Legal Malpractice, 1974; Defenses in Wrongful Death Cases, 1975; contbr. chpts. and articles to legal publs. Home: 1318 Woodcliff Dr SE East Grand Rapids MI 49506 Office: Dykema Gossett Spencer et al 200 Oldtown Riverfront Bldg Louis Campau Promenade NW Grand Rapids MI 49503

BAYAZES, GEORGIA, real estate and financial consultant; b. N.Y.C., Jan. 29, 1920; d. Prokop and Sappho (Galetsa) B.; B.A. in Bus. Adminstrn., Bklyn. Coll., 1941; postgrad. N.Y. U., 1958. Asst. to treas. Hubschman Factors Corp., N.Y.C., 1942-52; office mgr. Koeppel & Koeppel, N.Y.C., 1952-57; real estate mgr. Ramapo Estates, Inc., N.Y.C., 1957-77; real estate and fin. cons. Seth Evans & Aronson, Inc., N.Y.C., 1977—; Co-chairperson benefit luncheons Assn. for Help to Retarded Children, N.Y.C., 1976, Cooley's Anemia Found., N.Y.C., 1977, N.Y. Hosp. Cardiac Children's Fund, N.Y.C., 1978, St. Michaels Home, Yonkers, N.Y., 1975, Holy Cross Sem. of Brookline, Mass., 1973, St Basils Acad. of Garrison, N.Y., 1974; pres. Ladies Philoptochos Soc., Greek Orthodox Ch. of Assumption, Bklyn., 1972-77, sec. Archdiocesan Dist. Bd., 1980-81; pres. Hellenic Soc. Bklyn. Coll. Mem. Stats. Soc. Bklyn. Coll. Club: Hellenic Univ. (sec., treas., scholarship com.). Home: 639-80th St Brooklyn NY 11209 Office: PO Box 8174 FDR Station New York NY 10022

BAYBARS, ILKER, business educator; b. Gordes, Manisa, Turkey, Nov. 26, 1947; s. Tevfik and Emine (Basboga) B. BS, Middle East Tech. U., Ankara, Turkey, 1969; MS, Carnegie-Mellon U., 1972, PhD, 1979. Instr. Middle-East Tech. U., 1969-70; instr. Carnegie-Mellon U., Pitts., 1978-79, acad. dir. quantitative skills summer inst., 1980, vis. asst. prof. sch. urban pub. affairs, 1979-81, asst. prof. grad. sch. indsl. adminstrn., 1982-86, assoc. dean., dir. masters programs grad. sch. indsl. adminstrn., 1985—, assoc. prof. grad. sch. indsl. adminstrn., 1986—; cons. Par Ajans, Ankara, 1968-70, UN, N.Y.C., 1981—, AT&T , Bedminister, N.J., 1981—, Mellon Bank, Pitts., 1982—. Author: Graph Theory: A Self Place Text, 1976; contbr. articles to profl. jours. Served with Turkish Army, 1976. Recipient Carnegie-Mellon U. Limbach Teaching award, 1981; UN Traveling grantee, 1981, NSF grantee, 1980-82. Mem. Pitts. Turkish Am. Assn., Ops. Research Soc. Am., Inst. Mgmt. Sci., Am. Prodn. and Inventory Control Soc., Soc. Indsl., Applications of Math., Assn. Pub. Policy Analysis and Mgmt., Am. Friends of Turkey, Assembly of Am. Turkish Assns., Assn. Turkish Am. Scientists, Am. Prodn. and Inventory Control Soc., Sigma Xi. Home: 5133 Forbes Ave Pittsburgh PA 15213 Office: GSIA Carnegie Mellon U 5000 Forbes Ave Pittsburgh PA 15213

BAYBAYAN, RONALD ALAN, lawyer; b. Paia, Hawaii, July 4, 1946; s. Celedonio Ludrano and Carlina (Domingo) B.; m. Dianne Lea, June 14, 1969 (div. June 1985); children: Alycia Kay, Amber Lea; m. Sharyn Dee Huckins, Dec. 31, 1985. BA, Coe Coll., 1968; JD, Drake U., 1974. Bar: Iowa 1977, U.S. Dist. Ct. (so. dist.) Iowa 1977, U.S. Tax Ct. 1978, U.S. Dist. Ct. (no. dist.) Iowa 1980, U.S. Ct. Appeals (8th cir.) 1985, U.S. Supreme Ct. 1985, U.S. Dist. Ct. Hawaii 1986. Asst. law librarian Drake U., Des Moines, 1974-77; assoc. Law Office Mike Wilson, Des Moines, 1977-78; sole practice Des Moines, 1978—. Served with USAF, 1969-73. Mem. ABA, Iowa Bar Assn., Polk County Bar Assn., Am.-Filipino Assn. Iowa (bd. dirs. 1986), Bass Anglers Sportsman Soc. (Iowa chpt. pres. 1979-82). Republican. Mem. Wakonda Christian Ch. Club: Mid-Iowa Bassmasters (past pres., past v.p., past sec.) (Des Moines). Home: 1520 Birch Norwalk IA 50211 Office: 5609 Douglas Des Moines IA 50310

BAYERTZ, KURT, philosopher, educator; b. Dusseldorf, Fed. Republic Germany, Nov. 13, 1948; s. Heinrich and Anneliese (Behrendt) B.; 1 child, Charlotte. MA, U. Dusseldorf, 1974; PhD, U. Bremen, Fed. Republic of Germany, 1977. Prof. philosophy U. Bremen, 1979-83, U. Bielefeld, Fed. Republic of Germany, 1983—. Author 3 German books. Office: U Bielefeld, Postfach 8640, 4800 Bielefeld Federal Republic of Germany

BAYLES, SAMUEL HEAGAN, advertising agency executive; b. Port Jefferson, L.I., N.Y., Nov. 10, 1910; s. Edward Post and Mary Jane (Lerch) B.; m. Gladys Grinnell, Sept. 25, 1933 (dec. Dec. 1980); children: Elizabeth Jane (Mrs. Frederick Joseph Wheeler), Samuel Heagan, Christina Mary (Mrs. William Francis Callahan, III); m. Jane Curry, Feb. 11, 1984. Student, Stony Brook Prep. Sch., 1928; B.A., Dartmouth, 1933. With Ruthrauff & Ryan, Inc., 1933-46, v.p., dir., co-dir. radio and television, 1940-46; a prin., chief exec. officer, founder chmn. SSC & B, Inc. (formerly Sullivan, Stauffer, Colwell & Bayles, Inc.), N.Y.C., 1946—; mem. policy, ops. coms. SSC & B Lintas Internat., Ltd. Author and pub.: Modern Man's Quest for Identity, The Golden Book on Writing, The Power of Intersensory Selling; writer foreword to Slogans. Bd. overseers Hanover Inn, Dartmouth Coll.; chmn. bd. dirs. Advt. Research Found. Mem. Phi Beta Kappa, Psi Upsilon. Clubs: North Fork Country (Cutchogue, L.I., N.Y.); Manhasset Bay Yacht (Port Washington). Home: Sands Light Sands Point NY 11050 also: Nassau Point NY 11935

BAYLISS, DAVID, English government official, researcher; b. Cleveleys, Lancashire, Eng., July 9, 1938; s. Herbert and Anne Esther (Roper) B.; m. Dorothy Christine Crohill, Aug. 25, 1961; children—Mark Andrew, Jason Peter, Ruth Abigail. BS in Civil Engring., Manchester U., 1961, diploma in town planning, 1966; testamur Inst. Mcpl. Engrs., 1963, diploma in traffic engring., 1964. Registered chartered engr., U.K. Chief transport planner Greater London Council, 1972-84; dir. planning London Regional Transport, 1984—; bd. dirs. London Transport Internat.; expert advisor OECD, World Bank, European Conf. of Ministers of Transport, WHO. Author: Encyclopedia Brittanica Year Book (Transportation), 1978—. Contbr. numerous articles on urban and transport planning to profl. pubis. Fellow Inst. Civil Engrs., Royal Town Planning Inst., Chartered Inst. Transport, Inst. Hwys. and Transp., Inst. Transp. Engrs. (U.S.); mem. Sci. Research Council (chmn. transport com. 1978-80), Regional Studies Assn. (chmn. 1980-82), Brit. Parking Assn. (pres. 1987). Mem. Ch. of Eng. Home: 37 Ledborough Ln, Beaconsfield Bucks HP9 2DB, England Office: London Regional Transport, 55 Broadway, London SW1 H9B, England

BAYOL, IRENE S., information services specialist; b. Franklin County, N.C., Oct. 11, 1933; d. Walter Ernest and Nonie (Parrish) Sledge; m. Charlie Morton Hamlet, Aug. 23, 1950 (div. Mar. 1956, dec. 1981); 1 child, Marcia Jean; m. Jerome Stollenwerch Bayol, Aug. 9, 1958 (div. May 1972, dec. 1980); children: Jerome Jr., Susan Carol, Keenan Jules. Student, Louisburg (N.C.) Jr. Coll., 1952-53, U. Va., 1970, Northern Va. Community Coll., Alexandria, Va., 1984, Am. U., Washington, 1986—. Computer equipment analyst USAF, Washington, 1970-73; supr. GSA, Washington, 1973-84; computer equipment specialist GSA Inst. for Info. Tech., Washington, 1984-85; policy officer GSA, Washington, 1985-87, program mgr., 1987—; real estate agt., 1973—. Episcopalian. Clubs: Profl. Womens' Club, Toastmistress Club, Travel Club, Investments.

BAYRAKTAR, ALI ULVI, corporate sales executive; b. Eskisehir, Turkey, Sept. 6, 1955; s. Ali Erdoğan and Emine Ayser Bayraktar; m. Gülgün Özsahin, Sept. 26, 1987. BS, ME, Bosphorus U., Istanbul, Turkey, 1981. engr. Dogus Constr. Co., Istanbul, 1981; project officer Tech. Dept. Headquarters of Turkish Landforces, Ankara, 1982-83; sales mgr. Aymak Mak. Sanayii ve Ticaret A.S., Istanbul, 1984—; cons. Sadri Sener Constrn. Co., Istanbul, 1986. Author Insaat Dünyasi mag., 1986. Clubs: Uğur Tennis, Raket Tennis (Istanbul). Home: Lemi Atli Sokak #3 Bostanci, Istanbul Turkey Office: Aymak Makina Sanayii ve Ticaret AS, Ortaklar Cad Bahceler Sok No 13, Meciidyekoy Istanbul, Turkey

BAYS, JOHN THEOPHANIS, consulting engineer; b. Bklyn., July 17, 1947; s. Theophanis A. and Mildred Bays; B.S., N.Y. Inst. Tech., 1972; B.Arch., CCNY, 1974; cert. in solar design, Ohio State U., 1975; m. Mindy Giardina, July 8, 1973; 1 dau., Nina. Cert. energy mgr., energy auditor. Project mgr., head system designer Wormser Sci. Corp., Stamford, Conn., 1975-82, v.p. engring., 1982-85; prin. cons. E.E. Linden Assocs., Cons. Engrs., Darien, Conn., 1985—. Recipient awards in solar design. Mem. ASHRAE. Home: 1435 E 104th St Brooklyn NY 11236 Office: 5 Brook St Darien CT 06820

BAYS, ROBERT PAYNE, internist, educator; b. Woodland, Miss., Mar. 19, 1921; s. Fred Barry and Sara Louise (Payne) B.; B.S., Miss. State Coll., 1942; M.D., Vanderbilt U., 1945; m. Lilburn Catherine Sandoz, Dec. 13, 1946; children—Robert Payne, Bonnie Lee, Katherine Elizabeth. Intern, Gorgas Meml. Hosp., Ancon, C.Z., 1946-47, resident, 1946-47; asst. resident Strong Meml. Hosp., Rochester, N.Y., 1949-50; resident in internal medicine Scott and White Clinic, Temple, Tex., 1950; fellow pathology Strong Meml. Hosp., Rochester, 1948, fellow hematology, 1948-49; chief med. services U.S. Med. Center, Springfield, Mo., 1951-53; pvt. practice internal medicine, Shreveport, La., 1953—; pres., Bays and Herold Med. Corp., Shreveport, 1970—; clin. asso. prof. La. State U. Med. Sch., Shreveport, 1967—; bd. dirs. Doctors Hosp., Inc., Shreveport, 1963-67, vice chmn., 1967, exec. com., 1967-71; dir. Savs. Life Ins. Co., 1974—, med. dir., 1975—. Served with U.S. Army, 1942-45, 46-48; USPHS, 1950-53. Diplomate Am. Bd. Internal Medicine, Bd. Life Ins. Medicine, Fellow ACP; mem. Am. Soc. Internal Medicine, Am. Fedn. Clin. Research, Am. Heart Assn., AAAS, Am. Assn. Life Ins. Med. Dirs., La. Soc. Internal Medicine (pres. 1958-61). Contbr. articles to profl. jours. Home: 5513 Flagstone Dr Shreveport LA 71119 Office: 1121 Louisiana Ave Shreveport LA 71101

BAYS, STEPHEN, air cargo handling company executive; b. South Shields, County Durham, Eng., Feb. 8, 1948; s. Stephen and Nancy Anne (Foggon) B.; m. Susan Margaret Cockerill, Mar. 23, 1974; children: Daniel, Andrew. Postgrad. diploma in mgmt. studies, Newcastle-Upon-Tyne (Eng.) Poly. Coll., 1975-76. Apprentice fitter, machinist Rolls-Royce Aero Engine div., Sunderland, County Durham, 1964-69; fitter, turner Glacier Bearings and Thor Power Tools Ltd., Jarrow and North Shields, Tyne and Wear, Eng., 1970-72; med. physics dept. technician Gen. Hosp., Newcastle-Upon-Tyne, 1972-73; design draughtsman Brit. Die Casting Co. Ltd., North Shields, Northumberland, Eng., 1973-75, estimator, 1976-77; applications engr. Am. Air Filters Ltd., Cramlington, Northumberland, 1977-79; sales and estimating mgr. Weldwork Cargo Systems Ltd., London, 1979-87; sales mgr. Lodige Systems Internat. Ltd., London, 1987—. Mgr. football team Cub Scouts. Mem. Brit. Inst. Mgmt., World Wild Life Fund. Conservative. Lodge: Lions Internat. Home: 1 Cairngorm Pl, Farnborough Hampshire GU14 9HU, England Office: Lodige Systems Internat Ltd, The Mill Horton Rd, Stanwell Moor, Staines Middlesex TW19 GBJ, England

BAZEMORE, ALVAH WALKER, writer, editor educational materials; b. Butler, Ga., Oct. 3, 1920; s. Clarence Walker and Bertha Annie (Salzer) B. B.S., U. Ga., 1941; M.A., U. N.C., 1943, Ph.D., 1948; postgrad. Mc Gill U., 1955-56. Research assoc. Merck/Sharp & Dohme Inc., Rahway, N.J., 1947-59; mgr. med. ednl. design Xerox/Basic Systems Inc., N.Y.C., 1962-66; dir. SRI Press, Sci. Resources Inc., Union, N.J., 1967-71; project dir. Learning Systems/MIND, Inc., Cin., 1971-74; ednl. cons. EBASCO Services, Inc., N.Y.C., 1974-78; writer, editor, cons. Automatic Data Processing, Inc., Roseland, N.J., 1978—; cons. in field; mem. adv. bd. Ctr. for Adult Learning, Rutgers U., New Brunswick, N.J., 1982; dir. 1st Nat. Braintrust, Inc., Montclair, N.J., 1983—, pres., 1984. Author, editor numerous books; contbr. numerous articles to profl. jours. Recipient Pres.'s Excellence award, 1985. Mem. Nat. Soc. Performance and Instrn. (pres.'s award 1983), Am. Soc. Tng. and Devel., Soc. Applied Learning Tech., Assn. Ednl. Communications and Tech., AAAS, Mensa, Phi Beta Kappa, Sigma Xi. Democrat. Methodist. Home: 32B Tierney Dr Cedar Grove NJ 07009 Office: Automatic Data Processing Inc 1 ADP Blvd Roseland NJ 07068

BAZERMAN, STEVEN HOWARD, lawyer; b. N.Y.C., Dec. 12, 1940; s. Solomon and Miriam (Kirschenberg) B.; m. Christina Ann Gray, Aug. 28, 1981 (div. June 1988). BS in Math., BS in Engring., U. Mich., 1962; JD, Georgetown U., 1966. Bar: D.C. 1967, N.Y. 1968, U.S. Dist. Ct. (so. dist.) N.Y. 1970, U.S. Dist. Ct. (ea. dist.) N.Y. 1973, U.S. Claims Ct. 1976, U.S. Ct. Appeals (2d cir.) 1978, U.S. Cts. Customs and Patents Appeals 1981-82, U.S. Ct. Appeals (fed. cir.) 1982. Assoc. Arthur, Dry & Kalish, N.Y.C., 1967-80, Offner & Kuhn, N.Y.C., 1980-83; ptnr., head litigation dept. Kuhn, Muller & Bazerman, N.Y.C., 1983-87; ptnr. Moore, Berson, Lifflander, Eisenberg & Mewhinney, N.Y.C., 1987-88; of counsel Lerner, David, Littenberg, Krumholz & Mentlik, Westfield, N.J., 1988—. Vol. counsel community law offices Legal Aid Soc., N.Y.C., 1974-82, treas., 1979-82. Mem. Assn. of Bar of City of N.Y., Am. Intellectual Property Law Assn., N.Y. Patent, Trademark & Copyright Law Assn. Jewish. Home: 77 Park Ave New York NY 10016 Office: Lerner David Littenberg Krumholz & Mentlik 600 South Avenue W Westfield NJ 07090

BAZIN, PHILIPPE, photographer; b. Nantes, France, Sept. 1, 1954; s. Paul and Raymonde (Dulos) B.; m. Gwenolée Houdy, May 2, 1983; children: Camille, Bruno, Marie. Docteur en medecine, Techniques Medicales UER, 1983. Practice gen. medicine, Les Herbiers, France, 1983-86; photographer Ecole Nat. de la Photographie, Arles, France, 1986—. Represented in collections of Musée Nat. d'Art Moderne, Beaubourg, Musée d'Art Moderne de la Ville de Paris, La Galerie Mcpl. du Chateau d'Eau Toulouse, Le Fond Regional d'Art Contemporain Lyon, Bibliotheque Nationale, Paris.

BEACH, JOHNSTON, psychologist, army officer; b. Albany, N.Y., Apr. 21, 1945; s. Charles Addison Wilson and Eleanor (Johnston) B.; m. Maureen Ethel Brandow, June 17, 1967; children—Brandon Kirk, Amy Maureen, Emily Renee. B.A., U. Rochester, 1967; M.A., U. Maine, 1969, Ph.D., 1975. Enlisted in U.S. Army, 1969, advanced through grades to lt. col., 1982; assoc. prof. dept. behavioral scis. and leadership U.S. Mil. Acad., West Point, N.Y., 1981—. Decorated Bronze Star, Meritorious Service medal with 2 oak leaf clusters, Army Commendation medal. Mem. Am. Psychol. Assn., Assn. for Advancement Psychology. Republican. Presbyterian. Home: 216 C Barry Rd West Point NY 10996 Office: US Military Academy Dept Behavioral Sciences and Leadership West Point NY 10996

BEACH, LOUIS ANDREW, physicist; b. Greenville, Ind., June 2, 1925; s. George Covert and Clara (Kiesler) B.; B.S., Ind. U., 1944, M.S., 1947, Ph.D., 1949; m. Virginia Ann McHugh, Oct. 20, 1956; children—Andrew, Ann Marie, Ruth Christine, Covert John. Research asso. Lab. Nuclear Studies, Cornell U., 1949-51; physicist Naval Research Lab., Washington, 1951-87, head shielding sect., 1953-55, head nuclear reactions br., 1955-66, head physics I sect., cyclotron br., 1966-71, head nuclear physics sect., 1971-76, head radiation damage simulation sect., 1976-78, head radiation interactions sect., 1978-80, research physicist radiation detection sect., 1981-87; cons. Sachs/Freeman, Inc., Landover; lectr. grad. program nuclear engring. Catholic U. Am., 1960-66. Served with AUS, 1944-46. Fellow Washington Acad. Sci.; mem. Am. Phys. Soc., AAAS, Sigma Xi. Democrat. Roman Catholic. Home: 1200 Waynewood Blvd Alexandria VA 22308 Office: Code 4616 Naval Research Lab Washington DC 20375

BEACHELL, HENRY MONROE, agriculturalist; b. Waverly, Neb., Sept. 21, 1906; s. William Albert and Alice Leona (Degler) B.; m. Edna Mary Payne, Sept. 17, 1983 (dec. Dec. 1982). BS in Agr., U. Neb., 1930; MS in Plant Breeding and Genetics, Kans. State U., 1933; postgrad., Tex. A&M U., 1939; PhD Agr. (hon.), Seoul Nat. U., Korea, 1970, U. Neb., 1972. Rice breeder Agr. Research Service U.S. Dept. Agr., Beaumont, Tex., 1931-63, Rockefeller Found. Internat. Rice Research Inst., Los Banos, Philippines, 1963-72; rice breeder, cons. Internat. Rice Research Inst., Bagor, Indonesia, 1972-82, Farms Tex., Alvin, 1982—; cons. Brit. Supply Delegation, George Town, Brit. Guana, 1949, Atomic Energy Agy. UN, Internat. Rice Research Inst., Los Banos, 1983, Winrock Internat., Colombo, Sri Lanka. Breeder of numerous types of rice 1940-63. Recipient Indsl. Service Merit Bronze Tower award, Korea, 1978, Japan prize Sci. and Tech. Found. Japan, 1987, John Scott medal Honor City of Phila., 1969, award Internat. Rice Research Inst. Los Banos, 1972, Disting. Service award Tex. A&M U., 1981. Mem. AAAS (fellow), Am. Soc. Agronomy (fellow). Republican. Episcopal. Club: Golf Crest Country (Pearland, Tex.). Home: 2462 Country Club Dr Pearland TX 77581

BEACHLER, EDWIN HARRY, III, lawyer; b. Pitts., Nov. 21, 1940; s. Edwin H. and Mercedes S. B. B.A., Georgetown U., 1962; J.D., U. Pitts., 1965. Bar: Pa. 1965, U.S. Dist. Ct. (we. dist.) Pa. 1965, U.S. Ct. Appeals (3d cir.) 1966. Assoc., McArdle, McLaughlin, Paletta & McVay, Pitts., 1966-72; ptnr. Caroselli, Spagmolli & Beachler, Pitts., 1972—. Mem. ABA, Allegheny County Bar Assn., Allegheny County Acad. Trial Lawyers, Pa. Trial Lawyers Assn. (gov. 1982-83), Assn. Trial Lawyers Am. Home: 5660 Darlington Rd Pittsburgh PA 15217

BEACHLEY, MICHAEL CHARLES, radiologist; b. Harrisburg, Pa., Nov. 14, 1940; s. Kenneth Gumbert and Carolyn Elizabeth (Jones) B.; m. Deborah Rowe Samson, July 27, 1963; children: Kenneth, Barbara, William. A.B., Dartmouth Coll., 1962, B.M.S., 1963; M.D., Harvard U., 1965. Diplomate: Am. Bd. Radiology. Intern in surgery Med. Coll. Va., Richmond, 1965-66; resident in radiology Med. Coll. Va., 1966-69; instr. radiology 1970, faculty, 1972—, acting chmn. dept. radiology, 1976, prof., 1977-87, chmn. dept. radiology, 1977-82, prof. radiation scis., 1981-87, prof. biophysics, 1980-82, prof. physiology and biophysics, 1982-87, clin. prof., 1987—; clin. prof. radiology U. Pitts., 1988—; chmn. Dept. Radiology St. Margaret Meml. Hosp., Pitts., 1987—; cons. McGuire VA Hosp., 1977—; fellow in radiol. pathology Armed Forces Inst. Pathology, Washington, 1969. Contbr. chpt. to book, revs. and med. articles to profl. jours. Vice-pres. College Hills Civic Assn., 1975-77. Served as maj. M.C. U.S. Army, 1970-72. Fellow Am. Coll. Radiology (pres. Va. chpt. 1982-83), Am. Coll. Angiology; mem. AMA, Am. Heart Assn., Radiol. Soc. N.Am., Am. Roentgen Ray Soc., Pitts. Roentgen Soc., Pa. Radiol. Soc., Pa. Med. Soc., Allegheny Med. Soc. Clubs: Dartmouth of Western Pa. Home: Box 331 Heckert Rd Bakerstown PA 15007 Office: St Margaret Meml Hosp 815 Freeport Rd Pittsburgh PA 15215

BEADLE, GEORGE WELLS, biologist, emeritus educator; b. Wahoo, Nebr., Oct. 22, 1903; s. Chauncey Elmer and Hattie (Albro) B.; m. Marion Cecile Hill, Aug. 22, 1928 (div. 1953); 1 son, David; m. Muriel Barnett, Aug. 12, 1953; 1 stepson, Redmond James Barnett. B.S., U. Nebr., 1926, M.S., 1927, D.Sc., 1949; Ph.D., Cornell U., 1931; M.A., Oxford (Eng.) U., 1958, D.Sc. (hon.), 1959; D.Sc., Yale U., 1947, Northwestern U., 1952, Rutgers U., 1954, Kenyon Coll., 1955, Wesleyan U., 1956, Birmingham U., 1959, Pomona Coll., 1961, Lake Forest Coll., 1962, U. Rochester, 1963, U. Ill., 1963, Brown U., 1964, Kans. State U., 1964, U. Pa., 1964, Wabash Coll., 1966, Syracuse U., 1967, Loyola U., Chgo., 1970, Hanover Coll., 1971, Eureka Coll., 1972, Butler U., 1973, Gustavus Adolphus Coll., 1975, Ind. State U., 1976; LL.D., U. Calif. at Los Angeles, 1962, U. Miami, 1963, Brandeis U., 1963, Johns Hopkins U., 1966, Beloit Coll., 1966, U. Mich., 1969; D.H.L., Jewish Theol. Sem. Am., 1966, DePaul U., 1969, U. Chgo., 1969, Canisius Coll., 1969, Knox Coll., 1969, Carroll Coll., 1971, Roosevelt U., 1971; D. Pub. Service, Ohio No. U., 1970. Teaching asst. Cornell U., 1926-27, experimentalist, 1927-31; NRC fellow Calif. Inst. Tech., 1931-33, instr., 1933-35; guest investigator Institut de Biologie, physico-chimique, Paris, 1935; asst. prof. genetics Harvard U., 1936-37; prof. biology (genetics) Stanford U., 1937-47; prof. biology and chmn. div. biology Calif. Inst. Tech., 1946-60, acting dean faculty, 1960-61; pres., trustee, prof. biology U. Chgo., 1961-68, pres. emeritus, William E. Wrather Distinguished Service prof., hon. trustee, 1969-75, prof. emeritus, 1975; dir. Inst. Biomed. Research, AMA, Chgo., 1968-70; Eastman vis. prof. Oxford U., 1958-59; mem. Pres.'s Sci. Adv. Council, 1960; hon. pres. 12th Internat. Congress Genetics, 1968. Author: (with Alfred H. Sturtevant) An Introduction to Genetics, 1939, Genetics and Modern Biology, 1963, (with Muriel B. Beadle) The Language of Life, 1966 (Edison award best sci. book for youth 1967). Hon. trustee Mus. Sci. and Industry, Chgo.; trustee Calif. Inst. Tech., 1969-75; adv. bd. Robert A. Welch Found., 1971—. Recipient Lasker award, 1950, Dyer award, 1951, Emil C. Hansen prize Denmark, 1953; Albert Einstein Commemorative award in sci., 1958; Nobel Prize in medicine and physiology (with Edward L. Tatum and Joshua Lederberg), 1958; Am. Cancer Soc. award, 1959; Kimber Genetics award, 1960; Priestley Meml. award, 1967; Donald Forsha Jones medal, 1972; Order St. Olaf. Mem. Nat. Acad. Scis. (council 1969-72), Am. Philos. Soc., Royal Soc., Japan Acad. (hon.), Instituto Lombardo di Scienze e Lettre (Milan), AAAS (pres. 1946), Am. Acad. Arts and Scis., Genetics Soc. Am. (pres. 1955), Genetical Soc. Gt. Britain, Indian Soc. Genetics and Plant Breeding, Indian Nat. Sci. Acad. (hon.), Chgo. Hort. Soc. (pres. 1968-71, trustee 1971-76), Danish Royal Acad. Scis., Phi Beta Kappa (hon.), Sigma Xi. Home: 900 E Harrison Apt D-33 Pomona CA 91767

BEAL, PETER GEORGE, manuscript expert; b. Coventry, Eng., Apr. 16, 1944; s. William George and Marjorie Ena (Owen) B.; m. Gwyneth Morgan, July 24, 1974 (div. 1980); m. Sally Josephine Taylor, Nov. 19, 1982; 1 stepson, Jeffrey Taylor. BA in English with honors, U. Leeds, Eng., 1966, PhD, 1974. Research editor Bowker Mansell Pub. Co., London, 1974—; manuscript expert Sotheby's, London, 1980—. Compiler Index of English Literary Manuscripts, vol. I, 1980, vol. II, 1987; co-editor English Manuscript Studies 1100-1700 for Basil Blackwell Ltd., 1988—; gen. editor facsimile series seventeenth-century verse for Gregg Pub. Co. Ltd., 1988—; contbr. articles on manuscripts to profl. publs. Office: Sotheby's Manuscript Dept, 34-35 New Bond St, London W1A 2AA, England

BEAL, ROBERT LAWRENCE, real estate executive; b. Boston, Sept. 10, 1941; s. Alexander Simpson and Leona M. (Rothstein) B. B.S. cum laude, Harvard U., 1963, M.B.A., 1965. Vice pres., ptnr. Beacon Cos., Boston, 1965-76; ptnr. The Beal Cos.; exec. v.p. Beal and Co., Inc., Boston, 1976—; dir., mem. exec. com., mem. lending com. Provident Instn. Savs., 1983-86; dir., mem. exec. com. U.K.-Am. Properties; chmn., dir. Mass. Indsl. Fin. Agy., 1976—; instr. real estate Northeastern U., 1969-75. Bd. dirs. Boston Zool. Soc., 1972-86, pres., 1980, chmn. 1981-84, hon. chmn., 1985; mem. vis. com. Sch. Mus. Fine Arts, Boston; overseer Boys Club Boston, 1975—; mem. corp. Belmont Hill Sch.; trustee Beth Israel Hosp., 1981—, mem. bldg. and grounds com., 1976-82, 86; dir. Harvard Coll. Fund Council, 1972-73, capital fund dr. Class '63, 1979-85, co-chmn. 25th reunion; exec. bd. Boston chpt. Am. Jewish Com., 1987—; bd. dirs. Boston Mcpl. Research Bur., 1978—; trustee The Partnership, Inc., 1981—, New Eng. Aquarium, 1987—; bd. dirs. Boston Housing Partnership, Inc., 1983—; mem. adv. task force John F. Kennedy Library, 1982—; bd. govs. Mus. Fine Arts, Boston, 1988—; bd. overseers Mus. Fine Arts., Boston, 1988—. Mem. Nat. Realty Com. (dir., past sec., mem. exec. com. 1974—, v.p., vice-chmn.), Mass. Assn. Realtors (dir. 1979-81), Greater Boston Real Estate Bd. (dir. 1970-72, 76—, pres. 1978-79), Am. Soc. Real Estate Counselors, Bldg. Owners-Mgrs. Assn. Boston (dir. 1970-72), Ripon Soc. (co-founder, nat. treas. 1968-73, nat. governing bd. 1979—), Nat. Assn. Real Estate Appraiser (cert.), Mass. Taxpayers Found. (dir. 1980-86), Inst. Property Taxation (affliate), Internat. Assn. Assessing Officers (primary subscribing mem. 1982—), Beacon Hill Civic Assn. (dir. 1975-79), Greater Boston C. of C. (execs. club). Republican. Jewish. Home: 21 Brimmer St Boston MA 02108 Office: Beal and Co Inc 15 Broad St Suite 800 Boston MA 02109

BEALE, HELEN RUBY, insurance company brokerage administrator; b. Michigamme, Mich., Mar. 29, 1922; d. Edwin Martin and Katherine Mae (Rahilly) Stensrud; m. Roland Earl Beale, June 19, 1944 (dec.); children—John Robert, Ann Marie Beale Trachtenberg, James Edward. Student Mich. State U., St. Catherine's Coll., U. Wis., Platteville. Cert. adminstrv. mgr. Owner Beale Funeral Home, Michigamme, 1943-60; asst. to pres. Ind. Mgmt. Cons., Madison, Wis., 1966-73; sec. Sch. Dist. Office, Oregon, Wis., 1974-76; adminstrv. asst. Modern Kitchen Supply, Madison, 1976-81; agy. adminstrv. asst. Bankers Life, Madison, 1981—. State advisor U.S. Congl. adv. bd. Am. Security Council Found., Washington, 1983; mem. Sen. Robert Dole Exploratory Com. Mem. Adminstrv. Mgmt. Soc. (pres. 1981-82), Am. Mgmt. Assn., Nat. Tax Limitations Com., Madison Deanery (v.p. 1982-84, regents 1981-85). Roman Catholic. Club: Toastmasters.

BEALES, DEREK EDWARD DAWSON, historian, educator; b. Felixstowe, Eng., June 12, 1931; s. Edward and Dorothy Kathleen (Dawson) B.; m. Sara Jean Ledbury, Aug. 14, 1964; children: Christina Margaret, Richard Derek. BA, U. Cambridge, Eng., 1953, MA, PhD, 1957, LittD, 1988. Research fellow Cambridge U., 1955-58, fellow, 1958-62, asst. lectr., 1962-65, lectr., 1965-80, prof. modern history, 1980—; vis. prof. Harvard U., Cambridge, Mass., 1965. Author: England And Italy, 1859-60, 1961, From Castlereagh To Gladstone, 1969, The Risorgimento And The Unification of Italy, 1971, History And Biography, 1981, Joseph II, I: In The Shadow Of Maria Theresa, 1987; Editor (with Geoffrey Best): History, Society And The Churches, 1985, various hist. jours. Served as sgt. Royal Arty., Brit. army, 1949-50. Recipient Prince Consort prize U. Cambridge, 1960. Fellow Royal Hist. Soc. (council mem.). Anglican. Office: Cambridge U, Sidney Sussex Coll, Cambridge England

BEALL, DONALD RAY, manufacturing company executive; b. Beaumont, Calif., Nov. 29, 1938; s. Ray C. and Margaret (Murray) B. B.S., San Jose State Coll., 1960; M.B.A., U. Pitts., 1961; postgrad., UCLA. With Ford Motor Co., 1961-68; fin. mgmt. positions Newport Beach, Calif., 1961-66; mgr. corp. fin. planning and contracts Phila., 1966-67; controller Palo Alto, Calif., 1967-68; exec. dir. corp. fin. planning N.Am. Rockwell, El Segundo, Calif., 1968-69, exec. v.p. electronics group, 1969-71; exec. v.p. Collins Radio Co., Dallas, 1971-74; pres. Collins Radio Group, Rockwell Internat. Corp., Dallas, 1974-76, Electronic Ops., Dallas, 1976-77; exec. v.p. Rockwell Internat. Corp., Dallas, 1977-79; pres., chief operating officer Rockwell Internat. Corp., Pitts., 1979-88; chief exec. officer Rockwell Internat. Corp., El Segundo, Calif., 1988—; bd. dirs. Interfirst Corp.; mem. Pres.'s Export Council, 1981-85. Past Dallas met. chmn. Nat. Alliance Bus.; mem. Dallas Citizens Council; past bd. dirs. United Way of Met. Dallas, So. Methodist U. Found. Sci. and Engring.; bd. dirs. Dallas Council World Affairs; trustee U. Pitts.; gen. campaign chmn. Western Pa. affiliate Am. Diabetes Assn.; vice chmn. region IV Los Angeles County United Way, 1984-85; mem. Brit.-N.Am. com. Bus.-Higher Edn. Forum. Recipient award of distinction San Jose State U. Sch. Engring., 1980. Mem. Armed Forces Communications and Electronics Assn. (nat. dir.), Electronic Industries Assn., Aerospace Industries Assn. (chmn. bd. govs. 1987), Soc. Automotive Engrs., Soc. Mfg. Engrs. (hon.), Def. Preparedness Assn., Young Pres.'s Orgn., Navy League of U.S., Sigma Alpha Epsilon, Beta Gamma Sigma. Office: Rockwell Internat Corp 2230 E Imperial Hwy El Segundo CA 90245

BEALL, JAMES HOWARD, physicist, educator, poet; b. Grantsville, W.Va., May 12, 1945; s. Judson Harmon and Mary Lenore (Burns) B.; B.A. in Physics cum laude, U. Colo., 1972; M.S., U. Md., 1975, Ph.D., 1979; 1 dau., Tara Siobhan. Astrophysicist, Goddard Space Flight Center, NASA, Greenbelt, Md., 1975-78; Congressional Fellow U.S. Congress Office Tech. Assessment, Washington, 1978-79; project scientist sci. and analysis div. BKD, Rockville, Md., 1979-81; NAS/NRC resident research assoc. Naval Research Lab., Washington, 1981-83; mem. faculty St. John's Coll., 1983—; project adminstr. black oral history project Folger Shakespeare Library, Washington, 1981; moderator Library of Congress Symposium, 1981. Dir. edn. Environ. Action Com., Denver, 1971-72; bd. dirs. Partridgeberry Sch., Greenbelt, 1977-78; Poets-in-the Schs. participant Va. Public Schs., 1975—. Served in USAF, 1963-67. Nat. Endowment for Humanities grantee, 1976, 78; recipient Teaching Excellence award U. Md., 1974-75. Mem. AAAS, Am. Phys. Soc., Am. Astron. Soc., Md. Writers Council, Phi Beta Kappa, Sigma Xi, Sigma Pi Sigma. Democrat. Author: Hickey, the Days, 1980. Research in theoretical and observational astrophysics, renewable energy resources and public policy; discovered 1st concurrent radio and x-ray variability of active galaxy; made first prediction of inverse compton x-ray emission from supernovae, first prediction of detectable infrared and optical emission from accretion disks around black holes, first detection of a ring of x-ray light around the earth's equator. Home: 15606 Powell Ln Mitchellville MD 20716 Office: Naval Research Lab Code 4120 Washington DC 20375

BEAM, FRANK LETTS, communications corporation executive; b. Mount Vernon, Ohio, Apr. 10, 1942; s. James Alfred and Margaret Adele (Rudin) B. B.S.B.A., Northwestern U., Evanston, 1964. With advt. dept. ITT Bell and Gossett, Morton Grove, Ill., 1961-62; exec. trainee Leo Burnett Co., Chgo., 1964-65; acct. exec. Young and Rubicam, Chgo., 1965-67; prin., founder Frank L. Beam Co., Chgo., 1967-80; founder, pres. Beam Communications, Key Biscayne, Fla., 1981—; co-founder Beam Laser Systems, Inc., 1986, Allbev, Inc., Charlotte, N.C., 1986; v.p. MR Group, Inc., Key Biscayne, 1985—. Author: Effects of the Inner Six Outer Seven on Damlier-Benz ATG, 1961. Co-founder Key Biscayners for Responsive Govt., 1985; mem. steering com. Rep., 1972. Mem. Broadcast Pioneers, Nat. Assn. Broadcasters, Internat. Radio and T.V. Soc., Mayflower Desendents, SAR. Presbyterian. Clubs: Chig. Yacht; Key Biscayne Yacht, Surf (Miami). Avocations: boating, music, photography. Home: 201 Crandon Blvd Key Biscayne FL 33149 Office: Beam Communications Corp 50 W Mashta Dr Key Biscayne FL 33149

BEAM, JEROME CHRISTOPHER, psychologist; b. Canton, Ill., May 4, 1929; s. Louis Christopher and Ina Nell (Godwin) B.; B.A. in Psychology, Knox Coll., 1951; Ph.D. in Clin. Psychology (USPHS fellow), U. Ill., 1955. Cons. psychologist Miller Assos., Boston, 1955-58, Dunlap & Assos., Inc., Darien, Conn. and N.Y.C., 1958-67; cons. psychologist, v.p. subs. Clark Channell, Inc., v.p. parent co., Darien, 1958-63; cons. psychologist Stamford Hosp. Psychiat. Clinic, 1958-63, Narcotics Service Addiction Center of Fairfield County (Conn.), 1960-62; chmn. Drake-Beam & Assos., Inc., N.Y.C., 1967-81, Beam-Pines, Inc., N.Y.C., 1981—; pvt. practice clin. psychology, 1957—. Lic. clin. psychologist, N.Y. State, Conn.; diplomate in clin. psychology. Mem. Am. Psychol. Assn., Nat. Register Health Service Providers in Psychology, Phi Beta Kappa, Sigma Xi. Contbr. numerous articles to profl. jours. Office: 600 Third Ave New York NY 10016

BEAM, ROBERT CHARLES, lawyer; b. Phila., Dec. 21, 1946; s. Thomas Joseph and Jeannette Hortense (Templin) B.; m. Maureen McCauley, Aug. 21, 1976.; children—Davis McCauley B., Morgan McCauley B. BS in Commerce and Engring. Scis., Drexel U., 1970; JD, Temple U., 1977. Bar: U.S. Patent Office 1976, Pa. 1977, U.S. Dist. Ct. (ea. dist.) Pa. 1977, N.Y. 1978, D.C. 1979, U.S. Ct. Customs and Patent Appeals 1980, U.S. Ct.

Appeals (3d and fed. cirs.) 1982, N.J. 1983, U.S. Dist. Ct. N.J. 1983, Can. Patent Office 1985. Law clk. U.S. Dist. Ct., Phila., 1976-77; assoc. Firzpatrick, Cella, Harper & Scinto, N.Y.C., 1977-79; patent atty. Hercules Inc., Wilmington, Del., 1979-81, CPC Internat. Inc., Englewood Cliffs, N.J., 1981-83; patent counsel Congoleum Corp., Kearny, N.J., 1983-85, patent counsel and asst. gen. counsel, 1983-85; assoc. Paul & Paul, Phila., 1985-86; sr. atty. Armstrong World Industries, Lancaster, Pa., 1986-87; sole practice Blue Bell, Pa., 1987—. Mem. ABA, Phila. Bar Assn., D.C. Bar Assn., Phila. Patent Law Assn., Am. Intellectual Property Law Assn. Home and Office: 78 High Gate Ln Blue Bell PA 19422

BEAMER, SCOTT, consulting electrical engineer, lecturer; b. Berkeley, Calif., Apr. 2, 1914; s. Joseph H. and Louise (Scott) B.; B.S. in Elec. Engring., U. Calif., 1936; m. Alpha Mae Rogers, Oct. 21, 1939; children—Joan Louise, Scott, Ronald Laurence, Alexander Rogers, Deborah. Jr. elec. engr. Pacific Electric Motor Co., 1938-40; asso. elec. engr. Farm Sect. Adminstrn., U.S. Dept. Agr., 1940-42; cons. engr. with Clyde E. Bentley, 1946-47, Beamer & Tilson, 1949-51; with Beamer/Wilkinson & Assos.; 1966-76, Scott Beamer & Assos., 1977—; mem. faculty U. Calif., 1948-63, teaching regular classes architecture and engring. and extension classes at Oakland and San Francisco, 1948-59, also univ. research projects; lighting cons. Bay Area Rapid Transit Dist. Joint Ventures. Former chmn. adv. council Salvation Army Hosp.; former chmn. troop com., mem. exec. council Boy Scouts Am., elected to Order of Arrow; former trustee Children's Hosp. Med. Center Found.; bd. dirs. Oakland Mus. Assn., Heart-Lung Inst. East Bay; mem. adv. bd. Ladies Home Soc., Oakland. Served as maj. AUS, Office Chief of Ordnance, 1942-46, in Washington, France and Germany on Proximity Fuse project; mem. O.R.C., 1937-63. Decorated Bronze Star medal, Distinguished Service Wreath, Army Commendation medal. Registered profl. engr., Calif., Nev., Oreg. Fellow Illuminating Engring. Soc.; mem. IEEE (life), Nat. Acad. Forensic Engrs. (diplomate grade), Nat. Soc. Profl. Engrs. Clubs: Rotary (past pres.), Claremont Country, 100 (past dir.). Contbr. articles to profl. jours. Patentee neon dimming transformer; co-author of patent luminous bodies. Home: 36 King Ave Piedmont CA 94611 Office: Scott Beamer & Assocs 618 Grand Ave Oakland CA 94610

BEAN, ALAN LAVERN, space artist, retired astronaut; b. Wheeler, Tex., Mar. 15, 1932; s. Arnold H. B.; children: Clay, Amy. B.S. in Aero. Engring, U. Tex., 1955; grad., USN Test Pilot Sch.; Dr. Sci. (hon.), Tex. Wesleyan U., 1972, U. Akron; student, St. Mary's Coll., 1962; pvt. studies with various art tchrs. Commd. ensign U.S. Navy, 1955; advanced through grades to capt.; test pilot various aircraft U.S. Navy, Patuxent, Md., 1960-63; astronaut Manned Spacecraft Center, NASA, 1963—, lunar module pilot Apollo XII, 1969, ret., 1975; Mem. Internat. Adv. Bd. Frederic Remington Art Mus., Ogdensburg, N.Y., 1986. Exhibited in group shows at Bryant Galleries, Houston, 1974, Nat. Air and Space Mus., Smithsonian Inst., Washington, 1978-80; Astronaut/Cosmonaut art in LaGeode, Paris, 1985; Bus. in the Arts Awards, Hirshorn Mus. and Sculpture Garden, Washington, 1986; one man shows include Opera Assn., Ft. Worth, 1983, Meredith Long Gallery, Houston, 1984; represented in numerous pubs. including Aviation Space mag., Time mag., Art Gallery International mag.; host, narrator (video) The Safe and Succesful Use of Art Materials, 1986. Decorated D.S.M. with cluster, Navy Astronaut Wings; Navy Disting. Service medal with cluster; recipient Man of Yr. award Tex. Press Assn., 1969, Rear Adm. William S. Parsons award, 1970, Disting. Engring. Grad. award U. Tex., 1970, Godfrey L. Cabot award, 1970, Spl. Trustees award Nat. Acad. TV Arts and Scis., 1970, Yuri Gagarin award AIAA, 1974, Merit award N.Y. Art Dirs. Club, 1985. Fellow Am. Astron. Soc.; mem. Delta Kappa Epsilon. Home and Studio: 26 Sugarberry Circle Houston TX 77024

BEAN, MARVIN DAY, clergyman; b. Tampa, Fla., Sept. 8, 1921; s. Marvin Day and Lillian (Howell) B.; A.B., Fla. So. Coll., 1946, M.S. in Social Work, Vanderbilt U., 1948; postgrad. Ohio State U., 1951-52, Northwestern U., 1950; B.D., Garrett Theol. Sem., 1950; children: Bethany Louise, Thomas Holmes, Carol Sue. Ordained to ministry Methodist Ch., 1950; pastor, Lena Vista, Fla., 1946; asso. pastor San Marcos Meth. Ch., Tampa, 1947; pastor Cedar Lake (Ind.) Meth. Ch., 1948-50, Shepard Meth. Ch., Columbus, Ohio, 1951-68, Stonybrook Meth. Ch., Gahanna, Ohio, 1960-65, Obetz (Ohio) Meth. Ch., 1968-73, Neil Ave. Ch., Columbus, 1973-79, St. Andrew Ch., Columbus, 1979—. Asst. to exec. sec. Meth. Union in Ch. Extension, Columbus, 1965-74; v.p. com. info. and pub. relations Ohio Conf. Meth. Ch., 1964-68, vice chmn. health and welfare ministries, 1968-72, chmn. urban life com. Bd. Missions, 1968-70, asso. sec. Bd. Missions, 1968-72, chmn. Services to Children and Youth, 1962-72; chmn. research Ohio Area Study on Aging, Ohio area Meth. Ch., 1959-64; sec. Columbus dist. conf. Meth. Ch., 1960-68; chmn. sch. religion Columbus area Council Chs., 1953; sec. United Meth. Hist. Soc. of Ohio, 1984; trustee Meth. Retirement Ctr. Central Ohio, Columbus; trustee United Meth. Children's Home, Worthington, Ohio, 1973-74; chmn. bd. trustees Neil Ave. Found., 1973-79; chmn. W. Ohio Commn. Archives and History; conf. historian West Ohio Conf., United Meth. Ch.; pres. United Meth. Hist. Soc. Ohio. Served with AUS, 1943-46. Recipient Wolfley Found. recognition award for inner city work, 1961. Mem. Columbus Meth. Ministerial Assn. (pres. 1960-61), Ohio Council Chs. (rep. com. strategy and planning 1965-68). Nat. Assn. Social Workers, Acad. Cert. Social Workers. Author: A Guide to United Methodist Building, 1973; You Are on the District Board, 1974; Unto the Least of These, 1981; contbr. articles to profl. jours. Home: 122 W Henderson Rd Columbus OH 43214 Office: 1033 High St Worthington OH 43085

BEAR, LARRY ALAN, lawyer; b. Melrose, Mass., Feb. 28, 1928; s. Joseph E. and Pearl Florence B.; B.A., Duke U., 1949; J.D., Harvard U., 1953; LL.M. (James Kent fellow), Columbia U., 1966; m. 2d, Rita Maldonado, Mar. 29, 1975; children: Peter, Jonathan, Steven. Admitted to Mass. bar, 1953, N.Y. bar, 1967; trial lawyer firm Bear & Bear, Boston, 1953-60; cons. legal medicine P.R. Dept. Justice, also prof. law U. P.R. Law Sch., 1960-65; legal counsel, then commr. addiction services City N.Y., 1967-70; dir. Nat. Action Com. Drug Edn., U. Rochester (N.Y.), 1970-77; individual practice, N.Y.C., also public affairs radio broadcaster Sta. WABC, 1970-82; U.S. legal counsel Master Enterprises of P.R., 1982—; adj. prof. fin. Grad. Sch. Bus. Adminstrn. NYU, 1986—; spl. cons. to the Ctr. for New Era Philanthropy and Human Service Systems, Inc., 1987—; vis. prof. legal medicine Rutgers U. Law Sch., 1969; mem. alcohol and drug com. Nat. Safety Council, 1972-82; cons. in field. Mem. public policy com. Advt. Council, 1972—; mem.-at-large Nat. council Boy Scouts Am., 1972-85. Mem. Am. Bar Assn., N.Y. State Bar Assn., Forensic Sci. Soc. Gt. Britain, Acad. Colombiana de Ciencias Medico-Forenses. Club: Harvard (N.Y.C.). Author: Law, Medicine, Science and Justice, 1964; also articles. Home: 95 Tam O'Shanter Dr Mahwah NJ 07430 also: Ctr for New Era Philanthropy 7 Wynnewood Rd Wynnewood PA 19096

BEARAK, COREY B(ECKER), lawyer; b. Forest Hills, N.Y., Oct. 7, 1955; s. Stephen Irwin Bearak and Phyllis (Stone) Stark; m. Rachelle Pamela Confino, Mar. 24, 1985; 1 child: Jonathan Marc. BA in Polit. Sci., Hofstra U., 1977, JD, 1981. Bar: N.Y. 1982. Asst. to sec. of state N.Y. State, Albany and N.Y.C., 1978; sole practice Queens, N.Y., 1982—; counsel, chief staff Councilman Sheldon S. Leffler, N.Y.C., 1982—. Mem. Community Planning Bd. #13, Queens and N.Y.C., 1980—, N.Y. State Dems., 1986-88; alt. del. Dem. Nat. Convention, San Francisco, 1984, Queens Jewish Community Council, 1978—, dir. 1987—, del. 1985—, Northeast Queens Jewish Community Council, legis. chmn. 1987—, del. 1985—, N. Bellerose Civic Assn.; v.p. Greater N.Y. Raoul Wallenberg Com., N.Y.C., 1985—, trustee, 1983-84; assoc. v.p. Temple Sholom, Floral Park, 1986-88, brotherhood pres. 1984-86; trustee Lost Community Civic Assn., Floral Park and Hyde Park; 1st v.p. Queens County Line Dem. Assn., Glen Oaks, N.Y., 1980-82, pres. 1982-84, exec. sec. 1985—, other Dem. orgns. Recipient Cert. of Merit Boy Scouts Am., 1983; named one of Outstanding Young Men Am., 1985, 86. Mem. ABA (state and local govt. law sect.), N.Y. State Bar Assn. (legis. policy com., environ. law section), Queens Bar Assn. (assoc. editor jour. 1983-86, real property com.), N.Y. County Lawyers Assn. (legis. com., real property com.), Brandeis Assn. Home: 82-35 251st St Bellerose NY 11426 Office: 250 Broadway 22d Floor New York NY 10007

BEARD, HAROLD FINLEY, JR., insurance broker; b. Spokane, Wash., Apr. 25, 1943; s. Harold Finley and Kathleen Frances (Calkins) B.; m. Nancy Ann Canfield, June 17, 1966; children—Rebecca Kathleen, Malcolm Charles. B.A., U. Wash., 1966; postgrad., Byrn Mawr Coll., 1987—. C.L.U. Campus agt. Conn. Mut. Life Ins. Co., Seattle, 1965-66, sales mgmt. trainee, 1968-69; dist. agy. New Eng. Life Ins. Co., Yakima, Wash., 1969-75; sec.-treas. Beard, Bench & Mendenhall, Yakima, Wash., 1975-86, pres., 1986—. Contbr. articles to mags.; speaker profl. convs. Served with U.S. Army Spl. Forces, 1966-69. Life mem. Million Dollar Round Table, New Eng. Life's Hall of Fame, Ten Million Dollar Forum. Mem. Assn. Advanced Life Underwriters, Am. Soc. C.L.U.s, New Eng. Life Leaders Assn. (bd. dirs. 1985-86, sec., treas.), U. Wash. Alumni Assn. (bd. dirs., dist. gov. 1978-84). Republican. Episcopalian. Club: Rotary. Office: Beard Bench & Mendenhall 1100 Chinook Tower Box 4044 Yakima WA 98901

BEARD, JOHN HARVEY, exploration company executive; b. Pike City, Ark., Apr. 18, 1928; s. William Alexander and Nobia Gertrude (Head) B.; m. Delores Griffiths, Aug. 1949 (div. 1974); children—John Raymond, Nathan Lee, Rachel Johnell, Denise Louise, Morgan Louis; m. 2nd Laurel June McCarthy, Mar. 1974. B.S., U. Utah, 1957, M.S., 1959. Teaching asst. U. Utah, Salt Lake City, 1957-59; geologist Carter Oil Co., Salt Lake City, 1959-61, Humble Oil & Refining Co., Denver, 1961-62, Humble Prodn. and Research, Houston, 1962-63; geologist, micropaleontologist Humble Oil & Refining, Denver, 1963-66; sr. research geologist Exxon Prodn. Research Co., Houston, 1966-70, sr. research specialist, Houston, Singapore, 1970-72, Houston, 1972-74, Houston, 1975-79, Esso Prodn. Research, Bordeaux, France, 1974-75, Houston, 1974-75; sr. exploration geophysicist Exxon Co. U.S.A., Houston, 1979-81; exec. v.p., stockholder Zenith Exploration Co., Inc., Houston, 1981-87; dir., v.p. TDC Energy Corp., 1987—; dir., stockholder Kiowa Exploration, Houston; pres., stockholder, incorporator StrataVision Energy Inc., Houston, 1985—. Co-author (with others) The University of Kansas Paleontological Contribution-Article 62, 1975. Contbr. articles to profl. jours. Served with USN, 1945-49. Mem. Am. Assn. Petroleum Geologists (cert., author bull. 1968-69, 82), Soc. Exploration Geophysicists, Houston Geol. Soc., Geophys. Soc. Houston, Soc. Econ. Paleontologists and Mineralogists. Republican. Baptist. Avocations: fishing, golf. Home: 14135 Cardinal Ln Houston TX 77079 Office: TDC Energy Corp 15415 Katy Freeway 500 Houston TX 77094

BEARDMORE, JOHN ALEC, genetics educator, researcher; b. Burton on Trent, Staffordshire, Eng., May 1, 1930; s. George Edward and Anne Jean (Warrington) B.; m. Anne Patricia Wallace, Dec. 26, 1953; children: Anne Virginia, James Wallace, Hugo John, Charles Edward. BSc in Botany with 1st class hons., U. Sheffield, 1953; PhD in Genetics, 1956. Research demonstrator U. Sheffield, Eng., 1954-56, lectr., 1958-61; Harkness fellow Columbia U., N.Y.C., 1956-58; prof. genetics, dir. lab. U. Groningen, Netherlands, 1961-66; head Dept. Genetics U. Wales, Swansea, 1966-87; dir. Inst. Marine Studies, 1983-87; head Sch. Biol. U. Wales, 1988—; vis. asst. prof. Cornell U., 1958; research assoc. Rochester U., 1961; NSF fellow Pa. State U., 1966. Editor: (with B. Battaglia) Marine Organisms, 1977; contbr. numerous articles to profl. jours. Com. mem. Abbeyfield Homes, Swansea, 1987—. Recipient medal U. Helsinki, 1980. Fellow Inst. Biology (hon. sec. 1980-85); mem. Natural Environ. Research Council (aquatic life scis. com. 1982-87, chmn. 1984-87). Club: Athenaeum (London). Home: 153 Derwen Fawr Rd, Swansea SA2 8ED, Wales UK Office: U Wales, Sch Biol Scis, Swansea SA2 8PP, Wales UK

BEARDSLEY, THEODORE S(TERLING), JR., association executive; b. East St. Louis, Ill., Aug. 26, 1930; s. Theodore Sterling and Margaret (Kienzle) B.; m. Lenora J. Fierke, May 26, 1955; children: Theodore Sterling III, Mark A., Mary Elizabeth. B.S., So. Ill. U., 1952; M.A. (Max Bryant fellow), Washington U., St. Louis, 1954; postgrad., U. Heidelberg, Germany, 1955-56; Ph.D., U. Pa., 1961; linguistic research, Inst. Caro y Cuervo, Bogota, Colombia, summer 1973. Asst. in English Lycee Wilson, Chaumont, France, 1952-53; mem. faculty Rider Coll., 1957-61, chmn. dept. modern lang., 1959-61; asst. prof. Spanish So. Ill. U., 1961-62, U. Wis., 1962-65; dir. Hispanic Soc. Am., N.Y.C., 1965—; adj. prof. NYU, 1967-69, 80, Adelphi U., 1966, 68, Columbia U., 1969; Fulbright lectr., Ecuador, 1974; chmn. Museums Council N.Y.C., 1972-73; spl. cons. Hispanic bibliography Library of Congress, fall 1973, N.J. State Dept. Edn., spring 1975, Nat. Endowment for Humanities, 1978—. Narrator Spanish lang. recorded tours, Nat. Gallery Art, Met. Mus., Mus. Natural Sci., Boston Sci. Mus., Smithsonian Instn.; continuing series on Caribbean popular music in U.S, WBGO-FM, 1979; Xavier Cugat, 1980, USA Latino, 1981, Enrique Madriguera, Spanish Nat. Radio, 1985. Author: Hispano-Classical Translations, 1482-1699, 1970, Tomas Navarro Tomas, A Tentative Bibliography, 1908-1970, 1971; also articles; Recordings include: Charla con Camilo José Cela, 1966, Visita a la Hispanic Society, 1969; narrator-author: 4 part series Hispanic Immigration to the United States (text pub. 1976), CBS-TV, 1972; Librettist: Ponce de Leon, 1973; mem. adv. bd.: Hispanic Rev., Studia humanitatis, Boletin de ANLE, Hispanic Sem. of Medieval Studies. Served with AUS, 1954-56. Decorated Orden de Mérito Civil, Spain ; Fulbright grantee, 1952-53; Jusserand traveling fellow, 1962; research grantee Am. Council Learned Socs., 1964; travel grantee, 1974; Recipient Premio Bibliofilia Barcelona, Spain, 1973. Mem. Hispanic Soc. Am., Renaissance Soc. Am. (exec. council, acting dir. 1981-82), ASCAP, Academia Norteamericana de la lengua española, Internat. Inst. (Madrid), Internat. Linguistic Assn. (exec. council), Sigma Delta Pi, Sigma Tau Gamma; corr. mem. Royal Spanish Acad., Real Academia de Bellas Artes de San Carlos (Valencia), Academia Guatemalteca de la Lengua, Asociacion de Bibliofilos de Barcelona, Fundacion Santa Maria de la Rabida. Clubs: Grolier, Century. Office: 613 W 155th St New York NY 10032

BEARDSWORTH, DONALD EUGENE, college president; b. Clinton, Iowa, Jan. 2, 1921; s. Arthur E. and Hazel M. (Higgins) B.; student Northeastern State Coll., Tahlequah, Okla., 1939-41; m. Janyce Estelle McDorman, Feb. 3, 1968; children—Donald Eugene, Jerry Lee, Mary Carol Beardsworth Anderson. Vice pres., cashier Comml. Bank, Muskogee, Okla., 1946-52; v.p. Bank of N.Mex., Albuquerque, 1952-54; pres. Citizens Bank, Albuquerque, 1962-66, LSI/Draughon Sch. Bus., Oklahoma City, 1967-72, Nettleton Bus. Coll., Omaha, 1972-73; pres., chmn. bd., chief exec. officer Internat. Bus. Colls., El Paso, Tex., Las Cruces and Alamogordo, N.Mex., Lubbock, Tex. and Albuquerque; mem. proprietary adv. council Region VI, Office Edn., chmn. 1987—; dir. Tex. Commerce Bank, Border City; real estate and ins. agt., Albuquerque, 1955-62. Mem. City Council Muskogee, 1950-52; bd. mgrs. Thomason Gen. Hosp., El Paso, 1983—, chmn., 1987—; chmn. adv. bd., El Paso County Alcohol and Drug Abuse Treatment Ctr., 1987—. Served with AUS, 1943-46. Mem. Southwestern Comml. Schs. Assn. (pres. 1977—), Tex. Assn. Pvt. Schs. (dir., pres. 1980-81, pres.-elect 1988), Nat. Assn. Ind. Colls. and Schs., N.Mex. Assn. Pvt. Schs. (bd. dirs.), Tex. Tchrs. Assn., Nat. Rehab. Assn., Okla. Writers Guild, Am. Legion, Phi Sigma Epsilon. Democrat. Methodist. Clubs: El Paso, El Paso Internat., Kiwanis (pres. Highland-Albuquerque 1960, pres. El Paso 1983-84). Editor N.Mex. Realtor, 1962-63. Home: 9001 McFall St El Paso TX 79925 Office: 6501 Boeing Bldg I Suite 200 El Paso TX 79925

BEARE, GENE KERWIN, electric company executive; b. Chester, Ill., July 14, 1915; s. Nicholas Eugene and Minnie Cole (St. Vrain) B.; m. Doris Margaret Alt, Dec. 11, 1943 (dec.); children: Gail Kathryn, Joanne St. Vrain; m. Patricia Pfau Cade, Sept. 12, 1964. B.S. in Mech. Engring, Washington U., 1937; M.B.A., Harvard, 1939. Registered profl. engr., Ill. With Automatic Electric Co., Chgo., 1939-58, successively asst. to v.p. and gen. mgr., asst. to pres., mgr. internat. affiliated cos., gen. comml. mgr., 1939-54, v.p. prodn., 1954-58, dir., 1956-61; pres., dir. Automatic Electric Internat., Inc., Chgo., 1958-61; chmn., dir. Automatic Electric (Can.), Ltd., Chgo., Automatic Electric Sales (Can.), Ltd., 1958-61; pres., dir. Sylvania Internat., 1959-60; pres. Gen. Telephone & Electronics Internat., Inc., 1960-61, dir., 1960-72; also dir. numerous subs. in Gen. Telephone & Electronics Internat., Inc., Colombia, Mex., Venezuela, Argentina, Switzerland, Panama, Brazil, Bel; dir. Am. Research and Devel. Corp., 1967-74, Canadair Ltd., 1972-75; pres. Sylvania Electric Products, Inc., 1961-69, dir., 1961-72; exec. v.p. mfg., dir. Gen. Telephone & Electronics Corp., 1969-72; exec. v.p., dir. Gen. Dynamics Corp., St. Louis, 1972-77; pres. Gen. Dynamics Comml. Products Co., 1972-77; chmn. Asbestos Corp. Ltd., 1974-77; dir. Arkwright-Boston Mut. Ins. Co., Westvaco Corp., Emerson Electric Co., St. Joe Minerals Corp., Am. Maize-Products Corp., Datapoint Corp., Nooney Realty Trust, Inc. Served to lt. USNR, 1942-45. Mem. Pan Am. Soc., Nat. Elec. Mfrs. Assn. (bd. govs. 1963-72, v.p. 1964, pres. 1965-66), Armed Forces Communications and Electronics Assn., Nat. Security Indsl. Assn. (trustee 1969-72). Clubs: Wee Burn (Darien, Conn.) (gov. 1963-68); Union League (N.Y.C.), Econ. (N.Y.C.); St. Louis (dir. 1979—); Old Warson (Ladue, Mo.) (dir. 1979—). Home: 801 S Skinker Blvd Saint Louis MO 63105 Office: Pierre Laclede Center 7701 Forsyth Blvd Suite 545 Saint Louis MO 63105

BEARLEY, WILLIAM LEON, consulting company executive; b. Hays, Kans., June 6, 1938; s. William L. and Wilma M. (Sechrist) B.; B.S., U. Wyo., 1969, M.Ed., 1964; Ed.D., U. La Verne, 1983; M.H.R.D., Univ. Assos. Grad. Sch. Human Resource Devel., 1980; also grad. Lab. Edn. Intern Program; m. Diane Lee Kiser, Dec. 15, 1967. Tchr. math. Baldwin Park Unified Sch. Dist., Baldwin Park, Calif., 1961-64, chmn. dept. math, 1962-64; chmn. math. dept. Citrus Coll., Azusa, Calif., 1965-69, chmn. data processing dept., 1969-80, dir. computing and info. systems, 1972-80; pres. Computer Info. Assocs., Inc., Pasadena, Calif., 1980-82; prof. Edn. Mgmt., U. LaVerne, 1982—; v.p. Organizational Universe Systems, Valley Ctr., Calif., 1985—; cons., trainer info. resourse mgmt., 1981—. Mem. Data Processing Mgmt. Assn. (cert.), Am. Soc. Tng. and Devel., Acad. Mgmt., Am. Mgmt. Assn., Am. Guild Organists, Assn. Computing Machinery, Assn. Systems Mgmt. (cert.), Phi Delta Kappa. Author/co-author computer software, books and articles in field. Home: 12665 Cumbres Rd Valley Center CA 92082 Office: U La Verne 1950 3d St La Verne CA 91750

BEASLEY, JAMES EDWIN, lawyer; b. Buffalo, July 2, 1926; s. James Edwin and Margaret Ann (Patterson) B.; m. Helen Mary, Jan. 1, 1958 (div.); children—Pamela Jane, Kimberly Ann, James Edwin. B.S., Temple U., 1953, J.D., 1956. Bar: Pa. 1956. Law clk. to judge U.S. Dist. Ct. Ea. Dist. Pa., Phila., 1954-56; mem. Beasley, Casey, Colleran, Erbstein, Thistle, Kline & Murphy, 1966—; instr. law Temple U., 1979-81; mem. Philadelphia County Bd. Law Examiners; permanent del. 3d Cir. Jud. Conf.; chmn. com. standard jury instrns. Pa. Supreme Ct. Author: Products Liability and Unreasonably Dangerous Doctrine; contbr. articles to legal jours. Served with USN, 1943-45, USAR, 1951-57; ETO, PTO. Mem. Am. Judicature Soc., ABA, Pa. Bar Assn., Phila. Bar Assn., Fed. Bar Assn., Am. Law Inst., Phila. Trial Lawyers Assn. (pres. 1970-71), Pa. Trial Lawyers Assn. (pres. 1969-70), Aircraft Owners and Pilots Assn., Inner Circle of Advocates, Am. Trial Lawyers Assn., Phila. Trial Lawyers Assn. (Justice Michael Musmanno award), Am. Bd. Profl. Liability Attys., Temple U. Gen. Alumni Assn. (cert. of honor), Pa. Soc. Republican. Episcopalian. Clubs: Masons, Union League. Office: 21 S 12th St Philadelphia PA 19107

BEATIE, RUSSEL HARRISON, JR., lawyer; b. Lawrence, Kans., Jan. 20, 1938; s. Russel Harrison and Mary Louise (Zimmerman) B.; children—Benjamin Wilson Parkhill, Amy Wilder. B.A. cum laude, Princeton U., 1959, LL.B. cum laude Columbia U., 1964. Bar: N.Y., U.S. Dist. Ct. (so. and ea. dists.) N.Y., U.S. Ct. Appeals (2d cir.), U.S. Supreme Ct. Assoc., Dewey, Ballantine, Bushby, Palmer & Wood, N.Y.C., 1964-66, 68-72; assoc. Rogers & Wells, 1966-68; mem. Dewey Ballantine, 1972-83; sole practice, 1983—. Served to 1st lt., arty. U.S. Army, 1959-61. Mem. Assn. Bar City N.Y. Republican. Christian Scientist. Clubs: Union, University, Verbank Hunting and Fishing. Author: Road to Manassas—The Growth of Union Command in the Eastern Theatre from the Fall of Fort Sumter to the First Battle of Bull Run, 1961. Office: 10 E 53d St Suite 3200 New York NY 10005

BEATON, IAN KEITH, mechanical engineer; b. Yeovil, Somerset, Eng., July 16, 1942; s. Ralph Hubert and Ann (Ricketts) B.; m. Sally Pauline Belbin, May 14, 1966 (div. 1971); m. Pamela Margaret Grinnell, Dec. 27, 1973; children: Stephen James, Nicola Anne, Michael Jon. Diploma in Aero. Engring., Loughborough Coll., Eng., 1965. Chartered aero. engr., mech. engr. Aerodynamicist Brit. Aircraft Corp., Filton, Eng., 1965-73; plant engr. Edmund Nuttall Ltd., Kilsyth, Scotland, 1974-76, works mgr., 1976-81; group engr. Gloucestershire County Council, Scotland, 1982-84, chief mech. engr., 1985—. Mem. Royal Aero. Soc., Inst. Mech. Engrs., Inst. Road Transport Engrs., Royal Air Force Assn., Dean Forest Ry. Soc. (chmn. 1985—). Home: 10 Brimsome Meadow, Highnam GL2 8EW, England Office: Gloucestershire County Council, Shepherd Rd, Cole Ave, Gloucester GL2 6EW, England

BEATRIX, HER MAJESTY, Queen of The Netherlands; b. Soestdijk, Netherlands, Jan. 31, 1938; d. Queen Juliana and Prince Bernhard; D. Sociol., Juridical and Hist. Scis., U. Leiden, Netherlands; m. Prince Claus von Amsberg, Mar. 10, 1966; children: Prince Willem-Alexander of Orange, Prince Johan Friso, Prince Constantijn. Queen of The Netherlands, 1980—. Home: Paleis Huis Ten Bosch, The Hague The Netherlands

BEATRÍZ, DULCE, artist; b. La Habana, Cuba, Mar. 17, 1931, came to U.S. 1960, naturalized 1970; d. José Mariá and Dulce Amelia (Moreno de Ayala) Hernández; m. Leonardo Beatríz, Mar. 30, 1959. Grad. Tchr.'s Coll., Havana, 1949; M.A. in Music, Conservatory Peyrellade, Havana, 1953; M.F.A., San Alejandro, Havana, 1955. First tech. dir. Cuban dept. fine arts, prof. drawing and painting, mem. judging bd. City Hall, Havana, 1956-59. Exhibited in 61 one-man shows, more than 150 group shows; represented in permanent collections in N.Am., Central Am., S.Am., Europe. Recipient Hall of Fame Internat. award for painting and sculpture Hispanic Internat. Research Inst., New York, 1971, Internat. award Honor Al Merito, 1974, Royal Order of Isabel La Católica decoration for painting and sculpture, Spain, 1983, Gold Keys, Dade County, Fla., 1983; travel prize San Alejandro, Havana, 1956, Gold medal Havana City Hall, 1956, commendation City of Miami, 1970; Lincoln-Marti nat. award Dept. HEW, 1971; named Eminent Alumna, Conservatory Peyrellade, Havana, 1953; hon. ambassador, Dade County, Fla., 1977. Fellow Royal Soc. Arts, London, 1977. mem. Hispania Nostra, Spain, 1978, Circulo de Cultura Panamericana, 1978. Republican. Roman Catholic.

BEATTIE, DAVID STUART, former governor-general of New Zealand; b. Sydney, Australia, Feb. 29, 1924; s. Joseph Nesbitt B.; LLB, U. Auckland, 1948; m. Norma Macdonald; 7 children. Called to bar, 1949; ptnr. firm Grierson, Moody, Jackson and Beattie, 1953-58; individual practice law, from 1958; Queen's counsel, 1965; judge N.Z. Supreme Ct., 1969-80; gov.-gen. for N.Z., 1980-85; chmn. Royal Commn. on Cts., 1977-78; chmn. Sir Winston Churchill Meml. Trust Bd., 1975-80; chmn. rules com. Supreme Ct., 1977-79. Mem. exec. bd. Crippled Children's Soc., Auckland, 1963-69; chmn. Dilworth Trust Bd., 1966-69; treas. Auckland Cancer Soc., 1969; trustee Halberg Trust, Intellectually Handicapped Trust, 1971—, McKenzie Found., 1970—; chancellor Anglican Diocese of Auckland, 1967-69; former chmn. N.Z. Sports Found. Served with N.Z. Army, 1941-43, Royal N.Z. Naval Vol. Res., 1943-46. Mem. Auckland Dist. Law Soc. (pres. 1964). Home: 18 Golf Rd, Heretaunga, Wellington New Zealand *

BEATTIE, EDWARD JAMES, surgeon, educator; b. Phila., June 30, 1918; m. Nicole Mary; 1 son, Bruce Stewart. B.A., Princeton U., 1939; M.D., Harvard U., 1943. Diplomate Am. Bd. Surgery, Am. Bd. Thoracic Surgery (mem. bd. 1960-69, chmn. bd. 1967-69). Intern, surg. resident Peter Bent Brigham Hosp., Boston, 1942-46; Mosely traveling fellow (Harvard) to U. London, Eng., 1946-47; surg. fellow, Markle scholar George Washington U., 1947-52; chief thoracic surgery Presbyn. Hosp., 1952-54; chmn. dept. surgery Presbyn.-St. Luke's Hosp., 1954-65; cons. thoracic surgery Hines VA Hosp., 1953-65, Chgo. Tb San., 1954-65, Ill. Research and Edn. Hosp., 1956-65, Rockefeller U. Hosp., 1978—; prof. surgery U. Ill., 1955-65; prof. surgery Cornell U., 1965-83, emeritus, 1983—; prof. surgery, prof. oncology U. Miami, Fla., 1983-85; chief thoracic surgery Meml. Hosp., N.Y.C., 1965-75, chmn. dept. surgery, 1966-78, chief med. officer, 1966-83, emeritus, 1983—, gen. dir., chief operating officer, 1975-83; chief thoracic surgery, dir. Kriser Lung Cancer Ctr., dir. clin. cancer programs Beth Israel Med. Ctr., 1985—. Editorial bd. Jour. Thoracic and Cardiovascular Surgery, 1962-81, Pediatric Digest, 1962—, Jour. Surg. Oncology, 1972—, Cancer Clin. Trials, 1977, Internat. Advances in Surg. Oncology, 1977. Fellow A.C.S.; mem. Am. Assn. Thoracic Surgery, Am. Surg. Assn., Soc. Vascular Surgery, AMA, Central, Western surg. assns., Internat. Soc. Surgery, Soc. Clin. Surgery, Am. Radium Soc., Soc. Thoracic Surgeons, Transplantation Soc., Am. Assn. Med. Colls., Pan Am. Med. Assn., Am. Cancer Soc., Am. Fedn. Clin. Research, Soc. Surg. Oncology. Republican. Office: Beth Israel Med Ctr 1st Ave at 16th St New York NY 10003

BEATTY, HENRY PERRIN, Canadian government official; b. Toronto, Ont., Can., June 1, 1950; s. George Ernest and Martha Letitia (Perrin) B.; m. Julia Florence Carroll Kenny; 2 children. Grad., Upper Can. Coll.; BA, U. Western Ont., 1971. Mem. Ho. of Commons, Ottawa, Ont., Can., 1972—, minister of state for treasury bd., 1979-84, minister nat. revenue, 1984-85; solicitor gen. of Can. 1985-86; minister nat. def. Can., 1986—; Progressive Conservative Caucus spokesman on communications, 1980; chmn. Caucus Com. on Fed. Province Relations, 1983; Caucus spokesperson on Rev. Can., 1983; chmn. Progressive Conservative Caucus Task Force on Rev. Can., 1984. Office: House of Commons, Ottawa, ON Canada K1A 0A6

BEATTY, JOHN TOWNSEND, JR., investment banker; b. Evanston, Ill., Feb. 18, 1936; s. John Townsend and Jane (Confer) B.; m. Marila M. Miller, Sept. 8, 1962; children—John Townsend III, William Oeric, Emily Frances. B.A., Yale U., 1958; M.B.A., U. Chgo., 1966. Regional mgr. Allis-Chalmers Mfg. Co., Bangkok, Thailand, 1966-69; v.p. Halsey Stuart & Co., Chgo., 1969-72; 1st v.p. Smith Barney, Harris Upham & Co., Chgo., 1972-86; dir. Miss. Valley Airlines, 1981-85, dir. Green Tree Acceptance Corp., 1982-85 ; trustee CPL Real Estate Investment Trust, 1985-88. Sr. Warden St. James the Less Ch., Northfield, Ill., 1987; mem. sch. bd. Sunset Ridge Sch., 1976-83; dir. United Way, 1975-80. Served with U.S. Army, 1958-61. Clubs: Chgo., Econs. (membership com. 1987); Sunset Ridge Country.

BEATTY, LESTER ROBERT, telecommunications and information systems executive, b. Natrona Heights, Pa., Sept. 29, 1937; s. Lester R. and Virginia E. (Rumbaugh) B.; B.S., Carnegie Inst. Tech., 1960; M.B.A. magna cum laude, U. Bridgeport, 1970; m. Anita Ruth Ruben, July 27, 1963; children—Virginia, Sandra, Brian. Sci. programmer Carnegie Inst. Tech., Pitts., 1958-60; sci. programmer Allegheny Ludlum Steel, Natrona Heights, 1960-64; benefits programming project leader U.S. Steel, Pitts., 1964-66; software sr. analyst RCA, Palm Beach Gardens, Fla., 1966-68; NASDAQ applications project leader Bunker-Ramo, Trumbull, Conn., 1968-70; systems mgr. Champion Internat., Hamilton, Ohio, 1970-79; dir. mgmt. info. and computer systems Cin. Electronics, 1979-81; strategic systems cons. Armco, Inc., Middletown, Ohio, 1982-84; mgr. telecommunications and info. systems Cin. United Appeal and Community Chest, 1984—; instr. systems analysis Miami U., 1982; data processing cons.; 1968—; guest lectr. U. Cin., 1979. County bus. chmn. United Way, Ohio, 1975; speaker Nat. United Way Conv., 1986; data processing adv. Ohio Congressional campaigns, 1978—; publicity chmn. Cin. Renaissance Fair, 1980; speaker Cin. 2000 com. and conf., 1986; county chmn. Young Republicans, 1967-68; senate pres. Ohio Model Legislature, 1974; nat. honor guard Rep. Nat. Conv., 1968; mem. Hamilton County Republican Central Com., 1972-84. Served as 1st lt. Signal Corps, U.S. Army, 1960-61. Named outstanding state chmn. in U.S., U.S. Jaycees, 1968; outstanding local pres. in Pa., Pa. Jaycees, 1964; cert. data processor. Mem. Assn. Systems Mgmt. (dir.), Paper Industry Mgmt. Assn. (nat. EDP com.), Am. Water Ski Assn., Mensa (local editor 1975-76, nat. conv. com. 1978, nat. legis. coordinator 1983-84, Midwestern regional conv. chmn. 1986, nat. nominating com. 1986, pres. 1986—), SAR. Presbyterian. Clubs: Kiwanis, Masons (32 deg.), Shriners. Author: One Corporation, One System; programming rev. columnist Adventure Gaming mag. Home: 10224 Lochcrest Dr Cincinnati OH 45231 Office: 2400 Reading Rd Cincinnati OH 45202

BEATY, HARRY NELSON, internist, educator, university dean; b. Brookfield, Mo., June 25, 1932; s. William Harry and Agnes Marie (Walton) B.; m. Georgia Kay Luther, July 30, 1955; children: Christopher, Kara Lynn. Student, U. Wash., 1950-54, M.D., 1958. Intern in medicine U. Minn., Mpls., 1958-59; resident in medicine U. Wash., Seattle, 1962-63; NIH fellow in medicine 1963-65; instr. medicine U. Wash., 1965-67, asst. prof., 1967-71, assoc. prof., 1971-75, prof., 1975-77; prof., chmn. dept. medicine U. Vt., Burlington, 1977-83; prof., dean Med. Sch. Northwestern U., Chgo., 1983—; head infectious diseases Harborview Med. Ctr., Seattle, 1968-73; med. dir. Providence Med. Ctr., Seattle, 1973-77; chief med. service Med. Ctr. Hosp. Vt. Burlington, 1977-83; investigator Howard Hughes Med. Inst., 1965-66; dir. Becton, Dickinson & Co. Contbr. articles on infectious disease to med. to profl. jours., chpts. to med. textbooks. Served to lt. USN, 1959-63. Fellow ACP (sec. treas. Wash. chpt. 1975-76); mem. Assn. Profs. Medicine (chmn. task force manpower needs 1980-83), Infectious Diseases Soc. Am. (councillor 1979-82), Am. Soc. Clin. Investigation, Alpha Omega Alpha. Office: Northwestern U Med Sch 303 E Chicago Ave Chicago IL 60611 also: Northwestern U Med Sch 633 Clark St Evanston IL 60208

BEAUBIEN, ELAINE ESTERVIG, business educator, human relations consultant; b. Madison, Wis., Oct. 27, 1949; d. Raymond Knute and Hazel (Shultis) Estervig; m. Kenneth Charles Beaubien, Aug. 2, 1975. B.S., Wis. State U.-Platteville, 1971; M.B.A., U. Wis., 1975. Dept. mgr. J.C. Penney Co., Madison, 1971-74; instr., chmn. dept. econs. Detroit Coll. Bus., 1975-76; instr. bus., econs. Mercy Coll. of Detroit, 1976-78; lectr. mgmt. dept. U. Wis.-Whitewater, 1978-81; assoc. prof., chmn. dept. bus. Edgewood Coll., Madison, 1981—; cons. in human relations, 1978—; tng. coordinator, owner Mgmt. Tng. Seminars, 1980—; speaker, seminar leader on women in mgmt., 1980—. Mgmt. mem. Adv. Com. for Cert. Profl. Secs. Cert., 1982—. Recipient Outstanding Alumnus award Wis. State U.-Platteville, 1973, Appreciation cert. Madison Met. Distributive Edn. Assn., 1973; named An Outstanding Young Woman of Am., Gen. Fedn. Women's Clubs, 1982. Evjue scholar, 1970. Mem. Wis. Profl. Speakers Assn., Internat. Bus. Assn., Nat. Assn. Female Execs., Am. Mgmt. Assn., Am. Mktg. Assn., Nat. Speakers Bur. Methodist. Lodge: Order Eastern Star (trustee 1979-82). Home: Route 1 Box 66-E Waterloo WI 53594 Office: Edgewood Coll 855 Woodrow St Madison WI 53711

BEAUCAGE, SERGE LAURENT, biochemist; b. St. Hyacinthe, Que., Can., Jan. 11, 1951; came to U.S., 1978; s. Rene and Therese (Bernier) B.; m. Diane Marie Desrosiers, Sept. 6, 1975; 1 child, Brian. BSc in Chemistry, U. du Que., Montreal, 1974; PhD in Chemistry, McGill U., Montreal, 1978. Research assoc. U. Colo., Boulder, 1978-81, U. Mich., Ann Arbor, 1981-82; sr. staff scientist Smith-Kline Beckman, Palo Alto, Calif., 1982-87; research assoc. Sch. Medicine Stanford (Calif.) U., 1985—; cons. Genetics Inst., Boston, 1981-84. Patentee in field; contbr. articles to profl. jours. Postdoctoral fellow NRC of Can., 1979-81, Am. Cancer Soc., 1986-88. Mem. Am. Chem. Soc. Roman Catholic. Office: Stanford U Sch Medicine Dept Genetics S-337 Stanford CA 94305

BEAUCHAMP, FRANCIS JEAN, ophthalmologist; b. Rouen, France, Aug. 8, 1932; s. Charlemagne Ovide Beauchamp and Albertine Victoria Beauchamp Mayeu; m. Anick Marie-Jose De Queant, Dec. 18, 1957; children: Thierry, Frederic. MD, U. Bordeaux, 1957. Commd. health corps French Army, 1958, advanced through grades to col.; chief medicine 2d Bn. 75th Rima, Algiera, 1958-59, Circonscription Medicale Pala, Chad, 1959-60, Sous-Prefecture de Sud-Quaddai, Chad, 1960-62; specialist Hosp. Bouake, Ivory Coast, 1964-66, Hosp. Vientiane, Laos, 1968-75, Hosp. N'Djamena, Chad, 1975-77, Hosp. Militaire Instrn., Bordeaux, France, 1977-80; ret. French Army; practice medicine specializing in ophthalmology Toulon, France, 1980—; prof. Royal Faculty Medicine, Laos, 1968-75; ophthalmologist U. Marseille, 1968; dir. teaching clinic Faculty Medicine, U. Bordeaux, 1977-80. Decorated Ordre Valeur Militaire France, Chevalier Order Nat. du Merite, France, Chevalier Ordre Royal Loatian di Million d' Elephants, Order Nat. du Chad. Mem. Soc. Française Ophthalmologie. Republican. Mem. Reformed Ch. of France (pres. Toulon Ch. 1988). Home: 10 rue Henri Vienne, 83000 Toulon France Office: 7 Ave Vauban, 83000 Toulon France

BEAUDOIN, ROBERT LAWRENCE, small business owner; b. Newberry, Mich., Nov. 22, 1933; s. Leo Joseph and Edith Wilhelmina (Graunstadt) B.; m. Margaret Cecelia Linck, June 20, 1953; children: Eugene Robert, Kathleen Therese, Annette Marie, Suzanne Margaret. Student, Marquette U., 1952-53. With Fisher plant Gen. Motors, 1953; dock hand State of Mich., St. Ignace, 1953; sch. bus driver Engadine (Mich.) Consol. Schs., 1957; owner, operator Beaudoin's Texaco, Beaudoin's Cafe, Naubinway, Mich., 1956-82, Beaudoin's Cafe and Marathon, Naubinway, 1982-83, Beaudoin's Cafe, Naubinway, 1956—; bd. dirs. Naubinway Mchts. Inc., 1985—. Mem. Naubinway July 4th Com., 1954—; vol. fireman Garfield Twp. Fire Dept., Naubinway, 1980—; mem. recreation com. Garfield Twp. Bd., Engadine, 1983; support fellow N.G. and Res., support mem. U.S. Army Recruiting Main Sta., Detroit. Recipient Cert. of Appreciation, U.S. Army Recruiting Main Sta., Detroit, 1971, Statement of Support, N.G. and Res., 1976. Mem. West Mackinac C. of C., Nat. Fedn. Ind. Bus. (mem. adv. bd. 1971—, 20 yr. award 1985). Roman Catholic. Club: Hiawatha Sportsmans (mem. bd. govs. Engadine 1965-67). Lodges: KC (grand knight 1979-83, Mich. State Council mem., program dir. East Marquette diocese 1984—), Lions (3d v.p. Engadine club 1970-71). Home: PO Box 143 E Main St Naubinway MI 49762 Office: Beaudoins Cafe PO Box 143 US Hwy 2 Naubinway MI 49762

BEAUMONT, MONA MAGDELEINE, artist; b. Paris, Jan. 1, 1927; came to U.S., 1942, naturalized, 1945; d. Jacques Hippolyte and Elsie M. (Didisheim) Marx; BA, U. Calif., Berkeley, 1945, M.A., 1946; postgrad. Harvard U., Fogg Mus., Cambridge, postgrad. spl. studies Hans Hoffman Studios, N.Y.C., 1946; m. William G. Beaumont; children—Garrett, Kevin. One-woman shows at Galeria Proteo, Mexico City, Gumps Gallery, San Francisco, Palace of Legion of Honor, San Francisco, L'Armitiere Gallery, Rouen, France, Hoover Gallery, San Francisco, San Francisco Mus. Modern Art, Galeria Van der Voort, San Francisco, William Sawyer Gallery, San Francisco, Palo Alto (Calif.) Cultural Ctr., Galerie Alexandre Monnet, Brussels, Honolulu Acad. Arts, exhibited in group shows at San Francisco Mus. Modern Art, San Francisco Art Inst., DeYoung Meml. Mus., San Francisco, Grey Found. Tour of Asia, Bell Telephone Invitational, Chgo., Richmond Art Ctr., Los Angeles County Mus. Art, Galerie Zodiaque, Geneva, others; represented in permanent collections: Oakland (Calif.) Mus. Art, City and County of San Francisco, Hoover Found., San Francisco, Grey Found., Washington, Bulart Found., San Francisco; also numerous pvt. collections. Recipient Jack London Sq. Ann. Painting award; Purchase award Grey Found.; Ann. awards San Francisco Women Artists (2); Purchase award San Francisco Art Festival; One-Man Show award San Francisco Art Festival; included in Printworld Internat., 1982-88, Internat. Art Diary, N.Y. Art Review, Art in the San Francisco Bay area. Mem. Soc. for Encouragement of Contemporary Art, Bay Area Graphic Arts Council, San Francisco Art Inst., San Francisco Mus. Modern Art, Capp Street Project, Langton Street Ctr., Pro Arts Assn., others. Address: 1087 Upper Happy Valley Rd Lafayette CA 94549

BEAUMONT, TREVOR EDWARD, engineer, consultant; b. Leeds, Yorkshire, Eng., May 15, 1948; s. Roland and Dorothy (Blakely) B.; m. Valerie Hogg, May 4, 1974; 1 child, Sandra Dawn. BS, London U., 1969; MS, Sheffield U., 1970; MPhil, London U., 1973; PhD, Pacific Western U., 1988. Chartered engr., Eng. Demonstrator U. Reading, Eng., 1973-74; sr. sci. officer Transport & Road Research Lab., Crowthorne, Eng., 1974-78; mgr. Environment & Resources Consultancy, Clyde Surveys, Maidenhead, Eng., 1978-82; cons. Scott Wilson Kirkpatrick & Ptnrs., Cons. Engrs., Basingstoke, Eng., 1982—; lectr. U.N., N.Y.C.; cons. World Bank, Washington. Contbr. articles to profl. jours. Chmn. Caversham Park Village Assn., Reading, 1983—. Fellow Remote Sensing Soc.; mem. Instn. Hwys. and Transp., Instn. Mining and Metallurgy, Council Engring. Instns. (chartered engr.). Home: 17 Phillimore Rd, Reading Berkshire RG4 8UR, England Office: Scott Wilson Kirkpatrick, & Ptnrs, Basing View, Basingstoke RG21 2JG, England

BEAUZAMY, BERNARD M., mathematics; b. Paris, Jan. 8, 1949; s. Pierre E. and Ida (Moday) B.; m. Denise Pruvost; 1 child, Brigitte. PhD, U. Paris, 1976. Prof. U. Lyon, France, 1979—; researcher U. Paris, 1985—; bd. dirs. Inst. de Calcul Mathematique, Paris. Author: Espaces d'Interpolation, 1976, Introduction to Banach Spaces, 1982, 2d edit., 1985, Modèles Etalés, 1984, Operator Theory. Trustee Quality French Sci., Paris, 1986—. Mem. Am. Math. Soc., Société Mathématique de France. Home: 27 Ave Parmentier, 75011 Paris France

BEAVEN, PETER JAMIESON, architect; b. Christchurch, N.Z., Aug. 13, 1925; s. Eric Tamate and Maria Joan (Jamieson) B.; m. Anne Mary Beaglehole, 1952; 3 children. Student Christ's Coll., Christchurch, Univ. Coll., Auckland. Architect, Christchurch; founder N.Z. Civic Trust; chmn. Environ. Adv. Com., Christchurch City council; prin. Beaven Hunt Assocs., Christchurch. Author: Urban Renewal Report; (with others) New Zealand Architecture 1840-1970, 1973. Served with N.Z. Royal Naval Vol. Res., Far East. Recipient Gold medal N.Z. Inst. of Archtiects, 1966, numerous others. Office: Beaven Hunt Assocs, 22 Salisbury St PO Box 1766, Christchurch 1 New Zealand *

BEAVER, WILLIAM LEE, JR., electric company executive; b. Kuttawa, Ky., June 16, 1917; s. William Lee and Ida Melinda (Perryman) B.; grad. St. Louis U., 1939; m. Mary Eva Rodgers, June 18, 1940; children—Douglas Alden, Betsy Lee. With Price-Waterhouse & Co., St. Louis, 1936-42; treas., dir. Artophone Corp., St. Louis, 1946-62; v.p. fin., treas., dir. Sachs Elec. Co., St. Louis, 1962-83, Sachs Properties, Inc., 1968-83; exec. v.p., treas., dir. Sachs Holdings, Inc., 1973-82, vice-chmn., 1983-84; dir. Centerre Bank of Chesterfield, Chesterfield Village, Mo. Dist. chmn. Boy Scouts Am., 1963; area chmn. ARC, 1955-56; chmn. Health and Hosp. Panel, 1966-70; mem. cabinet United Fund, 1962; trustee, exec. com., chmn. fin. com., vice chmn. Mo. Bapt. Med. Ctr.; trustee, treas. Children's Home Soc. of Mo.; trustee, mem. exec. com. Southeastern Bapt. Theol. Sem., 1979—, chmn., 1983-84; mem. exec. com. Mo. Bapt. Convention, 1986—, v.p. 1987-88. Served with USAAF, 1942-45. Recipient citation for outstanding community leadership Religious Heritage of Am., 1978. Mem. Fin. Execs. Inst. (nat. dir. 1973-77, Midwest Area v.p. 1976-77), Am. Inst. C.P.A.s, Nat. Assn. Accts., Fin. Analysts Soc. Baptist (deacon, trustee). Clubs: Media, Mo. Athletic, Norwood Hills Country. Home: 1587 Milbridge Dr Chesterfield MO 63017 Office: 400 Chesterfield Rd Chesterfield MO 63017

BEAZLEY, KIM CHRISTIAN, government official; b. Perth, Australia, Dec. 14, 1948; s. Kim Edwards and Betty Beazley; m. Mary Paltridge, 1974; children: Jessica, Hannah. Student, U. Western Australia, Oxford (Eng.) U. Lectr. social polit. theory Murdoch U., Perth; M.P. 1980—, minister for aviation, minister assisting the minister for def., 1983, spl. minister of state, 1983-84, minister for def., 1984—. Co-author: The Politics of Intrusion, the Superpowers and the Indian Ocean. Rhodes scholar, Oxford U., 1973-76. Office: Ministry for Def, Parliament House, Canberra Australia *

BECH, HANS-PETER, marketing executive; b. Copenhagen, July 4, 1951; m. Susan Patricia Boylan; children: Daniel, Maria. Cand. Polit., U. Copenhagen, 1977. Economist Ministry of Labour, Copenhagen, 1977-78, sr. economist, 1978-80; sales rep. Control Data Corp., Copenhagen, 1980-83, sales mgr., 1983-85, v.p., 1985-86; exec. v.p. Dataco, Copenhagen, 1986—; asst. lectr. U. Copenhagen, 1975-78; lectr. Sch. Adminstrn., Copenhagen, 1977-79. Co-editor Information Tech. Mem. Economist Club. Home: Leerbjerg Lod 16, 3400 Hilleroed Denmark Office: Dataco, Thielsensve 22, 2100 Copenhagen Denmark

BECH, INGE V., interior design consultant; b. Aarhus, Denmark, June 29, 1912; arrived in U.S., 1939, naturalized, 1952; parents Philip Bech and Johanne (Schelde Bang) B. Student, Ecole Menagere, 1927-28, Upper Chine, 1931, Tech. Inst. Copenhagen, 1932-33. Interior decorator Bolighuset, Copenhagen, 1933-35; interior designer various archtl. and design firms, Denmark, 1935-39, 46-48; head dept. furniture and textile George Jensen, Inc., N.Y.C., 1941-44; window display rep. Eve Bruser Studios, N.Y., 1945; interior designer Jack Lessman Interior Design, N.Y., 1948-52, Intercontinental Hotels, N.Y., 1953; dir. interior design Hilton Internat. Hotels, N.Y. and Brussels, 1954-79; pvt. cons. Brussels, 1979—. Contbr. articles to profl. jours. Home and Office: 4 Ave Air Marshal Coningham, 1050 Brussels Belgium

BECHER, ULRICH, author; b. Berlin, Jan. 2, 1910; s. Richard and Elisa Ulrich (von Rickenbach) B.; m. Dana Roda, 1934; 1 son. Ed. Werner-Siemens-Gymnasium, Berlin, Freie Schulgemeinde Wickersdorf, Univs. Geneva, Berlin and Leipzig. Newspaper corr., Paris, Switzerland, Vienna, 1933-38, Zurich, 1938-41, Rio de Janeiro, 1941-43, Brazil, 1944, N.Y.C., 1945-48, Basle, Switzerland, 1949—. Author: Manner machen Fehler (short stories), 1932; Die Eroberer (short stories), 1936; Nachtigall will zum Vater fliegen (novel), 1950; Kurz nach 4 (novel), 1957; Manner machen Fehler, Geschichten der Windrose (collected short stories), 1958; Das Herz des Hais (novel), 1960; Brasilianischer Romanzero, 1962; author plays: Niemand, 1934; Der Bockerer (with Peter Preses), 1948; Der Pfeifer von Wien (with Peter Preses), 1950; Samba, 1951; Feuerwasser, 1952; Mädemoiselle Lowenzorn, 1954; Die Kleinen und di Grossen, 1957; Der Herr kommt aus Bahia, 1958; Makumba, 1969; Biene gib mir Honig, 1972; Murmeljagd (novel in 5 vols.) (Am. edit. Woodchuckhunt); Tote Zeit; Licht im See; Geisterbahn Geisterbahn 11; Die Strasse uber San Gian, 1969; Der schwarze H, 1972; Das Profil (novel), 1973; William's Ex-Casino (novel), 1974; Selective Indentification of Friend and Foe (essays). Recipient Drama prize German Stage Club, Cologne for Mademoiselle Lowenzorn, 1955; Swiss Schiller Found. prize, 1976. Address: Spalenring 95, Basle Switzerland *

BECHERT, JOHANNES STEFAN, linguist, educator; b. Munich, Fed. Republic Germany, Sept. 17, 1931; s. Karl Richard and Mignon Sibylle (Lepsius) B.; m. Eva Charlotte Büttner, Aug. 21, 1957; children: Ernst, Maja, Susanne, Anna Maria. PhD, U. Munich, 1964, habilitation, 1968. Asst. prof. linguistics U. Munich, 1964-68, lectr., 1968-71; locum tenancy of chair U. Bonn, Fed. Republic Germany, 1971; prof. linguistics U. Bremen, Fed. Republic Germany, 1971—. Co-author: Einführung in die generative Transformationsgrammatik, 1980; contbr. articles on linguistics to profl. jours. Mem. Indogermanische Gesellschaft, Soc. Linguistica Europaea, Linguistic Soc. Am., Deutsche Gesellschaft Sprachwissenschaft, Soc. Italiana Glottologia. Office: U Bremen, Postfach 33 04 40, D-2800 Bremen 33 Federal Republic of Germany

BECHETOILLE, BERNARD LAURENT, corporate executive; b. Montbrison, France, June 26, 1940; s. Regis Hugues and Mary Lucy (Bonnet) B.; m. Marie Antoinette Cholat, July 26, 1962; children—Florence, Sophie, Charlotte, Hugues. Student Ecole Polytechnique, Paris, 1960. Cons. Sema-Metra Internat., Paris, 1963-66; brain trust chmn. CIE Bancaire, Paris, 1966-72; founder Cardif SA, Paris, 1972-75; dir. credit Agricole, Paris, 1975-81; v.p. fin. UNISABI (MARS), 1981-82; dir. budget and fin. IAEA, Vienna, Austria, 1982-87; chief exec. officer Trans Expansion Vie, Paris, 1987—. Served with French Navy, 1962-63. Club: Yacht du Trieux. Office: 37 Rue de la Victoire, 75008 Paris France

BECHHOFER, FRANK, sociology educator, research director; b. Nuremberg, Fed. Republic Germany, Oct. 10, 1935; arrived in Eng., 1939; s. Ernest and Elisabeth (Hoffman) B.; m. Jean Barbara Conochie, Dec. 3, 1960; children: Kirsten Elisabeth, Sean Kenneth. BA in Mech. Scis., U. Cambridge, Eng., 1959. Research officer dept. applied econs. U. Cambridge, 1962-65; lectr. dept. sociology Edinburgh (Scotland) U., 1965-74, reader, 1974-87, prof. Research Ctr. for Social Studies, 1987—. Co-author: The Affluent Worker, vols. 1-3, 1968-69; editor: Population growth in the Brain Drain, 1968; co-editor: The Petite Bourgeoisie, 1981. Mem. Brit. Sociol. Assn. (vice chmn. 1983-84, chmn. 1984-86). Mem. Labor Party. Office: U Edinburgh, Research Ctr for Social Scis, 56 George Sq, Edinburgh EH8 9JU, Scotland

BECHLER, ADAM KRZYSZTOF, educator; b. Krakow, Poland, Jan. 31, 1945; s. Antoni and Helena (Michalska) B.; m. Lidia Pankiewicz, Apr. 12, 1970; 1 child, Paul. M in Edn., U. Warsaw (Poland), 1968, PhD, 1973, habilitation, 1986. Teaching asst. U. Warsaw, 1968-70, sr. asst., 1970-74, research assoc., 1974-87; vis. researcher U. Pitts., 1985-86, U. Heidelberg, Germany, 1986-87; asst. prof. U. Szczecin, Poland, 1987—; cons. U. Pitts., 1987. Contbr. articles to profl. jours. Mem. Am. Math. Soc., Polish Phys. Soc.

BECHTEL, STEPHEN DAVISON, JR., engineering company executive; b. Oakland, Calif., May 10, 1925; s. Stephen Davison and Laura (Peart) B.; m. Elizabeth Mead Hogan, June 5, 1946; 5 children. Student, U. Colo., 1943-44; BS, Purdue U., 1946, D. in Engring. (hon.), 1972; MBA, Stanford U., 1948; DSc (hon.), U. Colo., 1981. Registered profl. engr., N.Y., Mich., Alaska, Calif., Md., Hawaii, Ohio, D.C., Va., Ill. Engring. and mgmt. positions Bechtel Corp., San Francisco, 1941-60; pres. Bechtel Corp., 1960-73, chmn. of cos. in Bechtel group, 1973-80; chmn. Bechtel Group, Inc., 1980—; bd. dirs. IBM Co.; chmn. Bus. Council; life councillor, past chmn. Conf. Bd.; mem. policy com. Bus. Roundtable; mem. Labor-Mgmt. Group, Nat. Action Council on Minorities in Engring., from 1974. Trustee, mem., past chmn. bldg. and grounds com. Calif. Inst. Tech.; mem. pres.'s council Purdue U.; mem. adv. council Stanford U. Grad. Sch. Bus. Served with USMC, 1943-46. Decorated officer French Legion of Honor; recipient Disting. Alumnus award Purdue U., 1964, Disting. Alumnus award U. Colo., 1978; Ernest C. Arbuckle Disting. Alumnus award Stanford U. Grad. Sch. Bus., 1974; Man of Yr. Engring. News-Record, 1974; Outstanding Achievement in Constrn. award Moles, 1977; Disting. Engring. Alumnus award U. Colo., 1979; Herbert Hoover medal, 1980; Washington award Western Soc. Engrs., 1985, Chmn.'s award Am. Assn. Engring. Socs., 1982. Fellow ASCE (Engring. Mgmt. award 1979, Pres. award 1985), Instn. Chem. Engrs. (U.K., hon.); mem. AIME, Nat. Acad. Engring. (past chmn., chmn. industry adv. bd.), Calif. Acad. Scis. (hon. trustee), Am. Soc. French Legion of Honor (bd. dirs.), Fellowship of Engring (U.K., fgn. mem.), Chi Epsilon, Tau Beta Pi. Clubs: Pacific Union, Bohemian, San Francisco Golf (San Francisco); Claremont Country (Berkeley, Calif.); Cypress Point (Monterey Peninsula, Calif.); Thunderbird Country (Palm Springs, Calif.); Vancouver (B.C.); Ramada (Houston); Links, Blind Brook (N.Y.C.); Met. (Washington); Augusta (Ga.) National Golf; York (Toronto); Mount Royal (Montreal). Office: Bechtel Group Inc PO Box 3965 50 Beale St San Francisco CA 94119

BECHTOLD, JAMES HENRY, metallurgical engineer; b. Boonville, Mo., May 22, 1922; s. Henry Walter and Mabel (Oswald) B., m. Rosanne Calderwood, Aug. 25, 1951; children—Thomas E., Marcia A., J. Scott, Frederick A. B.S., U. Ill., 1947, M.S., 1949. Research engr. Westinghouse Research Labs., Pitts., 1949-55, mgr. metallurgy dept., 1955-62, assoc. dir. metall. and ceramics, 1962-64, dir. cons., 1964-69, dir. materials, 1969-79, div. mgr. chem. and mech. engring., 1979-84; dir. Metals Properties Council, 1975—. Patentee in field; contbr. articles to profl. jours. Fellow Am. Soc. Metals, Mem. AIME. Republican. Roman Catholic. Home: 1017 Orchid Oak Dr Vero Beach FL 32963

BECK, ANDREW JAMES, lawyer; b. Washington, Feb. 19, 1948; s. Leonard Norman and Frances (Greif) B.; m. Gretchen Ann Schroeder, Feb. 14, 1971; children: Carter, Lowell, Justin. BA, Carleton Coll., 1969; JD, Stanford U., 1972; MBA, Long Island U., 1975. Bar; Va. 1972, N.Y. 1973. Assoc. Casey, Lane & Mittendorf, N.Y.C., 1972-80, ptnr., 1980-82; managing ptnr. Haythe & Curley, N.Y.C., 1982—. Trustee Bklyn. Heights Synagogue, 1980-81, Bklyn. Heights Montessori Sch., 1988—. Mem. ABA, Va. State Bar Assn., New York State Bar Assn., Assn. of Bar of City of N.Y. Home: 71 Willow St Apt 1 Brooklyn NY 11201 Office: Haythe & Curley 437 Madison Ave New York NY 10022

BECK, DOROTHY FAHS, social researcher; b. N.Y.C.; d. Charles Harvey and Sophia (Lyon) Fahs; A.B., U. N.C., 1928; M.A., U. Chgo., 1932; Ph.D. (Gilder fellow), Columbia U., 1944, postdoctoral study, 1955-56; Am.-German Student Exchange fellow, Germany, 1928-29; m. Hubert Park Beck, Aug. 20, 1930; 1 child, Brenda E.F. Dir. econ. research ADA, 1929-32; social worker Emergency Relief Adminstrn. N.J., 1933-34; statistician N.J. State Emergency Relief Adminstrn., 1934-35, U.S. Office Edn., 1935-36; asso. social economist U.S. Central Statis. Bd., 1936-38; research supr., author Am. Coll. Dentists, 1940-42; statistician Am. Heart Assn., 1947-53, Cornell U. Med. Coll., part-time 1951-53; asst. prof. biostats. Am. U. Beirut, part-time 1954; dir. research Family Service Am., N.Y.C., 1956-81, dir. study counselor attitudes and feelings, 1982-87, evaluation research cons., 1982-87. Fellow Am. Sociol. Assn.; mem. Acad. Cert. Social Workers, Am. Assn. Marriage and Family Therapy (affiliate), Nat. Council Family Relations, Groves Conf., Am. Statis. Assn., Nat. Assn. Social Workers, Soc. Study Social Problems, Am. Pub. Health Assn., Phi Beta Kappa. Unitarian-Universalist. Author: Patterns in Use of Family Agency Service, 1962; Marriage and the Family Under Challenge, 1976; New Treatment Modalities, 1978; Counselor Characteristics: How They Affect Outcomes, 1988; co-author: Costs of Dental Care Under Specific Clinical Conditions, 1943; My-ocardial Infarction, 1954; Clients' Progress within Five Interviews, 1970; How to Conduct a Client Follow-Up Study, 1974, 2d enlarged edit., 1980; Progress on Family Problems, 1973. Home: 523 W 121 St Apt 63 New York NY 10027

BECK, EARL RAY, historian, educator; b. Junction City, Ohio, Sept. 8, 1916; s. Ernest Ray and Mary Frances (Helser) B.; m. Marjorie Culbertson, Nov. 7, 1944; children: Ann, Mary Sue. A.B., Capital U., 1937; M.A., Ohio State U., 1939, Ph.D., 1942. Instr. Capital U., 1942-43, Ohio State U., 1946-49; asst. prof. Fla. State U., Tallahassee, 1949-52; assoc. prof. Fla. State U., 1952-60, prof. history, 1960—, chmn. dept. history, 1967-72, chmn. grad.

studies, 1982-87; summer vis. prof. La. State U., 1955, Tulane U., 1959, Duke U., 1966. Author: Verdict on Schacht, 1956, The Death of the Prussian Republic, 1959, Contemporary Civilization I, 1959, On Teaching History in Colleges and Universities, 1966, Germany Rediscovers America, 1968, A Time of Triumph and of Sorrow: Spanish Politics During the Reign of Alfonso XII, 1874-1885, 1979, Under the Bombs: the German Home Front, 1942-1945, 1986. Served with AUS, 1946-49. Mem. Am. Hist. Assn. (del. European history sect. 1983—), So. Hist. Assn. (chmn. European history sect. 1983-84), German Studies Assn. (conf. group for Central European history, Soc. Spanish and Portuguese History. Presbyterian. Home: 2514 Killarney Way Tallahassee FL 32308

BECK, EUGEN ALEXANDER, physician; b. Basel, Switzerland, Nov. 27, 1933; s. Conrad Arthur Beck and Emma Jacot-Descombes; m. Charlotte Karrer, Mar. 12, 1964 (div.); children: Thomas, Michael, Catherine; m. Elsbeth Baertschi, June 14, 1984; 1 child, Anna. MD, U. Zurich, 1959, PhD, 1965. Mem. specialty bds. in Internal Medicine and Hematology. Intern U. Zurich Hosp., 1960-61, 62-63, Neumünster Hosp., Zurich, 1961-62; research fellow Johns Hopkins Hosp., Balt., 1963-65; resident U. Hosp., Basel, 1965-70; vice chmn. cen. hematology lab. U. Hosp., Bern, 1970-87; gen. practice medicine Lugano, Switzerland, 1987—; prof. med. U. Bern, 1987; cons. Swiss Nat. Sci. Found., U. Bern, 1986. Editor: Acta Haematologica, 1984-88; co-author Die einfachen hämatologischen Laboruntersuchungen, 1978. Chmn. Deutsche Arbeitsgemeinschaft Für Blutgerinnungs Forschung, 1984. Served as capt. Sanit, 1967. Postdoctoral fellow U.S. Nat. Health Service, 1963; research grantee Swiss Nat. Sci. Found., 1965, 87. Mem. Swiss Soc. Internal Medicine, Swiss Soc. Hematology, Swiss Soc. History of Medicine, Internat. Soc. on Thrombosis and Hemostasis, N.Y. Acad. Scis. Home: CP 52, CH-6966 Villa Luganese Ticino, Switzerland Office: Via Beltramina 7 A, CH-6900 Lugano Ticino, Switzerland

BECK, FRANCES JOSEPHINE MOTTEY (MRS. JOHN MATTHEW BECK), educator; b. Eleanora, Pa., July 12, 1918; d. George F. and Mary (Wisnieski) Mottey; B.S., Ind. State Tchrs. Coll., 1939; M.A., U. Chgo., 1955, Ph.D., 1980; m. John Matthew Beck, Aug. 23, 1941. Jr. visitor Pa. Dept. Pub. Assistance, 1940-41; asst. to the sec. dept. edn. U. Chgo., 1952-58, asst. sec., 1958, asst. dean of students Grad. Sch. Edn., 1958-75; asst. to dean Sch. Edn., De Paul U., Chgo., 1975-79, asst. prof., 1979-82; reading tchr. Bontemps Pub. Sch., Chgo., 1982-85, Chgo. Pub. Sch., 1985—; reading instr. Central YMCA, Chgo., 1958-61. Bd. dirs. Reading is Fundamental of Chgo., 1979—. Mem. Nat., Ill. assns. women deans and counselors, Internat. Reading Assn., Chgo. Area Reading Assn. (dir. 1980-85), Delta Kappa Gamma. Pi Lambda Theta (nat. v.p. 1966-70, 1st v.p. 1971-74), Sigma Sigma Sigma. Co-author: Extending Reading Skills, 1976; author articles in field. Office: 5832 Stony Island Ave Chicago IL 60637

BECK, GEORGE PRESTON, anesthesiologist, educator; b. Wichita Falls, Tex., Oct. 21, 1930; s. George P. and Amanda (Wilbanks) B.; m. Constance Carolyn Krog, Dec. 22, 1953; children: Carla Elizabeth, George P., Howard W. BS, Midwestern U., 1951; MD, U. Tex., 1955. Diplomate Am. Bd. Anesthesiology. Intern John Sealy Hosp., 1955-56; resident anesthesiology Parkland Meml. Hosp., Dallas, 1959-62, vis. staff, 1964—; practice medicine specializing in anesthesiology, Lubbock, Tex., 1964—; chief staff Meth. Hosp., Lubbock, 1967-68; asst. prof. anesthesiology Southwestern Med. Sch., Dallas, 1962-64, asst. clin. prof., 1964-71, assoc. clin. prof. anesthesiology U. Tex. Med. Br. at Galveston, 1971—; pres. Gt. Plain Ballistics Corp., 1967—; clin. prof. Tex. Tech. U. Sch. Medicine, 1986—, pres. found. bd., 1972-73. Author: The Ideal Anesthesiologist, 1960, Mnemonics as an Aid to the Anesthesiologist, 1961, Anterior Approach to Sciatic Nerve Block, 1962; inventor Beck Airway Airflow Monitor. Pres. Luth. Ch. council, pres. congregation, 1965-66. Served with USAF, 1956-59. Fellow Am. Coll. Anesthesiologists; mem. Am. Soc. Anesthesiologists, Tex. Soc. Anesthesiologists (pres. 1974) Tex. Med. Soc., Lubbock County Med. Soc., Lubbock Surg. Soc. (pres. 1969). Home: 4601 W 18th St Lubbock TX 79416 Office: PO Box 16385 Lubbock TX 79490

BECK, HANS, physicist; b. Zurich, Switzerland, Dec. 4, 1939; s. Hans and Marthy (Schnorf) B.; m. Ursula Urfer, Apr. 25, 1970. Diploma in Theoretical Physics, U. Zurich, 1967, Ph.D. in Physics, 1970. Postdoctoral fellow U. Zurich, 1970-72; research assoc. Cornell U., Ithaca, N.Y., 1973; postdoctoral fellow IBM Research Lab., Ruschlikan, Switzerland, 1974; lectr. U. Basel, 1975-78; prof. physics U. Neuchatel, Switzerland, 1978—, vice-rector, 1987—, dean faculty sci., 1983-85. Contbr. articles to sci. jours. Mem. Swiss Phys. Soc. (sec. 1981-83). Home: Peupliers 6, 2014 Bole, Neuchatel Switzerland Office: Inst de Physique, Rue Breguet 1, 2000 Neuchatel Switzerland

BECK, JOHN MATTHEW, educator; b. Rogoznig, Austria, Apr. 10, 1913; s. Matthias and Antoinette (Bukowski) B.; came to U.S., 1914, naturalized, 1942; B.S., Ind. State Coll. (Pa.), 1936; M.A., U. Chgo., 1947, Ph.D., 1953; m. Frances Josephine Mottey, Aug. 23, 1941. Tchr., Clymer (Pa.) High Sch., 1937-41; instr. history and philosophy of edn. De Paul U., 1948-53; instr. Chgo. State College, 1953-56, chmn. dept. edn., 1959-60, asst. dean, prof. edn., 1960-66, dean coll., 1966-67; dir. Chgo. Tchr. Corps, 1967—; exec. dir. Chgo. Consortium Colls. and Univs., 1968—; prof. urban tchr. edn. Govs. State U., 1972—; cons. U.S. Office of Edn., 1968—. Mem. Ill. State Advisory Com. on Guidance, 1963—, Citizens Schs. Com., Chgo., 1953—; chmn. curriculum adv. com. Ednl. Facilities Center, Chgo., 1971—; exec. bd. Cook County OEO, 1971—; adv. com. interstate interinstnl. cooperation Ill. Bd. Higher Edn., 1972—; mem. Chgo. Mayor's Adv. Commn. Sch. Bd. Nominations, 1975, Mayor's Adv. Council on Aging, 1976—, Exec. Service Corps. of Chgo., 1983—, Mayor Washington's Task Force on Edn., 1983. Bd. govs. Chgo. City Club, 1961—, v.p., 1962-63, 64-65; mem. Exec. Service Corps of Chgo., 1983—. Served with AUS, 1941-46. Decorated Bronze Star. Recipient W. Germany grant, 1972. Fellow AAAS, Philosophy of Edn. Soc.; mem. Am. Hist. Assn., Am. Edn. Research Assn., Ill. Edn. Assn. (pres. Chgo. div. 1960-62). Co-author: Extending Reading Skills, 1976. Editor: Chgo. Sch. Jour., 1964-65; co-editor: Teaching the Culturally Disadvantaged Child, 1966; contbr. articles to profl. jours. and encys. Home: 5832 Stony Island Ave Chicago IL 60637 Office: 95th and King Dr Suite 204 Chicago IL 60628

BECK, PATRICIA M., educational administrator; b. Oakdale, Nebr., Dec. 6, 1923; d. Elmer C. and Theo J. (Burner) Malm; m. Jack G. Elam, July 26, 1974; children—Karlyn Beck Edwards, Christine L. Proctor, Susan P. Gardner. Student Dallas Secretarial Inst., 1940-41; student various univ. courses, 1968-80. Sec., Anderson & Johnson, Midland, Tex., 1958-63; office mgr. C.C. Thomas, Midland, 1963-68; registrar Permian Basin Grad. Center, Midland, also dir.; 1968-69, dir. adminstrn. 1969-71, exec. dir., 1971-79, pres., 1979-86, pres. emeritus, 1986—; v.p. Naja Internacional S.A.; cons., tchr. office mgmt. and procedures, acctg.; v.p., dir. 2501 Corp. Mem. Mensa. Home: 2501 Princeton Midland TX 79701 Office: PO Box 195 Midland TX 79702

BECK, WILLIAM SAMSON, physician, educator, biochemist; b. Reading, Pa., Nov. 7, 1923; s. Myron Paul and Gertrude (Harris) B.; m. Helene Samuels, Oct. 24, 1947; children—Thomas Russell, Peter Dean; m. Hanne Troedsson, July 20, 1964; children—John Christopher, Paul Brooks. B.S. in Chemistry, U. Mich., 1943, M.D., 1946; A.M. (hon.), Harvard U., 1971. Diplomate Am. Bd. Internal Medicine. Instr., asst. prof. medicine UCLA, 1950-57; fellow in biochemistry NYU Coll. Medicine, 1955-57; mem. faculty dept. medicine Harvard U., Boston, 1957—; prof. Harvard U., 1979—, tutor in biochem. scis., 1957—; prof. div. health sci. and tech., chmn. admissions com. Harvard-MIT, 1971-88; dir. clin. labs. Mass. Gen. Hosp., Boston, 1957-75, chief hematology unit, 1957-72, dir. hematology research lab., physician, 1957—; mem. adv. council Nat. Inst. Arthritis, Metabolism and Digestive Diseases, NIH, 1971-74; mem. hematology study sect. NIH, 1967-71. Author: Modern Science and the Nature of Life, 1957, Human Design, 1971, Hematology, 4th edit. 1985; contbr. articles to profl. jours. Served with AUS, 1943-46. Mem. Am. Soc. Biol. Chemists, Am. Soc. Hematology (exec. com. 1979-84), Assn. Am. Physicians, Am. Soc. Clin. Investigation, Am. Assn. Cancer Research. Home: 85 Arlington St Winchester MA 01890 Office: Mass Gen Hosp Boston MA 02114

BECKER, GERT, diversified company executive; b. Kronberg, Aug. 21, 1933; s. Otto and Henriette (Syring) B.; m. Margrit Bruns, 1960; 2 children. Ed. Akademie fur Welthandel, Frankfurt, Germany. With sales dept. Degussa AG, Frankfurt, 1956-60, with rep. office, Teheran, Iran, 1960, with subs., Sao Paolo, Brazil, 1963-66, div. mgr., Frankfurt, 1966-71, dir., 1971-77, mng. dir. parent co., Frankfurt, from 1977, now pres., chief exec. officer. Office: Degussa AG, PO Box 11 05 33, 6000 Frankfurt am Main Federal Republic of Germany *

BECKER, JURGEN, author; b. Cologne, July 10, 1932; s. Robert and Else (Schuchardt) B.; m. Marie Becker, 1954 (div. 1965); 1 son; m. 2d, Rango Bohne, 1965; 2 stepchildren. Ed. U. Cologne. Freelance writer, contbr. to W. German Radio, 1959-64; reader Rowohlt Verlag, 1964-65; freelance writer, 1965—; dir. Suhrkamp-Theaterverlag, 1974; head drama dept. Deutschlandfunk Koln; mem. Akademie der Kunste, Berlin, Deutsche Akademie fur Sprache und Dichtung Darmstadt, PEN Club. Author: Phasen (Text and Typogramme with Wolf Vostell), 1960; Felder (short stories), 1964; Rander (short stories), 1968; Bilder, Hauser (radio play), 1969; Umgebungen (short stories), 1970; Schnee (poems), 1971; Das Ende der Landschaftsmalerei (poems), 1974; Erzahl mir nichts vom Kreig (poems), 1977; In der verbleibenden Zeit (poetry), 1979; editor Happenings (documentary with Wolf Vostell), 1965. Address: Am Klausenberg 84, 5000 Koln-Bruck Federal Republic of Germany *

BECKER, LARRY EUGENE, dermatologist; b. Sioux City, Iowa, Nov. 8, 1943; s. Lawrence and JoAn Denice (Rembe) B.; B.S. in Zoology, Iowa State U., 1966; M.D., U. Iowa, 1969; m. Dorothy Jean Smith, Aug. 13, 1966; children—Douglas Paul, Bradley David. Commd. 2d lt. M.C., U.S. Army, 1968, advanced through grades to col.; intern Tripler Gen. Hosp., Honolulu, 1969-70; flight surgeon Ft. Campbell (Ky.) Army Hosp., 1970-71; resident in dermatology Walter Reed Army Med. Center, 1971-74; staff dermatologist William Beaumont Army Med. Center, 1974-76; resigned, 1976; clin. assoc. prof. Tex. Tech. U. Med. Sch., 1975-76; asst. prof. medicine U. N.Mex. Med. Sch., 1976-79, assoc. prof., 1979-83, dir. div. dermatology, 1979-83; com. mem. N.Mex. Skin Cancer project, 1978-83; chief clin. investigation program div. HCSCIA, Health Services Command, Ft. Sam Houston, Tex., 1984-86, comdr., 1986-88, staff dermatologist Boerne Army Med. Ctr., 1988—. Bd. Dermatology (dermatopathology). Fellow Am. Acad. Dermatology, Royal Soc. Tropical Medicine and Hygiene, A.C.P.; mem. Soc. Investigative Dermatology, AMA, Pacific Dermatol. Assn. Republican. Baptist. Author or co-author papers in field. Home: PO Box 2741 Rt 2 Boerne TX 78006 Office: Dermatology SVC BAMC Attn HSHE-MDD Fort Sam Houston TX 78234

BECKER, MARY LOUISE, polit. scientist; b. St. Louis; d. W. R. and Evelyn (Thompson) Becker; B.S., Washington U., St. Louis, 1949, M.A. (Blewett fellow), 1951; Ph.D. (resident fellow 1952-56), Radcliffe Coll., 1957; postgrad. (Fulbright scholar) U. Karachi (Pakistan), 1953-54; div.; children—James, John. Intelligence research analyst Dept. State, Washington, 1957-59; internat. relations officer AID, Washington, 1959-64, community relations officer, 1964-66, sci. research officer, 1966-71, UN relations officer, 1971—; adviser U.S. dels. 19th, 21st, 23d, 25th, 26th, 28th, and 30th Governing Council sessions UN Devel. Program; adv. U.S. del. 3d prep. com. meeting World Conf. UN Decade for Women; lectr. internat. relations civic orgns., student groups, 1954—. Mem. adv. bd., chmn. student placement Washington Citizenship Seminar, Nat. YMCA-YWCA, Washington, 1961-71. Mem. Am. Polit. Sci. Assn., Soc. Internat. Devel., Assn. Asian Studies, Asia Soc., Am. Soc. Public Adminstrn., AAUW, Mo. Soc. Washington (sec. 1959-60), Mortar Bd., Chimes, Alpha Lambda Delta, Beta Gamma Sigma, Eta Mu Phi, Pi Sigma Alpha. Presbyterian. Clubs: International, Harvard (Washington). Author: Muhammed Iqbal, 1965. Contbg. editor: Concise Ency. of Middle East, 1973. Contbr. articles to govt. publs. Office: Agy for Internat Devel Washington DC 20523

BECKER, RALPH ELIHU, lawyer, diplomat; b. N.Y.C., Jan. 29, 1907; s. Max Joseph and Rose (Becker) B.; m. Ann Marie Watters; children: William Watters, Donald Lee, Pamela Rose, Ralph Elihu. LL.B., St. John's U., 1928; L.L.D., St. Johns U., 1983; LL.D. (hon.), South Eastern U., Washington. Bar: N.Y. 1929, U.S. Supreme Ct. 1940, D.C. 1949. Practice in Washington, 1948-76; spl. counsel to Landfield, Becker & Green, 1978—; gen. counsel, founding trustee John F. Kennedy Center for Performing Arts, 1958-76, hon. trustee, 1980—; U.S. ambassador to Honduras, 1976-77; cons. NASA; Disting. lectr. Strom Thurmond Inst., Clemson U., S.C.; assoc. mem. council NASA Task Force for the Comml. Use of Space. Author numerous booklets, articles on constl. law, ins., space law, atomic energy. Chmn. and former bd. dirs., gen. counsel Met. Washington Bd. of Trade, 1964-71; bd. dirs., gen. counsel, sec. Albert Schweitzer Found., 1955; pres. bd. dirs. Voice Found., 1976—, Friends of LBJ Library; adv. com. L.B. Johnson Meml. Grove on the Park; founding dir., former gen. counsel Wolf Trap Found., 1964-76; mem. adv. com. Sec. Interior Wolf Trap Farm Park for Performing Arts; dir. emeritus Nat. Bank Washington; rep. of Pres. L.B. Johnson with rank spl. ambassador Independence Ceremonies, Swaziland, 1968; mem. Arctic Expdn. for polar bears Washington Zoo, 1962, Antarctic-South Pole Operation Deepfreeze, 1963; nat. chmn. Young Republicans, 1946-49; mem. Rep. Nat. Exec. Com., 1948-51, Pres.'s Inaugural Com., 1953, 57, 69, 73, 80, 83, Vice Pres. Rockefeller Inaugural Medal Com., Rep. Senatorial Inner Circle, fin. com. Rep. Eagle, Presdl. Task Force; charter mem. Nat. Rep. Congl. Com.; donor collection polit. Americana to Smithsonian Instn., Dartmouth Coll., St. Albans Sch., L.B.J. Library, U. Tex., Austin., Strom Thurmond Inst., Clemson U. (S.C.); founder, dir. Inter-Am. Music Festival. Served to capt. AUS, 1942-45, ETO. Decorated Bronze Star medal U.S.; chevalier Legion of Honor; Croix de Guerre with palm France; Belgian Fourragere; Order Morazon 1st class Honduras; chevalier and officer So. Cross of Brazil; Knight's Cross Order of Dannebrog, Denmark; Gt. Cross for Meritorious Services to Austrian Republic; Royal Order de Vasa Sweden; Netherlands Resistance Meml. Cross; Order Rising Sun Japan; recipient Smithsonian Instn. Benefactor medal, 1975; Antarctic Service medal; honored with award by OAS, 1968. Fellow Corcoran Gallery Art, Aspen Inst. Humanistic Studies; mem. ABA (mem. major coms., del. Internat. Bar Assn. com. meeting Monte Carlo 1954, Oslo, 1956, chmn. Vienna post conv. Am. Bar Assn. meeting London 1957), D.C. Bar Assn., N.Y. State Bar Assn., Internat. Bar Assn., Fed. Bar Assn. (nat. council), Am. Law Inst. (life mem.), 30th Inf. Div. Assn. (pres. 1958), U.S. Capitol Hist. Soc. (founding dir.), N.Y. State Soc. (pres. 1963-64), Columbia Hist. Soc., Arctic Polar Inst. (hon.), Smithsonian Assn. (nat. mem.), Supreme Ct. Hist. Soc. (founding dir., mem. exec. com., chmn. ann. meetings 1978, 79, 80), Am. Fedn. Musicians (hon.), James Smithson Soc. of Smithsonian Assocs. (life), Friends of the Folger Library, Ctr. For Study of Presidency, Nat. Wildflower Research Ctr., Dacor-Bacon House Found., Am. Chamber Orch. Soc. (hon.), Choral Arts Soc. (hon.), Council Am. Ambassadors, Am. Fgn. Service Officers Assn., Am. Fgn. Service Assn., Diplomatic and Consular Officers Ret. Clubs: International, Capitol Hill; Bald Peak Colony (N.H.). Lodge: Masons. Home: 4000 Massachusetts Ave NW Washington DC 20016 Office: 1818 N St NW Suite 300 Washington DC 20036

BECKER, ROLF-WALTER, theological educator; b. Hamm, Westphalia, Fed. Republic Germany, Oct. 23, 1935; s. Juergen Echter and Erika (Kochs) B.; m. Jean Virginia Wissing, Mar. 16, 1963; 1 child, Jan Peter. Grad., Evang. Ch. of Westphalia, 1961, Evang. Ch. of Westphalia, 1965; ThD, U. Muenster, Fed. Republic Germany, 1966. Pastor Evang. Ch. Marl, Westphalia, 1965-74; docent Predigerseminar Evang. Ch. Westphalia, Soest, 1974-82, prin., 1982—. Author: Religion in Zahlen, 1968, Leben mit Terminen, 1981. Chgo. Theol. Sem. fellow, 1961-62.

BECKER, RONALD ISADORE, mathematician; b. Cape Town, Republic South Africa, Sept. 18, 1937; s. Myer and Bella (Milner) B.; m. Lily Hurwitz; children: Joanne, Cathryn, Deborah. BSc with honors, U. Cape Town, 1958; PhD, MIT, 1963. Asst. prof. Boston U., 1963-64; lectr. thru prof. math U. Cape Town, 1964—, head dept. math., 1985—. Contbr. articles to profl. jours. Recipient award of S. African Math. Soc. for distinction in research, 1984. Mem. S. African Math. Soc. (v.p.), Am. Math. Soc., Assn. for Computing Machinery, European Computer Sci. Soc. Jewish. Home: 8 Kamfer Rd, Wynberg 7800, Republic of South Africa Office: U of Cape Town, Rondebosch 7700, Republic of South Africa

BECKETT, MARTYN GERVASE, architect, artist; b. Yorkshire, England, Nov. 6, 1918; s. William Gervase and Marjorie Blanche (Greville) B.; m. Priscilla Leonie Brett, May 30, 1921; children: Lucy Caroline, Richard Gervase, Jeremy Rupert. BA, Cambridge U., 1939. Lic. Architect. Pvt. practice architecture, pvt. houses and scheduled bldgs. London, 1952—; architect Kings Coll. Cambridge U., 1961—; cons. Gordonstoun (Scotland) Sch., 1957-61, Savoy Hotel Group, London 1980—, Temple Bar Trust, 1982—, Charterhouse Sch., 1983—, Eton (Eng.) Coll., 1986—. One-man shows Royal Acad., Clarges Gallery, 1980, 83, Soan Gallery, 1986, 88, Grape Lane Gallery, York, 1988; represented in permanent collections Sudbury Lake House, Derbyshire, 1966, Bruern Abbey, Oxfordshir, 1972, Hunton Ct., Kent., 1979, Mortham Tower, Durham, 1972. Chmn. bd. trustees Wallace Collection, London, 1972—; trustee Brit. Mus., London, 1978—; chmn. Nat. Trust, Yorkshire Region, 1980-85; mem. mgmt. council Chatsworth House Trust, Derbyshire, Eng., 1981—. Served to capt. Brit. Army, 1939-46, ETO. Decorated Mil. Cross. Fellow Royal Soc. Arts; mem. Royal Inst. Brit. Architects. Club: Brooks (London). Home and Office: 3 St Albans Grove, London W8 5PN, England

BECKETT, SAMUEL, writer; b. Dublin, Ireland, Apr. 13, 1906; s. William Frank and Mary Roe Beckett; m. Suzanne Dechevaux-Dumesnil. B.A., Trinity Coll., Dublin, 1927, M.A., 1931, D.Litt. (hon.), 1959. Lectr. English Ecole Normale Superieure, Paris, 1928-30; lectr. French Trinity Coll., Dublin, 1930-32. Author: (poems) Whoroscope, 1930, Echo's Bones, 1935, Collected Poems in English and French, 1977; (essay) Proust, 1930; (short stories) More Pricks Than Kicks, 1934, Four Novellas, 1977; (novels) Murphy, 1938, Watt, 1944, Company, 1980; novels in French Molloy, 1956, Malone Dies, 1956, The Unnamable, 1949, How It Is, 1961, Imagination Dead Imagine, 1966, First Love, 1973, Mercier and Camier, 1974, Company, 1980, Worstward Ho, 1983; plays in French Waiting for Godot, 1952, Endgame, 1956; plays for radio All That Fall, 1956, Embers, 1958; (plays) Krapp's Last Tape and Other Dramatic Pieces, 1960, Happy Days, 1961, Play, 1963 (Obie award), Breath and Other Short Plays, 1972, Not I, 1973, Rockaby, 1980, That Time, Theater 1, Theater 2, 1985; short stories in French Nouvelle et Textes pour Rien, 1958, Poems in English, 1961, Cascando and Other Short Dramatic Pieces, 1964, Film, 1969, Six Residuq, 1979, Ill Seen Ill Said, 1981; radio plays All that Fall, 1957, Words and Music, 1961, No's Knife: Collected Short Prose, 1945-66, 67, Cascando, 1964; TV play Ghost Trio and...But the Clouds, 1977. Recipient Prix Formentor, 1961; Nobel prize for lit., 1969; Grand Priz National du Théâtre (France), 1975. Mem. Am. Acad. Arts and Scis. (hon.). Address: care Faber & Faber Ltd, 3 Queen Sq, London WC1, England also: Editions de Minuit, 7 rue Bernard Palissy, F-75006 Paris France *

BECKETT, THEODORE CHARLES, lawyer; b. Boonville, Mo., May 6, 1929; s. Theodore Cooper and Gladys (Watson) B.; m. Daysie Margaret Cornwall, 1950; children: Elizabeth Gayle, Theodore Cornwall, Margaret Lynn, William Harrison, Anne Marie. B.S., U. Mo., Columbia, 1950, J.D., 1957. Bar: Mo. 1957. Since practiced in Kansas City; mem. firm Beckett & Steinkamp; instr. polit. sci. U. Mo., Columbia, 1956-57; asst. atty. gen. State of Mo., 1961-64. Former mem. bd. dirs. Kansas City Civic Ballet; mem. City Plan Commn., Kansas City, 1976-80. Served to 1st lt. U.S. Army, 1950-53. Mem. Am., Mo., Kansas City bar assns., Lawyers Assn. Kansas City, Newcomen Soc. N.Am., SAR, Order of Coif, Sigma Nu, Phi Alpha Delta. Presbyterian. Clubs: Kansas City (Kansas City, Mo.), Blue Hills Country (Kansas City, Mo.). Office: Beckett & Steinkamp 1400 Commerce Trust Bldg PO Box 13425 Kansas City MO 64199

BECKETT, THEODORE CORNWALL, lawyer; b. Heidelberg, Fed. Republic of Germany, Nov. 21, 1952 (parents Am. Citizens); s. Theodore Charles and Daysie Margaret (Cornwall) B.; m. Patricia Anne McKelvy, June 18, 1983; children: Anna, Kathleen. B.A., U. Mo., 1975, J.D., 1978. Bar: Mo. 1978, U.S. Dist. Ct. (we. dist.) Mo. 1978. Ptnr. Beckett & Steinkamp, Kansas City, Mo., 1978—. Bd. dirs. Kans. Spl. Olympics, 1979-84. Mem. ABA, Mo. Bar Assn., Kansas City Bar Assn., Mo. Assn. Trial Attys., Assn. Trial Lawyers Am., Beta Theta Pi. Democrat. Presbyterian. Clubs: Kansas City, Carriage. Office: Beckett & Steinkamp 600 Commerce Bank Bldg PO Box 13425 Kansas City MO 64199

BECKEY, SYLVIA LOUISE, lawyer; b. Los Angeles, Feb. 8, 1946; d. Andrew Gabriel and Rita Jane (Mayer) B. B.A. with spl. honors, U. Tex.-Austin, 1968, postgrad., 1968-69; J.D., Duke U., 1971; M.A. candidate Johns Hopkins Sch. Advanced Internat. Studies, 1973-74; LL.M., NYU, 1981. Bar: D.C. 1972, N.Y. 1975, U.S. Dist. Ct. (so. and ea. dist.) N.Y. 1975, U.S. Supreme Ct. 1975, U.S. Ct. Appeals (2d cir.) 1980. Legis. atty. Am. law div. Congl. Research Service, Library of Congress, Washington, 1971-74; assoc. Cole & Deitz, N.Y.C., 1975-76, Milberg, Weiss, Bershad & Specthrie, N.Y.C., 1976-78; law. clk. to judge U.S. Dist. Ct. (so. dist.) N.Y., 1979-80; asst. chief div. comml. litigation Office of Corp. Counsel of City of N.Y., 1980-86; spl. master Supreme Ct. State of N.Y.-N.Y. County, 1984-86; spl. counsel-enforcement U.S. Securities and Exchange Commn., N.Y.C., 1986—; guest speaker U. Witwatersrand Sch. Law, Johannesburg, S. Africa, 1973; guest researcher Ct. Library, Nairobi, Kenya, 1973; pro bono Internat. League Human Rights, N.Y.C., 1974-75, 8th ann. Conf. for World Peace through Law, Abidjan, Ivory Coast, W. Africa, 1973. Co-author Handbook for Drafting Jury Instructions, U.S. Dept. Justice Civil Rights Div., 1970; assoc. editor The Constitution of the United States of America-Analysis and Interpretation, 1972; author legis. reports on Equal Credit Opportunity Act; referee Am. Bus. Law Jour., 1980-81. Bd. dirs. Chalon Cooperative Bldg., Washington, 1972-73; chmn. fine arts com., mem. bd. dirs. St. Bartholomew's Episcopal Ch., N.Y.C., 1982-83. Grantee Hinds Webbs Fund, 1967. Mem. Women's Bar Assn. City of N.Y., NYU Law Alumni Assn., Duke U. Law Alumni Assn., Fed. Bar Council, Am. Fgn. Law Assn., Consular Law Soc., Dramatists Guild. Protestant Lawyers Guild, English Speaking Union, Met. Mus. Art, Chelsea Block Assn. and Hist. Soc. Democrat. Home: 235 W 22d St New York NY 10011 Office: US SEC NY Regional Office 26 Federal Plaza New York NY 10278

BECKLER, DAVID ZANDER, U.S. government official, science administrator; b. Detroit, June 29, 1918; s. William J. and Thekla (Levy) B.; m. Harriet Levy, Aug. 1, 1943; children—Stephen, Paul, Rochelle. B.S. in Chem. Engring., U. Rochester (N.Y.), 1939; J.D., George Washington U., 1943. Bar: D.C. 1942. Patent atty. Pennie, Davis, Marvin & Edmonds, Washington, 1939-42; tech. aide fgn. liaison office, chief intelligence group Office Sci. Research and Devel., Exec. Office of Pres., Washington, 1942-45; patent atty. Eastman Kodak Co., Rochester, 1946; dep. tech. historian joint task force one Joint Chiefs of Staff, Washington, 1946; chief tech. intelligence br. Research and Devel. Bd., Office of Sec. of Def., Washington, 1947-49; mem. internat. sci. policy survey group Dept. of State, Washington, 1949-50; exec. dir. com. atomic energy Research and Devel. Bd., Washington, 1950-52; asst. dir. office indsl. devel. AEC, Washington, 1952-53; exec. officer Pres.'s Sci. Adv. Com., Washington, 1953-73; spl. asst. to dir. Office of Def. Mblzn., Washington, 1954-57; asst. to spl. asst. to pres. for sci. and tech. The White House, Washington, 1957-62; asst. to dir. Office Sci. and Tech., Exec. Office of Pres., Washington, 1962-73; asst. to pres. Nat. Acad. Scis., Washington, 1973-76; dir. sci., tech. and industry OECD, Paris, 1976-83; cons. on sci. and tech. policies, 1983—. Recipient cert. of appreciation War and Navy Depts., Washington, 1945. Fellow AAAS; mem. Council Fgn. Relations. Club: Cosmos (Washington). Home: 21 rue Spontini, 75116 Paris France

BECKMAN, JAMES WALLACE BIM, economist, business executive; b. Mpls., May 2, 1936; s. Wallace Gerald and Mary Louise (Frissell) B. B.A., Princeton U., 1958; Ph.D., U. Calif., 1973. Pvt. practice econ. cons., Berkeley, Calif. 1962-67; cons. Calif. State Assembly, Sacramento, 1967-68; pvt. practice market research and econs. consulting, Laguna Beach, Calif., 1969-77; cons. Calif. State Gov.'s Office, Sacramento 1977-80; pvt. practice real estate cons., Los Angeles 1980-83; v.p. mktg. Gold-Well Investments, Inc., Los Angeles 1982-83; pres. Beckman Analytics Internat., econ. cons. to bus. and govt., Los Angeles and Lake Arrowhead, Calif., 1983—. Served to maj. USMC 1958-67. NIMH fellow 1971-72. Fellow Soc. Applied Anthropology; mem. Am. Econs. Assn., Am. Statis. Assn., Am. Mktg. Assn., Nat. Assn. Bus. Economists (officer). Democrat. Presbyterian. Contbr. articles to profl. jours. Home: Drawer 2350 Crestline CA 92325

BECKMANN, LEO HEINRICH JOSEF FRANZ, research and development director; b. Ratingen, W. Ger., Feb. 12, 1930; s. Josef Hubert and Katharina Wilhelmine (Linnartz) B.; m. Ilse Dimigen, July 30, 1959; children: Martin, Stefan Heinrich. M.S., U. Freiburg, Germany, 1957, Ph.D., 1963. Asst., Inst. f. Elektrowerkst, Freiburg, Germany, 1959-65; physicist Opt. Industrie de Oude Delft, Delft, Netherlands, 1965-68, dir. research and devel., 1969—, adj. dir., 1979—; cons. Barnes Engring. Co., Stamford, Conn., 1961-65; adj. prof. fine mechanics Tech. U. Twente, 1984—. Patentee electro-optics. Contbr. articles to sci. jours. Mem. Optical Soc. Am., Deutsche Gesellschaft für angewandte Optik, Soc. Photo-Optical Instrumentation Engrs. Roman Catholic. Home: Willem de Merodestraat 9, 2624 LC Delft The Netherlands Office: NV Optische Industrie, van Miereveltlaan 9, Delft The Netherlands

BECKWITH, HENRY HOPKINS, construction company executive; b. Jacksonville, Fla., Oct. 18, 1935; s. Francis Judd and Marian (Hopkins) B.; m. Patricia Stonis, Apr. 30, 1960 (div. 1970); m. Madeleine Elmore, Mar. 15, 1971; children: Henry Hopkins Jr., Kathryn Ann, Michael E. Ingram, Thomas D. Ingram. BS, Fla. So. Coll., 1959. Project mgr. Henley & Beckwith, Jacksonville, Fla., 1954-61; v.p. Tompkins-Beckwith, Jacksonville, 1965, exec. v.p., 1972, pres., 1978, chmn. bd., pres., 1985—; chmn. bd. Somity Corp., 1988; bd. dirs. Fla. Nat. Banks of Fla., Turknett-MPS Engrs., Am. Surety & Casualty Co., Blue Cross and Blue Shield of Fla., Inc., Health Options, Inc. Charter mem. Liberty Mut. Ins. Co. Fla. Adv. Bd., 1987. Democratic candidate Fla. Ho. of Reps., 1962; bd. dirs. State Bd. Social Welfare, Fla., 1966-68, Fla. State Community Coll. Coordinating Bd.; 1981-83; mem. council the Fla. Sch. of Arts, 1985; pres. Gator Bowl Assn., 1985; pres. Jacksonville C. of C., 1981. Served with U.S. N.G., 1957-63. Named Man of Vision, Nat. Soc. to Prevent Blindness, Jacksonville, 1980; recipient Top Mgmt. award Sales and Mktg. Execs. of Jacksonville, 1983. Mem. Fla. Council of 100 (bd. dirs. 1987-88), ASME, ASHRAE, Am. Nuclear Soc., Mech. Contractors Assn. Am., Nat. Constructors Assn., U. So. Fla. Alumni Assn., TAPPI, Kappa Alpha, Delta Sigma Pi. Democrat. Episcopalian. Club: Capt. Jacksonville Quarterback. Lodge: Rotary (pres. Jacksonville 1978-79, dist. gov. 1982-83). Avocations: hunting, fishing. Office: Tompkins-Beckwith Inc 2160 McCoys Blvd Jacksonville FL 32203

BECKWITH, HERBERT L., educator, architect; b. Midland, Mich., Feb. 4, 1903; s. Herbert W. and Antoinette (Lynes) B.; m. Elizabeth McMillin, 1946; 1 dau., Suzanne. B.Arch., MIT, 1926, M.Arch., 1927. Registered architect, Del., Maine, Md., Mass., Mich., N.J., N.Y., Ohio, Va. Pvt. practice architecture Boston, 1930—; partner Anderson & Beckwith, 1938—; faculty Mass. Inst. Tech., 1927—, prof. architecture, 1947—, dir. exhibits, 1945-66, acting chmn. dept. architecture, 1956-57; Cons. architect George Mason Coll., U. Va., Copley Hill Devel., Charlottesville, others; Mem. corp. vis. com. Case Inst. Tech.; Served asst. to chmn. dept. physics Princeton and; exec. officer Princeton Sta., Div. 2, Nat. Def. Research Com., 1943-45; Cons. Mass. Civil Def. Agy.; Sec. Nat. Archtl. Accrediting Bd., 1949-54, pres., 1954-56. Works include exec. office bldg., Raytheon Mfg. Co., office bldgs., Town of Brookline, Mass., New Eng. Electric Service Co., Lab. for Life Scis., dormitory for women, Mass. Inst. Tech.; U. Va. bldgs. A.I.U. Bldg, Tokyo; Sci. Bldg., Boston campus, U. Mass., Am. Internat. Office Bldg, Bermuda, Fisk-Meharry Sci. Center, Nashville, Raytheon Hist. Mus; co-designer sci. complex, U. Rochester, swimming pool and radiation lab., John Thompson Dorrance Lab.; asso. architect: Kresge Auditorium and Chapel, Mass. Inst. Tech.; architect also bldgs. designed, Burma, P.I., P.R., Taiwan. Recipient Coll. of Fellows citation AIA, 1955; named hon. alumnus U. Rochester. Fellow AIA (nat. com. on edn. 1953-60, vice chmn. 1959-60, nat. com. on profession 1958—); mem. Boston Soc. Architects, Mass. Assn. Architects, Mus. Modern Art N.Y., Mus. Fine Arts Boston, Marine Hist. Assn. Mystic, Phi Kappa Psi. Episcopalian. Clubs: Somerset (Boston); Century Assn. (N.Y.C.), N.Y. Yacht (N.Y.C.); Royal Bermuda Yacht. Home: Indian Pond Rd Kingston MA 02364

BEDELL, BARBARA LEE, newspaperwoman; b. Annapolis, Md., July 10, 1936; d. Royal Lee and Kathryn Rosalee (Alton) Sweeney; m. Raymond Lester Bedell, July 1, 1955 (div. 1979); children—Patricia Bedell Pulito, Barbara Ann Bedell Porrini, Raymond, Robert. B.A., U. Wyo., 1967. Dir. woman's programming, host daily talk show Sta. KLME, Laramie, Wyo., 1962-68, Sta. WKIP, Poughkeepsie, N.Y., 1968-70; asst. society editor, feature writer Poughkeepsie Jour., 1968-70; dir. communications and publs. Spackenkill Sch. Dist., Poughkeepsie, 1970-73; columnist, feature writer Times Herald-Record Newspaper, Middletown, N.Y., 1973—; lectr. on various topics to civic, polit., religious, social orgns., 1961—. Mem. 75th Anniversary Com., Cheyenne, Wyo., 1965; mem. Republican Precinct Com., 1961-68, Albany County Bd. Electors, 1966-68; mem. com. history and heritage collection Orange County Community Coll., Middletown, 1984; mem. 100th Anniversary Com., Middletown, 1983-88. Recipient 1st in N.Y. feature writing award Am. Cancer Soc., 1973; Disting. Service award NAACP, 1980; Service awards from numerous service clubs and lodges, chs., assns.; named Mrs. Wyoming, Mrs. Am. Pageant, 1967; N.Y. State All-Am. Family, 1972. Mem. Nat. Fedn. Press Women (8 awards for feature writing 1967-70, top Wyo. state award for radio script writing 1966). Republican. Home: Basel Rd Walker Valley NY 12588 Office: Times Herald-Record Newspaper 40 Mulberry St Middletown NY 10940

BEDELL, GAYNELL PACK (MRS. F. KEITH BEDELL), Christian Sci. practitioner; b. Paintsville, Ky.; d. William Reaves and Iuka D. (Welch) Pack; grad. W.Va. Bus. Coll.; m. Charles T. Skeer, 1921 (dec. 1949); children—William Thom, Zoe (Mrs. A. G. Vecchione); m. 2d, Frederick Haller, July 25, 1953 (dec. Apr. 1957); m. 3d, F. Keith Bedell, Nov. 21, 1966. Mgr. fashion shops, 1942-46; star Claire Angrist radio fashion show, Huntington, W.Va., 1942-46; fashion cons., resident rep. Goode-Bridgeman, Inc., N.Y.C., 1946-54; mem. Christian Sci. Ch., registered practitioner, N.Y.C., 1931—. Pres., 1st Ch. of Christ Scientist, Huntington, reader, Flushing, N.Y., 1951-53. Mem. Nat. Fedn. Bus. and Profl. Women's Clubs (pres. Huntington). Home: 25 Sutton Pl S New York NY 10022 Office: 342 Madison Ave New York NY 10017

BEDELL, JAY DEE, educator, writer; b. Monterey, Calif., Oct. 20, 1946; s. John Dewhirst and Lucille (Huffman) B. BA, U. Calif.-Davis, 1968. Tchr. Antioch Schs., Calif., 1969-84, v.p., dir. Credit Union, 1979-81; owner Bedell Enterprises, 1986—; pvt. cons., 1985—; mem. Adv. Council for Spl. Edn., Antioch, Calif., 1979-81. Bd. dirs. Storyland Theater, Antioch, 1979. Writer poetry (Golden Poet awards World of Poetry Press, 1985, 86, 87, 88); author: (poems) The Golden Eagle, 1984, Dreams, 1986, Lady Liberty, 1986, Sierra-Nevada, 1986, Grand Canyon, 1986, Mother Teresa, 1987, The Eyes of a Child, 1988. Served with U.S. Army, 1971-73. Fellow Am. Biog. Assn. (life); mem. Internat. Platform Assn., Delta Upsilon. Democrat. Home: 1020 Claudia Ct Apt 11 Antioch CA 94509

BEDELL, RALPH CLAIRON, psychologist, educator; b. Hale, Mo., June 4, 1904; s. Charles E. and Jennie (Eaton) B.; m. Stella Virginia Bales, Aug. 19, 1929 (dec. 1968); m. Ann Barclay Sorency, Dec. 21, 1968 (dec. 1975); m. Myra Jervey Hoyle, Feb. 14, 1976. B.S. in Edn., Central Mo. State U., 1926; A.M., U. Mo., 1929, Ph.D., 1932. Diplomate in Counseling Am. Bd. Profl. Psychology. Tchr. Hale Pub. Schs., 1922-24; tchr. sci. and math. S.W. High Sch., Kansas City, Mo., 1926-30, 32-33; asst. prof. ednl. psychology N.E. Mo. State U., 1933-34, prof. ednl. psychology, 1934-37, dir. Bur. Guidance, 1934-37; dean, faculty and student personnel Cen. Mo. State U., 1937-38; freshman counselor, dir. reading labs., assoc. prof. ednl. psychology and measurements U. Nebr., 1938-46, prof., counselor, educator, 1946-50; chmn. dept., prof. psychology and edn. Sch. Social Scis. and Pub. Affairs, Am. U., Washington, 1950-52; dir. program planning and rev. br. internat. div. U.S. Office Edn., HEW, 1952-55; sec.-gen. South Pacific Commn. Noumea, New Caledonia, 1955-58; dir. counseling and guidance insts. br. U.S. Office of Edn., Washington, 1959-66; prof. edn., dir. nat. edn. studies U. Mo., Columbia, 1966-77, prof. emeritus, 1974—; research assoc. Ctr. for Ednl. Improvement, 1974-75; cons. faculty devel. Lincoln U. of Mo., 1976-77; mem. study group to Surinam, 1954; adviser U.S. del. UN, 1953, 62; U.S. del. Caribbean Commn. and West Indian Conf., 1952, 53; cons. Stephens Coll., Columbia, 1974, U.S. Office Edn., 1974; chmn. tech. com. access and retention for master planning Mo. Coordinating Bd. Higher Edn., 1976-78; edn. cons. Prince of Songkla U., Pattani, Thailand, 1980—. Author or co-author sch. textbooks and achievement tests in sci. and aviation, 1930-40; dir. tng. manuals preparation Chief of Naval Air Tng., 1941-45; contbr. articles to profl. jours. V.p., trustee Sigma Tau Gamma Found., 1972-74; founder Bedell Fund to Support Sch. Counseling; dean Sigma Tau Gamma Leadership Inst., 1973. Served as comdr. USNR, 1942-46. Named Honored Alumnus, Cen. Mo. State U., 1971, Disting. Alumnus Cen. Mo. State U., 1984, Outstanding Contbn. cert. Assn. Counselor Edn. and Supervision, 1967, Disting. Contbn. award Assn. Counselor Edn. and Supervision, 1984, Award of Merit, Mo. Assn. Sch. Librarians, 1971, Outstanding Achievement and Meritorious Service in Edn. citation U. Mo., Columbia Alumni Assn., 1979, Profl. award Mo. Coll. Personnel Assn., 1982, Appreciation award Prince of Songkla U., 1986. Fellow Am. Psychol. Assn. (disting. sr. contbr. to counseling psychology div. counseling psychology 1985), Royal Soc. Health; mem. NEA (life), Internat. Assn. Applied Psychology, Nat. Soc. for Study Edn. (life), Mil. Order of World Wars (perpetual), Am. Assn. Counseling and Devel. (life), Internat. Soc. Polit. Psychology, Am. Assn. for Higher Edn., N.Y. Acad. Scis., Mo. Tchrs. Assn., Mo. Guidance Assn. (award of merit 1971), Mo. Assn. Counseling and Devel., Kappa Delta Pi, Phi Kappa Phi, Phi Delta Kappa (life), Sigma Tau Gamma (Top Tau 1970, Wilson C. Morris fellow 1982, pres. Wilson C. Morris fellowship 1985-86, Soc. of Seventeen Disting. Achievement award 1985). Clubs: Explorers (N.Y.C.); Army and Navy (Washington); Country of Mo. Home: 106 S Ann St Columbia MO 65201

BEDI, SARJIVAN SINGH, physician; b. Patiala, India, Oct. 4, 1934; arrived in Eng. 1969; s. Gurdit Singh and Shanti Devi (Sodhi) B.; m. Dhanjit Malvai, Apr. 11, 1940; children: Mandeep, Rimmindeep. MBBS, Glancy Med. Coll., Amritsar, Punjab, 1959. Cert. F.P.A., IUD. Trainee gen. practice medicine Rugby, Warwickshire, Eng., 1969-70; gen. practice medicine Warks, Eng., 1971—; trustee Sikh Temple, Rugby, 1981—. Served to maj. Indian Army, 1961-68. Mem. Brit. Med. Assn. (chmn. Rugby div. 1986—), Amritsar Drs. and Dentists Assn. U.K. (founder, pres. 1980-84, sec. 1984—) Sikh Drs. Assn. U.K. (exec. com. 1987—). Conservative Party. Home: 33 Overslade Ln, Rugby Warwickshire, Midlands CV22 6DY, England Office: Drs Bedi Ahluwalia & Sripuram, 14 Clifton Rd, Rugby, Warks CV21 3QF, England

BEDJAOUI, M. MOHAMMED, judge, International Court Justice; b. Sidi Bel Abbes, Sept. 21, 1929; s. Benali and Fatima El-Oukili); Doctorate in Law, Grenoble U., diploma Polit. Studies Inst.; m. Leila Francis, Oct. 21, 1962; children: Amal, Assia. Lawyer, Appeal Ct., Grenoble; then, attache researches internat. law sect. Nat. Center Sci. Research, Paris; jur. counsellor provisional govt. Algeria; dir. Cabinet Pres. Nat. Constituent Assembly, Algiers, 1962; gen. sec. govt., 1962-64; pres. dir. Nat. Rys. Soc. Algeria, 1964; dean Faculty Law, Algiers, 1964-65; minister justice, 1964-70; ambassador to France, Paris, 1970-79; ambassador to UN, N.Y.C., 1979-82; judge Internat. Ct. Justice, The Hague, Netherlands, 1982—; mem. Internat. Law Commn., UN, 1965-82. Recipient decorations UAR, France, Morocco, algeria, Mali. Mem. Assn. Acad. Internat. Law. Author: International Civil Service, 1956. Fonction Publique internationale et influences nationales, 1958; La Revolution Algerienne et le Droit, 1961; Problèmes récents de Succession d'Etats, 1970; Non-alignement et droit international, 1976; Pour un nouvel ordre economique international, 1978; contbr. articles to profl. jours. Office: Internat Ct Justice, Peace Palace, KJ-2517 Hague The Netherlands

BEDNAREK, JANA MARIA, biochemist; b. Bratislava, Czechoslovakia, Mar. 8, 1934; came to U.S., 1966, naturalized, 1971; d. Rudolf and Helena (Lastovickova) Kozdera; m. Milan Kraus, June 23, 1957 (div. 1963); m. Milan B. Bednarek, Nov. 27, 1966; 1 child, Paula Helen. M.S., Charles U., 1959; postgrad. NYU, 1966-67; Ph.D., Med. Sch. Va., 1973. Fellow dept. biochemistry Med. Sch. Va., Charlottesville, 1973-75; research assoc. dept. chemistry U. S.C., Columbia, 1975-79; research assoc. dept. biochemistry, Med. Sch. S.C., Charleston, 1979-80; research chemist hematology and oncology service Walter Reed Army Med Ctr., Washington, 1981—. Contbr. articles to profl. jours. Mem. N.Y. Acad. Scis., Sigma XI. Democrat. Roman Catholic. Avocations: hiking; skiing; volleyball. Office: 9705 Corkran La Bethesda MD 20817

BEDNORZ, GEORG, physicist; b. May 16, 1950. Grad., U. Munster, Federal Republic of Germany, 1976; PhD, Swiss Federal Inst. Tech., ETH Zurich, 1982. Researcher IBM Zurich Research Lab., Ruschlikon, Switzerland, 1982—; lectr. Swiss Federal Inst. Tech. and U. Zurich, 1987—. Co-recipient Thirteenth Fritz London Meml. award, 1987, Nobel Prize in physics Royal Swedish Acad. Soc., 1987; recipient Dannie Heineman prize Minna James Heineman Stiftung, Acad. Scis. Gottingen, West Germany, 1987, Robert Wichard Pohl prize German Phys. Soc., 1987, Hewlett-Packard Europhysics prize, 1988, Marcel-Benoist prize Marcel-Benoist Found., 1986, APS Internat. prize for new materials reserach, 1988, Viktor Moritz Goldschmidt prize German Mineralogical Soc., 1987, Otto-Klung prize Otto-Klung Found., 1987. Office: IBM Zurich Research Lab, Saumerstrasse 4, CH-8803, Ruschlikon Switzerland *

BEDREGAL DE CONITZER, YOLANDA, writer; b. La Paz, Bolivia, Sept. 21, 1918; d. Juan Francisco and Carmen (Iturri) Bedregal; m. Gert Conitzer, Dec. 18, 1983; children: Rosangela, Juan-Gert. Attended Acad. Fine Arts, La Paz; attended Barnard Coll. of Columbia U. Instr. Sch. Fine Arts, La Paz, U. San Andrés, La Paz, Acad. de Artes Benavides, Suere, Bolivia; dep. mayor cultural affairs City of La Paz; mem. Cen. Com. on Childrens' Literature; cons. La Paz Ministry of Edn. Author 12 books of poetry, folklore, essays and novels (several Nat. Prizes); contbr. articles to mags. and newspapers. Mem. Acad. Boliviana de la Lengua Correspondiente, PEN, Inst. Cultural Bolivia-Israel, others (founder/pres. several bi-nat. instns.). Home and Office: Calle Goitia 17, Mejor Casilla 149, La Paz Bolivia

BEDREGAL GUTIERREZ, GUILLERMO, government official; b. La Paz, Bolivia; married. Degree in Law and Polit. Sci. summa cum laude, U. de Salamanca, Spain, 1950, JD, 1951; student, Diplomatic Sch., Spain, 1950-51, Inst. Polit. Studies, Madrid, 1951; Degree in Econs., Ruprecht Karl U., Heidelberg, Fed. Republic Germany, 1954. Pres. Customs Tribunal, Bolivia, 1955; under-sec. Ministry of Fin., 1955; minister, sec. to Pres. of the Republic Bolivia, 1956-58, minister of mining and petroleum, 1959; minister, pres. Bolivian Mining Corp., 1959-64; prof. law history U. Mayor de San Andrés, La Paz, 1964-65; prof. Inst. of Polit. Studies Cen. U. of Venezuela, Caracas, 1965-71, prof. Dept. of Econs., 1971-78; prof. econ. theory U. Nat. Federico Villarreal, Lima, Perú, 1973; tech. mgr. Planagro Cons. Corp., Venezuela, 1973-78; minister of fgn. affairs and worship Govt. of Bolivia, 1979, 86—, minister of planning and coordination, 1985; cons. Corporación Venezolana de Fomento, 1965-71, Corpoandes, Corporiente, 1971; advisor Ministry of Mining and Petroleum, 1965-71; vis. prof. Nat. U. of Colombia, 1966, Syracuse U., 1969, U. Nat. Autónoma de México, 1974, Rutgers State U., 1979. Contbr. articles to profl. jours. Office: Ministry of Fgn Affairs, La Paz Bolivia *

BEDROSSIAN, PETER STEPHEN, lawyer, business executive; b. Hoboken, N.J., Sept. 15, 1926; s. Nishan and Helen (Jamagotchian) B.; m. Jean M. Reynolds, Jan. 1951 (div. Oct. 1962); children: Peter, Alice Marie; m. JoAnn H. Thorpson, Nov. 16, 1962 (div. July 1986); children: Stephanie Ann, Jennifer Ann. B.B.A., St. Johns U., 1949, J.D., 1954. Bar: N.Y. 1954, Calif. 1973. Chief acct. Stauffer Chem. Co., N.Y.C., 1948-58; dir. taxes Stauffer Chem. Co., 1958-76, asst. treas., 1961-76; mem. firm Dobbs, Berger & Molinari, San Francisco, 1976-80; pres. Parrot Ranch Co., San Francisco, 1982—; v.p., dir. Stauffer Chem. Internat., Geneva, Switzerland, 1959-62; Vice chmn. Nitron Inc., Cupertino, Calif.; dir. Kali-Chemie Stauffer, Hannover, Germany, Stauffer Chem. Co. Internat. Served with AUS, 1944-46. Mem. Am., N.Y., Calif. bar assns., Tax Execs. Inst. (pres. N.Y. chpt.), Internat. Assn. Assessing Officers, Am. Electronics Assn., Am. Legion, Phi Delta Phi, Alpha Kappa Psi. Club: N.Y. Athletic (N.Y.C.); Beach and Tennis (Pebble Beach, Fla.). Address: PO Box 122 Pebble Beach CA 93953-0122

BEE, ALICE VIRGINIA, librarian; b. Brigham, Utah, Aug. 20, 1918; d. James William and Alice (Berg) Pett; m. Earl Sheldon Bee, Oct. 5, 1940 (dec.); children—Sheldon Wayne, Barbara Ann Bee Hutchason (dec.); m. Reece B. Robertson, Sept. 13, 1986. A.A., San Mateo Jr. Coll., 1940. Statis. clk. Proctor & Gamble Corp., San Francisco, 1939-41; payroll clk. Roberts Pub. Markets, Santa Monica, Calif., 1946-50; sec., treas. Roberts Liquor Stores, Santa Monica, 1953-77, Fred L. Roberts Enterprises, Santa Monica, 1953-77; asst. dir., head librarian Los Angeles Geneal. Library, 1980-83, dir., head librarian, 1983-87; retired 1987. Mem. Daus. Utah Pioneers. Democrat. Mormon. Home: 9027 David Ave Los Angeles CA 90034

BEECH, JOHNNY GALE, lawyer; b. Chickasha, Okla., Sept. 18, 1954; s. Lovell Gale and Lucille L. (Phillips) B.; m. Judy Carol Schroeder, Dec. 31, 1977. BS, Southwestern Okla. State U., 1977; JD, U. Ark., Little Rock, 1980; LLM in Energy-Environment, Tulane U., 1985. Bar: Okla. 1980, U.S. Dist. Ct. (we. dist.) Okla. 1982, U.S. Dist. Ct. (no. dist.) Tex. 1983, U.S. Dist. Ct. (no. dist.) Okla. 1986. Assoc. Meacham, Meacham and Meacham, Clinton, Okla., 1980-84, Ford & Brown, Enid, Okla., 1985-86, Wright & Sawyer, Enid, Okla., 1986-88, Phillips, McFall, McVay, Sheets, Lovelace, and Juris, Oklahoma City, 1988—; mcpl. judge town of Arapaho, Okla., 1982-84. bd. dirs. Jr. Achievement Garfield County, Enid, 1986—. Mem. ABA (real property, probate and trusts sect.), Assn. Trial Lawyers Am., Okla. Bar Assn., Garfield County Bar Assn. (treas. 1988—), Am. Bus. Club, Southwestern Okla. State U. Alumni Assn. (pres. 1983-86, exec. council 1986—), Southwestern Sch. Bus. Alumni Assn. (v.p. 1980—), Jaycees, Phi Alpha Delta (sec. 1979). Democrat. Methodist. Club: Am. Bus., Enid. Home: 702 N Cook Cordell OK 73632 Office: Phillips McFall McVay Sheets Lovelace and Juris 1001 NW 63rd Suite 205 Oklahoma City OK 73116

BEECHAM, CLAYTON TREMAIN, gynecologist; b. Ladd, Ill., Mar. 1, 1907; s. Horace King and Bessie (File) B.; m. Patricia Anne Miller, Dec. 25, 1979; children: Richard K., Jackson B., Nina Beecham Stratton. B.S., U. Minn., 1930, M.D., 1932. Intern U. Minn. Hosp., 1932-33; resident U. Kans. Hosp., 1933-34, Kensington Hosp. Women, Phila., 1934-36; instr. ob-gyn U. Pa. Sch. Medicine, 1936-40; prof. ob-gyn Temple U. Med. Sch., 1940-64, dir. tumor clinic, 1940-64; dir. ob-gyn Geisinger Med. Center, Danville, Pa., 1965-78, now sr. cons. gynecology; pres. Am. Assn. Obstetricians and Gynecologists Found., Inc., 1969-80; examiner Am. Bd. Obstetrics and Gynecology, in-tng. exams for residents. Author: (with others) Obstetrics and Gynecology, 3d edit, 1966, 5th edit., 1975; (as Clay Sheringham) Women and the knife, Goodbye Reds; editorial bd.: Obstetrics and Gynecology, 1968-71; cons. surgery: Year Book Cancer, 1965—. Bd. dirs. Solebury Sch., New Hope, Pa., 1951-53, Chestnut Hill Acad., Phila., 1955-57. Recipient Emeritus Prof. award Temple U. Sch. Medicine, 1986. Hon. fellow Kansas City (Mo.), N.J., Pitts., Seattle ob-gyn socs.; fellow A.C.S., Am. Assn. Obstetricians and Gynecologists (exec. bd. 1960-72, editor bull., pres. 1968); mem. Am. Coll. Obstetricians and Gynecologists (exec. bd. 1965-68, commr. edn. 1974-79, Disting. Service award 1988), Obstet. Soc. Phila. (exec. bd. 1963-66, pres. 1964-65), Soc. Pelvic Surgeons, Am. Cancer Soc. (dir. Phila. 1964). Home: Mile Post Rd RD 1 Sunbury PA 17801 Office: Geisinger Med Center Danville PA 17821

BEEK, CORNELIS ZEGER ANTONIUS, association executive; b. Rotterdam, Holland, May 17, 1932; arrived in the Republic of South Africa, 1966; s. Zeger Antonius and Frederika Theadora Maria (Hendriks) B.; m. Martina Maria Vloemans, Nov. 21, 1980; m. Cornelia Catharina Vloemans, Aug. 25, 1954 (div. 1980); children: Simone Adriënne, Alexandra Maria. Lic. helicopter pilot. Commd. pilot officer Royal Netherlands Air Force, 1952, advanced through grades to 1st lt., 1962; pilot Aero Contractors, Nigeria, 1964-65; pilot, area mgr. Autair cum Ct. Line Helicopters, Republic South Africa, 1966-74; helicopter sales mgr. African Aircraft Agys., 1974-78; exec. dir. Comml. Aviation Assn. of So. Africa, Republic South Africa, 1977—; also bd. dirs. Comml. Aviation Assn. of So. Africa. Editor Jour. So. African Aviation Safety Council, 1986—; contbr. numerous articles to profl. jours. Councillor So. African Aviation Safety Council, Pretoria, 1982—. Decorated New Guinea Cross. Fellow Aero. Soc. South Africa; mem. Chartered Inst. Transport, Inst. Transport So. Africa, Assn. Aviation Maintnence Orgns. (chief exec. officer 1978—), Helicopter Assn. So. Africa (chief exec. officer 1975—), Republic South Africa Gunowners Assn. Office: Comml Aviation Assn South Africa, RA 29 Bldg, Comair Ctr, Rand Airport, Transvaal 1419, Republic of South Africa

BEEKMAN, BERNADETTE THERESA, tax lawyer; b. N.Y.C., June 1, 1954; d. Augustus Anthony and Muriel Estelle (Gittens) B. BA, CUNY, 1977; JD, New Eng. Sch. Law, 1981; LLM, Boston U. Sch. Law, 1982. Bar: Mass. 1981, N.Y. 1983. Tax atty. IBM Corp., Armonk, N.Y. and Paris, 1982-85; adv. tax atty. IBM Europe, S/A, Paris, 1986—; mem. steering com. 12th Annual Conf. on Women and Law, Boston, 1981. Writer, editor (film) Three in the Park, 1972. Mem. Internat. Fiscal Assn., Am. Bar Assn., N.Y. State Bar Assn., Mass. Bar Assn.. Roman Catholic. Club: Am. of Paris. Home: 5 Tudor Pl New York NY 10017 Home: 15 Rue Saint Denis, 75001 Paris France

BEEM, JOHN KELLY, mathematician, educator; b. Detroit, Jan. 24, 1942; s. William Richard and June Ellen (Kelly) B.; m. Eloise Masako Yamamoto, Mar. 24, 1964; 1 child, Thomas Kelly. A.B. in Math., U. So. Calif., 1963, M.A. in Math., 1965, Ph.D. in Math., 1968. Asst. prof. math. U. Mo., Columbia, 1968-71, assoc. prof., 1971-79, prof., 1979—. Co-author: (with P. Y. Woo) Doubly Timelike Surfaces, 1969, (with P. E. Ehrlich) Global Lorentzian Geometry, 1981; condr. research in differential geometry and gen. relativity. NSF fellow, 1965, 68. Mem. Math. Assn. Am., Am. Math. Soc., Phi Beta Kappa. Home: 1906 Garden Dr Columbia MO 65202

BEER, OTTO F., author, journalist; b. Vienna, Sept. 8, 1910; s. Leopold J. and Emma (Pabst) B.; m. Gerty Mothwurf, 1949. Ed., U. Vienna. With Neues Wiener Journal and Neues Wiener Tagblatt until 1939; chief editor Salzburger Nachrichten, 1945; drama critic Welt am Abend, 1946-48, Der Standpunkt, Merano, 1948-52, Neues Osterreich, Vienna, 1952-67, Osterreichischer Rundfunk, 1967—, Suddeutsche Zeitung, 1967—. Author: Zehnte Symphonie, 1952; Wiedersehen in Meran, 1952; Ich-Rodolfo-Magier, 1965; Christin-Theres, 1967; author comedies: Man ist nur zweimal jung, 1955; Bummel durch Wien, 1971; Der Fenstergucker, 1974; Einladung nach Wien, 1977. Address: Lederergasse 27, Vienna VIII Austria *

BEERING, STEVEN CLAUS, university president, medical educator; b. Berlin, Germany, Aug. 20, 1932; came to U.S., 1948, naturalized, 1953; s. Steven and Alice (Friedrichs) B.; m. Catherine Jane Pickering, Dec. 27, 1956; children: Peter, David, John. B.S. summa cum laude, U. Pitts., 1954, M.D., 1958. Intern Walter Reed Gen. Hosp., Washington, 1958-59; resident Wilford Hall Med. Center, San Antonio, Tex., 1959-62; chief internal medicine, edn. coordinator Wilford Hall Med. Center, 1967-69; prof. medicine Ind. U. Sch. Medicine, Indpls., 1969—; asst. dean Ind. U. Sch. Medicine, 1969-70, assoc. dean, dir. postgrad. edn., 1970-74, dir. statewide med. edn. system, from 1970, dean, 1974-83; chief exec. officer Ind. U. Med. Center, 1974-83; pres. Purdue U. and Purdue U. Research Found., West Lafayette, Ind., 1983—; bd. dirs. Arvin Industries; cons. Indpls. VA Hosp., St. Vincent Hosp.; chmn. Ind. Commn. Med. Edn., 1973-83, Med. Edn. Bd. Ind., 1974-83, Liaison Com. on Med. Edn., 1976-81. Contbr. articles to jours. Sec. Ind. Atty. Gen.'s Trust., 1974-83. Served to lt. col. M.C. USAF, 1957-69. Fellow A.C.P.; mem. Am. Fedn. Clin. Research, Am. Diabetes Assn., Endocrine Soc., Assn. Am. Med. Colls. (chmn. 1982-83), Council Med. Deans (chmn. 1981-82), AMA (chmn. sect. on med. schs. 1976-78), Nat. Acad. Sci. Inst. of Medicine, Phi Beta Kappa, Sigma Xi, Alpha Omega Alpha, Phi Rho Sigma (U.S. v.p. 1976—). Presbyn. (elder). Clubs: Indpls. Athletic, Columbia, Skyline, Woodstock, Meridian Hills, University. Home: 575 McCormick Rd West Lafayette IN 47906 Office: Purdue U Office of Pres West Lafayette IN 47907

BEERMAN, BERNARD MARVIN, lawyer; b. N.Y.C., Apr. 23, 1936; s. Michael and Ester Flora (Goodman) B.; m. Frances Ann Ferrall; children: Rachel, Michael, David, Jenifer. BA, Princeton U., 1958; LLB, George Washington U., 1962. Bar: D.C. 1963, Md. 1983. Ptnr. Morison, Murphy, Abrams & Haddock, Washington, 1968-71, mng. ptnr., 1971-79; ptnr. Baker & Hostetler, Washington, 1979-82, Sills & Brodsky P.C., Washington, 1982-85, Stein, Stills & Brodsky, Washington, 1986—; cons. Strategic Resources, Inc., Stamford, Conn., 1985—; counsel The Nat. Burglar & Fire Alarm Assn., Washington, 1986—, Cen. Sta. Elec. Assn., 1986—; pres. Alarm Industry Telecommunications Cons., Washington, 1986—. Spl. counsel D.C. Rep. Com., Washington, 1965-66; mem. pvt. security adv. panel Law Enforcement Assistance Adminstrn., Washington, 1975-77; bd. dirs. Choral Arts of Washington, 1966—. Mem. ABA, Am. Judicature Soc., Princeton Terr. (bd. dirs. 1985—). Clubs: Princeton of N.Y., Princeton Terr. (bd. dirs. 1985—), Nassau of Princeton; Carmel Valley Racquet. Home: 27481 Schulte Rd Carmel CA 93923 Office: Nat Burglar & Fire Alarm Assn 1016 16th St NW 6th fl Washington DC 20036

BEETHAM, STANLEY WILLIAMS, consumer products executive; b. Montpelier, Idaho, Nov. 2, 1933; s. Harry Stanley and Mary (Williams) B.; 1 child, Lara Mary; m. Barbara Burnham Barnard, June 20, 1987. BA, Wesleyan U., 1956; MA, U. Amsterdam (Netherlands), 1957; postgrad. Harvard U., 1958-59, U. Wash., 1959-60. Internat. market mgr. U.S. Rubber/Uniroyal, N.Y.C., 1960-63; corp. mktg. cons. Gen. Electric Co., N.Y.C., 1963-65; assoc. dir. Benton & Bowles, Inc., N.Y.C., 1965-67; dir. corp. planning Esmark, Chgo., 1967-72; dir. corp. planning Consol. Packaging Co., Chgo., 1972-74; sr. cons. Booz Allen Hamilton/Hay Assocs., N.Y.C. and Phila., 1975-80; sr. v.p. U.S. Tobacco Co., Greenwich, Conn., 1981-87; pres. S.W. Beetham & Assocs., Ridgefield, Conn., 1987—. Contbr. articles in field. Candidate for U.S. Congress from 13th Ill. Dist., 1972, 74. Fulbright scholar, 1956, Marshall scholar, 1957; Woodrow Wilson fellow, 1958. Mem. N.Am. Soc. Corp. Planning, Nat. Assn. Bus. Economists, Council for Urban Econ. Devel., Internat. Soc. for Planning and Strategic Mgmt., Phi Beta Kappa. Home: 62 Old Branchville Rd Ridgefield CT 06877

BEFOURE, JEANNINE MARIE, writer, accounting and business consultant; b. N.Y.C., Aug. 6, 1923; d. Thomas James and Frances Marie (Thompson) Nicholson; m. Willard Rockne, Oct., 1940 (div. 1946); children—Rodger Lloyd, Lenore Irene; m. Jean Maure Befoure, Aug. 3, 1974. B.S. in Communications magna cum laude, Woodbury U., 1979, M.B.A., 1981. Audit clk. Sears Roebuck, Seattle, 1946-50; supr. materials U.S. Navy, Guam, 1951-52; self-employed acct., Nev., Calif., Ariz., 1953-68; pres. Yearound Bus. Services, Las Vegas, Nev., 1969-73; writer, cons. The JM People, San Gabriel, Calif., 1982—; TV producer Channel 20, El Monte, Calif., TV access producer Channel 3, El Monte, 1987—; instr. bus. and indsl. mgmt. Calif. Community Colls., 1979-82; mem. IRS/Tax Practioner Bd., Las Vegas, 1972-73; tutor Lauback Literacy Action, Los Angeles, 1981—. Author children's stories and poetry, bus. articles. Trainer Kellogg Found.-United Way, Los Angeles; founding sec. Homeowners of Golden Valley, Ariz., 1961. Mem. World Future Soc., Assn. M.B.A. Execs., Greater Los Angeles Press Club, Phi Gamma Kappa. Republican. Religious Scientist. Avocations: photography; poetry.

BEGELL, WILLIAM, publisher; b. Wilno, Poland, May 18, 1928; came to U.S., 1947, naturalized, 1953; s. Ferdinand and Liza (Kowarski) Beigel; m. Esther Kessler, May 27, 1948; children: Frederick Paul, Alissa Maya. B.Ch.E., CCNY, 1953; M.Ch.E., Poly. Inst. Bklyn., 1958; postgrad., Columbia U., 1958-59; Dr.Sci., Acad. Sci. BSSR, Minsk, 1984. Engring. mgr. heat transfer research facility dept. chem. engring. Columbia U., 1953-59; co-founder, exec. v.p. Scripta Technica, Inc., Washington, 1959-74; founder, pres. Hemisphere Publishing Corp., Washington, 1974—; lectr. pub. George Washington U., Washington, also N.Y. U.; cons. Heat Transfer Research Lab., Columbia U.; cons. in field. Editor 7 books; contbr. numerous articles on heat transfer to profl. jours. Mem. nat. adv. bd. Center for the Book, Library of Congress; chmn. exec. council Profl. and Scholarly Pubs. Recipient Benjamin Gomez award book pub. div. Anti-Defamation League, 1984. Mem. AAAS, Am. Inst. Chem. Engrs., Am. Soc. for Engring. Edn., ASME (policy bd.), Assn. Am. Publishers (dir.), N.Y. Acad. Scis. (publs. bd.), Internat. Centre for Heat and Mass Transfer, Washington Book Publishers (founder), Am. Assn. Engring. Socs. Jewish. Home: 46 E 91st St New York NY 10028 Office: Hemisphere Pub Corp 1010 Vermont Ave NW Washington DC 20005 also: 79 Madison Ave New York NY 10016

BEGGS, HARRY MARK, lawyer; b. Los Angeles, Nov. 15, 1941; s. John Edgar and Agnes (Kentro) B.; m. Sandra Lynne Mikal, May 25, 1963; children—Brendan, Sean, Corey, Michael. Student, Ariz. State U., 1959-61, Phoenix Coll., 1961; LL.B., U. Ariz., 1964. Bar: Ariz. 1964, U.S. Dist. Ct. Ariz. 1964, U.S. Ct. Appeals (9th cir.) 1973. Assoc. Carson Messinger, Elliott, Laughlin & Ragan, Phoenix, 1964-69, ptnr., 1969—; mem. Civil Practice and Procedure Com., State Bar of Ariz., 1969-80, Fin. Insts. Counsels Com., 1980-83; founding fellow Ariz. Bar Found. Recipient award for highest grade on state bar exam. Atty. Gen. Ariz., 1964; Fegtly Moot Ct. award, 1963, 64; Abner S. Lipscomb scholar U. Ariz. Law Sch., 1963. Mem. State Bar of Ariz., Maricopa County Bar Assn., ABA. (litigation, antitrust sects.), Ariz. Acad. Clubs: Plaza, LaMancha Racquet. Mem. editorial bd. Ariz. Law Rev. 1963-64; contbr. articles to profl. jours. Address: PO Box 33907 Phoenix AZ 85067

BEGGS, VERONICA DOLOURES, educator, vice principal; b. Stewartstown, County of Tyrone, Northern Ireland, Jan. 29, 1948; d. Joseph Gerard and Mary Alice (Maye) Logan; m. John James Beggs, Dec. 30, 1971; children: Claire Therese, Orla Catherine, David Vincent. Cert. tchr., No. Ireland. Asst. lectr. Tech. Coll., Bangor, No. Ireland, 1970-71; asst. tchr. St. Rose's Secondary Sch., Belfast, No. Ireland, 1971-72; asst. tchr. St. Luke's Primary Sch., Belfast, No. Ireland, 1972-88, vice prin., 1986—. Roman Catholic. Home: 40 Malone Hill Park, Malone Rd, Belfast Northern Ireland BT9 6RE Office: St Lukes Primary Sch, Glasvey Rise Twinbrook, Belfast Northern Ireland

BEGIN, MENACHEM, Israeli politician; b. Brest-Litovsk, Russia, Aug. 16, 1913; s. Zeev-Dov and Hassia Begin; MJ, U. Warsaw; m. Aliza Arnold; 3 children. Head Betar Zionist Youth Movement, Poland, from 1939; served with Polish Army; arrested by Russians, 1940, held in concentration camp in Siberia, 1940-41; released under Stalin-Sikorski agreement and joined Polish Army in USSR, discharged upon arrival in Palestine (now Israel), 1942; led freedom movement against Brit. rule in Palestine as comdr.-in-chief Irgun Zvai Leumi in Israel, 1942; co-founder Herut (Freedom) Movement in Israel, 1948, now chmn.; mem. Knesset, from 1948; minister without portfolio, 1967-70; prime minister, 1977-83; minister of def., 1980-81. Joint chmn. Likud (Unity) Party, 1973-84. Recipient Nobel Peace Prize, 1978. Author: The Revolt: Personal Memories of the Commander of Irgun Zvei Leumi, 1949, The White Nights. Address: 1 Rosenbaum St, Tel-Aviv Israel *

BÉGUÉ, PIERRE-CHARLES, pediatrics educator; b. Paris, May 15, 1939; s. Felicien and Lucienne Claire (Pica) B.; m. Marie Claude Genevieve Fraudet; children: Genevieve, Claire, Marie-Ann. MD, U. Paris, 1969. Fellow IHP Assistance Publique, Paris, 1965-70; asst. Faculty of Medicine U. Paris, 1966-70; chief clin. asst. Faculty St. Antoine Paris, 1970-74; prof. pediatrics Faculty of Medicine U. Lomé, France, 1974-79, U. Paris, 1979-81; chief of service Hosp. Trousseau, Paris, 1981—; mem. vaccinations com. Health Ministry, Paris, 1981—. Author: Drepanocytosis, 1985; editor: Antibiotics in Pediatrics, 1988; author film Nutrition of Children, 1987. Served to lt. French Army, 1865-75. Decorated Ordre of Mono, Togo, 1980, Encouragement au Progress Vermeil medal, 1984. Mem. French Soc. Pediatrics, French Soc. Infectious Diseases, Am. Soc. Microbiology, European Soc. Pediatric Infectious Diseases, French Group of Infectious Diseases of Children. Home: Denis Gogue, 92140 Clamart France Office: Trousseau Hopitaux, Pediatrics Dept, Ave A Netter, 75012 Paris France

BEGUIN, BERNARD AUGUSTE, columnist, retired broadcasting company executive; b. Sion, Valais, Switzerland, Feb. 14, 1923; s. Bernard and Clemence (Welten) B.; m. Antoinette Leonie Waelbroeck, Apr. 12, 1948; children—Pierre, Claude, Jean, Martine. Licence es lettres classiques, U. Geneva, 1945; postgrad. Grad. Inst. Internat. Studies, Geneva, 1945. Sec. World Student Relief, Geneva, 1945-46; editor Journal de Geneve, Geneva, 1947-59, editor-in-chief, 1959-70; UN corr. Fin. Times, Geneva, 1949-59; Radio and TV commentator Swiss Broadcasting, Geneva, 1955-70, dep. dir., 1970-86, sec. bd. dirs., 1980-86; vis. prof. profl. ethics U. Neuchatel, 1985—. Vice pres. Press Ctr., Geneva, 1954-55. U.S. Dept. State Smith-Mundt fellow, Washington, 1952. Mem. Swiss Press Assn. (pres. 1959-60, hon. mem. 1970—), Swiss Press Council (pres. 1986). Club: Cruising of Switzerland (Geneva).

BEHLING, DOROTHY CLARA, fashion professional; b. Scotia, N.Y., May 25, 1930; d. Paul Carl and Evelyn Elizabeth (Blinsinger) Bazar. m. William Herman Behling, May 21, 1949; children: Gary Paul, Bruce William, Corrine Elizabeth. Student profl. modeling Roemary Bischoff Studios, Milw., 1965. Cert. modeling instr., Wis. Payroll mgr. Sears, Roebuck & Co., Schenectady, N.Y., 1947-49; sec., treas. Maple Grove Oil Co., West Allis, Wis., 1957-70; staff instr. Rosemary Bischoff Studios, 1966-81, profl. model, 1966-85; staff model Boston Stores, Milw., 1967-68, Gimbel Stores, 1968-69; instr. Alyce Stoney Modeling Sch., 1969-70; free-lance fashion profl., Mequon, Wis., 1985—; cons. Max Factor, 1970; fashion model, cons. Alston Stores, Cedarburg, Wis., 1980—. Treas., PTA, Hales Corners, Wis., 1957-58; leader Hales Corners council Boy Scouts Am., 1962-63; chmn. Hales Corners council Girl Scouts Am., 1967-68; mem., coordinator Milw. Soc. Models for United Assn. for Retarded Citizens, 1972-76; mem. Ozaukee (Wis.) Humane Soc. Pet Therapy Program, 1986-87. Mem. Bus. and Profl. Women' Assn., River Oaks Assn. (sec. 1976). Republican. Roman Catholic. Club: Christian Women Orgn. Avocations: tennis; gardening. Home: 10635 N Ivy Ct Mequon WI 53092 also: 154 Palm Dr Naples FL 33962

BEHLMER, RUDY H., JR., writer, film educator; b. San Francisco, Oct. 13, 1926; s. Rudy H. and Helen Mae (McDonough) B.; 1 child, Curt. Student, Pasadena Playhouse Coll., 1946-49, Los Angeles City Coll., 1949-50. Dir. Sta. KLAC-TV, Hollywood, Calif., 1952-56; network TV dir. ABC-TV, Hollywood, 1956-57; TV comml. producer-dir., exec. Grant Advt., Hollywood, 1957-60; exec. producer-dir. Sta. KCOP-TV, Hollywood, 1960-63; v.p., TV comml. producer-dir. Hollywood office Leo Burnett USA, 1963-84; lectr. film Art Ctr. Coll. of Design, Pasadena, Calif., 1967—, Calif. State U., Northridge, 1984—, UCLA, 1988—. Author: Memo From David O. Selznick, 1972; (with Tony Thomas) Hollywood's Hollywood, 1975; America's Favorite Movies-Behind the Scenes, 1982, Inside Warner Bros., 1985; co-author The Films of Errol Flynn, 1969; text on Warner Bros. Fifty Years of Film Music, 1973; editor: The Adventures of Robin Hood,1979, The Sea Hawk, 1982 (Wis./Warner Bros. screenplay series); various articles on aspects of film history; writer and narrator audio essay for Criterion Laserdiscs, 1988. Served with AC, USNR, 1944-46. Mem. Dirs. Guild Am.

BEHNCKE, HORST, mathematics educator; b. Hamburg, Germany, Nov. 7, 1939; s. Robert Behncke and Lilli (Metzing) Kaminski; m. Karin Schreck; children: Kirsten, Helge, Christian. Degree, U. Hamburg, 1963; postgrad., Ind. U., Bloomington, 1964-66; PhD in Math and Physics, Ind. U., 1968; postgrad., U. Calif., Irvine, 1966-68. Instr. NYU, 1968-69; asst. prof. U. Heidelberg, Germany, 1969-71; assoc. prof. U. Bielefeld, 1971-73; mathematics prof. U. Osnabrück, 1973—. Mem. Am. Math. Soc., German Math. Soc. Office: U Osnabruck, Albrechtstr 28, 4500 Osnabruck Federal Republic of Germany

BEHNEY, CHARLES AUGUSTUS, JR., veterinarian; b. Bryn Mawr, Pa., Nov. 30, 1929; s. Charles Augustus and Victoria Parks (Wythe) B.; B.S., U. Wyo., D.V.M., Colo. State U., 1961; m. Judith Ann Boggs, May 26, 1979; children—Charles Augustus III, Keenan F. Owner, Cochise Animal Hosp., Bisbee, Ariz., 1961—; veterinarian, dir. S.W. Traildust Zoo, Bisbee, 1966—; owner Kazam Arabians, Bisbee, 1969—; asso. prof. Cochise Coll. Chmn., Comprehensive Health Planning, Cochise County, Ariz., 1968. Mem. Am. Vet. Med. Assn., Soc. for Breeding Soundness, Internat. Platform Assn. Republican. Episcopalian. Rotarian, Elk. Patentee ultrasound device and eye cover for treating infections, apparatus to alter equine leg conformation, external vein clamp, equine sanitation instrument; developer ear implant instrumentation system. Home and Office: PO Box 4337 Bisbee AZ 85603

BEHNKE, ROY HERBERT, physician, educator; b. Chgo., Feb. 24, 1921; s. Harry and Florence Alice (MacArthur) B.; m. Ruth Gretchen Zinszer, June 3, 1944; children: Roy, Michael, Donald, Elise. A.B., Hanover Coll., 1943; Ph.D. (hon.), 1972; M.D., Ind. U., 1946. Diplomate: Am. Bd. Internal Medicine. Intern Ind. U. Med. Center, 1946-47, resident, 1949-51, chief resident medicine, 1951-52; instr. medicine Ind. U. Sch. Medicine, Indpls., 1952-55, asst. prof. medicine, 1955-58, assoc. prof., 1958-61, prof., 1961-72; chief medicine VA Hosp., Indpls., 1957-72; prof. medicine, chmn. dept. U. South Fla. Coll. Medicine, Tampa, 1972—; AMA rep. to residency rev. com. in internal medicine, 1970-75; mem. exec. and adv. com. Inter-Soc. Commn. Heart Disease Resources, 1968-72, chmn. pulmonary study sect., 1969-72; chmn. career devel. com. VA, 1980-83. Mem. Met. Sch. Bd. Washington Twp., 1968-72, pres., 1971; bd. dirs. Southside Community Health Center, 1968; trustee Tampa Gen. Hosp. Found., 1979-85; mem. research coordinating com. Am. Lung Assn., 1983-85, chmn., 1985-87, bd. dirs., 1983-87. Served with AUS, 1943-45, 47-49. Recipient Clin. Tchr. of Year award Ind. U. Sch. Medicine, 1968, 69, 70, Clin. Tchr. of Year award U. South Fla. Coll. Medicine, 1977, Disting. Prof., 1983, also recipient Founders award, 1984, recipient Standard Oil Found. award Ind. U., 1971; Alumni Achievement award Hanover Coll., 1971; John and Mary Markle scholar, 1952, 57. Fellow ACP (gov. Fla. 1980-84), Am. Coll. Chest Physicians.; mem. AMA, Am. Fedn. Clin. Research, Central Soc. Clin. Research, So. Soc. Clin. Research, Alpha Omega Alpha. Home: 5111 Rolling Hill Ct Tampa FL 33617 Office: Dept Internal Medicine 12901 N 30th St Box 19 Tampa FL 33612

BEHR, HANS-JOACHIM, language educator; b. Hirschaid, Fed. Republic Germany, Jan. 18, 1949; s. Heinrich and Ellen-Gertraude (Wetzelt) B.; m. Ingrid Bennewitz, June 11, 1981. Grad., U. Erlangen, Federal Republic of Germany, 1973. Habilitation U. Münster, 1984. Scientist's asst. U. Erlangen, 1974-78; scientist's asst. U. Münster, Fed. Republic Germany, 1978-84, lectr., 1984-86, prof., 1986—. Author: Politische Realität und Literarische Selbstdarstellung, 1978; contbr. articles to profl. jours. Office: U Munster, Johannisstr 1-4, D-4400 Munster Federal Republic of Germany

BEHR, MARION RAY, artist, author, business executive; b. Rochester, N.Y., Sept. 12, 1939; d. Justin Max and Sophie Gusta (Koffler) Rosenfeld; B.Art Edn., Syracuse U., 1961, M.F.A., 1962; m. Omri Marc Behr, June 24, 1962; children—Dawn Marcy Yael, Darrin Justin Mason, Dana Marisa Jana. Freelance contbr. illustrations for stories, crafts, mag. covers and toy designs to nat. mags. including McCall's, Good Housekeeping, Lady's Circle, 1962-77; artist, works exhibited Contemporary Am. Artists, Scarsdale, N.Y., 1964, Am. Women Artists, Douglass Coll., 1977; one-woman show: Douglas Coll., 1983; creator survey Women Working Home—the Invisible Workforce, 1978; pres. Women Working Home, Inc., Edison, N.J., 1980—; condr. workshops; books include: (with others) Women Working Home: The Homebased Business Guide and Directory, 1981, 2d edit., 1983; illustrator: Jewish Holiday Book, 1977; extensive radio and TV appearances rep. Nat. Alliance Homebased Businesswomen. Mem. Kean for Gov. campaign, 1981; mem. White House Conf. on Free Enterprise Zones, 1982; trustee Women's Bus. Ownership Ednl. Conf., Inc., N.J., 1985; appointed to N.J. Devel. Authority for Small, Minority and Women's Bus. Commn., 1986; Presdl. del. White House Conf. on Small Bus., 1986. Recipient N.J. Women in Bus. Advocate of the Yr. award SBA, 1984; Woman of Yr. in Bus. and Industry award, 1985; Syracuse U. alumni grantee, 1957. Mem. Nat. Alliance Homebased Businesswomen (pres. 1980-82, legis. chair 1982-85; originator, founder), Women's Caucus for Art. Jewish. Home and Office: 24 Fishel Rd Edison NJ 08820

BEHRENDT, JOHN THOMAS, lawyer; b. Syracuse, Kans., Oct. 26, 1945; s. Thomas Franklin and Anna Iola (Carrithers) B. m. Martha Jean Montgomery, Dec. 28, 1967 (div.); children: Todd Thomas, Gretchen Jean; m. Theresa Ann Elmore, Oct. 27, 1985. BA, Sterling Coll.; J.D. cum laude, U. Minn. Bar: Calif. 1971, Tex. 1973. Assoc., then ptnr. Gibson, Dunn & Crutcher, Los Angeles, 1970-71, 1974—; lectr. Practicing Law Inst., Acctg. for Lawyers. Served to capt. JAGC, U.S. Army, 1971-74. Mem. ABA (law and acctg. com.), Los Angeles County Bar Assn, Order of Coif. Republican. Presbyterian. Clubs: Jonathan (Los Angeles); Union League (N.Y.); The Tuxedo (Tuxedo Park, N.Y.). Office: Gibson Dunn & Crutcher 333 S Grand Suite 5000 Los Angeles CA 90071 also: 200 Park Ave New York NY 10001-0193

BEHRENDT, LARS CHRISTIAN FREDERIK, hydraulic engineer; b. Dronninglund, Denmark, Oct. 4, 1958; s. Jan Christian Frederik and Hanne (Jessing) B. MSc in Civil Engring., Tech. U. Denmark, Copenhagen, 1983, PhD in Civil Engring., 1985. Research fellow Tech. U. Denmark, 1983-85; hydraulic engr. Danish Hydraulic Inst., Horsholm, 1985—. Mem. Indsl. and Applied Math. (activity group on supercomputing), Danish Assn. Civil Engrs., Wave Modelling Group (internat. research group on wave modelling), Scientific Com. Oceanic Research (working group 83 wave modelling). Office: Danish Hydraulic Inst, Agern Alles, DK-2970 Horsholm Denmark

BEHRENS, HENRY WILLIAM, international business educator, financial consulting firm executive; b. Scheessel, Germany, Aug. 4, 1935; came to U.S., 1955, naturalized, 1960; s. Claude William and Sophie Magdalena (Ellmers) B.; m. Eva Paeslack, June 12, 1960; children—Andrew M., Lawrence H. B.S., Columbia U., 1961, M.B.A., 1962; Ph.D., New Sch. for Social Research, 1969. Economist Exxon Internat., Inc., N.Y.C., 1962-65; vis. lectr. econs. Columbia U., N.Y.C., 1965; asst. prof. econs. and fin. Fairleigh Dickinson U., Rutherford, N.J., 1965-68; assoc. prof. econs. and fin. Union Coll. and U., Schenectady, 1968-72; pres. Algonquin Investors Corp., Niskayuna, N.Y., 1972-78; exec. dir. U.S.A.F.E.C., N.Y.C., 1979-81; prof. world bus. Am. Grad. Sch. Internat. Mgmt., Phoenix, 1982-84; prof. fin. and internat. bus. Nat. U., San Diego, 1984-85; mng. dir. The McCormack Group, San Diego, 1985—; pres., fin. cons. to corps. and fgn. govts. Behrens & Assocs., Phoenix and San Diego, 1982—. Author: The Effects of Monetary Policy on Commercial Banks, Thrift Institutions, and the Residential Mortgage Market, 1968; Export Guide, 1985; author research reports. Mem. U.S. Senate Club, Am. Mgmt. Assns., Am. Fin. Assn., Am. Econ. Assn., Acad. Internat. Bus., Alpha Kappa Psi. Club: Columbia U. (N.Y.C.). Office: Nat U 4007 Camino Del Rio S San Diego CA 92108

BEHRENS, HILDEGARD, soprano; b. Oldenburg, Fed. Republic of Germany, 1937. Student, Music Conservatory, Freiburg, Fed. Republic of Germany. Opera debut in Freiburg, 1971; resident mem. Deutsche Opera Am Rhein, Dusseldorf, Fed. Republic of Germany; appeared with Frankfurt (Fed. Republic of Germany) Opera, Teatro Nacional de San Carlo, Lisbon, Portugal, Vienna Staatsoper, Met. Opera, N.Y.C.; soloist Chgo. Symphony Orch., 1984. Office: care Columbia Artists Mgmt Inc 165 W 57th St New York NY 10019 *

BEHRENS, KENNETH CHARLES, wholesale importing and distributing company executive; b. St. Louis, Mar. 19, 1942; s. Miller Louis and Theresa Mary Behrens; m. Patricia Ann Edkstrnad, 1965; children: Cheryl Ann, Brian Charles. BS, S.E. Mo. State U., 1967. CPA, Mo. Acct. Coopers & Lybrand, St. Louis, 1967-70, Alexander Grant & Co., 1975; chief fin. officer Tacony Corp., 1975-88, sr. v.p. fin., 1976-86, sr. v.p. fin. and adminstrn., 1977-88. Trustee Employees Pension Plan and Employees Profit Sharing Plan, 1975-88; corp. bd. dirs., 1984-88. Served with U.S. Army, 1961. Recipient Most Outstanding Performance award Alexander Grant & Co., 1974, Service award Tacony Corp., 1985. Mem. Nat. Assn. Accts., Am. Inst. CPA's, Mo. Soc. CPA's, Sigma Chi. Home: 9569 Banyon Tree Ct Saint Louis MO 63126 Office: Tacony Corp 1760 Ginsinn Ln Fenton MO 63116

BEHRINGER, SAMUEL JOSEPH, JR., lawyer; b. Detroit, Oct. 6, 1948; s. Samuel Joseph and Evania Theresa (Cherry) B.; m. Linda Suzanne Gross, Sept. 7, 1979; 1 child, Kathryn Elizabeth. B.S. in Labor and Indsl. Relations, Mich. State U., 1970; J.D., U. Detroit, 1973. Bar: Mich. 1974, U.S. Dist. Ct. (eastern dist.) Mich. 1974, U.S. Ct. Claims 1975, U.S. Tax Ct. 1975, U.S. Ct. Appeals (6th circuit) 1974, U.S. Supreme Ct. 1980. Asst. U.S. atty. Ea. Dist. Mich., Detroit, 1974-80; group v.p., gen. counsel Mich. Nat. Bank Detroit, 1980-83; sole practice, Birmingham, 1983-87; with Mich. Consol. Gas Co., 1988—; chmn. young lawyers sect. 6th cir. admission ceremony State Bar Mich., 1975-83. Recipient Merit commendations U.S. Dept. Justice, 1977, 78; Spl. Commendation Outstanding Service U.S. Atty. Gen., 1979. Mem. ABA, Fed. Bar Assn. (chmn. chpt. host com. of nat. conv. Detroit, 1985, mem. exec. bd. Detroit chpt. 1979-81), Detroit Bar Assn., Comml. Law League Am., Oakland County Bar Assn., Am. Corp. Counsel Assn., Assn. Trial Lawyers Am., Nat. Rifle Assn., Phi Kappa Tau, Gamma Eta Gamma. Contbr. legal articles to profl. publs. Home: 333 McKinley Ave Grosse Pointe Farms MI 48236 Office: Box 36863 18640 Mack Ave Grosse Pointe Farms MI 48236

BEIDLER, PAUL HENRY, retired architect; b. Lehighton, Pa., Oct. 20, 1906; s. Lewis Mark and Edna Alice (Heiney) B.; m. Udon Kotwongjann, June 20, 1973; children—Penh, Siriporn, Theonor; m. Margaret Grant, Sept. 18, 1936 (div. 1964); children—Jo, Peter, Sue, Fran. B.Arch., U. Pa., 1931. Fellow, Taliesin, Spring Green, Wis., 1934-35; archeologist U. Pa. Mus., Phila., 1931-36; architect Beidler Assocs., Easton, Pa., 1937-55; regional engr. AID, Southeast Asia, 1955-73; dir. Northeon Forest, Easton, Pa.; prof. architecture Black Mountain Coll. (N.C.), 1941-43; capt. fishing fleet, Barnegat City, N.J., 1939-41. Author: (with E. Speiser) Excavation at Tepe Gawra, 1935. Republican. Club: Explorers (N.Y.C.). Home: 10200 N Camino Valdeflores Tucson AZ 85704 also: Northeon Forest Route 4 Easton PA 18042

BEIER, PAUL ANDREW, lutenist, educator; b. Salt Lake City, Feb. 23, 1954; arrived in Italy, 1981; s. Ernst Gunther and Franses (Redlich) B.; m. Jeanne Clausen. Degree in performance, Royal Coll. Music, London, 1977. Dir. Ensemble Galilei, Milan, 1978—; prof. of lute Civica Scuala Di Musica Di Milano, 1981—; lutenist Ensemble Concerto, Milan, 1982—. Published numerous recordings for radio, TV, and discograph, 1980—. Home: Viale Col Di Lana 8, Milan 20136, Italy

BEIG, ROBERT ERICH, physicist, educator; b. Vienna, Austria, Aug. 21, 1948; s. Herbert and Alice (Tichy) B.; m. Elisabeth Hubauer, July 21, 1975; children: Stefan, Daphne. PhD, U. Vienna, 1974. Univ. asst. Inst. for Theory Physics U. Vienna, 1975-82, univ. dozent, 1982—. Contbr. articles to sci. jours. Recipient Erich Schmid prize Austrain Acad. Scis., 1983. Mem. Am. Math. Soc. Office: U Vienna, Boltzmanngasse 5, 1090 Vienna Austria

BEIGEL, MICHAEL LEE, electronic executive; b. N.Y.C., Jan. 29, 1947; s. Jerome and Freda (Marks) B. BSEE, MIT, 1969, BS in Humanities, 1970. Pres., Identic Data Inc., Cambridge, Mass., 1969-70; cons. Guild Mus. Instruments, Elizabeth, N.J., 1970-72; v.p. Musitronics Corp., Rosemont, N.J., 1972-78; pres. Beigel Cons. Services, N.Y.C., 1978—; pres. EPD Tech. Corp., 1984-86; in-house cons. Amprobe Instrument div. Core Industries Inc., 1986—; pres. Measurement & Control Systems, Inc., 1988—; tech. counsel Sound and Communications Mag.; lectr. MIT, 1968-70, Boston Mus. Sch., 1969-70, also confs. Contbr. articles in field to profl. jours.; patentee electronic musical products, power control systems, ultrasonic measurement systems and electronic identification systems. Mem. IEEE, Audio Engring. Soc., Am. Mgmt. Assn., Am. Acoustical Soc. Home: 34 Echo Lane Warwick NY 10990 Office: Beigel Cons Services 60 E 12th St New York NY 10003

BEIGHTLER, CHARLES SPRAGUE, mechanical engineering educator; b. Cin., Mar. 18, 1924; s. Donald Sprague and Elizabeth (Bainer) B.; B.S., U. Mich., 1950, M.S., 1954; Ph.D., Northwestern U., 1961; m. Patricia Ann Thompson, Mar. 3, 1957; children—William John, Judith Ann, Susan Jeanne, Carol Lynn, Barbara Gail. Design engr. Aeronca Mfg. Co., Middletown, Ohio, 1950-51; research engr. Gen. Motors Research Lab., Detroit, 1954-55; ops. research analyst Caywood-Schiller Assocs., Chgo., 1956-57; dir. ops. research Ernst & Ernst, Chgo., 1957-58; asst. prof. mech. engring. U. Tex., Austin, 1961-65, asso. prof., 1965-68, prof., 1968—; Fulbright lectr. U. Freiburg (Germany), 1971-72; cons. Humble Oil Co., Houston, Office Gov. Tex. Served with inf. AUS, 1943-45, to 1st lt. arty., 1951-52. Decorated Bronze Star medal, Combat Inf. Badge; recipient Book of Yr. award Am. Inst. Indsl. Engrs., 1969. Mem. Ops. Research Soc. Am. (Lanchester prize 1967), Inst. Mgmt. Scis., N.Y. Acad. Scis., Sigma Xi, Pi Tau Sigma, Kappa Sigma. Author: (with Douglass J. Wilde) Foundations of Optimization, 1967, 2d edit. (with D. Phillips and D.J. Wilde), 1979; (with Donald Phillips) Applied Geometric Programming, 1976. Home: 7007 Edgefield Dr Austin TX 78731

BEIGL, WILLIAM, naturopath, hypnotist, consultant; b. Chgo., July 9, 1950; s. William C. Beigl and Mary Tomlinson; m. Mavis Johnson, Aug. 5, 1977. BA in Elem. Edn., U. S. Fla., 1971; D of Natural Medicine, Acad. Sci. of Man, Sussex, Eng., 1979. Pvt. practice hypnotherapy Chgo., 1977—, pvt. practice naturopathic medicine, 1979—; mem. research team Donsbach U., 1980; chief researcher disease prevention B.P.H. Corp.; bd. dirs. Mid-West Hypnosis Conv., 1983; cons. in field. Editor, pub. Portage Park News, 1980; originator of the Paramedic System, 1968 (honored by Pres. Johnson 1968, Pres. Nixon, 1969); contbr. articles on natural healing and hypnosis to newspapers and mags.; patentee in field. Assoc. bd. mgrs. Robert R. McCormick chpt. Chgo. Boy's Club, 1975. Served to capt. U.S. Army, Vietnam. Recipient award Congressman Sidney Yates, 1971, Disease Prevention award Beter Positive Health Found., 1979; named Chicagoan of Yr., Mayor Richard J. Daley, 1968, Chgo. Cath. of Yr., Cardinal John Cody, 1968, Illinoisan of Yr., Gov. Richard B. Ogilvie, 1968, one of Ten Outstanding Young Citizens, Chgo. Jaycees, 1980, Citizen of Week, Sta. WBBM, 1984; nominee for Nobel Prize, 1984. Mem. Internat. Naturopathic Assn. (cert., named Naturopathic Physician Yr. 1985), Nat. Assn. Naturopathic Physicians (cert.), Assn. Advance Ethical Hypnosis (cert., past v.p., past sec. Ill. chpt., bd. dirs. 1986, participant the biggest hypnosis conv., 1988), Minn. Assn. Naturopathic Physicians (cert.), Hemlock Soc., Chgo. Meml. Assn.,

Boy's Clubs Am. (life, named Nat. Boy of Yr. 1968). Lodge: Moose. Office: 2521 W Montrose Chicago IL 60618

BEIL, GERHARD, minister of foreign trade; b. Leipzig, Germany, May 28, 1926. Student, Berlin-Karlshorst U., German Democratic Republic, 1952; diploma in Econs., Berlin Humboldt U., German Democratic Republic, 1957; PhD. in Polit. Sci. and Law, Potsdam-Babelsberg U., German Democratic Republic, 1968. Mgr. industl. metal constn. co., mechanic; with Ministry Foreign Trade, German Democratic Republic, 1958—; with trade representation Govt. of German Democratic Republic, Vienna; dir.-gen. trade Govt. of German Democratic Republic, Western Europe, 1962-65; dep. minister Govt. of German Democratic Republic, 1965-68, state sec. Ministry Foreign Trade, 1968-77, member Council Ministers, 1977-86, minister Foreign Trade, 1986—; head German Democratic Republic delegation to Com. Fgn. Econ. Relations of Council Mutual Econ. Assistance; chmn. German Democratic Republic side in Mixed Govt. Commns. and Econ. Coms. with capitalist industrialized countries. Named to Karl Marx Order, Hero of Labour. Office: Ministry of Foreign Trade, Berlin German Democratic Republic

BEILIN, JOSEPH, government administrator; b. Petach Tikva, Israel, June 12, 1948; s. Zvi and Zehava (Bregman) B.; m. Helen Einhorn, Aug. 12, 1969; Gil, Ori. BA in Hebrew Lit., Tel Aviv U., MA in Polit. Sci., 1976, PhD in Polit. Sci., 1981. Journalist Davar newspaper, Tel Aviv, 1969-77; spokesman Israel Labour Party, Tel Aviv, 1977-86; sec. of govt. Office of Prime Minister, Jerusalem, 1984-86; dir. gen. fgn. affairs Israel Ministry Fgn. Affairs, Jerusalem, 1986—; instr., researcher Tel Aviv U., 1972-85. Author: Sons in their Fathers' Shadow, 1984, The Price of Unity, 1985, The Roots of Industry in Israel, 1987. Mem. Assn. Polit. Sci. Office: Israel Office Fgn Affairs, Romema, Jerusalem Israel

BEINHOCKER, GILBERT DAVID, investment banker; b. Phila., July 7, 1932; s. Joseph A. and Florence (Shlifer) B.; B.A., Pa. State U., 1954; M.S., U. Pa., 1958; D.Eng., U. Detroit, 1968; m. Barbara Broadley, Dec. 17, 1960; children—Eric David, Elizabeth Broadley, Robert Marc. Engring. dir. Epsco, Inc., 1958-61; pres. Syber Corp., Natick, Mass., 1961-64; div. mgr. Tech. Measurement Corp., 1964-65; dir. advanced planning Am. Optical Co., 1965-66; chmn. bd. Microdyne Instruments, Inc., Waltham, Mass., 1967-69; pres., chief exec. officer, dir. Mgmt. Scis., Inc., Cambridge, Mass., 1968—; dir. Nat. Info. Services Inc., Cambridge; chief exec. officer, dir. Eurocom Inc., Cambridge, 1975—; dir. corp. finance Moors and Cabot, Boston, 1976-82; v.p., treas., dir. First New Eng. Corp. Fin., Inc., 1982—; pres. Excalibur Ventures, Inc.; chmn. bd. Paragon Plastics Inc.; bd. chmn., chief exec. officer Regal Internat., bd. dirs. Waterman Industries Corp.; sr. lectr. U. Detroit, 1967-68. Recipient Nat. Fight for Sight citation Nat. Council to Combat Blindness, 1963. Mem. AAAS, IEEE, Assn. Computing Machinery, Internat. Fedn. Med. Electronics and Biol. Engring., Internat. Soc. Clin. Electroretinography, Assn. Research Ophthalmology, Am. Def. Preparedness Assn., Am. Mgmt. Assn., Instrument Soc. Am., Am. Assn. Med. Instrumentation, Pi Lambda Phi. Democrat. Author: Theory and Operation of Stardac Computers, 1960, also articles. Patentee in field. Home: 36 Beatrice Circle Belmont MA 02178 Office: Excalibur Ventures Inc 1 Boston Pl Suite 3400 Boston MA 02108

BEIRNE, MARTIN DOUGLAS, lawyer; b. N.Y.C., Oct. 24, 1944; s. Martin Douglas and Catherine Anne (Rooney) B.; m. Kathleen Harrington; children—Martin, Shannon, Kelley. B.S., Spring Hill Coll., 1966; J.D., St. Mary's Sch. Law, 1969. Bar: Tex. 1969, U.S. Dist. Ct. (ea. dist.) Tex. 1972, U.S. Dist. Ct. (so. dist.) Tex. 1971, U.S. Ct. Appeals (5th cir.) 1974, U.S. Dist. Ct. (ea. dist.) Calif., U.S. Supreme Ct. 1975, U.S. Dist. Ct. (no. dist.) Tex., U.S. Dist. Ct. (we. dist.) Tex. Ptnr. Fulbright & Jaworski, Houston, 1971-85; mng. ptnr. Beirne, Maynard & Parsons, Houston, 1985—. Editor in chief St. Mary's Law Rev. Served to capt. Signal Corps, U.S. Army, 1969-71. Fellow Tex. Bar Found.; mem. ABA, Tex. Bar Assn., Houston Bar Assn. Roman Catholic. Clubs: Coronado, Houston Athletic, Meml. Drive Country. Office: 1300 Post Oak Blvd 24th Floor 24th Floor First Interstate Tower Houston TX 77056

BEJART, MAURICE JEAN (MAURICE BERGER), ballet artistic director, choreographer; b. Marseilles, France, Jan. 1, 1927; s. Gaston Berger; attended lycee in Marseilles. With Marseilles Opera and Royal Opera, Stockholm, before founding Ballet de l'Etoile, Paris, 1954, dir., 1954-57; dir. Ballet Theatre de Paris, 1957-59, Ballet du 20th Siecle, Brussels, then Lausanne, 1959—, Brussels Opera, Theatre Royal de la Monnaie; prodns. include: Orphee, Le voyage, Le sacre du printemps, Les noces, Don Juan, Bolero, Symphonie pour un homme seul, Nijinsky, Clown of God (ballets); The Merry Widow, Tales of Hoffmann, Ode a la Joie (IXe symphonie), La damanation de Faust, Messe pour le temps present, Romeo et Juliette, Prospective, Baudelaire, Ni fleurs-ni couronnes, La tentation de St-Antoine, A la recherche de..., Le marteau sans maitre, La Traviata, Per la Dolce Memoria di quel Giorno, 1974, Ce que l'amour me dit, 1974, Chants d'amour et de guerre, 1975, Notre Faust, 1975, Petrushka, 1977, Don Giovanni, 1980, The Magic Flute, 1981, History of a Soldier, 1982, Salome, 1983, Fragments, 1984, 5 Modern No Plays by Mishima, 1984-85, The Bats, 1985, Arépo, 1986, The Kabuki, 1986, Martyr of St. Sebastian, 1986, Malraux, or the Metamorphosis of the Gods. Decorated chevalier de l'Ordre des Arts et des Lettres; recipient Grand Prix de la Musique, 1970, Malraux ou La Metramprphose Des Dieux, 1986. Author: (novel) Mathilde ou le temps perdu; (play) La Reine verte. Decorated grand officer Order of the Crown. Office: Ballet of 20th Century, 103 rue Bara, Brussels B-1070, Belgium *

BÉKÁSSY DE BÉKÁS, STEFAN PETER ADAM, banker; b. Stockholm, July 18, 1947; came to Switzerland, 1971; s. Adam Peter Elek and Marianne (Boijeaf Gennäs) B. de B.; m. Agneta Catharina Magnusson. Student, London Sch. Fgn. Trade, 1970, U. Fribourg, Switzerland, 1974. Ptnr. Gärdets Hälsokost AB, Sweden, 1971-80; sales mgr. Ebus SA, Switzerland, 1974-79; auditor Fin. UNHCR, Geneva, 1981-87; adminstrv. coordinator Banque Scandinave en Suisse, Zurich, Switzerland, 1988—; fin. advisor Toucom SA, Switzerland, 1976-87, Cashbox, Switzerland, 1984-87. Roman Catholic. Home: Obstgartenstrasse 20, 8136 Gattikon Switzerland Office: Banque Scandinave en Suisse, Schipfe 2, Zurich Switzerland

BEKELE, ASFAW, transportation company executive; b. Gimbi, Wellega, Ethiopia, June 19, 1930; s. Asfaw Bungule and Kenae Rikitu; m. Abebech Gizaw, May 7, 1960; children: Woubababa, Tsigereda, Andualem, Maskerem, Merone. Diploma in aero. engring., Aeronautica U., Chgo., 1958; BBA, Haile Selassie I U., Addis Ababa, Ethiopia, 1972. Supr. inspection Ethiopian Airlines, Addis Ababa, 1960-62, foreman inspection, 1962-66, contracts adminstr., 1966-70, fin. dir., 1970-78; gen. mgr. RRC Air Service, Addis Ababa, 1978—; pres. Ethiopian Nat. Credit Cooperative Soc., Addis, 1968-74. Mem. Ethiopian Red Cross, 1968—. Mem. Ethiopian Bible Soc. Lodge: Orthodox (fin. officer 1976—). Home: PO Box 90060, Addis Ababa Ethiopia

BEKKEDAHL, BRAD DOUGLAS, dentist; b. Williston, N.D., Nov. 23, 1957; s. Oliver Lawrence Jr. and Gudrun Joan (Sundby) B. BA, Jamestown (N.D.) Coll., 1979; BS, U. Minn., 1982, DDS, 1984. Gen. practice dentistry Williston, 1984—; dental staff Mercy Med. Ctr. Scoutmaster Boy Scouts Am., Williston, 1984-86; pastoral com. Gloria Dei Luth. Ch., Williston, 1986—; pres. Am. Legion Drum and Bugle Corps, Williston, 1986—, Williston Hockey Club, 1987—; bd. dirs. Basin Empire United Way, Williston, 1986; com. mem. dist. 1 Rep. Exec.; mem. strategic planning com. Williston Park Dist., also commr.; mem. exec. com. Raymond Family Community Ctr. Mem. ADA, N.D. Dental Assn., N.W. Dist. Dental Assn., N.D. Amateur Hockey Assn. (community rep.). Republican. Club: Williston Hockey (bd. dirs. 1986—). Lodge: Elks. Home: 2501 13th Ave W Williston ND 58801 Office: 115 2d Ave W PO Box 2443 Williston ND 58801

BEKKUM, OWEN D., gas company executive; b. Westby, Wis., Mar. 2, 1924; s. Alfred T. and Huldah (Storbakken) B.; m. Dorothy A. Jobs, Aug. 26, 1950. B.B.A., U. Wis., 1950; postgrad., Northwestern U. C.P.A. With Arthur Andersen & Co., 1951-57, Hertz Corp., 1957-62; with No. Ill. Gas Co., Aurora, 1963—, asst. comptroller, 1966-68, comptroller, 1968-70, adminstrv. v.p., 1970-73, exec. v.p., 1973-76, pres., 1976-87, chief exec. officer, also dir., 1981-87, vice chmn., 1988—; dir. NICOR Inc., New Eng. Energy Co. Bd. dirs. Jr. Achievement, Chgo., 1975-79, vice chmn., 1976-79; bd. dirs. Protestant Found. Greater Chgo., 1975—, pres., 1985-87; bd. dirs. Pace Inst., 1977-83, Andrew Corp., 1980—; bd. dirs. Am. Scandinavian Council, 1987—, chmn., 1988—. Served with AUS, 1943-46. Mem. Am. Mgmt. Assn., Am. Gas Assn. (dir. 1978-82, 83-87), Inst. Gas Tech. (dir. 1978-82), Gas Research Inst. (dir. 1982-88). Clubs: Economic, Comml., Mid-Day (Chgo.). Home: 46 Royal Vale Dr Oak Brook IL 60521 Office: No Ill Gas Co PO Box 190 Aurora IL 60507

BELAFONTE, HARRY, singer, concert artist, actor; b. N.Y.C., 1927; s. Harold George and Melvine (Love) B.; m. Julie Robinson, Mar. 8, 1957; children—Adrienne, Shari, David, Gina. Student pub. schs.; DHL (hon.), Park Coll., Mo., 1968; HHD (hon.), Park Coll.; Doctorate Liberal Arts (hon.), ArtsD (hon.), New Sch. Social Research; MusD (hon.), Morehouse Coll., 1987; DFA (hon.), SUNY, Purchase, 1987. Pres. Belafonte Enterprises, Inc., N.Y.C. Singer, actor in Broadway shows John Murray Anderson's Almanac (Tony award 1953), Three for Tonight, 1955; motion pictures Bright Road, 1952, Carmen Jones, 1954, Island in the Sun, 1957, The World, the Flesh and the Devil, 1958, Odds Against Tomorrow, 1959, The Angel Levine, 1969, Buck and the Preacher, 1971, Uptown Saturday Night, 1974; producer stage play To Be Young Gifted and Black, 1969; appeared in TV movie Grambling's White Tiger, 1981; producer TV spls. A Time for Laughter, 1967, Harry and Lena, 1969; TV program Tonight with Belafonte, 1960 (Emmy award); appeared on German TV spl. I Sing What I See, 1980; concert performances in Cuba, Jamaica, Europe, 1980, Australia, N.Z., U.S., Europe, 1981, Can., 1982, U.S., Europe and with Can. symphony orchs., 1983, U.S., 1985, U.S., Can., Japan, Europe, 1986; producer Strolling Twenties-TV; co-producer Beat Street, 1984; appeared at Golden Nugget, Atlantic City and Las Vegas, 1985, 86; initiator, performer rec. We Are the World, 1985 (Grammy award 1985); performer concert tours, U.S., Can. and Europe including 60 city tour, 1988. Appointed chmn. by Gov. N.Y. State Martin Luther King, Jr. Holiday Commn., 1987; appointed Goodwill Ambassador UNICEF, 1987. Recipient award of appreciation for initiation of and work for USA for Africa, Am. Music, 1986, Leader for Peace award Peace Corps, 1988.

BELAICHE, RAYMOND BERNARD, gynecologist, obstetrician; b. Tunis, Tunisia, Jan. 4, 1943; arrived in France, 1959; children: Frank, Luc. MD, U. Montpellier, France, 1969, cert. spl. study in gynecology, 1972, cert. in obstetrics, 1982. Faculty attache, asst. in physiology Faculty Medicine U. Montpellier, 1965-73, in charge teaching in physiology, 1965-75, in charge psychology, 1972-82; mem. of staff Montpellier Hosp., 1972-76; practice medicine specializing in gynecology and obstetrics Montpellier, 1972—; chief service Clinique Clementville, Montpellier, 1979—. Pres. Com. Ethics, Montpellier, 1984—. Mem. Syndicat National Gynecology Obstetrics France, French Soc. Gynecologie, French Soc. Colposcopy. Home: 3 Rue de la Colline, 34790 Grabels France Office: Clinique Clementville, 25 Rue de Clementville, 34000 Montpellier France

BELCHER, DONALD WILLIAM, engineering consultant; b. N.Y.C., July 13, 1922; s. Donald Ray and Mary Carver (Williams) B.; B.E. in Chem. Engring., Yale U., 1943; m. Dariel Keith, Mar. 23, 1946; children—Dariel Jean Belcher Sellers, Donald Richard, Susan Keith Belcher Penedos, David Todd, Jonathan Rockwood. Chem. supr. E. I. DuPont de Nemours & Co., Inc., muriatic acid dept., Grasselli, N.J., 1946, asst. dept. supt. silicate dept., 1946-48; project design engr. Bowen Engring. Inc. North Branch, N.J., now Somerville, N.J., 1948-51, mgr. functional design, 1951-57, v.p. and chief engr., 1957-72, v.p. and tech. dir., 1972-76, exec. v.p., dir., 1976-78, pres., dir., 1978-79, exec. v.p., dir., 1979-81; pres. Belcher Engring., Inc., 1982—, Drytec Coffee Inc., 1983—. Bd. dirs. YMCA, Westfield, N.J., 1959-64. Served in USNR, 1943-46. Registered profl. engr., N.J., La. Mem. Am. Inst. Chem. Engrs. Nat. Soc. Profl. Engrs., Assn. Cons. Chemists and Chem. Engrs. Home and Office: 550 Prospect St Westfield NJ 07090

BELCHER, FORREST RENFROW, management consultant; b. Tulsa, Mar. 5, 1922; s. John Cheslow and Sarah Blanche (Renfrow) B.; student Okla. State U., 1939-42, Okla. U., 1944; B.A. in Psychology, U. Tulsa, 1947, M.A. in Psychology, 1949; postgrad. in psychology U. Houston, 1950-52; m. Betty Dings, June 2, 1943; children—Forrest Ray, Gail, Michael, Lynne. With Amoco Prodn. Co., 1948-69, employee relations supr., Houston, 1955-57, tng. and devel. cons., Tulsa, 1957-69; mgr. tng. and devel. Amoco Corp., Chgo., 1970-78; pvt. practice mgmt. cons., Tulsa, 1978—; pres. Mega Cons., Inc., Tulsa, 1981—; adj. prof. Okla. State U.; gen. chmn. First Internat. Tng. and Devel. Conf., Geneva, 1972; chmn. First Inter Am. Tng. Conf., Caracas, Venezuela, 1971; cons., speaker First S.E. Asia Tng. Conf., Manila, 1974; speaker in field; founder, chmn. Woodlands Group, a tng. and devel. think tank; cons. to mgmt. groups, Europe, S.Am., Can., U.S. Served with inf. U.S. Army, 1942-45; ETO. Decorated Purple Heart. Mem. Am. Soc. Tng. and Devel. (life; pres. 1970, Gordon M. Bliss Meml. award 1979), Am. Assn. Humanistic Psychology, U. Tulsa Alumni Assn. Democrat. Unitarian. Author booklet: How to Form a National Training Society, 1971; contbr. articles to profl. jours. Office: 10 Lookout Ln Diamond Head Sand Springs OK 74063

BELCHER, NANCY FOOTE, land use planner, consultant; b. Rutherford, N.J., Nov. 13, 1921; d. Joseph W. and Helen L. (Maxcy) Foote; student Broughton Coll., 1939-40; student airphoto interpretation and geomorphology Cornell U., 1948-50; m. Donald J. Belcher, July 1, 1954; children—Marilyn K. Belcher Whisman, M. Candace Belcher Brann, Mathew B., Mark D., Neil F., Helen Stacey (dec.). Research asso. Arctic Inst. N. Am., Permafrost Research Program, 1947; adminstrv. asst. Cornell U. Center Aerial Photog. Studies, 1948-51; tech. asst. for hydrology UN Mission to Iran, 1950; research asso. ops. research office Johns Hopkins U., 1951; asso. dir. site selection group Capital Site Selection Project, Brazil, 1952-54; v.p. Donald J. Belcher & Assos. Inc., Ithaca, N.Y., 1952—. Editor reports in field. Home: 1044 Cayuga Heights Rd Ithaca NY 14850

BELDOCK, DONALD TRAVIS, corporation financial executive; b. N.Y.C., May 29, 1934; s. George and Rosa (Tribus) B.; m. Lucy Geringer, Apr. 23, 1971; children: John Anthony, Gwen Ann, James Geringer Christopher. B.A., Yale U., 1955. Mdse., fin. exec. R. H. Macy & Co., N.Y.C., 1955-60; mng. ptnr., fin. cons. D. T. Beldock & Co., N.Y.C., 1961-66; pres., chief exec. officer, chmn. fin. com. BASIX Corp. (formerly Basic Resources Corp.), N.Y.C., 1966-69; chmn. bd., pres., chief exec. officer BASIX Corp. (formerly Basic Resources Corp.), 1970—; chmn., dir. White Shield Greece Oil Corp., 1969—; bd. dirs. Winko-Matic Signal Co., Norcross, Ga., Phoenix; bd. dirs. Packard Press Corp., Phila., chmn., chief exec. officer, 1987—; pres., bd. dirs. Fundamental Properties Corp., N.Y.C., 1970—; founding ptnr. Transp. Infrastructure Adv. Group; chmn., dir. White Shield Greece Oil Corp., N.Y.C.;. Chmn. bd. trustees Strang Clinic-Preventive Medicine Inst., 1968—; mem. bd. advisors Chem. Bank, 1985-88; bd. dirs. Renewable Energy Inst., 1981-86; trustee Am. Symphony Orch., 1979—; chmn. bd. dirs. Teamwork Found., 1980—; mem. com. Nat. UN Day, 1978-87; mem. N.Y. commn. Voluntary Enterprise; chmn. N.Y. commn. subcom. Foster Care Ind. Living; bd. advisers U. Hawaii Free Fellowship Program, 1982-86; mem. pvt. sector adv. panel on infrastructure financing Senate Budget Com.; mem. exec. com. Yale Devel. Bd., 1984—, bd. govs. Honoree testimonial dinner United Jewish Appeal, 1960. Mem. Am. Mgmt. Assn., Fgn. Policy Assn., Assn. of Yale U. Alumni (nat. class rep. 1983-86, gov. 1986—). Clubs: Lotos, Yale, Westchester Country. Office: BASIX Corp 50 E 72nd St New York NY 10021

BELEGRADEK, OLEG VIL'GEL'MOVICH, mathematician; b. Chelyabinsk, USSR, Nov. 24, 1949; s. Vil'gel'm Karlovich Belegradek and Fanya Abramovna (Drusvyatskaya) A.; m. Ol'ga Jakovlevna Chaiko, Feb. 20, 1969; 1 child, Igor. Masters, Novosibirsk U., USSR, 1972, postgrad., 1972-74, candidate degree, 1975. Assoc. prof. Kemerovo U., USSR, 1974-77, head algebra and geometry dept., 1977-87, docent, 1987—. Contbr. articles to profl. jours.; cons. editor math. jours.; also reviewer. Mem. Am. Math. Soc. Home: 71-41 Sovetsky St, 650099 Kemerovo USSR Office: Kemerovo U, 6 Krasnaya, 650043 Kemerovo USSR

BELESON, ROBERT BRIAN, spirits and wine company executive; b. N.Y.C., Sept. 28, 1950; s. Abraham Gilbert and Ruth (Zirman) B. B.S., Cornell U., 1971; M.B.A., Harvard U., 1974. Personnel planning mgr. J.C. Penney Co., N.Y.C., 1971-72; product mgr. Gen. Foods Corp., White Plains, N.Y., 1974-79; v.p. mktg. Remy Martin Amerique, N.Y.C., 1979-81, pres., chmn., 1982—; v.p., mgmt. supr. Ogilvy & Mather, 1981-82. Bd. dirs. Alvin Ailey Am. Dance Theatre. Mem. Young Pres. Orgn. Republican. Jewish. Avocations: tennis, skiing, horseback riding, travel. Home: 15 Charles St #2C New York NY 10014 Office: Remy Martin Amerique 888 7th Ave New York NY 10106

BELEW, THOMAS EUGENE, musical instrument retailer, musician; b. Paris, Tex., Jan. 29, 1948; s. Eugene Maxwell and Gladys Emogene (Bolin) B. B.B.A. in Mktg., North Tex. State U., 1970. Pres., gen. mgr. Belew Music Co., Paris, Tex., 1970—; organist, choirmaster Central Presbyterian Ch., Paris, 1977—. Treas. Paris Downtown Devel. Assn., 1982-86; co-founder Paris Motet Choir, 1981—; pres. Paris Community Concert Assn., 1988—; mem. Paris Mcpl. Band, 1965—; mem. fine arts adv. com. Paris Jr. Coll., 1988—. Recipient award of merit Nat. Fedn. Music Clubs, 1971; Paul Harris fellow, 1987. Mem. Nat. Assn. Music Mchts., Choristers Guild, Am. Guild English Handbell Ringers, Am. Guild Organists (exec. com. Dallas 1977-79), Phi Mu Alpha Sinfonia. Lodge: Greater Paris Rotary (dir. 1978-80, Disting. Service award internat. 1977). Home: 3175 Clark Ln Paris TX 75460 Office: Belew Music Co 218 Bonham St Paris TX 75460

BELFIGLIO, VALENTINE JOHN, political science educator; b. Troy, N.Y., May 28, 1934; s. Edmond Liberato and Mildred Elizabeth (Sherwood) B.; B.S., Union U., 1956; M.A., U. Okla., Norman, 1967, Ph.D., 1970; 1 child, by previous marriage, Valentine Edmond. Grad. asst., instr. U. Okla., 1967-70; prof. polit. sci. Tex. Woman's U., Denton, 1970—. Reviewer textbooks in internat. politics Holbrook Press, Boston, 1973-75. Served with USAF, 1959-67. Tex. Woman's U. Instl. Research grantee, 1973-74, 76-77; postdoctoral fellow Republic of South Africa, 1976; Nat. Endowment for Humanities grantee, 1978; decorated knight Order of Merit, Republic of Italy; recipient Guido Dorso prize U. Naples, 1985. Mem. Internat. Studies Assn. (sec.-treas. region 1974-76), Am. Polit. Sci. Assn., Am. Italian Hist. Assn., AAUP, MENSA, Kappa Psi. Democrat. Roman Catholic. Author: The United States and World Peace, 1971; American Foreign Policy, 1979; The Italian Experience in Texas, 1983; The Best of Italian Cooking, 1985, Alliances, 1986, Go For Orbit, 1987. Contbr. numerous articles on internat. relations, Asian politics to profl. jours. Home: 704 Camilla Ln Garland TX 75040 Office: Tex Woman's U Box 23974 Denton TX 76204

BELFIORE, FRANCESCO, medical educator; b. Fiumefreddo, Catania, Italy, Oct. 14, 1932; s. Salvatore and Eleonora (Pirrone) B.; m. Silvia Iannello, July 31, 1974; children—Eleonora, Rosanna. M.D., U. Catania, 1957. Research assoc. U. Catania, 1959-65, asst. prof., 1966-79, assoc. prof. medicine, 1980—. Author: Enzyme Regulation and Metabolic Diseases, 1980. Contbg. author: Frontiers in Diabetes, book series, 1981—. Contbr. articles to profl. jours. Mem. European Assn. for Study of Diabetes. Home: Via XX Settembre 19, San Gregorio-Catania 95027, Italy Office: I Instituto Patologia Medica, Ospedale Garibaldi, 95123 Catania Italy

BELGUEDJ, MOURAD, hydrocarbon transportation company executive; b. Constantine, Algeria, Jan. 21, 1946; m. Chouakri Samia, July 18, 1985; children: Mohamed, Nadir. Diploma, Holborn Coll., London, 1969; BS, Boston U., 1972, MS, 1973; Am in Internat. Law and Diplomacy, Tufts U., 1974, MALD, 1975, PhD in Internat. Econ. Relations, 1977. Interpreter, tech. translator Geneva U., 1968; translator/conf. interpreter Sonatrach of Algeria, Algiers, 1969-70, head energy econs. and devel. planning, 1977-78, dir. gas exports, 1978-82; pres., dir. gen. SNTM-HYPROC, Arzew, Algeria, 1982—; prof. Algiers U., 1977-79; mem. council internat. com. Bur. Veritas, Paris, 1983; bd. dirs., nat. rep. Arab Maritime Petroleum Transp. Co., Kuwait, 1984; mem. adv. council on energy Fletcher Sch. Law and Diplomacy, Tufts U., Medford, Mass., 1985. Contbr. articles to profl. jours. Mem. Arab Fedn. Shipping, Arab Ctr. for Coordination and Maritime Consultation. Club: Algiers Flying. Home: 7 Ave du Premier Novembre, Algiers Algeria Office: SNTM-HYPROC, PO Box 60, Arzew Algeria

BELIN, DAVID WILLIAM, lawyer; b. Washington, June 20, 1928; s. Louis I. and Esther (Klass) B.; m. Constance Newman, Sept. 14, 1952 (dec. June 1980); children—Jonathan L., James M., Joy E., Thomas R., Laura R. B.A., U. Mich., 1951, M.B.A., 1953, J.D., 1954. Bar: Iowa 1954. Ptnr. Herrick & Langdon, 1955-62, Herrick, Langdon, Sandblom & Belin, 1962-66; sr. ptnr. Herrick, Langdon, Belin, Harris, Langdon & Helmick, 1966-78, Belin, Harris, Helmick, Tesdell, Lamson & McCormick, Des Moines, 1978—; dir. Kemper Mut. Funds.; counsel President's Commn. on Assassination of President Kennedy (Warren Commn.), 1964; exec. dir. Commn. on CIA Activities within the U.S. (Rockefeller Commn.), 1975; mem. Pres.'s Com. on Arts and Humanities, 1984—. Author: November 22, 1963: You Are the Jury, 1973, Final Disclosure, 1988. Bd. dirs. Des Moines Civic Music Assn., 1959-61, Des Moines Community Drama Assn., 1961-64, Des Moines Symphony, 1968-70, U. Mich. Alumni Assn., 1963-66. Served with AUS, 1946-47. Recipient Henry M. Bates Meml. award U. Mich. Law Sch., Brotherhood award NCCJ, 1978; hon. orator U. Mich., 1950. Mem. Soc. Barristers, Order of Coif, Phi Beta Kappa, Phi Kappa Phi, Delta Sigma Rho, Beta Alpha Psi. Club: Michigamua. Home: 1705 Plaza Circle Des Moines IA 50322 Office: 2000 Financial Ctr Des Moines IA 50309

BELJAN, JOHN RICHARD, university administrator, medical educator; b. Detroit, May 26, 1930; s. Joseph and Margaret Anne (Brozovich) B.; m. Bernadette Marie Marenda, Feb. 2, 1952; children: Ann Marie, John Richard, Paul Eric. B.S., U. Mich., 1951, M.D., 1954. Diplomate: Am. Bd. Surgery. Intern U. Mich., Ann Arbor, 1954-55, resident in gen. surgery, 1955-59; dir. med. services Stuart div. Atlas Chem. Industries, Pasadena, Calif., 1965-66; from asst. prof. to assoc. prof. surgery U. Calif. Med. Sch., Davis, 1966-74, from asst. prof. to assoc. prof. engring., 1968-74, from asst. dean to assoc. dean, 1971-74; prof. surgery, prof. biol. engring. Wright State U., Dayton, Ohio, 1974-83, dean Sch. Medicine, 1974-81, vice provost Sch. Medicine, 1974-78, v.p. health affairs Sch. Medicine, 1978-81, provost, sr. v.p., 1981-83; provost, v.p. acad. affairs, dean Sch. Medicine Hahnemann U., Phila., 1983-85, prof. surgery and biomed. engring., 1983-86, spl. adviser to pres., 1985-86; prof. anatomy, physiology and biomed. engring., v.p. acad. affairs Calif. State U., Long Beach, 1986—; prof. arts and scis., assoc. v.p. med. affairs Central State U., Wilberforce, Ohio, 1976-83 ; trustee Cox Heart Inst., 1975-77, Drew Health Center, 1977-78, Wright State U. Found., 1975-83, CSULB Found., 1986—, 49er Athletic Found., 1986—; trustee, regional v.p. Engring. and Sci. Inst. Hall of Fame, 1983—; bd. dirs. Miami Valley Health Systems Agy., 1975-82, UCI Ctr for Health Edn., 1987—; cons. in field. Author articles, revs., chpts. in books. Home 6490 Saddle Dr Long Beach CA 90815 Office Calif State U Long Beach CA 90840. Served with M.C. USAF, 1955-65. Decorated Commendation medal; Braun fellow, 1949; grantee USPHS, 1967—; NASA, 1968—. Fellow A.C.S., mem. Aerospace Med. Assn., AAUP, AMA (council on sci. affairs 1978-87), F.A. Coller Surg. Soc., Biomed. Engring. Soc., IEEE, Internat Soc. Am., Calif. Med. Assn., Los Angeles County Med. Assn., Phi Beta Delta, Phi Beta Kappa, Alpha Omega Alpha, Phi Eta Sigma, Phi Kappa Phi, Alpha Kappa Kappa. Clubs: Mich. Alumni (Dayton) (Outstanding Alumnus award 1976), Oakwood Fur, Fin and Feather. Lodge: Rotary. Home: 6490 Saddle Dr Long Beach CA 90815

BELL, (ERNEST) ARTHUR, botanist; b. Gosforth, Northumberland, Eng., June 20, 1926; s. Albert and Rachel Enid (Williams) B.; m. Jean Swinton Ogilvie, Sept. 3, 1952; children—Victoria Jane Bell Smith, Alasdair Gordon Simon, Robin Andrew. B.Sc., King's Coll., U. Newcastle, 1946; Ph.D., Trinity Coll., U. Dublin, 1950, M.A., 1953. Research chemist Imperial Chem. Industries, Billingham, Eng., 1946-47; asst. lectr. Trinity Coll., U. Dublin (Ireland), 1949-53; lectr., then reader King's Coll., U. London, 1953-68, prof. biology, dean of sci., 1972-81; prof. botany U. Tex., Austin, 1968-72; dir. Royal Bot. Gardens, Kew, Eng., 1981-88; vis. prof. biochem. and biology King's Coll., U. London and U. Tex., Austin, 1988— . Contbr. numerous articles on plant biochemistry to profl. publs.; co-editor: Secondary Plant Products, vol. 8 of Ency. of Plant Physiology, 1980. Fellow Royal Soc. Chemistry, Linnean Soc. of London (v.p. 1982—); mem. Phytochem. Soc. Europe (chmn.). Club: Athenaeum (London). Office: Royal Botanic Gardens, Richmond Surrey TW9 3AB, England

BELL, BRYAN, real estate, oil investment executive, educator; b. New Orleans, Dec. 15, 1918; s. Bryan and Sarah (Perry) B.; B.A., Woodrow Wilson Sch. Pub. and Internat. Affairs, Princeton, 1941; M.A., Tulane U.,

1962; m. Rubie S. Crosby, July 15, 1950; children—Rubie Perry Gosnell, Helen Elizabeth, Bryan, Beverly Saunders, Barbara Crosby. Pres., Tasso Plantation Foods, Inc., New Orleans, 1945-66; partner Bell Oil Cos., New Orleans, 1962—; gen. ptnr. 26 ltd. partnerships in oil, real estate and venture capital, 1962—; instr. econs. of real estate devel. Sch. Architecture, Tulane U., New Orleans, 1967—; instr. entrepreneurship, Univ. Coll. Mem. Garden Dist. Assn., 1964—. Bd. dirs. United Fund for Greater New Orleans Area, 1964-71, pres., 1968-69; chmn. Human Talent Bank Com., New Orleans, 1969—; mem. City Planning Commn., New Orleans, 1956-58; mem. bd. Met. Area Com., 1968—, pres., 1971—; bd. dirs. Bur. Govtl. Research, 1966—, pres., 1971—; chmn. com. Met. Leadership Forum, 1969—; mem. bd. New Orleans Area Health Council, 1966-70; bd. dirs. Tulane-Lyceum, 1947-51, Family Service Soc., 1951-58, pres., 1956-58; bd. dirs. St. Martin's Protestant Episcopal Sch., 1964-68, Metairie Park Country Day Sch., 1967-71; bd. dirs. Trinity Episcopal Sch., chmn., 1958-68; chmn. Trinity Christian Community, 1975—; bd. dirs. Christ Spirit of 76 Com., Fedn. Chs., 1975—, pres., 1984; bd. dirs. aux. Lighthouse for Blind; bd. dirs. Alton Ochsner Med. Found., 1983—. Served to 1st lt. AUS, World War II. Recipient Weiss Brotherhood award NCCJ, 1983, Times Picayune Loving Cup City of New Orleans, 1985. Mem. New Orleans C. of C., Princeton Alumni Assn. La. (pres. 1962-63), Fgn. Realtions Assn. Democrat. Episcopalian (vestry 1960—, jr. warden 1968-70, sr. warden 1970-72). Clubs: Internat. House, Boston, New Orleans Lawn Tennis, Wyvern, Lakeshore, Pickwick, New Orleans Country. Address: 1331 3d St New Orleans LA 70130

BELL, CHARLES EUGENE, JR., industrial engineer; b. N.Y.C., Dec. 13, 1932; s. Charles Edward and Constance Elizabeth (Verbelia) B.; B. Engring., Johns Hopkins U., 1954, M.S. in Engring., 1959; m. Doris R. Clifton, Jan. 14, 1967; 1 son, Scott Charles Bell. Indsl. engr. Signode Corp., Balt., 1957-61, asst. to plant mgr., 1961-63, plant engr., 1963-64, div. indsl. engr., Glenview, Ill., 1964-69, asst. to div. mgr., 1969-76, engring. mgr., 1976—; host committeeman Internat. Indsl. Engring. Conf., Chgo., 1984. Served with U.S. Army, 1955-57. Registered profl. engr., Calif. Mem. Am. Inst. Indsl. Engrs. (pres. 1981), Indsl. Mgmt. Club Central Md. (pres. 1964), Nat. Soc. Profl. Engrs., Ill. Soc. Profl. Engrs. Republican. Roman Catholic. Home: 1021 W Old Mill Rd Lake Forest IL 60045 Office: Signode Corp 3610 W Lake Ave Glenview IL 60025

BELL, CHARLOTTE RENEE, psychologist, researcher; b. St. Louis, Jan. 23, 1949. BA, Dillard U., New Orleans, 1970; MA, U. No. Colo., Greeley, 1973; EdD, U. No. Colo., 1976. Sch. psychologist Aurora (Colo.) Pub. Schs., 1974-76, Cherry Creek Schs., Englewood, Colo., 1976-78; psychologist Orangeburg (S.C.) Area Mental Health Ctr., 1978-79; prin. investigator 1890 research S.C. State Coll., 1979-83; private practice Columbia, S.C., 1983-87; research and program evaluator S.C. Inst. Poverty & Deprivation, 1987—; founder, chairperson Citizens Against Sexual Assault, O'burg, S.C., Columbia Coalition Black Concerns, Cola, S.C., 1987—; exec. dir. Project Soaring, Cola, 1986-87. Co-author: Discipline and Classroom Management, 1980, Added Dimensions in Fitness, 1984. Sec. Dem. Precinct Ward, Columbia, 1988. Home: 2307 Laurel St Columbia SC 29204

BELL, DAVID, steelmill company consultant; b. Dumfries, Scotland, Sept. 2, 1902; s. Edward and Isabella (Jardine) B.; m. Elizabeth Bell, Apr. 15, 1926; children: Heather, Edward. Student, Purdue U., Motherwell Tech. U., Scotland. With Colvilles, Scotland; asst. supt. Inland Steel Corp., Chgo., 1926-37; mgr. of mills Stewarts and Lloyds, Corby, England, 1937, British Steel, Corby, to 1967; cons. Dumfries, 1967—. Mem. Iron and Steel Inst. Presbyterian. Home: Glenburn Kettleholm, Lockerbie Dumfries Scotland

BELL, DENNIS ARTHUR, lawyer; b. Chgo., July 5, 1934; s. Samuel Arthur and Frances (Gordon) B.; m. Judith Gail Young, Nov. 6, 1977. B.S. in Accountancy, U. Ill., 1955; J.D., DePaul U., 1961. Bar: Ill. 1961, U.S. Supreme Ct., 1964. C.P.A., Ill., 1956. C.P.A. Peat, Marwick Mitchell, Chgo., 1957-62; staff acct., atty. SEC, Washington, 1957-62; capital devel. officer U.S. AID, Ankara, Turkey, 1966-68; pvt. cons., Chgo., 1968-70; group controller Nat. Student Mktg. Corp., Chgo., 1970-72; dir. corp. fin. dept. and house counsel Rothschild Securities Corp., Chgo., 1973-74; corp. sec., assoc. gen. counsel Midwest Stock Exchange, 1974-79; pres. Dennis A. Bell & Assocs. Ltd., Chgo., 1979—; dir., sec., treas. Joy Internat. Corp., 1977—, Lyric Internat. Corp., Chgo. and Hong Kong, 1983—. Bd. dirs. Mental Health Assn., Chgo. Clarence Darrow Community Ctr. Served with USAR, 1957-62. Mem. ABA, Fed. Bar Assn., Ill. Bar Assn., Ill. C.P.A. Soc., Am. Soc. Corp. Secs. Democrat. Jewish. Club: Attic (Chgo.); International (Chgo.). Home: 1325 N State Pkwy 10F Chicago IL 60610 Office: 140 S Dearborn St Suite 800 Chicago IL 60603

BELL, GRAHAM, airline executive; b. Whakatane, Bay of Plenty, New Zealand, June 16, 1937; s. Lorna (Fogarty) B.; m. Patricia Beverley South; children: Brendon, Hadyn. Grad. high sch., Whakatane. Electrician New Zealand Forest Products, Whakatane, 1953-68; mng. dir., pilot Bell-Air Intercity Commuter Airlines, Whakatane, 1968—; bd. dirs. Aero Hire Ltd., Whakatane, 1973—, Purse Seiner Services Ltd., Auckland, 1984—. Home and Office: 7 Tui St, Whakatane New Zealand

BELL, JAMES MILTON, psychiatrist; b. Portsmouth, Va., Nov. 5, 1921; s. Charles Edward and Lucy (Barnes) B.; student Va. State Coll., 1939-40; B.S., N.C. Central U. (formerly N.C. Coll.), 1943; M.D., Meharry Med. Coll., 1947. Rotating intern Harlem Hosp., N.Y.C., 1947-48; asst. physician to clin. dir. Lakin (W.Va.) State Hosp., 1948-51; fellow gen. psychiatry Menninger Sch. Psychiatry-Menninger Found., Topeka, 1953-56, tng. child psychiatry, 1957-58; resident Winter VA Hosp., Topeka, 1953-56; asst. sect. chief childrens unit Topeka State Hosp., 1956-58; clin. teaching staff Menninger Sch. Psychiatry, 1956-58; med. cons. psychiatry Irwin Army Hosp., Ft. Riley, Kans., 1957-58; clin. dir., psychiatrist Berkshire Farm Center and Services for Youth, Canaan, N.Y., 1959-86, sr. child and adolescent psychiatrist, 1986—; clin. asst. to clin. prof. psychiatry Albany Med. Coll., Union U., 1959—, mem. admission com., 1972-79; psychiatrist-in-charge Albany Home for Children, N.Y., 1959-77; staff psychiatrist Parsons Child and Family Center, 1977—; asst. dispensary to dispensary psychiatrist Albany Med. Center Clinic, 1960; trainee cons. Albany Child Guidance Center Psychiat. Service, Inc., 1961; cons. Astor Home for Children, Rhinebeck, N.Y., 1965; instrnl. staff Frederick Amman Meml. Inst. Delinquency and Crime, St. Lawrence U., 1965-70; cons. adolescence N.Y. State Div. Youth, 1966-76, mem. med. rev. bd., 1974-76; mem. Child Abuse Adv. Council, Albany; bd. dirs., v.p., mem. com. on proposed policy N.Y. Spaulding for Children; bd. dirs., exec. com. Gould Farm, Barrington, Mass. Served to capt. M.C., AUS, 1951-53; col. Res., ret.; comdg. officer 364th Gen. Hosp., USAR, Albany, 1967-76, assigned 344th Gen. Hosp., USAR, Ft. Totten, N.Y., 1976, 815th Sta. Hosp., Stewart Army Subport, Newburgh, N.Y., 1977; cons. Keller U.S. Army Hosp., U.S. Mil. Acad., West Point, N.Y. Decorated Army Commendation medal, Meritorious Service medal, others; nominated for Am. Psychiat. Assn. 1988 McGavin award; recipient awards; named Disting. Alumnus, Meharry Med. Coll., 1980; "A" Profl. Designation, Dept. Army Med. Dept., 1982; diplomate in psychiatry and child psychiatry Am. Bd. Psychiatry and Neurology (examiner 1980—), Pan. Am. Med. Assn. (council psychiatry sect.); cert. N.Y. State Dept. Mental Hygiene. Life fellow Am. Psychiat. Assn. (chmn. council nat. affairs 1973-75, past vice-chmn.), Am. Acad. of Child and Adolescent, Am. Orthopsychiatrist Assn., Am. Acad. Child Psychiatry (chmn. com. facilities for children and adolescence 1973-75), Am. Orthopsychiat. Assn. (past dir.); fellow AAAS, Soc. Adolescent Psychiatry, N.Y. Acad. Scis., Am. Coll. Psychiatrists (past mem. Stanley Dean award com.); mem. Group for Advancement of Psychiatry (com. on child psychiatry), Inst. Religion and Health (charter), Council for Exceptional Children, Nat. Assn. Tng. Schs. and Juvenile Agys., Assn. N.Y. Educators of Emotionally Disturbed, AMA, Nat., N.Y. State, Columbia Country med. assns., Am. Psychopath. Assn. (fellow), Child Care Workers (bd. dirs. N.Y.), Assn. Psychiat. Treatment of Offenders, N.Y. Acad. Scis., Am. Acad. Polit. and Social Sci., N.Y. State Soc. Med. Research, N.Y. Capitol Dist. Council Child Psychiatry (pres. 1974), Am. Med. Soc. on Alcoholism, Black Psychiatrists Am., NAACP (life), Alpha Omega Alpha. Rotarian. Contbr. numerous articles to profl. jours. Home: Hudsonview Old Post Rd N Croton-on-Hudson NY 10520 Office: Berkshire Farm Ctr & Services for Youth Canaan NY 12029

BELL, JOHN STEPHEN, clinical psychologist; b. Glasgow, Scotland, Jan. 7, 1951; s. Ronald and Dorothy (King) B. M.A., U. St. Andrew's, Fife, Scotland, 1972; M.Sc., U. Leeds (Eng.), 1974. Clin. psychologist Leeds Area Health Authority, Yorkshire, 1974-76; sr. clin. psychologist Royal Edinburgh Hosp. (Scotland), 1976-82; prin. clin. psychologist Lothian Health Bd., Edinburgh, 1982-87; head of dept. clin. psychology mental health service unit Grampian Health Bd., 1987—; hon. fellow Med. faculty U. Edinburgh, 1979-86; hon. sr. lectr. in mental health U. Aberdeen, 1987—. Contbr. articles, chpts. on enuresis, insomnia, sexual counselling, infertility, parenthood motivation, male infertility and psychogeriatric day care to profl. publs. Chmn. Lothian Area Clin. Psychology Adv. Group, 1985-86. Fellow Brit. Psychol. Soc. (assoc., mem. Scottish br. com. div. clin. psychology 1983-85, chmn. 1985-86); mem. Brit. Assn. Behavioural Psychotherapy (chmn. East Scotland br. com. 1978-81, mem. nat. exec. com. 1980-82). Office: Dept Clin Psychology, Royal Cornhill Hosp, Aberdeen Scotland

BELL, JOHN STEWART, physicist; b. Belfast, Ireland, July 28, 1928; s. John and Mary Ann (Brownlee) B. BSc, Queen's U., Ireland, 1948; PhD, U. Birmingham, England, 1955. Physicist United Kingdom Atomic Research Establishment, Harwell, 1949-60, CERN, Geneva, 1960—. Contbr. numerous articles to profl. jours. Office: CERN, 1211 Geneva 23 Switzerland

BELL, JOHN WRIGHT, lawyer; b. Pontiac, Mich., June 19, 1925; s. Robert William and Bernice Verdella (Hoskins) B.; m. Catherine Eloise Duffy, Jan. 16, 1946; children—Leslie Bell Maslowski, Dawson, Zachary, Hilary, Nicholas; m. 2d, Suzanne Elizabeth Conat, Aug. 28, 1970; Kimberly, Elizabeth. B.A., U. Rochester, 1946; J.D., U. Mich., Ann Arbor, 1949. Bar: Mich. 1949, U.S. Dist. Ct. (ea. dist.) Mich. 1949, U.S. Ct. Appeals (6th cir.) 1973, U.S. Supreme Ct. 1964. Twp. atty. Waterford, Independence and Springfield Twps., Mich., 1951-57; sole practice, Pontiac, 1949-56; ptnr. Bell & Hertler, P.C., Pontiac, also sec.-treas. Pres. Oakland County Young Republicans, 1952-54, Oakland County Animal Welfare Soc., 1950-52. Served to ensign, USN, 1943-46. Mem. Oakland County Bar Assn., Mich. Bar Assn., Def. Research Inst., Mich. Def. Trial Counsel. Office: Bell & Hertler PC Suite 1410 Pontiac State Bank Bldg Pontiac MI 48058

BELL, JULIE SUSAN, accountant, small business owner; b. Manchester, Lancashire, Eng., Mar. 17, 1958; d. Robert Alan and Joan (Cooke) B. BA in Bus. Studies with honors, U. London, 1980. Cert. acct. Sr. acct. Ernst & Whinney, London, 1980-84; assoc. Smith & Williamson, London, 1984-85; affiliate Arthur Young, London, 1985-87; sr. ptnr. accounts and fin. services practice Hammond Bell and Co., London; owner antiques sales and export firm, London; cons. Gad & Co., London, 1987—; bd. dirs. Property Co., London. Recipient Gold award of Duke of Edinburgh Scheme, 1977. Mem. London Soc., Manchester High Sch. Old Girls Fedn. (treas. 1985—). Mem. Conservative Party. Jewish. Home: 1 Devonshire Pl, London W1N 1PA, England Office: Hammond Bell & Co, PO Box 4TT, London W1N 4TT, England

BELL, LEO S., retired physician; b. Newark, Nov. 7, 1913; s. Alexander M. and Marie (Saxon) B.; A.B., Syracuse U., 1934; M.D., 1938; m. Edith Lewis, July 3, 1938; children—Jewyl Linn, David Alden. Intern, N.Y.C. Hosp., 1938, Bklyn. Hosp., 1939-40; resident in pediatrics Sea View Hosp., N.Y.C., 1940-41, N.Y.C. Hosp., 1941-42; practice medicine specializing in pediatrics, San Mateo, Calif., 1946-86; mem. staff Mills Meml. Hosp., San Mateo, Peninsula Hosp. & Med. Center, Burlingame, Children's Hosp., San Francisco; assoc. clin. prof. pediatrics U. Calif. Med Sch., San Francisco, Stanford Med. Sch. Palo Alto. Bd. dirs. Mills Hosp. Found., San Mateo, San Mateo County Heart Assn., Hillsborough Schs. Found. (Calif.), 1980-83. Served to capt. as flight surgeon USAAF, 1942-46. Recipient bronze and silver medals Am. Heart Assn.; diplomate Am. Bd. Pediatrics. Fellow Am. Acad. Pediatrics, Am. Pub. Health Assn.; mem. Calif. Fedn. Pediatric Socs. (pres.), Am. Fedn. Pediatric Socs. (pres.), Calif. Med. Assn., Am. Pub. Health Assn., Air Force Assn., AMA (alt. del. to ho. of dels.), Calif. (ho. of dels.), San Mateo County (sec.-treas.) med. assns., Internat., Hong Kong snuff bottle socs., World Affairs Council San Francisco. Clubs: Peninsula Golf and Country (San Mateo); Commonwealth (San Francisco). Contbr. articles to profl. jours. Home: 220 Roblar Ave Hillsborough CA 94010 Office: PO Box 1877 San Mateo CA 94401

BELL, MARY-KATHERINE, lawyer; b. Los Angeles, July 7, 1910; d. Weldon Branch and Vina (Cowan) Morris; m. Robert Collins Bell, Mar. 22, 1941; children—Robert Collins III, Marianne Bell Reifenheiser. B.A., Stanford U., 1934; J.D., George Washington U., 1943. Bar: D.C. 1943, N.Y. 1952, Conn. 1960. Atty., Cummings & Lockwood, Stamford, Conn., 1944-45, Shearman & Sterling, N.Y.C., 1948-77, Ivey, Barnum & O'Mara, Greenwich, Conn., 1978-83; asst. sec. to Assn. Bar City of N.Y., 1946-47; atty. to Conf. on Personal Fin. Law, N.Y.C., 1947-48; sole practice, New Canaan, Conn., 1983-84; mem. Tax Adv. Com. of Am. Law Inst. Co-editor: U.S. Bankruptcy Guide, 1948. Mem. Democratic Town Com., Conn. Bar Assn., Delta Gamma. Clubs: Cosmopolitan (N.Y.C.), Tokeneke (Darien). Home: 528 Main St New Canaan CT 06840 Office: 16 Forest St New Canaan CT 06840

BELL, MILDRED BAILEY, law educator; b. Sanford, Fla., June 28, 1928; d. William F. and Frances E. (Williford) Bailey; m. J. Thomas Bell, Jr., Sept. 18, 1948 (div.); children—Tom, Elizabeth, Ansley. A.B., U. Ga., 1950, J.D. cum laude, 1969; LL.M. in Taxation, N.Y. U., 1977. Bar: Ga. 1969. Law clk. U.S. Dist. Ct. No. Dist. Ga., 1969-70; prof. law Mercer U., Macon, Ga., 1970—; mem. Ga. Com. Constl. Revision, 1978-79. Mem. ABA, Ga. Bar Assn., Phi Beta Kappa, Phi Kappa Phi. Republican. Episcopalian. Bd. editors Ga. State Bar Jour., 1974-76; contbr. articles to profl. jours., chpts. in books. Home: 516 High Point North Rd Macon GA 31210 Office: Mercer U Law Sch Georgia Ave Macon GA 31207

BELL, RANDALL WILLIAM, ophthalmic surgeon; b. N.Y.C., Jan. 20, 1938; s. William Randall and Frances Veronica (Dwyer) B.; m. Carole Ann Gilligan, June 6, 1959; children: Randall, Deborah, Kevin, Thomas, James. BS, U.S. Mil. Acad., 1959; MD, Cornell U., 1966; grad., U.S. Army War Coll., 1983. Diplomate: Am. Bd. Ophthalmology, Nat. Bd. Med. Examiners. Commd. 2d Lt. U.S. Army, 1959, advanced through grades to brig. gen. Res., 1975; intern Walter Reed Gen. Hosp. U.S. Army, Washington, 1966-67, resident Walter Reed Gen. Hosp., 1967-70; chief ophthalmology Valley Forge (Pa.) Gen. Hosp. U.S. Army, 1970-72; practice medicine specializing in ophthalmology USAR 338th Med. Group, Wayne, Pa., 1972-83; comdg. gen. 2290th U.S. Army Hosp., Washington, 1981-85; mem. Surgeon's Gen.'s Adv. Council; mem. staff Scheie Inst., Presbyn. U. Pa. Med. Ctr., Wills Eye Hosp., Phila., Jefferson Hosp., Phila., Bryn Mawr (Pa.) Hosp.; sr. attending opthalmologist, mem. exec. com. Sacred Heart Hosp., Norristown; chief ophthalmology service Montgomery Hosp., Norristown; asst. prof. Thomas Jefferson U., Phila., 1972-76, U. Pa., 1978. Contbr. articles on ophthalmology to profl. jours. Fellow ACS, Pa. Acad. Opthalmology and Otolaryngology, Am. Acad. Opthalmology, Phila. Coll. Physicians; mem. AMA, Pa. Med. Soc., Del. County Med. Soc., Assn. Research in Vision and Ophthalmology, Soc. Contemporary Ophthalmology, Soc. Mil. Ophthalmologists, Ophthalmic Club Phila. (pres. 1981-83), West Point Soc. Phila. (bd. govs. 1975—, pres. 1981-82), Assn. U.S. Army (life), Soc. Med. Cons. Armed Forces. Clubs: Merion Cricket, Merion Golf, Union League of Phila, Cornell. Home: 124 Bloomingdale Ave Wayne PA 19087

BELL, REGINA JEAN, business owner; b. Lebanon, Mo.; d. Stephen S. and Ida M. (Reaves) B. B.A., Draughens U., 1948; postgrad., Butler U., 1958, Ind.-Purdue U., Indpls., 1970. Prodn. mgr. Howe Mfg. Co., Inc., Indpls., 1958-64; v.p. budgetary control Howe Engring. Co., Inc., Indpls., 1964-67; mgr. material control Nat. Aluminum Div., Indpls., 1968-84; now owner Brown County Letter Shop, Nashville, Ind. Mem. Indpls. Real Estate Assn.

BELL, RICHARD HARDING, II, venture capitalist; b. Columbus, Ohio, Dec. 26, 1946; s. Richard Harding and Cynthia May (Kyper) B.; m. Paulise G. Rossetti, Nov. 17, 1973; children: Christina, Carleigh, Richard III, Michael Jonathan. Student, Ohio Wesleyan U., Ohio Wesleyan U. and Franklin Coll., Lugano, Switzerland. Registered corp. agt., Del. Circulation dir. Rolling Stone mag., San Francisco, 1970-71; mgmt. cons. various nat. mags., 1972-79; bus. mgr. Enterprise Pub. Co., Wilmington, Del., 1980-81; pres., founder Harvard Bus. Services, Wilmington, 1981—, also bd. dirs.; bd. dirs. Highlights for Children mag., Columbus, Tripledge Wiper Corp., Bensalem, Pa.; founder, bd. dirs. Corp. Law Ctr. Del., Wilmington, 1985; mem. Del. Valley Venture Group. Chmn. venture capital task force Del. State C. of C., Wilmington, 1984-85, capital com. Del. Gov.'s High Tech. Task Force, Wilmington, 1986-87; mem. bidco rev. com. devel. office State of Del., gov.'s small bus. com., bus. and econ. devel. com.; fund raising chmn. Franklin Coll. Mem. Venture Capital Stock Market Assn. (bd. dirs. 1982-84, founding com.), Lyon's Eye Found. (life), Del. State C. of C., Del. Valley Venture Group, Wilmington Bus. Execs., Personal Computer Users Groups. Republican. Episcopalian. Club: Brandywine Country (Wilmington). Lodge: Lions. Office: Harvard Bus Services PO Box 392 Claymont DE 19703

BELL, ROBERT COLLINS, lawyer; b. St. Joseph, Mo., Sept. 19, 1912; s. Robert Cook and Mamie Burke (Collins) B.; m. Mary-Katherine Morris, Mar. 22, 1941; children—Robert III, Marianne. Student Carleton Coll., 1929-32; A.B., U. Minn., 1933; J.D., Harvard U., 1936. Bar: Minn. 1936, Conn. 1942, D.C. 1949, N.Y. 1953. Assoc. Fowler, Youngquist, Furber, Taney and Johnson, Mpls., 1936-37; atty. U.S. Wage and Hour Div.-Minn., N.D., S.D., Mont., 1939-40; chief tax amortization sect. War Prodn. Bd., 1940-42; assoc. Cummings and Lockwood, Stamford, Conn., 1942-52; ptnr. Smith Mathews, Bell and Solomon, N.Y.C., 1952-62; practice, New Canaan, Conn., 1962—; pros. atty., New Canaan, 1948-50. Mem. War Dept. Bd. Contract Appeals, Office of Under Sec. of War, 1944-45. Mem. ABA, Conn. Bar Assn., Internat. Bar Assn. Democrat. Congregationalist. Clubs: Harvard (N.Y.C.); Tokeneke (Darien, Conn.); Masons. Obtained judgments totalling over 25 million dollars on behalf of the Pottawatomi, Miami and Chippewa Indian Tribes in U.S. Ct. Claims and U.S. Indian Claims Commn. Home and Office: 528 Main St New Canaan CT 06840

BELL, WILLIAM HENRY, lawyer; b. Yenangyaung, Burma, Dec. 15, 1926; came to U.S., 1932; s. William R. and Beulah Joyce (Girsham) B.; m. Rita Ely, 1950; children: Sharon, Martin, David, Leta. BA, Duke U., 1947; BBA, Texas A&I U., 1950; JD, Tulsa U., 1954; DHL (hon.), Okla. Christian Coll., 1973. Bar: Okla. 1954, U.S. Dist. Ct. (no. dist.) 1954, U.S. Ct. Appeals (10th cir.). 1954, U.S. Supreme Ct. 1968. Assoc. John Rogers, Tulsa, 1954-64; ptnr. Rogers and Bell, Tulsa, 1964—; Bd. dirs. Bank Okla., Tulsa, Red River Oil Co. Trustee Hillcrest Med. Ctr., Okla., 1964—, Okla Med. Research Found., 1964—, Trinity U., 1967—, various colls. and univs.; past pres., chmn. Tulsa Area United Way; past pres. Tulsa Edn. Found., Tulsa Med. Edn. Found., others. Served with USNR, 1944-46. Recipient Disting. Service award U.S. Jr. C. of C., 1961, Medallion Boys Clubs Am., 1962; named Man of Yr. Downtown Tulsa Unlimited, 1973, Outstanding Layman Okla. State Med. Assn., 1983; named to Okla. Hall of Fame, 1974; Disting. Service award Trinity U., 1988. Fellow Am. Bar Found., Am. Coll. Probate Counsel, Southwestern Legal Found. , Okla. Bar Found. (past pres.); mem. ABA (resource devel. council), Fed. Energy Bar Assn., Okla. Bar Assn. (past pres.), Tulsa County Bar Assn. (past pres., outstanding jr. mem. 1960, outstanding sr. mem. 1972). Republican. Episcopalian. Clubs: So. Hills, Summit, Tulsa. Home: 4612 S Birmingham Ave Tulsa OK 74105

BELLAH, C. RICHARD, lawyer; b. San Antonio, Jan. 11, 1955; s. Max and Charlotte (Arant) B.; m. Erin P. Jones, Oct. 1987. BS in Gen. Bus. Adminstrn., Ariz. State U., 1977; JD, U. Ariz., 1980. Bar: U.S. Dist. Ct. Ariz. 1980, U.S. Ct. Appeals (9th cir.) 1981, U.S. Tax Ct. 1985, U.S. Supreme Ct. 1985. Law clk. to presiding justice Ariz. Supreme Ct., Phoenix, 1980-81; assoc. Crotts & Laird, Phoenix, 1981-82; ptnr. Charles, Smith & Bellah, Glendale, Ariz., 1982-86; sole practice Glendale, 1986—; councilman City of Glendale, 1984—; justice of peace pro tem Maricopa County Justice Ct., Glendale, 1985—; bd. dirs. Arrowhead Hosp. Committeeman precinct Maricopa County Reps.; bd. dirs. Glendale Youth Ctr., Faith House Women's Shelter. Recipient Outstanding Service award Am. Legion, 1979, Cert. of Appreciation Ariz. State Legis., 1979, Maricopa Services Commn., 1985, Phoenix of Realtors, 1985, Soroptimist Internat., 1985, City of Glendale, 1985, Glendale Sr. Ctr., 1986. Mem. ABA (Silver Key award 1979), Ariz. Bar Assn., Assn. Trial Lawyers Am., Ariz. Trial Lawyers Assn., Phi Alpha Delta (chpt. justice, vice justice alumni assn.). Baptist. Lodge: Rotary (chmn. installation banquet). Home: 4554 W Maryland Glendale AZ 85301 Office: 5724 W Palmaire Ave Glendale AZ 85301

BELLAMY, JOHN GILBERT, history educator; b. Nottingham, Eng., July 7, 1930; s. Alfred George and Gladys (Robinson) B.; m. Annette Sally Fearn, Aug. 6, 1960; children—Joanna Kate, Matthew Jonathan. B.A., U. Oxford, 1953; M.A., U. Nottingham, 1961, Ph.D., 1966. Head dept. history, grammar schs., Derbyshire and Cambridgeshire, Eng., 1955-61; lectr., sr. lectr. Loughborough Coll., Leicestershire, Eng., 1962-68; assoc. prof. Carleton U., Ottawa, Ont., Can., 1968-74, prof. history, 1974—; assoc. Clare Hall, U. Cambridge, 1972-73; assessor research projects in history Can. Council, 1969-75, Social Scis. and Humanities Research Council Can., 1981—. Author: The Law of Treason in England in the Later Middle Ages, 1970; Crime and Public Order in England in the Later Middle Ages, 1973; The Tudor Law of Treason, 1979, Criminal Law and Society in Late Medieval and Tudor England, 1984; Robin Hood: An Historical Enquiry, 1985. Mem. editorial bd. Florilegium jour., 1980—. Contbr. articles, book revs. to profl. pubs. Grantee Can. Council, 1969-75, Social Scis. and Humanities Research Council Can., 1981—; recipient Disting. Teaching award Carleton U., 1983. Mem. Selden Soc. Club: Ottawa Athletic. Avocations: tennis; golf. Home: 1261 Pebble Rd, Ottawa, ON Canada K1V 7S1 Office: Carleton U, Ottawa, ON Canada K1S 5B6

BELLANGER, SERGE RENÉ, banker; b. Vimoutiers, France, Apr. 30, 1933; s. René Albert and Raymonde Maria (Renard) B.; MBA, Paris Bus. Sch., 1957. With Citibank, 1966-73, Paris br., 1966-69, world corp. relations officer for Europe, N.Y.C., 1969-73, asst. v.p., 1969-71, v.p., 1972-73; sr. v.p., gen. mgr. N.Y. br. Crédit Industriel et Comml., 1973-79, exec. v.p., gen. mgr., 1979-84, exec. v.p., gen. mgr. CIC-Union Européenne Internat. et Cie, 1984—, also U.S. gen. rep. CIC Group, 1973-88; prof. banking French Banking Inst., 1961-64; mem. adv. com. French House, Columbia U., 1976—, mem. U.S. Com. Fgn. Trade Advisors for France, 1979-83, v.p. U.S. com., 1984-85, exec. v.p. 1985—. Chmn. internat. banking course New Sch. Social Research, N.Y.C., 1981-83. Served with French Air Force, 1958-60. Decorated Algeria Commemorative medal, chevalier Legion of Honor. Mem. French-Am. C. of C. (councillor 1973-74, exec. com. 1974-80, v.p. 1980-82, exec. v.p. 1982-83, nat. pres. 1983—, pres. N.Y. chpt. 1983—), French Overseas Assn., Inst. Fgn. Bankers (trustee 1975-77, v.p. 1977-79, chmn. legis. and regulatory com. 1977-79, chmn. 1979-80), Société Lyonnaise de Banque (bd. dirs. 1986—), Assn. for the Promotion of French Sci., Industry and Tech., 1986—, N.Y. Futures Exchange (dir. 1980-87, chmn. fgn. exchange steering com. 1981-82), N.Y. Cotton Exchange (bd. dirs. fin. instrument exchange div. 1985—), Bank Adminstrn. Inst. (editorial bd. World of Banking Mag. 1981—, clumnist 1986—). Clubs: Board Room, River (N.Y.C.); Automobile de France (Paris). Home: 860 UN Plaza Apt 23/24C New York NY 10017 Office: 520 Madison Ave New York NY 10022

BELLENGER, DOMINIC AIDAN, historian, monk; b. London, July 21, 1950; s. Gerald and Kathleen Patricia (O'Donnell) B. BA, Jesus Coll., Cambridge, Eng., 1972; MA, Cambridge (Eng.) U., 1975, PhD, 1978. Research historian U. Cambridge, 1972-78; asst. master Downside Sch., Bath, Eng., 1978-82; monk of Order of St. Benedict Downside Abbey, Bath, 1982—; mem. com. Benedictine History Symposium aand Commn. Eng., 1987. Author: English and Welsh Priests 1558-1800, 1984, The French Exiled Clergy in the British Isles, 1986, Opening the Scrolls: Essays in Catholic History, 1987; editor: South Western Catholic History; contbr. articles to profl. jours. Leverhulme Trust grantee, 1986. Fellow Royal Hist. Soc., Royal Soc. Arts, The Huguenot Soc.; mem. Ecclesiastical History Soc. Eng. (com. 1982-85). Roman Catholic. Home and Office: Downside Abbey, Stratton-on-the Fosse, Bath Somerset BA3 4RH, England

BELLES, ANITA LOUISE, health care administrator, advertising and marketing consultant, graphic arts executive; b. San Angelo, Tex., Aug. 30, 1948; d. Curtis Lee and Margaret Louise (Perry) B.; m. John Arvel Willey, July 13, 1969 (div. Aug. 1978); children: Suzan Heather, Kenneth Alan. BA, U. Tex., 1972; MS in Health Care Adminstrn., Trinity U., 1984. Registered emergency med. technician; cert. CPR instr., emergency med. technician tchr., La. Regional emergency med. service tng. coordinator Bur. Emergency Med. Service, Lake Charles, La., 1978-79; exec. dir. Southwest La. Emergency Med. Service Council, Lake Charles, 1979-83; project coordinator Tulane U. Med. Sch., New Orleans, 1982-83; dir. La. Bur. of Emergency Med. Service, Baton Rouge, 1982; pres. Computype, Inc., San Antonio, 1983-86, Emergency Med. and Safety Assocs., La. and Tex., 1982—; dir. family planning Bexar County Hosp. Dist., Tex., 1987; mgmt. engr. Inpatient Support Applications, 1987-88. Editor A.L.E.R.T., 1980-83, San Antonio Executive News, 1987—, Family Living, 1987-88; feature writer Bright Scrawl, 1985-86; contbr. numerous articles on emergency med. services to profl. jours. Bd. dirs. Thousand Oaks Homeowner's Assn., sec., treas., 1985; active Trinity U. Health Care Alumni Assn., Jr. League San Antonio, The Parenting Ctr., Baton Rouge, 1982-83, Jr. League Lake Charles, 1982, Campfire Council Pub. Relations Com., Lake Charles, 1982; newsletter editor Community Food Co-Op, Newsletter Editor, 1979; vol. Lake Charles Mental Health Ctr., 1974. Recipient Outstanding Service award La. Assn Registered Emergency Med. Technicians, 1983, Southwest La. Assn. Emergency Med. Technicians, 1983; named Community Leader KPLC TV, Lake Charles, 1981, regional winner Assn U. Programs in Health Adminstrn., HHS Sec's. Competitions for Innovations in Health, 1982. Mem. Nat. Assn. Emergency Med. Technicians., Tex. Assn. Emergency Med. Technicians, Am. Coll. Health Care Execs., Am. Assn. Automotive Medicine, Southwest La. Assn. Emergency Med. Technicians (founding mem., v.p. 1979-80, CPR com. chmn. 1980-81, pub. relations com. chmn. 1981-82, bd. dirs. 1980-82), Am. Mgmt. Assn., Nat. Soc. Emergency Med. Service Adminstrs., Nat. Coalition Emergency Med. Services, Am. Composition Assn. Methodist. Office: Bexar County Hosp Dist 4502 Medical Dr San Antonio TX 78284

BELLI, ARCANGELO, real estate development executive; b. Rome, Oct. 19, 1933; s. Francesco and Maria (Onori) B.; children: Paola, Francesca, Deborah, Frencesco; m. Luisa Mazzuca; 1 child, Elisabetta. Pres., chmn. Belli SA, Lugano, Switzerland, 1985—; past pres. and dir. numerous multinational companies. Named Cavaliere del Lavoro Pres. of the Republic, 1979, Hon. Citizen Tex., Utah, Houston. Clubs: Maxim Bus. (Paris), Dos Caicaras (Rio de Janeiro). Home: Via Guilding 3, 6900 Lugano Switzerland Office: Belli SA, Via San Gottardo 10, 6900 Lugano Switzerland

BELLINI, MARIO, architect; b. Milan, Italy, 1935. Degree in Architecture, Polytech. of Milan. Prof. Istito Superiore di Disegno Industriale, Venice, Italy, 1962-65; chief indsl. design cons. Olivetti, 1963—; practice architecture with Marco Romano 1963-73; research cons. Renault, 1978—; mem. archtl. list GESCAL, 1967—; instr. courses and seminars UCIMU, 1971, Art Internat. U., Florence, 1973, 76, Nat. Hoger Inst., Antwerp, 1977, Royal Coll. Art, 1978. Works include Civic Ctr. Paderno Dugnano, Info. Systems Dept. Ivrea; contbr. articles to profl. jours. Recipient Compasso D'Oro, 1962, 64, 70, 79, Bolaffi Design prize, 1973, Smau prize, 1978, Delta and Oro prize, 1977-79. Mem. Archtl. Assn. of Milan, Indsl. Design Assn. (v.p. 1969-71), Sci. Council for the Triennial Design Section. Office: Domus, Via Achille Grandi 5/7, I-20089 Rozzano Milan Italy *

BELLIS, ARTHUR ALBERT, financial executive, government official; b. Worcester, Mass., June 16, 1928; s. Frank Clayton and Ruth Porter (Gordon) B.; m. Barbara Swift, Feb. 22, 1952 (div. 1969); children—Bradford, Susan; m. E. Deborah Shea, May 28, 1972; children—Cynthia, Michael. B.S. in B.A., Boston U., 1952. Asst. credit mgr. Procter & Gamble, N.Y.C., 1955-56; asst. supr. capital budget Western Union, N.Y.C., 1956-58; corp. budget analyst CBS, N.Y.C., 1958-64; account exec. Edwards & Hanley, N.Y.C., 1964-66, Spencer Trask, Worcester, 1966-70; sr. securities compliance examiner SEC, Boston, 1970—. Advisor Explorer program Mohegan council Boy Scouts Am., 1966-70; mem. Worcester Rep. Com., 1952-53, Rep. Presdl. Task Force, 1984-85; mem. fin. com. Town of Yarmouth, 1982-86. Recipient Superior Performance award SEC, 1976, 1986; Medal of Merit, Pres. of U.S., 1985. Mem. Aircraft Owners and Pilots Assn., Internat. Platform Assn. Methodist. Lodge: Masons. Avocation: flying. Home: 14 Ice House Rd South Yarmouth MA 02664 Office: John McCormack Courthouse and Post Office Bldg 7th Floor Boston MA 02109

BELLOC, MARC HENRI, history and geography educator; b. Brest, Finistére, France, Sept. 27, 1922; s. Albert-Jacques and Marguerite Marie (Lehugeur) B.; m. Jeannine Madeleine de Brousse, Sept. 28, 1946; children: Emmanuelle, Pascale, Sabine, Vincent, Christophe. BA, Faculté des Lettres, Aix-en-Provence, 1942; MA, U. Aix-Marseille, Aix-en-Provence, 1943. Educator lycée level Laval, France, 1949-52, Guingamp, France, 1953-54; educator lycée level Lycée Bertrand d'Argentré, Vitré, France, 1954—. Author: History CAP 1, Chronologies 1914-45, 1973, Chronologies 1946-73, 1974. Active the Résistance force, France, 1941-44. Named Officier des Palmes Académiques Nat. Edn. Bd., 1975, Chevalier de l'Ordre Nat. du Mérite Nat. Edn. Bd., 1981. Mem. Breton Assn. History and Geography Tchrs. (pres. 1974-81). Roman Catholic. Home: 6 rue de Corbin, 35000 Rennes Ille et Vilaine, France Office: Lycee Bertrand d'Argentre, 15 rue du College, 35500 Vitre France

BELLOCCHI, NATALE H., U.S. ambassador to Botswana; b. Little Falls, N.Y., July 5, 1926; m. Sujr Lilan Liu; 2 children. B.S., Ga. Tech., 1948; M.A., Georgetown U., 1954. Indsl. engr. Burlington Mills Corp., 1948-50; joined Fgn. Service, Dept. State, 1955, diplomatic courier, 1955-60; adminstrv. asst. Fgn. Service, Dept. State, Hong Kong, 1960-61; gen. services officer Fgn. Service, Dept. State, Vientiane, Laos, 1961-63; asst. comml. attache Taipei, Taiwan, 1964-68; chief comml. unit Hong Kong, 1968-69; comml. attache Saigon, Vietnam, 1971-72; comml. counselor Tokyo, 1973-74; spl. asst. Office of Asst. Sec. for Internat. Affairs, Dept. Treasury, 1975-79; then econ. counselor New Delhi, India; dep. prin. officer Hong Kong, 1979-81; dep. asst. sec. for current analysis Bur. Intelligence and Research, Dept. State, 1981-85; U.S. ambassador to Botswana 1985—. Served with U.S. Army, 1950-53. Address: US State Dept US Ambassador to Botswana Washington DC 20520

BELLON, ERROL MANFRED, radiologist, educator, researcher; b. Beaufort West, South Africa, May 13, 1938; s. Michael and Roslyn (Sklaar) B.; m. Eveline Morgenstern, Apr. 5, 1962; children—Steven F., Richard J., Jennifer R. M.D., U. Cape Town (South Africa), 1961. Diplomate Am. Bd. Radiology. Intern Groote Schuur Hosp., Cape Town, 1962; resident in radiology Mpilo Central Hosp., Bulawayo, Rhodesia, 1963; resident in radiology Univ. Hosps. Cleve., 1964-67, asst. radiologist, 1967—; chief radiology service VA Hosp., Cleve., 1968-73; assoc. dir. dept. radiology Cuyahoga County Hosp., Cleve., 1973-76, dir. dept. radiology, 1976—; asst. prof. radiology Case Western Res. U., Cleve., 1968-73, assoc. prof., 1973-82, prof., 1982—; surveyor AMA Joint Rev. Com. on Edn. in Radiologic Tech., 1975—. James Picker Found. scholar, 1967-69. Fellow Am. Coll. Radiology; mem. Radiol. Soc. N.Am., Soc. Photo-Optical Instrumentation Engrs., Assn. Univ. Radiologists, Am. Roentgen Ray Soc., Am. Acad. Med. Dirs. Author: Radiologic Interpretation of ERCP: A Clinical Atlas, 1983 also sci. papers. Office: Dept Radiology 3395 Scranton Rd Cleveland OH 44109

BELLO-REUSS, ELSA NOEMI, physician, educator; b. Buenos Aires, Argentina, May 1, 1939; came to U.S., 1972; d. Jose F. and Julia M. (Hiriart) Bello; B.S., U. Chile, 1957, M.D., 1964; m. Luis Reuss, Apr. 15, 1965; children—Luis F., Alejandro E. Intern J.J. Aguirre Hosp., Chile, 1963-64; resident in internal medicine U. Chile, Santiago, 1964-66; practice medicine specializing in nephrology Santiago, 1967-72; Internat. NIH fellow U. N.C., Chapel Hill, 1972-74; vis. asst. prof. physiology U. N.C., Chapel Hill, 1974-75; Louis Welt fellow U. N.C.-Duke U. Med. Center, 1975-76; mem. faculty Jewish Hosp. St. Louis, 1976-83, asst. prof. medicine, physiology and biophysics Washington U. Sch. Medicine, St. Louis, 1976-86, assoc. prof. physiology dept. cell biology and physiology, 1986; assoc. prof. medicine U. Tex. Med. Br., Galveston, 1986—. Mem. Internat., Am. Socs. Nephrology, Royal Soc. Medicine, Nat. Kidney Found. of Southeast Tex. (med. adv. bd.), Council of Women in Nephronology, Tex. Med. Assn., Am. Fedn. Clin. Research, Am. Physiology Soc., Am. Heart Assn., Kidney Council, Soc. Gen. Physiologists, Math. Assn. Am., Gt. Houston and Gulf Coast Nephrology Assn., NIH Gen. Medicine B Study Sect. (mem. 1987—). Contbr. articles on nephrology and epithelial electrophysiology to med. and physiology jours., chpt. to nephrology text. Office: U Tex Med Br Dept Medicine Nephrology OJS 4 200 Galveston TX 66550

BELLOT-ROSADO, FRANCISCO, mathematics educator; b. Madrid, Dec. 28, 1941; s. Francisco Bellot-Rodriguez and Maria Rosado Alvarez de Sotomayor; m. Maria Ascensión López Chamorro, July 27, 1968. Lic. in Math., U. Madrid, 1964. Prof. math. I.N.E.M. Marqués de la Ensenada, Logroño, Spain, 1966-70, I.N.B. Emilio Ferrari, Valladolid, Spain, 1970—; charged of course Faculty of Scis., Valladolid, 1972-75; mem. jury Spanish Math. Olympiad, Valladolid, 1986-87; reviewer Zentralblatt Didaktik D. Math., Karlsruhe, Fed. Republic Germany, 1987—. Mem. jour. editorial staff Gaceta Matematica, 1987—; contbr. articles to profl. jours. Pres. Assn. de Catedráticos de Bachillerato, Valladolid, 1983—. Mem. Real Soc. Math. Española, Math. Assn. (Eng.), Math. Assn. Am., Assn. Profs. Math. de l'Enseignement Pub., N.Y. Acad. Scis. Office: INB Emilio Ferrari, La Sementera S/N, E-47009 Valladolid Spain

BELLOW, SAUL, writer; b. Lachine, Quebec, Can., June 10, 1915; s. Abraham and Liza (Gordon) B.; children: Gregory, Adam, Daniel. Student, U. Chgo., 1933-35; B.S., Northwestern U., 1937, Litt.D., 1962; Litt.D., Bard Coll., 1962, Harvard U., 1972, Yale U., 1972, McGill U., 1973, Brandeis U., 1974, Hebrew Union Coll.-Jewish Inst. Religion, 1976, Trinity Coll., Dublin, Ireland, 1976. Tchr. Pestalozzi-Froebel Tchrs. Coll., Chgo., 1938-42; faculty Princeton, N.Y. U., U. Minn.; faculty English dept. U. Chgo., 1963—, mem. com. on social thought, 1963—, chmn. com. on social thought, 1970-76, now Raymond W. and Martha Hilpert Gruiner Distinguished Services prof.; Tanner lectr. Oxford U. Author: Dangling Man, 1944, The Victim, 1947, The Adventures of Augie March, 1953 (Nat. Book award 1953), Seize the Day, 1956, Henderson the Rain King, 1959, Dessins, 1960, Herzog, 1964 (James L. Dow award 1964, Internat. Lit. prize 1965, Nat book award 1965, Soc. Midland Authors Fiction award 1976), (play) The Last Analysis, 1964, Mosby's Memoirs and Other Stories, 1968, Mr. Sammler's Planet, 1969 (Nat. Book award 1970), The Future of the Moon, 1970, Technology and the Frontiers of Knowledge, 1974, Humboldt's Gift, 1975 (Pulitzer prize 1976), To Jerusalem and Back, 1976, The Dean's December, 1982, More Die of Heartbreak, 1986; short stories Him With His Foot in His Mouth, 1984; contbr.: fiction to Esquire and lit. quarterlies; criticisms appear in New Leader, others; short story to Atlantic's 125th Anniversary Edit., 1982. Decorated Croix de Chevalier des Arts et Lettres France, Comdr. Legion of Honor France; recipient Nat. Inst. Arts and Letters award, 1952; Friends of Lit. Fiction award, 1960; Communicator of Yr. award U. Chgo. Alumni Assn., 1971; Nobel prize for lit., 1976; Medal of Honor for lit. Nat. Arts Club, 1978; O. Henry prize for short story A Silver Dish, 1980; Malaparte Lit. award, 1984; Guggenheim fellow, 1955-56; Ford Found. grantee, 1959-61. Mem. Am. Acad. Arts and Scis. Address: care Com Social Thought Univ of Chicago 1126 E 59th St Chicago IL 60637 *

BELLRICHARD, SUZANNE KAY, comparative literature educator; b. Janesville, Wis., July 4, 1947; d. Robert C. and Jean L. (McBeth) B. B.A., Ill. Wesleyan U., 1969; postgrad. Chinse lang. Taiwan Normal U., 1969-70; cert. in French, Sorbonne, Paris, summer 1970; postgrad. Am. U. Beirut, 1972-73; doctoral candidate McGill U., 1985. Dir., tchr. Ill. State U.-YMCA, Taipei, Taiwan, 1969-70, tchr. Am. U. Beirut, 1972-73, McGill U., Montreal, Que., Can., 1971-72, 75, College St.-Laurent, Que., 1975-83; tchr. Dawson Coll. Prison Program, Que., 1979; lectr. U. Wis. Rock County Ctr., 1986-87, U. Wis.-Oshkosh, 1987—; writer Can. Council, Ottawa, Ont., 1984-85; tutor and English cons. to Amin Gemayel (now Pres. Lebanon), 1972-73. Ford Found. grantee, 1970; Asia Found. grantee, 1969-70; McGill U. dean's grantee, 1976; Eli Williams scholar, 1967; Woodrow Willson fellow. Mem. MLA, Alpha Mu Gamma. Avocations: classical music; pianist; accompanist. Home: 1612 Holly Dr Janesville WI 53545 Office: U Wis-Oshkosh 800 Algoma Blvd Oshkosh WI 54901

BELLRINGER, ALAN WAYLAND, English language and literature educator; b. Croydon, Surrey, Eng., Aug. 26, 1932; s. Clarence Wayland and Edith Grace Maggie (Sayer) B.; m. Jean Wendie Taylor, July 5, 1965; children: Mark Wayland, Keith Taylor. MA, Glasgow U., Scotland, 1954; PhD, Aberdeen U., Scotland, 1968. Asst. Aberdeen U., 1960-63; asst. lectr. in English U. Coll. N. Wales, Bangor, 1963-64, lectr., 1964-74, sr. lectr., 1974—. Author: The Ambassadors, 1984; co-editor: The Victorian Sages, 1974, The Romantic Age in Prose, 1980. Office: U Coll No Wales, Bangor, Gwynedd LL57 2DG, Wales

BELMARES, HECTOR, chemist; b. Monclova, Coahuila, Mex., Feb. 21, 1938; s. Armando and Guadalupe (Sarabia) B.; B.Sc., Instituto Tecnológico de Monterrey (Mex.), 1960; Ph.D. (Todd fellow 1961-63), Cornell U., 1963; postdoctoral student Calif. Inst. Tech., 1965; m. Eleanor Johanna Wold, Aug. 28, 1965; children: Michelle Anne, Michael Paul, Elizabeth Myrna, Mary Eleanor. Sr. research chemist Rohm and Haas Co., Phila., 1965-71; gen. mgr. tech. and quality control Fibras Quimicas, S.A., Monterrey, Mex., 1972-75; sr. research chemist Centro de Investigación en Química Aplicada, Saltillo Coahuila, Mex., 1976-83, Sola Optical USA Inc., 1984—; mem. adv. panel Modern Plastics Mgmt., 1986-87; cons. on polymers for industry; cons. UN Indsl. Devel. Orgn. Community rep. Against Indsl. Air Pollution, Moorestown, N.J., 1968-70. Mem. Am. Chem. Soc., N.Y. Acad. Scis., AAAS, Sigma Xi. Mem. Christian Evangelical Ch. Patentee Plexiglas 70. Contbr. articles to profl. jours. Office: Sola Optical USA Inc 1500 Cader Ln Petaluma CA 94953

BELMONDO, JEAN-PAUL, actor; b. Nevilly-sur-Seine, France, Apr. 9, 1933; s. Paul Belmondo; student Ecole Alsacienne, Paris, Cours Pascal and Convervatoire nat. d'art dramatique, 1953-56. Appeared in plays L'hotel du libre-echange, Oscar, Tresor-Party, Medee, La megere apprivoisee; appeared in films Sois belle et tais-toi, A pied, a cheval et en voiture, les Tricheurs, Charlotte et son Jules, Drole de dimanche 1958, Les copains du dimanche, Mademoiselle Ange, A double toru, Classe tous risques, Au bout de souffle, L'Amour, La Novice, La Ciociara, Moderato Cantabile, Leon Morin Pretre, Le doulos, 1962, Dragees au poivre, l'Aine des Ferchaux, Pear de banane, 100,000 dollars au soleil, 1963; Two Women, The Man From Rio, Echappement libre, 1964, Les tribulations d'un Chinois en China, Pierrot le Fou, 1965, Paris, brule-t il?, 1966, Le Voleur, 1966, Casino Royale,1967, The Brain, 1969, La Sirene du Mississippi, 1969, Un Homme qui me plait, 1970, Borsalino, 1970, The Burglars, 1972, La Scoumoune, 1972, L'Heritier, 1972, Le Magnifique, 1972, Stavisky, 1974, Peur sur la ville, 1975, L'Incorrigible, 1974, L'Alpageur, Le corps de mon ennemi, 1976, L'Animal, 1977, Flic ou Voyou, 1979, Le Guignolo, 1980, Le Professionnel, 1981, L'As des As, 1982, Le Marginal, 1983, Les Morfalous, 1984. Decorated chevalier de l'Ordre nationale du Merite et des Arts et des Lettres; recipient Prix Citron, 1972. Mem. French Union Actors (pres. 1963-66). Author: 20 Ans et 25 Films, 1963. Address: Artmedia, 10 ave Georges V, 75008 Paris France *

BELMONTE, JOHN VIRGIL, surgeon; b. Chgo., Jan. 1, 1938; s. John Virgil and Anne (Izzo) B.; B.S., John Carroll U., 1956; M.D., Loyola U., Chgo., 1963; M.S., U. Ill., 1967; m. Sherill K. Premo, Sept. 26, 1964; children—John, Kristen Ann, Braden, Pamela. Intern, Cook County Hosp., Chgo., 1963-64; resident in surgery Hines VA Hosp., Ill., 1964-68; practice medicine specializing in surgery, 1968—; chief surgery dept. Good Samaritan Hosp., Downers Grove, Ill., Gottlieb Meml. Hosp.; mem. staff Oak Park Hosp. Served to maj. U.S. Army, 1968-70. Diplomate Am. Bd. Surgeons. Fellow A.C.S., Internat. Coll. Surgeons; mem. Ill. Med. Soc., DuPage County Med. Soc., Chgo. Med. Soc., AMA, Am. Trauma Soc., Am. Soc. Abdominal Surgeons, Pan-Pacific Surg. Soc. Roman Catholic. Home: One Pembroke Ln Oak Brook IL 60521 Office: 2340 Highland Ave Suite 280 Lombard IL 60148 also: 675 W North Ave Melrose Park IL 60160

BELOHLAVEK, JIRI, conductor; b. Prague, Feb. 24, 1946; s. Jiri and Anna (Nepomucka) B.; grad. Conservatoire in Prague, 1966, Acad. Music Arts, Prague, 1972; m. Anna Fejerova, Feb. 6, 1971; children—Susanna, Marie. Artistic dir., condr. Orch. Puellarum Pragensis, 1967-72; asso. condr. Czech Philharm. Orch., 1970-72; condr. Brno (Czechoslovakia) Philharm. Orch., 1972-77; chief condr. Prague Symphony Orch., 1977—; condr. Czech Philharm. Orch., 1981—. Winner first prize nat. competition young condrs. in Czechoslovakia, 1970; finalist H.V. Karajan Internat. Competition, 1971. Office: Prague Symphonic Orch FOK, Obecni Dum, 11000 Prague 1 Czechoslovakia

BELON, PHILIPPE-ETIENNE, dermatologist, pharmaceutical company research manager; b. Montauban, France, Apr. 6, 1949; s. Etienne-Marcel and Marie Thérèse (Pecquet) B.; m. Danielle Navarro; children: Elodie, Julien, Mathilde. MD, U. Lyon, France, 1975, D of Scis., 1976. Intern Hosp. Lyon, France, 1972-77, clinic chief, 1977-79; asst. U. Lyon, 1974-77; pvt. practice medicine specializing in dermatology Decines, France, 1979—; research mgr. Boiron, Sainte Foy, France, 1980—; expert in dermatology, angiology Ministry of Health, France, 1981—. Author: La Microcirculation, 1983, Aspect de la Recherche en Homéopathie, 1983; contbr. articles to sci. jours. Fellow Soc. Biol. Chemistry; mem. European Acad. Allergy, Am. Acad. Allergy, Am. Soc. Photobiol. Photochemistry, N.Y. Acad. Sci. Office: 261 Av Jean Jaurès, Decines France 69150

BELSKY, MARTIN HENRY, dean, law educator, lawyer; b. Phila., May 29, 1944; s. Abraham and Fannie (Turnoff) B.; m. Kathleen Waits, Mar. 9, 1985; 1 child, Allen Frederick. B.A. cum laude, Temple U., 1965; J.D. cum laude, Columbia U., 1968; cert. of study Hague (Netherlands) Acad. Internat. Law, 1968; diploma in criminology Cambridge (Eng.) U., 1969. Bar: Pa. 1969, Fla. 1983, U.S. dist. ct. (ea. dist.) Pa. 1969, U.S. Ct. Appeals (3d cir.) 1970, U.S. Supreme Ct. 1973, N.Y. 1987. Chief asst. dist. atty. Phila. Dist. Atty.'s Office, 1969-74; assoc. Blank, Rome, Klaus & Comisky, Phila., 1975; chief counsel U.S. Ho. of Reps., Washington, 1975-78; asst. adminstr. NOAA, Washington, 1979-82; dir. Ctr. for Govtl. Responsibility, assoc. prof. law U. Fla. Holand Law Ctr., 1982-86; dean Albany Law Sch., 1986—; bd. advs. Ctr. Oceans Law and Policy; mem. corrections task force Pa. Gov.'s Justice Commn., 1971-75; adv. task force on cts. Nat. Adv. Commn. on Criminal Justice Standards and Goals, 1972-74; mem. com. on proposed standard jury instrns. Pa. Supreme Ct., 1974-81; lectr. in law Temple U., 1971-75; mem. faculty Pa. Coll. Judiciary, 1975-77; adj. prof. law Georgetown U., 1977-81. Chmn. Phila. council Anti-Defamation League, 1975, mem. D.C. bd., 1977-78, now mem. nat. leadership Council. Stone scholar and Internat. fellow Columbia U. Law Sch. Mem. Phila. Bar Assn. (chmn. young lawyers sect. 1974-75), Pa. Bar Assn. (exec. com. young lawyers sect. 1973-75), ABA (del. young lawyers sect. exec. bd. 1973-75), Fla. Bar Assn., Fed. Bar Assn., Am. Judicature Soc., Nat. Dist. Attys. Assn., Am. Soc. Internat. Law, Am. Arbitration Assn., Temple U. Liberal Arts Alumni Assn. (v.p. 1971-75), Sword Soc. Jewish. Club: B'nai B'rith (v.p. lodge 1973-75). Author: (with Steven H. Goldblatt) Analysis and Commentary to the Pennsylvania Crimes Codes, 1973; Handbook for Trial Judges, 1976; contbr. articles to legal publs.; editor-in-chief Jour. Transnat. Law, Columbia Law Sch., 1968, now bd. dirs. Office: Albany Law Sch of Union U Office of the Pres 80 New Scotland Ave Albany NY 12208

BELSTEAD, LORD (JOHN JULIAN GANZONI), Lord Privy Seal, leader of House of Lords; b. Ipswich, Eng., Sept. 30, 1932; s. Francis John and Gwendoline (Turner) Ganzoni. Student, Eton U., England; MA, Christ Church, Oxford, England, 1961. Parliamentary Under-Secretary of State Dept. Edn. and Sci., England, 1970-73, No. Ireland Office, England, 1973-74, Home Office, England, 1979-83; minister of state Foreign and Commonwealth Office, England, 1982-83, Ministry of Agriculture, Fisheries and Food, England, 1983-87, Dept. Environ., England, 1987-88; Lord Privy Seal, leader House of Lords England, 1988—. Named Justice of Peace, Borough of Ipswich, 1962, Dep. Lt. Suffolk, 1979, Privy Councillor, 1983. Conservative. Clubs: MCC, All Eng. Lawn Tennis.

BELTRAO, ALEXANDRE FONTANA, coffee organization executive; b. Curitiba, Parana, Brazil, Apr. 28, 1924; s. Alexandre and Zilda (Fontana) B.; m. Anna Emilia, 1964; two children. Ed. Instituto Santa Maria, Curitiba, U. de Sao Paulo, Escola Nacional de Engenharia, Rio de Janeiro. Asst. engr. dept. soil mechanics Inst. de Pesquisas Tecnologicas, Sao Paulo, 1948; mem. staff Inst. Nat. d'Aerophotogrametrie, Ministere de la Reconstruction, Paris, 1950-51, Ministry of Works, London, 1950-51; founder, dir. Planning Services Ltd., 1954—; observer Govt. of State of Parana to UN Internat. Coffee Conf., 1962; spl. adviser to Pres., Brazilian Coffee Inst., 1964; chief Brazilian Coffee Inst. Bur., N.Y.C., 1965-67; pres. World Coffee Promotion Com. of Internat. Coffee Orgn., 1965-67; exec. dir. Internat. Coffee Orgn., 1968—. Author: Parana and the Coffee Economy, 1963; (essay) Economy of States of Parana, Para and Ceara, 1958. Decorated comdr. Order of Rio Branco. Address: Internat Coffee Orgn, 22 Berners St, London W1 England

BELTZNER, GAIL ANN, educator; b. Palmerton, Pa., July 20, 1950; d. Conon Nelson and Lorraine Ann (Carey) Beltzner; B.S. in Music Edn. summa cum laude, West Chester State U., 1972; postgrad. Kean State Coll., Temple U., Westminster Choir Coll., Lehigh U. Tchr. music Drexel Hill Jr. High Sch., 1972-73; music specialist Allentown Sch. Dist., Pa., 1973—; tchr. Corps Sch. and Community Developmental Lab., 1978-80, Corps Community Resource Festival, 1979-81, Corps Cultural Fair, 1980, 81. Mem. aux. Allentown Art Museum; mem. womans com. Allentown Symphony; bd. dirs. Allentown Area Ecumenical Food Bank. Mem. Allentown Fedn. Tchrs. (sec., exec. com.), Music Educators Nat. Conf., Pa. Music Educators Assn., Am. Orff-Schulwerk Assn., Soc. Gen. Music, Am. Assn. Music Therapy, Internat. Soc. Music Edn., Assn. Supervision and Curriculum Devel., Choristers Guild, Lenni Lenape Hist. Soc., Allentown Symphony Assn., Allentown 2d Civilian Police Acad., Nat. Sch. Orch. Assn., Lehigh County Hist. Soc., AAUW, Kappa Delta Pi, Phi Delta Kappa, Alpha Lambda. Republican. Lutheran. Home: PO Box 4427 Allentown PA 18105

BELZER, JEFFREY A., lawyer, automobile dealer and developer; b. Mpls., Sept. 8, 1941; s. Meyer S. and Kathleen (Bardin) B.; B.A., St. Cloud State U., 1963; J.D., Drake U., 1968; children—Steven, Michael, Anna, Jeffrey. Admitted to Minn. bar, 1968, U.S. Dist. Ct. bar., 1969; mem. firm Henretta, Muirhead, McGinty, Ltd., Mpls., 1968-71; pres., sr. atty. Belzer & Brenner Ltd., Mpls., 1971-80; pres., dir. Walesch Devel. Co., Mpls., 1969—, Walsch Estates, Inc., Mpls., 1971—, Jeff Belzer's Todd Chevrolet Inc., Lakeville, Minn., 1980—. Mem. Am., Hennepin County, Minn. bar assns., Phi Alpha Delta. Staff: Drake Law Rev., 1966-67. Office: PO Box 965 Hwy 50 and Cedar Ave Lakeville MN 55044

BEMANANJARA, JEAN ANDRIANARIBONE, minister of foreign affairs of Madagascar; b. Toamasina, Malagasy, Aug. 13, 1943; s. Jean de la Croix and Jeannette (Rabarone) B; m. Marie Pierrette Narove, Oct. 31, 1964; 6 children. Diploma, Institut des Hautes Etudes d'Outre Mer, Paris, 1966; diploma, Ecole D'Administration des Affaires Maritimes de Bordeaux, 1968. Div. chief Madagascar Navy, Tamatave, 1968-72; transp. dir. Govt. Madagascar, Antananrivo, 1972-75, minister of transp., 1975-76, minister of fgn. affairs, 1976, 83—, minister of transp., 1976-82, dir. Civil cabinet of the Pres., 1982-83; pres. bd. dirs. Port Autonome Tamatave, 1972-82, Societe Malgache Trans. Maritimes, Antananrivo, 1972-75, Societe Lima-Holding, Antananarivo, 1982—. Roman Catholic. Office: Ministry Fgn Affairs, Ampefiloha, Antananarivo Madagascar

BEMIS, HAL LAWALL, engineering and business executive; b. Palm Beach, Fla., Jan. 30, 1912; s. Henry E. and Elise (Lawall) B.; m. Isabel Mead, June 27, 1942; children—Elise, Carolyn, Claudia. B.S., M.I.T., 1935. With Campbell Soup Co., 1935-53; mgr., asst. to pres., v.p., dir. Campbell Soup Co., Ltd., 1946-53; organizer, pres. Mariner Corp., 1954—; v.p. Hosp. Food Mgmt., Inc., 1954-57; sec., treas. Bell Key Corp., 1955—; v.p. Coral Motel Corp., 1963—; pres. Jennings Machine Corp., 1957—; cons. Coopers & Lybrand, 1973—; dir., mem. exec. and audit coms. Publicker Industries; chmn., dir. Phila. Reins. Corp.; dir. Ott, Hertner, Ott & Assos., Colonial Savs. Bank. Past pres. Commn. Twp. Lower Merion, Pa.; bd. dirs., vice chmn. Spring Garden Coll.; exec. bd. Com. of 70; chmn. bd. Am. Cancer Soc.; bd. dirs. Delaware Valley area Nat. Council on Alcoholism; adv. bd. Salvation Army; past trustee Haverford Sch.; dir. Phila. Port Corp., West Phila. Corp., Phila. Indsl. Devel. Corp.; trustee United Fund, Young Men's Inst.; pres., trustee Greater Phila. Found.; bd. dirs. Am. Diabetes Assn., M.I.T. Devel. Found., Broad St. So. Com.; mem. corp. bd. Goodwill Industries, Garrett-Williamson Found. Served 1st lt. to lt. col. AUS, 1942-45. Decorated Legion of Merit with oak leaf cluster, Bronze Star medal; Croix de Guerre (France). Mem. Greater Phila. C. of C. (past chmn. bd., past pres.), SAR, S.R., Pa. Soc., Newcomen Soc., Mil. Order World Wars, Mil. Order Fgn. Wars, Am. Legion (past comdr.), Tau Beta Pi, Delta Psi. Clubs: Union League (pres.), Racquet, Rittenhouse, Penn, Philadelphia; St. Anthony (N.Y.C.), Merion Golf (Ardmore, Pa.); Merion Cricket (dir.) (Haverford, Pa.); Bachelor's Barge, IV Street, Pine Valley Golf, Sunday Breakfast, Right Angle, Toronto Golf, Royal Canadian Yacht, Brit. Officers. Home: 101 Cheswold Ln Haverford PA 19041 Office: 410 Lancaster Ave Haverford PA 19041

BENACERRAF, BARUJ, pathologist, educator; b. Caracas, Venezuela, Oct. 29, 1920; came to U.S., 1939, naturalized, 1943; s. Abraham and Henriette

(Lasry) B.; m. Annette Dreyfus, Mar. 24, 1943; 1 dau., Beryl. B. es L., Lycee Janson, 1940; B.S., Columbia U., 1942; M.D., Med. Sch. Va., 1945; M.A., Harvard U., 1970; M.D. (hon.), U. Geneva, 1980; D.Sc. (hon.), NYU, 1981, Va. Commonwealth U., 1981, Yeshiva U., 1982, U. Aix-Marseille, 1982, Columbia U., 1985. Intern Queens Gen. Hosp., N.Y.C., 1945-46; research fellow dept. microbiology Columbia U. Med. Sch., 1948-50; charge de recherches Centre National de Recherche Scientique Hospital Broussais, Paris, 1950-56; asst. prof. pathology NYU Sch. Medicine, 1956-58, asso. prof., 1958-60, prof., 1960-68; chief immunology Nat. Inst. Allergy and Infectious Diseases, NIH, Bethesda, Md., 1968-70; Fabyan prof. comparative pathology, chmn. dept. Harvard Med. Sch., 1970—; pres., chief exec. officer Dana-Farber Cancer Inst., 1980; mem. immunology study sect. NIH; pres. Fedn. Am. Socs. Exptl. Biology, 1974-75; chmn. sci. adv. com. Centre d'Immunologie de Marseille. Editorial bd.: Jour. Immunology. Trustee, mem. sci. adv. bd. Trudeau Found.; mem. sci. adv. com. Children's Hosp. Boston; bd. govs. Weizmann Inst. Medicine; mem. award com. Gen. Motors Cancer Research Found., also chmn. selection com. Sloan prize, 1980. Served to capt. M.C. AUS, 1946-48. Recipient T. Duckett Jones Meml. award Helen Hay Whitney Found., 1976; Rabbi Shai Shacknai lectr. and prize Hebrew U. Jerusalem, 1974; Waterford award for biomed. scis., 1980; Nobel prize for medicine or physiology, 1980. Fellow Am. Acad. Arts and Scis.; mem. Nat. Acad. Scis., Nat. Inst. Medicine, Am. Assn. Immunologists (pres. 1973-74), Am. Assn. Pathologists and Bacteriologists, Am. Soc. Exptl. Pathology, Soc. Exptl. Biology and Medicine, Brit. Assn. Immunology, French Soc. Biol. Chemistry, Harvey Soc., Internat. Union Immunology Socs. (pres. 1980—), Alpha Omega Alpha. Home: 111 Perkins St Boston MA 02130

BENAK, JAMES DONALD, lawyer; b. Omaha, Jan. 22, 1954; s. James R. and Norma Lea (Roberts) B.; m. Mari Lu Petersen, Sept. 15, 1979. BA, U. Nebr., 1977; JD, Creighton U., 1980. Bar: Nebr. 1980, U.S. Dist. Ct. Nebr. 1980. Assoc. Kennedy, Holland, DeLacy & Svoboda, Omaha, 1980-84; asst. gen. atty. Union Pacific R.R. Co., Omaha, 1984-87, gen. atty., 1987—. Fin. dir. Hugh O'Brian Youth Found., Omaha, 1983-84; co-incorporator Nebr. Leadership Seminar Inc., Omaha, 1984; bd. dirs. Combined Health Agencies Drive/Nebr., Omaha, 1985—. Mem. ABA, Nebr. Bar Assn., Omaha Bar Assn. (chmn. law day 1986—). Republican. Roman Catholic. Home: 15353 Page St Omaha NE 68154 Office: Union Pacific RR Co 1416 Dodge St Room 830 Omaha NE 68179

BEN ALI, ZINE AL-ABIDINE, president of Tunisia; b. Sousse, Tunisia, Sept. 3, 1936; Married; 3 children. Dir. mil. security Tunisia, 1958; mil. attaché Tunisian Embassy, Rabat, Morocco, 1974-77; Tunisian ambassador Poland, 1980-83; sec. state internal security Ministry of Interior, Tunisia, 1984, minister nat. security, 1985-86, minister of interior, 1986-87, prime minister, 1987, pres., 1987—. Office: Office of the Pres, Tunis Tunisia *

BENBEN, JOHN STEPHEN, emeritus educator; b. Chgo., Jan. 25, 1912; s. Stanley P. and Josephine (Siwek) B.; B.S., Northwestern U., 1934, M.A., 1938, Ph.D., 1953; m. Beverlee F. Brown, Jan. 21, 1949; children—Paul Leland, Stephen James, Nancy Ruth. Social service casework, Chgo., 1933-37, staff Hull House, Chgo., 1933-36; prin. schs., Midlothian, Ill., 1937-39, dist. supt., 1939-50; prof. No. Ill. U., 1953-56, head dept. edn., 1957-60; prof. ednl. adminstrn. N.Y. U., 1960-78, prof. emeritus, 1978—; lectr. Pace U., 1978-79; vis. prof., adv. U. P.R., 1979—; ednl. adviser Lago Community Schs., Aruba, Netherlands Antilles, Colombia, S.Am., 1976; adviser Korean Govt., 1948, V.I. Edn. Dept., 1965, U. P. R., 1966-68; cons. to P.R. sec. edn., 1967-68, 69-71, Presbyn. Hosp., 1968; dir. edn. UN Command program Prisoner of War Camp, Koje-Do, Korea, 1951-52; UNESCO adviser Sierra Leone, B.W.I., 1956-57. Mem. Bd. Edn., Ardsley, N.Y., 1963-67, adviser, 1978-79. Recipient Disting. Service award N.Y. U. Sch. Edn., 1977. Mem. Ill. Conf. Profs. Ednl. Adminstrn., Ill. Ednl. Assn., Ill. Prins. Assn., Ill. Supts. Assn., Round Table Chgo., Nat. Conf. Profs. Ednl. Adminstrn., Am. Assn. Sch. Adminstrs., Am. Assn. U. Profs., Univ. Council Ednl. Adminstrn., Comparative and Internat. Edn. Soc., African Resources Conf., Profs. World Peace Acad., Phi Delta Kappa. Author: History of Education, 1965, The Human Enterprises; Study N.Y.C. Personnel, 1965; For Educational Adminstrators, 1971, 73; Administration of Education in Puerto Rico: Its Tasks and Competencies and Designs for the Improvement of Administrative Skills, 1984; Planning, Development of Doctoral Studies Program, Sch. of Edn., U. P.R., 1981-84; Curriculum Umbrella, 1968. Home: El Monte Apt B 542 190 de Hostos Ave Hato Rey PR 00918 Office: U PR Sch Edn Rio Piedras PR 00931

BENBOW, ROBERT MICHAEL, biology educator; b. San Pedro, Calif., Nov. 10, 1943; s. Henry Robertson and Betty Lou (Pederson) B.; m. Lena Camilla Persson, Jan. 5, 1975; children—Wystan, Bronwen, Trefor, Evan, Lovisa, Byron, Lena. B.S., Yale U., 1967; Ph.D., Calif. Inst. Tech., 1972. Helen Hay Whitney postdoctoral research fellow Lab. Molecular Biology, Med. Research Council, Cambridge, Eng., 1972-75; asst. prof. Johns Hopkins U., Balt., 1975 81, assoc. prof. molecular biology, 1981-83; prof. Iowa State U., Ames, 1985—, also dir., 1986— ; mem. cell biology panel NSF, 1980—. Co-author: Biochemistry, 1981. NIH Research Career Devel. awardee, 1976. Mem. Am. Soc. Biol. Chemists, Am. Soc. Cell Biology, Am. Chem. Soc., Devel. Biology Soc., Sigma Xi. Republican. Roman Catholic. Research on control of DNA replication during embryogenesis in the frog, Xenopus laevis, molecular mechanisms of DNA replication in soybean, Glycine max. Home: 2901 Forest Hills Dr Ames IA 50010 Office: Iowa State U Nucleic Acid Facility Ames IA 50511

BENCHIMOL, ALBERTO, cardiologist, author; b. Belem, Para, Brazil, Apr. 26, 1932; s. Isaac I. and Nina (Siqueira) B.; came to U.S., 1957, naturalized, 1964; B.S., State Coll., Rio de Janeiro, Brazil, 1950; M.D., U. Brazil, 1956; m. Helena Lourdes Levy, Apr. 14, 1962; children—Nelson, Alex. Intern, U. Brazil Med. Center, Rio de Janeiro, 1956-57, resident in medicine, 1957; fellow in medicine U. Kans. Med. Center, Kansas City, 1958-60, Scripps Clinic, La Jolla, Calif., 1960-61; practice medicine specializing in cardiology, La Jolla, now Phoenix; research assoc. Inst. Cardiopulmonary Diseases, Scripps Clinic and Research Found., La Jolla, 1961-63, assoc., 1963-66; dir. Inst. Cardiovascular Diseases, Good Samaritan Med. Center, Phoenix, 1966-82; vis. prof. U. Brazil, 1966, Desert Hosp., Palm Springs, Calif., 1971; tutor U. Mo. Sch. Medicine, Kansas City, 1974-77, lectr., 1978-81; prof. in residence U. Oreg., Portland, 1975; vis. prof. Nagasaki U., Japan, 1970, Letterman Gen. Hosp., San Francisco, 1972. Haskell fellow in cardiology, 1957-59. Fellow ACP, Am. Coll. Cardiology, Am. Coll. Chest Physicians, Am. Coll. Angiology; mem. Am., Ariz. heart assns., Am. Physiol. Soc., Western Soc. Clin. Research, AMA, Biol. and Med. Scis. Research Club San Diego, Am. Fedn. Clin. Research. Author: Atlas of Vectorcardiography, 1971; Atlas of Phonocardiography, 1971; Vectorcardiography, 1973; Non-Invasive Diagnostic Techniques in Cardiology, 1977, 2d edit., 1981; Noninvasive Techniques in Cardiology for the Nurse and Technician, 1978; contbr. articles on cardiology and cardiography to profl. jours., chpts. to med. books; editorial bd. Am. Heart Jour., 1968-76, Am. Jour. Cardiology, 1969-76, Catheterization and Cardiovascular Diagnosis, 1974—, Chest, 1974; producer films on cardiography, 1962, 66. Home: 195 E Desert Park Ln Phoenix AZ 85020 Office: 1300 N 12th St Phoenix AZ 85006

BENCKENSTEIN, JOHN HENRY, lawyer; b. Detroit, Nov. 28, 1903; s. Leonard Fredrick and Genevieve (Peterson) B.; m. Agnes Merle Halpin, June 27, 1936; children: Mary Agnes Benckenstein Cain, Jacqueline Louise. JD, U. Va., 1928. Bar: Tex. 1928, U.S. Dist. Ct. (ea. dist.) Tex. 1928, U.S. Ct. Appeals (5th cir.) 1931, U.S. Dist. Ct. (we. dist.) La. 1948, U.S. Supreme Ct. 1952, U.S. Dist. Ct. (so. dist.) Tex. 1957, U.S. Dist. Ct. (ea. dist.) La. 1957, U.S. Dist. Ct. (we. dist.) Tex. 1980, U.S. Ct. Appeals (11th cir.) 1981. Ptnr. Benckenstein & Norvell, Beaumont, Tex., 1966-80; of counsel Benckenstein, Norvell, Bernsen & Nathan, Beaumont, 1981—; tchr. Interstate Commerce Practice & Procedure Lamar State Coll., Beaumont. Recipient Selective Service medal U.S. Congress. Fellow Tex. Bar Found.; mem. ABA (sr. lawyers sect.), Tex. Bar Assn., Jefferson County Bar Assn., Assn. Trial Lawyers Am., Fedn. Ins. Counsel, Tex. Assn. Def. Counsel, Thomas Jefferson Soc. Alumni U. Va., Phi Delta Phi. Republican. Episcopalian. Clubs: Beaumont (pres. 1980-81), Beaumont Country; Tower. Home: 2625 Gladys Beaumont TX 77702 Office: Benckenstein Norvell Bernsen & Nathan 2615 Calder Beaumont TX 77702

BENDELIUS, ARTHUR GEORGE, engineering firm executive; b. Passaic, N.J., May 21, 1936; s. Arthur Leopold and Lydia Ella (Flach) B.; m. Virginia Brown, June 21, 1958; children: Linda Ellen, Bonnie Sue, Heidi Ann. BE, Stevens Inst. Tech., 1958, MMS, 1966. Registered profl. engr., N.Y., N.J., Minn., Ga., Fla., Tex., Ala., Ky., N.C., S.C., Miss., Tenn., La., Ohio, Ark., Okla., Md., Utah lic. pilot. Engr. Syska & Hennessey, N.Y.C., 1958-60; engr. Parsons Brinckerhoff Quade & Douglas, Inc., N.Y.C., 1960-62, asst. dept. head, 1963-68, dept. head, 1968-70, project mgr., 1970-73; regional mgr. Parsons Brinckerhoff Quade & Douglas, Inc., Atlanta, 1973-76, asst. v.p., 1976-78, v.p., 1978-82, sr. v.p., 1982—; engr. Nat. Biscuit Co., N.Y.C., 1962-63; condr. seminars, moderator forums in computer usage and environ. design. Co-author: Tunnel Engring. Handbook, 1982; contbr. articles to profl. jours. Pres. Brookside Home Sch. Orgn., Westwood, N.J., 1972-73; co-v.p. Dunwoody Bank Booster Club, Ga., 1975-76, co-pres., 1976-77. Named Atlanta Engr. of Yr. in Pvt. Practice, 1978; recipient Harold R. Fee Alumni award, 1978. Fellow Soc. Am. Mil. Engrs. (pres. Atlanta post 1978-79, nat. bd. direction 1983-86); mem. Nat. Soc. Profl. Engrs., Ga. Soc. Profl. Engrs. (dir. 1976-78), Nat. Council Engring. Examiners (cert.), Ga. Engring. Found. (life, dir. 1977—, sec. 1979, v.p. 1980, pres. elect 1981, pres. 1982, 83), Stevens Alumni Assn., ASME, ASHRAE (chmn. tech. com. 1975-79, research promotion com. 1980-82), Australian Inst. of Refrigerating and Air Conditioning , Brit. Tunneling Soc., Transp. Assn. of S.C. (bd. dirs. 1987—, treas. 1987—), Electric Railroaders Assn., Aircraft Owners and Pilots Assn., Australian Tunneling Inst., Atlanta C. of C., Tau Beta Pi, Sigma Nu (pres. alumni assn. 1966-70, comdr. 1971-73). Lutheran. Clubs: Ansley Golf, Atlanta Stevens (pres. 1974—). Home: 1220 Witham Dr Dunwoody CA 30338 Office: 148 International Blvd Atlanta GA 30303

BENDER, BURWYN BOYNE, truck manufacturer; b. Columbus, Ohio, Oct. 2, 1929; s. Alfred Carl and Ethel May (Ryan) B.; m. Evelyn Juanita Roden, May 14, 1955; children: Kathy, Michael, Gregory. BSME, Case Inst. Tech., 1951; MS in Automotive Engring., Chrysler Inst. Tech., 1953; grad. advanced mgmt. program, Harvard U., 1978. Registered profl. engr., Mich. Mgr. advance prodn. planning missile div. Chrysler Corp., Sterling Heights, Mich., 1960-62; mgr., mfg. engr. space div. Chrysler Corp., New Orleans, 1962-68; ops. mgr. missile div. Chrysler Corp., Sterling Heights, 1968-70; v.p., gen. mgr. Cooper Bessemer div. Cooper Industries, Mt. Vernon, Ohio, 1970-80; group v.p. Gulf & Western Mfg. Co., Southfield, Mich., 1980-83; owner, chief exec. officer Ottawa (Kans.) Truck Corp., 1983—. Served with U.S. Army, 1954-56. Mem. Soc. Automotive Engrs. (New Orleans sect. chmn. 1963-65), Computer-Aided Systems Assn. of Soc. Automotive Engrs. (bd. dirs. 1978-80), Machine and Allied Products Inst. (mem. mktg. council 1986—), Soc. Mfg. Engrs. (bd. dirs. 1978-80). Republican. Lodge: Masons. Office: Ottawa Truck Corp 415 E Dundee Ottawa KS 66067

BENDER, DIANE LOUISE WOLF, lawyer; b. Evansville, Ind, Oct. 21, 1955; d. Thomas Joseph and Margaret Gertrude (Horn) Wolf; m. John Frederick Bender, June 15, 1985. BBA with highest honors, U. Notre Dame, 1977, JD cum laude, 1980. Bar: Ind. 1980. Ptnr. Kahn, Dees, Donovan & Kahn, Evansville, Ind., 1980—. Bd. dirs. Vis. Nurses Assn. of Southwestern Ind., Inc., 1983—, United Way of Southwestern Ind., Inc., 1984—, Health Skills, Inc., Evansville, 1984—, Cath. Press of Evansville, Inc., 1985—. Mem. ABA, Ind. Bar Assn., Evansville Bar Assn., Am. Inst. CPA's, Ill. CPA Soc. Home: PO Box 9164 Evansville IN 47710 Office: Kahn Dees Donovan & Kahn PO Box 3646 Evansville IN 47735-3646

BENDER, HENRY ELIAS, psychologist; b. Mineola, N.Y., Apr. 5, 1938; s. Max and Tanya (Galmitz) B.; B.A., Hofstra Coll., 1959, M.A., 1961; Ph.D., N.Y.U., 1970; M.B.A., Adelphi U., 1986; m. Judy Ziegler, May 30, 1976; children—Jara Dee, Adam Ziegler. Human factors engr. Gen. Dynamics Electronics, Rochester, N.Y., 1963-64; scientist Matrix Corp., L.I., 1965-69; prin. cons. Concept Applications, Ltd., N.Y.C., 1969—; assoc. prof. So. Ill. U., Carbondale, 1972-75; dir. research N.Y. State Legis. Inst., Baruch Coll., N.Y.C., 1975-77; dir. research Am. Mgmt. Assn., 1977-84; mem. tech. staff Bell Communications Research, Piscataway, N.J., 1984—; adj. assoc. prof. Hofstra U., Hempstead, N.Y., 1977—. Mem. Am. Psychol. Assn., Am. Soc. Tng. and Devel., Acad. Mgmt., Human Factors Soc. Home: 4 White Oak Tree Rd Laurel Hollow NY 11791 Office: Bell Communications Research 444 Hoes Ln RRC 1S-327 Piscataway NJ 08854

BENDER, JOEL CHARLES, lawyer; b. Bklyn., Dec. 12, 1939; s. Harry and Edna (Bogolowitz) B.; children: Andrew, Gary. BA, Cornell U., 1961; JD, NYU, 1964. Bar: N.Y. 1964, U.S. Supreme Ct. 1970, Fla. 1980. Ptnr. Bender & Bodnar, White Plains, N.Y., 1980—. Councilman Greenburgh, N.Y. 1976—; dep. supv., police commr. Greenburgh, 1979—. Fellow Am. Acad. Matrimonial Law; mem. ABA, N.Y. State Bar Assn., Fla. Bar, Westchester County Bar Assn. Democrat. Home: 4 Mohican Ln Irvington NY 10533 Office: Bender & Bodnar 11 Martine Ave White Plains NY 10606

BENDER, JOHN HENRY (JACK), JR., editor, cartoonist; b. Waterloo, Iowa, Mar. 28, 1931; s. John Henry and Wilma (Lowe) B.; m. Mary P. Henderson; children—Thereza, John IV, Anthony. B.A., U. Iowa, 1953; M.A., U. Mo., 1962; postgrad. Art. Inst. Chgo., Washington U., St. Louis. Art. dir., asst. editor Commerce Pub. Co., St. Louis, 1953-58; editor Florissant Reporter, 1958-61; editorial cartoonist Waterloo Courier, 1962-84, assoc. editor, 1975-83, sports editor, 1983-84; art. dir., editor Alpha VII Corp., Tulsa, 1984-86; instr. prodn. art Platt Coll., Tulsa, 1986—; sports cartoons Basketball Weekly, Baseball Digest Mag., U. Iowa, others. Author: Pocket Guide to Judging Springboard Diving; (with Dick Smith) Inside Diving; (with Ed Gagnier) Inside Gymnastics. Served with USAF, 1954-56, now col. Res. Recipient Best Editorial award Mo. Press Assn., 1960; Grenville Clark Editorial Page award, 1968, Freedoms Found. award, 1969, 71, 75. Mem. Assn. Am. Editorial Cartoonists, Nat. Cartoonists Soc., Sigma Chi. Home and Office: Rt 1 Box 540 Terlton OK 74081

BENDER, MILES DENNIS, oil company executive, management consultant; b. Buffalo, Feb. 26, 1937; s. Samuel Arthur and Adele Ida (Altman) B.; B.A., U. Buffalo, 1959, postgrad. Law Sch., 1959-60; postgrad. Harvard Bus. Sch., 1965; m. Sue Ellen Rolader, Apr. 12, 1975; children: Carolyn Gilbert, Melissa Joan, Jami Brett, Elizabeth Anne, Ashley Sue. Registered rep. Bache & Co., Buffalo, 1960-65; dir. public relations, asst. to pres. Internat. Life Ins. Co. of Buffalo, 1966-67; pres. Wunderest Industries, Inc., Buffalo, 1967-68; dir. mktg. Hard Co., Buffalo, 1968-70; pres., chmn. bd. Syncom Inc., Orchard Park, N.Y., 1970-79; pres. Miles Bender & Assocs., Inc., 1980—; gen. ptnr. Rio Colorado Mining Ltd., Atlanta, 1981-85; pres., chmn. bd. Compañia Minera Rio Tierra S.A., Lima, Peru, 1981-85, Compañia Minera Montaña de Oro, S.A., Lima, 1981-85; pres. Compania de Minas Pancominas, Medellin, Colombia, 1983-85, U.S. Sand & Gravel Co., Atlanta, 1984-87, Tierra Energy, Inc., Atlanta, 1984—, v.p. Vulture Petroleum Corp., Atlanta, 1986—; dir. Graphic Arts Supply, Inc., Rochester, N.Y., Graphic Arts Supply, Inc., Ft. Lauderdale, Fla. Mem. Erie County (N.Y.) Legislature, 1966-68; supr. 18th ward City of Buffalo, 1966-68;chmn. Erie County div. Am. Cancer Soc. corp. gifts div., 1975, 76, 77; mem. Pres.'s UN Day Com., 1977, 78; mem. exec. com. Erie County Republican Party, 1966-70, Ind. Petroleum Assn. Am. (bd. dirs. 1987—); lobbyist for Erie County, N.Y. State Legislature, 1968-70; chmn., founder Reps. for Constructive Policy, Buffalo, 1963-72; mem. Ga. Rep. Found. (vice-chmn., bd. govs., 1987), Ga. Oil & Gas Assn. (pres. 1987). Clubs: Orchard Park Country; Regatas (Lima, Peru). Home: 360 Balboa Ct Atlanta GA 30342 Office: 3340 Peachtree Rd NE 1770 Tower Pl Atlanta GA 30026

BENDETSEN, KARL ROBIN, business executive, lawyer; b. Aberdeen, Wash., Oct. 11, 1907; s. Albert M. and Anna (Bentson) B.; m. Billie McIntosh, 1938; 1 son, Brookes McIntosh; m. Maxine Bosworth, 1947; 1 dau., Anna Martha; m. Gladys Ponton de Arce Heurtematte Johnston, 1972. A.B., Stanford U., 1929, J.S.D., 1932. Bar: Calif., Oreg., Ohio, N.Y., Wash., D.C., U.S. Supreme Ct. Practiced law Aberdeen, Wash., 1932-40; mgmt. counsel 1946-47; cons. spl. asst. to sec. U.S. Dept. Def., 1948; asst. sec. Dept. Army, 1948-50, under sec., 1950-52; dir. gen. U.S. R.R.s, 1950-52; chmn. bd. Panama Canal Co., 1950-54; counsel Champion Papers, 1952-53, v.p. Tex. div., 1953-55, v.p. ops., 1955-60, chmn. bd., pres., chief exec. officer, 1960-67; dir. Westinghouse Electric, 1961-80; chmn., pres., chief exec. officer Champion Internat., 1967-72; dir. N.Y. Stock Exchange, 1972-82; chmn. exec. com. Champion Internat., 1973-75; spl. U.S. rep. with rank of ambassador to W.Ger., 1956, spl. U.S. ambassador to Philippines, 1956; chmn. adv. com. to sec. Dept. Def., 1962; vice chmn. Def. Manpower Commn., 1974-76; bd. overseers Hoover Instn.; chmn. panel on Strategic Def. Initiative for Pres. Reagan, 1980-84. Chmn. Strategic Def. Initiative panel for Pres. Reagan, 1980-84. Served to col. U.S. Army, 1940-46; spl. rep. sec. of war to Gen. MacArthur 1941. Decorated D.S.M. with oak leaf cluster, Silver Star, Legion of Merit with 2 oak leaf clusters, Bronze Star with 3 oak leaf clusters and Combat V, Army Commendation medal with 3 oak leaf clusters, medal of Freedom; Croix de Guerre with Palm; officer Legion of Honor (France); Croix de Guerre with palm (Belgium); mem. Order Brit. Empire; recipient Disting. Civilian Service medal. Mem. Theta Delta Chi. Episcopalian. Clubs: Links (N.Y.C.), Metropolitan (N.Y.C.), Brook (N.Y.C.); Chicago; Washington Athletic (Seattle); Bohemian (San Francisco), Pacific Union (San Francisco); F Street (D.C.), Georgetown (D.C.); Everglades (Palm Beach, Fla.), Bath and Tennis (Palm Beach, Fla.). Home: 2918 Garfield Terr NW Washington DC 20008 Office: Champion Internat 1850 K St Suite 1185 Washington DC 20006

BENDJABALLAH, HAMID, physiologist, educator, hospital administrator; b. L'arba, Algeria, 1940; s. Mohammed and Fetta (Chikh) B.; m. Fadila Terkmane; children: Amel, Asma. MD, U. Algiers, Algeria, 1967; degree in Specialized Chest Diseases, Med. Sch. Algiers, 1969; D of Advanced Medicine, Faculty of Sci., Orsay, France, 1971. Intern Mustapha Hosp., Algiers, 1965-69, dir. lab. of hemodynamics, 1977—; gen. practice medicine Algiers, 1967—; prof. physiology Med. Sch. Algiers, 1972—; mem. Internat. Ctr. Probation, Hémodynamics Lab. Henri Mondor Hosp., Creteil, France, 1969-73. Mem. Algerian Med. Assn. Muslim. Home: 18 Chemin des Glycines, Algiers Algeria Office: Mustapha Hosp, Algiers Algeria

BENDJEDID, CHADLI, president of Algeria; b. Bouteldja, Algeria, Apr. 14, 1929; m. Halima Bourokba; 6 children. Student Annaba. Joined F.L.N., 1954; joined Nat. Liberation Army, 1955, regional chief, 1956-57, dep. zone chief, 1957-58, capt. zone chief, from 1958, apptd. to operational command in no. mil. zone, 1960, comdr. 5th mil. region, 1962, chief 2nd mil. region, 1964; mem. Council of the Revolution; pres. of Algeria, minister of def., 1979—; sec.-gen. Nat. Liberation Front, 1979—. Office: Office of Pres, Algiers Algeria *

BENDURE, LEONA JENSEN, pianist, educator; b. Springtown, Tex., Sept. 27, 1912; d. James Daniel and Nettie Mae (Folley) Jensen; m. Lloyd Kenneth Bendure, Aug. 14, 1938 (dec. 1971); children: Lorene Joan Bendure Teed, Donald Wesley. MusB, U. Kans., 1934, B Music Edn., 1937; postgrad., Midwestern U., Wichita Falls, Tex., 1966-67. Tchr. music edn., Gove, Kans., 1937-38; tchr. Bible studies Ponca City (Okla.) High Sch., 1938-42; tchr. piano, Lawton, Okla., 1943—; bd. dirs. Lawton Symphony Soc., dir. childrens' concerts; pianist Meth. Youth camp, 1934-36; initiated study of music Lawton elem. schs., 1957; piano soloist Lawrence, Kans., Bonner Springs, Kans., Ponca City, Okla., Shawnee, Okla., Bartelville, Okla., Lawton, Tulsa. Mem. Citizens Edn. Council, Lawton, 1956-58; 3d v.p. Lawton's Woman's Forum, 1974-75, bd. dirs., 1976-79, 2d v.p., 1975-76, fine arts chmn., 1970-71, dir. fine arts and crafts dept., 1981-82; mem. Commn. on Missions Meth. Ch. Friends in Council scholar, Theodore Presser scholar, Howard Taylor scholar. Mem. Nat. Piano Guild, AAUW (chmn. Ednl. Found.), Okla. Music Tchrs. Assn. (pres. Lawton 1969-70), Am. Biog. Inst. (bd. advisors Raleigh N.C. chpt.), Nat. Assn. Music Tchrs., Mu Phi Epsilon (Scholar), Pi Kappa Lambda. Democrat. Club: Entre Nous (historian), Bus. and Profl. Women's (pianist). Avocations: reading, walking. Home and Office: 711 Euclid Lawton OK 73507

BENEDICT, GARY CLARENCE, educational administrator; b. Valley City, N.D., Oct. 22, 1938; s. Clarence Augustus and Mary Rae (Spink) B.; m. Carmen Jean Schreiner, May 29, 1965; children—Andrew Scott, Anne Kathleen. B.E., Wis. State U., 1964; M.S., U. Wis., 1968; Ed.D., Marquette U., 1978. Tchr., New Berlin (Wis.) Pub. Schs., 1960-67; supt. Merton (Wis.) Joint Sch. Dist. 9, 1967-75; dir. curriculum and instrn. Mukwonago (Wis.) Sch. Dist., 1975-84; adminstrv. asst. curriculum Shorewood Sch. Dist., 1984-87; supt. St. Louis Affton Sch. Dist., 1987—; adj. instr. Lakeland Coll., Sheboygan, Wis., 1988. Charles F. Kettering Found. fellow, 1981-86. Mem. Am. Assn. Sch. Adminstrs., Assn. Supervision and Curriculum Devel., Phi Delta Kappa. Contbr. articles in field to profl. jours. Home: 7549 Terri Lynn Dr Saint Louis MO 63123 Office: 8701 MacKenzie Rd Saint Louis MO 63123

BENEDICT, JAMES NELSON, lawyer; b. Norwich, N.Y., Oct. 6, 1949; s. Nelson H. and Helen (Wilson) B.; m. Janet E. Fagal, May 8, 1982. B.A. magna cum laude, St. Lawrence U., 1971; J.D., Albany Law Sch. of Union U., 1974. Bar: N.Y. 1975, U.S. Dist. Ct. (no., ea. and so. dists.) N.Y. 1975, U.S. Ct. Appeals (2d cir.) 1975, U.S. Ct. Appeals (8th cir.) 1977, U.S. Ct. Appeals (10th cir.) 1978, U.S. Ct. Appeals (11th cir.) 1982, U.S. Supreme Ct. 1978. Assoc. Rogers & Wells, N.Y.C., 1974-82, ptnr., 1982—. Mem. bd. contbg. editors and advisors The Corp. Law Rev., 1976-86. Contbr. articles to profl. jours. Bd. dirs. Reece Sch., N.Y.C., 1984—, Stanley Isaacs Neighborhood Ctr., N.Y.C., 1984—; trustee St. Lawrence U., Canton, N.Y., 1985—. Mem. ABA (chmn. securities litigation subcom. on 1940 Act matters 1984-86), Fed. Bar Council, N.Y. State Bar Assn., Assn. Bar City N.Y. (mem. fed. legislation com., fed. cts. com.) Am. Soc. Writers on Legal Subjects, Phi Beta Kappa. Clubs: Princeton, Sky (N.Y.C.); New Haven Country (Hamden, Conn.). Home: 435 E 79th St Apt 5-C New York NY 10021 Office: Rogers & Wells Pan Am Bldg 200 Park Ave New York NY 10166

BENEDIKTSSON, JAKOB, philologist; b. Fjall, Iceland, July 20, 1907; s. Benedikt Sigurdsson and Sigurlaug Sigurdardottir; m. Grethe Kyhl, 1936. Ph.D., D.Litt., U. Copenhagen. Asst. editor Old-Icelandic Dictionary, Copenhagen, 1939-46; librarian U. Copenhagen, 1943-46; editor-in-chief Icelandic Dictionary, U. Iceland, 1948-77. Author: Gisli Magnusson, 1939; Chronologie de deux listes des pretres kamireens, 1940; Jardabok Arna Magnussonar og Pals Vidalins, vols. VII, X, XI, 1940-43; Skardsbok (Corpus codicum Islandicorum XVI), 1943; Two Treatises on Iceland, 1943; Veraldar saga, 1944; Ferdabok Tomasar Saemundssonar, 1947; Ole Worm's Correspondence with Icelanders, 1948; G. Andresson, Deilurit, 1948; Persius rimur, 1949; Arngrimi Jonae Opera I-IV, 1950-57; Arngrimur Jonsson and his Works, 1957; Skardsarbok, 1958; Sturlunga Saga (Early Icelandic Manuscript I), 1958; Islenzk-donsk ordabok, Vidbaetir, 1963; Islendingabok, Landnamabok, 1968; Landnamabok, 1974; Romverjasaga (Early Icelandic Manuscript XIII), 1980, Hugtök og Heiti, 1983, Crymogaea, 1985, Laerdómslistir, 1987. Mem. Societas Scientiarum Islandica, Royal Danish Acad. Scis. and Letters, Norwegian Acad. Scis. and Letters, Swedish Acad. Address: 2 Stigahlid, Reykjavik Iceland

BENENSON, CLAIRE BERGER, investment and fin. planning educator; b. N.Y.C.; d. Nathan H. and Alice E. (Zeisler) B.; m. Lawrence A. Benenson; children—Harold, Gary. B.A., Wellesley Coll.; postgrad. N.Y. Inst. Fin., New Sch. Social Research, 1965-69. Security analyst Merrill Lynch, N.Y.C., 1940-43; research assoc. Conn. Coll., 1943-45; lectr. NYU Mgmt. Inst., N.Y.C., 1960-68; lectr. New Sch. for Social Research, N.Y.C., 1963-86, dir. annual conf. Wall St. and Economy, 1967-87, dir. annual conf. Futures and Options, 1979-86, chmn. dept. investment and fin. planning, 1974-86; cons. fin. confs., N.Y.C., 1987—; mem. adv. bd. The First Women's Bank, N.Y.C., 1984-86; dir. Drexel Burnham Fund, DBL Cash Fund, DBL Tax Free Cash Fund, Drexel Series Trust, N.Y.C., 1970—; trustee Simms Global Fund; pres. Money Marketeers, NYU, N.Y.C., 1979-80. Contbg. editor Exec. Jeweler, 1981-83; creator, moderator NBC-TV series, Wall St. for Everyone, 1967-68. Mem. bd. overseers Parsons Sch. of Design, N.Y.C., 1974—. Named Disting. Alumnae, Wellesley Coll., 1968, Durant Scholar, Wellesley Coll.; Alt. fellow in econs. Columbia U., 1938-39. Mem. Fin. Women's Assn. (bd. dirs., chair dirs. resource adv. com., co-chair Program Com., 1988—), Econ. Club N.Y., N.Y. Assn. Bus. Economists, Money Marketeers NYU, Women's Bond Club, Harmonie Club (mem. forum com.), Nat. Assn. Bus. Econs. Jewish.

BENENSON, EDWARD HARTLEY, realty company executive; b. N.Y.C., Mar. 27, 1914; s. Robert C. and Nettie B.; m. Gladys Steinberg, Apr. 5, 1962; 1 dau., Lisa; children by previous marriage: Thomas Hartley, James Stuart, Amy Roberta. B.A., Duke, 1934. Pres. Benenson & Co., Benenson Funding Corp., Yale Motor Inn, Conn., Yale Inn, Meriden, Conn., Benenson

Investment Corp., Greenwich Devel. Corp., Sedgefield Realty N.C., Thomas James Corp., Arbee Properties of Fla. Author: The Benenson Restaurant Guide, 1985, 86, 87, 88. Chmn. Urban Redevel. Commn., 1957-58; mem. Mayor's Youth Adv. Group, N.Y.C., 1956-58; chmn. Friends Duke U. Mus. Art; trustee emeritus Duke U.; overseer Albert Einstein Coll. Medicine; trustee Lebanon Hosp.; trustee, governing bd. Am. Ballet Theatre; trustee Fedn. Jewish Philanthropics N.Y., mem. exec. com., 1960-66; trustee Synagogue Council; mem. Republican Nat. Com. Am.; pres. YM-YWHA of Bronx, 1958-63, now bd. dirs.; exec. com. Donor Benenson Arts awards Duke U.; univ. rep. com. Corporate Support for Pvt. Univs.; mem. President's Citizens Com. Served to 2d lt. AUS, 1939-43. Decorated officier Ordre du Merite Agricole (France), knight Order St. John of Malta; recipient Legion of Merit of France, gold medal Renaissance Francaise, Bronze medal City of Paris. Mem. Real Estate Bd. N.Y., Am. Ballet Theatre, Confrerie des Chevaliers du Tastevin (grand sénéchal N.Y. commanderie, grand Camerlingue of Am.), Culinary Inst. Am. (trustee), Les Amis d'Escoffier Soc., Grand Jury Assn., Commerce and Industry Assn. N.Y., Nat. Bd. Realtors, Internat. Real Estate Fedn. (charter), Order of Lafayette, Profl. Engrs. Soc. France, Fedn. War Vets. (France) (former chmn.), Chaine des Rotisseurs (mem. Conseil d'Honneur), Am. Soc. Italian Legions Merit (cavaliere), Les Chevaliers de la Croix de Lorraine, Commanderie de Bordeaux, du Bailliage N.Am., Res. Officers Assn. Conseil de la Croix du Combattant de l'Europe, Vingt-six Soc. (chmn., founder). Clubs: Century Country, Harmonie (gov.), Presidents, Paris Am., Wines and Food, Noyac Country, Palm Beach Country, Southampton Golf, Princeton of N.Y. Home: 510 Park Ave New York NY 10022 also: Georgica Rd East Hampton NY 11937 also: 130 Sunrise Ave Palm Beach FL 33480 Office: 445 Park Ave New York NY 10022

BENETTI, FEDERICO JOSÉ, surgeon; b. Pascanas, Cordoba, Argentina, Nov. 29, 1947; s. Pablo Benetti and Marta Rossi; m. Ana Diaz de Brito, June 26, 1972 (div.); children: Ines Maria, Pablo Jose, Juan Ignacio; m. Silvia Fernandez, June 17, 1981; children: Justo, Bruno. MD, Rosario U., Argentina, 1971. Resident in heart surgery Medicine Sch. Sao Paulo, Brazil, 1972; chief heart surgery Spanish Hosp., Rosario, 1973-84, Inst. Cardiology, Rosario, 1973-84, Victor J. Vilella Children's Hosp., Rosario, 1975-78, Model Inst. Lanus, Buenos Aires, 1984—, Inst. "La Sagrada Familia", Buenos Aires, 1985—; surgeon Argentine Inst. Diagnosis and Treatment, Buenos Aires, 1982—; bd. dirs. Argentine Heart Inst., Buenos Aires, 1985-86. Author: How Does Your Heart Live?, 1981, Clinic Technical Surgery, 1985. Mem. Argentine Soc. Cardiovascular Surgeons, Internat. Cardiovascular Soc., Argentine Soc. Cardiology, Argentine Soc. Organs Transplantations, Argentine Med. Assn., Argentine Assn. of Surgery. Lodge: Rotary. Home: Basavilbaso 964, Buenos Aires 1428, Argentina Office: Heart Inst, Marcelo T de Alvear 2323 2C, Buenos Aires 1122, Argentina

BEN-GACEM, HAMIDA, finance executive; b. Beni-Kalled, Tunisia, Mar. 3, 1938; s. Mohamed Ben and Khadija (Boudjebel) Ben-Gacem; m. Naziha Chachia, Sept. 16, 1967; children—Leila, Hazem, Amira, Amir. Diplome Ingenieur des Statistiques, Institut des Statistiques, Rabat/-Marocco, 1963; M.P.A., Harvard U., 1973. Advisor to Minister of Planning Abu-Dhabi, United Arab Emirates, 1975-79; dir. statistics Arab Monetary Fund, Abu-Dhabi, United Arab Emirates, 1979-80, exec. dir., 1980-83, adv. to pres., 1983—; statistician Ministry of Planning, Tunis, Tunisia, 1963-65, chief nat. account, 1965-70, dep. dir. planning, 1970-75. Mayor, Municipality of Beni Khalled, Tunis, 1965-75; pres. Football Assn. Tunis, 1969. Decorated officier de l'Ordre de la République (Tunisia). Office: Arab Monetary Fund, PO Box 2818, Abu-Dhabi United Arab Emirates

BENGTSSON, INGEMUND, speaker of the Swedish Parliament; b. Veddinge, Sweden, 1919. Ed., County Coll., Halland, Sweden. Previously mgr. Halland County Labor Exchange, Sweden; mem. Parliament 1951—, cons. to Ministry for Health and Welfare, 1954-65; former v.p. Social Dem. Party Member's Council; Swedish del. to UN Gen. Assembly 1963-67; pres. UN Com. on the Human Environment, 1972-74; Minister of Agr. Sweden, 1969-73, Minister of Labor, 1973-76, Speaker of the Parliament, 1979—. Office: Riksdag, 10012 Stockholm Sweden *

BENHABIB, SEYLA, political philosophy educator; b. Istanbul, Turkey, Sept. 9, 1950; came to U.S., 1970; d. Nesim and Palomba Benhabib; m. Wolf Schaefer, Feb. 13, 1984; 1 child, Laura. BA, Am. Coll. for Girls, Istanbul, 1970, Brandeis U., 1972; PhD, Yale U., 1975, MPhil, 1977. Asst. prof. Yale U., New Haven, 1977-79; research fellow Max-Planck Inst., Starnberg, Fed. Republic Germany, 1979-81; asst. prof. philosophy Boston U., 1981-85; assoc. prof. govt. Harvard U., Cambridge, Mass., 1986—. Author: Critique, Norm and Utopia, 1986; editor: Feminism as Critique, 1987; translator: Hegel's Ontology and the Theory of Historicity, 1987; mem. editorial bd. Telos, 1982-85; editor in chief Praxis Internat., 1986—. Danforth fellow Yale U., 1974-77, Alexander von Humbold fellow, 1979-81. Mem. Am. Philos. Assn. (program com. 1985—), Soc. for Phenomenology and Existentialism (book rev. com. 1985-87), Phi Beta Kappa. Jewish. Office: Harvard U Dept Govt Littauer Ctr Cambridge MA 02138

BENINGTON, JONATHAN MICHAEL, museum curator; b. Portadown, No. Ireland, Sept. 23, 1959; arrived in Eng., 1978; s. John Michael and Christel Martha (Köhler) B.; m. Elizabeth Baldwin, July 26, 1985. BA in History of Art and German, U. London, 1981, MA in History of Art, 1982. Trainee curator Leeds (Eng.) City Art Galleries, 1982-84; asst. curator fine art Glasgow (Scotland) Art Gallery and Mus., 1984-87; asst. curator, exhbns. officer Cheltenham (Eng.) Art Gallery and Mus., 1987—; cons. picture authenticator, 1982—. Contbr. articles on Irish and Brit. art to profl. jours. Mem. Mus. Assn. Office: Cheltenham Art Gallery and Mus, Clarence St, Cheltenham GL50 3JT, England

BENINI, painter; b. Imola, Italy, Apr. 17, 1941; came to U.S., 1977; s. Paolo and Ida Benini; m. Lorraine Frances Link; children from previous marriage—Christopher, Elisa. Liceo Classico, Bologna, Italy, 1956, Evalc Assisi cum laude, 1958. Mgmt. positions with various firms, 1959-67; mng. ptnr. Green & Assoc., Grand Bahama, 1968-72; chmn. Space Bahamas Ltd., 1973-76; painter, solo exhibitions in numerous museums, 1985, galleries, pub. instns., insts., univs., 1965—; exhibited in solo exhbns. Charleston Heights Arts Ctr., Las Vegas, 1985, Landmark Ctr., Orlando, Fla., Jacksonville (Fla.) U., Daytona Beach (Fla.) Community Coll., 1985, Osceola (Fla.) Ctr. Arts, 1986, Portland (Oreg.) State U., 1987, Ft. Smith (Ark.) Art Ctr., 1987, U. Ill., 1988, Bridgewater (Mass.) State Coll., 1988, U. South Carolina, 1988, U.S.C., 1988; lectr. in visual arts. Served with Italian Army, 1960-63. Named Kiwanis Man of Yr., 1970-71. Researcher in visual arts, 1977—. Studio: 520 Central Ave Hot Springs AR 71901

BENIRSCHKE, KURT, pathologist, educator; b. Glueckstadt, Germany, May 26, 1924; came to U.S., 1949, naturalized, 1955; s. Fritz Franz and Marie (Luebcke) B.; m. Marion Elizabeth Waldhausen, May 17, 1952; children: Stephen Kurt, Rolf Joachim, Ingrid Marie. Student, U. Hamburg, Germany, 1942, 45-48, U. Berlin, Germany, 1943, U. Wuerzburg, Germany, 1943-44; M.D., U. Hamburg, 1948. Resident Teaneck, N.J., 1950-51, Peter Bent Brigham Hosp., Boston, 1951-52, Boston Lying-in-Hosp., 1952-53, Free Hosp. for Women, Boston, 1953, Children's Hosp., Boston, 1953; pathologist Boston Lying-in-Hosp., 1955-60; teaching fellow, assoc. Med. Sch. Harvard, 1954-60; prof. pathology, chmn. dept. pathology Med. Sch. Dartmouth, Hanover, N.H., 1960-70; prof. reproductive medicine and pathology U. Calif. at San Diego, 1970—; chmn. dept. pathology U. Calif. at San Diego (Sch. Med.), La Jolla, 1976-79; dir. research San Diego Zoo, 1975-86, trustee, 1986—; cons. NIH, 1957-70. Served with German Army, 1942-45. Mem. Am. Soc. Pathology, Internat. Acad. Pathology, Am. Coll. Pathology, Teratol. Soc., Am. Soc. Zool. Veterinarians. Home: 8457 Prestwick Dr LaJolla CA 92037 Office: U Calif at San Diego San Diego CA 92110

BENITEZ, CARLOS, mathematics educator; b. Madrid, Feb. 24, 1943; s. Teofilo Benitez and Elena Rodriguez; m. Esperanza Lopez, Aug. 16, 1968; children: Elena, Esperanza, Carlos, Pablo. Cert. in Math., U. Madrid, 1965; PhD in Math., U. Snatiago, 1971. Lectr. U. Madrid, 1965-67; assoc. prof. U. Santiago, Spain, 1967-79, sec. math. faculty, 1976-79; prof. U. Extremadura, Badajoz, Spain, 1979—, dean econ. faculty, 1983-84, chief dept. math., 1979—. Editor various books; contbr. articles to profl. jours. Mem. Real Soc. Math. EspaÑola (v.p. 1982—), Assn. Math EspaÑola, Am. Math. Soc. Home: Urb. Universitaria 10, 06006 Badajoz Spain Office: U Extremadura, Dept Math, 06071 Badajoz Spain

BENJAMIN, EDWARD BERNARD, JR., lawyer; b. New Orleans, Feb. 11, 1923; s. Edward Bernard and Blanche (Sternberger) B.; m. Adelaide Wisdom, May 11, 1957; children: Edward Wisdom, Mary Dabney, Ann Leith, Stuart Minor. B.S., Yale U., 1944; J.D., Tulane U., 1952. Bar: La. 1952. Since practiced in New Orleans; ptnr. firm Jones, Walker, Waechter, Poitevent, Carrere & Denegre; pres. Am. Coll. Probate Counsel, 1986-87, Internat. Acad. Estate & Trust Law, 1976-78; chmn. bd. Starmount Co., Greensboro, N.C., 1968-88. Editor-in-chief: Tulane U. Law Rev, 1951-52. Vice chmn. bd. trustees Southwestern Legal Found., 1980—; trustee Hollins Coll., 1966-87; chancellor Episcopal Diocese of La., 1984—, Trinity Ch., New Orleans, 1974—; mem. editorial bd., Community Property Journ.; mem. adv. bd. CCH Estate & Fin. Planning Service, 1982-88. Served to 1st lt. F.A., U.S. Army, 1943-46. Mem. Am. Coll. Tax Counsel, Am. Law Inst., La. Law Inst., ABA (sec. taxation sect. 1967-68, council 1976-79, council real property, probate and trust law sect. 1978-81), La. Bar Assn. (chmn. taxation sect. 1959-60). Clubs: New Orleans Country, Greensboro Country, So. Yacht, New Orleans Lawn Tennis. Home: 1837 Palmer Ave New Orleans LA 70118 Office: 201 St Charles Ave 51st Floor New Orleans LA 70170

BENJAMIN, ROBERT SPIERS, foreign correspondent, writer, publicist; b. Bklyn., Aug. 17, 1917; s. Harry Asher and Alice (Spiers) B.; m. Dorothy Calhoun, Apr. 25, 1945 (dec. 1961); children: Robert C. and Gordon R. (twins), Geraldine Benjamin Ameriks, Alan; m. Sarah Graves, Nov. 7, 1970 (div.); 1 dau., Diana Lee; m. Patricia Chamberlin, Aug. 16, 1986. Student Sch. Journalism, Rutgers U., 1940. Staff writer Panama Star & Herald, 1940; asst. editor Dodd, Mead & Co., 1941; chief publs., office coordinator Inter-Am. Affairs Dept. State, Washington, 1942-43; chief Time-Life Bur., Santiago, Chile, 1946-47, Buenos Aires, Argentina, 1947-48, Mexico City, 1949-51; corr., dir. Latin Am. ops. Vision Mag., 1951-56; stringer N.Y. Times, Mexico, 1951-56; founder, chief exec. officer Robert S. Benjamin & Assocs., Mexico City, 1957—. Author: Call To Adventure, 1934, (several fgn. edits.), The Vacation Guide, 1940, The Inside Story, 1940, Europa Para Todos, 1973; editor: Eye Witness, 1940, I'm An American, 1941; assoc. editor: New World Guide to the Latin American Republics, 1943; contbr. numerous articles to various publs.; lectr. on Inter-Am. affairs. Served with CIC, U.S. Army, 1943-46. Recipient Honor award Ohio U. Coll. Communications, 1971. Mem. Overseas Press Club (founder, hon. life mem.), Explorers Club, Pub. Relations Soc. Am. (v.p. internat. com. 1971-74, dir. 1975-76), Time-Life Alumni Assn., Interam. Fedn. Pub. Relations Assns. (v.p. 1973-75). Club: University (Mexico) (pres. 1977-78). Office: Homero 1933-2P, Mexico City Mexico 11510 also: 2502 Sunset Dr Tampa FL 33629

BENJENK, MUNIR P., banker; b. 1924. Student, English Lycee, Robert Coll., Istanbul, Turkey; BS, U. London Sch. Econs., 1949. Reader BBC, 1949-51; with OECD, Paris, 1953-63; mem. permanent mission to Washington OECD, 1955-57, dir. Sardinian Village Devel. project, 1957-60, asst. dir. devel. dept., 1962-63; with World Bank, Washington, 1963-84; head econ. adv. mission World Bank, Algeria, 1964; head North Africa div. World Bank, 1965-67, dep. dir. Middle East and North Africa dept., 1967-68, dep. dir. Europe, Middle East and North Africa dept., 1968-69, dir. dept., 1970-72, v.p. Europe, Middle East and North Africa region, 1972-80, v.p. external relations, 1980-84; sr. internat. advisor Standard Chartered Bank, London, 1984—. Decorated Ordine al Merito della Repubblica Itanliana, 1960, Order Cedars of Lebanon, 1971. Fellow Fgn. Policy Inst. Johns Hopkins U., 1986-87. Home and Office: 1308 28th St NW Washington DC 20007

BENJES, PETER JOHN, dairy products financial administrator; b. Castricum, Holland, July 13, 1933; arrived in N.Z., 1952; s. Hermanus Johannus and Veronica Alberdina (Huigen) B.; m. Jeanette Lillian Howe; children: Paul Andrew, Anthony Simon. B in Commerce, Canterbury U., Christchurch, New Zealand, 1961; postgrad., Harvard U., 1983. CPA, New Zealand. Cost acct. J. Gadsden and Co. Ltd., Chistchurch, 1957-60; br. acct. Turnbull and Jones Ltd., Chistchurch, 1960-64; dir. fin. Selco Ltd., Hong Kong, 1965-68; system engr. IBM, Adelaide, Australia, 1968-71; fin. controller Onkaparina Woollen Co Ltd., Adelaide, 1971-76; mgr. fin. Tecalemit Ltd., Adelaide, 1976-77; asst. gen. mgr. N.Z. Dairy Bd., Wellington, N.Z., 1977—; bd. dirs. N.Z. Dairy Packers Ltd., Hamilton, N.Z. Containers Ltd., Hamilton, Lactose C., Hawera, N.Z., Butter Canners Ltd., Wellington. Mem. N.Z. Soc. Accts., Australian Soc. Accts. (sr.), N.Z. Cost and Mgmt. Accts. Clubs: Wellington, Aorangi. Office: NZ Dairy Bd, 25 The Terrace, PO Box 417, Wellington New Zealand

BENKOW, JOSEF, parliament president; b. Trondheim, Norway, Aug. 15, 1924; s. Ivan and Annie Louise (Florence) B.; m. Annelise Høegh; 1 child from previous marriage, Annie. Diploma, Copenhagen Tech. Inst., 1949. Cert. master photographer, 1952. Owner photography studio, 1949—; chmn. Young Conservatives, Østfold County, 1951-54; mem. Baerum Mcpl. Council, 1959-67, alderman, 1963-69; dep. mem. Norwegian Parliament, 1961-65, mem., 1965—, pres., 1985—; mem. Cen. Bd. Conservative party, 1971—, chmn. Akershus County, 1971-75, vice-chmn., 1973-80, chmn., 1981-84, leader parliamentary group, 1981-85; del. UN Gen. Assembly, 1971. Author: From Synagogue to Løvebakken, 1985; editor Norwegian Photographic Peridica, 1949-69. Mem. exec. bd. Akershus County, 1962-66; mem. Nordic Council, 1973—, chmn. Norwegian delegation, 1981—, chmn. Cultural Found., 1980—, pres., 1983-84, dep. mem., 1971-73. Served as 2d lt. Swedish Air Force, 1944-46. Recipient Def. Participation medal. Office: Norwegian Parliament, 0026 Oslo 1, Norway

BENMBAREK, JILANI, business executive; b. Tunisia, July 8, 1947; s. M'Barek M.B. and Meryem (Boundka) B.; children: Islem, Malek, Donia. M in Physics, U. Tunis, 1968; AEA Thermodynamics U. Poitiers, France; postgrad. Ecole Nationale de Mecanique et Superieur d'Aeronautique, France, 1971.Journalist for sports newspaper, Tunisia, 1963-68; prin. engr. Tunis Air, Tunisia, 1971-73; resident rep. Tunis Air at Boeing Co., Seattle, 1973, Schweiser Aircraft Corp.; chmn. bd. Oasis Trade Agy.; mng. dir. Tunisavia and Most, Tunis, 1974—; pres. GEMS (Gen. Elec./Mech. Systems); rep. in Tunisia of TRW Reda Pumps Ltd. Mem. Airlines Orgn. Planning Adminstrn. Assn. (exec. com.). Home: 92 Ave Republique, Megrine Coteaux Tunisia Office: Immeuble Saadi Tourc, Tunis 2080, Tunisia

BENN, DOUGLAS FRANK, computer and telecommunications consulting and services company executive; b. Detroit, May 8, 1936; s. Frank E. and Madeline (Pond) B.; m. Shirley M. Flanery, July 16, 1955; children—Christopher, Susan, Kathy. A.A., Jackson Jr. Coll., 1956; student, U. Mich., 1957-58; B.S. in Math., Mich. State U., 1960, M.A., 1962; cert. data processing (NSF scholar), Milw. Inst. Tech., 1965; postgrad., U. Wis., 1965-66; Ed.Adminstrn., Washington U., 1972; M.S. in Computer Sci., So. Meth. U., 1982. Diecaster Diecast Corp., Jackson, Mich., 1955-60; tchr. math. and sci. Lansing (Mich.) Public Schs., 1960-64; chmn. computer sci. dept. Kenosha (Wis.) Area Tech. Inst., 1964-67, registrar, 1966-67, mgr. data processing, 1965-67; sr. systems analyst Abbott Labs., North Chicago, Ill., 1967-68, sr. project leader, 1968-69; dir. data processing div. St. Louis Public Schs., 1969-74; dir. div. info. systems dept. mental health State of Ill., Springfield, 1974-78; dir. data processing div. Med. Computer Systems, Inc., Dallas, 1978; dir. bus. adminstrn. Dallas County Mental Health Center, 1979-80; prof. computer sci. So. Meth. U., Dallas, 1979-82; sr. dir. corp. research and devel. Blue Cross & Blue Shield of Tex., Dallas, 1980-83; v.p. mgmt. info. services Western States Adminstrs., Fresno, Calif., 1984-88; chmn. bd., pres. The Benn Group, Inc., Merced, Calif., 1987—; lectr. and adv. Council of Great Cities Public Sch. Systems, 1969-74; cons. Ill. Med. Soc., 1976-78, Wis. Bd. Vocat., Tech. and Adult Edn., 1964-67; co-dir. mgmt. adv. group Ill. Dept. Mental Health, 1974-78; adv. Tex. Soc.'s Task on Mental Health, 1980. Contbr. articles on data processing systems to profl. publs. Dist. supt. Kenosha council Boy Scouts Am., 1965-66. Mem. Data Processing Mgmt. Assn., Assn. for System Mgmt. (Disting. Service award 1980, Merit award 1976, Achievement award 1978, chpt. pres. 1976-77), Am. Arbitration Assn. Presbyterian. Club: So. Meth. U. Faculty. Home: 646 E Magill St Fresno CA 93710

BENN, NILES S., lawyer; b. Phila., Feb. 18, 1945; s. Samuel and Rose (Singer) B.; m. Joyce Barmach, June 30, 1968; children—Merrick Jordan, Evan Samuel. B.S., Temple U., 1967; J.D., Dickinson Sch. of Law, 1972. Bar: Pa. 1972, U.S. Dist. Ct. (mid. dist.) Pa. 1973, U.S. Supreme Ct. 1983. Ptnr., Wiley & Benn, Dillsburg, Pa., 1973—. Bd. mgrs. Holy Spirit Hosp., 1978—, mem. fin. com., 1983—, asst. treas., 1983—, vice chmn. mental health ctr., 1983—; mem. legis. com. Phila. sect. Am. Cancer Soc., 1982—, bd. dirs. York unit, 1977—, pres., 1985—, mem. exec. com. Pa. div., 1981—, bd. dirs., 1981—, chmn. legacy and planned giving com., 1985—, chmn. pub. affairs com., 1982-85, vice chmn. Pa. div. bd., 1985—; chmn. Dillsburg Community Health Ctr., 1977—; bd. dirs. York Council Jewish Charities, 1985—, Capitol Engrng. Corp., 1985—; solicitor Lake Meade Mcpl. Authority, 1975-77, Carroll Twp. Zoning and Hearing Bd., 1980-82, Carroll Twp. Planning Commn., 1980-84, Carroll Twp. Bd. Suprs., 1983-84, No. York County Sch. Dist., 1973-84, Monaghan Twp. Planning Commn., 1973—, Monaghan Twp. Bd. Suprs., 1973—; vice chmn. Am. Cancer Soc., Pa., 1985-87, chmn. bd., 1987—. Named Vol. of Yr., Pa. div. Am. Cancer Soc., 1984. Mem. ABA (family law sect.), Pa. Bar Assn. (family law sect., com. on legal edn. and bar admission), York County Bar Assn. (chmn. ins. com., divorce rules com.), Assn. Trial Lawyers Am., Pa. Trial Lawyers Assn. Home: 1295 Detwiler Dr York PA 17404

BENNANI, AHMED, banker; b. Fes, Morocco, Dec. 12, 1926; s. Haj Driss and Khaddouj Bennani; m. Latifa El Kohen; children: Chakir, Omar, Myriem. Diplome d'enseignement supérieur, U. Paris, 1951, lic. droit, 1952. Sec. gen. Ministry of Finances, Morocco, 1963; sec. of state Ministry of Commerce and Industry, Morocco, 1964; gen. dir. Caisse Dépôt et Gestion, Morocco, 1965-66; sec. of state for econ. affairs Office Prime Minister, Morocco, 1967-68; vice gov. Bank of Morocco, 1968-85, gov., 1985—; vice chair UBAF, Paris, 1968; bd. dirs. UBAF, Ltd., London, UBAF Arab Am. Bank, N.Y.C., UBAE Rome. Named Officer, l'Ordre du Trône, 1970, Comdr., Ouissam Al Arch, 1987. Club: Dakar (Sénegal, Morocco). Home: 2 Rue de Khenifra, Rabat Morocco Office: Bank of Morocco, 227 Ave Mohamed V, Rabat Morocco

BENNE, KENNETH DEAN, educator; b. Morrowville, Kans., May 11, 1908; s. Henry and Bertha Alveen (Thrun) B. B.S., Kans. State Coll., 1930; A.M., U. Mich., 1936; Ph.D. (scholar Advanced Sch. Edn.), Columbia U., 1941; L.H.D. (hon.), Lesley Coll., Cambridge, Mass., 1969, Morris Brown Coll., 1971. Tchr. phys. and biol. scis. Concordia (Kans.) High Sch., 1930-35; tchr chemistry Manhattan (Kans.) High Sch., 1935-36; asso. social and philos. founds. edn. Columbia Tchrs. Coll., 1938-41; asso. prof. edn. and research asso. Horace Mann-Lincoln Inst., 1946-48; asst. prof. edn. U. Ill., 1941-46, prof. edn., 1948-53; editor Adult Leadership, 1952-53; Berenson prof. Boston U., 1953-73, prof. emeritus, 1973—; dir. Human Relations Center, 1953-61; pres. Staff and Orgn. Consultation, Inc., 1975—; Vice pres. Boston Adult Edn. Center, 1957-60; exec. bd. New Eng. Adult Edn. Inst., 1958-69. Author: A Conception of Authority, 1943, 71, Education for Tragedy, 1967, From Pedagogy to Anthropogogy, 1981; Co-author: Discipline of Practical Judgement, 1943, Mobilizing Educational Resources, 1943, Group Dynamics and Social Action, 1950, Improvement of Practical Intelligence, 1950, Theoretical Foundations of Education, 1952, Social Foundations of Education, 1955, The Planning of Change, 1961, 69, 76, 85, The University and the National Future, 1966, Philosophy and Educational Development, 1966, Teaching and Learning about Science and Social Policy, 1978, The Social Self, 1983; Co-editor: Reading in Foundations of Education, 2 vols., 1941, Essays for John Dewey's Ninetieth Birthday, 1950, Human Relations in Curriculum Change, 1951, Readings in Social Aspects of Education, 1951, T-Group Theory and Laboratory Method, 1963, The Laboratory Method of Changing and Learning, 1975, Society as Educator in an Age of Transition, 1987; editorial bd.: Progressive Edn., 1948-53, Jour. Applied Behavioral Sci., 1963-68; bd. cons. editors: Teachers College Record, 1962-64, Integrativ Therapie, 1973—. Mem. Mayor's Civic Unity Com., Boston, 1954-59; mem. Commn. Human Relations, 1957-65. Served to lt. comdr. USNR, 1942-46. Recipient Kilpatrick award for disting. contbn. to Am. Philosophy of Edn., 1943; Bode Meml. lectr. Ohio State U., 1961; Centennial prof. social scis. U. Ky., 1965. Fellow Nat. Council Religion in Higher Edn., Internat. Inst. Arts and Letters, AAAS, Am. Edn. Research Assn.; mem. Adult Edn. Assn. (pres. 1955-56, publs. com. 1956-59), Nat. Assn. Intergroup Relations Ofcl., Am. Sociol. Soc., Soc. for Psychol. Study Social Issues, Am. Philos. Assn., Philosophy of Edn. Soc. (pres. 1950-51), Am. Edn. Fellowship (pres. 1949-52), NEA (adj. staff, fellow Nat. Tng. Lab. 1959—, dir. 1959-62, 66-70), Internat. Assn. Applied Social Scientists (chmn. bd. 1971-73), Phi Delta Kappa, Phi Kappa Phi, Kappa Delta Pi. Home: 4000 Cathedral Ave NW Washington DC 20016 also: Center Lovell ME 04016

BENNETT, CARL MCGHIE, engineering company executive, consultant, national guard officer; b. Salt Lake City, Sept. 11, 1933; s. M. Woodruff and Sybil L. (McGhie) B.; m. Ardel Krantz, Aug. 10, 1954; children: Carlene, Matt, Brent, Dale, Hugh, Caren, Teri. BS, U. Utah, 1956; postgrad., U.S. Army Engr. Sch., 1964; M, Command and Gen. Staff Coll., 1974; postgrad., Indsl. Coll. Armed Forces, 1976. Commd. 2d. lt. ROTC U.S. Army, 1953; treas. and office mgr. Hercules Inc. and Data Source Corp., Salt Lake City and Los Angeles, 1963-70; controller Boise Cascade, Los Angeles, 1970-72; corp. controller Griffin Devel. Co., Los Angeles, 1972-75; controller Dart Industries, Dart Resorts, Los Angeles, 1975-78; chief fin. officer Ford, Bacon & Davis, Salt Lake City, 1978-87; pres. B&A Cons., 1987—; cons. Served to lt. col. U.S. Army Res., 1953-79, col. Utah N.G., 1985—. Recipient Meritorious Service medal Pres. of the U.S., 1979. Mem. Controllers Council, Nat. Assn. Accts. (v.p., bd. dirs. 1979-85). Republican. Office: Ford Bacon Davis 375 Chipeta Way Salt Lake City UT 84108

BENNETT, DAVID SPENCER, publishing executive; b. Chgo., Nov. 17, 1935; s. David Spencer and Edna Virginia (Hewling) B.; m. Charolotte Ann Nalley, Sept. 14, 1957 (div. Mar. 1979); children: Tucker David, Charles Roy, Ward Ross, Spencer Hill; m. Donna Mae Boeser, Feb. 8, 1981. Exec. v.p. Bennett Advt., Harlingen, Tex., 1958-63; account exec. Leo Burnett Advt., Chgo., 1963-65; editor, pub. M-G Publs., Inc., Chgo., 1965-66; exec. dir. mem. services Am. Bus. Press, N.Y.C., 1966-69; mgr. mktg. services Miller Pub. Co., Mpls., 1969-81; gen. mgr. Doane Pub., Control Data Corp., St. Louis, 1981—; bd. dirs. Finan Pub. Co. Co-author: New Heights for Journalism, 1969, A Guide to New Profit Opportunites, 1970; author: The Publication Marketing Plan, 1981. Nat. chmn. Am. Agr. Day, 1973, 1974, 1977; bd. dirs. Kirkwood (Mo.) Library, 1987-89. Served to capt, USAFR, 1957-65. Mem. Nat. Agrimarketing Assn. (dir. 1982-83, Workhorse of Yr. award 1977), Agr. Day Found. (pres. 1979-80), St. Louis Agr. Bus. Club., Sales and Mktg. Execs. (v.p., exec. com., bd. dirs. 1987—), Nat. Speakers Assn. Lodge: Rotary (v.p., bd. dir. Webster Groves 1986-88).

BENNETT, ELMER FRANK, lawyer; b. Longmont, Colo., Sept. 17, 1917; s. Herbert A. and Jessie C. (Wharton) B.; A.B., Colo. State Coll. Edn., 1938; LL.B., Stanford U., 1941; m. Gertrude A. Turner, Sept. 9, 1939 (dec. 1972); children—John H., Kathryn H.; m. Jewell Brooks Middleton, 1982. Admitted to D.C. bar, 1947; adminstrv. work War Dept., 1942-48; trial atty. FTC, 1948-51; legal adviser, exec. sec. U.S. Senator Eugene D. Millikin of Colo., 1951-53; legis. counsel Dept. Interior, 1953-56, asst. to sec. interior, 1956-57, gen. counsel Dept. Interior, 1957-58; undersec. Dept. Interior, 1958-61; mem. firm Ely, Duncan & Bennett, 1961-66; gen. counsel U.S. Pub. Land Law Rev. Commn., 1966-70; spl. asst. to dir. Office Emergency Preparedness, Exec. Office of Pres., Washington, 1970-71, gen. counsel, asst. dir., 1971-73; trustee pension and health benefit trusts, 1978—. Adminstrv. asst. to chmn. resolutions com. Republican Nat. Conv., 1952. Mem. Am. (chmn. mineral law sect. 1965-66), Fed. bar assns., Blue Key, Phi Alpha Delta, Phi Alpha Theta. Republican. Episcopalian. Home: 265 Locust Ln Roslyn Heights NY 11577 Office: 2020 K St NW Suite 800 Washington DC 20006

BENNETT, EUDORA SMITH, hospital administrator; b. W. Franklin, Pa., July 16, 1924; d. Merton Henry and Ruby-Estelle Grace (Allen) Smith; R.N., Robert Packer Hosp. Tng. Sch. Nurses, Sayre, Pa., 1945; m. Raymond Leslie Bennett, Dec. 21, 1946 (div. Jan. 1967); children—Ann Marie, Donald Hasbrouck, Stanley Douglas. Gen. duty nurse Robert Packer Hosp., 1945-46, supr. pediatrics, 1947-48; pvt. duty nurse Carbondale (Pa.) Gen. Hosp., 1948-49; supr. Monmouth Meml. Hosp., Long Branch, N.J., 1950-51; adminstr. Montrose (Pa.) Med. Center, 1951-87, also dir.; pres., chief exec. officer Montrose Gen. Hosp., 1987—; dir. Med. Arts Nursing Center, Montrose; a founder Med. Arts Clinic, Montrose Gen. Hosp. Inc. (formerly Med. Arts Hosp.), Med. Arts Nursing Ctr., Inc.; mem. exec. com. Pa. Statewide Health Coordinating Council, 1976-86. Bd. dirs., mem. exec. com. N.Y.-Pa.

Health Planning Council, 1969—, chmn. Susquehanna County chpt., 1971-72; mem. bd. Northeastern Human Parts Assn., 1971-76; mem. Susquehanna County Ambulance and Emergency Services Assn., 1971—. Named Spirit of Nursing, Robert Packer Hosp., 1945. Mem. Am. Hosp. Assn., Pa. Hosp. Assn. (dir. 1982-86, planning and devel. com. 1978—, small and rural hosp. com., trustee 1981—) hosp. assns., Hosp. Council N.E. Pa. (chmn. 1982-83), Health Care Facilities Assn. Pa. Republican. Presbyterian. Club: Y-Gradale (Montrose). Home: 42 Maple St Montrose PA 18801 Office: 3 Grow St Montrose PA 18801

BENNETT, HYWEL, actor; b. Garnant, Wales, Apr. 8, 1944; s. Gorden and Sarah Gwen (Lewis) B.; m. Cathy McGowan, 1970; 1 child. Student, Royal Acad. Dramatic Art, London. London stage debut in Ophelia, Youth Theatre's Hamlet, Queen's Theatre, 1959; played in repertory, Salisbury and Leatherhead, 1965; stage roles include Puck in A Midsummer Night's Dream, Edinburgh Festival, 1967, Prince Hal in Henry IV (Parts I and II), Mermaid, 1970, Antony in Julius Caesar, Young Vic, 1972, Stanley in The Birthday Party, Gardner Ctr., Brighton, 1973, Hamlet (touring South Africa), 1974, Danny in Night Must Fall, Sherman, Cardiff, 1974, Shaw, 1975, Jimmy Porter in Look Back in Anger, Belgrade, Conventry, 1974, Konstantin in the Seagull (on tour), Birmingham Repertory Co., 1974; other appearances Comedy Theatre, 1978, Terra Nova, Chichester, 1979, The Case of the Only Levantine, Her Majesty's, 1980; dir. several plays including Rosencrantz and Guildenstern are Dead, Leatherhead, 1975, A Man For All Seasons, 1976; films include The Family Way, 1966, Twisted Nerve, 1968, The Virgin Soldiers, 1969, Loot, 1970, Percy, 1971, Alice in Wonderland, 1972; TV appearances include Romeo and Juliet, The Idiot, Unman, Wittering and Zigo, A Month in the Country, Malice Afterthought (serial), Shelley (two series), Tinker, Tailor, Soldier, Spy (serial), 1979, Coming Out, Pennies From Heaven, Artemis '81, The Critic, The Consultant. Address: care James Sharkey Fraser, and Dunlop, 91 Regent St, London W1, England

BENNETT, JACK OLEN, aerospace engineer; b. Ebensburg, Pa., Dec. 19, 1914; s. Harry John and Gertrude Hixson (Shaeffer) B.; m. Marianne Alice Sattler, May 24, 1934; Olen Thomas, Ann Desireé. BS in Chemistry, Physics, Mech. Engring., Pa. State U., 1936; PhD in Aerodynamics, Technische Universitat Berlin, U. Pa. Med. Sch., 1938-39; postgrad., NYU, 1939-45. Research and devel. engr. United Airlines, Chgo., 1940-43; chief research engring. pilot Curtiss-Wright Corp., Columbus, Ohio, 1944; chief pilot ATC div. Am. Export Airlines, LaGuardia Field, N.Y., 1943-45; European dir., chief pilot Am. Overseas Airlines & Panam, Frankfurt, Fed. Republic Germany, 1945-53; supervisory bd. dirs., cons. Rockwell Internat., Pitts., 1957-79; engring. cons. various orgns., various, 1979-83; chief aircraft designer Arbonia-Forster Group, Arbon, Switzerland, 1983—; bd. dirs. ILO, Pinneberg, Fed. Republic Germany, 1957-62, chmn. bd., prin. Bedico Research & Mfr., Giessen-Lahn, Fed. Repub. Germany, 1955-58; prin. Bennett Machine & Scientific Co., Berlin, 1955—. Author: How to Fly an Airplane, 1942, 40,000 Hours in the Sky, 1982; contbr. articles to profl. jours.; patentee in field. Lectr. Polit. Edn. Ctr. for NATO Forces, Helmstedt, Fed. Republic Germany. Decorated German Cross of Honor medal Pres. Fed. Republic Germany, 1965; recipient Berlin Senate awards, 1965, 68, Ernst Reuter plaque Berlin Mayor, 1985; Rockefeller fellow MIT, Technische U. Berlin, U. Pa. Med. Sch. Mem. Soc. Automotive Engrs. (life), Karl Schurz Soc. (life), Alexander von Humboldt Soc. (life), Am. C. of C. (life), Quiet Birdmen (life), Kappa Sigma. Home and Office: Bennett Machine & Scientific Co, Trabenerstrasse 68A, D-1000 Berlin 33 Federal Republic of Germany

BENNETT, JACQUELINE BEEKMAN, school psychologist; b. Santa Paula, Calif., Sept. 4, 1946; d. Jack Edward and Margaret Blanche (MacPherson) Beekman.; m. Thomas LeRoy Bennett Jr., Aug. 5, 1972; children: Shannon, Brian, Laurie. BA, U. Calif., Davis, 1968; MS, Colo. State U., 1975, PhD, 1984. Histologist Sch. Veterinary Medicine, Davis, 1969-71; sch. psychologist Poudre Sch. Dist. R-1, Ft. Collins, Colo., 1983—. Nominating chmn. United Presbyn. Women, Timnath, Colo., 1982, pres., 1986; com. mem. Women and the Ch. Com., Boulder Presbytery, Colo., 1985-86; elder Timnath Presbyn. Ch., 1985—. Mem. Colo. Soc. Sch. Psychologists (cert.), Nat. Assn. Sch. Psychologists, NEA, Am. Psychol. Assn., Ft. Collins Parents of Twins (pres. 1977-78), Sigma Xi, Phi Kappa Phi. Democrat. Club: Squaredusters (Ft. Collins) (v.p. 1977-78). Home: 213 Camino Real Fort Collins CO 80524 Office: Poudre Sch Dist R-1 2407 Laporte Ave Fort Collins CO 80521

BENNETT, JAMES AUSTIN, animal science educator; b. Taber, Alta., Can., Jan. 29, 1915; came to U.S., 1945, naturalized, 1949; s. William Alvin and Mary (Walker) B.; m. Dolores Buttars, Sept. 18, 1940; children: James Ralph, Carl Robert and Calleen (twins), Marvin Charles and Marilyn (twins). B.S., Utah State U., 1940, M.S., 1941; Ph.D., U. Minn., 1957. Livestock asst. Dominion Dept. Agr., Swift Current, Sask., Can., 1941-45; asst. prof. Utah State U., 1945-50, prof., animal sci., 1950-73, 74—, head dept., 1950-73, 74-76, acting dept. head animal, dairy and vet. scis., 1983-84; coordinator sheep research Utah State U.-Ministry Agr. Iran, 1973-74. Contbr. numerous articles on animal breeding and genetics to profl. jours. Mem. AAAS, Am. Soc. Animal Sci., Am. Genetic Assn., Sigma Xi. Home: 307 E 5 N Logan UT 84321

BENNETT, MARGARET ETHEL BOOKER, psychotherapist; b. Spartanburg, S.C., June 15, 1923; d. Paschal and Ovie (Grey) Booker. B.S., N.C. A&T State U., 1944; M.S.W., U. Mich., 1947; Ph.D., Wayne State U., 1980. Caseworker, field instr. Family Services Soc. Met. Detroit, 1947-52; caseworker, field instr., casework supr. Wayne County Cons. Center, 1952-60, Psychiat. Social Service, Wayne County Gen. Hosp., 1960-62; psychotherapist, field instr., asst. dir. Wayne County Mental Health Clinic, 1962-76; asst. dir. psychiat. social service Wayne County Psychiat. Hosp., 1976-77; dir. med. social service Wayne County Gen. Hosp., 1977-78; treatment cons. Project Paradigm; pvt. practice psychotherapy, Detroit, 1965—; psychotherapist, pres. Booker Bennett & Assocs., 1980—; founder Consultation Center of Ecorse, Mich., 1961; instr. Immanuel Luth. Coll., 1944-45; lectr. U. Mich., 1975-76. Bd. dirs. Crossroads, 1980—; exec. council Episcopal Diocese of Mich., 1974-77, 80—, exec. com. 1982—; governing bd. Cathedral Ch. of St. Paul, Detroit, 1971-74, 76-77, 79-82, v.p. governing bd., 1977; bd. dirs. Cathedral Terrace, 1981—, U. Mich. Women, 1982—, Wayne State U. Sch. Social Work Alumni Assn., 1981—. Cert. marriage counselor, cert. social worker, Mich.; cert. Acad. Cert. Social Workers. Fellow Am. Orthopsychiat. Assn.; mem. Mich. Assn. Marriage and Family Therapy, Am. Assn. Marriage and Family Therapy, Mich. Assn. Clin. Social Worker's Nat. Assn. Social Workers, Phi Delta Kappa, Alpha Kappa Alpha. Democrat. Episcopalian. Co-author: The Handbook of Psychodynamic Therapy; contbr. articles to profl. jours. Home and Office: 1971 Glynn Ct Detroit MI 48206

BENNETT, MICHAEL, sales professional; b. Gravesend, Kent, Eng., Sept. 8, 1943; s. Charles David and Joan Liley (Howecroft) B.; m. Pamela Megan Bennett, Mar. 18, 1967; 1 child, Phillip Anthony Michael. Grad., Twickenham Coll. Advanced Tech., Middlesex, Eng., 1971. Research engr. EMI Ltd., Hayes, Middlesex, 1965-70; sr. engr. Ind. Broadcasting Authority, Winchester, Hampshire, Eng., 1971-79; broadcast mgr. Stancoil Ltd., Windsor, Berkshire, Eng., 1979-80; regional sales mgr. Sony Broadcast Ltd., Basingstoke, Hampshire, Eng., 1980—. Contbr. articles to profl. jours. Fellow Brit. Interplanetary Soc.; mem. IEEE (sr.) (exec. com. 1984—), Audio Engring. Soc. (conf. exhbn. coordinator 1987, chmn. Brit. Sec. 1987-88), Brit. Kine. Sound, and TV Soc., Inst. Electronic and Radio Engrs. Conservative. Roman Catholic. Home: 55 Valley Rd, Newbury Berkshire R914 6HN, England Office: Sony Broadcast Ltd, Belgrave House, Basingview, Basingstoke Hampshire R914 6HN, England

BENNETT, SAUL, public relations agency executive; b. N.Y.C., Oct. 21, 1936; s. Philip and Ruth (Weinstein) Ostrove; m. Joan Marian Abrahams, Aug. 15, 1965; children—Sara, Charles, Elizabeth. B.S. in Journalism, Ohio U., Athens, 1957. Engaged in public relations 1963—; account supr., then v.p. Rowland Co. (public relations), N.Y.C., 1965-74; v.p., then sr. v.p. Robert Marston and Assocs., N.Y.C., 1974-78; exec. v.p. Robert Marston and Assocs., 1978-86, partner, 1979—, sr. exec. v.p., 1986—. Served with USAR, 1958-59, 61-62. Office: Robert Marston & Assocs Inc 485 Madison Ave New York NY 10022

BENNETT, WILLARD HARRISON, physicist, emeritus educator; b. Findlay, Ohio, June 13, 1903; s. Harry and Elsie Mae (Ward) B.; m. Mona D. Sheets, Sept. 8, 1928; children: Willard Harrison, Barbara, Bruce, Steven; m. Helen Mae Sawyer, Oct. 24, 1948; children: Charles, Ward, Rebecca. Student, Carnegie Inst. Tech., 1921-22; A.B., Ohio State U., 1924; M.S., U. Wis., 1926; Ph.D., U. Mich., 1928. NRC fellow Calif. Inst. Tech., 1928-30; faculty Ohio State U., 1930-38; dir. research Electronics Research Corp., 1938-41; dir. applied research Inst. Textile Tech., 1945; physicist, sect. chief Nat. Bur. Standards, 1945-50; prof. physics U. Ark., 1950-51; br. head, div. cons. U.S. Naval Research Lab., 1951-61; Burlington prof. physics N.C. State U., 1961-76, prof. emeritus, 1976—; cons. Los Alamos Sci. Lab., 1953—. Contbr. articles to profl. jours.; co-author textbook. Served to lt. col. AUS, 1941-45. Fellow Am. Phys. Soc., Washington Acad. Sci. Presbyterian (ruling elder). Home: 2608 Saint Mary's St Raleigh NC 27609 *Died Dec. 28, 1987.*

BENNETT, WILLIAM JOHN, educator, former U.S. secretary of education; b. Bklyn., July 3, 1943; m. Mary Elayne Glover, May 29, 1982. BA, Williams Coll., 1965, LLD (hon.), 1983; PhD, U. Tex., 1970; JD, Harvard U., 1971; LittD (hon.), Gonzaga U., 1982; HHD (hon.), Franklin Coll., Ind., 1982, U. N.C., 1984, George Washington U., 1985, Gallaudet Coll., 1985, The Citadel, 1986; LHD (hon.), U. N.H., 1982, Manhattan Coll., 1983, Elon Coll., 1984, Loyola Coll., Md., 1984, Assumption Coll., 1985, Yeshiva U., 1986, Cen. State U., Wilburforce, Ohio, 1987; LD (hon.), Williams Coll., 1983, U. Notre Dame, 1984. Asst. to pres. Boston U., 1972-76; exec. dir. Nat. Humanities Ctr., Research Triangle Park, N.C., 1976-79, pres., dir., 1979-81; assoc. prof. N.C. State U., Raleigh, 1979-81, U. N.C., 1979-81; chmn. NEH, Washington, 1981-85; sec. U.S. Dept. Edn., 1985-88; with Dunnels, Duvall, Bennett and Porter, Washington, 1988—. Office: Dunnels Duvall Bennett & Porter 1220 19th St NW Washington DC 20036

BENNETT, WILLIAM RALPH, JR., educator, physicist; b. Jersey City, Jan. 30, 1930; s. William Ralph and Viola (Schreiber) B.; m. Frances Commins, Dec. 11, 1952; children: Jean, William Robert, Nancy. A.B., Princeton U., 1951; Ph.D., Columbia U., 1957; M.A. (hon.), Yale U., 1965; D.Sc. (hon.), U. New Haven, 1975. Research asst. physics Columbia Radiation Lab., 1952-54; mem. Pupin Cyclotron Group, 1954-57; mem. faculty Yale U., 1957-59, 62—, prof. physics and applied sci., 1965-72, Charles Baldwin Sawyer prof. engring. and applied sci., prof. physics, 1972—; fellow Berkeley Coll., 1963-81; master Silliman Coll., 1981-87, life fellow, 1981—; tech. staff Bell Telephone Labs., Murray Hill, N.J., 1959-62; Cons. Tech. Research Group, Melville, N.Y., 1962-67, Inst. Def. Analysis, Washington, 1963-70; vis. scientist Am. Inst. Physics Vis. Scientist Program, 1963-64; vis. prof. Brandeis Summer Inst. Theoretical Physics, 1969; cons. mem. bd. dirs. Laser Scis. Corp., Bethel, Conn., 1968-71; mem. adv. panels atomic physics and astrophysics Nat. Bur. Standards, 1964-69; cons. CBS Labs., Stamford, Conn., 1967-68, AVCO Corp., 1978-81; mem. lab. adv. bd. for research Naval Research Adv. Com., 1968-78; guest of, Soviet Union, 1967, 69, 79. Author: Introduction to Computer Applications, 1976, Scientific and Engineering Problem Solving with the Computer, 1976, The Physics of Gas Lasers, 1977, Atomic Gas Laser Transition Data: A Critical Evaluation, 1979; Editorial adv. bd.: also Jour. Quantum Electronics, 1965-69; guest editor: Applied Optics, 1965. Recipient Western Electric Fund award for outstanding teaching Am. Assn. Engring. Educators, 1977; Outstanding Patent award Research and Devel. Council N.J., 1977; Sloan Found. fellow, 1963-65; Guggenheim fellow, 1967. Fellow Am. Phys. Soc., Optical Soc. Am., IEEE (Morris Liebmann award 1965); mem. Sigma Xi. Office: Dunham Lab 10 Hillhouse Ave New Haven CT 06520

BENNETT, WILLIAM TAPLEY, JR., retired U.S. diplomat, lecturer, consultant; b. Griffin, Ga., Apr. 1, 1917; s. William Tapley and Annie Mem (Little) B.; m. Margaret Rutherfurd White, June 23, 1945; children: William Tapley, John Campbell White, Anne Barclay, Ellen Pierrepont Bennett Godsall, Victoria Ridgely. AB, U. Ga., 1937; postgrad., U. Freiburg, Germany, 1937-38; JD, George Washington U., 1948; DCL (hon.), Ind. State U., 1966. Instr. polit. sci. U. Ga., 1937; with Nat. Inst. Pub. Affairs, 1939-40; with U.S. Dept. of State, 1941-85, officer in charge Cen.Am. and Panama affairs, 1949-51, officer in charge Caribbean affairs, 1951, dep. dir. office S.Am. affairs, 1951-54, assigned to Nat. War Coll., 1954-55, spl. asst. to undersec. state, 1955-57; counselor embassy U.S. Dept. of State, Vienna, Austria, 1957-61, Rome, 1961; counselor with rank of minister U.S. Dept. of State, Athens, Greece, 1961-64; ambassador to Dominican Republic U.S. Dept. of State, 1964-66, ambassador to Portugal, 1966-69, advisor Air U., 1969-71, dep. permanent rep. to UN, ambassador UN Security Council, 1971-77, permanent rep. to NATO, 1977-83, asst. sec. for legis. and intergovtl. affairs, 1983-85; cons. Washington, 1985—; asst. U.S. del. organizing conf. UN, San Francisco, 1945; advisor U.S. del. UN Gen. Assembly, N.Y.C., 1950, alt. rep., 1971, 72, U.S. rep. 1973-76; sec. gen. 4th meeting of fgn. ministers of Am. States, Washington, 1951; mem. U.S. del. to inauguration Pres. Ibanez of Chile, 1952, Eisenhower mission to S.Am., 1953, U.S. del. 10th Inter-Am. Conf., Caracas, 1954, IAEA Confs., Vienna, 1957, 58; U.S. rep. UN Trusteeship Council, 1971-77, pres. 1972-73; chmn. UN vis. mission to Papua New Guinea, 1972; chmn. U.S. del. UN Devel. Conf., Geneva, 1973, 76, Econ. Commn. for Europe, Bucharest, 1974, UN Conf. on Indsl. Devel., Lima, Peru, 1975, Econ. Commn. for Asia and South Pacific, Bangkok, 1976; cons. Inst. Fgn. Policy Analysis Tufts Univ., Ctr. for Strategic and Internat. Studies, 1985—; adj. prof. internat. relations U. Ga., 1985—. Mem. adv. bd. Harvard U. Div. Sch., 1979—, bd. visitors Air U., 1987—. Served to lt. AUS, 1944-46, ETO. Recipient Carr award for disting. service Dept. State, Disting. Pub. Service medal Dept. Def. Fellow Inst. for Higher Def. Studies (sr.); mem. Am. Acad. Diplomacy, Council Fgn. Relations., So. Ctr. Internat. Studies, Am. Council on Germany, Ga. Bar Assn., Fgn. Policy Assn. (bd. dirs. 1987—), Atlantic Council (bd. dirs. 1985—), Pilgrims, Sphinx Soc., Phi Beta Kappa, Phi Kappa Phi, Omicron Delta Kappa, Sigma Chi, Phi Delta Phi. Presbyterian. Clubs Chevy Chase; Metropolitan (Washington).

BENNEY, DOUGLAS MABLEY, marketing executive, consultant; b. Cold Spring Harbor, N.Y., Aug. 7, 1922; s. William Mabley and Wilhelmina (Walters) B.; m. Eugenia Sammis, Sept. 30, 1944 (div. Jan. 1980); children—William Douglas, Barbara Gates, Robert Scott; m. Barbara Mueller, July 8, 1983; stepchildren—Gregory Carmichael, Andrew Carmichael. Navy air cadet U. N.C.-Chapel Hill, 1943, Cornell U., 1943; student in engring. Purdue U., 1939-41; A.B., Colgate U., 1946-49; postgrad. Columbia U., 1951-52; With Curtis Publs., Phila., 1950-63, editor, assoc. pub. Jack & Jill, 1960-63; mktg. mgr. edn. div. Doubleday & Co., N.Y.C., 1963-67; advt. and sales mgr. Hearst Book div. N.Y.C., 1967-68; v.p. creative services Nat. Liberty Corp., Valley Forge, Pa., 1968-72; v.p. mktg. Gerber Life Ins. Co., N.Y.C., 1972-75; sr. mktg. officer Internat. Group Plans, Washington, 1975-78; v.p. mktg. Maxon Adminstrs., Inc., Washington, 1978—. Patentee newspaper inserts, self-mailers. Served as ensign AC, USN, 1943-46; PTO. Recipient award Artists Guild Del. Valley, 1969, Direct Mail Mktg. Assn., 1965, Myasthenia Gravis Found., 1985. Mem. Direct Mktg. Assn., Direct Mktg. Assn. Washington, Direct Mktg. Creative Guild, Greater Washington Soc. Assn. Execs. Club: Woodlawn Country (Alexandria, Va.). Avocations: woodworking; sailing; photography; scuba diving.

BENNINGTON, MARCY MARIE, former school psychologist; b. South Bend, Ind., Feb. 1, 1949; d. John William, Jr. and Constance Dorothy (Weingartner) Truemper; A.B., Ind. U., Bloomington, 1971; M.Ed., U. Mo., St. Louis, 1976; Ph.D. (teaching asst./instr.), St. Louis U., 1981; m. Mark Ian Bennington, Sept. 7, 1968. Adminstrv. asst. Psychol. Service Center, St. Louis, 1974-75; personnel asst. Orchard Corp. Am., St. Louis, 1975-77; sch. psychology intern Pattonville Schs., Maryland Heights, Mo., 1978-79; diagnostician, eval. coordinator Wentzville Schs., Mo., 1979-80, dir. spl. edn., 1980-85. Speaker to community groups. Phi Beta Kappa scholar. Mem. Am. Psychol. Assn., Nat. Assn. Sch. Psychologists, Am. Assn. Counseling and Devel., Council Exceptional Children.

BENNIS, WARREN, business administration educator, author, consultant; b. N.Y.C., Mar. 8, 1925; s. Philip and Rachel (Landau) B.; m. Clurie Williams, Mar. 30, 1962 (div. 1983); children—Katharine, John Leslie, Will Martin; m. Mary Jane O'Donnell, Mar. 8, 1988. A.B., Antioch Coll., 1951; hon. cert. econs., London Sch. Econs., 1952; Ph.D., MIT, 1955; LL.D. (hon.), Xavier U., Cin., 1972, George Washington U., 1977; L.H.D. (hon.), Hebrew Union Coll., 1974, Kans. State U., 1979; D.Sc. (hon.), U. Louisville, 1977, Pacific Grad. Sch. Psychology, 1987. Diplomate Am. Ed. Profl. Psychology. Asst. prof. psychology MIT, Cambridge, 1953-56, prof., 1959-67; asst. prof. psychology and bus. Boston U., 1956-59; provost SUNY-Buffalo, 1967-68, v.p. acad. devel., 1968-71; pres. U. Cin., 1971-77; U.S. prof. corps. and soc. Centre d'Etudes Industrielles, Geneva, Switzerland, 1978-79; exec.-in-residence Pepperdine U., 1978-79; George Miller Disting. prof.-in-residence U. Ill., Champaign-Urbana, 1978; Disting. prof. Bus. Adminstrn. Sch. Bus., U. So. Calif., 1980—; vis. lectr. Harvard U., 1958-59, Indian Mgmt. Inst., Calcutta; vis. prof. U. Lausanne (Switzerland), 1961-62, INSEAD, France, 1983; bd. dirs. First Exec. Corp. Author: Planning of Change, 4th edit., 1985, Interpersonal Dynamics, 1963, 3d edit., 1975, Personal and Organizational Change, 1965, Changing Organizations, 1966, repub. in paperback as Beyond the Bureaucracy, 1974, The Temporary Society, 1968, Organization Development, 1969, American Bureaucracy, 1970, Management of Change and Conflict, 1972, The Leaning Ivory Tower, 1973, The Unconscious Conspiracy: Why Leaders Can't Lead, 1976, Essays in Interpersonal Dynamics, 1979; (with B. Nanus): Leaders, 1985, Why Leaders Can't Lead, 1988; columnist, chmn. bd. editors New Mgmt.; assoc. editor Jour. Transpersonal Psychology, Community Psychology; cons. editor Jour. Creative Behavior, Jour. Higher Edn., Jour. Occupational Behavior, Ency. of Econs. and Bus., Jour. Humanistic Psychology. Mgmt. Series Jossey-Bass Pubs. Mem. Pres.' White House Task Force on Sci. Policy, 1969-70; mem. FAA study task force U.S. Dept. Transp., 1975; mem. adv. com. N.Y. State Joint Legis. Com. Higher Edn., 1970-71; mem. Ohio Gov.'s Bus. and Employment Council, 1972-74; mem. panel on alt. approaches to grad. edn. Council Grad. Schs. and Grad. Record-Exam Bd., 1971-73; chmn. Nat. Adv. Commn. on Higher Edn. for Police Officers, 1976-78; adv. bd. NIH, 1978-84; trustee Colo. Rocky Mountains Sch.; bd. dirs. Am. Leadership Forum, Foothill Group, First Exec. Corp., Calif. Sch. Profl. Psychology; mem. vis. com. for humanities MIT. Served to capt. AUS, World War II. Decorated Bronze Star, Purple Heart; recipient Dow Jones award, 1987. Fellow Am. Psychol. Assn., AAAS, Am. Sociol. Assn.; mem. Am. Acad. Arts and Scis. (co-chmn. policy council 1969-71), Am. Soc. Pub. Adminstrn. (nat. council), Am. Mgmt. Assn. (dir. 1974-77), U.S. C. of C. (adv. group scholars). Office: Sch of Bus U So Calif University Park Los Angeles CA 90089-1421

BENOIST, JEAN-MARIE JULES, educator, author, journalist, researcher; b. Paris, Apr. 4, 1942; s. Jean Adrien and Suzanne (Guesde) B.; m. Nathalie Isabelle Bréaud, Oct. 16, 1964 (div. 1979); children: Fabrice, Alienor, Sylvain; m. 2d, Catherine Cecile Dewavrin, Sept. 27, 1979; children: Olivier Alexis, Alexis Emmanuel. B.A. in Philosophy, Sorbonne, 1963, B.A. in Arts, 1963, M.A., 1965, Agregation, 1966; student Ecole Normale Supérieure, Paris, 1963-66. Prof. philosophy, Lycee London, 1966-70; cultural attaché French Embassy, London, 1970-74; sr. lectr. College de France, Paris, 1974-81, assoc. prof., 1981—; dir. essay series Presses Universitaires de France, Paris, 1979—; founder Conservative Think Tank Forum, 1984, 1979; sr. research fellow Monde et Entreprise, 1983—; founder, chmn. CERIS (European Ctr. for Internat. Relations and Strategy), 1984; vis. lectr. Harvard U., NYU, Georgetown U., War Coll., Washington, others. Author: Marx est Mort, 1970; La Revolution Structurale, 1975 (French Acad. award, paperback 1980, pub. U.S. under title The Structural Revolution); Tyrannie du Logos, 1975; Pavane pour une Europe Defunte, 1976 (paperback 1978); Les Nouveaux Primaires, 1978; Un Singulier Programme, 1978; Chronique de Décomposition du PCF, 1979 (French Acad. award), La Génération Sacrifiee, 1980 (French Acad. award), Le Devoir D'Opposition, 1982; editor: John Donne, 1983; L'Identité , 1983; Figures de Baroque, 1983; Les Outils de la Liberté, 1985; SDI and Deterrence, 1987; Chirac: Homme d'Etat, 1988;; mem. editorial bd. La Revue des Deux Mondes, 1988; columnist: Le Quotidien de Paris, 1981—; contbr. articles to publs. including Le Figaro, le Monde, Le Quotidien de Paris, Critique, Wall Street Journal, Washington Port. Gen. election Union Democratie Française candidate against Marchais, Val de Marne, 1978; mem. Nat. Com. for Giscard's Re-election; mem. Nat. Council of Rally for French Republic; French mem. of Com. for Free World. Mem. Am. Legion. Roman Catholic. Clubs: Le Siècle, Savile (London), PEN (nat. com.); Travellers (Paris). Home: 3 Rond-Point, Saint-James, 92200 Neuilly sur Seine France Office: College de France, 11 Pl M Berthelot, 75006 Paris France

BENOIT, DONALD ANTHONY, agronomist; b. Beaverville, Ill., May 3, 1936; s. Donald O'Neil and Edith Maude (Giasson) B; m. Susanne Elisabeth Haller, Nov. 9, 1957 (div. Oct. 1975); children: Jeanette M., Jacqueline T., James P., Christine A., John A., Derryl A. (dec.); m. Linda Ruth Grundy, Nov. 3, 1978 (div. Feb. 1984); 1 child, Lorrie. Gen. equivalency diploma, USAF Inst. (Europe), U.S. Army, 1960. Commd. U.S. Army, 1954, advanced through grades to sgt.; communications specialist U.S. Army, Europe, 1954-65; resigned U.S. Army, 1965; fin. cons. Vega & Assocs., Rainy River, Ont., Can., 1965-66; communications specialist Uniroyal, Inc., Joliet, Ill., 1966-68; chmn., chief exec. officer Rainy River L&C, Ltd., 1972-84; chmn, chief exec. officer, investment cons. Agbank, Inc., Baudette, Minn., 1984—. Decorated Army Occupation medal U.S. Army, Germany, 1954, Nat. Def. Service medal, U.S. Army, Europe, 1954, Good Conduct medal, U.S. Army, Continental U.S., 1965. Mem. DAV, Am. Legion. Roman Catholic. Home and Office: AGBANK Inc Box 429 R R #1 Baudette MN 56623-0429

BENOÎT, HENRI CHARLES, physicist; b. Montpellier, France, July 11, 1921; s. Jean-Daniel and Henriette (Bois) B.; diploma physics Ecole Normale Superieure, Paris, 1945; D.Sc., U. Strasbourg, 1950; m. Marie-Therese Bigand, July 20, 1946; children—Nicole, Alain, Eric. Prof. physics U. Strasbourg, 1954—, dir. Macromolecular Lab., 1967-78; pres. div. macromolecular chemistry IUPAC, 1971-75; mem. nat. com. Centre Nat. Recherche Sci., 1967-75, pres. sect. phys. chemistry molecules and macromolecules, 1971-75. Decorated officer Palmes Academiques, 1962, comdr., 1974, chevalier Legion of Honor, 1963, officer Nat. Order Merit, 1968, officier Legion of Honor; comdr. Ordre National du Merite; officier de l'Ordre National de la Legion d'Honneur, 1978; recipient Silver medal Centre Nat. Recherche Sci., 1961, Gold medal Czech. Acad. Scis., 1969; Polymer Chemistry award Am. Chem. Soc., 1979; Witco award, 1979; Ford prize in high polymer physics Am. Phys. Soc., 1978; Alexander von Humboldt prize, 1986. Mem. French Chem. Soc. (pres. molecular and macromolecular phys. chemistry sect. 1971-75), Acad. Scis. (corr.). Contbr. numerous articles to profl. jours. Office: Inst Charles Sadron (CRM), 6 rue Boussingault, 67083 Strasbourg France

BENSAID, JULIEN, cardiologist, educator; b. Constantine, Algeria, Aug. 2, 1933; s. Albert and Berthe (Fassi) B.; m. Danieke Cohen, Mar. 20, 1975; children: Bruno, Eric. MD, U. Algiers, 1960. Resident in cardiovascular diseases Hosp. Fernand Widal, Hosp. Necker, Hosp. Lariboisiere, Hosp. Boucicaut, Paris, 1964-66; asst. in cardiology Boucicaut Hosp., Paris, 1966-73, prof. cardiology, 1974—; sub-chief Depuytren Hosp., Limoges, France, 1974-84; chief cardiology dept. Depuytren Hosp., Limoges, 1984—; cons. in cardiovascular diseases 1974—; prof. cardiology U. Limoges, 1984—, chief cardiology dept., 1984—; pres. Fondation Regionale de Cardiologie du Limousin, 1984. Contbr. articles to med. jours. Served as lt. French Health Service, 1963-64. Decorated chevalier Ordre des Palmes Academiques. Fellow Internat. Coll. Angiology; mem. Societe Francaise Cardiologie, Societe Europeenne Physiopathologie Respiratoire. Home: Garibaldi Ave 51, 87000 Limoges France Office: Dupuytren Hosp, Alexis Carrel Ave 2, 87042 Limoges France

BENSCHECK, WOLFGANG WERNER, electronic publishing company executive; b. Hoechst, Hessen, Federal Republic of Germany, Dec. 28, 1948; s. Karl and Gertrud (Schuster) B.; m. Beate Maria Wiesehof, Mar. 9, 1982; 1 child, Brian. Diplom-Kaufmann, U. Regensburg, 1976. Fin. analyst Verlag Hoppenstedt & Co., Darmstadt, 1976-77; credit analyst Chem. Bank, Frankfurt, 1978; mng. dir. Hoppenstedt Wirtschaftsdatenbank GmbH, Darmstadt, 1979—. Contbr. articles to profl. jours. Mem. adv. bd. Telematica, Stuttgart, 1987, Optical Info., Amsterdam, 1988—. Mem. Arbeitsgemeinschaft Fachinformation, Mktg. Club. Home: Zum Hartberg 24 Hoechst, 6128 Hessen Federal Republic of Germany Office: Hoppenstedt Wirtschaftsdatenbank, HavelstraBe 9 Darmstadt, 6100 Hessen Federal Republic of Germany

BENSEN, ANNETTE WOLF, graphic art company executive; b. Bklyn., Aug. 7, 1938; d. Isidor and Sylvia Wolf; m. Gene Bensen, Oct. 14,

1979. A.A.S., N.Y.C. Community Coll., 1958; postgrad., Pratt Inst., 1974-75. With Wagner-Ellsberg, Inc., N.Y.C., 1958-62; art dir. Island Pen Mfg. Inc., Stacie Pen, Curtis Rand Industries, Inc., N.Y.C., 1962-68; with G.S. Lithographers, Inc., N.Y.C., 1968-70; partner, pres. Rembrandt's Mother, Inc., N.Y.C., 1970-72; co-owner, pres. Film Comp., Inc., N.Y.C., 1972-75; mgr. Expertype, Inc., N.Y.C., 1975—; adj. lectr. N.Y.C. Community Coll., 1971-75. Mem. Advt. Women N.Y., Am. Printing History Assn., Assn. Graphic Arts , Club of Printing Women of N.Y. (pres.), Sales Assn. of the Graphic Arts, Typographers Assn. N.Y., Women in Prodn. Inc., Aircraft Owner and Pilots Assn. Office: Expertype Inc 44 W 28th St New York NY 10001

BENSEN, LLOYD, holding company chief executive Ultramar P.L.C., London. Address: Ultramar PLC Office Chmn, 141 Moorgate, London EC2M 6TX, England

BENSI, XING, philosopher, educator; b. Hangzhou, Zhejiang, People's Republic China, Nov. 7, 1929; parents: Xing Zhen Nan and Gui Yu Yin; m. Zhou Bang Yuan, Jan. 31, 1953; 1 child, Xing Yi. BA in Fgn. Languages, Beijing Coll., 1952; MA, Chinese Acad., Beijing, 1958. Asst., lectr., asst. research fellow Beijing Coll. Fgn. Lang., 1952-56; research prof. Inst. Philosophy, Beijing, 1954-85, dep. dir., 1978-82, dir., 1982—; com. mem. Chinese Acad. Social Scis., Beijing, 1982—; prof. Ginghua U., Beijing, 1984—; dep. gen. editor com. philosophy vol. Chinese Ency., Beijing, 1982—; trustee Ctr. Internat. Cultural Exchange, Beijing, 1984—. Author: Philosophy and Enlightenment, 1979 (Chinese Acad. Social Scis. award 1983); chief editor: Little Encyclopedia of Philosophy, 1987 (Chinese Library award 1987). Home: Zizhuyuan Changyungong, First Bldg, Beijing Peoples Republic of China Office: Chinese Acad Social Scis, Jiang Guomendajie, Beijing Peoples Republic of China

BENSON, BETTY JONES, educator; b. Barrow County, Ga., Jan. 11, 1928; d. George C. and Bertha (Mobley) Jones; B.S. in Edn., N. Ga. U., Dahlonega, 1958; M.Ed. in Curriculum and Supervision, U. Ga., Athens, 1968, edn. specialist in Curriculum and Supervision, 1970; m. George T. Benson; children—George Steven, Elizabeth Gayle, James Claud, Robert Benjamin. Tchr. Forsyth County (Ga.) Bd. Edn., Cumming, 1956-66, curriculum dir., 1966—; asst. supt. for instrn. Forsyth County Schs., 1981—. Active Alpine Center for Disturbed Children; chmn. Ga. Lake Lanier Island Authority; mem. N. Ga. Coll. Edn. Adv. Com., Ga. Textbook Com.; adv. Boy Scouts; Sunday sch. tchr. 1st Baptist Ch. Cumming. Mem. NEA, Ga. Assn. Educators (dir.), Nat., Ga. (pres.) assns. supervision and curriculum devel., Assn. Childhood Edn. Internat., Bus. and Profl. Women's Club, Internat. Platform Assn., Ga. Future Tchrs. Adv. Assn. (pres.), HeadStart Dirs. Assn., Forsyth County Hist. Soc. Home: Route 1 Box 12 Cumming GA 30130 Office: 101 School St Cumming GA 30130

BENSON, DAVID BERNARD, computer science educator; b. Seattle, Nov. 18, 1940; s. Allan I. and Martha (White) B.; B.S. in Engring., Calif. Inst. Tech., 1962, M.S. in E.E., 1963, Ph.D. (NASA fellow), 1967; m. Nancy Elaine Dollahite, Sept. 17, 1962 (div. Aug. 1986); children—Megan, Bjorn, Nils, Amy, Kjell, Ingri. Research engr. N. Am. Rockwell, Downey, Calif., 1963-64; asst. prof. U. N.C., Chapel Hill, 1967-70; vis. assoc. prof. U. Colo., Boulder, 1976-77; asst. prof. Wash. State U., Pullman, 1970-72, assoc. prof., 1972-79, prof. computer sci., 1979—; vis. computer scientist U. Edinburgh, Scotland, 1983; pres. BENTEC, 1985—. Precinct chmn. 72d Precinct, Whitman County, Wash., 1978-82; Whitman County Dem. Conv. del., 1972, 76. NSF grantee, 1969-87. Mem. Assn. Computing Machinery, Am. Math. Soc., Am. Assn. Computational Linguistics, IEEE Computer Soc., AAAS, AAUP, Sigma Xi. Mem. Soc. of Friends. Contbr. over 30 articles to profl. jours. Home: NE 615 Campus St Pullman WA 99163 Office: Computer Sci Dept Wash State Univ Pullman WA 99164-1210

BENSON, DAVID JOHN, mathematician; b. Farnborough, Eng., Dec. 3, 1955; s. John Cecil and Margaret Eve (Saxby) B.; 1 child, Christine Natasha Martens. BA in Math., Trinity Coll., Cambridge, Eng., 1977, 78, PhD in Math., 1982. Royal soc. exchange fellow Arhus (Denmark) U., 1981-82; Gibbs instr. Yale U., 1982-84; asst. prof. Northwestern U., 1984-86; new blood lectr. U. Oxford, 1986—. Author: Modular Representation Theory: New Trends and Methods, 1984; contbr. articles to profl. jours. Mem. London Math. Soc., Am. Math. Soc. Green Party. Office: Math Inst, 24-29 St Giles, Oxford OX1 3LB, England

BENSON, GEORGE LEONARD, telecommunications company executive; b. Seattle, Sept. 20, 1934; s. George and Gertrude (Rolph) B.; m. Kyleen Susan Gordon, Sept. 22, 1962; children—William, Barbara, Stephen, Kristin, Shanon, Pamela. B.A. in Bus., U. Wash., 1959. Sales rep. Bus. Systems, Inc., Los Angeles, 1959-64, sales mgr., 1964-66; mgr. Pacific div. NCR, San Francisco, Calif., 1966-69; br. mgr., Rochester, Minn., 1969-74, dist. dir., Milw., 1974-78; pres. Telecom North, Inc., Little Chute, Wis., 1979-87 ; ptnr., chief exec. officer Coradian Corp., Latham, N.Y., 1987—. Army, 1953-55. Mem. No. Wis. Telecom Assn. Republican. Methodist. Avocations: sports; reading; travel. Lodge: Rotary. Home: 6786 Pheasant Run Rd Hartford WI 53027 Office: Telecom N Inc 2301 Kelbe Dr Little Chute WI 54140

BENSON, GEORGE STUART, university chancellor; b. Okla. Ter., Sept. 26, 1898; s. Stuart Felix and Emma (Rogers) B.; m. Sallie Ellis Hockaday, July 2, 1925 (dec. 1980); children: Mary Ruth, Fannie Lois.; m. Marguerite O'Banion, Feb. 22, 1983. B.S., Okla. A. and M. Coll., Stillwater, 1924; A.B., Harding Coll., 1925, LL.D., 1932; M.A., U. Chgo., 1931; LL.D., Knox Coll., 1948, Waynesburg Coll., Okla. Christian Coll., 1968, Freed-Hardeman Coll., 1981. Tchr. rural schs. Okla., 1918-21; high sch. prin. 1924-25; missionary and tchr. South China, 1925-36; prof. English Nat. Sun Yat Sen U., Canton, China, 1929-30; editor Oriental Christian, Canton, 1929-36; founder, trustee and pres. Canton Bible Sch., 1930-36; pres. Harding Coll., 1936-65, pres. emeritus, 1965—; chancellor Okla. Christian Coll., 1956-67, Ala. Christian Coll., Montgomery, 1975—; Tchr., authority on Oriental religions and philosophy. Writer: syndicated weekly newspaper column Looking Ahead, 1942-85; producer: radio program Land of the Free (now Behind the News), 1942-85; Contbr. to religious publs. and secular mags. Pres. Ark. Pub. Expenditure Council, 1942-44, 52-56; dir. Nat. Thrift Com., Inc.; Mem. Nat. Com. for Religion and Welfare Recovery, 1939; appointed by Pres. Eisenhower to advisory bd. U.S. Mcht. Marine Acad., Kings Port, N.Y., 1953-56; pres. Nat. Edn. Program, Searcy, Ark., 1942-85; chmn. bd. Zambia Christian Secondary Sch., Kalomo, 1966-84; mem. nat. adv. bd. Am. Security Council, 1975—; mem. Pres. Reagan's Task Force. Recipient numerous awards Freedoms Found., Horatio Alger award, 1981; named to Okla. Hall of Fame, 1972, Arkansan of Year, 1953-54; others. Mem. C. of C., AIM, Pi Kappa Delta. Mem. Ch. of Christ. Club: Kiwanian. Home: 25 Harding Dr Searcy AR 72143 Office: Harding U Box 760 Searcy AR 72143

BENSON, JAMES CARL, accountant; b. Mpls., Aug. 24, 1935; s. Fritz L. and Annie C. (Nordstrom) B.; m. Ruth Ann Backlin, Sept. 10, 1960; 1 child, Emily Ruthann. BBS with distinction, U. Minn., 1960. CPA, Calif. Intern Greyhound Co., 1959, Haskins & Sells, 1960; with Arthur Andersen & Co., San Francisco, Brussels, San Jose, Calif., 1960—, ptnr., 1970—. Pres. Trinity Luth. Ch., Oakland, Calif., 1966, bd. dirs., 1978-80; pres. West Valley Aquatic Team, 1979-80; bd. dirs. Family Services Assn., Alexian Bros. Hosp. Found., 1977-82, pres., 1981-82; trustee Alexian Bros. Hosp., 1982—; mem. planning and allocations com. United Way of Santa Clara County, 1981-82; mem. council Prince of Peace Luth. Ch., 1977-79, 83—, pres., 1986-87; bd. dirs. San Jose Opera Assn., 1985-87, San Jose Mus. of Art, 1987—. Sloan scholar U. Minn. Mem. Am. Inst. CPA's, Nat. Assn. Accts., Calif. CPA Soc., Alliance Francaise of Saratoga (treas.), Beta Alpha Psi, Beta Gamma Sigma. Club: Am. Men's (Brussels). Lodge: Kiwanis (bd. dirs. West Valley chpt.).

BENSON, JERRY SANFORD, JR., computer industry executive; b. Syracuse, N.Y., Oct. 8, 1956; s. Jerry Sanford Sr. and Nancy (Burns) B.; m. Stephanie Mizutowicz, Feb. 20, 1982; children: Bethany Rae, Emma Leigh. BA in Pyschology cum laude, Duke U., 1979. With sales dept. Atlantic Richfield Oil Co., Waterbury, Conn., 1980-82; executive mktg. and sales Amdek Corp., Chgo., 1982-86; v.p. mktg. NEC Corp., Wood Dale, Ill., 1987—; lectr. in field. Robert L. Flowers scholar Duke U., 1976. Republican. Roman Catholic. Home: 35 W Hattendorf Ave Roselle IL 60172 Office: NEC Corp 1255 Michael Dr Wood Dale IL 60191

BENSON, JOHN SCOTT, lawyer; b. Atlanta, Sept. 17, 1947; s. Lawrence Walker and Betty Lamar (Chick) B.; m. Louise Kathryn Sweet, July 22, 1984; children: Nathaniel Michael, Elisabeth Sweet. BA magna cum laude, Vanderbilt U., 1969; JD, U. Va., 1974. Bar: Fla. 1974. Assoc. Martin, Ade, Birchfield & Johnson, Jacksonville, Fla., 1974-78, ptnr., 1978—; bd. dirs. Associated Unit Cos., Inc. Bd. dirs. Cerebral Palsy of Jacksonville, 1980-88, pres., 1986; mem. Fedn. Council YMCA Indian Guides, 1985-86; bd. dirs. Children's Services of Jacksonville, 1986-88. Served to 1st lt. U.S. Army, 1969-71, Vietnam. Decorated Air medal; named one of Outstanding Young Men in Am., 1979. Mem. ABA, Fla. Bar Assn., Jacksonville Bar Assn., Internat. Platform Assn., Phi Beta Kappa, Phi Kappa Sigma. Republican. Club: Fla. Yacht (Jacksonville). Office: Martin Ade Birchfield & Mickler 3000 Independent Sq Jacksonville FL 32202

BENSON, LAWRENCE KERN, JR., lawyer, real estate exec.; b. New Orleans, May 16, 1938; s. Lawrence Kern and Adele (Foster) B.; m. Alta Sarah Bechtel, June 10, 1961; children—Robert Foster, Andrew Thompson, Marion Alta. Student Washington & Lee U., 1956-58; B.A., Tulane U., 1960, J.D., 1962. Bar: La. 1962, U.S. Dist. Ct. (ea. and mid. dists.) La. 1962, U.S. Ct. Mil. Appeals 1963, U.S. Ct. Appeals (5th cir.) 1969, U.S. Supreme Ct. 1971, U.S. Dist. Ct. (we. dist.) La. 1977. Assoc. Milling, Benson, Woodward, Hillyer, Pierson & Miller, New Orleans, 1962-66, ptnr., 1966-85, asst. U.S. Atty. ea. dist., La., 1986—; adj. lectr. Tulane U. Law Sch., 1980. Served with USAR, 1963-64. Mem. ABA, La. Bar Assn. (ho. of dels. 1978-81), New Orleans Bar Assn. (exec. com. 1979-81), Order of Coif. Republican. Methodist. Clubs: City (New Orleans). Office: US Atty's Office Hale Boggs Fed Bldg New Orleans LA 70130

BENSON, MORTON, educator, lexicographer; b. Newark, Dec. 13, 1924; s. Jacob and Mollie (Ravin) B.; m. Evelyn Rose, July 3, 1955; children—Rebecca J., Miriam E. B.A., N.Y. U., 1947; Certificat, Grenoble U., France, 1948; student, Frankfurt (Germany) U., 1948-50; Ph.D., U. Pa., 1954. Asst. prof. Ohio U., 1954-60; mem. faculty U. Pa., Phila., 1960—, prof., chmn. dept. Slavic langs., dir. Slavic lang. and area center, 1966-74; mem. joint com. on Eastern Europe Am. Council Learned Socs., 1971-73. Author: Dictionary of Russian Personal Names, 2d rev. edit., 1967, Serbocroatian-English Dictionary, 1971, rev. edit., 1979, 1988, English-Serbocroatian Dictionary, 1978, rev. edit., 1984, 1988; co-author: Lexicographic Description of English, 1986, BBI Combinatory Dictionary of English: A Guide to Word Combinations, 1986; asso. editor: Slavic and East European Jour, 1960-70; mem. editorial bd.: Names, 1967-70; mem. adv. bd.: Am. Speech, 1961-62; contbr. articles to profl. jours. Served with AUS, 1943-46, 48-52. Fulbright-Hays research fellow, 1965-66; recipient Cert. Merit, English-Speaking Union, Buckingham Palace, London, 1987. Mem. Am. Assn. Tchrs. Slavic and East European Langs. (pres. 1964), Linguistic Soc. Am., Assn. Internat. des Langues and Litteratures Slaves (sec. 1963-66), European Assn. Lexicography, MLA, Dictionary Soc. N.Am. Home: 219 Myrtle Ave Havertown PA 19083 Office: Dept Slavic Langs Univ Pa Philadelphia PA 19104

BENSON, ROBERT CLINTON, JR., finance, development broker; b. Lynn, Mass., Dec. 8, 1946; s. Robert Clinton and Lillian M. (MacArthur) B.; B.S., Suffolk U., 1970; M.A., Boston U., 1979; M.B.A., N.H. Coll., 1982; m. Jo-Ann Murphy, Aug. 26, 1977 (div. Feb. 1987); children—Jarrod Grayson, Marissa Ashley. Planner, City of Lynn, Mass., 1972-73, asst. supt. parks, 1973-74, spl. asst. to mayor, 1974-75, dep. exec. dir. Dept. Community Devel., 1975-78; dir. econ. devel. City of Portsmouth (N.H.), 1978-80; founder Benson & Co., mgmt. cons., 1980—, Inst. for Fin. Planning ; founder Robert C. Benson, Inc., investment bankers, 1984—; dir. Sesame Tape Systems, Inc.; adj. faculty Golden Gate U. Bd. dirs. Portsmouth Community Health Services, 1980-82; chmn. Swampscott (Mass.) Conservation Commn., 1967-70; mem. Swampscott Town Charter Commn., 1968-69. Served with USNR, 1970-72. Lic. real estate broker, N.H., Maine, Mass.; lic. pvt. pilot; justice of peace, notary public, Mass. Mem. Am. Indsl. Devel. Council, Inc., Am. Planning Assn., Northeastern Indsl. Devel. Assn., Portsmouth C. of C. (dir.). Episcopalian. Club: Racquetball and Tennis (Portsmouth). Editor Cruiser-Destroyerman Mag., 1971; contbr. articles to profl. publs.; research on labor market in Portsmouth, 1978-80; drafter model environ. statutes Mass. Legislature, 1968. Office: 501 Islington St 3d Floor Suite 14 Portsmouth NH 03801

BENSON, THOMAS QUENTIN, lawyer; b. Grand Forks, N.D., Jan. 9, 1943; s. Theodore Quentin and Helen Marie (Winzenberg) B.; m. Mary Mangelsdorf, Aug. 3, 1968; children: Annemarie C., Thomas Quentin II, Mark W. B.A. U. Notre Dame, 1964; J.D., U. Denver, 1967. Bar: Colo. 1967, N.D. 1967, U.S. Dist. Ct. 1968, U.S. Circuit Ct. Appeals 1974, U.S. Mil. Ct. Appeals 1981. Legal counsel Denver Regional Council Govts., 1968-70; assoc. Schneider, Shoemaker, Wham & Cooke, Denver, 1970-72; prin. Thomas Quentin Benson, Denver, 1972-74, 76—; ptnr. Benson & Vernon, Denver, 1974-76; Mem. bd. Am. Health Planning Assn., 1973-77. Mem. bd. Mayor's Adv. Com. Community Devel., Denver, 1975-78; Republican precinct committeeman, 1972-78; mem. White House Advance for U.S. Pres., 1975; pres. Park Vista-Pine Ridge Homeowners Assn., 1971-73; mem. parish council Ch. of Risen Christ, Roman Catholic, 1978-80, chief lector, 1975-76; pres. M.P.B. Home and Sch. Assn. Served to capt. JAGC USNR. Cited for Leadership Denver C. of C., 1975-76. Mem. ABA, Colo. Bar Assn. (sect. chmn. 1975-78), Denver Bar Assn., Cath. Lawyers Guild Denver (pres. 1979-80). Republican. Clubs: U. Notre Dame (Denver) (pres. 1980-81), Univ. Hills Rotary (Denver) (dir. 1976-78, program chmn. 1978-81, pres. 1987-88), Eastmoor Swim and Tennis (Denver) (dir. 1973-74, 78-80), Serra Internat. (pres. club 1984-85, dist. gov. 1986-87, internat. membership com. 1985—, internat. bd. trustees 1988—). Office: 1600 S Albion St Suite 1100 Denver CO 80222

BENT, MICHAEL WILLIAM, realty company executive, consultant; b. Oakland, Calif., Mar. 7, 1951; s. William Camp and Lorene (Howson) B.; 1 child, J. Donovan; m. Laurie Sue Nelson, Dec. 15, 1984. Student Rutgers U., 1969-72. Lic. real estate broker. V.p. Century 21 Kato & Co., Denver, 1979-80; broker, mgr. Century 21 Hasz & Assocs., Denver, 1980-81; sec. Metro Brokers, Inc., Denver, 1982-83, v.p., 1983-84; sec., dir. Metro Brokers Fin. Services, Inc., 1984-85, dir., 1984-86, Metro Brokers, Inc., 1982-85 ; broker, owner Metro Broker M. Bent Realty & Mgmt. Co., Aurora, Colo., 1981—; dir. Metro Brokers, Inc.; past pres. Country Club Real Estate, Inc. Com. chmn., Boy Scouts Am., 1987—. Mem. Denver Bd. Realtors, Aurora Bd. Realtors, Realtors Nat. Mktg. Inst., Internat. Assn. Fin. Planners (Cert. Comml. Investment Mem.). Republican. Roman Catholic. Club: Optimist of Heather Ridge, (pres. 1982-84). Home: 17096 E Dorado Circle Aurora CO 80015 Office: Metro Brokers/M Bent Realty & Mgmt Co 2260 S Xanadu Way Suite 390 Aurora CO 80014

BENTEL, DWIGHT, emeritus journalism educator; b. Walla Walla, Wash., Apr. 15, 1909; s. Joseph Eugene and Kate (Essler) B.; m. Edna Fuller, Mar. 28, 1934 (div. Apr. 1956); 1 son, David; m. Genieva Record, Sept. 8, 1959. A.B., Stanford U., 1934, A.M., 1935; Ed.D. (Henry W. Sackett scholar 1943), Columbia U., 1950. Newspaperman San Jose and San Francisco, 1928-34; founder, head dept. journalism and mass communications Calif. State U., San Jose, 1934-69; prof., Journalism Calif. State U., 1947—, distinguished prof., 1968-74, prof. emeritus, 1974—; Mem. staff div. of edn. Am. Mus. Natural History, N.Y.C., 1942-43; lectr. Coll. Notre Dame, Columbia, 1943; mem. editorial staff Editor & Publisher mag., 1944-45, edn. editor, 1946-62; co-founder, dir. San Jose Savs. & Loan Assn.; dir. Am. Bank & Trust Co. Contbr. publs. on newspaper industry and journalism, edn. Mem. Am. Council Edn. for Journalism, 1954-58, Am. Council Radio and TV Journalism, 1958-62. Dwight Bentel Hall of Journalism and Mass Communication named in his honor Calif. State U., San Jose, 1982. Mem. Am. Acad. Advt., Am. Soc. Journalism Sch. Adminstrs. (pres. 1949-50), Nat. Press Photographers Assn., Assn. Edn. in Journalism, Calif. Newspaper Pubs. Assn. (sec. central coast div. 1947—, sec., pres. 1960), Kappa Tau Alpha, Sigma Delta Chi. Home: 1729 Santa Barbara Dr San Jose CA 95112

BENTLEY, ALAN FRANK, astrophysicist, educator; b. Bennington, Vt., Oct. 9, 1932; s. Frank Wilcox and Mildred Irene (Carey) B.; m. Patricia Eileen Manley, Sept. 7, 1952; children: Laura, Rosanna, Brenda, Marcia, Matthew, Carl. BS cum laude, U. Vt., 1953; MS, NYU, 1968; PhD, U. Wyo., 1980. Design engr. Block Engring., Cambridge, Mass., 1962-64, sr. systems engr., 1970-76; sr. electro-optical engr. Perkin-Elmer Corp., Norwalk, Conn., 1964-70; research assoc. U. Wyo., Laramie, 1976-80; prof. No. Ky. U., Highland Heights, 1980-82; prof. physics Ea. Mont. Coll., Billings, 1982—. Contbr. articles to profl. jours. USAF fellow, 1984; grantee NSF, USAF. Mem. Am. Astron. Soc. (Harlow Shapley lectr. 1984—), Astron. Soc. Pacific, Mont. Acad. Scis, Exptl. Aircraft Assn. (sec., treas., 1984-86, pres. 1986-88), Am. Indian Soc. Engrs. and Scientists, AAUP (sec. 1985-87), Pacific NW Assn. Coll. Physics (bd. dirs. 1988—), Sigma Xi. Republican. Lodge: Elks.

BENTLEY, CLARENCE EDWARD, savings and loan executive; b. Ranger, Tex., Oct. 9, 1921; s. Clarence Edward and Rosa Estelle (Bryant) B.; m. Gloria Gill, Oct. 9, 1943; children: Jon, Kitty, Perry (dec.). Student, McMurry Coll., Abilene, Tex., 1939-42. Pres. Abilene Savs. Assn., 1944-77, Southwestern Group Fin. Co., Houston, 1976-77; pres. United Savs. Assn. Tex., Houston, 1977-80; chmn. bd. United Savs. Assn. Tex., 1980-85; dir., chmn. bd. Sandia Fed. Savs. & Loan, Albuquerque, 1986—; chmn. bd. dirs. United Fin. Mortgage Co., Dallas, United Fin. Group, Inc., Houston, 1980-86; bd. dirs. Kaneb Services Inc., Investors Mortgage Ins. Co., Boston, Fed. Home Loan Bank Little Rock. Contbr. articles to profl. publns. Pres. Abilene Indsl. Found., 1970, United Fund Abilene, 1962; mem. bd. Tex. State Hosps., 1962-64; mem. Tex. Fin. Commn., 1964-76, chmn., 1971. Served with USAAF, 1942-43. Recipient Outstanding Citizen award City of Abilene, 1964, Disting. Alumnus award McMurry Coll., 1971. Mem. Nat. Savs. and Loan League (pres. 1970-71), Tex. Savs. and Loan League (pres. 1970-71), Assn. Thrift Holding Cos. (chmn. bd. 1985-87), Abilene C. of C. (pres. 1964). Episcopalian. Club: Abilene Country (pres. 1951). Home: 52 Rue Maison Abilene TX 79605 Office: 3030 LBJ Freeway Suite 1400 Dallas TX 75234

BENTLEY, ROBERT CLYDE, architect; b. Livermore, Calif., July 5, 1926; s. Clyde Edward and Doris Katherin (Taylor) B.; m. Patricia Ann Grant, Sept. 10, 1948 (div. 1974); children—Grant Patrick, Linda, William Clyde; m. Elizabeth Aldrin Hench, June 7, 1974; stepchildren—Anders Hench, Colleen Hench, Carolyn Hench. B.A., U. Calif.-Berkeley, 1950; grad. Anthony Sch. Real Estate, 1982. Registered architect, Calif. Pvt. practice architecture, Los Altos, Calif., 1959—; mng. employee Advanced Interiors, San Jose, 1982-83; interior contractor Red Lion Inn, San Jose, 1982-83; Marriott Hotel, San Jose, 1982-83; architect's rep. San Jose Airport, 1980-81; realtor El Monte Properties, Los Altos, 1980—; asst. city planner Yakima Wash., 1958-59; dir. Bentley Engrs., 1950-75; elec. takeoff estimator of tube Bay Area Rapid Transit, San Francisco, 1967-68. Mem. housing code commn. Yakima City Planning Dept., 1959. Served to lt. (j.g.) USNR, 1944-45. Recipient Spark Plug award, Oakland Jaycees, 1965. Mem. Calif. Council of AIA, Calif. Architects, Los Altos C. of C. Democrat. Unitarian. Clubs: Phi Delta Theta. Home: 595 Jay St Los Altos CA 94022 Office: 745 Distel Dr Los Altos CA 94022

BENTLEY, WILLIAM ARTHUR, engineer, consultant in electro-optics; b. Jan. 21, 1931; s. Garth Ashley and Helen (Dieterle) B.; m. Erika Bernadette Seuthe, Nov. 17, 1956; children: David Garth, Barbara Elizabeth. BS in Physics, Northwestern U., 1952; MS in Systems Engring., Calif. State U., Fullerton, 1972. Engr. N. Am. Aircraft, Downey, Calif., 1956-69; chief engr. Fairchild Optical, El Segundo, Calif., 1969-72; project engr. Hughes Aircraft Co., Culver City, Calif., 1972-75; sr. staff engr. Advanced Controls, Irvine, Calif., 1975-80; prin. Instrument Design Cons., Stanta Ana, Calif., 1978—; mgr. mfg. research and devel. Xerox Electro-Optical, Pomona, Calif., 1980-83; cons. Kasper Industries, Sunnyvale, Calif., 1977-78, Litton Industries, Woodland Hills, Calif., 1978, Lincoln Laser Co., Phoenix, 1983—, Coopervision, Irvine, 1984—, Triad Microsystems, 1985—. Patentee in field including interferometric lens assembly techniques, 1st automatic optical printed wiring board inspector. Served with U.S. Army, 1952-54. Mem. Soc. Photo-optical Instrumentation Engrs., Optical Soc. Am., Mensa. Democrat. Unitarian. Home: 170 The Masters Circle Costa Mesa CA 92627 Office: Instrument Design Cons PO Box 2203 Santa Ana CA 92707

BENTON, DONALD STEWART, publishing company executive; b. Marlboro, N.Y., Jan. 2, 1924; s. Fred Stanton and Agnes (Townsend) B.; B.A., Columbia U., 1947, J.D., 1949; LL.M., N.Y.U., 1953; student U. Leeds (Eng.), 1945. Admitted to N.Y. State bar, 1953; practiced in N.Y.C., 1953-56; atty. N.Y. State Banking Dept., 1954-55; v.p. Found. Press, Inc., Bklyn., 1957-60; exec. asst. to exec. v.p. N.Y. Stock Exchange, 1960-61; dir. reference book dept. and spl. projects editor Appleton Century Crofts, N.Y.C., 1962-71; sr. editor Matthew Bender & Co., Inc., N.Y.C., 1974-77; sr. legal editor Warren, Gorham & Lamont, Inc., N.Y.C., 1977—. Author: Federal Banking Laws, 3d edit., 1987. Real Estate Tax Digest, 1984, Criminal Law Digest, 3d edit., 1983, Modern Real Estate and Mortgage Checklists, 1979. Mem. Cresskill (N.J.) Zoning Bd. Adjustment, 1969-71, 82-83; 86—. Mem. Cresskill Planning Bd., 1971-74; councilman City of Cresskill, 1972-74. Served with AUS, 1943-46, 50-52. Decorated Bronze Star. Mem. Phi Delta Phi. Mem. Reformed Ch. in Am. Home: 117 Heatherhill Rd Cresskill NJ 07626 Office: Warren Gorham & Lamont Inc 1 Penn Plaza New York NY 10119

BENTON, NICHOLAS, theater producer; b. Boston, Oct. 18, 1926; s. Jay Rogers and Frances (Hill) B.; m. Kate Lenthal Bigelow, June 5, 1954; children: Frances Hill, Kate, Emily Weld, Louisa Barclay. Grad. Phillips Exeter Acad., 1945; A.B., Harvard, 1951. Promotion writer Life mag., N.Y.C., 1951-55, Fortune mag., 1955-56; staff writer Time Mag., 1956-57; advt. promotion mgr. Archtl. Forum, 1957-64; gen. promotion mgr. Time-Life Books, Alexandria, Va., 1965-68, public relations dir., 1968-83, v.p., 1977-83, lectr. pub. procedures course Radcliffe Coll., 1976-82; producing dir. Am. Kaleidoscope Theatre, 1983-85. Mem. Nat. Book Awards Com., 1971, co-chmn. Nat. Book Awards Week Com., 1975-79; vice chmn. Am. Book Awards, 1981-82. Author: A Benton Heritage, 1964; co-producer musical Salad Days, 1958, The Golden Age, 1984, The Perfect Party, 1986. Pres., E. 69th St. Assn., 1963-64; 1st v.p. Soc. Meml. Sloan-Kettering Cancer Center, 1963-64, asst. treas., 1964-66, treas., 1967-68; mem. exec. com. Friends of the Theatre Collection, Mus. of the City of N.Y.C., 1983-86, exec. com. 1984-87. Served with AUS, 1945-46. Mem. Pubs. Publicity Assn. (pres. 1970-71), New Eng. Historic Geneal. Soc. (trustee 1979-82, corr. sec. 1982-88, v.p. 1988—), N.Y. Geneal. and Biog. Soc., Assn. Am. Pubs. (freedom to read com. 1974-78, internat. freedom to pub. com. 1979-82), Soc. of Colonial Wars. Clubs: Harvard (bd. mgrs. 1971-73) (N.Y.C.); Bourne's Cove Yacht (Wareham, Mass.) (commodore, 1987-88). Home and Office: 129 E 82d St New York NY 10028

BENTON-BORGHI, BEATRICE HOPE, educational consultant; b. San Antonio, Nov. 7, 1946; d. Donald Francis and Beatrice Hope (Peche) Benton; A.B. in Chemistry, North Adams State Coll., 1968; M.Secondary Edn., Boston U., 1972; m. Peter T. Borghi, Aug. 12, 1980; children—Kathryn Benton Borghi, Sarah Benton Borghi. Tchr. chemistry Cathedral High Sch., Springfield, Mass., 1968-69; tchr. sci. and history Munich (W.Ger.) Am. High Sch., 1969-70; tchr. English, Tokyo, Japan, 1970-71; tchr. chemistry and sci. Marlborough (Mass.) High Sch., 1971-80; project dir., adminstr. ESEA, Marlborough Pub. Schs., 1976-77; project dir., proposal writer Title III, Title IX, U.S. Dept. Edn., 1975-76, 76-77; evaluation team New Eng. Assn. Schs. and Colls., 1974, 78; mem. regional dept. edn. com., 1977-78; ednl. cons., lectr., 1978—. Energy conservation rep. Marlborough's Overall Econ. Devel. Com., 1976; chmn. Marlborough's Energy Conservation Task Force, 1975; dir. Walk for Mankind, 1972; sec. Group Action for Marlborough Environment, 1975-76; bd. dirs. Girls Club, Marlborough, 1979; pres. Sisters, Inc., 1979-83. Mem. Council for Exceptional Children, Nat. Women's Health Network. Home and Office: 2449 Edington Rd Columbus OH 43221

BENTSEN, LLOYD, U.S. senator; b. Mission, Tex., Feb. 11, 1921; s. Lloyd M. and Edna Ruth (Colbath) B.; m. Beryl Ann Longino, Nov. 27, 1943; children: Lloyd M. III, Lan, Tina. J.D., U. Tex., 1942. Bar: Tex. 1942. Practice law McAllen, Tex., 1945-48; judge Hidalgo County, Tex., (hdqrs. Edinburg), 1946-48; mem. 80th-83d congresses from 15th Tex. Dist.; pres. Lincoln Consol., Houston, 1955-70; U.S. Senator from Tex. 1971—, chmn. senate fin. com.; mem. senate commerce, sci., transp. and intelligence, joint com. on taxation and congl. joint econ. com.; Democratic nominee for Vice Pres. U.S., 1988. Served to maj. USAAF, 1942-45. Decorated D.F.C., Air Medal with 3 oak leaf clusters. Home: Houston TX 77013 Office: 4026 Fed Bldg 515 Rusk St Houston TX 77002 also: 961 Fed Bldg Austin TX 78701 also: Earle Cabell Bldg Room 7C14 Dallas TX 75242 *

BENTZ, CLAUDE MARVIN, clinical psychologist, administrator; b. Long Beach, Calif., Feb. 21, 1929; s. Claude M. and Vilate (LeCheminant) B.; A.A., Compton City Coll., 1948; B.A., Brigham Young U., 1950; M.A., U. Utah, 1957; Ph.D., U.S. Internat. U., 1974; m. Arvilla Simpson, June 19, 1970 (dec. 1984); children—Dean, Vilate, Shelby; m. Janice Rushing, Apr. 11, 1987. Psychologist, counselor Lancaster Sch. Dist., 1957-60; clin. psychologist Pasadena (Calif.) Child Guidance Clinic, 1960-61; psychologist Kern County Sch., Bakersfield, Calif., 1961-64; coordinator guidance Supt. Schs. Office, Bakersfield, 1964-67 dir. guidance, 1967-79; staff psychologist Kern View Mental Health Center and Hosp., 1979, chief psychologist, 1979-80; psychol. cons. San Felipe Boys Home, 1969-78; pvt. practice as psychologist and marriage counselor, Bakersfield, 1961—. Tchr. Antelope Valley Coll., 1958-61, Fresno State Coll., Santa Barbara Extension, 1962-74, U. Calif. at Bakersfield, 1971—, Calif. Lutheran Coll., 1975. Vice-chmn. Kern County Human Resources Coordinating Council, 1969-80; pres. Kern County Mental Health Assn., 1971-72, chmn. mental health research com., 1965-71, 72-74; exec. council Bakersfield chpt. Big Bros. Am., 1968—; bd. dirs. Crises Center Hotline, 1970-80, Citizens Orgn. Against Drug Abuse, 1971-74; pres. Kern Child Abuse Prevention Counsel Inc., 1979-80; budget com. United Way, 1971—, allocation chmn., 1983—. Served to lt. U.S. Army, 1950-54. Mem. Am., Western, Calif., Kern County (past pres.) psychol. assns., Assn. Calif. Sch. Adminstrs. (adminstr. region II pupil personnel services 1971-73). Club: Elks. Home: 5207 Kent Dr Bakersfield CA 93306 Office: 3535 San Dimas Sq Suite 24 Bakersfield CA 93301

BENTZ, EDWARD JOSEPH, JR., energy, environment and transportation management consulting firm executive; b. N.Y.C., May 17, 1945; m. Carole. BS in Physics, Rensselaer Poly. Inst., 1966; vis. fellow Rockefeller Inst., 1966-67; MPhil., Yale U., 1969, PhD, 1971. Danmark-Amerika Fondet George C. Marshall fellow Neils Bohr Inst., Copenhagen, 1971-72; vis. fellow USSR Acad. Scis., 1972, mem. tech. staff David Sarnoff Research Center, RCA, Princeton, N.J., 1972-74; mem. policy staff EPA, Washington, 1974-77; Congl. fellow U.S. Senate com. Commerce, sci. and transp., Washington, 1976-77; dir. impact analysis Presidential-Congl. Nat. Transp. Policy Study Commn., Washington, 1977-79; exec. dir. Presidential-Congl. Nat. Alcohol Fuels Commn., Washington, 1979-80; pres. E.J. Bentz & Assocs., Inc., Springfield, Va., 1980—. appointed mem. Fairfax County Va. Wetlands Bd., 1986—, vice-chmn., 1988—. Author books; contbr. articles to profl. jours. Mem. N.Y. Acad. Scis., Transp. Research Bd. Va. Acad. Scis., Soc. Govt. Regulatory Economists, Sigma Xi, Sigma Pi Sigma. Office: EJ Bentz & Assocs Inc 7915 Richfield Rd Springfield VA 22153

BENVENUTO, GIUSEPPE MARINO, cardiologist; b. Copertino, Italy, June 11, 1955; s. Cosimo Benvenuto and Galignano Pasqualina; m. Carla Maria Battistelli, July 5, 1986. Degree in Medicine and Surgery, Med. U., Padua, Italy, 1980, cert. in cardiology, 1984, cert. in nutrition and dietetics, 1987. Resident div. cardiology Univ. Hosp., Padua, 1980-82, fellow, 1983; fellow Health Superior Inst., Rome, 1983; med. asst. cardiology div. Rovigo (Italy) Hosp., 1984-87; vice dir. Cardiology Service Hosp. Noventa Vicentina, Italy, 1988—; cons. Cardiology Found., Verbania, Italy, 1983-86. Mem. Internat. Soc. Cardiac Doppler, European Group Echocardiography, Italian Soc. Echocardiography, Italian Assn. Hosp. Cardiologists, Anti-Infarct Center of Rome. Home: Via A Meneghini 1, 35122 Padova Italy Office: Civic Hosp Cardiology Service, 36025 Noventa Vicentina Italy

BENYAMINA, MOHAMED, data processing executive; b. Beni-Hau, Tenes, Algeria, July 29, 1949; s. Djeloul and Fatma (Medjadji) B.; m. Aicha Ouchene, Feb. 18, 1953; children: Abdelkader-Nassim, Chahira, Nafissa, Mohamed-Mounir. Student, Algiers U., 1968-69, IBM Ednl. Ctr., Algiers, 1969-70, 71-73; FCE, U. Cambridge, Eng., 1982. Programmer Ministry of Fin., Algiers, Algeria, 1970-72; analyst-programmer Ministry of Agriculture, Algiers, Algeria, 1973-76; dept. head Buhlega Computer Services, Tripoli, Libya, 1977-79; project mgr. Abu-Dhabi (United Arab Emirates) Nat. Oil Co., 1979-82, 1983—; gen. sec. Labor Union Ministry of Agriculture, Algeria, 1974-76. Patentee in field. Mem. Assn. for Info. and Image Mgmt., Internat. Info. Congress, Inst. Profl. Mgrs. Club: Tourist (Abu-Dhabi). Home: PO Box 898, Abu-Dhabi United Arab Emirates Office: Abu-Dhabi Nat Oil Co, PO Box 898, Abu-Dhabi United Arab Emirates

BENYO, RICHARD STEPHEN, magazine editor, writer; b. Palmerton, Pa., Apr. 20, 1946; s. Andrew Joseph and Dorothy Rita (Herman) B.; m. Jill Wapensky, Apr. 29, 1972 (div. 1979). B.A. in English Lit., Bloomsburg (Pa.) State U., 1968. Mng. editor Times-News, Lehighton, Pa., 1968-72; editor Stock Car Racing mag., Alexandria, Va., 1972-77; sr. editor Stock Car Racing mag., 1977—; exec. editor Runner's World mag., Mountain View, Calif., 1977-84; editorial dir. Skier's mag. and Fit mag., Mountain View, 1980-84, Anderson World Books, Mountain View, 1980-84, Strength Tng. for Beauty mag., 1983-84; editor Corporate Fitness Report, Mountain View, 1980-84, Nat. Health & Fitness Report, 1982-84, Runner's World Quar., 1982-84; v.p. J.R. Anderson Enterprizes, Inc., 1982-84; pres., pub. Specific Publs., Inc., 1983—; fitness columnist San Francisco Chronicle, 1985—; columnist Sports Care and Fitness, 1988—; program dir. PTVC-TV, Palmerton, Pa., 1969-72. Author: The Grand National Stars, 1975, The Book of Richard Petty, 1976, Superspeedway, 1977, Return to Running, 1978, (with Rhonda Provost) The Indoor Exercise Book, 1980, (with Rhonda Provost) Advanced Indoor Exercise Book, 1981, (with Kym Herrin) Sexercise, 1981, Masters of the Marathon, 1983, (with Elaine LaLanne) Fitness After 50, 1986, (with Rhonda Provost) Feeling Fit in Your 40's, 1987, (with Elaine LaLanne), Dynastride!, 1988; editor: The Complete Woman Runner, 1978, Running for Everybody, 1981. Mem. racing panel of experts Union 76. Recipient 1st pl. award local column Pa. Newspaper Pubs. Assn., 1972; named Young Alumnus of Yr., Bloomsburg U., 1985. Mem. Am. Auto Racing Writers and Broadcasters Assn. (1st place award for tech. writing), Internat. Motor Press Assn., Athletic Congress, U.S. Ski Writers Assn., N.Y. Road Runners Club, Nat. Sportscasters and Sportswriters Assn., Track and Field Writers of Am., Internat. Sports Press Assn. Democrat. Roman Catholic. Home and Office: 107 Lilac Ln Saint Helena CA 94574

BEN-ZEEV, AARON, philosopher educator; b. Ein Hayam, Israel, July 30, 1949; s. Israel and Haika (Weinkrantz) B-Z.; m. Ruth Reichman, July 30, 1985; 1 child, Dean. BA, U. Haifa, Israel, 1975, MA with highest honors, 1978; PhD with honors, U. Chgo., 1981. Teaching asst. U. Haifa, 1975-78, lectr. philosophy, 1981-84, sr. lectr. philosophy, 1984—, chmn. dept. philosophy, 1986-88. Auhtor: Aristotle's On The Soul, 1989. Mem. Kibbutz Ein Carmel. Served to maj. Israeli army, 1968-72. Deutscher Akademescher Austauschdient scholar, 1976; Fulbright-Hays grantee, 1978; Rothschild fellow, 1980, Yigall-Allon Teaching fellow, 1981. Jewish. Home: Ein Carmel, Haifa 30860, Israel Office: U Haifa, Dept Philosophy, Haifa 31999, Israel

BERANEK, LEO LEROY, business and engineering consultant; b. Solon, Iowa, Sept. 15, 1914; s. Edward Fred and Beatrice (Stahle) B.; m. Phyllis Knight, Sept. 6, 1941 (dec. 11/7/82); children: James Knight, Thomas Haynes; m. Gabriella Sohn, Aug. 10, 1985. A.B., Cornell Coll., 1936, D.Sc. (hon.), 1946; M.S., Harvard U., 1937, D.Sc., 1940; D.Eng. (hon.), Worcester Poly. Inst., 1971; D.Comml. Sci. (hon.), Suffolk U., 1979; LL.D. (hon.), Emerson College, 1982; Dr. Pub. Service (hon.), Northeastern U., 1984. Instr. physics Harvard, 1940-41, asst. prof., 1941-43, dir. research on sound, 1941-45; dir. Electro-Acoustics and Systems Research Labs., 1945-46; assoc. prof. communications engring. MIT, 1947-58, lectr., 1958-81; tech. dir. Acoustics Lab., 1947-53; pres., dir., chief exec. officer Bolt Beranek & Newman, Cambridge, Mass., 1953-69; chief scientist Bolt Beranek & Newman, 1969-71, dir., 1953-84; pres., chief exec. officer, dir. Boston Broadcasters, Inc., 1963-79, chmn. bd., 1980-83; part-owner WCVB-TV, Boston, 1972-82; chmn. bd. Mueller-BBM GmbH, Munich, Germany, 1962-86; bd. dirs. Tech. Integration and Devel. Group, Inc., Billerica, Mass. Author: (with others) Principles of Sound Control in Airplanes, 1944, Acoustic Measurements, 1949, 2d edit., 1988, Acoustics, 1954, 2d edit., 1986, Music, Acoustics and Architecture, 1962; editor, contbr.: (with others) Noise Reduction, 1960, Noise and Vibration Control, 1971, 2d edit., 1988; editor: (with others) Noise Control mag, 1954-55; assoc. editor: (with others) Sound mag, 1961-63; mem. editorial bd.: (with others) Noise Control Engring, 1973-77; contbr. (with others) articles on acoustics, audio and TV communications systems to tech. publs. Mem. Mass. Gov.'s Task Force on Coastal Resources, 1974-77; charter mem. bd. overseers Boston Symphony Orch., 1968-80, chmn., 1977-80, trustee, 1977-87, v.p., 1980-83, chmn. bd. trustees, 1983-86, hon. chmn., 1987; mem. vis. com. Center Behavioral Scis., Harvard U., 1964-70, vis. com. biology and related research facilities, 1971-77, 86—, mem. vis. com. physics dept., 1983—, now bd. overseers univ.; mem. advisory com. mgmt. devel. Harvard Bus. Sch., 1965-71; mem. council for arts Mass. Inst. Tech., 1972—; pres. World Affairs Council Boston, 1975-78, vice chmn. bd., 1979-86; trustee Cornell Coll., 1955-71, Emerson Coll., 1973-79; bd. dirs. Opera Co. of Boston, pres., 1961-63, hon. chmn., 1987—; bd. dirs. Boston 200, 1975-77, United Way Mass. Bay, 1975-80, Flaschner Jud. Inst., 1977-81; mem. Mass. Commn. on Jud. Conduct, 1986—; chmn. Curtis-Saval Internat. Ctr., Boston, 1987—. Guggenheim fellow, 1946-47; recipient Presdl. certificate of merit, 1948; Cornell Coll. Alumni Citation, 1953; 1st Silver medal le Groupement des Acousticiens de Langue Francaise Paris, 1966; Abe Lincoln TV award So. Bapt. Conv., 1975; Media award NAACP, 1975; named Sta. WCRB Person of the Yr., 1987. Fellow Acoustical Soc. Am. (Biennial award 1944, exec. council 1944-47, v.p. 1949-50, pres. 1954-55, assoc. editor 1946-60, Wallace Clement Sabine Archtl. Acoustics award 1961, Gold medal award 1975), Nat. Acad. Engring. (dir. marine bd., com. pub. engring. policy, aeros. and space engring. bd.), Am. Acad. Arts and Scis., Am. Phys. Soc., AAAS, Audio Engring. Soc. (pres. 1967-68, Gold medal 1971, gov. 1966-71), IEEE (chmn. profl. group audio 1950-51); mem. Inst. Noise Control Engring. (charter pres. 1971-73, dir. 1973-75), Am. Standards Assn. (chmn. acoustical standards bd. 1956-68, dir. 1963-68), Mass. Broadcasters Assn. (dir. 1973-80, pres. 1978-79, Disting. Service award 1980), Boston Community Media Council (treas. 1973-76, v.p. 1976-77), Cambridge Soc. Early Music (pres. 1963-71, dir. 1961-79), Acad. Disting. Bostonians, Greater Boston C. of C. (dir. 1973-79, v.p. 1976-79, Disting. Community Service award 1980, 83), Phi Beta Kappa, Sigma Xi, Eta Kappa Nu. Episcopalian. Clubs: Mass. Inst. Tech. Faculty, St. Botolph, Harvard, City. Office: 975 Memorial Dr Suite 804 Cambridge MA 02138

BERARDI, RONALD STEPHEN, pathologist, educator; b. Rochester, Pa., Jan. 12, 1943; s. Desiderio John and Florence (Salvaggio) B.; m. Diane Lenore Wytaske, June 17, 1967; children: Lenore Christine, James Ronald, Anne-Marie. BS in Chemstry, U. Pitts., 1963; MD, Loyola U., Chgo., 1967. Diplomate Am. Bd. Pathology. Intern Presbyn.-St. Lukes Hosp., Chgo., 1967-68; resident in pathology Presbyn.-St. Lukes Hosp., Chgo., 1968-69, Malcolm Grow USAF Med. Ctr., Washington, 1969-71, New Eng. Deaconess Hosp., Boston, 1971-72, U. Pitts. Health Ctr. Hosp., 1972-73; Sarah Mellon Scaife fellow in immunopathology U. Pitts., 1973-74; assoc. pathologist Latrobe Area Hosp., Pa., 1974-80; chief pathologist, dir. labs., 1980—; co-dir. labs. Henry Clay Frick Community Hosp., Mt. Pleasant, Pa., 1974-80; assoc. instr. U. Ill., Chgo., 1967-69; teaching fellow U. Pitts., 1972-74, teaching faculty, 1974-76; instr. Thomas Jefferson Coll. Medicine, Phila., 1977—; med. dir. Sch. Med. Tech. Ind. U. Pa., 1980—; lab. insp. Coll. Am. Pathology, Chgo., 1980—; chmn. infection control com., tissue transfusion com., cancer registry, cost containment com. Latrobe Area Hosp., 1980—. Contbr. articles to profl. jours. Mem. Nat. Adv. Bd. Am. Security Council, Boston, 1985; mem. Rep. Presdl. Task Force, Washington, 1985-88; mem. Rep. Nat. Com., Washington, 1985. Senatorial scholar, 1961-63; mem. Rep. Senatorial Inner Circle, U.S. Senatorial Bus. Adv. Bd., 1988, state advisor to U.S. Congl. Adv. Bd.; U.S. Congressional Adv. Bd. (state advisor). Fellow Am. Soc. Clin. Pathologists, Coll. Am. Pathologists, U.S.-Can. Acad. Pathology Inc., Internat. Biographical Assn.; mem. Am. Assn. Blood Banks, AMA (Physicians Recognition award 1985), Am. Chem. Soc., N.Y. Acad. Scis., Internat. Platform Assn., Am. Biographical Inst. (disting. leadership award), Am. Inst. Chemists, Am. Med. Writers Assn., Westmoreland County Med. Soc. (editor bulletin), Phi Eta Sigma, Alpha Epsilon Delta. Roman Catholic. Clubs: Latrobe Country, Univ., U.S. Senatorial. Avocations: astronomy, golf, horseback riding, hunting, fishing. Home: 811 Spring St Latrobe PA 15650 Office: Latrobe Area Hosp W 2d Ave Latrobe PA 15650

BERAS ROJAS, OCTAVIO ANTONIO CARDINAL, former archbishop of Santo Domingo; b. El Seybo, Dominican Republic, Nov. 16, 1906; s. Octavio and Teresa (Rojas) B. Ordained priest Roman Catholic Ch.; pastor Cathedral of Santo Domingo; dir. Verdad Catolica Sem.; archbishop coadjutor of Santo Domingo, 1945-61, archbishop of Santo Domingo, 1961—; elevated to Sacred Coll. of Cardinals, 1976; founder Cath. Action, Santiago; pres. Tribunal; chancellor, then pro-vicar gen., Santo Domingo; sec.-gen. 1st Conf. Latin Am. Episcopate; mem. central commn. II Vatican Conf.; pres. Dominican Episcopal Conf., 1963-75. Office: Isabel La Catolica Esq, Pellerano Alfau Apartado 186, Santo Domingo Dominican Republic *

BERBARY, MAURICE SHEHADEH, physician, military officer, hosp. adminstr., educator; b. Beirut, Lebanon, Jan. 14, 1923; s. Shehadeh M. and Marie K. Berbary; came to U.S., 1945, naturalized, 1952; BA, Am. U., Beirut, 1943; MD, U. Tex., 1948; MA in Hosp. Adminstrn., Baylor U., 1970; diploma Army Command and Gen. Staff Coll., Leavenworth, Kan., 1963, Air Force Sch. Aerospace Medicine, 1964, Army War Coll., Carlisle, Pa., 1969; m. Bruennhild Hepp; children—Geoffrey Maurice, Laura Marie. Diplomate Am. Bd. obstetrics and gynecology. Intern, Parkland Meml. Hosp., Dallas, 1948-49, resident in obstetrics and gynecology, gen. surgery and urology, 1949-53; resident in obstetrics and gynecology Walter Reed Army Hosp., Washington, 1955-57; fellow in obstetric and gynecologic pathology Armed Forces Inst. Pathology, Washington, 1959-60; bd. obstetrics and gynecology, 1961;practice clin. medicine in obstetrics and gynecology, 1953—; capt. MC, U.S. Army, 1952, advanced through grades to col., 1968; chief dept. obstetrics and gynecology U.S. Army Hosp., Ft. Polk, La., 1957-59, Womack Army Hosp., Ft. Bragg, N.C., 1960-62; div. surgeon 1st. inf. div., Ft. Riley, Kans., 1963-64, 3d. Armored div., Germany, 1964-65; corps surgeon, V. Corps, Germany, 1965-67; corps surgeon 24th Army Corps, S. Vietnam Theater of Operation, 1970; comdr., hosp. adminstr. U.S. Army Hosp., Teheran, Iran, 1954-55; comdr. hosp. group complex, Vietnam, 1969-70; command surgeon U.S. Armed Forces Command and U.S. Army South, U.S. C.Z., Panama, 1970-73; comdr. 5th Gen. Hosp., U.S. Army, Stuttgart, West Germany, 1973-77, Munson Army Hosp., Ft. Leavenworth, Kans., 1977-81, sr. staff officer William Beaumont Army Med. Ctr., Ft. Bliss, Tex., 1981-83; ret., 1983; cons. health care adminstrn. and med.-legal affairs, 1984—; vis. lectr. obstetrics and gynecology pathology Duke U. Med. Center, Durham, N.C., 1960-62; clin. instr. obstetrics and gynecology U. Kans. Coll. of Medicine, Kansas City, 1963-80, clin. asst. prof. Dept. of Obstetrics & Gynecology, 1980—; instr. 5th Army NCO Acad., Fort Riley, Kans., 1963-64. Decorated Legion of Merit with three oak leaf clusters, Bronze Star medal, Army Commendation medal, Combat Air medal. Fellow A.C.S., Am. Coll. Obstetricians and Gynecologists; mem. AMA, Assn. of Mil. Surgeons, Soc. of U.S. Army Flight Surgeons, Am. Coll. Health Care Execs., Internat. Platform Assn., Am. Hosp. Assn., N.Y. Acad. Scis., Dallas County Med. Soc., Tex. State Med. Assn. Mason (32 deg.). Home and Office: 7923 Abramshire Ave Dallas TX 75231

BERBICH, ABDELLATIF, nephrologist, educator; b. Rabat, Morocco, May 17, 1934; s. Mohamed and Zaynab (Filal) B; m. Assia Chaouni Benabdallah; children: Omar, Ali, Mahdi. Doctorate degree, Sch. Medicine, Montpellier, France, 1961; specialty study in intensive care and nephrology, U. Paris, 1962-64. Head of reanimation Hôpital Avicenne, Rabat, Morocco, 1964—; prof. internal medicine Faculté de Medicine, Rabat, 1967—, dean, 1969-74, full prof., 1972—; chancellor Acad. Kingdom of Morocco, Rabat, 1980-82, permanent sec., 1982—; founder ctr. for hemodialysis through artificial kidney, 1976. Contbr. over 100 articles to profl. jours. Decorated Hassi Baida Mil. medal, Officer Order of Throne (Morocco), Officer Légion d'Honneur (France), Order Brit. Empire, Comdr. Royal Victorian Order (U.K.),. Mem. Moroccan Assn. Med. Scis., Internat. Assn. Urologists, High Commn. Accrediting Med. Specialists (chmn. 1972—), African Acad. Sci., Sci. Council French Speaking Med. Doctors. Office: Acad Kingdom of Morocco, Route des Zaers, BP 1380 Rabat Morocco

BERC, HAROLD THANE, lawyer; b. Chgo., Aug. 12, 1914; s. Abraham B. and Sarah D. (Glassberg) B.; m. Mary E. Amtman, June 21, 1938 (dec.). Student Northwestern U., 1934; J.D., DePaul U., 1937. Bar: Ill. 1937. Sole practice, Chgo., 1937—; of counsel Carroll, Sain and Epstein, Ltd., Chgo., 1975-87; participant panel and TV program in field. Spl. counsel to com. on cultural and econ. devel. City of Chgo., 1971-73; pres. local Cancer Research Founds., 1947-52; mem. exec. com. Citizens of Greater Chgo., 1978; U.S. rep. to gen. assemblies World Vets. Fedn., 1956-67. Served to lt. comdr. USNR, 1942-53; PTO. Mem. ABA, Ill. Bar Assn., Chgo. Bar Assn., 7th Fed. Circuit Bar Assn., World Peace Through Law Ctr. (charter), Am. Arbitration Assn. (arbitrator), Decalogue Soc. Lawyers (pres. 1970-71), Chgo.: Pres. Vets. Assn. (counsel), Am. Acad. Polit. Sci., U.S. Naval Inst., Navy League U.S., Naval Hist. Found., UN Assn. (v.p. Ill. 1970), Chgo. Press Vets. Assn. (bd. dirs., counsel), AMVETS (nat. comdr. 1959-60), Chgo. Maritime Soc., USS Chgo. Found. (charter; v.p. 1985). Clubs: City (pres. 1968-70), Chgo. Press (charter), Northwestern (Chgo.); Internat. Initiated legis. to complete U.S.S. Arizona Meml., Pearl Harbor, 1960. Probate, Real property, General corporate. Home: 2850 N Sheridan Rd Chicago IL 60657 Office: 55 E Monroe St Chicago IL 60603

BERDAHL, CLARENCE ARTHUR, educator; b. Baltic, S.D., June 14, 1890; s. Anders J. and Karen (Otterness) B.; A.B., St. Olaf Coll. 1914, LL.D., 1958; A.M., U. S.D., 1917, LL.D., 1961; Ph.D. (fellow), U. Ill., 1917-20; m. Evelyn Tripp, June 9, 1926. Clk. archives div. War Dept., Washington, 1914-15; asst. in periodicals div. Library of Congress, 1916; instr. polit. sci. U. Ill., 1920-22, asso., 1922-25, asst. prof., 1925-29, asso. prof., 1929-30, prof., 1930-61, prof. emeritus dept. polit sci., 1961—, chmn. div. social scis., 1935-39, chmn. dept. polit. sci., 1942-48; tchr. summers U. Tex., 1920, Tulane U., 1921, Ohio State U., 1923, U. Colo., 1928, Syracuse U., 1929, Columbia U., 1934, Stanford U., 1950; acting mng. editor Am. Polit. Sci. Rev., 1923; lectr. L'Institut Universitaire de Hautes Etudes Internationales, Geneva, 1932; vis. prof. govt. So. Ill. U., 1958-67; vis. prof. polit. sci. U. Del., 1965; chmn. bd. editors Ill. Studies in Social Scis., 1941-52; cons. U.S. Dept. State 1942-45; on London staff Office Strategic Services, 1944; mem. Internat. Secretariat, UN Conf., San Francisco, 1945; adv. com. on fgn. relations Dept. State, 1957-64, chmn., 1963-64, cons. hist. office, summer 1961; mem. exec. com. Commn. To Study Orgn. of Peace, 1953—; mem. European Conf. Tchrs. Internat. Law and Relations, Carnegie Endowment for Internat. Peace, summer 1926. Served in inf. U.S. Army, 1918. Social Sci. Research Council grantee for study abroad, 1931-32. Mem. Am. Polit. Sci. Assn. (exec. council 1932-35, 3d v.p. 1939, 2d v.p. 1944), Norwegian-Am. Hist. Assn., Am. Soc. Pub. Adminstrn. (council 1944-47), Ill. Hist. Soc., Midwest Polit. Sci. Assn. (pres. 1957-58), Am. Soc. Internat. Law (exec. council 1939-42, 43-46, 52-54), Fgn. Policy Assn., Soc. Advancement of Scandinavian Study, Geneva Research Center (adv. com. 1932-36), Conf. Tchrs. Internat. Law and Related Subjects (exec. com. 1933-42, 47-50), Internat. Studies Assn. (adv. com. 1965-69), Phi Beta Kappa (book award com. Ralph Waldo Emerson award 1966-68). Clubs: Univ., Cosmos (Washington). Author or co-author books including: War Powers of the Executive in the United States, 1921; The Policy of the United States with Respect to the League of Nations, 1932; Aspects of American Government, 1950; Toward a More Responsible Two-Party System, 1950; Presidential Nominating Politics, 1952; also articles. Home: Clark-Lindsey Village 101 W Windsor Rd Apt 4105 Urbana IL 61801

BERDING, HELMUT, historian, educator; b. Quakenbruck, Germany, Sept. 21, 1930; s. Wilhelm and Anna (Ostendorf) B.; m. Elli Piotrowski, Apr. 30, 1963; children: Dietrich, Susanne. Dr. phil., U. Cologne, Fed. Republic Germany, 1969; habilitation, U. Cologne, 1972. Asst. prof. U. Cologne, 1969-72; prof. history U. Giessen, Fed. Republic Germany, 1972—; vis. prof. Ecole des Hautes Etudes en Scis. Social, Paris, 1985-86. Author: Rationalismus und Mythos, 1969, Napoleonische Herrschaftspolitik, 1972, Moderner Autisemitismus in Deutschland, 1988; co-editor rev. Geschichte und Gesellschaft, 1972—, book collection Kritische Studien zur Geschichte, 1972—. Home: Birkenweg 40, D6301 Giessen-Wettenberg 3 Federal Republic of Germany Office: U Giessen, Ludwigstrasse 23, D6300 Giessen Hesse Federal Republic of Germany

BERECZ, FRIGYES, Hungarian government official; b. Budapest, Hungary, 1933. Grad., Tech. U., Budapest, 1964. Mem. Hungarian Socialist Workers' Party, 1962—, mem. cen. com., 1980; dept. leader, dir. Beloiannis Telecommunications Works, gen. mgr., 1981; dep. premier Hungary Council of Ministers, Budapest, 1987; minister industry Hungary, 1988—. Served with the Hungarian Armed Forces, 1949. Address: Ministry Industry, Budapest Hungary *

BEREGI, EDIT, physician; b. Brasso, Hungary, Mar. 3, 1926; d. Miklós and Ilona (Róth) B.; m. István Földes; children: István, Éva. MD, Med. U., Hungary, 1950, postgrad. specialization in pathology, 1956; C.M.Sc., Hungarian Acad. Sci., 1956, D.M.Sc., 1969. Asst. dept. pathology Med. U., Budapest, Hungary, 1950-53, 56-60, dir. research dept. gerontology, 1961-78, prof., dir. Gerontology Ctr., 1978—; head physician dept. pathology Semmelweis Hosp., Budapest, 1960-76; cons. on aging UN Network on Aging, Budapest, 1983-87. Author five books; contbr. numerous articles to profl. jours. Mem. Verzár Award Com., 1974—, Sandoz Found. for Gerontology Research, 1986—. Recipient Karger prize, 1970; Hungarian Acad. Sci. scholar, 1953-56. Mem. Fedn. Internat. Assns. Personnes Agées (sci. com. 1982—), Internat. Ctr. for Social Gerontology (bd. dirs. 1976—), Internat. Fedn. on Aging (exec. com. 1985—), Internat. Psychogerontol. Assn. (exec. com. 1985—). Home: Nemetvölgyi ut 69/b, 1124 Budapest Hungary Office: Gerontology Ctr, Med Univ, Somogyi Béla u 33., 1085 Budapest Hungary

BERENATO, ANTHONY FRANCIS, financial executive; b. Phila., Dec. 3, 1922; s. Frank A. and Eleanor A. (Siderio) B.; m. Dena Marie Marchione, Sept. 5, 1946; children—Anthony F., Mark Anthony. B.S. in Econs., Villanova U., 1949; postgrad., Am. U., Biarritz, France, 1945-46. C.P.A., Pa. Ptnr. Steinberg, Spiegel and Berenato, Springfield, Pa., 1956—; pres. Roger Fin. Corp., Phila., 1961-63, Sure Loan Corp., Phila., 1961-65, Cobbs Fla. Cupboard Inc., Bala Cynwyd, Pa., 1965-67, Phila. Arena Corp., 1961-65; chmn. Crescent Iron Works, Phila., 1974-86; chmn., chief exec. officer Custom Art Metals, Inc., Barrington, N.J., 1967—; founder, chmn. Crescent Cab Co., Phila.; founder, chmn., pres., chief exec. officer Custom Art Metals Puerto Rico Inc., 1987—. Trustee Anthony F. and Dena Marie Berenato Charitable Trust. Served with U.S. Army, 1942-49, ETO. Fellow Am. Inst. Mgmt., Navy League of U.S. (life member), Pa. Soc., Am. Inst. CPA's, Pa. Inst. CPA's, U.S. Naval Inst. (life), Am. Sec. Council. Republican. Roman Catholic. Clubs: Bala Golf (treas. 1974-76); Rio Mar Country (P.R.); Sands Country, Rolling Green Golf, Hamilton. Home: 411 Schollar Ln Springfield PA 19064 Office: Custom Art Metals Inc 181 E Gloucester Pike Barrington NJ 08007

BERENBERG, DANNY BOB, restaurateur; b. Mpls., Sept. 10, 1944; s. Morris and Theresa Clara B.; m. Christina Ann Thompson, Sept. 10, 1977; children—Jake Robert, Jena Thompson. B.A., U. Minn., 1966; J.D., 1970. Bar: Minn. 1970, U.S. Supreme Ct. 1976. Mem. firm Schermer, Schwappach, Borkon & Ramstead, Mpls., 1970-75; mgr. Lincoln Dels Restaurants, Bloomington, Minn., 1975-77, sr. exec., 1981—; vice chmn. Lincoln Baking Co., 1981—, Lincoln Dels Inc., 1981—. Founder Kaiser Roll Found. and Kaiser Roll, wheelcair and able-bodied race; bd. dirs. Bloomington Hospitality Assn., A.M. Miller & Assocs., Inc., Minn. chpt. U.S. Olympic Com., 1985—, Shattuck Sch., chmn. devel. com.; founder S.W. Hospitality Assn.; founder, pres., bd. dirs. 494 Ministry, 1982—, Cancer Kids Found., 1985—; mem. Minn. Conv. Facility Commn., 1984—, Minn. Internat. Trade Commn., 1984—. Served to 1st lt. AUS, 1968. Named Bloomington Man of Yr., Bloomington mag. 1982, Small Bus. of Yr. award, 1982; recipient Teamsters Law Enforcement Recognition award, 1982, merit award Minn. N.G., 1982; Omar Bonderud-Human Rights award City of Bloomington, 1983, Minn. Human Rights award, 1985, Good Neighbor award WCCO, 1986, Disting. Community Citizen award March of Dimes, 1986. Mem. Conv. Bur. (dir.), Minn. Restaurant Assn., Hennepin County Bar Assn., Minn. Bar Assn., Norwegian Home Guard Friends (founder). Jewish. Club: U. Minn. Touchdown (v.p.).

BEREND, DANIEL, mathematics scientist, educator; b. Kfar-Saba, Israel, July 12, 1954; s. Joseph and Lea Tova (Klein) B.; m. Tsafrira Weisenstern, Mar. 21, 1977; children: Judith, Orith, Hagai. BS, Tel-Aviv U., 1973, MA, 1975; PhD, Hebrew U., Jerusalem, 1982. Reader Tel-Aviv U., 1972-73, research asst., 1973; teaching asst. Hebrew U., Jerusalem, 1977-82; Hedrick asst. prof. U. Calif., Los Angeles, 1982-85; asst. prof. Ben-Gurion U., Beer-Sheva, Israel, 1985—. Contbr. articles to profl. jours. Served with Israeli mil., 1974-76. Grantee NSF, 1984-85, 85-86, Binat. Sci. Found., Israel-

U.S.A., 1987—, Israel Acad. Sci., 1987—; Rothschild fellow, Israel-France, 1982-83, 83-84. Mem. Israel Math. Union, Am. Math. Soc. Jewish. Office: Ben Gurion U, Dept Math, 84105 Beer-Sheva Israel

BEREND, IVAN T., economics educator; b. Budapest, Hungary, Dec. 11, 1930; s. Mihaly and Elvira (Gellei) B.; m. Rose Berend, Jan. 23, 1953; children—Zsuzsa, Nora. Ph.D., Karl Marx U. Econs., Budapest, 1951; Ph.D., L. Eotvos U. Faculty of Philosophy, Budapest, 1951-53. Asst. prof. Karl Marx U. Econs., 1953-60, assoc. prof., 1960-64, prof., 1964—, head dept. econ. history, 1967—, dir. Ctr. on East-Central Europe, 1981-85; rector Karl Marx U. Econs., 1973-79. Author: A Century of Economic Development, 1974, Italian edit., 1976; Economic Development of East Central Europe in the 19th and 20th Centuries, 1974, 2d edit., 1976, Japanese edit., 1978, Italian edit., 1978; East Central Europe in the 19th and 20th Centuries, 1977; The European Periphery and Industrialization 1780-1914, 1982; Maison des Sciences de l'Homme, 1982; Akademiai Kiado, 1982; Underdevelopment and Economic Growth, Studies in Hungarian Social and Economic History, 1979; The Decades of Crisis, An Interpretation of Interwar East Central European Economic Social Political Ideological and Cultural History, 1982, The Crisis Zone of Europe, 1986. All Souls Coll. fellow, 1980; Wilson Ctr. fellow, 1982-83. Mem. Hungarian Acad. Scis. (pres. 1985—), Royal Hist. Soc. (corr.), Internat. Econ. History Assn. (v.p.). Home: 13 Zsombolyai St, 1113 Budapest Hungary Office: Hungarian Acad Scis, 9 Roosevelt Sq, 1051 Budapest Hungary

BERENGO-GARDIN, GIANNI, photographer; b. Santa Margherita Ligure, Italy, Oct. 10, 1930; m. Caterina Stiffoni, 1957; children—Alberto, Susanna. Ed. Liceo Scientifico, Venice, Italy, until 1950. With tourist industry, Paris, Venice, 1950-60; photographer with La Gondola group of photographers, Venice, 1954; free-lance photojournalist, Venice, 1960-64, Milan, Italy, 1964—; founder-mem. Il Ponte group of photographers, Venice, 1958; one-man shows: Galleria Il Diaframma, Milan, 1968, (retrospective), 1972, 78, Napoli '81, Naples, 1981, Fotografi Centrum, Stockholm, Palazzo Stelline, Milan, Incontro Rimini, Rimini, Italy, 1983, FNAC Galerie, Paris, Bund Freischaffender Fotodesigner, Dusseldorf, 1984, Palazzo Dugnani, Milan, 1985; group shows include: Internat. Mus. Photography, Rochester, N.Y., 1965, Expo '67, Montreal, Que., Can., 1967, Galleria Il Diaframma, 1968, Victoria and Albert Mus., London (travelled to Nat. Gallery, Edinburgh, Scotland, Ulster Mus., Belfast, and Nat. Mus. Wales, Cardiff 1976), 1975, Biennale, Venice, 1976, Venezia '79, Venice, 1979, Palazzo Fortuny, Venice, 1980, Pinacoteca Provinciale, Bari, Italy, 1981, Galleria d'Arte Moderna, Bologna, Italy, 1985; represented in permanent collections: Università di Pisa (Italy), Bibliotheque Nationale, Paris, Mus. Modern Art, N.Y.C., Internat. Mus. Photography at George Eastman House, Rochester, N.Y., Mus. of Aesthetic Art, Beijing; photographer books: (text by Giorgio Bassani and Mario Soldati) Venise des Saisons, 1965; Toscana, 2 vols., 1966; (with introduction by Giorgio Soavi) Viaggio in Toscana, 1967; (with Introduction by Cesare Colombo) L'Occhio come Mestiere, 1970; Francia, 1975; Grecia, 1976; (with Cesare Zavattini) Un Paese, Venti Anni Dopo, 1976; England, Wales and Scotland, 1977; Dentro le Case, 1977; Dentro il Lavoro, 1978; Case Contadine, 1979; India, 1980; Spazi dell'Uomo, 1980, (with Antonio Romagnino and Magda Arduino) Cagliari, Marina, 1981; (text by Giorgio Soavi) Venezia, 1981; Germania, 1981; Scandinavia, 1983; Archeologia Industriale, 1983; I Navigli, 1984; Il Mondo, 1985; Veneto, 1985; Roma, 1986; Toscana, 1986. Recipient Artist award Internat. Fedn. Photog. Art, 1957. Office: Via San Michele del Carso 21, I-20144 Milan Italy *

BERENZWEIG, JACK CHARLES, lawyer; b. Bklyn., Sept. 29, 1942; s. Sidney A. and Anne R. (Dubowe) B.; m. Susan J. Berenzweig, Aug. 8, 1968; children—Mindy, Andrew. B.E.E., Cornell U., 1964; J.D., Am. U., 1968. Bar: Va. 1968, Ill. 1969. Examiner U.S. Pat. Off., Washington, 1964-66; pat. adviser U.S. Naval Air Systems Command, Washington, 1966-68; ptnr. William Brinks Hofer Gilson & Lione Ltd. and predecessor firm, Chgo., 1968—. Editorial staff Am. U. Law Rev., 1966-68; contbr. articles to profl. jours. Mem. Chgo. Bar Assn., Ill. State Bar Assn., ABA, Bar Assn. 7th Fed. Cir., Va. State Bar, U.S. Trademark Assn. (bd. dirs. 1983-85), Delta Theta Phi. Club: Meadow (Rolling Meadows, Ill.). Home: 4119 Terramere Ave Arlington Heights IL 60004 Office: One IBM Plaza Suite 4100 Chicago IL 60611

BERES, MARY ELIZABETH, management educator, organizational consultant; b. Birmingham, Mich., Jan. 19, 1942; d. John Charles and Ethel (Belenyesi) B. B.S., Siena Heights Coll., Adrian, Mich., 1969; Ph.D, Northwestern U., 1976. Joined Dominican Sisters, 1960; tchr., St. Francis Xavier Sch., Medina, Ohio, 1962-64, St. Edward Sch., Detroit, 1964-67; tchr. Our Lady of Mt. Carmel Sch., Temperance, Mich., 1967-69, asst. prin., 1968-69; tchr. math. St. Ambrose High Sch., Detroit, 1969-70; vis. instr. Cornell U., 1973-74; assoc. prof. orgn. behavior Temple U., Phila., 1974-84; assoc. prof. mgmt. Mercer U. Atlanta, 1984—; cons. in field. Contbr. chpts. to books; organizer of symposia in areas of corp. leadership and cross-cultural communication. Bd. trustees Adrian Dominican Ind. Sch. System (Mich.), 1971-79; bd. dirs. Ctr. for Ethics and Social Policy, Phila., 1980-84; mem. Atlanta Clergy and Laity Concerned, 1986—; mem. Econ. Pastoral Implementation Com. of Archdiocese of Atlanta, 1988—. Recipient Legion of Honor membership Chapel of the Four Chaplains, Phila., 1982; Disting. Teaching award Lindback Found., 1982, Cert. for Humanity, Mercer U., 1985; mem. program planning com. of interdepartmental group in bus. adminstrn. U. Ctr. in Ga., 1987—, chair, 1988—. Mem. Acad. Mgmt., Indsl. Relations Research Assn., Acad. Internat. Bus. (program com. southeast U.S. region 1987, chairperson mgmt. track 1988), The So. Mgmt. Assn., So. Ctr. Internat. Studies, Nat. Assn. Female Execs. Democrat. Roman Catholic. Office: Mercer U Sch Bus and Econs 3001 Mercer University Dr Atlanta GA 30341

BERESFORD, BRUCE, film director; b. Sydney, New South Wales, Australia, Aug. 16, 1940; s. Leslie and Lona (Warr) B.; m. Rhoisin Patricia Harrison, 1965; children: Benjamin, Cordella, Adam; m. Virginia Patricia Mary Duigan, 1985. BA, Sydney U., 1961. Films officer Brit. Film Inst., London, 1965-70; film advisor Arts Council of Great Britain, London, 1967-70. Dir. films Dons Party, 1976 (Best Dir. award Australian Film Inst.), The Getting of Wisdom, 1977, Money Movers, 1978, The Club, 1980, Tender Mercies, 1981, Puberty Blues, 1982, King David, 1984; dir., writer: Breaker Morant, 1980, Fringe Dwellers, 1985, Crimes of the Heart, 1986, (segment) Aria, 1988; producer, dir.: The Adventures of Barry McKenzie, 1972, Barry McKenzie Holds His Own, 1974. Mem. Dirs. Guild U.S.A. Office: care Leonard Hirshan William Morris Agy 151 El Camino Dr Beverly Hills CA 90212 also: care Cameron's Mgmt, 120 Victoria St, King Cross NSW 2011, Australia *

BERESFORD-HILL, PAUL VINCENT, headmaster; b. Dublin, Ireland, May 15, 1949; s. Francis John and Alexandra (de La Poer Beresford) H.; came to U.S., 1974, naturalized, 1978; Cert. in Edn., B.Ed., Oxford (Eng.) U., 1971; M.A., New Sch., 1979; m. Kathryn Elizabeth Ernyei, Apr. 11, 1976; 1 son, Christopher Tristram. Gov., Milton Keynes' Coll. Edn. (U.K.), 1969-71; curriculum co-ordinator Buckinghamshire Edn. Authority, Milton Keynes, Eng., 1971-74; lectr. Bletchley (Eng.) Coll. of Further Edn., 1972-74; headmaster Anglo-Am. Internat. Sch., N.Y.C., 1974—; pres. bd. dirs. Am. Home Study Inst., 1981—; dir. Wolsey Hall Oxford, N.Am. Ltd., 1981—; mem. grad. faculty New Sch. Social Research, 1979; pres. GAP Activity Project Inc., 1985—; chmn. Mountbatten Internship Program, 1985—. Mem. edn. com. Brit. Council Chs., 1970-74; bd. dirs. Internat. Baccalaureate N.Am. Inc., 1979—, Riverside Shakespeare Co., N.Y.C., 1984-87, Malignant Hyperthermia Assn. U.S., 1984—; vice chmn. Prew Sch. Bd. Trustees, Sarasota, 1987—, Internat. Sch. Found., London, 1984—; chmn. bd. dirs. Am. Friends of Shaftesbury Homes and Arethusa, 1987—; founder, mem. English speaking union U.S. Nat. Shakespeare Recitation Competition; founder, chmn. N.Y.C. Coalition Concerned Students. Fellow Royal Anthrop. Inst. (U.K.), Coll. Preceptors; mem. Royal Soc. Lit., Guild Ind. Schs. (bd. dirs. 1985—), European Council Internat. Schs., Oxford Union Soc., English-Speaking Union, St. George's Soc., Brit.-Am. C. of C., Brit. Schs. and Univs. Club N.Y. (dir.). Roman Catholic. Clubs: Metropolitan (N.Y.C.); Carlton (London). Home: 21 Sprain Rd Hartsdale NY 10530 Office: Anglo-Am Internat Sch 18 W 89th St New York NY 10024

BERESTON, EUGENE SYDNEY, dermatologist; b. Balt., Feb. 21, 1914; s. Arthur and Sarah Bertha (Hillman) B.; m. Marion Ableman, Jan. 15, 1942 (dec. May 1975); children: Linda Bereston Katz, David, Michael; m. Bertha G. Kaufman, June 7, 1980; stepchildren: Felix Kaufman, Bruce Kaufman. A.B., Johns Hopkins U., 1933; M.D., U. Md., 1937; M.Sc., U. Pa., 1945, D.Sc., 1955. Diplomate Am. Bd. Dermatology. Intern Meml. Hosp., Johnstown, Pa., 1937-38, Mercy Hosp., Balt., 1938-39; resident in dermatology U. Pa., Phila., 1939-40, Montefiore Hosp., N.Y.C., 1940-41; practice medicine specializing in dermatology Balt., 1946—; faculty U. Md., 1946—, prof. medicine in dermatology, 1972—; instr. dermatology Johns Hopkins U., 1946-60; chief dermatology Mercy Hosp., 1968—; part-time chief dermatology VA Hosp., Washington, 1977-83; cons. dermatology VA Hosp. Balt., 1951-76, Spring Grove State Hosp., 1952-82. Bd. dirs., chmn. Religious Sch., Temple Oheb Shalom, 1960-72, trustee, 1977-80. Served to maj. M.C. AUS, 1941-46, PTO. Recipient research grant U.S. Army, 1951-57, award Ner Israel Rabbinical Coll., 1970. Fellow ACP, Am. Acad. Dermatology, Royal Soc. Health (Eng.); mem. AMA, Am. Legion (comdr. 1971-73), Dermatology Found., Md. Dermatol. Soc., Royal Soc. Medicine (affiliate), Md., Balt. City med. socs. Clubs: Civitan (Balt.) (dir. 1964-78), Johns Hopkins (Balt.); Suburban Country, University. Home: 7 Slade Ave Apt 221 Baltimore MD 21208 Office: 22 E Eager St Baltimore MD 21202

BEREZANSKY, RICHARD FABIAN, transportation executive; b. New Brunswick, N.J., Apr. 10, 1948; s. Nicholas Peter and Lillian Catherine Berezansky; m. Donna Milchanoski, June 12, 1971; children: Nicholas A. Sr., Christopher. BS in Mgmt., Embry Riddle U., Daytona Beach, Fla., 1970. Cert. hazard control mgr., safety exec. and specialist. Sr. loss control rep. Allstate Ins. Co., Murray Hills, N.J., 1971-73; dir. safety ins. and claims Hermann Forwarding Co., New Brunswick, 1973-75; dir. safety and security Tose Inc., Bridgeport, Pa., 1975-76; dir. safety, security and claims William H.P. Inc./Burgmeyer, Phila., 1976-79; mgr. safety distbn. systems div. Ryder Systems Inc., Miami, Fla., 1979-86; dir. safety Scheduled Truckways, Rogers, Ark., 1986-88; ops. mgr. Rollins Transpn. Services, Teterboro, N.J., 1988—. CPR, 1st aid instr. Am. Heart Assn., ARC; dist. chmn. N.J. First Aid Council, 1977-79. Mem. Am. Soc. Safety Engrs., World Safety Orgn. (internat. bd. hazard control mgrs.), Am. Soc. Indsl. Security, Nat. Fire Protection Assn., Nat. Assn. Chiefs of Police, Am. Trucking Assn. (safety planning com. pvt. carrier conf. and common carrier conf.). Republican. Roman Catholic.

BEREZIN, ALEXANDRE, surgeon; b. Paris, Oct. 1, 1927; s. Berezin Simon and Fanny (Portnoi) B.; m. Nicole Lugan, Dec. 7, 1976; m. Denise Duval, June 6, 1956; children—Serge, Catherine. M.D., U. Paris. Resident Hosp. of Paris, 1955-59, asst., 1960-73; clinic chief U. Paris, 1960-61; chief ear/nose and throat dept. Hosp. Nanterre, 1973—; prof. U. Paris VII, 1975—. Author: Practical Book of Eye, Ear, Nose and Throat, 1985. Contbr. numerous articles, tech. revs. to profl. lit. Served with arty. French Army, 1947. Mem. Laryngology Soc. Paris, French Soc. Laryngology, French Soc. Plastic and Reconstructive Surgery. Avocations: sailing; photography. Home: 6 Ave Emile-Acollas, F-75007 Paris France

BERG, BENGT R., business executive, engineer; b. Helsingborg, Sweden, 1929. Grad., Gothenburg Tech. Coll., 1949; Degree in Aeronautical and Mech. Engring., Royal U. of Tech., 1955. Trainee ASEA AB, Sweden, 1950, then engr. and mgr.; research engr. AB Atomenergi, Sweden, 1958-59; chief engr. Fläkt AB, Sweden, 1959-60, exec. vp. sales, 1960-64, pres., 1964, vice-chmn., 1983—; chmn. Gadelius AB, Procordia AB, Swedish Bus. Group Japan. Served with Royal Swedish Air Force, 1949-50. Mem. AB Asea-Atom, Assn. Swedish Industry, Sweden-Japan Found. Research and Devel. Office: Flakt AB, Sickla Alle 13, S104 81 Stockholm Sweden *

BERG, IRWIN AUGUST, psychology educator; b. Chgo., Oct. 9, 1913; s. Bertil Sigfried and Clara (Anderson) B.; m. Sylvia Maria Taipale, Mar. 4, 1939; 1 dau., Karen Astrid (Mrs. A. C. Kirby). A.B. cum laude, Knox Coll., 1936; A.M., U. Mich., 1940, Ph.D., 1942. Asst. prof. psychology U. Ill., 1942-47; assoc. prof. Pomona Coll., 1947-48, Northwestern U., 1948-55; chmn. dept., prof. psychology La. State U., 1955-65, dean coll. arts and scis. emeritus, prof. psychology, 1965-79; Spl. cons. U.S. Dept. Labor, U.S. VA, La. State Dept. Hosps.; Mem. La. State Commn. on Law Enforcement and Adminstrn. Criminal Justice, 1968-73; mem. La. Bd. Licensing for Sanitarians. Author: Workbook in Psychology, 1961, Response Set and Personality Assessment, 1967; Co-editor: Conformity and Deviation, 1961, An Introduction to Clinical Psychology, 3d edit, 1966. Bd. dirs. Nat. Council on Arts and Scis., 1970-73. Mem. Am. Psychol. Assn. (pres. div. counseling psychology 1964), Southeastern Psychol. Assn. (pres. 1963), Southwestern Psychol. Assn. (pres. 1963-64), AAAS, AAUP, Phi Beta Kappa, Sigma Xi, Phi Kappa Phi, Phi Beta. Home: St James Pl 333 Lee Dr Apt G-17 Baton Rouge LA 70808

BERG, KAI-ERIK, insurance company executive; b. Turku, Finland, Oct. 21, 1927; s. Erik and Tyyni (Laakso) B.; m. Maire Sinikka Alakoski, 1951 (div. 1957); children: Kari-Erik, Kaisla-Kaarina, Kirsi-Maaret; m. Sirkka Judin; 1 child, Markku. Degree in Engring., Tech. U., Helsinki, Finland, 1952. Instr. U. Pori, Helsinki, 1953-55; tech. insp. Mutual Ins. Soc. TARMO, Helsinki, 1955-67, tech. dept. mgr., 1967-70; dept. mgr. Mutual Ins. Soc. SAMPO-TARMO, Helsinki, 1970-73; mng. dir. Non-Life Ins. Assn., Helsinki, 1977-83; tech. mgr. Automobile Ins. Assn., Helsinki, 1977-83; dir. Fedn. Finnish Ins. Co., Helsinki, 1983—. Author: Non-Life Insurance and Risk Management for Companies; contbr. articles to profl. jours. Served with Finnish Army. Mem. Fire Engrs., Am. Soc. Testing and Materials, Internat. Assn. Arson Investigators, Am. Soc. Indsl. Security, Nat. Fire Protection Assn., Internat. Assn. Cief Police, numerous other fire ins. orgns. Lutheran. Office: Fedn Finnish Ins Co, Bulevardi 28, 00120 Helsinki Finland

BERG, LASSE, writer; b. Sundsvall, Sweden, Jan. 7, 1943; s. Edvard and Ebba Berg; m. Lisa Edfelt, July 22, 1965 (div. 1982); children: Josefin, Mia; m. Ingrid Lofstrom, Mar. 9, 1982; 1 child, Linda. Author: Face to Face, 1971, Mat and Makt (Boerma award FAO 1979), Along the Ganges, 1986 (award 1987), Vem hjalper bistandet?, 1987 (award 1987). Recipient Lat Leva prize Tidningen Arbetet, Malmoe, 1979, Fackboks-priset Raben & Sjogren Pub., Stockholm, 1987. Office: Swedish Embassy, Pvt Bag, 0017 Gaborone Botswana

BERG, LOUIS LESLIE, investment executive; b. Vienna, Austria, Dec. 27, 1919; s. Gustav and Hedwig (Kohn) B.; came to U.S., 1938, naturalized, 1943; student U. Vienna, 1937-38, Coll. City N.Y., 1941-43; m. Minnette Whitman, Aug. 28, 1959; children: Sharon, Randee, Michel. Pres., Gt. Empire Corp., N.Y.C., 1946—, Bendalou Real Estate Corp., N.Y.C., 1950-60, Netherlands Securities Co., Inc., N.Y.C., 1959-62, Imported Automotive Parts, Ltd., L.I. City, N.Y., IAP Inc., Avenel, N.J., IAP West Inc., Los Angeles; bd. dirs., exec. com. Auto Internat. Assn.; advisor U.S. Congl. Adv. Bd. dir. Internat. Aviation Corp., Cosmos Industries, Kane-Miller Corp., Knickerbocker Toy Co., Inc., Vernitron Corp., Jet Aero Corp., Fidelity Am. Finance Corp., S.W. Fla. Enterprises, Sulray Inc., U.S. Airlines, Commuter Airlines, Aviation Equipment. Mem. Am. Mgmt. Assn. Club: Wings. Office: IAP Inc 26 Englehard Ave Avenel NJ 07001 also: IAP West Inc 2939 Bandini Rd Los Angeles CA 90023

BERG, PAUL, biochemist, educator; b. N.Y.C., June 30, 1926; s. Harry and Sarah (Brodsky) B.; m. Mildred Levy, Sept. 13, 1947; 1 son, John. B.S., Pa. State U., 1948; Ph.D. (NIH fellow 1950-52), Western Res. U., 1952; D.Sc. (hon.), U. Rochester, 1978, Yale U., 1978, Wash. U., St. Louis, 1986. Postdoctoral fellow Copenhagen (Denmark) U., 1952-53; postdoctoral fellow Sch. Medicine, Washington U., St. Louis, 1953-54; Am. Cancer Soc. scholar cancer research dept. microbiology Sch. Medicine, Washington U., 1954-57, from asst. to assoc. prof. microbiology, 1955-59; prof. biochemistry Stanford Sch. Medicine, 1959—, Sam, Lula and Jack Willson prof. biochemistry, 1970, chmn. dept., 1969-74; dir. Stanford U. Beckman Ctr. for Molecular and Genetic Medicine, 1985; non-resident fellow Salk Inst., 1973; adv. bd. NIH, NSF, M.I.T.; vis. com. dept. biochemistry and molecular biology Harvard U.; bd. sci. advisors Jane Coffin Childs Found. Med. Research, 1970-80; chmn. sci. adv. com. Whitehead Inst., 1984; internat. adv. bd. Basel Inst. Immunology. Contbr. profl. jours.; Editor: Biochem. and Biophys. Research Communications, 1959-68; editorial bd.: Molecular Biology, 1966-69. Served to lt. (j.g.) USNR, 1943-46. Recipient Eli Lilly prize biochemistry, 1959; V.D. Mattia award Roche Inst. Molecular Biology, 1972; Henry J. Kaiser award for excellence in teaching, 1972; Disting. Alumnus award Pa. State U., 1972; Sarasota Med. awards for achievement and excellence, 1979; Gairdner Found. annual award, 1980; Lasker Found. award, 1980; Nobel award in chemistry, 1980; N.Y. Acad. Sci. award, 1980; Sci. Freedom and Responsibility award AAAS, 1982; Nat. Medal of Sci., 1985; named Calif. Scientist of Yr. Calif. Museum Sci. and Industry, 1963; numerous spl. and disting. lectureships including Harvey lectr., 1972, Lynen lectr., 1977, Priestly lectrs. Pa. State U., 1978, Dreyfus Disting. lectrs. Northwestern U., 1979, Lawrence Livermore Dir.'s Disting. lectr., 1983, W.H. Stein Meml. lectr. Rockefeller U., 1984, Charles E. Dohme Meml. lectr. Johns Hopkins U., 1984, Weizmann Inst. Sci. Jubilee lectr., 1984, U. Houston Nobel Prize Winners Series, 1985. Mem. Inst. Medicine, Nat. Acad. Scis., Am. Acad. Arts and Scis., Am. Soc. Biol. Chemists (pres. 1974-75), Am. Soc. Microbiology, Am. Philos. Soc., Japan Biochem. Soc. (elected fgn. mem. 1978), French Acad. Sci. (elected fgn. mem. 1981). Office: Stanford Sch Medicine 838 Santa Fe Ave Stanford CA 94305

BERG, ROLAND, psychiatrist, educator; b. Stockholm, Oct. 31, 1943; s. Sven and Margareta (Strömhammar) B.; m. Gunilla Johansson, May 30, 1947; children: Ida, Sofia. Licentiate in Medicine, Karolinska Inst., Stockholm, 1970, PhD, 1983; psychoanalyst, Swedish Psychoanalytical Inst., Stockholm, 1984. Various positions in internal medicine, surgery and gynecology, Stockholm, 1967-70; practice psychiatry Karolinska Inst., Stockholm, 1970-83; head Child Psychiat. Outpatient Clinic, Nacka, 1983; asst. chief psychiatrist Ersta Hosp., Stockholm, 1984-87, head dept. psychiatry, 1987—; assoc. prof. Karolinska Inst., 1985—; expert in psychotherapy Nat. Swedish Bd. Health and Welfare, 1985—. Editor: Svensk Psykiatri, 1983-87; contbr. articles on psychiatry, psychotherapy and popular sci. Mem. Swedish Psychiat. Assn. (pres. 1987—), Swedish and Internat. Psychoanalytical Assn., Swedish Med. Soc., Swedish Med. Assn., World Psychiat. Assn., Scandinavian Soc. Psychology. Home: Dalagatan 42, S-11324 Stockholm Sweden Office: Ersta Hosp, Fjällgatan 44, S-11635 Stockholm Sweden

BERG, STANTON ONEAL, firearms and ballistics cons.; b. Barron, Wis., June 14, 1928; s. Thomas C. and Ellen Florence (Nedland) Silbaugh; student U. Wis., 1949-50; LL.B., LaSalle Extension U., 1951; postgrad. U. Minn., 1960-69; qualified as ct. expert witness in ballistics various cts.; m. June K. Rolstad, Aug. 16, 1952; children—David M., Daniel L., Susan E., Julie L. Claim rep. State Farm Ins. Co., Mpls., Hibbing and Duluth, Minn., 1952-57, claim supt., 1957-66, divisional claim supt., 1966-70; firearms cons., Mpls., 1961—; regional mgr. State Farm Fire and Casualty Co., St. Paul, 1970-84; bd. dirs. Am. Bd. Forensic Firearm and Tool Mark Examiners, 1980—; instr. home firearms safety, Mpls.; cons. to Sporting Arms and Ammunition Mfrs. Inst.; internat. lectr. on forensic ballistics. Adv. bd. Milton Helpern Internat. Center for Forensic Scis., 1975—; mem. bd. cons. Inst. Applied Sci., Chgo.; cons. for re-exam. of ballistics evidence in Sirhan case Superior Ct. Los Angeles, 1975; mem. Nat. Forensic Ctr., 1979—, internat. study group in forensic scis., 1985—; chmn. internat. symposiums on forensic ballistics, Edinburgh, Scotland, 1972, Zurich, 1975, Bergen, Norway, 1981. Served with CIC, AUS, 1948-52. Fellow Am. Acad. Forensic Sci.; mem. Assn. of Firearm and Tool Mark Examiners (exec. council 1970-71, Distinguished Mem. and Key Man award 1972, exam. and standards com., spl. honors award 1976, nat. peer group on cert. of firearms examiners 1978—), Forensic Sci. Soc., Internat. Assn. Forensic Scis., Internat. Assn. for Identification (mem. firearms subcom. of sci. and practice com. 1961-74, 87-88, chmn. firearm subcom. 1964-66, 69-70, lab. research and techniques subcom. 1980-81), Firearms Western Conf. Criminal and Civil Problems (sci. adv. com.), Am. Ordinance Assn., Nat. Rifle Assn., Minn. Weapons, Internat. Cartridge Collectors Assns., Internat. Reference Orgn. Forensic Medicine and Scis, Internat. Assn. Bloodstain Pattern Analysts, Internat. Study Group in Forensic Scis. Contbg. editor Am. Rifleman mag., 1973-84; mem. editorial bd. Internat. Microform Jour. Legal Medicine and Forensic Sciences, 1979—, Am. Jour. Forensic Medicine and Pathology, 1979—; contbr. articles on firearms and forensic ballistics to profl. publs. Address: 6025 Gardena Ln NE Minneapolis MN 55432

BERG, SVANTE HJALMAR, architect; b. Stockholm, July 3, 1943; s. Anders Ingvar and Karin Rut (Sander) B.; m. Kerstin Elisabeth Ericsson; children: Susanna, Sara, Stina. Degree in architecture, Royal Inst. Tech., Stockholm, 1968. Registered architect, Sweden, Eng. Architect Royal Swedish Nat. Bd. Pub. Bldg., Stockholm, 1969-73; asst. tchr. Royal Inst. Tech., Stockholm, 1971-73; sr. architect Edward Mills & Ptnrs., London, 1973-75; ptnr. Berg Arkitektkontor AB, Stockholm, 1975—, mng. dir., 1978—; bd. dirs. Berg Architects, Ltd., London, Berg & Ohman Architects, Ltd., London, Berg Assocs. Ltd., N.Y.C., Alfredeen-Rako Engring. Cons., Stockholm, Editech, Stockholm. 1st prize winner archtl. competition Stockholm Globe Arena, 1986. Mem. Nat. Assn. Swedish Architects, Swedish Assn. Practicing Architects, Royal Inst. British Architects. Home: Orrvägen 13, S-13553 Tyresö Sweden Office: Berg Arkitektkontor, Kommendorsgatan 30, 11448 Stockholm Sweden

BERG, THOMAS, business executive; b. Sparta, Wis., Dec. 28, 1914; m. Evelyn Sweet, Nov. 13, 1937; children: Barbara Caryl, James Richard. B.S.E.E., U. Wis., 1937. Engr. Gen. Electric Co., Schenectady, 1937-48; instr. Rensselaer Poly. Inst., Troy, N.Y., 1943-44; pres., owner, welding specialist, application engr. Arcway Equipment Co., Phila., 1948-58; pres. Airco Welding Products div. Air Reduction Co., N.Y.C., 1958-68; pres., chief exec. officer, dir. Friedrich Refrigerators Inc., San Antonio, 1968-75; chmn. Friedrich Refrigerators Inc., 1975-86; v.p., dir. Crutcher Resources Corp., Houston; v.p. Wylain Inc.; dir. Universal Bookbindery Inc.; v.p., dir. Ellison Industries Inc.; pres. Ray Ellison Devels. Inc.; bd. dirs., chmn. S.W. Research Inst.; founder Skills Tng. Center, San Antonio, 1971; dir. First Nat. Bank, San Antonio, Jim Berg Publs., Inc.; dir., chmn. exec. com., pres. J.E.T. Properties, Inc., San Antonio. Author: Aim for a Job in Welding, 1967. Adv. dir. Southwest Craft Center, San Antonio, 1975—; mem., dir. fed. policy com. Urban Land Inst., Washington, 1977—; trustee Myra Stafford Pryor chair of free enterprise, St. Mary's U., 1977—; chmn. adv. council Sch. Bus., 1976-77, San Antonio; chmn. bd. City Pub. Service Bd., San Antonio; bd. dirs. Prevent Blindness of San Antonio.; pres., bd. dirs. Nat. Myasthenia Gravis Found., N.Y.C., bd. dirs., San Antonio; pres. bd. dirs. Myastenia Gravis Found., N.Y., 1986—; founding dir. Tex. Research & Tech. Found., San Antonio. Named hon. citizen City of San Antonio, 1978. Mem. Am. Welding Soc. (founder annual Airco award 1965), Am. Inst. Elec. Engrs., San Antonio C. of C. (dir. 1972—, chmn. econ. devel. council 1973—), Trinity U. Assos. Presbyterian. Clubs: San Antonio Country, City, Argyle, Univ, Giraud, Plaza, St. Anthony, Rotary (dir.). Office: PO Box 5250 San Antonio TX 78201

BERGAMINI, EDUARDO WHITAKER, electrical engineer; b. Ribeirao Preto, Sao Paulo, Brazil, Apr. 30, 1944; s. Fausto A.B. and Eudoxia (Whitaker) B.; m. Zuleica Maria Nogueira, Mar. 5, 1969; children—Ana Luiza, Ana Cristina. Elec. Engr., Escola Politecnica da Universidade de Sao Paulo, 1967; M.Sc. in Space Sci., Instituto de Pesquisas Espacias, 1969; M.Sc. in Elec. Engring., Stanford U., 1971, Ph.D. in Elec. Engring., 1973, postdoctoral, 1973. Asst. research Instituto de Pesquisas Espaciais Brazil, S. J. Campos, Sao Paulo, 1968-69; research asst. elec. engring. dept. Stanford U., 1971-73, research assoc., 1973; head group Instituto de Pesquisas Espaciais, São José dos Campos, Sao Paulo, Brazil, 1974-78, head div., 1978-82, head dept., 1982-88, resp. dine of research and devel., 1988— ; cons. Financiadora de Estudios e Projetos, Conselho Nacional de Desenvolvimento Cientifico e Tecnologico, Brazil, 1984, Soc. Open Systems Interconnection-BRISA; head del. Consultative Com. for Space Data Systems, Washington, 1982—; exec. vice-dir. Laboratorio Nacional de Redes de Computadores, Sao Paulo, 1983—. NASA fellow Stanford U., 1969-71, Conselho Nacional de Desenvolvimento Cientifico e Tecnologico fellow Stanford U., 1969-72, Coordenacao do Aperfeicoamento Pessoal de Nivel Superior fellow Ministry Edn. Brazil, Stanford U., 1971-73. Mem. IEEE Computer Soc., IEEE Aerospace and Electronics Soc., Internat. Astronautical Fedn. (space exploration com.), Sociedade Brasileira de Computacao, Sociedade Brasileira de Telecomunicacoes, Stanford U. Alumni Assn. Roman Catholic. Club: Tenis (Sao Jose Campos, Sao Paulo). Avocations: tennis; swimming. Home: Rua Beatriz Sa de Toledo 38, San Jose dos Campos, Sao Paulo Brazil 12243 Office: Instituto de Pesquisas Espacias, Avenida dos Astronautas 17 58, San Jose dos Campos, Sao Paulo Brazil 12225

BERGAN, JAMES GARTH, food science and nutrition educator, researcher, administrator; b. Harvey, Ill., Apr. 4, 1938; s. John Francis and Ana Elizabeth (Modschiedler) B.; m. Barbara Ann Bruner, Aug. 15, 1957 (div. 1973); children—James, Richard, David, JoAnne; m. Monica G. Sierra, Apr. 14, 1984; children: Sean, Paul. B.S. in Agrl. Sci., U. Ill., 1966, Ph.D. in Nutrition, 1970. Student engr. Natural Gas Co. Am., Hersher, Ill., 1957-58; research assoc. U. Ill., Urbana, 1970-71; assoc. prof. food and nutrition U. R.I., Kingston, 1971-81, chmn. and prof. food sci. and nutrition, 1977-81; vis. lectr. Hawkesbury Agrl. Coll., Richmond, New South Wales, Australia, 1981-82, head dept. food tech., 1983—, assoc. dean, 1986—; cons. Found. Chile, Santiago, 1979-80. Contbr. to book; contbr. articles to publs. USPHS trainee NIH, 1967-70; Future Leader, Nutrition Found., Inc., N.Y.C., 1973. Mem. Am. Inst. Nutrition, Inst. Food Technologists (communicator 1977-81), Nutrition Found. Australia, Nutrition Soc. Australia. Club: Rotary. Home: 123 Terrace Rd, North Richmond New South Wales 2754, Australia Office: Hawkesbury Agr Coll, Sch Food Tech, Richmond New South Wales 2753, Australia

BERGAU, FRANK CONRAD, real estate executive; b. N.Y.C., Sept. 17, 1926; s. Frank Conrad and Mary Elizabeth (Davie) B.; B.A. in English, St. Francis Coll., Loretto, Pa., 1950; M.S. in Edn. and English, Potsdam (N.Y.) State U., 1969; m. Rita I. Korotkin; children—Mary, Rita, Francis, Theresa, Veronica. Tchr. English Gouverneur (N.Y.) Schs., 1962-81, dir. continuing edn., 1968-81, summer prin., 1974-80; project dir. St. Lawrence County (N.Y.) Bd. Co-op. Ednl. Services, Canton, 1974; pres. Irenicon Assos. Bd. dirs. St. Lawrence County Assn. Retarded Children, 1965—; pres. bd. dirs. Gouverneur Library. Mem. Gouverneur C. of C. (dir. 1963-66), Lake County Bd. Realtors, NEA, N.Y. Assn. Continuing Edn. (dir.). Certified as tchr., supr., adminstr., N.Y. Club: Gouverneur Luncheon. Lodge: Kiwanis (charter mem. Clermont).

BERGE, ODD, corporate professional; b. Bergen, Norway, Oct. 21, 1938; s. Annanias and Inga (Hanssen) B.; m. Ase Karset, July 11, 1938; children: Ole Andreas, Arne Petter. MSc, Norweigian Tech. U., 1963. Devel. engr. Stord Bartz A/S, Bergen, 1964-65, head research, 1967-72, mgr. sales and projects, 1972-83, mng. dir., 1983—; engring. supr. Hilmar Rekstens Rederi, Bergen, 1965-67; chmn. bd. dirs. Stord Bartz U.K., Aberdeen Scotland, Stord Bartz Ams., Greensboro, N.C., Stord Bartz Deutschland, Düsseldorf, Fed. Republic Germany, Stord Bartz Japan, Tokyo. Chmn. fishfarming com. Govt. Norway, Oslo, 1985—. Served with Norwegian Army, 1957-58. Mem. Norwegian Engrs. Orgn., Polyteknisk Foreing. Lodge: Rotary. Home: Kuven 5200, 5200 Oslo Norway Office: Stord Bartz A/S C, Sundtsgt 29, 500 Bergen Norway

BERGEN, THOMAS JOSEPH, lawyer, nursing home executive, association executive; b. Prairie du Chien, Wis., Feb. 7, 1913; s. Thomas Joseph and Emma Marilla (Grelle) B.; m. Jean Loraine Bowler, May 29, 1941 (dec. Aug. 1972); children—Kathleen Bergen McElwee, Eileen Bergen Bednarz, Patricia Bergen Buss, Thomas Joseph, Patrick Joseph, John Joseph. Student, U. Wis., 1930-32; J.D., Marquette U., 1937, postgrad., 1937-38. Bar: Wis. 1937, U.S. Supreme Ct. 1972. Practice law Milw., 1937—; exec. sec. Wis. Assn. Nursing Homes, 1957-71; legal counsel, exec. dir. Am. Coll. Nursing Home Adminstrs., Milw., 1967-68; sec., dir. Bayside Nursing Home, Milw., 1967—; pres., dir. N.W. Med. Ctrs., Inc., Milw., 1968—, Northland Med. Ctrs., Inc., Milw., 1968—; treas., exec. dir. Nat. Geriatrics Soc., Milw., 1971—; pres. Sen. Joseph R. McCarthy Found., Inc., 1983, pres. bd. dirs., 1979—; mem. program planning com. Nat. Conf. on Aging, del. to conf., 1974; panel speaker Nat. Justice Found. Conv., 1974. Editor: Silver Threads, Wis. Assn. Nursing Homes publ., 1963-71, News Letter, Am. Coll. Nursing Home Adminstrs., 1967-68; Views and News, Nat. Geriatrics Soc., 1971—; mem. editorial bd. Educational Gerontology, 1973-85; contbr. articles to nursing home publs. Bd. dirs., treas. Nat. Geriatrics Ednl. Soc., 1971—; bd. dirs., pres. Wis. Justice Found., 1971—. Served with AUS, 1943, 44. Recipient Merit award Wis. Assn. Nursing Homes, 1962, Outstanding Leadership award Nat. Geriatrics Soc., 1976. Mem. ABA, Wis. Bar Assn., Milw. Bar Assn. (pres., exec. dir.), Real Estate Profls. Assn. (pres. 1974—), Am. Med. Writers Assn., Delta Theta Phi, Delta Sigma Rho. Roman Catholic. Home: 10324 W Vienna Ave Wauwatosa WI 53222 Office: 212 W Wisconsin Ave Milwaukee WI 53203

BERGENDAHL, WALDEMAR, film producer; b. Gävle, Sweden, Apr. 18, 1933. Student, Stockholm Sch. Econs., Borgarskolan. Product mgr. Europa Film, Sweden, 1958-59, producer, 1960-69; free-lance producer Sweden, 1970-74; producer Svensk Film Industry, Sweden, 1974-82, head prodn., producer, 1982—. Office: Svensk Filmindustry, S-117, 88 Stockholm Sweden B1450

BERGER, BRIGITTE, neuroscientist; b. Paris, Apr. 7, 1932; d. Michel and Ida (Bajer) Hegedus; m. Roland Berger, June 2, 1962; children: Marc, Sandrine. MD, Faculté Paris, 1964; ScD, Faculté Pierre Et Marie Curie, Paris, 1973. Intern Paris Hosps., 1958-63; attache de recherche Nat. Inst. Health and Med. Research, Paris, 1964-68, chargé de recherche, 1968-73, maitre de recherche, 1973-84, dir. research, 1984—. contbr. 150 sci. articles to profl. jours. Grantee Med. Research Found., 1978, Found. Singer Polignac, 1987. Mem. French Neurol. Soc., French Neuropath. Club, European Neurosci. Assn.,Internat Soc. for Devel. Neurosci. Office: INSERM U106 Salpetriere, 47 Blvd de l'Hopital, 75651 Paris Cedex 13, France

BERGER, CHARLES LEE, lawyer; b. Evansville, Ind. Oct. 14, 1947; s. Sydney L. and Sadelle (Kaplan) B.; m. Leslie Lilly, Apr. 20, 1973; children—Sarah, Rebecca, Leah. B.A., U. Evansville, 1969; J.D. cum laude, Ind. U., 1972. Bar: Ind. 1972, U.S. Dist. Ct. (so. dist.) Ind. 1972, U.S. Ct. Appeals (7th cir.) 1972, U.S. Ct. Appeals D.C. 1975, U.S. Supreme Ct. 1977, U.S. Dist. Ct. (we. dist.) Ky. 1981, U.S. Ct. Appeals (6th cir.) 1984. Ptnr., Berger & Berger, Evansville, 1972—. Bd. dirs. Leadership Evansville, 1977. Fellow Ind. Bar Found.; mem. Ind. Bar Assn. (chmn. trial lawyers sect. 1982-83), Am. Bd. Trial Advocates, Ind. Trial Lawyers Assn. (bd. dirs. 1973-77, 77-84, v.p. 1984—). Jewish. Home: 723 SE Riverside Evansville IN 47713 Office: Berger & Berger 313 Main St Evansville IN 47708

BERGER, DAVID, lawyer; b. Archbald, Pa., Sept. 6, 1912; s. Jonas and Anna (Raker) B.; children—Jonathan, Daniel. A.B. cum laude, U. Pa., 1932, LL.B. cum laude, 1936. Bar: Pa. 1938, D.C., N.Y. Asst. to prof. U. Pa. Law Sch., Phila., 1936-38, spl. asst. to dean; law clk. Pa. Supreme Ct., Phila., 1939-40; spl. asst. to dir. enemy alien identification program U.S. Dept. Justice, Washington, 1941-42; law clk. U.S. Ct. Appeals, 1946; pvt. practice Phila., Washington and N.Y.C.; city solicitor Phila., 1956-63; former counsel Sch. Dist. Phila.; former chmn. adv. com. Pa. Superior Ct.; mem. adv. com. fed. rules evidence U.S. Supreme Ct.; lectr. on legal subjects including antitrust, securities, mass torts and class actions; founder, chmn. Berger & Montague, P.C. Author numerous articles on law. Nat. commr. Anti-Defamation League, B'nai B'rith; chmn. Anti-trust Inst.; mem. adv. bd. anti-trust and trade regulation report Bur. Nat. Affairs, Inc. Served to comdr. USNR, 1942-45. Decorated Silver Star, Presdl. Unit Citation. Fellow Am. Coll. Trial Lawyers, Internat. Acad. Trial Lawyers, Internat. Soc. Barristers; mem. ABA, Phila. Bar Assn. (pres., bd. govs., chancellor), Phila. Bar Found. (past pres.), Order of Coif. Home: One Breakers Row Palm Beach FL 33480 Office: Berger & Montague PC 1622 Locust St Philadelphia PA 19103

BERGER, HAROLD, lawyer, engineer; b. Archbald, Pa., June 10, 1925; s. Jonas and Anna (Raker) B.; m. Renee Margareten, Aug. 26, 1951; children: Jill Ellen, Jonathan David. B.S. in Elec. Engring, U. Pa., 1948, J.D., 1951. Bar: Pa. 1951. Since practiced in Phila.; judge Ct. of Common Pleas, Phila. County, 1971-72; Chmn., moderator Internat. Aerospace Meetings Princeton U., N.J., 1965-66; chmn. Western Hemisphere Internat. Law Conf., San Jose, Costa Rica, 1967; chmn. internat. Confs. on Aerospace and Internat. Law, Coll. William and Mary; permanent mem. Jud. Conf. 3d Circuit Ct. of Appeals; mem. County Bd. Law Examiners, Phila. County, 1961-71; chmn. World Conf. Internat. Law and Aerospace, Caracas, Venezuela, Internat. Conf. on Environ. and Internat. Law, U. Pa., 1974, Internat. Confs. on Global Interdependence, Princeton U., 1975, 79; mem. Pa. State Conf. Trial Judges, 1972-80, Nat. Conf. State Trial Judges, 1972—; chmn. Pa. Com. for Independent Judiciary, 1973—. Mem. editorial advisory bd.: Jour. of Space Law, U. Miss. Sch. of Law, 1973—; Contbr. articles to profl. jours. Mem. Bar Assn.We the People 200 Com. for Constn. Bicentennial. Served with Signal Corps AUS, 1946-48. Recipient Alumnus of Year award Thomas McKean Law Club, U. Pa. Law Sch., 1965, Gen. Electric Co. Space award, 1966, Nat. Disting. Achievement award Tau Epsilon Rho, 1972, Spl. Pa. Jud. Conf. award, 1981. Mem. Inter-Am. Bar Assn. (past chmn. aerospace law com.), Fed. Bar Assn. (chmn. class action and complex litigation com. Phila. chpt. 1986—, past nat. chmn. com. on aerospace law, pres. Phila. chpt. 1983-84, nat. exec. council, nat. chmn. fed. jud. com., Presdl. award 1970, Nat. Distinguished Service award 1978, nat. com. 1987 bi-centennial of U.S. Constn.), ABA (Spl. Presdl. Program medal 1975, past chmn. aerospace law com., mem. state and fed. ct. com., nat. conf. of state trial judges), Phila. Bar Assn. (chmn. jud. liaison com. 1975, past chmn. internat. law com. 1977), Assn. U.S. Mems. Internat. Inst. Space Law Internat. Astronautical Fedn. (dir.), Internat. Acad. Astronautics Paris (past v.p.). Office: 1622 Locust St Philadelphia PA 19103

BERGER, HARVEY ROBERT, psychologist; b. Quincy, Mass., Nov. 3, 1927; s. Joel Joseph and Helen Esther (Stone) B.; B.A., Tufts U., 1949, M.A., 1950; Ph.D., U. Mo., 1953; m. Thelma Lee Cohen, July 11, 1954. Psychologist, Marblehead (Mass.) Public Schs., 1953-79; dir. psychol. services Federally Assisted Programs, Salem (Mass.) Public Schs., 1967-76; cons. Revere (Mass.) Public Schs., 1979—; assoc. prof. Salem State Coll., 1963; clin. dir. North Shore Psychol. Counseling and Testing Center, 1963-75; pres. Paul Revere Savs. & Loan Assn., 1971-76, William Dawes Realty Corp.; nat. service officer Jewish War Vets. U.S.A., 1984—. Mem. Nat. Commn. on Safety Edn., 1952-54; capt., Mass. comdt. U.S. Naval Cadet Program, 1966—; col. Gov.'s staff Ky. N.G.; pres. Area Bd. on Mental Health and Retardation, 1975-78; vice chmn. Greater Lynn Council for Children, Mass. Office for Children, 1977-78; mem. governance bd. Greater Lynn Community Mental Health Center, 1977—. Auditor Republican City Com., Lynn, Mass., 1970-75; pres. Mass. Am. Legion Coll., 1964-66; pres. NEA Mut. Fund; chmn. bd. NEA Income Fund; trustee Ida C. Romanow Fund; pres. Congregation Chevra Tehillim. Served with AUS, 1945-47. Fellow Sch. Alcohol Studies, Yale, 1957. Diplomate Am. Bd. Examiners Profl. Psychology. Fellow Am. Assn. Mental Deficiency, Am. Orthopsychiat. Assn., Royal Soc. Health; mem. Am. Psychol. Assn., Soc. for Personality and Social Psychology, Nat. Assn. Sch. Psychologists, Nat. Assn. Sch. Counselors, Mass. Schoolmasters Club (life), Am. Psychology-Law Soc., Soc. for Advancement Social Psychology, Soc. for Psychol. Study Social Issues, Soc. Behaviorists, Religious Zionists Am. (life), Mass. Bar Assn., NEA (life), Am. Legion (life), VFW (life), Mil. Order Purple Heart (life). Navy League (life), U.S. Naval Inst. (life), Nat. Soc. Profs. (life), Am. Assn. Higher Edn. (life), Jewish War Vets. (life), DAV (life), Tufts Jumbo Club, Nat. Eagle Scout Assn., Phi Beta Kappa, Phi Delta Kappa. Clubs: Masons (32 deg.), Shriners (fire brigade chaplain), Order Eastern Star. Home: 31 Tudor St Lynn MA 01902 Office: John F Kennedy Fed Bldg Boston MA 02203

BERGER, HERBERT, retired internist, educator; b. Bklyn., Dec. 14, 1909; s. Louis and Augusta (Feldman) B.; m. Sylvia Berger, Oct. 1934; children: Leland S., Shelby L. (Mrs. William Jakoby). B.Sc., NYU, 1929; M.D., U. Md., 1932. Diplomate: Am. Bd. Internal Medicine. Intern Morrisania City Hosp., Bronx, N.Y., 1932-34; resident U.S. Naval Hosps., 1941-45; practice medicine 1934-88; cons. cardiologist Seaview Hosp., S.I., 1934-88; attending physician Flower-Fifth Ave. Hosp., Met. Hosp.; cons. USPHS Hosp.; prof. medicine N.Y. Med. Coll., 1962—; pres. med. staff, dir. medicine emeritus Richmond Meml. Hosp., 1975-88; dir. emeritus Group Health Ins., Inc.; med. lectr. in over 85 countries. Contbr. over 181 articles to med. jours., chpts. to med. text books. Cons. editor Internat. Jour. Addictions. Served to comdr. USNR, 1942-45. Recipient Gold medal U. Md., 1978. Fellow ACP, Am. Coll. Chest Physicians; mem. Internat. Coll. Angiology, N.Y. Acad. Medicine (v.p., mem. council, chmn. sect. on medicine, vice chmn. com. med. edn.), Brit. Soc. Health Edn., Richmond County Med. Soc. (past pres.), N.Y.C. Med. Soc. (past pres.), Med. Soc. State N.Y. (past v.p.), Blood Banks Assn. (past pres.), N.Y. Soc. Internal Medicine (past pres.), Am. Soc. Study Addictions (past pres.). Republican. Jewish. Clubs: Richmond County Country, Richmond County Yacht, Circumnavigators. Home: 25 Bloomingdale Rd Staten Island NY 10309

BERGER, JAMES CHARLES, research and information center administrator; b. Wilmington, Del., Nov. 9, 1941; s. Theodore and Grace (First) B.; m. Linda Simon, Oct. 24, 1975. BA, U. Del., 1965; MA, U. Mass., 1968; PhD, U. Conn., 1973. Asst. prof. Newton (Mass.) Coll., 1972-75; research assoc. Fairleigh Dickinson U., Teaneck, N.J., 1975-76; research dir. John Jay Coll. Criminal Justice, N.Y.C., 1976—, cons. Nat. Orgn. Black Law Enforcement Execs., Washington, 1977, Nat. Assn. Legal Assts., Tulsa, 1981, Ctr. Applied Research and Analysis in the Social Scis., Bklyn., 1981—. Author: Criminal Justice Education, 1980; also articles. Cons. Jewish Family Service of Del., Wilmington, 1974-75. Grantee NSF, 1974, Conn. Research Found., 1971-72; hon. mem. research bd. advisors Am. Biographical Inst., 1988. Mem. Am. Assn. Pub. Opinion Research, Am. Polit. Sci. Assn., Am. Soc. Pub. Adminstrn., Pi Sigma Alpha, Pi Alpha Alpha. Jewish. Home: 7 Olyphant Pl Morristown NJ 07960

BERGER, JOHN PETER, author, art critic; b. London, Nov. 5, 1926; s. S.J.D. and Miriam (Branson) B.; attended Central Sch. Art, Chelsea Sch. Art. Began career as painter, tchr. drawing; exhibited works at Wildenstein Gallery, Redfern Gallery and Leicester Gallery, London; art critic Tribune, New Statesman; scenario: (with Alain Tanner) La Salamandre, Le Milieu du Monde, Jonas (N.Y. Critics prize for best scenario of Yr. 1976); author: Marcel Frishman, 1958, A Painter of Our Time (novel), 1958, Permanent Red, 1960, The Foot of Clive (novel), 1962, Corker's Freedom (novel), 1964, The Success and Failure of Picasso, 1965, (with J. Mohr) A Fortunate Man; the story of a country doctor, 1967; Art and Revolution, 1969, Moments of Cubism and Other Essays, 1969; (essays) The Sense of Sight, 1985 (pub. in Eng. as The White Bird); essays and articles include: The Look of Things, 1972, G (novel), 1972 (Booker prize 1972, James Tait Black Meml. prize 1972), Ways of Seeing, 1972, (with J. Mohr) The Seventh Man, 1975 (Union of Journalists and Writers of Paris prize for best reportage 1977), Pig Earth (fiction), 1979; About Looking, 1980; (with J. Mohr) Another Way of Telling, 1982; work for theatre (with Nella Bielski) A Question of Geography, premiere Theatre National de Marseille, 1984; (non-fiction) My Heart, Brief as Photos, 1984; Once in Europa (fiction) 1987; translator: (with A Bostock) Poems on the Theatre (B. Brecht), 1960, Return to My Native Land (Aime Cesaire), 1969; numerous TV appearances, including: Monitor, two series for Granada TV. Office: Quincy, Mieussy, 74440 Taninges France also: care of Weidenfeld and Nicolson, 11 St John's #H-11, London SW11, England

BERGER, JULIE ANN, social worker, research analyst; b. Newark, Sept. 18, 1950; d. Murray M. and Estelle C. (Sperber) Monestersky. Student, U. Wis., 1968-70; BA, Tufts U., 1972; MSW, Rutgers U., 1974. Med. social worker dialysis unit VA Hosp., East Orange, N.J., 1974-76, med. social worker hosp.-based home-care program and outpatient clinic, 1976-77; med. social worker dialysis unit Morristown (N.J.) Meml. Hosp., 1977-81; social worker pvt. practice, 1981-84; asst./trainee Donna Aughey Ely and Assocs., Morristown, N.J., 1984; freelance market research, health care and telecommunications cons., 1984-86; telecommunications market researcher, assoc. editor Probe Research, Inc., Morristown, 1986-88; field instr. casework sequence Rutgers U. Grad. Sch. Social Work, 1978; social work rep. to N.J. Renal Network Council, Inc., 1979-81, mem. subcom. on allied health profl. practice, 1978-81, mem. by-laws com., 1978-79, sec. to full council, 1980-81. Social work vol. The Richmond Fellowship, Morristown, 1984. Mem. Acad. Cert. Social Workers, Nat. Assn. Social Workers, Register Clin. Social Workers, Am. Assn. Kidney Patients, Inc., Council Nephrology Social Workers, Nat. Assn. Female Execs., N.J. Dialysis and Transplant Assn. (sec. 1976-78, pres. 1978-80). Home: 7 Hamilton Rd Apt 4B Morristown NJ 07960

BERGER, KENNETH JAMES EDWARD, oceanographer, consultant; b. Astoria, N.Y., Mar. 14, 1951; s. Edward Berger and Helen Lucille (Roland) Manfredi. BS, Pace U., 1972; MS, NYU, 1974, postgrad., 1974-78; PhD in Environ. Sci. and Engring., UCLA, 1982; grad. cert., U. San Diego, 1984. Cert. community coll. instr., ESL tchr. Research asst. N.C. State U., Raleigh, 1972, Inst. for Marine and Atmospheric Sci., N.Y.C., 1973-74; oceanographer U.S. Dept. of Interior, N.Y.C., 1975-79; postgrad. reseacher II UCLA, 1979-82; sr. scientist IWG Corp., San Diego, 1980-81; assoc. prof. Chapman Coll., San Diego, 1982—; section mgr., systems scientist Computer Scis. Corp., San Diego, 1984-85; cons. in marine sci., San Diego, 1982—; adj. instr. Cen. Tex. Coll., Clark AFB, Philippines, 1983, U. LaVerne, San Diego, 1985—. Contbr. articles to profl. jours. Served with USCG aux., 1981. Recipient Unit Citation award U.S. Dept. of Interior, 1978, first place San Diego Brit. Car Club Council, 1980, second place San Diego Brit. Car Club Council, 1981; N.Y. State scholar, 1972; Pace U. Sci. scholar, 1972; UCLA fellow, SDSU scholr award, 1988. Mem. AAAS, Internat. Oceanographic Found., N.Y. Acad. Scis., Assn. Asian Studies, Kappa Mu Epsilon. Clubs: San Diego, San Diego MG (sec. 1983), San Diego MGA's (v.p. 1982), New Eng. MG "T" Register, Ltd. Home: PO Box 90314 San Diego CA 92109 Office: Chapman Coll REC Naval Tng Ctr Bldg 214 San Diego CA 92133

BERGER, KNUT BERNT, diplomat; b. Larvik, Norway, Dec. 23, 1932; s. Christian and Laura (Berntsen Gjone) B.; m. Gerd, Sept. 29, 1962; 1 child, Knut Erik. Grad., Norwegian Sch. Econs. and Bus. Adminstrn., 1957. Sec. Ministry Fgn. Affairs, Oslo, 1957-59; sec. Norwegian Embassy, Peking, China, 1959-61; vice consul Norwegian Consulate Gen., Rotterdam, Netherlands, 1962-64; first sec. Ministry Fgn. Affairs, Oslo, 1965-68, Permanent Delegation to OECD, Paris, 1968-71; Head of Div. Ministry of Fgn. Affairs, Oslo, 1972-79; minister counsellor Permanent Misson, Geneva, 1979-83; Ambassador Norwegian Embassy, Jakarta, Indonesia, 1984—.

BERGER, LANCE ALLEN, consulting firm executive; b. Bklyn., July 12, 1943; s. Henry and Ruth (Hirschhorn) B.; m. Dorothy Roberta Turk, June 13, 1965; children—Adam, Craig, Cheryl, Nancy. B.A., Bklyn. Coll., 1965, M.A., 1967. Mgr. mgmt. resources CPC Internat., Englewood Cliffs, N.J., 1976-77, dir. human resources, 1977-79; dir. orgn. devel. Continental Can, Stamford, Conn., 1979-80; prin. Hay Group, N.Y.C., 1980-81, sr. prin., 1981-83, ptnr. gen. mgr., Phila., 1983-85, exec. v.p., 1985—; vice chmn. Pequonnock Valley Mental Health, N.J., 1974-78; mem. Council of Bus. Advisors, Teaneck, N.J., 1975-78, Community Leadership Program, Phila., 1983—. Contbr. to profl. jours. Mem. Am. Soc. Personnel Adminstrn., Am. Soc Tng. Devel., Planning Forum, Manalapan Jaycees (sec. 1971-74). Home: 17 Courtney Circle Bryn Mawr PA 19010 Office: Hay Group 229 S 18th St Philadelphia PA 19103

BERGER, LEV ISAAC, physicist, educator; b. Rostov, USSR, June 23, 1929; came to U.S., 1978; s. Isaac Mark and Sara (Poltevsker) B.; m. Ninelle Rossine, July 2, 1956; 1 child, Yuri. MS in Physics, State U., Moscow, 1955; PhD in Physics, State U., Minsk, USSR, 1959; PhD in Tech. Scis., U. Steel Alloys, Moscow, 1968. Lectr. physics U. Nonferrous Metlas, Moscow, 1956-60; docent Physics U. Metallurgy, Moscow, 1960-62; prof. Poly. Inst., Moscow, 1962-77; sr. scientist New Eng. Research Ctr., Sudbury, Mass., 1979-81; lectr. physics Calif. State U., San Diego, 1981—; dir. div. Inst. Spl. Pure Substances, Moscow, 1962-71, Introscopy Research Inst., Moscow, 1971-77. Author: Ternary Diamond-like Semiconductors, 1969; contbr. articles to profl. jours.; patentee in field. San Diego State U. grantee, 1983. Mem. AAAS, Am. Phys. Soc., Am. Assn. Crystal Growth, Calif. Inst. Electronics and Materials Sci. (pres. 1981—), Inst. Electronics of San Diego State U. (bd. dirs. 1983—), Materials Research Soc. Home: 2115 Flame Tree Way Hemet CA 92343 Office: San Diego State U Dept Physics San Diego CA 92182

BERGER, MARCEL, scientific institution administrator; b. Paris, Apr. 14, 1927; s. Jacques and Paule (Lefebvre) B.; m. Odile Moufle, Sept. 8, 1951; children: Isabelle, Anne, Benoît. MA, Ecole Normale Sup Ulm, Paris, 1951; Doctorat État, U. Paris, 1954. Fellow Ecole Normale Supérieure, Paris, 1948-53; prof. Strasbourg U., France, 1955-64, U. Nice, France, 1964-66, U. Paris, 1966-74; research dir. Nat. Ctr. Sci. Research, Paris, 1974-85; prof. U. Calif., Berkeley, 1981-82; research assoc. MIT, Cambridge, 1956-57; dir. Inst. Hautes Et Sci., Bures, France, 1985—. Author: Geometry I and II, 1987, Differential Geometry, 1987, Problems in Geometry, 1986; mng. editor Springer Verlag, 1982—. Recipient Prix Julia, Paris, 1979, Prix Carriere, 1969, Prix Lecomte, 1978. Fellow Soc. Math. France (pres. 1979-81), Am. Math. Soc.; mem. Acad. Scis. Roman Catholic. Home: 11 Ave Suffern, 75007 Paris France Office: Inst Hautes Et Sci, 35 Route de Chartres, 91440 Bures sur Yvette France

BERGER, OSCAR, artist; b. Presov, Eperjes, Czechoslovakia, May 12, 1901; came to U.S., 1928, naturalized, 1955; s. Henry and Regina (Berger) B.; m. Ann Arany I. Varga, Feb. 9, 1937. Art study, in Europe. Cartoonist world celebrities drawn from life; sketched meetings at League of Nations, Geneva, 1925, House of Commons, London, 1935-45, San Francisco Conf. of UN for N.Y. Times and Daily Telegraph, London, 1943, UN confs., 1945-87, UN gen. assemblies, 1946-87; work represented in permanent collections Library of Congress, Nat. Portrait Gallery, Met. Mus., also pvt. collections and museums.; author: Tip and Top, 1933, A La Carte, 1948, Aesop's Foibles, 1949, Famous Faces, 1950, My Victims, 1952, I Love You, 1960, The Presidents, 1968; contbr. to Am., European publs. Club: Nat. Press (Washington). Address: Berkeley House 120 Central Park S New York NY 10019

BERGER, RITA ROSE, educator; b. Bronx, N.Y., Jan. 1, 1925; s. Jack Maurice and Helene (Abrevaya); B.Ed., U. Miami, 1949; M.A., U. South Fla., 1973; m. Nathaniel Leah Berger, Sept. 29, 1949; 1 son, Carl Franklin. Tchr., North Miami (Fla.) Christian Ch., 1960-61, East Zephyrhills (Fla.) Elem. Sch., 1962-63; tchr. spl. edn. Polk County, Fla., 1965-67, tchr., 1967-73, reading tchr., 1973-81, tchr. learning disabled Rochelle Elem. Sch., Lakeland, 1981—; reading tchr. Plant City (Fla.) campus Hillsborough Community Coll., 1974-75; sec.-treas. Nate's Bike and Mower Sales and Service, Inc., Lakeland, Fla., 1973—; sales assoc. Pre-paid Legal Services; West area dir. Polk Edn., 1970-71; sec. Polk County Schs. Title I Dist. Parent Adv. Council, 1980-81. Altar worker First Assembly of God Ch. Recipient award for meritorious service United Negro Coll. Fund, 1977; cert. in elem. edn., reading, and secondary social studies, also adminstrn. and supervision, specific learning disabilities, and gifted edn., Fla. Mem. Internat. Reading Assn. (treas., del. Gen. Assembly), Fla. Reading Council (life), Assn. Children with Learning Disabilities, Polk Edn. Assn. (chmn. human relations com.), Fla. Teaching Profession, NEA, Assn. Supervision and Curriculum Devel., Fla. Assn. Supervision and Curriculum Devel., Nat. Assn. Female Execs., Internat. Platform Assn., Kappa Delta Pi. Republican. Pentecostal. Club: Century of South Fla. Home: 811 Arietta Dr Auburndale FL 33823 Office: 1728 E Edgewood Dr Lakeland FL 33803

BERGER, SANDRA BETH, accountant; b. Phila., Dec. 26, 1939; d. Albert B. and Jeanne G. (Miller) B. B.S. cum laude, Temple U., 1961. C.P.A., Pa., N.J. Fin. reports unit U.S. Govt., Phila., 1961-62; staff acct. Alexander Grant & Co., Phila., 1962-63, various acctg. firms, Phila., 1963-65; prin. Sandra B. Berger, CPA, Huntingdon Valley, Pa., 1965—; asst. prof. Temple U., Phila. and Ambler, Pa., 1969-73; issue specialist White House Conf. on Small Bus., 1985. Mem. Dean's adv. council Sch. of Bus. Administrn., Temple U., 1983—; acctg. adv. council Temple U., 1987—; adv. council Community Accts., Phila., 1984—; pres. bd. mgrs. Sch. Bus. Adminstrn., Temple U. Alumni, 1982-84, now acting treas.; mem. Edn. Com. Greenberg Elem. Sch., Baldi Middle Sch.; mem. parents adv. counsel Mentally Gifted Program Sch. Dist. of Phila. Recipient Chapel of 4 Chaplains award, Phila., 1979; Disting. Alumni Cert. of Honor, Temple U., 1980; inducted into Acctg. Hall of Fame, 1985. Mem. Am. Inst. C.P.A.s, Pa. Inst. C.P.A.s (past dir., mem. exec. com. Greater Phila. chpt., Cert. of Appreciation 1984), N.J. Soc. C.P.A.s, Am. Women's Soc. C.P.A.s, Bucks Co. Assn. C.P.A.s, Montco C.P.A.s (Montco planning com., 1978-83), Gen. Alumni Assn. (acting treas. 1980-84). Office: Le Mont Plaza 603 County Line Rd Huntingdon Valley PA 19006 also: 504 Tearose Ln Cherry Hill NJ 08003

BERGER, SANFORD JASON, lawyer, securities dealer, real estate broker; b. Cleve., June 29, 1926; s. Sam and Ida (Solomon) B.; m. Bertine Mae Benjamin, Aug. 6, 1950 (div. Dec. 1977); children: Bradley Alan, Bonnie Jean. B.A., Case Western Res. U., 1950, J.D., 1952. Bar: Ohio 1952, U.S. Supreme Ct. 1979. Field examiner Ohio Dept. Taxation, Cleve., 1952; sole practice, Cleve., 1952—; real estate cons., Cleve., 1960—; investment cons., Cleve., 1970—. Contbr. author: Family Evaluation in Child Custody Litigation, 1982, Child Custody Litigation, 1986, The Parental Alienation Syndrome and the Differentiation Between Fabricated and Genuine Child Sex Abuse, 1987; Copyright 10 songs, 1977. Candidate police judge, East Cleve., 1955, Bd. Edn., Beachwood, Ohio, 1963, mayor, Beachwood, 1967, judge ct. common pleas, Cuyahoga County, Ohio, 1984, 1986. Successful lawyer in U.S. Supreme Ct. Case of Cleveland Bd. of Edn. vs. Loudermill, 1985.

Served with USMC, 1944-45; PTO. Recipient Cert. Appreciation Phi Alpha Delta, 1969, U.S. Supreme Ct. Chief Justice Warren E. Burger Healer award, 1987, Outstanding Ohio Citizen award Ohio Gen. Assembly, 1987. Mem. Ohio State Bar Assn. (family law com.). Republican. Jewish. Lodge: B'nai B'rith (editor 1968-70). Avocations: poet; lyricist; legal writer; drag racer; scuba diving. Home: 6809 Mayfield Rd Apt 972 Mayfield Heights OH 44124 Office: Berger and Fertel 1836 Euclid Ave #305 Cleveland OH 44115

BERGER, STANISLAW, nutritionist, educator; b. Lublin, Poland, Sept. 13, 1923; s. Adam and Zofia (Stepien) B.; M.Sc. in Agr., Lublin U., 1949, Ph.D., 1951; D.Sc., Warsaw Agrl. U., 1961; m. Hanna Stankiewicz, Apr. 27, 1959; children—Agnes, Christopher, Martin. Asst., Lublin U., 1946-49; research worker Warsaw Public Health Inst., 1950-57; mem. faculty Warsaw Agrl. U., 1954--, prof. nutrition, 1966—, founder, dir. Human Nutrition Inst., 1959-80, dean Faculty Human Nutrition and Rural Home Econs., 1977-84; staff FAO, Rome, 1967-71; nutrition expert, adviser FAO, WHO, UNICEF, UN; mem. various govt. sci. commns. and councils. Served as under-officer Polish Army, 1944-45; prisoner-of-war (severely wounded); Rockefeller fellow Cornell U., 1957-58. Mem. Food Engrs. Assn. Poland (v.p., dir. 1952—), Polish Biochem. Soc., Internat. Union Nutritional Scis. (council), Fed. European Nutrition Soc. (pres. 1987), Polish Acad. Scis. (pres. human nutrition com. 1978—), Group of European Nutritionists Council, Polish Soc. Nutritional Scis. (1st pres. 1980-88, hon. pres. 1988—), Soc. Nutrition Edn., Polono-Swiss Soc. (pres. 1984—). Roman Catholic. Author numerous papers, revs., articles in field; chief editor Food Industry monthly, 1972-78; co-editor several sci. jours. Office: Inst Human Nutrition, 166 Nowoursynowska, Warsaw 02766, Poland

BERGER, STEPHEN EDWARD, psychologist, consultant; b. Phila., Oct. 1, 1944; s. Harold Allen and Lilian Eleanor (Loev) B.; m. Diane Marilyn Klein, Dec. 24, 1967; children—Michael Allen, Gary David. Ph.D., U. Miami, 1971. Diplomate in Clin. Psychology, Am. Bd. Profl. Psychology. Asst. prof. psychology U. So. Calif., 1971-78; pvt. practice psychology, Mission Viejo, Calif., 1972—; chief occupational health psychologist Los Angeles County Dept. Health Services, Los Angeles, 1978-82. Contbr. articles to profl. jours. Mem. Am. Psychol. Assn., Western Psychol. Assn., AAAS, Calif. State Psychol. Assn., N.Y. Acad. Scis. Democrat. Jewish. Office: 23461 S Pointe Dr #190 Laguna Hills CA 92653

BERGER, WILHELM GEORG, composer, musicologist; b. Rupea, Brasov, Dec. 4, 1929. Studied violin Bucharest Conservatoire. Mem. Bucharest Philharmonic Orch., 1948-57; mem. Composers' Union Quartet, 1953-57; sec. Romanian Composers' Union, 1968—. Composer: eleven symphonies; chamber music including 12 string quartets, sonatas; author: Studies: Moduri si proportii; Structuri sonore si aspectele lor armonice (Modes and proportions; Sonorous structures and their harmonic aspects); Ghid pentru muzica instrumentala de camera (Guidebook for instrumental chamber music), 1965; Muzica simfonica (Baroque-Classical 1967, Romantic 1972, Modern 1974, Contemporary 1976); Quartetul de coarde de la Haydn la Debussy (The string quartet from Haydn to Debussy), 1970. Recipient Prince Rainier III of Monaco prize, Monte Carlo, 1964; Concours internat. de composition d'oeuvres pour quatuor a cordes prize, Liege, 1965; Reine Elisabeth de Belgique, Internat. Musical Contest prize, 1966; George Enescu prize of Romanian Acad., 1966; Composers' Union prize, 1969. Address: Uniunea Compozitorilor, Str Constantin Exarcu 2, Bucharest Romania *

BERGGREN, BO ERIK GUNNAR, paper company executive; b. Falun, Sweden, Aug. 11, 1936; s. Tage B. and Elsa (Hoglund) B.; m. Gunbritt Haglund, 1962; children: Erik, Karin, Charlotta, Klas. Degree in Metall. Engring., Royal Inst. Tech., Stockholm, 1962. Metall. engr. in research and devel. Stora Kopparbergs Bergslags AB, Borlange, Sweden, 1962-68, mill mgr., Soderfors, Sweden, 1968-74, v.p., Falun, 1975-78, pres., 1984—; pres. Incentive, Aktiebolag, Stockholm, 1978-84; dir. Garphyttan Industrier AB, Ovako Steel, LE Lundberg-foretagen AB; bd. dirs., Skandinaviska Enskilda Banken. Mem. Swedish Pulp and Paper Assn. (dir.), Fedn. Swedish Industries (dir.), Fedn. Swedish Forest Industries, Swedish Employers' Confedn. Office: Stora Kopparbergs, Bergslags AB, 79180 Falun Sweden

BERGGREN, RONALD BERNARD, surgeon, emeritus educator; b. S.I., N.Y., June 13, 1931; s. Bernard and Florence (Schmidt) B.; m. Mary Beth Griffith, Nov. 25, 1954; children: Karen Ann, Eric Griffith. BA, Johns Hopkins U., 1953; MD, U. Pa., 1957. Diplomate Am. Bd. Surgery, Nat. Bd. Med. Examiners, Am. Bd. Plastic Surgery (bd. dirs. 1982-88, chmn. 1987-88). Asst. instr. surgery U. Pa., 1958-62, instr., 1962-65; gen. surg. resident Hosp. U. Pa., 1958-62, resident plastic surgery, 1963-64, chief resident plastic surgery, 1964-65; sr. resident surgery Phila. Gen. Hosp., 1962-63; asst. prof. surgery Ohio State U. Sch. Medicine, 1965-68, dir. div. plastic surgery, 1965-85, assoc. prof. surgery, 1968-73, prof. surgery, 1973-86, emeritus prof. surgery, 1986—; attending staff Ohio State U. Hosps., chief of staff, 1983-85, hon. staff, 1986—; attending staff, dir. div. plastic surgery Children's Hosp., Columbus, Ohio; v.p. Plastic Surgery Ednl. Found., 1984-85, pres.-elect, 1985-86, pres., 1986-87; sec. Plastic Surgery Tng. Program Dirs., 1981-83, chmn., 1983-85; mem. med. adv. bd. Ohio Bur. Crippled Children's Services, 1974—. Trustee Mid Ohio Health Planning Fedn., 1979-82, 84, PSRO, 1980-84, Scioto Valley Health Systems Agy., 1985-87. Fellow ACS; mem. Central, Columbus surg. socs., Am. Soc. Plastic and Reconstructive Surgeons, Ohio Valley Plastic Surg. Soc., Am. Cleft Palate Assn., AMA, Am. Assn. Plastic Surgeons (treas. 1982-85, v.p. 1988—), Franklin County Med. Soc. (pres.-elect 1982-83, pres. 1983-84), Soc. Cryosurgery, Plastic Surg. Research Council Ohio, Soc. Cryobiology, N.Y. Acad. Scis., Am. Assn. Surgery Trauma, Assn. Acad. Surgery, Am. Burn Assn., Am. Trauma Soc., Am. Soc. Aesthetic Plastic Surgery, Am. Soc. Maxillofacial Surgery, Accreditation Council for Grad. Med. Edn. (resident rev. com. for plastic surgery, 1983—, vice chmn. 1988, designate chmn. 1988—), Council Med. Specialty Socs., Sigma Xi, Phi Kappa Psi, Alpha Kappa Kappa. Home: 1960 Hampshire Rd Columbus OH 43221 Office: 410 W 10th Ave Columbus OH 43210

BERGGREN, THOMMY, actor; b. 1937. Ed. The Pickwick Club, Atelierteatern, Stockholm, Gothenburg Theatre. With Gothenberg Theatre, 1959-63, Royal Dramatic Theatre, Stockholm, 1963—. Appeared in plays including: Gengangaren (Ibsen), 1962, Romeo and Juliet, 1962, Chembalo, 1962, Who's Afraid of Virginia Woolf, 1964; films include: Parlemor, 1961; Barnvagnen, (The Pram), 1962; Kvarteret Korpen (Ravens End), 1963; En sondag i september (A Sunday in September), 1963; Karlek 65 (Love 65), 1965; Elvira Madigan, 1967; The Black Palm Trees, 1969; The Ballad of Joe Hill, 1971. Address: co Svenska Filminstitutet, Kungsgatan 48, Stockholm Sweden *

BERGHAUS, GÜNTER, drama educator, lecturer; b. Hückeswagen, Nordrhein-Westfalen, Fed. Republic of Germany, Nov. 3, 1953; arrived in Eng., 1977; s. Hans Helmut and Margret (Biesenbach) B. PhD, Free U. Berlin, 1977. Lectr. Bedford Coll., U. London, 1978-83, U. Bristol, Eng., 1983—; mem. council mgmt. Bristol Dance Ctr., 1984—. Author 3 books; editor 1 book; contbr. articles to profl. jours. Recipient German Research Found. award, Bonn, 1982, Polish Acad. Sci. Research award, Warsaw, 1983, 88, Brit. Acad. Research award, London, 1984, 88. Mem. Internat. Nestroy Soc., Internat. Baroque Soc. Home: 20 Hughenden Rd, Bristol BS8 2TT, England Office: U Bristol Dept Drama, 29 Park Row, Bristol England

BERGLEITNER, GEORGE CHARLES, JR., investment banker; b. Bklyn., July 16, 1935; s. George Charles and Marie (Preitz) B.; m. Betty Van Buren, Oct. 29, 1966; children—George Charles III, Michael John, Stephen William. B.B.A., St. Francis Coll., Bklyn., 1959; M.B.A., Coll. City N.Y., 1961; Ph.D. in Bus. Adminstrn. (hon.), Colo. State Christian Coll. Dir. instl. sales A.T. Brod & Co., N.Y.C., 1965-66; dir. instl. sales Weis, Voisin & Cannon, Inc., N.Y.C., 1966-67, C.B. Richard, Ellis & Co., N.Y.C., 1967-68; pres. Stamford (N.Y.) Fin. Co., also bd. dirs.; pres. M.J. Manchester & Co., Fashion & Time, Inc., B.J.B. Graphics, Inc., First Coinvestors, Inc., Smart Fit Foundations, Inc., Jay Co., Computer Holdings Corp., Ltd., Delhi Mfg. Corp.; pres. Delhi Chems., Inc., Walton; chmn. bd. dirs. Delhi Industries, Delhi Mfg. Inc., Delhi Internat., Inc., Luxembourg, Bio-Life, Inc., Bio-Vite, Inc.; bd. dirs. Alpha Capital Corp., Am. Energy Mgmt. Corp., Stamford Fin., Leonia Enterprises, L.I. Venture Capital Group, L.I. Venture Group, N.Y. Venture Capital Group, N.Y. Venture Group, Maritime Transp. & Tech., Inc., Vital Signs Inc., Delaware County Real Estate Corp.; exec. v.p. Cove Abstract Corp., also bd. dirs.; mem. Nat. Stock Exchange, N.Y. Merc. Exchange, Phila.-Balt.-Washington Stock Exchange. Chmn. Franciscan Fathers Devel. Program, 1967-71; mem. President's Council, Franciscan Spirit award, 1959—; pres. South Kortright Central Sch.; chmn. No. Catskills Econ. Devel. Council.; Regent St Francis Coll.; bd. dirs. Econ. Devel. Council Delaware County, Printing Trade Sch., Community Hosp., Stamford, N.Y., Western Catskills Community Revitalization Council, Inc. Served with U.S. Army, 1952-55. Recipient St. Francis Coll. Alumni Fund award, 1965; John F. Kennedy Meml. award, 1972; Internat. award for service to investment comm., 1972; Paul Harris fellow Rotary Internat. Mem. Security Traders Assn. N.Y., Nat. Security Traders Assn., AIM, Cath. War Vets., Assn. Investment Bankers, Honor Legion N.Y.C. Police Dept., Coll. City N.Y. alumni assns. Republican. Club: Stamford Country. Lodges: KC, Moose, Rotary (pres. Stamford 1980-81, Paul Harris fellow). Home: Red Rock Rd Stamford NY 12167 Office: Stamford Fin Bldg Stamford NY 12167

BERGLUND, BRITA, journalist, editor, writer, translator; b. Liverpool, Eng., Apr. 20, 1909; d. Emil Augustin and Emmy Maria (von Haartman) Enhörning; m. Karl Axel Berglund, Mar. 25, 1936; children: Staffan, Ingela, Michaël. BA in English Edn, with honors, U. Stockholm, 1936. Consulate gen. to asst. mgr. Colombia Åhlén and Akerlund Pub., Stockholm, 1931-32; editor women's page Norbottenskuriren newspaper, Stockholm, 1947-48; editor women's page, reporter Året Runt mag. Åhlén, Åkerlund Pub., Stockholm, 1949-50; editor women's page, reporter Dagens Nyheter newspaper, Stockholm, 1950-56; reporter Dagens Nyheter newpaper, Stockholm, 1958-76, free-lance reporter, 1974—. Author: (guidebook) Gambia, 1973; contbr. articles, short stories to profl. jours.; translator into post-grad. sci. essays, travel guidebook. Mem. Swedish Journalist's Union (mem. election com. 1970-72), Swedish Press Assn., Swedish Bus. and Profl. Women's Fedn., Swedish Women's Ednl. Assn. Liberal. Home: Kampemntsgatan 24 8tr, 11538 Stockholm Sweden

BERGLUND, PAAVO ALLEN ENGELBERT, conductor; b. Helsinki, Finland, Apr. 14, 1929; s. Hjalmar and Siiri (Loiri) B.; m. Kirsti Kivekas, 1958; 3 children. Ed. Sibelius Acad., Helsinki. Violinist, Finnish Radio Symphony Orch., 1949-56, condr., 1956-62, prin. condr., 1962-71; prin. condr. Bournemouth Symphony Orch., 1972-79, Helsinki Philharmonic Orch., 1975-79; prin. guest condr. Scottish Nat. Orch., 1982-84. Recs.: Kullervo Symphony, 1971-77; Ma Vlast (Smetana), Shostakovich symphonies 5, 6, 7, 10, 11; numerous other recs.; author: A Comparative Study of the Printed Score and the Manuscript of the Seventh Symphony of Sibelius, 1970. Recipient State award for Music, 1972, Hon. Order Brit. Empire. Address: Munkkiniemenranta 41, 00330 Helsinki 33 Finland *

BERGMAN, BRUCE JEFFREY, lawyer; b. N.Y.C., May 15, 1944; s. Lawrence A. and Myrna (Coe) B.; m. Linda A. Cantor, May 30, 1971; children: Jennifer Dana, Jason Cole. BS, Cornell U., 1966; JD, Fordham U., 1969. Bar: N.Y. 1970, D.C. 1987, U.S. Dist. Ct. (so. dist.) N.Y. 1971, U.S. Supreme Ct. 1973, U.S. Dist. Ct. (ea. dist.) N.Y. 1973, U.S. Ct. Appeals (2d cir.) 1973. Assoc. law firm Jarvis, Pilz, Buckley & Treacy, N.Y.C., 1970-76; ptnr. law firm Pedowitz & Bergman, Garden City, N.Y., 1976-80; dep. county atty. Nassau County, Mineola, N.Y., 1980-84; counsel Jonas Libert & Weinstein, Garden City, 1981-84; ptnr. Roach & Bergman, 1984—; adj. assoc. prof. NYU Real Estate Inst., N.Y.C., 1981—. Author: New York Mortgage Foreclosures, 1983; contbr. numerous articles to legal jours.; contbg. editor: Mortgages and Mortgage Foreclosure in New York, 1982. Councilman, City of Long Beach, N.Y., 1980—. Mem. ABA, N.Y. State Bar Assn., Nassau County Bar Assn. (dir., chmn. real property law com.), Am. Coll. Real Estate Lawyers. Republican. Club: Cornell of L.I. (past pres.). Home: 12 Hawthorne Ln Lawrence NY 11516 Office: Roach & Bergman 600 Old Country Rd Garden City NY 11530

BERGMAN, HANS OTTO MAURITZ, psychology educator, alcohol use researcher; b. Stockholm, Sept. 16, 1938; s. Gösta Mauritz and Karin Johanna (Ålander) B.; m. Inger Kerstin Peterson, Nov. 27, 1965; children: Martin, Henrik. BA, U. Stockholm, 1964, MA, 1971, PhD, 1975. Psychologist St. Görans Hosp., Stockholm, 1964-68; research psychologist U. Stockholm, 1969-75; chief psychologist Karolinska Hosp., Stockholm, 1976-80, prof., 1981—. Contbr. approx. 100 articles in clin. psychology, especially within field of alcohol and alcoholism. Mem. Swedish Assn. Alcohol and Drug Research (com. mem. 1981-82, v.p. 1984). Home: Kungsholms hamnplan 2, S-11220 Stockholm Sweden Office: Clin Alcohol, and Drug Addiction Research, PO Box 60 500, S-104 01 Stockholm Sweden

BERGMAN, (ERNST) INGMAR, film writer, director; b. Uppsala, Sweden, July 14, 1918; m. Ingrid Karlebovon Rosen; 8 children. Ed., Stockholm U. Producer Royal Theatre, Stockholm, 1940-42; producer, writer Swedish Film Co., 1940-44; theatrical dir. Helsingborg, 1944-46, Gothenburg, 1946-49, Malmo, 1952-59; dir. Royal Dramatic Theatre, Stockholm, 1963-66. Writer screenplay: Torment, 1943; dir. films: Crisis, 1945, It Rains on Our Love, 1946, A Ship Bound For India, 1947, Music in Darkness, 1947, Port of Call, 1948, Prison, 1948, Thirst, 1949, To Joy, 1949, Summer Interlude, 1950, Summer with Monika, 1952, Sawdust and Tinsel, 1953, Lesson in Love, 1954, Journey into Autumn, 1955, Smiles of a Summer Night, 1956 (Cannes Film Festival award), The Seventh Seal, 1957 (Cannes Film Festival award), So Close to Life, 1958 (Cannes Film Festival award), The Magician, 1958, Wild Strawberries, 1958 (Berlin Film Festival award), The Virgin Spring, 1960 (Acad. award), The Devil's Eye, 1961, Through a Glass Darkly, 1961, Winter Light, 1962, The Silence, 1963, Now About All These Women, 1964, Persona, 1967, Hour of the Wolves, 1968, The Shame, 1969, The Passion of Anna, 1970, The Touch, 1971, Cries and Whispers, 1972 (Best Film award Nat. Soc. Film Critics 1972), Scenes from a Marriage (also TV), 1974, The Magic Flute (also TV), 1975, Face to Face (also TV), 1975, The Serpent's Egg, 1977, Autumn Sonata, 1978, Summer Paradise, 1978, Sally and Freedom, 1983, Fanny and Alexander, 1983 (Acad. Award Best Foreign Language Film Dir. 1984), After the Rehearsal, 1984; producer plays: Hedda Gabler, Cambridge, 1970, Slow, 1971; author plays: Four Stories, 1977, A Painting on Wood, The City, The Rite (TV play), The Lie (TV play); dir. plays: To Damascus, 1974, The Merry Widow, Twelfth Night, 1975, 80, Tartuffe, 1980, King Lear, 1985, John Gabriel Borkman, 1985, Miss Julie, 1986, Hamlet, 1986, others. Recipient Erasmus award for contbn. to arts, The Netherlands, 1965, Best Dir. award Nat. Soc. Film Critics, 1970, Goethe prize, 1976, Gold Medal of Swedish Acad., 1977; decorated Comdr. Legion of Honor, 1985. Address: Titurelstrasse 2, D-8000 Munich 8, Federal Republic of Germany *

BERGMAN, ROBERT SCRIBNER, toy manufacturing executive; b. Aurora, Ill., Nov. 23, 1934; s. Ross M. and Mary O. (Ochsenschlager) B.; B.S., Ill. Inst. Tech., 1956; postgrad., Stanford U., 1956-58; m. Patricia LeBaron, June 10, 1956; children: David C., Lynne M., Joseph R. With Hughes Aircraft Co., Culver City, Calif., 1956, Gen. Electric Co., Palo Alto, Calif., 1957, Sylvania, Mountain View, Calif., 1958-61; with Processed Plastic, Montgomery, Ill., 1961— , pres., 1969—; treas. Intertoy, Montgomery, 1977—, Graphic Label Co., Montgomery, Ill., 1977—; bd. dirs. Brunsport, Montgomery, Anthony Strodder (Leeds), Ltd.; chmn. bd. Lektro-Vend, Aurora, Ill.; chmn. bd., treas. Berkir Sales, Montgomery, 1986. Mem. Am. Phys. Soc., Toy Mfrs. Am. (dir. 1981-85). Republican. Mem. United Ch. of Christ. Club: Elks. Home: 1330 Monona Ave Aurora IL 60506 Office: 1001 Aucutt Rd Montgomery IL 60538

BERGMANN, ARTHUR M., writer, investor, yachtsman, former county official, former newspaperman; b. N.Y., Nov. 24, 1927; s. Augustus H. Bergmann; m. Ruth Naomi Liebman, July 1, 1982; children by previous marriage: Susan M., Joel M., Kathy G., Jonathan M. BS in Polit. Sci. and Pub. Adminstrn., Empire State Coll., SUNY, Old Westbury, 1974; M in Pub. and Gen. Adminstrn., L.I.U., 1979. With N.Y. Herald Tribune, 1945-63; asst. news editor Riverhead News, 1949-50; Suffolk County (N.Y.) corr. for N.Y.C. newspapers, 1949-63; news editor Moriches (N.Y.) Tribune, 1950-51; mem. staff Newsday, 1951-71, Suffolk County polit. editor, columnist, 1965-71; chief dep. Suffolk County Exec., Hauppauge, N.Y., 1972-79. Chmn., Suffolk Criminal Justice Coordinating Council, 1975-79, Arson Action Com.-Suffolk Arson Task Force, 1978-79; mem. Juvenile Justice Task Force, 1975-77, MTA Permanent Citizens Adv. Com., 1978-79; adv. council N.Y. State Crime Victims Compensation Bd., 1978-79; trustee Suffolk Acad. Medicine, 1976, Huntington Hist. Soc., 1988. Served with USAAF, 1946-47. Recipient Disting. Service award United Jewish Appeal, 1976; Public Adminstrn. award C. W. Post Coll., 1977; Disting. Service plaque L.I. Assn. Commerce and Industry, 1977; Exemplary Service award Empire State Coll., SUNY, 1981; nominated for Pulitzer prize (2). Mem. Acad. Polit. Sci., Soc. Silurians, Am. Soc. Public Adminstrn., Am. Legion, Sierra, Pi Alpha Alpha. Clubs: Moriches Yacht (past commodore) (Center Moriches, N.Y.); Huntington Yacht (N.Y.). Address: Pebble Hill 245 Little Neck Rd Centerport NY 11721

BERGNÄS, SVEN, corporate professional; b. Stockholm, Sweden, Apr. 15, 1940; children: Fredrik, Annika, Christina. Student, Coll. Europe, Bruges, 1964-65; law degree, Stockholm U., 1965. Gen. counsel, corp. sec. Armerad Betong Vägförbättringar AB, Stockholm, Sweden, 1981—. Office: Armerad Betong Vagforbattringar AB, Vallgatan 3, S-171 80 Solna Sweden

BERGOLD, ORM, medical educator; b. Nuremberg, Germany, Apr. 30, 1925; s. Friedrich and Wilhelmine (Schering) B.; M.D., Chgo. Med. Coll., 1974; D.Chemistry, Benjamin Franklin Inst., N.Y.C., 1976; M.Acupuncture, Old Chinese Acupuncture Acad., Hong Kong, 1978; D.Sc. (hon.), St. Andrew's Coll., London, 1965; m. Sylvia Patricia Sanchez, 1983; children: Heike, Timm. Pres., Orm Bergold Chemie, Langlau and Bochum, W. Ger., 1953-63; pres. Inst. Med. Biophysics and Biochemistry, Campione, Switzerland, 1963-82; pres. Inst. Med. Biophysics and Biochemistry, San Jose, Costa Rica, 1982—, Inst. Biocybernetic and Natural Therapy, San Jose, 1985—; v.p. Stress and Aging Control Ctr, Panama, Costa Rica, 1986—; prof. cybernetic medicine Academia Gentium Pro Pace, Rome, 1977—, senator, 1979—; prof. extraordinary U. Francisco Marroquin, Guatemala City, 1979—, senator, 1980—. Decorated grand cross Ordre Equestre de la San Croix de Jérusalem; chevalier du Tastevin. Author: Kybernetische Medizin, 1977; Cancer prophylaxis: a problem of early recognition and treatment, 1980; Cancer Treatment with Human Fibroblast Interferon, 1982; Cancer Treatment by Natural Remedies, 1983; also articles. Home: PO Box 359, CR-1250 Escazu Costa Rica Office: PO Box 257, 1005 Barrio Mexico, San Jose Costa Rica

BERGS, SUNE OLOF, industrial consultant; b. Falun, Dalarna, Sweden, 1941; m. Mari-Ann Bergs; children: Susanne, Tommy, Benny. Product mgr. Svenska Elektromagneter, Amal, Sweden, 1966-70, AB Abroga Maskiner, Sweden, 1970-73, AB Dellner-Malmco, Falun, 1973-78; pres. Dellner Couplers Ltd., Mississauga, Can., 1979-85, Dellner Couplers Inc., Bridgeport, Conn., 1980-85; mng. dir. Dellner Couplers B.V., Amsterdam, The Netherlands, 1981-85, Dellner Couplers Pty. Ltd., Victoria, Australia, 1983-85; dir. Dellner Kupplungen Gmbh, Dusseldorf, Fed. Republic Germany, 1983-85; pres. Bergs Engring. AB, Falun, 1985—, AB Air Control, Falun, 1986—; bd. dirs. Foreningsbanken, Falun. Bd. dirs., sec. Swedish Can. C. of C. in Can., 1980-82. Office: Bergs Engring AB, Skuggarvet 10, 790-15 Sundborn Sweden

BERGSMA, ALLE, business executive; b. Elsloo, Friesland, The Netherlands, Sept. 13, 1952; s. Heine and Richtje (Russcher) B.; m. Regina Johanna Riksma, July 6, 1973; children: Heine, Alle. Student, Nyenrode, The Netherlands, 1971-73, U. Oreg., 1973-74. With Celtona B.V., Cuyk, The Netherlands, 1976—, asst. to export mgr., 1976-79, nat. account mgr., 1979-83, export mgr., 1983-86, export dir., 1986-88; comml. dir. Hollandia-Coevorden B.V., Cuyk, The Netherlands, 1988—. Home: Everdrift 14, NL-5431 LV Cuyk The Netherlands Office: Hollandia-Coevorden BV, Robert Weg 2, NL-7741 KX Coevorden The Netherlands

BERGSTRAESSER, ROLAND, banker; b. Landau, Pfalz, Germany, July 6, 1926. Legal exam, U. Mainz, 1951, 2d legal exam, 1955. With Fed. Ministry Finance, Bonn, 1958-77; exec. bd. DG Bank, Frankfurt am Main, 1978—; dir. Coop AG, Frankfurt am Main, DG Capital Co. Ltd., Hong Kong, DG Diskontbank AG, Frankfurt and Main, Frankfurter Kredit-Bank GmbH, Frankfurt am Main, Deutsche Ausgleichsbank, Bonn-Bad Godesberg; dep. bd. dirs. Liquiditaets-Konsortialbank GmbH, Frankfurt. Office: Deutsche Genossenschaftsbank, Am Platz der Republik, Postfach 100651, D 6000 Frankfurt am Main Federal Republic of Germany

BERGSTROM, ALBION ANDREW, army officer; b. Salem, Mass., Sept. 2, 1947; s. Eric Hjalmar and Helen Lawrence (Andrew) B.; m. Yvonne Darlene Umfleet, Mar. 16, 1981. B.A. in Polit. Sci., Colo. State U., 1969; M.A. in Personnel Mgmt., Central Mich. U., 1978; grad. Command and Gen. Staff Coll., U.S. Army, 1982. Commd. 2d lt. U.S. Army, 1969, advanced through grades to lt. col., 1985; platoon leader, aide de camp, Vietnam, 1970-71; co. commdr., Ft. Hood, Tex., 1974-75; bn. exec. officer, Erlangen, W.Ger., 1980-81, bn. comdr., 1986—; assignment officer, Washington, 1983-85; sec. of gen. staff VII Corps, Stuttgart, W. Ger., 1985-86. Program chmn. Pinewood Forest Assn., Lake Ridge, Va., 1982-84; del. N.H. Republican conventions, 1966, 68. Decorated Bronze Star medal, Purple Heart medal. Mem. Armor Assn. (program chmn. Abrams chpt. 1984-85), Assn. U.S. Army, 1st Cavalry Div. Assn., Phi Sigma Delta, Zeta Beta Tau. Congregationalist. Lodges: Masons, Shriners. Avocations: photography, antique cars, cross-country skiing. Home: 3397 Ft Lyon Dr Woodbridge VA 22192 Office: CDR 1-35 Armor, APO New York NY 09066

BERGSTRÖM, INGVAR ERIK, art historian, educator; b. Gothenburg, Sweden, Dec. 16, 1913; s. Erik Oscar and Tonny Dagmar (Sðron) B.; Ph.D., U. Gothenburg, 1947; m. Adie Elisabeth Lundell, May 4, 1935 (dec. 1982); 1 dau., Lisbeth. Asst. at Röhss Mus. of Arts and Crafts, Gothenburg, 1937-46; asst. prof. history of art U. Gothenburg, 1947-58, research prof., 1958-80; Decorated Royal Swedish Order of the North Star, Gold medal for ser. to Sweden, Order of Orange-Nassau, King Haakon Cross of Liberty, Norway. Fellow Royal Soc. Arts and Scis. (Gothenburg), Cuisine Culinaire Nederland, recipient Bukowski prize, 1987; mem. Union of Swedish Profs. (bd. dirs. 1963—), Union of Research Profs. of Sweden (pres. 1963-82, hon. pres. 1983—). Author: Holländskt stillebenmåleri under 1600-talet, 1947; Dutch Still-Life Painting in the 17th Century, 1956; Revival of Antique Illusionistic Wall-Painting in Renaissance Art, 1957; Den Symboliska Nejlikan, 1958; Bodegones y floreros del siglo XVII, 1970; La Natura in Posa, 1971; co-author: La Grande Stagione Della Natura Morta Europaea, 1977; Interpretationes Selectae, 1978; co-author: Stilleben in Europa, 1979-80; (with Georg Flegel) Lucas van Valckenborch, 1983, Jacob Marrel's Earliest Tulip Book, 1984, Ludger tom Ring the Younger as a Painter of Birds and Beasts, 1987 and others. Home: 4 Gibraltargatan, 41132 Gothenburg Sweden Office: Forskningsinstitutet, for Atomfysik, Roslagvagen 100, 10405 Stockholm Sweden

BERGSTRÖM, K. SUNE D., biochemist; b. Stockholm, Jan. 10, 1916; s. Sverker B. and Wera (Wistrand) B.; m. Maj Gernandt, July 30, 1943. Docent physiol. chemistry, MD., Karolinska Inst., Stockholm, 1944, D.Med.Sci. in Biochemistry, 1944; Dr. h.c., U. Basel (Switzerland), 1960, U. Chgo., 1960, Harvard U., 1976, Mt. Sinai Med. Sch., 1976, Med. Acad. Wroclaw (Poland), 1976. Research fellow U. London, 1938, Columbia U., N.Y.C., 1940-41, Squibb Inst. Med. Research, New Brunswick, N.J., 1941-42; asst. biochem. dept. Med. Nobel Inst., Karolinsa Inst., Stockholm, 1944-47; research fellow U. Basel, 1946-47; prof. physiol. chemistry U. Lund (Sweden), 1947-58; prof. chemistry Karolinska Inst., 1958-80, dean med. faculty, 1963-66, rector, 1969-77; chmn. bd. dirs. Nobel Found., Stockholm, 1975—; pres. Royal Swedish Acad. Scis., from 1983; chmn. WHO Adv. Com. Med. Research, Geneva, 1977-82; La Madonnina lectr., Milan, Italy, 1972; Dunham Lectr. Harvard U., 1972; Dohme lectr. Johns Hopkins U., 1972-73; Merrimon lectr. U. N.C.-Chapel Hill, 1973; V.D. Mattia lectr. Roche Inst., 1974; Harvey lectr. Harvey Soc., N.Y.C., 1974; Gen. Amir Chand orator All India Inst., New Delhi, 1978; Cairlton lectr. U. Tex. Health Sci. Ctr., Dallas, 1979; mem. Swedish Med. Research Council, 1952-58, 64-70, Swedish Natural Sci. Research Council, 1955-62. Contbr. articles to sci. jours. Recipient Anders Jahre Med. prize, Oslo, 1972; Gairdner award U. Toronto, 1972; Louisa Gross Horwitz prize Columbia U., 1975; Francis Amory prize Am. Acad. Arts and Scis., 1975; Albert Lasker Basic Med. Research award, N.Y.C., 1977; Robert A. Welch award, Houston, 1980; Nobel prize, 1982. Mem. Royal Swedish Acad. Scis., Swedish Acad. Engring. Scis., Am. Acad. Arts and Scis., Am. Soc. Biol. Chemists, Acad. Scis. USSR, Academia Leopoldina (E.Ger.), Royal Soc. Edinburgh, Med. Acad. USSR, Finska Vetenskaps-Societeten, Swedish Soc. Med. Scis., sr. mem. Inst. of Medicine, Nat. Acad. Scis., fgn. assoc. Nat. Acad. Scis. Address: care Nobel

Found, Noblstiftelsen, PO Box 5232, Stockholm 10245, Sweden also: Karolinska Inst, Solnavagen I, PO Box 60400, 10401 Stockholm Sweden *

BERGSTROM, ROBERT WILLIAM, lawyer; b. Chgo., Nov. 8, 1918; s. C. William and Ellen (Anderson) B.; m. Betty Howard; children: Mark Robert, Philip Alan, Bryan Scott, Cheryl Lee, Jeffrey Alan. M.B.A., U. Chgo., 1947; LL.B., Ill. Inst. Tech.-Chgo. Kent Coll. Law, 1940, J.D., 1970. Bar: Ill. 1940, U.S. Supreme Ct. 1950. Ptnr. Bergstrom, Davis & Teeple (and predecessors), 1951—; founder Ill. Statewide Com. on Cts. and Justice, 1971—; bd. dirs. Ill. Com. for Constl. Conv., 1969, Ill. Constl. Research Group, 1970; spl. counsel Ill. Joint Legislative Com. to Investigate Met. San. Dist. of Cook County, 1967, Ill. Senate Mcpl. Corp. Com., 1970. Co-author: The Law of Competition in Illinois, 1962, Antitrust Developments, 1955-68, Antitrust Advisor, 1985; author Marxism, Senator Sherman, and Our Economic System, 1968, and numerous articles on antitrust, constl. law, and econs.; Editor: Chgo. Bar Record, 1971-72. Served to lt. USNR, 1941-46. Named Chicagoan of Yr. in Law and Judiciary Chgo. Jaycees, 1969; recipient medal Ill. Constl. Conv., 1970, Disting. Pub. Service award Union League Club, 1981. Mem. ABA, Ill. Bar Assn., Chgo. Bar Assn. (sec. 1969-71). Club: Union League (pres. 1971-72). Office: Bergstrom Davis & Teeple 39 S LaSalle St Suite 800 Chicago IL 60603

BERGSTROM, ROLF OLOF BERNHARD, manufacturing company executive; b. Helsingborg, Skaane, Sweden, Jan. 20, 1934; s. Curt and Inga (Stalbrand) B.; m. Ingrid Haggstrom, June 23, 1959; children—Eva, Anders, Mats. M.B.A., Gothenburg (Sweden) U., 1957. Vice pres. adminstrn. AB Ifoverken, Bromolla, Sweden, 1965-68; asst. fin. mgr. Industri AB Euroc, Malmo, Sweden, 1968-70; exec. v.p. Ifo AB, Bromolla, 1970-71, pres., 1971-76; exec. v.p. Industri AB Euroc, Malmo, Bromolla, 1976-77; pres. Dynapac AB, Solna, Sweden, 1977-86; pres. HeatTech. AB, Sundbyberg, Sweden, 1986— . Lutheran. Office: Heat Tech AB, PO Box 7097, Sundbyberg S 17027, Sweden

BERGSTROM-WALAN, MAJ-BRIHT, sexologist, psychotherapist, educator, writer, researcher; b. Stockholm, Nov. 17, 1924; d. Gustav Arvid and Hanna (Eriksson) Bergstrom; m. Bror Edvin Walan, Mar. 17, 1949 (div.); 1 son, Gustav. Midwife, Midwife Coll. Stockholm, 1947; MA in Nordic Langs., U. Stockholm, 1957, MA in Pedagogics, 1961, PhD in Psychology, 1963. Youth leader Swedish Mission Covenant Ch., 1941-50; midwife Maternity Hosps., Sweden, 1947-55; tchr. Nordic langs., sex edn., Stockholm, 1957-65; assoc. prof. sexology, psychology, Stockholm, 1957-70; sec. gen. Swedish State Commn. Sex Edn., Stockholm, 1965-68; founder, dir. Swedish Inst. Sexual Research, Stockholm, 1970—; cons. Swedish Central Com. Rehab., Stockholm, 1969—, Swedish Internat. Devel. Authority, Stockholm, 1970, Australian Commn. Sex Edn., Canberra, 1975; organizer Internat. Symposium Sex Edn. and Therapy, Stockholm, 1976. Author: The Swedish Hite Report, 1981; 9memoirs) Passions, 1987; also sex edn. books in several langs. and sex edn. films. Mcpl. del. Liberal Party, Stockholm, 1959-63. Swedish Social Sci. Research Council grantee, 1958-66; Royal Swedish Found. grantee, 1961; Swedish Med. Research Council grantee, 1965. Mem. Swedish Assn. Midwives (chmn. 1962-66), Swedish Assn. Writers Ednl. Material, Swedish Assn. Psychology, World Assn. Sexology, Swedish Assn. Sexology, Swedish Assn. Sexology (hon.). Home: Tystbergavagen 41, S-12241 Stockholm Sweden Office: Swedish Inst Sexual Research, Lästmakargatan 14-16, S-11144 Stockholm Sweden

BERING, EDGAR ANDREW, III, physicist; b. N.Y.C., Jan. 9, 1946; s. Edgar Andrew and Harriet Crocker (Aldrich) B.; m. Stacie Eden Cherniack, June 27, 1971 (div. 1979); m. Barbara Adele Clark, May 11, 1985. B.A., Harvard U., 1967; Ph.D., U. Calif.-Berkeley, 1974. Teaching asst. U. Calif., Berkeley, 1967-69, research assoc., 1969-74; research scientist physics dept. U. Houston, 1974-75, asst. prof., 1975-81, assoc. prof., 1981—; ptnr. I.F.&G. Tech. Cons., Bellaire, Tex., 1984—. Contbr. articles to profl. jours. Pres. Festival Angels, Inc., Houston, 1984, treas., 1983; bd. dirs. Gulf Coast World Affairs Council, Houston, 1982—. Recipient Antarctica Service medal NSF, 1981. Mem. Am. Astron. Soc., Am. Geophys. Union, AAAS, N.Y. Acad. Scis., Sigma Xi. Episcopalian. Home: 4622 Braeburn Dr Bellaire TX 77401

BERIO, LUCIANO, composer, conductor, educator; b. Imperia Oneglia, Italy, Oct. 24, 1925; s. Ernesto Filippo and Ada (Dal Fiume) B.; m. Cathy Berberian, Oct. 1, 1950 (div.); 1 dau., Christina Luisa; m. Susan Oyama, 1964 (div.); children: Marina, Stefano; m. Talia Pecker, 1977; children: Daniel, Jonathan. Student, Liceo Classico, 1936-43; grad. composition and orch. conducting, Conservatorio G. Verdi, Milan, 1951. Tchr. composition Berkshire Festival, 1960, Dartington Summer Sch., 1961, 62, Mills Coll., 1962, 63, Darmstadt Ferienkurse, 1963; tchr. at Juilliard Sch. Music, 1965, also seminars at; Harvard, 1966. Founder, 1954, Studio de Fonologia Musicale, for electronic music at Italian Radio; founder, 1954; musical rev. Incontri Musicali; Composer: Tre Liriche popolari, 1948, Magnificat, 1949-71, Due Pezzi, 1951, 5 Variazioni, 1951, Chamber Music, 1953, Variazioni, 1953, El Mar la Mar, 1952-53, Mimusique 1, 1953, Mimusique 2, 1953, Nones, 1954, Quartetto, 1955, Perspectives, 1956, Allelujah II, 1956-57, Serenata, 1957, Thema, 1958, Sequenza, I, 1958, Allez-Hop, 1952-59, Differences, 1958-59, Tempi Concertati, 1958-59, Circles, 1960, Momenti, 1960, Epifanie, 1959-61, Visage, 1961, Passaggio, 1962, Sequenza II, 1963, Rounds, 1965, Sincronie, 1963-64, Chemins, I, 1965, Sequenza III, IV, V, 1955-56, Folk Songs, 1964, Laborintus, 1965, Gesti, 1966, Chemins II, 1967-68, Chemins III, 1968, Sinfonia, 1968, Questo Vuol Dire Che, 1968-69, Opera, 1970, rev., 1977, Memory, 1971, Bewegung, 1971, Concerto, 1972-73, Still, 1973, A. Ronne, 1974, Chemins IV, 1955, Coro, 1975-76, IL Ritorno degli Snovidenia, 1976, La Vera Storia, 1979, Un re in Ascolto, 1982, Voci, 1985, Requies, 1985, Ricorrenze, 1985, Formazioni, 1986; also numerous recs. Address: Il Colombaio, Radicondoli, Siena Italy

BERISTAIN IPIÑA, ANTONIO, criminologist, lawyer, educator; b. Medina Rioseco, Spain, Apr. 4, 1924; s. Ignacio Beristain and Felisa Ipiña de Beristain; M.A., OñA, Burgos, Spain, 1950; LL.B., U. Valladolid (Spain), 1953; B.D., St. Georgen Coll., Frankfurt, Germany, 1957; LL.D., U. Madrid, 1961; LL.D. (hon.), U. Pau (France). Lectr. criminal law U. Deusto-Bilbao, Bilbao, Vizcaya, Spain, 1958-67; lectr. criminal law U. Valladolid, 1967-68, U. Madrid (Spain), 1968-70; prof. criminal law U. Oviedo (Spain), 1970-73, U. País Vasco, San Sebastián, Spain, 1973—; head dept. criminal law U. San Sebastian, Spain, 1973—; founder, head Basque Inst. Criminology, San Sebastián, 1976—; vis. prof. U. El Salvador, Buenos Aires, Argentina, 1980. Introduced Amnesty Internat. in Basque Country, 1977. Recipient 1st prize Inst. Young Persons for study juvenile delinquency and soc., Madrid, 1968. Mem. Internat. Assn. Criminal Law, Soc. de Estudios Vascos, Soc. Internat. de Crimininologie (cons. dir.). Roman Catholic. Club: Amnesty International. Author: Medidas penales en derecho contemporáneo, 1974; Crisis del derecho represivo, 1977; Cuestiones penales y criminológicas, 1979; coauthor: (with Larrea) Fuentes de derecho penal vasco (Siglos XI-XVI), 1980; Desbideraketa, Bazterketa eta Gizarte Kontrola, 1984; Presondegiak, Gazteen Gaizkintza, Drogoak, 1987; La Droga. Aspectos penales y criminológicos, Bogotá, 1986; Derecho penal y Criminología, Bogotá, 1986; Problemas criminológicos, Mex., 1985; El delincuente en la democracia, Buenos Aires, 1985; La pena-retribución y las actuales concepciones criminológicas, Buenos Aires, 1982, Los derechos humanos ante la Criminologia y el Derecho penal, 1986, La droga en la sodiedad actual, 1985. Editor: Estudios Vascos de Criminologia, 1982. Corr., Revue sci. criminal et droit penal comparé; Rev. de Droit Péal et de Criminologie, Brussels. Home: EUTG (Mundaiz), San Sebastian Spain Office: Facultad Derecho, San Sebastian Spain

BERKARDA, BULENT, internist, hematologist, oncologist; b. Duzce, Turkey, May 18, 1932; s. Kemal and Nadire Berkarda; m. Nevin Tirnakci, Sept. 4, 1959; children: Hulya, Kemal. MD summa cum laude, U. Istanbul, Turkey, 1956. Intern Haseki Therapeutics Clinic, Istanbul, Turkey, 1957-58; resident Haseki Therapeutics Clinic, 1958-61; succesively asst. prof. medicine, assoc. prof., head dept. hematology, prof. medicine, head dept. oncology, assoc. dean, dean Cerrahpasa Sch. Medicine, Istanbul, 1964-83, dir. dept. med. oncology, 1975—; spl. Wilson fellow in oncology U. Rochester, N.Y., 1973-74. Author book on hematology in Turkish, 1977; developer global coagulation test, 1964; contbr. research writings in field to profl. publs. Served as med. officer Turkish Navy, 1962-64. Decorated Ordre du Merite Nat., Legion d'Honneur, France. Mem. Internat. Soc. Chemotherapy, Internat. Soc. Hematology, Am. Soc. Cancer Edn., European Soc. Med. Edn., various local socs. Moslem. Home: Spor Cd 96 Besiktas, Istanbul Turkey Office: Cerrahpasa Sch Medicine, Dept Oncology, Istanbul Turkey

BERKE, JUDIE, publisher, editor; b. Mpls., Apr. 15, 1938; d. Maurice M. and Sue (Supak) Kleyman; student U. Minn., 1956-60, Mpls. Sch. Art, 1945-59. Free lance illustrator and designer, 1959—; pres. Berke-Wood, Inc., N.Y.C., 1971-80, Manhattan Rainbow & Lollipop Co. subs. Berke-Wood, Inc., 1971-80; pres. Get Your Act Together, club act staging, N.Y.C., 1971-80; pres. Coordinator Pubs.,Inc., 1982-87; pres., chief exec. officer, Health Market Communications, 1987—; pres. Pub. and Media Services, Burbank, 1987—; pub., editor Continuing Care Coordinator, Health Watch mags.; pres. Continuing Care Coordinator Convs. and Seminars; cons. to film and ednl. cos.; guest lectr. various colls. and univs. in Calif. and N.Y., 1973—; cons., designer Healthy Lifestyles mag.; writer, illustrator, dir. numerous ednl. filmstrips, 1972—, latest being Focus on Professions, 1974, Focus on the Performing Arts, 1974, Focus on the Creative Arts, 1974, Workstyles, 1976, Wonderworm, 1976, Supernut, 1977; author, illustrator film Fat Black Mack (San Francisco Ednl. Film Festival award, part of permanent collection Mus. Modern Art, N.Y.C.), 1970; designer posters and brochures for various entertainment groups, 1963—; composer numerous songs, latest being Time is Relative, 1976, Love Will Live On in My Mind, 1976, My Blue Walk, 1976, You Make Me a Baby, 1982, Let's Go Around Once More, 1983, Anytime Anyplace Anywhere, 1987, Bittersweet, 1987, Sometimes It Pays, 1987; composer/author off-Broadway musical Street Corner Time, 1978; producer: The Reals Estate TV Shows 1988—; contbr. children's short stories to various publs., also articles. Trustee The Happy Spot Sch., N.Y.C., 1972-75. Mem. Nat. Fedn. Bus. and Profl. Women, Nat. Assn. Female Execs., Am. Acad. Polit. and Social Sci. Home and Office: 958 N Vista St Los Angeles CA 90046

BERKELEY, FRANCIS LEWIS, JR., retired archivist; b. Albemarle County, Va., Apr. 9, 1911; s. Francis Lewis and Ethel (Crissey) B.; B.S., U. Va., 1934, M.A., 1940; m. Helen Wayland Sutherland, June 12, 1937. Tchr. Va. pub. schs., 1934-38; asst. curator manuscripts U. Va. Library, Charlottesville, 1938-41, curator and univ. archivist, 1946-63, asso. librarian, 1957-63, sec. of Rector and Visitors, 1953-58, exec. asst. to pres., 1963-74, archivist emeritus, prof. emeritus, 1974—; council Inst. Early Am. History and Culture. Fulbright research fellow U. Edinburgh, 1952-53; Guggenheim fellow U. London, 1961-62; sec. of navy adv. com. on naval history, 1958-74. Trustee Thomas Jefferson Meml. Found.; mem. adv. com. Papers of Thomas Jefferson, Papers of James Madison, Papers of George Washington; mem. Va. Com. on Colonial Records, 1955-71, Va. Commn. on Hist. Records, 1976—. Served with USNR, 1942-46; capt. ret. Fellow Soc. Am. Archivists; mem. Am. Antiquarian Soc., Mass., Va., (v.p. 1970-78, trustee 1979—), other hist. socs., Colonial Soc. Mass., Walpole Soc., Raven Soc., Phi Beta Kappa, Omicron Delta Kappa. Democrat. Episcopalian. Clubs: Colonnade (Charlottesville); Century (N.Y.). Editor and compiler: Dunmore's Proclamation of Emancipation, 1941; Annual Reports on Historical Collections, University of Virginia Library, 1945-50, with cumulative indexes, 1945, 50; Jefferson Papers of the University of Virginia, 1950; Papers of John Randolph of Roanoke, 1950; John Rolfe's True Relation. 1951; Introduction to Thomas Jefferson's Farm Book, 1953. Editorial bd. Va. Quar. Rev., 1961-74. Contbr. to Dictionary of Biography, Ency. Brit., Collier's Nat. Am. Cyclopedia; other reference works. Home: 227-16 Colonnade Dr Charlottesville VA 22901

BERKEMEIER, PAUL RICHARD, architect; b. Sydney, Australia, Feb. 20, 1952; s. Albert Georg and Mary Helena (Sullivan) B.; m. Geraldine Goodwin; children: Sophia, Helen. BArch, Sydney U., 1975; MArch, Harvard U., 1983. Chartered architect, Australia. Architect Govt. of Australia, 1975-85; assoc. Denton Corker Marshall, Sydney, 1985-87, assoc. dir., 1987—; vis. critic Sydney U., 1986-87. Mem. Royal Australian Inst. Architects. Club: Harvard of New South Wales. Home: 67 Milson Rd, 2090 Cremorne Point Australia Office: Denton Corker Marshall, 285 Clarence St, 2000 Sydney Australia

BERKENES, JOYCE MARIE POORE, family counselor; b. Des Moines, Aug. 29, 1953; d. Donald Roy and Thelma Beatrice (Hart) Poore; m. Robert Elliott Berkenes,Jan. 3, 1976; children: Tiffany Noelle, Cory Matthew. BA in Social Work and Biology, Simpson Coll., Indianola, Iowa., 1975. Resident counselor and group home mgr. Chaddock Boys Home, Quincy, Ill., 1976-78; social service dir. N. Adams Nursing Home, Mendon, Ill., 1978; home tchr. Head Start, Camp Point, Ill., 1978-79, home tchr. supr./edn. and parent involvement coordinator, 1979-82; family counselor Iowa Children's and Family Services, Des Moines, 1982-85; family counselor and vol. coordinator Luth. Social Services, Des Moines, 1985—; cons. in field, 1975-76. Mem. Iowa Soc. Autistic Children, Home Based Family Service Assn. (sec. 1984-87), Nat. Assn. Social Workers. Democrat. Methodist. Home: 2901 NE 80th St Altoona IA 50009 Office: Luth Social Services 2525 E Euclid Suite 110 Des Moines IA 50317

BERKLAND, JAMES OMER, geologist; b. Glendale, Calif., July 31, 1930; s. Joseph Omer and Gertrude Madelyn (Thompson) B.; A.A., Santa Rosa Jr. Coll., 1951; A.B., U. Calif., Berkeley, 1958; M.S., San Jose State U., 1964; postgrad., U. Calif., Davis, 1969-72; m. Janice Lark Keirstead, Dec. 19, 1966; children—Krista Lynn, Jay Olin. With U.S. Geol. Survey, 1958-64; engring. geologist U.S. Bur. Reclamation, 1964-69; cons. geologist, 1969-72; asst. prof. Appalachian State U., Boone, N.C., 1972-73; county geologist Santa Clara County, San Jose, Calif., 1973—; adj. prof. San Jose State U., 1975-76; mem. evening faculty San Jose City Coll.; West Valley legis. com., 1979; lectr. San Jose real estate bd. annual Deposit Receipt Seminar, 1980-85, San Jose State U. Gen. Edn. Conf.: Sci., Tech., Society, 1985-88; numerous TV and radio appearances including PBS, Frontline, Evening Mag., others. Treas. Creekside/Park Place Homeowners Group; v.p. West Coast Aquatics, Creekside/Park Place Swim Team; mem. various city and county adv. bds.; mem. Ctr. for Study Early Man, East Valley YMCA, Route 85 Task Force, Earthquake Watch, 1979-82, New Weather Observer. Registered geologist, Calif.; cert. engring. geologist, Calif. Fellow Geol. Soc. Am.; mem. Assn. Engring. Geologists (past vice chmn. San Francisco sect.), Seismol. Soc. Am., Chapparral Poets, Sierra Club, Santa Clara County Engrs. and Architects Assn. (v.p.), Mining Lamp, Citizens and Scientists Concerned About Damage to Environment, San Jose Hist. Mus. Assn., Western Council Engrs., Internat. Platform Assn., Nat. Jogging Assn., Nat. Geog. Soc., Calif. State Employees Assn., Calif. State Firemen's Assn., Youth Sci. Inst. Peninsula Geol. Soc. (past treas.), Earthquake Engring. Research Inst., AAAS, Saber Soc. (co-founder, past pres.), Bay Area Reviewing Geologists Assn., Sons of Norway, Sigma Xi. Democrat. Club: King of Clubs Lions (charter, 1st v.p. 1986-87, pres. 1987-88, dist. 4C-6 pub. relations officer 1987-88, Melvin Jones fellow Internat. Fedn.) (San Jose). Contbr. numerous articles to profl. jours.; originator seismic window theory for earthquake prediction. Home: 14927 East Hills Dr San Jose CA 95127 Office: Santa Clara County 70 W Hedding St San Jose CA 95110

BERKMAN, MILTON DAVID, orthodontist; b. Syracuse, N.Y., Nov. 8, 1940; s. Isaac and Sarah (Weinstein) B.; D.M.D., Tufts U., 1965, M.S., 1968; cert. in orthodontics Columbia U., 1972; cert. advanced gnathol. occlusion prins. and technique Found. Advanced Continuing Edn., 1981; diplomate Am. Bd. Orthodontics; m. Arlene Saltzman, Dec. 27, 1969; 1 child, Seth. Instr., U. Pa. Sch. Dental Medicine, 1969-70; asst. prof. dentistry Albert Einstein Coll. Medicine, Bronx, N.Y., 1972-77, asst. clin. prof., 1977—; practice dentistry specializing in orthodontics and temporomandibular joint disorders, Scarsdale, N.Y.; assoc. attending dentist Westchester Med. Center, Valhalla, N.Y., 1981—; orthodontist Center for Craniofacial Disorders, Montefiore Hosp., N.Y.C.; guest lectr. N.Y.U. Sch. Dentistry, 1981—. Served with Dental Corps, U.S. Army, 1968-70. Fellow Northeastern Gnathological Soc.; mem. Am. Assn. Orthodontists, Am. Cleft Palate Assn., ADA, Northeastern Soc. Orthodontists, N.Y. State Dental Soc., Northeastern Gnathol. Soc., Sigma Xi, Alpha Omega, Omicron Kappa Upsilon. Contbr, articles to profl. jours, contbr. chpts. to textbooks.

BERKON, MARTIN, artist; b. Bklyn., Jan. 30, 1932; s. Samuel F. and Sara (Hodes) B.; student Pratt Inst., 1952; B.A., Bklyn. Coll., 1954; M.A., N.Y. U., 1959; m. Eileen Phyllis Eichel, July 10, 1960. One man shows Smolin Gallery, N.Y.C., 1962, 20th Century West Gallery, N.Y.C., 1967, Soho Center for Visual Artists, N.Y.C., 1974, Genesis Galleries, N.Y.C., 1978, Adelphi U., Garden City, N.Y., 1983; exhibited in group shows Bklyn. Mus., 1958, Silvermine (Conn.) Guild Artists, 1963, Ohio U. Gallery, 1964, Ball State U., 1965, Wesleyan Coll. at Ga., 1965, Butler Inst. Am. Art, 1965, 67, 69, Aldrich Mus. Contemporary Art, Ridgefield, Conn., 1974, 75, 82, New Britain (Conn.) Mus., 1974, Am. Fedn. Arts traveling show, 1975-77, Meadowbrook Art Gallery Oakland U., Rochester, Mich., and Flint (Mich.) Inst. Art, 1975-76, Firehouse Gallery, Garden City, 1982, Barbara Walter Gallery, N.Y.C., 1982, Spaceport USA, Kennedy Space Ctr., 1985, 87, NASA collection traveling exhbn., Visions of Flight, 1988—; represented in permanent collection Aldrich Mus. Contemporary Art, Nat. Air and Space Mus., Smithsonian Inst., Washington, Texaco Inc., White Plains, N.Y., Pepsico Inc., Somers, N.Y., commd. NASA, 1984, 87 mem. adj. faculty Fairleigh Dickinson U., 1966, Nassau Community Coll., 1966-67; lectr. City Coll., CUNY, 1968-69; guest lectr. Middlebury Coll., 1977, Nassau Community Coll., 1982.; interviewed Long Island Art Scene, 1986. Home: 51-25 Van Kleek St Elmhurst NY 11373

BERKOVITZ, STANLEY, retail store executive; b. Boston, Nov. 9, 1943; s. Hyman and Jeanette Nyder (Jagoda) B.; married; children: Scott, Kim. B.S., N.H. Coll., 1966. With Zayre Corp., Framingham, Mass., 1966—, mgr. consumer affairs, 1971-77, v.p. consumer and community affairs, 1977—. Chmn. Mass. Bay March of Dimes, 1985-88; bd. dirs. South Middlesex United Way; trustee Greater Framingham Regional YMCA, 1984—; trustee Framingham Union Hosp., 1986—; chmn. bd. dirs. Eastern Mass./No. New Eng. Better Bus. Bur., 1981-83, mem. exec. com., 1979-83; chmn. Greater Framingham Red Cross, 1979-82, mem. adv. com., 1983—; bd. dirs. exec. com. Metro West United Way. Mem. Nat. Soc. Consumer Affairs Profls. (pres. 1982-83). Office: Zayre Corp Framingham MA 01701

BERKSON, ROBERT G., stockbroker; b. Bklyn., Feb. 14, 1939; s. Martin and Jeanne (Wolin) B.; B.S. in Econs., Hofstra U., 1960; m. Deanna Feinberg, Mar. 26, 1972. Sec./treas. Packer, Wilbur & Co., Inc., N.Y.C., 1961-70; pres. A.J. Carno Co., Inc., N.Y.C., 1971—; v.p. Berkson's Bldg. Corp., N.Y.C., 1961—, also dir.; pres. R.G. Berkson & Co., 1971—; with First Jersey Securities Inc., N.Y.C., 1975-80; chmn. bd. Fin. Communications Group Ltd., 1980—, The Triad Corp. Planning and Communications, Inc.; v.p. Rob-Len Amusement Corp. Trustee Children's Med. Fund. of N.Y.; assoc. trustee L.I. Jewish Hosp. Mem. N.Y. Merc. Exchange. Clubs: Pine Hollow Country, Whitehall. Home: 50 Georgian Ct East Hills NY 11576 Office: First Jersey Securities Inc 80 Broad St New York NY 10004

BERKUS, DAVID WILLIAM, computer company executive; b. Los Angeles, Mar. 23, 1941; s. Harry Jay and Clara S. (Widess) B.; m. Kathleen McGuire, Aug. 6, 1966; children: Eric, Matthew, Amy. BA, Occidental Coll., 1962. Pres. Custom Fidelity Inc., Hollywood, Calif., 1958-74, Berkus Compusystems Inc., Los Angeles, 1974-81; pres., chief exec. officer Computerized Lodging Systems Inc. and subs., Los Angeles, 1981—. Author: (software) Hotel Compusystem, 1979; creator 1st artificial intelligence-based yield mgmt. system, 1987. Council commr. Boy Scouts Am., San Gabriel Valley, 1986, mem. exec. council. Served to lt. USNR, 1963-72. Recipient Dist. award of merit Boy Scouts Am., 1986, INC. mag. 500 award, 1986, Silver Beaver award Boy Scouts Am., 1988. Mem. Am. Hotel-Motel Assn., Audio Engring. Soc. (chmn. Los Angeles sect. 1973-74). Democrat. Jewish. Office: Computerized Lodging Systems Inc 4800 Airport Plaza Dr #160 Long Beach CA 90815

BERLAGE, GAI INGHAM, sociologist, educator; b. Washington, Feb. 9, 1943; d. Paul Bowen and Grace (Artz) Ingham; m. Jan Coxe Berlage, Aug. 7, 1965; children: Jan Ingham, Cari Coxe. BA, Smith Coll., 1965; MA, So. Meth. U., 1968; PhD, NYU, 1979. Tchr. math. Piner Jr. High Sch., Sherman, Tex., 1968-69; asst. prof. sociology Iona Coll., New Rochelle, N.Y., 1971-83, assoc. prof., 1983-88, prof., 1988—, chmn. dept., 1981—, prof., 1988—; coordinator urban studies program, 1984—, gerontology program, 1985—. Author: Experience with Sociology: Social Issues in American Society, 1983, Understanding Social Issues: Sociological Fact Finding, 1987; contbr. articles to profl. jours. Commr. Wilton Commn. on Aging and Social Services, 1980-88, chmn., 1982-88; co-chmn. Wilton Task Force on Youth council, 1988; chmn. Wilton Task Force Comm. for Outreach Program, 1981-82, Wilton Task Force on Day Care, 1983—; mem. Wilton Task Force for Pub. Health Nursing Assn., 1981-82, Wilton Sport Council, 1985—; bd. dirs. Wilton Meals on Wheels, 1983—; fellow North Am. Faculty Network of Northeastern Univs.'s Ctr. for Study of Sport in Soc. NSF trainee, 1967-68. Mem. Am. Sociol. Assn., N.Y. State Sociol. Assn., N.Am. Soc. Sociology of Sport, Inst. Sport and Social Analysis, Internat. Com. Sociology of Sport, Wilton Assn. Gifted Edn. (pres. 1980-81), Internat. Soc. of Sport Psychology. Office: Iona Coll Dept Sociology New Rochelle NY 10801

BERLAND, KENNETH K., retail company executive; b. 1922; m. Gloria Berland; children: Alan Lance, Elizabeth Anne. Grad., CCNY. With Melville Corp., N.Y.C., 1953—, v.p. and treas., Miles Shoe div., 1957-64, corp. controller, 1964-65, treas. and controller, 1965-66, v.p., treas., controller, 1966-76, sr. v.p. fin. and adminstrn., treas., 1976-80, pres., 1980-86, vice chmn., 1986—, chief fin. officer, 1986-87, chief adminstrv. officer, 1987—, also dir.; Chmn. tax com. Volume FootWear Retailers Assn. Office: Melville Corp 3000 Westchester Ave PO Box 677 Harrison NY 10528 *

BERLEY, DAVID RICHARD, lawyer; b. Bklyn., Apr. 9, 1942; s. Alexander and Ruth (Ginsburg) B.; m. Sharon Lee Freeman, Aug. 10, 1964 (div. 1975); children—Steven N., Barbara Robin. B.S., Boston U., 1963; J.D., Boston Coll., 1966. Bar: Mass. 1966, Fla. 1977. Corp. and pvt. practice, 1966-77; gen. counsel Econocar Internat. Inc., Miami, Fla., 1976-77; v.p., gen. counsel Emergency Med. Services Assn., Inc., Miami, 1977-79; sole practice, Miami, 1979-85; ptnr. Berley & Littman, P.A., 1985— . Bd. dirs. Community Habilitation Ctr.; active Greater Miami Heart Assn., Jewish Fedn. Greater Miami. Mem. ABA, Mass. Bar Assn., Am. Trial Lawyers Assn., Fla. Bar Assn., Boston Coll. Law Sch. Alumni Assn. Office: 202 Brickell Exec Tower 1428 Brickell Ave Miami FL 33131

BERLIN, ALAN DANIEL, lawyer, oil company executive; b. Bklyn., Oct. 20, 1939; s. Joseph Jacob and Rose (Smith) B.; m. Renee Wellinger, Dec. 22, 1962; children—Nicole Suzanne, Allison Leigh. B.B.A., CCNY, 1960; LL.B., NYU, 1963, LL.M., 1968. Bar: N.Y. 1963. Assoc. Aranow, Brodsky, Bohlinger, Einhorn & Dann, N.Y.C., 1965-68; asst. counsel Gen. Electric Co., N.Y.C., 1968-70; tax counsel Norton Simon Inc., N.Y.C., 1970-77; pres. Belco Petroleum Corp., N.Y.C., 1977—; asst. prof. Pace U. Grad. Sch. Bus., 1977-85. Author monographs on fed. income tax. Bd. dirs. Mental Health Assn., Westchester; vice chmn. Briarcliff Manor (N.Y.) Peoples Caucus. Served with U.S. Army, 1963-65. Mem. Am. Bar Assn., N.Y. State Bar Assn., Assn. Bar City N.Y., Inter-Am. Bar Assn. Lodge: Masons. Office: 1 Dag Hammarskjold Plaza New York NY 10017

BERLIN, IRVING, composer; b. Russia, May 11, 1888; came to U.S., 1893; s. Moses and Leah (Lipkin) Baline; m. Dorothy Goetz, Feb. 1913 (dec. July 1913); m. Ellin Mackay (dec.), Jan. 4, 1926; children: Mary Ellin Berlin Barrett, Linda Berlin Emmet, Elizabeth Berlin Peters. Ed. pub. schs., N.Y.C.; hon. degrees, Bucknell U., Temple U., Fordham U. Pres. The Irving Berlin Music Corp. Writer, composer popular songs: Alexander's Ragtime Band, Oh How I Hate to Get Up in the Morning, When I Lost You, When I Leave the World Behind, What'll I Do?, All Alone, Remember, Reaching for the Moon, Always, Because I Love You, At Peace With the World, Russian Lullaby, Music Box Revues, Cocoanuts, Ziegfeld Follies, Me, Any Bonds Today, White Christmas; musical comedy revue This is the Army; film musical Easter Parade; stage musicals Annie Get Your Gun, Miss Liberty, Call Me Madam, Mr. President, 1962; also various others; total songs composed about 800. Served as sgt. Infantry, at Camp Upton, L.I. Recipient Presdl. Medal of Freedom, 1977, Medal of Merit for This Is The Army; Lawrence Langer award for disting. lifetime achievement in Am. theater, 1978; Congl. Gold medal for God Bless America; decorated Legion of Honor (France). Clubs: Lambs, Friars. Lodges: Masons, Shriners, Elks. Office: 1290 Avenue of the Americas New York NY 10104 *

BERLIN, ISAIAH, philosopher, author; b. Riga; b. June 6, 1909; s. Mendel and Marie B.; ed. St. Paul's Sch., London, 1922-28; scholar Corpus Christi Coll., Oxford (Eng.) U., 1928-32; LL.D. (hon.), Hull (Eng.) U.; D. Litt., univs. Glasgow, Cambridge, Oxford, East Anglia, Columbia, Duke,

Brandeis, Jerusalem, London, Liverpool, Johns Hopkins, Northwestern, N.Y., Sussex, N.Y. Theol. Sem., CUNY, D.Phil., Tel-Aviv U.; m. Aline de Gunzbourg, 1956. Fellow, All Souls Coll., Oxford U., 1932-38, 50-67, 75—, New Coll., 1938-50, lectr. philosophy New Coll., 1932-50, Chichele prof. social and polit. theory at univ., 1957-67, pres. Wolfson Coll., 1966-75; vis. prof. Harvard U., 1949, 52, 53, 61, Bryn Mawr Coll., 1952, Princeton U., 1965; Alexander White prof. U. Chgo., 1955; prof. humanities CUNY, 1966-71; first sec. Brit. embassy, Washington, 1942-46, Moscow, USSR, 1945. Mem. com. awards Commonwealth (Harkness) Fellowships, 1961-65, Kennedy Scholarships, 1965-87 ; bd. dirs. Royal Opera House, London, 1955-66, 75—; trustee Nat. Gallery, London, 1975—86; bd. govs. U. Jerusalem, 1955-80. Decorated comdr. Order Brit. Empire, 1946; created knight, 1957; recipient Order of Merit, 1971, Agnelli Internat. prize for Ethics, 1987. Fellow Brit. Acad. (pres. 1974-78); hon. fellow Corpus Christi Coll., Wolfson Coll., St. Anthony's Coll., Oxford, Wolfson Coll., Cambridge; hon. mem. Am. Acad. Arts and Scis., Am. Acad. Arts and Letters, Am. Philos. Soc. Author books and essays on lit., philosophy, other subjects. Address: All Souls Coll, Oxford U, Oxford England also: British Acad, 20-21 Cornwall Terrace, London NW1 4QP, England

BERLIN, JEROME CLIFFORD, lawyer, accountant, real estate developer; b. N.Y.C., Aug. 23, 1942; s. Benjamin R. and Muriel (Weintraub) B.; BSBA, U. Fla., 1964, JD, 1968; m. Gwen Tischler, July 30, 1977; children: Bret Jason, Sharon Nicole, Ashley Lauren. Acct., Peat, Marwick, Mitchell & Co., Houston, 1968-69; mem. law firm Jerome C. Berlin, Miami, Fla., 1969-71; pres. Sterling Capital Investments, Inc., Miami, 1971-80; pres., chief operating officer Robino-Ladd Co., Del., also Inprojet Corp., Miami, 1974-80; individual practice law, Miami, 1980—. Chmn., Dade County Zoning Appeals Bd., 1971-73; chmn. bd. Signature Gardens, 1984—; chmn. bd. Duex Michel, Inc. 1984—; vice chmn. bd. dirs. Anti-Defamation League, 1979-83 , chmn. Fla. regional bd., 1984-87, nat. commn. of Anti-Defamation League, 1981—; chmn. Fla. Com. of 100; mem. long-range planning com. Miami Children's Hosp., 1980— mem. citizens bd. Fla. Crime Prevention Commn., 1982; mem. world bd. dirs. Am. Israele Pub. Affairs Com., 1984-86, mem. exec. bd. dirs., 1987—; bd. dirs. Democratic Nat. Com., 1985—; bd. dirs., treas. Alexander Muss High Sch., Israel; nat. fin. chmn. Dem. Senatorial Campaign Com., 1987—; mem. exec. com. Dem. Nat. Fin. Council, 1985—; bd. dirs. Temple Beth Am., Miami; mem. exec. bd. Juvenile Diabetes Found., U. Miami Project Newborn; bd. overseers Hebrew Union Coll., 1983—. C.P.A., Fla., Tex. Mem. Am. Inst. C.P.A.s, Fla. Inst. C.P.A.s, Tex. Soc. C.P.A.s, Fla. Bar Assn., Am. Assn. Attys. and C.P.A.s, Fla. Thousand (chmn.), Fla. Soc. of Fellows (chmn.). Jewish. Home: 5425 SW 92d St Miami FL 33156

BERLINER, WILLIAM MICHAEL, business educator; b. Aug. 24, 1923; s. Samuel L. and Anna (Josephine) B.; m. Bertha A. Hagedorn, Apr. 27, 1946. B.S., N.Y. U., 1949, M.B.A., 1953, Ph.D., 1956. With Continental Casualty Co., 1941-42 45-46; retail div. mgr. B.F. Goodrich Co., 1949-50; asst. purchasing agt. Cutler-Hammer, Inc., 1950-51; mem. faculty N.Y. U., N.Y.C., 1951—; prof. mgmt. and orgnl. behavior, chmn. dept. mgmt. N.Y. U., 1965-74; dir., cons. OTI Services, Inc., 1958—; cons. Mfrs. Hanover Trust Co., 1956—; edn. adviser Am. Inst. Banking sect. Am. Bankers Assn., 1962—; Ford Found. cons. exec. program, N.Y.C. and Met. Area, 1961-65; mem. policy com. Regents Coll. Univ. of State of N.Y. Kellogg Found.; cons. exec. program Boys Clubs Am., 1962-67; faculty Stonier Grad. Sch. Banking, 1970—, Bank Personnel Grad. Sch., Am. Bankers Assn., 1980—; ednl. cons. Bank Adminstrn. Inst., 1976-81, Grad. Sch. Banking, U. Wis., 1982—, N.Y. State Bankers Assn., 1977—; policy and adv. com. Non-collegiate sponsored instrn. program, Univ. State of N.Y., 1983—, policy com. mem. Regents Coll. degrees, 1970—. Author: (with F.A. DePhillips and J.J. Cribbin) Management of Training Programs, 1960, (with W.J. McLarney (dec.) Management Practice and Training, Cases and Principles, 1974, Managerial and Supervisory Practice, 1979. Served to 1st lt. USAAF, 1942-45. Decorated D.F.C., Air medal with 6 oak leaf clusters, Purple Heart; Ford Found. grantee, 1960. Mem. Acad. Mgmt., Am. Soc. Personnel Adminstrn. (accredited personnel diplomate), Am. Mgmt. Assn., Am. Mktg. Assn., Beta Gamma Sigma, Alpha Kappa Psi. Home: 27 Perkins Rd Greenwich CT 06830 Office: NYU Grad Sch Bus Adminstrn 100 Trinity Pl New York NY 10006

BERLINGER, JOSEPH WILLIAM, building supply company executive; b. N.Y.C., May 27, 1933; s. Joseph Furth and Marjorie (Greenbaum) B.; m. Elissa Kopita, Apr. 29, 1956; children—Robert W., Joseph A. B.A., Cornell U., 1955. Zone mgr. Premier Indsl. Corp., Cleve., 1965-68; exec. v.p., dir. Gen. Casting Corp., Jefferson Valley, N.Y., 1968-72; pres. Millwood Industries, Inc., N.Y., 1972—; pres. Small Bus. Marketers, cons., Millwood, 1965—. Mem. Chappaqua Sch. Bd. Commn., N.Y., 1983-84. Served to 1st lt. QMC, U.S. Army, 1955-57. Mem. Am. Mgmt. Assn. Republican. Jewish. Club: Town (Chappaqua). Lodge: Masons. Home: 76 Taconic Rd Ossining NY 10562 Office: Millwood Industries Inc Millwood Rd Millwood NY 10562

BERLIOZ, GEORGES LOUIS, lawyer; b. Izieux, France, July 14, 1943; s. Louis Marie and Julie Marthe (Mollard) B.; B.A. with honors in Physics, U. Calif., Berkeley, 1963, B.A., LL.B., 1966; Lic. en Droit, U. Paris, 1969, D.E.S. Dr. Public, 1969, D.E.S. Dr. Prive, 1970, Dr. Droit with highest honors, 1971; m. Brigitte Anne Houin, July 4, 1974; 1 son, Pierre Roger Louis. Reader in physics U. Calif., Berkeley, 1961-63, research asst. law Boalt Hall, 1965-66; asst. U. Paris Law Sch., 1970-71; admitted to bar, 1969; prof. U. Lille Law Sch., 1971-75; lectr. U. Paris Law Sch., 1979—; avocat à la Cour de Paris, 1969—; sr. partner firm Berlioz, Ferry, David, Lutz, Rochefort, Paris, 1978—; mem. com. experts Codification Internat. Contracts, 1979; vis. lectr. internat. seminars. Sec.-gen., then pres. Union des Etudiants pour le Progrès, Paris, 1966-69. Maj. Walter Dinkelspiel scholar, 1964; John Woodman Ayer fellow, 1965. Mem. Internat. Bar Assn., Union Internat. des Avocats, Assn. des Docteurs en Droit, Assn. Droit et Commerce, Am. Tax Inst., Boalt Hall Alumni Assn. Author: Le Contrat d'Adhésion, 2d edit., 1976; co-author: L'Information et le Droit Privé , 1978; Les Eurocrédits, 1981; La loi française et l'activité internationale des entreprises; editor, Internat. Contract Law and Fin. Rev., 1980—; editorial advisor, corr. Jour. Bus. Law; contbr. articles to profl. jours. Home: 94 rue du Bac, Paris 75007 France Office: 68 Blvd de Courcelles, 75017 Paris France

BERLYNE, GEOFFREY MERTON, nephrologist, researcher; b. Manchester, Eng., May 11, 1931; came to U.S., 1976, naturalized, 1981; s. Charles Solomon and Miriam Hannah (Rosenthal) B.; m. Ruth Selbourne, June 7, 1969; children—Jonathan, Benjamin, Suzannah. M.B.Ch.B. with honors, Manchester U., 1954, M.D., 1966. Lectr. U. Manchester, 1961-62, sr. lectr., 1964-68, reader, 1969-70; prof. medicine and life scis. Negev U., Israel, 1970-79; prof. medicine SUNY-Bklyn., 1976—; chief nephrology sect. Brooklyn VA Med. Center, 1976—. Author: Course in Renal Diseases, 1966, Course on Electrolytes and Body Fluids, 1981. Fellow Am. Coll. Physicians, Am. Coll. Nutrition; mem. Japanese Nephrology Soc. (named distinguished nephrologist 1979), Assn. Physicians of G.B., Am. Fedn. Clin. Research. Republican. Jewish (chmn. 1970-74, pres. synagogue 1982—). Home: 27 Merrall Dr Lawrence NY 11559 Office: Bklyn VA Hosp 800 Poly Pl Renal Sect III 800 Poly Pl Brooklyn NY 11209

BERMAN, ARTHUR LEONARD, state senator; b. Chgo., May 4, 1935; s. Morris and Jean (Glast) B.; B.S. in Commerce and Law, U. Ill., 1956; J.D., Northwestern U., 1958; children—Adam, Marcy. Admitted to Ill. bar, 1958, since practiced in Chgo.; mem. firm White, White & Berman, Chartered, 1958-74, Maragos, Richter, Berman, Russell & White, Chartered, 1974-81, Chatz, Berman, Maragos, Haber & Fagel, 1981-82, Berman, Fagel, Haber, Maragos & Abrams, 1982-86, Karlin & Fleisher, 1986—; spl. atty. Bur. Liquidations, Ill. Dept. Ins., 1962-67; spl. asst. atty. gen. Ill., 1967-68; mem. Ill. Ho. of Reps., 1969-76, Ill. Senate, 1976—. Bd. dirs. Zionist Orgn. Chgo.; mem. Rogers Park, Edgewater, Northtown communtiy councils. Pres., 50th Ward Young Democrats, 1956-60; v.p. Cook County Young Dems., 1956-60, 50th Ward Regular Dem. Orgn., 1955—; exec. bd. Dem. Party, Evanston, Ill., 1973—. Bd. dirs. Bernard Horwich Jewish Community Center, North Town Community Council; bd. govs. State of Israel Bonds. Mem. Am., Ill., Chgo. (bd. mgrs. 1976-77) Bar Assns., Decalogue Soc. Lawyers (bd. mgrs. 1988—), Nat. Assn. Jewish Legislators (pres. 1987—), Am. Trial Lawyers Assn., John Howard Assn., Common Cause, Northwestern U., U. Ill. alumni assns., Phi Epsilon Pi, Tau Epsilon Rho. Home: 5855 N Sheridan Rd Chicago IL 60660

BERMAN, DANIEL LEWIS, lawyer; b. Washington, Dec. 13, 1934; s. Herbert A. and Ruth N. (Abramson) B.; children: Pricilla Decker, Jane, Katherine Ann, Sara Mark. B.A., Williams Coll., 1956; LL.B., Columbia U., 1959. Bar: N.Y. 1960, Utah 1962. Asso. firm Chadbourne, Parke, Whiteside & Wolff, N.Y.C., 1959-60; asst. prof. law U. Utah, 1960-62; practice Salt Lake City, 1962—; sr. ptnr. Berman & O'Rorke, 1981—; vis. prof. U. Utah, 1970, 74, 77; Mem. Utah Coordinating Council Higher Edn., 1965-68. Mem. Salt Lake County Merit Council, 1974-80; trustee Salt Lake Art Center, 1978-80; Democratic candidate for U.S. Senate from Utah, 1980. Mem. Am. Law Inst., Salt Lake Area C. of C. (bd. govs. 1976-79). Democrat. Jewish. Office: 50 S Main St Suite 1250 Salt Lake City UT 84144

BERMAN, MARGO RENEE, advertising executive; b. Jersey City, July 8, 1947; d. Jack H. and Blanche (Bram) Breitbart; m. Jack Robert Berman, June 25, 1978. MusB, U. Miami (Fla.), 1971, MusM, 1974, postgrad., 1977. Cert. tchr., Fla. Program host, producer Sta. WLRN-FM, 1977-78; copywriter, Ellman's, Atlanta, 1978-79; advt. supr. Mktg. Services, Hollywood, Fla., 1980-81; writer, account exec. WWJF, Ft. Lauderdale, Fla., 1981, WKQS, Ft. Lauderdale, 1981-82; producer, copywriter, dir. Hume, Smith, Mickelberry, Miami, Fla., 1982-83; sr. copywriter, dir., producer The Ad Team, North Miami Beach, Fla., 1983-84; prin. Madison Ave. Advt. Co., Inc., Miami Beach, 1984—; adjunct prof. in communications Fla. Internat. U., 1987-88; now pres. Margo Berman Creative Services, North Miami Beach; lectr. in field; judge Miami Herald Canny Awards, 1984, Clarion Awards, 1986, 87. Author TV and radio commls. Mem. Miami Citizens Against Crime, 1982; judge Calrion Awards, 1986-87. Recipient Bronze award Internat. Film Festival of N.Y., 1982, Nat. Advt. Agy. Network, 1982; Bronze Telly award TV Commls. Festival, 1982, Clarion award 1985; 1st place Angel award Fla. Advt. Fedn., 1982; John Caples award for Fla. Power & Light comml., 1983; Andy awards for Hilton Resort print campaign, 1983, Fla. Power & Light print ad, 1983, Pantry Pride Supermarkets radio campaign, 1983, 4 Nat. Silver Microphone awards, 1988; 8 FAME awards, 1987, 4 FAME awards, 1988. Mem. Women in Communications (profl. advisor 1982-83, rec. sec. Miami 1984-85, v.p. career devel. 1987, v.p. communications 1988), Nat. Acad. TV Arts and Scis. (judge Chgo. 1983), Miami Advt. Fedn., Nat. Assn. Women Bus. Owners, Nat. Assn. Female Execs., Phi Kappa Phi, Sigma Alpha Iota. Home: 3351 NE 164 St North Miami Beach FL 33160 Office: Margo Berman Creative Services 3909 NE 163d St Suite 301 North Miami Beach FL 33160

BERMAN, RONALD CHARLES, accountant; b. Chgo., July 7, 1949; s. Joseph and Helen (Neiderman) BBS with highest honors, U. Ill., 1971, JD with honors, 1974. Bar: Ill. 1974, Wis. 1976; CPA, Wis. Tax staff Grant Thornton, Chgo., 1974-76, tax supr., Madison, Wis., 1976-78, tax mgr., 1978-81; ptnr. tax dept. Grant Thornton, Madison, 1981—. Mem. editorial adv. bd. Physician's Tax Advisor Newsletter, 1986—; Scoutmaster Boy Scouts Am., Middleton, Wis., 1978—; fin. chmn. Mohawk Dist. Four Lakes council Boy Scouts Am., Madison, 1981-85, endowment fund chmn., 1984—, exec. bd., 1982—; bd. dirs. Scouts on Stamps Soc. Internat., 1986—, Madison Pension Council, 1986—. Recipient Bronze Tablet, U. Ill., 1971, Silver Beaver Boy Scouts Am., 1981. Mem. ABA (employee benefits com. taxation sect), Am. Inst. CPA's (Sells award hon. mention 1971), Wis. Soc. CPA's, State Bar of Wis., Ill. Bar Assn., Order of Coif, Alpha Phi Omega, Phi Kappa Phi, Phi Alpha Delta. Lodge: Optimist. Avocations: photography, philately, camping. Home: 3906 Rolling Hill Dr Middleton WI 53562 Office: Grant Thornton 2 E Gilman PO Box 8100 Madison WI 53708

BERMAN, TODD ROBERT, investment company executive; b. Buffalo, Apr. 16, 1957; s. Leonard and Judith (Goldenberg) B.; m. Susan Leslie Katz, Dec. 17, 1983. AB, Brown U., 1979; MBA, Columbia U., 1982. Assoc., Allen & Co., Inc., N.Y.C., 1979-81, Oppenheimer & Co., Inc., N.Y.C., 1983-84; v.p. Peterson, Jacobs & Co., N.Y.C., 1984-86; mng. dir. E.S. Jacobs & Co., 1986—; adviser Columbia U. Bus. Sch. Alumni Counselling Bd., N.Y.C., 1984—; bd. dirs. Memorex Telex N.V., Amsterdam, Westronix, Inc., Salt Lake City, Coordination Tech., Trumbull, Conn., Manhattan Toy Co., N.Y.C.; speaker in field. Mem. staff Office of Gov., Rhode Island, 1978-79. Recipient numerous internat. sailing awards, 1973—; elected to R.I. State Govt. Internship Program, 1978. Mem. Nat. Assn. Securities Dealers. Clubs: University. Office: ES Jacobs & Co 375 Park Ave Suite 3108 New York NY 10152

BERMES, ROBERT JOEL, physician; b. Oran, Algeria, Jan. 19, 1932; s. Marcel Julien and Germaine Eloise (Blanchard) B. D in Medicine, U. Lyon, France, 1962. Intern, resident Edouard Herriot Hosp. and Hôtel Dieu, 1952-60; practice medicine, Roquebrune sur Argens, 1962—. Inventor retative pump for artificial heart, 1979, sphygmo-circular motor, 1987. Club: Aero Club Grasse (Cannes, France). Home and Office: 1 Ave Jean Giono, 83520 Roquebrune sur Argens France

BERMOND, PIERRE GEORGES, physician, educator; b. Paris, France, Mar. 26, 1922; s. Jean Pierre and Thérèse Marie (Chauvin) B.; married, Sept. 17, 1946; children: Stéphanie, Caroline, Aude, Virginie. Cert. indsl. hygiene, Inst. Legal Medicine, Paris, 1948; MD, Faculté de Médecine, Paris, 1948. Gen. practice medicine Reims, France, 1948-53; cons. Cen. U. Hosp., Reims, 1953-69; pvt. practice medicine specializing in nutrition Reims, 1967-86; founder Nutrition Unit Cen. U. Hosp., 1957; cons. clin. research F. Hoffmann-la-Roche, Basel, Switzerland, 1967—, various locations; lectr. Inst. Nutrition, Nancy, France, 1972—. Contbr. over 200 articles to scholarly jours. Mem. Assn. Française des Spécialistes du Diabète et des Maladies Métaboliques, Internat. Cen. Vitaminology (mem. sci. com.), World Transport Users Fedn. (hon. pres. Transport 2000 Internat., dir. publ. Transport 2000 1975—), European Fedn. Transport Users (chmn.), French Fedn. Transport Users (1st vice chmn.), French Nat. Council of Transports (dep. mem.). Home: Binningerstrasse 12, 4123 Allschwil Switzerland Office: 72 rue de Talleyrand, 51100 Reims France

BERN, PAULA, communications training company executive; b. Pitts., July 27, 1934; m. Joseph Bern, Dec. 21, 1954; children—Bruce, Caryn, Marshall, Samuel, Rona. B.A., Pa. State U., 1956; M.A., U. Pitts., 1978, Ph.D., 1980. Editor-in-chief Jaffe Pub. Co., Los Angeles, 1958-63; on-air producer Sta. WQED-TV, Pitts., 1963-65; dir. univ. relations and devel. Robert Morris Coll., Pitts. and Coraopolis, 1965-69, Point Park Coll., Pitts., 1969-72; pres. Bern Assocs., Inc., 1972-87; chief exec. officer The Exec. TV Workshop, Pitts., 1987—; tchr. sr. exec. seminars Grad. Sch. Urban and Pub. Affairs, Carnegie Mellon U., 1985—. Author: Point Park College: A History, 1980; How to Work for a Woman Boss (Even if You'd Rather Not), 1987. Trustee Pitts. Ballet Theatre, Inc., 1973—; bd. dirs. Council for Internat. Visitors, 1975—, Exec. Women's Council, 1980—; mem. adv. council Internat. Poetry Forum, 1979—. Mem. Women in Communications, Pub. Relations Soc. Am., Delta Sigma Rho, Phi Beta Kappa. Home: 154 Inglewood Dr Pittsburgh PA 15243 Office: Exec TV Workshop Inc 475 Carnegie Dr Pittsburgh PA 15243

BERNACCHI, RICHARD LLOYD, lawyer; b. Los Angeles, Dec. 15, 1938; s. Bernard and Anne (Belluomini) B. B.S. with honors in Commerce (Nat. Merit Found. scholar), U. Santa Clara, 1961; LL.B. with highest honors (Legion Lex scholar, Jerry Geisler Meml. scholar), U. So. Calif., 1964. Bar: Calif. 1964. Since practiced in Los Angeles; partner firm Irell and Manella, 1964—; lectr. Am. Law Inst., 1972-73; lectr. data processing contracts and law U. So. Calif., Los Angeles, 1972, 78, 81; co-chmn. Regional Transp. Com., 1970-72; mem. adv. bd. U. So. Calif. Computer Law Inst., 1979—, Ariz. Law and Tech. Inst., 1982-86; U. Santa Clara Computer and High Tech. Law Jour., 1982—. Author: (with Gerald H. Larsen) Data Processing Contracts and the Law, 1974; (with Frank and Statland) Bernacchi on Computer Law, 1986; editor-in-chief: U. So. Calif. Law Rev., 1962-64; mem. adv. bd. Computer Negotiators Report, 1983—, Computer and Tech. Law Jour., 1984—, Computer Law Strategist, 1984—. Served to capt. AUS, 1964-66, PTO. Mem. Am. Bar Assn. (mem. adv. com. on edn. 1973-74, chmn. subcom. taxation computer systems of sect. sci. and tech. 1976-78), Los Angeles Bar Assn., Computer Law Assn. (bd. dirs. 1973-86, chmn. preconf. symposium on law and computers 1974-75, West Coast v.p. 1976-79, sr. v.p. 1979-81, pres. 1981-83, adv. bd. 1986—), Am. Fedn. Info. Processing Socs. (mem. spl. com. electronic funds transfer systems 1974-78), Order of Coif, Scabbard and Blade, Beta Gamma Sigma, Alpha Sigma Nu.

BERNAL, IGNACIO PIMENTEL, archaeologist; b. Mexico City, Feb. 13, 1910; s. Rafael Bernal and Rafaela Garcia Pimentel; m. Sofia Verea, Oct. 14, 1944; children—Ignacio, Rafaela, Carlos, Concha. LL.D., U. Mex., 1949; M.A., Cambridge (Eng.) U., 1975; M.A. hon. degrees, U. Calif., St. Mary's U., San Antonio, U. Americas. Prof. anthropology U. Mex., 1948-76; dir. Nat. Inst., Mexico City, 1968-71, Mus. Anthropology, Mexico City, 1962-77; vis. prof. anthropology U. Tex., 1954, U. Calif., 1958, Harvard U., 1961, Cambridge U., 1975-76, Sorbonne U., Paris, 1955-56, U. Madrid, 1964, U. Rome, 1966. Author: A History of Mexican Archaeology, The Olmec World, others; contbr. numerous articles on archaeology and history to profl. jours. Decorated officer Royal Order Orange-Nassau, Netherlands; officer Legion of Honor; comdr. Legion of Honor, France; comdr. Order of Merit, Italy; officer Order of Crown, Belgium; comdr. Order of Merit, Ger.; officer Royal Order of Danebrog, Denmark; comdr. Order of Merit, Senegal; comdr. Royal Victoria Order, Eng.; comdr. Star of Yugoslavia. Mem. U.S. Nat. Acad. Scis. (fgn. assoc.). Roman Catholic. Home: 65 Tres Picos, Mexico City Mexico 5 *

BERNARD, ALAIN MICHEL, radiologist; b. Marseille, France, Nov. 13, 1940; s. Henri-Jean and Michèle (Fauconnier) B.; married; children: Antoine, Olivier. MD, U. Paris, 1968. Intern. Internat. Hosp. of Paris, 1965-66, resident, 1967-68; sci. chief Diaconesse Hosp., Paris, 1970-74; dept. chief Foch Hosp., Paris, 1974-81, Ctr. Cardiologique Evecquement, Meulan, France, 1982-85, A Raré, Paris, 1985—; cons. Ministere Santé, Paris, 1975-84, Soc. Radiologie, Paris, 1985—. Contbr. articles to profl. jours. Med. advisor Amnesty Internat., London and Paris, 1978-86. Home: 12-14 Gen Koenig, 75017 Paris France Office: A Paré, 27 Blvd Victor Hugo, 92200 Neuilly Sur Seine France

BERNARD, BRUCE WILLIAM, lawyer; b. Erie, Pa., Feb. 3, 1951; s. Barney and Barbara Jean (Wurst) B.; m. Valerie Jean Noziglia, June 2, 1978 (div.); children: Elizabeth Anne, Brandon Wallace; m. Catherine Ann Blore, May 4, 1984. B.A., Case Western Res. U., Cleve., 1972, J.D., 1975. Bar: Pa. 1975, U.S. Dist. Ct. (we. dist.) Pa. 1975, U.S. Supreme Ct. 1980. Assoc. Silin, Eckert & Burke, Erie, 1975-77; ptnr. Ely & Bernard, Erie, 1978-85, Bernard & Stuczynski, Erie, 1985—; instr. Am. Inst. Banking, Erie, 1981—. Bd. dirs., Erie Civic Music Assn., 1976-83, Florence Crittendon Services, Erie, 1978-84, Meth. Towers, Erie, 1979—. Named Vol. of Yr., Erie chpt. ARC, 1982. Mem. ABA, Pa. Bar Assn., Erie County Bar Assn., Assn. Trial Lawyers Am., Pa. Trial Lawyers Assn., Comml. Law League Am., Phi Delta Phi. Republican. Methodist. Club: Kiwanis (bd. dirs. 1978-81, Disting. Service award 1976, 79). Home: 1211 St Mary Dr Erie PA 16509 Office: Bernard & Stuczynski 234 W 6th St Erie PA 16507-1319

BERNARD, DONALD RAY, lawyer, author; b. San Antonio, June 5, 1932; s. Horatio J. and Amber (McDonald) B.; children—Doren, Kevin; m. Elizabeth Priscilla Gilpin, 1986. Student U. Mich., 1950-52; B.A., U. Tex., 1954, J.D., 1958, LL.M., 1964. Bar: Tex. 1958, U.S. Ct. Mil. Appeals, U.S. Supreme Ct. Briefing atty. Supreme Ct. Tex., Austin, 1958-59; asst. atty. gen. State of Tex., Austin, 1959-60; ptnr. Bernard & Bernard, Houston, 1960-80; sole practice, Houston, 1980—; mem. faculty S.W. Sch. Real Estate, 1968-77; bd. dirs. Pulp Industries Co. Bd. dirs. Nat. Kidney Found., Houston, 1960-63; chmn. Bd. Adjustment, Hedwig Village, Houston, 1972-76, Third Am. Funding Group, Inc. Served to comdr. U.S. Navy, 1950. Mem. Lawyers Soc. Houston (pres. 1973-74), Houston Bd. Realtors, ABA, Inter-Am. Bar Assn., Tex. Bar Assn., Houston Bar Assn. (sec.-treas. internat. law sect.), Internat. Bar Assn., Lawyer-Pilot Bar Assn., Sons of the Republic of Tex., Alpha Tau Omega, Phi Delta Phi. Methodist. Clubs: St. James's (London); Masons, Shriners. Lic. comml. pilot. Author: Origin of the Special Verdict As Now Practiced in Texas, 1964; co-author: (novel) Bullion, 1982. Office: 1212 Main St Suite 851 Houston TX 77002

BERNARD, HENRI DESIRE, chemical company executive; b. Gerouville, Luxemburg, Belgium, Feb. 25, 1926; s. Desire and Martha (Thibe) B.; m. Andree Marini, Oct. 30, 1952; children: Michele, Annie, Alain, Brigitte. Civil Mining Engr., Univ., Brussels, Belgium, 1948, geologist, 1950. Registered profl. engr. Geologist Geomines Manono, Zaire, 1950-60; chief Tessenderlo Chemie, Flam, Belgium, 1960-71; mgr. L.V.M., Tessenderlo, 1971-83; gen. mgr. Pont Brule, Vilvoorde, 1983-86; dep. gen. mgr. Tessenderlo Chemie, Belgium, 1986—. Office: Tessenderlo Chemie, Stationsstraat, B-3980 Tessenderlo Belgium

BERNARD, JACQUES NIELS, venture capitalist; b. Lyons, Rhone, France, Sept. 27, 1938; s. Rene G. and Eliette S. (Granyi) B.; m. Sophie M. Blanc, Dec. 21, 1960; children: Jean-François, Laurence, Nicolas. M.Sc., Ecole Polytechnique, Paris, 1960; B.A., Faculté de Droit et Scis. Economiques, Paris, 1964. Mktg. mgr. Schlumberger, Mpls., Paris, 1965-69; planner, planning mgr. IBM Systems Devel. Div., Nice, France, Harrison, N.Y., 1969-74; product line mgr. IBM-Europe, Paris, 1974-78; dir. Consultronique, Paris, 1979-82, mng. dir., 1982—; geschaeftsfuhrer Consultronik, Frankfurt, W.Ger., 1983-87; gen. ptnr. Tech. Investment Ptnrs., 1988—. Served to lt. French Army, 1960-62. Recipient Medaille Commemorative Algerie, 1962. Mem. Institut de l'Enterprise (conf. bd.), Am. C. of C. (Frankfurt, Paris). Roman Catholic. Home: 8 Rue de Jarente, 75004 Paris France

BERNARD, JEAN-ANTOINE, ophthalmologist; b. Paris, Apr. 8, 1938; s. Georges and Stefanie B.; m. Julie Celia Gregory. MD, Faculté de Paris, 1969. Interne Hopitaux de Paris, Assistance Publique de Paris, 1969; asst. biophysique Faculté Médecine de Paris, 1965-69; chef Clinique Hôtel-Dieu de Paris, 1969-76; chmn. Diabeto-Ophthalmology dept., 1982—. Author: Les Voies Lacrymales, 1982. Mem. Societe Francaise d'Ophtalmologie (v.p. 1985—), Jules Gonin Club, European Eye Research Assn. Home and Office: 1 Rue Scheffer, 75116 Paris France

BERNARDI, GIORGIO, molecular biologist; b. Genova, Italy, Jan. 10, 1929; s. Guglielmo and Maria (Cappabianca) B.; M.D., U. Padova, 1952; D.Sc. Phys., U. Strasbourg, 1967; m. Riva Gabriella, Aug. 28, 1957; children: Guglielmo, Gregorio, Giacomo. Asst. prof. biochemistry U. Padova, U. Pavia, Italy, 1953-56; postdoctoral fellow Nat. Research Council, Ottawa, Can., 1957-59; mem. staff Centre National de la Recherche Scientifique as chargé, 1959-63, maître, 1963-68, dir. research, 1968—; head lab. molecular genetics Inst. Jacques Mohod, Paris, 1969—, dir. Inst., 1978-81; scholar Fogarty Internat. Center, Bethesda, Md., 1981-84. Served with Italian Air Force, 1952-53. Recipient K.A. Forster Prize Akademie der Wissenschaften und der Literatur, Mainz, Germany, 1973. Mem. Fedn. European Biochem. Socs. (chmn. advanced course com. 1978-86), European Molecular Biology Orgn. (chmn. standing adv. com. on recombinant DNA 1980—), Internat. Council Sci. Unions (chmn. com. on genetic experimentation 1982—). Editor: European Jour. Biochemistry, 1977—, Biochemistry Internat., 1980—, EMBO Jour., 1982-85, Trends in Genetics, 1985—, Nucleic Acids Res., 1986—. Office: Laboratoire de Genetique Moleculaire, Institut Jacques Monod, IRBM 2 Pl Jussieu, 75005 Paris France

BERNARDI, JAMES EDWARD, retail liquor merchant, real estate investor; b. Highland Park, Ill., July 26, 1946; s. Irving D. and Nell D. (Dimmitt) B.; m. Michelle DiCarlo, June 12, 1976; children—Jamie Elizabeth, Michael James. B.A., North Park Coll., 1969. Cert. real estate agt. Tchr., coach Carmel High Sch., Mundelein, Ill., 1969-75; gen. mgr. and officer Foremost Liquors, Mundelein, 1976—; owner, The Hair Designers, Libertyville, Ill, 1987—; real estate agt., Century 21. Mem. Com. Bus. Devel. Commn., Mundelein, ARC, Mundelein. Mem. Ill. High Sch. Assn. (ofcl. 1969—), No. Ofcls. Assn. (past pres., bd. dirs.). Roman Catholic. Officiated Ill. High Sch. Basketball Championship Series for past 14 yrs. Avocations: golf, officiating football and basketball. Home: 849 Braemar Mundelein IL 60060 Office: Foremost Liquors 425 Townline Rd Mundelein IL 60060

BERNARDIN, JOSEPH LOUIS CARDINAL, archbishop; b. Columbia, S.C., Apr. 2, 1928; s. Joseph and Maria M. (Simion) B. AB in Philosophy, St. Mary's Sem., Balt., 1948; MEd, Cath. U. Am., 1952. Ordained priest Roman Catholic Ch., 1952; asst. pastor Diocese of Charleston, S.C., 1952-54; vice chancellor Diocese of Charleston, 1954-56, chancellor, 1956-66, vicar gen., 1962-66, diocesan consultor, 1962-66, adminstr., 1964-65; aux. bishop Atlanta, 1966-68; pastor Christ the King Cathedral, 1966-68; sec., mem. exec. com. Nat. Conf. Cath. Bishops-U.S. Cath. Conf., gen. sec., 1968-72, pres., 1974-77; archbishop of Cin. 1972-82, of Chgo., 1982—; mem. Sacred Congregation Bishops, 1973-78; del., mem. permanent council World Synod of Bishops, 1974, 77—; mem. Pontifical Commn. Social Communications, Rome, 1970-72, Sacred Coll. Cardinals, 1983—. Mem. adv. council Am. Revolution Bicentennial, 1975, Pres.'s Adv. Com. Refugees, 1975. Mem. Nat. Cath. Edn. Assn. (chmn. bd. 1978-79). Home: 1555 N State Pkwy Chicago IL 60610 *

BERNARDO, FELICISIMO C., physician, consultant; b. Aliaga, Philippines, Aug. 23, 1937; s. Hoivesimo B. Bernardo and Ruperta G. Cruz; m. Edith Nicolas, Apr. 10, 1963; children: Butch, Ricky, Gladys, Fritz, Jason. MD, Far Eastern U., Manila, 1966; postgrad, Ednl. Council Fgn. Med. Grads., Phila., 1975. Resident, then clinics chief Isabela Provincial Hosp., Philippines, 1968-74; med. dir. John Rauch Meml. Hosp., Tabuk, Philippines, 1975-80; cons. Kalinga Integrated Hosp., Philippines, 1980-83; founder, med. dir. Med. Surg. Clinic, Tabuk, 1983—; cons. Devel. Bank Philippines, Coca-Cola Bottling Co. Author: Healing and Medicine, 1978. Advisor Provincial Peace and Order council; mem. Provincial Music and Cultural Affairs. Recipient Advisory award George Washington U., 1977-78, Bantayog award Concerned Citizens Philippines, 1980, Merit award Population Commn. Philippines, 1984. Fellow Acad. Family Physicians; mem. Philippine Med. Assn. (pres. 1983-85, Merit award 1985), Philippine Medicare Commn. Provincial Council (vice-chmn. 1983-85, Merit award 1985), Peace Coordinating Com. 1986-87. Mem. United Ch. Christ. Club: Isabella Badminton (pres. 1971-74). Lodge: Gideon's Internat. Office: Med Surg Clinic, 203 Molintas, Tabuk Kalinga Apayao 1401, Philippines

BERNARDO, JOSE MIGUEL, academic statistician, consultant; b. Valencia, Spain, Mar. 12, 1950; s. Gregorio and Lucrecia (Herranz) B.; m. Amparo Vercher, May 29, 1982; 1 child, Marina. BS, MS, U. Valencia, 1972, PhD, 1974; PhD in Stats., U. London, 1976. Lectr., U. Valencia, Spain, 1976-78, prof. biostats., head dept., 1978-86, prof. stats., 1987—; mem. European Com. Statisticians, 1980-85. Author: Bioestadistica, 1981; editor: Proceedings International Meetings in Bayesian Statistics, 1979, 83, 88. Recipient Nat. PhD award, Ministry of Edn., 1975. Fellow Royal Statis. Soc. U.K., Inst. Statisticians; mem. Internat. Statis. Inst., Am. Statis. Assn., Inst. Math. Stats., Spanish Statis. Soc. (v.p. 1984—). Socialist. Office: Dept Estadistica, Fac Matematicas, 46100 Burjassot, Valencia Spain

BERNASCONI, MARCO CORNELIO, aerospace company executive, researcher; b. Bellinzona, Ticino, Switzerland, July 13, 1950; s. Rinaldo and Cornelia (Necchi) B.; m. Cristina Ghirlanda, May 19, 1979; children: Alessandro Marco, Massimo Luca. ME, Fed. Inst. Tech., Zurich, Switzerland, 1974, DSc in Tech., 1979. Project engr., mgr. space dept. Contraves AG, Zurich, 1978-87, tech. supr. space dept., 1987—; pres. Euroavia Zurich, 1973-74; cons. Orbitine Unification Ring Satellite Project, Embrach, Switzerland, 1986—. Contbr. 20 tech. articles on space tech. to profl. jours., 1977—; patentee in field. Pres. Thomas Jefferson Assn., Vezia, Switzerland, 1971—. Served with Swiss Air Force. Fellow Brit. Interplanetary Soc.; mem. Am. Inst. Aeronautics and Astronautics. Roman Catholic. Home: Koeschenruetistr #139, 8052 Zurich Switzerland Office: Contraves AG/ Space Dept, Schaffauserstr 580, 8052 Zurich Switzerland

BERNAY, BETTI, artist; b. 1926; d. David Michael and Anna Gaynia (Bernay) Woolin; m. J. Bernard Goldfarb, Apr. 19, 1947; children: Manette Deitsch, Karen Lynn. Grad. costume design, Pratt Inst., 1946; student, Nat. Acad. Design, N.Y.C., 1947-49, Art Students League, N.Y.C., 1950-51. Exhibited one man shows at Galerie Raymond Duncan, Paris, France, Salas Municipales, San Sebastian, Spain, Circulo de Bellas Artes, Madrid, Spain, Bacardi Gallery, Miami, Fla., Columbia (S.C.) Mus., Columbus (Ga.) Mus., Galerie Andre Weil, Paris, Galerie Hermitage, Monte Carlo, Monaco, Casino de San Remo, Italy, Galerie de Arte de la Caja de Ahorros de Ronda, Malaga, Spain, Centro Artistico, Granada, Spain, Circulo de la Amistad, Cordoba, Spain, Studio H Gallery, N.Y.C., Walter Wallace Gallery, Palm Beach, Fla., Mus. Bellas Artes, Malaga, Harbor House Gallery, Crystal House Gallery, Internat. Gallery, Jordan Marsh, Fontainebleau Gallery, Miami Beach, Carriage House Gallery, Galerie 99, Pageant Gallery, Carriage House, Miami Beach, Rosenbaum Galleries, Palm Beach; exhibited group shows at Painters and Sculptors Soc., Jersey City Mus., Salon de Invierno, Mus. Malaga, Salon des Beaux Arts, Cannes, France, Guggenheim Gallery, Nat. Acad. Gallery, Salmagundi Club, Lever House, Lord & Taylor Art Gallery, Nat. Arts Gallery, Knickerbocker Artists, N.Y.C., Salon des Artistes Independants, Salon des Artistes Francais, Salon Populiste, Paris, Salon de Otono, Nat. Assn. Painters and Sculptors Spain, Madrid, Phipps Gallery, Palm Beach, Artists Equity, Hollywood (Fla.) Mus., Gault Gallery Cheltenham, Phila., Springfield (Mass.) Mus., Met. Mus. and Art Center, Miami, Fla., Planet Ocean Mus., Charter Club, Trade Fair Ams., Guggenheim Gallery, N.Y.C.; represented in permanent collections including Jockey Club Art Gallery, Miami, Mus. Malaga, Circulo de la Amistad, I.O.S. Found., Geneva, Switzerland, others. Bd. dirs. Men's Opera Guild; mem. adv. bd. Jackson Meml. Hosp. Project Newborn; mem. women's com. Bascon Palmer Eye Inst.; active Greater Miami Heart Assn., Alzheimer Grand Notable, 2d Generation Miami Heart Inst., Sunrisers Mentally Retarded, Orchid Ball Com. Recipient medal City N.Y., medal Sch. Art Leagues, N.Y.C., Prix de Paris Raymond Duncan, 1958, others. Mem. Nat. Assn. Painters and Sculptors Spain, Nat. Assn. Women Artists, Société des Artistes Français, Société des Artistes Independants, Fedn. Francais des Sociétés d'Art Graphique et Plastique, Artists Equity, Am. Artists Profl. League, Am. Fedn. Art, Nat. Soc. Lit. and Arts, Met. Mus. and Arts Center Miami. Clubs: Palm Bay, Jockey, Turnberry, Club of Clubs Internat. Address: 10155 Collins Ave Apt 1705 Bal Harbour FL 33154

BERNECKER, WALTHER LUDWIG, historian, educator; b. Dollnstein, Bavaria, Fed. Republic of Germany, July 17, 1947; s. Wendelin and Ingeborg (Kaersten) B. PhD, U. Erlangen, Fed. Republic of Germany, 1976; postgrad., U. Augsburg, Fed. Republic of Germany, 1986. Instr. U. Augsburg, Fed. Republic of Germany, 1979-84; assoc. prof. 1986—; visiting scholar U. Chgo., 1984-85. Author 10 books about spanish and late American history, 1977-87. Home: Ziehrerstrasse 7A, 8906 Gersthofen Federal Republic of Germany Office: Uni Augsburg, Universitatstrasse 2, 89 Augsburg Federal Republic of Germany

BERNHAGEN, LILLIAN FLICKINGER, school health consultant; b. Cleve., Oct. 1, 1916; d. Norman Henry and Bertha May (Rogers) Flickinger; m. Ralph John Bernhagen, Sept. 2, 1940; children: Ralph, Janet Bernhagen Smiley, Penelope Bernhagen Braat. Student, Ohio Wesleyan U., 1934-37; B.S., R.N., Ohio State U., 1940, M.A., 1958; postgrad., LaVerne Coll., 1972-73. Asst. dir. Kiwanis Health Camp for Underprivileged Children, Steubenville, Ohio, summer 1940; asst. dir. nurses Jefferson Davis Hosp., Houston, 1940-41; ARC instr. Ohio State U., 1943, 63, elem. edn. lectr., 1970; dir. health services Worthington (Ohio) City Schs., 1951-76; health edn. instr. Ohio State U., 1976-77; spl. cons. venereal disease and sex edn. Ohio Dept. Health, 1976-82; sch. health cons. 1976—; vice chmn. medicine/edn. com. on sch. and coll. health AMA, 1976-78, chmn., 1978-80. Author: Sex Education: Understanding Growth and Social Development, 1968, What A Miracle You Are-Boys, 1968, 3d rev. edit., 1986, What A Miracle You Are-Girls, 1968, 3d rev. edit., 1986, Toward a Reverance for Life, 1971, Personality, Sexuality and Stereotyping, 1974, (with others) Growth Patterns and Sex Education: A Suggested Curriculum Guide K-12, 1967, Sex Education: Understanding Growth and Social Development, 1968; contbr. articles to profl. jours., mags. Bd. dirs. Hearing and Speech Center of Columbus and Franklin County, 1954-57, sec., 1957; mem. nat. adv. com. Nat. Center for Health Edn., 1978-82; sec. Ohio Wesleyan U. Class of 38, 1968-78, 83-88; bd. dirs. V.D. Hotline Columbus and Franklin County, 1974-87, bd. expansion chmn., 1978-85, pres., 1985-86; mem. Worthington Hist. Soc., Doll Docent, 1982—, Meth. Chancel choir 1950—, Pastor Parish Relations Com., 1985-88, bd. trustees, 1989-92, edn. commn., 1982-85. Recipient Centennial award Sch. Nursing, Ohio State U., 1970, Outstanding Alumnae award Ohio State U., 1964, Disting. Service award Mich. Sch. Nurses Assn., hon. mention La Sertoma Internat. Woman of Yr., 1972. Fellow Am. Sch. Health Assn. (pres. 1976, governing council 1969-77, 1982—, chmn. health guidance in sex edn. com. 1963-67, 71-77, chmn. sr. adv. council 1983—, Disting. Service award 1969, Howe award 1979, cert. of merit, 1985), Am. Pub. Health Assn. (chmn. com. on urban health problems 1972); mem. Assn. for Advancement of Health Edn., Sex Edn. and Info. Council of U.S., NEA, Worthington Edn. Assn. (v.p. 1961-62, Tchr. of Year 1972-73), Central Ohio Tchrs. Assn. (chmn. sch. health services sect. 1963), Royal Soc. Health, AAUW, Chi Omega (pres. Columbus Alumnae chpt. 1947-49, fin. adv. Ohio Wesleyan U. 1964-76, Outstanding Alumna of Year, State of Ohio 1986), Pi Lambda Theta (citation award), Sigma Theta Tau, Phi Delta Kappa. Clubs: Monnett, Worthington Women's, Ohio State U. Women's Golf (chmn. (1973), Columbus Women's Dist. Golf Assn. (treas. 1985, sec. 1987). Home and Office: 5916 Linworth Rd Worthington OH 43085

BERNHARD, (LEOPOLD FREDERIK EVERHARD JULIUS COERT KAREL GODFRIED PIETER), Prince of the Netherlands, Prince zur Lippe-Biesterfeld; b. Jena, Germany, June 29, 1911; s. Prince Bernhard zur Lippe and Baroness Armgard von Sierstorpff-Cramm; referendar juris U. Berlin; LLD, State U. Utrecht, 1946, U. Montreal, 1958, U. B.C., 1958, U. Mich., 1965; D.Econs, Free U. Amsterdam, 1965; D.Tech. Scis., U. Advanced Tech., Delft, 1951; D. Natural Sci., U. Basel, 1971; m. Juliana Louise Emma Marie Wilhelmina, Princess of The Netherlands, Jan. 7, 1937; children—Beatrix Wilhelmina Armgard, Irene Emma Elizabeth, Margriet Francisca, Maria Christina. Royal commr. bd. Netherlands Trade and Industry Fair; hon. air marshal RAF, 1964—; ret. gen. Netherlands Army and Air Force; ret. adm. Netherlands Navy; founder, regent Prince Bernhard Fund, Praemium Erasmianum Found.; hon. mem. European Cultural Found.; founder, pres. World Wildlife Fund; councillor Netherlands Inst. Econs., Netherlands U. Econs., Rotterdam; hon. functions number over 200. Decorated knight grand cross Order of Bath, Royal Victorian Order, Order Brit. Empire; hon. commodore Royal N.Z. Air Force, 1973. Hon. mem. Royal Aeros. Soc., Royal Inst. Naval Architects, Aeromed. Soc., Royal Spanish Acad. Address: Soestdijk Palace, Baarn The Netherlands *

BERNHARD, ALEXANDER ALFRED, lawyer; b. New Orleans, Sept. 20, 1936; s. John Helanus and Dora (Solosko) B.; m. Martha Ruggles, Nov. 21, 1959 (div.); m. Joyce Harrington, Dec. 30, 1976 (div.); children—John, Jason, Frederic; m. Myra Mayman, Nov. 1986. B.S., MIT, 1957; LL.B., Harvard U., 1964; Assoc. Master, Harvard U., 1986; Bar: Calif. 1964, Oreg. 1965, Mass. 1966. Law clk. to judge U.S. Ct. Appeals (9th cir.), 1964-65; assoc. Johnson, Johnson & Harrang, Eugene, Oreg., 1965-66, Bingham, Dana & Gould, Boston, 1966-71, Hale and Dorr, Boston, 1971-73, jr. ptnr., 1973-75, sr. ptnr., 1975—. Trustee Mass. Eye and Ear Infirmary. Served to lt. USNR, 1957-61. Mem. ABA, Boston Bar Assn. Democrat. Clubs: Union Boat, Manchester Yacht, Longwood Cricket, Union Boston. Office: Hale and Dorr 60 State St Boston MA 02109

BERNHARDT, ARTHUR DIETER, housing consultant; b. Dresden, Germany, Nov. 19, 1937; came to U.S., 1966; s. Rudolf B. and Charlotte (Bernhardt). Dipl. Ing., U. Tech., Munich, W. Ger., 1965; postgrad., U. So. Calif., 1966-67; M. City Planning, MIT, 1969. In various postions with bldg. projects 1965-68; dir. Program in Industrialization of Housing Sector MIT, 1969-76, pres. Program in Industrialization of Housing Sector, 1977—; chief exec. officer, dir. ASI, Inc., 1984—; internat. housing industry cons., Cambridge, Mass., 1973—; asst. prof. MIT, 1970-76. Author book; contbr. articles to profl. jours. Mem. exec. com. Mass. Gov.'s Adv. Com. on Manufactured Housing, 1974-75; NRC del. 8th Gen. Assembly Internat. Council Bldg. Research, 1974. Fed. Republic Germany fellow, 1965, 66, 67, 68; MIT fellow, 1968, 69; MIT grantee, 1970; Fed. Republic Germany grantee, 1965; Alfred P. Sloan Found. grantee, 1970; Dept. Commerce grantee, 1972; HUD grantee, 1972, 74. Mem. Internat. Council Bldg. Research, Am. Acad. Polit. and Social Sci., Am. Planning Assn., Deutscher Hochschulverband, Am. Judicature Soc. (assoc.). Office: PO Box 2288 New York NY 10185

BERNIS, FRANCISCO, mathematics researcher; b. Lugo, Spain, May 10, 1946; s. Francisco and Cristina (Carro) B.; m. Carmen Clavijo, Jan. 25, 1984; 1 child, Maria. Licenciado, Complutense U., Madrid, 1968, PhD, 1982. Teaching asst. Complutense U., 1969-72; tchr. various high schs., Spain, 1972-78; asst. prof. math. Polytechnic U., Barcelona, Spain, 1978-85, assoc. prof. math., 1985-87; assoc. prof. math. Complutense U., Madrid, 1987—; chmn. calculus com. Polytechnic U., 1974-85, supr. algebra courses, 1983-85, dept. head math., 1983-85; reviewer #5291 Zentralblatt fur Mathematik, Berlin, 1984; prin. Sant Boi High Sch., Barcelona, 1975-77. Author: Mathematics (in Spanish), 1978; A Course in Mathematics Problems, 1979; contbr. articles to profl. jours. Served with Spanish Army, 1968-69. NSF grantee Purdue U., 1985-86. Mem. Nat. Com. of High Sch. Prins., Nat. Assn. High Sch. Tchrs. (treas. 1976-77), Real Sociedad Matematica Espanola, Real Sociedad Espanola de Fisica, Am. Math. Soc., Math. Assn. Am., N.Y. Acad. Scis. Office: Complutense Univ of Madrid, Dept Applied Math, Madrid Spain 28040

BERNOSKY, HERMAN GEORGE, retail gasoline dealer; b. Minersville, Pa., Aug. 16, 1921; s. Peter and Mary Bernosky; student Rider Coll., Trenton, N.J., 1947-48. With Bernosky's Exxon Sta., Llewellyn, Pa., 1940-42, 46—, owner, operator, 1949—. Treas. Minersville Area Bicentennial, 1976. Served with AUS, 1942-46; ETO. Decorated Bronze Star (3). Mem. Internat. Platform Assn., Am. Legion. Democrat. Roman Catholic. Club: Minersville Lions (past pres., dir. 1957—). Home: 622 Lytle St Minersville PA 17954 Office: PO Box 170 Llewellyn PA 17944

BERNS, H(ERMAN) JEROME, restaurateur; b. N.Y.C., Feb. 19, 1907; s. Abraham and Sophia (Bazin) B.; B.A., U. Cin., 1929, D.C.S. (hon.), 1962; m. Suzanne Tanzer Pogany, Mar. 3, 1977; children—Cecily Miller, Diane Stein (dec.). Drama critic, editor Cin. Enquirer, 1929-38; v.p., sec. 21 Club, Inc., N.Y.C., 1945—; sec. Iron Gate Products, Inc., N.Y.C., 1951—. Pres. Kriendler Berns Found., 1971—; trustee, U. Cin. Found., 1976-84; employer-trustee Hotel/Restaurant Employees Welfare and Pension. Decorated chevalier Merite d'Agricole (France); recipient Escoffier award Confrerie de la Chaine des Rotisseurs, 1968; William Howard Taft medal U. Cin., 1972; named to Hall of Fame Culinary Inst. Am.; diplomate Nat. Inst. Foodservice Industry. Mem. Restaurant League N.Y. (chmn. bd. 1958), Nat. (dir. 1966-76, hon. dir. 1976—), N.Y. State (mem. exec. com. 1960, v.p. 1962, sec.-treas. 1963) restaurant assns., N.Y. Conv. and Visitors Bur. (mem. exec. com. 1953, v.p. and treas. 1953-63, vice-chmn. 1986—), U. Cin. Alumni Assn. (regional v.p. 1963), Food and Wine Soc. N.Y. (Andre Simon award), Chaine de Rotisseur (founder U.S.A. group). Home: 14 E 75th St New York NY 10021 Office: 21 W 52d St New York NY 10019

BERNSTEIN, DAVID, surgeon; b. Minsk, Russia, Oct. 20, 1910; came to U.S., 1912, naturalized, 1932; s. George and Anna (Rossoff) B.; m. Dorothy Ashery, Sept. 2, 1937; children—Helen Miriam Berman Young, Herbert Jacob. B.S., N.Y. U., 1930, M.D., 1935. Intern Bellevue Hosp.-N.Y. U., N.Y.C., 1935-37; resident in ear, nose, throat and facial plastic surgery Bellevue Hosp.-N.Y. U., 1937-39; clin. prof. otorhinolaryngology, chief of plastic surgery N.Y. U. Med. Center, 1966—; chief otolaryngology service Maimonides Med. Center, 1966—; cons. otorhinolaryngol. plastic surgery VA Hosp., N.Y.C.; attending otolaryngologist plastic surgery Bellevue-N.Y. U. Hosp.; pres., exec. com. of med. staff Met. Geriatric Center, 1974-75, mem. joint com. bd. trustees, 1975—; cons. Coney Island Hosp. Contbr. articles to profl. jours., sci. papers to meetings. Served to maj. M.C. AUS, 1944-46. Recipient Meritorious Service award N.Y. U., 1977; named hon. police surgeon N.Y.C., 1979. Fellow Am. Acad. Ophthalmology and Otolaryngology, Am. Acad. Facial, Plastic and Reconstructive Surgery, Am. Assn. Cosmetic Surgeons, Internat. Coll. Surgeons; mem. N.Y., Vienna acads. medicine, N.Y. U. Med. Sch. Alumni Assn. (pres. 1974-75), N.Y. U. Alumni Fedn. (dir.), Phi Beta Kappa. Jewish (adv. com. to bd. trustees temple). Clubs: N.Y. U, Medallion (pres. 1980). Home and Office: 1342 51st St Brooklyn NY 11219 *Died Jan. 15, 1988.*

BERNSTEIN, DAVID MAURICE, computer company executive; b. Glasgow, Scotland, Aug. 14, 1938; s. Abraham Lewis and Tilly (Woolfson) B.; m. Jill Ambrose, Jan. 16, 1962; children: Michael, Peter, Richard, Andrew; m. Mae McGeachie, Feb. 24, 1978. BS with honors, Glasgow U., 1959. Tech. dir. Miles, Shoreham, Sussex, 1959-67; mng. dir. Intertechnique Ltd., Uxbridge, Middlesex, Eng., 1967-78, R.I.C. Ltd., High Wycombe, 1975-87, Ire U.K. Ltd., High Wycombe, 1979-85; U.K. mgr. Efisysteme, High Wycombe, 1975-85, 1987—; cons. NUMELEC, Paris, 1978—. Contbr. numerous articles to profl. jours. Fellow Inst. Profl. Sales Mgmt.; mem. Inst. Physics. Conservative. Jewish. Home: 34 Wordsworth Rd, High Wycombe HP11 2UR, England Office: Efisysteme, 32 High St, High Wycombe HP11 2AZ, England

BERNSTEIN, EDWIN S., judge; b. Long Beach, N.Y., Aug. 15, 1930; s. Harry and Lena (Strizver) B.; m. Mira Frost, Dec. 25, 1974; children—Debora, Andrea, David. B.A., U. Pa., 1952; LL.B., Columbia U., 1955. Bar: N.Y. 1955, U.S. Ct. Appeals (2d cir.) 1962, U.S. Dist. Ct. (ea. and so. dists.) N.Y. 1962, U.S. Tax Ct. 1962, U.S. Supreme Ct. 1964, Md. 1981, D.C. 1982. Mem. bd. contract appeals Dept. Army, Heidelberg, Fed. Republic Germany, 1968-72; regional counsel U.S. Navy, Quincy, Mass., 1972-73; adminstrv. law judge U.S. Dept. Labor, Washington, 1973-79, Fed. Mine Safety and Health Rev. Commn., Washington, 1979-81, U.S. Postal Service, Washington, 1981-87, U.S. Dept. Agriculture, Washington, 1987—; liaison rep. Administrv. Conf. of U.S., Washington, 1983-84; guest lectr. SUNY-Albany, 1978, U. Md., 1982, George Washington U., 1984. Author: U.S. Army Procurement Handbook, 1971; Establishing Federal Administrative Law Judges as an Independent Corps, 1984, also articles. Bd. dirs. Washington Hebrew Congregation, 1985-88. Recipient Meritorious Civilian Service award Dept. Army, 1972. Mem. ABA, Fed. Bar Assn., D.C. Bar Assn., Fed. Adminstr. Law Judges Conf. (pres. 1983-84), Papermill Assn. (pres. 1980-81). Lodge: Masons. Home: 5225 Pooks Hill Rd Bethesda MD 20814 Office: USDA 1049 South Bldg Independence Ave & 14th St SW Washington DC 20250

BERNSTEIN, JEFFREY IAN, economics educator, consultant; b. Montreal, Que., Can., Apr. 14, 1950; s. Abraham and Minnie (Shaffer) B.; m. Lidia Eva Baranski, Aug. 22, 1971; 1 child, Jasmine Elenora. B.A. in Econs. with honors, Sir George Williams U., Montreal, 1971; M.A. in Econs., U. Western Ont., London, Can., 1972, Ph.D. in Econs., 1975. Asst. prof. econs. U. Guelph, Ont., 1974-75, Concordia U., Montreal, 1975-78; assoc. prof. econs. McGill U., Montreal, 1978-81; assoc. prof. econs. Carleton U., Ottawa, Ont., 1981-86, prof., 1986—, dir. M.A. studies in econs., 1983-86; research assoc. Inst. Applied Econ. Research, Montreal, 1975-78; research adviser Informetrica Ltd., Ottawa, 1978-85; dir. Centre for Quantitative Social Scis., Ottawa. Author monographs: Costs of Compliance of Government Regulation, 1980; Research and Development, Patents and Production, 1984; Research and Development and Tax Incentives, 1986. On. scholar U. Western Ont., 1971-72; Can. Council fellow U. Western Ont., 1972-75; research fellow Nat. Bur. Econ. Research, Cambridge, Mass., 1984-85. Mem. Can. Econs. Assn., Am. Econs. Assn. Avocations: squash; swimming; music appreciation; percussion instruments. Office: Carleton U Dept Econs, Ottawa, ON Canada K1S 5B6

BERNSTEIN, JOSEPH, lawyer; b. New Orleans, Feb. 12, 1930; s. Eugene Julian and Lola (Schlemoff) B.; B.S., U. Ala., 1952; LL.B., Tulane U., 1957; m. Phyllis Maxine Askanase, Sept. 4, 1955; children—Jill, Barbara, Elizabeth R, Jonathan Joseph. Clk. to Justice E. Howard McCaleb of La. Supreme Ct., 1957; admitted to La. bar, 1957; asso. firm Jones, Walker, Waechter, Poitevent, Carrere & Denegre, 1957-60, partner, 1960-65; gen. practice New Orleans, 1965—; gen. counsel Alliance for Affordable Energy. Past pres. New Orleans Jewish Community Ctr., Met. New Orleans chpt. March of Dimes. Trustee New Orleans Symphony Soc.; past mem. adv. council New Orleans Mus. Art; past nat. exec. com. Am. Jewish Com. Served to 2d lt. AUS, 1952-54. Mem. Am., La., New Orleans bar assns., Phi Delta Phi, Zeta Beta Tau. Democrat. Jewish. Home: 3119 Prytania Ave New Orleans LA 70115

BERNSTEIN, LAWRENCE ALLEN, architect; York, Pa., Aug. 28, 1932; s. Phillip Gordon and Evelyn (Spielman) B.; m. Susan Hacket, Oct. 8, 1959; m. Johanna Navarro, Feb. 10, 1979; 1 child, Brenda Lena. Student indsl. engring. and architecture MIT, 1951-58. Registered architect, Calif., Va., D.C. Tallesin fellow with Frank Lloyd Wright, 1958; prin. L.A. Bernstein & Assos., Carmel, Calif., 1959-67; pres. Concepts LAB., Inc., N.Y.C., 1968; chief architect, dir. design center new town Linganore, Md., Frederick, Md., 1971-73; pres. bd. chmn., dir. architect and design, prin. The Advanced Design Ctr., San Antonio and Los Angeles, 1973-76, L.A. Bernstein, AIA, 1973-76; dir. design, Diker-Moe Assocs., Los Angeles, 1976-77; prin. Bernstein Assocs., Los Angeles, 1977-80; pres., chmn. bd. L.A. Bernstein Assocs., Inc., 1981—; dir. new product devel. Dart Advanced Design Ctr., N.Y.C. and Los Angeles, 1967-71. Contbr. numerous articles to various publs. Recipient awards including 1st award for engring. excellence Cons. Engrs. Council/USA for Lake Linganore Dam and Dams on Twin Lakes Anita, 1972; spl. recognition award Nat. Assn. Home Builders, 1973; 1st award for excellence Environ. Monthly Mag., 1974; 1st Honor award Monterey Bay chpt. AIA for Mira Obs., 1983. Mem. AIA, Soc. Plastics Engrs. Jewish. Home and Office: 6456 Surfside Way Malibu CA 90265

BERNSTEIN, LEONARD, conductor, pianist, composer; b. Lawrence, Mass., Aug. 25, 1918; s. Samuel Joseph and Jennie (Resnick) B.; m. Felicia Montealegre Cohn, Sept. 9, 1951 (dec. June 1978); children: Jamie, Alexander, Nina. A.B., Harvard U., 1939; grad., Curtis Inst. Music, 1941; studied conducting with, Fritz Reiner and Serge Koussevitzky; studied piano with, Helen Coates, Heinrich Gebhard, and Isabella Vengerova; numerous hon. degrees from various colls. and univs. Asst. to Serge Koussevitzky at Berkshire Music Center, 1942; asst. condr. N.Y. Philharmonic Symphony, 1943-44; condr. N.Y.C. Symphony, 1945-48; frequent condr. Israel Philharmonic Orch., 1947—, mus. adviser, 1948-49; faculty Berkshire Music Center, 1948-55, head conducting dept., 1951-55; prof. music Brandeis U., 1951-56; co-condr. with Dimitri Mitropoulos of N.Y. Philharmonic, 1957-58, music dir., 1958-69; Charles Eliot Norton prof. poetry Harvard, 1972-73. Condr. major orchs. of U.S., Europe in tours, 1946—, opera at La Scala, Milan, also Met. Opera, N.Y.C. and Vienna State Opera; shared transcontinental tour in U.S. with Serge Koussevitzky and Israel Philharmonic, 1951; toured Europe with Vienna Philharmonic Orch., 1970, gala Bicentennial tour, Am. and Europe with N.Y. Philharmonic, 1976; condr. 6-city tour of U.S., summer 1986; condr. Israel Philharm. Orch. in celebration of its 50th anniversary, N.Y.C., Sept. 1986, laureate condr., 1988, pres. English Bach Festival 1977—, London Symphony Orch. 1987—; works include Clarinet Sonata, 1942, Seven Anniversaries for Piano, 1942, Song Cycle, I Hate Music, 1943, Four Anniversaries for Piano, 1948, Song Cycle, La Bonne Cuisine, 1949, Symphony No.2-The Age of Anxiety, 1949, Symphony No. 3, Kaddish, 1; composer, librettist 1 act opera Trouble in Tahiti, 1952; also wrote speaker's text Chichester Psalms, for mixed chorus, boys' choir, orch., 1965; score for musical show On The Town; ballets Fancy Free, 1944, Facsmile, 1946; incidental score for prodn. Peter Pan, 1950, The Lark, 1957; mus. score for Broadway prodn. Wonderful Town, 1953; Broadway musicals Candide, 1956, West Side Story, 1957; film On the Waterfront, 1954; songs Afterthought, Silhouette, 1951, Two Love Songs, 1949, Serenade; for violin and string orch. with percussion, 1954, Five Anniversaries for Piano, 1964, Mass; theatre piece for singers, players and dancers, 1971; ballet score Dybbuk, N.Y.C. Ballet Co., 1974, Dybbuk Variations, Suites No. 1 and 2, from ballet by Jerome Robbins, 1974, Songfest; a cycle of Am. poems for six singers and orch., 1977; overture for orch. Slava!, 1977, Three Meditations, from Mass, for cello and orch., 1977, Divertimento for Orchestra, 1980, A Musical Toast for Orchestra, 1980 Halil, 1980, A Quiet Place (opera), 1983; author: The Joy of Music, 1959 (Christopher award), Leonard Bernstein's Young People's Concerts for Reading and Listening, 1962, rev. edit., 1970, The Infinite Variety of Music, 1966, The Unanswered Question: Six Talks at Harvard, 1976. Findings, 1982. Recipient Gold medal Britain Royal Philharmonic Soc., 1987, Grammy award for best cast show album West Side Story, 1986, Edward MacDowell medal, 1987, Johannes Brahms prize, 1988. Office: Amberson Enterprises 24 W 57th St New York NY 10019 *

BERNSTEIN, MERTON CLAY, lawyer, educator; b. N.Y.C., Mar. 26, 1923; s. Benjamin and Ruth (Frederica (Kleeblatt)) B.; m. Joan Barbara Brodshaug, Dec. 17, 1955; children: Johanna Karin, Inga Saterlie, Matthew Curtis, Rachel Libby. B.A., Oberlin Coll., 1943; LL.B., Columbia U., 1948. Bar: N.Y. 1948, U.S. Supreme Ct. 1952. Assoc. Schlesinger & Schlesinger, 1948; atty. NLRB, 1949-50, 50-51, Office of Solicitor, U.S. Dept. Labor, 1950; counsel Nat. Enforcement Commn., 1951, U.S. Senate Subcom. on Labor, 1952; legis. asst. to U.S. Sen. Wayne L. Morse, 1953-56; counsel U.S. Senate Com. on R.R. Retirement, 1958-59; spl. counsel U.S. Senate Subcom. on Labor, 1959; lectr., sr. fellow Yale U. Law Sch., 1960-65; prof. law Ohio State U., 1965-75; Walter D. Coles prof. law Washington U., St. Louis, 1975—; prin. cons. Nat. Commn. on Social Security Reform, 1982-83; vis.

prof. law Columbia U. Law Sch., 1967-68, Leiden U., 1975-76; mem. adv. com. to Sec. of Treas. on Coordination of Social Security and pvt. pension plans, 1967-68; mem. adv. com. research U.S. Social Security Adminstrn., 1967-68, chmn., 1969-70; cons. Twentieth Century Fund, 1966-67, Dept. Labor, 1966-67, Russell Sage Found., 1967-68, NSF, 1970-71, Center for Study of Contemporary Problems, 1968-71; mem. Bethany (Conn.) Planning and Zoning Commn., 1962-65, Ohio Retirement Study Commn, 1967-68. Author: The Future of Private Pensions, 1964, Private Dispute Settlement, 1969, (with Joan B. Bernstein) Social Security: The System That Works, 1988; contbr. articles to profl. jours. Bd. dirs. St. Louis Theatre Project, 1981-84; pres. bd. Met. Sch. Columbus, Ohio, 1974-75. Served with AUS, 1943-45. Fulbright fellow, 1975-76. Mem. ABA (sec. sect. labor relations law 1968-69), Internat. Assn. for Labor Law and Social Security (dir. U.S. sect. 1973-83), Fulbright Alumni Assn. (dir. 1976-78), Indsl. Relations Research Assn., Nat. Acad. Arbitrators, Am. Arbitration Assn. (mem. adv. com. St. Louis region 1987—), Nat. Acad. Social Ins. (founding mem., bd. dirs, 1986—). Democrat. Jewish. Office: Washington U Sch Law Campus Box 1120 Saint Louis MO 63130

BERNSTEIN, STEPHEN MICHAEL, lawyer, real estate developer; b. Bklyn., Feb. 10, 1941; s. Murray P. and Harriet L. (Rosenberg) B.; m. Lois Blitzer Kleinerman, July 15, 1984; 1 stepchild, Matthew. B.A., Bklyn. Coll., 1962; LL.B., Columbia U., 1965. Bar: N.Y. 1965. Atty. HUD, N.Y.C., 1966-69; asst. counsel N.Y. State Urban Devel. Corp., N.Y.C., 1969-72, assoc. dir. housing devel., 1972-75; practice law, N.Y.C., 1975—; real estate developer, N.Y.C., 1975—; vis. prof. real estate fin. Pratt Inst., 1985. Bd. dirs. Am. Cancer Soc., N.Y.C., 1980—; bd. dirs. Florence Court Corp., Bklyn., 1982—, pres., 1982—. Mem. Nat. Housing Conf., Citizens Housing and Planning Council, N.Y. State Bar Assn. Club: City N.Y. Avocations: baseball, history. Home: 187 Hicks St Brooklyn Heights NY 11201 Office: 10 E 40th St New York NY 10016

BERON, GAIL LASKEY, real estate analyst, consultant, appraiser; b. Detroit, Nov. 13, 1943; d. Charles Jack Laskey and Florence B. (Rosenthal) Eisenberg; divorced; children: Monty Charles, Bryan David. Cert. real estate analyst, Mich. Chief/staff appraiser Ft. Wayne Mortgage Co., Birmingham, Mich., 1973-75; pvt. practice fee appraiser S.C., Iowa, Mich., 1976-80; pres. The Beron Co., Southfield, Mich., 1980—; cons. ptnr. Real Estate Counseling Group Conn., Storrs, 1983—, Real Estate Counseling Group Am., prin., 1984—; lectr. real estate confs. Recipient M. William Donnally award Mortgage Bankers Assn. Am., 1975. Mem. Soc. Real Estate Appraisers (bd. dirs. Detroit chpt. 1980-82, nat. faculty mem. 1983—), Am. Inst. Real Estate Appraisers (bd. dirs. Detroit chpt. 1982-86, nat. faculty mem. 1984—), Nat. Assn. Realtors, Detroit Bd. Realtors, Southfield Bd. Realtors, Women Brokers Assn. (treas. Southfield chpt. 1981-83), Young Mortgage Bankers (bd. dirs. 1974-75). Lodge: B'nai Brith. Home: 7008 Bridge Way West Bloomfield MI 48322 Office: Beron Co 17228 W Hampton Rd Southfield MI 48075

BERQUEZ, GÉRARD PAUL, psychiatrist, psychoanalyst; b. Chateauroux, France, Nov. 23, 1945; s. Berquez Maurice and Josette (Bredy) B.; m. Rosemarie Saez, Aug. 22, 1970; children: Michael, Fabien. MD, U. Montpellier, France, 1978; diploma in psychopathology and psychoanalysis, U. Paris VII, 1978. Spl. studies cert. in psychiatry and childhood psychiatry. Intern Navarre Psychiat. Hosp., Evreux, France, 1974-77, Ville Evrard Psychiat. Hosp., Neuilly, France, 1978-80; psychiatrist Medico-Educative Inst., Ecouis, France, 1977-83, Children's Social Service Aid, Villepinte, France, 1980; asst. lectr. U. Paris-X-Nanterre, 1983—; mem. splty. and establishment commn. U. Paris VII, 1985. Author: Early Infantile Autism, 1983; contbr. articles to med. jours. Mem. French Analysis Psychology Soc., Evolution Psychiatrique (corr.), Univ. Tchrs. Psychology Assn. Home: 4 Rue Crevaux, 75116 Paris France Office: U Paris X Nanterre, 200 Ave de la Republique, 92001 Nanterre France

BERRADA, MOHAMMED, government official; b. Casablanca, Morocco, Nov. 3, 1944. Grad., U. Bordeaux. Lectr. Faculty Legal, Econ. and Social Scis., Rabat, Morocco, 1969; prof. Faculty Legal, Econ. and Social Scis., Casablanca, Morocco, 1971; former auditor Moroccan Tribunal; now minister fin. Morocco. Address: Ministry of Fin, Rabat Morocco *

BERREY, BEDFORD HUDSON, physician; b. Carrollton, Mo., Apr. 20, 1922; s. Robert Wilson and Elizabeth Mary (Hudson) B.; student Kansas City Jr. Coll., Mo., 1939-40, U. Kans., 1940-42; B.S. in Medicine, U. Mo., 1943; M.D., U. Colo., 1945; M.A. in Internat. Relations, Am. U., 1969; m. Marcia Lois Bagley, May 22, 1943; children—Elizabeth, Barbara, B. Hudson, Christopher, Michael. Intern, Kansas City Gen. Hosp., Mo., 1945-46; resident in pediatrics Denver Children's Hosp., 1946-47; practice medicine specializing in pediatrics, Kansas City, Mo., 1947-48, Harlingen, Tex., 1950-51; fellow in pediatrics Ochsner Clinic, New Orleans, 1949; commd. capt. U.S. Army, 1951, advanced through grades to col., 1967, ret., 1976; dep. asst. chief med. dir. VA, Washington, 1976-77; asst. state health commr. Va. Health Dept., Richmond, 1977-84; med. dir. Nat. Alliance Sr. Citizen, 1986—; Pres. South Tex. Amateur Athletic Union, 1962-63; pres. PTA, Berlin, 1954, Denver, 1952. Decorated Legion of Merit with 2 oak leaf clusters. Diplomate Am. Bd. Pediatrics. Fellow Am. Acad. Pediatrics, ACP, Am. Coll. Physician Execs.; mem. Am. Acad. Med. Dirs., Med. Soc. Va., Hudson Family Assn. (pres. elect). Richmond Acad. Medicine. Republican. Clubs: Army-Navy (Washington); Army and Navy Country (Arlington, Va.). Lodges: Masons (32 degrees), Shriners. Home: 4431 Old Fox Trail Midlothian VA 23113

BERREY, ROBERT WILSON, III, lawyer, judge; b. Kansas City, Mo., Dec. 6, 1929; s. Robert Wilson and Elizabeth (Hudson) B.; A.B., William Jewell Coll., 1950; M.A., U. S.D., 1952; LL.B., Kansas City U., 1955; LL.M., U. Mo. at Kansas City, 1972; grad. Trial Judges Coll., U. Nev., 1972; m. Katharine Rollins Wilcoxson, Sept. 5, 1950; children—Robert Wilson IV, Mary Jane, John Lind. Admitted to Mo. bar, 1955, Kans. bar, 1955, since practiced in Kansas City; asso. mem. firm Shugert and Thomson, 1955-56, Clark, Krings & Bredehoft, 1957-61, Terry and Welton, 1961-62; judge 4th Dist. Magistrate Ct., Jackson County, Mo., 1962-79; asso. cir. judge 16th Jud. Cir. Ct., Jackson County, Mo., 1979-81, cir. judge, 1981-83, mem. mgmt.-exec. com., 1979-83; judge Mo. Ct. Appeals-Western Dist., Kansas City, 1983—; mem. Supreme Ct. Com. to Draft Rules and Procedures for Mo.'s Small Claims Ct., 1976-86. Vol. legal cons. Psychiat. Receiving Center. Del. Atlantic Council Young Polit. Leaders, Oxford, Eng., 1965; Kansas City rep. to President's National Conference on Crime Control; del.-at-large White House Conf. Aging, 1972; former pack chmn. Cub Scouts Am.; counselor, com. mem. Boy Scouts Am., sponsor Eagle Scouts; vice chmn. water fowl com. Mo. Conservation Fedn., 1968-69, chmn. water fowl com., 1971-73; v.p. Cook PTA, 1967-68; mem. cts. and judiciary com. Mo. bar, 1969-73; mem. Midwest region adv. com. Nat. Park Service, 1973-78, chmn., 1973-78; mem. Mo. State Judicial Planning Commn., 1977; bd. dirs., founder Kansas City Open Space Found., 1976. Regional dir. Young Rep. Nat. Fedn., 1957-59, gen. counsel, 1959-61, nat. vice-chmn.; chmn. Mo. Young Rep. Fedn., 1960, nat. committeeman, 1959-60, 61-64; Mo. alternate at large Republican Nat. Conv., 1960, asst. gen. counsel, 1964, del. state and dist. convs., 1960, 64, 68. Bd. dirs. Naturalization Council, Kansas City, pres., 1973—, Native Sons of Kansas City, 1987; trustee Kansas City Mus., 1972-73, Hyman Brand Hebrew Acad., 1983—; hon. life dir. Rockhurst Coll. Mem. Mo. Bar (Disting. Service award 1973, agr. law com., com. council 1980-81), Kansas City Bar Assn., Urban League (exec. com., dir.), S.A.R., Kansas City Mus. Natural Sci. Soc. (charter), Tex. Longhorn Breeders Assn. (life), Am. Royal (bd. of govs.), Mo. Longhorn Breeders Assn. (life), Alpha Phi Omega, Delta Theta Phi, Pi Gamma Mu, Tau Kappa Epsilon. Mem. Christian Ch. Mason, mem. DeMolay Legion Honor. Clubs: Kansas City; Waldo Optimist (v.p. 1967-68); Capitol Hill (Washington); Ducks Unltd. (state com. 1981—, nat. trustee 1986—), The Explorers. Home: Rural Rt 2 Box 1078 Excelsior Springs MO 64024 Home (summer): Route 2 Battle Lake MN 56515 Office: Mo Ct Appeals Bldg 1300 Oak St Kansas City MO 64106

BERRY, ALASDAIR IAN, psychologist; b. Liverpool, Eng., Sept. 1, 1943; s. Edward Allan and Margaret Elizabeth (Gilchrist) B.; m. Carla Vivien Dennis, Aug. 11, 1967; children—Katherine Charlotte Jane, Christian David Gilchrist. B.A. with honors, Liverpool U., 1968; Dip. Ed. Psych., Manchester U., 1972, M.Sc., 1974. Tchr. Edn. Authority, Liverpool, Eng., 1966-69, ednl. psychologist, 1969-72, sr. ednl. psychologist, 1972-74, asst. prin. ednl. psychologist, 1974-75, head psychology and edn. of handicapped, 1975-80; prin. psychologist Health Authority, Tunbridge Wells, Kent, Eng., 1980-82; prin. psychologist, Clwyd, Wales, 1982-85, top grade psychologist, 1985—; hon. spl. lectr. edn. U. Manchester, 1974-75; hon. sr. clin. lectr. mental handicap U. Kent, Canterbury, 1980-82. Compiler psychol. test, 1976. Bd. govs. spl. schs., Liverpool, 1975-80, Kent, 1980-82; tutor Brit. Inst. Mental Handicap, 1981-82; chmn. Clwyd Joint Secretariat, 1986—, Mental Handicap Services Mgmt. Team, Clwyd, 1987—; sec. Welsh Clin. Psychology Adv. Com., 1987—. Research grantee Liverpool Edn. and Health Authority, 1976, North Wales Inst. Health Studies, 1983. Mem. Brit. Psychol. Soc. (assoc.). Home: Cobblestones Old Barnhill Broxton, Chester CH3 9JL, England Office: Broughton Hosp, Psychology Dept, Broughton NR Chester, Wales

BERRY, BREWTON, writer, editor; b. Orangeburg, S.C., Aug. 9, 1901; s. Joseph Andrew and Frances Deborah (Pike) B.; m. Margaret Foley Woods, Sept. 11, 1926; children—Margaret (Mrs. Forrest J. Curtin, Jr.), Deborah (Mrs. Douglas R. Houser). A.B., Wofford Coll., 1922; B.D. (Fogg scholarship, Day fellowship), Yale, 1925; Ph.D., U. Edinburgh, 1930. Asst. prof. sociology and anthropology U. Mo., 1931-37, asso. prof., 1937-45, vis. prof., summer 1950, dir. anthrop. collection, 1932-45; dir. Archeol. Survey Mo., 1932-45; prof., head sociology dept. U. R.I., 1945-46; prof. sociology and anthropology Ohio State U., Columbus, 1946-64. Author: You and Your Superstitions, 1940, 74, (with Seba Eldridge) Fundamentals of Sociology, 1950; Race Relations, 1951, Race and Ethnic Relations, 1958, rev. edit, 1965, 78, Almost White, 1963, rev. edit, 1969, The Education of American Indians, 1968, (with N.P. Gist, others) The Blending of Races, 1972; A Letter to the Grandchildren, 1983 also articles, essays, short stories.; Editor, Mo. Archaeologist, 1934-45, Ohio Valley Sociologist, 1947-52, assoc. editor, Am. Sociol. Rev., 1953-56, editorial bd., Ohio State U. Press, 1964-78. Julius Rosenwald fellow, 1943-44; recipient Anisfield-Wolf book award, 1952. Fellow Am. Anthrop. Assn., Am. Sociol. Assn.; mem. Mo. Archeol. Soc. (hon. life), Ohio Valley Sociol. Soc. (pres. 1954-55), SAR; Mem. South Caroliniana Soc. (life), S.C. Hist. Soc., Ohio Hist. Soc.; mem. Phi Beta Kappa (chpt. pres. 1965-66), Sigma Xi. Episcopalian. Clubs: Scioto Country; Torch (Columbus, Ohio) (chpt. pres. 1967-68), Faculty (Columbus, Ohio); Book and Bond (Yale). Home: 6000 Riverside B-257 Dublin OH 43017 Office: 300 Adminstrn Bldg 190 N Oval Mall Columbus OH 43210

BERRY, JAY, management consultant; b. N.Y.C., May 29, 1928; s. Joseph G. and Rose K. Berry; B.A., Yale U., 1947; children by previous marriage: Kristin Forsyth, Dana Stephens, Stewart Duffy, Daria Elisa; m. Eugenia Malokienko; children: Andrei Polosov, Alessandra Casati, Christopher Jay. Exec. v.p. Brooke Smith French & Dorrance, advt. agy., N.Y.C., 1949-57; pres. Alexander Internat. and Delta Films Internat., San Juan, P.R., 1957-63; mng. prin. McKinsey and Co., N.Y.C., Zurich, Switzerland and Milan, Italy, 1963-73; v.p. Europe, Bata Devel. Corp., London, 1974-75; pres. Airwick Industries, Carlstadt, N.J., 1975-82; exec. v.p. Macmillan Inc., N.Y.C., 1982-83; sr. ptnr. BGN Europe, Geneva, Milan, N.Y.C., 1984—; speaker for industry assns. Mem. Swiss-Am. C. of C., Am. C. of C. Italy, Yale Alumni Assn. (pres. 1971-73). Clubs: Metropolitan, Yale (N.Y.C.). European editor Journ. Mgmt. Consulting; contbr. articles to profl. publs., newspapers. Home: Via Nino, Bixio 11, Como Italy Office: BGN Europe, SrL Via Frua 22, 20146 Milan Italy

BERRY, JOHN CHARLES, clinical psychologist, educational administrator; b. Modesto, Calif., Nov. 29, 1938; s. John Wesley and Dorothy Evelyn (Harris) B.; A.B., Stanford, 1960; postgrad. Trinity Coll., Dublin, Ireland, 1960-61; Ph.D., Columbia, 1967; m. Arlene Ellen Sossin, Oct. 7, 1978; children—Elise, John Jordan, Kaitlyn. Research assoc. Judge Baker Guidance Center, Boston, 1965-66; psychology asso. Napa State Hosp., Imola, Calif., 1966-67, staff psychologist, 1967-75, program asst., 1975-76; program dir. Met. State Hosp., Norwalk, Calif., 1976-77; asst. supt. Empire (Calif.) Union Sch. Dist., 1977—. Mem. Am. Psychol. Assn., Assn. Calif. Sch. Adminstrs., Sigma Xi. Contbg. author: Life History Research in Psychopathology, 1970. Home: 920 Eastridge Dr Modesto CA 95355 Office: Empire Union Sch Dist 200 G St Empire CA 95319

BERRY, KEITH DAVID, micropaleontologist; b. Gladbrook, Iowa, Nov. 18, 1923; s. Fred Gordon and Grace Nadine (Strohm) B.; m. Barbara Ann Wisdom, June 20, 1948; children—David Scott, Ellen Suzanne, Margaret Elaine. B.S., Iowa State U., 1949, M.S. in Geology, 1951. Registered geologist, Calif. Geologist-paleontologist Standard Oil Co. Calif., Taft, 1951-53, Bakersfield, 1953-60, profl. specialist in paleontology, 1960-68, sr. paleontologist, 1968-71; Standard Oil Calif. and Chevron USA, San Francisco, 1971-80; staff paleontologist Chevron USA Inc., San Francisco and Concord, Calif., 1980-85; cons. in field, 1985—; mem. M.S. grad. adv. com. U. Nev., Reno, 1979; mem. Ph.D. grad. adv. com. U. Calif.-Santa Barbara, 1980-85; bd. govs. Calif. Well Sample Adv. Com., Bakersfield, 1980-84; com. mem. Correlation of Stratigraphic Units N.Am., San Francisco, 1979-82. Contbr. articles to profl. jours. Served with U.S. Army, 1943-45. ETO. Mem. Am. Assn. Petroleum Geologists, Soc. Econ. Paleontologists and Mineralogists (sec.-treas. Pacific sect. 1962-63, chmn. conv. program 1976, Best Paper award 1965), San Joaquin Geol. Soc., No. Calif. Geol. Soc., N.Am. Micropaleontol. Soc., Am. Inst. Profl. Geologists, DAV, Phi Delta Theta. Republican. Presbyterian. Home and Office: 745 San Gabriel Ct Concord CA 94518

BERRY, MICHAEL JAMES, chemist; b. Chgo., July 17, 1947; s. Bernie Milton and Irene Barbara (Lentz) B.; m. Julianne Elward, Apr. 28, 1967; children—Michael James, II, Jennifer Anne; m. Patricia Gale Hackerman, July 7, 1984. B.S. in Chemistry, U. Mich., 1967; Ph.D. (NSF predoctoral fellow), U. Calif., Berkeley, 1970. Asst. prof., then assoc. prof. chemistry U. Wis., Madison, 1970-76; mgr. photon chemistry dept., corp. research center Allied Chem. Corp. Morristown, NJ, 1976-79; Robert A. Welch prof. chemistry Rice U., Houston, 1979—; pres. Antropix Corp., Houston, 1982—; dir. Laser Applications Research Ctr., Houston Area Research Ctr., 1984—. Author research papers in field. Recipient Phi Lambda Upsilon Fresenius award, 1982; Air Force Office Sci. Research grantee, 1972-76, 85—, Office Naval Research, 1972-74; Camille and Henry Dreyfus Found. tchr.-scholar, 1974-76; Alfred P. Sloan research fellow, 1975-76; NSF grantee, 1975—. John Simon Guggenheim Meml. Found. fellow, 1981-82. Fellow AAAS; mem. Am. Chem. Soc. (pure chemistry award 1983), Am. Phys. Soc., AIAA, Optical Soc. Am., Am. Soc. Photobiology, Inter-Am. Photochem. Soc., Am. Soc. Laser Medicine and Surgery, Materials Research Soc., Sigma Xi. Home: 30 Meadowfair Ct The Woodlands TX 77381 Office: HARC 4802 Research Forest Dr The Woodlands TX 77381

BERRY, MICHEL ANDRE, radiologist; b. Poitiers, Vienne, France, June 1, 1937; s. Andre Leonce and Jeanne Helene (Roucher) B.; m. Nicolle Andree Guirand, July 13, 1960; 1 child, Sandrine. Diploma, U. Sci., Caen, France, 1959; MD, Med. U., Paris, 1968, diploma in radiology, 1969. Med. resident Oncology Ctr., Inst. Gustave Roussy, Villejuif, France, 1966-69; asst. radiologist Oncology Ctr., Ctr. Henri Becquerel, Rouen, France, 1969-71, dept. mgr., 1971—. Author numerous med. publs. Mem. Radiologist Oncology Ctrs. Group, Nat. Lodge Oncologist Physicians (treas. 1982—). Roman Catholic. Office: Ctr Luite Contre Cancer, H Becquerel, 1 rue d'Amiens, 76038 Rouen Seine Maritime, France

BERRY, PHILLIP SAMUEL, lawyer; b. Berkeley, Calif., Jan. 30, 1937; s. Samuel Harper and Jean Mobley (Kramer) B.; m. Michele Ann Perrault, Jan. 16, 1982; children—David, Douglas, Dylan, Shane, Matthew. A.B., Stanford U., 1958, LL.B., 1961. Bar: Calif. 1962. Ptnr., Berry, Davis & McInerney, Oakland, Calif., 1968-76; owner Berry & Berry, Oakland, 1976—, pres., sec., 1977—. Mem., Calif. State Bd. Forestry, 1974-86, vice-chmn., 1976-86. Trustee So. Calif. Ctr. for Law in Pub. Interest, 1970-87, Sierra Club Legal Def. Fund, 1971—; trustee Pub. Advs., 1971-86, chmn. bd., 1980-82. Served with AUS, 1961-67. Mem. ABA, Calif. State Bar Assn., Sierra Club (nat. pres. 1969-71, v.p. conservation law 1971—, v.p. polit. affairs 1983-85, John Muir award Club: Am. Alpine Office: Berry & Berry 505 14th St Oakland CA 94612

BERRY, ROBERT WORTH, lawyer, educator, retired army officer; b. Ryderwood, Wash., Mar. 2, 1926; s. John Franklin and Anita Louise (Worth) B. B.A. in Polit. Sci., Wash. State U., 1950; J.D., Harvard U., 1955; M.A., John Jay Coll. Criminal Justice, 1981. Bar: D.C. 1956, Pa. 1961, Calif. 1967, U.S. Supreme Ct. 1961. Research assoc. Harvard U., 1955-56; atty. Office Gen. Counsel U.S. Dept. Def., Washington, 1956-60; staff counsel Philco Ford Co., Phila., 1960-63; dir. Washington office Litton Industries, 1967-71; gen. counsel U.S. Dept. Army, Washington, 1971-74, civilian aide to sec. army, 1975-77; col. U.S. Army, 1978-87; prof., head dept. law U.S. Mil. Acad., West Point, N.Y., 1978-86; retired brigadier gen. U.S. Mil. Acad., 1987; mil. asst. to asst. sec. of army, Manpower and Res. Affairs Dept. of Army, 1986-87; asst. gen. counsel pub. affairs Litton Industries, Beverly Hills, Calif., 1963-67; resident ptnr. Quarles and Brady, Washington, 1974-78; dir., corp. sec., counsel G.A. Wright & Assocs., Denver, 1987—. Served with U.S. Army, 1944-46, 51-53, Korea. Decorated Bronze Star, Legion of Merit, Disting. Service Medal; recipient Disting. Civilian Service medal U.S. Dept. Army, 1973, 74, Outstanding Civilian Service medal, 1977. Mem. ABA, Fed. Bar Assn., Phi Beta Kappa, Phi Kappa Phi, Sigma Delta Chi. Methodist. Clubs: Army Navy, Army Navy Country, Nat. Lawyers.

BERRY, THOMAS CLAYTON, securities broker, brokerage owner, energy company owner; b. Roswell, N.Mex., May 23, 1948; s. Homer C. and Betty J. (Cronic) B.; m. Bonnie L. Shamas, May 30, 1969; children: Lisa C., Joshua E. AA, N.Mex. Mil. Inst., 1969; Assoc. course in real estate, 1984, NASD DPP rep. and prin. courses, 1983. Farmer Berry Farms, Dexter, N.Mex., 1969-72; sec., dir. Victor & Assoc., Phoenix, 1972-74; dir., foreman Berry Land & Cattle, Dexter, 1974-82; v.p., dir. Trinity Investment Corp., Roswell, 1982-83; pres., dir. Jordache Investments, Roswell, 1982-83; v.p., dir. Diamond Braich Realtors, Roswell, 1982-83; v.p., dir. Tierra Fin. Group, Roswell, 1985-86, pres., dir., 1986-87; v.p., dir. Tierra Capital Corp., Roswell, 1984-86, pres., dir., 1986—; pres., dir. Tierra Energy Corp., Roswell, 1987—. Deacon North Phoenix Bapt. Ch., Phoenix, 1973-74; bd. dirs. First Assembly of God Ch., Roswell, youth group sponsor, 1978—; coach Roswell Youth Soccer, 1978—. Named one of Outstanding Men of Am., 1982. Mem. Nat. Assn. Securities Dealers, Roswell Realtor Assn., N.Mex. Realtor Assn., Republican. Mem. Assembly of God. Home: 2010 Brazos Roswell NM 88201 Office: Tierra Fin Group Inc 400 N Pennsylvania Roswell NM 88201

BERRYMAN, ROSE WARREN, medical school administrator, researcher; b. Richmond, Va., Mar. 13, 1940; d. Maynard Warren and Bessie Virginia (Edwards) Berryman; children: William Warren Beville, Robert Berryman, William Joseph Berryman. AB, Randolph Macon Woman's Coll., 1962. Labor. mgr. Med. Sch., Tulane U., New Orleans, 1965-72, lab. adminstr., 1972-78, research asst., 1978-81, research assoc., 1981—. Contbr. articles to profl. jours. Recipient Mayor's Civic award, 1982. Mem. AAUW, La. Nature Ctr., Am. Soc. Microbiology, Kappa Alpha Theta. Episcopalian. Avocations: foreign travel, antiques, gardening. Home: 7020 Bamberry St New Orleans LA 70126 Office: Tulane U Med Sch 1430 Tulane Ave New Orleans LA 70112

BERSIA, JOHN CESAR, editor, editorial writer, international affairs analyst; b. Orlando, Fla., Nov. 23, 1956; s. Alfred and Rose-Marie (Idromasia) B. BA in Polit. Sci. and French, U. Cen. Fla., 1977; MA in Govt., Georgetown U., 1979; MS in Pub. Info. Adminstrn., Am. U., 1980; MSc, in Internat. Relations and Polit. Economy, London Sch. Econs., 1981. Distbr. Dexter Press Inc., Orlando, 1975-77; intern, analyst U.S. Dept. Labor, Washington, 1978-79; cons., staff assoc. Am. U., Washington, 1979-80; editor, cons. Global Perspectives and Transnat. Studies Assn., Orlando, 1981-83; pres. Global Perspectives Research Group Inc., Casselberry, Fla., 1983-85; editorial bd. mem. The Orlando Sentinel, 1985—; dir. Transnat. Studies Assn., Orlando, 1982-85; ind. assoc. Cons. Capacities Group Inc., Cold Spring Harbor, N.Y., 1983-86; coordinator U.S. A.I.D. Seminar, Winter Park, Fla., 1984-85; speaker in field; host to profl., world-wide visitors; del. editorial page editors and writers seminar Am. Press Inst., 1987. Author: Directory of Community Resources: Orlando, 1983. Editor-in-chief Global Perspectives: An Interdisciplinary Jour. Internat. Relations, 1982-85; bd. dirs. Alliance Francaise, Winter Park, 1987—. Contbr. articles to profl. jours. Active Orlando Sci. Ctr., 1978—, Cen. Fla. Police Benevolent Soc., Winter Park, 1983-85, Council Arts and Scis., Orlando, 1984-85; vol. Mid-Fla. Council Internat. Visitors, Winter Park, 1983-85, bd. dirs., 1985-86. Named to Outstanding Young Men Am., Jaycees, 1978. Mem. Am. Polit. Sci. Assn., Acad. Polit. Sci., London Sch. Econs. Soc., Am. Friends London Sch. Econs., Phi Kappa Phi, Omicron Delta Kappa. Roman Catholic. Avocations: canoeing; boating; marksmanship; hiking; travel. Home: 880 Heather Glenn Circle Lake Mary FL 32746 Office: The Orlando Sentinel Edit Bd 633 N Orange Ave Orlando FL 32801

BERST, JANET ROSE, data processing executive; b. Hammond, Ind., June 25, 1937; d. John Albert and Mary Ruth (Barnes) B.; B.A. in Speech, Taylor U., Upland, Ind., 1959; diploma in programming Internat. Data Processing Inst., Cin., 1967. Lead programmer analyst Midland Mut. Life Ins. Co., Columbus, Ohio, 1969-72, Ohio Dept. Edn., Columbus, 1972-75; sr. programmer analyst Ohio Youth Commn., Columbus, 1975-77; sr. devel. analyst Lincoln Nat. Life Ins., Fort Wayne, Ind., 1977-79; tech. analyst Washington Nat. Ins., Evanston, Ill., 1979—. Active, Evanston Hist. Soc.; bd. dirs. Mental Health Assn. Evanston. Fellow Life Mgmt. Inst.; mem. Assn. Systems Mgmt. (pres. Chgo. chpt.), Assn. Computing Machinery (pres. Central Ohio chpt.), Internat. Platform Assn., AAUW. Presbyterian. Club: Photography. Author: Christianity and the Real World. Office: 1630 Chicago Ave Evanston IL 60201

BERSTEIN, IRVING AARON, biotechnology and medical technology executive; b. Providence, Oct. 11, 1926; s. Robert Louis and Laura (Sperber) B.; Sc.B., Brown U., 1946; Ph.D. (teaching fellow), Cornell U., 1951; m. Suzanne D'Amico, Apr. 16, 1972; children—Jonathan, Robert Laurance. Pres., tech. dir. Controls for Radiation, Inc., Cambridge, Mass., 1957-68; dir. med. div., v.p. AGA Corp., Secaucus, N.J., 1969-71; asst. dir. research program devel. div. health sci. and tech. Harvard U.-MIT, 1972-86; chmn. bd. Hygeia Scis. Inc., 1980-87, pres., 1985-87, sr. sci. advisor, 1988—; pres. Berstein Tech. Corp., 1980—; dir. Collaborative Res., Inc., 1988—; cons. for mgmt. research and devel. new med. tech., 1971—. Francis Wayland scholar. Mem. World Bus. Council, Forty-Niners, Sigma Xi. Home and Office: 42 Buckman Dr Lexington MA 02173

BERT, CHARLES WESLEY, mechanical engineer, educator; b. Chambersburg, Pa., Nov. 11, 1929; s. Charles Wesley and Gladys Adelle (Raff) B.; m. Charlotte Elizabeth Davis (June 29, 1957); children: Charles Wesley IV, David Raff. B.S. in Mech. Engring, Pa. State U., 1951, M.S., 1956; Ph.D. in Engring. Mechanics, Ohio State U., 1961. Registered profl. engr., Pa., Okla. Jr. design engr. Am. Flexible Coupling Co., State Coll., Pa., 1951-52; aero. design engr. Fairchild Aircraft div. Fairchild Engine and Airplane Corp., Hagerstown, Md., 1954-56; prin. M.E. Battelle Inst., Columbus, Ohio, 1956-61; sr. research engr. 1961-62, program dir., solid and structural mechanics research, 1962-63, cons., 1964-65; assoc. prof. U. Okla., 1963-66, prof., 1966—; dir. Sch. Aerospace, Mech. and Nuclear Engring., 1972-77, Benjamin H. Perkinson chair prof. engring., 1978—; instr. engring. mechanics Ohio State U., Columbus, 1959-61; cons. various indsl. firms.; bd. dirs. Midwestern Mechanics Conf., 1971-79, chmn., 1973-75; Honor lectr. Mid-Am. State Univs. Assn., 1983-84; seminar lectr. Midwest Mechanics, 1983-84; Plenary lectr. 4th Internat. Conf. on Composite Structures, Paisley, Scotland, 1987. Mem. editorial bd.: Composite Structures jour., 1982—; assoc. editor: Exptl. Mechanics, 1982—, Applied Mechanics Revs., 1984—; contbr. chpts. to books, articles to profl. jours. Served from 2d lt. to 1st lt. USAF, 1952-54. Recipient Disting. Alumnus award Ohio State U. Coll. Engring., 1985. Fellow AAAS, AIAA (assoc., nat. tech. com. on structures 1969-72, vice chmn. Central Okla. sect. 1965-66, chmn. 1966-67), Am. Acad. Mechanics (dir. 1979-82), ASME (Central Okla. sect. exec. com. 1973-78, Region X mech. engring. dept. heads com. 1972-77, chmn. 1975-77), Soc. Exptl. Mechanics (monograph com. 1978-82, chmn. 1980-82, sec. mid-Ohio sect. 1958-59, chmn. 1959-60, adv. bd. 1960-63, 82); mem. Am. Soc. Engring. Edn., Japan Soc. for Composite Materials, Soc. Engring. Sci. (bd. dirs.), N.Y. Acad. Sci., Okla. Acad. Sci., NSPE, Okla. Soc. Profl. Engrs., Scabbard and Blade, Sigma Xi, Sigma Tau, Pi Tau Sigma, Sigma Gamma Tau (Disting. Engr. award), Tau Beta Pi (Disting. Engr. award). Home: 2516 Butler Dr Norman OK 73069 Office: Sch Aerospace Mech and Nuclear Engring U Okla 865 Asp Ave Norman OK 73019

BERT, CLARA VIRGINIA, home economics educator, administrator; b. Quincy, Fla., Jan. 29, 1929; d. Harold C. and Ella J. (McDavid) B. BS, Fla.

State U., 1950, MS, 1963, PhD, 1967. Cert. tchr., Fla.; cert. home economist. Tchr. Union County High Sch., Lake Butler, Fla., 1950-53, Havana High Sch., Fla., 1953-65; cons. research and devel. Fla. Dept. Edn., Tallahassee, 1967-75, sect. dir. research and devel., 1975-85, program dir. home econs. edn., 1985—; cons. Nat. Ctr. Research in Vocat. Edn., Ohio State U., 1978; field reader U.S. Dept. Edn., 1974-75. Author/editor booklets. U.S. Office Edn. grantee, 1976, 77, 78. Mem. Am. Home Econs. Assn. (state treas. 1969-71), Am. Vocat. Assn., Fla. Vocat. Assn., Fla. Vocat. Home Econs., Fla. Home Econs., Am. Vocat. Edn. Research Assn. (nat. treas. 1970-71), Nat. Council Family Relations, Am. Ednl. Research Assn., Fla. State U. Alumni Assn. (bd. dirs. home econs. sect.), Kappa Delta Pi, Omicron Nu (chpt. pres. 1965-66), Delta Kappa Gamma (pres. 1974-76), Sigma Kappa (pres. corp. bd.), Phi Delta Kappa. Club: Havana Golf and Country. Office: Fla Dept Edn Knott Bldg Tallahassee FL 32399

BERTAIN, G(EORGE) JOSEPH, JR., lawyer; b. Scotia, Calif., Mar. 9, 1929; s. George J. and Ellen Veronica (Canty) B.; m. Bernardine Joy Galli, May 11, 1957; 1 son, Joseph F. A.B., St. Mary's Coll. of Calif., 1951; J.D., Cath. U. Am., 1955. Bar: Calif. Assoc. Joseph L. Alioto, San Francisco, 1955-57, 59-65; asst. U.S. Atty. No. Dist. Calif., 1957-59; pvt. practice of law San Francisco, 1966—. Editor-in-chief, Law Rev. Cath. U. Am. (vol. 5), 1954-55. Chmn. San Francisco Lawyers Com. for Elections of Gov./Pres. Ronald Reagan, 1966, 70, 80, 84; spl. confidential adviser to Gov. Reagan for jud. selection, San Francisco, 1967-74; chmn. San Francisco Lawyers for Better Govt., 1978—; confidential adv. on jud. selection to Senator Hayakawa, 1981-82, to Gov. Deukmejian, 1983—; bd. regents St. Mary's Coll. of Calif., 1980—; mem. civilian adv. com. U.S. 6th Army, Presidio, San Francisco. Recipient De La Salle medal St. Mary's Coll. of Calif., 1951, Signum Fidei award St. Mary's Coll. of Calif., 1976. Mem. ABA, Calif. Bar Assn., Fed. Bar Assn. (del. 9th Circuit Jud. Conf. 1967-76), Am. Judicature Soc., St. Thomas More Soc. San Francisco, Calif. Acad. Scis., Mus. Soc., Assn. Former U.S. Attys. and Asst. U.S. Attys. of No. Calif. (past pres.), Supreme Ct. Hist. Soc., Western Assn. Republican. Roman Catholic. Clubs: Commonwealth, Commercial. Lodges: K.C., Order of Knights of Malta. Office: Alcoa Bldg Suite 1600 One Maritime Plaza San Francisco CA 94111

BERTAUX, JEAN-LOUP CHRISTIAN, research scientist; b. Toulouse, France, Jan. 8, 1942; s. Pierre and Denise Mercedes (Supervielle) B.; Grad., Ecole Polytechnique, 1961; Docteur es Sciences, U. Paris, 1974. Research asst. Centre National d'Études Spatiales, 1970-72, researcher, 1972-74, dep. dir., 1975—; cons. European Space Agy., NASA. Served as officer, cavalry, 1964. Decorated Knight Nat. Order of Merit; recipient Silver medal Centre National de la Recherche Scientifique; Louis Deslandres award Academie des Sciences. Author: De l'Autre Côté du Soleil; contbr. articles to profl. jours. Mem. Internat. Union Geodesy and Geophysics, Comite National Français de Geophysique et Geomagnetisme, Comité National Français d'Astronomie, Internat. Astron. Union. Prime investigator Spacelab 1, 1983. Home: 106 Rue Brancas, 92310 Sevres France Office: Service d'Aeronomie du Centre, Nat de la Recherche Scientefique,, 91370 Verrieres-le Buisson France

BERTELSEN, AKSEL BROCKHUSEN, psychiatrist; b. Fredericia, Denmark, July 25, 1936; d. Bertel and Clara (Brockhusen) B.; m. Kamma Gerner Olsen, Aug. 22, 1959; children: Sören, Erik. MD, Århus U., 1963. Intern Dept. Surgery and Medicine Århus U., Denmark, 1963-64, intern Dept. Neurology and Neurosurgery, 1965-68; jr. registrar Psychiat. Hosp., Århus, Denmark, 1969-70, sr. registrar, 1976-82, supt., 1982—; spl. adv. WHO, 1973, 79. Asst. Editor Acta Psychiatrica Scandinavia, 1976-82; contbr. articles to profl., acad. jours. Recipient James Shield Meml. award, 1985; research fellow WHO Collaborating Ctr., 1970—, inst. Psychiat. Demography, 1970-76. Mem. Den Alm Danske Laegeforening, Fgn. Speciallaeger, Danish Psychiatric Selskab, Internat. Soc. for Twin Studies (founding). Mem. Christian Peoples Party. Lutheran. Home: Rosenvej 26, 8240 Risskov Denmark Office: Århus Psychiat Hosp, Skovagervej 2, 8240 Risskov Denmark

BERTI, LUCIANO, art historian, museum director; b. Florence, Italy, Jan. 28, 1922; s. Ferdinando and Ines B.; m. Anna Maria Tinacci, 1959. Ed., U. Florence. With Superintendancy of Florence, 1949; arranger new museums: Casa Vasari, Arezzo, Italy, 1950; Palazzo Davanzati, 1955, Il Museo di Arezzo, 1958, Il Museo di S. Giovanni Valdarno, 1959, Mus. of Verna, 1961, Mus. of S. Croce, Florence, 1962; dir. mus. Arezzo, San Marco, Acad., Florence; dir. Museo Nazionale del Bargello; dir. Uffizi Gallery, Florence, 1969—; dir. monuments Pisa Gallery, 1973—; dir. galleries, Florence, 1974—; mem. Consiglio Superiore, 1976-80. Author: Filippino Lippi, 1957; Masaccio, 1964, English transl., 1967; Pontormo, 1964; Pontormo disegni, 1965; Il Principe dello Studiolo, 1967; Il Museo tra Thanatos ed Eros, 1973-74; Diario sugli Uffizi in Nuova Antologia, 1976; Coordinazione e introduzione Catalogo Generale e Uffizi, 1979; I disegni di Michelangelo in Casa Buonarroti, 1985; contbr. articles to profl jours. and catalogues. Decorated Silver medal Ministry of Pub. Edn.; Dott. Laurea in Lettere; Libera docenza in Stoira dell'Arte. Address: Galleria degli Uffizi, Piazzale degli Uffizi, I-50100 Florence Italy *

BERTIN, GILLES YVES, economist, educator; b. Fougeres, France, Aug. 9, 1933; s. Francis Henry and Paule Louise (Bagourd) B.; m. Chantal Alice de Riverieulx, July 10, 1961; children: Grégoire H., Denis F. Grad., Hautes Etudes Commerciales, Paris, 1956; doctorate, U. Rennes (France), 1962. Prof., U. Rennes, 1964-79; asst. prof., then prof. Centre National de la Recherche Scientifique, Rennes, 1965-79, sr. researcher, Paris, 1979—; assoc. prof. econs. U. Paris Dauphine, 1980—; dir. AREPIT, Paris, 1981—; cons. in field. Author: The Growth of Multinational Corporations, 1973, Les sociétés multinationales, 1975, Les choix exerieurs des Etats, 1981; contbr. articles to profl. jours. Recipient Bronze medal CNRS, 1958, 66. Mem. Am. Econ. Assn., Association de Sci. Economique (dir.). Home: 5 rue Leon Bonnat, 75016 Paris France

BERTINI, GARY, conductor, composer; b. Russia, May 1, 1927; s. Aaron and Berthe B.; Dipl., Conservatorio Verdi Milano, 1948; Dipl., Tel Aviv Music Edn. Coll., 1951; Dipl., 1st prize, Conservatoire Nat. Superieur Paris, 1954; Dipl., Ecole Normale de Musique, 1954; Dipl., Institut de Musicologie, Sorbonne, Paris, 1955; m. Rosette Berengole, Oct. 21, 1956; children: Orit, Michal. Music dir. Rinat Chamber Chorus, 1955-72; music dir. Israel Chamber Ensemble Orch., 1965-75; prin. guest condr. Scottish Nat. Orch., 1971-81; music dir. Jerusalem Symphony Orch., 1978-87; music advisor Detroit Symphony Orch., 1981-83; chief condr. Cologne Radio-Symphonie-Orch.; orch. gen. mgr., music dir. Frankfurt Opera, 1987; guest condr. prin. orchs. Opera Houses, Europe, U.S., Japan; artistic advisor Israel Festival, 1976-83; prof., Tel Aviv U., 1976; artistic dir., music dir. Frankfurt Opera. Served with Israeli Def. Forces, 1948-49. Recipient Israel State prize, 1978. Mem. Israel League Composers. Jewish. Composer symphonic, chamber, incidental music for theater, radio. Contbr. articles on music, conducting to musicol. jours. Office: care ICM Artists Ltd 40 W 57th St New York NY 10019

BERTINOTTI, DOMINIQUE, historian; b. Paris, Jan. 10, 1954; m. Pierre Bertinotti, Apr. 7, 1978; 1 child, Florent. Licence d'histoire, U. Paris, 1974; maitrise d'histoire comtemporary, U. Paris 13, 1975, agregation d' history, 1977; PhD, U. Paris 1, 1984. Prof. history, geography Edn. Nationale Estrees St. Denis, 1977-78, Coll. Dugny, 1978-84; asst. d'history du monde contemporain U. Picardie, Amiens, France, 1984—. Author: (article): Carrieres Feminines et Carrieres Masculines dans l'Administration des Postes et des Telegraphes a la Fin du XIXth Siecle, in Annales, No. 3, 1985. Mem. Assn. des Historiens Contemporaneistes de l'Enseignement Superieur et de la Recherche. Home: 6 ave Boutarel, 75004 Paris France Office: U Picardie, UFR Scis History and Geography, Rue Solomon Mahlangu, 80000 Amiens France

BERTOG, EUGENE TRACY, educator; b. Chgo., Nov. 29, 1930; s. Frank Carl and Grayce (Tracy) B.; B.S., Loyola U., Chgo., 1952, M.Ed., 1973; m. Elaine Kohl, June 25, 1955; children—Eugene, Elaine, Joseph, Steven, Robert. Dir. edn. and tng. Continental Casualty Co., Chgo., 1955-69; dir. ednl. services CNA Fin. Corp., Chgo., 1969-72; gen. mgr. Lake Shore Club Chgo., 1972-74; prof., chmn. dept. hotel mgmt. Oakton Community Coll., Des Plaines, 1974—. Mem. deans adv. council Loyola U., 1976—, also mem. citizens bd.; pres. PTA, 1971-73. Served as lt. AUS, 1953-55; Korea. Named Alumnus of Yr., Loyola U., 1967; mem. Loyola U. Athletic Hall of Fame; recipient service to youth through athletics awards, Teaching Effectiveness award Oakton Community Coll., Tchr. Yr. award Council Vocat. Edn. Mem. Hotel Sales Mktg. Assn. (dir.), Soc. Ins. Tng. Edn., Am. Acad. Polit. and Social Sci., Am. Soc. Tng. and Devel., U.S. Olympic Soc., Loyola U. Alumni Assn. (pres. 1969-72), Ill. Tng. Dirs. Assn., U.S. Navy League, Blue Key, Alpha Kappa Psi, Beta Gamma Sigma, Tau Kappa Epsilon. Clubs: North Shore Country; Lake Shore (pres. dir.), Executives (Chgo.); Internat. (Chgo.). Home: 2314 Sussex Ln Northbrook IL 60062 Office: 1600 E Golf Des Plaines IL 60016

BERTOLI, PAOLO CARDINAL, Cardinal, clergyman; b. Poggio, Lucca, Italy, Feb. 1, 1908; s. Carlo and Aride (Poli) B. Ordained priest Roman Catholic Ch., 1930; sec. Apostolic Nunciature, Belgrade, 1933-38, France, 1938-42; charge d'affaires, Apostolic Nunciature, Port-au-Prince, Haiti, 1942-46; counsellor Apostolic Nunciature, Berne, 1946-52; chargé mission for emigration to S. Am., 1947; titular archbishop Nicomedia, 1952—; apostolic del., Turkey, 1952-53; apostolic nuncio, Colombia, 1953-59, Lebanon, 1959-60, France, 1960-69; prefect Congregation for Causes of Saints, 1969-73; elevated Sacred Coll. of Cardinals, 1969; named Camerlingue of H.R.C., 1979; Suburbicarian bishop of Frascati, 1979. Address: Piazza della Città Leonina 1, 00193 Rome Italy *

BERTOLUCCI, BERNARDO, film director; b. Parma, Italy, Mar. 16, 1940; s. Attilio and Ninetta B.; m. Clare Peploe, 1978. Attended, Rome (Italy) U. Dir. films The Grim Reaper, 1962, Before the Revolution, 1964 (Young Critics award Cannes Film Festival), La Via del Petrolio, 1965, His Partner, 1968, The Conformist, 1969 (Nat. Film Critics Best Dir. award), The Spider's Strategem, 1970, Last Tango in Paris, 1972, 1900, 1975, Luna, 1979, Tragedy of a Ridiculous Man, 1981, The Last Emperor (Golden Globe award for Best Dramatic Picture, Best Dir., Best Screenplay, Best Original Score, Acad. award for Best Dir., Best Screenplay Adaptation) 1987; author: poems In Search of Mystery, 1962 (Viareggio prize, Italy). Office: care Minister of Tourism, Via della Ferratella #51, I-00184 Rome Italy also: care Larry Auerbach William Morris Agy 151 El Camino Beverly Hills CA 90212 *

BERTRAND, MICHEL EUGENE, cardiologist, educator; b. Lille, France, Apr. 30, 1935; s. Jean M. and Roberte N. (Deverly) B.; m. DeBlock Marie C., Oct. 4, 1958; children: Catherine, Fabienne. MD, Faculty of Medicine, Lille, 1964. Sr. resident U. Hosp. Lille, 1964-68, assoc. prof. medicine, 1972-78, chief div. cardiology, 1978-84, prof. medicine, 1984—. Served to capt. French army, 1960-62. Fellow Am. Coll. Cardiology, mem. French Cardiac Soc. (gen. sec. 1982), European Soc. Cardiology (councilor of the bd. 1984). Lodge: Rotary. Office: Hopital Cardiologique, Blvd PR, 59037 Leclerc France

BERTUCA, DANIEL ANTHONY, sales representative; b. Chgo., Apr. 26, 1948; s. Anthony Francis and Angeline Geraldine (Serritella) B. AA, Wenatchee (Wash.) Coll., 1971; BA, Northeastern Ill. U., 1977, MA, 1981; PhD, Pacific Western U., 1985. Coordinator Neighborhood Housing Devel Services, Chgo., 1978-79; counselor Dept. of Justice, Chgo., 1978-80; sales rep. Player Sports, Chgo., 1979—. Author: Cast A Runaway Smile, 1987. Pres., founder Louie's People Community Youth Orgn. and Action Group; mem. state's atty. Gang Task Force, 1986. Served with USMC, 1965-66. Recipient One of 10 Outstanding Young Chgo. Citizens award, 1986. Home: 1234 Castle Dr Glenview IL 60025

BERZINS, ERNA MARIJA, physician; b. Latvia, Nov. 27, 1914; d. Arturs and Anna (Steckenbergs) Meilands; came to U.S., 1951, naturalized, 1956; M.D., Latvian State U., 1940; m. Verners Berzins, Aug. 24, 1935; children—Valdis, Andis. Mem. pediatric faculty Latvian State U., 1940-44; intern Good Samaritan Hosp., Dayton, Ohio, 1951-52; resident in pediatrics Children's Hosp. of Mich., Detroit, 1953-55; practice medicine specialising in pediatrics, Detroit, 1956-60; with ARC, Cleve., 1961-63; physician pediatric outpatient dept. Cleve. Met. Gen. Hosp., 1963-84; asst. prof. emeritus Case-Western Res. U., Cleve. Mem. Am., Ohio med. assns., Acad. Medicine, No. Ohio Pediatric Soc., Am. Women's Med. Assn., Am. Med. Polit. Action Com. Lutheran. Address: 5460 Friar Circle Cleveland OH 44126

BESANCON, FRANCOIS JEAN, internist, gastroenterologist, educator; b. Paris, Sept. 16, 1927; s. Justin Louis and Madeleine Marie (Delagrange) B.; m. Béatrice Sabine Hoppenot, Apr. 4, 1951; children: Odile, Paul, Jean, Pascale, Hélène. MD, U. Paris, 1955, DSc, 1957, agrégé, 1963. Intern Hosp. Paris, 1951-56; chief clinic U. Paris, 1956-58; head of research Nat. Ctr. Sci. Research, Paris, 1958-61; internist various hosps., Paris, 1961-67; chief of staff Lauboiriere Hosp., Vaugirard Hosp., Paris, 1967-77, Hosp. Hôtel-Dieu, Paris, 1977—; prof. internal medicine U. Paris, 1973—; mem. med. faculty Broussais Hôtel-Dieu, 1973—. Author: L'anémie Pernicieuse, 1955, Votre Premiere Publication, 1973, 80, Contre-Indic des Exam Complé, 1983, Conseils du Médecin à ses Malades, 1985; contbr. more than 300 articles to profl. jours. Mem. Soc. Nat. Francaise Gastro-Entérologie, Soc. Biologie, Soc. Médicale Hosp. Paris, Soc. Thérapeutique, Soc. French Hydrologie et Climatologie Médicales, Sci. Soc. Belgium, Sci. Soc. Czechoslovakia, Sci. Soc. Poland, Sci. Soc. Bulgary. Roman Catholic. Home: 14 Bd Emile Augier, 75116 Paris France Office: Hosp Hotel-Dieu, 75181 Paris Cedex 04 France

BESHAR, CHRISTINE, lawyer; b. Paetzig, Germany, Nov. 6, 1929; came to U.S., 1952, naturalized, 1957; d. Hans and Ruth (vonKleist-Retzow) von Wedemeyer; m. Robert P. Beshar, Dec. 20, 1953; children: Cornelia, Jacqueline, Frederica, Peter. Student, U. Hamburg, 1950-51, U. Tuebingen, 1951-52; B.A., Smith Coll., 1953. Bar: N.Y. 1960, U.S. Supreme Ct. 1971. Assoc. firm Cravath, Swaine & Moore, N.Y.C., 1964-70; partner Cravath, Swaine & Moore, 1971—. Bd. dirs. Catalyst for Women Inc., 1977—; trustee Colgate U., 1978-84, Smith Coll., 1987—. Inst. Internat. Edn. fellow, 1952-53; recipient Disting. Alumnae medal Smith Coll., 1974. Fellow Am. Coll. Probate Counsel, Am. Bar Found.; mem. Assn. Bar City N.Y. (exec. com. 1973-75, v.p. 1985-86), N.Y. State Bar Assn. (ho. of dels. 1971-80, v.p. 1979-80), N.Y. State Bar Found. (bd. dirs. 1977—), UN Assn. (bd. dirs. 1975—), Fgn. Policy Assn. (bd. dirs. 1978-87). Presbyterian. Clubs: Wall St., Downtown Assn., Cosmopolitan, Gipsy Trail. Home: 120 East End Ave New York NY 10028 Office: Cravath Swaine & Moore 1 Chase Manhattan Plaza New York NY 10005 also: Stone House Farm Box 533 Somers NY 10589

BESPALOV, YURIY ALEKSANDROVICH, Soviet government official; b. 1939; married. D Tech. Scis., S. M. Kirov Chem. Technol. Inst., Kazan, USSR. Mem. Communist Party Soviet Union, 1967—; with chem. industry dept. Cen. Com. Communist Party Soviet Union, 1979-86; head Ministry Chem. Industry, Moscow, 1986—. Contbr. articles to profl. jours. Address: Ministry Chem Industry, Moscow USSR *

BESS, HAROLD LEON, osteopath; b. Atlantic City, Oct. 25, 1924; s. Edward and Lillian (Rubenstien) B.; m. Elaine Sabott, Aug. 22, 1948; children: Alan, Ronald, Barbara. A.B. cum laude, Rutgers U., 1950; D.O., Coll. Osteo. Physicians and Surgeons, 1954. Cert. in gen. practice, 1976. Intern Mass. Osteo. Hosp. Boston, 1954-55; resident Bristol Gen. Hosp. Bristol, Pa., 1955-57; chmn. dept. gen. practice Del. Valley Hosp., Bristol, Pa., also chmn. utilization com., chief of staff, dir. med. edn., 1971-74, pres. bd. dirs., 1976-77; med. dir. H.L. Bess Neuromuscular Pain Clin., Levittown, Pa., 1985—; pres. bd. dirs. Exit Drug Treatment Center, Del. Valley Hosp., 1976-78, lectr. on thermography with attn. to neck and low back injuries. Contbr. articles to profl. jours. Served with USNR, 1943-46. Decorated 3 bronze stars. Fellow Acad. Psychosomatic Medicine; mem. Am. Acad. Thermology, Royal Soc. Medicine, Internat. Assn. for Study of Pain, Am. Pain Soc., Am. Assn. Orthopaedic Medicine, Am. Coll. Neuropsychiatry, Internat. Soc. Comprehensive Medicine, Am. Osteo. Assn., AAAS, Soc. of Ultramolecular Medicine, Am. Coll. Gen. Practice, Am. Coll. of Gen. Practice in Osteo. Medicine and Surgery, Acad. of Neuro-Muscular Thermography, Am. Osteo. Acad. of Sports Medicine, Internat. Rehab. Medicine Assn., Am. Coll. Medicine, Can. Pain Soc., People to People Pain Mgmt. to Soviet Union, Intractable Pain Soc. of Gt. Britain and Northern Ireland, Internat. Soc. Gen. Semantics, Inst. Gen. Semantics, Internat. Soc. Transactional Psychiatry, Bucks County Osteo. Soc. (sec.-treas. 1959-62), Phi Sigma Gamma. Lodge: Masons. Address: 2 Red Rose Dr Levittown PA 19056

BESSE, PHILIPPE LUCIEN, physician; b. Rueil, Seine, France, Dec. 11, 1931; s. Lucien Besse and Léontine (parent B.; m. Thérèse Besse; children: Dominique, Laurent, Claire, Damien. B of Philosophy, 1952; MD, U. Paris, 1965. Extern Paris Hosps., 1959; practice medicine specializing in extracorporeal circulation and intensive care Hosp. Brousiais, Paris, 1963-69; practice medicine specializing in extracorporeal circulation Hosp. Marie Lannelongue, Paris, 1966-75; practice medicine specializing in extracorporeal circulation and intensive care Hosp. Foch, Suresenes, 1969-80; gen. practice medicine Rueil Malmaison, France, 1975—; practice medicine specializing in analytic psychotherapy Rueil Malmaison, 1983—. Mem. Soc. Reanimation de Langue Française. Home: 17-19 Rue de Buzenval, 92000 Nanterre France Office: 60 Rue Danton, 92500 Rueil Malmasion France

BESSE, ROBERT GALE, food technologist; b. Calgary, Alta., Can., Feb. 11, 1923 (parents Am. citizens); s. Rene A. and Doria (Bray) B.; student N.Mex. State Tchrs. Coll., 1941-42; B.S., Oreg. State Coll., 1948; m. Mary A. McKay, Sept. 11, 1948; children—Rene A., Madeleine E., Leon J., Alan G., Michele M., Marc P., Angelique C. Supt., also in quality control Alderman Farms Frozen Foods, Dayton, Oreg., 1948-50, plant supt., 1950-54; chief food technologist Kuner Empson Co., Brighton, Colo., 1954-60; food technologist Northwest Packing Co., Portland, Oreg., 1960-62; food technologist research and devel. Nat. Can Corp., San Francisco, 1962-67, mgr. Pacific Area tech. research service, 1967-70; mgr. tech. services Western Can Co., 1970-86 ; customer tech. services Continental Can Co., 1986-88; cons. to food and can industries, RGB Cons., 1988—; dir. Material Metrics. Pres. St. Gregory's Theatre Guild; vol. hunting safety instr. Calif. Fish and Game Dept., 1972-—. Served with Signal Corps, AUS, 1942-45. Mem. Soc. Plastic Engrs., Pacific Fish Tech. (pres.), Inst. Food Technologists (sec.-treas. Rocky Mountain sect.; exec. com. Oreg. sect.), Confraternity of Christian Doctrine Cath. (pres.), N.W. Canners and Packers, Packaging Inst. (profl. mem.), Nat. Canners Assn. (mem. Western lab. adv. com.), No. Calif. Metal Decorating Assn. (pres.), Western Packaging Assn.; Soc. Mfg. Engrs. Club: Elks. Home and Office: 264 Portola Dr San Mateo CA 94403

BESSIRE, HOWARD DEAN, foundation executive, consultant; b. Missouri Valley, Iowa, Mar. 1921; s. Howard Dean and Etta Blanche (Pound) B. B.S. in Bus. Adminstrn., U. Neb., 1948; grad. Organization Mgmt. Inst., Economic Devel. Inst., Sec. C. of C., Colby, Kans., 1948-49, exec. dir., Clinton, Iowa, 1949-53, El Paso County Texas Ind. Devel. Corp., 1962-66, Cofco Indsl. Found., Council Bluffs, Iowa, 1953-57; economic developer, chief operating officer Walla Walla County Port Dist., Washington, 1957-59; exec. v.p. Idaho East Oreg. Economic Devel. Council, Boise, 1959-62, Indsl. Devel., Inc., Wichita Falls, Tex., 1966-70; exec. dir., chief operating officer Indsl. Found., Inc., South Bend, Ind., 1973; sec. H & S Cons., Inc., South Bend, 1969—; pres. Econs. Devel. Assocs., Inc., 1986—; also dir.; dir. Am. Economic Devel. Council, Chgo.; chmn. Ind. Area Devel. Council, Indpls., 1979; v.p. Pacific Northwest Industrial Devel. Council, 1961. Author: Techniques of Industrial Development, 1964, Practice of Industrial Development, 1970, A Handbook for the 80s Industrial Development, 1981. Served as 1st sgt. U.S. Army, 1940-45, ETO. Fellow Am. Economic Devel. Council (bd. dirs. 1981—); mem. Ind. Area Devel. Council (chmn. 1979), Mid-Am. Econ. Devel. Council. Democrat. Lodges: Masons, Shriners. Avocations: writing; indsl. park and building designer. Office: Industrial Found Inc PO Box 4216 South Bend IN 46634

BESSMERTNOVA, NATALYA IGOREVNA, ballet dancer; b. July 19, 1941. Student Bolshoi Theatre Ballet Sch. Dancer Bolshoi Theatre Ballet, Moscow, 1961—, roles include: Mazurka and 7th Valsa in Chopiniana, Pas de trois in Swan Lake, variations in Baiadere, Giselle in Giselle, The Muse in Paganini, Florin in Sleeping Beauty, Leila in Leila and Madjnun, Shirin in Legend of Love, Odette-Odile in Swan Lake, Girl in Le Spectre de la Rose, Maria in The Fountain of Bakhtchisaray, Frigina in Spartacus, Juliet in Romeo and Juliet, Tsarina Anastasia in Ivan the Terrible. Recipient award of merit RSFSR, Gold medal, Varna competition, 1965; most recent award Lenin prize, 1986. Address: State Acad Bolshoi Theatre USSR, 1 Ploshchad Sverdlova, Moscow USSR *

BESSON, JOHN ALEXANDER, psychiatrist, researcher; b. New Amsterdam, Berbice, Guyana, June 29, 1944; arrived in Scotland, 1956; s. William Willesbert and Sheila Daphne (Davis) B.; m. Margaret Jean McFarlane, Aug. 9, 1969. BS with honors, Edinburgh U., Scotland, 1966, B in Surgery, 1969, diploma in psychol. medicine, 1973. Cons. psychiatrist Lothian Health Bd., Scotland, 1977-80; lectr. Aberdeen U., Scotland, 1980-81, sr. lectr., 1981—; external examiner U. Newcastle, Scotland, 1986—. Contbr. articles to profl. jours. Mem. Royal Coll. Psychiatrists (mem. panel specialists 1983-86, regional advisor 1987—, bd. examiners 1987—, cert.). Home: 20 Lochside Rd, Bridge of Don, Aberdeen AB28AE, Scotland Office: U Aberdeen, Foresterhill, Aberdeen Scotland

BEST, FRANKLIN L., JR., lawyer; b. Lock Haven, Pa., Dec. 14, 1945; s. Franklin L. and Hazel M. (Yearick) B.; m. Kimberly R., May 1, 1982. B.A., Yale U., 1967; J.D., U. Pa., 1970. Bar: Pa. 1970. Assoc. MacCoy, Evans & Lewis, Phila., 1970-74; asst. counsel Penn Mutual Life Ins. Co., Phila., 1974-77, asst. gen. counsel, 1978-84, assoc. gen. counsel, 1985—; counsel, asst. sec. Penn Ins. and Annuity Co., Phila., 1983—; lectr. Pa. Bar Inst. Bd. dirs. Center City South Neighborhood Assn., 1979-80; pres. Center City South Neighborhood Assn., 1978-79; mem. Com. of Seventy, 1978-84; sec. Washington Sq. Assn., 1977-87; mem. 30th Ward Republican Exec. Com., 1972-84, West Pikeland Twp. Open Spaces Com., 1987—. Mem. Phila. Bar Assn., ABA, Internat. Claim Assn. (exec. com. 1979-81, 1985-88). Presbyterian. Club: Yale of Phila. Author: Pennsylvania Life and Health Insurance Law, 1989; contbr. articles to profl. jours. Office: Penn Mutual Life Ins Co Independence Sq Philadelphia PA 19172

BEST, JAMES CALBERT, government agency administrator; b. New Glasgow, N.S., Can., July 12, 1926; s. Albert T. and Carrie Mae (Prevoe) B.; m. Barbara Doreen Phills, Oct. 17, 1957; children: Christene, Jamie, Stephen, Kevin. BA, King's Coll., Dalhousie U., Halifax, N.S., 1948, diploma in journalism, 1948; postgrad. in Polit. Sci. and Pub. Adminstrn., King's Coll., Dalhousie U., 1949. Nat. pres. Civil Service Assn., Can., 1957-66; dir. personnel and adminstrn. Office Comptroller of Treasury, Can., 1966-69; dir. gen. Dept. Supply and Services, Can., 1969-70, asst. dep. minister ops., 1970-73; asst. dep. minister adminstrn. Dept. Manpower and Immigration, Can., 1974-75; dir. applied studies in govt. progress Commonwealth Secretariat, London, 1975-77; spl. policy advisor to dep. minister/chmn. Can. Employment and Immigration Commn., 1978, exec. dir. immigration, 1978-85; Can. high commr. to Trinidad and Tobago 1985-88. Past mem. bd. govs. King's Coll. Recipient Centennial medal, 1967. Mem. Inst. Pub. Adminstn. Can., Fed. Inst. Gen. Mgmt. (bd. dirs.), Fed. Fin. Officers Inst. Anglican. Home: Box 500 PSPAN Sta A, Ottawa, ON Canada K1N 8T7 Office: Can High Commn, 72-74 S Quay, Port of Spain Trinidad and Tobago

BEST, PETER, trade association administrator; b. Berne, Switzerland, Apr. 10, 1925; s. Louis and Maria (Sulzer) B.; m. Marianne Lehnherr, Nov. 30, 1957. Notary of Canton of Berne Berne U., 1957; Notary Aarwangen, Switzerland, 1957-58; sec. Swiss Cheese Union, Inc., Berne, 1958-68, adminstrv. mgr., 1969-73, gen. mgr., 1973—. Contbr. articles to profl. jours. Pres. Stiftungsrat Nationales Milchwirtschaftliches Mus., 1965—, Commn. du Gruyere, 1971—, Fachausschuss Milch, 1978—. Lodge: Rotary. Office: Swiss Cheese Union Inc, Postfach, CH-3001 Berne Switzerland

BESTEHORN, UTE WILTRUD, librarian; b. Cologne, Fed. Rep. of Germany, Nov. 6, 1930; came to U.S., 1930; d. Henry Hugo and Wiltrud Lucie (Vincentz) B. BA, U. Cin., 1954, BEd, 1955, MEd, 1958; MS in Library Sci., Western Res. U. (now Case-Western Res. U.), 1961. Tchr. Cutter Jr. High Sch., Cin., 1955-57; tchr., supr. library Felicity (Ohio) Franklin Sr. High Sch., 1959-60; librarian sci. dept. Pub. Library Cin. and Hamilton County, 1961-78, librarian info. desk, 1978—; textbook selection com., Felicity-Franklin Sr. High Sch., 1959-60; supr. Health Alcove Sci. Dept. and annual health lectures, Cin. Pub. Library, 1972-77. Book reviewer Library Jour., 1972-77; author and inventor Rainbow 40 marble game, 1971, Condominium game, 1976; patentee indexed packaging and stacking device, 1973, mobile packaging and stacking device, 1974. Mem. Clifton Townb Mtg, 1988—. Recipient Cert. of Merit and Appreciation Pub. Library of Cin., 1986. Mem. Ohio Library Assn., Cin. Chpt. Spl. Libraries Assn. (archivist 1964-64, editor Queen City Gazette bull. 1964-69), Pub. Library

Staff Assn. (exec. bd., activities com. 1965, welfare com. 1966, recipient Golden Book 25 yr. service pin, 1986), Clifton Town Meeting, Friends of the Library, Greater Cin. Calligraphers Guild (reviewer New Letters pub. 1986—), Delta Phi Alpha (nat. German hon. 1951). Republican. Mem. United Ch. of Christ. Home: 3330 Morrison Ave Cincinnati OH 45220 Office: Pub Library Cin 800 Vine St Cincinnati OH 45202

BESTMAN, JOHN GEORGE, government official Liberia; b. Marshall, Liberia, Dec. 1, 1939; s. Wreh Sammy and Kini (Payne) B.; m. Beulah Jones, May 10, 1976; children: Nimley, Pennoh, John Jr. AA, Strayer Coll., 1968; BS, Syracuse U., 1972, MS, 1973. Dep. commr. maritime affairs Liberia Ministry Fin., Monrovia, 1975-77, asst. minister, 1977-79, dep. minister, 1979-85; dir.-gen. Bur. Budget, Monrovia, 1985-86; gov. Nat. Bank Liberia, Monrovia, 1986-87; minister fin. Liberia, Monrovia, 1987-88. Mem. Am. Acctg. Assn. Mem. Nat. Democratic Party Liberia. Office: Ministry Finance, Monrovia Liberia

BETANCUR, BELISARIO, former president of Colombia; b. Amaga, Antioquia, Feb. 4, 1923; married; 3 children. Grad. in law Bolivian U. of Medellin, 1974. Dep. to local Assembly, Antioquia; sec. ministry of nat. edn., 1947-48. Mem. Ho. of Reps.; former Senator; presdl. candidate Conservative Party, 1962, 70, 78; minister of labour, 1963; ambassador to Spain, 1974; pres. of Colombia, 1982-86. Address: Partido Conservador, calle 36, No 16-56, Bogota Colombia *

BETETA, ELIZABETH DE COU, social programs executive; b. Eugene, Oreg., Sept. 12, 1926; moved to Mexico, 1948, naturalized, 1953; d. Edgar E. and Elizabeth (Fox) De Cou; m. Ramon Beteta, Sept. 2, 1949 (dec. Oct. 1965); children—Ramon Eduardo, Isabel. B.A., U. Oreg., Eugene, 1947; M. cum laude of the Americas, Cholula, Mex., 1972. Regional council rep. MEXFAM/Internat. Planned Parenthood Fedn., Mexico City, 1968—, bd. dirs., 1970—; central council rep. Internat. Planned Parenthood Fedn. Internat., London, 1970-85; bd. dirs. C.B. Casa de Bolsa, Agro Indsl. Exportadora S.A. v.p. Mexican Family Planning Found., Mexico City., 1981—; pres. bd. Save the Children, Mexico, 1978—; Mexican ambassadress Mexican Govt., Rome, 1953-58. Author numerous poems; also articles. Avocations: music; tennis; swimming; cooking.

BETHE, HANS ALBRECHT, physicist, educator; b. Strassburg, Alsace-Lorraine, Germany, July 2, 1906; came to U.S., 1935; s. Albrecht Theodore and Anna (Kuhn) B.; m. Rose Ewald, 1939; children: Henry, Monica. Ed. Goethe Gymnasium, Frankfurt on Main, U. Frankfort; Ph.D., U. Munich, 1928; D.Sc., Bklyn. Poly. Inst., 1950, U. Denver, 1952, U. Chgo., 1953, U. Birmingham, 1956, Harvard U., 1958. Instr. in theoretical physics univs. of Frankfort, Stuttgart, Munich and Tubingen, 1928-33; lectr. univs. of Manchester and Bristol, Eng., 1933-35; asst. prof. Cornell U., 1935, prof., 1937-75, prof. emeritus, 1975—; dir. theoretical physics div. Los Alamos Sci. Lab., 1943-46; Mem. Presdl. Study Disarmament, 1958; mem. President's Sci. Adv. Com., 1956-60. Author: Mesons and Fields, 1953, Elementary Nuclear Theory, 1957, Quantum Mechanics of One-and Two-Electron Atoms, 1957, Intermediate Quantum Mechanics, 1964; Contbr. to: Handbuch der Physik, 1933, Reviews of Modern Physics, 1936-37, Phys. Rev. Recipient A. Cressy Morrison prize N.Y. Acad. Sci., 1938-40; Presdl. Medal of Merit, 1946; Max Planck medal, 1953; Enrico Fermi award AEC, 1961; Nobel Prize in physics, 1967; Nat. Medal of Sci., 1976; Vannevar Bush award NSF, 1985. Fgn. mem. Royal Soc. London; mem. Am. Philos. Soc., Nat. Acad. Scis. (Henry Draper medal 1968), Am. Phys. Soc. (pres. 1954), Am. Astron. Soc. Office: Cornell U Lab Nuclear Studies Ithaca NY 14853 *

BETHEA, BARRON, lawyer, elec. hardware mfr., former state legislator; b. Birmingham, Ala., May 20, 1929; s. Malcolm and Wilma (Edwards) B.; student U. of South, 1948-50; B.S., U. Ala., 1952, LL.B., 1953; m. Phyllis Parker, Sept. 8, 1967; children—Barron Augustus, Elizabeth Ann. Admitted to Ala. bar, 1953; practiced in Birmingham, 1953-54; founder Barron Bethea Co., Inc., elec. hardware mfrs., Birmingham, 1957, chmn., pres., sec., treas., 1957—. Mem. Ala. Democratic Exec. Com., 1958-62; mem. Ala. Ho. of Reps., 1962-66. Mem. mgmt. bd. Five Points YMCA, 1962. Served as 1st lt. USAF, 1954-56. Mem. Ala. State Bar, Birmingham Bar Assn., Asso. Industries Ala., Birmingham C. of C., Am. Judicature Soc., Scabbard and Blade, Phi Gamma Delta, Phi Alpha Delta. Methodist. Elk. Club: Downtown. Patentee in field. Home: 4963 Spring Rock Rd Birmingham AL 35223 Office: POB 2202 Birmingham AL 35201

BETHEA-SHIELDS, KAREN, lawyer; b. Raleigh, N.C., Apr. 29, 1949; d. Bryant William and Grace Louise (Parrish) Bethea; m. Kenneth R. Galloway, 1971 (div. 1976); m. Linwood B. Shields, Dec. 1984. AB in Psychology, East Carolina U., 1971; JD, Duke U., 1974. Bar: N.C. 1974. Ptnr. Paul, Keenan, Rowan & Galloway, Durham, N.C., 1974-77, Loflin, Loflin, Galloway, Leary & Acker, Durham, 1977-80; ct. judge 14th Judicial Dist., Durham, N.C., 1980-85; sole practice, Durham, 1986—; mem. faculty Nat. Inst. Trial Advocacy. Recipient Cert. of Recognition, City of Detroit, 1975, Award of Appreciation Delta Sigma Theta, 1977, Cert. of Appreciation N.C. State Assn. Black Social Workers, 1979, Disting. Achievement award NAACP, 1981; named one of Durham's First Black Women in their Chosen Professions Iota Phi Lambda. Mem. ABA, Am. Judicature Soc., Nat. Conf. Black Lawyers (Lawyer of Yr. 1977), Nat. Assn. Women Attys. (Award of Appreciation 1982), Nat. Assn. Black Women Attys., Internat. Platform Assn., N.C. Bar Assn., N.C. Assn. Women Attys. (award of appreciation 1982), N.C. Acad. Trial Lawyers, Nat. Assn. Women Judges, Delta Sigma Theta (contbr. for securing justice for black women), Iota Phi Lambda. Democrat. Baptist. Home and Office: 3525 Mayfair Rd Durham NC 27707

BETHEL, TAMARA ANN, psychiatric nurse, consultant; b. Granville, N.Y., Dec. 5, 1939; d. William Henry and Delphine Ann (McDonough) B. Diploma, Jeanne Mance Sch. Nursing, Burlington, Vt., 1961; BS, Boston Coll., 1968; MEd, Antioch Grad. Ctr., Cambridge, Mass., 1974; PhD, Walden U., Fla., 1981. RN, Mass. Head nurse Dept. Mental Health, Boston, 1961-63, supr., 1963-66; staff nurse VA Hosp., Brockton, Mass., 1966-68; mem. faculty Newton Wellesley Hosp. Sch. Nursing, Mass., 1968-84, chmn. med./surg./psychiat. nursing, 1984-87; exec. dir. Mass. chpt. Lupus Found. of Am., 1987—; cons. in curriculum; mem. adj. faculty in crisis intervention Inst. Open Edn., Cambridge Coll., Bridgewater State Coll.; developer, presenter workshops in mental health and psychiat. nursing, human sexuality ethics. Contbr. psychiat. nursing sect. Little Brown Rev. of Nursing, 1985, articles on lupus to profl. jours., including Lupus News, 1985—; columnist Jour. Nursing Care, 1979-82. Pres. Mass. chpt. Lupus Found. Am., 1985—; bd. dirs. Lupus Found. Am., 1985—. Fellow Am. Orthopsychiat. Assn.; mem. Diploma Nurses Assn. (treas. Mass.), Mass. Mental Health Nurses Assn., Am. Nurses Assn., Am. Med. Writers Assn., others. Home: 54 Mt Pleasant St Westboro MA 01581 Office: 215 California St Newton MA 02158

BETHELL, LESLIE MICHAEL, historian, educator; b. Leeds, Yorkshire, Eng., Feb. 12, 1937; s. Stanley and Bessie (Stoddart) B.; m. Valerie Wood, Sept. 24, 1961 (div. 1983); children: Ben, Daniel. BA, U. London, 1958, PhD, 1963. Lectr. in history U. Bristol, Eng., 1961-66; lectr. in history U. Coll. U. London, 1966-74, reader in history, 1974-86; prof. Latin Am. history U. London, 1986—, dir. Inst. Latin Am. Studies, 1987—. Author: The Abolition of the Brazilian Slave Trade, 1970; editor: The Cambridge History of Latin America, Vols. I and II-Colonial Latin America, 1984, Vol. III-From Independence to circa 1870, 1985, Vols. IV and V-Circa 1870 to 1930, 1986. Home: 2 Keats Grove, Hampstead, London NW3 2RT, England Office: Inst Latin Am Studies, 31 Tavistock Sq, London WC1 9HA, England

BETTELHEIM, BRUNO, psychologist, retired educator, author; b. Vienna, Austria, Aug. 28, 1903; came to U.S., 1939, naturalized, 1944; s. Anton and Paula (Seidler) B.; m. Trude Weinfeld, May 14, 1941; children: Ruth, Naomi, Eric. Ph.D., U. Vienna, 1938. Research assoc. Progressive Edn. Assn., U. Chgo., 1939-41; assoc. prof. psychology Rockford (Ill.) Coll., 1942-44; asst. prof. ednl. psychology U. Chgo., 1944-47, assoc. prof., 1947-52, prof., 1952-73, Stella M. Rowley Distinguished Service prof. edn., prof. psychology and psychiatry, 1963-73; head Sonia Shankman Orthogenic Sch., 1944-73. Author: (with Morris Janowitz) Dynamics of Prejudice, 1950, Love is Not Enough: The Treatment of Emotionally Disturbed Children, 1950, Symbolic Wounds, 1954, Truants from Life, 1955, The Informed Heart, 1960, Dialogues with Mothers, 1962, The Empty Fortress, 1967, The Children of the Dream, 1969, A Home for the Heart, 1974, The Uses of Enchantment, 1976, Surviving, 1979, (with Karen Zelan) On Learning to Read: The Child's Fascination with Meaning, 1982, Freud and Man's Soul, 1983, A Good Enough Parent, 1987; contbr. articles, essays to popular, profl. publs. Fellow Am. Psychol. Assn., Am. Orthopsychiat. Assn.; mem. Am. Philos. Assn., AAUP, Am. Sociol. Assn., Chgo. Psychoanalytic Soc., Am. Acad. Edn. Democrat. Home: 718 Adelaide Pl Santa Monica CA 90402

BETTENCOURT, JOSE FERNANDO SILVA CALDEIRA, corporate executive; b. Aveiro, Portugal, Sept. 18, 1938; s. Fernando Caldeira and Rosa Da Conceicão (Silva) B.; m. Olga Branca Pinto Madail Caldeira, Jan. 4, 1962; children: Maria Da Conceicã, Jose Miguel, Andre Bernardo. Engr., U. Oporto, Porto, Portugal, 1962. Engr. Soc. Tecnica de Fomento, Porto, 1962-66; br. mgr. Soc. Tecnica de Fomento, Lisboa, 1969-73; tech. mgr. Ind. Montagem Aut., Setubal, Portugal, 1973-74, personnel dir., 1974-87; mng. dir. Extrusal-Co., Portugaesa de Extrusão, Aveiro, 1978—; mgr. Crovan Ferramentas de Portugal, Illhavo. Mem. dist. com. Pardido Social Democrata, Aveiro, 1979-80. Mem. Ordem dos engenheiros, Assn. Portugesa de Anodizadores (gen. meeting chmn. 1982-85), European Anod. Assn. (exec. com.). Roman Catholic. Clubs: ACP (Lisboa); Galitos (Aveiro). Home: R de S Martinho 53 2 deg, 3800 Aveiro Portugal Office: Extrusal-Caompanhia, Portuguesa de Extrusão, SARL, PO Box 171, 3802 Aveiro Codex Portugal

BETTERSWORTH, JOHN KNOX, educator, writer; b. Jackson, Miss., Oct. 4, 1909; s. Horace Greely and Annie McConnell (Murphey) B.; m. Ann L. Stephens, Oct. 28, 1943; 1 child, Nancy Elizabeth. B.A. magna cum laude, Millsaps Coll., 1929; Ph.D., Duke U., 1937. Instr. Jackson (Miss.) Central High Sch., 1930-35; grad. fellow Duke U., 1935-37, vis. prof., summer 1940; vis. instr. Asheville (N.C.) Normal, summer 1937; instr. history Miss. State U., Mississippi State, 1937; asst. prof. 1938-42, asso. prof., 1945-48, prof., 1948—, head dept. history and govt., 1948-61; dir. Social Sci. Research Center, 1950-60; asso. dean for liberal arts Sch. Arts and Sci., 1956-61, acad. v.p., 1961-77, dean faculty, 1966-77, spl. cons. to pres., 1977-79, prof. and v.p. emeritus, 1978—; text editor Miss. Hist. Commn., 1948-68; chmn. Miss. Research Clearing House, 1953-55; pres. So. Conf. Deans Faculty and Acad. Vice Pres.'s, 1967-68. Author: The People and Policies of a Cotton State in Wartime, 1943, People's College: A History of Mississippi State, 1953, Mississippi: A History, 1959, Mississippi in the Confederacy: As They Saw It, 1961, Your Old World Past, 1960, Mississippi: Yesterday and Today, 1965, New World Heritage, 1968, Your Mississippi, 1975, People's University: The Centennial History of Mississippi State, 1980, Mississippi: The Land and The People, 1981; co-author: This Country of Ours, 1965, South of Appomattox, 1959; contbg. author: A History of Mississippi, 1973; contbr. articles to profl. publs.; founder, pub. The Miss. Quar., 1946-56. Pres. Mississippians for ETV, 1972-73; founding pres. Friends of the Arts in Miss., 1977-80; trustee Miss. Dept. Archives and History, 1955—; chmn. Miss. Hist. Preservation Rev. Bd., 1979—; mem. Miss. Commn. on Jud. Performance, 1979—. Served as lt. (j.g.) USNR, 1942-45; instr. Naval Indoctrination Sch. Tucson. Fellow Internat. Inst. Arts and Letters; mem. Miss. Hist. Soc. (dir. 1953—), (v.p. 1955-56), (pres. 1961-62), Am., Miss., So. hist. assns., Phi Beta Kappa, Omicron Delta Kappa, Phi Kappa Phi, Phi Alpha Theta, Alpha Tau Omega. Democrat. Episcopalian. Club: Starkville Rotary (pres. 1951-52). Home: 401 Broad St Starkville MS 39759 Office: Drawer B Mississippi State MS 39762

BETTI VAN DER NOOT, DINO ALFREDO, advertising executive; b. Rapallo, Italy, Sept. 18, 1936; s. Alfredo Enrico and Minnie (Debicke) E.; m. Titti Ernestina Fabiani, Nov. 5, 1964; children—Gian Lorenzo, Allegra Barbara. Degree in opinion research and econs., Bocconi U., Milan, 1959. Asst., Price Waterhouse, Milan, 1957-58; mktg. exec. Boston Chem. Co., Bollate, Italy, 1958-60; mng. ptnr. Studio B, Milan, 1960-70; pres. B Communications, Milan, 1970-76, chmn., 1976—. Composer, conductor albums Basement Big Band, 1977, A Midwinter Night's Dream, 1983, Here Comes Springtime, 1986, They Cannot Know, 1987 (Best Album in Italy award, 2d best album in U.S. award), A Chance for a Dance, 1988; contbr. articles in advt. to profl. jours. Mem Internat. Advt. Assn. (world v.p. 1982-88, world sec. 1988—, pres. Italy, bd. dirs., 1971-74), TecniciPubblicitari. Roman Catholic. Clubs: Clubino Milan, Yacht Italiano (Genoa). Home: Via Palermo 8, 20121 Milan Italy Office: B Communications, Via Palermo 8, 20121 Milan Italy

BETTS, BARBARA LANG (MRS. BERT A. BETTS), lawyer; b. Anaheim, Calif., Apr. 28, 1926; d. W. Harold and Helen (Thompson) Lang; B.A. magna cum laude, Stanford U., 1948; LL.B., Balboa U., 1951; m. Roby F. Hayes, July 22, 1948 (dec.); children—John Chauncey IV, Frederick Prescott, Roby Francis II; m. Bert A. Betts, July 11, 1962; 1 son, Bruce Harold; stepchildren: Bert Alan, Randy W., Sally Betts Joynt, Terry Betts Marsteller, Linda Betts Hansen, LeAnn Betts Hoffman. Admitted to Calif. bar, 1952, U.S. Supreme Ct. bar, 1978; pvt. practice law, Oceanside, Calif., 1952-68, San Diego, 1960—, Sacramento, 1962—; partner firm Roby F. Hayes & Barbara Lang Hayes, 1952-60; city atty., Carlsbad, Calif., 1959-63; v.p. Isle & Oceans Marinas, Inc., 1970-80, W. H. Lang Corp., 1964-69; sec. Internat. Prodn. Assos., 1968—, Margaret M. McCabe, M.D., Inc., 1977—. Chmn., Traveler's Aid, 1952-53; pres. Oceanside-Carlsbad Jr. Chambrettes, 1955-56; vice chmn. Carlsbad Planning Commn., 1959; mem. San Diego Planning Congress, 1959; v.p. Oceanside Diamond Jubilee Com., 1958; dir. No. San Diego County Chpt. for Retarded Children, 1957-58. Candidate Calif. State Legislature, 77th Dist., 1954; mem. Calif. Dem. State Central Com., 1958-66; co-chmn. 28th Congl. Dist., Dem. State Central Com., 1960-62; alt. del. Dem. Nat. Conv., 1960. Named to Fullerton Union High Sch. Wall of Fame, 1986. Mem. Am. Judicature Soc., Nat. Inst. Mcpl. Officers, ABA, Calif. Bar Assn., San Diego County Bar Assn., Oceanside C. of C. (sec. 1957, v.p. 1958, dir. 1953-54, 57-59), AAUW (legis. com. 1958-59; local pres. 1959-60; asst. state legis. chmn. 1958-59), No. San Diego County Assn. Chambers of Commerce (sec.-treas.), Bus. and Profl. Women's Club (So. dist. legislation chmn. 1958-59), DAR (regent Oceanside chpt. 1960-61), San Diego C. of C., U.S. Supreme Ct. Hist. Soc., San Diego Hist. Soc., Fullerton Jr. Assistance League, U.S. Supreme Ct. Hist. Soc., Calif. Scholarship Fedn., Loyola Guild of Jesuit High Sch., Phi Beta Kappa. Clubs: Soroptimist Internat. (pres. Oceanside-Carlsbad 1958-59, sec. pub. affairs San Diego, Imperial Counties 1954; pres. of pres.'s council San Diego and Imperial counties and Mexico 1958-59), Barristers, Stanford (Sacramento), Stanford Mothers. Author: (with Bert A. Betts) A Citizen Answers. Office: Betts Ranch PO Box 306 Elverta CA 95626 also: 3119-A Howard Ave San Diego CA 92104

BETTS, BERT A., former state treasurer; b. San Diego, Aug. 16, 1923; s. Bert A. and Alma (Jorgenson) B.; m. Barbara Lang; children: Terry Lou, Linda Sue, Sara Ellen, Bert Alan, Randy Wayne, LeAnn, John Chauncey, Frederick P., Roby F., Bruce H. BBA, Calif. Western U., 1950. CPA, Calif. Accountant John R. Gillette, 1946-48; ptnr. Gillette & Betts, 1949-50; pvt. accounting practice 1951-54; ptnr. Betts & Munden, Lemon Grove, Calif., 1954-57; sr. ptnr. Bert A. Betts & Co., 1958-59; treas. State of Calif., 1959-67; prin. Bert A. Betts & Assos., 1967-77; chief exec. officer Internat. Prodn. Assos., 1970-87; dir. Lifetime Communities Inc.; gen. partner Sacramento Met. Airport Properties 4, Ltd., 1970—. Mem. Lemon Grove Sch. Bd., 1954-57; Calif. chmn. Max Baer Heart Fund; state employees chmn. Am. Cancer Soc., 1962-64, bd. dirs. county br., 1963-69, Sacramento County campaign chmn., mem. exec. com., 1965; pres. Sacramento chpt., 1967-68. Served as 1st lt. USAAF, 1942-45. Decorated D.F.C., Air medal with four clusters; recipient Louisville award Municipal Finance Officers Assn. U.S. and Can., 1963; honored by Calif. Municipal Treas.'s Assn., 1964. Mem. Nat. Assn. State Auditors, Comptrollers and Treas.'s, Municipal Forum N.Y., Calif. Soc. C.P.A.'s, San Diego Squadron Air Force Assn. (past vice comdr.), Am. Legion, VFW, Native Sons Golden West, Foresters, Sigma Phi Epsilon, Beta Alpha Psi (hon.), Alpha Kappa Psi (hon.). Presbyn. Clubs: Eagles; Men's (Lemon Grove) (pres.), Lions (Lemon Grove) (treas.); Commonwealth. Home: 441 Sandburg Dr Sacramento CA 95819 also: Betts Ranch East Levee Rd Elverta CA 95626

BETTS, JAMES WILLIAM, JR., financial analyst, consultant; b. Montclair, N.J., Oct. 11, 1923; s. James William and Cora Anna (Banta) B.; m. Barbara Stone, July 28, 1951; 1 dau., Barbara Susan (dec.). B.A., Rutgers U., 1946; M.A., U. Hawaii, 1957. With Dun & Bradstreet, Inc., 1946-86, service cons., 1963-64, reporting and service mgr., 1964-65, sr. fin. analyst, Honolulu, 1965—; owner, operator Portfolio Cons. of Hawaii, 1979—. Served with AUS, 1942-43. Mem. Am. Econ. Assn., Western Econ. Assn., Atlantic Econ. Soc. Republican. Episcopalian.

BEUBE, FRANK EDWARD, periodontist, educator; b. Kingston, Ont., Can., July 1, 1904; s. Gabriel and Fannie Bessie (Florence) B.; L.D.S., D.D.S., U. Toronto, 1930; m. Edith Schweitzer, Oct. 5, 1930; children—Eric, Stephen. Came to U.S., 1930, naturalized, 1937. Clin. asst. div. periodontology Sch. Dental and Oral Surgery, Columbia, 1930-37, instr., 1937-41, asst. prof., 1941-46, assoc. prof., 1946-53, head div., 1948—, clin. prof. dentistry, 1953-84, clin. prof. emeritus, 1984—, emeritus prof.-spl. lectr., 1984—; head dept. periodontology Presbyn. Hosp., N.Y.C., 1941-70; lectr. dept. periodontology, Dental Sch. N.Y. U., 1973—; found. mem. Hebrew U. Recipient William J. Gies award, 1979; Disting. Alumnus award Columbia U. Periodontal Alumni Assn., 1984. Diplomate Am. Bd. Periodontology (dir., v.p. 1963-64). Fellow AAAS, Am. Coll. Dentists, Am. Acad. Periodontology (councilman 1962, chmn. edn. com. 1963, chmn. com. on coms. 1964, pres. 1964-65, chmn. exec. council 1965-66, Pres. award 1988); mem. ADA (chmn. periodontia sect. 1964-65), Western Soc. Periodontology (hon.), Academy Oral Pathology, So. Acad. Periodontology (hon.), Internat. Assn. Dental Research, First Dist. Dental Soc. (past pres. pathodontia sect.), Sigma Xi. Author: Periodontology: Diagnosis and Treatment, 1953; Prevention of Periodontal Diseases, 1956; Gingivectomy in the treatment of Periodontal Diseases, 1957; Disadvantages of Surgical Techniques, 1960; contbr. chpts. to books, articles to dental jours. Research in study of healing of cementum and bone, periodontal diseases and their treatment. Home: 10 London Terr New Rochelle NY 10804 Office: 933 Fifth Ave New York NY 10021

BEUTELSPACHER, ALBRECHT FRIEDRICH, computer scientist, researcher; b. Tübingen, Fed. Republic Germany, June 5, 1950; s. Hans F. and Ilserose (de Pay) B.; m. Monika Stäbler, Aug. 15, 1975; children: Christoph, Maria Corinna. Diploma, U. Tübingen, 1973; PhD, U. Mainz, Fed. Republic Germany, 1976, habilitation, 1980. Asst. prof. U. Mainz, 1973-83, prof. math., 1982-85; research mgr. Siemens AG, Munich, Fed. Republic Germany, 1986-88; prof. math. and computer sci. U. Giessen, 1988—. Author: Endliche Geometrie, 1982, Luftschlösser, 1986, Kryptologie, 1987; contbr. over 70 articles on math. and cryptology to profl. jours. Mem. Deutsche Mathematiker Vereinigung, Am. Math. Soc., Gesellschaft Für Informatik. Home: Landwehtweg 7, D-6305 Grossen-Buseck Federal Republic of Germany Office: U Giessen Math Institut, Arndtstr 2, D-6300 Giessen Federal Republic of Germany

BEUTLER, ARTHUR JULIUS, manufacturing company executive; b. LaCrosse, Wis., Sept. 2, 1924; s. Arthur Julius and Augusta Henrietta (Dobe) B.; m. Carolee Yvonne Crawford, Dec. 28, 1952; 1 child, Karen Elizabeth. BSEE, U. Wis., 1948, Grad. in EE, 1968. Registered profl. engr., Wis. Trainee inventor program Gen. Electric Co., Schenectady, N.Y., 1948-51; devel. engr. Gen. Electric Co., Milw., 1951-59, project engr., 1959-61, sr. engr., 1961-64; chief engr. Dings Magnetic Separator Co., Milw., 1964-67; pres., owner Creative Engring. Assocs., Inc., Greendale, Wis., 1967-72; v.p. mfg. Gettys Mfg. Co., Racine, Wis., 1972-79, v.p. internat., 1979-81; v.p. tech. planning div. motion control div. Gould, Inc. (formerly Gettys Mfg. Co.), Racine, 1981—. Patentee elec. controls. Served with U.S. Army, 1943-46, PTO. Mem. IEEE (sr., chpt. chmn. 1969-72), NSPE, Soc. Mfg. Engrs. (cert.), Tau Beta Pi, Eta Kappa Nu. Office: Gould Inc 2701 N Green Bay Rd Racine WI 53404

BEVAN, ROBERT LEWIS, lawyer; b. Springfield, Mo., Mar. 23, 1928; s. Gene Walter and Blanche Omega (Woods) B.; m. Ronice Diane Gartin, Jan 25, 1977; children: Matthew Gene, Lisa Ann. AB, U. Mo., 1950; LLB, U. Kansas City, 1957. Bar: Mo. 1957, D.C. 1969. Adminstrv. asst. U.S. Senator T. Hennings Jr., Washington, 1957-60; legis. asst. U.S. Senator E.V. Long, Washington, 1960-69; sr. govt. relations counsel Am. Bankers Assn., Washington, 1970-84; ptnr. Hopkins & Sutter, Washington, 1984—. Ghost author: The Intruders, 1967; contbg. editor U.S. Banker, 1985-88. Fieldman Dem. Nat. Com., 1968. Served with U.S. Army, 1946-47, 1951-53. Mem. ABA (adminstrv. law sect., bus. law sect., chmn. banking com.). Democrat. Methodist. Club: Exchequer (Washington). Home: 310 N Pitt St Alexandria VA 22314 Office: Hopkins Sutter Hamel & Park 888 16th St Washington DC 20006

BEVELACQUA, JOSEPH JOHN, physicist, researcher; b. Waynesburg, Pa., Mar. 17, 1949; s. Frank and Lucy Ann (Cataneo) B.; m. Terry Sanders, Sept. 4, 1971; children—Anthony, Jeffrey, Megan, Peter, Michael, Karen. B.S. in Physics, Calif. State Coll., 1970; postgrad., U. Maine, 1970-72; M.S. in Physics, Fla. State U., 1974, Ph.D., 1976. Cert. radiol. shield survey engr., Westinghouse Bettis Atomic Power Lab.; cert. health physicist (comprehensive and power reactors), nat. office mem. Am. Bd. Health Physics Comprehensive Panel of Examiners. Diplomate Am. Bd. Health Physics. Teaching/research asst. U. Maine, 1970-72, Fla. State U., 1973-76; research asst. NSF, 1975-76; nuclear engr. Bettis Atomic Power Lab., West Mifflin, Pa., 1973, sr. nuclear engr., 1976-78; ops. research analyst U.S. Dept. Energy, Oak Ridge, 1978-80, chief physicist advanced laser isotope separation program, 1980-83; sr. engr. GPU Nuclear Corp. (Three Mile Island Sta.-Unit 2), Middletown, Pa., 1983-84; Three Mile Island emergency preparedness mgr. GPU Nuclear Corp., Middletown, Pa., 1984-86, mgr. TMI-2 safety rev. group, 1986—; cons. U.S. Dept. Energy's Process Evaluation Bd. of Isotope Separation, Washington, 1981-82. Contbr. articles to profl. jours. including Physical Rev. Letters. Mem. Republican Presdl. Task Force, Nat. Rep. Senatorial Com. Recipient Outstanding Performance award Dept. Energy, 1982; grantee USAF, NSF; Von Humboldt fellow U. Hamburg. Mem. Am. Nuclear Soc., Am. Phys. Soc., Am. Acad. Health Physics, Susquehanna Valley Health Physics Soc. (mem. exec. com.), N.Y. Acad. Scis., Soc. Nuclear Medicine, Nuclear Utility Coordinating Group on Emergency Preparedness Implementation, Babcock and Wilcox Owners Group on Emergency Preparedness, Sigma Pi Sigma, Health Physics Soc. Republican. Lutheran. Club: Oak Ridge Sportsman's. Research on theoretical studies of light nuclei, few nucleon transfer reactions, radiation shielding, laser isotope separation, neutron nuclei, symmetry violations in nuclei, grand unification theories, quark models of nuclear forces, nuclear fuel cycle, laser fusion and gravitational collapse of stars, beta dosimetry, internal dosimetry, health effects of ionizing radiation; nuclear reactor safety. Home: 19 Merion Ln PO Box 166 Hummelstown PA 17036 Office: GPU Nuclear Corp 3 Mile Island Nuclear Generating Sta PO Box 480 Middletown PA 17057

BEVERIDO-DUHALT, FRANCISCO ALBERTO, theatre educator; b. Cordoba, Veracruz, Mex., July 14, 1949; s. Francisco and Bertha (Duhalt) Beverido. MA, U. Veracruzana, Xalapa, 1973. Editor Arte Nuevo U. Veracruzana, 1978-79, students drama coordinator, 1979-81, 85-87, dir. theatre inst., 1981-83, dir., researcher, 1987—; head theatre dept. Inst. Veracruzano de la Cultura, Veracruz, 1987—; theatre advisor Inst. Nat. de Bellas Artes, Mexico City, 1985-87; lectr., tchr., dir. internat. drama festivals at Copal, San Juan, P.R., 1979, U. Alta., Edmonton, Can., 1980, U. Kans., Lawrence, 1982, Festival Cervantino, Guanajuato, Mex., 1983. Author: Esquema Para un Taller de Actuacion, 1987; actor, dir. various stage and U. Veracruzana prodns.; guest dir. Co. de Teatro Estatal, Oaxaca, Mex., 1985, Inst. de Cultura de Aguascalientes (Mex.), 1986; contbr. articles to profl. jours. Office: Apartado Postal 462, 91000 Xalapa Mexico

BEVIER, JAMES HASBROUCK, consultant; b. Kingston, N.Y., Mar. 10, 1924; s. Gilbert Hasbrouck and Gertrude (Hancock) B.; m. Margaret Eleanor Grimm, Dec. 20, 1948 (div. Mar. 1966); children—James Gerret, Dan Grimm; m. Janet Lee Griffie, May 17, 1968. B.S., Springfield Coll., Mass., 1949, M.Ed., 1950; LL.B., LaSalle Extension U., Chgo., 1970; postgrad. Calif. Coast U., 1985—. Program dir. YMCA, Balt., 1956-59; Membership, Program sec., Dundalk Br., Wilmington, Del. YMCA, 1950-56; community relations mgr. Firestone, Harbel, Liberia, Africa, 1959-63, indsl. relations mgr., 1963-65, gen. services mgr., 1966-68; pvt. practice as bus. cons., Glasco, N.Y., 1969—. Editor jour. Adult Program Digest of the YMCAs of N.Am., 1956-59. Nat. bd. dirs. Boy Scouts Liberia, 1961-68. Served to sgt. USMC, 1942-45, PTO. Recipient Citation, YMCA of Balt., 1953, Boy Scouts Liberia, 1968. Avocations: reading, golf, crossword puzzles. Home and office: PO Box 217 Glasco NY 12432

BEW, PAUL ANTHONY, political science educator; b. Belfast, Northern Ireland, Jan. 22, 1950; s. Kenneth and Mary (Leahy) B.; m. Greta Jones,

Aug. 13, 1977; 1 child, John. MA, Pembroke Coll., Eng., 1971; PhD, Cambridge U., Eng., 1974. Lctr. Ulster Polytech., Belfast, 1975-79; lctr. Queen's U., Belfast, 1979-86, reader polit. sci. dept., 1986—; vis. lctr. U. Pa., Phila. 1982-3; commentator Irish affairs on British and Irish radio and TV. Author: Land and National Question in Ireland, 1978, C.S. Parnell, 1980, Conflict and Conciliation in Ireland, 1987; author: (with others) The Stte in Northern Ireland, 1979, Sean Lemass and the Making of Modern Ireland, 1982, The British State and the Ulster Crisis, 1985; contbr. articles to profl. jours. Office: Queens U Dept Polit Sci, Belfast Ireland BT7

BEWLEY, RONALD ANTHONY, economist, lecturer; b. Birkenhead, Cheshire, Eng., June 16, 1949; arrived in Australia, 1975; s. James and Doris (Lowres) B.; m. Roslyn Margaret Jasper, July 9, 1977; children: Laura Clare, Michael Stuart. BA, Sheffield (Eng.) U., 1971; PhD, U. New South Wales, Australia, 1982. Research fellow Sheffield U., 1971-74; lectr. econometrics Manchester (Eng.) U., 1974-75; lectr. U. New South Wales, 1975-83, sr. lectr., 1983—; cons. in field. Author: Allocation Models, 1986; contbr. articles to profl. jours. Mem. Econometric Soc., Econ. Soc. Australia. Anglican. Office: U New South Wales, PO Box 1, Kensington New South Wales 2033, Australia

BEXTERMILLER, THERESA MARIE, architect; b. St. Charles, Mo., Feb. 9, 1960; d. Charles Frederick and Loretta Joan (Unterreiner) B. BArch, Kans. State U., 1978-83; postgrad., Wash. U., St. Louis, 1985, Pratt Inst., 1988—. Grad. architect Fleming Corp., St. Louis, 1984-85; project architect, prototype mgr. Casco Corp., St. Louis, 1985-87; architect HBE Corp., St. Louis, 1987-88, Hal A. Dorfman, N.Y.C., 1988—. Mem. AIA. Roman Catholic. Home: Pratt Inst 215 Willoughby Ave #1612 Brooklyn NY 11205 Office: Hal A Dorfman Architects 145 W 45th St Suite 1115 New York NY 10036

BEYER, KAREN ANN, administrator; b. Cleve.; d. William and Evelyn Haynes; B.A., Ohio State U., 1965; M.S.W., Loyola U., Chgo., 1969; post-grad. Family Inst., Northwestern U., 1979; Diplomate clin. social work. With Cuyahoga County Div. Child Welfare, Cleve., 1965, Dallas County Child Welfare Unit, Dallas, 1966; with Lutheran Welfare Services Ill., Chgo., 1967-73; pvt. practice psychotherapy, family mediation, Schaumburg, Ill., 1975—; therapist Family Service Assn. Greater Elgin (Ill.), 1973-77, dir. profl. services, 1977-83; dir. HHS Village of Hoffman Estates, Ill., 1983—; fieldwork social work instr. for Loyola U., U. Ill., 1977-80. Bd. dirs. Talkline, 1982-85; mem. mental health adv. bd. Elgin Community Coll. Mem. Nat. Assn. Social Workers, Acad. Cert. Social Workers (clin. and approved supr.), Am. Assn. Marriage and Family Therapy, Am. Orthopsychiat. Assn. Unitarian. Home: 824 Brendon Dr Schaumburg IL 60194

BEYER, SUZANNE, advertising agency executive; b. N.Y.C., Dec. 28, 1928; d. Harry and Jennie Hillman; student Nassau Community Coll., 1963-65; grad. Conservatory of Musical Art, N.Y.C., 1947; m. Isadore Beyer, Oct. 19, 1947; children—Pamela Claire, Hillary Jay. Singer, tchr. piano, N.Y.C., 1947-66; asst. to v.p. media dir. Robert E. Wilson, Advt., N.Y.C., 1967-72; media planner, media buyer Frank J. Corbett div. BBDO Internat., N.Y.C., 1972-77; media planner, media buyer Lavey/Wolff/Swift div. BBDO Advt., N.Y.C., 1977-80, sr. media planner, 1980-83, media supr., 1983—; soprano Opera Assn. Nassau, 1976—; soprano United Choral Soc., Woodmere, L.I., 1970—, Armand Sodero Chorale, Baldwin, L.I., 1980-86, Rockville Centre Choral Soc., 1986—. Mem. Pharm. Advt. Council, L.I. Advt. Club, Health-care Bus. Women's Assn. Home: 66 Fonda Rd Rockville Centre NY 11570 Office: 488 Madison Ave New York NY 10022

BEYER-MEARS, ANNETTE, physiologist; b. Madison, Wis., May 26, 1941; d. Karl and Annette (Weiss) Beyer. B.A., Vassar Coll., 1963; M.S., Fairleigh Dickinson U., 1973; Ph.D., Coll. Medicine and Dentistry N.J., 1977. NIH fellow Cornell U. Med. Sch., 1963-65; instr. physiology Springside Inc., Phila., 1967-71; teaching asst. dept. physiology Coll. Medicine and Dentistry N.J., N.J. Med. Sch., 1974-77, NIH fellow dept. ophthalmology, 1978-80; asst. prof. dept. ophthalmology U. Medicine and Dentistry N.J., N.J. Med. Sch., Newark, 1979—, asst. prof. dept. physiology, 1980-85, assoc. prof. dept. physiology, 1986—, assoc. prof. dept. ophthalmology, 1986—; cons. Alcon Labs. Chmn. admissions No. N.J., Vassar Coll., 1974-79; mem. minister search com. St. Bartholomew Episcopal Ch., N.J., 1978, fund-raising chmn., 1978, 79; del. Episc. Diocesian Conv., 1977, 78; long range planning com. Christ Ch., Newark, 1985-87. Recipient NIH Nat. Research Service award, 1978—, Found. CMDNJ Research award, 1980; grantee Juvenile Diabetes Found., 1985-87, Pfizer, Inc., 1985-87. Mem. Am. Physiol. Soc., N.Y. Acad. Scis., Soc. for Neurosci., Am. Soc. Pharmacology and Exptl. Therapeutics, Assn. for Research in Vision and Ophthalmology, Internat. Soc. for Eye Research, AAAS, The Royal Soc. Medicine, Internat. Diabetes Found., Am. Diabetes Assn., Aircraft Owners and Pilots Assn., Civil Air Patrol, Sigma Xi. Contbr. articles in field of diabetic lens and kidney therapy to profl. jours. Office: NJ Med Sch Dept Physiology 185 S Orange Ave Newark NJ 07103

BEZAZIAN, PAUL D., advertising agency executive; b. Providence, Mar. 29, 1906; s. John B. and Daisy (Babasinian) B.; m. Florence Irene Bell, Sept. 9, 1933; children: John P., Paulette F., Harold A. BA, Oberlin Coll., 1927. Salesman Meyer Connor & Co., Chgo., 1927-31; sales mgr. Credit Firm, Chgo., 1931-36; ptnr. Bezazian & Sutherland, Niles Center, Ill., 1936-37; mgr., ptnr. Bezazian Bros., Chgo., 1937-40; mng. ptnr., treas. Burton Browne Advt., Chgo., 1941—. Club: Gaslight (chmn. bd. dirs., chmn. exec. com. 1975-76). Home: 5555 N Sheridan Rd Apt 1002 Chicago IL 60640

BEZIRJIAN, BERGE, shipping company executive; b. Beirut, Lebanon, Jan. 14, 1925; s. Diran and Rebecca (Dombourian) B. Degree, Coll. Des Freres, Beirut, 1944, Degree in Philosophy, 1945. Prof. Coll. Du Sacre-Coeur, Beirut, 1946-50; beginner apprentice then mgr-proxy L. Raissis Shipping Agy., Beirut, 1950-70; pvt. practice comml. broker Beirut, 1970-80; mgr. Marachart Shipping Co., Ltd., Piraeus, Greece, 1980—. Christian Orthodox. Home: Perikleous 15, 185 36 Piraeus Greece

BEZZOLA, EUGENIO LUIS, electronics company executive; b. Buenos Aires, Argentina, May 4, 1926; s. Ricardo Ramon and Elvira (D'Emilio) B.; m. Irene Teresa Laura Metivier, Sept. 19, 1951; children—Carlos Eugenio, Laura Victoria. Grad. Naval Acad., Rio Santiago, 1948; Telecommunications Engr., Engring. U., Buenos Aires, 1953. Commd. naval cadet Argentine Navy, 1944, advanced through grades to rear adm., 1980; head electronics hydrographic dept. Buenos Aires, 1964-67; dir. Naval Electronics Tech. Dept., Buenos Aires, 1968-70, 72-79; dir. Naval Welfare Bur., Buenos Aires, 1980, Naval Electronics Bur., Buenos Aires, 1981-82, Naval Logistic Bur., Buenos Aires, 1983-84, ret., 1984; pres. Sisteval S.A., Buenos Aires, 1984—; prof. Instituto Tecnologico, Buenos Aires, 1963-69. Author book and articles in field. Roman Catholic. Clubs: Naval, Military (Buenos Aires). Lodge: Lions. Avocations: journalism; photography; home and gardens planning; naval and military history. Home: Olavarria 671, 1714 Ituzaingo, Buenos Aires Argentina

BHAGAT, DHANRAJ, sculptor; b. Lahore, Pakistan, Dec. 20, 1917; s. B. Hargobind and Lakshmi (Done) B.; m. Kamla Devi, 1943; 4 children. Ed., Khalsa High Sch., Mayo Sch. Arts, Lahore. Tchr., Mayo Sch. of Arts, Lahore, 1939, 44; lectr. in sculpture Delhi Poly. Art Dept., 1946-60, sr. lectr., 1960-62, asst. prof., 1962-68, prof., 1968-73; numerous commissions throughout India; works in stone, wood, plaster, cement and metal-sheet; ten one-man sculpture shows in India, 1950-72; exhbns. in London and Paris, 1948, Eastern Europe, 1955, 58, U.S., 1954, Fed. Republic Ger., 1958, Sao Paulo, 1962, South Africa, 1965; works in Govt. Mus., Punjab, India, Nat. Gallery Modern Art, New Delhi, Lalit Kala Acad., Baroda Mus., Punjab U. Mus.; participant first, second triennial exhbn. of World Art, New Delhi. Recipient State award India, 1969. Mem. Nat. Com. Internat. Assn. Plastic Arts (Paris). Address: College of Art, 22 Tilak Marg, New Delhi India *

BHAGAT, PHIROZ MANECK, mechanical engineer; b. Poona, India, Oct. 28, 1948; came to U.S., 1970; s. Maneck Phirozshaw and Khorshed Eduljee (Batliwala) B.; m. Patricia Jane Steckler, Oct. 13, 1979; children—Kay, Sarah. B.Tech., Indian Inst. Tech.-Bombay, 1970; M.S.E., U. Mich., 1971, Ph.D., 1975. Research fellow in applied mechanics Harvard U., Cambridge, Mass., 1975-77; asst. prof. engring. Columbia U., N.Y.C., 1977-81, adj. asst. prof., 1981-84; staff engr. Exxon Research & Engring. Co., Florham Park, N.J., 1981-83, sr. staff engr., 1983-88, head sci. computing group, 1988—. Contbr. articles to profl. jours. K.C., Mahindra scholar, 1970; J.N. Tata scholar, 1970; Horace Rackham predoctoral fellow, 1973-74, 74-75. Mem. N.Y. Acad. Scis., Am. Inst. Chem. Engrs., ASME, Combustion Inst., Tau Beta Pi, Sigma Xi. Research on application of thermal scis. to model petrochemical processes, sci. computing, combustion, heat transfer, fluid mechanics, thermodynamics, computer modeling. Home: 519 Alden Ave Westfield NJ 07090 Office: Exxon Research & Engring Co Florham Park NJ 07932

BHALLA, MADHU BALA, physician; b. Agra, U.P., India, May 21, 1944; came to U.S., 1968; d. Gopal Singh and Brij Rani (Kakkar) Sarin; m. Vinod K. Bhalla, May 29, 1966; children—Niti, Jyoti, Varun Kumar. B.Sc., St. John's Coll., Agra, UP, India, 1962; M.B.B.S., S.N. Med. Coll., Agra, 1966; M.S. in Anatomy, U. Ga., 1972. Rotating intern S.N. Med. Coll., Agra, U.P., India, 1966; ob-gyn housemanship K.E.M. Hosp., Poona, India, 1967-68; postdoctoral fellow U. Ga., Athens, 1968-71; rotating intern Crawford W. Long Hosp., Atlanta, 1972-73; resident ob-gyn Ga. Bapt. Hosp., Atlanta, 1973-74; fellow in family planning Med. Coll. Ga., Augusta, 1974-75, resident ob-gyn, 1975-78; practice medicine specializing in ob-gyn, Augusta, 1978—; mem. med. staff Univ. Hosp., Augusta, 1978—, mem. D.R.G. review com., 1984; mem. med. staff St. Joseph Hosp., Augusta, 1978—, mem. infectious control com., 1980. Recipient Merit award in med. jurisprudence and toxicology S.N. Med. Coll., Agra, India, 1965; Good Samaritan award St. Joseph Hosp., Augusta, 1983—; postdoctoral fellow NIH Grant, U. Ga., Athens, 1968. Jr. fellow Am. Coll. Ob-gyn; mem. AMA, Med. Assn. Ga., So. Ob-Gyn Soc., Ob-gyn Soc. Augusta. Office: 2320 Wrightsboro Rd Augusta GA 30904

BHALLA, VIJAY KUMAR, construction executive; b. Patiala, Punjab, India, Mar. 11, 1946; s. B.K. and Lakshmi Bhalla; m. Sangeet Mehta, May 17, 1970; children: Rajan, Rajit. B of Engring., Punjab Engring. Coll., Chandigarh, India, 1967. Mktg. dir. Gospel India Mktg. Pvt. Ltd., Patiala, 1983—, also bd. dirs. Mem. Patiala Industries Assn. (sec. 1975077). Club: Rajendra and Gymkhana (Patiala). Home: 124-C Model Town, Patiala, Punjab 147001, India Office: Gospel India Mktg Pvt Ltd, Industrial Estate, Patiala, Punjab 147001, India

BHALLA, VINOD K., endocrinologist, biochemist, educator; b. Lahore, India, Aug. 4, 1940; came to U.S., 1968, naturalized, 1981; s. Lal C. and Shanti (Punga) B.; m. Madhu B. Sarin, May 29, 1966; children—Niti, Jyoti, Varun. B.S., St. John's Coll., Agra, India, 1962, M.S., 1964; Ph.D., Nat. Chem. Lab., Poona, India, 1968. Research assoc. U. Ga., Athens, 1969-72, Emory U., Atlanta, 1972-74; mem. faculty Med. Coll. Ga., Augusta, 1974—, prof. endocrinology, 1982—; regular mem. endocrine study sect. NIH, 1985—; speaker in field. Mem. editorial bd. Biology of Reproduction, 1978-83; reviewer Endocrinology Jour, 1980—, Alcoholism-Clinical and Exptl. Research, 1982—. Andrology Jour, 1982—. NSF grantee, 1976-79; NIH grantee, 1976—. Mem. Am. Soc. Biol. Chemists (endocring study sect.), Endrocine Soc., Soc. for Study Reprodn., N.Y. Acad. Sci., Am. Fertility Soc., Am. Chem. Soc. Research on polypeptide hormone action at testicular level, polypeptide hormone receptors, cAMP, mediation and testosterone prodn. Home: 3541 Westlake Dr Augusta GA 30907 Office: Med Coll Ga Endocrinology Dept Augusta GA 30912

BHANDARI, SUMAN, cardiologist; b. Bhiwani, Haryana, India, Oct. 9, 1955; s. Bharat Kumar and Bimla (Kohli) B.; m. Nita Chawla, Feb. 16, 1982; 1 child, Sonakshi. MBBS, Rohtak Med. Coll., Haryana, 1977, MD in Gen. Medicine, 1981; DM in Cardiology, All India Inst. Med. Scis., New Delhi, 1983. Med. diplomate, India. Sr. resident medicine All India Inst. Med. Scis., New Delhi, 1981-82, sr. resident cardiology, 1982-84, pool officer cardiology, 1985-86; cons. cardiologist Sir Granga Ram Hosp., New Delhi, 1986-88; cardiologist Escort's Heart Hosp., New Delhi, 1988—. Contbr. articles to profl. jours. Mem. Cardiol. Soc. India. Club: Panchshila (New Delhi). Home: B-10 Soami Nagar, New Delhi India Office: Escort's Heart Hosp, New Delhi India

BHARADWAJA, VIJAYA KUMAR, philosopher, educator; b. Rahimyarkhan, Punjab, India, Mar. 10, 1937; s. Dewan Chand and Droupadi Devi B. MA in Philosophy, U. Delhi, India, 1965; PhD in Philosophy, Indian Inst. Tech., Kanpur, India, 1969. Asst. lectr. U. Delhi, 1965-66, lectr. philosophy, 1969-80, reader philosophy, 1980—; research fellow Indian Inst. Tech., 1966-69. Author: Natural Ethical Theory, 1978, Form and Validity in Indian Logic, 1988; editor: Rationality and Philosophy, 1984; editorial bd. Indian Philosophical Quarterly, PARAMARSA. Mem. Indian Philos. Congress, Hindi Darshan Parishad (pres. logic, sci. section Chandigarh chpt. 1976, Jabbalpur chpt. 1981). Hindu. Office: U Delhi, Dept Philosophy, Univ Campus, Delhi 110 007, India

DHASKARAN, MEEMPAT, mathematics educator; b. Malappuram, Kerala, India, Aug. 6, 1935; came to Australia, 1968; s. Vellat Gopalan Nair and Meempat Ammukutty Amma; m. Raji Udumbath, June 1, 1963; children—Krishnakumar, Radhika, Sreekumar. B.A. with honors, U. Madras, India, 1956, M.A., 1961; Ph.D., 1965; M.Sc., Annamalai U., 1960. Instr. Sree Venkateswara U., Tirupati, India, 1963-64; research asst. Ramanujan Inst., U. Madras, 1964-66; vis. instr. U. Ill.-Urbana, 1966-67; vis. asst. prof. Mich. State U., East Lansing, 1967-68; lectr. U. New South Wales, Kensington, Australia, 1968-71; pvt. teaching and research, Australia, 1972—. Author articles in field. Mem. Ramanujan Math. Soc. Home: 48 Nalpa Way, Duncraig 6023, Australia

BHAT, KHANDIGE SHAMBHAT SUBRAHMANYA, cardiologist, educator; b. Perdala, India, May 11, 1939; s. K.S. and Sharada B.; m. Asha C. Moogoor, Mar. 5, 1969; children—Deepa, Shyam K. M.B.B.S., Bikram U. (India), 1961; D.T.C.D., Delhi U. (India), 1964, M.D., 1967. Fellow Royal Australasian Coll. Physicians. Med. officer Safdarjang Hosp., New Delhi, 1961-71; instr. medicine All India Inst. Med. Sci., New Delhi, 1965-70; sr. registrar, asst. lectr. Otago Med. Sch., Dunedin, N.Z. 1971-73; instr. medicine Univ. Coll. Med. Scis., New Delhi, 1973-74; cons. cardiologists, physician Central Hosp., Tripoli, Libya, 1974-84; assoc. prof. medicine and cardiology Al Fatah U., Tripoli, 1979=84, prof. cardiology, 1985; vis. prof. medicine HAL Hosp., Bangalore, 1986—; dir. Heart-Lung Clinic & Diagnostic Ctr., Bangalore, 1986—Research, publs. in field. Founder-mem., former chmn. Indian Sch., Tripoli; founder Research Ctr. for Prevention Heart Diseases. Mem. several sci., profl. and research orgns. Office: Heart-Lung Clinic, and Diagnostic Ctr, CMH Rd, Indiranagar, Bangalore 560038, India

BHAT, KRISHNA HILLEMANE, anthropologist, social worker; b. Kumbla, Kerala, India, Sept. 6, 1949; s. Venkateshwara Hillemane and Shankari Bhat; m. Indira Devi; 1 child, Sushruta. BSc, J.S.S. Sci. Coll., Dharwad, India, 1970; MA, Karnatak U., Dharwad, 1972, PhD, 1979. Research fellow Anthropol. Survey India, Calcutta, 1972-77; anthropologist Anthropol. Survey India, Shillong, 1981-82; coordinator research Indo-U.S. Subcommn. Community Diagnosis Project, Karnataka, India, 1979-80; lectr. in anthropology Northeastern Hill U., Shillong, 1982—. Contbr. articles to profl. jours. Life mem. Gandhi Meml. Leprosy Found. Mem. Soc. for Indian Med. Anthropology (life, sec. Srinagar 1985—), Soc. for Community Diagnosis and Rural Devel. (sec. Karnataka 1979—), North-East India Hist. Assn., North-East India Council Social Sci. Research, Ethnographic and Folk Culture Soc. (life). Home: Ayyankave Po Paraklayi, Anandashrama Kerala, India 670531 Office: Northeastern Hill Univ, Dept Anthropology, Shillong Meghalaya, India 793014

BHATHENA, SAM JEHANGIRJI, research chemist; b. Bombay, India, Sept. 18, 1936; s. Jehangirji and Pirojbai (Mistry) B.; m. Pauruchisty K. Kias, July 13, 1975. B.Sc. with honors, U. Bombay, 1961, M.Sc., 1964, Ph.D., 1970, Vis. fellow NIH, Bethesda, Md., 1971-73, vis. assoc., 1974; research biochemist VA Med. Ctr., Washington, 1975-82; asst. prof. Georgetown U., Washington, 1979-82; research chemist U.S. Dept. Agr., Beltsville, Md., 1983—. Contbr. articles and revs. to profl. jours., chpts. to books. Treas. Zorastrian Assn. Met. Washington, 1979-82; v.p. Assn. Indians in Am., Washington, 1979-82. Mem. Endocrine Soc., Am. Diabetes Assn., N.Y. Acad. Sci., Soc. for Exptl. Biology and Medicine, Am. Fedn. for Clin. Research, AAAS. Democrat. Home: 11912 Judson Ct Wheaton MD 20902 Office: Carbohydrate Nutrition Lab Beltsville Human Nutrition Ctr BARC East Beltsville MD 20705

BHATIA, RAVI, neurosurgery educator; b. London, June 2, 1938; s. Madan Lal and Svarna Lata Bhatia; m. Rita Mubayi, Jan. 19, 1969; children: Radhika, Madhavi. MBBS, All India Inst. Med. Scis., New Delhi, 1961, M.Ch. in Neurosurgery, 1971; MS in Surgery, Delhi U., 1966. Sr. house surgeon CMCH Vellore, India, 1963-64; demonstrator Lady Hardinge Med. Coll., New Delhi, 1964; post grad. Safdarjung Hosp., New Delhi, 1964-66; sr. house officer Willesden Gen. Hosp., London, 1966-67, St. Thomas Hosp., London, 1967; sci. pool officer Council of Sci. and Indsl. Research, New Delhi, 1969; post-doctoral fellow Ulleval Hosp., Oslo, 1972-74; intern All India Inst. Med. Scis., 1962, sr. registrar neurosurgery, 1969-72, lectr., 1974-76, asst. prof., 1976-80, assoc. prof., 1980-87, prof., 1987—. Trustee Spastic Soc. India, New Delhi. Mem. Neurol. Soc. India. Clubs: Delhi Gymkhana, Delhi Gliding. Office: AIIMS Campus, DII/29, Ansari, Nagar, New Delhi 110029, India

BHATTACHARYA, RABI SANKAR, physicist; b. Silchar, India, Feb. 19, 1948, came to U.S., 1980, naturalized, 1982; s. Ranajit Krishna and Sucharu Bhattacharya; m. Kabita Biswas, Mar. 13, 1979; children—Ratnesh, Debanjana. B.S., Gauhati U., India, 1967; M.S., India Inst. Tech., Kharagpur, 1969; A.S.I.N.P., Saha Inst., Calcutta, 1970; Ph.D., Calcutta U., India, 1975. Postdoctorial fellow Fom-Inst., Amsterdam, The Netherlands, 1975-77; guest prof. Giessen, Fed. Republic Germany, 1977-78; guest sci. Max Planck Inst., Munich, W. Ger., 1978-79; sr. research assoc. McMaster U., Hamilton, Can., 1979-80; sr. research assoc. U. Fla., Gainesville, 1980-81; sr. sci. Universal Energy, Dayton, Ohio, 1981—. Contbr. articles to profl. jours. FOM fellow, The Netherlands; Max Planck fellow, W.Ger. Mem. Am. Phys. Soc., Nat. Assn. Corrosion Engrs. Office: Universal Energy Systems Inc 4401 Dayton Xenia Rd Dayton OH 45432

BHATTACHARYA, SUBHRANSU SEKHAR, zoologist, educator; b. Uttarpara, India, Jan. 1, 1941; s. Sudhansu Sekhar and Anila Devi B.; m. Aruna Bahen Patel, June 26, 1966; 1 child, Ameet. BS, Ramnarain Ruia Coll., Bombay, 1962; MS, Inst. Sci., Bombay, 1964; PhD, Taraporevala Marine Biol. Research Sta., Bombay, 1972. Demonstrator in biology Siddharth Coll., U. Bombay, 1964-65, lectr. zoology, 1965-81, head dept. zoology, 1981—; mem. faculty sci. U. Bombay, 1983—, bd. studies zoology, 1983, sci. com. Nehru Sci. Ctr. Govt. India, Bombay, 1986—. Author: Biology Practicals, 1976, Zoology Practicals, 1976, Practicals in Zoology, 1978, A New Course in Biology, 1980, Second Course in Biology, 1982, Ecology of Mysidacea, 1983, others; contbr. articles to sci. jours. Fellow Norwegian Agy. Internat. Devel., 1982. Fellow Zool. Soc. London, Acad. Zoology; mem. Am. Soc. Limnology and Oceanography, Internat. Assn. Copepodologists, Bombay Biol. Assn. (pres. 1984-85). Office: Siddharth Coll, PT Marg, Bombay India 400001

BHATTACHARYA, SYAMAL KANTI, biomedical engineer, educator; b. Calcutta, West Bengal, India, Feb. 13, 1949; came to U.S., 1974, naturalized, 1983; s. Sudhir Chandra and Prabhabati B.; m. Keka Ghoshal, Dec. 11, 1969; children—Sumoulindra T., Julie, Syamal Dave. B.Sc. with honors, U. Calcutta, 1968; B.A. in English Lit, 1969; M.S., Murray State U., 1976; A.M., Washington U., St. Louis, 1978; Ph.D., Memphis State U., 1979. Diplomate; Am. Bd. Bioanalysis; cert. profl. chemist Nat. Cert. Commn. Chemistry and Chem. Engring.; licensed med. lab. dir. Tenn. Dept. Pub. Health. Instr. chemistry Netaji Shikshaytan, Calcutta, India, 1968-69; sr. instr. chemistry Bhabanath Instn., Calcutta, 1969-70; research and devel. chemist Swastik Household and Indsl. Products Pvt. Ltd., Bombay, India, 1970-74; sr. research technician Washington U. Med. Sch., St. Louis, 1976-77; research assoc. U. Tenn. Med. Ctr., Memphis, 1979-80, instr. medicine, 1980-82, mem. surgery faculty, 1983—, dir., surg. research labs; 1982—, dir. chemistry and nutrient data output lab., 1982—, instr. surgery, 1983-84, asst. prof. surgery, 1984-86, asst. prof. medicinal chemistry, 1985—, assoc. prof. surgery, 1986—; vis. prof. surgery Yale U. Sch. Med., 1985, pediatrics U. Cin. Med. Ctr. and Cin. Children's Hosp., 1985; vis. prof. pediatric surgery Johns Hopkins U. Sch. Medicine, 1987; Leginer Meml. lectr. in surgery, Rush-Presbyn.-St. Luke's Med. Ctr., Chgo., 1987, N.Y. Med. Coll., 1987; cons. in field; teaching asst. Murray State U., Ky. 1974-76; research/teaching fellow Washington U., 1976-78; visiting prof. of pediatric surgery Johns Hopkins U. Sch. of Medicine, 1987; Leginer Meml. lectr. in surgery Rush-Presbyn.-St. Luke's Med. Ctr., Chgo., 1987; visiting prof. of surgery N.Y. Med. Coll., 1987. Ad-hoc reviewer, contbr. articles to various profl. jours. Commr. Nat. Cert. Commn. in Chemistry and Chem. Engring., Washington, 1987—. Presdl. research fellow Memphis State U., 1978-79. Indian Nat. scholar Govt. India, New Delhi, 1965-69; Govt. India scholar Bank of India, 1974-75; Muscular Dystrophy Assn. Am. grantee, 1983-84; U. Physician's Found. research grantee, 1985-86, Varian Instrument Group of Am. Res. grantee, 1986-88. Research grantee Univ. Physician's Found., 1985-86, Varian Instrument Group Am., 1986-88, Am. Heart Assn., 1986-87, NIH, 1988-93; recipient Nat. Research Service award in medicine NIH, 1979-81. Contbr. to numerous publs. in biomed. and sci. jours.; contributor in nat., internat. sci. confs.; Ad-Hoc reviewer for numerous sci. and profl. jours. Fellow Am. Instn. Chemists (cert. profl. chemist 1980), Indian Chem. Soc.; mem. Royal Soc. Chemistry (chartered chemist 1981), Am. Fedn. Clin. Research, N.Y. Acad. Sci., Soc. Neurosci., Internat. Soc. Brain Research, AAAS, ACS, Am. Oil Chemists' Soc. Sigma Xi, Phi Kappa Phi. Club: U. Tenn. Faculty (Memphis). Home: 76 South Fernway Rd Memphis TN 38117 Office: U Tenn Med Ctr Dept Surgery 956 Court Ave Suite G215 Memphis TN 38163 also: U Calcutta, Coll St, Calcutta West Bengal 700073, India

BHATTACHARYYA, BHABATARAK, biologist, educator; b. Calcutta, West Bengal, India, Dec. 2, 1944; parents: Bhabaranjan and Malancha B.; m. Sikha Roychowdhuri, Nov. 24, 1974; children: Sudeshna, Sanchari. BSc with honors, Calcutta U., 1965, MSc, 1967, PhD, 1974. Vis. assoc. NIH, Bethesda, Md., 1972-76, vis. scientist, 1983-85; asst. prof. Bose Inst., Calcutta, 1978-82, assoc. prof., 1982—. Conbr. articles to 45 pubs. Indian Council Med. Research fellow, 1968-72; Indian Council of Scientific and Indsl. Research grantee, Indian Dept. Sci. and Tech. grantee; recipient P.S. Sarma Meml. award, 1987. Mem. Soc. Biol. Chemists. Home: 569B Lake Gardens, Calcutta 700 045, India Office: Bose Inst, Dept Biochemistry, Calcutta India 700 054

BHATTACHARYYA, MUKTI NATH, consultant physician, educator; b. Naihati, West Bengal, India, Jan. 22, 1935; came to Eng., 1962; s. Manju Gopal and Santilata (Mukherjee) B.; m. Brenda Kathleen Evans, Oct. 18, 1969; children—Neil, Robin. MBBS, U. Calcutta, 1959, DGO, 1961. Intern, R.G. Kar Med. Coll., Calcutta, 1959-61; resident in medicine, surgery, ob-gyn Teaching Hosp., Calcutta, 1959-62; registrar ob-gyn Wisbech Hosp., 1963-64; sr. house officer ob-gyn Huddersfield Hosp., 1964; registrar ob-gyn, Stockport, 1965-67; registrar in diagnostic radiology, Manchester, 1967-70; sr. registrar in venereology Royal Infirmary, Sheffield, 1971-73; cons. in genito-urinary medicine Royal Infirmary, Sheffield, 1973-79, Manchester Royal Infirmary, 1979—; lectr. in genito-urinary medicine U. Manchester, 1979—. Contbr. articles to profl. jours. Fellow Royal Coll. Obstetricians and Gynecologists, Med. Soc. for Study Venereal Diseases, Internat. Soc. for Study Vulvar Diseases, Manchester Med. Soc., North of Eng. Ob-Gyn Soc.; mem. Brit. Med. Assn. (sec. Manchester div. 1984-87, chmn. 1987—), Internat. Soc. Venereal Diseases and Treponamatoses, Internat. Soc. for Research into Sexually Transmitted Diseases, Genito-Urinary Medicine Adv. Subcom. N.W. Region Eng. Club: Astron. Soc. (Manchester). Lodge: Manchester Rotary (internat. and fellowship coms.). Hindu. Avocations: astronomy; music; sports; travel. Home: 56 Green Pastures, Heaton Mersey, Stockport Cheshire SK4 3RA, England Office: Manchester Royal Infirmary, Dept Genito-Urinary Medicine, Oxford Rd, Manchester England

BHATTACHARYYA, SANTOSH KUMAR, management consultant; b. Jharia, India, Jan. 8, 1927; s. Tridib Nath and Renubala B.; m. Gayatri Chakravarti, May 9, 1959; 1 child, Sanjoy. BS, Calcutta U., 1946, B in Commerce, 1949; postgrad., Harvard U., 1964. Account exec. Bird-Heiglers Group, Calcutta, India, 1952-56; acctg. adviser, registrar of cos. Dept. Co. Law Administrn. Govt. of India, New Delhi, 1956-64; prof. mgmt. Indian Inst. Mgmt., Ahmedabad, 1964-69, 71-78; vis. prof. MBA program Harvard U., Boston, 1969-70; assoc. cons. McKinsey & Co., Inc., N.Y.C., 1969-70; chief exec. Mgmt. Structure & Systems Pvt. Ltd., Bombay, 1978—; chmn. local adv. bd. Deutsche Bank Asia, Bombay; bd. dirs. Sandvik Asia Ltd.,

Poona, Nagarjuna Investment Trust Ltd., Hyderabad, Mktg. & Research Group Ltd., Bombay, Lakame Ltd., Bombay, VIP Industries Ltd., Bombay, Scindia Steamship Navigation Co. Ltd. Author: Management Planning and Information System, 1976; co-author: Accounting for Management: Text and Cases, 1976, Management Control Systems: A Framework for Resolution of Problems of Implementation, 1977, Managing Business Enterprises: Startegies, Structure and Systems (Escort award), 1983; contbr. articles on mgmt. to numerous publs. Mem. Indian Inst. Bankers (governing council). Home: B 502 Udyan Darshan, 92 Sayani Rd, Prabhadevi Bombay 400 025, India Office: Mgmt Structure & Systems Pvt Ltd, B 36 Jayent Apts, A Marathe Marg Opp Lucas Bldg, Bombay 400 025, India

BHAVE, PRAMOD RAGHUNATH, civil engineering educator; b. Surat, Gujarat, India, Feb. 24, 1932; s. Raghunath Vishnu and Kantabai Bhave; m. Kusum Mukund Sapre, Nov. 29, 1962; children: Suhas, Mohit. BSCE, U. Poona, Maharashtra, India, 1953; MSCE, M.S. Univ., Gujarat, 1962; PhD, Nagpur (India) U., 1978. Surveyor town planning and valuation depts. Ahmedabad and Vadodara, India, 1954-56; lectr. tech. and engring. M.S. Univ., Vadodara, 1956-62; asst. prof. Visvesvaraya Regional Coll. Engring., Nagpur, 1962-74, prof., 1974—. Author: Technical Writing, 1976, Fluid Mechanics, 1978; contbr. 5 vols. to Civil Engineering Practice, 1987; contbr. articles to profl. jours. Fellow UNESCO, 1967; recipient State Award Govt. Maharashtra, 1977; grantee Curriculum Devel. Program Govt. India, 1987. Fellow Indian Water Works Assn. (Best Paper awards 1978, 84, 85); mem. Instn. Engrs. India (hon. sec. Nagpur ctr. 1970, Sir Arthur Cotton Meml. Gold Medal 1970, Shrimati Saroma Sanyal Meml. Prize 1978). Hindu. Home: 3 Visvesvaraya Campus Apts, Nagpur Maharashtra, India 440 011 Office: Visvesvaraya Regional Coll, Engring, Nagpur Maharashtra, India 440 011

BHICHAI RATTAKUL, Thai government official, business executive; b. Bangkok, Thailand, Sept. 16, 1926; s. Bhisal and Vilai R.; m. Charoye R., Sept. 16, 1946; children: Bhichit, Patcharee, Anatchai. Sr. Cambridge Cert., St. Stephen's Coll., Hong Kong, 1941. Mgr., Bhisal Forestry Co., Pitsanuloke, Thailand, 1946-60, Pitsanuloke Forestry Co., 1960-65; gen. mgr., mng. dir. Jawarad Co., Ltd., Bangkok, 1960-77, Jaward Indsl. Corp., Ltd., Bangkok, 1978-83; chmn. 1st City Credit Co., Ltd., 1979-83, Indsl. Syndicate Co., Ltd., 1979-83, First City Investment Co., Ltd., 1981-83. Mem. Nat. Parliament Thailand, 1969, 75, 76, 83; fgn. minister Ministry Fgn. Affairs, 1975-76; dep. prime minister Govt. Kingdom Thailand, 1983—; chmn. Democrat Party. Decorated knight Grand Cordon Most Noble Order Crown Thailand (Spl. Class), knight Grand Cross (1st Class) Most Exalted Order White Elephant (Thailand); Order Diplomatic Service Merit Gwanghwa medal (Republic Korea). Buddhist. Clubs: Rotary of Dhonburi (pres. 1960-61, gov. 1963-64), Royal Bangkok Sports. Office: Royal Thai Govt, Govt House, Bangkok Thailand *

BHORA, YAHYA ABBAS, physician; b. Bombay, June 29, 1919; s. Abbas Sadek Ali and Mariam (Mariam) Bai; m. Mohtaram Shirazi, Apr. 3, 1933; children: Nisreen, Faizullah, Moez. BS in Medicine, Grant Med. Coll., Bombay, 1946. Resident J.J. Group of Hosps., Bombay, 1947-48; med. dir. Cen. Hosp., Karachi, Pakistan, 1960—. Fellow Royal Coll. Physicians, Royal Soc. Hygiene; mem. Pakistan Med. Assn. (life), Am. Coll. Chest Physicians, Assn. Pvt. Hosps. & Nursing Homes (pres. 1970-85). Muslim. Clubs: Karachi Gymkhana, Karachi, Karachi Boat. Home: 24-B Queens Rd St #2, 02 Karachi Pakistan Office: Central Hospital, 411 Frere Rd, 01 Karachi Pakistan

BHUMIBOL ADULYADEJ, HIS MAJESTY, King of Thailand; b. Cambridge, Mass., Dec. 5, 1927; s. Prince and Princess Mahidol of Songkhla; ed. Bangkok and Lausanne; m. Mom Rajawongse Sirikit, Apr. 28, 1950; children: Princess Ubol Ratana, Crown Prince Maha Vajiralongkorn, Princess Maha Chakri Sirindhorn, Princess Chulabhorn. Succeeded brother King Ananda Mahidol (dec.), 1946; coronation ceremony, May 5, 1950. Address: Chitralada Villa, Bangkok Thailand *

BIAGIOTTI, LAURA, fashion designer; b. Rome, Italy, Aug. 4, 1943; d. Giuseppe and Delia (Soldaini) B.; 1 dau., Lavinia. Student U. Rome. Worked in mother's ready-to-wear fashion bus., Rome, 1960's; co-founder Biagiotti Exports, from 1965; showed 1st collection, 1972; designer cashmere fashions. Address: Via Palombarese Km 17, 300 Guidonia, 100012 Rome Italy

BIAGO, ANTHONY JOSEPH, real estate corporation executive, accountant; b. Exeter, Pa., Feb. 24, 1938; s. Albert and Rose (Bianco) B.; m. Barbara Ellen Killiri, Oct. 8, 1960; children: Denise Ann, Anthony Joseph Jr. AS in Mgmt., Middlesex Coll., 1971; BS in Acctg., Rutgers U., 1974; MBA in Fin., La Salle U., 1980. Controller Tujax Industries, N.Y.C., 1969-72; pres. Porter Foods, Inc., Linden, N.J., 1973-79; v.p. fin. Eliz. Iron Works, Union, N.J., 1980-83; pres. Ace Brokers, Union, N.J., 1983—, ABBCO Devel. Corp., Kenilworth, N.J., 1983—; appraiser-cons. N.J. Cts., State of N.J., 1983—. Chmn. Boy Scouts Am., Cranford, N.J., 1979-80; com. mem. Rep. Party, Union, 1977-81; treas. Cranford Rep. Com., 1980-81; mem. Cranford Zoning Bd. Adjustments, 1980-82. Served with U.S. Army, 1956-59. Mem. Rutgers Alumni Assn., Delta Sigma Pi (pres. 1972-73). Roman Catholic. Lodge: KC (pres. 1960). Office: Ace Bus Brokers & ABBCO Devel Corp 1527A Stuyvesant Ave Union NJ 07083

BIBBO, MARLUCE, physician, educator; b. Sao Paulo, Brazil, July 14, 1939; d. Domingos and Yolanda (Ranciaro) B. M.D, U. Sao Paulo, 1963, Sc.D., 1968. Intern Hosps. das Clinicas, U. Sao Paulo, 1963; resident in ob-gyn 1964-66; instr. dept. morphology and ob-gyn U. Sao Paulo, 1966-68, asst. prof., 1968-69; asst. prof. sect. cytology dept. ob-gyn U. Chgo., 1969-73, asso. prof., 1973-77, asso. prof. pathology, 1974-77, prof. ob-gyn and pathology, 1978—; asso. dir. Cytology Lab., Approved Sch. Cytotech and Cytocybernetics, AMA-Am. Soc. Clin. Pathologists, 1970—; mem. research com. Ill. div. Am. Cancer Soc., 1976—. Contbr. numerous articles to profl. jours. Fellow Internat. Acad. Cytology (v.p. 1987, dep. editor Acta Cytologica), Am. Soc. Clin. Pathologists; mem. Am. Soc. Cytology (exec. com., pres. 1982-83), U.S. Acad. Pathology, Can. Acad. Pathology, Soc. Analytical Cytology. Home: 400 E Randolph St Apt 2009 Chicago IL 60601 Office: Univ Chgo 5841 S Maryland Ave Chicago IL 60637

BIBERGER, ERICH LUDWIG, editor, writer; b. Passau, Bavaria, Fed. Republic Germany, July 20, 1927; s. Franz Sales and Therese (Becherle) B.; m. Maria Ederer, 1965. Exam., Städt Wirschaftsaufbauschule, Passau, 1944; evening student, Volksschochschule, Passau. Editor newspapers in Passau, 1952-55, Tages-Anzeiger, Regensburg, 1956-73, Mittelbayerische Zeitung, Regensburg, 1973—. Author: (poems) Dreiklang der Stille, 1955, Denn im Allsein der Welt, 1966, Andere Wege bis Zitterluft, 1977, 82, Was ist hier Schilf, was Reiher?, 1984, Nichts als das Meer, 1984; (fairy tales of atomic age) Rundgang über dem Nordlicht, 1958; (novel) Die Traumwelle, 1962; (radio plays) Duadu oder der Mann im Mond, 1967; (prose anthology) Anthologie 2, 1969; (lyric anthologies) Quer, 1974, Anthologie 3 (in 47 langs.), 1979; (satirical verse) Gar mancher, 1975; (feuilletons) Zwei Pfund Morgenduft, 1975; also texts for numerous mus. compositions; included in anthologies. Decorated Bundersverdienstkreuz am Band; recipient Nordgaupreis für Dichtung, 1974, Hans-Huldreich-Büttner-Gedächtnis-Preis, 1979, Caballero y Yuste, 1979, medal Studiosis humanitatis, 1981, Excellence in Lit., 1981, Diploma di merito, 1982, AWMM-Buchpreis, 1983, Adolf-Georg-Bartels-Gedächtnispreis, 1986, Marc-Aurel Siegel, 1988. Mem. Regensburger Schriftstellergruppe Internat., Joint Assn. Authors in German Lang. Community (chmn. 1960—), Cultural Orgn. Bavarian Country Oberpfalz (co-founder, lit. adviser 1968-74, presiding bd. 1975—), Internat. Regensburger Literaturtage (initiator, leader 1967, 71, 75, 80, 84, 86), Internat. Authors Guild, Internationaler Jungautoren-Wettbewerb (initiator, leader 1972—), Kreis der Freunde, Austrian, English and Indian Authors Circles, German Authors Circles. Address: Reichstrasse 5, D-8400 Regensburg Federal Republic of Germany

BIBLE, FRANCES LILLIAN, mezzo soprano, educator; b. Sackets Harbor, N.Y.; d. Arthur and Lillian (Cooke) B. Student, Juilliard Sch. Music, 1939-47. Artist-in-residence Shepherd Sch. of Music Rice U., Houston, 1975—. Appeared throughout, U.S., Australia, Europe including, Vienna Staatsoper, Karlsruhe Staatsoper, Dublin Opera Co., N.Y.C. Opera, NBC-TV Opera, San Francisco Opera, Glyndebourne Opera, San Antonio Opera Festival, New Orleans Opera, Houston Grand Opera, Miami Opera, Dallas Opera; appeared in concert with major symphonies. Mem. Am. Guild Mus. Artists (past 3d v.p.), Sigma Alpha Iota (hon.), Beta Sigma Phi (hon.). Republican. Episcopalian. Home: 2225 Bolsover Houston TX 77005

BICE, DAVID ALLEN, writer, publishing company executive; b. Danbury, Conn., Aug. 12, 1940; children: Penny, Cheryl, Daniel, Jeffrey, Richard; m. Alice Ruth Skidmore. BS in Edn., W.Va. State Coll., 1963; MA in History, Marshall U., 1967. Cert. tchr., W.Va. Tchr. Kanawha County Schs., Charleston, W.Va., 1963-79; instr. W.Va. Coll. Grad. Studies, Institute, 1978-79; pres. Jalamap Publs., South Charleston, W.Va., 1983-86; gen. mgr. textbook div. Walsworth Pub. Co., Marceline, Mo., 1986-88; exec. editor, 1988—; cons. in field. Author: The Pringle Tree, 1977, A Panorama of West Virginia, 1979, 2d edit., 1985, The Legend of John Henry, 1980, Mad Anne Bailey, 1980, A Panorama of Florida, 1982, West Virginia and the Appalachians, 1983, A Panorama of Tennessee, 1984, A Panorama of North Carolina, 1987, Horizons of North Carolina, 1987, Spectrum of American Civics, 1987, People Make the Difference, 1988, A Panorama of Idaho, 1988, Horizons of Idaho, 1988, A Panorama of Florida II, 1989; contbr. articles to newspapers and mags. Recipient Outstanding Contbn. to Geog. Edn. award Nat. Council for Geography, 1980. Lodge: Rotary (recording sec.).

BICK, DAVID GREER, health care marketing; b. Toledo, June 29, 1953; s. James D. and Carol Jean (Hermann) B.; children: Jennifer Kelly, Jesse Quinn, Matthew Adam, Wylie Christine. BE, U. Toledo, 1975; cert. health cons. Purdue U., 1981. Dist. mgr. Blue Cross Northwest Ohio, Tiffin, 1977-79, regional mgr., Sandusky, 1979-81, dir. sales, Toledo, 1981-82; v.p. mktg. Blue Cross/Blue Shield Central N.Y., Syracuse, 1983; exec. dir. Preview-Health Benefits Mgmt. of Ohio, Toledo, 1984-87, chief mktg. exec. Medchoice/Dentachoice HMO Blue Cross and Blue Shield of Ohio, 1984-87, v.p. sales and support sevices, mut. health services, 1988—. Author: Paupers and Profiteers (poetry). Mem. Toledo Found. for Life, PTA, People's Med. Soc., The Park Ridge Ctr. Inst. for the Study of Health, Faith & Ethics, Toledo Zoological Soc., Toledo Mus. Art. Mem. Am. Coll. Utilization Rev. Physicians, Hastings Ctr./Inst. & Soc. of Ethics and Life, Am. Hosp. Assn., U.S. Tennis Assn., U. Toledo Alumni Assn., Toledo C. of C. Roman Catholic. Club: Boilermaker (Purdue (Ind.) U.). Lodge: Rotary. Avocations: photography, golf, basketball, skiing, tennis. Home: 4000 Sylvania Ave #58 Toledo OH 43623 Office: 3737 Sylvania Ave Toledo OH 43623

BICKFORD, GEORGE PERCIVAL, lawyer; b. Berlin, N.H., Nov. 28, 1901; s. Gershon Percival and Lula Adine (Buck) B.; m. Clara L. Gehring, Apr. 6, 1933 (dec. Dec. 1985); 1 dau., Louise G. Boyd; m. Jessie B. McGaw, May, 1986. A.B. cum laude, Harvard, 1922, LL.B., 1926. Bar: Ohio 1926. Since practiced in Cleve.; asso. firm Arter & Hadden, partner, 1940—; instr. Hauchung U., Wuchang, China, 1922-23; instr. taxation Western Res. Law Sch., 1940-47; lectr. Indian history and culture Cleve. Coll., 1948-50; gen. counsel FHA, Washington, 1958-59; hon. consul of India 1964—; Mem. Cleve. Moral Claims Commn., 1935-37. Mem. Cuyahoga County Rep. Exec. Com., 1948-58, 60—; Trustee Am. U. in Cairo; vis. com. fine arts dept. Harvard, 1962-68, 72-78; trustee, former v.p. Cleve. Mus. Art; trustee Cleve. Inst. Art.; mem. Nat. Com. for Festival of India in U.S., 1985; mem. adv. com. Asia Soc. Houston, 1986. Served with Ohio N.G., 1926-29; from capt. to lt. col. JAG dept. AUS, 1942-46. Decorated Legion of Merit. Mem. Am., Ohio, Cleve. bar assns., Cleve. Council World Affairs (trustee). Episcopalian (standing com. Diocese Ohio 1951-63, chancellor 1962-77). Clubs: Union (Cleve.), Rowfant (Cleve.); Army and Navy (Washington); Harvard (N.Y.C.). Home: 13415 Shaker Blvd Cleveland OH 44120

BICKHAM, CHARLES EDWARD, JR., radiologist, educator; b. Bude, Miss., Nov. 29, 1918; s. Charles Edward and Luda (Oglesby) B.; m. Melba Scrivner, Dec. 22, 1944; children—Charles Edward III, Martha, Melissa. B.A., U. Ala., 1943; M.D., Jefferson Med. Coll., 1946. Diplomate Am. Bd. Radiology. Intern U.S. Naval Hosp., Jacksonville, Fla., 1947; resident in radiology Doctors Hosp., Washington, 1949, Garfield Meml. Hosp. and Emergency Hosp., Washington, 1952; practice medicine specializing in radiology, Washington, 1952—; clin. assoc. prof. radiology Uniformed Services Univ. Health Scis. Med. Sch., Bethesda, Md., 1982—; cons. radiologist Armed Forces Inst. Pathology, Washington, 1960-68, U.S. Naval Hosp., Bethesda, 1958—, Washington Hosp. Ctr., 1958—; attending radiologist, vice chmn. dept. Doctors Hosp., 1958-73, chmn. dept., 1973-75; chmn. dept. radiology Suburban Hosp., Bethesda, 1975—; assoc. radiologist Sibley Meml. Hosp., Washington, 1968—; trustee Med. Service of D.C., 1966-75; mem. N-44 com. Am. Nat. Standards Inst. Contbr. articles to med. jours. Served with USN, 1943-45, 46-49, 50-51; lt. Res. ret. Fellow Am. Coll. Radiology (com. on Blue Shield program); mem. AMA (sect. council radiology 1978-79, adv. com. health policy agenda for the Am. people, 1983-86; physician's recognition award 1969, 72, 75, 79, 82), Med. Soc. D.C. (occupational health com., vice chmn. relative value com., mem. clin. efficacy rev. com.), Am. Roentgen Ray Soc. (exec. council 1972-77, fin. com. 1974-76, chmn. exec. council 1976-77, 2d v.p. 1977-79), Radiol. Soc. N.Am., So. Med. Assn. (chmn. elec. sect. radiology 1974), Pan Am. Med. Soc. (pres. 1978-79), Hippocrates Galen Med. Soc., Med. Arts Soc., William Earl Clark Gastroent. Soc., Eastern Radiol. Soc., Montgomery County Med. Soc. (affiliate), Med. and Chirurg. Faculty Md. Home: 5920 Sear Terr Bethesda MD 20816 Office: Suburban Hosp Dept Radiology 8600 Old Georgetown Rd Bethesda MD 20814

BIDDISON, JACK MICHAEL, oil company executive, geologist, engineer; b. Columbus, Ohio, Feb. 27, 1954; s. Jack Carpenter and Betty Yvonne (Mollette) B; m. Qiang Zhang, Oct. 25, 1986. B.S. in Geology and Mineralogy, Ohio State U., 1977; M.B.A., Kent State U., 1985. Cert. profl. geol. scientist. Geologist, Inland Drilling Co., Ravenna, Ohio, 1978-81; geol. engr. Gasearch, Inc., Girard, Ohio, 1981; geotech. engr. CER Corp., Las Vegas, Nev., 1981-82; mgr. petroleum engring. and geol. services Energy Devel. Ops., Gen. Electric Co., Kent, Ohio, 1982-87; chief div. oil and gas Ohio Dept. Natural Resources, Columbus, 1987—. Mem. Am. Inst. Profl. Geologists, Am. Assn. Petroleum Geologists, Soc. Petroleum Engrs., Ohio Geol. Soc., Beta Gamma Sigma. Methodist. Avocations: basketball; rock collecting; cross country skiing. Home: 1904 Judwick Dr Columbus OH 43229 Office: Ohio Dept Nat Resources Fountain Square Bldg A Columbus OH 43229

BIDDLE, LIVINGSTON LUDLOW, JR., former government official, author; b. Bryn Mawr, Pa., May 26, 1918; s. Livingston Ludlow and Eugenia (Law) B.; m. Cordelia Frances Fenton, Mar. 15, 1945 (dec. May 1972); children: Cordelia Frances, Livingston Ludlow IV; m. Catharina Van Beek Baart, Nov. 3, 1973. A.B., Princeton, 1940; L.H.D. (hon.), Mt. St. Mary's Coll., N.Y., 1978; LL.D. (hon.), Catholic U., 1979; D.F.A. (hon.), U. L.I., 1979, U. Cin., 1979, Providence Coll., 1980, U. Notre Dame, 1980; D.L. (hon.), Drexel U., 1980. Reporter Phila. Evening Bull., 1940-42; with Am. Field Service, Middle East, North Africa, Italy, France, Germany, 1942-45; spl. asst. to U.S. Senator Claiborne Pell, 1963-65; dep. chmn. Nat. Endowment for Arts, Washington, 1965-67; chmn. div. arts Liberal Arts Coll., Fordham U., Lincoln Center, N.Y.C., 1967-70; spl. asst. to Senator Claiborne Pell, 1973-74; liaison dir. Nat. Endowment for Arts, Washington, 1974-75; chmn. Nat. Endowment for Arts, 1977-81; staff dir. subcom. on edn. arts and humanities U.S. Senate, 1975-77. Author: Main Line, 1950, Debut, 1952, The Village Beyond, 1956, Sam Bentley's Island, 1960, Our Government and the Arts: A Perspective From Inside, 1988. Pres. Children's Service, Inc., Phila., 1960-62; chmn. bd. Pa. Ballet, 1971-72. Decorated Order of Leopold II Belgium, Jubilee medal, Bulgaria; recipient Phila. Athenaeum Best Novel award, 1956. Democrat. Episcopalian. Clubs: Chevy Chase, Washington, Merion Cricket (Phila.); Century Assn. (N.Y.C.). Home: 3050 P St NW Washington DC 20007

BIDE, SIR AUSTIN ERNEST, manufacturing and pharmaceutical company executive; b. London, Sept. 11, 1915; s. Ernest Arthur and Eliza (Young) B.; m. Irene Ward, June 26, 1940; children—Ann Bide Trowbridge, Susan Bide Payne, Patricia. Honours degree in Chemistry, U. London, 1939. Mem. staff Dept. Govt. Chemist, 1939-40; various positions Glaxo Labs. Ltd. (name changed to Glaxo Group Ltd. 1962, re-named Glaxo Holdings Ltd. 1972), Greenford, Eng., 1940-46, asst. to dep. mng. dir., 1946-51, factory mgr., Montrose, Eng., 1951-54, dep. sec., 1954-59, sec., 1959-65, chief exec. officer, 1973-80, chmn. bd., 1973-85, hon. pres., 1985—, also dir., chmn. subs. cos.; chmn. BL Pub. Ltd. Co., London, 1982-86, QCA Ltd., 1985—. Decorated knight bachelor Her Majesty Queen Elizabeth. Fellow Royal Soc. Chemistry, Instn. Chem. Engrs., Instn. Indsl. Mgrs., Inst. for Biotechnol. Studies; companion Brit. Inst. Mgmt. (Gold medal 1982; mem. Council Confedn. Brit. Industry. Club: Hurlingham (London). Avocations: fishing; handicrafts. Office: Glaxo Holdings plc, 6-12 Clarges St, London W1Y 8DH, England *

BIDEN, JOSEPH ROBINETTE, JR., U.S. senator; b. Scranton, Pa., Nov. 20, 1942; m. Jill Tracy Jacobs, June 17, 1977; children: Ashley Blazer, Joseph Robinette, Robert Hunter. A.B., U. Del.; J.D., Syracuse U. Bar: Del. 1968. Practice law Wilmington, 1968-72; U.S. senator from Del. 1972—; chmn. judiciary com., mem. foreign relations com.; mem. New Castle (Del.) County Council, 1970-72. Democrat. Office: Senate Bldg 489 Russell Washington DC 20510

BIDWELL, JAMES TRUMAN, JR., lawyer; b. N.Y.C., Jan. 2, 1934; s. James Truman and Mary (Kane) B.; m. Gail S. Bidwell, Mar. 6, 1965 (div.); children: Hillary Day, Kimberly Wade, Courtney E.; m. KatharineT. O'Neil, July 15, 1988. B.A., Yale U., 1956; LL.B., Harvard U., 1959. Bar: N.Y. 1959. Atty. U.S. Air Force, Austin, Tex., 1959-62; assoc. firm Donovan, Leisure, Newton & Irvine, N.Y.C., 1962-68, ptnr., 1968-84; ptnr. White & Case, N.Y.C., 1984—. Pres. Youth Consultation Service, 1973-78. Mem. ABA, Fed. Bar Assn., N.Y. State Bar Assn., N.Y. County Lawyers Assn. Episcopalian. Club: Ch. N.Y.C. (pres. 1983-87). Lodge: Am. Friends of St. George's (pres. 1987—). Office: White & Case 1155 Ave of the Americas New York NY 10036

BIDWELL, ROBERT ERNEST, inventor; b. Bklyn., Jan. 15, 1926; s. Ernest Martin and Helen (Hamilton) B.; degree in Archtl. Design, Pratt Inst., 1953; m. Patricia Murphy, July 1, 1950; children—Robert Bruce, Kerry Martin, Jane, James Patrick. Designer, Harrison & Abramovitz, Rockefeller Center, N.Y.C., 1955-58; pres. Robert Bidwell Assos., Farmingdale, N.Y., 1958-68; gen. mgr., dir. design Bioresearch, Inc., Farmingdale, 1968-80; founder, chmn. bd. Bidwell Vineyards and Winery, Cutchogue, N.Y. Served with AUS, 1944-46. Mem. Soc. Plastic Engrs. (sr.), Am. Soc. Metals, Assn. Advancement Med. Instrumentation, Def. Preparedness Assn., Bidwell Family Assn., U.S. Naval Inst., SAR, L.I. Grape Growers Assn. (com. on new by-laws). Republican. Mem. Christian Ch. Inventor, holder 103 patents. Home: 27 Montrose Pl Melville NY 11747 Office: Bidwell Vineyard Route 48 Cutchogue NY 11935

BIEDERMAN, DONALD ELLIS, lawyer; b. N.Y.C., Aug. 23, 1934; s. William and Sophye (Groll) B.; m. Marna M. Leerburger, Dec. 22, 1962; children: Charles Jefferson, Melissa Anne. AB, Cornell U., 1955; JD, Harvard U., 1958; LLM in Taxation, NYU, 1970. Bar: N.Y. 1959, Calif. 1977, U.S. Dist. Ct. (so. dist.) N.Y. 1967. Assoc. Hale, Russell & Stentzel, N.Y.C., 1962-66; asst. corp. counsel City of N.Y., 1966-68; assoc. Delson & Gordon, N.Y.C., 1968-69; ptnr. Roe, Carman, Clerke, Berkman & Berkman, Jamaica, N.Y., 1969-72; gen. atty. CBS Records, N.Y.C., 1972-76; v.p. legal affairs and adminstrn. ABC Records, Los Angeles, 1977-79; ptnr. Mitchell, Silberberg & Knupp, Los Angeles, 1979-83; sr. v.p. legal and bus. affairs Warner Bros. Music (now Warner/Chappell Music Inc.), Los Angeles, 1983—; adj. prof. law Southwestern U. Sch. Law, Los Angeles, 1982—, Pepperdine U., Malibu, Calif., 1985—. Editor: Legal and Business Problems of the Music Industry, 1980; co-author: Law and Business of the Entertainment Industries, 1987. Bd. dirs. Calif. Chamber Symphony Soc., Los Angeles, 1981—. Served to 1st lt. U.S. Army, 1959. Recipient Hon. Gold Record, Recording Industry Assn. Am., 1974, Trendsetter award Billboard Mag., 1976. Mem. N.Y. State Bar, State Bar Calif. Democrat. Jewish. Club: Riviera Country (Pacific Palisades, Calif). Home: 2406 Pesquera Dr Los Angeles CA 90049 Office: Warner Bros Music 9000 Sunset Blvd Los Angeles CA 90069

BIEGEN, ARNOLD IRWIN, lawyer; b. N.Y.C., Apr. 9, 1933; s. Sol and Eva (Trupine) B.; m. Anne R. Friedenberg, Feb. 19, 1967; children: Richard, Peter, Mathew, Elissa. B.A., Bklyn. Coll., 1954; J.D., N.Y.U., 1959. Bar: N.Y. 1959, U.S. Supreme Ct. 1964. Assoc., Booth, Lipton & Lipton, N.Y.C., 1959-63, ptnr., 1964-87, ptnr. Parker, Chapin, Flattau & Klimpl, 1987—; faculty Grad. Sch. John Jay Coll. Mem. casino gambling study panel, N.Y., 1979; trustee John Jay Coll. Criminal Justice, 1982; mem. Commn. on Jud. Nomination, 1983—; bd. dirs. N.Y. Urban League, 1984—; mem. adv. bd. PBS Channel 13, N.Y.C., 1983—. Served as cpl. U.S. Army, 1954-56. Mem. Assn. Bar City of N.Y. (commr. council on jud. adminstrn.), N.Y. State Bar Assn., N.Y.U. Sch. Law Alumni Assn. (dir. 1977-82). Democrat. Office: Parker Chapin Flattau & Klimpl 1211 Ave of the Americas New York NY 10036

BIELENBERG, KARL, government official; b. Hamburg, Germany, June 6, 1942; s. Helmut Ernst and Elfriede (Bartsch) B.; came to U.S., 1950; m. Kathleen Anne Daulton, Apr. 25, 1964 (div. 1981); children: Kathryn Lynn, Karl Steven; m. Nancy J. McKee, 1984. BA Rutgers U., 1967; grad. U.S.A. Command and Gen. Staff Coll., 1986. Co-owner, Friedel's Restaurant, Ft. Lee, N.J., 1958-64; supr. terminal ops. Associated Transport, Inc., Landover, Md., 1972-73; with Dept. Army, various locations, 1974—, project mgr. BASOPS-COM project Adj. Gen.'s Office, Washington, 1976-78, chief AR-STADS study group, 1978-79, dep. dir. Hdqrs. Adminstrv. Systems Directorate, 1979-82, dep. exec. sec., chief examiner Army Bd. for Correction of Mil. Records, Office of Sec. of Army, 1982-85, exec. sec. Army Bd. for Correction of Mil. Records, 1985-86; chief info. mgmt. Omaha Dist. U.S. Army C.E., 1986—. Served to capt. AUS, 1967-72, to lt. col. USAR, 1974—. Decorated Bronze Star; recipient Outstanding Performance award Dept. Army, 1978-86. Mem. Res. Officers Assn. of the U.S. (pres. Omaha chpt.), Assn. U.S. Army, Info. Resource Adminstrn., Conf., Fed. Govt. Micrographics Council, Fed. Govt. Word Processing Council, Armed Forces Stamp Exchange Club (exec. sec. 1971—). Designed and developed standard computer output microfiche throughout U.S. Army; 1st mechanized mail sorting system in fed. govt. Home: PO Box 1337 Omaha NE 68101 Office: Chief IMO Omaha Dist USA Corps Engrs 215 N 17th St Omaha NE 68102

BIELORY, ABRAHAM M., lawyer, financial executive; b. Modena, Italy, Sept. 20, 1946; came to U.S., 1948; s. Motel and Basia (Spielberg) B.; m. Beverly B. Berkowitz, Jan. 26, 1969; children—Jennifer Rebecca, Debra Elizabeth, David Ethan. BS, N.J. Inst. Tech., 1968; JD, U. Denver, 1973. Bar: N.J. 1974, U.S. Dist. Ct. N.J. 1974, U.S. Supreme Ct. 1979. Field engr. Control Data Corp., Mpls., 1968-69; assoc. Paschon & Feurey, Toms River, N.J., 1973-77; ptnr. Paschow & Feurey, 1978, VanSicle & Bielory, Toms River, 1978—; owner ABEV Fin. Service, Toms River, 1976—. Vice pres. Lakewood Hebrew Day Sch., N.J., 1975-82, pres., 1982-86 ; trustee Hillel High Sch., Deal, N.J., 1983—; v.p. Congregation Sons of Israel, Lakewood, 1984-86, pres. 1986-88. Served as sgt. USAF, 1969-73. Fellow ABA; mem. Assn. Trial Lawyers Am., N.J. State Bar Assn., Trial Atty. N.J., Ocean County Bd. Realtors, Ocean County Bar Assn. (chmn. ins. com. 1975), Hudson County Bar Assn. (sr. citizen com. 1984), Internat. Lawyers Assn. Jewish War Vets. Republican. Home: 1422 14th St Lakewood NJ 08701

BIENENSTEIN, KATHLEEN LINDA, engineering company executive; b. Detroit, June 20, 1951; d. Charles August and Emily Linda (Tomolillo) B.; m. Alfred Reginal Trainer, III, Sept. 11, 1970 (div. 1972). BA Oakland U., Mich., 1973; AA in Bus., Kellogg Community Coll., Battle Creek, 1980. Owner retail store, Livonia, Mich., 1973-75; designer Criterion Design, Royal Oak, Mich., 1975-77; designer Eaton Corp., Galesburg, Mich., 1977-81; v.p. engring. services Charles S. Davis & Assoc. Inc., Pontiac, Mich., 1981-87, gen. mgr., 1984-85; engring. group mgr. Ruecker Engring Ltd., 1987-88; chief exec. officer, pres. Celtech Inc., 1988— . Patentee camshaft bushing. Sponsor, Star Theatre, Flint, Mich., 1983-86. Mem. Soc. Automotive Engrs., Soc. Body Engrs., NOW, Nat. Assn. Female Execs. Democrat. Office: Celtech Inc 400 Monroe #400 Detroit MI 48226

BIENSTOCK, ERIC MARTIN, educator, consultant; b. N.Y.C., May 29, 1946; s. Herman Abraham and Fay (Bistreich) B.; B.S. (N.Y. State regents scholar), Bklyn. Coll., 1968; M.S., N.Y.U., 1973, Ph.D., 1980; hon cert. psychoanalysis Psychoanalytic Inst. Clin. Social Work, 1979; m. Jane Susan Barrow, Feb. 8, 1975; 1 dau., Elizabeth Barrow. Tchr. math. N.Y.C. Bd. Edn., 1968-79; adj. lectr. math. CUNY, 1973-80; adminstr. Triana & Assos., N.Y.C., 1973-80; adminstrv. cons. Psychoanalytic Inst. Clin. Social Work, N.Y.C., 1974-80; adj. prof. math. Baruch Coll., CUNY, 1980-84 , N.Y.U., 1982-83; mng. dir. Edward de Bono Sch. Thinking, N.Y.C., 1980-834; pres. Eric M. Bienstock & Assocs., 1980—. Bd. dirs. Cognitive Research and Tng.

Found., N.Y.C.; mem. U.S. Congl. Adv. Bd. Decorated Knight Knights of Malta Ecumenical, Order St. John of Jerusalem. Mem. Assn. Supervision and Curriculum Devel., Math. Assn. Am., Nat. Council Tchrs. Math., Doctorate Assn. N.Y. Educators, Play Schs. Assn. (exec. com.). Mil. Order Germania (capt.). Office: 231 E 76th St New York NY 10021

BIERHALTER, GÜNTER AXEL, writer; b. Pforzheim, Baden, Federal Republic of Germany, Sept. 9, 1949; s. Karl Albert and Margaretha (Kessler) B. Student, U. Karlsruhe, Fed. Republic Germany, 1976. Author sci. jours. for German and internat. publs. 1978—.

BIERI, HANSRUDOLF, corporate executive; b. Munsingen, Switzerland, Oct. 26, 1947. MME, Swiss Fed. Inst. Tech., Zurich, 1974; MBA, Babson Coll., Wellesley, Mass., 1978. Gen. mgr. Bieri Pumpenbau div. Biral Internat. Inc., Munsingen, 1979—. Mem. AMSE, Mass. Soc. Profl. Engrs. Office: Bieri Pumpenbau Biral Internat, 3110 Munsingen Switzerland

BIERINGA, LUITJEN HENDRIK, art gallery dir.; b. Groningen, Netherlands, Sept. 10, 1942; s. Lammert and Aaltina Cornelia (de Vries) B.; B.A., Auckland U., 1964, M.A. with honors in German, 1966, M.A. in Art History, 1971; m. Janet Ann Elizabeth Miller, May 19, 1967; children—Sven, Tanya, Kris. Substitute tchr., lang. tchr., Auckland, 1967-70; dir. Manawatu Art Gallery, Palmerston N., 1971-79; dir. Nat. Art Gallery, Wellington, N.Z., 1979—; part-time lectr. Palmerston N. Tchrs. Coll., 1971-79. Queen Elizabeth II Arts Council overseas study grantee, 1975. Mem. N.Z. Art Gallery Dirs. Council (chmn. 1978-80), Art Galleries and Mus. Assn. N.Z. (pres.), ICOM. Club: Photo-Forum (Wellington). Author: M.T. Woollaston: Works 1933-73, 1973; McCahon: Religious Works, 1975, Content/Context, A Survey of Recent NZ Art, 1986. Home: PO Box 467, Fax 857 157, Wellington New Zealand Office: Nat Art Gallery, Buckle St, Wellington New Zealand

BIERMAN, EVERETT EUGENE, ambassador; b. Hastings, Nebr., Aug. 16, 1924; s. Herbert Theodore and Lulu Alma (Girard) B.; m. Joyce Elizabeth Lear, June 25, 1950; children: James, Karen, Robert, Marta. BS, Purdue U., 1948; MA, Am. U., 1958. Info. officer USDA, Washington, 1948-51; info. dir. Nat. 4-H Club Found., Washington, 1951-59; pub. relations dir. Cen. Soya Co., Ft. Wayne, Ind., 1959-67; minority staff dir. com. on fgn. affairs U.S. House of Reps., Washington, 1967-86; ambassador Papua New Guinea and Solomon Islands, and Vanuatu, 1986—. Mem. Pres. Reagan's Transition Team, 1980. Served with U.S. Army, 1943-46. Mem. Sigma Delta Chi, Alpha Gamma Rho. Republican. Methodist. Clubs: Army-Navy; Internat. (Washington); Capitol Hill. Lodges: Masons, Lions. Home: 10425 Courthouse Dr Fairfax VA 22030 Office: Am Embassy Port Moresby US Dept State Washington DC 20520

BIERNAT, LILLIAN M. NAHUMENUK, interior designer; b. Phila., Apr. 27, 1931; d. Peter and Anna (Wolonick) Nahumenuk; m. Joseph Anthony Biernat, July 22, 1951; children: Joseph A., Daria Ann, Karen Marie, Mark Allen, Brent Hilary. Student, N.Y. Sch. Interior Design, 1955. Receptionist, sec. Mayer, Magaziner & Brunswick, Phila., 1950-53; owner Town House Interiors, Columbia, Conn., also Newton Square, Pa., 1956—, Lillian Biernat Interiors, Columbia and Avon, Conn.; bd. dirs. Conn. à la Carte Cook Book. Mem. fund raising com. Girl Scouts U.S., 1968; mem. exec. bd. Conn. Opera Guild, Hartford Ballet; pres. Friends of Hartford Ballet. Clubs: Womens, Garden (Newtown Square); Villagers Women's (Columbia); Avon Garden. Address: 30 Hurdle Fence Dr Avon CT 06001

BIERRING, OLE, Danish permanent representative to UN; b. Copenhagen, Nov. 9, 1926; s. Knud and Ester Marie (Lorck) B.; m. Bodil Elisabeth Kisbye, Mar. 2, 1960; children—Christina, Jens, Marie Louise, Arendse. LL.M., U. Copenhagen, 1951; postgrad. Princeton U., 1956. With Danish Ministry of Fgn. Affairs, Copenhagen, 1951, attache Danish Embassy, Washington, 1956-58, 1st sec., Vienna, 1960-63, head dept. Ministry Fgn. Affairs, Copenhagen, 1967-68; minister councellor and alt. permanent rep. Denmark to N. Atlantic Council, Brussels, Belgium, 1968-72; head dept. Ministry Fgn. Affairs, Copenhagen, 1972-74; dep. under-sec. state for polit. affairs, 1974-75, undersec., 1976-80, dep. permanent undersec., 1980; Danish ambassador to France, 1980-84; permanent rep. of Denmark to UN, 1984—; rep. of Denmark in security council, 1985-86. Decorated Grand Cross, Order St. Olav (Norway); comdr. Order of Dannebrog; Legion d'Honneur (France); Merite National (France), others. Address: Permanent Mission of Denmark to UN 2 UN Plaza 26th Floor New York NY 10017

BIERSTEDT, ROBERT, sociologist, author; b. Burlington, Iowa, Mar. 20, 1913; s. Henry F. and Bertha (Strauss) B.; m. Betty MacIver, Dec. 26, 1939; children: Peter, Karen, Robin. A.B., U. Iowa, 1934; A.M., Columbia U., 1935; Ph.D., 1950; fellow, Harvard U., 1936-37. Lectr. philosophy Columbia U., 1937-39, head men's residence halls, 1938-39; instr. social studies div. Bennington Coll., 1939-40; instr. philosophy Bard Coll., 1940-43; asst. prof. sociology U. Wash., summer 1946; asst. prof. Wellesley Coll., 1946-47; asst. prof. U. Ill., 1947-51, asso. prof., 1951-53; prof., chmn. dept. sociology and anthropology Coll. City N.Y., 1953-59; vis. prof. Stanford U., summer 1959; Fulbright lectr. U. Edinburgh, Scotland, 1959-60; Barnett lectr. Oxford U., 1960; head dept. N.Y. U., 1960-66, prof. sociology, 1960-72; mem. Center Advanced Studies, U. Va., 1972-74, prof. sociology, 1972-82, Commonwealth prof., 1982—, prof. emeritus, 1983—; Fulbright lectr. London Sch. Econs., 1966-67; Bd. dirs. Am. Council Learned Socs., 1979-87. Author: The Social Order, 1957, 4th edit., 1974, (with others) Modern Social Science, 1964, Emile Durkheim, 1966, Power and Progress, 1974, American Sociological Theory, 1981; Editor: The Making of Society, 1959, (with others) Florian Znaniecki, 1969; adv. editor: Internat. Jour. Sociology and Social Policy; contbr. articles to profl. lit. jours. Served from lt. (j.g.) to lt. USNR, 1943-46. Mem. Am. Sociol. Assn. (past v.p.), Eastern Sociol. Soc. (past pres.), Sociol. Research Assn., AAUP (pres. City Coll. chpt. 1958-59, council 1963-66), ACLU (dir. 1962-74, nat. adv. council 1975—), Phi Beta Kappa. Club: Harvard, Century Assn. (N.Y.C.). Home: 9 Old Farm Rd Charlottesville VA 22901 also: Chilmark MA 02535

BIES, DAVID ALAN, mechanical engineering educator, acoustical engineer; b. Los Angeles, Aug. 15, 1925; s. Milton Irving and Frances E. (Mitchel) B.; m. Helen Margret Ormerod, Nov. 24, 1954 (div. 1985); 1 dau., Carolyn Ann. B.A., UCLA, 1948, M.A., 1951, Ph.D., 1953. Staff physicist Bodine Soundrive, Los Angeles, 1954-59; cons. Bolt Beranek & Newman, Los Angeles, 1959-72; reader dept. mech. engring. U. Adelaide (Australia), 1972—. Contbr. articles to profl. jours. Fellow Acoustical Soc. Am.; mem. Inst. Noise Control Engrings., Australian Acoustical Soc., AAAS, Sigma Xi. Office: Dept Mech Engring, U Adelaide, Adelaide South Australia 5001, Australia

BIESELE, JOHN JULIUS, biologist, educator; b. Waco, Tex., Mar. 24, 1918; s. Rudolph Leopold and Anna Emma (Jahn) B.; m. Marguerite Calfee McAfee, July 29, 1943; children: Marguerite Anne, Diana Terry, Elizabeth Jane. B.A. with highest honors, U. Tex., 1939, Ph.D., 1942. Fellow Internat. Cancer Research Found., U. Tex., 1942-43, Barnard Skin and Cancer Hosp., St. Louis, also; U. Pa., 1943-44, instr. zoology, 1943-44; temporary research assoc. dept. genetics Carnegie Instn. of Washington, Cold Spring Harbor, 1944-46; research assoc. biology dept. Mass. Inst. Tech., 1946-47; asst. Sloan-Kettering Inst. Cancer Research, 1946-47, research fellow, 1947, assoc., 1947-55, head cell growth sect., div. exptl. chemotherapy, 1947-58, mem., 1955-58, assoc. scientist div., 1959-78; asst. prof. anatomy Cornell U. Med. Sch., 1950-52; assoc. prof. biology Sloan-Kettering div. Cornell U. Grad. Sch. Med. Scis., 1952-55, prof. biology, 1955-58; prof. zoology, mem. grad. faculty U. Tex., Austin, 1958-78; also mem. faculty U. Tex. (Coll. Pharmacy), 1969-71, prof. edn., 1973-78; cons. cell biology M.D. Anderson Hosp. and Tumor Inst., U. Tex. at Houston, 1958-72; dir. Genetics Found., 1959-78; mem. cell biology study sect. NIH, 1958-63; Sigma Xi lectr. N.Y. U. Grad. Sch. Arts and Scis., 1957; Mendel lectr. St. Peter's Coll., Jersey City, 1958; Mendel Club lectr. Canisius Coll., Buffalo, 1971; mem. adv. com. research etiology of cancer Am. Cancer Soc., 1961-64, pres. Travis County unit, 1966, mem. adv. com. on personnel for research, 1969-73; counsellor Cancer Internat. Research Coop., Inc., 1962—; mem. cancer research tng. com. Nat. Cancer Inst., 1969-72; Gen. chmn. Conf. Advancement Sci. and Math. Teaching, 1966. Author: Mitotic Poisons and the Cancer Problem, 1958; Editorial bd.: Year Book Cancer, 1959-72; editorial adv. bd.: Cancer Research, 1960-64; asso. editor, 1969-72; cons. editor: Am. Jour. Mental Deficiency, 1963-68; Contbr. articles sci. jours., books. Research Career award NIH, 1962, 67, 72, 77. Fellow N.Y., Tex. acads. scis., AAAS; mem. Am. Assn. Cancer Research (dir. 1960-63), Am. Soc. Cell Biology, Am. Inst. Biol. Scis., Phi Beta Kappa, Sigma Xi (pres. Tex. chpt. 1963-64), Phi Eta Sigma. Home: 2500 Great Oaks Pkwy Austin TX 78756

BIFFEN, JOHN, former British leader of House of Commons; b. Nov. 3, 1930; s. Victor W. B.; ed. Jesus Coll., Cambridge, Eng.; m. Sarah Drew Wood, 1979. M.P. for Oswestry dist., 1961-83; with Tube Investments Ltd., 1953-60; with Economist Intelligence Unit, 1960-61; chief sec. to treasury, 1979-81, sec. state for trade, 1981-82, lord pres. of council, 1982-83, leader House of Commons, 1982-87. Conservative. Office: House of Commoms, Westminster, London SW 1 England *

BIGALKE, RUDOLPH CARL, nature conservation educator; b. Kimberley, Cape Province, Republic South Africa, Feb. 24, 1932; s. Heinrich Carl and Elizabeth Catherine (Chatterton) B.; m. Ingeborg Dorothea Gaber, Dec. 4, 1957; children: Martin Carl, Michael Hermann). BS, Rhodes U., Grahamstown, South Africa, 1951, BS with hons., 1952, Univ. Edn. diploma, 1953; PhD, Goethe U., Frankfurt, Fed. Republic Germany, 1956. Biologist South African Adminstr., Etosha Game Res., 1956-58; dir. McGregor Meml. Mus., Kimberley, South Africa, 1958-64; prin. research Natal Parks Bd., Pietermaritzburg, South Africa, 1964-70; prof. nature conservation U. Stellenbosch, South Africa, 1970—, dean of forestry; vis. scientist Deutsche Akadamie Austauschdient Tech. U., Munich, 1974; overseas vis. scholar St. Johns Coll., Cambridge, 1981; trustee The Hans Merensky Found., Johannesburg, 1983—; council mem. South African Mus., Capetown, 1986—. Contbr. numerous articles to profl. jours. and chpts. to books. Pres. Habitat Council, Pretoria, 1984—. Fellow Royal Soc. South Africa (pres. 1984-86); mem. Zool. Soc. South Africa (pres. 1972-74), Bot. Soc. South Africa, South Africa Wildlife Mgmt. Assn. (hon.), South African Inst. of Forestry. Lutheran. Club: Kimberley. Home: 120 Merriman Ave, 7600 Stellenbosch Republic of South Africa Office: U Stellenbosch, Faculty of Forestry, Rondebosch 7600, Republic of South Africa

BIGELOW, DAVID SKINNER, III, management consultant; b. Orange, N.J., Apr. 19, 1931; s. Nelson Sylvester and Elizabeth Frances (Freeman) B.; m. Mary Elizabeth Nutting, Sept. 14, 1957; children: David Skinner IV, Seth, Hope N., Jonathon G.H. BS, U.S. Naval Acad., 1953; BCE, Rensselaer Poly. Inst., 1956; MBA, U. Chgo., 1960. Commd. ensign U.S. Navy, 1953, advanced through grades to lt. comdr., 1960; ret., 1960; mgmt. cons. McKinsey & Co. Inc., Chgo., 1960-64; cost mgr. Worldwide Massey-Ferguson Ltd., Toronto, Ont., Can., 1964-66; comptroller Massey Ferguson U.K., Ltd., Coventry, 1966-68, dir. tech. ops., 1968-70, dir. farm machinery mfg. worldwide, 1970-73; mng. dir. Motores Perkins SA, Sao Paulo, Brazil, 1973-75; sr. v.p. corp. ops. J.I. Case Co., Racine, Wis., 1975-78; dir. gen. Poclain S.A., Belleville, France, 1978-81; v.p. Tenneco Inc., Houston, 1982-83; pres. Poclain S.A., Belleville, France, 1983-87; dir. D.M.L. Mgmt. Cons., N.Y.C., 1987—; adj. prof. Rensselaer Poly. Inst. and Ecole Superioure des Scis Economiques et Commerciales, France. Decorated chevalier Nat. Order Merit (France). Registered profl. engr. Mem. ASCE, Am. Inst. Indsl. Engrs. (sr.). Clubs: Interalliee (Paris), Pilgrims. Home: 226 Langrove Londonderry VT 05148 Office: 420 Lexington Ave, Suite 406, New York France also: 50 Rue de Bourgogne, Paris France

BIGELOW, MARY D., electrical company executive, photographer; b. Perry, N.Y.; d. Albert E. and Rebecca Ann (Miller) Davis; student Rochester Bus. Inst., Am. Inst. Banking, 1938, Woodbury Coll., 1944, UCLA, 1945; m. Richard Harned Bates, Oct. 4, 1940 (div. Sept. 1947); m. 2d, Floyd Burget Bigelow, 1948 (div. May, 1952); 1 dau., Judith Lynne Bigelow McMullen; m. 3d, Rudy Gray Burton, Nov. 17, 1962. Various positions, 1931-36, banking, 1936-41, advt., oil bus., 1944-50; sec.-treas. Emerald Bay Community Assn., Laguna Beach, Calif., 1950-52, Tel-I-Clear Systems, Inc., Laguna Beach, 1952-54; owner, operator Bigelow Bus. Services, Laguna Beach, 1954—; co-owner, mgr. Burton Electric, Laguna Beach, 1963—; owner Meri-Bee Originals, 1980—; photographer Div. II, U.S. Coast Guard Aux., Flotilla 25, 1983—. Asst., bd. dirs. Three Arch Bay Dist., South Laguna, 1957-73; bd. dirs. Girls Club Laguna Beach; com. mem. Lyric Opera and Opera League Laguna Beach, 1968—; mem. U. Calif., Irvine Friends of Library; bd. dirs. Joe Thurston Found., 1957-64, First Nighters. Recipient various civic and photog. awards; named Leading Lady in Bus., Laguna News-Post, 1971. Mem. Nat. Soc. Public Accts., Nat., Inland assns. tax cons., Soc. Calif. Accts., Nat. League Am. Pen Women, Dana Point Power Squadron, World Affairs Council Los Angeles and Orange County, Laguna Beach C. of C. Mermaids (info. chmn. Festival of Arts 1966, 67, 68), Cousteau Soc. Clubs: Altrusa (treas., dir.) (Laguna Beach); West Coast Yacht (staff photographer); Riviera, Anchorettes, Dana Point Yacht. Address: 697 Catalina St Laguna Beach CA 92651

BIGELOW, PAUL UPHAM, stock exchange executive; b. N.Y.C., Aug. 20, 1932; s. Horace Ransom and Cecile (Coudert) B.; m. Cecilia T. McDonough, Nov. 23, 1962; children—Margaret, Frank. B.A. in Philosophy, St. Vincent Coll., 1955; postgrad. NYU. With Deloitte, Haskins & Sells, C.P.A.s, N.Y.C., 1955-62, semi-sr., 1959-62; founder, dir. internal auditing dept. Dean Witter & Co. (now Dean Witter Reynolds, Inc.), 1962-72; examiner, coordinator, div. resources adminstr. N.Y. Stock Exchange, Inc., 1972—; internal auditor Port Alert Inc., 1973-76. Served with AUS, 1956-58. C.P.A., N.Y. State. Mem. Am. Inst. C.P.A.s, Securities Industries Assn. (founder internal auditing div.), N.Y. State Soc. C.P.A.s (ethics com. 1984-86). Address: 19 Revere Rd Port Washington NY 11050

BIGGERS, WILLIAM JOSEPH, corporation executive; b. Great Bend, Kans., Mar. 16, 1928; s. William Henry and Frances (Jack) B.; m. Eathil Bonner, Nov. 17, 1956 (div. July 1981); children: Frances, Patricia; m. Diane McLaughlin, Feb. 14, 1983. B.A., Duke U., 1949. C.P.A., Ga. Pub. acct. 1949-55; sec.-treas. Parker, Helms & Langston, Inc., Brunswick, Ga., 1955-59, Stuckey's, Inc., Eastman, Ga., 1959-60; sec.-treas., v.p. finance Curtis 1000 Inc., 1961-69; v.p. Am. Bus. Products, Inc., Atlanta, 1969-73, chief exec. officer, 1973-88, chmn. bd., 1983—; also dir.; trustee ABP Profit Sharing Trust; Trustee Ga. Council Econ. Edn.; mem. mgmt. conf. bd. Emory U. Grad. Sch. Bus.; bd. dirs. Com. Publicly Owned Cos., Carriage Industries, Inc., Vt. Am. Corp., Joint Council on Econ. Edn.; mem. listed co. adv. com. N.Y. Stock Exchange. Bd. visitors Berry Coll.; bd. dirs. Atlanta Area council Boy Scouts Am. Served with USNR, 1946; Served with AUS, 1950-52. Mem. Am. Inst. C.P.A.s, Ga. Soc. C.P.A.s, Fin. Execs. Inst., Am. Mgmt. Assn., Phoenix Soc. Atlanta, Conf. Bd., NAM, Phi Kappa Psi. Clubs: Capital City, Georgian, Marietta County. Lodge: Rotary. Office: Am Bus Products Inc 2100 Riveredge Pkwy Suite 1200 Atlanta GA 30328

BIGGS, BARBARA ELLEN, clinical psychologist; b. Bayonne, N.J., Aug. 30, 1931; d. Joseph Michael and Sylvia (Rosenthal) Silverman; B.A., Adelphi U., 1953; M.A., N.Y.U., 1954; Ph.D., UCLA, 1971; m. Sidney Sonenblum, Nov. 22, 1973; children—Michael Patrick, Jonathan David. Speech pathologist Upper Darby (Pa.) Sch. Dist., 1954-55; asst. prof. communicative disorders U. Calif. at Northridge, 1968-69; dir. acad. studies student devel. center Mt. St. Mary's Coll., 1969-71; vis. prof. psychobiology U. So. Calif., 1971-73; clin. psychologist, marriage, family and child counselor; co-dir. Center for Interpersonal Studies, Los Angeles, 1971-86; co-founder Mediation Inst. Am., 1983-85, asso. clin. prof. psychology UCLA, 1981-86; co-founder, clin. psychologist, mediator, mediation trainer Spectrum Psychological Resources, Los Angeles, 1986—; cons. Profl. Tng. Workshops for Tchrs., Claremont Colls., Immaculate Heart Coll., Rio Hondo Coll., Center in Amsterdam, Quaesitor in London, 1969-75; founding mem., bd. dirs. Westside Children's Ctr., 1984—; cons. St. John's Hosp., VA Outpatient Clinic, Assn. Social Workers, Japanese Counseling Assn., Tokyo, Center, Amsterdam, Quaesitor, London, Cold Mountain Inst., Vancouver, B.C., 1969-75; dir. hearing officers tng. program Los Angeles City Atty.'s Office, 1975-76; cons. Clackamas County (Oreg.) Dist. Atty.'s Office, 1976, State Calif. Office Adminstrv. Hearings, 1976; cons. Southwestern U. Law Sch., 1976, Humanistic Law Inst., 1976-78; condr. tng. workshops Beverly Hills Barristers, Calif. Bar Assn.; condr. mediation tng. programs Venice Mar Vista Neighborhood Justice Center, City of Los Angeles Landlord-Tenant Mediation Bd., 1977, 78, exhibited in photography shows Gallery La Porte, Los Angeles, 1979-81, Garendo Gallery, 1979-80, La Art Gallery , Soho, N.Y.C., 1986, Brand Library Glendale, Calif., 1988. Recipient Public Service award VA, 1966. Mem. state central com. Democratic party, 1964. Mem. Am., Calif., Los Angeles County psychol. assns., Group Psychotherapy Assn. So. Calif. (mem. bd. 1970-74, membership sec. 1972-73), Los Angeles Soc. Clin. Psychologist (pres. 1976), Calif. Assn. Psychology Providers (bd. dirs. 1984—; pres. 1985-86), Children's Design, 1983—. Author: (with Gary Felton) Up From Under-Achievement, 1977; contbr. articles to profl. jours. Home: 1340 Linda Flora Dr Los Angeles CA 90049 Office: Spectrum Psychological Resources 10780 Santa Monica Blvd #450 Los Angeles CA 90025

BIGGS, FREDERICK WILLIAM, real estate executive; b. Adelaide, Australia, Apr. 8, 1927; s. Frederick Ernest and Gladys (Nicholls) B.; m. Roslyn Claire Biggs, July 2, 1949 (div. 1984); children: Susan Claire, Christine Michelle, John Frederick William; m. Vera Klara Diana Lukic, Sept. 28, 1984. Joint mng. dir. Woodham Biggs Proprietary Ltd., Adelaide, 1959-69, chmn., mng. dir., 1969—; bd. dirs. Florence Lock Proprietary Ltd., Ceywood Proprietary Ltd., FWB Proprietary Ltd., WBS Proprietary Ltd., WB Holdings Proprietary Ltd., WB Mgmt. Proprietary Ltd., Vee Holdings Proprietary Ltd., Harvard Securities Proprietary Ltd. Active Heart Found., Adelaide Cen. Mission, Bedford Industries. Served with Australian mil., 1945-47. Mem. Real Estate Inst., Auctioneers and Appraisers, Real Estate Employer's Fedn. Liberal. Anglican. Clubs: Kooyonga Golf, Mt. Lofty Golf, Stock Exchange, Tattersalls, Naval and Mil., S.A. Jockey. Home: 132 Strangways Terr, North Adelaide 5006, Australia Office: Woodham Biggs Proprietary Ltd, 91 Currie St, Adelaide 5000, Australia

BIGGS, NANCY GENE, businesswoman; b. Memphis, Sept. 28, 1923; d. Raynor H. and Genevieve (Tarrant) Chisholm; B.S., Memphis State U., 1961, M.A., 1962, Ed.D., 1969; m. Jack Clayton Biggs, Jan. 21, 1965; children—Charles C. Shoaf III, Raynor G. Shoaf, Robert J. Burnett, John A. Burnett. Tchr., Memphis City Schs., 1961-71, math. cons., 1971-84. Recipient Woman's award Memphis State U., 1961; 1st woman to receive doctorate from Memphis State U. Mem. Nat. Council Tchrs. Math., Nat. Council Suprs. Math. (1st v.p., 1981—), Assn. Supervision and Curriculum Devel., Tenn. Math. Tchrs. Assn., Memphis Area Council Tchrs. Math., Gen. Fedn. Women's Clubs (local pres. 1982-83), Delta Kappa Gamma (chpt. pres. 1982-84). Republican. Baptist. Clubs: Stage Set, Gavel (sec., 1981, 1st v.p. 1983, pres. 1985), Twentieth Century (pres. 1980—), Quota (pres. Memphis, 1977-78). Editor 9 books for individualized math. Home and Office: 1330 Brookfield Memphis TN 38119

BIGGY, MARY VIRGINIA, college dean; b. Boston, Oct. 15, 1924; d. John J. and Mary C. (Dwyer) B. B.S., Boston U., 1945, Ed.M., 1946, Ed.D., 1953. Tchr. bus. edn. Needham (Mass.) High Sch., 1944-45; reading cons. Plainville (Conn.) Public Schs., 1946-47; coordinator elem. edn. Concord (Mass.) Public Schs., 1947-62; dir. N.E. instrnl. TV project, dir. instrnl. TV Eastern Ednl. Network, Boston, 1962-67; asst. supt., supr. Concord Public Schs. and Concord Carlisle Regional Sch. Dist., 1967-69; prof. edn. U. Lowell, Mass., 1969—; dean U. Lowell (Coll. Edn.), 1979—; pres. (Designs for Edn.), 1969—; cons. Corp. Pub. Broadcasting; mem. Acton Boxborough (Mass.) Regional High Sch. Dist. Sch. Com., 1963-66; chmn. Mass. Bd. Library Commrs., 1973-78; project dir. criteria for funding major initiatives Corp. Pub. Broadcasting, 1981-85. Author: Independence in Spelling, 1966, (with others) Spell Correctly, 1965-86, 5th edit., 1986. Recipient Ida M. Johnston award Boston U., 1981. Mem. NEA, Am. Assn. Sch. Adminstrs., Am. Ednl. Research Assn., Assn. Supervision and Curriculum Devel., AAUP, Internat. Reading Assn., New Eng. Reading Assn., Pi Lambda Theta (nat. pres. 1961-65, 83 Disting. Pi Lambda Thetan award), others. Democrat. Roman Catholic. Home: 162 Park Ln Concord MA 01742 Office: U Lowell Coll Edn Lowell MA 01854

BIGLEY, WILLIAM JOSEPH, JR., control engineer; b. Union City, N.J., May 8, 1924; s. William Joseph and Mary May (Quigley) B.; B.M.E., Rensselaer Polytech. Inst., 1950; M.S. in Elec. Engring., N.J. Inst. Tech., 1962, M.S. in Computer Sci., 1973; Ed.D., Fairleigh Dickinson U., 1984; m. Hannelore Hicks, June 24, 1950; children—Laura C., William Joseph IV, Susan J. Project engr. Tube Reducing Corp., Wallington, N.J., 1953-58, Flight Support, Inc., Metuchen, N.J., 1958-59, Airborne Accessories, Inc., Hillside, N.J., 1959-61; sr. staff engr. in control engring. Lockheed Electronics Co. div. Lockheed Aircraft, Inc., Plainfield, N.J., 1961—. Prof. engring. electronics Newark Coll. Engring., 1961-62; prof. cons. engr. Automatic Control Systems, 1958—. Mem. council Boy Scouts of Am., Scotch Plains, N.J., 1960-63. Served with AUS, 1943-44; served with USNR, 1944-46. Named Engr.-Scientist of Yr., Lockheed Electronics Co., Inc., 1980, recipient Robert E. Gross award for tech. excellence, 1980; Achievement Honor Roll award N.J. Inst. Tech. Alumni Assn., 1982; registered profl. engr., N.Y., N.J., Calif. Mem. Nat. Soc. Profl. Engrs., IEEE, AAAS, ASME, Instrument Soc. Am., Am. Mgmt. Assn., Nat. Rifle Assn., Tau Beta Pi (eminent engr. 1986). Contbr. articles to profl. jours. Home: 1641 Terrill Rd Scotch Plains NJ 07076 Office: Lockheed Corp Hwy 22 Plainfield NJ 07060

BIGLIERI, EDWARD GEORGE, physician; b. San Francisco, Jan. 17, 1925; s. Ned and (Mignacco) B.; m. Beverly A. Bergesen, May 16, 1953; children: Mark, Michael, Gregg. Student, U. San Francisco, 1942-43, Gonzaga U., 1943-44; B.S. in Chemistry summa cum laude, U. San Francisco, 1948, D.Sc. (hon.), 1985; M.D., U. Calif., 1952. Diplomate Am. Bd. Internal Medicine (endocrine test com. 1971-76). Intern U. Calif., San Francisco Med. Center, also, VA Hosp., San Francisco, 1952-54; resident VA Hosp., 1954-56; clin. assoc. and research physician NIH, 1956-58; also metabolic unit U. Calif., 1958-61, asst. prof. medicine, 1962-65, assoc. prof., 1965-71, prof., 1971—; program dir. gen. clin. research, also chief endocrinology service San Francisco Gen. Hosp., 1962—; vis. prof. Monash U., Melbourne, Australia, 1967; NATO vis. prof., Italy, 1983; mem. study sect. NIH, 1971-74, 82-87. Contbr. articles on endocrinology ahd hormones in hypertension to profl. jours. Served to lt. (j.g.) USN, 1944-46. NIH grantee, 1972-73. Mem. Am. Soc. Hypertension (pres.-elect 1988—, Robt Tigerstedt award for defining role of adrenal steriods in hypertension), Endocrine Soc., F.A.C.P., Am. Soc. Clin. Investigation, Am. Heart Assn. (council high blood pressure research), Assn. Am. Physicians, Western Assn. Physicians, Am. Fedn. Clin. Research. Home: 129 Convent Ct San Rafael CA 94901 Office: San Francisco Gen Hosp San Francisco CA 94110

BIGORNIA, RODOLFO ROMAN TUPAS, internist; b. Cebu City, Philippines, Feb. 28, 1950; s. Jovencio Bandayrel and Pacita Bollozos (Tupas) B.; m. Lydia Lipango Almadro; children: Lyll Karen, Liza Kristine, Lovell Kimberly, Lianne Karla, Lesley Kyna. BS, Velez Coll., 1969; MD, Cebu Inst. Medicine, 1974. Diplomate Philippine Bd. Internal Medicine, Philippine Bd. Pulmonary Medicine. Intern Cebu Doctors' Hosp., Cebu City, 1974-75; rural intern No. Mindanao Regional Tng. Hosp., Cagayan de Oro City, Philippines, 1975; asst. chief resident dept. internal medicine Cebu Doctors' Hosp., 1978; jr. fellow pulmonary services Philippine Heart Ctr. Asia, Quezon City, Philippines, 1979; chief fellow Philippine Heart Ctr. Asia, Quezon City, 1980, sr. house officer, 1981, jr. cons., 1981; officer-in-charge critical care and ICU Cortes Gen. Hosp. and Cebu Velez Gen. Hosp., Cebu City, 1984; chief pulmonary sect., dept. medicine Chong Hua Hosp., Cebu City, 1985-87, chmn. dept. medicine, 1988—. Contbr. to profl. publs. Chmn. Emergency Rescue Unit Found., Philipppines, 1987—; mem. regional coordinating body Nat. Convenors Group for Presdl. Consultative Vis., 1987. Served as sgt. Philippine Army Res. Mem. Philippine Med. Assn., Philippine Coll. Physicians, Philippine Coll. Chest Physicians and Surgeons, Philippine Assn. Boehringer-Ingelheim Fellows, YMCA. Roman Catholic. Lodge: Rotary. Home: 39 President Roxas St, Villa Aurora Mabolo, Cebu City 6000, Philippines Office: Chong Hua Hosp Fuente Osmena, Suite 209A, Cebu City 6401, Philippines

BIGOT, JEAN-MICHAEL ROGER, educator, radiologist; b. Paris, Nov. 7, 1935; s. Alfred Georges and Simone (Cornevin) B.; m. Anne Le Guennec, Mar. 5, 1965; children: Eric Christophe, Justine Alexandra. Student, Janson de Sailly, Le Harve, France, 1950-52; MD, U. Paris, 1952-68. Externe Hosp. Paris., 1956-62, intern, 1964-68, chief clinic, 1968-74; radiologist Hosp. St. Antoine, Paris, 1974-76; chief radiology service Hosp. Tenon, Paris, 1976—; prof. U. Paris, 1974—. Contbr. over 210 artices to French and fgn. med. jours. Mem. various French and European med. socs., Radiol Soc. N.Am., Am. Roentgen Ray Soc., European Congress Radiology (sci. sec. 1983), Internat. Congress Radiology (sec. gen.). Home: 16 rud des Fosses St Jacques, 75005 Paris France Office: Hopital Tenon, 4 rue de la Chine, 75020 Paris France

BILAL, ALI MUSTAFA, psychiatrist, educator; b. Omdurman, Khartoum, Sudan, Oct. 29, 1938; s. Mustafa and Amna (Suleiman) B.; m. Leila Salman Elaqib, Nov. 20, 1966; children: Limya, Luai, Alya, Shayma, Ahmed. MBBS, Khartoum U., 1964, Dip. Psycholog. Medicine. Intern Sudan Govt., Khartoum, 1964-65, med. officer, 1965-69, psychiat. registrar, 1969-70, jr. psychiatrist, 1972-73; clin. asst. Inst. Psychiatry Springfield Hosp., Maudsley Hosp., Eng., 1970-72; psychiatry Dept. Health and Social Security, Eng., 1973-75; asst. prof. U. Khartoum, 1975-76; cons. psychiatrist Ministry of Health, United Arab Emirates, 1976-82; asst. prof. psychiatry U. Kuwait, 1982—. Contbr. articles to profl. jours. Mem. Royal Coll. Physicians and Surgeons, Royal Coll. Psychiatrists, Soc. Study of Addiction to Alcohol and Other Drugs. Muslim. Home: Villa 6 ST15 Block 1, Sulaibikhat Jahra Kuwait Office: Kuwait U Faculty of Medicine, PO Box 24923, Safat 13110 Kuwait

BILES, DAVID, criminologist; b. Wembley, Eng., Dec. 18, 1932; s. Sidney John and Kathleen Georgina (Litera) B.; m. Julie Teresa Kelly, Jan. 22, 1955; children—Roselynne Jane, Amanda Louise. B.A., U. Melbourne, 1963. B.Ed., 1968; M.A., Latrobe U., 1971. Edn. officer, State Prisons Victoria, 1954-64; lectr. psychology Tchrs. Colls., Victoria, 1965-66; lectr. criminology U. Melbourne, 1967-72, sr. lectr., 1973; asst. dir. research Australian Inst. Criminology, Canberra, 1974-84, dep. dir., 1984-88; cons. criminologist, head research Royal commn. into Aboriginal deaths in custody, 1988— . Mem. criminal law and penal methods reform com. South Australia, 1971-75; mem. Sentencing Alternatives Com. Victoria, 1978-82; mem. Com. of Inquiry into Victoria Police, 1982-85. Editor: Crime in Papua New Guinea, 1976, Crime and Justice in Australia, 1977; contbr. articles to profl. jours. Fulbright sr. scholar, U. Calif., 1981; U. Calif. Irvine Regents lectr., 1985. Mem. Austalia and N.Z. Soc. Criminology (v.p., past pres.); Australian Crime Prevention Council (v.p. 1973-75), Australian Psychol. Soc., Am. Soc. Criminology. Club: Canberra. Avocation: Squash; reading; spear fishing. Home: 25 Kidston Crescent, Curtin ACT 2605, Australia Office: PO Box 28, ACT 2606 Woden Australia

BILITCH, MICHAEL, medical educator, physician; b. Belgrade, Yugoslavia, Feb. 8, 1932; came to U.S., 1949; s. Sasha Alexander and Oona Mary (Ball) B.; m. Mary Jo Ann Minges, June 19, 1956 (dec. 1966); children—Bonnie, Kimberly, David; m. Nancy Ann Neher, Sept. 3, 1967 (div. 1982); children—Kendal, Dawn, Robert, Susan, Douglas; m. Alexis Donath, June 19, 1983; 1 son, Eric. A.B., San Jose State Coll., 1954; M.A., Miami U., 1956; M.D., U. So. Calif., 1960. Teaching asst. San Jose State Coll., 1952-54; teaching asst. Miami U., Oxford, Ohio, 1954-56; research asst. U. So. Calif., Los Angeles, 1958-60, instr. medicine, 1964-67, asst. prof. medicine, 1967-71, assoc. prof., 1971—, dir., 1970—; vis. prof. U. Groningen, Netherlands, 1978; cons. Cardiac Pacemakers, St. Paul, 1978—. Author: A Manual of Cardiac Arrhythmias, 1971; co-author: Heart Block, 1972; contbr. articles to profl. jours; patentee leadless pacemaker. Los Angeles County Heart Assn. fellow, 1965-67. Fellow ACP, Am. Coll. Cardiology; mem. Assn. Advancement of Med. Instrumentation (chmn. pacemaker com. 1971-77), N.Am. Soc. Pacing and Electrophysiology (founding mem., exec. com.), Am. Fedn. Clin. Research, AAAS, N.Y. Acad. Scis., Royal Soc. Health. Home: 1420 San Pablo St Apt C-201 Los Angeles CA 90033 Office: U So Calif Sch Medicine 2025 Zonal Ave Los Angeles CA 90033

BILL, MAX, architect, sculptor, painter; b. Winterthur, Switzerland, Dec. 22, 1908; s. Erwin and Marie (Geiger) B.; student Zurich Sch. Art and Craft, 1924-27, Dessau Bauhaus, 1927-29; Dr. HC U. Stuttgart, 1979; m. Binia Spoerri, 1931. Pvt. practice architecture and graphic artist, Zurich, 1929—; publicist, Zurich, 1936; dir. Inst. for Design, Ulm, Germany, 1951-56; chief architect educating and creating sect. Swiss Nat. Exhbn., Lausanne, 1961-64; mem. Swiss Parliament, Berne, 1967-74; over 200 one-man shows include Albright-Knox Art Gallery, Buffalo, N.Y., 1974; represented in permanent collections Kunstmuseum, Basle, Kunstmuseum, Berne, Art Inst. Chgo., Hirshhorn Mus., Washington, Musee d'Art Moderne, Paris, Gallery Naz d'Arte Moderna, Rome, Kunsthaus, Zurich; prof. environ. design Inst. fine Arts, Hamburg, 1967-74. Mem. Zurich City Council, 1961-67. Recipient Grand Prix Triennale Milan, 1936, 51, Biennale Sao Paulo, 1951, 1st prize, City of Goslar, 1982, Kandinsky prize, 1949, Gold medal Italian Chamber of Deps., Verucchio, 1966, 1st prize Internat. Biennale of Small Sculpture, Budapest, 1971, Internat. Leonardo prize, 1987, Marconi prize, 1988; named Comdr. of the Ordre of Arts and Letters, France, 1985. Fellow AIA (hon.); mem. Acad. Arts (Berlin). Address: Albulastrasse 39 III, CH-8048 Zurich Switzerland

BILLÉ, JEAN-GEORGES, neurologist; b. Marseille, France, Nov. 12, 1931; s. Francois and Victoria (Guilerme) B.; m. Mathilde Gavalda, June 6, 1959; children: Jacques, Francoise, Dominique. Grad., Faculté de Medecine, Marseille. Interne Hopitaux de Marseille, 1958-63; chef de clinique Faculté de Medecine, Marseille, 1963—, dr. en medecine, 1963—, laureat, chargé de cours; médecine-chef du service de neurologie L'Hosp. St. Joseph, Marseille; organizer neurogeriatric and gerontopsychiatric congres. Editor: Le Cerveau du 3ème Age, 1976, Le Cerveau du 3è Age, 1979. Mem. Soc. Française de Neurologie, Internat. Psychogeriatric Assn. Roman Catholic. Home: Ave Talabot, 13007 Marseille France Office: 255 Ave du Prado, 13008 Marseille France

BILLERBECK, MARGARETHE, classicist, educator; b. Basel, Switzerland, Dec. 13, 1945; d. Wilhelm and Marie (Werdenberg) Billerbeck; m. Bruce Karl Braswell, Oct. 10, 1978. MA, Free U., Berlin, 1972; PhD, Free U., 1974, Oxford U., 1981. Lectr. Free U., Berlin, 1975-78; sr. lectr. Fribourg (Switzerland) U., 1978-87, prof., 1987—; Chmn. ancient studies Fribourg U., 1986. Cusanuswerk fellow, Bonn, Fed. Republic Germany, 1973-74, British Council fellow, Oxford, 1975-76. Mem. Swiss Classical Assn. (auditor 1986—), Classical Assn. Can., Roman Soc., Assn. Guillaume Budé. ROMAN CATHOLIC. Home: Rt Joseph Chaley 33, CH-1700 Fribourg Switzerland Office: U Fribourg, Rue Pierre Aeby 190, CH-1700 Fribourg Switzerland

BILLIGHEIMER, RACHEL VICTORIA, literature educator; b. Makassar, Dutch East Indies, Feb. 10, 1932; arrived in Can., 1961; d. Jonah and Regina (Minie) Gubbay; m. Claude Elias Billigheimer, Aug. 8, 1955. B.A., Queen's U., Kingston, Ont., Can., 1969; M.A., U. Guelph, Ont., Can., 1972; Ph.D., York U., Toronto, Ont., 1980; B.Ed., U. Toronto, 1982. Lectr. McMaster U., Hamilton, Ont., 1982—. Contbr. articles to profl. lit. Mem. Can. Assn. for Irish Studies, Internat. Assn. for Study Anglo-Irish Lit., MLA, N.E. Modern Lang. Assn., Soc. for Study Narrative Lit., Am. Com. for Irish Studies. Lodge: B'nai B'rith. Avocations: music; drama. Home: 103 Traymore Ave, Hamilton, ON Canada L8S 1R8 Office: McMaster U, 1280 Main St W, Hamilton, ON Canada L8S 4L9

BILLINGS, THOMAS NEAL, computer and publishing executive; b. Milw., Mar. 2, 1931; s. Neal and Gladys Victoria (Lockard) B.; A.B. with honors, Harvard U., 1952, M.B.A., 1954; m. Barta Hope Chipman, June 12, 1954 (div. 1967); children—Bridget Ann, Bruce Neal; m. Marie Louise Farrell, Mar. 27, 1982. Vice pres. fin. and adminstrn. Copley Newspapers Inc., La Jolla, Calif., 1957-70; group v.p. Harte-Hanks Communications Inc., San Antonio, 1970-73; exec. v.p. United Media, Inc., Phoenix, 1973-75; asst. to pres. Ramada Inns, Inc., Phoenix, 1975-76; exec. dir. Nat. Rifle Assn., Washington, 1976-77; pres. Ideation Inc., Washington, 1977-81; chmn. Bergen-Billings Inc., N.Y.C., 1977-80; pres. The Assn. Service Corp., San Francisco, 1978—; pres. Recorder Printing and Pub. Co. Inc., San Francisco, 1980-82; v.p. adminstrn. Victor Techs. Inc., Scotts Valley, Calif., 1982-84; mng. dir. Saga-Wilcox Computers Ltd., Wrexham, Wales, 1984-85; chief exec. officer Oberon Internat. Ltd., 1985-86; dir., chief exec. officer Insignia Solutions group, High Wycombe, England, Cupertino, Calif., 1986—; guest lectr. in field. Bd. dirs. Nat. Allergy Found., 1973—, The Wilderness Fund, 1978—, San Diego Civic Light Opera Assn., 1965-69; chief exec. San Diego 200th Anniversary Expn., 1969. Served with U.S. Army, 1955-57. Recipient Walter F. Carley Meml. award, 1966, 69. Fellow U.K. Inst. Dirs.; mem. Am. Newspaper Pubs. Assn., Nat. Assn. Accts., Inst. Internal Auditors, Inst. Newspaper Controllers, Am. Assn. V.P.s (dir.), Sigma Delta Chi. Republican. Clubs: West Side Tennis, LaJolla Country; Washington Athletic; San Francisco Press; Harvard (N.Y.C.); Elks. Author: Creative Controllership, 1978; editor The Vice Presidents' Letter, 1978—; pub. The Microcomputer Letter, 1982—. Office: 1255 Post St Suite 625 San Francisco CA 94109 Other: 500 Chesham House, 150 Regent St, London W1R 5FA, England

BILLMAN, IRWIN EDWARD, publishing company executive; b. Manhattan, N.Y., July 7, 1940; s. Herman Frank and Ruth (Dutchen) B. B.S. in Econs, Wharton Sch., U. Pa., 1962. Asst. controller Whelan Drug Co., 1965-66; v.p., treas. Curtis Circulation Co., Phila., 1966-71; exec. v.p., chief operating officer Penthouse, Omni and Forum mags., 1971-81; pres., publisher Oui Mag., N.Y.C., 1981-82; pres. Billman Media Group; ptnr. Mag. Communications Cons. Mem. Periodical and Book Assn. Am. (pres. 1977-81). Clubs: Friars, A.C.E.S. Home: PO Box 350 Westhampton NY 11977 Office: 136 E 55th St New York NY 10022

BILLSON, EDWARD FIELDER, III, architect; b. Melbourne, Australia, May 28, 1960; s. Edward Fielder Jr. and Margaret Jessie (McPherson) B. BArch, U. Melbourne, 1982. Registered architect, Victoria, Australia. Architect Billson Sawley Architects, Adelaide, Australia, 1983, Otis Elevator Co., Montvale, N.J., 1983, Goldberg, O'Connor Architects, N.Y.C., 1984, John Burgee Architects, N.Y.C., 1984-85; prin. Edward F. Billson & Assocs., Melbourne, 1986—; bd. dirs. Kemple Investments P/L, Melbourne. Mem. Royal Australian Inst. Architects, AIA (assoc.). Clubs: Melbourne, Melbourne Cricket, Moonee Valley Racing. Office: 106 Jolimont Rd, Melbourne 3002, Australia

BILSKI, PETER, music publishing company executive; b. Archbald, Pa., Jan. 9, 1918; s. Michael and Mary (Shereda) B.; student Villanova Coll., 1939-40, Akron U., 1943-44, CCNY, 1960; m. Oct. 10, 1942; children—Peter, Andrew, Christopher, Victoria. Owner, Re-Nu Bowling Pin Co., Ozone Park, N.Y., 1947-60, B & M Wood Co., Ozone Park, 1949-51; prop. Anton Hotel, Salisbury Mills, N.Y., 1951-52; ptnr. Festive Music Pub. Co., N.Y.C., 1975—; v.p. Final Vinyl Record Co., 1982—, Stampede Record Co., 1983—, Loose Tongue Pub. Co., 1983—. Co-chmn. Rockland Pub. Edn. and Religious Liberty, dir. exec. com. N.Y. State chpt. Served with USAAF, WW II. Decorated Air medal with oak leaf cluster. Mem. Internat. Platform Assn. Home: 126 Cara Dr Pearl River NY 10965

BILSKY, EARL, textile/apparel company executive; b. Fall River, Mass., Sept. 26, 1928; s. David and Rose (Nulman) B.; B.S., S.E. Mass. U., 1952; M.S. (research fellow), Inst. of Textile Tech., 1954; m. Betty Ann Funk, Dec. 5, 1954; children—Edward Scott, Karen Lee, Matthew Kolman. Engr. specialist Goodyear Aerospace Corp., Akron, Ohio, 1960-62; merchandise mgr. apparel and indsl. Am. Cyanamid Co., N.Y.C. and Wayne, N.J., 1962-71; exec. v.p. Aileen, Inc., N.Y.C. and Abilene, Tex., 1971-76, also dir.; pres. Eagle Knitting Mills, Milw., 1976—. Bd. dirs. United Way, Abilene, 1975-76, YMCA, Abilene, 1973-76, Abilene Art Mus., 1974-75, Milw. Council on Drug Abuse, 1981-83. planning/zoning commr. City of Abilene, 1975-76. Served with USMC, 1946-48. Patentee in field. Office: Eagle Knitting Mills 507 13 S 2d St Milwaukee WI 53204

BILTIS, MARVIN, food retailing executive; b. Montreal, Que., Can., Nov. 11, 1941; s. Charles Arthur and Ida (Segal) B.; m. Pamela Treves, June 25, 1963; children: Gary, Linda, Lorne. B in Commerce, Concordia U., Montreal, 1967; postgrad., Harvard U., 1982. Market research analyst Steinberg, Inc., Montreal, 1960-64, buyer, 1964-68, sales mgr., 1968-72, sales dir., 1972-77, v.p. mktg., 1977-80, v.p., gen. mgr., 1980-84, corp. v.p., gen. mgr., 1984-88; pres. farmer jack supermarket div. Berman, Inc., 1988—. Mem. Harvard Bus. Sch. Alumni. Lodge: B'nai Brith (exec. com. 1975—, bd. dirs. 1978-83). Home: 8030 Guelph Ave, Cote Saint Luc, PQ Canada H4W 1H8 Office: Steinberg Inc, 3500 De Maisonneuve W, Westmount, PQ Canada H32 143

BILYI, MIKHAIL ULIANOVICH, physicist, university administrator; b. Moskali, Chernigov Oblast, USSR, 1922. Grad. Kiev State U., 1948. Tchr., lectr., chmn. exptl. physics Kiev State U., 1951—, dean faculty, 1962—, prof. physics and math., rector, 1970—. Mem. Supr. Soviet Ukranian SSR, 1971—, dep. chmn., 1971-72, chmn., 1972-80. Mem. USSR-Can. Soc. (chmn. Ukranian br. 1971—), Ukranian Acad. Scis. Address: Kiev T G Shevchenko State U, Vladimirskaya 64, Kiev 252071 Ukraine, USSR *

BINA, GIAN CARLO, fashion design executive; b. T. Monate, Italy, Dec. 8, 1935; s. Aldo and Ernestina (Lenta) B.; m. Emma M. Cavazzoni, Aug. 28, 1965; children: Michele A., Olivia C. Student, mktg. and lang. courses; PMD, Harvard U., 1972. Export employee SNIA Viscosa Spa, Milan, 1965-66; export mgr. Anic Spa, Milan, 1965-66, Sai Spa, Saronno, Italy, 1967-70; div. mgr. Basseti Group, Milan, 1971-76; gen. mgr. Inco SpA-E. Zegnagr, Novara, Italy, 1977-80, Stima SpA-E. Zegnagr, Trivero, Italy, 1981-85; mgr. Andre Spa, Milan, 1986—; pres., chief exec. officer Claudio La Viola Spa, Milan, 1986—. Home: Via dei Rospigliosi 3, 20151 Milan Italy Office: Claudio La Viola Spa, Via S Pietro All'Orto 5, 20122 Milan Italy

BINBASGIL, SEDA, feminine hygiene product company executive; b. Istanbul, Turkey, Sept. 12, 1959; d. Nashih and Esin (Erman) Tumay; m. Hakan Binbasgil, Aug. 17, 1983. BS in Mktg., Bosphorus U., 1983; MBA, La. State U., 1985. Trainee life ins. dept. Basler, Frankfurt, Fed. Republic Germany, 1981, 82; asst. quantitative bus. analysis dept. La. State U., Baton Rouge, 1984-85, instr. mktg., 1985-86; product mgr. Tambrands, Inc., Istanbul, 1986—. Mem. Turkish Diabetic Assn. Club: Florya Country (Istanbul). Home: Tuatpasa sok Yogurtcubasi, cikmazi 4/13 Fenerbahce-Dalyan, Istanbul 813030, Turkey Office: Sanipak Tambrands Inc, Buyukdere cad 193/3, Istanbul Levent Turkey

BINDER, DAVID FRANKLIN, lawyer, author; b. Beaver Falls, Pa., Aug. 1, 1935; s. Walter Carl and Jessie Maivis (Bliss) B.; m. Deana Jacqueline Pines, Dec. 25, 1971; children—April, Bret. B.A., Geneva Coll., 1956; J.D., Harvard U., 1959. Bar: Pa. 1960, U.S. Ct. Appeals (3d cir.) 1963, U.S. Supreme Ct. 1967. Law clk. to chief justice Pa. Supreme Ct., 1959-61; counsel Fidelity Mut. Life Ins. Co., Phila., 1964-66; ptnr. Bennett, Bricklin & Saltzburg, Phila., 1967-68; mem. Richter, Syken, Ross, and Binder, Phila., 1969-72, Raynes, McCarty, Binder, Ross and Mundy, Phila., 1972—; mem. faculty Pa. Coll. Judiciary; lectr., course planner Pa. Bar Inst. Recipient Disting. Alumnus award Geneva Coll., 1981. Mem. ABA, Pa. Bar Assn., Phila. Bar Assn., Assn. Trial Lawyers Am. (lectr.), Pa. Trial Lawyers Assn. (lectr.), Phila. Trial Lawyers Assn., Harvard Law Sch. Assn. Clubs: Peale, Union League. Author: Hearsay Handbook, 1975, ann. supplements, 2d edit., 1983. Office: 1845 Walnut St Suite 2000 Philadelphia PA 19103

BINDER, JAMES KAUFFMAN, computing consultant; b. Reading, Pa., Nov. 20, 1920; s. Paul Burdette and Edna (Kauffman) B.; B.A., Lehigh U., 1941; M.A., Johns Hopkins U., 1952; profl. cert. in systems mgmt. U. Calif.-San Diego, 1976; A.S. in Data Processing, San Diego Evening Coll., 1979, A.A. in Fgn. Lang., 1979; A.A. in Spanish, Mira Costa Coll., Oceanside, Calif., 1981. Instr. English, Notre Dame U., South Bend, Ind., 1948-49; prof. English, Athens (Greece) Coll., 1950-51; CARE rep., Greece, 1951-52; reporter, staff writer Athens News, 1952-53; dir. lang. tng. World Council Chs. Refugee Service, Athens, 1953-54; co-editor Am. Overseas Guide, N.Y., West Berlin, 1957-58; lectr. English, U. Md. Overseas Program, European and Far East divs., 1958-66; successively supr. Cen. Info. Ctr., supt. documents, sr. systems analyst GA Techs., Inc., La Jolla, Calif., 1968-85. Recipient Williams Prize, Lehigh U., 1939, 41; Johns Hopkins U. Grad. Sch. Pres. scholar, 1945-48. Mem. San Diego Opera Assn., Friends of U. Calif.-San Diego Library, IEEE Computer Soc., Assn. Computing Machinery. Roman Catholic. Clubs: Tudor and Stuart, Automobile of So. Calif. Author: The Correct Comedy, 1951; contbg. translator Modern Scandinavian Poetry, 1948; editor: (with Erwin H. Tiebe) American Overseas Guide, 1958.

BINDER, LEO OTTO, chemistry educator; b. Linz, Austria, July 13, 1946; s. Leopold Florian and Anna (Hamberger) B.; m. Helga Zeipelt, Feb. 12, 1983; Claudia, Veronika. PhD, Tech. U., Graz, 1971-86. Cert. chem. engring. Univ. asst. Tech. U., Graz, 1971-86, asst. prof., 1986—. Contbr. articles to profl. jours. Roman Catholic. Office: Tech U, Stremayrgasse 16, A-8010 Graz Austria

BINDER, LEONARD JAMES, magazine editor; b. Jackson, Mich., June 21, 1926; s. Leonard George and Ethel Cecile (Lilly) B.; m. Margery Elizabeth Rose, Sept. 6, 1950; children: Timothy James, Michael Paul, Douglas Harold. B.S., Central Mich. U., 1952. Editor Wingfoot Clan, Goodyear Tire & Rubber Co., 1952-54, Wayne (Mich.) Eagle, 1954-55; news editor Pontiac (Mich.) Press, 1955-57; editor, newsman AP, 1957-60; state editor Detroit News, 1960-67; editor-in-chief Army mag., Washington, 1967—; corr., book reviewer Nat. Observer, 1962-67; Bd. dirs. Central Mich. U. Devel. Fund. Contbr. articles to various publs. Served with USNR, 1944-46; with USAR, 1950-54. Recipient George Washington Honor medal Freedoms Found., 1975, George Washington award editorial, 1974, 76. Mem. Am. Soc. Mag. Editors, Assn. U.S. Army., Sigma Delta Phi. Methodist. Clubs: Cosmos, Nat. Press, Detroit Press, Ends of Earth. Home: 304 Lewis St Vienna VA 22180 Office: Army Magazine 2425 Wilson Blvd Arlington VA 22201-3385

BINDER, WOLFGANG, humanities educator; b. Esslingen, Fed. Republic Germany, July 3, 1941. Student, U. Tübingen, Fed. Republic Germany, 1961-67; PhD, U. Erlangen, Fed. Republic Germany, 1973; postgrad., various univs., Mex., U.S., France, Spain. Faculty U. Erlangen, 1976—; prof. humanities Inst. for English and Am. Studies, Erlangen, 1973. Reviewer books Nurnberger Zeitung, 1975—; author: Europäisches Drama, 1974; editor Anglos Are Weird People..., 1979, America is My Country Too, 1983, Entwicklungen im karibischen Raum, 1985, Contemporary Chicano Poetry, 1986, Westward Expansion in America, 1987. Organizer art exhibits cultural office City of Erlangen, 1975—. Research fellow Am. Council Learned Socs., N.Y.C., 1978-79; research grantee John F. Kennedy Inst., Free U. Berlin, 1980, 86. Mem. German Assn. for Am. Studies, European Assn. for Am. Studies, Caribbean Studies Assn., German Assn. Hispanists, Nat. Assn. Interdisciplinary Ethnic Studies, Soc. for Study Multi-Ethnic Lit. of U.S. Office: Inst Anglistik und Amerikanistic, U Erlangen Bismarckst 1 C, 8520 Erlangen Federal Republic of Germany

BINDSEIL, REINHART WERNER MARTIN, diplomat; b. Liegnitz, Sept. 19, 1935; m. Baerbel Denzin, Apr. 30, 1966; 2 children. LLB, Heidelberg (Fed. Republic Germany) U., 1958, LLD, 1965; postgrad., Lucknow U., India, 1959; LLM, Singapore U., 1962. With Fgn. Service, Fed. Republic Germany, 1966; consulate gen. Madras, India, 1967-71, German Embassy, Tokyo, 1971-74, Fgn. Office, Bonn, Fed. Republic Germany, 1974-77, 80-84; ambassador Bangui, Central African Republic, 1977-80, Rwanda, 1984-88. Office: Embassy Fed Republic Germany, 8 rue de Bugarama, Kigali BP 355, Rwanda

BINFIELD, JOHN CLYDE, historian, educator; b. Fulmer Chase, Buckingham, Eng., Dec. 5, 1940; s. Edward John and Margaret Florence (Goodfellow) B.; m. Noreen Helen Maycock, June 18, 1969; children: Emma Victoria, Anna Alexandra. BA, Emmanuel Coll., Cambridge, Eng., 1961, MA, PhD, 1965. Asst. lectr. U. Sheffield, Eng., 1964-67, lectr., 1967-74, sr. lectr., 1974-84, reader, 1984—, dept. head, 1988—. Author: George Williams and YMCA, 1973, So Down to Prayers, 1977, Pastors and People, 1984; editor Jour. United Reformed Ch. History Soc., 1976—. Vice chmn. Nat. Council YMCA's, London, 1982—; mem. Exec. World Alliance YMCA's, Geneva, 1985—; chmn. bd. govs. Silcoates Sch., Wakefield, Eng., 1983—. Fellow Royal Hist. Soc., Soc. Antiquaries. Mem. Social and Liberal Democrats. Club: Royal Overseas League (London). Office: U Sheffield, Dept History, Western Bank, Sheffield S10 2TN, England

BINGAMAN, JEFF, senator; b. Silver City, N.Mex., Oct. 3, 1943; s. Jesse and Beth (Ball) B.; m. Anne Kovacovich, Sept. 13, 1968. Ed., Harvard U., 1965; J.D., Stanford U., 1968. Bar: N.Mex. 1968. Partner firm Campbell, Bingaman & Black, Santa Fe, 1972-78; atty. gen. State of N.Mex., from 1979; now U.S. senator from N.Mex. Democrat. Methodist. Home: PO Box 5775 Santa Fe NM 87501 Office: 502 Hart Senate Bldg Washington DC 20510

BINGEMAN, JOHN MERVYN, retired military officer, nautical archaeologist; b. London, Dec. 27, 1933; s. Alfred Mervyn and Grace Marjorie (Lanchester) B.; m. Jean Heather Sturgess (div. Mar. 1982); children: Michael John, Robin Mervyn; m. Jane Elizabeth Lucas Evans, June 1, 1982. Grad., Royal Naval Coll., Dartmouth, Eng., 1951, Royal Naval Engring. Coll., Plymouth, Eng., 1957. Chartered engr., Eng. Commd. ensign British Royal Navy, 1951; sr. engr. H.M.S. Daring, 1960-61; tech. officer Ghana Navy Base, Takoradi, 1966-67; tradesmaster Royal Naval Dockyard, Chatham, Eng., 1968-69; gen. mgr. Nigerian Naval Dockyard, Lagos, 1970-71; chief engr. H.M.S. Exmouth, 1972-73, H.M.S. Fearless-Intrepid, 1975-77; project mgr. Royal Naval Dockyard, Portsmouth, Eng., 78-80; staff officer Ministry of Def. Navy, London, 1981-84; ret. British Royal Navy, 1986; diving dir. historic British shipwreck sites, 1986—; lectr. on nautical archaeology; contbr. articles to profl. jours. Mem. Inst. Mech. Engrs., Council Nautical Archaeology (hon. sec. 1982-83), Nautical Archaeology Soc. (hon. sec. 1983-86). Home: 5 Rumbolds Close, Chichester PO19 2JJ, England

BINGER, WILSON VALENTINE, civil engineer; b. Greenwich, N.Y., Feb. 28, 1917; s. George and Blanche (Wilson) B.; m. Barbara Ridgway, May 19, 1947 (dec. 1984); children—Wilson Valentine, Mary Blanche, Julia Ridgway; m. Jane E. Schwarz, Apr. 24, 1986. A.B. cum laude, Harvard, 1938, M.S. in Engring, 1939. Registered profl. engr., N.Y., Ohio. Soils engr. U.S. Army Engrs., Wilmington, Del., 1939-40; soils and found. engr. Gatun 3d Locks project, Panama Canal, 1940-43; soils engr., resident engr. Parsons Brinckerhoff, Hogan & MacDonald, Caracas, Venezuela, 1945-46; chief soils engr. Parsons Brinckerhoff, Hogan & MacDonald, Caracas, Buenos Aires, Argentina, 1948-49; chief soils and found. sect. Isthmian Canal Studies, Panama Canal, 1946-47; chief soils br. Mo. River div. U.S. Army Engrs., Omaha, 1947-48; v.p. Porterfield-Binger Constrn. Co., Youngstown, Ohio, 1950-52; regional mgr. Tippetts-Abbett-McCarthy-Stratton, Bogota, Colombia, 1952-56; assoc. partner Tippetts-Abbett-McCarthy-Stratton, N.Y.C., 1957-61, partner, 1962-84; chmn. Tippetts-Abbett-McCarthy-Stratton, 1975-84, cons., 1985—. Author papers in field. Pres., trustee Chappaqua (N.Y.) Library, 1967-69; trustee Robert Coll., Istanbul, Turkey, 1970—, vice chmn., 1974-78; bd. dirs. Regional Plan Assn., N.Y., 1983-88. Served to 2d lt. C.E. AUS, 1943-45. Recipient Disting. Citizen award Warren (Ohio) Met. Area Assn., Steinmetz award Consulting Engr. Mag. Fellow ASCE, Inst. Civil Engrs. (Eng.), Am. Cons. Engrs. Council (v.p. 1973-75); mem. Nat. Acad. Engring., Fellowship of Engring. U.K. (fgn. mem.), Am. Inst. Cons. Engrs. (councillor 1971-73, pres. 1973), Nat. Soc. Profl. Engrs., Harvard Engring. Soc., U.S. Com. Large Dams (exec. com. 1964-69, sec. 1962-78), Internat. Com. Large Dams (v.p. 1978-81), N.Y. Assn. Cons. Engrs. (v.p., dir. 1964-65), Moles, Internat. Road Fedn. (dir. 1975-82, exec. com. 1975-82), Fedn. Internationale des Ingenieurs Conseils (exec. com. 1976-83, treas. 1976-79, v.p. 1980-81, pres. 1981-83), Am. Arbitration Assn., N.Y. Acad. of Sci. Congregationalist (chmn. bd. deacons 1960-65, trustee 1985-88). Clubs: Century (N.Y.C.), Harvard (N.Y.C.), Univ. (N.Y.C.); St. Stephen's (London). Home: PO Box 225 Chappaqua NY 10514 Office: 655 3d Ave New York NY 10017

BIN HASSAN, ABDULAZIZ AHMAD, automobile agency executive; b. Almajmaah, Saudi Arabia, Mar. 31, 1933; s. Ahmed Mohammad and Munirah (Ahmed) Bin H.; m. Hussah Abdulaziz Alyahya, Dec. 25, 1964; children: Mohammed, Ahmed, Manal, Ziad. Student, Egyptian Mil. Acad., Cairo, 1953-54, Command and Gen. Staff Coll., Ft. Leavenworth, Kans., 1966-67, Beiruth Arab U., 1969. Cert. in law. Commd. 2d lt. Arabian Army, 1954, advanced through ranks to Col., 1970, served in planning and ops., units commdg., mil. attache in Spain, ret., 1970; self-employed in bus. Riyadh, Saudi Arabia, 1970-75; exec. v.p. Arabian Auto Agy., Jeddah, 1975. Office: Arabian Auto Agy, PO Box 2223, Jeddah 21451, Saudi Arabia

BINNIE, MYRNA LORRAINE, medical technologist, microbiologist; b. Cheyenne, Wyo., Sept. 18, 1941; d. John William and Estella Christina (Stewart) Hart; B.S. with honors in Med. Tech., U. Wyo., 1964; M.S. in Microbiology, Ariz. State U., 1972; m. Ronald C. Bugh, Dec. 29, 1964 (div. Aug., 1972); 1 son, Robert Hart; m. 2d, Thomas G. Binnie, Apr. 18, 1980. Med. technologist Laramie County Meml. Hosp., Cheyenne, 1964; med. technologist Mesa (Ariz.) Luth. Hosp., 1965-73, supr. bacteriology dept., 1973-76, co-ordinator microbiology, 1976-81, lab. coordinator, 1981—; instr. microbiology Maricopa Tech. Coll., 1980. Mem. Am. Soc. Microbiology, Am. Soc. Clin. Pathologists (registered mem.), DAR, Sigma Xi, Sigma Pi Sigma, Beta Beta Beta. Republican. Club: Samoyed Am. Home: 617 N Ash St Mesa AZ 85201 Office: 525 W Brown Rd Mesa AZ 85201

BINNIG, GERD KARL, physicist, educator; b. July 20, 1947; m. Lore Binnig, 1969; 2 children. Dip. in Phys., Goethe U., Frankfurt, Fed. Republic Germany, PhD. Research staff mem. IBM Zurich Research lab., 1978—, group leader, 1984—; group leader IBM Almaden Research Ctr.,

San José, 1985-86; prof. Physics U. Munich, 1987—; vis. prof. Stanford U., 1986. Co-recipient Nobel prize in Physics, 1986; recipient Physics prize, German Phys. Soc., 1982, Otto Klung prize, 1983, Joint King Faisal Internat. prize for Sci. and Hewlett-Packard Europhysics prize, 1984, Elliot Cresson medal, Franklin Inst., Phila., 1987, Grosses Verdienstkreuz mit Stern und Schulterband des Verdienstordens, 1987. Office: IBM Research Physics Group, Sektion Physik der Universitat, Schellingstrasse 4, 8000 Munich 40 Federal Republic of Germany *

BINNING, BETTE FINESE (MRS. GENE HEDGCOCK BINNING), athletic association official; b. Brandon, Man., Can., Sept. 20, 1927 (father Am. citizen); d. Henry Josiah and Beatrice Victoria (Harrop) Ames; grad. Brandon Collegiate, 1944; student Brandon, U., 1944-46; m. Gene Hedgcock Binning, May 3, 1952; children—Gene Barton, Barbara Jo, Bradford Jay. Exec. sec. to mgr. Gardner-Denver Co., Denver, 1950-52; mem. age group swimming com. Amateur Athletic Union U.S., 1966-68, 70-72, women's swimming com., 1968-69, 72—, age group swimming objectives subcom., 1970-71, del. conv., 1971, 72, 73, 74, 75, 76, 77, 79, 80; Okla. state chmn. age group swimming Amateur Athletic Union, 1966-68, 70-72, chmn. women's swimming com., 1968-69, 72-79, mem. Okla. exec. bd. for all amateur sports, also registration com., 1971-79; mem. U.S. Olympic com., 1972-80; nat. dir. swimming records, 1972-81; U.S. rep. to records com. Amateur Swimming Assn. Ams., 1975-83, dir. records com., 1975-83; dir., sec. records com. Union Amateur de Natacion de las Americas, 1979-83; tech. ofcl. Pan Am. Games, Mexico City, 1975, San Juan, P.R., 1979; ofcl. XXI Olympiad, Montreal, Que., Can., 1976; mem. interim organizing com. U.S. Olympic Festival, 1986; athletic adv. dir. U.S. Olympic Festival '89, 1987-88. Team capt. YMCA fund drives, 1966-78; active Community Chest, Cancer, Muscular Dystrophy fund drives, Okla. Horse Shows. Mem. Kiwanis Ladies, Youth Study Club (treas. 1971-72). Presbyn. Clubs: Kerr-Mcgee Swim (dir. 1968-75), Quail Creek Golf and Country, Oklahoma City Ski (Oklahoma City); La Quinta Golf (Calif.); Vail Athletic (Colo.). Home: 3101 Rolling Stone Rd Oklahoma City OK 73120

BINNS, WALTER GORDON, JR., automobile manufacturing company executive; b. Richmond, Va., June 8, 1929; s. Walter Gordon and Virginia Belle (Matheny) B.; A.B., Coll. William and Mary, 1949; A.M., Harvard U., 1951; M.B.A., N.Y. U., 1959; m. Alberta Louise Fry, Apr. 1, 1972; 1 dau., Amanda; 1 stepdau., Clarissa. Trainee, Chase Nat. Bank, N.Y.C., 1953-54; with Gen. Motors Corp., N.Y.C., 1954—, asst. treas., 1974-82, chief investment funds officer, 1982—, v.p. 1986—; bd. dirs. Gen. Motors Acceptance Corp., Motors Ins. Corp., Futures Industry Assn.; investment adv. com. N.Y. State Common Retirement Fund; mem. pension mgrs. adv. com. N.Y. Stock Exchange. Trustee ARC Retirement System, Citizens Budget Commn., N.Y.C., Joint Council Econ. Edn., Fin. Execs. Research Found.; bd. dirs. Alcoholism Council Greater N.Y., Community Fund of Bronxville, Eastchester Tuckahoe, Inc. Served with U.S. Army, 1951-53. Mem. Futures Industry Assn. (bd. dirs. 1987—), Fin. Execs. Inst. (chmn. com. on employee benefits 1977-80, com. on investment of employee benefit assets, 1985—), Am. Pension Conf., Economic Club of N.Y., Phi Beta Kappa, Beta Gamma Sigma. Clubs: Bronxville (N.Y.) Field; Harvard (N.Y.C.); Recess (Detroit). Home: 21 Crows Nest Rd Bronxville NY 10708 Office: 767 Fifth Ave New York NY 10153 also: Gen Motors Corp Gen Motors Bldg Detroit MI 48202

BINSWANGER, CLAUS PAUL, logistics consultant; b. Berne, Switzerland, Nov. 15, 1934; s. Paul Edward and Maria (Huber) B.; m. Elsbeth Steiner, Aug. 22, 1941; children: Benedikt, Simone. Licentiate, Hochschule, St. Gallen, Switzerland, 1958. Logistics engr. Galactina, Belp, Switzerland, 1960-63; project mgr. logistics Nestle Co., Montreux, Switzerland, 1964-65; mgr. Elcon, Zug, Switzerland, 1966-68; exec. v.p. Omega, Biel, Switzerland, 1969, 76; chief exec. officer Hibetag, Zug, 1970-75, Greiner, Langenthal, Switzerland, 1977-83; pvt. practice cons. Zug, 1984-87; pres. EGBE, Zug, 1971—, Marolo, Zug, 1983—; cons. MBB, Toyota, Flachg, Fed. Republic Germany, 1983—; v.p. Datormark, Zug, 1975—. Author: Packing in Food Industry, 1956. Served to 1st lt. Swiss inf. Res., 1958—. Home: Aberenterrasse 1, CH-6340 Baar (Zug) Switzerland Office: Datormark Terrassenweg 1 c, CH-6300 Zug Switzerland

BIOBAKU, SABURI OLADENI, historian, educator; b. June 16, 1918. m. Muhabat Folasade Agusto, 1949; 4 sons. Ed. Govt. Coll., Ibadan, Higher Coll., Yaba, Nigeria, Univ. Coll. Exeter, Trinity Coll., Cambridge U.; Ph.D., Inst. Hist. Research, London. Master, Govt. Coll., Ibadan, 1941-44, ednl. officer, 1947-50; asst. liaison officer for Nigerian students in U.K., Colonial Office, London 1951-53; registrar Univ. Coll., Ibadan, 1953-57; sec. to premier Exec. Council, West Nigeria, 1957-61; pro-vice chancellor U. Ife, 1961-65, dir. insts. African Studies and Pub. Adminstrn., 1961-65; vice chancellor designate U. Zambia, 1965; vice-chancellor U. Lagos, 1965-72, prof., dir. African studies, 1965; research prof., dir. Inst. African studies, U. Ibadan, 1976-83; chair Mgmt. Cons. Services Ltd., 1972—; chair Com. Vice-Chancellors, Nigeria, 1967-70; mem. standing com. Ency. Africana, 1968—; creator: Balogun of Iddo, 1981; Agbaakin of Igbore, Abeokuta, 1972, Baapitan Egba, 1981. Author: The Origin of the Yoruba, 1955; The Egba and Their Neighbours, 1957; African Studies in an African University, 1963; Sources of Yoruba History, 1972; Living Cultures of Nigeria, 1977. Named Chief Maye of Ife, Chief Baapitan of Egbaland. Fellow Nigerian Inst. of Man, Hist. Soc. Nigeria (pres. 1968-71), West African Assn. Surgeons (hon.); mem. Assn. African Univs. (exec. bd. 1967-72). Address: PO Box 47741, Lagos Nigeria

BIOKO, CRISTINO SERICHE, prime minister of Equatorial Guinea, army officer. Second v.p., Minister of Health, Equatorial Guinea, 1981-82, Prime Minister, 1982—, Minister of Govt. Coordination, Planning, Econ. Devel. and Fin., 1982-86. Address: Oficina del Primer Ministro, Malabo Equatorial Guinea *

BIÖRCK, GUNNAR CARL WILHELM, physician; b. Gothenburg, Sweden, Apr. 4, 1916; s. Wilhelm K. A. and Louise (Petterson) B.; med. licentiate Karolinska Inst., Stockholm, 1942, M.D., 1949; M.D. honoris causa, U. Helsinki, 1981; m. Margareta Lundberg, May 26, 1944; children—Eva, Anders, Lena, Hans, Marie. Asst. prof. cardiology Karolinska Inst., 1949, prof. medicine, 1958-82, emeritus, 1982—; asst. prof. internal medicine U. Lund (Sweden), 1950-58; head dept. medicine Serafimer Hosp., Stockholm, 1958-80, physician in chief, 1961-77; sr. physician Karolinska Hosp., 1980-81; physician to Royal Family, 1965-85, 1st physician to King Gustaf VI Adolf of Sweden, 1968-73, to Crown Prince Carl Gustaf of Sweden, 1970-73, to King Carl XVI Gustaf, 1973-85, to Queen Silvia and Princess Lilian, 1976-85, to Prince Bertil, 1984-85; mem. Parliament, 1976-87; sci. adviser Royal Med. Bd., 1960-81, Mil. Med. Bd., 1960-86; mem. WHO Expert Adv. Panel, 1960-86; chmn. Nobel Assembly, Karolinska Inst., 1981. Decorated grand cross Royal Order of Polar Star, 1973; King's Gold medal, 1981; knight comdr. Iranian Houmayon Order, 1965; gt. officer Order of Falcon (Iceland); grand cross Order of Merit (Germany); grand cross Order of Lion of Finland; Knight comdr. Royal Victoria Order; gt. officer Order of Yugoslav Flag; gt. officer Order of Civil Merit (Spain); gt. officer Nat. Order of Merit (France); gt. officer of Dannebrogen (Denmark). Fellow Royal Coll. Physicians, London; hon. fellow ACP; mem. Am. Acad. Arts and Scis. (hon. fgn.); hon. mem. Swedish Soc. Cardiology, Swedish Soc. Internal Medicine, Swedish Soc. Clin. Pharmacology. Author: Our People and Its Future, 1940; Myoglobin in Man, 1949; If Your Heart Troubles You, 1953; Medicine for Politicians, 1953; Man's Possibilities, 1956; Conditions of Medical Care, 1966; Soul and Heart, 1967; Record 67, 1967; The Physician in Modern Society, 1968; At the Other Side of the Corridor, 1970; Honestly Said, 1972; To the Defense of the Serafimer Hospital, 1974; Unity and Diversity, 1974; With Stethoscope and Sword, 1974; speeches at closing of the Serafimer Hosp., 1980, 10 yrs. speeches in Parliament, 1986; research, numerous publs. on biochemistry, physiology, clin. manifestations, epidemiology and rehab. of heart disease. Home: Vaestra Ekedal, Gustavsberg Sweden

BIRCH, GRACE MORGAN, library administrator, educator; b. N.Y.C., June 3, 1925; d. Milton Melville and Adeline Ellsdale (Springer) Morgan; m. Kenneth Francis Birch, Oct. 26, 1947; children—Shari R., Timothy F. B.A., U. Bridgeport, 1963; M.L.S., Pratt Inst., 1968. With Bridgeport Pub. Library, Conn., 1949-66; asst. town librarian Fairfield Pub. Library, Conn., 1966-69; dir. Trumbull Library System, Conn., 1969—; lectr. Housatonic Community Coll., Bridgeport, 1970—. Judge, Barnum Festival Soc. Bridgeport, 1971-73. Mem. ALA, New Eng. Library Assn., Conn. Library Assn. (pres. 1972), Southwestern Conn. Library Council (pres. 1975-77), Fairfield Library Adminstrs. Group (pres. 1976-77), Nat. Assn. Female Execs. Democrat. Episcopalian. Avocations: sketching; dancing; traveling. Home: 175 Brooklawn Ave Bridgeport CT 06604 Office: The Trumbull Library 33 Quality St Trumbull CT 06611

BIRCH, LOUIS CHARLES, biology educator; b. Melbourne, Victoria, Australia, Feb. 8, 1918; s. Harry Milton and Honoria Eleanor (Hogan) B. B of Agrl. Sci., U. Melbourne, 1939; DSc, U. Adelaide, 1948. Research officer Waite Agrl. Research Inst., Adelaide, 1939-45; research fellow U. Chgo., 1946, Bur. Animal Population, Oxford, Eng., 1947; sr. lectr. biology U. Sydney, 1948-54, reader, 1954-60, Challis prof. biology, 1960-83, emeritus prof., 1984—; vis. prof. biology U. Sao Paulo, Brazil, 1955. Author: Nature and God, 1965, Confronting The Future, 1976, (with others) The Distribution and Abundance of Animals, 1954, The Liberation of Life, 1981, The Ecological Web, 1984. Vice-moderator dept. ch. and soc. World Council Chs., Geneva, 1970—. Fellow AAAS, Australian Acad. Sci.; Brit. Ecol. Soc. (hon. life mem.), Indian Acad. Environ. Biology (v.p. 1980—), Club of Rome, Biol. Soc. Am. (hon. life mem.). Home: 5A/73 Yarranabba Rd, Darling Point New South Wales 2027, Australia

BIRCHAM, DERIC NEALE, photographer; b. Wellington, N.Z., Dec. 16, 1934; s. Stanley Ernest and Rita Muriel (Sanvig) B.; student St. Patricks Coll., Silverstream, N.Z., BA, MBA, Calif. U., PhD (hon.), DLitt, Marquis Guiseppe Scicluna; DLitt, Would U., Aeterna Lucina U. Patricia Frances Simkin, Apr. 18, 1960; children—Venessa Frances, Patricia Frances (dec.), Melanie Elenor. Sr. photographer Ministry of Works and Devel., 1954-78; chief photographer Nat. Publicity Studios, 1976, N.Z. Public Service, 1976; pres. Deric Bircham & Assos., Wellington, 1978—; head med. photography U. Otago, 1979—, head med. illustration, 1981-84; author: Seeing New Zealand, 1971, 4th edit., 1975, Tuttle edit., 1975; Towards a More Just World, 1973; Waitomo Tourist Caves, 1975; Table Tennis, 1976; New Zealanders of Destiny, 1977; I Shall Pass This Way but Once, 1982; Old St. Paul's Cathedral, 1982; Day in the Life of New Zealand, 1983; Dunedin: New Zealand's Best Kept Secret, 1984, Rhapsody, 1984, St. Joseph's Cathedral, 1986, Works of Sottfried Lindauer, 1986, Golf Course Design X Turf Care, 1988; commd. by prime minister to portray Queen Elizabeth II, Prince Philip, Duke and Duchess of Kent; portrayed N.Z. prime minister, former prime ministers, gov. gens., knights of realm, others; exhibited photography in U.S.A., U.K., Can., S.E. Asia, Fiji, Australia, N.Z.; dir. Summer Sch. of Photography; cons. Poly. Sch. Design, pvt. firms; lectr. seminars. Recipient Albert Einstein Peace medal, 1986, Named Knight Order of White Cross, Chevalier Grand Star with status Order Souverain et Militaire et la Milice du St. sepulcre, Chevalier Grand Commr. Cordon Bleu du St. Esprit, conferred royal warrant by appointment official photographer to a monarchy. Fellow N.Z. Profl. Photographers Assn. (chmn. qualifications bd. 1974-76, dir. 1970-82, trustee 1970-80; chmn. Wellington Dist. Council 1974-76; nat. chmn. sci. and tech. group 1967-71, chmn. internat. conf. 1976), Royal Photog. Soc., Royal Soc. Arts, Internat. Inst. Community Service, Internat. Inst. Profl. Photographers (hon.), Brit. Inst. Profl. Photography; mem. Fedn. Internationale de l'Industrie Phonographique, Profl. Photographers Am. N.Z. Inst. Mgmt. (assoc.), Confed. Chivalry, Confed. Monarchy. Club: Univ. Otago. Lodge: Rotary. Home: 130 Easther Crescent, Kew, Dunedin New Zealand

BIRD, CAROLINE, author; b. N.Y.C., Apr. 15, 1915; d. Hobart Stanley and Ida (Brattrud) B.; m. Edward A. Menuez, June 8, 1934 (div. Dec. 1945); 1 dau., Carol (Mrs. John Paul Barach); m. John Thomas Mahoney, Jan. 5, 1957; 1 son, John Thomas. Student, Vassar Coll., 1931-34; BA, U. Toledo, 1938; MA, U. Wis., 1939; LHD (hon.), Keene State U., 1988. Desk editor N.Y. Jour. Commerce, 1943-44; editorial researcher Newsweek mag., N.Y.C., 1942-43, Fortune mag., N.Y.C., 1944-46; with Dudley-Anderson-Yutzy, pub. relations, N.Y.C., 1947-68; Froman Disting. prof. Russell Sage Coll., 1972-73; Mather prof. Case-Western Res. U., 1977. Author: The Invisible Scar, 1966, Born Female, 1968, rev. edit., 1970, The Crowding Syndrome, 1972, Everything a Woman Needs To Know To Get Paid What She's Worth, 1973, rev., 1982, The Case Against College, 1975, Enterprising Women, 1976, What Women Want, 1979, The Two-Paycheck Marriage, 1979, The Good Years, 1983; chief writer: The Spirit of Houston, 1978; also articles in nat. mags. Mem. review bd. Dept. State, 1974. Mem. Soc. Journalists and Authors, Am. Sociol. Assn. Home: 31 Sunrise Ln Poughkeepsie NY 12603

BIRD, FRANCIS MARION, lawyer; b. Comer, Ga., Sept. 4, 1902; s. Henry Madison and Minnie Lee (McConnell) B.; m. Mary Adair Howell, Jan. 30, 1935; children—Francis Marion, Mary Adair Bird Kennedy, Elizabeth Howell Bird Hewitt, George Arthur. A.B., U. Ga., 1922, LL.B., 1924; LL.M., George Washington U., 1925; LL.D., Emory U., 1980, U. St. Andrews, 1982. Bar: Ga. bar 1924, D.C. bar 1925. Since practiced in Atlanta; with U.S. Senator Hoke Smith, 1925; individual practice 1930-45; mem. firm Bird & Howell, 1945-59, Jones Bird & Howell, 1959-82, Alston & Bird, 1982—; served as part-time U.S. referee in bankruptcy, 1945-54; spl. asst. to U.S. atty. gen. as hearings officer Nat. Selective Service Act.; Mem. commn. for preparation plan of govt. City of Atlanta and county area; mem. permanent rules com. Ga. Supreme Ct.; mem. Met. Atlanta Commn. Crime and Juvenile Delinquency, chmn., 1969-70; formerly Ga. co-chmn. Tech.-Ga. Devel. Fund.; Trustee Young Harris Coll., U. Ga. Found., Atlanta Lawyers Found., Interdenominational Theol. Center; trustee, past mem. exec. com. Emory U., Atlanta.; Chmn. Ga. Bd. Bar Examiners, 1954-61. Mem. permanent editorial bd.: Uniform Comml. Code, 1962-77, Fed. Jud. Conf., 5th Circuit, Fed. Jud. Conf., 11th Circuit, 1960-81, 1981—. Recipient Distinguished Service citation U. Ga. Law Sch.; Distinguished Service award Atlanta Bar Assn., 1977; Pres.'s award Assn. Pvt. Colls. and Univs., 1979. Fellow Am. Bar Found; mem. Am. Judicature Soc. (past dir.), Am. Law Inst. (council 1949-82, emeritus, past chmn. com. membership), ABA, Ga. (past pres.), Atlanta Bar Assns., N.Y.C. Bar Assn., Atlanta C. of C. (past pres., Atlanta Civic Service award 1957), U. Ga. Alumni Assn. (past pres., certificate of merit 1952), George Washington U. Alumni Assn. (achievement award 1965), Phi Kappa Phi, Sigma Chi, Phi Delta Phi. Methodist. Clubs: Peachtree Golf, Atlanta Athletic (past pres.), Kiwanis, Piedmont Driving, Capital City, Lawyers (past pres.), Augusta (Ga.) Nat. Golf (gov.). Home: 89 Brighton Rd NE Atlanta GA 30309 Office: 1200 The Citizens and So Nat Bank Bldg Atlanta GA 30335

BIRD, MERLE KENDALL, steel processing company executive; b. Mt. Pleasant, Iowa, July 1, 1927; s. Eugene Clifford and Freida Fern (Kerr) B.; m. Helen Marie Hohn, June 16, 1951; children: Stephen Kent, Cynthia June, David Kurt, Kim Marie, Kevin Lee, Rebbecca Susan. Student, U. Minn., 1945-46; B.S. in Edn., Western Ill. U., 1949; M.S. in Edn., No. Ill. U., 1956. Basketball ofcl. Ill. High Sch. Assn., Colusa and Crystal Lake, Ill., 1949-67, football ofcl., 1952-67; tchr., coach, athletic dir. Sch. Dist. 311, Colusa, 1949-52, Sch. Dist. 47, Crystal Lake, 1952-57; prodn. mgr. TC Industries, Inc., Crystal Lake, 1957-65, personnel mgr., 1965-74, dir. employee and pub. relations, 1974—, dir. employee relations TC Industries Can., TC Industries Europe Ltd., 1985—. Pres. McHenry County Tuberculosis Assn., 1962-65, St. Thomas Sch. Bd., 1967-68, DuPage-McHenry Lung Assn., 1968-71, Crystal Lake Park Dist., 1970, 73, Four Colonies Townhouse Assn., 1981-83; marshall 4th of July Parade, Crystal Lake; campaign exec. United Way; cubmaster Blackhawk Area council Boy Scouts Am., 1964-66; sec. McHenry Hosp. Bd., 1974-79; v.p. Am. Lung Assn. Ill., 1980, 83, 87. Served with USN, 1945-46. Mem. McHenry County Mfg. Assn. (pres. 1961), McHenry County Personnel Mgrs., Crystal Lake Jr. C. of C. (pres. 1960-61, awards 1959, 62), Am. Legion. Republican. Roman Catholic. Club: Lions. Editor, Terra Cotta Newsletter, 1966—. Home: 601 Cress Creek Crystal Lake IL 60014 Office: TC Industries Inc PO Box 477 Crystal Lake IL 60014

BIRD, VERE CORNWALL, SR., prime minister of Antigua and Barbuda; b. Dec. 9, 1909; ed. St. John's Boys' Sch., Salvation Army Tng. Sch., Trinidad. Served with Salvation Army in Grenada; founding mem. exec. bd. Antigua Trades and Labor Union, 1939, pres., 1943-67; elected mem. Legis. Council Antigua, 1945, mem. exec. council, 1951, also chmn. coms., 1956; minister trade and prodn., 1956-60; chief minister Antigua, 1960-67; led del. to U.K. that achieved assoc. statehood for Antigua, 1966; premier of Antigua, 1967-71, 76-81, led del. that gained full Antiguan independence from Gt. Britain, 1980; prime minister ind. Antigua and Barbuda, 1981—, minister of planning, external affairs, def. and energy, 1981-82, minister of fin., 1982-84, also minister of def. Participant Caribbean Union Confs., Trinidad, 1945, St. Kitts, 1946, Jamaica, 1947, West Indian Govt. Confs., London, 1953, 56; founder (with reps. from Barbados and Guyana) Caribbean Free Trade Assn., 1965; leader Antigua Labor Party. Address: Office of Prime Minister, Saint John's Antigua *

BIRD, WENDELL RALEIGH, lawyer; b. Atlanta, July 16, 1954; s. Raleigh Milton and R. Jean (Edwards) B.; m. Celia Ann Reed, Dec. 22, 1978; 1 child, Courtenay Asheton. BA summa cum laude, Vanderbilt U., 1975; JD, Yale U., 1978. Bar: Ga. 1978, Calif. 1981, Fla. 1982, Ala. 1980, U.S. Supreme Ct. 1983, U.S. Ct. Appeals (3rd, 4th, 5th, 7th, 8th, 9th, 11th cirs.). Law clk. to judge U.S. Ct. Appeals (4th cir.), Durham, N.C., 1978-79, U.S. Ct. Appeals (5th cir.), Birmingham, Ala., 1979-80; atty. Parker, Johnson, Cook & Dunlevie, Atlanta, 1982-86; sr. ptnr. Law Offices of Wendell R. Bird, Atlanta, 1986—; adj. prof. Emory U. Law Sch., Atlanta, 1985—; lectr. Washington Non-Profit Tax Conf., 1982, 84-86, 88, 89. Author: Home Education and Constitutional Liberties, 1984, The Origin of Species Revisited, 2 vols., 1987; bd. editors Yale U. Law Jour., 1977-78, others; contbr. articles to profl. jours. including Yale U. Law Jour., Harvard U. Jour. Law and Pub. Policy. Bd. govs. Council for Nat. Policy, Washington, 1983—; bd. dirs. Transnat. Assn. Christian Schs., Dallas, 1985—; mem. nat. adv. council Nat. Ctr. for Privatization, Wichita, 1984—. Recipient Egger Prize Yale U., 1978. Mem. Am. Law Inst., ABA, Assn. Trial Lawyers Am., Phi Beta Kappa. Republican. Baptist. Office: 3414 Peachtree Rd NE 1150 Monarch Plaza Atlanta GA 30326

BIRDMAN, JEROME M., drama educator, dean; b. Phila., Dec. 4, 1930; s. Morris Schiowitz and Minerva B.; m. Evanira Pereira Mendes, July 1, 1959; children: Julia, Beatrice. B.S., Temple U., 1956; A.M., U. Ill., 1957, Ph.D., 1970; mem. seminar for Arts Trustees, Harvard U., 1975. Mem. editorial staff Accent Quar. of New Lit., 1957-58; dir. cultural programming for Am. Forces, U.S. Info. Service, Northeast Italy, 1958-61; mem. faculty theatre dept. So. Ill. U., Edwardsville, 1961-71; acad. program officer So. Ill. U., 1972-73; prof. dramatic arts, dean Coll. Fine Arts, U. Nebr., Omaha, 1973-78, Sch. Fine Arts, U. Conn., Storrs, 1978—; adv. bd. Nebr. Alliance for Arts Edn., 1976-78; lectr. USIS, Brazil, 1964; arts commr. Nat. Assn. State Univs. and Land Grant Colls., 1979—, chmn., 1983—; panelist NEH, 1976—, Nat. Endowment Arts, 1983—; adv. Conn. Dept. Edn., 1980—; accreditor New Eng. Assn. Schs. and Colls.; cons. to various colls. and univs. in arts adminstrn. Contbr. articles on theatrical art to various profl. publs.; originator exhibit: Artists Who Teach, Washington, 1987; producer or director more than 40 plays, musicals and concerts at universities, 1963-76; translator Six Ccharacters in Search of an Author, U. Mo., 1987-88. Mem. Mayor's Task Force on the Arts, Omaha, 1977-78; bd. dirs. Dance Concert Soc., St. Louis, 1970-73, New Music Circle, 1971-73, Prelude Civic Ballet, Ill., 1971-73, Omaha Opera Co., 1973-75, Omaha Symphony Assn., 1973-78, Stamford Ctr. for the Arts, 1984—, Met. Arts Council, Omaha, 1976-78, Omaha Children's Mus., 1976-78. Served with U.S. Army, 1952-54. Recipient merit citation Provincia di Vicenza, 1961. Mem. Am. Theatre Assn., Internat. Fedn. Theatre Research, Am. Soc. Theatre Research, Internat. Council Fine Arts Deans, Soc. Theatre Research Great Britain., Societé d'Histoire du Theâtre, Nat. Assn. State Universities and Land-Grant Colls., Am. Theatre Assn./Assn. for Theatre in Higher Edn. Home: 76 Charles Ln Storrs CT 06268 Office: U Conn Sch Fine Arts U-128 Room 202 875 Coventry Rd Storrs CT 06268

BIRENDRA BIR BIKRAM SHAH DEV, HIS MAJESTY, King of Nepal; b. Kathmandu, Nepal, Dec. 28, 1945; s. King Mahendra Bir Bikram Shah and Crown Princess Indra Ravaj Laxmi Devi Shah; ed. St. Joseph's Coll., Darjeeling, India, Eton (Eng.) Coll., U. Tokyo, Harvard U.; LL.D. (hon.), U. Delhi; m. Queen Aishwarya Rajya Laxmi Devi Rana, Feb. 27, 1970; children: Crown Prince Dipendra Bir Bikram Shah Dev, Princess Shruti Rajya Laxmi Devi Shah, Prince Nirajan Biv Bikram Shah. Grandmaster, col.-in-chief Royal Nepalese Army, 1964, supreme comdr.-in-chief, from 1972; became king, Jan. 31, 1972, crowned, 1975. Chancellor, Tribhuvan U.; chief scout Nepal Boy and Girl Scouts; chmn. Nepal Assn. Arts. Avocations: painting, swimming, riding. Address: Narayanhiti Royal Palace, Kathmandu Nepal Office: Tribhuvan U, PO Box 3757, Kathmandu Nepal *

BIRK, ROBERT EUGENE, physician, educator; b. Buffalo, Jan. 7, 1926; s. Reginald H. and Florence (Diebolt) B.; m. Janet L. Davidson, June 24, 1950; children—David Eugene, James Michael, Patricia Jean, Thomas Spencer, Susan Margaret. A.B., Colgate U., 1948; M.D., U. Rochester, 1952. Diplomate Am. Bd. Internal Medicine. Intern, resident Henry Ford Hosp., Detroit, 1952-57, chief 2d med. div., 1961-66, asst. to chmn. dept. medicine, 1965-66; practice medicine specializing in internal medicine Grosse Pointe, Mich., 1966—; sr. active staff St. John Hosp., 1966—, chief dept. medicine, 1967-70, dir. health edn., dir. grad. med. edn., 1975-86, exec. dir. continuing med. edn., 1975-86; dir. med. affairs St. Clair Ambulatory Care Corp., St. Clair Home Care Services, 1980—; v.p. clin. affairs St. Clair Health Corp., 1985—; assoc. prof. medicine Wayne State U., 1969—. Contbr. articles to profl. jours. Mem. trustee's council U. Rochester, 1973-75, Med. Ctr. alumni council, 1974-75; corp. mem. bd. Boys Clubs Met. Detroit, 1973—; trustee Mich. Cancer Found., 1980—, bd. dirs., 1982-85. Served with U.S. Army, 1943-46. Fellow ACP, Detroit Acad. Medicine; mem. AMA, Assn. Hosp. Med. Edn. (trustee region IV 1986-87), Mich Assn. Med. Edn. (trustee 1985-86), Am. Soc. Internal Medicine, Am. Acad. Med. Dirs., Alpha Tau Omega. Republican. Episcopalian. Clubs: Grosse Pointe (Mich.); Carleton (Chgo.). Home: 10 Stratford Pl Grosse Pointe MI 48230 Office: 22151 Moross Rd Suite G3 Detroit MI 48236

BIRK, ROGER EMIL, federal mortgage association executive; b. St. Cloud, Minn., July 14, 1930; s. Emil S. and Barbara E. (Zimmer) B.; m. Mary Lou Schrank, June 25, 1955; children: Kathleen, Steven, Mary Beth, Barbara. BA, St. John's U., 1952. Mgr. Merrill Lynch, Pierce, Fenner and Smith, Inc., Ft. Wayne, Ind., 1964-66, Kansas City, Mo., 1966-68; asst. div. dir. Merrill Lynch, Pierce, Fenner and Smith, Inc., N.Y.C., 1968-70, div. dir., 1971-74, pres., 1974-76, chmn., 1980-85; pres. Merrill Lynch & Co., N.Y.C., 1976-81, chmn., chief exec. officer, 1981-85, chmn. emeritus, 1985—; chmn. bd. Internat. Securities Clearing Corp., N.Y.C., 1986-87; pres., chief operating officer Fed. Nat. Mortgage Assn., Washington, 1987—; dir. N.Y. Stock Exchange, 1981-85, vice chmn., 1983-85; mem. Bus. Roundtable, 1981-85, Pres.'s Commn. on Exec. Exchange, 1981-85, Pres.'s Pvt. Sector Survey on Cost Control, 1982-85. Chmn. nat. adv. council St. John's U., 1975-76, bd. regents, 1975-78; trustee U. Notre Dame, 1981—. Served with AUS, 1952-54. Mem. Nat. Assn. Securities Dealers (mem. long-range planning com. 1975-78), Council on Fgn. Relations. Club: Navesink Country (Middletown, N.J.). Office: Fed Nat Mortgage Assn 3900 Wisconsin Ave NW Washington DC 20016

BIRKETT, JENNIFER, French studies educator; b. Doncaster, Eng., Mar. 26, 1946. BA with honors, St. Hilda's Coll., 1968, MA (hon.), 1973; DPhil, Linacre Coll., 1973. Lectr. Dundee (Scotland) U., 1971-87; prof. French studies Strathclyde U., Glasgow, Scotland, 1988—. Author: The Body and the Dream, 1983, The Sins of the Fathers: Decadence in France, 1986, Samuel Beckett, 1987; contbr. articles to profl. jours. Mem. steering com. Standing Conf. of Faculties of Arts and Social Scis. in Univs. Research grantee Brit. Acad., 1987. Mem. Assn. Univ. Tchrs., Assn. Univ. Profs. French (exec. com.), Soc. French Studies, Assn. Study Modern and Contemporary France, Brit. Soc. for Eighteenth-Century Studies. Mem. Labour Party. Office: U Strathclyde, 26 Richmond St, Glasgow Scotland

BIRKITT, JOHN CLAIR, aerospace engineer; b. Inglewood, Calif., Aug. 20, 1941; s. Clair Willis and Helene Blanche (Gille) B.; m. Constance Ellen May, June 4, 1966; m. 2d, Linda Ann Aylmer, Sept. 13, 1980; children—Andra, Robert, Danielle, William. B.S. in Aerospace Engring., Calif. Poly. State U., 1969. Engr., Aerojet Mfg. Co., Fullerton, Calif., 1969-74; with TRW, 1974-83, engr. def. and space systems group, Redondo Beach, Calif., 1974-79, plant mgr. advanced ground systems engring., Long Beach, Calif., 1979-83, test condr. Capistrano test site, San Clemente, Calif., 1975-83; tech. mgr. Ford Aerospace and Communications Corp., Newport Beach, Calif., 1983-86; gen. mgr. White Missile Range Ops., W.J. Schafer Assocs., Inc., Arlington, Va., 1986—. Vice pres., treas., tng. officer El Cariso Vol. Fire Dept., 1978—. Served with USMC, 1959-65. Mem. AIAA (sr.), Nat. Assn. Watch and Clock Collectors, Nat. Mgmt. Assn., Nat. Defense Preparedness Assn., Musical Box Soc. Internat. Home: James Canyon Rt PO

Box 935 Cloudcroft NM 88317 Office: Bldg 23106 High Energy Laser Lab Nike Rd White Sands Missile Range NM 88002

BIRKITT, LINDA ANN AYLMER, physical therapist; b. Oakland, Calif., Feb. 8, 1946; d. William Stanley and Phyllis Jane (King) Aylmer; student U. Md. at Munich, W.Ger., 1967-68; B.S., Calif. State Poly. U., 1963-69; M.A. (HEW scholar), U. So. Calif., 1973; m. John C. Birkitt, Sept. 13, 1980; children: Andra, Robert, Lowell, Danielle, William. Staff phys. therapist Valley Presbyn. Hosp., Van Nuys, Calif., 1973-75; chief therapist Ingleside Mental Health Center, Rosemead, Calif., 1975-79; mem. Speakers Bur., 1976-79; lectr. Santa Monica City Coll., 1976-79; asst. chief phys. therapist Alhambra (Calif.) Community Hosp., 1979-81; pvt. practice phys. therapy, San Juan Capistrano, Calif., 1981—; dir. ops. Healthtech Rehab., Inc., Irvine, Calif., 1985-88; adminstr. Mariners Rehab. Inc., Santa Ana, Calif., 1988—. Vol. fire fighter, El Cariso Village, Calif., 1979—; mem. sch. improvement council San Juan Elem. Sch.; mem. guild Capistrano Ballet. Contbr. articles to profl. jour. Mem. AAUW, Nat. Assn. Female Execs., Nat. Mgmt. Assn. Episcopalian. Research in motivation as a factor in performance of phys. skill, verticality perception distortion in hemiplegic patients. Home: James Canyon Star Rt Cloudcroft NM 88317

BIRLA, GANGA PRASAD, family business owner; b. Calcutta, West Bengal, India, Aug. 2, 1922; s. Braj Mohan and Rukmani (Tapuriah) B.; m. Nirmala Devi, Jan. 31, 1952; children: Chandralekha, Chandrakant. BS, Presidency Coll., Calcutta, 1940. Chmn. Hindustan Motors Ltd., Calcutta, Orient Paper & Industries Ltd., Calcutta, Nigeria Engring. Works Ltd., Port Harcourt; dir. Pan African Consultancy Services, Lagos, Nigeria; mng. dir. Birla Bros. Pvt. Ltd., Calcutta; chmn. bd. govs. Birla Inst. Tech., Ranchi, Bihar, India, Birla Inst. Sci. Research, Calcutta, Calcutta Med. Research Inst. Active Indian Red Cross Soc., Calcutta, Nat. Sports Club India. Home: 8/9 Alipore Rd, 700 027 Calcutta India Office: Hindustan Motors Ltd, 9/1 RN Mukherjee Rd, Calcutta 700 001, India

BIRMINGHAM, STEPHEN, writer; b. Hartford, Conn., May 28, 1931; s. Thomas J. and Editha (Gardner) B.; m. Janet Tillson, Jan. 5, 1951 (div.); children: Mark, Harriet, Carey. B.A. cum laude, Williams Coll., 1950; postgrad., Univ. Coll., Oxford (Eng.) U., 1951. Advt. copywriter Needham, Harper & Steers, Inc., 1953-67. Author: Young Mr. Keefe, 1958, Barbara Greer, 1959, The Towers of Love, 1961, Those Harper Women, 1963, Fast Start, Fast Finish, 1966, Our Crowd: The Great Jewish Families of New York, 1967, The Right People, 1968, Heart Toubles, 1968, The Grandees, 1971, The Late John Marquand, 1972, The Right Places, 1973, Real Lace, 1973, Certain People: America's Black Elite, 1977, The Golden Dream: Suburbia in the 1970's, 1978, Jacqueline Bouvier Kennedy Onassis, 1978, Life at the Dakota, 1979, California Rich, 1980, Duchess, 1981, The Grandes Dames, 1982, The Auerbach Will, 1983; The Rest of Us, 1984, The LeBaron Secret, 1986, Americas Secret Aristocracy, 1987; contbr. numerous articles to numerous periodicals. Served with AUS, 1951-53. Mem. New Eng. Soc. of City N.Y., Phi Beta Kappa. Democrat. Episcopalian. Club: Coffee House (N.Y.C.). Address: care Brandt & Brandt 1501 Broadway New York NY 10036

BIRMINGHAM, WILLIAM JOSEPH, lawyer; b. Lynbrook, N.Y., Aug. 7, 1923; s. Daniel Joseph and Mary Elizabeth (Tighe) B.; m. Helen Elizabeth Roche, July 23, 1955; children: Deirdre, Patrick, Maureen, Kathleen, Brian. ME, Stevens Inst. Tech., 1944; MBA, Harvard U., 1948; JD, DePaul U., Chgo., 1953. Bar: Ill. 1953, U.S. Patent and Trademark Office, 1955, U.S. Dist. Ct. (no. dist.) Ill. 1960, U.S. Supreme Ct. 1961, U.S. Ct. Appeals (7th cir.) 1962, U.S. Ct. Appeals (3d cir.) 1968, U.S. Ct. Appeals (D.C. cir.) 1973, U.S. Ct. Mil. Appeals 1973, U.S. Ct. Appeals (fed. cir.) 1982, U.S. Ct. Claims 1986; registered profl. engr., Ill., Ind. Chem. engr. Standard Oil Co. Ind., Chgo., 1948-53, patent atty., 1953-59; assoc. Neuman, Williams, Anderson & Olson, Chgo., 1959-60, ptnr., 1961—. Served to capt. USNR, 1942-75. Mem. ABA, Ill. Bar Assn., Chgo. Bar Assn., Bar Assn. Seventh Fed. Cir., Fed. Cir. Bar Assn. Am. Intellectual Property Law Assn., Patent Law Assn. Chgo. (bd. mgrs. 1976-77), Internat. Trade Commn. Trial Lawyers Assn., Internat. Patent and Trademark Assn., Licensing Execs. Soc., ASME. Clubs: Mid-Day (Chgo.); Harvard Bus. Sch. of Chgo. (officer, bd. dirs.). Home: 233 Pine St Deerfield IL 60015 Office: Neuman Williams Anderson & Olson 77 W Washington St Chicago IL 60602

BIRNBAUM, PHILIP HARVEY, business administrator educator; b. San Diego, Jan. 21, 1944; s. Louis and Ruth Laureen (Bay) B.; m. Marlin Sue Van Every, Dec. 26, 1964; 1 child, Brian Philip. BA, U. Calif., Berkeley, 1965; PhD, U. Wash., 1975. Personnel analyst Los Angeles County Civil Service Commn., 1965-67; teaching assoc. U. Wash., Seattle, 1972-74; asst. prof. bus. adminstrn. Ind. U., Bloomington, 1975-80, assoc. prof., 1980-85; prof. Ind. U., Bloomington, 1986, U. So. Calif., 1986—; resident dir. J.F.K. Inst., Tiburg U., The Netherlands; vis. scholar Polish Acad. Scis. Co-author: Organization Theory: A Structural and Behavioral Analysis, Modern Management Techniques for Engineers and Scientists; assoc. editor IEEE Transaction on Engring. Mgmt. jour.; contbr. articles to profl. jours., book revs., sects. to books, invited papers Germany, Poland, Eng., Can., Thailand, Hong Kong. Served with USAF, 1967-71. Recipient DBA Assn. Teaching award Ind. U., 1978; NSF fellow, 1974-75, N.Y. Acad. Scis. fellow, 1981; U. Hong Kong Sr. Fulbright scholar, 1981-82. Mem. Acad. of Mgmt., AAAS, Am. Inst. for Decision Scis., Am. Sociol. Assn., Soc. for Social Study of Sci., Engring. Mgmt. Soc., Inst. of Mgmt. Sci., Internat. Assn. for Study of Interdisciplinary Research, Beta Gamma Sigma, Beta Alpha Psi, Sigma Iota Epsilon. Methodist. Office: U So Calif Grad Sch Bus Admistrn Los Angeles CA 90089-1421

BIRNBAUM, PIERRE, political science educator; b. Lourdes, France, July 19, 1940; s. Jacob and Ruth (Kupferman) B.; children: Juliette, Jean, Lea; m. Judith Lamberger. LittD, U. Sorbonne, 1975. Assoc. prof. U. Bordeaux, France, 1966-70; assoc. prof. polit. sci. U. Sorbonne, Paris, 1970-75; prof. U. Sorbonne, 1975—; prof. Inst. Study of Politics, Paris, 1970—; vis. prof. U. Chgo., NYU, New Sch. Social Research, U. Geneva, U. Jerusalem, U. Ind., Oxford U., Edinburgh U., U. Florence, U. Rome, U. Bogota, others. Author: Sociologie de Tocqueville, 1969, La fin du politique, 1975, Les sommets de l'Etat, 1977, Le peuple et les gros Histoire d'un mythe, 1979, La Logique de l'Etat, 1982, The Heights of Power, 1981, Sociology of the States, States and Collective Action, 1988, On Indidivualism, 1988; mem. editorial bd. Brit. Jour. Polit. Sci., 1978-82; corr. editor Theory and Soc., 1984—; contbr. to numerous profl. publs. Home: Corvisart 50, 75013 Paris France Office: U Sorbonne, 14 rue Cujas, Paris France

BIRNEY, (ALFRED) EARLE, writer; b. Calgary, Alta., Can., May 13, 1904; s. William George and Martha Stout (Robertson) B.; m. Esther Bull, Mar., 1940 (div. 1978); 1 son, William Laurenson. B.A., U. B.C., 1926; postgrad., U. Calif.-Berkeley, 1927-30; M.A., U. Toronto, 1927, Ph.D., 1936; postgrad., U. London, 1934-35; LL.D., U. Alta., 1965; D.Litt., McGill U., 1979, U. Western Ont., 1984, U. B.C., 1987. Summer sch. lectr. U. B.C., 1927-37; instr. U. Utah, 1930-32, 33-34; lectr. U. Toronto, 1936-40, asst. prof., 1940-42; prof. English U. B.C., 1946-62, head dept. creative writing, 1963-65; writer-in-residence U. Toronto, 1965-67, U. Waterloo, Ont., 1967-68, U. Western Ont., 1981-82; Regents prof. U. Calif. at Irvine, 1968; supr. fgn. lang. broadcasts to Europe Radio Can., 1945-46; vis. prof. creative writing U. Oreg., 1961; lit. adviser Can. Council, 1965-67. Author: poetry David, 1942, Near False Creek Mouth, 1964, Memory No Servant, 1968, Pnomes, Jukollages and other Stunzas, 1969, Rag and Bone Shop, 1971, What's So Big About Green?, 1973, Bear on the Delhi Road, 1973, Collected Poems, 2 vols, 1975, The Rugging and the Moving Times, 1976, Alphabe-ings; poems-drawings, 1976; selected poems Ghost in the Wheels, 1977; new poems Fall by Fury, 1978, The Mammoth Corridors; selected poems, 1980, others; novels Turvey, 1949, Down the Long Table, 1955; short stories Big Bird in the Bush; play Damnation of Vancouver, 1952; lit. theory The Creative Writer, 1966, The Cow Jumped Over the Moon, 1972; lit. criticism Spreading Time/Remarks on Canadian Writing and Writers, 1980; editor-in-chief: lit. criticism Canadian Poetry mag, 1946-48, Prism Internat, 1963-65; lit. editor: lit. criticism Canadian Forum, 1937-40; adv. editor: Selected Poems of Malcolm Lowry, 1962; lit. criticism New Canadian and Am. Poetry, 1964-68. Served with Canadian Army, 1942-45. Decorated officer Order of Can.; recipient Gov.-Gen.'s medals for poetry, 1943, 46, Stephen Leacock medal for humor, 1949, Borestone Mt. poetry 1st prize, 1951, Pierce medal for lit., 1953, Can. Council medal for services to arts, 1968; Canadian Govt. fellow France, 1953; Nuffield fellow Eng., 1958-59; Can. Council travelling fellowships and grants to Latin Am., 1962-63; Can. Council travelling fellowships and grants to Latin Am. Australia and New Zealand, 1968; West and East Africa, 1972; Europe and South Asia, 1974-75. Fellow Royal Soc. Can. Address: RR 3, Uxbridge, ON Canada L0C 1K0

BIRNKRANT, MICHAEL CHARLES, JR., investor; b. Chgo., Feb. 27, 1942; s. Michael Charles and Cecele June (Greenfield) B.; m. Susan Frances Delaney, Jan. 23, 1971; 1 child, Michael Charles III. A.B., Stanford U., 1964. Prin. Michael C. Birnkrant, Jr., Chgo. Contbr. articles to real estate jours. Vice chmn. sustaining fellows and major gifts, collectors group Art Inst. Chgo. Republican. Clubs: Saddle and Cycle, Standard (Chgo.). Office: 200 W Adams Suite 2000 Chicago IL 60606

BIROLI, MARCO, mathematical analysis educator; b. Vigevano, Lombardy, Italy, May 7, 1945; s. Mino and Fiorella (Anzani) B.; m. Margherita Fabbri, July 31, 1972; 1 child, Giulio. Laureate, U. Milan, Italy, 1968; DSc, U Paris VI, 1973. Scholarship holder Consiglio Nazionale delle Richerche-NATO, Paris, 1968-73; asst. prof. U. Parma, Italy, 1974; full prof. math. analysis Politecnico di Milano, 1974—. Editor: Rivista de Matematica, 1980—; contbr. over 100 articles on math. to profl. jours. internationally. Mem. Unione Matematica Italiana, Am. Math. Soc. Office: Dept Math-Politecnico, Piazza Leonardo da Vinci 32, 20133 Milan Italy

BIRUS, HENDRIK KARL, German literature educator; b. Kamenz, Saxony, Germany, Apr. 16, 1943; s. Karl Christian and Ilse Dora (Ködder) B.; m. Barbara Siegrun Schauer; children: Anna Katharina, Marie Christiane. MA, Univ., Heidelberg, Fed. Republic of Germany, 1972, PhD, 1977; PhD Habilitation, Univ., Göttingen, Fed. Republic of Germany, 1984. Acad. asst. Dept. Germanic Philology Univ., Göttingen, Fed. Republic of Germany, 1972-83, asst., 1983-85, prof., 1985-87, 1987—; head Dept. Comparative Lit. U., Munich, Fed. Republic of Germany, 1987—. Mem. Lessing Soc., Jean-Paul-Gesellschaft. Home: Kaiserstr 40, D-8000 Munich Federal Republic of Germany

BIRY, YVES GEORGE, international development organization and mangement consultant; b. Nancy, France, Aug. 12, 1926; came to U.S., 1949; m. George M. and Georgette P. (Dinot) B.; m. Yvonne Clavery, Sept. 8, 1951; children: Yvonne G., Marie C., George R., Pierre. Ingenieur, Ecole Centrale, Paris, 1949; MS in Elec. Engring., Columbia U., 1950; postgrad., MIT, 1962-63. Lic. engr., P.R. Cons. engr. Transitron Electronic Corp., Wakefield, Mass., 1960-62; project engr. missiles and space div. AVCO, Wilmington, Mass., 1962-67; indsl. exec. ITT-Europe, Brussels, 1968-70; pres. internat. Mgmt. & Devel. Co., Waterloo, Belgium, 1971—; cons. UN Indsl. Devel. Orgn., Vienna, 1971—, OECD, Paris, 1973, UN Conf. on Trade and Devel., Geneva, 1983-85, Internat. Trade Ctr., Geneva, 1986—; guest and keynote speaker in field. Author: Commerce in Mali, 1985; contbr. articles to profl. jours. Mem. Ecole Centrale Alumni Assn., Columbia U. Engring Alumni Assn., Internat. House Alumni Assn. Roman Catholic. Club: Columbia of Belgium (Brussels). Home and Office: Ave Prince Royal 12, B-1410 Waterloo Belgium

BISCIGLIA, ANTHONY FRANK, junior high school administrator; b. Kenosha, Wis., May 28, 1938; s. Joseph Thomas and Marie (Bruno) B.; m. Rita Frances Savaglio, Aug. 22, 1964; children—Anthony J., Susan M., Linda A. B.S. in History, U. Wis.-Madison, 1960; M.S. in Guidance, Marquette U., 1968, doctoral student in Sch. Adminstrn., 1980—. Elem. tchr. Milw. Pub. Schs., Wis., 1962-68, elem. sch. guidance counselor, 1968-69; elem. sch. principal Kenosha Unified Sch. Dist., Wis., 1969-75, jr. high sch. prin., 1975—; bd. mem. Wis. Dept. Pub. Insts. State Superintendents Adv. Com. on the Deaf, 1984—; sch. chmn. Effective Schs. Research Lance Jr. High Sch., Kenosha, 1984—; chmn. human resources com. Kenosha Compass, 1988; co-chmn. Modern Tech. Conf. for Educators, U. Wis., 1983. Bd. dirs. Kenosha United Way, 1972-79, pres., 1975-76, campaign chmn., 1974-75; campaign chmn. Archbishop's Funds Appeal, Kenosha, 1970-71; mem. commonwealth parent com. Carthage Coll., 1984, co-chmn. devel. campaign, 1987-88; v.p. pub. relations Kenosha Civic Vet.'s Parade com., 1984, v.p., 1985, 87; chmn. Kenosha Plus Task Force, 1985. Recipient Distng. Service award Girl Scouts of U.S., Kenosha, 1974, Award of Merit Boy Scouts Am., 1988. Mem. Kenosha Schs. Administrn Assn. (pres. 1976), Kenosha Industrial Task Force (bd. mem. 1984—), Kenosha Econ. Devel. Commn., Nat. Soc. Study Edn., Wis. Assn. Middle Level Educators, U. Wis. Alumni Club (pres. 1977), Rotary West Found. (bd. dirs. 1981-86), Marquette U. Alumni Assn. (rep. for Kenosha, 1982), Phi Delta Kappa, Delta Sigma Phi. Roman Catholic. Lodge: Rotary (pres. 1982, Paul Harris award 1983, bd. mem. 1973—, rep. SE Wis. in New South Wales, Australia 1972). Home: 4470 Harrison Rd Kenosha WI 53142 Office: Bullen Jr High Sch 2804 39th Ave Kenosha WI 53142

BISHARA, LOUIS YOUSIF, chemist, textile technologist; b. Tanta, Egypt, May 7, 1939; s. Yousif and Farha (Mina) B.; B.Sc. in Chemistry, Ein Shams U., 1959; m. Amal Adly Georgy, Aug. 1, 1965; children—Marie, Nelly, Yasmin. Textile chemist Citex Co., Cairo, 1959-61; founder, owner Zeitoun Printers, Cairo, 1961-70, Amiria Dyers, Cairo, 1970—, BTM Bishara Textile Mfg., Ramadan City, 1981—, Weaving, 1983—, Garments, 1984—, Marie Louis Co. for Fashon Garments Printing and Dying, 1988, Ladies Wear, 1989 . Mem. Sci. Vocations Syndicate Union of Egyptian Industries, Dyers and Finishers Assn. Christian. Clubs: Rotary of Heliopolis (bd. dirs., chmn. community service com. 1980, Paul Harris fellow, pres. elect, 1987-88), Shams Sporting. Home: 15 Ahmed Mahmod Heliopolis, Cairo Egypt Office: 5 Masane St, Amiria, Cairo Egypt

BISHOP, BARRY RHETT, newspaper publisher, rancher; b. Stevens Point, Wis., Aug. 7, 1940; s. Rexford Ernest and Bernice Marie (Whiting) B.; student UCLA, 1960-61; B.S., U. Wis., Madison, 1962; postgrad. U Puget Sound, Tacoma, 1963-64, U. Calif., San Jose, 1973-74; m. Gael Lucette Briggs, Oct. 28, 1966; children—Terri, Steve, Heidi, Barbra, Robert. With Stars and Stripes, 1964; editor Wis. State Farmer, 1965; editor, advt. dir. Manawa (Wis.) Adv., 1965-66, editor, pub., owner, 1966-69; editor The Ariz. Currents, writer/reporter Milw. Jour., also editor, pub. Sierra Vista (Ariz.) Herald-Dispatch, 1969-74; editor, pub., owner The Paper, Sierra Vista, 1974—; pub. Huachuca Scout, 1982—, Desert Airman, 1984—, Friday Times, 1985—; v.p. Sulphur Springs Valley Elec. Coop.; tchr. journalism Cochise Coll. Bd. dirs. Sierra Vista Bd. Edn.; sec.-treas. Sierra Vista Indsl. Devel. Authority. Chmn. Border Relations Commn., Utilities Commn., City of Sierra Vista; fin. chmn. Catalina council Boy Scouts Am.; cubmaster Pack 464, Sierra Vista, also troop chmn. mem. Gov.'s Commn. Ariz.-Mex.; del. Gov.'s Commn. Small Bus. Served to capt. U.S. Army, 1962-64. Recipient Spoke award Wis. Jaycees; winner numerous nat., state awards including editorial award Wis. br. Am. Automobile Assn., Ariz. Dept. Edn.; named Small Businessman of Year, also Citizen of Yr., City of Sierra Vista, 1979. Mem. Nat. Assn. Advt. Publs., Western Pubs. Assn., Western Newspaper Found., Nat. Newspaper Assn., Wis. Newspaper Assn., Ariz. Newspaper Assn., Wis. Press Photographers Assn., Ariz. Interscholastic Assn., Nat. Sch. Bd. Assn., Sierra Vista C. of C. (past pres., bd. dirs.), Full Gospel Businessmen's Internat. Assn. (bd. dirs.), Assn. U.S. Army (dir.), Nat. Guard Employer-Employee Com., Kappa Sigma. Republican. Mem. Christ Tabernacle Ch. Clubs: Sierra Vista Rotary (pres., gov.'s rep. dist. 550), Lions (past mem. Wis. dist. cabinet), U. Wis. Lettermen's, U. Ariz. Wildcat, Masons. Home: 2500 Quail Run Sierra Vista AZ 85635 Office: 200 E Wilcox Dr Sierra Vista AZ 85635

BISHOP, GEORGE FRANKLIN, political social psychologist, educator; b. New Haven, July 26, 1942; s. George Elwood and Mary Bridget (Trant) B.; m. Lucille C. Minervini, Aug. 14, 1971; 1 child, Kristina. B.S. in Psychology, Mich. State U., 1966, M.A., 1969, Ph.D., 1973. Instr. Multidisciplinary Social Sci. program Mich. State U., East Lansing, 1972-73; asst. prof. dept. sociology and anthropology U. Notre Dame, Ind., 1973-75; research assoc. behavioral sci. lab U. Cin., 1975-77, sr. research assoc., 1977—, co-dir. Greater Cin. Survey, 1978-81, dir. Greater Cin. Survey, 1981—, assoc. prof. polit. sci., 1982-87, prof., 1987—; assoc. dir. Ohio Poll, 1981—; guest prof. Zentrum für Umfragen, Methoden und Analysen, Mannheim, Fed. Republic Germany, Aug.-Oct., 1985. Sr. editor The Presdl. Debates: Media, Electoral and Policy Perspectives, 1978; sr. author various articles in profl. jours.; editorial bd. mem. Pub. Opinion Quar., 1987—. Served with U.S. Army N.G., 1960-63. NSF grantee, 1977-84. Mem. Midwest Assn. Pub. Opinion Research (pres. 1977-78), Am. Assn. Pub. Opinion Research, Am. Polit. Sci. Assn., Soc. Advancement of Social Psychology, World Assn. Pub. Opinion Research (treas. 1983-85). Home: 459 Karenlaw Ln Cincinnati OH 45231 Office: ML132 Univ Cin Cincinnati OH 45221

BISHOP, GEORGE WILLIAMS, III, supply company executive; b. Williamson, W.Va., May 11, 1936; s. George W. and Dorothy Ann (Scott) B.; B.E.E., Va. Mil. Inst., 1958; postgrad. U. Va., 1959; m. Nancy Lee Long, Dec. 4, 1976; 1 dau., Rebecca Lee; children by previous marriage—George Williams IV, Angela, Brett, Dale Scott. Mgr. elec. div. Buchanan Williamson Supply Co., Grundy, Va., 1962-64, exec. v.p., 1964-77, pres., chmn., 1977-85 , dir., 1964-85 ; v.p., gen. mgr. Wingfield & Hundley, Inc., Richmond, Va., 1966-69, pres., 1969-72; chmn. Grundy Coal and Dock Co., 1977-85 , Royal Mgmt. Cons., 1983-86. Served to capt. USAF, 1959-62. Republican. Presbyterian. Lodge: Rotary (local pres. 1965-66). Home: 710 Sharon Dr Johnson City TN 37601 Winter Home: 1020 Ponce de Leon Dr Fort Lauderdale FL 33316

BISHOP, JAMES DREW, editor; b. London, June 18, 1929; s. Patrick and Vera (Drew) B.; m. Brenda Pearson, June 5, 1959; children—Edward James, William John. B.A., Cambridge U., 1953. Fgn. corr. The Times, London, 1957-64, fgn. news editor, 1964-66, features editor, 1966-71; editor The Illustrated London News, 1971-87; editor-in-chief, 1987—; dir. Internat. Thomson Pub. Ltd., London, 1980-85; mem. adv. bd., author Am. sect. The Annual Register, London, 1970—. Author: The Social History of Edwardian Britain, 1977; The Social History of First World War, 1982; co-author: The Story of the Times, 1983; editor: The Illustrated Counties of England, 1985. Mem. Assn. Brit. Editors (chmn. 1987—). Clubs: United Oxford and Cambridge, MCC. Office: The Illustrated London News, 20 Upper Ground, London SEWI 9PF, England

BISHOP, JAMES KEOUGH, foreign service officer; b. New Rochelle, N.Y., July 21, 1938. B.S., Coll. Holy Cross, 1960; grad. exec. seminar in nat. and internat. affairs, Fgn. Service Inst., 1977; M.I.I.P., Johns Hopkins U., 1981. With Fgn. Service, Dept. State, 1960—; press officer Dept. State, 1961-63; vice consul Auckland, N.Z., 1963-66; econ. officer Beirut, 1966-68, Yaounde, 1968-70; internat. relations officer Bur. African Affairs, 1970-74; dep. dir. Office West African Affairs, 1974-76; dir. North African Affairs, Dept. State, 1977-79; AEP, Republic of Niger, 1979-81; dep. asst. sec. state African Affairs Bur., 1981-87; U. S. ambassador to Liberia, Washington, DC, 1987—. Office: US Ambassador to Liberia Am Embassy APO NY 09155

BISHOP, JOYCE ANN, financial planner; b. West Mansfield, Ohio, June 16, 1935; d. Frederic J. and Marjorie Vere (Stephens) Armentrout; m. Belinda Lee, Thomas James. AB, Albion Coll., 1956; MA, Western Mich. U., 1969, postgrad., 1972-87. Cert. social worker. Tchr. phys. edn., health and cheerleading Walled Lake (Mich.) Jr. High Sch., 1956-58; instr. slimnastics adult edn. Milw. Pub. Schs., 1959-65; demonstrator, co. rep. Polaroid Corp., Cambridge, Mass., 1960-81; research asst. fetal electrocardiography Marquette U., Milw., 1962-64; tchr. phys. edn., health and cheerleading Brown Deer (Wis.) High Sch., 1963-65; instr. slimnastics adult edn., instr. volleyball Lakeview High Sch., Battle Creek, Mich., 1966—; dir. student activities, counselor, asst. prof. Kellogg Community Coll., Battle Creek, 1971-87, transfer counselor; asst. prof. Olivet (Mich.) Coll., 1969-71. Sec. adult bd. Teens, Inc., 1965-68; bd. dirs. Battle Creek Day Care Ctrs., sec., 1984, pres., 1984-86; team capt. United Way Awareness Week, 1984, United Arts Fund Dr., 1985, chmn., 1986; mem. Battle Creek Leadership Acad. Recipient Master Teaching award Lakeview Schs., 1969, 87. Mem. Mich. Assn. Collegiate Registrars and Admissions Officers (pres. 1979-80, historian 1984-87), Am. Assn. Collegiate Registrars and Admissions Officers (mem. com. 1984-87), Am. Personnel and Guidance Assn., Am. Coll. Personnel Assn., Mich. Personnel and Guidance Assn., Mich. Coll. Personnel Assn., Mich. Assn. Women Deans, Adminstrs. and Counselors, Mich. Assn. Coll. Admissions Counselors, AAUW, Alpha Chi Omega, Beta Beta Beta. Clubs: Battle Creek Road Runners (v.p. 1983-85), Battle Creek Altrusa. Home: 721 Eastfield Dr Battle Creek MI 49015 Office: Richard M Groff Assocs Inc 5320 Holiday Terr Kalamazoo MI 49009

BISHOP, SID GLENWOOD, union official; b. Gladehill, Va., Nov. 11, 1923; s. Clarence Glenwood and Lillian Helen (Onks) B.; grad. U.S. Naval Trade Sch., 1942; certificate in coll. labor relations Concord Coll., Athens, W.Va., 1961; m. Margaret Lucille Linkous, June 6, 1947. Telegraph operator Virginian R.R., 1946-47, C & O R.R., 1947-62; local chmn. Order R.R. Telegraphers, 1960-62, gen. chmn. C & O-Virginian R.R.'s, 1962-68; 2d v.p. Transp-Communication Employees Union, St. Louis, 1968-69; v.p. communication-transp. div. Brotherhood Ry. and Airline Clks., Rockville, Md., 1969-73, asst. internat. v.p., 1973—; mem. subcom. Labor Research Adv. Council, Dept. Labor, 1975, mem. com. on productivity, tech., growth Bur. Labor Statistics, 1975-77. Served with USN, 1941-46. Mem. AFL-CIO, Canadian Labor Congress, Hunting Hills Home Owners Assn., VFW. Democrat. Clubs: Chantilly Nat. Golf and Country. Lodge: Elks, Masons, K.T., Shriners. Home and Office: 5211 Chukar Dr SW Roanoke VA 24014

BISHOP, SUSAN KATHARINE, search company executive; b. Palm Beach, Fla., Apr. 3, 1946; d. Warner Bader Bishop and Katharine Sue (White) McLennan; m. Robert Uchitel, Dec. 27, 1973 (div. 1979); 1 child, Rachel. B.A., Briarcliff Coll., 1968; M.B.A., Fordham U., 1985. Actress, N.Y.C., 1968-72; producer, hostess Sta. KIMO-TV, Anchorage, 1972-74; dir. programming Visions Pay TV, 1974-79; recruiter Joe Sullivan & Assocs., N.Y.C., 1980-82; prin. Johnson, Smith & Knisely, 1982-87, ptnr., 1988—. Mem. Cable TV Adminstrn. and Mktg. Soc., Women in Cable. Office: Johnson Smith & Knisely 475 Fifth Ave New York NY 10017

BISHOP, THOMAS RAY, mechanical engineer, retired; b. Hutchinson, Kans., Oct. 26, 1925; s. Orren E. and Myrtle (Dale) Bish; student California (Pa.) State Tchrs. Coll., 1947-48; B.S., U. Houston, 1953; postgrad. U. Wash., 1960-61; grad. Alexander Hamilton Bus. Inst., 1972; m. Mary Lou Nesmith, Sept. 1, 1951 children—Thomas Ray II, Frances Joann. Research engr. Boeing Co., Seattle, 1953-64, research engr. Apollo program, 1964-69; asst. chief engr. Product div. Bowen Tools, Inc., Houston, 1969-75, chief engr., 1975-77, chief engr. research and devel., 1977-86; cons. engr., Tom Bishop Enterprises, 1986—; asso. ABC Mech. Engr. Cons. Precinct committeeman King County (Wash.) Democratic Com., 1960; pres. Tom Bishop Enterprises. Served with USMCR, 1944-46. Decorated Purple Heart; named Engr. of Year, Boeing Aerospace Co., 1966; recipient Excellence in Engring. citation A.I.S.I., 1975. Registered profl. engr., Ala., La., Tex. Mem. Tex. Soc. Profl. Engrs. Unitarian. Mason. Contbr. articles to profl. jours.; multipatentee oil field equipment field. Home and Office: 2202 Viking Dr Houston TX 77018

BISHOP, VIRGINIA WAKEMAN, librarian, humanities educator; b. Portland, Oreg., Dec. 28, 1927; d. Andrew Virgil and Letha Evangeline (Ward) Wakeman; m. Clarence Edmund Bishop, Aug. 23, 1953; children: Jean Marie Bishop Johnson, Marilyn Joyce. BA, Bapt. Missionary Tng. Sch., Chgo., 1949; BA, Linfield Coll., McMinnville, Oreg., 1952, MEd, 1953; MA in Librarianship, U. Wash., 1968. Ch. worker Univ. Bapt. Ch., Seattle, 1954-56, 59-61; pre-sch. tchr. parent coop presch., Seattle, 1965-66; librarian Northwest Coll., Kirkland, Wash., 1968-69, U. Wash. undergrad. library, Seattle, 1970; librarian, instr. Seattle Central Community Coll., 1970—. Leader Totem council Girl Scouts U.S., 1962-65; pres. Wedgwood Sch. PTA, Seattle, 1964-65; chairperson 46th Dist. Democratic Orgn., Seattle, 1972-73; candidate Wash. State Legislature, Seattle, 1974, 80. Recipient Golden Acorn award Wedgwood Elem. Sch., 1966. Mem. Wash. Commn. for Humanities (Humanist scholar 1979-80), Wash. Library Assn. (legis. rep. 1972), U. Wash. Grad. Sch. Library and Info. Sci. Alumni Assn. (1st v.p. 1986-87, pres. 1987—), Community Coll. Librarians and Media Specialists, Seattle Community Coll. Fedn. Tchrs., LWV. Unitarian. Avocations: swimming, hiking, reading. Home: 3032 NE 87th St Seattle WA 98115 Office: Seattle Cen Community Coll 1701 Broadway Seattle WA 98122

BISPO, ANTONIO ALEXANDRE, musicologist, architect; b. São Paulo, Brazil, Mar. 17, 1949; arrived in Fed. Republic Germany, 1974.; s. Antonio and Ermelinda (Rego) B. Lic. in Mus. Edn., Inst. Mus. de São Paulo, 1972, Lic. Condr., 1973; Diploma Architect, U. São Paulo, 1972; D Musicology, U. Cologne, Fed. Republic Germany, 1979. Dir. Conservatorio Jardim Am.,

São Paulo, 1971-73; lectr. Faculdade de Musica, São Paulo, 1973-74; researcher Institut für Hymnologische und Musikethnologische Studien Maria Laach, Cologne, 1979—; dir. Musikschule der Stadt, Leichlingen, Fed. Republic Germany, 1981-84; mem. council Consociato Internationalis Musicae Sacrae, Rome, 1980-85. Author: Die Katholische Kirchenmusik in der Provinz São Paulo, 1979, Zur Formung Musikkultur ij der Katholischer Welt der Neuzeit, 1988; contbg. author: Collectanea Musicae Sacrae Brasiliensis, 1981; contbr. articles to profl. jours. Mem. Soc. Brasileira de Musicologia (bd. dirs. 1981—), Acad. Paulistana de Historia. Roman Catholic. Home: Theodor Heuss Ring 14, 5000 Cologne Federal Republic of Germany

BISSADA, NABIL KADDIS, urologist, professor; b. Cairo, Egypt, Sept. 2, 1938; s. Kaddis B. and Negma Bissada; m. Samia Shafik Henain, July 23, 1967; children—Sally, Nancy, Mary, Amy, Andrew. M.D., Cairo U., 1963. Diplomate Am. Bd. Urology. Intern, Cairo Univ. Hosp., 1964-65; resident in urology U. N.C. Hosp., 1970-73; asst. prof. urology U. Ark., 1973-77, assoc. prof., 1977-79; cons. urologist King Faisal Specialist Hosp., Riyadh, Saudi Arabia, 1979-87; prof. urology Med. U. S.C., 1987— ; frequent speaker to regional, nat. and internat. med. groups. Fellow ACS, Internat. Coll. Surgeons; mem. AMA, Am. Urol. Assn., Sigma Xi. Author: Lower Urinary Tract Function and Dysfunction: Diagnosis and Management, 1978; Pharmacology of the Urinary Tract and the Male Reproductive System, 1982; numerous articles in field. Address: Med Univ of SC Med Ctr 171 Ashley Ave Charleston SC 29425-2280

BISSELL, ELAINE, novelist, writer; b. Chgo., Oct. 18; d. Harold Whitney and Edwinna Stuart (Biederman) Faulkner; m. John Cooper McMahon, May 31, 1941 (div. 1959); children—Mary Jane McMahon Christofferson, Kathleen Conroy, Susan; m. Nicol Bissell, Dec. 18, 1965. Student Goodman Theatre Sch. Drama, NYU. Reporter Daily Times, Mamaroneck, N.Y., 1956-61; woman's editor Standard-Star, New Rochelle, N.Y., 1961-74; social editor Gannett-Westchester Newspapers, White Plains, N.Y., 1974-77, lifestyles editor, 1977-84, restaurant critic, 1984—; author, novelist St. Martin's Press, N.Y.C. Author: Women Who Wait, 1978; As Time Goes By, 1983; Family Fortunes, 1985, Empire, 1988. Bd. dirs. Iona Coll. Inst. for Arts, New Rochelle, 1961-75. Recipient Penney-Mo. Journalism award U. Mo., 1978. Mem. Authors League of Am., Authors Guild, Overseas Press Club.

BISSON, ANDRE, management executive; b. Trois-Rivieres, Que., Can., Oct. 7, 1929; s. Roger and Marcelle (Morin) B.; m. Reine Levesque, June 13, 1953; children—Helene, Isabelle. BA, Laval U., Que., 1950, M.Commerce, 1953; MBA, Harvard U., 1955, LHD (hon.), U. Du Quebec, 1985. Asst. prof. bus. adminstrn. Laval U., 1955-63, assoc. prof., 1963-66; dir. Inst. Can. Bankers, Montreal, Que., 1966-71; gen. mgr. Bank of N.S., Montreal, 1971-77, v.p., gen. mgr., 1977-83, sr. v.p., gen. mgr., 1983-87; pres. Logistec Corp., 1987—, Donohue Inc., Columbia Computing Services Inc.; bd. dirs. Rougier Inc., Miron Inc., Power Fin. Corp., L'Union Can. Cie d'Assurance, Que; bd. dirs. Cercle des chefs mailleurs du Quebec. Chmn. bd. Notre Dame Hosp., Montreal, 1977—, Fondation canadienne de perfectionnement en affaires; bd. dirs. U. Montreal, 1979—, Fondation de l'Universitié du Québec à Montréal, Montreal Bd. Trade, Théâtre du Noveau Monde, European Inst. Bus. Adminstrs., Fontainebleau, France, 1977—. Named Man of Month, Revue Commerce, Montreal, 1979; mem. Order of Can., Gov. Gen., Ottawa, 1982; recipient medal Gloire de l'Escolle, Laval U. Alumni Assn., Que., 1982. Fellow Inst. Can. Bankers (hon.), mem. French C. of C. in Can. (pres. 1983-85), International Fin. Ctrs. Orgn. Montreal, Société d'Investissement Jeunesse, Province of Que. C. of C. (exec. com. 1976-80). Roman Catholic. Clubs: Mount Royal (com. 1987), St. James (com. 1975-78), Canadian of Montreal, Harvard Bus. Montreal (pres. 1971), St.-Denis (bd. 1984) (Montreal).

BISTRIAN, BRUCE RYAN, internist, educator; b. Southampton, N.Y., Oct. 22, 1939; s. Peter and Mary Laura (Ryan) B.; m. Eleanor Alice Dix, Sept. 3, 1964; children—Tennille Ryan, Jordan Brooke, Britton Perry. B.A., NYU, 1961; M.D., Cornell U., 1965; M.P.H., Johns Hopkins U., 1971; Ph.D., MIT, 1975. Diplomate: Am. Bd. Internal Medicine; bd. cert. Critical Care Medicine. Intern Cornell U., N.Y.C., 1965-66; metabolism fellow U. Vt., Burlington, 1968-69, resident in medicine, 1969-70; mem. faculty Harvard U. Med. Sch., Boston, 1975—; clin. assoc. physician research resources div. NIH, 1975-78; lectr. MIT, 1981-84. Contbr. over 120 sci. articles to profl. publs. Served to capt. U.S. Army, 1966-68. Grantee Nat. Inst. Gen. Med. Scis., 1977-80; Nat. Inst. Arthritis, Metabolism and Digestive Disease, 1979-83, Nat. Inst. Arthritis, Diabetes, Digestive and Kidney Diseases, 1985—, Nat. Cancer Inst., 1984—. Fellow Am. Coll. Nutrition, ACP; mem. Fedn. Am. Soc. Exptl. Biologists, Am. Soc. Clin. Nutrition, Am. Fedn. Clin. Research, Am. Soc. Parenteral and Enteral Nutrition, Mass. Med. Soc. Presbyterian. Subspecialties: Nutrition (medicine); Biochemistry (medicine). Current work: Protein calorie malnutrition; total parenteral nutrition; nutrition and infection; treatment of obesity. Home: Argilla Rd Ipswich MA 01938 Office: New Eng Deaconess Hosp 194 Pilgrim Dr Boston MA 02215

BITTANTI, SERGIO, mathematics and engineering educator; b. Milan, Jan. 7, 1947; s. Giulio Piero and Vittorina (Scida) B. D in Electronic Engring., Poly. U. Milan, 1970; D in Math., U. Milan, 1978. Researcher Poly. Milan, 1971, 73, asst. prof., 1974-78, assoc. prof., 1979-85, full prof., 1986—. Contbr. articles to profl. jours. Mem. IEEE, Assn. Mex. Control Automatico, Soc. Brasileira Automatico, Society for Indsl. and Applied Math., Unione Matematica Italiana. Office: Politecnico Milano, Piazza Leonardo da Vinci 32, 20133 Milan Italy

BIVAS, ROBERT, chemical company executive; b. Paris, May 29, 1940; s. Albert and Laure (Dinar) B.; m. Michele Eripret, Sept. 7, 1963; children: Pierre, Philippe. BS in Engring., Ecole Poly., Paris, 1960; DSc, Facult'46 de Scis., Paris, 1968. Researcher Centre Nat. d'Etudes Spatiales, Paris, 1963-68; cons. Sligos, Puteaux, France, 1969-81; group info. systems mgr. Rhône Poulenc, Courbevoie, France, 1983—; cons. in field, 1981-82; adminstr. Club Informatique des Grandes Enterprises Françaises. Contbr. articles to profl. jours. Mem. Com. for Space Research, Internat. Union Geodesy and Geophysics. Home: Clos St Michel Damply, Montalet Le Bois, F78440 Gargenville France Office: Rhone Poulenc Group, 25 quai Paul Doumer, 92408 Courbevoie France

BIXBY, R. BURDELL, lawyer; b. Schenectady, Oct. 11, 1914; s. Raymond O. and Mabel A. (Rumsey) B.; m. Anne M. Hardwick, Oct. 25, 1941; 1 son, Robert Hardwick. A.B., Colgate U., 1936; LL.B., Albany Law Sch., 1940, J.D., 1968. Bar: N.Y. 1940. Partner firm Dewey, Ballantine, Bushby, Palmer & Wood, N.Y.C., 1955—; Asst. sec. gov. State N.Y., 1948-50, exec. asst., 1950-52, sec., 1952-54; sec.-treas. N.Y. State Thruway Authority, 1950-60, chmn., sec., treas., 1960-61, chmn., sec., 1961-74; permanent pres. N.Y. State Electoral Coll. of 1972. Trustee Hudson City Savs. Instn., N.Y.; treas. N.Y. State Republican Com., 1959-61. Served with USAAF, 1942-46. Mem. ABA, Am. Legion. Lodge: Masons. Home: 7 Joslen Pl Hudson NY 12534 Office: Dewey Ballantine Bushby et al 140 Broadway New York NY 10005

BIYA, PAUL, president of Cameroon; b. Mvomeko, Cameroon, Feb. 13, 1933; Licence en Droit Public, U. Paris, 1960; diplome Institut d'Etudes Politiques Paris, 1961; diplome Institut des Hautes Etudes d'Outre-Mer, 1962; diplome Etudes Superieures en Droit Public, 1963; m. Jeanne Atyam; 1 child. Head, Dept. Fgn. Devel. Aid, 1962-63; dir. cabinet in Ministry Nat. Edn., 1964-65; mem. goodwill mission to Ghana and Nigeria, 1965; sec.-gen. Ministry Edn., Youth and Culture, 1965-67; dir. Civil Cabinet of Head of State, 1967-68; sec.-gen. to pres., 1968; minister of state, sec.-gen. to pres., 1968-75; prime minister, 1975-82; president Republic of Cameroon, 1982—. Decorated chevalier Order de la Valeur Cemerounaise; comdr. Nat. Order Fed. Republic Germany, Nat. Order Tunisia; Grand-Croix Nat. Order of Merit Senegal; grand officer Legion of Honor (France). Mem. Union Nat. Camerouaise. Address: Office of President, Yaounde Cameroon *

BJARNASON, GUDMUNDUR, minister of health and social security; b. Húsavik, Northern, Iceland, Oct. 9, 1944; s. Bjarni Stefánsson and Jakobina Jónssdóttir; m. Vigdis Funnarsdóttir, Dec. 25, 1965; children: Jakobina, Arna, Silja Rún. Grad., Co-operative Coll., Bifröst, Iceland, 1963. With Coop. Soc., Húsaviik, 1963-67, Coop. Bank of Iceland, Húsavik, 1967-77; dir. br. Keflavík, Iceland, 1977-80; member Althingi-Progressive Party, NE Constituency, 1979—; minister of health and social security Govt. of Iceland, 1987—. Office: Heilbrigôisráôuneytiô, Laugavegi 116, 150 Reykjavík Iceland

BJARNASON, MATTHIAS, former government offical; b. Isafjorour, Iceland, Aug. 15, 1921; s. Bjarni and Audur (Johannestottir) B.; m. Kristin Ingimundardottir; 2 children. Grad. Comml. Coll. Iceland, 1939. Dir. Djupbatur Ltd., 1942-68, Kogur Fishing Co. Ltd., 1956-66, Isafjorour Shipping Ins. Co.; town counsellor Isafjorour, 1946-70, pres. council, 1950-52; rep. Western Iceland, Althing, 1963—, minister of fisheries, health and social security, 1974-78, minister of communications, 1983-87; editor Western Iceland weekly, 1953-59. Chmn. youth assn. Independence party, Isafjorour, 1945-50; chmn. bd. dirs. Isafjorour Mcpl. Electricity Distbn. System, 1946-51; chmn. Independence Party Assn. Western Iceland, 1955-61, chmn. bd. reps., 1960-68, mem. central com., 1970—. Mem. Union of Icelandic Fishing Vessels (dir. 1962-74), Icelandic Fishing Vessels Joint Ins. Inst. (chmn. 1967-74), Icelandic Fishing Industries Fund (dir. 1969-74), Econ. Devel. Inst. Iceland (dir. 1972-74). Address: Ministry of Communications, Reykjavik Iceland *

BJERCKE, ALF RICHARD, business executive; b. Oslo, May 30, 1921; s. Richard and Birgit (Brambani) B.; student Mass. Inst. Tech., 1939-41; m. Berit Blikstad, Mar. 15, 1946; children—Leif Richard, Haakon Richard, Ingerid, Berit. With Alf Bjercke A/S, Oslo, 1945—, partner, 1950—, vice chmn., 1966-69, chmn., 1969—; dir. A/S. Jotungruppen, 1972-83, chmn. corp. council, 1983—; chmn. bd. Nydalens Compagnie, 1982—; with Addis Ababa, Nat. Chem. Ind. Ltd., 1966-75; chmn. Norwater (Norske Vannkilder A/S.), ABC Produkter A/S, Scanpump A/S, 1972-78, Vallenova, Inc., Oslo, 1984—; chmn., dir. Oplandske Dampskibsselskab, 1981—; dir. Norwegian Shipping & Trade Jour., 1962-81, Atheneum Forlag, Vallenova Inc.; chmn. Jotungruppen A/S, Kolding, Denmark; vice chmn. Akershus Broiler Co., chmn. Chilinvest A/S., Pan Art Gallery; dir. Atheneum Pub. Co., Mosvold Overseas Trading Co., Atheneum Communications, Inc., Mosvold Internat., Inc., Alamo Co. Hon. consul gen. Tunisia in Norway, City Gruppen A/S; vice chmn. Norwegian Spring Water Assn.; chmn. council Kofoed Sch., 1962-80; mem. Norway's Olympic Com., 1971-74; mem. exec. com. Norwegian UNIDO Council, del. conf.; Norway del. Econ. Commn. for Africa; mem. Norwegian Arbitration Bd. for Competitive Questions; chmn. Soc. for Protection Ancient Towns, Soc. for Reconstrn. of Old Christiania, 1968-78; mem. council Norsk Sjofartsmuseum; chmn. bd. Norway's Bus. Mus., 1980—; Norwegian mem. adv. com. Sail Tng. Assn., London; past chmn. Nordic Adv. Council for Industry; mem. Commn. 3 CIOR, Norwegian chmn. Rotary Internat. Campaign Polio Plus (eradicating polio). Mem. campaign com. Norwegian Conservative party, 1974, council mem. Oslo'dagere '86; bd. dirs. Artists Gallery of Oslo, 1957-69; vice chmn. East Norway Sailing Sch. Ship Assn., 1961-78; chmn. Norwegian-Ethiopian Soc., 1954-70; chmn. council Norway-Am. Assn.; chmn. fin. com. Norwegian World Wild Life Fund Bd. Reps.; Norwegian rep. Operation Sail 76; bd. dirs. A Smoke-free Generation, 1980; chmn. Norwegian Ch. Council, 1984; bd. dirs. Case (Norway), 1984, Norwegian Orgn. Asylum Seekers, 1984; Served with Royal Norwegian Air Force, 1941-45; maj. Res. Mem. Norwegian Assn. Industries (past dir.), Color Council Norway (chmn. 1958-69, 72-81), Norwegian Paint Mfrs. Assn. (past chmn.), Norway Athletic Assn. (chmn. 1968-72), Wine and Food Soc., World Wildlife Fund 1001 Club. Clubs: Rotary (dist. gov. 1980-81, vice chmn. world community service); Oslo Bus. Men's (dir. 1968-70). Pub.: From the Diplomatic World, 1983. Contbr. articles in several fields to profl. jours.; columnist jour. Farmand. Home: 14 President Harbitzgate 0259, Oslo 2 Norway Office: Solliveien 2a, 1324 Lysaker Norway

BJORK, ROBERT DAVID, JR., lawyer; b. Evanston, Ill., Sept. 29, 1946; s. Robert David and Lenore Evelyn (Loderhose) B.; m. Linda Louise Reese, Mar. 27, 1971; children: Heidi Lynne, Gretchen Anne. BBA, U. Wis., 1968; JD, Tulane U., 1974. Bar: La. 1974, U.S. Dist. Ct. (ea. dist.) La. 1974, U.S. Ct. Appeals (5th cir.) 1974, U.S. Dist. Ct. (mid. dist.) 1975, U.S. Supreme Ct. 1977, U.S. Dist. Ct. (we. dist.) 1978, U.S. Ct. Appeals (11th cir.) 1981, Calif. 1983, U.S. Dist. Ct. (no. dist.) Calif. 1983, U.S. Dist. Ct. (ea. dist.) Calif. 1984. Ptnr. Adams & Rees, New Orleans, 1974-83; assoc. Crosby, Heafey, Roach & May, Oakland, Calif., 1983-85; ptnr. Bjork, Fleer & Lawrence, Oakland, 1985—; instr. paralegal studies Tulane U., New Orleans, 1979-82. Mem. Tulane U. Law Rev., 1973-74; editor Med. Malpractice newsletter, 1983—. Bd. dirs. Piedmont (Calif.) Council of Camp Fire, 1984—, pres. 1987—; treas. Couhig Congl. Com., New Orleans, 1980-82. Served to lt., USNR, 1968-71. Mem. ABA, Calif. Bar Assn., La. Bar Assn. (chmn. young lawyers sect. 1982-83), Am. Soc. Law and Medicine. Home: 1909 Oakland Ave Piedmont CA 94611 Office: Bjork Fleer & Lawrence 192 Tenth St Oakland CA 94607

BJORKLUND, JANET VINSEN, speech pathologist; b. Seattle, July 31, 1947; d. Vernon Edward and Virginia Lea (Rogers) B.; m. Dan Robert Young, Dec. 04, 1971; children: Emery Allen, Alanna Vinsen, Marisa Rogers. Student, U. Vienna, Austria, 1966-67; BA, Pacific U., 1969; student, U. Wash., 1970-71; MA, San Francisco State U., 1977. Cert. clin. speech pathologist, audiologist. Speech pathologist, audiological cons. USN Hosp., Rota, Spain, 1972-75; traineeship in audiology VA Hosp., San Francisco, 1976; speech pathologist San Lorenzo (Calif.) Unified Schs., 1975-77, 78-81; dir. speech pathology St. Lukes Speech and Hearing Clinic, San Francisco, 1977-78; audiologist X.O. Barrios, M.D., San Francisco, 1977-81; cons. Visually Impaired Infant Program, Seattle, 1981-82; speech pathologist Everett (Wash.) Schs., 1982—; cons. Madison House, Kirkland, Wash., 1983-88, NW Devel. Therapists, Everett, 1985-87, Pediatric Diagnostic and Treatment Ctr., Everett, 1985—, Pacific Hearing and Speach, 1988—. Author: (with others) Screening for Bilingual Preschoolers, 1977, (TV script), Clinical Services in San Francisco, 1978, Developing Better Communication Skills, 1982. Coordinator pre-sch. Christian edn. Kirkland Congl. Ch., Wash., 1983-85; organizer Residents Against Speeding Drivers, Madison Park, Seattle, 1985-87. Mem. Am. Speech and Hearing Assn., Am. Speech and Hearing Found., Wash. Speech and Hearing Assn. (regional rep. 1985-86, chair licensure task force 1986-88), Phi Lambda Omicron (pres. Pacific U. chpt. 1968). Congregational. Office: Everett Sch Dist 2 202 Alder Everett WA 98203

BJÖRNER, ANDERS, mathematician, educator; b. Örnsköldsvik, Sweden, Dec. 17, 1947; s. Arne and Maud (Ocklind) B.; m. Christine Kast, Apr. 29, 1967; children: Edward, Katja, Siri, Elise. PhD, U. Stockholm, 1979. Asst. prof. U. Stockholm, 1980-84; asst., assoc. prof. MIT, Cambridge, Mass., 1984-87; prof. Royal Inst. Tech., Stockholm, 1987—. Contbr. articles to profl. jours. Recipient Letterstedt prize Royal Swedish Acad. Scis., 1982, G. Polya prize Soc. Indsl. Applied Math, 1983. Mem. Swedish Math. Soc. (sec. 1980-82), Am. Math. Soc. Office: Royal Inst Tech, Dept Math, S-10044 Stockholm Sweden

BJORNESETH, HELGE JOHAN, finance executive; b. Aalesund, Sunnmore, Norway, June 9, 1943; s. Johan Peter and Hjordis (Eidem) B.; m. Brit Lied; children: Gisle Johan, Torje-Bendik, Froy-Birte. Mktg. 1st Level, Aalesund Highs; Mktg. High Level, Norwegian Sch. Mgmt. Mktg. sec. A/S Porolon, Aalesund, 1963-67, Eriksens Oljeklade, Aalesund, 1967-69; export cons. Norwegian Govt. Scheme Textile, Oslo, 1969-70; sales mgr. Westnofa-Infi Internat., London, 1970-72; export mgr. Stoknes Trikotasje, Aalesund, 1972-74, Stok Food, Aalesund, 1974-75; dir. Highland Stokfood, Iverness, Scotland, 1975-77, Breasclete Fishing Co., Aberdeen, Scotland, 1975-79; new bus. mgr. Aalesund Sparebank, 1979-82; regional dir. Norsk Finans, Aalesund, 1982-84, A.S. Factoring Finans, Aalesund, 1985—. Mem. Alesund Handels Forening, Aalesund, 1975, Polyteknisk Forening Export, Oslo, 1977; pres. Eksportklubben Sunnmere, Aalesund, 1980; bd. dirs. Norwegian Sch. Mgmt. Campus More, Aalesund, 1985—. Conservative. Club: Norwegian (London). Lodge: Old Fellows. Home: Svartskjerveien 10, Aalesund Sunnmore N-6017, Norway Office: AS Factoring, Finans Notenesgt 14 PO Box 570, Aalesund N-6001, Norway

BJORNSSON, SIGURDUR, physician; b. Princeton, N.J., June 5, 1942; s. Bjorn Sigurdsson and Una (Johannesdottir) S.; m. Gudny Stefania Kristjansdottir, June 11, 1966; children—Kristin, Bjorn, Signy Sif. M.D., U. Iceland, 1968. Diplomate Am. Bd. Internal Medicine. Intern U. Iceland Hosp., Reykjavik, 1969; resident New Britain Gen. Hosp., Conn., 1972; fellow Roswell Park Meml. Inst., Buffalo, 1974; sr. cancer research internist Roswell Park Meml. Inst., Buffalo, 1974-78; research asst. prof. medicine SUNY, Buffalo, 1977-78; cons. med. oncologist City Hosp., Reykjavik, Iceland, 1978—; attending physician internal medicine and oncology St. Joseph's Hosp., Reykjavik, 1978—; cons. med. oncologist U. Hosp., Reykjavik, 1978—; lectr. medicine and oncology U. Iceland, Reykjavik, 1978—. Bd. dirs. Icelandic Cancer Soc., Reykjavik, 1980, Icelandic Physicians for the Prevention Nuclear War, Reykjavik, 1983. Mem. Am. Soc. Clin. Oncology, Am. Assn. Cancer Research, Icelandic Med. Assn., Icelandic Soc. Internal Medicine, World Med. Assn. Home: Bergstadastraeti 78, 101 Reykjavik Iceland Office: St Joseph's Hosp, Tungata, Reykjavik Iceland

BJORNVIG, THORKID STRANGE, poet, writer; b. Feb. 2, 1918; s. Adda and Theodor B.; m. Grete Damgaard Pedersen, 1946; m. Birgit Hornum, 1970; 3 children. Ed. Cathedral Sch., Aarhus, Denmark; Dr.Phil., U. Aarhus. Author: Stjaernen bag gavlen, 1947; Anubis, 1955; Figur og Ild, 1959; Vibrationer, 1966; Ravnen, 1968; Udvalgte digte, 1970; Morgenmorke, 1977; (essays) Rilke og tysk Tradition, 1959; Begyndelsen, 1960; Kains Alter, 1964; Opror mod neonguden, 1970; Virkeligheden er til, 1973; Pagten mit venskab med Karen Blixen, 1974; Delfinen, 1975; Stoffets Krystalhav, 1975; Det religiose menneskes ansigter, 1975; Ogsa for naturens skyld, 1978; Bernet og dyret i industrisamfundet, 1979; Abeguder Miljodigte 1975-80, 1981; The Pact: My Friendship with Isak Dinesen, 1983. Mem. Danish Acad., 1960. Recipient numerous prizes for excellence in writing. Address: Issehoved, 8795 Nordby Denmark *

BJORUM, HALVDAN, mining company executive; b. Oslo, July 23, 1926; s. Haakon Johan and Julie (Bing) B.; m. Mette Margrethe Bergh, Nov. 30, 1962; children: Rolf M., Haakon Johan, Annette Julie. BSc, Purdue U., 1951. Sales engr. H. Bjorum, Oslo, 1952-57, sales mgr., 1958-62, mng. dir., 1962-68, chmn., mng. dir., 1968—; chmn. bd. EB, Oslo, 1974-86, M. Peterson & Son, Moss, 1970—, Sarpsborg Papp A/S, 1975—, Saab Norge A/S, 1979—, Vingreiser A/S, Oslo, 1976—; vice chmn. bd. Lovenskiold-Vakero A/S, 1980—; dir. D.N.L. A/S, Vingresor AB, Stockholm, Scanair A/B, Scandinavian Airlines. Mem. fin. com. Conservative party, 1982-87. Served to lt. Air Force, 1951-56. Mem. Am. Inst. Mining. Lutheran. Clubs: Norske Selskab, Royal Aero (London). Home: Holmenkollvn 120B, 0391 Oslo Norway Office: H Bjorum, Kirkevn 7, PB 5683, 0209 Oslo Norway

BLACHFORD, PETER CARL HOWARD, medical executive, health care consultant; b. North Bay, Ont., Can., Apr. 28, 1949; s. Howard Arnold and Mary Greenlees (Rous) B.; children: Courtney Patricia, Lauren Alexandra. BBA, York U., Toronto, Can., 1972, MBA, 1973. Owner, mgr. B&C Services Ltd., Landscape Cons., Oakville, Ont., Can., 1968-73; sr. corp. planner Imperial Oil Ltd., Toronto, Can., 1973-75; sr. mgmt. cons. Toronto Gen. Hosp., 1975-76; asst. adminstr. Oaklands Regional Ctr., Oakville, 1976-78; sr. mgt. cons. Woods Gordon (Arthur Young Can.), 1978-80; pres., chief exec. officer Queensway Gen. Hosp., Etobicoke, Ont., Can., 1980-86; pres., chief exec. officer Toronto East Gen. & Orthopaedic Hosp. Inc., 1986—, also bd. dirs., sec. bd.; bd. dirs. Centennial Linen Services, Toronto; guest lectr. U. Toronto Faculty of Medicine, 1981—. Contbr. articles on health care mgmt. to profl. pubs. Bd. dirs. Toronto East Gen. & Orthopaedic Hosp. Found. and Research Found., 1986-87; mem. Town Planning Bd. Adv., Oakville, 1976-78, Muskoka (Ont.) Lakes Assn., 1967-87; preceptor Masters of Health Care Service Students, U. Toronto, 1981—. Mem. Can. Coll. Health Service Execs. (cert.); C.H.E., 1984. Anglican. Clubs: Badminton & Racquet, Boulevard (Toronto). Home: 2373 Conquest Dr, Mississauga, ON Canada L5C 2Z1 Office: Toronto E Gen & Ortho Hosp, 825 Coxwell Ave, Toronto, ON Canada M4C 3E7

BLACHLY, JACK LEE, oil company executive, lawyer; b. Dallas, Mar. 8, 1942; s. Emery Lee and Thelma Jo (Budd) B.; m. Lucy Largent Rain, Jan. 15, 1972; 1 son, Michael Talbot. B.B.A., So. Meth. U., 1965, J.D., 1968. Bar: Tex. 1968, U.S. Ct. Appeals (5th cir.) 1969, U.S. Supreme Ct. 1975, U.S. Tax Ct. 1977. Trust officer InterFirst Bank Dallas, N.A., 1968-70; ptnr. firm Reese & Blachly, Dallas, 1970-71; assoc. firm Rain Harrell Emery Young & Doke, Dallas, 1971-76; staff atty. Sabine Corp., Dallas, 1976-77, mgr. legal dept., 1977-80, v.p., gen. counsel, 1980—. Mem. ABA, Tex. Bar Assn., Dallas Bar Assn., Am. Soc. Corp. Secs. Baptist. Clubs: Chaparral, Dallas Gun, Northwood, Dallas Petroleum (Dallas). Office: 1000 Trammell Crow Ctr 2001 Ross Ave Dallas TX 75201

BLACK, ALEXANDER, lawyer; b. Pitts., Nov. 19, 1914; s. Alexander and Ruth (Hay) B.; m. Jane Mevay McIntosh, Apr. 23, 1955; children: F. Kristin Hoeveler, Kenneth M., Elizabeth H. Black Watson. AB, Princeton U., 1936; LLB, Harvard U., 1939. Bar: Pa. 1940, U.S. Supreme Ct. 1955, U.S. Ct. Appeals (3d cir.) 1957, U.S. Ct. Claims 1959, U.S. Ct. Appeals (Fed. cir.) 1982. Law clk. Buchanan, Ingersoll P.C. and predecessors, Pitts., summers 1936-39, assoc., 1939-51, ptnr., 1951-85, shareholder, 1980-85, of counsel, 1985—. Served to lt. USNR, 1942-46, PTO. Mem. ABA, Pa. Bar Assn., Allegheny County Bar Assn., Am. Law Inst., Am. Coll. Trial Lawyers, Am. Coll. Real Estate Lawyers, Am. Bar Found., Pa. Bar Found., Am. Judicature Soc., Comml. Panel Arbitrators, Am. Arbitration Assn. Republican. Presbyterian. Clubs: Harvard/Yale/Princeton, Duquesne (Pitts.); Princeton (N.Y.C.); Edgeworth (Sewickley, Pa.). Home: 1309 Beaver Rd Sewickley PA 15143 Office: Buchanan Ingersoll PC 600 Grant St 57th Floor Pittsburgh PA 15219

BLACK, CHARLES HENRY, industrialist; b. Atlanta, Sept. 12, 1926; s. Charles Henry and Elfrida Elizabeth (Peterson) B.; m. Bonnie Nicksic; children: Charles Henry, Richard Swanton; stepchildren—Laura Branch, Peter Branch. B.S., U. So. Calif., 1950. Engr. Hughes Aircraft Co., Culver City, Calif., 1950-53; mgr. budgets Lockheed Missiles & Space Div., Van Nuys, Calif., 1954-57; dir. fin. control and adminstrn., guidance and control div. Litton Industries, Inc., Beverly Hills, Calif., 1958-65; v.p. fin., profl. services and equipment group Litton Industries, Inc., 1965-70, corp. treas., 1971—, treas., v.p., 1976-80; exec. v.p. Great Western Fin. Corp. and Great Western Savs. & Loan Assn., Beverly Hills, Calif., 1980-82; sr. v.p. Kaiser Steel Corp., 1982-84, exec. v.p., dir., 1984-85; vice chmn. Pertron Controls Corp., Chatsworth, Calif., 1985-86; pvt. investor and corp. cons. Pacific Palisades, Calif., 1987—; dir. Investment Co. Am., Fundamental Investors Inc., Pertron Controls Corp., James Mitchell & Co., Interdyne Co.; bd. govs. Pacific Stock Exchange; trustee Am. Pathway Fund, Inc. Served with AC USNR, 1944-46. Mem. Fin. Execs. Inst., Phi Kappa Psi. Clubs: Los Angeles Country, California.

BLACK, DAVID, writer, educator; b. Boston, Apr. 21, 1945; s. Henry Arnold and Zelda Edith (Hodosh) B.; m. Deborah Hughes Keehn, June 22, 1968; children: Susannah Haden and Tobiah Samuel McKee. B.A. cum laude, Amherst Coll., 1967; M.F.A., Columbia U., 1971. Freelance writer, 1971—; writer-in-residence Mt. Holyoke Coll., South Hadley, Mass., 1982-86. Author: (novels) Minds, 1982, Like Father (Notable Book of Yr. N.Y. Times 1978, One of 7 Best Novels of Yr. Washington Post), 1978, Peep Show, 1986, (non-fiction) Ekstasy, 1975, The King of Fifth Avenue (Notable Book of Yr. N.Y. Times 1981), Murder at the Met, 1984, Medicine Man, 1985, The Plague Years, 1986; contbr. articles and stories to various mags.; author screenplays for Disney, Michael Douglas, Highgate, Paramount, miniseries for Chris-Rose/CBS/Viacom; writer teleplay "More Skinned Against Than Skinning", "Death and The Lady", "Days of Swine and Rose", others; story editor Hill Street Blues, 1986-88, Miami Vice, 1987-88; others; producer The Lou Gossett Show, 1988; contbg. editor Rolling Stone, 1986—. Recipient Atlantic "Firsts" award Atlantic Monthly, 1973, Playboy's Best Article of Yr. award Playboy mag., 1979; Nat. Assn. Sci. Writers award, 1985, hon. mention for Best Essay of Yr., 1986, Nat. Mag. award in reporting, 1986; Nat. Endowment Arts grantee, 1979; nominee for Best Episodic Drama of Yr. Writers Guild ann. awards, 1988. Mem. Mystery Writers Am. (nominated for Edgar-Best Fact Crime 1984), Author's Guild, PEN, Writer's Guild East. Democrat. Jewish. Home: 150 W 95th St Apt 5B New York NY 10025

BLACK, EDWARD PARTRIDGE, engineer, business executive; b. Tooele, Utah, Jan. 21, 1946; s. Elliot R. and Agnes (Partridge) B.; m. Marybeth Raynes, Feb. 27, 1968 (div. 1977); children—Teriesa, Nathan Jeffery, Sara, Melissa; m. Ardith Lynore Ashpole, Apr. 17, 1980; children—Camille Marie, Emily Jane. B.S., Ariz. State U., 1971; B.S.E.E., U. Utah, 1974, Ph.D., 1980. Instrument mgr., dept. chemistry Rice U., Houston, 1977-78; systems engr. Intel Corp., Phoenix, 1978-80; electromagnetic compatability cons. Chris

Kendall Cons., Running Springs, Calif., 1980-83; founder, pres. Certitech Labs., Inc., Running Springs, 1983—; founding ptnr. CAD Values, Pomona, Calif.; corp. sec. The Wellness Inst., Lake Arrowhead, Calif; founding ptnr. DBW Enterprises, Mariposa, Calif. Contbr. articles to profl. jours. Chmn. Democratic Legis. Dist. Com., Salt Lake City, 1974; mem. State Dem. Central Com., Salt Lake City, 1975-76; operator So. Calif. Emergency Response Radio Net, Colton, 1984—. Served with USAR, 1963—. NSF, grantee 1978. Mem. IEEE. Mormon.

BLACK, JAN KNIPPERS, political scientist; b. Lawrenceburg, Tenn., Mar. 10, 1940; d. Ottis J. and Opal (Moody) Knippers; B.A. in Art and Spanish, U. Tenn., 1962; M.A. in Latin Am. Studies, Am. U., 1967, Ph.D. in Internat. Relations, 1975; m. John D. Black, 1967 (dec. 1974); m. Martin C. Needler, 1976; stepchildren—John D., II, Marc Black, Steve Needler, Dan Needler; 1 foster dau., Mary Marfise. Singer, pianist, 1954-58; comml. artist Sta. WSM-TV, Nashville, 1960; vol. Peace Corps, Chile, 1962-64, mem. staff, 1965; research polit. scientist div. fgn. area studies Am. U., 1968-75, chmn. Latin Am. research team, editor area handbooks for Latin Am., 1975-76; program coordinator State Dept. funded study Latin Am. petroleum policies U. N.Mex., 1976-78, sr. research assoc. div. inter-Am. affairs, 1976—, coordinator interdisciplinary courses Latin Am. Inst., research assoc. prof. Div. Public Adminstrn., 1979-85; research prof. 1986— ; mem. faculty World Campus Afloat, 1966, Dag Hammarskjold Coll., 1974, George Mason U., 1975-76, semester-at-sea program U. Pitts., 1988; cons. in field; TV appearances include MacNeil-Lehrer Report, 1976. Del., Nat. Young Democrats Conv., 1965, N.Mex. Dem. Conv., 1978, 80, 82, 84, 86, 88; ward chmn. New Mex. Dem. Com., 1985—, State Cen. Com., 1987—; v.p. N.Mem. Dem. Council, 1983-87; exec. com. N.Mex. Progressive Polit. Action Com., 1984-87, pres., 1987—; mem. fgn. policy adv. team Dem. Presdl. Campaign., 1972; mem. Mayoral Transition Team, City of Albuquerque, 1977; mgr. various polit. campaigns. Recipient Outstanding Dissertation award Am. U., 1967, Choice Book of the Yr. Citation award, 1987. Mem. Latin Am. Studies Assn. (chmn. subcom. ethical guidelines 1976-78), Inter-Am. Council Washington (v.p. 1975-76), Am. Polit. Sci. Assn., Internat. Studies Assn., Phi Kappa Phi. Contbg. author of 14 anthologies, edited texts, and reference books; co-author 17 books in Area Handbook series, 1969-75; author: United States Penetration of Brazil, 1977; The Dominican Republic; Politics and Development in an Unsovereign State, 1986; Sentinels of Empire; The United States and Latin American Militarism, 1986; editor books on Latin Am. and Caribbean, including: Area Handbook for Cuba, 1976; Area Handbook for Trinidad and Tubago, 1976; Latin America: Its Problems and Its Promise, 1984. contbr. numerous articles to profl. jours., popular publs. Home: 421 Solano Dr SE Albuquerque NM 87108 Office: U NMex Dept Polit Sci Albuquerque NM 87131

BLACK, LOUIS ECKERT, travel bureau executive; b. Cleve., Sept. 6, 1942; s. Louis Eckert and Leonie Louise (Young) B.; B.A., Coll. of Wooster, 1965; M.A.T., U. Fla., 1966; m. Susan Sims Harrell, Dec. 28, 1966. Adminstrv. asst. USIA, Barranquilla, Colombia, 1963-64; chmn. dept. fgn. langs. Ribault Jr. High Sch., Jacksonville, Fla., 1967-69; field claim rep. State Farm Ins. Co., Jacksonville, 1969-70; account exec. Hayden, Stone, Inc., Jacksonville, 1970-74; pres. Avondale Travel Bur., Inc., Jacksonville, 1974—; adv. bd. Eastern Airlines, Pan Am. World Airways, Norwegian Caribbean Cruise Lines, Bahamas Tourism Council; instr. Am. Soc. Travel Agts. Seminars at Sea. Charter mem. Jacksonville Sports and Entertainment Commn., 1980-82; mem. nat. polit. action com. Am. Soc. Travel Agts; bd. dirs. Goodwill Industries. Mem. Am. Soc. Travel Agts. (Crest award 1981, 82, 83), Fla.-Ga. Football Ofcls. Assn., So. Assn. Basketball Ofcls. Democrat. Episcopalian. Clubs: Skal, Rotary, Jacksonville Quarterback, Ponte Vedra, River, Amelia Island Plantation, Sales and Mktg. Execs. of Jacksonville, Timuquana Country. Home: 3530 St Johns Ave Jacksonville FL 32205 Office: 3651 St Johns Ave Jacksonville FL 32205

BLACK, PAGE MORTON, civic worker; b. Chgo.; d. Alexander and Rose Morton; m. William Black, Mar. 27, 1962. Student, Chgo. Mus. Coll. Singer, pianist, Pierre Hotel, N.Y.C., Warwick Hotel, One Fifth Ave. Sherry Netherland Hotel; singer radio show and comml. Chock Full o' Nuts Corp., now hon. chmn.; rec. artist Atlantic Records; co-founder Page and William Black Post-Grad. Sch. Medicine, Mt. Sinai Med. Sch., 1965—; chmn., mem. exec. bd. Parkinsons' Disease Found., Columbia U. Med. Ctr. Recipient Ann. award Parkinsons' Disease Found., 1987. Home: Premium Point New Rochelle NY 10801

BLACK, ROBERT ALLEN, lawyer; b. Ocala, Fla., Aug. 15, 1954; s. Allen Harrison and Rose Marie (Dupree) B. BA, U. Tex., El Paso, 1977; JD summa cum laude, Tex. Tech U., 1980. Bar: Tex. 1980, U.S. Ct. Appeals (5th and 11th cirs.) 1980, U.S. Supreme Ct. 1985. Ptnr. Mehaffy, Weber, Keith & Gonsoulin, Beaumont, Tex., 1980—; adj. prof. law Lamar U., Beaumont, Tex., 1981-84. Case note editor Tex. Tech Law Rev., 1979-80. Pres. Humane Soc. Southeast Tex., Beaumont, 1983-89; bd. dirs. YMCA, Beaumont, 1985-87; host TV show Pets on Parade, Beaumont, 1986-87; mem. Beaumont City Planning and Zoning Commn., 1987—. Named one of Outstanding Young Men of Am., Jaycees, 1982. Mem. ABA, Tex. Young Lawyers Assn (treas. 1983-84), Tex. Assn. Def. Counsel, Jefferson County Young Lawyers Assn. (bd. dirs. 1982-83, treas. 1983-84), Tex. Bar Assn. Democrat. Episcopalian. Home: 601 22d St Beaumont TX 77706 Office: Mehaffy Weber Keith & Gonsoulin 2615 Calder Beaumont TX 77702

BLACK, ROBERT DENIS COLLISON, economics educator; b. Dublin, Ireland, June 11, 1922; s. William Robert and Rose Anna (Reid) B.; m. Frances Mary Weatherup, Aug. 29, 1953; children: Rosemary Joy, Terence Robert William. BA, B of Commerce, U. Dublin, 1941, MA, 1943, PhD, 1945; DSc in Econs. (hon.), Queen's U., Belfast, 1988. Dep. prof. econs. U. Dublin, 1943-45; from asst. lectr. to reader in econs. Queen's U., Belfast, Ireland, 1945-62, prof. econs., 1962-85, prof. emeritus, 1985—; vis. prof. Yale U., 1964-65; chmn. Com. for Social Sci. Research in Ireland, Dublin, 1973-80; pro vice chancellor Queens U., 1971-75. Author: Economic Thought and the Irish Question, 1817-1870, 1960; editor: Papers and Correspondence of W.S. Jevons, 7 vols., 1972-81, Ideas in Economics, 1986; contbr. numerous articles to internat. econ. jours. Mem. Northern Ireland Indsl. Ct., 1963-72; chmn. Commn. Inquiry into Wages in the Catering Industry, 1964, Commn. Inquiry into Angling, 1979-81. Named Hon. Fellow Trinity Coll. U. Dublin, 1982, Disting. Fellow History of Econs. Soc. U.S., 1987; research fellow Japan Soc. for the Promotion of Sci., 1980; postdoctoral fellow Rockefeller Found., 1950-51. Fellow Brit. Acad., Royal Irish Acad.; mem. Royal London Econ. Soc. (exec. council 1963-81), Dublin Econ. and Social Research Inst. (exec. council 1963-85), Statis. and Social Inquiry Soc. Ireland (pres. 1983-86, v.p. 1986-88). Office: Queen's U Belfast, University Rd, Belfast BT7 1NN, Northern Ireland

BLACK, ROBERT L., JR., state judge; b. Cin., Dec. 11, 1917; s. Robert L. and Anna M. (Smith) B.; m. Helen Charfield, July 27, 1946; children—William C., Stephen L., Luther F. A.B., Yale U., 1939; LL.B., Harvard U., 1942. Bar: Ohio 1946, U.S. Ct. Appeals (6th cir.) 1947, U.S. Supreme Ct. 1955. Sole practice, Cin., 1946-53; ptnr. Graydon, Head & Ritchey, Cin., 1953-72; judge Ct. Common Pleas, Cin., 1973-77, Ct. Appeals, Cin., 1977—; chmn. jury instrns. com. Ohio Jud. Conf. 1973-86 (chmn. 1986—), chmn. Supreme Ct. Com. on Ct. Tech., 1988—; Councilman Village Indian Hill (Ohio), 1953-65, mayor, 1959-65; chmn. Cin. Human Relations Commn., 1967-70. Served to capt. U.S. Army, 1942-45. Decorated Bronze Star. Mem. Cin. Bar Assn., Ohio Bar Assn., ABA, Am. Judicature Soc., Nat. Legal Aid and Defender Assn., Ohio Cts. of Appeals Judges Assn. Republican. Episcopalian. Clubs: Queen City, Camargo, Commonwealth (Cin.). Contbr. articles on law to profl. jours. Home: 5900 Drake Rd Cincinnati OH 45243 Office: 300 Hamilton County Courthouse Cincinnati OH 45202

BLACK, ROBERT STITT, public utility executive; b. Newport News, Va., Oct. 31, 1951; s. William Holmes and Catherine Louise (Stitt) B.; B.A. cum laude in Econs., Kenyon Coll., 1973; M.B.A. in Fin., U. Mich., 1975; m. Christine Carr, Aug. 17, 1974; children—Robert Stitt II, Michael Todd. Regulatory affairs analyst El Paso Natural Gas Co. (Tex.), 1975-76; asst. to pres. Waterville Gas and Oil Co. (Ohio), 1976-77, pres., 1977—; spokesman for gas cos. at legis. and regulatory agy. hearings, 1978—. Mem. Ohio Gas Assn. (trustee 1981—, v.p. 1983-84, pres. 1984-85), Waterville C. of C. (dir. 1977-78, pres. 1983). Republican. Episcopalian. Clubs: Toledo, Waterville Rotary (bd. dirs. 1981-84, pres. 1985-86), Belmont Country, Masons. Home: 26623 W River Rd Perrysburg OH 43551 Office: PO Box 259 Waterville OH 43566

BLACK, SHIRLEY NORMAN, lawyer, retired museum official, retired air force officer; b. Gardner, Mass., Sept. 26, 1916; s. Henry Warren and Ella (Thompson) B.; m. Kathryn Mary Linser, Mar. 19, 1947; 1 son, Peter Norman. B.S. in Commerce and Bus. Adminstrn., U. Ala., 1938; M.B.A. with distinction, Harvard U., 1954; postgrad. George Washington U., 1955; grad. Air U., 1959; J.D., Western State U., 1978. Commd. 2d lt., USAF, 1938, advanced through grades to col. U.S. Air Force, 1953; exec. dir. fin. Hdqrs., U.S. Air Force, 1951-52; dep. chief staff, comptroller hdqrs. Crew Tng., 1955-57; dir. acctg. and fin. Hdqrs. Air Tng. Command, 1957-58, Hdqrs. Pacific Air Force, 1959-60; dep. chief staff, comptroller Hdqrs. 5th Air Force, 1960-62; comptroller, asst. treas. Art Inst. Chgo., 1963-72, v.p. adminstrv. affairs, 1972-75; treas. Restaurant Food Buyers, Inc., 1972—, also dir.; pres. Restaurant Food Buyers Investment Co., 1972—. Commr. Far East Council Boy Scouts Am.; dir. Far East Little League, 1960-61. Decorated Bronze Star, Commendation medal with oak leaf cluster. Mem. Air Force Assn., Ret. Officers Assn., Am. Mgmt. Assn., Am. Soc. Mil. Comptrollers (outstanding achievement cert. 1959), Chgo. Assn. Commerce and Industry, Harvard Bus. Sch. Assn. So. Calif. Heroes of '76, Nat. Sojourners. Clubs: Army Navy Country (Arlington, Va.); Yorba Linda Country; Toastmasters (pres. Scott AFB chpt. 1954). Lodges: Masons, Shriners. Home: 6151 Sandy Hill Ln Yorba Linda CA 92686 Office: Bldg E 1801 E Parkcourt Pl Suite 102 Santa Ana CA 92701

BLACK, WARREN JOHN, lawyer; b. N.Y.C., July 14,1929; s. Charles Warren and Gladys Belle (Lord) B.; m. Dorothy Windle, Oct. 29, 1955; children —Neal S., Warren L. B.A., NYU, 1949; LL.B., St. John's U., 1952. Bar: N.Y. 1954, U.S. Supreme Ct. 1970. Sole practice, N.Y.C., 1954—; also lectr. Fellow Am. Acad. Matrimonial Lawyers (bd. mgrs.); mem. N.Y. State Bar Assn., Internat. Soc. Family Law, N.Y. Criminal and Civil Cts. Bar Assn., Internat. Platform Assn. Men of Achievment. Presbyterian. Office: 4930 Broadway New York NY 10034

BLACK, WILLIAM BRUCE, retired chemist; b. Indpls., Feb. 25, 1923; s. Paul and Vivian Love (Rothgeb) B.; B.A. in Chemistry, U. Va., 1950, M.S. in Organic Chemistry (Philip Francis duPont research fellow 1952-53), 1953, Ph.D. in Organic Chemistry (duPont postgrad. fellow 1953-54), 1954; m. Marie Christoffersen, Sept. 20, 1945; children—Linda Bruce Black Willson, John Christoffer. Research chemist Chemstrand Research Corp., Decatur, Ala., 1954-59, Chemstrand Research Center, Inc., Research Triangle Park, N.C., 1959-69; with Monsanto Textiles Co., Pensacola, Fla., 1969—, sr. group leader, 1969-80, sr. fellow, 1980-85; owner Photography by Black, Pensacola, 1971—. Served to 1st lt. USAAF, 1943-46. Decorated Air medal; recipient President and Visitors prize U. Va., 1954. Mem. Am. Chem. Soc., Fiber Soc., Sigma Xi. Presbyterian. Author, patentee in field. Co-editor: High-Modulus Wholly Aromatic Fibers, 1973; Stress-Induced Crystallization, Part II, 1979. Home: 2300 N Whaley Ave Pensacola FL 32503

BLACKBURN, ALAN GEOFFREY, college adminstrator, consultant; b. Hopetown, Australia, Aug. 21, 1943; s. Geoffrey Herbert and Edna Eireen (Atkins) B.; m. Jasenka Maria Zivkovic, Jan. 26, 1970; children—Sanja Emily, Anthony Alan. B. Agr. Sc., U. Melbourne, Victoria, Australia, 1965; Dip. Agr. Econ., U. New England, Australia, 1966; M.A. in Bus. Analysis, U. Lancaster, Eng., 1974. Sheep and wool officer Dept. Agr., Victoria, 1967-70; lectr. farm mgmt. Marcus Oldham Coll., Victoria, 1970-74, sr. lectr., 1974-85, dir. external studies, 1978—, dep. prin., 1985—; leader cons. team Nat. Australia Bank, Victoria, 1984—, Weternport Environ. Survey, Victoria, 1977. Editor: The Management of Booms and Busts, 1976, 84. Mem. Australian Inst. Agr. Sci., Agr. Econ. Soc., Australian Farm Mgmt. Soc., Victorian Rural Discussion Group (sec. 1984—). Mem. Uniting Ch. Club: Apex (Belmont, Australia). Lodge: Rotary (Belmont). Avocations: woodworking; running; coach. Home: 15 Darling St, East Geelong Victoria 3219, Australia Office: Marcus Oldham Coll, Pvt Bag 116, Geelong 3221, Australia

BLACKBURN, CATHERINE ELAINE, lawyer, pharmacist; b. Columbus, Ohio, Nov. 5, 1953; d. Robert Jerome and Patricia Ann (Buchman) B. BS in Pharmacy with high distinction U. Ky., 1978; JD with honors, Ohio State U., 1982. Bars: Ohio 1982, U.S. Dist. Ct. (so. dist.) Ohio 1983. Chief pharmacist Louisa Community Hosp., Ky., 1978; pharmacist Riverside Meth. Hosp., Columbus, Ohio, 1978-82; law clk. Michael F. Colley Co., L.P.A., Columbus, 1980-82, assoc., 1982-87; asst. prof. law U. Louisville Sch. Law, 1987—; workshop leader Ohio Drug Studies Inst., Columbus, 1982, 83, 14th Nat. Conf. on Women and the Law, Washington, D.C., 1983, 15th Nat. Conf., 1985; lectr./speaker Iowa Trial Lawyers Assn., Iowa City, 1984; speaker Nat. Assn. for Rights Protection and Advocacy, Nat. Conf., Boston, 1986; speaker Nat. Assn. of Protection and Advocacy Systems; lectr. legal writing Coll. Law Ohio State U., 1986; mem. aids edn. task force, subcom. on legal ethical issues U. Louisville, 1988—; speaker nat. conf. Nat. Assn. Protection and Advocacy Systems, Washington, 1988; cons. Ohio Legal Rights Service, 1985—, Mich. Protection and Advocacy Service, 1988—. Contbr. article to profl. jour. Staff writer, editor Ohio State U. Law Jour., 1980-82. Trustee Women's Outreach for Women, Columbus, 1982-85, Amethyst, Inc., 1985-87; incorporator Columbus Career Women Inc., 1986-87, treas., 1986-87. Fellow Am. Soc. Pharmacy Law; mem. ABA, Assn. Trial Lawyers Am. (lectr./speaker 1982—), Order of Coif, Phi Beta Kappa, Rho Chi Soc. Democrat.

BLACKBURN, JACOB FLOYD, computer scientist; b. Newton., N.C., Nov. 27, 1918; s. Julius Walter and Lottie Mae (Lael) B.; m. Beverley England, Mar. 29, 1944; 1 son, Gregg Scott. B.A., Lenoir-Rhyne Coll., 1940; certificate, N.Y.U., 1942; M.A., Duke U., 1947; Ph.D., U. N.C., 1953. Asst. prof. The Citadel, Charleston, S.C., 1947-50; mem. Inst. for Advanced Study, Princeton, N.J., 1953-54; assoc. prof. USAF Acad., 1955-56; various mgmt positions IBM, Cranford, N.J., 1956-77, Geneva, Switzerland, 1956-77, Brussels, Belgium, 1956-77; dir. Office Tech. Policy and Space Affairs, Dept. State, Washington, 1977-79; exec. dir. computer sci. bd. Nat. Acad. Scis., 1980-82; liaison scientist Office Naval Research, London, Eng., 1982—. Contbr. articles to profl. jours. Pres. Brussels Am. Club, 1974; pres. Brussels Toastmasters, 1972-73, Paris Toastmasters, 1975-76, Dresden Condominium Assn., Washington, 1978-82. Served to capt. USAAF, 1941-46; to lt. col. USAF, 1951-56. Decorated Air medal.; Recipient Computer Pioneer award Nat. Computer Conf., 1975; Alumnus of Yr. award Lenoir-Rhyne Coll., 1981. Mem. Assn. Computing Machinery, Am. Math. Soc. Democrat. Club: Grosvenor Sq. Toastmasters (London) (pres. 1983). Home: 12A Redcliffe Sq, London SW10, England Office: 223 Old Marylebone Rd, London NW1, England

BLACKBURN, JAMES ROSS, JR., corporate executive, airline pilot; b. Lakeland, Fla., Feb. 28, 1930; s. James Ross and Esther Louise (Flagle) B.; student Davidson Coll., 1948-49; B.B.A., U. Miami, 1953, postgrad., 1968-69; m. Joyce Gaynelle Green, Aug. 29, 1960 (div. 1988); children—Linda Marie, Lisa Joyce. Pilot, Eastern Air Lines, 1957—, capt., 1969-88; mktg. cons. Comrex Corp., 1967-72; pres. Surete Ltd., 1973; pres. J.R. Blackburn & Assos., 1974-76; pres. Blackburn Assos., Inc., (a Del. Corp.), Miami, Fla., 1977-81; pres., chief exec. officer Aerodynetics Corp., (name changed to Aerodyne Corp., 1988) Miami, 1981—. Mem. steering com., chmns. com. U.S. Senatorial Bus. Adv. Bd., Washington, 1980-83; co-founder Republican Presdl. Task Force, 1981; mem. Rep. Senatorial Inner Circle, 1983—, dir. circle Aviation Research and Edn. Found., 1986—. Served to 1st lt. USAF, 1953-57. Mem. Air Line Pilots Assn., First Flight Soc., AMS/Oil Dealers Assn., Geneal. Soc. Greater Miami (past treas.), Am. Hall Aviation History (founding mem.) Quiet Birdmen, Soc. So. Families, Mil. Order Stars and Bars, Internat. Platform Assn., Nat. Aero. Assn., Fedn. Aeronautique Internationale, Greater Miami Aviation Assn., Smithsonian Air and Space (charter), SAR, Sons Confederate Vets. (past comdr.), Am. Security Council, Nat. Rifle Assn. (life), Alpha Phi Omega. Sigma Chi. Republican. Baptist. Clubs: Masons, Country Club of Coral Gables; Flamingo Dinner (dir.). Home: 6765 Miami Lakes Dr Miami Lakes FL 33014 Office: PO Box 59-2032 AMF Miami FL 33159-2032

BLACKBURN, JOHN LEWIS, consulting engineer; b. Kansas City, Mo., Oct. 2, 1913; s. John Ealy and Lela (Garnett) B.; m. Margaret Bailey, Sept. 12, 1943; children—Susan T., Joan Blackburn Krist, Margot A. Blackburn Jahns. BSEE with high honors, U. Ill., 1935. With Westinghouse Electric Corp., Newark, 1936-78, cons. engr., 1969-78; pvt. practice as cons. engr., Bothell, Wash., 1979—; adj. prof. Poly. Inst. N.Y., 1949-65, Poly. Inst. N.J., Newark, 1958-71; spl. lectr. IEEE Ednl. Activities, 1952—. Author, editor: Applied Protective Relaying, 1978; author: Protective Relaying Principles and Application, 1987. Trustee, treas. Millington Bapt. Ch., N.J., 1952-69. Recipient Order of Merit award Westinghouse Electric Corp., 1971, Attwood Assocs. award U.S. Nat. Com. Internat. Conf. for Large High Voltage Electric Systems, 1986. Fellow IEEE (chmn. publ. dept. Power Engrng. Soc. 1972-76, sec., 1977-79, chmn. power system relaying com. 1969-70, Disting. Service award 1978, Outstanding Service award IEEE ednl. bd. 1979, Centennial medal 1984); mem. Sigma Xi, Tau Beta Pi, Eta Kappa Nu, Phi Kappa Phi. Club: China Stamp Soc., Inc. (pres. 1979—), Am. Soc. Polar Philatelists (dir., treas. 1967—). Home: 21816 8th Pl W Bothell WA 98021

BLACKBURN, NORMAN, mathematics educator; b. Huddersfield, Eng., May 27, 1930; s. Ernest and Janet Elsie (Warwick) B.; m. Joan Pamela Herbert, Sept. 3, 1960; children: Virginia Ellen, Caroline Mary. BA, PhD, Trinity Coll., Cambridge, Eng., 1957; MSc (hon.), U. Manchester, Eng., 1978. Lectr. U. Manchester, 1958-65, Fielden prof. math., 1975—; prof. math. U. Ill., Chgo., 1965-75. Author: (with B. Huppert) Finite Groups, 1981. Mem. London Math. Soc., Am. Math. Soc., Deutsche Mathematiker Vereinigung. Office: U Manchester Dept Math, Manchester M13 9PL, England

BLACKBURN, WILLIAM EWART, sales executive; b. Preston, Lancashire, Eng., July 22, 1929; s. Thomas and Marion Sterling (Ewart) B.; m. June Yvonne Wicks, Dec. 22, 1967; children: Rebecca Jane, Mark William. With outward freight dept. Herbert Watson & Co. Ltd., Manchester, Eng., 1949-53; U.K., Ireland rep. Booth Steamship Co., Ltd., Liverpool, Eng., 1953-57; U.K. rep. Ulster Ferry Transport Ltd., Belfast, 1957-62; U.K. dir. J & A Line/Bellferry Ltd., Dublin, Preston, 1963—; sales mgr., trustee group pension scheme U.K. north nat. Bell Lines Ltd. (formerly J&A Line, Bellferry Ltd.), Dublin, Preston, 1963—. Mem. The Eng.-Speaking Union of Commonwealth (chmn. hon. treas., North Lancashire Br. 1973—). Conservative. Anglican.

BLACKEBY, JEREMY GARWOOD, sales executive; b. Uckfield, Sussex, Eng., Jan. 3, 1935; s. Donald Herbert and Marjorie Olga (Chapman) B.; m. Valarie Mary Coutts, July 18, 1959; children: Adrian Paul, Angela Mary, Anne Catherine. Asst. site engr. Brit. Insulated Callender's Constrn. Co. Ltd., Edinburgh, Scotland, 1957-60; from computer trainee to ops. supr. U.K. Atomic Energy Authority, Eng., 1960-67; mgr. computer U. Coll. Swansea, Eng., 1967-75; mgr. computer services Australian Nat. U., Canberra, 1975-77; sales exec. Dacoll Ltd., Bathgate, Eng., 1978-79; prin. sales exec. Prime Computer Ltd., Leeds, Eng., 1980—. Mem. Brit. Computer Soc. Conservative. Roman Catholic. Office: Prime Computer UK Ltd, Stockdale House, 8 Victoria Rd, Leeds LS6 8PF, England

BLACKEN, JOHN DALE, U.S. ambassador; b. Everett, Wash., Aug. 26, 1930. BA, Wash. State U., 1955; student Portuguese, Fgn. Service Lang. Sch., Rio de Janeiro, 1967. Sales exec. Encyclopedia Britannica, San Francisco, 1956-58; mgmt. analyst Office Sec. of Agr., Washington, 1958-61; entered fgn. service 1961; 3d sec. Dar es Salaam, Tanzania, 1961-63; cultural affairs officer Bur. Edn. and Cultural Affairs, Dept. State, Washington, 1964-67; polit. officer U.S. Consulate Gen., Sao Paulo, Brazil, 1967-70; John Quincy Adams lectr. U. Mass., 1970-71; Panama desk officer Dept. State, 1971-73; polit. counselor Panama, 1973-76; dep. chief mission Georgetown, Guyana, 1976-78; dep. poli. counselor U.S. Mission to UN, N.Y.C., 1978-80; dir. Office Cen. Am. Affairs, Dept. State, Washington, 1980-81; dep. chief mission Santa Domingo, 1981-84; dep. coordinator Office Pub. Diplomacy for Latin Am. and Caribbean, Dept. of State, Washington, 1984-86; U.S. ambassador to Guinea-Bissau, 1986—. Served with U.S. Army, 1950-52. Office: Embassy of Guniea-Bissau care Dept State 2201 C St NW Washington DC 20520 *

BLACKFAN, CYRUS LINTON, specialty chemicals company executive; b. Phila., Sept. 10, 1935; s. Cyrus Linton and Ethel Carrel (Hobensack) B.; m. Barbara Lee Hance, Dec. 17, 1960; children—Barbara May, John Cyrus, David Lyle. B.S., Lafayette Coll., 1957; postgrad. Northwestern U., 1973, MIT, 1982. Sales engr. Union Carbide, N.Y.C., Cleve., 1957-66; product mgr. B.F. Goodrich, Cleve., 1967-72, mgr. new products, 1972-74, mgr. corp. planning, Akron, Ohio, 1974-75, dir. planning, Cleve., 1977-78, v.p. mktg., Akron, 1978-80, v.p., gen. mgr., 1980-82; pres. Chemionics Corp., Tallmadge, Ohio, 1982—. Mem. Akron Regional Development Bd., 1982—. Served to 1st lt. U.S. Army, 1957-59. Mem. Comml. Devel. Assn., Am. Chem. Soc. Republican. Presbyterian. Club: Cascade. Contbr. articles to profl. jours.

BLACKHAM, ANN ROSEMARY (MRS. J. W. BLACKHAM), realtor; b. N.Y.C., June 16, 1927; d. Frederick Alfred and Letitia L. (Stolfe) DeCain; m. James W. Blackham Jr., Aug. 18, 1951; children: Ann C., James W. III. AB, Ohio Dominican Coll., 1949; postgrad., Ohio State U., 1950. Mgr. br. store Filene & Sons, Winchester, 1950-52; broker Porter Co. Real Estate, Winchester, 1961-66; sales mgr. James T. Trefrey, Inc., Winchester, 1966-68; pres., founder Ann Blackham & Co. Inc., Realtors, Winchester, Mass., 1969—. Mem. bd. econ. advisors to Gov., 1969-74; participant White House Conf. on Internat. Cooperation, 1965; mem. Presdl. Task Force on Women's Rights and Responsibilities, 1969; mem. exec. council Mass. Civil Def., 1965-69; chmn. Gov.'s Commn. on Status of Women, 1971-75; regional dir. Interstate Assn. Commn. on Status of Women, 1971-74; mem. Gov. Task Force on Mass. Economy, 1972; mem. Gov.'s Judicial Selection Com., 1972, Mass. Emergency Fin. Bd., 1974-75; corporator, trustee Charlestown Savs. Bank, 1974-84; corporator Winchester Hosp., 1983—; mem. design rev. commn. Town of Winchester; bd. dirs. Phoenix Found., Bay State Health Care, Mass. Taxpayers Found., Speech and Hearing Found.; mem. regional selection panel White House Fellows, 1973-74; mem. com. on women in service U.S. Dept. Def., 1977-80; 2d v.p. Doric Dames, 1971-74, bd. dirs., 1974—; pres. Mass. Fedn. Rep. Women, 1964-69; sec. Nat. Fedn. Rep. Women, 1967-71, 2d v.p., 1972-78; New Eng. regional dir., 1967-78; pres. Women's Rep. Club Winchester, 1960-62, 83-84; dep. chmn. Mass. Rep. State Com., 1965-66; sec. Mass. Rep. State Conv., 1970, del., 1960, 62, 64, 66, 70, 72, 74, 78; state vice chmn. Mass. Rep. Fin. Com., 1970; alt. del.-at-large Rep. Nat. Conv., 1968, 72, del., 1984; v.p. Rep. Club Mass., 1980—; pres. Scholarship Found., 1976-78, Mass. Fedn. Women's Clubs; mem. Winchester 350th Aniversary Commn. Recipient Pub. Service award Commonwealth of Mass., 1978, Merit award Rep. Party, 1969, Pub. Affairs award Mass. Fedn. Women's Clubs, 1975; named Civic Leader of Yr., Mass. Broadcasters, 1962. Mem. Greater Boston Real Estate Bd. (bd. dirs.), Mass. Assn. Real Estate Bds. (bd. dirs.), Nat. Assn. Real Estate Bd. (women's council). Brokers Inst., Council Realtors (pres. 1983-84), Winchester C. of C. (bd. dirs.), Greater Boston C. of C., Nat. Assn. Women Bus. Owners, Million Dollar Club (life), ENKA Soc. Republican. Clubs: Capitol Hill (Washington); Ponte Vedra, Winchester Boat, Winchester Country, Wychemere Harbor, Womens City Boston, Winton (sec., bd. dir.). Home: 60 Swan Rd Winchester MA 01890 Office: 11 Thompson St Winchester MA 01890

BLACKMUN, HARRY ANDREW, associate justice U.S. Supreme Court; b. Nashville, Ill., Nov. 12, 1908; s. Corwin Manning and Theo H. (Reuter) B.; m. Dorothy E. Clark, June 21, 1941; children: Nancy Clark, Sally Ann, Susan Manning. B.A. summa cum laude in Math, Harvard U., 1929, LL.B., 1932; numerous hon. degrees. Bar: Minn. 1932. Law clk. to presiding justice U.S. Ct. Appeals (8th cir.), St. Paul, 1932-33; assoc. Dorsey, Colman, Barker, Scott & Barber, Mpls., 1934-38, jr. ptnr., 1939-42, gen. ptnr., 1943-50; instr. St. Paul Coll. Law, 1935-41, U. Minn. Law Sch., 1945-47; resident counsel Mayo Clinic, Mayo Assn., Rochester, 1950-59; mem. sect. adminstrn. Mayo Clinic, 1950-59; judge 8th Circuit U.S. Ct. of Appeals, 1959-70; assoc. justice U.S. Supreme Ct., 1970—; chmn. faculty Salzburg Seminar in Am. Studies, July 1977; Mem. bd. members Mayo Assn. Rochester, 1953-60; mem. adv. com. on jud. activities Jud. Conf., 1969-79; co-moderator seminar on justice and soc., Aspen (Colo.) Inst., 1979-88, seminar on constl. justice and soc., Aspen Inst. Italia, Rome, 1986; vis. instr. Constl. Law, La. State U. Law Sch., Summer Session at Aix-en-Provence, France, 1986; participant seminar on the role of cts. in soc. Hebrew Univ., 1986. Contbr. articles to legal, med. jours. Bd. dirs., mem. exec. com. Rochester Meth. Hosp., 1954-70; trustee Hamline Univ., St. Paul, 1964-70, William Mitchell

Coll. Law, St. Paul, 1959-74; jud. mem. Nat. Hist. Publs. and Records Commn., 1975-82, 86—; participant Franco-Am. Colloquium on Human Rights, Paris, 1979. Mem. ABA, Minn. Bar Assn., Olmsted County Bar Assn., 32 Jud. Dist. Bar Assn., Phi Beta Kappa. Office: Supreme Ct US 1 First St NE Washington DC 20543

BLACKSTOCK, LEROY, lawyer; b. El Reno, Okla., Apr. 19, 1914; s. Herbert Austin and Ethel Mae (Gwin) B.; m. Virginia Lee Lowman, Dec. 29, 1939; children: Craig, Priscilla, Birch, Lore, Trena. Grad., Draughon's Bus. Inst., Tulsa, 1933; LL.B., U. Tulsa, 1938. Bar: Okla. 1938. With Phillips Petroleum Co., Tulsa, 1933-41; asst. credit mgr. Phillips Petroleum Co., 1939-41; practiced in Tulsa, 1941-74; now of counsel firm Blackstock Joyce Pollard & Montgomery; dir., gen. counsel Tulsa Homebuilders Assn., 1959-68; dir. Fourth Nat. Bank, Tulsa, 1969-76, Owasso 1st State Bank, Okla., 1967-70; pres. Skelly Stadium Corp., 1964-70; pres., trustee Gt. Western Investment Trust; mem. nat. adv. com. Practising Law Inst., 1969-70; pres. Jud. Reform Inc., 1966-70; lectr. law office mgmt., econs. U. Tulsa Coll. Law, 1970-75; chmn. Okla. Council on Jud. Complaints, 1974-84; Pres. Tulsa Sci. Center, 1968-73; chmn. Tulsa U. Law Schs. Com., 1960-74, Citizens Adv. Com. County Commrs., 1963-66; pres., bd. dirs. Tulsa County Bar Found., 1962-66; patron Okla. Bar Found., trustee, 1966; mem. Gov.'s Acad. for State Govt., 1966-68; chmn. Okla. Supreme Ct. Bar Com., 1966. Author: Managing Partner Approach, Paper Dolls and Lawyers' Fees. Pres. Tulsa council Camp Fire Girls, 1971-72; pres. Tulsa Baptist Laymen's Corp., 1962-66; Bd. dirs. Tulsa County Mental Health Assn., 1963-70, Tulsa Psychiat. Found., 1964-67; pres. Tulsa County Legal Aid Soc., 1961-62, bd. dirs., 1958-66. Served with USNR, 1943-46. Recipient Disting. Citizens award Okla. Psychol. Assn., 1963; Disting. Alumni award U. Tulsa, 1969, 78; Disting. Alumni award Tulsa U. Coll. Law, 1978; Boss of Year award Tulsa County Assn. Legal Secs., 1978. Fellow Am. Coll. Probate Counsel; mem. ABA (ho. dels. 1965-67, mem. spl. com. on nat. coordination of disciplinary enforcement 1969-72, standing com. profl. discipline 1973-77), Okla. Bar Assn. (bd. govs. 1965-67, pres. 1966), Tulsa County Bar Assn. (pres. 1962, Outstanding Atty. award 1961), World Assn. Lawyers (charter mem.), Tulsa County Hist. Soc. (founding mem.), Photog. Soc. Am., Soc. Amateur Cinematographers, Phi Alpha Delta. Republican. Baptist (chmn. deacons 1962, chmn. bldg. com. 1951-53). Club: Petroleum (dir. 1974-77). Home: 7213 S Atlanta Tulsa OK 74136 Office: 515 S Main Mall Tulsa OK 74103

BLACKWELL, EARL, publisher, writer; b. Atlanta, May 3, 1913; s. Samuel Earl and Carrie (Lagomarsino) B. Student, Culver Mil. Acad., 1928; A.B., Oglethorpe U., 1933; student, Columbia U.; D (hon.), 1980. Co-founder, Celebrity Service Inc. (offices N.Y.C., London, Paris, Rome, Hollywood), pres., 1939-85, chmn., 1985—; editor-in-chief Celebrity Register; contbg. editor Town & Country mag., N.Y.C., 1964—; now editorial cons. Town & Country mag.; pres. Embassy Found., Inc., 1958-67, French-Am. Found. Med. Research, 1987; radio commentator Celebrity Table, 1955-56; founder, v.p. Doubles Club, N.Y.C.; lectr. on celebrities, 1963—. Author: play Aries is Rising, 1939; novels Crystal Clear, 1978, Skyrocket, 1980; contbr. articles on celebrities to mags. Producer Pres. Kennedy's Birthday Celebration, Madison Sq. Garden, 1962; Founder, pres. Nine O'Clocks of N.Y.; dir. Mayor N.Y.C. Com. for Scholastic Achievement, 1957-65; bd. dirs. Soldiers, Sailors, Airmen's Club, N.Y.C.; organizer, pres. Theater Hall of Fame; organizer Salute to Israel's 25th Anniversary. Decorated Knight of Malta. Mem. Pi Kappa Phi, The Boar's Head. Republican. Roman Catholic. Clubs: N.Y. Athletic (N.Y.C.); Tamboo (Bahamas). Office: 171 W 57th St New York NY 10019

BLACKWELL, RONALD EUGENE, breed registry executive; b. Lexington, Okla., Feb. 15, 1933; s. Elight and Vee B.; m. Carolyn Crawford, Jan. 17, 1959; children—Scott, Stacy, Steven, Shanda. B.S. in Animal Sci, Okla. State U., 1954. Hog buyer Wilson Packing Co., Chgo., Galesburg, Ill., 1954-55; mng. editor Poland China World, Chgo., Galesburg, 1955; exec. sec. Tex. Angus Assn., Fort Worth, 1957-60; fieldman, asst. exec. sec. Am. Angus Assn., St. Joseph, Mo., 1960-69; dir. public relations Am. Quarter Horse Assn., Amarillo, Tex., 1969-76; exec. v.p., chief operating officer Am. Quarter Horse Assn., 1976-87; mem. exec. com. Am. Horse Council, 1976—. Bd. dirs. United Way, Tri-State Fair Assn. (1st. v.p.), Panhandle Provider Orgn. Served with U.S. Army, 1955-57, ETO. Recipient animal sci. grad. of distinction award Okla. State U., 1981. Mem. Nat. Soc. Livestock Record Assns. (past pres.), Am. Soc. Assn. Execs., Amarillo C. of C. (bd. dirs.). Republican. Baptist. Office: 2701 I-40 E Amarillo TX 79168

BLADE, MELINDA KIM, educator, researcher, archaeologist; b. San Diego, Jan. 12, 1952; d. George A. and Arline A. M. (MacLeod) B. BA, U. San Diego, 1974, MA in Teaching, 1975, MA, 1975, EdD, 1986. Cert. secondary tchr., Calif.; cert. community coll. instr., Calif.; registered profl. historian, Calif. Instr. Coronado Unified Sch. Dist., Calif., 1975-76; head coach women's basketball U. San Diego, 1976-78; instr. Acad. of Our Lady of Peace, San Diego, 1976—, chmn. social studies dept., 1983—, counselor, 1984—, co-dir. student activities, 1984-87, coordinator advanced placement program, 1986—; mem. archaeol. excavation team U. San Diego, 1975—, hist. researcher, 1975—; lectr., 1981—. Author hist. reports and research papers. Editor U. San Diego pubs. Vol. Am. Diabetes Assn., San Diego, 1975—; coordinator McDonald's Diabetes Bike-a-thon, San Diego, 1977, 78. Mem. Nat. Council Social Studies, Calif. Council Social Studies, Soc. Bibl. Archeology, Assn. Supervision and Curriculum Devel., Assn. Scientists and Scholars Internat. for Shroud of Turin, Medieval Acad. Am., Medieval Assn. Pacific, Am. Hist. Assn., Western Assn. Women Historians, Renaissance Soc. Am., San Diego Hist. Soc., Phi Alpha Theta (sec.-treas. 1975-77), Phi Delta Kappa. Office: Acad Our Lady of Peace 4860 Oregon St San Diego CA 92116

BLAICH, ROBERT IAN, manufacturing executive; b. Syracuse, N.Y., Feb. 25, 1930; arrived in The Netherlands, 1980; s. William V. and Eleanor (McGillivary) B.; m. Janet Streithof; children: Robert Jared, David Scott, James Cameron. BFA, Syracuse U., 1952; Advanced Mgmt. Course, U. Va., 1978, EMI, Geneva, Switzerland, 1985. V.p. corp. design and communications Herman Miller, Inc., Zeeland, Mich., 1953-79; mng. dir. N.V. Philips Co., Eindhoven, The Netherlands, 1980—; bd. dirs. London Sch. Bus. Design, Design Mgmt. Inst., Boston; frequent speaker. Mem. environ. arts panel NEA, Washington, 1968-70; chmn. Design Mich., 1972-79, Mich. Environ. Arts Panel, 1971-79; past v.p. Grand Rapids (Mich.) Art Mus.; jury Forma Finlandia Competition, Helsinki, Finland, 1987, Osaka (Japan) Internat. Design Competition, 1987. Recipient Mich. Gov.'s Award, 1978. Fellow Indsl. Designers Soc. Am.; mem. Internat. Council Soc. Indsl. Design (pres. 1987—), Am. Inst. Graphics, Internat. Council Graphic Arts (Pres.' award 1983). Office: NV Philips Corp, CID-BLD SX 2, Eindhoven The Netherlands

BLAINE, DOROTHEA CONSTANCE RAGETTÉ, lawyer, b. N.Y.C., Sept. 23, 1930; d. Robert Raymond and Dorothea Ottilie Ragetté; B.A., Barnard Coll., 1952; M.A., Calif. State U., 1968; Ed.D., UCLA, 1978; J.D., Western State U., 1981; postgrad. in taxation Golden Gate U. Bar: U.S. Dist. Ct. (ea., so. and cen. dists.) Calif., 1986—. Mem. tech. staff Planning Research Corp., Los Angeles, 1964-67; asso. scientist Holy Cross Hosp., Mission Hills, Calif., 1967-70; career devel. officer and affirmative action officer County of Orange, Santa Ana, Calif., 1970-74, sr. adminstrv. analyst, budget and program coordination, 1974-78; spl. projects asst. CAO/Spl. Programs Office, 1978-80, sr. adminstrv. analyst, 1980-83; admitted to Calif. bar, 1982; sole practice, 1982—; instr. Am. Coll. Law, Brea, Calif., 1987. Bd. dirs. Deerfield Community Assn., 1975-78, Orange YMCA, 1975-77. Mem. Assn. Trial Lawyers Am., Calif. Trial Lawyers Assn., Orange County Trial Lawyers Assn., Calif. Women Lawyers, Nat. Women's Polit. Caucus, ABA, Calif. Bar Assn., Orange County Bar Assn., Orange County Women Lawyers Assn. ACLU, Delta Theta Phi, Phi Delta Kappa. Office: 17541 17th St Suite 201 Tustin CA 92680

BLAINEY, GEOFFREY NORMAN, historian, educator; b. Melbourne, Australia, Mar. 11, 1930; s. Samuel and Hilda (Lanyon) B.; m. Ann Heriot, Feb. 15, 1957; 1 child, Anna. Free-lance author Australia, 1951-61; reader econ. history U. Melbourne, 1962-68, prof. econ. history, 1968-76, Ernest Scott prof., 1977—; prof. Australian studies Harvard U., 1982-83; chmn. Australia Council, 1977-81, Govts. Australia-China Council, 1979-84, Australian Selection Com. Harkness Fellowships, 1983—; pres. council Queen's Coll., U. Melbourne, 1971—. Author The Tyranny of Distance, 1966, The Causes of War, 1973, A Land Half Won, 1979. Decorated Officer Order of Australia, 1975; recipient Gold medal Australian Lit. Soc., 1965. Fellow Australian Acad. Humanities, Australian Acad. Social Scis.;. Office: U Melbourne, Parkville, 3052 Victoria Australia

BLAIR, DAVID FAIRLIE, barrister, solicitor; b. Tonbridge, Kent, Eng., Mar. 15, 1955; s. Ronald Edward and Miriam Phipps (Baker) B.; m. Paule Champoux, Sept. 7, 1985; 1 child, Eric Fairlie. DEC, St. Lawrence Coll., Quebec City, Can.; LLB, U. Laval, Quebec City, Can., 1979. Bar: Que. 1980. Assoc. Sirois Blanchard Beaudet and Assocs., Quebec City, 1981; assoc. Gagné, Letarte, Sirois, Beaudet and Assocs., Quebec City, 1985-87, ptnr., 1987—; bd. dirs. Elliot-Fairlie Inc., Que. Mem. Citadel Charity Found., 1985 (bd. dirs. 1988—); pres. Voice of English Que., 1987; bd. dirs. Jeffrey Hale Found., J.H. Meml. Found. Mem. Can. Transport Lawyers Assn. (provincial dir.), Can. Bar Assn. Club: Garrison (Quebec City); Little Saguenay Fish and Game (Portneuf county). Home: 271 Ave Royale St Jean, Ile D'Orléans, PQ Canada G0A 3WD Office: Gagné Letarte Sirois Beaudet, & Assocs, 2 Ave Chauveau, 4th Floor, Quebec City, PQ Canada G1R 4R3

BLAIR, FREDERICK DAVID, interior designer; b. Denver, June 15, 1946; s. Frederick Edward and Margaret (Whitely) B. BA, U. Colo., 1969; postgrad. in French, U. Denver, 1981-82. Interior designer The Denver, 1969-76, store mgr., 1976-80; v.p. Hartley House Interiors, Ltd., Denver, 1980-83; pvt. practice interior design Denver, 1983—; com. mem. Ice House Design Ctr., Denver, 1985-86, Design Directory Western Region, Denver, 1986. Designs shown in various mags. Mem. Rep. Nat. Com. Mem. Am. Soc. Interior Designers (co-chmn. com. profl. registration 1986), Denver Art Mus., Nat. Trust for Hist. Preservation, Hist. Denver, Inc. Christian Scientist. Office: 1961 Wazee St Suite 3005 Denver CO 80202

BLAIR, GRAHAM KERIN, lawyer; b. Shirley, Mass., Aug. 20, 1951; s. Joseph William and Ruth Marilyn (Shore) B.; children: Elizabeth Bryson; m. Frances Marie Oalton. B.A., So. Meth. U., 1973; J.D., U. Tex.-Austin, 1976. Bar: Tex. 1976, U.S. Ct. Appeals (5th cir.) 1977, U.S. Dist. Ct. (so. dist.) Tex. 1977. Assoc. Bracewell & Patterson, Houston, 1976-79; ptnr., co-chmn. litigation sect. Chamberlain, Hrdlicka, White, Johnson & Williams, Houston, 1979-82; sr. ptnr., chmn. litigation sect. Boyar, Norton & Blair, Houston, 1982—. Served to lt. (j.g.) USNR, 1973-76. Dir. advocacy, bd. advocates U. Tex. Sch. Law, Austin, 1976. Mem. ABA, Houston Bar Assn., Houston Young Lawyers Assn., State Bar Tex., Am. Arbitration Assn., Alpha Tau Omega. Democrat. Methodist. Office: Boyar Norton & Blair 4th Floor Five Post Oak Park Houston TX 77027

BLAIR, ROBERT ALLEN, lawyer, savings and loan executive; b. Suffolk, Va., June 25, 1946; s. Thomas Francis Jr. and Ossie (Southern) B.; m. Linda Britt, Dec. 27, 1970; children—Robert Allen II, Thomas Edward. B.A. in Math., Coll. William and Mary, 1968; J.D., U. Va., 1973. Bar: Mass. 1974, U.S. Dist. Ct. Mass. 1974, U.S. Ct. Appeals (D.C. cir.) 1976, U.S. Dist. Ct. D.C. 1980. Assoc. Goodwin, Procter & Hoar, Boston, 1973-74; assoc. Surrey & Morse, Washington, 1974-78, ptnr., 1979-81; mng. ptnr. Anderson, Hibey, Nauheim & Blair, Washington, 1981—; vice-chmn. Enterprise Fed. Savs. & Loan Assn., Clearwater, Fla., 1984-87, chmn. 1987—; dir. Palmer Tech. Services, Inc., Washington; pres., dir. Performance Evaluation Assocs., Inc., Va. Editorial bd. Law Rev. U. Va., 1971. Chmn. Inst. on Terrorism and Subnat. Conflict, Washington, 1982—; active Dupont Circle Citizens Assn., Washington, 1982—, 1700 S St. Assn., Washington, 1982-87; co-counsel Citizens for Democratic Alternatives in 1980, Washington, 1979-81; mem. adv. panel on fgn. policy, def. and arms control Dem. Nat. Com., Washington, 1982-85; mem. drafting team for fgn. policy, def. and arms control issue workshop Dem. Nat. Conf., Phila., 1982; mem. exec. com. Senate Dem. Roundtable, Washington, 1983—; mem. Senate Dem. Leadership Circle, Washington, 1983—; vice chmn. Potomac Group, Washington, 1983-84, chmn., 1984-85; mem. adv. council Dem. Platform Com., Washington, 1984; spl. counsel 1984 Dem. Nat. Conv., San Francisco, 1984; spl. counsel to nat. fin. chmn. Dem. Nat. Com., Washington, 1984-85, mem. fin. bd. dirs., 1982-85 ; mem. Nat. Dem. Club; vice chmn. Washington Fgn. Affairs Soc., 1984—; mem. Gov.'s Econ. Adv. Council, Va., 1986—; bd. dirs. Operation Up and Coming, Washington, 1984-86, Project Accessibility, Washington, 1984-86, Youth Leadership Inst., Washington, 1984-86. Named to Outstanding Young Men Am., U.S. Jaycees, 1976. Mem. Am. Soc. Internat. Law, ABA. Roman Catholic. Club: University (Washington). Home: 4936 Rodman St NW Washington DC 20016 Office: Anderson Hibey Nauheim & Blair 1708 New Hampshire Ave NW Washington DC 20009

BLAIR, ROBERT RUSH, oil company executive; b. Rawlins, Wyo., Sept. 22, 1928; s. James Scott and Ellen Scott (Rush) B.; B.S., Okla. State U., 1950; m. Carine Naveau de la Hault, Apr. 28, 1967; 1 dau., Tracy Catherine. With Sinclair Oil Corp., various locations, 1950-70, product coordinator Eastern Hemisphere, Brussels, 1964-67, gen. mgr., Algiers, 1967-70; v.p. Delhi Internat. Oil Corp., Dallas, 1970—; v.p., dir. Delhi Pacific Minerals Corp., Dallas, 1970—, exec. v.p. Delhi Internat. Oil Corp., Dallas, 1979—; chmn. bd., pres. CINCO Drilling Co., 1979—; chmn. bd. Enviromaster Internat., Inc.; pres. Magnolia Exploration Co.; dir. Natural Gas Pipeline Authority South Australia, Australian Mineral Found. Vice chmn. Dallas Arboretum and Bot. Soc. Served with AUS, 1951-53; Korea. Registered profl. engr., Tex. Mem. Ind. Petroleum Assn. Am., Am. Petroleum Inst., Australian Petroleum Exploration Assn. (dir.), Soc. Petroleum Engrs., Am. Inst. Mgmt., Am. C. of C. in Australia, Australian Am. Assn. Methodist. Clubs: Dallas Petroleum, Univ., Northwood, Commerce South Australia, South Australian Cricket Assn. Home: 4506 Kelsey Rd Dallas TX 75229 Office: 2 Energy Sq Suite 440 4849 Greenville Ave Dallas TX 75206

BLAIR, SIDNEY ROBERT, petroleum company executive; b. Port of Spain, Trinidad, Aug. 13, 1929; s. Sidney Martin and Janet (Gentleman) B.; m. Lois Wedderburn, June 13, 1953; children: Megan, James, Robert, Martin, Charlotte. BS, Queens U., 1951. Field engr., mgr. constrn. of gas and oil pipe lines and refineries 1951-58; dir. gas ops. and purchasing Alta. (Can.) and So. Gas Co. Ltd. and affiliates, 1959-69; exec. v.p. The Alta. Gas Trunk Line Co. Ltd., 1969-70, pres., chief exec. officer, from 1970; past chmn., chief exec. officer Nova, an Alta. (Can.) Corp., Calgary; former pres., chmn. bd. dirs. Husky Oil Ltd. subs. Calgary; chmn., chief exec. officer, dir. Nova Corp. Alta., Calgary, 1988—. Office: Nova Corp of Alta, 801 Seventh Ave SW, Calgary, AB Canada T2P 2N6 *

BLAIR, THOMAS S., steel company executive; b. New Castle, Pa., Apr. 15, 1922; s. George Dike, Jr. and Hazel (Slingluff) B.; m. Phyllis Emmerich, Sept. 17, 1946; children: Joan Dix, George Dike, Hadden Slingluff. A.B., Williams Coll., 1943. With Manhattan Project, 1942-47; asso. editor Iron Age mag., 1947-49; former pres. Blair Strip Steel Co., New Castle, chmn. bd., 1949—; dir. Columbia Gas System, Inc., Columbia Gas Pa., Inc., Columbia Gas Md., Inc., Tuscarora Plastics, Inc., Matflo Corp., Southeastern Plastics Corp. Home: 2906 Old Plank Rd New Castle PA 16105 Office: Blair Strip Steel Co New Castle PA 16107

BLAIR, VIRGINIA ANN, public relations executive; b. Kansas City, Mo., Dec. 20, 1925; d. Paul Lowe and Lou Etta (Cooley) Smith; m. James Leon Grant, Sept. 3, 1943 (dec. July 1944); m. 2d, Warden Tannahill Blair, Jr., Nov. 7, 1947; children—Janet, Warden Tannahill, III. B.S. in Speech, Northwestern U., 1948. Free-lance writer, Chgo., 1959-69; writer, editor Smith, Bucklin & Assocs., Inc., Chgo., 1969-72, account mgr., 1972-79, account supr., 1979-80, dir. pub. relations, 1980-85; pres. GB Pub. Relations, 1985—; judge U.S. Indsl. Film Festival, 1974, 75; instr. Writer's Workshop, Evanston, Ill., 1978; dir. Northwestern U. Library Council, 1978—. Emmy nominee Nat. Acad. TV Arts & Scis., 1963; recipient Service award Northwestern U., 1978, Creative Excellence award U.S. Indsl. Film Festival, 1976, Gold Leaf merit cert. Family Circle mag. and Food Council Am., 1977. Mem. Pub. Relations Soc. Am. (counselors acad.), Women's Advt. Club Chgo. (pres.), Publicity Club Chgo., Nat. Acad. TV Arts & Scis., Zeta Phi Eta (Service award 1978), Alpha Gamma Delta. Author dramas (produced on CBS): Jeanne D'Arc: The Trial, 1961; Cordon of Fear, 1961; Reflection, 1961; If I Should Die, 1963; 3-act children's play: Children of Courage, 1967. Home and Office: 463 Highcrest Dr Wilmette IL 60091

BLAIS, ROGER NATHANIEL, physics educator, researcher, consultant; b. Duluth, Minn., Oct. 3, 1944; s. Eusebe Joseph and Edith Seldina (Anderson) B.; m. Mary Louise Leclerc, Aug. 2, 1971; children—Christopher Edward, Laura Louise. B.A. in Physics and French Lit., U. Minn., 1966; Ph.D. in Physics, U. Okla., 1971; cert. in computer programming Tulsa Jr. Coll., 1981; cert. in bus. UCLA, 1986. Registered profl. engr., Okla. Instr. physics Westark Community Coll., Ft. Smith, Ark., 1971-72; asst. prof. physics and geophys. scis. Old Dominion U., Norfolk, Va., 1972-77; asst. prof. engring. physics U. Tulsa, 1977-81, assoc. prof., 1981—, assoc. dir. Artificial Lift Projects, 1983—, chmn. physics, 1986— . Contbr. articles to profl. jours. Mem. Am. Phys. Soc., AAAS, Am. Geophys. Union, Nat. Soc. Profl. Engrs., AAUP, Soc. Petroleum Engrs., Instrument Soc. Am., N.Y. Acad. Sci., Iron Wedge Soc., Phi Beta Kappa, Sigma Xi, Sigma Pi Sigma, Tau Beta Pi. Home: 5348 E 30th Pl Tulsa OK 74114-6314 Office: U Tulsa Physics Dept 600 S College Ave Tulsa OK 74104-3189

BLAIZE, HERBERT AUGUSTUS, prime minister of Grenada; b. Feb. 26, 1918, Island of Carriacou; s. James and Mary Blaize; m. Venetia Blaize, 1946; 6 children. Ed. Grenada Boys' Secondary Sch., Law Soc. Eng. Solicitor; M.P., after 1957, minister for trade and prodn., 1957-60, chief minister, 1960-61, 62-67, premier, 1967, mem. opposition to Coup of 1979, prime minister, 1984—. Office: Office of Prime Minister, Tanteen, Saint George's Grenada *

BLAKE, BARRY JOHN, educator; b. Melbourne, Victoria, Australia, Sept. 5, 1937; s. John Douglas and Kathleen Clare (Dolan) B.; m. Marie Therese Quilty, Nov. 18, 1963; children: Laurence, Hilary, Alice, Celia. BA with honors, U. Melbourne, 1958; MA, Monash U., Australia, 1967, PhD, 1975. Research fellow Monash U., Australia, 1966-67; lectr. Monash U., Clayton, Victoria, Australia, 1970-72, sr. lectr., 1973-81, assoc. prof., 1982-87; lectr. U. Sydney, New South Wales, Australia, 1968-69; prof. La Trobe U., Victoria, Australia, 1988—. Author: Case in Australian Languages, 1977, Australian Aboriginal Languages, 1981, Australian Aboriginal Grammar, 1987; co-author Language Typology, 1981; co-editor Handbook of Australian Languages, 1979-81, 83.

BLAKE, DARLENE EVELYN, political worker, consultant, educator; b. Rockford, Iowa, Feb. 26, 1947; d. Forest Kenneth and Violet Evelyn (Fisher) Kuhlemeier, m. Joel Franklin Blake, May 1, 1975; 1 child, Alexander Joel. AA, N. Iowa Area Community Coll., Mason City, 1967; BS, Mankato (Minn.) State Coll., 1969; MS, Mankato (Minn.) State U., 1975. Cert. profl. tchr., Iowa; registered art therapist. Tchr. Bishop Whipple Sch., Faribault, Minn., 1970-72; art therapist C.B. Wilson Ctr., Faribault, 1972-76, Sedgwick County Dept. Mental Health, Wichita, Kans., 1976-79; cons. Batten, Batten, Hudson & Swab, Des Moines, 1979-81; pres. Blake Seminars, Des Moines, 1984—; polit. cons. to Alexander Haig for Pres., 1987-88, mem. adv. bd. Alexander Haig for Pres. Exhibited in one-woman show at local library, 1970. Chmn. U.S. Selective Service Bd. #27, Polk County, Iowa, 1981—; sustaining mem. Rep. Nat. Com.; Rep. candidate Polk County Treas., Des Moines, 1982; chmn. Polk County Rep. Party, 1985-88; commr. Des Moines Commn. Human Rights and Job Discrimination, 1984—; mem. Martin Luther King Scholarship Com., 1986—; mem. Iowa State Bd. Psychology Examiners, 1983—; mem. nat. adv. bd. Alexande Haig for Pres. Mem. Am. Art Therapy Assn., (cert., standards com. 1986—), Am. Soc. Tng. Devel., Iowa Art Therapy Assn. (pres. elect. 1984-85, founder). Lutheran. Clubs: Des Moines Garden (pres. 1984-85), Saylorville Yacht (Des Moines) (social chair 1983), Polk County Rep. Women (pres. elect 1983-85). Home: 2802 SW Caulder Des Moines IA 50321

BLAKE, GARY BOMAN, advertising executive; b. San Diego, Apr. 1, 1947; s. Ross Clifford and Cecily Anne (Boman) B.; m. Susanne Rosling (div. Sept. 1985); 1 child:, Ashley Lauren; m. Lynette Gaye Holland, Sept. 7, 1985; 1 child, Ryan Winslow. BA in Polit. Sci. and Psychology, Whittier (Calif.) Coll., 1969; postgrad., U. Copenhagen, 1970-71. Mktg., mdse. cons. J. Walter Thompson, Copenhagen, 1969-72, Warner/Electra/Atlantic, San Francisco, 1972-74, Warner Bros. Records, Burbank, Calif., 1976-79; creative dir. Lambert & Blake, Inc., San Francisco, 1979-81; pres. The Blake Agy., Inc., San Francisco, 1981—; bd. dirs. Transam. Trading Corp., Salinas, Kans. Fund raiser Mt. Diablo council Boy Scouts Am., 1985-86; mem. adv. council Berkeley Pub. Edn. Found., 1987-88. Recipient CLIO award for radio commercial Meaningful Details, 1981, Award of Excellence, Mead Ann. Report Show, 1986, Cable Car award San Francisco Ad Club, 1986, Merit award San Francisco Art Dirs. Show, 1986, Cert. of Merit, BPAA West-Zitel Ann. Report, 1987. Mem. San Francisco Art Dirs. Club (v.p. 1982-83, pres. 1983-84), San Francisco Advt. Club (civic affairs com.), Western States Advt. Club. Republican. Methodist. Lodge: Rotary. Home: 32 The Plaza Dr Berkeley CA 94705 Office: The Ice House 151 Union St Suite 451 San Francisco CA 94111

BLAKE, GEORGE ROWLAND, soil science educator, water resources research administrator; b. Provo, Utah, Mar. 14, 1918; s. Samuel Henry and Annie Matilda (Bevan) B.; m. Kathryn M. Sumsion, Feb. 26, 1941; children—Carla Paul, Rowland, Lorraine Blake Phillips, Henry; m. Helen M. Patten, May 25, 1985. B.A., Brigham Young U., 1943; Ph.D., Ohio State U., 1949. Missionary Ch. of Jesus Christ of Latter-day Saints, Germany, 1937-39; with FBI, Washington, 1941-42; research fellow, teaching asst. Ohio State U., Columbus, 1946-49; asst. prof., asst. research specialist Rutgers U., New Brunswick, N.J., 1949-55; assoc. prof. dept. soil sci. U. Minn., St. Paul, 1955-60, prof., 1960—, dir. Water Resources Research Ctr., 1979-84; NSF sr. postdoctoral fellow, Braunschweig, Fed. Republic Germany, 1962-63; Fulbright guest prof. U. Hohenheim, Fed. Republic Germany, 1970-71; Ford Found. cons., Chile, 1967; guest prof. U. Kesthely, Hungary, 1974, U. Warsaw, Poland, 1981; USAID cons., Morocco, 1979-88; adj. prof. Institut Agronomique et Veterinaire Hassan II Rabat Morocco 1982—; guest prof. Humboldt U., Berlin, German Democratic Republic, 1986. Contbr. articles to profl. jours. Recipient Georgicon award U. Kesthely, 1974. Fellow Am. Soc. Agronomy, Soil Sci. Soc. Am.; mem. Internat. Soc. Soil Sci., Soil Sci. Soc. Am., Soil Conservation Soc. Am., Sigma Xi, Gamma Sigma Delta, Omicron Delta Kappa. Mormon. Home: 1579 Burton St Saint Paul MN 55108 Office: U Minn 150 Borlaug Hall Saint Paul MN 55108

BLAKE, GERALD HENRY, geography educator; b. Southampton, Eng., Feb. 11, 1936; s. Geoffrey Thomas and Grace (Dibben) B.; m. Brenda Jane Peach, Apr. 17, 1965; children: Robert Thomas, Carolyn Rachel, Julia Louise. MA, Oxford U., 1960; PhD, Southampton Coll., 1964. Tchr. St. John's Coll., Johannesburg, South Africa, 1960-61; lectr., sr. lectr. U. Durham, Eng., 1964-84, reader in geography, 1985—; prin. Collingwood Coll., Eng., 1987—. Co-author: The Middle East, 1976, Cambridge Atlas of the Middle East, 1987, Political Geography of the Middle East and North Africa, 1985; editor: Maritime Boundaries and Ocean Resources, 1987. Justice of the Peace, County of Durham, 1973—; vice chmn. parochial ch. council St. Nicholas Ch., Durham, 1985—. Fellow Royal Geog. Soc., Brit. Soc. for Middle Eastern Studies; mem. Marine Conservation Soc., Soc. for Libyan Studies, Soc. for Mediterranean Studies, Inst. Brit. Geographers. Anglican. Clubs: Leander, Durham Amateur Rowing. Home: Collingwood Coll, South Rd, Durham DH1 3LT, England Office: U Durham, Dept of Geography, Durham DH1 3LE, England

BLAKE, JOHN FREEMAN, financial lawyer; b. Santa Clara, Calif., June 29, 1950; s. Freeman Dawes and Teresa (Seneker) B.; m. Linda Humphlett, Aug. 27, 1977; children: William, Braden. AB cum laude, U. Calif., Berkeley, 1972; postgrad., Tufts U., 1973-74; JD, U. San Francisco, 1979. Bar: Calif., D.C. Asst. v.p., fin. counselor Bank Am., San Francisco, 1974-79; assoc. McCutchen, Doyle, Brown & Enersen, San Francisco, 1979-80, Trembath, McCabe, Schwartz, Evans & Levy, Concord, Calif., 1980-83, Silverstein & Mullens, Washington, 1983-87; sole practice Washington, 1987—; mem. Joint Adv. Com. Calif. Continuing Edn. of Bar, 1981-83; adj. prof. estate planning Golden Gate U., San Francisco, 1982-83, George Washington U., Washington, 1984—; numerous seminars, lectures, forums. Author: Tax Management Financial Planning (4 vols.), 1985, also exec. editor; author and editor: Introduction, Financial Planning After the Tax Reform Act of 1986; prepared numerous manuals, pamphlets on Calif. probate laws, estate planning; contbr. articles to Money mag., profl. jours. Active Washington Estate Planning Council. Mem. ABA, Calif. State Bar Assn., Internat. Assn. Fin. Planning (nat. bd. dirs. 1985—), Registry of Fin.

Planning Practitioners, Phi Beta Kappa. Office: 1101 Connecticut Ave NW Suite 1202 Washington DC 20036

BLAKE, STANFORD, lawyer; b. Detroit, Sept. 13, 1948; s. Morris and Betty (Yaffe) B.; m. Ellen Perkins, Mar. 5, 1978; children—Cary, Brandon, Stephanie. B.S., U. Fla. 1970; J.D., U. Miami, 1973. Bar: Fla. 1973, U.S. Dist. Ct. (so. dist.) Fla. 1973, U.S. Supreme Ct. 1980, U.S. Ct. Appeals (5th and 11th cirs.) 1981. Asst. pub. defender Dade County, Miami, Fla., 1973-78; ptnr. Todd, Rosinek & Blake, Miami, 1978-84, Rosinek & Blake, Miami, 1984-86; sole practice, Miami, 1986—. Chmn. Jr. Maccabiah Games S. Fla., Miami, 1984—. Co-chmn. Dade County Outstanding Citizen award, 1986; v.p. congregation Bet Breira, 1987—. Mem. ABA, Fla. State Bar Assn. (chmn. grievance com. 1987), Fed. Bar Assn., Nat. Assn. Criminal Def. Lawyers, Fla. Criminal Def. Attys. Assn. (pres. 1982-83), so. Miami Kendall Bar Assn. (pres. 1984-85). Lodge: B'nai B'rith (pres. 1980-81). Democrat. Jewish. Home: 7810 SW 164th St Miami FL 33157 Office: 9200 S Dadeland Blvd Suite 617 Miami FL 33156

BLAKEMORE, COLIN BRIAN, neurophysiologist, educator; b. Stratford-on-Avon, England, June 1, 1944; s. Cedric Norman (dec.) and Beryl Ann B.; m. Andree Elizabeth Washbourne, 1965; three daus. Student Cambridge U.; Ph.D. (Harkness fellow), U. Calif.-Berkeley. Univ. demonstrator Physiol. Lab., Cambridge U., 1968-72, lectr. in physiology, 1972-79; fellow, dir. med. studies Downing Coll., 1972-79; vis. prof. NYU, 1970, MIT, 1971; Locke research fellow Royal Soc. Eng., 1976-79; Waynflete prof. physiology Oxford (Eng.) U., 1979—, professorial fellow Magdalen Coll., 1979—; BBC Reith lectr., 1976; Lethaby prof. R.C.A., London, 1978; Storer lectr. U. Calif.-Davis, 1980; Macallum lectr. U. Toronto, 1984. Author: Educational Handbook of Psychobiology, 1975; Mechanics of the Mind, 1977; Mindwaves, 1987, The Mind Machine, 1988Images and Understanding, 1989; editor-in-chief IBRO News, 1986; contbr.: Constraints on Learning, 1973; Illusion in Art and Nature, 1973; The Neurosciences Third Study Program, 1974; contbr. articles to profl. jours.; editorial bd. Perception, 1971—; Behavioral and Brain Scis., 1977—, Jour. Developmental Physiology, 1978-86, Exptl. Brain Research, 1979—, Lang. and Communication, 1979—, News in Physiol. Scis., 1986—, Clin. Vision Scis., 1986—; editorial adv. bd. Trends in Neuroscis., 1977-83, Chinese Jour. of Physiol. Scis.; lectr. Common Sense, Christmas Lectures for Young People, Royal Inst., 1982; presenter BBC TV series The Mind Machine, 1988. Mem. nat. com. Brain Research Assn., 1973-77; mem. exec. com. and governing council Internat. Brain Research Orgn., 1973—; mem. com. BBC Sci. Cons. Group, 1975-79; mem. sci. adv. bd. Cognitive Neuroscis. Inst. N.Y., 1981—; Rationalist Press Assn (hon. assoc. 1986), IRL Press (U.K. pub. adv. panel). Leverhulme fellow, 1974-75; recipient Robert Bing prize Swiss Acad. Med. Scis., 1975; Dr. Robert Netter prize Académie Nationale de Médicine, Paris, 1984; Cairns medal, 1986; named Man of Yr., Royal Soc. Disability and Rehab., 1978. Mem. European Brain and Behaviour Soc. (com. 1974-76), Cambridge Philos. Soc. (council 1975-79), Physiol. Soc., Exptl. Psychology Soc., Soc. Neurosci., European Neurosci. Assn. Address: Univ Lab Physiology, Parks Rd, Oxford OX1 3PT, England

BLAKENEY, ROGER NEAL, educator, psychologist; b. Deatur, Tex., Sept. 16, 1939; s. C.B. and Flora M. (McAnelly) B.; BS in Psychology, Tex. A&M U., 1964; MA in Indsl. Psychology, U. Houston, 1967, PhD in Indsl. Psychology, 1969; m. Jenifer Blakeney; children—Christopher Alan, Benjamin G. Teaching fellow dept. psychology U. Houston, 1965-68, instr. mgmt., 1968-69, asst. prof. behavioral mgmt. sci., 1969-72, dir. masters program, 1970, coordinator Human Resources Center, 1971-72, assoc. prof. behavioral mgmt. sci., 1972-74, assoc. prof. organizational behavior and mgmt. Coll. Bus. Adminstrn., 1974—, dir. Ctr. Exec. Devel. 1986—; indsl. psychology intern Exxon U.S.A., 1967-68; adj. prof. Houston Bapt. U., 1978-1984; pres. Blakeney & Assocs., 1972-86, Organizational Tech., Inc., 1973-78; dir. Self-Dimensions, Inc., 1983—. cons. to various govt., labor and bus. orgns. Served with AUS, 1960-62. Mem. Am., Southwestern, Tex., Houston psychol. assns., Am., Southwestern acads. mgmt., Internat. Transactional Analysis Assn., Sigma Xi, Beta Gamma Sigma, Alpha Kappa Delta, Alpha Zeta, Sigma Iota Epsilon. Past mem. of editorial bd. Employee Responsibility and Rights Jour. Author: (with E.C. Bell) Building Effective Local Unions; Course XV of the Labor Education Program of District 37 United Steelworkers of America, 1972, Advanced Leadership: Course XIII of the Labor Education Program of District 37 United Steelworkers of America, 1972; Introduction To Management By Objectives, 1974; Developmental Supervision: Performance Review and Career Planning with Dan & Billie Duncan; That Special Person is Me, 1983; I Have the Power, 1983; Early Start, 1984. Editor: (with M.T. Matteson and D.R. Domm) Contemporary Personnel Management, 1972; (with D.R. Domm, R.W. Scofield and M.T. Matteson) The Individual and the Organization: A book of readings, 1971; Current Issues in Transactional Analysis, 1977; contbg. author: Certificate in Management Accounting Review, 1978; editorial bd. Transaction Analysis Jour.; contbr. articles to profl. publs. Office: U Houston Ctr Exec Devel Coll Bus Adminstrn Houston TX 77204-6283

BLAKEWAY, MARTIN IVAN, educator; b. Southampton, Hampshire, Eng., Nov. 12, 1930; s. Francis Henry and Esther (Messe) B. BA, Cambridge U., Eng., 1954, MA, 1958. Adventurer, tchr., 1949—; lectr. Sophia and Waseda U., Tokyo, Japan, 1972—; ind. fgn. cons., 1972—; pres. Lynx Internat. KK, 1988—. Contbr. articles to profl. jours. Mem. Marco Polo Soc. (pres. 1974-75), South Seas Soc. (gov. 1976—), The Embassy of Man (founder 1957). Address: 101 Sunnyside Flats, 2-20-4 Kohinata, Bunkyo-ku, Tokyo 112, Japan

BLAKLEY, BENJAMIN SPENCER, III, lawyer; b. DuBois, Pa., Sept. 1, 1952; s. Benjamin Spencer Jr. and Mary Jane (Campney) B.; 1 child, Benjamin Spencer IV. BA, Grove City Coll., 1974; JD, Duquesne U., 1977. Bar: Pa. 1977. Ptnr. Blakley & Jones, DuBois, 1977—; pub. defender Clearfield (Pa.) County, 1977-84; instr. Pa. State U., DuBois, 1979-85. Bd. dirs. Salvation Army Pa. Corp., DuBois, 1978—, pres., 1988—, DuBois Area Youth Aid Panel, 1984-87, Citizens for Effective Govt., DuBois, 1985—; trustee DuBois Vol. Fire Dept., 1986-87, treas., 1987—. Mem. ABA, Pa. Bar Assn., Clearfield County Bar Assn., Nat. Assn. Criminal Def. Lawyers. Democrat. Methodist. Office: Blakley & Jones 406 Deposit Bank Bldg DuBois PA 15801

BLAKLEY, JOHN CLYDE, administrator; b. Bogota, Colombia, Sept. 14, 1955; came to U.S., 1964; s. Arthur C. and Dorothy M. (Balcome) B.; m. Jean M. Padden, May 21, 1983. BS, U. Miami, 1977, MEd, 1979. Notary at large, Fla. Mgr., adminstrv. asst. U. Miami Student Union, Coral Gables, Fla., 1977-79; mgr. Aladdins Castle, Inc., South Miami, Fla., 1979-80; adminstrv. mgr., cons. Lexow Brackins, CPA's, Hollywood, Fla., 1981-84; firm adminstr., cons. Lexow, Brackins, Koffler, CPA's, Hollywood, 1985—; pres. Miami Apple Users Group, 1983; cons. YMCA, 1983. Chmn. Multiple Sclerosis Project Dance Marathon, Coral Gables, 1977-79; coordinator United Way Miami, 1975-79. Recipient Whitten award Assn. Coll. Unions, 1977, Outstanding Leadership award C. of C., 1973, Outstanding Vol., United Way, 1975, Outstanding Alumni award U. Miami, 1986. Mem. Assn. Acctg. Adminstrs., Fla. Inst. CPA's, Assn. Coll. Unions Internat. (chmn. region 6, 1975-77), U. Miami Young Alumni Club (bd. dirs., pres.), U. Miami Alumni Assn. (bd. dirs.). Club: Hurricane. Home: 11531 SW 98th St Miami FL 33176 Office: Lexow Brackins Koffler CPA's 2611 Hollywood Blvd Hollywood FL 33020

BLAMEY, THOMAS EDWARD, transportation executive; b. Melbourne, Victoria, Australia, June 24, 1945; came to U.S., 1988; s. Thomas R. and Georgia C. (Roberts) B. B in Applied Sci. with honors, U. Melbourne, 1967; MBA, Harvard, 1970. Product mgr. Bristol-Myers Co., N.Y.C., 1970-71; mgr. new products Bristol-Myers Co., Auckland, New Zealand, 1972; gen. mgr. Clairol div. Bristol-Myers Co., Sydney, Australia, 1973-75; cons. McKinsey & Co. Inc., Sydney, Melbourne, London, 1975-79; mng. dir. Sitmar Cruises, Sydney, 1979-87; pres. Sitmar Internat., Los Angeles, 1988—; bd. dirs. Bounty Voyages Pty. Ltd., Sydney, 1985-87. Leader Scout Assn. Australia, Sydney and Melbourne; trustee Com. Econ. Devel. Australia, 1986-87. Fellow Australian Mktg. Inst. Clubs: Am. Nat. (Sydney); Royal Melbourne Golf. Office: Sitmar Cruises 10100 Santa Monica Blvd Los Angeles CA 90067

BLAN, KENNITH WILLIAM, JR., lawyer; b. Detroit, Dec. 15, 1946; s. Kennith William and Sarah Shirley (Shane) B.; m. Rebbeca Jo McCraken, Mar. 6, 1981; 1 son, Noah Winton. B.S., U. Ill., 1968, J.D., 1971. Bar: Ill. 1972, U.S. Supreme Ct. 1978. With Office State's Atty., Vermilion County, Ill., 1971-72; atty. Chgo. Title & Trust Co., 1972; asso. firm Graham, Meyer, Young, Welsch & Maton, Chgo., Springfield and Danville, Ill., 1972-74; individual practice law, Danville, 1975—; spl. asst. atty. gen. Ill., 1974-76; atty. City of Georgetown, Ill., 1985—, Village of Westville, Ill., Village of Belgium, Ill. Chmn. Vermilion County Young Rep. Club, 1975-77; founding sponsor Civil Justice Found.; capt. CAP; mem. Christian Businessmen's Com. Mem. ABA, Ill. Bar Assn., Vermilion County Bar Assn., Lawyer-Pilots Bar Assn., Assn. Trial Lawyers Am., Ill. Trial Lawyers Assn., Ind. Trial Lawyers Assn., Am. Soc. Law and Medicine, Gideons Internat., Aircraft Owners and Pilots Assn. Mem. Ch. of Christ. Lodge: Elks. Office: PO Box 1995 Danville IL 61834-1995

BLANCH, STUART YARWORTH, archbishop; b. Blakeney, Gloucestershire, Eng., Feb. 2, 1918; s. William Edwin and Elizabeth Blanch; m. Brenda Gertrude Coyte, 1943; children—Susan, Hilary, Angela, Timothy, Alison. BA, Oxford U., 1948, MA, 1952; LLD, Liverpool U., 1975; DD (hon.), Hull U., 1977, Wycliffe Coll., Toronto, 1979, U. Manchester, 1984; D (hon.), U. York, 1979. Ordained priest Ch. of Eng. With Law Fire Ins. Soc. Ltd., 1936-40; curate, then vicar chs. in Oxford, 1949-57; vice prin. Wycliffe Hall, 1957-60; Oriel canon Rochester Cathedral, warden Rochester Theol. Coll., 1960-66; bishop of Liverpool, 1966-75; archbishop of York, 1975-83; prochancellor Hull U., 1975-83, York U., 1977-83; mem. House of Lords, 1972—, privy counsellor, 1975—, subprelate Order St. John, 1975—. Served as navigator RAF, 1940-46. Hon. fellow St. Catherine's Coll., Oxford, 1975, St. Peter's Coll., Oxford, 1983; decorated Baron, 1983. Mem. Royal Commonwealth Soc. Author: The World Our Orphanage, 1972; For All Mankind, 1976; The Christian Militant, 1978; The Burning Bush, 1978; The Trumpet in Morning, 1979; The Ten Commandments, 1981; Living by Faith, 1983; Way of Blessedness, 1985, Encounters with Jesus, 1988. Address: Bishopthorpe, York YO2 1QE England

BLANCHARD, JAMES J., governor of Michigan; b. Detroit, Aug. 8, 1942; divorced; 1 son, Jay. B.A.,, Mich. State U., Lansing, 1964; MBA, Mich. State U., 1965; J.D., U. Minn., 1967; J.D. (hon.), Mich. State U., U. Mich., 1985, Wayne State U., 1985, Oakland U., 1984, Alma Coll., 1987; JD (hon.), Grand Valley State U., 1988. Bar: Mich. 1968. Legal aid elections bur. Office Sec. State, State of Mich., 1968-69; asst. atty. gen. State of Mich., 1969-74, adminstrv. asst. to atty. gen., 1970-71, asst. dep. atty. gen., 1971-72; mem. Congress from 18th Mich. Dist., 1974-82; gov. State of Mich., 1983—; mem. Pres.'s Commn. on Holocaust, Nat. Govs. Assn. Exec. Com.; chmn. Dem. Nat. Platform Com., Dem. Govs. Assn. Mem. Oakland County exec. club Mich. State U.; bd. advisors Ctr. for Policy Research. Recipient Oustanding Achievement award U. Minn., Tree of Life award Jewish Nat. Fund.; named one of Outstanding Young Men Am., U.S. Jaycees, 1987, a Michiganian of Yr. Detroit News mag., 1980. Mem. Assn. Asst. Attys. Gen., Ferndale Jaycees, State Bar Mich., Am. Bar Assn., LWV, Nat. Gov's. Assn. (chmn. legal affairs com. 1987, mem. finance com., human resources com.), Dem. Gov's. Assn. (chmn., 1988)U. Minn. Law Sch. Alumni Club, U. Detroit Titan Club. Democrat. Office: Office of the Governor State Capitol Lansing MI 48933

BLANCHARD, THOMAS EARLE, business owner, consultant; b. Schenectady, Mar. 14, 1943; s. Edward W. and Elanor A. (Butler) B.; m. Janet Lee Marsh, Oct. 10, 1946; children: Marcy Lee, Michael Thomas. AAS, Paul Smith's Coll., 1964. Regional credit ctr. mgr. W.T. Grant Co., Albany, N.Y., 1964-72, store mgr., 1972-75; distbn. mgr. Central Warehouse Corp., Albany, 1975-80; gen. mgr. Toledo Cold Storage Inc., 1980-81; chmn., pres. Great Lakes Cold Storage Inc., Toledo, 1981—, Blanchard Oil Co., 1984—, Jiffy Mart Inc., 1983—, cons. Served with Air N.G., 1964-70. Mem. Internat. Assn. Refrigerated Warehouses, Toledo Chamber of Commerce, Maumee Valley Petroleum Dealers Assn., Ohio Petroleum Mktg. Assn., Toledo Area Small Bus. Assn. Home: 2383 Hubbard Rd Monroe MI 48161

BLANCHARD WILDMAN, SUZANNE, composer, educator; b. Boston, Jan. 4, 1940; d. Wells and Helen Lane Blanchard; grad. San Francisco Conservatory Music, Vocal major, 1957; A.B., Classics, Stanford U., 1958; m. Ben. H. Wildman, July 28, 1952 (div. 1958); children—Helen LeRoy, Benjamin Henry, Ludwig Altmann. Concert pianist, performing at Palace of Legion of Honor, San Francisco, 1961, Temple Emmanuel, San Francisco, 1961, Meml. Ch., Stanford U., 1962; tchr. elem. piano San Francisco Conservatory, 1963-64. Foster parent Operation Happy Child, Taiwan; active Met. Opera Raffle, UNICEF; mem. Republican Town Com., Manchester, Mass. Mem. Am. Security Council, Manchester Hist. Soc., Stanford U. Alumni Assn. Republican. Christian Scientist. Clubs: Pebble Beach (Carmel, Calif.); Singing Beach Beach (Manchester); Revolutionary Ridge Book (Concord, Mass.). Composer: The Governor Proposes, 1962, additional scenes, 1985; Five Christmas Duets for Teacher and Beginner, Preludes 1-3, Fugue, 1962, Prelude 4, 1984, Julia Song Cycle for Robert Herrick North Shore Community Coll. Sch. of Music, 1984, ballet suite The Leonardo, 1987, (background music for TV prodn.) Preview of Shakespeare in Camelot, 1988. Home: 27 Pine St Manchester-by-the Sea MA 01944 Office: University Ln Manchester MA 01944

BLANCHE, ERNEST EVRED, mathematical statistician; b. Passaic, N.J., Oct. 22, 1912; s. John and Stella (Haluschak) B.; A.B. magna cum laude, Bucknell U., 1938, A.M., 1938; Ph.D., U. Ill., 1941; m. Judith Waypa, Nov. 24, 1938; children—Patricia Irene, John Jacob. Teaching asst. U. Ill., Urbana, 1938-41; instr. math. and statistics Mich. State U., East Lansing, 1941-42; statis dir. engring. Curtiss-Wright Corp., Buffalo, 1942-43, head, math. and statistics, research lab., 1943-44; prin. statistician Fgn. Econ. Adminstrn., Washington, 1944-45; civilian instr. Army U., Florence, Italy, 1945; prin. analyst Army Service Forces, Washington, 1946-47; chief statistician, research and devel. div. Army Gen. Staff, 1947-48, chief statistician, logistics div., 1948-54; v.p. Frederick Research Corp., Bethesda, Md., 1954-55; pres. Ernest E. Blanche & Assos., Kensington, Md., 1955-68; prof. Capitol Inst. Tech., Kensington, 1970-71, acting pres., 1971-72, chmn. bd. trustees, 1972-74; pres. Ernest E. Blanche Cons., Chevy Chase, Md., 1974—. Mem. Am. Math. Soc., Inst. Math. Statistics, Am. Statis. Assn. Math. Assn. Am., Biometric Soc., Washington Statis. Soc., Phi Beta Kappa, Sigma Xi, Pi Mu Epsilon, Delta Phi Alpha, Tau Alpha Pi. Roman Catholic. Clubs: Lions, Manor Country, Inverrary Country (Lauderhill, Fla.). Author: Off to the Races, 1947; You Can't Win, 1949; contbr. articles to profl. jours. Home: 14818 Carrolton Rd Rockville MD 20853 Office: 10335 Kensington Pkwy Kensington MD 20895

BLANCHETTE, JAMES EDWARD, psychiatrist; b. Syracuse, N.Y., Aug. 28, 1924; s. Joseph M. and Margaret (Vincent) B.; m. Shirley Ruth Brisco, Sept. 1, 1948 (dec. May 1981). BA, Syracuse U., 1950; MD, SUNY-Syracuse Sch. Med., 1953. Intern, St. Vincent's Hosp., N.Y.C., 1953-54; resident Patton (Calif.) State Hosp., 1954-55, Met. State Hosp., Norwalk, Calif., 1957-59; pvt. practice psychiatry, Redlands, Calif., 1959—; chief profl. edn. Patton State Hosp., 1960-64, tchg. cons., 1964-69; asst. clin. prof. psychiatry Loma Linda Med. Sch.; mem. staffs San Bernardino Community Hosp., St. Bernadine Hosp. (both San Bernardino), Charter Hosp. Redlands, Calif.; cons. psychiatry Redlands Community Hosp. Served with USAAF, 1945-47. Diplomate Am. Bd. Med. Examiners, Am. Bd. Psychiatry and Neurology. Fellow Am. Psychiat. Assn., AAAS, Pan-Am. Med. Assn.; mem. AMA, Calif. Med. Assn., San Bernardino Med. Soc., Internat. Platform Assn., So. Calif. Psychiat. Soc. (pres. Inland chpt. 1963-64, pres. 1983-84), Royal Soc. Health, Am. Med. Soc. Vienna, Phi Mu Alpha Symphonia, Nu Sigma Nu. Home: 972 W Marshall Blvd San Bernardino CA 92405 Office: 236 Cajon St Redlands CA 92373

BLANCK, DAG ANTON, research center executive; b. Uddevalla, Sweden, Dec. 18, 1956; s. Herman Anton and Tania (Gullers) B. BA, Augustana Coll., 1978; grad., Uppsala U., Sweden, 1983, postgrad., 1984—. Instr. history Scandinavian Augustana Coll., Rock Island, Ill., 1980-81, dir. Swenson Swedish Immigration Ctr., 1985—; mem. undergrad. scholarship selection com. Sweden-Am. Found., 1983—. Editor: Scandinavia Overseas, 1986; contbr. articles to profl. jours. Mauritszon fellow Sweden-Am. Found., 1976-78, Thor-Gray fellow, 1983; doctoral fellow Uppsala U., 1985—. Mem. Swedish Hist. Assn., Orgn. Am. Historians, Swedish-Am. Hist. Soc. (editorial bd. 1986—), Augustana Hist. Soc. Office: Augustana Coll Swenson Swedish Immigration Research Ctr Box 175 Rock Island IL 61202

BLANCO, MANUEL MENDOZA, surgical dressings company executive, management consultant; b. Pasay City, Metro Manila, Philippines, Dec. 9, 1947; s. Jaime Resurreccion and Purita Mata (Mendoza) B.; m. Stephania De Guzman Bernardo, Oct. 7, 1972; children—Anna Katrina, Manuel Jr., Mark Philip. B.S. Bus. Adminstrn., De La Salle U., Manila, 1969, M.B.A., 1971. Real estate broker. Treas., Adamson & Adamson, Inc., Makati, Manila, 1972-73, exec. v.p., treas., 1973—, also dir.; treas., dir. Adamson Mgmt. Corp., Makati, 1973—; v.p., dir. Adamson Realty Corp., 1979—, pres., chmn. Strand Mktg. Corp., 1972—; exec. v.p., dir. JRB Realty Corp., 1971—. Roman Catholic. Mem. De La Salle Alumni Assn., Club: Manila Polo. Lodge: Rotary. Avocation: Reading. Home: 2096 Lumbang St, Dasmarinas Village, Makati Metro Manila 3117, Philippines Office: Adamson & Adamson Inc, Adamson Centre 121, Alfaro St, Salcedo Village, Makati Metro Manila 3117, Philippines

BLANE, JOHN, diplomat; b. Birmingham, Ala., July 15, 1929; s. John and Floy (Stewart) B.; m. Elizabeth Kubin, Dec. 26, 1953; children: Sharon, John Patrick; m. 2d Dianne Metzger, Dec. 19, 1970. B.A., U. Tenn.-Knoxville, 1951, M.A., 1956; student, U. Vienna, 1952-53, Northwestern U., 1962-63. Fgn. service officer Dept. of State, 1956—; consular and polit. officer Dept. of State, Mogadishu, 1957, Asmara, 1958-60, Salzburg, 1960-62; polit. officer Yaounde, 1963-66; country officer Togo, Dahomey, Chad and Gabon, 1966-68; acting chief of No. and Eastern Africa Bur. Intelligence and Research, 1969; dept. chief of mission Ft. Lamy, 1969-72; policy planning officer Bur. African Affairs, 1972-75; acting staff dir. Nat. Security Council Interdeptl. Group, 1972-75; dir. bilateral programs div. Office of Internat. Activities, EPA, 1975-77; dep. chief of mission Nairobi, 1977-80; mem. Exec. Seminar in Nat. and Internat. Affairs Fgn. Service Inst., 1980-81; mem. U.S. delegation to 36th session UN Gen. Assembly, N.Y.C., 1981; spl. projects officer Bur. African Affairs, 1982; U.S. ambassador to Rwanda 1982-85, U.S. ambassador to Chad, 1985—. Served with U.S. Army, 1953-55. Fulbright scholar, 1952-53. Mem. Am. Fgn. Service Assn., Alpha Tau Omega. Episcopalian. Lodge: N'Djamena Rotary. Home: Greenview IL 62642

BLANK, A(NDREW) RUSSELL, lawyer; b. Bklyn., June 13, 1945; s. Lawrence and Joan B.; children—Adam, Marisa. Student U. N.C., 1963-64; B.A., U. Fla., 1966, postgrad. Law Sch., 1966-68; J.D., U. Miami, 1970. Bar: Ga. 1971, Fla. 1970; cert. civil trial advocate Nat. Bd. Trial Advocacy. Law asst. Dist. Ct. Judge, Atlanta, 1970-72; ptnr. Blank and LaChance, 1972—. Contbr. articles to profl. jours. Mem. pub. adv. com. Atlanta Regional Commn., 1972-74. Recipient Merit award Ga. Bar Assn., 1981. Mem. Atlanta Bar Assn., Ga. Bar Assn., Ga. Trial Lawyers Assn. (officer), Lawyers Club Atlanta, ABA, Assn. Trial Lawyers Am., Fla. Bar Assn., Am. Bd. Trial Advocates (advocate, pres. Ga. chpt.). Office: 230 Peachtree St NW Suite 800 Atlanta GA 30303

BLANK, GEORGE WILLIAM, III, entrepreneur, consultant; b. Phila., June 1, 1945; s. George W. and Betty Marion (Drinnan) B.; m. Linda Kay Cotten, Aug. 19, 1967; children: George W. IV, Robert Alan. AB, Eastern Coll., St. Davids, Pa., 1971; MDiv, Princeton Theol. Sem., 1974. Ordained to ministry Presbyn. Ch., 1975. Pastor Calvary Presbyn. Ch., Leechburg, Pa., 1975-79; editor-in-chief Softside Pubs., Milford, N.H., 1979-81; editorial dir. Creative Computing, Morris Plains, N.J., 1981-82; pres. NuClas Corp., Denville, N.J., 1982—; cons. Office Tech. Assessment, U.S. Congress, Washington, 1981; founder, bd. dirs. Computer Action Learning, Summit, N.J., 1983—; speaker Nat. Computer Conf., Houston, 1981. Author: The Creative Atari, 1981, (computer program) Wordscope, 1985; editor: Pathways Through the ROM. Pres. Leechburg Ministerium, 1977-79; v.p. Meals on Wheels, Leechburg, 1976-79; asst. scoutmaster, Boy Scouts Am., Coatesville, Pa., 1969-71, Morris Plains, 1985-86, dist. commr. Morris County, 1986—. Served with U.S. Army, 1965-68. Office: NuClas Corp 239 Fox Hill Rd Denville NJ 07834

BLANK, LAWRENCE FRANCIS, computer consultant; b. Detroit, Oct. 4, 1932; s. Frank A. and Marcella A. (Pieper) B.; m. Carol Louise Mann, Oct. 12, 1963; children: Ann, Steven, Susan, Lori. BS, Xavier U., 1954. Asst. engr. Gen. Electric Co., Evendale, Ohio, 1956-60; research engr. Gen. Dynamics Corp., San Diego, 1960-62; mem. tech. staff Computer Scis. Corp., El Segundo, Calif., 1962-64; programming mgr. IBM, Los Angeles, 1964-69, Xerox Corp., El Segundo, 1969-74; ind. computer cons., Torrance, Calif., 1974—. Mem. Assn. Computing Machinery, Ind. Computer Cons. Assn. Home and Office: 212 Via Eboli Newport Beach CA 92663

BLANK, WALLACE JAMES, manufacturing executive; b. Neenah, Wis., Apr. 16, 1929; s. Julius August and Caroline Ann (Werner) B.; B.S. in Mech. Engring., U. Wis., 1952; m. Margaret Mary Schultz, June 7, 1958. Registered profl. engr., Wis. Staff engr. Fairbanks Morse & Co., Beloit, Wis., 1952-59; sr. engr. Thiokol Chem. Co., 1960, N. Am. Aviation Atomics, internat. div., 1961; dir. mil. engring. FWD Corp., Clintonville, Wis., 1962-68; tech. dir. Oshkosh Truck Corp. (Wis.), 1968-74, v.p. engring., 1974—. Patentee in field of truck suspensions and transmissions. Mem. Soc. Auto Engrs., Am. Def. Preparedness Assn., Assn. U.S. Army, Air Force Assn. Roman Catholic. Home: 5352 Iahmaytah Rd Oshkosh WI 54901 Office: 2300 Oregon St Oshkosh WI 54903

BLANKENBAKER, RONALD GAIL, physician; b. Rensselaer, Ind., Dec. 1, 1941; s. Lloyd L. and Lovina (Anderson) B. B.S. in Biology, Purdue U., 1963; M.D., Ind U., 1968, M.S. in Pharmacology, 1970. Diplomate: Am. Bd. Family Practice. Intern Meth. Hosp. Grad. Med. Center, Indpls., 1968-69; resident in family practice Meth. Hosp. Grad. Med. Center, 1969-71; med. dir. Indpls. Home for Aged, 1971-77, Am. Mid-Town Nursing Center, Indpls., 1974-77, Home Assn., Tampa, Fla., 1977-79; asst. prof. family practice Ind. U., Indpls., 1973-77, clin. prof., 1980—, clin. prof. sch. nursing, 1986—; asst. dean for St. Vincent Hosp., Ind. U., Indpls., 1985—; v.p. med. affairs St. Vincent Hosp. and Health Care Ctr., 1984—; prof. dept. family medicine U. South Fla., Tampa, 1977-79, chmn. dept., 1977-79; health commr. State of Ind.; sec. Ind. State Bd. Health, Indpls., 1979-84; dir. family practice edn. Meth. Hosp. Grad. Med. Center, 1971-77; family practice editor Reference and Index Services, Inc., Indpls., 1976-77, sr. editor, 1977-79; legis. lobbyist Ind. Acad. Family Physicians, 1973-77; med. advisor New Hope Found. Am., Inc., 1974-79. Bd. dirs. Meals on Wheels, Inc., Peoples Health Center Indpls., Marion County Cancer Soc., Indpls. Alliance Health Promotion, Marion County Med. Soc., Ind. Sports Corp., Life Leadership Devel. Inc., Sch. Sci. Alumni Assn. Purdue U.; mem. Ind. Gov.'s Council Phys. Fitness and Sports Medicine, Nat. Com. on Vital and Health Stats., 1984—, chmn., 1986—, Marion County Heart Assn.; mem. med. commn. Pan Am. Sports Orgn., 1985—; pres., bd. dirs. Hoosier Safety Council, 1985-87, Hoosiers for Safety Belts, 1986-88; med. coordinator Nat. Sports Festival IV, 1983; chief drug control team U.S. Olympic Com., 1986—; co-chmn. med. services Pan Am. Games X, 1987. Served to col. USAFR, 1971—. Recipient Disting. Service award, Commendation medal, award Ind. Pub. Health Assn., 1984; Decorated Meritorious Service medal; recipient Service to Mankind award Sertoma Club, 1975, Outstanding Alumnus award Mt. Ayr (Ind.) High Sch., 1976, Sen. Lugar's Health Enhancement award, 1983, Pub. Health excellence award Marion County Health Dept., 1984; named a Sagamore of the Wabash by Gov. of Ind., 1980, 84. Fellow Am. Acad. Family Physicians, Am. Coll. Preventive Medicine, Soc. Prospective Medicine (pres., dir.); mem. AMA, Ind. State Med. Assn., Marion County Med. Soc. (bd. dirs.), Ind. Acad. Family Physicians (v.p. 1977, bd. dirs., pres. 1987-88), Ind. Allied Health Assn. (pres. 1973-74), Ind. Acad. Sci., Ind. Pub. Health Assn., Soc. Tchrs. Family Medicine, Ind. Assn. Pub. Health Physicians, Ind. Arthritis Found. (bd. dirs.), Orgn. Am. States, World Med. Assn., Aerospace Med. Assn., Ptnrs. for the Ams., Ind. Lung Assn. (bd. dirs.), Assn. Am. Med. Colls., Assn. Depts. Family Medicine, Fla. Acad. Family Physicians (bd. dirs.). Republican. Office: St Vincent Hosp 2001 W 86th St PO Box 40970 Indianapolis IN 46240-0970

BLANKENSHIP, EDWARD G., architect; b. Martin, Tenn., June 22, 1943; s. Edward G. and Martha Lucille (Baldridge) B. B.Arch., Columbia U., 1966, M.Sc. in Architecture, 1967; M. Litt. Arch., Cambridge U., 1971. Registered architect, N.Y., Calif. Sr. v.p. Thompson Cons. Internat., Los

Angeles. Author: The Airport-Architecture, Urban Integration, Ecological Problems, 1974. William Kinne fellow, 1966; alt. Fulbright fellow to Eng., 1967. Mem. AIA. Episcopalian. Clubs: United Oxford and Cambridge U.; Meadow (Southhampton), Am. Friends of Cambridge U. (sec. Los Angeles chpt.). Lodge: Rotary Internat. Home: 4260 Via Arbolada #207 Monterey Hills CA 90042 Office: 8929 S Sepulveda Blvd Los Angeles CA 90045

BLANTON, HOOVER CLARENCE, lawyer; b. Green Sea, S.C., Oct. 13, 1925; s. Clarence Leo and Margaret (Hoover) B.; m. Cecilia Lopez, July 31, 1949; children: Lawson Hoover, Michael Lopez. J.D., U. S.C., 1953. Bar: S.C. 1953. Assoc. Whaley & McCutchen, Columbia, S.C., 1953-66; ptnr. Whaley & McCutchen Blanton & Rhodes, and precessors, Columbia, 1967—; dir. Legal Aid Service Agy., Columbia, chmn. bd., 1972-73. Gen. counsel S.C. Republican party, 1963-66; pres. Richland County Rep. Conv., 1962; del. Rep. State Conv., 1962, 64, 66, 68, 70, 74; bd. dirs. Midlands Community Action Agy., Columbia, vice chmn., 1972-73; bd. dirs. Wildewood Sch., 1976-78; mem. Gov.'s Legal Services Adv. Council, 1976-77, Commn. on Continuing Legal Edn. for Judiciary, 1977-84, Commn. on Continuing Lawyer Competence, 1988—; ordained deacon Baptist Ch. Served with USNR, 1942-46, 50-52. Mem. S.C. Bar (ho. of dels. 1975-76, chmn. fee disputes bd. 1977-81), ABA, Richland County Bar Assn. (pres. 1980), S.C. Def. Trial Attys. Assn., Def. Research Inst., Assn. Def. Trial Attys. (state chmn. 1971-77, 80—, exec. council 1977-80), Am. Bd. Trial Advs., Phi Delta Phi. Clubs: Toastmasters (pres. 1959), Palmetto. Home: 3655 Deerfield Dr Columbia SC 29204 Office: 1414 Lady St Columbia SC 29201

BLAQUIER, NELLY ARRIETA DE, association executive; b. Buenos Aires, Nov. 11, 1931; d. Herminio and Paulette (Wollmann) Arrieta; m. Carlos Pedro Blaquier, Sept. 12, 1951; children: Maria Elena, Carlos H., Alejandro, Santiago, Ignacio. Cert., Buenos Aires. V.p. Friends of Nat. Mus. Fine Arts, Buenos Aires, 1966-77, pres., 1977—. Mem. council Found. of Colon Theatre, Buenos Aires, 1978—, internat. council Mus. Modern Art, N.Y.C. Recipient Dama di Grazia Magistrale Sovereign Order of Malta, 1984, prize Order San Martin De Tours, 1986. Mem. Fedn. Friends of Mus. (v.p. 1983—). Roman Catholic. Office: Friends of Fine Arts Mus, Ave Figueroa Alcorta, 2280, Buenos Aires Argentina

BLASCO, ALFRED JOSEPH, business and financial consultant; b. Kansas City, Mo., Oct. 9, 1904; s. Joseph and Mary (Bevacqua) B.; m. Kathryn Oleno, June 28, 1926; children: Barbara Blasco Lowry, Phyllis Blasco O'Connor. Student, Kansas City Sch. Accountancy, 1921-25, Am. Inst. Banking, 1926-30; Ph.D. (hon.), Avila Coll., 1969. From office boy to asst. controller Commerce Trust Co., Kansas City, Mo., 1921-35; controller Interstate Securities Co., Kansas City, 1935-45; v.p. Interstate Securities Co., 1945-53, pres., 1953—, chmn. bd., 1961-68; sr. v.p. ISC Fin. Corp., 1968-69, hon. chmn. bd., 1970-77, pres., 1979-88; chmn. bd. Red Bridge Bank, 1966-72; Mark Plaza State Bank, Overland Park, Kans., 1973-77; spl. lectr. consumer credit Columbia U., N.Y.C., 1956, U. Kans., Lawrence, 1963-64. Contbr. articles to profl. jours. Pres. Cath. Community Library, 1955-56; Mem. Fair Public Accomodations Com., Kansas City, Mo., 1964-68; ward committeeman, 1972-76; pres., hon. bd. dirs. Baptist Med. Ctr., 1970-74; chmn. bd. dirs. St. Anthony's Home, 1965-69; chmn. bd. trustees Avila Coll., 1969—. Decorated papal knight Equestrian Order Holy Sepulchre of Jerusalem, 1957, knight comdr., 1964, knight grand cross, 1966, knight of collar, 1982, lt. No. Lieutenancy U.S., 1970-77, vice gov.-gen., 1977-82; named Bus. Man of Yr. State of Mo., 1957, Man of Yr. City of Hope, 1973; recipient Community Service award Rockne Club Notre Dame, 1959, wisdom award of honor, 1979; Brotherhood award NCCJ, 1979. Mem. Soc. St. Vincent de Paul (pres. 1959-67), Am. Instl. Bankers Assn. (pres. 1956-57), Am. Inst. Banking (chpt. pres. 1932-33), Bank Auditors and Controllers Assn. (chpt. pres. 1925-26), Fin. Execs. Inst. (chpt. pres. 1928-29), Nat. Assn. Accts. Clubs: Rotary, Kansas City, Hillcrest Country, Serra (pres. 1959-60). Office: 8080 Ward Pkwy Kansas City MO 64114

BLASKE, E. ROBERT, lawyer; b. Battle Creek, Mich., June 4, 1945; s. Edmund Robert and Wilma Jayne (Hill) B.; m. Vicki Lyn Rayner, Aug. 11, 1968. BA with distinction, U. Mich., 1966, JD cum laude, 1969. Bar: Mich. 1969, U.S. Dist. Ct. (we. dist.) Mich. 1970, U.S. Ct. Appeals (6th cir.) 1983. Ptnr. Blaske & Blaske, Battle Creek, 1969—; mem. Mich. Bd. Law Examiners, 1976—, drafting com. for rules to implement Mich. mental health code, 1978-79, multi-state bar exam. com. Nat. Conf. Bar Examiners, 1983-85, multi-state profl. responsibility exam. com., 1985—; instr. trial advocacy program steering com. U.S. Dist. Ct. (we. dist.) Mich., 1982—; lectr. Inst. Continuing Legal Edn., 1983—; mediator U.S. Dist. Ct. (we. dist.) Mich., 1985—, Calhoun County Cir. Ct. Mich., 1984—; arbitrator U.S. Dist. Ct. (we. dist.) Mich., 1987—. Mem. U. Mich. Law Rev., 1968-69. Bd. dirs. Calhoun County Legal Aid Soc., Battle Creek, 1976, Mich. Audubon Soc., Kalamazoo, 1981, Blaske-Hill Found., Battle Creek, 1983—; bd. govs. Lawyers Club U. Mich. Law Sch., 1985—. Mem. ABA, State Bar Mich., Calhoun County Bar Assn. (pres. 1977-78), Assn. Trial Lawyers Am., Mich. Trial Lawyers Assn., Order of Coif. Roman Catholic. Home: 25001 Battle Creek Hwy Bellevue MI 49021 Office: Blaske & Blaske 1509 Comerica Bldg Battle Creek MI 49017

BLASS, GERHARD ALOIS, educator; b. Chemnitz, Germany, Mar. 12, 1916; came to U.S., 1949, naturalized, 1955; s. Gustav Alois and Anna (Mehnert) B.; m. Barbara Siegert, July 16, 1945; children—Andrew, Marcus, Evamaria, Annamaria, Peter. Abitur, Oberrealschule Chemnitz, 1935; Dr. rer. nat., Universität Leipzig, 1943. Asst. Institut für Theoretische Physik, Leipzig, 1939-43; research cons. Siemens & Halske, Berlin, 1943-46; dozent math. and physics Oberrealschule, Nuremberg, 1946-47, Ohm Polytechnikum, Nuremberg, 1947-49; prof. physics Coll. St. Thomas, St. Paul, 1949-51; prof. physics U. Detroit, 1951-81, chmn. dept., 1962-71. Author: Theoretical Physics, 1962, Weil Hiersein viel ist Poems in German, 1987. Fellow AAAS; mem. Soc. Asian and Comparative Philosophy, Esperanto League N.Am., Sigma Pi Sigma. Roman Catholic. Home: 4441 Stewart Rd Metamora MI 48455

BLASS, NOLAND, JR., architect; b. Little Rock, May 28, 1920; s. Noland and Isabel (Ringelhaupt) B.; m. Elizabeth Weitzenhoffer, Oct. 21, 1947; children: Elizabeth Victoria, Wendy Blass Dilivio. BArch., Cornell U., 1941. Registered architect, Ark. Designer-prin. Blass Chilcote Carter & Wilcox, Little Rock, 1940-71, pres.-prin., 1971—; pres. Blass Chilcote and partners (and predecessor firms), 1980—; bd. dirs. Ottenheimer Found., Little Rock, 1985—; mem. Fifty for the Future, Little Rock, 1965— (pres. 1985-87). Prin. works include Worthen Bank bldg., 1969, Supreme Ct. bldg., State of Ark., 1972, Edn. Lab. for Med. Scis., U. Ark., 1974. Pres. Ark. Arts Center, 1972; mem. Little Rock Planning Commn., 1960-69; pres. Pulaski Met. YMCA, 1967-68; mem. Gov.'s Inauguration Com., 1971; pres. Ark. Orch. Soc., 1976; trustee A.I.A. Ednl. Endowment Fund; bd. dirs. Leo N. Levi Hosp., Mid-Am. Arts Alliance, 1980—; pres. Levi Found., 1983. Served with AUS, 1941-45. Fellow AIA (pres. Ark. 1958-59); mem. Tau Beta Pi, Zeta Beta Tau. Democrat. Jewish. Lodge: Masons (33 deg.). Home: 217 Normandy Little Rock AR 72207 Office: Blass Chilcote Carter & Wilcox 303 W Capitol Little Rock AR 72201

BLATT, MORTON BERNARD, medical illustrator; b. Chgo., Jan. 9, 1923; s. Arthur E. and Hazel B. Student Central YMCA Coll., 1940-42, U. Ill., 1943-46. Tchr., Ray-Vogue Art Schs., Chgo., 1946-51; med. illustrator VA Center, Wood, Wis., 1951-57, Swedish Covenant Hosp., Chgo., 1957-76; med. illustrator Laidlaw Bros., River Forest, Ill., 1956-59; cons., artist health textbooks, 1956-59; illustrator Standard Edn. Soc., Chgo., 1960; art editor Covenant Home Altar, 1972-83, Covenant Companion, 1958-82. Served with USAAF, 1943-44. Mem. Art Inst. Chgo. Club: Chgo. Press. Illustrator: Atlas and Demonstration Technique of the Central Nervous System, also numerous med. jours.; illustrator, designer Covenant Hymnal, books, record jackets. Address: PO Box 489 Mill Valley CA 94942

BLATTNER, MEERA MCCUAIG, educator; b. Chgo., Aug. 14, 1930; d. William D. McCuaig and Nina (Spertus) Klevs; m. Minao Kamegai, June 22 1985; children: Douglas, Robert, William. B.A., U. Chgo., 1952; M.S., U. So. Calif., 1966; Ph.D., UCLA, 1973 . Research fellow in computer sci. Harvard U., 1973-74; asst. prof. Rice U., 1974-80; asso. prof. applied sci. U. Calif. at Davis, Livermore, 1980—; adj. prof. U. Tex., Houston, 1977—; vis. prof. U. Paris, 1980; program dir. theoretical computer sci. NSF, Washington, 1979-80. NSF grantee, 1977-81. Mem. Soc. Women Engrs., Assn. Computing Machinery, IEEE Computer Soc. Contbr. articles to profl. jours. Office: U Calif Davis/Livermore Dept Applied Sci Livermore CA 94550

BLATTY, WILLIAM PETER, writer; b. N.Y.C., Jan. 7, 1928; s. Peter and Mary (Mouakad) B.; children: Christine Ann, Michael Peter, Mary Joanne, Billy, Jennifer, Peter Vincent. A.B., Georgetown U., 1950; M.A., George Washington U., 1954; L.H.D., Seattle U., 1974. Publicity dir. U. So. Calif., 1957-58; public relations dir. Loyola U., Los Angeles, 1959-60. Editor: USIA, 1955-57; author: Which Way To Mecca, Jack?, 1959, John Goldfarb, Please Come Home, 1962, I, Billy Shakespeare, 1965, Twinkle, Twinkle "Killer" Kane, 1966 (Golden Globe award as best movie screen play 1981), The Exorcist, 1970, I'll Tell Them I Remember You, 1973, The Exorcist: From Novel to Film, 1974, The Ninth Configuration, 1978, Legion, 1983; writer screenplays: The Man From the Diner's Club, 1961, John Goldfarb, Please Come Home, 1963, Promise Her Anything, 1962, The Great Bank Robbery, 1967, Gunn, 1967, What Did You Do In The War, Daddy?, 1965, A Shot In The Dark, 1964, Darling Lili, 1968, The Exorcist, 1973, Twinkle, Twinkle, Killer Kane, (The Ninth Configuration), 1981. Served to 1st lt. USAF, 1951-54. Recipient Academy award Acad. Motion Picture Arts and Scis., 1973, Gabriel award and blue ribbon for Insight TV series script Am. Film Festival, 1969, Golden Globe award, 1980. Roman Catholic. Office: care William Morris Agy 151 El Camino Blvd Beverly Hills CA 90212

BLAUSTEIN, ALBERT PAUL, law educator, author; b. N.Y.C., Oct. 12, 1921; s. Karl Allen and Rose (Brickman) B.; m. Phyllis Migden, Dec. 21, 1948; children—Mark Allen, Eric Barry, Dana Blaustein Epstein. A.B., U. Mich., 1941; J.D., Columbia U., 1948. Bar: N.Y. 1948, N.J. 1962. Reporter, rewriteman Chgo. Tribune and City News Bur., Chgo., 1941-42; ptnr. Blaustein and Blaustein, N.Y.C., 1948-50, 52-55; asst. prof. law N.Y. Law Sch., N.Y.C., 1953-55; assoc. prof. law Rutgers U., Camden, N.J., 1955-59; prof. law Rutgers U., 1959—; mem. Civil Rights Reviewing Authority, U.S. Dept. Edn., 1984—; chief exec. officer sec. gen., Phila. Found., pres. Constns. Research Ctr., Fribourg, Switzerland; v.p., chmn. adv. bd. Internat. Ctr. Constitutions Studies, Athens, Greece, 1984—; pres., chmn. Constns., Assocs., N.Y.C., 1979—; pres., Blaustein Assocs. Ltd.; counsel/ advisor, draftsman Constns. of Bangladesh, Brazil, Mozambique, Cambodia, Liberia, Niger, Peru, Uganda, Zimbabwe, 1966—; cons. law sch. devel. Internat. Legal Ctr. and Asia Found., Nigeria, Liberia, Ethiopia, Kenya, Vietnam, Taiwan, Tanzania, Uganda, Zaire, 1963-73; cons. U.S. CRC, Washington, 1962-63, N.J. Div. Civil Rights, Trenton, 1971-72; pres., chmn. Human Rights Advocates Internat., N.Y.C., 1979—; academico honoris causa La Academia Mexicana de Derecho Internacional; Miembro correspondiente (hon.), Revista Uruguaya de Derecho Constitucional; sr. assoc. Jerusalem Ctr. for Pub. Affairs; prof. Miembro (hon.) Inst. Derecho Politico y Constn., Argentina; founder Law Day. Author or co-author: Public Relations for Bar Associations, 1953; The American Lawyer, 1972, Fiction Goes to Court, 1954, 1977; Desegregation and the Law, 1957, 2d edit., 1962, 85; Doctors' Choice, 1957; Deals with the Devil, 1958; Invisible Men, 1960; Civil Affairs Legislation, Selected Cases and Materials, 1960, Fundamental legal Documents of Communist China, 1962; Manual on Foreign Legal Periodicals and their Index, 1962; Civil Rights U.S.A.: Public Schools in Cities in the North and West, Philadelphia, 1962; Human and Other Beings, 1963; Civil Rights U.S.A., 1963; Public Schools in Camden and Environs, 1964; Civil Rights and the American Negro, 1968; Civil Rights and the Black American, 1970; Law and the Military Establishment, 1970; Cataloging Manual for Use in Vietnamese Law Libraries, 1971; Constitutions of the Countries of the World, 18 vols., 1971—; Housing Discrimination in New Jersey, 1972; Human Rights and the Bangladesh Trials, 1973; A Bibliography on The Common Law in French, 1973; Intellectual Property: Cases and Materials (1960-70), 1973; Constitutions of Dependencies and Special Sovereignties, 7 vols., 1975—; Independence Documents of the World, 2 vols., 1977; The Arab Oil Weapon, 1977; The First 100 Justices: Statistical Studies on the Supreme Court of the U.S., 1978; The Military and American Society, 1978, 2d edit., 1984; Disinvestment, 1985; Influence of the U.S. Constitution Abroad, 1986; Resolving Language Conflicts: A Story of the World's Constitutions, 1986; Human Rights Sourcebook, 1987; Constitutions That Made History, 1988, The Role of the Military in Modern Government: A Constitutional Analysis, 1988. Editor-in-chief Influence of the U.S. Constitution Abroad. Served to maj. U.S. Army, 1942-46, 1950-52. Fellow Ford Found., 1962, Centre Internat. Studies, London Sch. Econs., 1984-85. Mem. World Bar Assn. for Peace Through Law (chmn. com. constns. 1982—), Nat. Ctr. Constl. Studies (adv. bd.), Scribes (co-founder), Internat. Bar Assn., Internat. Law Assn., ABA, Assn. Bar City N.Y., Soc. Mil. Law and Law of War, Internat. Assn. Jewish Lawyers and Jurists (UN rep. 1975—). Republican. Jewish. Clubs: Chemists (N.Y.C.); Woodcrest Country (Cherry Hill, N.J.). Home: 415 Barby Ln Cherry Hill NJ 08003 Office: Sch of Law Rutgers U Camden NJ 08102

BLAXTER, KENNETH LYON, agriculturist; b. June 19, 1919; s. Gaspard Culling and Charlotte Ellen B.; attended U. Reading (Eng.), U. Ill.; B.Sc. in Agr.; Ph.D.; D.Sc.; NDA (hons.); D.Sc. (hon.), QUB, 1974, Leeds, 1977; D.Agr. (hon.), Agrl. U. Norway; LL.D. (hon.), U. Aberdeen, 1981; D.Sc. (hon.), U. Newcastle, 1984; m. Mildred Lillington Hall, 1957; 3 children. Sci. officer Nat. Inst. for Research in Dairying, 1939-40, 41-44; research officer Ministry Agr. Vet. Lab., 1944-46; Commonwealth fellow U. Ill., 1946-47; head dept. nutrition Hannah Inst., Ayr, Scotland, 1948-65; chmn. Individual Merit Promotion Panel, Cabinet Office, 1965—; dir. Rowett Research Inst., Bucksburn, Aberdeen, Scotland and cons. dir. Commonwealth Bur. Nutrition (formerly Animal Nutrition), 1965-82; vis. prof. dept. agrl. biochemistry U. Newcastle-upon-Tyne, 1982—; pres. Inst. Biology, 1986—. Served with RA, 1940-41. Created knight; recipient Thomas Baxter prize and Gold medal, 1960; Gold medal RASE, 1964, Wooldridge Gold medal Brit. Vet. Assn., 1973, De Laval medal Royal Swedish Acad. Engring. Scis., 1976, Messel medal Soc. Chem. Industry, 1976; Massey Ferguson award, 1977; Wolf Found. Internat. prize, 1979. Fellow Royal Soc., RSE (Keith medal and prize 1977, pres. 1979—); mem. Brit. Soc. Animal Prodn. (pres. 1970-71), Nutrition Soc. (pres. 1974), Lenin Acad. Agrl. Scis. (fgn.), French Acad. Agrl. Sci. (fgn.), Am. Inst. Nutrition (hon.), Dutch Soc. Scis. (fgn.), Royal Coll. Vet. Sci. (hon.). Author: Energy Metabolism of Ruminants, 1962; Energy Metabolism, 1965; People, Food and Resources, 1986; contbr. articles to profl. jours.; research in vet. sci. and other profl. fields. Home: Stradbroke Hall, Stradbroke, Suffolk 1P21 5HH, England Office: care Royal Society, 6 Carlton House Terrace, London SW1Y 5AG, England

BLAŽEKOVIC, ZDRAVKO, musicologist, librarian; b. Zagreb, Yugoslavia, May 13, 1956; parents: Zvonimir and Marija (Sumelic) B. BA in Musicology, U. Zagreb, 1980, MA in Musicology, 1983. Editor Music Info. Ctr., Zagreb, 1983; asst. Musicological Inst. Acad. Music, Zagreb, 1980; asst. Inst. Musicological Research Yugoslav Acad. Scis. Arts, Zagreb, 1980-81, researcher, 1984—; librarian in chief Croatian Music Inst., Zagreb, 1985—; mem. nat. com. Répertoire Internat. de Lit. Musicale, N.Y., U.S.A., Répertoire Internat. des Sources Musicales, Frankfurt, Fed. Republic Germany. Editor, contbr. articles profl. jours. Served with Yugoslav mil. 1983-84. Mem. Internat. Musicological Soc., Croatian Composers' Soc., Am. Musicological Soc. Home: Zigroviceva 1, 41000 Zagreb Yugoslavia Office: Inst Musicological Research, Maticina 2, 41000 Zagreb Yugoslavia

BLECHA, KARL, minister of interior Austria; b. Vienna, Austria, Apr. 16, 1933; s. Karl-Matthias and Rosa Blecha; m. Rosa Nimmerrichter. Ed. U. Vienna. Mng. dir. Inst. Empirical Social Sci. Research, Vienna, 1963-75; M.P. Austrian Socialist Party for Lower Austrian constituency, 1970-83; chmn. drafting com. Austrian Socialist Party program, 1978, gen. sec. hdqrs., 1976-81, chmn. exec. com., from 1977, dep. chmn. parliamentary group, 1979-83, dep. chmn. of party, 1981—; minister of interior Austria, 1983—. Author: Der durchleuchtete Wahler; Opinion Leaders in Austria; Recht und Menschlichkeit; Die Nationalratswahl. Office: Ministry of Interior, Vienna Austria *

BLECK, MICHAEL JOHN, lawyer; b. Michigan City, Ind., Apr. 8, 1950; s. Eugene and Joan (Mathias) B.; m. Sally Bulleit, Aug. 19, 1972; children—Andrew, Erica. A.B. with distinction, DePauw U., 1972; J.D. cum laude, Ind. U., 1975. Bar: Ind. 1975, Minn. 1977, U.S. Dist. Ct. Ind. 1975, U.S. Dist. Ct. Minn. 1977, U.S. Ct. Appeals (8th cir.) 1978. Law clk. to judge U.S. Ct. Appeals (8th cir.), Des Moines, 1975-76; assoc. Oppenheimer, Wolff & Donnelly, Mpls., 1977-82, ptnr. 1983—. Articles editor Ind. Law Rev., 1974-75. Trustee Mayflower Community Congregational Ch. Mem. Minn. State Bar Assn. (ct. rules com. 1981—), Hennepin County Bar Assn. (ct. rules com. 1981—), Ind. State Bar Assn., Ramsey County Bar Assn., ABA (civil litigation sect.). Democrat. Home: 4650 W 44th St Edina MN 55424 Office: Oppenheimer Wolff & Donnelly 4800 IDS Ctr Minneapolis MN 55402

BLECKMANN, PAUL WILHELM, chemistry educator; b. Muenster, W.Ger., Jan. 16, 1937; s. Paul Theodor and Elisabeth (Kaussen) B.; m. Ingrid Karla Kreutz, Nov. 19, 1965; children—Ulrike, Gregor, Gernot, Elke. B.S., Westfaelische Wilhelms U., 1965, Dr. rer. nat., 1969. Dep. head dept. molecular spectroscopy Inst. fur Spektrochemie, Dortmund, W.Ger., 1969-72; lectr. spectroscopy U. Dortmund 1972-75, univ. lectr., 1975-79, assoc. prof., 1979-83, prof., 1983—. Contbr. articles to sci. jours. Mem. Gesellschaft Deutscher Chemiker, Hochschullererverband. Roman Catholic. Club: Gesellschaft der Freunde der Universitat Dortmund. Home: Von Corfey Str 36, 4400 Muenster Nordrhein-Westfalen, Federal Republic of Germany Office: Universitat Dortmund Abteilung, Chemie, 50 Postfach, 46 Dortmund 50 05 00, Federal Republic of Germany

BLEDSOE, (ELLEN) ALENE, retired physician; b. Linden, Tex., May 5, 1914; d. Joseph Sidney and Clyde (Harkey) Bledsoe; B.A., Columbia Union Coll., 1941, postgrad; M.D., Loma Linda U., 1950. Intern, Bridgeport (Conn.) Hosp., 1949-50; resident home obstetrics Chgo. Maternity Center, 1950, Jacksonville (Ill.) State Psychiatry Hosp., 1951-52; resident in pathology St. Joseph's Hosp., Marshfield, Wis., 1952-53, City of Hope Med. Ctr., Duarte, Calif., 1953-54, Ill. Masonic Hosp., Chgo., 1954, Jewish Hosp., Cin., 1955, Kern County Hosp., Bakersfield, Calif., 1956, Gorgas Hosp., C.Z., 1957, Sacramento County Hosp., 1960; gen. practice medicine Skagway, Alaska, 1951; pathologist Ft. Bragg and Mendicino, Calif., 1961-69; regional Cumberland, N.S., Can., 1970-72; quality control physician Cutter's Intake Labs., Stockton and Oakland, Calif., 1974-75; med. dir. Clinica de Salud para Familias, Hollister, Calif., 1975-76; practice medicine specializing in family medicine, Ft. Bragg, Calif., 1978-84, ret., 1984. Diplomate Am. Bd. Anat. and Clin. Pathology. Fellow Coll. Am. Pathologists (emeritus), Am. Soc. Clin. Pathologists (emeritus fellow); mem. N.Y. Acad. Scis. (life mem.), Pan-Am. Med. Assn. (diplomate), World Med. Assn. (asso. mem.), Am. Cancer Soc., Am. Heart Assn., Am. Lung Assn., Calif. Acad. Scis. (sr. mem.). Republican. Adventist. Author: Resident's Manual of Clinical Pathology, 1955; contbr. articles on pathology to profl. jours. Home: 33201 Jefferson Way Fort Bragg CA 95437

BLEICHER, SHELDON JOSEPH, endocrinologist, medical educator; b. N.Y.C., Apr. 9, 1931; s. Max and Fannie (Klieger) B.; m. Anne C. M. Ames, July 28, 1967; children: Erick Max, Phillip Thaddeus Samuel. A.B., NYU, 1951; M.S., Western Ill. U., 1952; M.D., SUNY Downstate Med. Center, Bklyn., 1956. Intern L.I. Jewish Hosp. Ctr., New Hyde Park, N.Y., 1956-57; resident Boston City Hosp., 1959-60; research fellow in medicine Harvard-Thorndike Meml. Lab., Boston, 1960-63; chief metabolic research unit Jewish Hosp. Med. Center, Bklyn., 1963-67; chief div. endocrinology and metabolism Jewish Hosp. Med. Center, 1967-77; practice medicine specializing in endocrinology and diabetes Bklyn. and Upper Brookville, N.Y., 1963—; prof. medicine SUNY Downstate Med. Center, 1975—; chmn. dept. internal medicine Bklyn.-Cumberland Med. Center, 1978-83, Bklyn.-Caledonian Med. Ctr., 1983—; cons. IAEA, Vienna, 1966—. Contbr. articles to profl. jours. Vice pres. Locust Valley Central Sch. Bd., 1981-82, pres., 1982-85. Served to capt. M.C. USNR, 1957—. NIH fellow, 1960-63; NIH research career devel. award, 1970-75; recipient Torch of Liberty award Anti-Defamation League of B'nai Brith, 1982, Diabetes Achievement award Am. Diabetes Assn., 1986. Fellow ACP; mem. Am. Diabetes Assn. (dir. 1979-85), N.Y. Diabetes Assn. (bd. dirs. 1965—, pres. 1976-78), L.I. Diabetes Assn. (pres. 1978-81), N.Y. State Soc. Internal Medicine (state bd. dirs., treas. Bklyn. chpt., chmn. continuing edn. com.), Bklyn. Soc. Internal Medicine (treas. 1983-85, sec. 1985-87, pres. 1987—), Am. Fedn. Clin. Research, Endocrine Soc., AAAS, Harvey Soc. Jewish. Club: Sagamore Yacht (L.I.) (fleet surgeon 1983-86). Office: 121 DeKalb Ave Brooklyn NY 11201

BLEICHNER, WILLIAM RICHARD, advertising agency executive; b. Pitts., Sept. 16, 1927; s. William Joseph and Agatha Elizabeth (Davidson) B. B.A. in Journalism, Duquesne U., 1949; postgrad. U. Pitts., 1955-57. Cert. bus. communicator. Asst. account exec. Ketchum, MacLeod & Grove, Pitts., 1945-50; coordinating foreman Bleichner Sign & Display, Pitts., 1950-51; asst. account exec. Pub. Relations Research, Pitts., 1951-52; advt. mgmt. positions Rockwell Mfg. Co., Pitts., 1952-68, advt. prodn. mgr., 1959-68; 1st v.p. W.S. Hill Co., Pitts., 1968-85; pres., owner Bleichner Advt. and Cons., Pitts., 1986—. Served with U.S. Army, 1952-55, Europe. Mem. Bus. Press Advt. Assn., Pitts. Advt. Prodn. Assn. (past pres.), Pitts. Club Printing House Craftsmen, Duquesne U. Alumni Assn. (founding pres. Penn Hills Duchy, Pitts.), Cath. Alumni Club (pres. Pitts. 1968—), Am. Legion. Roman Catholic. Clubs: Pitts. Press, Pitts. Advt., University (Pitts.).

BLENKO, WALTER JOHN, JR., lawyer; b. Pitts., June 15, 1926; s. Walter J. and Ardis Leah (Jones) B.; m. Joy Kinneman, Apr. 9, 1949; children—John W., Andrew W. BS, Carnegie-Mellon U., 1950; JD, U. Pitts., 1953. Bar: Pa. 1954. Practice law, Pitts., 1954—; ptnr. Eckert, Seamans, Cherin & Mellott. Active Churchill Vol. Fire Co., 1970-82; charter and hon. mem. Wilkinsburg Emergency Med. Service. Served with U.S. Army, 1944-46, ETO. Decorated Bronze Star. Fellow Am. Coll. Trial Lawyers; mem. ABA, ASME, Pa. Bar Assn., Allegheny County Bar Assn., Am. Patent Law Assn., Patent Law Assn. Pitts. (pres. 1977-78), Assn. Bar City of N.Y., Engrs. Soc. Western Pa., Internat. Patent and Trademark Assn. Clubs: Duquesne, Univ., Rolls-Royce Owners (bd. dirs. 1982-84, v.p. publs. 1984-87, treas. 1987—). Avocation: old cars. Home: 4073 Middle Rd Allison Park PA 15101 Office: Eckert Seamans Cherin & Mellott 600 Grant St Pittsburgh PA 15219

BLESCH, CHRISTOPHER JOHN, systems engineer; b. Whittier, Calif., Jan. 9, 1958; s. William Robert and Beverly Jean (Schurman) B.; m. Melinda Catherine Lewis, Aug. 25, 1979. B.S. in Mech. Engring., Ohio State U., 1979, M.S. in Mech. Engring., 1981, M.B.A., 1985. Registered profl. engr., Mich. Engr. Owens-Corning Fiberglas, Granville, Ohio, 1980-85; systems engr. Electronic Data Systems, Dallas, 1985—. Mem. ASME. Republican. Methodist. Avocations: reading; photography; bicycling. Home: 3353 Millcrest Dr Lake Orion MI 48035 Office: Electronic Data Systems 750 Tower Dr Troy MI 48007-7019

BLEWETT, ROBERT NOALL, lawyer; b. Stockton, Calif., July 12, 1915; s. Stephen Noall and Bess Errol (Simard) B.; m. Virginia Weston, Mar. 30, 1940; children—Richard Weston, Carolyn Blewett Lawrence. LL.B., Stanford U., 1936, J.D., 1939. Bar: Calif. bar 1939. Dep. dist. atty. San Joaquin County, 1942-46; practice law Stockton, 1946—; mem. firm, pres. Blewett, Garretson & Hachman, Stockton, 1971—. Chmn. San Joaquin County chpt. ARC, 1947-49; v.p. Goodwill Industries, 1967-68; vice chmn. Stockton Sister City Commn., 1969-70; adv. bd. bus. adminstrn. dept. U. Pacific; trustee San Joaquin Pioneer and Haggin Galleries. Fellow Am. Coll. Probate Counsel, Am. Bar Found.; mem. State Bar Calif. (mem. exec. com. of conf. of dels. 1969-72, vice chmn. 1971-72), Am. Bar Assn., Am. Judicature Soc., Am. Law Inst., Stockton C. of C., Delta Theta Phi, Theta Xi. Republican. Clubs: Rotary, Yosemite, San Francisco Comml, Masons, Shriners. Home: 3016 Dwight Way Stockton CA 95203 Office: 141 E Acacia St Stockton CA 95202

BLINDER, CAIO KRAISER, journalist; b. São Paulo, Brazil, Aug. 14, 1957; s. David and Flora (Kraiser) B.; m. Alma Carina Abaya-Pajar, Oct. 20, 1984. BA in Journalism, Faculdade de Comunicação Cásper Libero, São Paulo, Brazil, 1977; MA in Internat. Affairs, Ohio U., 1984. Reporter Shalom Mag., São Paulo, Brazil, 1977-78; editor TV Bandeirantes, São Paulo, 1978-79, Journal de Hoje, Campinas, Brazil, 1980; with Folha de São Paulo, 1980—, roving correspondent, 1986-87, editor, 1987—; prof. U. São Paulo, 1985-87. Speaker Rotary, Ohio, W.Va., 1982-86, Congregação Israelita Paulista, São Paulo, 1985—. World Press Inst. fellow, 1986; scholarships Ohio U., 1982, Orgn. Am. States, 1983-84, Rotary, 1963. Mem. Phi Kappa Phi Soc. (outstanding student 1984). Jewish. Club: São Paulo Athletic. Home: Rua Brasilio Machado 380/400, Sao Paulo SP Brazil 01230 Office: Folha de S Paulo, Al Barao de Limeira 425, Sao Paulo SP Brazil 01202

BLINDER, MARTIN S., publishing company executive; b. Bklyn., Nov. 18, 1946; s. Meyer and Lillian (Stein) B.; m. Janet Weiss, Dec. 10, 1983. BBA, Adelphi U., 1968. Account exec. Bruns, Nordeman & Co., N.Y.C., 1968-69; v.p. Blinder, Robinson & Co., Westbury, N.Y., 1969-73; treas. BHB Prodns., Los Angeles, 1973-76; pres. Martin Lawrence Ltd. Edits., Van Nuys, Calif., 1976—, also chmn. bd. dirs.; pres., dir. Corp. Art Inc., Visual Artists Mgmt. Corp., Art Consultants Inc.; lectr. bus. symposia. Contbr. articles to mags. and newspapers; appeared on TV and radio. Mem. Dem. Nat. Com.; patron Guggenheim Mus., N.Y.C., Mus. Modern Art, N.Y.C., Los Angeles County Mus. Art, Los Angeles Mus. Contemporary Art (hon. founder), Whitney Mus. Am. Art, Palm Springs Mus. Art, Hirschhorn Mus., Washington, Skirball Mus., Los Angeles, Diabetes Found. of City of Hope, B'nai B'rith Anti-Defamation League, Very Spl. Arts, read into Congressional Record, 1988 ; mem. Citizens for Common Sense; bd. dirs., pres. Research Found. for Crohns Disease. Read into Congl. Record, 1981, 83, 86, 88; recipient resolution of commendation Los Angeles City Council, 1983; State of Calif. resolution for contbn. to arts in Calif., 1983; County of Los Angeles Bd. Suprs. resolution for Contbn. to arts in So. Calif., 1983, Gov. of R.I. resolution for contbns. to arts, 1985. Nov. 18, 1985 declared Martin S. Blinder Day in Los Angeles in his honor by Mayor Tom Bradley. Office: Martin Lawrence Ltd Edits 16250 Stagg St Van Nuys CA 91406

BLISH, JOHN HARWOOD, lawyer; b. Racine, Wis., May 9, 1937; s. Wesley Wainwright and Lois Margaret (Jensen) B.; m. Edith Josephine Smith, Aug. 5, 1961; children—Geoffrey Harwood, Catherine Elizabeth. A.B., Brown U., 1959; J.D., U. Mich., 1965. Bar: R.I. 1965, U.S. Dist. Ct. R.I. 1967, U.S. Ct. Appeals (1st cir.) 1973, U.S. Ct. Appeals (Fed. cir.) 1985. Assoc. Edwards & Angell, Providence, 1965-73, ptnr., 1973-86, Blish & Cavanagh, Providence, 1986—. Bd. overseers Moses Brown Sch., Providence, 1978-81; bd. dirs., past pres. Sophia Little Home, Cranston, R.I.; trustee Providence Country Day Sch., East Providence, R.I. Served to lt. j.g. USN, 1959-62. Fellow Am. Coll. Trial Lawyers; mem. R.I. Bar Assn., ABA, Am. Judicature Soc., Assoc. Alumni Brown U. (past bd. dirs., sec.), Order of Coif, Phi Delta Phi. Clubs: Univ., Brown of R.I. (trustee, past pres.) (Providence); Agawam Hunt (East Providence); Acoaxet (Westport, Mass.). Home: 66 Catlin Ave Rumford RI 02916 Office: Blish & Cavanagh 30 Exchange Terr Providence RI 02903

BLITZER, ANDREW, otolaryngologist, educator; b. Pitts., Apr. 25, 1946; s. Martin Hollander and Lyrene Iris (Lave) B.; m. Patricia Volk, Dec. 21, 1969; children: Peter Morgen, Polly Volk. BA, Adelphi U., 1967; DDS, Columbia U., 1970; MD, Mt. Sinai Sch. Medicine, 1973. Diplomate Am. Bd. Otolaryngology. Resident in gen. surgery Beth Israel Hosp., N.Y.C., 1973-74; resident in otolaryngology Mt. Sinai Hosp., N.Y.C., 1974-77; asst. prof. otolaryngology Coll. Phys. & Surg., Columbia U., N.Y.C., 1977-82, assoc. prof. otolaryngology and oral surgery, 1982-84, prof. clin. otolaryngology and oral surgery, 1984—; dir. div. head and neck surgery Columbia-Presbyn. Med. Ctr., N.Y.C., 1980—, dir. residency edn., 1978—; lectr. dept. otolaryngology Mt. Sinai Sch. Medicine, N.Y.C., 1977—. Co-Author several books; assoc. editor: Oncology Times; contbr. chpts. to books, articles to profl. jours. Recipient award for excellence Am. Assn. Orthodontists, 1970, Tchr.-Investigator award Nat. Inst. Neurol. Communicative Disorders and Strokes, 1978-83. Fellow ACS, N.Y. Acad. Medicine, Am. Soc. Head and Neck Surgery, Am. Acad. Facial Plastic and Reconstructive Surgery, Am. Laryngol. Assn., Am. Larynol., Rhinol. and Otol. Soc., Am. Acad. Otolaryngology-Head and Neck Surgery, Am. Broncho-esophagological Assn. Home: 1136 Fifth Ave New York NY 10028 Office: Columbia U Coll Physicians and Surgeons Dept Otolaryngology 630 W 168th St New York NY 10032

BLIVEN, BRUCE, JR., writer; b. Los Angeles, Jan. 31, 1916; s. Bruce and Rose (Emery) B.; m. Naomi Horowitz, May 26, 1950; 1 son, Frederic Bruce. A.B., Harvard U., 1937. Reporter Manchester (Eng.) Guardian, 1936; editorial asst. New Republic mag., 1937-38; editorial writer N.Y. Post, 1939-42; contbr. to New Yorker (other nat. mags.), 1946—; Tchr. Ind. U. Writers Conf., 1955, 66. Author: The Wonderful Writing Machine, 1954, Battle for Manhattan, 1956, Under the Guns, 1972, Book Traveller, 1975, Volunteers, One and All, 1976, The Finishing Touch, 1978, New York: A Bicentennial History, 1981; juveniles The Story of D-Day, 1956, The American Revolution, 1958, From Pearl Harbor to Okinawa, 1960, From Casablanca To Berlin, 1965, (with Naomi Bliven) New York: The Story of the World's Most Exciting City, 1969. Served from pvt. to capt. F.A. AUS, 1942-45. Decorated Bronze Star with oak leaf cluster. Mem. Am. Soc. Journalists and Authors, Authors Guild (council 1970—), P.E.N., Soc. Am. Historians (exec. bd. 1975—). Office: care The New Yorker 25 W 43d St New York NY 10036

BLIX, HANS MARTIN, intergovernmental organization executive; b. Uppsala, Sweden, June 28, 1928; s. Gunnar and Hertha (Wiberg) B.; m. Eva Kettis, Mar. 17, 1962; children—Marten, Goran. LL.B., U. Uppsala, 1951; Ph.D., Cambridge U., 1959; LL.D., Stockholm U., 1960. Assoc. prof. U. Stockholm, 1960; legal adviser Ministry Fgn. Affairs, Stockholm, 1963-76, under sec. of state in charge of internat. devel. corp., 1976-78, 79-81; minister fgn. affairs Sweden, 1978-79; dir. gen. IAEA, Vienna, Austria, 1981—; mem. Swedish Del. UN Gen. Assembly, N.Y., 1961-81, Swedish Del. Conf. Disarmament, Geneva, 1962-78. Author: Treaty Making Power, 1959; Statsmyndigheternas Internationella Forbindelser, 1964; Sovereignty, Aggression and Neutrality, 1970; The Treaty Maker's Handbook, 1974. Mem. Inst. de Droit Internat. Office: Internat Atomic Energy Agy, Wagramerstrasse 5, POB 100, A-1400 Vienna Austria

BLOCH, ANTOINE, cardiologist; b. Lausanne, Switzerland, Aug. 9, 1938; s. Paul and Herta (Sonnenfeld) B.; M.D., U. Lausanne, 1963; m. Josee Sánchez, Aug. 25, 1973. Intern, U. Lausanne Hosp., 1964-66; med. resident St. Antonius Hosp., Utrecht, Netherlands, 1966-67, univ. hosps., Lausanne and Geneva, 1967-70; chief resident Univ. Cardiac Center of Geneva, 1970-73, physician, 1975-80; cardiac fellow Mass. Gen. Hosp., Boston, 1973-75; privat-docent Geneva Med. Sch., 1975-80, charge de cours, 1980—; chief cardiac unit Hopital de la Tour, Geneva, 1981—. Swiss Nat. Fund grantee, 1977-79. Fellow Am. Coll. Cardiology; mem. Am. Heart Assn., Am. Soc. Echocardiography, Swiss Med. Assn., Swiss Soc. Cardiology, French Soc. Cardiology, Swiss Soc. Intensive Care, Swiss Soc. Ultrasound. Author books, including: L'echocardiographie, 1978; L'infarctus du myocarde, 1979; contbr. numerous articles to profl. publs. Home: 33 Crêt-de-Choully, CH-1242 Choully Switzerland Office: Hosp de la Tour, Cardiac Unit, Geneva CH-1217, Switzerland

BLOCH, KONRAD EMIL, biochemist; b. Neisse, Germany, Jan. 12, 1912; came to U.S., 1936, naturalized, 1944; s. Frederick D. and Hedwig (Steimer) B.; m. Lore Teutsch, Feb. 15, 1941; children—Peter, Susan. Chem.Eng., Technische Hochschule, Munich, Germany, 1934; Ph.D., Columbia U., 1938. Asst. prof. biochemistry U. Chgo., 1946-50, prof., 1950-54; Higgins prof. biochemistry Harvard U., Cambridge, Mass., 1954—. Recipient Nobel prize in physiology and medicine, 1964; Ernest Guenther award in chemistry of essential oils and related products, 1965. Fellow Am. Acad. Arts and Scis.; mem. Nat. Acad. Scis., Am. Philos. Soc. Office: Harvard U Dept Biochemistry 12 Oxford St Cambridge MA 02138 *

BLOCH, SUSAN LOW, law educator; b. N.Y.C., Sept. 15, 1944; d. Ernest and Ruth (Frankel) Low; m. Richard I. Bloch, July 10, 1966; children—Rebecca, Michael. B.A. in Math., Smith Coll., 1966; M.A. in Math., U. Mich., 1968, M.A. in Computer Sci., Ph.C., 1972, J.D., 1975. Bar: D.C. 1975. Law clk. to chief judge U.S. Ct. Appeals, Washington, 1975-76; law clk. to assoc. justice Marshall, U.S. Supreme Ct., Washington, 1976-77; assoc. Wilmer, Cutler & Pickering, Washington, 1978-82; assoc. prof. Georgetown U. Law Ctr., Washington, 1983—; contbr. Mich. Law Rev., Wis. Law Rev., Georgetown Law Rev., Supreme Ct Preview, 1984, Voice of Am., 1983. Active Common Cause, ACLU, Women's Legal Def. Fund. Mem. ABA, D.C. Bar (Bicentennial of Constn.)Assn., Soc. Am. Law Tchrs., Inst. Pub. Representation (bd. dirs.), Order of Coif, Phi Beta Kappa, Sigma Xi. Home: 4335 Cathedral Ave NW Washington DC 20016 Office: Georgetown U Law Ctr 600 New Jersey Ave NW Washington DC 20001

BLOCK, AXEL, photographer; b. Velbert, Fed. Republic Germany, July 13, 1947; s. Hans H. and Helga (Thielenhaus) B. Grad., Sch. TV and film, Munich, Fed. Republic Germany, 1972. Dir. photography: (films) Schlaf Der Vernunft, 1983 (Deutscher Kamerapreis award), Zabou, 1986, Welcome to Germany, 1987, La Amiga, 1987. Mem. Bundesverband Kamera. Home and Office: Naumann St 13, 1000 Berlin 62 Federal Republic of Germany

BLOCK, ISAAC EDWARD, association executive; b. Phila., Aug. 8, 1924; s. Louis Emanuel and Stella Florence (Goodman) B.; m. Marline Beryl Lewin, June 16, 1957; children—Nancy Anne, Kathie Sue, Stephen Edward. B.S. in Physics, Haverford Coll., 1944; M.A. in Math., Harvard U., 1947, Ph.D. in Math., 1952. Math. cons. Philco Corp., Phila., 1951-54; mgr. computer ctr. Burroughs Corp., Phila., 1954-59; mgr. engrng. computer ctr. Univac div. Sperry Rand Corp., Phila., 1959-61; mgr. applied math. systems Univac div. Sperry Rand Corp., Blue Bell, Pa., 1961-64; tech. advisor Auerbach Corp., Phila., 1964-65; mgr. Auerbach Info. Inc., Phila., 1965-67, v.p., gen. mgr., 1967-72; v.p., dir. product planning and devel. Auerbach Pub. Inc., Phila., 1972-76; mng. dir. Soc. for Indsl. and Applied Math., Phila., 1976—; Sec., 1951-53, chmn. pubs. com., 1954-63, v.p., 1964-74, council, 1957-65, trustee, 1971-75, chmn. bd. trustees, 1974-75; lectr. Computation Lab, Wayne State U., summers 1954-55. Served with USNR, 1944-45. Mem. Assn. for Computing Machinery, Am. Math. Soc., Math. Assn. Am., Phi Beta Kappa, Sigma Xi. Home: 7904 Cobden Rd Laverock PA 19118 Office: Soc for Indsl and Applied Math 117 S 17th St Suite 1400 Philadelphia PA 19118

BLOCK, ROBERT MICHAEL, endodontist, educator, researcher; b. Ann Arbor, Mich., Oct. 15, 1947; s. Walter David and Thelma Violet (Levine) B.; m. Anne Powell Marshall, Sept. 4, 1977. BA, DePauw U., 1969; DDS, U. Mich.-Ann Arbor, 1974; cert. in endodontics, Va. Commonwealth U., 1977; MS in Pathology, Va. Commonwealth U., 1978. Diplomate Am. Bd. Endodontics. Clin. instr. Va. Commonwealth U., 1975-77, instr. pathology, 1977-78; research assoc. endodontics U. Conn.-Farmington, 1975—; vis. sr. scientist Nat. Med. Research Inst., Bethesda, Md., 1976-78; research assoc. McGuire Vets. Hosp., Richmond, Va., 1975-78; vis. research scientist U. Conn.-Farmington, 1978—; lectr. endodontics Flint Community Schs.; bd. dirs. Republic Bancorp, Oakland. Contbr. articles profl. jours., chpt. in book. Exec. mem. campaign com. candidate for U. Mich. Bd. Regents, 1980; candidate for Mich. State Bd. Edn., 1982. HEW and NIH summer research fellow, 1970-71; research grantee McGuire Vets. Hosp., 1976-78. Mem. Internat. Assn. Dental Research (Edward P. Hatton award 1977), Am. Assn. Dental Research, Am. Assn. Endodontists (Meml. Research award 1977), Lapeer Dental Study Club (treas. 1978-82), ADA (Preventive Dentistry award 1973). Club: Bourben Barrell Hunt (Imlay City, Mich.). Office: 3163 Flushing Rd Suite 212 Flint MI 48504

BLOCK, SANFORD LEE, oral surgeon; b. Chgo., Aug. 30, 1943; s. Harry Leo and Sophie (Dombek) B.; m. Noal S. Blender, May 30, 1966; children—Jared Gavin, Darren Randall, Nicole Suzanne. Student U. Ill., 1964; D.D.S., Loyola U., Chgo., 1969; LL.B., Blackstone Law Sch., 1973. Cert. Am. Bd. Dental Examiners. Asst. prof. oral surgery U. Ill. Coll. Dentistry, Chgo., 1972—, clinic coordinator Temporomandibular Joint and Facial Pain Research Ctr., 1974-84; dir. dentistry/oral surgery Swedish Covenant Hosp., Chgo., 1976—; cons. Office of Med. Examiner Cook County, Chgo., 1980—. Co-author: The Temporomandibular Joint, 1980. Contbr. articles to profl. jours. C.V. Mosby scholar, 1969; Marcus Levy scholar Chgo. Jewish Fedn., 1967-68; Alpha Omega scholar, 1969. Fellow Acad. Implants and Transplants, Internat. Coll. Oral Implantologists, Am. Coll. Oral Implantologists; mem. ADA, Ill. Dental Soc., Chgo. Dental Soc., Am. Assn. Dental Research, Internat. Assn. Study of Pain, Blue Key. Avocations: archeology; computers; guitar. Office: Swedish Covenant Hosp 5145 N California Ave Chicago IL 60625

BLODGETT, ANNE WASHINGTON, artist; b. N.Y.C., Apr. 17, 1940; d. Thomas Peabody and Martha (Allen) B.; m. Thomas Noyes Blodgett, Sept. 15, 1962; children—Joanne Washington, Laura Landon, Thomas Noyes, Jr. M.A., Smith Coll., 1961; postgrad. Sch. Mus. Fine Arts, 1961-62. One woman shows include Caravan Gallery, N.Y.C., 1971, 74, Berkshire Mus., Pittsfield, Mass., 1971, N.E. Harbor Library, Maine, 1973, 75, 1974, Bodley Gallery, N.Y.C., 1976-82, Medici Gallery, London, 1973, Carspecken-Scott Gallery, Wilmington, Del., 1978, Marbella Gallery, N.Y.C., 1985, 88, Millbrook (N.Y.) Gallery, 1988; exhibited in group shows New Grafton Gallery, London, 1972, Red Barn, Fishers Island, N.Y., 1974, 76, Pioneer Gallery, Cooperstown, N.Y., 1976, 78, Wingspread Gallery, Northeastern Harbor, 1979, Feguson Gallery, Hartford, Conn., 1980, Erikson Gallery, N.Y.C., 1981, Tomlyn Gallery, Jupiter, Fla., 1982, Wunderlich Gallery, Chgo., 1987; represented in permanent collections Fitswilliam Coll., Cambridge, Eng., Berkshire Mus., Heublein Co., Farmington, Conn., Competence Assurance Systems, Cambridge, Mass., Energy Absorptions Systems, Inc., Chgo., Charles River Partnership II, Boston, Bernstein, Obstfeld & Schwed Co., N.Y.C., Wilson Learning Co., Mpls., Mancom Co., Princeton, N.J., Quixote Co., Inc., Chgo., United Mining Co., N.Y.C., Respuestos Automotrices, Mexico City, Davis, Polk & Wardell, Inc., N.Y.C., Ins. Co. N.Am., Phila., InnerAsia, San Francisco, Ford Electronic Corp., Dearborn, Mich. Home and Office: 55 72d St New York NY 10021

BLODGETT, FORREST CLINTON, economics educator; b. Oregon City, Oreg., Oct. 6, 1927; s. Clinton Alexander and Mabel (Wells) B.; B.S., U. Omaha, 1961; M.A., U. Mo., 1969; Ph.D., Portland State U., 1979; m. Beverley Janice Buchholz, Dec. 21, 1946; children—Cherine (Mrs. Jon R. Klein), Candis Melis, Clinton George. Joined C.E., U.S. Army, 1946, commd. 2d lt., 1946, advanced through grades to lt. col., 1965; ret. 1968; engrng. assignments Japan, 1947-49, U.K., 1950-53, Korea, 1955-56, Alaska, 1958-60, Vietnam, 1963; staff engr. 2d Army Air Def. Region, Richards-Gebaur AFB, Mo., 1964-66; base engr. Def. Atomic Support Agy., Sandia Base, N.Mex., 1966-68; bus. mgr., trustee, asst. prof. econs. Linfield Coll., McMinnville, Oreg., 1968-73, assoc. prof., 1973-83, prof., 1983—; pres. Blodgett Enterprises, Inc., 1983-85; founder, dir. Valley Community Bank, 1980-86, vice chmn. bd. dirs., 1985-86. Commr., Housing Authority of Yamhill County (Oreg.), chmn., 1980-83; mem. Yamhill County Econ. Devel. Com., 1978-83; bd. dirs. Yamhill County Found., 1983—. Decorated Army Commendation medal with oak leaf cluster; recipient Joint Service Commendation medal Dept. of Def. Mem. Soc. Am. Mil. Engrs. (pres. Albuquerque post 1968), Am. Econ. Assn., Western Econ. Assn. Internat., Nat. Retired Officers Assn., Res. Officers Assn. (pres. Marion chpt. 1976), SAR (pres. Oreg. soc. 1985-86), Urban Affairs Assn., Pi Sigma Epsilon, Pi Gamma Mu, Omicron Delta Epsilon (Pacific NW regional dir. 1978—). Republican. Episcopalian. Lodge: Rotary (pres. McMinnville club 1983-84). Office: Linfield Coll McMinnville OR 97128

BLODGETT, RALPH HAMILTON, economist, educator; b. North Adams, Mass., Dec. 25, 1905; s. Charles Raymond and Lillian (Morits) B.; m. Loretta Neunfeldt, June 14, 1930 (dec. Dec. 1957); children: Moyra Loretta (Mrs. James F. Schaeffner), Sandra Elizabeth (Mrs. Stuart A. McIntosh); m. Margaret Adkins, July 18, 1958. B.S. in Econs, U. Vt., 1927; A.M., Syracuse U., 1928; Ph.D., U. Pa., 1933. Grad. asst. econs. Syracuse U., 1927-28; instr. econs. Valparaiso U., 1928-29; instr., asst. prof. econs. U. Pa., 1929-37; asst. prof. econs. U. Ill., 1937-41, assoc. prof., 1941-45, prof., 1945-50; prof. econs. U. Fla., 1950-76, prof. emeritus, 1976—, acting head econs. dept., 1964-65; bd. editors U. Fla. Social Sci. Monograph Series; vis. prof. econs. U. So. Calif., summer, 1949; econ. cons., expert witness various law firms; econ. cons. TVA, 1959-61, NASA, 1964-65, HUD, 1965-67. Author: Cyclical Fluctuations in Commodity Stocks, 1935, Principles of Economics, 1941, rev. edit., 1946, 51, Comparative Economic Systems, 1944, 49, Our Expanding Economy: An Introduction, 1955; co-author: An Economic Question Book, 1931, Contemporary Economic Problems, 1932, Getting and Earning, 1937, Economics: Principles and Problems, 1937, rev. edits., 1942, 48, Current Economic Problems, 1939, 1947, Comparative Economic Development, 1956, Fluctuations in General Business, 1977; Author numerous articles and monographs in econs. Mem. Am. Econ. Assn., So. Econ. Assn., Midwest Econ. Assn. (v.p. 1946-47), AAUP, Univ. Profs. for Acad. Order, Am. Contract Bridge League (life master), Phi Beta Kappa, Omicron Delta Epsilon, Sigma Alpha Epsilon, Alpha Kappa Psi, Beta Gamma Sigma. Democrat. Episcopalian. Clubs: U. Fla. Bridge, Gainesville Golf and Country, Heritage. Home: 2358 NW 13th Pl Gainesville FL 32605

BLOEDE, MERLE HUIE, civic worker; b. Brady, Tex., May 4, 1921; d. Hulon William and Anna (Lohn) Huie; student San Angelo Bus. Coll., 1944; m. Victor G. Bloede III, Mar. 11, 1945; children—Dee Anna Smith (Mrs. Jerry Willis), Victor G. IV, Susan Lohn Quaid. Asst supr. Office Censorship, San Antonio, 1942-43, Patroness North Shore Hosp., Manhasset, N.Y., 1954-56, 67-68; vol. Waldorf Sch. Scholarship Fund, Garden City, N.Y., 1957; asst. treas., exec. bd., mem. art com. Meml. Sloan-Kettering Cancer Ctr. Soc., N.Y.C., chmn. pub. relations com., 1982-83 Mem. North Shore So. Soc. (pres. 1963-65). Republican. Mem. Community Reformed Ch. Clubs: Coral Beach and Tennis (Bermuda); Sands Point (N.Y.) Golf, Flower Hill Garden (chmn. community service com. 1967), Manhasset Bay Yacht, Delray Dunes (Fla.) Golf and Country, Harbour Ridge Golf (Stuart, Fla.). Home: 4923 King Palm Circle Boynton Beach FL 33436 also: 19 Duke of Gloucester Manhasset NY 11030

BLOEDE, VICTOR GUSTAV, retired advertising executive; b. Balt., Jan. 31, 1920; s. Victor Gustav, Jr. and Helen (Yoe) B.; m. Merle Huie, Mar. 11, 1945; children—Victor Gustav, Susan Lohn. Student, St. John's Coll., Annapolis, Md., 1937-39, U. Md., 1941. Vice pres., copy chief French & Preston, N.Y.C., 1947-50; with Benton & Bowles, Inc., N.Y.C., 1950-83; v.p., creative dir. Benton & Bowles, Inc., 1957-61, sr. v.p., 1961-62, sr. v.p. charge creative services, 1962-63, exec. v.p., 1963-68, chmn. plans bd., 1963-67, pres., chief exec. officer, 1968-71, chmn. bd., 1971-83, chief exec. officer, 1971-74; mem. Nat. Advt. Rev. Bd., 1975-79, mem. steering com., 1976-78; mem. pvt. sector mktg. com. U.S. Info. Agy., 1980—; guest lectr. Duke U., 1987, Fla. Atlantic U., 1988. Author: the Full Service Advertising Agency, 1983; contbg. author: The Copy Writer's Guide, 1958, Ency. International, 1978. bd. dirs. Travelers Aid Soc. N.Y., 1966-83; bd. dirs. Am. Cancer Soc., 1976—, exec. com., 1985-87, chmn. pub. info. com., 1984-87; bd. visitors and govs. St. John's Coll., 1972-78, 79-84. Served to capt. USAAF, 1942-45. Decorated Air medal with 6 oak leaf clusters. Mem. Am. Assn. Advt. Agys. (dir.-at-large, vice chmn. 1972-73, chmn. 1973-74, chmn. adv. council 1975—), Am. Advt. Fedn. (bd. dirs., vice chmn. 1977-79), Nat. Outdoor Advt. Bur. (bd. dirs.), N.Y.C. C. of C. (pub. service adv. com. 1979—, chmn. nat. adv. com. 1987—), Profl. Golf Assn. Am. (nat. adv. com. 1979—, chmn. 1987—, bd. dirs. 1987—, pres. nat. golf fund 1987—), Phi Sigma Kappa. Clubs: Sands Point Golf (L.I.) (gov. 1975-80), Delray Dunes Golf and Country. Home: 4923 King Palm Circle Boynton Beach FL 33436

BLOEMBERGEN, NICOLAAS, physicist, educator; b. Dordrecht, The Netherlands, Mar. 11, 1920; came to U.S., 1952, naturalized, 1958; s. Auke and Sophia M. (Quint) B.; m. Huberta D. Brink, June 26, 1950; children: Antonia, Brink, Juliana. B.A., Utrecht U., 1941, M.A., 1943; Ph.D., Leiden U., 1948; M.A. (hon.), Harvard, 1951. Teaching asst. Utrecht U., 1942-45; research fellow Leiden U., 1948; mem. Soc. Fellows Harvard, 1949-51, assoc. prof., 1951-57, Gordon McKay prof. applied physics, 1957—, Rumford prof. physics, 1974, Gerhard Gade univ. prof., 1980; vis. prof. U. Paris, 1957, U. Calif., 1965, Collège de France, Paris, 1980; Lorentz guest prof. U. Leiden, 1973; Raman vis prof. Bangalore, India, 1979; Fairchild disting. scholar Calif. Inst. Tech., 1984. Author: Nuclear Magnetic Relaxation, 1948, Nonlinear Optics, 1965; also articles in profl. jours. Recipient Buckley prize for solid state physics Am. Phys. Soc., 1958, Dirac medal U. New South Wales (Australia), 1983; Stuart Ballantine medal Franklin Inst., 1961; Half Moon trophy Netherlands Club N.Y., 1972; Nat. medal of Sci., 1975; Lorentz medal Royal Dutch Acad., 1978; Frederic Ives medal Optical Soc. Am., 1979; von Humboldt sr. scientist award Munich, 1980; Nobel prize in Physics, 1981; Guggenheim fellow, 1957. Fellow Am. Phys. Soc., Am. Acad. Arts and Scis., IEEE (Morris Liebmann award 1959, Medal of Honor 1983); hon. fellow Indian Acad. Scis.; mem. Optical Soc. Am. (hon.), Nat., Royal Dutch acads. scis., Nat. Acad. Engring., Am. Philos. Soc., Deutsche Akademie der Naturforscher Leopoldina, Koninklyke Nederlandse Akademie von Wetenschappen (corr.), Paris Acad. Scis. (fgn. assoc.). Office: Harvard U Dept Physics Pierce Hall Cambridge MA 02138

BLOEMHOF, RINZE, pharmaceutical company executive; b. The Hague, The Netherlands, Sept. 29, 1935; s. Teake and Johanna (van Seyl) B.; m. Willemina J.M. van der Sys, Nov. 24, 1960; children: Take Jan F.M., R.J. Maarten. Degree in chemistry, Higher Tech. Sch., Dordrecht, The Netherlands, 1960, MBA, 1964. Prodn. mgr. Optilon, Winschoten, The Netherlands, 1964-70; trainer/cons. I.S.W., The Hague, 1970-78; internat. tng. mgr. H.V.A., Amsterdam, The Netherlands, 1978-82, Duphar Pharms. BV, Weesp, The Netherlands, 1982—. Bd. dirs., sec. Democraten '66, The Hague, 1967-74. Mem. Dutch Soc. for Tchrs., Tutors and Trainers (bd. dirs., v.p. 1984—, jour. publicist). Office: Duphar Pharms BV, CJ van Houtenlaan, 1381 CP Weesp The Netherlands

BLOEMSMA, MARCO PAUL, investor; b. Heemstede, Netherlands, July 20, 1924; s. Philippus and Wilhelmina Geertruida (Bonebakker) B.; LLM, Leyden U., 1948; m. Mieke Harten, Sept. 23, 1955; children: Marco Reinier, Barbara Patricia, Michiel Alexander. Lawyer firm van der Feltz, Voûte & Riechelmann, 1948-49; assoc., then ptnr. Blackstone, Rueb & van Boeschoten, 1951-72; pres. C. Harten Holding B.V., The Hague, 1972-85; pres. NEBIM Handelmaatschappij B.V.; hon. chmn. KTI-group; chmn. Ten Doesschate-group; dir. Volvo Bedryfswages B.V., Mauritshuis Found.; positions held include: dir., pres. chmn. Patino-group; chmn. Lips United-group, ICL Nederland B.V., Auto-Palace-group; dir. Mobil Chemie B.V., Ambac B.V., Ned. Mij. Mijnbouwkundige Werken N.V., Polak & Schwarz N.V., Lockheed Europe N.V., Vulcaansoord N.V., Merck Sharp en Dohme Nederland N.V., Svenska Metallverken/Granges Nederland B.V., Volvo Bedryfswagens B.V., Mauritshuis Found., Staalglas B.V. Author nat. reports on fiscal and corp. subjects. Served with Dutch Naval Reserve, 1949-51. Hon. Ky. col. since 1962. Mem. Internat. Law Assn., Internat. Fiscal Assn. Clubs: Cercle Interalliée (Paris); Amstel (Amsterdam); Wittenburg (Wassenaar); Royal Bachelors (Gothenborg); Cercle Litteraire (Lausanne). Home: 5 Ave de Crousaz, 1010 Lausanne Switzerland

BLOFIELD, DAVID, marketing executive; b. Letchworth, Eng., Jan. 30, 1946; s. Clement Charles and Ellen Elizabeth (Church) B.; m. Cheryl Elizabeth Males, June 14, 1969; children: Robert David, Rodger James. Student electronic engring., Mander Coll., 1963-67. Sci. asst. Ministry Def., Henlow, Eng., 1963-67; sect. leader Internat. Computers Ltd., Letchworth, 1967-70, MSL Calibration Ctr., Bedfordshire, Eng., 1970-77; mktg. mgr. Wentworth Labs. Ltd., Bedfordshire, Eng., 1979—. Mem. Brit. Inst. Mgmt., Internat. Soc. Hybrid Microelectronics. Home: 25 Gorst Close, Letchworth SG6 3HA, England Office: Wentworth Labs Ltd, Sunderland Rd, Sandy Bedfordshire SG19 1RB, England

BLOKHIN, NIKOLAI NIKOLAEVITCH, medical research scientist; b. May 4, 1912. Grad. Gorky Med. Inst., 1934. Surgeon, oncologist, prof. Med. Inst. Gorky, 1947—; dir. Inst. Exptl. and Clin. Oncology (now All Union Cancer Research Ctr.), Acad. Med. Scis. USSR, Moscow; mem. council Internat. Union Against Cancer, governing council Internat. Agy. for Research on Cancer. Chmn. com. Internat. Lenin prize for Strengthening of Peace among Nations; pres. Inst. Soviet-Am. Relations, 1960—. Decorated Order of Lenin (4), Order of Red Star, Order of October Revolution, Order of Labour Red Banner; named Hero Socialist Labour. Mem. Acad. Sci. USSR, (pres. 1960-68, 77-87), Polish Acad. Scis., Am. Assn. Cancer Research, N.Y. Acad. Sci., Cancer Soc. Italy. Researcher on malignant neoplasms treatment; organizer of med. scientists for internat. coop. in field. Mem. Communist Party, 1948. Address: All Union Cancer Research Ctr, Acad Med Sci USSR, Kashirskoye sh 24, 115478 Moscow USSR

BLOM, DANIEL CHARLES, lawyer, investor, insurance company executive; b. Portland, Oreg., Dec. 13, 1919; s. Charles D. and Anna (Reiner) B.; m. Ellen Lavon Stewart, June 28, 1952; children: Daniel Stewart, Nicole Jan. B.A. magna cum laude, U. Wash., 1941, postgrad., 1941-42; J.D., Harvard U., 1948; postgrad., U. Paris, 1954-55. Bar: Wash. bar 1949. Teaching fellow speech U. Wash., 1941-42; law clk. to justice Supreme Ct. Wash., 1948-49; since practiced in Seattle; assoc. Graves, Kizer & Graves, 1949-51; gen. counsel Northwestern Life Ins. Co., 1952-54; partner Case & Blom, 1952-54; assoc., ptnr. Ryan, Swanson & Cleveland, 1956—; exec. v.p., gen. counsel Family Life Ins. Co., 1977-85, spl. counsel, 1985—; vice chmn. Wash. Bd. Bar Examiners, 1970-72, chmn., 1972-75; mem. industry adv. com. Nat. Assn. Ins. Commrs., 1966-68; pres. Wash. Ins. Council, also Ins. Fund Found., 1971-73, gen. counsel, 1975-78; bd. dirs. Family Life Ins. Co., 1964-85. Editor: Wash. State Bar Jour, 1951-52; assoc. editor: The Brief, 1975-76; Author: Life Insurance Law of the State of Washington, 1980. Chmn. jury selection Wash. Gov.'s Writer's Day Awards, 1976; bd. dirs.

Crisis Clinic; trustee Bush Sch., 1971-79, v.p., 1976-77; trustee, v.p. Frye Mus., Seattle, 1976-82, World Affairs Council Seattle, 1972—, Friends of Freeway Park, 1976—; trustee Friends of Seattle Pub. Library, 1982—; bd. visitors U. Wash. Library, 1988—. Served to 2d lt. AUS, 1942-45, PTO. Decorated Bronze Star. Mem. ABA (vice chmn. com. on life ins. law, sect. ins., negligence and compensation law 1971-76, chmn. 1976-78, sect. program chmn. 1978-79, mem. council 1979-83, chmn. pub. relations com. 1981-83, chmn. com. on profl. independence of the lawyer 1984-85, chmn. com. on scope and correlation 1985-86, del. ABA to Union Internat. Des Avocats 1986—, policy coordinator Tips sect. 1986—), Wash. Bar Assn. (award of merit 1975, chmn. legal edn. liason com. 1977-78), Seattle Bar Assn., Union Internat. Des Avocats (v.p. 1987—), N.Am. Found. for Internat. Legal Practice (pres. 1987—), Wash. Ins. Council (pres. 1971-73, trustee 1971-85), Am. Judicature Soc., Assn. Life Ins. Counsel, Harvard Law Sch. Assn., Am. Council Life Ins. (legis. com. 1982-85), Am. Arbitration Assn., Harvard Assn. Seattle and Western Wash. (trustee 1976-77), Phi Beta Kappa, Tau Kappa Alpha. Club: Rainier (Seattle), Harvard of Seattle, Western Washington. Home: 2424 Magnolia Blvd W Seattle WA 98199 Office: Ryan Swanson & Cleveland 3201 Bank of Calif Ctr Seattle WA 98164

BLOMQVIST, HANS CHRISTER WALDEMAR, professor of economics; b. Pernå, Finland, Mar. 11, 1947; s. Oiva Valdemar and Gerda Viola (Tennberg) B.; m. Clara Benita Strandberg, Dec. 18, 1971; children: Anna-Clara Maria, Johan Andreas Waldemar. BS in Econs., Swedish Sch. Econs., Helsinki, Finland, 1970; MS in Econs., Swedish Sch. Econs., 1971, D of Econs., 1982. Asst. lectr. Swedish Sch. Econs., 1970-77, researcher in econs., 1977-80, acting prof. econs., 1980—, acting prof. mktg., 1981; vice rector Swedish Sch. Econs., 1983-87, dept. head, 1983—. Author: Studies on Inflation in Small Open Economies, 1981; contbr. articles to prol. jours. Home: Lappviksgatan 6 H 89, 00180 Helsinki Finland

BLOMSTEDT, HENRIK LENNART, former Finnish diplomat; b. 1921; m. Ulla Westin, 1960; 1 child. LL.B., U. Helsinki, 1947. With Finnish Fgn. Service, 1947-88 ; ambassador to Ethiopia, 1965-69, Kenya, Tanzania, Uganda, Zambia, 1965-69; head legal dept. Fgn. Ministry, 1970-73; ambassador to Netherlands and Ireland, 1973-78; Ambassador to Japan and Republic of Korea, 1978-84, The Philippines, 1978-80; ambassador to Norway, 1984-88 . Named Comdr. 1st class of the Order of the White Rose of Finland, 1982, Comdr. 1st class of the Order of the Lion of Finland, 1976, Memory medal of War 1941-45, Grand Knight Cross with Star of the Order of Icelandic Falcon, 1972, Grand Cross of Order of Orange-Nassau of Netherlands, 1974, The First Order of Merit with Grand Cordon of Rising Sun of Japan, 1984, Order of Diplomatic Service Merit, 1977, Heung-In medal of Republic of Korea, 1984, Comdr. of Order of North Star of Sweden, 1966, Knight of Order of Dannebrog of Denmark, 1966; decorated 2d class Order of Tudor Vladimirescu of Romania. Address: Mellstens-vägen 9F2, 02170 Esbo Finland

BLONDIN, ANTOINE, writer; b. Paris, Apr. 11, 1922; s. Pierre and Germaine (Ragoulleau) B.; m. Sylviane Dollfus; 2 children; m. Francois Barrere. Student Lycee Louis-le-Grand, U. of Paris. Author scenarios for films La route Napoleon, Obsession, La foire aux femmes; author: L'Europe buissonnere, 1949; Les enfants du bon Diev, 1952; L'humeur vagabonde, 1955; Un Singe en Hiver (Prix Interallie 1959), 1959; Un garcon d'honneur, 1960; (with Paul Grimard) Detrompez-Vous, 1966; Quat saisons, 1975; Vivre a Paris, 1976; Certificals d'etudes, 1977; Monsieur Jadis ou l'ecole du Soir; Nous reviendrons a pied. Recipient Prix des Deux-Magots, 1949, Grand Prix littiraire prince Pierre de Monaco, 1971, Grand Prix Academie Francaise, 1979. •

BLOODWORTH, A(LBERT) W(ILLIAM) FRANKLIN, lawyer; b. Atlanta, Sept. 23, 1935; s. James Morgan Bartow and Elizabeth Westfield (Dimmock) B.; m. Elizabeth Howell, Nov. 24, 1967; 1 child, Elizabeth Howell. A.B. in History and French, Davidson Coll., 1957; J.D. magna cum laude with 1st honors, U. Ga., 1963. Bar: Ga. 1962, U.S. Supreme Ct. 1971. Asst. dir. alumni and pub. relations Davidson Coll., N.C., 1959-60; assoc. Hansell & Post, Atlanta, 1963-68, ptnr., 1969-84; ptnr. Bloodworth & Nix, Atlanta, 1984—; counsel organized crime com. Met. Atlanta Commn. on Crime, 1965-67; asst. sec., counsel Met. Found. Atlanta, 1968-76. Bd. dirs. Atlanta Presbytery, 1974-78; trustee Synod of Southeast, Presbyn. Ch. in U.S.A., Augusta, Ga., 1982-87; trustee Big Canoe Chapel, Ga., 1983-86, chmn. bd. trustees, 1985-86. Served to 1st lt. Intelligence Corps, USAR, 1957-59. Recipient Jessie Dan MacDougal Scholarship award U. Ga. Found., 1963, Outstanding Student Leadership award Student Bar Assn., U. Ga., 1963. Fellow Am. Coll. Probate Counsel; mem. ABA, State Bar Ga., Atlanta Bar Assn., Atlanta Estate Planning Council, N. Atlanta Estate Planning Council, Phi Beta Kappa, Phi Kappa Phi, Omicron Delta Kappa, Alpha Tau Omega (pres. chpt. 1957), Phi Delta Phi (grad. of yr. 1963, pres. chpt. 1963). Republican. Presbyterian (elder). Clubs: Capital City, Lawyers (Atlanta); Sphinx, Gridiron (Athens, Ga.). Home: 3784 Club Dr NE Atlanta GA 30319 Office: Bloodworth & Nix 3414 Peachtree Rd Suite 706 Monarch Plaza Atlanta GA 30326

BLOOM, CLAIRE, actress; b. London, Feb. 15, 1931; d. Edward Max and Elizabeth (Grew) Blume; m. Rod Steiger, Sept. 19, 1959 (div. Jan. 1969); 1 child, Anna Justine. Student, Badminton Sch., Bristol, Eng., Fern Hill Manor, New Milton, Eng., Guildhall Sch. Music and Drama, London. Appeared as Ophelia, Stratford-Upon-Avon, 1948; plays include also Ring Around the Moon, London, 1949-51, Romeo and Juliet, also as Juliet in Old Vic tour of U.S.; film roles in Richard III, 1956, Alexander the Great, 1956, The Brothers Karamazov, 1958, Look Back in Anger, 1958, The Brothers Grimm, 1962, The Chapman Report, 1962, The Haunting, 1963, 80,000 Suspects, 1963, Alta Infidelita, 1963, Il Maestro di Vigeuono, 1963, The Outrage, 1964, The Spy Who Came in from the Cold, 1965, The Illustrated Man, 1969, Three into Two Won't Go, 1969, A Severed Head, 1971, A Doll's House, 1973, Islands in the Stream, 1976, Clash of the Titans, 1981, Always, 1984, Sammy and Rosie, 1987; Broadway prodns. include Rashomon, 1959; other theatre appearances include Altona, Royal Court Theatre, London, 1960, A Doll's House, Hedda Gabler, 1971, Vivat! Vivat Regina!, 1972; N.Y. appearance The Innocents, 1976; London appearances A Doll's House, 1973, A Streetcar Named Desire, 1974, Rosmersholm, 1977, The Cherry Orchard, 1981, These are Women, 1982-83; many roles Brit. and U.S. TV including In Praise of Love, 1975, A Legacy, 1975, Henry VIII, 1979, Hamlet, 1979, The Ghost Writer, 1983, Cymebeline, 1983, King John, 1983, Brideshead Revisited, 1981, Shadowlands, 1984, Time and the Conways, 1985, Queenie, 1987, Anastasia, 1987, Shadow in the Sun, 1988; author: Limelight and After, 1982. Recipient Evening Standard award, London, 1974, Brit. Film and TV award, London, 1984. Office: William Morris Agy 1350 6th Ave New York NY 10019

BLOOM, EUGENE CHARLES, physician; b. Tupelo, Miss., June 3, 1933; s. Robert Harold and Anna Esther (Kronick) B.; m. Joan Ellen Margoles, July 22, 1956; children: Marjorie Wynne Bloom Albert, Stacey Bloom Schlafstein, Robin Hilary. Student, Emory U., 1951-55, U. Fla., 1955-56; MD, U. Miami, 1960. Intern Cook County Hosp., Chgo., 1960-61; resident in internal medicine Jackson Meml. Hosp., 1961-63; resident in gastroenterology Coral Gables VA Hosp., 1963-64; research fellow dept. medicine, div. gastroenterology U. Miami (Fla.) Sch. Medicine, 1964-65, research scientist, 1964-66, instr. medicine, 1964-74, clin. asst. prof. medicine, 1974—; gen. practice medicine, Miami, 1966—; mem. staff Bapt. Hosp. Miami, sec.-treas. med. staff, 1979-80, chief of staff, 1980-82. Contbr. articles to profl. jours. Bd. dirs. Jewish Vocat. Service. Served to capt. M.C., U.S. Army, 1963-67, Vietnam. Mem. AMA, So. Med. Assn., Fla. Med. Assn., Dade County Med. Assn. (alt. del. Fla. Med. Assn. 1974), Am. Acad. Sci., U. Miami Med. Alumni Assn. (chmn. Dade County chpt. 1972-75, nat. pres. 1975-77, v.p. pub. relations com. 1987—, v.p. 1987—), Gen. Alumni U. Miami (bd. dirs. 1973-77, 88—), Fla. Gastroent. Soc., Greater Miami Jewish Fedn. (chmn. physicians div. 1979-80), Alpha Omega Alpha, Omicron Delta Kappa. Democrat. Club: King's Bay Yacht and Country. Office: 9045 SW 87 Ct Miami FL 33176

BLOOM, MICHAEL EUGENE, communications executive; b. Pittsburg, Calif., Jan. 16, 1947; s. Benjamin Bernard and Mildred (Haims) B.; m. Deborah Ann Bresler, Aug. 6, 1977; children—Benjamin Solomon Bresler, Miriam Hannah Bresler. B.A. in Sociology, U. Calif.-Santa Barbara, 1969, postgrad. elec. engring., 1969-71; M.B.A., Stanford U., 1979. Broadcaster, Sta. KCSB-FM, Santa Barbara, 1964-68, gen. mgr., 1968-69; broadcaster KKIS-AM, Pittsburg, Calif., 1965, KMUZ-FM, Santa Barbara, 1965-67, KTMS-AM-FM, Santa Barbara, 1967-69; mem. tech. staff Gen. Research Corp., Santa Barbara, 1970-72; mgmt. scientist, cons. Sci. Applications, Inc., LaJolla, Calif., 1973-74, Planning and Mgmt. Cons. Corp., Cleve., 1974, Bloom Enterprises, Santa Monica, Calif., 1975-77; project team leader, sr. programmer Bendix Field Engring. Corp., Sunnyvale, Calif., 1977; retail product planner Crocker Nat. Bank, San Francisco, 1978; dir. corp. devel. Am. TV & Communications Corp., Englewood, Colo., 1979-82, dir. new bus. devel., 1983-84, dir. bus. and tech. devel., 1984-85; dir. video services devel. Pacific Bell, San Francisco, 1985-86, dir. product strategy and devel., San Ramon, Calif., 1986-87, dir. market strategy group, 1987-88, NTT task force, 1988—; chmn. communications bd. U. Calif.-Santa Barbara; v.p., dir. Intercollegiate Broadcasting System, Inc., 1967-70; founder, dir. U. Calif. Radio Network, 1967-69; chmn. systems standards task force on teletext Nat. Cable TV Assn., 1980-81. Adv. council Coll. Info. Studies, U. Denver, 1982-85. Recipient Pres.'s merit award U. Calif., 1965. Mem. IEEE, Assn. MBA Execs., Am. Mktg. Assn. (exec.), Soc. Cable TV Engrs., Soc. Broadcast Engrs., Nat. Cable TV Assn., U. Calif.-Santa Barbara Alumni Assn. (life), Stanford U. Bus. Sch. Alumni Assn. (program chmn. Rocky Mountain chpt. 1982-85), Stanford U. Alumni Assn. (life). Author: (with L.A. Sibley) Carrier Current System Design, 1967. Office: Pacific Bell 2600 Camino Ramon Room 4 South 054 San Ramon CA 94583

BLOOM, RICHARD FREDRIC, behavioral scientist, psychologist; b. Bklyn., Oct. 23, 1931; s. Morris and Mary (Schur) B.; m. Myra R. Thal, Dec. 27, 1956 (div.); children—Laura A.; David T.; m. Susan Davies, May 30, 1981; stepchildren—David Y. Redford II, Hugh T. Redford. BS, Bklyn. Coll., 1953; AE, Newark Coll. Engring., 1959, MS, 1962; PhD, NYU, 1969. Lic. psychologist, Conn., Fla., Pa. Physicist U.S. Nat. Bur. Standards, Washington, 1953; electronics engr. ITT Fed. Labs., Nutley, N.J., 1955-65; behavioral scientist Dunlap & Assocs., Inc., Norwalk, Conn., 1965—, dir., 1984-87; pvt. practice psychologist, New Canaan, Conn., 1970—; co-dir. Psychotherapy & Counseling Assocs., New Canaan, 1981—; co-founder, dir. Mental Health Benefits Corp., North Haven, Conn., 1985—, TriSource Group Inc., New Rochelle, N.Y., 1985—; research cons. Silver Hill Found. Hosp., New Canaan, 1972-75. Author tech. reports and research papers. Bd. dirs. Am. Cancer Soc., Darien, Conn., 1981—. Served with U.S. Army, 1953-55; Korea. Fellow Soc. Clin. and Exptl. Hypnosis; mem. Am. Psychol. Assn., IEEE, Soc. Psychophysiol. Research. Jewish. Home: 45 Silvermine Rd New Canaan CT 06840 Office: Dunlap & Assocs 17 Washington St Norwalk CT 06854

BLOOM, WALTER RUSSELL, mathematics educator; b. Auckland, New Zealand, Dec. 2, 1948; came to Australia, 1960; s. Harry and Norma (Morris) B.; m. Lynette Myra Butler, Nov. 3, 1971; 1 child, Alyson Claire. BSc with honors, I, U., Tasmania, 1971; PhD, Australian Nat. U., 1974. Tchr. of math. Hobart Matriculation Coll., Tasmania, Australia, 1967; lectr. in math. U. Tasmania, 1974; lectr. in math. Murdoch U., Perth, Western Australia, 1975-81, sr. lectr., 1982-87, assoc. prof. math., 1988—; vis. Fulbright scholar U.Wash., 1976-77; vis. prof. U. Tübingen, Fed. Republic Germany, 1980, 87. Contbr. articles to profl. jours. Alexander von Humboldt research fellow, 1987. Mem. Australian Math. Soc. (sec. 1980-88), Am. Math. Soc., Australian Assn. Math. Tchrs., Royal Soc. Western Australia, Deutsche Math. Vereinigüng. Clubs: Perth Numismatic, Royal Numismatic. Office: Murdoch Univ, Perth 6150, Australia

BLOUSTEIN, EDWARD J., college president; b. N.Y.C., Jan. 20, 1925; s. Samuel and Celia (Einwohner) B.; m. Ruth Ellen Steinman, Oct. 6, 1951; children: Elise, Lori. B.A., N.Y. U., 1948; B. Phil. (Fulbright Scholar), Wadham Coll., Oxford (Eng.) U., 1950; Ph.D., Cornell U., 1954, J.D., 1959. Bar: N.Y. 1959, Vt. 1971. Polit. analyst State Dept., 1951-52; instr. logic and philosophy Cornell U., 1954-55; prof. law N.Y. U. Law Sch., 1961-65; pres. Bennington (Vt.) Coll., 1965-71, Rutgers U., 1971—. Address: 1245 River Rd Piscataway NJ 08854

BLOW, DAVID MERVYN, biophysics educator; b. June 27, 1931; s. Edward Mervyn and Dorothy Laura Blow; m. Mavis Sears, 1955; 2 children. PhD, Cambridge U. Med. Research Council Unit for Study of Molecular Biol. Systems at Cambridge U., 1959-62, Cambridge Lab. Molecular Biology, 1962-77; lectr. and fellow Trinity Coll.-Cambridge U., 1968-77; prof. biophysics Imperial Coll.-U. London, 1977—; dean Royal Coll. Sci. London, 1981-84. Contbr. articles and revs. to sci. jours. Fulbright scholar NIH and MIT, 1957-59; recipient CIBA medal Biochemistry Soc., 1967, Charles Léopold Meyer Prize, 1979, The Wolf Prize in Chemistry, 1987. Mem. Brit. Crystallographic Assn. (pres. 1984—). Office: U London Imperial Coll, Blackett Lab, London SW7 2BZ, England •

BLOWER, BRUCE GREGORY, social service administrator; b. Bklyn., May 9, 1937; s. Howard and Elisabeth (Bernstein) B.; children—C. Elizabeth, Bruce Gregory II, Erin. B.B.A., Hofstra U., 1958. Investigator, claims adjustor Liberty Mut. Ins. Co., Lynbrook, N.Y., 1958-59; real estate salesman Vigilant Assocs., Inc., Huntington, N.Y., 1963-64; advt. salesman L.I. Comml. Rev., Plainview, N.Y., 1965-66; spl. corr. The Long-Islander, Huntington, 1966-76; legis. aide N.Y. State Assembly, Albany, 1976-80; dir. handicapped services County of Suffolk, Hauppauge, N.Y., 1980—; v.p. Nassau-Suffolk Health Systems Agy., Inc., Plainview, 1987—; chmn. bd., pres. Huntington Community First Aid Squad, Inc., 1969-73, 78; mem. Gov.'s Task Force on Emergency Med. Services, 1979; chmn. N.Y. State Emergency Med. Services Council, 1979-80; chmn. L.I. regional council Internat. Year of Disabled Persons, 1981-82; chmn. Suffolk County Emergency Med. Services Task Force, 1986—; mem. citizens adv. council N.Y. State Assembly Task Force on Disabled, 1982—; nat. pres. Assn. of Local Govtl. Agys. for Disabled, 1983-88; v.p. Nassau-Suffolk Health Systems Agy., Inc., Plainview, N.Y., 1987—; mem. met. adv. bd. N.Y. State Senate Select Com. on Disabled, 1983-86; adv. council N.Y. State Senate Select com. on Disabled, 1987—; mem. client assistance program adv. council N.Y. State Commn. on Quality of Care for Mentally Disabled, 1983—; mem. Suffolk Regional adv. council N.Y. State Div. Human Rights, 1983—; bd. dirs. L.I. Ctr. for Ind. Living, Inc., Levittown, N.Y., 1983—, Suffolk Ind. Living Orgn., Inc., Medford, N.Y., 1985—, Huntington (N.Y.) Community 1st Aid Squad, Inc., 1988—; chmn. employability com. N.Y. State Edn. Commr.'s Adv. Council on Vocat. Rehab., 1984—; treas. Long Island chpt. Medic Alert Found. Internat., 1986—. Served to 2d lt. U.S. Army, 1959-60. Named hon. fire chief Town of Huntington, 1974; recipient pub. service award Suffolk County Traffic Safety Bd., 1974, Spl. award N.Y. State Vol. Ambulance Assn., 1980, Outstanding Achievement in Govt. award Suffolk Community Council, 1983, Good Deed award F.D.R. div. Suffolk County council Boy Scouts Am., 1984. Mem. DAV (life), Eastern Paralyzed Vets. Assn. (life). Republican. Lodge: Elks. Avocation: ambulance volunteer. Home: 3 Mcroke Ct Huntington Station NY 11746 Office: Suffolk County Office Handicapped Services 65 Jetson Ln Central Islip NY 11722

BLUECHER, VIGGO G(RAF) VON, sociology educator, researcher; b. Flensburg, Germany, Aug. 15, 1914; came to Switzerland, 1974; s. Ulrich Graf von Bluecher and Fanny Elisabeth (Graefin Moltke) Graefin von Bluecher; m. Lia Romanow, Aug. 9, 1952; children—Dorothee-Elisabeth, Ulrich-Reimar, Ulrich. Dr. phil., U. Hamburg (W.Ger.), 1955. Pub. opinion researcher N.W. German Radio network, Hamburg, 1954-56; social researcher Institut Infratest, Hamburg and Munich, W.Ger., 1956-60; head dept. social research EMNID-Institut, Bielefeld, W.Ger., 1960-74; lectr. in field Bielefeld U., 1969-84; prof. empirical sociology Inst. Sociology, U. Berne (Switzerland), 1984—; mem. faculty Salzburg Seminar for Am. Studies, 1980; sci. adviser Deutsche Gesellschaft für Freizeit, Frankfort and Dusseldorf, 1968-71; chief methodological edn. BVM (Profl. Assn. Mktg. Research Germany), 1978-84; dir. seminar VSMF Swiss Mktg. Assn., 1982—. Author: Freizeit in der Industriellen Gesellschaft, 1956; Generation der Unbefangenen, 1966; contbr. numerous articles to profl. jours.; author numerous research reports. Served to maj. Gen. Staff, German Army, 1942-45. Mem. Deutsche Gesellschaft für Soziologie (methodensektion 1961-88), World Assn. Pub. Opinion Research, Berufsverband Deutscher Marktforscher, Verband Schweizer Marktforscher (v.p.), Study Circle for Tourism. Lutheran. Club: Grande Société Berne. Lodge: Order St. Joan Europe (Rechtsritter). Home: Bottigenstrasse 250, CH-3019 Berne Switzerland Office: Institut für Soziologie, Speichergasse 39, CH-3001 Berne Switzerland

BLUESTEIN, PAUL HAROLD, management engineer; b. Cin., June 14, 1923; s. Norman and Eunice D. (Schullman) B.; m. Joan Ruth Straus, May 17, 1943; children: Alice Sue Bluestein Greenbaum, Judith Ann. B.S., Carnegie Inst. Tech., 1946, B.Engring. in Mgmt. Engring., 1946; M.B.A., Xavier U., 1973. Registered profl. engr., Ohio. Time study engr. Lodge & Shipley Co., 1946-47; adminstrv. engr. Randall Co., 1947-52; partner Paul H. Bluestein & Co. (mgmt. cons.), 1952—, Seinsheimer-Bluestein Mgmt. Services, 1964-70; gen. mgr. Baker Refrigeration Co., 1953-56; pres., dir. Tabor Mfg. Co., 1953-54, Bluejay Corp., 1954—, Blatt & Ludwig Corp., 1954-57, Jason Industries, Inc., 1954-57, Hamilton-York Corp., 1954-57, Earle Hardware Mfg. Co., 1955-57, Hermas Machine Co., 1956—, Panel Machine Co., Ermet Products Corp., 1957-86, Tyco Labs., Inc., 1968-69, All-Tech Industries, 1968; gen. mgr. Hafleigh & Co., 1959-60; sr. v.p., gen. mgr. McCauley Ind. Corp., 1959-60; gen. mgr. Am. Art Works div. Rapid-Am. Corp., 1960-63; sec.-treas., dir. Liberty Baking Co., 1964-65; pres. Duguesne Baking Co., 1964-65, Goddard Bakers, Inc., 1964-65; pub. Merger and Acquisition Digest, 1962-69; partner Companhia Engenheiros Indsl. Bluestein Do Brasil, 1970-84; v.p., gen. mgr. Famco Machine div. Worden-Allen Co., 1974-75; exec. v.p., gen. mgr. Peck, Stow & Wilcox Co., Inc., 1976-77; mem. Joint Engring. Mgmt. Conf. Com., 1971-78. Com. mem. Cin. Art Mus. Served with AUS, 1943-46. Mem. ASME, Internat. Inst. Indsl. Engrs., Am. Soc. Engring. Mgmt., N.Am. Mgmt. Council; C.I.O.S.-World Council Mgmt. (dir., 1982-87). Home and Office: 3420 Section Rd Amberley Village Cincinnati OH 45237

BLUETT, THOMAS BYRON, SR., child psychologist; b. Milw., May 29, 1931; s. Byron Walter and Ida Mae (Mineau) B.; m. Daina Lauretta Kubilius, Sept. 21, 1974; children: Thomas Jr., Elizabeth, William, Martha, Dorothea (dec.), Byron. BS, U. Wis., 1953, MS, 1955, PhD, 1971. Reg. psychologist Nat. Health Service Providers. Counselor Appleton (Wis.) Pub. Schs., 1955-57; psychologist Green Bay (Wis.) Pub. Schs., 1957-65; exec. dir. United Cerebral Palsy, Green Bay, 1965-68; dir. pupil services Cooperative Edn. Service Agy., Wis., 1968-71; child psychologist Pediatrics Beaumont Clin., Green Bay, 1972—; sec., treas. Tri-State Testing Service, Inc., DePere, Wis., 1958—; child psychologist Sta. WTMJ-TV and Radio, Milw., 1981—, Sta. WOAI, San Antonio, 1986—; lectr. child devel., U. Wis., Green Bay, 1968-73. Author, presenter (TV series) In-Charge Parenting, 1982, (book, audio tapes) In-Charge Parenting Kit, 1983; author: Conquering Low Impulse Control, 1984; co-author: Youth Tutoring Youth, 1970. Bd. dirs. United Cerebral Palsy, N.Y.C., 1957-65; mem. Wis. Day Care Adv. Bd., Wis., 1960-65; exec. dir. Nat. Early Childhood Edn. Fund., Wis., 1971-80. Served to corp. U.S. Army, 1953-55, Korea. Grantee Rural Pupil Services, HEW, Washington, D.C., 1969, Early Childhood Edn. , ESEA, Madison, 1970. Fellow Am. Assn. Mental Deficiency, Nat. Assn. Mental Deficiency; charter mem. Wis. Soc. Clin. Cons. Psychologists (co-chmn. publicity 1986—), Nat. Gen. Psychol. Services Corp., Nat. Assn. Sch. Psychologists (charter), Brown County Clin. Cons. Psychologists (treas. 1985-87), Phi Delta Kappa (pres. 1958-60). Episcopalian. Club: Packer Monday Night Quarterback. Lodges: Elks (handicapped children's chmn. 1958-68), Optimist (youth chmn. 1957-68). Home: E5315 7th Rd Alaska Lake Algoma WI 54201 Office: Beaumont Clinic Ltd 1821 S Webster Ave Green Bay WI 54301

BLUITT, KAREN, infosystems engineer; b. N.Y.C., Oct. 25, 1957; d. James Bertrand and Beatrice (Kaufman) B.; BS, Fordham U., 1979; MBA, Calif. State Poly. U., 1982; m. Kenneth Mark Curry, Nov. 24, 1979. Software engr. Hughes Aircraft Co., Fullerton, Calif., 1979-81; microprocessor engr. Beckman Instruments Co., Fullerton, 1981-82, Singer Co., Glendale, Calif., 1982-83; sr. software engr. Sanders Assoc., Nashua, N.H., 1983-85; software project mgr. GTE Corp., Billerica, Mass., 1985-86; sr. software engr. Wang Labs, Lowell, Mass., 1986—. Served to 1st lt. USAR, 1979—. Scholarship Gov. N.Y. Scholarship Com., 1975-79; Beta Gamma Sigma scholar, 1978—. Served with USAR, 1979—. Mem. Nat. Assn. Female Execs., Assn. MBA Execs., Res. Officers Assn. NOW, Civil Affairs Assn., LWV, AAUW, Boston Computer Soc. Execs., Res. Officers Assn. Office: Wang Labs 1 Industrial Ave Lowell MA 01851

BLUM, IRVING RONALD, lawyer; b. Phila., Mar. 3, 1935; s. William and Dorothy B.; m. Rochelle S. Klempner, June 17, 1956; children—Loren, Karen, Jill, Jason. B.A., Wayne State U., 1956; J.D., Detroit Coll. Law, 1959. Bar: Mich. 1959, U.S. Dist. Ct. (ea. dist.) Mich. 1959. Ptnr., Akerman, Kaplan & Blum, Detroit, 1959-62, Blum, Brady & Rosenberg, Detroit, 1962—. Fellow Assn. Trial Lawyers Am. Republican. Jewish. Home: 4681 Cove Rd West Bloomfield MI 48033

BLUM, ROBERT EDWARD, business executive; b. Bklyn., May 8, 1899; s. Edward C. and Florence (Abraham) B.; m. Ethel Mildred Halsey, Aug. 15, 1928; children: John Robert Halsey, Alice Elizabeth Packard (Mrs. Robert H. Yoakum). AB, Yale, 1921; LittD (hon.), L.I. U., 1959; LLD (hon.), Pratt Inst., 1986. Joined Abraham and Straus, Inc., Bklyn., 1922; v.p. Abraham and Straus, Inc., 1930-37, 42-64, sec., 1936-60; former dir. Equitable Life Assurance Soc. U.S., Bklyn. Union Gas Co., Church & Dwight Co., Inc.; past trustee Dime Savs. Bank N.Y.; hon. v.p., former pres. Bahamas Nat. Trust; mem. N.Y. State Bd. Social Welfare, 1954-64; former mem. Temp. N.Y. State Commn. on Edn. Finance. Hon trustee Am. Mus. Nat. History; hon. trustee N.Y. Zool. Soc.; former trustee, v.p. Bklyn. Public Library; former dir. N.Y. World's Fair Corp., 1964-65; bd. dirs., former pres. Am. Friends of Bahamas Found., Inc.; gen. chmn. Prospect Park Centennial, 1966; mem. Mayor's Com. for Cultural Affairs, N.Y.C., 1967; v.p., dir. Bklyn. War Meml., Inc.; dir. emeritus, past treas. Lincoln Center Performing Arts; vice chmn., mem. Bklyn. Sports Center Authority; mem., past pres. Art Commn. City of N.Y.; advisor, former mem. distbn. com. N.Y. Community Trust; mem. adv. bd. Maine Community Fedn., Berkshire Taconic Fedn.; life trustee Coll. of Atlantic, Bar Harbor, Maine; trustee emeritus Wendell Gilley Mus. Served as 2d lt. F.A., AUS, World War I; maj. Ordnance Dept. AUS, World War II. Mem. Bklyn. Inst. Arts and Scis. (pres. 1951-60, trustee 1936-72, hon. trustee 1972—, past chmn. governing com. Bklyn. Mus., hon. trustee, hon. chmn. adv. bd.), Bklyn. C. of C. (past v.p., dir.), Better Bus. Bur. N.Y.C., Downtown Bklyn. Assn. (former pres., dir.). Clubs: Yale (N.Y.C.); Century Assn, Bar Harbor, Pilgrims, Sharon Country. Home: Ore Mine Rd Box 95 RR 1 Lakeville CT 06039 also: Indian Point Mount Desert ME 04660

BLUM, ULRICH CHRISTIAN, economics professor; b. Munich, Fed. Republic of Germany, May 19, 1953; s. Eberhard Peter and Lonny Gabriele (von Gusmann) B.; m. Melanie Pollert, Sept. 18, 1981; 1 child, Elisa-Victoria. Diploma in Econs. and Indsl. Engring., U. Karlsruhe, 1979, doctorate degree, 1982, Habilitation, 1986. Research fellow U. Karlsruhe, Fed. Republic of Germany, 1979-86; prof. Econs. U. Bamberg, Fed. Republic of Germany, 1987—; vis. prof. U. Montreal, 1986-87; cons. in field. Author: Regionale Wirkungen von Infrastrukturinvestitionen, 1982 (Lösch Price of Regional Science 1982), Volkswirtschaftslehre, 1985, 2d edit., 1987, Raumwirkungen des Budgets der Gesetzlichen Rentenversicherung, 1986; contbr. articles to profl. jours. Mem. Regional Sci. Assn., Gesellschaft für Regionalforschung. Home: Truschenhof, 8601 Untermerzbach Federal Republic of Germany Office: Univ of Bamberg, Faculty Social Scis & Econs, PO Box 1549, 8600 Bamberg Federal Republic of Germany

BLUMBERG, ARNOLD, historian, educator; b. Phila., May 9, 1925; s. Louis and Rose Y. (Bleecher) B.; B.S., U. Pa., 1947, M.S., 1948, Ph.D. in European Diplomatic History, 1952; m. Thelma Lillian Alpert, Dec. 26, 1954; children—Raphael David, Eva Rebecca, Michael Seth. Tchr. social studies Phila. Public Schs., 1950-58; faculty Towson State U., Balt., 1958—, prof. history, 1964—; vis. lectr., library cons. Mohawk Valley Community Coll., Utica, N.Y., summers 1963, 64; vis. prof. history U. R.I., summer 1967; researcher public and pvt. archives U.S., Gt. Brit., France, Israel. Bd. mem., historian Congregation Shearith Israel, Balt. Served with U.S. Army, 1943-45. Danforth Found. grantee, 1961; grantee Johnson Fund, Am. Philos. Soc., 1966; ann. research grantee research com. Towson State U., 1963-85. Mem. Am. Hist. Assn. (life), So. Hist. Assn. (life mem. European Div.), Soc. French Hist. Studies, AAUP, Phi Alpha Theta (charter Theta Beta chpt.), DAV (life). Democrat. Editorial cons. publs. including Am. Hist. Rev., Historian, Pacific Coast Hist. Rev.; reviewer, abstracter various jours.; author: Diplomacy of the Austro-Sardinian War of 1859, 1952; Diplomacy of the Mexican Empire, 1863-1867, 71, 87, 2d edit., 1987; A View from Jerusalem, 1849-1858, 1980; Zion before Zionism, 1838-1880, 1985; contbr.

articles to jours. Home: 3901 Glen Ave Baltimore MD 21215 Office: Towson State U Linthicum Hall 119C Baltimore MD 21204

BLUMBERG, BARBARA SALMANSON (MRS. ARNOLD G. BLUMBERG), state housing official; b. Bklyn., Oct. 2, 1927; d. Sam and Mollie (Greenberg) Salmanson; B.A., De Pauw U., 1948; postgrad. New Sch. for Social Research, N.Y.C.; m. Arnold G. Blumberg, June 19, 1949; children—Florence Ellen Schwartz, Martin Jay, Emily Anne. Pub. relations Nate Fein & Co., N.Y.C., 1948-51; free lance, 1960—; councilwoman, North Hempstead, 1975-82; adviser to energy com. N.Y. State Assembly, 1982-84; dir. spl. needs housing Div. Housing and Community Renewal, State of N.Y. Pres., UN Assn. Great Neck, N.Y., 1967-69, chmn. China Study Workshop, 1966-67; pres. Shalom chpt. Hadassah, 1955-57; exec. v.p. Lakeville P.T.A., Great Neck, 1963-65; exec. v.p. Great Neck S. Jr. High Sch., 1965-66; co-chmn. Great Neck UNICEF, 1968-70, mem. speakers bur., 1971—; v.p. Herricks Community Life Center, 1976-77, B'nai B'rith, Lake Success, N.Y.; coordinator, 6th Congl. Dist., N.Y. McGovern for Pres.; bd. dirs. New Democratic Coalition of Nassau, Am. Jewish Congress, Am. Jewish Com., Day Care Council of Nassau County; v.p. Reform Dem. Assn. Great Neck; bd. dirs. Citizen's Sch. Com., Great Neck; mem. platform com. Nassau Dem. Com.; mem. adv. com. to speaker N.Y. State Assembly. Recipient award Anti-Defamation League, New Hyde Park, N.Y., 1975, Alumni award DePauw U., 1977, Hadassah New Life award, 1980. Mem. N.Y. Alumni Club DePauw U. (trustee), North Shore Archeol. Assn. (chmn. study group), Women in Communication, Internat. Platform Assn., L.I. Women's Network (co-convenor), Alpha Lambda Delta. Home: 12 Birch Hill Rd Great Neck NY 11020 Office: HFA 3 Park Ave New York NY 10016

BLUMBERG, BARUCH SAMUEL, research center executive; b. N.Y.C., July 28, 1925; s. Meyer and Ida (Simonoff) B.; m. Jean Liebesman, Apr. 4, 1954; children: Anne, George, Jane, Noah. B.S., Union Coll., Schenectady, 1946; M.D., Columbia U., 1951; Ph.D., Balliol Coll., Oxford U., Eng., 1957; 16 hon. doctoral degrees. Intern, resident Columbia div. Bellevue Hosp., N.Y.C., 1951-53; fellow in medicine Columbia-Presbyn. Med. Ctr., N.Y.C., 1953-55; chief geog. medicine and genetics sect. NIH, Bethesda, Md., 1957-64; assoc. dir. clin. research Fox Chase Cancer Ctr., Phila., 1964-86, v.p. population oncology, 1986—; Univ. prof. medicine and anthropology U. Pa.; George Eastman vis. prof. Balliol Coll., Oxford U., 1983-84; Raman vis. prof., Bangalore, India, 1986; Ashland vis. prof. U. Ky., Lexington, 1986, 87. Contbr. articles to profl. jours. Served to ensign USNR, 1943-46. Recipient Albion O. Berstein, M.D. award Med. Soc. State of N.Y., 1969, Grand Sci. award Phi Lambda Kappa, 1972, Ann. award Eastern Pa. br. Am. Soc. Microbiology, 1972, Passano award Williams & Wilkens Co., 1974, Modern Medicine Disting. Achievement award, 1975, Internat. award Gairdner Found., 1975, Karl Landsteiner Meml. award Am. Assn. Blood Banks, 1975, Nobel prize in physiology or medicine, 1976, Scopus award Am. Friends of Hebrew U., 1977, Strittmatter award Philadelphia County Med. Soc., 1980, Disting. Service award Pa. Med. Soc., 1982, Zubrow award Pa. Hosp., 1986, Achievement award Sammy Davis Jr. Nat. Liver Inst., 1987. Fellow ACP, Royal Coll. Physicians; mem. Nat. Acad. Scis., Assn. Am. Physicians, Am. Soc. Clin. Investigation, Am. Soc. Human Genetics, Am. Assn. Phys. Anthropologists, John Morgan Soc., Chesapeake and Ohio Canal Soc. Clubs: Provincetown Yacht, Atheneum. Office: Fox Chase Cancer Ctr 7701 Burholme Ave Philadelphia PA 19111

BLUMBERG, JULIA BAUM, community leader, educator; b. Hazleton, Pa.; d. Benjamin and Ida Ruth (Lurie) Baum; Ph.B. summa cum laude, Muhlenberg Coll., Allentown, Pa.; postgrad. NYU, Columbia U.; m. Dr. Leo Blumberg, Aug. 9, 1938. Mem. faculty Bethleham (Pa.) Sr. High Sch., dir. placement comml. grads., 1938-46. Life mem. B'nai B'rith Women, organized Bethlehem group, 1938, pres. Bethlehem, 1938-39, pres. Dist. 3, 1945-46, mem. nat. exec. bd., 1957-59, rep. nat. orgn., 1957-59, chmn. nat. vocat. guidance, 1957-59, chmn. dist. 3 Klutznick scholarship award, 1966-69, mem. bd. B'nai B'rith Women of Wilmington, pres. vocational service bd., 1962-64; life mem. Temple Beth Emeth Sisterhood, mem. bd., 1949-59, 70-88; treas. Dist 8, Nat. Fedn. Temple Sisterhoods, 1952-56; mem. nat. exec. bd. nat. fedn., 1953-57; gen. chmn. Dist. 8 conv., Wilmington, 1957; pres. community adv. bd. Hillel Counselorship, U. Del., 1979-88; mem. bd. Wilmington City Fedn. Women's Clubs and Allied Orgns., 1951—, 1st v.p., 1961-63, pres., 1963-65; mem. bd. mgrs. Florence Crittendon Home of Del., 1955-61; mem. Women's div. Brandeis U.; life life mem. Aux. Kutz Home for Aged, also bd. dirs. aux., 1972-88, named Hon. Life Chmn. Bd., 1983; mem. Nat. Commn. Vocational Service, 1957-59, Mayor's Com. for Christmas, Mayor's Com. for UN; mem. bd. UNICEF, 1972-82; mem. steering com. CARE, Inc., 1971-82; mem. Del. Nature Edn. Soc., Inc., 1963-88, Del. Council on Crime and Justice; chmn. bldg. and furniture com., dedication com. Hillel Found. at U. Del., 1963-64, hon. life chmn. community adv. bd. B'nai B'rith Hillel Counselorship, U. Del.; mem. women's div. Jewish Fedn. Del.; mem. bldg. fund com. St. Francis Hosp., 1973; v.p. bd. dirs. Kutz Home Aux. Appointed chmn. survey com. for accreditation Bethlehem (Pa.) Sr. High Sch. Author accrediting guide: The Philosophy and Aims & Objectives of Secondary Education. Mem. Nat. Council Jewish Women (life), Greater Wilmington Fedn. Women's Orgns. (dir. 1965-69, 69-73, 73-77, 77-86, pres. Past Officers Club 1965-67, historian 1973-75, dir. 1975—), Del. Mental Health Assn., Crippled Children and Adults Soc. Del., Hadassah (life), B'nai B'rith Women (life), Phi Sigma Iota. Jewish (life mem., pres. Sisterhood 1952-53, mem. bd. 1970-88, dir. temple 1952-55). Clubs: Widener U. Faculty Wives (hon. life), Wilmington New Century (internat. relations com. 1978-88, edn. com. 1978-86). Home: 1401 Pennsylvania Ave Apt 406 Wilmington DE 19806

BLUMBERG, NATHAN(IEL) BERNARD, journalist, emeritus educator, writer and publisher; b. Denver, Apr. 8, 1922; s. Abraham Moses and Jeannette B.; m. Lynne Stout, June 1946 (div. Feb. 1970); children: Janet Leslie Blumberg Knedlik, Jenifer Lyn Blumberg Loeb, Josephine Laura Blumberg Loewen; m. Barbara Farquhar, July 1973. B.A., U. Colo., 1947, M.A., 1948; D.Phil. (Rhodes scholar), Oxford (Eng.) U., 1950. Reporter Denver Post, 1947-48; assoc. editor Lincoln (Nebr.) Star, 1950-53; asst. to editor Ashland (Nebr.) Gazette, 1954-55; asst. city editor Washington Post and Times Herald, 1956; from asst. prof. to assoc. prof. journalism U. Nebr., 1950-55; asso. prof. journalism Mich. State U., 1955-56; dean, prof. Sch. Journalism, U. Mont., 1956-68, prof. journalism, 1968-78, prof. emeritus, 1978—; pub. Wood FIRE Ashes Press, 1981—; vis. prof. Pa. State U., 1964, Northwestern U., 1966-67, U. Calif., Berkeley, 1970; Dept. State specialist in Thailand, 1961, in Trinidad, Guyana, Surinam and Jamaica, 1964. Author: One-Party Press?, 1954; The Afternoon of March 30: A Contemporary Historical Novel, 1984, also articles in mags. and jours.; co-editor: A Century of Montana Journalism, 1971; editor: The Mansfield Lectures in International Relations, Vols. I and II, 1979; founder: Mont. Journalism Rev, 1958—. Served with arty. U.S. Army, 1943-46. Decorated Bronze Star medal. Mem. Assn. Am. Rhodes Scholars, Nat. Conf. Editorial Writers, Kappa Tau Alpha (nat. pres. 1969-70). Home: PO Box 99 Big Fork MT 59911

BLUMBERG, PHILIP FLAYDERMAN, real estate developer; b. Miami, Fla., Nov. 10, 1957; s. David and Lee (Dickens) B.; m. Lina Esther Waingortin, Apr. 13, 1986. BBA, U. N.C., 1979; MBA, Harvard U., 1983. Mng. ptnr. Banyan Reach ltd., Cutler Ridge, Fla., 1979; pres. Real Data Systems, Inc., Miami, Fla., 1984, Fort Dallas Assocs., Miami, 1985, Am. Ventures Corp., Miami, 1979—; bd. dirs. Profl. Savs. Bank, Coral Gables, Fla., chmn. exam. com., 1985—. Trustee Colony Performing Arts Theater, Miami Beach, 1985; bd. advs. New World Sch. Arts, Miami, 1985; mem. U. Miami Venture Council, Coral Gables, 1984; co-chmn. Japan-Miami Bus. Council, 1987—; trustee Beacon Council, 1988—. Clubs: City (founding mem.), Bankers, Harvard (Miami). Home: 2430 Brickell Ave Apt 306-A Miami FL 33129 Office: Am Ventures Corp 1443 S Miami Ave Miami FL 33130

BLUME, MARSHALL EDWARD, finance educator; b. Chgo., Mar. 31, 1941; s. Marshall Edward Blume and Helen Corliss (Frank) Gilbert; m. Loretta Ryan, June 25, 1966; children—Christopher, Caroline, Catherine. S.B., Trinity Coll., Hartford, Conn., 1963; M.B.A., U. Chgo., 1965, Ph.D., 1968; M.A. (hon.), U. Pa., 1970. Lectr. applied math. Grad. Sch. Bus., U. Chgo., 1966, instr. bus. fin. and applied math., 1967; lectr. fin. U. Pa., Phila., 1967, asst. prof., 1968-70, assoc. prof., 1970-74, prof., 1974-78, Howard Butcher prof., 1978—, chmn. dept., 1982-86, assoc. dir. Rodney White Ctr., 1978-86; dir. Rodney White Ctr., 1986—; prof. fin. European Inst., Brussels, 1975-76, New U. Lisbon, Portugal, 1982; vis. prof. Stockholm Sch., spring 1976, U. Brussels, 1975. Author: Mutual Funds and Other Institutional Investors, 1970; The Changing Role of the Individual Investor, 1978; The Structure and Reform of the U.S. Tax System, 1985; editor: Encyclopedia of Investments, 1982; The Complete Guide to Investment Opportunities, 1984; assoc. editor Jour. Fin. and Quantitative Analysis, 1967-76, Jour. Fin. Econs., 1976-81, Jour. of Portfolio Mgmt., 1985—; mng. editor Jour. Fin., 1977-80, assoc. editor, 1985—. Contbr. articles to profl. publs. Trustee Trinity Coll., Hartford, Conn., 1980-86. Mem. Am. Fin. Assn. (officer 1977-80), Am. Econs. Assn. Home: 204 Woodstock Rd Villanova PA 19085 Office: U Pa White Ctr for Fin Research 3250 Steinberg Hall Philadelphia PA 19104

BLUMENFELD, THEODORE, museum director, engineer; b. Tiganasi, Tassy, Romania, Aug. 28, 1915; s. Adolf and Fani (Horowitz) B.; m. Madeleine Blumenfeld Altain, Dec. 22, 1942. Diplomate in Engring., Politechnia, Tassy, 1938. Tchr. Jewish Secondary Sch., Tassy, 1940-42; engr. Romanian Railway, Tassy, 1942-44, 1st engr., 1944-49; pro-rector Railway Inst., Bucharest, Romania, 1949-51; vice minister Dept. Transport and Communications, Bucharest, 1951-61, permanent undersec., 1961-76; pres., dir. The Jewish Mus., Bucharest, 1976—. Author: The Scientific Organization of the Construction of the Banages Roads and Railway, 1950. Recipient numerous govtl. awards. Home: Bul Alex J Cuza ar 10, 78131 Bucharest Romania Office: Comunictatea Erreibr, Str Lapusna ar 9-11, Bucharest Romania

BLUMENTHAL, MICHAEL, ophthalmologist; b. Tiberias, Israel, Nov. 11, 1935; s. Zvi Hans and Ruth (Erlich) B.; m. Naomi Grönbaum; children: Daria, Uri, Boaz. Lectr. Hadassah Med. Sch., Jerusalem, 1966-68; sr. lectr. Hadassah Med. Sch., 1972-74; assoc. prof. faculty health scis. Ben Gurion U. Negev. Beer-Sheba, Israel, 1974-76; assoc. prof. Tel Aviv U., 1977—, head of ophthamology dept., 1984, prof. ophthamology, 1985; head of eye care Fgn. Aid to Africa Ministry Fgn. Affairs, Malawi, 1964, Dar-es-Salaam, Tanzania, 1964-65. Editor in chief The Eye: The Journal of the Israeli Ophthalmol. Soc., 1985. Cons. Ministry of Health, Jerusalem. Ophthalmology fellow Hadassah Med. Sch., 1968-70; Am. Coll. Surgeons grant, San Francisco, 1969, XXI Internat. Congress Ophthalmology, Mex., 1970, Internat. Congress Regional Ophthalmology, Can., 1970, Am. Acad. grant, 1975. Mem. Israeli Eye Soc., Internat. Intraocular Lens Club, Am. Intraocular Implant Soc., European Intraocular Implant Lens Council (present sec.), French Ophthalmology Soc. Home: 2 Haegoz St, Ramat Efal 52960, Israel

BLUMENTHAL, W. MICHAEL, manufacturing company executive, former secretary Treasury; b. 1926. BS, U. Calif., Berkeley, 1951; MA, MPA, Princeton U., 1953, PhD, 1956. Research assoc. Princeton U., 1954-57; v.p., also bd. dirs. Crown Cork Internat. Corp., 1957-61; dep. asst. sec. for econ. affairs Dept. State, 1961; apptd. Pres.'s dep. spl. rep. for trade negotiations with rank of ambassador 1963-67; pres. Bendix Internat., 1967-70; also bd. dirs. Bendix Corp., 1967-77, vice chmn., 1970-71, pres., chief operating officer, 1971-72, chmn., pres., chief exec. officer, 1972-77; sec. of Treasury Washington, 1977-79; also bd. dirs. UNISYS Corp. (formerly Burroughs Corp.), Detroit, 1979—; vice chmn., chief exec. officer Unisys Corp. (formerly Burroughs Corp.), Detroit, 1980-81, chmn., chief exec. officer, 1981—; bd. dirs. Tenneco, Inc., Pillsbury Co., Chem. N.Y. Corp. and subs. Chem. Bank. Bd. dirs. Detroit Renaissance, New Detroit, Detroit Symphony Orch.; v.p., bd. dirs. Detroit Area council Boy Scouts Am.; v.p., bd. dirs., mem. exec. com. United Found. Detroit. Mem. Bus. Council, Bus. Roundtable, Am. Econ. Assn., Rockefeller Found. (trustee). Club: Economic of Detroit (bd. dirs.). Office: Unisys Corp PO Box 418 Detroit MI 48232

BLUMROSEN, RUTH GERBER, lawyer, educator, arbitrator; b. N.Y.C., Mar. 7, 1927; d. Lipman Samuel and Dorothy (Finklebrand) Gerber; m. Alfred William Blumrosen, July 3, 1952; children—Steven Marshall, Alexander B. B.A. in Econs., U. Mich., 1947, J.D., 1953. Bar: Mich. 1953, U.S. Supreme Ct. 1967, U.S. Ct. Appeals (3d cir.). Sole practice, Detroit, 1953-55; cons. civil rights litigation, 1958-65; acting chief advice and analyses, acting dir. compliance EEOC, Washington, 1965; asst. dean Howard U., Washington, 1965-67; consul to chmn. EEOC, 1979-80; expert EEO HHS, Washington, 1980-81; assoc. prof. Grad. Sch. Mgmt., Rutgers U., Newark, 1972-87. Adviser, N.J. Commn. on Sex Discrimination in the Statutes, 1983—. Mem. ABA, Fed. Bar Assn., Indsl. Relations Research Assn., Nat. Com. Pay Equity. Author: (with A. Blumrosen) Layoff or Worksharing: The Civil Rights Act of 1964 in the Recession of 1975; The Duty to Plan for Fair Employment Revisited: Worksharing in Hard Times, 1975; Wage Discrimination, Job Segregation and Title VII of Civil Rights Act of 1964, 1979; Wage Discrimination and Job Segregation: The Survival of a Theory, 1980; An Analysis of Wage Discrimination in N.J. State Service, 1983; Worksharing, STC and Affirmative Action in Shorttime Compensation: A Formula for Work-sharing; Remedies for Wage Discrimination., 1987. Home: 54 Riverside Dr New York NY 10024

BLUNDELL, WILLIAM RICHARD C., electric company executive; b. Montreal, Apr. 13, 1927; s. Richard C. and Did Aileen (Payne) B.; m. Monique Audet, Mar. 20, 1959; children: Richard, Emily, Michelle, Louise. B.A.Sc., U. Toronto, 1949. Registered profl. engr., Ont. Sales engr. Can. Gen. Electric Co., Toronto, 1949-51, travelling auditor, 1951, various fin. positions, 1951-66, treas., 1966-68, v.p.-fin., 1968-70, v.p., exec. consumer div., 1970-72; v.p., exec. apparatus div. Can. Gen. Electric Co., Lachine, Que., 1972-79; pres., chief exec. officer Camco Inc., Weston, Ont., 1979-83; pres., chief operating officer Can. Gen. Electric Co. Ltd., Toronto, 1983-84; chmn., chief exec. officer Gen. Electric Can. Inc., 1985—; bd. dirs. Alcan Aluminium Ltd. Home: 45 Stratheden Rd, Toronto, ON Canada M4N 1E5 Office: Gen Electric Can Inc, 2300 Meadowood Blvd, Mississauga, ON Canada L5N 5P9

BLUNK, FORREST STEWART, lawyer; b. Doniphan, Mo., July 22, 1913; s. Forest Stanley and Margaret Anna (Stewart) B.; m. Mary Williams, July 10, 1971; children—Scott Stewart, Sally Jo. B.A., U. Mo., 1936; J.D., U. Wyo., 1940. Bar: Ill. bar 1946, Colo. bar 1953. Asso. firm Vogel & Bunge, Chgo., 1946-50; assoc. January & Yegge, Denver, 1953-55; ptnr. Blunk and Johnson, Denver, 1955—; pres., dir. Williams Land & Livestock Co., Tie Siding, Wyo. Served with AUS, 1941-46, ETO. Mem. Fed., Am., Ill., Wyo., Colo., 5th Dist., 10th Circuit bar assns., Colo. Def. Bar Assn. (pres. 1969-70), Lawyer-Pilots Bar Assn., Internat. Assn. Ins. Counsel, Denver Bar, Am. Bd. Trial Advs. (pres. Colo. chpt. 1974-75, nat. sec. 1975-76), Legal Club Chgo. Republican. Clubs: Masons, Elks, Rotary, Ft. Collins Country, Denver Athletic. Home: 2909 Terry Lake Rd Fort Collins CO 80524 Office: 2696 S Colorado Blvd Suite 595 Denver CO 80222

BLUNT, PETER, organizational psychologist; b. Athens, Greece, Feb. 19, 1948; came to Australia, 1976, naturalized; s. Harold William and Elly (Sfalangacos) B.; m. Marla Pauline Skartvedt, Apr. 1, 1973. B.A., U. Natal, Durban, South Africa, 1969, B.A. with honours, 1970; M.Sc., U. Bath, Eng., 1980. Lectr. U. Nairobi, Kenya, 1973-75; lectr. U. Adelaide, Australia, 1976-80, sr. lectr. mgmt., 1981—; vis. sr. research fellow U. Zambia, Lusaka, 1982-84; assoc. prof., dean faculty mgmt. and adminstrv. study, U. Brunei, 1986—; cons. to pub. and pvt. orgns., Eng., Africa, Australia. Author: Organizational Theory and Behaviour: An African Perspective, 1983; Personnel Management in Africa, 1985; human resource mgmt., 1986. Internat. cons. editor Jour. Applied Behavioural Sci., 1982—. Contbr. articles to profl. and sci. jours. Mem. African Studies Assn. of Australia and the Pacific, Am. Acad. Mgmt. Avocations: squash; rugby football; chess; bridge; game viewing. Office: U Brunei, Faculty Management, Bandar Seri Begawan Brunei

BLUTTER, JOAN WERNICK, interior designer; b. London, July 6, 1929; naturalized, 1948; d. Samuel and Bertha (Cohn) Wernick; m. Melvyn Blutter, Oct. 29, 1948; 1 child, Janet Lesley. Student, Northwestern U., 1944. Pres. Blutter Shiff Design Group, Chgo., 1955—; ptnr. Mel Blutter Co., Chgo.; partner Designers Collaborative, San Francisco, 1975—; design cons. Reed, Ltd., Toronto, Can., Exec. House Ltd., Chgo.; bd. dirs. Fashion Group. Contbr.: articles to Interior Design; others. bd. dirs. United Cerebral Palsy. Fellow Am. Soc. Interior Designers (past pres. Ill. chpt., past nat. sec., nat. chmn. industry 1978-79, nat. chmn. Design Interest program 1981-82, recipient Gold Key award, design award, Presdl. citation, Designer of Year 1979); mem. Nat. Soc. Interior Design (past chpt. pres., sec., bd. chmn.), LWV, Nat. Home Fashions League, Mchts. and Mfrs. Club, Art Inst. Chgo., Mus. Contemporary Art. Home: 2801 N Sheridan Rd Chicago IL 60657 Office: 1648 Merchandise Mart Chicago IL 60654 also: 85 Blvd Berthier, Paris 17 France

BLYTHE, DAVID ARMSTRONG, advertising executive; b. Birkenhead, Cheshire, Eng., Nov. 30, 1935; s. Joseph and May Armstrong (Smith) B.; m. Priscilla Alexandra Bird, June 21, 1958; children: Susan Alexandra, Helen Gillian. M.CAM., Birkenhead Sch., 1945-52. Dir. Royds McCann, Manchester, Eng., 1963-68; mng. dir. Brunnings, Manchester, 1968-74; dep. mng. dir. Bowden Dyble Hayes & Ptnrs., Manchester, 1974—. Served as bombadier Royal Arty., 1954-56. Fellow Inst. Practitioners in Advt. (council 1986—); mem. Communications, Advt. and Mktg. Assn. (chmn. N.W. chpt. 1986-87), Assn. No. Advt. Agys. (chmn. Manchester 1983-87). Conservative. Mem. Ch. of England. Club: First Friday (Manchester) (v.p. 1984-87). Office: Bowden Dyble Hayes & Ptnrs, Oakland House Talbot Rd, Manchester M16 0AX, England

BLYTHE, JAMES DAVID, II, lawyer; b. Indpls., Oct. 20, 1940; s. James David and Marjorie M. (Horne) B.; m. Sara S. Frantz, Nov. 21, 1974; 1 child, Amanda Renee. BS, Butler U., 1962; JD, Ind. U., 1966; diploma Ct. Practice Inst., 1974. Bar: Ind. 1966, U.S. Dist. Ct. (so. dist.) Ind. 1966. U.S. Congressional staff asst., 1965-69, also majority atty. Ind. Ho. of Reps., 1967, 69; dep. prosecutor Marion County Prosecutor's Office, 1966, 68; travel agt. Skyline Travel, Inc., 1972-87; sole practice, Indpls., 1966—; assoc. Butler, Brown & Blythe, 1984—; mem. com. on character and fitness Ind. Supreme Ct., 1974—; host TV show Ask a Lawyer, 1977-79. Bd. dirs. Marion County chpt. Am. Cancer Soc., 1971-76, pres., 1975-76.; Ind. chmn. West Indies Ambassador Exchange, Jaycees, 1972-73; bd. dirs. Cen. Ind. council Boy Scouts Am., 1969-72, exec. com., 1969-71, bd. dirs. Crossroads of Am. council, 1972-87, exec. com., 1976-84, pres., 1979-81; mem. lawyers fund raising com. Indpls. Mus. Art, 1973-74; co-membership chmn. Friends of Channel 20, 1975; bd. dirs. Salvation Army, 1976—, vice chmn., 1986, chmn., 1987, 88. Recipient cert. of Merit Am. Cancer Soc., 1971, 74-75, Outstanding Service award Indpls. br. Am. Cancer Soc., 1972-73, Richard E. Rowland award Jaycees, 1971-72, Stanley K. Lacy Meml. award Jaycees, 1974, Disting. Service award Jaycees, 1974, Silver Beaver award Boy Scouts Am., 1981, commendation Gov. State of Ind., 1973; named Man of Yr., Am. Cancer Soc., 1974; Jim Blythe Day named in his honor, Mayor of Indpls., 1976; named Sagamore of the Wabash, 1981. Mem. Indpls. Bar Assn. (bd. mgrs. 1978-81, chmn. grievance com. 1980-88), Kappa Sigma, Phi Delta Phi. Republican. Presbyterian. Lodge: Kiwanis (v.p. Indpls. 1986-87, pres. 1987, 88). Home: 11028 Lakeshore Dr E Carmel IN 46032 Office: 155 E Market St Suite 301 Indianapolis IN 46204

BO, KETIL, productivity support executive; b. Valle, Norway, Mar. 20, 1940; s. Asmund and Ingeborg (Aamli) B.; m. Aasta Berntsen, July 3, 1965; children—Bjornar, Bjarte. Tchr., Kristiansand, 1962; Master, U. Trondheim, 1972, Ph.D., 1983. Tchr. secondary sch., Trondheim, 1966-70; researcher Runit, Trondheim, 1970-72, group leader, 1972-77, 78-80; vis. prof. So. Meth. U., Dallas, 1977-78; Cad/Cam coordinator SINTEF, Trondheim, 1980-82; pres. SIU (Found for Indsl. Devel.) Trondheim, 1982-85; pres. Productivity Support AS, 1985-88, PS Partner A/S, 1988—; internat. program chmn. Eurographics 78, Bologna, Italy, 1978; conf. chmn. IFIP WG.5.2. Work Conf., 1982, CAD, 1984-87; internat. program chmn. Eurographics 84, Copenhagen, 1984, 86, Cape '86. Author: Grafisk Databehandling, 1975; contbr. articles to profl. jours.; guest editor IEEE Computer Jour., 1982; editor; CAD System Framework, 1983. Served to lt., Norwegian Army, 1962-64. Specialist Exchange grantee, Hungary/Norway, 1976, Italy/Norway, 1978; NTNF grantee, 1979-82; BMFT grantee, 1980-82. Office: PO Box 2865, Trondheim 7001, Norway

BOALT, GUNNAR RUDOLF, sociologist, educator; b. Ljustero, Sweden, Aug. 26, 1910; s. Anton and Ruda (Brodin) B.; Ph.D., U. Stockholm, 1947; m. I. Carin Akerman, June 1, 1935; children—Siv Boalt Boethius, Birgitta Boalt Alexius, Kaj Boalt Akerman, Ake, Arne; m. Pian Halden, Aug. 8, 1957; 1 dau., Margareta; m. Bibbi Petterson, Apr. 27, 1974. Mem. faculty U. Stockholm, 1948—, prof. sociology, 1954-77, dean social sci. faculty, 1965-71; adj. prof. So. Ill. U., Carbondale, 1967. Chmn. Union Social Work, 1956-72; mem. sci. council Royal Social Bd., 1963-78. Author: Family and Marriage, 1965; Educational Research, 1968; The Sociology of Research, 1969; Universities and Research, 1970; European Orders of Chivalry, 1971; Resources and Production of University Departments, 1971; The Academic Pattern, 1972; Communication and Communication Barriers in Sociology, 1975; Sociologists in Search of their Intellectual Domain, 1978; Professionalization and Democratization, 1980; Political Value Patterns and Parties in Sweden, 1981; The Political Process, 1983; 1981; Competing Belief Systems, 1983. Office: 160B Fiskartorpsvagen, 10691 Stockholm Sweden

BOAND, CHARLES WILBUR, lawyer; b. Bates County, Mo., Aug. 19, 1908; s. Albert and Edith Nadine (Pipes) B.; m. Phoebe Bard, Aug. 2, 1980; children: Bard, Barbara. AA, Jr. Coll. Kansas City; JD summa cum laude, U. Mo., Kansas City; MBA, LLB cum laude, U. Chgo. Bar: Mo. 1931, D.C. 1936, Ill. 1937, U.S. Supreme Ct. 1935, U.S. Ct. Appeals (1st, 2d, 5th, 6th, 7th, 9th, 10th, 11th and D.C. cirs.), trial bar of U.S. Dist. Ct. (no. dist.) Ill. Assoc. Moore & Fitch, St. Louis, 1933; atty. Gen. Counsel's Office, U.S. Treasury Dept., 1933-36; assoc. Wilson & McIlvaine, 1937-42, ptnr., 1945-88, chmn. exec. com., 1974-86, sr. ptnr., 1982-88, spl. counsel, 1988—; mem. Nat. Conf. Lawyers and CPA's, 1976-82. Mem. grad. sch. bus. council U. Chgo., 1961-68, citizens bd., vis. com. to libraries, 1985—; trustee Muskingum Coll., 1965-79; stated clk. Presbyn. Ch. Barrington, 1962-65. Served as officer USNR, 1942-45, lt. comdr. Res. (ret.). Mem. ABA, Ill. Bar Assn. (chmn. exec. com. corp. securities law sect. 1954-56), Chgo. Bar Assn. (chmn. com. corp. law 1963-64), Fed. Bar Assn., 7th Circuit Bar Assn., U. Chgo. Alumni Assn. (pres. 1975-80, alumni cabinet 1964-70, 72-80, v.p. 1973-74, 1st Alumni Disting. Service award 1981), U. Chgo. Law Sch. Alumni Assn. (pres. 1968-70, bd. dirs. 1950-72), Order of Coif, Beta Gamma Sigma, Sigma Chi, Phi Alpha Delta. Clubs: Chgo., Mid-Am., Met., Law, Legal (Chgo.); Barrington Hills (Ill.) Country (bd. dirs. 1947-55); Los Caballeros Golf (Ariz.). Home: 250 W County Line Rd PO Box 567 Barrington Hills IL 60011 Office: 135 S LaSalle St Chicago IL 60603

BOARDMAN, ROSANNE VIRGINIA, military science executive; b. Twin Falls, Idaho, Oct. 4, 1946; d. Gordon Ross and Garnet Othalia (Peterson) Tobin; m. Lowell Jay Boardman, May 12, 1973. BA cum laude, Occidental Coll., 1968; MA with honors, Columbia U., 1969; postgrad., U. Calif., Irvine, 1971-72, U. Calif., Santa Barbara, 1973-74. Cert. jr. coll. tchr., Calif., cert. secondary tchg., Calif. Instr. U. Calif., Irvine, 1971-72, Ventura (Calif.) Community Coll., 1973-77; engring. analyst John J. McMullen Co., Ventura, 1978-80; sr. logistics specialist Raytheon Co., Ventura, 1977-78, 80-83; civilian tech. writer, editor USN, Port Hueneme, Calif., 1983-84, civilian logistics mgr., 1984—. Author numerous manuals and logistics guides. Internat. fellow Occidental Coll., 1967; recipient Outstanding Performance award Naval Ship Weapon Systems Engring. Sta., 1985, 86. Mem. Soc. Logistics Engrs., Phi Beta Kappa.

BOARDMAN, BARON THOMAS GRAY, banker; b. Jan. 12, 1919; s. John Clayton and Janet (Houston) B.; m. Norah Mary Deirdre Gough, 1948; 3 children. Grad., Bromsgrove Sch.; solicitor, 1947. Served Northants Yeomanry, 1939-45, commdr., 1956; M.P. Leicester Leicester SW, 1967-74, Leicester S., 1974; minister for industry 1972-74; chief sec. to Treasury, 1974; joint hon. treas. Conservative Party, 1981-82; chmn. Nat. Westminster Bank, 1983—; chmn. Chamberlain Phipps Ltd., 1958-72, The Steetly Co. Ltd., 1978-83; vice-chmn. Allied Breweries Ltd., 1975-76. High Sheriff, Northamptonshire, 1978, DL, 1977—. Decorated MC 1944, TD 1952. Mem. Assn. Brit. C. of C. (pres. 1977-80), Exec. Assn. Cons. Peers. Club: Cavalry and Guards. Home: 29 Tufton Court, Tufton St, London SW1P 3QH, England also: The Manor House, Welford, Northamptonshire England *

BOAZ, NOEL THOMAS, museum director; b. Martinsville, Va., Feb. 8, 1952; s. Thalma Noel and Elena More Anson (Taylor) B.; m. Dorothy Dechant, June 17, 1978. B.A., U. Va., 1973; M.A., U. Calif.-Berkeley, 1974, Ph.D. in Phys. Anthropology, 1977. Sr. mus. scientist (paleoanthropology) U. Calif.-Berkeley, 1975-77; lectr. anthropology UCLA, 1977-78; adj. asst. prof. anatomy N.Y. U. Sch. Medicine, 1978-81, asst. prof. anthropology,

1978-84; dir. Va. Mus. Natural History, 1984—; dir. Internat. Sahabi Research Project, 1976—, Semliki Research Expdn., 1982—, research assoc. prof. biology U. Va., 1986—. Sr. editor Neogene Paleontology and Geology of Sahabi, Libya, 1987; contbr. articles to profl. jours. Apptd. Va. Commn. Historic Landmarks, 1987. NSF grantee, 1976, 1980-82, 85-86, 86—; Nat. Geog. Soc. grantee, 1978, 84, 86—; Presdl. fellow, 1981; Wenner-Gren Found. grantee, 1982, 85; Fulbright sr. research fellow, Zaire, 1983-84; L.S.B. Leakey Found. grantee, 1984-85, 86—. Mem. Am. Assn. Phys. Anthropologists, Am. Anthrop. Assn., AAAS, Royal Anthrop. Inst., Soc. Vertebrate Paleontology, Am. Assn. Mus., Internat. Council. Mus., Explorers Club. Democrat. Episcopalian. Office: Va Mus Natural History 1001 Douglas Ave Martinsville VA 24115

BOCCHINO, ROBERT LOUIS, marketing communications consultant, actor; b. Phila., May 28, 1936; s. Daniel and Gertrude Rita (LaBattaglia) B.; student Fordham U., 1959-60; B.A., Temple U., 1964, M.B.A., 1973; m. Nancy Lee Keeler, Dec. 20, 1969; children—Robert Louis, Steven Robert. Gen. assignment reporter, news writer Westinghouse Broadcasting Co., Phila.; prin. Robert L. Bocchino, exec. communications cons., Haverford, Pa., 1973—; freelance TV, comml. and movie actor bicentennial prodns. Independence, 1975, Adams Chronicles, 1976; producer, announcer (radio, TV spots) Bartram's Garden, 1984—, Woodford Mansion, 1986—. Past mem. energy adv. com., econ. adv. com. PENJERDEL; pres., treas. Mansard House Condominium Assn., Haverford, Pa., 1981-82; mem. The N.Y. Pub. Library Mus. of Broadcasting; bd. dirs. Main Line YMCA, Ardmore, Pa., 1980. Mem. Greater Phila. C. of C. (life mem. Hall of Fame; awards 1978, 79), Screen Actors Guild (N.Y. local on-camera comml. performers com., N.Y. nat. telecommunications com.), AFTRA, Phila. Orch. Assn., Franklin Inst., Independence Nat. Hist. Park, Nat. Trust for Hist. Preservation, Nat. Acad. TV Arts and Scis. (membership com. N.Y. chpt.), Phila. Mus. Art, John Bartram Assn. (bd. dirs., past chmn. mktg./communications com., 1986), Haverford Civic Assn. Club: Vesper. Office: PO Box 99 Haverford PA 19041

BOCHMANN, KLAUS WALTER, linguist, educator; b. Dresden, Saxony, Germany, June 8, 1939; s. Walter Ernst and Margarete Ida (Kaule) B.; m. Renate Erika Krüger; children: Martin, Benjamin. Diploma in romance philology, U. Karl Marx, Leipzig, German Dem. Republic, 1962, PhD, 1967, D of Philos. Sci., 1976. Sci. asst. U. Karl Marx, 1962-69, asst. prof. romance linguistics, 1972-78, full prof. dept. theoretical and applied linguistics, 1978—, dir. research, 1981-85, dir. dept. romance linguistics, 1985—; asst. prof. dept. linguistics and lit. U. Martin Luther Halle, Saale, German Dem. Republic, 1969-72, vice dir. research, 1969-72; pres. romanistics com. German Dem. Republic, 1979—. Author: Romanian Sociopolitic Vocabulary, 1979, (with others) Romanian Grammar, 1986, Minority Languages in France, Spain and Italy, 1987; editor: Sociolinguistic Aspects of Romanian, 1980, also various projects Coll. Sociolinguistics Studies; co-editor: Beiträge for romanischen Philologie, 1986—. Fellow Soc. Italian Linguistics, Internat. Assn. Catalan Linguistics and Lit.; mem. European Ctr. Research in Social Scis. (co-dir. projects 1985—). Office: U Karl Marx, Karl Marx Platz, 7010 Leipzig German Democratic Republic

BOCKELIE, TORE HELSETH, management consulting company executive; b. Tromsø, Norway, Feb. 1, 1940; s. Thorleif Aug and Gunnvor (Helseth) B.; m. Jorunn Wahlberg, Aug. 3, 1963; children: Kristin, Marianne. Exam artium, Tromsø Off. Høgre Alm. Skole, 1960; cand mag., U. Oslo, 1966, mag. art, 1969. Student advisor, ednl. cons. U. Oslo, 1966-68, asst. dir. personnel, 1969-74; dir. personnel Collett-Marwell Hauge A/S, Asker, Norway, 1974-81, Norconsult, Sandvika, Norway, 1981-87; mng. dir. Norconsult/ISOT A/S, Sandvika, Norway, 1987—; sr. mgmt. advisor NPC Consult, 1988—. Editor NO Newsletter, 1981-87. Bd. dirs. Nat. Fedn. Employers, 1977-81, Peoples U., Asker, 1978—, Com. of Environ., 1978-85. Mem. Norwegian Inst. Personnel Adminstrn., Norwegian Ctr. Personnel Devel. Office: Norconsult/ISOT, Kiorboveien 20, 1300 Sandvika Norway

BOCKELMAN, JOHN RICHARD, lawyer; b. Chgo., Aug. 8, 1925; s. Carl August and Mary (Ritchie) B. Student, U. Wis., 1943-44, Northwestern U., 1944-45, Harvard U., 1945, U. Hawaii, 1946; B.S. in Bus. Adminstrn, Northwestern U., 1946; M.A. in Econs, U. Chgo., 1949, J.D., 1951. Bar: Ill. 1951. Atty.-advisor Chgo. ops. office AEC, 1951-52; asso. firm Schradzke, Gould & Ratner, Chgo., 1952-57, Brown, Dashow & Langeluttig, Chgo., 1957-59, Antonow & Weissbourd, Chgo., 1959-61; partner firm Burton, Isaacs, Bockelman & Miller, Chgo., 1961-69; individual practice law Chgo., 1970—; prof. bus. law Ill. Inst. Tech., Chgo., 1950-82; lectr. econs. DePaul U., Chgo., 1952-53; Beale Travel Service, Inc; dir., sec. Arlington Engring. Co.; dir., v.p. Universal Distbrs., Inc. Pres. 1212 Lake Shore Dr. Condo Assn. Served with USNR, 1943-46. Mem. Am. Bar Assn., Ill. Bar Assn., Chgo. Bar Assn., Cath. Lawyers Guild Chgo., Phi Delta Theta. Clubs: Lake Point Tower (Chgo.), Barclay Ltd. (Chgo.), Whitehall (Chgo.), Internat. (Chgo.); Anvil (East Dundee, Ill.). Home: 1212 Lake Shore Dr Chicago IL 60610 Office: Suite 808 104 South Michigan Ave Chicago IL 60603

BOCKIAN, JAMES BERNARD, computer systems executive; b. Jersey City, Sept. 16, 1936; s. Abraham and Evelyn (Skner) B.; m. Donna M. Hastings; children: Vivian Shifra, Adrian Adena, Lillian Tova. B.A., Columbia U., 1953; M.Pub. Adminstrn., U. Mich., 1955; M.A., Yale U., 1957. Vice-consul, 3d sec. Embassy, Dept. State, Washington and abroad, 1957-61; sr. systems analyst J.C. Penney Co., N.Y.C., 1961-67; mgr. systems services, head dept. systems projects adminstrn. McDonnell Douglas Automation Co., East Orange, N.J., 1967-76; prin. James B. Bockian & Assocs., Inc., Morristown, N.J., 1976—; dir. info. systems Comml. Computer Systems, Inc., Norwalk, Conn., 1976-80; v.p. mgmt. info. systems Thomas Cook, Inc., 1980-83, exec. cons. to Thomas Cook Group; lectr. in field. Grad. fellow Yale U., 1957. Mem. Internat. Assn. Cybernetics, Assn. Computing Machinery, Data Processing Mgmt. Assn., Am. Mgmt. Assn., Systems and Procedures Assn. Democrat. Jewish. Clubs: Yale (N.Y.); Royal Danish Yacht (Copenhagen). Author: Management Manual for Systems Development Projects; Project Management for Systems Development, 1979; AT&T User Guide to Information Systems Development, 1980. Contbr. treatises and articles to profl. publs. Home: 26 Farmhouse Ln Morristown NJ 07960 Office: Olde Forge E Suite 26-5B Morristown NJ 07960

BOCKOVEN, DONALD NORMAN, JR., engineer; b. Dover, N.J., July 3, 1959; s. Donald Norman Sr. and Kathleen Regina (Armitage) B.; m. Laura Ann Shortall, May 30, 1981; 1 child, Donald Norman Bockoven III. B of Engring., Stevens Inst. Tech., 1981; postgrad., Villanova U., 1984-85. Engr. E.I. DuPont, Newark, Del., 1981-83; devel. engr. E.I. DuPont, Wilmington, Del., 1983-85; contractor liaison engr. E.I. DuPont, Zoetermeer, The Netherlands, 1985-87; field liaison engr. E.I. DuPont, Contern, Luxembourg, 1987—. Coach Am. Baseball Fedn., Wassenaar, The Netherlands, 1986-87. Recipient Outstanding Student Participation N.J. Soc. Profl. Engrs., Newark, 1981. Mem. Am. Soc. Mech. Engrs. Republican. Home: 51 Rue Henri Entringer, 1467 Howald Luxembourg Office: EI DuPont de Nemours SA, L2984 Luxembourg Luxembourg also: 37 Mt View Ave Long Valley NJ 07853

BODDEN, JAMES MANOAH, II, investment consultant; b. Port Arthur, Tex., Nov. 15, 1951; s. James Manoah and Dorothy Mae (Foreman) B.; m. Lana Arline Jackson, May 1, 1981; children—James Manoah, III, Natasha Arline. A.A.S. in Banking, Internat. Coll. Cayman Islands, 1976, B.A. in Bus. and Econs., 1976. Sr. cert. valuer; registered property mgr. Mgr. Bodden Motors, Ltd., Grand Cayman, 1969-73; asst. mgr. J.M. Bodden & Co. Ltd., Grand Cayman, 1973-77; v.p. J.M. Bodden & Son Internat. Ltd., Grand Cayman, 1977-81; pres., chmn. bd. Internat. Fin. Cons., Ltd., Grand Cayman, 1981-83; pres., mng. dir. Select Internat. Properties, Ltd., 1983—. Founding mem. Jr. C. of C. Cayman Islands, 1971; mem. Cayman Islands Tourism Adv. Bd., 1979. Mem. Ind. Cons. Am., Cayman Islands Real Estate Assn. (founding mem., v.p. 1987—) Internat. Middle East Assn., Internat. Orgn. Real Estate Appraisers, Internat. Inst. (internat. mem.). Office: PO Box 499, Grand Cayman Islands British West Indies

BODDIE, DON O'MAR, recording company executive, producer, recording artist; b. St. Louis, Nov. 22, 1944; s. George Palmer and Lucille (Owens) Johnson-Boddie; m. Martha Lee Brown, Oct. 11, 1970 (div. Dec. 1979); children: Don O'Mar, Anthony, Shawn, Shellie. BS in Bus. Mgmt. Tarkio Coll., 1988; BS in Mgmt., 1988, St. Louis Music Inst., 1968. Rec. artist Bamboo Records, St. Louis, 1966-70; producer, writer Puzzletown Prodns., St. Louis, 1970-77, James Earl World Prodns., East St. Louis, Ill. and Memphis, 1975-79, Hi Records, Memphis, 1975-79, Motown Records, Los Angeles, 1976-78; owner, producer, writer, artist Chrome Records, St. Louis, 1978—; cons. Archway Studios, St. Louis, 1970-85, Music Assocs. in Mo. Corp, Jefferson City, Mo., 1978—, JD Mgmt., St. Louis, 1978—; v.p. Scorpio Prodns., Pine Lawn, Mo., 1980-82, music producer, 1980-84. Producer: Lets Be Lovers, 1985 (Heritage award), The Legend, 1986 (Heritage award); rec. artist Can't Stop the Fire, 1987 (Heritage award). Mem. entertainment com. to elect Irene Smith, St. Louis, 1982. Democrat. Roman Catholic. Avocations: basketball, martial arts. Home: Chrome Records 6112 Hancock Saint Louis MO 63134

BODE, CARL, writer, educator; b. Milw., Mar. 14, 1911; s. Paul and Celeste Helene (Schmidt) B.; m. Margaret Lutze, Aug. 3, 1938 (dec.); children: Barbara, Janet, Carolyn; m. Charlotte W. Smith, 1972. Ph.B., U. Chgo., 1933; M.A., Northwestern U., 1938, fellow, 1940-41, Ph.D., 1941. Tchr. Milw. Vocat. Sch., 1933-37; asst. prof. English UCLA, 1946-47; prof. English U. Md., College Park, 1947-82, emeritus, 1982—; exec. sec. Am. Civilization program U. Md., 1950-57; cultural attache Am. embassy, London, 1957-59 (on leave from U. Md); chmn. U.S. Ednl. Commn. in U.K., 1957-59; vis. prof. Calif. Inst. Tech., Claremont Colls., Northwestern U., U. Wis., Stanford. Author: (poems) The Sacred Seasons, 1953, The Man Behind You, 1959, Practical Magic, 1981; (books) The American Lyceum, 1956, The Anatomy of American Popular Culture, 1840-1861, 1959 (repub. as Antebellum Culture, 1970), The Half-World of American Culture, 1965; Mencken, 1969, 73, re-issue 86, Highly Irregular (newspaper columns), 1974, Maryland: A Bicentennial History, 1978; Maryland (photographs by Steve Uzzell), 1983; editor: Collected Poems of Henry Thoreau, 1943, enlarged edit., 1964, The Portable Thoreau, 1947, rev. edit., 1964, 82, 87; American Life in the 1840s, 1967, The Selected Journals of Henry David Thoreau, 1967, The Best of Thoreau's Journals, 1971, Ralph Waldo Emerson, A Profile, 1969, Midcentury America: Life in the 1850's, 1972, The Young Mencken, 1973, The New Mencken Letters, 1977, Barnum, Struggles and Triumphs, 1982; Alger, Ragged Dick & Struggling Upward, 1985; co-editor: American Heritage, 2 vols., 1955, The Correspondence of Henry David Thoreau, 1958, American Literature, 3 vols, 1966, The Portable Emerson, 1981; editor, contbr. The Young Rebel in Am. Lit., 1959, The Great Experiment in Am. Lit., 1961; editor: The Bluenose and the Prostitute: H.L. Mencken's History of the "Hatrack" Censorship Case, 1988; contbr. articles to encys., poetry and revs. to Brit. and Am. jours.; Columnist: Balt. Evening Sun. Mem. Md. State Arts Council, 1971-79, chmn., 1972-76; mem. Md. Humanities Council, 1981—, chmn., 1984-86; mem. Marshall Scholarship Adv. Council, 1960-69. Served with AUS, 1944-45. Ford Found. fellow, 1952-53; Newberry Library fellow, 1954; Guggenheim Found. fellow, 1954-55. Fellow Royal Soc. Lit. U.K. (hon.); mem. AAUP (council 1965-68), Am. Studies Assn. (founder, 1st pres. 1952), Modern Lang. Assn., Thoreau Soc. Am. (dir. 1955-57, pres. 1960-61), Popular Culture Assn. Am. (v.p. 1972-75, pres. 1978-79), Mencken Soc. (founder, 1st pres. 1976-79), Phi Beta Kappa (hon.), Alpha Tau Omega. Democrat. Episcopalian. Clubs: Cosmos (Washington); Hamilton St. (Balt.). Home: 7008 Partridge Pl College Heights Estates Hyattsville MD 20782 Office: U Md Dept English College Park MD 20742

BODE, CHRISTOPH, literature educator; b. Siegen, Fed. Republic Germany, May 13, 1952; s. Adolf and Ute (Kuss) B. PhD, Phillips U., Marburg, Fed. Republic Germany, 1978. Habilitation Christian-Albrechts U., Kiel, Fed. Republic Germany, 1986. Asst. prof. Christian-Albrechts U., 1977-86, assoc. prof., 1986—. Author: William Wordsworth, 1977, Intellektualismus, 1979, Lyrik und Methode, 1983, Aldous Huxley, 1985, Ein Lehrer, 1987, Aesthetik der Ambiguitaet, 1988. Mem. MLA, Deutscher Anglistentag, Deutsche Shakespeare Assn., Assn. fuer Englische Romantik. Home: Am Bloecken 72, D-2300 Kiel 1 Federal Republic of Germany Office: Christian-Albrechts U, Olshausenstr 40-60, D-2300 Kiel 1 Federal Republic of Germany

BODEI, REMO GIUSEPPE, philosopher, educator; b. Cagliari, Sardinia, Italy, Aug. 3, 1938; s. Orazio G. and Eleonora M. (Carta) B.; m. Gabriella I. Giglioni, June 26, 1966; children: Chiara, Lisa. Laurea in Filosofia, Scuola Normale Superiore, Pisa, Italy, 1965; Diploma Perfezionamento, U. Pisa (Italy), 1961. Assoc. prof. Scuola Normale Superiore, 1969—; from asst. prof. philosophy to prof. U. Pisa, 1965—, dean dept. philosophy, 1984—; vis. prof. Ruhr U., Bochum, Fed. Republic Germany, 1977-80 (Humboldt fellow), King's Coll., Cambridge U., 1980, Ottawa U., 1983, NYU, N.Y.C., 1985—. Author: Sistema ed epoca in Hegel, 1975, Multiversum, 1983, Scomposizioni, 1987; mem. editorial bd. Laboratorio Politico; mem. rev. bd. Il centauro-Materiali, 1980—; contbr. 200 articles to profl. jours. Scuola Normale Superiore fellow, 1969—. Mem. Istituto Gramsci (dir. philosophy sect. 1983—). Home: Lungarno Gambacorti 31, I-56100 Pisa Italy Office: Pisa U Dept Philosophy, Piazza Torricelli 3A, I-56100 Pisa Italy

BODENHEIMER, ARTHUR, publishing executive; b. Frankfurt am Main, Germany, Jan. 3, 1921; came to U.S., 1938, naturalized, 1945; s. Louis and Bertha (Schoemann) B.; B.B.S., Mercantile Coll., Frankfurt, 1938; grad. Goethe Jr. Coll., Frankfurt, 1938; m. Suzanne Ottenheimer, Aug. 20, 1950; 1 dau., Joan Sandra. Circulation mgr. Saturday Rev. Lit., 1938-42, 45-46; circulation promotion dir. Scholastic Mags., asst. dir. Teen-Age Book Club, 1946-56; sales promotion mgr. Pocket Books, Simon & Schuster, 1956-87; v.p. mktg. The Benjamin Co., Inc., Elmsford, N.Y., 1956-57. Democratic dist. capt. N.Y.C.; mem. pub. div. Anti-Defamation League, B'nai B'rith, 1980—; mem., trustee Sr. Residence of River Edge. Served with U.S. Army, 1942-45. Decorated Bronze Star. Mem. Mktg. Communications Execs. Internat. Contbr. articles to profl. pubs. Home: 22 Eastbrook Dr River Edge NJ 07661 Office: 1 Westchester Plaza Elmsford NY 10523

BODI, LESLIE, language educator; b. Budapest, Hungary, Sept. 1, 1922; arrived in Australia, 1957; s. Bruchsteiner Istvan and Klara (Pongracz) Werheimer; m. Marianne Marton, June 10, 1950; 1 child, Anna. PhD, U. Budapest, 1948, Diploma in Edn., 1949. Tutor, lectr. dept. German U. Budapest, 1946-57; tchr. grammar sch. Melbourne, Australia, 1957-58; lectr. in German Newcastle (New South Wales, Australia) U. Coll., 1958-60; sr. lectr. in German Monash U., Clayton, Victoria, Australia, 1961-63, prof., chmn. dept., 1963-87, prof. emeritus, 1988—. Author: Heinrich Heine, 1951, Tauwetter in Wien, 1977; co-editor: Das Problem Osterreich, 1982, The German Connection, 1985; contbr. numerous articles to scholarly jours. Recipient Officer's Cross, Order of Merit, Fed. Republic Germany, 1973, Order for Art and Lit., Republic of Austria, 1976; Festschrift published in his honor Antipodean Enlightenments, 1987. Mem. Internat. Assn. Germanists, Australian Langs. and Lit. Assn., Heinrich Heine Soc., 18th Century Austrian History Soc., PEN, Australian and South Pacific Assn. Comparative Lit., Modern Lang. Tchrs. Assn. Victoria. Home: 25 Beddoe Ave, Clayton, Victoria 3168, Australia Office: Monash U Dept German, Clayton, Victoria 3168, Australia

BODINAGODA, RANAPALA, newspaper company excutive; b. Colombo, Sri Lanka, Jan. 28, 1916; m. Malinie Mangalika Hettiarachi, June 1, 1949; children: Urmila, Kaushaliya. Student, Ananda Coll., Colombo, 1930-38. Sec. to Minister Fin., Minister Agr. Colombo, 1947-56; mgr. Associated Newspapers Ceylon Ltd., Colombo, 1957-76, chmn., mng. dir., 1977—. Recipient Medal Merit Boy Scouts Sri Lanka, 1983. Mem. Press Trust Ceylon Ltd. (chmn.), Commonwealth Press Union, Internat. Press Inst. (chmn. Sri Lanka Br.), Press Found. Asia (v.p.). Buddhist. Clubs: Sri Lanka Chaess Fedn. (pres.), Sri Lanka Magic Circle (pres.). Home: #17 Don Carolis Rd, Colombo 5 Sri Lanka Office: Associated Newspaper Ceylon Ltd, # 35 D R Wijewardene Mawatha, Colombo 10 Sri Lanka

BODINSON, HOLT, conservationist; b. East Orange, N.J., Nov. 14, 1941; s. Earl Herdien and Hermoine (Holt) B.; B.A., Harvard, 1963; m. Ilse Marie Maier, Feb. 29, 1970. Sr. asso. Am. Conservation Assn., Inc., N.Y.C., 1966-70; dir. Office of Policy Analysis, N.Y. State Dept. Environ. Conservation, Albany, 1970-71, dir. div. ednl. services, 1971-77; dir. Ariz.-Sonora Desert Mus., 1977-78; exec. dir. Safari Club Internat./Safari Club Internat. Conservation Fund, Tucson, 1980—. Committeeman, Montgomery Twp. Conservation Commn., 1967-70. Served with arty. AUS, 1964-66. Mem. Stony Brook-Millstone Watershed Assn. (dir.), Safari Club Internat. (dir. Ariz. chpt.), N.Y. Outdoor Edn. Assn. (dir.), Outdoor Writers Assn. of Am., N.Y. State Rifle and Pistol Assn. (dir.). Episcopalian. Club: Harvard of So. Ariz. (pres.). Author: (with Clepper and others) Leaders in American Conservation, 1971. Contbg. editor Jour. Environmental Edn., 1968-88; dir. Conservationist mag. 1971-77, N.Y. State Environment newspaper, 1971-74. Home: 4525 Hacienda del Sol Rd Tucson AZ 85718 Office: 4800 West Gate Pass Rd Tucson AZ 85745

BODKIN, JEAN FLETCHER, psychiatric social worker; b. Jackson Heights, N.Y., Oct. 4, 1919; d. William M. and Lillian (Pastor) Fletcher; m. Richard E. Bodkin, Oct. 4, 1952 (dec. 1983); children—Karen, Alec, Andrew. B.A., U. Chgo., 1942; M.S.W., U. Conn.-West Hartford, 1959; postgrad. Met. Inst. for Psychoanalytic Studies, N.Y.C., 1963-66. Reporter, City Press, Chgo., 1942-43, Times Picayune, New Orleans, 1943-44; promotion and advt. staff Knopf Pub., N.Y.C., 1949-52; psychiatric social worker Fairfield Family Service, Conn., 1959-62, Bridgeport Child Guidance Clinic, Conn., 1963-65; psychotherapist Norwalk Hosp. Psychiat. Clinic, Conn., 1965-85; psychiat. cons. Elderhouse, Norwalk, 1980-82; field work faculty U. Conn., W. Hartford, 1974-81, N.Y. U., 1982-83; guardian ad litem cir. cts., Sanford, Fla., 1987; sec. Assn. Psychiat. Clinics of Conn., 1981-82. Legislator Rep. Town Meeting, Westport, Conn., 1977-83, R.T.M. Fin. Com., Westport, 1981-83, Environ. Com., Library Com., Westport, 1979-81; bd. dirs. Dept. Social Services, Westport, 1975-76; commn. mem. Westport Housing Authority, 1984-85. Fellow Am. Orthopsychiat. Assn.; mem. Acad. Cert. Social Workers, Nat. Assn. Social Workers, Conn. Soc. Clin. Social Workers. Democrat. Unitarian.

BODKIN, LAWRENCE EDWARD, inventor, research development company executive, gemologist; b. Sapulpa, Okla., May 17, 1927; s. Clarence Elsworth and Lillie (Moore) B.; m. Ruby Emma Pate, Jan. 15, 1949; children: Karen Bodkin Snead, Cinda, Lawrence Jr. Student, Fla. State U., 1947-50; grad., Gemological Inst., 1969. Chief announcer, program dir., mgr. various radio stations, Winter Haven, Fla., Tallahassee and Jacksonville, Fla., 1947-60; ind. jewelry salesman and appraiser Underwood Jewelers, 1961-87; pres. Bodkin Jewelers and Appraisers, Jacksonville, 1984—, Telanon, Jacksonville, 1981—, Bodkin Co., Jacksonville, 1974—; chmn., chief exec. officer Bodkin Corp., Jacksonville, 1975—; cons. gem and mineral groups, Jacksonville, 1960—, numerous corps. and industries (on inventions); lectr. in field. Author: Dual Imagery of Ultra Speed Bodies, 1971, Miniatures, 1976; contbr. articles to sci. publs.; inventor Universal-Fault Circuit-Interrupter, 1973; holder of over 15 U.S. and fgn. patents. Mem. Jacksonville Mus. Sci. and Hist., 1981—, Jacksonville Symphony Assn., 1985—, Cummer Gallery Art, Jacksonville, 1985—. Served with U.S. Army, 1945-47, ETO. Mem. Am. Gem Soc. (cert.), Fla. State U. Alumni Assn, Mensa Internat. Clubs: San Jose Country (Jacksonville); Ponte Vedra Country (Fla.). Home: 1149 Molokai Rd Jacksonville FL 32216 Office: Bodkin Jewelers and Appraisers at Wells Jewelers 4452 Hendricks Ave Jacksonville FL 32207

BODKIN, RUBY PATE, corporate executive, real estate broker, educator; b. Frostproof, Fla., Mar. 11, 1926; d. James Henry and Lucy Beatrice (Latham) P.; m. Lawrence Edward Bodkin Sr., Jan. 15, 1949; children: Karen Bodkin Snead, Cinda, Lawrence Jr. BA, Fla. State U., 1948; MA, U. Fla., 1972. Lic. real estate broker. Banker Lewis State Bank, Tallahassee, 1944-49; ins. underwriter Hunt Ins. Agy., Tallahassee, 1949-51; tchr. Duval County Sch. Bd., Jacksonville, Fla., 1952-76; pvt. practice realty Jacksonville, 1976—; tchr. Nassau County Sch. Bd., Jacksonville, 1978-83; sec., treas., v.p. Bodkin Corp., R&D/Inventions, Jacksonville, 1983—; pvt. practice tutoring, Jacksonville; substitute tchr. Duval County Sch. Bd., 1980—. Mem. Jacksonville Symphony Guild, 1985—, Mus. Sci. And History Guild, Jacksonville, 1959—, Southside Woman's Club, Jacksonville, 1957—, Garden Club Jacksonville, 1976—. Recipient 25 Yr. Service award Duval County Sch. Bd., 1976, Tchr. of Yr. award Bryceville Sch., 1981. Democrat. Baptist. Clubs: San Jose Country; Ponte Vedra Oceanfront Resort. Home: 1149 Molokai Rd Jacksonville FL 32216 Office: Bodkin Jewelers and Appraisers PO Box 16482 Jacksonville FL 32216

BODNER, SOL RUBIN, engineering educator; b. N.Y.C., Mar. 7, 1929; s. Irving and Nettie (Finkelstein) B.; BCE, Poly. Inst. Bklyn., 1950, PhD, 1955; MS, N.Y. U., 1953; m. Nechama Vardi, Nov. 1, 1952; children—Nir, Alan, Oran, Bettina. Sr. engr. Republic Aviation Corp., N.Y.C., 1955-56; sr. scientist Avco Research and Devel., Mass., 1956, cons., 1956-64; asst. prof., asso. prof. Brown U., Providence, 1956-64; prof. engring. Technion-Israel Inst. Tech., Haifa, 1964—; vis. prof. Cambridge U., 1962, Weizmann Inst., 1962-63, U. Calif., 1970, U. Ill., 1975, 79, ETH, Zurich, Switzerland, 1983. Recipient Rothschild prize, 1982. Guggenheim fellow, 1962. Mem. AAAS, ASME, AIAA, N.Y. Acad. Sci., Rheology Soc., Soc. Engring. Sci., Sigma Xi. Contbr. articles to profl. jours. Home: 62 Sea Rd, Haifa 34744, Israel Office: Material Mechanics Lab, Technion, Haifa 32000, Israel

BODOH, PATRICIA ANN, nurse; b. Quincy, Ill., Nov. 26, 1941; arrived in Brazil, 1975; d. Irwin A. and Dorothy Elizabeth (Rapp) Heinecke; m. Edward Clarence Bodoh, Aug. 4, 1962; children: Kimberly Anne, Katherine Lynn, Keith Douglas, Kent Matthew. Grad., Barnes Hosp. Sch. Nursing, 1961; student, Washington U., St. Louis, 1961, Wayne State U., 1962-64, 65-67, U. Minn., 1972-74, U. Ind., 1988—. RN, Mo., Mich., Minn. Head nurse ophthalmology, ear, nose and throat Barnes Hosp., St. Louis, 1961-62; nurse med. and surg. pediatrics Oakwood Hosp., Dearborn, Mich., 1962-63; nurse clin. and emergency U. Minn., Mpls., 1973-75; pvt. nurse Sao Paulo, Brazil, 1975—. Editor: Taste and Tell, 1979, 82. Instr., trainer affiliate Am. Heart Assn., Sao Paulo, 1982—; instr. ARC, 1987—; active Jr. League. Mem. Assn. Escola Graduada (bd. dirs., sec.). Club: Edina Federated Women's (Minn.) (officer, v.p., pres. 1971-75).

BODZENTA, ERICH, sociology educator; b. Vienna, Austria, May 7, 1927; s. Peter and Augustine (Suchy) B.; m. Martha Matyas, July 6, 1954; children—Maria, Johanna, Birgitt, Markus, Philipp. Dr.Phil., U. Vienna, 1952, Dozent Sociology, 1962. Asst. ICARES (Internat. Cath. Research Inst.), Den Haag, Netherlands, 1952-56, dir., Vienna, 1957-60; dir. Pastoralsoz Inst., Essen, 1961; profl U. Linz, Austria, 1965-70, Senator, 1965-68, dean Law Faculty, 1968-70; prof. U. Vienna, 1971—. Pres. Aktion besseres Wien, Vienna, 1973-88. Decorated Great Silver Decoration of Republic of Austria, 1987; recipient Chamber of Workers award, Vienna, 1953; Hampel Found. award Austrian Geographers Soc., Vienna, 1960; City of Vienna award, 1963; Kardinal Innitzer award, 1984. Mem. Austrian Sociol. Assn. (pres. Vienna 1968-72), German Soc. of Sociologists, Austrian Soc. of Sociologists. Roman Catholic. Contbr. articles to profl. jours. Home: Ferstelgasse 1/9, A-1090 Vienna Austria Office: Inst fur Sociology, Neutorgasse 12, A-1013 Vienna Austria

BOE, ALF, museum director; b. Bergen, Hordaland, Norway, July 8, 1927; s. Johannes and Dagny (Godager) B.; m. Kari Faerden, 1955 (div.); children: Ole Johannes, Elisabeth; m. Ulla Tarras-Wahlberg, 1972; 1 child, Stefan Tarras. MLitt, Oxford U., Eng., 1954; degree in Art, Oslo U., Norway, 1954. Asst. Mus. Applied Art, Oslo, 1955-59; curator Mus. Applied Art, Trondheim, Norway, 1959-62; asst. dir. Mus. Applied Art, Oslo, 1962-67; exec. dir. Norwegian Design Ctr., Oslo, 1968-73; asst. prof. Art History Oslo U., 1973-76; exec. dir. City Art Collections, Oslo, 1976—; chargé de mission Dept. des Objets d'Art, Louvre, Paris, 1956-57. Author: From Gothic Revival to Functional Form: A Study in Victorian Theories of Design, 1957, Norsk/Norwegian Cultural Design, 1963, Porsgrunds Porselaensfabrik, 1967, The Norwegian Design Prize: The First Seven Years, 1969. Chmn. Oslo City Soc. Recipient Das Grosse Silberne Ehrenseichen für Verdienste um die Republik Österreich Govt. Austria, Grande-Oficial da Ordem do Infante Dom Henrique Govt. Portugal, Chevalier of the Order of Isabel la Catolica Govt. Spain. Mem. Norwegian Assn. for Craft and Design (pres.), Scandinavian Mus. Assn. (chmn. Norwegian sect. 1985—), Norwegian Assn. Art Cultural History Museums (chmn. 1982-86). Office: Oslo Kommunes Kunstsamlinger, PO Box 2812, Toyengaten 53, 0578 Oslo 5 Norway

BOE, MYRON TIMOTHY, lawyer; b. New Orleans, Oct. 30, 1948; s. Myron Roger and Elaine (Tracy) B. BA, U. Ark., 1970, JD, 1973; LLM in Labor, So. Methodist U., 1976. Bar: Ark. 1974, Tenn. 1977, U.S. Ct. Appeals (4th, 5th, 6th, 7th, 8th, 9th, 10th, 11th cirs.) 1978, U.S. Supreme Ct. 1978. City atty. City of Pine Bluff, Ark., 1974-75; sec.-treas. Ark. City Atty. Assn., 1975; labor atty. Weintraub-Dehart, Memphis, 1976-78; sr. ptnr. Rose Law Firm, Little Rock, 1980—. Author: Handling the Title VII Case

Practical Tips for the Employer, 1980; contbr. book supplement: Employment Discrimination Law, 2d edit., 1983. Served to 2d lt. USAR, 1972-73. Recipient Florentino-Ramirez Internat. Law award, 1975. Mem. ABA (labor sect. 1974—, employment law com. 1974—), Ark. Bar Assn. (sec., chmn. labor sect. 1978-81, ho. of dels. 1979-82, Golden Gavel award 1983), Def. Research Inst. (employment law com. 1982—), Am. Trial Lawyers Assn., Ark. Trial Lawyers Assn., Ark. Assn. of Def. Counsel, Ark. Bd. of Legal Specialization (sec. 1982-85, chmn. 1985—, labor, employment discrimination, civil rights). Office: Rose Law Firm 120 E Fourth St Little Rock AR 72201

BOECK, HARALD CHRISTIAN ANANDO VON HAMM, cement company executive, cement consultant; b. Ringkoebing, Jutlandia, Denmark; Apr. 9, 1925; s. Philip Lewin von Beck Boeck and Eva Sophie Constantia von Hamm; m. Ellen Marie Lassen, Apr. 2, 1953 (div. Aug. 1984); children—Eva Margot von Hamm, Henrik von Hamm; m. Remedios Dueno Sanico, Mar. 1, 1985; 1 child, Philip Christian von Hamm Sanico. Mech. Engr., Copenhagen Higher Tech. Inst. Engring., 1955. Engr., supervision and commissioning F.L. Smidth & Co Ltd., Denmark, 1955-70; chief engr. Hasle Klinker & Chamottestensfabrik Ltd., Denmark, 1970-71; cement cons., U.N. Indsl. Devel. Orgn., Vienna, Austria, World Bank, Washington, Internat. Fin. Corp., Washington, Inter-Am. Devel. Bank, Washington, Asian Devel. Bank, Metro Manila, Philippines, Arab Funds Econ. and Social Devel., Kuwait, 1971-83; mng. dir., chief exec. Benue Cement Co., Nigeria, 1983-86. Served to first lt. Arty., 1953-58. Fellow Internat. Biographical Assn. (life). Conservative. Avocations: do-it-yourself activities; gardening; travel. Home: Byskellet 9, DK 2960 2960 Rungsted Kyst Denmark

BOEHM, GÜNTHER, pediatrician; b. Gerstungen, German Dem. Republic, Oct. 24, 1946; s. Heinz Werner and Ingeborg (Fräbel) B.; m. Margaret Kessner, Apr. 7, 1968 (div. 1980); children: Andreas, Steffen; m. Heidi Dippe, July 2, 1981; 1 child, Alexander. MD, Karl Marx U., 1972. Pediatrician Karl Marx U., Leipzig, German Dem. Republic, 1972-86, sr. physician dept. neonatology, 1986—; guest prof. Gondar (Ethopia) Coll. Med. Scis., 1981-82. Patentee in field; contbr. numerous articles to profl. jours. Recipient prize European Assn. Prenatal Medicine, 1986; neonatology fellow U. Milan, 1987, pediatric fellow U. Lund, 1984, 86, 87, fellow WHO. Mem. Pediatric Soc. German Dem. Republic, Soc. Perinatale Medicine German Dem. Republic. Office: Karl Marx U, Pediatric Clinic, Univ Ostrasse 21-25, 7050 Leipzig German Democratic Republic

BOEHM, MARY MAGDALENE, interior designer, space planning consultant; b. Bluffton, Ohio, June 23, 1944; d. Marvin George and Martha Leoda (von Stein) B. B.S. in Interior Design, U. Cin., 1967. Designer, Taylor Designs, Cin., 1967-68, Space Design/Interior Architecture, Cin., 1968-74, Caudill, Rowlett, Scott, Houston, 1974-76; dept. head interior design, The Klein Partnership, Houston, 1977-80; propr. Boehm Design Assocs., Houston, 1980—; expert witness Tex. Health Facilities Comm.; tchr. interior design Jewish Community Ctr., Cin., 1968. Contbr. articles on interior design to profl. jours., newspapers. Recipient Hexter award, 1969, 76, Nat. award Inst. Bus. Designers, 1974, Burlington House award Burlington House Corp., 1974. Mem. Neartown Civic Assn., Preservation Alliance, Tex. Soc. Architects, Houston chpt. AIA; assoc. mem. AIA.

BOEHME, HORST, chemist; b. Berlin, May 30, 1908; s. Arthur and Adele (Meyer) B.; m. Ines Meyer-Belitz, Aug. 3, 1935; children: Jochen, Angelika Boehme Moeller. Grad. in Pharmacy, U. Munich, 1931, diploma in Chemistry, 1933; PhD, U. Berlin, 1934, grad. in Food Chemistry, 1935; Dr. Rer. Nat. H.C., Free U., Berlin, 1968, Tech. U., Brunswick, 1981. Docent U. Berlin, 1938-43, prof., 1943-45; head div. Kaiser-Wilhelm Inst. for Physical Chemistry and Electrochemistry, Berlin-Dahlem, 1943-45; dir. Inst. Pharmaceutical Chemistry and Food Chemistry U. Marburg, Fed. Republic Germany, 1946-76, prof., rector, 1961-62. Editor: (with K. Hartke) Commentaries German European Pharmacopeia, 1968, 4th edit., 1979, (with H.G. Viehe) Iminium Salts in Organic Chemistry, 1976, part 2, 1979; contbr. over 420 articles to profl. jours. Recipient Carl-Mannich medaille German Pharm. Soc., 1969, Sertürner-Medaille in gold, German Pharm. Soc., 1986, Grosses Verdienstkreuz, Fed. Republic Germany, 1973, (co-recipient) 78. Mem. Deutsche Akademie de Naturforscher Leopoldina. Home: von Harnack-Str 21, 3550 Marburg/Lahn Federal Republic of Germany Office: Inst Pharm Chemistry, Marbacher Weg 6, 3550 Marburg/Lahn Federal Republic of Germany

BOEHMER, JAN PHILIP, control valves manufacturing company executive; b. Utrecht, The Netherlands, May 7, 1937; arrived in Fed. Republic of Germany, 1969; s. Petrus Johannes and Adriana Antoneta (Van Brussel) B.; m. Christine Jasiek, Apr. 20, 1963; 1 child, Martin. Diploma cum laude, Dutch Inst. for Internat. Bus. Adminstrn. and Mgmt., 1958. Cert. in internat. mktg. mgmt. Regional export mgr. Contam (Exports) Lt., London, 1961-63; gen. mgr. Rosenthal China Corp., Brussels, 1964-68; treas., v.p. Rosenthal China Corp., N.Y.C., 1968-69; export mgr. J. Gerhardt Wines, Nierstein, Fed. Republic Germany, 1969-71, P.W.A. AG, Mannheim, Fed. Republic Germany, 1971-74; export mktg. mgr. MNG & Co. GmbH, Arnsberg, Fed. Republic Germany, 1974—; lectr. U. Mainz, 1958-59; mng. dir. Jakob Gerhardt-France, Paris, 1969-71, MNG-France, Paris, 1986—. Author: Ein Bisschen Glasnost, 1987. Served with Dutch Army, 1959-61. Roman Catholic. Home: Zur Alten Ruhr 8, D-5760 Arnsberg 1 Federal Republic of Germany Office: MNG & Co GmbH, PO Box 2040, D-5760 Arnsberg 1 Federal Republic of Germany

BOEHNEN, DAVID LEO, lawyer; b. Mitchell, S.D., Dec. 3, 1946; s. Lloyd L. Boehnen and Mary Elizabeth (Buche) Roby; m. Shari A. Bauhs, Aug. 9, 1969; children—Lesley, Michelle, Heather. A.B., U. Notre Dame, 1968; J.D. with honors, Cornell U., 1971. Bar: Minn. 1971. Assoc. firm Dorsey & Whitney, Mpls., 1971-76, ptnr., 1977—; sec. Supercomputer Systems, Inc., Eau Claire, Wis., Helix BioCore, Inc., Equimed Corp.; FilmTec Corp., Mpls., 1979-85 , Pandex Labs., Inc., Mundelein, Ill., 1982-86 ; sec., dir. Immuno Nuclear Corp., Stillwater, Minn., 1980-83; sec. London Diagnostics, Inc., Mpls., 1985—; vis. prof. law Cornell U. Law Sch., Ithaca, N.Y., fall 1982. Adv. Council Cornell U. Law Sch., 1983—, chmn. council 1986, 87. Mem. ABA (bus. law sect., fed. regulation of securities com.), Minn. State Bar Assn. (chmn. bus. law sect., 1986). Roman Catholic. Clubs: Mpls. Athletic; Town and Country, St. Paul. Home: 71 Otis Ln Saint Paul MN 55104

BOEHNER, LEONARD BRUCE, lawyer; b. Malvern, Iowa, Apr. 19, 1930; s. Bruce and Flora (Kruse) B. A.B., Harvard U., 1952, J.D., 1955. Bar: N.Y. 1956, U.S. Dist. Ct. (so. dist.) N.Y. 1963, U.S. Ct. Appeals (2d cir.) 1963, U.S. Supreme Ct. 1964. Assoc. Dewey, Ballantine, Bushby, Palmer & Wood, N.Y.C., 1959-66; ptnr. Clare & Whitehead, N.Y.C., 1966-73, Morris & McVeigh, N.Y.C. 1973—. Served to lt. USN, 1955-59. Mem. Assn. Bar City N.Y. Club: Union (N.Y.C.). Office: 767 3d Ave New York NY 10017

BOEKER, PAUL HAROLD, diplomat; b. St. Louis, May 2, 1938; s. Victor W. and Marie Dorothy (Bernthal) B.; m. Margaret Macon Campbell, Nov. 25, 1961; children: Michelle Renee, Kent Elliott, Katherine Madison. A.B., Dartmouth Coll., 1960; postgrad., Princeton U., 1961; M.A. in Econs., U. Mich., 1967. Joined Dept. State, 1961; vice consul Duesseldorf, Germany, 1962-63; 2d sec. Am. embassy, Bogotá, Colombia, 1964-66; mem. White House Task Force on Internat. Devel., 1969; dir. Office Devel. Fin., Dept. State, 1970; 1st sec. Am. embassy, Bonn, Germany, 1971-73; mem. policy planning staff Dept. State, 1974, dep. asst. sec. state for internat. fin. and devel., 1975, sr. dep. asst. sec. state for econ. and bus. affairs, 1976; ambassador to Bolivia, 1977-80; dir. Fgn. Service Inst., Washington, 1980-81; mem. Sec.'s Planning Council, Washington, 1983-84; ambassador to Jordan 1984-87. Recipient Arthur S. Fleming award for outstanding young people in fed. service, 1976, Presdl. Disting. Service award, 1985, 87.

BOEMI, A. ANDREW, banker; b. N.Y.C., Mar. 3, 1915; s. S. and Marietta (Boemi) B.; B.C.E., Coll. City N.Y., 1936, M.C.E., 1938; m. Flora Dorothy DeMuro, Apr. 26, 1941; children—Andrew A., Marcia Rosamond Buchanan. Engr., Gibb & Hill, Cons. Engrs., N.Y.C., 1937; city planner N.Y. Planning Comm., 1938-41; cons. U.S. Bur. Budget, Exec. Office of President, Washington, 1942; asst. loan officer, planning cons., asst. v.p., v.p. First Fed. Savs. & Loan, Chgo., 1946-57; pres., chief exec. officer Madison Bank & Trust Co., Chgo., 1957-84, chmn. bd., 1974—; pres., chmn. bd. Madison Fin. Corp., Chgo., 1974-84, chmn. bd., chief exec. officer, 1985-87, chmn. bd., 1988— ; chmn. bd. Madison Nat. Bank of Niles (Ill.), 1976—, 1st Nat. Bank of Wheeling (Ill.), 1978—, MFC Mortgage Co., 1983—. Mem. exec. com. Archdiocesan Commn. Human Relations and Ecumenism, 1969-72; mem. Mayor's Commn. Landmarks Preservation Council, 1972-75. Bd. dirs. Met. Housing and Planning Council, 1950—, pres., 1975-76; mem. Elem. Sch. Bd., Park Ridge, Ill., 1953-59, pres., 1956-59; citizens bd. Loyola U. Chgo.; chmn. Joint Action Com. Civic Assns. for location Chgo. campus U. Ill., 1960-61; chmn. Gateway Com., Chgo., 1958-63; bd. dirs. Duncan YMCA, 1964-77. Served to lt. comdr. USNR, 1942-46. Recipient commendation ribbon from sec. navy, World War II; decorated Knight Order Holy Sepulchre of Jerusalem. Mem. Am. Bankers Assn., Ill. Bankers Assn. (fed. legis. and regulation com.), ASCE, Am. Inst. Planners, Navy League U.S., Newcomen Soc. N.Am., Am. Legion, Lambda Alpha, Alpha Beta Gamma. Republican. Roman Catholic. Clubs: Economic, Bankers, University (Chgo.); Park Ridge Country. Lodge: Knights of Malta (decorated). Home: 1110 N Lake Shore Dr Apt 7-S Chicago IL 60611 Office: 400 W Madison St Chicago IL 60606

BOERI, RENATO RAIMONDO, neurologist; b. Milano, Italy, May 15, 1922; s. Giovanni Battista and Pierina (Martinelli) B.; m. Cini Mariani, Sept. 14, 1950 (div. 1969); children—Sandro, Stefano, Tito; m. 2d Maria Grazia Casiraghi, Sept. 15, 1978. Liceo, Beccaria, Milano, Italy, 1940; M.D., U. Milano, 1947. Diplomate Neurology and Psychiatry, Univ. Milan, 1951. Intern, resident Istituto Neurologico C. Besta, Milano; clin. and sci. dir. Instituto Neurologico Carlo Besta, Milano, 1977—. Editor Italian Jour. Neurol. Scis., 1980—. Mem. Italian Soc. Neurology (v.p. 1982), Am. Acad. Neurology, Societe Francaise de Neurologie, N.Y. Acad. Scis. Home: Via Senato 18, 20121 Milano Italy Office: Via Sant'Andrea n5, 20121 Milano Italy

BOERNER, WILKO HERMANN, insurance company executive; b. Hamburg, Fed. Republic Germany, Oct. 20, 1937; m. Hilke Schuldt; 3 children. MBA, Harvard U., 1963. Mem. mgmt. bd. Agrippina Reinsurance Co., Cologne, Fed. Republic Germany, 1965-70, Wuerttembergische Fire Ins. Co., Stuttgart, Fed. Republic Germany, 1971-83, Aachen-Munich Ins. Co., 1983-88; chmn. mgmt. bd. Aachen-Munich Life Ins. Co., 1988—. Office: Aachen Munich Life Ins Co, PO Box 26, D-5100 Aachen Federal Republic of Germany

BOES, DIETER JOSEF, economist, educator; b. Prague, Czechoslovakia, Aug. 4, 1940; arrived in Austria, 1945; s. Josef Heinrich and Margret (Ressel) B.; m. Emoeke Bady, Dec. 1, 1966; children: Ursula, Monika, Leonhard, Dominik. JD, U. Vienna, Austria, 1963, D of Rerum Politicarum, 1968. Asst. prof. U. Vienna, 1965-71, prof. econs., 1975-79; prof. U. Graz, Austria, 1971-75, U. Bonn, Fed. Republic of Germany, 1979—; vis. prof. Sch. Econs., U. London, 1976—; mem. bd. Internat. Seminar in Pub. Econs., 1986—. Author: Economic Theory of Public Enterprise, 1981, Public Enterprise Economics, 1986; co-editor (with Bergson and Meyer) Entrepreneurship, 1984; mng. editor: Jour. of Econs., 1973—. Mem. European Econ. Assn. (mem. council), Nat. Econ. Assn. (bd. dirs. Austrian sect.), Am. Econ. Assn. Roman Catholic. Home: Baumschulallee 3, D 5300 Bonn Federal Republic of Germany Office: U Bonn, Adenauerallee 24-42, D 5300 Bonn Federal Republic of Germany

BOESAK, ALLAN AUBREY, religious organization adminstrator, pastor; b. Kakamas, N.W. Cape, Republic of South Africa, Feb. 23, 1946; s. Willem Andreas and Sarah Helena (Mannel) B.; m. Dorothy Rose Martin, June 21, 1969; children: Lieneke, Belèn, Pulane, Allan Jr. Diploma in theology, Theol. Sem. U. West Cape, Bellville, 1967; ThM, Theol. Sem. Reformed Chs., Kampen, The Netherlands, 1974, ThD, 1976; DD (hon.), Victoria U., Toronto, Ont., Can., 1983, Yale U., 1984; ThD, Geneva U., 1986. Pastor N.G. Sendingkerk Immanuel, Paarl, Republic of South Africa, 1968-70; campus minister U. Western Cape, Bellville, Republic of South Africa, 1976-85; sr. pastor N.G. Sendingkerk Bellville, 1986—; assessor synod N.G. Sendingkerk (Dutch Reformed Mission Ch.), 1982-86, moderator synod, 1986—; pres. World Alliance Reformed Chs., 1982—; founder Found. for Peace and Justice, Bellville, 1986—. Author: Farewell to Innocence, 1976, The Finger of God, 1982, Black and Reformed, 1984, Comfort and Protest, 1987. Patron, co-founder United Dem. Front, Republic of South Africa, 1983—. Recipient Kaj Munk award Ch. Denmark, 1983, Humanitarian award R.F. Kennedy Found., 1985, Humanitarian award Congl. Black Caucus, 1985, M.L. King Jr. award So. Christian Leadership Conf., 1986. Mem. Assn. Christian Students in So. Africa (pres. 1980—).

BOESBY, STEEN, surgeon, lecturer, researcher; b. Odense, Denmark, July 5, 1944; s. Thorkild and Bodil Magdalene (Schmidt) B.; m. Karen Jorgensen, Feb. 14, 1970; children—Lene, Dorte. Cand. med., Aarhus U., Denmark, 1971; M.D. Odense U., Denmark, 1979. Registrar Kjellerup Hosp., Denmark, 1971-72, Odense Hosp., Denmark, 1972-73; research fellow Odense U., 1973-76; registrar Odense U. Hosp., 1976-79; sr. registrar Svendborg Hosp., Denmark, 1979-81, Hammersmith Hosp., London, 1981-83, Rigshospitalet, Copenhagen, 1983-86, 87—, Herlev Hosp., 1986-87; resident surg. officer Hammersmith Hosp., 1982-83. Contbr. chpts. to books, articles to profl. jours. Mem. Danish Surg. Soc., Danish Soc. Gastroenterology (sec.-gen. 1987—), Danish Assn. for the Study of the Liver (bd. dirs. 1986—), Danish Esophagus Assn., Brit. Soc. Gastroenterology, European Histamine Research Soc., European Motility Soc. Protestant. Avocations: sailing; gardening; badminton. Home: Fuglevadsvej 48, 2800 Lyngby Denmark Office: Rigshospitalet, Dept C Blegdamsvej 9, 2100 Copenhagen Denmark

BOESEL, MILTON CHARLES, JR., lawyer, business executive; b. Toledo, July 12, 1928; s. Milton Charles and Florence (Fitzgerald) B.; m. Lucy Laughlin Mather, Mar. 25, 1961; children—Elizabeth Parks, Charles Mather, Andrew Fitzgerald. B.A., Yale, 1950; LL.B., Harvard, 1953. Bar: Ohio bar 1953, Mich. bar 1953. Of counsel firm Ritter, Boesel and Robinson, Toledo, 1956—; pres., dir. Michabo, Inc.; dir. 1st Nat. Bank of Toledo. Served to lt. USNR, 1953-56. Episcopalian. Clubs: Toledo, Toledo Country; Leland Country (Mich.). Home: 2268 Innisbrook Rd Toledo OH 43606 Office: 240 Huron St Toledo OH 43604

BOETSCH, URS, real estate broker; b. Basel, Switzerland, Aug. 20, 1943; s. Ernst and Ruth B.; m. Maja Boetschi, May 26, 1972; children: Tina, Aisha. BS, U. Basel, 1966; cert. BA, U. Mass, 1968. With Swiss Credit Bank, Basel, 1964-66; asst. br. mgr. Friden-Singer Corp., Basel, Zurich, 1966-69; mgr. renting dept. L. Cron Real Estate, Basel, 1969-71; mgr. sales dept. Zentra Ver Real Estate, Basel, 1971-80; chmn. U. Boetsch Real Estate, Basel, 1980—; cons. Rio-Basel, 1981. Mem. Switzerland-Internat. Real Estate Fedn. (pres. 1982), Swiss Real Estate Fedn. (v.p. 1979), Fiabci Real Estate Fedn. (counselors pres.). Democrat. Clubs: Nazdar, Basle Lawn Tennis, Casino. Home: Rennweg 86, Basel Switzerland Office: Urs Boetsch Real Estate Corp, Angensteiner St 21, Basel 4020, Switzerland

BOFILL, RICARDO, architect; b. Barcelona, Spain, 1939. Ed. Ecole Francaise, Barcelona; then student architecture U. Geneva, 1957-60. Designer and planner for urban structures, especially residential complexes, beginning in 1960; works include: City in Space designs, Walden 7, Barcelona suburbs, La Petite Cathedrale complex, France, La Citadelle renovations, France; exhbns.: Venice, 1976, Paris, 1978, Berlin, N.Y.C., 1979, Archtl. Assn., London, 1981, Mus. Modern Art, N.Y.C., 1985; author books; contbr. articles to profl. jours.; founder Taller de Arquitectura, Barcelona, 1960. Recipient ADIFAD prize, 1964, Schumacher prize Hamburg U., 1968, Internat. Design award ASID, 1978. Office: care Taller de Arquitectura, Avenida la Industria 14, Santjustdesvern, Barcelona Spain *

BOGAERTS, COUNT ARTHUR FLORENT, scientist; b. Gent, Belgium, Dec. 30, 1937; s. Count Francois and Countess Ludovica (Verselole de Wondelgem) B.; m. Countess Patricia Koeb. B.Sc.M.E., Belgian Mil. Acad., 1960; M.Sc., Case Western Res. U., 1963; Ph.D., MIT; M.D., Harvard U.; Ph.D., U. London; Ph.D. (hon.), So. U., 1978, Am. U., 1978. Lic. physician, Ger., India, Nepal, Guatamala, Panama; cert. profl. engr., U.S., U.K., Germany, Belgium. Chmn., Fla. Interstate, Jacksonville, from 1972; v.p. Heather Corp., N.Y.C., 1983—; chmn. Heraldic Research Corp., Albert Schweitzer Soc., St. Lazarus Med. Corps.; dir. internat. coordination for Missions Unltd. Corp., Jasper, Ala.; pres. Jignum Fidei Med. Air Corps; adviser, expert in sci. and medicine to numerous countries; vis. prof., lectr., cons. to numerous profl. and ednl. instns. Author numerous books on acoustics, solar energy, leprosy and missionary work; contbr. articles to profl. jours. Past v.p. Liberal Party, Belgium; co-founder, 1st dean applied sci. European U., Antwerp (affiliated U. Dallas). Served to col. Belgium Army, 1956-61, reserve 1961—. Decorated knight Order of St. Lazarus; knight Order of Constantine St. George; knight Order of Swan, knight Order of Lion, officer Order of St. John (Eng.), numerous other decorations including Zaire, Poland, Leberia; comdr. Order of Merit (Italy); named Hon. Citizen of cities of Rome, Jasper, Cordova, states of Tenn., Ala., Ga., Okla., Miss., La.; recipient Royal Sci. award Belgium, 1976, Cult award, 1978, Royal medal, 1986; recipient numerous civic and profl. awards. Fellow World Acad. Arts and Scis., Brit. Acoustical Soc., Inst., Inst. Aeros. and Astronautics, Inst. Dirs. (U.K.), Acad. Sci. Pro Pace Vatican, Acad. Sci. Flandriensis; mem. N.Y. Acad. Scis., Acad. Sci. Rome, AMA, German Med. Soc., Internat. Leprosy Found., Germna Leprosy Found., AIAA, Physics, IEEE (sr. mem.; editorial bd. Spectrum, The Institute 1978-84, 85—); numerous others. Clubs: Royal Yacht (Belgium), Royal Golf (Belgium and Hannover); Exec. Royal Travel (chmn.); Royal Safari (chmn.); Mt. Kenya Safari (bd. dirs.); Mt. Crest County (S.C.); St. Johns (London). Home: 116 Central Park S Apt 7C New York NY 10019 also: The Circus 20, Bath/ Avon England Office: Missions Unltd Corp/ The Albert Schweitzer Soc PO Box 929 Jasper AL 35502

BOGAERTS, JACQUES LOUIS, transportation executive; b. Uccle, Belgium, Mar. 23, 1926; s. Andre H. Bogaerts and Jeanne Ferryn; m. Denise L. Missal, Nov. 20, 1952; children: Jacques G., Anne-Françoise, Laurent A. Grad., milit. sch., Belgium, 1946. Commd. armed forces, Belgium, 1944, advanced through grades to commdr., 1957, ret., 1957; mng. dir. Sabena, Belgium, 1957—, Abelag, Belgium, 1964—, Interaction, Belgium, 1986—. Named to Order of Leopold, Belgian armed forces, 1950, Order of the Crown, Belgian armed forces, 1951; decorated Milit. Cross, Belgian armed forces, 1944; others. Home: Pont-A-Lesse, 5500 Dinant-Anseremme Belgium

BOGARDE, DIRK (DEREK NIVEN VAN DEN BOGAERDE), actor; b. Mar. 28, 1921; s. Ulric Jules and Margaret (Niven) Van den B.; student Allan Glen's Sch., Glasgow, Univ. Coll. Sch., London, Chelsea Poly.; Litt.D. (hon.), St. Andrews U., 1985. Appeared in plays Cliff in Power without Glory, 1947, Orpheus in Point of Departure, 1950, Nicky in The Vortex, 1953, Alberto in Summertime, 1955-56, Jezebel, 1958; films include Hunted, Appointment in London, They Who Dare, The Sleeping Tiger, Doctor in the House, Doctor at Sea, Doctor at Large, The Spanish Gardener, Cast a Dark Shadow, Ill Met by Moonlight, A Tale of Two Cities, The Wind Cannot Read, The Doctor's Dilemma, Libel, Song Without End, The Angel Wore Red, The Singer Not the Song, Victim, H.M.S. Defiant, Password Is Courage, The Mind Benders, I Could Go on Singing, The Servant, Doctor in Distress, High Bright Sun, King and Country, Accident, Our Mother's House, Sebastian, Justine, The Fixer, Upon This Rock, The Serpent, The Night Porter, The Damned, Death in Venice, Providence, A Bridge Too Far, Despair, The Patricia Neal Story (CBS), 1981. Served with Brit. Army, 1940-46. Decorated chevalier Ordre des Arts et des Lettres (France). Author: A Postillion Struck by Lightning, 1977; Snakes and Ladders, 1978; A Gentle Occupation, 1980; Voices in the Garden, 1981; (autobiography) An Orderly Man, 1983, Backcloth, 1986; (novel) West of Sunset, 1984. Office: Duncan Heath Assocs, 162 Wardour St, London W1, England *

BOGARD-REYNOLDS, CHRISTINE ELIZABETH, stock brokerage executive; b. Aberdeen, Md., Apr. 15, 1954; d. Charles Francis and Donna June (Mosbaugh) Bogard; divorced; 1 child, Zachary Kagan. Student, U. Colo., 1972-73. Adminstrv. asst. Lange Co., Broomfield, Colo., 1973-74; field sales and service rep. Bowman Products Div., Denver, 1974-75; cashier Regency Inn, Denver, 1975-76; gen. mgr., sec.-treas., Edison Agy. Inc., Denver, 1976-81; gen. mgr. Edison Press, Inc., Englewood, Colo., 1979-80, 81; advt. dir. Blinder, Robinson & Co., Englewood, 1981—. Active fundraising Passages, Inc., Contacts for Kids Sake, Denver, 1987—, Blinder Research Found. for Crohn's Disease (bd. dirs.), Rocky Mountain Multiple Sclerosis Ctr.; mem. Direct Mktg. Assn., Denver Advt. Fedn., Am. Mgmt. Assn. Home: 6860 S Bannock #H Littleton CO 80120 Office: Blinder Robinson & Co 6455 S Yosemite Englewood CO 80111

BOGART, KEITH CHARLES, neurologist; b. Lorain, Ohio, Apr. 12, 1936; s. Lloyd William and Evelyn (Overmyer) B.; m. B. Diane Seigel, June 8, 1967; children: Keith Charles Jr., Catherine Michelle; m. Alice Craib, July 21, 1976; 1 child, Matthew William. BA, Ohio State U., 1958, MD, 1961. Diplomate Am. Bd. Psychiatry and Neurology, Am. Bd. Qualification in EEG. Asst. prof. neurology U. Wis., Madison, 1968-69, Creighton U., Omaha, Nebr., 1975-78; chmn. neurology Gunderson Clinic, Lacrosse, Wis., 1969-75; clin. neurologist Mansfield (Ohio) Neurology, Inc., 1978—; med. dir. rehab. unit Mansfield Gen. Hosp., 1988—; cons. neurology VA Hosp., Omaha, 1977-78. Mem. christian edn. com. First Congl. Ch., Mansfield, 1986; bd. dirs. Boy Scouts Am., Mansfield, 1986. Served to lt. comdr. USPHS, 1963-65. Fellow Am. Acad. Neurology, Am. EEG Soc. (mem. lab. accreditation bd. 1984—); mem. AMA (Physician's Recognition award 1969, 72, 77, 82), Cen. Assn. EEGers (pres. 1977-78), Nebr. Epilepsy League (pres. 1976-78), Wis. Med. Soc. (chmn. neurology sect. 1975), Wis. Neurol. Soc. (pres. 1973), Richland County Med. Soc. (sec.-treas. 1986—), Knights of Magic (pres. 1986-87, Magician of Yr. 1984, 85, 86), Internat. Brotherhood Magicians (v.p. ter. 1986—, Presdl. Citation 1988). Lodge: Rotary. Home: 730 Woodhill Mansfield OH 44907 Office: Mansfield Neurology Inc 222 Marion Ave Mansfield OH 44903

BOGART, PAUL, film director; b. N.Y.C., Nov. 21, 1919; s. Benjamin and Molly (Glass) B.; m. Alma Jane Gitnick, Mar. 22, 1941; children: Peter Gareth, Tracy Katherine, Jennifer Jane. Ed. pub. schs., N.Y.C. Puppeteer, actor Berkeley Marionettes, 1946-48; stage mgr., assoc. dir. NBC, 1950-52; freelance dir. film and TV 1952—; lectr. New Sch. Social Research, 1960, ANTA, 1960, U. Memphis, 1968—, U. Calif., Irvine, 1979, UCLA, 1979, Loyola Marymount, 1981. TV prodns. include U.S. Steel Hour, Kraft Theatre, Armstrong Circle Theatre Goodyear Playhouse, Hallmark Hall of Fame, 1953-60, The Defenders, 1963 (Emmy award 1964-65), Dear Friends (Emmy award 1967-68), Shadow Game (Emmy award 1969-70) Ages of Man, 1965, Final War of Ollie Winter, 1966, All in the Family, 1975-79 (Emmy award 1977-78), The Golden Girls (Emmy award 1985-86), The War Widow (PBS), The Shady Hill Kidnapping (PBS), Weekend (PBS), Nutcracker: Money, Madness and Murder, 1987, Natica Jackson, 1987; films include Marlowe, 1968, Halls of Anger, 1969, Skin Game, 1971, Class of '44, 1973, Mr. Ricco, 1975; Oh, God! You Devil, 1984, The Canterville Ghost, 1986, Torch Song Trilogy, 1988. Served with USAAF, 1944-46. Recipient Christopher award 1955, 73, 75, Human Arts award Community Relations Conf. So. Calif., 1964, Humanitas award, 1977-78, Golden Globe award, 1977, So. Calif. Motion Picture Council award, 1979, Film Adv. Bd. award, 1979. Mem. Dirs. Guild Am. (nat. dir. 1962, 79, 80-81, 87—, award 1977, 78), Writers Guild Am., Am. Film Inst., Acad. Motion Picture Arts and Scis. (bd. govs. 1979-81), Acad. TV Arts and Scis., Soc. Stage Dirs. and Choreographers. Office: Tiber Prodns Inc 760 N LaCienega Blvd Los Angeles CA 90069

BOGART, VINCENT LAVAUGHN, lawyer; b. Kirwin, Kans., June 8, 1922; s. Leroy Lindsey and Maude Winifred (Wickwar) B.; m. Julia Ruth Henry, Aug. 23, 1952; children—Candace, Lee, Celeste, Cynthia. B.S., Kans. State U., 1953; LL.B., Washburn U., 1955, J.D., 1955. Bar: Kans. 1955, U.S. Dist. Ct. Kans. 1955, U.S. Ct. Appeals (10th cir.) 1955, U.S. Supreme Ct. 1960. Practice law, Wichita, Kans., 1955—; mem. Kans. Legislature, 1955-57; mem. Wichita City Commn., 1963-67; mayor City of Wichita, 1964-65; legis. liaison State of Kans., 1967-68; spl. asst. atty. gen. State of Kans., 1972-74, 76-77. Chmn., Sedgwick County Democratic Com., Wichita, 1960; mem. Nat. Dem. Platform Com., 1968; del. Nat. Dem. Conv., 1968; chmn. State Dem. Platform Com., 1966-67; trustee Wichita State U., 1968; mem. Kans. Bd. Regents, 1969; trustee Wichita Art Mus., 1983—, pres. 1988—. Served to 1st lt. USAAF, 1943-46. Decorated Asiatic Pacific Ribbon and Victory medal. Mem. ABA, Kans. Bar Assn., Wichita Bar Assn. (bd. govs. 1985-88), Assn. Trial Lawyers Am., Kans. Trial Lawyers Assn., VFW, Sigma Nu. Presbyterian. Home: 227 N Belmont Wichita KS 67208 Office: PO Box 1801 Wichita KS 67201

BOGDANOR, VERNON, political science educator; b. London, July 16, 1943; s. Harry and Rosa B.; m. Judith Evelyn Beckett, July 23, 1972; 2

sons. BA, Oxford U., 1964, MA, 1968. Fellow Brasenose Coll., Oxford, 1966—; sr. vis. fellow Ctr. for European Political Studies Policy Studies Inst., London, 1983-86; mem. ct. Essex U., Eng., 1982-84. Author: Devolution, 1979, The People and the Party System, 1981, Multi-Party Politics and the Constitution, 1983, What is Proportional Representation?, 1984. Mem. Hansard Soc. for Parliamentary Govt., London, 1984—, Nat. Com. for Electoral Reform, London, 1983—. Office: Oxford U, Brasenose Coll, Oxford OX1 4AJ, England

BOGDANOV, MICHAEL, artistic director; b. London, Dec. 15, 1938; s. Francis Benzion and Rhoda Rees (Bogdin); m. Patricia Ann Warwick, Dec. 17, 1966; children: Jethro, Malachi, Ffion. Student, U. Paris Sorbonne, 1958, U. Munich, 1962; MA in Modern Lang., Trinity Coll., Dublin, Ireland, 1963. Producer, dir. TV Radio Telefis Eireann, Dublin, 1966-68; asst. dir. Royal Shakespeare Co., Stratford, Eng., 1970-71; assoc. dir. Tyneside Theatre Co., Newcastle, Eng., 1971-73; artistic dir. Phoenix Theatre, Leicester, Eng., 1973-77, The Young Vic Theatre, London, 1978-80; assoc. dir. The Nat. Theatre Great Britain, London, 1980—; founder, artistic dir. The English Shakespeare Co., London, 1986—; assoc. dir. The Nat. Theatre Hamburg, Fed. Republic Germany, 1986—, intendant, 1988-93; assoc. dir. The Abbey Theatre, Dublin, 1986—. Dir. numerous plays including The Taming of the Shrew, 1979 (Best Dir. award Soc. West End Theatre 1979), Romeo and Juliet, 1984 (Best Dir. award Tokyo Critics 1984), Hamlet, 1984 (Best Dir. award Dublin Critics 1984). Recipient Outstanding Achievement award Drama Mag., Manchester Critics award, 1986-87. Office: The English Shakespeare Co, 60 Paddington St, London W1, England

BOGDEN, GEORGE ANDREW, publisher; b. Paterson, N.J., Apr. 15, 1932; s. George John and Rose (Clemis) B.; m. Carolyn Siegle, Nov. 25, 1955 (dec.); children—Margaret, Kathleen, George, Suzanne; m. Jeannette Parry, July 20, 1988. B.S. in Bus. Mgmt, Fairleigh Dickinson U., 1955. Editor-in-chief sci. publns. Allyn & Bacon, Boston, 1959-67; co-founder, pub. Bogden & Quigley, Inc., Tarrytown, N.Y. and Belmont, Calif., 1967-74; officer, dir. Springer Verlag N.Y., Inc, N.Y.C., 1974-77; co-founder, pub. K.G. Saur Pub., N.Y., Inc., N.Y.C., 1977-80; pres., chief exec. officer George A. Bogden & Son, Inc. (pubs. and distbrs. sci. and med. publs.), Ridgewood, N.J., 1980—; founder, pres. Multimedia Internat., Ho-Ho-Kus, N.J., 1982—; co-founder, dir. MED AV Pub. Co., Hawthorne, N.J., 1985—; dir. pub. Parthenon Pub. Group, Inc., Park Ridge, N.J., 1986—. Active fund raising Ridgewood Scholarship Com. Served to 1st lt. USMCR, 1955-58. Mem. Sci., Tech. and Med. Pubs., Am. Pubs. Assn., Internat. Fedn. Lit. Assns., N.Y. Library Assn. Club: Benefactor Lituanus. Office: 300 AIA Ocean Parks (J301) Jupiter FL 33477

BOGDON, GLENDON JOSEPH, orthodontist; b. Green Bay, Wis., Sept. 23, 1935; s. Joseph Frank and Anne Marie (Jacklin) B.; m. Susanne Ellen Daley, Aug. 8, 1959; 1 child, Amy Sue. BS, St. Norbert Coll., DePere, Wis., 1957; DDS, Marquette U., 1971, MS in Clin. Dentistry, 1973. Officer IRS, Chgo., 1958; social worker Cath. Welfare Bur., Milw., 1958-59; tchr. secondary sch. So. Door County Schs., Brussels, Wis., 1959-67; practice dentistry specializing in orthodontics Milw., 1973—; pres. So. Orthodontic Services, Milw., 1986—. Contbr. articles to profl. jours. Served with U.S. Army, 1957-58. Mem. Greater Milw. Dental Assn. (Continuing Edn. award 1971-73), Wis. Dental Assn. (Continuing Edn. award 1971-74, 79-81), ADA (Continuing Edn. award 1976-78), Royal Soc. Health, Wis. Soc. Orthodontists, Midwestern Soc. Orthodontists, Am. Assn. Orthodontists. Democrat. Roman Catholic. Office: 3044 S 92d St West Allis WI 53227

BOGER, DAN CALVIN, economics educator, statistical and economic consultant; b. Salisbury, N.C., July 9, 1946; s. Brady Cashwell and Gertrude Virginia (Hamilton) B.; m. Gail Lorraine Zivna, June 23, 1973; children—Gretchen Zivna, Gregory Zivna. B.S. in Mgmt. Sci., U. Rochester, 1968; M.S. in Mgmt. Sci., Naval Postgrad. Sch., Monterey, Calif., 1969; M.A. in Stats., U. Calif.-Berkeley, 1977, Ph.D. in Econs., 1979. Cert. cost analyst; cert. profl. estimator. Research asst. U. Calif.-Berkeley, 1975-79; asst. prof. econs. Naval Postgrad. Sch., Monterey, Calif., 1979-85, assoc. prof., 1985—; cons. econs. and statis. legal matters CSX Corp, others, 1977—. Assoc. editor The Logistics and Transportation Rev., 1981-85; mem. editorial rev. bd. Jour. Tranp. Research Forum, 1987—; contbr. articles to profl. jours. Served to lt. USN, 1968-75. Flood fellow Dept. Econs., U. Calif.-Berkeley, 1975-76; dissertation research grantee A.P. Sloan Found., 1978-79. Mem. Am. Econ. Assn., Am. Statis. Assn., Econometric Soc., Math. Assn. Am., Inst. Mgmt. Sci., Ops. Research Soc. Am. (sec., treas. mil. applications sect. 1987—), Sigma Xi. Home: 61 Ave Maria Rd Monterey CA 93940 Office: Naval Postgrad Sch Code 54Bo Monterey CA 93943

BOGER, WILLIAM PIERCE, III, ophthalmologist; b. Phila., Oct. 16, 1945; s. William Pierce Jr. and Mae Elizabeth (Shelton) B.; m. Barbara Crawford, Aug. 10, 1968; children—Matthew, Andrew, John. A.B. in Biophysics magna cum laude with honors, Amherst Coll., 1967; M.D., Harvard U., 1971. Diplomate Am. Bd. Ophthalmology. Intern in medicine and pediatrics U. Va. Hosp., Charlottesville, 1971-72; resident in ophthalmology Mass. Eye and Ear Infirmary, Boston, 1972-75; fellow in pediatric ophthalmology and strabismus Children's Hosp. Med. Ctr., Boston, 1976, assoc. in ophthalmology, full-time staff, 1976-80; practice medicine specializing in ophthalmology Lexington Eye Assocs., Mass., 1980—; mem. staff Boston Children's Hosp. Med. Ctr., Beth Israel Hosp., Boston, Emerson Hosp., Concord, Mass., Choate-Symmes Health Services Inc., Arlington and Woburn, Mass.; instr. Harvard U., 1976—; lectr. in field. Contbr. articles, chpts. to profl. publs. Served to capt. M.C., USAR, 1971-81. Pathology grantee Mass. Gen. Hosp., Boston, summer 1969; clin. fellow in ophthalmology Harvard U., 1974-76. Mem. Assn. Research in Vision and Ophthalmology, Am. Acad. Ophthalmology, Mass. Soc. Eye Physicians and Surgeons, New Eng. Ophthalmol. Soc., AAAS, Pan Am. Assn. Ophthalmology, Am. Assn. for Pediatric Ophthalmology and Strabismus, Mass. Med. Soc. (Middlesex Central dist.), N.Y. Acad. Scis., Research to Prevent Blindness, Phi Beta Kappa, Sigma Xi. Home: 357 Nashawtuc Rd Concord MA 01742 Office: Lexington Eye Assocs 99 Waltham St Lexington MA 02173

BOGERTS, BERNHARD, psychiatrist, researcher; b. Stromberg, Rheinland-Pfalz, Fed. Republic of Germany, June 1, 1948; s. Ludwig and Maria (Pauly) B.; m. Dorothee Roedel, June 8, 1982; children: Anna, Lisa. MD, U. Duesseldorf, 1975. Staff psychiatrist Psychiat. Hosp., Schleswig, Fed. Republic of Germany, 1976-78; researcher Vogt Inst. Brain Research, Duesseldorf, 1978-84; sr. physician Dept. Psychiatry U. Duesseldorf, 1984—. Contbr. articles to profl. jours. Recipient Kurt Schneider prize German Assn. Psychiatry, 1948. Mem. German Soc. Biol. Psychiatry. Home: Dunantstrasse 37, D-4040 Neuss Federal Republic of Germany Office: U Duesseldorf, Dept Psychiatry, Postfach 12 0510, D-4000 Duesseldorf Federal Republic of Germany

BOGESKOV-JENSEN, OLE, hearing aid company executive; b. Copenhagen, Apr. 6, 1939; s. Helge and Kirstine (Hoegh) B.; m. Else Lilholt, Dec. 1, 1962; children: Tom, Anders. MBA, Handelshøjskolen, Copenhagen, 1963. Export asst. Esmarch's Successors, Copenhagen, 1960-62, Brdr. Vestergard, Copenhagen, 1962-65; regional sales mgr. Oticon AS, Copenhagen, 1965-70, mktg. mgr., 1970-76, v.p., 1976-80, group dir., 1980-86, v.p., group secretariat, 1986—; bd. dirs. Oticon Corp., Oticon West Corp., Oticon France S.A., Oticon Ltd., Oticon Italia, Oticon KK; dir. gen. Oticon S.A., Switzerland, Oticon France S.A. Lutheran. Office: Oticon AS, 9 Klaedemaalet, 2100 O Copenhagen Denmark

BOGGS, JOSEPH DODRIDGE, pediatric pathologist; b. Bellefontaine, Ohio, Dec. 31, 1921; s. Walter C. and Birdella Z. (Coons) B.; m. Donna Lee Shoemaker, June 12, 1964; 1 son, Joseph Dodridge. A.B., Ohio U., 1941, Litt.D., 1966; M.D., Jefferson Med. Coll., 1945. Intern Jefferson Med. Coll. Hosp., Phila., 1945-46; resident Peter Bent Brigham Hosp., Boston, 1946-48; asso. pathologist Peter Bent Brigham Hosp., 1947-51; instr. pathology Harvard Med. Sch., Boston, 1948-51; with Children's Meml. Hosp., Chgo., 1951—; dir. labs. Children's Meml. Hosp., 1951—; prof. pathology Northwestern U., Chgo., 1952—; dir. BSP Ins. Co., Phoenix. Contbr. articles to profl. jours. Mem. med. adv. bd. Ill. Dept. Corrections, Springfield, 1971-77; bd. dirs. Blood Services, Phoenix, 1972, Community Hosp., Evanston, Ill., 1958-61, Lorreto Hosp., Chgo., 1971-72. Served to capt. M.C. U.S. Army, 1948-51. Mem. Am. Soc. Study of Liver Disease, N.Y. Acad. Scis., Midwest Soc. Pediatric Research, Inst. Medicine, Ill. Soc. Pathologists (pres. 1965), Ill. Assn. Blood Banks (pres. 1969-70). Home: 1448 N Lake Shore Dr Chicago IL 60610 Office: Children's Meml Hosp 2300 Children's Plaza Chicago IL 60614

BOGOSIAN, RICHARD WAYNE, diplomat; b. Boston, July 18, 1937; s. Karekin Jacob and Arshalous (Najarian) B.; m. Claire Marie Mornane, June 25, 1961; children—David, Jill, Catherine. A.B. in History, Tufts U., 1959; J.D., U. Chgo., 1962. Bar: Mass. 1962. With U.S. Fgn. Service, Dept. State, 1962—; economic counselor U.S. Fgn. Service, Dept. State, Kuwait, Kuwait, 1972-76; dep. chief mission U.S. Fgn. Service, Dept. State, Khartoum, Sudan, 1976-79; chief aviations negotiations div. U.S. Fgn. Service, Dept. State, Washington, 1979-82, dir. East African Affairs, 1982-85; ambassador to Niger U.S. Fgn. Service, Dept. State, 1985—. Recipient Superior Honor award State Dept., 1971; Meritorious Honor award State Dept., 1974; Superior Honor award State Dept., 1985; Meritorious Performance award State Dept., 1985, 86. Mem. Am. Fgn. Service Assn. Office: Dept State US Ambassador to Niger Washington DC 20520 *

BOGUE, BRUCE, insurance agent; b. Los Angeles, Sept. 24, 1924; s. Charles Luther and Viola (Adam) B.; m. Tays Myrl Tarvin, Dec. 18, 1945; children: Tays Elizabeth, Charles Luther II. BA, U. Calif. at Los Angeles, 1947; grad. Inf. Staff and Command Sch. U.S. Army, 1948. Agt. Mut. Benefit Life Ins. Co., Los Angeles, 1948-55, prodn. mgr., 1955-62; gen. agt. Guardian Life Ins. Co., Los Angeles, 1962-85, agt., 1985—; tchr. ins. UCLA. Contbr. articles to profl. jours. Precinct capt., poll watcher, hdqrs. chmn., fund raising chmn., campaign chmn. for Rep. party. Served to capt. inf. AUS, 1942-46, ETO. Recipient Man of Affairs award Los Angeles Wilshire Press, Los Angeles Mirror News, 1958, Nat. Mgmt. award 1980-85. Mem. Million Dollar Round Table (life), Am. Soc. CLUs, Assn. Advanced Life Underwriters, Nat. Assn. Life Underwriters, U. Calif. at Los Angeles Alumni Assn. (life). Congregationalist. Clubs: Annandale Golf (Pasadena, Calif.); Monrovia Tennis, Calif. (Los Angeles). Home: 2200 Homet Rd San Marino CA 91108 Office: 617 S Olive St #1000 Los Angeles CA 90014

BOGUTZ, JEROME E., lawyer; b. Bridgeton, N.J., June 7, 1935; s. Charles and Gertrude (Lahn) B.; m. Helene Carole Ross, Nov. 20, 1960; children—Marc Lahn, Tami Lynne. B.S. in Finance, Pa. State U., 1957; J.D., Villanova U., 1962. Assoc. Dash & Levy, Phila., 1962-63; assoc. Abrahams & Loewenstein, Phila., 1963-64; dep. dir., chief of litigation Community Legal Services, Phila., 1964-68; sole practice law Phila., 1968-71; ptnr. Bogutz & Mazer, Phila., 1971-81, Fox Rothschild O'Brien & Frankel, Phila., 1981—; adj. clin. prof. law Villanova U., Pa., 1969-72, lectr., 1987—; pres., dir. Internat. Mobile Machines, Phila., 1974-81; dir., sec. Jefferson Park Hosp., Phila., 1982—; bd. consultors Villanova Law Sch., 1983—; ABA/JAD Lawyers Conf., 1987—, exec. council, 1986—, vice chmn., 1987-88, chmn., 1988—. Commr., chmn. ABA Commn. on Advt., 1988—, bd. dirs. Am. Friends Hebrew U. Served with USAR, 1955-60. Fellow Am. Bar Found. (life), Pa. Bar Found. (pres. 1986—, dir. 1983—); mem. Phila. C. of C. (dir. 1980-83), ABA (ho. of dels., 1980-84, 86—, credentials and admissions com., chair ABA/JAD bench bar com., vice chmn. lawyer's conf. 1987-88, co-chair mid-yr. meeting com. 1987-88), Am. Judicature Soc. (life), Pa. Bar Assn. (pres. 1985-86), Phila. Bar Assn. (pres. 1980), Phila. Bar Found. (pres. 1981), House of Delegates (life, trustee 1981—), Nat. Met. Bar Leaders (founder, pres. 1979-82), Nat. Conf. Bar Pres.' (exec. council 1981-84). Republican. Jewish. Home: 509 Hamilton Rd Merion PA 19066 Office: Fox Rothschild O'Brien and Frankel 2000 Market St 10th Floor Philadelphia PA 19103

BOHAN, MARC, fashion designer; b. Paris, France, Aug. 22, 1926; s. Alfred and Genevieve (Baudoux) B.; m. Dominique Gaborit, Feb. 23, 1950 (dec. June 1962); 1 child, Marie Anne. Received baccalaureat. Asst. designer Piquet, Paris, 1945-49, Molyneux, 1949-51; designer Patou,, Paris, 1951-58, Christian Dior, London, 1958-60; chief designer, artistic dir. Christian Dior S.A., Paris, 1960—; also designer for theatre and film 1960—.

BOHLER, TORSTEIN, consulting company executive; b. Oslo, Aug. 4, 1934; s. Thorvald Johannes and Petra (Gaarder) B.; m. Liv Hanevik, Sept. 8, 1962; children—Line Beate, Tove Cathrine. Dipl. Ing. M.E., Tech. U., Karlsruhe, W. Ger., 1960. Project engr. Reactor Centrum Nederland, Petten, Netherlands, 1961-65; sr. engr. Inst. Atomic Energy, Kjeller, Norway, 1965-69, Bechtel Corp., San Francisco, 1969-70; div. leader Scandpower A/S, Oslo, 1971-76, asst. dir., 1976-80; mng. dir., pres. Scandpower A/S Norway, Scandpower Inc., Washington, 1980—. Contbr. articles on quality assurance and risk mgmt. to profl. jours.; patentee in field. Mem. City Bd., Skedsmo Municipality, 1976-80, mem. energy utility bd., 1980-88, mem. ISO tech. com. quality assurance, 1980—. Served with Signal Corps, Norwegian Army, 1953-54. Mem. Norwegian Poly. Soc., Norwegian Petroleum Soc. Conservative. Lutheran. Club: Lions (pres. 1980-81) (Skedsmo). Office: Scandpower A/S, 2007 Kjeller Norway

BOHLIM, RICHARD CHARLES, civil engineer; b. Michigan City, Ind., Sept. 5, 1952; s. George A. and Margaret (Elias) B.; BSCE, Ind. Inst. Tech., 1974. Registered profl. engr., Kans.; lic. pvt. pilot. Service engr. Combustion Engring., Martins Creek, Pa., 1974, Boston, 1974-75, St. Louis, 1975-76, lead service engr. for combustion engring., Lawrence, Kans., 1976-78, resident service engr., Overland Park, Kans., 1978-80, resident supr. tech. services Kansas City Dist., 1980-87, dist. mgr. tech. services, Kansas City, 1981-87, Englewood, Colo., 1987—. Mem. ASCE (citation award 1974), Alpha Sigma Phi. Roman Catholic. Club: Moose. Home: 205 Corby Ct Castle Rock CO 80104 Office: 23 Inverness Way E Suite 110 Englewood CO 80112

BOHLIN, DANIEL JAMES, air force officer; b. Elgin, Ill., Apr. 17, 1949; s. Wallace Bernard and Lillian Elsie (Schock) B.; m. Gwendolyn Joan Flynn, Apr. 21, 1973 (div.); 1 dau., Adrienne. BS, U.S. Air Force Acad., 1971; Disting. grad. Squadron Officers Sch., 1976, Def. Lang. Inst., 1978, Armed Forces Staff Coll., 1985; postgrad. Inst. d'Etudes Politiques U. Grenoble, 1978-80; MA in Polit. Sci., Ariz. State U., 1981. Commd. 2d lt. U.S. Air Force, 1971, advanced through grades to lt. col., 1987; forward air controller O-2A, Vietnam, 1973; co-pilot KC-135, Loring AFB, Maine, 1973-75, aircraft comdr., 1975-77, aircraft comdr., instr. pilot, flight comdr., evaluation br. chief, March AFB, Calif., 1981-84; Air Attache, W. Africa, 1985-87; research assoc. Hoover Inst., 1987-88; Internat. Pol.-Mil. Affairs, HQ USAF, 1988—. Contbr. articles to profl. jours., chpt. to book. Decorated Air Force Meritorious Service medal, Commendation medal, with oak leaf cluster. Recipient Olmsted Found. scholarship, 1978. Mem. Air Force Assn., Assn. Grads. U.S. Air Force Acad. Home: 1523 Highland Ave Elgin IL 60123 Office: care Jean Devericks 11015 Becontree Lake Dr #301 Reston VA 22090

BOHLKE, GARY LEE, lawyer, playwright; b. Yakima, Wash., Mar. 9, 1941; s. Francis Douglas and Laura Mae (Bianchi) B. B.A., U. Wash., 1963; J.D., Am. U., 1966; LL.M., U. London, 1967; diploma London Inst. of World Affairs, 1967. Bar: D.C. 1967. Assoc. firm Mason, Fenwick & Lawrence, Washington, 1967-70; atty.-advisor U.S. C.E., Washington, 1972-74; asst. solicitor environ. law U.S. Dept. Interior, Washington, 1974-83, asst. solicitor for environ. and realty, 1983-86, sr. atty. environ. protection, 1986—. Author: (plays) The Crime Tetraology consisting of Double Cross, 1982, Obsession, 1984, Judgment, 1985, Act of Justice, 1987, Echoes of Forgotten Time, 1988. Vice chmn. com. on environ. and transp. Washington, Adv. Neighborhood Commn. 4C, 1980—. Recipient outstanding service award Office of Solicitor, Dept. Interior, 1979, 80, 81, 83, 84, 85, 86, Spl. Achievement award 1981, 86. Mem. D.C. Bar Assn. (chmn. environ. law com. 1977-78, ABA del. 1978-79). Lutheran. Home: 4617 Arkansas Ave NW Washington DC 20011 Office: Dept Interior 18th and E Sts NW Washington DC 20240

BOHM, PETER JAN GUNNAR, economist; b. Stockholm, Mar. 30, 1935; s. Stellan G. and Marta Bohm; children: Helena, Katarina, Petra, Martin, Paula. PhD, Stockholm U., 1970. Asst. prof. econs. Stockholm U., 1962, assoc. prof., 1970-75, prof., 1975—; judge Mkt. Ct., 1971; research fellow U. Calif., 1964-65. Author: External Economics in Production, 1964, Resource Allocation and the Credit Market, 1967, Pricing of Copper, 1967, Social Efficiency, 1974, 87; editor: Swedish Jour. Econs., 1968-72; assoc. editor Jour. Pub. Econs.; contbr. articles to profl. jours. Recipient Lindahl Found. award 1962; Am. Council Learned Socs. fellow, 1964. Mem. Am. Econ. Assn. Home: 6D Odenvagen, Upplands Vasby Sweden Office: U Stockholm, Dept Econs, Stockholm Sweden

BÖHM, TOMAS A.W., psychoanalyst; b. Stockholm, Apr. 20, 1945; s. Paul and Clary (Weingeist) B.; m. Karin Mattsson; children: Felix, Anna; m. Suzanne Kaplan; 1 child, Paula Nomi. MD, Karolinska Inst., Stockholm, 1971. Sr. physician Stockholm Psychotherapeutic Inst., 1974—; pvt. practice psychoanalysis 1975—. Author: The Mountain Trip, 1980, After Falling in Love, 1984, On Infidelity, 1987; contbr. articles on psychology to profl. jours.

BOHN, ROBERT HERBERT, lawyer; b. Austin, Tex., Sept. 2, 1935; s. Herbert and Alice (Heinen) B.; m. Gay P. Maloy, June 4, 1957; children—Rebecca Shoemaker, Katherine, Robert H., Jr. B.B.A., U. Tex., 1957, LL.B., 1963. Bar: Tex. 1963, Calif. 1965. Ptnr. Boccardo Law Firm, San Jose, Calif., 1965-87 ptnr. Alexander & Bohn, 1987—; speaker Calif. Continuing Edn. of Bar; judge pro tem Superior Ct. of Calif., San Jose, 1975-86. Sustaining mem. Republican Nat. Com., Washington, Nat. Rep. Senatorial Com., Washington, Rep. Presdl. Task Force, Washington. Mem. Calif. Trial Lawyers Assn., Assn. Trial Lawyers Am., Santa Clara County Bar Assn., Calif. State Bar Assn., Internat. Platform Assn., Phi Gamma Delta. Home: 14124 Pike Rd Saratoga CA 95070 Office: 55 S Market St Suite 1080 San Jose CA 95113

BOHNEN, KLAUS, language educator; b. Ratingen, Fed. Republic of Germany, Aug. 17, 1940; arrived in Denmark, 1970; s. Peter and Katharina (Hoffmann) B. Student, U. Cologne, Fed. Republic of Germany, 1961-62, 66-68, U. Vienna, Austria, 1963, U. Poitiers, France, 1964-65; PhD, U. Cologne, Fed. Republic Germany, 1970. Research scholar U. Cologne, 1968-70; assoc. prof. German lit. U. Copenhagen, 1970-82; prof. U. Aalborg, Denmark, 1982—. Author several books and 70 articles in field; editor: (jours.) Kopenhagener Kolloquien zur deutschen Literatur, 1977—, Text and Context, 1978—, Beiträge zur Literaturvermittlung im Fremdsprachenunterricht, 1980—, also books. Mem. Lessing Acad., Gesellschaft zur Erforschung des 18 Jahrhunderts, Brandes Gesellschaft, Harro-Harring Gesellschaft. Office: U Aalborg, Langagervej 6, 9100 Aalborg Denmark

BOHORFOUSH, JOSEPH GEORGE, retired physician; b. Birmingham, Ala., Dec. 20, 1907; s. George and Susan (Joseph) B.; A.B., Vanderbilt U., 1929, M.D., 1933; m. Agravene M. Bohorfoush; children—William, David. Intern Hillman Hosp., Birmingham, 1933-34; resident Waverly Hills (Ky.) Sanatorium, 1934-35; asst. med. dir. Lake View Sanatorium, Madison, Wis., 1936-41; med. dir. Jefferson Sanatorium, Birmingham, 1946-47; instr. medicine U. Ala. Med. Coll., 1946-48; chief profl. services VA Hosp., Memphis, 1947-51; asst. prof. medicine U. Tenn., Memphis, 1947, 51; clin. prof. medicine Med. Coll. Ga., 1951-60; chief medicine VA Hosp, Augusta, Ga., 1951-60. Served as maj. M.C., AUS, 1941-45; col. M.C. ret. Diplomate Am. Bd. Internal Medicine, Am. Bd. Pulmonary Diseases. Fellow A.C.P., Am. Coll. Chest Physicians; mem. AMA, So. med. assns., Ret. Officers Assn. Home: 1300 Beacon Pkwy Apt 608 Birmingham AL 35209

BOHR, AAGE NIELS, physicist; b. June 19, 1922; Ph.D., U. Copenhagen (Denmark), 1954; Dr. honoris causa, Manchester U., 1961; hon. degrees Oslo U., 1969, Heidelberg U., 1971, Trondheim U., 1972, Uppsala U., 1975; m. Marietta Bettina Soffer (dec. 1978); 3 children: m. Bente Meyer Scharff, 1981. Jr. sci. officer Dept. Sci. and Indsl. Research, London, 1943-45; research asso. Inst. Theoretical Physics, U. Copenhagen, from 1946, prof. physics, 1956—; dir. Niels Bohr Inst., 1962-70; mem. bd. Nordita, 1958-74, dir., 1975-81. Recipient Dannie Heineman prize, 1960; Pope Pius XI medal 1963; Atoms for Peace award, 1969; H.C. Ørsted medal, 1970; Rutherford medal, 1972; John Price Wetherill medal, 1974; Nobel prize in physics, 1975; Ole Römer medal, 1976. Mem. Danish, Norwegian, Yugoslavian, Polish, Swedish acads. scis., Royal Physiograph. Soc. Lund, Sweden, Am. Acad. Arts and Scis., Nat. Acad. Scis. (U.S.), Deutsche Akademie der Naturforscher Leopoldina, Am. Philos. Soc., Finska Vetenskaps-Societeten, Pontifical Acad. Author: Rotational States of Atomic Nuclei, 1954; (with Ben R. Mottelson) Nuclear Structure, Vol. 1, 1969, Vol. 2, 1975. Research quantum physics; specialist nuclear physics. Office: Niels Bohr Inst, Blegdamsvej 15-17, DK-2100 Copenhagen Denmark *

BOHR, NIELS KARSTEN, corporate executive; b. Hellerup, Denmark, Apr. 11, 1946; s. Erik and Ulla (Meyer) B.; m. Lis Christiansen, Mar 22, 1968; children: Betina, Babette. BBA, Copenhagen U., 1968, MBA, 1971; MBA, Stanford U., 1974. Group acct. Minn. Mining and Mfg., Copenhagen, 1969-71; personal asst. to pres. F.L.S. Overseas A/S, Copenhagen, 1974-76; pres. De Forenede Vognmandsforretninger A/S, Copenhagen, 1976-78, J.E. Lau A/S, Copenhagen, 1978-79, FJC, Barcelona, Spain, 1979-80, Pedershaab Maskinfabrik, Brønderslev, Denmark, 1981-84, Kongskilde, Sorø, Denmark, 1984—; chmn. Kongskilde Group Cos., Denmark and internat., 1984—; dir. Kores Nordic Holding A/S, 1987. Co-author: Industriens Indtjening og finansiering, 1977. Mem/ Dansk Arbejdsgiverforenings lokalafdeling i Sorø. Home: Skaelskørvej 45, 4180 Sorø Denmark Office: Kongskilde Koncernselskab A/S, Skaelskørvej, 4180 Sorø Denmark

BOHTLINGK, JORGE ERNESTO, banker; b. Buenos Aires, Aug. 5, 1945; s. Heriberto and Leonor Luisa (Sackmann) B.; m. Guillermina Moreno Bunge, Sept. 26, 1948; children: Jorge Jose, Isabel, Nicolas Herbert, Alexander. Litentiate in Social Sci. and Econs., Argentine Cath. U., 1969. Asst. acct. Citibank N.A., Buenos Aires, 1968-70; resident v.p. Citibank N.A., Sao Paulo, Brazil, 1974-79; v.p. Citibank N.A., Buenos Aires, 1979—; mgr. Rural Adminstrns., Las Rosas, Argentina, 1970-73; mng. ptnr. Las Chilquitas SCA, Buenos Aires, 1970—; syndic Carlos Casado SA, Buenos Aires, 1986—. Mem. Soc. Rural Argentina, Soc. Argentina, Soc. Argentina Horticulture. Roman Catholic. Clubs: Yacht, Ski, Jockey (Buenos Aires). Office: Citibank NA, B Mitre 530, Buenos Aires 1036, Argentina

BOICE, CRAIG KENDALL, management consultant; b. Portland, Oreg., June 25, 1952; s. Charles A. and Audrey (Larson) B.; m. Jacinta E. Remedios, Nov. 21, 1979. BA summa cum laude, Beloit Coll., 1973; MA, Yale U., 1974, M.Phil., 1976, M in Pub. and Pvt. Mgmt., 1979. Instr. fellow philosophy Yale U., New Haven, 1978-79; economist Overseas Pvt. Investment Corp., Washington, 1978; sr. cons. Coopers and Lybrand, Washington and London, 1979-81; v.p. ops. Internat. Licensing Network, N.Y.C., 1981-82; pres., chmn., chief exec. officer Boice Dunham Group, N.Y.C., 1983—; adj. asst. prof. NYU, 1984—. Cons. Lake Placid Olympic Organizing Com., (N.Y.), 1979, New Haven Homesteading Program, 1979. Mem. Computer and Automated Systems Assn., Soc. Mfg. Engrs., Corp. Growth Assn., Soc. Photog. Scientists and Engrs., Planning Forum., World Future Soc., Internat. Platform Assn. Democrat. Office: Boice Dunham Group 437 Madison Ave New York NY 10022

BOILEAU, OLIVER CLARK, JR., aerospace company executive; b. Camden, N.J., Mar. 31, 1927; s. Oliver Clark and Florence Mary (Smith) B.; m. Nan Eleze Hallen, Sept. 15, 1951; children: Clark Edward, Adrienne Lee, Nanette Erika, Jay Marshall. B.S. in Elec. Engring., U. Pa., 1951, M.S., 1953; SM in Indsl. Mgmt., MIT, 1964. With Boeing Aerospace Co., 1953-79, mgr. Minuteman, v.p., 1968, pres., 1973-79; pres. Gen. Dynamics Corp., 1980—, also bd. dirs.; bd. dirs. Centerre Bank; trustee The Conf. Bd.; mem. vis. com. aeronautics and astronautics MIT, Lincoln Lab. Adv. Bd. Mem. corp. Lawrence Inst. Tech.; trustee Ranken Tech. Inst.; v.p. exec. bd. St. Louis Area council Boy Scouts Am.; bd. overseers U. Pa.; trustee St. Louis U. Served with USN, 1944-46. Sloan fellow, MIT, 1963-64. Mem. AIAA, Navy League, Air Force Assn., Am. Def. Preparedness Assn., Assn. U.S. Army, Nat. Aeros. Assn., Nat. Space Club, Naval War Coll. Found., Nat. Acad. Engring. Office: Gen Dynamics Corp Pierre Laclede Ctr Saint Louis MO 63105

BOIMAN, DONNA RAE, art academy executive; b. Columbus, Ohio, Jan. 13, 1946; d. George Brandle and Donna Rae (Rockwell) Hall; m. David Charles Boiman, Dec. 8, 1973. BS in Pharmacy, Ohio State U., 1969; student, Columbus Coll. Art & Design, 1979-83. Registered pharmacist, Ohio. Pharmacist, mgr. various retail stores, Cleve., 1970-73, Columbus, 1973-77; owner L'Artiste, Reynoldsburg, Ohio, 1977-81; pres. Cen. Ohio Art

Acad., Reynoldsburg, 1981—; cons. to Mayor City of Reynoldsburg, 1986-87. Represented in permanent collections including Collector's Gallery Columbus Mus. Art, Gallery 200, Columbus, Art Exchange, Columbus, The Huntington Collection, Dean Witter Reynolds Collection, Zanesville Art Ctr. Author: Anatomy and Structure: A Guide for Young Artists, 1988; represented in permanent collections Mt. Carmel East Hosp., Columbus, Corp. 2005, Radisson Hotels, Mich. and Ohio, Fifth 3d Bank, Bexley, Ohio, On Line Computer Library, Dublin, Ohio, Cintas Corp. Recipient John Lennon Meml. Award for the Arts, Internat. Art Challenge com., 1987. Mem. Pa. Soc. Watercolorists, Nat. Soc. Layerists in Multimedia, Columbus Art League, Cen. Ohio Watercolor Soc. (pres. 1983-84), Am. Quarter Horse Assn., Ohio Quarter Horse Assn., Allied Artists of Am. (assoc.), Licking County Art Assn., Nat. Wildlife Fedn., Ohio State U. Alumni Assn., Ohio State U. Pharmacy Alumni Assn. (charter). Office: Cen Ohio Art Acad 7297 E Main St Reynoldsburg OH 43068

BOINEM, MAURICE MICHEL, walnut wood specialist; b. Liege, Belgium, July 3, 1922; s. Francois and Anne Rosa (Deprez) B.; m. Jeanine Cremers, July 14,1972. Mem. Fedn. Industries Du Bois Belgium. Home: Voie De Liege 148, B 4920 Embourg Belgium Office: Maison Boinem, 101 103 Rue Hayeneux, B 4400 Herstal Belgium

BOISBOUVIER, JEAN-PAUL ROBERT, real estate executive; b. Monaco, Feb. 19, 1958; s. Paul Henri and Jocelyn (Benyayer) B. BA in Math. and Physics with honors, Lycee Albert Ier, Monaco, 1976; MBA, Ecole Sup. Commerce Lyon, France, 1979, U. Conn., 1980. Asst. planning mgr. Thyssen Bornemisza, Monaco, 1979-1980; asst. mktg. mgr. Duchef Fancy Food, N.Y.C., 1980-81; asst. merchandsising. mgr. Calvin Klein Menswear, N.Y.C., 1981-82; pres. Internat. Reality and Ins. Sales, Monte Carlo, 1983—. Mem. Assn. Internat. Etudiants Scis. Economiques et Commerciales (treas. 1978), Monaco Jr. C. of C. (1985-86), Jaycees, USA Assn (sec. 1986-87). Lodge: Rotary (pres. 1979). Home: 33 Saint Charles, Monte Carlo Monaco MC98000 Office: Internat Reality and Ins Services, 4 Rue des Iris, Monte Carlo Monaco MC98000

BOISSEVAIN, MATTHIJS GIDEON JAN, mechanical engineer; b. Amsterdam, Netherlands, Apr. 24, 1916; came to U.S., 1935, naturalized, 1941; s. Walrave and Romelia Abr (Kalff) B.; S.B. in Mech. Engring., M.I.T., 1938, postgrad., 1938-42; M.S. in Adminstrv. Sci., Rensselaer Poly. Inst., 1979; m. Helen Richmond Fisk, Mar. 15, 1939 (dec. Oct. 1979); children—Robert, Romelia Boissevain Bayer, Bruce (dec.), Pamela Boissevain Wilkinson, Lance, Kimberley Boissevain Buck, Mia; m. Ethel Stodgell Knobloch, Oct. 1, 1983. Instr., M.I.T., 1938-42; with Stone & Webster Engring. Corp., 1942-44; asst. prof. Pratt Inst., 1949-51; with Electric Boat div. Gen. Dynamics Corp., 1951-82, chief tech. ops., 1954-82; with Stone & Webster Engring. Corp., 1982-83; cons., 1982-83; pres. Computer Country Corp., 1983—; pres. Highland Orchards Resort Park, Inc. Chmn. Bd. Edn. North Stonington (Conn.), 1956-68; mem. Westerly Community Chorus, 1966, 67, 79-81; chmn. Republican Town Com. North Stonington, 1978, 79. Registered profl. engr., Conn., Mass. Mem. Electric Boat Mgmt. Assn. (dir. profl. devel.), Soc. Preservation and Encouragement Barber Shop Quartet Singing Am. (pres. New London chpt. 1979-80), Nat. Campground Owners Assn. (dir. 1981), Conn. Campground Owners Assn. (pres. 1975-76). Christian Scientist. Clubs: Lions, Masons, Elks. Patentee in field. Address: 216 Prospect Hill Rd Noank CT 06340

BOJAXHIU, AGNES GONXHA See TERESA, MOTHER

BOJIN, JACQUES, management consultant; b. Paris, July 25, 1939; s. Simon and Genevieve (Chabaud) B.; m. Daniele Perrin, Dec. 20, 1971; children: Marie-Helene, Severine. M.E., Ecole Nationale superieure d'Arts and Métiers, Paris, 1961; M.A., Institut d'Etudes Politiques, Paris, 1963; M.S. in Mgmt., MIT, 1964. Analyst, First Nat. Bank Boston, 1964-65, asst. rep., Paris, 1967-68, internat. officer, Boston, 1968-69, asst. v.p. (BOFC), 1969-70; mgmt. cons. McKinsey & Co., Paris, 1970-74, J.B. & Associés. Paris, 1975—; pres. Terrin Group, Marseilles, France, 1977-78; chmn. The A.B.C. Group, Paris, 1979—. Served as ops. research officer French Navy, 1965-67. Clubs: Interallié, Paris Country. Home: 5 Avenue Erlanger, 75016 Paris France Office: ABC Group, 70 Rue Anatole France, 92300 Levallois France

BOK, DEREK, university president; b. Bryn Mawr, Pa., Mar. 22, 1930; s. Curtis and Margaret (Plummer) B.; m. Sissela Ann Myrdal, May 7, 1955; children: Hilary Margaret, Victoria, Tomas Jeremy. B.A., Stanford U., 1951; J.D., Harvard U., 1954; M.A., George Washington U., 1958. Fulbright scholar Paris, 1954-55; faculty Harvard U. Law Sch., Cambridge, Mass., 1958—, prof., 1961—, dean, 1968-71; pres. Harvard U., Cambridge, 1971—. Editor: (with Archibald Cox) Cases and Materials on Labor Law, 1962; author: (with John T. Dunlop) Labor and the American Community, 1970, Beyond the Ivory Tower: Social Responsibilities of the Modern University, 1982, Higher Learning, 1986; contbr.: In the Public Interest, 1980. Served to 1st lt. AUS, 1956-58. Fellow Am. Acad. Arts and Scis., Nat. Assn. Ind. Colls. and Univs. (bd. dirs.); mem. Inst. Medicine, Am. Philos. Soc., Nat. Commn. on the Pub. Service Forum, Bus.-Higher Edn. Human Capital Task Force, Phi Beta Kappa. Office: Harvard U Massachusetts Hall Cambridge MA 02138

BOKLUND-LAGOPOULOS, KARIN MARGARETA, English educator; b. Uppsala, Sweden, Dec. 14, 1948; arrived in Greece, 1976; d. Karl Gunnar and Gjördis Vanja (Sandin) Boklund; m. George Coffer, 1970 (div. 1976); m. Alexandros Phaedon Lagopoulos, July 24, 1979. BA in French, U. Colo., 1969, MA in Comparative Lit., 1971, PhD in Comparative Lit., 1975; BA in English, U. Thessaloniki, Greece, 1980. Teaching assoc. dept. English U. Colo., Boulder, 1971-75; postdoctoral fellow Ctr. Humanities, Wesleyan U., Middletown, Conn., 1977-78; lectr. Dept. English, U. Thessaloniki, 1981-84, asst. prof., 1984-85, assoc. prof., 1985—. Editor: (books) Semiotics and Society, 1980, Dynamics of Sign, 1986; guest editor: (jour.) Signs of the Past, 1986; contbr. articles to profl. jours. Regents scholar U. Colo., 1965-69; grantee Fulbright Found., 1987; fellow Mellon Found., 1977-78. Mem. MLA, Internat. Assn. Semiotic Studies, Hellenic Semiotic Soc. (sec. 1985-87). Office: U Thessaloniki, Dept English, 540 06 Thessaloniki Greece

BOKOR, PAL, journalist; b. Budapest, Hungary, May 2, 1942; s. Mihaly and Rozsa (Steiner) B.; m. Aleftina Sirjajeva; children: Klara, Julia, Marton, Katalin. Student, Budapest Sch. Journalism, 1961-62, U. Marxizm, Budapest, 1963-65, U. Lomonosov, Moscow, 1964-66. Journalist Hungarian News Agy., Budapest, 1960-64, Moscow, 1971-77; correspondent Hungarian News Agy., Washington, 1980-84; mng. fgn. editor Magyar Hirlap, Budapest, 1986—. Author: Vladivostok, Kamchatka, Szahalin, 1978, A Chinese Summer, 1980, Washington, 1984, The Panda (novel), 1985, The Silver Malibu, 1988. Mem. MSZMP Communist Party, 1970. Recipient Excellence award Hungarian TV, 1982. Mem. Hungarian Assn. of Journalists (v.p. control com. 1985, excellence award 1987). Home: Beregszasz u 68, 1116 Budapest Hungary Office: Magyar Hirlap, VII Lenin krt, 9-11 Budapest Hungary

BOKROSS, AGNES HELEN, educator documentalist; b. Budapest, Hungary, Jan. 9, 1922; came to Can., 1957, naturalized, 1962; d. Lajos Ferenc and Andrea (Tömöry) Szakonyi; B.A. with honors in English, Sir George Williams U., Montreal, Que., Can., 1970; Ph.D. in Comparative Lit. (Woodrow Wilson fellow 1970-71, Ford fellow 1970-71, Can. Council doctoral awards 1972-74), McGill U., Montreal, 1974; m. Béla E. Bokross, 1943 (div. 1945); 1 dau., Apollonia Elizabeth Bokross Schofield. Indexer and archivist Internat. Civil Aviation Orgn., Montreal, 1957-72; lectr. in English lit. Concordia U., Montreal, 1974-80; multilingual annotator Nat. Library Can., Ottawa, Ont., 1975-81; documentalist Public Service Commn. Can., Ottawa, 1981—; tchr., cons. in field. Recipient Gold medal Gov. Gen. Can., 1970; McGill U. travel research grantee, 1973. Mem. MLA, Can. Soc. Comparative Study Civilizations, Nat. Geog. Soc. Roman Catholic. Author Nat. Library of Can. Annotations Manual, 1979; contbr. essays to lit. jours.; papers to confs. Office: Public Service Commn L'Esplanade Laurier West Tower, B1123 300 Laurier W, Ottawa, ON Canada K1A 0M7

BOKSENBERG, ALEXANDER, astronomer; b. Mar. 18, 1936; s. Julius and Ernestina (Steinberg) B.; m. 1960, Adella Coren; 2 children. B.Sc., Ph.D., Dept. Physics and Astronomy, U. London. Research ass. U. Coll. London, 1960-65, lectr. physics, 1965-75, head optical and ultraviolet astronomy research group, 1969-81; reader in physics 1975-78; SRC sr. fellow, 1976-81; prof. physics, dir. Royal Greenwich Obs., 1981—; vis. pro dep. physics and astronomy UCL, 1981—, Astronomy Centre, U. Sussex, 1981—. Contbr. articles to profl. jours. Dr. H.C., l'Observatoire de Paris, 1982. Address: Royal Greenwich Observatory, Herstmonceux Castle, Hailsham East Sussex BN27 1RP, England

BOLAJI, ROTIMI MICHAEL, accountant, operational research consultant; b. Okemesi-Ekiti, Nigeria, Mar. 3, 1952; s. Ibiloye Ezekiel and Ojuolade Abigael (Ojo-Odide) B.; m. Aduke Janet Adeoti, Nov. 4, 1981; children: Oluwatola Peter, Oluwafunmilola Deborah, Paul Oluwatuyi. Ordinary Nat. Diploma in Acctg., Poly. Ibadan, Nigeria, 1975, Higher Nat. Diploma in Acctg., 1976. Acctg. supr. Nigerian Nat. Petroleum Co., Lagos, 1979-82; acct., co. sec. Tixo Ltd., Ibadan, 1982-83, Abdulai & Amimolo Co. Ltd., Ibadan, 1983-84; internal auditor Ekiti-Akoko Agrl. Devel. Projects, Ikole-Ekiti, Nigeria, 1984-85; fin. mgr. Nigerian Telecommunications Ltd., Lagos, 1985-86; mng. dir. Mgmt. & Profl. Services Ltd, Ibadan, 1986—; audit mgr./cons. Opeabayomi & Co., Ibadan, 1986; bd. dirs. Profl. Edn. Ctr., Jos., Nigeria. Mem. Brit. Inst. Mgmt., Inst. Chartered Accts. Nigeria (assoc., chartered), Am. Mgmt. Assn. Clubs: Christian Pen Witness (Ibadan) (pres. 1977-86, editor newsletter 1977). Home: Obala Compound, PO Box 18, Okemesi-Ekiti Nigeria Office: Mgmt & Profl Services Ltd, N6/390B Polytechnic Rd, PO Box 15304, Ibadan Nigeria

BOLAK, HALIL DOGAN, petroleum company executive; b. Istanbul, Turkey, Oct. 14, 1961; s. Ahmet Aydin and Ayse Selma (Gürsan) B.; m. Ümit Nazli Alplay, Aug 10, 1984. BS in Engring., U. Rochester, 1983, MBA, 1985. With, bd. dirs. Türkpetrol T.A.S., Istanbul, Marmara Petrol A.S., Istanbul, Turtel A.S., Istanbul, Tüdas A.S., Istanbul; cons. in field. Mem. Beta Gamma Sigma. Office: Turkpetrol TAS, Muallim Naci Cad 100, Istanbul Turkey

BOLAN, THOMAS ANTHONY, lawyer; b. Lynn, Mass., May 30, 1924; s. Thomas J. and Margaret (Cremin) B.; m. Marie T. Gerst, Nov. 25, 1950; children: Sean, Douglas, Mary, Jacqueline, William. B.A. summa cum laude, St. John's U., 1952, LL.B. summa cum laude, 1950, LL.D. (hon.), 1985. Bar: N.Y. 1951. Assoc. firm Burroughs & Brown, N.Y.C., 1951-53; asst. U.S. atty. Dept. Justice, N.Y.C., 1953-57; assoc. Roy M. Cohn, N.Y.C., 1957-59; mem. firm Saxe, Bacon & Bolan, N.Y.C., 1960-71; counsel Saxe, Bacon & Bolan, 1972-87; ptnr. Bolan, Lang, Biancone, Tiffenberg, P.C., N.Y.C., 1987—; lectr. law St. John's U., 1957-61; pres., chmn. bd. 5th Ave. Coach Lines, N.Y.C., 1967-68, Championship Sports, Inc., N.Y.C., 1961—; treas., exec. dir. Feature Sports, Inc., 1959-61; chmn. bd. Merc. Nat. Bank, Chgo., 1967-68, Gateway Nat. Bank, Chgo., 1966-67; sec. Balt. Paint and Chem. Corp., N.Y.C., 1966-68, TelePro Industries Inc., N.Y.C., 1966-68; sec., dir. B.S.F. Co., N.Y.C., 1966-68, Defiance Industries, N.Y.C., 1966-68; v.p. Am. Steel and Pump Corp., N.Y.C., 1966-68, WRNJ Assocs., Atlantic City, 1961-68, Harrisburg Broadcasting Co., Palmyra, Pa., 1966-68; sec., treas., dir. Berwick Broadcasting Corp., Reading, Pa., 1967-68; dir. Overseas Pvt. Investment Corp., 1982-86. Bd. editors: Nat. Law Jour., 1983—; Contbr. articles to legal jours. Co-chmn. N.Y. Reagan Fin. Com., 1980, N.Y. Reagan-Bush Campaign Com., 1984; founder law chmn., mem. exec. com. Conservative Party, N.Y. State, 1962—; chmn. E. Side Conservative Club, N.Y.C., 1973—; v.p. Crusade for Am., Rockville Center, N.Y., 1957-62; bd. regents St. Francis Coll., Bklyn., 1968—; treas. Ednl. Reviewer, 1960—; pres. Cambria Heights (N.Y.) Parish Council, 1968-70; pres., dir. Pro Ecclesia Found., 1972-73; trustee Cambria Heights Boys Club Assn., 1968-72, St. John's U., 1987—, deans bd. of visitors Sch. of Law, 1987—; v.p., dir. Heiser Found., 1955-73; mem. Com. to Restore Internal Security, 1979—; bd. govs. Council for Nat. Policy, 1983—; mem. Am. Council on Germany, 1983—, U.S. Commn. for UNESCO, 1983-85; bd. visitors Eureka Coll., 1983—; nat. adv. council Actors Youth Fund, 1982—; mem. U.S. Senator Alfonse D'Amato's Jud. Screening Com., 1980—; bd. dirs. Global Econ. Action Inst., 1986—. Served with USAF, 1943-45. Decorated Air medal with 5 oak leaf clusters; recipient Medal of Honor The 52 Assn., 1981, Bella V. Dodd Meml. award N.Y. County Conservative Party, 1981, Ann. award Bronx County Conservative Party, 1984, Charles Edison award Conservative Party N.Y. State, 1987, Disting. Service award Nat. Cath. War Vets., 1985. Mem. Fed. Bar Council, Am., N.Y. State, N.Y. County bar assns., Am. Judicature Soc., Cath. Lawyers Guild, Nat. Assn. Coll. and Univ. Attys., Cath. War Vets. (Queens County judge advocate 1965—, nat. judge advocate 1984—, Service award Queens County chpt. 1968, 77, elected to Order St. Sebastian, nat. assn. 1981), Am. African Affairs Assn. (sec., dir. 1975—), Internat. Assn. Jurists, Ret. Officers Assn. (Knickerbocker chpt.). Club: Knights of Malta. Office: Bolan Lang et al 645 Madison Ave New York NY 10022

BOLAND, GERALD LEE, financial executive; b. Harrisburg, Pa., Apr. 2, 1946; s. Vincent Harry and Alice Jane (Geiste) B.; m. Elaine Frances Glenn, Oct. 25, 1980; 1 child, Peter Alexander. BS, Lebanon Valley Coll., 1968. Acctg. trainee Armstrong Cork Co., Millville, N.J., 1968; payroll supr., plant ops. accountant, 1969-70; sr. fin. acct. Lancaster (Pa.) Gen. Hosp., 1970-71, mgr. gen. acctg., 1972; corp. acctg. mgr. HMW Industries, Inc., Lancaster, 1972; corp. controller Fleck-Marshall Co. subs. Gable Industries, Lancaster, 1973-74, sec.-treas., 1974-75; controller Dominion Psychiat. Treatment Center, Falls Church, Va., 1975-76; controller, dir. fin. Miller & Byrne, Inc., Rockville, Md., 1976-79; v.p. internal auditing Medlantic Healthcare Group, 1979-88; gen. mgr. ops. Kapner Wolfberg & Assocs., Van Nuys, Calif., 1988—. Mem. Am. Acctg. Assn., Nat. Assn. Accts., Hosp. Fin. Mgmt. Assn., Eastern Fin. Assn., Am. Hosp. Assn., Am. Mgmt. Assn., Fin. Mgmt. Assn., Inst. Internal Auditors. Methodist. Home: 6309 Gallery St Bowie MD 20715

BOLAS, STAMATIOS SOCRATES, tannery executive; b. Alexandria, Egypt, Sept. 21, 1928; came to Greece, 1932; s. Socrates Stamatios and Urania Constantine (Kyrlagitsi) B.; m. Kyriaki Leonidas Kolybaki, Nov. 30, 1963; children: Anni, George, Mary. Master in Fin. and Comml. Studies, Superior Sch., Athens, 1952; Degree, U. Athens, 1966, Master in Fin. and Polit. Sci., 1967. Acct. N. Zafirakis & Sons S.A., Chios, Greece, 1952-54, dir., 1954-62; mng. dir. N. Zafirakis & Sons S.A., Athens, 1962—; mng. dir. Soc. Anonyme des Exploitations Immobilieres, Athens, 1955. Served with Greek mil., 1951-52. Decorated Silver Cross of Phenix, Ministry of Justice, 1963. Mem. Athens C. of C. and Industry, Econ. Chamber Greece, Hellenic Tanners Assn. (pres.). Home: 4 Alkaiou St, 115 28 Athens Greece Office: N Zafirakis & Son SA, 3 Emm Benaki St, 105 64 Athens Greece

BOLDT, HEINZ, aerospace engineer; b. Schönfeld Krs. Friedberg, Germany, July 12, 1923; s. August and Marie (Hamann) B.; diploma in engring., Technische Universität, Berlin, 1951; m. Christa Friebel, Mar. 25, 1965; children: Pierre, Manon. Tech. dir. Borsig AG, Berlin, 1951-66; gen. mgr., dir. Messerschmitt-Werke Flugzeug-Union Sud, München-Augsburg, Fed. Republic Germany, 1967-70; gen. proxi Klöckner-Humboldt-Deutz, Köln, Fed. Republic Germany, 1970-72; mem. exec. bd. for devel., constrn. and prodn. FAHR AG, Gottmadingen, Fed. Republic Germany, 1970-72; pres. VDI-Bodenseebezirksverein, Friedrichshafen, Fed. Republic Germany, 1971-76; mem. exec. bd. Dornier GmbH, Munich, 1972-77; pres. Deutsche Industrieanlagen Gesellschaft mbH, Berlin, 1978-82; rep. Machinoexport. Served with German Army, 1942-45. Mem. Am. C. of C. Club: Club der Luftfahrt. Home: 4 Paartalweg Merching, Bayern 8901 Federal Republic of Germany

BOLES, CHRIS A., advertising executive; b. Purdy, Mo., Feb. 4, 1944; d. Alvin J. and Wilma Agnes (Parrigan) Ceselski; m. James Hugh Boles, July 6, 1963; children—Tammy Jo, Rana Dawn, Russell James. Student Wichita Bus. Coll., Crowder Coll. With Farm and Ranch World, Tulsa, 1971-81; stringer Country World, Tulsa, Joplin Globe, 1972-82; columnist Calif. Horse Rev., Fla. Horse Country, Tex. and So. Quarter Horse Jour., Horses Unltd., Valley Horse News, Continental Horseman; contbr. over 1200 articles to horse mags.; advt. cons.; press sec. Mo. Parimutuel Horse Racing, 1983—; pub. relations chairperson Quarter Horse Racing Assn. Mo., 1981—; owner, adminstr. Hook Up Communications Advt. Agy., Fairview, Mo., 1987—; regional dir. Quarter Horse Racing Owners Am., Ft. Worth. Home: PO Box 225 Stark City MO 64866 Office: Hook Up Communications PO Box 161 Fairview MO 64842

BOLGER, JAMES BRENDAN, politician, farmer; b. New Zealand, 1935; m. Joan Bolger; nine children. MP for King Country Nat. Party, 1972—; with Govt. Ministry of Fisheries, 1977-78; assoc. minister of agri. New Zealand, 1977-78, minister of labour, 1978-84, minister of immigration, 1978-84, dep. leader of opposition, 1984-86, leader of opposition, 1986—. Pres. Internat. Labour Orgn., 1983. Office: Parliament Bldgs, Wellington New Zealand

BOLIN, VERNON SPENCER, microbiologist, consultant; b. Parma, Idaho, July 9, 1913; s. Thadeus Howard Bolin and Jennie Bell Harm; m. Helen Epling, Jan. 5, 1948 (div. 1964); children—Rex, Janet, Mark; m. Barbara Sue Chase, Aug. 1965; children—Vladimir, Erik. B.S., U. Wash., 1942; M.S., U. Minn. 1949. Teaching asst. U. Minn.-Mpls., 1943-45; research assoc. U. Utah, Salt Lake City, 1945-50, fellow in surgery, 1950-52; research virologist Jensen-Salsbery Labs., Inc., Kansas City, Mo., 1952-57; research assoc. Wistar Inst. U. Pa., 1957-58; research virologist USPHS, 1958-61; founder Bolin Lab., 1959; dir. Bolin Labs., Inc., Phoenix. Contbr. articles to profl. jours. Served with U.S. Army, 1931-33. Mem. N.Y. Acad. Scis., Phi Mu Chi. Home: 4812 W Greenway Rd Glendale AZ 85036

BOLING, HAROLD EDWARD, software company executive, consultant; b. Portsmouth, Ohio, June 17, 1939; s. Andrew Edward and Ruth Lucille (Stratton) B.; m. Virginia Lee Lowman, Dec. 27, 1962; children—Constance, Edward. B.S. in Bus. and Edn., Va. Commonwealth U., 1974; postgrad. U. Ark., 1978-79. Br. campus registrar Ohio U., 1968-69; registrar Wesleyan U., Middletown, Conn., 1969-70, Va. Commonwealth U., 1970-75; pres. Edn. Data Mgmt., Richmond, Va., 1975-77; registrar U. Ark., Little Rock, 1977-79; dist. sales mgr. Westinghouse Info. Service, Richardson, Tex., 1979-83; dist. sales mgr. Info. Assocs., Inc., Richardson, 1984—, v.p., Plano, Tex., 1984—; owner Am. Internat. Computer Systems, Inc., Plano, 1981—; bd. dirs. Universal Algorithms, Inc., Portland, Oreg., 1983-87. Author, coordinator workshop On-Line Registration and Data Base Mgmt., 1979. Mem. adv. council Salvation Army, Athens, Ohio, 1965-67; coach YMCA Basketball, 1979, 1980-81; scoutmaster Boy Scouts Am., 1980-82, mem. council, 1980-82. Recipient Super Salesman award Internat. Computer Programs, 1982-83; Ark. Traveler award, 1982; cert. of appreciation So. Assn. Coll. Registrars and Admissions Officers, 1985. Republican. Methodist. Office: Info Assocs Inc 4100 Alpha Rd Suite 1000 Dallas TX 75234

BOLING, JEWELL, retired government official; b. Randleman, N.C., Sept. 26, 1907; d. John Emmitt and Carrie (Ballard) Boling; student Women's Coll., U. N.C., 1926, Am. U., 1942, 51-52. Interviewer, N.C. Employment Service, Winston-Salem, Asheboro, 1937-41; occupational analyst U.S. Dept. Labor, Washington, 1943-57, placement officer, 1957-58, employment service adviser, 1959-61, occupational analyst, 1962, employment service specialist counseling and testing, 1963-69, manpower devel. specialist, from 1969. Recipient Meritorious Achievement award U.S. Dept. Labor, 1972. Mem. AAAS, N.Y. Acad. Scis., Am. Assn. Counseling and Devel., Nat. Career Devel. Assn., Am. Rehab. Counseling Assn. (archivist 1964-68), Assn. Measurement in Counseling and Devel., Assn. Humanistic Psychology, Planetary Soc., Smithsonians, Sierra Club, Nature Conservancy, Internat. Platform Assn., Audubon Naturalist Soc., Nat. Capital Astronomers (editor Star Dust 1949-58). Author: Counselor's Handbook, 1967; Counselor's Desk Aid, Eighteen Basic Vocational Directions, 1967; Handbook for New Careerists in Employment Security, 1971; contbr. articles to profl. publs. Address: Route 2 Box 176 Randleman NC 27317

BOLING, PATRICIA ANN, political science educator, researcher, writer; b. Ft. Sill, Okla., Feb. 14, 1953; d. Victor LeRoy and Dorothy Mildred (Collins) B.; m. Mark Campbell Tilton, Sept. 21, 1981; children: Ellen, Clio, Andrew. BA in Politics, U. Calif., Santa Cruz, 1975; MA in Polit. Sci., U. Calif., Berkeley, PhD, 1984. Teaching asst. U. Calif., Berkeley, 1977-80, teaching assoc., 1981-82; asst. prof. Trinity U., San Antonio, Tex., 1984-86; freelance writer, researcher Tokyo, 1986—; spl. research fellow Social Sci. Research Inst., Internat. Christian U., Tokyo, 1988—. Sponsor Campub NOW, Young Democrats, Trinity U., 1985-86. Summer research fellowship Trinity U., 1985, 86; grad. fellowship U. Calif., Berkeley, 1981-82. Democrat. Clubs: Internat. Friendship (Tokyo).

BOLINGER, DWIGHT LEMERTON, language educator; b. Topeka, Aug. 18, 1907; s. Arthur Joel and Gertrude (Ott) B.; m. Louise Ida Schrynemakers, July 1, 1934 (dec. Apr. 1986); children: Bruce Clyde, Ann Celeste Bolinger McClure. BA, Washburn Coll., 1930, LittD (hon.), 1963; MA, U. Kans., 1932; PhD, U. Wis., 1936; MA (hon.), Harvard U., 1963. Instr. U. Wis., Madison, 1936, Kansas City (Mo.) Jr. Coll., 1937; assoc. prof. Washburn Coll., Topeka, 1937-44; from asst. prof. to prof. U. So. Calif., Los Angeles, 1944-60, head dept. Spanish, Italian and Portuguese, 1947-59; prof. Spanish U. Colo., Boulder, 1960-63; prof. Romance langs. and lits. Harvard U., Cambridge, Mass., 1963-73, prof. emeritus, 1973—; vis. prof. emeritus Stanford (Calif.) U., 1977—. Author: Interrogative Structures of American English, 1957, Forms of English, 1965, The Phrasal Verb in English, 1971, Degree Words, 1972, Meaning and Form, 1977, Language: The Loaded Weapon, 1980 (George Orwell award Nat. Council Tchrs. English 1981), Intonation and its Parts, 1986, (with others) Modern Spanish, 1960. Sterling fellow in linguistics Yale U., 1943-44, research fellow in speech Haskins Labs., 1956-57, fellow Ctr. for Advanced Study in Behavioral Scis., 1969-70.

BOLLACK, CLAUDE GERARD, surgery educator, urological surgeon; b. Strasbourg, France, Nov. 29, 1925; s. Edmond and Yvonne (Daniel) B.; children—France, Yves, Josee. M.D., U. Strasbourg, 1952. Chief resident Med. Sch., U. Strasbourg, 1952-56, assoc. prof. surgery, 1962-68, prof., chmn. dept. surgery; hon. prof. Med. Sch., U. Cordoba, Argentina, 1978. Author: Cancer of the Kidney, 1980; Male Potency, 1983; Seminal Vesical, 1984. Mem. Internat. Surg. Soc., Internat. Urol. Soc., Am. Urol. Assn., European Urol. Soc., Acad. Medicine Buenos Aires (hon.). Home: 12 Rue Offendorf, 67000 Strasbourg France Office: Centre Hospitalier, 1 Place Hospitalier, 67000 Strasbourg France

BOLLAR, MARJORIE ODESSA, nurse; b. N.Y.C., July 25, 1923; d. Charles Whitmore and Glenfield Ernesta (Griffith) Heath; grad. Central Islip Sch. Nursing, 1948; B.S. Edn. and Health, Coll. Oneonta, 1973; M.A., SUNY, Stony Brook, 1977; m. Wilbur B. Bollar, July 11, 1944; children—Diane Seaman, Ronald. Head nurse Central Islip (N.Y.) State Hosp., 1949-70; acting nurse adminstr. Central Islip Psychiat. Center, 1970-77, nurse adminstr., 1977-81, dir. nursing services, 1981-83, coordinator for geriatrics, 1980-83, overtime coordinator, 1980—, mem. com. quality of care for memtally disabled, 1985, mem. instl. rev. com. on research proposals, 1975—, mem. bd. visitors, 1985—, supr. research programs, tng. activities, tchr. affiliating nursing students and therapy aides div. research, chmn. unit med. records rev. com.; examiner N.Y. State Civil Service, 1982. Sec. bd. Christian edn. Faith Bapt. Ch., Coram, N.Y., 1985, treas., 1986. Recipient 8th ann. Community Service award Eastern Suffolk Fed. Credit Union, 1980; cert. sch. nurse tchr., in-service edn. medication trainer and lectr., N.Y. Mem. Am. Public Health Assn., L.I. Minority Educators Assn., Internat. Platform Assn., Nat. Council Negro Women, N.Y. State Nurses Assn., Am. Film Industry Assn., Central Islip, Stony Brook alumnae, Centereach (N.Y.) C. of C., N.Y. Acad. Scis., NAACP, Delta Sigma Theta (chmn. social actions com. Nassau alumni chpt.). Research on follow up of geriatric subjects, discharged alcoholics and disturbed children, on geriatric hyperbaric oxygen therapy. Home: 218 N Washington Ave Centereach NY 11720 Office: Central Islip Psychiat Ctr Cen Islip NY 11722

BOLLERER, FRED L., banker. Pres. First City Nat. Bank Houston subs. First City Bancorp Tex. Inc. Office: 1st City Nat Bank Houston 1001 Main St PO Box 2557 Houston TX 77252 *

BOLMAN, PIETER SIMON HEINRICH, publishing company executive, physicist; b. Groningen, The Netherlands, Apr. 4, 1941; s. Jan and Engelina (Schulte) B.; m. Jacqueline A. Reeves, Nov. 2, 1968; children: Paul V.J., Justin A. Doctoral degree, U. Groningen, 1966; PhD, U. Southampton, 1973. Acquisition editor Elsevier Sci. Publs. Besloten Vennootschap, Amsterdam, The Netherlands, 1972-76, dep. mng. dir., 1976-78, div. dir., 1981—; v.p. Elsevier Sci. Pub. Co. Inc., N.Y.C., 1978-81. Home: Frederik Hendriklaan 32, 2012 SJ Haarlem The Netherlands Office: Elsevier Sci Publs BV, 25 Sara Burgerhartstraat, 1055 KV Amsterdam The Netherlands also: PO Box 103, 1000 AC Amsterdam The Netherlands

BOLSTER, JACQUELINE NEBEN (MRS. JOHN A. BOLSTER), cosmetic company executive; b. Woodhaven, N.Y.; d. Ernest William Benedict and Emily Claire (Guck) Neben; student Pratt Inst., Columbia U.; m. John A. Bolster, May 8, 1954. Promotion mgr. Photoplay mag., 1949-53; merchandising mgr. McCall's, N.Y.C., 1953-64; dir. promotion and merchandising Harper's Bazaar, N.Y.C., 1964-71; dir. advt. and promotion Elizabeth Arden Salons, N.Y.C., 1971—; dir. creative services Elizabeth Arden, Inc., 1976-78, dir. communications Elizabeth Arden Salons, 1978—. Recipient Art Director's award 1961, 66. Mem. Fashion Group, Fashion Execs. Roundtable, Inner Circle, Advt. Women N.Y. (life), Mag. Promotion Assn. Home: 8531 88th St Woodhaven NY 11421 Office: Elizabeth Arden Inc 55 E 52d St New York NY 10022 also: Halsey Neck Ln Southampton NY 11968

BOLT, PAUL BOUDEWYN EDWARD, pharmaceutical company executive; b. Groningen, Holland, Mar. 9, 1943; s. Simon and Elsina Jantina (Nap) B.; m. Jennifer Susan Bell, Feb. 1, 1975. Lab. asst. Royal Women's Hosp., Melbourne, Australia, 1965-66; med. rep. CIBA Australia Ltd., Melbourne, 1966-70; mktg. coordinator Ciba-Geigy, Ltd., Switzerland, 1970-71; mktg. mgr. Ciba-Geigy Nigeria, Ltd., Lagos, 1971-72; regional mgr. Ciba-Geigy East Africa, Ltd., Nairobi, Kenya, 1972-75; area mgr. Ciba-Geigy MTS, Ltd., Taipei, Taiwan, 1975-79; gen. mgr. Ji Kang Co., Ltd., Taipei, 1979-81; div. mgr. Ciba-Geigy Pakistan, Ltd., Karachi, 1981-83, Ciba-Geigy Hellas, Ltd., Athens, Greece, 1983—. Club: American. (bd. dirs. 1980-81) (Taipei). Office: Ciba-Geigy Hellas SA, PO Box 8282, 10010 Athens Greece

BOLT, RICHARD HENRY, science educator, business executive; b. Peking, People's Republic of China, Apr. 22, 1911; s. Richard Arthur and Beatrice (French) B.; m. Katherine Mary Smith, June 24, 1933; children: Beatrice Bolt Scribner, Richard Eugene, Deborah Bolt Zieses. A.B. in Architecture, U. Calif.-Berkeley, 1933, A.M. in Physics, 1937, Ph.D. in Physics, 1939. Assoc. in physics U. Ill., 1940; NRC fellow in physics M.I.T., Cambridge, 1939-40; research assoc. MIT, 1941-43, assoc. prof. physics, 1946-54, prof. acoustics, 1954-64, adj. prof. acoustics, 1983-85, lectr. polit. sci., 1964-70, dir. acoustics lab., 1946-57; assoc. dir. NSF, 1960-63; prin. cons. biophysics and biophys. chemistry study sect. NIH, Bethesda, Md., 1957-59; chmn. bd. Bolt, Beranek & Newman, Inc., Cambridge, 1953-76; chmn. emeritus Bolt, Beranek & Newman, Inc., 1976—; vis. scientist Mass. State Legislature, 1977; guest lectr. Inst. Acoustics, Academia Sinica, Peking and Xian, China, 1981; Sci. liaison officer OSRD, London, 1943-44; chief tech. aide Nat. Def. Research Com., 1944-45; mem. Armed Forces-Nat. Research Council chmn. com. on hearing and bio-acoustics, 1953-55; pres. Internat. Commn. on Acoustics, 1951-57; chmn. com. on sound spectrograms NRC, 1976-79; chmn. adv. panel on White House tapes U.S. Dist. Ct. D.C., 1973-74. Author: (with other) Sonics, 1959; also numerous articles in sound, acoustics, noise control, sci. and public policy. Fellow Center for Advanced Study in Behavioral Sciences, Stanford, 1963-64; Phi Beta Kappa vis. scholar, 1979-80; New Eng. award Engring. Socs. New Eng., 1980. Fellow Acoustical Soc. Am. (pres. 1949-50, Biennial award 1942, Gold medal 1979), IEEE, Am. Acad. Arts and Scis., AAAS (dir. 1969-77), Inst. Noise Control Engring., Nat. Acad. Engring., Mass. Engrs. Council (chmn. 1975-77), Am. Inst. Physics (gov. bd. 1957-63), Phi Beta Kappa, Sigma Xi, Eta Kappa Nu. Club: Cosmos (Washington). Home: Tabor Hill Rd Lincoln MA 01773 Office: 50 Moulton St Cambridge MA 02138

BOLT, ROBERT OXTON, playwright; b. Manchester, Eng., Aug. 15, 1924; s. Ralph and Leah (Binnion) B.; m. Celia Anne Roberts, Nov. 1948 (div. 1967); children—Sally, Benedict, Joanna; m. Sarah Elizabeth Miles, 1967 (div. 1975); 1 son, Thomas; m. Ann Zane, 1980 (div. 1985). B.A. with honors in History, Manchester U., 1949; LL.D., Exeter U., 1977. Office-boy ins. office, Manchester, 1941-42; tchr. village sch., Bishopsteignton, Devonshire, 1950-51, Millfield Sch., Sommerset, 1951-58; playwright, screen script writer, 1958—. Served with RAF and British Army, 1943-46, Author: (plays) Flowering Cherry, 1957; The Critic and the Heart, 1957; The Tiger and the Horse, 1960; A Man for All Seasons, 1960; Gentle Jack, 1963; (for children) The Thwarting of Baron Bolligrew, 1966; Brother and Sister, 1967; Vivat! Vivat! Regina!, 1970; State of Revolution, 1977; (screenplays) Lawrence of Arabia, 1962, Dr. Zhivago, 1965, A Man for All Seasons, 1967 (Acad. award 1966, N.Y. film critics award 1966, Brit. Film Acad. award), Ryan's Daughter, 1970, Lady Caroline Lamb (also dir.), 1972, The Bounty, 1984; numerous TV and radio plays. Decorated comdr. Order Brit. Empire. Address: care Margaret Ramsay Ltd, 14A Goodwins Ct, St Martins Ln, London WC 2, England *

BOLTANSKI, CHRISTIAN, painter, photographer; b. Paris, Sept. 6, 1944; s. Etienne and Annie (Lauran) B. Profl. photographer and artist, Paris, 1969—. One-man shows include: Sonnabend Gallery, N.Y.C., 1973, 75, 79, 82, Musée d'Art Moderne, Paris, 1970, 76, (retrospective) 1981, Mus. Modern Art, Oxford, 1973, Israel Mus., Jerusalem, 1973, Louisiana Mus., Hamleback, Denmark, 1974, Centre Nat. d'Art Contemporian, Paris, 1974, Kunsthalle, Kiel, W.Ger., 1975, Centre d'Art Contemporain, Geneva, 1975, Landesmuseum, Bonn, W.Ger., 1976, Mus. Contemporary Art, La Jolla, Calif., 1977, Galleria Bruno Soletti, Milan, 1977, Musée de Peinture, Calais, 1980, Carpenter Art Ctr., Harvard U., Cambridge, Mass., 1980, Centre Georges Pompidou, Paris, 1984, Kunsthaus, Zurich, Switzerland, 1984, Galerie Crousel-Hussenot, Paris, 1985, Kunstverein, Munich, 1986, Photographer's Gallery, London, 1986; group shows include Documenta 5, Kassel, Germany, 1972, Venice Biennale, 1980, Westkunst, Cologne, Germany, 1981; represented in permanent collections including: Musée d'Art Moderne, Paris, Kunsthalle, Hamburg, W.Ger., Neue Gallerie, Aachen, W.Ger., Louisiana Mus., Hamleback, Boymans-van Beuningen Mus., Rotterdam, Netherlands, Mus. Fine Arts, Lodz, Poland, Israel Mus., Jerusalem, Art Inst. Chgo.; author: Reconsitutions des Gestes, 1971, 10 Portraits Photographiques, 1972, Album Photographique, 1972, Inventaire, 1973, Quelques Interpretations, 1974, 10 Regles et Technique, 1975, Les Morts pour Rire, 1975; (with others) Modellbilder, 1976. Address: 100 rue de Grenelle, 75007 Paris France Other: 420 W Broadway New York NY 10012 *

BOLTÉ, BROWN, investment executive; b. Winnetka, Ill., Dec. 23, 1908; s. John Willard and Jessie (Brown) B.; m. Bernice Nicholson, Jan. 4, 1930 (dec.); 1 child, Celia (Mrs. John William Griesé, Jr.); m. Baronessa Erminia Amaru-Landau, 1987. Student, Butler U., 1930, U.S. Army Sch. for Spl. Services, Washington and Lee U., 1943. Western and So. sales mgr. Rytex Co., Indpls., 1930-35; asst. to pres. mktg. Beecham Products, Inc., Bloomfield, N.J., 1935-39; from account exec. to exec. v.p., chmn. plans bd. Benton & Bowles, Inc., N.Y.C., 1939-57; pres. SSC&B, Inc., 1958-60, vice chmn. bd., 1965; owner Bolté Advt. Cos., N.Y., Conn., Tex., 1961-73; chmn. Bolté-Lukin & Assocs., Inc., Palm Beach, 1970—; v.p., dir. World of Plastics, Inc., Ft. Pierce, Fla., 1973—. Inventor, writer, composer. Trustee Norwalk Hosp. Assn., 1958-65, YMCA, New Canaan, 1967—; bd. dirs. New Canaan chpt. ARC, 1953-54, New Canaan YMCA, 1967—, Eleanor Roosevelt Cancer Found., 1961, Child Welfare League Am., 1962-63, Community Mental Health Center, West Palm Beach, 1961, hon. dir., 1963—; bd. govs. Gulfstream Goodwill Industries, 1973—; trustee Palm Beach-Martin County Med. Center, Inc., Jupiter, Fla., 1974—, life mem., 1977—; bd. dirs. Boys Club of Palm Beach County, 1973—, pres., 1985-88, chmn., 1988. Served from 2d lt. to maj. AUS, 1942-46. Mem. Am. Assn. Advt. Agys. (gov. 1956, chmn. eastern region 1957), Inst. Outdoor Advt. (dir., chmn. bd. 1967-68), Advt. Council (dir. 1966—), Nat. Def. Transp. Assn. (bd. dirs., exec. com. 1956-58), ASCAP, Am. Guild Authors and Composers, SAR, Sigma Chi (Significant Sig.). Clubs: Sailfish (Palm Beach); Old Port Yacht, (North Palm Beach); Governor's, Wellington (West Palm Beach); Lotos (N.Y.C.); Club Limited. Home: 369 South Lake Dr Palm Beach FL 33480 also: 46 Quai Gustav Ador, Geneva Switzerland Office: Bolté Investment Group 630 U S Hwy 1 North Palm Beach FL 33408

BOLTON, CLIVE STUART, sales director; b. Tripoli, Lebanon, July 26, 1953; arrived in U.K., 1959; s. Malcolm Stewart and Joan Anne (Lewis) B.; m. Alexandra Gail Allan, Sept. 29, 1974 (div. Nov. 1985). Student, Brighton (Eng.) Sci. Poly. Coll., 1969-70. Clk., computer operator Paymaster Gen.'s Office, Crawley, Eng., 1970-71; computer operator Crusader Ins. Co., Reigate, Eng., 1971-72; shift leader computer unit Brit. Caledonian Airways, Gatwick Airport, Eng., 1972-74, Advance Linen Services, Brighton, 1974-76; rep. sales K&J Wespac Ltd., London, 1976-87, dir. sales, 1987—; Chmn., company sec. Steelhaven Ltd., London, 1987. Mem. Inst. Sales and Mktg. Mgmt. Mem. Ch. of Eng. Home: 21 Turners Meadow Way, Beckenham Kent England Office: Wespac Ltd, 154/8 Shoreditch High St, London EI 6HU, England

BOMAN, JAN, consultant; b. Copenhagen, June 29, 1962; s. Mogens and Kirsten Elisabeth (Petersen) B. B of Commerce in Logistics, Copenhagen Bus. Sch., 1987. With OP Reproduktioner A/S, Copenhagen, 1981-82; asst. controller Ginge-Kerr A/S, Copenhagen, 1982-85; controller DFDS A/S, Copenhagen, 1985-86; mgr. procurement Intersupply A/S, Copenhagen, 1986-87; cons. A/S Enator, Copenhagen, 1987—; mem. permanant program com. IHS, The Danish Aspen Inst., Copenhagen, 1986—; mem. exec. bd. for research project The Bus. Economist in the Yr. 2000; bd. dirs. Civilokonomernes Forlag A/S, Copenhagen, 1986—. Mem. editorial bd. Civilokonomen mag., 1985—; contbr. articles on info. tech. and mgmt. to profl. jours. Vice chmn. for planning logistics edn. Copenhagen Bus. Sch., 1984-85. Recipient Jenle Prisen Danish Soc. Civil Engrs. and Ingenioren mag., 1982. Mem. Assn. Danish Bus. Economists (council, various commns.). Home: Ragnhildgade 34, Copenhagen 0 DK-2100, Denmark

BOMBERGER, RUSSELL BRANSON, lawyer, educator; b. Lebanon, Pa., May 1, 1934; s. John Mark and Viola (Aurentz) B.; divorced; children—Ann Elizabeth, Jane Carmel. B.S., Temple U., 1955; M.A., U. Iowa, 1956, U. Iowa, 1961; Ph.D., U. Iowa, 1962; M.S., U. So. Calif., 1960; LL.B., J.D., LaSalle U. Bar: Calif. also various fed. cts., U.S. Supreme Ct. Mem. editorial staff Phila. Inquirer, 1952-54; lectr. U. Iowa, 1955-57, U. So. Calif., 1957-58; asst. prof. U.S. Naval Postgrad. Sch., Monterey, Calif., 1958-62; assoc. prof. U.S. Naval Postgrad. Sch., 1963-75, prof., 1975—; practice law 1970—; free lance writer, 1952—, communications cons., 1963—; safety cons. internat. program U. So. Calif. Inst. Safety and Systems Mgmt., 1983—; cons. Internat. Ctr. for Aviation Safety, Lisbon, 1984—. Author: broadcast series The World of Ideas; motion picture Strokes and Stamps; abstracter-editor: Internat. Transactional Analysis Assn. Served to capt. USNR, 1966—. Am. Psychol. Found. fellow Columbia U., 1954-55; CBS fellow U. So. Calif., 1957-58. Office: PO Box 8741 Monterey CA 93943

BOMPEY, STUART HOWARD, lawyer; b. Bridgeport, Conn., Aug. 30, 1940; s. Samuel and Freida (Rifkin) B.; m. Cynthia Kupferberg, Aug. 15, 1965; children—Sheri Ann, Mitchell Scott, Nanci Beth. B.S. in Bus. Adminstrn., Boston U., 1962, J.D. cum laude, 1965. Bar: Conn. 1965, U.S. Dist. Ct. Conn. 1966, U.S Ct. Appeals (2d cir.) 1966, N.Y. 1971, U.S. Dist. Ct. (ea. and so. dists.) N.Y. 1971; U.S. Supreme Ct., 1980. Atty., NLRB, Washington and N.Y.C., 1965-69; assoc. Proskauer Rose Goetz & Mendelsohn, N.Y.C., 1969-72; ptnr. Baer, Marks & Upham, N.Y.C., 1972—; speaker various seminars. Mem. ABA (chmn. subcom. dealing with EEO com.), Nat. Assn. Coll. and Univ. Attys. (chmn. personnel, tenure and retirement com., co-chmn. 1981 Mid-winter Conf.), N.Y. State Bar Assn. (charter mem. labor relations sect., equal employment opportunity com., past mem. task force to study N.Y. State Human Rights Commn.), N.Y. Mgmt. Attys. Conf., Nat. Assn. Broadcasters. Republican. Jewish. Clubs: Orienta Beach & Yacht (Mamaroneck, N.Y.), Mario Polo (N.Y.C.). Editor: Boston U. Law Rev.; co-author: Wrongful Termination: A Prevention Approach C.P.L. I, 1986; contbr. articles on employee discrimination to profl. jours. Home: 277 Rockingstone Ave Larchmont NY 10538

BONAN, SEON PIERRE, real estate developer; b. N.Y.C., Feb. 6, 1917; s. Salvator and Matilda (Fox) B.; m. Janet Ross, Apr. 22, 1948; children: Mrs. Elizabeth Bertin-Boussu, Charles Sauveur, Mrs. Andrew E. Adelson. B.S., Columbia U., 1938; LL.B., Bklyn. Law Sch., 1946. Bar: N.Y. State 1946. Gen. partner Charles River Park, Boston, 1956—, Capital Place Assocs., Trenton, N.J., 1972—, others; chmn., chief exec. officer Royal Bus. Funds Corp., N.Y.C., 1978. Served as lt. USNR, 1941-46. Recipient Congressional Record tribute, 1966. Mem. World Bus. Council, Met. Presidents Orgn. Clubs: Union League (N.Y.C.).; Burning Tree Country (Greenwich, Conn.). Home: Palm Beach FL 33480 Office: 60 E 42d St New York NY 10165

BONANG, GERARD HOK-GIE, university administrator, microbiology educator; b. Makassar, South Sulawest, Indonesia, Oct. 5, 1935; s. Anton and Maria Theresia (Sambuaga) B; m. Engelina Tanzil, May 17, 1964; children; Joe, Theresia, Catharina, Anton. MD, U. Indonesia, 1962, grad. microbiology, 1968. Asst. Sch. Dentistry U. Indonesia, Jakarta, 1962-63, jr. lectr., 1963-65, vice dean adminstrn. and student affairs, 1964-66, lectr., 1965-72; lect. dept. head microbiology Sch. Medicine Atma Jaya Cath. U., Jakarta, 1972-80, sec., vice dean, 1974-76, vice rector, 1981-82, rector, 1982-87; dir. Pub. Health Ctr., St. Kristoforus, West Jakarta, 1978—, Ctr. Devel. Tourism Atma Jaya, South Jakarta, 1983—. Author: Mikrobiologi Kedokteran, 1982. Mem. Indonesian Scouts Movement, Makassar, Jakarta, 1949—, chmn, South Jakarta,, Atma Jaya, 1985; councilor Internat. Fedn. Cath. Univs., Paris, 1983-88; chmn. Dharmasih Praharana Found., Central Jakarta, 1986—. Mem. Indonesian Med. Assn. (treas. 1980-82), Indonesian Soc. Microbiology, Indonesian Soc. Clin. Microbiology. Golkar. Roman Catholic. Lodge: Lions (pres. 1987-88). Home: Kapling Polri Blok F, 1415 Jelambar, West Jakarta 11460, Indonesia Office: Atma Jaya Cath U, Jalan Jendral Sudirman 49A, South Jakarta 12930, Indonesia

BONAR, ROLAND BIRT, educational administrator; b. El Paso, Tex., Jan. 24, 1934; s. Bernard E. and Dorothy L. (Birt) B.; student Calif. Inst. Tech., 1951-54, U. Tex. at El Paso, 1957-62; L.H.D., Lincoln Meml. U., 1968; Ph.D., Columbia U., 1972; children: Robert James, Marla Lynn, Michael G. Vice-pres., gen. mgr. Western GMC Truck Co., El Paso, 1955-60; tchr. Dale Carnegie courses N.Mex. and W. Tex., 1960-66; prin. Roland B. Bonar & Assos., presenting Dale Carnegie courses, Balt., 1966-73, Denver, 1973—; past pres. Dale Carnegie Internat. Sponsors Assn.; guest lectr. U. Md., 1968-74; chmn. bd. Explorex Oil Co., Houston, 1975—; past chmn. First Savs. & Loan of Orland Park, Chgo.; dir. Transportes de Ref de Mex. S.A., Bombas Turbinas de Mex. S.A., B & M Oil Co., N.Mex. Vice pres. Denver area Boy Scouts Am., 1973—; past chmn. fin. Denver area council; fin. dir., 1974-75; mem. Pres. Johnson's Council on Mental Retardation, 1965-68; mem. cabinet Mile Hi United Way, 1978—; bd. dirs. Balt. Cystic Fibrosis Found., 1966-70, U. Colo. Health Scis.; trustee Lincoln Meml. U., 1969-85. Served with USAF, 1950-54; Korea. Decorated D.F.C., Air medal; named outstanding citizen Albuquerque, 1972; Group Pres.'s awardee Dale Carnegie & Assos., 1974-76. Mem. Am. Soc. Tng. Dirs., Am. Mgmt. Assn., U. Tex., Columbia, Lincoln Meml. U. alumni assns., Denver C. of C., Colo. Assn. Commerce and Industry (chmn. fin.), Civil War Round Table. Republican. Lutheran. Clubs: Rolling Hills Country; Denver Rotary, Masons. Office: 210 University Blvd Suite 820 Denver CO 80206

BONAVENTURA, LEO MARK, gynecologist, educator; b. East Chicago, Ill., Aug. 1, 1945; s. Angelo Peter and Wanda D. (Kelleher) B.; student Marquette U., 1963-66; M.D., Ind. U., 1970; married; children—Leo Mark, Dena Anne, Angela Lorena, Nicole Palmira, Leah Michelle, Adam Xavier. Intern in surgery, Cook County Hosp., Chgo., 1970-71; resident in ob-gyn., Ind. U. Hosps., 1973-76, fellow in reproductive endocrinology and infertility, 1976-78; asst. prof. ob-gyn., Ind. U., 1976—, asst. head sect. reproductive endocrinology and infertility, 1978-80, head sect., 1980-81. Served with USN attached to USMC, 1971-73. Named Intern of Yr., Cook County Hosp., 1971. Diplomate Am. Bd. Obstetrics and Gynecology, Am. Bd. Reproductive Endocrinology and Infertility. Mem. Central Assn. Ob-Gyn., Am. Coll. Obstetricians and Gynecologists, Am. Fertility Soc., Can. Fertility Soc., Soc. Reproductive Endocrinologists, Soc. Reproductive Surgeons. Roman Catholic. Contbr. articles to profl. jours. Office: 8091 Townshipline Rd Indianapolis IN 46260

BOND, ALAN, land developer, yacht racing syndicate executive; b. Apr. 22, 1938; s. Frank and Kathleen Bond; m. Eileen Hughes, 1955; 4 children. Chmn. Swan Brewery Co., Ltd., Pacific Copper Ltd., Leighton Mining N.L., Swan TV and Radio Broadcasters Ltd., Airship Industries Ltd., Castlemaine Tooheys Ltd., Throughbred Racing and Breeding Australia Ltd.; exec. chmn., dir. Bond Corp. Holdings Ltd.; dir. Bond Corp. Internat. Ltd., Bond Media U.K. Ltd., Bond Univ. Ltd., North Kalgurli Mines Ltd., Dallhold Investments Pty Ltd; head of syndicate that owns the yacht Australia Ltd.; head of syndicate that owns the yacht Australia II, winner of 1983 America's Cup. Decorated officer Order of Australia. Clubs: Royal Perth Yacht, Cruising Yacht, Claremont Yacht, Fremantle Sailing, South Fremantle Football, Richmond Football. Address: 89 Watkins Rd, Dalkeith Western Australia 6009, Australia *

BOND, CHRISTOPHER SAMUEL, U.S. senator, lawyer; b. St. Louis, Mar. 6, 1939; s. Arthur D. and Elizabeth (Green) B.; m. Carolyn Reid, May 13, 1967; 1 child, Samuel Reid. B.A. with honors, Princeton U., 1960; LL.B., U. Va., 1963. Bar: Mo. bar 1963, U.S. Supreme Ct. bar 1967. Law clk. to chief judge U.S. Ct. of Appeals, 5th Dist., Atlanta, 1963-64; assoc. firm Covington & Burling, Washington, 1965-67; practice law Mexico, Mo., 1968; asst. atty. gen., chief counsel consumer protection div. State of Mo., 1969-70; auditor 1971-73; gov. State of Mo., 1973-77, 81-85; ptnr. law firm Gage & Tucker, Kansas City and St. Louis, 1985-87; U.S. senator from Mo., 1987—; pres. Gt. Plains Legal Found., Kansas City, Mo., 1978-81; chmn. Republican Govs. Assn.; chmn. Midwestern Govs. Assn.; exec. com. Nat. Govs. Conf., chmn. com. on econ. and community devel., 1981-83, chmn. com. on energy and environment, 1983-84. Republican. Presbyterian. Office: Russell Senate Bldg Room 293 Washington DC 20510

BOND, CORNELIUS COMBS, JR., investment advisor; b. Balt., Sept. 21, 1933; s. Cornelius Combs and Pauline Woodruff (Sanford) B.; m. Johann Hodges, June 12, 1956; children: Margaret J. Simon, Cornelius Combs III, Katherine K. B.S. in E.E, Princeton U., 1956; postgrad., Johns Hopkins U., 1960. Research analyst T. Rowe Price Assos., Balt., 1960-68; v.p. T. Rowe Price Assos., 1968-82, dir., 1972-82, chmn. fin. com., 1979-82; dir., chmn. adv. com. T. Rowe Price Growth Stock Fund, 1974-79, pres., 1976-79; pres., chmn. bd. TRP Ventures, Inc.; gen. ptnr. New Enterprise Assocs.; dir. Charles Center Properties, Inc. Bd. dirs. Historic Annapolis; asso. trustee U. Pa. Served to capt. USAF, 1957-64. Mem. Balt. Soc. Security Analysts. Episcopalian. Clubs: Los Angeles Yacht; Bachelors Cotillion; St. Francis Yacht, Bankers (San Francisco). Home: 1070 Green St Apt 1801 San Francisco CA 94133 Office: 235 Montgomery St Suite 1025 San Francisco CA 94104

BOND, EDWARD, playwright; b. London, July 18, 1934; m. Elizabeth Pable, 1971. Resident theatre writer U. Essex, 1982-83. D.Litt. (hon.), Yale U., 1977. Author plays: Saved, 1965; Narrow Road to the Deep North, 1968; Early Morning, 1968; The Pope's Wedding, 1971; Passion, 1971; Black Mass, 1971; Lear, 1972; The Sea, 1973; Bingo, 1974; The Fool, 1976; A* America! (Grandma Faust and The Swing), 1976; Stone, 1976; The Bundle, 1978; The Woman, 1979; The Worlds and The Activist Papers, 1980; Restoration, 1981; Summer: A Play for Europe, 1982; Derek, 1983; The War Plays, Red Black and Ignorant, The Tin Can People, Great Peace, 1985; Author librettos: We Come to the River, 1977; The English Cat, 1982; Human Cannon, 1982; Orpheus, 1982; Theatre Poems and Songs, 1978-85, 87. Recipient George Devine award, John Whiting award, 1968; No. Arts Lit. fellow, 1977-79. Address: care Margaret Ramsay Ltd, 14A Goodwin's Ct, St Martin's Ln, London WC2N 4LL, England

BOND, EPPERSON ELLIS, chemist; b. Nashville, Apr. 5, 1923; s. Epperson Porter and Margaret (Reed) B.; m. Marian Ruth Philips, June 9, 1950; 1 child, Michael Ellis. B.A., Fisk U., 1944, postgrad., 1945; postgrad., DePaul U., 1946. Research assoc. Glidden Co., Chgo., 1946-47; research assoc. Med. Sch., U. Ill., Chgo., 1947-50, Northwestern U., Chgo., 1950-53; chemist VA Hosp., Hines, Ill., 1953—, now research chemist; Chmn. credit com. Hines Fed. Credit Union, 1963-73, pres., 1973—; chmn. EEO com. Hines Hosp.; chmn. EEO program council Med. Dist. 17. Bd. dirs., pres. Roseland Heights Community Assn.; mem. community adv. council Chgo. State U., 1984—. Fellow Am. Inst. Chemists; mem. Am. Assn. Clin. Chemists (bd. dirs.), Am. Chem. Soc., Ill. Kidney Found., Alpha Phi Alpha. Methodist (vice chmn. bd. stewards). Club: Men's (Chgo.). Home: 9835 Forest Ave Chicago IL 60628 Office: PO Box 41 Hines IL 60141

BONDARCHUK, SERGEY FEDOROVICH, actor, director; b. Byelozerka, Odessa Region, Russia; Sept. 25, 1920. Student All Union State Inst. Cinematography. Appeared as Othello, Shevchenko in Taras Shevchenko, Valko in the Young Guard, Dymov in The Grasshopper, Yershov in An Unfinished Tale, Ivan Franko in Ivan Franko, Matvei Krylov in The Soldiers Go On, Sokolov in Destiny of a Man, Korostylov in Seryozha, Pierre Bezukhov in War and Peace, Astrov in Uncle Vanya, Sergey Tutarinov in Gold Star Winner, Fyodor in It Was Night in Rome, Martin Evens in The Silence of Doctor Evens, Ivan Nikolayevich in This High Mountain, Kurchatov in Choosing the Goal, Zvyagintsev in They fought for the Motherland, Emelyan in Steppe; dir. films including Destiny of a Man, War and Peace, 1962-67, Waterloo, 1970, Uncle Vanya, 1974, They Fought for the Motherland, 1975, Steppe, 1979, Father Sergius, 1979; Mexico in Flames, 1982. Recipient numerous awards including: Order of Lenin (2), People's Artist of USSR, Order of Red Banner, Hero of Soviet Labour, 1980, USSR State prize, 1984. Author: Intimate Thoughts, 1979. Address: Gorky St 9, 1075 Moscow 9 USSR *

BONDI, HERMANN, mathematician; b. Vienna, Austria, Nov. 1, 1919; s. Samuel and Helene (Hirsch) B.; B.A., Trinity Coll., Cambridge (Eng.) U., 1940, M.A., 1944; D.Sc. (hon.), U. Bath, 1974, U. Sussex, 1974, U. Surrey, 1974, U. York, 1980, Southampton U., 1981, U. Salford, 1982, U. St. Andrews, 1985l; m. Christine Mary Stockmann, Nov. 1, 1947; children: Alison, Jonathan, Elizabeth, David, Deborah. Lectr. math. U. Cambridge, 1948-54; prof. applied math. King's Coll., U. London, 1954—; vis. prof. Cornell U., Ithaca, N.Y., 1960; dir. gen. European Space Research Orgn., 1967-71; chief sci. adviser Ministry Def., 1971-77; chief scientist Dept. of Energy, 1977-80, chmn. Offshore Energy Bd., 1977-80; chmn., chief exec. Nat. Environ. Research Council, 1980-84; master Churchill Coll., Cambridge, 1983 chmn. astronomy policy and grants com. Sci. Research Council, 1965-67; chmn. Nat. Com. for Astronomy, 1964-67; pres. Internat. Com. on Gen. Relativity and Gravitation, 1965-68; mem. adv. council Sci. Policy Found.; pres. Inst. Math. and Its Applications, 1974-75; mem. Adv. Council on Research and Dept. for Fuel and Power, 1977-80, Severn Barrage Com., 1978-81. Created knight (K.C.B.), 1973. Fellow Royal Soc., 1959, Royal Astron. Soc., Cambridge Philos. Soc. Author: Cosmology, 1960; The Universe at Large, 1961; Relativity and Common Sense, 1964; Assumption and Myth in Physical Theory, 1968; also numerous articles. Research in constn. of stars, structure and evolution of universe, gen. relativity, especially propagation of gravitational distburbances; known for steady state theory of expanding universe. Office: The Master's Lodge, Churchill Coll, Cambridge England also: care Royal Soc, 6 Carlton House Terr, London SW1Y 5AG England

BONES, ROGER ALEC, engineer; b. East Molesey, Surrey, Eng., Feb. 8, 1928. BS with 1st hons., U. London, 1949, PhD, 1954. Lectr. U. Hong Kong, 1955-58; dep. dir. research Govt. of Nigeria, 1958-60; head contracts lab. Wayne Kerr Labs., New Malden, Eng., 1960-63; various positions STC plc, London and home counties, 1963-83; dir. indsl. projects City and Guilds of London Inst., 1983-86; sr. ptnr. RAB Assocs., Claygate/Surrey, Eng., 1987—. Recipient award Freeman City of London. Fellow Instn. Elec. Engrs.; mem. Inst. Physics, Inst. Dirs., Inst. Chartered Secs. and Adminstrs. (assoc.), Worshipful Co. Horners (liveryman). Office: RAB Assocs, 5 Derwent Close, Claygate, Surrey KT10 0RF, England

BONET, JOSE, mathematics educator, researcher; b. Valencia, Spain, June 18, 1955; s. Jose Bonet and Pilar Solves; m. Encarna Giner, Sept. 26, 1986. B in Math., U. Valencia, 1977, D in Math., 1980. Asst. U. Valencia, 1977-83; asst. prof. Poly. U., Valencia, 1983-86, prof., 1987—. Author: Espacios Tonelados, 1980, Barrelled Locally Convex Spaces, 1987; also articles. Recipient 1st Nat. Prize Ministery Edn. Spain, 1978; Real Soc. Math. Spain grantee, 1972-77. Mem. The Math. Assn. Am., Am. Math. Soc. Home: Sequia Rascanya 2-6, 46120 Alboraya, Valencia Spain Office: Poly U, Dept Math, 46022 Valencia Spain

BONFIELD, ANDREW JOSEPH, tax practitioner; b. London, Jan. 26, 1924; s. George William and Elizabeth Agnes B.; came to U.S., 1946, naturalized, 1954; m. Eleanor Ackerman, Oct. 16, 1955; children—Bruce Ian, Sandra Karen. Gen. mgr. Am. Cushion Co., Los Angeles, 1948-50, Monson Calif. Co., Redwood City, 1951-58; mfrs. mktg. rep., San Francisco, 1958-62; tax practitioner, bus. cons., Redwood City, San Jose, Los Gatos, Calif., 1963—. Past treas., dir. Northwood Park Improvement Assn.; mem. exec. bd. Santa Clara County council Boy Scouts Am., 1971—, past council pres., mem. Nat. council; mem. Santa Clara County Parks and Recreation Commn., 1975-81, 82-86; mem. County Assessment Appeals Bd., 1978-86.

Served with Brit. Royal Navy, 1940-46. Decorated King George VI Silver Badge; recipient Silver Beaver award, Vigil honor award Boy Scouts Am.; enrolled to practice before IRS. Mem. Nat. Soc. Public Accts., Nat. Assn. Enrolled Agts., Calif. Soc. Enrolled Agts., Royal Can. Legion (past state parliamentarian, past state 1st vice comdr.). Club: Rotary (pres. San Jose E. 1977-78). Home: 760 S Kihei Rd #215 Kihei HI 96753

BONFIELD, PETER LEAHY, information technology executive; b. Letchworth, Eng., June 3, 1944; s. George Robert and Dora Patricia (Talbot) B.; m. Josephine Houghton, Mar. 9, 1968. B.Tech., Loughborough u., Eng., 1962-66. Various positions with Tex. Instruments, Bedford, Eng., 1966-68, Bedford and Dallas, 1968-81; mktg. dir. world-wide ops. Internat. Computers Ltd., 1981-84; mng. dir. STC Internat. Computers Ltd., London, 1984—, chmn., 1986—; dep. chief exec. STC PLC, London, 1987—; dir. of tech. Loughborough U., 1988. Mem. Brit. Inst. Mgmt. (companion), Confedn. Brit. Industry. Club: Royal Automobile (London). Office: STC Internat Computers Ltd, Putney Bridge Approach, London SW6 3JX, England

BONFIL, (REUBEN) ROBERT, historian, educator; b. Karditsa, Greece, Apr. 30, 1937; s. David and Bijou (David) B.; m. Eva Rechtschaffen, Nov. 4, 1959; children: Ruchama, David, Alisa. D, U. Turin, Italy, 1960; PhD, Hebrew U., Jerusalem, 1976. Ordained rabbi, 1959. Rabbi Jewish Community of Milan, 1959-68; librarian Jewish Nat. Univ. Library, Jerusalem, 1969-73; lectr. Jewish history Ben Gurion U., Beer Sheva, Israel, 1973-80; prof. Jewish history Hebrew U., 1980—. Author: The Rabbinate in Renaissance Italy, 1979. Office: Hebrew U, Dept Jewish History, Jerusalem Israel

BONGARTZ, WALTER, psychologist, educator; b. Regenburg, Fed. Republic Germany, Feb. 19, 1946; s. Franz and Anna (Bongartz) Hellwanger; m. Bärbel Küpker, Sept. 22, 1986. Diploma psychology, U. Bochum, Fed. Republic Germany, 1972; PhD, U. Konstanz, Fed. Republic Germany, 1978. Lectr. U. Konstanz, 1975-79; post doctoral fellow U. Calif., Santa Barbara, 1979-80; head research project exptl. hypnosis U. Konstanz, 1980-85, head research project psychoimmunology, 1986—. Author: Tachistoscopic Processing, 1979; editor Experimental Klin. Hypnose, 1984—; contnr. articles to profl. jours. Mem. German Soc. Hypnosis (v.p. 1982-86, pres. 1986—), European Soc. Hypnosis (pres. 1988—), Am. Soc. Clin. and Exptl. Hypnosis, Swedish Soc. Hypnosis. Home: Breitenstein, CH-8272 Ermatingen Switzerland Office: U Konstanz, D-7750 Konstanz Federal Republic of Germany

BONGIORNI, DOMENIC FRANK, lawyer; b. Essex, Conn., June 19, 1908; s. Gaetano and Esterina (Carini) B.; B.S., U. Conn., 1933; Ph.D., Johns Hopkins U., 1936; LL.B., Fordham U., 1944. Research chemist Gen. Chem. Co., 1936-39, spl. cons., 1940; staff mem. patent dept. Union Carbide & Carbon Research Labs., Inc., 1941-42; research chemist Bakelite Corp., 1942; chem. research asst. Columbia U., 1942-44; admitted to N.Y. bar, 1944; asso. patent lawyer Campbell, Brumbaugh, Free & Graves, 1944-51; patent lawyer Gen. Aniline & Film Corp., 1951-52; counsel Sci. Design Co., Inc., N.Y.C., 1952-55; patent counsel Johnson & Johnson, 1955-60; cons., 1960—. Mem. Am. Chem. Soc., Internat. Patent Agreement. Address: Essex Po Box 291 Ivoryton CT 06442

BONGO, ALBERT-BERNARD (OMAR), president of Gabon; b. Lewai, Franceville, Gabon, Dec. 30, 1935; ed. Tech. Coll., Brazzaville; married; 2 children. Civil servant; served with Air Force, 1958-60; entered Ministry Fgn. Affairs, 1960; dir. Office of Pres. Leon M'Ba, 1962, charge of Info., 1963-64, Nat. Def., 1964-65; minister-del. Presidency in charge Nat. Def. and Coordination, Info. and Tourism, 1966-67; v.p. Republic Gabon, 1967, pres., 1967—, minister nat. def., 1967-81, minister of info., 1967-80, minister of planning, 1967-77, prime minister 1967-75, minister of the interior, 1967-70, minister of devel., 1970-77, minister of women's affairs, 1976-77; founder, sec.-gen. Parti Democratique Gabonais, 1968. Decorated High Chancellor Ordre Nat. de l'Etoile Equatoriale, Grand Cross Ordre Nat. de Cote d'Ivoire, Ordre Nat. du Niger, high officer Ordre Nat. Centrafricain, comdr. Ordre Nat. Francais du Merite, officier du Merite Combattant, Grand Cross Nat. Order of Chad, Grand Cross Nat. Order of Cameroon, Grand Cross Nat. Order of Togo, Grand Ribbon Nat. Order Leopard (Congo). Address: Office of President, Boite Postale 546, Libreville Gabon *

BONGO, MARTIN, Gabonese minister foreign affairs; b. Lekei, Gabon, July 4, 1940; student Ecole Normale de Mitzic. Formerly sch. dir., Franceville, then insp. for primary instrn. Upper-Ogooue Region; former dir. of cabinet of v.p.; dep. dir. cabinet to pres., 1968-69; commr.-gen. info., 1969; sec. of state to presidency for pententiary services, 1969-70, for nat. edn. charge spl. missions, 1970-72; head of state's personal rep., 1972-73; minister edn. and sci. research, 1973-75, minister of nat. edn., 1975-76, minister of fgn. affairs and cooperation, 1976—. Decorated comdr. Order Equatorial Star, grand officer Nat. Order of Merit (Mauritania); grand officer Order of Merit (Italy); comdr. Ordre Nat. du Merite. Address: Ministry of Fgn Affairs, and Cooperation, Libreville Gabon *

BONHAG, THOMAS EDWARD, insurance executive, financial consultant; b. Bronxville, N.Y., Jan. 19, 1952; s. Herman Arthur and Anne Elizabeth (Sage) B.; m. Noreen Patricia Early, Apr. 24, 1976 (div. Dec. 1981); m. Cornelia Hackett Lyons, Oct. 8, 1983. BS, Fordham U., 1973; MBA, St. John's U., 1979; postgrad., Am. Coll., 1979-84. CLU; Chartered Fin. Cons. Field sales rep. Colgate-Palmolive Co., N.Y.C., 1973-74; employee relations officer The Chase Manhattan Bank, N.Y.C., 1974-78; agt., dist. mgr. The Equitable Life Assurance Soc., N.Y.C., 1979-83; N.Ea.regional dir. mktg. ops. The Equitable Life Assurance Soc., Edison, N.J., 1984—; fin. cons. Am. Geriatrics Soc., N.Y.C., 1983—. Mem. Hoboken (N.J.) Environ. Com., 1983—. Am. Soc. CLU's, Nat. Assn. Life Underwriters, Internat. Assn. Fin. Planning, Assn. for MBA Execs. Republican. Roman Catholic. Home: 2 Marine View Plaza Hoboken NJ 07030

BONHAM, TERRENCE JAMES, lawyer, hearing officer; b. Richmond, Calif., June 8, 1938; s. Harry L. and Helen G. (Gately) B.; m. Joyce E. Trout, July 28, 1968; 1 dau., Teresa J. B.A. in Econs., St. Mary's Coll., 1960; J.D., U. Calif., Hastings Coll. Law, San Francisco, 1963. Bar: Calif. 1964, U.S. Dist. Ct. (no. dist.) Calif. 1964, U.S. Ct. Mil. Appeals 1964, U.S. Ct. Appeals (9th cir.) 1964, U.S. Supreme Ct. 1983. Assoc. Halde, Battin, Barrymore & Stevens, Santa Barbara, Calif., 1968-73; ptnr. Barrymore, Stevens & Bonham, Santa Barbara, 1973-74; mem. Riley, Holzhauer, Denver & McClain, Santa Barbara, 1974-80; ptnr. Lawler & Ellis, Ventura, Calif., 1980-85, ptnr. Lawler, Bonham & Walsh, 1985—; judge protem Santa Barbara-Goleta Mcpl. Ct., Ventura County Superior Ct.; hearing officer County of Santa Barbara Civil Service Com., Santa Barbara Bd. Retirement; lectr. Bridging the Gap, Ventura County; lectr. to assns. Mem. Civil Arbitration Panel Ventura County, 1979—; mem. Republican Presdl. Task Force, Nat. Rep. Senatorial Com. Served to capt. U.S. Army, 1964-68. Decorated Bronze Star. Mem. Assn. So. Calif. Def. Counsel, Am. Bd. Trial Advs. (pres. 1984-85), Ventura County Bar Assn. (formerly exec. com., co-chmn. atty./client com., now mem. cts.-bar com.), ABA, Am. Soc. Law and Medicine. Roman Catholic. Clubs: KC (past faithful navigator) (Santa Barbara); Elks (Ventura). Home: 2851 Seahorse Ave Ventura CA 93001 Office: PO Box 1269 Ventura CA 93002

BONHAM-YEAMAN, DORIA, law educator; b. Los Angeles, June 10, 1932; d. Carl Herschel and Edna Mae (Jones) Bonham; widowed; children—Carl Q., Doria Valerie-Constance. B.A., U. Tenn., 1953, J.D., 1957, M.A., 1958; Ed.S. in Computer Edn., Barry U., 1984. Instr. bus. law Palm Beach Jr. Coll., Lake Worth, Fla., 1960-69; instr. legal environment Fla. Atlantic U., Boca Raton, 1969-73; lectr. bus. law Fla. Internat. U., North Miami, 1973-83, assoc. prof. bus. law, 1983—. Editor: Anglo-Am. Law Conf., 1980; Developing Global Corporate Strategies, 1981; editorial bd. Attys. Computer Report, 1984-85, Jour. Legal Studies Edn., 1985—. Contbr. articles to profl. jours. Bd. dirs. Palm Beach County Assn. for Deaf Children, 1960-63; mem. Fla. Commn. on Status of Women, Tallahassee, 1969-70; mem. Broward County Democratic Exec. Com., 1982—; pres. Dem. Women's Club Broward County, 1981; mem. Marine Council of Greater Miami, 1978—, Service award, 1979. Recipient Faculty Devel. award Fla. Internat. U., Miami, 1980; grantee Notre Dame Law Sch., London, summer 1980. Mem. U.S. Council for Internat. Bus., Am. Bus. Law Assn., No. Dade C. of C., Am. Acctg. Assn., AAUW (pres. Palm Beach County 1965-66), Alpha Chi Omega (alumnae club pres. 1968-71), Tau Kappa Alpha. Episcopalian. Office: Fla Internat Univ North Miami FL 33181

BONI, ALBERT, rheumatologist; b. Schanis, Switzerland, Jan. 10, 1912; s. Albert and Emma (von Kraaz) B.; student U. Zurich (Switzerland), 1933-39, U. Berlin, 1936-37, U. Hamburg (Germany), 1936; m. Rosmarie, Jan. 30, 1942; children—Lucas, Martin. Intern, Klinik Bergli Luzer, 1939-40, Bezirkspital Muri, 1940-41; resident in phys. medicine and rheumatology Lund-Schweder, 1947-48; prof. Universitä ts-Rheumaklinik and Institut fur physikalische Therapie mit Poliklinik, Zurich, 1949-80, hon. pro. 1980—, dir. clinic, 1950—; mem. Fed. commn. Rheumatology. Recipient Van Bremen medal Holländ Gesellschaft für Rheumatologie, 1978, Purkeney medal Tschech. Wiss. Vereinigung, 1965. Mem. European League Against Rheumatism (pres. 1975-78), Verdinst-kreuz, Klasse der B.R.D.; hon. mem. 20 rheumatology leagues. Contbr. numerous articles on rheumatology and phys. therapeutics to profl. publs.; co-editor: Klinik der rheumatischen Erkrankungen, 1968. Home: Enzenbuhlstrasse 44, 8008 Zurich Switzerland

BONI, ROBERT EUGENE, industrial company executive; b. Canton, Ohio, Feb. 18, 1928; s. Frank and Sara Boni; m. Janet Virginia Klotz, Aug. 16, 1952; children: Susan, Leslie. B.S. in Metall. Engring, U. Cin., 1951; M.S., Carnegie Inst. Tech., 1954, Ph.D., 1954. Research engr. Armco Inc., Middletown, Ohio, 1956-61, sr. research engr., 1961-68, mgr. applied sci., 1968-70, dir. metall. research, 1970-75, asst. v.p. research and tech., 1976, v.p. research and tech., 1976-78, group v.p. material resources and strata energy, 1978-80, group v.p. steel group, 1980-82, exec. v.p., chief operating officer, 1982-83, pres., chief exec. officer, 1985-86; chmn., chief exec. officer Armco Inc., Parsippany, N.J., 1986—. Bd. dirs. N.C. Cen. U., Alexander and Alexander Services, Inc. Served with U.S. Army, 1954-56. Recipient Disting. Engring. Alumnus award U. Cin., 1970. Mem. AIME (Fairless award Iron & Steel Soc. of AIME 1987), Indsl. Research Inst., Am. Iron and Steel Inst., Am. Iron and Steel Engrs., ASTM, Welding Research Council. Office: Armco Inc 300 Interpace Pkwy Parsippany NJ 07054

BONIFAZI, STEPHEN, chemist; b. Hartford, Conn., Oct. 31, 1924; s. Camillo and Carrie (Mortensen) B.; BS, Trinity Coll., Hartford, 1947; postgrad. Okla. U., 1943-44, Rensselaer Poly. Inst., 1955-58; m. Joan Rose Dunlop, Dec. 19, 1959; 1 dau., Karen Stephanie. Sr. chemist Pratt & Whitney Aircraft Co., East Hartford, Conn., 1950-56, supr. chemistry, 1956-58, project chemist, West Palm Beach, Fla., 1958-63, gen. supr. chemistry, 1963-78, fuels and lubricants specialist, 1978-86, cons. 1986—. Served with inf. AUS, 1943-45; ETO. Decorated Bronze Star medal. Mem. Am. Chem. Soc., Am. Soc. Lubrication Engrs., Internat. Assn. for Hydrogen Energy, ASTM, Coordinating Research Council, Sigma Pi Sigma. Contbr. articles to sci. jours. Home and Office: 516 Kingfish Rd North Palm Beach FL 33408

BONNEFOY, YVES JEAN, author; b. Tours, France, June 24, 1923; s. Elie and Hélène (Maury) B.; licentiate in Lit., Faculty Sci. and Letters, Paris, also degree advanced studies in Philosophy; m. Lucille Vine, 1968; 1 child, Mathilde. Author poetry, essays, including: Du mouvement et de l'immobilité de Douve, 1953; Peintures murales de la France gothique, 1954; Hier régnant désert, 1958; L'Improbable, 1959; Arthur Rimbaud, 1961; Pierre écrite, 1965; Un rêve fait à Mantoue, 1967; Rome 1630, 1970; L'Arrière-Pays, 1972; Dans è Leurre du Seuil, 1975; L'Ordalie, 1975; Le Nuage Rouge, 1977; Rue Traversière, 1977; Poemes 1946-1974, 1978; Entretiens sur la Poésie, 1981; La Présence et l'image, 1983; Ce Qui Fut Sans Lumière, 1987; Récits en Rêve, 1987; assoc. prof. Univ. Ctr. Vincennes, 1969-70, U. Nice, 1973-76, Provence U., Aix-en-Provence, 1979; prof. Collège de France, Paris, 1981; translator Shakespearean plays performed Theatre de France, French TV, festivals. Recipient Prix des Critiques, 1971, Lauréat de l'Académie Francaise, 1973, Prix Montaigne, 1978, Prix Florence Gould, 1987, Grand Prix de la Société des Gens de Lettres, 1987. Address: 63 rue Lepic, 75018 Paris 18e France

BONNER, ASA WALTHALL, SR., business executive; b. Lexa, Ark., Nov. 3, 1901; s. Thomas Elbert and Susie (Vaughan) B.; m. Helen Gertrude Tucker, Feb. 7, 1925 (dec. 1974); children—Asa Walthall, Ben Vaughan; m. Margaret Armbruster, Nov. 3, 1982 (dec. Dec., 1984); m. Edna M. Baum, Dec. 9, 1985. Various courses in mech. engring. and bus. mgmt. Internat. Correspondence Sch.; D.Sc. in Mech. Engring., Lawrence Inst. Tech., 1952. Apprentice operator and set-up Burroughs Adding Machine, Detroit, 1918-21; foreman, supt. M.B. Fetcher Co., Detroit, 1921-24; automobile salesman C.K. Miller Co., Wayne, Mich., 1924-28; supt. McLaren Screw Products, Detroit, 1928-34; v.p., gen. mgr. M.B. Fetcher Co., 1935-55, pres., chief exec. officer, 1955—; founder, pres., chief exec. officer A.T. and G. Co., Inc., Farmington Hills, Mich., 1942—, Lexbon Enterprises, Inc., Detroit, 1943—; founder, chmn. bd., chief exec. officer Approved Mfg. Co., Farmington Hills, 1939-65; field supr. N.R.A.-Five Man Code Authority, 1934-35, chief field ops., Chmn. 1934-35. Chmn. Office Price Adminstrn., Industry Adv. Com., Washington, 1942-46; commr. Civil Service Bd., Ferndale, Mich., 1945-48. Recipient, Merit cert. Office of Price Adminstrn., 1946; Leading Citizen award City of Detroit, 1954; Merit cert. Nat. Screw Machine Assn., 1954; Recognition award Helena 150 Celebration, 1983. Life mem. Soc. Automotive Engrs., ASME; mem. Nat. Screw Machine Products Assn. (exec. bd. 1946-48, v.p. 1952-53, pres. 1953-54). Republican. Methodist. Clubs: Detroit Athletic, Detroit Golf, Oakland Hills Country. Lodges: York Rite, Scottish Rite, Shriners. Died Dec. 6, 1987. Home: 299 Vester Ave Ferndale MI 48220 Office: AT&G Co Inc 30790 W 8 Mile Rd Farmington Hills MI 48024

BONNER, JACK WILBUR, III, psychiatrist; b. Corpus Christi, Tex., July 30, 1940; s. Jack Wilbur and Irldene (Turner) B.; A.A., Del Mar Coll., 1960; B.A. with honors U. Tex., 1961, M.D., S.W. Med. Sch., U. Tex., 1965; m. Myra Lynn Taylor; children—Jack Wilbur, IV, Katherine Lynn, Shelley Bliss. Intern, U. Ark. Med. Center, 1965-66; resident Duke U. Med. Center, 1966-69; asso. in psychiatry Highland Hosp. div. Duke U. Med. Center, Asheville, N.C., 1971, asst. prof. psychiatry, 1972-80, dir. outpatient services, 1972-75, med. dir., 1975-81; chmn. bd. dirs. The Highland Hosp., Asheville, N.C., chief exec. officer, 1981—; asst. clin. prof., Duke U. Med. Ctr., Durham, N.C., 1982-87, cons. prof. psychiatry, 1987—; clin. assoc. prof. U. N.C. Sch. Medicine, Chapel Hill, 1986—; chmn. bd. dirs. The Highland Found., 1980—; bd. dirs. Western N.C. Med. Peer Rev. Found., 1975-78,; trustee La Amistad Found., Maitland, Fla., 1985—, N.C. Symphony, 1987—. Served to maj. M.C., USAF, 1969-71. Diplomate Am. Bd. Psychiatry and Neurology. Fellow Am. Psychiat. Assn., So. Psychiat. Assn. (v.p. 1984-85), Am. Coll. Psychiatrists; mem. Am. Group Psychotherapy Assn., AMA, Buncombe County (N.C.) Med. Soc. (pres.-elect 1982, pres. 1983), N.C. Psychiat. Assn. (pres.-elect 1981-82, pres. 1982-83), Nat. Anorexic Aid Soc. (nat. anorexia adv. council 1979-86), So. Med. Assn. (sec. sect. on neurology, neurosurgery and psychiatry 1977-80, chmn. elect 1980-81, chmn. 1981-82), Central Neuropsychiat. Hosp. Assn. (councillor 1981-85, pres.-elect 1982-83, pres. 1983-84), Group Advancement Psychiatry, N.C. Inst. Medicine, Phi Theta Kappa. Author: (with others) The Psychology of Discipline, 1983, Unmasking the Psychopath: Antisocial Personality and Related Syndromes, 1986. Contbr. articles to profl. jours. Home: 125 Patton Mountain Rd Asheville NC 28804 Office: Highland Hosp PO Box 1101 Asheville NC 28802

BÖNNER, KARL HEINZ, clinical psychologist; b. Essen, Germany, Feb. 6, 1932; s. Bernhard Theodor and Ida Helene (Freiburg) B.; Diplom-Psychologe, U. Cologne, 1964, Dr.rer.pol., 1970; m. Hildegard Scheitzbach, Feb. 17, 1978; children: Natascha, Bertine, Benjamin. Tchr., Cologne, 1956-59; tchr., counselor, Munich, 1959-62; tchr., counseling psychologist, Cologne, 1962-64; research asst. U. Cologne, 1964-67; pvt. practice psychotherapy, 1967-73; prof. psychology U. Marburg, 1973—; dir. Research Center for Psychosocial and Psychosomatic Prevention and Rehab. Pres. Aktion Suchthilfe, 1971—. Mem. Deutsche Akad. Suchttherapie (pres. 1975—), Gesellschaft Psychosomatische Therapie (pres.), Berufsverband Deutscher Psychologen, Gesellschaft Sozialtherapie. Author: Deutschlands Jugend und das Erbe Ihrer Väter, 1967; Nicht Autoritäre Erziehung, 1971; Die Geschlechterrolle, 1973; co-editor Jour. Demokratische Erziehung, 1975-84, Schriften reihe des Instituts für Konfliktforschung, 1977-85, Beitrage zur Praxis der Verhaltens-Medizin; editor FPR-REHA, Praxis der Psychosozialen Pravention und Rehabilitation, 1982—. Home: 39 An der Haustatt, Marburg 355, Federal Republic of Germany Office: 50 Schwanallee, 355 Marburg Federal Republic of Germany

BONNET, ANDRE, physician; b. St. Etienne, Loire, France, Jan. 28, 1953; s. Charles and Marcelle (Six) B.; m. Peillet Françoise, Sept. 13, 1975; children: Geraldine, Alice, Juliette. Mmed. Thesis, U. St. Etienne, France, 1981. With Assn. de Formation Practice in Manual Medicine, Paris, 1983-85; gen. practice medicine St. Etienne, 1981—. Fellow Assn. Formation Practice Manual Medicine. Home and Office: 23 Rue Du 11 Novembre, 42100 Saint Etienne France

BONNET, JEAN MARIE MARCEL, English educator; b. Douai, France, July 18, 1944; s. Georges and Madeleine (Messene) B.; div.; children—Corinne, Marie Laure. Licence es Lettres, U. Nancy (France), 1966, Maitrise es Lettres, 1968; Agregation d'anglais, U. Paris, 1969; Doctorat es Lettres, U. Lyons, 1978. Asst. lectr. U. Keele, Eng., 1966-67; lectr. U. Nancy, France, 1970-78, prof., 1979—; dir. Nancy U. Press; v.p. internat. affairs U. Nancy, 1981—. Author books. Contbr. numerous articles to profl. jours. Pres. Clubs Perspectives et Realites, 1983. Recipient award Am. Council Learned Socs., 1973. Mem. Centre Regional de Lorraine pour l'Enfance Inadaptee (pres. 1984), Assn. Francaise d'Etudes Ams. (v.p. 1984), Assn. Francaise des Presses d'U. (pres. 1981). Roman Catholic. Lodge: Rotary. Office: Presses U de Nancy, 25 rue Baron Louis, Nancy France

BONNETBLANC, JEAN-MARIE, dermatologist; b. Chatelus-Le-Mazcheix, France, Nov. 25, 1948; s. Andre and Francoise (Schmautz) B.; m. Francoise Sindou, Dec. 1987. Cert. immunology, U. Paris, 1975, cert. dermatology, 1979; MD, U. Limoges, 1976. Intern U. Hosp., Limoges, 1972-77, chief clin. asst. in internal medicine, 1977-78, clin. asst. in dermatology, 1978-81, prof. dermatology, 1981—, head dept. dermatology, 1983—. Author: Dermatology for Students, 1988; contbr. articles to profl. jours. Served as capt. French armed forces, 1977. Mem. French Soc. Dermatology, European Soc. Dermatol. Research, N.Y. Acad. Scis., French Soc. Dermatol. Research. Roman Catholic. Office: Ctr Hosp Universitaire, 2 Ave Alexis Carrel, 87000 Limoges France

BONSANTI, GIORGIO, museum director; b. Florence, Tuscany, Italy, Sept. 25, 1944; s. Alessandro and Marcella (del Valle) B.; m. Donata Orsi Battaglini, Mar. 15, 1969; children: Maria, Marta. Asst. to dir. Casa Buonarroti, Florence, 1968-74; mus. dir. Galleria Estense, Modena, Italy, 1974-79, Cappelle Medicee, Florence, 1979-82, Museo di S. Marco, Florence, 1979—, Galleria dell' Accademia, Florence, 1979—; dir. Ufficio Restauri div. Bur. for Conservation, Florence, 1979—; mem. sci. bd. U. Internat. dell'Arte, Florence, 1986—, Archivio Vieusseux, Florence, 1985—. Author: Galleria Estense, 1977, Restauri Fra Modena e Reggio, 1978, Giotto, 1985; editor: Donatello e i Sudi, 1986. City counselor City of Florence, 1985—; v.p. Commn. for Culture City of Florence, 1985—. Mem. Associazione Funzionari Soprintendenze (nat. counselor 1978-85). Italian Communist Party. Home: Via S Marta 17, 50139 Florence Italy Office: Soprintendenza per i Beni, Via Della Ninna S, 50122 Florence Italy

BONSKY, JACK ALAN, chemical company executive, lawyer; b. Canton, Ohio, Mar. 12, 1938; s. Jack H. and Pearl E. Bonsky; A.B., Ohio U., 1960; J.D., Ohio State U., 1964; m. Carol Ann Portmann, Sept. 2, 1960; children—Jack Raymond, Cynthia Lynn. Bar: Ohio 1964, U.S. Dist. Ct. (so. dist.) Ohio 1969. With Metcalf, Thomas & Bonsky, Marietta, Ohio, 1964-69, Addison, Fisher & Bonsky, Marietta, 1969-70; asst. counsel GenCorp., Inc. (formerly Gen. Tire & Rubber Co.), Akron, Ohio, 1970-75, assoc. gen. counsel, 1975-86, asst. sec., 1977-86, v.p. and sec., 1986; v.p., sec., gen. counsel DiversiTech Gen., Inc., 1986-87; v.p., gen. counsel GenCorp Polymer Products, 1988—; solicitor City of Marietta, Ohio, 1966-67; legal advisor City of Marietta Bd. of Edn., 1966-67; police prosecutor, Belpre, Ohio, 1969-70; comml. law instr. Am. Inst. Banking, 1969; dir. Frontier Holdings, Inc., Denver, Frontier Airlines, Denver, 1985 (merged with People Express Airlines, 1985). Mem. Marietta Income Tax Bd. of Rev., 1966-67; mem. Traffic Commn., 1966-69, chmn., 1967; mem. Civil Service Commn., 1969; trustee Urban League, 1978-81, pres., 1980-81; trustee Akron Community Service Ctr., 1978-81, United Way of Summit County, 1982—; bd. dirs. Washington County Soc. for Crippled Children, 1964-70; bd. dirs. S.E. Ohio unit Arthritis Found., 1967-70, chmn., 1968-70; mem. Washington County Health Planning Com., 1968-70; mem. ho. of dels. Ohio Easter Seal Soc., 1968-70. Recipient Akron Community Service Ctr. and Urban League Leadership award, 1981. Mem. Ohio Bar Assn. Home: 4234 Idlebrook Dr Akron OH 44313 Office: GenCorp Polymer Products 350 Springside Dr PO Box 3545 Akron OH 44309-3545

BONVENTRE, JOSEPH VINCENT, physician, scientist, medical educator; b. Bklyn., May 13, 1949; s. Vincent and Philomena (Orsino) B.; m. Kristina Brenn Cannon, Oct. 12, 1974; children—Joanna, Andrew. BS with distinction, Cornell U., 1970; MD, Harvard U., 1976, PhD, 1979. Diplomate Am. Bd. Internal Medicine, Am. Bd. Nephrology. Intern, asst. resident Mass. Gen. Hosp., Boston, 1976-78, clin. asst. medicine, 1980-81, asst. medicine, 1981-85, asst. physician, 1985—; clin., research fellow Harvard U. Med. Sch., Boston, 1976-80, instr. medicine, 1980-81, asst. prof. medicine, 1981—, assoc. prof., 1988—; mem. NE regional rev. com. Am. Heart Assn.; mem. spl. study sect., 1983-87; cons. mem. adv. bd. Nat. Kidney and Urol. Diseases; mem. editorial bd. Am. Jour. Physiology. Author: Key References in Nephrology, 1983. Contbr. scientific articles to profl. jours. Recipient Pres. award Microbeam Soc., 1975, fellow Nat. Kidney Found., 1978, New Investigator Research award NIH, 1980-83, Am. Heart Assn. (Established Investigator 1987-92). Mem. Am. Soc. Clin. Investigation, Am. Soc. Nephrology, Internat. Soc. Nephrology, Am. Physiol. Soc., Am. Fedn. Clin. Research, N.Y. Acad. Sci. Club: Salt and Water. Home: 101 Boston Post Rd Wayland MA 01778 Office: Renal Unit MA Gen Hosp Fruit St Boston MA 02114

BONYNGE, RICHARD, opera conductor; b. Sydney, Australia, Sept. 29, 1930; s. C.A. Bonynge; m. Joan Sutherland, 1954; 1 child. Trained as pianist; specialist in bel canto repertoire. Debut as condr. Santa Cecilia Orch., Rome, 1962, as opera condr. Faust, Vancouver, Can., 1963; condr. world opera houses and Edinburgh Festival, Vienna Festival, Florence Festival; prin. condr., artistic and mus. dir. various cos. including: Sutherland-Williamson Internat. Grand Opera Co., 1965, Vancouver Opera, 1974-78, Australian Opera, 1975-85; opera recs. include: Beatrice di Tenda, Norma, I Puritani, La Sonnambula, Lakme, L'Elisir D'Amore, La Fille du Régiment, Lucia di Lammermoor, Lucrezia Borgia, Maria Stuarda, Faust, Alcina, Giulio Cesare, The Merry Widow, L'Oracolo, Esclarmonde, Le Roi de Lahore, Thérèse, Les Hugenots, Don Giovanni, Les Contes d'Hoffmann, Suor Angelica, Semiramide, Die Fledermaus, Hamlet, I Masnadieri, Rigoletto, La Traviata, Il Trovatore; ballet recs. include: Le Diable a Quatre, Giselle, Marco Spada, La Péri, Coppelia, Sylvia, Le Carillon, La Cigale, Le Papillon, La Boutique Fantasque, Aschenbrödel, The Nutcracker, Sleeping Beauty, Swan Lake; others; recital discs with Sutherland, Tebaldi, Tourangeau, Pavarotti, orchestral and ballet anthologies. Decorated comdr. Order Brit. Empire; officer Order Australia. Office: Ingpen and Williams, 14 Kensington Ct, London W8 5DN, England also: care Colbert Artists Mgmt Inc 111 W 57th St New York NY 10019 *

BOO, JÖRGEN HANS, computer software executive, educator; b. Borås, Sweden, May 11, 1961; s. Lars-Ove and Birgitta Kristina (Persson) B. Engr. degree, Sven Erikson Sch., Borås, 1981; postgrad., U. Gothenberg, Sweden, 1987—. Tchr. TBV, Sweden, 1983-86, head tchr., 1986—; exec. programmer, systems developer Svensk Programtjänst, Hillared, Sweden, 1985—. Bd. dirs. Hillared Dept. Centern, 1987. Served with Swedish Air Force, 1981-84. Home: Åsalund Hillared, S-51200 Svenljunga Sweden Office: Svensk Programtjänst, P1 Åsalunnd Hillared, S-51200 Svenljunga Sweden

BOODELL, THOMAS JOSEPH, JR., lawyer; b. Chgo., Sept. 29, 1935; s. Thomas J. and Mary Elizabeth (Houze) B.; m. Beata Bergman Boodell, Aug. 4, 1962; children—Beata, Mary, Peter, David. A.B., Princeton U., 1957; J.D., Harvard U., 1964. Bar: Ill. 1964. Assoc. Boodell, Sears et al. Chgo., 1964-68; fellow Adlai Stevenson Inst. Internat. Affairs, Chgo., 1968-71; ptnr. Boodell, Sears, Giambalvo & Crowley, Chgo., 1971-84; ptnr. Keck, Mahin & Cate, Chgo., 1984—. Publisher, contbr. articles New City Mag., 1967-71. Pres. bd. dirs. Chgo. Children's Choir, 1979—; bd. dirs. Wendy Will Case Cancer Fund, 1983—, Law in Am. Soc. Found., Chgo., 1972—; trustee Chi Psi Ednl. Trust, Chgo., 1978-84. Served to lt. (j.g.) USN, 1957-60. Recipient Disting. Service award Chi Psi 1984, Disting. Service award Princeton Club

Chgo., 1979. Fellow Am. Bar Found.; mem ABA, Chgo. Bar Assn., Ill. Bar Assn., Law Club City Chgo., Legal Club Chgo., Democrat. Clubs: University, Metropolitan. Home: 1229 E 56th St Chicago IL 60637 Office: Keck Mahin & Cate 8300 Sears Tower Chicago IL 60606

BOODOOSINGH, VISHNU, petroleum executive; b. Siparia, St. Patrick, Trinidad, Nov. 12, 1952; s. Bachan and Dhanee (Chadeesingh) B.; m. Abiya Sheikh, July 23, 1978; children: Nilesh, Ashwin, Aarti. Diploma in acctg., S.W. London Coll., 1976. Chartered acct. Tchr. Ministry of Edn. Govt. of Trinidad and Tobago, Port of Spain, Trinidad, 1970, acct. III, 1977-78, project mgr., 1979-80; trainee acct. Catelli Primo Ltd., Port of Spain, 1971-73; fin. controller Palmiste Ltd., San Fernando, Trinidad, 1980-83; chief exec. officer Ramco Industries Ltd., San Fernando, 1984—, also bd. dirs. Fellow Chartered Assn. Cert. Accts.; mem. Inst. Charteted Accts. of Trinidad and Tobago. Hindu. Club: Beach Camp (Palo Seco, Trinidad). Home: 145 De Montagnac Dr, Palmiste, San Fernando Trinidad Office: Ramco Industries Ltd, Shafik Dr, San Fernando Trinidad

BOOGAERTS, JOHN JOSEPH, JR., architect, map publisher; b. Alexandria, La., Mar. 30, 1934; s. John Joseph and Eunice Loenie (Muse) B.; m. Florence May Macdonald, June 1, 1961; children: Charrette, Whitmore, Pieter, Wijngaert. BArch, Tulane U., 1962; MS in Urban Planning, Columbia U., 1965. Project planner Milan Engring. Ltd., Belize, Brit. Honduras, 1960-62; planner, mem. staff New Orleans City Planning Commn., 1962-63; architect Skidmore Owings & Merrill, 1966-68; prin., urban designer N.Y.C. Housing and Devel. Adminstrn., 1968-74; pres. Boogaerts & Assocs. PC, N.Y.C. and Riyadh, Saudi Arabia, 1975—, Middle East Info. Co., Stamford, Conn. and Al Kohbar, Saudi Arabia, 1978—; cons. UN, 1975, 77, Cen. Planning Orgn., Yemen Arab Republic, 1975, Ministry of Mcpl. and Rural Affairs and Ministry of Info., Kingdom of Saudi Arabia, 1977-78; guest lectr. Columbia U., 1969, NYU, 1975-76, Princeton (N.J.) U., 1975-76. Producer pub. series of guide maps of cities and countries of Middle East. Mem. Manhattan Community Bd. 8, 1968-75, chmn. E. 86th St. corridor com., 1968-75; Republican candidate Ho. of Reps. 18th Congl. Dist., 1974; mem. steering com. Carnegie Hill Neighbors, Inc., 1968-75, N.Y. Mcpl. Art Soc., 1968—; speakers bur. N.Y.C. Charter Revision Commn., 1975; pres. Columbia Archtl. and Planning Alumni, 1974-76; active Rep. Town Com., Greenwich, Conn., 1988—. William Kinne Fellows travel grantee, 1964. Mem. AIA, Am. Inst. Cert. Planners, Greenwich (Conn.) Rep. Town Com. Republican. Roman Catholic. Clubs: Union (N.Y.C.), N.Y. Road Runners, Riyadh Scuba Divers. Home: 315 Valley Rd Cos Cob Greenwich CT 06807-1814

BOOIJ, LEO, anesthesiologist; b. Dordrecht, The Netherlands, Oct. 27, 1946; s. Willem and Maria (Luyten) B.; m. Maria Soetekouw, Jan. 17, 1967; children: Josquin, Celesta, Marie-Leon. MD, Cath. U., Nijmegen, The Netherlands, 1973. Jr. assoc. resident physiology dept. Cath. U. Nijmegen, The Netherlands, 1967-72; resident in anesthesiology Cath. U. Nijmegen, 1973-77, staff dept. anesthesiology, 1977-82; anesthesiologist Free U. Hosp., Amsterdam, The Netherlands, 1982-88, prof. chmn. dept. anesthesiology, 1982-88; prof., chmn. dept. anesthesiology Cath. U. Nijmegen, Amsterdam, 1988%. Mem. Town Council, Beuningen, 1970-78. Served to capt. The Netherlands Army, 1973-74. Mem. Dutch Soc. Anesthesiology, Am. Soc. Anesthesiologists, European Acad. Anesthesiology, (senator 1986—), Biophysics Holland. Home: Kerkstr 23, 6551 2X Weurt The Netherlands Office: Catholic Univ, Dept Anesthesiology, PO Box 9101, Nijmegen The Netherlands

BOOIJ, THIJS, Semitic languages educator; b. Beilen, Drenthe, The Netherlands, Feb. 2, 1933; s. Jan Elbert Booij and Alida Voorbij. D Div., Free U., Amsterdam, The Netherlands, 1978; kandidaat Semitische taal-en letterkunde, U. Amsterdam, 1982. Librarian Free U., Amsterdam, 1978, instr. Semitic langs., 1971—. Home: Lomanstraat 32 B, 1075 RC Amsterdam The Netherlands Office: Vrije Universiteit, Faculteit der Letteren, De Boelelaan 1105, 1081 HV Amsterdam The Netherlands

BOOK, JAN ARVID, medical geneticist; b. Malmo, Sweden, Nov. 4, 1915; s. Arvid and Wivi (Haag) B.; Ph.D., U. Lund (Sweden), 1943, M.D., 1949; D.M.S., U. Uppsala (Sweden), 1954; Dipl.Sci., Salerno (Italy) Med. Sch., 1961; m. Greta Malmberg, 1943; 1 son, Sven; m. Ruth Kerstin Alskog, May 31, 1947; children—Eva Christine, Kerstin Mariane, Marie Jeanette. Research asst. Inst. Genetics, U. Lund, 1940-46, dir. med. genetics research unit, 1946-49; spl. research fellow NIMH, USPHS, U. Minn., 1949-51; asst. dir. State Inst. Human Genetics, Uppsala, 1951-55, dir., 1955-57; asso. prof. med. genetics U. Uppsala, 1954-57, prof. med. genetics, 1957-80; mem. expert panel on human genetics WHO, 1961—; Galton lectr., London, 1964; mem. sci. adv. bd. Research Inst. Human Reprodn. and Fetal Devel., Tel Aviv U. Med. Sch., 1972—; mem. various nat. and internat. expert coms. on genetics in relation to human populations, public health, radiation hazards and mental health UN, UNESCO, WHO, 1952—. Decorated Knight North Star; recipient King's Gold medal 1977, G. Dahlberg Gold medal, 1980. Fellow Internat. Soc. Twin Studies, Royal Swedish Physiographic Soc.; mem. Swedish Soc. Med. Genetics (pres. 1957-80). Author: A Genetic and Neuro-Psychiatric Investigation of a North Swedish Population, 1953; co-editor: Jour. Clin. Genetics, 1970—; contbr. articles on clin. genetics and cytogenetics to profl. jours. Home and Office: Le Hameau du Chateau, 23 Rue de la Cour, 74000 Annecy-le-Vieux France Other: Axinos, 35300 Stylidos Greece

BOOKOUT, JOHN FRANK, JR., oil company executive; b. Shreveport, La., Dec. 31, 1922; s. John Frank and Lena (Hagen) B.; m. Mary Carolyn Cook, Dec. 21, 1946; children: Beverly Carolyn, Mary Adair and John Frank III (twins). Student, Iowa Wesleyan Coll., 1943, Centenary Coll., 1946-47; LLD (hon.), Centenary Coll., 1987; BSc, U. Tex., 1949, MA, 1950; DSc (hon.), Tulane U., 1978. Geologist Shell Oil Co., Tulsa, 1950-59, div. exploration mgr., 1959-61; area exploration mgr. Shell Oil Co., Denver, 1961-63, The Hague, Netherlands, 1963-64; mgr. exploration and prodn. econs. dept. Shell Oil Co., N.Y.C., 1965, v.p. Denver exploration and prodn. area, 1966; v.p. Southeastern exploration and prodn. region Shell Oil Co., New Orleans, 1967-70; pres., chief exec. officer, dir. Shell Can. Ltd., Toronto, Ont., 1970-74; exec. v.p., dir. Shell Oil Co., Houston, 1974-76, pres., chief exec. officer, dir., 1976-88; Bd. dirs. Irving Trust Co., Royal Dutch Shell, Shell Petroleum, Inc.; chmn. adv. bd. Inst. Bioscis. and Tech. Tex. A&M U. Active chancellors council U. Tex.; bd. dirs. Meth. Hosp., Houston; mem. regional adv. bd. Inst. Internat. Edn.; mem. U.S. Fish and Wildlife Found. Served with USAAF, 1942-46. Decorated Air medal with 3 oak leaf clusters; comdr. Order of Orange-Nassau, (The Netherlands), 1988; recipient Disting. Service award Nat. Assn. Secondary Sch. Prins., John Rogers award Southwestern Legal Fedn., 1986; named Outstanding Chief Exec. Domestic Integrated Oil Co. Wall St. Transcript, 1982-84, Disting. Alumnus U. Tex., 1981. Mem. Am. Assn. Petroleum Geologists, Nat. Petroleum Council (former chmn.), Houston C. of C., The Conf. Bd. (bd. dirs.), Am. Petroleum Inst. (bd. dirs., past chmn. bd., mgmt. com.), 25 Year Club Petroleum Industry (bd. govs. SW dist.), Internat. C. of C. (U.S. Council; trustee), Council on Fgn. Relations Inc., All-Am. Wildcatters Assn., Bus. Roundtable (mem. policy com.), Am. Council on Edn. (bus.-higher edn. forum), Nat. Fish and Wildlife Found. (bd. dirs.). Home: PO Box 2463 Houston TX 77252 Office: One Shell Plaza Houston TX 77001

BOOLELL, SIR SATCAM, government official; b. New Grove, Mauritius, Sept. 11, 1920; 3 children. LLB. with honors, London Sch. Econs., 1952. Mem. Legis. Council for Moka-Flacq, 1953; minister agriculture and natural resources Mauritius, 1959-67, 68-82, minister edn., 1967-68, minister econ. planning and devel., 1983-84; pres., leader Mauritius Labour Party, from 1983; dep. prime minister, atty.-gen., minister justice, minister external affairs and emigration Mauritius, 1986—; official spokesman ACP group of countries on sugar; rep. Mauritius at internat. confs. Decorated knight, 1977. Address: Office Atty Gen, Port Louis Mauritius *

BOON, PIETER JACOB SJIRK, data processing executive; b. Alkmaar, The Netherlands, June 12, 1942; s. Jacob and Orselle (Wyma) B.; m. Marie Catherine van Wyk, June 14, 1968; 1 child, Sjirk Niels. MO-Wiskunde degree, U. Staatsexamen Amsterdam, 1969; degree in Stats., Vereniging voor Statistiek, 1972. Registered informaticus. Data processing mgr. Ultra Centrifuge Project RCN, Amsterdam, 1965-73; analyst Reactor Centrum Nederland, Petten, The Netherlands, 1973-75; sci. applications mgr. Univ. Computing Ctr., Nymegen, 1975-77; applications mgr. Univ. Computing Ctr., 1977-85; data processing mgr. Acad. Hosp., Maastricht, The Netherlands, 1985—; founder, tchr. Curs. Info. Onderwys, Arnhem, The Netherlands, 1981-85; tchr. Econ. Inst. Tilburg, Arnhem, Nymegen, Maastricht, 1976—; cons. ABC i.o., Nymegen, Maastricht, 1975—. Mem. Share European Assn. (bd. dirs. Nymegen 1976-84), Gemeenteraad Alkmaar - VVD (council mem. 1974-75), Ver van Register Informatici. Club: Hobby Computer (bd. dirs. 1977-79). Home: Tongerseweg 320-C, 6215 AC Maastricht, Limburg The Netherlands Office: Akademisch Ziekenhuis DA, Postbus 1918, 6201 BX Maastricht The Netherlands

BOONE, JAMES VIRGIL, engineering executive; b. Little Rock, Sept. 1, 1933; s. Virgil Bennett and Dorothy Bliss (Dorough) B.; m. Gloria Marjorie Gieseler, June 5, 1955; children—Clifford B., Sandra J. Smyser, Steven B. B.S. in Elec. Engring., Tulane U., 1955; M.S.E.E., Air Force Inst. Tech., Ohio, 1959. Assoc. elec. engr. Martin Co., Balt., 1955; research and develop. engr. U.S. Air Force, 1955-62; electronics engr. Nat. Security Agy., Ft. Meade, Md., 1962-77, dep. dir. for research and engring., 1978-81; spl. asst. to gen. mgr. Mil. Electronics div. TRW, Inc., San Diego, 1981-83, asst. gen. mgr., 1983-85, dir. program mgmt. and group devel. TRW Electronic Systems Group, 1985-86, v.p., dir. program mgmt. and group devel, 1986-87; v.p., gen. mgr. Defense Communications div. TRW Electronic Systems Group, 1987; Served to capt. USAF, 1955-62. Recipient Nat. Security Agy. Exceptional Civilian Service award, 1975. Mem. IEEE (sr.), AIAA. Republican. Presbyterian (elder). Contbr. articles to profl. jours. Home: 3030 Deluna Dr Rancho Palos Verdes CA 90274 Office: One Space Park Redondo Beach CA 90278

BOONE, PATRICIA NEEF, account manager, investment company associate; b. Houston, Mar. 7, 1952; d. William G. and Hazel Eve (Mouton) Neef; m. Ronald W. Boone, June 4, 1982; children: Amy Marie, Alicia Catherine. BA, U. Southwestern La., 1974, M of Elem. Edn., 1977, postgrad. in ednl. sci., 1980-82. Cert. tchr., La. Tchr., head English dept. Acad. of Sacred Heart, Grand Coteau, La., 1974-75; coordinator high sch. relations U. Southwestern La., Lafayette, 1975-80; tchr. academically gifted St. Mary's Parish Sch. Bd., Franklin, La., 1980-82; dir. Chapman Coll. Residence Edn. Ctr., Holloman AFB, N.Mex., 1982-84; dir. tng. The Acacia Group, San Antonio, 1985—, PACE instr., Washington, 1987. Editor: The Acacia Bull., 1986-87. Mem. San Antonio Child Abuse Resources and Edn. Services, 1985-87, sch. bd. St. Pius X Sch.; coordinating chair Case Worker Luncheon, 1988. Mem. Nat. Assn. Life Underwriters, Tex. Assn. Life Underwriters, San Antonio Assn. Life Underwriters, Internat. Bd. Cert. Fin. Planners (assoc.), Kappa Delta (panhellenic del. 1985-87). Democrat. Roman Catholic. Club: San Antonio Panhellenic (del. 1985-87). Avocations: studying Acacian culture, travel, entertaining, gardening. Office: The Acacia Group 7550 Interstate Hwy 10 W Suite 1000 San Antonio TX 78229

BOONSHAFT-LEWIS, HOPE JUDITH, public relations executive; b. Phila., May 3, 1949; d. Barry and Lorelei Gail (Rienzi) B. B.A., Pa. State U., 1972; postgrad. Del. Law Sch., Kellogg Inst. Mgmt. Tng. Program writer Youth Edn., N.Y.C., 1972; legal aide to judge, Phila., 1973; dir. spl. projects Guiffre Med. Center, Phila., 1975; Arlen Specter senatorial campaign fin. dir., Phila., 1975; fin. dir. Jimmy Carter Presdl. Campaign, Atlanta, 1976; nat. fin. dir. Democratic Nat. Com., 1977-78; dir. devel. World Jewish Congress, N.Y.C., 1978; dir. devel. Yeshiva U., Los Angeles, 1979; dir. communications Nat. Easter Seal Soc., Chgo., 1979-83; chief exec. officer Boonshaft-Lewis & Savitch Pub. Relations and Govt. Affairs, Los Angeles, 1983—; spl. adv. community relations The White House, 1977-80; guest lectr. U. Ill., 1982, May Co.'s Calif. Women in Bus. Bd. dirs. Los Angeles Arts Council, Hollywood Heritage Council. Named 1 of 6 Non Stop Achievers, GermaineMonteil. Mem. Nat. Soc. Fundraisers, Am. Inst. Wine and Food (bd. dirs.), Women's Nat. Dem. Club, Alpha Chi Omega. Home: 1234 N Wetherly Dr Los Angeles CA 90069 Office: 1888 Century Park E Suite 330 Los Angeles CA 90067

BOOR, MYRON VERNON, psychologist, educator; b. Wadena, Minn., Dec. 21, 1942; s. Vernon LeRoy and Rosella Katharine (Eckhoff) B. BS, U. Iowa, 1965; MA, So. Ill. U., 1967, PhD, 1970; MS in Hygiene, U. Pitts., 1981. Lic. psychologist, Kans., Ky., R.I. Research psychologist Milw. County Mental Health Ctr., 1970-72; asst. prof. clin. psychologist Ft. Hays State U., Hays, Kans., 1972-76; assoc. prof. Ft. Hays State U., Hays, 1976-79; NIMH postdoctoral fellow in psychiat. epidemiology U. Pitts., Western Psychiat. Inst. and Clinic, 1979-81; research psychologist R.I. Hosp. and Butler Hosp., Providence, 1981-84; clin. psychologist Newman Meml. County Hosp., Emporia, Kans., 1985—; clin. psychologist Ft. Hays State U., 1972-79; asst. prof. psychiatry and human behavior Brown U., Providence, 1981-84; adj. faculty Emporia State U., 1985—. Contbr. articles to profl. jours. U.S. Pub. Health Service fellow, 1965-67, NIMH fellow 1979-81. Mem. Am. Psychol. Assn., Soc. for Psychol. Study of Social Issues, Internat. Soc. for Study of Multiple Personalities (charter). Home: 2225 Prairie Emporia KS 66801 Office: Newman Meml County Hosp 12th & Chestnut Emporia KS 66801

BOORMAN, JOHN, film director, producer, screenwriter; b. Shepperton, Middlesex, Eng., Jan. 18, 1933; s. George and Ivy (Chapman) B.; m. Christel Kruse, 1957; 4 children. Broadcaster, critic BBC Radio; film editor ITN London, 1955-58; dir., producer So. TV, 1958-60. Contbr. articles to Manchester Guardian and mags.; 1950-54; head documentaries, Bristol, BBC-TV; dir. documentary The Citizens series The Newcomers, 1960-64; dir. films Catch Us If You Can, 1965, Point Blank, 1967, Hell in the Pacific, 1968, Leo the Last, 1969, Deliverance, 1970, Zardoz, 1973, The Heretic, 1976, Excalibur, 1981, Emerald Forest, 1985, Hope and Glory, 1987 (Golden Globe award 1988 and Nat. Soc. Film Critics award); founder: TV mag. Day by Day; author: fiction The Legend of Zardoz, 1973. Recipient Best Dir. prize Cannes Festival, 1970. Office: care Edgar Gross Internat Bus Mgmt 9696 Blvd #203 Culver City CA 90232 *

BOORSTIN, DANIEL J., librarian, emeritus history educator, writer; b. Atlanta, Oct. 1, 1914; s. Samuel and Dora (Olsan) B.; m. Ruth Carolyn Frankel, Apr. 9, 1941; children: Paul Terry, Jonathan, David West. A.B. summa cum laude, Harvard U., 1934; B.A. with first class honors (Rhodes scholar), Balliol Coll., Oxford U., 1936, B.C.L. with first class honors, 1937; postgrad., Inner Temple, London, 1934-37; J.S.D. (Sterling fellow), Yale U., 1940; Litt.D. (hon.), Cambridge U., 1967; numerous other hon. degrees. Bar: Admitted as barrister-at-law Inner Temple 1937, Mass. bar 1942. Instr., tutor history and lit. Harvard and Radcliffe Coll., 1938-42; lectr. legal history Harvard Law Sch., 1939-42; asst. prof. history Swarthmore Coll., 1942-44; asst. prof. U. Chgo., 1944-49, assoc. prof., 1949-56, prof. Am. History, 1956-64, Preston and Sterling Morton Disting. Service prof., 1964-69; Walgreen lectr. Am. instns., 1952; dir. Nat. Mus. History and Tech., Smithsonian Instn., Washington, 1969-73; sr. historian Nat. Mus. History and Tech., Smithsonian Instn., 1973-75; Librarian of Congress Library of Congress, 1975-87, Librarian of Congress Emeritus, 1987—; Fulbright vis. lectr. Am. history U. Rome, Italy, 1950-51, Kyoto U., Japan, 1957; cons. Social Sci. Research Center, U. P.R., 1955; lectr. for U.S. Dept. State in, Turkey, Iran, Nepal, India, Ceylon, 1959-60, Indonesia, Australia, New Zealand, Fiji, 1968, India, Pakistan, Iceland, 1974, Philippines, Thailand, Malaysia, India, Egypt, 1975; 1st incumbent of chair Am. history U. Paris, 1961-62; Pitt prof. Am. history and instns. U. Cambridge, 1964-65; Shelby and Kathryn Cullom Davis lectr. Grad. Inst. Internat. Studies, Geneva, 1973-74; sr. fellow Huntington Library, 1969; mem. Commn. on Critical Choices for Ams., 1973—, Dept. State Indo-Am. Joint Subcommn. Edn. and Culture, 1974-81, Japan-U.S. Friendship Commn., 1978-84; Mem. Am. Revolution Bicentennial Commn.; sr. attorney Office Lend Lease Adminstr., Dept. Justice, Washington.; Fellow Trinity Coll., 1964-65. Author: The Mysterious Science of the Law, 1941, Delaware Cases, 1792-1830 (3 vols.), 1943, The Lost World of Thomas Jefferson, 1948, The Genius of American Politics, 1953, The Americans: The Colonial Experience, 1958 (winner Bancroft award 1959), America and the Image of Europe, 1960, The Image or What Happened to the American Dream, 1962, The Americans: The National Experience, 1965 (Francis Parkman prize 1966), The Landmark History of the American People, 2 vols., 1968, 70, 87, The Decline of Radicalism, 1969, The Sociology of the Absurd, 1970, The Americans: The Democratic Experience, 1973 (Pulitzer prize 1974), (Dexter prize 1974), Democracy and Its Discontents, 1974, The Exploring Spirit, 1976, The Republic of Technology, 1978; (with Brooks M. Kelley) A History of the United States, 1981, The Discoverers, 1983 (Watson-Davis Prize 1986), Watson-Davis Prize of the History of Society for the Discoverers, 1986, Hidden History, 1987; editor: An American Primer, 1966, American Civilization, 1972, Am. history, Ency. Brit, 1951-55; author articles, book reviews; bd. editors Ency. Brit., 1981—. Trustee Colonial Williamsburg, Kennedy Center, Cafritz Found., Woodrow Wilson Center, Thomas Gilcrease Mus.; bd. visitors U.S. Air Force Acad., 1968-70. Recipient Bowdoin prize Harvard, 1934, Jenkins prize, Younger prize Balliol Coll., 1935, 36. Fellow Am. Geographical Soc. (hon.); mem. Colonial Soc. Mass., Orgn. Am. Historians, Am. Acad. Arts and Scis., Am. Philos. Soc., Am. Antiquarian Soc., Am. Studies Assn. (pres. 1969-71), Internat. House Japan, Royal Hist. Soc. (corr. fellow), Phi Beta Kappa. Jewish. Clubs: Nat. Press, Cosmos; Elizabethan (Yale). Home: 3541 Ordway St NW Washington DC 20016 Office: Library of Congress Washington DC 20540

BOOSALIS, ELSIE, real estate management executive; b. Cedar Rapids, Iowa, Dec. 1, 1913; adopted dau. of Peter and Rose (Halleck) B.; student Phoenix Bus. Coll., 1943-44, Northwestern U., 1952-53, U. Minn. Property mgr. Peter Boosalis Bldg. Trust, Mpls., 1953—, trustee, 1960—. Bd. dirs. Greater Lake St. Council; sustaining mem. council Girl Scouts U.S.A.; bus. mem. Powderhorn Devel. Corp.; donor Guthrie Theater; active ARC, YWCA, WAMSO. Mem. Mpls. Soc. Fine Arts, Minn., Hennepin County hist. socs., Mpls. C. of C., Minn. Orch. Assn. (guarantor, chmn.), English Speaking Union, Am. Swedish Inst. Home: 4551 Dupont Ave S Minneapolis MN 55409 Office: 2951 Chicago Ave Minneapolis MN 55407

BOOTH, BONNIE NELSON, human resources administrator; b. Lynn, Mass., Aug. 28, 1942; d. Vincent Carl and Merchelle Romaine (Eastman) Nelson. Student, Mary Washington Coll., 1960-61, Columbia U., 1965, Carnegie-Mellon U., 1962, 78-80; EdM in Adminstrn., Planning and Social Policy, Harvard U., 1979. Exec. sec. Kenyon and Eckhardt, Inc., N.Y.C., 1964-65; exec. sec., asst. to assoc. dir. Am. Press. Inst., Columbia U., 1965; prin. sec. to chief housing sect. UN Hdqrs., N.Y.C., 1965-68; adminstrv. asst. sec. UN Mission, Magadiscio, Somalia, 1968, Tripoli, Libya, 1968-69; research asst. Stockholm Sch. Econs., 1970; adminstrv. sec. to dep. dir. UN Conf. Trade and Devel./GATT, Geneva, 1970; adminstrv. asst. Harvard U., 1970-74, personnel officer dept. psychology and social relations, 1974-75; adminstrv. asst. Dravo Corp., Pitts., 1975-76; assoc. dir. admissions Chatham Coll., Pitts., 1976-77, acting dir. admissions, 1977-78; mgmt. devel. trainer and adminstr. Westinghouse Credit Corp., Pitts., 1981-86, human resources adminstr., 1986—. Dem. committeewoman 7th Ward, Pitts., 1980—. Recipient Hon. diploma for outstanding performance Internat. Seminar on Rural Housing and Community Facilities, Venezuelan Govt., 1967, Outstanding Quality Circle Facilitator award Westinghouse Electric Corp., 1985. Mem. Am. Soc. for Tng. and Devel., Internat. Assn. Quality Circles (pres. Pitts. chpt. 1985—), Am. Soc. Exec. Women. Episcopalian. Lodge: Rotary. Avocations: literature, art, music, film, arranging silk flowers. Home: 5825 5th Ave Pittsburgh PA 15232 Office: Westinghouse Credit Corp 1 Oxford Ctr 7th Floor Pittsburgh PA 15219

BOOTH, GEORGE WARREN, artist, advertising executive; b. Omaha, July 6, 1917; s. George H. and Rae (McGrady) B.; A.B., summa sum laude, Ohio U., 1940, M.A., 1942; postgrad. John Huntington Poly. Inst., 1941, Chouinard Sch. Art, 1945-46; m. Nancy Jane Schuele, Dec. 6, 1968; children—George Geoffrey, Katherine Ellen, Robert Alan. Art dir. J.Walter Thompson Co., N.Y.C., 1947-58, Gardner Advt. Co., N.Y.C., 1958-60, Ted Bates Co., N.Y.C., 1960-64; exhibited numerous one-man shows in N.Y.C., Calif., Washington, Md., 1972—, group shows: NAD, N.Y.C., Am. Water Color Soc., N.Y.C., Allied Artists Am., Calif. Watercolor Soc., Los Angeles, Los Angeles Mus. Art, San Francisco Mus. Art, Butler Art Inst., others; represented in permanent collections, galleries in N.Y.C., Washington, Palm Beach, Middleburg, Va.; teaching fellow photography Ohio U., Athens, 1941-42, cons. in field. Served with Signal Corps, U.S. Army, 1942-44. Recipient Art Dirs. Club N.Y.'s gold medal, 1954, Kerwin H.Fulton medal, 1954. Mem. Soc. Illustrators N.Y.C., N.Y. Artists Equity, Art Dirs. Club N.Y., Fla. Thoroughbred Breeders Assn. Club: Golden Hills Golf and Turf (Ocala, Fla.). Home: 1771 SW 55th Rd Ocala FL 32674

BOOTH, GORDON DEAN, JR., lawyer; b. Columbus, Ga., June 25, 1939; s. Gordon Dean and Lois Mildred (Bray) B.; m. Katherine Morris Campbell, June 17, 1961; children: Mary Katherine, Abigail Kilgore, Sarah Elizabeth, Margaret Campbell. B.A., Emory U., 1961, J.D., 1964, LL.M, 1973. Bar: Ga. 1964, U.S. Supreme Ct. 1973. Practice law Atlanta, 1964-80; ptnr. Kilpatrick & Cody, Atlanta, 1980—; dir., v.p. Stallion Music, Inc., Nashville, Computer Microfilm Corp., Atlanta. Contbr. articles to profl. jours. Trustee Met. Atlanta Crime Commn., 1977-80, chmn., 1979-80; mem. assembly for arts and scis. Emory Coll., 1971—, chmn., 1983. Mem. Atlanta Bar Assn., ABA, Internat. Bar Assn. (council sec. bus. law 1974—, chmn. aero. law com. 1971—), Am. Soc. Internat. Law Assn. Bar City N.Y., State Bar Ga., Lawyers Club Atlanta, Sigma Chi. Clubs: Capital City (Atlanta); University, Wings (N.Y.C.). Home: 580 Old Harbor Dr Atlanta GA 30328 Office: Kilpatrick & Cody 3100 Equitable Bldg Atlanta GA 30043

BOPP, EDWARD SIDNEY, lawyer, pharmacist; b. New Orleans, Nov. 28, 1930; s. Edward Sidney and Eunice (Demoulette) B.; m. Patricia Lynette Planche, July 3, 1952; children—Sydney, Felix, Michael, Eric, Kelly. B.S. in Pharmacy, U. Miss., 1955; LL.B., Loyola U., New Orleans, 1963. Bar: La. 1963; registered pharmacist, La. Pharmacist, St. Bernard Drugs, Arabi, La., 1959-64; v.p. Albert and Wegman Drugs, Inc., 1965-80; v.p. St. Bernard Bank, Arabi, 1963—, dir., 1956—; sole practice law, Arabi, 1963—; adj. prof. Northeastern and Xavier Pharmacy Sch., New Orleans; owner Contesta Apts., Inc., 1971—. Mem. La. Ho. of Reps., 1977—; pres. La. State Bd. Elem. and Secondary Edn., 1972-77; bd. adminstrn. Charity Hosp. of La., New Orleans, 1964-72; exec. com. New Orleans council Boy Scouts Am., 1969-79; mem. Holy Cross Found.; St. Bernard Parish chmn. March of Dimes, 1979; bd. dirs. Tulane Med Ctr., 1984—. Named Pharmacist of Yr., La. Pharm. Assn., 1981; recipient Meritorious Service award NE La. U., 1979, Bowl of Hygeia award A.H. Robins, 1969, Good Turn award Boy Scouts Am., 1971. Served with USNR, 1948-52. Fellow Am. Soc. for Pharmacy Law; mem. La. Bar Assn. (ho. of dels.), ABA, Assn. Trial Lawyers Am., La. Trial Lawyers Assn., 34th Jud. Dist. Bar Assn., Am. Pharm. Assn., Nat. Assn. Retail Druggists (nat. legis. chmn. 1978), La. State Pharm. Assn. (pres. 1967-68), Am. Banking Assn., La. Banking Assn. Democrat. Roman Catholic. Clubs: Lions, New Orleans Young Mens Bus. Assn., Rotary. Lodge: KC (4th deg.). Home: 14 Pamela Pl Arabi LA 70032 Office: 6725 St Claude Ave Arabi LA 70032

BORAI, AMR MAHMOUD, petroleum engineer; b. Alexandria, Egypt, May 25, 1949; s. Mahmoud Borai and Souad Ahmed Chokry; m. Heba Salem, May 6, 1982; children: Inji, Haidi. BS in Mech. Engring., Alexandria U., 1972. Petroleum engr. Gulf of Suez Petroleum co., Ras Shokair, Egypt, 1977-79; petroleum engr. Abu Dhabi Marine Operating Co., Abu Dhabi, United Arab Emirates, 1979-87, sr. petroleum engr., 1987—. Contbr. papers in field; reveiwer profl. mags. Served to lt. Egyptian Air Defense, 1972-76. Mem. Soc. Petroleum Engrs. (treas. 1979-82, vice chmn. 1982-85), Egyptian Syndicate Engrs, Soc. Profl. Well Log Analysts. Office: Abu Dhabi Marine Operating Co, PO Box 303, Abu Dhabi United Arab Emirates

BORCH, KURT ESBEN, surgeon, educator; b. Ny Osted, Denmark, Nov. 4, 1944; arrived in Sweden, 1978; s. Erik Esben Hansen and Ulla Borch; m. Gerd Gunilla Bjorkblom, Mar. 1, 1985; children: Daniel Visti, Lau Esben, Bjorn Andreas, Eric Olof, Michael Erik. MD, U. Copenhagen, 1978; PhD in Surgery, U. Linkoping, 1985. Intern Cen. Hosp., Eskilstuna, Sweden, 1978-79, resident in surgery, 1980-84, staff surgeon, 1984-85; staff surgeon U. Hosp., Linkoping, Sweden, 1985-87, asst. prof. surgery, 1987—. Contbr. articles to med. jours. Mem. Swedish Assn. Surgery, Swedish Soc. Gastroenterology, Swedish Soc. Gastrointestinal Endoscopy, Swedish Med. Assn., Danish Med. Assn. Home: Fridsbergsgatan 10, S-58247 Linköping Sweden

BORDALO, GABRIELA HAUSER DA COSTA-SANTOS, mathematics educator; b. Lisbon, Portugal, Mar. 23, 1949; d. Paulo Belmarco and Carmen (Hauser) da Costa-Santos. M in Math., U. Lisbon, 1971, PhD in Math., 1983. Research fellow U. Liège, Belgium, 1976-77; teaching asst. U. Lisbon, 1977-83, prof. math. dept., 1983—; research fellow Nat. Inst. Sci. Research, Lisbon, 1977-83; participated in numerous internat. seminars, confs. and meetings. Mem. Portuguese Math. Soc., Am. Math. Soc. Home: R Filipe Magalhaes 4 7D, 1700 Lisbon Portugal Office: U Lisbon Dept Math, R Ernesto Vasconcelos BL C1, 1700 Lisbon Portugal

BORDCOSH, LEILA COSTANDI, insurance executive; b. Jaffa, Palestine, June 9, 1942; d. Costandi Elias and Laurice George (Abdelnour) B.; B.A., Beirut Coll. for Women, 1964. With Arab Comml. Enterprises Group of Cos., Athens, Greece, 1964—, adminstrv. asst., 1965-67, mgr., 1967-71, group coordinator, 1971-75, asst. v.p., 1975-78, group v.p., 1978-86, sr. group v.p., 1986-87, v.p. Fred S. James & Co., N.Y., 1987—. Office: Fred S James & Co 1290 Avenue of the Americas New York NY 10104

BORDEN, SANDRA MCCLISTER, day care center administrator, dancer; b. Trenton, Oct. 18, 1946; d. Harry Arthur and Ruth West McClister; m. Robert Stetson Borden, Mar. 23, 1968; children: Robert Freeman, Randolph McClister, David Buckley, Christian Delano. BA, Eastern Nazarene Coll., Quincy, Mass., 1968; MA, Nova U., 1986. Tchr. kindergarten Doves Nest Day Care Ctr., Rockland, Mass., 1979-84, owner, adminstr., 1979—; owner, adminstr. Dove's Nest Day Care Ctr., Weymouth, Mass., 1980-82, Abington, Mass., 1980-83; owner, editor Barter & Trade Jour., Rockland, 1980-83; owner Dove's Nest Family Day Care System, Rockland, 1984—; co-owner Carriage House Day Care Ctr., Brockton, Mass., 1986—, Commonwealth Child Care Cons., 1987—, Bevell Assocs., Stoughton, Mass., 1987—, Beginning Roots Day Care Ctr., Stoughton, 1987—. Dancer Foggs Dancers, Boston, 1980—; dir. Country Dance Soc., Boston, 1982—, v.p. 1986—, dancer, 1984-85, pres. 1988; co-founder, dancer Rapscallion Rapper Sword Team, 1985—. Bd. dirs. LWV, Rockland, 1972-73. Mem. Nat. Assn. Young Children, Royal Scottish Dance Soc., Country Dance Soc. (pres. elect 1987), Nat. Assn. Female Execs., Assn. for Childhood Edn. Internat. Baptist. Clubs: Women Aglow (sec., bd. dirs.) (Brockton); New Eng. Folk Festival Assn. (Boston). Home: 1040 Plymouth St Abington MA 02351 Office: The Dove's Nest Day Care Ctr 1040 Plymouth St Abington MA 02351

BORDES, LOUIS RENÉ, physician, educator; b. Balaruc, Herault, France, June 28, 1926; s. Louis Marius and Marcelle (Dufour) B.; m. Carratier Mireille, July 18, 1948 (div. 1958); 1 child, Marie Christine; m. Janine Du Queroix, Dec. 6, 1975; 1 child, Lauriane. MD, U. Toulouse, France, 1951. Flight surgeon USAF, San Antonio, 1953; asst. in oto-rhino-laryngology Val de Grace Hosp., Paris, 1955-58; chief of oto-rhino-laryngology dept. Robert Picqué Hosp., Bordeaux, France, 1958-59; chief of oto-rhino-laryngology, head and neck surgery dept. Versailles (France) Dominique Larrey Hosp., 1960-79; prof. clin. an surgical oto-rhino-laryngology French Sch. Aviation and Space Medicine, Paris, 1964-79; practice specializing in oto-rhino-laryngology Sceaux, France, 1979—; clin. health expert French Pub. Health Office, Paris, 1964—; Ct. of Appeal, Versailles, 1973; cons. in field. Contbr. more than 200 published works in field. Served to brigadier gen. French Air Force, 1978. Named Officer of National merit, 1966, Chevalier of French Legion honor, 1970, Chevalier of Acad. Palms decoration of Edn. Ministry, 1971, Army Health Service medal, 1972, Air Service medal, 1973. Mem. Oto-rhino-laryngology Soc. Paris Hosps., French Soc. Oto-rhino-laryngology and Head and Neck Surgery, French Soc. Aviation and Space Medicine. Home: Rue du Ranelagh No 49, 75016 Paris France Office: ORL Med Office, No 135 Rue Houdan, 92330 Sceaux France

BORDES, PHILLIPE ANDRÉ, museum director, art historian; b. St. Michel-en-Greve, Côtes-du-Nord, France, July 13, 1949; s. Pierre Paul and Yvette Marie (Berger) B. BA, Stanford U., Calif., 1970; MA, U. London, 1972; PhD, U. Sorbonne, Paris, 1981. Asst. prof. U. Montpellier, France, 1975-84; dir. Musée de la Revolution Française, Vizille, France, 1984—; sci. com. bicentennial of French revolution, 1986—; mem. commn. CNRS bicentennial, 1983—. Author books on J.L. David, 1983, 88; editorial bd. Cahier Mus. Nat. d'Art Moderne, Paris, 1987—; author articles. Office: Mus de la Revolution Francaise, Chateau de Vizille, 38220 Vizille France

BORDIGA, BENNO, automotive parts manufacturing company executive; b. Vienna, Austria, July 25, 1923; came to U.S., 1940; s. Adolph and Grace V. (Blaustein) B.; m. Edna Bordiga, Feb. 5, 1944 (div. 1960); children—Robert S., Jeffrey S.; m. Melva E. Leftwich (div. 1986). B.S. in Mech. Engring., U. Vienna, 1938. v.p. mfg. Olympic Radio and TV, L.I., 1943-58; pres., chmn. bd. Allomatic Industries, Woodside, N.Y., 1958—, Allstar Automotive Co., Hyde Park, N.Y., 1962-80, All-O-Matic Instrument and Systems, New Hyde Park, N.Y., 1967-79; pres. William R. Davis Fine Arts Ltd., Woodside, 1957—; v.p., dir. Hotel Commander, N.Y.C., 1955—; pres., dir. Fogel Mfg. Corp., Bklyn., 1959-64, W&B Industries, 1961-68; dir. Hotel Endicott, N.Y.C., Allomatic U.K. Ltd., Parzen Research Co. Contbr. articles to profl. jours. Pres., bd. dirs. Franz Bader Gallery, Washington, 1968-86, 1050 Park Ave Tenants Assn., 1985—. Served with U.S. Army, 1944-46. Home: 1050 Park Ave New York NY 10028 also: 3095 N Course Dr Pompano Beach FL 33069 Office: Allomatic Industries Inc 30-30 60th St Woodside NY 11377

BORDOGNA, JOSEPH, educator, engineer; b. Scranton, Pa., Mar. 22, 1933; s. Raymond and Rose (Yesu) B. B.S. in Elec. Engring., U. Pa., 1955, Ph.D., 1964; S.M., MIT, 1960. With RCA Corp., 1958-64; asst. prof. U. Pa., Phila., 1964-68; assoc. prof. U. Pa., 1968-72, prof., 1972—, assoc. dean engring. and applied sci., 1973-80, acting dean, 1980-81, dean, 1981—; dir. Moore Sch. Elec. Engring., 1976—, Alfred Fitler Moore chair, 1979—, also bd. dirs., Weston Inc., Univ. City Sci. Ctr.; master Stouffer Coll. House, 1972-76; Cons. industry, govt., founds. Author: (with H. Ruston) Electric Networks, 1966; (with others) The Man-Made World, 1971; chmn. editorial bd. Engring. Edn., 1987—. Served with USN, 1955-58. Recipient Lindback award for distinguished teaching U. Pa., 1967; George Westinghouse award Am. Soc. Engring. Edn., 1974; Engr. of Yr. award Phila., 1984. Fellow IEEE, (chmn. Phila. sect. 1987-88), fellow AAAS; mem. Franklin Inst., Sigma Xi, Eta Kappa Nu, Tau Beta Pi. Home: 1237 Medford Rd Wynnewood PA 19096

BOREL, JACQUES, writer; b. Paris, Dec. 17, 1925; s. Pierre and Lucie (Dubee) B.; m. Christiane Idrac, Sept. 25, 1948; children: Denis, Anne, Helene, Claude, Claire. Licence es Lettres, Sorbonne, U. Paris, 1948, Maitrise Lettres, 1949. Cert. tchr., France. Tchr., Lycee Blaise Pascal, Clermont-Ferrand, France, 1952-54, Lycee Paul Lapie, Courbevoie, France, 1954-56, Lycee Rodin, Paris, 1956-67; lit. adviser Editions Gallimard, Paris, 1969-75, Editions Balland, Paris, 1979-82; vis. prof. Middlebury Coll. (Vt.), summer 1966, U. Hawaii, Honolulu, 1968-69, Portland State U. (Oreg.), summer 1967, U. Calif.-Irvine, fall 1969, U. Calif.-Riverside, fall 1980, NYU, N.Y.C., 1983. Author: (novels) L'Adoration (The Bond), 1965, Le Retour, 1970; Histoire de mes Vieux Habits, 1979; Petite Histoire de mes Reves, 1981; (diary) La Depossession, 1973; (essays) Marcel Proust, 1972; Commentaires, 1974; Poesie et Nostalgie, 1979; Un Voyage Ordinaire, 1975, Paroles Écrites; playwright Tata ou de L'education, 1967; translator James Joyce's Collected Poems, 1967; editor Verlaine's Complete Works, 1958, 1962, 1972. Decorated officier Ordre National Des Arts et Lettres; recipient prix Goncourt, Academie Goncourt, Paris, 1965. Mem. PEN Club. Office: Cultural Attaché, Embassy of France in Belgium, Brussels Belgium

BOREL, JAMES DAVID, physician; b. Chgo., Nov. 15, 1951; s. James Albert and Nancy Ann (Sieverson) B. BS, U. Wis., 1973; MD, Med. Coll. of Wis., 1977. Diplomate Am. Bd. Anesthesiology, Nat. Bd. Med. Examiners, Am. Coll. Anesthesiologists. Research asst. McArdle Lab. for Cancer Research, Madison, Wis., 1972-73, Stanford U. and VA Hosp., Palo Alto, 1976-77; intern. The Cambridge (Mass.) Hosp., 1977-78; clin. fellow in medicine Harvard Med. Sch., Boston, 1977-78, clin. fellow in asaesthesia, 1978-80, clin. instr. in anaesthesia, 1980; resident in anesthesiology Peter Bent Brigham Hosp., Boston, 1978-80; anesthesiologistt Mt. Auburn Hosp., Cambridge, 1980; fellow in anesthesiology Ariz. Health Scis. Ctr., Tucson, 1980-81; research assoc. U. Ariz. Coll. Medicine, Tucson, 1980-81, assoc. in anesthesiology, 1981—; active staff Mesa (Ariz.) Luth. Hosp., 1981—; courtesy staff Scottsdale (Ariz.) Meml. Hosp., 1982—; vis. anaesthetist St. Joseph's Hosp., Kingston, Jamaica, 1980. Contbr. numerous articles to profl. jours. Mem. AMA, AAAS, Mass. Anesthesia Council on Edn., Ariz. Anesthesia Alumni Assn., Ariz. Soc. Anesthesiologists, Am. Soc. Regional Anesthesia, Can. Anesthetists' Soc., Internat. Anesthesia Research Soc., Am. Soc. Anesthesiologists. Office: Valley Anesthesia Cons 2950 N 7th St Phoenix AZ 85014

BOREN, DAVID LYLE, senator; b. Washington, Apr. 21, 1941; s. Lyle H. and Christine (McKown) B.; m. Molly Shi, Dec. 1977; children: David Daniel, Carrie Christine. B.A. summa cum laude, Yale, 1963; M.A. (Rhodes scholar), Oxford (Eng.) U., 1965; J.D. (Bledsoe Meml. prize as outstanding law grad.), U. Okla., 1968. Bar: Okla. 1968. Asst. to dir. liaison Office Civil and Def. Moblzn., Washington, 1960-62; propaganda analyst Soviet affairs USIA, Washington, 1962-63; mem. Speakers Bur., Am. embassy, London, Eng., 1963-65; mem. residential counseling staff U. Okla., 1965-66; practiced in Seminole, 1968-74; mem. Okla. Ho. of Reps., 1966-74; gov. Okla., 1975-79; mem. U.S. Senate from Okla., 1979—; mem. Senate Fin. Com., Senate Agrl. Com., Senate Small Bus. Com.; chmn. Senate Select Com. on Intelligence, govt. dept. Okla. Bapt. U., 1969-74. Del. Democratic Nat. Conv., 1968, 76, 84. Named U.S. Army ROTC Disting. Mil. Grad.; One of 10 Outstanding Young Men in U.S. U.S. Jaycees, 1967. Mem. Assn. U.S. Rhodes Scholars, Phi Beta Kappa, Sigma Delta Rho. Methodist. Office: Office of the Senate 453 Russell Senate Bldg Washington DC 20515 *

BOREN, HOLLY LYNN, writer; b. Renton, Wash., Nov. 29, 1951; d. Samuel Alexander and Ernetta Marie (Fox) B.; m. Paul William Reast. BA with honors in Eng. Lit., New Coll., Sarasota, Fla., 1973. Jr. account exec. pub. relations dept., David S. Wachsman Assn., Inc., N.Y.C., 1977-79, account exec. pub. relations dept., 1979-82, v.p. pub. relations, 1982-85; pub. relations writer, cons. Abingdon, Eng., 1986—; cons. Janevale Direct Response and Mktg., Abingdon, 1987—, Brookwood Mktg., Kidlington, 1986-87. Author numerous poems. Mem. Amnesty Internat. Democrat. Home and Office: Wick Hall #9, Radley Rd, Abingdon OX14 3NF, England

BORENSTEIN, MILTON CONRAD, manufacturing company executive; b. Boston, Oct. 21, 1914; s. Isadore Sidney and Eva Beatrice B.; m. Anne Shapiro, June 20, 1937; children: Roberta, Jeffrey. A.B. cum laude, Boston Coll., 1935; J.D., Harvard U., 1938. Bar: Mass. 1938, U.S. Dist. Ct. 1939, U.S. Ct. Appeals 1944, U.S. Supreme Ct. 1944. Gen. practice law Boston, 1938—; officer, dir. Sweetheart Paper Products Co., Inc., Chelsea, Mass., 1944-61, pres., 1961-83, chmn. bd., 1984; with Sweetheart Plastics, Inc., Wilmington, Mass., 1958—, v.p., 1958-84, also dir.; v.p. Md. Cup Corp., Owings Mills, 1960-77, exec. v.p., treas., 1977-84, also dir.; Bd. dirs. Am. Assocs. Hebrew U., 1968—. Trustee Boston Coll., 1979-87, assoc. trustee, 1987—, chmn. estate planning council, 1981-83, mem. council exec. com., 1984—; trustee Combined Jewish Philanthropies, Boston, 1969—, N.E. Sinai Hosp., Stoughton, Mass., 1974—, Ben-Gurion U., 1975-85, 87—; bd. overseers Jewish Theol. Sem. Am., 1971—; mem. pres.'s council Sarah Lawrence Coll., 1970-79; pres. Congregation Kehillath Israel, Brookline, Mass., 1977-79, hon. pres., 1979—; mem. pres.'s council Brandeis U., 1979-81, fellow, 1981—; v.p. Assoc. Synagogues of Mass., 1980-81; bd. dirs. nat. governing council Am. Jewish Congress, 1984—. Recipient Community Service award Jewish Theol. Sem. Am., 1970. Mem. ABA, Boston Bar Assn. (bicentennial com. 1986-87), Mass. Bar Assn., Chelsea C. of C. (dir.). Clubs: Harvard (Boston and N.Y.C.), Harvard Faculty, 100, Masons, Shriners. Home: 273 Eliot St Chestnut Hill MA 02167 Office: 1 Devonshire Pl Suite 2912 Boston MA 02109

BORER, EDWARD TURNER, investment banker; b. Phila., Nov. 30, 1938; s. Robert Chamberlin and Helen Elizabeth (Clawges) B.; B.S., U. Pa., 1960; m. Amy Hamilton Ryerson, Aug. 8, 1959; children—Edward Turner, Catherine Hamilton, Elizabeth Taft. Rep., Hopper Soliday & Co., Inc., Phila., 1960-67, v.p. research, 1967-73, sec., 1971-85, sr. v.p., 1973-82, exec. v.p., 1982-84, pres., 1984—, also bd. dirs.; dir. Manchester Gas Co. (N.H.), 1965—, pres., 1970, chmn. bd., chmn. exec. com., 1970-82; chmn. bd. EnergyNorth, Inc., 1982—; dir., sec. Disaster Control, Inc., 1981-83, Omni Oil & Gas Mgmt. Co., 1981-84; dir. Hopper Soliday Corp., 1988—; founder, treas., sec., dir. Creative Information Systems, Inc., Chadds Ford, Pa., 1967-77; v.p. Sovereign Investors, 1980-86 ; dir. Gas Service, Inc., Concord Natural Gas Co., Energy North Propane, Inc. (formerly Rent-A-Space of New Eng., Inc.), Hopper Soliday Corp. Chmn. West Met. Area-Wide Com., Regional Med. Program, 1969-70. Pres. Swarthmore Home and Sch. Assn., 1973; bd. dirs. Freedom Valley council Girl Scouts U.S.A., 1974-75, also chmn. finance com.; bd. dirs., chmn. fin. com. Planned Parenthood Southeastern Pa., 1980-85, dir. 1986; treas., trustee George W. South Meml. Ch. of the Adv., Phila., 1978-88. Served to 1st lt., Q.M.C., AUS, 1961-62. Chartered fin. analyst. Mem. Fin. Analysts Fedn., Phila. Securities Assn. (dir. 1979-83, v.p. 1980-81, pres. 1981-82), Nat. Assn. Securities Dealers (arbitrator 1982—, chmn. dist. 11 and bus. conduct com. 1986), Fin. Analysts Phila. (treas. 1976-77), N.Y. Soc. Security Analysts, Delta Upsilon. Episcopalian (vestryman 1970-73, 74-77, 85-88). Club: Union League (Phila.). Home: 125 Guernsey Rd Swarthmore PA 19081 also: Box 643 Saint John VI 00830 Office: 1401 Walnut St Philadelphia PA 19102

BORFIGA, JEAN BERNARD, biotechnology company executive; b. Casablanca, Moroco, France, May 13, 1945; s. Elysee and Estelle (Simon) B.; m. Annie Audebert, Sept. 13, 1968 (div. 1986); children: Laurence, Philippe, Estelle. MS in Chemistry, Sorbonne Coll., Paris, 1968; diploma, Inst. Adminstrn. Entreprises, 1971; PMD, Harvard Bus. Sch., 1977. Engr. Mobil Oil Framce, Frontignan, 1969-74; from mgr. to dir. Internat. Devel. Montenay SA, Frontignan, 1974-78; gen. mgr. Corning Tech. Internat., Paris, 1978-84; chmn., chief exec. officer BioEurope, Paris, 1984—. Served to pvt. France Artillery, 1968-69. Recipient Chevalier Du Merite Agricole, French Govt., 1986. Mem. Assn. Anciens Eleves Ecole Nationale Chimie Paris (com. mem.), Harvard Club France. Office: BioEurope 6/8 Rue Chardin, F-75016 Paris France

BORG, ANNE, ballet company director; b. Sept. 28, 1936. Student Gerd Kjolaas and Rita Tori, Oslo, 1950-57, Cleo Nordi and Mari Rambert, London, 1957-58, Dudinskaya and Pushkin, Leningrad, USSR, 1965, Joffrey Sch., Sch. Am. Ballet, 1966. Soloist, Norsk Operaselskap, Oslo, 1957-59; soloist, then prin. dancer Norwegian Nat. Ballet, Oslo, 1960-75, artistic ballet dir., 1971-77, 83—; head tchr. ballet State Acad. Ballet, Oslo, 1979-83. Recipient various grants, State of Norway, City of Oslo.

BORG, BJORN, professional tennis player; b. Sodertlage, Sweden, June 6, 1956; s. Rune and Margaretha Borg; 1 child, Robin. Mem. Sweden's Davis Cup Team; joined World Championship Tennis circuit, 1974. Named World Champion of Men's Tennis Internat. Tennis Fedn., 1978. Office: care Internat Mgmt Group 1 Erieview Plaza Cleveland OH 44114

BORG, FINN, management consultant; b. Tottarp, Malmoe, Sweden, Sept. 24, 1955; came to Switzerland, 1959; s. Bjorn and Anna-Greta (Andersson) B.; m. Helena Ulrika Hellbrand, Aug. 4, 1984; 1 child, Malin Annika. B.A. in Econs. cum laude, Claremont Men's Coll., 1978; M.B.A., U. Chgo., 1980. Asst. mgr. Citibank N.A., Zurich, Switzerland, 1980-83; pvt. practice mgmt. cons., Zurich, 1983—. Mem. Internat. Tax Planning Assn. Clubs: Ski (Arosa, Switzerland); Club 88 (Zurich). Avocations: marathon, triathlon; skiing; squash; food and wine. Office: Breitingerstrasse 19, 8002 Zurich Switzerland

BORG, KIM, basso; b. Helsinki, Finland, Aug. 7, 1919; s. Kaarlo and Hilkka (Stenius) B.; student Inst. Tech., Helsinki, 1937-45; M.Sc., Sibelius-Acad., Helsinki, 1948-49; m. Ebon Ringblom, Feb. 10, 1950; children—Mette, Matti. Engaged as scientist, 1945-48, as photographer, 1948-49, as singer, 1949—; debut, Helsinki, 1947; with Finnish Nat. Opera, Royal Theatre, Copenhagen, 1952-70; tours in Europe, N.Am., South Am., Asia, Australia, Africa; operatic appearances Met. Opera Co., State Opera Hamburg (Germany), Royal Opera, Stockholm, Sweden; guest appearances Bolshoi Theatre, Moscow, USSR, State Opera Vienna (Austria); composer orchestral and chamber music; prof. Royal Conservatory, Copenhagen, 1972—. Bd. dirs. Danish-Finnish Soc. Served to 1st lt. with Finnish Army, 1940-44. Decorated Cross of Liberty, Pro Finlandia medal, knight White Rose (Finland); hon. cross for scis. and arts (Austria); knight Dannebrog (Denmark); comdr. North Star (Sweden). Composer: String Quartet, 1968; Trios, 1974, 75, 76; Concerto for Trombone, 1977, String Sextet, 1977, Concerto for Double Bass, 1983; Trombone Quartet, 1983; String Quartet II, 1984; Quintet for Wood Winds, 1985; Suite for Flute and Harp, 1987. Decorated Sibelius medal (Sweden). Author: Suomalainen Laulajanaapinen, 1972. Office: Det Kgl danske Musikkonservatorium, Copenhagen Denmark

BORG, STEFAN LENNART, psychiatrist, educator; b. Stockholm, May 15, 1945; s. Lennart and Inga B.; m. Lena, Feb. 21, 1945; children: Charlotte, Niklas. MD, Karolinska Inst., Stockholm, 1971; PhD, Karolinska Inst., 1975. Asst. prof., sr. registrant Karolinska Inst. and Hosp., Stockholm, 1980; assoc. prof. Karolinska Inst., 1985—; program dir. Methadon Maintenance Treatment, Stockholm, 1985—, Treatment Program Hypnotic-Sedative Dependence, Stockholm, 1980—; cons. Swedish Nat. Bd. Health and Welfare. Contbr. numerous articles to profl. jours. Grantee Swedish Med. Research Council, Swedish Ministry Health. Mem. Swedish Med. Assn.(sec. alcohol pol. program, 1980), Swedish Psychiatrie Assn., Nat. Swedish Sci. Council, Nat. Bd. Health and Welfare, Swedish Psychiatric Assn. (bd. dirs. 1976-84).

BORGEAUD, PIERRE, executive; married; 3 children. Chief exec. officer Sulzer Group. Address: Sulzer Bros Ltd, Zurcherstrasse 9, CH 8401 Winterthur Switzerland

BORGERT, LEIF ÅKE, small business owner; b. Orsa, Dalarna, Sweden, Sept. 2, 1943; s. Eric A. and Randi V.W. (Renstrøm) B.; m. Birgitta K.M. Mårthen, June 26, 1966; children: Lisa, Sofia, Johan. BS in Econs., Stockholm Sch. Econs., 1968. Orgn. cons. Swedish Fedn. Local Communities, Stockholm, 1969-72; personnel, ops. directive mgr. County Council Norrbotten, Luleå, Sweden, 1972-75; ops. directive mgr. Billeruds AB, Säffle, Sweden, 1975-79; mgr., chief exec. officer Leif Borgert Konsult AB, Falun, Sweden, 1979—; bd. dirs. Daladatorer AB, Falun, 1985—. Author: Ledarskap Begriper Vi Oss På Det?, 1977, Att Utveckla Organisationen, 1982. Served as sgt. inf. Swedish army, 1963-64. Fellow Krilongruppen. Liberal. Home and Office: Engelbredtsgatan 2G, S-79151 Falun Sweden

BORGES, JACOBO, painter; b. Nov. 28, 1931; student Escuela de Artes Plásticas Cristóbal Rojas, Caracas, Ecole des Beaux Arts, Paris. One-man shows: Galería Lauro, Caracas, 1956, Museo de Bellas Artes, Caracas, 1956, Galería G, Caracas, 1963, Galería Techo, Caracas, 1965, CDS Gallery, N.Y.C., 1983; group shows include: São Paulo Bienal, 1957, 63, 65, Venice Biennale, 1958, Brussels World Fair, 1958, Guggenheim Mus., N.Y.C., 1964, 65; represented in permanent collections; illustrator of mags. and record covers, Paris, 1951-56; prof. scenography and plastic analysis Escuela de Artes Plásticas Cristóbal Rojas, 1958-65; prof. scenography Theatre Sch. Valencia, dir. Exptl. Art Centre U. Central de Venezuela, 1966—. Recipient Nat. Painting prize, 1963; Armando Reverón Bienal prize, 1965. Mem. Young Painters Group. Office: care Museo de Bellas Artes, Avenida los Caobos, Caracas Venezuela *

BORGOGNINI TARLI, SILVANA MARIA, anthropology educator; b. Florence, Tuscany, Italy, June 8, 1940; d. Roberto and Paolina (Giani) Borgognini; m. Roberto Raffaello Tarli, Mar. 12, 1969; 1 child, Fiammetta. M in Biology, U. Florence, 1963; PhD in Anthropology, Scuola Normale Superiore, Pisa, 1970. Vol. asst. prof. anthropology U. Pisa, Italy, 1966-67, asst. prof. phys. anthropology, 1967-80, prof., 1980—, instr. phys. anthropology, 1966-69, lectr. human biology, 1969-73, assoc. prof. human biology, 1973-77, assoc. prof. phys. anthropology, 1977-80; pres. faculty council for natural sci. U. Pisa, Italy, 1978-79; lectr. anthropometry U. Milan, Italy, 1970-72; tchr. Internat. Sch. Human Biology, Erice, Italy, 1972. Co-author: Antropologia e Antropometria, 1987; editor: Man and Environment between Mesolithic and Neolithic, 1989; asst. editor Internat. Jour. Anthropology, 1986—; reviewer Jour. Human Evolution, 1983-85; contbr. articles to profl. jours. Bd. dirs. Inst. Anthropology and Human Paleontology, Pisa, 1985—; mem. Unione Scienziati per il Disarmo, Italy, 1984. Grantee Italian Nat. Research Council, 1968, 73, 77-79, Italian Ministry Edn., 1980-86. Mem. Societa' Italiana Antropologica Etnologica, Internat. Assn. Human Biologists (founding), Unione Antropologica Italiana (v.p. 1983-85), European Anthrop. Assn., Current Anthropology (assoc.). Roman Catholic. Home: Via A Grandi #33, 56010 Pisa, Tuscany Italy Office: Inst Anthropology and Paleontology, Via S Maria #55, 56100 Pisa, Tuscany Italy

BORG OLIVIER, ALEXANDER GEORGE, diplomat, ambassador, lawyer; b. Sliema, Malta, Jan. 28, 1946; s. George and Alexandra (Mattei) Borg Olivier; m. Kathleen Bonello, Jan. 22, 1972; children: Nicholas George, Karina Maria. BA, Royal U. Malta, 1968, LLD, 1971; LLM, Columbia U., 1973. Lawyer Chamber of Advocates, Malta, 1971; assoc. Paterson, Belknapp and Webb, N.Y.C., 1973; ambassador, sr. legal advisor office of legal counsel UN, N.Y.C., 1973-87, ambassador and permanent rep. of Malta, 1987—; legal advisor UN Internat. Conf. on Question of Palestine, Geneva, 1983, UN Internat. Conf. on Population, Mexico City, 1984, The World Conf. on UN Decade for Women, Nairobi, 1985, Internat. Conf. on Drug Abuse and Illicit Trafficking, Vienna, 1987; sec. credentials com. UN Gen. Assembly, N.Y.C., 1980-87. Office: Permanent Mission Malta to UN 249 E 35th St New York NY 10016

BORIE, BERNARD SIMON, JR., physicist, educator; b. New Orleans, June 21, 1924; s. Bernard Simon and Ruth (Lastrapes) B.; B.S., U. S.W. La., 1944; M.S., Tulane U., 1949; Ph.D., M.I.T., 1956; Fulbright fellow U. Paris, 1956-57; m. Martine Edith Descamps, May 2, 1957 (div. May 1964); children—Kathleen, Fabienne, Marianne. Research physicist metall. div. Oak Ridge Nat. Lab., 1949-53, group leader x-ray diffraction Metals and Ceramics Div., 1957-60, head fundamental research sect., 1960-69, sr. scientist, 1969-85 ; prof., U. Tenn., 1963—; vis. prof. Cornell U., 1971-72, U. Calif., Berkeley, 1980. Served to lt., USNR, 1944-45. Fellow AAAS; mem. AIME, Am. Soc. Metals, Am. Crystallographic Assn., Sci. Research Soc. Am. Research in diffraction effects of thermal motion, x-ray diffraction studies of imperfect solids; order-disorder effects in solid solutions. Home: 13 Brookside Dr Oak Ridge TN 37830 Office: U Tenn Materials Sci & Engring Dept Dougherty Hall Knoxville TN 37996-2200

BORINSTEIN, DENNIS IVAN, management consultant; b. Detroit, Feb. 1, 1949; s. Morris Z. and Dora (Denenberg) B.; m. Carole M. Haveman, June 22, 1973; 1 child, David Michael. B.A., Mich. State U., 1970; A.M., U. Chgo., 1972, Ph.D. 1976. Clin. practice psychology, Ill., 1973-75, N.Y., 1975-80; pres. MDI Systems, Inc., N.Y.C., 1980—; cons. in field. Contbr. articles to profl. jours. Mem. Am. Psychol. Assn., N.Y. State Psychol. Assn., Am. Soc. Tng. and Devel., Assn. Behavior Analysis, Nat. Soc. Performance and Instrn. Home and Office: 139 N Lapeer Dr Beverly Hills CA 90211

BORISEVICH, NIKOLAI ALEXANDROVICH, physicist; b. Berezino, Minsk, USSR, Sept. 21, 1923; s. Alexander Andreevich and Maria Semenovna B.; m. Irina Pavlovna; children: Alexei, Andrei. Cert. in physics, Byelorussian State U., Minsk, USSR, 1950; postgrad., State Optica Inst., Leningrad, USSR, 1951-54; D in Physics and Math., Byelorussian State U., Minsk, USSR, 1965; PhD (hon.), Yena U., German Dem. Republic, 1985. Cert. professor. Dep. dir. Inst. Physics Byelorussian Soviet Socialist Republic Acad. Scis., Minsk, 1955-69, pres., 1969-87, head lab Inst. Phys., 1957—; head lab. Phys. Inst. USSR Acad. Scis., Moscow, 1987—; asst. prof. Byelorussian State U., Minsk, 1955-64. Author: Excited States of Complex Molecules in the Gas Phase, 1967, Infrared Filters, 1971; contbr. 180 articles to profl. jours. Dep. Supreme Soviet USSR, Moscow, 1969; mem. cen. com. Communist Party Byelorussian Soviet Socialist Republic, Minsk, 1971—. Recipient 2 orders of Red Star, 1944, 45, 2 orders of Patroitic War, I, II degree, 1945, 85, Order of Red Banner of Labor, 1967, 4 orders of Lenin, 1971, 75, 78, 83, Order of October Revolution, 1973, Hero of Socialist Labor medal Supreme Soviet USSR, 1978, Lenin Prize, 1980, USSR State prize, 1973. Mem. Czechoslovakian Acad. (fgn. mem.), Slovenian Acad. (fgn. mem.). Home: Ya Kupala 7-80, 220030 Minsk USSR Office: Phys Inst, Leninski prospekt 53, 117924 Moscow USSR

BORJA CEVALLOS, RODRIGO, president of Ecuador; b. June 19, 1935; m. Carmen Calisto; 4 children. Founder Dem. Left Party, 1970; pres. Ecuador, Quito, 1988—. Address: Office of Pres, Quito Ecuador *

BORJA NAVARRETE, GILBERTO, civil engineering executive; b. Mexico City, Sept. 1, 1929; s. Angel Borja Osorno and Maria Teresa Navarrete Salas; m. Gloria Suarez Garcia, May 17, 1958; 1 child, Gilberto Borja Suarez. Licentiate, U. Nacional Autonoma de Mex., 1951. Pres. bd. dirs. Empresas ICA, Sociedad Controladora, S.A. de C.V. (now EMICA), holders 119 constrn., engring., capital goods, tourism, cement, automobile parts, electronics, mining, petrochems., and maritime transport cos.; pres. bd. dirs. Empresas Industria del Hierro, Transmisiones y Equipos Mecánicos, S.A., Productos Industriales Metálicos, S.A., Automanufacturas, S.A. de C.V.

Borg and Beck de México, S.A. de C.V., Automatización y Tracción; mem. Banco Obrero, Grupo Tolteca, Banco Nac. de Méico, Fundacion Mexicana para la Salud; mem. exec. com. Seguros Am., S.A.; mem. Found. Instituto Tecnologico de la Construccion. Mem. Hosp. Infantil de México, Am. Brit. Cowdray Hosp., Sistema Nacional para el Desarrollo Integral de la Familia. Mem. or assoc. Colegio Nacional de Educacion Profesional Tecnica, Fundacion Javier Barros Sierra, Asociacion Mexicana de Caminos, Academia de Musica del Palacio de Mineria, Consejo Mexicano de Hombres de Negocios, Orquesta Filarmónica de la UNAM, Com. sobre el Futuro de las Relaciones México-Estados Unidos, Sociedad Mexicana de Ingenieros, Sociéte des Ingénieurs et Scientifiques de France, Soc. de Exalumnos de la Facultad de Ingenieria de la UNAM (pres.), Camara Franco-Mexicana de Comercio e Industria (pres.), Assoc. U. Nacional Football Soccer Club (pres.). Home: Mineria No 145, Mexico City 11800, Mexico Office: Grupo ICA SA, Mineria 145, Mexico City 11800, Mexico

BORJESON, LENA, publisher, writer; b. Kalmar, Sweden, May 7, 1940; d. Erik and Martha (Edgren) B.; m. K.G. Wettermark (div.); m. Klas R. Gustavii; children: Bjorn, Asa. MA, Uppsala (Sweden) U., 1962. Research asst. Harvard U., Boston, 1961-62; organizational cons., dir. Statskontoret, FRI and SIPU, Stockholm, 1962-82; mng. dir. METODA Cons. and Pubs., Huddinge, Sweden, 1982—. Author several books and novels; editor newsletter. Mem. Inst. Social Inventions, Swedish Authors Assn. Home: Marmorvagen 3, 14139 Huddinge Sweden Office: METODA, PO Box 2033, 14102 Huddinge Sweden

BORLAND, BARBARA DODGE (MRS. HAL BORLAND), author; b. Waterbury, Conn.; d. Harry G. and Grace (Cross) Dodge; student Oberlin U., 1922-23, Columbia U. Sch. Journalism, 1923; m. 2d, Hal Borland, Aug. 10, 1945 (dec. Feb. 1978); 1 dau., Diana (Mrs. James C. Thomson, Jr.). Editorial cons. various pubs., 1923-35; condr. Writers Workshop, N.Y.C., 1934-38; writer, also collaborator with husband, fiction for Colliers, McCalls, Good Housekeeping, Cosmopolitan, Redbook, others, 1946-56; garden columnist Berkshire Eagle, Pittsfield, Mass., 1960. Recipient Distinguished Alumna award St. Margaret's Sch., 1972. Congregationalist. Mem. Authors League Am. Author: The Greater Hunger, 1962 (chosen Ambassador Book, English Speaking Union 1963); This is the Way My Garden Grows ... and This is the Way My Garden Cooks, 1986; contbr.: New England: The Four Seasons, 1980; editor: Twelve Moons of the Year (by Hal Borland), 1979. Address: Weatogue Rd Salisbury CT 06068

BORLAND, BRUCE HENNINGER, transportation equipment management and leasing company executive; b. Butler, Pa., Dec. 28, 1929; s. Bruce Sylvester and Mary Elizabeth (Henninger) B.; m. Beatrice Anne Buckler, Nov. 25, 1952; children—Cheryl Borland McClure, Bruce David. B.S., Northwestern U., 1951. Sales promotion staff Bell & Howell, Chgo., 1952-53; mgr. Hotpoint Co., Chgo., 1956-58; sales rep. GATX Corp., Chgo., 1958-60, dist. mgr., 1960-79, sales mgr., 1979-80; pres., chmn., chief exec. officer Temco Corp., Lake Bluff, Ill., 1981—; dir. Omnicard Internat., Wheeling, Ill.; mem. Shippers Adv. Bd. Mem. U.S. Congl. Adv. Bd. Served with JAGC, U.S. Army, 1952-54. Mem. Am. Petroleum Inst., Chgo. Traffic Club, Covered Hopper Car Shippers Assn., Fertilizer Inst., Traffic Clubs Internat., Internat. Platform Assn., Am. Mgmt. Assn., Am. Legion, R.R. Progress Inst. Republican. Clubs: Forge; Evanston (Ill.) Golf; Union League (Chgo.), Post and Paddock, Market; Stonebridge. Home: 2801 Orange Brace Rd Riverwoods IL 60015 Office: Temco Corp 100 E Scranton Lake Bluff IL 60044

BORLAUG, NORMAN ERNEST, agricultural scientist; b. Cresco, Iowa, Mar. 25, 1914; s. Henry O. and Clara (Vaala) B.; m. Margaret G. Gibson, Sept. 24, 1937; children: Norma Jean (Mrs. Richard H. Rhoda), William Gibson. BS in Forestry, U. Minn., 1937, MS in Plant Pathology, 1940, PhD in Plant Pathology, 1941; ScD (honoris causa), Punjab (India) Agrl. U., 1969, Kanpur U., India, Royal Norwegian Agrl. Coll., Luther Coll., 1970, Mich. State U., Univ. de la Plata, Argentina, Uttar Pradesh Agrl. U., India, 1971; Sc.D. (honoris causa), U. Ariz., 1972, U. Fla., 1973, Univ. Católica de Chile, 1974, Univ. Hohenheim, Fed. Republic Germany, 1976, U. Agr., Lyallpur, Faisalabad, Pakistan, 1978, Columbia U., N.Y.C., 1980, Ohio State U., 1981, U. Minn., 1982, U. Notre Dame, 1987; L.H.D., Gustavus Adolphus Coll., 1971; LL.D. (hon.), N.Mex. State U., 1973; D. Agr. (hon.), Tufts U., 1982; D. Agrl. Scis. (hon.), U. Agrl. Scis., Hungary, 1980, Tokyo U. Agr., 1981, Univ. Nacional Pedro Henriques Turena, Dominican Republic, Univ. Cen. del Estes, Dominican Republic, 1983; D. Honoris Causa, Univ. Mayor de San Simón, Bolivia, Univ. de Buenos Aires, 1983, Univ. de Cordoba, Spain, Univ. Politécnica de Catalunya, Barcelon, Spain, 1986. With U.S. Forest Service, 1935-38; instr. U. Minn., 1941; microbiologist E.I. DuPont de Nemours, 1942-44; research scientist in charge wheat improvement Coop. Mexican Agrl. Program, Mexican Ministry Agr. Rockefeller Found., Mexico, 1944-60; assoc. dir. assigned to Inter-Am. Food Crop Program Rockefeller Found., 1960-63; dir. wheat research and prodn. program Internat. Maize and Wheat Improvement Ctr., Mexico City, 1964—; cons. Internat. Maize and Wheat Improvement Ctr., 1982—; cons., collaborator Inst. Nacional de Investigationes Agricolas, Mexican Ministry Agr., 1960-64; cons. FAO, North Africa and Asia, 1960; ex-officio cons. wheat research and prodn. problems to govts. in, Latin Am., Africa, Asia.; Mem. Citizen's Commn. on Sci., Law and Food Supply, 1973—, Commn. Critical Choices for Am., 1973—, Council Agr. Sci. and Tech., 1973—, Presdl. Commn. on World Hunger U.S.A., 1978-79; dir. Population Crisis Com., 1971; asesor especial Fundacion para Estudios de la Poblacion A.C., Mexico, 1971—; mem. adv. council Renewable Natural Resources Found., 1973—; A.D. White Disting. prof.-at-large Cornell U., 1983—; Disting. prof. Internat. Agr., Dept. Soil & Crop Scis., Tex. A&M U., Jan.-May, 1984—; advisor The Population Inst., U.S.A., 1978; bd. trustees Winrock Internat. U.S.A.; life fellow Rockefeller Found., 1983—. Recipient Disting. Service awards Wheat Producers Assns., and state govts. Mexican States of Guanajuato, Queretaro, Sonora, Tlaxcala and Zacatecas, 1954-60; Recognition award Agrl. Inst. Can., 1966; Recognition award Instituto Nacional de Tecnologia Agropecuaria de Marcos Juarez, Argentina, 1968; Sci. Service award El Colegio de Ingenieros Agronomos de Mexico, 1970; Outstanding Achievement award U. Minn., 1959; E.C. Stakman award, 1961; named Uncle of Paul Bunyan, 1969; recipient Disting. Citizen award Cresco Centennial Com., 1966; Nat. Disting. Service award Am. Agrl. Editors Assn., 1967; Genetics and Plant Breeding award Nat. Council Comml. Plant Breeders, 1968; Star of Distinction Govt. of Pakistan, 1968; citation and street named in honor Citizens of Sonora and Rotary Club, 1968; Internat. Agronomy award Am. Soc. Agronomy, 1968; Distinguished Service award Wheat Farmers of Punjab, Haryana and Himachal Pradesh, 1969; Nobel Peace prize, 1970; Diploma de Merito El Instituto Tecnologico y de Estudios Superiores de Monterrey, Mexico, 1971; medalla y Diploma de Merito Antonio Narro Escuela Superior de Agricultura de la U. de Coahuila, Mexico, 1971; Diploma de Merito Escuela Superior de Agricultura Hermanos Escobar, Mexico, 1973; award for service to agr. Am. Farm Bur. Fedn., 1971; Outstanding Agrl. Achievement award World Farm Found., 1971; Medal of Merit Italian Wheat Scientists, 1971; Service award for outstanding contbn. to alleviation of world hunger 8th Latin Am. Food Prodn. Conf., 1972; Nat. award for Agrl. Excellence in Sci. Nat. Agri-Mktg. Assn., 1982, Disting. Achievement award Council for Agrl. Scis. and Tech., 1982; inaugural lectr., medal recipient Dr. S.B. Hendrick's Meml. Lectureship., 1981, other honored lecturships; named to Halls of Fame Oreg. State U. Agrl., 1981, Agrl. Nat. Ctr., Bonner Springs, Kans., 1984, Scandinavian-Am., U.S.A., 1986; dedicated in his name Norman E. Borlaug Centro de Capitación y Formación de Agrs., Santa Cruz, Bolivia, 1983, Borlaug Hall U. Minn., 1985, Borlaug Bldg. Internat. Maize and Wheat Improvement Ctr., 1986; numerous other honors and awards from govts., ednl. instns., citizens groups. Hon. fellow Indian Soc. Genetics and Plant Breeding; mem. Nat. Acad. Sci., Am. Soc. Agronomy (1st Internat. Service award 1960, 1st hon. life mem.), Am. Assn. Cereal Chemists (hon. life mem., Meritorious Service award 1969), Crop Sci. Soc. Am. (hon. life mem.), Soil Sci. Soc. Am. (hon. life mem.), Sociedad de Agronomia do Rio Grande do Sul Brazil (hon.), India Nat. Sci. Acad. (fgn.), Royal Agrl. Soc. Eng. (hon.), Royal Soc. Edinburgh (hon.), Hungarian Acad. Sci. (hon.), Royal Swedish Acad. Agr. and Forestry (fgn.), Academia Nacional de Agronomia y Veterinaria (Argentina); hon. academician N.I. Vavilov Acad. Agrl. Scis. Lenin Order (USSR.), Am. Council on Sci. and Health (trustee 1978—), Internat. Food Policy Research Inst. (trustee 1976-82), Royal Soc. Office: Tex A&M Univ Dept Soil & Crop Sci College Station TX 77843

BORMAN, FRANK, airlines company executive, former astronaut; b. Gary, Ind., Mar. 14, 1928; s. Edwin Borman; m. Susan Bugbee; children: Fredrick, Edwin. B.S., U.S. Mil. Acad., 1950; M. Aero. Engring, Calif. Inst. Tech., 1957; grad., USAF Aerospace Research Pilots Sch., 1960, Advanced Mgmt. Program, Harvard Bus. Sch., 1970. Commd. 2d lt. USAF, advanced through grades to col., 1965, ret., 1970; assigned various fighter squadrons U.S. and Philippines, 1951-56; instr. thermodynamics and fluid mechanics U.S. Mil. Acad., 1957-60; instr. USAF Aerospace Research Pilots Sch., 1960-62; astronaut With Manned Spacecraft Ctr., NASA, until 1970; command pilot on 14 day orbital Gemini 7 flight Dec. 1965, including rendezvous with Gemini 6; command pilot Apollo 8, 1st lunar orbital mission, Dec. 1968; sr. v.p. for ops. Eastern Air Lines, Inc., Miami, Fla., 1970-74, exec. v.p., gen. operations mgr., 1974-75, pres., chief exec. officer, 1975-85, chief exec. officer, 1975-86, chmn. bd., 1976-86; vice chmn., dir. Tex. Air Corp., Houston, 1986—. Recipient Distinguished Service award NASA, 1965; Collier Trophy. Nat. Aeros. Assn., 1968. Office: Tex Air Corp 4040 Capital Bank Plaza Houston TX 77002 *

BORMANN, KARL WILHELM, philosophy educator; b. Monheim, Germany, Nov. 23, 1928; s. Gerhard and Gertrud (Goebbels) B.; m. Gertrud Gladbach, July 26, 1956; children—Diana, Markus. Ph.D., U. Cologne (W.Ger.), 1955. Researcher U. Cologne, 1955-59, asst. prof., 1959-66, acad. lectr., 1967-70, prof. philosophy, 1970—. Author: Parmenides, 1971; Plato, 1973; contbr. articles on Plato, Aristotle, the Stoics, Proclus, Cusanus and Parmenides to profl. publs., 1968—; editor: The Works of Nicholas Cusanus, 1972—. Mem. Heidelberger Akademie der Wissenschaften (mem. Cusanus commn. 1970—), Internat. Ctr. for Platonic and Aristotelian Studies (Athens). Roman Catholic. Home: Weststrasse 6A, 4018 Langenfeld Federal Republic of Germany Office: Thomas-Inst, Universitaetstrasse 22, 5000 Cologne 41 Federal Republic of Germany

BORNSTEIN, LAURA LEE, artist; b. Cleve., Nov. 9, 1948; d. Andrew Clark Lee and Beatrice Laura (Barna) Robinson; m. Miguel Andres Bornstein, Apr. 16, 1983; children: Michael Andrew, Nicolas Lee, Isabel. BFA, Miami U., Oxford, Ohio, 1970. Designer Avon Cosmetics, Liancour, France, 1970-72; ptnr., designer Harbinger Studio, Aspen, Colo., 1972-74; freelance graphic designer Los Angeles, 1974-80; art dir. ABC Leisure mags., N.Y.C., 1980-84; freelance artist, painter, book designer Buenos Aires, 1984—. Editor newsletter Corage, 1987—. Home: Callao 1685, Buenos Aires Argentina

BORNSTEIN, ROBERT JOSEPH, hospital administrator; b. Rockaway Beach, N.Y., Nov. 11, 1937; s. Joseph I. and Marjorie (Hogan) B.; BA, Adelphi U., 1959; MPA, N.Y.U., 1972; PhD, Columbia Pacific U., 1980; postgrad. in law Touro Coll., 1987—; m. Ingrid F.; 1 dau., Debra E. Asso. dir. Goldwater Meml. Hosp., Roosevelt Island, N.Y., 1970-73; adminstr. Massapequa Gen. Hosp., Seaford, N.Y., 1973-74, Lydia E. Hall Hosp., Freeport, N.Y., 1974-76, Central Gen. Hosp., Planview, N.Y., 1977—; preceptor hosp. adminstrn. program U. Buffalo and Ithaca Coll., C.W. Post Coll., SUNY, Stony Brook, NYU, Hofstra U., 1979—; prof., preceptor St. Joseph's Coll., Patchogue, N.Y., 1978-83. Chmn. bd. Am. Cancer Soc., 1979—; mem. Community Planning Bd., Queens, N.Y., 1973-76; vice chmn. Comprehensive Health Planning Agy., 1974-76; bd. mgrs. Blue Ridge Condominiums/Coventry Home Owners Assn., 1977-85; mediator Community Mediation Center, 1982—; cons. Ret. Police Assn. of N.Y. Served with U.S. Army, 1959-65. Recipient Outstanding Community Service award United Fund, 1968. Fellow Am. Acad. Med. Adminstrs., Royal Soc. Health, Am. Coll. Health Care Adminstrs.; mem. Am. Coll. Osteo. Hosp. Adminstrs., Am. Hosp. Assn., N.Y. State Public Health Assn. Club: Mensa. Contbr. articles to profl. jours. Office: 888 Old Country Rd Plainview NY 11803

BOROCHOFF, CHARLES ZACHARY, manufacturing company owner; b. Atlanta, Apr. 11, 1921; s. Isadore and Pauline (Reisman) B.; m. Ida Dorothy Sloan, Jan. 11, 1942; children—Lynn Borochoff Gould, Toby Ann Borochoff Bernstein, Jean Sue Borochoff Shapiro, Lance Mark. LLB, Atlanta Law Sch., 1941. Exec v.p. So. Wire & Iron Works, Atlanta, 1936-63; pres. Borochoff Properties, Inc., real estate, Atlanta, 1954—, Designs Unlimited, Inc., Atlanta, 1964—, Scottdale Enterprises, Atlanta, 1972—; chmn. Borochoff Realty; exec. v.p. Imperial SE; pres. CDR Mfg. Co. Mem. High Museum of Art (patron 1955—), Corcoran Gallery (patron); Nat. Conf. Christians and Jews, 1967—, Planned Parenthood, 1970—. Trustee Atlanta Playhouse, 1971—; bd. dirs. Little Miss Ga. Pageant, Little Mr. Dogwood Festival Pageant; mem. program com. Nat. UN Day, 1977, 78; mem. nat. adv. bd. Am. Security Council. Mem. DeKalb C. of C. (econ. devel. com. 1975), Nat. Retail Wholesale Furniture Assn., Internat. Home and Furniture Reps. Assn., Am. Mgmt. Assn. (Presdl. Club), String & Splinter Club Inc., Nu Beta Epsilon. Jewish. Lodges: Masons, Shriner (32 deg.), B'nai B'rith. Clubs: Atlanta Music, Progressive, Jockey. Home: 3450 Old Plantation Rd NW Atlanta GA 30327 Office: 733 Glendale Rd NE Scottdale GA 30079

BOROCHOFF, IDA SLOAN, real estate executive, artist; b. July 29, 1922; d. Louis and Eva (Bistrick) Sloan; ed. U. Ga., 1939-40, Ga. State U., 1940, Chgo. Sch. Interior Decorating, 1966, Allegro Sch. Ballet, Chgo., Atlanta Ballet, 1948-54, Emory U., 1971-72; m. Charles Zachary Borochoff, Jan. 11, 1942; children—Lynn Borochoff Gould, Jean Sue Borochoff Shapiro, Toby Ann Borochoff Bernstein, Lance Mark. Investor and owner real estate, 1941—; v.p. Designs Unltd., Inc., Atlanta, 1964—; pres. Sloan Borochoff Gallery, Atlanta, 1970—; art lectr. Met. Ednl. Service; tchr. Ga. Inst. Tech.-Free U.; producer live talk health show on cable TV, Atlanta, 1983—; exhibited several one-woman shows, 1961-71, including Lovett Sch., 1972, 75, Ga. Inst. Tech., 1972, 75, Atlanta Mdse. Mart; art rev. columnist Northside Neighbor Newspapers. Bd. dirs. Atlanta Ballet, 1950-57; bd. dirs. Atlanta Music Club, also co-editor Newsletter; hostess Atlanta Arts Festival; capt. Heart Fund, 1968-76, area chmn. dr.; active various multi-media groups; artistic dir. Atlanta Playhouse Theatre, Little Miss Ga. Pageant, Little Mr. Dogwood Festival Pageant; active Dogwood Festival; chmn., trustee Atlanta Playhouse Theatre; mem. U.S. Congl. adv. bd. Am. Security Council, 1983—. Recipient several art awards; Caber award, 1984; named hon. alumnus Atlanta Art Inst., 1968, One of Ten Leading Ladies of Atlanta, J.C. Singles, 1976; City grantee, 1985. Mem. Atlanta Press Club, Atlanta Writers Club (membership com.), Atlanta Artists Club, Atlanta Women's C. of C. (chmn. fine arts 1977-78), LWV, High Mus. Art, Ga. Writers Assn., Arts High Mus. (patron), Corcoran Gallery (patron), Nat. Mus. Women in Arts (charter mem.), Internat. Platform Assn. Mem. B'nai B'rith Women (pres. chpt. 1975, mem. SE regional bd.), AAUW, Women in the Arts. Clubs: Jockey, Progressive. Home: 3450 Old Plantation Rd NW Atlanta GA 30327 Office: 733 Glendale Rd Scottdale GA 30079

BOROVIK-ROMANOV, VIKTOR-ANDREY STANISLAVOVICH, physicist; b. Leningrad, USSR, Mar. 18, 1920; s. Stanislav Antonovich and Tatiana Fedorovna (Romanova) B.; m. Tatiana Ptrovna Belicova, Sept. 30, 1947; 1 child, Alexei. Diploma of Sci. in Physics, Moscow State U., 1947; PhD, Inst. for Measurement, Moscow, 1950; DSc, Inst. for Phys. Problems, Moscow, 1960. Research assoc. Inst. for Phys. Problems, Moscow, 1947-48, sr. research worker, 1956-62, dep. dir., 1962-84, dir., 1984—; research assoc. Inst. for Measurement and Measuring Instruments, Moscow, 1948-55; sr. research worker Inst. for Phys.-Tech. and Elec. Measurement, Moscow, 1955-56; prof. Phys.-Tech. U., Moscow, 1956—. Editor Jour. Exptl. and Theoretical Physics, 1984—, Jour. Exptl. and Theoretical Physics Letters, 1965-87; contbr. articles on low temperature physics and magnetism to profl. jours. Dep. Moscow Council, 1969-73. Decorated Order Red Bannez Labour, 1972, Order Labour Silver Degree Govt. Hungary, 1974, Order of Lenin, 1980. Mem. USSR Acad. Scis. (corr. mem. 1966-72, Lomonosov prize 1972), Deutsche Akademie der Naturforscher Leopoldina. Home: Ul Gubkina 4/7, 117333 Moscow USSR Office: Inst Phys Problems, 2 Ul Kosygina, 117334 Moscow USSR

BORRAS CARRERA, CARLOS ALBERTO, investment company executive; b. Buenos Aires, Argentina, Apr. 30, 1952; s. Eugenio Borras Granata and Elsa Carrera Copello. Degree in indsl. engring., Nat. U. Buenos Aires, 1975; MBA, Inst. de Estudios Superiors de la Empresa, Barcelona, Spain, 1979. Chief indsl. systems Alpargatas Co., Buenos Aires, 1976-77; treas. Metro Radio, Barcelona, 1978-79; asst. to pres. Trust Propiedades, Buenos Aires, 1980; asst. to minister commerce Ministry of Commerce, Buenos Aires, 1981; asst. to pres. Gobenia Co., Buenos Aires, 1982-85; co-founder MBA profl. program, Inst. de Altos Estudios Empresariales, Buenos Aires, 1980, prof., 1980-85; advisor to econ. minister Ministry of Economy of Province of Chaco, 1976; controller Lago Electric Co., Buenos Aires, 1982-85, Badaracco Co., Buenos Aires, 1982-85, Vasoplast Co., Buenos Aires, 1983-86, Cafetti Co., Buenos Aires, 1984-85; ptnr. Overseas Ventures Capital Co., Buenos Aires, 1986—. Asst. to editor: Criterio, Buenos Aires, 1980; author agrl. control system, 1986. Mem. Consejo Profesional Ing. Industry, IESE (Agrupacion de Miembros, Spain, 1979, Co-founder Assn. de Miembros en Argentina, 1986, v.p., 1986). Roman Catholic. Clubs: Buenos Aires Rowing, Olivos Yacht (Buenos Aires). Home: Callao 1727 7, 1024 Buenos Aires Argentina

BORRELLI, JOHN FRANCIS, architect; b. Buffalo, Nov. 6, 1955; s. Peter and Maria (Raimondo) B. BS in Civil Engring., Columbia U., 1977; postgrad. Pratt Inst., 1977-81. Registered architect, N.Y., N.J., Conn., Nat. Council Archtl. Registration Bds. Project coordinator C. Raimondo and Sons, Ft. Lee, N.J., 1971-78; project mgr. DAT Consultants, N.Y.C., 1978-81, Litchfield Grosfeld Assocs., N.Y.C., 1981-83; project architect Design Mgmt., Inc., N.Y.C., 1983-87; ptnr. Systems Collaborative, Inc., N.Y.C., 1987-88, Davis-Borrelli Assocs., 1987—, Karco-Davis Inc., 1987—, Rampart Constrn. Assocs., 1987—. Recipient 1st prize Gabriel Industries, 1976; Columbia U. scholar, 1973-77. Mem. AIA, Nat. Trust for Hist. Preservation, ASCE (assoc.). Avocations: woodworking; antique collecting; book collecting; gardening; tennis. Home: 96 Fifth Ave Apt 11-K New York NY 10011 Office: Davis Borelli Assocs 52 Duane St New York NY 10007

BORRELLI, MARIO ALFREDO, sociologist; b. Naples, Italy, Sept. 19, 1922; s. Gennaro and Lucia (Morvillo) B.; Licentiate in theology Theol. U. Naples, 1965; postgrad. Tufts U., 1967-68; M. Social Adminstrn. and Social Work Studies, London Sch. Econs., 1970; m. Jilyan West, Sept. 19, 1971; 1 dau., Luciana. Dir., Casa dello Scugnizzo, 1950-70, Centro Communitario Materdei, 1970-77; pres. Italian Peace Research Inst., Naples, 1977—; prof. sociology U. Md., 1973-76. Hon. mem. Kiderschutzbund; recipient Lane Bryant Internat. Vol. citation, 1963, Stella della Bonta, 1963, Penna d'argento, 1981. Mem. Pontaniana Acad. Naples, Associazione Italiana della Stampa. Author 40 works in field. Home: 100A Via Vecchia San Gennaro, Pozzuoli, Naples Italy Office: 3/A Largo San Gennaro, a Materdei, Naples Italy

BORSAY, PETER NIGEL, historian, educator; b. Sale, Cheshire, Eng., Jan. 9, 1950; s. James and Gladys (Woodcock) B.; m. Anne Howard, Apr. 12, 1980; 1 child, Clare. BA, Lancaster U., Eng., 1972, PhD, 1981. Lectr. history St. David's U. Coll., Lampeter, Dyfed, Wales, 1975—. Editorial bd. Urban History Yearbook, 1987—; contbr. articles and book revs. to profl. jours. Mem. Ct. U. Wales, 1985-88; mem. com. Pre-Modern Towns Group, Eng., 1984—. Mem. Social History Soc. U.K., Econ. History Soc., Lampeter Assn. Univ. Tchrs. (pres. 1984-85), Brit. Soc. for Eighteenth-Century Studies, Georgian Group. Office: St David's Univ Coll, Lampeter, Dyfed Wales

BORSODY, ROBERT PETER, lawyer; b. N.Y.C., Oct. 6, 1937; s. Benjamin F. and Edith Nora (Corcoran) B.; m. Paula Jane Bercutt, Oct. 14, 1973; children: Lisa M., Daniel B., Sarah E., Alexander S. B.E.E., U. Va., 1961, LL.B., 1964; diploma, U. Teheran, Iran, 1959. Bar: N.Y. 1965, D.C. 1978. Asso. firm Sullivan & Cromwell, N.Y.C., 1964-69; dir. Legal Services for Elderly Poor, 1969-71, Community Health Law Project, 1971-73; individual practice law N.Y.C., 1973-78; partner firm Epstein Becker Borsody & Green, N.Y.C., 1978-87, of counsel, 1987—; bd. dirs. Health Law Project, Phila., 1971-73; adj. prof. Manhattan Coll., 1978-82, Pace Unvi. Sch. Law, 1986—; mem. N.Y. State Council Health Care Financing, 1978—; sec. N.Y. Statewide Health Coordinating Council, 1978-87; chmn. bd. dirs. N.Y. Bus. Group on Health. Bd. dirs. Mental Health Assn. Bronx and Manhattan. Mem. N.Y. State Bar Assn. (chmn. pub. health com.), Assn. Bar N.Y.C., Am. Bar Assn., Am. Assn. Hosp. Attys., Nat. Health Lawyers Assn., Hosp. Fin. Mgmt. Assn. Club: Univ. Home: 23 Winged Foot Dr Larchmont NY 10538 Office: 250 Park Ave New York NY 10017

BORTOLUZZI, PAOLO, ballet dancer, choreographer; b. Genoe, Italy, May 17, 1938; m. Jaleh Kerendi, 1970; 2 children. Student of Ugo Dell'Ara, Genoe, 1954. With Del Balletio Italiano, Milan, 1957, Leone Massine's Festival de Nervi, 1960, Maurice Béjart's Ballet of the 20th Century, 1960-72; permanent guest artist Am. Ballet Theater, 1972, La Scala, Milan, Dusseldorf Opera; artistic adviser, choreographer La Scala, Milan. Repertoire includes Romeo and Juliet, Les Sylphides, Giselle, The Sleeping Beauty, Orpheo, The Nutcracker, Cinderella, Swan Lake, Firebird, Nomos Alpha, Apollo. Musagète, Albinoni Adagio, L'Aprés-midi d'un faune, Sheherazade, Spectre-de-al-Rose, Mess Baudelaire, IXe Symphonie. Address: Nuovo Corso Torino 11, Rivoli, I-10098 Turin Italy *

BORUM, RODNEY LEE, corporation executive; b. nr. High Point, N.C., Sept. 30, 1929; s. Carl Macy and Etta (Sullivan) B.; m. Helen Marie Rigby, June 27, 1953; children: Richard Harlan, Sarah Elizabeth. Student, U. N.C., 1947-49; B.S., U.S. Naval Acad., 1953. Design-devel. engr. Gen. Electric Co., Syracuse, N.Y., 1956-58; design-devel. engr. Gen. Electric Co., Cape Kennedy, Fla., 1956-58, missile test condr., 1958-60, mgr. ground equipment engr., 1960-61, mgr. eastern test range engring., 1961-65; adminstr. Bus. and Def. Services Adminstrn.-Dept. Commerce, 1966-69; pres. Printing Industries Am., Arlington, Va., 1969-85, staff cons., 1985-86, mem. exec. com., 1969-85, dir.; pres. W.H. Rigby Cons., 1985-86; exec. v.p. Amasek Inc., Cocoa, Fla., 1986-87; assoc. Fin. Services Orgn., 1987—; sec. Graphic Arts Show Corp.; dir. Inter-Comprint Ltd., Strangers Cay, Ltd.; mem. governing bd. Comprints Internat. Mem. exec. council Cub Scouts Am., 1965; bd. dirs. Brevard County United Fund (Fla.), 1964-65, v.p., 1964-65; bd. dirs. Brevard Beaches Concert Assn., 1965; mem. edn. council bd. dirs. Graphic Arts Tech. Found., Pitts., 1970-86; trustee, founder Graphic Arts Edn. and Research Trust Fund, Arlington, Va., 1978-85. Served to 1st lt. USAF, 1953-56. Named Boss of Yr., C. of C., 1965; recipient Bausch and Lomb Sci. award, 1947, Am. Legion award, 1952. Mem. U.S. Naval Inst., U.S. Naval Acad. Alumni Assn., Graphic Arts Council N.Am. (bd. dirs. 1977—), Phi Eta Sigma. Methodist.

BORYSEWICZ, MARY LOUISE, editor; b. Chgo.; d. Thomas J. and Mabel E. (Zeien) O'Farrell; B.A., Mundelein Coll., 1970; postgrad. in English lit. U. Ill, 1970-71; grad. exec. program U. Chgo., 1982; m. Daniel S. Borysewicz, June 11, 1955; children—Mary Adele, Stephen Francis, Paul Barnabas. Editor sci. publs. AMA, Chgo., 1971-73; exec. mng. editor Am. Jour. Ophthalmology, Chgo., 1973—; asst. sec., treas Ophthalmic Pub. Co., 1985—; guest lectr. U. Chgo. Med. Sch., 1979, Harvard U. Med. Sch., 1978, Northwestern U. Med. Sch., 1979, Am. Acad. Ophthalmology, 1976, 81. Mem. Am. Soc. Profl. and Exec. Women, Council Biology Editors (fin. com. 1985—, bd. dirs. 1988—), Bus. Vols. for the Arts (1988—), Internat. Fedn. Sci. Editors Assns., Art Inst. Chgo. dept. vols. Contbr. articles to sci. publs.; editor: Ophthalmology Principles and Concepts, 6th edit., 1986. Home: 4415 N California Ave Chicago IL 60625 Office: 435 N Michigan Ave Chicago IL 60611

BOSCHWITZ, RUDY, senator; b. Berlin, 1930; m. Ellen; children: Gerry, Ken, Dan, Tom. Student, Johns Hopkins U., 1947-49; B.S. in Bus, N.Y. U., 1950, LL.B., 1953. Bar: N.Y. State bar 1954, Wis. bar 1959. Founder, owner, operator Plywood Minnesota (do-it-yourself bldg. materials chain), 1963—; mem. U.S. Senate from Minn., 1979—; Del. Minn. Republican Conv., 1966-78, Republican Nat. Conv., 1972-76. State chmn. Am. Cancer Soc.; state chmn. Minn. Mental Health Assn., Minn. Kidney Found., Lubavitch House, St. Paul. Served with Signal Corps U.S. Army, 1954-55. Office: 506 Hart Senate Bldg Washington DC 20510

BOSE, SAM C., aerospace engineer, system scientist, consultant; b. Calcutta, India, July 28, 1953; came to U.S., 1969; s. Amaresh Chandra and Renuka (Sen) B. B.S. summa cum laude in Elec. Engring., Poly Inst. of Bklyn., 1973, M.S., 1974; Ph.D. in Engring., UCLA, 1980. Mem. tech. staff Computer Scis. Corp., Mountain View, Calif., 1974-76; mem. tech. staff Litton Guidance and Control Systems, Woodland Hills, Calif., 1976-82; pres. and chief exec. officer Applied Sci. Analytics Inc., Canoga Park, Calif., 1982—; cons. and lectr. in field; chmn. sessions nat. and internat. confs. Rotary Internat. and Danforth Found. fellow; Oceanographic Inst. fellow; Polytech. Inst. of Bklyn. fellow. Mem. IEEE, AIAA, Inst. of Nav., Internat. Fedn. of Automatic Control, Am. Geophys. Union, Eta Kappa Nu, Tau

Beta Pi, Sigma Xi. Contbr. articles in field to profl. jours. Home: 7101 Farralone Ave 156 Canoga Park CA 91303 Office: 7049 Owensmouth Ave Canoga Park CA 91303

BOSERUP, ANDERS, sociology educator, peace researcher; b. Copenhagen, Jan. 15, 1940; s. Mogens and Ester (Borgesen) B.; m. Danielle Zemour, 1974 (div. 1983); children: Nicolai, Oliver. MS in Physics, U. Copenhagen, 1965. Research fellow Inst. Peace and Conflict Research, Copenhagen, 1966-73; research assoc. Stockholm Internat. Peace Research Inst., 1967-71; assoc. prof. sociology U. Copenhagen, 1973—; cons. disarmament UN Secretariat, N.Y.C., 1977-85, Danish Ministry Fgn. Affairs, 1978-84; co-chmn. Danish Commn. on Security and Disarmament Policy, Copenhagen, 1980-83; project dir. Ctr. Peace and Conflict Research, Copenhagen, 1985—; co-covener Pugwash Study Group on Conventional Forces in Europe, 1984—; mem. Ind. Commn. on World Security Altenatives, 1984—. Author: CBW and the Law of War, 1971, War without Weapons, 1972; editor various vols. and collections; contbr. numerous articles to jours. and readers. Mem. Soc. for Peace and Security Policy (chmn. Copenhagen 1985—). Home: 13 Onsgaardsvej, 2900 Hellerup Denmark Office: Ctr Peace and Conflict Research, 5 Vandkunsten, 1467 Copenhagen Denmark

BOSQUET, ALAIN (ANATOLE BISK), writer, critic; b. Odessa, Russia, Mar. 28, 1919; s. Alexander and Berthe (Turiansky) Bisk; m. Norma E. Caplan, 1954. Ed. Free U. Brussels, Sorbonne, U. Paris. With Allied Control Council, Berlin, from 1945, Dept. State, to 1951; literary art critic various dailies and revs.; prof. French lit. Brandeis U., 1958-59; prof. Am. lit. U. Lyons (France), 1959-60; v.p. Acad. Mallarme; mem. juries Theophraste-Renaudot and Max Jacob prizes. Author books of poetry: A la memoire de ma planète, 1948; Langue morte (prix Guillaume Apollinaire 1952), 1951; Quel royaume oublié, 1955; Premier Testament (prix Sainte-Beuve 1957), 1957; Deuxième Testament (prix Max Jacob 1959), 1959; Maître objet, 1962; Quatre Testaments et autres poemes (grand prix de Poésie de l'Academie Franç aise 1967), 1966; 100 notes pour une solitude, 1970; Notes pour un Amour, 1972; Notes pour un pluriel, 1974; Le livre du doute et de la grace, 1977; Poemes, Un (1945-1967), 1979, Deux (1970-1974), 1981; Sonnets pour une Fin de Siècle, 1981; Un Jour Après La Vie, 1984, Le Tourment de Dieu, 1987; (essays) Saint-John Perse; Emily Dickinson; Walt Whitman; Anthologie de la poésie americaine, 1946; 35 jeunes poetes americaines, 1961; Verbe et vertige (on contemporary poetry) (prix Femina-Vecaresco 1962), 1961; Entretiens avec Salvador Dali, 1967; Le Middle West, 1967; (novels) La grande eclipse, 1952; Le mecréant, 1960; Un besoin de malheur, 1963; Les petites eternités, 1964; La confession mexicaine (prix Interallié), 1965; Les tigres de papier, 1968; Chicago oignon sauvage, 1971; Monsieur Vaudeville, 1973; L'amour bourgeois, 1974; Les bonnes intentions, 1975; Une mere russe, 1978 (Grand Prix for novels of French Acad.); Jean-Louis Trabart; Médecin, 1981; L'enfant que tu etais, 1982 (Prix Marcel Proust); Ni Guerre Ni Paix, 1983; Les Fetes Cruelles, 1984, Lettre à mon père qui aurait eu cent ans (Prix Saint-Simon) 1987; (short stories) Un homme pour un autre, 1985. Recipient Prix Chateaubriand for entire body of works, 1987. Served with Belgian, French and U.S. armies, 1940-45.

BOSSANO, JOSEPH JOHN, Gibraltan government official; b. Gibraltar, June 10, 1939; s. Oscar Maria Teresa (Tosso) B.; m. Judith Baker, 1967 (div. 1988); children: David, John, Joseph, Maresa; m. Rose Torilla, Aug. 1988. BS in Econs., U. London, 1969; BA, Birmingham (Eng.) U., 1972. Seaman Brit. Mcht. Marines, 1960-64; laborer various factories, London, 1964-68; mem. House of Assembly Govt. Gibraltar, 1972—, leader of opposition House of Assembly, 1976-77, 84-88; leader Transport and Gen. Workers' Union, Gibraltar, 1974-88. Leader Gibraltar Socialist Labour Party, 1976—. Mem. Assn. Gibraltar Br. (v.p. 1984—). Lodge: Order of Odd Fellows (sec. 1980—). Office: Gibraltar Govt, 6 Convent Pl Gibraltar

BOSSANYI, ERVIN ASHOKA, wind energy specialist, consultant; b. Whitley Bay, Northumberland, Eng., Apr. 13, 1954; s. Jo and Lucie Marie (Gevaert) B. BA in Physics with honors, Cambridge (Eng.) U., 1975, PhD in Energy Econs., 1979, MA (hon.), 1979. Research fellow U. Reading (Eng.), 1978-83, Sci. & Engring. Research Council, Eng., 1983-86; engring. analyst Wind Energy Group Ltd., Southall, Eng., 1986—; cons. US DoE, Solar Energy Research Inst., Golden, Colo., 1981, Sir Robert McAlpine Ltd., London, 1984-86; course tutor Open U., Milton Keynes, Eng., 1986. Contbr. articles to profl. jours. Newsletter editor and task leader Berkshire (Eng.) Conservation Vols., 1985—. Scholar St. John's Coll., 1972-75. Mem. British Wind Energy Assn. Office: Wind Energy Group, Taywood House 345 Ruislip Rd, Southall, Middlesex UB1 2QX, England

BOSSARD, JEAN-CLAUDE, psychiatrist; b. Montargis, France, Oct. 27, 1946; s. Georges and Marcelle (Bijoux) B.; m. Genevieve Rousiot; children: Francois-Xavier, Alexis, Amihan. MD, U. Paris, 1978, PhM in Ethnology, 1988. Cert. in pub. health and tropical medicine. Resident physician psychiat. hosps. Paris, 1972-76; child psychiatrist Ednl. Orientation Ctr., Melun, France, 1972-73; psychiatrist Medico-Psychol. Clinic for Clergy, Melun, 1975-80; child psychiatrist Multisector for Children Health and Social Dept. Services, Creteil, France, 1975-80; child psychiatrist Exptl. Psycho Pedagogical Ctr., Val de Marne, France, 1975-80; psychiatrist Ministry of Nat. Edn., Paris, 1987—; pvt. practice psychiatry Paris, 1979—; tchr. various schs., 1969-76; staff hosps. in Cameroun, Algeria, Congo. Contbr. articles to profl. jours. Mem. Internat. Cath. Child Bur., 1987; founder French Agy. for Coop. with Cameroonian Hsops., Nat. Assn. for Campaign Against Drug Abuse, Research and Care of Children with Sch. Difficulties. Mem. World Psychiat. Assn., Psychiat. Evolution. Roman Catholic. Home and Office: 32 Rue Lacepede, Paris France 75005

BOSSHARDT, HANS-GEORG, research psychologist; b. Salzburg, Austria, July 15, 1944; s. Georg and Edith (Mildenberger) B.; m. Petra Eckensberger, 1967 (div. 1975). Diploma in Psychology, U. Berlin, 1969; Ph.D., Ruhr U. Bochum, 1973. Research asst. Ruhr U., Bochum, 1969—. Author: Subjektive Realität und Konzeptuelles Wissen: Sprachpsychologische Untersuchung zum Begriff der Belastigung, 1986; editor Perspektiven und Sprache: Interdisciplinäre Beiträge zum Gedenken an Hans Hörmann; author articles on exptl. psychology and psycholinguistics. Recipient Dissertation award Ruhr U., 1973. Mem. Deutsche Gesellschaft für Psychologie, Internat. Soc. Applied Psycholinguistics. Office: Ruhr Univ Bochum, Postfach 102148, D-4630 Bochum Federal Republic of Germany

BOSSHARDT, MARCIA PATRICIA, foundation administrator; b. Lima, Peru, July 20, 1960; d. Hans Jacob and Marcia Judith (Hernando) B. BA in internat. relations, polit. sci., The Cath. U. Am., Washington, 1982. Supr. U.S. Senate Parking, Washington, 1982-83, spl. projects officer, 1983; recruitment asst. Internat. Vol. Services, Washington, 1984, asst. dir. fundraising, 1984-86; assoc. dir. Internat. Vol. Services, La Paz, Bolivia, 1986—. Vol. intern Am.'s Watch, Washington, 1984, literacy tchr. Spanish Am. Cath. Ctr., 1983-84. Democrat. Roman Catholic. Home: Casilla 20190, La Paz Bolivia Office: Internat Vol Services 1424 16th NW #204 Washington DC 20036

BOSSI, MARIO, cardiologist; b. Milan, Dec. 23, 1938; s. Cesare and Enrica (Cremonesi) B.; m. Maria Adriana Rossi; children: Irene Maria, Michele. MD, U. Milan, 1965, cert. in cardiology, 1968, cert. in anesthesiology, 1975. Asst. cardiologist Ospedale Maggiore, Milan, 1965-70, Ospedale Niguarda "de Gasperis", Milan, 1970-78; cons. cardiologist Ospedale St. Carlo Borromeo, Milan, 1978-88; chief cardiology dept. Ospedale Civile, Saronno, Italy, 1988—. Mem. Assn. Nat. Medici, Cardiologi Ospedalieri. Home: Via Francesco Sforza 3, 20122 Milano Italy Office: Ospedale Civile, Piazza Borella, 1-21047 Saronno Italy

BOSSON, CHELL ERIC, mechanical engineer; b. Cannon Falls, Minn., Oct. 31, 1924; s. Nils Evert and Asta Viola (Ahnfors) B.; m. Doris Richards, Mar. 23, 1951 (div. 1976); children—Darryl Winslow, Charles Elliott, Karin Lynne. Diploma in engring., Inst. Tech., Stockholm, Sweden, 1946; B.S. with distinction in M.E., U. Minn., 1950. Registered profl. engr., Wis. Project engr. Calif. Ordnance Research Corp., Altadena, 1953-54; sr. research engr. N.Am. Aviation, Downey, Calif., 1954-60; supr. research engring. N.Am. Rockwell, Anaheim, Calif., 1962-72; sr. engring. specialist Rockwell Internat., Anaheim, 1973—; pres. Chell of Calif. City pub. works commr. La Mirada, Calif. Served with AUS, Honor Guard SHAEF, 1946-48. Mem. Nat. Mgmt. Assn., ASME, IEEE (gyro and accelerometer tech. panel), Vasa Order Am., Pi Tau Sigma. Home: 14209 Jalisco Rd La Mirada CA 90638 Office: 3370 Miraloma Ave Anaheim CA 92803

BOSSON, PIERRE ANTOINE, psychoanalyst; b. Billom, France, Nov. 4, 1943; s. Rene and Marie-Eugenie (Olloix) B.; m. Josette Diot, July 6, 1966; children: Sebastien, Benedicte. B, Lycee Blaise Pascal, France, 1960; MD, U. Clermont-Ferrand, France, 1972. Intern Chru Hosp., Clermont, 1967-71, attache des hosp., 1972—; pvt. practice medicine specializing in psychiatry and psychoanalysis Clermont, 1972—; cons. A.L.E.F.P.A. Served to capt. French Army Res. Mem. Ecole de la Cause Freudienne. Address: 32 Rue Bonnabaud, Clermont-Ferrand 63, France

BOST, CECILE ROWE, journalist, producer; b. Newton, N.C., Nov. 28, 1924; d. Marcus Marion and Myrtle Cidy (Gross) Rowe; A.B. cum laude, Catawba Coll., 1946; m. Robert Preston Bost, Apr. 28, 1946; 1 son, William Stephen. Tchr. English, Rock Springs High Sch., Denver, N.C., 1947-48; women's editor, producer, newscaster Sta. WNNC, Newton, N.C., 1948-53; editor, producer, air personality Sta. WIRC, Hickory, N.C., 1953-63; freelance broadcaster, writer, producer Cecile Bost Reporting, 1963-83; spl. corr. WBTV News, Charlotte, N.C., 1970—; owner Cecile Bost Prodns., 1984—; reporter-producer documentary Cherokee Child (awards), 1977; chosen for Broadcast Pioneers Library, Washington, 1982; lectr. in field; columnist. Recipient N.C. Sch. Bell award, 1966; N.C. AP 1st pl. broadcast news awards women's news, 1966, 68, 70, state news, 1968, documentary-pub. affairs, 1970; named Catawba County's Leading Citizen in Communications, Catawba News-Enterprise, Newton's Woman of Yr., 1953; recipient Disting. Service award Catawba Coll., 1975, award for bicentennial TV show Freedoms Found., 1976. Mem. Catawba Coll. Alumni Assn. (1st woman pres. 1964-66), Am. Women in Radio and TV (pres. N.C. chpt. 1964-66), N.C. Lit. and Hist. Soc., Hist. Preservation Found. N.C. Author short stories, one-act plays; contbr. articles to mags. and newspapers. Home and Office: 1304 N Main Ave Newton NC 28658

BOSTIAN, DAVID BOONE, JR., financial company executive; b. Charlotte, N.C., Feb. 12, 1943; s. David Boone and Clara Edna (Kanoy) B.; A.B. (Disting. Mil. grad.), Davidson Coll., 1964; M.B.A. (Bus. Found. scholar), U. N.C., 1965; m. Mary Rodgers Hunter, Sept. 11, 1965; 1 son, Robert Boone. Dir. market services Hayden, Stone Inc., N.Y.C., 1967-72; v.p., dir. market research Loeb, Rhoades & Co., N.Y.C., 1972-76; pres. Bostian Research Assos., Inc., N.Y.C., 1977—; lectr. Wharton Bus. Sch., Columbia U., N.Y. Inst. Fin., New Sch., Conf. Bd.; expert witness U.S. Senate Fin. Com., U.S. Gold Commn., Joint Econ. Com.; econ. advisor to Exec. Office of the Pres., U.S. Treasury Dept., Fed. Reserve. Mem. Republican Nat. Com.; mem. U.S. Senate Bus. Adv. Bd., Pres.' Econ. Policy Advisory Bd. Served to lt. U.S. Army, 1965-67. Named one of Outstanding Young Men Am., 1978. Mem. Am. Fin. Assn., N.Y. Soc. Security Analysts (govt. relations com.), Inst. Chartered Fin. Analysts, Fin. Analysts Research Found., Blue Chip Economists, Nat. Assn. Bus. Economists, N.Y. Assn. Bus. Economists, Nat. Bur. Econ. Research, Ne Ultra Soc. of Davidson Coll., Ballet Theater Found., Internat. Platform Assn., Internat. Assn. Bus. Economists, Pres.'s Assn. Am. Mgmt. Assn., World Future Soc., U. N.C. Alumni Assn. (trustee), N.C. Society of N.Y. (trustee), Alpha Phi Omega. Republican. Presbyterian. Clubs: U.S. Senatorial; Economic (N.Y.C.). Author: (with others) Methods and Techniques of Business Forecasting, Encyclopedia of Stock Market Techniques, A Question of National Economic Security, Toward a Synthesis of Random Walk and Market Analysis, Market Analysis and Portfolio Strategy, The New American Boom. Home: Suffolk Ln Tenafly NJ 07670 Office: 360 Madison Ave New York NY 10017

BOSTIN, MARVIN JAY, hospital and health services consultant; b. Toronto, Ont., Can., July 3, 1933; s. Samuel and Rose (Mandel) B.; came to U.S., 1956; B.S., U. Toronto, 1955; M.S. in Hosp. Adminstrn., Columbia U., 1958; Ph.D. in Pub. Adminstrn. (Gottlieb Meml. scholar), N.Y.U., 1972; 1 son, Shepard Craig. Pharmacist, New Mount Sinai Hosp., Toronto, 1953-56; asst. adminstr. L.I. Jewish Hosp., New Hyde Park, N.Y., 1958-62; asso. dir. Mt. Sinai Med. Center, Miami Beach, Fla., 1962-65; exec. v.p. E.D. Rosenfeld Assos. Inc., hosp. and health services cons. White Plains, N.Y., 1965-78; pres. M. Bostin Assos., Inc., Elmsford, N.Y., 1979—; guest scholar Brookings Instn., Washington, 1965; lectr. Sch. of Pub. Health and Adminstrv. Medicine, Columbia U., N.Y.C., 1965-78, Grad. Sch. of Pub. Adminstrn., N.Y.C., 1967; lectr. Grad. Sch. of Architecture and Planning, Columbia U., N.Y.C., 1975-78; cons. to Bur. of Hearings and Appeals, Social Security Adminstrn., HEW, 1967-68; spl. cons. to Office of Equal Health Opportunity, Office of Surgeon Gen., USPHS, 1966-67. Mem. Dade County (Fla.) Welfare Planning Council, Miami, 1962-65; bd. dirs. South Fla. Hosp. Council, Miami, 1963-65. Fellow Royal Soc. Health (London), Am. Pub. Health Assn., Am. Assn. Healthcare Consultants (chmn. monograph series com. 1970-71, exec. com. 1972-75, profl. standards com. 1974-76), mem. Am. Hosp. Assn., Forum for Health Care Planning (dir. 1982—, Am. Coll. Healthcare Execs., AIA (mem. com. on architecture for health 1974—), Canadian Coll. Health Service Execs. (fgn. affiliate), Internat. Hosp. Fedn., Can. Pharm. Assn. Address: 45 Knollwood Rd Elmsford NY 10523

BÖSTMAN, OLE MIKAEL, orthopedic surgeon; b. Helsinki, Finland, Dec. 12, 1950; s. Erik Willehard and Anita Margareta (Manner) B. M.D., Helsinki U., 1975, D.Med.Sci., 1983. Intern, Helsinki U. Central Hosp., 1974-75, resident in gen., thoracovascular, orthopaedic surgery, 1979-84, orthopaedic surgeon, 1984—; gen. practice, 1975-78; surgeon mem. Accident Bd. Helsinki, 1984—. Contbr. articles to profl. jours. Swedish Med. Soc. of Finland research grantee, 1981-84. Fellow Internat. Coll. Surgeons; mem. Scandinavian Orthopaedic Assn. (regional sec. 1984—), Finnish Orthopaedic Assn. Office: Töölö Hosp, Helsinki Univ, Topeliuksenkatu 5, Helsinki SF-00260, Finland

BOSTON, ROBERT MCCAULEY, hospital administrator; b. Ballymacarratt, Ireland, Jan. 14, 1911; s. Robert and Sara (McCauley) B.; came to U.S., 1928, naturalized, 1939; student Carnegie Inst. Tech., 1930-33; m. Olive May Miller, June 8, 1940; children—Judith Findley Boston Skillman, Olive Lawrence Boston Davidson. Prevention of blindness dir. Center for Blind, Phila., 1953-72; dir. devel. and community relations Wills Eye Hosp., Phila., 1973-75. Cons. Pa. Acad. Ophthalmology and Otolaryngology, 1958-86, adminstr. Sci. and Edn. Found., 1982-86; adminstr. Interspity. Med. Polit. Action Com., 1981-86; pres. Rudolphy Residence for Blind, 1977-85; mem. Pa. Gov.'s Com. for Blind, 1964-72, vice chmn., 1968, chmn., 1969-70; exec. com. Comprehensive Rehab. Study, 1967-74; bd. dirs. Southeastern Pa. chpt. Nat. Kidney Found., 1973-76, Pa. Indsl. Home for Blind, 1973-76, pres., chmn. bd., 1977—; cons. Sci. for the Blind, 1973-75; cons., TV producer Telegroup, Inc., 1973-77. Bd. dirs. Chapin Meml. Home for Aged Blind, 1979—. Served with USNR, 1943-46. Named hon. mem. Penn. Acad. Ophthalmology and Otolaryngology, 1986. Mem. Nat. Aid to Visually Handicapped (chmn. tech. adv. com. 1961-70, vice chmn. 1970-71), Nat. Soc. Prevention of Blindness (state rep. 1957-72), Am. Assn. Workers for Blind (dir. Pa.-Del. chpt. 1970-72), Pa. Council Blind, Phila. County Med. Soc. (rep. of eye sect. 1956-86), Pa. Soc., Scotch-Irish Soc. Presbyterian. Home: 120 Birch Ave Bala-Cynwyd PA 19004

BOSWELL, SIR ALEXANDER (CRAWFORD SIMPSON), career military officer; b. Aug. 3, 1928; s. Alexander Boswell Simpson and Elizabeth Burns (Park) B.; m. Jocelyn Leslie Blundstone Pomfret, 1956; 5 sons. Student, RMA, Sandhurst, Eng. Enlisted Brit. Army, 1947; commd. Argyll and Sutherland Highlanders, 1948; regimental appts. Hong Kong, Korea, U.K., Suez, Guyana, 1949-58, Camberley, 1959; mil. asst. to GOC Berlin, 1960-62; co-comdr., then second in command 1A and SH, Malaya and Borneo, 1963-65; directing staff Staff Coll., Camberley, 1965-68; CO 1A and SH, 1968-71; col. GS Tng. Army Strategic Command, 1971; brig. comdg. 39 Inf. Brigade, 1972-74; COS 1st Brit. Corps, 1974-76; NDC (Can.) 1976-77; GOC 2nd Armed Div., 1978-80; dir. TA and Cadets, 1980-82; GOC Scotland and gov. Edinburgh Castle 1982-85; hon. col. Tayforth Univs OTC, 1982-86; col. comdt. Scottish Div., 1982-86; comdr.-in-chief Guernsey, 1985—. Decorated KCB, 1982, CBE, 1974, OBE, 1971, MBE, 1962. Clubs: Army and Navy, New (Edinburgh). Office: care Bank of Scotland, Palmerston Pl Branch, 32 West Maitland St, Edinburgh EH12 5KZ, Scotland •

BOSWELL, ALFRED CHESTER, JR., communication management company executive; b. Washington, May 7, 1947; s. Alfred Chester and Gladys (Amos) B.; m. Cecilia Diane Baker, June 3, 1967 (div. 1982); children: Cameron David, Amy Dulane. BFA, Md. Inst., 1969. Publs. rev. editor U. Md., College Park, 1969; pres., chmn. bd. dirs. Boswell Prodns., Silver Spring, Md., 1964—; pres., chmn. bd. dirs., founder Graphica Internat., Washington, 1974-80; chmn. Image Info. Processing, Inc., 1978—, Dream Team, Inc., 1983-86; pres., chmn. bd. dirs. Market Design Internat. Inc., 1984—; supr., distbr. Herbalife Internat., 1984-86; mktg. dir. Adventures in Home Bldg., Ltd., 1984—; pres. Boswell Puppets, 1964—, Edits., Ltd., 1977—, Creative Environs., 1979—, daVelli Internat., 1979—, Rustic Wall Plaques, 1979—, MasterWorks, 1980—, MediaWorks, 1981—; pres., chmn. The Boswell Co., Inc., 1980—; exec. v.p., bd. dirs. Point of View Photography; pres. City Gate West Assn., 1985-86; moderator Debtbuster Megathon Thinktank sponsored by Roosevelt Ctr. for Am. Policy Studies, 1986; keynote speaker The Mktg. Forum, What The Chief Exec. Officer Needs to Know About Mktg., 1987, 88, mem. bd. dirs., mktg. Mindventures, Inc. Author: (musical comedy) Don't Steal a Meal, 1969. Bd. dirs., mktg. dir. Columbia Baptist Fellowship, 1979-80; m. Nat. Symphony Orch.; mem. adv. council Lifespring, 1978-79; mem. steering com. Annapolis (Md.)-Anne Arundel County Tourism Council, 1987—. Served with USAF, 1969-73. U.S. Senatorial scholar, 1967. Mem. Printing Industries Am. (judge graphic arts award competition 1977—), Hampton Roads Hort. Soc., Greater Annapolis C. of C. Lodge: Rotary. Office: 1939 Baltimore Annapolis Blvd Annapolis MD 21401

BOSWELL, DAN ALAN, health maintenance organization executive, health care consultant; b. Upland, Calif., July 25, 1947; s. Paul Leslie and Jana Delores (Thompson) B.; m. Lona Kathalene Bentley, Dec. 26, 1969; children: Bethanie Laurel, Daniel Alan II. Grad. in Mktg. and Sales Mgmt., UCLA. Mktg. dir. Maxicare Co., Los Angeles, 1974-78; v.p. Gen. Med. Santa Ana, Calif., 1978-81; exec. v.p. IMC Health Maintenance Orgn., Miami, Fla., 1981-83, Protective Health Providers, San Diego, 1981-83; chief exec. officer U.S. Health Plan, San Diego, 1982-84; pres., chief exec. officer Serra Health Plan, Sun Valley, Calif., 1984-85, Serra Health Plan (name changed to Amerimed 1985), Burbank, Calif.; pres. The Wellstarr Group, Inc., Upland, Calif., 1986—; faculty fellow Nat. Health Maintenance Orgn. George Washington U., 1982-83; teaching asst. expert market devel., fed. reviewer health maintenance qualification HHS, Rockville, Md., 1982-84. Active governing body Healthsystems Agy., San Diego and Imperial Counties, Calif., 1981-85; pres. Trauma Task Force, HSA, San Diego, 1984; mem. adv. bd. Calif. Med. Asst. Commn., San Fernando Valley, Calif., 1986. Served to sgt. USMC, 1967-70, Vietnam. Mem. Am. Mgmt. Assn. Am. Mktg. Asssn., Group Health Assn. Am., Marine Corps Assn. Am. Republican. Clubs: El Prado Men's (Chino, Calif.) (bd. dirs. 1985-86); Towns (Pomona, Calif.). Home: 851 Emerson Upland CA 91786 Office: The Wellstarr Group Inc 245 E Foothill Blvd Suite 290 Upland CA 91786

BOSWELL, GEORGE MARION, JR., orthopedist, health care facility administrator; b. Dallas, May 12, 1920; s. George Marion and Viola (Scarbrough) B.; m. Veta M. Fuller, Oct. 30, 1958; children: Brianna Boswell Brown, Kama, Maia. BS, Tex. Tech U., 1940; MD, U. Tex., Southwestern Dallas, 1950. Diplomate Am. Acad. Orthopaedic Surgery. Intern Parkland Hosp., Dallas, 1950-51; resident gen. surgeryand orthopedic surgery Parkland, Baylor and Scottish Rite Hosps., Dallas, 1951-55; practice medicine specializing in orthopedics Dallas, 1955—; v.p. med. affairs Baylor Health Care System, Dallas, 1982—; pres., owner Bee Aviation Inc., Dallas, 1968—, Boswell Realty Inc., Dallas, 1971—; lectr., cons. on health care delivery. Contbr. articles to profl. jours. Fellow ACS; mem. AMA, Am. Acad. Orthopaedic Surgery (Key Man U.S. Congress 1980—), Am. Hosp. Assn., Tex. Hosp. Assn. (Key Man Tex. Legislature 1980—, council on hosp. staffs), Flying Physicians (pres. Tex. 1960-64). Republican. Methodist. Club: Cresent (Dallas). Home: 4849 W Lawther Dr Dallas TX 75214 Office: Baylor Health Care System 3201 Worth St Dallas TX 75226

BOSWORTH, ROSWELL SEWELL, JR., publisher; b. Bristol, R.I., Sept. 2, 1926; s. Roswell S. and Edith H. (Howard) B.; student U. Mass., 1944; AB, U. R.I., 1949; m. Sarah Hodgman, May 26, 1951; children: Barbara, Peter; m. Marcia Walls, Feb. 15, 1975; stepchildren: Matthew D. Hayes, Jonathan W. Hayes. Founder Barrington Times, Warren Times-Gazette and Sakonnet Times; pres., pub. Phoenix-Times Pub. Co., Bristol, R.I., 1969—. Chmn., Bristol Charter Commn., 1969-70; chmn. Harbor Devel. Commn., Bristol, 1955-70; trustee U.R.I. Found.; chmn. beautification com. U.R.I.; trustee Roger Williams Coll., 1973-76. Served with USAAF, 1944-45. Recipient U. R.I. award, 1969; decorated officer Order of Prince Henry (Portugal). Mem. New Eng. Press Assn. (pres. 1958-59, recipient Disting. Service award), Suburban Newspapers Am. (pres. 1977-78), Bristol County C. of C. (pres. 1980-82), Sigma Delta Chi. Episcopalian. Mason. Clubs: University (Providence); Bristol Yacht. Lodge: Rotary. Home and Office: 1 Bradford St Bristol RI 02809

BOSWORTH, THOMAS LAWRENCE, architect, educator; b. Oberlin, Ohio, June 15, 1930; s. Edward Franklin and Imogene (Rose) B.; m. Abigail Lumbard, Nov. 6, 1954 (div. Nov. 1974); children: Thomas Edward, Nathaniel David; m. Elaine R. Pedigo, Nov. 23, 1974. B.A., Oberlin Coll., 1952, M.A., 1954; postgrad., Princeton U., 1952-53, Harvard U., 1956-57; M.Arch., Yale U., 1960. Draftsman Gordon McMaster AIA, Cheshire, Conn., summer 1957-58; resident planner Tunnard & Harris Planning Cons., Newport, R.I., summer 1959; designer, field supr. Eero Saarinen & Assocs., Birmingham, Mich., 1960-61, Hamden, Conn., 1961-64; individual practice architecture Providence, 1964-68; asst. instr. architecture Yale U., 1962-65, vis. lectr., 1965-66; asst. prof. R.I. Sch. Design, 1964-66, asso. prof., head dept., 1966-68; prof. architecture U. Wash., Seattle, 1968—, chmn. dept., 1968-72; chief architecture Peace Corps Tng. Program, Tunisia, Brown U., summers 1965-66; archtl. cons., individual practice Seattle, 1972—; dir. multidisciplinary Rome Studies program U. Wash., Rome, Italy, 1984-86; vis. lectr. Kobe U., Japan, Oct. 1982; bd. dirs. N.W. Inst. for Architecture and Urban Studies in Italy, 1983—, pres., 1983-85; mem. Seattle Model Cities Land Use Rev. Bd., 1969-70, Tech. Com. Site Selection Wash. Multi-Purpose Stadium, 1970; chmn. King County (Wash.) Environ. Devel. Commn., 1970-74; mem. Medina Planning Commn., 1972-74; chmn. King County Policy Devel. Commn., 1974-77; mem. steering adv. com. King County Stadium, 1972-74. Dir. Pilchuck Sch., Seattle, 1977-80, trustee, 1980—. Served with U.S. Army, 1954-56. Winchester traveling fellow Greece, 1960; asso. fellow Ezra Stiles Coll. Yale U.; mid-career fellow in architecture Am. Acad. in Rome, 1980-81. Fellow AIA; mem. Soc. Archtl. Historians, AAUP, Tau Sigma Delta. Home: 4532 E Laurel Dr NE Seattle WA 98105 Office: U Wash Dept Architecture Seattle WA 98195

BOTERO, FERNANDO, artist; b. Medellin, Colombia, Apr. 19, 1932; s. David and Flora B.; m. Cecilia Botero, 1964; 4 children. Student, Academia San Fernando, Madrid, 1952, Prado Museum, Madrid, 1952; student in art history, Univ. Florence, Italy, 1953-54. Numerous one-man shows, including first solo show at Gallery Leo Matiz, Columbia, 1957, Pan-Am. Union, Washington, 1957, Marlborough Gallery, N.Y.C., 1982, Hooks-Epstein Gallery, Houston, 1982, Hokin Gallery, Chgo., 1982, Benjamin Mangel Gallery, Phila., 1982, Galería Quintana, Bogotá, Colombia, 1982, Thomas Gal Gallery, Boston, 1983, Palazzo Grassi, Venice, Italy, 1983, Marlborough Gallery, London, 1983, Fondation Veranneman, Kruishoutem, Belgium, 1983, Adler Gallery, Los Angeles, 1984, Everhard Mus., Sranton, Pa., 1984, Hokkaido Mus. Modern Art, Japan, 1986; retrospective exhibition Hirshhorn Mus. and Sculpture Garden, 1979; represented numerous permanent collections, including Museo Nacional, Bogotá, Walrat-Richarts Mus., Cologne, Germany, Museo d'Arte Moderna del Vaticano, Rome, Museo de Arte Contemporáneo, Madrid, Hirshhorn Mus. and Sculpture Garden, Washington, Mus. Modern Art, N.Y.C., Solomon R. Guggenheim Mus., N.Y.C., Nat. Mus., Tokyo, Met. Mus. Art, N.Y.C. Decorated Order Andrés Bello (Venezuela); recipient Guggenheim Nat. prize for Colombia, 1960. Office: care Marlborough Fine Arts 40 W 57th St New York NY 10019 •

BOTHA, PIETER WILLEM, executive state president of Republic South Africa; b. Paul Roux, Jan. 12, 1916; s. Pieter Willem and Hendriena Christina (De Wet) B.; student U. Orange Free State, PhD (hon.), 1981; Dr. Mil. Sci. (hon.), U. Stellenbosch, 1976; m. Anna Elizabeth Rossouw, Mar. 13, 1943; children: Elanza, Amelia, Pieter Willem, Rozanne, Rossouw. M.P., 1948—; dep. minister of interior, 1958; minister of comml. devel. and

Coloured affairs, 1961; minister of public works, 1964; minister of def., 1966; leader House Assembly, 1975; prime minister, 1978-84, state pres., 1984—. Leader, Nat. Party, Cape Province, 1966—. Decorated Grand Cross of Mil. Orders of Christ (Portugal); Decoration for Meritorious Service; Star of South Africa; Order of Propitious Clouds with Spl. Grand Cordon (Taiwan). Dutch Reformed Ch. Home: Westbrooke, Rondebosch Cape Province 7700, Republic South Africa Office: Office of the State Pres, Pvt Bag x 193, Cape Town 8000, Republic South Africa *

BOTHMA, JOHN ALLISON, food scientist; b. East London, South Africa, Aug. 15, 1936; s. Johannes Jacobus and Freda Wilhemina (Schwartz) B.; m. Penelope Ann Mackay, Dec. 6, 1961; children—Katherine, Michael, Belinda, Nicholas. B.S., Rhodes U., Grahamstown, South Africa, 1960; M. Bus. Leadership, U. South Africa, 1970. Chemist, African Explosives, Modderfontein, 1955-56; works chemist Schweppes S.A. Ltd., Johannesburg, 1961-62; devel. chemist South African Breweries, Johannesburg, 1962-66; devel. mgr. Keartlands, Johannesburg, 1966-70; dir. Epic Oil Mills Pty. Ltd., Johannesburg, 1970-83; mng. dir. Southbakels Pty. Ltd., Johannesburg, 1984—; chmn. Bakels R&D Com.; mem. adv. com. Nat. Food Research Inst., 1981—; mem. exec. com. South African Food Standards Adv. Council, 1982—. Author tech. papers on oil chemistry and sunflower processing. Organizer Jr. Achievement, Johannesburg; com. mem. South African Schs. Rowing Fedn. Served to lt. South African Army, 1955-56. Mem. South African Chem. Inst. (exec. com. 1982-83), South African Inst. Prodn. Mgmt., South African Assn. Food Sci. and Tech. (com. 1976-77), Am. Oil Chemists Assn., Am. Inst. Food Technologists, Assn. of Cereal Chemists, Am. Oil Mill Superintendents Assn. Methodist. Clubs: Wemmer Pan Rowing (Johannesburg) (sec. 1962-63); Royal Cape Yacht (Cape Town). Home: 9 Riepen Ave, Riepen Park, Sandton 2196 Republic of South Africa Office: PO Box 9583, Johannesburg 2000 Republic of South Africa

BOTSAI, ELMER EUGENE, architect, university dean; b. St. Louis, Feb. 1, 1928; s. Paul and Ita May (Cole) B.; m. Patricia L. Keegan, Aug. 28, 1955; children: Donald Rolf, Kurt Gregory.; m. Sharon K. Kaiser, Dec. 5, 1981; 1 dau., Kiana Michelle. AA, Sacramento Jr. Coll., 1950; A.B., U. Calif.-Berkeley, 1954. Registered architect, Nev., Hawaii, Calif. Draftsman, then asst. to architect So. Pacific Co., San Francisco, 1953-57; chief designer J.H. Ferguson Co., San Francisco, 1955; project architect Anshen & Allen Architects, San Francisco, 1957-63; prin. Botsai, Overstreet & Rosenberg, Architects and Planners, San Francisco, 1963-79, Elmer E. Botsai FAIA, Honolulu, 1979—; chmn. dept. architecture U. Hawaii at Manoa, 1976-80, dean Sch. Architecture, 1980—; instr. seismic safety Summer Inst. Architecture at Stanford U., Calif., 1977; lectr. U. Calif., Berkeley, 1976; dir. Nat. Archtl. Accrediting Bd., 1972-73, 79; adminstrv. and tech. cons. wood building research ctr., U. Calif., Berkeley, 1985—; mem. Profl. Preparation Project Com. at U. Mich., Ann Arbor, 1986-87; co-creator Water Infiltration Seminar Series for Bldg. Owners and Mgrs. Research Ctr., 1986-87; chief investigator effects of Guatemalan earthquake for NSF and AIA, Washington, 1976; steering com. on structural failures Nat. Bur. Standards, 1982-84; chmn. and dir. gen. services Adv. Com. of the State of Calif., 1969; extensive speaker to profl. orgns., univs., corps. Co-author: Architects and Earthquake, Research Needs, 1976, ATC Seismic Standards for National Bur. of Standards, 1976, Architects and Earthquakes: A Primer, 1977, Seismic Design, 1978; contbr. articles and reports to profl. jours.; prin. works include expansion of Nuclear Weapons Tng. Facility at Lemoore Naval Air Station, Calif., LASH Terminal Port Facility Archtl. Phase, San Francisco, Incline Village (Nev.) Country Club, 1365 Columbus Ave. Bldg., San Francisco, Marina View Redevel., Pittsburg, Calif., modernization of Stanford Court Hotel, San Francisco; monument area constrn. several Calif. cemeteries. Served with U.S. Army, 1946-48. Recipient Cert. Honor Fedn. Archtl. Colls. Mex. Republic, 1984; NSF grantee for investigative workshop project, San Diego, 1974-80. Fellow AIA (treas. San Francisco chpt. 1972-73, bd. dirs., 1966-71, treas. No. Calif. chpt. 1968-69, pres. 1971, nat. v.p., 1975-76, nat. pres. 1978, pres. Hawaii 1985); hon. fellow Royal Can. Inst. Architects, N.Z. Inst. Architects, Royal Australian Inst. Architects, La Societed de Arquitectos Mexicano; mem. Earthquake Engring. Research Inst., Archtl. Secs. Assn. (hon.), Forest Products Research Soc., Soc. Wood Sci. and Tech., Internat. Conf. Bldg. Ofcls., AAAS, Nat. Fire Protection Assn., Am. Arbitration Assn. Home: 321 Wailupe Circle Honolulu HI 96821 Office: 2560 Campus Rd GA B2 Honolulu HI 96822

BOTT, HAROLD SHELDON, accountant; b. Chgo., Dec. 12, 1933; s. Harold S. and Mary (Moseley) B.; m. Audrey Anne Connor, May 15, 1964; children: Susan, Lynda. AB, Princeton U., 1955; MBA, Harvard U., 1959; postgrad., U. Chgo., 1960-62. Adminstrv. asst. to exec v.p. Champion Paper, Hamilton, Ohio, 1959-61; mgmt. cons. Arthur Andersen & Co., Chgo., 1961-65, mgr., 1965-71, ptnr., 1971—; mng. dir. mgmt. info. cons., ptnr. strategic services; vice chmn. The Assn. of Mgmt. Cons. Firms; pres., bd. dirs. Inst. Mgmt. Cons. Officer, dir. Urban Gateways; pres., dir. sch. bd.; pres. Kenilworth Caucus, Kenilworth United Fund; dir. Orchestra of Ill. Served with USN, 1955-56. Mem. Ill Soc. CPA's, Am. Inst. CPA's, Harvard Bus. Sch. Assn. (officer, bd. dirs.), Am. Mktg. Assn. Republican. Congregationalist. Clubs: Kenilworth Sailing (commodore), Kenilworth (officer, dir.), Indian Hill, Mid Am.; Univ. (Chgo.). Home: 305 Kenilworth Ave Kenilworth IL 60043 Office: Arthur Andersen & Co 33 W Monroe St Chicago IL 60603

BOTTERO, PHILIPPE BERNARD, general practitioner; b. Villecresnes, France, May 21, 1940; s. Pierre and Hetty (Saltiel) B. SPCN, Faculty Scis., Paris, 1959; studies of medicine, Faculty Medicine, Paris, 1959-65; MD, 1977. Intern Montfermeil Hosp., Coulommiers Hosp., Meaux Hosp., 1965-66, Necker Enfants Malades Hosp., Paris, 1970-73; gen. practice medicine Nyons, France, 1978—. Contbr. articles to profl. jours. Home: Venterol, 26110 Nyons France Office: 10 Ave Henri Rochier, 26110 Nyons France

BOTTI, OTTAVIO SILVIO VIRGINIO, civil engineer, consultant; b. Salsomaggiore, Italy, Oct. 13, 1921; arrived in Uganda, 1958; s. Giuseppe and Maria Maddalena (Rondani) B.; m. Renata Bacciocchi, 1951. Dott. Ingegnere, Politecnico U., 1947. Registered profl. engr. Soil machinist, dir. Stirling Astaldi, Arusha & Dares Salaam, 1949-52; chief engr., mgr. M. Gonella & Co., Dar Es Salaam, 1952-54; cons. engr., Milan, Italy, 1954-58; mng. dir., cons. Westomat Group in East Africa, Kampala, Uganda, Nairobi, Kenya, Dar Es Salaam, Tansania. Fellow Inst. of Dir., Uganda Inst. Profl. Engrs. (v.p. 1968—); mem. Uganda Nat. Research Council, Italian Assn. Engrs., Uganda Nat. Sci. Research Council. Roman Catholic. Lodge: Rotary. Home: PO Box 3188, Kampala Uganda Office: PO Box 45154, Nairobi Kenya

BOTTINI, ERNESTO ENRIQUE, urodynamist; b. Baires, Argentina, June 6, 1947; s. Ernesto Eugenio and Dora (Tomassini) B.; m. Margarita C. Rodriguez; children: Ernesto, Eugenia, Enriqueta, Estefania. MD, U. Buenos Aires, 1970. Diplomate Bd. Urodynamics. Resident Childrens Hosp., Buenos Aires, 1975-77, head urodynamic dept., 1978-79, chief urodynamic dept., diagnostic medicine, 1980-; chief urodynamic dept. Italian Hospital, Buenos Aires, 1979-80; cons. pediatric dept. Italian Hosp., 1980, Nat. Childrens Hosp., 1986. Mem. Soc. Pediatric Research in Latin Am. Roman Catholic. Club: BAC (Buenos Aires). Home: Conesa 2079, 1428 Buenos Aires Argentina

BOTTOMLEY, BRIAN ROGERS, mechanical engineer; b. Salford, Lancashire, Eng., Dec. 12, 1927; s. Harry and Ivy (Wragg) B.; m. Kathleen Neville, Apr. 1, 1950; children—Nigel Rogers. Student pub. schs., Cheshire, Eng. Chartered engr. Tech. dir. Churchill Machine Tool Co., Ltd., Altrinchan, Eng., 1968-73; mng. dir. T. I. Matrix Ltd., Coventry, Eng., 1973-81; mng. dir. Staveley Machine Tools, Ltd., Altrincham, Eng., 1981-84; chmn. and mng. dir. Kearns-Richards Ltd., Altrincham, 1984—; chmn. K.R.S. Ltd.; chmn., mng. dir. Kearns-Richards Ltd., Trafford Mfg. Ltd. Fellow Instn. Mech. Engrs., Instn. Prodn. Engrs. Office: Kearns-Richards Ltd, Atlantic St, Broadheath Altrincham Cheshire England

BOTTOMLEY, F. DAVID, advertising executive; b. Barkisland, Yorkshire, Eng., July 28, 1931; s. Frank and Alice (Buchanan) B.; m. Irene Jean Allan, Apr. 14, 1962; children: Bruce, Ruth, Kate. MA with honors, U. Edinburgh, Scotland, 1956. Account exec. Osborne Peacock, Ltd., London and Manchester, Eng., 1956-57, T.B. Browne, Ltd., London, 1957-58; advt. exec. John Mackintosh & Sons, Ltd., Norwich, Eng., 1958-61, advt. mgr., 1961-69; advt. mgr. Europe Rowntree Mackintosh, Norwich and York, Eng., 1969-87; internat. advt. mgr. Rowntree PLC, York, 1987—. Mem. council Brafferton Parochial Ch., 1984—. Served to capt. Royal Artillery Territorial Army, 1950-70. Mem. Internat. Advt. Assn. (lectr. edn. com. 1980—), Inst. Mktg., World Fedn. Advertisers (del., chmn. communications), Inc. Soc. Brit. Advertisers (del.). Office: Rowntree PLC, Haxby Rd, York YO1 1XY, England

BOTZ, GERHARD, historian, educator; b. Schaerding, Austria, Mar. 14, 1941; s. Anton and Maria (Parzer) B.; m. Maria Antonakou-Mavromichali, 1965; children—Aurel, Daniel, Fabian. Student, Acad. Music and Univ., Vienna, Austria, 1959-67; PhD, U. Vienna, 1967. Archivist, Chamber of Labour, Vienna, 1966-68; asst. prof. U. Linz, Austria, 1968-79, assoc. prof., 1979-80; prof. history U. Salzburg, Austria, 1980—; dir. Ludwig-Boltzmann Inst. Social Sci. History, Salzburg, 1982—; vis. prof. U. Minn., Mpls., 1985, Stanford U., 1986, 87. Author: Die Eingliederung Oesterreichs in das Deutsche Reich, 1972, 76, 88; Wohnungspolitik und Judendeportation in Wien, 1938-45, 1975, Gewalt in der Politik, 1976, 83; Wien vom Anschluss zum Krieg, 1978, 80, 88, Der 13 Maerz 38 und die Anschlussbewegung, 1978, 81, M. Glas-Larsson: Ich will reden, 1982, Krisenzonen einer Demokratie, 1987; series editor Studien zur Historischen Sozialwissenschaft; co-author, editor numerous books; contbr. articles to profl. publs. Alexander von Humboldt Found. grantee, 1976-77, Fulbright grantee, 1985. Mem. Wissenschaftliche Kommission zur Erforschung der Geschichte Oesterreichs, QUANTUM Working Group Austrian History (chmn.), Internat. Commn. for Application of Quantitative Methods in History (exec. bur.), Internat. Oral History Soc. (Austrian rep.), Dokumentationsarchiv des oesterreichischen Widerstands (trustee). Club: Naturfreunde (Vienna). Office: U Salzburg, Hist Inst, Mirabellplatz 1, A-5020 Salzburg Austria

BOUCÉ, PAUL-GABRIEL, literature educator; b. Versailles, France, Jan. 26, 1936; s. Gabriel and Andrée B.; children: Hugh, Anne. Lic., Lyons (France) U., 1957, DES, 1958, Agrégation, 1960; LittD, U. Sorbonne, 1970. Asst. prof. U. Sorbonne, Paris, 1963-67, assoc. prof., 1968-71; prof. lit. Sorbonne Nouvelle, Paris, 1972—. Author: Smollett's Novels, 1976; editor: Sexuality in 18th Century Britain, 1982, Roderick Random, 1979; editor-in-chief Etudes Anglaises, Paris, 1980-86. Served to lt. French navy, 1960-62. Mem. Internat. Assn. U. Prof. English, Societé des Anglicistes de l'Enseignement Supérieur, Coll. Franco-Britannique (dir. 1987—), Wolfson Coll. Cambridge. Home: 9B Blvd Jourdan, 75014 Paris France Office: Sorbonne Nouvelle Paris III, 5 rue de l'Ecole de Médecine, 75006 Paris France

BOUDART, MICHEL, chemist, chemical engineer; b. Belgium, June 18, 1924; came to U.S., 1947, naturalized, 1957; s. Francois and Marguerite (Swolfs) B.; m. Marina D'Haese, Dec. 27, 1948; children: Mark, Baudouin, Iris, Philip. BS, U. Louvain, Belgium, 1944, MS, 1947; PhD, Princeton U., 1950; D honoris causa, U. Liège, U. Notre Dame, U. Nancy, U. Ghent, Belgium. Research asso. James Forrestal Research Ctr., Princeton, 1950-54; mem. faculty Princeton U., 1954-61; prof. chem. engring. U. Calif. - Berkeley, 1961-64; prof. chem. engring. and chemistry Stanford U., 1964-80, William J. Keck prof. chem. engring., 1980—; cons. to industry, 1955—; co-founder Catalytica, Inc.; Humble Oil Co. lectr., 1958, Am. Inst. Chem. Engrs. lectr., 1961, Sigma Xi nat. lectr., 1965; chmn. Gordon Research Conf. Catalysis, 1962. Author: Kinetics of Chemical Processes, 1968, (with A. Djéga-Mariadassou) Kinetics of Heterogeneous Catalytic Reactions, 1983; editor: (with J.R. Anderson) Catalysis: Science and Technology, 1981; adv. editorial bd. Jour. Internat. Chem. Engring., 1964—, Advances in Catalysis, 1968—, Catalysis Rev., 1968—, Accounts Chem. Research, 1978—. Belgium-Am. Ednl. Found. fellow, 1948; Procter fellow, 1949; recipient Curtis-McGraw research award Am. Soc. Engring. Edn., 1962, R.H. Wilhelm award in chem. reaction engring., 1974. Fellow AAAS; mem. Am. Chem. Soc. (Kendall award 1977, E.V. Murphee award in Indsl. & Engring. Chemistry 1985), Catalysis Soc., Am. Inst. Chem. Engrs., Chem. Soc., Nat. Acad. Sci., Nat. Acad. Engring.; fgn. assoc. Académie Royale de Belgique. Home: 512 Gerona Rd Stanford CA 94305 Office: Dept Chem Engring Stanford Univ Stanford CA 94305

BOUDOULAS, HARISIOS, physician; b. Velvendo-Kozani, Greece, Nov. 3, 1935; married; 2 children. MD, U. Salonica, Greece, 1959. Resident in medicine Red Cross Hosp., Athens, Greece, 1960-61; resident in medicine U. Salonica First Med. Clinic, 1962-64, resident in internal medicine, 1964-66, resident in cardiology, 1967-69, lectr., 1969-70; postgrad. fellow, instr. div. cardiology Ohio State U. Coll. Medicine, Columbus, 1970-73, 75, asst. prof. medicine, 1975-78, assoc. prof., 1978-80, dir. cardiac non-invasive lab., 1978-80, prof. medicine div. cardiology, 1983—, prof. pharmacy, 1984—, dir. cardiovascular research div., 1983-86; prof. medicine div. cardiology Wayne State U., Detroit, 1980-82, chief clin. cardiovascular research, 1980-82, acting dir. div. cardiology, 1982; chief cardiovascular diagnostic and tng. center VA Med. Ctr., Allen Park, Mich., 1980 83; acting chief sect. cardiology Harper-Grace Hosps., Detroit, 1982; co-dir. Overstreet Teaching and Research Labs. Contbr. numerous articles to med. jours. Named Disting. Research Investigator, Cen. Ohio chpt. Am. Heart Assn., Columbus, 1983. Fellow ACP, Am. Coll. Angiology, Am. Coll. Clin. Pharmacology, Council Clin. Cardiology, Am. Coll. Cardiology; mem. Am. Heart Assn., Greek Heart Assn., Greek Com. Against Hypertension, Central Soc. Clin. Research, Am. Fedn. Clin. Research. Office: Ohio State U Div Cardiology 1655 Upham Dr Columbus OH 43210

BOUDOURESQUES, GÉRARD JACQUES, neurologist; b. Marseille, France, May 5, 1947; s. Jacques and Christiane (Olivier) B.; divorced; 1 child, Nicolas; m. Nathalie Ceccaldi, 1988. MD, U. Marseille, 1975. Cert. neurologist. Intern Pub. Hosp., Marseille, 1971; practice medicine specializing in neurology Marseille, 1982—; sr. hosp. lectr. neurology Faculty Medicine, Marseille, 1975-76, 77-82, lectr., 1982—; sr. hosp. lectr. Hopital Salpetriere, Paris, 1977; neurology attache Chutimone, Marseille, 1982—. Success at the Agregation, 1979; contbr. articles to profl. jours. Mem. French Neurology Soc. Roman Catholic. Club: Tennis (Marseille). Home: 77 Rue Jean Mermoz, 13008 Marseille France Office: 36 Ave du Prado, 13006 Marseille France

BOUDREAU, A. ALLAN, museum director, historian; b. Albany, N.Y., Aug. 1, 1936; s. Alexander and Lillian (Allan) B.; children: Kirstin Rosamund, Andrew Allan. BS, Russell Sage Coll., 1958; MBA, NYU, 1964, PhD, 1973; MS, Columbia U., 1972. Jr. adminstrv. asst. N.Y. State Dept. Edn., 1958-59; adminstrv. officer N.Y. State Library, 1959-62; asst. dir. NYU Libraries, 1962-73; sr. research assoc. NYU, 1973-74; sec. Library Trustees Found., 1973—; dir. library and mus. Grand Lodge Masons N.Y., 1974—; pub. acct. N.Y. State, 1961—; cons. libraries, mus., research orgns., mfrs., architects, state and local govtl. units; lectr. colls. and profl. groups. Author: The Library and Scholarly Research, 1964, The Research Resources at Washington Square, 1831-1970, 1972, 200 Years of Freemasonry in New York, 1981, George Washington in New York, 1988; contbr. articles to profl. jours. N.Y. State Exempt vol. fireman; trustee Allan Found., 1970—; trustee Livingston Library, 1983—. Served with AUS, 1953-55. Recipient Founder's Day award NYU, 1973. Mem. ALA (life), N.Y. Library Assn., N.Y. State Assn. Library Bds. (bd. dirs. 1973—), Am. Assn. State and Local History, Am. Legion. Club: N.Y. Athletic. Lodge: Masons. Home: 1 Washington Sq Village New York NY 10012 Office: 71 W 23d St New York NY 10010

BOUDREAU, EDWARD DAVID, JR., physician; b. Hartford, Conn., Nov. 21, 1951; s. Edward David Sr. and Margaret (Murphy) B.; m. Susan Kathleen Giblin, Sept. 17, 1978; children—Kristen, Michael. B.S. in Chemistry, Bates Coll., 1973; D.O., Mich. State U., 1977. Diplomate Am. Bd. Emergency Medicine. Intern Doctors Hosp., Columbus, Ohio; staff physician emergency dept. Point Pleasant Hosp., N.J., 1981-82; dir. emergency dept. Doctors Hosp., Columbus, 1982—, chmn. dept. emergency medicine, 1984-85; vice chmn. dept. emergency medicine St. Ann's Hosp., Westerville, Ohio, 1986—; asst. clin. prof. preventive medicine Ohio State U., Columbus, 1986; pres. Immediate Health Assocs., Inc., 1987. Served to capt. U.S. Army, 1978-81. Dana scholar Bates Coll., 1970. Fellow Am. Coll. Emergency Physicians; mem. Phi Beta Kappa. Roman Catholic. Avocation: sailing catamaran. Home: 5205 Ashford Rd Dublin OH 43017 Office: St Ann's Hosp Emergency Dept 500 Cleveland Ave Westerville OH 43281

BOUEY, GERALD KEITH, economic consultant, retired banker; b. Axford, Sask., Can., Apr. 2, 1920; s. John Alexander and Inez Amanda B.; m. Anne Margaret Ferguson, Aug. 8, 1945; children—Kathryn, Robert. Hon. B.A., Queen's U., Kingston, Ont., Can., 1948. Bank clk. Royal Bank of Can., Sask., 1936-40; with Bank of Can., Ottawa, Ont., 1948-87; gov. Bank of Can., 1973-87. Served with RCAF, 1941-45. Mem. United Ch. Can. Clubs: Can., Rideau, Royal Ottawa Golf.

BOULEZ, PIERRE, composer, conductor; b. Montbrison, nr. Clermont-Ferrand, France, Mar. 26, 1925; s. Leon and Marcelle (Calabre) B. Pupil, Olivier Messiaen at Paris Conservatory; pupil (recipient 1st prize 1945). Apptd. dir. music Jean-Louis Barrault's Theater Co., 1948; now tchr., lectr., condr.; musical adviser, prin. guest condr. Cleve. Symphony Orch., 1970-71; musical dir. N.Y. Philharmonic Orch., 1971-77; dir. I.R.C.A.M., 1976—. Toured, Orient, Europe, North and South Am., (with Barrault), conducting appearances include, Edinburgh Festival, 1965, Bayreuth Festival, 1966, 76-80; Compositions include Sonatina for flute and piano, 1946, Three Piano Sonatas, 1946, 50, 57, Le Soleil des Eaux for voice and orchestra, 1948, Structures, 1952, Le Marteau sans maitre, 1955, Deux improvisations sur Mallarme, 1957, Doubles for orchestra, 1958, Tombeau, (on text of Mallarmé), 1959, Pli selon pli, 1960, Structures II, 1962, Eclat, 1964, Domaines, 1968, Multiples, 1970, Cummings ist der Dichter, 1970, Explosante/Fixe, 1973, Rituel, 1975, Messagesquisse, 1977, Notations, part I, 1980; Répons, 1981, Dialogue de l'Ombre double, 1986, Mémoriale, 1986; author: musical criticism and analysis, including Penser la Musique d'Aujourd'hui. Address: Postfach 22, Baden-Baden Federal Republic of Germany Office: IRCAM, 31 rue St Merri, 75004 Paris France

BOULGER, WILLIAM CHARLES, lawyer; b. Columbus, Ohio, Apr. 2, 1924; s. James Ignatius and Rebecca (Laughlin) B.; m. Ruth J. Schachtele, Dec. 29, 1954; children—Brigid Carolyn, Ruth Mary. A.B., Harvard Coll., 1948; LL.B., Law Sch. Cin., 1951. Bar: Ohio, 1951, U.S. Dist. Ct. (so. dist.) Ohio 1952, U.S. Supreme Ct. 1957. Ptnr. with Thomas A. Boulger, Chillicothe, Ohio, 1951-73; sole propr. Law Offices of William C. Boulger, Chillicothe, 1974—. Pres. Ross County Welfare Assn., Chillicothe, 1954-60; mem. Chillicothe. ARC, 1958-84, chmn., 1959-63, 1985—; mem. Democratic Exec. Com., Chillicothe, 1950s. Served as pfc. U.S. Army, 1943-45, ETO. Mem. Ross County Bar Assn. (pres. 1971), Ohio Bar Assn., ABA. Roman Catholic. Clubs: Sunset, Symposiarchs (pres.). Avocations: tennis, golf. Home: 31 Club Dr Chillicothe OH 45601 Office: 10-14 Foulke Block Chillicothe OH 45601

BOULLATA, ISSA JOSEPH, Arabic literature and language educator; b. Jerusalem, Feb. 25, 1929; came to U.S., 1968, Can., 1975; s. Joseph Issa and Barbara (Atallah) B.; m. Marita Joan Seward, Aug. 12, 1960; children—Joseph, Barbara, David, Peter. B.A. with honors, U. London, 1964, Ph.D., 1969. Sr. tchr. Arabic lit. and lang. DeLaSalle Coll., Jerusalem, Jordan, 1949-52, Ahliyyah Coll., Ramallah, Jordan, 1952-53, St. George's Sch., Jerusalem, 1953-68; prof. Arabic lit. and lang. Hartford Sem., Conn., 1968-75, McGill U., Montreal, 1975—. Author: Al-Rumantiqiyya, 1960; Al-Sayyab, 1971. Translator, editor: Modern Arab Poets, 1976; Ahmad Amin: My Life, 1978; Critical Perspectives on Modern Arabic Literature, 1980, Flight Against Time (Emily Nasrallah) 1987. Editor: The Muslim World, 1970-80, Al-Arabiyya, 1978-82; (with Muhsin Mahdi, Salih J. Altoma and David Partington) Mundus Arabicus, 1981—; Oral Tradition (spl. issue on Arab oral tradition), 1988. Contbr. articles to profl. jours. Recipient Arberry Meml. prize Pembroke Arabic Research Group, Cambridge U., 1972. Fellow Middle East Studies Assn., Am. Assn. Tchrs. of Arabic (bd. dirs. 1976-78, 85-87, pres. 1983); mem. Am. Comparative Lit. Assn., Internat. Comparative Lit. Assn., Internat. Assn. Mid. Ea. Studies, Assn. of Arab-Am. Univ. Graduates, Arab-Am. Anti-Discrimination Com., Arab Orgn. for Human Rights. Eastern Orthodox. Club: McGill Faculty. Avocations: chess; reading; music. Home: 4070 Madison Ave, Montreal, PQ Canada H4B 2T7 Office: McGill Univ, Inst Islamic Studies, 3485 McTavish St, Montreal, PQ Canada H3A 1Y1

BOULOUBASSIS, ARIS PANAYIOTIS, cosmetic and pharmaceutical company executive; b. Longos, Aigion, Greece, Feb. 14, 1941; s. Panayotis and Alexandra (Cristodoulos) B.; m. Despina Tsiros, Dec. 18, 1967. M in Polit. Sci., U. Athens, 1966. Research supr. Minos Advt. Co., Athens, 1960-65; product mgr. Fix Brewery Co., Athens, 1966-67; mgr. sales Adel Food Distbn. Co., Athens, 1968-70; sales supr. consumer div. Bristol Hellas SA subs. Bristol Meyers Co. U.S.A., Athens, 1970-72, sales mgr., 1973-74, sales and mktg. mgr., 1975-80, dir. consumer div., 1981-84; v.p. cosmetics Lavipharm SA, Athens, 1984—; mgr. mktg. Bristol Hellas SA, Athens, 1970-84; cons. Lavico SA, Athens, 1984—. Contbr. articles to profl. jours. Mem. Byron Longos, 1958—. Served as master sgt. Greek Air Force, 1965-66. Mem. Greek Mgmt. Assn., Greek Inst. Mktg., Greek Advertisers Assn., Greek Chamber Econs., Alexander Hamilton Inst. Democrat. Greek Orthodox. Club: Aris Sports (Figon). Home: A Papanastasiou 14B', 15127 Melissia Greece Office: Lavipharm SA, Agias Marinas, 19002 Peania Greece

BOULT, REBER FIELDING, lawyer; b. Hollandale, Miss., July 8, 1907; s. Richard Ward and Ida Louise (Collum) B.; m. Olivia Stephenson Weaver, July 23, 1935; children—Reber Fielding, Ann (Mrs. C.D. Walling Jr.). BA, Vanderbilt U., 1927, JD, 1929. Bar: Tenn. 1929. Practice law, Nashville; sr. ptnr., mem. firm Boult, Cummings, Conners & Berry, 1949—; dir. Peoples Bank & Trust Co., Tupelo, Miss., Dominion Bank of Mid. Tenn. Past pres., Nashville Symphony Assn., United Givers Fund; bd. dirs. Nashville Pub. Library; pres. adv. bd. St. Thomas Hosp., 1965-70; trustee Vanderbilt U., sec. bd.; past pres., trustee Cumberland Mus. and Sci. Ctr.; trustee George Peabody Coll.; founding trustee So. Calif. Sch. Theology; chmn. nat. com. on wills and trusts Vanderbilt U. Served with USNR, 1944-46. Fellow Am. Coll. Probate Counsel; mem. Nat. Vanderbilt U. Law Alumni (past pres.), Alpha Tau Omega. Methodist (past pres. bd. trustees). Clubs: Belle Meade Country (past pres.), Coffee House (past pres.), Cumberland. Lodge: Kiwanis (past pres.). Home: 3701 West End Ave No 8 Whitehall Nashville TN 37205 Office: 222 3d Ave N PO Box 198062 Nashville TN 37219

BOUMA, JOHN JACOB, lawyer; b. Fort Dodge, Iowa, Jan. 13, 1937. B.A., U. Iowa, 1958, J.D., 1960. Bar: Iowa 1960, Wis. 1960, Ariz. 1962, U.S. Supreme Ct. 1975. Assoc. Foley, Sammond & Lardner, Milw., 1960; assoc. Snell & Wilmer, Phoenix, 1962-66, ptnr., 1967—. Chmn. Phoenix Human Relations Commn., 1973-75; mem. Phoenix Commn. on LEAP, 1971-72; bd. dirs. Phoenix Legal Aid Soc., 1970-76; trustee Ariz. Opera Co. (v.p. 1987—). Served to capt. JAGC, U.S. Army, 1960-62. Fellow Am. Coll. Trial Lawyers; mem. Maricopa County Bar Assn. (pres. 1977-78), Nat. Conf. Bar Pres. (exec. council) Ariz. Bar Assn. (pres. 1983-84), Ariz. Bar Found. (pres. 1987—), Iowa Bar Assn., Wis. Bar Assn., ABA, Phoenix Assn. Def. Counsel (pres. 1972), Attys. Liability Assurance Soc., Ltd. (bd. dirs. 1987—), Iowa Law Sch. Found. (bd. dirs.), Ariz. State Coll. Law Soc. (bd. dirs.), Order of Coif, Phi Beta Kappa. Home: 800 E Circle Rd Phoenix AZ 85020 Office: 3100 Valley Center Phoenix AZ 85073

BOUMAH, AUGUSTIN, Gabon government official; b. Libreville, Gabon, Nov. 7, 1927; married; 10 children. Ed., French Inst. Overseas Studies, Coll. Medene de Libreville, Ecolé des Cadres Supériers, Brazzaville, Gabon. Minister youth, sports and cultural affairs Gabon, 1967, minister justice, keeper of the seals, 1967, minister interior and justice, 1967-68, minister fin. and the budget, 1968-72, minister state at presidency in charge of planning and devel. and land adminstrn., 1972-75; pres. Gabon Supreme Ct., 1975-80, Nat. Assembly Gabon. Address: care Supreme Ct, BP 1043, Libreville Gabon *

BOUMENDIL, ROGER FOURCROY, advertising agency consultant; b. Algiers, Algeria, Nov. 30, 1922; s. Henri and Germaine (Nebot) B.; m. Danielle Dautigny, July 24, 1940; children: Laurent, Sophie. BA, U. Algiers, 1940; postgrad., State Advt. Sch., Paris, 1950-52. Pvt. practice advt. cons. Paris, 1952-63; chmn. Rb-Ideas Agy., Paris, 1964-84, advt. cons., 1984—. One-man shows include Paris, Versailles, Vichy; exhibited in group shows at Salon D'Automne, Paris, Salon des Independants, Salon Des Artistes Francais, 1958-87. Served with French Army, 1942-45. Decorated War Cross with Star, Vol. Corps Cross. Mem. French Assn. Agys., State Advertisers Assn. Home: 15 Ave Gambetta, 92410 Ville D'Avray France Office: Agence RB Idees, 18 Rue Four Croy, 75017 Paris France

BOUMIS, EVANGELOS, cement company personnel executive, management and training consultant; b. Athens, Greece, Mar. 25, 1937; s. Demosthenes and Ekaterini (Triantafillou) B.; m. Avra Tsagli, June 17, 1967; children—Ekaterini, Demosthenes. Diploma in Mining and Metall. Engring., Tech. Univ., Athens, 1960; cert. Bus. Adminstrn., Univ., Nancy, France, 1961; grad. in Econs., Univ. Athens, 1975. Prodn. engr. Halivourgik S.A., Elefsis, Greece, 1964-65; inspector quarries and mines, Ministry of Industry, Athens, 1965-66; orgn. and tng. officer Titan Cement Co. S.A., Elefsis, 1966-70, fin. adminstr., 1970-74, indsl. engring. mgr., Athens headquarters, 1974-78, personnel corp. mgr., 1978—. Author: Mineral Wealth of Greece, 1978; contbr. articles to profl. jours. Bd. dirs. Manpower Employment Orgn., Athens, 1982—, Ctr. de Formation Professionelle, Berlin, 1981—; mem. Adv. Com. Vocat. Tng. EEC, Brussels, 1981—; gen. sec. Companies' Assn. Vocat. Tng., Athens, 1980—. Mem. Tech. Chamber Greece, Assn. Mining Engrs., Comml. and Indsl. Chamber, Econ. Chamber Greece. Greek Orthodox. Home: 10 Agiou Andrea Str, 171 22 Nea Smyrni Greece Office: Titan Cement Co SA, 8 Dragatsaniou Str, 105 59 Athens Greece

BOUNDS, SARAH ETHELINE, historian; b. Huntsville, Ala., Nov. 5, 1942; d. Leo Deltis and Alice Etheline (Boone) Bounds; A.B., Birmingham-So. Coll., 1963; M.A., U. Ala., Tuscaloosa, 1965, Ed.S. in History, 1971, Ph.D., 1977. Tchr. social studies Huntsville City Schs., 1963, 65-66, 71-74; residence hall adv., dir. univ. housing U. Ala., Tuscaloosa, 1963-65, 68-71; instr. history N.E. State Jr. Coll., Rainsville, Ala., 1966-68; instr. history U. Ala., Huntsville, 1975, 78-80, 85—, dir. Weeden House Mus., 1981-83; asst. prof. edn., supr. student tchrs. U. North Ala., Florence, 1978. Mem. AAUW, Assn. Tchrs. Educators, Nat. Council Tchrs. Social Studies, NEA, Ala. Hist. Assn., Ala. Assn. Historians, Ala. Assn. Tchrs. Educators, Huntsville Hist. Soc., Historic Huntsville Found., Alpha Delta Kappa, Kappa Delta Pi, Phi Alpha Theta. Methodist. Club: Huntsville Pilot. Home: 1100 Bob Wallace Ave SE Huntsville AL 35801

BOUNDY, RAY HAROLD, chemical engineer; b. Brave, Pa., Jan. 10, 1903; s. George W. and Anetta (Cather) B.; m. Geraldine McCurdy, Nov. 27, 1926; children: Richard Ray, Lois Cather. B.S. in Chemistry, Grove City Coll., Pa., 1924; B.S., Case Western Res. U., 1926, M.S. in Chem. Engring, 1930; D.Sc. in Chemistry (hon.), Grove City (Pa.) Coll., 1961. With Dow Chem. Co., Midland, Mich., 1926-68; v.p., dir. research, corp. dir. Dow Chem. Co., 1951-68, cons. mgmt. of research, 1968—; vol. Internat. Exec. Service Corps., Taiwan and Iran, 1968—. Co-editor: Styrene, Its Polymers and Copolymers, 1951; Contbr. articles to profl. jours. Bd. dirs. Grove City Coll., Saginaw Valley State Coll. Recipient Gold medal Indsl. Research Inst., 1967; Alumni Achievement award Case Western Res. U., 1967; Alumni Achievement award Grove City Coll., 1968. Mem. NAM, Modern Pioneers in Creative Industry, Nat. Acad. Engring., Am. Chem. Soc., Am. Inst. Chem. Engrs., Sigma Xi. Clubs: Kiwanis, Torch, Midland Country, Boca Raton Hotel. Address: 600 S Ocean Blvd Apt 1503 Boca Raton FL 33432

BOUNKOULOU, BENJAMIN, diplomat; b. Kinkengue, Peoples Republic Congo, Sept. 25, 1942; m. Jacqueline Nzouzi, Apr. 20, 1967; 4 children. Lycee, Savorgnan of Brazza, Brazzaville, Peoples Republic Congo, 1963; postgrad., Congo Cen. Adminstrn., 1963-65; student, Internat. Inst. Pub. Adminstrn., Paris, 1965-67. Dir. African div. Peoples Republic Congo Ministry Fgn. Affairs, 1967-69; polit. dir. Ministry Fgn. Policy, 1969-71; gen. sec. Ministry of the Republic, 1971-75; itinerant ambassador, diplomatic advisor to Pres. Govt. of Peoples Republic Congo, 1975-76; ambassador to Angola 1976-79, ambassador in Algeria, Libya, Arab Republic Egypt, Mauritania, Tunisia, 1979-83, ambassador to Ethiopia, 1983-87, ambassador of Peoples Republic of Congo to U.S., 1987—. Office: Embassy of Peoples Republic of the Congo 4891 Colorado Ave NW Washington DC 20011

BOUQUET, FRANCIS LESTER, physicist; b. Enterprise, Oreg., Feb. 1, 1926; s. Francis Lester and Esther (Johnson) B.; m. Betty Jane Davis, Sept. 26, 1979; children: Tim, Jeffrey, Janet; stepchildren: John Perry, Peggy Korv. AA, U. Calif., Berkeley, 1948, BA, 1950; MA, UCLA, 1953. Physicist U.S. Radiol. Def. Lab., San Francisco, 1953-55; engr., mgr. Lockheed Aircraft Co., Burbank, Calif., 1955-74; physicist Jet Propulsion Lab., Pasadena, Calif., 1974—; cons. in field. Author: Solar Energy Simplified, 1984, 2d edit., 1987, Radiation Damage in Materials, 1985, Radiation Effects on Electronics, 1986, 2d edit., 1987, Introduction to Materials Engineering, 1986, 2d edit., 1987, Introduction to Seals, O-Rings and Gaskets, 1987; writer numerous govt. and industry reports; contbr. articles to sci. jours. Elder 1st Presbyn. Ch., Van Nuys, Calif. 1970-81. Served with U.S. Army, 1944-46, with Signal Corps U.S. Army, 1951-52, PTO. Recipient Eagle Scout Award Boy Scouts Am., 1940, Performance commendations Lockheed Aircraft Co., 1964, 66, Mgmt. Achievement Program award, 1973, 15 NASA awards, 1980-88; named to Honor Roll of Inventors, 1966. Mem. N.Y. Acad. Sci., Calif. Soc. Profl. Engrs., Nat. Soc. Profl. Engrs., IEEE (chmn. Los Angeles chpt. Nuclear and Plasma Scis. Soc. 1973-74), Am. Inst. Physics, AIAA, Nat. Mgmt. Assn., Air Force Assn., Lockheed Mgmt. Club, Caltech Mgmt. Club. Republican. Office: Jet Propulsion Lab 4800 Oak Grove Dr Mail Stop 89-1 Pasadena CA 91109

BOURBAN, ROGER ARSENE, restaurateur, athlete; b. Sion, Valais, Switzerland, May 10, 1948; came to U.S., 1972, naturalized, 1980; s. Marcel and Jeanne (Schmelzbach) B. Apprenticeship of cook, Restaurant/Hotel Touring, Sion, 1964-66, Ecole Hoteliere, De La Societe, Lausanne, 1967-69; student Nelson Sch., London, 1970. Sommelier, waiter Gitana Grill Room, Geneva, 1968; maitre D' Hotel De La Tête Noire, Rolle, Switzerland, 1970; sommelier Surfer's Paradise, Australia, 1971; mgr. New and Old El Camino Real, Sydney, Australia, 1972; chef La Chaumiere, Beverly Hills, Calif., 1972-74; capt. L'Ermitage, Los Angeles, 1974-75, Le Restaurant, Los Angeles, 1975-77; asst. dir. Habitation Leclerc Hotel, Port Au Prince, Haiti, 1978; capt. Ma Maison, Los Angeles, 1979-80; proprietor Cafe Monet Bistro, Los Angeles, 1980-82; gen. mgr. Nicky Blair's Restaurant, Hollywood, 1985-87; v.p., gen. ptnr. JCW Restaurant Devel. Group, 1987—; cons., actor in films, TV and commls.; product spokesperson; guest chef internat. TV appearances, 1980—; lectr and speaker in field; judge, ofcl. Running Waiters Races, worldwide, 1976—. Celebrity/fundraiser Calif. Spl. Olympics, 1980—, United Cerebral Palsy/Spastic Children's Found., 1980—, Am. Diabetes Assn., 1983— . Recipient 1st place award Open Judo Championship, Sydney, Australia, 1970; completed numerous waiter marathons. Mem. AFTRA, Screen Actors Guild. Roman Catholic. Home: PO Box 2992 Beverly Hills CA 90213 Office: care The Press Connection 320 N LaPeer Dr Suite 103 Beverly Hills CA 90211

BOURCIER, JACQUES ADAIR, communications executive; b. Paris, July 23, 1927; s. Georges Edmond and Violet Adair (Maitland) B.; m. Elizabeth Beatrice Ward-Jackson, Dec. 20, 1966; children—Simon, Catherine, Hugo. Student Malvern Coll., 1941-42, Harrow Sch., 1942-44. Journalist, various locations, 1946-59; press asst. to chmn. The Thomson Orgn., Can., 1955-59; mng. dir. The Newspaper Service Ltd., London, 1959-72; chmn. bd. Internat. Press Europe, London, 1972—; dir. Universal-PA. Conservative. Roman Catholic. Office: Internat Press Europe, 46-47 Pall Mall, London SW1 England

BOURDAIS DE CHARBONNIERE, ERIC, banker; b. Boulogne sur Seine, France, July 1, 1939; s. Roger and Edithe (Chesnot) BdeC.; m. Jill Hollister Adams, Aug. 30, 1968. BA, Lycée Michelet, Paris; MBA, Ecole des Hautes Etudes Commerciales, Jouy-en-Josas, France, 1963. With Morgan Guaranty Trust Co., Paris, 1965-73; with Morgan Guaranty Trust Co., N.Y.C., 1974-79; v.p., head treas. Morgan Guaranty Trust Co., Paris, 1979-81, v.p., mgr. gal, 1981-83, sr. v.p., area head, 1983-85, sr. v.p., group exec., 1985-87, exec. v.p., head Europe, Middle East and Africa, 1987—; bd. dirs. IBM World Trade Europe MEA, Paris, IBM World Trade Europe, Mid. East and Africa Corp.; pres. Morgan & Cie S.A., 1981—. Recipient Chevalier des Arts et Lettres award Ministry of Culture, Paris, 1985. Club: Automobile (Paris). Office: JP Morgan Guaranty Trust Co NY, 14 Place Vendôme, 75001 Paris France

BOURDILLON, MICHAEL FRANCIS CHARLES, social anthropology educator; b. Kasama, Zambia, Oct. 3, 1942; s. Victor Edmund and Marjorie Caroline Agnes (Robson) B. Student, St. George's Coll., Harare, Zimbabwe, 1953-60; diploma in Sociology and Anthropology, Oxford (Eng.) U., 1972, M in Letters, DPhil, 1972; Lic. Phil, Heythrop Coll., Chipping Norton, Eng., 1966. Lectr. U. Rhodesia, Harare, 1972-75; sr. lectr. U. Calabar, Nigeria, 1977-80; reader, assoc. prof. sociology U. Zimbabwe, Harare, 1980—. Author: Shona Peoples, 1976, 87, Christianity South of the Zambezi, 1977, Sacrifice, 1980, Studies of Fishing on Lake Kariba, 1986; contbr. numerous articles to profl. jours. Fellow Royal Anthropol. Inst., Assn. Social Anthropologistsof the Commonwealth, Current Anthropology; mem. Internat. African Inst. Roman Catholic. Office: U Zimbabwe, Dept Sociology, Box MP167, Harare Zimbabwe

BOURG, BONNIE JEAN, university administrator; b. New Orleans, Feb. 17, 1927; d. Francis Floyd and Malvin Marguerite (Boudreaux) Bourg; B.A., H. Sophie Newcomb Coll. of Tulane U., 1947; M.S., La. State U., 1948, Ph.D., 1979. Instr. in health and phys. edn. F.T. Nicholls Jr. Coll., La. State U. (name later changed to Nicholls State U.), 1947-50, head dept. women's health and phys. edn. 1950-63, dean women, 1963-77, dean student devel., 1977, asst. v.p. student affairs, 1977-83, asst. v.p. acad. affairs, dean freshman div., 1983-86, v.p. student affairs, 1986—, also prof. edn.; dir. Intracoastal Co., 1973—; adv. bd. Schriever br. 1st Nat. Bank of Houma (La.), 1978-88. Mem. City of Thibodaux (La.) Planning Commn., 1967-75; bd. dirs. Le Petit Theatre de Terrebonne, 1955-65, pres., 1958; State Chair La. Cath. Bishops Task Force on Women. Recipient Pres.'s award Nicholls State U., 1975, named Hon. Alumna, 1975, Disting. Service award, 1980, Bishop's Service award Diocese of Houma-Thibodaux, 1984, Vol. Activist award, 1987; Delta Kappa Gamma Soc. Internat. Epsilon State scholar, 1975-76, Internat. scholar, 1978-79; certified tchr., counselor, La. Mem. Nat., La. assns. women deans, adminstrs. and counselors Am., Assn. Counseling and Devel., Nat. Assn. Student Personnel Adminstrs., Am. Coll. Personnel Assn. La. Folklore Soc., Terrebonne Hist. Soc., Delta Kappa Gamma, Phi Delta Kappa, Phi Mu, Delta Psi Kappa, Alpha Psi Omega, Phi Kappa Phi. Office: Box 2008 Nicholls State U Thibodaux LA 70301

BOURGEOIS, LOUISE, sculptor; b. Paris, Dec. 25, 1911; came to U.S., 1938, naturalized, 1953; d. Louis and Josephine (Fauriaux) B.; m. Robert Goldwater, Sept. 12, 1938; children: Michel, Jean-Louis, Alain. Baccalaureat Ecole des Beaux Artis, U. Paris, 1934; postgrad., Ecole du Louvre, 1936, 37, 38, Academie Ranson (Atelier Bissiere), 1936-37, Academie de la Grand Chaumiere (Atelier Vlerick), 1937-38, Academie Julian; also with, Fernand Legar, 1938; D.F.A. (hon.), Yale U., 1977. Docent Louvre, 1937-38; teaching asst. Atelier Yves Brayer, Grande Chaumiere, 1937, 38; tchr. Great Neck (NY) Schs., program, 1960, Bklyn. Coll., 1963-68; tchr. Pratt Inst., 1965-67, Goddard Coll., 1970. One-woman shows include, Norlyst Gallers, 1947, Peridot Gallery, 1949, 50, 53, Allan Frumkin Gallery, Chgo., 1953, White Art Mus., Cornell U., Ithaca, N.Y., 1959, Stable Gallery, 1964, Rose Fried Gallery, 1964, Mus. Modern Art, N.Y.C., 1982, Akron Art Mus., 1983, Contemporary Art Mus., Houston, 1983, Daniel Weinberg Gallery, Los Angeles, 1984, Robert Miller Gallery, 1984, Serpentine Gallery, London, 1985, Naeght-Lelong, Zurich, 1985, Paris, 1985; exhibited in numerous group shows, U.S., Europe, including 64th Whitney Biennial, 1987; represented in permanent collections Mus. Modern Art, N.Y.C., Whitney Mus,, R.I. Sch. Design, NYU, also pvt. collections; works reproduced in Contemporary Sculpture (Giedion Welker), 1955, Sculpture of This Century (Michel Seuphor), 1959, Form and Space (Trier), 1961, A Concise History of Modern Sculpture, (Herbert Read), 1964, Modern American Sculpture (Dore Ashton), 1968, History of Modern Art (H.H. Arnason), 1968, What is Modern Sculpture, 1969, Sculpture in Wood (J.C. Rich), 1970, numerous others, also various mags. Recipient Pres.'s Fellow award R.I. Sch. Design, 1984. Mem. Sculptors Guild, Am. Abstract Artists, Coll. Art Assn., Women's Caucus (Outstanding Achievement award 1980), La Jeune Sculpture, Paris. Address: care Robert Miller Gallery 41 E 57th St New York NY 10022-1908 *

BOURGEOIS-PICHAT, JEAN LOUIS ERNEST, demography educator; b. Lizy-sur-Ourcq, France, June 21, 1912; s. Maurice and Marguerite (Tetu) B.; m. Rita Pichat, June 19, 1942; 1 child, Yolande. Ph.D. equivalent, Ecole Poly., 1933. Research worker Foundation Française pour l'etude des problemes humains, Paris, 1944, 45; research dir. Inst. Nat. d'etudes Demographiques, 1945-53; dep. dir. Population div. N.Y. of UN, 1953-62; dir. I.N.E.D., Paris, 1962-71; chmn. com. for internat. coop. in Nat. Research in Demography, 1972—; prof. demography Inst. d'Etudes Politiques, Paris, 1978—. Mem. Internat. Union for Sci. Study of Population, Internat. Stats. Inst. Roman Catholic. Home: 30 rue Montrosier, 92200 Neuilly sur Seine France Office: CICRED, 27 rue du Commandeur, Paris France

BOURGERY, MARC EDMOND CLEMENT, advertising executive; b. Tientsin, China, May 8, 1941; came to France, 1952; s. Edmond Marc and Marjorie Phyllis (Pearson) B.; m. Chantal Anne Bergeault, June 6, 1986; 1 child, Luc. Diploma, Hautes Etudes Commerciales, Paris, 1966. Researcher Secodip, Paris, 1969-72; group head Feldman Calleux Assocs., Paris, 1972-74, comml. mgr., 1974-75, mng. dir., 1975—; v.p. mng. dir. Group FCA, Suresnes, France, 1983—. Office: FCA, 26 Rue Salomon de Rothschild, 92150 Suresnes France

BOURGUIBA, HABIB BEN ALI, former president of Tunisia; b. Monastir, Aug. 3, 1903; student U. Paris, Faculty of Law, Ecole Libre des Sciences Politiques; m. Ouassila Ben Ammar, May 1962; 1 son, Habib. Mem. Destour Party, 1921; writer for The Voice of the Tunisian, 1930-32; founded The Tunisian Action, 1932; formed Neo-Destour Party, 1934; imprisoned by French, 1934-36, 38-42; exiled 5 years; toured to promote Tunisian independence, 1945-49; imprisoned, 1952; released from imprisonment 1954; pres. Tunisian Nat. Assembly, prime minister, pres. council, minister fgn. affairs and def., 1956; pres. Republic of Tunisia, 1957-87, named pres. for life, 1975; mem. 11th Gen. Assembly UN. Address: Office of the Pres, Tunis Tunisia *

BOURKE, WILLIAM OLIVER, metals company executive; b. Chgo., Apr. 12, 1927; s. Robert Emmett and Mable Elizabeth (D'Arcy) B.; m. Elizabeth Philbey, Sept. 4, 1970; children: William Oliver, Judith A., Andrew E., Edward A. Student, U. Ill., 1944-45; B.S. in Commerce, DePaul U., 1951. With Ford Motor Co., Dearborn, Mich., 1956-60, nat. distbn. mgr., 1960-64; gen. sales mgr. Ford Can., Toronto, Ontario, 1964-67; asst. mng. dir. Ford Australia, Melbourne, 1967-70, mng. dir., 1970-71; pres. Ford Asia-Pacific and South Africa, Inc., Melbourne, 1971-72, Ford Asia-Pacific, Inc., Melbourne, 1972-73; pres. Europe, Inc., 1973-75, chmn. bd., 1975-80; exec. v.p. Ford N.Am. Automotive Ops., Dearborn, 1981-83, also bd. dirs.; exec. v.p. Reynolds Metals Co., Richmond, Va., 1981-83, pres., chief operating officer, 1983-86, pres., chief exec. officer, 1986-88, chief exec. officer, chmn. of the bd., 1988—, also bd. dirs.; bd. dirs. Kraft, Inc., Merrill Lynch, U.S. C. of C. Served to 1st lt. MI U.S. Army, 1944-48. Mem. U.S. C. of C. Office: Reynolds Metals Co 6601 Broad St Rd Richmond VA 23261 also: Can Reynolds Metals Co Ltd, 420 Sherbrooke St W, Montreal, PQ Canada H3G 1K9

BOURNE, KENNETH, historian, educator; b. Wickford, Eng., Mar. 17, 1930; s. Clarence Arthur and Doris (English) B.; m. Eleanor Anne Wells, Jan. 1, 1955; 2 children. BA, Exeter U., 1951; PhD, London Sch. Econs., 1955. Research fellow Inst. Hist. Research, London, 1955-56, Reading (Eng.) U., 1956; lectr. internat. history London Sch. Econs., 1957-69, reader, 1969-76, prof., 1976—, bd. govs., 1986—; sr. research fellow Fulbright/Brit. Assn. for Am. Studies, Washington, 1961-62; vis. lectr. U. Calif., Davis, 1966-67; Scaife disting. lectr. Kenyon Coll., Gambier, Ohio, 1971; Kratter prof. Stanford (Calif.) U., 1979; Harrison prof. Coll. William and Mary, Williams-burg, Va., 1984-85; vis. prof. U. Colo., 1988; mem. Inst. for Advanced Study, Princeton. Author: Britain and Balance of Power in North America, 1967 (Corey prize 1969), Foreign Policy of Victorian England, 1970, Palmerston, 1983; co-editor: British Documents on Foreign Affairs, 1983. Bd. govs. Wilson's Grammar Sch., London, 1970-75, Wilson's Sch., Sutton, Eng., 1972-84; senator U. London, 1987—. Fellow Royal Hist. Soc., Brit. Acad. Home: 15 Oakcroft Rd, London SE13 7ED, England Office: London Sch Econs, Houghton St, London WC2A 2AE, England

BOURNE, MARY BONNIE MURRAY (MRS. SAUL HAMILTON BOURNE), music publishing company executive; b. Salix, Iowa, Sept. 13, 1903; d. Thomas William and Kathryn (McDermott) Murray; student Morningside Normal Coll., 1922-23; student Am. Banking Inst., N.Y.C.; m. Saul Hamilton Bourne, Apr. 12, 1928; 1 dau., Mary Elizabeth. Appeared with George White Scandals, Ramblers, Cocoanuts, Ziegfield Follies, 1925-28; owner, mgr. Bourne Co., N.Y.C., 1960—. Mem. social work recruiting com. United Hosp. Fund. Trustee S.H. Bourne Found., Coll. New Rochelle; trustee N.Y. Infirmary, 1945—, chmn. social service youth bd., 1947—, bd. visitors Sch. Music, Catholic U. Am., Washington. Mem. A.S.C.A.P. (dir., pubs. adv. com.). Home: 14 E 75th St New York NY 10021 Office: 5 W 37th St New York NY 10016

BOURQUE, JEAN-JACQUES, psychiatrist; b. Windsor, Que., Can., Sept. 22, 1937; s. Hervé and Jeanne (Frédette) B.; BA, Laval U., Qué., 1959, MD, 1964; diploma in psychiatry McGill U., Montreal, Que., 1972; m. Marguerite Danièle Houle, Jan. 2, 1961; children: Dominique, Pierre. Intern, Hôtel Dieu, Quebec City, 1963-64; resident in psychiatry Royal Victoria Hosp., Montreal, 1968, Douglas Hosp., Montreal, 1969, Albert Prévost Inst., Montreal, 1970, Ste. Justine's Hosp., Montreal, 1971; practice medicine specializing in psychiatry, Montreal, 1972-76; dir. outpatient team for adolescence, Charles LeMoyne Hosp., Montreal, 1974-80, dir. child and adolescence service, 1980-86; dir. adolescent service Allan Meml. Inst. Royal Victoria Hosp., 1975; demonstrator McGill U., 1975; clin. demonstrator U. Montreal, 1977—; assoc. Richardson Mgmt. Assocs. Ltd., 1988—. Served officer M.C., Can. Army, 1964-68. Fellow Royal Coll. Physicians (Can.); mem. Soc. Québécoise des Psychiatres de L'Adolescence (pres. 1978-82), Am. Soc. Adolescent Psychiatry, Que. Psychiatrists Assn. (pres. 1984-88), Can. Med. Assn., Assn. French Physicians Que. Roman Catholic. Office: Hopital Charles LeMoyne, 121 Boul Taschereau, Greenfield Park, PQ Canada J4V 2H1

BOUSEMAN, JOHN KEITH, entomologist, naturalist; b. Clinton, Iowa, Aug. 11, 1936; s. Thomas Elmer and Kathryn Teresa (Van Buer) B.; m. Barbara Ann Busby, Aug. 21, 1956; children—Karen, David, Thomas, Lynn, Paul; m. 2d, Tamara Faye Moore, Oct. 15, 1977; 1 child, William. B.S. in Entomology, U. Ill., 1960, M.S. in Entomology, 1962. Registered profl. entomologist, Ill. Expdn. entomologist Am. Mus. Natural History, Uruguayan Expdn., 1963, Bolivian Expdn., 1964, 65; instr. U. Ill., Urbana, 1965-66; asst. entomologist agrl. entomology Ill. Agrl. Expt. Sta., Urbana, 1972—; asst. entomologist Ill. Natural History Survey, Champaign, 1972-84, assoc. entomologist, 1984—; entomol. expdns. to Bolivia, Brazil, Paraguay, Zambia, Uruguay, Venezuela, W.I., Mex.; cons. Zambia Ministry Agr. and Water Devel., 1984; mem. tech. adv. com. on mgmt. Ill. Nature Preserves Commn., 1985—. Sci. Research Soc. Am. grantee, 1961; NSF grantee, 1982. Mem. Am. Entomol. Soc., Coleopterists Soc., N.Y. Acad. Sci., N.Y. Entomol. Soc., Internat. Soc. Hymenopterists, Mich. Entomol. Soc., Torrey Bot. Club, Entomol. Soc. Washington, Kans. Entomol. Soc., Sigma Xi. Club: Ill. Field Entomologists (Champaign). Contbr. numerous publ. to profl. jours. Office: Ill Natural History Survey 607 E Peabody Champaign IL 61820

BOUSTANY, SALADIN YOUSSEF, publisher, writer; b. Cairo, Apr. 7, 1927; s. Cheikh Youssef T. and Victoria Boustany; m. Venus, Feb. 24, 1963; children—Fadwa, Fida, Tamer. M.A., Am. U. Cairo, 1951. Journalist, al-Muqattam, Cairo, from 1947, Al-Ahram, Cairo, Le Journal d'Egypte, Cairo, al-Zaman, Cairo, to 1954; pub. Arab Bookshop, Cairo, 1951—; importer/exporter of books; agt. Library of Congress, Cairo, 1960—. Author: The Press During the French Expedition in Egypt, 1798-1801; Proverbs from East and West; The Wall of Shame in Berlin; Beethoven; Wagner; The Journals of Bonaparte in Egypt, 1798-1801; Bonaparte's Egypt in Picture and Word 1789-1801; Canal Zone Suez Battle 1951-52; The Secret British Military Press of the Canal Zone Battle 1951-51; editor: Pan Islamism: al' Urwat al-Wuthqa of Gamal al-Din al-Afghani and Muhammad 'Abduh. Rotary Internat. Paul Harris fellow, 1978. Roman Catholic. Lodge: Rotary. Office: Arab Bookshop, 28 Faggalah St PO Box 32, Faggalah Cairo Egypt

BOUTARIC, JEAN-JOSE ETIENNE, physician, writer; b. Tours, France, Jan. 11, 1938; s. Philippe Louis and Marthe Marie Julie (Dou) B.; m. Michele Annick Salaun; Nov. 5, 1966; children: Anne, Jean-Philippe, François. MD, U. Lyon, 1962, Lauréat, 1963; cert. specialized study in anesthesiology, U. Paris, 1971; Diplôme d'Etudes Approfondies d'Histoire et Philosophie des Scis., U. Paris, Sorbonne, 1987. Physician French Air Force, 1964-69; anesthesiologist Hopitaux de l'Assistance Pub., Paris, 1969-71; anesthesiologist at pvt. clinic Paris, 1971-80; gen. practice medicine Brunoy, France, 1980—; sec. gen. de Assn. Sauver les documents en Péril de la Bibliothéque Nat., 1988—. Author essays, novels, case studies, short stories. Served to capt. French Health Service, 1966-69. Recipient Cesare Pavese prize, 1987. Mem. Groupement des Ecrivains Medecins (adj. sec. gen. 1987—). Roman Catholic. Home and Office: 17 Rue de Cercay, 91800 Brunoy France

BOUTERSE, DESIRE, government official of the Republic of Suriname. Army officer, co-founder and head (Nationale Militaire Raad-NMR), 1980—, lead mil. coup, 1982, head of state, 1982-88, comdr.-in-chief of Nat. Army, Paramaribo, 1982-88. Office: Office of Head of State, Paramaribo Suriname *

BOUTILLIER, ROBERT JOHN, accountant; b. Newark, Jan. 1, 1924; s. William and Millicent (Davies) B.; m. Marie C. Humphries, June 24, 1945; children: Robert Allan, Suzanne Marie. B.S., Rutgers U., 1948. C.P.A., N.J. With Peat, Marwick, Mitchell & Co., 1943-82, ptnr., 1955-82, ptnr. charge Newark office, 1960-70, mem. adv. com. and Eastern area, ptnr., 1965-70, ptnr. in charge U.S. ops., 1970-77, vice-chmn., 1977, ret., 1982; lectr. Rutgers U.; dir. Prudential Ins. Co. Am., Howard Savs. Bank. Bd. dirs. Newark YM-YWCA.; trustee Rutgers, The State U. Mem. Am. Inst. C.P.A.s, N.J. Soc. C.P.A.s, Newark Jaycees (pres. 1956-57, Outstanding Young Man of Yr. 1957), Newark Assn. Commerce and Industry, Delta Sigma Pi, Beta Gamma Sigma. Republican. Presbyterian. Clubs: Rotary of N.Y, Baltusrol Golf (past pres., gov.), Echo Lake Country, Seaview Country, Ocean Reef. Home and Office: 920 Minisink Way Westfield NJ 07090

BOUVENG, NILS HARALD, aluminum executive; b. Stockholm, Apr. 26, 1929; s. Nils Erik and Elsa Marianne (Hojer) B.; m. Kerstin Berlin, May 10, 1956; children—Kristian, Susanna, Helena, Katarina. M.S. in Mech. Engring., U. Chalmers, Sweden, 1956. Project mgr. Rosengren AB, Gothenburg, Sweden, 1956-58; design engr. Green Bay Paper Converting Machine (Wis.), 1958-60; research engr. Nat. Anilin Div., Hopewell, Va., 1960-62; vice mng. dir. Skandinaviska Aluminum Profiler AB, Vetlanda, Sweden, 1963-77, mng. dir., 1977-88, chmn., 1988—; bd. dirs. Granges Aluminum, Stockholm. Office: Skandinaviska Aluminium, Profiler AB, 57481 Vetlanda Sweden

BOUVIER, CHRISTIAN RENÉ, audit manager, administration educator; b. Paris, Nov. 13, 1940; s. Raymond and Charlotte (Mirault) B.; m. Jacqueline Boulard, Nov. 4, 1968; children: Romuald, Aldric, Thibault, Astrid. Capitaine au long Cñurs, 1967; CPA, France. Mate and fist mate Mcht. Navy, 1960-68, with mktg. dept., then fin. dept. IBM, Paris, 1969-84; audit dir. Hutchinson then Nouvelles-Galeries, 1984-88. Author: Audit and Computer, 1983. Served with French Navy, 1961-62. Mem. Inst. Internal Auditors. Roman Catholic. Home: 68 Rue de l'Ermitage, 95320 Saint-Leu-la-Forêt France Office: 66 Rue des Archives, 75003 Paris France

BOUVIER, JOHN ANDRE, JR., lawyer, corporate executive, legal and financial consultant; b. nr. Ocala, Fla., May 16, 1903; s. John Andre and Ella (Richardson) B.; m. Helen A. Schaefer, June 6, 1928 (dec. 1983); children: Helen Elizabeth (Mrs. William Spencer), John Andre III, Thomas Richardson; m. Barbara Carney; children: Mark B. Carney, Kevin P. Carney. Student, Davidson Coll., 1922-24; AB, U. Fla., 1926, LLB, 1929, JD, 1969; MBA, Northwestern U., Evanston, Ill., 1930; LHD (hon.), Windham Coll., 1977; D of Commerce (hon.), Ft. Lauderdale Coll., 1985. Bar: Fla. bar 1929. Practiced in Gainesville, 1929, Miami, 1930—; specialist corp., real estate and probate law, cons. atty.; gen. counsel Patterson & Maloney, Ft. Lauderdale; chmn. exec. com. Permutit Co., 1964-73; chmn. bd. Prosperity Co.; vice chmn. bd. Ward Indsl. Corp.; chmn. bd., pres. Pantex Mfg. Corp., Nat. Leasing Inc., Miami; pres. Knaust Bros., Inc., K-B Products Corp., Iron Mountain Atomic Storage Vaults, Inc., West Kingsway, Inc., East Kingsway, Inc., South Kingsway, Inc.; pres., dir. Ace Solar Constrn. Co., Southport Apts., BMB Devel. Co., Hendricks Devel. Corp.; sec. 50th St. Heights, Inc., Knight Manor, Inc., Dade Constrn. Co. (all Miami), Karen Club Apt. Hotel, Ft. Lauderdale, C&S Banking Corp., Landmark Banking Corp. Fla., Farquhar Machinery Co. Author monographs, newspaper articles in field. Bd. dirs. Syracuse Govtl. Research Bur.; dir., sec. Wilson Garden Apts. Inc. Commr., Dade County council Boy

Scouts Am.; chmn. Malecon Com. Dade County; mem. Planning Council Zoning Bd. Miami; chmn. Coxsackie-Athens Area Redevel. Com.; vice chmn. Nat. Parkinson Found.; bd. dirs., trustee Miami Boys Clubs; trustee Windham Coll., Westminster Manor, Gateway Terrace. Mem. Internat. Platform Assn., Am. Judicature Soc., Am., Fla., Dade County, Broward County bar assns., Miami C. of C., Sigma Chi (Order of Constance). Presbyterian. Clubs: Miami Beach Rod and Reel, Riviera Country, Ft. Lauderdale Yacht, Skaneateles (N.Y.) Country, Ponte Vedra Country, Tower, Capitol Hill. Lodge: Masons, Shriners, Elks, Rotary. Home: 608 Intracoastal Dr Fort Lauderdale FL 33304 Office: 6888 NW 7th Ave Miami FL 33150 also: Bienvenue Blowing Rock NC 28605 also: Box 14 Climax NY 12042 Mailing Address: Box 7254 Fort Lauderdale FL 33338

BOUVIER, MARSHALL ANDRE, lawyer; b. Jacksonville, Fla., Sept. 30, 1923; s. Marshall and Helen Marion B.; m. Zepha Windle, July 11, 1938; children—Mark A., Marshall Andre III, Debra Bouvier Zanetti, Michael A., Jennifer Lynn, John A. Bouvier (dec.), Wendy Karen. A.B., Emory U., LL.B., 1949. Bar: Ga. 1948, Nev. 1960. Commd. U.S. Navy, 1949; naval aviator, judge advocate; ret., 1959; atty. State of Nevada, 1959-60; sole practice law, Reno, 1960-82; dist. atty. Storey County (Nev.), 1982—. Mem. Judge Advocates Assn., Phi Delta Phi, Sigma Chi. Clubs: Ancient and Honorable Order Quiet Birdmen, Rotary, E Clampus Vitus.

BOUVILLE, LUC, physician; b. Boreaux, Gironde, France, June 18, 1950; s. Jules and Nicheline (Dubo) B.; m. Beatrice Daney, June 17, 1985 (div. 1985); children: Antoine, Alexia, Amandine; m. Monique Neveu, June 1, 1987; 1 child, Pierre-Arthur. Baccalaureat, U. Paris, 1968. Docteur de Travaux Protiques Societe Medicale de Biotherapie, Paris, 1976-77, prof. d'acupuncture, v.p., 1977-86; prof. L'Academie Medicale d'Acupuncture, 1981-86; secretaire gen. L'Union Syndicale des Medecines Acupunctures, France, 1984—. v.p. de l'amociation de Repherchez et etudes du l'acupuncture, Toulouse, France, 1985—. Served to capt. French Armed Forces, 1976-77. Lodge: Rotary. Home: 25 Rue Rolland, 33000 Bordeaux Gironde France Office: Institut Helio Marin, 8 Rue Franklin, 33000 Bordeaux Gironde France

BOUWELS, LEON HENRI ROBERT, cardiologist; b. Budel, Brabant, The Netherlands, Oct. 26, 1952; m. Van Ool Agmj, 1980; children: Ronald, Thomas, Caspar. MD, U. Nymegen, 1981. Intern St. Joseph Hosp., Eindhoven, The Netherlands, 1979, U. Hosp., Nymegen, The Netherlands, 1980; resident Acad. Hosp., Maastricht, The Netherlands, 1982-87; cardiologist Canisius Wilhelmina Hosp., Nymegen, The Netherlands, 1987—. Contbr. articles to profl. jours. Mem. Dutch Med. Assn., Dutch Cardiology Assn. Office: Canisius Wilhelmina Hosp, Annastraat, Nijmegen Holland The Netherlands

BOUYGUES, FRANCIS GEORGES, industrialist; b. Paris, Dec. 5, 1922; Dipolma in E.C.P. Sch. of Engring, diploma in C.P.A. Bus. Tng. Ctr., diploma of C. of C., Paris; s. Georges B. and Edmee nee Regnault (Marr) B.; m. Monique Teze, Oct. 26, 1946; children: Corinne, Nicolas, Martin, Olivier. Founder Bouygues Group, Clamart, France, 1951; v.p. found. pour entreprendre. chmn. chief exec. officer Bouygues Co., first French TV Sta. Decorated Officer of the Legion of Honour, Comdr. of Nat. Order of Merit. Ach. yachting, hunting, fishing. Home: 14 rue des Sablons, F 75116 Paris France Office: 1 ave Eugene Freyssinet, 78061 Saint Quentin en Yvelines France

BOUZAR, WADIE, writer, educator; b. Rabat, Morocco, Aug. 14, 1938; parents: Abdelkader and Catherine (Martinelli) B. Licence ès Lettres, U. Strasbourg, France, 1969; D d'Etat ès Lettres et Scis. Humaines (Sociologie), U. Tours, France, 1980, lettres u sciences humaines (sociologie), 1980. Prof. French High Schs., Algeria, France, 1963-71; from asst. prof. to titular prof. U. Algiers, Algeria, 1971-84; with Inst. des langues étrangères U. Algiers, Bouzaréa, 1988—. Author: La Culture en Question, 1982, La Mouvance et la Pause, 1983, Lectures Maghrébines, 1984, Les Fleuves ont Toujours deux Rives, 1986 (Prix de L'Afrique Méditerraneénne award, Paris); contbr. numerous articles and papers in field. Mem. Pen Club, Assn. des Ecrivains de Langue FranÇaise, Assn. Internat. des Sociologues de Langue FranÇaise, Lab. de Sociologie-U. Paris, Arab Sociol. Assn. Home: 98 Ave Ali Khodja, Algiers Algeria Office: Inst des Lang étrangères, U d'Alger, Bouzaréa, Alger Algeria

BOVA, VINCENT ARTHUR, JR., lawyer, consultant; b. Pitts., Apr. 25, 1946; s. Vincent A. and Janie (Pope) B.; m. Breda Murphy, Mar. 20, 1971; 1 dau., Kate Murphy. B.A. in Bus. Adminstrn., Alma Coll., 1968; M.P.A., Ohio State U., 1972; J.D., Oklahoma City U., 1975. Bar: Okla. 1975, N.Mex. 1976, U.S. Dist. Ct. 1976, U.S. Tax Ct., 1976, U.S. Ct. Appeals (10th cir.) 1976, U.S. Supreme Ct. 1979. Mktg. and systems rep., computer systems div. RCA, 1968-70; research analyst Research Atlanta, 1972-73; assoc. Threet, Threet, Glass, King & Maxwell, 1976-78; ptnr. Lill & Bova, P.A., 1978-81; sole practice, Albuquerque, 1981—. Bd. dirs. Salvation Army. Served with Air N.G., 1969-75. Recipient Pacesetters award Ohio State U., 1972; named one of Outstanding Young Men of Am., 1975, 76. Mem. Assn. Trial Lawyers Am. (advanced grad. Nat. Coll. Advocacy), Ct. Practice Inst. (advanced diplomate), ABA, N.Mex. Bar Assn., N.Mex. Trial Lawyers Assn., Internat. Assn. Fin. Planners, Nat. Assn. Social Security Claimants Reps. (past state chmn.), Business Round Table, Albuquerque Bar Assn., Fumilan Investment Club (past pres.), N.Mex. Fin. Planning Assn., Sole Practitioners Assn., Internat. Credit Assn. (lectr.), Phi Alpha Delta, Sigma Tau Gamma. Democrat. Presbyterian. Clubs: Toastmasters, Bare Bulls, Ltd., Millionaires Tip. Address: 5716 Osuna NE Albuquerque NM 87109

BOVET, DANIEL, physiologist; b. Neuchatel, Switzerland, 1907; s. Pierre and Amy (Babut) B.; m. Filomena Nitti, 1938; 1 son. Dr.Sci., U. Geneva; hon. doctorates U. Palermo, U. Rio de Janeiro, others. Asst. in physiology U. Geneva, 1928-29; asst. Inst. Pasteur, Paris, 1929-39, dir. lab., 1939-47; dir. labs. therapeutic chemistry Istituto Superiore di Sanità, Rome, 1947-64; prof. pharmacology U. Sassari, 1964-71; prof. psychobiology U. Rome, 1971-82, hon. prof., 1982—; dir. lab. psychobiology and psychopharmacology Consiglio Nazionale della Richerche, 1969-75. Author: (with others) Structure chimique et activité pharmacodynamique des medicaments du système nerveux vegetatif, 1948; (with others) Curare and Curare-like Agents, 1959; (with others) Controlling Drugs, 1974. Recipient Nobel prize for physiology and medicine, 1957; decorated grand officer Order Italian Republic. Mem. Accademia Nazionale dei Lincei, Royal Soc. (Eng.) (fgn.). *

BOVON, FRANCOIS, professor; b. Lausanne, Vaud, Switzerland, Mar. 13, 1938; s. André and Hélène (Mayor) B.; m. Thurneysen Annegreth; children: Pierre, Martin. BTh, U. Lausanne, 1961; ThD, U. Basel, Switzerland, 1965. Pastor Eglise Réformée, Canton de Vaud, Switzerland, 1965-67; prof. U. Geneva, 1967—; co-editor Revue de Theologie et de Philosophie, Lausanne, 1977-86, Studia Biblica, Leiden, The Netherlands, 1983—. Author: (patristics and New Testament) De Vocatione Gentium, 1967, Luc le Théologien, 1968, Lukas in Neuer Sicht, 1985, L'oeuvre de Luc, 1987. Mem. Studiorum Novi Testamenti Societas, Assn. pour L'étude de la Littérature Apocryphe Chrétienne (pres. 1981-87), Soc. Suisse de Théologie (pres. 1973-77). Home: Chemin de la Paix, CH 1261, Genolier Switzerland Office: U Geneva, Faculté de Théologie, 1211 Geneva Switzerland

BOVY, JEAN-CLAUDE PIERRE, cardiologist; b. Paris, Mar. 22, 1934; s. Roger Felix and Marie-Helene (Laurent) B.; m. Monique Mazzoli, July 1, 1978; children: Marie Caroline, Frederic, Julie, Magali, Hadrien. BS Physics, Chemistry and Biology, 1954, MD, 1957. Externe des hopitaux Assistance Publique, Paris, 1957-61; practice medicine specializing in cardiology Cassis, 1961—; doctor Prefecture Bouches du Rhône, Marseille, 1985—. Served to capt. French Med. Corps, 1961-63. Club: Cercle Nautique de Cassis.

BOWATER, MARIAN LARSON, retired art gallery director; b. Emmons, Minn., Sept. 5, 1924; d. James Melvin and Hannah Elvira (Olson) Larson; student Gustavus Adolphus Coll., 1941-42; m. John J. Bowater, Jan. 22, 1945; children—Christine, Julianna, John James. Owner, dir. Bowater Gallery of Fine Art, Los Angeles, 1975-86; active mus. shows; lectr. art clubs. Mem. Art Dealers Assn. So. Calif. Home: 1168 Wales Pl Cardiff-by-the-Sea CA 92007

BOWDEN, ANN, bibliographer, educator; b. East Orange, N.J., Feb. 7, 1924; d. William and Anna Elisabeth (Herrstrom) Haddon; m. Edwin Turner Bowden, June 12, 1948; children: Elisabeth Bowden Ward, Susan Turner, Edwin Eric; m. 2d, William Burton Todd, Nov. 23, 1969. BA, Radcliffe Coll., 1948; MS in Library Services, Columbia U., 1951; PhD, U. Tex., 1975. Cataloger, reference asst. Yale U., 1948-53; manuscript cataloger, rare book librarian, librarian Humanities Research Ctr., librarian Acad. Ctr., U. Tex., Austin, 1958-63, lectr., sr. lectr. Grad. Sch. Library and Info. Sci., 1964-85, 88—; coordinator adult services Austin Pub. Library, 1963-67, asst. dir., 1967-71, dep. dir., 1971-77, assoc. dir., 1977-86; bd. dirs. Tex. Info. Exchange, Houston, 1977-78; bd. dirs. AMIGOS Bibliog. Council, Dallas, 1978-82, chmn. bd., 1980-81, trustee emeritus, 1986—; chmn. AMIGOS '85 Plan, 1984-86; scholar in residence Rockefeller Found. Villa Serbelloni, Bellagio, Italy, 1986. Author (with W.B. Todd) Tauchnitz International Editions in English, 1988; editor: T.E. Lawrence Fifty Letters: 1921-1935, 1962; Maps and Atlases, 1978; assoc. editor Papers of the Bibliographical Soc. Am., 1967-82; contbr. articles to profl. jours. Served as cpl. USMC Women's Res., 1944-46. Mem. ALA (council 1975-79), Assn. Coll. and Research Libraries (chmn. rare book and manuscript sect. 1975-76), Tex. Library Assn. (chmn. publs. com. 1965-71), Bibliog. Soc. Am., Phi Kappa Phi, Kappa Tau Alpha. Club: Grolier (N.Y.C.).

BOWDEN, THOMAS JEFFERSON, engineer; b. Jacksonville, Fla., Aug. 14, 1919; s. Frederick Harrison and Lula Letty (Fouraker) B.; B.M.E., Drexel U., 1950; m. Almira Schwartz, June 20, 1942; children—M. Ruth Bowden Coleman, Thomas Frederick. Designer, Gen. Electric Co., Phila., 1940-43, Fleetwings div. Kaiser Corp., Bristol, Pa., 1943-44; devel. engr. Franklin Inst., Phila., 1946-55; sr. engr. RCA, Camden, N.J., 1955-69; prin. T.J. Bowden PE Assos., cons. engr., Cherry Hill, N.J., 1969-81; pres. Bowden Corp. Archtl. Engrs., Cherry Hill, 1982—. Served with U.S. Army, 1944-46; PTO. Registered profl. engr., N.J., Pa., Md. Baptist. Home and Office: 1307 Paddock Way Cherry Hill NJ 08034

BOWELL, WILLIAM DAVID, cruise and excursion company executive, river boat captain; b. St. Paul, Feb. 14, 1921; s. Ralph Raymond and Leone C. (Padelford) B.; m. 1946; children—William D., Shelley Ann Bowell Kosmo, Beth Ann. B.A., Macalester Coll., 1949, postgrad. in journalism, 1952. Curator Minn. State Hist. Soc., St. Paul, 1949-51; liaison engr. Studebaker Corp., South Bend, Ind., 1952-55; account exec. Edwards & Deustch Litho, Chgo., 1956-61; exec. v.p. United Sci., St. Paul, 1962-69; pres. Miller Farms, St. Paul, 1969-70, Stillwater Tug & Salvage, Minn., 1969-76; founder, pres. Padelford Packet Boat Co., Inc., St. Paul, 1970—; founder, co-pub. United Airline Mainliner Mag., 1956; co-pub. Oldsmobile Rocket Circle mag., 1956; co-pub. Holiday Inns Am. mag., 1956. Patentee binaural earphone, 1958. Grand marshall Aquatennial Boat Parade, St. Paul/Mpls., 1972, East Side Parade, St. Paul, 1979; bd. dirs. Metroland, St. Paul, 1972-84. Served with Paratroopers, U.S. Army, 1942-45; ETO. Decorated Bronze Star, Purple Heart; recipient award for top tourist attraction Gov. Minn., 1972. Mem. Sons and Daus. Pioneer Rivermen, Am. Sternwheel Assn., Nat. Passenger Vessel Assn. (pres. 1970-77), Minn. Hist. Soc. (life), Ramsey County Hist. Soc. (dir. 1984). Home: 3540 James Ave S Minneapolis MN 55408 Office: Padelford Packet Boat Co Inc Harriet Island Saint Paul MN 55107

BOWEN, JEFFREY LOUIS, dental materials researcher; b. Wooster, Ohio, July 1, 1960; s. Edward Brooks and Ruth (Sanderson) B. B.S. in Geology, Mary Washington Coll., 1982. Researcher, Arlington, Va., 1982—. Recipient Eagle Scout award Boy Scouts Am., 1976. Mem. Geol. Soc. Am., Sigma Gamma Epsilon.

BOWEN, LIONEL FROST, government official Australia. LL.B. Minister for mfg. industry Australia, 1975-78, spl. minister of state, minister assisting Prime Minister, 1974-75, dep. leader fed. opposition, 1978-83, dep. prime minister, minister for trade, 1983-84, fed. atty.-gen., 1984—. Office: Office of Atty Gen, Parliament House, Canberra 2600, Australia

BOWEN, MARCIA KAY, customs house broker; b. Bradford, Pa., July 20, 1957; d. George W. Allen Jr. and Katherine (Jema) Allen; m. Glenn Edward Rollins, June 26, 1975 (div. 1979); m. Michael James Bowen, Dec. 27, 1983; 1 child, James Derek. Student Houston Community Coll., 1978-81; student Am. Mgmt. Assn., 1984-85. Lic. customs house broker. Asst. mgr. W.R. Zanes & Co. of La., Inc., Houston, 1975-76; sec. Westchester Corp., Houston, 1973-75; import br. mgr. Schenkers Internat., Inc., Houston, 1976-85; br. mgr. F.W. Myers & Co., Inc., El Paso, 1985—. Mem. Houston Customs House Brokers Assn. (sec. 1977-79, mem. U.S. customs com. 1979-83), El Paso Customs House Brokers Assn., Houston Freight Forwarders Assn., El Paso Fgn. Trade Zone Assn., Nat. Assn. Female Execs., Soc. Global Trade Execs., El Paso/Juarez Transp. and Distbn. Assn., Inc. Roman Catholic. Office: FW Myers & Co Inc 9801 Carnegie St El Paso TX 79925

BOWEN, OTIS RAY, federal agency administrator, former governor Indiana, physician; b. nr. Rochester, Ind., Feb. 26, 1918; s. Vernie and Pearl (Wright) B.; m. Elizabeth A. Steinmann, Feb. 25, 1939 (dec. Jan. 1981); children: Richard H., Judith I. McGrew, Timothy R., Robert O.; m. Rose May Hochstetler, Sept. 26, 1981. A.B. in Chemistry, Ind. U., 1939, M.D., 1942, LL.D. (hon.); LL.D. (hon.), Anderson Coll., 1973, Valparaiso U., 1973, Butler U., 1973; LL.D., S.C. U. Med. Ctr., 1986; LL.D. (hon.), Vincennes U., Tri-State Coll., Calumet Coll., U. Evansville, Ind. U., 1987, Ind. State U., Ball State U., U. Notre Dame, Rose-Hulman Inst., St. Joseph Coll., Calumet Campus of Purdue U., Manchester Coll., Hanover Coll., St. Mary's Coll., Bethel Coll., Marian Coll.; LL.D.(hon.), U. Md., Balt., 1987; LL.D. (hon.), Baylor U., 1987; LL.D (hon.)degree, Wabash U., 1987, NYU Med. Coll., 1987. Intern, Meml. Hosp., South Bend, Ind., 1942-43; practice gen. medicine Bremen, Ind., 1946-72; past mem. staff Bremen Community Hosp., Parkview Hosp., Plymouth, Ind., St. Joseph's and Meml. Hosp., South Bend, St. Joseph Hosp., Mishawaka, Ind.; clin. prof. family medicine Sch. Medicine, Ind. U., 1976-85; coroner Marshall County, Ind., 1952-56; mem. Ind. Ho. of Reps., 1956-58, 60-72, minority leader, 1965-67, speaker of house, 1967-72; vice chmn. legis. council Ind. (Gen. Assembly), 1967-68, chmn., 1970-72; gov. Ind. 1973-81; mem. staff dept. family medicine Long Hosp., Indpls., 1981-85; mem. Council State Govts., 1973-81, mem. exec. com.; sec. Health & Human Services Dept., 1985—; mem. Edn. Commn. States, 1973-81, chmn.-elect, 1976-77, chmn., 1977-78; mem. Midwest Govs. Conf., 1973-81, vice chmn., 1977-78, chmn., 1978; mem. Republican Govs. Conf., 1973-81, chmn., 1978; mem. Nat. Govs. Conf., 1973-81, chmn., 1979; past chmn. com. on crime reduction and pub. safety, mem. energy com.; past mem. Pres.'s Commn. Fed. Paperwork, Pres.'s Commn. Sci. and Tech.; mem. Pres.'s Commn. Federalism, 1981-82; past chmn. Interstate Mining Commn.; past med. services dir. Marshall County CD; mem. Midwest Govs. Gt. Lakes Caucus; former mem. adv. com. on curricula Vincennes U.; hon. dir. Center for Pub. Service, Anderson Coll.; chmn. Adv. Council Social Security, 1982; chmn. adv. council BACCHUS, 1979-85. Contbr. articles to med. jours. Past trustee Ancilla Coll.; trustee Valparaiso U., 1978-85; past mem. adv. council United Student Aid Fund; mem. adv. bd. Indpls. chpt. Fellowship Christian Athletes; mem., past chmn. Lutheran Sch. Bd., Bremen; past v.p. congregation, past fin. bd. chmn. St. Paul's Lutheran Ch., Bremen.; bd. govs. Riley Meml. Assn., 1981-85; bd. dirs. Greater Indpls. Council Alcoholism, 1982-85, Lilly Endowment Found. Served from 1st lt. to capt. M.C., AUS, 1943-46, PTO. Recipient Merit award Ind. Pub. Health Assn., 1971, Presdl. Citation, NYU, Maynard K. Hine award Ind. Dental Assn.; named Alumni of Year, Ind. U. Med. Sch., 1971; Disting. Service award Future Farmers Am., 1976; Public Service award Ind. Soc. Public Adminstrn, George F. Hixson award Kiwanis Internat., 1987. Mem. AMA (Dr. Benjamin Rush award 1973), Ind. Med. Assn. (legis commn. 1958-71, 13th dist. councilor 1965-71), 13th Dist. Med. Assn. (past pres.), Marshall County Med. Assn. (past pres.), Am. Gen. Practice Assn., Ind. Gen. Practice Assn., 13th Dist. Gen. Practice Assn., Farm Bur., Marshall County Tb Soc. (past v.p.), Bremen C. of C., Am. Legion, VFW, Alpha Omega Alpha, Phi Beta Pi, Delta Chi (Delta Chi of Yr. 1986). Lutheran. Club: Kiwanis (past pres., George F. Hixon award 1987). Home: Bremen IN 46506 Office: Dept Health & Human Services 200 Independence Ave Washington DC 20201

BOWEN, RICHARD SANGER, construction executive; b. London, May 23, 1947; s. John Sanger and Dorothy Winifred (Jones) B.; m. Patricia Margaret Skinner, Sept. 6, 1969; children: Andrew Sanger, Christopher George, Robert John. Diploma in bldg., Hammersmith Coll., London, 1968. Site engr. Wimpey Constrn., Eng., 1967-69; asst. mgr. Gilbert Ash, Eng., 1969-73; asst. mgr., then contracts mgr. W.S. Try Ltd., Eng., 1973-78; sr. contracts mgr. Try Internat. Ltd., Eng. and Saudi Arabia, 1978-83, Try Hounslow Ltd., Eng., 1983-86; mgr. mktg. Try Build Ltd., Eng., 1986; dir. group mktg. Try Constrn. Group, Middlesex, Eng., 1986—. Contbr. articles to profl. jours.; author brochures. Recipient Silver medal London Constrn. Industry Bd., 1969. Fellow Chartered Inst. Bldg.; mem. High Wycombe Round Table (officer, chmn.), Catenian Assn. Roman Catholic. Home: 270 Hughenden Rd, High Wycombe HP13 5PE, England

BOWEN, W. J., gas company executive; b. Sweetwater, Tex., Mar. 31, 1922; s. Berry and Annah (Robey) B.; m. Annis K. Hilty, June 6, 1945; children: Shelley Ann, Barbara Kay, Berry Dunbar, William Jackson. B.S., U.S. Mil. Acad., 1945. Registered profl. engr., Tex. Petroleum engr. Delhi Oil Corp., Dallas, 1949-57; v.p. Fla. Gas Co., Houston, 1957-60; pres. Fla. Gas Co., Winter Park, Fla., 1960-74; pres., chief exec. officer Transco Cos., Inc., Houston, 1974-81; chmn. Transco Cos., Inc. (name changed to Transco Energy Co.), Houston, 1976—; chief exec. officer Transco Energy Co., Houston, 1981-87, also bd. dirs.; dir. Crown Zellerbach Corp., S.W. Bancshares, Inc. Chmn. Houston Clean City Commn.; chmn. bd. dirs. YMCA, Houston; bd. dirs. Houston Mus. Fine Arts. Served with AUS, 1945-49. Mem. Am. Gas Assn., Houston C. of C. (dir.), Delta Kappa Epsilon. Episcopalian. Office: Transco Energy Co 2800 Post Oak Blvd Houston TX 77251 *

BOWEN, WILLIAM GORDON, economist, educator, foundation administrator; b. Cin., Oct. 6, 1933; s. Albert A. and Bernice (Pomert) B.; m. Mary Ellen Maxwell, Aug. 25, 1956; children: David Alan, Karen Lee. B.A., Denison U., 1955; Ph.D., Princeton U., 1958. Mem. faculty Princeton (N.J.) U., 1958—, prof. econs., 1965—, dir. grad. studies Woodrow Wilson Sch. Pub. and Internat. Affairs, 1964-66, provost, 1967-72, pres., 1972-87; pres. Andrew W. Mellon Found., N.Y.C., 1988—; bd. dirs. Reader's Digest Inc., NCR Corp., Merck and Co., Inc., Am. Express. Co. Author: The Wage-Price Issue; A Theoretical Analysis, 1960, Wage Behavior in the Postwar Period; An Empirical Analysis, 1960, Economic Aspects of Education: Three Essays, 1964, (with W. J. Baumol) Performing Arts: The Economic Dilemma, 1966, (with T.A. Finegan) The Economics of Labor Force Participation, 1969. Trustee Ctr. for Advanced Study in Behavioral Scis., 1978-84, 86—; bd. regents Smithsonian Instn.; mem. Council on Fgn. Relations. Mem. Am. Econ. Assn., Indsl. Relations Research Assn., Council on Foreign Relations, Phi Beta Kappa. Club: University. Office: Andrew W Mellon Found 140 E 62d St New York NY 10021

BOWER, MARVIN D., insurance company executive; b. Stanford, Ill., July 20, 1924; s. Charles Howard and Marjorie Dale (Garst) B.; m. Mari Morrissey, June 1, 1946 (dec. 1981); children: Stacie (Mrs. John Killian), Jim, Pete, Molly (Mrs. Christopher Miller), Tom, John.; m. Carolyn Paine Newland, Apr. 24, 1983; stepchildren: Linda (Mrs. Bradford Gleason), Lori (Mrs. Paul Lorenz), Leslie, William, David. Ph.B., Ill. Wesleyan U., 1948. C.L.U. Agt. Northwestern Mut. Life, Bloomington, Ill., 1949-52; with State Farm Life Ins. Co., 1952—; sec. for Can. State Farm Life Ins. Co., Toronto, 1955-58; exec. v.p., sec. State Farm Life and Accident Assurance Co., 1961—, also bd. dirs.; v.p. health State Farm Mut. Auto Ins. Co., 1968—; exec. v.p. State Farm Life Ins. Co., Bloomington, Ill., 1973—, chmn. bd., 1985—, also dir. Served to capt. AUS, 1943-46. Fellow Life Office Mgmt. Inst.; mem. Phi Gamma Delta. Home: 49 Country Club Pl Bloomington IL 61701 Office: State Farm Life Ins Co One State Farm Plaza Bloomington IL 61710

BOWERS, LEOLA DELEAN, educator, nurse; b. Birmingham, Ala., May 5, 1919; d. Jasper Wiley and Lonie (Dunsford) B. Diploma Carraway Methodist Hosp. Sch. Nursing, Birmingham, 1946, Brook Army Med. Ctr. Sch. Anesthesia, Ft. Sam Houston, Tex., 1953; student U. Ga., 1954, U. Md., 1955; B.S.N., U. Ala.-Tuscaloosa, 1959; class B cert. in secondary edn. Jacksonville State U., 1960, M.S. in Edn., 1961; postgrad. Spring Hill Coll., 1962, U. Ala.-Mobile, 1963; cert. Nat. Respiratory Disease Course for Nurses, New Orleans, 1969; postgrad. Pepperdine U., 1971-74; cert. health occupation edn. U. Ala., Birmingham, 1975. R.N., Ala.; cert. secondary tchr., Ala. Hosp. supr. Citizens Hosp., Talladega, Ala., 1946-47, surg. nurse, 1949-50; gen. duty nurse Sylacauga Hosp. (Ala.), 1948; instr. med.-surg. nursing Sylacauga Sch. Nursing, 1963-71; tchr. health occupations Talladega City Vocat. Ctr., 1971—, coordinator Health Occupation Edn. Student Clin. Citizens Hosp. and Nursing Home, 1971—. Instr. ARC, Talladega, 1975—; CPR instr. Am. Heart Assn., Talladega, 1979—, adv. projects, 1978-83; mem. telephone com. for election legislators, Talladega, 1982. Served as capt. Nurses Corps, U.S. Army, 1950-58; ETO. Recipient CD cert. State Ala., 1980, cert. service City of Talladega, 1983; named Tchr. of Yr., Talladega City Vocat. Ctr. and Health Occupation Edn., 1979, 83, 84, Outstanding Ala. Tchr., Ala. Vocat. Dept., 1983, 84. Mem. Am. Nurses' Assn., Ala. Nurses' Assn., Bus. and Profl. Women's Club, Talladega Nurses' Assn., Health Occupation Students Am. (adviser local club 1976—, adviser Dist. III Ala. 1981-85). Methodist. Lodge: Order Eastern Star. Home: Route 4 Box 239 Talladega AL 35160 Office: Talladega City Vocat Ctr 110 Picadilly Circle Talladega AL 35160

BOWERS, RAYMOND VICTOR, sociology educator; b. Victoria, B.C., Can., June 19, 1907; s. Samuel Victor Bowers and Beulah Dodds Bowers Ramsey; student Victoria Coll., 1923-25; A.B., U. Kans., 1927; A.M., Northwestern U., 1930; Ph.D., U. Minn., 1934; m. Virginia Dallam Wallis, June 30, 1933; children—Sally Virginia Bowers Wittliff, Katherine Mary Bowers Arrell. Instr. dept. sociology U. Minn., 1930-34; Social Sci. Research Council postdoctoral fellow Inst. Human Relations, Yale U., 1934-35; asst. prof. dept. sociology U. Rochester, 1935-42, acting chmn., 1938-42, chmn., 1942; asst. chief research and stats. div. Nat. Hdqrs. SSS, Washington, 1942-44, chief, 1946-47; dep. exec. dir. com. on human resources R&D Bd., Office Sec. Def., Washington, 1947-48, exec. dir., 1948-49; dir. Human Resources Research Inst., Air U., Maxwell AFB, Ala., 1949-52; tech. adviser social scis. Air R&D Command, USAF, 1952-55; dir. Office Social Sci. Programs, Air Force Personnel and Tng. Research Ctr., San Antonio, 1955-57, tech. dir., 1957-58; prof., head dept. sociology and anthropology, chmn. social scis. div. U. Ga.-Athens, 1958-62; prof. sociology U. Ariz., Tucson, 1962-75, prof. emeritus, 1975—, head dept., 1962-71; vis. scholar London Sch. Econs. and Polit. Sci., 1970; cons. AT&T, HEW, Dept. Air Force, NSF. Research leader morale div. U.S. Strategic Bombing Survey, Japan, 1945-46; expert cons. sociol. and pub. opinion surveys G.H.Q., SCAP, Japan, 1946-47. Served as lt. USNR, 1944-46; col. USAFR, 1951—. ret. Recipient Army and Navy commendations, Selective Service medal. Fellow AAAS, Am. Sociol. Assn.; mem. Sociol. Research Assn., Phi Beta Kappa, Delta Tau Delta. Co-author: ARDC Studies in Personnel and Organizational Effectiveness, 1956; editor, contbr.: Studies in Organizational Effectiveness, 1962, Studies on Behavior in Organizations, 1966; contbr.: The Uses of Sociology, 1967; contbr. articles to profl. jours. Home: 2702 Kiva Pl Tucson AZ 85715

BOWERSOCK, GLEN WARREN, historian; b. Providence, Jan. 12, 1936; s. Donald Curtis and Josephine (Evans) B. A.B., Harvard U., 1957; B.A., Oxford U., Eng., 1959, M.A. and D.Phil., 1962. Lectr. ancient history Oxford U., 1960-62, vis. lectr., 1966; instr. Harvard U., 1962-64, asst. prof., 1964-67, assoc. prof. classics, 1967-69, prof. Greek and Latin, 1969-80, chmn. dept. classics, 1972-77, assoc. dean faculty arts and scis., 1977-80; prof. hist. studies Inst. Advanced Study, Princeton, N.J., 1980—; sr. fellow Dumbarton Oaks Ctr. for Byzantine Studies, Washington, 1984—; cons. Ednl. Services, Inc., 1964, NEH, 1971—; sr. fellow Center for Hellenic Studies, Washington, 1976—; mem. Internat. Colloquium on the Classics in Edn., 1964-66; vis. prof. Australian Nat. U., 1972, Princeton U., 1986-87; syndic Harvard U. Press, 1977-81; mem. editorial bd. Berytus, Am. Jour. Philology. Author: Augustus and the Greek World, 1965, Pseudo-Xenophon, Constitution of the Athenians, 1968, Greek Sophists in the Roman Empire, 1969, Julian the Apostate, 1978, Roman Arabia, 1983; editor: Philostratus' Life of Apollonius, 1970, Approaches to the Second Sophistic, 1974, (with J. Clive, S. Graubard) Edward Gibbon and the Decline and Fall of the Roman Empire, 1977; mem. editorial bd. Am. Scholar, 1981—. Trustee Am. Schs. Oriental Research, 1984—. Rhodes scholar, 1957-60. Fellow Am. Acad. Arts and Scis., Am. Numis. Soc. (council); mem. Am. Philol. Assn., Archeol. Inst. Am., Leschetizky Assn. Am., Soc. Promotion Roman and Hellenic Studies, German Archaeol. Inst. (corr.), The Johnsonians, Phi Beta Kappa. Clubs: Knickerbocker (N.Y.C.), Century (N.Y.C.). Office: Sch Hist Studies Inst Advanced Study Princeton NJ 08540

BOWERSOX, THOMAS LLOYD, business executive; search consultant; b. Troy, Ohio, Aug. 7, 1934; s. Van L. and Julia Fay (Wimmer) B.; B.A. in Bus. Adminstrn. (Danforth Found. fellow), Carthage Coll., Kenosha, Wis., 1957; m. Jeanette Erkert, Aug. 11, 1956; children—Michael T., Sue Ann, Kathy Lynn. Asst. dist. traffic mgr. Ill. Bell Telephone Co., Chgo., 1957-61; mgr. labor relations Martin-Marietta Corp., Rapid City, S.D., 1961-63; regional dir. indsl. relations U.S. Envelope Co., Waukegan, Ill., 1963-64; prin. Fry Cons., exec. search, Chgo., 1964-69; owner, pres. Bowersox & Assocs., Inc., Des Plaines, Ill. and La Jolla, Calif., 1969—; lectr. bus. topics. Pres., Civic Assn., Des Plaines, 1958-60; founder Bauersachs Geneal. Soc., 1975, chmn., exec. dir., 1976—. Mem. Am. Soc. Personnel Adminstrn., Am. Mgmt. Assn. (Pres.'s Assn.), Am. Foundrymans Soc. Republican. Lutheran. Clubs: Meadow (Rolling Meadows, Ill.); River Trails Tennis Center (Arlington Heights, Ill.). Author: Executive In-Depth Interview Guide, 1979; How to Market Yourself, 1983; contbr. articles to bus. publs. Home: 8880-201 Villa La Jolla Dr La Jolla CA 92037

BOWES, FLORENCE (MRS. WILLIAM DAVID BOWES), writer; b. Salt Lake City, Nov. 19, 1925; d. John Albreckt Elias and Alma Wilhelmina (Jonasson) Norborg; student U. Utah, 1941-42, Columbia, 1945-46, N.Y. U., 1954-55; grad. N.Y. TV Workshop, 1950; m. Samuel Ellis Levine, July 15, 1944 (dec. July 1953); m. 2d, William David Bowes, Mar. 15, 1958 (dec. 1976); 1 son, Alan Richard. Actress, writer Hearst Radio Network, WINS, N.Y.C., 1944-45; personnel and adminstrv. exec. Mut. Broadcasting System, N.Y.C., 1946-49, free-lance editor, writer, 1948-49; freelance writer NBC and ABC, 1949-53; script editor, writer Robert A. Monroe Prodns., N.Y.C., Hollywood, Calif., 1953-56; script and comml. dir. KUTV-TV, Salt Lake City, 1956-58; spl. editor, writer pub. relations dept. U. Utah, Salt Lake City, 1966-68, editor, writer U. Utah Rev., 1968-75; author: Web of Solitude, 1979; The MacOrvan Curse, 1980; Interlude in Venice, 1981; Beauchamp, 1983. Mem. Beta Sigma Phi. Home: 338-K St Salt Lake City UT 84103

BOWES, KENNETH EBERLE, consulting company executive; b. Montreal, Que., Can., May 16, 1937; s. David Proctor and Corine (Eberle) B.; came to U.S., 1943, naturalized, 1955; m. Mary Priscilla Mohlhenrich, Aug. 10, 1958; children—Kenneth William, Douglas Proctor, Ann Eberle. BS, Fla. State U., 1959. Advt. writer Atlanta Gas Light Co., 1959-64, advt. mgr., 1964-66; with Liller Neal Battle & Lindsey, Atlanta, 1966-72, v.p., 1969-72; pres. Bowes/Hanlon Advt., Atlanta, 1972-87; chmn. Bowes/Hanlon/Yarbrough Pub. Relations Inc., The Project Group, Strategic Research Ctr., 1985-87; pres., chief exec. officer Auric Group Inc., 1985-87; exec. v.p. Gillis, Townsend, Bowes, Hanlon, Inc., Atlanta, 1987-88; pres. Wanamaker Assocs., Inc., Atlanta, 1988—. Bd. dirs. Kidney Found. Ga., Atlanta Area council Boy Scouts Am., Hub Family Crisis Ctr.; pres. Ga. Youth and Family Network. Mem. Ga. C. of C., Friends of the Alphabet. Republican. Mem. Moravian Ch. Clubs: Cherokee Country. Home: 5290 Antelope Ln Stone Mountain GA 30087 Office: Wanamaker Assocs Inc 3340 Peachtree Rd NE Suite 1776 Atlanta GA 30026

BOWKER, MICHAEL, chemist, researcher; b. Manchester, Eng., Sept. 27, 1952; s. Ronald James and Joyce (Byrne) B.; m. Sheelagh Mary Macaulay; children: Laurel Jessica, Holly Zofia, Richard Michael. B.Sc. with honors, U. East Anglia, Norwich, Norfolk, Eng., 1974; PhD, Liverpool (Eng.) U., 1977. Research assoc. dept. chem. engring. Stanford (Calif.) U., 1977-79; sr. research scientist I.C.I. P.L.C., Runcorn, Cheshire, Eng., 1979-87; asst. dir. Leverhulme Ctr. for Innovative Catalysis, Liverpool U., 1987—. Contbr. articles to profl. jours. Mem. Royal Soc. Chemistry. Office: U Liverpool Leverhulme, Ctr for Innovative Catalysis, Liverpool L69 3BX, England

BOWLBY, JOHN MOSTYN, psychiatric consultant; b. London, Feb. 26, 1907; s. Anthony Alfred and Maria Bridget (Mostyn) B.; m. Ursula Longstaff, Apr. 14, 1938; children: Mary, Richard, Pia, Robert. BA, U. Cambridge, Eng., 1928, MA, 1932, MD, 1939, ScD (hon.), 1977; LittD (hon.), U. Leicester, Eng., 1971. Staff psychiatrist London Child Guidance Clinic, London, 1937-40; cons. psychiatrist Tavistock Clinic, London, 1946-72, hon. cons. psychiatrist, 1972—; fellow Ctr. Advanced Study Behavioral Scis., Stanford, Calif., 1957-58; sci. staff Med. Research Council, London, 1963-72; vis. prof. Stanford U. Med. Ctr., 1968; Freud prof. psychoanalysis University Coll., London, 1981; cons. Word Health Orgn., Geneva, 1950-57, Nat. Inst. Mental Health, Bethesda, Md., 1958-61. Author: Maternal Care and Mental Health, 1951, Attachment and Loss vol. 1, 1969,, 2d edit. 1982, vol. 2, 1972, vol. 3, 1980. Served to lt. col. Royal Army Med. Corps., 1940-45. Recipient Salmon medal N.Y. Acad. Med., 1984; named Comdr. Order British Empire, Her Majesty's Govt., 1972; Royal Soc. Medicine fellow (hon.), 1987. Fellow Royal Coll. Psychiatrists (hon. 1980), British Psychol. Soc.; mem. Am. Acad. Arts and Scis. (hon. 1981), British Psychoanalytical Soc., Internat. Assn. Child Psychiatry (pres. 1962-66). Ch. of Eng. Office: Tavistock Clinic, 120 Belsize Ln, London NW3 5BA, England

BOWLBY, RACHEL HELENA, English educator; b. Billingham, Eng., Jan. 29, 1957; d. Ronald Oliver and Elizabeth Trevelyan (Monro) B.; m. Geoffrey Peter Bennington, July 18, 1987. MA in English, Oxford U., 1979; PhD in Comparative Lit., Yale U., 1983. Lectr. English Sch. Cultural and Community Studies Sussex U., Brighton, Eng., 1984—. Author: Just Looking: Consumer Culture in Dreiser, Gissing and Zola, 1985, Virginia Woolf: Feminist Destinations, 1988. Lurcy Found. fellow, 1982-83. Home: 45 Hendon St, Brighton BN2 2EG, England Office: Sussex U, Arts Bldg B, Falmer, Brighton BN1 9QN, England

BOWLBY, RICHARD ERIC, computer systems analyst; b. Detroit, Aug. 17, 1939; s. Garner Milton and Florence Marie (Russell) B.; m. Gwendoline Joyce Coldwell, Apr. 29, 1967. B.A., Wayne State U., 1962. With Ford Motor Co., Detroit, 1962-65, 66—, now computer systems analyst; pres. 1300 Lafayette East-Coop., Inc., 1981-82. Mem. Antiquaries, Friends Detroit Pub. Library, Friends Orch. Hall. Club: Founders Soc. (Detroit). Office: Ford Motor Co 300 Renaissance Ctr Suite 3000 Box 43314 Detroit MI 48243

BOWLEY, NEWELL LYNN, accountant; b. Lexington, Nebr., Oct. 7, 1958; d. John William and Frances Kay (Leibhart) B. BS, Kearney State Coll., 1981. CPA, Nebr.; cert. mgmt. acct., Nebr. Staff auditor Touche Ross & Co., Lincoln, Nebr., 1981-82, sr. auditor, 1982-84; sr. fin. analyst Mut. of Omaha Ins. Co., Omaha, 1984-86, corp. cost acctg. supr., 1986-87; fin. cons., sec. Mutual Omaha Internat. Ltd. UK, Bournemouth, Eng., 1987—. Mem. Am. Inst. CPA's, Nebr. Soc. CPA's (mem. com.). Home: 8655 S Plaza Omaha NE 68127 Office: Mutual of Omaha Ins Co Mutual of Omaha Plaza Omaha NE 68175 also: Mutual Omaha Internat Ltd, Richmond House Richmond Hill, Bournemouth, Dorset BH2 6EQ, England

BOWLEY, ROY, mining engineer; b. Sheffield, Yorkshire, Eng., July 6, 1952; s. James and Phoebe (Taberner) B.; Denise Farthing, Aug. 14, 1976; children: Gareth James, Peter John, Stacey Ann. Diploma in Mining Engring., Doncaster Met. Inst. of Higher Edn., South Yorkshire, Eng., 1976. Student apprentice Barnsley area Nat. Coal Bd., South Yorkshire, 1971-76, engring. trainee Barnsley area, 1976-77, tech. asst. Houghton Main Colliery, 1977-78, asst. undermgr. Dearne Valley Colliery, 1978-80, undermgr. Kiveton Park Colliery, 1980-85; undermgr. Manton Colliery British Coal, Nottinghamshire, 1985—. Mem. Instn. Mining Engrs., Council Engirng. Instns. (chartered 1983). Mem. Ch. Eng. Home: 3 Rotherham Rd, Dinnington, South Yorkshire S31 7RG, England Office: British Coal Corp, Manton Colliery, Retford Rd Manton, Worksop, Nottinghamshire England

BOWLING, JAMES CHANDLER, consultant; b. Covington, Ky., Mar. 29, 1928; s. Van Dorn and Belinda (Johnson) B.; m. Ann Jones, Oct. 20, 1951; children: Belinda, Nancy, James Jr., Stephanie. B.S., U. Louisville, 1951; LL.D. (hon.), Murray U., 1976, U. Ky., 1981. Various positions from campus rep. to v.p. sales and corp. relations Philip Morris, Inc., N.Y.C.; then exec. v.p., group v.p., dir. marketing, asst. to chmn. bd., sr. v.p., dir., now cons.; dir. Miller Brewing Co., Seven Up Co.; bd. dirs., mem. exec. com. Tobacco Inst., Washington.; sr. adv. bd. Burson-Marsteller; advisor USIA; bd. dirs. Cherokee Farms, Union Trust, Darien, Conn., Centurion, Inc., Centurion Stables, Inc.; chmn. bd. Prnews.; chmn. Bowling Investments, Inc. Author: How To Improve Your Personal Relations, 1959. Mem. nat. council Boy Scouts Am., 1961—; trustee Boy Scout Mus.; justice of peace, Rowayton, Conn., 1960-68; vice-chmn. Clean World Internat.; chmn. Pub. Affairs Council, Washington; bd. overseers U. Louisville; bd. dirs., former pres., former chmn., Keep Am. Beautiful; bd. dirs. Nat. Automatic Merchandising Assn.; trustee Berea Coll., Midway Jr. Coll.; bd. dirs. Ky. Ind. Coll. Found., Nat. Tennis Found. and Hall of Fame, U. Ky. Devel. Council., Lambda Chi Alpha Found. Served with AUS, World War II, PTO. Recipient Kolodny award as outstanding young exec. in tobacco industry, 1963; named U.S. Young Businessman of Year St. John's U., 1967, Outstanding Alumnus U. Louisville, 1970, 86, Kentuckian of Year, 1977; elected to Tobacco Industry Hall of Fame, 1976. Mem. Nat. Assn. Tobacco Distbg. (dir. exec. mgmt. div.), Pub. Relations Soc. Am., Sales Execs. Club N.Y., The Kentuckians (past pres.), Laymen's Nat. Bible Assn. (v.p., dir.), World Press Inst. Episcopalian. Clubs: Wee Burn Country; Union League (N.Y.C.). Home: 13 Tokeneke Trail Darien CT 06820 Office: 230 Park Ave S New York NY 10003

BOWLING, WILLIAM GLASGOW, language professional, educator; b. St. Louis, May 7, 1902; s. William Walter and Mary Susan (Glasgow) B.; m. Violet Whelen, Aug. 3, 1933; 1 son, Townsend Whelen. A.B., Washington U., St. Louis, 1924, A.M., 1925; postgrad., Harvard U., 1930-31. Instr., asst. prof., asso. prof. English, Washington U., 1925-70, prof. emeritus, 1970—, asst. to dean, acting dean, dean Univ. Coll., 1928-42, dean Coll. Liberal Arts, 1942-46, dean of men, 1942-44; civilian adminstr. pre-profl. unit Army Specialized Tng. Program, Washington U., 1943-44, dean admissions, 1946-65, univ. grand marshal, 1960-68, univ. historian, 1965—; part time drama critic St. Louis Times, 1929-30. Contbr. articles to profl. jours. Recipient Washington U. Alumni award for disting. service, 1960. Mem. Am. Assn. Collegiate Registrars and Admissions Officers (hon.; book rev. editor quar. jour. Coll. and Univ. 1955-66), Greater St. Louis Council Tchrs. of English (pres. 1936-39, exec. sec. 1939-41), Washington U. Assn. Lecture Series (exec. sec. 1940-47), St. Louis Audubon Soc. (dir. 1944—, pres. 1950-52), Phi Delta Theta, Omicron Delta Kappa, Phi Beta Kappa. Republican. Episcopalian. Club: University (St. Louis). Address: 7408 Washington Ave Saint Louis MO 63130

BOWMAN, MONROE BENGT, architect; b. Chgo., Aug. 28, 1901; s. Henry William and Ellen Mercedes (Bjork) B.; m. Louise Kohnmann, Nov. 1944; 1 son, Kenneth Monroe; B.Arch., Ill. Inst. Tech., 1924. Registered architect, Ill., Wis., Ind., Ohio, Colo. Asso., Benjamin H. Marshall, Chgo., 1926; exhibited models and photographs of Bowman Bros. comtemporary designs at Mus. Modern Art, N.Y.C., 1931; pvt. practice architecture, Chgo., 1941-44; asso. Monroe Bowman Assos., Chgo., 1945—; cons. Chgo. Dept. City Planning, City of Sparta (Wis.), Alfred Shaw, Architect. Mem. Navy League U.S. Important works include Boeing Aircraft bldgs., Wichita, Kans., Emerson Electric bldgs., St. Louis, Maytag Co., Newton, Iowa, Douglas Aircraft bldgs., Park Ridge, Ill., Shwayder Bros. bldgs., Denver, Clark Equipment Co., Buchannon, Mich., Radio-TV Sta. WHO, Des Moines, Foote, Cone & Belding offices, Chgo., Burridge Devel., Hinsdale, Ill., Yacht Club and recreational facilities, Lake Bemiji, Minn., United Airlines offices downtown Chgo., Automatic Sprinkler Corp., Chgo., King Machine Tool div. Am. Steel Foundries, Cin., Marine Terr. Apts., Chgo., Dorchester Park Apts., Chgo., Manteno (Ill.) State Hosp., No. Ill. Gas Co. bldgs., LaGrange, Joliet, Streator and Morris, 1340 Astor St. Apt. Bldg., Burnham Center, Chgo., NSF, Green Bank, W.Va., Naval Radio Research Sta., Sugar Grove, W.Va., Columbus Boy Choir Sch., Princeton, N.J., office bldg. and hotel, Charleston, W.Va. Home: 730 Ridge Ave Evanston IL 60201

BOWMAN, NED DAVID, medical administrator; b. Chattanooga, July 15, 1948; s. Ned Turner and Ernie (White) B.; stepmother Charlotte (Bramlett) B.; m. Linda Carol Eggers, Sept. 18, 1970; children: Bob, Jean, Beth, Scott, Ben. BS, U. Tenn., 1971, MBA, Vanderbilt U., 1982. Adminstr. Oak Ridge Orthopedic Clinic, 1971—; cons. med. adminstrn. Mem. Oak Ridge Human Resources Bd., 1975; past pres. Anderson County Health Council, 1980-81; adv. com. vocat. edn. Oak Ridge city schs., 1977; treas. UN Com. Oak Ridge, 1977, 81. Bd. dirs. Oak Ridge Boys Club; mem. wood badge patrol, advisor to explorer post Boy Scouts Am. Recipient certs. of appreciation City of Oak Ridge, Oak Ridge City Schs. Mem. AAAS, UN Assn. U.S., Soc. Advancement Mgmt. (cert. appreciation 1975, v.p. 1975), Nat. Audubon Soc., Oak Ridge C. of C. (past bd. dirs.), N.Y. Acad. Sci., Med. Group Mgmt. Assn. (past pres. Tenn. chpt.), Am. Coll. Med. Group Adminstrs., Nat. Assn. Orthopedic Clinic Adminstrs., Tenn. Secondary Schs. Athletic Assn., Tenn. Med. Group Mgmt. Assn. Nat. Fedn. Interscholastic Ofcls. Assn., Tenn. Conservation League, Orthopedics Overseas. Mormon. Lodge: Rotary. Avocation: basketball ofcl. Home: 502 Delaware Ave Oak Ridge TN 37830 Office: 145 E Vance Rd Oak Ridge TN 37830

BOWMAN, WILLIAM POWELL, advertising executive; b. Leeds, Eng., Oct. 22, 1932; s. George Edward and Isabel Conyers (Dix) B.; student public schs., Uppingham, Eng.; m. Patricia Elizabeth McCoskrie, Apr. 21, 1956; children—Jonathan William Powell, Edward Normand. Sales mgr. Goodall Backhouse & Co. Ltd., Leeds, 1953-59; sales mgr. Cheeseboro Ponds Ltd., London, 1959-60; mktg. mgr. Dorland Advt., London, 1960-63, United Biscuits (U.K.) Ltd., 1963-65, controller overseas devel., 1965-66, export dir., 1966-72; mng. dir. United Biscuits Internat. Ltd., London, 1972-77; group personnel dir. United Biscuits (Holdings) PLC, London, 1977-83; chmn. bd. Carr's of Carlisle, 1978-83; chmn. Royds Advt. Group, 1984-85; chmn. Royds McCann Ltd., 1986-87; chmn. Forum for Occupational Counselling and Unemployment Services, 1986—, Vanderhaas BV, 1987—, Brit. Food and Farming, Buckshire County, Eng., 1987—; dir. Meiji McVitie, Japan, United Biscuits Can., UB Denmark, 1978-83, The Extel Group P.L.C., Twyman Fishlock Ltd., Harvey Bergenroth Ptnrs., Saladin Ltd.; chmn. Covent Garden Market Authority, 1988—. Royal warrant holder Her Majesty the Queen and Her Majesty the Queen Mother, 1978-83; founder, chmn. British Food Export Council, 1970-72; vice chmn. Project Trident, 1979-83, gov., 1984—, chmn., 1985—; chmn. Industry and Parliament Trust, 1981-83; sec. U.K. Com., Humbert H. Humphrey Inst. of Pub. Affairs, 1980—; bd. mgmt., fellow Zoological Soc. London. Served with RAF, 1951-53, Royal Aux. Air Force, 1953-58. Officer, Order of British Empire. Fellow Inst. Dirs.; mem. Cake and Biscuit Alliance (chmn. 1976-78), Inst. Mktg., Inst. Mgmt., Inst. Personnel Conservative. Ch. of England. Clubs: White Elephant, Royal Air Force. Office: Covent House, New Covent Garden Market, London SW8 5NX, England

BOWMAN-DALTON, BURDENE KATHRYN, educator, computer consultant; b. Magnolia, Ohio, July 13, 1937; d. Ernest Mowles and Mary Kathryn (Long) Bowman; B.M.E., Capital U., 1959; MA in Edn., Akron U., 1967, postgrad. 1976—; m. Louis W. Dalton, Mar. 13, 1979. Profl. vocalist, various clubs in the East, 1959-60; music tchr. East Liverpool (Ohio) City Schs., 1959-62; music tchr. Revere Local Schs., Akron, Ohio, 1962-75, elem. tchr., 1975-80, elem. team leader/computer cons., 1979-85, tchr. middle sch. math., gift-talented, computer literacy, 1981—, dist. computer specialist, 1987—; local and regional dir., Olympics of the Mind, also World Problem Captain for computer problem, 1984-86; cons., workshop presenter State of Ohio, 1987—. Mem. Citizen Com., Akron, 1975-76; profl. rep. Bath Assn. to Help, 1978-80; mem. Revere Levy Com. 1986; audit com. BATH, 1977-79; volunteer chmn. Antique Car Show, Akron, 1972-81; dist. advisor MidWest Talent Search, 1987—; dist. statistician of standardized test results. Martha Holden Jennings Found. grantee, 1977-78; Title IV ESEA grantee, 1977-81. Mem. Assn. for Devel. of Computer-Based Instructional Systems, Assn. Supervision and Curriculum Devel., Ohio Assn. for Gifted Children, Phi Beta. Republican. Lutheran. Home: 353 Retreat Dr Akron OH 44313 Office: 3195 Spring Valley Rd Bath OH 44210

BOWRON, EDGAR PETERS, art museum director; b. Birmingham, Ala., May 27, 1943; s. James Edgar Bowron and Dorothe Peters Lowles; m. Lornagrace Thomas Grenfell, Aug. 20, 1966 (div. 1981); children: James Edgar III, Clara Beatrice, St. John Grenfell. B.A. in English Lit., Colgate U., 1965; M.A. in History of Art, NYU, 1969, Ph.D. in History of Art, 1979. Edn. lectr. Met. Mus. Art, N.Y.C., 1969-70; registrar Mpls. Inst. Arts, 1970-73; curator Renaissance and Baroque art Walters Art Gallery, Balt., 1973-78; adminstrv. asst. to dir. and curator Renaissance and Baroque art Nelson Gallery-Atkins Mus., Kansas City, Mo., 1978-81; dir. N.C. Mus. Art, Raleigh, 1981-85; Elizabeth and John Moors Cabot dir., prof. fine arts Harvard U. Art Museums, Cambridge, Mass., 1985—. Author: Renaissance Bronzes in the Walters Art Gallery, 1978, Pompeo Batoni (1708-87), 1982, Pompeo Batoni and His British Patrons, 1982; co-author: The J. Paul Getty Collection, 1972; editor: Selected Writings of Anthony M. Clark: Studies in Eighteenth Roman Painting, 1981, The North Carolina Museum of Art: Introduction to the Collections, 1983, Anthony M. Clark, Pompeo Batoni, A Complete Catalogue of his Works with an Introductory Text, 1985; contbr. articles to jours. in field. Fellow Ford Found., 1967-69; fellow Nat. Endowment for Arts, 1975-76; Am. Acad. in Rome grantee, 1979-85. Mem. Assn. Art Mus. Dirs. (trustee, bd. dirs.), Master Drawings Assn. Office: Harvard U Art Mus 32 Quincy St Cambridge MA 02138

BOWSER, EMILIE LOUISE, nurse, educator, dress designer; b. Newark, Ohio, July 16, 1941; d. James Elbert and Geraldine Mae (Utts) Drumm; m. Gary L. Bowser, June 6, 1964 (div. July 1980); children—Deborah, Diana, David. B.S.N. in Nursing, Ohio State U., 1964; M.S. in Nursing, Wayne State U., 1984. R.N., Ohio. Charge nurse West Paces Ferry Hosp., Atlanta, 1972-73; clin. instr. St. Vincent's Hosp., Toledo, Ohio, 1976; staff nurse Toledo Hosp., part time 1976—; staff nurse Flower Hosp., Toledo, 1978-79; clin. instr. U. Toledo, 1979; assoc. prof. nursing Owens Tech. Coll., Toledo, 1979—, cons. continuing edn., 1981-87; owner Emilie's Original Bridal Creations; advisor Nat. Student Nurses Assn., Toledo, 1981-87. Cub scout com. chmn. Wolverine council Boy Scouts Am., 1983-86; mem. youth com., tchr., acolyte advisor Trinity Episcopal Ch. Mem. Ohio Nurses Assn. (publicity com. 1980-82), Bedford Band Boosters, Alpha Delta Pi. Republican. Club: Tamaron Country (Toledo). Office: Owens Tech Coll Oregon Rd Toledo OH 43699

BOWYER, ALLEN FRANK, cardiologist, administrator; b. Milw., Aug. 9, 1932; s. Charles Maynard and Mildred Berniece (Haagensen) B.; m. Carolyn Isabel Gramlich, June 5, 1954; children—Sylvia Renee, Susan Rayleen. B.A., Pacific Union Coll., 1955; M.D., Loma Linda U., 1959. Diplomate: Am. Bd. Cardiology. Resident in medicine Rush-Presbyn., St. Luke's Hops., Chgo., 1960-63, fellow in cardiology, 1963-66; extramural fellow Nat. Heart Inst., Bethesda, Md., 1963-66; instr. in medicine U. Ill. Sch. Medicine, Chgo., 1960-65; asst. prof. Loma Linda (Calif.) U., 1966-72, assoc. prof., 1972-73; prof. medicine W. Va. U., Morgantown, 1973-78, East Carolina U., Greenville, 1978-86; pres. East Carolina Heart Inst., 1986—; chmn. East Carolina Heart Specialists, 1986—; research physician Rush-Presbyn. Hosp., 1965-66; dir. cardiovascular research lab. Loma Linda U., 1970-73; dir. cardiac catheterization lab. W.Va. U. Sch. Medicine, 1973-78; dir. cardiac labs. East Carolina U. Sch. Medicine, 1975-81. Author and producer: Computer Graphics Film, Heart Motion by Computer Graphics, 1968 (1st prize for research at Internat. Film Festival 1970), Teaching Heart Function by Computer Graphics, (sci. film award Australia, New Zealand Sci. Film Festival 1970). Pres. Monoghalia County Heart Assn., Morgantown, 1974, 75; trustee Columbia Union Coll., Takoma Park, Md., 1976-78; pres. Pitt County Unit Am. Heart Assn., Greenville, N.C., 1983; dir. W. Va. Heart Assn., Charleston, 1974, 75. Recipient Golden Eagle ward Council on Internat. Non-theatrical Events, 1969, 1970; MacNeal award for Med. Research Rush-Presbyn. Hosp., 1963. Mem. IEEE, Instrument Soc. Am., Am. Fedn. for Clin. Research, Assn. for Computing Machinery, Sigma Xi. Democrat. Adventist. Home: 315 King George Rd Greenville NC 27834 Office: East Carolina Heart Inst East Carolina Heart Specialists PA 2000 Venture Tower Dr Greenville NC 27834

BOXER, DAVID WAYNE, museum director, artist; b. Kingston, Jamaica, Mar. 17, 1946; s. Dudley Dussard and Gloria Ingle (Forbes) Pinto B. AB, Cornell U., 1969; MA, Johns Hopkins U., 1973, PhD, 1975. Film dir. Jamaica Broadcasting Corp., Kingston, 1970-71; asst. prof. George Mason U., Fairfax, U., 1974-75; dir., curator Nat. Gallery Jamaica, Kingston, 1975—; council mem. Inst. Jamaica, Kingston, 1981—; bd. dirs. Jamaica Sch. Art, Kingston, 1981—. Author: Jamaican Art 1922-82, 1983; one man shows include Inst. of Jamaica, Kingston, Museum of Modern Art of Latin Am., Washington, N.Y.C., Los Angeles; exhibited in group shows Nat. Gallery of Jamaica, Kingston, Commonwealth Inst., London, Wadsworth Athaneum, Hartford, Conn., Palace of Fine Arts, Mexico City, Museum of Afro-Am. Artists, Boston, Nat. Museum of Haiti, Port-au-Prince, Bass Museum, Miami; film dir. documentaries for Jamaican TV. Recipient Centenary medal Inst. Jamaica, 1978. Methodist. Office: Nat Gallery Jamaica, 12 Ocean Blvd, Kingston Mall, Kingston Jamaica West Indies

BOXER, JEROME HARVEY, accountant; b. Chgo., Nov. 27, 1930; s. Ben Avrum and Edith (Lyman) B.; A.A. magna cum laude, East Los Angeles Coll., 1952; A.B. with honors, Calif. State U., Los Angeles, 1954; m. Sandra Schaffner, June 17, 1980; children by previous marriage—Michael, Jodi. Lab. instr. Calif. State U., Los Angeles, 1953-54; staff accountant Dolman, Freeman & Buchalter, Los Angeles, 1955-57; sr. accountant Neiman, Sanger, Miller & Beress, Los Angeles, 1957-63; partner firm Glynn and Boxer, C.P.A.s, Los Angeles, 1964-68; v.p., sec. Glynn, Boxer & Phillips Inc., CPA's, Los Angeles and Glendale, 1968—; pres. Echo Data Services, Inc., 1978—; instr. data processing Los Angeles City Adult Schs.; tchr. lectr., cons. wines and wine-tasting; instr. photography. Mem. ops. bd. Everywoman's Village; bd. dirs. So. Calif. Jewish Hist. Soc.; co-founder Open Space Theatre; former officer Ethel Josephine Scantland Found.; past post adviser Explorer Scouts, Boy Scouts Am., also Eagle Scout. Recipient Youth Service award Mid-Valley YMCA, 1972-73; C.P.A., Calif., cert. systems profl. Mem. Am. Inst. C.P.A.s, Calif. Soc. C.P.A.s, Assn. for Systems Mgmt., Data Processing Mgmt. Assn., Am. Fedn. Musicians, Friends of Photography, Los Angeles Photog. Ctr., Acad. Model Aeros., Nat. Model Railroad Assn., Maltese Falcons Home Brewing Soc., San Fernando Valley Silent Flyers, San Fernando Valley Radio Control Flyers, Associated Students Calif. State U., Los Angeles (hon. life), Acad. Magical Arts, Internal Brotherhood of Magicians, Soc. Preservation of Variety Arts, Les Amis du Vin, Knights of the Vine, Soc. Wine Educators, Soc. Bacchus Am., German Shepherd Dog Club Am., German Shepherd Dog Club Los Angeles County, Blue Key, Alpha Phi Omega. Clubs: Verdugo, Kiwanis (pres. Sunset-Echo Park 1968), Braemar Country, Pacific Mariners Yacht, S.Coast Corinthian Yacht (Former dir., officer), B'nai B'rith. Cons., contbr. Wine World Mag., 1974—. Home: 15534 Morrison St Sherman Oaks CA 91403 Office: Glynn Boxer & Phillips Inc CPA's 1000 N Central Ave Glendale CA 91202

BOXER, TIM, photographer, journalist; b. Winnipeg, Man., Can., May 12, 1934; s. Gabriel and Annie (Gampel) B.; m. Nina Naham, June 12, 1977; children—Gabriel Paul, David Michael. Student United Coll., Can., 1951-52, Herzl Jr. Coll., 1952-54, Northwestern U., 1954-55, Hebrew Theol. Coll., 1952-56. News editor Nat. Jewish Post, Chgo., 1956-57; reporter City News Bur., Chgo., 1957-59; city editor Sentinel of Chgo., 1958-60; asst. pub. relations dir. Israel Bonds of Chgo., 1960; publicist for Dick Gregory, Chgo., 1960-61; Eastern publicity mgr. Playboy mag. and Playboy Club of N.Y., 1961-62; freelance pub. relations specialist, 1963-67; asst. to Earl Wilson, N.Y.C., 1967-83; freelance photographer, 1967—; columnist Jewish Week of N.Y., 1978—, United Feature Syndicate, 1984-85; N.Y. Post, 1979-86 ; producer Manhattan Cable TV, 1974-77. Author: Jewish Celebrity Hall of Fame, 1987. Served with AUS, 1957. Recipient Community Service award Dov Revel Yeshiva, Forest Hills, N.Y. Mem. Internat. Platform Assn., Young Israel, Zionist Orgn. Am., Jewish War Vets., B'nai B'rith, Bnai Zion, Am.-Israel Friendship League. Home and Office: 73-34 173d St Hillcrest NY 11366

BOXWILL, FRANK E., psychologist; b. Georgetown, Guyana, June 25, 1926; s. Isaac and Stella (Bunbury) B.; came to U.S., 1946, naturalized, 1960; children: Frank E., Eric, Yvette, Francyne, André. Student, Howard U., 1947-48; BS, Wagner Coll., 1953; postgrad., New Sch. Social Research, 1954, LIU, 1956-58, U. Oreg., 1958-59; PhD, East Coast U., 1971. Fellow in psychology Bklyn. Psychiat. Ctr., 1959-61; clin. psychologist Kings County Hosp., Bklyn., 1961-65; psychotherapist Bklyn. Ctr. Psychotherapy, 1964-66; psychotherapist Bleuler Ctr. Psychotherapy, Forest Hills, N.Y., 1967-81; psychologist Brentwood (N.Y.) Pub. Schs., 1965-66, Amityville (N.Y.) Pub. Schs., 1967-84; chmn. bd. Family Inst. for More Effective Living Inc., Wilmington, Del., 1985—; sr. research assoc. Tng. Resources for Youth, Bklyn., 1965-66; coordinator research Harlem Psychiat. Rehab. Ctr., Columbia U., N.Y.C., 1966-67; dir. Family Inst. for More Effective Living, Westbury, 1973; founder Parent Adolescent Relations Inst., Inc., 1980—; cons. Child Abuse Agy.; cons. in child devel., learning, marital and family relations, tchr., trainer. Author: the Troubled Youngster in the Classroom, 1971,

Understanding Ego Development of the Troubled Youngster, 1972, Learning Disabilities, A Multi-disciplinary Approach, 1973. Mem. Rep. Presdl. Task Force, 1983—. Fellow Royal Soc. Health (Eng.), Am. Orthopsychiat. Assn.; mem. Nat. Assn. Sch. Psychologists, Nat. Council Family Relations, Am. Soc. Tng. and Devel., Am. Mgmt. Assn., N.Y. Soc. Clin. Psychologists.

BOYA, LUIS JOAQUIN, theoretical physics educator; b. Zaragoza, Spain, June 17, 1936; s. Luis and Engracia (Balet) B.; widower; children: Patricia, Fernanco. Licenciado en Ciencias Fisicas, U. Zaragoza, 1958; PhD, U. Barcelona, 1964. Asst. prof. physics U. Barcelona, Spain, 1964-68; assoc. prof. U. Valladolid, Spain, 1968-73; assoc. prof. theoretical physics U. Zaragoza, Spain, 1973-76; prof. physics, head dept. U. Salamanca, Spain, 1976-81; prof. U. Zaragoza, Spain, 1881-83, head dept., 1983-87. Author: Differential Geometry, 1977, Supersymmetry Quantum Mechanics, 1987. Fellow Real Sociedad Fisica y Quimica; mem. Am. Phys. Soc. Roman Catholic. Home: Plaza E Carlos 1, 50009 Zaragoza Spain Office: Univ Zaragoza, Departamento de Fisica Teorica, Facultad de Ciencias, 50009 Zaragoza Spain

BOYADJIAN, HAIG JOHN, banker, writer; b. Jerusalem, Feb. 13, 1935; s. HaRouTune Panos and Mary (Karakashian) B. BA in Internat. Affairs, Swarthmore Coll., 1957; MA in Internat. Econs., Fletcher Sch. Law and Diplomacy, 1958. From exec. mgmt. trainee to v.p. and div. exec. Chase Manhattan Bank N.Am., N.Y.C., 1961-77; v.p., sr. lending officer Berliner Handels Und Frankfurter Bank, 1977-79, sr. v.p. credit policy and bus. planning, 1979-82; sr. v.p. Midland Bank PLC, N.Y.C., London and Fed. Republic of Germany, 1982-83, asst. gen. mgr., controller of lending, 1983-86, head global commodities and securities industries, 1987—. Author: Risks: Reading Corporate Signals, 1987. Served with M.I. Corps, U.S. Army, 1959-61. Republican. Episcopalian. Office: Midland Bank PLC, 47 Cannon St, London EC4, England

BOYAR, ROBERT LEE, architect, educator; b. N.Y.C., Jan. 4, 1935; s. Benjamin and Sadie (Geller) B.; m. Joan Rhoda Lederer, June 16, 1957; children—Michele Fern and Howard Evan (twins). B.Arch., Rensselaer Poly. Inst., 1957; postgrad. NYU, 1959-60. Draftsman, Harrison & Abramovitz, 1959-60; designer, draftsman Joseph Douglas Weiss, Architect, 1960-64; ptnr. Joseph Douglas Weiss & Assocs., 1964-66; ptnr. Joseph D. Weiss, Whelan & Boyar, N.Y.C., 1967-68; dir. ambulatory facilities design City N.Y. Health Services Adminstrn., 1968-70; dir. capital planning and budgeting N.Y.C. Health and Hosps. Corp., 1970-72, dir. master planning, 1973-74; hosp. cons., dir. bldg. consultation Anthony J.J. Rourke, Inc., Harrison, N.Y., 1974-79; dir. facilities planning and constrn. L.I. Jewish Med Ctr., 1979-85; v.p. Master Plan Facilities, St. Luke's/Roosevelt Hosp. Ctr. 1985—; adj. prof. Columbia U. Sch. Pub. Health, N.Y.C., 1985—; panelist Dept. Health and Human Services conf. on future of hosp. design, NIH, Bethesda, Md., 1984. Contbr. articles on hosp. planning and constrn. to profl. publs. Served with AUS, 1957-59. Mem. AIA, N.Y. State Assn. Architects, N.Y. Soc. Architects, Am. Arbitration Assn., Am. Health Planning Assn., N.Y. Soc. Health Planning, Phi Sigma Delta. Prin. works include Friedman Pavilion Hosp. for Elderly, N.Y.C., Kittay House, Isabella Home, Hebrew Home for Aged, Hartford; owner's rep. Schneider Children's Hosp., Queens, N.Y. Lodge: K.P. Home: 869 Fiske St Woodmere NY 11598 Office: 425 W 59th St New York NY 10019

BOYD, CLARENCE ELMO, surgeon; b. Leesville, La., Nov. 2, 1911; s. Isaac Clarence and Ada Lee (Stakes) B.; m. Emma Kittredge Sims, Aug. 13, 1937; children: Charles Elmo, Marjorie Emily (Mrs. James O. Hudson), Frances Ada (Mrs. Thomas H. Thigpen), James E. B.A., U. Tex., 1932, M.D., 1935. Diplomate Am. Bd. Abdominal Surgeons (a founder 1959). Intern Charity Hosp., New Orleans, 1935-36; resident North La. Sanitarium (now Doctors Hosp.), Shreveport, 1936-37; founding dir., med. dir. Doctor's Hosp., Shreveport, 1959—, chmn. bd., 1959-80, vis. surgeon, 1937—; gen. practice medicine 1937-42; jr. vis. surgeon Charity Hosp., Shreveport, 1937-42; practice medicine specializing in surgery Shreveport, 1942—; sr. vis. surgeon Confederate Meml. Hosp., 1942—; 1st v.p. vis. staff 1943-44; sr., founding mem. C. E. Boyd Clinic Ltd., 1942—; clin. asst. prof. surgery La. State U., Shreveport, 1957-67; clin. asst. prof. surgery, co-founder La. State U. Sch. Medicine, Shreveport, 1967—; Founding dir. Shreveport Bank & Trust Co., 1954, chmn. investment com., 1954-78, chmn. bd., 1961-87. Author numerous articles; producer films in field. Bd. dirs. Volunteers Am., 1950-58, chmn. bd., 1955-57; trustee Pub. Affairs Research Council La., 1959-79; mem. nat. adv. bd. We, The People, 1964—; mem. sponsors com. Shreveport United Fund, 1962-66; Guest speaker Dean's lecture La. State Med. Sch., 1955, 57; founder, chmn. Student Loan Fund, 1942—. hon. col. Gov. La. staff, 1964. Fellow A.C.S., Internat. Coll. Surgeons, Southeastern Surg. Congress, Am. Soc. Abdominal Surgeons (a founder 1959, pres. 1966-67, mem. teaching faculty 1962—, Gold medal 1962—); mem. AMA (chmn. surg. sect. 1965, 67, mem. surg. sect. 1969-71, alternate del. gen. surg. council 1972-78, mem. surg. council 1972-78, del. 1978-79, Recognition award 1966-69, 70-72, 73-75, 76-78, 79-81, 82-84), Assn. Am. Physicians and Surgeons (del. 1960-72, chmn. La. membership com. 1950-72, pres. La. chpt. 1972-73), Internat. Acad. Proctology, Surg. Assn. La., Am. Mastology Assn., La. State Med. Soc. (Ho. of Dels. 1945-59, chmn. pub. policy and legis. com. 1954-57, chmn. surg. sect. 1957, councilor 1959-66, 1st v.p. 1967-68, chmn. com. on hosps. 1968-71, vice chmn. socio-econs. 1970-71, first chmn. com. medicine and religion 1964-66), Shreveport Med. Soc. (Gold medal 1956-57, pres. 1956-57, 1st chmn. med. progress 1957-59), Am. Cancer Soc. (bd. dirs. Caddo br. 1952-59, vice chmn. bd. 1957-58), So. Med. Assn. (asst. councilor 1959-68), Pan-Pacific Surg. Assn. Episcopalian (vestryman 1966-69; Gold medal Bible Class 1965). Clubs: Mason (32 deg.), Shriner, Rotarian (pres. South Shreveport Chpt. 1940-41, founder 1942, student loan com.). Home: 401 Delaware St Shreveport LA 71106 Office: 1128 Louisiana Ave Shreveport LA 71101

BOYD, DAVID PRESTON, business educator; b. Amsterdam, N.Y., Oct. 19, 1943; s. David Preston and Mignon (Finch) B. BA in English Lit., Harvard U., 1965; DPhil in Behavioral Scis., Oxford U., 1973. Asst. headmaster Dedham Country Day Sch., Mass., 1965-69; co-owner The Old Cambridge Co., Mass., 1973-77; instr. Coll. Bus. Adminstrn., Northeastern U., Boston, 1977-78, asst. prof., 1978-82, assoc. prof., 1982-87, prof., 1987—, acting dean, 1987, dean, 1987—; Patrick F. and Helen C. Walsh research prof., 1985-86, chmn. human resources mgmt. dept., 1986-87, mem. univ. editorial bd., 1984-89. Author: Elites and Their Education, National Foundation for Educational Research, 1973, also numerous articles. Recipient Excellence in Teaching award Northeastern U., 1980; Northeastern U. grantee, 1982-84, Control Data Corp., 1983, NYU, 1985. Home: 65 Grove St Wellesley MA 02181 Office: Northeastern U 101 Hayden Hall Boston MA 02115

BOYD, EDWARD LEE, physicist, computer scientist; b. Mexico, Mo., Nov. 27, 1932; s. Lee Moore Boyd and Billy (Richter) Boyd Falk; m. Irene Howe Crossman, July 26, 1969; children—Sloane Victoria, Ashton Lee. B.A. in Physics, Lehigh U., 1954; D.S. in Materials Sci., Kyoto U., Japan, 1967. Engr. Beva Labs., Trenton, 1953-54, Associated Enrs., Poughkeepsie, N.Y., 1954-55; physicist in research IBM, Yorktown Heights, N.Y., 1955-66, physicist in components, Poughkeepsie, N.Y., 1966-76, sr. staff mem. corp. hdqrs., Armonk, N.Y., 1976-79, sr. engr. gen. tech. div., East Fishkill, N.Y., 1979-88, sr. tech. staff mem., 1988—. Contbr. chpt., articles on physics of magnetism to profl. publs. Patentee in field. Bd. dirs. various cultural orgns. Served as pfc. USAR, 1957-69. Mem. Am. Phys. Soc., Am. Assn. Physics Tchrs., AAAS. Episcopalian. Office: IBM Rt 52 Hopewell Junction NY 12533

BOYD, JOHN KENT, advertising executive; b. Portsmouth, Ohio, Oct. 17, 1910; s. Lambert Thomas and Faery Ann (Ritter) B.; student Tulane U., New Orleans, 1927-29; m. Jeanne Marie Dunlap, Dec. 26, 1935; children—John Kent, Barbara Ann. Mem. staff advt. dept. Am. Rolling Mill Co., Middletown, Ohio, 1929-31; advt. mgr. Pitts. and Midway Coal Mining Co., Kansas City, Mo., 1932-35; v.p. Ferry-Hanly Co., 1935-44; partner Bruce B. Brewer & Co., Kansas City and Mpls., 1944-66; pres., chief exec. officer Bruce B. Brewer Co., Inc., 1967-72, chmn. bd., chief exec. officer, 1972-75; dir. Marco Mfg. Co.; past pres., dir. Quivira, Inc.; pres. Kaybee, Inc. Co-chmn. United Funds publicity com., 1953; dir. United Cerebral Palsy Assn. of Kansas City; active Boy Scouts Am.; bd. govs. Starlight Theatre Assn., YMCA, Quiet Birdmen; bd. dirs. Kansas City Crime Commn. Control adv. com. FAA Kanas City Air Traffic. Named Man of Yr. in Gen. Aviation, 1969; recipient silver medal Am. Advt. Fedn., 1972. Mem. AIM, Nat. Aero. Assn., Am. Legion, Kansas City Sr. Golf Assn., Kansas City Promotion Com., Airplane Owners and Pilots Assn. (nat.). Am. Mktg. Assn. (dir. Kansas City chpt.), Am. Royal Assn. (gov.), C. of C., Snipe Class Internat. Racing Assn., Nat. Pilots Assn. (dir.) Am. Bonanza Soc., Air Force Assn., Silver Wings. Clubs: Kansas City, Advt., Sales Execs., Quivira Country, Mission Hills Country, Aero of Kansas City, OX5 of Am.; Capital Hill (Washington); Quivira Sailing (past commodore); Diamondhead Yacht and Country; Bay-Waveland Yacht. Author: Jerry Dalrymple, 1931, Crowded Skies, 1969. Home: 3400 Yacht Club Circle Bay Saint Louis MS 39520 Office: 6512 Maple Dr Mission KS 66202

BOYD, LEONA POTTER, former social worker; b. Creekside, Pa., Aug. 31, 1907; d. Joseph M. and Belle (McHenry) Johnston; grad. Ind. Normal Sch., 1927; student Las Vegas Normal U., N.Mex., summer 1933; postgrad. Carnegie Inst. Tech. Sch. Social Work, summer 1945, U. Pitts. Sch. Social Work, 1956-57; m. Edgar D. Potter, July 16, 1932 (div.); m. Harold Lee Boyd, Oct. 1972. Tchr., Creekside (Pa.) pub. schs., 1927-30, Papago Indian Reservation, Sells, Ariz., 1931-33; caseworker, supr. Indiana County (Pa.) Bd. Assistance, 1934-54, exec. dir., 1954-68, ret. Bd. dirs. Indiana County Tourist Promotion; former bd. dirs. Indiana County United Fund, Salvation Army, Indiana County Guidance Ctr., Armstrong-Indiana Mental Health Bd.; cons. asso. Community Research Assos., Inc.; mem. Counseling Center Aux., Lake Havasu City, Ariz., 1978-80; mem. Western Welcome Club, Lake Havasu City, Sierra Vista Hosp. Aux., Truth or Consequences, N.Mex. Recipient Jr. C. of C. Disting. Service award, 1966, Business and Profl. Women's Club award, Indiana, Pa., 1965. Mem. Am. Assn. Ret. Persons, Daus. Am. Colonists, Internat. Platform Assn., Sierra County hist. socs. Lutheran. Club: Hot Springs Women's. Home: 507 N Foch St Truth or Consequences NM 87901

BOYD, MAURICE, history educator; b. Guthrie, Ky., Apr. 3, 1921; s. Charles Hayden and Lorena (Shelton) B.; m. Shirley Mereness, Mar. 5, 1944 (dec. 1970); children: James, Robert, Jon Christopher, Thomas; m. Sarah Bernhardt, 1980. AB, U. Mo., 1943; MA, U. Mich., 1948, PhD, 1951. Teaching fellow U. Mich., 1949-50; instr. Bradley U., Peoria, Ill., 1950-52, asst. prof., 1952-54, assoc. prof., 1954-56, dir. gen. edn., 1953-56; assoc. prof. humanities U. Fla., Gainesville, 1956-57, chmn. dept. social sci., 1957-61, prof. social scis., 1959-64, prof. humanities, 1961-64; prof. history Tex. Christian U., Ft. Worth, 1964—, chmn. dept., 1974-80. Author: Cardinal Quiroga: Inquisitor General of Spain, 1955, Eight Tarascan Legends, 1958, American Civilization, 1964, William Knox and Abraham Lincoln, 1966, Contemporary America: Issues and Problems, 1968, Tarascan Myths and Legends, 1969, Reflections of a Young Woman, 1980, Kiowa Voices, Vol. I: Dance, Music and Song, 1981, Kiowa Voices, Vol II: Myths, Legends and Folktales, 1982, The Flemish Art of Frans De Cauter, 1988; also articles. Mem. Am. Hist. Assn., So. Hist. Assn., Western Hist. Assn., NEA, Phi Alpha Theta, Pi Sigma Alpha. Home: 4025 Glenwood Dr Fort Worth TX 76109

BOYD, ROBERT EDWARD LEE, II, mechanical engineer; b. Wheeling, W.Va., Nov. 12, 1914; s. Robert E. Lee and Mary (Bachtler) B.; m. Julia Eleanor Beal, Jan. 1, 1938; children—Mary Eleanor Boyd Eads, Barbara Ann Boyd Hall, Robert E. Lee III. A.B. in Physics, Kenyon Coll., 1936. With Westinghouse Co., 1937-38; mech. contractor, 1939; with Houston Lighting and Power Co., 1940-42; heat pump contractor, 1946-48; with Airtemp Corp., 1948-51, contractor, 1951-53; with Electromode Corp., 1953-57; tech. dir. Edwin L. Wiegand Co., Pitts., 1957-66; engring. cons. climate control div. Singer Co., Auburn, N.Y., 1966-71; asso. prof. air-conditioning tech. State U. N.Y. Coll., Alfred, 1971-74; asso. tech. dir. Sheet Metal and Air Conditioning Contractors' Nat. Assn., Vienna, Va., 1974-76; sr. mech. engr. NAHB (Nat. Assn. Home Builders) Research Found., Inc., Rockville, Md., 1976-78, ret., 1978. Contbr. numerous articles on heating and air conditioning application engring. to trade and profl. pubs.; patentee in field. Served to 1st lt. C.E., AUS, 1942-46. Fellow ASHRAE; mem. Engrs. Joint Council, Engrs. of Distinction, Am. Assn. Ret. Persons, Phi Beta Kappa, Tau Kappa Alpha. Home: 413 Brewers Creek Ln Carrollton VA 23314

BOYD, WILLIAM ANDREW MURRAY, novelist, screenwriter; b. Accra, Ghana, Mar. 7, 1952; s. Alexander Murray and Evelyn (Smith) B.; m. Susan Anne Wilson, Sept. 4, 1975. Diploma of French Studies, U. Nice (France), 1971; MA in English Philosophy, Glasgow (Scotland) U., 1971-75; postgrad., Oxford U., 1975-80. lectr. in English St. Hilda's Coll. Oxford U., 1980-83. Author: A Good Man in Africa, 1981, An Ice Cream War, 1982, Stars and Bars, 1984, The New Confessions, 1987. Recipient the Whitbread prize, 1981, Somerset Maugham award, 1982, John Llewelyn Rhys prize, 1982. Fellow Royal Soc. Literature. Club: 2 Bridges Place (London).

BOYD, WILLIAM DOUGLAS, JR., library science educator, clergyman; b. Pulaski, Tenn., Dec. 15, 1929; s. William Douglas and Lula May (Scott) B.; m. Margaret Woolfolk, July 16, 1966; 1 child, Julia Woolfolk. BA, Rhodes Coll., 1952; BD, Union Theol. Sem., N.Y.C., 1955; ThM, Princeton Theol. Sem., 1958; MLS, Ind. U., 1972, PhD, 1975. Ordained to ministry, 1956. Pastor First Presbyn. Ch., Mt. Pleasant, Tenn., 1956-63; asst. pastor Ind. Presbyn. Ch., Birmingham, Ala., 1963-67; asst. law librarian Ind. U., Bloomington, 1972-73; asst. prof. library sci. U. So. Miss., Hattiesburg, 1973-77, assoc. prof., 1977—; reviewer pub. library program NEH, 1978. Translator: (L. Buzás) German Library History 800 1945, 1986. Contbr. articles to profl. jours. Mem. ALA,SAR, (sec. Miss. 1985-88, 2nd v.p. 1988—), Tenn. Library Assn. (vice-chmn. trustees and friends sect. 1962-63), Miss. Library Assn., Am. Assn. Adult and Continuing Edn., Miss. Inst. Arts and Letters, Presbytery of Miss., Mil. Order Stars and Bars, Krewe of Zeus, Omicron Delta Kappa, Beta Phi Mu. Democrat. Club: Hattiesburg Country. Home: 104 Lee Circle Hattiesburg MS 39401 Office: U So Miss Hattiesburg MS 39406-8238

BOYDEN, RICHARD, JR., finance executive; b. Bklyn., July 27, 1945; s. Richard John and Rebecca Lee (Wright) B.; A.A.S., Manhattan Community Coll., 1971; B.S., St. John's U., 1973; M.B.A., L.I.U., 1978. Cert. mgmt. acct. In-charge auditor Ernst & Ernst, C.P.A.s, N.Y.C., 1973-76; staff acct. Belco Petroleum Corp., N.Y.C., 1976-77; sr. internal auditor Am. Standard, Inc., N.Y.C., 1977-79; internal audit supr. Colgate Palmolive Co., N.Y.C., 1979-83, acctg. mgr. 1983—. Served with U.S. Army, 1965-67. C.P.A., N.Y.C. Mem. Am. Inst. C.P.A.s, Nat Assn. Accts., Inst. Internal Auditors, Council Concerned Black Execs., Nat. Black M.B.A. Assn., Nat. Assn. Black Accts., Inst. Mgmt. Acctg., One Hundred Black Men, Inc., N.Y. State Soc. C.P.A.s. Home: 94 Hampden Dr Norwood MA 02062 Office: 300 Park Ave New York NY 10022

BOYER, LAURA MERCEDES, librarian; b. Madison, Ind., Aug. 3, 1934; d. Clyde C. and Dorcas H. (Willyard) Boyer. A.B., George Washington U., 1956; A.M., U. Denver, 1959; M.L.S., George Peabody U., 1961. Pub. sch. tchr., Kankakee, Ill., 1957-58; asst. circulation librarian U. Kans., Lawrence, 1961-63; asst. reference librarian U. of Pacific Library, Stockton, Calif., 1963-65, head reference dept., 1965-84, coordinator reference services, 1984-86; reference librarian Calif. State U.-Stanislaus, Turlock, 1987—. Compiler of Play Anthologies Union List, 1976. Author article in profl. jour. Mem. Am. Soc. Info. Sci., ALA, Calif. Library Assn., AAUP, Nat. Assn. Female Exes., Nat. Assn. Vietnamese Am. Educators, DAR, Daughters of the Am. Colonists, Phi Beta Kappa, Kappa Delta Pi, Beta Phi Mu. Republican. Episcopalian. Home: 825 Muir Rd Modesto CA 95350

BOYES, JON L., association executive; b. Oakland, Calif., July 5, 1921; s. Gordon McBoyes; m. Nancy Mitchell, Oct. 23, 1970; children: Jan Brooke, Christopher Lynne, Virginia Leigh. B.S., U.S. Naval Acad., 1943; M.A., U. Md., 1960, Ph.D., 1970; M.A., U. Hawaii, 1963; M.S., U.S. Naval Postgrad. Sch. Messenger Am. Trust Co., 1940-41; commd. ensign U.S. Navy, 1943; advanced through grades to vice adm.; destroyer and submarine duty; 1st comdr. underice Arctic ops., also nuclear attach squadron Navy Command and Con U.S. Navy (Navy Command and Control System); later dep. dir. gen. NAT; ret.; now pres. Nat. Sci. Ctr. Found.; mem. faculty U. Md. Grad. Sch.; dir. Andrew Corp., Miltope Corp., SAMA Corp., Andrulis Resch Corp., Andrew Corp., SOTAS Corp. Author tech. articles. Decorated D.S.M., Legion of Merit (4), Purple Heart; recipient Gold medal Armed Forces Communications and Electronics Assn., Distinguished Service medal. Mem. IEEE, Armed Forces Communications and Electronics Assn., Electronic Warfare Assn., NATO Service Club. Republican. Episcopalian. Club: Lions. Home: 11807 Wayland St Oakton VA 22033 Office: 4400 Fair Lakes Ct Fairfax VA 22033-3899

BOYHUS, ELSE-MARIE, museum director; b. Nykøbing, Denmark, Dec. 20, 1935; d. Tage Mikkelsen and Sørine (Skøtt) B.; m. Finn Ragn-Hansen, Jan. 25, 1958; children: Henrik, Hanne. MA, U. Copenhagen, 1963. Dir. Lolland-Falsters Stifts Mus., Maribo, Denmark, 1963—; chmn. Danish Bd. Museums, 1977-81. Contbr. articles to profl. jours. Fellow Danish Soc. for Agrl. History, Danish Gastronomique Acad.; mem. Danish Agrl. Found. for Culture (bd. dirs.). Home: Sdr Blvd 1, 4930 Maribo Denmark Office: Stiftsmuseet, Museumsgade 1, 4930 Maribo Denmark

BO YIBO, government official; b. Dingxiang, Shanxi, People's Republic of China, 1908; m. Hu Ming. Mem. Chinese Communist Party, from 1925, Chinese Communist Party Cen. Com., from 1945; vice-chmn., minister of fin. Fin. and Econ. Affairs Com., 1949-53; mem. State Planning Commn., 1952-54, vice-chmn., 1954; dir. 3d staff office State Council, 1954-59; chmn. Economy Commn., 1956-66; alt. mem. Chinese Communist Party Politburo, 1956; vice-premier 1956-66, 79-82; mem. State Fin. and Econ. Commn., 1979-81, Chinese Communist Party 11th Cen. Com., 1979-82; minister State Machine Bldg. Industry Commn., 1980-82; state councillor 1982-83; vice-minister State Commn. Restructuring Econ. System, 1982; mem. Presidium, 12th Party Congress, 1982; vice-chmn. Cen. Adv. Commn. Chinese Communist Party Cen. Com., from 1982, vice-chmn. Cen. Commn. for Guiding Party Consolidation, 1983—. Address: Chinese Communist Party, Vice-chmn Cen Adv Com, Beijing Peoples Republic of China *

BOYKEN, IMMO, architect, historian; b. Oldenburg, Fed Republic Germany, Dec. 2, 1943; s. Ernst Henry and Annemarie (Ostendorf) B.; m. Inge Heinzelmann, Mar. 9, 1978. Diploma in Engring., U. Karlsruhe, Fed. Republic Germany, 1972, DEng, 1984. Lic. architect, Baden-Württemberg. Pvt. practice architecture Baden-Württemberg, Fed. Republic Germany, 1979—; research worker Inst. Baugeschichte U. Karlsruhe, Fed. Republic Germany, 1979—, Sonderforschungsbereich Soc. Preservation of Historically Important Bldgs., Structures, Constrn. and Bldg. Materials, Fed. Republic Germany, 1985—; instr., researcher Inst. Baugeschichte, Sonderforschungsbereich, Karlsruhe, 1979—. Author books, articles on history of modern architecture. Mem. Architektenkammer Baden-Württemberg, Koldewey Gesellschaft. Home: Neuhauser Strasse 16a, 7750 Konstanz Federal Republic of Germany Office: Inst Baugeschichte, Englerstrasse 7, 7500 Karlsruhe Federal Republic of Germany

BOYKIN, FRANCES LEWIS, retired social worker; b. Boston; d. Joel Randolph and Frances Virginia (Kenney) Lewis; m. Herbert Charles Boykin Jr., Dec. 23, 1951 (div. 1958). BS, Simmons Coll., 1945, MS, 1946. Cert. social worker, N.Y. Caseworker Family Service of Orange County, Maplewood, N.J., 1946-47; child welfare worker Riverdale Children's Assn., N.Y.C., 1946-51; supr., casework coordinator Assoc. Day Care Services of Greater Boston, 1952-53; caseworker, advancing to sr. caseworker Salvation Army-Family Service, N.Y.C., 1955-74; psychiat. researcher, 1957-62; student supr. NYU Sch. Edn., 1969-74, field supr. student unit, 1976-79; field supr. for student unit Salvation Army Corps and Community Ctrs., N.Y.C., 1974-79, adv. orgn. mem. Salvation Army N.Y. State, 1979-86 (meritorious service award); adj. asst. prof. NYU Sch. Social Work, 1977-79. Bd. dirs. Assn. Bronx Community Orgns., 1964-73, v.p., 1968-69, treas., 1970-73; bd. dirs. N.Y.C. region NCCJ, 1976-85, mem. exec. com., 1977-85; mem. Bronx adv. com. Urban League, 1966-69; pres. corp. body 12th Ch. Christ Scientist, N.Y.C., 1988; active mother ch. 1st Ch. Christ Scientist, Boston. Recipient Service plaque for 30 yrs. with Salvation Army N.Y.C., 1986. Mem. Nat. Assn. Social Workers, Acad. Cert. Social Workers, Internat. Conf. Social Work (del. 1964-84). Home: 2235 Fifth Ave New York NY 10037

BOYKIN, HARTFORD EDWIN, JR., corporate planning executive; b. Wilmington, N.C., Apr. 18, 1952; s. Hartford Edwin and Eunice Elizabeth (Neal) B.; m. Aysegül Erginay, Oct. 9, 1987. BS, Cornell U., 1975, postgrad., 1974-75. Loan officer Wachovia Bank & Trust Co. N.A., Raleigh, N.C., 1976-77; cons., dir. tech. commercialization U.S. Dept. Commerce, Raleigh, 1977-79; cons., dir. tech. commercialization Long Beach, Calif., 1979-81, Los Angeles, 1981-82; sr. cons. Spectrum Internat., Inc., Culver City, Calif., 1982-84; mgr. info. planning Saudi Arabian Ailines, Jeddah, 1984—; pres. Tech. Transfer Soc., Los Angeles, 1980-82; chmn. bd. Tech. Research & Commercialization, Los Angeles, 1982-84. Corp. vol. Jr. Achievement, Raleigh, 1976-77; mem. adv. council Tech. Utilization Ctr., Ga. Inst. Tech., Atlanta, 1980-82. Mem. Planning Forum, Cornell U. Soc. Engrs., Profl. Assn. Diving Instrs. Club: Diving Ventures Internat. (Santa Ana, Calif.). Home: 353 S Kerr Ave Wilmington NY 28403

BOYLAN, BRIAN RICHARD, author, theatre/film director, photographer; b. Chgo., Dec. 11, 1936, s. Francis Thomas and Mary Catherine (Kane) B.; student Loyola U., 1954-58; children—Rebecca, Gregory, Ingrid. Editor, Jour. AMA, Med. World News, The Statesman, 1956-64; author, 1965—; works include: The New Heart, 1969; Infidelity, 1971; Benedict Arnold: The Dark Eagle, 1973; A Hack in a Hurry, 1980; Final Trace, 1983; works include 12 books, 3 plays, 2 screenplays; photographer, 1966—; theatre dir., 1970—; works include 31 plays, videotapes and films. Home: 1530 S 6th St Minneapolis MN 55454

BOYLAN, WILLIAM ALVIN, lawyer; b. Marshalltown, Iowa, Sept. 18, 1924; s. Glen D. and Dorothy I. (Gibson) B.; m. Nancy Dickson, Aug. 5, 1950; children: Ross, Laura. Student, U. Iowa, 1943-44; B.A., Drake U., 1947; LL.B., Harvard U., 1950. Bar: Ill. 1950, N.Y. bar 1952. Practiced in N.Y.C., 1952—; bd. dirs. Tribune Oil Corp. Contbr. articles to profl. jours. Served with USAAF, 1943-46. Mem. ABA, N.Y. State Bar Assn., Assn. Bar City N.Y., Fed. Bar Council, Phi Beta Kappa, Sigma Alpha Epsilon. Episcopalian. Clubs: Harvard, The Down Town Assn. Home: 108 E 82d St New York NY 10028 Office: Gould & Wilkie 1 Wall St 34th Floor New York NY 10005

BOYLE, DANIEL EDWARD, JR., real estate and oil investor; b. Pueblo, Colo., Feb. 11, 1931; s. Daniel Edward and Claire M. Boyle; m. Patricia Ann Bellamah, Jan. 9, 1954; children: Daniel Edward, III, Patricia Elaine Boyle Wilken, Cynthia Kay. B.A. in English, N.Mex. Mil. Inst., Roswell, 1953. With Dale J. Bellamah Corp. and related entities, Albuquerque, 1956-81, pres., 1970, chmn. bd., 1972-81; chmn. bd. Oilsearch Corp., 1983, D.E. Boyle Cos., Liberty Land Co., 1984; bd. dirs. First Interstate Bank Albuquerque, United Southwest Corp., Phoenix, First Am. Asset Mgmt. Bd. dirs. Southwest Community Health Services, Albuquerque. Served as officer U.S. Army, 1953-56. Methodist. Clubs: Rio Rancho, Tanoan Country. Home: 1425 Stagecoach Rd SE Albuquerque NM 87123 Office: One Coronado Pl 6201 Uptown Blvd NE Suite 204 Albuquerque NM 87110

BOYLE, IAIN THOMSON, medical educator, physician; b. Glasgow, Scotland, Oct. 7, 1935; s. Dugald Thomson and Annie Ross (McPhail) B.; m. Elizabeth Johnston Carmichael, Aug. 28, 1964; children—Catriona, Alison, Douglas. B.Sc. with honors, Glasgow U., 1959, M.B.Ch.B., 1962. House officer in medicine and surgery Glasgow Royal Infirmary, 1962-63, jr. research fellow, 1963-64; lectr. in medicine U. Glasgow, 1964-70, sr. lectr., 1973-84; reader in medicine U. Glasgow, 1984—; cons. physician. Contbr. articles on bone and vitamin D metabolism to profl. jours.; editor Scottish Med. Jour., 1977-83, chmn. bd. mgmt., 1988—; co-editor Bone, 1984—; mem. editorial bd. Clin. Sci., 1988—. Pres. Caledonian Philatelic Soc., Glasgow, 1983-84. Research fellow U. Wis.-Madison, 1970-72. Fellow Royal Coll. Physicians (Glasgow, councillor 1984—), Royal Coll. Physicians (London), Scottish Soc. Antiquaries; mem. Scottish Soc. Physicians (sec. 1983—), Scottish Soc. Exptl. Medicine (sec. 1983—), Assn. Physicians U.K. and Ireland, Bone and Tooth Soc. (treas. 1988—). Home: 7 Lochbrae Dr, Burnside, Glasgow G73 5QL, Scotland Office: Univ Dept Medicine, Glasgow Royal Infirmary, 10 Alexandra Parade, Glasgow G73 2ER, Scotland

BOYLES, PATRICIA ANN, real estate executive; b. Cleve., Mar. 7, 1951; d. Charles William and Ann Marie (Galla) B. Student, Douglass Coll., 1969-72, Camden County Coll., 1976-77, Temple U., 1978. Mgr. advt., dir.

pub. relations W.T. Grant Co., Somerset, N.J., 1972-73; staff announcer Sta. WGAY, Washington, 1973; freelance in broadcast prodn. Phila., 1973-75; dir. adminstrn. Houser Demolition Inc., Camden, 1975-76; exec. coordinator Capp Realty Co., Lindenwold, N.J., 1977-80; rep. sales Ryland Group Inc., Cherry Hill, N.J., 1980-87; corp. sec. Security Mortgage and Investment Co., 1977-80; dir. field sales Ryland Group Inc., Marlton, 1987-88; mgr. div. sales Ryland Group Inc., Marlton, N.J., 1988—. Mem. Nat. Assn. Female Execs., Nat. Assn. Realtors, N.J. Assn. Realtors, Camden County Bd. Realtors, Am. Soc. Notaries, Am. Soc. Profl. and Exec. Women, Kings Grant Civic Assn. Home: 48 Queen Anne Ct Marlton NJ 08053 Office: Ryland Group Inc Delaware Valley Div 5 Greentree Ctr Suite 213 Marlton NJ 08053

BOYNE, WALTER JAMES, writer, former museum director; b. East St. Louis, Ill., Feb. 2, 1929; s. Walter William and Emily (Campbell) B.; m. Jeanne Quigley, Dec. 26, 1952; children: Mary Louise, Katherine Elizabeth, William James, Margaret Ann. B.B.A., U. Calif., Berkeley, 1958; M.B.A., U. Pitts., 1963. Commd. 2d lt. USAF, 1952, advanced through grades to col., retired, 1974; asst. curator Nat. Air and Space Mus., Washington, 1974-75, curator, 1975-78, exec. officer, 1978-80, asst. dir., 1980-82; dep. dir. Nat. Air and Space Mus., 1982-83, dir., 1983-86; retired 1986. Author: Boeing B-52, 1981, Messerschmitt Me-262, 1980, Treasures of Silver Hill, 1982, Flying, 1979, Jet Age, 1979, De Havilland DH-4, 1983, McDonnell Douglas F-4, 1983, Vertical Flight, 1983, Leading Edge, 1986, (novel) The Wild Blue, 1986; contbg. author numerous articles. Recipient Best Fgn. Book award Aero Club de France, 1982, Robert A. Brooks award Smithsonian Instn., 1980, Best Fiction and Non-Fiction awards Aviation Space Writers, 1987. Mem. Daedalians, Am. Aviation Hist. Soc. (nat. advisor), Sons of the Desert. Club: Cosmos, Explorers. Home: 11175 Lake Chapel Ln Reston VA 22091

BOYNTON, FREDERICK GEORGE, lawyer; b. Yokohama, Japan, May 9, 1948; s. Fred Wenderoth and Buelah Eleanor (Nygaard) B.; m. Nancy Jeanne McLendon, Aug. 3, 1985. BA, The Citadel, 1970; JD, Tulane U., 1973. Bar: SC 1973, Ga. 1976, U.S. Dist. Ct. Ga. 1976, U.S. Ct. Appeals (5th and 11th cirs.). Assoc. Smith, Gambrell & Russell, and predecessors, Atlanta, 1976-82, ptnr., 1982-88; sole practice, Atlanta, 1988—. Author: Criminal Defense Techniques, 1976. Mem. exec. com. Southside Progress Assn., Atlanta, 1983-84; deacon, Westminster Presbyn. Ch., Atlanta. Served to capt. JAGC, U.S. Army, 1973-76. Articles editor Tulane Sch. Law Rev. Fellow Ga. Bar Found.; mem. Fed. Bar Assn. (pres. Atlanta chpt. 1981-82, dep. chmn. adminstrv. law sect. 1986-87, bd. dirs. younger lawyers div. 1981-84, v.p. 11th Cir. 1985-87), ABA, State Bar Ga. (chmn. adminstrv. law sect. 1987-88), Lawyers Club of Atlanta, Order of Coif. Republican. Presbyterian. Home: 4860 Northway Dr NE Atlanta GA 30342 Office: 5871 Glenridge Dr NE Suite 230 Atlanta GA 30328

BOYNTON, WYMAN PENDER, retired lawyer; b. Portsmouth, N.H., Oct. 8, 1908; s. Harry Edwin and Helen Catherine (Pender) B.; m. Mildred Elizabeth Ballard, Feb. 1, 1935; children: Elizabeth Ballard Boynton Larsen. BS, MIT, 1931; LLB, U. Mich. 1936. Bar: N.H. 1936, U.S. Dist. Ct. 1946; registered profl. engr. Clk. Granite State Fire Ins. Co., 1926-27; with C.E. Walker & Co., 1931-33; jr. acct. J. Ben Hart, 1934; mem. Jeremy R. Waldron, 1936-39, Waldron & Boynton and successors Boynton, Waldron, Doleac, Woodman & Scott, P.A., Portsmouth, N.H., 1940-86; trustee Portsmouth Coop. Bank, 1946-81, chmn. bd. 1976-81. Asst. scoutmaster, then scoutmaster Boy Scouts Am., 1931-33, mem. troop com. and dist. com. 1936-40, mem. council exec. bd. 1951-60, council commr., 1953-54, council pres. 1957-58; mem. Portsmouth Athenaeum, N.H. Hist. Soc., Soc. for Preservation of New England Antiquities; trustee Portsmouth Hist. Soc., 1940-86, v.p., 1946-85, 87—, pres., 1985-87; trustee Mark H. Wentworth Home for Chronic Invalids, 1948-81, pres. 1950-81; pres. Chase Home for Children, 1950-77, trustee 1946—; trustee Portsmouth YWCA, 1949-70; pres. Portsmouth Athenaeum, 1977-80; trustee Portsmouth Pub. Library, 1955-70; trustee N.H. Indsl. Sch., Manchester, 1955-66, chmn. 1958-66; mem. Portsmouth Spl. Water Com., 1958-62; mem. Portsmouth City Mgr. Charter Com., 1947-49; mem. N.H. Hos. of Reps., 1933-34; mem. Portsmouth City Council, 1937-38; county atty. Rockingham County, 1947-50; mem. Portsmouth Sch. Bd., 1954-58, 62-70; del. Rep. Nat. Conv., Chgo., 1952; mem. N.H. Constl. Conv., 1974. Commd. 2d lt. USAR, 1931 C.E., U.S. Army, 1940-45, ETO; col. res., 1945-61. Decorated Bronze Star; recipient Silver Beaver award Daniel Webster Council Boy Scouts Am., 1958; Portsmouth C. of C. Community Service award, 1978. Mem. ABA, N.H. Soc. Profl. Engrs., NSPE, N.H. Land Surveyors Assn., Soc. Am. Mil. Engrs. Republican. Congregationalist. Clubs: Rotary (Paul Harris award 1985), Wentworth Fairways, Pease AFB Golf. Home: 668 Middle St Portsmouth NH 03801

BOYOM, BODIE MICHEL NGUIFFO, mathematics educator, consultant; b. Bandjoun, Cameroon, Nov. 29, 1940; came to France, 1960; s. Bodie Tapiaptie Boyom and Jeannette (Kapche) Njiumkam; m. Marie Therese Kamga; children—Claude Valerie Njiukoua, Patrick Roger Kamga, Jacques Yves Boyom, Muriel Carole Youbi, Vincent Michel Foamkom. B.S. in Math., U. Grenoble, 1965, postgrad. 1967; M.S., 1968; Ph.D. in Math., U. Paris XI, 1976. Asst. prof. U. Grenoble, France, 1967-70; vis. prof. U. Sao Paulo, Brazil, 1972, 78, 79, U. Brasilia, Brazil, 1972; prof. math. U. Montpellier, France, 1979—; lectr. in field; cons. FRALAM, Paris, 1983—, Minister of Equipment, Yaounde, 1983—, SI-Informatique, Douala, Cameroon, 1983—. Contbr. articles to profl. jours. Fellow Sao Paulo State Found for Research, Nat. Council for Research CNPQ, FINEP; mem. Societe Math. de France, Am. Math. Soc. Avocations: tennis; golf; walking. Home: 3 Rue du Dahomey, 34000 Montpellier France Office: Univ des Sci and Tech, du Languedoc Place, Eugene Bataillon, 34000 Montpellier France

BOZIC, JORGE CARLOS, manufacturing company executive; b. Buenos Aires, Argentina, July 9, 1954; s. Justino and María (Suban) B.; m. Cecilia Verónica Marinelli, Nov. 20, 1983; 1 child, Carolina Lía. Licentiate in Bus. Adminstrn. with honours, Sch. Econs. Scis. U. Buenos Aires, 1975. CPA, Argentina. Mem. auditory team Arthur Andersen and Co., Buenos Aires, 1975-78; adminstr. and fin. mgr. Fademac Argentina S.A., Buenos Aires, 1978-84, fin. mgr., 1984-86; fin. mgr. Nicoll Eterplast S.A., Buenos Aires, 1984-86, also bd. dirs.; fin. mgr. Eternit Argentina S.A., Buenos Aires, 1984-86, gen. mgr., 1986—, also bd. dirs.; asst. lectr. fin. statements Sch. Econ. Scis. U. Buenos Aires, 1979-86, planning adviser dept. acctg. theory, 1987. Mem. Argentinian Belgo-Luxembourgian C. of C. (adviser 1987), Buenos Aires Profl. Council Econ. Scis.

BOZICEVIC, JURAJ, electrical engineer, educator; b. Vrbovsko, Croatia, Yugoslavia, Oct. 7, 1935; s. Emil and Antonija (Crnkovic) B. Diploma in Elec. Engring., U. Zagreb, also Ph.D.; m. Biserka Vitez, Dec. 27, 1961; children—Hrvoje, Zrinka. Research asst. Faculty Elec. Engring., U. Zagreb, 1961-63, lectr., then asst. prof. Faculty Tech., 1964-71, prof. measurement and control, 1972—, head postgrad. study systems sci. and tech. cybernetics, 1972-82; research fellow Tech. U. Eindhoven (Netherlands), 1971; vis. prof. U. Trondheim (Norway), 1977; hon. prof. U. Split; founder Internat. Sch. of Measurement, 1980—; UNESCO cons. Rizal Technol. Coll., Manila, 1986—. Mem. Yugoslav Assn. Measurement, Control and Automation (chmn. exec. com. 1974-80), Internat. Measurement Confedn. (gen. council 1976-77, chmn. tech. com. meteorol. requirements in devel. countries 1978—, Disting. Service award 1985), Union Internat. Tech. Assn. (chmn. working group metrology 1986—), Internat. Assn. Cybernetics, Yugoslav Assn. Inventors, ISA, UKSS. Author: Automatic Process Control, 1971; Automatic Control Fundamentals I, 1978, 7th rev. edit, 1987, II, 1979, 7th rev. edit., 1987; also articles; editor books, proc.; patentee Measurement transducers. Home: 18 Trg kralja Tomislava,, Zagreb 41000, Yugoslavia Office: 6 Pierottieva, Zagreb 41000,, Yugoslavia

BRAAKMAN, TED CORNELIS, insurance company executive, member parliament; b. The Hague, The Netherlands, May 13, 1926; m. Cornelia Maria van Leeuwen, Aug. 20, 1954; children: Ted, Joan. D in Math., U. Leiden, 1952. Sci. asst. Math. Ctr., Amsterdam, The Netherlands, 1952-54; sci. staff mem. Tech. U., Delft, The Netherlands, 1954-55; mathematician Royal Dutch Shell, Delft, 1955-60; staff mem. The Netherlands Ins. Group, The Hague, 1960-63; staff mem. Nationale-Nederlanden N.V., The Hague, 1963-68, mgr. life ins., 1968-74, mem. exec. bd., 1974-85, chmn. exec. bd., 1985—; chmn. bd. dirs. Lips en Gispen B.V., Dordrecht, The Netherlands, Joh. Enschedé en Zonen, Haarlem, The Netherlands; mem. adv. bd. Amsterdam-Rotterdam Bank N.V., 1984—. Mem. First Chamber Parliament Liberal Party, The Hague, 1987. Decorated officer Order Orange-Nassau (The Netherlands). Mem. The Netherlands Soc. Industry and Trade (dep. chmn. 1987—). Home: JF Kennedylaan 245, 2285 AJ Rijswijk The Netherlands Office: Nationale-Nederlanden NV, Pr Beatrixlaan 15, 2595 AK The Hague The Netherlands

BRABOURNE, JOHN ULICK KNATCHBULL, film and television producer; b. Nov. 9, 1924; s. 5th Baron and Lady Doreen Geraldine Browne; m. Lady Patricia Edwina Victoria Mountbatten, 1946; 6 children. Ed. Eton, Oxford. Producer: Harry Black, 1958, Sink the Bismarck, 1959, HMS Defiant, 1961, Othello, 1965, The Mikado, 1966, Romeo and Juliet, Up the Junction, 1967, Dance of Death, 1968, Tales of Beatrix Potter, 1971, Murder on the Orient Express, 1974, Death on the Nile, 1978, Stories from a Flying Trunk, 1979, The Mirror Crack'd, 1980, Evil Under the Sun, 1982, A Passage to India, 1984, Little Dorrit, 1987; TV series include: National Gallery, 1974, A Much-Maligned Monarch, 1976; dir. Thames Television, 1978—, Thorn EMI, 1981-86; gov. Brit. Film Inst., 1979—, Nat. Film Sch., 1980—. Mem. Brit. Screen Adv. Council, trustee Brit. Acad. Film and TV Arts, Sci. Mus.; pres. Kent Trust for Nature Conservation; chmn. council Caldecott Community; gov. Norton Knatchbull Sch., Wye Coll., Gordonstoun Sch., United World Coll., dep. pro-chancellor U. Kent. Address: Newhouse Mesham Ashford, Kent TN25 6NQ England

BRACETE, JUAN MANUEL, judge; b. Mayaguez, P.R., Sept. 10, 1951; s. Manuel and Norma (Mari) B.; m. Sonia Rivera, Apr. 5, 1974. BS in Bus. Adminstrn. summa cum laude, Georgetown U., 1971; JD magna cum laude, U. P.R., Rio Piedras, 1976. Bar: P.R. 1976, D.C. 1976, U.S. Tax Ct. 1978, Fla. 1986, U.S. Ct. Internat. Trade 1988. Mgmt. trainee First Fed. Savs., San Juan, P.R., 1972; pro mgr. CitiBank, N.A., San Juan, 1972-74; law clk. U.S. Dept. Justice, Washington, 1975; atty., advisor Bd. of Immigration Appeals, Washington, 1976-78; assoc. Goldman & Antonetti, San Juan, 1979-84; immigration judge U.S. Dept. Justice, Miami, 1985—; treas. Am. Immigration Lawyer's Assn. Puerto Rico chpt., 1982-84, chairperson, 1984. Contbr. articles to profl. jours. Sec., supr. Dept. Justice Fed. Credit Union, Washington, 1976-78; sec. real estate commn.; Alliance Francaise, San Juan, 1980-84; treas. Magdalena 1305 Owners Assn., San Juan, 1983-84; alt. bd. dirs. Harbour Club Villas, Miami, 1986. Recipient Sustained Achievement award U.S. Dept. Justice, Washington, 1977, Spl. award Fed. Credit Union, Washington, 1979; German-Marshall Fund Immigration fellow, 1987. Mem. ABA (vice chmn. immigration, naturalization and aliens com. 1987—), Fed. Bar Assn., P.R. Bar Assn., Canon Law Soc. Am., The Fla. Bar, The D.C. Bar, Nat. Assn. Immigration Judges (sec. 1985—), Internat. Platform Soc. Republican. Roman Catholic. Office: Office of the Immigration Judge 7880 Biscayne Blvd 8th Floor Miami FL 33138

BRACHER, KARL DIETRICH, history and political science educator; b. Stuttgart, Ger., Mar. 13, 1922; m. Dorothee Schleicher, May 3, 1951; children: Christian, Susanne. Dr.Phil., U. Tuebingen, 1948; postgrad. Harvard U., 1949-50; Dr.H.C.Lett., Fla. State U., 1973; Dr.Jur.H.C., U. Graz, 1985. Research assoc. Inst. Polit. Sci., Berlin, 1950-58; lectr. Hochschule fur Politik, Berlin, 1954-58; privatdozent, Free U. Berlin, 1955-58, prof., 1958; prof. history and polit. sci. U. Bonn, 1959—; vis. prof. Oxford, Tel Aviv, Seattle, Japan, Sweden; fellow Inst. Advanced Studies, Stanford, Princeton, Washington. pres. Commn. of Parliamentarism, Bonn, 1962-68, v.p. 1972—; bd. dirs. chmn. Inst. Contemporary History, Munich, 1980—. Author: The Dissolution of the Weimar Republic, 1955, 6th edit. 1978, The Nazi Seizure of Power, 1960, 3d edit., 1974; The German Dictatorship, 1969, 6th edit. 1979, The Age of Ideologies, 1982-84, The Crisis of Europe 1917-1975, 1976-79, The German Dilemma, 1971-74, History and Violence, 1981; The Totalitarian Experience, 1987; Progress and Decline in Early Roman Thought, 1987; editor: Vierteljahrshefte für Zeitgeschichte. Recipient Premio Storia Acqui, City of Acqui, 1973, European Prix Adolphe Bentinck, 1981. Fellow Brit. Acad.; mem. Am. Acad. Arts and Sci. (hon.), Am. Philos. Soc., Austrian Acad. Sci., German Acad. Lang. and Poetry, Rhenish-Westfalian Acad. Sci., PEN Club of Germany. Home: Stationsweg 17, Bonn Federal Republic of Germany Office: Univ Bonn, Am Hofgarten 15, Bonn Federal Republic of Germany

BRACKENRIDGE, ELOISE WILSON, industrial communications consultant specializing in technology transfer; b. Taylor, Tex., Oct. 22, 1939; d. John Adams III and Eloise (Wilson) B. BFA in Communications, U. Tex., 1961, MA in Communications, 1969. Fgn. service staff officer U.S. Dept. State, Washington, 1961-66; campaign aide Rep. George Bush, Houston, 1970; communications cons. Austin (Tex.), Houston, and Washington, 1970-73; pub. relations mgr. Tex. Internat. Airlines, Houston, 1973-75; communications mgr. Dresser Industries Inc., Houston, 1975-83; v.p. corp. communications CRS Sirrine Inc., Houston, 1983-86; indsl. communications cons. Houston, 1986—; mng. ptnr. Brackenridge and Eilert, Houston and Austin, 1972—; bd. dirs. Hobby Community Bank, Houston. Author: Mota Bonita, 1979; editor: Anthology of Communication Theory, 1967; prod. and dir. ednl. and indsl. film series, 1970-73; contbr. articles to profl. jours. Mem. selection bd. USIA, Washington, 1971; active Houston Council Performing Arts, Houston Econ. Devel. Forum; patron Houston Jr. League, 1974—. Recipient Meritorious Honor award U.S. Dept. State, 1964, Best Nat. Trade Show Exhibit award U.S. Trade Show Assn., 1982, Nat. Excellence award Soc. Mktg. Profl. Services, 1985, numerous awards for advt. and speaking. Mem. Internat. Platform Assn., Phi Kappa Phi, Alpha Epsilon Rho. Republican. Episcopalian. Club: Houston Forum. Home: 3524 Greystone Dr #199 Austin TX 78731

BRACKHAHN, DONALD GARLAND, university administrator; b. Kansas City, Mo., Nov. 2, 1936; s. James Alexander and Mary Jeannette (Garland) B.; B.A., U. Mo., Kansas City, 1958, M.A. in History, 1965; m. Nancy Lee Dunbar, Feb. 24, 1962; children—Dawn Renee, Diane Michelle. Grad. asst. history dept. U. Kansas City, 1958-60; social sci. tchr. Kansas City (Mo.) Sch. Dist., 1960-66, athletic dir., tennis coach, 1964-66; asst. dir. devel. U. Mo., Kansas City, 1966-70, dir. devel., alumni and constituent relations, 1970-80, dir. alumni and constituent relations, asst. to pres. for alumni relations, 1980-84; exec. dir. alumni relations U. Mo., Rolla, 1985—. Trustee, Kansas City Mus. History and Sci., 1972-80, Johnson County (Kans.) Library, 1972-73; mem. Johnson County Charter Commn., 1974-76; bd. dirs. Shawnee Civic Band, 1971-85; pres. Johnson County Friends of Library, 1976-78; mem. transition com., nominating com., chmn. speakers bur. Heart of Am. United Way; bd. dirs., pres. Johnson County United Community Services, 1980-82; bd. dirs. United Fund, Rolla, Mo.; sec., pres. standing com. Episcopal Diocese of Kans., 1980-83; mem. vestry, lay reader, liturgical asst., lay pastor Christ Ch., Overland Park, Kans.; lay reader Christ Ch., Rolla. Served with USNG, 1959-65. Mem. ALA, Kansas City Council for Social Studies (pres. 1965-66), Greater Kansas City Council on Philanthropy (pres. 1980-81), Council for Advancement and Support of Edn., Assn. of Vol. Bds., U. Mo. Kansas City Internat. Alumni Assn. (pres. 1965), Kansas City C. of C., Omicron Delta Kappa (faculty advisor), Phi Delta Kappa, Phi Mu Alpha Sinfonia, Tau Kappa Epsilon. Republican. Club: Rockhill Tennis. Lodge: Rotary. Home: Route 4 Box 319 Rolla MO 65401 Office: U Mo Rolla 106 Harris Hall Rolla MO 65401

BRADBURN, DAVID DENISON, retired air force officer, engineer; b. Hollywood, Calif., May 27, 1925; s. Clarence Earl and Florence Lyle (Easton) B.; m. Bertha Evelyn Stout, Nov. 3, 1956; children: Carol (Mrs. Patrick V. Navagato), Susan (Mrs. John A. Fitzpatrick), David Stout, Robert Easton. B.S., U.S. Mil. Acad., 1946; M.S.E., Purdue U., 1952; M.S. in Internat. Affairs, George Washington U., 1966. Commd. 2d lt. U.S. Army, 1946; advanced through grades to maj. gen. USAF, 1974; pilot, flight comdr. Korea, 1950-51; research and devel. staff officer Balt., 1952-57; mil. space research project officer Los Angeles, 1957-65; space program mgr. 1966-71; dir. space systems Washington, 1971-73; dir. spl. projects Office Sec. Air Force, Los Angeles, 1973-75; vice-comdr. Electronic Systems Div., Boston, 1975-76; ret. 1976. Mem. U.S. del. Joint Chiefs Staff rep. to U.S.-Soviet Anti-Satellite Negotiations, Helsinki, 1978, Bern, Vienna, 1979; sr. staff scientist TRW Def. Systems Group, 1980-84, dir. engring., 1984-87; chmn. bd. Beach Cities Symphony Assn., 1978-84, pres., 1984-87. Decorated D.S.M. (2), Legion of Merit (3), D.F.C., Meritorious Service medal, Air medal (4). Mem. Sigma Xi, Tau Beta Pi, Eta Kappa Nu. Mem. United Ch. of Christ. Home: 421 2d St Manhattan Beach CA 90266

BRADBURY, JAMES HOWARD, chemistry educator; b. Bendigo, Australia, Sept. 7, 1927; s. Joseph Ayrton and Lucy Augusta B.; m. Ruth Marian McComb, Sept. 13, 1952; children: Joanne Ruth, Annette Lyn, Meredith Gaye. BSc, Melbourne (Australia) U., 1948, MSc, 1950, DSc, 1968; PhD, Birmingham (Eng.) U., 1953; DSc, Australian Nat. U., 1981. Overseas research study Birmingham U., Eng., 1951-53; postdoctoral fellow Harvard U., Cambridge, Mass., 1953-54; sr. research officer Commonwealth Scientific and Indsl. Research Orgn., Geelong, Australia, 1954-60; sr. lectr. Australian Nat. U., Canberra, 1961-65, reader in phys. chemistry, 1965—; sr. fellowship European Molecular Biology Orgn., Oxford, Eng., 1972; vis. prof. Cornell U., Ithaca, N.Y., 1964-65; project leader Australian Centre for Internat. Agrl. Research, Canberra, 1983-88; aid assignment Australian Devel. Assistance Bur., Canberra, 1979; mem. com., 1985-88. Author: Chemistry and Nutrition of Tropical Root Crops, 1988; contbr. articles to profl. jours.; editorial bd. Journal of Applied Polymer Science, N.Y.C., 1976—; editor Bulletin of Magnetic Resonance, 1979-82. Mem. council Burgmann Coll., Australian Nat. U., Canberra, 1970-80; area organiser Australian Red Cross Soc, Canberra, 1977—. Recipient Fulbright Travel award Australian-Am. Edn. Found., Canberra, 1965, David Syme Research prize Melbourne U., 1970. Fellow Royal Australian Chem. Inst. (pres. Canberra br. 1979-80; mem. nat. exec. council, 1980-82; chmn. 7th nat. conv. 1982, chmn. nat. polymer div. 1973-74; recipient Rennie Meml. medal, 1957, H.G. Smith Meml. medal, 1975); mem. Royal Soc. Chemistry, Australian and New Zealand Assn. for Advancement of Sci. (chmn. Canberra section 1985-86), Australian Biochem. Soc. Home: 118 Vasey Crescent, Campbell 2601, Australia Office: Australian Nat U, Chemistry Dept, Canberra 2601, Australia

BRADBURY, JOHN DANIELS, advertising executive; b. N.Y.C., Apr. 9, 1941; s. Warren Ball and Mary Elizabeth (Brennemann) B.; A.B., Harvard U., 1963; m. Judith Barrett Horowitz, July 17, 1969; children—Douglas, Mitchell, Kristin, Andrew. Partner, W.B. Bradbury Co., N.Y.C., 1963-74; pres., owner Mil. Media Inc., N.Y.C., 1974—. Pres., Bentley Sch. PTA, 1972-73; sec. 257 Central Park W. Inc., 1980-82; vice chmn. Phillips Exeter Fund Raising Campaign for Manhattan, 1980. Mem. Am. Logistics Assn., Nat. Assn. Pubs. Reps., The Chief Execs. Officers Club. Club: Harvard of N.Y.C. Office: Mil Media Inc 1 Lincoln Plaza New York NY 10023

BRADBURY, JOHN MICHAEL, banker; b. Stockport, Cheshire, Eng., Feb. 1, 1943; s. John Fildes and Elsie (Moorby) B.; m. Christine Judith Fletcher, Aug. 13, 1966; children: Sara Jane, John Fletcher. BA in Econ., U. Manchester, Eng., 1969. Asst. mgr. Nat. Westminster Bank, Liverpool, Eng., 1974-76; mgr. shipping Nat. Westminster Bank, London, 1976-78, mgr. corp. fin., 1978-79, mgr. mktg. and coordination, 1979, mgr. forfaiting, 1980-81; head syndications and forfaiting Scandinavian Bank Ltd., London, 1981-84; dir. Prudential Bache Trade Fin. Ltd., London, 1984-88; bus. devel. dir. Elders Fin. Group Ltd, London, 1988—. Mem. Chartered Inst. Bankers. Office: Elders Fin Group Ltd, 40 Dukes Pl, London EC3A 5BX, England

BRADBURY, MALCOLM STANLEY, educator, author; b. Sheffield, Yorks, Eng., Sept. 7, 1932; s. Arthur and Doris Ethel (Marshall) B.; m. Elizabeth Salt, 1959; 2 sons. Ed. Univ. Coll., Leicester (Eng.), Queen Mary Coll.; M.A., U. London; Ph.D., U. Manchester; D.Litt. (hon.), U. Leicester, 1986. Staff tutor in lit. and drama dept. adult edn. U. Hull, 1959-61; lectr. in English, lang. and lit. U. Birmingham (Eng.), 1961-65; lectr., later sr. lectr. and reader Sch. English and Am. studies U. East Anglia, Norwich, Norfolk, Eng., 1965-70, prof. Am. studies, 1970—; vis. prof. U. Zurich, 1972, Washington U., St. Louis, 1982, U. Queensland, 1983. Author: Eating People is Wrong (novel), 1959; Evelyn Waugh, 1962; E.M. Forster: A Collection of Critical Essays (editor), 1965; Stepping Westward (novel), 1965; What is a Novel?, 1969; A Passage to India: A Casebook, 1970; A Penguin Companion to Literature: Vol. III, American Literature (with E. Mottram), 1971; The Social Context of Modern English Literature, 1972; Possibilities: Essays on the State of the Novel, 1973; (novel) The History Man (Royal Soc. Lit. prize), 1975; Modernism (with J.W. MacFarlane), 1976; Who Do You Think You Are? (short stories), 1976; The Novel Today (editor), 1977; An Introduction to American Studies (editor) (with H. Temperley), 1981; The After Dinner Game (TV plays), 1982; Saul Bellow, 1982; All Dressed Up and Nowhere to Go, 1982; (novel) Rates of Exchange (Shortlisted, Barker prize), 1982; The Modern American Novel, 1983; Why Come to Slaka?, 1986; Cuts, 1987; Mensonge, 1987; (collected essays) No, Not Bloomsbury, 1987; Unsent Letters (1988); The Modern World: The Great Writers, 1988; (tv adaptations of Alison Lurie) Imaginary Friends and Tom Sharpe, Porterhouse Blue (Internat. Emmy award 1987). Hon. fellow Queen Mary Coll., London, 1984. Office: Sch English and Am Studies, U East Anglia, Univ Plain, Norwich Norfolk, England

BRADDOCK, JOHN WILLIAM, safety engineer; b. Phila., May 23, 1947; s. John Thomas and Joan Betty (Faulkner) B. BS in Commerce and Engring., Drexel U., 1970; MS in Organizational Behavior, U. Hartford, 1976. Cert. safety profl., hazard control mgr. Asst. plant mgr. N.J. Silica Sand Co., Millville, 1972-73; lead safety engr. Pratt & Whitney Aircraft Co., East Hartford, Conn., 1973-78; mgr. occupational safety and indsl. hygiene Sikorsky Aircraft Co., Stratford, Conn., 1978-86; sr. cons. Occupational Safety United Techs. Corp., Hartford, Conn., 1987—; instr. Hartford Grad. Ctr., 1977. Warden St. John's Episc. Ch., also Vestry, 1985. Served to 1st lt. U.S. Army, 1970-72. Mem. Indsl. Health Found. (trustee 1988), Am. Soc. Safety Engrs., Am. Indsl. Hygiene Assn., Nat. Fire Protection Assn., Res. Officers Assn., Bushnell Park Carousel Soc., Lambda Chi Alpha. Author: (lyrics) The Carousel Song. Club: Corvair Soc. Am. Lodge: Knights of Malta. Home: 247 Natchaug Dr Meriden CT 06450 Office: United Techs Hartford CT 06101

BRADEMAS, JOHN, university president, former congressman; b. Mishawaka, Ind., Mar. 2, 1927; s. Stephen J. and Beatrice Cenci (Goble) B.; m. Mary Ellen Briggs, July 9, 1977. B.A. magna cum laude (Vets. nat. scholar), Harvard, 1949; D.Phil. (Rhodes scholar), Oxford (Eng.) U., 1954; LL.D. (hon.), U. Notre Dame, Middlebury Coll., Tufts U. (others); L.H.D., Brandeis U., CCNY (others). Legislative asst. to U.S. Senator Pat McNamara; adminstrv. asst. U.S. Rep. Thomas L. Ashley, 1955; exec. asst. to presdl. nominee Stevenson 1955-56; asst. prof. polit. sci. St. Mary's Coll., Notre Dame, Ind., 1957-58; mem. 86th-96th Congresses from 3d Ind. Dist.; chief dep. majority whip 93d-94th Congresses; majority whip 95th-96th Congresses; mem. com. house adminstrn., com. on edn. and labor, joint com. on Library of Congress; pres. NYU, 1981—; chmn. Fed. Res. Bank N.Y.; dir. RCA/NBC, Loew's Corp., Scholastic, Inc., N.Y. Stock Exchange, Rockefeller Found.; Past mem. bd. visitors John F. Kennedy Sch. Govt.; bd. overseers Harvard U.; mem. overseers' com. to visit Grad. Sch. Edn.; trustee, mem. adv. council Coll. Arts and Letters U. Notre Dame; bd. visitors dept. polit. sci. M.I.T.; bd. advs. Dumbarton Oaks Research Library and Collection, Woodrow Wilson Center Internat. Scholars; mem. Central Com. World Council Chs.; past mem. Nat. Hist. Publs. Commn., Nat. Commn. on Financing Post-Secondary Edn.; mem. Nat. Commn. Student Fin. Assistance, Study Nat. Needs Biomed. and Behavioral Research NRC, Nat. Acad. Sci. Com. Relations between Univs. and Govt.; bd. dirs. Am. Council Edn. Served with USNR, 1945-46. Recipient Disting. Service award Inst. Internat. Edn., 1966, Disting. Service award NEA, 1968, Disting. Service award Tchrs. Coll., Columbia U., 1969; Merit award Nat. Council Sr. Citizens, 1972; Disting. Service award Council of State Adminstrs. of Vocat. Rehab., 1973; Disting. Service award Conservation Edn. Assn., 1974; Caritas Soc. award for outstanding contbns. in field of mental retardation, 1975; Gold Key award Am. Congress Rehab. Medicine, 1976; named Humanist of Year Nat. Assn. Humanities Edn., 1978; award for disting. service to arts AAAL, 1978; George Peabody award, 1980. Fellow Am. Acad. Arts and Scis.; mem. Am. Legion, Phi Beta Kappa (Senator). Methodist. Clubs: Masons, Ahepa. Office: NYU Office of Pres 70 Washington Square S New York NY 10003 *

BRADEN, WALDO W., emeritus speech educator; b. Ottumwa, Iowa, Mar. 7, 1911; s. Wilbern C. and Stella (Warder) B.; m. Dana Crane, Aug. 18, 1938; 1 child, Helen Dana. B.A., Penn Coll., 1932; M.A., U. Iowa, 1938, Ph.D., 1942. Tchr. Fremont (Iowa) High Sch., 1933-35, Mt. Pleasant High Sch., 1935-38; tchr. speech Iowa Wesleyan Coll., 1938-40, dean students, 1942-43, 45-46; asso. prof. speech La. State U., Baton Rouge, 1946-51; prof. La. State U., 1951-73, Boyd prof., 1973-79, Boyd prof. emeritus, 1979—, chmn., 1958-76; vis. prof. Washington U., summer 1952, Mich. State U., summer 1953, U. Pacific, summer 1965, Calif. State Coll., Fullerton, 1969. Author: (with Gray) Public Speaking, 1951, rev. edit., 1963, (with Brandenburg) Oral Decision-Making, 1955, (with Gehring) Speech Practices, 1958, Public Speaking: Essentials, 1966, (with Thonssen and Baird) Speech Criticism, 1970; Editor: Speech Methods and Resources, 1961, rev. edit., 1972, The Speech Teacher, 1967-69, Oratory in the Old South, 1970, Oratory in the New South, 1979, Representative American Speeches, 1970-80, Oral Tradition in the South, 1983; Contbr. articles to speech and hist. jours. Served with AUS, 1943-45. Mem. Speech Communication Assn. (council 1954—, exec. sec. 1954-57, pres. 1962, Disting. Ser. award 1978), So. Speech Assn. (pres. 1969-70), Pi Kappa Delta, Delta Sigma Rho, Tau Kappa Alpha, Omicron Delta Kappa. Methodist. Home: Terrace Reirement Apts W201 1408 Business 70 W Box 21 Columbia MO 65202

BRADEN, WILLIAM EDWARD, trading company executive, consultant; b. Milw., Dec. 29, 1919; s. Armond Edward and Eve Ninette (Fuller) B.; AB, Harvard U., 1941; m. Sonoyo Matsuda, Jan. 23, 1950 (dec.); children: Amy, Wythe Edward, Robert Fuller, William Samuel; m. Margaret Peterson Bowen, Oct. 16, 1987. Foreman, Procter & Gamble Mfg. Co., Quincy, Mass., 1941-42; civilian employee War Dept., Changchun, Manchuria, 1946-47; pres. Pacific Projects Ltd., Tokyo, 1948—; pres. Taihei Boeki Co., Ltd., Tokyo, 1955-80, chmn. bd., 1980-86; dir. Ferro Far East Ltd., Hong Kong, Ferro Enamels (Japan) Ltd., Osaka, Nissan Ferro Organic Chem. Co., Ltd., Tokyo, Palace Housing Co., Ltd., Tokyo, Taiwan Longson Co. Ltd., Taipei. Served with AF, USNR, 1943-45. Mem. Am. Japan Soc., Am. C. of C. in Japan, Japan Am. Soc. Honolulu, Pacific and Asian Affairs Council Honolulu (gov. 1984—), Chamber Music Soc. Hawaii (dir. 1984—), Asia Soc. N.Y.C. Clubs: Harvard (N.Y.C., Tokyo, Honolulu); Tokyo Am.; Fgn. Correspondents (Japan) (asso. mem.).

BRADFORD, DAVID GALEN, air force officer; b. Graham, Tex., July 20, 1948; s. Leo Galen and Elizabeth Arline (Younger) B.; m. Irene Carol Boehning, June 2, 1972; children: Emily Neumann, Scott Galen. AA, Howard Coll., 1968; BA, S.W. Tex. State U., 1970; MA, U. No. Colo., 1974; diploma, U.S. Army Comdr. and Gen. Staff Coll., 1985. Commd. 2d lt. USAF, 1972, advanced through grades to lt. col., 1987; logistics plans officer USAF, Vandenberg AFB, Calif., 1980-82; exec. officer dep. chief of staff logisitics Strategic Air Command, USAF, 1982-83, exec. officer dep. chief of staff plans Strategic Air Command,, 1983; staff officer long range planning staff Strategic Air Command, USAF, Omaha, 1983-84; plans officer N.E. Asia div. Comdr. in Chief Pacific Command, USAF, Hawaii, 1985-87, strategist, asst. fgn. policy adv. to Comdr-in-Chief Pacific Command, 1987—; mem. adj. faculty English, History and Bus., Wayland Bapt. U., Honolulu, 1986—. Mem. USAF Assn., East-West Ctr. Hawaii, World Future Soc., Japan-Am. Soc. Honolulu., Internat. Churchill Soc. Republican. Baptist. Home: 302-A Travis Ave Honolulu HI 96818 Office: USCINCPAC/FPA Camp Smith HI 96861

BRADLEY, BILL, U.S. senator; b. Crystal City, Mo., July 28, 1943; s. Warren W. and Susan (Crowe) B.; m. Ernestine Schlant, Jan. 14, 1974; 1 dau., Theresa Anne. B.A., Princeton U., 1965; M.A. (Rhodes scholar 1965-68), Oxford (Eng.) U., 1968. Player N.Y. Knickerbockers Profl. Basketball Team, 1967-77; U.S. senator from N.J., 1979—; mem. fin., energy coms., spl. com. on aging, select com. on intelligence. Author: Life on the Run, 1976, The Fair Tax, 1984. Served with USAFR, 1967-78. Democrat. Office: Senate Bldg 731 Hart Washington DC 20510

BRADLEY, CHARLES MACARTHUR, architect; b. Chgo., Sept. 26, 1918; s. Harold Smith and Helen Frances (MacArthur) B.; B.A. in Architecture, U. Ill., 1940; m. Joan Marie Daane, July 27, 1946; children—Mary Barbara, Nancy Ann, Sally Joan, William Charles. With Holabird & Root, architects, Chgo., 1940-41, Giffels & Vallet, architects and engrs., Detroit, 1941-45; partner, corp. pres. Bradley & Bradley, architects and engrs., Rockford, Ill., 1947—; pres. Bradley Bldg. Corp., 1962—; sec.-treas. Mchts. Police, 1972—; pres. Westshore Plaza Inc., 1979—. Active, Blackhawk council Boy Scouts Am. Served with C.E., U.S. Army, 1945-46. Decorated Bronze Star; recipient Meritorious Service award Ill. Assn. Sch. Bds., 1976. Mem. AIA (pres. No. Ill. chpt. 1962, treas. Ill. council 1973-74), Ill. Soc. Architects (pres. 1974), Edn. Facilities Planners Inst., Ill. Assn. Sch. Bd. Officers. Republican. Congregationalist. Clubs: Rotary, Union League, University, Midday (Chgo.). Lodges: Shriners, Moose. Prin. works include North Sheboygan (Wis.) High Sch. and addition, 1960-68, J.F. Kennedy Middle Sch., Rockford, 1968, Singer Health Clinic, Rockford, 1964, Jacobs High Sch., Algonquin, Ill., 1976, Atwood plant, Rockford, 1977, Admiral Home, Chgo., 1978, Bushnell (Ill.) Jr. High Sch., 1980, Bloom High Schs., 1983, Evenglow Lodge, 1984. Author papers on life cycling old schs., roofing procedures. Home: 3203 Landstrom Rd Rockford IL 61107 Office: 924 N Main St Rockford IL 61103

BRADLEY, CHARLES WILLIAM, podiatrist; b. Fife, Tex., July 23, 1923; s. Tom and Mary Ada (Cheatham) B.; student Tex. Tech., 1940-42; D. Podiatric Medicine, Calif. Coll. Podiatric Medicine U. San Francisco, 1949, MPA, 1987; D.Sc. (hon.), Calif. Coll. Podiatric Medicine; m. Marilyn A. Brown, Apr. 3, 1948 (dec. Mar. 1973); children—Steven, Gregory, Jeffrey, Elizabeth, Gerald. Practice podiatry, Beaumont, Tex., 1950-51, Brownwood, Tex., 1951-52, San Francisco, San Bruno, Calif., 1952—; chief of staff Calif. Podiatry Hosp., San Francisco; mem. surg. staff Sequoia Hosp., Redwood City, Calif.; mem. podiatry staff Peninsula Hosp., Burlingame, Calif.; chief podiatry staff St. Luke's Hosp., San Francisco; pres. Podiatry Ins. Co. Am.; cons. VA. Mem. San Francisco Symphony Found.; mem. adv. com. Health Policy Agenda for the Am. People, AMA. Chmn. trustees Calif. Coll. Podiatric Medicine, Calif. Podiatry Coll., Calif. Podiatry Hosp. Mem. Am. Podiatric Med. Assn. (trustee, pres. 1983-84), Calif. Podiatry Assn. (pres. No. div. 1964-66, state bd. dirs., pres. 1975-76, Podiatrist of Yr. award 1983), Nat. Council Edn. (vice chmn.), Nat. Acads. Practice, Am. Legion, San Bruno C. of C. (dir. 1978—). Clubs: Elks, Lions, Commonwealth of Calif., Olympic (San Francisco). Served with USNR, 1942-45. Home: 2965 Trousdale Dr Burlingame CA 94010 also: 560 Jenevein Ave San Bruno CA 94066 Office: 2469 Mission St San Francisco CA 94110

BRADLEY, FLOYD HENRY III, computer executive; b. Orange, N.J., Mar. 6, 1951; came to Eng. in 1976.; s. Floyd Henry Jr. and Carol Georgette (Lake) B.; m. Amanda Jane Urmston June 30, 1984. BA in Econs. amgna cum laude, Yale Coll., 1973; MBA, Harvard U., 1975. Cons. Boston Cons. Group, 1975-76; case leader Boston Cons. Group, London, 1976-79; mgr. Bain and Co., London, 1979-81; v.p. Europe Computer Pictures Corp., London, 1981-82; dir. internat. mktg. Cullinet Software Inc., Stanmore, Eng., 1982-84; v.p. internat. Optionware Inc., London, 1984-85; mng. dir. Lotus Devel. (U.K.) Ltd., Windsor, Eng., 1985-87; v.p. Europe Ashton Tate Corp., Maidenhead, Eng., 1987—. Fellow Inst. Dirs.; Inst. of 1770. Clubs: Royal Blackheath Golf (Kent, Eng.), Mory's Assn. (New Haven), Hasty Pudding (Cambridge, Mass.). Home: 18 Mulberry Walk, London SW3 6DY, England Office: Ashton-Tate Corp, Oaklands 1 Bath Rd, Maidenhead, Berkshire SL6 4UH, England

BRADLEY, GEORGE HAVIS, lawyer; b. Warren, Ark., May 31, 1937; s. James Harvey Hawley and Dixie (Stringer) B.; children: Hai Minh Le, Tuan Minh Le. AB, Mercer U., 1959; JD, U. Tenn., 1971. Atty. estate tax IRS, Wilmington, Del., 1972-75; tax law specialist legis. and regulations div. office of chief counsel IRS, Washington, 1975—; fed. register liaison officer IRS, Washington, 1977—. Pres. Literacy Council No. Va., Alexandria, 1980-81, v.p., 1982; sec. Alexandria Community Mental Health Ctr., 1978; literacy tutor Refugee Edn. and Employment Program, Arlington, Va., 1985—, Refugee Unaccompanied Minors Program, 1986—; vol. Learning Program, Fairfax, 1978—. Served to lt. USN, 1962-66. Recipient Outstanding Service award, Literacy Council No. Va., 1980-83, Vol. Learning Program, 1978-81, Alexandria Community Mental Health Ctr., 1978-81, Refugee Unaccompanied Minors Program, 1986-87. Mem. ABA, Tenn. Bar Assn., Phi Alpha Delta. Episcopalian. Home: 1301 N Courthouse Rd #1603 Arlington VA 22201 Office: IRS Legis and Regulations Div Office of Chief Counsel 1111 Constitution Ave NW Washington DC 20224

BRADLEY, JOHN EDMUND, physician, emeritus educator; b. Balt., Oct. 31, 1906; s. Charles Edward and Mary (Henry) B.; m. Kathryn Davis Strong, Sept. 21, 1933; children—Mark, Marcia. B.S., Loyola Coll., 1928; M.D., Georgetown U., 1932; postgrad. in pediatrics, Harvard, 1933-34. Intern Mercy Hosp., Balt., 1932-33; practice medicine specializing in pediatrics Balt., 1935-47; chmn. med. bd. St. Gabriel's Home, 1957-1966; chief pediatrics Luth. Hosp., 1956-66; instr., asst. prof., then assoc. prof. pediatrics U. Md. Sch. Medicine, 1934-46, prof., head pediatrics, 1948-66, emeritus prof. pediatrics, 1966—; dir. Pediatrics Permanente Found., 1947-48; now hon. cons. Childrens' Health Center, San Diego.; Mem. Md. Bd. Health and Mental Hygiene, 1961-1971; mem. adv. bd. Childhood Study Center Md. Editorial bd.: Current Medical Dialog; Contbr. articles to med. jours. Mem. adv. com. Md. Civil Def., 1941-46; mem. health council Md. Conf. Social Welfare; mem. Maternal Child and Welfare Med. Care Com.; mem. nat. adv. com. SSS.; Bd. dirs. Mental Hygiene Soc. Md.; trustee Hosp. Council. Recipient 6 gold medals for gen. acad. excellence, gold medal for sci. in schs.; J. Edmund Bradley prize named in his honor; Bradley Pediatric Soc. and Bradley Pediatric Library named in his honor at U. Md. Sch. Medicine. Fellow Am. Acad. Pediatrics; mem. AMA, Am. Pediatric Soc., Alpha Omega Alpha. Home: Sintonte and Mirasol Rds Rancho Bernardo San Diego CA 92128

BRADLEY, MARTHA WASHINGTON NUTTER (MRS. GEORGE WASHINGTON BRADLEY), educator; b. East St. Louis, Ill.; d. Cecil Grafton and Mabel (Hunt) Nutter; B.S. in Edn., U. Va., 1951, M.Ed., 1960; diplome de la langue Française, Alliance Française, Paris, 1958; Ph.D. (NDEA fellow), Syracuse U., 1967; m. George Washington Bradley, Feb. 20, 1960 (dec.). Tchr. elem. sch., East St. Louis, 1951-53, Long Beach, Calif., 1953-54, U.S. Army Dependent Schs., Europe, 1954-59, 60-61; reading cons. public schs., Fredericksburg, Va., 1961-62; instr. U. Va. Sch. Gen. Studies, 1962-63; asst. prof. edn. E. Tenn. State U., Johnson City, 1967-70, assoc. prof. edn., 1970-76, prof., 1976—, chmn. univ. publs. com., 1979-80, chmn. univ. acad. honor day com., 1980-81, 84-87, bd. dirs. Christian Student Fellowship, 1978-80; faculty adv. Student NEA, 1968-71. Trustee, George and Martha Washington Bradley Found., Johnson City, 1968-81; bd. dirs. Sister City Town Affiliation, Johnson City, 1971—, 2d v.p., 1972-76, pres., 1986-88; mem. Robert Young Cabin com. City of Johnson City, 1975-85; vol. service nat. appointee VA, 1973-80, 86—; bd. dirs. Appalachian Dist. council Girl Scouts U.S., 1978-79, U. Va. Edn. Found., 1983-87; bd. assocs. Emmanuel Sch. Religion, 1987—. Recipient Kappa Delta Pi honor key, 1983. Mem. Nat. (life), Tenn., East Tenn. (pres. East Tenn. State U. unit 1977-78) edn. assns., Conf. English Edn. (evaluator com. to evaluate documents 1968—), Nat. Council Tchrs. English, DAR (chmn. service for vet. patients Tenn. 1971-74, 76-77, chpt. vice regent 1974-77, regent 1977-80, pres. Tenn. regents' club 1978-79, chpt. dir. 1980-83, 1986—, chpt. mag. advt. chmn. 1980—), Daus. Am. Colonists (rec. sec. 1973-76, 1st vice regent 1976-79, 88—, regent 1985-88, state 1st vice regent 1988—, state chmn. pages com. 1985—, chmn. Tenn. Soc. Assembly 1986, southern sect., patriotic edn., nat. soc.), Internat. Reading Assn. (upper East Tenn. council research chmn. 1969-70), Bus. and Profl. Women's Club (chmn. nominating com. Tenn. fedn. 1972-73; dist. dir. 1974-75, fin. chmn. 1976-77, treas. 1977-78, local chmn. personal devel. com. 1969-70, local pres. 1971-72, 2d v.p. 1972-73; local chmn. by-laws com. 1973-75, chmn. young careerist com. 1975-76, legis. com. 1976-79), Am. Ednl. Research Assn., Nat. Soc. Study of Edn., AAUW (publicity chmn. 1968-70, corp. del. 1976-79, br. pres. 1976-80), Unaka Rock and Mineral Soc. (pres. 1969-70), Friends of the Reece Mus. (mem. edn. com. 1973-75), Assn. for Preservation Tenn. Antiquities, Mensa (East Tenn. proctor 1975-79), Phi Kappa Phi (life, charter pres. East Tenn. State U. chpt. 1970-72), Kappa Delta Pi (life, counselor Zeta Iota chpt. 1968-80), Delta Kappa Gamma (1st v.p. 1972-74), Phi Delta Kappa (life). Mem. Christian Ch. (pres. Women's council 1970-72, edn. com. 1970—, dir. Bible sch. 1971-73; mem. missions com. 1982—, personnel com. 1982-83, bequest com. 1984—). Clubs: Wednesday Morning Music (yearbook com. 1971-74, chmn. Music Week com. 1974—), E. Tenn. State U. Women's Faculty (co-chmn. book com. 1969-70), v.p. 1971-72, pres. 1972-73). Office: East Tenn State U Box 20110A Johnson City TN 37614

BRADLEY, NOLEN EUGENE, JR., personnel executive; educator; b. Memphis, Nov. 29, 1925; s. Nolen Eugene and Anice Pearl (Luther) B.; B.S., Memphis State U., 1951, M.A., 1952; Ed.D., U. Tenn., 1966; m. Eloise Mullins, Jan. 7, 1947; children—Sharon (Mrs. Brabson), Diana (Mrs. Wiley M. Rutledge), Nolen Eugene III, David Lee. Instr. polit. sci. Memphis State U., 1951-52; tchr. English, Messick High Sch., Memphis, 1952-56; asst. dean admissions Memphis State U., 1956-64; dir. State Agy. for Title I, Higher Edn. Act 1965, Div. Continuing Edn., U. Tenn., 1966-70; dean instrn. Vol. State Community Coll., Gallatin, Tenn., 1970-78; tutor, ednl. cons., 1978-79; personnel asst. Hoeganaes Corp., Gallatin, 1979-80, personnel mgr., 1980-82; dir. personnel Music Village U.S.A., Hendersonville, Tenn., 1984—. Served with AUS, 1944-46, ETO. Mem. Am. Assn. Sch. Adminstrs., Tenn. Adult Edn. Assn., Tenn. Edn. Assn., Omicron Delta Kappa, Pi Delta Epsilon, Phi Delta Kappa, Phi Kappa Phi. Contbr. articles to profl. jours. Democrat. Baptist (deacon 1966—). Lion. Avocations: writing, travel, movies, reading. Home: 907 Harris Dr Gallatin TN 37066

BRADLEY, RAMONA KAISER, curator; b. Hamilton County, Ohio, Aug. 9, 1909; d. Oliver Barnard and Grace Lytle (Edwards) Kaiser; student Oakhurst Coll., Cin., 1926-28, Schuster-Martin Sch. Drama, 1931-33; m. Judson M. Bradley, Sept. 4, 1954. Sec. to patent atty., Cin., 1939-54; curator Sherman Indian Mus., Riverside, Calif., 1970—; cons. Title IV Project, Indian edn. Riverside Sch. Dist. Bd. dirs. Riverside Library, 1966-74, Riverside Cultural Heritage, 1974-80. Recipient Appreciation award Sherman Indian High Sch., 1977, honored for civic service City and County Riverside, 1980, honor award D.A.R., 1981. Mem. Nat. League Am. Pen Women, D.A.R., Daus. Am. Colonists, Printing House Craftsmen, Inland Empire Mus. Consortium. Republican. Methodist. Club: Citrus Belt (hon.). Author: Glimpses Into the Past, 1940, Weavers of Tales, 1965. Home: 9130 Andrew St Riverside CA 92503 Office: 9010 Magnolia Ave Riverside CA 92503

BRADLEY, THOMAS AUGUSTUS, communications educator; b. Danville, Va., Mar. 5, 1939; s. Augustus and Annie (Leake) B.; B.S., The Citadel, 1961; M.A., U. N.C., 1971; m. Patsy Jean Griswold, Aug. 27, 1967; children—Patricia Jean, Thomas Augustus. Tchr., media specialist Richland Dist. I Sch. System, Columbia, S.C., 1965-82, instr. communications U. S.C., Columbia, 1983-84; ednl. cons. Distinctive Ednl. Ctr., Columbia, 1983-84; instr. Columbia Jr. Coll., 1984-87; tutor Epworth Children's Home, Columbia, 1985-86. Mem. adminstrv. bd. St. Mark United Meth. Ch., 1980-81. Served with U.S. Army, 1961-64. Club: Garden Dale Swim and Racquet.

BRADLEY, WANDA LOUISE, librarian; b. Havre de Grace, Md., June 6, 1953; d. William Smith and Josephine Viola (Miller) B. B.A. (scholar), U. Md., 1975; M.S.L.S. (scholar), Atlanta U., 1976; postgrad. Cath. U.; M.P.A. (scholar), U. Balt., 1986. Librarian, Harford County Pub. Library, Bel Air, Md., 1976, Harford County Bd. Edn., Bel Air, 1977-81, Nat. Grad. U., Arlington, Va., 1982, Md. State Dept. Edn., Balt., 1982-83, U.S. Dept. Labor, Washington, 1984, Balt. Gas and Electric Co., 1984-85, Morgan State U., Balt., 1985, Coppin State Coll., Balt., 1985-86, Montgomery County Pub. Sch. System, Rockville, Md., 1985-86, Community Coll. Balt., 1987—; acad. advisor George Mason U., Fairfax, Va., 1981-82. Dept. Edn. fellow, 1983-84; U. Balt. Merit scholar, 1984. Mem. ALA, Md. Library Assn., Spl. Libraries Assn., Med. Library Assn., ASIS. Methodist.

BRADSHAW, CARL JOHN, lawyer, consultant; b. Oelwein, Iowa, Nov. 1, 1930; s. Carl John and Lorraine Lillian (Thiele) B.; m. Katsuko Anno, Nov. 5, 1954; children: Carla K. Bradshaw Marder, Arthur Herbert, Vincent Marcus. BS, U. Minn., 1952, JD, 1957; LLM, U. Mich., 1958; MJur, Keio U., Tokyo, 1962. Bar: Minn. 1961, U.S. Supreme Ct., 1981, Calif. 1985. Assoc. Graham, James & Rolph, Tokyo, 1961-63; assoc. prof. law U. Wash., Seattle, 1963-64; sr. v.p. Oak Industries, Inc., Crystal Lake, Ill., 1964-84, dir. internat. ops., 1964-70, dir. corp. devel., 1970-72, pres. communications group, 1972-78, chief legal officer, 1979-84; counsel Seki & Jarvis, Los Angeles, 1985-87, Bell, Boyd & Lloyd, Los Angeles, 1987; now prin. The Pacific Law Group, Los Angeles, Tokyo and Palo Alto, Calif. Contbr. articles to legal and bus. jours. Bd. dirs. Japan-Am. Soc., Chgo., 1966-72; bd. dirs., fin. dir. San Diego Symphony Orch. Assn., 1980-81. Served to lt. (j.g.) USN, 1952-55. Fellow Radio Club Am.; mem. Minn. Bar Assn., Calif. Bar Assn., ABA, Am. Soc. Internat. Law, Internat. Fiscal Assn. Club: Regency (Los Angeles). Home: 12958 Robleda Cove San Diego CA 92128 Office: The Pacific Law Group 1875 Century Park E 8th Floor Los Angeles CA 90067

BRADSHAW, CYNTHIA HELENE, educator; b. S.I., N.Y., May 9, 1954; d. Frederick Thomas and Audrey Helene (Stetter) B. B.S. in Elem. Edn., Wagner Coll., 1975; M.S. in Edn., U. Miami, 1979. Cert. elem. tchr., adminstr., and supr. Tchr. Young Scholars Montessori Sch., S.I., 1975-76, Lutheran Schs., Mo. Synod, S.I., 1976, Hialeah and N. Miami, Fla., 1976-80, Dade County pub. schs., Miami, 1980-88, Rahway (N.J.) pub. schs., 1988—; reliability study subject Fla. Dept. Edn., Tallahassee, 1984—. Sch. chairperson United Way, Miami, 1983—. Recipient Cert. of Recognition Dade County Pub. Schs., 1984. Mem. United Tchrs. Dade, United Tchrs. Dade Polit. Orgn., U. Miami Sch. Edn. Allied Professions Alumni Assn. (mem. alumni telephone funding campaign 1984), Alpha Delta Kappa. Republican. Lutheran. Lodge: Order Eastern Star. Avocation: Music. Home: 34 Douglas Ave Staten Island NY 10310 Office: Roosevelt Elem Sch 811 Saint Georges Ave Rahway NJ 07065

BRADSHAW, THORNTON FREDERICK, business consultant; b. Washington, Aug. 4, 1917; s. Frederick and Julia V. (See) B.; m. Sally Davis, 1940 (div. 1974); children: Nancy M. (Mrs. Thomas Poor), Priscilla W. (Mrs. Richard Page, Jr.), Jonathan G.; m. Patricia Salter West, May 11, 1974; children: Jeffrey D. West, Nicholas S. West, Andrew P. West, Eric R. West. AB, Harvard U., 1940, MBA, 1942; DCS, Harvard, 1950; LLD (hon.), Pepperdine U., 1974, Southampton Coll., 1983; DSocial Sci. (hon.), Villanova U., 1975; LLD (hon.), Dickinson Coll., 1986. Assoc. prof. Grad. Sch. Bus. Adminstrn., Harvard U., Cambridge, Mass., 1942-52; ptnr. Cresap, McCormick & Paget, N.Y.C., 1952-56; v.p., dir. Atlantic Richfield Co. (formerly Atlantic Refining Co.), Los Angeles, 1956-62, exec. v.p., 1962-64, pres., 1964-80, mem. exec. com., 1966-81; chmn. bd. RCA Corp., N.Y.C., 1981-86; bd. dirs. NBC, First Boston, Inc., Brooks Fashion Stores, Inc., Gen. Electric Co.; overseer Harvard Coll., 1978-84. Trustee Conservation Found.; trustee Rockefeller Bros. Fund, Inst. Internat. Edn., Inst. Advanced Study; chmn. bd. Aspen Inst. Humanistic Studies Aspen Inst.; chmn. Ctr. for Communication, The Lauder Inst. of Mgmt. and Internat. Studies; chmn. vis. com. The Loeb Drama Ctr. Harvard U.; chmn. bd. dirs. John D. and Catherine T. MacArthur Found. Served to lt. (j.g.) USNR, 1943-45. Mem. Am. Petroleum Inst. Office: 570 Lexington Ave New York NY 10022

BRADY, HARRY ALBERT, former printing company executive; b. Bellevue, Iowa, Feb. 7, 1925; s. John Albert and Evangeline Lucille (Mace) B.; m. Doris Aileen, Apr. 5, 1946 (div. June 1985); children: Evangeline Pell, Marshall, Byron, Yvonne Perry; m. Sue Pipes, July 5, 1985. BS, Yale U., 1950. Engr. R.R. Donnelley, Chgo., 1950-55; salesman R.R. Donnelley, Los Angeles, 1956-58, west coast sales mgr., 1958-62; western regional mgr. R.R. Donnelley, Chgo., 1962-67; v.p., sales dir. Western Pub. Co., Racine, Wis., 1967-70, Meredith/Bunda Inc., Lynchburg, Va., 1971-81; sr. v.p. mktg. Meredith/Bunda Inc., Des Moines, 1981-86. Served to 1st sgt. USMC, 1942-46, PTO. Republican. Presbyterian. Clubs: Pine Valley (Clementon, N.J.); Yale (N.Y.C.). Home: 1301 Wakefield Lynchburg VA 24503

BRADY, LUTHER W., JR., physician, radiology educator; b. Rocky Mount, N.C., Oct. 20, 1925; s. Luther W. and Gladys B. A.A., George Washington U., 1944, A.B., 1946, M.D., 1948. Diplomate: Am. Bd. Radiology (treas. 1980-82, v.p. 1982-84, pres. 1984-86). Intern Jefferson Med. Coll. Hosp., Phila., 1948-50; resident in radiology Jefferson Med. Coll. Hosp., 1954-55; resident radiology Hosp. U. Pa., Phila., 1955-56; fellow Nat. Cancer Inst., 1953-57, 1957-59; practice medicine, specializing in radiation therapy and oncology Phila.; asst. instr. radiology Jefferson Med. Coll. Hosp., 1954-55, U. Pa., Phila., 1955, instr., 1956-57, assoc. radiology, 1957-59; asst. prof. radiology Coll. of Physicians and Surgeons, Columbia U., N.Y.C., summer, 1959; assoc. prof. radiology Hahnemann Med. Coll. and Hosp., Phila., 1959-62, prof., 1963—, chmn. dept. radiation oncology, 1970—; asst. prof. radiology Harvard Med. Sch., Boston, 1962-63; mem. med. radiation adv. com. Bur. Radiation Health, HEW, 1971-74; cons. radiation therapy various hosps.; mem. U.S. del. to Interam. Congress Radiology, 1975, Internat. Congress of Radiology, 1981; sec. gen. Internat. Congress Radiology, 1985; med. adv. radiation therapy, dir. Pa. Blue Shield, Camp Hill. Author: Tumors of the Nervous System, 1975, Cancer of the Lung, Clinical Applications of the Electron Beam; editor Cancer Clin. Trials (Am. Jour. Clin. Oncology), (with C. Perez) Principles and Practice of Radiation Oncology; editorial bd. Cancer; assoc. editor: Gynecologic Oncology, Am. Jour. Roentgenology, Cancer Research; sr. editor: Internat. Jour. Radiol. Oncology; contbr. articles on radiation therapy to profl. jours. Bd. dirs. Assn. Artists Equity of Phila., Welcome House, 1974—, Settlement Music Sch., 1973—, Phila. Art Alliance, 1977-84; trustee Phila. Mus. Art, also mem. oriental art com., 1974—, chmn. exec. com., 1968-72, mem. print, contemporary art and Indian art coms., 1974—. Served to lt. M.C. USN, 1950-54. Recipient Grubbe award Chgo. Radiol. Soc., 1977; Gold medal Gilbert Fletcher Soc., 1984; Albert Soiland Gold medal U. So. Calif., 1985; del Regato Gold medal, 1986. Fellow Am. Coll. Radiology (chmn. commn. radiation therapy 1975-81, bd. chancellors 1975-81, Gold Medal 1983), Royal Coll. Radiology (hon.), Deutsches Roentgengesellschaft (hon.), Italian Radiology Soc. (hon.); mem. Radiol. Soc. N.Am. (bd. dirs. 1977-84, chmn. bd. dirs. 1982 83, pres. 1984-85 chmn. refresher course com. com. 1971-75, Erskine lectr. 1979), Pa. Radiol. Soc. (dir. 1970-77, councilor to Am. Coll. Radiology 1971-77), Am. Radium Soc. (pres. 1976-77, dir., Janeway medal 1979, Janeway lectr. 1980), Am. Cancer Soc. (pres. Phila. div. 1976-78, dir. 1968—, exec. com. 1976-78, mem. breast cancer task force 1974—), Am. Soc. Therapeutic Radiologists (pres. 1971-72), Assn. U. Radiologists, Am. Roentgen Ray Soc., Am. Assn. for Cancer Research, Radiation Research Soc., Am. Fedn. Clin. Oncologic Soc. (exec. com.), Am. Soc. Clin. Oncology, Phila. Roentgen Ray Soc. (pres. 1976-77, mem. exec. com. 1976-78), Am. Fedn. Clin. Research, Coll. Physicians Phila., James Ewing Soc., Assn. Pendergrass Fellows, Philadelphia County Med. Soc., AMA (chair residency rev. com. for radiology 1982-84), Med. Soc. State Pa., Internat. Skeletal Soc., Council Acad. Socs., Soc. Chairmen Acad. Radiation Oncology Programs (pres. 1977-79), Soc. Chairmen Acad. Radiology Depts. (pres. 1974-75), Gynecologic Oncology Group (exec. com. 1971-85, assoc. chmn. 1971-85), Radiation Therapy Oncology Group (chmn. 1980-87), Internat. Club Radiotherapists, Nat. Cancer Inst. (bd. sci. counselors, com. for radiation therapy studies 1971-84, chmn. cancer clin. trails com.), Smith-Reed-Russell Soc., Alpha Omega Alpha, Phi Lambda Kappa. Clubs: Merion Cricket; Racquet, Union League (Phila.), Phila., Peale. Office: 230 N Broad St Philadelphia PA 19102

BRADY, MELVIN MICHAEL, engineer, writer; b. San Francisco, Dec. 15, 1933; arrived in Norway, 1962; s. Robert Alexander and Dorothy Elizabeth (Stahl) B.; m. Marianne Hadler, Aug. 11, 1978; 1 child, Thomas Hadler. BEE, George Washington U., 1956; MS, MIT, 1958; Degree Engr., Stanford U., 1962. Mem. staff Nat. Bur. Standards, Washington and Boulder, Colo., 1952-56; research engr. MIT, 1956-58, Stanford U., Calif., 1959-62, Norwegian Def. Research Establishment, 1958-59, 62-65; project engr., chief editor Norconsult, Oslo, 1968-74; cons. engr. Oslo, 1975—, freelance writer, editor, 1975—; guest faculty mem. U. Rochester (N.Y.), 1975, U. Ottawa (Ont., Can.), 1979-80. Author: Nordic Touring and Cross-Country Skiing, 1966, Waxing for Cross-Country Skiing, 1971, Cross-Country Ski Gear, 1979, The Complete Ski Cross-Country, 1982; co-author Citizen Racing, 1982, Sequence Training, 1984; translator books; contbr. articles to profl. jours., mags. Fulbright fellow, 1958-59; Norwegian Council Sci. and Indsl. Research fellow, 1962-65. Mem. IEEE (sr.). Office: PO Box 8236 Hammersborg, N-0129 Oslo Norway

BRADY, PEGGY JOE, oil company executive, consultant; b. Grimsley, Tenn., May 24, 1941; d. Paul Earl and Daisy Elease (Demonbreun) Stults; m. Robert Collins Whited, Oct. 9, 1959 (dec. July 1975); children—Paula Diane, Robert Wayne, Wesley Dale (dec.); m. James Dexter Brady, Mar. 10, 1984. A.B., U. Tenn., 1972-73. Insp. Colonial Mfr., Jamestown, Tenn., 1957-60; clk. Frisch's, Inc., Dayton, Ohio, 1960-64, Tenn. Dept. Pub. Health, Nashville, 1967-69; acct. Tenn. Dept. Safety, Nashville, 1969-73; service rep. IRS, Nashville, 1973-74; pvt. practice acctg., Crossville, Tenn., 1977-79; exec. asst. Vol. Energy, Inc., Crossville, 1979-82; owner Brady Enterprises; corp. officer H. Stonewell Service, Inc., Crossville, 1982—; cons. to oil and gas industries. Com mem. Young Democrats, Nashville, 1967-69; officer/del. PTA, Nashville, 1966-68; counselor Wautauga council Boy Scouts Am., 1968-69; bd. dirs. Community Action Services, Crossville, 1985-86, 86-87, 87-88; advisor Am. Inst. for Cancer Research, 1984. Mem. Tenn. Oil and Gas Assn., Nat. Assn. Female Execs. Club: Order Eastern Star. Office: Harold Stonewell Service Inc Hwy 127 PO Box 2768 Crossville TN 38557 also: Brady Enterprises Hwy 127 PO Box 2646 Crossville TN 38557

BRADY, WILLIAM MILNER, oil company executive, geophysicist; b. Mex., Nov. 26, 1945; came to U.S., 1947; s. William Connolly and Kathryn (Annis) B.; m. Ruth Annette Hartmann, Sept. 18, 1970 (div. 1986); m. L.C. Ochoa Munoz, 1987; 1 child, William Michael. Student, U. So. Calif., 1962-64, U. Mich., 1964-65; B.S. in Geology, U. Tex., 1969; postgrad. UCLA, 1974-76. Geophysicist, Eltres/Richard Brewer & Assocs., 1978-80; gen. ptnr. Alpine Resources, Tex., 1980-85, Ashton Resources Ltd., Houston, 1983—; cons. Katana Belize Ltd., Denver, 1982-85, D&S Belize Ltd., Calgary, Can., 1982-85, Fairfield Indsl. Belize, Houston, 1978-80, Basic Resources Ltd., N.Y.C., 1973-78. Patentee in field. Mem. IEEE, AAAS, Am. Assn. Petroleum Geologists, Soc. Am. Inventors, Soc. Computer Aided Design Eng. Clubs: St. Anthony (San Antonio); Soc. War 1812 (New Orleans).

BRAFFORD, WILLIAM CHARLES, chemical company executive; b. Pike County, Ky., Aug. 7, 1932; s. William Charles and Minnie (Tacket) B.; m. Katherine Jane Prather, Nov. 13, 1954; children—William Charles III, David A. J.D., U. Ky., 1957; LL.M. (fellow), U. Ill., 1958. Bar: Ky. bar 1957, Ga. bar 1965, Tax Ct. bar U.S 1965, Ct. Claims bar 1965, Ohio bar 1966, U.S. Ct. Appeals bar 1966, U.S. Supreme Ct. bar 1970, Pa. bar 1973. Trial atty. NLRB, Washington and Cin., 1958-60; atty. Louisville & Nashville R.R. Co., Louisville, 1960-63, So. Bell Telephone Co., Atlanta, 1963-65; asst. gen. counsel NCR Corp., Dayton, Ohio, 1965-72; v.p., sec., gen. counsel Betz Labs., Inc., Trevose, Pa., 1972—; dir. Betz Process Chems., Inc., Betz, Ltd. U.K., Betz Paper Chem. Inc., Betz Energy Chems., Inc., Betz S.A. France, B.L. Chems., Inc., Betz GmbH, Germany, Betz Entec, Inc., Betz Ges. GmbH, Austria, Betz NV Belgium, Betz Sud S.p.A., Italy, Betz Internat. Inc., Betz Europe Inc., Primex Ltd., Barbados. Served as 1st lt. C.I.C. AUS, 1954-56. Mem. Am. Soc. Corp. Secs., Nat. Assn. Corp. Dirs., Atlantic Legal Found. Republican. Presbyterian. Office: Betz Labs Inc 4636 Somerton Rd Trevose PA 19047

BRAGA, DANIEL, management consultant; b. Oporto, Portugal, Feb. 14, 1946; s. Daniel Sr. and Teresa (de Meireles) B.; m. Monika Bäuerle; 1 child, Diana. Grad., Inst. Superieur des Scis. Econs. et Commerciales, Paris, 1979, Ctr. de Perfectionnement aux Affaires, Paris, 1982. Inventory mgr. D.A.F. France, Survilliers, 1970-73; asst. to v.p. ops. Manpower France, Paris, 1973-79; personnel dir. Erom France, Paris, 1980-84; dir. ops. Ordinter, Paris, 1984-85; pvt. practice in mgmt. cons. Paris, 1985—; v.p. Assn. pour la Promotion des Entreprises, La Celle Saint-Cloud, 1985—; bd. dirs. Syndicat des Profls. du Marche du Travail Temporaire Work Services Fedn., Paris, 1985-86. V.p. Centro de Pesquisas Espaciais, Porto, Portugal, 1966—. Home and Office: 100 Blvd Massena, 75013 Paris France

BRAGANZA, NIRMALA MARIE, librarian; b. Moradabad, India, July 15, 1949; d. Victor Sylvester and Therese Enid (Lobo) B. BA, Loreto Coll., Lucknow, India, 1968; EdB, Tilak Coll., Poona, India, 1970; BLS, Poona U., 1976, MLS, 1983. Tchr. St. Patrick's High Sch., Poona, 1968-69, Loreto Convent, Darjeeling, India, 1971-72; tchr. St. Vincent's High Sch., Poona, 1970-71, librarian, 1973-78; documentation asst. Philips India, Ltd., Poona, 1978-80; librarian Tata Mgmt. Tng. Ctr., Poona, 1983—; cons. Ishwani Kendra, Poona, 1982. Mem. Indian Assn. Spl. Libraries and Info. Centres, Univ. Women's Assn. (sec. 1985-87). Roman Catholic. Home: 37 St Patricks Town, Poona 411 013, India Office: Tata Mgmt Tng, Ctr 1 Mangaldas Rd, Poona 411 001, India

BRAGG, MICHAEL ELLIS, lawyer; b. Holdrege, Nebr., Oct. 6, 1947; s. Lionel C. and Frances E. (Klinginsmith) B.; m. Nancy Jo Aabel, Jan. 19, 1980; children: Brian Michael, Kyle Christopher. BA, U. Nebr., 1971, JD, 1975. Bar: Alaska 1976, U.S. Dist. Ct. Alaska 1976, Nebr. 1976, U.S. Dist. Ct. Nebr. 1976. Assoc. White & Jones, Anchorage, 1976-77; field rep. State Farm Ins., Anchorage, 1977-79, atty. corp. law dept., Bloomington, Ill., 1979-81, sr. atty., 1981-84, asst. counsel, 1984-86, counsel dept. corp. law, 1986-88, claims counsel dept. gen. claims, 1988—; lectr., contbr. legal seminars. Contbr. articles to legal and ins. jours., also editor various publs. Bd. dirs. Friends of Arts, Bloomington, 1984-85, McLean County Crime Prevention Com., 1988—. Served with USNG, 1970-76. Mem. ABA (vice chmn. property ins. com. 1986—, corp. counsel and antitrust coms., various offices tort and ins. practices sect. 1987—), Am. Corp. Counsel Assn., Internat. Platform Assn., Defense Research Inst. Republican. Mem. Unitarian Ch. Club: Crestwicke Country. Office: State Farm Ins Cos 112 E Washington Suite 12N Bloomington IL 61701

BRAHA, THOMAS I., business executive; b. Austin, Tex., Sept. 3, 1947; s. Jacob and Valentine (Capone) B.; m. Nancy Elizabeth Rowe, Mar. 31, 1973; children—Nancy Elizabeth, Jeanne Valentine, Travis Ian. B.S.M.E., U. Tex., 1969; M.B.A., Temple U., 1971; postgrad., N.Y. U., 1971-73. Engr. Davis Electronics, Inc., Austin, 1967, Whirlpool Corp., Evansville, Ind., 1968; project engr. ITE Imperial Corp., Phila., 1969-71; sr. supply analyst Mobil Oil Corp., N.Y.C., 1971-74; pres. Western Hemisphere Bulk Oil (U.S.A.), Inc., N.Y.C., 1974-75; pres., chief exec. officer Braha Oil Inc., Braha Oil Ltd., Braha Oil B.V., Braha Estates, Inc., Braha Farms, Braha Profit and Pension Trusts. Mem. Am. Mgmt. Assn., ASME, Inst. Petroleum (U.K.), Nat. Petroleum Refining Assn., Am. Petroleum Inst. Office: Braha Holding Co PO Box 13442 Philadelphia PA 19101

BRAHAM, DELPHINE DORIS, government accountant; b. L'Anse, Mich., Mar. 16, 1946; d. Richard Andrew and Viola Mary (Niemi) Aho; m. John Emerson Braham, Sept. 23, 1967 (div. Dec. 1987); children: Tammy, Debra, John Jr. BS summa cum laude, Drury Coll., 1983; M in Mgmt., Webster U., St. Louis, 1986. Bookkeeper, Community Mental Health Ctr., Marquette, Mich., 1966-68; credit clk. Remington Rand, Marietta, Ohio, 1971-72; acctg. technician St. Joseph's Hosp., Parkersburg, W.Va., 1972-74; material mgr. U.S. Army, Ft. Leonard Wood, Mo., 1982-86, accountant, 1986—;instr., adjunct faculty Columbia Coll., 1987—; Park Coll., 1988—. Leader Girls Scouts U.S., Williamstown, W.Va., 1972-74, Hanau, W.Ger., 1977-79. Mem. AAUW (treas. Waynesville br. 1986—), Nat. Assn. Female Execs., Assn. Govt. Accts., Am. Soc. Mil. Comptrollers. Home: RT 2 Box 248L #28 Waynesville MO 65583

BRAHIMI, ABDELHAMID, prime minister of Algeria; b. Constantine, Algeria, April 2, 1936; one child. Officer, Nat. Liberation Army, 1956-62; govt. rep. Annaba province, Algeria, 1963-65; dir. Algerian-French Bd. for promotion of indsl. coop., 1968-70; prof. econs. U. Algiers, 1970-75; chmn. SONATRACH Inc., U.S.A., 1976-78; minister of planning and regional devel., Algeria, 1979-83, prime minister, 1984—. Office: Office of the Prime Minister, Algiers Algeria *

BRAIBANTI, RALPH JOHN, political scientist, educator; b. Danbury, Conn., June 29, 1920; s. Daniel Vincent and Jane Helena B.; m. Lucy Kauffman, Feb. 19, 1943; children—Claire, Ralph Lynn. B.S., Western Conn. State U., 1941; A.M., Syracuse U., 1947, Ph.D., 1949. Asst. prof. polit. sci. Kenyon Coll., 1949-52, assoc. prof., 1952-53; asst. dir. Am. Polit. Sci. Assn., Washington, 1950-51; cons. Govtl. Affairs Inst., 1950-51; assoc. prof. polit. sci. Duke U., Durham, N.C., 1953-58; prof. Duke U., 1958-68, James B. Duke prof. polit. sci., 1968—; dir. Islamic and Arabian devel. studies, 1977—; scholar-in-residence Rockefeller Found. Bellagio Ctr., Italy, 1967; cons. AID, 1958-59, Ford Found., 1972, UN, 1974, Govt. Saudi Arabia, 1974—, UNESCO, 1977, Islamic Secretariat, 1980, World Bank, 1987; vis. prof. U. Kuwait, 1984; adviser on adminstrv. reform Pakistan, Malaysia, South Africa, Lebanon, Morocco, Saudi Arabia, Bangladesh; bd. advisors Nat. Council U.S.-Arab Relations, Moroccan-Am. Found., Am.-Arab Affairs Council, Nat. Council Study Islamic Socs.; trustee Am. Inst. Pakistan Studies, Am. Inst. Yemeni Studies; chmn. nat. selection com. Joseph J. Malone Postdoctoral Fellowships in Arabian Affairs. Author: Research on the Bureaucracy of Pakistan, 1966; co-author, editor: Political and Administrative Development, 1969, Pakistan: The Long View, 1976, Asian Bureaucratic Systems Emergent from the British Imperial Tradition, 1966, Tradition, Values and Socio-Economic Development, 1961, Administration and Economic Development in India, 1963; gen. editor 7 vol. series on comparative adminstrn., 1968-73; bd. editors: Arab Affairs, Jour. South Asian and Middle Eastern Studies, Comparative Politics, Politikon, Asian Forum, Jour. Pakistan Studies. Served to capt. U.S. Army, 1942-47. Recipient citation outstanding prof. Duke Student Assn., 1972, Alumni award disting. undergrad. teaching, 1979; Maxwell fellow Syracuse U., 1949, Ford Found. fellow, 1955-56, Social Sci. Research Council fellow, 1955-56. Mem. Internat. Studies Assn.-South (pres.), Am. Inst. Pakistan Studies (founding pres. 1975-77, pres. 1986—), Internat. Cultural Soc. Korea (hon.), Am. Council for Study Islamic Socs. (bd. dirs.). Republican. Episcopalian. Home: 3805 Darby Rd Durham NC 27707 Office: Duke Univ 2114 Campus Dr Durham NC 27706

BRAIN, PAUL FREDRIC, zoology educator; b. Manchester, Eng., July 1, 1945; s. Frederick Ernest and Ada (Squirell) B.; m. Sonja Strijbos, July 4, 1975; children: Ilka, Vincent Fredric, Daniel Robert. BS with 1st class honors, U. Hull, 1967, PhD, 1971. Postdoctoral fellow U. Sheffield (Eng.), 1970-71; lectr. zoology U. Wales, Swansea, 1971-78, sr. lectr., 1978-83, reader, 1983-87, prof., 1987—; cons. ICI, Macclesfield, Eng., 1983-85; vis. prof. psychology U. Hawaii at Manoa, Honolulu, 1986. Co-editor: The Biology of Aggression, 1981, Ethopharmacology in..., 1987; editor: Alcohol and Aggression, 1986; assoc. editor Aggressive Behavior, 1974. Bd. govs. Casllwchr Sch., 1986—; advisor on animal experimentation Brit. Govt., 1986—. Recipient internat. prize for medicine UNESCO/WHO, 1980; project grantee Med. Research Council, 1976-78, Brit. Council, 1985—. Mem. Internat. Soc. for Research on Aggression (pres. 1982-84), Assn. for Study Animal Behaviour, Soc. for Endocrinology, Inst. Biology. Home: 8 Landor Dr, SA4 2GL Loughor Nr Swansea England Office: U Coll Swansea Biol Scis, Singleton Park, Swansea SA2 8PP, Wales

BRAINE, RAYMOND GERMAINE MARIE HENRI, chemistry educator; b. Liege, Belgium, Sept. 7, 1926; s. Jean A. and Raymonde Braine; m. Jacqueline Ramakers, Nov. 10, 1959; children: Emmanuel R. Licencie Sciences Chimiques, U. de l'Etat a Liege, 1950, Docteur en Sciences, Groupe Des Sciences Chimiques, 1954. Prof., Ecole Normale Moyenne de Liege, 1950-69; prof. indsl. chemistry Hautes Etudes Commerciales Liege, 1969—. Pres., Groupement des Ingenieurs Commerciaux H.E.C., Liege, 1981—. Contbr. articles to profl. jours. Decorated chevalier de l'Ordre des Palmes Academiques (France); Order of Crown, officier Ordre Léopold II (Belgium). Mem. Societe Chimique de Belgique, Association Belge des Professeurs de Chimie et de Physique, Association des Chimistes Sortis de U. Liege. Home: Quai Churchill 19, 4020 Liege Belgium Office: Hautes Etudes Commerciales, Rue Sohet 21, 4020 Liege B Belgium

BRAITHWAITE, EUSTACE ADOLPHE, author, former diplomat; b. June 27, 1922. Ed. NYU; M.Sc., Cambridge U. Sch. tchr., London, 1950-57; welfare officer London County Council, 1958-60; human rights officer World Vets. Found., Paris, 1960-63; lectr., ednl. cons. UNESCO, Paris, 1963-66; permanent rep. of Guyana to UN, 1967-68; ambassador to Venezuela, 1968-69; Author: To Sir, With Love (Ainsfield Wolff Lit. award), 1959 (film 1967)); A Kind of Homecoming, 1961; Paid Servant, 1962; A Choice of Straws, 1965; Reluctant Neighbours, 1972; Honorary White, 1976. Served with RAF, World War II. *

BRAKE, CECIL CLIFFORD, diversified manufacturing executive; b. Ystrad, Mynach, Wales, Nov. 14, 1932; came to U.S., 1967; s. Leonard James and Ivy Gertrude (Berry) B.; m. Vera Morris, Aug. 14, 1954; children—Stephen John, Richard Colin, Vanessa Elaine. Chartered engr.; B.Sc. in Engring., U. Wales, 1954; M.Sc., Cranfield Inst., Bedford, Eng., 1957; grad. A.M.P., Harvard U. Sch. Bus., 1985. Mgr. research and devel. Schrader Fluid Power, Wake Forest, N.C., 1968-70, engring. mgr., 1970-75; mng. dir. Schrader U.K. Fluid Power, 1975-77; v.p., gen. mgr. Schrader Internat., 1977-78; group v.p. Schrader Bellows, Fluid Power, Akron, Ohio, 1978-82; exec. v.p. Scovill, Inc., Waterbury, Conn., 1982-86; pres. Yale Security, Inc. subs. Scovill, Inc.; group exec. Eagle Industries, Inc., Chgo., 1986—; chief operating officer Mansfield (Ohio) Plumbing Products Inc., Hart and Cooley Inc., Holland, Mich., Chemineer Inc., Dayton, Ohio, Pulsafeeder Inc., Rochester, N.Y., Clevaflex Inc., Cleve., Equality Specialties Inc., N.Y.C., De-Vilbiss Co., Toledo. Mem. Royal Aero. Soc., Allied Products Inst. (bd. dirs.), Nat. Fluid Power Assn. (bd. dirs. 1981—). Office: Eagle Industries Inc 2 N Riverside Plaza Chicago IL 60606

BRAM, LEON LEONARD, publishing company executive; b. Chgo., Sept. 20, 1931; s. Samuel and Rose (Rosenbloom) B.; m. Doris A. Hebel, Apr. 29, 1961 (div. 1972); children—Mark James, Alexander Anton; m. Joanne Frances Casino, Sept. 30, 1978; 1 child, Victoria Lynn. B.Sc., DePaul U., 1967. Various positions Chgo. Pub. Library, 1949-55; various positions E.E. Compton Co., Chgo., 1955-63; dir. editorial research Standard Ednl. Corp., Chgo., 1963-69; exec. editor E.E. Compton Co., Chgo., 1969-74; v.p., editorial dir. Funk and Wagnalls Inc., N.Y.C., 1974—. Mgr. Ill. Ballet Co., Chgo., 1959-68; bd. dirs. Assn. Am. Dance Cos., N.Y.C., 1966-72; v.p. Performing Arts Dance Fund, N.J., 1976-85. Mem. ALA. Home: 235 E 22d St Apt 4E New York NY 10010 Office: Funk and Wagnalls Inc 70 Hilltop Rd Ramsey NJ 07446

BRAMBLE, RONALD LEE, business and legal consultant; b. Pauls Valley, Okla., Sept. 9, 1937; s. Homer Lee and Ethyle Juanita (Stephens) B.; m. Kathryn Louise Seiler, July 2, 1960; children: Julia Dawn, Kristin Lee. AA, San Antonio Coll., 1957; BS, Trinity U., 1959, MS, 1964; JD, St. Mary's U., 1975; DBA, Ind. No. U., 1973. Mgr., buyer Fed-Mart, Inc., San Antonio, 1959-61; tchr. bus. San Antonio Ind. Sch. Dist., 1961-65, edn. coordinator, bus. tng. specialist, 1965-67; assoc. prof., chmn. dept. mgmt. San Antonio Coll., 1967-73; prin. Ron Bramble Assocs., San Antonio, 1967-77; pres. Adminstrv. Research Assocs., Inc., 1977-82; v.p. PIA, Inc., 1982-83; v.p. fin. Solar 21 Corp., 1983-84, sr. staff Ausburn, Astoria & Seale, 1984—; lectr. bus., edn. and ch. groups, 1965—. Cons. editor: Prentice-Hall, Inc., Englewood Cliffs, N.J., 1969-71; contbr. articles to profl. jours. Cert. lay speaker Meth. Ch. Served with AUS, 1959. Recipient Wall Street Jour. award Trinity U., 1959, U.S. Law Week award, 1975. Mem. ABA, San Antonio C. of C., Adminstrv. Mgmt. Soc. (pres. 1966-68, Merit award 1968), Bus. Edn. Tchrs. Assn. (pres. 1964), Sales and Mktg. Execs. San Antonio (bd. dirs. 1967-68, Disting. Salesman award 1967), Internat. Platform Assn., Internat. Assn. Cons. to Bus., Nat. Assn. Bus. Economists, Acad. Mgmt., Christian Legal Soc., Comml. Law League Am., San Antonio Advt. Club, Phi Delta Phi. Republican. Lodge: Lions. Home: 127 Palo Duro San Antonio TX 78232

BRAMHALL, ROBERT RICHARD, financial consultant; b. Ft. Smith, Ark., Oct. 30, 1927; s. Richard Marion and Ima Lucille (Stovall) B.: A.B., Harvard U., 1951, M.B.A., 1960; m. Mary Margaret Bundy, Aug. 10, 1957; children—Robert Richard Jr., Laura Louise. With Gen. Electric Co., Fairfield, Conn., 1954-66, Philco-Ford subs. Ford Motor Co., Phila., 1966-68, Warwick Electronics subs. Whirlpool Corp., Niles, Ill., 1968-70; prin. Bramhall Assocs., Lake Forest, Ill., 1970—; cons. to Rockwell Internat., Bunker-Ramo Corp., Dan River Inc., Molex, Spartan Mills, Rollins, Inc., Lubrizol Corp., Sears (Can.) Ltd., Northrop Corp. Pres. Chgo. Tennis Patrons, Inc., 1974-75. Served with U.S. Army, 1946-48. Winner Singles and Doubles Vt. State Tennis Championship, 1956; runner-up U.S. Clay Ct. Doubles' Championships (with Bobby Riggs). Republican. Presbyterian. Club: Harvard of Chgo. Home: 855 Buena Rd Lake Forest IL 60045 Office: 222 Wisconsin Bldg Box 783 Lake Forest IL 60045

BRANCA, JOHN GREGORY, lawyer, consultant; b. Bronxville, N.Y., Dec. 11, 1950; s. John Ralph and Barbara (Werle) B. AB in Polit. Sci. cum laude, Occidental Coll., 1972; JD, UCLA, 1975. Bar: Calif. 1975. Assoc. Kindel & Anderson, Los Angeles, 1975-77, Hardee, Barovick, Konecky & Braun, Beverly Hills, Calif., 1977-81; ptnr. Ziffren, Brittenham & Branca, Los Angeles, 1981—; cons. N.Y. State Assembly, Mt. Vernon, 1978-82, various music industry orgns., Los Angeles, 1981—; bd. dirs. Michael Jackson Prodns., Los Angeles. Editor-in-Chief UCLA-Alaska Law Rev., 1974-75; contbr. articles to profl. jours. Cons. United Negro Coll. Fund; bd. dirs. Michael Jackson Burn Ctr., UCLA Law Sch. Com. Recipient Bancroft-Whitney award; named Entertainment Lawyer of Yr. Am. Lawyer mag., 1981. Mem. ABA (patent trademark and copyright law sect.), Calif. Bar Assn., Beverly Hills Bar Assn. (entertainment law sect.), Phi Alpha Delta, Sigma Tau Sigma. Office: 2121 Avenue of the Stars 32d Floor Los Angeles CA 90067

BRANCH, GARY LEO, college president, consultant; b. Birmingham, Ala., Sept. 25, 1942; s. Leo Frank and Mable (Tibbet) B.; m. Janis Dianna Miller, Nov. 1, 1945; children—Gary Leo, Tracy Dianna. B.S., U. Ala., 1965, M.A., 1967; LL.D., Livingston U., 1981. Counselor to men, U. Ga., Athens, 1967-68; asst. dir. student affairs Floyd Jr. Coll., Rome, Ga., 1970-71; assoc. dean student affairs Troy State U. (Ala.), 1971-75, dean enrollment and counseling services, 1975-78; pres. Brewer State Jr. Coll., Fayette, Ala., 1979-81; pres. James H. Faulkner State Jr. Coll., Bay Minette, Ala., 1981—; cons. services in higher edn. Mem. Ala. Postsecondary Policy Adv. Com.; mem. Regional Employment and Tng. Adv. Council; pres. Fayette County Heart Assn.; chmn. Troy Recreation and Day Care Bd.; chmn. sustaining membership drive for Pike County, Ala. council Boy Scouts Am. Named Outstanding Young Man Fayette County, 1980. Mem. Nat. Assn. Student Personnel Adminstrs., So. Coll. Personnel Assn., Am. Assn. Collegiate Registrars and Admissions Officers, So. Assn. Collegiate Registrars and Admissions Officers, Ala. Assn. Collegiate Registrars and Admissions Officers, Ala. Council Jr. and Community Coll. Presidents, Ala. Jr. and Community Coll. Assn. (pres.-elect 1984-85), Ala. Assn. Coll. Adminstrs. (pres.-elect 1984-85), Bay Minette C. of C. (bd. dirs.), North Baldwin County Ministerial Assn. (pres. 1983), Omicron Delta Kappa (nat. editor The Circle 1978-80, Meritorious Service award 1979, Disting. Service Key 1980), Delta Chi. Mem. Assembly of God. Home: College Dr Bay Minette AL 36507 Office: Faulkner State Jr Coll Hwy 31 S Bay Minette AL 26507

BRANCH, JOHN ELLISON, lawyer; b. Atlanta, Sept. 17, 1915; s. William Harllee and Bernice (Simpson) B.; m. Jean McKay, Nov. 19, 1938; children—Jean Elizabeth, Barbara Ann, Patricia Elaine, John Ellison Jr. B.S., Davidson Coll., 1937; J.D., Emory U., 1940. Bar: Ga. 1939. Assoc., Gambrell and White, Atlanta, 1940-49; ptnr. Wilson, Branch and Barwick, Atlanta, 1949-70; sr. ptnr. Branch and Swann, Atlanta, 1970-81; of counsel Ogletree, Deakins, Nash, Smoak and Stewart, Atlanta, 1981—; guest lectr. Ga. State U. Atlanta, 1960-70; employer mem. U.S. del. ILO, Geneva, 1960-62. Bd. dirs. Ga. Hospitality and Travel Assn.; past trustee Atlanta council Boy Scouts Am.; mem. governing bd. Bus. Council Ga. Served to maj. U.S. Army, 1942-45. Mem. ABA, State Bar Ga., Atlanta Bar Assn., Lawyers Club Atlanta, U.S. C. of C. (past mem. employee relations com.), Council State Chambers Commerce (chmn. employee relations com.), Ga. C. of C. (mem. governing bd.), Atlanta C. of C. (past bd. dirs., chmn. govt. affairs dept.), Phi Beta Kappa, Omicron Delta Kappa. Presbyterian. Clubs: Capital City, Commerce, Cherokee, Athletic (Atlanta); University Yacht (Lake Lanier, Ga.); Amelia Plantation (Amelia Island, Fla.). Author: (with J.P. Swann) The Wage and Hour Law Handbook, 1980. Home: 3648 Peachtree Rd NE 1G Atlanta GA 30319 Office: 3800 One Atlantic Ctr 1201 W Peachtree St NW Atlanta GA 30309

BRANCH, LAURENCE GEORGE, health policy researcher, educator, gerontologist; b. Cleve., Oct. 31, 1944; s. John Howard and Mercedes (Brachle) B.; m. Patricia Mary Skalski, June 24, 1967; children—Kathryn Helen, Carolyn Mercedes, Daniel Laurence. BA, Marquette U., 1967; MA, Loyola U., Chgo., 1969, PhD, 1971. Program dir. Ctr. Survey Research, Boston, 1973-79; Assoc. prof. Harvard Med. Sch., 1978-86, Harvard Sch. Pub. Health, 1980-86; exec. com. div. aging Harvard Med. Sch., 1979-86; assoc. dir. Geriatric Research Edn. and Clin. Ctr. West Roxbury VA Outpatient Clinic, 1982-86; prof, chief health services, Boston U. sch. pub. health, 1986—; prof., Boston U. sch. medicine, 1986—; staff GRECC Bedford VA Hosp, 1986—; trustee, pres. North Hill Life Care Community, Wellesley, Mass., 1980—; trustee, pres. Mercy Services for Aging, Farmington Hills, Mich., 1984—; mem. profl. staff Brigham & Women's Hosp., Boston, 1981—; cons. Robert Wood Johnson Found., Princeton, N.J. Mem. editorial bd. Jour. Gerontology, 1981, Jour. Community Health, 1980, Gerontologist, 1982. Served to lt. col. USAR, 1968—. Fellow Gerontol. Soc. Am.; Mem. Am. Pub. Health Assn. (sect. chmn. 1983-84), Am. Psychol. Assn., AAAS. Home: 20 Hammondswood Rd Chestnut Hill MA 02167 Office: Boston U Sch Pub Health 80 E Concord St Boston MA 02116

BRANCH, RAYMOND LEE, nursing home administrator; b. Balt., Aug. 3, 1928; s. Augustus Lee Branch and Irene Frances (Colbert) Branch Gilmore; B.S. in Health Care Adminstrn., Wichita State U., 1980; m. Idaline Clark, Dec. 27, 1963; children—Joan L. Branch Roberts, Pamela L. Branch Gilyard, Pamela J. Branch Whitaker, Bonnie F. Branch Marshall. Served as enlisted man U.S. Air Force, 1947-74, advanced through grades to master sgt., 1971; various supervisory positions in personnel and records, U.S., Korea, Eng. and Vietnam, 1951-72; personnel supt., chief customer service center 81st Combat Support Group RAF Bentwaters, Eng., 1972-74; ret., 1974; data intern Health Systems Agy. S.E. Kans., Wichita, 1978-79; asst. adminstr. Stafford Homes, Wichita, Kans., 1980-81; nursing home adminstr. Medicalodg South of Kansas City (Kans.), 1981-82, Spl. Care Devel. Ctr., Haven, Kans., 1982-83, Heartland Care Ctr., Belleville, Kans., 1983-84, Directions Unltd., Winfield, Kans., 1985, Hill Haven of Wichita, 1985-86, Medicalodge of Goddard, Kans., 1987—. Decorated Bronze Star medal, Meritorious Service medal, Air Force Commendation medal with oak leaf cluster. Democrat. Baptist. Club: Am. Legion. Home: 615 E Maywood Wichita KS 67216 Office: 501 Easy St Goddard KS 67052

BRANCH, WILLIAM TERRELL, urologist, educator; b. Paragould, Ark., Dec. 7, 1937; s. William Owen and Mary Rose (Dempsey) B.; m. Mary Fletcher Cox, Dec. 11, 1965; 1 child, Ashley Tucker. BS, Ark. State U., 1964; BS, U. Ark., 1966, MD, 1971. Diplomate Am. Bd. Urology. Adminstrv. asst. mental retardation planning project State of Ark., Little Rock, 1964-66; intern U. South Fla. Sch. Medicine Affiliated Hosps., Tampa, 1971-72, resident in surgery, 1972-73, resident in urology, 1973-75, chief resident in urology, 1975-76, clin. assoc. prof. urology, 1976—, mem. adv. bd. Suncoast Ednl. Telecommunications Systems, 1982; practice medicine specializing in urology, Tampa, 1976—; mem. staff, sec. urology Tampa Gen. Hosp., 1976-78, vice chief urology, 1978-80, chief urology, 1980-82; mem. staff, co-chief surgery Meml. Hosp. Tampa, 1978-80, vice chief med. staff, 1980-82, chief med. staff, 1982-84, trustee, 1983-88, also bd. dirs., vice chmn. bd. dirs. 1987-88; cons. in urology James A. Haley VA Hosp., Tampa, 1978—; mem. staff St. Joseph's Hosp., Tampa, 1982—; cons. staff Women's Hosp. Tampa; adv. bd. Glendale Fed. Savs., 1983-85, Beneficial Harbour Island Savs. Bank, 1985-87, South Trust Bank, 1988—. Author: (with others) Mental Retardation in Arkansas 1964-66: A Demographic Study, 1966; cons. editor Jour. Fla. Med. Assn., 1978—. Bd. dirs. Tampa Ballet, 1980, Tampa Charity Horse Show bd. dirs. Assn., 1985-87; United Way, Tampa, 1983—, mem. exec. com., 1984—; mem. med. adv. bd. Nat. Kidney Found. of Fla., Inc., 1983—. Fellow ACS (credit com. Region IV, Fla. chpt. 1982—, exec. com. Fla. chpt. 1985—, sec./treas. 1987-88); mem. AMA (physician recognition award 1977, 80, 83, 85, 88), Am. Urol. Assn., Royal Soc. Medicine (affiliate), Fla. Med. Assn. (del. 1983, 88—), Fla. Urol. Soc. (Milton Copeland award 1976, exec. com. 1978-82), Hillsborough County Med. Assn. (exec. com. 1978-81, treas. 1981-82, sec. 1983-84), Southeastern Surg. Congress, Greater Tampa C. of C. (dir. 1982-86, 87—, chmn. med. meetings task force, 1983—, Super Star award 1983), Tampa Hist. Soc., Hillsborough County Med. Soc. (pres. polit. action com. 1986-87, 88—). Clubs: Tampa Yacht and Country (gov. 1984-87), Centre of Tampa (founding mem. 1985, bd. dirs., chmn. membership com.), University, Ye Mystic Krewe of Gasparilla (bd. dirs., 1st lt. 1988—). Home: 909 Golf View Tampa FL 33609 Office: 2919 Swann Ave Suite 303 Tampa FL 33609

BRÂNCUSI, PETRE, composer, musicologist, educator; b. Targu-Jiu, Gorj, Romania, June 1, 1928; s. Vasile and Paulina Brâncusi; m. Maria Brâncusi, July 1950; children: Cristian-Dorel, Valentin. Ed. Ciprian Porumbescu Acad. Music, Bucharest, 1950-55, M.A., 1955, D Musicology, 1975. Mng. dir. Music Pub. House, Bucharest, 1959-62; asst. lectr., reader, prof. Acad. Music, Bucharest, 1959, 62, 70, 76; music dir. Romanian RTV, Bucharest, 1968-72; prin. Ciprian Porumbescu, Acad. Music, Bucharest, 1972-81; pres. Union of Composers, Bucharest, 1977-82; mng. dir. Romanian Opera, Bucharest, 1982. Co-author: Music in Romania After August 23, 1944, 1964; Romanian Music History, 1969; Music in Socialist Romania, 1973; George Breazul and the Unwritten History of Romanian Music, 1976; Romanian Music and its Grand Transformations vol. I, 1978, vol. 2, 1980; Monuments of Romanian Musical Culture, Vol. I, 1986, Vol. II, 1988. Composer choral poems: Branch Under the Sun; Spring Song; At the Springs of a Dream; I am Leaving, Mother. Rep., Grand Nat. Assembly of the S.R. of Romania, 1975-80. Recipient prize Acad. Romania, 1965, Union Composers Romania, 1969, 73, 76; named Laureate, Nat. Festival Cintarea Romaniei, 1979. Mem. Romanian Composers Union (dir. 1968—), Internat. Assn. Lyric Theatres (leading bd.), Santa Cecilia Acad. (Rome) (corr.). Office: C Porumbescu Acad Music, Stirbei-Voda 33, Bucharest 70732, Romania

BRAND, JOSEPH LYON, lawyer; b. Urbana, Ohio, Aug. 11, 1936; s. Vance and Katherine (Lyon) B.; children: Elizabeth Brand Schell, Stephanie

Lyon, Joseph Howard (dec. 1983). AB, U. Mich., 1958; MA, Ohio State U., 1959; JD with honors, George Washington U., 1963. Bar: Ohio and D.C. 1963. Ptnr. Patton, Boggs & Blow (and predecessor), 1967—; professorial lectr. comparative law George Washington U. Nat. Law Ctr., 1983—; mem. adv. bd. Internat. and Comparative Law Ctr., Southwestern Legal Found. Trustee Urbana U., 1981-83. Mem. ABA (chmn. com. banking and fin. sect. internat. law 1971-72), Washington Inst. Fgn. Affairs, Washington Fgn. Law Soc., Internat. Bar Assn., D.C. Bar Assn., Am. Soc. Internat. Law, George Washington Law Alumni Assn. (pres. 1988-89), Order of Coif (chpt. pres. 1970-71). Home: PO Box 540 Great Falls VA 22066 Office: Patton Boggs & Blow 2550 M St NW Washington DC 20037

BRAND, RAY MANNING, lawyer; b. N.Y.C., May 6, 1922; s. David and Mary (Honigman) B.; m. Edythe Bernstein, Sept. 17, 1928; children—Clifford, David, Patrice, Allison. LL.B., St. John's U., 1946. Bar: N.Y. 1946, U.S. Dist. Ct. (ea. and so. dists.) N.Y. 1947, U.S. Supreme Ct. 1961. Sr. ptnr. Brand & Brand, Garden City, N.Y., 1949—; lectr. criminal law Nassau County Bar Assn. Mem. exec. com. Nassau County Democratic County Com., 1960—; chmn. Democratic Town Com., 1955-58. Served as capt. USAF, 1943-46. Decorated Air medal with 5 oak leaf clusters. Mem. N.Y. State Bar Assn., Nassau County Bar Assn., Assn. Trial Lawyers Am., N.Y. State Trial Lawyers Assn., Nassau County Criminal Bar Assn. (past pres.), Nat. Assn. Criminal Def. Attys., Internat. Platform Assn. Clubs: Pine Hollow Country (East Norwich, N.Y.); Frenchmens Creek (North Palm Beach, Fla.); Masons. Office: 100 Ring Rd W Garden City NY 11530

BRANDEIS, BARRY, management consultant; b. Phila., May 3, 1946; s. Norman and Jennie (Yousin) B.; B.S. in Psychology, Pa. State U., 1968, M.B.A. in Mgmt., 1970; M.B.A. in Fin., Baruch Coll., CUNY, 1974, postgrad. in bus., 1975; m. Renee Riesenberg, Apr. 4, 1971; children—Adam, Marisa. Account exec. Meridian Securities Co., Bala Cynwyd, Pa., 1968-70; instr. Pace U. Grad. Sch., also Baruch Coll., 1968-75; asst. to chmn. Wasko Gold Products Corp., N.Y.C., 1975-77, v.p. fin., 1977-80, exec. v.p., 1980-83; mem. U.S. Senate Bus. Adv. Bd.; adj. assoc. prof. Pace U. Grad. Sch. Bus.; group exec. Holding Capital Group, 1984-85; chief exec. officer Budoff, Inc., 1985—. Mem. AAUP, Internat. Precious Metals Inst. (charter), Assn. M.B.A. Execs., P.R. C. of C. in U.S. (bd. dirs.), Internat. Platform Assn., N.Y. Acad. Scis., Omicron Delta Kappa, Psi Chi. Home: 15 Cooper Dr Great Neck NY 11023 Office: 685 Fifth Ave New York NY 10022

BRANDENBURG, HENRY LEE, manufacturing company executive; b. Secaucus, N.J., Feb. 5, 1925; s. Henry Herman and Nathalie Estelle (Ackerman) B.; student Fairleigh Dickinson U., 1946-47, U. Colo., 1947-48, Cleve. State U., 1968-72; m. Sherrill Ann Overton, June 23, 1973; children—Sherry Lee, Henry Lance, Kim Bowen, Kit Archer, Kevin Dixon, Heidi Lalani. Project engr. Gibson Refrigerator Co., Greenville, Miss., 1952-61; mgr. def. products Mueller Brass Co., Port Huron, Mich., 1961-63; mgr. Ordnance Devel. Center, TRW, Cleve., 1964-68; dir. Tech. & Bus. Services, Cleve. State U., 1968-73, also lectr.; pres. Prontour Co., Dennison, Ohio, 1973—; dir. Lashle Enterprises, Dover, Ohio, 1972—, First Name, Inc., Ft. Pierce, Fla. Pres., Small World Credit Union, Dennison, 1981—; indsl. dir. Dennison Growth Assn., 1976—; candidate State Senate 30th Dist., 1988. Served with USAAF, 1943-46. Mem. Cleve. Engring. Soc., AIAA, Buckeye State Sheriff's Assn., Full Gospel Businessmen's Fellowship Internat. (pres.). Republican. Methodist. Club: Kiwanis. Patentee in field. Home: 635 N Water St Uhrichsville OH 44683 Office: PO Box 269 Dennison OH 44621

BRANDENBURG, MICHELE, advertising executive; b. Algiers, Algeria, Dec. 21, 1942; arrived in France, 1960.; d. Georges and Jacqueline (Bégué) Corvino; Richard Brandenburg, July 4, 1970; children: Guillaume, Eve. Lic. in Scis. Econs., U. Paris, 1967, diploma in polit. sci., 1968. Product mgr. Havas, Paris, 1969-72; mgr. mktg. C.E.P., Paris, 1972-78; dir. advt. Excelsior Pub Interoleco, Paris, 1978-86, Hachette Régie 7, Paris, 1986—. Home: 1 Rue Andre Colledeboeuf, 75016 Paris France Office: 27 Rue de Boetie, 75008 Paris France

BRANDENBURG, ROBERT FAIRCHILD, JR., lawyer, business executive; b. Oklahoma City, Mar. 6, 1938; s. Robert Fairchild and Lorraine (Harkey) B.; m. Heidi Harper, Sept. 28, 1962; children: Robert Fairchild III, John Harper, Adam Charles. BA, U. Okla., 1961, JD, 1966. Bar: Okla. 1966, U.S. Dist. Ct. (we. dist.) Okla. 1968, U.S. Tax Ct. 1969, U.S. Ct. Appeals (10th cir.) 1972, U.S. Ct. Claims 1977. Sole practice, Norman, Okla., 1968-75; ptnr. Floyd & Brandenburg and predecessors, Norman, 1975—; pres. Brandenburg Enterprises, 1970—, also bd. dirs.; pres., bd. dirs. Cumberland Heights Inc., 1973-77; Robert F. Brandenburg, Jr. Atty. at Law P.C., 1979—; v.p., bd. dirs. Great SW Health Care Systems, Inc., 1987—; instr. dept. continuing edn. U. Okla., 1978; co-trustee John B. Brandenburg Trust, 1971—. Bd. dirs., mem. exec. com. Norman Alcohol Info. Ctr., Inc., 1972—, past pres., sec.; trustee Okla. Resource Found. for Alcoholism & Chem. Dependency, 1975—, vice chmn., chmn.; mem. vestry St. Michael's Episcopal Ch., Norman, 1976-78, 83-85; sec. vestry St. John's Epicopal Ch., Norman, Okla., 1972-73, mem. 1973-76; pres., dir. SW Inst. Human Relations Inc., 1978—; co-pres., bd. dirs. Norman Athletic Assn., 1987-88; bd. dirs. Phi Delta Theta Ednl. Found. Inc., 1982-85, Phi Delta Theta Endowment Fund, 1982-85, Cleveland County Family YMCA, 1988—. Served to lt. USNR, 1961-70. Mem. ABA, Okla. Bar Assn., Cleveland County Bar Assn., Nat. Assn. Bond Lawyers, Phi Alpha Delta. Republican. Episcopalian. Address: 116 E Main St Norman OK 73069

BRANDI, JAY THOMAS, finance educator; b. Bennington, Vt., Feb. 9, 1947; s. Joseph Andrew and Lillian Ruth (Docherty) B. BS, Kans. State U., 1975; MBA, Tex. Christian U., 1976; PhD, U. Ariz., 1985. Supr. fin. investigations Fla. Div. of Securities, Tallahassee, 1976-77, asst. dir., 1977-79; asst. prof. fin. U. Louisville, 1982-88, assoc. prof. fin., 1988—; cons. Ky. Revenue Cabinet, Frankfort, 1984-85; pres. and cons. Finplan Assocs., Louisville, 1982—; acad. coordinator Equine Industry Program, U. Louisville, 1987; adj. faculty U. Denver Coll. for Fin. Planning. Contbr. numerous articles to profl. jours. Curriculum coordinator, mem. steering com. Project Build, Louisville, 1985—; lobbyist Office of Controller, Fla., 1977-79. Served with U.S. Army, 1967-69, 1971-74. Mem. Internat. Assn. Fin. Planning (v.p., bd. dirs. Ky. chpt. 1986—), Fin. Mgmt. Assn., Acad. Fin. Socs., Am. Fin. Assn., Eastern Fin. Assn., So. Fin. Assn., Southwestern Fin. Assn., Louisville C. of C. (devel. fin. steering com., venture capital/capital gains preference task force), Am. Legion, VFW, Phi Kappa Phi, Beta Gamma Sigma, Delta Sigma Pi, Alpha Phi Omega. Democrat. Roman Catholic. Home: 1030 Stivers Rd Louisville KY 40207 Office: U Louisville Sch Bus Louisville KY 40292

BRANDIN, ALF ELVIN, retired mining and shipping company executive; b. Newton, Kans., July 1, 1912; s. Oscar E. and Agnes (Larsen) B.; m. Marie Eck, June 15, 1936 (dec. 1980); children: Alf R., Jon, Erik, Mark.; m. Pamela J. Brandin, Jan. 28, 1983. A.B., Stanford U., 1936. With Standard Accident of Detroit, 1936-42; bus. mgr. Stanford U., Calif., 1946-52; bus. mgr., exec. officer for land devel. Stanford U., 1952-59, v.p. for bus. affairs, 1959-70; sr. v.p., dir., mem. exec. com. Utah Internat. Inc., San Francisco, from 1970; pres. Richardson-Brandin, 1964-86, also bd. dirs.; bd. dirs. Hershey Oil Co.; vice chmn. bd. dirs. Doric Devel. Inc. Bd. govs. San Francisco Bay Area Council; trustee Reclamation Dist. 2087, Alameda, Calif.; bd. overseers Hoover Instn. on War, Revolution and Peace, Stanford. Served as comdr. USNR, 1942-46. Mem. Zeta Psi. Clubs: Elk, Stanford Golf, Bohemian, Pauma Valley Country, Silverado Country; Royal Lahaina. Home: 668 Salvatierra St Stanford CA 94305 Office: 550 California St San Francisco CA 94104

BRANDON, ELVIS DENBY, JR., financial planner; b. Sheridan, Ark., Nov. 28, 1927; s. Elvis Denby and Hazel Ione (Davidson) B.; m. Helen Holt Deupree, Apr. 25, 1953; children: Elvis Denby III, Raymond Wilson. BA with honors, Rhodes Coll., Memphis, 1950; MA, Duke U., 1952. CLU, chartered fin. cons. Fin. planner, pres. Denby Brandon Orgn., Inc./Branco Planning Co., Inc., Memphis, 1952—; chmn. Brandon Underwriting Specialists, Inc., Memphis, 1969—; mem. adj. faculty Coll. Fin. Planning, Memphis, 1982-87. Author: A New Beginning, 1979, A Seventh Call to Action. Elder, tchr. A.W. Dick Meml. class, 2d Presbyn. Ch., Memphis; chmn. Presbyn. Peacemaking corps. Named Young Man of Yr., Memphis Jaycees, 1953. Mem. Inst. Cert. Fin. Planners (cert.), Internat. Assn. Fin. Planning, Internat. Bd. Standards and Practices of Cert. Fin. Planners, Am. Soc. Chartered Life Underwriters, Nat. Assn. Securities Dealers, Phi Beta Kappa. Clubs: Econ. of Memphis, Racquet (Memphis). Lodge: Rotary. Home: 5711 The Forest Gate Rd Memphis TN 38119 Office: Denby Brandon Orgn Inc 3100 Walnut Grove Rd #404 Memphis TN 38111

BRANDON, INMAN, lawyer; b. Atlanta, May 14, 1906; s. Morris and Harriet Frances (Inman) B.; m. Louise Courts Glancy, Nov. 14, 1932 (dec. Mar. 21, 1982); children: Louise (Mrs. Robert Castle), Shane, Christopher Inman.; m. Ruth Woltz Alford, Dec. 14, 1983. B.A. magna cum laude, U. Ga., 1927; LL.B., Yale U., 1930. Bar: Ga. 1930. Since practiced in Atlanta; partner firm Hansell & Post (and predecessors), 1946—. Co-chmn. Atlanta Community Chest drive, 1956, chmn. budget com., 1957, pres., 1958; chmn. Atlanta United Appeals, Community Chest-A.R.C., 1959; pres., dir. Family Service Soc. Atlanta, 1960-61, hon. dir., 1963—; co-chmn. joint Tech.-Ga. Devel. Fund drive, 1957-58; Co-finance chmn. Ga. Central Republican Com., 1958-62, hon. finance chmn., 1963; Trustee, sec. bd. U. Ga. Found., 1957-61, chmn. trustees, 1961-70, trustee emeritus, 1977—. Served to lt. comdr. USNR, 1942-45, PTO. Recipient Distinguished Alumni award U. Ga., 1961. Mem. Am., Fed., Ga., Atlanta bar assns., Lawyers Club Atlanta, Nat. Lawyers Club, Am. Judicature Soc., Sphinx (hon. mem. U. Ga.), Phi Beta Kappa, Phi Kappa Phi, Phi Delta Phi., Lion (charter pres. Buckhead club 1941-42). Clubs: Commerce (Atlanta), Piedmont Driving (Atlanta), River Bend Gun (Atlanta) (pres. 1965-66), Capital City (Atlanta) (dir. 1961-63); Fla. Yacht (Jacksonville, Fla.), River (Jacksonville, Fla.); University Yacht (Lake Lanier, Ga.); ZENAX, The Nine O'Clocks. Home: 3488 Knollwood Dr NW Atlanta GA 30305 Office: First Nat Bank Tower Atlanta GA 30303

BRANDON, SYDNEY, psychiatry educator; b. Washington, Eng., Sept. 20, 1927; s. Thomas and Rhoda May (Rook) B.; m. Joanne Watson, Apr. 5, 1950; children: Helene Anne, Victoria Jane. Grad., Rutherford Coll., Newcastle upon Tyne, Eng., 1944, Queen's U., Belfast, Northern Ireland, 1945; MBBS, U. Durham, Eng., 1954, MD, 1960. Nuffield research fellow in child health U. Durham, 1953-59; sr. registrar, lectr. U. Newcastle, Eng., 1959-63, Nuffield sr. lectr., 1965-69; vis. fellow in psychiatry Columbia U., N.Y.C., 1963-65; reader in psychiatry U. Manchester, Eng., 1969-73; prof. psychiatry U. Leicester, Eng., 1973—; chmn. Tng. Adv. Group on Sexual Abuse of Children, London, 1986—; pub. orator U. Leicester, 1979-81, 87—. Co-author: Growing Up in Newcastle upon Tyne, 1974, Sexual Abuse in the Family, 1985; contbr. articles to profl. jours. Served with RAF, 1981—. Fellow Royal Coll. Physicians, Royal Coll. Psychiatrists, Royal Soc. Medicine (v.p. psychiatry sect.); mem. Assn. Univ. Tchrs. Psychiatry (chmn. 1980-86). Home: 19 Homfield Rd, Leicester LE2 1SD, England Office: U Leicester Dept Psychiatry, Royal Infirmary, PO Box 65, Leicester LE2 7LX, England

BRANDON, WILLIAM CLINT, agri-business consultant; b. Chancellor, Ala., Oct. 9, 1918; s. John W. and Bess (Broxson) B.; B.S. in Agr. with high honors, U. Fla., 1942, M.A., 1948; postgrad. Northwestern U., 1955-56, U. Mich., 1961, Harvard U., 1964; m. Ethel I. Pool, Aug. 23, 1963; children—Deborah Jean, Eric Bradley, Michael Clint, William Wade. Terr. mgr. Swift & Co., Miami, Fla., 1948-54, mgr. advt. and merchandising, Chgo., 1954-58, Midwest mktg. and ops. mgr., Cleve., 1958-59, dir. personnel, tng. and devel., Chgo., 1960-70; mgr. Sales and Mktg. Services Cons., Chgo., 1970-71; owner, pres. Agri-Bus. Tng. & Devel., Roswell, Ga., 1971—, Brandon Assos., Roswell, 1977—; cons. in field. Nat. pres. Danforth Found., 1942. Served with U.S. Army, 1942-47; mem. Res. Recipient Danforth Found. award, 1942; Fla. Blue Key Leadership award, 1976. Mem. Am. Feed Mfg. Assn. (cons. personnel devel.), Ga. Agri-Bus. Council, Nat. Speakers Assn., Ga. Speakers Assn. (dir.), Can. Feed Industry Assn. (cons. personnel devel.), Phi Gamma Delta (life, Loyal Fiji), Alpha Zeta (chancellor), Phi Eta Sigma, Phi Kappa Phi. Baptist. Author: Professional Selling in Agri-Business, 1972; Building and Developing Your Work Force, 1972; Motivation: Roots of Human Behavior, 1972, 80; Train-the-Trainer, 1977; Managerial Work Organization and Time Management in the Sales Territory, 1979; Closing Sales in Agri-Business, 1979; editor-in-chief U. Fla. Mag., 1941-42; contbr. numerous articles to profl. jours. Home and Office: 9370 Rivera Rd PO Box 1757 Roswell GA 30077

BRANDRUP, DOUGLAS WARREN, lawyer; b. Mitchel, S.D., July 11, 1940; s. Clair L. and Ruth M. (Wolverton) B.; m. Patricia R. Tuck, Dec. 20, 1986; children—Kendra, Monika, Peter. A.B. in Econs., Middlebury Coll., 1963; J.D., Boston U., 1966. Bar: N.Y. 1969, U.S. Dist. Ct. (so. dist.) N.Y. 1970, U.S. Ct. Appeals (2d cir.) 1970. Assoc. Donovan, Leisure, Newton & Irvine, N.Y.C., 1968-72; ptnr. Griggs, Baldwin & Baldwin, N.Y.C., 1972—, sr. ptnr., 1980—; dir. Equity Oil Co., A.T. Info. Products Inc. Mem. Govs. Security Adv. Com., State of N.J., 1975—. Served to capt. U.S. Army, 1966-68. Mem. N.Y. County Bar Assn., N.Y. State Bar Assn., ABA. Republican. Episcopalian. Clubs: World Trade Ctr., Met. (bd. govs.) (N.Y.C.); Club de Mar (Palma, Majorca Spain). Office: Griggs Baldwin & Baldwin 1 Wall St New York NY 10005

BRANDS, DAVID, electrical engineer; b. Greenock, Scotland, Nov. 14, 1960; s. Thomas Douglas and Rachael (Marlin) B.; m. Helen Elizabeth Paterson, July 26, 1982. BEE honors, U. Strathclyde, Glasgow, Scotland, 1982. Registered profl. eng., UK. Engr. relay application GEC Measurements, Stafford, Eng., 1982-84; GEC Can. Ontario, 1984-85; mgr. UK area sales GEC Measurements, Harrogate, Eng., 1985-87; mgr. export sales GEC Measurements, Stafford, 1987—. Mem. IEEE. Office: GEC Measurements, St Leonards Ave, Stafford England ST17 4LX

BRANDSLUND, IVAN, hospital administrator, educator; b. Sonderso, Denmark, 1947. Cand. Med. Et. Chir., Odense U., 1974, MD, 1978, D of Med. Sci., 1986. Cert. specialist chem. pathology. Resident Odense (Denmark) U. Hosp., 1974-78, sr. resident, 1981-85, assoc. prof., 1986—; researcher Odense U., 1978-81; vis. investigator NIH U.S. Dept. Health and Human Services, 1985-86; dir., head clin. labs. Vejle County Hosp., Denmark, 1986—; cons. Hosp. Assn. Vejle County, Denmark, 1986—. Contbr. articles to profl. jours. Recipient Poul Astrup prize, Radiometer, Copenhagen, 1983; USPHS Internat. research fellow NIH, 1984. Mem. Danish Assn. Clin. Chemistry (chmn. edn. com., 1986—). Office: Vejle County Hosp, DK-7100 Vejle Denmark

BRANDT, JOE ANN MARIE, clinical psychologist; b. Mpls., Jan. 8, 1952; d. Henry Aimar and Estelle Ann (Smith) B.; B.A. cum laude, U. Ga., 1974; M.A., U. Ark., 1977, Ph.D., 1980; postgrad. U. Ala. Med. Center, 1981; m. William Arthur Dickinson, Apr. 4, 1981; 1 dau., Ashley Lauren Brandt. Mem. interdisciplinary team in adolescent medicine U. Ala., 1978-79, intern, 1978-79, instr. psychology, 1979-80; pvt. practice clin. psychology Savannah Psychol. Cons. (Ga.), 1981—; cons. St. Joseph's Hosp., Candler Gen. Hosp., Charter Hosp. of Savannah, Meml. Hosp., Bethesda Home for Boys, St. Mary's Home, Vietnam Vet.'s Ctr., Victims Witness Assistance Optifast Program at St. Joseph's Hosp., Personal Performance Cons., Coastal Behavior Medicine, Victim Witness Assistance; appointee Ga. State Health Planning Agy. Mem. Ga. Conservancy, Hist. Savannah Assn., Am. Soc. Clin. Hypnosis, Assn. Advancement Psychology, Coastal Assn. Lic. Psychologists, Am. Psychol. Assn., Assn. Women Psychologists, Ga. Psychol. Assn., Sierra Club, Citizens for Clean Air. Roman Catholic. Research on predictors of effective family functioning, neuropsychol. correlates of degenerative brain disorders, effects of sexual misconceptions on marital happiness and satisfaction. Home: 106 Dutch Island Dr Savannah GA 31406 Office: 1 St Joseph's Profl Plaza Savannah GA 31419

BRANDT, REINHARD, chemist; b. Konigsberg, Germany, Nov. 14, 1932; s. Melchior Sebastian and Ruthilt (Mannesmann) B.; diplom chemiker Frankfurt U., 1959; Ph.D., U. Calif., Berkeley, 1963; m. Magdalene Brandt-Geller, Nov. 6, 1961; children—Johann-Friedrich, Dorothea Desiree. Postdoctoral fellow CERN, Geneva, 1963-68; mem. faculty Marburg (Germany) U., 1968—, prof. chemistry, 1971—; mem. Adv. Commn. Nuclear Research Fed. Govt., 1976-83; sci. visitor Weizmann Inst., Rehovoth, Joint Inst. Nuclear Research, Dubna, USSR, Los Alamos Nat. Lab., Lawrence Berkeley Lab., CERN. Mem. Am. Chem. Soc., Gesellschaft deutscher Chemiker. Mem. Free Democratic Party. Contbr. articles to profl. jours.; mem. editorial bd. Nuclear Tracks, 1979—. Research in heavy ion nuclear chemistry concentrating on anomalons. Office: Kernchemie Philipps U, 355 Marburg Federal Republic of Germany

BRANDT, WILLY, former chancellor Federal Republic of Germany; b. Lübeck, Germany, Dec. 18, 1913; student Latin Sch., Lübeck; student history, U. Oslo (Norway); arbitur Johanneum; Dr. (hon.) U. Pa., Harvard, Yale, St. Andrews, Oxford U. LL.D., U. Md., 1960; m. Carlotta Thorkildonn, 1941; 1 dau., Ninja; m. 2d, Rut Hansen, 1948; children: Peter, Lars, Matthias; m. 3d, Brigitte Seebacher, 1983. Journalist, Norway, Sweden, 1933-45; journalist Scandinavian newspapers, press cooperator diplomatic rep., Berlin, 1945-47; chief editor Berlin Stadtblatt, 1950-51; mem. House of Reps., Berlin, from 1950, 1955-57; governing mayor, West Berlin, 1957-66; fgn. minister, dep. chancellor, 1966-69, chancellor Fed. Republic of Germany, Bonn 1969-74. Mem. German Bundestag, 1949-57, 69—; pres. German Bundesrat, 1957-58, v.p., 1958-59; pres. Deutscher Staedtetag (Conf. German mayors), 1958-63; mem. European Parliament, 1979-83. Chmn. bd. dirs. Berliner Bank. Rep. in Berlin, directive com. Social Dem. Party, 1948-49, mem. provincial com., Berlin, 1950-63, dep. chmn., 1954-58, 1950-70, chmn., 1958-63, dep. chmn., Germany, 1962-64, party chmn., 1964-87, candidate for chancellorship, 1961, 65; pres. Socialists Internat., 1976—; chmn. Ind. Commn. on Devel. Issues, 1977. Hon. pres. provincial com. German Red Cross; chmn. governing bodies Free U. Tech. U. Berlin. Decorated Grosses Verdienstkreuz (Germany); Star of Uprising 1st Class (Jordan); grand cross Order of St. Olaf (Norway); grand cross Order of King of Greece; recipient Freedom House award, 1961, Nobel Peace prize, 1971, Reinhold Niebuhr award, 1972, Aspen Inst. Humanities Studies prize, 1973, numerous others. Mem. S.S. Soc. Berlin, Soc. Germany Indivisable (exec. com.), German Hort. Soc., Bonn Germann Soc. Fgn. Politics, Soc. Christian-Jewish Coop., Ernest Reuter Soc., German Soc. UN, Max Planck Gesellschaft (senator). Author: Peace Politics in Europe, 1968; The Ordeal of Co-Existence, 1963; Begegnung mit Kennedy, 1964; People and Politics 1960-1975, 1978; Frauenheute, 1978; Links und Frei, 1982. Office: Sozialdemokratische Partei Deutschlands, Erich-Ollenhauer Haus, 5300 Bonn Federal Republic of Germany *

BRANEA, IOAN DOREL, internal medicine and cardiology educator; b. Sibiu, Romania, Dec. 12, 1938; s. Ioan Ioan and Eugenia (Bălan) B.; m. Stela Simon, 1966 (div. 1986); children: Horea, Ioan; m. Felicia Munteanu, 1987; 1 child, Eugenia. Student, Inst. Medicine, Timosoara, Romania, 1957-63, PhD, 1973. Intern, then resident in internal medicine Clin. Hosp. #2, Timisoara, 1962-68, instr. internal medicine and cardiology, 1969-80; asst. prof. Inst. Medicine, Timisoara, 1971-80, prof., 1981—; prof. med. Polyclinic Inst. Medicine, Timisoara, 1981. Author: Medical Polyclinic, 1980, Chronic Myocardopathies, 1987; conbr. 82 articles in field to profl. jours. Sec. med. rev. Timisoara Medicală, 1978. Mem. Romanian Union Med. Scientists, Romanian Soc. Cardiology, Timisoara Commn. Cardiology (v.p. 1981). Mem. Romanian Communist Party. Greek Orthodox. Home: Bd Cetatii 11, 1900 Timisoara Romania Office: Inst Medicine, Bd 23 August 12, 1900 Timisoara Romania

BRANN, DONALD LEWIS, JR., superintendent schools; b. Los Angeles, Nov. 1, 1945; s. Donald Lewis and Shirley June (Scott) B.; m. Sari Ellen Donohoe, June 17, 1967; children—Shanonn, Rebecca. A.A. in Bus. Adminstrn. El Camino Coll., 1966; B.S. in Bus. Adminstrn. U. So. Calif.-Los Angeles, 1968, Ed.D. in Ednl. Adminstrn., 1982; M.A. in Elem. Edn., Calif. State U.-Los Angeles, 1972. Cert. tchr., sch. adminstr., Calif. Tchr. El Segundo Unified Sch. Dist., Calif., 1970-72, reading specialist, 1972-76, program coordinator, 1976-79; prin. Wilsona Sch. Dist., Lancaster, Calif., 1979-81, supt., 1981-84; supt. Old Adobe Union Sch. Dist., Petaluma, Calif., 1984—; bd. dirs. Schs. Committed To Reducing Utility Bills, Sacramento, 1983—; mem. State Supts. Small Sch. Adv. Com.; coordinator El Segundo Jr. Olympics, 1972; bd. dirs. Antelope Valley Fedn. Tchrs. Credit Union, Lancaster, 1983; v.p., bd. dirs. Friends of Antelope Valley Indian Mus., Lancaster, 1982. Named One of Top 100 Sch. Execs. in N.Am., Exec. Educator, 1985. Mem. Am. Assn. Sch. Adminstrs., Sonoma County Supts. Gang of 13, Assn. Calif. Sch. Adminstrs., Small Sch. Dist. Assn. (founder; treas. 1983—), Alpha Kappa Psi. Home: 18 Weatherby Ct Petaluma CA 94952 Office: Old Adobe Union Sch Dist 845 Crinella Dr Petaluma CA 94952

BRANNAN, DAVID ALEXANDER, mathematics educator; b. Cowdenbeath, Fife, Scotland, Sept. 15, 1942; m. Margaret Philomena McAuley, Apr. 1, 1970; children: David, Joseph, Michael. BSc, Glasgow (Scotland) U., 1964; PhD, U. London, 1967. Asst. prof. U. Md., 1967-68; lectr. Glasgow U., 1968-70, U. London, 1970-78; prof. Open U., 1979—; bd. dirs. LMS Pub. Ltd. Author, editor: Aspects of Contemporary Complex Analysis, 1980. Chmn. govs. St. Gregory's Roman Cath. Middle Sch., Bedford, Eng., 1985—. Mem. London Math. Soc. (gen. sec. 1971-81, publs. sec. 1986—), Am. Math. Soc. Roman Catholic. Office: Open U, Walton Hall, Milton Keynes MK7 6AA, England

BRANSCOMB, ANNE WELLS, lawyer, communications consultant; b. Statesboro, Ga., Nov. 22, 1928; d. Guy Herbert and Ruby Mae (Hammond) Wells; m. Lewis McAdory Branscomb, Oct. 13, 1951; children: Harvie Hammond, Katharine Capers. B.A., Ga. State Coll. Women, 1949; BA, U. N.C., 1949; postgrad., London Sch. Econs., 1950; MA, Harvard U., 1951; JD with honors, George Washington, 1962. Bar: D.C. 1962, Colo. 1963, N.Y. 1973, U.S. Supreme Ct. 1972. Research assoc. Pierson, Ball and Dowd, Washington, 1962; law clk. to presiding judge U.S. Dist. Ct., Denver, 1962-63; assoc. Williams & Zook, 1963-66; sole practice Boulder, 1963-69; assoc. Arnold and Porter, Washington, 1969-72; communications counsel Teleprompter Corp., N.Y.C., 1973; v.p. Kalba-Bowen Assocs. Inc., communication cons., Cambridge, Mass., 1974-77, chmn. bd., 1977-80, sr. assoc. dir., 1980-82; pres. The Raven Group, Concord, Mass., 1986—; trustee Pacific Telecommunications Council, 1981-83, 86—; Inaugural fellow Gannett Ctr. Media Studies, Columbia U., 1985; mem. tech. adv. bd. Dept. Commerce, 1977-81; WARC adv. com. Dept. State, 1978-79; mem. Carnegie Corp. Task Force on Pub. Broadcasting, 1976-77; mem. overseers, vis. com. Harvard U. Office of Info. Tech., 1977-83; vis. scholar Yale U. Law, 1981-82; mem. program on information resources and pub. policy Harvard U., 1986—; chmn. program com. Legal Symposium Telecom '87, Internat. Telecommunications Union, 1986-87; bd. dirs. Pub. Interest Radio, 1986—; adj. prof. internat. law Tufts U., 1988—; mem. adv. bd. Atwater Inst., Ottawa, Can. Contbr. articles to profl. jours.; mem. editorial bd.: Info. Soc.; editor: Toward a Law of Global Communications Networks; contbg. editor: Jour. Communications, 1980—. Housing commr. Boulder Pub. Housing Authority, 1969-70; bd. dirs. Nat. Pub. Radio, 1975-78; trustee EDUCOM, Interuniv. Communications Council Inc., 1975-78; vice chmn. Colo. Dem. State Central Com., 1967-69; del., mem. permanent orgn. com. Dem. Nat. Conv., 1968; trustee, exec. com. Rensselaer Poly. Inst., 1980—. Recipient Alumni Achievement award Ga. Coll., 1980; recipient Rotary Found. fellowship, 1950-51; inaugural fellow Gannett Ctr. for Media Studies Columbia U., 1985. Mem. ABA (Nat. Conf. Lawyers and Scientists ABA/AAAS 1985—, chmn. communications com. sci. and tech. sect. 1980-82, chmn. communications law div. 1982-84, mem. council sci. and tech. sect. 1981-85), Am. Polit. Sci. Assn., Internat. Communications Assn., Internat. Inst. Communications, Soc. Preservation of First Wives and First Husbands (nat. pres. 1981—), Order of Coif, Valkyries, Phi Beta Kappa, Alpha Psi Omega, Chi Delta Phi, Pi Gamma Mu. Home: 5 Hidden Oak Ln Armonk NY 10504

BRANSCOMB, LEWIS CAPERS, JR., librarian, educator; b. Birmingham, Ala., Aug. 5, 1911; s. Lewis Capers and Minnie Vaughn (McGehee) B.; m. Marjorie Berry Stafford, Jan. 15, 1938; children—Lewis Capers III, Ralph Stafford, Carol Jean, Lawrence McGehee. Student, Birmingham-So. Coll., 1929-30; A.B., Duke U., 1933; A.B. in L.S, U. Mich., 1939, A.M. in L.S, 1941; postgrad., U. Ga., 1940; Ph.D., U. Chgo., 1954. Clk. Young & Vann Supply Co., Birmingham, 1933-38; order librarian U. Ga., 1939-41; librarian Mercer U., 1941-42; librarian, prof. library sci. U. S.C., 1942-44; asst. dir. pub. service depts., asso. prof. library sci. U. Ill., 1944-48; assoc. dir. libraries, prof. library adminstrn. 1948-52; dir. libraries, prof. library adminstrn. Ohio State U., Columbus, 1952-71; prof. Thurber studies Ohio State U., 1971-81, prof. emeritus, 1981—, mem. faculty compensation and benefits com., 1981—; mem. Ohio Commn. to Abolish Capital Punishment, 1960-69; bd. dirs. Center for Research Libraries, 1953-64, exec. com., 1954-56, chmn. bd., 1961-62, mem. council, 1965-71; chmn. bd. trustees Ohio Coll. Library Center, 1968-70, vice chmn., 1970-72; chmn. adv. council on Library Services and Constrn. Act, Ohio, 1967-70; cons. Punjab Agrl. U., India, 1967, Mansfield (Ohio) Pub. Library, 1977; mem. adv. council Hitachi Found. Editor: The Case for Faculty Status for Academic Librarians, 1970; contbr. articles to profl. jours. Mem. AAUP (sec.-treas. 1947-48, Ohio State U. sec.-treas. U. Ill. 1948-52, pres. 1953-54, nat. council 1952-55, co-author History of the

Ohio Conf. 1949-74, chmn. com. E 1979—, mem. exec. com. 1981—), ALA (chmn. nominating com. 1954-55), Assn. Coll. and Research Libraries (dir. 1953-55, v.p. 1957-58, pres. 1958-59), Ohio Library Assn. (chmn. coll. and univ. sect. 1952-53, chmn. library adminstrn. sect. 1969-70, chmn. local conf. com. 1970, chmn. awards and honors com. 1974-75, chmn. notable Ohio librarians com. 1978-79, award of merit 1971, Hall of Fame 1982), Franklin County Library Assn., Acad. Library Assn. Ohio, ACLU (exec. com. Central Ohio chpt. 1958-60, 64-66), Common Cause, Thurber Circle, Thurber House (bd. trustees 1985—), Friends of Ohio State U. Libraries, Ohio State U. Retirees Assn. (exec. bd. 1983—), Beta Phi Mu (exec. council 1955-58), Sigma Alpha Epsilon. Democrat. Clubs: Torch (dir. 1958-59, 72-74, pres. 1971-72); Faculty (Columbus); Crichton. Home: 3790 Overdale Dr Columbus OH 43220 Office: Ohio State Univ Main Library Columbus OH 43210

BRANSON, HARLEY KENNETH, lawyer; b. Ukiah, Calif., June 10, 1942; s. Harley Edward and Clara Lucile (Slocum) B.; 1 child, Erik Jordan. AA, San Francisco City Coll., 1963; BS in Acctg. and Fin., San Jose State U., 1965; JD, Santa Clara U., 1968. Bar: Calif. 1969, U.S. Dist. Ct. (so. dist.) Calif. 1969, U.S. Ct. Appeals (9th cir.) 1969, U.S. Tax Ct. 1969, U.S. Ct. Customs and Patent Appeals 1970, U.S. Supreme Ct. 1973. Law clk. to judge U.S. Ct. Appeals (9th cir.), San Diego, 1968-69; ptnr. Klitgaard & Branson, Inc., San Diego, 1969-72; assoc. Jennings, Engstrand & Henrikson, San Diego, 1972-76, ptnr., 1976-78; div. counsel Ralston Purina Co., San Diego, 1978-83; group gen. counsel Castle & Cooke, Inc., San Diego, 1983-85; gen. counsel, corp. sec. Bumble Bee Seafoods, Inc., San Diego, 1985—, also bd. dirs., exec. v.p. Editor Santa Clara Law Rev., 1967-68. Mem. Mission Valley Unified Planning com., 1978; bd. dirs. Mission Valley Council, San Diego, 1977-78; coach Peninsula YMCA Soccer, San Diego, 1978-79. James B. Emery scholar and Farmers Ins. Group scholar Santa Clara U., 1966-68. Mem. ABA (corp., banking and bus. law, and internat. law sects.), Calif. Bar Assn., Am. Soc. Corp. Secs., Nat. Food Processors Assn. (lawyer com., claims com.), Am. Corp. Counsel Assn. (pres. San Diego County 1987-88). Republican. Club: San Diego Tennis and Racquet. Office: Bumble Bee Seafoods Inc 5775 Roscoe Ct San Diego CA 92123

BRANSTAD, TERRY EDWARD, governor of Iowa, lawyer; b. Leland, Iowa, Nov. 17, 1946; s. Edward Arnold and Rita (Garl) B.; m. Christine Ann Johnson, June 17, 1972; children: Eric, Allison, Marcus. BA, U. Iowa, 1969; JD, Drake U., 1974. Bar: Iowa. Sr. ptnr. firm Branstad-Schwarm, Lake Mills, Iowa, until 1982; farmer Lake Mills; mem. Iowa Ho. of Reps., 1973-78; lt. gov. Iowa 1979-82; gov. State of Iowa, 1983—; Bd. dirs. Am. Legion of Iowa Found. Served in U.S. Army, 1969. Mem. Nat. Govs. Assn. (chmn. agrl. com.), Midwestern Govs. Assn. (chmn.), Am. Legion, Farm Bur. Republican. Roman Catholic. Lodges: Lions, KC. Office: Office Gov Statehouse Des Moines IA 50319 *

BRANTINGHAM, CHARLES ROSS, podiatrist; b. Long Beach, Calif., Feb. 14, 1917; m. Lila Carolyn Price; children: Paul Jeffery, John Price, Charles Ross, James William. Student, Long Beach City Coll., 1935; D in Podiatric Medicine, Calif. Coll. Podiatric Medicine, 1939, cert. foot surgery, 1947. Resident in podiatry San Francisco, 1939-40; pvt. practice podiatry Long Beach, 1946-56; podiatrist, dir. Podiatric Group, Long Beach, 1956-71, Los Alamitos (Calif.) Podiatric Group, 1971-86; chmn. podiatry dept. orthopedics Los Alamitos Med. Ctr., 1983—; clin. asst. prof. medicine U. So. Calif., Los Angeles, 1965—; adj. prof. Calif. State U., Long Beach, 1972—; cons. Specified Products Co., El Monte, Calif., 1968—, Armstrong World Industries, Lancaster, Pa., 1983—. Contbr. articles to profl. jours., chpts. to books. Bd. dirs. Diabetes Assn. of So. Calif., Los Angeles, 1964-67; cons., bd. dirs. Comprehensive Health Planning Assn., Los Angeles, 1969-72; pub. improvement and adv. cons. Long Beach City Council and Office of Mayor, 1957-67. Served to lt. comdr. USN, 1941-46. Named Disting. Practitioner in Podiatry Nat. Acad. Practice, 1982. Fellow Am. Assn. Hosp. Podiatrists (pres. 1958-60), Am. Pub. Health Assn. (council 1986—, Steven Toth award 1982), Am. Soc. Podiatric Medicine, Internat. Acad. for Standing and Walking Fitness (pres. 1963—); mem. Am. Podiatric Med. Assn. (exec. council 1957-59, Hall of Sci. award 1973), Assn. Mil. Surgeons of U.S. (life), Res. Officers Assn. of U.S. Republican. Mormon. Clubs: Exchange (Long Beach) (pres. 1948-49), Ind. Bus. (pres. 1958). Home: 11386 Holder St Cypress CA 90630 Office: 3791 Katella Ave Suite 207 Los Alamitos CA 90720

BRATBY, JOHN, painter, author; b. July 19, 1928; s. George Alfred and Lily (Randall) B.; m. Jean Cooke, 1953 (div.); 4 children; m. Patti Prime, 1977. Ed. Kingston Art Sch., Royal Coll. Art, London. Works in: Tate Gallery, London, Nat. Gallery Can., Nat. Gallery New South Wales, Mus. Modern Art, N.Y.C., Walker Art Gallery, Arts Council, Glasgow Mus. Art, numerous others; numerous one-man exhbns.; rep.: Pittsburgh Internat. Festival, 1955, 57, Venice Biennale, 1956; executed painting for film The Horse's Mouth, 1958; author: Breakdown, 1960; Breakfast and Elevenses, 1961; Brake-Pedal Down, 1962; Break 50 Kill, 1963; Stanley Spencer, 1969; The Devils, 1984, Apocryphal Letters by Edward Lowerby, 1985. Recipient Guggenheim Nat. award, 1956, 58. *

BRATITCH, EDWARD NICOLAS, chemical products company executive; b. Smyrne, Turkey, Sept. 4, 1918; s. Nicolas P. and Emily C. (Missir) B.; Dipl. Chemist, U. Athens (Greece), 1940; m. Catherine Germeni, Jan. 28, 1950; children—Helen, Nicolas. Prodn. mgr. Phoebus, textile, dying and finishing co., Athens, 1947-52; founder, chief exec. officer E.N. Bratitch & Co., household and chem. products mfr., Athens, 1952-74; chmn. bd., chief exec. officer Trylet S.A., Athens, 1974—. Mem. Greek Chemist's Assn., Am. Chem. Soc., Nat. Geog. Soc., Hellenic Assn. Environ. Pollution, Greek Club Sea Shell Collectors. Home: Kifissia 145, 63 Athens Greece Office: Metamorphissis, 150 Tatoiou St, 144 52 Athens Greece

BRATT, BENGT ERIK, academic administrator, engineer, consultant; b. Willstad, Sweden, May 18, 1922; came to U.S., 1956, naturalized, 1962; s. Victor A. and Elsa (Modeen) B.; m. Gerlinde Froehner, Nov. 10, 1966; 1 son, Stephen Mark. M.E., Tech. Coll. Gothenburg, Sweden, 1946; B.S. in Bus. Adminstrn. and Econs, Malmo (Sweden) Coll., 1950; postgrad., U. Stockholm, 1955, U. San Diego, 1960; M.S. in Systems Engring, West Coast U., 1966, M.S. in Ops. Research, 1970; D.Sc., Western Colo. U., 1977. Registered profl. engr., Calif., Colo., Europe. Marine engr. Kockums Shipbldg. Corp., Malmo, 1947-51; project engr. De Laval Steam Turbine Co., Stockholm, 1951-55; thermodynamics engr. Convair div. Gen. Dynamics Corp., San Diego, 1956-60; sr. scientist Research Inst. Nat. Def., Stockholm, 1961; sr. systems engr. Northrop Space Labs., Hawthorne, Calif., 1962-63; sr. research scientist Lockheed Research Center, Burbank, Calif., 1963-67; engr. long range planning Met. Water Dist. So. Calif., Los Angeles, 1967-85; cons. engr. 1985—; lectr. Calif. State U., Los Angeles; mem. adv. bd. Western Colo. U., Town Hall Calif. Contbr. articles in thermodynamics, space propulsion and systems engring. to profl. jours. Fellow AAAS, ASCE; mem. Ops. Research Soc. Am., Coll. Planning, Inst. Mgmt. Scis., Svenska Teknolog- foreningen (Sweden), West Coast U. Alumni Assn. (pres. 1972). Office: 1942 Lemoyne St Los Angeles CA 90026

BRATT, PETER CHRISTIAN, publishing executive; b. Katrineholm, Sweden, Feb. 3, 1942; s. Eldon and Lizzie (Olauson) B.; m. Roma Stocka, June 12, 1976; children: Michael, Maximilian. MBA, Stockholm Econ. Sch., 1972. Sales rep. IBM, Stockholm, 1968-72; owner, pub. Bratt Mktg. AB, Stockholm, 1972—. Office: Bratt Mktg AB, Grev Turegatan 60, 11738 Stockholm Sweden

BRATTELI, OLA, mathematician, educator; b. Oslo, Norway, Oct. 24, 1946; s. Trygve Martin and Randi Helene (Larssen) B.; m. Rungnapa Neumpiem, Aug. 29, 1986; 1 child, Kitidet. PhD, U. Oslo, 1974. Lectr. U. Oslo, 1978-80; full prof. U. Trondheim, Norway, 1980—; research fellow, vis. fellow or vis. prof. various instns. since 1971, including NYU, CNRS, Marseille, U. Bielefeld, U. New South Wales, U. Warwick, Kyoto U., U. Toronto. Author: Derivations, Dissipations and Group Actions on C* Algebras, 1986; (with others) Operator Algebras and Quantum Statistical Mechanics, I and II, 1979, 81; editor: Mathematica Scandinavica, Aarhus, Denmark, 1987—; also approx. 60 articles in sci. jours. Mem. Am. Math. Soc., Internat. Assn. Math. Physics, Det Kongelige Norske Videnskabers Selskab. Office: U Trondheim, N-7034 Trondheim NTH, Norway

BRATTEN, THOMAS ARNOLD, lawyer, cons. engr.; b. Dayton, Ohio, Sept. 11, 1934; s. Samuel Arnold and Helen Jeannette (Wonderly) B.; m. Glenna Mary Bratten, Apr. 20, 1963; children—Charles, Christina, Thomas. M.E., U. Cin., 1957; J.D., Chase Coll., Cin., 1968. Bar: Ohio, 1968, Fla., 1968, U.S. Supreme Ct., 1972; cert. civil trial lawyer Fla. Bar, Nat. Bd. Trial Advocacy; Engr. in tng. Gen. Motors Corp., 1953-57, test engr., 1957-59, project engr., 1963-68, sr. project engr., 1968; design engr. Pratt & Whitney Aircraft, 1959-61; gen. mgr. Auto-Technia, Inc., 1961-63; with Pub. Defender's Office, 1968-75, chief trial atty., 1970-72, chief Capital div., 1972-75; ptnr. Campbell, Colbath, Kapner & Bratten, West Palm Beach, Fla., 1969-72; prin. Bratten & Harris, P.A., West Palm Beach, 1973-86; of counsel Easley, Massa & Willits, P.A., West Palm Beach, Fla., 1986—; spl. master, 1973-85 ; faculty Nat. Inst. Trial Advocacy, U. Fla., 1978—; nat. panel arbitrators Am. Arbitration Assn., 1970-78. Mem. Palm Beach County Republican Exec. Com., 1971-80, county campaign chmn., 1974. Mem. Fla. Bar Assn. (exec. com. criminal law sect. 1978-81), Acad. Fla. Trial Lawyers, Assn. Trial Lawyers Am., Palm Beach County Bar Assn., Fla. Engring. Soc., Soc. Automotive Engrs., Nat. Acad. Forensic Engrs. (diplomate), Pi Tau Sigma. Author: Criminal Lawyers Trial Notebook, 1977; Florida Criminal Procedure, 1981. Inventor, 6 U.S. and 9 fgn. patents. Home: 8623 Thousand Pines Ct West Palm Beach FL 33411 Office: Forum III 1655 Palm Beach Lakes Blvd West Palm Beach FL 33401

BRATTER, THOMAS EDWARD, psychologist, educator; b. N.Y.C., May 18, 1939; s. Edward Maurice and Marjorie (Polikoff) B.; B.A., Columbia Coll., 1961, M.A., 1963, Ed.M., 1969; Columbia U., Ed.D., 1974; m. Carole Ann Jaffe, Aug. 25, 1963; children—Edward Philip, Barbara Ilyse. Youth resources dir. Village Scarsdale (N.Y.), 1970-72; dir. City Island Methadone Clinic, Bronx, N.Y., 1972-74; instr. dept. health edn. Tchrs. Coll., Columbia U., N.Y.C., 1969—; pres., founder John Dewey Acad., Gt. Barrington, Mass., 1984—; prof. Union Grad. Sch., Ohio, 1975-81; pvt. practice psychotherapy, 1970-84; cons. Dept. Probation City N.Y., 1973-77, Pan Am Commodities Corp., 1975-78, N. Castle Police Dept., 1978—; adolescent group psychotherapy cons. Pelham (N.Y.) Guidance Council, 1973-79. Bd. dirs. Odyssey Inst., N.Y.C., 1975-77, Nat. Health Inst., Inc., 1974-76; trustee Daytop Village, Inc., N.Y.C., 1972-84, Forest Inst. Profl. Psychology, Des Plaines, Ill., 1981-84, Gabelli Equity Fund, N.Y.C., 1986—; troop master Boy Scouts Am., Scarsdale; varsity basketball coach Sarah Lawrence Coll., 1977-78. Served with NG, 1960-61. Mem. Kappa Delta Pi, Phi Delta Kappa. Author: (with A. Bassin and R.L. Rachin) Reality Therapy Reader, 1976; (with R. and N. Kolodny) How to Survive Your Adolescent's Adolescence, 1984, (with G. Forrest) Alcoholism and Substance Abuse: Strategies for Clinical Intervention, 1985, (with N. and R. Kolodny) Smart Choices, 1986; also over 100 articles on adolescent substance abuse and alcoholism treatment, individual and group psychotherapy and edn.; assoc. editor Jour. Drug Issues, 1970-78; mem. editorial bd. Jour. Corrective and Social Psychiatry, 1974-78, Addiction Therapist, 1975—, Jour. Specialists in Group Work, 1975-78, Jour. of Mental Health Counseling Assn., 1979-82, Jour. Reality Therapy, 1980-85, Jour. Counseling and Devel., 1983-88. Home: 166A Under Mountain Rd Salisbury CT 06068-9802

BRATTON, IDA FRANK, educator; b. Glasgow, Ky., Aug. 31, 1933; d. Edmund Bates and Robbie Davis (Hume) Button; m. Robert Franklin Bratton, June 20, 1954; 1 son, Timothy Andrew. B.A., Western Ky. U., 1959, M.A., 1962. Cert. secondary tchr., Ky. Tchr. math. and sci. Gottschalk Jr. High Sch., Louisville, 1959-65; tchr. math. Iroquois High Sch., Louisville, 1965-79, Waggener High Sch., Louisville, 1979—. Mem. NEA, Ky. Edn. Assn., Jefferson County Tchrs. Assn., AAUW. Democrat. Methodist. Avocations: travel; needle crafts. Home: 304 Paddington Ct Louisville KY 40222 Office: Waggener High Sch 330 S Hubbards Ln Louisville KY 40207

BRATTSTRÖM, GUDRUN BIRGITTA, mathematican, educator; b. Helsingborg, Sweden, Mar. 23, 1954; d. Carl Edwin and Anna-Lisa (Brattström) B. Fil kand, U. Lund, Sweden, 1975; PhD, Cornell U., 1981. Postdoctoral fellow Swedish Natural Sci. Research Council, Orsay, France, 1981-83; Bunting sci. scholar Mary Ingraham Bunting Inst., Cambridge, Mass., 1983-85; assoc. prof. Stockholm U., 1985—. Contbr. articles to profl. jours. Mem. Am. Math. Soc., Soc. Math. France, Svenska Matematikersamfundet. Office: Stockholm U Dept Math, Box 6701, S-113 85 Stockholm Sweden

BRAUCH, CHARLES P., banker; b. Everett, Wash., May 29, 1937; s. Cyril Peter and Marie Alice (Aldrich) B.; m. Ruthann Volk; children—Aaron C., Shawn V. B.A. cum laude, U. Wash., 1967; M.B.A., Cornell U., 1969. Mgr. Chase Manhattan Bank, Tokyo, 1970-72; pres. United Chase Mcht. Bankers Ltd., Singapore, 1972-74; gen. mgr. Asia Fin. Devel. Group, Hong Kong, China, 1975-76; pres. Chase Manhattan Asia Ltd, Hong Kong, 1976-80, Chase Banco Lar Ltd., Rio de Janeiro, Brazil, 1980-84; sr. v.p. Chase Manhattan Corp., N.Y.C., 1982—; sr. managing dir. client relations and new bus. Chase Investment Bank, N.Y.C., 1984-86; sr. v.p., head securities Chase Manhattan Bank, Tokyo, 1987—; pres. Chase Manhattan Securities Japan, Tokyo, 1987—. Bd. dirs. Community Action Program, Rio de Janeiro, 1982-84. Mem. Am. Mgmt. Assn., Japan Mgmt. Assn. (assoc.), Am. C. of C. (bd. dirs., 1st v.p. Japan chpt. 1983-84). Club: Tokyo Am. Office: Chase Manhattan Securities Japan, New Tokio Kaijo Bldg 1F, 1-2-1 Marunouchi, Chiyoda-ku Tokyo 100, Japan

BRAUER, ERICH, artist; b. Vienna, Austria, Jan. 4, 1929; s. Simon Moses and Hermine Brauer; m. Naomi Dahabani, 1957; three children. Student, Wiener Kunstakademie. after studies in Vienna travelled in Africa, France, Spain, Austria, Greece and Israel, 1950-58, U.S.A., E. Africa, Ethiopia, Japan, 1965-74; guest lectr. Int. Summer Acad. for Fine Arts, Salzburg 1982—, 83. One-man exhbns., 1956—, in Austria, Germany, Switzerland, France, Denmark, Liechtenstein, Italy, Can., Sweden, Yugoslavia, Bulgaria, Norway Japan, Israel and U.S.A.; world travelling exhbns., 1979—; group exhbns. including travelling exhbns. with Wiener Schule des Phantastischen Realismus, 1962—, in We. Europe, U.S.A., S. Am., Poland, Yugoslavia, Israel, Iran, Turkey, Japan; Scenery for The Seven Mortal Sins (Vienna 1972), Bomarzo (Zürich 1970); scenery and customes for Media (Vienna 1972), The Magic Flute (Paris 1977); book, design and costumes for Sieben auf einen Streich (Vienna 1978); mural design for Univ. of Haifa, Israel 1982—; two gold records for Erich Bauer LP (poetry, music and songs), 1971. Publs: Zigeunerziege, 1976, Runde Fliegt, 1983. Address: care Joram Harel Mgmt, PO Box 28, A-1182 Vienna Austria

BRAUER, HARROL ANDREW, JR., broadcasting executive; b. Richmond, Va., Oct. 17, 1920; s. Harrol Andrew and Bertie (Gregory) B.; m. Elizabeth Anne Hill, May 18, 1946; children: Harrol Andrew III, William Lanier, Gregory Hill. BA, U. Richmond, 1942; LLD, Christopher Newport Coll. Chief announcer, program dir., account exec. various radio stas. in Va., 1939-42, 45-49; assoc. WVEC radio, Hampton, Va., 1949-80; v.p., dir. sales Sta. WVEC-TV, Hampton, 1953-82; v.p. Peninsula Cable Corp., 1966-82; chmn. Wyatt Bros., 1983—; bd. dirs. Peninsula Broadcasting Corp. Pres. Hampton Community Chest, 1951-52; crusade chmn. Peninsula unit Am. Cancer Soc., 1960—. Mem. Hampton Sch. Bd., 1963—, vice chmn., 1964-68, chmn., 1968-70; active Hampton Parking Authority; bd. dirs. YMCA, Va. U.S.O.; bd. dirs., vice chmn. Va. Pub. Telecommunications Bd., chmn. 1985—; chmn. Hampton Parking Authority, 1988—, Soc. Founders of Mace Christopher Newport Coll., 1988—; chmn. bd. trustees Hampton Roads Ednl. TV Assn., 1965-70; rector Christopher Newport Coll., 1976-82; co-chmn. for 375th Anniversary Celebration City of Hampton, 1985; v.p., founder Chesapeake Acad., 1988—. Served as lt. USNR, 1942-45. Recipient Disting. Service medallion Christopher Newport Coll., NCCJ award, Disting. Citizen award City of Hampton. Mem. Hampton Retail Mchts. Assn. (past pres., bd. dirs.), Chesapeake Acad. Found. (vice-chmn. 1988—), Jamestowne Soc., Peninsula C. of C. (past bd. dirs.), Broadcast Pioneers, Sigma Alpha Epsilon. Clubs: Commonwealth, Indian Creek Yacht and Country, James River Country, Hampton Yacht, Peninsula Exec.'s (past pres., bd. dirs.); Town Point. Lodge: Kiwanis (past bd. dirs., pres., lt. gov.). Home: 35 N Boxwood St Hampton VA 23669

BRAUER, STEPHEN FRANKLIN, manufacturing company executive; b. St. Louis, Sept. 3, 1945; s. Arthur John, Jr. and Jane (Franklin) B.; m. Camilla Cary Thompson, June 12, 1971; children—Blackford Fitzhugh, Rebecca Randolph, Stephen Franklin. Student Washington and Lee U., 1963-64; B.A., Westminster Coll., 1967. Sales and mktg. ofcl. Hunter Engring. Co., St. Louis, 1971-78, exec. v.p., 1978-81, pres., 1981—. Dir. Centerre Trust Co., St. Louis, 1986—. Trustee St. Louis Art Mus., St. Louis Country Day Sch. Mo. Botanical Garden. Served to 1st lt. C.E., AUS, 1968-70. Republican. Episcopalian. Clubs: St. Louis Country, St. Louis, Log Cabin. Home: 9630 Ladue Rd Saint Louis MO 63124 Office: 11250 Hunter Dr Bridgeton MO 63044

BRAUMILLER, ALLEN SPOONER, oil and gas exploration company executive, geologist; b. Texarkana, Tex., Feb. 1, 1934; s. Jack and Jennie (Spooner) B.; student Tulane U., 1952-53; B.S., U. Miss., 1955; M.S., U. Ill., 1957; m. Patsy L. McCoy, Dec. 23, 1955; children: Allen Spooner, Dana R., Adrienne Brevard, Colin McCoy. Exploration geologist Carter Oil Co. (merged into Humble Oil & Refining Co. 1961), 1957-69; with Helmerich & Payne, Inc., Tulsa, 1969—, v.p., exploration geologist, 1977—. Mem. Am. Assn. Petroleum Geologists, Geol. Soc. Am., Ill. Geol. Soc., Okla. City Geol. Soc., Tulsa Geol. Soc., Internat. Wine and Foods Soc. Republican. Presbyterian. Club: Petroleum. Home: 4979 E 113th St S Tulsa OK 74137 Office: Helmerich & Payne Inc 1579 E 21st St Tulsa OK 74114

BRAUN, BARBARA DICKEY, nurse; b. Washington, Apr. 22, 1933; d. William Kinchley and Helen Bertha (Randall) Dickey; m. James Milton Bruan, Feb. 13, 1953; children—James Milton, Jr., Jon Mark. Lic. Practical Nurse, Savannah Vocat. Sch., 1967; A.S., Brunswick Jr. Coll., 1975. R.N., Ga. Indsl. nurse Interstate Paper Co., Riceboro, Ga., 1968-72; nurse Liberty Meml. Hosp., Hinesville, Ga., 1972—; dir. nursing Midway Nursing Inn, Ga., 1980-81, Savannah Health Care, Ga., 1982-83; vol. nurse for indigent patients Liberty Meml. Hosp. and Liberty Manor Nursing Inn, Midway, 1972—; owner, operator Jims Oyster Bar, Midway, 1983—. Republican. Baptist. Home: PO Box 57 Lake Gale Midway GA 31320

BRAUN, BRIAN ALAN, lawyer; b. Chgo., Jan. 21, 1947; s. Jerome and Lillian (Schuster) B.; m. Terre J. Tibbles, Dec. 18, 1980; children: David Joshua, Aaron Jonathan. BS, U. Ill., 1969; JD, DePaul U., 1975. Bar: Ill. 1975, U.S. Dist. Ct. (cen. and so. dists.) Ill. 1983, U.S. Ct. Appeals (7th cir.) 1987. Gen. counsel Ill. Assn. Sch. Bds., Springfield, 1977-82; ptnr. Miller, Tracy, Braun & Wilson, Ltd., Monticello, Ill., 1982—; lectr. Ill. State U., 1981, East Ill. U., 1983, Bradley U., 1985, U. Ill., 1988. Author: Teacher Salaries and Fringe Benefits, 1980; contbr. numerous articles to profl. jours. Mem. ABA, Ill. Bar Assn., Piatt County Bar Assn., Am. Arbitration Assn., Phi Alpha Delta, Sigma Alpha Mu. Jewish. Home: 6 Eton Ct Champaign IL 61820 Office: Miller Tracy Braun & Wilson Ltd PO Box 112 Monticello IL 61856

BRAUN, DANIEL CARL, physician; b. San Diego, July 2, 1905; s. Daniel Jacob and Frida (Lorch) B.; m. Hazel Winfield Beckley, Aug. 10, 1929. Student, Carnegie Inst. Tech., 1923-31; B.S., U. Pitts., 1933, M.D., 1937; postgrad., L.I. Coll. Medicine, 1942, Columbia U., 1945. Diplomate Am. Bd. Preventive Medicine. Intern Mercy Hosp., Pitts., 1937-38; practice medicine specializing in occupational medicine Pitts., 1938—; med. dir. Pitts. Coal Co., 1944-50, cons. occupational medicine, 1950-52; med. dir. Indsl. Hygiene Found., Pitts., 1952-58, Homestead dist. works U.S. Steel Corp., Munhall, Pa., 1958-61; asst. med. dir. U.S. Steel Corp., 1961-70; mgr. occupational medicine services Indsl. Health Found., 1970-72, pres., 1972—; lectr. indsl. hygiene U. Pitts. Sch. Medicine, 1948—; lectr. occupational medicine Grad. Sch. Pub. Health U. Pitts., 1950—. Contbr. articles to profl. jours. Mem. Mayor Pitts. Com. Reorgn. Pitts. Dept. Health, 1948-50, President's Com. Employment Handicapped, 1958-80; mem. SSS appeal bd. Western Fed. Jud. Dist. Pa., 1962-68; active, Allegheny council Boy Scouts Am.; Bd. dirs. St. Clair Meml. Hosp.; trustee Indsl. Health Found. Am. Fellow Am. Coll. Chest Physicians, Am. Acad. Occupational Medicine (chmn. standards com. 1967-70), Am. Occupational Med. Assn. (dir. 1950-52), Am. Coll. Preventive Medicine, Am. Inst. Chemists; mem. AMA (recognition award 1976), Pa., Allegheny County med. socs., Alpha Omega Alpha. Club: University (Pitts.). Lodge: Masons. Home: 750 Washington Rd Pittsburgh PA 15228 Office: Indsl Health Found Inc 34 Penn Circle W Pittsburgh PA 15206

BRAUN, JEAN DANIEL, engineer; b. Strasbourg, France, Apr. 6, 1938; s. Andre and Lucienne (Weil) B.; m. Chantal Grienenberger, July 4, 1974 (div. 1983); children—Deborah, Maxime. Engr., E.T.H., Zurich, 1961. Engr., Hayek Engring., Zurich, Switzerland, 1965-67; cons., pres. J.D. Braun Engring., Strasbourg, France, 1967—; arbitrator Ct. Justice France, 1978—; adminstr. Industequip, Strasbourg, 1982—. Pres., Conseil Departemental Jeunesse, Strasbourg, 1968, S.V.P. Jeunesse, Strasbourg, 1969, Centre des Jeunes Dirigeants, Strasbourg, 1978. Served with French Army, 1962-63. Mem. Assn. Tech. de Fonderie, Assn. des Ingenieurs d'Alsace, Assn. des Anciens E.T.H. Zurich, Circle Europeen. Jewish. Home: 6 rue Himmerich, 67000 Strasbourg France Office: Cabinet Braun SA, 22 Rue La Fayette, Strasbourg France

BRAUN, JEROME IRWIN, lawyer; b. St. Joseph, Mo., Dec. 16, 1929; s. Martin H. and Bess (Donsker) B.; m. Dolores F. Braun; children: Aaron Hugh, Susan Lori, Daniel Victor. AB with distinction, Stanford U., 1951, LLB, 1953. Bar: Mo. 1953, Calif. 1953, U.S. Dist. Ct. (no. dist.) Calif., U.S. Tax Ct., U.S. Ct. Mil. Appeals, U.S. Supreme Ct., U.S. Ct. Appeals (9th cir.). Assoc. Long & Levit, San Francisco, 1957-58, Law Offices of Jefferson Peyser, 1958-62; founding ptnr. Farella, Braun & Martel (formerly Elke, Farella & Braun), San Francisco, 1962—; instr. San Francisco Law Sch., 1958-69; lectr. in field; speaker various State Bar Conventions in Calif., Ill., Nev., Mont. Editor: Stanford U. Law Rev.; contbr. articles to profl. jours. Mem. Jewish Welfare Fedn. of San Francisco, Marin County and Peninsula (past pres.), 1979-80, San Francisco United Jewish Community Ctrs. Served to 1st lt. JAGC, U.S. Army, 1954-57. Recipient Lloyd W. Dinkelspiel Outstanding Young Leader award Jewish Welfare Fedn., 1967. Mem. ABA, Calif. Bar Assn. (chmn. adminstrn. justice com. 1977, lawyer reps. to 9th cir. jud. conf. (chmn. 1982), frequent moderator continuing edn. of the bar programs), Bar Assn. San Francisco (past chmn. spl. com. on lawyers malpractice and malpractice ins.), State Bar Mo., San Francisco Bar Found. (past trustee), Calif. Acad. Appellate Lawyers (past pres.), Am. Judicature Soc., Stanford Law Sch. Bd. of Visitors, Am. Coll. Trial Lawyers, Mex.-Am. Legal Def. Fund (honoree), Order of Coif.

BRAUN, ROBERT CLARE, association and advertising executive; b. Indpls., July 18, 1928; s. Ewald Elsworth and Lila (Inman) B.; B.S. in Journalism-Advt., Butler U., 1950; postgrad. Ind. U., 1957, 66. Reporter, Northside Topics Newspaper, Indpls., 1949, advt. mgr., 1950; asst. mgr. Clarence E. Crippen Printing Co., Indpls., 1951; corp. sec. Auto-Imports, Ltd., Indpls., 1952-53; pres. O. R. Brown Paper Co., Indpls., 1953-69; pres., chief exec. officer Robert C. Braun Advt. Agy., 1959-70, Zimmer Engraving Inc., Indpls., 1964-69; former chmn. bd. O. R. Brown Paper Co., Zimmer Engraving, Inc.; advt. cons. Rolls-Royce Motor Cars, 1957-59; exec. dir., chief exec. officer Historic Landmarks Found., Ind., 1969-73; exec. v.p., Purchasing Mgmt. Assn. Indpls., 1974-85; cen. dist. coordinator Ind. Regional Minority Supplier Devel. Council, 1985—; pres. A.P.S. Industries, Inc., 1979—; nat. v.p. Associated Purchasing Publs., 1981-85; gen. mgr. Midwest Indsl. Show, 1974-85, Midwest Office Systems and Equipment Show, 1974-85, Grand Valley Indsl. Show, 1974-85, Evansville Indsl. Show, 1982-85, Ind. Bus. Opportunity Fair, 1985—. Chmn., Citizens' Adv. Com. to Marion County Met. Planning Dept., 1963; pres. museum com. Indpls. Fire Dept., 1966—; mem. adv. com. Historic Preservation Commn. Marion County, 1967-73; Midwestern artifacts cons. to curator of White House, Washington, 1971-73; mem., chmn. Mayor's Contract Compliance Adv. Bd., 1977—; mem. Mayor's Subcom. for Indpls. Stadium, 1981—; adv. bd., exec. com. Inpls. Office Equal Opportunity 1982—; mem. Ind. Minority Bus. Opportunity Council, 1985—; mem. Met. Mus. Art, Indpls. Mus. Art. Bd. dirs. Historic Landmarks Found. Ind., 1960-69; dir., sec. Ind. Arthritis and Rheumatism Found., 1960-67, pres., 1969, dir., 1970—, dir. Asso. Patient Services, 1976—; pres. Amanda Wasson Meml. Found., 1961-72, Huggler-Ault Meml. Trust, 1961-72. Recipient Meritorious Service award St. Jude's Police League, 1961; citation for meritorious service Am. Legion Police Post 56, 1962; Tafflinger-Holiday Park appreciation award, 1973; Nat. Vol. Service Citation, Arthritis Found., 1979; Margaret Egan Meml. award Ind. Arthritis Found., 1980; Indpls. Profl. Fire Fighters meritorious service award, 1982. Mem. Marion County Hist. Soc. (dir. 1964—, pres. 1965-69, 74-76, 1st v.p. 1979), Am. Guild Organists (mem. Indpls. chpt., charter mem. Franklin Coll. br.), Indpls. Humane Soc., Ind. Museum Soc. (treas., dir. 1967-74), Internat. Fire Buff Assos., Indpls. Second Alarm Fire Buffs (sec.-treas. 1967, pres. 1969), Ind. Hist. Soc., Nat. Hist. Soc., Nat. Trust Historic Preservation, Smithsonian Assn., Soc. Archtl. Historians, Am. Heritage Soc., N.A.P.M. Editors Group (nat. sec. 1979-81, nat. chmn./pres. 1981—), Am. Assn. State and Local History, Decorative Arts Soc. Indpls., Ind. Soc. Assn. Execs., Nat. Assn. Purchasing Mgmt. (W.L. Beckham internat. pub. relations award 1983), Purchasing Mgmt. Assn. Indpls. (dir. 1974—), Victorian Soc. Am. (nat. sec. 1971-74), Lambda Chi Alpha, Alpha Delta Sigma, Sigma Delta Chi, Tau Kappa Alpha. Club: Indpls. Press, Rolls-Royce Owners. Author: The Mr. Eli Lilly that I Knew, 1977. Editor: Historic Landmarks News, 1969-74; Hoosier Purchasor mag., 1974-85, I.R.M.S.D.C. News, 1985—. Contbr. articles to profl. jours. Home: 1415 W 52d St Indianapolis IN 46208 Office: 300 E Fall Creek Pkwy ND Suite 403 Indianapolis IN 46205

BRAUN, ROBERT DUNCAN, architectural/landscape photographer; b. Buffalo, Apr. 7, 1939; s. Norman Wilbur and Jean (Duncan) B.; student Brooks Inst. Photography, Santa Barbara, Calif., 1959-61; m. Margaret Mary Woods, July 14, 1962; 1 dau., Sandra Jean. Photographer Union Carbide Corp., Buffalo, 1962-67; resort brochure photographer Hannau-Robinson Color Prodns., Orlando, Fla., 1967-69; free-lance photographer, Orlando, 1969-70; co-owner Esquire Studios, Orlando, 1970-72; free-lance archtl. photographer, Orlando, 1972—. Recipient PPG Archtl. Photographers invitational award, 1973. Mem. Fla. Assn. AIA (Photographer of Yr. award 1981), Am. Soc. Mag. Photographers. Photographs pub. in mags. and books including Archtl. Digest, Archtl. Record, Housing, Better Homes, Fla. Architect, Fla. Designers Quar., A&U (Japan), Builder, Remodeling, Zelo, Fla. Home & Garden, Profl. Builder, Flowers, Form & Function. Office: PO Box 547755 Orlando FL 32854

BRAUN, STEPHEN HUGHES, clinical and consulting psychologist; b. St. Louis, Nov. 20, 1942; s. William Lafon and Jane Louise B.; B.A., Washington U., St. Louis, 1964, M.A., 1965; Ph.D. (USPHS fellow in Clin. Psychology), U. Mo., Columbia, 1970; m. Penny Lee Prada, Aug. 28, 1965; 1 son, Damian Hughes. Asst. prof. psychology Calif. State U., Chico, 1970-71; dir. social learning div. Ariz. State Hosp., Phoenix, 1971-74; chief bur. planning and evaluation Ariz. Dept. Health Services, Phoenix, 1974-79; pres. Braun and Assocs., human service program cons.'s, Scottsdale, Ariz., 1979—; also pvt. clin. practice; asst. prof. psychology Ariz. State U., 1971-79, vis. asst. prof. Ctr. of Criminal Justice, 1974-79, Ctr. for Public Affairs, 1979-81; cons. Law Enforcement Assistance Adminstrn., NIMH, Alcohol, Drug Abuse, and Mental Health Adminstrn., Ariz. Dept. Health Services, Ariz. Dept. Corrections, Ariz. Dept. Econ. Security, local and regional human service agys. NIMH research grantee, 1971-74; State of Calif. research grantee, 1971; cert. clin. psychologist, Ariz. Mem. Am. Psychol. Assn., Sigma Xi. Editorial cons.; contbr. articles to profl. publs. Home: 6122 E Calle Tuberia Scottsdale AZ 85251 Office: 7125 E Second St Scottsdale AZ 85251

BRAUN, WARREN LLOYD, consulting company executive; b. Postville, Iowa, Aug. 11, 1922; s. Karl William and Cornelia (Mueller) B.; B.S.E.E., Valparaiso Tech. Inst., 1940-41, Capitol Engring. Inst., 1953, Alexander Hamilton Inst., 1953, DSc (hon.) Shenandoah Coll.; m. Lillian Cooke Stone, May 24, 1942; children: Warren L. (dec.), Dikki Carol. Chief engr.Sta. WKEY, 1941; chief engr. Sta. WSVA, 1941, later gen. mgr. Sta. WSVA-AM-FM-TV; v.p. EWSP Corp.; E.S.M.W.T.P. sect. head, 1942-45; charge installation Stas. WSIR, WTON, WSVA-FM, WJMA, TV stas. WAAM-TV and WSVA-TV, Blue Ridge TV cable facilities, 1945-60; asst. gen. mgr., dir. engring. WSVA AM-FM-TV, 1959-63; owner Warren Braun Cons. Engrs., 1957—; v.p. Market Dimensions, Inc.; pres., chief exec. officer ComSonics, Inc., 1972—, Shenandoah Valley Devel. Corp., 1972—. (Chmn Engr. Student Officer Program, Washington, 1984—); panel 4 mem. TV Allocations Study Orgn.; chmn. Harrisonburg-Rockingham County Recreational Study Commn.; chmn. Upper Valley Regional Park Authority. Recipient Rietzke award, Capitol Radio Engring. Inst., 1985. Fellow Audio Engring. Soc., Soc. Motion Picture and TV Engrs, Inst. of Electricalurg Chambertical Soc. Am of Commerce, v.p. Harrisonburg-Rockingham County Community Concert Assn., winner Businessman of the Year); mem. SE USA and Japan Bd. Trade Assn. Va., 1972—; bd. dirs. Richmond Regional Export Council, Va. Cultural Laureate Found.; bd. dirs. Employee Stock Ownership Council Am., 1977—, vice-chmn., 1984-85, pres. 1985-87, chmn. 1987. Recipient Jefferson Davis medal, 1961; A.S.E. Internat. award, 1969. Registered profl. engr., Va., S.C. Fellow Audio Engring. Soc., Internat. Consular Acad. (Reitzke award 1972), mem. Nat. Assn. Broadcasters (nat. chmn. tape standards com., engring. adv. com. 1966), IEEE, Va. Assn. Professions (v.p) . 1972-73, pres. 1974-75), Ohio River Valley Water Sanitation Com. Lutheran. Lodge: Elks. Soc. Profl. Engrs. (dir., pres. Skyline chpt.; named Engr. of Year 1965, Distinguished Service award 1974), Acoustical Soc. Am., Soc. Motion Picture and Television Engrs., Am. Soc. Heating Refrigerating and Air Conditioning Engrs., Nat. Soc. Profl. Engrs. (mem. air pollution control task force), Electronics Industry Assn. (mem. broadband communications standards com.), Harrisonburg-Rock County C. of C. (pres. 1965, Harrisonburg-Rockingham Man of Year 1965, Exec. of Yr. 1983, Businessman of Yr. 1985), Am. Soc. Testing and Materials, Va. Acad. Scis. (dir., exec. com.), Va. C. of C. (chmn. world trade com. 1969-71, dir. 1973-77, v.p. 1975-77). Clubs: Elks (Richmond). Office: ComSonics Inc 1350 Port Republic Rd Harrisonburg VA 22801

BRAUTBAR, NACHMAN, physician, educator; b. Haifa, Israel, Oct. 22, 1943; came to U.S., 1975; s. Pinhas and Sabine (Lohite) B.; m. Ronit Aboutboul, Mar. 25, 1968; children—Sigalit, Shirley, Jaques. M.D., Med. Sch. Jerusalem, 1968. Diplomate Am. Bd. Internal Medicine, Am. Bd. Nephrology. Intern, Rambam Hosp., Haifa, 1968-69; resident in internal medicine Hadassah Med. Center, Jerusalem, 1972-75; fellow in nephrology UCLA Med. Sch., 1975-77, asst. prof. medicine, 1977-78; asst. prof. medicine U. So. Calif., Los Angeles, 1978-80, assoc. prof. medicine, pharmacology and nutrition, 1980—, dir. Ctr. for Toxicology and Chem. Exposure; chmn. nephrology sect. Hollywood Presbyn. Med. Center, 1980—. Author: Cellular Bioenergetics, 1985. Contbr. numerous articles, papers to scientific publs. Chmn. research com., pub. relations com. Kidney Foundation Los Angeles, 1980—. Named Hon. Citizen, Los Angeles City Council, 1984; Grantee Am. Heart Assn., 1980—, NIH, 1983. Mem. Am. Soc. Nephrology, Am. Soc. Bone and Mineral Research, Am. Physiol. Soc., Am. Chem. Soc., Am. Soc. Parenteral Nutrition, Am. Coll. Nutrition, Israeli Soc. Nephrology (hon.). Office: U So Calif 2025 Zonal Ave Los Angeles CA 90023

BRAVERMAN, DONNA CARYN, fiber artist; b. Chgo., Apr. 4, 1947; d. Samuel and Pearl (Leen) B. Student, U. Mo., 1965-68; BFA in Interior Design, Chgo. Acad. Fine Arts, 1970. Interior designer Ascher Dental Supply-Healthco., Chgo., 1970-72, Clarence Krusinski & Assocs. Ltd., Chgo., 1972-74, Perkins & Will Architects, Chgo., 1974-77; fiber artist Fiber Co-op Fibrecations, Chgo., 1977, Scottsdale, Ariz., 1977—. Exhibited in group shows at Mus. Contemporary Crafts, N.Y.C., 1977, James Prendergast Library Art Gallery, Jamestown, N.Y., 1981, Grover M. Herman Fine Arts Ctr., Marietta, Ohio, 1982, Okla. Art Ctr., 1982, Middle Tenn. State U., Murfreesboro, 1982, Redding (Calif.) Mus., 1983, Tucson Mus. Art, 1984, 86, The Arts Ctr., Iowa City, 1985, The Wichita Nat., 1986; in traveling exhibitions Ariz. Archtl. Crafts, 1983, Clouds, Mountains, Fibers, 1983; represented in permanent collections Phillips Petroleum, Houston, Metro. Life, Tulsa, Directory Hotel, Tulsa, Keys Estate Ariz. Biltmore Estates, Phoenix, Sohio Petroleum, Dallas, Reichold Chem., White Plains, N.Y., Rolm Telecommunications, Colorado Springs, Mesirow & Co., Chgo., Exec. House Hotel, Chgo., Cambell Estate, Ariz.; contbr. articles to profl. jours. Home and Office: 7920 E Camelback Rd #511 Scottsdale AZ 85251

BRAVERMAN, SAMUEL, chemistry educator; b. Falticeni, Romania, May 23, 1934; arrived in Israel, 1952; s. Herscu and Rivka (Smilovici) B.; m. Bitya Auerbach, Aug. 11, 1976; 1 child, Ayala Rivka. BSc, Bar-Ilan U., Ramat-Gan, Israel, 1960; PhD, U. Alta., 1963. Lectr. Bar-Ilan U., Ramat-Gan, 1963-67, sr. lectr., 1067-75, assoc. prof., 1975—; vis. prof. Cornell U., Ithaca, N.Y., 1976-77; vis. scientist U. Ill., Urbana, 1980-81. Editor: Chemistry of Allenes, 1985; contbr. chpts. to books, articles to profl. jours. Mem. Israel Chem. Soc. Home: 65 Harei Yehuda, Ganei Tiqva 55900, Israel Office: Bar-Ilan U, Chemistry Dept, Ramat Gan 52100, Israel

BRAYMAN, HAROLD, public relations consultant; b. Middleburgh, N.Y., Mar. 10, 1900; s. Channing and Minnie C. (Feeck) B.; m. Martha Witherspoon Wood, Jan. 25, 1930; children: Harold Halliday, Walter Witherspoon. A.B., Cornell U., 1920; LL.D. (hon.), Gettysburg Coll., 1965. Tchr. English and history Ft. Lee (N.J.) High Sch., 1920-22; reporter Albany (N.Y.) Evening Jour., 1922-24; asst. legislative corr. N.Y. Evening Post, 1924-26, corr., 1926-1928, Washington corr., 1928-33; Washington corr. Phila. Evening Ledger; writer syndicated column Daily Mirror of Washington, 1934-40; Washington corr. Houston Chronicle and other newspapers, 1940-42; spl. corr. in, London, 1925, covered all nat. convs. and nat. polit. campaigns, 1928-40; asst. dir., public relations dept. E.I. du Pont de Nemours & Co., 1942-44, dir., 1944-65; corporate exec. in residence Am. U., 1968; bd. visitors Sch. Pub. Relations and Communications, Boston U., chmn., 1961-71. Editor: Pub. Relations Jour, 1956; author: Corporate Management in a World of Politics, 1967, Developing a Philosophy for Business Action, 1969, (with A.O.H. Grier) A History of the Lincoln Club of Delaware, 1970, The President Speaks Off-the-Record, 1976. Mem. Cornell U. Council, chmn., 1961-63; mem. Cornell Centennial planning com., also chmn. adv. council grad. sch. bus. and pub. adminstrn., 1960-65; Trustee emeritus Gettysburg Coll.; Trustee Found. for Pub. Relations Research and Edn., 1956-62, Wilmington Med. Center.; Mem. sponsoring com. Pub. Relations Seminar, 1952-61. Recipient citation Pub. Relations Soc. Am., 1963; Golden Plate award Am. Acad. Achievement, 1965. Mem. U.S. C. of C. (com. on taxation 1954-60, com. on govt. ops. and expenditures 1964-66), Am. Acad. Achievement (v.p. 1966-74), Mfg. Chemists Assn. (pub. relations adv. com. 1951-56, chmn. 1951-53), Mencken Soc. of Del. (pres. 1980-81), Ams. for the Competitive Enterprise System (life bd. dirs.). Clubs: University (N.Y.C.); Gridiron (pres. 1941), Nat. Press (pres. 1938), Overseas Writers (Washington); Wilmington, Wilmington Country (dir. 1952-64), Greenville Country (Wilmington, Del.). Lodge: Rotary. Home: 810 Park Plaza 1100 Lovering Ave Wilmington DE 19806 Office: 5726 Montchanin Bldg Wilmington DE 19801

BRAZ, EVANDRO FREITAS, management consultant; b. Rio de Janeiro, Apr. 20, 1943; came to U.S., 1966; s. Jose Nunes and Edir (Freitas) B.; B.S. in Mech. Engring., Rio de Janeiro U., 1965; M.S. in Indsl. Engring., Columbia U., 1967, M.B.A. (OAS fellow), 1968; m. Darline Kristina Ryther, Dec. 28, 1968; children—Erica Denise, Daniel William, Max Elliot. Assoc. engr., Mass Transit Authority, Rio de Janeiro, 1964; prodn. engr. Gen. Electric Corp., Rio de Janeiro, 1965-66; cons. mgmt. cons. services Coopers & Lybrand, N.Y.C., 1968-72, mgr. mgmt. cons. services, 1972-76, prin., partner mgmt. cons. services, 1976-81, prin. partner nat. office, 1981-85, N.Y. Office, 1986—. Registered profl. engr., Brazil. Mem. Inst. Mgmt. Cons. (cert.), Inst. Mgmt. Scis., Nat. Assn. Accts., Am. Prodn. and Inventory Control Soc., Am. Arbitration Assn., Am. Constrn. Owners Assn. Roman Catholic. Club: Mt. Kisco (N.Y.) Country. Home: 14 Whitlaw Close Chappaqua NY 10514 Office: Coopers & Lybrand 1251 Ave of Americas New York NY 10020

BRDAR, GOJKA BRANKO, surgeon; b. Bjelaj, Yugoslavia, Apr. 7, 1935; s. Jovana Gojko and Milka (Ciganovic) B.; m. Dragica Jaric, Dec. 25, 1961; children: Mirela, Sasa. Dr.Med., U. Sarajevo, Yuguslavia, 1961. Rot. med. tng. Gen. Hosp., Zenica, Yugoslavia, also Univ. Clinic, Sarajevo; physician Ironworks, Zenica, 1962-64; confidential physician Nat. Health Ins., Zenica, 1965-66, 68-70; ward and resident physician Marien Hosp., Siegen, W.Ger., 1966-68; resident physician Dist. Hosp., Wangen, W.Ger., 1970; resident physician Elisabeth Hosp., Rheydt-M. Gladbach, W.Ger., 1970-73, sr. surgeon, prin. surgery, 1973-75; prin. surgeon, vice chief Marien Hosp., Letmathe, W.Ger., 1975-76; prin. surgeon, vice chief surgery dept. Elisabeth Hosp., Recklinghausen, W.Ger., 1976; prin. surgeon Dist. Hosp., Lubbecke, W.Ger., 1976; prin. surgeon, vice chief Johanniter Hosp., Oberhausen, Sterkrade, W.Ger., 1976-77; sr. surgeon Mil. Hosp., Novi Sad, Yugoslavia, 1978; surgeon, physician in charge Organ Transplantation Inst., Sarajevo, 1978-79; physician in charge, head sect. surgery Med. Ctr., Novi Knezevac, Yugoslavia, 1979-80; sr. surgeon Weiz Hosp., Austria, 1981-87; sr. surgeon, vice chief Gen. Hosp., Hainburg, Austria, 1987—.Served with Yugoslav Nat. Army, 1964-65. Home: Lole Ribara 44, 11060 Beograd-Slanci Yugoslavia Office: Gen Hosp, Hofmeisterstrasse 78 A, 2410 Hainburg Donau Austria

BREAKEY, LISA KATHERINE, speech pathologist; b. Los Angeles, Oct. 21, 1945; d. Melvin Harvey and Inez (Rey) Smith. BA in Speech Pathology and Audiology, U. Calif., Santa Barbara, 1967; MA in Speech Pathology, San Jose State U., 1975. Cert. community coll. spl. edn. tchr., Calif. Speech pathologist Manitoba (Can.) Rehab. Hosp., 1968-69; speech pathologist Kingston (Ont.) Health Unit, Can., 1969-70, dir. speech therapy, 1970-73; pvt. practice San Jose, Calif., 1975—; cons. Atari Inc., Sunnyvale, Calif., 1977-79, Evergreen Valley Community Coll., San Jose, 1977-80, Los Gatos (Calif.) Rehab. Hosp., 1977—, VA Med. Ctr., Livermore, Calif., 1979-83, Irwin Lehrhoff and Assocs., Beverly Hills, Calif., 1985-86; profl. staff priviledges Santa Teresa Hosp., San Jose, 1981—, Mission Oaks Hosp., San Jose, 1982—, Good Samaritan Hosp., San Jose, 1983—; presenter numerous seminars, workshops in adult communication disorders, 1979—; guest lectr. San Jose State U., 1975-88. Contbr. articles to profl. jours. Mem. Am. Speech Lang. and Hearing Assn. (legis. counselor 1986—, congl. action contact 1985, cert. appreciation 1983, 84), Calif. Speech Lang. Hearing Assn. (chmn. printing com. 1977, mem. conf. commn. 1982-84, task force on occupational therapy, 1983-84, hospitality com. 1984, legis. handbook com. 1985, state nominating com. 1986-88, editor newsletter 1985, dist. dir. elect 1985, Outstanding Achievement award 1986), Calif. Speech Pathologists and Audiologists in Pvt. Practice (v.p. 1979-81, pres. 1983-85, chmn. speakers bur. 1981, 82, current trends workshop 1980, pvt. practice workship 1978-80, rev. course in preparation com. 1978-81, 83, 85-86, govt. affairs com. 1983—, nomination com. 1985—, cert. appreciation 1982), Santa Clara County Speech-Lang.-Hearing Assn. (bd. dirs. 1987—), Calif. Assn. Post Secondary Educators of Disabled, Profl. Group for Adult Communication Disorders (1st pres. 1977), Bay Area Group for Non-Oral, Bay Area Neurolinguistic Group, Bay Area Pvt. Practitioners Speech Pathology and Audiology (1st pres. 1977), Washington Sq. Soc.-San Jose State U., Phi Kappa Phi. Democrat. Roman Catholic. Office: 2444 Moorpark Ave Suite 300 San Jose CA 95128

BREAM, JULIAN, classical guitarist; b. London, Eng., July 15, 1933; s. Henry G. B. Ed., Royal Coll. Music; hon. degree, U. Surrey, Eng., 1968. First recital, 1946, London debut, 1950, U.S. debut, 1958; formed Julian Bream Consort, 1960; concerts in Europe; tours of Japan, Australia; frequent radio and TV appearances; recorded Malcolm Arnold's Guitar Concerto (RCA Victor). Served with Brit. Army, 1952-55. Decorated Order Brit. Empire. Recipient Grammy award for Classical Performance: An Evening of Elizabethan Music, 1963. Office: care Harold Shaw Concerts Inc 1995 Broadway New York NY 10023 also: care Harold Holt Ltd, 31 Sinclair Rd, London W14 0NS, England *

BREAUX, JOHN B., U.S. senator, former congressman; b. Crowley, La., Mar. 1, 1944; s. Ezra H., Jr. and Katherine (Berlinger) B.; m. Lois Gail Daigle, Aug. 1, 1964; children: John B., William Lloyd, Elizabeth Andre, Julia Agnes. B.A. in Polit. Sci, U. Southwestern La., 1964; J.D., La. State U., 1967. Bar: La. 1967. Ptnr. Brown, McKernan, Ingram & Breaux, 1967-68; legis. asst. to Congressman Edwin W. Edwards, 1968-69, dist. asst., 1969-72; mem. 92d-99th Congresses from 7th Dist. La., 1971-87; U.S. Senator from La. Washington, 1987—; mem. Commerce com., Environ., Agri., and Pub. Works com., Spl. Com. on Aging, Nat. Ocean Policy Study; U.S. del. World Food Conf., Dem. Leadership Council, Dem. Nat. Com.; chmn. Nuclear Regulation subcom., Mcht. Marine subcom., Nat. Water Alliance. Hon. chmn. La. March of Dimes. Recipient Am. Legion award; Moot Ct. finalist La. State U., 1966; Neptune award Am. Oceanic Orgn., 1980. Mem. La. Bar Assn., Acadia Parish Bar Assn., Internat. Rice Festival Assn. (dir.), Crowley Jr. C. of C., La. Jr. C. of C., Pi Lambda Beta, Phi Alpha Delta, Lambda Chi Alpha. Democrat. Office: US Senate Washington DC 20150

BREDFELDT, JOHN CREIGHTON, air force officer; b. Great Bend, Kans., Oct. 31, 1947; s. Willis John and Geraldine Elizabeth (Creighton) B.; m. Barbara Elaine Gutow, June 6, 1984; 1 child, Jason Caulter. B.B.A., Wichita State U., 1969, M.A. in Econs., 1971; grad. Air Command and Staff Coll., 1984. Dir. Brennan Halls, Wichita State U., 1969-71; commd. 2d lt. U.S. Air Force, 1971, advanced through grades to lt. col. 1987; budget/cost ananlyst Aero. System div., Dayton, Ohio, 1971-76; insp. Air Force IG, Andrews AFB, Md., 1976-79; chief economist Dir. Programs AF/PRP, Pentagon, Va., 1979-83; chief cost analyst div. U.S. Air Force Europe, 1985-87; dep. dir. program control, engine program office, Dayton, 1987—; instr. econs. Wichita State U., 1969-71; bus. prof. Bowie State Coll., 1980-83; econs. instr. European div. U. Md., Germany, 1985-87. Contbr. articles to profl. jours. Rep., Sunday sch. tchr. Ramstein Protestant Parish Council Germany, 1984-86; asst. scout master Ramstein council Boy Scouts Am., 1984-87. Mem. Inst. Cost Analysis, Nat. Estimating Soc., Am. Soc. Milit. Comptrollers, Internat. Platform Assn., Omicron Delta Epsilon. Lutheran. Avocations: micro-economics, golfing, tennis, racquetball, reading.

BREDIN, J(OHN) BRUCE, real estate executive; b. Wilmington, Del., June 1, 1914; s. Robert and Margaret (Starrett) B.; student Coll. William and Mary, 1932-34, U. Pa., 1938-40, LLD (hon.) Coll. William and Mary; m. Octavia M. duPont, Aug. 4, 1945; children—Stephanie S. du P. B. Speakman, Margaretta Starrett Bredin Brokaw, Jonathan Bruce, Alletta Bredin-Bell, Laura L. Bredin Hussey, Antonia duPont Massie. Civilian employee U.S. Govt., 1934-38; with E.I. du Pont de Nemours & Co., 1939-45, 49-52, Texaco, 1945-46; pres. Bredin Realty Co., 1950-81; Participant in Smithsonian expdns. to Africa and West Indies; mem. spl. fine arts com. Dept. State; chmn. Fund for the Diplomatic Reception Found., Dept. State; mem. adv. com. Longwood Found.; mem. devel. com. Woods Hole Oceanographic Inst.; pres. Bredin Found.; founding chmn. Henry Francis Du Pont Collectors Circle; emeritus bd. dirs. Med. Center of Del.; trustee Unidel Found., Henry Francis du Pont Winterthur Mus.; trustee, vice chmn. Endowment Assn. Coll. William and Mary; hon. trustee Foxcroft Sch. (life); exofficio trustee U. Del. Research Found.; chmn. bd. trustees U. Del.; bd. dirs. U. Del. Library Assocs.; vice chmn. Bartol Research Inst. U. Del.; lifetime trustee & dir. Med. Ctr. Del. Hosp. Found.; Hon. fellow Smithsonian Instn.; mem. Del. Acad. Medicine (dir.), Hist. Soc. Del. (trustee), Am. Competitive Enterprise System (hon. life dir.), Nantucket Cottage Hosp., Confrerie des Chevaliers du Tastevin. Clubs: Vicmead Hunt, Greenville Country, Wilmington, Wilmington Country; Corinthian Yacht (Phila.); Everglades, Soc. of Four Arts (Palm Beach, Fla.); Gulf Stream Bath and Tennis, Gulf Stream Golf (Delray Beach, Fla.); Nantucket Yacht, Sankaty Head Golf (Nantucket); Met. (Washington). Home: PO Box 87 Wilmington DE 19899 Office: PO Box 87 5724 Montchanin Bldg Wilmington DE 19899

BREE, PETER, oboist, radio producer; b. Driebergen-Rijsenburg, Netherlands, Sept. 23, 1949; s. Jan Hendrik, and Adriana (Hoogenboezem) B.; student English lang. and lit. U. Groningen, 1967-73, MO-A degree, 1972-73; oboe student with Han de Vries, Amsterdam Muzieklyceum (now Sweelinck Conservatoire), 1973-79, diplomas in Teaching, Orchestral, Soloist, Cor Anglais, Chamber Music, 1979-81; student with Neil Black (Dutch Cultural Ministry scholar, London), 1980-81. Master of English, grammar schs., Amsterdam, 1973-77; MusD (honoris causa) Marquis Giuseppe Seicluna Internat. U. Found., Delaware, U.S.A.; prin. oboist NOS-radio, Hilversum, 1977-79; freelance oboist, mainly solo and chamber music, 1979—; producer AVRO-radio programme Liever de Lucht in and Kurhaus concert series, 1980-83; producer, announcer Veronica Radio, Hilversum, 1983—; debut, 1964; London debut, Purcell Room, 1979; founder, vice chmn. bd. Live Music Now the Netherlands, 1980-85; recitalist, Netherlands, Belgium, U.K., France; rec. artist for Dutch radio with various pianists, ensembles and orchestras, 1977—; pub. with Dr. Bernard Rose Devienne Oboe Sonatas, 1987; recordings include: Fasch double concerto for oboe and flute, Amsterdam Conservatory Chamber Orchestra, 1975, Telemann Trio Sonata and Suite, 1981, Marais, Rheinberger, Handel, Koetsier, Pierné works for oboe/cor anglais and organ, 1981, Britten, Rubbra, Röntgen and Grabert pieces for oboe, cor anglais and piano, 1981, Louis Andriessen Sonatina, 1981, Huggens Treble Concerto with Wegenbouwkapel Nederland, 1983. Recipient Silver Vriendenkrans award Soc. of Friends of Concertgebouw and Concertgebouw Orch., Amsterdam, 1981. Home: 378 bel Marnixstraat, Amsterdam 1016 XX The Netherlands Office: Veronica Omroep Organisatie, 75 Laapersveld, Hilversum 1213VB, The Netherlands

BREEN, JAMES LANGHORNE, obstetrician, gynecologist; b. Chgo., Sept. 5, 1926; s. John J. and Lucrece Breen Hudgins (Bilisoly) B.; m. Doris Johnson, Dec. 1, 1951; children: Michael, Nash, Anne, Laura, Barbara, Beth. Diploma, Balt. City Coll., 1945; B.S., Johns Hopkins U., 1946; M.D., Northwestern U., 1952. Diplomate: Am. Bd. Obstetrics and Gynecology. Intern Walter Reed Army Hosp., Washington, 1953; resident obstetrics and gynecology Walter Reed Army Hosp., 1954-58, asst. chief, 1957-58; asst. chief Second Gen. Hosp., Landstuhl, Germany, 1958-60; acting chief Second Gen. Hosp., 1959-60; attending, assoc. prof. obstetrics and gynecology N. J. Coll. Medicine and Dentistry, Newark, 1969-75; clin. prof. obstetrics and gynecology Jefferson Med. Coll., Phila., 1975; chmn. dept. obstetrics and gynecology Newark City Hosp., 1963-69, St. Barnabas Med. Center, Livingston, N.J., 1969—; fellow in obstetric, gynecologic and breast Pathology Armed Forces Inst. Pathology, 1960-61; clin. prof. obstetrics and gynecology N.J. Med. Sch., 1987—. Served with M.C. U.S. Army, 1952-61. Fellow Am. Coll. Obstetricians and Gynecologists (sect. and dist. chmn. Dist. III 1971-73, v.p. 1981-82, pres. 1983-84, past pres. 1984-85), A.C.S., Internat. Acad. Pathology, Internat. Coll. Surgeons (regent 1965, chmn. dist. III 1977-80), Soc. Colposcopists and Colpomicroscopists (founding fellow 1965), Armed Forces Instn. Pathology, Acad. Medicine N.J., N.Y. Obstet. Soc., N.J. Obstet. and Gynecol. Soc., N.J. Soc. Surgeons; mem. Am. Soc. Cytology, Vienna Med. Soc. (life), Assn. Mil. Surgeons of U.S., AMA (Meritorious Service award 1966), N.Y. Acad. Scis., Essex County Med. Assn., Assn. Med. Writers, Assn. Profs. Obstetricians and Gynecologists, N.J. Hosp. Assn., Internat. Soc. Cybernetic Medicine, Am. Soc. Clin. Pathologists (asso.), Internat. Soc. for Study Vulvar Disease. Club: Mid-Eastern Travel (N.Y.C.). Home: 9 Kermit Rd Maplewood NJ 07040 Office: Old Short Hills Rd Livingston NJ 07039

BREEN, PATRICIA HELEN HALL, financial consultant; b. Detroit, Sept. 15, 1926; d. John William and Ethel Viola (Mardian) Hall. BBA, U. Mich., 1949; postgrad. U. Mich.-Detroit, 1953-54. Policy and procedure sec. Gen. Motors Central, Detroit, 1949-50; trust investment analyst Nat. Bank of Detroit, 1950-51; investment analyst Baxter & Co., Cleve., 1952; sr. fin. cons. Merrill Lynch, Farmington Hills, Mich., 1957—; founder, chmn., pres., chief exec. officer Good Food Co., Livonia, Mich.; radio and TV lectr. Mem. Nat. Assn. Female Execs. (pres. Oakland County 1985-87), U. Mich. Alumnae Assn. (bd. dirs. 1973-74). Republican. Roman Catholic. Club: Detroit Boat (Belle Isle, Mich.). Avocations: silversmithing, oil painting, writing, water and snow skiing, golf. Home: 17959 University Park Dr Livonia MI 48152 Office: Merrill Lynch Pierce Fenner & Smith Inc Triatria Bldg Suite 260 32255 Northwestern Hwy Farmington Hills MI 48018

BREFFEILH, LOUIS ANDREW, ophthalmologist, educator; b. Shreveport, La., Sept. 14, 1913; s. John Hypolite and Louise Claire (DeRichi(Marmouget)) B.; m. Marianna Franklin, Aug. 13, 1949; children—George Richard, Andrew Louis. Student, Loyola U. South, New Orleans, 1932-34; M.B., La. State U., 1938, M.D., 1939. Diplomate Am. Bd. Ophthalmology, Am. Acad. Ophthalmology and Otolaryngology, A.C.S., Internat. Coll. Surgeons. Intern Shreveport Charity Hosp., 1938-39; practice medicine specializing in ophthalmology Shreveport, 1950—; staff Confederate Meml. Med. Center, 1950—, pres., 1966-67; staff Schumpert Meml. Hosp., 1950—, pres., 1971-72; clin. instr. dept. ophthalmology Sch. Medicine, La. State U., New Orleans, 1946-50; asst. clin. prof. Sch. Medicine, La. State U., 1950-51; clin. prof. La. State U. Postgrad. Sch. Medicine, Shreveport, 1951-64; head dept., prof. Sch. Medicine, La. State U., Shreveport, 1970—; sr. cons. USAF, 1950—, VA Hosp., 1950—. Contbr. articles to profl. jours. Pres. Breffeilh and Texada Med. Found., 1971—. Served to maj. M.C. AUS, 1941-46; now lt. col. USAFR. Mem. Am., So. med. assns., Pan Am. Ophthal. Soc., La., Miss., Ophthal. and Otol. Soc., Shreveport Med. Soc. (v.p. 1969-70). Club: Shreveport Yacht. Home: 439 Springlake Dr Shreveport LA 71106 Office: 2515 Line Ave Shreveport LA 71104

BREGEON, CHRISTIAN HENRI, rheumatologist, educator; b. Somloire, France, June 1, 1934; s. Henri Joseph and Germaine (Cochard) B.; m. Anne Marie Perrau, July 5, 1963; children: Christine, Elisabeth, Marie Dominique, Eric, Claire, Thomas. Baccalaureat in Philosophy. Diplomate Agregation of Rheumatology. Intern Angers (France) U., 1962-66, asst., 1966-70, prof. rheumatology, 1971—; asst. Clinic of Rheumatology Ctr. Hosp. U., Angers, 1971-80, chief of service phys. medicine and rehab., 1981; med. and jud. specialist, Angers, 1967-74. Mem. Jeune Chambre Econ., Angers, 1967-74, Perspectives and Realities, Angers, 1981—. Served to 1st lt. French Artillery, 1956-58. Mem. French Soc. de Rheumatology (bd. dirs. 1986—), Ctr. Cath. des Medecins Francais. Roman Catholic. Home: 56 Blvd Strasbourg, 49000 Angers France Office: Ctr Hosp Univ Angers, 49040 Cedex France

BREGER, HERBERT JOSEPH, dentist, communications executive; b. N.Y.C., Nov. 21, 1920; s. Alvin Carl and Bertha Florence (Goodman) B.; B.A., N.Y. U., 1939, D.D.S., 1942; m. Anita Blankfein, Oct. 20, 1947 (div. Sept. 1963); children—Bruce, Kenneth; m. Joanne Sue Spector, Sept. 27, 1963; children—Jonathan, Beth. Pvt. practice dentistry, Long Island City, N.Y., 1946—; attending oral surgeon Horace Harding Hosp., 1949-59; asst. attending oral surgeon St. John's Long Island City Hosp., 1947-49, Queens Gen. Hosp., 1950-62; pres. Telecom Plus of P.R., Inc., 1975-84; sec. treas. Triboro Communications, 1983-85; pres. A Plus Info. Processing Corp., 1982—, Telecom Plus Shared Tennants Services, 1984-86, Integrated Communications Ltd., 1987—. Served with Dental Corps, AUS, 1942-47; CBI. Mem. Queens County Dental Soc. (pres. 1958), Phi Sigma Delta. Home: 75 East End Ave New York NY 10028 Office: 25-15 Bridge Plaza N Long Island City NY 11101 also: 885 3d Ave New York NY 10022

BREHENY, JAMES ERNEST, physician, medical editor; b. Melbourne, Australia, Jan. 11, 1936; s. Ernest Patrick and Gladys Therese (Holzer) B.; m. Maureen Anne Walsh, Dec. 19, 1960; children—Katherine, Nicholas, Camilla. B.Medicine and B.Surgery, U. Melbourne, 1960. Medical Chief resident Royal Children's Hosp., Melbourne, 1968, dep. med. dir., 1969; med. dir. Mercy Maternity Hosp., Melbourne, 1970-86; nat. dirs. Health Econs. Cons. Deloitte Haskins & Sells, 1986—; med. editor Australian Family Physician Jour., 1983-86; assoc. physician genetics Royal Children's Hosp., 1975-86.Contbr. articles to profl. jours. Exec. mem., pres. Victoria br. Australian Med. Assn., 1974-83; hon. sec. Australian Cath. Health Care Assn., 1978-84 ; mem. Victoria Nursing Council, 1974-86. Fellow Royal Australian Coll. Physicians, Royal Australian Coll. Med. Adminstrs., Australian Med. Assn. (hon. fellow); mem. Australian Coll. Health Services Adminstrs., Australian Coll. Paediatrics, Paediatric Soc. Victoria (pres. 1984-85), Harvard Bus. Sch. Assn. Australia, Australian Guild Realist Artists. Roman Catholic. Clubs: Kew Golf, The Australian, Victoria Racing. Home: 15 Riverside Ave, North Balwyn, Melbourne 3104, Australia Office: Deloitte Haskins & Sells, 461 Bourke St, Melbourne Australia 3000

BREHENY, PATRICK JOSEPH, oil company executive; b. Dec. 30, 1944; s. Patrick Joseph and Mary Catherine (Curran) B.; B.S. magna cum laude, Seton Hall U., South Orange, N.J., 1966, M.B.A., 1968; m. Carole Aielli, Apr. 27, 1969; children—Jennifer Marie, Natalie Catherine. Staff acct. Arthur Andersen & Co., C.P.A.s, Newark, 1966; with Exxon Corp., and affiliates, 1970—, mgr. acctg. and fin. services Exxon Chem. Co., 1977-79, mgr. corp. acctg. Exxon Corp., Florham Park, N.J., 1979—. Served to lt.col. USAR, 1968—, including Vietnam. Decorated Bronze Star, Army Commendation medal; Alpha Kappa Psi scholar, 1966; C.P.A., N.J. Mem. Am. Inst. C.P.A.s, Inst. Mgmt. Acctg., N.J. Soc. C.P.A.s, Res. Officers Assn., Civil Affairs Assn., Assn. U.S. Army. Office: 180 Park Ave Bldg 103 Rm D113 Florham Park NJ 07932

BREIDENBACH, CHERIE ELIZABETH, lawyer; b. Aberdeen, S.D., Aug. 20, 1952; d. Neil Allen and Portia Elizabeth (Bradner) Johnson; m. Steven Theodore Breidenbach, Aug. 9, 1975. BS, U. S.D., 1975, JD, 1979. Bar: S.D. 1979, Calif. 1981; CPA, Calif. Sole practice La Jolla, Calif., 1982-84; assoc., acct. Law Offices of Larry Siegel, San Diego, 1984-86; ptnr. Fout, Breidenbach & Chin, San Diego, 1986-88, Rose, Munns & Fout, Coronado, Calif., 1988—. Mem. ABA, Calif. Bar Assn., S.D. Bar Assn., Phi Delta Phi. Republican. Methodist.

BREINER, AVISHAI, engineer, educator; b. Haifa, Israel, Mar. 15, 1952; s. Ephraim Breiner and Miryam (Shpitz) Berlovite; m. Shoshana Katz, Mar. 27, 1973; 1 child, Omer. BS, Technion-Israel Inst. Tech., Haifa, 1977, MS, 1982, DSc, 1987. Research engr. dept. research and devel. Technion-Israel Inst. Tech., 1977-81, instr. indsl. engring., 1983-87, lectr., 1987—; researcher policy analysis Neaman Inst., Haifa, 1982—; mem. com. on electricity forecasts Ministry Energy, Jerusalem, 1985-86, mem. com. on electricity generation, 1987; cons. Israel Chems., Ltd., Tel-Aviv, 1983-84. Contbr. articles and papers to profl. publs. Served to sgt. Israel Army, 1970-73. Mem. Operation Research Soc. Israel. Office: Technion-Israel Inst Tech, Indsl Engring and Mgmt Dept, Technion City, Haifa 32000, Israel

BREININ, GOODWIN M., physician; b. N.Y.C., Dec. 10, 1918; s. Louis and Mary (Mirsky) B.; m. Rose-Helen Kopelman, June 22, 1947; children: Bartley James, Constance. B.S., U. Fla., 1939, A.M., Emory U., 1940, M.D., 1943. Diplomate Am. Bd. Ophthalmology (dir., vice chmn., cons.). Intern U.S. Marine Hosp., Stapleton, N.Y., 1944; resident ophthalmology N.Y. U.-Bellevue Med. Center, 1947-51, sr. Heed fellow ophthalmology, 1954, Daniel B. Kirby prof. research ophthalmology, 1958, Daniel B. Kirby prof., chmn. dept. ophthalmology, 1959—, chmn. med. bd., 1975-77; dir. eye service Bellevue and U. Hosps., N.Y.C., 1959—; chmn. vision research tng. com. Nat. Insts. Neurol. Diseases and Blindness, 1963-64; chief cons. Manhattan VA Hosp.; cons. Manhattan Eye, Ear and Throat, St. Vincent's, Beth Israel hosps., N.Y. Eye and Ear Infirmary, Lenox Hills Hosp.; surg. gen. USPHS; chmn. Nat. Res. Rev. Com., 1976-77; vis. prof., cons. Hailie Selassie I Univ. Found., 1972; lectr. Mem. various adv. coms. relating to field, mem. med. adv. bd. Nat. Council to Combat Blindness; pres. Council for U.S./USSR Health Exchange, 1977; mem. Am. com. Internat. Agy. for Prevention of Blindness, 1980—; pres. 2d Internat. Symposium in Visual Optics, Tucson, 1982. Author: The Electrophysiology of Extraocular Muscle, 1962; editor: Advances in Diagnostic Visual Optics, 1983; mem. editorial bd. Investigative Ophthalmology, Archives of Ophthalmology; Contbr. articles to profl. jours. Served as capt., M.C. AUS, 1944-46. Recipient Knapp Medal for contbn. ophthalmology A.M.A., 1957; Edward Lorenzo Holmes lectr. citation and award for contbns. to med. sci. Inst. Medicine Chgo., 1959; Gifford lectr. and award Chgo. Ophthal. Soc., 1970; Heed Ophthalmic Found. award, 1968; Wright lectr. U. Toronto, 1972; Lloyd lectr. Bklyn. Opthal. Soc., 1971; May lectr. N.Y. Acad. Medicine, 1974. Fellow Am. Acad. Ophthalmology and Otolaryngology (v.p. 1979), A.C.S., N.Y. Acad. Medicine (sec. sect. ophthalmology 1962-63, chmn. sect. 1967-68); mem. AMA (sec. sect. on ophthalmology 1966-69, chmn. 1970-71), Research Ophthalmology, Am. Ophthal. Soc., N.Y. Ophthal. Soc. (pres. 1980), Harvey Soc., AAAS, Am. Commn. for Optics and Visual Physiology (chmn. 1970—), Am. Orthoptic Council, Assn. Univ. Profs. Ophthalmology, Pan. Am. Assn. Ophthalmology, Sigma Xi, Alpha Omega Alpha. Clubs: Cosmos (Washington); Grolier, Century Assn., Practitioners, Charaka (N.Y.C.). Home: 912 Fifth Ave New York NY 10021 Office: 550 1st Ave New York NY 10016

BREITBART, BARBARA RENEE, research institute executive, psychologist, editor; b. N.Y.C., July 2, 1935; d. Bernard John and Sally Etta (Horwitz) Garson; m. Sheldon Lewis Breitbart, Mar. 16, 1954; children—Stacey Jana, Kevin Harrison. A.B., Syracuse U., 1973; M.A., Adelphi U., 1975, Ph.D., 1978. Lic. psychologist, N.Y. Pres. Research Inst. Psychophysiology, Inc., N.Y.C., 1982—; cons. on wellness; editor Who's Who in the Biobehavioral Scis., N.Y.C., 1984—; columnist, lectr. on behavioral medicine and psychophysiology, 1978—; guest on radio talk shows; psychophysiological therapist, N.Y., 1978—. Mem. Am. Psychol. Assn., Biofeedback Soc. Am., Eastern Psychol. Assn., N.Y. Acad. Sci., Am. Acad. Arts and Scis. Avocations: chess, classical music, tennis. Office: Research Inst of Psychophysiology 2 Park Ave New York NY 10016

BREITBARTH, S. ROBERT, manufacturing company executive; b. Newark, N.J., July 15, 1925; s. Jacob and Rose (Brandman) B.; m. Laurel Patricia Stroh, Oct. 30, 1949; children: Meredith Jane, Jill Gretchen. B.E.E., Cornell U., 1949. Vice pres. Gen. Cable Corp., Greenwich, Conn., 1966-77; exec. v.p. Gen. Cable Corp., 1976-78; pres. Gen. Cable Internat., Inc., 1978-85, also dir.; v.p. GK Technologies, Inc., 1979-82; pres. Waterbury (Conn.) Wire Inc., 1987—, also bd. dirs.; bd. dirs. Bankest Capital Corp., Miami. Treas. Stony Point Assn., Westport, Conn., 1973-75, pres., 1975-76. Served with USAAF, 1944-46. Mem. Council of Americas (mem. adv. bd.), U.S. Investment in Spain Com. (chmn. 1977-80), Spain-U.S. C. of C. (bd. dirs.), Wire Assn., IEEE, Cornell Soc. Engrs., Center for Inter-Am. Relations. Home: 2 Stony Point Westport CT 06880

BREIVIK, HARALD PETTER, anesthesiology educator; b. Ålesund, Norway, May 30, 1940; s. Peder and Kjellaug (Hellesylt) B.; m. Ellen Gerd Berge; children: Else, Øyvind, Anders. MD, U. Oslo, 1965, PhD, 1972. Asst. prof. anesthesiology U. Oslo, 1973-77; prof., chmn. dept anesthesiology U. Oslo, Nat. Hosp., 1984—, U. Trondheim, Norway, 1977-84. Served as lt. Norwegian Navy, 1969-71. Intensive care medicine and anesthesiology fellow U. Pitts., 1971-73. Mem. Internat. Assn. for Study of Pain (councillor). Office: Nat Hosp Dept Anesthesiology, Pilestredet 32, N-0027 Oslo 1 Norway

BREKLE, HERBERT ERNST, linguist, educator; b. Stuttgart, Fed. Republic Germany, June 11, 1935; s. Ernst and Maria (Kuhfuss) B.; m. Jutta Wagner, May 9, 1961 (dec. 1981); children: Barbara, Mathias. Dr Phil., U. Tubingen, 1963, Habilitation, 1969. Asst. prof. linguistics U. Tubingen, Fed. Republic Germany, 1963-69; prof. linguistics U. Regensburg, Fed. Republic Germany, 1969, chmn. dept., 1969—. Author: Semantik, 1974, Satzsemantik, 1976, Geschichte der Sprachwissenschaft, 1985; editor: Grammatica Universalis, 20 vols., 1966-88. Mem. Regensburg City Council, 1972-78, Regional Council Oberpfalz, 1978-82; pres. Bund Naturschutz, Regensburg, 1977-85. Mem. Deutsche Gesellschaft fur Sprachwissenschaft (sec. 1978-79, v.p. 1983-84, pres. 1984-86). Mem. Sozialdemokratische Partei Deutschlands. Home: Spessartstrasse 17A, D-8400 Regensburg Federal Republic of Germany Office: U Regensburg, Universitatsstrasse 31, D-8400 Regensburg Federal Republic of Germany

BREMER, DONALD DUANE, school administrator; b. Sioux City, Iowa, June 19, 1934; s. Donald Forbes and Irma Marjorie (Schaller) B.; m. Carol Louise Rankin, May 3, 1955; children—Douglas Duane, Robert Alan, Kevin Ray. B.A., Nebr. State U., 1958; M.A. sch. adminstr., Los Angeles State U., 1962; postgrad., U. Iowa, 1966, U. Calif., Riverside, 1967. Cert. tchr., Calif. Math. tchr. Chino Unified Sch. Dist., Calif., 1958-66; tchr. Chaffey Jr. Coll., Alta Loma, Calif., 1961-63; prin. summer sch., Chino Schs., 1966-67; vice prin. Ramona Jr. High Sch., Chino, 1967-77; prin. Boys Republic High Sch., Chino, 1978—, chmn. accreditation com., 1981-82. Com. chmn., asst. cubmaster Mt. Baldy council Boy Scouts Am., 1966-68. Grantee NSF, 1964. Served with U.S. Army, 1954-56. Mem. NEA, Calif. Tchrs. Assn., Assn. Calif. Sch. Adminstrs., Chino Adminstrs. Assn. (treas. 1971-73, pres. 1973-74, Am. Legion, Chino C. of C., Republican Senatorial Com. Club: Toastmasters. Lodges: Rotary Internat., Masons, Elks. Home: 12183 Dunlap Pl Chino CA 91710 Office: Boys Republic High Sch Chino CA 91709

BREMER, JOHN PAUL, management consultant; b. St. Louis, Apr. 11, 1926; s. Jesse Currier and Eunice Sibylla (Schaus) B.; student U. Ill., 1946-47, U. Lausanne, 1947-48, Sorbonne, Paris, 1948; M.B.A., U. Chgo., 1955. Sales, tech. rep. IBM Corp., Washington, 1955-58; sr. data processing cons. Vaule & Co., Providence, 1958-63; co-founder, pres. Systemation, Inc., Boston, 1963-71; sr. cons., mgr. Mgmt. Cons. Group, Keane Assos., Wellesley, Mass., 1971-74; pres. Bremer Assos., Inc., Boston, 1974—. Bd. dirs. Concert Opera Co., Boston. Served with AUS, 1944-46. Lutheran. Clubs: Charles River Yacht, University (Boston), Algonquin. Home: 191 Commonwealth Ave Boston MA 02116 Office: 575 Boylston St Boston MA 02116

BREMNER, JAMES GAVIN, educator; b. Rhu, Scotland, June 27, 1949; s. James Arthur and Bertha (McQuat) B.; m. Margaret Ellen Lucking; children: Andrew John, Edward James. BSc, St. Andrew's U., Scotland, 1974; D in Philosophy, Oxford U., England, 1978. Lectr. psychology U. Lancaster, Eng., 1977—. Author: Infancy, 1988; editor Infant Development, 1988. Grantee Social Sci. Research Council, 1979-82, Econ. and Social Research Council, 1988—, Lancaster U. Research Found., 1984-85. Fellow Brit. Psychol. Soc. (hon. sec. devel. sect. 1987—). Mem. Labour party. Mem. Ch. of Scotland. Home: 9 Belle Vue Terrace, Lancaster LA1 4TY, England Office: U Lancaster Dept Psychology, Bailrigg, Lancaster LA1 4TF, England

BREMOND, ANDRE SERGE, insurance broker; b. El Jadida, Morrocco, May 29, 1934; came to France, 1953; s. Albert and Rose (Levy) B.; m. Nadia Hachuel, June 28, 1958; children—Dominique Sandra, Pierre Francois (dec. 1971), Stephanie Vanessa. Diplome de l'Ecole des Hautes Etudes Commerciales, Paris, 1956; Licencie en Droit, Faculte de Droit, Paris, 1956; Diplome de l'Institut d'Etudes Politiques, Paris, 1959; diplome Centre d'Etudes Superieures de Banque, Paris, 1959. Officer Banque Nat. Paris, 1957-63; mng. dir. Moyse Lowndes Lambert, Paris, 1963-81, Franchelli et Louvet, Paris, 1981—; dir. Groupement Europeen de Souscription, Paris, 1984. Served to under lt. Med. Corps, French Army, 1960-62. Mem. Rassemblement pour la Republique. Avocations: tennis; swimming. Home: 1 Allée des Robichons, La Celle Saint Cloud 78170, France Office: Franchelli et Louvet, 7/13 Rue de Bucharest, 75008 Paris France

BREMOND, HENRY PELLAT, investor; b. Paris, France, Nov. 30, 1927; s. Pierre Bremond Pons and Marcelle (Martel) Pellat; m. Martha Santacruz, Sept. 13, 1952; children: Madeleine, Michele, Henri. Student, St. Louis Gonzague, Paris, 1947, Capitan de Barco, Mex., 1957. Chmn. El Puerto de Liverpool S.A., Mexico City, 1960—, Hotel Guadalajara--Carlton, Grupo Polaris S.A. de C.V., Mexico City, 1961—, Liceo Franco Mexicano, A.C. Instituto Tecnologico, A.C. Recipient Chevalier de la Legión d'Honneur, France, Officier des Palmes Academiques, France. Mem. Internat. Capitulo Mexicano C. of C., Fundación Mexicana para la Salud. Roman Catholic. Clubs: Banquer's of Mex., Yacht France, Industriales Jalisco, Yates de Acapulco. Home: 2289 Paseo Reforma, Mexico City 11020, Mexico Office: 755 Palmas, Mexico City Mexico

BREMS, HANS JULIUS, economist, educator; b. Viborg, Denmark, Oct. 16, 1915; s. Holger and Andrea (Golditz) B.; m. Ulla Constance Simoni, May 20, 1944; children: Lisa, Marianne, Karen Joyce. Cand. polit., U. Copenhagen, 1941, dr. polit., 1950; Hedersdoktor (hon.), Svenska Handelshögskolan, Helsinki, Finland, 1970. Asst. prof. U. Copenhagen, 1943-51; lectr. U. Calif., Berkeley, 1951-54; mem. faculty U. Ill., Champaign-Urbana, 1954-86; prof. U. Ill., 1955-86; vis. prof. U. Calif., Berkeley, 1959, Harvard U., 1960, U. Kiel, (W.Ger.), 1961, U. Colo., 1963, U. Göttingen, (W.Ger.), 1964, U. Hamburg, (W.Ger.), 1967, U. Uppsala, (Sweden), 1968, U. Stockholm, 1980, U. Zurich, 1983, others. Author: Product Equilibrium under Monopolistic Competition, 1951, Output, Employment, Capital, and Growth, 1959, 2d edit., 1973, Quantitative Economic Theory, 1968, Labor, Capital, and Growth, 1973, Inflation, Interest, and Growth—A Synthesis, 1980, Dynamische Makrotheorie—Inflation, Zins und Wachstum, 1980, Fiscal Theory Government, Inflation and Growth, 1983, Pioneering Economic Theory, 1630-1980, A Mathematical Restatement, 1986; contbr.: articles to profl. jours. and Ency. Americana. Rockefeller fellow, 1946-47; Fulbright prof., 1961, 64. Mem. Am. Econ. Assn., Royal Econ. Soc., Danish Acad. Scis. and Letters (fgn.). Home: 1103 S Douglas Ave Urbana IL 61801 Office: U Ill Dept Econs 330 Commerce Bldg W Box 111 1206 S Sixth St Champaign IL 61820

BREMSER, GEORGE, JR., manufacturing company executive; b. Newark, May 26, 1928; s. George and Virginia (Christian) B.; m. Marie Sundman, June 21, 1952 (div. July 1979); children: Christian Fredrick II, Priscilla Suzanne, Martha Anne, Sarah Elizabeth; m. Nancy Kay Woods, Oct. 27, 1983. BA, Yale U., 1949; postgrad., U. Miami, 1959; MBA, NYU, 1962. With McCann-Erickson Inc., N.Y.C., 1952-61; asst. gen. mgr. McCann-Erickson Inc., Bogota, Columbia, 1955, gen. mgr., 1955-57; account supr. McCann-Erickson Inc., N.Y.C., 1958; v.p., mgr. McCann-Erickson Inc., Miami, Fla., 1959-61; with Gen. Foods Corp., White Plains, N.Y., 1961-71; v.p., gen. mgr. internat. div. Gen. Foods Europe, White Plains, N.Y., 1967; pres. Gen. Foods Internat., White Plains, 1967-71; group v.p. Gen. Foods Corp., White Plains, 1970-71; chmn., pres., chief exec. officer Texstar Corp., Grand Prairie, Tex., 1971-81; exec. v.p. Shaklee Corp., San Francisco, 1981-82; chmn., pres., chief exec. officer Etak Inc., Menlo Park, Calif., 1983—; bd. dirs. Butler Internat. Inc., PBI Industries Inc. Trustee Union Ch., Bogota, 1956-57; Dem. county committeeman, Ridgewood, N.J., 1962-63; mem. New Canaan (Conn.) Town Council, 1969-73; founder, past pres. Citizens Com. for Conservation, New Canaan. Served to 2d lt. USMC 1950-52, capt. Res. Mem. Phi Beta Kappa, Beta Gamma Sigma, Beta Theta Pi. Congregationalist. Clubs: New Canaan Country; Brook, Metropolitan, Yale (N.Y.C.); Block Island; Casino (Nantucket, R.I.). Home: 215 Chestnut St San Francisco CA 94133 also: Mansion Beach Rd Block Island RI 02807 Office: 1455 Adams Dr Menlo Park CA 94025

BRENDEL, ALFRED, concert pianist; b. Wiesenberg, Austria, Jan. 5, 1931; s. Albert and Ida (Wieltschnig) B.; m. Iris Heymann-Gonzala, 1960 (div. 1972); m. Irene Semler, 1975; 1 son, 3 daus. Studied piano under Sofija Dezelic, Zagreb, Yugoslavia; under Ludovika V. Kaan, Graz, Austria; under Edwin Fischer, Lucerne, Switerland; under Paul Baumgartner, Basel, Switzerland; under Edward Steuermann, Salzburg, Austria; studied composition under A. Michl, Graz, Austria; studied harmony under Franjo Dugan, Zagreb; D.Mus. hon., U. London, 1978; D.Litt. hon., Sussex U., 1981; D.Mus. (hon.), Oxford U., 1983. First piano recital, Graz, 1948, concert tours through, Europe, Latin Am., N. Am., 1963—, Australia, 1963, 66, 69, 76, appeared at many music festivals including Salzburg, 1960—, Vienna, Edinburg, Aldeburgh, Athens, Granada, P.R.; has performed with most of major orchs. of Europe and U.S., also others; performed all Beethoven piano sonatas in concert cycle, Paris, London, Berlin, Amsterdam, Vienna, Hamburg, Basel, Dusseldorf, Freiburg, Vevey, N.Y.C., 1983; recorded complete piano works of Beethoven, Schubert's piano works of 1822-28; complete piano concertos of Mozart Works of Hayden, Liszt; author: Musical Thoughts and After-thoughts, 1976, 2d edit., 1982; contbr. essays on music to profl. jours. Recipient Premio Citta de Bolzano Concorso Busoni, 1949; recipient Grand Prix du Disque, 1965, 84, Edison prize, 1973, 84, 87, Grand Prix des Disquaires de France, 1975, Deutscher Schallplatenpreis, 1976, 77, Wiener Flotenuhr, 1976, 77, 79, 82, 84, 87, Gramaphone award, 1978, 80, 82, 84, Japanese Grand Prix, 1978, Franz Liszt prize, 1980, 82, 83, Frankfurt Music award 1984. Mem. Royal Acad. Music (hon.), Comdr. des Arts et Letters. Office: care Colbert Artists Mgmt Inc 111 W 57th St New York NY 10019 also: care Ingpen & Williams, 14 Kensington Court, London W8, England *

BRENDEL, THOMAS CHRISTIAN, consulting mechanical engineer; b. Vienna, Austria, Sept. 16, 1945; s. Hubert and Christiane (Kobé) B.; m. Angelika Maria Thamm, Apr. 24, 1981 (div. May 1984); 1 child, Nicholas. Diploma Engring., Tech. U., Darmstadt, Fed. Republic Germany, 1969, Dr. rer Polit., 1975. Engr. Deutsche Lufthansa AG, Frankfurt, Fed. Republic Germany, 1969-70; exec., engr. Ing. Büro Brendal & Güttler, Frankfurt, 1972-75; pres. SWD Software Design GmbH, Frankfurt, 1976-84; prin. IDB Dr. Brendel Cons. Engring., Frankfurt, 1985—; cons. Commn. European Countries, Brussels, 1972—, Ministry Research and Tech., Bonn Fed. Republic Germany; examining expert C. of C. and Industry, Darmstadt, 1981—. Author: Qualitatsrecht, 1976; contbr. articles to tech. jours. Deutsche Forschungs Gemeinschaft, 1970-72. Mem. ASHRAE, Verband Beratender Ingenieure. Avocations: bridge, music, tennis, sailing. Office: Ingenieurbüro Dr. Brendel Cons Engring, Reichsforststrasse 20, D-6000 Frankfurt Federal Republic of Germany

BRENIERE, JEAN-CLAUDE, marketing executive; b. Pont-St-Vincent, France, Aug. 10, 1943; s. Lucien and Alice (Picard) B.; m. Annelies Van Der Matten, Dec. 19, 1969; children: Stephan, Laurene. Degree in bus. mgmt., U. Bordeaux, France, 1966. Sales trainee films div. Deutsch Goodyear GmbH, Cologne, Fed. Republic Germany, 1971-72; area mgr. Paris, 1972-75; mgr. films div. Phillipsburg, Fed. Republic Germany, 1975-85, mktg. mgr. Europe, 1985—. Served to 1st lt. French Air Force, 1968-69. Home: Raimundstrasse 3, 6839 Oberhausen Federal Republic of Germany

BRENNAN, BERNARD FRANCIS, retail chain store executive; b. Chgo., 1938; married. B.A., Coll. St. Thomas, 1964. With Sears, Roebuck & Co., Chgo., 1964-76; with Sav-A-Stop, Inc., 1976-82, group v.p.-service mdse. group, 1976-78, pres., chief operating officer, 1978-79, pres., chief exec. officer, 1979-82, chmn., 1982; exec. v.p. Montgomery Ward & Co., Inc., Chgo., 1982-83, pres., chief exec. officer, 1985—; pres. Household Merchandising Inc., Des Plaines, Ill., 1983-85. Served with U.S. Army, 1958-60, 62. Office: Montgomery Ward & Co Inc 1 Montgomery Ward Plaza Chicago IL 60671 *

BRENNAN, CIARAN BRENDAN, accountant, independent oil producer; b. Dublin, Ireland, Jan. 28, 1944; s. Sean and Mary (Stone) B. BA with honors, Univ. Coll., Dublin, 1966; MBA, Harvard U., 1973; MS in Acctg., U. Houston, 1976. Auditor Coopers & Lybrand, London, 1967-70; sr. auditor Price Waterhouse & Co., Toronto, Ont., Can., 1970-71; project acctg. specialist Kerr-McGee Corp., Oklahoma City, 1976-80; controller Cummings Oil Co., Oklahoma City, 1980-82; chief fin. officer Red Stone Energies, Ltd., 1982, Hibernia Oil Inc., 1980—; treas., chief fin. officer Leonoco, Inc., 1982-87, JKJ Supply Co., 1983-87, Saturn Investments Inc., 1983-87, JFL Co., 1984-87, Little Chief Drilling & Energy Inc., 1984-85; chief fin. officer St. Regis Resources Corp., Culver City, Calif., 1988—; pres. Ciaran Brennan Corp., 1980—; bd. dirs., cons. small oil cos.; adj. faculty Okla. City U., 1977-86; vis. faculty Cen. State U., 1977-86. Contbr. articles to profl. jours. Mem. Inst. Chartered Accts. England and Wales, Inst. Chartered Accts. Can., Inst. Chartered Accts. in Ireland, Am. Inst. CPA's, Tex. Soc. CPA's, Okla. Soc. CPA's. Republican. Roman Catholic.

BRENNAN, HENRY HIGGINSON, architect; b. Chgo., Nov. 25, 1932; s. Henry D. and Ann (Higginson) B.; m. Margaret Butler, 1960; children—Jennifer Margaret, Henry Higginson Jr., Kathryn Ann, Martin Timothy. B.Arch., U. Ill., 1958. Registered architect in 12 states. Draftsman, Westchester Constrn., White Plains, N.Y., 1958-59; job capt. Ketchum & Sharp, N.Y.C., 1959-61, project architect, dir. prodn., 1961-73; sr. v.p., dir. N.Y. office Welton Becket, 1973-84; ptnr. Brennan Beer Gorman/Architects, 1984—. Prin. works include master plan and design of maj. office bldgs., hotels, retail and mixed-use complexes. Mem. AIA. Clubs: Union League (N.Y.C.); Apawamis (Rye, N.Y.). Office: Brennan Beer Gorman Architects 515 Madison Ave New York NY 10022

BRENNAN, JAMES THOMAS, radiologist; b. St. Louis, Jan. 12, 1916; s. James Thomas and Ellen Loretta (Hayes) B.; children by previous marriage: Martha Ellen, James Thomas; m. Elizabeth Bast Gagné, Aug. 23, 1975; stepchildren: William Roderick, Philip Bast, Elizabeth Lower. B.A. in Philosophy, U. Ill., 1939; M.D., U. Minn., 1943; M.A. (hon.), U. Pa., 1972. Diplomate Am. Bd. Radiology. Commd. 1st lt., M.C. AUS, 1943; advanced through grades to col. U.S. Army, 1959; intern St. Mary's Group Hosps., St. Louis, 1943; bn. surgeon 101st Airborne div., Europe, 1944-45; engaged in radiation hazard control and radiobiology research Los Alamos Labs., 1948-52; chief biophysics dept. Walter Reed Army Inst. Research, 1952-54; resident radiology Walter Reed Army Hosp., 1954-57; cons. radiol. def. to chief surgeon U.S. Army, Europe, 1957-60; chief radiation therapy Walter Reed Gen. Hosp., 1960-61; dir. Armed Forces Radiobiology Research Inst., 1961-66; ret. 1966; vis. lectr. radiology U. Pa. Med. Sch., Phila., 1966-67; Matthew J. Wilson prof. research radiology U. Pa. Med. Sch., 1967-78, prof. emeritus, 1968—; cons. in field, 1965—. Decorated Bronze Star, Legion of Merit, D.S.M. Mem. Radiol. Soc. N.Am., AMA, AAUP, AAAS. Home: 1211 East Butler Pike Ambler PA 19002

BRENNAN, MICHAEL JOSEPH, marketing executive; b. Waterford, Ireland, Mar. 20, 1950; s. James Joseph and Bridget (O'Gorman) B.; children: Alison Bridget, nicolas James; m. Eileen Marie Brennan, Apr. 14, 1979. MA, Dublin U., Ireland, 1973. Asst. audit mgr. Unilever, Merseyside, Eng., 1973-75; mktg. advisor Irish Export Bd., Dublin, Ireland, 1975-76, Brussels, 1976-78; mgr. engring. Irish Export Bd., Dublin, 1978-82; mgr. Irish Export Bd., Amsterdam, The Netherlands, 1982-86; mgr. Benelux Lithographic Universal, Brussels, Belgium, 1986-87; mktg. mgr. Waterford Crystal Europe, Brussels, Belgium, 1987—; cons. EEC, Brussels, 1983-85. Mem. Irish Mgmt. Inst., Irish Mktg. Inst., Trade Devel. Inst. Ireland (founding mem.). Home: Memlingdreef 69, 1900 Overijse Belgium Office: Waterford Crystal, Leuvensesteenweg 326, 1940 Saint Stevens Belgium

BRENNAN, PAUL JOSEPH, civil engineer, educator; b. Auburn, N.Y., June 29, 1920; s. William Henry and Hannah Frances (Murphy) B.; m. Virginia Ann Burns, Sept. 8, 1951; children: Patricia Ann., Margaret Mary, Maureen Ellen, William Henry II, Elizabeth Ann, Kathleen Ann, John Robert, Nancy Eileen, Virginia Ann, Mary Eileen. B of Archtl. Engring. cum laude, U. Detroit, 1943; MCE, Yale U., 1944, DEng in Civil Engring., 1951. Registered profl. engr., N.Y., Conn. Asst. prof. civil engring. Yale U., New Haven, 1948-53; prof. U. Del., Newark, 1953-58, chmn. dept. civil engring., 1953-58, chmn. dept. engring. mechanics, 1957-58, dir. hwy. research program, 1953-58; prof., chmn. dept. civil engring. Syracuse (N.Y.) U., 1958-74, David Rutty prof. engring., 1974—, assoc. dean for research and grad. affairs coll. engring., 1988—; cons. in field; bd. dirs. Mt. St. James

Corp., Syracuse. Contbr. articles to profl. jours. Chmn. planning bd. and zoning commn. Town of Onondaga, N.Y., 1962-86. Served to lt. (j.g.) USN, 1944-46. Mem. ASCE, Transp. Research Bd., Tau Beta Pi, Sigma Xi, Alpha Sigma Nu, Chi Epsilon, Phi Kappa Phi. Roman Catholic. Home: 4243 Wolf Hollow Rd Syracuse NY 13219 Office: Syracuse U 232 Hinds Hall Dept Civil Engring Syracuse NY 13244

BRENNAN, T. CASEY, writer; b. Port Huron, Mich., Aug. 11, 1948; s. William James and Mildred Alice (Goodrich) B. Free-lance writer Avoca, Mich., 1969—. Leader of campaign to ban smoking portrayals in comic books and other children's pubs. Subject hon. resolution Mich. State Legislature, 1987. Democrat. Roman Catholic. Home: 4238 Bricker Rd Avoca MI 48006-9615 Office: care Neil Staebler 202 E Washington #308 Ann Arbor MI 48104-2121

BRENNAN, THOMAS JOHN, city official, consultant, educator; b. Bklyn., Mar. 23, 1923; s. Thomas Joseph and Violet Emma (Jurgens) B.; m. Margaret Karen Jensen, Sept. 18, 1948; children—Debra Gail, Mark Kevin, Laurie Kathleen. A.B., Wittenberg Coll., 1949; M.G.A., Fels Inst. of Local and State Govt., Wharton Grad. Sch., 1950. Dep. sec. for adminstrn. Dept. Welfare, Commonwealth Pa., Harrisburg, 1957-59, dep. sec. for state properties Pa. Dept. Property and Supplies, 1959-64; exec. officer Del. Dept. Mental Health, Dover, 1965-67; v.p. Exec. Mgmt. Service, Arlington, Va., 1967-76; exec. dir. Gov.'s Justice Commn. and Pa. Commn. on Juvenile Delinquency, 1976-79; dir. water utility City of New Brunswick, N.J., 1983—; adj. assoc. prof. Rider Coll., Lawrenceville, N.J., 1983-84, 84-85; hearing officer N.J. Dept. Civil Service, Trenton, 1976—, cons. exam. constrn., 1985; cons. to staff com. UN, 1982-84; cons. various municipalities and agys.; presenter papers to profl. orgns. Bd. dirs. Bucks County Opera, Pa., 1975-80, Bucks County Play House, New Hope, Pa., 1970s; active mem. Bucks County Hist. Soc., Doylestown, Pa., 1983—, Merrill's Marauders. Decorated Silver Star, Bronze Star with oak leaf cluster, Combat Infantry badge; recipient various plaques; Fels scholar U. Pa., 1948. Mem. Internat. Personnel Mgmt. Assn., Am. Pub. Works Assn. (dist. rep. Eastern Pa. bldg. and grounds com.), Am. Water Works Assn., Internat. Chiefs of Police Assn., Nat. Conf. State Justice Planning Adminstrn. (regional chmn., mem. exec. com.), Criminal Justice Tng. Inst. (chmn. planning com. 1978, 79). Club: Huntington Valley Hunt (Bucks County) (bd. dirs. 1975-80), Wharton Alumni (Phila.), U. Pa. Faculty. Lodge: Fraternal Order of Police. Avocations: fox hunting; pleasure riding. Home: 327 Pineville Rd Newtown PA 18940 Office: Water Dept City of New Brunswick New Brunswick NJ 08901

BRENNEMAN, HUGH WARREN, JR., federal magistrate; b. Lansing, Mich., July 4, 1945; s. Hugh Warren and Irma June (Redman) B.; m. Katrina Cup Kindel, Apr. 30, 1977; children: Justin Scott, Ross Edward. B.A., Alma Coll., 1967; J.D., U. Mich., 1970. Bar: Mich. 1970, D.C. 1975, U.S. Dist. Ct. (we. dist.) Mich. 1974, U.S. Dist. Ct. Md. 1973, U.S. Ct. Mil. Appeals 1971, U.S. Ct. Appeals (6th cir.) 1976, U.S. Ct. Appeals (D.C. cir.) 1981, U.S. Supreme Ct. 1980. Law clk. Mich. 30th Jud. Cir., Lansing, 1970-71; asst. U.S. atty. Dept. Justice, Grand Rapids, Mich., 1974-77; assoc. Bergstrom, Slykhouse & Shaw, P.C., Grand Rapids, 1977-80; U.S. magistrate U.S. Dist. Ct. (we. dist.) Mich., Grand Rapids, 1980—. Mem. exec. bd. West Michigan Shores council Boy Scouts Am., 1984-87, adv. council, 1987—. Served to capt. JAGC, U.S. Army, 1971-74. Mem. State Bar Mich. (rep. assembly 1984—), D.C. Bar, Fed. Bar Assn. (pres. Western Mich. chpt. 1979-80, nat. del. 1980-84), Grand Rapids Bar Assn. (chmn. U.S. Constn. Bicentennial com.), Nat. Council U.S. Magistrates, ABA, Phi Delta Phi, Omicron Delta Kappa. Congregationalist. Clubs: Peninsular, Rotary (dir., pres.), Econ. of Grand Rapids (past dir.). Office: 580 Fed Bldg Grand Rapids MI 49503

BRENNEN, STEPHEN ALFRED, international business consultant; b. N.Y.C., July 7; s. Theodore and Margaret (Pembroke) B.; m. Yolanda Alicia Romero, Sept. 28, 1957; children—Stephen Robert, Richard Patrick. A.B. cum laude, U. Americas, Mexico City, 1956; M.B.A., U. Chgo., 1959. Supr. Montgomery Ward, Chgo., 1956; credit mgr. Aldens, Chgo., 1956-59; gen. mgr. Purina de Guatemala, 1964-66; pres. Purina Colombiana, Bogotá, 1967-69, Living Marine Resources, Inc., San Diego, 1969-70; mng. dir. Central and S. Am. Ralston Purina, Caracas, Venezuela, Coral Gabels, Fla., 1970-74; pres. Van Camp Seafood Co., San Diego, 1974-79; chmn. P.S.C. Corp., Buena Park, Calif., 1979-81; pres. Inter-Am. Cons. Group, San Diego, 1981-85; chmn. Beta Enterprises Inc., 1986—. Author: Successfully Yours. Mem. adv. bd. Mexican-Am. Found. Served with USAF. Mem. Am. Soc. Profl. Cons. Republican. Roman Catholic. Club: U. Chgo. in San Diego (past pres.).

BRENNEN, WILLIAM ELBERT, management consultant; b. Mo., Sept. 30, 1930; s. William E. and Frances (Andrew) B.; m. Natalia Summers, Nov. 14, 1958 (div. 1979); children: William, Natalia Jane, Elizabeth; m. Sharon Russell, Aug. 8, 1987. BS, U.S. Mcht. Marine Acad., 1952; MBA, U. Chgo., 1961. Ship's officer, traffic and ops. mgr. States Marine Lines Inc., Korea and Japan, 1952-61; with Case & Co./Stevenson Jordan & Harrison, Inc. Mgmt. Cons., Chgo. and N.Y.C., 1961-68; dir. internat. materials mgmt. Internat. Minerals & Chems., Skokie, Ill., 1968-71, Abbott Labs., North Chicago, Ill., 1971-73; pres. W.E. Brennen Cons., Inc. (name changed to Brennen Cons. Inc. 1987), 1978-88—. Mgmt. Cons. South Bend, Ind., Evanston, Ill., 1973-88; v.p., mng. prin. Fry Cons., 1982—. Served to lt. USNR, 1953-55. Mem. Am. Mktg. Assn. (pres. Chgo. chpt. 1982-83), Bus. Mktg. Council, Mktg. News editorial rev. bd., Mgmt. Inst. Assn. Cons., South Bend/Mishawaka C. of C., Elkhart C. of C. Episcopalian. Office: 300 N Michigan South Bend IN 46601

BRENNER, EDGAR H., lawyer; b. N.Y.C., Jan. 4, 1930; s. Louis and Bertha B. (Guttman) B.; m. Janet Maybin, Aug. 4, 1979; children from previous marriage—Charles S., David M., Paul R. B.A., Carleton Coll., 1951; J.D., Yale U., 1954. Bar: D.C. 1954, U.S. Ct. Claims 1957, U.S. Supreme Ct. 1957. Mem. 2d Hoover Commn. Legal Task Force, Washington, 1954; trial atty. U.S. Dept. Justice, Washington, 1954-57; assoc. Arnold & Porter, Washington, 1957-62, ptnr., 1962—. Contbr. articles to profl. jours. Commr. Fairfax County Econ. Devel. Corp., Va., 1963-78; v.p., bd. dirs. Stella and Charles Guttman Found., N.Y.C. Mem. ABA (chmn. arbitration com. litigation sect. 1984-87), D.C. Bar Assn. Democrat. Clubs: Yale, Explorers (N.Y.C.). Home: PO Box 145 Route 1 Washington VA 22747 Office: Arnold & Porter 1200 New Hampshire Ave NW Washington DC 20036

BRENNER, EDWARD JOHN, lawyer; b. Wisconsin Rapids, Wis., June 26, 1923; s. Edward Charles and Lillian (Hephner) B.; m. Jane Segrest, June 1, 1951; children: Beverly, Douglas, Carolyn, Mary. B.S. in Chem. Engring, U. Wis., 1947, M.S., 1948, J.D., 1950. Bar: Wis. bar 1950, D.C. bar 1970, Va. bar 1971. Chem. engr. Esso Standard Oil Co., 1950-53; with Esso Research and Engring. Co., 1953-64, asst. dir. legal div., 1960-64; U.S. commr. patents 1964-69; v.p., asst. to pres. Gen. Instrument Corp., 1969-70; pvt. practice patent law Arlington, Va., 1970—. Served with U.S. Army, 1944-46. Mem. Am., Wis., Va. bar assns., Bar Assn. D.C., Am., N.J. patent law assns., Am. Chem. Soc. Home: 4 Ocean Dr Punta Gorda FL 33950 Office: 4 Ocean Dr Punta Gorda FL 33950

BRENNER, GÜNTER, jurist; b. Mainz, Fed. Republic of Germany, Feb. 27, 1928; s. Jakob and Louise (Stulz) B.; m. Ruth Höhle, 1964; children: Björn, Lutz. Studium der Rechtswissenschaften, Soziologie und Philosophie, U. Frankfurt und Mainz, Fed. Republic of Germany; Dr. jur., U. Frankfurt, Fed. Republic of Germany, 1956. Juristisches Assessorexamen, 1958. Wissenschaftlicher Asst. u. Syndikus; Generalsekretär der Akademie der Wissenschaften und der Literatur, Mainz; Geschäftsführer der Konferenz der Akademien der Wissenschaften der Bundesrepublik Deutschland. Lehrbücher und Veröffentlichungen in Fachzeitschriften zu Naturrecht und politischer Ordnung, Medizin und Recht. Kirchliche und kulturelle Vereinigungen. Home: Am Marienpfad 3, 6500 Mainz Federal Republic of Germany Office: Akademie der Wissenschaften, Geschwister Scholl Strasse 2, 6500 Mainz Federal Republic of Germany

BRENNER, MARSHALL LEIB, lawyer; b. N.Y.C., Aug. 8, 1933; s. Samuel and Ruth (Novak) B.; m. Gwen A. Krakower, Aug. 9, 1959; children: Scott David, Louri Ann, Robin Lynn. BA, St Lawrence U., Canton, N.Y., 1955; JD, Bklyn. Law Sch., 1959. Bar: N.Y. 1960, U.S. Dist. Ct. (no. and ea. dists.) N.Y. 1960, U.S. Ct. Claims 1964, U.S. Supreme Ct. 1964, U.S. Dist. Ct. (so. dist.) N.Y. 1969. Assoc. Spitz & Levine, Poughkeepsie, N.Y., 1960-62; sr. ptnr. Brenner, Gordon & Lane, Poughkeepsie, 1977—; chief appeals sect. Dutchess County Pub. Defenders Office, Poughkeepsie, 1966-78; tchr. law Marks Realtors/Appraisors, Poughkeepsie and Fishkill, N.Y., 1968-72, Robert-Mark Realtors, Hopewell Junction, N.Y., 1979—; lectr. Dutchess County Realty Bd. for Sales/Broker Lic. Applicants, 1985—. Contbr. articles to profl. jours. Pres., bd. dirs. Sloper-Willen Community Ambulance, Wappingers Falls, N.Y., 1966-79; bd. dirs. Poughkeepsie Jewish Community Ctr., 1980-82. Served to capt. U.S. Army, 1956-63. Mem. N.Y. State Bar Assn., Dutchess County Bar Assn., N.Y. State Trial Lawyers Assn. Republican. Jewish. Clubs: Harding (Poughkeepsie) (pres. 1968-69); County Players (Wappingers Falls) (bd. dirs. 1963-74). Lodges: Masons, Rotary (pres. 1973-74, 78-79, Govs. Trophy 1978). Home: 30 Robin Rd Poughkeepsie NY 12601 Office: Brenner Gordon & Lane 35 Market St Poughkeepsie NY 12601

BRENNER, THEODOR EDUARD, academic administrator; b. Zurich, Switzerland, May 9, 1942; s. Eduard and Wally Frieda (Thiele) B.; m. Vivienne Frances Shaw, June 11, 1966; children: Benedikt Eduard, Tristan Mark. Diploma, Kantonale Handelsschule, Zurich, 1962; LHD (hon.), Pace U., 1986. Dir. summer programs Am. Sch. Switzerland, Montagnola, 1963-65; dir. Inst. for European Studies Fleming Coll., Lugano, Switzerland, 1967-69; adminstrv. dean Franklin Coll., Lugano, 1970-78, pres., 1979—. Contbr. articles to profl. jours. Apptd. rep. Consiglio Comunale, Novaggio, Switzerland, 1976-80; mem. Am. Swiss Assn., Inc., N.Y.C., 1985—. Mem. Assn. Internat. Colls. and Univs. (v.p. 1984—), Swiss-Am. C. of C. (mem. steering com. Ticino chpt. 1987—). Republican. Club: Canottieri (Lugano). Lodge: Lions (charter). Office: Franklin Coll, Via Ponte Tresa 29, 6924 Sorengo, Lugano Switzerland

BRENNER, YEHOJACHIN SIMON, economics educator; b. Dec. 24, 1926; s. Albert and Rosel (Hilb) B.; m. Nancy Golomb; children: Eliezer, Yael. MA, Hebrew U., Jerusalem, 1956. Lectr. in econs. U. Meryland, Eng., 1961-62; sr. lectr. in econs. U. Cape Coast, Ghana, 1962-67; prof. econs. Inst. Social Studies, The Netherlands, 1967-69, Middle East Tech. U., Ankara, Turkey, 1969-72, U. Utrecht, The Netherlands, 1972—; cons. Orgn. for Econ. Cooperation and Devel., Turkey, 1969-72. Author: Theories of Economic Development and Growth, 1966, Looking into the Seeds of Time, 1979, Capitalism, Competition and Economic Crisis, 1984. Served with Israeli mil., 1948-49. Mem. History of Econs. Soc. (exec. 1986—). Home: Mozartlaan 23, 3723 JL Bilthoven The Netherlands Office: U Utrecht, Heidelberglaan 1, 3508 TC Utrecht The Netherlands

BRENNWALD, JURG WERNER, surgeon; b. Zurich, Switzerland, Dec. 8, 1940; s. Hermann and Martha (Moth) B.; children: Andreas, Lukas. M.D., U. Zurich, 1969; Private Dozent, U. Basel, 1983; F.M.H. Surgery, Med. Sch. Basel, 1979. Research fellow Swiss Research Inst., Davos, Switzerland, 1963-72; resident Hosp. Davos, 1969-72; resident U. Hosp., Basel, Switzerland, 1972-74, head miscrosurgery dept., 1978, Oberarzt hand surgery dept., 1980—; cons. Assn. for Study Internal Fixation, Bern, 1982—. Contbr. med. articles to profl. jours. Served to cpl. Arty., Swiss Army. Mem. European Soc. Surg. Research, Am. Soc. Surgery of the Hand, Internat. Soc. Surgery, Schweizerische Gesellschaft für Chirurgie der Hand, Internat. Soc. Reconstructive Microsurgery, Verbindung Schweizer Arzte, Zurcher Hochschulverein, Schweizerische Gesellschaft für Unfallmedizin und Berufskrankheiten, Schweizerische Gesellschaft fur Chirurgie, Deutschsprachige Arbeitsgemeinschaft fur Handchirugie. Freisinnig. Club: Zurcher Segel (Zurich); Modellfluggruppe (Oberwil). Avocations: swimming; cross country skiing. Office: Lab Expermental Surgery, Swiss Research Inst, CH-7270 Daros Switzerland

BRENOT, PHILIPPE-HENRI, psychiatrist, anthropologist; b. Bordeaux, France, May 6, 1948; s. Jean-Pierre and Jacqueline (Laclide) B.; m. Beatrice Marie Bessieres; children: Eleonore, Bastien. MA, U. Bordeaux, 1974, MD, 1975, spl. studies in indsl. medicine, 1976, spl. studies in gen. linguistics, 1976, cert. in human ecology, 1977, spl. studies in psychiatry, 1980, PhD in Anthropology, 1982. Hosp. cons. Pellegrin Hosp., Bordeaux, 1975—; intern various psychiat. hosps. Gironde, 1976-80; lectr. U. Bordeaux, 1982—. Author: (poetry) Mots sans Faim, 1985, Les Mots du Corps, 1987, Les Mots du Sexe, 1988; contbr. numerous articles in anthropology to profl. jours. Recipient design award for space sta. European Space Agy., 1985, Silver medal City of Bordeaux, 1986. Mem. Anthrop. Soc. Paris, Inter-Teaching Hosp. Assn. Sexology, Union Scientifique d' Aquitaine (vice chmn. 1986), Société Internationale d'Ecologie Humanie (chmn. 1984). Roman Catholic. Home: 2 rue de Marseille, 33000 Bordeaux France Office: Centre Vital-Carles, 38 rue Vital-Carles, 33000 Bordeaux France

BRENT, PAUL LESLIE, educator; b. Douglass, Okla., July 3, 1916; s. Paul Leslie and Ruth (McKee) B.; m. Aledo Render, May 29, 1938; children: Carolyn J., Paul Richard; m. E. Ferne McCoy, Nov. 19, 1984. BS, Central State U., 1938; MEd, U. Okla., 1949, EdD, 1959. Tchr. math. and sci. public schs. Adair, Okla., 1938-40; prin. Alden Public Schs., Carnegie, Okla., 1940-43; supt. Alden Public Schs., 1950-58; tchr. public schs. Cooperton, Okla., 1946-47; prin. high sch., public schs. Washita, Okla., 1947-48; supt. 1948-50; asst. prof. Calif. State U., Long Beach, 1959-63, assoc. prof. edn., 1963-72, asst. to chmn. div. edn., 1961-67, prof. instructional media, 1972-86, coordinator graphics support sect. dept. mech. engring., 1981-86; mem. Baptist Edn. Study Task, 1966-67; trustee Calif. Bapt. Coll., 1969-74. Co-Author: Point, Line, Plane and Solid, 1984. Served with USNR, 1943-46. Mem. Calif. Faculty Assn. (pres. elect), NEA, Calif. Media and Library Educators Assn., Am. Assn. Sch. Adminstrs., Congress of Faculty Assns., Phi Delta Kappa, Kappa Delta Pi, Phi Kappa Phi, Phi Beta Delta. Democrat. Baptist. Home: 11112 Bos Pl Cerritos CA 90701 Office: 1250 Bellflower Blvd Long Beach CA 90840

BRENTANI, PAOLO GIORGIO, metallurgical engineer; b. Trieste, Italy, Aug. 9, 1929; arrived in Brazil 1938, naturalized 1983; s. Ottone and Margherita (Goldberger) B.; m. Beatriz Souza Aguiar, 1958. CE, Mackenzie U., São Paulo, Brazil, 1954, EE, 1958, Degree econs., 1970, MetE, 1975; BMA, FGV, 1961. Archivist Banco Federal Crédito, São Paulo, 1949; engr. Arno S.A., São Paulo, 1954-56, sales engr., 1956-57, purchasing mgr., 1957-61, supply mgr., 1961-76; supply mgr. Metal Leve S.A., São Paulo, 1976—. Mem. Assn. Brasileira do Aluminio (bd. dirs. 1975—), Assn. Brasileira do Cobre, Assn. Brasileira de Fundicão, Conselho Regional de Engenharia e Arquitetura, Soc. Harmonia de Têis (bd. dirs. 1978-85), Brazil-Canadá C. of C. (bd. dirs. 1976—). Club: Harmonia; C.P.T. (São Paulo). Home: Rua Para 241 Apt 82, 01243 Sao Paulo Brazil Office: Metal Leve SA, Rua Brasilio Lux 535, 04746 Sao Paulo Brazil

BRESCIA, ANTHONY JOSEPH, federal agency administrator; b. Jersey City, Sept. 26, 1950; s. Anthony Joseph and Josephine (Russo) B.; m. Donna Mae Kremers, Apr. 5, 1974; children: Anthony Joseph, Brandon Michael. AA, Coll. of Sequoias, 1972; student, Calif. State U., Fresno, 1975-78; cert. in mgmt. devel., Ariz. State U., 1982. Supr. U.S. Postal Service, Hanford, Calif., 1973-78; sta. mgr. U.S. Postal Service, Bakersfield, Calif., 1978-80; mgr. stations and brs. U.S. Postal Service, Phoenix, 1980-83; dir. customer services U.S. Postal Service, Fresno, Calif., 1983-88, dir. city ops., 1988—. Bd. dirs. Woodward Park Homeowner Assn., Fresno, 1985—. Served with USN, 1968-72. Mem. Fed. Exec. Assn., Am. Legion, U.S. Jaycees (external dir. 1975-76). Republican. Roman Catholic. Office: US Postal Service 1900 E St Fresno CA 93706-9996

BRESEE, WILMER EDGAR, department store executive; b. Oneonta, N.Y., May 8, 1910; s. Lynn Harmon and Mary (White) B.; m. Esther Bartow, Aug. 14, 1935. B.A., Hamilton Coll., 1931; postgrad. NYU, 1932; L.H.D., Hamilton Coll., 1981. Buyer, dept. head Bresee's Oneonta Dept. Store (N.Y.), 1932-43, advt. mgr., 1932-43, mdse. mgr., dir. 1945-67, pres., 1967-73, chmn. bd., 1973—; chmn. bd. Preferred Mut. Ins. Co., New Berlin; sec., dir. Chestnut & Dietz Land Co. Oneonta, 1932—. Author: Along Masonic Trails, 1961; Trails from the East South and West, 1963; Masonic Trails of Early New York State, 1984. Mem. Civil Service Commn., Oneonta, 1935-36; mem. Bd. Pub. Safety, Oneonta, 1936-40; trustee Hartwick Coll., 1978-87. Served with U.S Army, 1943-46. Mem. Phi Beta Kappa, Eta Mu Pi. Republican. Methodist. Lodges: Rotary (pres. 1950; Paul Harris fellow 1973), Elks, Masons. Home: 160 East St Oneonta NY 13820 Office: Bresees Oneonta Dept Store 155-165 Main St Oneonta NY 13820

BRESSER PEREIRA, LUIZ CARLOS, government official; b. Sao Paulo, Brazil, 1934. MBA, Mich. State U., 1961; D. of Econs., U. Sao Paulo, 1972. Prof. bus. adminstrn. Getulio Vargas Found., 1959-66, with dept. econs., 1966-73, prof., 1973; adminstrv. dir. Pao de Acúcar Group, 1963-83; pres. Sao Paulo State Bank, 1983; sec. of state Sao Paulo, 1985-87; minister of fin. Govt. of Brazil, 1987; vis. prof. U. Paris Sorbonne, 1977. editor Jour. of Polit. Economy, 1981—; author: (books) Crisis and Development in Brazil 1930-67, 1968, Technobureaucracy and Contention, 1972, Businessmen and Administration in Brazil, 1974, The State and Industrialized Undevelopment, 1977, The Collapse of a Class Alliance, 1978, The State Society and the Technobureaucracy, 1981, Inflation and Recession, 1984, Political Pacts, 1985. Mem. Brazilian Ctr. Analysis and Research. Office: Ministry of Fin, Brasilia Brazil *

BRESSLER, RICHARD MAIN, railroad executive; b. Wayne, Nebr., Oct. 8, 1930; s. John T. and Helen (Main) B.; m. Dianne G. Pearson, Apr. 17, 1981; children: Kristin M., Alan L. B.A., Dartmouth Coll., 1952. With Gen. Electric Co., 1952-68; v.p., treas. Am. Airlines Inc., 1968-72, sr. v.p., 1972-73; v.p. finance Atlantic Richfield Co., Los Angeles, 1973-75, sr. v.p. fin., 1975-77; pres. Arco Chem. Co., 1977-78, exec. v.p., 1978-80; pres., chief exec. officer, dir. Burlington No., Inc., St. Paul, 1980—; chmn. Burlington No., Inc., Seattle, 1982—; dir. Baker Internat., El Paso Co., Seafirst Corp., Honeywell Inc., Gen. Mills, Inc.; trustee Penn Mut. Life Ins. Co. Office: Burlington No Inc 999 3d Ave Seattle WA 98104 *

BRESSON, ROBERT, film producer and director; b. Bromont-Lamothe, Sept. 25, 1901; s. Leon and Marie-Elizabeth (Clausels) B.; m. Leidia Van der Zee, Dec. 21, 1926 (dec.); m. Marie-Madeleine vander Mersch, Dec. 14, 1979. Student Lycee Lakanal a Sceaux. Started as painter; made 1st film, 1934; films produced and directed include: Anges du Peche, 1943, Les Dames du Bois de Boulogne, 1945, Journal d'un Cure de Campagne, 1951, Un Condomne a Mort s'est echappe, 1956, Pickpocket, 1959, Le Proces de Jeanne d'Arc, 1962, Lancelot du Lac, 1965, Au Hasard, Balthasar, 1966, Mouchette, 1966, A Gentle Creature, 1969, Quatre nuits d'un rêveur, 1971, le Diable Probablement, 1977, L'Argent, 1983 (Grand Prix Cannes Film Festival 1983). Decorated officier Legion d'Honneur, comdr. des Artes et Lettres, grand officier de l'Ordre National du Merite; recipient Grand Prix du cinema francais, 1943, 51, Prix Louis Oelluc, 1950. Grand Prix internat. de la Biennale de Venice, 1951, Grand Prix du film d'avant garde, 1950, Prix du meillieur film de l'annee for Pickpocket, 1959, Prix spl. du jury Cannes Festival for Jeanne d'Arc, 1960; spl. mention 1966 Venice Film Festival and Panama Festival for Au hasard Balthasar, Grand Prix Nat. des Arts et des Lettres, 1978. Mem. Soc. French Producers (hon. pres. 1968), Soc. Film Dirs. (hon. pres. 1968). Address: 49 Quai de Bourbon, F-75004 Paris France *

BREST VAN KEMPEN, GUSTAAF F., architect; b. Jakarta, Indonesia, Apr. 11, 1939; came to U.S., 1954; s. Carel Pieter and Maria Herbertina (Jakobs) Brest van K.; m. Helen Dorothy Burn, Dec. 26, 1969; children: Gillian Ann Charlotte, Katherine Elisabeth. BArch, U. Pa., 1964. Registered profl. architect, Ill. Architect U.S. Peace Corps, Tunis, Tunisia, 1964-66; from asst. to assoc. prof. architecture U. Utah, Salt Lake City, 1966-70, 71-75; resident project mgr. Skidmore, Owings and Merrill, Algiers, Algeria, 1976-78; project mgr., assoc. Skidmore, Owings and Merrill, Chgo., 1978-83; architect, prin. Evanston, 1983—; design cons., Salt Lake City, 1966-75; visiting prof. architecture U. Tunis, 1970-71; cons. Perkins & Will Internat., Chgo., 1983; cons. The World Bank, Algeria, Haiti, Jamaica, Morocco, Tunisia, Yemen Arab Republic, 1985—. Chief editor Utah Architect, 1973-75. JGB adv. council Chgo. Symphony Orchestra, 1980—; bd. dirs. Evanton Symphony Orchestra, 1988—. Benjamin Franklin nat. scholar U. Pa., 1964; NEA grantee, 1986-87; Council for Internat. Exchange of Scholars Fulbright Research grantee, 1985-86. Mem. AIA.

BRETH, HARRIS GEORGE, industrial consultant; b. Clearfield, Pa., Apr. 8, 1905; s. Joseph Ambrose and Clara (Hammond) B.; student Temple U., 1925, U. Pa., 1926-28; m. Mary Katherine Hall, Oct. 26, 1940; 1 son, Harris George. Operator, Harris G. Breth advt. and pub. relations agy., Clearfield, Pa., 1929-38; outdoor editor Pitts. Sun-Telegraph, 1939-57; radio commentator KDKA, Pitts., 1940-57; pres. radio sta. WNCC, Barnesboro, Pa., 1949-57; pres. Outdoor Adventurers, Inc., Brookville, Pa., 1957—; exec. sec. Clearfield C. of C., exec. dir. Clearfield Found., 1962-82; pres. Audio-Video-Arts, Inc., Pitts., 1965—; mem. Pa. Ho. of Rep., 1940-42, 1947-62, chmn. conservation com., mem. rules com., 1955-60, chmn. Joint State Govt. Commn., 1961-62; editor Pa. Sportsman's Digest, Clearfield, 1941-43. Sec. com. All-Am. City, Clearfield, 1966-68; mem. County Indsl. Devel. Authority; commr. Clearfield County, 1972-80; chmn. 16 County Water Mgmt. Com., 1978-80. Mem. Screen Actors Guild, AFTRA, Outdoor Writers Assn., Am. Wildlife Soc., Pa. Indsl. Devel. Execs. Roman Catholic Lodges: Moose, Elks, K.C. Home: 830 Ogden Ave Clearfield PA 16830 Office: Box 459 Clearfield PA 16830

BRETT, (PETER) JEREMY (WILLIAM HUGGINS), actor; b. Nov. 3, 1935; s. H.W. and Elizabeth Huggins; m. 1958 (divorced); 1 son; m. 1978; 1 son. Student, Central Sch. of Drama, Eton, Eng. With Nat. Theatre, 1967-71. Performances include (plays) As You Like It, Love's Labour's Lost, Hedda Gabler, The Merchant of Venice, Macrune's Guevara, Voyage round my Father, Haymarket, Eng., 1972, Design for Living, Phoenix, 1973-74, The Way of the World, Stratford, Ont., 1976, The Tempest, Toronto, 1982, Martha Graham ballet, N.Y.C., 1985, Aren't We All, Broadway, 1985; (films) War and Peace, 1955, My Fair Lady, 1965; (TV) Rebecca, 1978, On Approval, 1980, The Good Soldier, 1981, Macbeth the Last Visitor, 1982, The Barretts of Wimpole Street, 1982, William Pitt the Younger, 1983, The Adventures of Sherlock Holmes, 1984, The Return of Sherlock Holmes, 1986, Florence Nightingale, 1986, Deceptions, 1986. Club: Woodmen of Arden. Office: 9538 Brighton Way Suite 322 Beverly Hills CA 90210 *

BRETT, RICHARD JOHN, speech pathologist; b. Chgo., Sept. 5, 1921; s. Richard J. and Emily (Salter) B.; BEd, No. Ill. State Tchrs. Coll., 1943; MS, U. Ill., 1947; student U. Amsterdam (Holland), 1949, U. Chgo., 1948-49, 62, 66-67, Northwestern U., 1967. Speech supr. Summer Residential Clinic, U. Ill., Urbana, 1948, 50, 52; speech pathologist Waukegan (Ill.) High Schs., 1946—; chmn. Chgo. Regional Interviewing Com. for Exchange of Tchrs., U.S. Info. Agy., 1962-86; del. to Internat. Fedn. of Free Tchr. Unions, Switzerland, 1953. Founder, Pub. Sch. Caucus, Chgo., 1973, chmn., 1973-76. Served with U.S. Army, 1943-45. Fellow Am. Speech-Lang.-Hearing Assn. (membership com. 1975-77, conv. program com. 1974, 77, internat. affairs com. 1987—, mem. congl. affairs network 1988—); mem. Ill. Speech and Hearing Assn. (chmn. legis. com. 1964-65, treas. 1977-78, v.p. bus. affairs 1978-79), Internat. Council Exceptional Children (pres. Chgo. suburban chpt. 1949-50), Am. (co-chmn. internat. relations com. 1952-63), Ill. (chmn. profl. standards com. 1952-57), Lake County (pres. 1949-51, 64-67) fedns. tchrs., U.S.-China Peoples Friendship Assn. (v.p. Chgo. chpt. 1987—), UN Assn., Mus. Contemporary Art, ACLU, Common Cause, Art Inst. Chgo., Chgo. Symphony Soc. Club: National Travel. Compiler: World Study and Travel for Teachers, 1952-85; editor Five-O-Format, 1951-56, 66-69. Home: 616 4th St Waukegan IL 60085 Office: Waukegan East High Sch 1101 Washington St Waukegan IL 60085

BRETT-MAJOR, LIN, lawyer; b. N.Y.C., Sept. 21, 1943; d. B.L. and Edith H. Brett; children from previous marriage: Dania S., David M. BA, U. Mich., 1965; JD cum laude, Nova Law Ctr., 1978. Bar: Fla. 1978, U.S. Dist. Ct. (so. dist.) Fla. 1978, U.S. Ct. Appeals (5th and 11th cirs.) 1981, U.S. Tax Ct. 1981, U.S. Dist. Ct. (middle and no. dists.) Fla. 1982, U.S. Supreme Ct. 1984, U.S. Dist. Ct. (mid., no. dists.). Internat. communications asst. Mitsui and Co., Ltd., N.Y.C., 1962; with dept. pub. relations and devel. St. Rita's Hosp., Lima, Ohio, 1965-66; reporter The Lima News, 1969-70; intern U.S. Atty.'s Office, Miami, 1977; sole practice Ft. Lauderdale, Fla., 1980—; participant Gov.'s Conf. on World Trade, Mia and Jacksonville, Fla., 1984—; speaker Bus. Owners Conf., Hollywood, Fla., 1986, Nova U. Law Ctr. 1988, ABA Nat. Conv., Toronto, 1988. Mem. Ft. Lauderdale Opera Soc., 1985—, Ft. Lauderdale Mus. of Art, 1985—. Recipient Silver Key award ABA, 1977. Mem. Assn. Trial Lawyers Am., Fed. Bar Assn., Fla. Bar Assn., Broward County Bar Assn., Univ. Mich. Alumni Assn., U. Mich. Gold

Coast Alumni Assn. (pres. 1988—). Club: Propeller of U.S. (Port Everglades, Fla.) (nat. del. 1981—). Office: Galleria Profl Bldg 915 Middle River Dr Fort Lauderdale FL 33304

BRETZFIELD, HENRY, retired government official; b. N.Y.C., Dec. 3, 1912; s. George Ruggles and Sophia (Greenberg) B.; m. Anita Maurer, Apr. 27, 1957; children—Anne Sophia, Jane Elizabeth. B.A., Cornell U., 1934. Account exec., v.p. Lawrence Fertig & Co., Inc., N.Y.C., 1934-62; v.p. Lennen & Newell, Inc., N.Y.C., 1962-64; dir. Prescription Hearing, Rye, N.Y., 1964-68; head publs. br. Dept. Edn., HEW, Washington, 1968-80; head publs. Office Legis. and Pub. Affairs, U.S. Dept. Edn., Washington, 1980-84, dir. editorial policy div., 1984-88. Author: Liquor Marketing and Liquor Advertising, 1955. Pulitzer scholar Columbia U., 1930. Mem. Phi Beta Kappa, Phi Kappa Phi. Clubs: Nat. Press, Cornell (Washington). Home: 10501 Grove Ridge Pl Rockville MD 20852

BREUER, STEPHEN ERNEST, temple executive; b. Vienna, Austria, July 14, 1936; s. John Howard and Olga Marion (Haar) B.; came to U.S., 1938, naturalized, 1945; BA cum laude, UCLA, 1959, gen. secondary credential, 1960; m. Gail Fern Breitbart, Sept. 4, 1960 (div. 1986); children—Jared Noah, Rachel Elise; m. Nadine Bendit, Sept. 25, 1988. Tchr. pub. high schs., Los Angeles, 1960-62; dir. Wilshire Blvd. Temple Camps, Los Angeles, 1962-88; exec. dir. Wilshire Blvd. Temple, 1980—; dir. Edgar F. Magnin Religious Sch., Los Angeles, 1970-80. Instr. edn. Hebrew Union Coll., Los Angeles, 1965-76; field instr. San Francisco State U., 1970-80, Calif. State U., San Diego, Hebrew Union Coll., 1977-81. Vice pres. Los Angeles Youth Programs Inc., 1967-77; youth adviser Los Angeles County Commn. Human Relations, 1969-72. Bd. dirs. Community Relations Conf. So. Calif., 1965-85, Union Am. Hebrew Congregations; bd. dirs. Alzheimer's Disease and Related Disorders Assn., 1984—, v.p. Los Angeles County chpt., 1984-86, pres., 1986-88, nat. bd. regional rep 1987—, Calif. state chpt. pres. 1988—; mem. goals program City of Beverly Hills, Calif., 1985-86; bd. dirs. Echo Found., Wilshire Stakeholders, treas. Wilshire Community Prayer Alliance; active United Way. Recipient Service awards Los Angeles YWCA, 1974, Los Angeles County Bd. Suprs., 1982, 87, Ventura County Bd. Suprs., 1982, 87, Weinberg Chai Achievement award Jewish Fed. Council Los Angeles, 1986. Mem. So. Calif. Camping Assn. (dir. 1964-82), Nat. Assn. Temple Adminstrs., Nat. Assn. Temple Educators (nat. bd. mem. 1987—), Los Angeles Assn. Jewish Edn. (dir.), Profl. Assn. Temple Adminstrs. (pres. 1985-88), Assn. Supervision and Curriculum Devel., Am. Mgmt. Assn., So. Calif. Conf. Jewish Communal Workers, Jewish Profl. Network, Amnesty Internat., Jewish Resident Camping Assn. (pres. 1976-82), UCLA Alumni Assn., Wilderness Soc., Center for Environ. Edn., Wildlife Fedn., Los Angeles Countyt Mus. Contemporary Art, People for the Am. Way, Assn. Reform Zionists Am., Union of Am. Hebrew Congregations (bd. dirs. Pacific SW region). Office: Wilshire Blvd Temple 3663 Wilshire Blvd Los Angeles CA 90010

BREVIGNON, JEAN-PIERRE, research and development manager, physicist; b. St. Leu la Foret, France, Feb. 18, 1948; s. Andre Louis and Claudie Marie (Lemarchand) B.; m. Beatrice B. Arbis, Jan. 28, 1984; children: Thomas J., Eleonore M. D in Physics, Paris VII U., 1976. Process engr. Companie Internationale pour l'Informatique, Orsay, France, 1975-77, Thomson Sescosem, Orsay, 1977-79; devel. sect. head Thomson Etude et Fabrication de Circuits Integres Speciaux, Grenoble, France, 1979-82; process devel. supr. Fairchild Semiconductor, San Jose, Calif., 1982-83; engring. mgr. Hyundai-Modern Electronics Inc., Santa Clara, Calif., 1983-84, Thomson Semiconducteur, Grenoble, 1984-86; research and devel. mgr. L'Air Liquide, Jouy-en-Josas, France, 1986-88; liaison officer electronics L'Air Liquide, Paris, 1988—. Patentee semiconductor processing. Mem. IEEE, Electrochem. Soc., Internat. Soc. Optical Engring., Inst. Environ. Sci. Home: 4 Rue des Tulipes, 78960 Voisins le Bretonneux France Office: L'Air Liquide, BP 126, 78350 Jouy-en-Josas France

BREWER, CHARLES MOULTON, lawyer; b. Washington, June 9, 1931; s. Charles M. and Monemia (Moulton) B.; m. Lavon Brown, June 14, 1958; children: Charles Robert, Lisa Ann, John Brian. B.A., U. Md., 1953; J.D., George Washington U., 1957. Bar: Ariz. 1959. Since practiced in Phoenix; law clk. to Chief Justice Ariz. Supreme Ct. Levi S. Udall, 1958-59; pvt. practice 1959—; pres. Charles M. Brewer Ltd.; guest lectr. Stanford U. Law Sch., Ariz. State U. Law Sch. (Charles M. Brewer professorship of trial advocacy established 1985). Contbr. articles to profl. jours. Bd. visitors Ariz. State U. Law Sch. Served as capt. (airline transport pilot) USAF, 1954-56. Mem. Am., Ariz., Maricopa County bar assns., Am. Judicature Soc., Am., Calif., Ariz., Tex. trial lawyers assns., Am. Bd. Trial Advs., Internat. Med. Soc. of Paraplegia. Office: 1400 First Interstate Bank Plaza Phoenix AZ 85003

BREWER, EDWARD CAGE, III, lawyer; b. Clarkdale, Miss., Jan. 20, 1953; s. William G. III and Elizabeth (Alford) Little; children: Katherine Martin, Julia Blair. BA, U. of South, 1975; JD, Vanderbilt U., 1979. Bar: Ala. 1980, U.S. Dist. Ct. (so. dist.) Ala. 1981, U.S. Ct. Appeals (5th and 11th cirs) 1981, Ga. 1982, U.S. Dist. Ct. (no. dist.) Ga. 1982, U.S. Ct. Appeals(3d and 8th cirs.) 1983. Law clk. to chief judge U.S. Dist. Ct. (so. dist.) Ala., Mobile, 1979-81; law clk. to judge U.S. Ct. Appeals (5th and 11th cirs.), Atlanta, 1981-82; assoc. Ford & Harrison, Atlanta, 1982-85, Smith, Gambrell & Russell, Atlanta, 1985—; coach moot ct. team Emory U., Atlanta, 1985. Contbr. articles to profl. jours. Mem. St. Philip's and Evensong Choirs, Cathedral of St. Philip, Atlanta, 1984—. Mem. ABA (labor and employment law sect., project editor com. on railway and labor law, 1984—), State Bar of Ga. (labor and employment, young lawyers sects., treas. internat. law com. 1985—), Phi Beta Kappa, Omicron Delta Kappa. Episcopalian. Home: 1435 Benning Pl NE Atlanta GA 30307 Office: Smith Gambrell & Russell 2400 1st Atlanta Tower Atlanta GA 30383

BREZILLON, CLAUDE LÉON, clothing executive; b. Fontenay, France, July 21, 1920; m. Jacqueline M. Desnos de Kerjean, Feb. 15, 1947; children: Thierry, Didier, Olivier. Grad., Ecole Supérieure de Commerce de Paris, 1940, Hautes Etudes Commerciales, Paris, 1941. Gen. sec. S.A. Haut Ogoué, Paris, 1948-49; mng. dir. S.A. Orgaminer, Casablanca, Morocco, 1950-54; mgr. adminstrn. and fin. S.A. Filtres Philippe, Paris, 1954-64; gen. mgr. S.A. Belle Jardinière, Paris, 1964-85; chmn. S.A. Pierre Balmain, Paris, 1986—. Editor Caravelle, 1945-47. Served to 1st lt. Cavalery French mil., 1943-47. Decorated Chevalier Legion of Honor, Croix de Guerre. Roman Catholic. Home: 9 ave Le Verrier, 75006 Paris France Office: SA Pierre Balmain, 44 rue François 1er, 75008 Paris France

BRICEL, MARK LEON, marketing executive; b. Ljubljana, Slovenia, Yugoslavia, Apr. 11, 1929; s. Ivan John and Ivanka (Kregar) B.; m. Liselotte Liane, Mar. 10, 1951; children: Gary, Tania. Student, Air Force Acad, Mostar, Yugoslavia, 1948, Nautical Acad., Rijeka, Yugoslavia, 1949. Lic. pvt. pilot. Supr. G.M. Plastic Corp., Granby, Quebec, Can., 1964-66; gen. sales mgr. G.M. Plastic Corp./GMP Sports Ltd., Granby, 1966-70, G.M.P. Sports, Inc., Westport, Conn., 1967-70; exec. v.p. House of Colonial Furniture Ltd., Montreal, 1970-75; gen. sales agt. Arcese Bros. Furniture Ltd., Missisauga, Ont., Can., 1976—; pres. M.L. Bricel Agys. Ltd., Missisauga, 1984—; dir. mktg. and sales Arcese Bros. Furniture Ltd., Mississauga, 1981—. Served to lt. Yugoslav Air Force, 1946-48. Recipient Silver Medal award FIS, 1947. Mem. Can. Owners and Pilots Assn., Royal Can. Flying Clubs Assn. (Blue Seal 1984). Roman Catholic. Club: Brampton Flying. Home: 2160 Stillmeadow Rd, Mississauga, ON Canada L5B 1X3 Office: Arcese Bros Furniture Ltd, 6124 Shawson Dr, Mississauga, ON Canada L5T 1E5

BRICKELL, CHARLES HENNESSEY, JR., marine engineer; b. Memphis, Apr. 13, 1935; s. Charles Hennessey and Mary Ellen (Viau) B.; m. Barbara Virginia Davis, Jan. 4, 1958; children: David Brian, Patricia Ellen, Susan Elizabeth, Timothy Paul, Joel Howard. BS in Marine Engring., U.S. Merchant Marine Acad., 1957; MA in Bus. Mgmt., Cen. Mich. U., 1980. Enlisted USNR, 1953, commd. ensign, 1957; advanced through grades to rear adm. USN, 1984; dir. research and devel. Undersea and Strategic Warfare, and Nuclear Energy, 1984-87; dir. USN Strategic Def. Initiative Program, 1984—; dep. dir. Navy Research Devel., Test and Evaluation, 1987—. Decorated Def. Superior Service Medal, Legion of Merit with two Gold Stars, Meritorious Service Medal with two Gold Stars. Roman Catholic. Home: 5503 Teak Ct Alexandria VA 22309 Office: Dept of Defense Navy Dept Research Dev & Test The Pentagon Washington DC 20350

BRICKHILL, JOHN ARTHUR, consulting company executive; b. Odenton, Md., Oct. 15, 1947; s. Arthur Joseph and Eloise (Gay) B.; children—Michael, David. B.A., U. Va., 1969; M.B.A., Am. U., 1972. Fin. analyst Foster Assocs., Inc., Washington, 1968—, exec. v.p., 1983—; cons. Allied Corp., Morristown, N.J., 1980—, Bishop Apeline, Tulsa, 1981—, Consol. Edison Co., N.Y.C., 1982—, Mark Producing Co., Houston, 1983—. Contbr. to profl. publs. Treas. Pinehurst Heights Civic Assn., Annandale, Va., 1976-78; soccer commr. Annandale Boy's Club, 1976-79. Mem. Soc. Petroleum Engrs., Am. Econ. Assn., Internat. Assn. Energy Economists. Home: 2019 Arlington Ridge Rd Arlington VA 22202 Office: Foster Assocs Inc 1101 17th St NW Washington DC 20036

BRICKNER, GERALD BERNARD, highway construction company executive; b. Minot, N.D., Dec. 6, 1938; s. Harry Jerome and Cathern Elizabeth (Doyle) B.; divorced; 1 child, Derek. BSCE, S.D. Sch. Mines and Tech., 1961. With Everetts & Assocs. Inc., Jamestown, N.D., 1958-65, owner, engr., 1965—. Served with U.S. Army, 1962-64. Mem. Associated Gen. Contractors. Republican. Roman Catholic. Lodge: Eagles. Home: 408 Holiday Park Jamestown ND 58401 Office: Everetts & Assocs Inc West End 5th St NW Jamestown ND 58402

BRIDE, JOHN WILLIAM, communications executive, entrepreneur; b. Boston, Sept. 12, 1937; s. William T. and Elsie Francis (Duffy) B.; m. Marjorie McHenry, May 13, 1966 (div. 1984); children: John Hambleton, Christopher McHenry; m. Mary Eileen Kiniry, Feb. 15, 1985. BA, in Econs., Norwich U., 1960; LLB, U. Maine, 1964; Owner/Pres. Mgmt. degree, Harvard Bus. Sch., 1980. staff atty. FCC, Washington, 1964-66; account exec. Sta. KDKA-TV, Pitts., 1966-70; pres. Bride Broadcasting, Inc., Portland, Maine, 1970-86, Chandler Broadcasting, Inc., 1970-86, Greater Portland Radio, Inc., 1972-86, B-T Satellite, 1980—, Triangle Properties, 1980-85, Bride Communications, Inc., 1980—, Portland Broadcast, Inc., 1987—; trustee John W. Duffy Trusts, Boston, 1978—. Mem. com. fgn. relations, Portland, 1976—; mem. adv. com. Back Cove Improvement Project, Portland, 1984—; mem. adv. bd. Lifeline U. So. Maine, Portland, 1983—; pres. Bride Charitable Found., Portland, 1978—; instr. Jr. Achievement, Portland, 1980; treas., bd. dirs. ABC Talkradio Affiliates, N.Y.C., 1983—. Served with U.S. Army, 1960-61. Mem. Maine Bar Assn. Democrat. Episcopalian. Clubs: Harvard Bus. (v.p. 1984—); Pitts. Golf. Avocation: triathlons. Home: 83 West St Portland ME 04102 Office: Bride Communications Inc 2320 Congress St Portland ME 04102-1908

BRIDGEFORD, MICHAEL ANGUS, engineering company executive; b. Liverpool, Eng., Dec. 17, 1943; s. Robert Angus Bridgeford and Honora Wood McGibbon; m. Carole Mary Bridgeford, Nov. 11, 1968; children: Samantha Louise, Tamara Robyn, Vanessa Gabrielle. BS in Mech. Engring, U. Witwatersrand, Johannesburg, Republic of South Africa, 1969; MBA, U. Cape Town, Johannesburg, Republic of South Africa, 1977. Registered profl. engr., Republic of South Africa. Engr. Gold Fields Mines, Carletonville, Republic South Africa, 1976-78; project mgr. Gold Fields So. Africa Ltd, Johannesburg, 1978-79; mktg. dir. Heat Exchangers Africa Ltd, Johannesburg, 1979-81; mng. dir. Tesco Tube & Flange, Johannesburg, 1981-84; prin. Bridgeford Engring., Johannesburg, 1985; mng. dir. Duncan Bayne Proprietary Ltd, Johannesburg, 1984-87; dist. mgr. Otis Elevator Co., Johannesburg, 1987—. Mem. South African Inst. Mech. Engrs., South African Inst. Minings Metallurgy, South African Inst. Mktg. Presbyterian. Clubs: Round Table (chmn. Carletonville chpt. 1975-76, treas. Johannesburg chpt. 1978). Home: 20 Hampton Court Rd, Gallo Manor, Johannesburg 2052, Republic of South Africa Office: Otis Elevator Ltd, PO Box 2729, Johannesburg 2000, Republic of South Africa

BRIDGES, PAUL KENNETH, psychiatrist, consultant; b. London, July 24, 1931; s. Albert Charles and Alice Elizabeth (Paul) B. B Medicine, Surgery, U. London, 1956, DPM, 1960, MD, 1965, PhD, 1969. Psychiat. registrar, research fellow Royal Free Hosp., London, 1960-63, sr. lectr., 1965-70; sr. psychiat. registrar Kings Coll. Hosp., London, 1963-65; cons. psychiatrist Guys Hosp., London, 1970—, Brook Gen. Hosp., London, 1970—; sr. lectr. Guy's Hosp. Med. Sch., U. London, 1970—; examiner med. degrees U. London, 1982-86; assessor Nat. Health and Med. Research Council Australia, 1984—. Author: Psychiatric Emergencies, 1971, (with others) Psychiatry for Students, 1988. Served to maj., M.C., Royal Army, 1957-60. Fellow Royal Coll. Psychiatrists, Royal Soc. Medicine (pres. sect. psychiatry 1983-84); fellow Brit. Assn. Psychopharmacology (hon. sec. 1981-83), Brit. Med. Assn. Club: Royal Automobile (London). Office: Guy's Hosp, London SE1 9RT, England

BRIDGEWATER, WALTER CLEVELAND, educator, guidance consultant, accountant; b. Scottsburg, Ind., Mar. 11, 1938; s. Walter Scott and Mabel Clarice (White) B. BA, Wabash Coll., 1960; MA, Ind. U., 1961; postgrad., Purdue U., 1967-69. Cert. English tchr., reading specialist, sch. counselor. Reading specialist Ind. U. Ctr. for Child Study, Bloomington, 1960-61; English tchr. Crawfordsville (Ind.) Community Schs., 1961-66, reading specialist, 1966-68, 69-71, guidance counselor, 1971-77; instr. English Purdue U., West Lafayette, Ind., 1968-69; reading specialist Indpls. Pub. Schs., 1977-78; adminstrv. asst to supt. Scott County Schs. Dist. 2, Scottsburg, 1978-87, dir. gifted, talented edn. program, 1983-85, in-service dir., 1983-87; acct. Peyron Assocs., Clarksville, Ind., 1987-88; dept. mgr. Montgomery Ward at Lafayette Sq., Indpls., 1988; instr. St. Catharine (Ky.) Coll., 1988—; vol. admissions cons. for 7 colls. and 2 prep schs.; liaison Nat. Inst. Edn. Contbr. articles to edn. jours. Active Boy Scouts Am., Crawfordville and Scottsburg, 1961-86; cert. lay speaker United Meth. Ch., So. Ind. Conf., 1973—. Hon. fellow Truman Library Inst. Internat. Affairs, Independence, Mo., 1968; recipient Dist. Award of Merit, Boy Scouts Am., New Albany, Ind., 1982. Mem. Nat. Edn. Assn. (life), Internat. Reading Assn., Ind. State Tchrs. Assn., Phi Delta Kappa (life, 2d v.p. 1982-83). Lodges: Optimists, Masons (chaplain local club 1968-69). Office: St Catharine Coll Hwy 150 Saint Catharine KY 40061 also: Montgomery Ward & Co 3919 Lafayette Rd Indianapolis IN 46254

BRIDGFORTH, ROBERT MOORE, JR., aerospace engineer; b. Lexington, Miss., Oct. 21, 1918; s. Robert Moore and Theresa (Holder) B.; student Miss. State Coll., 1935-37; B.S., Iowa State Coll., 1940; M.S., M.I.T., 1948; postgrad. Harvard U., 1949; m. Florence Jarnberg, November 7, 1943; children—Robert Moore, Alice Theresa. Asst. engr. Standard Oil Co., of Ohio, 1940; teaching fellow M.I.T., 1940-41, instr. chemistry, 1941-43, research asst., 1943-44, mem. staff div. indsl. cooperation, 1944-47; asso. prof. physics and chemistry Emory and Henry Coll., 1949-51; research engr. Boeing Airplane Co., Seattle, 1951-54, research specialist 1954-55, sr. group engr., 1955-58, chief propulsion systems sect. Systems Mgmt. Office, 1958-59, chief propulsion research unit, 1959-60; chmn. bd. Rocket Research Corp. (name now Rockcor, Inc.), 1960-69, Explosives Corp. Am., 1966-69. Fellow Brit. Interplanetary Soc., AIAA (asso.), Am. Inst. Chemists; mem. Am. Astronautical Soc. (dir.), AAAS, Am. Chem. Soc., Am. Rocket Soc. (pres. Pacific NW 1955), Am. Ordnance Assn., Am. Inst. Physics, Am. Assn. Physics Tchrs., Tissue Culture Assn., Reticuloendothelial Soc., N.Y. Acad. Scis., Combustion Inst., Sigma Xi. Home: 4325 87th Ave SE Mercer Island WA 98040

BRIEM, SIGURDUR, aluminum plant engineer; b. Reykjavik, Iceland, Aug. 25, 1936; s. Gunnlaugur and Halldora M. (Gudjohnsen) B.; m. Thora Gudrun Moeller, Aug. 30, 1969; children—Dora Kristin, Gunnar Jakob, Gunnlaugur Thor. Grad. Elec. Engring., Royal Inst. Tech., Sweden, 1962. Elec. engr. Reykjavik Elec. Power Works, Iceland, 1963-66; head dept. electricity Icelandic Aluminum Co. Ltd., Straumsvik, Iceland, 1967-80, head dept. electrolysis, 1981-84, plant engr., 1984—. Mem. Assn. Chartered Engrs. Iceland. Club: Rotary. Home: Markarflot 27, 210 Gardabaer Iceland Office: Icelandic Aluminum Co Ltd, PO Box 244, Straumsvik, 222 Hafnarfjordur Iceland

BRIERLEY, PETER WILLIAM, charitable foundation administrator; b. London, Oct. 30, 1938; s. Joseph Clifford and Anne Sophia (New) B.; m. Cherry Antoinette Goatman, Apr. 3, 1965; children: Stephen, Timothy, Kim, Michael. BSc in Stats., U. London, 1961, diploma in theology, 1964. Sci. officer War Office, London, 1961-62; tchr. Edn. Authority, Southampton, Eng., 1965-67; statistician Ministry of Def., London, 1967-70, Cabinet Office, London, 1970-78; program dir. Brit. Fgn. Bible Soc., London, 1978-83; European dir. MARC Europe, London, 1983—; chmn. SE Asian Outreach, Gravesend, Eng., 1985—; mem. fin. com. Evang. Union S.Am., London, 1970-82, Eng. and Wales aux. Leprosy Mission, London, 1970-76, Brit. Inst. Mgmt. Council, 1985—, mgmt. com. Evang. Missionary Alliance, 1983—, exec. com. 1985—, com. meetings, 1987—, Market Research Soc., 1978—. Author: Mission to London Phase I, II, 1984, 85; editor: U.K. Christian Handbook, 1972, 77, 81, 83, 85-86, 87-88, 89-90; compiler: Prospects for the Eighties Vols. 1, 2, 1980,83, Prospects for Wales, 1983, Prospects for Scotland, 1985, several MARC monographs, 1984—. Mem. Inst. Charity and Fundraising Mgrs. (steering com. 1982-83), Royal Statis. Soc. (social sect. 1980-82), Social Research Assn. (exec. com. 1979-82), Christian Booksellers Assn. (bd. dirs. 1984-88), Spinnaker Trust (council of reference 1987—). Mem. Ch. of Eng. Home: 58 Alexandra Crescent, Bromley BR1 4EX, England Office: MARC Europe, Cosmos House, 6 Homesdale Rd, Bromley BR2 9EX, England

BRIGGS, ANTHONY DAVID, educator; b. Sheffield, Eng., Mar. 4, 1938; s. Horace and Doris Lily (Peach) B.; m. Pamela Anne Metcalfe, July 28, 1962; children: Fiona, ANtonia, Julian. BA, U. Cambridge, Eng., 1961, MA, 1965; PhD, U. London, 1968. Lectr. Russian U., Bristol, England, 1969-74, lectr. in charge Russian, 1974-80, sr. lectr. in charge Russian, 1980-83, reader in Russian studies, 1984; William Evans vis. prof. U. Otago, New Zealand, 1985; prof. Russian lang. and Lit. U. Birmingham, Eng., 1987—. Author: Vladimir Mayakovsky: A Tragedy, 1979, Alexander Pushkin: A Critical Study, 1983. Home: Over Moreton Breach Hill Chew Stoke, Bristol BS18 84A, England Office: U Birmingham, Dept Russian Lang and Lit, PO Box 363, Birmingham B15 2 TT, England

BRIGGS, DONALD JOHN, sales and marketing executive; b. London, May 16, 1935; s. Leonard James and Edith Lilian (Adcock) B.; m. Janette Constance Webb, Sept. 13, 1958 (div. 1971); children: Christina, Lawrence. Hon. Nat. Degree mech. and prodn. engr., Enfield Coll. Advanced Tech., London, 1958. Chartered engr. Designer Brit. Insulated Callenders Cables Ltd, London, 1960-63; apprentice Standard Telephones and Cables Ltd, London, 1951-58, devel. engr., 1963-68; applications engr. Hawker Siddeley Dynamics Ltd., Hatfield, Eng., 1968-73; indsl. engr. ITT, Brussels, 1973-76; mgr. product sales Gardner Denver Co., Brussels, 1976-81; pvt. practice U.K., 1982-84; mgr. sales and mktg. Dynapert Ltd., Colchester, Eng., 1984—. Mem. Inst. Prodn. Engrs. Conservative. Mem. Ch. Eng. Office: Dynapert Ltd, Mason Rd Cowdray Ctr, Colchester Essex CO1 1BX, England

BRIGGS, EVERETT ELLIS, ambassador; b. Havana, Cuba, Apr. 6, 1934; s. Ellis Ormsbee and Lucy (Barnard) B.; m. Sally Soast, Sept. 9, 1955; children—Everett B., Catherine Briggs Towsend, Allen T., Lucy Briggs Bassert, Church E. A.B., Dartmouth Coll., 1956; M.S., George Washington U., 1972. Fgn. service officer Dept. State, Washington, 1956; consul gen. U.S. Consulate Gen., Luanda, Angola, 1972-74; dep. chief mission U.S. Embassy, Asuncion, Paraguay, 1974-78, Bogota, Colombia, 1978-79; dir. Mexican Affairs Dept. State, Washington, 1979-81, dep. asst. sec. state for inter-Am. affairs, 1981-82; ambassador to Panama, 1982-86, ambassador to Honduras, 1986—. Mem. Sr. Fgn. Service Officers Assn. Republican. Universalist. Club: Met. (Washington). Home: 3 Pleasant St Hanover NH 03755 Office: Dept State US Ambassador to Honduras Washington DC 20520 •

BRIGGS, GEORGE MADISON, civil engineer; b. Albany, N.Y., May 4, 1927; s. Franklin H. and Emma E. (Briggs) B.; B.S. in C.E., Purdue U., 1952; M.P.A., SUNY, Albany, 1968; m. Jean M. Cully, Oct. 31, 1954; children—George Madison, Barbara Jean. Engr., N.Y. State Dept. Public Works, Albany, 1952-56, asst. planning and location engr. dist. 1, 1956-60, resident engr. Saratoga County, 1961-64; asso. civil engr. N.Y. State Dept. Transp., Albany, 1965-67, dir. hwy. maintenance, 1968-72, dir. maintenance, 1972-80, asst. commr. ops., 1980-83; pres. Briggs Enginring., P.C., Greenwich, N.Y., 1983—; exec. dir. N.Y. Bituminous Distbrs. Assn.; v.p. Transpo Industries, New Rochelle, N.Y.; mem. coms. Transp. Research Bd., Nat. Acad. Scis.; instr. Fed. Hwy. Adminstrn.'s Course in bridge maintenance for state DOT bridge maintenance technicians and suprs. Co-author Am. pub. works assn. Roads and Streets Manual. Chmn. transp. com. 1980 Olympic Winter Games; cons. FHWA , Saudi Arabia, 1983, OAS, Caracas, Venezuela, 1984. Mem. Planning Bd. Town of Easton. Served with AUS, 1945-47. Registered profl. engr., N.Y. Mem. Nat. Soc. Profl. Engrs., N.Y. State Soc. Profl. Engrs. (pres. Tri-County chpt.), Am. Public Works Assn., Nat. Inst. Transp. (exec. council), Nat. Assn. State Hwy. and Transp. Ofcls. (vice chmn. maintenance com., task force leader bridge maintenance), SAR (v.p. chpt.), Soc. Mayflower Descs. Mem. Soc. Friends. Clubs: Masons, Shriners, Elks. Contbr. articles to profl. publs. Home and Office: Burton Rd #1 Box 401M Greenwich NY 12834

BRIGGS, PHILIP JAMES, political science educator, author, lecturer; b. N.Y.C., July 28, 1938; s. Philip Edward and Florence Marie (Fullam) B.; m. Candace Rae Kohn, Jan. 30, 1971; children—Nicola Fullam, Adam Kohn. B.S., SUNY-Oswego, 1960; M.A., Maxwell Sch. Citizenship and Pub. Affairs, Syracuse U., 1962, Ph.D., 1969. Asst. prof. social sci. SUNY Agrl. and Tech. Coll., Delhi, 1963-65; part-time admissions counselor Syracuse U. (N.Y.), 1967; assoc. prof. polit. sci. East Stroudsburg, U. (Pa.), 1968-72, prof. polit. sci., 1972—, dept. grad. coordinator, 1977—, dept. chmn., 1977—, faculty Fulbright adviser, 1981-82; book cons. McGraw-Hill Book Co., N.Y.C., 1981; reviewer books Mid-Am.: An Hist. Rev., Chgo., 1979; manuscript referee Armed Forces and Society, Chgo., 1979; Foxhowe lectr., Foxhowe Assn., 1980; Commonwealth speaker Pa. Humanities Council, 1984-86; invited discussant Sci. Research Council, Acad. Sci. USSR, 1979; invited participant seminar Georgetown U., 1983; invited scholar Presdl. Conf. Com., Hofstra U., 1984, 85, 87; panel co-chair Internat. Polit. Sci. World Congress, Paris, 1985. Editor: Politics in America: Readings and Documents, 1972; contbr. articles to publs. in field. Lectr. Young Democrats Monroe County, Stroudsburg, 1980, DAR, 1979, civic groups/polit. commentator, 1980. Served with USCG, 1962, with USCGR, 1962-70. Fellow Inter-Univ. Seminar on Armed Forces and Society; mem. Acad. Polit. Sci., Lyman L. Lemnitzer Ctr. NATO Studies (assoc.), Research Com. on Armed Forces and Soc. (exec. sec. 1985—), Pa. Polit. Sci. Assn., Pi Sigma Alpha (charter, co-advisor East Stroudsburg U.). Democrat. Unitarian. Office: East Stroudsburg U Dept Polit Sci East Stroudsburg PA 18301

BRIGHT, DONALD BOLTON, environmental consultant; b. Ventura, Calif., Nov. 28, 1930; s. Claude Wilson and Ruby Thelma (Bolton) B.; m. Patricia Jean McLaughlin, Nov. 25, 1955; children: Debra Ann, Steven Allan. BA in Zoology, U. So. Calif., 1952, MS in Biology, 1957, PhD in Biology, 1967; postdoctoral studies, Ariz. State U., 1974. Instr. Fullerton (Calif.) Coll., 1960-67; prof., chmn. dept. biol. scis. Calif. State U., Fullerton, 1967-77; dir. commerce Port of Long Beach, Calif., 1977-78, dir. environ. affairs, 1975-78; exec. v.p. EFS, Inc., Los Angeles, 1978-79; pres. Bright & Assocs., Anaheim, Calif., 1979—; chief exec. officer Environ. Audit Inc., Placentia, Calif., 1987—. Mem. Marine Sci. Coast Guard Adv. Com., Washington, 1977-80. Editor: Proc. National Magazine Science Edmc., 1970, Proc. Southern California Coastal Zone Supervisor, 1972; sci. advisor Am. Scientist mag., 1975-77; contbr. articles to profl. jours. Chmn. Calif. Regulatory Coastal Commn., Long Beach, 1973-75. Served to 1st lt. U.S. Army, 1952-55. Grantee NSF, 1969-75. Mem. Am. Inst. Planners, So. Calif. Acad. Sci. (v.p. 1975-78, fellow 1975), Western Soc. Naturalists, Sierra Club, Sigma Xi, Phi Sigma. Democrat. Presbyterian. Home: 921 Finnell Way Placentia CA 92670 Office: Bright & Assocs 1200 N Jefferson Suite B Anaheim CA 92807

BRIGHT, HARVEY R., oil producer; b. Muskogee, Okla., Oct. 6, 1920; s. Christopher R. and Rebecca E. (Van Ness) B.; m. Mary Frances Smith, May 27, 1943 (dec. Apr. 1971); children—Carol (Mrs. James B. Reeder), Margaret (Mrs. Jerry R. Petty), Christopher R., Clay Van Ness; m. Peggy Braselton, Dec. 15, 1972. B.S., Tex. A&M U., 1943. Partner Bright & Co. (oil producers), Dallas; bd. dirs. State Fair of Tex., Dallas, Dallas Market Center Co., Reynolds Penland Co., Southwestern Pub. Service Co., Bright Mortgage Co., Dallas; gen. ptnr. Dallas Cowboys Football Club; pres. Tex. Stadium Corp.; chmn. bd. dirs. Bright Truck Leasing Corp., Dallas; chmn. bd. dirs., chief exec. officer Bright Banc Savs. Assn., Dallas. Dir. State Fair of Tex., Dallas; chmn. bd. Children's Health Services of Tex., Dallas. Served with AUS, World War II. Home: 4500 Lakeside Dr Dallas TX 75205 Office: 2355 Stemmons Bldg Dallas TX 75207

BRIGHTON, JOHN TREVOR, historian, educator; b. Chesterfield, Eng., Mar. 17, 1936; s. Harry John B. and Alice Mary (Fern) B.; m. Patricia Wood, Aug. 24, 1936; children: Mark, Clare. BA with honors, Univ. Coll., London, 1958; Postgrad. Cert. in Edn., U. Nottingham, 1959; MA, U. Hull, 1968; PhD, U. York, 1978. Asst. master Hawarden Sch., Chester, Eng., 1959-61; sr. history master Kingston High Sch., Kingston upon Hull, Eng., 1961-64; sr. lectr. history St. John's Coll., York, Eng., 1964-69; head dept. history Matlock Coll., Derbyshire, Eng., 1969-72; head dept. art history City Poly., Sheffield, Eng., 1972-83, head faculty of art and design, 1979-83; head Bishop Otter Coll., Chichester, Eng., 1983—; dep. dir. Inst. Higher Edn., West Sussex, Eng., 1983—; adviser York Glaziers' Trust, 1980—. Author, editor designer various books, articles and illustrations. Fellow Royal Soc. Arts, Soc. Antiquaries. Home: College House College Ln, Chichester PO19 4PE, England Office: West Sussex Inst, The Dome, Bognor Regis England

BRIGHT-WHITE, JUNE LOUISE, project engineer, program manager; b. Dover, N.J., June 17, 1956; d. Richard Otten and Lois Ann (Preuss) B. BSCE, Bucknell U., 1978; MBA, Fla. Inst. Tech., 1984. Civil engr. Interpace Corp., Parsippany, N.J., 1978-79; mech. engr. Dept. Def. munitions systems div., Dover, N.J., 1979-82, systems engr. Infantry and Armor, 1981-84, recruitment cons., 1979-84, systems engr., advanced tactical programs, 1984-85, asst. program mgr. project engr. space and strategic div. Hughes Aircraft Co., 1985-87; mgr. program control advanced communications tech.satellite GE Astro Space Div., 1987—. Recipient Outstanding Young Employee Fed. Exec. Bd., 1981. Mem. Am. Def. Preparadeness Assn., Assn. U.S. Army, Tech. Mktg. Soc. Am. Republican. Lutheran. Home: 4 Colebrook Ct Princeton NJ 08540 Office: GE Astro PO Box 800 Princeton NJ 08543

BRIHAT, DENIS, photographer; b. Paris, Sept. 16, 1928; s. Georges and Rose (Guasco) B.; m. Solange Robert, July 8, 1967; children: Anne, Pierre. Profl. photographer, Paris, 1947-52, Biot, France, 1952-56, Provence, France, 1958—; dir. Brihat Ann. Photography Workshops, Provence, 1969—; co-founder, instr. dept. photography Marseille-Provence U., 1975-77; one-man shows Brihat Studio, Biot, 1952, Société Française de Photographie, Paris, 1957, 88, Galerie Montaigne, Paris, 1962, Galerie Pierre Coren, Aixen-Provence, France, 1962, Galerie La Proue, Lyon, France, 1963, Galerie Les Contards, Lacoste, France, 1965, Mus. Modern Art, N.Y.C., 1967, Orly Airport Gallery, Paris, 1968, Galerie La Lampe à Huile, Marseilles, France, 1971, Galerie La Demeure, Paris, Witkin Gallery, N.Y.C., Art Ctr., Washington, Conn., 1972, Fondation Grand Cachot de Vent, Neuchatel, Switzerland, 1973, Galleria 291, Milan, 1974, Photo-Galerie Fiolet, Amsterdam Galerie Paule, Pia, Antwerp, 1976, Musé e d'Angouleme, France, 1976, Galerie Agathe Gaillard, Paris, 1977, 82, Galerie Jean Dieuzaide, Toulouse, France, 1977, Musé e Nicephore Niepce, Chalon-sur-Saone, France, 1977, Galerie Photo-Art, Basle, 1978, Galerie Portfolio, Lausanne, 1979, 82, 86, Galerie Municipale à Chateau d'Eau, Toulouse, 1980, Musé e des Beaux Arts, Neuchatel, Switzerland, 1981, Musé e d'Orange, France, 1982, Galerie de la Salle, St. Paul de Vence, France, 1982, 85, Galerie Photogramme, Montreal, 1982, Espace Canon, Paris, 1982, Galerie L. d'Alessandro, Torino, Italy, 1983, Ctr. for Photography, Santa Fe, 1983, Galerie S. Kuepfer, Bienne, Switzerland, 1983 Wooster Art Ctr., Danbury, Conn., 1985, Musé e Henri Fabre, Montpellier, France, 1986, Galerie Suisse, Paris, 1986, Photographer's Gallery, Palo-Alto, Calif., 1988; represented in permanent collections: Bibliothèque Nationale, Paris, Musé e Reattu, Arles, France, Musé e Nicephore Niepce, Chalon-sur-Saone, Musé e d'Angouleme, France, Het Sterckshof Mus., Antwerp, Mus. Modern Art, N.Y.C., Ctr. Creative Photography, U. Ariz., Tucson, Fond Nat. d'Art Contemporain, Paris, Moderna Museet, Stockholm. Recipient Niepce prize Société des Gens d'Images, 1957; medal of Vermeil, Ville de Paris.

BRILL, RICHARD GEORGE, explorer; b. Danzig, Free State, Feb. 29, 1924, came to U.S., 1948, naturalized, 1953; s. Gustave and Peggy Brill; grad. U. Bologna, 1948; m. Brigitte Beglaiter, May 24, 1951; children—Elaine, Michael. Explorer jungles of the Amazon and West Africa, 1948—, also pres. Amazon/African Explorers, Inc., Parlin, N.J., 1957—; former interpreter UN; discoverer paintings and temple at Sierra Macarena, the Amazon; producer several films for TV. Served with French Fgn. Legion, Brit. Army and AUS, 1940-45. Mem. Am. Soc. Travel Agts., Outdoor Writers Am., African Travel Assn., S.Am. Tour Operators. Clubs: Rotary, Explorers. Amazon editor Travel Guides; photographer travel films. First to map Amazon region; linguist 8 langs. Office: 499 Ernston Rd Parlin NJ 08859

BRILLIANDE, ROBERT, insurance executive; b. Paris, France, Sept. 14, 1909; s. Isiah and Sophia (Gerine) B.; B.A., U. Hawaii, 1935; m. Irvine Tewksbury Baptiste, June 25, 1938; children—Robert Irving II, Gary Shawn, Timothy Wayne, Michael Bruce, Karen Joy. Editor, pub. Waikiki Pictorial News, 1935-37; engaged in ins. bus., 1937—; pres., treas. Brilliande Ins. Agy., Ltd., 1944-79, emeritus, 1979—; founder Financial Security Life Ins. Co., Ltd., Honolulu, 1950, pres., from 1950, chmn., from 1950, now emeritus chmn. and pres.; pres., treas. Reliable Investment Corp., Ltd., 1953—, Hawaii Underwriting Co., Ltd., 1953-79. Founder-patron Chamber Music Soc. Honolulu, Hawaiin Opera Theatre; patron Royal Circle of Honolulu Symphony Soc., Commedia, Inc., repertory theatre. Bd. dirs. Inst. Orch. and Ensemble Hawaii, Honolulu Community Theatre. Served with U.S. Army, 1930-36. Mem. Nat. Assn. Life Underwriters (life mem. Million Dollar Round Table), Ins. Accounting and Statis. Assn., Life Office Mgmt. Assn., Nat. Assn. Life Cos., Am. Mgmt. Assn., Gen. Agts. and Mgrs. Assn. Hawaii, Assn. Life Underwriters Hawaii, Hawaii Claims Assn., Am. Risk and Ins. Assn., Internat. Monetary and Fin. Soc. Hawaii (founder, 1st pres.), First Hawaii Shakespearean Soc. (pres. 1974), Nat. Skeet Shooting Assn., U.S. Tennis Assn. (past exec. com.), Hawaii Tennis Assn. (founder, 1st pres.) Lawn Tennis Assn., AAU (bd. mgrs. for weightlifting, organizer, 1st pres. weightlifting assn. Hawaii), Honolulu Acad. Arts, U. Hawaii Theater Guild, Honolulu Community Theater (dir. 1979—), U. Hawaii Alumni Assn., Hist. Soc. Bishop Mus. Assn., N.Y. Shavians, African Soc. Denmark (hon. life), Game Conservation Internat., East African Profl. Hunters Assn. (hon. life), Internat. Platform Assn., Internat. Shakespeare Assn., African Soc. Denmark (life), Bernard Shaw Soc. N.Y., Alliance Francaise, Phi Delta Phi. Clubs: Masons (K.T., 32d deg.), Safari Internat. (founder, 1st pres. Hawaii chpt., mem. internat. bd.), Aloha Skeet and Trap Hawaii (hon. life), Club de Regatas Corona Fishing (Tampico, Mexico), Hickam Rod and Gun (hon. life), Sailfish and Tarpon Mexico, Haura Marlin de Tahiti (founder), Hawaii, Kona Big Game Fishing, Honolulu Automobile, Honolulu Press (life). Home: 3671 Diamond Head Rd Honolulu HI 96816

BRIMHALL, JOHN CLARK, editor, composer, arranger; b. Huntington Park, Calif., Nov. 22, 1928; s. John Clark and Nora Louise (Baffa) B.; m. Virgin Mae Ravain, Apr. 1, 1951; children—James, Mary, Anthony. Mus.B. cum laude, Loyola U., 1950; M.A., Calif. State U.-San Francisco, 1952. Tchr., Corcoran (Calif.) High Sch., 1953-55; supr. music Corcoran Union Sch. Dists., 1955-56; instr. Porterville (Calif.) Coll., 1956-59, Orange Coast Coll., Costa Mesa, Calif., 1959-61; chief editor Hansen Publs., Inc., Miami Beach, Fla., 1962-78; pres. Brimhall Publs., Inc., Las Vegas, 1978—; composer, arranger, numerous books, sheet music; composer primary series John Brimhall Piano Method, John Brimhall Organ Method; author: (theory notebook) Young Adult Piano Course. Recipient La Croix de Commandeur, Merite et Devouement Francais (France), 1973. Mem. ASCAP, Am. Coll. Musicians (faculty mem.), Nat. Assn. of Music Merchants, Am. Fedn. Musicians, Music Educators Nat. Conf. Home: 106 Matterhorn Way Mount Charleston NV 89124

BRIMMEKAMP, CARL GERD, foreign trade company executive; b. Hamburg, Germany, Aug. 7, 1928; s. Carl and Charlotte Eugenie (Steinwachs) B.; student U. Hamburg; B.A. in Econs., Bklyn. Coll., 1955; postgrad. N.Y. U., 1955-56; M.B.A., U. Calif., Berkeley, 1961; m. Ruth M. Lingg, Sept. 5, 1953; children—Thomas L., Susanne L., Kristina S. Sales engr. Ferrostaal Overseas Corp., N.Y.C., 1952-56; gen. mgr., sec.-treas. Ferrostaal Pacific Corp., San Francisco, 1957-62; pres. Carl G. Brimmekamp Co., San Francisco, N.Y.C., 1962-73; pres., chief exec. officer Krupp Internat., Inc., Harrison, N.Y., 1970-79, Carl G. Brimmekamp & Co., Inc., Stamford, Conn., 1979—; chmn. Brimmekamp Corp., San Rafael, Calif., 1980—. Co-founder, German-Am. Round Table, San Francisco, 1958; founder German-Am. Trade Adv. Bd., 1962-66; bd. dirs. Gulf Atlantic Machine and Tool Co., Inc., Mobile, Ala., Koch Material Handling Systems, Inc., Stamford, Conn. Served with U.S. Army, 1953-55. Mem. TAPPI, Wire Industry Assn., German-Am. C. of C. (dir. 1971-74, 76-79, exec. com. 1976-79). Republican. Presbyterian. Clubs: Landmark (Stamford); World Trade, Univ. (San Francisco); Greenwich (Conn.) Country; Met. Opera, Met. (N.Y.C.); Fripp Island (S.C.); Duquesne (Pitts.); Deutscher Verein. Office: 102 Hamilton Ave Stamford CT 06901

BRING, LUIZ JARLSSON, equipment sales company executive; b. Recife, Pernambuco, Brazil, June 2, 1951; s. Göran Jarl and Josita (Campello) B.; m. Maria Elisabeth Bring, Apr. 4, 1974; children: Marcus Jarl, Anna Maria, Anna Sophia. Degree in mech. engring., The Royal Inst. of Tech., Stockholm, 1977. Sales engr ASEA AB, Vasteras, Sweden, 1977-80, regional sales mgr. Africa, 1980-82; gen. mgr. regional office So. Africa ASEA, Harace, Zimbabwe, 1982-85; pres. ASEA de Colombia, Bógota, 1985—. Club: Los Lagartos (Bógota). Office: ASEA de Colombia, Calle 45 A #102-48, Int 5 Apartado, 6195 Bogota Colombia

BRINGHAM, WILLIAM TALBERT, fraternal organization executive; b. Normal, Ill., Dec. 16, 1924; s. Russell Wilson and Sarah E. (Talbert) B.; m. Ruth Irene Jaeger, Jan. 10, 1947; 1 son, William Talbert. Ph.B., Ill. Wesleyan U., 1948; J.D., Vanderbilt U., 1951; grad. trust devel. sch., Northwestern U. Sch. Commerce, 1953. Spl. agt. FBI, 1951-52; exec. v.p. Sigma Chi frat., Wilmette, Ill., 1954—; v.p. Sigma Chi Found., 1956—, also sec.; sec. bd. grand trustees Sigma Chi; exec. v.p., sec., exec. com., sec. grand council Sigma Chi Corp.; bd. dirs., v.p. Nat. Interfrat. Found.; bd. dirs. Found. ASAE. Author booklet on alumni relations Sigma Chi; chmn. editorial com. Visitation Manuel for College Fraternities. Del. Ill. Republican Conv.; former mem. Cook County Rep. Cen. Com.; committeeman Northfield Twp. Rep. Com.; del. Sch. Bd. Caucus; past chmn. Fire and Police Commn., Wilmette; mem. corp. Kendall Coll., past trustee, Wilmette; bd. visitors Ill. Wesleyan U. Served with USNR, 1942-46. Recipient Significant Sig and Order of Constantine awards Sigma Chi, 1975. Mem. Am. Personnel and Guidance Assn., Am. Soc. Assn. Execs. (cert.; v.p. awards com., dir. found., Key award 1973), Chgo. Soc. Assn. Execs. (past pres.), Nat. Assn. Student Personnel Adminstrs. (pres. 1984-85), Am. Council on Edn., Council for Advancement and Support Edn., Fraternity Execs. Assn. (pres., mem. exec. com.), Assn. Alumni Advisors, Assn. Fraternity Advisors, Internat. Platform Assn., Wilmette Hist. Soc., Evanston Hist. Soc., Travelers Protective Assn., U.S. C. of C., Evanston C. of C. (past bd. dirs.), Am. Legion, SAR, Soc. Golden Key, Omicron Delta Kappa, Phi Delta Phi. Clubs: Univ. (Evanston) (pres.); Westmoreland Country (Wilmette). Lodges: Masons (33 deg.), Shriners, KT, Kiwanis (past pres.), Royal Order of Scotland; Red Cross of Constantine. Home: 4020 Bunker Ln Wilmette IL 60091 Office: Sigma Chi 1714 Hinman Ave Evanston IL 60204

BRINK, ANDRÉ PHILIPPUS, author, educator; b. Vrede, S. Africa, May 29, 1935; s. Daniel and Aletta (Wolmarans) B.; m. Estelle Naude, Oct. 3, 1959 (div.); m. Salomi Louw, Nov. 28, 1965 (div.); children—Anton, Gustav; m. 3d Sophia Albertina Miller, July 17, 1970 (div.); children—Danie, Sonja. B.A., Potchefstroom U., 1955, M.A., 1957, M.A., 1959; D.Litt., Rhodes U., 1975; D.Litt. (hon.) Witwatersrand U., 1985. Lectr. Rhodes U., Grahamstown, 1961-73, sr. lectr., 1973-75, asst. prof., 1976-79, prof., 1980—. Decorated chevalier de Legion d'Honneur (France), Officier de l'Ordre des arts et des Lettres (France); recipient Martin Luther King award, 1980; prix Medicis étranger, 1980. Author: Looking on Darkness, 1974; An Instant in the Wind, 1976; Rumors of Rain, 1978; A Dry White Season, 1979; A Chain of Voices, 1982; The Wall of the Plague, 1984; The Ambassador, 1985; States of Emergency, 1988.

BRINK, ANDRIES J., medical scientist; b. Potchefstroom, Transvaal, Republic of South Africa, Aug. 29, 1923; s. Andries J. and Petronella J. (Havenga) B.; m. Maria Ruskovich, Oct. 28, 1949; children: Paul A., Maryna, Annalise, Justinus. MB, BChir., U. Witwatersrand, Johannesburg, Republic South Africa, 1946; MD, U. Pretoria, Republic South Africa, 1951; DSc., U. Stellenbosch, Republic South Africa, 1971; DSc. (hon.), U. Natal, Durban, Republic South Africa, 1976, U. Poschefstroom, 1985. Resident, lectr. med. depts. U. Witwatersrand, U. Pretoria, 1948-50; registrar medicine U. London, 1951; fellow in pediatric cardiology Johns Hopkins U., 1952; sr. lectr. in internal medicine U. Pretoria, 1953-56; chief physician and cardiologist U. Stellenbosch, 1956-71, dean faculty medicine, 1971-85; pres. South Africa Med. Research Council, Cape Town, 1969—; cons. South Africa Def. Force, 1964—; bd. dirs. Pvt. Hosps., Cape Town. Author: Dictionary Afrikans Med. Lang., 1979 (Gold Medal 1980), Heart Disease, 1980, (with others) Heart and Lung Med. Terms, 1974 (trophy 1974); contbr. numerous articles to profl. jours. Andries Brink Chair in Cardiology at U. Stellenbosch named in his honor, 1983; reciepient Decoration for Meritorious Service, 1982, Merit award Claude Leon Harris Found., 1984; named hon. col. 2d Med. Bn. South African Def. Fource, 1985. Fellow Am. Coll. Cardiology, Royal Coll. Physicians; mem. South African Med. Assn., Council South African Acad. Arts and Scis. (Havenga prize 1967), Council U. Stellenbosch, Com. Heads of Sci. Councils (chmn. 1987—), Internat. Medlars Policy Adv. Group, South African Botan. Soc., Arts Soc. Durbanville. Home: 13 Lindenberg Ave, Durbanville Cape Province 7550, Republic of South Africa Office: So African Med Research Council, PO Box 70, Tygerberg 7505, Republic of South Africa

BRINKER, THOMAS MICHAEL, finance executive; b. Phila., Sept. 8, 1933; s. William Joseph and Elizabeth C. (Feeley) B.; m. Doris Marie Carlin, Oct. 11, 1958; children—Thomas Michael, James E., Joseph F., Diane M. Student, St. Joseph's U., U. Pa.; M.S. in Fin. Services, Am. Coll., 1980. Registered investment advisor. With Ice Capades, 1951-52, 56; with Casa Carioca, Garmisch, Fed. Rep. Germany, 1954-56; profl. ice skating tchr. and mfrs. rep. Ridley Park, Pa., 1956-60; agt., div. mgr. Prudential Ins. Co., Phila., 1960-65; gen. agt. Mut. Trust Life Ins. Co., 1965-70; pres., founder Fringe Benefits Inc., Havertown, Pa., 1970—, Fin. Foresight Ltd., Havertown, Pa., 1983—; adj. prof. Pa. State U., 1984—, St. Joseph's U., 1985—. Host. weekly radio show: Financial Forum, WWDB-FM, 1982—; author: Hi, I'm Tom Brinker, You're on WWDB, 1987; columnist: Financially Yours, 1983—; ghostwriter: Nat. Assn. Life Underwriters' Fin. Fitness campaign, 1985; contbr., author, conductor of seminars on fin. planning; contbr. articles to profl. jours. Pres., Delaware County Estate Planning Council, 1979-80, Pipeline Inc., Springfield, Pa., 1970-71; dir. nat. council Invest-in-Am., 1986. Served with US Army, 1954-56. Recipient Nat. Quality awards Nat. Assn. Life Underwriters, 1966—, Nat. Sales Achievement awards, 1970—. Mem. C.L.U. (chartered fin. cons.), Delaware County Life Underwriters (pres. 1975-76, 82-83), Am. Coll. Life Underwriters, Nat. Assn. Life Underwriters, Million Dollar Round Table (life and qualifying mem.), Internat. Platform Assn., Internat. Assn. Fin. Planners (admitted registry fin. planning practitioners 1984, v.p. Del. Valley chpt. 1986-88, pres.-elect Del. Valley chpt. 1988—). Roman Catholic. Clubs: Lake Naomi (v.p. bd. govs. 1982, pres. 1986), The Manor, Knights of Columbus. Home: 115 Locust Ave Springfield PA 19064 Office: 1 N Ormond Ave Township Line Rd Havertown PA 19083 also: Rt 940 PO Box 219 Pocono Summit PA 18346

BRINKERHOFF, LORIN C., nuclear engineer, federal official; b. St. Anthony, Idaho, June 4, 1929; s. James Byron and Bessie Hazel (Miller) B.; m. Donna Lee Lords, Nov. 27, 1951; children—Kathleen Rae, Diane Lee, Sandra Lynne, Bonnie Jo, Dirk Lorin, Michael Lorin. B.S. in Chem. Engring., U. Utah, 1955; postgrad. MIT, 1970, Safety and Reliability Directorate (Eng.), 1974, Nuclear Power Devel. Establishment (Scotland), 1981. Research specialist Gen. Electric Co., Hanford, Wash., 1952-53; reactor ops. foreman Phillips Petroleum Co., Idaho Falls, Idaho, 1955-58; critical facility mgr. Lawrence Radiation Lab., Nevada Test Site, 1958-62; sr. nuclear engr. Aerojet Gen. Corp., Nevada Test Site, 1962-69; sr. reactor safety specialist AEC, Germantown, Md., 1969-81; chief reactor safety br. U.S. Dept. Energy, Germantown, 1981-86; mgr. tech. safety appraisal team, 1986—. Served with U.S. Army, 1950-51. Mem. Am. Nuclear Soc. (standards com. 1980—), Am. Nat. Standards Assn. (standards com. 1978-85). Democrat. Mem. Ch. of Jesus Christ of Latter-day Saints (bishop). Home: 14921 Bauer Dr Rockville MD 20853 Office: Office Nuclear Safety Dept of Energy EH33 Washington DC 20545

BRINKLEY, DAVID, news commentator; b. Wilmington, N.C., July 10, 1920; s. William Graham and Mary (West) B.; m. Ann Fischer, Oct. 11, 1946; children: Alan, Joel, John; m. Susan Adolph, June 10, 1972; 1 child, Alexis. Reporter Wilmington (N.C.) Star-News, 1938-41; reporter, bur. mgr. United Press Assns., various So. cities, 1941-43; news writer, broadcaster radio and TV NBC, Washington, 1943—; Washington corr. NBC, 1951-81; anchorman ABC This Week, 1981—. Recipient duPont award, Peabody award, Sch. Bell award, other journalism awards. Club: Cosmos (Washington). Office: ABC News 1717 DeSales St NW Washington DC 20036

BRINKLEY, GEORGE ARNOLD, JR., educator; b. Wilmington, N.C., Apr. 20, 1931; s. George Arnold and Ida Bell (West) B.; A.B., Davidson Coll., 1953; M.A., Columbia U., 1955, Ph.D., 1964; m. Ann Mae Kreps, Aug. 9, 1959; 1 dau., Heidi Ann. Instr. polit. sci. Columbia U., N.Y.C., 1957-58; with dept. govt. U. Notre Dame, 1958—, prof., 1970—, dir. Program of Soviet & East European Studies, 1969—, chmn. dept., 1969-77, dir. Inst. Internat. Studies, 1975-78. Ford Found. fellow, 1954-57; Internat. Affairs fellow Council on Fgn. Relations, 1968-69. Mem. Am. Assn. Advancement of Slavic Studies (chmn. membership com. 1978-81); Midwest Slavic Assn. (chmn. exec. com. 1979-81), Phi Beta Kappa. Methodist. Author: The Volunteer Army and Allied Intervention in South Russia, 1917-1921, 1966. Office: U Notre Dame Dept Govt Notre Dame IN 46556

BRINKLEY, WILLIAM CLARK, writer; b. Custer, Okla., Sept. 10, 1917; s. Daniel Squire and Ruth (Clark) B. Student, William Jewell Coll., 1936-37; B.A., U. Okla., 1940; spl. student, Yale Drama Sch., 1961-62. Reporter Daily Oklahoman, Oklahoma City, 1940-41, Washington Post, 1941-42, 49-51; successively corr., asst. editor, staff writer Life mag., 1951-58. Author: Quicksand, 1948, The Deliverance of Sister Cecilia, 1954, Don't Go Near the Water, 1956, The Fun House, 1961, The Two Susans, 1962, The Ninety and Nine, 1966, Breakpoint, 1978, Peeper, 1981, The Last Ship, 1988. Served to lt. USNR, 1942-46. Recipient Citation for Achievement award William Jewell Coll., 1986. Mem. Phi Beta Kappa. Club: Nat. Press (Washington). Address: 500 Wichita St No 79 McAllen TX 78501

BRINKMANN, RICHARD A., German language educator; b. Elberfeld, Germany, June 16, 1921; s. Richard and Margarete B.; PhD, U. Tübingen, 1948; m. Ursula Roser, Apr. 4, 1947; children: Ursula, Fritz, Brigitte. Asst. prof. U. Tübingen, 1948-55, assoc. prof., 1955-59, prof., 1959—; vis. prof. German, U. Calif., Berkeley, 1966, prof. German, 1968; vis. prof. U. N.Z., 1963, U. Tex., Austin, 1963, Columbia U., 1964. Mem. Internationale Vereinigung für Germanische Sprach-und Literaturwissenschaft (v.p. 1975-80), Senatskommission für Germanistische Forschung der Deutschen Forschungsgemeinschaft (chmn. 1975-80), Austrian Acad. Scis. (corr.), Acad. Scis. Heidelberg (ord.). Author: Wirklichkeit und Illusion, 1957, 3d edit., 1977; Expressionismus-Probleme, 1961; Theodor Fontane, 1967, 2d edit., 1977, Expressionismus, 1980; Wirklichkeiten. Essays zur Literatur, 1982; others. Contbr. articles to profl. jours. Editor: Deutsche Vierteljahrsschrift für Literaturwissenschaft und Geistesgeschichte, Germanistik Studien z. dt. Literatur. Home: 30 Rotbad, D-7400 Tubingen Federal Republic of Germany Office: 50 Wilhelmstrasse, D-7400 Tübingen 1, Federal Republic of Germany also: 5317 Dwinelle Hall Berkeley CA 94720

BRINSON, DONALD EDWARD, data processing executive; b. Ponca City, Okla., Sept. 6, 1953; s. Merwyn Glen and Mildred Colleen (Good) B.; B.S. in Math., U. Okla., 1980. With Sta. KGOU, Norman, Okla., 1971-73; lab. instr. ELS Lang. Center, Norman, 1972-74; computer programmer Oscar Rose Jr. Coll., Midwest City, Okla., 1974-78; systems programmer Okla. Tax Commn., Oklahoma City, 1978-80; dir. computer center Rose State Coll., Midwest City, 1980-85; systems specialist Hertz Corp., Oklahoma City, 1985—; cons. Organizer, activities coordinator Single Adult Persons, 1977-79. Mem. Assn. Computing Machinery, Hewlett-Packard Internat. Users Group (pres. Central Okla. Regional Users Group 1982-83). Democrat. Methodist. Club: Order of Foresters. Home: 308 Draper Dr Midwest City OK 73110 Office: Hertz Corp 5601 Northwest Expressway Oklahoma City OK 73132

BRINSON, GAY CRESWELL, JR., lawyer; b. Kingsville, Tex., June 13, 1925; s. Gay Creswell and Lelia (Wendelkin) B.; children from former marriage: Thomas Wade, Mary Kaye; m. Bette Lee Butler, June 17, 1979. Student, U. Ill.-Chgo., 1947-48; B.S., U. Houston, 1953, J.D., 1957; cert. civil trial law, personal injury trial law and family law, Tex. Bd. Legal Splzn. Bar: Tex. 1956, U.S. Dist. Ct. (so. dist.) Tex. 1957, U.S. Dist. Ct. (ca. dist.) Tex. 1959, U.S. Dist. Ct. (we. dist.) Tex. 1965, U.S. Ct. Appeals (5th cir.) 1962, U.S. Supreme Ct. 1974; diplomate: Am. Bd. Trial Advocates. Spl. agt. FBI, Washington and Salt Lake City, 1957-59; trial atty. Liberty Mut. Ins. Co., Houston, 1959-62; assoc. Horace Brown, Houston, 1962-64; assoc. Vinson & Elkins, Houston, 1964-67, ptnr., 1967—; lectr. U. Houston Coll. Law, 1964-65, Tex. Coll. Trial Advocacy, Houston, 1978-86; prosecutor Harris County Grievance Com.-State Bar Tex., Houston, 1965-70. Served with AUS, 1943-46, ETO. Fellow Tex. Bar Found. (life); mem. Tex. Acad. Family Law Specialists (cert. trial specialist), Tex. Assn. Def. Counsel, Fedn. Ins. Counsel, Nat. Assn. R.R. Trial Counsel, Phi Delta Phi. Clubs: Houston Center, Beaumont (Tex.). Home: 2938 San Felipe Houston TX 77019 Office: Vinson & Elkins 3300 First City Tower 1001 Fannin Houston TX 77002

BRISCOE, ANNE M., scientist, educator; b. N.Y.C., Dec. 1, 1918; M.A., Vassar Coll., 1945; Ph.D. (Sterling jr. fellow, USPHS fellow), Yale U., 1949; m. William A. Briscoe, Aug. 20, 1955. From research asso. to asst. prof. Cornell U. Med. Coll., 1950-56; faculty Columbia U. Coll. Physicians and Surgeons, N.Y.C., 1956—, prof. emeritus, 1987, spl. lectr., 1987—; lectr. Harlem Hosp. Center Sch. Nursing, 1968-77; adj. asst. prof. Hunter Coll., 1951-64, 73-75. Mem. N.Y.C. Commn. on Status of Women, 1979—, vice chairperson, 1982—; non-govtl. orgn. del. to UN; mem. adv. council Inst. Nuclear Power Ops., 1979-84. Fellow Am. Inst. Chemists (sec. N.Y. chpt. 1981-83). Recipient Yale medal, 1986 N.Y. Acad. Scis. (chairperson women in sci. com. 1978—, bd. govs. 1981); mem. AAAS (mem. council 1982-85), Am. Chem. Soc., Am. Soc. Clin. Nutrition, Am. Fedn. Clin. Research, Harvey Soc., Fedn. Orgns. for Profl. Women (treas. 1978-80), Assn. Women in Sci. Ednl. Founds. (pres. 1978-82), Assn. Women in Sci. (editor newsletter 1971-74, nat. pres. 1974-76), Assn. Yale Alumni (assembly rep. 1978—, bd. govs. 1982-85), Yale Grad. Sch. Alumni Assn. (pres. 1981-82). Contbr. articles to profl. jours.). Contbr. articles to profl. jours. Home: 2 Peter Cooper Rd New York NY 10010 Office: Harlem Hosp Ctr Dept Medicine New York NY 10037

BRISCOE, JACK CLAYTON, lawyer; b. Bradford, Pa., July 23, 1920; s. Park Harry and Elsie Gertrude (Woodward) B.; m. Dorothy Lillian Shaw, Sept. 3, 1949; children: Jacqueline Kamp, Jeffrey S., Joan Ryd. BS in Econs. U. Pa., 1943; LLB Harvard U., 1948. Bar: Pa. 1950. Assoc. Robert C. Duffy, Phila., 1950-66; ptnr. Briscoe, Haggerty & Howard, Phila., 1966-85, Briscoe & Howard, Phila., 1985—; instr. U. Pa., 1950-56; bd. dirs. SonMark Books and Gifts Inc. Treas. Phila. Flag Day Assn., Mark Brodns. Ltd.,; Pa. Bible Soc., Mark Prodns., Ltd.; chmn. bd. Community Christian Fellowship Ctr. Inc.; elder United Presbyn. Ch. Manoa; active Fellowship Christian Athletes; mem. Rep. Task Force. Served with USAAF, 1943-46. Branch Ricky Assocs. award; Cert Achievement award compulsory arbitration div. Phila. County Ct. Fellow Harry S. Truman Library Inst.; mem. ABA, Pa. Bar Assn., Phila. Bar Assn., Pa. Trial Lawyers Assn., Am. Arbitration Assn. (panel), Internat. Platform Assn. (Pa Soc.), Harvard Law Sch. Assn., Friendly Sons of St. Patrick, Gideons Internat., Chapel of Four Chaplains (legion hon. mem.). Clubs: Harvard, Lawyers (Phila.), Union League. Office: Briscoe & Howard 1608 Walnut St Suite 1700 Philadelphia PA 19103

BRISKIN, MADELEINE, paleoceanographer, paleoclimatologist, micropaleontologist; b. Paris, Sept. 4, 1932; came to U.S., 1951, naturalized, 1956; d. Michel and Mina B.; B.S., CCNY, 1965; M.S., U. Conn., 1967; Ph.D., Brown U., 1973. Assoc. prof. geology Geology/Physics Bldg. Old Tech. U. Cin., 1980—. Recipient award Research Support, 1971-72, NSF Support award, 1978, Old Tech. U. Cin. Dean's award, 1978, U.C. Research Council award, 1978. Mem. Climap, Am. Geophys. Union, Am. Quaternary Assn., AAAS, Paleontologist Soc., Cin. Engrs. and Scientists Soc., Woods Hole Oceanographic Instn., Lamont-Doherty Geol. Obs., N.Y. Acad. Sci., Sigma Xi. Contbr. articles to profl. jours. Office: Dept Geology U Cin Cincinnati OH 45221

BRISTOW, ROBERT O'NEIL, writer, educator; b. St. Louis, Nov. 17, 1926; s. Jesse Reuben and Helen Marjorie (Utley) B.; children by previous marriage—Cynthia Lynn, Margery Jan Wu, Gregory Scott, Kelly Robert. B.A. in Journalism, U. Okla., 1951, M.A. in Journalism, 1965. Asst. advt. mgr. Altus (Okla.) Times Democrat, 1951-53; free-lance writer Altus, 1951-60; prof. English Winthrop Coll., Rock Hill, S.C., 1960-87, prof. emeritus, 1987—. Author: Time for Glory, 1968, Night Season, 1970, A Faraway Drummer, 1973, Laughter in Darkness, 1974. Served with USNR, 1944-45. Recipient award for lit. excellence U. Okla., 1969, award for novel Friends of Am. Writers, 1974. Mem. Alpha Tau Omega. Home: 613 1/2 Charlotte Ave Rock Hill SC 29730

BRITO, GILBERTO OTTONI, neuroscientist, physician; b. Rio de Janeiro, Brazil, May 24, 1951; s. Ney P. and Herbene I. (Ottoni) B.; m. Linda; children—Alexandre, Bianca. M.D., State U. Rio de Janeiro, 1974; Ph.D., U. Rochester. Postdoctoral fellow Center for Brain Research, U. Rochester Med. Center, 1981; asst. prof. Center for Brain Research U. Rochester Med. Center, 1982—; assoc. prof. Instituto Biomedico, Universidade Federal Fluminense, 1983—. Contbr. articles to profl. publs. Co-investigator NIH. Mem. AAAS, Soc. Neurosci., Internat. Brain Research Orgn., Internat. Neuropsychol. Soc., N.Y. Acad. Scis., Assn. Child Psychology and Psychiatry, Sigma Xi. Home: Rua Rego Lopes 30, casa 12, RJ 20520 Rio de Janeiro Brazil Office: Rua Conde de Bonfim 232, sala 401, RJ 20520 Rio de Janeiro Brazil

BRITO, JOSE DOMINGOS, librarian; b. Jupi, Brazil, Aug. 9, 1950; s. João Domingos de Brito and Olidina Cordeiro de Barros; m. Feb. 5, 1975; children: Juliana Correia, Jonas. MS in Social Studies, U. Garulhos SP, Brazil, 1973; MS in Librarian, Sc. Sociol. and Polit. Faculty Librarianship, Brazil, 1976. Librarian-chief Comp. Engenharia de Tráfego, São Paulo, 1976-80; documentation analyst Abril Cultural S.Am., Sãa Paulo, 1981-83; librarian-chief Comp. Mcpl. Transp. Coletivos, São Paulo, 1983-86, Found. Getulio Vargas, São Paulo, 1986—; tchr., Tereza D'avila, São Paulo, 1981, Tereza Martin, São Paulo, 1984-85. Contbr. articles to profl. jours. Pres. Syndicate of Librarians, São Paulo, 1986—. Mem. Assn. Paulista de Bibliotecários (named Librarian Yr. 1987). Roman Catholic. Home: Rua Vicente 10, 02084 São Paulo Brazil Office: FGV/EAESP, Ave 9 de Julho, 2029, 01327 São Paulo Brazil

BRITS, JACOB PIETER, educator; b. Christiana, Republic South Africa, Jan. 14, 1945; s. Rudolf Martinus and Anna Catharina (Du Toit) B.; m. Sophia Elizabeth Marais, Dec. 21, 1968; children: Rudolf Marthinus, Gert Lodewicus Marais. BA, U. Orange Free State, 1967; BA (hon.), Potchefstroom U., 1969, MA, 1971; D. Litt. et Phil., U. South Africa, 1978. Tchr. dept. edn. Orange Free State, Parys and Bloemfontein, Republic South Africa, 1967-72; researcher Human Scis. Research Council, Pretoria, Republic South Africa, 1972-80; sr. lectr. history U. South Africa, Pretoria, 1980-87, assoc. prof., 1988—. Author: Tielman Roos: Political Prophet or Opportunist?, 1987; contbr. articles to profl. jours.; editor mag. Kleio, 1987. U. South Africa grantee, 1986, Human Sci. Research Council grantee, 1986. Mem. South African Hist. Soc. Office: U South Africa, Muckleneuk Ridge, Pretoria 0001, Republic of South Africa

BRITT, DAVID PAUL, biomedical sciences educator; b. Beckenham, Eng., Jan. 9, 1939; s. Bertram Stanley and Edith Hannah (Jefferies) B.; m. Shirley Margaret Glenville, Mar. 28, 1964. Tchr.'s Cert., U. Leicester, 1967; BA, Open U., 1973; MSc., Salford U., 1978; PhD, Liverpool U., 1984. Med. lab. sci. officer King's Coll. Hosp., London, 1956-63; sr. med. lab. sci. officer Charing Cross Hosp. Med. Sch., London, 1963-64; asst. master for biology Vale of Catmose Village Coll., Oakham, Eng., 1967-68; lectr. med. lab. sci. North East Liverpool Tech. Coll., 1968-74; adviser Nat. Vet. Research Inst., Vom, Nigeria, 1974-77; researcher/demonstrator vet. preventive medicine Liverpool U., 1979-81; sr. research fellow Liverpool Sch. Tropical Medicine, 1982-86; asst. prof. allied health scis. and nursing Kuwait U., 1986—. Contbr. articles on sci. and animal welfare to profl. jours. Winston Churchill Meml. Trust travelling fellow, 1984. Fellow Royal Soc. Tropical Medicine and Hygiene, Inst. Med. Lab. Scis.; mem. Freshwater Biol. Assn. (life), Inst. Biology, Wirral Soc. (exec. com. 1985-86). Home: Nelson Cottage 15 Station Rd, Parkgate South Wirral, Cheshire L64 6QJ, England Office: Kuwait U Faculty Allied Health Scis and Nursing, PO Box 31470, 90805 Sulaibikhat Kuwait

BRITT, JAMES THOMAS, lawyer; b. Kansas City, Mo., Feb. 27, 1904; s. Aylett T. and Katherine B. (Henderson) B.; LL.B., Washington U., St. Louis, 1926; m. Ruth E. Burgin, Sept. 18, 1930; children—Thomas Burgin, Robert McCammon. Bar: Mo. 1926. Practiced in Kansas City, 1926—; sr. ptnr. firm Spencer, Fane, Britt & Browne, 1951—; instr. Real Estate Bd. Inst., 1945-66; mem. bar com. 16th Jud. Circuit Mo., 1942-49; legal adviser local SSS, 1939-75; sec., dir. Commonwealth Theatres, Inc., 1965-77. Mem. bd. visitors Jackson County, 1948-53; chmn. Recreation Adv. Com. Kansas City, 1955-62; chmn. citizens adv. bd. City-County Office of Aging, 1969-72; co-founder, dir. Nat. Council on Alcoholism, Kansas City, area pres., 1966-67, exec. v.p., 1967-68; bd. dirs. Kansas City Social Health Agy., 1969-72; mem. Mo. Adv. Council Alcoholism and Drug Abuse, 1965-77; bd. dirs., mem. exec. com., pres. Starlight Theatre Assn., 1977-79. Mem. Am., Mo., Kansas City bar assns., Lawyers Assn. Kansas City, Kappa Alpha, Phi Delta Phi. Clubs: Rotary, Kansas City, River. Contbr. articles to legal jours. Home: 409 W 58th Terr Kansas City MO 64113 Office: 1400 Commerce Bank Bldg Kansas City MO 64106

BRITT, RONALD LEROY, manufacturing company executive; b. Abilene, Kans., Mar. 1, 1935; s. Elvin Elbert and Lona Helen (Conn) B.; B.S.M.E., Wichita State U., 1963; m. Judith Ann Salter, June 29, 1957; children—Brett Gavin, Mark Damon, Melissa Ann. Product engr. to product planner Hotpoint div. Gen. Electric Co., Chgo., 1963-68; product planner Norge Co., Chgo., 1968; product mgr., asst. dir. engring. Leigh Products Inc., Coopersville, Mich., 1968-74; mgr. research and devel. MiamiCarey div. Jim Walter Corp., Monroe, Ohio, 1974-84; v.p. mfg. and engring. div. SICO, Belvidere Co., Belvidere, Ill., 1984—; industry rep. for electric fans Underwriters Labs. Active, Boy Scouts Am., 1970-73, PTA, 1973—; exec. adviser Jr. Achievement, 1984-85, Boone County chmn., 1986—. Served with U.S. Army, 1958-60. Recipient Inventor's award Gen. Electric Co., 1967. Mem. ASME, Home Ventilation Inst. (engring. com. 1975-84), Belvidere C. of C. (bd. dirs. 1986—). Republican. Congregationalist. Clubs: Free Blown Glassblowing, Carnival and Art Glass Collectors. Lodge: Rotary. Patentee in field. Home: 11858 Limetree Ln Belvidere IL 61008 Office: 725 Columbia Ave Belvidere IL 61008

BRITTAIN, LAURA READING, dancer, educator; b. Longmont, Colo., July 25, 1945; d. David R. and Jeanne (McKibbin) Reading; AA in Theatre, Bakersfield Jr. Coll., 1965; BA in Theatre Arts, UCLA, 1968, MA in Dance, 1971; m. Darryl A. Brittain, June 28, 1969 (div.). Dancer, Gus Solomons Dance Co., N.Y.C., 1971-73; asso. prof. dance and dance edn., artist-in-residence N.Y.U., 1973—, dir. N.Y. U. Washington Sq. Repertory Dance Co.; performer Michelle Berne Dance Co., Marjorie Gamso & Dancers, Linda Diamond Dance Co.; choreographer; regional co-dir. Am. Coll. Dance Festival, N.Y.C., 1980; guest lectr. Jerusalem Rubin Acad. Music and Dance, 1982, 83. Recipient Prof. of Yr. award N.Y.U. Sch. of Edn., 1984; Mem. Nat. Dance Assn., N.Y. State Dance Assn., Am. Assn. Univ. Profs. Presbyterian. Democrat. Office: NYU 35 W 4th St New York NY 10003

BRITTAIN, MAX GORDON, JR., lawyer; b. Glens Falls, N.Y., Dec. 22, 1947; s. Max Gordon and Eloise (Wilbur) B.; m. Teresa Ann Hochreiter, Sept. 28, 1984; children by previous marriage: Matthew Greer, Amanda Kelly. B.S., Bradley U., 1969; J.D. cum laude, Loyola U., Chgo., 1976. Bar: Ill. 1976, U.S. Dist. Ct. (no. dist.) Ill. 1976, U.S. Ct. Appeals (7th cir.) 1978, U.S. Supreme Ct. 1980, U.S. Ct. Appeals (fed. cir.) 1984. Assoc., Schiff Hardin & Waite, Chgo., 1976-79, Kovar & Smetana, Chgo., 1979-82; ptnr. Kovar, Nelson & Brittain, Chgo., 1982—; instr. Loyola U., Chgo., 1981—; lectr. on labor law. Mng. editor Loyola Law Rev., 1975-76; author: Wrongful Discharge Claims. Mem. ABA, Ill. Bar Assn. Republican. Methodist. Club: Union League (Chgo.). Home: 515 S Beverly Ln Arlington Heights IL 60005 Office: Kovar Nelson & Brittain 500 Marquette Bldg 140 S Dearb orn St Chicago IL 60603

BRITTAIN, ROBERT DAMERON, chemist; b. Birmingham, Ala., Jan. 11, 1949; s. George Marshall and Bettysu (Bozeman) B.; m. Cynthia Jane Elsberry, Dec. 18, 1971. B.S., Furman U., 1971, M.S., 1974; Ph.D., U. Fla., 1979. Sr. phys. chemist SRI Internat., Menlo Park, Calif., 1979—. Contbr. articles to profl. jours. Mem. Am. Chem. Soc., AIME, Am. Ceramic Soc., Electrochem. Soc., Sierra Club. Home: 10451 Lansdale Ave Cupertino CA 95014

BRITTAN, LEON, member British Parliament, lawyer; b. London, Sept. 25, 1939; s. Joseph and Rebecca B.; m. Diana Paterson, 1980; ed. Trinity Coll., Cambridge U., Yale U. Called to Inner Temple bar, 1962; chmn. Bow Group, 1964-65; contested N. Kensington seat Parliament, 1966, 70; vice chmn. govs. Isaac Newton Sch., 1968-71; M.P. for Cleveland and Whitby, Govt. of England, 1974-83, M.P. for Richmond, Yorkshire, 1983—; vice chmn. Parliamentary Conservative Party Employment Com., 1974-76, opposition spokesman on devolution, 1976-78, on employment, 1978-79, minister state home office, 1979-81, chief sec. to treasury, 1981-83, home sec., 1983-85, sec. of state for trade and industry, 1985-86. Author: (with others) Millstones for the Sixties, Rough Justice, Infancy and the Law, How to Save Your Schools, A New Deal for Health Care, 1988, Defence and Arms Control in a Changing Era, 1988. Address: House of Commons, London SW1 England

BRITTAN, SAMUEL, commentator, editor; b. London, Dec. 29, 1933; s. Joseph and Kiva (Lipetz) Brittan. BA in Econs. with 1st class honors, Cambridge U., 1955, MA, 1955; DLitt (hon.), Heriot-Watt U., 1985. With Fin. Times, London, 1955-61, prin. econs. commentator, 1966—, asst. editor, 1978—; econs. editor Observer, London, 1961-64; advisor Dept. Of Econ. Affairs, 1965; research fellow Nuffield Coll., 1973-74, vis. fellow, 1974; vis. prof. Chgo. Law Sch., 1978; mem. Peacock Com. on Fin. BBC, 1985-86. Author: Left or Right: The Bogu Dilemma, 1968, Steering the Economy, 3d edit., 1971, The Price of Economic Freedom: A Guide to Flexible Rates, 1970, Is There an Economic Consensus?, 1973, Capitalism and the Permissive Society, 1973, The Delusion of Incomes Policy, 1977, The Economic Consequences of Democracy, 1977, Role and Limits of Government: Essays in Political Economy, 1983, Jobs, Pay, Unions and the Ownership of Capital, 1984; Second Thoughts on Full Employment Policy (with Peter Lilley), 1975. Recipient Sr. Wincott Found. award, 1971, George Orwell prize Penguin Books, 1981. Office: The Fin Times, Bracken House, 10 Cannon St, London EC4, England

BRITTENHAM, RAYMOND LEE, investment company executive; b. Moscow, Russia, Feb. 8, 1916; s. Edward Arthur and Marietta (Wemple) B.; m. Mary Ann Stanard, Nov. 3, 1956; children—Edward C., Carol. A.B., Principia Coll., Elsah, Ill., 1936; postgrad., Kaiser Wilhelm U., Berlin, Germany, 1937; LL.B., Harvard, 1940. Bar: Ill. 1940, N.Y. 1946. Assoc. firm Pope & Ballard, Chgo., 1940-42, Mitchell Carroll, N.Y.C., 1947-56; v.p., gen. counsel ITT (and subs.), 1962-68; sr. v.p. law, counsel ITT (and subs.'s), 1968-80, dir., 1965-80; with Lazard Freres & Co., N.Y.C., 1980—; pres. Spanish Inst., 1980-82, vice chmn., 1982—; sec. U.S. sect. Internat. Fiscal Assn., 1950-57; bd. dirs. Nat. Fgn. Trade Council, 1961-80. Served to maj. AUS, 1942-46. Decorated Bronze Star medal; Croix de Guerre France and Belgium; chevalier Ordre de Leopold Belgium). Mem. ABA, Council Fgn. Relations. Club: University (N.Y.C.). Home: 925 Park Ave New York NY 10028 Office: 1 Rockefeller Plaza New York NY 10020

BRITTO, PAULO FERNANDO HENRIQUES, translator; b. Rio de Janeiro, Dec. 12, 1951; s. Wilson Da Silveira and Leda (Marques Henriques) B. Licenciatura in English, U. Santa Úrsula, 1974; Licenciatura in English and Portuguese, Pontifícia U. Católica, Rio de Janeiro, 1978, MA, 1982. Tchr. Inst. Brasil-Estados Unidos, Rio de Janeiro, 1974-79; inst. Pontifícia U. Católica, Rio de Janeiro, 1978-81; aux. prof. translation Pontifícia U. Católica, Rio de Janeiro, 1981—. Author: Liturgia da Matéria, 1982; translator Voss (Patrick White), 1985, Miss Lonelyhearts and the Day of the Locust (Nathanael West), 1985, To the Finland Station (Edmund Wilson) 1986, The Fall of America (Allen Ginsberg), 1987; editor, translator: Poems (Wallace Stevens), 1987. Home: R Mário Portela 161/bIA/402, 22241 Rio de Janeiro Brazil Office: Pontifícia U Católica, R Marques de S Vicente 209, 22451 Rio de Janeiro Brazil

BRITTON, CLAROLD LAWRENCE, lawyer; b. Soldier, Iowa, Nov. 1, 1932; s. Arnold Olaf and Florence Ruth (Gardner) B.; m. Joyce Helene Hamlett, Feb. 1, 1957; children: Laura, Eric, Val, Martha. B.S. in Engring., U. Mich., Ann Arbor, 1958, J.D., 1961. Bar: Ill. 1961, U.S. Dist. Ct. (no. dist.) Ill. 1962, U.S. Ct. Appeals (7th cir.) 1963, U.S. Supreme Ct. 1970. Assoc., Jenner & Block, Chgo., 1961-70, ptnr., 1970-88. Lectr. DePaul U., 1988—. Served to comdr. USNR, 1952-57. Fellow Am. Coll. Trial Lawyers; mem. Chgo. Bar Assn. (past chmn. fed. civil procedure, judiciary and computer law coms., civil practice com.,), Ill. State Bar Assn. (chmn. Allerton House Conf. 1984, 86, chmn. rule 23 com. 1985-87, chmn. civil practice and procedure council 1987-88, antitrust com.), ABA (litigation sect., antitrust com., discovery com., past regional chmn. 7th cir. 1961—), 7th Cir. Bar Assn., Def. Research Inst. (com. on aerospace 1984), Ill. Soc. Trial Lawyers, Order of Coif, Alpha Phi Mu, Tau Beta Pi. Republican. Lutheran. Clubs: Law (Chgo.); Racine Yacht (Wis.). Lodge: Masons. Asst. editor Mich. Law Rev., 1960.

BRITZ, DIANE EDWARD, investment company executive, chemical trader; b. York, Pa., June 15, 1952; d. Everett Frank and Billie Jacqueline (Sherrill) B.; m. Marcello Lotti, Sept. 9, 1978; children: Ariane Elizabeth, Samantha Alexis. BA, Duke U., 1974; MBA, Columbia U., 1982. Asst. mgr. Columbia Artists, N.Y.C., 1974-76; gen. mgr. Eastern Music Festival, Greensboro, N.C., 1977-78; v.p. Britz Cobin, N.Y.C., 1979-82; pres. Pan Oceanic Mgmt., N.Y.C., 1983, also bd. dirs.; pres. Pan Oceanic Advisors, Ltd., 1988—, also bd. dirs; bd. trustees Turtle Bay Music Sch. Mem. Bus. Vols. For Arts; class chmn. Duke U. Ann. Fund Drive. Mem. NOW, Fin. Women's Assn., Internat. Platform Assn., Columbia Bus. Sch. Clubs: Quaker, Doubles, Wings (N.Y.C.). Office: Pan Oceanic Mgmt Ltd 122 E 42d St Suite 205 New York NY 10168

BRIX, JAMES ALEXANDER, accountant; b. Seattle, Aug. 30, 1913; s. James S. and Edith (Seedorff) B.; B.A. in Bus. Adminstrn. magna cum laude, U. Wash., 1954; m. Sigrid Lena Forsberg, Feb. 13, 1935; children—Joan Lenea (Mrs. Jack Carter), James Alexander, Julee Karen (Mrs. George E. Barber). Asst. personnel supr. Dept. Lighting, Seattle, 1937-41, 44-49, accountant Haskins and Sells, C.P.A.'s, 1954-56; partner Brix and Shank, C.P.A.'s, Poulsbo, Wash., 1956-58, pvt. practice pub. accountant, 1958—; gen. partner BHL W & Co.; v.p., dir. Fairview Estates, Inc.; dir. Jensen, Richards and Olhava, Inc. Served to capt., AUS, 1940-44. President's medalist U. Wash., 1954. Mem. Am. Inst. C.P.A.'s, Wash. Soc. C.P.A.'s, Am. Legion, Disabled Officers World Wars, Ret. Officers Assn., C. of C. (past treas.), Phi Beta Kappa, Beta Gamma Sigma, Beta Alpha Psi, Alpha Kappa Psi. Mason. Lutheran (past treas.). Clubs: Collins Lake Community (past v.p., dir.); Emerald Lake Community (past pres., dir.); Poulsbo Yacht (past treas.). Home: PO Box 823 Poulsbo WA 98370

BRO, KENNETH ARTHUR, plastic manufacturing company executive; b. Tsingdao, Shandung, China, Aug. 28, 1921 (parents Am. citizens); s. Albin Carl and Marguerite (Harmon) B.; m. Patricia Welch, May 6, 1944; children—William, Peter, Kenneth M., Patricia, Elizabeth, A. Charles. B.S., Northwestern U., 1949. Purchasing agent Welch Mfg. Co., Chgo., 1950-56; v.p. Welch Sci. Co., Chgo., 1957-64; v.p., co-owner Webb Plastic Co., Northbrook, Ill., 1965-87 . Chmn. bd. trustees Northland Coll., Ashland, Wis., 1957, 70-74; pres. bd. dirs. Chgo. Commons Assn., 1962, 70-74; dist. chmn. bd. dirs. Jr. Achievement, Chgo., 1970, 72-74; pres. Found. for Sci. Relaxation, 1965—. Served to pvt. 1st class U.S. Army, 1944-46, ETO. Decorated Bronze Star, Purple Heart. Mem. Am. Vaccum Soc., Am. Assn. Physics Tchrs. Republican. Congregationalist. Clubs: Indian Hill (Winnetka, Ill.); University, Chgo. Yacht, Economic, Executive (Chgo.). Avocations: sailing; flying; travel. Home: 375 Sheridan Rd Winnetka IL 60093 Office: PO Box 583 Wilmette IL 60091

BROADBENT, DONALD E., experimental psychologist; b. Birmingham, Eng., May 6, 1926; s. Herbert Arthur and Hannah Elizabeth B.; m. Margaret Elizabeth Wright, June 23, 1949 (div. 1972); children: Patricia Anne, Judith Elizabeth (dec.); m. Margaret Hope Pattison Gregory, Nov. 11, 1972. BA, U. Cambridge, Eng., 1949, ScD, 1965; Doctorate (hon.), U. Southampton, Eng., 1974, U. York, Eng., 1979, U. Loughborough, Eng., 1982, U. Brussels, 1985. Mem. sci. staff applied psychology unit Med. Research Council, Cambridge, 1949-58, dir., 1958-74; mem. external staff Med. Research Council, Oxford, 1974—; fellow Pembroke Coll., Cambridge, 1965-74, Wolfson Coll., Oxford, 1974—. Author: Perception and Communication, 1958, Behaviour, 1961, Decision and Stress, 1971, In Defence of Empirical Psychology, 1973. Served as cpl. RAF, 1944-47. Named Comdr. Order Brit. Empire, Queen of Eng., 1974; recipient Disting. Sci. Contbn. award Am. Psychol. Assn., 1975. Fellow Royal Soc. London (mem. council 1978-80), Brit. Psychol. Soc. (hon., pres. 1964-65); mem. U.S. Nat. Acad. Sci. (fgn. assoc.), Ergonomics Soc. (hon., founder), Exptl. Psychology Soc. (pres. 1973-74). Office: Dept Exptl Psychology, South Parks Rd, Oxford OX1 3UD, England

BROADBRIDGE, HANNA DORETE AGNETE, English educator; b. Langaa, Denmark, Apr. 4, 1945; d. Carl Ring and Lydia Maria (Holm Larsen) Graabech; m. Edward John Broadbridge, Sept. 2, 1967; children: Lisa Maria, Helena Tara. MA in English, Aarhus U., Denmark, 1970, BA in Japanese, 1977. Tchr. English County High Sch., Randers, Denmark, 1970—; lectr. Royal Acad. Edn., Skive, Denmark, 1978—, Ministry Edn., Aarhus, 1980-85; freelance course organizer, lectr. Author ednl., religious drama material. Councillor Luth. Ch., Randers, 1984—, fiscal com. Aarhus Diocese, 1985; instigator Refugee Integration Program, Randers, 1984—. Fulbright scholar U. Mich., 1985. Mem. English Tchrs. Assn. Denmark (bd. dirs. 1986—). Mem. Liberal Party. Home: Granvaenget 4, 8900 Randers Denmark Office: Amtsgymnasiet i Paderup, Apollovej, 8900 Randers Denmark

BROADHURST, AUSTIN, JR., executive recruiter; b. Boston, Aug. 9, 1947; s. Austin and Deborah (Lowell) B.; B.A., Williams Coll., 1969; M.B.A., Harvard U., 1972; m. Janine Boyajian, June 15, 1974; children—Robert James, Lauren Cox. With sec.'s office HEW, Washington, 1972-76; asst. to corp. exec. v.p. Travenol Labs., Deerfield, Ill., 1976-78, group product mgr., 1978-79; dir. corp. planning Nat. Med. Care, Boston, 1979-80, corp. v.p., 1980-83; sr. v.p. UHA Enterprises, N.Y.C., 1983-84; pres., chief exec. officer, dir. OcuSystems, Inc., 1985-86; exec. dir. Russell Reynolds Assn. 1986-88, mng. dir., 1988—. Corporator New Eng. Bapt. Hosp., 1982-83; active Squam Lakes Assn., N.H. Episcopalian. Clubs: Harvard of N.Y., Milbrook. Home: 45 Patterson Ave Greenwich CT 06830 Office: 3 Landmark Sq Stamford CT 06901

BROADWAY, NANCY RUTH, landscape design and construction company executive; b. Memphis, Tenn., Dec. 20, 1946; d. Charlie Sidney and Patsy Ruth (Meadows) Adkins. B.S. in Biology and Sociology cum laude, Memphis State U., 1969; postgrad. Tulane U., 1969-70; M.S. in Horticulture, U. Calif.-Davis, 1976. Lic. landscape contractor, Calif. Claims adjuster Mass. Mut. Ins., San Francisco, 1972-73; community garden coordinator City of Davis, Calif., 1976; supr. seed propagation Bordier's Wholesale Nursery, Santa Ana, Calif., 1976-78; owner, contractor Calif. Landscape Co., Stockton, Calif., 1978—, Design and Mgmt. Cons., Wallace, Calif.; NDEA fellow Tulane U., 1969-70. Mem. Am. Hort. Soc., Net. Assn. Gen. Contractors, Calif. Native Plant Soc., Stockton C. of C. Democrat. Office: Calif Landscape Co/Design & Mgmt Cons PO Box 122 Wallace CA 95254

BROADWELL, RICHARD DOW, neurocytologist, neuropathologist, researcher, educator; b. Oak Park, Ill., Nov. 4, 1945; s. Robert and Dorothy Jane (Dow) B. B.A., Knox Coll., 1967; M.S., U. Wis., Madison, 1971, D. Phil., 1974. Staff fellow in neurocytology/neuropathology Nat. Inst. Neurol. and Communicable Diseases and Stroke, NIH, Bethesda, Md., 1974-80; assoc. prof. pathology and neurol. surgery, head Lab. Exptl. Neuropathology and Labs. Neuro-Oncology and Cerebrovascular Studies (Neurol. Surgery), U. Md. Sch. Medicine, 1980—; dir. molecular and cellular neurobiology program NSF, Washington, 1987—; cons. in field. Contbr. numerous articles, chpts. on brain and neurocytology to profl. publs. Recipient Undergrad. Research award NSF, 1966-67; Japanese Soc. for Promotion of Sci. fellow, 1980-81; NIH Nat. Inst. Neurol. and Communicable Diseases and Stroke grantee, 1982—. Mem. Neurosci. Soc., Am. Soc. Cell Biology, Histochem. Soc., Chesapeake Electron Microscopy Soc. Republican. Presbyterian. Home: 10939 Brewer House Pl Rockville MD 20852 Office: U Md Dept Pathology 10 S Pine St Baltimore MD 21201

BROCK, ANDREW DUNCAN, accountant; b. Prestwick, Scotland, Oct. 16, 1925; arrived in Zimbabwe, 1955; s. James and Edna Mary (McCulloch) B.; m. Elizabeth Crawford Blackwood, June 10, 1948; children: Anne Elizabeth, Iain Duncan. Grad., Inst. Chartered Acctg. of Scotland, 1951, Inst. Chartered Secs. Poly., Zimbabwe, 1972; postgrad diploma in mgmt. studies, Harane Polytechnic, 1974. Acct., sec. Tobacco Research Bd., Harare, Zimbabwe, 1955-75; with T.A. Holdings Ltd., Harare, 1975—. Fellow Zimbabwe Inst. Mgmt. (v.p. 1983-85), Inst. Chartered Secs. and Adminstrs.; mem. Inst. Chartered Accts. Zimbabwe, Inst. Chartered Accts. Scotland. Home: 5 Norest Heights Quinton Rd, Greystone Park, PO Box 1069, Harare Zimbabwe

BROCK, CHARLES LAWRENCE, lawyer, business executive; b. Ottumwa, Iowa, Mar. 7, 1943; s. Charles Harlan and Betty Arlene (Ream) B.; m. Mary Jane Hipp, June 17, 1978; children: William Walker, Susanna Lawrence. BA with highest distinction, Northwestern U., 1964; JD, Harvard U., 1967; postgrad. (Rotary Found. fellow), U. Delhi (India) and India Law Inst., 1967-68; grad., Advanced Mgmt. Program, Harvard Bus. Sch., 1979. Bar: N.Y. State bar 1968. Asso. firm Sullivan & Cromwell, N.Y.C., 1969-74; v.p., corp. sec., gen. counsel Scholastic Mags., Inc. (now Scholastic, Inc.), N.Y.C., 1974-80; interim chief fin. and chief ops. officer Scholastic Mags., Inc., 1975-76, pub. internat. div., 1976-80; pres. Scholastic Tab Publs. Ltd., Can., 1976-80, Ashton-Scholastic Pty. Ltd., Australia, 1976-80, Ashton-Scholastic Ltd., N.Z., 1976-80; chmn. Scholastic Publs. Ltd., U.K., 1976-80; sr. v.p., mgmt. dir. Compton Communications, 1980-82; mgr. subsidiaries Compton Advertising, 1980-82; counsel Drinker, Biddle & Reath, N.Y.C., Phila., Washington, 1982-84; ptnr. Carter, Ledyard & Milburn, 1984—; bd. dirs. B&H Bulk Carriers Ltd., B&H Ocean Carriers Ltd. Anniversary gift chmn. Harvard Law Sch. Fund, 1967-68, vice chmn., 1975-77; council Nat. Harvard Law Sch. Assn., 1983-85, sec., 1988—, mem. exec. com., 1986—, chmn. membership com., 1987—; trustee Harvard Law Sch. Assn. N.Y.C., 1982-85, chmn. placement com., 1983-86, v.p., 1985-86, originator, chmn. summer reception, 1982; trustee, treas. Family Dynamics, 1981—; mem. Harvard Bus. Club of N.Y., v.p. 1984-86, chmn. Harvard Community Ptnrs., 1984-86; trustee, mem. exec. com., chmn. nominating com. Guild Hall, 1986—; deacon Brick Presbyn. Ch., N.Y.C., 1973-76. Mem. Am. Bar Assn., N.Y. State Bar Assn., N.Y. County Lawyers Assn., Assn. Bar City N.Y., Assn. Am. Pubs., Harvard Law Sch. Assn., Phi Beta Kappa, Kappa Sigma. Clubs: Union (N.Y.C.), Harvard (N.Y.C.), N.Y. Yacht (N.Y.C.), Metropolitan (N.Y.C.), Down Town (N.Y.C.); Piping Rock (Locust Valley, N.Y.); Maidstone (East Hampton, N.Y.). Home: 765 Park Ave New York NY 10021 Office: Carter Ledyard & Milburn 2 Wall St New York NY 10005

BROCK, CHARLES MARQUIS, lawyer; b. Watseka, Ill., Oct. 8, 1941; s. Glen Westgate and Muriel Lucile (Bubeck) B.; m. Elizabeth Bonilla, Dec. 17, 1966; children—Henry Christopher, Anna Melissa. A.B. cum laude, Princeton U., 1963; J.D., Georgetown U., 1968; M.B.A., U. Chgo., 1974. Bar: Ill. 1969, U.S. Dist. Ct. (no. dist.) Ill. 1969. Asst. trust counsel Continental Ill. Nat. Bank, Chgo., 1968-74; regional counsel Latin Am., Can. Abbott Labs., Abbott Park, Ill., 1974-77, regional counsel, Europe, Africa and Middle East, 1977-81, div. counsel, 1981—; sec. mgmt. com. TAP Pharms., 1985—. Served with Inter-Am. Def. Coll., U.S. Army, 1964-66. Mem. ABA, Chgo. Bar Assn., Phi Beta Kappa. Republican. Clubs: Princeton (Chgo.); Princeton (N.Y.C.), Mich. Shores (Wilmette, Ill.) Home: 1473 Asbury Ave Winnetka IL 60093 Office: Abbott Labs Abbott Park IL 60064

BROCK, JOHN HEDLEY, mining company director; b. Kelly Bray, Cornwall, Eng., Jan. 18, 1912; s. John and Mary (Priest) B.; m. Vera Wonnacott, June 6, 1940 (dec. Feb. 1972); 1 child, John David; m. Ann Laity, Feb. 8, 1973. Student, Callington Sch., Cornwall, Eng. Mgr. Lloyds Bank PLC, Plymouth, Eng., 1950-74; dir. Coverack (Eng.) Harbour Co. Ltd., 1970—; chmn. China Clay Council, St. Austell, Eng., 1972—; exec. Cornish Chamber of Mines, 1985—. Served to lt. comdr. Royal Navy, 1940-46.

Decorated Order of the Brit. Empire, Her Majesty The Queen, 1976. Fellow Chartered Inst. Bankers; mem. Cornish Mining Devel. Assn. (pres. 1975—). Conservative. Methodist. Home: Chy An Mor, Coverack, Helston Cornwall TR12 6SZ, England

BROCK, JUDITH ANNE, publisher, magazine editor, marketing consultant, graphics designer; b. McAlester, Okla., July 8, 1950; d. Eddie W. and Irene Laverne (Hicks) Lee; m. James Lavern Hodge, Jan. 30, 1970 (div. Dec. 1977); 1 child, Joshua Lee; m. Paul Edward Brock, May 31, 1980. AA in Bus., Crowder Coll., 1972; BA, Boston U., 1988. Pres. J.L.I., Neosho, Mo., 1981—; v.p., mktg. The Brock Corp., Neosho, 1982—; founder, editor In..Joplin (Mo.) Met. Mag., 1984—; founding pres. The Apricotery, Neosho and Boston, 1987—; founder The Epicenter, Joplin, Mo., 1987—; dir. mktg. TechMark, Ltd.; entrepreneur, mktg. cons. Neosho, 1980—. inventor card games Josh, 1982, E.W. Lee, 1988. Pres. Neosho PTA, 1982-84. Named Woman of Yr., Beta Sigma Phi, Neosho, 1983-84; recipient Bringing Out Your Best award Budweiser Light, 1983. Mem. Am. Mktg. Assn. (exec.), Neosho C. of C. (retail dir. 1983-84), Gifted Assn. (pres. 1985—), Mensa. Lodge: Soroptimist (treas. 1984-85). Office: The Brock Corp 317 Fairground Rd Neosho MO 64850

BROCK, PATRICK LAURENCE, rector; b. Bromley, Kent, England, July 7, 1918; s. Laurence George and Ellen Margery (Williams) B.; m. Patricia Addinsell Walton, June, 1950; children: Jonathan Simon, Penelope Rachel, Jeremy Benjamin. Degree, Oxford U., 1945. With Ministry of Civil Aviation and Cabinet Office U.K. Home Civil Service, London, 1946-55; asst. curate Ch. of Eng., Malvern and London, 1957-62; vicar St. Peter, Belsize Park, London, 1962-72; rector of Finchley London, 1972—; area dean Ctl. Barnet, London, 1980-85; staff, council, exec. com. Coll. of Preachers, 1971—; prebendary St. Paul's Cathedral, 1980—. Author: Worship Beyond the Mind, 1987; booklet: A Theology of Church Design, 1984. Served to maj. with Brit. Army, 1939-45. Named Mem. of the Order of the British Empire His Majesty the King, 1944. Home and Office: St Marys Rectory, Rectory Close, Finchley, London England N3 1TS

BROCK, WARREN RICHARD, lawyer; b. Buffalo, Mar. 30, 1919; m. Kathryn Brock; children: Rick (dec.), Jeff, Bonnie. BA, U. Mich., 1940; JD, U.Ariz., 1952. Bar: Ariz. 1952, N.Y. 1952. Sole practice, Tucson, 1952—; spl. ct. commr., Tucson, 1975; chmn. law sch. brief contest U. Ariz., 1966. Active Anti-Defamation Council; del. Democratic Nat. Conv., 1976; mem. character guidance com. Tucson YMCA. Named Tucson Community Leader, Tucson Sun newspaper, 1954. Mem. Am. Arbitration Assn. (panel arbitrators 1972-84), So. Ariz. Claimants compensation Attys. Assn. (co-founder, treas. 1959-63), Nat. Assn. Claimant's Counsel Assn. (former treas. local chpt.), ABA, Ariz. Bar Assn., N.Y. State Bar Assn., Assn. Trial Lawyers Am., Ariz. Trial Lawyers Assn., Calif. Trial Lawyers Assn., Pima County Trial Lawyers Assn., Am. Judicature Soc., Phi Alpha Delta, Phi Epsilon Pi. Contbr. weekly sports column to Green Valley News; editor Pleasure Mag., 1946-48. Clubs: Alianza, Arizona Wildcat, Golden Baton. Lodges: Masons, Elks. Home: 5242 N Genematas St Tucson AZ 85704 Office: 244 W Drachman St Tucson AZ 85705

BROCK, WILLIAM EMERSON, former secretary Department of Labor; b. Chattanooga, Nov. 23, 1930; s. William E. and Myra (Kruesi) B.; m. Laura Handly, Jan. 11, 1957 (dec. 1985); children: William, Oscar, Laura, John; m. Sandra Schubert Mitchell, Dec. 5, 1986. B.S., Washington and Lee Coll., 1953. V.p. Brock Candy Co., 1957-62; mem. U.S. Congress from Tenn., 1963-70, U.S. Senate from Tenn., 1971-77; chmn. Rep. Nat. Com., Washington, 1977-81; U.S. trade rep. Washington, 1981-85; sec. U.S. Dept. Labor, Washington, 1985-87; owner Wm. Brock Assocs., Washington, 1987—. Chmn. Nat. Endowment for Democracy, Kirkpatrick Forum; counselor Ctr. Stategic and Internat. Studies. Served to lt. (j.g.) USN, 1953-56. Named Outstanding Young Man of Yr., Tenn. Jaycees, 1965; recipient Disting. Service award Jaycees, Chattanooga, 1966, award for outstanding service Teenage Reps., 1967. Presbyterian. Office: William Brock Associates 1800 K St NW Suite 400 Washington DC 20006

BROCKERT, JOSEPH PAUL, government executive, writer, editor, design consultant; b. Tipp City, Ohio, Sept. 17, 1954; s. Paul Edwin and Mary (Aten) B.; m. Deborah Sue Schaefer, Apr. 10, 1976; children: Jonathan Andre, Jason Anthony. BS in Journalism with honors, Ohio U., 1975. Sr. editor Linn's Stamp News, Sidney, Ohio, 1976-84; sr. stamp program specialist U.S. Postal Service, Washington, 1984-87, program mgr. for stamp design, 1987—; coordinator Citizens' Stamp Adv. Com., 1985; art dir. U.S. stamps and stationery, 1986—, designer, 1988—; agy. rep. Commn. Bicentennial of U.S. Constn., 1986—. Author: Basic Knowledge for the Stamp Collector, 1978, 4th revised edit., 1983 (Silver medal Am. Philatelic Soc. 1979, Internat. Bronze medal 1986), (with Elaine Durnin Boughner) Stamp Collecting Made Easy, 1984, 3d revised edit., 1986; contbr. articles to profl. and hobby jours. Chmn. publicity Gunston (Va.) Elem. PTA, 1985, pres., 1986-87; Lorton Little League Coach, 1987—. Mem. Mensa. Roman Catholic. Avocations: music, collecting stamps, photography, composing. Home: 8456 Gold Sky Ct Springfield VA 22153

BROCKHAUS, ROBERT HEROLD, SR., business educator, consultant; b. St. Louis, Apr. 18, 1940; s. Herold August and Leona M (Stutzke) B.; m. Joyce Patricia Dees, June 13, 1970; children—Cheryl Lynn, Robert Herold. B.S. in Mech. Engring., U. Mo.-Rolla, 1962; M.S.I.A., Purdue U., 1966; Ph.D., Washington U., St. Louis, 1976. Mgr. Ralston-Purina, St. Louis, 1962-69; pres. Progressive Mgmt. Enterprises, Ltd., St. Louis, 1969—; asst. prof. mgmt. sci. St. Louis U., 1972-78, assoc. prof., 1978-84, prof., 1984—; dir. Small Bus. Inst., St. Louis U., 1976-86; dir. Inst. Entrpreneurial Studies, 1987—; state adminstr. Mo. Small Bus. Devel. Ctrs., St. Louis, 1982-86, state dir., 1987—; Schoen prof. entrepreneurship Baylor U., 1981; McAninch prof. entrepreneurship Kans. State U., 1985-87 . Co-author: Encyclopedia of Entrepreneurship, 1982; Building A Better You, 1982; Nursing Concepts for Health Promotion, 1979, Art and Science of Enterpreneurship, 1985; editor Journal of Consulting, 1988—; also contbr. articles to profl. jours. Bd. dirs. City Venture, St. Louis, 1982-86; del White House Conf.on Small Bus., 1986. Recipient Disting. Service award Pi Kappa Alpha, 1972; Fulbright fellow, U. Waikato, N.Z., 1985. Fellow Internat. Council for Small Bus. (sr. v.p. 1981-83, internat. pres. 1983-84, bd. dirs. 1983, v.p. 1986, exec. dir. 1987—), Nat. Small Bus. Inst. Dirs. Assn. (nat. v.p. 1980-82, nat. pres. 1982-83); mem. Acad. Mgmt. (nat. program chmn. 1977-78), Fenton Jaycees (treas.). Mem. United Ch. of Christ. Club: Executive (St. Louis) (moderator 1973-86). Avocations: swimming; sailing; camping. Home: 10000 Hilltop Dr Saint Louis MO 63128

BROCKSBANK, ROBERT WAYNE, retired oil company executive; b. Hudson, N.Y., June 2, 1924; s. Harold Ten Eyck and Helen (Beeler) B.; m. Grace Mary Wright, June 24, 1944 (div. 1976); children—Leslie B. Lucas, Stephanie B. Rodgers, Sydney B. Kirchner; m. Karin Paulson, Oct. 6, 1979. B.S. in Commerce, Drexel U., 1947. Varsity athletic coach Friends Central Prep. Sch., Phila., 1946; with Socony Vacuum Oil (now Mobil), Paulsboro, N.J., 1947-55; staff asst., mfg. employee relations Socony Mobil Oil (now Mobil), N.Y.C., 1955-57; asst. employee relations mgr. Mobil Oil, N.Y.C., 1957-59, mgr. coll. relations, 1959-85. Contbr. articles to profl. jours. Cons., Council on Career Devel. for Minorities, Dallas, 1964—, bd., 1968—, chmn., 1981—, chmn. emeritus, 1988—. Nat. Urban League Summer Fellowship and Career Awareness Program, 1966-81; dir. Southeastern Econ. Devel. Found., Atlanta, 1976-85; trustee Tougaloo (Miss.) Coll., 1977—; exec. adv. council Soc. Hispanic Profl. Engrs., Los Angeles, 1977—; chmn. bus. adv. com. Hampton (Va.) Inst., 1978-81, mem., 1978-86; mem. minority engring. corp. adv. bd. U. Md., 1979-85, chmn., 1979-81; mem. bd. visitors Drexel U. Sch. Bus., Phila., 1980—; dir. Nat. Consortium for Grad. Degrees for Minorities in Engring., South Bend, Ind., 1981-84. Served to maj. USMC 1942-46, 50-52. Named Friend of the Univ., Va. State U., 1981; Mem. Emeritus, N.C. Central U. Bus. Adv. Council, 1983; Trustee of Edn., League of Latin Am. Citizens, 1983 Robert W. Brocksbank endowed scholarship fund established in his honor, 1985; recipient Pericles award Nat. Employment Mgrs. Assn., 1986, Martin Luther King Dream award Nat. Assn. Negro Profl. and Bus. Women's Clubs, Inc., 1988. Mem. Am. Assembly Coll. Schs. of Bus. (dir. 1980-82, com. Upward Mobility for Minorities in Bus.), Coop. Edn. Assn., Am. Soc. Engring. Edn., Mexican-Am. Engring. Soc., Western Coll. Placement Assn., Southern Coll. Placement Assn., S.W. Coll. Placement Assn., Tex. Assn. Chicanos in Higher Edn., Internat. Platform Assn., Am. Indian Sci. and Engring. Soc. (adv. bd. 1982—, chmn. 1985), Midwest Coll. Placement Assn. (mem. emeritus), Middle Atlantic Placement Assn. (hon., dir. 1963-65), Eastern Coll. Personnel Officers (dir. 1961-63). Republican. Presbyterian. Clubs: Marine Meml. Club (San Francisco); Marine Officers Assn. (Quantico, Va.). First Person to be featured 3 times on page 1 of Wall Street Journal. Office: Mobil Oil Corp 150 E 42d St New York NY 10017

BRODATY, YVES JACQUES, physician, educator; b. Paris, Dec. 21, 1944; s. Serge Samuel and Françoise (Gottesfeld) B.; m. Christine Rachel Bourdier, Oct. 9, 1980; children: Marion Catherine, Sophie Agnes. MD, Faculté Medecine, Paris, 1970. Resident in rhumatology Faculté Medecine, Paris, 1970-73; practice medicine specializing in rhumatology Paris, 1974—; rhumatologist Clinic at Hosp. St. Antoine and Pitié Salpetrière, Paris, 1974—; cons. RhonePoulenc Farmacy, Paris, 1972-78; asst. prof. Dept. Geriatry Faculté Medecine, 1979. Office: 48 rue de Malte, Paris France 75011

BRODER, PATRICIA JANIS, art historian, writer, lecturer; b. N.Y.C., Nov. 22, 1935; d. Milton W. and Rheba (Mantell) Janis; m. Stanley H. Broder, Jan. 22, 1959; children: Clifford James, Peter Howard, Helen Anna. Student, Smith Coll., 1953-54; B.A., Barnard Coll., Columbia U., 1957; postgrad., Rutgers U., 1962-64. Stock brokerage trainee A.M. Kidder & Co., N.Y.C., 1958; registered rep. Thomson & McKinnon, N.Y.C., 1959-61; ind. registered investment advisor 1962-64. Art cons., art investment advisor; writer on art history: books include Bronzes of the American West (Hebert Adam Meml. medal Nat. Sculpture Soc. 1975), 1974 (Gold medal Nat. Acad. Western Art 1975), Great Paintings of the Old American West, American Indian Painting and Sculpture, Taos: A Painter's Dream (Western Heritage Wrangler award, Border Regional Library Assn. award 1980), Hopi Painting: The World of the Hopis, Dean Cornwell: Dean of Illustrators, The American West: The Modern Vision (new award 1984, Trustees award Nat. Cowboy Hall of Fame 1984). Recipient Western Heritage Wranglers award for best article on Am. West, 1975; Gold medal Nat. Acad. Western Art. Mem. Western History Assn., AAUW. Home: 488 Long Hill Dr Short Hills NJ 07078

BRODERICK, HAROLD CHRISTIAN, interior designer; b. Oakland, Calif., Apr. 8, 1925; s. Harold Christian and Laura Jane (Lloyd) B. BA, U. Tex., 1947. A founder Arthur Elrod Assos., Inc., Palm Springs, Calif., 1954, now pres. Mem. Planning Commn., City of Palm Springs, 1972-74; trust Palm Springs Desert Mus.; mem. devel. com. Barbara Sinatra Children's Ctr. Mem. Am. Soc. Interior Designers. Republican. Office: Arthur Elrod Associates Inc 850 N Palm Canyon Dr Palm Springs CA 92262

BRODIE, HARLOW KEITH HAMMOND, university president; b. Stamford, Conn., Aug. 24, 1939; s. Lawrence Sheldon and Elizabeth White (Hammond) B.; m. Brenda Ann Barrowclough, Jan. 26, 1967; children: Melissa Verduin, Cameron Keith, Tyler Hammond, Bryson Barrowclough. AB, Princeton U., 1961; MD, Columbia U., 1965; LLD hon., U. Richmond, 1987. Diplomate Am. Bd. Psychiatry and Neurology. Intern Ochsner Found. Hosp., New Orleans, 1965-66; resident in psychiatry Columbia-Presbyn. Med. Center, N.Y.C., 1966-68; clin. assoc. intramural research program NIMH, 1968-70; asst. prof. psychiatry, dir. gen. clin. research center Stanford U. Med. Sch., 1970-74; prof. psychiatry, chmn. dept. Duke U. Med. Sch., 1974-82, James B. Duke prof. psychiatry and law, 1981—, adj. prof. psychology, 1980—; psychiatrist-in-chief Duke U. Med. Center, 1974-82; chancellor Duke U., 1982-85, pres., 1985—. Co-author: The Importance of Mental Health Services to General Health Care, 1979, Modern Clinical Psychiatry, 1981; co-editor: American Handbook of Psychiatry, vols. 6, 7 and 8, 1975, 81, 86, Controversy in Psychiatry, 1978; assoc. editor: Am. Jour. Psychiatry, 1973-81. Chmn. Durham Area Mental Health, Mental Retardation and Substance Abuse Bd., 1981-82; pres., trustee Durham Acad., 1985-87. Recipient Disting. Med. Alumni award Columbia U., 1985; Disting. Alumnus award Ochsner Found. Hosp., 1984, Strecker award Inst. of Pa. Hosp., 1980. Mem. Am. Psychiat. Assn. (sec. 1977-81, pres. 1982-83), Inst. Medicine, Royal Coll. Psychiatrists, Soc. Biol. Psychiatry (A.E. Bennet research award 1970). Home: 63 Beverly Dr Durham NC 27707 Office: Duke U Office of Pres 207 Allen Bldg Durham NC 27706

BRODNAX-WATSON, SHIRLEY JEAN, microbiologist; b. Norfolk, Va.; d. John B. and Louise (Booker) Holloway; m. Jack Leon Brodnax, July 31, 1976; children: Melodie, Tracey, Maisha. AA, Contra Costa Coll., 1978; BS in Cell and Molecular Biology, San Francisco State U., 1985. Jr. accountant Philco Corp., Phila.; sec., supr. U.S. Govt., Phila. and San Francisco, 1968-76; research asst., microbiologist Kelly Tech. Services, Oakland, Calif., 1986; microbiologist Nabisco Brands, Inc., Oakland, 1986—. Kennedy King scholar Contra Costa Coll., 1978-80. Mem. Internat. Platform Assn. Roman Catholic. Home: 1537 Hellings Ave Richmond CA 94801 Office: Nabisco Brands Inc 98th Ave Oakland CA 94630

BRODSGAARD, JORGEN, contractor; b. Gentofte, Denmark, July 18, 1922; s. Andreas Flensborg and Betty Helene (Sorensen) B.; m. Kirsten Palsboll, May 27, 1949; children—Peter Andreas, Jette, Trine. M.S. in Civil and Structural Engring., Danish Tech. U., 1947. Engr., Anglo-Iranian Oil Co., Copenhagen, 1947-49; engr. Cia Alcasan Construtora Minas Gerais, Belo Horizonite, Brazil, 1949-51; chief engr. Centrais Electricas de Belo Horizonte, 1951-60; project engr. Hanstholm Konsortiet, Copenhagen, 1960-70; mng. dir. Topsoe-Jensen & Schroder, Copenhagen, 1970—; dir. H. Meisner-Jensen, Copenhagen, 1964—, Humudan, Copehagen, 1976—; bldg. and civil engring. expert to Ct. Arbitration, 1979—. Mem. Assn. Danish Civil Engrs. Lutheran.

BRODSKY, IOSIF ALEXANDROVICH, poet; b. Leningrad, USSR, May 24, 1940; expelled from Russia, came to U.S., 1972; s. Alexander I. and Maria (Volpert) B. Student, Russian secondary schs., until 1956; D.Litt. (hon.), Yale U., 1978. Began writing poetry 1955; poet-in-residence U. Mich., Ann Arbor, 1972-73, 74-79; Andrew W. Mellon prof. lit. Mount Holyoke Coll., South Hadley, Mass., 1986—; vis. prof. Smith Coll., Amherst Coll., Queens Coll., Hampshire Coll., 1981-86; fellow N.Y. Inst. Humanities, NYU; assoc. Russian Inst., Columbia U., N.Y.C. Works include poetry in Russian and English, A Christmas Ballad, 1962, Elegy for John Donne, 1963, Isaac and Abraham, 1963, Verses on the Death of T.S. Eliot, 1965, Song Without Music, 1969, Selected Poems, 1973, A Part of Speech, 1980, History of the Twentieth Century, 1986; essays Less than One, 1981 (U.S. Nat. Book Critics' award, 1986), Urania: A New Book of Poems, 1984. John D. and Catherine T. MacArthur Found. fellow, 1981. recd. Nobel Prize for literature, 1987. Mem. AAAL, Bavarian Acad. Scis. (corr.). Jewish. Office: Mount Holyoke Coll Dept of Lit South Hadley MA 01075-1496 *

BRODY, DAVID A., lawyer; b. Bklyn., June 24, 1916; s. Samuel and Lily (Robinson) B.; m. Beatrice K. Brody, Mar. 11, 1943; children—Ann, Michael. B.S.S., CCNY, 1936; LL.B., Columbia U., 1940. Bar: N.Y. 1940, D.C. 1951, U.S. Supreme Ct. 1969, U.S. Ct. of Appeals, D.C., 1951. Atty., Office of Solicitor, U.S. Dept. Agr., 1940-49; Washington counsel Anti Defamation League of B'nai B'rith, 1949—; sole practice, Washington, 1953—; mem. rules adv. com. D.C. Ct. Appeals, 1978—, Bicentennial Commn. of U.S. CLaims Ct., 1986—, mem., 1986—; voting del. Jud. Conf. D.C., 1978—. Served with USN, 1943-46, legis. officer, 1944-46. Mem. Bar Assn. D.C. (chmn. com. trademarks 1975-76), ABA, U.S. Trademark Assn. (mem. internat. trademark com. 1981—), Fed. Cir. Bar Assn., Fed. Bar Assn., Fed. Cir. Bar Assn., Phi Beta Kappa. Jewish. Club: Nat. Lawyers (Washington). Legis. editor Columbia Law Rev., 1939-40; mem. adv. bd. BNA Patent, Trademark and Copyright Jour., 1970—. Home: 3001 Veazey Terr NW #202 Washington DC 20008 Office: 1050 17th St NW Washington DC 20036 also: 1640 Rhode Island Ave NW Washington DC 20036

BRODY, ELAINE, musicologist, educator; b. N.Y.C., Apr. 21, 1923; d. S. Lawrence and Helen (Golding) B.; m. David Silverberg, July 4, 1966; 1 dau. by previous marriage, Sue Shapiro. Student, Vassar Coll., 1940-41; A.B. with honors in Russian History, NYU, 1944; Ph.D. in Musicology, N.Y. U., 1964; A.M. in Musicology, Columbia U., 1960. Grad. asst., teaching fellow Washington Square Coll., NYU, 1961-63, instr., 1963-65, asst. prof., 1965-67, assoc. prof., 1967-70, prof. music history, 1970—; chmn. dept. music Univ. Coll., N.Y. U., 1965-73; instr. Sunrise Semester CBS-TV, 1975; lectr. 92d St. Y, 1977, also; NYU Med. Sch., Inst. Fine Arts, NYU, Cosmopolitan Club, Leo Baeck Inst.; condr. biography seminar N.Y. Inst. for Humanities, 1984-85; ednl. com. Met. Opera Guild, 1977—; music cons. N.Y. U. Press; organizer symposium Paris 1900/New York Today, 1980. Author: Music in Opera, 1970, (with R.A. Fowkes) The German Lied and Its Poetry, 1971, (with Claire Brook) The Music Guide to Great Britain, 1975, The Music Guide to Austria and Germany, 1975, The Music Guide to Belgium, Holland, Switzerland, 1977, The Music Guide to Italy, 1978, The Music Guide to France, Spain and Portugal, 1984, Paris: The Musical Kaleidoscope, 1870-1925, 1987; contbr. numerous articles, revs. to profl. jours. William Randolph Hearst Found. grantee, 1972-77; NYU Challenge grantee Humanities Council, 1978. Mem. Internat. Musicological Soc., Am. Musicological Soc. (chmn. Greater N.Y.C. chpt. 1974-76, nat. council) musicological socs.), Music Library Assn., Internat. Music Library Assn., Consortium Comparativists, Phi Beta Kappa (sec. Beta chpt. 1963-71). Home: 35 E 84th St New York NY 10028

BRODY, ROBERT, dermatologist; b. Cleve., June 15, 1948; s. Melvin and Nancy Elizabeth Brody; A.B. with distinction, Stanford U., 1970; M.D., U. Mich., 1974. Intern in internal medicine, Cleve. Clinic, 1974-75, resident in dermatology, 1975-78; practice medicine specializing in dermatology, Cleve., 1978—; staff physician Kaiser-Permanente Med. Center, 1978-82, mem. profl. edn. com., 1978-82, chmn., 1980-82, also sec. exec. com., 1980; pvt. practice, 1982—; asst. clin. prof. Case Western Res. U. Med. Sch., 1978-80, 83—, clin. instr., 1980-83, dermatology dept. rep. to gen. faculty, 1980-82; asst. physician Univ. Hosps. Cleve., 1979—. Sec., Cleve. Play House Men's Com., 1979-82; mem. ann. fund com. Stanford U., 1978—, regional co-chmn., 1981-82. Diplomate Am. Bd. Dermatology. Mem. Am. Acad. Dermatology, Cleve. Acad. Medicine. Contbr. articles to med. jours. Club: Cleve. Skating. Home: 13415 Shaker Blvd Cleveland OH 44120 Office: 3461 Warrensville Ctr Rd Shaker Heights OH 44122

BROEK, HENRI VAN DEN, minister foreign affairs The Netherlands; b. Paris, Dec. 11, 1936; m. J.A.A. Van Den Broek; 2 daus. Ed. The Alberdingk Thymlyceum, Utrecht U. Lawyer, Rotterdam, 1965-68; sec. mng. bd. ENKA B.V., Arnhem, 1969-73, comml. mgr., 1973-76; mem. Lower House, The Hague, 1976-81; state sec. Ministry Fgn. Affairs, 1981-82, minister fgn. affairs, 1982—; mem. mcpl. council Rheden, 1970-74. Exec., Cath. People's party, 1978-81. Office: Ministry of Fgn Affairs, Bezuidenhoutseweg 67, PO Box 20061, 2500 EB The Hague The Netherlands *

BROEKHUIS-NEHLS, JEANETTE LOUISE, computer and English educator; b. Toledo, June 27, 1942; d. Lester Henry James and Alice E. (Sauer) Nehls; m. Siemen Broekhuis, July 31, 1965; children: Robert, Frederick. BA, Heidelberg Coll., Tiffin, Ohio, 1964; M Secondary Edn., Nutsacademie, Rotterdam, The Netherlands, 1974; PhD, U. Leyden, The Netherlands, 1977. Tchr. English Nutsacademie, Rotterdam, 1974—; dir. PC Tng. Ctr., Rotterdam, 1985—. Author 12 ednl. books including Drama Survey, Reading Right, Memo Series. Home: Achterdijk 2, 3161 EC Rhoon The Netherlands Office: PC Tng Centre, Groenendaal 221, 3011 ST Rotterdam The Netherlands

BROEKMAN, JAN MAURITS, philosophy educator; b. Voorburg, The Netherlands, Feb. 16, 1931; s. Jan Maurits and Elisabeth (Koornstra) B.; m. Anne M.J.J. Van den Troost, Sept. 4, 1950; 1 child, Annelies. Diploma in sociology, U. Leiden, 1955; PhD, U. Gottingen, Fed. Republic Germany, 1961. 2d dir. Hague Social Acad., The Netherlands, 1961-65; asst. prof. Amsterdam (The Netherlands) U., 1965-68; prof. Catholic U. Leuven, Belgium, 1968—, Free U. Amsterdam, 1980—. Author books, sci. articles in 8 langs. Mem. profl. orgns. Home: Vant Sestichlaan 34, 3009 Leuven Belgium Office: Tiensestr 41, 3000 Leuven Belgium

BROERING, NAOMI CORDERO, librarian; b. N.Y.C., Nov. 24, 1929; d. Julius and Emily (Perez) Cordero; B.A., Calif. State U., 1961, M.A. in history, 1963; postgrad. UCLA, 1964, M.L.S. in Library Sci., 1966, postgrad. (NIH fellow), 1967; postgrad. U. West Los Angeles, 1970; m. Arthur J. Broering, 1971. Acquisitions and reference librarian U. So. Calif., 1967-68; chief librarian Children's Hosp., Los Angeles, 1968-71; asst. librarian Walter Reed Gen. Hosp., Washington, 1972; chief reader services, grant officer VA, Washington, 1972-75; assoc. librarian Med. Ctr., Georgetown U., Washington, 1975-78, librarian, 1978—, Med. Ctr. librarian Dahlgren Meml. Library, dir. Biomed. Info. Resources Ctr., 1986—; mem. adj. faculty Cath. U. Mem. ALA, Med. Library Assn. (dir. 1979-82), Am. Soc. Info. Sci., AAAS, Assn. Acad. Health Sci. Library Dirs., Spl. Library Assn., Am. Assn. Med. Systems and Informatics, MLA. Contbr. articles to profl. jours. Office: Georgetown Univ Med Ctr Library 3900 Reservoir Rd NW Washington DC 20007

BROGAN, JOHN ANDREW, III, international business consultant; b. Jersey City, Mar. 5, 1924; s. John Andrew Jr. and Marie Jeannette (Ferris) B.; m. Edith Maria Eyermann, Oct. 25, 1952; children: Jeannette Gräfin Beissel von Gymnich. Student, Biarritz Am. U., France, 1945; BS in Fgn. Service, Georgetown U., 1948. Fgn. rep. King Features Syndicate, Mex., Colombia, Argentina, France, Sweden, 1948-50; fgn. service officer Dept. of State, Washington, 1951-85, asst. French desk officer, 1957-60, dir. ops. ctr., 1968-70, sr. mem. bd. of examiners, 1971, sr. examiner, 1979-85; spl. asst. to U.S. High Commr., Vienna, Austria, 1951-52; press officer U.S. High Commn., Bonn, Fed. Republic Germany, 1952-54; vice consul Am. Consulate, Edinburgh, Scotland, 1954-56; first sec. Am. Embassy, Buenos Aires, 1960-65; Allied Press spokesman U.S. Mission, Berlin, 1965-68; consul gen. Am. Consulate Gen., Hamburg, Fed. Republic Germany, 1972-76; advisor on political and security affairs Spl. Session U.N. Gen. Assembly, N.Y.C., 1977-78; dir. Amerika Gesellschaft, Hamburg, Fed. Republic Germany, 1985—. Served with U.S. Army Air Corps, 1942-46, Europe. Named Hon. citizen of Quito, Ecuadorian Govt.; Decorated Knight Sovereign Mil. Order of Malta. Mem. Am. C. of C., Am. Club, English Speaking Union. Roman Catholic. Clubs: Hamburg Golf, Übersee (Hamburg), Metropolitan (Washington), Diplomatic and Consular Officers, Ret. (Washington), Williams (N.Y.C.). Office: Brogan and Co, Schwanenwik 10, 2000 Hamburg 76 Federal Republic of Germany

BROGARD, JEAN-MARIE, internist, physician; b. Strasbourg, Alsace, France, Dec. 26, 1935; s. Paul and Isabelle (Ganter) B.; m. Christiane Meyer, July 7, 1960; children: Michel, Yves-Francois, Catherine, Anne-Florentine. MD, U. Strasbourg, 1965. Diplomate Bd. Internal Medicine. Extern Civil Hosp. Strasbourg, 1955-58, intern, 1958-65; chief clinic, hosp. asst. Ctr. Hosp., U. Strasbourg, 1965-72, chief of works, 1972-75, prof. internal medicine, 1975—. Served with French Army, 1960-62. Mem. European Assn. Internal Medicine (gen. sec. 1977-85). Home: 17 Rue de l'Observatoire, 67000 Strasbourg France Office: Med Clinic B Hospices Civil, 1 Place l'Hopital, 67091 Strasbourg France

BRØGGER, SUZANNE PREIS, writer; b. Copenhagen, Nov. 18, 1944; d. Ove and Lilian (Henius) Preis; m. Keld Zeruneith Brøgger, Feb. 19, 1985; 1 child, Luzia Zeruneith. BA in Russian and French, U. Copenhagen, 1966. Author: Deliver Us from Love, 1973, Ways and Byways of Love, 1975, Creme Fraiche, 1976, Love from Løve, 1975, Brew, 1980, Tone, 1981, Yes, 1984, The Spicy Whizz, 1986, Edvard and Elvira, 1988. Recipient prize for beautiful and useful scis. Danish Acad. Lit., 1981, named Golden Laureate, 1982. Mem. Danish-Tibetan Cultural Soc. (vice chmn).

BROGGI, MICHAEL, marketing executive; b. Los Angeles, June 19, 1942; s. Roger Edward and Thelma Cecile (Marchal) B.; m. Sharon Boyd; children: Michael Jr., Stephen. AA in Journalism, Los Angeles Valley Coll., 1961; grad., USAF Sch. Medicine, Montgomery, Ala., 1962; BA in Mktg. and Communications, Calif. State U., Northridge, 1967; cert. bus. and real estate, San Bernardino Coll., 1975; postgrad., Lincoln U. Law Sch., San Jose, Calif., 1975-76; PhD in Bus. Adminstrn., Calif. Pacific U., 1988. Newswriter, reporter Sta. KGIL, San Fernando, Calif., 1963-67; mem. corp. mktg. staff Walt Disney Prodns., Burbank, Calif., 1967-70; mgr. pub. relations Magic Mountain Amusement Park, Valencia, Calif., 1970-72; exec. v.p., gen. mgr. Lake Arrowhead, Calif., 1972-75; dir. adminstrv. services Marriott Corp. Gt. Am. Theme Park, Santa Clara, Calif., 1975-78; v.p., dir. mktg. Mktg. and Fin. Mgmt. Enterprises, Inc., Encino, Calif., 1978—; lectr. Calif. Poly. State U., Pomona, Calif. State U., Northridge, Moorpark (Calif.) Community Coll., Los Angeles Valley Coll., U. So. Calif., Acad. Ambulatory Surgery, Scottsdale, Ariz., Los Angeles Publicity Club, San Francisco Advt. Club, Orange County Advt. Club. Mem. Fire Commn., Spl. Dep. Commn., San Bernardino County. Mem. Am. Mktg. Assn., Cultural Found., Internat.

Platform Assn., Am. Soc. Profl. Cosn., Journalism Alumni Assn. Office: Mktg and Fin Mgmt 6320 Canoga Ave Woodland Hills CA 91367

BROICH, ULRICH, English literature educator; b. Köln, Fed. Republic of Germany, May 30, 1932; s. Karl and Irmgard (Clewinghaus) B.; m. Christine Hett, June 28, 1963; children: Cornelia, Alexander, Susanne. PhD, U. Bonn, 1957; habilitation, U. Erlangen, 1966. Lektor U. St. Andrews, Scotland, 1957-58; tchr. various schs. Siegburg and Bonn, Fed. Republic of Germany, 1958-60; lektor U. Göttingen, Fed. Republic of Germany, 1960-63; asst. prof. U. Erlangen, Fed. Republic of Germany, 1963-67; prof. U. Bochum, Fed. Republic of Germany, 1967-76, U. München, Fed. Republic of Germany, 1976—; vis. prof. U. Minn., 1987. Author: (with others) Studien zum literarischen Patronat, 1962, Science Fiction, 1981, Intertextualität, 1985; author: Studien zum komischen Epos, 1968, Gattungen des modernen englischen Romans, 1975. Mem. Anglistentag (pres. 1984-86), Deutsche Shakespeare-Gesellschaft West, Deutsche Gesellschaft für Allgemeine und Vergleichende Literaturwissenschaft. Roman Catholic. Home: Kufsteiner St 24a, 8012 Riemerling Federal Republic of Germany Office: Ludwig-Maximilians-Univ, Schellingstr 3, 8000 München Federal Republic of Germany

BROIHAHN, MICHAEL ALLEN, infosystems educator; b. Cuba City, Wis., June 2, 1948; s. Lester E. and Shirley L. (Bendorf) B.; m. Cynthia Barbara Andreas, May 29, 1982; children: David Michael, Matthew Allen. BS, U. Wis., 1972; MBA, U. Wis., Milw., 1973, MS, 1976. CPA, Wis., Fla.; cert. mgmt. acct.; cert. fin. planner, cert. gemologist Gemological Inst. Am. Auditor Price Waterhouse & Co., Milw., 1976-78; portfolio controller Fox & Carskadon Fin. Corp., San Mateo, Calif., 1979-82; corp. controller Computerland Corp., Hayward, Calif., 1982-84; v.p. fin. Computers Unltd./ Computer Bay, Milw., 1985-88; assoc. prof. Barry U., Miami, Fla., 1988—; lectr. U. Wis., Milw., 1977-78, Keller Grad. Sch., Mgmt., Milw., 1986-88. Fellow Wis. Inst. CPA's; mem. Am. Inst. CPA's, Nat. Assn. Accts. (bd. dirs., 1981-85), Inst. Cert. Mgmt. Accts., U. Wis. Alumni Assn., Kappa Sigma. Republican. Lutheran. Office: Barry U 11300 NE 2d Ave Miami Shores FL 33161

BROKAW, CLIFFORD VAIL, III, investment banker, business executive; b. N.Y.C., Sept. 17, 1928; s. Clifford Vail and Audrey (Stransom Joel) B.; m. Elizabeth Stokes Rogers, June 29, 1960; children—Clifford Vail, George Rogers. B.A., Yale U., 1950; JD, U. Va., 1956. Bar: N.Y. Assoc. White & Case, N.Y.C., 1956-59; assoc. Blyth & Co., Inc., N.Y.C., 1959-61; assoc., then gen. ptnr. W.E. Hutton & Co., N.Y.C., 1961-67; gen. ptnr., sr. v.p. Eastman Dillon Union Securities & Co. and successor firm Blyth, Eastman, Dillon & Co., Inc., N.Y.C., 1967-77; chmn., chief exec. officer Invail Capital, Inc., N.Y.C., 1977—; chmn. bd., chief exec. officer IRT Corp., 1986—; bd. dirs., chmn. fin. com. Brazos River Gas Co., Mineral Wells, Tex., 1962—. Bd. advisors Marine Mil. Acad., Harlingen, Tex., 1985—; mem. alumni assn. council U. Va. Sch. Law, 1976-79; founder Brokaw chair corp. law U. Va. Sch. Law, 1985; mem. indsl. adv. com. Sch. Engring. and Applied Sci. U. Va., 1987—; vestryman French Ch. du St. Esprit, 1986—. Served to lt. col. USMCR, 1950-73. Decorated Purple Heart. Mem. ABA, N.Y. Bar Assn., Pilgrims U.S., Mil. Order Carabao, Ends of the Earth, Huguenot Soc. Am. (council 1974-80, v.p. 1986—). Republican. Episcopalian. Clubs: Beaver Dam Winter Sports (Mill Neck, N.Y.); Brook Hollow Golf (Dallas); Burning Tree (Bethesda, Md.); Farmington Country (Charlottesville, Va.); Lyford Cay (Bahamas); Meadow Brook (Jericho, N.Y.); Piping Rock (Locust Valley, N.Y.); The Meadow, Southampton Beach (Southampton, N.Y.); River (N.Y.C.); Union. Lodges: Masons, Shriners. Office: Invail Capital Inc 767 3d Ave New York NY 10017

BROKENBOUGH, WILLA MAE, caterer; b. Clio, S.C., Dec. 5, 1921; d. Joseph and Rebecca (Ales) Burch; student Va. State U., 1940-41; m. John Robert Brokenbough, Feb. 4, 1942; children—Jack, Russell Allen, Diane Elaine Brown. Caterer, Elk's Lodge, Vineland, N.J., 1939-40; cafeteria mgr. Gen. Floor Co., Los Angeles, 1960-63, Schick Safety Razar Co., Culver City, Calif., 1963-66; owner, pres. Willa Brokenbough Parties, Los Angeles, 1963—. Recipient award SBA, 1978, 79, 81; Hennessy trophy USAF. Mem. Nat. Restaurant Assn., Calif. Restaurant Assn., Internat. Food Service Execs. Assn. Lutheran. Clubs: Eastern Star, Heroines of Jericho. Office: 4853 Crenshaw Blvd Los Angeles CA 90043

BROMAN, SIV, publisher; b. Stockholm, Dec. 28, 1930; d. Sven and Märta (Elfström) Thorelius; m. Sven Broman, June 8, 1957. Book club mgr., pub. The Bonnier Group, Stockholm, 1973-83; mng. dir. Bokförlaget Viva, Stockholm, 1984—. Home: Surbrunnsgatan 56, 11348 Stockholm Sweden Office: AB Bokförlaget Viva, Sveavägen 56, 10363 Stockholm Sweden

BROMBERG, ALAN ROBERT, lawyer, educator, writer; b. Dallas, Nov. 24, 1928; s. Alfred L. and Juanita (Kramer) B.; m. Anne Ruggles, July 26, 1959. A.B., Harvard U., 1949; J.D., Yale U., 1952. Bar: Tex. 1952. Assoc. firm Carrington, Gowan, Johnson, Bromberg and Leeds, Dallas, 1952-56; atty. and cons 1956-76; of counsel firm Jenkens & Gilchrist, 1976—; asst. prof. law So. Meth. U., 1956-58, assoc. prof., 1958-62, prof., 1962-83, Univ. Disting. prof., 1983—, mem. presdl. search group, 1971-72; faculty adviser Southwestern Law Jour., 1958-65; sr. fellow Yale U. Law Faculty, 1966-67; vis. prof. Stanford U., 1972-73; mem. adv. bd. U. Calif. Securities Regulation Inst., 1973-78, 79-87; counsel Internat. Data Systems, Inc., 1961-65, sec., dir., 1963-65; mem. Tex. Legis. Council Bus. and Commerce Code Adv. Com., 1966-67. Author: Supplementary Materials on Texas Corporations, 3d edit, 1971, Partnership Primer-Problems and Planning, 1961, Materials on Corporate Securities and Finance—A Growing Company's Search for Funds, 2d edit, 1965, Securities Fraud and Commodities Fraud, Vols. 1-5, 1967-86, Crane and Bromberg on Partnership, 1968; mem. ednl. publs. adv. bd., Matthew Bender & Co., 1977—, chmn., 1981—; contbr. articles and revs. to law and bar jours.; adv. editor: Rev. Securities Regulation, 1969—, Securities Regulation Law Jour, 1973—, Jour. Corp. Law, 1976—. Sec., bd. dirs. Community Arts Fund, 1963-73; gen. atty. Dallas Mus. Contemporary Arts, 1956-63; bd. dirs. Dallas Theater Center, 1955-73, sec., 1957-66, fin. com., 1957-65, mem. exec. com., 1957-70, 79-85, life, 1973—, v.p., trustee endowment fund, 1974-85. Served as cpl. U.S. Army, 1952-54. Mem. Am. Bar Assn. (coms. commodities, partnerships, fed. regulation securities), Dallas Bar Assn. (chmn. com. uniform partnership act 1959-61, library com. 1981-83), State Bar Tex. (chmn. sect. corp. banking and bus. law 1967-68, vice-chmn. 1965-67, com. corp. law revision 1957—, mem. com. securities and investment banking 1965-69, chmn. 1965-69, mem. com. partnership 1957—, chmn. 1979-81), Am. Law Inst., Southwestern Legal Found. (co-chmn. securities com. 1982-85), AAUP (exec. com. chpt. 1962-63, chmn. acad. freedom and tenure com. 1968-70, 71-72), Nat. Assn. Corp. Dirs. Office: So Meth U Law Sch Dallas TX 75275 also: 3200 Allied Bank Tower Dallas TX 75202-2711

BROMBERG, MYRON JAMES, lawyer; b. Paterson, N.J., Nov. 5, 1934; s. Abraham and Elsie (Baker) B.; m. Lisa Murtha, Nov. 28, 1988; children—Kenneth Karl, Eric Edward, Bruce Abraham. B.A., Yale U., 1956; LL.B., Columbia U., 1959. Bar: N.J. bar 1960, N.Y. bar 1981. Law asst. to dist. atty. N.Y. County, 1958; law asst. U.S. atty. So. Dist. N.Y., 1958-59; asso. mem. firm Ralph Porzio, Morristown, N.J., 1960-61; partner firm Porzio, Bromberg & Newman, Morristown, 1961-77, 80—, Porzio & Bromberg, 1977-80; atty. Morris County Bd. Elections, 1963-64; town atty., Town of Morristown, 1965-67; lectr. trial practice Rutgers Inst. Continuing Legal Edn., 1965—. Chmn. fund and membership Morristown chpt. ARC, 1965; chmn. retail div. Community Chest Morris County, 1963; chmn. Keep Morristown Beautiful Com., 1963; mem. Morris Twp. Com., 1970-72; committeeman Morris County Democratic Com., 1962-63, 72-77; lay trustee Delbarton Sch., Morristown, 1972-75; trustee Morris Mus., 1973-79. Fellow Am. Coll. Trial Lawyers, Am. Bar Found.; mem. ABA, N.J. Bar Assn. (named outstanding young lawyer 1970, chmn. joint conf. com. with N.J. Med. Soc. 1970-72), Morris County Bar Assn., Am. Judicature Soc., Trial Attys. N.J. (pres. 1976-77), Internat. Soc. Barristers, Internat. Assn. Def. Counsel, Andover Alumni Assn. of N.Y.C., Columbia U. Law Sch. Assn. of N.J. (bd. dirs. 1986—), Chi Phi, Phi Delta Phi. Jewish. Clubs: Nat. Lawyers (Washington); Yale (N.Y.C. and Central N.J.); Morristown (N.J.). Home: 9 Thompson Ct Morristown NJ 07960 Office: 163 Madison Ave Morristown NJ 07960

BROMKE, ADAM, political scientist, educator; b. Warsaw, Poland, July 11, 1928; s. Waclaw and Rolualda (Beckmann) B.; m. Alina B. Kosmider, June 7, 1958 (div. 1985); m. Ewa Boniecka, Dec. 30, 1986. M.A., St. Andrews U., 1950; Ph.D., U. Montreal, 1953, McGill U., 1964. Lectr. U. Ottawa, Ont., Can., 1952-53; lectr. U. Montreal, 1952-54; editor-in-chief Polish Overseas Project, Free Europe Com., N.Y.C., 1955-57; conf. leader, lectr. McGill U., Montreal, 1957-60; research fellow Russian Research Ctr. Harvard U., Cambridge, Mass., 1960-62; asst. prof. polit. sci. Carleton U., 1962, chmn. Soviet and European Studies program, 1963-66, assoc. prof., 1964-67, prof., 1967-73, chmn. dept., 1968-71; prof. polit. sci. McMaster U., Hamilton, Ont., Can., 1973—; chmn. dept. McMaster U., 1973-79; columnist on internat. affairs The Toronto Star, 1986-87. Author: Poland: The Last Decade, 1981; Poland's Politics, Idealism vs. Realism, 1967; editor: The Communist States at the Crossroads, 1965; (with Philip E. Uren) The Communist States and the West, 1967; (with Teresa-Rakowska-Harmstone) The Communist States in Disarray, 1965-71, 1972; (with John W. Strong) Gierek's Poland, 1973; (with Derry Novak) The Communist States in the Era of Detente, 1971-77, 1978; Poland: The Protracted Crisis, 1983; Eastern Europe in the Aftermath of Solidarity, 1985; The Meaning and Uses of Polish History, 1987. Served with Polish Underground Army under Brit., 1944-45. Decorated Polish Army medal, Cross of Warsaw Uprising, Cross of Polish Home Army. Mem. Can. Assn. Slavists (v.p. 1966-68, pres. 1968-69), Can. Polit. Sci. Assn., Am. Assn. Advancement Slavic Studies, Internat. Polit. Sci. Assn., Internat. Com. Soviet and European Studies (pres. 1974-80). Office: Vista Communications Inc Pheasant Run Newtown Indsl Commons Newtown PA 18940

BROMSEN, MAURY AUSTIN, bibliographer, historian, antiquarian bookseller; b. N.Y.C., Apr. 25, 1919; s. Herman and Rose (Eisenberg) B. B.S.S. cum laude with spl. honors, CCNY, 1939; M.A., U. Calif.-Berkeley, 1941; Carnegie Endowment for Internat. Peace and U.S. Govt. exchange fellow, U. Chile, 1942; M.A., Harvard U., 1945; Harvard Woodbury Lowery Travelling fellow, 1946-47, Social Sci. Research Council fellow, 1946-48; doctoral postgrad. in history, Harvard U., 1945-50; L.H.D. (hon.), Northeastern U., 1987. Vis. lectr. Am. history Cath. U., Santiago, Chile, 1942; instr. history CCNY, 1943-44; founding editor Inter-Am. Rev. Bibliography, 1950-53; editor, sect. chief dept. cultural affairs Pan Am. Union, Washington, 1950-54; adv. editor, U.S. rep. Inter-Am. Rev. Bibliography, 1956—; founder, dir. Maury A. Bromsen Assocs. (rare book, manuscript and fine art dealers), Boston, 1954—; pres., treas. Maury A. Bromsen Assocs., Inc. (rare book, manuscript and fine art dealers), 1963—; hon. curator Latin Am. collections Boston Pub. Library, 1977—; vis. prof. U. Chile, Santiago, 1947; editor, sect. chief dept. cultural affairs Pan. Am. Union, Washington, 1950-53, on leave, 1953-54; exec. sec. Medina Centennial Celebration, Washington, 1952; mem. adv. council univ. libraries U. Notre Dame, 1981-84, emeritus adviser, 1984—; bd. govs. Am. Jewish Hist. Soc., 1987—. Author: Simón Bolívar: A Bicentennial Tribute, 1983; Editor: José Toribio Medina, Humanist of the Americas: an Appraisal, 1960, Spanish transl., 1969; Research and publs. in history and bibliography of Ams., Established Medina and Harrisse rare book collections, U. Fla. Library, 1958, 63. Endowed Archibald Bromsen Meml. scholarship, CCNY, 1964; endowed Bromsen lectureship in Humanistic Bibliography, Boston Pub. Library, 1970, Maury A. Bromsen Latin Am. Acquisitions Fund, 1976, Bromsen Fund, 1983, Mass. Gen. Hosp., 1983. Named Knight Comdr. Orden al Mérito Bernardo O'Higgins, (Chile), Orden de Francisco de Miranda, First Class, (Venezuela); recipient Bromsen Endowment, Mass. Gen. Hosp., 1983; elected Colonial Soc. Mass., 1985. Mem. Antiquarian Booksellers Assn. Am., Am. Hist. Assn., ALA, Bibliog. Soc. Am., Manuscript Soc. (charter), Conf. on Latin Am. History, Academia Nacional de la Historia, Buenos Aires (corr.), Latin Am. Studies Assn., Sociedad de Historia Argentina (corr.), Pan Am. Soc. New Eng. (patron), Bibliog. Soc. (London), Bibliog. Soc. U. Va., Boston Athenaeum, Harvard Coll. Library Friends, Boston Pub. Library Assocs. (hon.), Boston U. Library Assocs. (life), Iowa Library Assocs. (patron), Bell (Minn.) Library Assocs., Ky. Library Assocs., Miami Library Assocs., Clements (Mich.) Library Assocs., Yale Library Assocs., Am. Hist. Soc., Am. Jewish Hist. Soc., Va. Hist. Soc. (life), Fla. Hist. Soc., Mo. Hist. Soc., N.Y. Hist. Soc., Sociedad Chilena de Historia y Geografia, Filson Club (life), Phi Beta Kappa. Clubs: Harvard (Boston), Boston Athenaeum (Boston). Address: 770 Boylston St Boston MA 02199

BRONFENBRENNER, MARTIN, economics educator; b. Pitts., Dec. 2, 1914; s. Jacques Jacob and Martha (Ornstein) B.; m. Jean Knowlton Andrus, June 6, 1940 (div. Nov. 1949); m. Teruko Okuaki, Nov. 13, 1951. AB, Washington U., St. Louis, 1934; PhD, U. Chgo., 1939. Asst. prof. econs. Cen. YMCA Coll., Chgo., 1938-40; econs. analyst U.S. Treasury Dept., Washington, 1940-41; fin. economist Fed. Res. Bank, Chgo., 1941-47; assoc. prof., then prof. U. Wis., Madison, 1947-57; prof. U. Minn., Mpls., 1957-62, Carnegie-Mellon U., Pitts., 1962-71; Kenan prof. Duke U., Durham, N.C., 1971-84; prof. internat. econs. Aoyama Gakuin U., Tokyo, 1984—; vis. fellow Ctr. for Advanced Study in Behavioral Scis., Stanford, Calif., 1966-67, Inst. for Devel. Studies, Brighton, Eng., 1978. Author: Income Distribution Theory, 1971, Macroeconomics Alternatives, 1979; contbr. 200 articles to profl. jours. Mem. Am. Econs. Assn. (past v.p.), So. Econs. Assn. (past pres.), Atlantic Econs. Assn. (past pres.), History Econs. Soc. (past pres.), Am. Assn. Asian Studies, Mt. Pelerin Soc. Home: 2-20-15 Shimouma, 154 Setagaya-ku, Tokyo Japan Office: Aoyama Gakuin U, 4-4-25 Shibuya, 150 Shibuya-ku, Tokyo Japan

BRONFMAN, EDGAR MILES, distillery executive; b. Montreal, Que., Can., June 20, 1929; s. Samuel and Saidye (Rosner) B. Student, Williams Coll., 1946-49; B.A., McGill U., 1951; LHD (hon.), Pace U., 1982; LLD (hon.), Williams Coll., 1986. Chmn. adminstrv. com. Joseph E. Seagram & Sons, Inc., 1955-57, pres., 1957-71; chmn., chief exec. officer, pres. Distillers Corp.-Seagram Ltd., Montreal, 1971-75; now chmn., chief exec. officer Seagram Co. Ltd. and Joseph E. Seagram & Sons Inc.; bd. dirs. Am. Technion Soc., Internat. Exec. Service Corps, E.I. duPont de Nemours & Co.; mem. internat. adv. bd. Columbia U. Sch. Internat. and Pub. Affairs, also mem. planning com. Citizens Com. for N.Y.C., U.S.-USSR Trade and Econ. Council; pres. Samuel Bronfman Found., World Jewish Congress; mem. exec. com. Am. Jewish Congress, Am. Jewish Com.; chmn. Anti-Defamation League N.Y. Appeal; bd. dirs. Am. com. Weizmann Inst. Sci., Israel; chmn. planning com., mem. adv. council Sch. of Internat. and Pub. Affairs, Columbia U. Named Chevalier de la Légion d'Honneur French Govt. Mem. Ctr. for Inter-Am. Relations, Council Fgn. Relations, Hundred Year Assn. N.Y., United Jewish Appeal, Fedn. Jewish Philanthropies (hon. chmn.), Com. for Econ. Devel., Nat. Urban League, Fgn. Policy Assn., Bus. Com. for Arts, Inc., Union Am. Hebrew Congregations (bd. dels.), B'nai B'rith Internat. (bd. overseers). Office: Joseph E Seagram & Sons Inc 375 Park Ave New York NY 10152 also: Seagram Company Ltd, 1430 Rue Peel, Montreal, PQ Canada H3A 1S9

BRONN, DONALD GEORGE, radiation oncologist, medical researcher; b. Karlsruhe, W.Ger., Oct. 12, 1948; s. Count Jakov Ivanovich and Agnes (Pervak) Broschnovsky; came to U.S., 1950; m. Leslie Joan Boyle, Aug. 21, 1973; children—Jacob Alexander, Natasha Nisa. B.A., Ohio State U., 1972, M.S., 1976, Ph.D. in Cell Physiology, 1979, M.D., 1982. Grad. research assoc. in surgery Ohio State U., 1975-79, research coordinator Lab for Breast Cancer Research, Ohio State U. Hosps., 1977-85, research assoc. ultrasound and nuclear medicine divs., dept. radiology, 1980-82; asst. prof. radiation oncology Wayne State U., 1986-87; asst. prof. radiation therapy Med. Coll. Ohio; attending radiation oncologist Children's Hosp. Mich., Hutzel Hosp., Detroit Med. Ctr., Med. Coll. Ohio Hosps., Toledo, Samuel J. Roessler Found. Med. Research fellow, 1980-82; Cancer Soc. fellow in clin. oncology, 1985-86; clin. instr. dir. of radiation oncology, dept. radiology Ohio State U., 1982-85. Named to Landacre Soc. Ohio State U. Coll. Med., 1979, Outstanding Research Presentation, 1979; pres., 1981-82; grantee Am. Cancer Soc., Elsa U. Pardee Found., Bremer Found., 1975-85; recipient Nat. Student Research Forum 1st prize, 1979; Mead Johnson Excellence of Research award, 1979; Surgery award Ohio State U. Coll. Medicine, 1982, Robert M. Zollinger Research award, 1982; Am. Radium Soc. young oncologist travel grantee, 1985. Fellow Royal Micros. Soc.; mem. AAAS, AMA, Am. Soc. for Cell Biology, N.Y. Acad. Scis., Am. Coll. Radiology, Radiol. Soc. N. Am., Soc. for Magnetic Resonance Imaging, Am. Soc. Clin. Oncology, Radiation Research Soc., Am. Soc. Therapeutic Radiology and Oncology, Mich. State Med. Soc., Mich. Soc. Therapeutic Radiologists, Oio State Med. Assn., Wayne County Med. Soc., Sigma Xi. Author: The Hormonal Characterization of Breast Cancer By Oxygen Consumption Levels, 1979; contbr. articles on cancer biology and medicine to profl. publs.; inventor Bronn intraoperative treatment unit for Microtron generated long distance electron beam radiation in the operative suite. Home: 4901 Susans Way Bloomfield Hills MI 48013 Office: Med Coll of Ohio Radiation Therapy Dept CS # 10008 Toledo OH 43699

BRONNER, GUY, otolaryngologist; b. Strasbourg, France, July 2, 1948; s. Albert and Marie (Rebmeister) B. MD, U. Strasbourg, 1968. Extern U. Hosp. Ctr., Strasbourg, 1968; resident CHU, Strasbourg, 1974-78, chief of clinic, 1979-83; asst. to affiliated hosps. Strasbourg, 1979-83; attache Paul Strauss Anti-Cancer Ctr., Strasbourg, 1983—; practice medicine specializingin cervicofacial surgery Strasbourg, 1983—. Contbr. articles to sci. jours. Pres. Soc. Conservation Monuments Hist. d'Alsace, 1985. Served with French Army, 1974-75. Mem. French Soc. Otorhinolaryngology. Home: 6 Pierre Bucher, 67000 Strasbourg France Office: 16 Ave de la Paix, 67000 Strasbourg France

BRONOCCO, TERRI LYNN, telecommunications company executive; b. San Antonio, Jan. 7, 1953; d. Lawrence and Jimmie Doris (Mears) B.; m. Martin L. Lowy, July 5, 1975 (div. Jan. 1979). Student in communications U. Tex.-Austin, 1970-73. Pub. relations mgr. Assocs. Corp., Dallas, 1976-79; editor-in-chief Nat. Tax Shelter Digest, Dallas, 1979; fin. editor Dallas/Ft. Worth Bus., Dallas, 1979-80; pub. affairs dir. Gen. Telephone Co., Lewisville, Tex., 1980-82; pub. info. mgr. GTE Corp., Stamford, Conn., 1982-83, media communications mgr., 1983-84, media relations and communications mgr., 1984-86; v.p. external affairs U.S. Sprint Communications Co., Dallas, 1986-88; v.p. external affairs U.S. Sprint, Washington, 1988—. Fundraiser, pub. relations counsel Am. Shakespeare Theatre, Stratford, Conn., 1984-86; bd. dirs. Music Found. for the Handicapped, Bridgeport, Conn., 1984-86; precinct chmn. Dallas County Dem. Party, 1982; bd. dirs. Far Mill River Assn., Stratford, 1983-86; mem. adv. commn. State Tex. Emergency Communications, 1987—. Recipient award for Newspaper Series Dept. Transp., 1980. Mem. Internat. Assn. Bus. Communicators (Best Photograph award 1977), Women in Communications (Matrix award 1985), Women in Mgmt., Am. Mgmt. Assn., Dallas C. of C. (telecommunications com. 1987, Spl. Recognition award 1978). Roman Catholic. Home: 1600 N Oak St Arlington VA 22201 Office: US Sprint Communications Co 2002 Edmund Halley Dr Reston VA 22091

BRONSON, PATRICIA ANN, mathematics educator; b. Leesville, La., Mar. 15, 1931; d. Glenn Cecil and Allie Lee (Copeland) Packer; student Northwestern State U., 1948-51; B.A., George Peabody Coll., 1960, M.A., 1962; m. John Orville Bronson, Jr., June 11, 1966; children—Richard Wayne McCoy, Victoria Patricia Elizabeth, Glenn Charles Stephen. Tchr., Nashville Met. Schs., 1962-65, Calhoun Tech. Jr. Coll., Decatur, Ala., 1965-67; asst. prof. math. Chesapeake Coll., Wye Mills, Md., 1967—. Mem. Math. Assn. Am., Nat. Council Tchrs. Math., AAUP, Miss., S.C. hist. socs., La. Hist. Assn., Am. Math. Assn. Two-Yr. Colls., Md. Math. Assn. Two-Yr. Colls., Theta Sigma Upsilon, Delta Kappa Gamma. Democrat. Episcopalian. Club: Order Eastern Star. Author: Index of the Census of 1850, Orangeburg and Pickens Districts, S.C., 1974. Home: Hopkins Hall Box 81 Wye Mills MD 21679

BRONSTEIN, MELVIN, ophthalmic surgeon; b. Yonkers, N.Y., Apr. 9, 1924; s. Harry and Betty (Mandel) B.; A.B., Columbia U., 1948, M.A., 1949; M.D., N.Y. Med. Coll., 1953; m. Gloria Liebman, May 20, 1956; children—Charles, Glen, Adam, Wendy. Intern, N.Y. Med. Coll., 1953-54; resident in ophthalmology Montefiore Hosp., Bronx, N.Y., 1954-56, asso. surgeon, 1970—; practice medicine, specializng in ophthalmic surgery, Yonkers, 1960—; chief of staff, attending ophthalmic surgeon, dir. ophthalmology dept. St. John's Riverside Hosp., Yonkers, 1970—; attending in ophthalmic surgery Bronx Mcpl. Hosp. Center, Westchester Med. Center; asso. clin. prof. ophthalmology Albert Einstein Coll. Medicine, 1976—, N.Y. Med. Coll., Valhalla, 1970—; cons. in field. Bd. dirs. Family Service Soc., 1970-73; pres. Yonkers Cancer Soc., 1976-78. Served with Ordnance Dept., U.S. Army, 1942-46. Decorated Bronze Star with cluster; diplomate Am. Bd. Ophthalmology, examiner, 1970-72, councillor, 1986—. Fellow Am. Acad. Ophthalmology, ACS (counselor 1974-82), Internat. Coll. Surgeons, N.Y. Acad. Medicine; mem. Assn. Research in Vision and Ophthalmology, Intraocular Lens Implant Soc., N.Y. Acad. Scis., N.Y. State Ophthal. Soc. (bd. dirs. 1986—), Yonkers Acad. Medicine (pres. 1971-72), AAAS, AMA, Nat. Soc. Prevention of Blindness, Westchester Acad. Medicine (pres. eye sect. 1982-86), Vitreous Soc., N.Y. State Ophthalmol. Soc. (bd. dirs. 1986—), Phi Delta Epsilon. Contbr. articles to profl. publs. Office: 984 N Broadway Yonkers NY 10701

BROOK, ELAINE ISABEL, travel guide, writer; b. London, May 23, 1949; d. Alec and Isabel May (Stanley) Turner; m. Lhakpa Sherpa, Apr. 19, 1986. Degree in Art Edn., Loughborough Coll., 1971; degree in Ecology, Leicester U., 1973. Art tchr. Castleton Sch., Derbyshire, Eng., 1973-75; mountain guide Fantasy Ridge Alpinism, Colo., 1975-78; dir. Himalayan Travel Co., Buxton, Eng., 1987—. Author: The Windhorse, 1986, Land of the Snow Lion, 1987; contbr. articles to profl. publs. Fellow Royal Geog. Soc.; mem. Tibetan Community in Britain. Buddhist. Office: Jonathan Cape Pub, 32 Bedford Sq, London WC1B 3EL, England

BROOK, GREVILLE BERTRAM, metallurgist; b. Nottingham, Eng., July 30, 1926; s. Bertram Frederick and Frances Emily (Weldon) B.; m. Mary Rose Saunders, Sept. 12, 1953; children: Adrian Kevin, Deborah Clare, Julian Simon. BMet with honors, U. Sheffield, Eng., 1947; MUniv (hon.), U. Surrey, Eng., 1980. Busar B.N.F.M.R.A., London, 1947-49; investigator Fulmer Research Inst., Stoke Poges, Eng., 1949-56, prin. metallurgist, 1956-75; dir. Fulmer Research Labs., Stoke Poges, 1975-87; asst. dir. Fulmer Ltd., Stoke Poges, 1987—; vis. reader U. Surrey, Guildford, Eng., 1974-86. Contbr. articles to profl. jours. Fellow Inst. Metals (council 1983-86), Fellowship Engring. Home: 9 Whitfield Rd, Hughenden Valley High, Wycombe Bucks HP14 4NZ, England Office: Fulmer Ltd, Hollybush Hill, Stoke Poges SL2 4QD, England

BROOK, PETER LESLIE, marketing executive; b. Dewsbury, West Yorkshire, Eng., Dec. 3, 1946; s. Sidney and Kathleen Mary (Wilkinson) B.; m. Therese Mary Stack, Sept. 7, 1974; children: Lara Michelle, Natalie Yvonne. BA in Geography, Manchester U., 1968; diploma in mktg., Inst. Mktg., 1972. Product mgr. Evode, Ltd., Stafford, Eng., 1970-75; mgr. mktg. De La Rue Systems, Portsmouth, Eng., 1975-80; divisional mgr. Data Card Internat., Havant, Eng., 1980-84; dir. mktg. and sales McCorquodale Security Cards, Ltd., Reigate, Eng., 1984—; lectr. West Sussex Adult Edn., Eng., 1985—. Mem. Inst. Mktg. Roman Catholic. Home: Shapansay 5 West Ave, Middleton on Sea Bognor, Regis England

BROOK, ROBERT LESLIE, accountant, airplane pilot; b. Bondon, Dec. 31, 1922; s. Henry Robert Jo and Doris Lillian (Rumbelow) B.; m. Ella Christine Curtis, Dec. 8, 1951; children: Brook, Robert, Joseph, Oliver. Student pub. schs. Bookkeeper Thorne Lancaster & Co., London, 1937-40; auditor accounts Brit. European Airways, 1947-51; with Sta. Garages Acctg., 1947-51; comml. pilot Scottish Airline, Brit. West Indian, Trinidad, 1952-55; ferry, survey pilot Eagle Fairey Handley Page, 1956-75; with Dan-Air Bristow Helicopters, 1956-75; survey pilot Skyways Schedules, 1976-77; exec. pilot Nchanga Consolidated Copper, Mines, Lusaka, Zambia, 1977-79; airline air freight scheduler Brit. Islands, 1980-81; pvt. practice estate acctg., Fleet, Hampshire, Eng., 1981—. Served with RAF, 1941-46. Decorated Mil. Campaign medal (Eng.). Mem. Brit. Airline Pilots Assn., Arnold Scheme Register, Spitfire Soc., III Squadron Royal Air Force Assn. Mem. Ch. of Eng. Home: 31 Crookham Rd, Fleet Hampshire GU13 8DP, England

BROOKE, CHRISTOPHER NUGENT LAWRENCE, historian, educator; b. Cambridge, Eng., June 23, 1927; s. Zachary Nugent and Rosa Grace (Stanton) B.; m. Rosalind Beckford Clark, 1951; 3 children. BA, Cambridge U., 1945, MA, 1952, DLitt, 1973; D (hon.), U. York, Eng., 1984. Fellow Gonville and Caius Coll., Cambridge U., 1949-56, 77—; univ. asst. lectr. Cambridge U., 1953-54, lectr., 1954-56, Dixie prof. ecclesiastical history, 1977—; prof. mediaeval history U. Liverpool, Eng., 1956-67; prof. history Westfield Coll., U. London, 1967-77. Author: The Dullness of the Past, 1957, From Alfred to Henry III, 1961, The Saxon and Norman Kings, 1963, Europe in the Central Middle Ages, 1964, Time the Archsatirist, 1968, The Twelfth Century Renaissance, 1969, Structure of Medieval Society, 1971, Medieval Church and Society, 1971, Marriage in Christian History, 1978, A

History of Gonville and Caius College, 1985, The Church and the Welsh Border, 1986; (with W. Swaan) The Monastic World, 1974; (with G. Keir) Lond, 800-1216, 1975; (with Rosalind Brooke) Popular Religion in the Middle Ages, 1000-1300, 1983; (with A. Morey) Gilbert Foliot and His Letters, 1965, (with R. Highfield, W. Swan) Oxford and Cambridge, 1988; part editor: the Book of William Morton, 1954; co-editor: The Letters of John of Salisbury, vol. 1, 1955, Vol. II, 1979, Carte Nativorum, 1960, The Letters and Charters of Gilbert Foliot, 1967; (with D. Knowles and V. London) Heads of Religious Houses, England and Wales 940-1216, 1972; (with D. Whitelock and M. Brett) Councils and Synods I, 1981; (with R. A. B. Mynors), rev. edit. of Walter Map, De nugis Curialium, 1983; contbg. author: A History of St. Paul's Cathedral, 1957, A History of York Minster, 1977; gen. editor: Oxford (formerly Nelson's) Medieval Texts, 1959-87; contbr. articles and revs. to profl. jours. Mem. Royal Commn. on Hist. Monuments, Eng., 1977-84; mem. rev. com. on Export of Works of Art, 1979-82. Fellow Brit. Acad., 1970. Fellow Royal Hist. Soc., Soc. Antiquaries (pres.), Medieval Acad. Am. (corr.), Monumenta Germaniae Historica (corr.), Societa Internat. Studi Francescani. Office: Faculty of History, West Rd, Cambridge CB3 9EF, England

BROOKE, CHRISTOPHER ROGER ETTRICK, financial services company executive; b. Hove, Sussex, Eng., Feb. 2, 1931; s. Ralph and Marjorie (Lee) B.; m. Nancy Belle Lowenthal, Nov. 25, 1936; children: Jenny, Christopher, Kenneth, Stephen. MA with honors, U. Oxford, 1954. Diplomat Her Majesty's Embassies, Bonn, Washington, 1955-66; dep. mng. dir. Indsl. Reorgn. Corp., London, 1966-69; mng. dir. Scienta S.A., Brussels, 1969-71; exec. dir. Pearson Group, London, 1971-79; group mng. dir. EMI, London, 1979-80; chief exec. Candover Investments PLC, London, 1980—; dir. Slough Estates PLC, London, Tech. Project Services PLC. Author: Santa's Christmas Journey, 1983. Councillor Royal Borough Kensington and Chelsea, London, 1973-79. Club: Brooks. Home: 99 Flood St, London SW3, England Office: Candover Investments PLC, 8-9 E Harding St, London EC4A 3AS, England

BROOKE, JOHN HEDLEY, historian, educator; b. Retford, Eng., May 20, 1944; s. Hedley Joseph and Margaret (Brown) B.; m. Janice Marian Heffer, Aug. 30, 1972. BA with honors, U. Cambridge, 1965, MA, 1966, PhD, 1969. Research fellow Fitzwilliam Coll. U. Cambridge, Eng., 1967-68; tutorial fellow U. Sussex, Brighton, Eng., 1968-69; lectr. dept. history, sr. lectr. history of sci. U. Lancaster, Eng., 1969—; sr. tutor Bowland Coll., U. Lancaster, 1978-80, prin. 1980-84; cons. The Open U., Milton Keynes, 1973-74. Contbr. articles to profl. jours. Grantee The Royal Soc., 1981. Mem. Brit. Soc. for History of Sci., Internat. History Sci. Soc., Soc. for History of Alchemy and Chemistry, Royal Soc. Nat. Com. for History of Sci., Medicine and Tech. (editor British Jour. for the History of Sci., 1988—). Mem. Church of England. Home: Pear Tree Cottage, Scorton, Lancaster PR3 1AP, England Office: Univ Lancaster, Dept of History, Lancaster LA1 4YG, England

BROOKE, MARTIN MONTAGUE, investment consultant; b. London, Aug. 25, 1923; s. Montague and Sybil Katharine (Martin) B.; m. Judith Mary Tanqueray, Sept. 9, 1950; children—Anthony Martin, Katharine Mary, Samuel Truman. M.A., Cambridge U., 1947. With Guinness Mahon & Co. Ltd., London, 1947-72, dir. 1963-72; chmn. Druidale Securities Ltd., London, 1972—; dir. Emperor Fund N.V., Curacao. Mem. Council Distressed Gentlefolks Assn., London, 1969—. Served to lt. Royal Navy, 1942-46. Anglican. Club: Naval (London). Home: 53 Chantry View Rd, Guildford GU1 3XT, England Office: Druidale Securities Ltd, 41/42 King William St, London EC4R 9ET, England

BROOKE, MICHAEL ZACHARY, writer, consultant; b. Cambridge, Eng., May 11, 1921; s. Zachary Nugent and Rose Grace (Stanton) B.; m. Hilda Gillatt, July 25, 1953; children: Jacqueline, Robert Zachary, Martin. MA, Cambridge U., 1946, U. Manchester, 1966; PhD, U. Manchester, 1969. Indsl. chaplain Ch. of Eng., Sheffield, 1948-57, Manchester, 1957-61; lectr. mgmt. scis. Inst. Sci. and Tech. U. Manchester, 1966-72, sr. lectr., 1972-84; mng. dir. Brooke Assocs. Ltd., Manchester, 1984—; vis. prof. U. S.C., 1975-76, Queen's U., Kingston, Ont., Can., 1980-81. Author: Frederic Le Play: Engineer and Social Scientist, 1970, Centralization and Autonomy, 1984, Selling Management Service Contracts in International Business, 1985, International Management, 1986, South Pennine Escort, 1987; (with others) The International Firm, 1977, The Strategy of Multinational Enterprise, 1970, 2d edit., 1978 (tranlated into French and Spanish), A Bibliography of International Business, 1977, International Corporate Planning, 1979, International Financial Management Handbook, 2 vols., 1983, International Travel and Tourism Forecasts, 1985, Handbook of International Trade, 1988; co-editor: The Schoolmaster in the EEC, 1973. Fellow Acad. Internat. Bus. (chmn. European region), Inst. of Export; mem. Soc. Authors (chmn. no. region). Mem. Labour Party. Club: Fox House (London). Home: 21 Barnfield, Urmston M31 1EW, England Office: Falkner House, 45 Station Rd, Urmston M31 1JG, England

BROOKE, PETER LEONARD, chairman Conservative and Unionist Party; b. England, Mar. 3, 1934; m. Joan Margaret Smith, 1964 (dec. 1985); 3 sons (1 dec.). Student, Marlborough; MA, Baliol Coll., Oxford; MBA, Harvard Bus.Sch. Commonwealth Fund fellow 1957-59; research asst. IMEDE, Lausanne, Switzerland, 1960-61; with Spencer Stuart & Assocs., Mgmt. Cons., 1961-65, dir., 1965-79, chmn., 1974-79; asst. govt. whip 1979-81; lord commr. HM Treasury, 1981-83; Parliamentary under-sec. of state Dept. Edn. & Sci., 1983-85; chmn. Conservative and Unionist Party 1987—; pres. Inc. Assn. of Prep. Schs., 1980-83; trustee Dove Cottage, 1976—, Cusichaca Project, 1978—. Lay advisor St. Paul's Cathedral, 1980—. Sen. fellow RCA, 1987. Clubs: Brooks's, City Livery, MCC, I Zingari, St. George's (Hanover Sq.), Conservative. Address: House of Commons, London SW1 England *

BROOKINS, DOUGLAS GRIDLEY, geochemist, educator; b. Healdsburg, Calif., Sept. 27, 1936; s. Rex McKain and Ellyn Caroline (Hitt) B.; m. Barbara Flashman, Sept. 16, 1961; children: Laura Beth, Rachel Sarah. A.A., Santa Rosa Jr. Coll., 1956; A.B., U. Calif.-Berkeley, 1958; Ph.D., MIT, 1963. Geologist Bear Creek Co., San Francisco, 1957-59; research asst. MIT, Cambridge, 1958-63; physicist Avco Corp., Wilmington, Mass., 1961; asst. prof. geology Kans. State U., Manhattan, 1963-65; assoc. prof. Kans. State U., 1965-70; prof. geology U. N.Mex., Albuquerque, 1971—; acting chmn. U. N.Mex., 1972, chmn. dept., 1976-79. Author: Earth Resources, Energy and the Environment, 1980, Geochemical Aspects of Radioactive Waste Disposal, 1984, Physical Geology, 1982, Eh-ph Diagrams for Geochemists, 1987, Earth and Energy Resources and Their Environmental Impact, 1988, The Geological Disposal of High Level Radioactive Wastes, 1988; contbr. 500 articles to profl. jours. Bd. dirs. Jewish Community Council Albuquerque, 1974; trustee Congregation Albert, 1975-81 , v.p., 1983-84, pres., 1985-87. Named Researcher-Tchr. of Year, 1971. Fellow Geol. Soc. Am., Am. Inst. Chemists, Mineral Soc. Am., Explorers Club; mem. Geochem. Soc., Meteoritical Soc., Am. Geophys. Union, N.Y. Acad. Sci., AAAS, AAUP, Albuquerque Geol. Soc. (pres. 1973), N.Mex. Geol. Soc., N.Mex. Inst. Chemists (councillor 1974-75), Am. Assn. Petroleum Geologists, Internat. Assn. Geochemistry and Cosmochemistry, Mineral Soc. Am., Soc. Economic Geologists, Soc. Exploration Geochemists, Materials Research Soc., Am. Chem. Soc., Am. Nuclear Soc., Phi Beta Kappa (pres. Alpha Assn. Kans. 1967-68), Sigma Xi. Mem. B'nai B'rith faith (fin. sec. 1974-75). Address: Dept Geology Univ NMex Albuquerque NM 87131

BROOKMAN, ANTHONY RAYMOND, lawyer; b. Chgo., Mar. 23, 1922; s. Raymond Charles and Marie Clara (Alberg) B.; m. Marilyn Joyce Brookman, June 5, 1982; children—Meribeth Brookman Patrick, Anthony Raymond, Lindsay Logan. Student Ripon Coll., 1940-41; B.S., Northwestern U., 1947; J.D., U. Calif.-San Francisco, 1953. Bar: Calif. 1954. Law clk. Calif. Supreme Ct., 1953-54; ptnr. Nichols, Williams, Morgan, Digardi & Brookman, 1954-68; sr. ptnr. Brookman & Hoffman, Inc., San Francisco, 1968—. Pres., Young Republicans Calif., San Mateo County, 1953-54. Served to 1st lt. USAF. Mem. ABA, Alameda County Bar Assn., State Bar Calif., Lawyers Club Alameda County, Alameda-Contra Costa County Trial Lawyers Assn., Assn. Trial Lawyers Am., Calif. Trial Lawyers Assn. Republican. Clubs: Masons, Athenian Nile, Crow Canyon Country, Shriners. Pub. Contra Costa New Register. Office: Brookman and Hoffman 901 H St Suite 200 Sacramento CA 95814 also: 1990 N California Blvd Walnut Creek CA 94596

BROOKMAN, RUDOLF, health facility administrator; b. Amsterdam, The Netherlands, June 10, 1932; s. Wonter C. and Anna C. (Hofman) B.; m. Myrna Kloprogge, Apr. 12, 1957; children: Yvette, Kim. Cert. secondary teaching, Mcpl. Coll. of Edn., Amsterdam, 1953. Univ. tchr. Ac. Hosp. Amsterdam, 1962-69; hosp. dir. Hosp. St. Jan-Hoog-Laren, The Netherlands, 1969-71; gen. dir. Leo Polak-Huis, Amsterdam, 1971-72, Reinalda-Huis, Haarlem, The Netherlands, 1972—; cons. in field. Author: Calculating Injections, 1968. Mem. Assn. Dirs. Nursing Homes (chmn. 1977), Assn. Cooperating Nursing Homes (vice-chmn. 1975). Office: Reinalda-Huis, Leonard Springerlaan 1, Haarlem The Netherlands

BROOKNER, ANITA, writer, educator. d. Newson and Maude Brookner. Ed., King's Coll., U. London, Courtauld Inst., Paris. vis. lectr. U. Reading, 1959-64; Slade prof. U. Cambridge, 1967-68; lectr. Courtauld Inst. of Art, 1964. Author: Watteau, 1968, The Genius of the Future, 1971, Greuze: The Rise and Fall of an Eighteenth Century Phenomenon, 1972, Jacques-Louis David, 1980, (novels) A Start in Life, 1981, Providence, 1982, Look At Me, 1983, Hotel du Lac, 1984 (Booker McConnell Prize); Family and Friends, 1985; A Misalliance, 1986; contrib. articles to mags. Office: Courtauld Inst Art, 20 Portman Sq, London W1H OBE, England

BROOKS, BARRY HEWITT, diplomat; b. Wellington, New Zealand, Dec. 27, 1932; m. Joan Aroha Kermode, Nov. 3, 1961; 3 children. MA, Victoria U., Wellington. Clk. Dept. Fgn. Affairs, New Zealand, 1952-54, Dunlop New Zealand Ltd., 1954-57, Ministry of Fgn. Affairs, Wellington, 1957-58; adminstrv. and consular attache Ministry of Fgn. Affairs, Kuala Lumpur, Malaysia, 1959-60; attache Ministry of Fgn. Affairs, Jakarta, Indonesia, 1960-61; registrar Ministry of Fgn. Affairs, Wellington, 1962-63; 2d and 1st sec. Ministry of Fgn. Affairs, Washington, 1963-67; acting and dep. head econ. div. Ministry of Fgn. Affairs, Wellington, 1968-69, 74-75; 1st sec. econ. affairs Ministry of Fgn. Affairs, Paris, 1969-73; dep. high commr. Ministry of Fgn. Affairs, Suva, Fiji, 1975-77, Ottawa, Can., 1977-81; high commr. Ministry of Fgn. Affairs, New Delhi, Bangladesh, 1981-82; ambassador to Nepal, 1981-82, Baghdad, Iraq, 1983-85, Santiago, Chile, 1985-88, Brazil, 1988—, Lima, Peru, 1988—, Argentina, Colombia, Ecuador, and Bolivia. Recipient Gold medal Men's Vocal Championship/Wellington Competitions, 1958, Soc. Australian Tchrs. Ballroom Dancing, 1958. Address: New Zealand Embassy, Casilla 5587, Lima 100, Peru

BROOKS, GEORGE ANDREW, lawyer, educator; b. N.Y.C., May 11, 1900; s. George H. and Mary Agnes (Winifred (O'Hara) B. A.B. with sr. class hons., Fordham U., 1924, J.D. (LL.B.) cum laude, 1927, LL.D. (hon.), 1952; LL.M., NYU, 1951; LL.D. (hon.), Scranton U., 1953. Bar: N.Y. 1928, U.S. Dist. Ct. (so. and no. dists.) N.Y. 1938, U.S. Dist. Ct. (no. dist.) Ind. 1939, U.S. Ct. Appeals (2d cir.) 1941, U.S. Dist. Ct. (ea. dist.) N.Y. 1946, U.S. Tax Ct. 1947, U.S. Ct. Appeals (3d cir.) 1949, U.S. Supreme Ct. 1958. Tchr. Regis High Sch., N.Y.C., 1924-27; Seton Hall High Sch., South Orange, N.J., 1924-30; practice, N.Y.C. and Tuckahoe, N.Y., 1928-34; with Gen. Motors Corp., N.Y.C., 1934-65, dir. N.Y. legal staff, 1941-65, corp. sec., 1947-65, sec. fin. policy com., 1947-58, sec. fin. com., 1958-65; lectr. law Fordham U., N.Y.C., 1929-35, adj. asst. prof., 1965-70, adj. assoc. prof., 1970-72, adj. prof. law, 1972—; prof. Seton Hall Coll., South Orange, N.J., 1924-34; atty. Union Free Sch. Dist. 1, Town of Eastchester, Westchester County, N.Y., 1930-56; legal cons., prodn. div. Nat. Def. Adv. Commn., Washington, 1940; arbitrator Nat. Assn. Securities Dealers, Inc. Bd. dirs. Legal Aid Soc. Westchester County, 1964-75, sec., 1965-72, pres., 1972-74; bd. dirs. Lavelle Sch. for Blind, N.Y.C., 1956—, v.p. 1971-78, pres., 1978-80, pres. emeritus; trustee emeritus Fordham U.; bd. dirs. Westchester Legal Services, Inc., 1967-85, N.Y. County Lawyers Assn., 1965-71, Rose Hill Housing Devel. Fund Corp.; trustee St. Agnes Hosp., White Plains, N.Y., 1982-87. Served with U.S. Army, 1918. Created knight of Malta; recipient Alumni Achievement award Fordham Coll., 1959, Encaenia award Fordham Coll., 1959, medal of Achievement Fordham Law Alumni Assn., 1968, Bene Merenti medal Fordham U., 1979, Law Sch. award Fordham U., 1984. Fellow N.Y. Bar Found.; mem. U.S. Cath. Hist. Soc. (bd. dirs. 1958-84, v.p. 1964-66, pres. 1966-68), ABA, Fed. Bar Assn., Comml. Law League of Am., Westchester County Bar Assn., Cath. Lawyers Guild (bd. dirs. 1958-61), N.Y. State Bar Assn. (ho. of dels. 1972-77), Fordham U. Alumni Fedn. (bd. dirs. 1955-64), Fordham Law Alumni Assn. (bd. dirs. 1960-75), Assn. Bar City N.Y., Fordham Coll. Alumni Assn. (pres. 1948-52). Republican. Clubs: University, N.Y. Athletic (N.Y.C.). Home: Eton Hall 127 Garth Rd Apt 5A Scarsdale NY 10583

BROOKS, GWENDOLYN, writer, poet; b. Topeka, June 7, 1917; d. David Anderson and Keziah Corinne (Wims) B.; m. Henry L. Blakely, Sept. 17, 1939; children: Henry L., Nora. Grad., Wilson Jr. Coll., Chgo., 1936; L.H.D., Columbia Coll., 1964. Instr. poetry Columbia Coll., Chgo., Northeastern Ill. State Coll., Chgo.; mem. Ill. Arts Counci; cons. in poetry Library of Congress, 1985-86. Author: poetry A Street in Bronzeville, 1945, Annie Allen, 1949, Maud Martha; novel, 1953, Bronzeville Boys and Girls; for children, 1956, The Bean Eaters; poetry, 1960, Selected Poems, 1963, In the Mecca, 1968, Riot, 1969, Family Pictures, 1970, Aloneness, 1971, To Disembark, 1981; autobiography Report From Part One, 1972, The Tiger Who Wore White Gloves, 1974, Beckonings, 1975, Primer for Blacks, 1980, Young Poets' Primer, 1981, Very Young Poets, 1983, The Near-Johannesburg Boy, 1986, Blacks, 1987. Named One of 10 Women of Year Mademoiselle mag., 1945; recipient award for creative writing Am. Acad. Arts and Letters, 1946; Guggenheim fellow for creative writing, 1946, 47; Pulitzer prize for poetry, 1950; Anisfield-Wolf award, 1969; named Poet Laureate of Ill., 1968. Mem. Soc. Midland Authors. Home: 7428 S Evans Ave Chicago IL 60619

BROOKS, JERRY CLAUDE, textile company executive; b. College Park, Ga., Apr. 23, 1936; s. John Bennett and Mattie Mae (Timms) B.; B.S., Ga. Inst. Tech., 1958; m. Peggy Sue Thornton, Feb. 26, 1961; children—Apryll Denise, Jerry Claude, Susan Vereen. Safety engr. Cotton Producers Assn., Atlanta, 1959-64, dir. safety and loss control, 1964-70; dir. corporate protection Gold Kist, Inc., Atlanta, 1970-81; dir. corporate safety J.P. Stevens, 1981-84, dir. Safety and Security, 1984-86, dir. health and safety, 1986—; instr., Ga. Safety Inst., Athens, Ga., 1971—. Bd. dirs. Greater Lithonia (Ga.) Homeowners Assn., Ga. Soc. Prevention of Blindness, Ga. Safety Council. Served with AUS, 1958-59. Mem. Am. Soc. Safety Engrs. (chpt. pres. 1968-69, regional v.p. 1974-76), Nat. Safety Council (gen. chmn. fertilizer sect. 1969-70, gen. chmn. textile sec. 1985—), So. Safety Conf. (v.p. bus. and industry 1968-74, pres. 1974), Am. Soc. Indsl. Security, Ga. Bus. and Industry Assn. (dir.; named outstanding mem. 1981), Internat. Assn. Hazard Control Mgrs. (chpt. pres. 1979—). Clubs: Masons, Rosicrucians; Exchange (pres. 1969-70; Book of Golden Deeds award 1981) (Lithonia). Home: 222 Rusty Ln Easley SC 29640 Office: 400 E Stone Ave Greenville SC 29602

BROOKS, JOHN CHRISTOPHER GEORGE, editor; b. London, Jan. 11, 1927; s. Cyrus Harry and Winifred Amy (White) B.; m. Gladys Sylvia Brown, July 26, 1947; children: David George, Leonora Mary Petrou, Katharine Sylvia. BSc, London Sch. Econs., U. London, 1950. Library asst. Westminster Pub. Libraries, London, 1951-52; sr. library asst. Holborn Pub. Libraries, London, 1952-55; research librarian Bank of London and S.Am. Ltd., London, 1956-62; research officer Bank of London and S.Am. Ltd., Rio de Janeiro, 1962-64; regional economist Latin Am. Bank of London and S.Am. Ltd., London, 1968-86; dep. chief econ. adviser Lloyds Bank Plc (formerly Bank of London and S.Am. Ltd.), London, 1986-87; editor Bolsa Review, London, 1964-83, South American Handbook, London, 1972—; broadcaster British Broadcasting Co. World Service, 1964—; Brazilian corr. Fin. Times Newspaper, Rio de Janeiro, 1962-64. Contbr. articles to profl. jours.; lectr. in Latin Am. field. Served as cpl. in British Army, 1945-48. Recipient Best Guidebook prize Thomas Cook Ltd. and Nat. Book League, London, 1981. Mem. Soc. Latin Am. Studies (vice chmn. 1973-79), Anglo-Brazilian Soc. (council mem. 1987—), Robert Simpson Soc. (joint sec. 1980—), Canning House Ctr. Mem. Social and Liberal Democratic Party. Home and Office: 3 Engel Park, London NW7 2HE, England

BROOKS, LARRY L(EROY), geologist, consultant; b. Albuquerque, Dec. 31, 1952; s. Jerry R. and Ruth N. (Burkholder) B.; m. Barbara A. Travland, June 26, 1985; 1 child, James Lawrence. AS, N.Mex. Highlands U., 1977, BS, 1978. Emergency room technician Las Vegas, Hosp. (N.Mex.), 1973-74; hydrologic technician U.S. Geol. Survey, Albuquerque, 1976-78; engr. technician State Engrs. Office, Albuquerque, 1978-79; dist. geologist N.Mex. Oil Commn., Artesia, 1979-86; exploration geologist Harvey E. Yates Co., Artesia, 1985—; guest lectr. Ea. N.Mex. U. Oil Field Tng. Ctr., Roswell, 1984—. Author jour. Geology of the Pecos Slope, 1982; contbr. articles to mags., profl. jours. Col.-aide de camp Dem. Party, Santa Fe, 1978—; sci. fair judge N.Mex. Highlands U., 1978-83; staff loss control officer Energy and Minerals Dept., Santa Fe, 1984. Served with U.S. Army, 1970-72. Recipient Exemplary Performance award N.Mex. Energy and Minerals Dept., 1983; named hon. sec. state N.Mex., 1984. Mem. Artesia C. of C. (bd. dirs. 1984—), Artesia Jaycees (pres. 1984), Am. Assn. Petroleum Geologists, Roswell Geol. Soc., N.Mex. Geol. Soc., N.Mex. Waterflood Assn., Sigma Gamma Epsilon, Tau Kappa Epsilon. Republican. Mem. Soc. of Friends. Lodge: Moose. Office: Harvey E Yates Co PO Box 1933 Roswell NM 88201

BROOKS, LEONARD, retired finance executive; b. Sheffield, Eng., May 11, 1930; s. Leonard and Daisy (Bell) B.; m. Sheila Mary Marcroft, Sept. 16, 1957; children: Ian David, Niall Richard, Stuart Andrew. Diploma Pub. Adminstrn., Sheffield U., 1953. With Sheffield County Borough Council, 1946-65, chief establishment asst., 1965-73; chief superannuation officer South Yorkshire County (Eng.) Council, 1973-86; chief superannotation officer South Yorkshire Residuary Body, 1986-87; ret. 1987; chmn. Yorkshire and Humberside Superannuation Officers Group, 1981-87. Author: (booklets) Paying for Retirement, 1978, Unreduced Lump Sum Benefits, 1979. Mem. Inst. Chartered Secs. and Adminstrs., Pensions Mgmt. Inst. Mem. Ch. of Eng. Home: 54 Hollins Ln, Sheffield S6 5GR, England

BROOKS, MARY JEANETTE TIDWELL, lobbyist; b. Dallas, July 14, 1951; d. Earl Carl Edwin and Leta Virginia (McDonald) Tidwell; m. Eldon Lloyd Brooks, Mar. 18, 1972 (div.); children: Kari Rene, Chad Ryan. BA in History cum laude, U. Tex., Arlington, 1973; MA in Social Sci., U. Okla., 1978. Tchr., Hurst (Tex.) Pub. Schs., 1975, Lawton (Okla.) Pub. Schs., 1976; research analyst Okla. Legis. Council, Oklahoma City, 1979; legis. rep. state govt. affairs Texaco USA, Houston, 1980-83; sr. rep. state govt. affairs Panhandle Eastern Corp., Houston, 1983-84, mgr. state govt. affairs, 1984—. Author: (with others) Agencies, Boards and Commissions of Oklahoma, 1979. Mem. Internat. Platform Assn., Ohio Gas Assn. (legis. com., regulator com.), Ill. C. of C. (energy com.), Ill. Mfrs. Assn. (energy com.), Ohio C. of C. (pub. affairs com.), Ohio Mfrs. Assn. (govt. affairs com.), Arlington Alumni Assn., U. Okla. Alumni Assn., Alpha Chi, Phi Alpha Theta, Sigma Delta Pi. Methodist. Club: Third House (Ill.). Home: 5107 Westerham Houston TX 77069 Office: Panhandle Eastern Pipe Line Co 3000 Bissonnet Houston TX 77005

BROOKS, NICHOLAS PETER, historian, educator; b. Virginia Water, Surrey, Eng., Jan. 14, 1941; s. William Donald Wykeham and Phyllis Kathleen (Juler) B.; m. Chloë Carolyn Willis, Sept. 16, 1967; children: Carolyn Ebba, Crispin Edmund Hartley. BA, Oxford U., Eng., 1962, MA, PhD, 1969. Lectr. medieval history U. St. Andrews, Fife, Scotland, 1964-77, sr. lectr., 1977-85; prof. U. Birmingham, Eng., 1985—; adviser Toronto (Univ.) Old English Dictionary, 1982—; bd. dirs. St. Andrews Univ. Excavations. Author: The Early History of the Church of Canterbury, 1984; editor: Studies in the Early History of Britain (series), 1977—; contbr. articles to profl. jours. Trustee St. Andrews Preservation Trust, 1971-85, chmn. 1977-81; active Council for Mus. and Galleries of Scotland, Edinburgh, 1982-85. Fellow Royal Hist. Soc., Soc. Antiquaries London. Office: Birmingham Univ, Sch of History, PO Box 363, Birmingham B15 2TT, England

BROOKS, ROBERT DEAN, university official; b. St. Louis, Oct. 24, 1934; s. Arthur Lee and Bessie Lois (Hill) B.; divorced; children: Andrea Lee, Heather Ann, Alexis Pauline, Robert C., Sarah Hill. BA, Washington U., St. Louis, 1959; MA, Cornell U., 1961, PhD, 1965. Asst. prof. San Diego State U., 1963-64, U. Ill., Urbana, 1964-69; vis. prof. U. Wis., Madison, 1969-70; assoc. prof. orgnl. and polit. communication Northwestern U., Evanston, Ill., 1970-74; prof., chmn. dept. U. South Fla., Tampa, 1974-79, dir., 1978-79; guest prof. U. Cologne, Fed. Republic of Germany, 1980-81; dir. Webster U., Vienna, Austria, 1981-88; dean, dir. New Eng. Coll., Arundel, Eng., 1988—; cons. Tampa Electric Co., 1974-80, Am. Mgmt. Assn., 1975-80, Westinghouse Electric Co., 1978-80, ALCOA, 1979-80. Contbg. author: Principles of Speech Communication, 1969, Readings in Psychologyof Adjustment, 1971, Studies in Applied Linguistics, 1977, Advances in Medical Education, 1981. Trainer/advisor United Fund, NCCJ, NAACP, Tampa, 1974-80; chmn. fund raising Boy Scouts Am., Austria, 1982-85, Reps. Abroad, Vienna, 1987. Recipient Gold Record for fund raising United Fund, Tampa, 1979; Fulbright-Hays Commn. Sr. Research award, 1980; grantee NSF, NEH, Fla. Endowment for Humanities. Mem. Popular Culture Assn. (chmn. German sect. 1976), Speech Communication Assn. (assoc. editor 1975, commn. chmn. 1979), Internat. Communication Assn., Soc. for Intercultural Edn., Tng. and Research. Office: New Eng Coll, Arundel, Sussex England

BROOME, ALBERT EDWARD, surgeon; b. Lund, Sweden, Nov. 10, 1926; s. Gustav and Elsa (Odhnoff) B.; m. Birgitta Klingspor, Sept. 20, 1958; children—Helena, Staffan, Erik, Ulrika. M.D., U. Lund, 1952; Ph.D., U. Gothenburg, 1969. Resident dept. surgery U. Helsingborg Hosp., Sweden, 1953-57; resident dept. surgery U. Lund, 1958, asst. prof. surgery, 1970-71, dept. plastic surgery, 1972; resident dept. hand surgery U. Gothenburg Hosp., 1959; chief resident dept. surgery Central Hosp., Boras, Sweden, 1960-69; asst. chief surgeon Central Hosp., Helsingborg, 1973-74, chief surgeon, 1975—; practice gen. vascular and plastic surgery, Helsingborg, 1975—. Author: Correction and Reconstruction of the Breast, 1986; 50 articles in surg. jours. Served to capt. Swedish Navy, 1963. Mem. Swedish Surg. Soc., Nordic Surg. Soc., Internat. Soc. Surgery, Internat. Soc. for Cardiovascular Surgery, European Soc. for Cardiovascular Surgery, Swedish Soc. for Plastic and Reconstructive Surgery. Lodge: Rotary. Avocations: tennis, hunting, windsurfing, music. Home: Johan Baners Gata 22, Helsingborg S-25233 Sweden Office: Central Hosp, S-25187 Helsingborg Sweden

BROOMFIELD, JOHN ROBERT, business consultant; b. Malta, Aug. 11, 1949; s. Harry Escourt Broomfield and Yvonne (Bathard) Gilbert; m. Mary Elizabeth Edwards, July 23, 1974; children: Laura Clare, Megan Clare, Glen Thomas. MS in Constrn. Mgmt., U. Tech., Loughborough, Eng., 1983. Instr. Royal Sch. Mil. Engring., Rochester, Eng., 1972-74; materials engr. Haggie Patterson & Assocs., Dartford, Eng., 1974-75; dep. resident engr. Render, Palmer & Tritton, Falklands Islands, 1975-77; sr. constrn. engr. Bechtel, Inc., Saudi Arabia, 1977-81; head corp. planning and devel. Harry Stanger Ltd., Elstree, Eng., 1984-87; dir. Quality Mgmt. Internat. Ltd., Luton, Eng., 1987—; sr. research fellow Reading (Eng.) U., 1986-88. Author: Quality Management Workshop, 1986. Fellow Inst. Quality Assurance; mem. Inst. Corrosion Sci. and Tech., Assn. Project Mgrs., Chartered Inst. Arbitrators (assoc.). Mem. Conservative Party. Home and Office: 5 Claydown, Luton LU1 4DU, England

BROOTEN, KENNETH EDWARD, JR., lawyer; b. Kirkland, Wash., Oct. 17, 1942; s. Kenneth Edward Sr. and Sadie Josephine (Assad) B.; m. Patricia Anne Folsom, Aug. 29, 1965 (div. April 1986); children: Michelle Catherine, Justin Kenneth. Diploma, Lewis Sch. Hotel, Restaurant and Club Mgmt., Washington, 1963; student, U. Md., 1964-66; AA, Sante Fe Community Coll., Gainesville, Fla., 1969; BS in Journalism with highest honors, U. Fla., 1971, MA in Journalism and Communications with highest honors, 1972, JD with honors, 1975; law student, U. Idaho, 1972-73; diploma, Inst. Legal Scis., Polish Acad. Scis., Warsaw, 1974; student, Trinity Coll., U. Cambridge, England, 1974. Bar: Fla., D.C., U.S. Dist. Ct. (no., mid. and so. dists.) Fla., U.S. Dist. Ct. D.C., U.S. Tax Ct., U.S. Ct. Appeals (5th, 9th, 11th and D.C. circs.), U.S. Supreme Ct., Trial Counsel Her Majesty's Govt. of United Kingdom. Asst. to several Congressmen U.S. Ho. of Reps., Washington, 1962-67; adminstrv. asst. VA Cen. Office, Washington, 1967; adminstrv. officer VA Hosp., Gainesville, Fla., 1967-72; ptnr. Carter & Brooten, P.A., Gainesville, Fla., 1975-78, Brooten & Fleisher, Chartered, Washington and Gainesville, Fla., 1978-80; sole practice Washington and Gainesville, 1980-86, Washington, 1987-88, Orlando, Fla., 1988—; permanent spl. counsel, acting chief counsel, dir. Select Com. Assassinations

U.S. Ho. of Reps., 1976-77; counsel Her Majesty's Govt. of U.K. (in U.S.). Author: Malpractice Guide to Avoidance and Treatment, 1987; writer episode TV series Simon & Simon; nat. columnist Private Practice, official pub. of Congress of County Med. Socs.; contbr. 70 articles to profl. jours. Served with USCGR, 1960-68. Named one of Outstanding Young Men Am., U.S. Jaycees, 1977. Mem. ABA, Fla. Bar Assn., D.C. Bar Assn., Am. Coll. Legal Medicine, Sigma Delta Chi. Roman Catholic. Office: 615 E Princeton St Suite 525 Orlando FL 32803

BROSHEARS, KEITH MACER, dentist; b. Terre Haute, Ind., Dec. 14, 1948; s. Kenneth P. and Geraldine (Macer) B.; m. Donnetta Jean Yenne, Dec. 10, 1982; children: Shelly L'Dee, James Lee, Robert Evan, Brian Keith. BA, DePauw U., 1971; DDS, Ind. U., 1976. Dentist Linton (Ind.) Dental Clinic, 1976—; prin. Linton Dental Lab., 1979—; pres. Bio-Systems Internat., 1988; medical staff Greene County Gen. Hosp., Linton, 1976—; dental cons. PSC, Inc., Madison, Wis., 1983—; lectr. in field. Author: How Tibbar Learned to Fly, 1971 (Lit. Excellance award 1971), TM Joint Systems Medical Manager for the Dental Office, 1988, Bio-Systems International Medical Manager for the Dental Office, 1988. Councilman Greene County, Bloomfield, 1978-82. DePauw U. scholar, 1967-71; State of Ind. Hoosier scholar, 1967-71; Robert Woods Johnson fellow, 1971-76. Mem. ADA, Internat. Coll. Oral Implantology, Ind. Dental Assn., Greene Dist. Dental Soc. Republican. Lodge: Rotary, Elks, Moose. Home: PO Box 144 Linton IN 47441 Office: Linton Dental Clinic 290 A St SE PO Box 675 Linton IN 47441-0675

BROSKY, JOHN G., judge; b. Scott Twp., Pa., Aug. 4, 1920; m. Rose F. Brosky, June 24, 1950; children—John C., Carol Ann, David J. B.A., U. Pitts., 1942, LL.B., 1949, J.D., 1968. Bar: Pa. 1950. Asst. county solicitor, Allegheny County, Pa., 1951-56; judge County Ct. Allegheny County, 1956-61; adminstrv. judge family div. Common Pleas Ct. Allegheny County, 1961-80; judge, sec. Superior Ct. Pa., 1980—; mem. faculty Pa. Coll. Judiciary. Chmn. Operation Patrick Henry, Boy Scouts Am.; pres. Scott Twp. Sch. Bd., 1946-56; 1st pres. Chartiers Valley Joint Sch. Dist., Allegheny County, Pa.; pres. Greater Pitts. Guild for Blind. Served with U.S. Army, 1942-46; maj. gen. (ret.) USAF-Pa. N.G. Recipient Disting. Jud. Service award Pa., Mason Juvenile Ct. Inst., Man of Yr. award in law Pitts. Jr. C. of C., 1960, Humanitarian award New Light Men's Club, 1960, Loyalty Day award VFW, 1960, Four Chaplains award, 1965; Man of Yr. award Cath. War Vets., 1960, 62; Service award Alliance Coll.; ; Disting. Citation, Mil. Order World Wars; Humanitarian award Variety Club, 1974; Jimmy Doolittle fellow award Aerospace Edn. Found., 1975; Pa. Meritorious Service medal Pa. N.G., 1976; State Humanitarian award Domestic Relations Assn. Pa., 1978; Man of Yr. award Am. Legion, 1978; Pa. Disting. Service medal; Disting. Service award Pa. N.G. Assn., 1980; Exceptional Service award USAF, 1982; General Ira Eaker fellow, 1981; Brotherhood of Man award Fraternal Socs. of Greater Pitts., 1987; Community Service award Chartiers Valley Commn. on Human Relations, 1988; named Pitts. Polonian of Yr., 1988. Mem. Am. Judicature Soc., ABA, Pa. Bar Assn. (co-chmn. professionalism com. 1987-88), Assn. Trial Lawyers Am., Inst. Jud. Adminstrn., Inc., Internat. Platform Assn., Air Force Assn. (nat. dir., nat. pres., chmn. bd., presidential citation 1974, 80, 81), Am. Acad. Matrimonial Lawyers, N.G. Assn. of Pa. (pres.), Pa. Conf. State Trial Judges (past pres.), Pa. Joint Family Law Council. Clubs: Press, Variety, Aero (past pres.) (Pitts.). Home: 29 Greenview Dr Carnegie PA 15106 Office: 2703 Grant Bldg Pittsburgh PA 15219

BROSNAN, CAROL RAPHAEL SARAH, musician, arts reports specialist; b. Paterson, N.J., July 19, 1931; d. Basil Roger Warnock and Mary Ellen Carroll (McDonald) Brosnan; student George Washington U., Washington, 1956-61, U. Va., 1975, U. Oxford (Eng.), 1975; B.A. in History, George Washington U., 1981, postgrad., 1983-87; pupil Iris Brussels, Helen Yakobson. Adminstrv. clk. Dept. of Army, Def., Pentagon, Office of asst. chief of staff intelligence, Washington, 1955-58; clk. fgn. sci. info. program NSF, Washington, 1958-60, adminstrv. clk., 1960-65, adminstrv. fellowship clk. grad. fellowship program, 1965-72; deputy chmn. for mgmt. Nat. Found. Arts and Humanities, Nat. Endowment for Arts, Washington, 1972—; music tchr. piano, Paterson, N.J., 1945-53; piano recitalist U.S., Heidelberg, W. Ger. Served with WAC, 1953-55. Recipient Young People's Concerts award, 1945. Hon. fellow Harry S. Truman Library Inst. Nat. and Internat. Affairs, 1975. Fellow Intercontinental Biog. Assn.; mem. Am. Assn. for Advancement Slavic Studies, Am. Hist. Assn., Am. Philol. Assn., Acad. Polit. Sci. (contbg.), Am. Classical League, Friends of Bodleian Library (Oxford U.), Luther Rice Soc. of George Washington U. (life), Phi Alpha Theta. Home: 4338 Carmelo Dr Apt #202 Annandale VA 22003 Office: NEH 1100 Pennsylvania Ave NW Washington DC 20506

BROSS, JOHN ADAMS, government official; b. Chgo., Jan. 17, 1911; s. Mason and Isabel Foster (Adams) B.; m. Priscilla Prince, June 1936; children: Wendy, John, Justine; m. Joanne Bass, Oct. 28, 1947; 1 son, Peter F. AB, Harvard U., 1933, LLB, 1936. Bar: N.Y. 1938. Sole practice N.Y.C., 1936-42, 46-49; assoc. firm Parker & Duryee, N.Y.C.; ptnr. Parker & Duryee, 1941—; asst. gen. counsel U.S. High Commr. to Germany, 1949-51; U.S. govt. cons. fgn. affairs 1951-57, 60—; advisor, coordinator Am. embassy, Bonn, Germany, 1957-59; dep. to dir. of central intelligence for programs evaluation 1963-71; staff mem. task force on nat. mil. establishment Hoover Commn., 1948. Chmn. bd. dirs. Cen. Atlantic Environment Ctr., 1971—; trustee Conservation Found., 1986—; bd. dirs. World Wild Life Fund U.S. Conservation Found. Served to col. USAAF, 1942-46. Decorated Legion of Merit, Bronze Star medal; Order Brit. Empire; King Christian X Medal of Liberty. Mem. Assn. Bar City N.Y. (chmn. com. state legislation 1946-49), Council on Fgn. Relations N.Y. Clubs: Metropolitan (N.Y.C.), Harvard (N.Y.C.); Alibi. Home: 1261 Crest Ln McLean VA 22101

BROSS, STEWARD RICHARD, JR., lawyer; b. Lancaster, Pa., Oct. 25, 1922; s. Steward Richard and Katherine Mauk (Hoover) B.; m. Isabel Florence Kenney, May 10, 1943; 1 dau., Donna Isabel Bross Cunneff. Student, McGill U., Montreal, Can., 1940-42; LL.B., Columbia U., 1948. Bar: N.Y. 1948. Since practiced in N.Y.C.; partner firm Cravath, Swaine & Moore, 1958—; adv. com. fgn. direct investment program Office of Sec. Dept. Commerce, 1969; adv. com. regulations Office Fgn. Direct Investment, 1968-70. Mem. Warden Trinity Ch., N.Y.C.; regent and trustee The Cathedral Ch. of St. John the Divine, N.Y.C. Served as officer Canadian Navy, 1942-45. Mem. Am., N.Y. State, Internat. bar assns., Assn. Bar City N.Y., Am. Soc. Internat. Law, Union Internat. des Avocats, Pilgrims U.S., Econ. Club N.Y. Clubs: Union (N.Y.C.), Wall Street (N.Y.C.), Board Room (N.Y.C.), Down Town Assn. (N.Y.C.). Home: 215 E 68th St New York NY 10021 also: Ashgrove 130 Litchfield Rd Norfolk CT 06058 Office: Cravath Swaine & Moore 1 Chase Manhattan Plaza New York NY 10005

BROSTRÖM, GÖRAN ROLF AXEL, mathematical statistics educator; b. Umeå, Sweden, Apr. 27, 1942; s. Rolf Theodor and Karin Charlotta (Harnesk) B.; m. Kristina Eva Ingvarson, Dec. 27, 1968; children: Anders, Kalle. PhD, Umeå U., Sweden, 1979. Researcher Demographic Data Base, Umeå, 1979-82; lector dept math. stats. Umeå U., 1982-86, docent, 1987—. Contbr. articles to profl. jours. Mem. Bernoulli Soc., Biometric Soc., Swedish Assn. Statisticians, Swedish Demographic Assn. Club: Universum (Umeå) (sec. 1982-86, chmn. 1986—). Home: Kopparvagen 45C, Umea S-90243, Sweden Office: Umea Univ, Dept Math Stats, Umea S-90187, Sweden

BROTCHNER, DOROTHY GOLDBLUM, civic worker; b. Mpls.; d. Hal and Emma (Shapere) Goldblum; student Macalester Coll., 1935-36, U. Minn., 1936-38; m. Robert Brotchner, Apr. 3, 1943; children—Richard Raymond, Leslie Alison Zentner. Mem. bd. Ramsey County (Minn.) Med. Aux., 1947-51, rec. sec., 1950-51; mem. bd. Rheumatic Diagnostic Clinic, St. Paul, 1949-51; unit chmn. LWV, St. Paul, 1950; mem. U. Minn. Faculty Wives' Club, 1949-51; mem. bd. univ. sect. Newcomers, 1949-51; mem. various local and council bds. Calif. PTA, 1951-64, hon. life mem., 1956—; mem. aux. bd. Queen of Angels Hosp., Los Angeles, 1953-62; den mother Cub Scouts, Los Angeles, 1952-54; patrol sponsor Boy Scouts Am., Los Angeles, 1954-55; Brownie leader Girl Scouts U.S.A., Los Angeles, 1954-58, troop leader, 1959; bd. dirs. Wilshire and Los Angeles council, 1955-59; mem. U. So. Calif. Med. Faculty Wives' Club, 1960-80 ; bd. dirs. met. sect. Los Angeles County Med. Aux., 1960, mem. bd. West Valley sect., 1969-70; pres. Gamma Phi Beta Mothers' Club, 1963-64, assoc., 1969-75; bd. dirs. bd. UCLA Intersorority Mothers' Club, 1964-69; vol. Los Angeles Youth Employment Service, 1962; mem. The Affiliates of UCLA, 1970—, life mem., 1971—, bd. dirs., 1973—, pres., 1974-75; mem. Arts Council, UCLA, 1974—, Valley Heart Guild of Children's Hosp.; mem. exec. bd. Alumni Council, UCLA, 1973-74; mem. counterpoint com. Partners for Los Angeles Music Center; bd. dirs. Design for Sharing, UCLA, 1982-86; mem. Encino (Calif.) Republican Women's Club, 1965-75 , bd. dirs., 1969-70. Recipient certificate for Outstanding Pub. Service, Civil Def. and Disaster Corps. Mem. Town Hall of Calif., Town and Gown (U. So. Calif.) (life), Los Angeles Mus. Art, Los Angeles Natural History Mus., Los Angeles World Affairs Council, Assistance League of So. Calif. (life), Calif. Museum Found. (The Muses), Los Angeles County Mus. of Sci. and Industry, Friends of Robinson Gardens. Clubs: Westwood Women's Bruin (dir. 1969—, pres. 1972-74, 78-79), UCLA Gold Shield (hon., bd. dirs. 1986—), Westside Trojan, Westside Bruin, Braemar Country, Riviera Country, Club 100 of Music Center. Home: 15604 Royal Woods Pl Sherman Oaks CA 91403

BROTCHNER, ROBERT JACOB, cardiologist; b. St. Paul, Apr. 3, 1912; s. Harry M. and Henrietta B. (Birnberg) B.; B.S., U. Minn., 1935, M.B., 1935, M.D., 1936, M.S., 1939; m. Dorothy Goldblum, Apr. 3, 1943; children—Richard Raymond, Leslie Alison Zentner. Intern, fellow Hennepin County Hosp., U. Minn., 1935-40; pvt. practice specializing in internal medicine, St. Paul, 1947-52, Los Angeles, 1952—; chmn. dept. medicine Ross-Loos Hosp., Los Angeles, 1974-76; mem. staff Good Hope Found., 1952—; chmn. dept. medicine, partner Ross-Loos Med. Group, 1956-77, emeritus chmn. dept. medicine, 1978—; chief of cardiology, 1954-72; chmn. dept. medicine Queen of Angeles Hosp., Los Angeles, 1957-58, 64, mem. active staff, from 1952; emeritus clin. asst. prof. medicine U. So. Calif. Served to lt. col. M.C., AUS, 1940-47; PTO. Diplomate Am. Bd. Interal Medicine. Fellow A.C.P., Am. Coll. Chest Physicians, Am. Coll. Cardiology; mem. AMA, Los Angeles County Med. Assn., Am. Heart Assn., Calif. Med. Golfers Assn. (pres. 1966), U. Minn. Med. alumni assns., Mus. Natural History, Am. Legion, Mus. Sci. Industry, Affiliates of UCLA, Sigma Xi, Alpha Omega Alpha. Clubs: Riviera Country (Pacific Palisades); Braemar Country (Tarzana); Westside Bruin; Big Ten (Los Angeles). Contbr. articles profl. jours. Home: 15604 Royal Woods Pl Sherman Oaks CA 91403

BROTHERTON, DAVID IAN, landscape designer, educator; b. Leeds, Yorkshire, Eng., Nov. 6, 1941; s. Frank Dudley and Jean Amice (Robertson) B.; m. Jennifer Margaret Clarkson, Dec. 30, 1964; children—Simon Guy, Vanessa Clare. M.A., U. Cambridge, 1963; M.Sc., U. London, 1970, Ph.D., 1974. Chartered engr. Engring. Council London. Civil engr. Taylor Woodrow Constrn. Ltd., London, 1964-69; environ. researcher Countryside Commn., London, 1970-74; prin. planner Yorkshire Dales Nat. Park, Bainbridge, North Yorkshire, Eng., 1974-76; sr. lectr. landscape design U. Sheffield (Eng.), 1976—; dir. Landscape Research Group Ltd., London, 1982-85; ptnr. Brotherton Oulsnam and Assocs., Bakewell, Derbyshire, Eng., 1982—. Editor Landscape Research Jour., 1980-86. Contbr. numerous articles to profl. jours. Mem. exec. com. Council for Protection Rural Eng., Sheffield, 1980—, Yorkshire Rural Community Council, York, Eng., 1981—. Fellow Royal Soc. Arts; mem. Instn. Civil Engrs., Brit. Ecol. Soc., Landscape Inst. (assoc.). Home: Lathkill Old Farmhouse, Over Haddon, Bakewell DE4 1JE, England Office: U Sheffield, Dept Landscape Architecture, Sheffield S10 2TN, England

BROTT, WALTER HOWARD, cardiac surgeon, educator, retired army officer; b. Alamosa, Colo., Sept. 5, 1933; s. Walter Hugo and Viola Helen (Roscher) B.; m. Marie Helen Kuzniewski; children: Cheryl Marie, Michelle Marie, Kevin Walter. B.A., Yale U., 1955; M.D., U. Kans., 1959. Diplomate Am. Bd. Surgery, Am. Bd. Thoracic Surgery. Commd. 1st. lt. U.S. Army, 1959, advanced through grades to col., 1974; intern Walter Reed Army Med. Ctr., Washington, 1959; resident in gen. surgery William Beaumont Gen. Hosp., El Paso, Tex., 1960-64; resident in thoracic surgery Fitzsimmons Army Med. Ctr., Denver, 1967-69; comdr. 3d Surg. Hosp., Vietnam, 1969, 18th Surg. Hosp., 1970; asst. chief thoracic and cardiovascular surgery Walter Reed Army Med. Ctr., 1971-76, chief cardiothoracic surgery, 1977-84; ret. U.S. Army, 1982; chief surg. cons. Surgeon Gen. Army, Washington, 1976-77; prof. surgery Uniformed Services U. Health Scis., 1976-84; assoc. clin. prof. surgery U. Tenn., Knoxville, 1984—; mem. joint rev. com. Council for Perfusion Edn. and Accreditation, 1981-87. Contbr. articles to profl. jours.; chmn.: NATO editorial bd. Emergency War Surgery Handbook, 1977-82. Decorated Legion of Merit with oak leaf cluster; decorated Bronze Star (U.S.), Cross of Gallantry (Vietnam); recipient Cert. of Achievement Surgeon Gen. U.S., 1978. Fellow ACS (grad. edn. com. 1977-78); mem. Soc. Thoracic Surgeons, Washington Med. Soc., Thoracic and Cardiovascular Surgeons, Thoracic Surgery Program Dirs. Assn., Am. Assn. Thoracic Surgeons, Assn. Med. Cons. to Armed Forces, AMA (cons. panel council allied health edn. accreditation 1981-87), Knoxville Acad. Medicine (grad. edn. com.), Assn. Mil. Surgeons, Internat. Platform Assn., Alpha Omega Alpha. Lutheran. Clubs: Yale (Washington); Marine Meml. Office: Dept Surgery U Tenn Meml Hosp Knoxville TN 37920

BROUE, MICHEL JEAN, mathematician, educator; b. Paris, France, Oct. 28, 1946; s. Pierre Broue and Simone Paulette (Charras) Lemarchand; m. Marie-Claude Cidere, Sept. 10, 1966; children—Isabelle Sandrine, Caroline Severine. Maitrise/DEA/Doct. 3e c., Ecole Normale Super., 1970, Agregation de Math., 1969; Doctorat d'Etat es. Sc., Universite Paris 7, 1975. Cert. univ. prof. Eleve-professeur Ecole Normale Super., Saint-Cloud, France, 1966-70; attache de recherche CNRS, Paris, 1970-75, charge de recherche, 1975-80; prof. Universite Paris 7, 1980-83, prof. lere classe, 1983—; dir. service math. Ecole Normale Super. de Jeunes Filles, France, 1983—; dir. math. dept. and Info. Ecole Normale Superieure, 1986—. Contbr. numerous articles to profl. jours. Sec. Com. Mathematicians, Paris, 1974—. Mem. Societe Mathematique de France, Am. Math. Soc. Home: 9 rue Brezin, 75014 Paris France Office: Ecole Normale Superieure, 45 rue d Ulm, 75005 Paris France

BROUWER, HARRY JOSEPHUS, food company executive; b. Delft, Netherlands, July 7, 1958; s. Wilhelmus Adrianus and Wilhelmina (van Vlijmen) B.; m. Marjolein Paulina G. Rietbergen, May 16, 1986. D in Economics and Bus. Adminstrn., Erasmus U., 1983; postgrad. in mktg. and advt., Mich. State U., 1983; postgrad. in advt. S.R.M., Ultrecht, Netherlands, 1985. Mgr. H.B. Party Service, Delft, 1981-82; project cons. Prodis, Rotterdam, Netherlands, 1982-83; product mgr. C.P.C.-Benelux (Knorr), Utrecht, 1983-84, sales mgr., 1984-86, mktg. mgr., 1987—; pub. relations cons. to lawyer, Rotterdam, 1985—. Author: In Detail Getreden, 1984. Chmn. bd. real estate owners, Rotterdam, 1986—. Recipient 1st prize for best publs. on retail devels. VIVO-Nederland, 1984. Mem. Dutch Mktg. Inst. (exam. corrector 1985—), Dutch Mich. State U. Alumni Assn. Roman Catholic. Home: JJ Slauerhoffstraat 45, 3069 JV Rotterdam The Netherlands

BROWALDH, TORE, banker; b. Vasteras, Sweden, Aug. 23, 1917; s. Ernfrid and Ingrid (Gezelius) B.; B.A., Stockholm U., 1941, LL.M., 1942; Dr.Eng. h.c., Engring U. Stockholm, 1967; m. Gunnel Ericson, June 30, 1942; children—Dag, Suzanne, Lars, Mikael. Asst. sec. Com. for Post-War Econ. Planning, 1944-45; sec. Indsl. Research Inst., 1944-45; v.p. Svenska Handelsbanken, 1946-48, cons., head econ., social and cultural div. Gen. Secretariat of Council of Europe, Strasbourg, France, 1949-51; dep. mng. dir. Swedish Employers Assn., 1951-54; dir. Svenska Handelsbanken, 1954, pres., 1955-66, chmn. bd. dirs., 1966-77, vice chmn., 1977-88, hon. chmn. 1988— ; vice chmn. bd. Volvo; chmn. Svenska Cellulosa AB, dir. IBM World Trade Corp., N.Y.C., Unilever adv. bd., Rotterdam; chmn. IBM Swedish Div., Swedish Unilever Ltd. Former mem. Labor Market Inst. Govt. Econ. Planning Commn., UN Study Group Multi-nat. Corps., 1973. Bd. dirs. Dag Hammarskjold Meml. Fund Found.; dep. chmn. Nobel Found. Mem. Royal Swedish Acad. Scis. Home: 14 Sturegatan, Stockholm Sweden Office: 8 Kungstraedgaardsgatan, Stockholm Sweden

BROWDER, FELIX EARL, mathematician, educator; b. Moscow, July 31, 1927; s. Earl and Raissa (Berkmann) B.; m. Eva Tislowitz, Oct. 5, 1949; children: Thomas, William. S.B., Mass. Inst. Tech., 1946; Ph.D., Princeton U., 1948. C.L.E. Moore instr. math. MIT, 1948-51, vis. assoc. prof., 1961-62, vis. prof., 1977-78; instr. math. Boston U., 1951-53; asst. prof. Brandeis U., 1955-56; from asst. prof. to prof. math. Yale U., 1956-63; prof. math. U. Chgo., 1963-72, Louis Block prof. math., 1972-82, Max Mason Disting. Service prof. math., 1982-87, chmn. dept., 1972-77, 80-85; v.p. for research Rutgers U., New Brunswick, N.J., 1986—; univ. prof. math. Rutgers U., New Brunswick, 1986—; vis. mem. Inst. Advanced Study, Princeton, 1953-54, 63-64; vis. prof. Instituto de Matematica Pura e Aplicada, Rio de Janeiro, 1960, Princeton U., 1968; Fairchild disting. visitor Calif. Inst. Tech., 1975-76; sr. research fellow U. Sussex, Eng., 1970, 76; vis. prof. U. Paris, 1973, 75, 78, 81, 83, 85. Served with AUS, 1953-55. Guggenheim fellow, 1953-54, 66-67, Sloan Found. fellow, 1959-63, NSF sr. postdoctoral fellow, 1957-58. Fellow Am. Acad. Arts and Scis.; mem. Nat. Acad. Scis., Am. Math. Soc. (editor bull. 1959-68, 78-83, council mem. 1959-72, 78-83, mng. editor 1964-68, 80, exec. com. council 1979-80), Math. Assn. Am., AAAS (chmn. sect. A 1982-83), Sigma Xi (pres. chpt. 1985-86).

BROWER, DAVID JOHN, lawyer, urban planner, educator, administrator; b. Holland, Mich., Sept. 11, 1930; s. John J. and Helen (Olson) B.; m. Lou Ann Brown, Nov. 26, 1960; children—Timothy Seth, David John, II, Ann Lacey. B.A., U. Mich., 1956, J.D., 1960. Bar: Ill. 1960, Mich. 1961, Ind. 1961, U.S. Supreme Ct. 1971. Asst. dir. div. community planning Ind. U., Bloomington, 1960-70; assoc. dir. Ctr. for Urban and Regional Studies, U. N.C., Chapel Hill, 1970—; pres. Coastal Resources Collaborative, Ltd., Chapel Hill, 1980—; counsel Robinson & Cole, Hartford, Conn., 1986—. Author: (with others) Contitutional Issues of Growth Management, 1978; Growth Management, 1984, Special Area Management, 1985. Mem. ABA, Am. Planning Assn. bd. dirs. 1982-85, chmn.-founder planning and law div. 1978), Am. Inst. Cert. Planners. Democrat. Episcopalian. Home: 612 Shady Lawn Chapel Hill NC 27514 Office: U NC 108 Battle Ln Chapel Hill NC 27514

BROWN, ANTHONY B., aerospace executive; b. Mpls., Apr. 5, 1922; s. Wayland Hoyt and Adele (Birdsall) B.; m. Mary Alice Ann Anderson, July 28, 1956. BS, Rutgers U., 1949; postgrad. U. So. Calif., 1968-69; PhD, U. Beverly Hills, 1986. Cert. data processor, systems profl. Sr. system analyst Thrifty Corp., Los Angeles, 1957-69; system engr. Informatics Gen., Inc., Los Angeles, 1969-73; contract instr. computer software York U., 1970, McGill U., U. Victoria, 1971, USMC, Boston U., W.Va. U., U. Guelph, 1972; sr. system engr. Jet Propulsion Lab., La Canada, Calif., 1974-76; sr. system engr. Informatics Gen., Inc., Anchorage, Los Angeles, Washington, 1976-78; supr. project control Hughes Aircraft Co., Los Angeles, 1978-81; mgr. fin. Contel Corp., Redondo Beach, Calif., 1981-88. Author: A Century of Blunders--America's China Policy 1844-1949. Rep. precinct capt., presdl. election, 1964; chmn. bd. govs. La Brea Vista Townhouses, 1967-68; active numerous animal welfare orgns. Served with Finance Corps, U.S. Army, 1951-57. Decorated Bronze Star. Fellow Brit. Interplanetary Soc.; mem. AAAS, The Planetary Soc., Nature Conservancy, Town Hall of Calif., Assn. Computer Machinery (chpt. sec. 1973-74), Assn. Systems Mgmt., Mensa, Intertel, Armed Forces Communications and Electronics Assn., Assn. Inst. Cert. Computer Profls., Am. Assn. Fin. Profls., Am. Def. Preparedness Assn., Washington Legal Found., Am. Security Council (mem. nat. adv. bd.), Calif. Soc., SAR, Mil. Order World Wars, Aircraft Owners and Pilots Assn., Internat. Platform Assn., Theodore Roosevelt Assn., Res. Officers Assn., Delta Phi Epsilon. Republican. Club: Los Angeles Athletic. Lodges: Masons, Shriners, Nat. Sojourners. Home: 4333 Redwood Ave Marina del Rey CA 90292

BROWN, BRITT MURDOCK, banker; b. Wichita, Kans., Aug. 1, 1952; s. Harry Britton Jr. and Ann Louise (McCarthy) B.; m. Sally Melissa Andrews, Nov. 26, 1982; children: Aaron Britton, Jacqueline Lea, Ruse Murdock. B of Bus. Adminstrn. and Econs., Wichita State U., 1974. Investment officer Fourth Nat. Bank, Wichita, 1974-80; investment broker A.G. Edwards & Sons, Wichita, 1980; v.p., trust officer Kans. State Bank and Trust Co., Wichita, 1980-83, sr. v.p, trust officer, 1983-86, exec. v.p., trust officer, 1986-87, exec. v.p., sr. trust officer, 1987—; exec. v.p. Kans. State Fin. Corp., Wichita, 1987—; sec., treas. Sun Eagle Enterprises, Wichita, Britt Brown Ptnrship., Wichita, M. M. Murdock, Wichita. Advisor Senator Robert Dole, Washington, 1983—; chmn. bd. dirs. Holy Family Ctr., Wichita, 1974—, Sedgewick County Civil Service Bd., 1985—; bd. govs. Wichita State U., 1980—; bd. dirs. Police and Fire Retirement Bd., Wichita, 1985—; mem. Kans. State Political Action com., 1987—, Wichita Crime commn., pres., 1988. Named one of Outstanding Young Men Am., 1981. Mem. Am. Inst. Banking, Kans. Ind. Oil and Gas Assn., Wichita Estate Planning Council (v.p. 1984—), Wichita C. of C., Nat. Conf. Christians and Jews (bd. dirs. 1986—), Paul Revere Found. Republican. Roman Catholic. Clubs: Wichita (bd. dirs. 1985—), Wichita Country. Office: Kans State Bank & Trust Co 123 N Market Wichita KS 67202

BROWN, CAMERON, insurance company consultant; b. Chgo., Sept. 29, 1914; s. George Frederic and Irene (Larmon) B.; m. Dorothea Fruechtenicht, May 10, 1947 (div. Feb. 1965); children: Reid L., Deborah Sue; m. Jean McGrew, Dec. 22, 1965; 1 dau., Sophia Lyn. A.B., U. Ill., 1937; grad., Indsl. Coll. Armed Forces, 1941. Vice pres. R. B. Jones & Sons, Inc., 1938-41; dir. Geo. F. Brown & Sons, Inc., Chgo., 1947-79; v.p. Geo. F. Brown & Sons, Inc., 1947-50, exec. v.p., 1950-53, pres., 1953-64, chmn., chief exec. officer, 1964-76; dir. Interstate Nat. Corp., 1968-79, pres., 1968-74, chmn., 1970-76; dir. Nat. Student Mktg. Corp., 1970-79, pres., 1970-72, chmn., 1970-75; dir. Interstate Fire & Casualty Co., 1952-79, exec. v.p., 1953-56, pres., 1956-74, chmn., 1970-76; dir. Chgo. Ins. Co., 1957-79, pres., 1957-74, chmn., 1970-76; dir. Interstate Reins. Corp., 1957-79; pres. Cameron Brown Ltd., 1976—; underwriting mem. Lloyd's of London, 1971—; sec., dir. Ill. Ins. Info. Service, 1967-76. Contbg. author: Property and Liability Handbook, 1965. Pres., Chgo. area Planned Parenthood Assn., 1969-72; vis. com. U. Chgo.; governing mem. Shedd Aquarium; bd. dirs. Planned Parenthood Fedn. Am., 1976-79; mem. Exec. Service Corps, Chgo., 1978—, John Evans Club, Northwestern U., U. Ill. Pres.'s Club, U. Ill. Found., U. Chgo. Pres.'s Club.; Fellow Aspen Inst. Humanistic Studies, 1976—. Served from 2d lt. to lt. col. Gen. Staff Corps AUS, 1941-45. Decorated Bronze Star with oak leaf cluster. Mem. Lloyd's Brokers Assn. (chmn. 1959-60), Nat. Assn. Ind. Insurers (bd. govs. 1961-77), Ill. St. Andrews Soc., Internat. Wine and Food Soc. (Chgo.), Surplus Line Brokers Assn. (chmn. 1954), Confrerie des Chevaliers du Tastevin (officier-comdr.), Commanderie de Bordeaux (Maitre honoraire), Conseiller de Bordeaux, Santa Barbara Wine & Food Soc. Psi Upsilon. Clubs: Chgo., Attic, Exec., (dir. 1969-73, 1st v.p. 1970-71), Econ., Mid-Am., Casino (Chgo.); Army-Navy Country (Arlington, Va.), Old Elm, Shoreacres, Onwentsia (Lake Forest, Ill.), Pine Valley Golf (Clementon, N.J.), Birnam Wood Golf, The Valley, (Montecito, Calif.), Hon. Co. Edinburgh Golfers (Muirfield, Scotland), Royal and Ancient Golf St. Andrews (Scotland). Home (summer): 1400 N Green Bay Rd Lake Forest IL 60045 Home (winter): 2004 Sandy Pl Santa Barbara CA 93108 Office: 222 E Wisconsin Ave Lake Forest IL 60045

BROWN, CAROL ANN, magazine editor; b. Nassau, The Bahamas, Jan. 11, 1951; d. David Moon and Joan Marjorie (Lightburn) Lightbourn; m. Geoffrey Brown, Dec. 3, 1978 (div. Sept. 1982); 1 child, Jonathan David. BA, Rollins Coll., 1973. Assoc. editor, advt. dir. Brice Advt. and Pub. Co. Ltd., Nassau, 1975—. Mem. pub. relations com. Free Nat. Movement, Nassau, 1987. Recipient award Acad. Am. Poets, 1972-73. Mem. Nassau Poetry Soc., Nassau Players Drama Soc. (sec. 1975-78, 84-85, chmn. 1988—), Bahamas Writers' Assn. Methodist. Clubs: Royal Nassau Sailing, Nassau Lawn Tennis, Nassau Garden. Home: PO Box N 431, Nassau The Bahamas Office: Brice Advt Co Ltd, PO Box N 4181, Nassau The Bahamas

BROWN, CAROL ANNE, manufacturers' representative; b. Detroit, Feb. 26, 1947; d. Bruno Walter and Irene Sabina (Derengowski) Siedlarz; student Los Angeles City Coll., 1971, DeAnza Community Coll., 1973; m. Leonard Brown, Apr. 24, 1976; 1 son, David. Sec., Fairchild Semicondrs., Detroit, 1965-69, inside sales rep., Mountain View, Calif., 1969-74; sales rep. Calif. Circuit Engring., Sunnyvale, 1974-76; owner, operator Brown Sales Co., Mission Viejo, Calif., 1976-79; pres., gen. mgr. S.W. Contemporary Sales, Inc., Scottsdale, Ariz., 1979—. Mem. Bus. and Profl. Women Am., Network Female Execs. Republican. Roman Catholic. Home and Office: 12580 N 84th Pl Scottsdale AZ 85260

BROWN, CHARLES ASA, lawyer; b. Woodsfield, Ohio, Oct. 17, 1912; s. Charles A. and Anna Miriam (Hayes) B.; A.B. Va. Mil. Inst., 1931-35;

student U. Mich., 1937; J.D., Western Res. U., 1938 children—Charles A. III, Ridgley. Bar: Ohio, 1938. Pvt. practice Portsmouth, 1938—; asst. atty. gen. State of Ohio, 1963; owner Raven Rock Farm and Feurt Farm, Scioto River Farm Tract, Winters Farm. Lectr. Indian lore. Active Boy Scouts Am., 1946—, serving as merit badge counsellor, exec. bds. Scioto Area council, Portsmouth dist. commr., scout master troop 12, 1966-80; developer, adviser Indian dance team Portsmouth dist., 1964-78, v.p. Scioto Area council, 1967-68, nat. rep. Nat. council, 1967-68; adv. council Girl Scouts of Am., 1947-48; adv. Indian Tribes, 1961-63; councilman Western Black Elk Keetowah, Cherokee Nation, 1964—; mem. Cedar River Tulsa Muskogee Band. Bd. dirs. Portsmouth Little League Baseball Assn., 1957-58, Scioto County unit Am. Cancer Soc., 1973-80; adv. bd. Practical Nurses Assn., 1960-61; sr. warden Episcopal Ch., lay reader, 1950-76; lay reader Anglican Orthodox Ch., 1976-77, Anglican Ch. N. Am., 1977-81. Served from 1st lt. to capt. U.S. Army, 1941-46; lt. col. Res. (ret.). Decorated Bronze Star with oak leaf cluster, Purple Heart, Am. Defense medal, Victory medal, Occupational medal, European theatre ribbon, 3 battle stars; named Ky. Col.; recipient Silver Beaver award Boy Scouts Am., 1968, Vigil Order of Arrow, 1971. Mem. Am. Indian Bar Assn., Ohio Bar Assn., Portsmouth Bar Assn. (trustee 1966-71), Am. Legion, VFW, DAV, Nat. Rifle Assn., Ohio Farm Bur., various Am. Indian orgns. Club: Daniel Boone Muzzle Loading Rifle. Lodges: Odd Fellow, Mason (32 deg., master of lodge 1965, past sovereign master, Allied Masonic degrees); Shriner (past comdr., trustee lodge 1966-71, excellent high priest chpt. 1976-77, illustrious master council 1978-79, pres. 5th dist. Royal Arch Masons 1979, arch adjutant 6th arch council 1979-81, dist. dep. grand high priest 1980-83, anointed high priest RAM, recipient silver trowel), Royal Order Scotland, Knight Masons Ireland, Nat. Sojourners, Order of Corks, Tall Cedars Lebanon, York Cross of Honour, HRAKTP, Knight Masons of USA, Order of the Bath, K.P. (grand tribune Ohio 1961, past chancellor comdr.), Red Br. of Erie, Ohio Masonic Vets., Philalethes Soc., Fraternal Order of Police, Order Eastern Star (patron 1966, trustee 1967-70), White Shrine of Jerusalem. Delineator flood wall, Portsmouth, Ohio, 1936. Office: 721 Washington St Portsmouth OH 45662

BROWN, CHARLES IRVING, financial consultant; b. Bombay, India, Jan. 14, 1932; s. Charles Irving and Frances Belcher (Woods) B. (parents Am. citizens); B.A. in Geology, Williams Coll., 1954; M.B.A. with distinction, Harvard U., 1959; m. Kathleen Mae Shrum, July 2, 1960; children—Dana Scott, Tracy Ann, Kelly Mae. Asst. mgr. credit dept. First Nat. City Bank of N.Y., Rio de Janeiro, Brazil, 1954-57; v.p. fin. Western Nuclear Inc., Denver, 1959-73, also dir.; v.p. fin. and mktg. Energy Fuels Corp., Denver, 1974-82, also dir.; fin. cons., 1982—; dir. Rawlins Nat. Bank (Wyo.), Am. Nat. Bank, Laramie, Wyo., Original Sixteen-to-One Mine, Allegheny, Calif., Clinical Diagnostics, Colo.; Trustee Colo. Outward Bound, Colo. State U. Research Found. Mem. Am. Inst. Mining Engrs., Fin. Execs. Inst. Clubs: Univ., Denver Athletic, Am. Alpine. Home: 2691 Pinehurst Dr Evergreen CO 80439 Office: One Tabor Ctr 1200 17th St Suite 2450 Denver CO 80202

BROWN, CHET (CHESTER ARTHUR), JR., sales executive; b. Boston, Oct. 14, 1938; s. Chester Arthur and Anna Hilda (Smith) B.; m. Marcie K. Brown; children—Patricia, Linda, Stephen, Christopher, Laura, Edward, Beth Ann. B.A. in Chemistry, Boston U., 1960; M.B.A. in Mktg., Northeastern U., 1962. Vice pres., sales and mktg. High Voltage Engring. Corp., Burlington, Calif., 1961-72; founder/ptnr. Ferro Fluidics Corp., Burlington, 1972-75; mgr. West Coast Office, Alpha Industries, San Jose, Calif., 1976-78; internat. mktg. mgr. Network Products Operation, Beckman Instruments, Fullerton, Calif., 78-80; group v.p. communications and subsystems Western Digital Corp., Irvine, Calif., 1980; sr. v.p. Imaging, pres. Paradise Systeme, Inc.; bd. dirs. Dual Systems Corp. Paradise Systems, Inc. Mem. IEEE, Am. Mgmt. Assn., Assn. Old Crows. Republican. Recipient Assn. Indsl. Advertisers award, 1967; Bus. Press Assn. awards; patentee in field. Office: Western Digital Corp Paradise Systems Inc 99 S hull Rd Brisbane CA 95004

BROWN, CLIFFORD CAPERTON, mathematician; b. Atlantic City, Aug. 14, 1928; s. John Wilson and Rose Gaston (Caperton) B.; m. Hannelore Adelheid Soltau; children: Esther, Isabella. BA, Princeton U., 1953; D rer. nat., Göttingen U., Fed. Republic of Germany, 1963; habilitation, Erlangen U., Fed. Republic of Germany, 1976. Mathematician Northrop Aircraft Corp., Hawthorne, Calif., 1953-56, Instrumentation Lab. MIT, Cambridge, Mass., 1956-59; mitarbeiter D.F.G. Deutshe Forschungsgemeinschaft, Fed. Republic of Germany, 1963-65; wiss. mitarbeiter Erlangen U., Fed. Republic of Germany, 1965-68; research stipendiat Battelle Inst., Geneva, 1968-69; wiss. mitarbeiter Erlangen U., Fed. Republic of Germany, 1969-76; prof. Free U., Berlin, 1976—; dep. adminstrv. dir. Math Inst. III Free U., Berlin, 1986—. Contbr. articles to profl. jours. Served with USAF, 1946-49. Mem. Deutsche Mathematiker-Vereinigung, Konferenz der Hochschullehrer der Mathematischen Statistik. Office: U Berlin Math Inst III, Arnimallee 2-6, 1-33 Berlin Federal Republic of Germany

BROWN, DANIEL, independent art consultant, critic; b. Cin., Nov. 4, 1946; s. Sidney H. and Genevieve Florence (Elbaum) B.; m. Ellen Neveloff, May 24, 1970; m. 2d, Jane Felson, Sept. 14, 1980; stepchildren—Christopher Minton, Scott Minton. A.B. cum laude, Middlebury Coll., 1968; A.M., U. Mich., 1970; postgrad. Princeton U., 1971-72. Dir. cultural events U. Cin., 1972, spl. asst. to pres., 1973; v.p., corp. sec. Brockton Shoe Trimming Co., Cin., 1974—; prin. Daniel Brown, Inc.; curator KZF Gallery, Cin., 1987—; art critic Cin. Mag., 1980-83, Cin. Art Acad. Newsletter; art commentator Sta. WKRC-TV, Cin., art and movie critic Sta. WCPO-TV, Cin., 1986; instr. Art Acad. Cin., 1988—; guest curator Non Art from Academe: An Overview The Cen. Exchange, Kansas City, Mo., 1988; guest co-curator Cincinnati Yesterday and Today Tangeman Fine Arts Gallery U. Cin., 1987; frequent guest lectr. on arts; permanent curator The KZF Art Gallery, Cin., 1987—; corr. editor: Dialogue Mag., 1986, art reviewer 1983— . Recipient The Critic's Purse award, Dialogue mag., 1985. Mem. exhbns. com. Contemporary Arts Ctr.; mem. membership com. Cin. Art Mus.; sec., bd. dirs. Mercantile Library, 1985—, treas. 1986, chmn. programs com., 1987—, Young Wing; trustee Contemporary Arts Ctr. 1984—, co-chmn. artists adv. bd., 1987, Vocal Arts Ensemble, 1984, Enjoy the Arts, 1985—, v.p. 1986; mem. bd. advisors Cin. Artists Group Effort, 1986—; guest curator Carnegie Arts Ctr., Covington, Ky., 1986—; juror art competitions Cin. and Columbus, Ohio, 1986-87. Mem. Shoe and Leather Club, Two-Ten Nat. Found., Internat. Platform Assn. Club: University (Cin.). Home: 3900 Rose Hill Ave Apt 401B Cincinnati OH 45229 Office: Brockton Shoe Trimming Co 212 E 8th St Cincinnati OH 45202

BROWN, DAVID, motion picture producer, writer; b. N.Y.C., July 28, 1916; s. Edward Fisher and Lillian (Baren) B.; m. Liberty LeGacy, Apr. 15, 1940 (div. 1951); 1 son, Bruce LeGacy; m. Wayne Clark, May 25, 1951 (div. 1957); m. Helen Gurley, Sept. 25, 1959. AB, Stanford U., 1936; MS, Columbia U., 1937. Apprentice San Francisco News and Wall St. Jour., 1936; night editor, asst. drama critic Fairchild Publs., 1937-39; editorial dir. Milk Research Council, 1939-40; assoc. editor Street & Smith Publs., 1940-43; assoc. editor, exec. editor, editor-in-chief Liberty mag., 1943-49; editorial dir. Nat. Edn. Campaign, A.M.A., 1949; assoc. editor, mng. editor Cosmopolitan mag., 1949-52; mng. editor, story editor, head scenario dept. 20th Century-Fox Film Corp. Studios, Beverly Hills, Calif., 1952-56, mem. studio exec. com., 1956-60, producer, 1960-62; v.p., dir. story operation 20th Century Fox Film Corp., Beverly Hills, Calif., 1964-69, exec. v.p. creative operations, 1969-70, dir., 1968-70; exec. v.p. creative operations, dir. Warner Bros., 1971-72; ptnr. Zanuck/Brown Co., N.Y.C., 1972—; exec. story editor, head scenario dept., editorial v.p. New Am. Library World Lit., Inc., 1963-64; final judge for best short story pub. in mags. Benjamin Franklin Mag. ann. awards, 1955-58. Author: Brown's Guide to Growing Gray, 1987; contbr. articles to Am. mag., Collier's, Harpers, Sat. Evening Post, others; editor: I Can Tell It Now, 1964, How I Got That Story, 1967; contbr.: Journalists in Action, 1963; producer: (films) The Sting, 1973, The Sugarland Express, 1974, The Eiger Sanction, 1975, Jaws, 1977, MacArthur, 1977, Jaws II, 1978, The Island, 1980, Neighbors, 1981, The Verdict, 1982, Target, 1985, Cocoon, 1985. Trustee com. on film Mus. Modern Art, N.Y.C. Served as 1st lt., M.I. AUS, World War II. Mem. Acad. Motion Picture Arts and Scis., Producers Guild Am., Am. Film Inst. (vice-chmn., trustee, mem. exec. com.). Clubs: Players (N.Y.C.), Dutch Treat (N.Y.C.), Century Assn. (N.Y.C.), Overseas Press (N.Y.C.); Nat. Press (Washington); Coffee House (N.Y.C.). Office: The Manhattan Project Ltd 711 Fifth Ave New York NY 10022

BROWN, DENISE SCOTT, architect, urban planner; b. Nkana, Zambia, Oct. 3, 1931; came to U.S., 1958; d. Simon and Phyllis (Hepker) Lakofski; m. Robert Scott Brown, July 21, 1955 (dec. 1959); m. Robert Charles Venturi, July 23, 1967; 1 child, James C. Student, U. Witwatersrand, South Africa, 1948-51; diploma, Archtl. Assn., London, 1955; M of City Planning, U. Pa., 1960, MArch, 1965; DFA (hon.), Oberlin Coll., 1977, Phila. Coll. Art, 1985, Parsons Sch. Design, 1985; LHD (hon.), N.J. Inst. Tech., 1984. Registered architect, U.K. Asst. prof. U. Pa., Phila., 1960-65; assoc. prof., head urban design program UCLA, 1965-68; with Venturi, Rauch and Scott Brown, Phila., 1967—, ptnr., 1969—; vis. prof. architecture U. Calif., Berkeley, 1965, U. Pa., 1982-83; vis. prof. architecture Yale U., 1967-70, 87; mem. vis. com. MIT, 1973-83; mem. adv. com. Temple U. Dept. Architecture, 1980—; policy panelist design arts program Nat. Endowment for Arts, 1981-83. Co-author: Learning from Las Vegas, 1972, rev. edit., 1977, A View from the Campidoglio: Selected Essays, 1953-84, 1985; contbr. numerous articles to profl. jours. Mem. curriculum and adult edn. com. Phila. Jewish Children's Folkshul, 1980-86; mem. bd. advisors Architects, Designers and Planners for Social Responsibility, 1982—; mem. capitol preservation com. Commonwealth of Pa., Harrisburg, 1983-87; bd. dirs. Cen. Phila. Devel. Corp., 1985—, Urban Affairs Ptnrship., Phila., 1987—; trustee Chestnut Hill Acad., Phila., 1985—. Recipient numerous awards, citations, commendations for design, urban planning, Chgo. Architecture award, 1987, order of merit Republic of Italy, 1987. Mem. Am. Planning Assn., Archtl. Assn. London, Alliance Women in Architecture N.Y., Soc. Archtl. Historians (bd. dirs. 1981-84), Royal Inst. Brit. Architects. Democrat. Jewish. Office: Venturi Rauch and Scott Brown 4236 Main St Philadelphia PA 19127

BROWN, DONALD RICHARD, capacitor engineer; b. Milw., Sept. 25, 1925; s. Edwin Frances and Loretta Ethlyn (Howard) B.; m. Dorothy Jane (Carey), Sept. 5, 1947; children: Donald R. Jr., Kenneth Allen. BS in Physics and Math., Monmouth (Ill.) Coll., 1950. Dept. chief engring. Western Electric, Cicero, Ill., 1951-85; pres. D.R.B. Tech. Services, Ltd., Downers Grove, Ill., 1985—. Patentee in field. Pres. Bruce Lake Home Owners Assn., 1960, Downer's Grove PTA, 1962. Served with USAF, 1944-45. Named one of top 100 technologists in western world by Tech. Mag., 1981.

BROWN, DONALD WESLEY, lawyer; b. Cleve., Jan. 2, 1953; s. Lloyd Elton Brown and Nancy Jeanne Hudson. AB summa cum laude, Ohio U., 1975; JD, Yale U., 1978. Bar: Calif. 1978, U.S. Dist. Ct. (no. dist.) Calif. 1978. Assoc. Brobeck, Phleger & Harrison, San Francisco, 1978-85, ptnr., 1985—. Democrat. Home: 1 Roble Rd Berkeley CA 94705 Office: Brobeck Phleger & Harrison Spear St Tower 1 Market St San Francisco CA 94105

BROWN, EDGAR HENRY, JR., mathematician, educator; b. Chgo., Dec. 27, 1926; s. Edgar Henry and Viola (Offen) B.; m. Gail Hamilton, June 13, 1954; children: Jessica, Nicholas. B.S., U. Wis., 1949; M.S., Wash. State U., 1951; Ph.D., Mass. Inst. Tech., 1954. Instr. Washington U., St. Louis, 1954-55, U. Chgo., 1955-57; Office Naval Res. fellow Brown U., 1957-58; faculty Brandeis U., 1958—, prof. math., 1963—. Served with USNR, 1944-46. NSF fellow, 1962-63; Guggenheim fellow, 1965-66; Brit. Sci. Research Council fellow, 1973-74, 82-83; sr. research fellow Jesus Coll., Oxford, 1986-87. Mem. Am. Math. Soc., Am. Acad. Arts and Sci. Home: 32 Fisher Ave Newton MA 02161 Office: Math Dept Brandeis Univ Waltham MA 02154

BROWN, EDWARD JAMES, utility executive; b. Fort Wayne, Ind., Sept. 30, 1937; s. William Theodore and Jane Elizabeth (Dix) B. B.A., Yale U., 1959; M.A., Fordham U., 1962; Fin. writer E.F. Hutton & Co., N.Y.C., 1970-71; economist N.Y. Power Authority, N.Y.C., 1971-74, prin. economist, 1974-80, mgr., customer services, 1980-83, mgr. spl. projects, 1983-86, dir. strategic planning, 1986—. Pres., Park Ave. Methodist Trust, N.Y.C., 1981—, Friends of the Shakers, Inc., Sabbathday Lake, Maine, 1982-84; trustee John St. Methodist Episcopal Trust Soc., N.Y.C., 1982—; mem. investment com. Methodist Home, Riverdale, N.Y., 1983—; mem. Customer Policy com. N.Y. Power Pool, Albany, 1984—; dir. Yorkville Emergency Alliance, N.Y.C., 1982—. Mem. N.Y. Soc. Security Analysts, Inst. Chartered Fin. Analysts (chartered fin. analyst). Home: 40 E 89th St New York NY 10128 Office: New York Power Authority 10 Columbus Circle New York NY 10019

BROWN, EDWIN LEWIS, JR., lawyer; b. Parker, S.D., Mar. 15, 1903; s. Edwin Lewis and Lucy Elizabeth (Lowenberg) B.; m. Faye Hulbert, May 8, 1926; children—Betty Lou Brown Trainer, Lewis Charles. J.D., U. Nebr., 1926. Bar: Nebr. bar 1926, Ill. bar 1933, U.S. Supreme Ct. bar 1960. Practiced in Chgo., 1933-85; partner firm Brown, Cook, Hanson, 1950-85; Mem. Nat. Conf. Lawyers and Collection Agys., 1964-74. Mem. wills and bequests com. Shriners Crippled Children's Hosp., Chgo.; pres. H.P. & S. Crowell Found. Named Time mag.-NADRA Man of Year, 1974. Mem. ABA, Ill. Bar Assn. (sr. counsellor 1976), Chgo. Bar Assn., Am. Judicature Soc., Comml. Law League Am. (pres. 1963-64), Comml. Law Found. (treas. 1969-74), Nat. Conf. Bar Presidents, Phi Alpha Delta. REPUBLICAN. PRESBYTERIAN. LODGES: MASONS (32 DEG.), K.T. SHRINERS. CLUBS: UNION LEAGUE (CHGO.); WESTMORELAND COUNTRY (WILMETTE, ILL.). Home: 2617 Hurd Ave Evanston IL 60201 Office: 135 S LaSalle St Chicago IL 60603

BROWN, ELIZABETH MYERS, publishing company executive; b. Bklyn., Dec. 31, 1915; d. Garry Cleveland and Caroline (Clark) Myers; B.S., Cornell U., 1937; M.A., Case Western Res. U., 1960; m. Kent Louis Brown, June 26, 1940; children—Karen Elizabeth Brown Johnson, Kent Louis, David Stuart, Garry Myers. Tchr., Walden, N.Y., 1937-38, Auburn, N.Y., 1938-39, Cleveland Heights, Ohio, 1939-40; asst. Erie County (N.Y.) home demonstration agt. govt. extension service Cornell U., Ithaca, N.Y., 1940-42; editorial asst. Highlights for Children, Columbus, Ohio, 1962-64, asst. editor, 1964-66, asso. editor, 1966-83, sr. editor, 1983—, asst. sec., 1968—, dir., 1960—; dir. Zaner-Bloser Co., Skillcorp Pub. Co. Mem. Metro Writers Workshop, Cleve., 1970-83; trustee New Day Press, Cleve., 1972-79; bd. dirs. Fedn. Cornell Women's Clubs, 1955-57, Fedn. Women's Clubs of Cleve., 1968-71, Nutrition Assn. Greater Cleve., 1964-68, Parent and Child Resource Ctr., 1982—; trustee YWCA Westfield, N.Y., 1985—. Mem. Assn. Continuing Edn. (treas. 1959-61, pres. 1961-63), Women's Aux. Acad. Med. Cleve. (pres. 1969-70), Woman's Aux. Ohio Med. Assn. (chmn. mems.-at-large com. 1970-71, dir. 5th dist. 1975-77), Women's Nat. Book Assn. (dir. Cleve. chpt. 1978-82), Am. Soc. Mag. Editors. Home: 148 S Portage St Westfield NY 14787 Office: 803 Church St Honesdale PA 18431

BROWN, ELLEN RUTH, theoretical physicist; b. N.Y.C., June 15, 1947; d. Aaron Joseph and Grace (Presser) B. B.S., Mary Washington Coll., 1969; M.S., Pa. State U., 1971; Ph.D. (Govs. fellow), U.Va., 1981. Physicist, Naval Weapons Lab., Dahlgren, Va., 1969; instr. physics Lord Fairfax Community Coll., Middletown, Va., 1971-74; summer faculty fellow NASA, Langley, Va., 1974-75; engr. EG&G Washington Analytical Services Center, Dahlgren, Va., 1979—, head dept. analysis and evaluation, 1982-86; v.p. Windy Knoll Enterprises, Inc., Magnolia, Tex., 1981—. First violinist Coll. and Community Orch., Fredericksburg, Va., 1981— . NSF Summer Sci. Faculty fellow, 1973; IEEE Summer Sci. Faculty fellow NASA, 1974-75. Mem. Am. Phys. Soc., Sierra Club, Sigma Xi. Club: Barry Lee Bressler Science (pres.). Home: PO Box 1397 Fredericksburg VA 22402 Office: EG&G PO Box 552 Dahlgren VA 22448

BROWN, ERIC JOSEPH, chemist, educator; b. Grenoble, France, Sept. 2, 1939; s. Douglas William and Lucienne (David) B.; Ingenieur des Industries Chimiques, Ecole Nationale Superieure des Industries Chimiques, Nancy, 1961; Ph.D., Cambridge (Eng.) U., 1964; D.Sc., U. Caen, 1967; m. Françoise Dumas, Apr. 13, 1966; children: Peggy, Marjorie. Research asst. Nat. Center Sci. Research, Caen, 1966-68; maitre de confs. U. Le Mans, 1968-73, prof. organic chemistry, 1973—; dir. Ecole Nationale Supérieure de Chimie de Rennes, 1980-83; cons. Pharmuka Co., 1975—. Laureate, French Chem. Soc., 1973, French Acad. Scis., 1977; recipient Protex prize for applied chemistry, 1981. Mem. Chem. Soc. France, Royal Soc. Chemistry (London). Roman Catholic. Lodge: Rotary (Le Mans). Author, patentee in field; inventor trisacryls polymers and other reagts. Home: Le Grand Roux Trange, 72650 La Milesse France Office: Univ du Maine, Route de Laval, BP 535 Le Mans 72017, France

BROWN, EVA BARBARA, journalist, editor; b. Budapest, Hungary, Oct. 20, 1933; arrived in New Zealand, 1957.; d. La'szlo and Vilma (Palko) Pala'sti; m. Denis Brown, 1963; 1 child, Stephen. BA, Eotuos Lorand U., Budapest, 1956; grad., San Francisco State U., 1962. Editor Russell Rev., New Zealand, 1977—. Author: Bluewater Cookbook, 1979.

BROWN, FRED, virologist; b. Clayton, Eng., Jan. 31, 1925; s. Fred and Jane Ellen (Fielding) B.; m. Audrey Alice Doherty, May 1, 1948; children: Roger, David. BS in Chemistry, U. Manchester, Eng., 1944, MSc, 1946, PhD, 1948. Asst. lectr. U. Manchester, 1946-48; lectr. U. Bristol, Eng., 1948-50; sr. sci. officer Hannah Dairy Research Inst., Scotland, 1950-53; sr. research assoc. Christie Hosp., Manchester, 1953-55; head biochemistry Animal Virus Research Inst., Pirbright, Eng., 1955-83; head virology Wellcome Found., Kent, Eng., 1983—. Editor-in-chief: Jour. Gen. Virology, 1975-80; contbr. sci. papers to various jours. and chpts. to books. Fellow Royal Soc. London, Inst. Biology; mem. Soc. Gen. Microbiology. Home: Syndal Glaziers Ln, Normandy GU3 2DF, England Office: Wellcome Found, Langley Ct, Beckenham England

BROWN, FREDERICK HAROLD, insurance company executive; b. Troy, N.Y., Apr. 21, 1927; s. Harold Lamphere and Maida Adelaide (Wooden) B.; m. Mary Lee Lamar, Aug. 12, 1950; children: Deborah Elaine Wright, Frederick Harold. BS in Mech. Engring., Bucknell U., 1949. Registered profl. engr., Wis., Pa., Tenn. With INA Corp. and Subs., Phila., 1949-73, asst. v.p., 1970-71, v.p., 1971-73; founder, pres., chief exec. officer Jersey/Internat. Group, Cherry Hill, N.J., 1973-84 ; pres., chief exec. officer Admiral Ins. Co. subs. W.R. Berkeley Corp., Greenwich, Conn., 1979-84; sr. v.p. W.R. Berkley Corp., Greenwich, 1984-87; chmn., pres. and chief exec. officer Investors Ins. Holding Corp. and all subs., 1987—. Contbr. articles to profl. jours. Mem. Phila. Fire Prevention Com., 1958-68; exec. treas. Camden County (N.J.) Rep. Orgn., 1968-73; clk. bd. chosen freeholders of Camden County, 1969-73; active United Fund, Boy Scouts Am. Served with USNR, 1944-46. Named Citizen of Yr., INA, 1970. Mem. Soc. Fire Protection Engrs., Nat. Fire Protection Assn., Conf. Spl. Risk Underwriters, U.S. Jaycees (hon. life, Outstanding State V.P. 1961, Outstanding Nat. Dir. 1962). Episcopalian. Clubs: Tavistock (N.J.) Country; St. James's; Crockford's (London). Lodge: Kiwanis (Haddonfield). Home: 45 Ocean Ave 4-B Monmouth Beach NJ 07750 Office: 100 Metro Park South CN-007 Laurence Harbor NJ 08878

BROWN, FREDERICK LEE, health care executive; b. Clarksburg, W.Va., Oct. 22, 1940; s. Claude Raymond and Anne Elizabeth (Kiddy) B.; m. Mary Ruth Price, Aug. 22, 1964; children—Gregory Lee, Michael Owen-Price. B.A. in Psychology, Northwestern U., 1962; M.B.A. in Health Care Adminstrn., George Washington U., 1966. Vocat. counselor Cook County Dept. Pub. Aid, Chgo., 1962-64; adminstrv. resident Meth. Hosp. Ind., Inc., Indpls., 1965-66, adminstrv. asst., 1966, asst. adminstr., 1966-71, assoc. adminstr., 1971-72, v.p. ops., 1972-74; exec. v.p., chief operating officer Meml. Hosp. DuPage County, Elmhurst, Ill., 1974-82, Meml. Health Services, Elmhurst, 1980-82; pres., chief exec. officer Christian Hosp. NE-NW, St. Louis, 1982—, Christian Health Care Systems, Inc., St. Louis, 1983—, CH Allied Services, Inc., St. Louis, 1983-85, Christian Health Services, St. Louis, 1986—; adj. instr. Washington U. Sch. of Medicine, St. Louis, 1982—; dir. Health Link, Inc., mem. exec. com. 1986; pres., chief exec. officer Village North, Inc., 1986—; bd. dirs. Am. Healthcare Systems, Inc., chmn. shareholder communications com. 1985—; bd. dirs. Commerce Bank St. Louis. Contbr. articles to profl. jours. Co-chmn. hosp. div. United Way Greater St. Louis, 1983, chmn. health services div., 1984, chmn., 1985—, bd. dirs., 1986; bd. dirs. Kammergild Chamber Orch., 1984—, v.p., 1985—; trustee, mem. adminstrv. bd. United Methodist Ch. Webster Grove, Mo., 1984—; chmn. emergency room services task force St. Louis Regional Med. Ctr., 1985; chmn. bd. Alton Meml. Hosp., 1987—. Fellow Am. Coll. Healthcare Execs. (chmn. credentials com. 1978, task force governance and constituencies 1986—; mem. Gold Medal award com. 1985, chmn. task force on governance and constituencies 1986-87); mem. Am. Acad. Med. Adminstrs. (life), Internat. Health Econ. and Mgmt. Inst., Hosp. Pres.'s Assn., Advt. Club Greater St. Louis, Am. Hosp. Assn. (council on mgmt. 1986), Am. Pub. Health Assn., George Washington U. Alumni Assn. for Health Services Adminstrn. (pres. 1979-80, Alumnus of Yr. award 1981), Hosp. Assn. Met. St. Louis (bd. dirs. 1984—, chmn. bd. 1988—, sec. 1985-86, treas. 1987—, chmn. council on pub. affairs and communications 1985, vice chmn. 1987—, various coms.), Mo. Hosp. Assn. (chmn. council on research and policy devel. 1983, chmn. council on multi-instnl. hosps. 1986, mem. dist. council pres.'s 1986, bd. dirs. 1988—), Central Eastern Mo. Profl. Rev. Orgn. (bd. dirs. 1982-85, various coms.), Am. Protestant Health Assn. (bd. dirs. 1987—). Republican. Clubs: Norwood Hills Country, Arena, Stadium (St. Louis). Lodge: Rotary. Home: 115 Mason Webster Groves MO 63119 Office: Christian Hosps NE-NW 11133 Dunn Rd Saint Louis MO 63136

BROWN, GARRETT EDWARD, JR., lawyer; b. Orange, N.J., Mar. 20, 1943; s. Garrett E. and Josephine L. (Raul) B.; m. Carolyn Powling, Apr. 12, 1985; children: Victoria, Rebecca Garrett. B.A., Lafayette Coll., 1965; J.D., Duke U., 1968. Bar: N.J. 1968, D.C. 1972, U.S. Supreme Ct. 1972, N.Y. 1980. Law sec. N.J. Supreme Ct., 1968-60; asst. U.S. atty., Dist. N.J., 1969-73, dep. chief criminal div., 1971-72, exec. asst., 1972-73; assoc. Stryker, Tams & Dill, Newark, 1973-75, ptnr., 1976-81; gen. counsel GPO, Washington, 1981-83; chief counsel Maritime Adminstrn., 1983-85; judge U.S. Dist. Ct., N.J., 1985—; mem. trial advocacy faculty Practising Law Inst., 1979-81; lectr. Inst. Continuing Legal Edn., 1975, 81. Editor, contbr.: Attorneys Fees: Recoverability and Deductability, 1981; Legislative History of Title 44 of the U.S. Code, 1982; issue editor Antitrust Law Jour. Counsel Union County Republican Com., 1981; spl. litigation counsel Union County Bd. Chosen Freeholders, 1981. Recipient Atty. Gen.'s Meritorious Service award, 1971, Pub. Printer's Gold medal for Disting. Service, 1983. Mem. ABA, Fed. Bar Assn., N.J. Bar Assn., D.C. Bar Assn. Republican. Clubs: Essex (Newark). Office: US Ct House 402 E State St Trenton NJ 08608

BROWN, GEORGE LESLIE, manufacturing company executive, former lieutenant governor of Colorado; b. Lawrence, Kans., July 1, 1926; s. George L. and Harriett Alberta (Watson) B.; m. Modeen; children: Gail Brown Chandler, Laura Nicole, Kim Doreen, Cynthia Renee, Ronnie, Carol, Angela, Sharolyn, Nyra. B.S. in Journalism, U. Kans., 1950; postgrad., U. Colo., 1950-51; A.M.P., Harvard Bus. Sch., 1980. Mem. writing staff Denver Post, 1950-65; asst. exec. dir. Denver Housing Authority, 1965-69; exec. dir. Met. Denver Urban Coalition, 1969-75; lt. gov. Colo. Denver, 1974-79; v.p. Grumman Corp., N.Y., 1979—; Bd. dirs. Davis and Elkins Coll., Washington Trade Ctr., Joint Ctr. for Polit. Studies. Mem. Colo. Ho. of Reps., 1955, Colo. Senate, 1956-74; chmn. bd. Nat. Urban Coalition; mem. exec. com. Bus. Council Nat. Dem. Com. Served with USAAF, 1944-46. Recipient Adam Clayton Powell award for polit. achievement, 1975, Opportunities Industrialization Center Nat. Govt. award, 1975; George Brown Urban Journalism scholarship established at U. Kans. William Allen White Sch. Journalism, 1976. Mem. Kappa Alpha Psi. Office: Grumman Corp 1000 Wilson Blvd Suite 2100 Arlington VA 22209

BROWN, GEORGE STEPHEN, physicist; b. Santa Monica, Calif., June 28, 1945; s. Paul Gordon and Frances Ruth (Moore) B.; m. Nohema Fernandez, Aug. 8, 1981; 1 child, Sonya. BS, Calif. Inst. Tech., 1967; MS, Cornell U., 1968, PhD, 1973. Mem. tech. staff Bell Labs., Murray Hill, N.J., 1973-77; sr. research assoc. Stanford (Calif.) U., 1977-82, research prof. applied physics, 1982—; assoc. dir. Stanford Synchrotron Radiation Lab., Stanford, 1980—. Mem. editorial bd. Rev. Sci. Instruments, 1983-86; contbr. articles to profl. jours. Fellow Am. Phys. Soc. Home: 740 Alameda Redwood City CA 94061 Office: SSRL Bin 69 PO Box 4349 Stanford CA 94305

BROWN, GERALDINE REED, lawyer; b. Los Angeles, Feb. 18, 1947; d. William Penn and Alberta Vernice (Coleman) Reed; m. Ronald Wellington Brown, Aug. 20, 1972; children—Kimberly Diana, Michael David. B.A. summa cum laude, Fisk U., 1968; J.D., Harvard U., 1971, M.B.A., 1973. Bar: N.Y. 1974, U.S. Dist. Ct. (so. and ea. dists.) N.Y. 1974, U.S. Ct. Appeals (2d cir.) 1974, U.S. Supreme Ct. 1977. Assoc. firm White & Case, N.Y.C., 1973-78; atty. J.C. Penney Co., Inc., N.Y.C., 1978—. Bd. dirs. Council Concerned Black Execs., N.Y.C., 1977—, Studio Mus. in Harlem, N.Y.C., 1980-81; mem. Montclair Devel. Bd., ad hoc com. on Montclair Econ. Devel. Corp. Mem. Women's Econ. Roundtable, Harvard Bus. Sch. Club, Harvard Law Sch. Assn., Coalition 100 Black Women, ABA (several coms. sect. corp., banking and bus. law, sect. internat. law and practice), Assn. Bar City N.Y. (corp. law com. 1978-81), N.Y. County Lawyers Assn. (corp. law com.), N.Y. State Bar Assn. (vice chmn., exec. com. of corp. counsel sect., chmn. com. on SEC, fin., corp. law and governance),, Harvard Bus. Sch. Black Alumni Assn., Harvard Law Sch. Black Alumni Assn., Phi Beta Kappa, Delta Sigma Theta (chair social action com. Montclair alumnae chpt., chair bylaw com., parlimentarian). Club: Harvard (N.Y.C.). Home: 180 Union St Montclair NJ 07042 Office: JC Penney Co Inc 1301 Ave of Americas New York NY 10019

BROWN, GILES TYLER, educator, lecturer; b. Marshall, Mich., Apr. 21, 1916; s. A. Watson and Ettroile (Kent) B.; m. Crysta Beth Cosner, Nov. 21, 1951. AB, San Diego State Coll., 1937; MA, U. Calif.-Berkeley, 1941; PhD, Claremont Grad. Sch., 1948; post-doctoral seminar, U. Edinburgh, Scotland, 1949. Tchr., counselor, Binet intelligence tester San Diego City Schs., 1937-46; chmn. social sci. div. Orange Coast Coll., Newport Beach, Calif., 1948-60; prof. history, chmn. social sci. div. Calif. State U., Fullerton, 1961-66; also chmn. history dept., dean grad. studies Calif. State U., 1967-83, assoc. v.p. acad. programs, 1979-83; pub. lectr. nat., internat. affairs, 1951—; also cons. gerontology; participant Wilton Park Conf., Eng., 1976; mem. instl. research bd. So. Calif. Coll. Optometry, 1980—; moderator Behind the Headlines Forum, Orange Coast Coll.; lectr. Laguna Hills Leisure World Forum; past chmn. Hist. Landmarks Com. Orange County; mem. nat. task force Assement Quality Masters' Degree, Council Grad. Schs., 1981-83. Author: Ships That Sail No More, 1966; Contbr. to: Help in Troubled Times, 1962; contbr. articles, book reviews to profl. jours. Trustee, past pres. and chmn. bd. World Affairs Council Orange County; past pres. U. Calif.-Irvine Friends Library; nat. bd. dirs., past nat. pres. Travelers Century Club; mem. grad. fellowship adv. com., State of Calif., 1980, Orange County Bd. NCCJ, 1984—; bd. dirs. Pacific Symphony Orch. Served to lt. USNR, 1942-46. Recipient Pacific History award Pacific Coast br. Am. Hist. Assn., 1950; hon. medal DAR, 1977; named Outstanding Prof. Calif. State U., 1966, Hon. Citizen of Orange County, 1969; hon. medal Nat. Soc. Daus. Colonial Wars, 1984. Mem. AAAS, Am. Hist. Assn., Western Assn. Grad. Schs. (exec. com. 1981-83), SAR, Phi Beta Delta, Phi Beta Kappa, Phi Delta Kappa, Phi Alpha Theta, Kappa Delta Pi. Baptist. Clubs: Explorers, Masons. Home: 413 Catalina Dr Newport Beach CA 92663

BROWN, GLADYS SADDLER, educator; b. Memphis, Jan. 27, 1923; d. Henry Rutherford and Edith Estee (Hawkins) Mahone; m. Joseph L. Brown, Nov. 10, 1950; children—Lorelle Joan, Karen Renee. B.S. in Edn., Central State U., 1947; M.S. in Counseling, Chgo. State U., 1968. Asst. to library film advisor ALA, Chgo., 1947-53; sec. to sec. Musicians Union Local 208, Chgo., 1953-60; tchr. Chgo. Bd. Edn., 1960-68; asst. prof. Chgo. City Coll., 1968—, mem. adv. council Olive-Harvey campus, 1978-82; sr. sponsor Hyde Park High Sch., Chgo., 1964-68, coordinator coop. edn., 1967-68. Mem. Chgo. Bus. Tchrs. Assn., Ill. Edn. Assn., Am. Fedn. Tchrs., Phi Beta Lambda, Alpha Kappa Alpha. Democrat. Episcopalian. Club: Merry Eight Bridge. Office: Olive Harvey Coll 10001 S Woodlawn Chicago IL 60628

BROWN, G(LENN) WILLIAM, JR., lawyer; b. Waynesville, N.C., June 9, 1955; s. Glenn William Sr. and Evelyn Myralyn (Davis) B.; m. Amy Margaret Moss, Apr. 14, 1984. BS in Biology and Polit. Sci., MIT, 1977; JD, Duke U., 1980. Bar: N.Y. 1981. Assoc. Donovan Leisure Newton & Irvine, N.Y.C., 1980-84; assoc. Sidley & Austin, N.Y.C., 1984-87, ptnr., 1988—. Editorial bd. Duke Law Jour. Mem. ABA (sect. internat. law com., internat. fin. and comml. transactions, and pvt. internat. law. 1988—), Assn. of Bar of City of N.Y. (uniform state laws com. 1984-87), coms. on internat. comml. transactions, internat. fin. transactions and pvt. internat. law. Democrat. Mem. Dutch Reform Ch. Home: 171 State St Brooklyn Heights NY 11201 Office: Sidley & Austin 520 Madison Ave New York NY 10022

BROWN, HARLAN JAMES, acquisition and industrial studies executive; b. Altoona, Pa., Dec. 16, 1933; s. Lindsey A. and E. Grace (Ackerman) B.; m. Christina L. Chapman, July 17, 1987; 1 child, Harlan James II. M in Engring., Colo. Sch. Mines, 1957; MBA, George Washington U., 1967. Field engr. Beckman Instruments, Arlington, Va., 1957-59; ptnr. Shaheen, Brown & Day, Denver, 1959-60; v.p. Nat. Engring. Service subs. NES, Inc., Washington, 1960-63; pres. NSC Internat., Washington, 1963-67; chmn. bd., chief exec. officer Harlan Brown & Co., Inc., McLean, Va., 1967—; seminar and video lectr. various corps. Mem. IEEE, Am. Soc. Metall. Engrs., Am. Chem. Soc., Am. Mgmt. Assn., Blue Key, Theta Tau, Sigma Delta Psi, Alpha Tau Omega. Methodist. Clubs: Regency Sport. Author: (with Mock and Shuckett) Financing for Growth, 1971. Home: 1800 Old Meadow Rd McLean VA 22102 Office: 6861 Elm St McLean VA 22101

BROWN, HELEN GURLEY, writer, editor; b. Green Forest, Ark., Feb. 18, 1922; d. Ira M. and Cleo (Sisco) Gurley; m. David Brown, Sept. 25, 1959. Student, Tex. State Coll. for Women, 1939-41, Woodbury Coll., 1942. Exec. sec. Music Corp. Am., 1942-45, William Morris Agy., 1945-47; copywriter Foote, Cone & Belding (advt. agy.), Los Angeles, 1948-58; advt. writer, account exec. Kenyon & Eckhardt (advt. agy.), Hollywood, Calif., 1958-62; editor-in-chief Cosmopolitan mag., 1965—; editorial dir. Cosmopolitan internat. edits., 1972—. Author: Sex and the Single Girl, 1962, Sex and the Office, 1965, Outrageous Opinions, 1966, Helen Gurley Brown's Single Girl's Cook Book, 1969, Sex and the New Single Girl, 1970, Cosmopolitan's Love Book: A Guide to Ecstacy in Bed, 1978, Having It All, 1982. Recipient Francis Holmes Achievement award for outstanding work in advt., 1956-59, Disting. Achievement award U. So. Calif. Sch. Journalism, 1971, Spl. award for editorial leadership Am. Newspaper Woman's Club, Washington, 1972, Disting. Achievement award in Journalism Stanford U., 1977; named 1 of 25 most influential women in U.S. World Almanac, 1976-81. Mem. Authors League Am., Am. Soc. Mag. Editors, AFTRA, Eta Upsilon Gamma. Office: Cosmopolitan The Hearst Corp 224 W 57th St New York NY 10019

BROWN, HERBERT CHARLES, chemistry educator; b. London, May 22, 1912; came to U.S., 1914; s. Charles and Pearl (Gorinstein) B.; m. Sarah Baylen, Feb. 6, 1937; 1 son, Charles Allan. A.S., Wright Jr. Coll., Chgo., 1935; B.S., U. Chgo., 1936, Ph.D., 1938, D.Sc., 1968, hon. doctorates, 1968; hon. doctorates, Wayne State U., 1980, Lebanon Valley Coll., 1980, L.I. U., 1980, Hebrew U. Jerusalem, 1980, Pontificia Universidad de Chile, 1980, Purdue U., 1980, U. Wales, 1981, U. Paris, 1982, Butler U., 1982, Ball State U., 1985. Asst. chemistry U. Chgo., 1936-38; Eli Lilly post-doctorate research fellow 1938-39, instr., 1939-43; asst. prof. chemistry Wayne U., 1943- 46, asso. prof., 1946-47; prof. inorganic chemistry Purdue U., 1947-59, Richard B. Wetherill prof. chemistry, 1959, Richard B. Wetherill research prof., 1960-78, emeritus, 1978—; vis. prof. U. Calif. at Los Angeles, 1951, Ohio State U., 1952, U. Mexico, 1954, U. Calif. at Berkeley, 1957, U. Colo., 1958, U. Heidelberg, 1963, State U. N.Y. at Stonybrook, 1966, U. Calif. at Santa Barbara, 1967, Hebrew U., Jerusalem, 1969, U. Wales, Swansea, 1973, U. Cape Town, S. Africa, 1974, U. Calif., San Diego, 1979; Harrison Howe lectr., 1953, Friend E. Clark lectr., 1953, Freud-McCormack lectr., 1954, Centenary lectr., Eng., 1955, Thomas W. Talley lectr., 1956, Falk-Plaut lectr., 1957, Julius Stieglitz lectr., 1958, Max Tishler lectr., 1958, Kekule-Couper Centenary lectr., 1958, E. C. Franklin lectr., 1960, Ira Remsen lectr., 1961, Edgar Fahs Smith lectr., 1962, Seydel-Wooley lectr., 1966, Baker lectr., 1969, Benjamin Rush lectr., 1971, Chem. Soc. lectr., Australia, 1972, Armes lectr., 1973, Henry Gilman lectr., 1975, others; chem. cons. to indsl. corps. Author: Hydroboration, 1962, Boranes in Organic Chemistry, 1972, Organic Synthesis via Boranes, 1975, The Nonclassical Ion Problem, 1977; Contbr. articles to chem. jours. Bd. govs. Hebrew U., 1969—. Served as co-dir. war research projects U. Chgo. for U.S. Army, Nat. Def. Research Com., Manhattan Project, 1940-43. Recipient Purdue Sigma Xi research award, 1951; Nichols medal, 1959; award Am. Chem. Soc., 1960; S.O.C.M.A. medal, 1960; H.N. McCoy award, 1965; Linus Pauling medal, 1968; Nat. Medal of Sci., 1969; Roger Adams medal, 1971; Charles Frederick Chandler medal, 1973; Chem. Pioneer award, 1975; C.U.N.Y. medal for sci. achievement, 1976; Elliott Cresson medal, 1978; C.K. Ingold medal, 1978; Nobel prize in chemistry, 1979; Priestley medal, 1981; Perkin medal, 1982; Gold medal award Am. Inst. Chemists, 1985; G.M. Kosolapoff medal, 1987; Nat. Acad. Scis. Award in Chem. Scis., 1987. Fellow Royal Soc. Chemistry (hon.), AAAS, Indian Nat. Sci. Acad. (fgn.); mem. Am. Acad. Arts and Scis., Nat. Acad. Scis., Chem. Soc. Japan (hon.), Pharm. Soc. Japan (hon.), Am. Chem. Soc. (chmn. Purdue sect. 1955-56), Ind. Acad. Sci., Phi Beta Kappa, Sigma Xi, Alpha Chi Sigma, Phi Lambda Upsilon (hon.). Office: Purdue Univ Dept of Chemistry West Lafayette IN 47907

BROWN, HORACE LUDWIG, civil engineer; b. Newark, Ohio, Dec. 20, 1906; s. Horace Randolph and Mary Anna (Steubs) B.; m. Ruth Elizabeth Anne, Nov. 28, 1936. Registered profl. engr., Ohio; profl. land surveyor. Rodman Chmn. City of Newark, 1928-41, engr. surveyor, 1945—, design engr., 1950—; surveyor Indsl. Gas Corp., Newark, 1941-45; pvt. practice engring.-surveying, Licking County, Ohio, 1944-75. Poet, writer and composer vocal, piano and symphonic music. Contbr. Devel. Fund, Ohio State U., Columbus; mem. N.Y. Philharmonic Soc., Friends of N.Y. Philharmonic, Met. Opera Guild of N.Y. Mem. Am. Congress Surveying-Mapping (life). Republican. Avocations: microscopy; astronomy; photography; electricity; electronics. Home: 135 N 21st St Newark OH 43055 Office: City of Newark 40 W Main St Newark OH 43055

BROWN, JAMES MARSTON, lawyer; b. Aberdeen, Wash., Feb. 5, 1950; s. Donald Matthew and Jeanette Marie (Phillips) B.; m. Coleen Tina Chin, July 6, 1974; children—William Lester, Peter James. Student U. Wash., 1968-72, Calif. State U.-Fullerton, 1975-76; B.S. in Laws, Western State U., Fullerton, 1977, J.D., 1978. Bar: Calif. 1979, U.S. Dist. Ct. (no. dist.) Calif. 1979, Wash. 1981, U.S. Dist. Ct. (we. dist.) Wash. 1982. Law clk. Orange County Superior Ct., Santa Ana, Calif., 1977-78; assoc. Gladys & Phillips, Aberdeen, 1979-81; ptnr. Phillips & Brown, Aberdeen, 1981—; lectr. Grays Harbor Coll., Aberdeen, 1983—. Bd. dirs. Channel 10 Ministries, Aberdeen, 1980-83; trustee Aberdeen Pub. Library Bd., 1979—. Mem. ABA, Wash. Bar Assn. (bar examiner 1982-83), Wash. State Trial Lawyers Assn. (chmn. Grays Harbor round table 1984-85), Assn. Trial Lawyers Am., Christian Legal Soc., Delta Theta Phi. Republican. Baptist. Home: 527 W 6th St Aberdeen WA 98520 Office: Phillips & Brown 525 Seattle First Nat Bank Bldg Aberdeen WA 98520

BROWN, JAMES NELSON, JR., accountant; b. Bronx, N.Y., Apr. 17, 1929; s. James Nelson and Agnes Mary (Cummins) B.; B.S. in Bus. Adminstrn., Drake U., Des Moines, 1956; m. Lila Barbara Watt, Dec. 12, 1950; children—Constance Ellen Brown Buttacavole, Nelson Arthur, Richard John. Sr. Acct. Arthur Andersen & Co., N.Y.C., 1956-61; asst. v.p., dir. internal auditing Salomon Inc, N.Y.C., 1961-86, asst. v.p., dir. projects mgmt. dept., 1986—. Com. chmn. Cub Scouts, 1973-75; troop com. chmn. Boy Scouts Am., Carteret, N.J., 1976-77, com. mem., 1978—. Served to sgt., AUS, 1947-52. C.P.A.; cert. internal auditor. Mem. Am. Mgmt. Assn., Am. Inst. C.P.A.s, N.J. Soc. C.P.A.s, Inst. Internal Auditors, Am. Legion. Republican. Roman Catholic. Club: Elks. Home: 47 Pinho Ave Carteret NJ 07008 Office: 2 New York Plaza New York NY 10004

BROWN, JAMES THOMPSON, JR., computer information scientist; b. Orange, N.J., Jan. 3, 1935; s. James Thompson and Marjorie (Hale) B.; m. Alice Beasley, Oct. 3, 1959; children—Kathryn, James. B.M.E., Cornell U., 1957; M.S., Stanford U., 1964. Applied sci. rep. IBM Corp., Schenectady, N.Y., 1957-59, corp. staff mem., White Plains, N.Y., 1960-68; cons. Case & Co., Stamford, Conn., 1969-74, dir., 1975-83, pres., 1983-84; pres. Tom Brown & Co., Wilton, Conn., 1985—. Mem. Internat. Assn. Chain Stores (adviser, speaker 1971—), Nat. Grocers Assn. (adviser 1983—), Am. Inst. Indsl. Engrs. (sr. mem.), Inst. of Mgmt. Scis. Republican. Home: 119 Middlebrook Farm Rd Wilton CT 06897 Office: Tom Brown & Co PO Box 431 Wilton CT 06897

BROWN, J'AMY MARONEY, journalist; b. Los Angeles, Oct. 30, 1945; d. Roland Francis and Jeanne (Wilbur) Maroney; m. James Raphael Brown, Jr., Nov. 5, 1967 (dec. July 1982); children—James Roland Francis, Jeanne Raphael. B.A., U. So. Calif., 1967. Reporter Los Angeles Herald Examiner, 1966-67, Lewisville Leader, Dallas, 1980-81; editor First Person Mag., Dallas, 1981-82; journalism dir. Pacific Palisades Sch., Los Angeles, 1983-84; free-lance writer, media cons., 1984-88; press liaison U.S. papal visit, Los Angeles, 1987. Auction chmn. Assn. Pub. Broadcasting, Houston, 1974, 75; vice chmn. Dallas Arts Council, 1976-80; vice chmn. Met. March of Dimes, Dallas, 1980-82; del. Dallas Council PTAs, 1976-80. Recipient UPI Editors award for investigative reporting, 1981. Mem. Women Meeting Women, Women in Communications, Am. Bus. Women's Assn. Republican. Roman Catholic. Home: 13101 Nimrod Pl Los Angeles CA 90049

BROWN, JAY ALLEN, news syndicate executive; b. Hartford, Mar. 14, 1935; s. Sidney Alfred and Sydney (Rabinovitz) B.; m. Phyllis Smiley, Aug. 29, 1965; children—Barbara, Richard. B.A. in Journalism, Calif. State U., Los Angeles, 1963. Reporter, The Valley Times, North Hollywood, Calif., 1963-64; aid to U.S. Congressman Tom Rees, Los Angeles, 1964-66; reporter-editor Sacramento (Calif.) Bee, 1966-68; reporter-editor Hartford Times, corr. Time Mag., 1968-72; pub. relations mgr. Am. Cyanamid, Shell Oil Co., 1972-80; pres. Cineman Syndicate, Middletown, N.Y., 1975—; lectr. pub. relations Bernard Baruch Coll., N.Y.C. Author: Rating The Movies, 1982; contbr. articles to profl. jours. Served with USN, 1956-58. Mem. Overseas Press Club, Am. Radio Relay League, Toastmasters. Home and Office: 7 Charles Ct Middletown NY 10940

BROWN, SIR JOHN (GILBERT NEWTON), publisher; b. July 7, 1916; s. John and Molly B.; m. Virginia Braddell, 3 children. Ed. Lancing Coll., Hertford Coll.; M.A. in Zoology, Oxford U. With Bombay br. Oxford Univ. Press, 1937-40, 46-49, sales mgr., 1949-56, pub., 1956-80; chmn. Univ. Bookshops Ltd., Oxford; dir. Book Tokens Ltd., Willshaw Booksellers Ltd., Manchester, Eng.; chmn. B.H. Blackwell Ltd., dir. Blackwell Group Ltd., 1980-87; pres. Pubs. Assn., 1963-65; mem. nat. libraries com. EDC for Newspapers, Printing and Pub. Industry, 1967-70; mem. Adv. Com. Sci. and Tech. Info., 1969-73; mem. communication adv. com. U.K. nat. com. UNESCO; asst. treas. Royal Lit. Fund; bd. dirs. Brit. Library, 1973-79; mem. Royal Soc. Sci. Info.; past mem. bd. Brit. Council. Commd. Royal Arty., 1941, served, 1941-46, Japanese prisoner of war, 1942-45. Professorial fellow Hertford Coll., Oxford U., 1974-80.

BROWN, KATHARINE EISENHART, artist; b. Princeton, N.J., Mar. 21, 1921; d. Luther P. and Katharine S. (Schmidt) Eisenhart; B.A., Vassar Coll., 1942; M.S. in Journalism, Columbia U., 1944; spl. studies in sculpture, Corcoran Gallery, Washington; pottery workshop, Boston Mus. Sch.; m. W. Danforth Compton, June 13, 1942 (dec.); children—John, Christina; m. 2d, Robert P. Brown, Apr. 3, 1959. Exhbns. include: Main Gallery Boston City Hall, 1978, Copley Art Assn., Boston, 1980, Clark Gallery, Lincoln, Mass., Cambridge (Mass.) Art Assn., 1981, Currier Art Gallery, Manchester, N.H., 1981, Hyatt Art Gallery, Cambridge, 1983, Simmons Coll., Boston, 1986, various art assns.; one person shows include: Cambridge Art Assn., 1976, 87, Episcopal Theol. Sch. Library, Cambridge, 1973, 78, 88, Hilles Library of Radcliffe Coll., 1975, 82, 85, Frameworks Gallery, Cambridge, 1977, Johnson (Vt.) State Coll., 1977, Vassar Coll., 1977, Harvard Law Sch. Library, 1978, Stonehill Coll., Easton, Mass., 1979, World Affairs Council, Boston, 1981, Wordsmith Gallery, Cambridge, 1983, Marion (Mass.) Art Ctr., 1983, ATrium Gallery, Boston, 1988; exhibited in group shows at Concord (Mass.) Art Assn., 1984, Copley Soc. Fed. Reserve, Boston, 1985, Cambridge Art Assn., 1985, Am. Stage Festival, N.H., 1986, Obsidian Gallery, Tucson, Ariz., 1986, Simmons Coll., Boston, 1986; many pvt. collections including Boston Globe, Bank Am., First Nat. Bank of Boston, Hearthstone Ins. Co. of Mass., Charleston Savings Bank, others in Mich., Ariz., N.Mex.; founder, dir. Martin St. Collage Dance Group, Cambridge. Recipient 1st prize Cambridge Art Assn., 1986, Quincy Coop. Bank award South Shore Art Center, 1977, hon. mention Sudbury Art Assn., 1979, hon. mention Concord Art Assn., 1979, juror's choice award, 1980, juror's award Cambridge Art Assn., 1981; Best of Show, medal of honor Concord Art Assn., 1983, Crumbacher Award, Concord, 1984, others. Mem. Boston Visual Artists Union, Cambridge Art Assn., Copley Soc. Boston, Mass. (Best in Show, 1986), Craftsmen's Council, Concord Art Assn., Sharon Art Center, N.H. Art Assn., Phi Beta Kappa. Democrat. Episcopalian. Home: 16 Avon St Cambridge MA 02138

BROWN, KENNETH, publisher; b. Spittal, Eng., June 30, 1919; came to U.S., 1921, naturalized 1927; s. William and Alice Ann (Huddleston) B.; m. Geraldine L. Schmid, Feb. 13, 1945 (div. 1971); children—Kenneth R., Richard L.; m. 2d Ethel I. Smith, July 16, 1977. B.Sc. in Mech. Engring., U. N.Mex., 1947; M.Sc. in Mech Engring., U. So. Calif., 1950; Ph.D., Calif. Western U., 1974; D. Communications (hon.), 1975. Editor, John Wiley & Sons, Los Angeles, 1960-67; pres. Tinnon-Brown, Inc., Los Angeles, 1967-69; pub. cons., Los Angeles, 1969-72; mgr. collection devel. Xerox Univ. Microfilm, Los Angeles and Washington, 1972-78; database mktg. mgr. Carrollton Press, Arlington, 1978-81; pres. Assoc. Faculty Press, Port Washington, N.Y. 1981-84, Huddleston-Brown Pub., Port Washington, 1984—. Author: Package Design Engineering, 1959. Author, editor: Ballistic Missiles, 1960; Ground Support Syctems, 1960; Space Logistics, 1961; editor: Greenwood Annual Index and Abstract of Legal Dissertations and Theses, 1986. Served to capt. USAF, 1941-45. Recipient Nat. Packaging Achievement award Nat. Assn. Packaging Engrs., 1961. Mem. Pi Tau Sigma, Tau Beta Pi. Republican. Methodist. Office: Huddlestone-Brown Pub 18 Lewis Ln Port Washington NY 11005

BROWN, LLOYD GEORGE, oil company executive; b. Falmouth, Trelawny, Jamaica, Feb. 25, 1944; s. Benjamin Louis and Rosa Maud (McCook) B.; m. Joanna Agatha Nyack, July 4, 1970; children: Donovan George, Keena Monique. Diploma in agr., Jamaica Sch. Agr., Spanish Town, 1965; BS, Tuskegee (Ala.) Inst., 1969; MBA, Columbia U., 1971. Citrus officer Citrus Growers Assn. Ltd., Kingston, Jamaica, 1965-67; budget officer CUNY, 1971-72; mkt. planning mgr. Massey-Ferguson, Inc., Des Moines, 1972-73; indsl. sales rep. Esso Standard Oil SA Ltd., Kingston, 1973-74, asst. to sales mgr., 1974-76; sales coordinator Esso West Indies Ltd., Kingston, 1976-77, refinery coordinator, 1977-78, econ. planning adv., 1978-82; econ. planning adv. Petrojam Ltd., Kingston, 1982—; cons. Dimpex Assocs., Inc., N.Y.C., 1971, MBA Mgmt. Cons., Inc., N.Y.C., 1970-71. Mem. Kay Kourt Assn. (pres. 1983—). Anglican. Lodges: Rotary (com. chmn.), Masons. Office: Petrojam Ltd, PO Box 241, 96 Marcus Garvey Dr, Kingston Jamaica

BROWN, LOUIS DANIEL, lawyer, corporation executive; b. San Francisco, Aug. 31, 1908; s. Louis Thomas and Rose Ella (Kelly) B.; m. Felice Stamper, Sept. 9, 1932; children—Lawrence Louis, Ronald Stamper, Carol Felice. A.A., U. San Francisco, 1929; A.B., Stanford U., 1931; postgrad. U. Calif.-Hastings Coll. Law, San Francisco, 1934-36; J.D., Southwestern U., 1944. Bar: Calif. 1944, U.S. Supreme Ct. 1950, U.S. Ct. Claims 1950. Ptnr., Romer, Brown, San Francisco and Los Angeles, 1944-72; sole practice, Los Angeles, 1972—; judge pro tem Mcpl. Ct., 1980, 82, 83, 84. Active Boy Scouts Am., La. Zool. Assn., Republican Nat. Com. Mem. Calif. State Guard. Mem. Calif. Bar Assn., Los Angeles County Bar Assn., Los Angeles Bar Assn., Lawyers Club Los Angeles, Am. Judicature Soc., U. San Francisco Alumni (past pres.), U. San Francisco Law Soc., Stanford Alumni (life), Stanford Law Soc., Southwestern U. Alumni Assn. Roman Catholic. Lodges: Lions, Elks, Friars and Friarettes. Contbr. articles to profl. jours. Address: 3030 Temple St Los Angeles CA 90026

BROWN, LOUIS M., lawyer, law educator; b. Los Angeles, Sept. 5, 1909; s. Emil and Anna B.; m. Hermione Kopp, 1937; children: Lawrence David, Marshall Joseph, Harold Arthur. A.B. cum laude, U. So. Calif., 1930; J.D., Harvard U., 1933; LL.D., Manhattan Coll., Riverdale, N.Y., 1977. Bar: Calif. 1933, U.S. Supreme Ct. 1944. Practiced in Los Angeles, 1933-35; with Emil Brown & Co., Dura Steel Products Co., both Los Angeles, 1936-41; counsel RFC, Washington, 1942-44; ptnr. firm Pacht, Warne, Ross and Bernhard, Los Angeles, Beverly Hills, Calif., 1944-47, Irell & Manella, Los Angeles, 1947-69; counsel Irell & Manella, 1969-72; Lectr. in law Southwestern U. Law Sch., Los Angeles, 1939-41, U. Calif. at Los Angeles, 1944-46; lectr. in law U. So. Calif., 1950-51, lectr., adj. prof. law, 1960-74, prof. law, 1974-80, prof. emeritus, 1980—, acad. dir. program for legal para-profls., 1970-77; mem. planning com. Tax Inst., 1948-69; vis. prof. law Loyola-Marymount Law Sch., Los Angeles, 1977-82; Disting. vis. prof. Whittier Coll. Sch. Law, 1980—; mem. nat. panel arbitrators Am. Arbitration Assn., 1956-63; chmn. bd. trustees Nat. Ctr. for Preventive Law, U. Denver Coll. Law, 1987—. Author: Preventive Law, 1950, How to Negotiate a Successful Contract, 1955, Lawyering Through Life: The Origin of Preventive Law, 1986; also case books, articles profl. jours.; co-author: Planning by Lawyers: Materials on a Non-Adversarial Legal Process, 1978; Editor: Major Tax Problems, 3 vols, 1948-51; Mem. Am. Community Symphony Orch., European Tour, 1968. Mem. com. Jewish Personnel Relations Bur., Community Relations Com., 1950-60; founder, adminstr. Emil Brown Fund Preventive Law Prize Awards, 1963-85, Hermione and Louis Brown Found., 1985—; founder, adminstr. Client Counseling Competition, 1968-73, cons., 1973-74; pres. Friends of Beverly Hills Pub. Library, 1960. Recipient Merit award U. So. Calif. Gen. Alumni Assn., 1979; Disting. Service award Beverly Hills Bar Found., 1985. Fellow Am. Bar Found., Soc. for Values in Higher Edn.; mem. ABA (chmn. standing com. legal assistance for servicemen 1969-72, mem. accreditation com. sect. legal edn. and admissions to bar 1978-81), Beverly Hills Bar Assn. (pres. 1961, Disting. Service award 1981), Los Angeles County Bar Assn. (chmn. prepaid legal services com. 1970-71), State Bar Calif., Am. Judicature Soc., Am. Bus. Law Assn., Internat. Assn. Jewish Lawyers and Jurists, Town Hall Los Angeles, Order of Coif. Jewish. Clubs: Mason (mem.), B'nai B'rith, Harvard Southern Calif. Home: 606 N Palm Dr Beverly Hills CA 90210 Office: 1901 Ave of Stars Suite 850 Los Angeles CA 90067

BROWN, MABEL ESTLE, retired educator; b. Muscatine County, Iowa, Oct. 6, 1907; d. Chester Millar and Mayme (Bell) Estle; m. Robert G. Brown, Dec. 30, 1931; children—Patricia Jane Brown Hoback, Linnaeus Estle. B.A., U. Iowa, 1929; M.S., Iowa State U., 1953. Cert. secondary tchr., guidance counselor, sch. librarian, Iowa. High sch. tchr., Conesville, Iowa, 1930-32, 42-48, Nichols, Iowa, 1949-50; grad. asst. journalism Iowa State U., Ames, 1950-53; tchr., librarian Lone Tree High Sch., (Iowa), 1953-60, guidance counselor, 1960-70; chmn. Carrie Stanley Scholarship Com., Lone Tree, 1962-70. Author: The Fork of the Rivers: History Is People, 1978. Chmn., Muscatine County Farm Bur. Women, Muscatine, Iowa, 1938-42; judge, clk. Twp. Election Com., Conesville, 1970-84. Mem. NEA (life), Iowa Edn. Soc. (life), ALA, Iowa Acad. Sci., Theta Sigma Phi. Republican. Home: Rural Route Conesville IA 52739

BROWN, MARCUS GORDON, foreign language educator; b. Miami, Fla., Mar. 14, 1908; s. David Chappel and Lula (Bell) B.; A.B., Columbia Union Coll., 1927; M.A., Emory U., 1936; Docteur ès Lettres, U. Dijon (France), 1939; Doctor en Filosofia y Letras, U. Madrid (Spain), 1940. Tchr. fgn. langs. high sch., Jacksonville, Fla., 1927-30, Boys' High Sch., Atlanta, 1930-36; instr. English and French, U. Fla., 1936-38; asst. prof. fgn. langs. Ga. Inst. Tech., Atlanta, 1940-42, assoc. prof., 1942-43, prof., 1943-50; specialist U.S. Office Edn., 1944-46; cultural attache Am. embassy Bogotá, Colombia, 1950-52, Rio de Janeiro, Brazil, 1952-54; asst. chancellor Univ. System Ga., Atlanta, 1954-57; fgn. lang. coordinator Ga. State Dept. Edn., Atlanta, 1957-62; assoc. prof. Romance langs. Memphis State U., 1963-67, prof., 1967-71, prof. modern langs., 1971-73; summer vis. prof. Duke U., 1941-44, U. Havana, 1943, U. Ga., 1947, U. Mont., 1948; vis. prof. Ft. Lewis Coll., 1975, Henderson State U., 1976-77; lectr. U.S. Dept. State, Latin Am., 1948-49, Spain and Portugal, 1957-58; lectr. numerous instns. and orgns. U.S. and abroad. Recipient Anchieta medal Municipality of Rio de Janeiro, Brazil, 1954; medals for excellence in French lang. and lit. French Govt., 1936. Mem. Sociedad Bolivariana de Colombia, Am. Assn. Tchrs. Spanish and Portugese, Am. Assn. Tchrs. French, Am. Assn. Tchrs. Italian, Am. Assn. Tchrs. German, AAUP, MLA, S. Central MLA, Phi Sigma Iota, Sigma Delta Pi, Pi Delta Phi, Delta Phi Alpha. Author: Les Idées Politiques et Religieuses de Stendhal, 1939; La Vida y Las Novelas de Emilia Pardo Bazán, 1940; (with J. Russell) Bibliography for the Teaching of English to Foreigners, 1947; also translations, articles, condensations of Brazilian novels.

BROWN, MICHAEL STUART, geneticist; b. N.Y.C., Apr. 13, 1941; s. Harvey and Evelyn (Katz) B.; m. Alice Lapin, June 21, 1964; children: Elizabeth Jane, Sara Ellen. B.A., U. Pa., 1962, M.D., 1966. Intern, then resident in medicine Mass. Gen. Hosp., Boston, 1966-68; served with USPHS, 1968-70; clin. assoc. NIH, 1968-71; asst. prof. U. Tex. Southwestern Med. Sch., Dallas, 1971-74; Paul J. Thomas prof. genetics, dir. Center Genetic Diseases, 1977—. Recipient Pfizer award Am. Chem. Soc., 1976, Passano award Passano Found., 1978, Lounsbery award U.S. Nat. Acad. Scis., 1979; Lita Annenberg Hazen award, 1982, Albert Lasker Med. Research award, 1985, Nobel Prize in Medicine or Physiology, 1985. Mem. Nat. Acad. Scis., Am. Soc. Clin. Investigation, Assn. Am. Physicians, Harvey Soc. Office: Univ of Tex Health Sci Ctr Internal Medicine-Biophysics 5323 Harry Hines Blvd Dallas TX 75235 *

BROWN, MURIEL WINDHAM, librarian, writer; b. Dallas, Nov. 19, 1926; d. Charles Wyatt and Gladys Mae (Patman) Windham; m. George W. Brown, II, Jan. 28, 1951; children—Laurence Windham, David Mitchum, Leslie Ann. B.A., So. Meth. U., 1949, M.A., 1950; M.L.S., North Tex. State U., 1974, postgrad., 1974—. Library assoc. Dallas Pub. Library, 1964-66, librarian lit. and history, 1966-66 children's librarian, 1966-72, head children's dept., 1967-69, children's selection new brs., 1972-77, children's lit. specialist, 1977—; cons. in field. Author: Books for You, 1981; co-author: Notable Children's Books 1976-1980, 1986; compiler bibliographies for Behind the Covers, 1984, Behind the Covers II, 1988; contbr. chpt. to School Library Media Annual, 1987. Mem. presch. edn. com. Am. Heart Assn., Dallas, 1982-83. Jesse Jones fellow, 1949. Mem. ALA (children's Notable books re-evaluation com. 1983—, Newberry award com. 1984-85), Tex. Library Assn. (chmn. children's round table, Siddie Joe Johnson Children's Librarian award 1988), So. Meth. U. Alumni Assn. (sec. 1972-73), Alpha Theta Phi, Beta Phi Mu, Alpha Lambda Sigma. Democrat. Unitarian. Home: 10415 Church Rd Dallas TX 75238 Office: Dallas Pub Library 1515 Young St Dallas TX 75201

BROWN, PAUL, export marketing executive; b. Sheffield, Yorkshire, Eng., Nov. 5, 1959; s. Thomas Peter and Betty (Sharman) B. BS with honors, U. Manchester Inst. Sci. and Tech., 1981. Polymer technologist Plascoat Systems Ltd., Farnham, Surrey, Eng., 1982-86; export mktg. exec. CIBA Geigy Indsl. Chems., Manchester, 1986—. Mem. Ch. of Eng. Club: Woking 18 Plus (vice chmn. 1983-84). Office: CIBA Geigy Indsl Chems, Tenax Rd, Trafford Park, Manchester M17 1WT, England

BROWN, PETER CAMPBELL, lawyer; b. Aug. 12, 1913; s. Peter P. and Ellen (Campbell) B.; m. Joan Gallagher, June 8, 1943; children: Peter Campbell, Patricia, Thomas, Michael, Robert. A.B., Fordham Coll., 1935, LL.B., 1938; LL.D., St. Bonaventure U., New York, 1951. Bar: N.Y. 1938. Practiced in Bklyn., 1938-41; asst. U.S. atty. for Eastern Dist. of N.Y., Bklyn., 1946; 1st. asst. criminal div. Dept. of Justice, 1947-48; exec. asst. to atty. gen. U.S. 1948, spl. asst. to atty. gen., 1949-50, mem. subversive activities control bd. (under the Internal Security Act of 1950), 1950-53, chmn., 1952-53; commr. investigation N.Y.C., 1954-55; corp. counsel City of N.Y., 1955-58; mem. Manning, Hollinger & Shea, 1958-65; ptnr. Brown, Carlino & Emmanuel, 1965-72; counsel Winer, Neuburger & Sive, 1972-78; sole practice N.Y.C., 1978—; dir. Thomas Pub. Co., Fedn. Bank & Trust Co. Bd. dirs. St. Mary's Coll., South Bend, Ind. Served to maj. AUS, 1942-45, ETO. Decorated 6 Battle Stars on European African Middle Eastern ribbon, Fourragere of Belgium for Battle of Ardennes (The Bulge); named Knight Holy Sepulchre Knight Malta. Fellow Am. Coll. Trial Lawyers, Bar Supreme Ct. U.S., Fed. Dist. Cts., U.S. Ct. Appeals, Am., N.Y. State bar assns., V.F.W., Legion, Catholic Lawyers Guild, Assn. Bar City of N.Y., St. Patrick Soc. Bklyn. (past pres., dir.), Friendly Sons St. Patrick City N.Y., Fordham Coll. Alumni Assn. (past pres.). Democrat. Roman Catholic. Clubs: Lawyers (Bklyn.), Montauk (Bklyn.); Manhattan (N.Y.C.), New York Athletic (N.Y.C.), Pinnacle (N.Y.C.); Army-Navy (Washington); Pelham Country; Westchester Country (Rye, N.Y.). Home: 275 N Ridge St Rye Brook NY 10573

BROWN, ROBERT J., JR., electronics company executive; b. Welsh, La., Aug. 15, 1921; s. Robert J. and Lavinia (McCollister) B.; B.S. in Elec. Engring., U. Southwestern La., 1942; m. Virginia Sewall, June 30, 1943; children—Robert J. III, Kenneth E. Electronics engr. Gen. Electric Co., Schenectady, 1942-44, sales engring. rep., 1946-50, mgr. dist. office Electronics div., Washington, 1950-54, mgr. sales heavy mil. electronics dept., Syracuse, N.Y., 1954-59, mgr. mktg., 1959-61, gen. mgr., 1961-62, gen. mgr. def. programs div. Washington, 1962-64; chmn. bd. Gen. Electric Tech. Services Co. Washington, 1963-64, Apparaten Industrie Def. Electronics, NV, The Hague, Netherlands, 1963-64; v.p., gen. ops. mgr. The Magnavox Co., Ft. Wayne, Ind., 1964-67; exec. v.p. Maxson Electronics Corp., L.I., N.Y., 1967-69; dir., 1969; v.p. Hazeltine Corp., Greenlawn, N.Y., 1969-72; sr. v.p. Potter Instrument Co. Inc., Plainview, N.Y., 1972-76; pres. Barry Miller Ordnance, Gardena, Calif., 1967-69; v.p. Lundy Electronics & Systems, Inc., 1975-78; chmn., pres., chief exec. officer Teletimer Internat., Inc., Boca Raton, 1986—. Served with USNR, 1944-45. Registered profl. engr., D.C. Mem. Assn. Energy Engrs., Assn. U.S. Army, Navy League U.S., Mil. Order of Carabao. Home: 6688 Serena Ln Boca Raton FL 33433 Office: 1801 Clint Moor Rd Boca Raton FL 33487-9987

BROWN, RONALD MALCOLM, engineer, corporation executive; b. Hot Springs, S.D., Feb. 21, 1938; s. George Malcolm and Cleo Lavonne (Plumb) B.; m. Sharon Ida Brown, Nov. 14, 1964 (div. Apr. 1974); children: Michael, Troy, George, Curtis, Lisa, Brittney. AA, Southwestern Coll., 1970; BA, Chapman Coll., 1978. Commd. USN, 1956, advanced through grades to master chief, 1973, ret., 1978; engring. mgr. Beckman Inst., Fullerton, Calif., 1978-82; mech. engring. br. mgr. Northrop Corp., Hawthorne, Calif., 1982-83; dir. of ops. Transco, Marina Del Rey, Calif., 1983-85; v.p. ops. Decor Concepts, Arcadia, Calif., 1985-87; design mgr. Lockheed Aircraft, 1987—. Mem. Soc. Mfg. Engrs., Inst. Indsl. Engrs., Nat. Trust for Hist. Preservation, Fleet Res. Assn., Am. Film Inst., Nat. Mgmt. Assn.

BROWN, RONALD OSBORNE, telecommunications and office information systems consultant; b. Winchester, Mass., Apr. 9, 1941; s. Herbert Walcott and Madeleine Louise (Osborne) B.; children—Melinda E., Jeffrey J. B.Sc. with distinction, U. Maine, 1963; M.Sc., Tufts U., 1965; Ph.D., Queens U., Kingston, Ont., 1972. Mem. tech. staff RCA Corp., Burlington, Mass., 1965-66; research assoc. Queen's U., Kingston, Ont., 1966-71; mem. sci. staff BNR, Ottawa, Ont., 1971-72; sr. systems engr. GTE Corp., Needham, Mass., 1973-83; mgr. Coopers & Lybrand, Boston, 1983-87, nat. dir, 1987—; program coordinator Northeastern U., Boston, 1976—; cons. Bell Can., 1968-71; tech. adv. bd. TP & T Mag., Littleton, Mass., 1984—; faculty adv. council Nat. Communications Forum, 1986—; mem. faculty adv. com. Nat. Communications Forum. Contbr. articles to profl. jours. Mem. IEEE, Assn. Profl. Engrs. Ont., Tau Beta Pi, Phi Kappa Phi, Eta Kappa Nu. Home: Quaker Ridge Rd PO Box 470 South Casio ME 04077 Office: Coopers & Lybrand 1 Post Office Sq Boston MA 02109

BROWN, RONALD WILLIAM, airline executive; b. Perth, Australia, Apr. 14, 1951; s. William Harrison and Norma Mavis (Kinghorn) B.; m. Ramona Concita Masiello, Sept. 2, 1977; children: Tracey Louise, Matthew Christopher. Grad. high sch., Perth. Traffic officer MacRobertson Miller Airlines, Karratha, Australia, 1971-74; traffic officer MacRobertson Miller Airlines, Paraburdoo, Australia, 1974-75, sr. traffic officer, 1975-76; br. mgr. Tom Price, Australia, 1976-77, Kununurra, Australia, 1977-81; br. mgr. Airlines Western Australia, Kununurra, 1984; mgr. Ansett Western Australia Airlines, Kununurra, 1984-87; field sales mgr. Ansett Airlines, Perth, 1987—. Contbr. articles to profl. jours. Hon. treas. Kununurra Visitors Ctr., 1977-87; pres. Kununurra C. of C., 1979-80; founding chmn. Celebrity Tree Park Mgmt. Commn., Kununurra, 1983-87; councillor Shire of Wyndham/East Kimberley, Kununurra, 1985-87. Named Citizen of Yr. City of Kununurra, 1987. Lodge: Rotary (pres.-elect 1986-87, Youth Leadership award 1969). Home: 41 Harrison St, Balcatta, 6021 Perth Australia

BROWN, SHARON GAIL, data processing executive, consultant; b. Chgo., Dec. 25, 1941; d. Otto and Pauline (Lauer) Schumacher; B.G.S., Roosevelt U.; m. Robert B. Ringo, Aug. 2, 1984; 1 dau. by previous marriage, Susan Ann. Info. analyst Internat. Minerals & Chems., Northbrook, Ill., 1966-71, programmer analyst, 1971-74; programmer analyst Procon Internat. Inc. subs. UOP Inc., Des Plaines, Ill., 1974-76, systems analyst, 1976-77, project leader, 1977-78; mgr. adminstrv. services, 1978-82; spl. cons. to pres. IPS Internat., Ltd., 1982-83; spl. cons. to pres. CEI Supply Co. div. Sigma-Chapman, Inc., 1984-87, ptnr. and co-founder Brown, Ringo & Assocs., 1987—; data processing cons. Mem. Buffalo Grove (Ill.) Youth Commn., 1978-82; mem. adv. com. UOP Polit. Action Com., 1979-82; Mem. Rep. Senatorial Com. Inner Circle. Mem. Am. Mgmt. Assn., Chgo. Council on Fgn. Relations, Lake Forest-Lake Bluff Hist. Soc. Home: 550 E Deerpath Lake Forest IL 60045

BROWN, SHERWIN OLIVIER, manufacturing executive; b. St. Ann, Jamaica, Dec. 1, 1944; s. Aston Wilmot and Reines Ulive (Shand) B; m. Nerissa Lee-Ann Sammott, June 16, 1979; children: Lisa Marie, Keri Gaye. BS in Engring., Univ. W.I., Trinidad and Tobago, 1969. Projects engr. Alcan, Jamaica, 1969-74, sr. projects engr., 1974-76, sr. maintenance engr., 1976-78, maintenance mgr., 1978-83; pres. Jamtrac Ltd. subs. Alcan, Jamaica, 1983-87, Alcan-Sprostons Ltd. subs. Alcan, Jamaica, 1987—. Served to capt. Jamaican Nat. Res., 1970—. Mem. Jamaica Inst. Engrs., Jamaica Inst. Mgmt. Adventist. Clubs: Jamaica, Liguanea. Office: Alcan-Sprostons Ltd, 379 Spanish Town Rd, 11 Kingston Jamaica

BROWN, STEVEN HARRY, corporation health physicist, consultant; b. Phila., Sept. 16, 1948; s. Robert Martin and Vera Ethel (Lipovsky) B.; m. Kathryn Helena Vassie, May 24, 1970; children—Chad, Joshua, Sean. A.B.S., Temple U., 1970, B.S., 1971; M.A., West Chester (Pa.) U., 1974. Cert. Am. Bd. Health Physics. Health physicist Temple U., Phila., 1969-71; tchr. phys. sci. Phila. Sch. Dist., 1971-76; mgr. radiation protection Westinghouse Electric Corp., Lakewood, Colo., 1976-80; mgr. western regional office Radiation Mgmt. Corp., Phila., 1980-82; prin. safety analysis engr. Rockwell Internat., Golden, Colo., 1982-83, program mgr. waste isolation pilot project, 1983-85; sr. project mgr. West Valley Demonstration Project, Dames and Moore, West Valley, N.Y., 1985—; cons. Westinghouse Electric Corp., Lakewood, Colo., 1981, Earth Scis. Inc., Golden, 1982, Radiation Mgmt. Corp., Chgo., 1982, U.S. Dept. Energy, 1985-88, Rockwell Internat., 1988, Atlantic Richfield, 1988; U.S. rep. Internat. Conf. on Radiation Hazards in Mining, Beijing, 1986. Mem. Nat. Health Physics Soc. (pres. Rocky Mountain chpt. 1982-83), Am. Nuclear Soc., Nat. Mgmt. Assn. Office: Dames and Moore 1626 Cole Blvd Golden CO 80401

BROWN, STEVEN RAY, language professional; b. Hayward, Calif., July 5, 1952; s. Curtis Ray and Clara Belle Brown. BA, U. Calif., 1974; MA, San Diego State U., 1979. Cert. tchr. adult edn., Calif. Tchr. Castro Valley (Calif.) Sch. Dist., 1979-81; instr. Tohoku Fgn. Language Sch., Sendai, Japan, 1981-82, Tohoku Gakuin U., Sendai, Japan, 1984-86; instr. James English Sch., Sendai, Japan, 1982-84, head tchr., 1984-86; instr. Japan program U. Pitts. English Lang. Inst., Tokyo, 1986-87, asst. dir., 1987-88, dir., 1988—; instr. MA TESOL program Columbia U. Tchrs. Coll., Tokyo, 1988—. Mem. Japan Assn. of Lang. Tchrs. (program chmn. 1985-86), Internat. Assn. Tchrs. English as a Fgn. Lang., Tchrs. English to Speakers of Other Langs. Democrat. Unitarian. Home: 3-6-22-401 Sekiguchi, Bunkyo-ku, 112 Tokyo Japan Office: U Pitts Eng Lang Inst, 2-6-12 Fujimi Chiyoda-ku, 102 Tokyo Japan

BROWN, SUZANNE WILEY, museum executive; b. Cheyenne, Wyo., Aug. 28, 1938; d. Robert James and Catharine Helen (Schroeder) Wiley; B.S. with honors, U. Wyo., 1960, M.S., 1964; postgrad. U. Cin. Med. Sch., 1965-66, U. Ill., 1969-72; m. Ralph E. Brown, July 19, 1968; 1 dau., Nina M. Research asst. Harvard Med. Sch., 1962-63; research asst. U. Cin. Med. Sch., 1964-65; sr. lab. asst. U. Chgo., 1966-67; research assoc. U. Colo. Med. Sch., 1968; teaching asst. U. Ill., 1971-73; exec. asst. Chgo. Acad. Scis., 1974-82, asst. dir., 1982-84, assoc. dir., 1984—. NDEA fellow, 1960-62. Mem. Mus. Educators of Greater Chgo., Am. Assn. Museums, Internat. Council Museums, Brookfield Zool. Soc. (bd. govs.), Pub. Relations in Service to Musuems, Midwest Mus. Conf., Phi Beta Kappa, Sigma Xi, Phi Kappa Phi. Office: 2001 N Clark St Chicago IL 60614

BROWN, THOMAS HUNTINGTON, neuroscientist; b. N.Y.C., June 13, 1945; s. Thomas Huntington and Elvira R. (Crandall) B.; m. Patricia Ann Carson, Aug. 10, 1968. BA in Molecular Biology, Calif. State U.-San Jose, 1972; MA in Psychology, 1972; PhD in Neurosci., Stanford U., 1977. Postdoctoral fellow Stanford U., Calif., 1977-79; asst. research scientist Beckman Research Inst., City of Hope, Duarte, Calif., 1979-82, assoc. research scientist, 1982-86, research scientist, 1986—; adviser NIH, NIMH study sections, 1982-83; Mem. editorial bd. Behavioral Neurosci. jour., 1983—. Contbr. articles to sci. jours., 1976—. Recipient Epilepsy Found. Am. award, 1980, McKnight Found. Scholar's award, 1981; McKnight Found. Career Devel. award, 1984; Muscular Dystrophy Found. fellow, 1978, NIH fellow, 1979; grantee in field, 1980—. Mem. AAAS, Soc. Neurosci., Internat. Neural Network Soc. Office: Yale U Dept Psychology PO Box 11A Yale Station New Haven CT 06520

BROWN, WADE EDWARD, lawyer; b. Blowing Rock, N.C., Nov. 5, 1907; s. Jefferson Davis and Etta Cornelia (Suddreth) B.; m. Gilma Baity; children—Margaret Rose Johnson, Wade Edward, Sarah Baity. Student Mars Hill Coll., 1928; J.D., Wake Forest U., 1931. Bar: N.C. 1930. Sole practice, Boone, N.C., 1931—; chmn. N.C. Bd. Paroles, Raleigh, 1967-72; cons. Atty. Gen., N.C. Dept. Justice, 1973, mem. N.C. Senate, 1947-49; mem. N.C. Ho. Reps., 1951-53; mayor Town of Boone, 1961-67; with student legal services, Appalachian State U. Chmn., Watauga County Hosp.; active Boone Merchants Assn.; mem. gen. bd. Bapt. State Conv. N.C.; trustee Wake Forest U., Appalachian State U., Bapt. Found. N.C. Bapt. State Conv. Served to lt. USN, 1944-46. Recipient N.C. State Bar cert. appreciation. Mem. N.C. Bar Assn., 24th Jud. Bar Assn., Am. Legion (comdr. post), Boone C. of C. (past pres.). Democrat. Baptist. Club: Boone Lions. Office: 221 W King St PO Box 1776 Boone NC 28607

BROWN, WALSTON SHEPARD, lawyer; b. Darien, Conn., Jan. 20, 1908; s. Clarence Shepard and Alma Mary (Mitchell) B.; m. Ellen F. Regan, August 13, 1955. A.B., Leland Stanford U., 1930; student, L'Ecole Libre des Science Politiques, Paris, 1931-32; LL.B., Harvard U., 1935. Bar: D.C. 1936. Atty. various govt. depts. 1935-40; asst. gen. counsel U.S. Maritime Commn., also mem. various adv. coms. on drafting and adminstrn. mem. various adv. coms. on drafting, reconversion and contract termination legislation, 1940-45; practiced in N.Y.C., 1945—; ptnr. Willkie Farr & Gallagher and predecessors. Mem. Newcomen Soc. N. Am., Am. Bar Assn., S.R., Phi Beta Kappa. Unitarian. Clubs: University, River (N.Y.C.); Tuxedo (N.Y.). Home: Mountain Farm Rd PO Box 772 Tuxedo Park NY 10987 Office: 153 E 53d St New York NY 10022

BROWN, WALTER FREDERICK, lawyer; b. Los Angeles, July 28, 1926; s. Walter Andrew and Emily Anna (Weber) B.; m. Barbara Mae Porter Stahmann, Aug. 6, 1950; children: Jeffrey David, Kendall Paul, David Walter. BA, U. So. Calif., 1949, JD, 1952; MA, Boston U., 1961; MLS, U. Oreg., 1975. Bar: Calif. 1952, Oreg. 1981, U.S. Tax Ct. 1974, U.S. Supreme Ct. 1975; cert. Am. Assn. Law Librarians. Assoc. prof. and law librarian Northwestern Sch. Law Lewis and Clark Coll., Portland, Oreg., 1970-80; senator Oreg. Legis. Assembly, Salem, 1975-87; gen. counsel Oreg. Consumer League, Portland, 1987—; bd. dirs. Oreg. Consumer League, 1972—; chmn. Senate Agrl. and Forestry Com., 1985, Senate Task Force Vet.'s Home Loans, 1985-87; chmn. capitol constrn. subcom. Joint Ways and Means Com., 1983; chmn. Senate Bus. and Consumer Affairs Com., 1981; senate co-chmn. Joint Legis. Counsel Com., 1979-87; mem. Legis. Emergency Bd., 1983-84; senate co-vice chmn. Joint Trade and Econ. Devel. Com., 1985-87; commr. Gov.'s Commn. Sr. Services, 1985-87; vice chmn. Judiciary Com., 1975, 79, 81, 83, 85, Labor Com., 1983, Elections, 1981. Contbr. articles to law jours. Pres. Clackamas County Citizens Assn., Oreg., 1971-74; mem. Oreg. Environ. Council, Oreg. Natural Resources Council, NW Coalition for Alternatives to Pesticides, Nat. Pro-Life Democrats. Served to comdr. JAGC, USN, 1944-70. Recipient Oreg. Civil Liberties Union award, 1983, Oreg. Environ. Council award, 1975, 79, 81, 83, 85, Trout Unltd. award Oregon City, 1975, Liberty award Oreg. Conf. Seventh-day Adventists, 1985. Mem. Nature Conservancy, Citizens Utility Bd. Oreg., Citizens for Tax Justice, Natural Resources Defense Council, Oreg. Common Cause, Nat. Eagle Scout Assn., Oreg. Meml. Assn., Am. Legion (award 1981, 82), VFW, Oreg. Small Woodlands Assn., Ctr. Environ. Edn., Sierra Club, Oreg. State Grange, Mazamas, Nat. Farmers Union. Democrat. Unitarian-Universalist. Lodges: Kiwanis, Masons. Home: 3710 SE Concord Rd # 95 Milwaukie OR 97267 Office: Oreg Consumer League 909 NE 114th Ave Portland OR 97220

BROWN, (ROBERT) WENDELL, lawyer; b. Mpls., Feb. 26, 1902; s. Robert and Jane Amanda (Anderson) B.; m. Barbara Ann Fisher, Oct. 20, 1934; children: Barbara Ann (Mrs. Neil Maurice Travis), Mary Alice (Mrs. Alfred Lee Fletcher). A.B., U. Hawaii, 1924; J.D., U. Mich., 1926. Bar: Mich. 1926, U.S. Supreme Ct 1934, U.S. Ct. Appeals (6th cir.) 1952, U.S. Dist. Ct (ea. dist.) Mich. 1927, U.S. Dist. Ct. (we. dist.) Mich. 1931, U.S. Bd. Immigration Appeals 1944, U.S. Tax Ct 1973. Lawyer firm Routier, Nichols & Fildew, Detroit, 1926, Nichols & Fildew, 1927-28, Frank C. Sibley, 1929, Ferguson & Ferguson, 1929-31; asst. atty. gen. Mich., 1931-32; with legal dept. Union Guardian Trust Co., Detroit, 1933-34; sole practice law Detroit, 1934-81, Farmington Hills, Mich., 1981—; Legal adviser Wayne County (Mich.) Graft Grand Jury, 1939-40; asst. pros. atty. civil matters Wayne County, 1940; spl. asst. city atty. to investigate Police Dept. Highland Park, Mich., 1951-52. Chmn. citizens com. to form Oakland County (Mich.) Community Coll., 1962-63; Pres. Farmington (Mich.) Sch. Bd., 1952-56; chmn. Oakland County Republican County Conv., 1952; trustee Farmington Twp., Oakland County, 1957-61; pres. Oakland County Lincoln Rep. Club, 1958; Treas., bd. dirs. Friends of Detroit Library, 1943-44; bd. dirs. Farmington Friends of Library, Inc., 1952-58, pres., 1956-57; Hon. mem. Farmington Hist. Soc., 1966, St. Anthonys Guild, Franciscan Friars, 1975. Recipient Recognition award for assisting formation 25 years ago Farmington Hist. Soc., 1987, plaque for pioneering efforts on behalf Farmington Community Library, 1987, Kenneth R. Glide award for exemplary service as vol. legal advisor The Samaritan Counseling Ctr. Southeastern Mich., 1987. Mem. Am. Bar Assn., State Bar Mich. (chmn. or mem. various coms. 1935-52, 77-80), Oakland County Bar Assn., Detroit Bar Assn. (bd. dirs. 1939-49, pres. 1948-49). Presbyn. (elder). Home: 29921 Ardmore St Farmington Hills MI 48018 Office: Quakertown Plaza 32969 Hamilton Ct Suite 115 Farmington Hills MI 48018

BROWN, WILLIAM ALLEY, law educator; b. La Grange, Tex., Sept. 5, 1921; s. Leon Dancy and Mary (Alley) B.; m. Ann Dyke Shafer, June 27, 1953; children—Ann Lenora, William Alley. B.B.A., U. Tex., 1942; Indsl. Adminstr., Harvard Bus. Sch., 1943; J.D., U. Tex., 1948. Bar: Tex. 1948, U.S. Dist. Ct. (we. dist.) Tex. 1950, U.S. Dist. Ct. (so. dist.) Tex. 1959, U.S. Ct. Appeals (5th cir.) 1950, U.S. Ct. Appeals (11th cir.) 1983. Assoc., ptnr. Powell, Wirtz Rauhut, Austin, Tex., 1950-58; ptnr. Powell, Rauhut, McGinnis, Reavley & Brown, Houston, 1958-61; assoc. gen. counsel Brown & Root, Inc., Houston, 1961-76, v.p., gen. atty., 1976-83; prof. constrn. law Tex. A&M U., College Station, 1983—. Served to 1st lt. U.S. Army, 1942-46, ETO. Mem. Sons of Rep. of Tex., Alpha Tau Omega. Republican. Episcopalian. Clubs: Frisch Auf Country (La Grange, Tex.), Plaza (Bryan, Tex.). Home: 2710 Pinehurst St Bryan TX 77802 Office: Tex A & M Univ Constrn Sci Dept College Station TX 77843

BROWN, WILLIAM ANDREAS, U.S. ambassador; b. Winchester, Mass., Sept. 7, 1930; m. Helen Melpomene Coutchavlis; 4 children. BA magna cum laude, Harvard U., 1952, MA, 1955, PhD, 1963; postdoctoral in Russian lang. studies, Fgn. Service Inst., 1965-66, Nat. War Coll., 1972. With U.S. Fgn. Service, 1956—; with U.S. Dept. State, 1956-57; consular and comml. officer U.S. Dept. State, Hong Kong, 1957-59; lang. student U.S. Dept. State, Taichung, Taiwan, 1959-61; polit. officer U.S. Dept. State, Singapore, 1961-64; prin. officer U.S. Dept. State, Kuching, Sarawak, 1964-65; polit. officer U.S. Dept. State, Moscow, USSR, 1966-68, New Delhi, India, 1968-70; dep. dir. Office Asian Communist Affairs U.S. Dept. State, 1970-72; student of Mongolian U.S. Dept. State, Leeds, Eng., 1972-73; spl. asst. to the adminstr., EPA, 1974-76; polit. counselor U.S. Dept. State, Moscow, USSR, 1977-78; dep. chief Mission U.S. Dept. State, Taipei, Taiwan, 1978-79, first acting dir. Am. Inst in Taiwan, 1978-79; dep. chief Mission U.S. Dept. State, Tel Aviv, Israel, 1979-82; vis. prof. U. N.H., 1982-83; prin. dep. asst. sec. East Asian and Pacific Affairs U.S. Dept. State, 1983-85; U.S. ambassador Dept. State, Bangkok, Thailand, 1985—. Served with USMC, 1952-54, capt. Res. Office: US Embassy, 95 Wireless Rd, Bangkok Thailand

BROWN, WILLIAM HILL, III, lawyer; b. Phila., Jan. 19, 1928; s. William H. Jr. and Ethel L. (Washington) B.; m. Sonya Morgan, Aug. 29, 1952 (div. 1975); 1 child, Michele D.; m. D. June Hairston, July 29, 1975; 1 child, Jeanne-Marie. B.S., Temple U., 1952; J.D., U. Pa., 1955. Bar: Pa. 1956, U.S. Ct. Appeals (3d cir.) 1959, U.S. Supreme Ct. 1960, D.C. 1972, U.S. Dist. Ct. (D.C.) 1972, U.S. Ct. Appeals (4th cir.) 1978, U.S. Ct. Appeals (10th cir.) 1986. Assoc. Norris, Schmidt, Phila., 1955-62; ptnr. Norris, Brown, Hall, Phila., 1962-68, Schnader, Harrison, Segal & Lewis, Phila., 1974—; chief of frauds Dist. Atty.'s Office, 1968, dep. dist. atty., 1968; commr. EEOC, Washington, 1968-69; chmn. EEOC, 1969-73; lectr. S.W. Legal Found., Practising Law Inst., Nat. Inst. Trial Advocacy; dir. United Parcel Service, Inc., 1983—; dir. Lawyers Com. Civil Rights Under Law, Pub. Interest Law Ctr.; chmn. Phila. Spl. Investigation Commn. MOVE; pres. Nat. Black Child Child Devel., Inc., 1986. Contbr. articles to profl. jours. Bd. dirs. Middle State Assn. Colls. and Secondary Schs.; bd. govs. Am. Heart Assn. (southeastern Pa. chpt.); life mem. NAACP (bd. dirs. legal def. and edn. fund). Served with USAF, 1946-48. Recipient award of merit Fed. Bar Assn., Columbus, 1971, NAACP award, 1971. Fellow Am. Law Inst.; mem. Phila. Bar Assn., D.C. Bar Assn., Pa. Bar Assn., ABA, Fed. Bar Assn., Inter-Am. Bar Assn., Assn. Trial Lawyers Am., World Assn. Lawyers (founding mem.),Am. Arbitration Assn. (former bd. dirs.), Barristers' Assn. Phila. Inc. (J. Austin Norris award 1987), Citizens Commn. Civil Rights, Alpha Phi Alpha (award of recognition 1969). Republican. Episcopalian. Office: Schnader Harrison Segal & Lewis 1600 Market St Suite 3600 Philadelphia PA 19103

BROWN, WILLIAM TED, biology educator, physician; b. Missoula, Mont., Feb. 18, 1946; s. C. W. and H. F. B.; m. Barbara Blegen, Mar. 31, 1967 (div. Jan. 1982); 1 child, Vanessa. BA, Johns Hopkins U., 1967, MA, 1969, PhD, 1973; MD cum laude, Harvard U., 1974. Diplomate Am. Bd. Internal Medicine, Am. Bd. Med. Genetics. Intern Roosevelt Hosp., N.Y.C., 1974-75, resident in medicine, 1975-77; Nat. Inst. on Aging postdoctoral fellow in genetics Cornell U. Med. Sch., N.Y.C., 1977-78, asst. prof., 1978-82; chmn. dept. human genetics N.Y. State Inst. Basic Research in Devel. Diseases, N.Y.C., 1982—; asst. attending physician N.Y. Hosp., N.Y.C., 1981—; asst. prof. Rockefeller U., N.Y.C., 1981—; prof. biophysics, anatomy & cell biology SUNY Health Sci. Ctr., Bkln., 1987—; mem. Nat. Inst. Aging Resources Adv. Panel. Contbr. chpts., articles on aging, genetics, mental retardation to profl. jours.; editorial bd.: Review Biol. Research in Aging. Recipient Andrew W. Mellon Tchr.-Scientist award. 1979; NSF research fellow Johns Hopkins U., 1967-69. Fellow Gerontilogical Soc. Am.; mem. Am. Soc. Human Genetics, Gerontol. Soc., Am. Fedn. Clin. Research, Harvey Soc., N.Y. Acad. Scis. Subspecialties: Genetics and genetic engineering (medicine); Gerontology. Current work: Genetic diseases affecting aging, progeria, mental retardation, fragile X syndrome, and Downs syndrome. Office: NY State Inst Basic Research in Devel Diseases 1050 Forest Hill Rd Staten Island NY 10314

BROWN, WILSON GORDON, physician, educator; b. Bosworth, Mo., Jan. 18, 1914; s. Arthur Grannison and Clemma (Frock) B.; m. Anne Buckalew; 1 child, Gordon Alan. A.B., William Jewell Coll., 1935; M.D., Washington U., St. Louis, 1939. Diplomate: Am. Bd. Clin. Pathology, Am. Bd. Anatomic Pathology. Intern pathology Barnes Hosp., St. Louis, 1939-40; resident in pathology St. Louis City Hosp., 1940-41; instr. pathology Washington U., 1945-51; clin. assoc. prof. Baylor U. Coll. Medicine, Houston, 1951—; clin. prof. U. Tex. Med. Sch. at Houston, 1972—; Pathologist, dir. labs. Hermann Hosp., Houston, 1951-71, apptd. disting. physician, 1986; dir. labs. Twelve Oaks Hosp., Houston, 1965—, Polly Ryon Hosp., Richmond, Tex., 1954—, Park Plaza Hosp., Houston, 1975—, Bellville Hosp., Ft. Bend Hosp., Katy Community Hosp., Navasota Regional Hosp., Parkway Hosp., Sharpstown Hosp.; ptnr. Brown & Assocs. Med. Labs., Houston, 1954—; mem. Anderson Assocs., U. Tex.; mem. adv. bd. Living Bank, Houston, 1968—; mem. adv. bd. InterFirst Fannin-Bank, mem. devel. bd., 1987; founding mem., trustee Mus. Med. Sci., Houston, 1969—, pres. bd. trustees, 1974-75; bd. dirs. Ewing Ctr. Inc., Am. Cancer Soc. Harris County (Tex.) Br., 1952, pres, 1967-68. Contbr. articles to med. publs. Mem. William Greenleaf Elliott Soc. Washington U. Sch. Medicine. Served to maj. M.C. AUS, 1942-46, ETO, MTO. Decorated Bronze Star medal. Mem. Am., Tex. med. assns., Harris County Med. Soc., Coll. Am. Pathologists, Am. Soc. Clin. Pathology, Houston, Tex. socs. pathologists, Sigma Xi, Beta Beta Beta, Theta Chi Delta, Aeons, Phi Gamma Delta. Clubs: Warwick (Houston), Forum (Houston). Home: 3518 Westridge St Houston TX 77025 Office: 220 Park Plaza Profl Bldg Houston TX 77004

BROWNE, ALAN KINGSTON, bank consultant; b. Alameda, Calif., Nov. 12, 1909; s. Ralph Stuart and Etta E. (Bouve) B.; m. Elisabeth Leone Henrotte, Feb. 7, 1942. Student, U. Calif., 1929. With Bankamerica Co. (formerly securities div. Nat. Bank Italy Co.), 1929-41; successively clk., mgr. mcpl. bond dept., asst. v.p.; with Bank of Am. Nat. Trust & Savs. Assn., 1941-71, asst. cashier, 1941-42, asst., v.p., mgr. mcpl. bond dept., 1946-52, v.p., 1952-65, sr. v.p., 1965-71, head investments, 1964-71; cons. 1971-72; sr. v.p., dir. Drexel Firestone Inc., N.Y.C., 1972-73; dir. Drexel Burnham & Co., Inc., 1973; cons. 1974—; past pres., dir. San Francisco Stadium, Inc., Candlestick Park; trustee Calif. Muni Fund; mem. arbitration panel N.Y. Stock Exchange, Inc., Nat. Assn. Securities Dealers; dir., bd. dirs. 2d Walnut Creek Mutual, Rossmoor and Walnut Creek, Calif. Contbr. articles to profl. jours. Mem. San Francisco Mus. Art, The Museum Soc.; past chmn. bd., past pres. Friends of San Francisco Pub. Library; chmn. adv. bd. on financing San Francisco Bay Area Rapid Transit Dist.; chmn. San Francisco Bay Area Rapid Transit Commn.; bd. dirs. Adminstrv. Bldg. Corp.; past dir. Golden Rain Found., Rossmoor and Walnut Creek, Calif.; past mem. Presdl. Adv. Com. Fed. Debt Mgmt.; past bd. dirs. Calif. State Tchrs.' Retirement System. Served from pvt. to maj. AUS, 1942-46. Recipient Disting. Citizens award Nat. Mcpl. League, 1964; recipient Wheeler Oak award U. Calif.-Berkeley, 1984. Mem. San Francisco C. of C. (past pres.; chmn. sr. council), Mcpl. Fin. Forum Washington, San Francisco Mcpl. Forum, Air Force Assn., Calif. Alumni Assn., Calif. Geneal. Soc., Calif. Hist. Soc., Friends Bancroft Library, Investment Bankers Assn. Am. (now Securities Industry Assn.) (past gov., v.p. mcpl. div.), SAR, Navy League, Mechanics Inst., Am. Legion, Phi Kappa Sigma. Clubs: Bond (past pres., outstanding investment banker of yr. award 1958), Olympic (50-year Mem.), Merchants Exchange , Commonwealth, Municipal Bond, Engrs. (all San Francisco); Faculty (Berkeley). Lodge: Rotary. Home: 1113 Singingwood Ct 6 Walnut Creek CA 94595

BROWNE, JOSEPH PETER, librarian; b. Detroit, June 12, 1929; s. George and Mary Bridget (Fahy) B.; A.B., U. Notre Dame, 1951; S.T.L., Pontificium Athenaeum Angelicum, Rome, 1957, S.T.D., 1960; M.S. in L.S., Cath. U. Am., 1965. Joined Congregation of Holy Cross, Roman Cath. Ch., 1947, ordained priest, 1955; asst. pastor Holy Cross Ch., South Bend, Ind., 1955-56; librarian, prof. moral theology Holy Cross Coll., Washington, 1959-64; mem. faculty U. Portland (Oreg.), 1964-73, 75—, dir. library, 1966-70, 76—, dean Coll. Arts and Scis., 1970-73, asso. prof. library sci. 1967—, regent, 1969-70, 77-81, chmn. acad. senate, 1968-70, 1987-88; prof., head dept. library sci. Our Lady of Lake Coll., San Antonio, 1973-75; chmn. Interstate Library Planning Council, 1977-79. Mem. Columbia River chpt. Huntington's Disease Soc. Am., 1975—, pres., 1979-82. Recipient Culligan award U. Portland, 1979. Mem. Cath. Library Assn. (pres. 1971-73), ALA, Cath. Theol. Soc. Am., Pacific N.W. Library Assn. (pres. 1985-86), Oreg. Library Assn. (pres. 1967-68), Nat. Assn. Parliamentarians, Oreg. Assn. Parliamentarians (pres. 1985-87), Archdiocesan Hist. Commn. (pres. 1985—), Mensa Internat., All-Ireland Cultural Soc. Oreg. (pres. 1984-85). Democrat. Club: KC. Home: 5410 N Strong St Apt 8 Portland OR 97203 Office: U Portland 5000 N Willamette Blvd Portland OR 97203

BROWNE, RICHARD CULLEN, lawyer; b. Akron, Ohio, Nov. 21, 1938; s. Francis Cedric and Elizabeth Ann (Cullen) B.; m. Patricia Anne Winkler, Apr. 23, 1962; children—Richard Cullen, Catherine Anne, Paulette Elizabeth, Maureen Frances, Colleen Marie. B.S. in Econs., Holy Cross Coll., 1960; J.D. Catholic U. Am., 1963. Bar: Va. 1963, U.S. Ct. Claims 1963, U.S. Ct. Customs and Patent Appeals 1963, D.C. 1964, U.S. Ct. Mil. Appeals, 1963, U.S. Ct. Appeals (D.C. cir.) 1964, U.S. Supreme Ct. 1966, U.S. Ct. Appeals (fed. cir.) 1982, U.S. Ct. Appeals (9th cir.) 1983. Assoc. Browne, Beveridge, DeGrandi & Kline, Washington, 1963-68, ptnr., 1968-72; ptnr. Shaffert, Miller & Browne, Washington, 1972-74; sr. counsel Office of Enforcement, EPA, Washington, 1974-76; asst. chief hearing counsel U.S. Nuclear Regulatory Commn., Washington, 1976-78; sole practice, Washington, 1978-80; ptnr. Bishop, Cook, Purcell & Reynolds and predecessor firms, Washington, 1980—; lectr. U. R.I., 1975, Washburn U., 1978, Legal Inst., CSC, 1975-78, Hofstra U., 1987—. Del., Montgomery County Civic Fedn., 1970-74; chmn. Citizens Adv. Com. on Rockville Corridor, 1972-77; bd. dirs. Nat. Inst. for Urban Wildlife, 1988—; mem. Montgomery County Potomac River Basin Adv. Com., 1972-74. Served to capt. USAF, 1963-66. Named Disting. Mil. grad. Holy Cross Coll., 1960. Mem. ABA, Fed. Bar Assn., D.C. Bar Assn., Va. State Bar, Coll. Holy Cross Alumni Assn. (bd. dirs. 1971-78, alumni senate 1978—). Republican. Roman Catholic. Clubs: Holy Cross (pres. Washington 1968-69, 1973-74), Nat. Lawyers, Advt., Capitol Hill, Kenwood (Md.). Bd. editors Cath. U. Law Rev., 1962-63. Home: 7203 Old Stage Rd Rockville MD 20852 Office: 1400 L St NW Washington DC 20005

BROWNELL, EDWIN ROWLAND, banker; b. Tampa, Fla., Sept. 19, 1924; s. Clarence DeWolf and Helen Lucy (Hill) B.; m. Helen Marie Kegel, Jan. 22, 1948 (dec. Apr. 1967); 1 child, Nancy; m. Blanche Rosina Parisi, Dec. 26, 1967; children: Elizabeth, Elaine, Evelyn. BCE, U. Fla., 1947. Registered profl. surveyor, Fla., Ark., Ga., Miss., Nev., N.D., S.D., S.C., Tenn., W.Va. Cadastral engr. City of Miami, Fla., 1948-53; pres., real estate salesman E.R. Brownell & Assocs., Inc., Miami, 1953—; pres., chief exec. officer, chmn. Brickellbanc Savs. Assn., Miami, 1985—, also bd. dirs.; chmn. surveying adv. com. U. Fla., Gainesville, 1974—; mem. degree accrediation team Nat. Council Engring. Examiners, S.C., 1985—; chmn. engring. adv. com. Fla. State Bd. Regents, Tallahassee, 1982-85. Elected county surveyor State of Fla., Dade County, 1956-60; chmn. Zoning Bd. Adjustment, Coral Gables, Fla., 1978-87; vice chmn. Coral Gables Planning and Zoning Bd., 1987—; bd. dirs. Boys Club of Miami, 1980-83; mem. Com. of 100, Miami, Fla. Fellow Am. Congress Surveying and Mapping (pres. 1980-81, Surveying Excellence award 1977), NSPE (pres. 1978-79), Fla. Soc. Profl. Surveyors (hon., Fla. Land Surveyor of Yr. 1973, pres. 1978-79), Dade County Chpt. Fla. Soc. Profl. Surveyors (pres. 1965-69); mem. Am. Soc. Photogrammetry (Presdl. citation 1982), Am. Soc. Photogrammetry Found. (vice chmn. 1985-87), Am. Mil. Engrs., Am. Planning Assn., Miami Bd. Realtors, Fla. Planning and Zoning Assn. (S. Fla. chpt.), Fla. Assn. Cadastral Mappers, Bus. Inc., Sierra Club (pres. 1977), NSF, Com. of 100, Bus. Inc., Lambda Alpha Internat., Kappa Alpha. Republican. Roman Catholic. Clubs: Coral Gables Country, Riviera Country (Coral Gables); Holly Hills Country (Sapphire, N.C.). Lodges: KC, Kiwanis. Home: 1207 Sorolla Ave Coral Gables FL 33134 Office: E R Brownell & Assocs Inc 3152 Coral Way Miami FL 33145

BROWNE-RIBEIRO-FILHO, HENRIQUE, mathematician, software consultant; b. Recife, Brazil, Sept. 24, 1948; m. Valeria Tedeschi; children—Gustavo Browne-Ribeiro, Anna Tedeschi Browne-Ribeiro. B.Sc., Pontificia Universidade Catolica, Rio de Janeiro, Brazil, 1970, M.Sc., 1971; Ph.D., MIT, 1977. Instr., Pontificia Universidade Catolica, Rio de Janeiro, 1970-71, asst. prof., 1977—; teaching asst. MIT, Cambridge, Mass., 1971-75. Author: Fibrados Conexoes e Geometria, 1982. Home: Est Barra da Tijuca, 1006/204-PH, 22641 Rio de Janeiro Brazil Office: Pontificia Universidade Catolica, Marq Sao Vicente 225, 22453 Rio de Janeiro Brazil

BROWNING, JESSE HARRISON, entrepreneur; b. Kingsville, Mo., July 27, 1935; s. Jesse Harrison and Anna Love (Swank) B.; m. Vicki Carol Thompson, Dec. 21, 1957; children: Caroline Kaye, Marcia Lynn, Nanci Ann, Susan Louise. Student, U. Wash., 1955-61, U. So. Calif., 1987—. Cert. mfg. engr. Field engr. The Boeing Co., Los Angeles, 1961-64; gen. mgr. SPI, Los Angeles, 1964-70; chmn. Browning Inc., Los Angeles, 1970—, Indsl. Systems, Los Angeles, 1979-87, Vapor Engring., Los Angeles, 1979-87. Patentee in field. Mem. Palos Verdes Breakfast Club, Los Angeles C. of C., Am. Helicopter Soc., Am. Electroplaters Soc., Soc. Mfg. Engrs. Lutheran. Home and Office: 4217 Via Pinzon Palos Verdes Estates CA 90274

BROWNING, PETER CRANE, packaging company executive; b. Boston, Sept. 2, 1941; s. Ralph Leslie and Nancy (Crane) B.; m. Carole Ann Shegog, Dec. 14, 1963 (div. 1974); children: Christina, Jennifer; m. Kathryn Ann Klucharich, July 27, 1974; children: Kimberly, Peter. AB in History, Colgate U., 1963; MBA, U. Chgo., 1976. Salesman, mktg. rep. White Cap div. Continental Can, Northbrook, Ill., 1964-75; mgr. mktg. Conally Venture div. Continental Can, 1975-79; gen. mktg. and sales mgr. Bondware div. Continental Can, 1979-81, v.p., gen. mgr., 1981-84; v.p. gen. mgr. White Cap. div. Continental Can, 1984-86, exec. v.p., operating officer, 1986—; bd. dirs. Conn. Chemical Ltd., Toronto, Can. Bd. dirs. Keep Am. Beautiful. Mem. Am. Mktg. Assn., Norwalk C. of C. Republican. Episcopalian. Clubs: Meadow (Rolling Meadows, Ill.), Carlton (Chgo.), Field (New Canaan, Conn.). Home: 11 Silver Ridge Rd New Canaan CT 06840 Office: Continental Can Co Inc 800 Connecticut Ave Norwalk CT 06856

BROWNLEE, DENIS NORMAN, geologist; b. Belfast, No. Ireland, May 18, 1947; came to U.S., 1983; s. Thomas Norman and Jeanetta (McKay) B.; m. Pamela Joan McCormick, Mar. 31, 1975; children: Denby, Joanna, Robert, Samantha. BSc with honors, Queens U. (Belfast), 1970; MSc, Imperial Coll. (London), 1971, DIC (hon.), 1971. Geologist, Burmah Oil Co./Anglo Ecuadorian Oil Fields Ltd., London and Quito, Ecuador, 1971-73; geologist Cities Service Oil Co., London, 1973-75, Jakarta, Indonesia, 1975-77, London, 1977-78, chief geologist, Manila, Philippines, 1978-83; area geologist Occidental Exploration and Prodn. Co., Bakersfield, Calif., 1983-84, spl. projects geologist, 1984-86, chief geologist Mid. East Petroleum Adv. Group, Oxford, Eng., 1986-87, Tullow Oil Plc, Dublin, Ireland, 1987—. Contbr. articles to profl. jours. Pres., St. Patrick's Soc., Manila, 1982-83. Fellow Geol. Soc. London; mem. Am. Assn. Petroleum Geologists. Methodist. Club: Old Wesley RFC (Dublin), Nomad Sports (sec. 1979-80, Manila).

BROWNLEE, THOMAS MARSHALL, lighting manufacturing company executive; b. Omaha, Oct. 11, 1926; s. John Templeton and Reed (Marshall) B.; m. Olive Ann Gettman, Sept. 13, 1950; children: Linda Sue, Thomas John, Curtis Marshall, Reed Ann. B.S. in Bus. Adminstrn, U. Nebr., 1950. Asst. mgr. Daytona Beach (Fla.) C. of C., 1950, Tampa (Fla.) C. of C., 1952-53; exec. mgr. Tallahassee C. of C., 1953- 58; exec. v.p. Greater Columbia (S.C.) C. of C., 1959-63, Winston-Salem (N.C.) C. of C., 1963-64, Orlando Area (Fla.) C. of C., 1964-78; pres. Brownlee Lighting Co., Orlando, 1978—; mem. energy policy com. Orange County (Fla.) Schs.; mem. Fla. Energy Action Com.; mem. energy com. Nat. League Cities. Contbr. articles to profl. jours. Bd. dirs. Loch Haven Art Mus.; bd. dirs. Chamber Inst., U. Ga.; mem. Orlando City Council.; pres. Christian Service Ctrs. Daily Bread. Served with USNR, 1944-46; as 1st lt. AUS, 1951-52. Mem. Fla. Energy mgmt. Assn. (pres.), Illuminating Engring. Soc. (pres. Cen. Fla. chpt.), Am. C. of C. Execs. Assn. (pres. 1966); Mem. (v.p., treas. So. Assn.), S.C. C. of C. Execs. Assn., Fla. C. of C. Execs Assn. (pres. 1971), Better Bus. Bur. Cen. Fla. (chmn.), Phi Delta Theta. Presbyterian (deacon). Clubs: Rotarian, Country of Orlando, University, Citrus. Office: Brownlee Lighting Co 2634 Taft Ave Orlando FL 32804

BROWNLIE, IAN, barrister, educator; b. Sept. 19, 1932; s. John Nason and Amy Isabella (Atherton) B.; B.A. (Gibbs scholar), Oxford (Eng.) U., 1953; postgrad. (Humanitarian Trust student) Cambridge (Eng.) U., 1955; D.Phil., Oxford U., 1961, D.C.L., 1976; m. Jocelyn Gale, 1957; 1 son, 2 daus.; m. 2d, Christine Apperley, 1978. Called to bar Gray's Inn, 1958, apptd. Queen's counsel, 1979; lectr. Nottingham (Eng.) U., 1957-63; fellow and tutor in law Wadham Coll., Oxford U., 1963-76, lectr., 1964-76; prof. internat. law U. London, 1976-80; Chichele prof. pub. internat. law U. Oxford, 1980—; fellow All Souls Coll., Oxford, 1980—; dir. studies Internat. Law Assn., 1982—; reader public internat. law Inns of Ct. Sch. Law, 1973-76; vis. prof. U. East Africa, 1968-69, U. Ghana, 1972, U. Florence (Italy), 1977; lectr. Hague (Netherlands) Acad. Internat. Law, 1979. Recipient Japan Found. award, 1978. Fellow Brit. Acad.; mem. Inst. Internat. Law. Author: International Law and the Use of Force by States, 1963; Principles of Public International Law (cert. of Merit, Am. Soc. Internat. Law 1976), 1966, 2d edit., 1973; Russian edit., 1977, 3d edit., 1979; The Law Relating to Public Order, 1968; Basic Documents on Human Rights, 1971, 2d edit., 1980; Basic Documents on African Affairs, 1971; African Boundaries, a legal and diplomatic encyclopedia, 1979; State Responsibility, Part I, 1983. Editor Brit. Year Book Internat. Law, 1974—. Office: All Souls Coll, Oxford OX1 4AL, England also: 2 Hare Ct Temple, London EC4Y 7BH, England

BROWNSTEIN, MARTIN HERBERT, dermatopathologist, educator; b. N.Y.C., Aug. 20, 1935; s. Samuel C. and Florence (Sturm) B.; m. Ann Lehman, June 23, 1964; children: Sara Leah, Michael Ari. A.B., Harvard U., 1956; M.D., Albert Einstein Coll. Medicine, 1961. Intern Lenox Hill Hosp., N.Y.C., 1961-62; resident in internal medicine VA Hosps., N.Y.C., 1962-65; resident in dermatology NYU, N.Y.C., 1965-66; practice medicine specializing in dermatopathology N.Y.C., 1970-72, Great Neck, N.Y., 1972-84, Port Washington, N.Y., 1984—; Osborne fellow Armed Forces Inst. Pathology, Washington, 1968-69; asst. clin. prof. dermatology N.Y. Med. Coll., N.Y.C., 1970-73, clin. assoc. prof. dermatology, 1973-78, clin. prof. dermatology, 1978-83, clin. asst. prof. pathology, 1971-83; clin. prof. dermatology Mt. Sinai Med. Ctr., N.Y.C., 1983—. Chief editor Jour. Cutaneous Pathology, 1984; contbr. articles to profl. jours. Trustee North Shore Hebrew Acad., Great Neck, N.Y., 1979-80; hon. trustee Great Neck Synagogue, 1986—. Served with M.C. U.S. Army, 1966-68. Recipient Pres.'s award Union Orthodox Jewish Congregations of Am., 1983. Mem. Am. Soc. Dermatopathology (pres. 1983-84), Soc. Investigative Dermatology, N.Y. State Soc. Dermatology, Am. Acad. Dermatology (chmn. com. on pathology 1980-82), Internat. Soc. Tropical Dermatology, Med. Soc. N.Y. State, Med. Soc. N.Y. County, AMA, ACP, Dermatol. Soc. Greater N.Y. (pres. 1978-79), L.I. Dermatology Soc. (treas. 1986—), N.Y. Acad. Medicine. Home: 2 N Plandome Rd Port Washington NY 11050 Office: 2 N Plandome Rd Port Washington NY 11050

BROYER, MICHEL JEAN-CLAUDE, pediatrics educator; b. Paris, Apr. 30, 1933; s. Franck Andre and Nina Marie (Lureau) B.; m. Rosy G. Cabanes; children: Murielle, Frederic, Delphine. Licence Scis., Sci. Faculty, Paris, 1961; MD, Medicine Faculty, Paris, 1965. Intern Paris Hosp. System, 1959-65; resident in pediatrics Necker Enfants Malades Hosp., Paris, 1966-71, assoc. prof. pediatrics, 1971-78, prof., dir. pediatrics-nephrology dept., 1978—. Contbr. articles to profl. jours. Mem. European Dialysis and Transplant Assn. (registry com. 1981-88), French Soc. for Pediatric Nephrology, Paris Kidney Transplant Assn. Office: Hopital Necker Enfants Malades, 149 Rue de Sevres, 75015 Paris France

BROYHILL, ROY FRANKLIN, manufacturing executive; b. Sioux City, Iowa, June 20, 1919; s. George Franklin and Effie (Motes) B.; B.B.A., U. Nebr., 1940; m. Arline W. Stewart, Jan. 30, 1943; children—Lynn Diann (dec.), Craig G., Kent Bryan, Bryce Alan. Trainee mgr. Montgomery Ward Co., 1940; semi-sr. acct. L. H. Keightley, 1941-42; chief accountant Army Exchange Service, Sioux City, 1942-46; pres. Broyhill Co., 1946-86, chmn., 1946—; pres., dir. Star Printing & Pub. Co., South Sioux City, 1949—; pres. Broyhill Corp., 1953-86, chmn., 1953—; v.p. Broyhill Mfg. Co., 1978-87, pres., 1987—; pres., chmn. bd. Broyhill Inc.; dir. 1st Nat. Bank, Sioux City. Mem. U.S.A. Exec. Res.; mem. Nebr. dist. adv. council SBA, 1971—. Mayor of Dakota City, 1951-53; mem. Nebr. Republican Central Com., 1954-56. Past mem. local sch. bd. Trustee U. Nebr., U. Nebr. Found. Served with AUS, 1940-41. Mem. Nitrogen Solutions Assn. (dir. 1956-60), Farm Equipment Mfrs. Assn. (dir., pres. 1971-72), Atokad Racing Assn. (past dir.), N.A.M., U.S., South Sioux City chambers commerce, Nebr. Assn. Commerce and Industry (dir. 1972-73), Alumni Assn. U. Nebr. (past dir.), Am. Legion (life), Beta Theta Pi, Alpha Kappa Psi. Presbyn. (elder). Club: U. Nebr. Chancellor's. Lodges: Masons (Shrine), Kiwanis. Home: 1610 Broadway Dakota City NE 68731 also (winters): 2185 Ibis Isle Rd Palm Beach FL 33480 Office: Broyhill Co N Market Sq Dakota City NE 68731

BROZOVIC, DALIBOR, educator; b. Sarajevo, Yugoslavia, July 28, 1927; s. Andrija and Olga (Čabrajic) B.; m. Nevenka Košutic, Nov. 26, 1952; children: Lada, Dunja, Hrvoje. BA, U. Zagreb, Yugoslavia, 1951, Dr. Sc., 1957. Teaching asst. Acad. Theater Art, Zagreb, 1952-53; lectr. Slavic U. Ljubljana, Yugoslavia, 1953-56; teaching asst. Slavic dept. U. Zadar, Yugoslavia, 1956-58, asst. prof., 1958-62, assoc. prof., 1962-67, prof., 1967—; vis. prof. U. Mich, Ann Arbor, 1969, U. Regensburg, Fed. Republic Germany, 1971; guest Chinese Acad. Scis., 1979, Govt. Austria, Vienna U., 1982, Govt. Norway, U. Oslo, 1982. Author: Standardni jezik, 1970, Rječnik jezika ili jezik rječnika, 1969; mem. editorial bd. All Slavic Linguistic Atlas, 1964—, Atlas Linguarum Europae, 1982—; contbr. 300 sci. studies to internat. jours. Mem. Yugoslav Acad. Scis. Arts, Macedonian Acad. Scis. Arts, Matica Hrvatska, Matica Srpska. Roman Catholic. Home: Marka Oreskovica 2, 57000 Zadar Croatia Yugoslavia Office: Filozofski fakultet, Titova obala 2, 57000 Zadar Dalmatia Yugoslavia

BRUBAKER, KAREN SUE, tire manufacturing company executive; b. Ashland, Ohio, Feb. 5, 1953; d. Robert Eugene and Dora Louise (Camp) B. BSBA, Ashland Coll., 1975; MBA, Bowling Green State U., 1976. Supr. tire ctr. ops. B.F. Goodrich Co., Akron, Ohio, 1976-77, supr. tire ctr. acctg., 1977-79, asst. product mgr. radial passenger tires, 1979-80, product mgr. broadline passenger tires, 1980-81, group product mgr. broadline passenger and light truck tires, 1981-83, mktg. mgr. T/A high tech radials, 1983-86; product mgr. B.F. Goodrich T/A radials, The Uniroyal Goodrich Tire Co., Akron, 1986—. Sect. chmn. indsl. div. United Way, Akron, 1983-86. Recipient Alumni Disting. Service award Ashland Coll., 1986; Alpha Phi Clara Bradley Burdette scholar, 1975. Mem. Am. Mktg. Assn. (pres. Akron/Canton chpt. 1982-83, Highest Honors award 1983, v.p.-elect bus. mktg., elected to nat. bd. dirs. 1984-86, v.p. profl. chpts., 1987—), Susan B. Anthony Soc. of Akron Women's Network, Nat. Assn. Female Execs., Beta Gamma Sigma, Omicron Delta Epsilon. Lodge: Zonta. Home: 1862 Indian Hills Trail Akron OH 44313 Office: The Uniroyal Goodrich Tire Co 600 S Main St Akron OH 44397-0001

BRUBECK, ANNE ELIZABETH DENTON, artist; b. Beardstown, Ill., Mar. 5, 1918; d. Harry B. and Helen Jean (Gibbs) Denton; student Christian Coll., 1935-36; B.Design, Newcomb Coll., Tulane U., 1939; postgrad. Art Inst. Chgo., 1939-40; A.A. (hon.), Wabash Valley Coll., 1981; m. William E. Brubeck, Dec. 14, 1940; children—Jean Brubeck Stayman, William E. Instr. painting Wabash Valley Coll., Mt. Carmel, Ill., 1962-67; painter; one-man shows include N.Y.C., 1961, 63-67, Evansville, Ind., 1963-69; retrospective, Wabash Valley Coll., 1980; juried exhbns. include: Evansville Mus., 1963, 64, 65, Swopes Gallery, Terre Haute, Ind., 1964, 68, Nashville, 1967. Trustee, Mt. Carmel Pub. Library, 1954—, chmn., 1975-6; mem. cultural events com. Wabash Valley Coll., 1976-80. Brubeck Art Center named in her and her husband's honor, 1976; named to Mt. Carmel High Sch. Centennial Hall of Fame, 1982. Mem. Ill. Library Assn., Nat. League Am. Penwomen, PEO. Methodist. Club: Reviewers Matinee. Home and Office: 729 Cherry St Mount Carmel IL 62863

BRUBECK, DAVID WARREN, musician; b. Concord, Calif., Dec. 6, 1920; s. Howard and Elizabeth (Ivey) B.; m. Iola Whitlock, Sept. 21, 1942; children: David Darius, Michael, Christopher, Catherine, Daniel, Matthew. BA, U. Pacific, 1942; PhD (hon.), U. Pacific, Fairfield U.; Ph.D. (hon.), U. Bridgeport; postgrad., Mills Coll., 1946-49, Ph.D. hon. Formed trio, 1950; bookings throughout U.S. in jazz nightclubs; formed Dave Brubeck Quartet, 1951, concert tours, U.S. Colls., festivals, etc., 1958—, 3 month tour, Europe and Middle East for U.S. State Dept., many tours, Europe and S. Am., Australia and Japan, European tour as soloist with Cin. Symphony, 1969; affiliated with, Atlantic Record Co., Columbia Record Co., Decca, Horizon, Concord Jazz, Fantasy Records; Composer: (oratorios) Beloved Son, The Light in the Wilderness; (cantatas) La Fiesta de la Posada, Gates of Justice, Truth; (orchestral) They All Sang Yankee Doodle, Elementals; (ballets) Points on Jazz and Glances, Tritonis (for flute and guitar), Festival Mass to Hope, chorus with soloists; (chorus and orch.) Pange Lingua; (oratorio) The Voice of the Holy Spirit, (chorus) Four New England Pieces, (chorus and orch.) Lenten Triptych, and over 100 jazz compositions. Recipient first place in popularity poll, 1953-55, 1st place in critics poll, Downbeat mag., 1953, winner jazz polls conducted by Downbeat, Melody Maker, Cashbox, Billboard, Playboy mags., 1962, Compostela Humanitarian award, 1986, State of Conn. Arts award, 1987; named Editor's Choice, Metronome mag., 1952, one of Calif.'s 5 outstanding young men, 1957; Duke Ellington fellow Yale U. Fellow Internat. Inst. Arts and Scis; mem. Broadcast Music, Inc. (Jazz Pioneer award 1985), Phi Mu Alpha. Office: Derry Music Co 601 Montgomery St San Francisco CA 94111 also: care Sutton Artists Corp 119 W 57th St New York NY 10019 •

BRUCE, CLEMONT HUGHES, geologist, consultant; b. Central City, Ky., Sept. 5, 1921; s. Ezra Clemont and Nancy (Woodson) B.; m. Bettie J. Kemp, June 11, 1949; children—Lynette, Byron. B.S., U. Ky., 1948, M.S., 1949. Exploration and prodn. geologist Mobil Oil Corp., Mount Vernon, Ill., 1949-53, regional and exploration geologist, Dallas and Jackson, Miss., 1953-65, geol. specialist Gulf Coast, Corpus Christi, Tex., 1965-72, staff geologist Alaska and Gulf Coast, Denver, Houston, 1972-76, spl. projects and research geologist, Dallas, 1976-84, ret., 1984; cons. geology, Carrollton, Tex., 1985—. Contbr. articles to profl. jours. Served to sgt. USAAF, 1942-45, ETO. Mem. Am. Assn. Petroleum Geologists (disting. lectr. 1973-74, v.p. exec. com. 1985-86, George C. Matson award 1983), Geol. Soc. Am., Dallas Geol. Soc., Houston Geol. Soc., Geol. Soc. Ky., Rocky Mountain Assn. Geologists, Pacific Sect. Am. Assn. Petroleum Geologists. Sigma Xi, Sigma Gamma Epsilon.

BRUCE, THOMAS ALLEN, physician, philanthropic administrator; b. Mountain Home, Ark., Dec. 22, 1930; s. Rex Floyd and Dora Madeline (Fee) B.; m. Dolores Fay Montgomery, May 28, 1960; children: T.K. Montgomery, Dana Fee. B.S.M., M.D., U. Ark., 1955. Intern Duke Hosp., 1956-57; resident medicine Bellevue Hosp., N.Y.C., 1957, Meml. Center Cancer and Allied Diseases, N.Y.C., 1958, Parkland Meml. Hosp., Dallas, 1958-59; cardiopulmonary trainee Southwestern Med. Sch. of U. Tex., 1959-60; cardiac research fellow Hammersmith Hosp. and U. London Postgrad. Med. Sch., London, 1960-61, Harvard Bus. Sch., 1974; from instr. to prof. medicine Wayne State U., 1961-68, also asst. dean Sch. of Medicine; prof. medicine, head cardiovascular sect. U. Okla. Med. Center, 1968-74; prof. medicine, dean Coll. Medicine, U. Ark. Med. Scis., 1974-85; med. dir. Barton Research Inst., 1974-85; coordinator Sino-Am. Med. Exchange Program, 1979-85; mem. ednl. adv. com. Nat. Fund Med. Edn., 1982-85; mem. research support rev. com. NIH, 1983-85; program dir. in health W.K. Kellogg Found., U.S., Latin Am., So. Africa, 1985—. Bd. dirs. Grantmakers in Health. Recipient Ark. Gov.'s Meritorious Achievement award. Fellow A.C.P., Am. Coll. Cardiology; mem. Assn. Univ. Cardiologists, Central Soc. Clin. Research, Soc. for Human Values in Medicine, Am. Pub. Health Assn., Mich. State Med. Soc., Nat. Rural Health Assn. (nat. cabinet 1978-82), Battle Creek His. Soc., Ark. Caduceus Club, Leila Arboretum Soc. (bd. dirs.), Sigma Xi, Alpha Omega Alpha. Home: 621 Jennings Ln Battle Creek MI 49015 Office: 400 North Ave Battle Creek MI 49017

BRUCH, REINHARD FRANK, physics educator; b. Berlin, Nov. 28, 1941; came to U.S., 1984; s. Walter Heinz and Ruth Hildegard (Jeskulke) B.; m. Karin Siglinde Falge, Aug. 1, 1980 (div. Dec. 1983); one child, Jan Frederik. Vordiplom, Technische U., Hanover, Fed. Republic Germany, 1966, Diplom, 1970; Dr. Rer. Nat., Freie U., West Berlin, 1976. Lectr. Medizinische Hochschule, Hanover, 1969-70; research assoc. Freie U., West Berlin, 1970-76; research scientist Arhus (Denmark) U., 1976-77; group leader U. Freiburg, Fed. Republic Germany, 1978-83; assoc. prof. physics U. Nev., Reno, 1984—; research scientist Argonne (Ill.) Nat. Lab., 1982. Contbr. articles to profl. jours. Grantee Deutsche Forschungs Gemeinschaft, 1970-83, Land Baden-Württenberg Wissenschaftliche Gesellschaft, 1978-83, Research Corp., 1986, NSF 1987, Industry, 1987. Mem. Am. Phys. Soc., Deutsche Physikalische Gesellschaft, Sigma Xi, Sigma Pi Sigma. Lutheran. Home: 685 College Dr Reno NV 89503 Office: U Nev-Reno Dept Physics Reno NV 89557

BRUESCHKE, ERICH EDWARD, physician, researcher, educator; b. nr. Eagle Butte, S.D., July 17, 1933; s. Erich Herman and Eva Johanna (Joens) B.; m. Frances Marie Bryan, Mar. 25, 1967; children: Erich Raymond, Jason Douglas, Tina Marie, Patricia Frances, Susan Eva. B.S. in Elec. Engring, S.D. Sch. Mines and Tech., 1956; postgrad., U. So. Calif., 1960-61; M.D., Temple U., 1965. Diplomate Am. Bd. Family Practice, also recert. Intern Germantown Dispensary and Hosp., Phila., 1965-66; mem. tech. staff Hughes Research and Devel. Labs., Culver City, Calif., 1956-61; practiced gen. medicine Fullerton, Calif., 1968-69; dir. research Ill. Inst. Tech. Research Inst., Chgo., 1970-76; research asst. prof. Temple U. Sch. Medicine, 1965-69; mem. staff Mercy Hosp. and Med. Center, Chgo., 1970-76; vis. prof. Rush Med. Coll., Chgo., 1974-76; prof., chmn. dept. family practice Rush Med. Coll., 1976—, program dir. Rush. Christ family practice residency, 1978—; trustee Anchor HMO, 1976—, v.p. med. and acad. affairs, 1981—; sr. attending Presbyn.-St. Luke's Hosp., Chgo., 1976—; med. dir. Chgo. Bd. of Health West Side Hypertension Center, 1974-78; Bd. dirs. Comprehensive Health Planning Met. Chgo., 1971-74. Assoc. editor: The Female Patient, 1979—; asso. editor: Primary Cardiology, 1979—; cons. editor for family practice Hosp. Medicine, 1986—; contbr. articles to profl. jours. Served with USAF, 1966-68. Named Physician Tchr. of Yr. Ill. Acad. Family Physicians, 1988. Fellow Am. Acad. Family Physicians, Inst. of Medicine of Chgo.; mem. IEEE (chmn. Chgo. sect. Engring. in Medicine and Biology group 1974-75), Am. Fertility Soc., Am. Occupational Med. Assn. (recipient Physician's recognition award 1969, 72, 75), Chgo. Med. Soc., Am. Heart Assn., Assn. for Advancement Med. Instrumentation, N.Y. Acad. Scis., Sigma Xi, Phi Rho Sigma, Eta Kappa Nu. Home: 314 N Lincoln St Hinsdale IL 60521 Office: Rush-Presbyn St Luke's Med Center W Congress Pkwy Chicago IL 60612

BRUHN, ARNOLD RAHN, JR., clinical psychologist, personality theorist; b. Bklyn., Dec. 30, 1941; s. Arnold Rahn and Paula Bruhn; m. Arlene Corinne Palmer, June 23, 1967 (div. Dec. 1986); children—Alexis Pamela, Erika Kerstin. Asst. prof. psychology George Washington U., 1976-82; asst. research prof. psychiatry and behavioral scis. George Washington Med. Center, 1980-83; staff psychologist Alexandria Community Mental Health Center (Va.), 1977-85, Woodmont Psychiat. Assocs., Bethesda, Md., 1982-86; Arnold R. Bruhn Assocs., 1986—. Fellow Soc. Personality Assessment; mem. Am. Psychol. Assn. USPHS fellow, 1972-76. Contbr. research and theoretical papers on personality and earliest childhood memories to profl. jours. Home: 4704 Hunt Ave Chevy Chase MD 20815 Office: Arnold R Bruhn & Assocs 7910 Woodmont Ave #1300 Bethesda MD 20814

BRUHN, HANS-JUERGEN, auditor, consultant; b. Hamburg, Federal Republic Germany, Jan. 13, 1940; s. Hans Friedrich and Herta Catherina (Iden) B.; m. Ursula Leu, May 12, 1967; children: Urte, Anke, Silke. Inspector Fed. Post-Telephone-Telecommunication Adminstrn., Hamburg, 1960-68; group leader EDP Post-Telephone-Telecommunications Research Plant, Darmstadt, Fed. Republic Germany, 1968-71; audit officer EDP Fed. Audit Office, Frankfurt, Fed. Republic Germany, 1971-81; sr. audit officer Fed. Audit Office, Frankfurt, Fed. Republic Germany, 1986—; project mgr. Ministry of Fin., Ankara, Turkey, 1981-85; chief cons. Hendrikson Associated Cons., Eschborn, Fed. Republic Germany, 1981-85. Author: Engagement of Computer Capacity in Terms of Commercial Efficiency, 1973, Audit Aspects in the Utilization of EDP, 1974, Manual of EDP Audit, 1975. Pres. German Folk Music Soc., Wehrheim, 1976. Grantee Minister Posts and Telecommunications, Bonn, 1969. Mem. Verband der Beamten der Obersten Bundesbehörden EV im Deutschen Beamtenbund. Lutheran. Home: Steinweg 8, D-6393 Wehrheim 3 Federal Republic of Germany Office: Bundesrechnungshof, Berliner Strasse 51, D-6000 Frankfurt Federal Republic of Germany

BRULEY, DUANE FREDERICK, academician, engineering consultant, tennis professional instructor; b. Chippewa Falls, Wis., Aug. 3, 1933; s. Casper Sepharald and Hazel Ella (Kuehn) B.; m. Suzanne Bigler, June 14, 1959; children: Scott, Randall, Mark. Student, Eau Clare (Wis.) State U., 1951-53; BS in Chem. Engring., U. Wis., 1956; student, Oak Ridge (Tenn.) Sch. of Reactor Tech., 1957; M in Mech. Engring., Stanford U., 1959; PhD in Chem. Engring., U. Tenn., 1962. Registered profl. engr., S.C. Nuclear engr. Union Carbide Nuclear Co., Oak Ridge, Tenn., 1956-59; prof. chem. engring., head tennis coach Clemson (S.C.) U., 1962-73; head chem. engring., head tennis coach Tulane U., New Orleans, 1973-77; head tennis profl. Timberlane Country Club, Gretna, La., 1973-76; v.p. acad. affairs, asst. tennis coach Rose Hulman Inst. Tech., Terre Haute, Ind., 1977-81; head biomed. engring., dir. rehab. engring. ctr. La. Tech. U., Ruston, 1981-84; dean sch. of engring. Cal Poly U., San Luis Obispo, 1984-87; program dir. Biochem. and Bus. Engring. NSF, Washington, 1987—; pres. Synthesizer, Inc., 1988—; vis. prof. Princeton (N.J.) U., fall 1970, U. Yamagata (Japan), U. Hokkaido, summer 1975; cons. Wesvaco, Charleston, S.C., 1964-67, DuPont, Ponchartrain, La., 1974-79, Am. Enka Corp, 1970-71, Milliken and Co., 1978-79, Exxon, Baton Rouge, La., 1978-79, El Paso Products Co., 1980-82, Electronics Assocs., Inc., Long Branch, N.J., 1984—. Author: (chpt.) Mathematics of Microcirculation, 1980; editor: Oxygen Supply, 1973, Oxygen Transport to Tissue, 1973, 83, 88, Hyperthermia, 1982. Narrator five part TV series on Biomed. Engring., 1982, TV Biomed. Engring. Sta. WEAU, Eau Clare, Wis., 1982; keynote speaker First Cray Acad.; recorded for Wis. Pub. TV Network Biotechnology/Bioengineering. Mem. Interna. Soc. on Oxygen Transport to Tissue (co-founder 1973, pres. 1983), Am. Inst. Chem. Engrs., Calif. Soc. of Profl. Engrs., Soc. Automotive Engrs. (Ralph R. Teetor Ednl. award 1986), NSPE, Am. Soc. of Engring. Edn. (1st Pl. Research award 1967), La. Engring. Soc. (Charles M. Kerr Pub. Relations award 1983). Home: 5904 Mount Eagle Dr #1509 Alexandria VA 22303 Office: NSF 1800 G St NW CBTE/BBE Room 1126 Washington DC 20550

BRUMAGIM, DUANE T., civil engineer; b. Terra Bella, Calif., Sept. 4, 1914; s. Joseph A. and Lolita L. (Couch) B.; B.C.E., Syracuse (N.Y.) U., 1952; m. Bette Romans, July 5, 1949; children—Marcia, William, Mark. Area engr. duPont Co., Aiken, S.C., 1952; project mgr. Caltex Co., Bahrain, Australia and N.Y.C., 1953, A.M. Kinney, Inc., Cin., 1964-75; project engr. Pandullo, Quirk Assos., Wayne, N.J., 1975-77; chief project engr. Apollo Chem. Corp., Whippany, N.J., 1977-83; supervising engr. Essex County Dept. Pub. Works, 1983—; chmn. bd. Brumagim & Assos., Assocs., 1971-75. Served to capt. C.E., AUS, 1943-47. Registered profl. engr., N.J., 8 other states. Mem. Nat. Soc. Profl. Engrs., N.J. Soc. Profl. Engrs., Order Ky. Cols. Republican. Lutheran. Club: Odd Fellows. Home: B10 A10 151 Route 206 Flanders NJ 07836 Office: 900 Bloomfield Ave Verona NJ 07044

BRUMIT, LAWRENCE EDWARD, III, oil field service company executive; b. Brunswick, Ga., Feb. 5, 1950; s. Lawrence Edward Jr. and Felicite (Smith) B.; m. Leila Ann Parker, Feb. 21, 1976; 1 child, Mary Louise. BS in Petroleum Engring., Mont. Tech., 1974. Field engr. Dowell, Farmington, N. Mex., 1974; service engr. Dowell Schlumberger, Warri, Nigeria, 1975, mgr., Cork, Ireland, 1976, tech. engr., Galeota, Trinidad, 1977, mgr., San Fernando, Trinidad, 1978-79, tng. ctr. mgr., Pau, France, 1980, div. mgr. S.W. Africa, Luanda, Angola, 1981-82, tech. mktg. mgr., Paris, 1983-84, v.p. region mgr., Paris, 1984-86, pres. compagnie de services, 1985—, mgr., v.p. Europe Africa, 1986-88; dir. personnel Schlumberger Ltd. Drilling and Pumping Services, Paris, 1988—. Recipient All Conf. Baseball Outstanding Coll. Athlete of Am. award Frontier Conf., 1969-71, 72, No. 1 Player and Capt. award, 1971. Mem. Soc. Petroleum Engrs. Episcopalian. Avocations: flying; golf. Home: 44 rue de Vinde, Pavilion 11, 78170 Lacelle Saint-Cloud France Office: Schlumberger Ltd, 42 rue St-Dominique, 75007 Paris France

BRUMMEL, STEVEN WILLIAM, foundation administrator; b. Los Angeles, Feb. 17, 1946; s. Henry William and Claudia (Borja) B.; m. Shari Marie Reville; children: Michael, Christopher, John William; stepson Netha Olive (Barlow) B.; BA in Govt. and Journalism with honors, Calif. State U., Sacramento, 1972, MA in Govt., 1975. Newsman, Sta. KNTV-TV, San Jose, Calif., 1969-71, Sta. KCRA-TV, Sacramento, 1971-73; cons. Calif. Assembly, 1973; dist. rep. U.S. Congressman Leo J. Ryan, 1973-75; pres. Pacific Cons., San Francisco, 1975, ELS, Inc., Santa Cruz, Calif., 1975-82; tchr., counselor Operation SHARE, 1970-71; pres., Elvirita Lewis Found. Geriatric Health and Nutrition, Palm Springs, Calif., 1976—; v.p. San Jose Ecology Action, 1970-71; pres., chmn. bd. dirs. Verde-Mar, Ltd., La Quinta, Calif., 1978—. Publicity chmn. Santa Clara County Easter Seals, 1970-71; bd. dirs. La Qunita Classic Jazz Festival, 1987—; mem. Rep. Nat. Com., Senatorial Inner Circle, Calif. Rep. Golden Circle; mem. Gov.'s Adv. Task Force on Long Term Care; mem. Santa Cruz County Housing Adv. Commn., 1976-81. Served with USN, 1964-67; Vietnam. Mem. Am. Acad. Polit. and Social Scientists, Nat. Council on Aging, Am. Soc. Aging (chmn. communications com., editorial bd., bd. dirs. 1986—), World Affairs Council San Francisco, Calif. Council on Internat. Trade, Calif. Farm Bur., Export Mgrs. Assn., Nat. Rifle Assn., Am. Assn. Internat. Aging (bd. dirs., treas.), Acad. Polit. Sci., Coachella Valley Mex.-Am. C. of C. (bd. dirs., treas. 1988—), Smithsonian Instn., Am. Mus. Natural History, Gerontol. Soc., Internat. Council Nat. Founds. on Aging (bd. dirs.), Nat. Hispanic Council on Aging (bd. dirs. 1986—), Sigma Delta Chi (Journalism award 1972, 73), Pi Sigma Alpha. Clubs: Commonwealth (San Francisco); La Quinta Tennis (Los Angeles). Address: Elvirita Lewis Found Suite 144 255 N El Cielo Rd Palm Springs CA 92262

BRUMMET, RICHARD LEE, accounting educator; b. Ewing, Ill., Mar. 16, 1921; s. George Otto and Iva Talitha (Smith) B.; m. Nellie Eldora Riddle, Aug. 6, 1942; children—Carmen, John. B.E., Ill. State U., 1942; M.S., U. Ill., 1947; Ph.D., U. Mich., 1956. Prof. Cornell U., 1954-55; prof. U. Mich., 1955-69, dir. mgmt. edn., 1966-68; Willard J. Graham distinguished prof. U. N.C., 1970-86, dir. M in Acctg. degree program, 1984-86, prof. emeritus, 1986—; cons. Ford Found., Cairo, Egypt, 1963-64; vis. prof. Netherlands Sch. Econs., 1969, U. South Africa, 1974, U. New South Wales, Australia, 1976; cons. in field. Author: Overhead Costing, 1957, Cost Accounting for Small Manufacturers, 1953; 1971, Record Keeping for Small Home Builders, 1952, The Metal Finishing Industry, 1966; Contbr. articles to profl. jours. articles. Served to capt. AUS, 1942-46. Mem. Am. Inst. C.P.A.'s (council 1975-77), Am. Acctg. Assn. (treas. 1967-69, pres. 1974-75), Nat. Assn. Accts. (v.p. 1970-71, pres. 1979-80, chmn. 1980-81). Home: 810 Kenmore Chapel Hill NC 27514

BRUN, GEORGES HARRIS, gynecologist; b. St. Cyr, Dordogne, France, Oct. 29, 1931; s. Emile and Marie Therese (Golfier) B.; m. Anquetil Suzanne, Dec. 31, 1960. BS In Physics, Chemistry, Biology, U. Scis. Poitiers, France, 1951; MD, Faculté de Medicine, Bordeaux, 1966. Cert. gynecologist. Intern 1953-62; physician, chef de clinique CHR, Bordeaux, France, 1962; prof. Agregé Coop., Marroco, France, 1966-70; chmn. gynecology Nat. Edn. Health Service, Bordeaux, 1970—. Numerous articles on gynecology to profl. jours. Mem. French Col. Ob-Gyn (adminstrv. council), Soc. French Gynecologists, Soc. French Pelvic Surgeons, French Soc. Ob-Gyn., Order of Academic Palms. Office: Hosp St André, 1 Rue Jean Burguet, 33075 Bordeaux France

BRUN, THORVALD GORGAS, educator, consultant; b. Bergen, Norway, 1953; s. Thorvald S. and Ellen J. Brun; m. Oddny Brun. BA in Engring., NKI Sch. of Engring., 1981; BA in Econs., U. Bergen, 1980, M. in Law, 1978. Economist Norwegian Petroleum Cons., Bergen, 1982-83, mgr., cons., economist, 1983-85; v.p., gen. mgr. E.B. Nera Satellite Communications, Bergen, 1985-87; pres. INTERPRO Cons., Bergen, 1986—; asst. prof. Norwegian Sch. of Econs.; bd. chmn. Norwegian Indsl. Council for Space Related Activities, 1986-87. Served with the Norwegian Army, 1972-73. Office: INTERPRO as, PO Box 85, N 5061 Kokstad Norway

BRUNALE, VITO JOHN, aerospace engineer; b. Mt. Vernon, N.Y., July 2, 1925; s. Donato and Antoinette (Wool) B.; AAS, Stewart Aero. Inst., 1948; BSAE, Tri-State U., 1958; MSME, U. Bridgeport, 1966; DSc, Nev. Inst. Tech., 1973; DSc in Engring., Pacific Western U., 1984; PhD (hon.) Internat. U., Spain, 1987; m. Joan Florence Montuori, Apr. 23, 1949; 1 son, Stephen. Research engr. Norden Labs., White Plains, N.Y., 1948-55; instr. Tri-State U., Angola, Ind., 1955-58; engring. cons. Norden Div. United Aircraft, Norwalk, Conn., 1958-67; chief engring. cons. Singer-Kearfott Corp., Pleasantville, N.Y., 1967-73; chief engr. Diagnostic/Retrieval systems Mt. Vernon, N.Y., 1973-76; tech. problem mgr. Fairchild Republic Co., Farmingdale, N.Y., 1977-87; sr. tech. expert, Sikorsky Aircraft, 1987—; cons. in field; engring. tutor to coll. students; v.p. Lithoway, Inc., 1969-73; lectr. in field. Served with USAAF, 1943-45. Decorated Purple Heart (3), Air medals, D.F.C. Tri-State U. teaching fellow, 1955-58; recipient Aircraft Design award, 1948; Inst. Aero. Sci. Lecture award, 1948; Norden Research award, 1963, Cost Reduction award, 1965, Fairchild outstanding achievement award, Fairchild award of excellence, 1984, Am. Biographical Inst. and Research Assn. Outstanding Performance award, 1985, Aircraft Recognition award, 1986, citation N.Y. State Assembly, 1988, Conspicuous Service Cross N.Y. State, 1988, others. Mem. AIAA, U.S. Naval Inst., Air Force Assn., Am. Ordnance Assn., Inst. Environ. Sci., Nat. Space Inst. Roman Catholic. Clubs: K.C., VFW, DAV, Newman, Internat. Students Assn., Internat. Platform Assn., World Inst. of Achievement. Contbr. articles to profl. jours. Home: 459 Bronxville Rd Bronxville NY 10708 Office: Conklin St Farmingdale NY 11735

BRUNDTLAND, GRO HARLEM, prime minister of Norway; b. Oslo, Norway, Apr. 20, 1939; d. Gudmund and Inga (Brynolf) Harlem; m. Arne Olav Brundtland, 1960; children: Knut, Kaja, Ivar, Jorgen. M.D., Oslo U., 1963; M.P.H., Harvard Sch. Pub. Health, 1965. Med. officer Nat. Directorate of Pub. Health, Oslo, 1965-67, asst. med. dir. Sch. Health Services, Oslo, 1968-74, Minister of Environment, Norwegian Govt., 1974-79, mem. Parliament from Oslo, 1977—, mem. standing com. on finance, chmn. standing com. on fgn. and constitutional affairs, 1979-81, dep. leader Labour Party's Parliamentary Group, 1979-81, leader Labour Party and Parliamentary Group, 1981—, standing com. on fgn. and constl. affairs, 1981-86, prime minister, Norway, 1981, 1986—. Contbr. scientific work in child growth and devel. Mem. Ind. Commn. on Disarmament and Security Issues, UN, 1980; chmn. World Commn. on Environment and Devel., 1983; bd. dirs. Better World Soc., 1985. Address: Office of the Prime Minister, PO Box 8001, Dep, N-0030 Oslo 1 Norway

BRUNER, LINDA POLLARD, management information consulting company executive; b. Sarasota, Fla., July 1, 1948; d. Donald Dunsmore and Elizabeth (Murley) Polland; m. G. Evans Bruner IV, June 7, 1969; children—John Evans, Leah Robinson. BA in Edn. and History, Erskine Coll., 1969; MA in Math., Fairfield U., 1979. Tchr., St. Thomas Sch., Tucson, 1971-73; tchr. math. West Rocks Mid. Sch., Norwalk, Conn., 1977-79; computer instr. Norwalk High Sch., 1979-81; cons. Bruner Consulting Associates, Inc., Bridgeport, Conn., 1981-83, v.p., 1983—. Author: Teaching Children Basic, 1980; contbr. articles to profl. jours. Mem. adv. bd. Notre Dame High Sch., Fairfield, 1985-86; bd. dirs. LWV, Bridgeport, 1978-82. Mem. Ind. Computer Cons. Assn. (bd. dirs. 1983-85), Fairfield Network of Exec. Women (chmn. bd. dirs. 1986-88, treas. 1984-85, pres. 1988), Data Processing Mgmt. Assn. (bd. dirs. 1987—, pres. 1988-89). Republican. Episcopalian. Club: Brooklawn Country (Fairfield). Avocations: golf, bridge. Office: Bruner Consulting Assocs Inc 112 Prospect St Stamford CT 06901

BRUNER, PHILIP LANE, lawyer; b. Chgo., Sept. 26, 1939; s. Henry Pfeiffer and Marjorie (Williamson) B.; A.B., Princeton U., 1961; J.D., U. Mich., 1964; M.B.A., Syracuse U., 1967; m. Ellen Carole Germann, Mar. 21, 1964; children—Philip Richard, Stephen Reed, Carolyn Anne. Admitted to Wis. bar, 1964, Minn. bar, 1968. Mem. Briggs and Morgan P.A., Mpls., St. Paul, 1967-83; sr. ptnr. Hart & Bruner, P.A., Mpls., 1983—; adj. prof. William Mitchell Coll. Law, St. Paul, 1970-78, 81; lectr. law seminars univs.; bar assns. and industry. Mem. Bd. Edn., Mahtomedi Ind. Sch. Dist. 832, 1978-86. Served to capt. USAF, 1964-67. Recipient Disting. Service award St. Paul Jaycees, 1974; named One of Ten Outstanding Young Minnesotans, Minn. Jaycees, 1975. Fellow Nat. Contract Mgmt. Assn.; mem. Internat. Am., Fed., Minn., Wis., Ramsey, Hennepin bar assns., Internat. Assn. Ins. Counsel, Am. Arbitration Assn. (nat. panel arbitrators). Club: Mpls. Athletic. Contbr. articles to profl. jours. Home: 8432 80th St N Stillwater MN 55082 Office: 1221 Nicollet Mall Minneapolis MN 55403

BRUNER, RALPH CLAYBURN, testing services company executive; metallurgist; b. Oklahoma City, Apr. 22, 1921; s. Ralph Sylvester and Macil Gladys (Stroup) B.; m. Cicely Louise Fidler, July 3, 1954; children—Martha Ellen, David Ralph. B.A. in Chemistry, Calif. State U.-Fullerton, 1965. Registered profl. engr., Okla. Research engr. N.Am. Aviation, Inc., Los Angeles, 1947-52, supr. metallurgy, Columbus, Ohio, 1952-56; chief chem. lab. Autonetics, Anaheim, Calif., 1956-65; mng. labs. Rockwell Internat., Tulsa, 1965-76; pres. Metlab Testing Services, Inc., Tulsa, 1976—. Contbr. articles to profl. meetings. Mem. Am. Soc. Metals, ASME, Am. Welding Soc., Am. Foundrymen's Soc. Automotive Engrs., Nat. Assn. Corrosion Engrs., Soc. for Advancement of Materials and Process Engring. Republican. Roman Catholic. Research on metall. forensic analysis; patentee in field. Office: 6825 E 38th St Tulsa OK 74145

BRUNET, JEAN CHRISTOPHE, corporate treasurer; b. Tunis, Tunisia, Nov. 9, 1951; arrived in France, 1956; s. Marc and Jacqueline (Gesweiller) B.; m. Pascaline Berthon; children: Joanna, Antonin. Diploma, Hautes Etudes Commls., 1975. Asst. br. mgr. Union de Banques à Paris, 1976-78, br. mgr., 1978-80; asst. treas. Becton Dickinson, Grenoble, France, 1980-84, treas. for Europe, 1984—. Club: Des Sources. Office: Becton Dickinson, 5 Chemin des Sources, F-38240 Meylan France

BRUNET, ROGER, geographer, researcher; b. Toulouse, France, Mar. 30, 1931. Agrégation de géographie, U. Toulouse, 1953; LittD, U. Toulouse, France, 1965. M. de Conf. U. Toulouse, Toulouse, France, 1957-66; prof. U. de Reims Champagne-Ardenne, Reims, France, 1966-76; dir. de recherche Cen. Nat. de la Recherche Sci., Paris, 1976-84, Montpellier, France, 1984—; bd. dirs. Groupement d'Intérêt Pub. Reclus & Maison de la Géographie, Montpellier, L'Espace Géographique, Mappemonde; conseiller tech. Ministere de la Recherche, Paris, 1981-84. Author several books and articles; editor several book collections including, Atlas de France, Géographie Universelle. Pres. Com. de Liaison pour L'Aménagement de la Marne, Reims, 1971-73. Office: Maison de la Geographie, 17 R Abbe de l'Epee, 34000 Montpellier France

BRUNHAMMER, YVONNE SUZANNE, curator; b. Belfort, France, Oct. 22, 1927; d. Fernand E. Brunhammer and Marie-Louise Arbeit. Diploma, Ecole du Louvre, Paris, 1954. With Mus. Decorative Arts, Paris, 1952—, asst. curator, 1963-69, curator, 1969-85, chief curator, 1985—. Named Chevalier of Arts and Letters. Office: Mus des Arts Decoratifs, Palais du Louvre, 107 rue de Rivoli, Pavillon de Marsan, 75001 Paris France

BRUNHART, HANS, head of government Liechtenstein; b. Balzers, Liechtenstein, Mar. 28, 1945; s. Andreas and Rosa (Frick) B.; diploma Lyceum Gutenberg, Balzers, 1966; student Germanic philology, Freiburg and Basel, Switzerland; m. Bernadette Biedermann, Nov. 18, 1972; children: Patrick, Ines, Andreas. Dir. Liechtenstein Nat. Library, also Liechtenstein State Archives, Vaduz, 1972-74; dep. head govt. Liechtenstein, 1974-78, head govt., 1978—. Decorated grand cross, comdr.'s cross with star Liechtenstein Order of Merit. Mem. Fatherland Union Party. Roman Catholic. Author articles in field. Office: Govt Bldg, 9490 Vaduz Liechtenstein

BRUNIE, CHARLES HENRY, investment manager; b. N.Y.C., July 17, 1930; s. Charles Henry and Olive (Swanston) B.; m. Jean Isbell Corley, June 23, 1965; stepchildren: William Corley, Jean Corley Yankus, Ellen Corley. B.A., Amherst Coll., 1952; M.B.A., Columbia, 1956. Analyst N.Y. Life Ins. Co., N.Y.C., 1956-60; sr. analyst firm Faulkner, Dawkins & Sullivan, 1960-63; sr. analyst Oppenheimer & Co., N.Y.C., 1963-65; gen. partner Oppenheimer & Co., 1965-82, mem. exec. com., sr. partner, 1969-82; chmn. Oppenheimer Capital Corp., 1977—, Manhattan Inst., 1980—. Served with AUS, 1952-54. Mem. N.Y. Soc. Security Analysts, Chartered Financial Analysts, Mont Pelerin Soc., Delta Upsilon. Clubs: Knickerbocker (N.Y.C.); Bronxville Field (Bronxville), Siwanoy Country (Bronxville). Home: 21 Elm Rock Rd Bronxville NY 10708 Office: Oppenheimer Capital Corp Oppenheimer Tower World Financial Ctr New York NY 10281

BRUNK, MAX EDWIN, emeritus marketing educator; b. Roswell, N.Mex., Sept. 12, 1914; s. Miller Michael and Susan Virginia (Sandy) B.; m. Letta Olga Reck, Mar. 30, 1941; children: Norma Marie Brunk Sullivan, Kathryn Sue Brunk Brennan. Student, Clemson Coll., 1934-35; B.S., U. Fla., 1938; M.S., Cornell U., 1941, Ph.D., 1947. Asst. agrl. economist U. Fla., 1941-44, assoc., 1944-45; assoc. prof. mktg. Cornell U., 1947-51, prof., 1951-82, prof. emeritus, 1983—; pres. Eastern Market Research Service, Inc., Ithaca, N.Y., 1954—; chmn. Beef Task Force for Council of Agrl. Sci. and Tech., Internat. Conf. Beef Producers, 1975—. Author: (with L.B. Darrah) Marketing Agricultural Products, 1954; Contbr. articles in field to profl. jours. Dir. Tompkins County Area Devel. Corp.; Award trustee, bd. govs. Livestock Merchandising Inst., 1979—. Recipient Research award Nat. Apple Inst., 1954, 64, 83; Research award Found. for Floriculture, 1964; award for disting. service to Am. agr. Am. Farm Bur., 1965; Klinck lectr. Agrl. Inst. Can., 1975. Mem. Am. Farm Econs. Assn., Internat. Conf. Agrl. Economists, N.Y. Agrl. Soc. (Disting. Service citation 1986). Republican. Presbyterian. Clubs: Cornell of N.Y., Statler, Tower, Lake Wales Country (Fla.). Home: 103 Terraceview Dr Ithaca NY 14850 Office: Cornell U 410 Warren Hall Ithaca NY 14853

BRUNKE, SCOTT MOORE, plastic manufacturing company executive; b. Evanston, Ill., June 14, 1947; s. Wallace Charles and Janice Marie (Moore) B.; m. Susan Virginia Lund, Oct. 21, 1967; children—Eric Moore, Aaron Mart, Adam Paul, David Ryan. Student Western Ill. U., 1965-66, Coll. of DuPage, 1966-67, Central YMCA Coll., 1967-68. With research and devel. dept. Am. Can Co., Batavia, Ill., 1967-69; plant engr. Borse Plastic Products, Hinsdale, Ill., 1969-71; plant mgr. A&G Plastic Products, Sturgis, Mich., 1971-75; plant mgr. Leon Plastics div. U.S. Industries, Grand Rapids, Mich., 1975-79; co-owner, exec. v.p. B&G Plastics Inc., Grand Rapids, Mich., 1979-86, B&G Industries, 1983-86; co-owner B&G Helicopter Co., 1982-86, B&G Machinery Co., 1982-86, B & G Export, 1981-85, Royal Am. Travel Inc., Grand Rapids, 1984-86, Cachia & Brunke Constrn. Co., Yucca Valley, Calif., 1983—; pres. Scott Industries, Inc., Yucca Valley, Calif. Mem. Soc. Plastics Industry, Soc. Plastics Engrs. (sr.), Aircraft Owners and Pilots Assn., Grand Rapids C. of C. Republican. Mem. Ch. of Christ. Patentee in field. Office: 56563 Golden Bee Dr Yucca Valley CA 92284

BRUNNER-TRAUT, EMMA K(ATHARINA), egyptologist; b. Frankfurt, Fed. Republic of Germany, Dec. 25, 1911; d. Adam and Katharina (Mechnig) Traut; m. Hellmut Brunner, Mar. 20, 1937. PhD, Univ., Münich, 1937. Hon. prof. 1973. Author numerous books on Egyptology. Mem. Deutsches Archäologisches Inst. of Berlin, Internat. Soc. Folk Narrative Research, Internat. Assn. for History of Religions, Assn. Internat. des Egyptologues. Clubs: Volkacher Bund (pres. Stuttgart chpt. 1984-85), Privatstudiengesellschaft (Stuttgart). Home: Bei der Ochsenweide 8, 74 00 Tübingen Federal Republic of Germany

BRUNO, MICHAEL, economics educator; b. Hamburg, Germany, July 30, 1932; came to Israel, 1933; s. Hans Walter and Lotte (Samson) B.; m. Ofra Hirshenberg, Oct. 27, 1958; children: Yael Ido, Asa. BA, King's Coll., Cambridge, Eng., 1957; PhD, Stanford U., 1962. Joint dir. research Bank of Israel, Jerusalem, 1957-65; lectr. Hebrew U., Jerusalem, 1963-65, sr. lectr., 1965-67, assoc. prof., 1967-70, prof. econs., 1970—, vis. prof. econs. Harvard U., Cambridge, Mass., 1965-56, 70-71, 76-77, 81, MIT, 65-66, 70-71, 76-77, 81; research assoc. Nat. Bur. Econ. Research, Cambridge, 1979—; sr. econ. policy advisor Minister of Fin., Jerusalem, 1975-76; cons. World Bank, Washington; dir. research Falk Inst. Econ. Research in Israel, 1973-75. Coauthor: Economics of Worldwide Stagflation, 1984; contbr. articles to profl. jours. Apptd. gov. Bank of Israel, 1986—, planning team by Israeli P.M., 1985-86. Recipient Rothchild prize for Social Sci., 1974. Fellow Econometric Soc. (council mem. 1967-69, 2d v.p. 1984-85, pres.); mem. Israel Acad. Sci., Israel Econ. Assn. (pres. 1975-77); fgn. hon. mem. Am. Acad. Arts and Sci. Office: Bank Israel, PO Box 780, Jerusalem 91007, Israel

BRUNO, THOMAS ANTHONY, lawyer; b. Berwyn, Ill., Feb. 8, 1954; s. Alexander Nicholas and Mildred Mary (Biciste) B.; m. Elizabeth Ann Matthias, June 12, 1976; children: Anthony Alexander, Evan Stanley. B.A., U. Ill. 1976, J.D., 1979. Bars: Ill. 1980, U.S. Dist. Ct. (cen. dist.) Ill. 1980, U.S. Supreme Ct. 1985. Prin. Thomas A. Bruno and Assocs., Urbana, Ill., 1980—; lectr. U. Ill. Law Sch., Urbana, 1981—; host TV show Legal-Ease. Author (newspaper column) Honest Lawyer, 1983. Bd. dirs. Devel. Services Ctr., Champaign, Ill., 1979-82; vice chmn. bd. Disabled Citizens Found., Champaign, 1982—; mem. Humane Soc. Champaign County, 1984, Chgo. Zool. Soc. Ill. Legis. scholar, 1972-76. Mem. ABA, Ill. Bar Assn., Champaign County Bar Assn., Assn. Trial Lawyers Am., Champaign County Assn. Criminal Defense Lawyers (past pres. Champaign chpt. 1982—), Nat. Assn. for Prevention Child Abuse (v.p. Champaign county chpt.), Phi Eta Sigma. Democrat. Roman Catholic. Clubs: U. Ill. Quarterback, U. Ill. Rebounder. Lodges: K.P., Kiwanis. Home: 1109 W Park Ave Champaign IL 61821 Office: Thomas A Bruno and Assocs 301 W Green St Urbana IL 61801

BRUNON, JACQUES MARIE, neurosurgeon; b. St.-Etienne, Loire, France, Nov. 20, 1944; s. Adrien and Helene (Robert) B.; m. Anne-Marie Thoiron, Oct. 10, 1966; children: Lise-Helene, Guillaume, Amandine. MD, U. Lyon, France, 1973. Cert. neurosurgeon, 1975. Resident U. Hosp. Lyon, 1967-73; asst. chief Neurol. Hosp., Lyon, 1973-79; sub-chief neurosurg. dept. U. St.-Etienne, 1979-85, chief med. officer neurosurg. dept., 1985—; prof. neurosurgery U. St. Etienne, 1985; chmn. med. consultative com. Bellevue Hosp., St.-Etienne, 1985; mem. adminstrv. com. Regional U. Hosp., St.-Etienne, 1987. Author: Vertebro Basilary Insufficiency, 1974; contbr. numerous articles to profl. jours. Mem. French Soc. Neurosurgery (chmn. 1985-87), Neurosurgery Soc. French Language, European Assn. Neurosurgeons (exec. co. 1987). Union pour la Démocratie Francaise. Roman Catholic. Lodge: Rotary.

BRUNS, BILLY LEE, consulting electrical engineer; b. St. Louis, Nov. 21, 1925; s. Henry Lee and Violet Jean (Williams) B.; B.A., Washington U., St. Louis, 1949, postgrad. Sch. Engring., 1959-62; EE, ICS, Scranton, Pa.; m. Lillian Colleen Mobley, Sept. 6, 1947; children—Holly Rene, Kerry Alan, Barry Lee, Terrence William. Supt., engr., estimator Schneider Electric Co., St. Louis, 1950-54, Ledbetter Electric Co., 1954-57; tchr. indsl. electricity St. Louis Bd. Edn., 1957-71; pres. B.L. Bruns & Assos., cons. engrs., St. Louis, 1963-72; v.p., chief engr. Hosp. Bldg. & Equipment Co., St. Louis, 1972-76; pres., prin. B.L. Bruns & Assos. cons. engrs., St. Louis, 1976—; tchr. elec. engring. U. Mo. St. Louis extension, 1975-76. Mem. Mo. Adv. Council on Vocat. Edn., 1969-76, chmn., 1975-76; leader Explorer post Boy Scouts Am., 1950-57. Served with AUS, 1944-46; PTO, Okinawa. Decorated Purple Heart. Registered profl. engr., Mo., Ill., Wash., Fla., La., Wis., Minn., N.Y.,

N.C., Iowa, Pa., Miss., Ind., Ala., N.C. Mem. Nat., Mo. socs. profl. engrs., Profl. Engrs. in Pvt. Practice, Am. Soc. Heating, Refrigeration and Air Conditioning Engrs., Illuminating Engrs. Soc., Am. Mgmt. Assn. Baptist. Club: Masons. Tech. editor The National Electrical Code and Blueprint Reading, Am. Tech. Soc., 1959-65. Home: 1243 Hobson Dr Ferguson MO 63135 Office: 10 Adams Suite 111 Ferguson MO 63135

BRUNS, EDWARD ALBERT, osteopath; b. St. Louis, Feb. 8, 1941; s. Edward F. and Thelma A. (Siekerman) B.; m. Mary Lou Kelley, Oct. 7, 1961; children: Cynthia K., Catherine L., Chris M. BS, N.E. Mo. U., 1964; DO, Kirksville Coll. Osteo. Medicine, 1968. Diplomate Am. Osteo. Bd. Internal Medicine. Asst. prof. medicine Kirksville Coll. Osteo. Medicine, 1968-72; attending physician Buenger Clinic, Memphis, Mo., 1972-74, Med. Specialists, St. Louis, 1974—; bd.dirs. Normandy Osteopathic Hosp., 1987—. Fellow Am. Coll. Utilization Rev. Physicians, Am. Coll. Osteo. Internists; mem. Am. Osteo. Assn. Methodist. Home: 12928 Briar Fork Ct Saint Louis MO 63131 Office: Med Specialists Inc 456 N New Ballas Rd Saint Louis MO 63141

BRUNTON, BRUCE WHITNEY, city official; b. Maple Creek, Sask., Can., Aug. 24, 1931; s. Clarence Alexander and Evelyn Gertrude (Whitney) B.; m. Mary Elizabeth Ankcorn, Oct. 13, 1929; children: Jane, Anne. Diploma in Civil Engring., U. Man., 1953. Registered profl. engr., Ont. Jr. engr. City of Oshawa (Ont.), 1953-55; project engr. Town Planning Cons. Ltd., Toronto, 1955-57; city engr. City of Owen Sound (Ont.), 1958-62; chief tech. engr. City of Sudbury (Ont.), 1962-73; dep. borough engr. City of Etobicoke (Ont.), 1973, commr. works, 1974—. Mem. Am. Pub. Works Assn. (pres. 1986). Office: City of Etobicoke, 399 The West Mall, Etobicoke, ON Canada M9C 2Y2

BRUSIS, OTTO ANTON, health science facility administrator, cardiologist; b. Munich, Feb. 12, 1935; came to U.S., 1966; s. Anton and Erika Barbara (Hippeli) B. m. Kimberly Smith, Apr. 24, 1964; children: Johannes M., Angela B. MD, U. Munich, 1960; MPH, Harvard Sch. Pub. Health, 1970. Intern Munich Kingston (Can.) Gen. Hosp., 1960-62; intern, resident in medicine De Goesbriand Meml. Hosp., U. Vt., Burlington, 1963-64; resident in cardiology Nat. Inst. Cardiology, Mexico City, 1966; research fellow U. Vt., 1966-67, asst. prof. dept. community medicine, 1967-71; asst. dept. nutrition Harvard Sch. Pub. Health, Boston, 1970-72; asst. in medicine Peter Bent Brigham Hosp., 1971-72; assoc. med. dir. Cen. for Cardiac Rehab. and Reconditioning, Waldkirch i Breisgau, Fed. Republic of Germany, 1972-77; med. dir., chief of service Cen. for Cardiac and Pulmonary Rehab., Albert Schweitzer Klinik, Konigsfeld, Fed. Republic of Germany, 1977—; sec. German Council of Cardiac Prevention and Rehab.; pres. Bad-Württemberg State Soc. Cardiology Rehab., 1985—. Pres. cardio-pulmonary work group ASK, Königsfeld, 1978—. Fellow Am. Coll. Cardiology; mem. Am. Pub. Health Assn., Am. Coll. Sports Medicine, German Mycological Soc. Am., Mexican Soc. Mycology, German Coll. Internal Medicine, German Soc. Sports Medicine, German Soc. Cardiovascular Research, German Soc. Intensive Care Medicine, German Soc. of Tuberculosis and Pulmonary Disease. Roman Catholic. Club: Harvard. Lodge: Lions. Office: Albert Schweitzer Klinik, Parkstr 10, D 7744 Königsfeld Federal Republic of Germany

BRUSKI, PAUL STEVEN, public relations executive; b. Kansas City, Mo., Mar. 10, 1949; s. Paul and Elizabeth Ann (Cravens) B.; m. Mary Margaret Williams, May 3, 1980. BS in Journalism, U. Berlin, Fed. Republic Germany, 1972. With engring. mgmt. Storage Tech. Corp., Louisville, 1973-77; dir. IMC, Denver, 1977-79; ptnr. Flack and Bruski Advt., Denver, 1979-81; dir. tech. Services D. J. Moore Advt., Guilderland, N.Y., 1983; dir. mktg. The Software Group, Ballston Lake, N.Y., 1984-86; dir. corp. communications Informix Software, Inc. (formerly Innovative Software, Inc.), Lenexa, Kans. and Menlo Park, Calif., 1986—; cons. publ. Brodock Press Inc., Utica, N.Y., 1983-86; computer cons. and free-lance journalist, 1974—. Author: Collected Works, 1977. Served with U.S. Army, 1968-72. Mem. Pub. Relations Soc. Am. (bd. dirs. Greater Kansas City chpt.). Office: Informix Software Inc 16011 College Blvd Lenexa KS 66219

BRUSS, CAROL LOUISE, educator, actress; b. Milw., May 30; d. Walter Julius and Erna Caroline (Pieplow) Bruss. B.A., Carthage Coll., 1951; post-grad. Alverno Coll.-Milw., 1971-72. Life cert. secondary tchr., Wis. Personnel clk. Sears & Roebuck Co., 1951-55; mgr. Security Nat. Ins. Agy., Milw., 1955-60; student, dir., producer Sta. WMUS, Milw. Area Tech. Coll., 1960-65; office mgr. Stat Tab Corp., Milw., 1965-71; career specialist Milw. Pub. Schs., 1971—; theatre career specialist, 1977-84; tchr. English and speech Bay View High Sch., 1984—; actress, dir. Milw. community theatres; soprano soloist Lake Park Ch., Milw. Active South Div. Civic Assn., Milw.; mem. Marquis Library N.Y Soc.; life mem. (hon.) Lutheran Ch. Women. Recipient producer's award for best program Channel 10 Milw. Area Tech. Coll., 1962; Best Artistic award Act One Theatre Co., Milw. Pub. Schs., 1981. Mem. Wis. Theatre Assn., Impresarios-Milw. Performing Arts Ctr., AAUW, South Div. Civic Assn., Milw. Zool. Soc., Phi Lambda Omega, Alpha Mu Gamma, Alpha Psi Omega. Club: Coll. Women's. Home: 2216 S 28th St Milwaukee WI 53215

BRUST, DAVID, physicist; b. Chgo., Aug. 24, 1935; s. Clifford and Ruth (Klapman) B.; B.S., Calif. Inst. Tech., 1957; M.S., U. Chgo., 1958, Ph.D., 1964. Research assoc. Purdue U., Lafayette, Ind., 1963-64; research assoc. Northwestern U., Evanston, Ill., 1964-65, asst. prof. physics, 1965-68; theoretical research physicist U. Calif., Lawrence Radiation Lab., Livermore, Calif., 1968-73; cons. Bell Telephone Lab., Murray Hill, N.J., 1966. Campaign co-ordinator No. Calif. Scientists and Engrs. for McGovern, 1972. NSF travel grantee, 1964; NSF research grantee, 1966-68. Mem. Am. Phys. Soc., Am. Assn. Coll. Profs., Internat. Solar Energy Soc., Pacific Assn. of AAU, Sierra Club, Sigma Xi. Office: PO Box 13130 Oakland CA 94661

BRUTIAN, GEORG ABEL, philosopher, researcher, educator; b. Sev kar, Idjevan, USSR, Mar. 24, 1926; s. Abel Michael and Mariam Arshak (Khachatrain) B.; m. Hranoush Ara Markarian, May 26, 1955; children: Lilit, Narine, Ara. Degree in engring., Poly. Inst., Yerevan, USSR, 1947; degree in history internat. relations, Yerevan U., 1950; D in Philos. Scis., Moscow U., 1962. Assoc. prof. Yerevan U., 1951-62, chmn. philosophy, 1970—; chmn. philosophy Yerevan Brussov Inst., 1962-70. Author: Logic, 1957, 4th rev. edit., 1987, Philosophy and Language, 1972, Transformatory Logic, 1983, Argumentation, 1984; editor-in-chief Philos. Yearbook, 1982—; internat. serie Argumentation, Belgium, 1988—; editorial bd. Philos. Scis., 1972-87, Philosophy and Rhetoric, 1970-72; hon. mem. European Ctr. for Study of Argumentation, 1987. Recipient Order of Friendship of Peoples award Presidium Supreme Soviet, 1986, Komenski medal Univ. Bratislava, 1971; named hon. citizen Masterton Borough Council, New Zealand, 1966. Mem. Acad. Scis. (academician 1982, sec. philosophy and philology div. 1977—, presidium mem. 1977—), Philos. Soc. USSR (presidium mem. Moscow div. 1982, pres. Armenian div. 1977—), Assn. USSR-Spain (pres. Armenian div. 1986). Home: Pushkin St 40, Apt 90, Yeravan, Armenian SSR 375010, USSR Office: Acad Scis, Marshal Baghramian Ave 24, Yerevan, Armenian SSR 375019, USSR

BRUTON, JOHN MACAULAY, association executive; b. Mexico City, Nov. 13, 1937; s. Edmund Macaulay and Byrd (Grant) B.; m. Frances McMillan Marks, Nov. 25, 1960; children—Alexander, Macaulay, Brinley. B.A., Duke U., 1959. Pres., gen. mgr. Grant Advt. de Panama, Panama City, 1970-72, Mexico City, 1972; communications dir. Am. C. of C. of Mex., Mexico City, 1972-74, gen. mgr., 1974-77, exec. v.p., 1977—, v.p. exec. mgmt., L.A., Washington, 1985-88, v.p. membership service, 1988—. Bd. dirs. Am. Benevolent Soc., Mex., 1964-68, Am. Soc., Mex., 1975-78, 80-84; adv. bd. Jr. League Mexico City, 1978—; founder, bd. dirs. Jr. Achievement Mex., 1977—; bd. govs. Am.-Brit.-Cowdray Hosp., 1986—. Episcopalian. Clubs: Univ. of Mex. (bd. dirs. 1979-83, pres. 1981-82); Internat. of Washington. Home: Ameyalcalli, Ocotepec 74, 10200 Mexico City Mexico Office: Am C of C of Mexico, Lucerna 78, 06600 Mexico DF Mexico

BRUYNES, CEES, manufacturing company executive; b. The Netherlands, Aug. 3, 1932; s. Arie and Petronella (Borst) B.; m. Elly Nagel, Feb. 1, 1963; children: Irene W., Jan Paul. Grad., Chr. Lyceum, Arnhem, Netherlands, 1951. With N.V. Philips' Gloeilampenfabrieken, Netherlands, 1953-71; pres., chief exec. officer Philips Can., 1971-74; exec. v.p. N. Am. Philips Corp., N.Y.C., 1975-78, pres., chief operating officer, 1978—, chief exec. officer, 1981—, chmn., 1985—. Served with Dutch Air Force, 1951-53. Clubs: Sky (N.Y.C.), Netherlands (N.Y.C.), Greenwich (Conn.) Country, Lyford Cay, Round Hill. Home: Khakum Wood Greenwich CT 06830 Office: N Am Philips Corp 100 E 42d St New York NY 10017 *

BRYAN, ARTHUR ELDRIDGE, JR., lawyer; b. Webster City, Iowa, July 28, 1924; s. Arthur Eldridge and Grace Lillian (Glassburner) B.; B.A., State U. Iowa, 1949, J.D., 1951; m. Elizabeth Ann Stubbings, Oct. 18, 1958; children—Elizabeth Grace, Arthur Eldridge III, John Milner, Daniel Franklin. With U.P. R.R. Co., Omaha, 1942-54; capital ptnr., mem. mgmt. com., chmn. tax dept. McDermott, Will & Emery, Chgo., 1954—; dir. Gits Bros. Mfg., Chgo., 1967-68; dir., v.p., sec. Yuma Mesa Devel. Co., Yuma, Ariz., 1967-79; chmn. bd. dirs., chief exec. officer Lake Arrowhead Devel. Co. (Calif.), 1971-80. Lectr. taxation U. Chgo., Marquette U., No. Ill. U. Mem. com. on legis. action New Trier (Ill.) High Sch., 1974-78; active Boy Scouts Am., Glencoe, Ill., 1968-74; mem. adv. bd. United Settlement Appeal, Chgo., 1962. Bd. dirs., treas., pres. chmn. fin. com. Erie Neighborhood House, Chgo., 1958—; trustee N. Cen. Coll., Naperville, Ill., 1974-79; sec., chmn. bd. trustees, sec. prudential bd. Glencoe Union Ch., 1969-79. Served with inf. AUS, 1942-46; ETO, PTO. Decorated Bronze Star, Combat Inf. badge. Fellow Am. Coll. of Tax Counsel; mem. ABA (chmn., spl. adviser sect. taxation com. on comml. banks and financials 1966-74), Ill. Bar Assn., Iowa Bar Assn., Chgo. Bar Assn., Chgo. Fed. Tax Forum., Ill. C. of C. (chmn. fed. tech. tax com. 1970), Chgo. Assn. Commerce and Industry (fed. appropriations and expenditures com. 1968—), Nat. Council Farmer Coops. (Legal Tax Acctg. com. 1974—, chmn. net operating loss, netting, tracing, tax controversies, patronage v. non-patronage subcoms. 1976-86), Am. Soc. of Accts. for Coops. (tax. com. 1976-86). Clubs: Chgo., Mid-Day, Monroe (Chgo.); Skokie Country (Glencoe, Ill.); Quail Creek Country (Naples, Fla.). Contbr. articles to profl. jours. Home: 1004 Pine Tree Ln Winnetka IL 60093 Office: McDermott Will & Emery 111 W Monroe St Chicago IL 60603

BRYAN, JACK YEAMAN, former diplomat, author, photographer; b. Peoria, Ill., Sept. 24, 1907; s. James Yeaman and Regina (Gibson) B.; m. Margaret Gardner, June 21, 1934; children: Joel Yeaman, Guy Kelsey, Donna Gardner, Kirsten Stuart (Mrs. Winkle-Bryan). Student, U. Chgo., 1925-27; B.A. with high distinction, U. Ariz., 1932, M.A., 1933; postgrad. (fellow philosophy), Duke U., 1933-35; Ph.D., U. Iowa, 1939. Research analyst Fed. Emergency Relief Adminstrn., Washington, 1935-36; from instr. English to prof., head dept. journalism U. Md., 1936-48; pub. relations adviser OCD, 1942-43; dir. pub. relations Welfare Fedn. Cleve., 1943-45; pub. info. officer UNRRA, 1945-46; cultural attaché Am. Embassy, Manila, 1948-51; chief program planning Internat. Exchange Service, State Dept., 1951-53; pub. affairs officer USIS, Bombay, India, 1953-54, Bangalore, India, 1954-55; cultural affairs officer embassy Cairo, Egypt, 1956, Tehran, Iran, 1956-58; cultural attaché, chief cultural affairs officer embassy Karachi, Pakistan, 1958-63; personnel officer for Africa USIA, 1964-65; officer in charge Project AIM, U.S. Dept. State, Washington, 1965; officer-in-charge spl. recruitment program Bur. Edn. and Cultural Affairs, 1965-67; chief cultural affairs adviser USIA, 1968; ret. 1968; lectr. creative photography U. Calif. at Riverside, 1968-80. Author: novel Come to the Bower, 1963, 1986, Cameras in the Quest for Meaning, 1986; contbr. short stories, articles, photographs to numerous mags.; Photog. exhibits one man shows, Pakistan, 1961-62, U.S., 1964, 66, Perspectives Eastward on tour U.S., 1968-71. Chmn. publs. bd. U. Md., 1946-48; chmn. bd. dirs. U.S. Ednl. Founds, Philippines, 1949-51, Pakistan, 1958-63; exec. dir. Iran Am. Soc. in Tehran, 1956-58; founder, exec. dir. Pakistan-Am. Cultural Center, 1959-60, 62-63. Recipient ann. prize for best novel Tex. Inst. Letters, 1964, Summerfield Roberts award, 1964, award for best short story, 1974. Mem. Am. Soc. Mag. Photographers, Friends of Ctr. for Tex. Studies, Tex. Inst. Letters, Tex. Hist. Assn., Am. Mus. Natural History, Am. Fgn. Service Assn., Wilderness Soc., Nature Conservancy, Audubon Soc., Sierra Club, Phi Delta Theta, Delta Sigma Rho, Phi Gamma Mu. Home: 3594 Ramona Dr Riverside CA 92506

BRYAN, JOHN HENRY, JR., food and consumer products company executive; b. West Point, Miss., 1936. B.A. in Econs. and Bus. Adminstrn, Rhodes Coll., Memphis, 1958. With Sara Lee Corp. (formerly known as Consol Food Corp.), Chgo., 1960—, exec. v.p. ops., 1974-75; pres., chief exec. officer Sara Lee Corp. (formerly known as consol food corp.), Chgo., 1975-76, chmn. bd., chief exec. officer, 1976—; also dir. Sara Lee Corp. (formerly known as consol food corp.); dir. Amoco Corp., First Chgo. Office: Sara Lee Corp 3 First National Plaza Chicago IL 60602-4260

BRYAN, JOSEPH MCKINLEY, insurance company executive; b. Elyria, Ohio, Feb. 11, 1896; s. Bart and Caroline (Ebert) B.; ed. Mt. Hermon Sch.; LL.D., Belmont (N.C.) Abbey Coll., U. N.C., Greensboro, Duke U.; Litt.D., Sacred Heart Coll.; L.H.D., N.C. A&T Coll.; m. Kathleen Marshall Price, Nov. 1927 (dec. 1984); children—Kay (Mrs. Bryan Edwards), Nancy Ann Faircloth, Joseph McKinley. Mem. N.Y. Cotton Exchange, 1923-31; with Jefferson Standard Life Ins. Co., 1931-61, now dir., mem. exec. com.; dir., mem. exec. com. Jefferson Pilot Broadcasting Co., owners and operators Jefferson Prodns., radio stas. WBT-AM, WBCY-FM, also TV sta. WBTV, Charlotte, other radio, TV stas, 1968—, also hon. chmn. bd.; hon. chmn. dir. exec. com. Pilot Life Ins. Co. Chmn. fin. sect. Am. Life Conv., 1949-50, pres., 1955-56. Chmn. N.C. Bd. Elections, 1960-61. Bd. govs. Shriner's Hosp. for Crippled Children, Greenville, 1945-72. Served with U.S. Army, World War I; AEF. Mem. Southeastern Shrine Assn. (past pres.), Sigma Chi. Clubs: Bath and Tennis, Everglades, Greensboro Country, Greensboro City, Sedgefield Country (Greensboro); Rolling Rock (Ligonier, Pa.); Nat. Golf (Augusta, Ga.); Metropolitan (Washington); Lyford Cay (Nassau, Bahamas). Lodges: Masons, Shriners, Rotary. Home: 711 Sunset Dr Greensboro NC 27408 Office: PO Box 21008 Greensboro NC 27420

BRYAN, MILDRED GOTT, lawyer, real estate broker; b. Washington, Oct. 20; d. Howard Seymour and Cora Elizabeth (Norris) Gott; m. Ernest R. Bryan, Sept. 15, 1952; (dec.); 1 dau., Carolyn Bryan Goodrich. Student Mt. Holyoke Coll., 1924-26; A.B. magna cum laude, Trinity Coll., 1928; J.D. cum laude, George Washington U., 1932. Bar: D.C. 1932. Atty. real estate div. War Dept., Dept. Def., Washington, 1942-46; sole practice, Washington, 1952—; pres. Eastland Gardens, Inc. Mem. women's com. Nat. Symphony Orch.; trustee World's Christian Endeavor Union, Met. Meml., Nat. Meth. Ch., Washington; patron Met. Opera Assn. Mem. ABA, Inter Am. Bar Assn., D.C. Bar Assn., English Speaking Union, Internat. Bar Assn., Nat. Trust for Historic Preservation, World Peace Through Law Assn., Smithsonian Assn., Friend of Nat. Zoo. Democrat. Methodist. Clubs: Columbia Country, Army-Navy, Spring Valley Garden. Home: 4840 Quebec St NW Washington DC 20016 Office: 1819 H St NW Suite 440 Washington DC 20006

BRYAN, RICHARD H., governor of Nevada; b. Washington, July 16, 1937; married; 3 children. B.A., U. Nev., 1959; LL.B., U. Calif.-San Francisco, 1963. Bar: Nev. 1963, U.S. Supreme Ct. 1967. Dep. dist. atty. Clark County, Nev., 1964-66; public defender Clark County, 1966-68; counsel Clark County Juvenile Ct., 1968-69; mem. Nev. Assembly, 1969-71, Nev. Senate, 1973-77; atty. gen. State of Nev. 1979-82, gov. Nev., 1982—. Bd. dirs. March of Dimes; former v.p. Nev. Easter Seal Soc.; former pres. Clark County Legal Aid Soc. Served with U.S. Army. Mem. ABA, Clark County Bar Assn., Am. Judicature Soc., Nat. Gov.'s Assn. (com. econ. devel. and technol. innovation, com. internat. trade and fgn. relations, task force on adult literacy, task force on jobs growth and competitiveness, chmn. subcom. tourism), Council of State Govts. (past pres.), Phi Alpha Delta, Phi Alpha Theta. Democrat. Clubs: Masons, Lions, Elks. Office: Office of Gov Capitol Complex Carson City NV 89710

BRYAN, ROBERT RUSSELL, lawyer; b. Shelbyville, Tenn., Mar. 14, 1943; s. Russell Duval and Auda Mai (Ellis) B. Student U. So. Miss., 1961-62; student Samford U., 1962-63, J.D., 1967; student George Washington U., 1964. Bar: Ala. 1967, U.S. Dist. Ct. (no. dist.) Ala. 1967, U.S. Supreme Ct., 1971, U.S. Tax Ct. 1972, U.S. Dist. Ct. S.D. 1973, U.S. Dist. Ct. (ea. dist.) Wis. 1975, Calif. 1978, U.S. Dist. Ct. (no. dist.) Calif. 1978, U.S. Ct. Appeals (5th and 9th cirs.) 1979, U.S. Ct. Appeals (4th cir.) 1980, U.S. Ct. Appeals (3d cir.) 1982, N.Y. 1983. Asst. to v.p. DeHavilland Aircraft of Can., Ltd., Toronto, Ont., Can., 1967; ptnr. Lindbergh, Lindbergh, Leach & Bryan, Birmingham, Ala., 1968-73; sr. counsel Law Offices of R.R. Bryan, Birmingham, 1973-75; ptnr. Bryan, Wiggins, Quinn & Appell, Birmingham, 1975-77; sr. ptnr. Law Offices of Robert R. Bryan, San Francisco, 1978—. Chair, mem. exec. bd. Nat. Coalition to Abolish the Death Penalty, Washington, 1984—; mem. adv. council Native Ams. and Death Penalty, 1988—; bd. dirs. Mill Valley Community Ctr., Calif., 1984-85, No. Calif. Coalition Against Death Penalty. Recipient Presdl. award Assn. to Advance Ethical Hypnosis, 1984. Fellow Am. Bd. Criminal Lawyers; mem. Nat. Assn. Criminal Def. Attys., N.Y. Assn. Criminal Def. Lawyers, Assn. Trial Lawyers Am., Calif. Trial Lawyers Assn., Criminal Trial Lawyers Assn., Calif. Bar (criminal law sect.), San Francisco Bar Assn., Nat. Lawyers Guild, Am. Acad. Forensic Scis., Calif. Attys. for Criminal Justice (death penalty com.), Amnesty Internat., NAACP (life), ACLU. Democrat. Baptist. Clubs: Press, Commonwealth (San Francisco). Office: 2020 Union St San Francisco CA 94123

BRYAN, SHARON ANN, medical writer, editor; b. Kansas City, Mo., Dec. 18, 1941; d. George William and Dorothy Joan (Henn) Goll; children: Lisa Ann, Holly Renee. BJ, U. Mo., 1963; diploma Stanford Radio and TV Inst., 1961; postgrad. NYU Sch. Arts and Sci., 1963-64; Personal Fin. Planning profl. designation UCLA, 1986; student U. So. Calif. Law Ctr., 1986—. Proofreader, copy editor Cadwalader, Wickersham, and Taft, N.Y.C., 1963-64; manuscript editor, writer nonsci. sects. N.Y. State Jour. Medicine, Med. Soc. State of N.Y., N.Y.C., also mng. editor Staffoscope, 1965-66; manuscript editor Transactions, also editor Perceiver, Am. Acad. Ophthalmology and Otolaryngology, Rochester, Minn., 1969-72, hist. writer, 1972-82; writer publicity articles Ft. Lee (Va.) Community Theatre. Mem. vol. honor roll Soc. of Meml. Sloan-Kettering Cancer Center; active N.Y. Hosp. Women's League, 1965-67 ; docent Los Angeles County Mus. Natural History. Mem. Am. Med. Writers Assn. (editor conv. bull. 1966), AAAS, Internat. Platform Assn., N.Y. Acad. Scis., NOW, Women's Lawyers Assn. of Los Angeles, Kappa Tau Alpha, Kappa Alpha Theta (chmn. membership com. N.Y. chpt. 1966). Club: Stanford. Author: Pioneering Specialists: History of the American Academy of Ophthalmology and Otolaryngology. Home: 533 Via del Monte Palos Verdes Estates CA 90274

BRYANT, DONALD LOUDON, pharmaceutical company executive; b. N.Y.C., June 25, 1908; s. Mortimer D. and Florence (Loudon) B.; m. Elizabeth Sheetz, 1956 (dec. 1983); m. Cynthia Ramsey, 1984. B.A., Williams Coll., 1930; grad., Advanced Mgmt. Program, Harvard U., 1962. With Fed. Advt. Agy., N.Y.C., 1931-35, Publ. Corp., N.Y.C., 1935-45; with Warner Lambert Pharm. Co., Morris Plains, N.J., 1945-59; with Richard Hudnut div. Warner Lambert Pharm. Co., 1953-55, pres. Ciro Perfumes div., 1957, v.p., asst. to pres., 1956-59; pres., dir. Q-Tips, Inc., L.I., N.Y., 1959-63; with Miles Labs., Inc., Elkhart, Ind., 1963-76; group v.p., dir. consumer products div., mem. exec. and finance coms. Miles Labs., Inc., 1964-73, sr. v.p., 1972-73, dir., 1964-76. Mem. Proprietary Assn. (exec. com. 1964-73, v.p.), World Fedn. Proprietary Medicine Mfrs. (founding chmn. 1970-73), Assn. Ex-mems. Squadron A, Elkhart C. of C., Delta Kappa Epsilon. Presbyn. Clubs: Williams (N.Y.C.); Gulfstream Golf, Delray Beach, Harvard Bus. Sch. S. Fla. Home: 86 MacFarlane Dr Delray Beach FL 33444 Office: 1127 Myrtle St Elkhart IN 46514

BRYANT, JOHN, economist, researcher; b. Bedford, Eng., Sept. 21, 1944; s. Jack Ronald and Bessie Muriel (Bates) B.; m. m. Alison Jean Minister; children: Fiona, Amanda, James, Christopher. Mgr. corp. devel. S.K.F., Luton, Eng., 1969-72; personal asst. to mng. dir. gen. engring. div. Babcock Engring. Group, London, 1972-75, mgr. bus. planning Power div., 1975-78; group economist Babcock Internat., London, 1978-80; economist, investment analyst Smith Keen Cutler, London, 1980-81; mng. dir. Mgmt. Insight Internat. Ltd., Harpenden, Eng., 1981—. Mem. Inst. Mech. Engrs., Soc. Bus. Economists, Strategic Planning Soc. Home: 3 Medlows, Hertfordshire, Harpenden AL5 3AY, England

BRYANT, STEVEN HARRY, design engineer; b. Des Moines, Nov. 28, 1946; s. Harry Kenneth and Hannah Levey B. AA in Engring., Fullerton Coll., 1968; BA in History, Calif. State U., Long Beach, 1970. Practice design engr. So. Calif., 1966—; pres. Hawkeye Enterprises, Cathedral City, Calif., 1986—. Contbr. polit. commentary to local newspapers, 1979-82. Commr. San Bernardino County, Calif.; mem. Calif. Dem. State Cen. Com., 1979-85, county sec. 1985; alt. del. Dem. Nat. Conv., 1984; 39th Congl. dist. campaign coordinator Jimmy Carter Dem. Presdl. campaign, 1976; 35th Congl. dist. campaign coordinator Gary Hart Dem. Presdl. campaign, 1984; fin. contbr. Calif. Dems., Dem. Nat. Com.; charter mem. Statue of Liberty Ellis Island Found., 1984—; service area com. for area 19, Chino Hills, 1979-82.

BRYCE, WILLIAM DELF, lawyer; b. Georgetown, Tex., Aug. 7, 1932; s. D. A. Bryce and Frances Maxine (Wilson) Bryce Bakke; m. Sarah Alice Riley, Dec. 20, 1954; children—Douglas Delf, David Dickson. B.A., U. Tex., 1955; LL.B., Yale U., 1960. Bar: Tex. 1960, U.S. Dist. Ct. (we. dist.) Tex. 1963, U.S. Ct. Claims 1964, U.S. Supreme Ct. 1971. Briefing atty. Tex. Supreme Ct., Austin, 1960-61; sole practice, Austin, 1961—; lectr. U. Tex., 1965-66. Editor The Tex. Supreme Ct. Jour., 1962. Served to 1st lt. USAF, 1955-57. Fellow Tex. Bar Found. (sustaining, life); mem. Travis County Bar Assn., State Bar Tex., ABA. Clubs: Argyle (San Antonio); Headliners, Met. (Austin). Home: 308 E University Ave Georgetown TX 78626 Office: 709 Brown Bldg Austin TX 78701

BRYDON, DAVID JOHN, manufacturing company executive; b. Melbourne, Australia, Nov. 6, 1929; s. Rupert James and Isa Mary (Watts) B.; m. Catherine Patricia Smith, Apr. 4, 1953; children—Anthony David, Lisa Ellen, Peter James. Student Scotch Coll., 1941-46. Sales exec. 3M Australia, Melbourne, 1954-65, mktg. dir., Sydney, Australia, 1966-73; mktg. dir. mineral products div. 3M, St. Paul, 1974-75; mng. dir. 3M Brazil, Sao Paulo, 1976-80; packaging systems gen. mgr. 3M St. Paul, 1981-82, v.p., 1982-83; mng. dir. ACI Internat., Melbourne, 1983—. Office: ACI Internat Ltd, 200 Queen St, Melbourne 3000, Australia

BRYDON, HAROLD WESLEY, entomologist, writer; b. Hayward, Calif., Dec. 6, 1923; s. Thomas Wesley and Hermione (McHenry) B.; m. Ruth Bacon Vickery, Mar. 28, 1951 (div.); children: Carol Ruth, Marilyn Jeanette, Kenneth Wesley. AB, San Jose State Coll., 1948; MA, Stanford U., 1950. Insecticide sales Calif. Spray Chem. Corp., San Jose, 1951-52; entomologist, fieldman, buyer Beech-Nut Packing Co., 1952-53; mgr., entomologist Lake County Mosquito Abatement Dist., Lakeport, Calif., 1954-58; entomologist, adviser Malaria Eradication Programs ICA (name changed to AID), Kathmandu, Nepal, 1958-61, Washington, 1961-62, Port-au-Prince, Haiti, 1962-63; dir. fly control research Orange County Health Dept. Santa Ana, Calif., 1963-66; free-lance writer in field, 1966—; research entomologist U. N.D. Sch. Medicine, 1968; developer, owner Casierra Resort, Lake Almanor, Calif., 1975-79; owner Westwood (Calif.) Sport Shop, 1979-84; instr. Lassen Community Coll., Susanville, Calif., 1975—; mem. entomology and plant pathology del. People to People Citizen Ambassador Program, China, 1986. Research and publs. on insecticides, mech. methods for dispersing insecticides, biol. control parasites of houseflies. Served with USNR, 1943-46. Recipient Meritorious Honor award for work in Nepal, AID, U.S. Dept. State, 1972. Mem. Entomol. Soc. Am., Am. Mosquito Control Assn., Pacific Coast Entomol. Soc., Am. Legion. Republican. Methodist. Club: Commonwealth of California. Lodges: Masons, Rotary. Home: PO Box 312 Westwood CA 96137

BRYNJOLFSSON, ARI, nuclear physicist; b. Akureyri, Iceland, Dec. 7, 1926; came to U.S., 1965, naturalized, 1970; s. Brynjolfur and Gudrun (Rosinkarsdottir) Sigtryggsson; m. Marguerite Reman, Dec. 22, 1950; children: Ariane, Olaf, Erik, John, Alan. Cand. Phil., U. Copenhagen, 1949, Cand. Mag., 1954, Mag. Scien., 1954; D.Phil., Niels Bohr Institut Theoretical and Exptl. Nuclear Physics, U. Copenhagen, 1973; post grad., Advanced Mgmt. Program, Harvard U., 1971. Dir. radiation research Danish Atomic Energy Research Establishment, Roskilde, 1957-65; chief radiation research U.S. Army Natick (Mass.) Lab., 1965-72; dir. food irradiation program, 1972-80, spl. asst. for physics, 1980-88; lectr. M.I.T., 1980-88; project dir. Internat. Facility for Food Irradiation Tech., Wageningen, Netherlands, 1988—. Contbr. articles to profl. jours. Recipient Mollers Found. award for exceptional service to Danish industry, 1965; spl. scholar NRC and U. Iceland, 1954-55; Alexander von Humboldt scholar U. Göttingen, W.Ger., 1955-57. Mem. Am. Physi Soc., Radiation Research Soc., Am. Nuclear Soc.,

Am. Soc. Physicists in Medicine, Inst. Food Technologists. Subspecialties: Nuclear physics; radiation biology. Current work: Astrophysics, theoretical physics, general theory of relativity. Biological effects of radiation. Home: 7 Bridle Path Wayland MA 01778 Office: PO Box 230, 6700AE Wageningen The Netherlands

BRYSON, VERN ELRICK, nuclear engineer; b. Woodruff, Utah, May 28, 1920; s. David Hyrum and Luella May (Eastman) B.; m. Esther Sybil de St Jeor, Oct. 14, 1942; children: Britt William, Forrest Lee, Craig Lewis, Nadine, Elaine. Commd. 2d lt. USAAF, 1941; advanced through grades to lt. col. USAF, 1960, ret., 1961; pilot, safety engr., civil engr., electronic engr., nuclear engr., chief Aeronaut. Systems div., Aircraft Nuclear Propulsion Program, Wright-Patterson AFB, Ohio, 1960-61; chiefRadiation Effects Lab., also chief Radiation Effects Group Boeing Airplane Co., Seattle, 1961-65; nuclear engr. Aerospace Corp., San Bernardino, Calif., 1965-68; service engr., also head instrumentation lab., Sacramento Air Logistic Ctr. USAF, McClellan AFB, Calif., 1968-77; owner, mgr. Sylvern Valley Ranch, Calif., 1977—; Mem. panel Transient Radiation Effects on Electronics, Weapons and Effects Bd., 1959-61. Contbr. research articles on radiation problems to profl. pubs. Decorated D.F.C. with oak leaf cluster, Air medal with 12 oak leaf clusters. Mem. IEEE. Mem. Ch. Jesus Christ of Latter-day Saints. Home: 1426 Caperton St Penryn CA 95663

BRYSON, WILLIAM NORMAN, art historian; b. Glasgow, Scotland, Aug. 4, 1949; s. Edward James and Mary Craig (Bendon) B. BA, Cambridge (Eng.) U., 1970, MA, 1972, PhD, 1976. Fellow King's Coll., Cambridge, 1976-87; prof. comparative arts Rochester (N.Y.) U., 1988—. Author: Word and Image, 1981, Vision and Painting, 1984, Tradition and Desire, 1985, Cambridge New Art History, 1988—. Recipient Prix de la Confederation des Negociantes en Oeuvres D'Art, Brussels, 1981.

BRZEZANSKI, JAY MARIAN, financial executive; b. Washington, Jan. 24, 1947; s. Henry Julian and Janina (Kamecki) B.; m. Rosemarie Raimo, Mar. 8, 1980; children: Jennifer, Jonathan. BS, U. Md., 1968; MBA, U. Va., 1970; MMAS, Command and Gen. Staff Coll., 1982. Internal auditor IBM, Armonk, N.Y., 1970-73; sr. staff acct. Gen. Cable Corp., Bayonne, N.J., 1973; sr. staff internal auditor K-Mart Corp., North Bergen, N.J., 1973-77; dir. internal audit Robert Hall Clothes, N.Y.C., 1977, asst. controller, 1977; loss prevention mgr./dir. systems Abraham & Straus, Bklyn., 1977-81; spl. asst. to treas., sr. v.p. fin. Gimbels-N.Y, Batus, N.Y.C., 1981-83, group fin. mgr. and asst., 1983; chief fin. officer, controller Krauszer's Food Stores, Edison, N.J., 1983-84; chief fin. officer D.B. Brown, Perth Amboy, N.J., 1984-86; v.p., chief fin. officer, treas., corp. sec. Tangent Internat., N.Y.C., 1986—. Commr. Boy Scouts Am., 1970-74, explorer advisor, 1971-75; mem. City Council Clifton, 1978, mem. Planning Bd., 1979; mem. Police Aux., CD, Clifton, 1975-78. Founding charter mem. Rep. Nat. Task Force, 1984—. Served with U.S. Army, 1966-69; lt. col. USAR, 1988—. Decorated Order of St. George, Order of Merit, Italy; comdr. Order Brit. Empire; recipient DAR Citizens award, 1970, CD award, 1974, Disting. Service Order, 1985, others. Mem. Inst. Internal Auditors (cert.), Assn. U.S. Army, Systems Mgmt. Assn., Res. Officers Assn., Am. Mgmt. Assn. Roman Catholic. Lodges: KC (4th deg.), Knights of Malta (Comdr. 1988). Home: 16 Hover Dr Mount Arlington NJ 07856 Office: 30 Broad St 44th Floor New York NY 10004

BRZEZINSKI, ZBIGNIEW, political science educator, author; b. Warsaw, Poland, Mar. 28, 1928; came to U.S., 1953, naturalized, 1958; s. Tadeusz and Leonia (Roman) B.; m. Emilie Ann Benes, June 11, 1955; children: Ian, Mark, Mika. B.A. with 1st class honors in Econs. and Polit. Sci., McGill U., 1949, M.A. in Polit. Sci., 1950; Ph.D., Harvard U., 1953. Inst. Govt. and research fellow Russian Research Center, Harvard U., 1953-56; asst. prof. govt., research asso. Russian Research Center and Center Internat. Affairs, Harvard U., 1956-60; asso. prof. public law and govt. Columbia U., 1960-62, prof., 1962-77, 81—; dir. Research Inst. Internat. Change (formerly Research Inst. Communist Affairs), 1962-77; mem. faculty Russian Inst., 1960-77; dir. Trilateral Commn., 1973-76; asst. to Pres. U.S. for nat. security affairs, 1977-81; ofcl. Nat. Security Council, 1977-81; counsellor Ctr. Strategic and Internat. Studies, 1981—; mem. policy planning council Dept. State, 1966-68, President's Fgn. Intelligence adv. bd., 1987—; Mem. joint com. contemporary China, Social Sci. Research Council, 1961-62; guest lectr. numerous pvt. and govt. instns., 1953—, participant internat. confs., 1955—. Author: The Permanent Purge-Politics in Soviet Totalitarianism, 1956, The Soviet Bloc—Unity and Conflict, 1960, Ideology and Power in Soviet Politics, 1962, Alternative to Partition, 1965, Between Two Ages, 1970, The Fragile Blossom, 1971, Power and Principle, 1983, Game Plan, 1986; co-author: Totalitarian Dictatorship and Autocracy, 1957, Political Power: USA/USSR, 1964 (German edit. 1966), also numerous articles.; editor, co-author, contbr.: Political Controls in the Soviet Army, 1954; Editor, co-author, contbr.: Africa and the Communist World, 1963, Dilemmas Of Change In Soviet Politics, 1969, Dilemmi Internationazionali In Un-epoca. Tecnotronica, 1969, columnist: Newsweek, 1970-72. Mem. hon. steering com. Young Citizens for Johnson, 1964. Guggenheim fellow, 1960; Ford Found. fellow, 1970. Fellow Am. Acad. Arts and Scis.; mem. NAACP, Council Fgn. Relations. Club: Internat. (Washington). Office: Ctr Strategic & Internat Studies 1800 K St NW Washington DC 20006

BUBB, HENRY AGNEW, savings and loan association executive; b. Williamsport, Pa., Mar. 26, 1907; s. Harry A. and Marjorie (Wheeler) B.; m. Elizabeth Black, June 26, 1929; 1 child, Barbara Elizabeth (Mrs. John C. Dicus). Student, U. Kans., 1924-27; D.B.A. in Bus. (hon.), Washburn U. Chmn. bd. Capitol Fed. Savs. and Loan Assn., Topeka; former chmn. and dir. Mortgage Guaranty Ins. Corp. of Milw.; chmn. emeritus MGIC Investment Corp., Milw.; dir. Columbian Nat. Title Ins. Co., Topeka, Capitol Funds, Inc., Topeka, Security Benefit Group Cos., Topeka; former chmn. Fed. Home Loan Bank of Topeka; former vice chmn. MGIC Indemnity Corp., N.Y.; former dir. MGIC Fin. Corp., MGIC Mortgage Co., Milw.; past pres. Mid-West Savings and Loan Conf.; past trustee Am. Savs. and Loan Inst.; mem. adv. com. of savs. and loan bus. Treasury Dept.; past mem. task force Fed. Home Loan Bank Bd., Washington. Past sr. mem., chmn. Kans. State Bd. Regents; past chmn. Kans. Edn. Commn.; past chmn. Higher Edn. Loan Program; former dir. Shawnee County ARC, former chmn. numerous charitable drives, chmn., mem. war loan and victory fund coms.; past vice chmn., mem. Topeka Planning Bd.; past chmn. Topeka Housing and Planning Com.; mem. Fiscal Adv. Bd. Topeka; chmn. United Fund; bd. regents Washburn U.; nat. chmn. Young Republican Nat. Fedn., 1937-38; del. Rep. Nat. Conv., 1964; nat. chmn. Citizens for Reagan, 1968; former trustee Inst. Fiscal and Polit. Edn., N.Y.C.; trustee U. Kans. Endowment Assn.; bd. dirs., past pres. Downtown Topeka, Inc. Recipient award Treasury Dept., 1946, Wisdom award of honor, Disting. Service citation, Higher Edn. Leadership prize, Fred Ellsworth medal U. Kans., Disting. Kansan award Native Sons and Daus., 1974, Bubb Light Circle Washburn U., 1980, others. Disting. fellow Internat. Union Bldg. Socs. and Savs. and Loan Assns.; mem. U.S. League Savs. Instns. (chmn. legis. com. 1954-63, legis. cons., exec. com. 1949-63, pres. 1949-50), Kans. Savs. and Loan League (past pres.), U.S. League Savs. Assns. (sr. adv. group com. on polit. action), Topeka C. of C. (past pres., dir.), Kans. U. Alumni Assn. (past nat. pres.), Newcomen Soc. N. Am., S.A.R., 35th Div. Assn., Sigma Chi (past pres. alumni chpt., named Significant Sig 1977), Alpha Kappa Psi. Episcopalian (past sr. warden). Lodges: Masons (Disting. Service award 1968, 33 deg., potentate), Jester (past dir., grand cross Ct. Honor), Rotary (Paul Harris fellow 1986), Sojourners. Clubs: Topeka Country (past pres., past dir.); Cabiri; Garden of the Gods (Colorado Springs, Colo.); Paradise Valley Country (Ariz.). Home: 2323 Mayfair Pl Topeka KS 66611 Office: Capitol Fed Savs and Loan Assn 700 Kansas Ave Topeka KS 66603

BUBNOV, IGOR D., diplomat; b. 1931. Official Soviet Ministry for Fgn. Affairs, 1955-59, 64-66, 71-74, 79-82; official Soviet Embassy, U.S., 1959-64, 1st sec. to counselor, 1971-74, counselor, 1974-79; ambassador to Surinam, 1982. Office: Embassy of USSR, Anton Dragtenweg 17, Paramaribo Suriname

BUCCHIERI, PETER CHARLES, accountant; b. Bristol, Conn., Nov. 2 1955; s. Carmelo Charles and Josephine Maria (Winzereth) B.; B.S., Central Conn. State U., 1978; m. Karen O'Connell., Oct. 11, 1975 (div. 1987); 1 child, Sara; m. Lorinda Carol Smart, July 8, 1988. Pres. Bucchieri & Lochet, Inc., Orleans, Mass., 1978; pres. Investment Timing and Research Inc., 1982—, pres. Eastham Travel, 1986—. Mem. Orleans Bd. Trade, 1978—. Cert. fin. planner. Mem. Internat. Assn. Fin. Planners, Inst. Cert. Fin. Planners, Nat. Assn. Security Dealers, Investment Cos. Inst. and Securities Industry Assn. Republican. Roman Catholic. Contbr. articles to various newspapers. Avocations: skiing, reading. Home: 8 Prides Path Orleans MA 02653 Office: Bucchieri & Lochet Inc 12 Main St Orleans MA 02653

BUCH, FRED NEWTON, manufacturing consultant; b. Lancaster, Pa., Nov. 19, 1937; s. Robert Ray and Helen Hacker B.; Mus.B., Westminster Choir Coll., 1959; m. Ruth Ranck, Oct. 15, 1966; 1 dau., Katrina Melissa. Founder, pres. Buch Church Organ Co., Ephrata, Pa., 1957—; sales cons. Aeolian/Skinner Organ Co., Boston, 1968-72; adminstr. Buch Properties Mgmt., Ephrata, 1977—. Trustee, Westminster Choir Coll., Princeton, N.J., 1980-83; pres. Ephrata Pub. Library, 1979, 80, bd. dirs., 1976-82; bd. dirs. Hist. Soc. Cocalico Valley 1976—, pres., 1980-82, v.p. endowment and devel., 1984—; mem. Zoning Hearing Bd. Ephrata, 1978—, vice-chmn., 1984—; bd. dirs. Old Zion Ch. Hist Site, 1982—, Lancaster County Hist. Preservation Trust, 1987—. Mem. Nat. Assn. Music Mchts., Piano Technicians Guild, Organ Hist. Soc., Am. Theatre Organ Soc., Hist. Soc. Cocalico Valley, Lancaster County Hist. Soc., Lancaster Mennonite Hist. Soc., Hist. Soc. Berks County, Valley Forge Hist. Soc. Republican. Methodist. Office: 1391 W Main St Ephrata PA 17522

BUCHAN, RONALD FORBES, physician; b. Concord, N.H., Sept. 24, 1915; s. Robert and Mary Jean (Forbes) B.; A.B., U. N.H., 1936; M.D., C.M., McGill U., 1940; m. Maureen O'Regan, June 17, 1940; children—Robert Bruce, Joan Dallas (Mrs. Fleming), Ian Forbes Morgan. Reporter, Concord Daily Monitor, 1936; asst. exec. sec. Unemployment Compensation Commn., N.H. Dept. Labor, 1937; sanitarian City of Concord, and Eastern Health Dist. N.H., 1938; chief, med. unit Bur. Indsl. Hygiene, Conn. Dept. Health, 1943-46; dir. Hartford Small Plant Indsl. Med. Service, 1946; clin. dir. Yale U. Inst. Occupational Medicine and Hygiene and asst. prof. indsl. medicine, 1946-48; assoc. clin. prof. indsl. medicine N.Y.U. Bellevue Post Grad. Med. Sch., 1948-57; assoc. med. dir. Prudential Ins. Co. Am., 1948-49, dir. employee health, 1949-57; med. dir., v.p. med. services Prudential Ins. Co. of Am., Boston, 1957-74, cons. occupational medicine and toxicology, 1974—; chief med. dir., v.p. Mediscreen, 1974—; propr. Portsmouth (N.H.) Athenaeum; asso. clin. prof. preventive medicine Tufts U. Sch. Medicine, 1958-74. Chmn. research adv. com. Brattleboro (Vt.) Retreat, 1960-70; mem. sci. adv. bd. Office Chief Staff USAF, chmn. life scis. human factors facilities, 1960-65, protocol rank, lt. gen.; cons. R.I. Group Health Assn., 1973-75. Bd. dirs. Met. Boston chpt. ARC, 1971-73, chmn. com. on safety, 1972-74. Sr. asst. surg., USPHS, 1943-46; surgeon-lt. York (Maine) Militia-Gov.'s Footguard, 1971—; trustee Miles Meml. Hosp., Damariscotta, Maine, , 1988—. Recipient Honor award Wisdom Soc., 1970. Diplomate Nat. Bd. Med. Examiners, Am. Bd. Preventive Medicine. Fellow Am. Acad. Occupational Medicine (past pres.), Am. Coll. Preventive Medicine (chmn. com. on clin. procedures 1972-74), Am. Occupational Med. Assn. (editorial bd. 1958-74); mem. Acad. Medicine N.J. (past pres.), Am. Indsl. Hygiene Assn., Am. Pub. Health Assn., Assn. Life Ins. Medical Directors, AMA (assoc. editor Archives environmental Health), Assn. Internationale Pour La Medicine Du Travail (permanent commn. 1965-74), Mass. Med. Soc., Ramazzini Soc., Academie Europeene des Arts, Sciences et des Lettres, Am. Assn. Sr. Physicians, N.Y. Acad. Scis., Planetary Soc., AAAS, Nat. Trust Historic Preservation, Soc. for Preservation of New Eng. Antiquities, John Buchan Soc. (Edinburgh), Soc. for Protection of N.H. Forests, North Country Authors and Scientists League (past pres.), Newcomen Soc. N.Am., St. Andrew's Soc. of Maine, Clan Buchan U.S.A., Clan Forbes U.S.A., Lowland Clans and Families U.S.A., U. N.H. Alumni Assn. (gen. awards com. 1987—). Author: Industrial Tooxicology. Contbr. Oxford Medicine, Current Therapy, Occupational Medicine, Encyclopedie-Medico-Chirurgicale (Paris); also numerous profl. texts and jours. Home: Thistle Downs Box 846 Damariscotta ME 04543

BUCHANAN, BRENDA J., computer manufacturing executive; b. San Diego; d. Fred and Annie M. (Winston) B. BS in Math., Physics and Chemistry, U. Denver; MA in Math., Washington U., 1973; postgrad. McGill U., 1973-75, U. Cologne, Fed. Republic Germany. Math. instr. Washington U., St. Louis, 1969-71; programmer/analyst United Aircraft of Can., Longueil, Que., 1971-73; ops. research analyst Consol. Bathurst Ltd., Montreal, Que., 1973-76; corp. new product planning mgr. Digital Equipment Corp., Maynard, Mass., 1976-80, new product program mgr., Springfield, Mass., 1980-84, tapes bus. mgr., 1984-88, corp. purchasing program office mgr., Northboro, Mass., 1986-88; dist. mfg. mgr., Marlboro, Mass., 1988—; mem. Digital Equipment Women's Adv. Com., 1986—. Leader, Can. Girl Guides, Montreal, 1972-74; mem. mayor's blue ribbon com. Dept. Pub. Works, Springfield, 1983. Fulbright fellow, Fed. Rep. Germany; recipient Experiment in Internat. Living award Fed. Republic Germany, 19. Mem. Can. Ops. Research Soc., LWV (bd. dirs.), Strathmore Shire Assn. (bd. trustees 1987—), The Profl. Council (Boston), Alpha Kappa Alpha (Basileus, Ivy of Yr., Denver chpt.). Democrat. Baptist. Club: Links, Inc. (Springfield) (treas. 1984-86). Home: 4E Strathmore Shire PO Box 49 North Uxbridge MA 01538 Office: Digital Equipment Corp 3 Results Way (MR03-2/J20) Marlboro MA 01752-9103

BUCHANAN, JAMES MCGILL, economist, educator; b. Murfreesboro, Tenn., Oct. 2, 1919; s. James McGill and Lila (Scott) B.; m. Anne Bakke, Oct. 5, 1945. B.S., Middle Tenn. State Coll., 1940; M.A., U. Tenn., 1941; Ph.D., U. Chgo., 1948; Dr.h.c., U. Giessen, 1982, U Zurich, 1984, George Mason U., U. Valencia, New U. Lisbon, 1987. Prof. econs. U. Tenn., 1950-51; prof. econs. Fla. State U., 1951-56; prof. econs. U. Va., 1956-62, Paul G. McIntyre prof. econs., 1962-68, chmn. dept., 1956-62; prof. econs. U. Calif., Los Angeles, 1968-69; univ. disting. prof. econs. Va. Poly. Inst., 1969-83, George Mason U., 1983—; dir. Ctr. for Pub. Choice, 1969—; Fulbright research scholar, Italy, 1955-56, Ford Faculty research fellow, 1959-60; Fulbright vis. prof. Cambridge U., 1961-62. Author: (with C.L. Allen and M.R. Colberg) Prices, Income and Public Policy, 954, Public Principles of Public Debt, 1958, The Public Finances, 1960, Fiscal Theory and Political Economy, 1960, (with G. Tullock) The Calculus of Consent, 1962, Public Finance in Democratic Process, 1966, The Demand and Supply of Public Goods, 1968, Cost and Choice, 1969, (with N. Devletoglou) Academia in Anarchy, 1970; Editor: (with R. Tollison) Theory of Public Choice, 1972, (with G.F. Thirlby) LSE Essays on Cost, 1973, The Limits of Liberty, 1975, (with R. Wagner) Democracy in Deficit, 1977, Freedom in Constitutional Contract, 1978, What Should Economists Do?, 1979, (with G. Brennan) The Power to Tax, 1980; (with G. Brennan) The Reason of Rules, 1985; Liberty Market and State, 1985, Economics: Between Predictive Science and Moral Philosophy, 1987; contbr. articles to profl. jours. Served as lt. USNR, 1941-46. Decorated Bronze Star medal. Recipient Nobel Prize in Economics, 1986. Fellow Am. Acad. Arts and Scis.; mem. Am. Econ. Assn. (exec. com. 1966-69, v.p. 1971, dist. fellow 1983—, Seidman award 1984), So. Econ. Assn. (pres. 1963), Western Econ. Assn. (pres. 1983), Mt. Pelerin Soc. (pres. 1984-86). Home: PO Box G Blacksburg VA 24063 Office: George Mason U Dept Econs 4400 University Dr Fairfax VA 22030

BUCHANAN, JOHN ROBERT, physician, educator; b. Newark, Mar. 8, 1928; s. John Hamilton and Elsie (Castles) B.; m. Susan Townsend Carver, Oct. 27, 1962; children: Ross, Allyn. A.B. cum laude, Amherst Coll., 1950; M.D., Cornell U., 1954; student, Inst. Arthritis and Metabolic Diseases, USPHS, 1956-57, 60-61. Diplomate: Am. Bd. Internal Medicine, Nat. Bd. Med. Examiners. Intern, asst. resident physician N.Y. Hosp., N.Y.C., 1954-58; physician to outpatients N.Y. Hosp., 1956-57, 60-62, from asst. to assoc. attending physician, 1962-71, attending physician, 1971-76, asso. dir. welfare med. care project, 1961-64; vis. asst. physician Rockefeller Inst. Hosp., N.Y.C., 1960-61; assoc. vis. physician Bellevue Hosp., N.Y.C., 1965-68; instr. medicine Cornell U., 1961-63, asst. prof. medicine, 1963-67, asst. dir. comprehensive care and teaching program, 1961-64, asst. to chmn. dept. medicine, 1964-65; assoc. dean Cornell U. (Med. Coll.), 1965-69, dean, 1969-76, clin. assoc. prof. medicine, 1967-69, asso. prof., 1969-71, prof., 1971-76; pres. Michael Reese Hosp. and Med. Center, Chgo., 1977-82; prof. medicine Pritzker Sch. Medicine, U. Chgo., 1977-82, assoc. dean, 1978-82; gen. dir. Mass. Gen. Hosp., Boston, 1982—; prof. medicine Harvard U. Med. Sch., Boston, 1982—; mem. com. on sci. policy Sloan-Kettering Inst., 1969-76; mem. State of Ill. Med. Determination Bd., 1980—; sr. program cons. prepaid managed health care program Robert Wood Johnson Found., 1982—; mem. adminstrv. bd. Council Teaching Hosps., 1984—; dir. Bank of New Eng., N.A.; bd. dirs. Charles River Breeding Labs., 1987—. Chmn. nat. adv. council Children's Television Workshop, 1974-75; Bd. dirs. Pub. Health Research Inst. of N.Y.C., 1969-76, Winnifred Masterson Burke Relief Found., 1972-80, 82—; trustee Cornell U., 1970-76; trustee China Med. Bd. of N.Y., Inc., 1970—, vice chmn.; bd. mgrs. Meml. Hosp., 1969-76; mem. adv. com. Edwin L. Crosby and W.K. Kellogg Found. Fellowships, 1979-80; trustee Center for Effective Philanthropy, 1981-85. Served as AUS, 1958-60. Fellow A.C.P., Am. Pub. Health Assn.; mem. Harvey Soc., N.J. State, N.Y. County med. socs., N.Y. Acad. (council deans 1969-76, exec. council 1971-76), Assn. Am. Med. Colls. (vice chmn. liaison com. on med. edn. 1982-83, chmn. 1983; chmn.-elect council of teachng hosps. 1986), Assn. Med. Schs. N.Y. and N.J. (trustee 1970-76, pres. 1972-76), Inst. Medicine-Nat. Acad. Scis., Ill. Hosp. Assn. (chmn. 1979-80), N.Y. Acad. Medicine, Royal Soc. for Promotion Health, Sigma Xi. Home: 25 Commonwealth Ave Boston MA 02116 Office: Mass Gen Hosp Boston MA 02114

BUCHBINDER, DARRELL BRUCE, lawyer, b. N.Y.C., Oct. 17, 1946; s. Julian and Bernice (Levy) B.; m. Janet Grey McLean, Jan. 22, 1977; children: Julian Bradford, Andrew Grey. BA in Politics with honors, NYU, 1968, JD, 1971. Bar: N.Y. 1972, U.S. Dist. Ct. (so. and ea. dists.) N.Y. 1973. Sole practice, N.Y.C., 1972-79; atty. Port Authority of N.Y. and N.J., N.Y.C., 1979-83, prin. atty., 1983-86, dep. chief fin. div. Law Dept., 1986—. Served with USNR, 1968-70. Mem. Nat. Assn. Bond Lawyers, Bar Assn. of City of N.Y., Pi Sigma Alpha. Republican. Club: Larchmont Shore. Office: Port Authority NY and NJ 1 World Trade Ctr New York NY 10048

BUCHBINDER, RUDOLF, pianist, educator; b. Leitmeritz, Austria, Dec. 1, 1946; m. Agnes Rado, Dec. 30, 1965; children—Susan, Michael. Prof. music U. Bzsel, Switzerland, 1976—; concert appearances through the world; rec. artist. Recipient Mozart Interpretation prize Austrian Ministry of Culture, 1970; Grand Prix de Disque, Academie Charles Cros-Paris, 1976. Address: Wilbrandtgasse 1, A-1190 Vienna Austria

BUCHER, JACQUES PIERRE, obstetrician; b. Mortagne, Orne, France, June 22, 1923; s. Robert Luc and Suzanne Marie (Fromont) B.; m. Therese Henriette Leruste, Oct. 12, 1946; children: Gilles, Marc, Christophe. PhB, St Francois de Sales U., 1942; MD, Paris Faculty, 1952. Gen. practice medicine specializing in ob-gyn Clinique St. Damien, Sarthe, France, 1953—. Mem Soc. Obstetrics and Gynecology Paris. Office: 20 Rue de Des Pompes, 7200 Le Mans, Sarthe France

BUCHERRE, VERONIQUE, development company executive, international cultural consultant; b. Casablanca, Morocco, Nov. 20, 1951; came to U.S., 1967; d. Maurice Daniel Bucherre and Lucette Jaqueline Piani; m. Douglas Lee Frazier. Diploma Para Profesores, Gregorio Maranon, Madrid, 1972; MA, San Francisco State U., 1974; PhD, U. Paris, 1980; diploma in conf. interpreting, London Sch. of Poly., 1983. Instr. French Peace Corps, Baker, La., 1968; editorial asst. Newsweek mag., San Francisco, 1970-72; mem. faculty San Francisco State U., 1972-74, 77; conf. interpreter-translator, France and U.S., 1974-85; rural developer, France and U.S., 1976-86; pres. Bucherre & Assocs., Washington, 1985-88, inventor The Rainbank Group, 1988—; bd. dirs. Rainbank Project; pres. Rainbank Group Ltd.; bd. dirs. Rainbank Group Ltd.; mem. bd. mgmt. Institut des Hautes Etudes de L'Amerique Latine, Paris, 1975-76; mem. Lab III, Centre National de Recherche Scientifique, Paris, 1975-77; mem. Interamerican Def. Inst. Civilian Personnel Assn. (pres. 1988—). Author: Florence, 1979, Uruguay, 1980. Club: Droit Humain, G.I.T.E. (Paris).

BUCHIN, STANLEY IRA, management consultant; b. N.Y.C., Sept. 7, 1931; s. K. and Bertha (Handman) B.; S.B., M.I.T., 1952; M.B.A., Harvard U., 1956, D.B.A., 1962; m. Jacqueline Thurber Chase, Sept. 14, 1957; children—Linda C., David L., Gordon T. Asst. to treas. Bay State Abrasives, 1956-58; research asst. Harvard Bus. Sch., 1958-59, research assoc., 1959-60, instr., 1960-61, lectr., 1961-62, asst. prof., 1962-66, asso. prof., 1966-69; pres. Applied Decision Systems, Wellesley, Mass., 1969-78; v.p. Temple, Barker & Sloane, Inc., Lexington, Mass., 1975-80, sr. v.p., 1980—, also dir.; dir. Wellesley Volkswagen, Capital Formations Corp., Diamond Machining Tech. Multicomp. Trustee, treas. Human Relations Service, 1973-82; trustee Gould Farm; mem. adv. com. Mass. Dept. Mental Health. Served in Chem. Corps, U.S. Army, 1952-54. IBM fellow, 1962-63; George F. Baker scholar, 1956. Mem. Am. Mktg. Assn., Inst. Mgmt. Sci., Fin. Mgmt. Assn., Tau Beta Pi. Republican. Congregationalist. Clubs: Stage Harbor Yacht, Harvard (Boston), Cambridge Boat. Home: 65 E India Row Boston MA 02110 Office: Temple Barker and Sloane 33 Hayden Ave Lexington MA 02173

BUCHOLZ, PETER, educator; b. Saarbrüken, Germany, Feb. 6, 1941; arrived in South Africa, 1981; s. Günther and Ilse (Schmidt) B.; m. Birkhild Utta, May 22, 1968. MA, U. Münster, 1966, PhD, 1968; Habilitation, U. Kiel, 1977. Research asst. U. Münster, Fed. Republic Germany, 1964-68; lectr. U. South Africa, Pretoria, 1969-71, sr. lectr., 1981—; sr. research fellow U. Kiel, Fed. Republic Germany, 1972-81. Contbr. articles to profl. jours. Recipient Disting. Leadership award, ABI, 1986. Mem. Internat. Vereinigung Für Germanische Sprach-und Literaturwissenschaft, Internat. Soc. for Folk Narrative Research, Soc. for Advancement of Scandinavian Studies, Folklore Soc. Home: 4 Finus Rd, Valhalla, Pretoria 0185, Republic of South Africa Office: U South Africa, Pretoria Republic of South Africa

BUCHWALD, ART, columnist, writer; b. Mt. Vernon, N.Y., Oct. 20, 1925; s. Joseph and Helen (Kleinberger) B.; m. Ann McGarry, Oct. 11, 1952; 3 children. Student, U. So. Calif., 1945-48. Syndicated columnist, 550 newspapers throughout world; columnist Los Angeles Times Syndicate. Author: Paris After Dark, 1950, Art Buchwald's Paris, 1954, The Brave Coward, 1957, A Gift From the Boys, 1959, More Caviar, 1958, Un Cadeau Pour Le Patron (Prix de la Bonne Humeur 1958), Don't Forget to Write, 1960, Art Buchwald's Secret List to Paris, 1963, How Much Is That in Dollars?, 1961, Is It Safe to Drink the Water?, 1962, I Chose Capitol Punishment, 1963, And Then I Told the President, 1965, Son of the Great Society, 1966, Have I Ever Lied To You, 1968, The Establishment Is Alive and Well in Washington, 1969, Counting Sheep, 1970, Getting High in Government Circles, 1971, I Never Danced at the White House, 1973, The Bollo Caper, 1974, I Am Not a Crook, 1974, Irving's Delight, 1975, Washington is Leaking, 1976, Down the Seine and Up the Potomac, 1977, The Buchwald Stops Here, 1978, Laid Back in Washington, 1981, While Reagan Slept, 1983, You CAN Fool All of The People All The Time, 1985, I Think I Don't Remember, 1987. Served as sgt. USMCR, 1942-45. Recipient Pulitzer prize for outstanding commentary, 1982. Mem. Am. Acad. and Inst. Arts and Letters, Am. Acad. Humor Columnists. Club: Anglo-American Press (Paris). Office: 2000 Pennsylvania Ave NW Washington DC 20006

BUCK, CHRISTIAN BREVOORT ZABRISKIE, ind. oil operator; b. San Francisco, Oct. 18, 1914; s. Frank Henry and Zayda Justine (Zabriskie) B.; student U. Calif., Berkeley, 1931-33; m. Natalie Leontine Smith, Sept. 12, 1948; children—Warren Zabriskie, Barbara Anne. Mem. engrng. dept. U.S. Potash Co., Carlsbad, N.Mex., 1933-39; ind. oil operator, producer, Calif., 1939-79, N.Mex., 1939—; owner, operator farm, ranch, Eddy County, N.Mex., 1951-79; dir. Belridge Oil Co. until 1979; dir. Buck Ranch Co. (Calif.). Served with RAF, 1942-45. Democrat. Episcopalian. Club: Riverside Country (Carlsbad). Home: 108 W Alicante Rd Santa Fe NM 87501 Office: PO Box 2183 Santa Fe NM 87504

BUCK, GERALD STEPHEN, architect; b. N.Y.C., July 4, 1946; s. Arthur and Dorothy F. (Coyne) B. B.Bldg. Sci., Rensselaer Poly. Inst., Troy, N.Y., 1968, B.Arch., 1968. Vol., Peace Corps, Puerto La Cruz, Venezuela, 1968-71; archtl. designer Bonsignore, Brignati, Goldstein & Mazzotta, N.Y.C., 1972; architect Edelman & Salzman, N.Y.C., 1972-78; ptnr. The Edelman Partnership/Architects, N.Y.C., 1979—; Co-author: Hospital, 1967; Neighborhood, 1968. Recipient nat. historic commendation Republic of Venezuela, 1970; urban planning award Mcpl. Govt. of Puerto La Cruz. 1971; award of merit N.J. chpt. Am. Concrete Inst., 1980; Albert S. Bard award for merit in architecture and urban design City Club of N.Y., 1982; pub. service award for excellence in archtl. services Settlement Housing Fund, N.Y.C., 1983. Mem. AIA (historic bldgs. com. N.Y. chpt.), N.Y.C. Mcpl. Arts Soc. (cert. of merit 1983), Nat. Trust for Historic Preservation (honor award 1983), Architects for Social Responsibility, Soc. for Mktg. Profl. Services. Roman Catholic. Office: Edelman Ptnrship/Architects 434 6th Ave New York NY 10011

BUCK, GURDON HALL, lawyer, real estate broker; b. Hartford, Conn., Apr. 10, 1936; s. Richard Saltonstall and Aloha Frances (Hall) B.; m. Sharon Smith, Dec. 27, 1958; children—Keith Saltonstall, Frances Josephine, Daniel Winthrop. B.A. in English, Lehigh U., 1958; J.D., U. Pa., 1965. Bar: Conn. 1965, U.S. Dist. Ct. 1966, U.S. Ct. Appeals (2d cir.) 1966. Assoc. Shipman & Goodwin, Hartford, 1965-67; v.p./counsel R. F. Broderick & Assocs., Hartford, 1968-69; ptnr. Pelgrift, Byrne, Buck & Connolly, Hartford and Farmington, Conn., 1969-75, Byrne, Buck, & Steiner and predecessor Byrne & Buck, Farmington, 1975-79; chmn. real estate dept. Robinson & Cole, Farmington and Hartford, 1980—. Served to lt. (s.g.) USCGR, 1958-62. Recipient Disting. Service award Glastonbury (Conn.) Jaycees, 1968. Mem. ABA (com. on coms., chmn. condominium com. Sect. Real Property and Probate, adv. Uniform Planned Community Act, Model Real Estate Coop. Act and Uniform Common Interest Ownership Act), Conn. Bar Assn., Hartford County Bar Assn., Internat. Bar Assn. (panelist common ownership consumer protection 1987), Hartford Bd. Realtors, Am. Coll. Real Estate Lawyers (bd. govs., chmn. common ownership com.), Am. Land Devel. Assn., Anglo-Am. Real Property Inst. (common ownership com.), Community Assns. Inst. (nat. trustee; chmn. lawyers council, pres. Conn. chpt. 1980-83, sec. 1986—, pres. Research Found. 1980-82, Byron Hanke Disting. Service award), Acad. of Authors. Club: Century, Hartford. Prin. co-author: The Connecticut Condominium Manual, 1972; Real Estate Brokers Community Associations Handbook, rev. edit., 1982; Connecticut Common Interest Ownership Manual, 1984; The Alaska Common Interest Ownership Manual, 1985; contbr. numerous articles on zoning, condominiums, planned unit devels. to profl. jours.; Condo Sense columnist Stamford Adv. and Greenwich Time. Office: 1 Commercial Plaza Hartford CT 06103

BUCK, JAMES ARNOLD, utility official, consultant; b. Evanston, Ill., Dec. 7, 1948; s. Arnold Queese and Carol Jean (Tait) B.; children: Marguerite Josephine, Lea Christine. BS in Journalism, So. Ill. U., 1972. Site rep. N. Anna Nuclear Power Sta., 1976-77, sr. pub. relations rep. corp. hdqrs., Richmond, Va., 1977-78, supr. community relations Bath County pumped storage project, Mountain Grove, Va., 1978-80, dir. media/community relations, No. Va. Power, 1980-86; pres., chief exec. officer McQuistan Assocs., 1986-87; loaned exec., speechwriter to Inst. of Nuclear Power Ops., 1986-88; sr. writer Ill. Poer Co.; guest lectr. energy, pub. relations, legis. affairs. Chmn. legis. affairs com., lobbyist Fairfax County C. of C., 1982-84. treas. Springfield Breakfast Rotary Club, 1981-84; active Fairfax Com. of 100; pres. Highland County Jaycees, 1978-80; sec. Monterey Lions Club, 1979-80. Served with USN, 1972-76. Mem. No. Va. Press Club (sec. 1982-84), Soc. Consumer Affairs Profls., Pub. Relations Soc. Am. (accredited mem.). Anglican Catholic. Lodge: Rotary (dir., treas. 1981-86). Home: 9 Powers Lane Pl Decatur IL 62522 Office: 500 S 27th St Decatur IL 62525

BUCK, NATALIE SMITH, former state ofcl.; b. Carlsbad, N.Mex., Jan. 10, 1923; d. Milton R. and Rosa Adele (Binford) Smith; student Coll. William and Mary, 1940-41; B.B.S., U. Colo., 1943; postgrad. U. Tex., 1945-46; m. C. B. Buck, Sept. 12, 1948; children—Warren Z., Barbara Anne. Chief clk., State Senate, N.Mex., 1951-53; sec. of state, N.Mex., 1955-59; chief personnel adminstr. N.Mex. Health and Social Services Dept., 1959-73. Democrat. Home: 108 W Alicante Rd Santa Fe NM 87501

BUCK, ROBERT REINHART, lawyer; b. Oklahoma City, Dec. 29, 1928; s. Arthur M. and Margaret A. (Rinehart) B.; m. Anne S. Scharlach, July 29, 1957; children—Carol, Alison, Monica, Leslie; m. 2d, Betty R. Cain, Dec. 27, 1978. B.S., Okla. State U., Stillwater, 1951; LL.D., U. Okla., 1956. Bar: U.S. Dist. Ct. (we. dist.) Okla. 1958, U.S. Supreme Ct. 1975. With Buck & Crabtree, Oklahoma City; to 1979; ptnr. Buck & Hoyt, Ltd., Oklahoma City, 1979—; lectr. U. Okla. Law Sch., Oklahoma City U., Law Sch., Tulsa U. Law Sch., Law Sci. Inst., Okla. Trial Lawyers, Okla. Hwy. Safety Office. Former dir. Urban League of Oklahoma City; leader Boy Scouts Am.; family life dir. diocese, Roman Catholic Ch.; Served to capt. USAF, 1951-63. Mem. ABA, Oklahoma Bar Assn., Oklahoma County Bar Assn., Assn. Trial Lawyers Am. (former state del.), Okla. Trial Lawyers Assn. (v.p. 1972, pres. elect 1973, pres. 1984). Democrat. Roman Catholic. Office: 1400 N Shartel Oklahoma OK 73103

BUCKLES-DEANS, DELORA ELIZABETH, educational diagnostician, consultant; b. Houston, Apr. 19, 1940; d. Joseph Bernhardt and Helen Elizabeth (Phillips) Blazek; m. Richard George Buckles, June 26, 1962 (div. Oct. 1969); children—Gregory, Deborah; m. 2d, Harry Alexander Deans, Jan. 1, 1975; 1 dau., Catherine; stepchildren—Laurie, Daniel, Melissa, Andrew. B.A., U. Tex., 1962; postgrad. Cornell U., 1962; M.Ed., Boston U., 1966, cert. advanced grad. study, 1966; Ed.D., U. Houston, 1981. Instr., Boston U., 1964-66; coordinator Harris County Dept. Edn., Houston, 1969-72; dir. resource services Klein Ind. Sch. Dist., Spring, Tex., 1972-75; coordinator, ednl. diagnostician area 6 Houston Ind. Sch. Dist., 1975-78; inservice coordinator Coll. Edn. U. Houston, 1979-81; ednl. diagnostician Vocat. Evaluation Ctr. for Handicapped, Houston, 1981-84; coordinator ednl./vocat. evaluation Houston Ind. Sch. Dist., 1984-86; cons. Aldine Ind. Sch. Dist., Houston, 1981-82, Harlingen Ind. Sch. Dist. (Tex.), 1982-83, Humble Ind. Sch. Dist., 1986—, ednl. diagnostician, 1986—; adj. prof. U. Houston at Clearlake, 1984—. Contbr. articles to profl. jours.; patentee in field. Campaign worker Democratic Party Tex., Houston, 1979-86. Named Outstanding Student, U. Tex., Austin, 1962. Mem. Council Ednl. Diagnostics Services (sec. 1981-83), Tex. Council Exceptional Children (chmn. 1980-82), Tex. Ednl. Diagnostics Assn. (pres. 1981-82), Tex. Div. for Career Devel. (pres. 1986—), Phi Delta Kappa, Zeta Tau Alpha. Democrat. Episcopalian. Home: 1931 Wroxton St Houston TX 77005

BUCKLEY, EDWARD JOSEPH, retired college dean; b. Belleville, Ont., Can., Aug. 28, 1920; s. William John and Mary Jane (Conlin) B. B.A., U. Ottawa (Ont.), 1952, M.A., 1958. Teaching master, Ont. Coll. Edn., Toronto. Treas., Famous Players Can. Corp., Belleville, 1940-60; dir. Fed. Govt. Adult Tng. Program, Belleville, 1960-70; dir. tech. div. Loyalist Coll. Applied Arts and Tech., Belleville, 1970-75, dean continuing edn., 1976-85. Author: History of St. Michael's Parish, 1829-1979, 1983. Mem., chmn. Belleville Separate Sch. Bd., 1943-60; mem. Belleville Retarded Children Authority, 1952-59; mem., chmn. bd. dirs. Belleville Dept. Health, 1949-56. Decorated Knight Equestrian Order Holy Sepulchre, Knight Sovereign M.I. Order Maltn. Liberal. Roman Catholic. Lodge: K.C. (state dep. Ont. 1978-80, dir. New Haven 1983—). Home: 153 Dundas St W, Belleville, ON Canada K8P 1A7

BUCKLEY, EDWARD RICHARD, chemical company executive; b. Wilmington, Del., Dec. 10, 1934; s. Edward Joseph and Hannah Jane (Shellady) B.; student U.S. Naval Acad., 1953-54; B.A., King's Coll., 1963. Salesman, DuPont Co., Chgo., 1963-67; mgr. graphic arts industry products Tex. Instruments, Attleboro, Mass., 1967; graphic arts products sales mgr. Du Pont Co., Cleve., Atlanta and Wilmington, Del., 1968-73, nat. sales mgr., Wilmington, 1973-77, mktg. mgr., 1977-82; nat. sales mgr. P.D. Magnetics affiliate Du Pont Co., 1982-84, v.p. ops., 1984-86; mktg. mgr. Du Pont Co., 1986—; bd. dirs. Del. Safety Council, 1985—. Mem. Internat. Tape Assn. (bd. dirs. 1984—), Mensa, Am. Film Inst. Republican. Roman Catholic. Clubs: Kennett Square Country (Pa.); Rehoboth Beach (Del.) Country; University and Whist (Wilmington). Home: 1016 S Hilton Rd Wilmington DE 19803 Office: DuPont Co BMP 301254 Wilmington DE 19898

BUCKLEY, JACK BOYD, mechanical and electrical engineer; b. Fort Wayne, Ind., Feb. 6, 1926; s. Chauncey Jason and Ruth W. (Boyd) B.; m. Helen C. Sartwelle, Jan. 18, 1952; children: Elizabeth Ann (Mrs. Christopher Till), James S., Steven B., William H. Student, Ind. State U., 1944, Kans. State U., 1944-45, Purdue, 1947; BCE, Rice Inst., 1948; postgrad., U. Houston, 1948-49. Registered profl. engr., Tex. Vice chmn. bd. I.A. Naman Assocs., Inc. and I.A. Naman Assocs. West, Inc., Houston, 1949—, also bd. dirs.; pres. Internat. Engrs., Inc., Houston; bd. dirs. Port City Stockyard, Tex. Agribus. Co., Inc.; mem. Houston Air Conditioning Bd., 1974-78; mem. Houston Gen. Appeals Bd., 1978—, chmn., 1987—. Cons. editor: Specifying Engr. mag., 1974—; contbr. articles to profl. jours.Mem. Aldine (Ind.) Sch. Bd., 1954-55; adv. council Am. Arbitration Assn.; bd. dirs. Goodwill Industries. Served with USNR, 1944-46. Fellow ASHRAE (chpt. pres. 1961); mem. Constrn. Specifications Inst. (chpt. pres. 1973-74), NSPE, Tex. Soc. Profl. Engrs., Am. Hosp. Assn., Nat. Fire Protection Assn. (mem. 90A and 92A coms.), Illuminating Engring. Soc., Smoke Control Assocs., Am. Cons. Engr. Council, Houston Livestock Show and Rodeo (life), Nat. Rifle Assn. (life), Am. Forestry Assn., Am. Mgmt. Assn., Constrn. Industry Council Houston, Soc. Fire Protection Engrs., Cease Fire Club Houston, Houston Zool. Soc. (bd. dirs. 1969-73). Club: 100 (life, dir. 1975) (Houston). Lodge: Rotary (Paul Harris fellow). Home: 10047 Del Monte Dr Houston TX 77042 Office: 2 Greenway Plaza 5th Floor Houston TX 77046

BUCKLEY, JOHN HOWARD, accountant; b. Preston, Lancashire, Eng., Aug. 7, 1947; s. Jack and Margorie (Simpson) B.; m. Helen Diana Young, Aug. 23, 1969; 1 child, Oliver John. LLB, Queens U., Belfast, 1971. Staff acct. Arthur Andersen & Co., London, Manchester, Eng., 1971-76; controller fin. group Whitecroft PLC, Manchester, 1976-80; dir. fin. planning Bassett Foods PLC, Sheffield, Eng., 1980-86; dir. fin. Pittard Garnar PLC, Yeovil, Eng., 1986—. Office: Pittard Garnar PLC, Sherborne Rd, Yeovil BA215BA, England

BUCKLEY, JOHN JOSEPH, JR., healthcare executive; b. Evanston, Ill., Oct. 5, 1944; s. John Joseph and Mary Ruth (Smith) B.; m. Sarah Amelia Puceloski, May 16, 1970; children—Ruth Mary, Patricia Kimberly, John Joseph III. A.B., Kenyon Coll., 1966; M.B.A., George Washington U., 1969. Asst. adminstr. Maricopa County Gen. Hosp., Phoenix, 1969-71; asst. adminstr. St. Joseph's Hosp. and Med. Ctr., Phoenix, 1971-74, assoc. adminstr., 1974-76, v.p., 1976-79, pres., 1984—; pres. St. Anthony's Hosp., Amarillo, Tex., 1979-84, St. Anthony's Devel. Corp., Amarillo, 1982-84; chief operating officer Harrington Cancer Ctr., Amarillo, 1982-84. Active Amarillo Alliance of Community Service Execs., Amarillo Area Acad. Health Ctr. Corp., Amarillo Area Hosp. Home Care, Amarillo Found. Health and Sci., Panhandle chpt. Tex. Soc. to Prevent Blindness, Amarillo Jr. League, Children's Oncology Services of Tex. Panhandle; Amarillo diocesan coordinator health affairs; mem. adminstrv. com. Amarillo; pres. Mercy Services Corp., 1984—; bd. dirs. Greater Phoenix Affordable Health Care Found. Fellow Am. Coll. Healthcare Execs. (regent Ariz. 1984-88); mem. Tex. Hosp. Assn. (trustee 1983-84), Phoenix C. of C. (bd. dirs. 1985-88), Cath. Health Assn. U.S. (bd. dirs., services com., trustee 1985—), Ariz. Kidney Found. (trustee com. on govt. relations 1985-88). Republican. Roman Catholic. Home: 6834 E Belmont Circle Paradise Valley AZ 85253 Office: St Joseph's Hosp & Med Ctr PO Box 2071 Phoenix AZ 85001

BUCKLEY, PETER JENNINGS, economics educator; b. Ashton-under-Lyne, Lancashire, Eng., July 11, 1949; s. Robert and Florence (Jennings) B.; m. Ann Patricia Kelland; children: Alice Louise, Thomas Robert. BA in Social Scis. with honors, U. York, Eng., 1970; MA, U. East Anglia, Norwich, Eng., 1971; PhD, U. Lancaster, Eng., 1975. Esme Fairbairn research asst. U. Reading, Eng., 1973-74; lectr. internat. bus. U. Bradford (Eng.) Mgmt. Ctr., 1974-80, sr. lectr., 1980-84, prof. econs., 1984—; vis. prof. U. Reading, 1987-88; cons. numerous firms and orgns. Author: The Future of the Multinational Enterprise, 1976, others; editor Handbook of Internat. Trade, 1983; contbr. numerous articles to profl. jours. Fellow Acad. Internat. Bus. (chmn. U.K. Region 1985—); mem. Royal Econ. Soc. Mem. Church of England. Club: Shibden Valley Soc. (vice chmn. 1983-1897). Office: U Bradford Mgmt Centre, Emm Ln, Bradford England BD9 4JL

BUCKLEY, THOMAS HUGH, historian, educator; b. Elkhart, Ind., Sept. 11, 1932; s. Bernard Leroy and Martha B. (Swoveland) B.; m. Julie Griffith; children: Christopher, Kathryn, Elizabeth, Thomas, Barbara. Student, Northwestern U., 1950-53; A.B., Ind. U., 1955, M.A., 1956, Ph.D. (grad. fellow), 1961; postdoctoral fellow, Stanford U., 1968, U. Wis., 1983, Brown U., 1986. From instr. to prof. U. S.D., 1960-69; vis. prof. Ind. U., 1969-71; prof., chmn. dept. U. Tulsa, 1971-81, chmn. humanistic studies, 1975-81, Jay Walker research chair Am. History, 1981—; cons. on overseas edn. to Nat. Edn. Corp. Author: The United States and the Washington Conference, 1921-1922, 1970 (award as best first book by an historian 1971); co-author: American Foreign and National Security Policies, 1914-1945, 1987; editor: Research and Roster Guide of Soc. Historians of Am. Fgn. Relations, 1980-86; contbr. chpts. in books. Fulbright fellow, U. Western Australia, 1986. Mem. Orgn. Am. Historians, Soc. Historians of Am. Fgn. Relations, Tulsa Com. Fgn. Relations, Phi Alpha Theta, Lambda Chi Alpha. Republican. Methodist. Home: 1301 Terrace Dr Tulsa OK 74104 Office: Univ of Tulsa Dept of History Tulsa OK 74104

BUCKLEY, WILLIAM FRANK, JR., magazine editor, writer; b. N.Y.C., Nov. 24, 1925; s. William Frank and Aloise (Steiner) B.; m. Patricia Taylor, July 6, 1950; 1 child, Christopher T. Student, U. Mexico, 1943; BA, Yale U., 1950; LHD (hon.), Seton Hall U., 1966, Niagara U., 1967, Mt. St. Mary's Coll., 1969, U. S.C., 1985; LLD (hon.), St. Peter's Coll., Syracuse U., Ursinus Coll., 1969, Lehigh U., 1970, Lafayette Coll., 1972, St. Anselm's Coll., 1973, St. Bonaventure U., 1974, U. Notre Dame, 1978, N.Y. Law Sch., 1981, Colby Coll., 1985; DScO (hon.), Curry Coll, 1970; LittD (hon.), St. Vincent Coll., 1971, Fairleigh Dickinson U., 1973, Alfred U., 1974, Coll. William and Mary, 1981, William Jewell Coll., 1982, Albertus Magnus Coll., Coll. St. Thomas, Bowling Green State U., 1987. Assoc. editor Am. Mercury, 1952; editor-in-chief Nat. Rev., N.Y.C., 1955—; syndicated columnist 1962—; host weekly TV show Firing Line, 1966—; Froman Disting. prof. Russell Sage Coll., 1973. Author: God and Man at Yale, 1951, (with L. Brent Bozell) McCarthy and His Enemies, 1954, Up from Liberalism, 1959, Rumbles Left and Right, 1963, The Unmaking of a Mayor, 1966, The Jeweler's Eye, 1968, The Governor Listeth, 1970, Cruising Speed, 1971, Inveighing We Will Go, 1972, Four Reforms, 1973, United Nations Journal, 1974, Execution Eve, 1975, Saving the Queen, 1976, Airborne, 1976, Stained Glass, 1978, A Hymnal, 1978, Who's On First, 1980, Marco Polo, If You Can, 1982, Atlantic High, 1982, Overdrive, 1983, The Story of Henri Tod, 1984, See You Later Alligator, 1985, Right Reason, 1985, High Jinx, 1986, Racing Through Paradise, 1987, Mongoose R.I.P., 1988; editor: The Committee and Its Critics, 1962, Odyssey of a Friend, 1970, American Conservative Thought in the Twentieth Century, 1970; contbr. to Racing at Sea, 1959, The Intellectuals, 1960, What is Conservatism?, 1964, Dialogues in Americanism, 1964, Violence in the Streets, 1968, The Beatles Book, 1968, Spectrum of Catholic Attitudes, 1969, Great Ideas Today Annual, 1970, Essays on Hayek, 1976; also periodicals. Mem. USIA Adv. Commn., 1969-72; pub. mem. U.S. del. to 28th Gen. Assembly UN, 1973. Served to 2d lt., inf. AUS, 1944-46. Recipient Bellarime medal, 1977; Am. Journalism award Friends of Haifa U., 1980; Creative Leadership award NYU, 1981. Fellow Soc. Profl. Journalists, Sigma Delta Chi; mem. Council on Fgn. Relations, Mont Pelerin Soc. Clubs: New York Yacht, Century, Bohemian. Office: 150 E 35th St New York NY 10016

BUCKNELL, PETER DAVID, executive recruiting specialist; b. Southend, Essex, Eng., May 4, 1956; s. Hal and Patricia (Butler) B. BSc in Polit. Sci. and Sociology with honors, U. Bristol, Eng., 1979. Cons. SOS Sr. Appointments Ltd., Bristol, 1980-82; sr. cons. Hugh Symons Mgmt. Services Ltd., Bristol, 1982-83; dir. Harrison Cowley Ltd., Bristol, 1983—. Home: The Cottage, Upper Castle Combe, Near Chippenham SN14 7HD, England Office: Park House High St, Thornbury BS12 2AQ, England

BUCKNER, BONNIE R(EYNOLDS), director of operations; b. Atlanta, Oct. 29, 1948; d. William Gerald and Betty Louise Reynolds; m. George Buckner II, Jan. 22, 1971 (div. 1974). B.A., West Ga. Coll., 1970, M.S., 1971. Chmn. sci. dept. Mt. Zion (Ga.) High Sch., 1971-74; indsl. engr. Milliken & Co., Spartanburg, S.C., 1974-76; mgr. indsl. engring. Burlington Industries, Wilson, N.C., 1976-78; sr. indsl. engr. Arcata Corp., Kingsport, Tenn., 1978-81; corp. indsl. engring. mgr. Baxter Travenol, Deerfield, Ill., 1981-86; mgr. Ernst & Whinney, Chgo., 1986-87; dir. ops. Biotherapeutics, Inc., 1987—. Advisor Jr. Achievement, Tenn., 1979, 80. Mem. Inst. Indsl. Engrs., Soc. Am. Value Engrs., Soc. Women Engrs., Soc. Mfg. Engrs., Computer and Automated Systems Assn., Robotics Internat., Nat. Assn. Female Execs. Episcopalian. Home: 902 Harpeth Trace Dr Nashville TN 37221 Office: Biotherapeutics Inc 357 Riverside Dr Franklin TN 37065

BUCKNER, LINDA IVERSON, insurance, software, and marketing consultant, author; b. Lincoln, Nebr., July 14, 1950; d. Joseph Thomas and Henrietta Mae (McClure) Fisher; m. David Lynn Iverson, Dec. 29, 1967 (div. May 1980); children: Rachelle, Meggan, Elyssa; m. John David Buckner, Apr. 17, 1981. BS in Bus., U. S.D., 1974; student in Direct Mktg., Northwestern U., 1986-87. Lic. life, accident and health ins. agt., 1980, property and casualty agt., 1985. Mktg. rep. ESCO, Northfield, Ill., 1975-76; sales mgr. Safecom, Inc., Schaumburg, Ill., 1976-79; account exec. CNA, Inc., Chgo., 1979-81; mktg. mgr. Computer Sci. Corp., Chgo., 1981-83; ptnr., v.p. mktg. Buckner & Assocs., Wheaton, Ill., 1981—; account exec., mgr. nat. accounts devel. Marsh-McLennan Group, 1984-87; pres. Buckner & Assocs., 1987—; cons. Ins. Agy. Automation, 1979-81, CARA Corp., Lombard, Ill., 1983-84. Dem. election judge, DuPage County, Ill., 1977—; mem. DuPage County Citizens Adv. Com., 1978-80; mem. Hoffman Hallmark Choir, 1978-80, fundraiser Acad. Performing Arts, Chgo., 1981—. Mem. Nat. Assn. Female Execs., Nat. Assn. Ins. Women, Soc. Mgmt. Info. Systems (assoc.), Data Processing Mgmt. Assn., Am. Mgmt. Assn., Am. Soc. Assn. Execs., Chgo. Soc. Assn. Execs. Home and Office: Buckner & Assocs 505 W Union St Wheaton IL 60187 Office: 222 S Riverside Plaza Chicago IL 60606

BUCKY, PETER STERN, psychologist; b. Berlin, Mar. 28; naturalized U.S. citizen, 1942; s. Franz and Ellen (Bucky) Stern; B.A., N.Y.U., 1955; M.S., CCNY, 1957; M.A., Columbia U., 1965, Ph.D. (fellow), 1972; children—Debra A., Janet L. Staff and chief psychologist U.S. Air Force, Dayton, Ohio, 1957-60; psychologist various N.J. public schs., 1960-72; dir., mgr., psychologist Meridian Learning Center, Meridian, Miss., Phoenix and San Diego, Calif., 1972-75; psychologist and psychotherapist in pvt. practice, North Bergen, N.J., 1960—; instr. Rutgers U., 1968-69, Fairleigh Dickinson U., 1970-71. Served to capt. USAF, 1957-60. Mem. Am. Psychol. Assn. Home: 5 Horizon Rd Apt 2002 Fort Lee NJ 07024 Office: 8600 Boulevard E Apt 1H North Bergen NJ 07047

BUDAI, LIVIA, opera singer; b. Esztergom, Hungary, June 23, 1950; d. Ferenc Budai and Martha Koszegi; m. Julius Batky. Grad. with honors, Ferenc Liszt Acad. Music, Budapest, 1973. Mem. artistic staff Budapest State Opera, 1973-75, Gelsenkirchen (Fed. Republic of Germany) Music Theater, 1977-80, Munich State Opera, 1980-83; bd. dirs. J.B. EM Services, Inc., St. Laurent, Montreal, Can. Appearances with Brussel Opera House, Covent Garden London Opera House, Paris Opera House, Can. Opera Co., Met. Opera, N.Y.C., San Francisco Opera House; appeared on TV in Europe; rec. artist Devon label, Hungaroton label, CBS label. Recipient Ravel prize, Paris, 1974, Erkel Voice Competition 1st Place award, Budapest, 1975. Office: JBS Mktg, 4280 rue Sere, Saint Laurent, PQ Canada H6T 1A6

BUDD, EDWARD HEY, insurance executive; b. Zanesville, Ohio, Apr. 30, 1933; s. Curtis Eugene and Mary (Hey) B.; m. Mary Goodrich, Aug. 24, 1957; children: Elizabeth, David, Susan. B.S. in Physics, Tufts U., 1955. With The Travelers Cos., Hartford, Conn., 1955—; v.p., then sr. v.p. The Travelers Cos., 1967-76, pres., chief operating officer, 1976-82, chief exec. officer, 1982—, chmn. bd., 1982—, also dir., pres., 1985—; bd. dirs. Delta Air Lines, GTE Corp., The Inst. of Living. Fellow Casualty Actuarial Soc.; mem. Bus. Roundtable, Am. Acad. Actuaries, Am. Ins. Assn. (immediate past chmn., dir., exec. com.), Bd. Overseers Inst. for Civil Justice. Episcopalian. Office: Travelers Indemnity Co 1 Tower Sq Hartford CT 06183

BUDD, ISABELLE AMELIA, financial consultant, research economist; b. Granite City, Ill., Feb. 8, 1923; d. Floyd Harry and Amelia Frederica (Bradvogel) Marx; B.S., U. Mo., 1944; postgrad. U. Wis., 1946; m. Louis John Budd, Mar. 3, 1945; children—Catherine Lou, David Harry. Research economist Ralston Purina Co., St. Louis, 1945-46; govtl. adminstr., Durham, N.C., 1975-79; fin. and govtl. cons., Durham, 1972—. Troop leader Girl Scouts U.S.A., 1955-61; mem. environ. concerns com. Duke U., Durham, 1972-77, co-chmn., 1974-75; mem. Durham City Council, 1975-79; Durham del. Council Govts., 1976-78; mem. exec. com. regional govt. criminal justice com., 1976-78; chmn. personnel policy com. regional govt., 1977-78; bd. dirs. Durham County Sr. Citizens Coordinating Council, 1982-85, Raleigh-Durham Airport Authority, 1983-85; chmn. bd. trustees Raleigh-Durham Firemen's Relief Fund, 1983—. Mem. N.C. Center for Public Policy Research, AAUW (life), Greater Durham C. of C., S.W. Durham Assn. (charter mem., treas. 1973-76), Mark Twain Circle of Am. (founding mem., govt. advisor), Nat. Trust for Historic Preservation, Historic Preservation Soc. Durham (charter mem.), N.C. Mus. Life and Sci., Friends of Duke U. Library (life). Home: 2753 McDowell St Durham NC 27705

BUDENHOLZER, ROLAND ANTHONY, mechanical engineering educator; b. St. Charles, Mo., Nov. 24, 1912; s. Joseph P. and Mary (Willey) B.; m. Florence C. Christiansen, Nov. 28, 1941; children: Francis Edward, John Christopher, Robert Joseph. B.S. in Mech. Engring, N.Mex. State U., 1935; M.S. in Mech. Engring, Calif. Inst. Tech., 1937, Ph.D., 1939. Grad. asst. Calif. Inst. Tech., 1935-39; research fellow Am. Petroleum Inst., 1939-40; faculty Ill. Inst. Tech., 1940—, prof. mech. engring., 1947-78, prof. emeritus, 1978—; resident research assoc. Argonne Nat. Lab., summer 1961; cons. IIT Research Inst., 1946—; dir. Midwest Power Conf., 1949-52; dir. Am. Power Conf., 1952-78, chmn., 1978-88; rep. Am. Power Conf. to World Energy Conf., 1965-84; bd. dirs. U.S. nat. com. World Energy Conf., 1972-78, mem. exec. com., 1973-78. Author handbooks; contbr. to encys., profl. jours. Recipient George Westinghouse gold medal Am. Soc. M.E., 1968, award Chgo. Tech. Socs. Council, 1975, Disting. Alumni award N.Mex. State U., 1981. Hon. mem. ASME (sec., exec. com. power div. 1967-68, chmn. 1970-71); mem. Am. Nuclear Soc., Am. Soc. Engring. Edn., Nat. Soc. Profl. Engrs., Western Soc. Engrs. (dir. 1969-72), AAUP (pres. Ill. Inst. Tech. chpt. 1963-64), Sigma Xi (pres. Ill. Inst. Tech. chpt. 1948-49), Tau Beta Pi, Pi Tau Sigma, Tau Kappa Epsilon, Triangle. Club: Armour Faculty. Home: 306 Harris Ave Clarendon Hills IL 60514 Office: Ill Inst Tech Chicago IL 60616

BUDER, EUGENE HAUCK, lawyer; b. St. Louis, Mar. 3, 1917; s. Oscar Edward and Eugenia Antonia (Hauck) B.; m. Jutta Zelle, June 9, 1956; children—Eugene, Annette Sanburn, Beatrice Clemens, Stella. A.B. cum laude, Harvard U., 1938, J.D., 1941. Bar: Mo. 1941, U.S. Dist. Ct. (ea. dist.) Mo. 1941, U.S. Ct. Appeals (8th cir.) 1954, U.S. Supreme Ct. 1948. Assoc. Oscar Edward Buder, St. Louis, 1945-50; ptnr. Stockham, Roth, Buder & Martin, St. Louis, 1953-60, Buder and Martin, St. Louis, 1960-63; assoc. Harold C. Hanke and Benjamin Roth, St. Louis, 1964-85; assoc. Benjamin Roth and Green, Hennings & Henry, 1985—; consul of Netherlands, St. Louis, 1963-87; trustee Nat. Urban League, 1962-68; gen. counsel Urban League Met. St. Louis, 1975—. Active St. Louis br. ACLU, 1946—. Served with Q.M.C., AUS, 1941-45, to maj. USAF, 1950-52. Decorated D.F.C., officer Order Orange-Nassau (Netherlands); recipient Civil Liberties award ACLU of Eastern Mo., 1972, Urban League St. Louis award, 1972. Mem. ABA, Mo. Bar, Bar Assn. Met. St. Louis. Democrat. Clubs: Mo. Athletic, Noonday. Office: 314 N Broadway Suite 1830 Saint Louis MO 63102

BUDGE, SANDRA KAY, accountant; b. Olds, Alta., Can., May 5, 1948; d. Robert Thomas and Laurel Mae (King) Hallett; m. Robert Wayne Budge, Apr. 6, 1968 (div. Dec. 1981); children: Melinda Rae, Susan Dale. Cert. mgmt. acctg., Red Deer Coll., 1976. CPA. Acct. John H. Grant, Stettler, Alta., Can., 1976-80; mgr. Kingston & Ross Accts., Edmonton, Alta., Can., 1980—. Grantee Govt. Alta, 1966, R. Willis Meml., 1966, Govt., 1976. Mem. Soc. Mgmt. Accts. Home: 3512 42 A Ave, Edmonton, AB Canada T6L-4N7 Office: Kingston Ross Chartered Accts, #2760 10180 - 101 St, Edmonton, AB Canada T5J #S4

BUDIG, GENE ARTHUR, university chancellor; b. McCook, Nebr., May 25, 1939; s. Arthur G. and Angela (Schaaf) B.; m. Gretchen VanBloom, Nov. 30, 1963; children: Christopher, Mary Frances, Kathryn Angela. B.S., U. Nebr., 1962, M.Ed., 1963, Ed.D., 1967. Exec. asst. to gov. Nebr., Lincoln, 1964-67; adminstrv. asst. to chancellor, asst. prof. ednl. adminstrn. U. Nebr., Lincoln, 1967-70; asst. vice chancellor acad. affairs, prof. ednl. adminstrn. U. Nebr., 1970, asst. v.p., dir. pub. affairs, 1971; v.p., dean univ. Ill. State U., Normal, 1972; pres. Ill. State U., 1973-77, W.Va. U., Morgantown, 1977-81; chancellor U. Kans., Lawrence, 1981—. Author: (with Dr. Stanley G. Rives) Academic Quicksand: Expectations of the Administrator, 1973; Editor, contbr.: chpts. Perceptions in Public Higher Education, 1970, Dollars and Sense: Budgeting for Today's Campus, 1972, Higher Education—Surviving the 1980s, 1981; editorial cons.: chpts. Phi Delta Kappan, 1976—; Contbr. articles to profl. jours. Mem. Intergovtl. Council on Edn., 1980-84; trustee Nelson-Atkins Mus. Art, Kansas City, Mo.; bd. dirs. Truman Library Inst.; bd. dirs. Midwest Research Inst., University Field Staff Internat. Serving as maj. gen. Air N.G., asst. to comdr. Air Tng. Command USAF, 1985—. Named one of ten outstanding young persons Ill. Jaycees, 1975; one of top 100 leaders in Am. higher edn. Change mag. and Am. Council on Edn., 1979; one of 75 outstanding young men and women educators of Am. Phi Delta Kappa, 1981. Home: 1532 Lilac Ln Lawrence

KS 66044 Office: U of Kans Cen Office Office of Chancellor Lawrence KS 66045

BUECHEL, WILLIAM BENJAMIN, lawyer; b. Wichita, Kans., July 27, 1926; s. Donald William and Bonnie S. (Priddy) B.; m. Theresa Marie Girard, Nov. 3, 1955; children—Sarah Ann, Julia Elaine. Student U. Wichita, 1947-49; B.S., U. Kans., 1951, LL.B., 1954. Bar: Kans., 1954, U.S. dist. ct. (Kans.), 1954. Sole practice, Concordia, Kans., 1954-56; stockholder Paulsen, Buechel, Swenson, Uri & Brewer, Chartered, and predecessors, Concordia, 1971-75, sec.-treas., 1975-77, pres., 1977—; dir. Cloud County Bank & Trust, Concordia, 1971—. Bd. dirs. Cloud County Community Coll. Endowment and Scholarship Assn., 1983—. Mem. ABA, Kan. Bar Assn. (exec. council 1966-68, chmn. adv. sect. profl. ethics com. 1974-76), Cloud County Bar Assn. (pres. 1984-86). Republican. Methodist. Clubs: Concordia Country, Elks, Moose, Rotary (pres. 1969-70). Home: 325 W 10th St Concordia KS 66901 Office: Paulsen Buechel et al 613 Washington St PO Box 327 Concordia KS 66901

BUEDINGEN, WILLIAM M., paper mill executive; b. Milw., Nov. 10, 1925; s. Wilmer Edward and Clara Alma (Kroening) B.; m. Mary Frances Valiquette, Dec. 18, 1949; children: Kim Keri, Todd. Student engring., Marquette U., 1946-48; BS in Phys. Edn., U. Wis., LaCrosse, 1951. Tchr., coach Tomahawk (Wis.) High Sch., 1951-55; supt. paper mill Nekoosa Packaging Co. (formerly Owens-Ill. Inc.), Big Island, Va., 1955-56, Valdosta, Ga., 1956-65, mgr. mill, Big Island, 1965-68, Valdosta, 1968-70, Tomahawk, 1970—; v.p. bd. trustees, mem. exec. com. Paper Sci. Found., Stevens Point, Wis., 1975—; bd. dirs. Bradley Bank. Contbr. articles to trade mags. V.p. Tomahawk Area Corp., 1971—; bd. dirs., mem. exec. com. Wis. Valley Improvement Co., Wausau, 1971—; trustee U. Wis. Found. Bd., LaCrosse, 1975-85; trustee, mem. exec. com., chmn. scholarship com. Pulp and Paper Sci. Sch., U. Wis., Stevens Point, 1980—; former bd. dirs. Tomahawk Civic Ctr. Assn., Trees for Tomorrow, Eagle River, Wis. Recipient Community Leader award Sta. WDEZ, 1975, 78. Mem. Tomahawk C. of C. (bd. dirs. 1975, Disting. Service award 1976), Wis. Paper Council (vice chmn. 1983-84, chmn. 1984-85), Paper Industry Mgmt. Assn., Tech. Assn. Pulp and Paper Industry. Republican. Congregationalist. Lodges: Lions (bd. dirs. 1974-78), Optimist (v.p. 1975-76). Avocations: lapidary, coin collecting, golf, swimming, water skiing. Office: Nekoosa Packaging Co N9090 Hwy E Tomahawk WI 54487

BUELL, EUGENE F(RANKLIN), lawyer; b. Elrama, Pa., Dec. 3, 1916; s. Frank Currey and Altina (Ecklund) B.; m. Elizabeth Ellen Foster, Dec. 28, 1940; children: Ellen E. (dec.), Erik Foster. B.S., St. Vincent's Coll., 1938; grad., Carnegie Inst. Tech., 1938-40, U. Pitts., 1941, Johns Hopkins U., 1942; J.D., Duquesne U., 1944. Bar: D.C. 1949, Canadian Patent Office 1949, U.S. Supreme Ct. 1952. Chemist U.S. Steel Corp., 1938-42; chief chemist Homestead works, 1942-45; with Stebbins, Blenko & Webb, 1945-48; partner firm Blenko, Hoopes, Leonard & Glenn, 1949-52; Blenko, Hoopes, Leonard & Buell Pitts., 1953-66; Blenko, Leonard & Buell 1966-72; partner firm Blenko, Buell, Ziesenheim & Beck (P.C.), 1973-79; pres., chmn. Buell, Blenko, Ziesenheim & Beck, P.C., 1979-84, Tartan Industries Inc.; chmn., pres. Buell, Ziesenheim, Beck & Alstadt, P.C., 1984—; treas. Pitts. Performance Products, Inc.; instr. Law Sch. U., Pitts., 1954-59, adj. prof. law, 1959—. Past pres. Richland Com. for Better Govt., Babcock Sch. Dist. Dirs.; chmn. Richland Sch. Authority; mem. Sch. Bd. Richland Twp. Mem. Am. Bar Assn., Am. Patent Law Assn., Engrs. Soc. Western Pa., Pa. Soc., Assn. Bar City N.Y., Licensing Exec. Soc., Am. Arbitration Assn., Am. Soc. Metals, Interam. Bar Assn., Am. Judicature Soc., Pa. Bar Assn., Allegheny County Bar Assn., U.S. Trademark Assn., Chartered Inst. Patent Agts., Asia-Pacific Lawyers Assn., Assn. Internationale pour la Protection de la Propriete Industrielle, Order of Coif. Clubs: Duquesne, Elks, Masons, Press, Allegheny, Rivers, Amen Corner. Office: Buell Ziesenheim Beck & Alstadt 322 Blvd of the Allies Pittsburgh PA 15222

BUELL, TEMPLE HOYNE, architect; b. Chgo., Sept. 9, 1895; s. Charles Clinton and Modrea (Hoyne) B.; children: Callae Mackey Buell Gilman, Temple Hoyne, Beverly Milne Buell More, Marjorie Daphne Buell Groos. Grad., Lake Forest Acad., 1912; BS, U. Ill., 1916; MS, Columbia U., 1917, DHL (hon.), 1986; DHL (hon.), U. Colo., 1987. Registered architect, Colo., N.Mex., Tex., Wyo., Nebr., Utah. Founder, pres. Buell & Co., architects & engrs., Denver, 1923—, Buell Devel. Corp., 1949—; doing bus. as Buell & Co. (real estate devel.), 1985—; pres. Sandex Equities, Ltd., 1985—. Spl. works include univ. bldgs. secondary and elementary schs., municipal, state and fed. bldgs., shopping ctrs., housing devels., others. Chmn. Cherry Hills Planning Commn., 1937—, Arapahoe County Planning Commn., 1939—, Tri-County Planning Commn. and Upper Plate Valley Planning Commn., 1940-42; founder Temple Hoyne Buell Found., 1963. Served to 1st lt. U.S. Army, 1917-19. Recipient Alumni medal Columbia U., 1932, Deans medal Sch. Architecture, 1938; Alumni Achievement award U. Ill., 1977, Disting. Service award U. Colo., 1985. Fellow AIA; Mem. Colo. Soc. Engrs., Soc. Mil. Engrs., Nat. Council Archtl. Registration Bds., Chi Psi (pres. 1967—). Clubs: Denver, Denver Athletic, Country, City (Denver); Cherry Hills Country (pres. 1943); Metropolitan (N.Y.C.); Camp Fire of Am. (Chappaqua, N.Y.); Regency (N.Y.C.); California (Los Angeles). Lodges: Masons (32 deg.); Shriners; K.T; Jesters; Rotary. Office: Buell & Co 106 S University Blvd Denver CO 80209

BUENO-DELGADO, RODRIGO, printing company executive; b. Cali, Valle, Colombia, Mar. 4, 1943; s. Hernando and María (Delgado) Bueno; m. María del Mar Piñeros, Dec. 10, 1966; 1 child, Eduardo J. MBA in Econs., Javeriana U., Bogotá, Colombia, 1966, PhD in Law, 1969. Gen. mgr. Bank of Am., Cali, Columbia, 1970-75; v.p. Bank of Am., Guayaquil, Ecuador, 1976-80; treas. Carvajal, S.A., Cali, 1980-86, mgr. gral. exports, 1986—; bd. dirs. Progreso Corp. Financiera, Bogotá, Molino Dagua, S.A., Cali. Founder Cali Zool. Soc.; bd. dirs. Fundación Valle del Lili, Cali, Fundación Educación Superior, Cali. Serving as lt. Colombian Air Force Res., 1985—. Mem. Assn. Abogados Javerianos, Assn. Exportadores Colombian (bd. dirs.), Am.-Colombian C. of C. (treas., bd. dirs.). Roman Catholic. Clubs: Campestre, Colombia (Cali). Lodge: Rotary. Home: Avenida 4 No 10-30, Cali, Valle Colombia Office: Carvajal SA, PO Box 46, Cali, Valle Colombia

BUENVIAJE, ELIZABETH REYES, physician; b. Manila, Sept. 14, 1954; d. Celso Javier and Zenaida (Reyes) Buenviaje. BS in Med. Tech., Far Eastern U., Manila, 1972-76; MD, Far Eastern U., 1977-81. Cert. Bd. Med. Tech., 1976, Bd. Medicine, 1982. Intern St. Luke's Hosp., Quezon City, Philippines, 1981-82; gen. practice medicine Rural Health Unit, Santa Cruz, Laguna, Philippines, 1982, Cainta, Rizal, Philippines, 1983—; med. officer Mcpl. Health Service, Cainta, 1986—; gen. practice medicine City of Refuge Children's Home, Quezon City, 1985—, Cainta Health Vols. Assn., 1984—, Community Outreach Med. Mission, Cainta, 1986—. Recipient cert. appreciation United Ch. Christ Disciples, 1985—. Mem. Far Eastern U. Nicanor Reyes Med. Found. Alumni Soc., Taytay-Angono-Cainta Med. Soc., Rizal Med. Soc., Philippine Med. Assn. Home: 41 M H del Pilar St, Corner A Bonifacio Ave, 1900 Cainta, Rizal Philippines Office: Mcpl Health Office, Amang Rodriguez St, 1900 Cainta, Rizal Philippines

BUER, JUTTA, writer; b. Cologne, Germany, Apr. 3, 1943; d. Carl Heinz and Ingeborg (Oetelshofen) B.; div. 1967; children: Michael, Christian. Student, U. Cologne. Author: Gekochte Geshenke, 1985; (with Winkler) Dreisterne-Küche für Zuhause, 1984, Besser Golf Spielen, 1987. Home and Office: Ismaninger Strasse 88, 8000 Munich 80 Federal Republic of Germany

BUERGER, DAVID BERNARD, lawyer; b. Phila., Dec. 1, 1909; s. Charles B. and Ada (Fischel) B.; m. Anne M. Fortun, June 30, 1946; 1 son, David C. A.B., U. Pitts., 1928, A.M., 1929; LL.B., Columbia U., 1932, J.D., 1969. Bar: Pa. 1932, U.S. Supreme Ct. Since practiced in Pitts.; mem., sr. ptnr. Buchanan, Ingersoll, Rodewald, Kyle & Buerger (and predecessors), 1932-83; sole practice, litigation in 48 states 1983—; lectr. taxation and corp. law Com. Continuing Legal Edn., Am. Law Inst., 1951—; pres., dir. Fourteen Bell Corp., Jersey City Investment Co.; dir. Don Irwin, Inc., O. Hommel Co., Munroe, Inc., Gestion Milway; sec. Elmhurst Co.; sec., dir. Vantage Broadcasting Co., Heritage Hills Realty, Howley Resources Inc., Pitts. Stage, Inc., Howley Resources Inc.; Gen. counsel Davis & Elkins Coll., Magee Womens Hosp., Hunt Found., Roy A. Hunt Found.; Allegheny Acad., Hampton Civic Assn.; trustee Helen Clay Frick Found., Davis & Elkins Coll. Editor: Columbia Law Rev, 1930-32. Pres. Hampton Civic Assn., 1956-57. Fellow Am. Bar Found.; mem. Am. Law Inst. (life), Am. Arbitration Assn., Am. Judicature Soc., ABA, Sigma Alpha Mu, Omicron Delta Kappa, Delta Sigma Rho. Club: Wildwood Golf (hon.). Home: 3000 McCully Rd Allison Park PA 15101 Office: 600 Grant St Rm 5600 Pittsburgh PA 15219

BUERO VALLEJO, ANTONIO, playwright; b. Guadalajara, Spain, Sept. 29, 1916; s. Francisco and Cruz B.V.; student High Sch. Acad. Fine Arts; m. Victoria Rodriguez, 1959. Mem. Ateneo de Madrid, Circulo de Bellas Artes de Madrid, Sociedad General de Autores de Espana, Internat. Com. of Theater, Hispanic Soc. Am., Real Academia Española. Author: (plays) Story of a Staircase, 1949; In the Burning Darkness, 1950; Today is a Holiday, 1956; The Cards Face Down, 1957; A Dreamer for a People, 1958; The Ladies-in-Waiting, 1960; Concert at St. Ovide, 1962; The Basement Window, 1967; The Sleep of Reason, 1970; The Foundation, 1974; The Detonation, 1977; The Weaver of Dreams, 1952; Irene or the Treasure, 1954; Dawn, 1953; Words in the Arena, 1949; Adventure in Gray, 1963; The Gods Arrival, 1972; The Double Case History of Doctor Valmy, 1976; Alligator, 1981; Judges in the Night, 1979; Secret Dialogue, 1984, Lazarus in the Labyrinth, 1986. Recipient Lope de Vega prize, 1949; Maria Rolland prize, 1956, 58, 60; Nacional de Teatro prize, 1957, 58, 59, 80; Fundacion March prize, 1959; Critica de Barcelona prize, 1960; El Espectador y la Critica prize, 1967, 70, 74, 76, 77, 81, 84, 86; Leopoldo Cano prize, 1968, 72, 74, 75, 77; Mayte prize, 1974; Cervantes prize, 1986; others. Office: Gen Diaz Porlier, 36 Madrid Spain

BUESSELER, JOHN AURE, ophthalmologist, management consultant; b. Madison, Wis., Sept. 30, 1919; s. John Xavier and Gerda Pernille (Aure) B.; m. Cathryn Anne Hansen, Dec. 26, 1959; 1 child, John McGlone. Ph.B., U. Wis., 1941, M.D., 1944; M.S. in Bus. Adminstrn., U. Mo., 1965. Intern Cleve. City Hosp., 1944-45; resident U. Pa. Hosp., 1948-51; practice medicine specializing in ophthalmology Madison, 1953-59; prof., founding chief ophthalmology U. Mo., Columbia, 1959-66; exec. officer Mo. Crippled Children's Service, 1967-70; exec. dir. Kansas City Gen. Hosp. and Med. Ctr., 1969-70; founding dean Tex. Tech U. Sch. Medicine, Lubbock, 1970-73, v.p. health affairs Univ. Complex, 1970-75, prof. dept. ophthalmology, prof. health orgn. mgmt., 1971—, chmn. dept. health orgn. mgmt., 1972-75, prof. grad. sch. faculty, 1972-80, chmn. dept. ophthalmology, 1973-75; Univ. prof. (distinguished and multidisciplinary) Univ. Complex, 1973—; founding v.p. health scis. Tex. Tech Univ. Health Scis. Center, 1972-74; pres. Radiol. Testing Lab., Inc., Madison, 1956-59; dir. House of Vision, Inc., Chgo., 1973-82; v.p. Madison Radiation Center, Inc., 1956-59; cons. NASA, mem. space medicine adv. group on devel. Orbiting Space Lab., Washington, 1963-66; cons. AEC, mem. Asso. Midwestern Univs.-Argonne Nat. Lab. biology com., Argonne, Ill., 1965-69; cons. to pres. Argonne Univs. Assn., Chgo., 1967-68; comdr. 94th Gen. Hosp., U.S. Army Res., Mesquite, Tex., 1973-75; co-founder, incorporator, bd. dirs., past pres. Joint Commn. on Allied Health Personnel in Ophthalmology, Inc.; mem. Residency Rev. Com. for Ophthalmology, 1974-80, chmn., 1978-80; sr. cons., chief exec. officer, founder Health Orgn. Mgmt. Systems Internat., 1978—. Contbr. articles to profl. jours. Served to capt. AUS, World War II, ETO; to maj. USAF, Korea; to col. USAR, Vietnam. Decorated Air medal with cluster, Legion of Merit; recipient Gold Medallion award for distinguished achievement in ophthalmology Mo. Ophthal. Soc., 1967, Tex. Tech U. Bd. Regents Resolution of Congratulations, 1973, Cert. of Citation Tex. Ho. of Reps., 1973, 87, Disting. Alumnus Citation U. Wis. Sch. Medicine, 1987. Fellow A.C.S., Am. Acad. Ophthalmology (Distinguished Service in Edn. award 1969); mem. AMA, Tex. Med. Assn., Soc. Mil. Ophthalmologists, Mo. Ophthal. Soc. (founder, past sec.-treas., pres., dir.), Acad. Mgmt., Soc. U.S. Army Flight Surgeons, Soc. Med. Cons. to Armed Forces, Sigma Xi., Alpha Omega Alpha. Home: 3313 23d St Lubbock TX 79410

BUESSER, ANTHONY CARPENTER, lawyer; b. Detroit, Oct. 15, 1929; s. Frederick Gustavis and Lela (Carpenter) B.; m. Carolyn Sue Pickle, Mar. 13, 1954; children: Kent Anderson, Anthony Carpenter, Andrew Clayton; m. Bettina Rieveschl, Dec. 14, 1973. B.A. in English with honors, U. Mich., 1952, M.A., 1953, J.D., 1960. Bar: Mich. 1961. Assoc. Chase, Goodenough & Buesser, Detroit, 1961-66; ptnr. Buesser, Buesser, Snyder & Blank, Detroit and Bloomfield Hills, Mich., 1966-81; sole practice Birmingham, Mich., 1981—. Trustee, chmn. bd. Detroit Country Day Sch., Birmingham, Mich., 1970-82, 84-87; bd. chmn. emeritus, chmn. nominating com., 1987—. Served with AUS, 1953-55. Recipient Avery Hopwood award major fiction U. Mich., 1953. Mem. ABA, Mich. Bar Assn., Detroit Bar Assn. (pres. 1976-77), Oakland County Bar Assn., Am. Judicature Soc., Am. Arbitration Assn., Alpha Delta Phi, Phi Delta Phi. Clubs: Detroit, Thomas M. Cooley (Detroit). Home and Office: 32908 Outland Trail PO Box 090159 Birmingham MI 48009

BUESSER, FREDERICK GUSTAVUS, III, lawyer; b. Detroit, Apr. 30, 1941; s. Frederick Gustavus and Betty A. (Rohal) B.; B.A., U. Mich., 1964, J.D., 1966; m. Julia Forsyth Guest, June 28, 1963; children—Jennifer, Katherine, Frederick. Admitted to Mich. bar, 1966; asso. firm Buesser, Buesser, Snyder & Blank, Detroit, Bloomfield Hills, 1966, partner, 1967—; lectr. and mem. faculty legal seminars. Fellow Am. Bar Found.; mem. Am. Bar Assn., State Bar of Mich., Am. Judicature Soc., Sigma Chi, Phi Delta Phi. Episcopalian. Home: 242 N Glengarry St Birmingham MI 48009 Office: 4190 Telegraph St Bloomfield Hills MI 48013

BUFFET, BERNARD, painter; b. Paris, July 10, 1928; s. Charles Buffet and Blanche-Emma Colombe; m. Agnes Nanquette, 1948 (div.); m. Anabelle Schwob, 1958; 3 children. Student Lycée Carnot, Ecole Nat. Supérieure des Beaux-Arts. Shows: ann. exhbn. Galerie Drouant-David, 1949-56, Galerie David & Garnier, 1957-67, Galerie Maurice Garnier, 1968—; retrospective exhbns., Paris, 1958, Berlin, 1958, Belgium, 1959, Tokyo, 1963; illustrator books, engraver, lithographer and state designer; mem. Acad. des Beaux-Arts, 1974—. Decorated chevalier Légion d'honneur; officier Ordre des Arts et des Lettres; recipient grand prix de la Critique, 1948. Address: Galerie Maurice Garnier, 6 avenue Matignon, Paris 75008 France

BUFFINGTON, FRANCIS STEPHAN, engineering educator, consultant, researcher; b. Allegany, N.Y., May 14, 1916; s. Henry Clay and Marguarite Ann (Stephan) B.; m. Marjorie Irma Hills, Aug. 26, 1939; children—Francis Stephan, Roger Hills. B.S., MIT, 1938, D.Sc., 1951. Registered profl. engr., Calif. Mem. research staff MIT, Cambridge, 1940-41, research asst., 1947-51; from asst. prof. to prof. Calif. Inst. Tech., Pasadena, Calif., 1951—; assoc. dean Calif. Inst. Tech., Pasadena, 1975-84; cons. in field. Contbr. chpt. to book, articles to profl. jours. Served to capt. U.S. Army, 1942-45. Mem. Am. Phys. Soc., Am. Soc. for Metals, Sigma Xi (pres. chpt. 1962-67). Republican. Clubs: Athenaeum. Home: 3870 Madison Rd Flintridge CA 91011 Office: Calif Inst Tech 1201 E California Blvd Pasadena CA 91125

BUFFINGTON, RALPH MELDRIM, architect; b. White Sulphur, Ga., Feb. 7, 1907; s. Marion Cook and Frances Louvinia (Moss) B. B.S. in Architecture, Ga. Inst. Tech., 1928; scholar pvt. study, Europe, 1929-30; also, Ecole Speciale d'Architecture. Registered profl. architect, Tex., Ga. Practice architecture as Ralph M. Buffington, Houston, 1939-42, 1946-66, 76-83; assoc. Buffington & McAllister, Houston, 1966-75; cons. Bapt. fgn. mission projects, Hawaii, Hong Kong, Taiwan, Thailand, Philippines, Indonesia, Mexico, Santo Domingo, Barbados, Antigua Barbados, and, Venezuela. Prin. archtl. works include Chinese Bapt. Evangelistic Temple; 8 Houston schs., Taipeh Bapt. Sem, Taiwan, schs.; designer 1st Bapt. Ch., Curitiba, Brazil, Bapt. Theol. Sem., Belo Horizonte, Brazil; other instns. and residences; author: Buffington Family in America, 1965. Served with AUS, 1942-45, PTO. Recipient Outstanding Service commendation Houston C. of C., 1962; named Architect Emeritus, State of Tex., also various archtl. awards. Mem. AIA, Tex. Soc. Architects, Nat. Geog. Soc. Nat. Council Archtl. Registration Bds. Democrat. Baptist. Home: Route 1 Box 1450 Pendergrass GA 30567

BUFFORD, RODGER KEITH, psychologist, educator; b. Santa Rosa, Calif., Dec. 23, 1944; s. John Samuel and Evelyn A. (Rude) B.; m. Kathleen A. Parson; children—Heather, Brett. B.A., King's Coll., 1966; M.A., U. Ill., 1970; Ph.D., 1971. Lic. psychologist, Oreg., Va. Psychologist, Adolph Meyer Zone Ctr., Decatur, Ill., 1969-70; asst. prof. psychology Am. U., Washington, 1971-76; asst. prof., chmn. dept. psychology Huntington (Ind.) Coll., 1976-77; assoc. prof. Psychol. Studies Inst., Atlanta, 1977-81; psychologist Atlanta Counseling Ctr., 1980-82; assoc. prof., chmn. dept. psychology Western Baptist Sem., Portland, Oreg., 1982-86, prof. and chmn., 1986—; pvt. practice psychology, 1973—; allied health care profl. Portland Adventist MEd. Ctr., 1982—, Cedar Hills Hosp., 1984—, Woodland PArk Hosp., 1988—; dir. Mental Health Assn., Huntington, Ind., 1976-77; acad. adv. bd. Family Research Council of Am. V.p. Minirth and Meier Found., 1988—, bd. dirs., 1986—; elder, Chapel Woods Presbyterian Ch., 1983. USPHS trainee, 1967-68, 70-71; Am. U. Faculty Research grantee, 1972. Mem. Am. Psychol. Assn., Western Psychol. Assn., Christian Assn. Psychol. Studies, Am. Sci. Affiliation, Oreg. Psychol. Assn. Author: The Human Reflex: Behavioral Psychology in Biblical Perspective, 1981; contbg. editor Jour. Psychology and Theology, Jour. Psychology and Christianity; contbr. chpts. to texts, numerous articles to profl. jours. Home: 19505 Hidden Springs Rd West Linn OR 97068 Office: 5511 SE Hawthorne Blvd Portland OR 97215

BUFKIN, ISAAC DAVID, energy diversified company executive; b. Haynesville, La., May 16, 1922; s. Floran E. and Pauline E. B.; m. Lee Elmo Renfrow, Apr. 23, 1944; children: Peggy Bufkin Gerst, David Michael. BS, La. Tech. U., 1948. Mech. engr. NACA, Langley Field, Va., 1948-49; with Tex. Eastern Transmission Corp., Houston, 1949-79, v.p. gas mktg. and rates, 1968-71, v.p. gas ops., 1971-79; exec. v.p. Tex. Eastern Corp., Houston, 1979, pres., chief operating officer, 1979-80, pres., chief exec. officer, 1980-86, chmn. bd., chief exec. officer, 1980-87, chmn. bd. dirs., 1987—; bd. dirs. Conf. Bd.; mem. Interstate Oil Compact Commn. Bd. dirs. Stehlin Found. for Cancer Research; life bd. dirs. La. Tech. Engring Found. Served with USAAF, 1943-46. Mem. La. Engring. Soc., Nat. Soc. Profl. Engrs., Soc. Gas Lighting, Gas Men's Roundtable Washington, Newcomen Soc. N. Am. Baptist. Office: Tex Eastern Corp PO Box 2521 Houston TX 77252

BUGGIE, FREDERICK DENMAN, management consultant; b. Toledo, Mar. 27, 1929; s. Horace and Loraine (Denman) B.; B.A., Yale U., 1956; M.B.A., George Washington U., 1961; m. Betty Jo Chilcote, Sept. 7, 1951; children—Martha Louise Buggie Kenney, John Chilcote. Sales engr. Alcoa, Balt. and Phila., 1956-66; pres. Gt. Lakes Research Inst., Erie, Pa., 1967-69; mktg. mgr. Technicon Instruments, Tarrytown, N.Y., 1969-71; program mgr. Innotech, Norwalk, Conn., 1971-76; pres. Strategic Innovations Internat., Lake Wylie, S.C., 1976—, SII Strategic Innovations A.G., Zurich, Switzerland; founder, chmn. Strategic Innovations Internat. Ltd., Bedford, England, Strategic Innovations B.V., Amsterdam, The Netherlands; conf. leader, lectr.; adj. prof. various univs. Served with USAF, 1950-54. Mem. Assn. Corp. Growth, The Planning Forum, C.D.A., EVAF, Inst. of Dirs. Clubs: Weston Field; Yale N.Y.C.; Yale London. Author: New Product Development Strategies, 1981. Home: 8 Sunrise Point Lake Wylie SC 29710 Office: 12 Executive Ct Lake Wylie SC 29710

BUGGS, CHARLES WESLEY, microbiologist, educator; b. Brunswick, Ga., Aug. 6, 1906; s. John Wesley and Leonora Vane (Clark) B.; m. Maggie Lee Bennett, Dec. 27, 1927; 1 dau., Margaret Leonora. A.B., Morehouse Coll., Atlanta, 1928; M.S. (Rosenwald scholar 1931-34), U. Minn., 1932, Ph.D. (Shevlin fellow medicine 1933), 1934. Prof. biology, chmn. div. scis. Dillard U., 1935-43, 49-56; from instr. to asso. prof. bacteriology Sch. Medicine, Wayne U., 1943-49; prof. microbiology Sch. Medicine, Howard U., 1956-71, chmn. dept., 1958-70; emeritus prof. microbiology; project dir. Faculty Allied Health Scis. Charles R. Drew Postgrad. Med. Sch., Los Angeles, 1969-72; dean Faculty Allied Health Scis. Charles R. Drew Postgrad. Med. Sch., 1972; interim program dir. Calif. Regional Med. Program, Area IX, 1970-71; vis. prof. microbiology U. Calif. at Los Angeles, 1969-72, U. So. Calif., 1969-76; prof. microbiology Calif. State U., Long Beach, 1973-83; spl. research resistance bacteria to antibiotics. Author: Premedical Education for Negroes, 1949. Del. 1st three confs. on med. edn. for liberal arts colls. Buck Hill Farms, 1950, 52, 58; NSF del. Bryn Mawr Conf. on biol. research in liberal arts colls., 1954; former mem. med. and sci. com. So. Calif. chpt. Arthritis Found., 1971-73; mem. State Alcoholism Adv. Council, 1972-73; bd. dirs. Comprehensive Health Planning Assn. Los Angeles County, 1972-73. Recipient awards for Outstanding Achievements in Field Howard U. Coll. Medicine, 1971, Watts-Willowbrook Regional Health Com., 1972, Nat. Med. Assn. Found., 1972, Nat. Med. Found., 1985, Nat. Soc. Allied Health, 1985, Mid-Cities Alliance Black Sch. Educators, 1985; recipient Presdl. award Nat. Soc. Allied Health, Cert. Spl. Congl. Recognition, 1985, Mayor's Cert. Appreciation City of Los Angeles, 1985, Los Angeles City Council Resolution, 1985, Resolution Calif. Senator Diane E. Watson, 1985; named Man of Yr. NAACP, Elsinor, 1984-85; inducted into Educators Hall of Fame. Fellow Am. Acad. Microbiology; mem. Am. Soc. Microbiology, Sigma Xi, Alpha Phi Alpha, Sigma Pi Phi; past fellow AAAS, Washington Acad. Scis.; past mem. Am. Assn. Dental Schs., Am. Public Health Assn., Assn. Am. Med. Colls., Assn. Schs. Allied Health Professions, Nat. Assn. Standard Med. Vocabulary, N.Y. Acad. Scis., Soc. Exptl. Biology and Medicine. Home: 5600 Verdun Ave Los Angeles CA 90043-2124

BUHAGIAR, CHARLES LAWRENCE, business executive; b. Vittoriosa, Malta, July 14, 1955; s. Vincent and Antonia (Borg) B.; m. Rita Magro. B in Engring. and Arch., U. Malta, 1977. Architect, Pub. Works Dept., Malta, 1977-79, A. Zammit & Assocs., Malta, 1979-80; civil engr. Malta Shipbldg. Co., Ltd., 1980-81, Gatt Bros. Co., Ltd., Malta, 1981-82; architect, mng. dir. Charles Buhagiar, Malta, 1982-83; chmn., mng. dir. Charles Buhagiar Assocs., Malta, 1983—; mng. dir. Med. Design Co., Ltd., Malta, 1983—, Hercules Group of Cos., Malta, 1987—. Author: Ferrocement, 1979. Editor Atrium Jour., 1980. Contbr. articles to profl. jours. Mem. Parliament Malta Labour Party, 1987—. Roman Catholic. Avocation: collection of books about Malta. Office: Charles Buhagier Assocs, Hercules House, Saint Mark St, Valletta Malta

BUHL, CYNTHIA MAUREEN, foreign policy educator and advocate; b. Los Angeles, Apr. 14, 1952; m. Albert Buhl and Dorothy Jane (Loth) Henry. B.A., Lewis & Clark Coll., 1974. Dir., Resource and Counseling Ctr., Portland Youth Advs., Oreg., 1971-72; resource coordinator S.E. Youth Service Ctr., Portland Action Coms. Together, 1975-77; sec., asst. Human Rights Office, Nat. Council Chs. Christ, N.Y.C., 1977-78; human rights coordinator Coalition for a New Fgn. and Mil. Policy, Washington, 1978-85; cons. Fgn. Policy Edn. Fund, Washington, 1986; nat. adv. bd. U.S. Student Assn. Peace Program, Washington, 1984—, West-Central Am. Network, Stanford, Calif., 1985—, Nat. Network in Solidarity with Guatemalan People, Washington, 1985—, Caribbean Basin Info. Project, 1983-85; bd. dirs., legis. dir. Pax Am.'s/Priorities-PAC, 1986—. Co-editor: Central America 1985: Basic Information and Legislative History on U.S.-Central American Relations, 1985. Contbr. articles to various jours., mags. Co-chmn. Human Rights Working Group, Washington, 1978-81, chmn., 1982-85; chmn. Central Am. Lobby Group, 1983-85; mem. Commn. on U.S.-Central Am. Relations, 1983—. Office: 122 Maryland Ave NE 3d Floor Washington DC 20002

BÜHM, GOTTFRIED, architect, educator; b. Offenbach am Main, Fed. Republic Germany, Jan. 23, 1920; s. Dominikus B; m. Elisabeth Haggenmüller, 1948; children: Stefan, Markus, Peter, Paul. B. in Engring., Technische Hochschule, Munich, 1946; student, Acad. of Sculptural Art, Munich, 1947. Asst. architect Dominikus Bühm, Cologne, Fed. Republic Germany, 1947-50, Rudolph Schwarz, Cologne, Fed. Republic Germany, 1950, C. Baumann, N.Y.C., 1951; pvt. practice Cologne, 1952—; prof. architecture Inst. Tech., Aachen, Fed. Republic Germany, 1963—. Works exhibited at Internationale Design Zentrum, Berlin, 1979, Museum of Modern Art, N.Y.C., 1979, Internationale Bauausstellung, Berlin, 1984, Art Gallery of Ontario, 1985; works include St. Columba's Ch., Cologne, 1949, St. Christopher's Ch., Oldenburg, 1958, Grodesburg Castle renovations, 1960, Bensberg Town Hall, 1962, Children's Village at Refrath, Bensberg, 1963, Housing complex, Chorweiler, Cologne, 1969, State Bur. for Data Processing and Statistics, Düsseldorf, 1969, City Hall and Cultural Ctr., 1973, Community Ctr., Kettwig, Esen, 1977, Municipal Hall, Bergisch-Gladbach, 1980, Single-Family Terraced Housing, Porz-Zündorf, 1981, Foyer of the Opera House, Stuttgart, 1984; contbr. articles to profl. jours. Served with German Army, 1938-42. Recipient Gold medal Acad. d'Architecture, Paris, 1983, Pritzker prize for Architecture, 1986; named hon. prof. U. Lima, Peru, 1979. Fellow AIA (hon.); mem. Akademie der Künste, German Acad. Urban and Regional Planning. Office: Architekturburo Bohm, Auf dem Romerberg 25, 5000 Cologne 51 (Marienburg) Federal Republic of Germany *

BUI, HUONG QUOC, neuropsychiatrist; b. Bac-Kan, Vietnam, Aug. 31, 1924; arrived in France, 1970; s. Tuong Phat and San Thi (Han) B.; m. Marie Thuc Thi Vu, July 16, 1954; children: Claude Hinh, Phillipe Hung, Pierre-Andre Hien. MD, Faculty of Medicine, U. Hanoi, Vietnam, 1952; cert. neuropsychiatry, diploma malariology, Faculty of Medicine, U. Paris, 1957, agregation in neuropsychiatry, 1962. Clinic chief Faculty of Medicine, Hanoi U., 1953, asst. prof., 1953-54; asst. prof. Faculty of Medicine, Paris, 1954-56; assoc. prof. Faculty of Medicine, Saigon, Vietnam, 1957-63, maitre de conference, 1963-65, prof. neurology and psychiatry, 1965-69; practice medicine specializing in neuropsychiatry Paris, 1977—; vis. prof. Georgetown U. Hosp., Washington, 1969, researcher, 1970-76. Contbr. articles to profl. jours. Recipient Nat. Sci. Research prize Ministry Culture Vietnam-Unesco, 1966. Mem. World Fedn. Neurology, Soc. Francaise de Neurology (fgn. hon. 1964, assoc. 1987). Confucian. Home: 7 Rue Nicolas Roret, Gobelin, 75013 Paris France Office: 14 Rue Pirandello, 75013 Paris France

BUIE, BENNETT FRANK, geologist, educator; b. Patrick, S.C., Jan. 9, 1910; s. Daniel Franklin and Mary Julia (Smith) B.; B.S., U. S.C., 1930; M.S. (research fellow 1930-32), Lehigh U., 1932; M.A., Harvard U., 1934, Ph.D., 1939; grad. Command and Gen. Staff Coll.; m. Susanna Townsend Peirce, Aug. 9, 1938; children—Susanna (Mrs. Susanna Matthews), Julia (Mrs. Julia B. Steinitz), Carolyn (Mrs. Carolyn B. Erdener, Margaret (Mrs. J. Duncan Keppie). Asst. in geology Harvard, 1932-37, resident adv., proctor, 1935-37; mem. Shaler Meml. Expdn., summers 1933-35; geologist subs. Seaboard Oil Co. in Iran and Afghanistan, 1937-38, subsidiaries Standard Oil Co. Calif. in Brit. India and Tex., 1939-42; prof. geology U. S.C., also geologist S.C. Devel. Bd., 1946-56; chief geologist Resources Devel. Corp., Iran, 1952; geologist U.S. Geol. Survey, 1953-57; prof. geology Fla. State U., 1956-81, emeritus prof., 1981—, chmn. dept., 1956-64; cons. geologist J.M. Huber Corp., 1958-88. Condr. del. geologists to USSR and Middle East, People-to-People Internat. Citizen Ambassador Program, 1979. Served to maj. C.E., AUS, 1942-46; col. Res. ret. Decorated Bronze Star and Order Red Star for work in Persian Gulf Command (USSR); recipient Algernon Sydney Sullivan award U. S.C. Fellow Geol. Soc. Am., Explorers Club, Mineral. Soc. Am.; mem. Soc. Econ. Geologists, AIME, Soc. Mining Engrs., Am. Assn. Petroleum Geologists, Geol. Soc. Washington, Carolina Geol. Soc. (pres. 1958), Acad. Sr. Profls. Eckerd Coll., Sigma Xi, Omicron Delta Kappa. Episcopalian. Research on world resources of kaolin and phosphate. Home: 124 College Harbor 4650 54th Ave S Saint Petersburg FL 33711

BUILTA, HOWARD CLAIRE, real estate development company executive; b. Lawton, Okla., Apr. 29, 1943; s. Howard Phillip and Alice Ann (Stimpert) B.; m. Claudia Lynn Mastalio, Sept. 3, 1966; children—Jeffrey B., Lindsey M. B.S., U. Ill., 1965; M.B.A., No. Ill. U., 1967. Project adminstr. Seay & Thomas, Chgo., 1969-71; v.p. Rauch & Co., Chgo., 1971-77; v.p., gen. mgr. The Whiston Group, Chgo., 1977-79; v.p. Marathon U.S. Realties, Chgo., 1979—. Mem. adv. council Lutheran Social Services, Chgo., 1976-81, Salvation Army Community Counseling Service, Chgo., 1982-86; trustee Palatine Twp. Govt., Ill., 1979-81; bd. dirs. Palatine Twp. Republican Orgn., 1979-81. Served to 1st lt. U.S. Army, 1967-69, Vietnam. Decorated Bronze Star, Army Commendation medal. Mem. Inst. Real Estate Mgmt. (cert. property mgr.), Bldg. Owners and Mgrs. Assn. Internat. (real property adminstr., pres. Suburban Chgo., Des Plaines, 1977-79, pres. North Central region 1984), Urban Land Inst., Chgo. Real Estate Bd. (pres. 1987—), Ill. Assn. Realtors (bd. dirs. 1985, dist. v.p. 1987—), Lambda Alpha (pres. Ely chpt. 1984), Am. Legion. Club: Attic (Chgo.). Lodge: Masons. Avocations: reading; fishing. Home: 2316 Sunset Rd Palatine IL 60074 Office: Marathon US Realties 3 1st National Plaza Suite 5700 Chicago IL 60602

BUIST, RICHARDSON, banker; b. Bklyn., Aug. 8, 1921; s. George Lamb and Adelaide (Richardson) B.; student Yale U.; m. Jean Mackerley, Oct. 2, 1948; children—Peter Richardson, Jean Morford Buist, Mary Elizabeth Buist Flores. Advt. copy writer Ecloss Co., Sparta, N.J., 1946-48; advt. mgr. Sussex County Ind., 1948-50, Dover Advance, 1950-53; bus. mgr. N.J. Herald, Newton, 1953-70; dir., v.p. The N.J. Herald, Inc., 1958-70, pub., 1967-70; dir. N.J. Press Assn., 1966-70; asst. sec., asst. treas. Morford Co., 1965-72, pres., 1986— ; trust officer Midlantic Nat. Bank/Sussex & Mchts., Newton, 1971-88, Midlantic Nat. Bank, Edison, N.J., 1972-86, cons., 86—; bd. dirs. North Jersey Health Care Corp. Pres. Sussex County chpt. Am. Cancer Soc., 1956-58, Sussex County Music Found., 1959-61; mem. Morris-Sussex Area Health Facilities Planning Council, 1965-68, bd. govs., 1962-88; v.p. Sussex County Council Arts, 1971-73. Chmn. pub. relations Morris-Sussex Area Council Boy Scouts Am., 1986-88; trustee Sussex County Music Found., 1955-75; v.p., chmn. fin. devel. com. Newton Meml. Hosp., 1966-68, bd. govs. 1962-88, pres. bd. govs., 1968-71, chmn., 1971-73, bd. govs. 1962-88; founding incorporator, trustee NW Jersey Health Care, 1971-76; trustee, mem. exec. com. regional health planning council Health Systems Agy., 1976-82, 1984-87, v.p., 1978-79; trustee United Way of Sussex County, 1984—, spl. gifts chmn., 1984-88; dir. N. Jersey Health Care Corp., 1988—. Mem. N.J. Vet. Med. Soc. Aux. (del. 1979-82, 88), Am. Vet. Med. Soc. Aux. (nat. chmn. legis. com., 1986-88). Clubs: Morristown (N.J.). Lodge: Rotary (pres. 1967-68, Paul Harris Fellow award 1988). Home: Rural Rt 2 Sand Pond Rd 668-A Hamburg NJ 07419 Office: 93 Spring St Newton NJ 07860

BUITA, SEVERINO GREGORIO, finance systems and procedures consultant; b. Jakarta5, Indonesia, May 15, 1925; s. Marcos Buita and Manuela (Gregorio) B.; m. Remedios Padilla, Jan. 6, 1967; children: Grace Glenda, Gloria. BS cum laude, Far Ea. U., Manilla, 1952. CPA. Audit mgr. SGV Nathalang & Co., Bangkok, 1967-75; ptnr., advisor DRS Utomo & Co., Jakarta, 1983—. Mem. Philippine Inst. C.P.A.s (dir. 1965). Club: Petroleum. Lodge: Lions (bd. dirs. 1965). Home: JL MSD D 31, Komplex Bangon, Jakarta, Cipta Sarana Indonesia Office: PT Internat Salim Corp, BCA Bldg 25 Jalan Asemka, Jakarta Indonesia

BUKHARI, S. HAIDER SHAH, physician; b. Shikarpur, Pakistan, Aug. 1, 1939; s. S. A. B. Majeed Shah and Hussna Majeed (Husna) B.; m. Sughra Bibi, Dec. 18, 1964; children: Najeeb, Tahmeena, Farah, Sajjad, Saima, Shahzad, Bahzad. M Medicine and Sci., Liaquat Med. Coll., Hyderabad, Pakistan, 1962. House surgeon Liaquat Med. Coll., 1962-63; asst. dist. health officer Provincial Health Service, Larkana, Pakistan, 1963-67; med. officer Civil Officer, Kot Samaba, Pakistan, 1967-69; resident med. officer Rbut Hosp., Shikarpur, Pakistan, 1968-69; med. advisor Agrl. Bank of Pakistan, Shikarpur, 1974-84; chief Najeeb Family Clinic, Shikarpur, 1968—. Mem. Pakistan Med. Assn. (pres. 1985-86). Islam. Office: Najeeb Clinic, Dadwai Rd, Shikarpur Pakistan

BUKMAN, PIET, government official; b. Delft, Zuid-Holland, The Netherlands, Feb. 7, 1934; m. Carolien Helena Boon; children: Bert, Kees, Arien, Johanna, Marc. Diploma in Social Geography, Amsterdam U., 1959. Info. officer Netherlands Protestant Farmers' & Market Gardeners' Fedn., Hague, 1961, sec. horticultural div., nat. chmn., 1975-79; chmn. Christian Dem. Alliance, Hague, 1980-85; minister for Devel. Coop., Hague, 1986—. Vice chmn. European People's Party, Hague, 1980, chmn., 1985; mem. Upper House of Parliament, 1981, M.P. chmn. standing com. on fgn. affairs, 1983. Served to 1st lt. Royal Netherlands Air Force. Office: Christen-Democratisch Appel, Dr Kuyperstraat 5, 2514 BA The Hague The Netherlands also: care Ministry of Fgn Affairs, PO Box 20061, 2500 EB The Hague The Netherlands

BUKOVSKY, VLADIMIR, scientist, author; b. Belebey, Dec. 30, 1942; s. Konstantin and Nina Bukovsky. Student, Moscow State U., 1961; B.A. in Psychology, Cambridge U., 1981. Mem. staff Moscow Centre of Cybernetics; arrested for possessing banned lit., 1963, confined to Leningrad Psychiat. Prison Hosp. for 15 months; arrested demonstration on behalf Soviet writers, 1965, confined 8 months in psychiat. instns.; arrested for civil rights work, 1967, on trial, Sept. 1967, sentenced 3 yrs. corrective labor; arrested for delivering info. on psychiat. abuse to West, 1971, on trial 1972, sentenced to 2 yrs. in prison, 5 in labor camp and 5 in exile; after world-wide campaign for his release, was exchanged for Chilean Communist Party leader Luis Corvelan, Zurich, 1976; fellow in neuroscis. Stanford U., from 1982. Contbr. short stories Russia's Other Writers, 1970; Opposition-Eine neue Geisteskrankheit in der USSR (German edition), 1972; author (with Semyon Gluzman) A Manual on Psychiatry for Dissenters, 1974; To Build a Castle: My Life as a Dissenter, 1978 (trans. into Swedish, Italian, Spanish, French and German); Cette lancinante douleur de la liberte, 1981; The Peace Movement and the Soviet Union, 1982, 70 Choose Freedom, 1987. Mem. (hon.) several human rights orgns., several PEN clubs. Address: care 1172 Clayton St San Francisco CA 94117 •

BUKOWINSKI, ANDRES, film director; b. Warsaw, Poland, Mar. 15, 1940; s. Mieczyslaw and Apolinara (Sniegocka) B.; m. Lisete Laghetto, June 28, 1944; 1 child, Paula. Dir., owner Delta Films, Buenos Aires, 1961-63; dir. photography Lowe Argentina, Buenos Aires, 1963-68; dir., ptnr. Lowe Interamericana, Buenos Aires, 1968-71, Andres Bukowinski ASC., Buenos Aires, 1971-72, ABA Prodns., Sao Paulo, Brazil, 1972—. Dir. Grupo "S", Cannes, 1969-70. Recipient 1st and 2d prize Screen Advt. World Assn., Venice, 1964, Golden Lion awards, Cannes and Venice Film Festivals, 1969, 70, 71, 75, 76, 81, 82, Silver Lions, 1973, 75, 77, 82, Bronze Lions, 1970, 78, 86. Mem. Clube de Criaçao-São Paolo, 1977. Office: ABA Prodns, Av Angelica 2.601, 01227 Sao Paulo Brazil

BUKRY, JOHN DAVID, geologist; b. Balt., May 17, 1941; s. Howard Leroy and Irene Evelyn (Davis) Snyder. Student, Colo. Sch. Mines, 1959-60; B.A., Johns Hopkins U., 1963; M.A., Princeton U., 1965, Ph.D., 1967; Postgrad., U. Ill., 1965-66. Geologist U.S. Army Corp Engrs., Balt., 1963; research asst. Mobil Oil Co., Dallas, 1965; geologist U.S. Geol. Survey, La Jolla, Calif., 1967-84, U.S. Minerals Mgmt. Service, La Jolla, 1984-86, U.S. Geol. Survey, Menlo Park, Calif., 1986—; research assoc. dept. geol. research div. U. Calif.-San Diego, 1970—; cons. Deep Sea Drilling Project, La Jolla, 1967-86; lectr. 3d. Internat. Planktonic Conf., Kiel, Ger., 1974. Author: Leg I of the Cruises of the Drilling Vessel Glomar Challenger, 1969, Coccoliths from Texas and Europe, 1969, Leg LXIII of the Cruises of the Drilling Vessel Glomar Challenger, 1981; editor: Marine Micropaleontology, 1976-83; editorial bd. Micropaleontology, 1985—. Mobil Oil, Princeton U. fellow, 1965-67; Am. Chem. Soc., Princeton U. fellow, 1966-67. Fellow AAAS, Geol. Soc. Am., Explorer's Club; mem. Hawaiian Malacological Soc., Paleontol. Research Inst., Am. Assn. Petroleum Geologists, Soc. Econ. Paleontologists and Mineralogists, Sigma Xi, Ida and Gecil Green Faculty Club. Club: San Diego Shell, San Diego Ida, Cecil Green Faculty, U. So. Calif. Office: US Geol Survey MS-915 345 Middlefield Rd Menlo Park CA 94025

BULAJIC, RADOSLAV PAVLE, steel company executive, educator; b. Niksic, Yugoslavia, May 19, 1935; s. Pavle Cetko and Ljubica Bozo (Pavlovic) B.; m. Zdenka Gabrijel Selec, Nov. 4, 1961; children—Ana, Pavle. Grad. Elec. Engring., Belgrade U., 1959, D.Tech. Scis., 1979. Cert. electroheating engr. Lomonosov U., Moscow, USSR. Chief of maintenance, Zeljezara Boris Kidric, Niksic, Yugoslavia, 1960-64, mgr. electroheat application, 1964-68, dir. devel., 1968-78, v.p., 1978-82, pres., 1982—; prof. Veljko Vlahovic U., Titograd, Yugoslavia, 1978; v.p. Assn. of Steel Industry, Belgrade, 1982, pres., 1985; bd. dirs. Internat. Union for Electroheat, Paris, 1979; pres. Yugoslav Com. for Electroheat, Belgrade, 1982. Author: Electric Circuit of Arc Furnace (N. Tesla prize 1980), 1979; Modernization Program (prize/diploma 1984), 1976-82; Thermal and Electrical Characteristics of Arc Furnace, 1986; Fundamentals of Electricity, 1988; contbr. articles to publs. in field. Pres. Football Assn. Montenegro, 1983; bd. dirs. Yugoslav Football Assn., 1981; mem. central com. Communist Party of Yugoslavia, 1982—, Montenegro, 1982-86, Nigoslavia, 1986—. Recipient September 18th prize Jury of Niksic Town Assembly, 1974, July 13th prize, Jury of Socialist Republic of Montenegro Assembly, Titograd, 1975; Prize Yugoslav C. of C., Belgrade, 1984; Gold medal Industriaimport, Titograd, 1985; decorated Order for Work Merits, Belgrade, 1975. Mem. Yugoslav Assn. Engrs. (bd. dirs. 1979—, N. Tesla prize 1980). Yugoslav C. of C. (bd. dirs. 1981, diploma for invention 1976). Home: Serdara Scepana S-70, YU 81400 Niksic Yugoslavia Office: Zeljezara Boris Kidric, Vuka Karadzica bb, YU 81400 Niksic Yugoslavia

BULBECK, MARGARET CACHILLA, social sciences educator; b. Adelaide, South Australia, Australia, June 23, 1951; d. Francis Paul an Paquita Margaret (Platten) B. B of Econs., U. Adelaide, 1972; postgrad., Australian Nat. U., 1975, PhD in Sociology, 1979. Clk. Australian Bur. Stats., Canberra, 1973-74; staff devel. officer Industries Asstance Commn., Canberra, 1974-75; sr. teaching fellow Griffith U., Brisbane, Queensland, Australia, 1979, lectr., 1983—; tutor Murdoch U., Perth, Western Australia, 1980, 81-83; sr. lectr. Griffith U., Brisbane, 1987—. Contbr. articles to profl. jours. Coordinator Nat. Register Unusual Monuments Project, Australian Bicentennial Authority, Queensland, 1987-89. Mem. Australian and New Zealand Sociol. Assn. (co-organizer conf. 1985), Australian Polit. Studies Assn., British Sociol. Assn. Club: Bardon Squash (Brisbane). Office: Griffith U Sch Humanities, Nathan, 4000 Brisbane Australia

BULL, OLE BORNEMANN, hospital architect; s. Carl Albert and Hildur Jenny Marie (Knudsen) B.; student Norwegian Tech. High. Sch.; m. Oct. 24, 1946 (div. 1965); children: Marit, Cecilie. Asst., then partner Ole Övergaard, hosp. architect, 1951-57; pvt. practice architecture specializing in hosps., Oslo, 1957—; leader tech. hosp. symposiums for Norske Siviling. Forening. Recipient various prizes, 1957-64, including 1st prize competition Alesund Fylkessykehus, 1957. Mem. Norske Arktekters Landsforbund, Den Norske Sykehusforening, Forum for Sykehusarkitekter. Mem. Norwegian State Ch. Contbr. articles on hosp. bldg. to profl. jours. Home: Gyssestadkollen 10, 1312 Slependen Norway Office: Rudsletta 38, 1351 Rud Norway

BULL, PETER ANTHONY, geography educator; b. Bristol, Eng., July 4, 1950; s. Francis Peter and June Rosemary (Symons) B.; m. Pauline Ann Linieres, Aug. 10, 1985; children: Adrian, Victoria, Charlotte. BSc, U. Wales, 1973, MSc, 1976, PhD, 1976; MA, Oxford U., Eng., 1985. Tutor in geography U. Wales, Swansea, 1976-78; research lectr. U. Oxford, 1978-85, univ. lectr., 1985—; cons. in field. Contbr. research papers, articles to profl. publs. Recipient Sir Dudley Stamp award U. Wales, 1973, E.K. Tratman award Brit. Cave Research Assn., 1985, Cuthbert Peek award Royal Geographic Soc., 1986. Fellow Royal Geog. Soc., Geol. Soc. London; mem. Quaternary Research Assn., Brit. Cave Research Assn., Brit. Geomorphol. Research Group. Club: Un-named Club (Bristol). Office: U Oxford Hertford Coll, Catte St, Oxford OX1 3BW, England

BULL, PETER TOWNLEY, consultant anesthetist; b. Wrexham, Clwyd, North Wales, U.K., Nov. 23, 1943; s. Mervyn Robert and Ethel (Lloyd) B.; m. June 26, 1968 (div. 1980); 1 child, Jeremy; m. Elayne Salter, Sept. 2, 1981; children—Andrew, Suzanna. M.B., Ch.B., Liverpool U., 1967. Commd. surg. lt. Royal Navy, 1968, advanced through grades to surgeon comdr., 1980; med. officer Royal Navy, 1968-83, HMS Ark Royal, 1976-77; hon. sr. registrar anesthetics Cambridge U., Eng., 1978-79; sr. anesthetist South Atlantic, Hosp. Ship, Uganda, Falklands War, 1982; cons. anesthetist Trent Regional Authority, Mansfield, Nottinghamshire, 1983—; sr. med. officer HMS Sherwood, Nottingham, 1984—. Recipient Pask Cert. of Honor, Assn. Anesthetists, London, 1983. Fellow Faculty Anesthetists, Royal Coll. Surgeons; mem. Med. Defence Union. Conservative. Mem. Ch. of England. Avocations: gardening; reading; cricket; tennis; bridge; photography. Home: Kota Tinggi, Mansfield Rd, Farnsfield NG22 8HG, England Office: Anesthetic Dept, West Hill Dr, Mansfield NG18 1PH, England

BULLARD, ETHEL MUNDAY, musician, music educator; b. Cranston, R.I.; d. Alfred James and Martha Jane (Walker) Munday; Mus. B., Am. Conservatory Music, Chgo., then postgrad.; postgrad. Northwestern U.; attended master classes Am. Conservatory of Music and Chgo. Mus. Coll.; m. Henry Messenger Bullard, Apr. 22; 1 son, Thomas Robert. Tchr. piano, Oak Park, Ill.; piano accompanist Oak Park Musical Theatre, 1967—, music dir., 1971-79; author, compiler music appreciation course Hadley Sch. for Blind, Winnetka, Ill., 1967; cons. in field. Afternoon chmn. Beye Elem. Sch. PTA, Oak Park, 1957, evening v.p., 1958. Recipient Steinway award, 1967; cert. for service to blind Sigma Alpha Iota, 1968. Mem. Soc. Am. Musicians, Music Tchrs. Nat. Assn. (master tchr. cert. 1984), Ill. State Music Tchrs. Assn. (Chgo. chmn. 1961-65, 71-72, piano chmn. 1968, Service award 1979), Nat. Fedn. Music Clubs, Am. Fedn. Musicians, Nat. Guild Piano Tchrs., Am. Music Scholarship Assn., MacDowell Artists Assn. Oak Park (Appreciation plaque 1985), Sonneck Soc., Sigma Alpha Iota (editorial bd. 1970-73, nat. editor 1973-79, dir. meml. Library at Music Library at U. Mich. 1973—, honor awards). Congregational. Club: Eastern Star. Address: 228 N Lombard St Oak Park IL 60302

BULLEN, JOHN BARRINGTON, English educator; b. Cardiff, Eng., Oct. 11, 1942; s. Kenneth Frederick and Majorie (James) B.; m. Mary Martine Brant, May 12, 1952. BA, Pembroke Coll., Cambridge, Eng., 1970, PhD, 1975. Andrew Bradley fellow in English Balliol Coll., Oxford, Eng., 1970-75; lectr. Reading (Eng.) U., 1975-87, reader in English, 1987—; vis. prof. English U. Ill., 1981-82. Author: The Expressive Eye, 1986; editor: Roger Fry: Vision and Design, 1982, Clive Bell: Art, 1987, The Sun is God, 1987. Mem. Amnesty Internat. Home: 344 Banbury Rd, Oxford England OX2 7PR Office: Reading U, Whiteknights, Reading England RG6 2AA

BULLIER, ANTOINE JEAN, law educator, political scientist; b. Paris, Oct. 26, 1946; s. Paul Alfred and Marie-Rose (Watin) B.; m. Françoise Jeanne Picard, Jan. 7, 1984. LLM, U. Mich., 1974; DSc, U. Paris Sorbonne, 1977, U. Paris II, 1977; LittD, U. Paris Sorbonne Nouvelle, 1987. Lectr. U. Potchefstroom, South Africa, 1975-77, U. of Witwatersrand, Johannesburg, South Africa, 1977-78, U. Natal, Durban, South Africa, 1978-81; maître asst. U. Réunion, St. Denis Réunion, France, 1981-86; maître de Conférences U. Panthéon-Sorbonne, Paris, 1986—. Author: Géopolitique de l'Apartheid, 1982, Le Parler franco-mauricien au Natal, 1983, Partition et Répartition, 1988; contbr. more than 40 articles to various internat. acad. jours. Brit. Council scholar, 1970, Franco-Am. scholar, 1973; recipient scholarship South African Govt., 1976; named to Am. Acad. Internat. Law, 1974. Office: U Pantheon Sorbonne, 12 place du Panthéon, 75231 Cédex 05 Paris France

BULLOCK, KEVIN EDWARD, analytical chemist; b. Clifton, N.J., Sept. 16, 1951; s. Edward Fitzgerald and Joan Valerie (Batura) B.; m. Lea Doerr, July 22, 1978. B.S. in Chemistry, Memphis State U., 1973; Ph.D., U. New Orleans, 1978. Sr. analytical chemist Monsanto Research Corp., Dayton, Ohio, 1978-81; research specialist Monsanto Ind. Chem., St. Louis, 1981-82, Monsanto Nutrition Chem. Co., St. Louis, 1982-85; group leader Monsanto Animal Scis. div. Monsanto Co., St. Louis, 1986—. Author of more than 70 proprietary analytical methods, 1981—. Mem. Am. Chem. Soc., N.Y. Acad. Scis. Roman Catholic. Home: 239 Aspen Village Dr Ballwin MO 63011

BULLOCK, PETER BRADLEY, tool company executive; b. Tipton, Eng., June 9, 1934; s. William Horace Bradley and Catherine (Garner) B.; B.Sc., U. London; m. Joyce Rea, Nov. 1, 1958; children—Claire Elizabeth Bradley, Penelope Jane Bradley. With Nat. Coal Bd., 1959-65, Thomas Potterton Ltd., 1966-67, Fibreglass Ltd., 1965-66, 67-69; pres., mng. dir., Flymo Ltd.; dir. Electrolux Ltd.; joint mng. dir. Electrolux Group UK; group chief exec. James Neill Holdings PLC, 1983—, Spear & Jackson Internat. PLC, 1986—; chmn. Neill Tools Ltd., 1983—; ; pres., dir. gen. AMV (France), 1986—; bd. dirs. 600 Group. Served with Brit. Army, 1956-58. Chartered engr., U.K. Mem. Inst. Energy, Inst. Mktg., Inst. Dirs. Conservative. Mem. Ch. of Eng. Clubs: Arts of London, Leander, Phyllis Court. Home: The Cottage, Queenwood, Watlington, Oxford OX9 5HW, England other: The Mill Cottage, Edale, via Sheffield, Derbyshire S30 2ZE, England Office: Handsworth Rd, Sheffield S13 9BR, England

BULMAN, WILLIAM PATRICK, data processing exec.; b. Corona, N.Y., Jan. 11, 1925; s. William T. and Bridget A. (Gibbons) B.; A.B.S., U. Upper N.Y., 1947; B.B.A., Syracuse (N.Y.) U., 1949; m. Jane G. Jones, June 30, 1952. In systems/programming Mohawk Airlines, Utica, N.Y., 1951-55; data processing mgr. Gold Medal Packing, Utica, 1956-59, West End Brewing, Utica, 1960-73; coordinator on-line data processing systems Sperry-Univac, Utica, 1973-76, data processing mgr., 1976-77; programmer/analyst MDS, Herkimer, N.Y., 1977-86; sr. programmer, analyst, Momentum Techs., Herkmer, N.Y., 1986—. Served with USN, 1941-46. Mem. Data Processing Mgmt. Assn. (v.p., treas.), Assn. Systems Mgmt. Address: 35 Ashwood Ave Whitesboro NY 13492

BUMBERY, JOSEPH LAWRENCE, diversified company executive; b. St. Louis, May 30, 1929; s. John Andrew and Lillian Belle (DeVinney) B. B.S., St. Louis U., 1951. Asst. comptroller Magic Chef, Inc., St. Louis, 1955-57; dir. audits and systems Bemis Corp., St. Louis, 1957-62; asst. comptroller Studebaker Corp., South Bend, Ind., 1962-65; with ITT, N.Y.C., 1965-86; v.p. ITT, 1979—, asst. comptroller, 1969—. Served to 1st lt. USAF, 1951-53. Decorated Comdr. Order St. John of Jerusalem (U.K.); St. Louis U. scholar, 1947-51.

BUMP, PARIS LOUIS, JR., management executive; b. Attleboro, Mass., Oct. 13, 1928; s. Paris Louis and Annie Dorothy (Booth) B.; m. Anita Merkt, Sept. 3, 1975. B.S.C., U. R.I., 1953; postgrad. Columbia U., 1953-54, Case Inst. Tech., 1954. Gen. mgr. New Bedford Cordage Co. (Mass.), 1955-58; pres. Venture Engring. Corp., Warren, R.I., 1958-64; mng. assoc. Booz Allen & Hamilton, N.Y.C., London and Bangkok, 1964-70; dir. ops. ITT Automotive Group, Brussels, 1970-76; v.p. product line mgmt. Bendix, Paris, 1977-78; chmn. bd., pres. Berkt Mgmt. Inc., Windsor, Conn., Zurich and Paris, 1978—; dir. Berkt Italiana, Milan; chmn. bd. Berkt France, 1982—; chmn. bd., pres. Berkt Mgmt., Inc., Berkt Cons. AG; chmn. Coval Shares Inc., Windsor, Conn., 1986—. Asst. dir. United Fund, New Bedford, 1956-57; cons. Vt. Gov.'s Indsl. Devel. Council, 1962. Mem. Soc. for Advancement of Mgmt. (dir. 1955-58), Soc. Automotive Engrs. Republican. Clubs: Circle Foch (Paris); Bristol Yacht (R.I.). Office: Berkt Consult AG, Strassburgstrasse 15, Zurich 8004, Switzerland

BUMPERS, DALE L., senator, former governor of Arkansas; b. Charleston, Ark., Aug. 12, 1925; s. William Rufus and Lattie (Jones) B.; m. Betty Lou Flanagan, Sept. 4, 1949; children: Dale Brent, William Mark, Margaret Brooke. Student, U. Ark., 1943, 46-48; J.D., Northwestern U., 1951. Bar: Ark. 1952. Pres. Charleston Hardware and Furniture Co., 1951-66; pvt. practice Charleston, 1952-70; operator Angus cattle farm, 1966-70; gov. of Ark., 1970-74; U.S. senator from Ark. 1975—. Pres. Charleston Sch. Bd., 1969-70. Served with USMC, 1943-46. Mem. Charleston C. of C. (pres.). Methodist. Home: Charleston AR 72933 Office: Office of the Senate 229 Dirksen Senate Bldg Washington DC 20510 •

BUNCE, DONALD FAIRBAIRN MACDOUGAL, II, physician, anatomist; b. Harrisburg, Pa., July 15, 1920; s. Wesley Hibbard and Jean (Fairbairn) B.; m. Lorraine Pelch, May 1, 1954 (dec. Nov. 1975); children: Chip Gregory Alan, Dale Graham Alison; m. Suzanne Brockman, July 13, 1978. B.S., U. Miami, 1951; M.S.c., U. Ill., 1959, Ph.D., 1960; D.O., Coll. Osteo. Medicine and Surgery, 1973. Pres., Bunce Sch. Lab. Technique, Coral Gables, Fla., 1945-48; clin. physiologist Armour Labs., Chgo., 1953-56; dir. research Chgo. Pharmacal Co., 1956-57; instr. anatomy Tulane Sch. Medicine, 1960-62; research prof. physiology Coll. Osteo. Medicine and Surgery, Des Moines, 1962-67; dir. grad. sch. Coll. Osteo. Medicine and Surgery, 1962-73, prof. pathology, acting chmn. dept., 1966-68, prof. physiology, chmn. dept., 1967-73; intern, house physician Des Moines Gen. Hosp., 1973-74; gen. practice medicine Forest City, Iowa, 1974-78, Dubuque, Iowa, 1978-80; clin. assoc. prof. dept. medicine U. Ala. Sch. Medicine, Tuscaloosa, 1982—; chief of staff Forest City Hosp., 1977-78; chief physician Acute Med. Care Unit, Bryce Hosp., Tuscaloosa, Ala., 1980—; vice-chief of staff Bryce Hosp., 1984-85, chief staff, 1985—; pres. med. staff Hale Meml. Hosp., 1986—; former mem. staff Mercy, Finley and Xavier hosps., Dubuque; now mem. staff depts. internal medicine Hale and Druid City hosps., Tuscaloosa; vis. fellow Inst. Exptl. Surgery, Copenhagen, 1962; vis. prof. Karolinska Inst., Stockholm, 1965, Edinburgh, Scotland, 1966, Kennedy Inst. Rheumatology, London, 1969-70; travelling fellow NSF-Internat. Union Physiology; program dir. grad. tng. program in med. scis. NIH; ofcl. del. 4th Internat. Congress Angiology. Editorial bd.: Angéiologie, Paris, 1960—, Jour. Psychiat. Medicine, 1984—; author: Laboratory Guide to Microscopic Anatomy, 1964, The Nervous System in Canine Medicine, 3d edit., 1968, Atlas of Arterial Histology, 1973; also articles. Bd. dirs. Mus. Sci. and Industry, Des Moines, 1971-75. Recipient Billups Meml. Research award La. Heart Assn., 1960. Fellow Am. Coll. Angiology, AAAS, N.Y., Iowa acads sci., Royal Soc. Medicine; mem. AMA, Iowa Med. Soc., Dubuque County Med. Soc., Ala. Med. Assn., Tuscaloosa County Med. Soc., Am. Osteo. Assn., So. Med. Assn, Am. Assn. Anatomists, Anat. Soc. Gt. Britain, So. Soc. Anatomists (exec. sec. 1960-62), Path. Soc. Gt. Britain, Soc. Exptl. Biology and Medicine, Am. Assn. U. Profs., Instn. Nuclear Engrs., L'Union Internationale d'Angéiologie, Société Français d'Angéiologie et d'Histopathologie, Mensa, Sigma Xi, Sigma Alpha Epsilon. Club: Mason. Home: 3203 Arbor Lane Tuscaloosa AL 35405

BUNDGAARD, KJELD, corporate director; b. Lynge, Denmark, Dec. 30, 1930; 1 child, Steen. B.Com., Comml. U. Copenhagen, 1962; M.Sc. in Chem. Engring., Royal Tech. U. Copenhagen, 1957. Gen. mgr. Holger Andreasen A/S, Copenhagen, 1959-63; mng. dir. Unifos Kemi A/S, Copenhagen, 1963-

72; exec. v.p. Novo Industri A/S, Copenhagen, 1972-74; pres. Scandinavian Mgmt. Council, Copenhagen, 1974-77; exec. v.p. The Danish Ferrosan Group, Copenhagen, 1977-80; chmn. bd., dir. Danish Cos., 1980—; examinor The Comml. Univs. of Denmark, 1968—. Author: Industrial Marketing, 1971; Industrial Marketing and Management: Problems and Solutions, 1978; contbr. articles to profl. jours. Served to 1st lt. Danish Navy, 1957-59. Mem. Danish Engrs. Postgrad. Inst. (dir. 1969-75), Danish Plastics Assn. (dir. 1972-73), Danish Mktg. Execs. Council (vice chmn. 1970-73), Danish Mgmt. Soc. (vice chmn. 1973-79). Home: Vejlesoparken 10, DK 2840 Holte Denmark

BUNDY, CHRISTOPHER, publishing executive; b. Bishops Stortford, Hertfordshire, Eng., Oct. 7, 1945; m. Wendy Constance Crook; children: Dominic, Philippa, Prudence. Chartered acct. Group fin. acct. Caravans Internat., Saffron Walden, Eng., 1970-73; fin. dir. Lex Service Group (and subs.), London, 1973-81; group mng. dir. E.J. Arnold and Son Ltd, Leeds, Yorkshire, Eng., 1981—; bd. dirs. Hollis Fin. and Profl. Services, London. Fellow Inst. Chartered Accts.; mem. Brit. Ednl. Equipment Assn. (chmn. 1987—). Office: E J Arnold & Son Ltd, Parkside Lane, Dewsbury Rd, Leeds LS11 5TD, England

BUNDY, KENNETH ALVIN, newspaper editor, publisher; b. Alliance, Neb., Dec. 16, 1910; s. A. Floyd and Carolyn (Southard) B.; B.A. in Journalism, U. Colo., 1935; m. Virginia L. Carr, July 6, 1938; children—Stephen Allen, Paul Emerson. Editor, Estes Park Trail, 1935-36; advt. Fort Collins (Colo.) Express-Courier, 1936; reporter Boulder (Colo.) Daily Camera, 1936-37; reporter and photographer Denver Rocky Mountain News, 1937-42; owner, editor Gunnison (Colo.) Courier, 1945-55; mng. editor Cervi's Journal, 1955-56; pub., elected editor Aurora (Colo.) Star and Adams County News, 1956-70, pres. Star Publs., 1970—. Editor plant newspaper, shell plant Kaiser Industries, Denver for War Manpower Bd., 1943-44. Mem. Colo. State Planning Commn., 1949-52; bd. regents U. Colo., 1950-56; bd. sec. Ridges Metro Dist., 1988—. Mem. Colo. Press Assn. (hon. life), Kappa Tau Alpha, Sigma Delta Chi. Democrat. Congregationalist. Club: Rotary. Home: The Ridges in Redlands 382 1/2 Ridgeview Dr Grand Junction CO 80503-1644 Office: 1336 Glenarm Pl Denver CO 80204

BUNDY, MCGEORGE, educator, former government official; b. Boston, Mar. 30, 1919; s. Harvey Hollister and Katharine Lawrence (Putnam) B.; m. Mary Buckminster Lothrop, June 10, 1950; children: Stephen, Andrew, William, James. A.B., Yale, 1940. Polit. analyst Council Fgn. Relations, 1948-49; vis. lectr. Harvard, 1949-51, assoc. prof. govt., 1951-54, dean faculty arts and scis., 1953-61, prof., 1954-61; spl. asst. to the President for nat. security 1961-66; pres. Ford Found., 1966-79; prof. history NYU, N.Y.C., 1979—. Author: (with Stimson) On Active Service, 1948, The Strength of Government, 1968; Editor: Pattern of Responsibility, 1952. Mem. Am. Polit. Sci. Assn., Phi Beta Kappa. Office: NYU Dept History 19 University Pl New York NY 10003

BUNN, CHARLES NIXON, consultant; b. Springfield, Ill., Feb. 8, 1926; s. Joseph Forman and Helen Anna Frieda (Link) B.; student U. Ill., 1943-44; B.S. in Engring., U.S. Mil. Acad., 1949; M.B.A., Xavier U., Cin., 1958; m. Cecine Cole, Dec. 26, 1951 (div. 1987); children—Sisene, Charles; m. Marjorie F. Tzmaurice, Apr. 5, 1988. Flight test engr. Gen. Electric Co., Cin., also Edwards AFB, Calif., 1953-59; sr. missile test engr., space systems div. Lockheed Aircraft Corp., USAF Satellite Test Center, Sunnyvale, Calif., 1959-60, 63-70, economist, advanced planning dept., 1961-63; economic and long-range planning cons., Los Altos, Calif., 1970-73; head systems planning, economist, strategic bus. planning, Western Regional hdqrs. U.S. Postal Service, San Bruno, Calif., 1973-78; strategic bus. planning cons., investment analysis cons., 1978-79; strategic bus. planning Advanced Reactor Systems dept. Gen. Electric Co., Sunnyvale, Calif., 1979-84; strategic planning cons., 1984—. Served with inf. paratroops U.S. Army, 1944-45, with inf. and rangers, 1949-53; Korea. Decorated Battle Star (5). Mem. Nat. Assn. Bus. Economists, World Future Soc., Sigma Nu. Episcopalian. Home and Office: 222 Incline Way San Jose CA 95139

BUNNAG, SRICHITRA CHAROENCHARAMPORN, endocrinologist, educator; b. Bangkok, July 25, 1933; d. Charoen and Som (Vajarastien) Charoencharamporn; M.D., Chulalongkorn Hosp., 1957; S.M., U. Chgo., 1961, Ph.D., 1964; m. Sirotma Bunnag, Mar. 15, 1962; children—Sara, Dan. Asst. prof. depts. medicine and pathology U. Chgo. Hosps. and Clinics, 1965; faculty, chief div. endocrinology and metabolism Chulalongkorn Hosp. Med. Sch., Bangkok, 1966—, prof. medicine, 1979, head dept. medicine, 1984-87, council mem. Faculty of Medicine, 1979-81; chmn. dept. medicine, faculty of medicine Chulalongkorn U., 1983—, assoc. dean, 1987-88; mem. Med. Council Thailand, 1983—; mem. bd. examiners Thai Bd. Internal Medicine; mem. div. hormone research, dept. med. scis. Anandamahidol Found., Chulalongkorn Hosp., 1974—. Anandamahidol scholar, 1959-65. Fellow Internat. Coll. Angiology, Royal Coll. of Physician of Thailand; mem. ASEAN Fedn. of Endocrine Socs. (exec.) (pres. 1982-83, assoc. editor jour.), Endocrine Soc., Am. Diabetes Assn., Am. Fedn. Clin. Research, U. Chgo. Alumni Assn., European Microcirculatory Soc., Women's Med. Assn. Thailand (council), Thailand Med. Assn., Sigma Xi. Contbr. articles to med. jours. Home: 38 Sukumvit Soi 89/1, Sukumvit Rd, Bangkok 10250 Thailand Office: Chulalongkorn U Hosp, Medicine Faculty Dept Medicine, Bangkok 10500, Thailand

BUNTROCK, R. DIK, management consultant; b. Grafton, Wis., June 24, 1938; s. Albert Julius and Ida Marie (Scherer) B.; m. Judith E. Kabke, July 27, 1963; 1 child, Sara Ruth. BS, U. Wis., Oshkosh, 1963; MA, Cardinal Stritch Coll., 1969. Tchr. elem. sch. Lompoc, Calif., 1963-65, West Bend, Wis., 1965-75; mgmt. cons. West Bend, 1975—; pvt. tutor, West Bend, 1963—; home decorator, West Bend, 1969—; speaker in field. Author: The Blue Beer Stein, 1986. Dir. Washington County Mental Health, Wis., 1973—, West Bend Econ. Devel. Corp., 1983—. Served in USAF, 1956-57. Mem. Soc. Mfg. Engrs., Nat. Geographic Soc., West Bend C. of C. (ambassador). Club: Toastmasters (hon. doctorate). Home and Office: 640 S 15th Ave West Bend WI 53095

BUNTS, FRANK EMORY, artist; b. Cleve., Mar. 2, 1932; s. Alexander Taylor and Mary (Corbin) B.; m. Norah Jean Grassle, Aug. 1, 1964. Student, Yale U., 1951-53, 55-57; diploma, Cleve. Inst. Art, 1964; M.A., Case Western Res. U., 1964. Instr. Cleve. Inst. Art, 1963-64, Ark. State U., 1965-67; mem. faculty U. Md., 1967-77, prof., 1973-77, dir. grad. art studio program, 1972-77. Exhibited in one-man shows Comara Gallery, Los Angeles, 1967, 68, Franz Bader Gallery, Washington, 1969, 73, 75, St. John's Coll., Annapolis, Md., 1972, Deson Zaks Gallery, Chgo., 1972, Gallery 118, Mpls., 1974, Nat. Acad. Scis., Washington, 1976, Cath. U. Am., Washington, 1978, Plum Gallery, Washington, 1979, Street Exhbn., Moscow, 1982, Flatiron Studio, N.Y.C., 1987, Maryanne McCarthy Fine Art, N.Y., 1988; group shows: San Francisco Mus. Art, Cleve. Mus. Art, Corcoran Gallery Art, Indpls. Mus. Art, Fine Arts Gallery San Diego, Gallery K, Washington, Studio Gallery, Washington, Modern Mus. Art, Rijenka, Yugoslavia, Brooks Meml. Art Gallery, Memphis, Limelight (painting and videos), N.Y.C., 1988, Maryanne McjCarthy Fine Art, N.Y., 1988; represented in collections Phila. Mus. Art, Cleve. Mus. Art, Mus. Holography, N.Y.C., Fine Arts Gallery, San Diego, Library of Congress, Corcoran Gallery Art, Washington, Cooperstown Art Assn., N.Y., Chinese Artists Assn., Beijing, Flatiron Studio, N.Y.C., 1987; works reproduced in jours.; videos: Callanetics, 1986, Portrait of an Artist by Konrad Gylfason, 1986; New York Art Review, 1988, 3rd edition. Address: 15 W 24th St 7th fl New York NY 10010

BUONPANE, GUERIN, lawyer; retired consultant; b. New Castle, Pa., Jan. 17, 1905; s. Elpidio and Mary Jane (Rizzuto) B.; m. Grace Marie Ross, Aug. 17, 1948; children—Anita Buonpane Hartmann, Elissa, James. B.A., Ohio No. U., 1927; student law pvt. attys., 1922-28. Bar: Ohio 1928, U.S. Dist. Ct. (no. dist.) Ohio 1929. Practice, Cleve., 1928—; mem. Buonpane & Buonpane, 1928-36; sole practice, 1936—; trial referee Ohio Indsl. Commn., 1936-42; gov.'s appointee Cleve. dist. Ohio Workers' Compensation Dist. Bd. Claims, 1942-55; gov.'s appointee, chmn. Ohio Workers' Compensation Bd. Rev., 1955-79; lectr. law Case-Western Res. U., 1961-67; legal cons. Indsl. Advisors Bur., Cleve., 1979-88; lectr. in field. Contbr. numerous articles to profl. publs. Govt. appeal agt. World War II, U.S. Govt., Cleve., 1942-45; mem. Beachwood Zoning Bd. Appeals, Ohio, 1954-55, Beachwood Zoning and Planning Commn., 1956-57. Recipient 50-Yr. Meritorious Service award Cleve. Assn. Compensation Attys., 1978; Outstanding Pub. Service award Ohio Acad. Trial Lawyers, 1979; honoree Cleve. Assn. Trial Attys., 1979; Outstanding Profl. Service award Employers Self Insurers Group of Ohio Inc., 1979. Democrat. Home: 3283 Somerset Dr Beachwood OH 44122

BURACZEWSKI, ADAM TADEUSZ, mathematician, educator; b. Zimodry, Vilnius/Vilejka, Poland, Apr. 14, 1926; s. Adam Buraczewski and Zofia Buraczewska; m. Janina Theodora Komorowska, Sept. 18, 1965 (div. 1976); children: Martha, Monika; m. Anna Krefft Buraczewska, Sept. 29, 1983; 1 child, Silvia. Cert. in math., Physical Lyceum, Luban Slaski, Poland, 1946-48; MS, Warsaw U., Poland, 1953; PhD, Math. Inst., Warsaw, 1961; DSc, Warsaw Tech. U., 1975. Cert. math. tchr. Asst. Warsaw Tech. U., 1952-62; sr. lectr. U. Sci. and Tech., Kumasi, Ghana, 1962-64, assoc. prof., 1964-65, prof., 1965-75; assoc. prof., dept. head Higher Pedagogical Inst., Olsztyn, Poland, 1976-80; prof., dept. head U. Papua New Guinea, Port Moresby, 1980-83; prof. Sebha U., Libya, 1983-86; assoc. prof. Higher Pedagogical Inst., Olsztyn, 1986—; vis. prof. U. Nairobi, Kenya, 1972. Contbr. numerous articles to profl. jours. Served as cpl. artillery, 1944-46, ETO. Decorated Gold Cross of Merit (Warsaw); recipient Higher Edn. Minister's award research achievements 1980, ednl. achievements, 1978. Mem. Polish Math. Soc., Am. Math. Soc., Assn. Combatants. Roman Catholic. Club: New Zealand. Office: Higher Pedagogical Inst, Zolnierska 14, 10-561 Olsztyn Poland

BURAS, BRENDA ALLYNN, public affairs executive; b. New Orleans, May 1, 1954; d. Allen Anthony and Gloria Violet (Short) B. BA in Commerce, Loyola U., New Orleans, 1976, MBA, 1984. Stenographer Texaco Inc., New Orleans, 1974-76, engr.'s asst., 1976-78, natural gas contracts analyst, 1978-80, pub. affairs asst., 1980-83, pub. and govt. affairs coordinator S.E. region, 1983—; owner Achievements Unltd.; cert. lectr. Silva Method Mind Devel. and Stress Control. Loaned exec. United Way Greater New Orleans, 1978-79, mem. speakers bur., 1979-83; cons. Jr. Achievement Project Bus., 1979-80; voting commr. St. Bernard Parish, 1976-80; mem. Friends of Audubon Zoo, Sta. WYES-(PBS) TV, New Orleans Mus. Art; mem. membership and pub. relations comms. Emergency Food Bank New Orleans, Vol Leadership Devel. Program United Way, 1987; chmn. subcom. United Way Corp. Recognition/Thank-You, 1988—; speaker Boy Scouts Explorers program. 1984—; active media com. Rep. Convention, 1988; host, media com. for Rep. Conv. 1988. Mem. Pub. Relations Soc. Am., Women in Communications, Inc., Press Club New Orleans, Inst. Noetic Scis., Assn. for Humanistic Psychology, People to People Internat. Inc. Republican. Clubs: U.S. Figure Skating Assn., Dixieland Figure Skating, Heritage Plaza Health. Office: Texaco Inc 400 Poydras St New Orleans LA 70160

BURBECK, ELIZABETH LOUISE, police superintendent; b. Taupo, New Zealand, Feb. 5, 1953; arrived in Gt. Britain, 1955; d. Adam Matthew and Mary Hallam (Cousins) Neville; m. John Burbeck; children: Matthew Edward, Katherine Mary. MA, Oxon U., 1973; PhD, London U., 1987. Constable Met. Police Force, London, 1973-76, sgt., 1976-78, insp., 1978-86; insp. Thames Valley Police Force, Reading, England, 1986-87; chief insp. Thames Valley Police Force, Cowley, England, 1987-88, supt., 1988—. Contbr. articles to profl. jours. Office: Thames Valley Police, Force Hdqrs, Kidlington Oxon, England

BURBIDGE, FREDERICK STEWART, transportation company executive; b. Winnipeg, Man., Can., Sept. 30, 1918; s. Frederick Maxwell and Susan Mary (Stewart) B.; m. Cynthia Adams Bennest, Apr. 27, 1942; children: John Bennest, George Frederick. B.A., U. Man., 1939, LL.B., 1946. Called to Bar of Manitoba, 1946. With law dept. Canadian Pacific Ltd., Winnipeg, 1947-50; served in various capacities Canadian Pacific Ltd., pres., 1972, chmn., chief exec. officer, 1981, chmn., 1985-86; dir., exec. com. Bank of Montreal; dir. Amca Internat. Ltd., Pan Can. Petroleum Ltd., C.I.L., Marathon Realty Co., Ltd., Can. Pacific Ltd., Soo Line R.R. Co.; mem. adv. bd. Ams. N.Am., ICI Americas Inc. Bd. dirs. Montreal Neurol. Inst.; chmn. corp. Montreal Neurological Hosp., bd. dirs.; bd. govs. McGill U. Served to lt. Royal Can. Navy, 1941-45. Club: Mt. Royal. Office: Canadian Pacific Ltd, Place du Canada Suite 800, Montreal, PQ Canada H3C 3E4 also: PO Box 6042 Sta A, Montreal, PQ Canada H3C 3E4

BURCH, CRAIG ALAN, electronics executive; b. Geneva, Nebr., May 13, 1954; s. J.J. and R. Eleanor (Bean) B. BS in Elec. Engring., BS in Biology, MIT, 1977. Product specialist Siemens Med., Iselin, N.J., 1977-79, product mgr., 1979-80, nat. sales mgr. computer tomography, 1986—; sr. sales specialist Siemens Med., Phila., 1981-85; pres. Micro Devices Corp., Princeton, N.J., 1985-88; v.p. Intelligent Prodn. Systems Inc., Deerfield Beach, Fla., 1988—. Methodist. Home: 2-14 Hunters Glen Dr Plainsboro NJ 08536 Office: Siemens Med 186 Wood Ave S Iselin NJ 08830

BURCH, JOHN THOMAS, JR., lawyer; b. Balt.; s. John T. and Katheryn Estella (Peregoy) B.; m. Linda Anne Shearer, Nov. 1, 1969; children: John Thomas, Richard James. B.A., U. Richmond, 1964, J.D., 1966; LL.M., George Washington U., 1971. Bar: Va. 1966, D.C. 1974, U.S. Supreme Ct. 1969, Mich. 1983. Pvt. practice Richmond, 1966, Washington, 1974-77; pres. firm Burch, Kerns and Klimek, 1977-82, Burch & Assocs., P.C., 1982-83, Burch & Bennett, P.C., 1983-85; ptnr. Barnett & Alagia, 1985—; pres. Internat. Procurement Cons. Ltd., Washington, 1977-85; Republican committeeman, City of Alexandria, Va., 1975—, a.d.c. to gov., State of Va., 1976—; alternate del. Rep. Nat. Conv., 1988; chmn. Nat. Vietnam Vets. Coalition. Served to maj. JAGC, U.S. Army, 1966-74, Vietnam. Decorated Bronze Star, Meritorious Service medal, others; named Ky. Col. Mem. ABA (sec. public contract law sect. 1976-77), Fed. Bar Assn. (nat. council, dep. sec. 1982-83), Am. Arbitration Assn., Am. Legion, VFW (dep. comdr. 1986-87), Spl. Forces Assn., Nat. Vietnam Vets (nat. chmn. 1983—), Va. Soc. SAR (pres. 1975-76, Patriots medal 1978, Good Citizenship medal 1970), Sons Confederate Vets., Scabbard and Blade, Phi Alpha Delta, Phi Sigma Alpha. Republican. Episcopalian. Home: 1015 N Pelham St Alexandria VA 22304 Office: 1000 Thomas Jefferson Pl Suite 600 Washington DC 20007

BURCH, JOHN WALTER, mining equipment company executive; b. Balt., July 14, 1925; s. Louis Claude and Constance (Boucher) B.; B.S. in Commerce, U. Va., 1951; postgrad. U.S. Coast Guard Acad., 1951; m. Robin Neely Sinkler, Apr. 19, 1952; children—John C., Robert L., Charles C., Anne N. With Procter & Gamble Co., Phila., 1953-65, sales mgr., 1960-65; v.p. Warner Co., Phila., 1965-73; chmn. bd., chief exec. officer S.S. Keely Co., Phila., 1973-75; pres., chmn. bd., chief exec. officer Burch Materials Co., Inc., Wayne, Pa., 1975—; dir. Eagle's Eye, Inc., Wayne. Bd. dirs. Nat. Multiple Sclerosis Soc., 1970-81, v.p., mem. exec. com., 1974-77; bd. dirs. Pa. Sports Hall of Fame, 1974—, v.p., mem. exec. com., 1974-79; chmn. Am. Legion Tennis Tournaments for State of Pa., 1975-82; mem. U.S. Congl. Adv. Bd., 1982—; bd. dirs. Eagle's Eye Lacrosse Club, 1982—. Served with USN, 1943-46, USCG, 1951-53. Mem. Am. Mgmt. Assn., Soc. Advancement of Mgmt., Internat. Platform Assn. Republican. Roman Catholic. Clubs: Merion Cricket, Merion Golf. All-Am. in lacrosse, 1949. Home: 412 Conestoga Rd Wayne PA 19087 Office: Burch Materials Co Inc 685 Kromer Ave Berwyn PA 19312

BURCHAM, RANDALL PARKS, lawyer, farmer; b. Union City, Tenn., July 20, 1917; s. John Simps and Myrtle Caldwell (Howard) B.; m. Hellon Owens, Sept. 30, 1945; children—Randall Parks Jr., Susan. Student Murray State Coll. (Ky.), 1934-38, U. Miss., 1938-39; LL.B., Cumberland U., Lebanon, Tenn., 1940; J.D., Samford U., Birmingham, 1969. Bar: Tenn. 1941. Sole practice, Union City, 1941; atty. U.S. Govt., Nashville, 1945-49; owner Interstate Oil Co., Fulton, Ky., 1949-53; ptnr. Burcham & Fox, Union City, 1953—. Del., Tenn. Constitutional Conv., Nashville, 1971. Served to comdr. U.S. Navy, 1941-45. Fellow Am. Coll. Probate Counsel; mem. ABA, Tenn. Bar Assn. (bd. govs. 1969-72). Democrat. Methodist. Home: 1130 Ethridge Ln PO Box 188 Union City TN 38261 Office: Burcham & Fox 505 S 3d St Union City TN 38261

BURCHARD, ELLEN WILLIAMS, actress, producer, artist, writer; b. Newport, R.I., June 13, 1913; d. Clarence Raymond and Mary Christine (Stewart) Williams; m. John Church Burchard, Feb. 6, 1943; 1 child, John Church. Studied painting with William Van Dresser, 1943, Stephen Olszewski, 1975-85; studied acting U. Wis., 1944, Stella Adler Studio, 1954-56, Herbert Berghof Studio, 1957-65, Harold Clurman's Profl. Acting Classes, N.Y.C., 1960-62. Actress on Broadway, films and TV, also in Rome and London; founder Carriage House Theatre, Little Compton, R.I., 1958, producer, artistic dir., actress Pro Summer Repertory Co., 1958-76; off-Broadway producer, N.Y.C., 1958-76; producer, artistic dir. Actors Repertory Co., Little Compton, 1976-85; actress R.I. Playwrights Theatre Summer Festival, Providence, 1985; lyricist Morning Song, 1979; playwright Marguerite, 1978, Scenes from the Past, 1979; off-Broadway roles include Journey to Endor, 1987-88; editor (poetry) To Diana, 1985. Founder, pres. Young Women's Rep. Club, Newport, 1935-37, 46-54, Little Compton Rep. Club, 1946-57, Newport Players Guild, 1936-42, 46-52; founder, 1st v.p. New Eng. Council Young Reps., 1932-37; Young Nat. Committeewoman Rep. Nat. Com., 1932-43. Mem. Actors Equity Assn., Screen Actors Guild, AFTRA, R.I. Short Story Club (pres. 1982-85), R.I. Water Color Soc., Newport Art Mus., Westport Art Club, Bus. Womens Club (charter, Newport). Congregationalist. Club: Mosaic (founder) (Newport).

BURCHARDT, LOTHAR, historian, educator; b. Frankfurt, Germany, Feb. 7, 1939; s. Hans H. and Ruth E. (Bergenthum) B.; m. Monika Müller-Pilgram, May 14, 1966; children: Christian, Ulrich, Erik. MA, U. Heidelberg, 1964, PhD, 1966. Asst. U. Heidelberg, Fed. Republic Germany, 1965-67, Mannheim U., Fed. Republic Germany, 1967-69; asst. U. Konstanz, Fed. Republic Germany, 1969-73, dozent, 1973-77, assoc. prof., 1977-79, prof. dept. history, 1979—; vis. prof. U. Mass., 1987. Author: Friedenswirtyschaft, 1968, Wissenschaftspolitik, 1975, Hitler n. die historische Grösse, 1979. Mem. Allensbach-Kaltbrunn Town Council, 1975. Grantee Internat. Com. History of Tech., 1974, Brit. Council, 1980, Fulbright Commn., 1987. Mem. Verband der Historiker Deutschlands, Deutsche Gesellschaft für Sozial u Wirtschaftsgeschichte. Home: Zur Breite 18, 7753 Allensbach Federal Republic of Germany Office: Univ Konstanz, Postfach 5560, 7750 Konstanz Federal Republic of Germany

BURCHELL, ROBERT ARTHUR, historian, educator; b. Plymouth, Eng., Mar. 31, 1941; s. Arthur Thomas and Mary Leonora (Symons) B. BA, U. Oxford, 1960, MA, 1967, BLitt, 1969. Asst. lectr. Am. history and instns. U. Manchester, Eng., 1965-68, lectr., 1968-80, sr. lectr., 1980—. Author: Westward Expansion, 1974, San Francisco Irish, 1980. Mem. Brit Assn. for Am. Studies (treas. 1979-84, sec. 1984—), Orgn. Am. Historians, St. Anselm Hall Assn. (chmn. 1987—), European Assn. for Am. Studies (sec. 1988—). Office: U Manchester, Dept Am Studies, Manchester M13 9PL, England

BURCHFIELD, HARRY PHINEAS, JR., biochemistry consultant; b. Pitts., Dec. 22, 1915; s. Harry Phineas and Florence Faye (Fearl) B.; m. Eleanor Emerett Storrs, Nov. 29, 1963; children: Sarah Storrs, Benjamin Hyde. A.B., Columbia U., 1938, M.A., 1938, Ph.D., 1956. Chemist, Nat. Oil Products Co., Harrison, N.J., 1938-40; research scientist Uniroyal Corp., Naugatuck, Conn., 1940-50; dir. plantations research dept. Uniroyal Corp., Indonesia and Malaysia, 1951-52; asso. dir. Boyce Thompson Inst. Plant Research, Yonkers, N.Y., 1952-61; inst. scientist, mgr. S.W. Research Inst., San Antonio, 1961-65; chief pesticides research lab. USPHS, Perrine, Fla., 1965-67; sci. dir. Gulf South Research Inst., New Iberia, La., 1967-76; adj. prof. chemistry U. Southwestern La., 1967-77; prof. chemistry, head div. molecular biology Med. Research Inst., Fla. Inst. Tech., Melbourne, 1977-81; charter mem. Soc. Univ. Fellows, 1978; prin. scientist Research Assos., 1976—; trustee Gulf Univs. Research Consortium, 1971-76; mem. carcinogenesis panel of secs. HEW Commn. on Pesticides, 1969; mem. nat. tech. adv. com. pesticides EPA, 1971-72, project reviewer research grants, 1972; cons. carcinogenesis Nat. Cancer Inst., 1965-67; cons. leprosy Pan Am. Health Orgn., WHO, 1974, EPA, 1976—. Author: (with Eleanor E. Storrs) Biochemical Applications of Gas Chromatography, 1962, (with D.E. Johnson and Eleanor Storrs) Guide to the Analysis of Pesticide Residues, 1965; contbr. chpts. to books, articles to profl. jours. Recipient award Chgo. Rubber Group, 1946; EPA grantee, 1969-76; Nat. Inst. Environ. Health Scis. grantee, 1977—. Mem. Am. Chem. Soc., Soc. Toxicology, Am. Inst. Biol. Scis., AAAS. Episcopalian. Office: 72 Riverview Terr Indialantic FL 32903

BURCHFIELD, JAMES RALPH, lawyer; b. Vincennes, Ind., Feb. 6, 1924; s. James R. and Doris (Marchal) B.; m. Dorothey Alice Underwood, July 31, 1949; children—Susan Burchfield Holliday, J. Randolph, Stephanie D. B.A., Ohio State U., 1947, J.D., 1949. Bar: Ohio 1949, U.S. Supreme Ct. 1960. Sole practice, Columbus, Ohio, 1949-77; ptnr. Burchfield & Burchfield, Columbus, 1978—; pres. Ohio Bar Liability Ins. Co., 1978—, also dir. Exec. dir. Franklin County Eisenhower Orgn., Ohio, 1952; mem. Mayor's Spl. Com. on Transit, Columbus, 1955-58; trustee Columbus Goodwill, 1970; mem. Ohio Soc. Colonial Wars, 1972. Served with USAF, 1943-45. Recipient Outstanding Young Man award Columbus Jaycees, 1956, Mil. Hon. award, Scabbard & Blade, 1948. Mem. Bexley Am. Legion (post comdr. 1954), Columbus Bar Assn., Am. Arbitrator's Assn., ABA, Ohio State Bar Assn. (chmn. 1970—), Am. Jud. Assn., Eastside Bus. Assn. (pres. 1955); fellow Ohio State Bar Found.; mem. Phi Alpha Theta. Republican. Clubs: Sertoma Internat. (pres. 1967), Sertoma Found. (pres. 1977-79). Lodges: Masons (treas. 1952—), Shriners. Avocations: world travel; hiking; fishing; reading. Home: 9330 White Oak Ln Westerville OH 43081 Office: Burchfield & Burchfield 1313 E Broad St Columbus OH 43205

BURCHFIELD, ROBERT WILLIAM, language professional, educator; b. Wanganui, New Zealand, Jan. 27, 1923; arrived in Eng., 1949; s. Frederick and Mary Lauder (Blair) B.; m. Ethel May Yates, July 2, 1949 (div. 1976); children: Jennifer Catherine, Jonathan Robert, Elizabeth Jane; m. Elizabeth Austen Knight, Nov. 5, 1976. Student, Wanganui Tech. Coll., New Zealand, 1934-39, Victoria U. Coll., Wellington, New Zealand, 1940-41, 46-48; MA, Victoria U. Coll., Wellington, New Zealand, 1948; student, Oxford U., Eng., 1949-53, BA, 1951, MA, 1955; LittD (hon.), Liverpool, 1978, Wellington, N.Z., 1983. Jr. lectr. English Magdalen Coll. Oxford U., Eng., 1952-53, lectr. English Christ Ch. Coll., 1953-57, lectr. St. Peter's Coll., 1955-63, sr. research fellow, 1963-79; editor Oxford U. Press, London, 1957—; chief editor The Oxford English Dictionaries, London, 1971-84. Author: The Spoken Word, 1981, The English Language, 1985; editor: A Supplement to the Oxford English Dictionary, 1972-86, The New Zealand Pocket Oxford Dictionary, 1986, Studies in Lexicography, 1987; contbr. articles to lit. mags. Served as sgt. in New Zealand Army, 1941-46. Named Commdr. of the Order of the British Empire by the Queen of Eng., 1975; New Zealand Rhodes Scholar, 1949. Fellow Inst. Linguists; mem. Am. Acad. Arts and Scis., English Assn. (pres. 1978-79), Early English Text Soc. (hon. sec. 1955-68, mem. council 1968-80). Home: The Barn, 14 The Green, Sutton Courtenay, Oxford OX14 4AE, England Office: St Peter's Coll, New Inn Hall St, Oxford OX1 2DL, England

BURDEN, JAMES EWERS, lawyer; b. Sacramento, Oct. 24, 1939; s. Herbert Spencer and Ida Elizabeth (Brosemer) B.; m. Kathryn Lee Gardner, Aug. 21, 1965; children—Kara Elizabeth, Justin Gardner. B.S., U. Calif.-Berkeley, 1961; J.D., U. Calif.-Hastings Coll. Law, 1964; postgrad. U. So. Calif., 1964-65. Bar: Calif. 1965, Tax Ct. U.S. 1969, U.S. Supreme Ct. 1970. Assoc. Elliott and Aune, Santa Ana, Calif., 1965, White, Harbor, Fort & Schei, Sacramento, 1965-67; assoc. Miller, Starr & Regalia, Oakland, Calif., 1967-69, ptnr., 1969-73; ptnr. Burden, Aiken, Mansuy & Stein, San Francisco, 1973-82; ptnr. James E. Burden, Inc., San Francisco, 1982—; ptnr. Austex Oil & Gas Co., Luling, Tex., Judgment Oil and Gas Co., Lockhart, Tex., Northpoint Investment Co., San Francisco; underwriting mem. Lloyds of London, 1986—; corp. sec. Doric Devel., Inc., Alameda, Calif.; sec. Harbor Bay Isle Assocs., Alameda; instr. U. Calif.-Berkeley, 1968-75, also Merritt Coll. Mem. ABA. Clubs: Claremont Country (Oakland), San Francisco Grid, San Francisco Comml., Commonwealth of Calif.; American (London). Contbr. articles to profl. jours. Office: 451 Jackson St 2d Floor San Francisco CA 94111

BURDEN, JEAN (PRUSSING), poet, writer, editor; b. Waukegan, Ill., Sept. 1, 1914; d. Harry Frederick and Miriam (Biddlecom) Prussing; m. David Charles Burden, 1940 (div. 1949). B.A., U. Chgo., 1936. Sec. John Hancock Mutual Life Ins. Co., Chgo., 1937-39, Young & Rubicam, Inc., Chgo., 1939-41; editor, copywriter Domestic Industries, Inc., Chgo., 1941-45; office mgr. O'Brion Russell & Co., Los Angeles, 1948-55; adminstr. pub. relations Meals for Millions Found., Los Angeles, 1955-65; editor Stanford Research Inst., South Pasadena, Calif., 1965-66; propr. Jean Burden & Assocs., Altadena, Calif., 1966-82; lectr. poetry to numerous colls. and univs., U.S., 1963—; supr. poetry workshop Pasadena City Coll., Calif., 1961-62, 66, U. Calif. at Irvine, 1975; also pvt. poetry workshops. Author: Naked as the

Glass, 1963, Journey Toward Poetry, 1966, The Cat You Care For, 1968, The Dog You Care For, 1968, The Bird You Care For, 1970, The Fish You Care For, 1971, A Celebration of Cats, 1974, The Classic Cats, 1975, The Woman's Day Book of Hints for Cat Owners, 1980, 84; Poetry editor: Yankee Mag, 1955—; pet editor: Woman's Day Mag, 1973-82; Contbr. numerous articles to various jours. and mags. MacDowell Colony fellow, 1973, 74, 76; Recipient Silver Anvil award Pub. Relations Soc. of Am., 1969, 1st prize Borestone Mountain Poetry award, 1963. Mem. Poetry Soc. Am., Acad. Am. Poets, Authors Guild. Address: 1129 Beverly Way Altadena CA 91001

BURDICK, GLENN ARTHUR, university dean, physicist, electrical engineer; b. Pavilion, Wyo., Sept. 9, 1932; s. Stephen Arthur and Mary Elizabeth (McClerg) B.; m. Joyce Mae Huggett, July 14, 1951; children—Stephen Arthur, Randy Glenn. B.S., Ga. Inst. Tech., 1958, M.S., 1959; Ph.D., MIT, 1961. Reg. profl. engr., Fla. Office mgr. Statewide Contractors, Las Vegas, Nev., 1955-56; spl. tool designer Ga. Inst. Tech., Atlanta, 1954-55, instr., 1956-59; sr. mem. research staff Sperry Microwave, Oldsmar, Fla., 1961-65; prof. elec. engring. U. So. Fla., Tampa, 1965—, dean Coll. Engring., 1979-86, prof. elec. engring., 1965-86, disting. prof. engring., 1986—, dean emeritus, 1986—. Invented underground pipeline leak detector, 1956, sail boat mast insulation, 1981. Mem. Tampa Bay Fgn. Affairs Com., 1981—, Pinellas County (Fla.) High Speed Rail Task Force, 1982—, Gov. of State of Fla. Energy Task Force, 1980-85; vice chmn. Fla. Task Force for Sci. Energy and Tech. Service to Industry, 1981-82. Tex. Gulf scholar, 1957-58; NSF fellow, 1958-61; Woodrow Wilson fellow, 1958-59; named Engring. Faculty Mem. of Yr. State of Fla., 1986. Mem. Fla. Engring. Soc. (Engr. of Yr. award 1981), Internat. Soc. Hybrid Microelectronics (nat. pres. 1974), IEEE (sr. mem., Engr. of Yr. award 1980), Am. Ry. Engring. Assn., N.Y. Acad. Sci., Am. Soc. Engring. Edn., U.S. Profl. Engrs. Edn. (vice-chmn. SE region, 1986—). Clubs: Clearwater Tennis (pres. Fla. chpt. 1965, 69), Downtown.). Lodge: Rotary. Home: 1005 Curlew Pl Tarpon Springs FL 34689 Office: Univ So Fla Coll Engring Tampa FL 33620

BURDICK, QUENTIN NORTHROP, U.S. senator; b. Munich, N.D., June 19, 1908; s. Usher Lloyd and Emma (Robertson) B.; m. Marietta Janecky, Mar. 18, 1933 (dec. Mar. 1958); children: Jonathan, Jan, Mary, Jennifer, Jessica; m. Jocelyn Birch Peterson; 1 son, Gage (dec.); stepchildren: Leslie, Birch. B.A., U. Minn., 1931, LL.B., 1932. Bar: N.D. 1932. Practiced in Fargo, 1932-58; mem. 86th Congress, N.D. at large, 1958-60; U.S. senator from N.D. 86th-100th Congresses, 1960—, chmn. Senate environ. and pub. works com., agr. appropriations subcom.; candidate for lt. gov., 1942, for gov., 1946, for U.S. senator, 1956. Mem. Sons of Norway, Sigma Nu. Democrat. Congregationalist. Clubs: Mason, Elk, Eagle, Moose. Office: 511 Hart Senate Bldg Washington DC 20510-3401

BURDUS, JULIA ANN, marketing researcher; b. Alnwick, Eng., Sept. 4, 1933; d. Gladstone and Julia Wilhelmina (Booth) Beaty; m. Ian Buchanan Robertson. BA in Psychology, St. Mary's, Durham, Eng., 1956. Research exec. O&M, London, 1961-67; dir. research Garland Compton, London, 1967-71; dir. research McCann Erickson, London, 1971-77, N.Y.C., 1977-79; chmn. McCann & Co., London, 1979-81; dir. strategic planning I.P.G., N.Y.C., 1981-83; dir. AGB Research, London, 1983—; chmn. Econ. Devel. Com., London, 1983-87. Dep. chmn. Health Edn. Authority, London, 1987—. Fellow Inst. Practitioners Advt.; mem. Advt. Assn. (chmn. 1981-82). Club: WACL. Office: AGB Research, 76 Shoe Ln, London EC4, England

BURGARD, HORST, banker; b. Federal Republic of Germany, Jan. 28, 1929. Mem. bd. mng. dirs. Deutsche Bank AG, 1987—; chmn., dep. chmn., and mem. supervisory bds. of numerous major companies. Address: Taunusanlage 12, D-6000 Frankfurt am Main Federal Republic of Germany

BURGER, HENRY G., anthropologist, educator, publisher; b. N.Y.C., June 27, 1923; s. B. William and Terese R. (Felleman) B. B.A. with honors (Pulitzer scholar), Columbia Coll., 1947; M.A., Columbia U., 1965, Ph.D. in Cultural Anthropology (State Doctoral fellow), 1967. Indsl. engr. various orgns. 1947-51, Midwest mfrs. rep., 1952-55; social sci. cons. Chgo. and N.Y.C., 1956-67; anthropologist Southwestern Coop. Ednl. Lab., Albuquerque, 1967-69; assoc. prof. anthropology and edn. U. Mo., Kansas City, 1969-73; prof. U. Mo., 1973—, founding mem. univ.wide doctoral faculty, 1974—; lectr. CUNY, 1957-65; Adj. prof. ednl. anthropology U. N.Mex., 1969; anthrop. cons. U.S. VA Hosp., Kansas City, 1971-72. Author: Ethno-Pedagogy, 1968, 2d edit., 1968; compiler, pub.: The Wordtree, a Transitive Cladistic for Solving Physical and Social Problems, 1984; contbr. to anthologies, articles to profl. jours., cassettes to tape libraries. Mem. editorial bd. Council on Anthropology and Edn., 1975-80. Served to capt. AUS, 1943-46. NSF Instl. grantee, 1970. Fellow AAAS, Internat. Union Anthrop. and Ethnol. Scis., World Acad. Art and Sci., Am. Anthrop. Assn. (life), Royal Anthrop. Inst. Gt. Britain (life); mem. Soc. for Linguistic Anthropology, European Assn. for Lexicography, Assn. for Computational Linguistics, Cosmep, Dictionary Soc. N.Am. (life mem.; terminology com.), Assn. internationale de terminologie, Académie européenne des sciences, arts et lettres (corr. mem.), Soc. Conceptual and Content Analysis by Computer, Phi Beta Kappa. Office: The Wordtree 10876 Bradshaw Overland Park KS 66210-1148 also: U Mo Kansas City MO 64110-2499

BURGESS, ANTHONY, author; b. Manchester, Eng., Feb. 25, 1917; s. Joseph and Elizabeth (Wilson) B.; m. Llewela Isherwood Jones, Jan. 23, 1942 (dec. 1968); m. Liliana Macellari, 1968. B.A. with honours, Manchester U., 1940, LLD; D. Litt., Birmingham U. Lectr., schoolmaster 1946-54; edn. officer in Malaya and Borneo, 1954-59; composer 1933—, play producer, 1947—, jazz pianist, 1941—; vis. fellow Princeton U., 1970-71; Disting. prof. CCNY, 1972-73. Author: The Right to an Answer, 1961, Devil of a State, 1962, The Wanting Seed, 1963, A Clockwork Orange, 1963, Honey for the Bears, 1964, Nothing Like the Sun, 1964, The Long Day Wanes, 1965, Language Made Plain, 1965, Re Joyce, 1965, The Doctor is Sick, 1965, Tremor of Intent, 1966, The Novel Now, 1967, Enderby, 1968, Urgent Copy, 1969, Shakespeare, 1970, MF, 1971, Cyrano de Bergerac-a version for the modern stage, 1971, Oedipus the King, 1972, Napoleon Symphony, 1974, The Clockwork Testament, 1974, Moses, 1976, A Long Trip to Teatime, 1976, Beard's Roman Women, 1976, ABBA ABBA, 1977, Nineteen Eighty-Five, 1978, World of Hemingway, 1978, Man of Nazareth, 1980, Earthly Powers, 1980, On Going to Bed, 1982, This Man and Music, 1982, The End of the World News, 1982, Enderby's Dark Lady, 1984, The Clockwork Testament, 1984, The Kingdom of the Wicked, 1985, The Pianoplayers, 1986, Little Wilson and Big God, 1987, Homage to Qwert Yuiop, 1986 (essays). Served with British Army, 1940-46. Address: 44 Rue Grimaldi, Monte Carlo Monaco also: land 2 Prazza Padella, Bracciano Italy also: 168 Trig Il-Klira, Lija Malta •

BURGESS, DAVID, lawyer, government official; b. Detroit, Nov. 30, 1948; s. Roger Edward and Claire Theresa (Sullivan) B.; m. Rebecca Culbertson Stuart. BS in Fgn. Service, Georgetown U., 1970, MS in Fgn. Service, 1978, JD, 1978. Research asst. Gerogetown U. Sch. Bus. Adminstrn., Washington, 1975, asst. to dean, 1975-76; research asso., prof. Acad. in the Public Service, Washington, 1976-79; asst. editor Securities Regulation Law Report; legal editor Internat. Trade Reporter, Bur. Nat. Affairs, 1978-79; atty. Cadwalader, Wickersham & Taft, Washington, 1979-81; mng. editor Bur. Nat. Affairs, Washington, 1981-82; dir. U.S. Peace Corps, Niamey, Niger, 1982-84, Rabat, Morocco, 1984-85; dir. policy planning, mgmt. Peace Corps, Washington, 1985-87; dir. Bur. Human rights and Humanitarian Affairs U.S. Dept. of State, Washington, 1987—; speaker workshops Minority Legis. Edn. Program, Ind. Assn. Cities and Towns, Georgetown U. Continuing Edn. Program, Communications Workers Am., Colo. State U., U. Wis. Alumni rep. Internat. Sch. Bangkok, 1972-74. Author: Financing Local Government, 1977, 2d edit., 1978, Preparation of the Local Budget, 2 vols., 1976, 2d edit., 1978, Local Government Accounting Fundamentals, 2d edit., 1977, Understanding Federal Assistance Programs, 2d edit., 1978, The POW/MIA Issue: Perspectives on the National League of Families, 1978; contbr. articles to publs. Served with USAF, 1970-74. Mem. ABA, D.C. Bar Assn., Wash. Internat. Trade Assn., Am. Soc. Internat. Law, Am. Acad. Arts and Scis., Acad. Polit. Sci., Washington Fgn. Law Soc., Amnesty Internat., U.S. Assn. Internat. Commn. Jurists, Internat. Platform Assn., Republican Nat. Lawyers Assn., World Affairs Council, Georgetown U. Alumni Assn. (bd. govs. 1975—, class rep. 1971—). Roman Catholic. Clubs: Nat. Press, Pres.'s.

BURGESS, ERIC, high technology company executive, writer; b. Stockport, Cheshire, Eng., May 30, 1920; came to U.S., 1956, naturalized 1962; s. William and Lily B.; m. Lilian Slater, Aug. 9, 1947; children—Janis Marie, Stephen Roy, Howard John. B.A., Coll. Commerce, Manchester, Eng., 1940; B.Sc., Coll. Tech., Manchester, 1950. Vice-pres. Mellonics Inc., Tucson and Northridge, La., 1959-62; sr. tech. staff mem. Informatics Inc., Sherman Oaks, Calif., 1962-65; dep. dir. Wolf Research & Develop Co., Encino, Calif., 1965-68; sci. correspondent The Christian Sci. Monitor, Boston, 1968-71; pvt. practice cons. space mission, high tech., satellite communications, Santa Rosa and Los Angeles, 1971-81; sr. v.p. corp. devel. Space Microwave Labs. Inc., Santa Rosa, Calif., 1981-86; pres. Am. Only, Inc., Sebastopol, Calif., 1983—. Author: Rocket Propulsion, 1952, Frontier to Space, 1954, Rockets & Spaceflight, 1956, Guided Weapons, 1957, Long-Range Ballistic Missiles, 1961, Assault on the Moon, 1966; Author with Bruce Murray: Flight to Mercury, 1977; Author: To The Red Planet, 1978; (with James Dunn) The Voyage of Mariner 10, 1978; (with R.O. Fimmel, James A Van Allen) First to Jupiter, Saturn and Beyond, 1981, By Jupiter, 1982, Celestial Basic, 1982; (with R.O. Fimmel and Lawrence Colin) Pioneer Venus, 1983; (with H.J. Burgess) Timex, Sinclair 1000: Astronomy, 1983; Venus, 1985; Uranus and Neptune, 1987; Into the Thermosphere, 1988; contbr. numerous articles to profl. jours. Fellow Royal Astron. Soc., Brit. Interplanetary Soc. (chmn. 1946-47), AIAA; mem. Nat. Assn. Sci. Writers. Address: 13361 Frati Ln Sebastopol CA 95472

BURGESS, HAROLD DEMPSTER, lawyer; b. Dundee, Ill., July 10, 1894; s. John W. and Sadie E. (Dempster) B.; m. Mary Ellen Evans, Sept. 16, 1964. Ed. pub. schs., Beatrice, Nebr.; student, U. Colo., 1913-14, U. Nebr., 1914-17; A.B. in absentia, U. Nebr., 1920; student, U. Chgo., 1920-21. Bar: Ill. 1921. Since practiced in Chgo; of counsel Keck, Mahin, Cate. Mem. Am., 7th Circuit, Ill., Chgo. bar assns., Legal Club Chgo., Law Club. Republican. Episcopalian. Clubs: Metropolitan (Chgo.); Edgewood Valley Country (LaGrange). Home: 300 E Claymoor Hinsdale IL 60521 Office: 233 S Wacker Dr 8300 Sears Tower Chicago IL 60606

BURGESS, HAYDEN FERN, lawyer; b. Honolulu, May 5, 1946; s. Ned E. and Nora (Lee) b.; m. Puanani Sonoda, Aug. 28, 1968. B in Polit. Sci., U. Hawaii, JD, 1976. Bar: Hawaii 1976, U.S. Tax Ct., U.S. Ct. Appeals (9th cir.). Sole practice Waianae, Hawaii, 1976—; v.p. World Counsel of Indigenous Peoples Before UN, 1984—, human rights adv.; exec. dir. Pacific and Asia Council of Indigenous Peoples; cons. on indigenous affairs, 1984—, indigenous expert to Internat. Labor Orgn. Conv. Trustee Office of Hawaiian Affairs, Honolulu, 1982-86; mem. Swedish Nat. Commn. on Museums. Mem. Law Assn. Asia and Western Pacific (steering com. on human rights). Office: 86-630 Puuhulu Rd Waianae HI 96792

BURGESS, MICHAEL, library science educator, publisher; b. Fukuoka, Kyushu, Japan, Feb. 11, 1948; came to U.S., 1949; s. Roy Walter and Betty Jane (Kapel) B.; m. Mary Alice Wickizer, Oct. 15, 1976; stepchildren—Richard Albert Rogers, Mary Louise Reynnells. AB with honors, Gonzaga U., 1969; MS In Library Sci., U. So. Calif., 1970. Periodicals librarian Calif. State U.-San Bernardino, 1970-81, chief cataloger, 1981—, prof., 1986—; editor Newcastle Pub. Co., North Hollywood, Calif., 1971—, publisher Borgo Press, San Bernardino, 1975—; adv. editor Arno Press, N.Y.C., 1975-78. Author 50 books, including: Cumulative Paperback Index, 1973, Things to Come, 1977, Science Fiction and Fantasy Literature, 1979, Tempest in a Teapot, 1984, Lords Temporal & Lords Spiritual, 1985, Futurevisions, 1985, Contemporary Science Fiction & Fantasy Authors III, 1988, Dictionary of Arms Control Disarmament and Military Security, 1989; editor 15 scholarly series, including Milford Series: Popular Writers of Today (40 vols.), Science Fiction (63 vols.), Stokvis Studies in Historical Chronology and Thought (10 vols.), editor 6 reprint series, 2 jours.; author over 100 articles. Named Title II fellow U. So. Calif., 1969-70. Mem. NEA, AAUP, Calif. Tchrs. Assn., Kent Hist. Soc., Sci. Fiction Writers Am., Calif. Faculty Assn. (mem. state-wide librarians task force 1986—, editor newsletter 1987—), Sci. Fiction Research Assn., Horror Writers of Am. Home: PO Box 2845 San Bernardino CA 92406 Office: Calif State U Library 5500 University Pkwy San Bernardino CA 92406

BURGESS, ROBERT BLUNDON, JR., manufacturing company executive; b. Washington, June 3, 1934; s. Robert Blundon and Kathryn (Roberts) B.; A.B. in Bus. and Indsl. Mgmt., Johns Hopkins, 1956; postgrad. McCoy Coll., 1959; m. Alice Lee Tomlin, Mar. 5, 1960; children—Sarah Watt, Robert Blundon III. Indsl. engr. Armco Steel Co., Balt., 1956-61; project mgr. Brunswick Corp., Marion, Va., 1962-63; internat. cons. Wofac Co., U.K., South Africa, Germany, Moorestown, N.J., 1963-71; group v.p. internat. Joy Mfg. Co., N.Y.C., 1971-75; sr. v.p. United Techs. Internat., Hartford, 1975-77, pres., 1977-80; pres. Support Systems, 1980-82; pres. Aviquipo, Lyndhurst, N.J., 1982-83; chmn., chief exec. officer W.S. Kirkpatrick Internat., 1983-84; pres. Eutectic Castolin, Flushing, N.Y., 1984-87, Societe Generale de Surveillance Govt. Programs, N.Y.C., 1987—. Commr. Blue Ridge dist. Boy Scouts Am., 1962-63; chmn. Smythe County Republican Com., 1963; mem. Zoning Commn., Farmington, Conn., 1980—; mem. adv. council Johns Hopkins U. Served to lt. inf. AUS, 1957-58; Korea. Mem. Work Factor Assocs. East Coast (dir. 1971-81), Nat. Fgn. Trade Council (dir. 1977-81), Phi Gamma Delta. Clubs: University, Wings, Links (N.Y.C.), Johns Hopkins Faculty (Balt.), Hartford, Hartford Gun, University (Hartford), Farmington (Conn.) Country, Farmington Field (pres. 1981), Aero of France, Sandanona Gun (Milbrook, N.Y.). Contbr. articles to German bus. publs. Home: 535 Smith Ridge Rd New Canaan CT 06840

BURGMAN, DIERDRE ANN, lawyer; b. Logansport, Ind., Mar. 25, 1948; d. Ferdinand William Jr. and Doreen Yvonne (Walsh) B. BA, Valparaiso U., 1970, JD, 1979; LLM, Yale U., 1985. Bar: Ind. 1979, D.C., 1988, U.S. Dist. Ct. (so. dist.) Ind. 1979, N.Y. 1982, U.S. Dist. Ct. (so. dist.) N.Y. 1982, U.S. Ct. Appeals (7th cir.) 1982, U.S. Ct. Appeals (D.C. cir.) 1984, U.S. Ct. Appeals (2d cir.) 1984, U.S. Supreme Ct. 1985, D.C. 1988. Law clk. to chief judge Ind. Ct. Appeals, Indpls., 1979-80; prof. law Valparaiso (Ind.) U., 1980-81; assoc. Dewey, Ballantine, Bushby, Palmer & Wood, N.Y.C., 1981-84, Cahill Gordon & Reindel, N.Y.C., 1985—. Note editor Valparaiso U. law rev., 1978-79; contbr. articles to law jours. Mem. bd. visitors Valparaiso U. Sch. Law, 1986—. Ind. Bar Found. scholar, 1978. Mem. ABA (trial evidence com., profl. liability com.), Assn. Bar N.Y.C., N.Y. County Lawyers Assn. (asst. chmn. com. Supreme Ct. 1987—, Outstanding Service award 1988). Home: 164 E 61st St New York NY 10021 Office: Cahill Gordon & Reindel 80 Pine St Suite 1700 New York NY 10005

BURGOS MARIN, JUAN LUIS, manufacturing company executive; b. Portugalete, Spain, July 3, 1932; s. Luis Burgos and Paula Marin; m. Angelica O. Tamendi, Aug. 4, 1959; children: Angelica, Carmen, Esmeralda, Juan Luis, Ignacio, Maria Jose. Degree in Law, U. Valladolid, 1955; degree in Econs., U. Deusto, Bilboa, Spain, 1955. Sec. gen. Electra De Salamanca (Spain) S.A., 1956-59; gen. acct. Altos Hornos De Vizcaya S.A., Baracaldo, Spain, 1959-68, controller, 1968-78, treas., 1978-79, chmn., chief exec. officer, 1979—; chmn. Union Empresas Siderurgicas, Madrid, vice-chmn. Assn. Progreso Direccion, Bilboa. Contbr. articles to newspapers and mags. Roman Catholic. Office: Altos Hornos De Vizcaya SA, Carmen 2, Baracaldo Spain

BURGOYNE, JOHN ALBERT, lawyer, management consultant; b. Malden, Mass., May 4, 1914; s. Albert M. and Anna M. (Bagley) B.; m. Juliet M. Moran, Oct. 12, 1940; children—J. Albert, Robert F. A.B., Boston Coll., 1936; J.D., Georgetown U., 1946; postgrad. advanced mgmt. program Harvard U. Grad. Sch. Bus. Adminstrn., 1965. Bar: Mass. 1946, D.C. 1946, U.S. Dist. Ct. Mass. 1950, U.S. Supreme Ct. 1961. Vice pres. Liberty Mut. Ins. Cos., 1936-68, State Farm Ins. Cos., 1968-72, Met. Life Ins. Co., 1972-79; chmn., chief exec. officer Met. Property and Liability Ins. Co., 1972-79; of counsel Coombs and Ryan, Boston, 1980—; instr. law Boston Coll. Law Sch., 1958-68. Served to lt. USNR, 1943-46. Mem. ABA. Clubs: Rockport Golf, Sandy Bay Yacht. Home: 15 Prospect St Rockport MA 01966

BURGUN, J. ARMAND, architect; b. Rochester, Pa., Nov. 19, 1925; s. Paul John and Wilda (Whitehill) B.; m. Muriel Ann DePowel, Dec. 30, 1944; children: Douglas Armand, Bruce Eric. B.Arch., Columbia U., 1950. Designer Ferrenz & Taylor, architects, N.Y.C., 1950-55; asst. dir. N.Y. State Joint Hosp. Planning Commn., Albany, 1955-60; assoc. Rogers Burgun Shahine & Deschler, architects, N.Y.C., 1960-63, ptnr., 1963—; spl. lectr. Grad. Sch. Med. Adminstrn. N.Y. Med. Coll. Author: Handbook-Hospital Construction, 1958, Institutional Fires, 1977; contbr. articles to profl. jours. Archtl. cons. Hosp. Council Greater N.Y., 1957—; archtl. cons. USPHS, VA; mem. Pres.'s Com. Mental Retardation, N.Y. State Bldg. Code Council; trustee N.Y. Sch. for Deaf. Served to lt. comdr. USCG, 1942-44. Decorated Purple Heart. Fellow AIA; mem. N.Y. Soc. Architects, N.Y. State Assn. Architects, Am. Hosp. Assn., Nat. Fire Protection Assn. (dir., chmn. bd.); mem Internat. Hosp. Fedn.; mem. Am. Assn. Hosp. Planning (pres.), N.Y. Bldg. Congress, Res. Officers Assn. Clubs: Winged Foot Country, Union League. Home: 235 Manville Rd Pleasantville NY 10570 Office: Rogers Burgun Shahine & Deschler Inc 215 Park Ave S New York NY 10003

BURHOE, RALPH WENDELL, educator of religion and science; b. Somerville, Mass., June 21, 1911; s. Winslow Page and Mary Trenaman (Stumbles) B.; m. Frances Bickford, Aug. 4, 1931 (dec. Aug. 1967); children: Winslow Newton, Laura Jean Burhoe Maier, Thomas Allen, Diana May Burhoe Chase; m. Calla Crawford Butler, Apr. 6, 1969. Student, Harvard, 1928-32, Andover Newton Theol. Sch., 1934-36; Sc.D., Meadville Lombard Theol. Sch., Chgo., 1975; L.H.D., Rollins Coll., 1979. Observer, research asst., librarian, asst. to dir. Blue Hill Meteorol. Harvard, 1936-47; asst. sec. Am. Meteorol. Soc., Milton, Mass., 1936-47; treas. Am. Meteorol. Soc., 1942-47; exec. officer Am. Acad. Arts and Sciences, Boston, 1947-64; research prof. theology and scis. Meadville Theol. Sch., Chgo., 1964-74; emeritus Meadville Theol. Sch., 1974—; founder, dir. Ctr. Advanced Study in Religion and Sci., 1964—, sec., sr. fellow, 1972—; co-founder (1954), hon. pres. Inst. Religion in an Age of Sci.; co-founder (1988), assoc. Chgo. Ctr. for Relgion and Sci. Author-editor: (with Hudson Hoagland) Evolution and Man's Progress, 1962; Author, editor: Science and Human Values in the Twenty-first Century, 1971, Toward a Scientific Theology, 1981; Editor: Zygon, Jour. Religion and Sci, 1965-79, founding editor, 1979—; Contbr. to profl. jours. and books. 1st Am. recipient Templeton prize for progress in religion, London, 1980. Fellow World Acad. Art and Sci., Am. Acad. Arts and Scis., AAAS; mem. Am. Acad. Religion, Am. Theol. Assn., Soc. Sci. Study Religion (treas. 1965-70, 1st recipient Disting. Career Achievement award 1984), Inst. Theol. Encounter with Sci. and Tech. Office: 1524 E 59th St Chicago IL 60637

BURILLO, PEDRO JESUS, mathematics professor; b. Zaragoza, Aragon, Spain, Dec. 20, 1945; s. Pedro Burillo Macipe and Gloria Lopez Garcia; m. Maria Isabel Sanchez, March 25, 1972; children: Miriam, Tania, Elisabet. PhD, U. Zaragoza, Spain, 1974; postgrad, U. Zaragoza, 1968. Chmn. math. dept. U. Cordoba, Spain, 1974-78, U. Politecnica Valencia, Spain, 1978-83; vice chancellor U. Alcala de Henares, 1984-86, chmn. math. dept., 1987—. Contbr. numerous articles to prof. jours. Mem. Am. Math. Soc., French Math. Soc., Internat. Fuzzy Sets and Systems Assn. Roman Catholic. Home: Cruz de Guadalajara 1 3D, Alcala de Henares, 28805 Madrid Spain Office: U Alcala de Henares, Math Dept, Alcala Henares, 28805 Madrid Spain

BURK, SYLVIA JOAN, petroleum landman, free-lance writer; b. Dallas, Oct. 16, 1928; d. Guy Thomas and Sylvia (Herrin) Ricketts; m. R. B. Murray, Jr., Sept. 7, 1951 (div. Jan. 1961); children—Jeffery Randolph, Brian BeVaughn; m. Bryan Burk, Apr. 26, 1973. B.A., So. Meth. U., Dallas, 1950, M.L.A., 1974; postgrad. U. So. Calif., 1973-74. Landman, E. B. Germany & Sons, Dallas, 1970-73; asst. mgr. real estate Atlantic Richfield Co., Los Angeles, 1973-74; landman GoldKing Prodn. Co., Houston, 1974-76; oil and gas cons./landman, co-owner Burk Properties, Burk Ednl. Properties, Houston, 1976—. Author: Petroleum Lands and Leasing, 1983 ; contbr. articles to jours. and photographs. Mem. The Author's Guild, Inc., Foremost Women 20th Century, Am. Assn. Petroleum Landmen (dir. 1980-82, 2d v.p. 1982-83), Houston Assn. Petroleum Landmen (dir. 1978-79), The Authors Guild, Inc., Nat. Writer's Club, Women's Inst. Houston. Republican. Presbyterian. Clubs: Dallas Woman's, Sugar Creek Country. Office: Burk Ednl Properties 1605 Parkway Blvd Title USA Bldg Sugar Land TX 77478

BURKAN, HAMED-SHARIF, diplomat, political economist; b. Benghazi, Cyrenaica, Libya, Dec. 22, 1944; s. Mahmoud Sharif and Salma (Mutturdi) B.; m. Huguette E. Consolin; Dec. 30, 1982. BS, Calif. State U., Fresno, 1971, MA, 1974; PhD, U. San Diego, 1977; postgrad., U. Calif., Berkeley, 1978-79. Dir. personnel Esso Atandard Libya, Inc. subs. Exxon, Marsa Brega, 1965-69; research fellow dept. econs. U. Calif., Berkeley, 1978-79; prof. U.S. Internat. U., San Diego, 1979-83; U.N. official U.N. Indsl. Devel., Vienna, Austria, 1983—; energy cons. Orgn. Petroleum Exporting Countries, Viennaand Kuwait, 1984-85; acad. dir. Saudi Arabian Ednl. Mission to U.S., Houston, 1980-81; sports attaché for Libya, Los Angeles summer Olympics, 1980. Author: OPEC and the World Econ. Order, 1980, Mgmt. and Coordination of World Economy, 1987, Politics of War and Peace, 1988. Esso Standard Libya, Inc. scholar, 1969. Mem. Am. Econ. Assn., Third World Econs. Assn., Internat. Econs. Assn. Home: Medlergasse 5, 1190 Vienna Austria Office: UN Indsl Devel, PO Box 400, Vienna Austria

BURKARD, PETER HUBERT, lawyer; b. Ottobeuren, Germany, Mar. 26, 1940; s. Peter and Ruth (Klein) B.; m. Barbara A. Sadowski, June 24, 1966; children—Melissa, Elizabeth, Amy. A.B., Harvard U., 1962; J.D., U. Mich., 1965; Dr. Jur., U. Heidelberg (W.Ger.), 1969. Bar: Mich. 1968, N.Y. 1971, Conn. 1979. Atty., Dow Chem. Co., Midland, Mich., 1968-70, Gen. Foods Corp., White Plains, N.Y., 1970-72; counsel Xerox Corp., Stamford, Conn., 1972-80, Rank Xerox Ltd., London, 1975; assoc. gen. counsel Burndy Corp., Norwalk, Conn., 1981; counsel European and Japanese region Eastman Kodak Co., Rochester, N.Y., 1982—. Club: Harvard of N.Y.C. Home: 280 Allens Creek Rd Rochester NY 14618 Office: Eastman Kodak Co 343 State St Rochester NY 14650

BURKE, CHARLES RICHARD, accountant; b. Chgo., June 21, 1949; s. Victor Lark and Virginia Cleta (O'Neil) B.; m. Judith Lynn Wolsic, June 27, 1970; children: Christopher, David, Amanda, Gregory, Laura. BS in Bus. Adminstrn., Marquette U., 1971. CPA, Ill. Staff supr. Robert W. Baird & Co., Milw., 1971-72; staff acct. Miedema, Lemna CPA's, Kankakee, Ill., 1972-77; ptnr. Lemna Burke & Downing, Kankakee, 1977-86; pvt. practice acctg. Kankakee, 1986—. Mem. Ill. CPA Soc., Am. Inst. CPA's, Nat. Assn. Accts. (pres. Kankakee Valley chpt. 1985-86, 87-88, Mem. Achievement award 1986). Home: 61 Briarcliff Ln Bourbonnais IL 60914 Office: Charles R Burke CPA Suite 515 One Dearborn Sq Kankakee IL 60901

BURKE, DANIEL MARTIN, lawyer; b. Casper, Wyo., Sept. 9, 1946; s. Michael Joseph and Mary Josephine (Sirridge) B.; B.A., U. Wyo., 1968, J.D., 1970; m. Ellen Arden, July 3, 1970; children—Daniel Martin III, Kathleen Ellen, Brendan Arden, Anne Mary, Susan Theresa. Bar: Wyo. 1970. Law clk. to judge U.S. 10th Cir. Ct. Appeals (10th cir.), Cheyenne, Wyo., 1970; spl. asst. atty. gen. State of Wyo., Cheyenne, 1970-71; instr. Casper Coll., 1971-75; county and pros. atty. Natrona County, Casper, 1975-79; mem. Burke, Horn & Lewis, Casper, 1975-79; pres. Burke & Horn, P.C., Casper, 1979-82, Burke & Brown, P.C., Casper, 1983-86; pres. Daniel M. Burke, 1986— ; chmn. bd., pres. Rocky Mountain Communications Network, Inc., 1982—; v.p., dir. Evco, Inc., 1982—; dir. Guaranty Fed. Bank, First Nat. Bank Evanston (Wyo.), Wyo. Fin. Services, Inc.; gen. partner Bantry Bay Co.; pres. The Chrysostom Corp.; sec. Shamrock Ranch Co., Casper, 1969—; asst. city atty. City of Casper, 1971-74. Mem. council St. Anthony Parish; mem. St. Anthony Parochial Sch. Bd.; bd. arbitrators Am. Arbitration Assn., Mem. ABA, Wyo. State Bar (sec. 1973-75), Natrona County bar assns., Am. Judicature Soc., Nat. Assn. Dist. Attys. (dir. 1977-78), Wyo. Assn. County Attys. (pres. 1977-78), Casper C. of C. Republican. Roman Catholic. Clubs: Casper Country, KC. Home: 1008 S Wolcott St Casper WY 82601 Office: 100 W "B" St Suite200 Casper WY 82601

BURKE, EDWARD NEWELL, radiologist; b. Wakefield, Apr. 28, 1916; s. Charles Edward and Laura Cecilia (Doherty) B.; B.S., Holy Cross Coll., 1938; M.D., C.M., McGill U., 1942; postgrad. Brit. Postgrad. Med. Sch., 1946, Johns Hopkins Sch. Public Health, 1943; m. Mary A. Bryon, Nov. 26, 1949; children—Laureen, Martha, Newell, Laurence. Resident in pathology Mallory Inst., Boston City Hosp., 1942-43; intern Salem (Mass.) Hosp., 1946-47, resident in radiology, 1947-50; resident in supervoltage Therapy

Lahey Clinic and MIT, 1949; assoc. radiologist Mass. Meml. Hosp., Boston, 1951-56; lectr. radiologic tech. Northeastern U., 1953-65; radiologist Lawrence Meml. Hosp., also Charles Choate Hosp., Medford, Mass., 1956—; individual practice medicine specializing in radiology Medford, 1956—; radiologist St. Joseph's Hosp., Lowell, Mass., 1956-64, Hooper Infirmary, Tufts Coll., Medford, 1971-80; chmn., chief depts. radiology Lawrence Meml. Hosp., 1961-85, assoc. chief radiology, 1985—; chief dept. Charles Choate Meml. Hosp., 1963-82; assoc. prof. radiology Boston U., 1951-56; asst. clin. prof. radiology Tufts U., 1971-81, assoc. clin. prof., 1981—; pres. Charles Choate Hosp. med. staff, 1974-76, incorporator, trustee, 1974-81; incorporator Lawrence Meml. Hosp., 1972—, pres. med. staff, 1980-82; lectr., dir. Carroll Ctr. for the Blind. Served to maj. M.C., U.S. Army, 1943-46. Diplomate Am. Coll. Radiology. Radiology wing dedicated in his honor Choate Hosp., 1982. Decorated Sovereign Mil. Order Malta. Fellow Am. Coll. Radiology; mem. AMA, Am. Roentgen Ray Soc., New Eng. Roentgen Ray Soc., Radiol. Soc. N.Am., N.Y. Acad. Scis., Mass. Radiol. Soc., Soc. Nuclear Medicine, Am. Inst. Ultrasound Medicine, New Eng. Ultrasound Soc., Mass. Med. Soc. Roman Catholic. Clubs: Clover Boston, Winchester Country. Contbr. articles to med. publs. Home: 40 Pine Ridge Rd West Medford MA 02155 Office: 170 Governors Ave Medford MA 02155

BURKE, JAMES EDWARD, manufacturing company executive; b. Rutland, Vt., Feb. 28, 1925; s. James Francis and Mary (Barnett) B.; B.S. in Econs., Holy Cross Coll., 1947; M.B.A., Harvard U., 1949; m. Alice Eubank, Apr. 27, 1957 (dec.); children—Mary Clotilde, James Charles; m. 2d, Diane W. Burke, Nov. 7, 1981. Sales rep., then asst. brand mgr., brand mgr. Procter & Gamble, 1949-52; product dir. Johnson & Johnson, 1953-54, dir. new products, 1954-57, dir. advt. and merchandising, 1957-58, v.p. advt. and merchandising, 1958-62, gen. mgr. Baby Products Co. div., 1962-64, exec. v.p. mktg., 1964-65, gen. mgr. Johnson & Johnson Products Co. div., 1965-66, pres. 1966-70, chmn. bd., 1970-71, corp. dir., mem. exec. com., 1973-76, dir., mem. exec. com. parent co., 1965—, vice-chmn. exec. com., from 1971, chief exec. officer, chmn. bd. parent co., 1976—; dir. IBM, Prudential Ins. Co. Mem. vis. com. bd. overseers Harvard Coll. Med. Sch. and Sch. Dental Medicine; bd. dirs. United Negro Coll. Fund; vice-chmn. Corp. Fund Kennedy Ctr.;mem. policy and planning commn. Bus. Roundtable; mem. Pres.'s Commn. Exec. Exchange, Pres.'s Pvt. Sector Survey on Cost Control in Fed. Govt.; mem. Trilateral and Nat. Commns. on Pub. Service; vice chmn. bus. council bd. dirs. Council on Fgn. Relations. Served as ensign USN, World War II; PTO. Mem. Conf. Bd. (vice chmn.). Office: Johnson & Johnson One Johnson & Johnson Plaza New Brunswick NJ 08933 *

BURKE, JOHN FREDERICK, writer; b. Rye, Sussex, Eng., Mar. 8, 1922; s. Frederick Goode and Lilian Gertrude (Sands) B.; m. Joan Morris, Sept. 13, 1941 (div. May 1963); children: Bronwen, Jennifer, Sara, Jane, Joanna; m. Jean Williams, June 29, 1963; children: David Martin, Owen Edmund. Grad. high sch., Liverpool, Eng. Editorial mgr. Paul Hamlyn Books for Pleasure, London, 1957-59; publicity media exec. Shell Internat. Petroleum, London, 1959-63; European story editor 20th Century Fox Prodns., London, 1963-66. Author: Swift Summer, 1949, Illustrated History of England, 1974, Musical Landscapes, 1983, Roman England, 1983, Illustrated Dictionary of Music, 1988. Served with RAF and REME, 1940-45. Recipient Atlantic award in Lit. Rockefeller Found., 1948. Mem. Soc. Authors. Club: Danish. Home: 8 North Parade, Southwold IP18 6LP, England

BURKE, (THOMAS) KERRY, government official; b. Christchurch, New Zealand, Mar. 24, 1942; m. Helen Paske, Oct. 1984; 1 child, Thomas; children from previous marriage: Dillon, Connell. BA in History, U. Canterbury, 1960-63; diploma of teaching, Christchurch Teacher's Coll., 1964. Tchr. Rangiora High Sch., New Zealand, 1967-72, Greymouth High Sch., New Zealand, 1976-78; M.P. Rangiora, New Zealand, 1972-75, West Coast, New Zealand, from 1978; shadow minister Labour and State Services, New Zealand, 1979-80, employment and technology and state services, New Zealand, 1981, employment, technology, immigration, regional devel. and tourism, New Zealand, 1982; head regional devel. and the South 'island, New Zealand, 1983; now speaker Ho. of Reps., New Zealand; mem. labour and edn. Parliamentary select coms., labour, employment, primary prodn., overseas trade, regional devel., small towns, primary resources and mktg. caucus coms. Chmn. Rangiora branch PPTA, 1969-71; mem. Lincoln Coll. Council, 1973-78; factory del. Labourers Union, Auckland, New Zealand, 1966. Mem. Labour Party. *

BURKE, LAURENCE DECLAN, chemistry educator; b. Cork, Ireland, July 5, 1939; s. Lawrence and Elizabeth (O'Connell) B.; m. Susan Elizabeth Allen, June 11, 1966; children: Vivienne, John, Alan. BSc, Univ. Coll., Cork, Ireland, 1959, MSc, 1961; PhD, Queen's U., Belfast, Ireland, 1964. Asst. lectr. chemistry Univ. Coll., Cork, 1965-80, lectr., 1980-83, assoc. prof., 1983—. Contbr. numerous articles to profl. jours. Alexander von Humboldt Stiftung fellow, Fed. Republic Germany, 1966-67. Mem. Internat. Soc. Electrochemistry. Roman Catholic. Home: Templehill, Carrigrohane, Cork Ireland Office: Univ Coll Dept Chemistry, Cork Ireland

BURKE, PAUL STANLEY, JR., insurance company executive; b. St. Paul, Aug. 5, 1926; s. Paul Stanley and Loretta Josephine (Bertrang) B.; B.B.A., U. Minn., 1956; m. Irene Marie Wagner, Apr. 22, 1950; children—John, Steven, Nancy, Lawrence, Linda, James, Thomas. Regional mgr. Minn. Mutual Life Ins. Co., Los Angeles, 1950-61; pres. Paul Burke & Assos., Inc., ins. consultants and adminstrs., Mpls., 1961-73, Trust Life Ins. Co. Am., Scottsdale, Ariz., 1968-73, Purchase & Discount Buying Service Corp., 1977-80, Am. Reliance Corp., 1967-85, Fingertip Facts, 1987-88; chmn. bd. Larson & Burke Inc., 1980—, N. Am. Outdoor Group Inc., 1987—, Wildlife Forever, 1988—; dir. Lindbom & Assos., Inc., St. Paul. Pres., Boys Clubs of Mpls., 1974-76. Served with USAAF, 1944-47. Mem. Pilots Internat. Assn. (pres. 1966-73). Republican. Roman Catholic. Clubs: Interlachen Country, N. Am. Hunting (chmn. bd. dirs. 1978—), N. Am. Fishing (chmn. bd. dirs. 1988—). Home: 27 Circle W Edina MN 55436

BURKE, RAPHAEL (RAY), Irish government official; b. Dublin, Ireland, Sept. 30, 1943; s. Patrick and Catherine (Carty) B.; m. Anne Fassfender, Nov. 1972; 2 daughters. Mem. Dail (House of Reps.), Dublin, 1973; minister state at dept. industry, commerce, tourism Ireland, Dublin, 1978-80, minister environment, 1980-81; leader of the house Fianna Field, 1982; minister energy, communications and forestry Ireland, 1987—; mem. Dublin County Council, 1967, chmn. 1985-87. Address: Ministry Energy and Communications, Dublin Ireland *

BURKE, RICHARD SYLVESTER, administrator, former Irish parliamentarian; b. N.Y.C., Mar. 29, 1932; s. David and Elizabeth (Kelly) B.; m. Mary Burke, Apr. 4, 1961; children: Mary, David, Audrey, Richard, Avila. MA, U. Coll., Dublin, Ireland, 1960; barrister at law, King's Inns, 1973. Chief whip Fine Gael Party, Ireland, 1969-72; spokesman on posts, telegraphs Govt. of Ireland, 1972-73, minister for edn., 1973-76; v.p. Commn. of European Communities, Brussels, 1977-85; pres. Canon Found. in Europe, Brussels, 1988—; mem. Dublin County Council, 1967-73, chmn., 1972-73. Fellow Ctr. for Internat. Affairs, Harvard U., 1981. Clubs: Elm Park Golf, Portmarnock Golf, Royal Golf of Belgium. Office: Ave Louise 300 Bte 6, 1050 Brussels Belgium

BURKE, ROBERT HARRY, surgeon, educator; b. Cambridge, Mass., Dec. 22, 1945; s. Harry Clearfield and Joan Rosalyn (Spire) B.; m. Margaret Cauldwell Fisher, May 4, 1968; children: Christopher David, Catherine Cauldwell. Student, U. Mich. Coll. Pharmacy, 1964-67; DDS, U. Mich., 1971, MS, 1973; MD, Mich. State U., 1980. Diplomate Am. Bd. Oral and Maxillofacial Surgery. Practice medicine and dentistry specializing in oral and maxillofacial surgery Ann Arbor, Mich., 1976—; house officer oral and maxillofacial surgery U. Mich. Sch. Dentistry, U. Mich. Hosp., Ann Arbor, 1973-76; clin. asst. prof. dept. oral surgery U. Detroit Sch. Dentistry, 1976-77; adj. asst. research scientist Ctr. Human Growth and Devel. U. Mich., 1976-77, adj. research investigator, 1982-85; clin. asst. prof. Mich. State U., East Lansing, 1978-80, 1987—; house officer surg. emphasis St. Joseph Mercy Hosp., Ann Arbor, 1980-81; adj. research investigator dept. anatomy U. Mich. Med. Sch., 1982-85; clin. asst. prof. oral and maxillofacial surgery U. Mich., 1984-86; lectr. U. Detroit Sch. Dentistry, 1986, assoc. clin. prof. oral and maxillofacial surgery, 1987—; asst. clin. prof. Coll. Human Medicine Mich. State U., 1987—; cons., lectr. dept. occlusion U. Mich. Sch. Dentistry, 1986; head sect. dentistry and oral surgery dept. gen. surgery St. Joseph Mercy Hosp., 1982-87, mem. exec. com. dept. gen. surgery, 1984-87; chmn. com. emergency care rev. Beyer Meml. Hosp., Ypsilanti, Mich., 1986, also courtesy staff, 1987; active staff St. Joseph Meml. Hosp.; courtesy staff Saline (Mich.) Community Hosp., 1978-88; Chelsea (Mich.) Med. Ctr., 1978—, McPherson Community Hosp., Howell, Mich., 1984-87. Mem. editorial bd. Topics in Pain Mgmt., 1985—. Campaign chmn. med. and dental sects. United Way Washtenaw County, Ann Arbor, 1982, dental sect. 1983; profl. adv. com. March of Dimes Genesee County Valley Chpt., Flint, 1979; pres. Huron Pkwy. Plaza Condominium, 1984—. Fellow Internat. Coll. Surgeons (U.S. Sect.), Am. Assn. Oral and Maxillofacial Surgeons, Mich. Soc. Oral and Maxillofacial Surgeons, Am. Coll. Oral and Maxillofacial Surgeons (v.p. 1987-88, chmn. orthognathic standardization com., chmn. membership com.); mem. ADA, AMA, Chalmers Lyons Acad. Oral Surgery, European Soc. Oral and Maxillofacial Surgeons (assoc.), Southeastern Mich. Surg. Soc., Great Lakes Soc. Oral and Maxillofacial Surgeons, Mich. Dental Assn. (cons., legis. com., vice chmn. com. health planning, hosp. and instl. services 1987-88, cons. and mem. com. cancer control, hosp. and instl. dental services 1984-86), Washtenaw County Med. Soc. (exec. com., del. to Mich. Med. Soc., alternate del. to Mich. State Soc., sec. 1987, 88), Mich. Med. Soc., Washtenaw County Dental Soc. (chmn. publications com., chmn. hosp. com., delta dental rep. 1987, liaison to Mich. dental polit. action com. 1987), Inst. Study Profl. Risk (bd. dirs. 1985—), Omicron Kappa Upsilon. Republican. Congregationalist. Clubs: Barton Hills Country, Ann Arbor Racquet, Victor's, Pres.'. Home: 3575 Stanton Ct Ann Arbor MI 48105 Office: 2260 Huron Pkwy Ann Arbor MI 48104

BURKE, THOMAS GEORGE, psychology educator; b. Bklyn., Mar. 16, 1947; s. George Joseph and Dorothy (Hohl) B.; B.A. in Psychology (State Regents scholar), St. John's U., 1968, M.A. in Clin. Psychology, 1971; postgrad. New Sch. Social Research, 1973—; m. Alice C. Heron, Aug. 29, 1976; children—George Albert, Jonathan Patrick. Tchr., student drug counselor St. John's Prep. High Sch., Bklyn., 1969-72; psychologist New High Sch., Bklyn., 1972-73; adj. instr. dept. psychology St. John's U., Jamaica, N.Y., 1973-78, S.I. Community Coll. (N.Y.), 1973-78; dir. Human Resources Devel. Center, assoc. prof. psychology N.Y. Inst. Tech., Old Westbury, 1974—, v.p., 1983-86, sr. v.p., 1987—; psychotherapist Personal Awareness Center, 1977-78. Vol. psychologist Creedmoor State Mental Hosp., Queen's Village, N.Y., 1972-76. Mem. Am. (asso.) N.Y. State (asso.) psychol. assns., N.Y. State Doctoral Assn. (v.p.), Delta Sigma Phi. Roman Catholic. Author: Contemporary Issues in Abnormal Psychology and Mental Illness, 1976; contbr. article to profl. jour. Composer (with Charles Frazer): Jack in the Box, 1969. Home: 71-32 Manse St Forest Hills NY 11375 Office: NY Inst Tech Tower House Old Westbury Campus Old Westbury NY 11568

BURKE, TIMOTHY JOHN, lawyer; b. Syracuse, N.Y., June 5, 1946; s. Francis Joseph and Alice Marie Burke; 1 child, Ryan Alexander; m. 2d, Denise Kay Blied, Mar. 18, 1978; 1 child, Aimee Noel. B.A. with distinction, Ariz. State U., 1967, J.D. cum laude, 1970. Bar: Ariz. 1970, U.S. Dist. Ct. Ariz. 1970, U.S. Ct. Appeals (9th cir.) 1974. Trial atty. Antitrust div. U.S. Dept. Justice, Washington, 1970-72, asst. to dir. ops., 1972-74; assoc. Fennemore Craig, Phoenix, 1974—, dir., 1978—; part-time instr. in legal writing Ariz. State U., 1974-75. Mem. panel rev. bd. Phoenix United Way, 1975-76; bd. dirs. Florence Crittenton Services, Phoenix, 1980—, pres 1985-87. Recipient Spl. Commendation award U.S. Dept. Justice, 1973. Mem. ABA (antitrust and litigation sects.), State Bar Ariz. (council antitrust sect., chmn. 1985-88), Fed. Bar Assn., Maricopa County Bar Assn. Club: Arizona (Phoenix). Office: 2 N Central Ave Suite 2200 Phoenix AZ 85004-2390

BURKE, WILLIAM TEMPLE, JR., lawyer; b. San Antonio, Oct. 30, 1935; s. William Temple and Adelaide H. (Raba) B.; m. Mary Sue Johnson, June 8, 1957; children: William Patrick, Michael Edmond, Karen Elizabeth. B.B.A., St. Mary's U., San Antonio, J.D., 1961. Bar: Tex. Practice law Dallas; dir. Phil Ross Realtors, Inc., MB Valuation Systems, Inc. Pres., founder Dallas Assn. KC, 1968-69; v.p., co-founder Dallas KC Credit Union, 1966-69; grand knight, trustee Dallas Council 799 KC, 1964-69; dist. exemplar 4th degree KC, 1968—; pres., dir. Dallas County Small Bus. Devel. Center, 1965-66; v.p. Dallas County Hist. Survey Com., 1966; pres. Dallas Mil. Govt. Assn., 1962-63; pres. men's club St. Patrick's Parish Roman Catholic Ch., 1963, prin. jr. high sch. Christian devel. program, 1970, chmn. scout troop com., 1976-78, chmn. fin. com., 1976-77, 84-86, mem. bldg. com., 1978-87, chmn. bd. consultors, 1978-81; bd. dirs. Dallas County War on Poverty, 1965-66. Served to 1st lt. AUS, 1958-60; capt. Res. ret. Recipient Man of Yr. award Dallas Assn. KC, 1969-70. Mem. ABA, Tex. Bar Assn., Dallas Bar Assn. (chmn. bankruptcy and comml. law sect. 1977-78, 1986-87, lectr. 1985—), Phi Delta Phi (magister 1960-61), Tau Delta Sigma (pres. 1956). Clubs: Seroco-Empire Toastmasters (past pres.), Dallas Optimist (past v.p., President's award 1968), 2001, Park Cities, Internat. Order Alhambra (dist. exemplar 1980—). Home: 9751 Larchcrest St Dallas TX 75238 Office: Suite 1201 Sherry Lane National Bank Bldg Dallas TX 75225

BURKEE, IRVIN, artist; b. Kenosha, Wis., Feb. 6, 1918; s. Omar Lars and Emily (Quardokas) B.; diploma Sch. of Art Inst. Chgo., 1945; m. Bonnie May Ness, Apr. 12, 1945; children—Brynn, Jill, Peter (dec.), Ian. Owner, silversmith, goldsmith Burkee Jewelry, Blackhawk, Colo., 1950-57; painter, sculptor, Aspen, Colo., 1957-78, Cottonwood, Ariz., Pietrasanta, Italy, 1978—; instr. art U. Colo., 1946, 50-53, Stephens Coll., Columbia, Mo., 1947-49. John Quincy Adams travel fellow, Mex., 1945. Executed copper mural of human history of Colo. for First Nat. Bank, Englewood, Colo., 1970, copper mural of wild birds of Kans. for Ranchmart State Bank, Overland Park, Kans., 1974; exhibited Art Inst. Chgo., Smithsonian Instn. (award 1957), Milw. Art Inst., Krannert Mus., William Rockhill Nelson Gallery, St. Louis Art Mus., Denver Art Mus.; represented in permanent collections several southwestern galleries, also pvt. collections throughout U.S.; work illustrated in books Design and Creation of Jewelry, Design through Discovery, Walls. Address: Box 2071 Rio Verde Acres Cottonwood AZ 86326

BURKET, GAIL BROOK, author; b. Stronghurst, Ill., Nov. 1, 1905; d. John Cecil and Maud (Simonson) Brook; A.B., U. Ill., 1926; M.A. in English Lit., Northwestern U., 1929; m. Walter Cleveland Burket, June 22, 1929; children—Elaine (Mrs. William L. Harwood), Anne, Margaret (Mrs. James Boyce). Pres. woman's aux. Internat. Coll. Surgeons, 1950-54, now bd. dirs. Mus.; nat. vice chmn. Am. Heritage of DAR, 1971-74; pres. Northwestern U. Guild, 1976-78; sec. Evanston women's bd. Northwestern U. Settlement, 1979-81, pres., 1984-86; mem. cen. com., 1986—. Recipient Robert Ferguson Meml. award Friends of Lit., 1973. Mem. Nat. League Am. Pen Women (Ill. state pres. 1952-54, nat. v.p. 1958-60), Soc. Midland Authors, Poetry Soc. Am., Women in Communications, AAUW (pres. N. Shore br. 1961-63), Ill. Opera Guild (bd. dirs. 1982—, 1st v.p. 1986—), Daus. Am. Colonists (state v.p. 1973-76), Colonial Dames Am. (chpt. regent 1974-80), Phi Beta Kappa, Delta Zeta. Author: Courage Beloved, 1949; Manners Please, 1949; Blueprint for Peace, 1951; Let's Be Popular, 1951; You Can Write a Poem, 1954; Far Meadows, 1955; This is My Country, 1960; From the Prairies, 1968. Contbr. articles, poems to lit. publs. Address: 1020 Lake Shore Dr Evanston IL 60202

BURKET, RICHARD EDWARD, agriprocessing executive; b. Sandusky, Ohio, Apr. 25, 1928; s. Firm C. and Marie (Bock) B.; m. Carolyn Anne McMillen, Feb. 22, 1951 (div. 1979); children: Leslie, Buffie, Lynn Murphy Burket. B.A., Oberlin Coll., 1950. Tech. sales mgr. Rhoades Equipment Co., Ft. Wayne, Ind., 1954-55; with Chemurgy div. Central Soya Co., Ft. Wayne, Ind., 1955-69; dir. mktg. Chemurgy div. Central Soya Co., Chgo., 1966-69; v.p. protein specialties Archer Daniel Midland Co., Decatur, Ill., 1969-74, v.p., asst. to pres., 1974-80; v.p., asst. to chmn. Archer Daniel Midland Co., Decatur, 1980—; mem. Gov.'s Task Force on Future Rural Agriculture. Bd. dirs. Decatur Area Arts Council, 1972-84; bd. dirs. Macon County United Way, 1974-77, Boys Club, Decatur, 1979-86, Decatur Metro C. of C., 1982-87; mem. Millikin U. Assocs., Macon County Econ. Devel. Found., St. Mary's Hosp. Adv. Bd., Ill. Agriculture Export Adv. Com. Served to 1st lt. U.S. Army, 1974-77. Mem. Inst. Food Technologists, Am. Mgmt. Assn., Soy Protein Council (chmn. 1974-76), Gov.'s Rural Affairs Council, U.S. Sweetener Producers Group, Ill. Agrl. Export Adv. Com., Ill. 4-H Found. Bd. Clubs: Decatur, Decatur Country. Home: Route 1 Box 84A Blue Mound IL 62513 Office: Archer Daniels Midland Co 4666 Faries Pkwy Decatur IL 62525

BURKETT, WILLIAM ANDREW, banker; b. nr. Herman, Nebr., July 1, 1913; s. William H. and Mary (Dill) B.; m. Juliet Ruth Johnson, Oct. 5, 1940; children: Juliet Ann Burkett Hooker, Katherine C. Burkett Congdon, William Cleveland. Student, U. Nebr., 1931-32, Creighton U. Law Sch., 1932-33; LL.B., U. Omaha, 1936. Sr. spl. agt., intelligence unit Treasury Dept., 1945-50; exec. v.p. Calif. Employers Assn. Group, Sacramento, 1950-53; dir. Calif. Dept. Employment, 1953-55; supt. banks, chmn. Dept. Investments Calif., 1955-59; dir. Liquidation Yokohama Specie Bank; also Sumitomo Bank, San Francisco, 1955-59; cons. Western Bancorp, San Francisco, 1959-61; chmn. bd., pres. Security Nat. Bank Monterey County, Monterey-Carmel, Calif., 1961-66, Burkett Land Co., Monterey, 1966—; chmn. bd. Securities Properties Corp., Monterey. Author: Mount Rushmore National Memorial's History of America, 1776-1904, 1971. Dir. banking and investments, cabinet gov., Calif., 1953-59; dir. Calif. Emergency Manpower Commn., 1953-55; chmn. Gov. Calif. Com. Refugee Relief, 1953-55; mem. Calif. Securities Commn., 1955-59; mem. financial bd. Pine Manor Jr. Coll., Chestnut Hill, Mass., 1967—; mem. Monterey County Hist. Commn., Nat. Trust Found., Royal Oak Found.; bd. dirs. Monterey Symphony Assn.; chmn. bd. trustees Nat. Hist. Found.; trustee Monterey Mus. Art, Bishop Kip Sch., Carmel Valley, Calif.; co-chmn., trustee Mt. Rushmore Hall of Records Commn., 1987; mem. adv. bd. Robert Louis Stevenson Sch., Pebble Beach, Calif., 1971—, candidate for gov. Calif., 1978. Served as officer USCGR, 1943-45. Mem. Am., Calif., Ind. bankers assns., Nat. Assn. Supts. State Banks (pres. 1958-59), Monterey History and Art Assn., Mt. Rushmore Nat. Meml. Soc. (life mem., trustee), Amvets (dept. comdr. Calif. 1947, nat. vice comdr. 1948), Soc. Calif. Pioneers. Episcopalian. Clubs: Monterey Peninsula Golf and Country (Pebble Beach), Beach and Tennis (Pebble Beach), Stillwater Yacht (Pebble Beach); Carmel Valley Golf and Tennis; Commonwealth (San Francisco), Rotary (San Francisco); Sutter Lawn (Sacramento). Home: PO Box 726 Pebble Beach CA 93953 Office: Viscaino Rd Pebble Beach CA 93953

BURKHARD, MICHAEL FRANZ, physics researcher; b. Frankfurt, Hessen, Fed. Republic Germany, Aug. 25, 1954; s. Franz Joseph and Sophie (Schneider) B.; m. Ulrike Hoos, June 12, 1985. Diploma in Physics, J.W. Goethe U., Frankfurt, 1983, D. Philosophicus Naturalis, 1987. Researcher Ministry Research, Frankfurt, 1984-86; project leader Kraftwerk Union, Offenbach, Fed. Republic Germany, 1987—. Contbr. articles to profl. jours. Delegate mem. Freie Demokratische Partei vis. People's Republic of China, 1978. Office: Kraftwerk Union, Berliner St 295-303, 6050 Offenbach, Hessen Federal Republic of Germany

BURKHARDT, CHARLES HENRY, author, association executive, lecturer, consultant; b. Bklyn., June 17, 1915; s. Adolph Michael and Mildred (Herman) B.; B.S., St. Johns U., 1938; postgrad Pratt Inst., 1947-48; m. Lillian Sanders, Jan. 31, 1942; children—Gregory Charles, Christopher Michael. Service mgr., asst. sales mgr. Concord Oil Corp., N.Y.C., 1939-43; instr. heat engring. Walter Hervey Jr. Coll., N.Y.C., 1947-49; dir. edn. Perfex Corp., Milw., 1949-51; gen. mgr. Paragon Maintenance Co., Mineola, N.Y., 1951-55; mng. dir., sec.-treas. Oil Heat Inst. Am., N.Y.C., 1955-60; v.p. Nat. Oil Fuel Inst., N.Y.C., 1960-62; exec. v.p. New Eng. Fuel Inst. Boston, 1962-81, pres., 1981-86; cons. Standard Oil Co. N.J., 1957-58, Bacharach Instrument Co., 1947, Richfield Mfg. Co., 1948, Arthur D. Little Inc., 1987, Global Petroleum Inc., 1986-87, Centennial and Atlantic Mutual Ins. Cos., 1984-88, Scully Signal Co., 1986-88, Nutter, McClennan & Fish, Boston, 1987—, Rich, May, Bilodeau & Flaherty, Boston, 1988—, Minshaw, Culbertson, Moelmann, Hoban & Fuller, Chgo., 1988—; mem. Mktg. Viability Task Force, U.S. Dept. Energy, 1977, also mem. fuel oil mktg. adv. com., residential conservation task force; del. New Eng. Energy Congress, 1978, White House Conf. on Small Bus.; chmn. fuel oil marketers' fin. viability task force SBA; mem. Mass. state residential conservation adv. com.; trustee St. Elizabeth's Hosp., Brighton, Mass., 1985—; nat. coordinator 1985 Oil Heat Centennial Celebration. Pres. New Eng. Fuel Inst. Edn. Found., 1983-86, cons. 1987, 88. Served to capt. AUS, 1943-46. Granted Knighthood Equestrian Order of the Holy Sepulchre, Jerusalem, 1986; recipient Disting. Achievement award New Eng. Oil Heat Industry, 1972; certs. of commendation Conn. Petroleum Assn., 1974, 80; Oil Man of New Eng. award Better Home Heat Council N.H., 1975; Certificate of Appreciation, Soc. Mfg. Engrs., 1976; 15th Anniversary commendation New Eng. Fuel Inst., 1977; Man of Yr. award Met. Energy Council, 1984. Mem. Am. Soc. Heating, Refrigeration and Air Conditioning Engrs. (life), Am. Soc. Assn. Execs., Nat. Soc. Bus. Economists, Paulist League. Republican. Roman Catholic. Author: Residential and Commercial Air Conditioning, 1959, Baseboard Heating, 1952, Domestic and Commercial Oil Burners, 1969. The Oil Heating Technician, 1957. Home: 770 Boylston St Boston MA 02199

BURKHARDT, DOLORES ANN, library consultant; b. Meriden, Conn., July 28, 1932; d. Frederick Christian and Emily (Detels) Burkhardt; B.A., U. Conn., 1955; M.S., So. Conn. State Coll., 1960; postgrad. Cen. Wash. State Coll., 1962, Columbia, 1964—; 6th yr. diploma U. Conn., 1972. Asst. librarian So. Conn. State Coll. Library, summers 1960, 62; sch. library tchr. Farmington High Sch., Unionville, Conn., 1955-65; library cons.; media specialist East Farms Sch., Farmington, Conn., 1967-70; sch. library coordinator K-12, Durham-Middlefield, Conn., 1970-72; media specialist regional dist. 10, Burlington-Harwinton, Conn., 1972-78; ednl. media cons., 1978—. Instr. Boston U. Media Inst. Spl. cons. Conn. Dept. Edn., 1965—. Mem. AAUW (sec. 1956-58), NEA, Conn. Edn. Assn., New Eng. (pres. 1969-70), Conn. (2d v.p. 1965—, chmn. sch. library devel.; chmn. standards com. 1970-72, chmn. instructional materials selection policy com. Region 10) sch. library assns., Am. Assn. Sch. Librarians, New Eng. Sch. Devel. Council, Phi Delta Kappa. Lutheran. Home and Office: 812 Savage St Southington CT 06489

BURKHARDT, HANS GUSTAV, artist; b. Basel, Switzerland, Dec. 20, 1904; came to U.S., 1924, naturalized, 1930; s. Gustav and Anna (Schmidt) B.; m. Louise Thile, Mar. 25, 1929 (div. 1938); 1 dau., Elsa Burkhardt Brown; m. Thordis Olga Westhassel, June 18, 1955. Student, Cooper Union, 1924-25, Grand Central Sch. Art, N.Y.C., 1928-29; pvt. student, with Gorky, 1930-37. Assoc. prof. art Long Beach State U., 1959; prof. art U. So. Calif., 1959-60; parttime instr. UCLA, 1960-63; asso. prof. U. Calif., Northridge, 1963-73, Chouinard Art Inst., 1962—; prof. emeritus Calif. State U., Northridge. Collaborator: (with Ray Bradbury) Man Dead? Then God is Slain, prints, 1977; (with William Everson) prints Rattlesnake August, 1978, (with Ray Bradbury) The Kiss, 1983; One-man exhbns. include, Los Angeles County Mus., Oreg. State U., Museo de Bellas Artex, Guadalajara, Mexico, Occidental Coll., Inst. de Allende, San Miguel de Allende, Mexico, Mt. St. Mary Coll., Palos Verdes Community Art Assn., Pasadena Art Mus., Valley Jr. Coll., Van Nuys, Santa Monica Pub. Library, Glendale Pub. Library, Whittier Art Assn., U. So. Calif., Santa Barbara Mus. Art, Palace Legion of Honor, Los Angeles Municipal Art Gallery, La Jolla Art Center, Pierce Coll., Los Angeles, Freie Schule, Basel, Switzerland, San Fernando Valley State Coll., Bay City Jewish Community Center, Laguna Beach Mus. Art, San Diego Art Inst. (forty year retrospective), ACA-American Masters Gallery, Los Angeles, San Diego Fine Arts Gallery, Michael Smith Gallery, Los Angeles, Long Beach Mus. Art (retrospective 1950-72), Calif. State U., Northridge, 1973, 75, Santa Barbara Mus. Art, Pasquale Ianetti, San Francisco, 1977, Palm Springs Desert Mus., 1979, Robert Schoelkopf Gallery, N.Y.C., 1979, Alana Gallery, Oslo, Norway, 1978, 80, C.H. Wenger Gallery, Basel, 1981, Jack Rutberg Fine Arts, Los Angeles, 1982, 83, 84, 87, Sid Deutsch Gallery, N.Y.C., 1987; group shows, Los Angeles Inst. Contemporary Art, San Francisco Mus. Art, numerous others; represented in permanent collections, Mus. Modern Art Stockholm, Oakland Mus., Palm Springs Desert Mus., Corcoran Gallery, Washington, Guggenheim Mus., N.Y.C., St. Louis Mus. Art, Tamarin Inst., U. N.Mex., Los County Art Mus., Pasadena Art Mus., Santa Barbara Mus. Art, Long Beach Art Mus., La Jolla Art Mus., San Diego Fine Art Center, Jocelyn Art Center, Lincoln, Nebr., Kunstmuseum, Basel, Switzerland, Ahmanson collection, Hirshhorn Mus.; subject documentary film Hans Burkhardt: The Artist's World, 1987. Recipient purchase prize in oil Los Angeles County Mus., 1946, cash awards, 1954, 57; award Terry Art Inst., Miami, Fla., 1951; purchase prize Santa Barbara Mus. Art, 1957; award Calif. Watercolor Soc., 1961; purchase oil Los Angeles All-City Show, 1958,61; purchase watercolor, 1961; purchase watercolor Long Beach Mus.; purchase watercolor Pasadena Art Mus.;

purchase watercolor Los Angeles County Mus.; purchase watercolor Santa Barbara Mus. Art; purchase watercolor La Jolla Art Center; purchase watercolor Emily and Joe Lowe Meml.; Outstanding Tchrs. award Calif. State U., Northridge, 1973. Mem. Santa Barbara Mus. Art, Los Angeles Art Assn., Long Beach Art Mus., Kappa Pi, Phi Kappa Phi (hon.). Address: Jack Rutberg Fine Arts Inc 357 N La Brea Ave Los Angeles CA 90036

BURKSTRAND, C. CLAYTON, retail discount company executive; b. Kimball, Minn., Mar. 11, 1934; s. Clarence and Evelyn Ida B.; m. Linda Kay Hardas, Nov. 15, 1973; children: David, Jeff, Steve, Beth. Student, U. Minn., 1952-54, U. Alaska. Trainee, ops. mgr. Target, Mpls., 1962-64, mdse. mgr., 1964-65, store mgr., 1965-68, dist. mgr., sr. dist. mgr. then regional mgr., 1968-74; v.p. ops. Globe div. Walgreen Drug Co., Inc., Houston, 1975, pres. Globe div. and v.p. parent co., 1975-78; pres., chief operating officer Pamida, Inc., Omaha, 1978-81, chmn., pres., chief exec. officer, 1981—, also bd. dirs. Past mem. bd. advisors Discount Store News. Mem. fin. com. Hal Daub Senatorial campaign, 1987; active Nebr. Rep. Party; participant local membership drive Ak-Sar-Ben. Served with AUS, 1954-56. Named Man of Yr. Boys and Young Men's Apparel Lodge B'nai B'rith, 1982. Mem. Nat. Mass Retailing Inst. (bd. dirs. 1986). Lutheran. Office: Pamida Inc 8800 F St Omaha NE 68127

BURLAND, BRIAN BERKELEY, novelist, poet, scenarist playwright; b. Paget, Bermuda, Apr. 23, 1931; s. Gordon Hamilton and Honor Alice Croydon (Gosling) B.; m. Edwina Ann Trentham, 1962 (div. 1979); children—Susan, Anne, William, Benjamin. Grad., Aldenham Sch., Elstree, Eng., 1948; student, U. Western Ont., Can., 1948-51. Mng. dir. Burland Estates, Ltd., Gosling Estates, Ltd.; 1st v.p. G.H. Burland & Co., Ltd., 1951-56; assoc. editor Bermudian Mag., 1957; lectr. Am. Sch., London, 1974, Washington and Lee U., Va., 1973; writer in residence So. Sem., Va., 1973, Bermuda Writers Conf., 1978, U. Hartford, Conn., 1981-82; guest fellow Yale U., 1982-83; vis. prof. Conn. Coll., 1986-87; judge P.E.N. Syndicated Fiction Project, 1985; narrator stories and poems BBC, 1968—. Author: A Fall from Aloft, 1968, A Few Flowers for St. George, 1969, Undertow, 1970, The Sailor and the Fox, 1973, Surprise, 1975, Stephen Decatur, The Devil and the Endymion, 1975, the Flight of the Cavalier, 1980, Love Is a Durable Fire, 1985, What Wanderwith, 1988, (childrens book) St. Nicholas and the Tub, 1964, (poetry) To Celebrate a Happiness that is America, 1971. Served with Brit. Mcht. Service, 1944. Conn. Commn. Arts grantee, 1984. Fellow Royal Soc. Lit.; mem. Authors Guild, Authors League Am., P.E.N. Am. Ctr., Soc. Authors (London). Club: Chelsea Arts (London); Royal Yacht (Bermuda). Home: Book Hill Essex CT 06426 Office: care Carol E Rinzler Rember & Curtis 19 W 44th St New York NY 10036 also: Robin Lowe, 200 Fulham Rd, London England MLR LN also: care Murray Pollinger, Literary Agt, 4 Garrick St, London WC2E 9BH, England

BURLAUD, ALAIN JEAN, management educator, consultant; b. Paris, Jan. 30, 1946; s. Paul Andre and Odile Aimee (Schouller) B.; m. Genevieve Huguette Imbert, July 12, 1967; children: Sophie, Denis. Docteur d'Etat es sciences de gestion, U. Paris, Sorbonne, 1976. Asst. prof. Ecole Supérieure de Commerce de Paris, 1969-72; secondary sch. tchr. Lycee Paul Langevin, Suresnes, France, 1972-73; lectr. Institut Universitaire de Technologie, Villetaneuse, France, 1973-74, U. Paris, Sorbonne, 1974-80; prof. U. Tours, France, 1980-83; U. Paris Val de Marne, 1984—; chmn. exam. bd. Diplôme d'expertise comptable, 1985—. C.P.A., France. Author: Comptabilité et Inflation (Prix de l'Academie de Comptabilité 1979), 1979; (with R. Laufer) Public Management, 1980; (with C. Simon) Couts/Controle, 1981; (with Raimbault and Saussois) Approche Systémique des relations etat-industrie: la relation d'aide, 1984; mem. editorial bd. Politics and Public Management, 1982—, Sciences de gestion, 1984—. Fellow Assn. Française de Comptabilité; mem. Compagnie des Commissaires aux Comptes, Ordre des experts comptables, Internat. Fedn. Accts. (edn. com., French rep.). Home: 19 Allee Courbet, F 93190 Livry-Gargan France Office: U Paris Val de Marne, 58 ave Didier, 94210 La Varenne Saint Hilaire France

BURLEIGH, BRUCE DANIEL, JR., biochemist, endocrinologist; b. Augusta, Ga., June 23, 1942; s. Bruce Daniel and Billie Ann (Carter) B.; m. Dorothy Jean Roskos, Sept. 4, 1962 (div. 1981); 1 son, Michael Eugene. B.S., Carnegie-Mellon U., 1964; M.S., U. Mich., 1967, Ph.D., 1970. With MRC Lab, Cambridge, Eng., 1970-73; asst. prof. biochemistry M.D. Anderson Hosp., U. Tex. Cancer Ctr., Houston, 1973-79, assoc. biochemist, 1979-81; research scientist Internat. Mineral & Chem. Corp., Terre Haute, Ind., 1981-82, sr. research scientist, 1983—. NIH fellow, 1968-70; Am. Cancer Soc. fellow, 1970-72; Robert A. Welch grantee, 1979-81. Mem. Am. Chem. Soc., Am. Soc. of Biol. Chemists, Endocrine Soc., AAAS, N.Y. Acad. of Sci., Sigma Xi, Tau Beta Pi, Phi Lambda Upsilon. Episcopalian. Contbr. articles to profl. jours. Home: 075 Oak Ave Oak Terr Div Mundelein IL 60060 Office: Internat Minerals & Chem Corp R & D Div Biochem Sect 1810 Frontage Rd Northbrook IL 60062

BURLESON, KAREN TRIPP, lawyer; b. Rocky Mount, N.C., Sept. 2, 1955; d. Bryant and Katherine Rebecca (Watkins) Tripp; m. Robert Mark Burleson, June 25, 1977. BA, U. N.C., 1976; JD, U. Ala., 1981. Bar: Tex. 1981, U.S. Dist. Ct. (so. dist.) Tex. 1982, U.S. Ct. Appeals (fed. cir.) 1983. Law clerk Tucker, Gray & Espy, Tuscaloosa, Ala., 1978-81, to presiding justice Ala. Supreme Ct., Montgomery, summer 1980; atty. Exxon Prodn. Research Co., Houston, 1981-86, coordinator tech. transfer, 1986-87; assoc. Arnold, White and Durkee, Attys. at Law, Houston, 1988—. Contbr. articles to profl. jours. Recipient Am. Jurisprudence award U. Ala., 1980, Dean's award, 1981. Mem. Houston Bar Assn. (internat. transfer tech. com. 1983-84), Houston Intellectual Property Lawyers Assn. (outstanding inventor com. 1982-84, chmn. student edn. com. 1986, sec. 1987-88, bd. govs., chmn. awards com. 1988-89), Tex. Bar Assn. (antitrust law com. 1984-85, chmn. Internat. Law com. of Intellectual Property Law Sect. 1987-88), ABA, Am. Intellectual Property Lawyers Assn. , Phi Alpha Delta (clerk 1980). Republican. Methodist. Office: Arnold White & Durkee PO Box 4433 Houston TX 77210

BURLINGAME, JOHN FRANCIS, retired electrical equipment company executive; b. Somerville, Mass., June 18, 1922; s. John Francis and Irene Mae (Walsh) B.; m. Genevieve Keohane, July 21, 1947; children: Susan M., Janet E., Mary E., Elizabeth A. B.S., Tufts U., 1942. With Gen. Electric Co., 1946-85; v.p., gen. mgr. computer systems div. Gen. Electric Co., Phoenix, 1969-71; v.p. employee relations Gen. Electric Co., N.Y.C., 1971-73; v.p., group exec. internat. group Gen. Electric Co., 1973-77; sr. v.p., internat. sector exec. Gen. Electric Co., Fairfield, Conn., 1977-79; vice chmn. Gen. Electric Co., 1979-85; bd. dirs. Eastman Kodak, Hershey Foods, Merrill Lynch. Served with USNR, 1943-46. Mem. AAAS, Conf. Bd., Am. Arbitration Assn. (dir. 1973-81), Fgn. Policy Assn. (dir. 1976-80), C. of C. of U.S. (dir. 1980-83), Sigma Pi Sigma. Home: 45 Hancock Ln Darien CT 06820 Office: General Electric Co Fairfield CT 06431

BURMAN, DAVID, pediatrician, researcher, educator; b. Bath, Somerset, Eng., Dec. 21, 1926; s. Alan Richard and Ada Bessie (Dyer) B.; m. Evelyn May Taylor, July 16, 1951; children—Helen Mary, Mark Richard. B.Sc., Kings Coll., London, 1947; M.B., B.S., Charing Cross Hosp., London, 1950, M.D., 1960. Med. officer Colonial Med. Service, Singapore, 1952-55; sr. pediatric registrar Charing Cross Hosp., London, 1955-60; research fellow dept. pediatrics, Iowa City, 1958-59; sr. pediatric registrar St. Marys Hosp., London, 1960-63; cons. pediatrician Derbyshire Childrens Hosp., Derby, 1963-64, Bristol Childrens Hosp., 1964-87, adminstrv. med. officer South Western Regional Health Authority, 1987—; vis. cons. WHO, Bangladesh, 1977-78; med. advisor Phenylketonuric Soc., London, 1980-84; chmn. med. com. Bristol and Weston Health Authority, 1982-84; examiner Royal Coll. Physicians, London, 1980—. Editor, author: Textbook of Pediatric Nutrition, 2d edit., 1982. Editor: Inherited Disorders of Carbohydrate Metabolism, 1980, founder, editor Pediatric Revs. and Communications, 1985—. Fulbright travel grantee, 1958, Heinz fellow British Pediatric Assn., East Africa, 1962, research grantee Med. Research Council, Bristol, 1965-68. Fellow Royal Soc. Medicine; mem. Brit. Pediatric Assn. (mem. council 1975-78), Nutrition Soc., Assn. for Study of Inborn Errors of Metabolism. Mem. Ch. of England. Avocations: sailing; theatre. Home: 2 Chew Ct Farm Chew Magna, Bristol England BS18 8 SF Office: South Western Regional Hosp, 26/27 Kings Sq House, Kings Sq, BS2 8EF Bristol England

BURMAN, MARSHA LINKWALD, lighting manufacture executive, marketing and management development trainer; b. Balt., Jan. 9, 1949; d. William and Lena (Ronin) Linkwald; m. Robert Schlosser, July 2, 1972 (div. 1980); m. John R. Burman, June, 1986; children—Melanie, David, Heather, Richard. B.S. cum laude in Edn., Kent State U., 1970, M.A. summa cum laude in Sociology, 1971. Cert. secondary edn., Ohio. Spl. project dir. Tng. and Research Ctr., Planned Parenthood, Chgo., 1978; with mgmt. edn. ctr. Gould, Inc., Chgo., 1979, program adminstr., 1979-80; systems trainer Lithonia Lighting, 1981, mgr. tng. and edn., 1981-86, dir. mktg., tng. and devel., 1986—. Author: (booklet) Putting Your Best Foot Forward (award Am Soc. Tng. and Devel.), 1982. Facilitator single parenting interaction group, Atlanta, 1984-85. U.S. Office Edn. grantee, 1971. Mem. Lithonia Lighting Mgmt. Club (v.p. 1982-83), Am. Soc. of Tng. and Devel. (bd. dirs. 1982, spl. projects. dir. Atlanta chpt. 1982, Vol. of Yr., Community Leader Am. 1987). Avocation: reading. Office: Lithonia Lighting Div of Nat Service Industries 1400 Lester Rd Conyers GA 30207

BURNARD, LOUIS DERYCK, computer executive; b. Birmingham, Eng., Dec. 9, 1946; s. David Chance and Josephine Moira (Nathan) B.; m. Marie Anne Lilette Toussaint, Dec. 23, 1972; children: Belinda Daphne, Sarah Daisy, Elisabeth Rose. BA in English Lang. Lit. Hons., Balliol Coll., Oxford, 1968, MPHIL in English Studies, 1977, MA, 1978. Lectr. U. Malawi, 1972-73; programmer U. Oxford, 1974—; dir. Oxford Text Archive, Oxford, 1976—; cons. in field, 1980—. Contbr. articles to profl. jours., book reviews. Fellow Max Planck Inst. Geshichte; mem. Assn. History and Computing, Assn. Literary and Linguistic Computing, Wolfson Coll. Jewish. Office: Oucs, 13 Banbury Rd, Oxford OX2 6NN, England

BURNASH, ROBERT JOHN CHARLES, hydrologist; b. Bklyn., Aug. 17, 1931; s. James Francis and Marion Josephine (Olifiers) B.; B.S., Bucknell U., 1953; postgrad. Naval Postgrad. Sch., 1954; m. Jeanne Carolyn Mack, July 11, 1953; children—Charles, Kathleen, Mary, Elizabeth, David, Daniel. Hydrologist, Nat. Weather Service River Forecast Center, Cin., 1957-62, prin. asst., Sacramento River Forecast Center, 1963-71, hydrologist in charge Calif.-Nev. River Forecast Center, 1972-87, retired 1987—; guest lectr. hydrologic systems Australian Water Resources Council, Melbourne, Perth, Brisbane, Sydney, 1984; World Meteorological Orgn. lectr. U. Calif., Davis, 1983-86; prin. organizer Internat. Tech. Conf. on Mitigation of Natural Hazards through Real-Time Data Collection and Hydrological Forecasting, World Meteorol. Orgn., Sacramento, 1983; cons. Hydrologic Services, 1987—. Served with USNR, 1953-56. Recipient Bronze medal Dept. Commerce, 1970, Silver medal, 1975, Gold medal, 1980; Outstanding Public Service award NOAA, 1978. Fellow Am. Meteorol. Soc. (Outstanding Forecaster award 1979, Robert E. Horton meml. lectr. 1983); mem. Am. Geophys. Union, AAAS, N.Y. Acad. Scis., Western Snow Conf., Assn. State Flood Plain Mgrs., Delta Mu Delta, Phi Lambda Theta. Author: (with others) The Sacramento Model. Contbr. articles to profl. jours. Originator real time event reporting telemetering systems and ALERT flood warning system. Home: 3539 Ridgeview Dr El Dorado Hills CA 95630

BURNET, THORNTON WEST, marketing executive; b. Cin., Aug. 27, 1917; s. David and Agnes McClung (West) B.; B.S. in Commerce, U. Va., 1940; m. Mary Elizabeth Charlton, Aug. 14, 1948; 1 son, Thornton West. Asst. treas. Lincoln Service Corp., Washington, 1941-50, v.p., sec., 1950-59; v.p. mktg. Am. Fin. Mgmt. Corp., Silver Spring, Md., 1959-76; v.p., treas., dir. Monet Constrn. Co., Fairfax, Va., 1962-84; v.p. mktg. Am. Directory Service Agy., Silver Spring, 1976-83; sec., treas., dir. Worldwide Yellow Pages, 1979-87. Committeeman, Boy Scouts Am., 1945—; trustee W. C. Westlake Found., 1960—, Children's Mission, Pitts., 1980-83; pres. bd. trustees Fletcher Meml. Library, 1962-86. Served with U.S. Army, 1940-43. Mem. Alpha Kappa Psi. Republican. Episcopalian (vestryman, past sr. warden). Home: 10800 Hunters Valley Rd Vienna VA 22180 Office: 1398 Lamberton Dr Silver Spring MD 20902

BURNETT, ALFRED DAVID, librarian; b. Edinburgh, Scotland, Aug. 15, 1937; s. Alfred Harding and Jessie Miller (Scott) B. Scottish Leaving Cert., George Watson's Boys' Coll., Edinburgh, 1955; MA with honors in English lang. and lit., U. Edinburgh, 1959; Associateship of Library Assn., U. Strathclyde, Glasgow, 1964. Library asst. U. Glasgow Library, 1959-64; asst. librarian Durham U. Library, 1964—; Author numerous poems; contbr. articles to profl. jours. Recipient Patterson Bursary in Anglo-Saxon award U. Edinburgh, 1958, Kelso Meml. prize in bibliography U. Strathclyde, 1964, Sevensma prize Internat. Fedn. Library Assns., 1971. Mem. Library Assn. (com. Internat. and Comparative Librarianship Group 1973—, Essay prize 1966), Bibliog. Soc., Pvt. Libraries Assn. Socialist. Presbyterian. Club: Colpitts Poetry (Durham) (com. mem. 1975—). Home: 33 Hastings Ave, Merry Oaks, Durham DHI 3QG, England Office: Durham U Library, Palace Green, Durham DH1 3RN, England

BURNETT, JAMES HOLDEN, engineer, consultant; b. Newark, May 20, 1911; s. James Brown and Elizabeth W. (Holden) B.; B.S. in Engring., Princeton U., 1932, E.E., 1933; m. Anne Seely, May 16, 1940; children—Barbara Anne Burnett Dwyer, James Bruce, Carol Elizabeth (dec.). Vice pres. Electrons, Inc., Newark, 1945-60; mktg. mgr. F.L. Moseley Co. div. Hewlett Packard Co., Pasadena, Calif., 1960-65; v.p. Edwards Co. unit Gen. Signal Corp., Norwalk, Conn., 1965-71; pres. James H. Burnett Co., Wilton, Conn., 1971—; dir. Essex Engring. Co. (Conn.); cons. on indsl. electronic controls, 1971—. Trustee, Boys Club of Newark, 1945-50; mem. grad. council Princeton U., 1955-57; mem. adv. bd. U. Bridgeport, 1969-73, Norwalk State Coll., 1968-71; mem. steering U.S. Senate Bus. Adv. Bd., 1981—. Mem. IEEE (life), Sigma Xi, Tau Beta Pi. Congregationalist. Club: Princeton (N.Y.C.). Joint author: Control Engineers Handbook, 1958; contbr. articles to tech. publs. Patentee in field. Home: 100 River Rd Wilton CT 06897 Office: PO Box 504 Wilton CT 06897

BURNHAM, DAVID HENDERSON, management consultant; b. Quincy, Mass., Mar. 4, 1942; s. Roger Appleton and Phyllis Katherine (Kline) B.; m. Frances Margarita Parry, Feb. 15, 1964; children: Amery Appleton, Hugh Tebault Ramseyer. BA, Northeastern U., 1964; MBA, Harvard U., 1969. Assoc. Sterling Inst., Boston, 1969; v.p., treas. McBer and Co., Boston, 1970-72, pres., 1972-77; pres. David H. Burnham and Assocs., orgn. devel. cons., Boston and London, 1977—; cons. Govt. of Singapore, 1978-86, St. Ivel's Ltd., 1982—, Unigate Dairies, Ltd., London, 1980—, U.S. Navy, Washington, 1975-77, Mattel, Inc., Los Angeles, 1971-75, UN Indsl. Devel. Orgn., Vienna, 1970-77, World Bank, Washington, 1978-80. Producer film: Motives Moving Business (Am. Film Festival award 1975), 1974; contbr. articles to profl. jours. Treas., v.p. Children's Mus. Boston, 1972-81; pres., chief exec. officer, 1981-83, chmn., 1984-86, hon. trustee, 1988—; pres. Cavalier King Charles Spaniel Club, Louisville, 1972-78; dir. Children's Mus., London, 1984-86 Mental Health Found., U.K., Drive for Youth Programme, U.K., 1986—; com. Derby Acad. Council, Hingham, Mass., 1974-81. Mem. Orgn. Devel. Network, Am. Soc. Tng. and Devel., Am. Assn. Mus. Trustees, Internat. Com. Mus. Episcopalian. Clubs: Somerset, Harvard (Boston); Cohasset Golf, Cohasset Yacht (Mass.); Lansdowne (London). Home: 30 Atlantic Ave Cohasset MA 02025 Office: David H Burnham & Assocs, 102 Ebury Mews, London SW1 W9NX, England

BURNHAM, HAROLD ARTHUR, pharmaceutical company executive, physician; b. Boston, Nov. 6, 1929; s. Howard Rowland and Edna Adelaide (Teachout) B.; m. Lucienne Jeanne Seas, June 28, 1952; children—Philippe Henri, Isabelle Jeanne. B.S., Union Coll., 1951; M.A., Middlebury Coll., 1952; postgrad., Albany State Tchrs. Coll., 1953-54, Adelphi U., 1958-59, Nassau Community Coll., 1961-62; M.D., U. Md., 1966. Diplomate Am. Bd. Med. Examiners, Am. Bd. Family Practice (charter). Tchr. sci., French and track team coach S. Glens Falls Central High Sch., N.Y., 1952-54; med. rep., hosp. salesman Upjohn Co., Bklyn., 1956-62; intern S. Balt. Gen. Hosp., 1966-67; resident Glen Cove Community Hosp., N.Y., 1967-69; practice family medicine Glen Cove, 1969-75; assoc. med. dir. Winthrop Labs. div. Sterling Drug Inc., N.Y.C., 1975-76, med. dir. Glenbrook Labs. div., 1977, v.p. med. affairs, sr. v.p. Winthrop Product Inc., 1977—; v.p. med. affairs, sr. v.p. Winthrop Product Inc. Sterling Drug Inc., N.J., 1977—, Sydney Ross Co. and Sterling Products Internat., N.Y.C., 1977—; v.p., med. dir. Glenbrook Labs. div. Sterling Drugs, Inc., N.Y.C., 1980—; med. dir. Choay Labs. Inc., N.Y.C., 1980-82; spl. cons. Labs. Choay, S.A., Paris, 1982—; asst. med. dir. United Presbyn. Residence, Woodbury, N.Y., 1983—; instr. Sch. Practical Nursing, Glen Cove Community Hosp., 1970-75; instr. geriatrics in coop. with Glen Cove Community Hosp. Family Practice Residency Program, 1983—; cons., clinician in medicine Nassau County Pub. Health Dept., 1975—; med. cons. Webb Inst. Naval Architecture and Marine Design, Glen Cove, N.Y., 1970—. Scoutmaster Boy Scouts Am., Glens Falls, N.Y., 1953-54, com. mem., 1968—, merit badge counsellor for first aid, pub. health emergency care, chemistry and mammals for Sagamore Dist., 1968—; lay reader St. John's of Lattingtown Episcopal Ch., N.Y., 1968—, vestryman, 1983—, ck. of vestry, 1986—; trustee Hawley Found., 1984—; del. to 120th conv. Episcopal Diocese of L.I. Served with U.S. Army, 1954-56. Mem. AMA (6 Continuing Edn. awards), Pan Am. Med. Soc., N.Y. State Med. Soc., Nassau County Med. Soc., Am. Acad. Family Physicians, Am. Fertility Soc., L.I. Scottish Clans Assn. (trustee 1984—, piper to chief 1986—), Am. Geriatric Soc., Nu Sigma Nu. Episcopalian. Office: United Presbyn Residence 378 Syosset-Woodbury Rd Woodbury NY 11797

BURNHAM, LEAH LUCILLE, medical technologist; b. Fergus Falls, Minn., July 31, 1947; d. Dresden Gordon and Helen Lucille (Keller) Taylor; B.S., Millikin U., 1969; M.S., U. Vt., 1972; m. Frederick R. Burnham, II, Dec. 8, 1973; children—Russell Adam, Laurel Helene. Blood bank technologist Luth. Hosp., Cleve., 1969-70; gen. technologist Lake Forest (Ill.) Hosp., 1970; teaching fellow U. Vt., Burlington, 1970-72; edn. coordinator Tucson Med. Center Sch. Med. Tech., 1972-74; sr. technologist in clin. toxicology U. Ariz. Health Sci. Center, Tucson, 1974-87, chief med. technologist chemistry, clin. pathology, 1987—; conductor workshops in field. Mem. Am. Soc. Clin. Pathologists. Contbr. articles to profl. jours. Office: Ariz Health Sci Ctr Clin Pathology Univ Tucson AZ 85724

BURNISON, BOYD EDWARD, lawyer; b. Arnolds Park, Iowa, Dec. 12, 1934; s. Boyd William and Lucile (Harnden) B.; m. Mari Amaral; children: Erica Lafore, Alison Katherine. BS, Iowa State U., 1957; JD, U. Calif., Berkeley, 1961. Bar: Calif. 1962, U.S. Supreme Ct. 1971, U.S. Dist. Ct. (no. dist.) Calif. 1962, U.S. Ct. Appeals (9th cir.) 1962, U.S. Dist. Ct. (ea. dist.) Calif. 1970. Dep. counsel Yolo County, Calif., 1962-65; of counsel Davis and Woodland (Calif.) Unified Sch. Dists., 1962-65; assoc. Steel & Arostegui, Marysville, Calif., 1965-66, St. Sure, Moore & Hoyt, Oakland, 1966-70; ptnr. St. Sure, Moore, Hoyt & Sizoo, Oakland and San Francisco, 1970-75; v.p. Crosby, Heafey, Roach & May, P.C., Oakland, 1975—, also bd. dirs. Adviser Berkeley YMCA, 1971—; adviser Yolo County YMCA, 1962-65, bd. dirs. 1965; bd. dirs. Easter Seal Soc. Crippled Children and Adults of Alameda County, Calif., 1972-75, Moot Ct. Bd., U. Calif., 1960-61; trustee, sec., legal counsel Easter Seal Found., Alameda County, 1974-79, hon. trustee, 1979—. Fellow ABA Found.; mem. ABA (labor relations and employment law sect., equal employment law com. 1972—), State Bar Calif. (spl. labor counsel 1981-84, labor and employment law sect. 1982—), Nat. Assn. Bar Pres., Alameda County Bar Assn. (chmn. memberships and directory com. 1973-74, 80, chmn. law office econs. com. 1975-77, assn. dir. 1981-85, pres., 1984, vice chmn. bench bar liaison com. 1983, chmn. 1984, Disting. Service award 1987), Yolo County Bar Assn. (sec. 1965), Yuba Sutter Bar Assn., Bar Assn. San Francisco (labor law sect.), Indsl. Relations Research Assn., Sproul Assoc. Boalt Hall Law Sch. U. Calif. Berkeley, Iowa State Alumni Assn., Order Knoll, Pi Kappa Alpha, Phi Delta Phi. Democrat. Club: Round Hill Country. Lodge: Rotary. Home: 2500 Caballo Ranchero Dr PO Box 743 Diablo CA 94528 Office: Crosby Heafey Roach and May 2300 Lake Merritt Plaza Bldg 1999 Harrison St Oakland CA 94612

BURNLEY, JAMES H., IV, government official; b. High Point, N.C., July 30, 1948; s. James Horace and Dorothy Mary (Rockwell) B.; m. Jane Nady. B.A. magna cum laude, Yale U., 1970; J.D., Harvard U., 1973. Assoc. Brooks, Pierce, McLendon, Humphrey & Leonard, 1973-75; ptnr. Turner, Enochs, Foster, Sparrow & Burnley, P.A., 1975-81; dir. VISTA, 1981-82; assoc. dep. atty. gen. Dept. Justice, Washington, 1982-83; gen. counsel Dept. Transp., Washington, 1983, dep. sec., 1983-87, sec., 1987—. Office: Dept Transp 400 7th St SW Washington DC 20590 •

BURNS, CORNELIUS, management consultant; b. L.I., N.Y., Jan. 11, 1951; s. Warren Harding and Martha Jesus (Payen) B.; I.B.A., U. de Mexico, 1973; D.B.A./PhD, Pacific Western U., 1983; instructional cert. U. of the Ams., 1972-73. Investments cons. Olavaretta-Ortiz, S.A., Mexico City, 1968-73; bus./fin. mgr., spl. cons. Salas Estrade, Mexico City, 1969-77; master instr. internat. bus. mgmt. U. of the Ams., Mexico City, 1972-73; chief cons. Cornelius Burns & Assos., El Paso, Tex., and Denver, 1976—; exec. trustee/adminstrv. coordinator Garcia Internacional, S.A., 1978—. Staff dir. Goodwill Industries of El Paso, 1977; student adv. com., dpet. fin. and econs. U. Tex., El Paso, 1973-74. Recipient Cert. of Appreciation, Dept. Commerce, Mexico, 1975; U. de Las Americas teaching fellow, 1971-74. Cert. managerial acct., internat. auditor, fin. adviser, purchasing mgr. Mem. Am. Mgmt. Assn., Ind. Businessman of Am., Internat. Assn. Profl. Adminstrs., Am. Mgmt. Soc. Roman Catholic. Clubs: Internat. Skyriders of Am., Lulac. Home: 7736 Phoenix Ave El Paso TX 79915 Office: 7736 Phoenix Ave B Level El Paso TX 79915 Office: 15390 E Arizona Ave #206 Aurora CO 80017

BURNS, DAN W., manufacturing company executive; b. Auburn, Calif., Sept. 10, 1925; s. William and Edith Lynn (Johnston) B.; 1 son, Dan. Dir. materials Menasco Mfg. Co., 1951-56; v.p., gen. mgr. Hufford Corp., 1956-58; pres. Hufford div. Siegler Corp., 1958-61; v.p. Siegler Corp., 1961-62, Lear Siegler, Inc., 1962-64; pres., dir. Electrada Corp., Culver City, Calif., from 1964; now chmn. Sargent Industries and related cos.; chmn., chief exec. officer Arlington Industries, Inc.; dir. Gen. Automotive Corp., Dover Tech. Internat., Inc., Monitor Techs., Inc. Bd. dirs. San Diego Aerospace Mus. Served to capt. U.S. Army, 1941-47; prisoner of war Japan; asst. mil. attache 1946, China; a.d.c. to Gen. George C. Marshall 1946-47. Mem. Orgn. Am. States Sports Com. (dir.). Clubs: Los Angeles Country, St. Francis Yacht, Calif., Conquistadores del Cielo, Garden of the Gods. Home: 10851 Chalon Rd Bel Air Los Angeles CA 90077 Office: Sargent Industries 1901 Bldg Suite 1251 Century City Los Angeles CA 90067

BURNS, DANIEL HOBART, management consultant; b. Atlanta, Jan. 26, 1928; s. Hobart H. and Florence (Kuhn) B.; B.A., U. Ala., 1949; grad. Armed Forces Staff Coll., 1966, Air Command and Staff Coll., 1969, Air War Coll., 1972; postgrad. U. S.C., 1975, Regent Coll., U. B.C., 1978-79, Trinity Episcopal Sch. for Ministry, 1979-80; m. Barbara Ann Grimsley, Jan. 15, 1949 (div. July 1974); children—Eric Grimsley, Daniel Hobart, Barbara Bennett, Arlene Chester; m. 2d, Ann Lyn Horrell, Sept. 28, 1979; children: Jessica Florence, Stephen John. Account exec. Sta. WCOS, Columbia, S.C., 1949-51; sales mgr. sta. WIS, Columbia, 1951-57; ins. agt. Aetna Life Ins. Co., Columbia, 1957-60; propr. Daniel H. Burns Co., mgmt. cons., broker, Columbia, 1960—; pres., dir. Nat. Search, Inc., 1966—, Indsl. Surveys, Inc., 1968—; Alliance Bldg. Industries, 1971-84; cons., Ednl. TV Network, govts. of Israel, Greece, W. Ger., Fed. Grants Projects, S.C. Ednl. TV Network; guest lectr. U. S.C.; cons. sales mgmt. and market analysis, analytical and conceptual problem solving; owner Western Rare Books-Fine Art Assocs., 1983—. Pres., Schneider Sch. PTA, 1963-66; supr. registration City of Columbia, 1962-69; asst. project dir., statewide law enforcement edn. through TV, 1966-69; cons. Pitts. Leadership Found., 1980-81; dist. commr. Boy Scouts Am.; pres., chmn. ward 15 Republican Party; pres., bd. dirs. Internat. Communications Resources Found.; bd. dirs. Travelers Aid Assn. Am., Nat. Council USO; Columbia Sch. Theology for Laity; bd. dirs., exec. com. Consol. Agys. of United Funds; Richland County chpt. Nat. Found. Served with USAAF, 1943-46; lt. col. USAF Res. ret. Mem. S.C. Football Ofcls. Assn., Columbia Real Estate Bd., Air Force Assn., Am. Y-Flyer Yacht Racing Assn., AAUP, Am. Mgmt. Assn., Nat. Assn. Ednl. Broadcasters, Soc. for Advancement Mgmt., Am. Soc. Real Estate Appraisers, Interprofl. Cons. Council, Nat. Assn. Security Dealers, Soc. Am. Archivists, Nat. Hist. Soc., Internat. Platform Assn., Hist. Columbia Found., S.C. Press Assn., Columbia C. of C., Am. Soc. Personal Adminstrn., Sierra Club, Columbia Lyric Opera, Internat. Christian Leaders, Fellowship Christian Athletes, English Speaking Union, N. Am. Yacht Racing Union, Sigma Phi Epsilon. Episcopalian/Anglican. Clubs: Charleston (S.C.) Yacht; Yachting of Am., Workshop Theatre, First Nighters, Columbia Squash Racquets, Town Theatre, Masons (Shriner), Lions. Author publs. in field. Home: 2130 11th St Boulder CO 80302 Office: PO Box 1725 Boulder CO 80306 Other: 46 Punga Grove, Whangarei New Zealand

BURNS, GLADYS KING, political scientist, author; b. Gadsden, Ala., Feb. 7, 1927; d. Leslie Cooper and Gladys (Angle) King; B.A., Huntingdon Coll.,

Montgomery, Ala., 1963; M.A., Auburn (Ala.) U., 1965; Ph.D., U. Ala., 1977; m. J.A. Burns, 1946 (div. 1963); 1 child, Elizabeth King. Mem. faculty N.E. State Jr. Coll., Rainesville, Ala., 1965-66; prof. polit. sci. Jefferson State Coll., Birmingham, Ala., 1966—, dir. Women's Center, 1980, dir. sex. discriminaton Ala. Gen. Assistance Center, U. Ala., 1975-77. Mem. Ala. Hist. Assn., Internat. Platform Assn., DAR, Phi Alpha Theta, Kappa Delta Pi. Home: 1163 Montclair Rd Birmingham AL 35213 Office: Jefferson State Jr Coll 2601 Carson Rd Birmingham AL 35215

BURNS, GLENN RICHARD, dentist; b. Marietta, Ohio, Mar. 23, 1951; s. Alphas Gale Burns and Elma June (Sayres) George; m. Linda Edith Bailey, June 10, 1978; children: Geoffrey William, Katharine May. BS in Zoology, Ohio U., 1973; DDS, Ohio State U., 1980. Gen. practice dentistry Lancaster, Ohio, 1980—. Bd. dirs. Lancaster YMCA, Fairfield County, 1985—. Served to sgt. U.S. Army, 1973-77. Mem. ADA, Ohio Dental Assn., Hocking Valley Dental Soc. (chmn. children's dental health month 1983-86), Acad. Gen. Dentistry, Xi Psi Phi (v.p. 1984—), Doctors With A Heart. Republican. Presbyterian. Lodge: Kiwanis. Home: 3931 Mudhouse Rd NE Lancaster OH 43130 Office: 204 N Columbus St Lancaster OH 43130

BURNS, IKUKO KAWAI, artist; b. Tokyo, Japan, Jan. 1, 1936; came to U.S., 1959, naturalized, 1965; d. Ichiro and Asa (Sato) Kawai; m. Padraic Burns, Oct. 19, 1959; children—Kenneth C., Amelia P., Margaret A. B.A., Yamagata U., 1958; postgrad. Sch. Mus. Fine Arts, 1961-64. Announcer Hokkaido Broadcasting Co., Sapporo, Japan, 1958-59; instr. Japanese Yale U., 1960; free lance sculptor, 1975—; foundry asst. David Phillips Bronze Art Casting, Somerville, Mass., 1980—; lectr. U. Mass., Boston, 1982-83. Exhibited Gallery 355, 1979, Bentley Coll. Gallery, 1979, Copley Soc. Boston, 1980, Fed. Res. Bank, John Hancock, Boston City Hall, 1981, Yamagata Matsuzakaya Gallery, 1985, Japan Soc. Boston, Inc., 1985, Wako Gallery, Ginza, Tokyo, 1987, City Hall Gallery, Sapparo, Japan, 1987. Prin. works include Hopkins Meml. plaque Dartmouth Coll., Hanover, N.H., standing figure Yamagata City Hall, Japan. Meml. plaque Kagasuka, Can. Mem. Copley Soc. Boston, Fort Point Arts Community, Cambridge Art Assn., Japanese Assn. of Greater Boston, Japan Soc. Boston (bd. dirs. 1980—). Home: 9 Downing Rd Brookline MA 02146 Studio: 311 Walnut St Wellesley Hills MA 02181

BURNS, JOHN JOSEPH, consultant, retired aerospace executive, retired air force officer; b. Jersey City, June 28, 1924; s. Walter Joseph and Gertruce Agnes (Leslie) B.; m. Patricia Ann Boyle, Oct. 21, 1945; children: John Joseph, Jeffrey A., Judith P. B.S. in Math., U. Omaha, 1964. Commd. 2d lt. USAAF, 1943; advanced through grades to lt. gen. USAF, 1974; comdr. 522d tactical fighter squadron Bergstrom AFB, Tex., 1957-59; comdr. 91st and 92d Tactical Fighter Squadrons Bentwaters, Eng., 1959-62; asst. dir. ops., later dir. ops. 4th Tactical Fighter Wing Seymour Johnson AFB, N.C., 1962-64; comdr. Detachment 2, Hdqrs. 831st Air Div. Edwards AFB, Calif., 1964-65; asst. dir., dir. requirements Directorate of Ops., Tactical Air Command Langley AFB, Va., 1965-67; dep. comdr. ops. 8th Tactical Fighter Wing Ubon Royal Thai AFB, Thailand, 1967; vice comdr. 8th Tactical Fighter Wing 1967-68; comdr. 4525th Fighter Weapons Wing Nellis AFB, Nev., 1968-69; comdr. 58th Tactical Fighter Tng. Wing Luke AFB, Ariz., 1969-70; dep. dir. Gen. Purpose Forces, Directorate Operational Requirements and Devel. Plans, Hdqrs. USAF 1970-72, dir., 1972-73; comdr. 12th Air Force, Bergstrom AFB, 1973, Air Force Test and Evaluation Center, Kirtland AFB, N.Mex., 1974, U.S. Support Activities Group, 7th Air Force, Nakhon Phanom Royal Thai AFB, 1974-75; dep. comdr. in chief U.S. Forces Korea/UN Command Korea, Seoul, 1975-77, U.S. Readiness Command, MacDill AFB, Fla., 1977-79; ret. 1979; v.p. advanced engring. McDonnell Aircraft Co., St. Louis, 1979-84, v.p., gen. mgr. advanced tactical fighter and spl. projects, 1984-86; cons. 1986—. Decorated D.S.M. with 2 oak leaf clusters, Silver Star, Legion of Merit with oak leaf cluster, D.F.C. with 2 oak leaf clusters, Bronze Star, Meritorious Service medal with 2 oak leaf clusters, Air medal with 33 oak leaf clusters, Air Force Commendation medal. Mem. Order Daedalians. Home: 23 Southwind Ct Niceville FL 32578

BURNS, MARVIN GERALD, lawyer; b. Los Angeles, July 3, 1930; s. Milton and Belle (Cytron) B.; m. Barbara Irene Fisher, Aug. 23, 1953; children: Scott Douglas, Jody Lynn, Bradley Frederick. B.A., U. Ariz., 1951; J.D., Harvard U., 1954. Bar: Calif. 1955. Mem. De Castro, West, Chodorow & Burns, Inc., Los Angeles. Served with AUS, 1955-56. Clubs: Beverly Hills Tennis, Sycamore Park Tennis. Home: 10350 Wilshire Blvd PH4 Los Angeles CA 90024 Office: 10960 Wilshire Blvd Suite 1800 Los Angeles CA 90024

BURNS, MICHAEL KENT, educator, chemical dependency counselor; b. Sarasota, Fla., Jan. 4, 1945; s. Richard Andrew and Lilian Ida (Kent) B.; BA (Univ. scholar), Capital U., 1967; MA, Ohio State U., 1969; ednl. staff personnel adminstrv. specialist cert., Cleve. State U., 1978; cert. sch. counselor Cleve. State U., 1982, chem. dependency counselor. Grad. teaching fellow Ohio State U., 1967-69; instr. Wright State U., 1969-70; tchr. Spanish, social studies Euclid (Ohio) High Sch., 1970—, tchr. social studies, 1977—; summer intern Euclid Fisher Body Plant, Gen. Motors Corp., 1978; fellow Taft Inst. Govt., 1978, 79; career guidance inst. intern Cleve. Met. Jobs Council, 1980; tchr. Cleve. State U., 1980-81; group facilitator insight and aftercare chem. dependency programs, peer counseling co-facilitator, 1981; chem. dependency counselor Glenbeigh Adolescent Hosp., Cleve., 1983—; coordinator summer youth employment and tng. program City of Euclid, Ohio, 1987—; mental health therapist Lorain County Council on Alcoholism and Drug Abuse, Inc., 1988—. Cert. drug counselor. Mem. Euclid Tchrs. Assn. (v.p. 1974-76, pres. 1977-78), Ohio Edn. Assn., NEA, Assn. Supervision and Curriculum Devel., World Future Soc., Penticulus, Pi Lambda Theta. Democrat. Unitarian. Home: 21215 Detroit Rd #213C Cleveland OH 44116-2221 Office: 711 E 222nd St Euclid OH 44123

BURNS, MONIQUE L., publishing executive; b. Bklyn., Dec. 9, 1955; d. William Wesley and Etta (Mason) B. BA in History and Lit. cum laude, Harvard U., 1977. Assoc. editor Essence mag., N.Y.C., 1977-79; assoc. editor Travel & Leisure mag., N.Y.C., 1979-85, sr. editor, 1985-87; creative dir. Travellers Design, Ltd., London, 1987—. Episcopalian. Clubs: Harvard (N.Y.C.); Signet Soc. (Cambridge, Mass.). Office: Travellers Internat, 110 Buckingham Palace Rd, London Sw1 9SA, England

BURNS, RICHARD OWEN, lawyer; b. Bklyn., Nov. 16, 1942; S. James I. and Ida (Shore) B.; m. Lynda Gail Birnbaum, Dec. 24, 1967; children—Marc Adam, Lisa Ann, Susan Danielle. B.S., Wilkes Coll., 1964; J.D., Bklyn. Law Sch., 1967. Bar: N.Y. 1967, U.S. Dist. Ct. (so. dist.) N.Y. 1969, U.S. Dist. Ct. (ea. dist.) N.Y. 1979. Assoc. Clune & O'Brien, Mineola, N.Y., 1967-73, Clune, Burns, White & Nelson, Harrison, N.Y., 1973-78; ptnr. Schurr & Burns, P.C., Spring Valley, N.Y., 1978—. Bd. dirs. Rockland County unit Am. Cancer Soc., West Nyack, N.Y., 1979-85, 86—, pres., 1981-83; bd. dirs. Hudson Valley Health System Agy., Sterling Park, N.Y., 1979, Vets. Meml. Assn., Congers, N.Y., 1980-86. Recipient Reese D. Jones award Wilkes Coll. Jr. C. of C., 1964. Mem. Rockland County Bar Assn., N.Y. State Bar Assn., N.Y. State Trial Lawyers Assn. Democrat. Jewish. Home: 140 Waters Edge Congers NY 10920 Office: Schurr & Burns PC 4 N Main St PO Box 202 Spring Valley NY 10977

BURNS, ROBERT EDWARD, editor, publisher; b. Chgo., May 14, 1919; s. William Joseph and Sara (Foy) B.; m. Brenda Coleman, May 15, 1948; children: Maddy F., Martin J. Student, De Paul U., 1937-39; Ph.B., Loyola U., Chgo., 1941. Pub. relations dir. Cath. Youth Orgn., Chgo., 1943-45, 47-49; exec. dir. No. Ind. region Nat. Conf. Christians and Jews, 1946; exec. editor U.S. Cath. mag.; gen. mgr. Claretian Publs., Chgo., 1949-84. Author: The Examined Life, 1980, Catholics on the Cutting Edge, 1983. Bd. dirs. Thomas More Assn. Home: Route 2 Box 277 #J Montello WI 53949-9802

BURNS, ROBERT MICHAEL, marketing executive; b. Monmouth, Ill., Dec. 8, 1938; s. Robert McNamera and Kathryn (Lutrell) B.; m. Shirley Ann Meyer, May 21, 1963; children: Robin, Robert, Tammy, Amy, Julie, Mark. Student, Knox Coll., 1956, U. Ark., 1957-58; BA, Mo. State U., 1965; postgrad., U. Md., 1973. Pvt. practice gen. agt. 1968-72; v.p. Swift & Co. Ins. Group, Chgo., 1972-77; regional dir. Realty World Corp., Washington, 1977-78; exec. v.p. Ptnrs. Internat., Washington, 1978-80; pres. Breakthru Mktg., Inc., Milw., 1980—; cons. Red Carpet/Guild, San Diego, 1986—; co-founder Strategic Mgmt. Inst., Milw., 1988; bd. dirs. Ptnrs. Internat., Cedar Rapids, Iowa, 1979-81. Author: The Sales Process, 1986; co-author The Psychology of Winning, 1983; inventor computer closed-loop mgmt. system. Served with U.S. Army, 1963-65. Recipient numerous awards for Outstanding Sales, Mktg. and Mgmt. ins., real estate and franchising. Republican. Methodist. Home: 16560 W Nancy Ln Brookfield WI 53005 Office: Breakthru Mktg Services Inc 21675 Doral Rd Waukesha WI 53186

BURNS, SANDRA K., lawyer, educator; b. Bryan, Tex., Aug. 9, 1949; d. Clyde W. and Bert (Rychlik) B.; 1 son, Scott. BS, U. Houston, 1970; MA, U. Tex.-Austin, 1972, PhD, 1975; JD, St. Mary's U., 1978. Bar: Tex. 1978; cert. tchr., adminstr., supr. instrn., Tex. Tchr. Austin (Tex.) Ind. Sch. Dist., 1970-71; prof. child devel./family life and home econs. edn. Coll. Nutrition, Textiles and Human Devel. Tex. Woman's U., Denton, 1974-75; instrnl. devel. asst. Office of Ednl. Resources div. instrnl. devel. U. Tex. Health Sci. San Antonio, 1976-77; legis. aide William T. Moore, Tex. Senate, Austin, fall, 1978, com. clk.-counsel, spring, 1979; legal cons. Colombotti & Assocs., Aberdeen, Scotland, 1980; corp. counsel 1st Internat. Oil and Gas, Inc., 1983; contracted atty. Humble Exploration Co., Inc., Dallas, 1984; assoc. Smith, Underwood, Dallas, 1986-88; sole practice, Dallas, 1988—; atty. contracted to Republic Energy Inc., Bryan, Tex., 1981-82, ARCO, Dallas, 1985; vis. lectr. Tex. A&M U., fall 1981, summer, 1981; lectr. home econ. Our Lady of the Lake Coll., San Antonio, fall, 1975. Mem. ABA, State Bar of Tex., Phi Delta Kappa. Methodist. Contbr. articles on law and edn. to profl. jours. Office: 12126 Forestwood Circle Dallas TX 75244

BURNS, TOM R(EARDEN), sociologist; b. Dallas, Feb. 27, 1937; s. Tom Russell and Vivien (King) B.; m. Inga Elisabeth Kjellberg; children: Nicholas, Hanna. BS in Physics, Stanford U., 1959, MA in Sociology, 1962, PhD in Sociology, 1969. Asst. prof. George Washington U., Washington, 1965-67; asst. prof. U. N.H., Durham, 1968-73, assoc. prof., 1973-76; vis. prof. U. Oslo, Norway, 1975-76, U. Lund, Sweden, 1976-77, U. Stockholm, Sweden, 1978-80; prof. U. Oslo, Norway, 1979-82, Uppsala U., Sweden, 1982—; Robinson Disting. univ. prof. George Mason U., Fairfax, Va., 1987—; co-dir. theory program Swedish Collegium for Advanced Study in Social Sciences, Uppsala, Sweden, 1985—; sr. cons. Scandinavian Inst. for Adminstrv. Research, Lund and Stockholm, Sweden, 1976-82. Author: Work and Power, 1979, Technological Development, 1985, Man, Decisions, Society, 1985, Shaping of Socio-economic Systems, 1986, Shaping of Social Organization, 1987, Creative Democracy, 1988. Mem. AAAS, Internat. Sociol. Assn., Am. Sociol. Assn. Social Democrat. Office: Uppsala U Sociol Inst, PO Box 513, 75120 Uppsala Sweden

BURNSIDE, WALDO HOWARD, department store executive; b. Washington, Nov. 5, 1928; s. Waldo and Eleanor B.; m. Jean Mae Culbert, June 24, 1950; children: Diane Louise, Leslie Ann, Arlene Kay, William Howard. B.S., U. Md., 1949. With Woodward & Lothrop, Washington, 1949-80; divisional mdse. mgr. Woodward & Lothrop, 1957-65, v.p., gen. mdse. mgr., 1965-74, exec. v.p., 1974-78, pres., 1978-80; also dir.; vice chmn., chief operating officer Carter Hawley Hale Stores, Inc., Los Angeles, 1980-83, pres., chief operating officer, 1983—; dir. Security Pacific Corp. Trustee Md. Ednl. Found.; trustee St. John's Hosp. and Health Ctr. Found.; trustee, past chmn. U. Md. Alumni Internat. Mem. Ind. Colls. So. Calif. (bd. dirs.), Los Angeles Area C. of C. (bd. dirs.), Automobile Club So. Calif. (bd. dirs.), Phi Kappa Phi, Sigma Chi. Episcopalian. Clubs: California, Los Angeles Country, N.Y. Athletic. Office: Carter Hawley Hale Stores Inc 550 S Flower St Los Angeles CA 90071

BURNTON, STANLEY JEFFREY, barrister; b. London, Oct. 25, 1942; s. Harry and Fay (Levy) B.; m. Gwenyth Frances Castle; children: Abigail, Simon, Rebecca. MA, U. Oxford, 1964. Office: 1 Essex Court Temple, London EC4Y 9AR, England

BURPEE, JON CHARLES, ophthalmologist; b. Alexandria, Va., Nov. 14, 1941; s. William and Margaret Jane (Evans) B; m. Jean Louise Davis, Aug. 22, 1964; children—John Evans, Mark Davis, Heather Jean. B.A. in Biology cum laude, Whitman Coll., 1964; M.D. cum laude, U. Oreg., 1968. Diplomate Am. Bd. Ophthalmology. Intern Fitzsimons Army Hosp., Denver, 1968-69, resident in ophthalmology, 1969-72; practice medicine specializing in ophthalmology, Roseburg, Oreg., 1975—; mem. staff Mercy Med. Ctr., Roseburg, 1975—, sec. staff, 1980, v.p. staff, 1981, chief staff, 1982. Bd. dirs., safety chmn. Oregon Trail council Boy Scouts Am., 1983-86, chmn. Douglas Fir dist., 1984-86. Served to maj. M.C., U.S. Army, 1967-75. Paul Harris fellow, 1982. Mem. Am. Acad. Ophthalmology, AMA, Oreg. Med. Assn., Oreg. Acad. Ophthalmology, Order of Wailatpu, Phi Beta Kappa, Alpha Omega Alpha, Beta Theta Pi. Republican. Episcopalian. Lodge: Rotary (bd. dirs. Roseburg 1978-80, pres. 1981). Home: 1435 Quail Ln Roseburg OR 97470 Office: Mercy Med Ctr 341 Medical Loop Roseburg OR 97470

BURR, RICHARD MARSHALL, municipal government administrator; b. Woodbury, N.J., Apr. 22, 1943; s. Samuel Marshall and Erna Louise (Fierke) B.; m. Janet Eileen Enzman, Apr. 10, 1976; children—Sarah Elizabeth, Richard Marshall. B.S., Phila. Coll. Pharmacy and Sci., 1966; M.S., U. Del., 1968; postgrad. U. Mont., 1968-69, Utah State U., 1968-73. Registered mcpl. clk., cert. mcpl. fin. officer, N.J. Treas., Borough of Westville, N.J., 1976—, borough clk., 1980—, registrar vital stats.; 1980—, borough adminstr., 1983—; certifying agt. for state pension systems, hospital service plan of N.J., 1977—. Contbr. articles to hist. and ornithol. publs. Treas., Westville Bd. Edn., 1977—, mem. vocat. edn. adv. com., 1984; coordinator United Way, 1983—; chmn. Salvation Army, 1980—; asst. librarian Genealogy Br. Library, Cherry Hill, N.J., 1983—; mem. Westville Plan Bd., 1979. Commr., sec. Westville Environ. Comm., 1987; active Westville Emergency Mgmt. Council, 1987—. Research fellow, U. Del., 1966-68, U. Mont., 1968-69. Mem. N.J. Mcpl. Fin. Officers Assn. (exec. bd. 1983—, 2d v.p. 1984, 1st v.p. 1985—, pres. 1987—), Gov. Fin. Officers Assn., Descendants the Family Bruce in Am., Townsend Family Assn., Wychoff Family Assn. (N.J. state registrar, 1987—), Flagon and Trencher (Descendents of Colonial Tavern Keepers), The Baronial Order of the Magna Charta, The Descendants of the Founders of Hartford, Descendants of Founders of N.J., Tax Collectors and Treasurers Assn. N.J., Tri-County Assn. Tax Collectors and Treasurers (v.p. 1981-82), Mcpl. Clks. Assn. N.J., Gloucester County Mcpl. Clks. Assn., Internat. Inst. Mcpl. Clks., N.J. State Police Office of Emergency Mgmt., N.J. Mcpl. Mgrs. Assn., Gloucester County Hist. Soc. (bull. editor 1981-87, trustee 1981—, membership chmn. 1987—), SAR (v.p. Haddonfield, N.J. 1983-84, pres. 1985-87 N.J. bd. mgrs. 1987—), Genealogy Soc. Pa., Westville Republican Club (treas. 1978—), Westville Concerned Citizens (environ. com.), Alpha Zeta, Alpha Phi Omega. Mormon. Lodge: Rotary (v.p. 1984-86, pres. 1986-87, RYLA chmn. 1987—). Home: 222 Elm St Westville NJ 08093 Office: Borough of Westville 114 Crown Point Rd Westville NJ 08093

BURRELL, CRAIG DONALD, physician, educator; b. Gravesend, Kent, Eng., July 5, 1926; came to U.S., 1960, naturalized, 1968; m. Mary Elizabeth Granger, 1960; children—Catherine, Sarah, Craig, Walter, David. M.B., B.Surgery, U. N.Z., 1951; D.Sc. (hon.), Ricker Coll., 1975; LL.D. (hon.), Union Coll., 1975. Rotating intern Wellington (N.Z.) Hosp., 1951-52; locum sr. house officer pediatrics Nottingham (Eng.) Children's Hosp., 1953; house physician gen. medicine and endocrinology Hammersmith Hosp. and Royal Postgrad. Med. Sch. Gt. Britain, London, 1954; sr. house officer endocrinology Hammersmith Hosp. and Royal Postgrad. Med. Sch. Gt. Britain, 1954-56; registrar gen. medicine Royal Infirmary and Welsh Nat. Sch. Medicine, Cardiff, Wales, 1957-60; asst. prof. medicine and medicine in psychiatry Cornell U. Med. Sch., 1960-61; dir. clin. labs. Payne Whitney Psychiat. Clinic, 1960-61; with Sandoz Pharms., Inc., East Hanover, N.J., 1961-72; v.p. med. affairs Sandoz Pharms., Inc., 1969-72; v.p., dir. external affairs Sandoz, Inc., East Hanover, 1973-85, Sandoz Corp., N.Y.C., 1985—; asst. attending physician Cornell 2d Div., Bellevue Hosp., 1966-68; clin. asso. prof. medicine Coll. Medicine and Dentistry N.J., Newark, 1968—; clin. prof. dept. community and family medicine U. Calif.-San Diego Sch. Medicine, 1982—; participant numerous internat. profl. confs.; mem. tech. com. White House Conf. on Aging, 1980-81. Mem. editorial bd.: Internat Jour. of Addictions; editor: Drug Assessment in Ferment, 1976, Primary Health Care in Industrialized Nations, 1978, Second Colloquium in Biol. Scis., 1986, Medical Journalism, 1987; contbr. articles to profl. jours. Vice pres. Sandoz Found.; trustee Union Coll. of Ky., Essex County Coll., N.J.; bd regents St. Peter's Coll., N.J. Fellow Am. Sch. Health Assn. (hon.), N.Y. Acad. Scis. (pres. 1984), Royal Soc. Medicine, Am. Sch. Health Assn. (hon.); mem. AAAS, Am. Coll. Clin. Pharmacology and Therapeutics, A.M.A., Endocrine Soc., European Soc. for Study Drug Toxicity, Sierra Club, Delaware County (N.Y.), Conservation Assn. Presbyterian (elder). Office: Sandoz Corp 608 Fifth Ave New York NY 10020

BURRELL, DONALD JAMES, photofinishing company executive; b. Gary, Ind., Oct. 31, 1936; s. Frank and Anna (Bonko) B.; m. Alice M. Shema, Oct. 3, 1959; children—John J., James A., Mary A., Robert M., Donna M. Cert. profl. photographer N.Y. Inst. Photography, 1958. Photographer, Spasoff Studio, Gary, 1956-57; indsl. photographer Rockwell Internat., East Chicago, Ind., 1957-59; owner DNJ Color Lab., Gary, 1959-69; gen. mgr. KMS Industries, Ann Arbor, Mich., 1969-73; owner Burrell Colour Inc., Crown Point, Ind., 1973—; owner, cons. mgr. D & S Color Inc., Bradenton, Fla., 1980—; owner, Sound Color Corp., Edmonds, Wash.; bd. dirs. Citizens Fed., Hammond, Ind. Bd. dirs. St. Anthony Hosp., Crown Point, 1970-78; mem. lay adv. bd. St. Matthias Catholic Ch., Crown Point, 1975-78. Recipient outstanding photography award Profl. Photographers Assn., 1959. Mem. Assn. Profl. Color Labs. (founder, pres. 1970-71), Photo Mktg. Assn. (trustee, pres.), Profl. Photographers Am., Crown Point C. of C. (dir. 1967-69). Lodge: Rotary (Crown Point). Office: Burrell Colour Inc 1311 Merrillville Rd Crown Point IN 46307

BURRELL, MICHAEL PHILIP, actor, writer; b. Harrow, Eng., May 12, 1937; s. Frederick Albert and Dora Edith (Jones) B.; B.A., Peterhouse, Cambridge U., 1961, M.A., 1965. Mem. Royal Shakespeare Co., 1961-64; dir. King's Lynn Festival, 1965, Chichester Festival Co., 1966, 68; asso. dir. Royal Lyceum Theatre, Edinburgh, Scotland, 1966-68, Derby Playhouse, 1974-76; dir. Wells Centre Ltd., 1982-86; chmn. KBE Ltd., 1983—; star theatrical prodn. Hess, London, 1978, N.Y.C., 1979. Stage appearances in 35 countries and numerous TV appearances, 1963—. Author: (plays) Hess, 1978 (TV adaptation, lead player, Bronze award N.Y. Film Festival 1986, Capital Critics citation as best actor, Ottawa, 1986), Love Among the Butterflies, 1984, Borrowing Time, 1986. Served with Brit. Army, 1956-58. Recipient Obie award, 1980; best actor and best show awards Edmonton Theatre Festival, Can., 1984; best actor award for Burrell on the Bard, Edmonton, 1985. Office: care Internat Artistes Ltd, 235 Regent St, London W1R 8AX, England

BURRI, RENE R., photographer, filmmaker; b. Zurich, Switzerland, Apr. 9, 1933; s. Rudolphe and Berta (Haas) B.; m. Rosellina H. Bischof, Dec. 18, 1963; children: Yasmine, Oliver. Diploma, Kunstgewerbeschule, Zurich. Free-lance photojournalist for various publs., including Life, Look, Paris, Match, Stern, Fortune, Epoca, Geo; pres. Europe, Magnum Photos, Paris, N.Y.C. One-man shows: Galene Form, 1965, Art Inst. Chgo., 1967, Galene Rencontre, Paris, 1971, Raffi Photo Gallery, N.Y.C., 1972, Galleria Diaframina, Milan, Italy, 1972, Mus. Folkwang, Essen, Germany, 1980, Galerie Kicken, Cologne, Germany, 1981, Stedelijk Mus., Amsterdam, Netherlands, 1982, Kunsthaus, Zurich, 1984, Musée d'Art Modern, Paris, 1984; represented in permanent collections: Mus. Modern Art, N.Y.C., Kunsthaus, Zurich, Art Inst. Chgo., Folkwang Mus., Essen, Bibliothèque Nationale, Paris, Internat. Ctr. Photography, Rochester, N.Y.; films include: Zurich Art School, 1953, The Two Faces of China, 1965, After the Six-Day War, 1967, Braccia Si-uomini no!, 1967, What's it all About, 1967, The Great Team, 1967, Indian Summer, 1971, French Wine, 1973. Recipient Internat. Film and TV Festival award, N.Y., 1967. Office: Magnum Photos, 20 rue des Grands Augustins, 75006 Paris France *

BURRIDGE, ROBERT, former mathematics educator, scientific consultant; b. Essex, Eng., Dec. 6, 1937; came to U.S., 1971; s. Sydney Stanmore and Phebe Mercy (Raven) B.; B.A. (Major scholar King's Coll.), U. Cambridge, 1959, M.A., 1962, Ph.D., 1963, Sc.D., 1980; m. Elizabeth Nelson Bingham, Sept. 22, 1962 (dec.); children—Rosalind, Lucinda, Robert; m. Marylyn Louise Sexton, Aug. 29, 1987. Research fellow Calif. Inst. Tech., Pasadena, 1963-64; research geophysicist UCLA, 1964-65; asst. lectr. U. Cambridge, 1965-67; research fellow U.K. Atomic Energy Authority, 1967-71; fellow King's Coll., Cambridge, 1965-71; assoc. prof. math. NYU, N.Y.C., 1971-75, prof., 1975-86; sci. cons. Schlumberger-Doll Research Ctr., Ridgefield, Conn., 1986—; cons. seismic studies, fracture phenomena and exploration geophysics. Recipient Adams prize in math. U. Cambridge, 1971; NSF research contract in earthquake mechanism studies, 1971—. Fellow Cambridge Philos. Soc., Explorers Club; mem. Am. Geophys. Union, Seismol. Soc. Am., Soc. Exploration Geophysicists. Mem. editorial bd. Soc. Indsl. and Applied Math., Wave Motion (Internat.); contbr. papers on applied math., theoretical seismology and wave propagation to tech. jours. Home: 15 Rockwell Rd Ridgefield CT 06877 Office: Schlumberger-Doll Research Ctr Old Quarry Rd Ridgefield CT 06877

BURROUGHS, JOHN TOWNSEND, lawyer; b. Akron, Ohio, May 27, 1926; s. Ralph and Helen (Townsend) B.; m. Laverne Casey, Nov. 23, 1966; 1 child, Brien C. BA cum laude, Brown U., 1946; MD, Harvard U., 1950; JD with honors, Calif. Western Sch. Law, 1978. Bar: Calif. 1979, U.S. Ct. Claims 1979, U.S. Dist. Ct. (ea. dist.) Wis. 1981, Wis. 1982, U.S. Dist. Ct. (cen. dist.) Calif. 1982; diplomate Am. Bd. Surgery, Am. Bd. Thoracic Surgery; lic. surgeon Calif., Wis. 1982, Colo. 1986, La. Intern, then resident Johns Hopkins Hosp., Balt., 1950-52; fellow Mayo Clinic, Rochester, Minn., 1954-56; resident in surgery UCLA Med. Ctr., 1956-58, asst. in surgery, 1958-59; asst. prof. dept. surgery UCLA Med. Sch., 1959-63; practice medicine specializing in thoracic and cardiovascular surgery Los Angeles, 1961-72; practice medicine specializing in thoracic, cardiovascular and coronary bypass surgery Milw., 1972-75, Baton Rouge, 1975-76; staff, chief med. legal research div. dept. legal medicine Armed Forces Inst. Pathology, Washington, 1979-82; ptnr. Joling, Rizzo, Willems, Oleniewski, Stern & Burroughs, S.C., Kenosha, Wis., 1982-85; sole practice Salem, Wis., 1985-88, San Diego, 1988—; vis. surgeon in cardiovascular surgery U. Free Berlin, 1959; asst. prof. dept. surgery UCLA Med. Sch., 1960-63; clin. assoc. prof. U. Calif., Irvine, 1963-72; adj. prof. law Antioch Sch., Washington, 1980; chief sect. thoracic surgery VA Hosp., Los Angeles, 1959-63; lectr. on law and medicine, 1979—. Contbr. articles to profl. jours. Chmn. Edn. com. Inglewood C. of C., 1968-69, chmn. drug com., 1969-71, bd. dirs. 1970-72; chmn. CPR Tng. Milw. Heart Assn., 1972-74, Community Programs Council, Inglewood, 1970-72, southwestern br. Los Angeles County Heart Assn., 1968-70, CPR Tng. Progam, Los Angeles Heart Assn., 1969-72; med. dir. Program in Inglewood Unified Sch. Dist. on Narcotics and Smoking, 1968-72, Narcotics edn. dist atty.'s advisory council, Los Angeles, 1968-70; trustee Centinela Valley Community Hosp., 1971-72; bd. dirs. Associated Centinela Services, 1971-72. Served to lt. M.C., USNR, 1952-54. Recipient Award of Merit Los Angeles County Heart Assn., 1967-70, Heart Recognition award Los Angeles County Heart Assn., 1971, Disting. Service award Los Angeles County Heart Assn., 1972, Cert. Commendation Los Angeles County, 1972, Cert. Merit Inglewood Unified Sch. Dist., 1969. Fellow Am. Coll. Surgeons, Am. Coll. Cardiology, Am. Coll. Legal Medicine, Am. Acad. Forensic Scis.; mem. ABA, Calif. Bar Assn., Wis. Bar Assn., Assn. Trial Lawyers Am., Soc. Thoracic Surgeons (founding), Am. Coll. Chest Physicians, Am. Bd. Law in Medicine (diplomate), Am. Bd. Profl. Liability Attys. (diplomate), Am. Trauma Soc. (founding), Sigma Xi.

BURROUGHS, WALTER LAUGHLIN, journalist, editor, publisher; b. Bridgewater, S.D., Aug. 21, 1901; s. William S. and Bertha (Laughlin) B.; m. Hazel Georgia Sexsmith, June 1, 1925 (dec. Oct. 1970); 1 child, Toni (Mrs. Philip Schuyler Doane); m. Lucy Bell, Feb. 28, 1972. BA, U. Wash., 1924; postgrad., U. Calif., Berkeley, 1925-28. Dir. publs. U. Calif., Berkeley, 1925-28; gen. mgr. North Pacific Gravure Co., Seattle, 1928-30; gen. mgr. Crocker Union Lithograph and Pub. Co., Los Angeles, 1930-41; co-founder Bantam Books, Los Angeles, 1938; ind. book pub. with Merle Armitage, 1938-42; Pacific coast rep. H.W. Kaster & Sons, Los Angeles, 1941-42; exec. v.p. Eldon Industries Los Angeles, 1946-62; corp. pres., pub. Orange Coast Daily Pilot, Newport Beach, Costa Mesa, Huntington Beach, Calif., 1948-65, chmn. bd., 1965-68; pres. Orion Mgmt. Corp. Chmn. bd. dirs. emeritus Children's Hosp. Orange County; trustee Jefferson Trust, Western World Med. Found., Irvine, Calif.; active Ctr. for the Performing Arts. Served to col. U.S. Army, 1942-45. Honored (with late E.J. Power) for role in bringing U. Calif. to Irvine with dedication of Founders Ct. on campus, 1978. Mem. Soc. Profl. Journalists, Sigma Delta Chi (nat. pres.). Clubs: Bohemian (San Francisco); Jonathan (Los Angeles); Newport Harbor Yacht, Newport Beach Country; Center (Costa Rica); Nat. Press (Washington). Lodge: Rotary.

Home: 260 Cagney Ln Apt 313 Newport Beach CA 92663 Office: 1670 Westminster Ave Costa Mesa CA 92627

BURROWAY, EDWARD CHARLES, technical service engineer; b. Pitts., May 29, 1947; s. William Madison and Louise Elizabeth (Shields) B.; m. Joanne Marie Gillner, June 3, 1972, 1 child, Alicia Lynn. Grad. high sch., Etna, Pa. Prodn. worker Inmont Corp., Pitts., 1968-70, lab. technician, 1970-74, prodn. mgr., 1974-84; tech. service engr. United Techs.-Inmont, Strongsville, Ohio, 1984-86, BASF-Inmont, 1986—. Served to lance cpl. USMC, 1966-68. Republican. Methodist. Home: 41 Washington St Pittsburgh PA 15223

BURROWS, EVA EVELYN, civic organization administrator; b. Newcastle, Australia, Sept. 15, 1929; d. Robert John and Ella Maria (Watson) B. BA, Queensland U., 1950; postgrad. cert. in edn., U. London, 1952; MEd, Sydney U., Australia, 1959; PhD (hon.), EWHA Woman's U., Seoul, Korea, 1988. Missionary educator Howard Inst., Zimbabwe, 1952-67; prin. Usher Inst., Zimbabwe, 1967-69; vice prin. Internat. Coll. for Officers, London, 1970-73, prin., 1974-75; leader Women's Social Services of Great Britain and Ireland, 1975-77; territorial comdr. Salvation Army, Sri Lanka, 1977-79, Scotland, 1979-82, Australia, 1982-86; Gen. (Internat. Leader) The Salvation Army, London, 1986—. Named Officer Order of Australia, 1986. Office: Salvation Army Internat Hdqrs, 101 Queen Victoria St, Box 249, London EC4P 4EP, England

BURROWS, ROBERT ALLEN, business development and infosystems specialist; b. Bracebridge, Ont., Can., July 7, 1954; s. Robert Keith and Norma M. (Small) B. BS in Elec. Engring., U. Waterloo, Can., 1978; MS in Bus. Mgmt., MIT, 1982. Design engr. Prime Computer, Natick, Mass., 1978-80, bus. devel. assoc., 1981-82; bus. devel. analyst Motorola Info. Systems, Mansfield, Mass., 1982-84; dir. bus. devel. Motorola Info. Systems, Brampton, Ont., 1984—. Office: Motorola Info Systems, 9445 Airport Rd, Brampton, ON Canada L6S 4J3

BURRY, WILLIAM CHARLES, physician, surgeon; b. Pitts., Aug. 9, 1911; s. Edward John and Ada Elizabeth (Simon) B.; m. Virginia Price Swaine, Oct. 26, 1940; children—William Charles III, Ronald Swaine, James Richard. B.A., Pa. State U., 1933; postgrad. U. Ariz., 1934, U. Pitts., 1935; M.D., Jefferson Med. Coll., 1939; grad. Army War Coll., 1958. Intern, Allegheny Gen. Hosp., Pitts., 1939-40; resident in surgery Gorgas Gen. Hosp., Ancon, Canal Zone, 1948-50; commd. 1st lt., M.C., U.S. Army, 1940, advanced through grades to col., 1950; dir. office sci. Dept. Def., Washington, 1950-57; surgeon USEUCOM, Paris, 1958-61; surgeon, comdr. USA Hosp., West Berlin, 1967-70; ret., 1970; med. dir. Tobyhanna Army Depot, Pa., 1972-77; staff mem. Pocono Med. Ctr., East Stroudsburg, Pa., 1979—; mem Speakers Bur., Pocono Med. Ctr., East Stroudsburg, 1985—; chief sch. physician Pocono Mountain Sch. Dist., 1981-86; cons. sports medicine, hosp. adminstrn., Mountainhome, Pa., 1981—. Mem. med. exec. com. Pocono Hosp., 1979-84; v.p. Monroe County Mus. Assn., 1984—; bd. dirs. Monroe County Hist. Soc., 1984—; chmn. adminstrv. bd. Methodist Ch., Mountainhome, 1980-83; mem. planning com. arts and museum, 1973-75; mem. physicians' review com. Monroe County Nursing Homes, 1980—; med. cons. to planning bd. Army Retirement Found., Fort Belvoir, Va. Decorated Bronze Star, Legion of Merit with oak leaf cluster, Army Commendation medal, European medal (four battle stars), Vietnam Service medal (1 star). Fellow Chgo. Surg. Soc., Phila. Coll. Physicians; mem. Ret. Officers Assn. (pres. chpt. 1975), Monroe County Med. Soc. (pres. 1984-86, mem. exec. com.), Sigma Pi, Alpha Kappa Kappa, Alpha Omega Alpha, AMA. Republican. Lodges: Masons, Shriners. Avocations: Music; photography; history; genealogy; golf; model railroading. Home: PO Box 240 Mountainhome PA 18342

BURSAC, ELLEN, literary translator; b. Boston, July 27, 1952; d. Peter and Marjorie (Forbes) Elias; m. Milorad Bursac, Feb. 23, 1974; children: Sara, Rachel. BA, Macalester Coll., 1973, Zagreb U., Yugoslavia, 1978. With Assn. of Lit. Translators of Croatia, Zagreb, 1979—; cons. Assn. Colls. of the Midwest, Chgo., 1979—. Contbr. articles to profl. jours. Mem. Soc. Lit. Translators of Croatia, Community of Freelance Artists of Croatia. Home and Office: Aleja V Popovica 5/70, Zagreb Yugoslavia 41020

BURSLEY, GILBERT EVERETTE, former college president, former state senator, former army officer; b. Ann Arbor, Mich., Feb. 28, 1913; s. Philip Everett and Flora (Peters) B.; m. Vivette Mumtaz, Jan. 15, 1949; 1 son, Philip. A.B., U. Mich., 1934; M.B.A., Harvard U., 1936; postgrad. in internat. relations George Washington U., 1953-54. Commd. 1st lt. U.S. Army, 1940, advanced through grades to lt. col., 1954; mil. attache, Istanbul, Turkey, 1946-49; with Joint U.S. Mil. Missions, Athens, 1949-52, UN Truce Supervision Orgn., Palestine, sr. mil. advisor Israel-Jordon and Israel-Egypt Mixed Armistice Commns., 1954; Am. consul, pub. affairs officer in charge USIA program, Belgian Congo, French Equatorial Africa, Ruanda, Urundi, Cameroons, Angola, 1955-57; cons. World Wide Broadcasting Found., 1957; asst. dir. U. Mich. Devel. Council, 1957-64; mem. U.S. Trade and Investment Mission to Cameroons and Ivory Coast, 1968; pres. Cleary Coll., Ypsilanti, Mich., 1978-83, chancellor, 1984, trustee, 1985—, pres. and chancellor emeritus, 1985—, vis. prof., 1988. Adviser policy com. Nat. Assessment Edn. Progress, 1976-83, Mich. Higher Edn. Capital Investment, 1980, Fund for Improvement Postsecondary Edn., 1976-79; mem. Interstate Migrant Edn. Task Force, 1976-81; mem. Edn. Commn. of States, 1973-85; chmn. Mich. Edn. Council, 1973-79; mem. Mich. Bicentennial Commn., 1976; mem. Mich. Ho. of Reps., 1960-64; mem. Mich. Senate, 1964-78, asst. pres. pro tem, 1974-78, asst. majority leader, 1970-74, also chmn. 15 legis. coms.; pres. Mich. Internat. Council, 1978-80; chmn. Mich. UN Day, 1970-80; bd. dirs. Mich. Artrain, 1974-83, Washtenaw County Hospice, 1980, Ann Arbor Citizens Council, Mich. Council on Arts; chmn. Mich. Vocat. Edn. Task Force, 1980; pres. Gulf Pines Home Owners Assn., Sanibel, 1984-85. Recipient award of merit Mich. Agrl. Conf., 1968; commendation Mich. Senate, 1973, 85; Disting. Service award Assn. Ind. Colls. and Univs. in Mich., 1976, Edn. Commn. of States, 1978; Ednl. Leadership award Mich. Assn. Elem. Prins., 1978. Mem. Mich. Hist. Soc., Mich. Soc. Mayflower Descs. (gov. 1965-71), SAR (past pres. Washtenaw chpt.), Sanibel Com. of The Islands (pres. 1984-85), Fgn. Policy Assn., Ann Arbor C. of C. (legis. com. 1982-85, Disting Service award 1978), VFW, Am. Legion, Soc. Am. Magicians. Republican. Episcopalian. Clubs: Harvard Bus. Sch., Economic (Detroit); U. Mich. Alumni, Ann Arbor. Lodge: Rotary (Paul Harris fellow). Contbr. articles on edn. and fgn. commerce to profl. publs. Home: 2065 Geddes Ave Ann Arbor MI 48104 also: 900 Snowberry Ln Sanibel FL 33957 Office: 2107 Washtenaw Ave Ypsilanti MI 48197

BURSNALL, PAUL, sales executive, consultant; b. Hayes, Middlesex, Eng., Mar. 17, 1948; s. George Herbert and Vera Lillian (Goddard) B.; m. Linda Gaye Williams, July 26, 1975; children: James, Thomas. Tech. cert., Southall (Eng.) Tech. Sch.; diploma, Slough (Eng.) Coll. Toolmaker Alston Tool & Gauge Co., West Drayton, Eng., 1964-69; project engr. Superflexit Ltd., Slough, 1970-79; standards engr. M. L. Aviation, Maidenhead, Eng., 1979-80; sales engr. Exem Lighting, Crewkerne, Eng., 1980-84, mgr. sales and adminstr., 1986—; area sales mgr. Victor Products, Newcastle, Eng., 1984-86; sales exec. Fliteline, Ltd., Slough, 1986—. Inventor isoclip tooling. Sec. Cippenham ward br. Conservative Party, 1986-87; bd. dirs. East Berkshire (Eng.) Health Authority, 1984. Mem. Inst. Engring. Designers, Inst. Technician Engrs., Brit. Triathlon Assn., Brit. Standards Inst. Mem. Ch. of England. Office: Celab-Exem, Woolmer Way, Bordon, Hampshire England

BURSSENS, ADOLF, orthopedist; b. Keerbergen, Belgium, Jan. 9, 1930; d. Walter Frans Louisa and Maria Francisca Margareta (Van Eynde) B.; m. Josephine Boets, Sept. 25, 1951; children: Rudiger, Werner, Godelieve, Gerda, Anne-Marie, Carla, Frank. MD, Cath. U. Leuven, Belgium, 1956. Practice medicine specializing in orthopedics 1956—; lectr. Cath. U. Leuven, 1986. Contbg. author: Nederlands Leerboek der Orthopedic, 1977, Tumor Prosthesis for Bone and Joint Reconstruction, 1983. Served to lt. col. Belgian Army, 1956-58. Mem. Belgische Vereniging Voor Orthopedie, N.Y. Acad. Scis. Roman Catholic. Home: 11 Oudebaan, 3010 Wilsele Belgium Office: Dept Orthopaedics, Weligerveld 1, 3041 Pellenberg-Lubbeek Belgium

BURSTALL, CLARE, research institute director; b. Rochester, Eng., Sept. 3, 1931; d. Alfred and Lily (Humphrys) Wells; m. Michael Lyle Burstall, Sept. 24, 1955 (div. 1977); children: Frances Everett, Lindsay Clare. BA with honors in French, U. London, 1953, BA with honors in psychology, 1963, PhD in Psychology, 1973; DSc (hon.), U. Hull, Eng., 1988. Project leader Nat. Found. Ednl. Research, Slough, Berkshire, Eng., 1964-68; sr. research officer Nat. Found. Ednl. Research, Slough, 5, Eng., 1968-72, dep. dir., 1972-83, dir., 1983—. Author: French from Eight: A National Experiment, 1968, French in the Primary School: Attitudes and Achievement, 1970, Primary French in the Balance, 1974; contbr. articles to jours. Fellow Brit. Psychol. Soc., Coll. of Preceptors (hon.); mem. Am. Ednl. Research Assn. Club: Royal Over-Seas League. Home: Flat 2, 26 Lennox Gardens, London SW1X ODQ England Office: Nat Found Ednl Research, The Mere, Upton Park SL1 2DQ, Berkshire England

BURSTEIN, STEPHEN DAVID, neurosurgeon; b. Bklyn., Apr. 10, 1934; s. Moe and Anna (Bloch) B.; m. Ronnie Sue Deutsch, Oct. 8, 1972; 1 dau., Alissa Aimee. B.A. with distinction, U. Mich., 1954; M.D., SUNY-Bklyn., 1958; M.S. in Neurosurgery, U. Minn.-Rochester, 1965. Diplomate Am. Bd. Neurol. Surgery. Surg. intern Johns Hopkins Hosp., Balt., 1958-59; neurosurgery fellow Mayo Clinic, Rochester, 1961-65; chief dept. neurosurgery South Nassau Community Hosp., Oceanside, N.Y., 1980—, pres. med. staff, 1980-82; chief dept. neurosurgery Franklin Gen. Hosp., Valley Stream, N.Y., 1980—; prin. Neurol. Surgery & Neurology, P.C., Freeport, N.Y., 1965—. Contbr. articles to med. jours. Bd. dirs. South Nassau Community Hosp., 1978—. Served to lt. USNR, 1959-61. Recipient Neurosurg. Travel award Mayo Found., 1966. Fellow ACS; mem. L.I. Hearing and Speech Soc. (bd. dirs.), N.Y. State Neurosurgeons Soc. (bd. dirs.), N.Y. State Neurosurg. Soc. (pres. 1981-82), Sigma Xi, Alpha Omega Alpha. Hebrew. Avocations: theatre; travel. Home: 19 Bridle Path Roslyn NY 11576 Office: Neurol Surgery & Neurology 88 S Bergen Pl Freeport NY 11520

BURSTON, RICHARD MERVIN, business executive; b. Brookline, Mass., Oct. 31, 1924; s. Mark and Anita (Andrews) B.; m. Phoebe Harvey Hopkins, Aug. 29, 1958; children—Abby Lyn, Seth Hopkins, Joshua Craig, Mark Andrews, Amanda Lee. B.A., Bowdoin Coll., 1949; M.B.A., Harvard U., 1952. Mgr. beauty dept. Kendall Co., Boston, 1953-58; regional sales mgr. M. Pier Co., Ft. Lauderdale, Fla., 1958-59; nat. sales mgr. Ozon Products, Inc., Bklyn., 1959-63; v.p., co-founder Burston/Larkin Assocs., Stamford, Conn., 1964—; pres., chief exec. officer Excalibur, Inc., Stamford, 1981—; founder, pres. Burston Inc., Stamford, 1987—; dir. Nat. Beauty and Barber Reps. Assn., N.Y.C., 1973-74, Louv Yacht Yard, Norwalk, Conn., 1969-73; cons. Ruckel Mfg., Inc., N.Y.C., 1969-87. Dir. Roxbury Babe Ruth, Stamford, 1969-85; pres., dir. Roxbury-Riverbank Little League, Stamford, 1971-82; trustee Miramichi Rod & Gun Club, Lyttleton, New Brunswick, Can., 1980—; fund raiser Bowdoin Coll., Brunswick, Maine, 1984—. Served to lt. USNR, 1943-46, PTO. Recipient Man of Yr. award United Beauty Supply Corp., Bridgeport, Conn., 1983. Mem. Beauty and Barber Supply Inst., Am. Beauty Assn. Republican. Jewish. Clubs: Landmark, North Stamford Exchange (dir. 1984-86), Miramichi Rod & Gun, Bowdoin (Southwest Conn.); Spartan. Lodge: Masons. Avocations: fly fishing; sailing, commemorative plates, oriental rugs. Home: 156 Riverbank Dr Stamford CT 06903 Office: Burston Inc 300 Broad St #804 Stamford CT 06901

BURT, DAVID LYNDON, finance company executive; b. London, Jan. 13, 1930; s. R. Frederick and Wanda E.M. (Porter) B.; m. Prunella M. Antrobus; children: Nicola K., Lyndon. Grad. high sch., Kent, Eng. Mng. dir. Ross Taylor NVK, Indonesia, 1953-55, Wilson, Smithett and Cope, Ltd., London, 1956-87, Burt Taylor and Co., Ltd., London, 1966-85, Lewis and Peat Ltd., London, 1972-85; dep. chmn. Guiness Peat Ltd., London, 1975-82. Mem. Lloyds of London. Club: Cavalry. Home: Silton, Peaslake, Surrey G45 9SR, England

BURT, JEFFREY AMSTERDAM, lawyer; b. Phila., Apr. 27, 1944; s. Samuel Matthew and Esther (Amsterdam) B.; m. Sandra Cass, Dec. 17, 1967; children—Stephen, Daniel, Jonathan, Andrew. B.A., Princeton U., 1966; LL.B., Yale U., 1970, M.A. in Econs., 1970. Bar: Md. 1971, D.C. 1971. Law clk. to judge U.S. Ct. Appeals (4th cir.), Balt., 1970-71; assoc. firm Arnold & Porter, Washington, 1971-77, ptnr., 1978—; adj. prof. law Georgetown U.; faculty Internat. Law Inst.; frequent lectr. Pres., Green Acres, Inc., Ind. Sch., Rockville, Md., 1984. Author: (with others) International Joint Ventures, 1986. Office: Arnold & Porter 1200 New Hampshire Ave NW Washington DC 20036

BURT, RICHARD REEVES, ambassador; b. Sewell, Chile, Feb. 3, 1947; s. Wayne and Dorothy Burt; m. Gahl Lee Hodges, Jan. 2, 1985. BA, Cornell U., 1969; MA, Fletcher Sch. Law and Diplomacy, 1972. Former research assoc., then asst. dir. Internat. Inst. for Strategic Studies, London; dir. Bur. Politico-Mil. Affairs Dept. State, Washington, 1981-82, asst. sec. state for European and Can. affairs, 1982-85; ambassador to Fed. Republic Germany Bonn, 1985—. Mem. Council on Fgn. Relations. Republican.

BURTIS, THEODORE ALFRED, oil company executive; b. Jamaica, N.Y., May 17, 1922; s. Theodore Alfred and Florence Angela (Whalen) B.; m. Billie Joyce King, June 2, 1945; children: Barbara, Theodore, Pamela. B.S., Carnegie Inst. Tech., 1942; M.Sc., Tex. A&M Coll., 1946; D.Sc., Ursinus Coll., 1972, Villanova U., 1981; LL.D., Widener U., 1983. With Magnolia Petroleum Co., 1943-45, Owens-Corning Fiberglass Corp., 1946-47; with Houdry Process Corp., Phila., 1947—, pres., 1956-62, chmn., pres.; v.p. Air Products & Chems. Inc., 1962-67; dir. comml. devel. Sun Co. Inc., Radnor, Pa., 1967-68, adminstrv. dir. research and engring., 1969-70, v.p. research and devel., 1970-72, v.p. mktg., 1970-72, pres. products group, 1974-75, exec. v.p., 1975—, pres., 1976—, chief exec. officer, 1978-85, chmn. bd., 1979-86, now bd. dirs. Fellow Am. Inst. Chem. Engrs. (pres. 1967); mem. Am. Chem. Soc., Kappa Sigma, Tau Beta Pi. Clubs: Union League (Phila.); Philadelphia Country (Gladwyne, Pa.). Office: Sun Co Inc 100 Matsonford Rd Radnor PA 19087

BURTON, AL, producer, director, writer; b. Chgo., Apr. 9, 1928; s. D. Chester and Isabelle (Olenick) G.; m. Sally Lou Lewis, Jan. 8, 1956; 1 dau., Jennifer. B.S. cum laude, Northwestern U., 1948. Exec. v.p. creative affairs Norman Lear-Embassy Communications, Inc., 1973-83; exec. producer-cons. Universal TV, 1983—; bd. dirs. Pilgrim Group Funds; mem. Second Decade council Am. Film Inst., adv. bd. Samantha Smith Found. Producer various youth-oriented TV series, 1949-52; producer Johnny Mercer's Mus. Chairs, 1952-55, Oscar Levant Show, 1955-61; creative producer Teen-Age Fair, 1962-72; exec. producer Charles in Charge, CBS-TV, 1984-85, Tribune Entertainment, 1986—, Together We Stand, CBS-TV, 1986-87, Nothing Is Easy, 1987-88; creative supr. Mary Hartman, Mary Hartman; prodn. supr. One Day At a Time, Facts of Life, Silver Spoons, The Jeffersons, Square Pegs, Diff'rent Strokes. Composer-lyricist theme songs for Facts of Life, Diff'rent Strokes, Charles in Charge, Together We Stand, Nothing Is Easy; Cons. Domestic Life, CBS-TV, 1983-84, Alan King Show, 1986. Recipient Emmy award for outstanding comedy series All in the Family, 1978-79, Producers award Nat. Council for Families and TV, 1984; honored for Diff'rent Strokes, NCCJ, 1979-80, honored for Facts of Life, Calif. Gov.'s Com. for the Employment of the Handicapped, 1981-82. Mem. Caucus for Producers, Writers and Dirs., Dirs. Guild Am., Writers Guild Am., AFTRA, Acad. of TV Arts and Scis., Acad. Magical Arts. Office: Universal Studio Universal City CA 91608

BURTON, JOHN LLOYD, dermatologist, author; b. Buxton, Derbyshire, Eng., Aug. 29, 1938; s. Lloyd and Dorothy (Pacey) B.; m. Patricia Anne Crankshaw, Sept. 12, 1964; children—John Benjamin, Jane Mary, Helena Catherine. B.Sc., Manchester U., 1961, M.B., Ch.B., 1964, M.D., 1970. Intern Manchester Royal Infirmary, 1964; resident Hammersmith Hosp., London, 1965, Edinburgh Royal Infirmary, 1966-68; sr. registrar Newcastle Royal Infirmary, Eng., 1969-73; sr. lectr. Bristol U., Eng., 1973-82, reader in dermatology, 1982—. Author: Aids to Postgraduate Medicine, 5th edit., 1988, Aids to Undergraduate Medicine, 4th edit., 1984, Essential Medicine, 2d. edit. 1981, Essentials of Dermatology, 2d edit., 1985; co-editor: Rook's Textbook of Dermatology (3 vols.), 1986; editor Brit. Jour. Dermatology, 1980-85; contbr. about 200 articles to profl. jours., chpts. to books. Recipient Dickson Research prize N.E. Regional Health Authority, 1971. Fellow Royal Coll. Physicians (Parkes-Weber lectr. 1988), Royal Soc. Medicine (v.p. dermatology sect. 1986—, Dowling Orator 1980); mem. Brit. Assn. Dermatologists (chmn. therapeutic trials group), Brit. Soc. Investigative Dermatology, European Soc. Dermatol. Research, Swedish Dermatol. Assn. (corr.). Avocation: fine book binding. Home: Norland House, 33 Canynge Rd, Bristol England BS8 3LD Office: Bristol Royal Infirmary Dermatology Dept, Maudlin St, Bristol England BS3 8HW

BURTON, PETER FREDERICK, retail executive; b. Weston Favell, Eng., Oct. 16, 1940; s. Frederick Stephen and Gladys (Williams) B.; m. Barbara Bouchard, Mar. 6, 1971; children: Richard David, Andrew Mark. Student pub. schs. Service mgr. Aperfield Garage Ltd., Biggin Hill, Kent, Eng., 1971-72; mng. dir. Aperfield Ct. Garage Ltd., Biggin Hill, 1972—, System-Network Ltd., Biggin Hill, 1986—. Served with RAF, 1958-67. Mem. Inst. of Motor Industry, Brit. Inst. Mgmt. Conservative. Mem. Ch. of England. Lodge: Endeavour. Office: Aperfield Ct Garage, 141/43 Main Rd, Biggin Hill England

BURTON, RICHARD JAY, lawyer; b. N.Y.C., May 4, 1949; s. Melvin F. Burton and Shirley (Burton) Silber; m. Truly Demetra Dourdis, June 11, 1972; 1 child, Marc Aaron. BA, George Washington U., 1971; JD, U. Miami, 1974. Bar: Fla. 1974, D.C. 1976, U.S. Supreme Ct. 1979. Adminstrv. aide Fla. Legis., 1973-74; gov. affairs liaison Dade County Fla. Legis., 1974; assoc. Richard H.W. Maloy and Assocs., Coral Gables, Fla., 1974-76; atty., advisor FAA, Washington, 1976-77; assoc. Pompan, Rumizen & Reynolds, Washington, 1978-79, Donald M. Murtha and Assocs., Washington, 1978-79; ptnr. Schoninger, Siegfried, Kipnis, Burton & Sussman PA, Miami, Fla., 1979-82; sole practice Miami, 1982—; guest lectr. U. Miami Sch. of Law, Coral Gables, 1982. Mem. Am. Arbitration Assn. Constr. law panel, 1974—, Builders Assn. S. Fla., legis. com. 1980—, Builder Industry Polit. action com.; elected fire commr. Met. Dade County, 1988. Mem. ABA, D.C. Bar Assn., Fed. Bar Assn., Fla. Bar Assn. (constr. law com.). Democrat. Jewish. Office: 13899 Biscayne Blvd North Miami Beach FL 33181

BURTON-BRADLEY, BURTON GYRTH, psychiatrist; b. Sydney, Australia, Nov. 18, 1914; s. Godfrey and Ruby Malvina (Drayton) MB ; BS, U. Sydney, 1946; diploma in Tropical Medicine and Hygiene, 1963, diploma in Anthropology, 1964; diploma in Psychol. Medicine, U. Melbourne, 1956; M.D., U. New South Wales, 1969; m. Ingeborg Roeser, Oct. 7, 1950 (dec.). Med. officer Australian mil. mission to Germany, 1949-50, Psychiatric Services, Queensland, 1951-57; psychiatrist Colombo Plan, Singapore, 1957-58; lectr. psychol. medicine U. Malaya, 1957-59; chief, mental health Dept. Public Health, Papua New Guinea, 1959-75; cons. psychiatrist Govt. of Papua New Guinea, 1975—; prof. psychiatry U. Papua New Guinea, 1978—; Rockefeller-WHO vis. scholar Villa Serbollini, Lake Como, Italy, 1979. Wenner-Gren Found. research fellow in psychol. anthropology, 1970; adv. in ethnopsychiatry S. Pacific Commn., 1967—; mem. expert adv. panel on mental health WHO, 1978—, advisor, Solomon Islands, 1979; mem. Constl. Adv. Com. on Power of Mercy, 1977—; M.D. external examiner dept. tropical medicine U. Sydney, Australia; Ph.D. external examiner dept. psychiatry Madurai U., India. Recipient Benjamin Rush bronze medal Am. Psychiat. Assn., 1974, Officer of the Order of the British Empire, 1982. Author 5 books, 200 sci. articles. Fellow Royal Coll. Psychiatrists, Internat. Coll. Psychosomatic Medicine (v.p. 1977—), Am. Anthrop. Assn., Pacific Rim Coll. Psychiatrists, Organisation Internationale de Psychophysiologie; mem. Papua New Guinea Psychiat. Assn., (pres. 1979—), World Assn. Social Psychiatry, Soc. Internat. de Nuevas Ciencias de la Conducta (hon.), Soc. Internat. D'Historie de la Médecine (Papua New Guinea del. 1985). Author: South Pacific Ethnopsychiatry, 1967; Mixed-Race Society in Port Moresby, 1968; Psychiatry and the Law in the Developing Country, 1970; Longlong, 1973; Stone Age Crisis, 1975. Home: PO Box 111, Port Moresby Papua New Guinea

BURTT, EVERETT JOHNSON, economic consultant; b. Jackson, Mich., Aug. 6, 1914; s. Everett Johnson and Eve Mildred (Meisenhelter) B.; m. Cynthia Webb, June 15, 1940; children—Michael Coburn, Judith. A.B., Berea Coll., 1935; M.A., Duke, 1937, Ph.D., 1950. Instr. econs. U. Me., 1939-41; instr. Denver U., 1941-42; labor market analyst War Manpower Commn., 1942-43; employment analyst U.S. Bur. Labor Statistics, Boston, 1946-47; asst. prof. Boston U., 1947-52, asso. prof., 1952-57, prof. econs., 1957-80, prof. emeritus, 1980—; chmn. dept. Boston U. (Coll. Liberal Arts and Grad. Sch.), 1952-68, chmn. all-univ. dept., 1956-68, acting chmn. dept. econs., 1971-74; asso. dir. Manpower Inst., 1974-75. Author: Labor Markets, Unions and Government Policies, 1963, Plant Relocation and the Core City Worker, 1967, Social Perspectives in the History of Economic Theory, 1972, Labor in the American Economy, 1979; Contbr. profl. periodicals, reports. Served with U.S. Army, 1943-46. Mem. Am. Econ. Assn., Indsl. Relations Research Assn. (pres. Boston 1966-67), AAUP, Phi Beta Kappa (hon. Boston U. chpt. 1981—). Address: 9 Mary Dyer Ln North Easton MA 02356

BURY, JOHN, theatre designer, consultant; b. Aberystwyth, Wales, U.K., Jan. 27, 1925; s. Charles Rusely and Emily Frances (Adams) B.; m. Margaret Liela Greenwood, 1947 (div. 1964); 1 son, Christopher Rugely; m. Elizabeth Margaret Duffield, Jan. 1966; children: Adam Charles, Abigail Frances, Matthew John. Student, Univ. Coll., London. Theatre designer London, 1947—; head of design Royal Shakespeare Theatre, London, 1964-68; head of design Nat. Theatre, London, 1973-85, assoc. designer, 1988—; chmn. Soc. Brit. Theatre Designers, 1966-86. Stage design: Amadeus. Served to lt. Brit. Royal Navy, 1942-45. Comdr. Order Brit. Empir. Fellow Royal Soc. Arts. *

BURZYNSKI, STANISLAW RAJMUND, internist; b. Lublin, Poland, Jan. 23, 1943; s. Grzegorz and Zofia Miroslawa (Radzikowski) B.; came to U.S., 1970; M.D. with distinction, Med. Acad., Lublin, 1967, Ph.D., 1968. Teaching asst. Med. Acad. Lublin, 1962-67; intern, resident in internal medicine, Med. Acad., 1967-70; research asso. Baylor U., 1970-72, asst. prof., 1972-77; pvt. practice specializing in internal medicine, Houston, 1977—; dir. Burzynski Research Lab., 1977-83; pres. Burzynski Research Inst., Inc., 1983—. Nat. Cancer Inst. grantee, 1974 West Found. grantee, 1975. Mem. AAAS, Am. Assn. Cancer Research, AMA, Fedn. Am. Scientists, Harris County Med. Soc., Polish Nat. Alliance (pres. Houston chpt. 1974-75), Soc. Neurosci., Tex. Med. Assn., Sigma Xi. Roman Catholic. Contbr. articles profl. jours. Discoverer of antineoplastons components of biochem. def. system against cancer; described structure of Ameletin, 1st substance known to be responsible for remembering sound in animal's brain. Home: 20 W Rivercrest Dr Houston TX 77042 Office: 6221 Corporate Dr Houston TX 77036

BUSAYAPOKA, THAKSA, glove manufacturing company executive; b. Bangkok, Thailand, Dec. 19, 1950; s. Watana and Lorsi B.; m. Charuwan Pruekthivilai, Feb. 2, 1977; children—Thanita, Suthira, Thanat. B. Commerce in Mktg. with honors, Chulalongkorn U., 1975. Sales promoter, Borneo (Thailand) Co., Bangkok, 1970; stenographer/clk. Econ. Commn. for Asia and the Far East (UN), Bangkok, 1970-73; export mgr. Watanakachorn Trading Co., Bangkok, 1973-74; mng. dir. Thai Glove Co., Bangkok, 1974—; exec. dir. Muang Thong Aluminium Industry Co., Bangkok, 1981-85; exec. dir. Thai Interseat Co., Bangkok, 1986—; dir. Modernform Furniture Co., Bangkok, Thai Plaspac Co., Bangkok. Office: Thai Interseat Co Ltd, 123 Mu 1, Bangkhunthien Rd, Bangkhunthien 10150, Thailand

BUSBY, JAMES LOUIE, electronics company executive; b. Mobile, Ala., Oct. 1, 1946; s. Louie Barton and Betty Jean (Snowden) B.; B.S.E.E., U. Ala., 1969; M.B.A., U. South Ala., 1982; m. Shawn Michele; children—Jimmy Barton, Brent Edward, Jeffrey Snowden, Kent Bertram. Sr. systems engr. Scott Paper Co., Mobile, 1973-77; project engr. Internat. Paper Co., Mobile, 1972-73; founder; pres., chmn. QMS, Inc., Mobile, 1977—. Bd. dirs. Salvation Army, Mobile Area C. of C., Colonial Bank. Served as officer, Signal Corps, U.S. Army, 1969-72. Decorated Meritorious Service medal; recipient Citizen award Optimist Club, 1958; Small Bus. Innovation Adv. of Yr., SBA, 1982; Ala. Exec. of Year, 1985, Engr. of Year, 1985. Mem. Pres.'s Assn., C. of C. Patentee in field. Office: One Magnum Pass Mobile AL 36618

BUSCAGLIA, ELVIRA ISABEL, association director; b. Buenos Aires, Oct. 13, 1939; d. Marcelo Giardini and Piedad Rodriquez Novoa; m. Alberto Buscaglia, Feb. 4, 1965; children: Mariana, Carola, Romina. Dir. The King's English Internat. Corp., Buenos Aires, 1972-82; propietary dir. Orgn. Privada de Extension Cultural, Bueno Aires, 1983—; organizer Congress,

Buenos Aires, 1978-80, Santiago, Chile, 1982, Guaruya, Brazil, 1983, Lima, Peru, 1983. Editor: Idiomatic Expressions, 1972, various textbooks, grammar books, 1973. Mem. Union of the Democratic Ctr. Party. Roman Catholic. Club: Hipico Argentino (Buenos Aires). Office: Orgn Privada de Extension Cultural, Piedras 77 8th, Buenos Aires Argentina 1070

BUSCH, AUGUST ADOLPHUS, III, brewery executive; b. St. Louis, June 16, 1937; s. August Adolphus and Elizabeth (Overton) B.; m. Susan Marie Hornibrook, Aug. 17, 1963 (div. 1969); children: August Adolphus IV, Susan Marie II; m. Virginia L. Wiley, Dec. 28, 1974; children: Steven August, Virginia Marie. Student, U. Ariz., 1957-58, Siebel Inst. Tech., 1960-61. With Anheuser-Busch, Inc., St. Louis, 1957—, sales mgr., 1962-64, v.p. mktg. ops., 1964-65, v.p., gen. mgr., 1965-74, pres., 1975-79, chief exec. officer, 1975—, chmn. bd., 1977—; chmn., pres. Anheuser Busch Cos., Inc., St. Louis, 1979—, also bd. dirs.; v.p. Busch Properties, Inc., St. Louis; bd. dirs. St. Louis Nat. Baseball Club, Mfrs. Railway Co., Southwestern Bell Corp., Gen. Am. Life Ins. Co., Emerson Electric Co.; trustee St. Louis Refrigerator Car Co. Mem. adv. bd. St. John Mercy Med. Ctr.; bd. dirs. United Way Greater St. Louis, St. Louis Symphony Soc.; bd. overseers Wharton Sch., U. Pa.; mem. exec. bd. Boy Scouts Am. Clubs: St. Louis, Frontenac Racquet, St. Louis Country, Racquet (St. Louis); Noonday, Log Cabin, Stadium. Office: Anheuser-Busch Cos Inc 1 Busch Pl Saint Louis MO 63118

BUSCH, HANS PETER, radiologist; b. Kiel, Fed. Republic of Germany, Feb. 6, 1949; s. Kelmens and Dorothea (Dettlaff) B.; m. Hildegard Winter, June 13, 1947; children: Stephanie, Thomas. Diploma in physics, U. Mainz, Fed. Republic of Germany, 1975, diploma in medicine, 1981. Physicist Inst. Physics, U. Mainz, 1975-81; radiologist Inst. Radiology, U. Heidelberg, Fed. Republic of Germany, 1981—, chief resident, 1986—, lectr., 1987—. Contbr. articles on digital radiology, radiology and med. physics to profl. jours. Home: Neuhofenerstrasse 53, 6703 Limburgerhof Federal Republic of Germany Office: U Heidelberg Inst Radiology, Klinikum Mannheim, Theodor-Kutzer Ufer, 6800 Mannheim Federal Republic of Germany

BÜSCHGES, GÜNTER, sociology educator; b. Weidenau, Germany, Sept. 4, 1926; s. Hermann and Eugenie (Sieps) B.; m. Margarete Felix; children: Beatrix, Birgitta, Ansgar. Diploma, Kaufmann U., Cologne, Fed. Republic Germany, 1952; Dr Rer Pol, U. Cologne, 1961. Ind. asst. 1947-49, ind. personnel mgr., 1952-68; asst. prof. sociology U. Regensburg, Fed. Republic Germany, 1968-70; prof. orgnganizational sociology U. Bielefeld, Fed. Republic Germany, 1970-75; prof. social research U. Essen, Fed. Republic Germany, 1975-80; prof. social sci. U. Distance Edn., Hagen, Fed. Republic Germany, 1980; prof. sociology U. Erlangen-Nurnberg, Fed. Republic Germany, 1982—; dir. Institut fur Freie Berufe, Nurnberg, 1983, Institut fur Empirische Soziologie, 1983. Author: Aspekte der Berufswahl, 1975, Organisationssoziologie, 1983, Organisationsforschung, 1977; editor Organisation und Herrschaft, 1975. Mem. Deutsche Gesellschaft fur Soziologie, Internat. Indsl. Relations Assn. Roman Catholic. Club: Neudeutschland. Lodge: Lions. Office: Sozialwissensschaftliches, Institut Findelgasse 7-9, Nurnberg Federal Republic of Germany

BUSCHKÜHL, MATTHIAS, librarian; b. Hamburg, Fed. Republic Germany, Apr. 28, 1953; s. Hans Alfred and Katharina Maria (Mausolf) B. Student, Trinity Coll., Dublin, Ireland, 1977-78; PhD, U. Hamburg, 1979. Reference librarian State Library Prussian Cultural Resources, Berlin, 1979-81; councillor library Cath. U., Eichstatt, Fed. Republic Germany, 1981—, librarian, 1983—. Author: Disraeli's "Lothair" (1870), 1981, Heilige Schrift Konnersreuth Widerstand Franz Xaver Wutz 1882-1938, 1982, Great Britain and the The Holy See, 1983, Seminar und Hochschule in Eichstatt unter dem National Sozialismus, 1984, Franz Xaver Mayr, 1987. Mem. Am. Cath. Hist. Assn., Verein Deutscher Bibliothekare, Societas Internationalis Historiae Conciliorum Investigandae, Arbeitsgemeinschaft Katholisch-Theolog. Bibliotheken (counsellor 1987—). Mem. Christian Social Union. Clubs: Budo (treas. 1987—), Unitas Franconia. Home: Pfahlstrasse 19, 8078 Eichstatt Federal Republic of Germany Office: Cath U Library, Universitatsallee 1, 8078 Eichstatt Federal Republic of Germany

BUSH, DAVID FREDERIC, psychologist, educator; b. Watertown, N.Y., July 12, 1942; s. Frederic Ralph and Charlotte Mary (Ellingworth) B.; B.A., U. South Fla., 1965; M.A., U. Wyo., 1968; Ph.D., Purdue U., 1972; 1 dau., Lara A. Instr. psychology Hiram Scott Coll., Scottsbluff, Nebr., 1967-69, Purdue U., West Lafayette, Ind., 1971-72; asso. prof. psychology West Chester (Pa.) State Coll., 1972-73; asst. prof., chmn. grad. program psychology Villanova (Pa.) U., 1972-77, assoc. prof., 1978-84, prof., 1984—, assoc. dir. human resource devel., grad. program in human orgn. sci.; instr. seminar Am. Coll., Bryn Mawr, Pa., 1976—; ptnr. Westminster Group; cons. in field. Mem. council Unitarian fellowship Lafayette, Ind., 1970-72; bd. dirs. Ars Moriendi, Dennis Burton Day Care Center, 1971-72, Life Guidance Services, Inc., 1977-82; pres. Bush Assocs. NDEA fellow 1969-71, David Ross summer fellow, 1972; Villanova U. grantee, 1974, 77, 83. Mem. Am., Eastern, Midwestern psychol. assns., Soc. Psychol. Study Social Issues, Internat. Communication Assn., Human Resources Profl. Assn. (bd. dirs.), Internat. Communication Assn., Acad. Mgmt., Am. Soc. for Personnel Administrn., Sigma Xi, Psi Chi. Author: Human Development: The Psychology of the Life-Span, 1974; Canterbury Press Memory Improvement Course. Editor: Social Sci. Rev. Researcher doctor-patient communication, decision making and communication, orgn. behavior, human resource mgmt. Home: 2392 Pineview Dr Malvern PA 19355 Office: Villanova U Dept Psychology Villanova PA 19085

BUSH, GEOFFREY, composer, pianist, educator, musicologist; b. London, Mar. 23, 1920; s. Christopher and Winifred (Chart) B.; m. Julie Kathleen McKenna, Apr. 15, 1950; children: Andrew, Paul. MA (Nettleship scholar), Oxford U., 1940, MusD, 1946. Lectr. U. Oxford, 1947-52; tutor U. London, 1952-64, sr. tutor, 1964-80; vis. prof. King's Coll., U. London, 1969—; music advisor John Ireland Trust, 1969—; mem. music adv. panel Arts Council Gt. Britain, 1963-69. Composer symphonies, operas, songs, instrumental music; editor Musica Britannica, vols. 37, 43, 49, 52; writer Musical Creation and the Listener, 1954; Left, Right and Centre, 1983. Recipient Royal Philharm. prize for overture Yorick, 1949; Guest Composer of Year, Music Tchrs. Assn., 1962. Hon. fellow U. Coll. of Wales; mem. Composers Guild Gt. Britain (council), Performing Rights Soc. Gt. Britain Fund (chmn.). Labour Party. Anglican.

BUSH, GEORGE HERBERT WALKER, Vice President of U.S.; b. Milton, Mass., June 12, 1924; s. Prescott Sheldon and Dorothy (Walker) B.; m. Barbara Pierce, Jan. 6, 1945; children: George W., John E., Neil M., Marvin P., Dorothy W. BA in Econs., Yale U., 1948; BA hon. degrees, Adelphi U.; B.A. hon. degrees, Austin Coll., No. Mich. U., Franklin Pierce Coll., Allegheny Coll., Beaver Coll. Co-founder, dir. Zapata Petroleum Corp., 1953-59; pres. Zapata Off Shore Co., Houston, 1956-64; chmn. bd. Zapata Off Shore Co., 1964-66; mem. 90th-91st congresses, 7th Dist. Tex., 1967-71, Ways and Means com.; U.S. ambassador to UN, 1971-72; chmn. Rep. Nat. Com., 1973-74; chief U.S. Liaison Office Peking, People's Republic China, 1974-75; dir. CIA, 1976-77; adj. prof. Rice U.; v.p. of U.S., 1981—; Rep. candidate for Pres. of U.S., 1988. Chmn. Rep. Party Harris County, Tex., 1963-64; del. Rep. Nat. Conv., 1964, 68; Rep. candidate U.S. senator from Tex., 1964, 70. Served to lt. (j.g.), pilot USN, World War II. Decorated D.F.C., Air medals (3). Office: The White House 1600 Pennsylvania Ave Washington DC 20501

BUSH, MARGERY PECK, clinical social worker; b. Bristol, Conn., Mar. 22, 1934; d. Seymour Roe and Margery (Earl) Peck; B.A. in Psychology, Wells Coll., Aurora, N.Y., 1956; M.S.W., U. Conn., 1975; m. Edward Wallace Bush, Jr., Feb. 28, 1958; children—Kimberly, Barbara, David. Diplomate in clin. social work, Conn. Intern, Family Service Soc., Hartford, Conn., 1973-74, Inst. Living, Adult Outpatient Clinic, Hartford, 1974-75; cons., sch. social worker East Hartford Bd. Edn., 1976; family counselor Family Service, Inc., New Britain, Conn., 1976-79; family Therapist Youth and Family Resource Center, Glastonbury, Conn., 1980-82. pvt. practice individual, marital, and family counseling, West Hartford, 1979-86; pvt. practice counseling, Noank, 1987—; instr. program Living in Fuller Effectiveness (LIFE), 1979—. Corporator, Oak Hill Sch. Blind, 1968—; trustee Larrabee Fund Assn., 1970-73, chmn. Hartford com., 1970-72; bd. dirs. Hartford Interval House, 1977-78. Mem. Nat. Assn. Social Workers, Acad. Cert. Social Workers, Conn. Soc. Clin. Social Workers, Hartford Audubon Soc., Internat. Platform Assn. Congregationalist. Club: Hartford Ski. Address: 28 Church St Noank CT 06340

BUSH, MARJORIE EVELYNN TOWER-TOOKER, educator, media specialist, librarian; b. Atkinson, Nebr., Mar. 12, 1925; d. Albert Ralph and Vera Marie (Rickover) Tower-Tooker; m. Louis T. Genung, Feb. 2, 1944 (dec. Jan. 1982); 1 son, Louis Thompson; m. Laurence Scott Bush, Sept. 22, 1984; 1 stepson, Roger A. Bush. Student U. Nebr.,1951, Wayne State Coll., 1942-47; BA Colo. State Coll., 1966, U. No. Colo., 1970; postgrad. Doane Coll., 1967-68, U. Utah, 1973-74, PhD (hon.), 1973. Elem. tchr. Atkinson Public Schs., 1958-69; adminstr. libraries and audiovisual communications Clay County Dist. I-C, Fairfield, Nebr., 1972-81; media specialist Albion (Nebr.) City Schs., 1981—; mem. Neb. Gov.'s White House Conf. on Libraries. Chmn. edn. adminstrv. bd. Park Hill United Meth. Ch., Denver, also pres.; sec. Denver Symphony Guild. Mem. NEA (life), Nebr., Colo. edn. assns., Assn. Childhood Edn. Internat., ALA, Nebr., Mountain Plains library assns., Nat. Council Tchrs. English, AAUW, Nebr. Ednl. Media Assn., Assn. Supervision and Curriculum Devel., Assn. Ednl. Communications and Tech., Internat. Visual Literacy Assn., Nat. Council Exceptional Children, Alumni Assn. U. No. Colo. (life charter), Women Educators Nebr., United Meth. Women (pres.), Am. Legion Aux., Nebr. Lay Citizens Edn. Assn. (exec.), Am. Nat. Cowbelles, Nebr. Cowbelles, DAR (regent 1971, dist. treas. 1968-71), Internat. Platform Assn., LWV, Women's Soc. Christian Service, Ak-Sar-Ben. Club: Windsor Gardens (Denver). Lodges: Opti-Mrs. (pres.), Optimists Internat., Columbine Optimists (pres. 1987-88), Eastern Star. Home: 9655 E Center Ave Denver CO 80231

BUSH, MELINDA JOHNSON, publisher; b. Champaign, Ill., June 14, 1940; d. Maurice R. and Margaret B. Johnson; BS, U. Colo., 1962; postgrad. NYU, 1962-64, London Sch. Econs. and Polit. Sci.; postgrad. Advanced Mgmt. Program, Harvard U., 1984. With J. Walter Thompson, advt., N.Y.C., 1962-64, Paul Bradley Assns., public relations, N.Y.C., 1964-66; with Ziff-Davis Publishing Co., N.Y.C., 1966—, mktg. dir. photographi div., 1966-74, asst. to pres., 1974-76, pub. Hotel & Travel Index, 1976—, v.p. bus. div., 1983-85; v.p. Murdoch Mags. div., pub. Hotel & Travel Index, News Group Publs., Inc., N.Y.C., 1985—; sr. v.p., group publisher Murdoch Mags., News America, Inc., N.Y.C., 1987—. advisor Cornell U. Hotel Sch., Lausanne Hotel Sch.; advisor tourism programs U. Mass., New Sch. for Social Research, Culinary Inst. Am. (also mem. corp. bd.); columnist, frequent speaker and panelist at industry assns. and convs. Nat. photography coordinator Pres.'s Council Model Cities Task Force, 1970-72; founder, chmn. Photography Youth Found., 1973-76; mem. nat. bd. dirs. Am. Univ., Washington., Sun Resorts Inc., Master Media, Inc. Named Woman of Year in Travel, Travel Industry Assn. Am., 1980. Fellow Inst. Cert. Travel Agts. (bd. dirs., trustee); mem. Hotel Sales Mgmt. Assn. Internat. (dir.), Am. Hotel and Motel Assn., Advt. Women N.Y., Com. of 200. Club: Wings (mem. com. of 200) (N.Y.C.). Author articles in field. Office: Murdoch Mags div News Group Publs Inc 2 Park Ave New York NY 10016

BUSH, MICHAEL GRAHAM, musician; b. Aughton, Lancashire, Eng., Oct. 8, 1932; s. James Graham and Josephine Mary (Adamson) B.; m. Marie-Louise Simpson, July 26, 1986; grad. Royal Manchester Coll. Music, 1954, Royal Acad. Music, 1957. Asst. music master Beaumont Coll., Old Windsor, Berkshire, 1958-62; singing master Convent Sacred Heart, Woldingham, 1959-67; mem. music staff N.E. Essex Tech. Coll., Colchester, 1962-68; prof. jr. exhibitioners dept. Royal Acad. Music, 1964-68; asst. music adv. Liverpool Edn. Com., 1968-82, music adv., 1982-86; condr. operas and pageant at music festivals and spl. celebrations. Mem. Incorp. Soc. Musicians (dist. councillor Liverpool 1977-83). Address: 11 Wynstay Rd, Meols, Wirral Merseyside L47 5AR England

BUSH, WENDELL EARL, lawyer; b. Little Rock, Dec. 10, 1943; s. David J. and Anne (Hampton) B. A.B., Philander South Coll., 1965; postgrad. Atlanta U., 1966; J.D., Emory U., 1969. Bar: Ga. 1971, Ind., Tenn. Atty., Emory U. Law Ctr., Atlanta, 1969-71, Indpls. Legal Aid Soc., 1969-72, EEOC, Memphis, 1973—. Bd. dirs. Boy Scouts Am., Memphis. Hal S. Clark fellow, 1968; Reginald Hebersmitt fellow, 1969-71. Mem. ABA, Nat. Bar Assn., Omega Psi Phi, Phi Alpha Delta (treas.). Methodist. Home: 3685 Winchester Park Ctr #8 Memphis TN 38118

BUSHNELL, CATHARINE, marketing consultant, licensing, marketing representation, consultation and production company executive; b. Pullman, Wash, July 2, 1950; d. David and Catharine Howe (Goodfellow) B.; m. H. Michael Sisson, Oct. 31, 1975. B.S. in Speech, Northwestern U., 1972. Prodn. mgr. Mike White Advt., Chgo., 1972; stage actress, Chgo., 1972-73; ptnr., dir. photography Mome, Raths & Outgrabe, Chgo., 1973-75; exec. v.p. Sisson Assocs., N.Y.C., 1975—; pres. Illusion Gallery, Creative Resource Co., N.Y.C., 1981—, The Sisson Group Inc., 1986—; faculty New Sch.-Parsons Sch. of Design, 1985-86. Photographer motion picture stills for various films, N.Y.C., 1975—; author: Raggedy Ann and Andy in the Tunnel of Lost Toys, 1980; Raggedy Ann and Andy and the Pirates of Outgo Inlet, 1981; Linda's Magic Window, 1981; Frannie's Magic Kazoo, 1982. Judge ann. student photog. portfolio rev. High Sch. of Art and Design, N.Y.C., 1979-83. Mem. Licensing Industry Assn., Internat. Photographers of Motion Picture Industry, Internat. Soc. Photography (charter), Actors Equity Assn., Northwestern U. Alumnae Assn., Delta Zeta. Office: The Sisson Group Inc 300 E 40th St New York NY 10016

BUSHNELL, RODERICK PAUL, lawyer; b. Buffalo, Mar. 6, 1944; s. Paul H. and Martha A. Bushnell; m. Suzann Y. Kaiser, Aug. 27, 1966; 1 son, Arlo P. B.A., Rutgers U., 1966; J.D., Georgetown U., 1969. Bar: Calif. 1970, U.S. Supreme Ct. 1980. Atty. dept. water resources Sacramento, 1969-71; ptnr. Bushnell, Caplan & Fielding, San Francisco, 1971—; chmn. bd. dirs. Bread & Roses, Inc., 1983-86. Bd. dirs. Calif. Lawyers for the Arts. Mem. Bar Assn. of San Francisco, Calif. Bar Assn., Lawyers Club of San Francisco, Calif. Trial Lawyers Assn., San Francisco Trial Lawyers Assn., No. Calif. Criminal Trial Lawyers Assn. Democrat. Clubs: San Francisco Bay, Commonwealth (San Francisco). Office: Bushnell Caplan & Fielding 901 Market St Suite 230 San Francisco CA 94103

BUSHO, ELIZABETH MARY, nurse, educator; b. Ellendale, Minn., Feb. 26, 1927; d. Ruben Oscar and Lillian Katherine (Gahagan) Busho. R.N., Kahler Hosps. Sch. of Nursing, 1948. R.N., Minn. Operating room staff nurse, Minn., Calif., Colo., 1948-53; operating room head nurse, Mt. Sinai Hosp., Mpls., 1953-61; asst. supr. operating room St. Barnabas Hosp., Mpls., 1961-71; asst. dir. surg. services St. Mary's Hosp., Rochester, Minn., 1971-80, dir., 1980—; instr. Rochester Community Coll. Mem. editorial bd. Perioperative Nursing Quar. Adv. bd. Rochester Area Vocat. Tech. Inst., Rochester Community Coll., Sigma Theta Tau. Republican. Methodist. Developer course in operating room nursing. Office: St Mary's Hosp 1216 2d St Rochester MN 55901

BUSICK, DENZEL REX, lawyer; b. Council Bluffs, Iowa, Oct. 16, 1945; s. Guy Henry and Selma Ardith (Woods) B.; m. Cheryl Ann Callahan, June 17, 1967; children—Elizabeth Colleen, Guy William. B.S. in Bus. Adminstrn., U. Nebr.-Omaha, 1969; J.D., Creighton U., 1971. Bar: Nebr. 1971, U.S. Dist. Ct. Nebr. 1971, U.S. Ct. Apls. (8th cir.) 1975, U.S. Sup. Ct. 1974; civil diplomate Nat. Bd. Trial Advocacy. Law clk., U.S. Dist. Ct. Nebr., 1970-72; mem. Fraser, Stryker, Veach, Vaughn, Meusey, Olsen & Boyer, Omaha, 1972-78; assoc. Kay & Satterfield, North Platte, Nebr., 1979-80; ptnr. Luebs, Dowding, Beltzer, Leininger, Smith & Busick, Grand Island, Nebr., 1980—. Mem. ABA, Assn. Trial Lawyers Am., Nat. Inst. Trial Advocacy, Am. Judicature Soc., Nebr. State Bar Assn., Nebr. Assn. Trial Attys., Mensa, Phi Alpha Delta. Republican. Club: Kiwanis (Grand Island). Contbr. to publs. in field. Home: 3027 Brentwood Pl Grand Island NE 68801 Office: Wheeler at First St PO Box 790 Grand Island NE 68802

BUSKE, NORMAN L., consulting scientist, energy researcher; b. Milw., Oct. 11, 1943; s. Gilbert and Genevieve (Strutt) B.; m. Patricia Teller, June 10, 1965; children—Heather, Alisyn, Robin; m. Linda S. Josephson, Aug. 25, 1980. B.A. in Physics, U. Conn., 1964, M.A., 1965; M.S. in Oceanography, Johns Hopkins U., 1967. Oceanographer Ocean Sci. & Engring., Inc., Rockville, Md., 1968-71; prin. Sea-Test Co., Laie, Hawaii, 1972-76; sr. scientist/engr. Van Gulik & Assocs., Lake Oswego, Oreg., 1976-77; dir. research Pacific Engring. Corp., Portland, Oreg., 1977-78; prin. Search Technical Services, Davenport, Wash., 1978—; sci. advisor Greenpeace, 1983—. Inventor internal pressure engine. Mem. ASME, ASTM, AAAS, IEEE, N.Y. Acad. Scis., Soc. Automotive Engrs. Discoverer temporal mechanical description of reality. Home and Office: Star Route Box 17 Davenport WA 99122

BUSKIRK, PHYLLIS RICHARDSON, economist; b. Queens, N.Y., July 19, 1930; d. William Edward and Amy A. Richardson; m. Allen V. Buskirk, Sept. 13, 1950; children: Leslie Ann, William Allen, Carol Amy, Janet Helen. AB cum laude, William Smith Coll., 1951. Research asst. W.E. Upjohn Inst. for Employment Research, Kalamazoo, 1970-75, research assoc., 1976-83, sr. staff economist, 1983-87. Co-editor Bus. Conditions in the Kalamazoo Area, Quar. Rev., 1979-84, asst. editor Bus. for Western Mich., 1984-87. Mem. Civil Service Bd. City of Kalamazoo, 1977—, chmn., 1981—; trustee First Presbyn. Ch., Kalamazoo, 1984-87, chmn., 1985, 86, mgr. adminstrn. and fin., 1987—; trustee Sr. Citizens Fund, Kalamazoo, 1984—, corp. restructuring com. 1985-86. exec. bd. 1986-88; bd. dirs. Heritage Community Kalamazoo, 1988—; pres. bd. dirs. Westland Meadows, 1988—. Mem. Indsl. Relations Research Assn., Nat. Assn. Bus. Economists, Nat. Assn. Ch. Bus. Adminstrn., Presbyn. Ch. Bus. Adminstrn. Assn. Clubs: P.E.O., Kalamazoo Network. Office: 321 W South St Kalamazoo MI 49007

BUSNELLI, FRANCO, industrialist; b. Meda, Milan, Italy, Dec. 28, 1931; s. Giuseppe and Maria (Ponzoni) B.; m. Graziella Martinoli, June 6, 1956; children: Cristina, Giuseppe. Pres. Nuovo Bosco Co., Novedrate, Italy, Finmisinto Co., Desio, Italy, Busnelli Edizioni S.p.A., Misinto, Italy; pres. mng. dir. Gruppo Industriale Busnelli S.p.A., Misinto, Italy. Mem. Federlegno Arredo, Assarredo. Roman Catholic. Clubs: Sporting (Milan); Yacht of Costa Smeralda (Sassari). Lodge: Rotary. Home and Office: Kennedy 34, 20020 Misinto Milan Italy

BUSS, GERALD VERE AUSTEN, educator, clergyman; b. Canterbury, Kent, Eng., May 17, 1936; s. Humphrey Austen and Angela (Horne) B.; m. Vivian Margaret Buss; children: Celina Lucie Buss Harris, Sofie Maria, Chloe Susanna Austen. Diploma in theology, St. Stephen's House, Oxford, Eng., 1963; PhD, Cambridge U., 1987. Trader messrs. Holiday, Cutler, Bath and Co., Singapore, 1956-59; asst. priest St. Peter's Ch., Petersham, Surrey, Eng., 1963-66, Holy Trinity Ch., London, 1966-70; sr. chaplain, lectr. modern history Hurstpierpoint Coll., Hassocks, Eng., 1970—; mem., part-time researcher Keston Coll., Kent, 1980—. Author: The Bear's Hug: Religious Belief and the Soviet State 1917-86, 87. Served to lt. inf. Brit. Army, 1954-56. Airey Neave Meml. scholar Ho. of Commons, 1984. Mem. Nat. Assn. Soviet and East European Studies. Club: Nikaean (London). Home: Souches The Street, Albourne BN6 9DJ, England Office: Hurstpierpoint Coll, Hassocks BN6 9JS, England

BUSSE, KONRAD ERICH WALTER, personnel consultant; b. Hannover, Germany, Aug. 1, 1929; s. Kurt and Elisabeth (Wilson) B.; m. Perella C. Busse, Mar. 14, 1955; children—Nicole, Christian, Andrea, Robin, Leslie. B.A., U. Iowa, 1952; Dr.Phil., U. Bonn, 1955. Mgr., German Acad. Exchange Service, Bonn, 1956-59; personnel officer UNESCO, Paris, 1959-61; dep. personnel mgr. World Bank, Washington, 1961-71; personnel dir. Kreditanstalt fur Wiederaufbau, Frankfurt, 1971-83; personnel cons. Kreditanstalt fur Wiederaufbau, The World Bank, European Investment Bank, 1983—. Contbr. articles to profl. jours. Fulbright scholar U. Iowa, 1951-52. Mem. German Soc. Personnel Mgmt.

BUSSON, CAMILLE J-C, construction company executive, consultant; b. France, Apr. 6, 1933; s. Jean B. and Celina (Puron) B.; m. Maud Turmel, July 20, 1960. Diploma in Engring., Ecole des Ponts et Chaussees, Paris, 1956; MS, U. Calif., Berkeley, 1957. Project engr. Campenon Bernard Co., Paris, 1960-63, project mgr., 1964-66, chief engr., 1967-69, dir. ops., 1969-72, v.p. overseas, 1973-74; v.p. overseas Societe Gen. d'Enterprise, Paris, 1975-80, exec. v.p., 1980-86; mng. dir. Consortium S.S.C., Paris, 1986—; bd. dirs. Soc. Aux. d'Enterprise, Paris, Analyse Mgmt. Innovations Cons.; mng. dir. Consortium Sainrapt et Brice Internat. Societe Aux. D'Entreprises Colas, Paris, 1986—. Mem. ASCE, French Com. on Large Dams, French Assn. Underground Works, Com. Ecole des Ponts et Chausees. Home: 20 Rue Corbon, Paris France 75015 Office: SSC, 21 Rue de la Vanne, Montrouge France 92120

BUSTAMANTE VASCONCELOS, EDUARDO, lawyer; b. Oaxaca, Mexico, Oct. 12, 1904; s. Manuel Bustamante and Luz Vasconcelos; m. Cuca Davila (dec. 1971); m. Maria Luisa Bascaran, June 2, 1973. Abogado, Escuela Nacional De Jurisprudencia, Mex., Profesor Extraordirio Derecho Fiscal (hon.), Universidad Benito Juarez, Oaxaca, 1959. Lawyer Diplomate Universidad Nacional Autonoma de Mexico. Tech. officer Sria. de Hacienda, Fed. Govt., 1925-30, Under Sec., 1946-48, sec. Sria. de Patrimonio Nacional, Fed. Govt., 1958-64; dir. Banca Confia, Mexico, D.F., 1952-82; mem. bd. Bancomer, Mexico, D.F., 1964-82. Decorated Oficial de la Legión de Honor; Gran Cruz de la Orden de la Corona de Bélgica y Gran Cruz de la Orden de Jorge Primero, Govts. of France, Belgium and Greece. Mem. Barra Mexicana. Roman Catholic. Club: Campestre de la Ciudad de Mexico. Home: Palmas 805 Torre 1 piso 6, Lomas de Chapultepec DF 11000, Mexico

BUSTANI, MYRNA, business executive; b. Beirut, Dec. 20, 1937; d. Emile and Laura B.; degree Coll. Protestant Francais, Beirut, 1954; licence es lettres psychology and philosophy Ecole Superieure des Lettres, Beirut, 1958; m. Fouad el Khazen, 1958 (div. 1970); children—Jamil, Laura. Mem. Lebanese Parliament, 1963-64; ptnr. C.A.T. Contracting Co., 1963—; dir. Société Hoteliere pour le Tourisme, Beirut, Banque de l'industrie et du Travail, Beirut, Banque de Financement et d'Investissement, Geneva. Trustee Am. U. Beirut, 1980; gov. Centre Lebanese Studies, Oxford. Mem. Arab Brit. C. of C. (dir. 1976—), Mid. East Assn. (London), Brit. Lebanese Assn. (London). Mem. Christian Ch. Office: PO Box 11-1036, Beirut Lebanon also: care Incotes Ltd, 1 Great Cumberland Pl, London W1 England

BUSTER, EDMOND BATE, metal products company executive; b. Whitt, Tex., Oct. 20, 1918; s. Edmond Bate and Emma Lee (Johnston) B.; m. Beatrice Keller, Oct. 24, 1939; children: John Edmond, Robert William, Susan Lynn, Steven K., James L., Brian R. A.A., Menlo Jr. Coll., 1937; B.S. in Mining Engring, U. Calif. at Berkeley, 1940. With Tex. Co., Santa Paula, Calif., 1937-40, Tidewater Asso. Oil Co., Ventura, 1940-42; supr. mfg. and engring. Douglas Aircraft Co., Long Beach, 1942-45; pres. Pacific Rivet and Machine Co., Alhambra, 1945-52, Pacific Fasteners, inc., Alhambra, 1951-54; v.p. Milford Rivet and Machine Co., Alhambra, 1952-54; sales mgr. S & C Electric Co., Chgo., 1954-56; v.p. West Coast ops. Townsend Co., Santa Ana, 1956-67; exec. v.p. West Coast ops. Townsend Co., 1967-82; pres. Cherry Textron, 1982-85, chmn., 1985-86; profl. cons. engr., 1954—; pres. Camalisa, Panama, 1965—; dir. Morehouse Engring. Corp., 1968-74, Orange County regional bd. U.S. Nat. Bank, 1969-73, First Fed. Savs. & Loan Assn., 1974-82; mem. regional bd. Calif. Fed. Savs. and Loan, 1982—; cons., bd. dirs. Airdrome Parts Co., Long Beach, Calif., 1987—. Mem. adv. bd. Calif. State U., Fullerton, 1961-81, chmn., 1971-81; chmn. Disneyland awards Com., 1971-72; trustee St. Joseph Found., 1970-76, 78-82, chmn., 1982; trustee Chapman Coll., Orange, 1972—, exec. vice chmn., 1976—; trustee Calif. Coll. Medicine of U. Calif. at Irvine, 1973—, vice chmn., 1976-79, chmn., 1979—; chmn. Community Airport Council, 1974-86. Recipient Outstanding Humanitarian award NCCJ, 1980. Mem. IEEE, Nat. Aeros. Assn., Mchts. and Mfrs. Assn. (v.p., bd. dirs., chmn. 1985, chmn. exec. com. 1986), Airplane Owners and Pilots Assn., Nat. Pilots Assn., Am. Mgmt. Assn., Theta Tau. Clubs: Santa Ana Country, Balboa Bay, Pacific. Home: 1841 Beverly Glen Dr Santa Ana CA 92705 Office: 1224 E Warner Santa Ana CA 92707

BUSTERUD, JOHN ARMAND, lawyer, environmental consultant; b. Coos Bay, Oreg., Mar. 7, 1921; s. Herbert Armand and Mary (Kruse) B.; m. Anne Witwer, Apr. 18, 1953; children—John, James, Mary. B.S. with honors in Econs., U. Oreg., 1943; LL.B., Yale U., 1949. Bar: Calif. 1950, U.S. Ct. Appeals (9th cir.) 1950, U.S. Dist. Ct. (no. dist.) Calif. 1950, U.S. Supreme Ct. 1969, D.C. 1977, U.S. Ct. Appeals (D.C. cir.) 1977. Assoc., Thelen, Marrin, Johnson & Bridges, San Francisco, 1949-53; of counsel John W. Broad, San Francisco, 1953-57; ptnr. Broad, Busterud & Khourie, San Francisco, 1957-70, Busterud, Draper & Adams, San Francisco, 1970-71; sr.

counselor Ecology & Environment, Inc., Palo Alto, Calif., 1981—; instr. Duke U. Sch. Forestry; spl. counsel in constl. revision Calif. State Assembly, 1963-64; mem. Council on Environ. Quality, Exec. Office of Pres., 1972-77, chmn., 1976-77; dep. asst. sec. of def., 1971-72; mem. Internat. Council Environ. Law, 1978-81; adj. prof. Hastings Coll. Law. Mem. Calif. State Assembly, 1957-62, Calif. Constl. Revision Commn., 1965-77; pres. Headlands, Inc., 1969-71, RESOLVE, Ctr. Environ. Conflict Resolution, 1978-81; del. UN Law of Sea Conf., 1973-76; chmn. legal project US-USSR Environ. Agreement, 1973-77. Served to lt. col. AUS, 1943-46. Decorated Bronze Star. Recipient Benjamin N. Cardozo prize Yale Law Sch., 1947; Civilian Service award Dept. of Def., 1972; research scholar Internat. Inst. Applied Systems Analysis, Austria, 1977. Fellow Am. Acad. Polit. Sci.; mem. ABA, Phi Beta Kappa. Republican. Episcopalian. Clubs: Bohemian, Commonwealth of Calif. (past pres.) (San Francisco); Chevy Chase, Cosmos (Washington); Rotary (Palo Alto, Calif.), Yale (N.Y.). Bd. editors Yale Law Jour., 1948-49; contbr. articles to profl. jours. Office: 60 Hamilton Ct Palo Alto CA 94301

BUSWELL, DAVID HASTINGS, automobile manufacturing executive; b. Chgo., June 25, 1934; s. Otis Leroy and Eleanor Josephine (Haser) B.; student U. Ill., 1952-54; B.S., No. Ill. U., 1957, postgrad., 1959-60; postgrad. U. Md., 1962; m. Susan Rowe, Oct. 15, 1960 (div. 1985); children—Janice, Scott Rockwood; m. Yoko Ogata, Apr. 11, 1986. Sr. editor Martin Marietta Corp., Middle River, Md., 1960-62; sr. editor The Asphalt Inst., College Park, Md., 1962-64; public info. officer Nat. Acad. Scis., Washington, 1964-70; dir. public affairs FTC, Washington, 1970-73; partner Kornmeier Ladd & Buswell, Washington, 1973-77; dir. govt. affairs Fiatallis N.Am., Inc., dir. govt. relations, Fiat U.S.A., Inc., Washington, 1977-88, v.p. Fiat Washngton Inc., 1988— . Mem. Md. Republican State Central Com., 1966-70; trustee Howard County (Md.) Gen. Hosp., 1976-80. Served with USCGR, 1957-59, USNR, 1966—. Recipient Disting. Service award FTC, 1973. Mem. Nat. Fgn. Trade Council, Constrn. Industry Mfrs. Assn., Nat. council U.S. China Trade, Washington Export Council, Public Relations Soc. Am., Res. Officers Assn., Naval Res. Assn., Am. Def. Preparedness Assn. Mem. United Ch. of Christ. Clubs: Internat., Capitol Hill, Mason. Home: 3007 Meeting St Falls Church VA 22044 Office: 1919 Pennsylvania Ave NW Washington DC 20006

BUSZKO, HENRYK BRONISLAW, architect; b. Lwow, Poland, Sept. 3, 1924; s. Jan and Henryka (Luczek) B.; m. Jozefa Brzoza, July 17, 1948; children—Marta Maria, Jan Pawel. M.Arch., Tech. U., Cracow, Poland, 1949. Architect, town planner, Katowice, Poland, 1949-58; mem. leading team Archtl. Atelie, Katowice, 1958—; interior and exhbn. designer Fine Art Studios, Katowice; asst. to prof. Sch. Architecture, Wroctaw, Poland, 1949-50; lectr. Tech. U., Gliwice, Poland, 1970-78; mem. Cons. Commn. Architecture, Katowice, 1954—; mem. com. State awards Archtl. sect., Warsaw, 1969—; mem. cons. Central Commn. for Town Planning, Warsaw, 1982—; mem. juries numerous archtl. competitions. Archtl. works include: Trade Unions Centre House, Regional Theatre, Rybnik, Poland, 1000-Year Urban Housing Devel., Mt. Health Resort Ustron Zawodzie, Roman Cath. Ch. in Katowice, Polish Cath. Ch. in Czestochowah, many others; author: My Meditations About Housing, 1982. Recipient awards Com. of Architecture and Town Planning 1959, 61, 62; Archtl. award Ministry of Bldg, 1969, 73; Sci. award Sci. and High Schs. Ministry, 1973; Tech. award Fedn. Engrs. Assn., 1973; Artistic award of Silesia region. Mem. Assn. Polish Architects (pres. 1965-75, hon. award 1975), AIA (hon.), Mexican Architects Assn., Counsel of Internat. Union Architects, Polish Acad. Sci. (com. for architecture and urbanism). Roman Catholic. Office: Pracownia Projektow Budowon Ogoln, Marchlewskiego 19, P-40-530 Katowice Poland *

BUSZKOWSKI, WOJCIECH PAWEL, mathematics educator; b. Poznan, Poland, Oct. 17, 1950; s. Leszek Stanislaw and Aleksandra (Langner) B.; m. Joanna Grazyna Mroczkowska, 1978; children: Eliza, Izabela. M in Mathematics, Adam Mickiewicz U., Poznan, Phd in Mathematics, 1982. Assistant Adam Mickiewicz U., Poznan, 1973-76, asst. lectr., 1976-82, lectr., 1982—; coordinator research Inst. Philosophy and Sociology Polish Acad., Warsaw, Poland, 1986—; supr. research Dept. Logic Warsaw U., 1986—. Assoc. editor jour. Studia Logica, 1985—, also adv. bd., 1988—; editor Categorial Grammar; contbr. articles to profl. jours.; speaker in field. Recipient sci. prize Ministry Sci. and Higher Edn., Warsaw, 1986; grantee Polish govt., Warsaw, 1986—. Mem. Polish Math. Soc., Polish Semiotic Soc. Avocations: philosophy, hiking, cycling, belles lettres. Home: Osiedle Rusa 6/52, 61-245 Poznan Poland Office: Adam Mickiewicz U Inst Math, Matejki 48/49, 60-769 Poznan Poland

BUTCHER, RUSSELL DEVEREUX, author, photographer; b. Bryn Mawr, Pa., Feb. 8, 1938; s. Devereux and Mary Frances (Taft) B.; student Colo. State U., 1957-58; B.A., U. Colo., 1960; postgrad. U. Mich. Law Sch., 1960-61; m. Pamela Richards, Apr. 12, 1967; 1 dau., Wendy Nan; children by previous marriage—Pamela Marie (dec.), Neill Devereux. Research editor Sierra Club, San Francisco, 1961-65; editorial writer N.Y. Times, 1963-79; publicity writer Save-the-Redwoods League, San Francisco, 1963-65; conservation specialist Nat. Audubon Soc., N.Y.C., 1965-66, also mem. editorial bd. Audubon mag.; chief of public relations and publs. Mus. of N.Mex., Santa Fe, 1967-69; free-lance writer, photographer and author, 1969-80; conservation zoning cons. Town of Mount Desert (Maine), 1978-79, SW and Calif. rep. Nat. Parks and Conservation Assn., 1980—. Mem. Ariz. Strip Dist. adv. council U.S. Bur. Land Mgmt. Mem. Save-the-Redwoods League (life), Nat. Parks and Conservation Assn., Maine Audubon Soc. (pres. Down East chpt. 1978-80, trustee 1979-80), Sierra Club (life). Episcopalian (vestryman 1978-81). Author: Maine Paradise, 1973; New Mexico: Gift of the Earth, 1975; The Desert, 1976; Field Guide to Acadia National Park, Maine, 1977; contbr. articles to environ. jours. Home and Office: Box 67 Cottonwood AZ 86326

BUTENANDT, ADOLF FRIEDRICH JOHANN, physiological chemist; b. Bremerhaven, Germany, Mar. 24, 1903; s. Otto and Wilhelmine (Thomfohrde) B.; Ph.D.; ed. Oberrealschule Bremerhaven, U. Marburg, U. Göttingen; m. Erika von Ziegner, 1931; 2 sons, 5 daus. Sci. asst. Chem. Inst., Göttingen U., 1927-30, docent in organic and biol. chemistry, 1931; prof. chemistry, dir. Organic Chemistry Inst., Danzig (Ger.) Inst. Tech., 1933-36; dir. Kaiser Wilhelm Inst. Biochemistry, Berlin, Max Planck Inst. Biochemistry, Munich, 1936-72; prof. physiol. chemistry Munich U., 1956-71, prof. emeritus, 1971—. Recipient Nobel prize for chemistry, 1939; Adolf von Harnack medal Max Planck Soc., 1973; decorated Orden pour le Mérite, 1962, comdr. Légion d'Honneur, Ordr Palmes Académiques; Österreichisches Ehrenzeichen für Wissenschaft und Kunst. Mem. Max Planck Soc. (pres. 1960-72, hon. pres. 1972), Acad. Scis. Paris (fgn.). Author: Biochemie der Wirkstoffe; also articles.

BUTERA, LUIGI, architect, educator; b. Naples, Italy, Feb. 26, 1946; came to U.S., 1977; s. Remigio and Adele (Zucchetti) B. Maestro d'Arte, Istituto d'Arte Academe Fine Arts, Venice, Italy, 1964; Maturita Artistica, Liceo Artistico, Naples, 1964; Dr. Arch., U. Venice, 1969. Registered architect, Italy. Asst. prof. U. Venice, 1971-77; vis. assoc. prof. Clemson U. (S.C.), 1977; prof. Archtl. Ctr., Boston, 1978, Ryerson Poly. Inst., Toronto, 1978-79; Ont. Coll., Toronto, Can., 1978-79; assoc. prof. Iowa State U., Ames, 1979-80; prof., chmn. EDP Roger Williams Coll., Bristol, R.I., 1980-86, Pa. State U., 1987, Tex. Tech U., 1988—; designer, cons. 3M Co., Milan, Italy, 1972, Fin-Mar Co., Milan, 1975-76, Barry Koretz Assocs., Boston, 1977-78; chief designer AM&A Assocs., Providence, 1980-81; prin. DLB Designs, Providence, 1980—; lectr. in field. Author: Architettura Acustica, 1973; contbr. articles to profl. jours. Seminar leader Henschede Technische Hogesch., Holland, 1970, S.I.E.I.C., Paris, 1972; advisor Fulbright Commn., Rome, 1974; founder pres. New CIAM, Toronto, 1979. Profl. design work illustrated at 3d Internat. Exhbn. of Architecture, 1985, and in collection of hist. archives of Biennale of Venice. Recipient 1st prize Lido Hosp. City of Venice, 1974; prize Excellence Design NERC, 1982; Acoustics and Architecture award U. Venice, 1971; project selected for Galveston (Tex.) Festival, 1988. Mem. ODA (Italian Architects Guild), SIAE (Italian Writers Guild), AIA (assoc. mem.), Boston Archtl. Ctr. Assocs., Nat. Trust for Hist. Preservation. Clubs: Architecture (advisor Ryerson 1978-79) (advisor Roger Williams Coll. 1980—). Home: Via Milano, 25 Mestre, Venice 30172, Italy Office: 10 Thayer St Providence RI 02906

BUTKOVIC, MIRKO, mechanical engineer, researcher, educator; b. Karlovac, Yugoslavia, Sept. 21, 1936; s. Valentin and Katarina (Sostarac) B.; m. Barbara Jarnevic, Jan. 6, 1962; children—Mladen, Goran. B.S.M.E., Zagreb U. (Yugoslavia), 1961, M.S.M.E., 1971, Ph.D. in Mech. Engring., 1976; M.S., Washington U., St. Louis, 1972. Designer Jugoturbina, Karlovac, Yugoslavia, 1962-65, lab. chief, 1965-69, dir. research and devel., 1970-80, pres. research and devel., 1980—; asst. Coll. of Karlovac, 1962-65, lectr., 1965-80, prof., 1980—; lectr. Zagreb U., 1978—. Author: Mechanics Handbook, 1978; contbr. articles to jours. and publs. in field. Mem. Reform Commn. of Ministry Edn., Zagreb, 1980—, Nuclear Commn., Jumel, Belgrade, 1981—. Recipient Town award Town of Karlovac, 1968, work medal Govt. of Yugoslavia, 1965. Mem. Internat. Fedn. for Theory of Machines and Mechanisms (pres. Croatia br. 1981-83), Assn. Engrs. and Technicians of Yugoslavia, Zagreb C. of C. (energy commn. 1980—). Home: 8 Divizije 1, 47000 Karlovac Yugoslavia Office: Jugoturbina, 155 Mala Svarca, 47000 Karlovac Yugoslavia

BUTLER, ARTHUR WILLIAM, parliamentary and political consultant; b. London, Jan. 20, 1929; s. Frederick and Ella (Waller) B.; m. Evelyn Mary Luetchford, May 3, 1959. BSc in Econs., U. London, 1952. Journalist Kemsley Newspapers, Middlesborough and London, Eng., 1952-56; polit. corr. News Chronicle, London, 1956-60; polit. editor Reynolds News, London, 1960-62; polit. corr. Daily Express, London, 1963-69; polit. editor Daily Sketch, London, 1969-71; parliamentary cons. Partnerplan, London, 1971-73, John Addey Assocs., London, 1973-76; parliamentary cons. Charles Barker Watney & Powell, London, 1976—, mng. dir., 1977-87, vice chmn., 1988—; sec. All Party Motor Industry Group, London, 1979—, Parliamentary Info. Tech. Com., London, 1980-84, Parliamentary and Sci. Com., London, 1977—; mem. Freeman City of London, Liveryman Tobacco Pipemakers Co. Co-author: No Feet To Drag, 1973, The First Forty Years, 1979; (booklet) Lobbying in the British Parliament, 1986. Sec. Roads Campaign Council, London, 1973-86. Served to capt. Brit. Army, 1946-48, with Res. 1952-62. Mem. Royal Instn., Nat. Union Journalists. Mem. Ch. of Eng. Home: 30 Chester Way, Kennington, London SE11 4UR, England Office: Charles Barker Watney & Powell, 30 Farringdon St, London EC4A 4EA, England

BUTLER, CHARLES HENRY, hospital administrator; b. N.Y.C., Oct. 12, 1932; s. Charles Henry and Theresa Edith (Simmons) B.; A.A.S., N.Y. City Community Coll., 1960; B.S., L.I. U., 1962; M.P.A., N.Y. U., 1970; m. Lois Evelyn Belle, Jan. 14, 1956; children—Charles Henry, Craig Aron. Advt. claims adjuster N.Y. Times, N.Y.C., 1950-65; br. office mgr. Bklyn. Union Gas Co., 1965-67; corp. personnel specialist Endicott Johnson Corp., Endicott, N.Y., 1967-69; sr. indsl. relations rep. Kennecott Copper Corp., N.Y.C., 1969-70; dir. personnel N.Y.C. Health & Hosps. Corp., 1970-83, Greenpoint Hosp., 1970-75, Queens Hosp. Center, 1975-78, Cumberland Hosp., Bklyn., 1978-83; evening adminstr. Woodhull Med. and Mental Health Ctr., Bklyn., 1983—; mem. faculty Marymount Coll., Tarrytown, N.Y., 1975-76. Pres. PTA, N.Y.C., 1966-67; chmn. adv. com. Citizens Affirmative Action, N.Y.C., 1974-76; state adviser U.S. Congl. Adv. Bd.; layreader St. Paul's Episcopal Ch., Spring Valley, N.Y. Served with USNR, 1953-55; lt. col. NY Air NG Res. Recipient Certificate of Appreciation, N.Y.C. Bd. Edn., 1967; award N.Y. State Dept. Mental Hygiene, 1975. Mem. Am. Mgmt. Assn., Res. Officers Assn., NAACP, Soc. Advancement of Mgmt., N.Y. U. Alumni Assn., 100 Black Men, Council Concerned Black Execs., N.Y. Orgn. Devel. Network, Assn. Mil. Surgeons U.S. Presbyterian. Contbr. article to profl. jours. Home: 6 Foxcroft Dr Nanuet NY 10954 Office: Woodhull Med & Mental Health Ctr 760 Broadway Brooklyn NY 11206

BUTLER, DAVID ALLEN, typesetting company executive; b. Pasadena, Calif., Mar. 13, 1944; s. Franklin Pierce and Leora Ruby (Westbrook) B. B.A., Pasadena Coll. (name changed to Point Loma Nazarene Coll.), 1966. Proofreader, Los Angeles Times, 1967-68, 71-72; tchr. Pasadena City Schs., 1968; typesetter Freedmen's Orgn., Los Angeles, 1972—, small bus. pres., 1977—. Served with U.S. Army, 1968-71, ETO. Republican. Mem. Ch. of Nazarene. Office: Freedmens Orgn 3311 Beverly Blvd Los Angeles CA 90004

BUTLER, EDWARD SCANNELL, organization executive; b. New Orleans, Mar. 11, 1934; s. Edward Scannell and Unola (Perrin) B.; m. Elizabeth Gay Bringier Rivet, Dec. 30, 1957 (div. Jan. 1972); children: Edward Scannell IV, Nola Elizabeth, Matthew Franklin Thomson; m. Rosanne Marie Clarkston, Nov. 18, 1972 (div. 1981); children: Dawn Marie, Clarkston James. Student, Loyola U., New Orleans, 1955-57, Nat. Art Acad., Washington, 1959. Account exec. Brown-Friedman Advt., New Orleans, 1960; dir. staff Info. Council of Ams., New Orleans, 1961-62, exec. v.p., 1963-69, v.p. communications, 1970, exec. v.p., 1971-77, pres., 1978—; pres. Scannell Assocs., Inc., 1967—; Sr. cons. to chmn. bd. Eversharp Inc., 1966-70, Technicolor Inc., 1966-70; speaker to nat. and local bus. edn. and profl. groups, also appearances on radio and TV, 1961—; Mem. nat. adv. com. Cold War Council, 1963-66; mem. adv. com. Friends of Free Asia, 1966-67; mem. adv. bd. Young Ams. for Freedom, 1967-69; Bd. dirs. World Youth Crusade for Freedom, 1967-68. Producer: record album Oswald: Self-Portrait in Red, 1964, Oswald Speaks, 1967; TV spl. Hitler in Havana!, 1967; host: TV spl. Oswald: Self-Portrait, 1968; TV series The Square World of Ed Butler, 1969-70; host, exec. producer: TV series Spirit '76, 1975-76; radio-TV series Spirit U.S; Author: Revolution Is My Profession, 1968; Contbr. articles to trade, profl. and popular publs. Served with AUS, 1957-59. Mem. Young Men's Bus. Club Greater New Orleans (def. bur. chmn. 1962, editor Action 1963, Americanism award 1963), New Orleans Jaycees (editor Forward 1963, Distinguished Service award, Outstanding Young Man in New Orleans award 1969), Am. Security Council (cold war victory com. 1966-68). Roman Catholic. Clubs: Bienville, Bogalusa Country. Office: care INCA 800 Audubon Bldg New Orleans LA 70112

BUTLER, ELAINE RUTH MARJORIE MALLORY (MRS. HAROLD ARTHUR BUTLER), civic worker, author; b. North Bergen, N.J., July 2; d. Eugene Lester and Adele May (Reeder) Mallory; A.B., Barnard Coll., 1930; postgrad. Montclair Coll., 1932; M.S., N.Y. Sch. Social Work, 1935; postgrad. Seton Hall U., 1939, 53; M.S., Newark State Coll., 1959; postgrad. U. San German (P.R.), 1959, No. Ariz. U., 1978, Scottsdale Community Coll., 1979; Ph.D. (hon.), Hamilton U., 1974; m. Harold Arthur Butler, Feb. 17, 1928; 1 dau., Dellamay Dorothy Butler Seibold. Tchr. Horace Mann Sch., Tchrs. Coll., N.Y.C., 1926; statistician, confidential sec. Boy Scouts Am., N.Y.C., 1926-30; investigator Tenement Housing Authority, N.Y. Assembly, 1927; tchr., asst. to prof. Montclair (N.J.) Coll., 1932-37; social worker Dept. Instns. and Agys., Trenton, N.J., 1937-48; adminstrv. sec. N.J. Heart Assn., Newark, 1948-51; tchr. specialist Montclair Pub. Schs., 1953-64; free lance writer, artist, 1964—. Worker, Gompers Rehab. Inst., Phoenix, 1966; mem. aux. Goodwill Industries, Phoenix, 1968—; chmn. Fun for Funds and Bridge Builders, Phoenix, 1966—; active Community Orgn. for Drug Abuse Control, Phoenix, 1969—; corp. sec. 7th Step Found., 1974-75, 79-84, bd. dirs., 1974-84; bd. dirs. Ariz. Corrections Project; v.p. Ariz. Citizens' Com. Self Help Now; adv. bd. Save-A-Child League, Loretta Young Youth Project. Sec., Democratic Club, New Brunswick, N.J., 1939; campaign mgr. South Orange Village Council, 1955; treas. Valley of Sun chpt. Northwood Inst., Midland, Mich.; bd. dirs. No. Regional Council of Prisons; adv. bd. Nat. Security Council. Recipient numerous awards latest including Ariz. Dept. Corrections for Vol. Work, cert. honor Bd. Edn., Montclair, N.J. Fellow Internat. Biog. Assn.; mem. AAUW (chmn. Scottsdale br. 1977), Nat. Assn. Ret. Fed. Employees (sec. Phoenix 1965-69, sec.-treas. Ariz. Fedn. 1969-71, charter mem. Scottsdale 1972—, sec.-treas. 1972-73, news editor 1979—, nat. 2d v.p. 1981—), Seven Coll. Conf., Nat., N.J., Montclair edn. assn., Franklin Mint Soc. (charter), Friends of Mexican Art, Friends for Terros Aux. (charter), Internat. Platform Assn., Scottsdale YWCA Triangles Aux., Valley Artists League, Ariz. Poets, Musicians and Artists Assn., Ariz. Women in Transition (charter, treas.), Scottsdale Artists League, Nat. Bus. and Profl. Women, Barnard Coll. Bus. and Profl. Women, Internat. Platform Assn., Heritage Assn., Women in Patrnership in Recognition of Outstanding Committment through Career AAUW, Phoenix Art Mus., Heard Mus. Presbyterian (fellowship chmn. 1965-66, coordinator for Involvement in Action 1966-68); one of 150 women chosen to attend 1st Ariz. Women's Town Hall. Clubs: Orange Lawn Tennis (South Orange, N.J.), Scottsdale College; College of the Oranges (West Orange, N.J.). Home: 4015 E Sierra Vista Dr Paradise Valley AZ 85253 also: Las Conchas, Puerto Penasco Sonora, Mexico

BUTLER, FREDERICK GEORGE, retired drug company exective; b. Greenwich, Conn., Mar. 25, 1919; s. Harold Nassau and Rosa (Rhinhart) B.; m. Sarah Lou Allred, Sept. 23, 1945; children: Pamela Sue, Frederick Houston. A.B., Middlebury (Vt.) Coll., 1941; M.B.A., Columbia U., 1947. C.P.A., N.Y. With Price Waterhouse & Co. (C.P.A.'s), 1941-42, 47-49; with McKesson & Robbins, Inc., N.Y.C., 1949-63; asst. comptroller McKesson & Robbins, Inc., 1952-61, comptroller, 1961-63; controller Bristol-Myers Co., N.Y.C., 1963-66; v.p., controller Bristol-Myers Co., 1966-69, v.p. ops., 1970-76. Village mayor, Briarcliff Manor, N.Y., 1969-71; treas., trustee Phelps Meml. Hosp., North Tarrytown, N.Y., 1976-78. Served to comdr. USNR, 1942-46, 51-52. Mem. Fin. Execs. Inst., Chi Psi. Congregationalist. Club: Marco Island (Fla.) Country. Home: 58 N Collier Blvd Apt 2103 Marco Island FL 33937

BUTLER, FREDERICK GUY, poet; b. Cradock, Cape, South Africa, Jan. 21, 1918; s. Ernest Collett and Alice Eyre (Stringer) B.; m. Jean Murray Satchwell, Dec. 10, 1940; children: Patrick, Jane, David, Christopher. BA, Rhodes U., Grahamstown, Republic of South Africa, 1938, MA, 1939; BA with honors, Oxford U., Eng., 1947, MA, 1951; LittD (hon.), U. Natal, Durban, Republic of South Africa, 1970, Witwatersrand U., Johannesburg, Republic of South Africa, 1984. Tchr. St. Johns Coll., Johannesburg, 1940; lectr. English U. Witwatersrand, Johannesburg, 1948-50; sr. lectr. Rhodes U., Grahamstown, 1951, prof., head dept. English, 1952-78, prof., head dept. speech and drama, 1966-72, research prof., 1984-86, hon. research fellow, 1987—. Author: (poems) Stranger to Europe, 1952, South of the Zambezi, 1966, On First Seeing Florence, 1968, Selected Poems, 1975, Songs and Ballads, 1978, Pilgrimage to Dias Cross, 1987, Out of the African Ark, Animal Poems, 1988; (prose) An Aspect of Tragedy, 1953, Karoo Morning: An Autogiography 1918-35, 1977, Bursting World: An Autogiography 1936-45, 1983; (plays) The Dove Returns, 1956, Cape Charade, 1968, Richard Gush of Salem, 1984, others; editor: A Book of South African Verse, 1959, When Boys Were Men, 1969, others; contbr. articles to profl. jours. Mem. Commn. Inquiry into Creative Arts, Pretoria, Republic of South Africa, 1981-84; mem. governing bd. South African Nat. Theatre Orgn., 1952-54; mem. council 1820 Settlers, 1967, chmn. Festivals Com., organizer conf. English-Speaking South Africa, 1973; mem. drama com. Cape Performing Arts Bd., 1965-75; planner Nat. Shakespeare Festival, 1976, 84. Served to capt. Army Edn. Services, South Africa Def. Force, 1940-45. Alfred Metcalfe scholar, 1935, U. South Africa scholar, 1939, Queen Victoria scholar, 1939; Nuffield Found. fellow, 1954, vis. fellow, Cambridge U., Eng., 1977; Carnegie Travel grantee, 1958; recipient 1st and 2d prizes, S.A.B.C. Poetry Competitions, 1949, 53, 1st prize van Riebeeck Tercentenary Found., 1953, Cen. News Agy. award, 1976, Cape Tercentenary Found. Lit. award, 1981. Mem. English Acad. South Africa (hon. life pres.), Shakespeare Soc. So. Africa (nat. pres. 1985). Progressive. Anglican. Office: Rhodes U, Dept English, Grahamstown 0461, Republic of South Africa

BUTLER, JAMES LEE, agricultural engineer, researcher; b. Sevierville, Tenn., Jan. 8, 1927; s. James Lawson and Dora Mae (Fox) B.; m. Jane Isabell Hollis, Nov. 20, 1948; children: Kathryn Jo, Nancy Lee, Benjamin Hollis. BS, U. Tenn., 1950, MS, 1951; PhD, Mich. State U., 1958. Asst. agrl. engr. U. Ga., Experiment, 1951-56, assoc. agrl. engr., 1958-60; grad. asst. Mich. State U., East Lansing, 1956-58; agrl. engr. Agrl. Research Service, USDA, Tifton, Ga., 1960-62, research investigations leader, 1962-80, research leader, 1985—; mgr. So. Agrl. Energy Ctr., Tifton, 1980-85. Assoc. editor Peanut Sci., 1974-80; mem. editorial bd. Energy in Agriculture, 1982-87; contbr. numerous articles to profl. publs. Served to cpl. AC, U.S. Army, 1944-46. Recipient Golden Peanut Research award Nat. Peanut Council, 1979, Ga. Research and Edn. award. 1988; USDA Merit cert. 1980, 82, 86. Fellow Am. Soc. Agrl. Engrs. (bd. dirs. 1980-82, 87-89, best paper award 1960, Ga. sect. Engr. of Yr. 1981); mem. Am. Peanut Research and Edn. Soc. (pres. 1982-83, Bailey award 1978), NSPE, Council Agrl. Sci. and Tech. Baptist. Home: 2823 Rainwater Rd Tifton GA 31794 Office: USDA-ARS PO Box 748 Tifton GA 31794

BUTLER, JAMES ROBERTSON, JR., lawyer; b. Cleve., May 29, 1946; s. James Robertson and Iris Davis (Welborn) B.; m. Laurie Jean Smith, June 26, 1979; 1 child, Brandy Valentine. AB magna cum laude, U. Calif., Berkeley, 1966, JD, 1969. Bar: Calif. 1970, U.S. Tax Ct. 1977, U.S. Supreme Ct. 1980. Sr. corp. and securities ptnr., chmn. Fin. Instns. Dept. Jeffer, Mangels & Butler, Los Angeles and San Francisco; speaker and panelist Robert Morris Assocs. 28th Western Regional Conf., San Diego, 1985; frequent TV appearances as expert on securities, real estate and banking, 1985-88. Author: Arbitration in Lending, A Robert Morris Associates State of the Art Book, 1988, Lending Liability: A Practical Guide, A BNA Special Report, 1987; editor Banking Law Report Capital Adequacy series, 1985, Calif. Law Rev.; co-chmn. adv. council Money and Real Estate: The Jour. of Lending, Syndication, Joint Ventures, and the Third Market; contbr. chpt., Mapping the Minefield--Lender's Liability to book, The Workout Game, Solutions to Problem Real Estate Loans, 1987; contbr. articles to profl. jours. Mem. Am. Arbitration Assn., Comml. Arbitration Panel; founding dir. Liberty Nat. Bank; Charter Adv. bd. dirs., Adv. Council of the Banking Law Inst. Recipient Kraft Prize U. Calif., 1966; Bartley Cavenaugh Crum scholar U. Calif. Sch. Law, 1969. Mem. ABA (corp., banking and bus. law sect., taxation sect.), Los Angeles County Bar Assn., Beverly Hills Bar Assn., Calif. League of Savs. Instns. (chmn. arbitration com. 1987, 88), Order of Coif, Phi Beta Kappa, Pi Sigma Alpha. Office: Jeffer Mangels & Butler 2121 Ave of the Stars Los Angeles CA 90067 also: One Sansome St 12th Fl San Francisco CA 94104

BUTLER, MICHAEL A., corporate executive; b. Garrett, Ind., Sept. 26, 1956; s. Donald F. and Retha D. (Manon) B.; m. V. Catherine Button, Oct. 30, 1984; children: Kenneth W. Button, Jessica M. Butler, Gregory M. Butler. BBA in Mktg., Ind. U., 1978. Asst. dir. Auburn (Ind.) Cord Duesenberg Mus., 1974-78; gen. mgr. State Theatres Inc., Westland, Mich., 1978-86; pres. Westwood Co., Dearborn Heights, Mich., 1984—; exec. v.p. Kruse Internat., Auburn, 1986—. Republican. Roman Catholic. Clubs: Auburn Automotive Heritage, Rolls Royce Owners, Mercedes Benz Owners. Home: 717 Brentwood Circle Auburn IN 46706 Office: Kruse Internat 5400 CR 11-A at 69 Auburn IN 46706

BUTLER, PERCY JAMES, accountant, business executive; b. Bath, Avon, Eng., Mar. 15, 1929; s. Percy Ernest and Phyllis Mary (Bartholomew) B.; m. Margaret Prudence Copland, June 26, 1954; children: Elizabeth Anne Hillier, Susan Margaret, David James. Student Marlborough Coll. (Eng.), 1942-47; MA in Math. with honors, Clare Coll. (Eng.), 1952. With Peat Marwick McLintock, London, 1952—, mng. ptnr., 1981-85, sr. ptnr., 1986—; mem. exec. com. and council Klynweld Peat Marwick Goerdeler, 1987—; dir. Mersey Docks & Harbour Co., Liverpool, Eng. Mem. Marlborough Coll. Council, 1975—, chmn. fin. com., 1983—; chmn. Local Conservative Assn., Ticehurst, Eng., 1980-85; treas. Pilgrims Soc., London, 1981—. Decorated comdr. Order of Brit. Empire. Fellow Inst. Chartered Accts. in Eng. and Wales. Mem. Ch. of England. Club: Carlton. Home: Crawley House, Littleton SO21 2QF, England Office: Peat Marwick McLintock & Co, 1 Puddle Dock Blackfriars, London EC4V3PD, England

BUTLIN, MARTIN RICHARD FLETCHER, art gallery curator; b. July 29, 1929; s. Kenneth Rupert and Helen Mary (Fletcher) B.; m. Frances Caroline Chodsko, 1969. Student, Rendcomb Coll., Eng., 194--42, Trinity Coll., Cambridge, 1949-52; MA, Cambridge U.; BA, Courtbauld Inst. of Art, London U., 1955; DLit, London U., 1984. Asst. keeper Hist. Brit. Collection, Tate Gallery, London, 1955-67, keeper Hist. Brit. Collection, 1967—. Author: A Catalogue of the Works of William Blake in the Tate Gallery, 1957, 2d edit. 1971, Samuel Palmer's Sketchbook of 1824, 1962, Turner Watercolours, 1962, (with Sir John Rothenstein) Turner, 1964, (with Mary Chamot and Dennis Farr) Tate Gallery Catalogues: The Modern British Paintings, Drawings and Sculpture, 1964, The Later Works of J.M.W. Turner, 1966, William Blake, 1966, The Blake-Varley Sketchbook of 1819, 1969, (with E. Joll) The Paintings of J.M.W. Turner, 1977, 2d edit. 1984 (Mitchell Prize for the History of Art 1979), The Paintings and Drawings of William Blake, 1981, Aspects of British Painting 1550-1800, From the Collection of the Sarah Campbell Blaffer Foundation, 1988; selected paintings and prepared catalogues for various exhbns., including: (with Andrew Wilson and John Cage) Turner, 1775-1851, 1974, William Blake, 1978; contbr. articles to Burlington Mag., Connoisseur, Master Drawings, Blake Newsletter and others. Office: Tate Gallery, Millbank, London SW1P 4RG, England

BUTOR, MICHEL, author, educator; b. Mons-en-Baroeul Nord, France, Sept. 14, 1926; s. Emile Butor and Anne Brajeux; m. Marie-Josephe Mas, 1958; 4 children. Degree, U. Paris. Tchr., Sens, France, 1950, Minieh, Egypt, 1950-51, Manchester, Eng., 1951-53, Slonica, Greece, 1954-55, Geneva, 1956-57; vis. prof. Bryn Mawr Coll. and Middlebury Coll., 1960, Northwestern U., Evanston, Ill., 1965, U. N.Mex., Albuquerque, 1969-70, 1973-74, Nice and Geneva, 1974-75; assoc. prof., Vincennes, 1969, Nice, 1970-73; prof. modern French, U. Geneva, from 1975. Author novels including: Passage de Milan, 1954; L'emploi du temps, 1956; La modification, 1957; Degrees, 1960; Intervalle, 1973; (essays) Le Genie du lieu, 1958; Repertoire, 1960; Histoire extraordinaire, 1961; Mobile, 1962; Reseau aerien, 1963; Description de San Marco, 1963; Les oeuvres d'art imaginaires chez Proust, 1964; Repertoire II, 1964; Portrait de l'artiste en jeune singe, 1967; Repertoire III, 1968; Essai sur les essais, 1968; Les mots dans la peinture, 1969; La rose des vents, 1970; Le genie du lieu II, 1971; Dialogue avec 33 variations de L. Van Beethoven, 1971; Repertoire IV, 1974; Matière de reves, 1975; Second sous-sol, 1976; Troisiè me dessous, 1977; Boomerang, 1978; Quadruple Fond, 1981; Repertoire V, 1982; (poetry) Illustrations, 1964; 6,801.00 litres d'eau par second, 1965; Illustrations II, 1969; Travaux d'approche, 1972; Illustrations III, 1973; Illustrations IV, 1976; Envois, 1980; Brassee d'Avril, 1982; Expres, 1983, A Change of Heart, 1984. Decorated chevalier Ordre Nationale deu Mérite; Ordre des Arts et des Lettres; prix Felix Feneon, 1957; prix Renaudot, 1957; grand prix de la critique litteraire 1960. *

BUTRUILLE, DANIEL, antibiotic manufacturing company executive; b. Reims, France, Oct. 8, 1944; arrived in Mex., 1968; s. Edmond and Francoise Louise (Ducancel) B.; m. Virginia Martinez, Jan. 29, 1970; children—Gabriela, Etienne. B., Coll. St. Joseph, Reims, 1961; B.Sc. in Chemistry, Sorbonne, 1964; Chem. Engr., E.S.C.O.M., Paris, 1965; Ph.D. in Chemistry, Laval U., 1968. Tech. expert French Embassy, Mex., 1968-76; prof. Instituto Tecnoló gico y de Estudios Superiores de Monterrey, Mex., 1977; devel. mgr. Fermentacionesy Sintesis, Monterrey, 1978-80; operation mgr. Grupo Indsl. Benavides, Monterrey, 1980-84; gen. dir. Centro Indsl. Bioquimico, Monterrey, 1984—. Contbr. chpts. to textbooks, articles to profl. jours. Com. mem. Alianza Francesa, Monterrey, 1977. Mem. Inst. Mexicano de Ingenieros Quimicos. Avocations: bridge; tennis; reading. Home: Missouri ote 224, Col del Valle Garza Garcia, Nuevo Leon Mexico 66220

BUTTERFIELD, BRUCE SCOTT, publishing company executive; b. N.Y.C., Feb. 4, 1949; s. Richard Julian and Mary (Hart) B.; m. Karin Lynn Wittlinger, June 20, 1986; 1 child, Elizabeth Holly. B.A. cum laude, Amherst Coll., 1971; M.A., Harvard U., 1972; M.B.A., U. Conn., 1977; advanced cert. in journalism and creative fiction, Newspaper Inst. Am, 1981. Adminstrv. asst. Golden Press div. Western Pub. Co., N.Y.C., 1972; editor, coordinator Golden Press div. Western Pub. Co., 1973-74, sr. editor, 1975-76, mng. editor, adminstr., 1977; gen. mgr. Decisions Publs., 1978; assoc. pub. Scholastic Inc., N.Y.C., 1979-80, v.p., pub., 1981-83; exec. v.p. Longman Inc., N.Y.C., 1984; pres. Longman Inc., 1985—, also bd. dirs.; bd. dirs. Pitman Pub. Inc., Longman Inc., Ind. Sch. Press, Angel Entertainment Inc. Author: Fantasy and the Free School Thought: E.B. White and His Literature for Children, 1971; A Plea for Fantasy, 1972; Our Real Work Can't Be Drudgery, 1979; editor various books including: ABC's Wide World of Sports, 1975; Buccaneers, 1975; Book of the Mysterious, 1976; Chroma-Schema, 1977; Calculator Games, 1977; Children's Bible Stories, 1978; Oh Heavenly Dog, 1980; The Watcher in the Woods, 1980. Named Most Valuable Pitcher, Bergen Highlanders, 1969, All New Eng. Amateur Baseball Pitcher, 1971, All Am. Amateur Baseball Pitcher, 1971; recipient Wall St. Jour. Achievement award, 1978; Nat. Fedn. Music award, 1963; J.F. Kennedy Brotherhood Essay award, 1967; Gardener Fletcher fellow, 1972; St. Clair Meml. fellow 1972; Amherst Coll. fellow, 1972. Mem. Am. Acad. Arts and Scis., Am. Acad. Polit. and Social Scis., Assn. Am. Pubs., Children's Book Council, M.B.A. Execs., Internat. Platform Assn., Beta Gamma Sigma, Phi Delta Kappa, Phi Delta Sigma. Republican. Christian Scientist. Clubs: Forum, Harvard (N.Y.C.). Home: 189 Parish Rd S New Canaan CT 06840 Office: Longman Inc 95 Church St White Plains NY 10601

BUTTERFIELD, JEFFREY, athletic society administrator; b. Cleckheaton, Yorkshire, Eng., Aug. 9, 1929; s. George and Hilda (Metcalf) B.; m. Barbara Kirton, Mar. 28, 1956; 1 child, Giles Dickon. Diploma in phys. edn., Loughborough (Eng.) Coll., 1951. Tchr. Wellingborough (Eng.) Grammar Sch., 1951-54, Worksop (Eng.) Coll., 1954-60; with Coating Contractors Ltd, Buckingham, Eng., 1960-67; property devel. Mackenzie Hill Ltd., Eng., 1967-73; dir. The Rugby Club, London, 1972—; Eng. selector Rugby Football Union, London, 1968-72. Served as sgt. Brit. mil., 1949-50. Recipient Brit. Lion South Africa, 1955, Australia and New Zealand, 1959. Home: Red Stack Wicken, Milton Keynes MK19 6B4, England Office: The Rugby Club London, 49 Hallam St, London W1N 5LJ, England

BUTTERS, GORDON, polymer scientist, chemical engineering educator; b. Lancaster, Eng., Oct. 2, 1936; s. John Stevenson and Mary Ann Steven (Munro) B.; m. Patricia Maureen Denton, Nov. 1, 1958; 1 child, Michael. Grad. Royal Inst. Chemistry, Lancaster and Morecambe Coll. Further Edn., 1962. Chartered chemist; chartered engr. Chief chemist Somic Ltd., Preston, Eng., 1962-65; sr. devel. chemist Mobil Chems. Ltd., Stroud, Eng., 1965-68; various tech. mgmt. positions BP Chems. Ltd., Barry, Eng., 1968-84; group leader processing and particle tech. BP Chems. Ltd., Grangemouth, Scotland, 1984—; hon. prof. chem. and process engring. Heriot-Watt U., Edinburgh, Scotland, 1986—. Editor, joint author: Plastics Pneumatic Conveying and Bulk Storage, 1981; editor: Particulate Nature of PVC, 1982. Dir. music Queensferry Parish Ch. Fellow Royal Soc. Chemistry (solids and materials processing award 1981), Plastics and Rubber Inst., Instn. Chem. Engrs.; mem. Brit. Inst. Mgmt. Lodge: Rotary (internat. chmn. South Queensferry 1986—). Home: 6 Ashburnham Gardens, South Queensferry West Lothian EH30 9LB, Scotland Office: BP Chemicals Ltd, Bogness Rd Grangemouth, Stirlingshire FK3 9XH, Scotland

BUTTLE, EDGAR ALLYN, judge; b. N.Y.C., May 7, 1903; s. Norman Alexander and Ella Tice (Collins) B.; m. Erika Lucille Heydolph, Aug. 9, 1931; 1 dau., Dagmar Jo Ann. A.B., Columbia U., 1928; J.D., N.Y. U., 1931, J.S.D., 1935; postgrad., Princeton U., 1945. Bar: N.Y. 1933, D.C. 1948. Spl. asst. atty. gen. N.Y. State, 1933; law assoc. George Gordon Battle, 1936-49; N.Y. regional counsel War Assets Adminstrn., 1946-48; spl. asst. to atty. gen. of U.S., antitrust div., 1950-52; trial counsel Finch & Schaefler, N.Y.C., 1952-56; adminstrv. law judge FTC, 1959-73, lectr. fed. trial practice; sr. fed. adminstrv. law judge, U.S.; presiding hearing officer adminstrv. trials Dade County, Fla.; chmn. bd. Buttle-Baker Chem. Corp., 1953-56; mem. adv. com. on vets. re-employment Dept. Labor; fed. referee Appeals Council Social Security Adminstrn., 1956-59. Author: The Perplexities of Trade Regulation, 1956, The Search for Administrative Justice, published 1958, A Guide to the Law and Legal Literature of Peru, (in collaboration with Library of Congress), 1947, Trial Problems in Antitrust Litigation, 1953; also articles to law jours. Served as comdr. USNR, 1942-45; navy liaison officer Selective Service Hdqrs., 1943-45, N.J. and Del. Decorated Army Commendation medal; recipient Distinguished Service award FTC; named hon. adm. Tex. Navy. Mem. S.R., SAR, Fed. Adminstrv. Law Judges Conf. (pres. 1961-62), World Assn. Judges, ABA, Fed. Bar Assn. (exec. council 1947-48, chmn. adminstrv. law com. 1962-63, 65-66), VFW, Delta Sigma Phi, Phi Delta Phi. Episcopalian. Club: Princeton of South Fla. Home: 100 Bayview Dr Apt 2115 North Miami Beach FL 33160

BUTTNER, JEAN BERNHARD, publishing company executive; b. New Rochelle, N.Y., Nov. 3, 1934; d. Arnold and Janet (Kinghorn) Bernhard; m. Edgar Buttner, Sept. 13, 1958 (div.); children: Janet, Edgar Arnold, Marianne. BA, Vassar Coll., 1957; cert. bus. adminstrn., Harvard U., 1958; Montessori diploma, Coll. Notre Dame, Belmont, Calif., 1967. Past v.p. Buttner Cos., Oakland, Calif.; pres., chief operating officer Value Line Inc. (subs. Arnold Bernhard & Co.), N.Y.C., 1985-88, chmn., chief exec. officer, 1988—, also bd. dirs. Trustee Williams Coll., Williamstown, Mass., Coll. Prepartory Sch., Oakland; mem. adv. council Stanford Bus. Sch.; mem. visitation com. for bd. overseers Harvard Bus. Sch. Mem. Com. 200. Republican. Unitarian. Office: Value Line Inc 711 3d Ave New York NY 10017

BUTTON, FORD LINCOLN, cartoonist; b. Wellsboro, Pa., June 22, 1924; s. Howard Henry and Beatrice Charlotte (Larson) B.; BS Edn., Mansfield U., 1952; postgrad. Buffalo State U., N.Y. U., Rochester Inst. Tech.; m. Joyce Marie Fullagar, Aug. 5, 1956; children: Lisa, Sally, Connie, Jeffrey, Christopher. Tchr. art Ramapo Central Sch. #2, Spring Valley, N.Y., 1952-56, Churchville (N.Y.) Chili Central Sch., 1956-62; art cons. Gates Chili Central Sch., 1962-69, tchr. art, 1962-83; ret., 1983; freelance cartoonist Good Housekeeping, Nation's Bus., Christian Sci. Monitor, Phi Delta Kappan, Nat. Sch. Bds. Assn., Am. Assn. Sch. Adminstrs., others, 1956—; editorial cartoonist Sch. Bd. News; illustrator Dryden Press, MacMillan Pub. Co., Allyn & Bacon, Simon and Shuster; Exhibited Internat. Salon Cartoons, Montreal. Author book of cartoons, 1985. Served with AUS, 1943-45; ETO. Mem. N.Y. United Tchrs. Presbyterian. Home and Office: 3398 Chili Ave Rochester NY 14624

BUTTON, KENNETH JOHN, economist, educator; b. Shoreham, Eng., Nov. 14, 1948; s. Frank Alfred Arthur and Joyce Daphne (Tapson) B.; m. Elizabeth Ruth Hallas, Aug. 3, 1974; 1 child, Alexandra Elizabeth. BA, East Anglia U., 1970; MA, Leeds U., 1971; PhD, Loughborough U., 1981. Lectr. Loughborough (Eng.) U., 1973-81, sr. lectr., 1982-84, reader, 1984—; vis. assoc. prof. U. B.C., Vancouver, Can., 1982; bd. dirs. Pearce, Sharp and Assocs., Birmingham, Eng.; dir. Applied Microecons. Research Group, 1984—. Author 22 books on transport econs., regional econs. and econ. policy; contbr. over 100 papers to learned jours. Mem. Royal Econ. Soc., Am. Econs. Assn., Regional Sci. Assn., Western Econs. Assn. Midwest Econs. Assn. Office: U Loughborough, Dept Econs, Loughborough LE11 3TU, England

BUTTON, RENA PRITSKER, public relations company executive; b. Providence, Feb. 15, 1925; d. Isadore and Esther (Kay) Pritsker; m. Daniel E. Button, Aug. 16, 1969; children by previous marriage: Joshua, Bruce, David Posner. Student, Pembroke Coll., 1942-45; B.S., Simmons Coll., 1948; postgrad., Albany Law Sch., Union U., 1968-69. Spl. asst. to U.S. Rep., 1967-69; spl. projects coordinator United Jewish Appeal, 1971-74; exec. dir. Nat. Council Jewish Women, Inc., N.Y.C., 1974-76; pres. Button Assos., N.Y.C., 1976—; exec. v.p. Catalyst, N.Y.C., 1980-82; pres. Button & Button, Albany, N.Y., 1982—; mem. adv. council N.Y. State Senate Minority, 1980—. Co-producer, moderator: TV pub. affairs program Speak For Yourself, Albany, N.Y., 1963-66. Past mem. Mohawk-Hudson Council on Edni. TV.; chmn. pub. affairs com. Marymount Manhattan Coll.; Past bd. dirs. Albany YWCA, Albany Council Chs. Devel. Corp., World Affairs Council, Planned Parenthood Assn. Albany; trustee Jerusalem Women's Seminar, Citizen's for Family Planning, N.Y. Com. Integrated Housing, Hist. Albany Found.; pres. Sr. Service Ctr. Albany Area. Clubs: Siasconset Casino (Siasconset, Mass.), Univ. (Albany). Home: 16 Spruce Ct Delmar NY 12054 Office: 289 State St Albany NY 12210

BUTTRAM, PRESTON LEE, oil and gas exploration company executive; b. Oklahoma City, Feb. 24, 1954; s. Dorsey Randal and Phyllis Green (Barnes) B.; m. Lianne Nelson, Aug. 18, 1979. Student Okla. U., 1972-74, Okla. City U., 1976. Gen. ptnr. PLB Ltd., Oklahoma City, 1977-79; propietor The Buttram Co., Edmond, Okla., 1980-85; pres., dir. Buttram Oil Properties Inc., Edmond, 1985—. Vol. Oklahoma City Festival of Arts, 1976-83, YMCA and YWCA, Oklahoma City, 1979, Oklahoma City Symphony, 1979-84, assoc. bd., 1980; sponsor Liberty Coll., Lynchburg, Va., 1983; vol. Chamber Music Orchestra, Oklahoma City, 1984; provider, counselor Metrochurch Ctr. Family Ministries, Edmond, 1985; precinct chmn. Republican Party, Edmond, 1985; county del. Rep. County Conv., Oklahoma City, 1985; del. Rep. State Conv., Oklahoma City, 1985. Mem. Oklahoma City Assn. Petroleum Landmen, Sigma Nu. Fundamentalist. Club: Bachelors (Oklahoma City) (pres. 1978-79). Office: Buttram Oil Properties Inc 6303 Waterford Blvd Suite 230 PO Box 54813 Oklahoma City OK 73154

BUTTROSS, ERNEST LOUIS, businessman; b. New Orleans, Aug. 7, 1922; s. David and Freada (Saab) B.; m. Mariam Boustany, Sept. 28, 1947; children—Miriam, Ernest, Susan, Martha, John, Annette, Cynthia, Rebecca. B.S. in Bus. Adminstrn., Miss. State Coll., 1943. Owner Buttross Dept. Store, Canton, Miss., 1947—; dir. First Fed. Savs. & Loan, Canton, Miss., 1976-83; adv. dir. Magnolia Fed. Bank, Canton, 1983—; commr. Canton Municipal Utilites, 1960—, chmn., 1973—. Past pres. Parish Council of Sacred Heart Cath. Ch.; chmn. Madison County chpt. ARC, 1959-69; bd. dir. Cen.Miss. Planning and Devel. Dist., Jackson, 1968—, pres., 1979-81. Served with USN, 1943-46. Named Madison County Man of Yr., Madison C. of C., 1961, chmn. bd. Cen. Miss. Planning and Devel. Co., 1981-86. Mem. Madison County C. of C. (pres. 1957-58, 1985-86, Business person of Yr. 1985), VFW (dist. comdr. 1950-52). Lodge: Rotary. Home: 421 E Center St Canton MS 39046 Office: Buttross Dept Store PO Box 545 Canton MS 39046

BUUR TRAERUP, MICHAEL, paper company executive; b. Copenhagen, Feb. 15, 1957; m. Mette Buur Traerup, Jan. 6, 1985; children: Line, Jacob. BCom, Copenhagen Bus. Sch., 1984. Export mgr. De Forenede Papirfabrikker, Copenhagen, 1986—. Home: Naeldebjerg Alle 42, 2670 Greve Denmark Office: De Forenede Papirfabrikker, Bormester Christiansens, Gade 40, 2450 Copenhagen Denmark

BUXRUD, ULF, computer software company executive; b. Skien, Norway, Apr. 19, 1942; came to Sweden, 1945; s. Lars Peter and Elsa Linnea (Anderson) B.; m. Birgitta Ulla Ingvarsson, Nov. 6, 1965; children—Petra, Jill. Computer programmer Bull-Gen. Electric, Malmoe, Sweden, 1963-65; system analyst Byggmastereforening, Stockholm, 1965-67; pres. DataAnalys Group, Stockholm, 1967—. Initiator, Software Suppliers Scandinavia, Stockholm, 1977. Recipient Million Dollar award ICP/USA, 1981; created TD G-L. Mem. Computer Assn. Sweden, Internat. Wine and Food Soc., Commanderie de Bordeaux a Malmoe. Moderaterna. Lutheran. Club: Sallskapet (Stockholm). Home: Amicitiagatan 33, Malmo 21618, Sweden Office: DataAnalys AB, Sturegatan 6, Stockholm 11435, Sweden

BUXTON, RICHARD MILLARD, financial executive; b. Denver, July 8, 1948; s. Charles Roberts and Janet (Millard) B.; m. Consuelo Gonzalez, June 15, 1974; children—Richard Fernando. B.A. with distinction, Stanford U., 1970; M.B.A., Harvard U., 1975. Mgr. ops. planning Western Fed. Savs., Denver, 1975-78; sr. fin. analyst Rocky Mountain Energy Co., Denver, 1978-83; dir. fin. analysis, treas. Frontier Devel. Group, Inc., Denver, 1983-85; treas. Frontier Holdings, Inc., Denver, 1985-86; dir. fin. services K N Energy, Inc., Denver, 1986—. Mem. Colo. Harvard Bus. Sch. Club, Rocky Mountain Stanford Club (bd. dirs. 1982-84). Presbyterian. Club: Columbine Country. Home: 17 Wedge Way Littleton CO 80123 Office: K N Energy Inc PO Box 15265 Lakewood CO 80215

BUXTON, SIMON CAMPDEN, television editor; b. Oxford, Eng., Apr. 9, 1943; s. Rufus Alexander and Helen Nancy (Connal) Noel-Buxton; m. Alison Dorothy Liddle, July 6, 1954; children: Katherine, Christopher. BA with honors, Oxford U., 1964. Researcher on ednl. programs Redifussion TV, London, 1965-68; coordinator religious programs Thames TV, London, 1968-71, producer arts programs, 1971-76, producer adult edn. programs, 1976-78, producer help programs, editor social action programs, 1976—. Contbr. articles to profl. jours. Trustee Noel-Buston Trust, London, 1985—, mem. com. Arts Access. Liberal. Mem. Ch. Eng. Club; Lords Cricket (London). Home: Abbotsmead, 55 East St, Coggeshall Essex C06 15J, England Office: Thames TV, 306 Evston Rd, London England

BUYERS, MARGARET, health society administrator, nurse; b. Buckie, Scotland, Apr. 22, 1927; d. James and Jamesina (Smith) Jappy; m. Donald Morison Buyers, Sept. 3, 1955; children: Donna Margaret, Mark James. State R.N., registered fever nurse, state cert. midwife. Staff nurse City Hosp., Aberdeen, Scotland, 1952-53, St. Alfege's Hosp., London, 1953-54, research unit, Maternity Hosp., Aberdeen, 1959-67; adminstr., sec., sr. counsellor Aberdeen and Dist. Council on Alcoholism, 1975-80; founder, adminstr., sr. counsellor Aberdeen Soc. for Prevention of Alcoholism, 1982—. Home: 96 Gray St, Aberdeen AB1 6JU, Scotland Office: Aberdeen Soc Prevention Alcoholism, 10 Belmont St, Aberdeen AB1 1JE, Scotland

BUYOYA, PIERRE, president of Burundi. Pres., minister of def. Burundi, 1987—. Address: Office of Pres, Bujumbura Burundi *

BUYSSE, PAUL HENRI, trading company executive; b. Antwerp, Belgium, Mar. 17, 1945; s. Eugene and Germaine (Van Hecke) B.; m. Myriam Wellens; children—Frank, Pia, Ann. Grad., Antwerp Mktg. Inst., 1963. Trainee, Ford Motor Co., Antwerp, 1964-65, pub. relations officer, 1966-76; pub. relations and mktg. cons. Robert Maillard, Brussels, 1965-66; asst. to mng. dir., gen. mgr. Brit. Leyland, Antwerp, 1976-79; gen. mgr. Poclain Belgium, Aartselaar, 1979-81; mng. dir. Tenneco Belgium N.V., Aartselaar, 1981-88 ; regional dir. J I Case Benelux, 1984-86; regional dir. J I Case Europe North, 1986-88 ; chmn. Sigma, Brussels, 1981-88 , Somadoc N.V., Aartselaar, 1980-88 ; group mng. dir. Hansen Transmissions Internat., Edegem, 1988—; founder, chmn. NEA, 1982—; regional dir. J.I. Case Benelux, 1984-86; dir. real estate Hugo Ceusters N.V., 1984—; judge Comml. Ct. Contbr. articles to profl. jours. Served with Belgian Armed Forces, 1963-64. Mem. Automobile Trade Assn. Belgium (dir. 1983-88), Belgian Assn. Importers Agrl. Equipment (bd. dirs.). Club: Orde van den Prince. Home: Pater Nuyenslaan 21, 2232 Schilde's Gravenwezel Belgium Office: Hansen Transmissions Internat, Leonardo da Vincilaan, 2550 Edegem Belgium

BYAM, SEWARD GROVES, JR., financial executive; b. Bridgeport, Conn., Jan. 9, 1928; s. Seward Groves and Marjorie W. (Cotton) B.; student Princeton U., 1949, U. Del., 1951; m. Constance Patricia Randell, Feb. 28, 1981; children—Pamela E. Byam Tinsley, John T. Mktg. exec. duPont Co., 1951-67; bus. mgr. Dow Badische Co., 1967-76; mktg. dir. Borg Textile Corp., 1976-79; v.p. Tower Securities Inc., 1979-81; pres., prin., Seward, Groves, Richard & Wells, Inc., 1985—; pres. Randell-Byam Assocs., Inc., Rye, N.Y., 1987—; mng. dir. Fiduciary Counsel Inc., 1981—, Econ. Analysts, Inc., 1983—. Chmn. Williamsburg (Va.) Sch. Bd., 1973-76. Served with USMC, 1946-47, USMCR, 1947-51. Mem. Mensa, SAR. Episcopalian. Clubs: Union League, Princeton (N.Y.C.); Nassau (Princeton, N.J.), Apawamis (Rye). Home: 472 Grace Church St Rye NY 10580 Office: Seward, Groves, Richard & Wells 40 Wall St New York NY 10005

BYCHKOV, SEMYON, conductor; b. Leningrad, USSR, Nov. 30, 1952; came to U.S., 1975; s. May and Doroteya (Kreizberg) B.; m. Tatiana Rozina, July 3, 1973; children: David, Elizabeth Rachel. Diploma of honor, Clinka Choir Sch., 1970; student, Leningrad Conservatory, 1970-74; diploma, Mannes Coll. Music, N.Y.C., 1976. Music dir. Bonch-Bruyevich Inst. Chorus, Leningrad, 1970-72; condr. Leningrad Conservatory Symphony and Opera Orch., 1972-74; assoc. condr., then music dir., Mannes Coll. Music Orch., 1976-80; music dir./condr., Grand Rapids (Mich.) Symphony, 1980-85; assoc. condr., Buffalo Philharm. Orch., 1979—, prin. guest condr., 1985—, music dir., 1985—; music dir. Oachertu de Paris, 1987—; guest condr. Berlin Philharm., London Philharm., Philharmonia, Orchestre de Paris, Vienna Symphony, Bayerische Rundfunk, NDR Hamburg, Bamberg Symphony, Boston Symphony, Phila. Orch., Toronto Symphony, Montreal Symphony, Balt. Symphony, BBC Symphony, Royal Philharm. Orchestre de la Suisse Romande, Israel Chamber Orch., N.Y. Philharm., Spoleto Festival, Concertebouw Orch., Art Park Festival, Cin. Symphony, San Remo Symphony, Aix-en-Provence Music Festival, Tivoli Symphony, Indpls. Symphony, Bournemouth Symphony, Chautaqua Symphony, Columbus Symphony, Lyon Opera, Seattle Symphony, L.I. Philharm., Minn. Orch., CBS Chamber Orch., Syracuse Orch., Can. Nat. Arts Center Orch., Detroit Symphony, summers 1981-83, N.Y.C. Opera, fall 1981, Monte Carlo Philharmonic, Strasbourg Philharmonic; recordings for Philips Records. Recipient 1st prize Rachmaninoff Conducting Competition, 1973. Mem. Am. Fedn. Musicians.

BYCZYNSKI, EDWARD FRANK, lawyer, financial executive; b. Chgo., Mar. 17, 1946; s. Edward James and Ann (Ruskey) B.; children—Stefan, Suzanne. B.A., U. Wis., 1968; J.D., U. Ill., 1972; Certificat de Droit, U. Caen, France, 1971. Bar: Ill. 1972, U.S. Dist. Ct. (no. dist.) Ill. 1972, U.S. Supreme Ct. 1976. Title officer Chgo. Title Ins. Co., 1972-73; asst. regional counsel SBA, Chgo., 1973-76; pres. Alderstreet Investments, Portland, Oreg., 1976-82; pres. Nat. Tenant Network, Portland, 1981—, Bay Venture Corp., Portland, 1984—; ptnr. Haley, Pirok, Byczynski. Chgo., 1973-76. Contbr. articles to profl. jours. Mem. ABA, Ill. Bar Assn. Democrat. Roman Catholic. Home: 47 Hillshire Dr Lake Oswego OR 97034 Office: 525 SW 1st Suite 105 Lake Oswego OR 97034

BYEFF, PETER DAVID, hematologist, oncologist; b. Newark, Nov. 27, 1948; s. Herbert Isaac and Ruth Helen (Wolfe) B.; B.A., U. Pa., 1970; M.D., Johns Hopkins U., 1974; m. Gail Schneider, Apr. 2, 1982. Intern, Georgetown U. Hosp., Washington, 1974-75, resident in internal medicine, 1975-77; vis. fellow in hematology and oncology Columbia-Presbyn. Med. Center, N.Y.C., 1977-81, Damon Runyon-Walter Winchell oncology fellow, 1977-81; instr. Coll. Physicians and Surgeons, Columbia U., N.Y.C.; asst. prof., attending physician U. Conn.; attending physician Bradley Meml. Hosp., Southington, Conn., New Britain (Conn.) Gen. Hosp. Diplomate Am. Bd. Internal Medicine (subcert. in med. oncology and hematology), Nat. Bd. Med. Examiners. Office: Bradley Med Bldg Suite 1-A 55 Meriden Ave Southington CT 06489 also: 40 Hart St New Britain CT 06050

BYER EISENBERG, KAREN SUE, nurse; b. Bklyn., Mar. 11, 1954; d. Marvin and Florence (Beck) Byer; 1 child, Carly Beth; diploma nursing L.I. Coll. Hosp. Sch. Nursing, 1973; B.S. in Nursing, L.I. U., 1976, M.Profl. Studies, 1977; m. Howard Eisenberg, May 11, 1974. Nurse recovery room and surg. intensive care unit Downstate Med. Center, Bklyn., 1973-75; utilization rev. analyst Bezallel Health Related Facility, Far Rockaway, N.Y., 1975-76; utilization rev. analyst, R.N. supr. Seagirt Health Related Facility, Far Rockaway, 1976; staff nurse neurosurg. and rehab. nursing Downstate Med. Center, Bklyn., 1978, nurse intensive care unit, 1978-79, asst. nursing dir. pathology, clin. research asso. Research Found., 1979—. Mem. Oncology Nursing Soc., Am. Nurses Assn., N.Y. State Nurses Assn., N.Y. Acad. Scis., L.I. Coll. Hosp. Alumnae Assn. Contbr. articles to profl. jours. Office: 450 Clarkson Ave Box 25 Brooklyn NY 11203

BYERS, WILLIAM SEWELL, electrical engineer, educator; b. Ironton, Ohio, Oct. 3, 1925; s. William T. and Anna M. (Sewell) B.; B.E.E., Ohio State U., 1951; M.B.A., Rollins Coll., 1966; M.Eng., Pa. State U., 1969, M.Ed., 1972; Ed.D., Nova U., 1976; LL.D. (hon.), Frank Ross Stewart U., 1981; m. Marjorie E. Reidel, Dec. 28, 1946; children—Thomas William, Robert M., Catherine G. Broadcast engr. Crosley Broadcasting Corp., Columbus, Ohio, 1949-51; dist. engr. Gen. Elec. Co., Syracuse, N.Y., 1951-55; staff engr., engring. mgr. Martin Marietta Aerospace Corp., Orlando, Fla., 1955-75; asso. prof. elec. engring. tech. U. Ala., Tuscaloosa, 1975-81, prof. and coordinator elec. engring. tech., 1981-83; prof., chmn. engring. tech. Murray State U. (Ky.), 1983-84, U. Central Fla., Cocoa, 1984—; academic advisor tech. Institut National d'Electricitie et d'Electronique at Boumerdes, Algeria, 1977-78; former adj. faculty Seminole Jr. Coll., Fla. So. Coll., Valencia Community Coll. Amateur radio operator. Nat. Sci. Found. grantee, 1968-69. Registered profl. engr., Fla., Ala., Mem. Soc. Wireless Pioneers (life), AAUP, Am. Soc. for Engring. Edn. (vice chmn. engring. tech. div., chmn. internat. div.), Mensa, IEEE (sr.), Capstone Engring. Soc., Pa. State Amateur Radio Club (hon. life), Tau Alpha Pi, Eta Kappa Nu. Home: 301 Westchester Dr Cocoa FL 32926 Office: U Central Fla 1519 Clearlake Rd Cocoa FL 32922

BYKOV, VALERY ALEXEEVICH, Soviet government official; b. Kuibyshev, USSR, Dec. 19, 1938. MA in Mech. Engring., Kuibyshev Indsl. Inst., 1961, PhD. Plant operator, dep. chief mechanic Petrochem. Processing Plant, Kirishi, Leningrad, 1961-71, dir. biochem. plant, 1971-76; mem. Communist Party Soviet Union, 1966—; 1st sec. of Kirishi City Com. of USSR Communist Party, 1976-79; head microbiology div. Chem. Industry Dept., USSR, 1979-85; head Ministry Med. and Microbiological Industry, Moscow, USSR, 1985—. Dep. USSR Supreme Soviet, mem. Supreme Soviet Parliamentary Group, Cen. Inspection Commn. USSR. Address: Ministry Med and Microbiol Industry, 2 proyezd Khudozhestvennogo theara, 103823 Moscow USSR *

BYLINA, STANISLAW JAN, historian, educator; b. Kielce, Poland, Apr. 4, 1936; s. Stefan and Irena (Domaniewska) Bylina; m. Elzbieta Wilamowska; children: Katarzyna, Malgorzata. M in Slavic Philology, U. Warsaw, Poland, 1959, D in Hist. Scis., 1964, Habilitation in Hist. Scis., 1972. Asst. Inst. Slavic Research Polish Acad. Scis., Warsaw, 1960-64, adjunctus, 1964-72; prof. Inst. History Polish Acad. Scis., Warsaw, 1972—. Author: Konrad Waldhauser and His Connections with Poland, 1966, Social Visions in the

Medieval Heretic Movements, 1974, Etudes sur L'Histoire de la Culture de L'Europe Centrale. 1980; contbr. articles to profl. jours. Mem. Solidarnosc. Roman Catholic. Home: Ul Askenazego 2 M 6, 03-580 Warsaw Poland Office: Inst History, Rynek St Miasta 29/31, Warsaw Poland

BYRD, HARVEY CLIFFORD, III, information management company executive; b. Durham, N.C., July 4, 1947; s. Harvey Clifford and Sarah Elizabeth (Morgan) B.; m. Mary Elizabeth Bell, Dec. 27, 1969; children—Harvey Clifford, IV, Kevin Michael. B.S. in Psychology, Old Dominion U., 1969; M.A. in Urban Planning, Morgan St. U., 1976. Chief program devel. planning Exec. Dept. St. Md., Towson, 1972-80; mgmt. analyst-Nat. Criminal Justice Reference Service, Aspen Systems Corp., Rockville, Md., 1980-81, dir., 1981—, dir. govt. ops., 1983-85, v.p. govt. ops., 1985-86; v.p. and gen. mgr. Cons. Group, 1986—; pub. Educating for Citizenship curriculum guides, 1983. Pres. Towson Loch Raven Community Council, 1980; pres. Loch Raven Community Assn., Towson, 1978-80. Mem. Info. Industry Assn., Am. Soc. Assn. Execs., Md. Bar Assn. (law edn. com.). Democrat. Episcopalian. Home: 12894 Eagles View Rd Phoenix MD 21131 Office: Aspen Systems Corp 1600 Research Blvd Rockville MD 20850

BYRD, LINWARD TONNETT, lawyer, rancher; b. Hamburg, Ark., June 25, 1921; s. Charley E. and Arrie (Montgomery) B.; m. Reba Ann Rowe, Dec. 22, 1965; 1 child, Jana Lynn. LL.B., U. Tex., 1950. Bar: Tex. 1950, U.S. Dist. Ct. (we. dist.) Tex. 1956, U.S. Ct. Appeals (5th cir.) 1965, U.S. Ct. Appeals (11th cir.) 1981. Sr. ptnr. Byrd, Davis & Eisenberg, Austin, Tex., 1959—. Served with USN, 1942-43. Fellow Am. Trial Lawyers Found., Tex. Bar Found., Am. Coll. Trial Lawyers; mem. Assn. Trial Lawyers Am., Am. Bd. Trial Advs. (adv.), Tex. Trial Lawyers Assn., Travis County Bar Assn., State Bar Tex. Baptist. Home: 3110 Maywood Ave Austin TX 78703 Office: Byrd Davis & Eisenberg 707 W 34th St Austin TX 78705

BYRD, ROBERT CARLYLE, senator; b. North Wilkesboro, N.C., Nov. 20, 1917; s. Cornelius Sale and Ada (Kirby) B.; m. Erma Ora James, May 29, 1937; children: Mona Carole (Mrs. Mohammad Fatemi), Marjorie Ellen (Mrs. John Moore). Student, Beckley Coll., Concord Coll., Morris Harvey Coll., 1950-51, Marshall U., 1951-52; J.D., Am. U., 1963. Elected mem. W.Va. Ho. of Dels., 1946-50; mem. 83d-85th Congresses from 6th W.Va. dist.; U.S. senator from W.Va. 1950-52, 59—, Senate majority leader, 1977-79, Senate minority leader, 1980-87, Senate majority leader, 1987-88. Named Most Influential Mem. U.S. Senate, U.S. News and World Report Poll, 1979. Mem. Country Music Assn. (hon.). Democrat. Baptist. Lodge: Masons (33 degree). Office: Office of the Senate 311 Hart Senate Bldg Washington DC 20510 *

BYRD, THOMAS SWAYNE, architect; b. Dec. 14, 1933. Student, U. Mo., 1952-54, Washington U., St. Louis, 1954-57, U. Ill., Urbana, 1957; B in Architecture, Washington U., 1958. Registered architect, Mo. With Lee Potter Smith & Assocs., Paducah, Ky., 1960-61; mgr. br. office Lee Potter Smith & Assocs., Carbondale, Ill., 1961-64; supr. bus. James L. Byrd Lumber Co., 1964-65; mgr. James L. Byrd Lumber Co., Charleston, 1967-75; pvt. practice architecture Charleston, Mo., 1965-67, Sikeston, Mo., 1975—. Mem. Nat. Council Archtl. Registration Bds. Home: 102 S Ingram Rd Sikeston MO 63801

BYRDAM-HANSEN, ORLA SVEND, airline executive; b. Copenhagen, Dec. 14, 1931; s. Paul Bertram and Gudrun (Nielsen) H.; m. Ingrid Christensen, Dec., 1954; children—Per Bertram, Michael. Student Copenhagen Navigation Sch., 1947-49. Sales dir. Danfoss Aviation, Sonderborg, Denmark, 1960-84; exec. Cimber Air A/S, Sonderborg, 1984—. Served to flight comdr. Danish Air Force, 1951-60. Home: Alssundvej 21, 6400 Sonderborg Denmark Office: Cimber Air A/S, Lufthavnen, 6400 Lutfhavnen, Sonderborg Denmark

BYRNE, GEORGE MELVIN, physician; b. San Francisco, Aug. 1, 1933; s. Carlton and Esther (Smith) B.; B.A., Occidental Coll., 1958; M.D., U. So. Calif., 1962; m. Joan Stecher, July 14, 1956; children—Kathryne, Michael, David; m. 2d, Margaret C. Smith, Dec. 18, 1982. Diplomate Am. Bd. Family Practice. Intern, Huntington Meml. Hosp., Pasadena, Calif., 1962-63, resident, 1963-64; family practice So. Calif. Permanente Med. Group, 1964-81, physician-in-charge Pasadena Clinic, 1966-81; asst. dir. Family Practice residency Kaiser Found. Hosp., Los Angeles, 1971-73; clin. instr. emergency medicine Sch. Medicine, U. So. Calif., 1973-80; v.p. East Ridge Co., 1983-84, sec., 1984; dir. Alan Johnson Porsche Audi, Inc., 1974-82, sec., 1974-77, v.p., 1978-82. Bd. dirs. Kaiser-Permante Mgmt. Assn., 1976-77; mem. regional mgmt. com. So. Calif. Lung Assn., 1976-77; patron Los Angeles County Mus. Art, The Southwest Mus., 1988; mem. pres.'s circle Occidental Coll., Los Angeles Drs. Symphony Orch, 1975-80. Fellow Am. Acad. Family Physicians (charter); mem. Am., Calif., Los Angeles County Med. Assns., Calif. Acad. Family Physicians, Internat. Horn Soc., Friends of Photography, Am. Radio Relay League (Pub. Service award). Clubs: Sierra (life mem.). Home: 528 Meadowview Dr La Canada Flintridge CA 91011

BYRNE, JOHN F(RANCIS), editor; b. Chgo., June 18, 1934; s. Robert E(mmet) and Margaret Mary (Heck) B. Student Loyola U., Chgo.; B.A., St. John's U., Minn.; postgrad. U. Madrid, 1961. Book translator, 1960-64; asst. editor Common Market Bus. Reports, Madrid, 1967, editor-in-chief Spanish Bus. Reports, 1967—; pub. relations cons. Fellow Internat. Bus. Assn. Cambridge, Royal Dublin Soc., Spanish Inst. N.Y.; mem. Club Internacional de Prensa Madrid, Asociacion Iberoamericana de Corresponsales de Prensa Madrid. Democrat. Roman Catholic. Clubs: Chgo. Press, Casino de Madrid, Ateneo. Home: General Diaz Porlier, 45 (7-C), 28001 Madrid Spain

BYRNE, JOHN PATRICK, state official, retired army officer; b. Detroit, May 25, 1929; s. George Arnold and Opal Vere (Cooper) B.; BS, Johns Hopkins U., 1958; MBA with high distinction, U. Mich., 1961; grad. Army War Coll., 1971; m. Dolores Ann Meyer, Aug. 11, 1951; children: John Patrick, David Michael, Richard Terrence, Kevin Francis. Commd. 2d lt. Chem. Corps, U.S. Army, 1950, advanced through grades to col., 1970; served with Far East Command in Japan, 1951-54; various logistic assignments Army Chem. Center, Md., 1954-58; assigned to Chem. Corps Hdqrs. and Dept. of Army, The Pentagon, Washington, 1961-65; U.S. Army exchange officer to Brit. Army, Eng., 1965-68; comdr. 2d chem. bn. Ft. McClellan, Ala., 1968-70; chief of staff Cam Ranh Support Command in Vietnam, 1970-71, dep. comdr., 1971-72; dep. comdr. Bayern Support Dist., Germany, 1972-73, exec. to comdg. gen. of Theater Army Support Command, 1973-74, dep. comdr. of 1st. Support Brigade, 1974-75; comdr. Rocky Mountain Arsenal, Denver, 1975-78; dir. emergency preparedness Denver County, 1978-79; dir. disaster emergency services State of Colo., Golden, 1979—; dir. St. Vincent DePaul Stores, Denver, 1979—. Pres. Brookland Estates Citizens Assn., Alexandria, Va., 1963-65; bd. advisors Natural Hazards Research and Applications Info. Ctr., U. Colo., 1984—; bd. visitors Emergency Mgmt. Inst. at Nat. Emergency Tng. Ctr., 1987—, chmn., 1987; hon. bd. dirs. Mile High chpt. ARC. Decorated Legion of Merit, Bronze Star; Vietnam Cross of Gallantry with palm. Mem. Nat. Emergency Mgmt. Assn. (pres. 1983-84), Assn. of U.S. Army (sec. Gallant Pelham chpt. 1969-70), Nat. Def. Preparedness Assn., Nat. Ret. Officers Assn., Denver C. of C. (mil. affairs com. 1975—), Colo. Emergency Mgmt. Assn. (sec.-treas. 1978-80), Emergency Med. Technicians Assn. of Colo. (adv. 1980-87), Beta Gamma Sigma, Delta Sigma Pi, Phi Kappa Phi. Roman Catholic. Clubs: Rotary, Denver Execs. Home: 7679 Waverly Mountain Littleton CO 80127 Office: State of Colorado Div Disaster Emergency Services Camp George West Golden CO 80401

BYRNE, MICHAEL JOSEPH, business executive; b. Chgo., Apr. 3, 1928; s. Michael Joseph and Edith (Lueken) B.; B.Sc. in Mktg., Loyola U., Chgo., 1952; m. Eileen Kelly, June 27, 1953; children—Michael Joseph, Nancy, James, Thomas, Patrick, Terrence. Sales engr. Emery Industries, Inc., Cin., 1952-59; with Pennsalt Chem. Corp., Phila., 1959-60; with Oakton Cleaners, Inc., Skokie, Ill., 1960-70, pres., 1960-70; pres. Datatax Inc., Skokie, 1970-74, Midwest Synthetic Lubrication Products, 1978—, Pure Water Systems, 1984—, Superior Tax Service, 1984—. Served with ordnance U.S. Army, 1946-48. Mem. A.I.M., VFW, Alpha Kappa Psi. Club: Toastmasters Internat. Home: 600 Grego Ct PO Box 916 Prospect Heights IL 60070

BYRNE, NOEL THOMAS, sociologist, educator; b. San Francisco, May 11, 1943; s. Joseph Joshua and Naomi Pearl (Denison) B.; m. Elizabeth Carla Rowlin, Nov. 5, 1966 (div.); 1 child, Ginger Butler. BA in Sociology, Sonoma State Coll., 1971; MA in Sociology, Rutgers U., 1975, PhD in Sociology, 1987. Instr. sociology Douglass Coll., Rutgers U., New Brunswick, N.J., 1974-76, Hartnell Coll., Salinas, Calif., 1977-78; research dir. mgmt. grads. survey projects Sonoma State U., Rohnert Park, Calif., 1983-86, family bus. research project, 1987-88; lectr. depts. sociology and mgmt. Sonoma State U., 1978—. Contbr. articles and revs. to profl. lit. Recipient Dell Pub. award Rutgers U. Grad. Sociology Program, 1976, Louis Bevier fellow, 1977-78. Mem. AAAS, Am. Sociol. Assn., Pacific Sociol. Assn., Am. Mgmt. Assn., N.Y. Acad. Sci., Soc. for Study Symbolic Interaction (rev. editor Jour. 1980-83), Soc. for Study Social Problems. Democrat. Club: Commonwealth. Home: 548 Racquet Club Circle Rohnert Park CA 94928 Office: Sonoma State U Sch Bus and Econs Rohnert Park CA 94928

BYRNE, RICHARD JOHN, architect, playwright; b. Castlebar, Ireland, Nov. 11, 1935; s. Richard Joseph and Jeanne Millicent (Clampett) B.; m. Irene Frawley, Oct. 30, 1961 (separated 1982); children: Richard David, Derval Anne. Cert. in art, Tech. Coll., Galway, Ireland, 1953. Playwright-in-residence, designer, dir. Taibhdhearc Nat. Gaelic Theatre Ltd., Galway, 1952-78; apprentice S.J. Kelly and Co. Architects, Galway, 1954-59; asst. art dir. Ardmore Film Studios, Bray, 1959-60; design cons. Potez Industries Ltd., Paris, Galway, 1961-63; architect Ed Ralph Ryan Assocs, Galway, 1963-65, Hession Construction, Galway, 1965-68, R.J. Byrne Cons., Galway, 1968—; freelance architect Galway, 1978—, freelance playwright, 1978—. Author 19 Gaelic plays, 1962-78, including Auld Dacency, 1984. Active Social Service Com. Claddagh Village, Galway, 1981-84; speaker Clifden Community Arts Group, Galway, 1987. Served with Irish military, 1950-55. Mem. Nat. Union Journalists, Mechanics Inst. Galway. Mem. Progressive Democratic Party. Roman Catholic. Club: Galway Flying (sec. 1979-82). Home and Studio: Mill House Caherdangan, Craughwell, Galway Ireland

BYRNSIDE, OSCAR JEHU, JR., association executive; b. Huntington, W.Va., June 2, 1935; s. Oscar Jehu and Eula (Bayliss) B.; m. Patricia Ann Oxley, Aug. 1, 1954; children: Barbara Ann, Brenda Gail, Bethany Lynne. B.S., Concord Coll., Athens, W.Va., 1960; M.S., Va. Poly. Inst. and State U., Blacksburg, 1961; Ph.D., Ohio State U., Columbus, 1968. Tchr. bus. Kanawha County schs., Charleston, W.Va., 1960; coordinator vocat. edn. Danville (Va.) public schs., 1961-63; asst. prof. bus., dir. data processing Longwood Coll., Farmville, Va., 1963-65; state dir. bus. edn. W.Va. Bd. Edn., 1965-66; research assoc., cons. Ohio State U., 1966-68; exec. dir. Nat. Bus. Edn. Assn., Reston, Va., 1968—, Future Bus. Leaders Am.-Phi Beta Lambda, Inc., 1968-73; vis. prof. Va. Poly. Inst. and State U., 1969-70, Catholic U. Am., 1969-82, U. Wyo., 1988—; pres. Center Ednl. Assns., Reston, 1976-77, 83-84; treas., bd. dirs. Alliance Assns. Advancement Edn., 1973-74; bd. dirs., exec. v.p. Found. for Teaching Free Enterprise, 1979—; pres. Assn. Data Mgmt., Inc., Reston, Va.; chmn. Trust for Insuring Educators, 1981—; mem. nat. task force edn. and tng. minority bus. enterprise HEW, 1971-74; trustee Joint Council on Econ. Edn., 1985—;. Editor: Bus. Edn. Forum, 1968-79, pub., 1979—. Bd. dirs. Reston Soccer Assn., 1979-81, commr. girls travel div., 1979-82; exec. bd. Washington Area Girls Soccer League, 1978-81; co-dir. Reston Internat. Soccer Festival, 1979; bd. dirs. Bus. Edn. Hall of Fame, 1978—; mem. Policies Commn. for Bus. and Econ. Edn., 1968—. Served with USMC, 1953-56. Recipient Centennial award Ohio State U., 1970. Mem. Nat. Bus. Edn. Assn., Am. Vocat. Assn. (life), NEA (life), Internat. Council Small Bus., Am. Soc. Assn. Execs., Nat. Assn. Secondary Sch. Prins., Am. Assn. Sch. Adminstrs., Assn. Supervision and Curriculum Devel., Internat. Soc. Bus. Edn., Phi Kappa Phi, Phi Delta Kappa, Pi Omega Pi, Delta Pi Epsilon, Kappa Delta Pi. Baptist. Home: 2053 Eakins Ct Reston VA 22091 Office: 1914 Association Dr Reston VA 22091

BYSTRYN, JEAN-CLAUDE, dermatologist; b. Paris, May 8, 1938; s. Iser and Sara Bystryn; came to U.S., 1949, naturalized, 1958; B.S., U. Chgo., 1958; M.D., N.Y. U., 1962; m. Marcia Hammill, May 14, 1972; children—Anne, Alexander. Intern, Montefiore Hosp., N.Y.C., 1962-63, resident in medicine, 1963-64; resident in dermatology N.Y. U. Sch. Medicine, N.Y.C., 1966-69, USPHS postgrad. tng. fellow in immunology, 1968-72, asst. prof. clin. dermatology, 1971-72, asst. prof., 1972-76, assoc. prof., 1976-84, prof., 1984—; asst. dispensary physician Albany Med. Coll., 1964-66; asst. attending physician Univ. Hosp., N.Y.C., 1969—; asst. vis. dermatologist Bellevue Hosp. Center, N.Y.C., 1969—; dir. Melanoma Program and Melanoma Immunotherapy Clinic, NYU Kaplan Cancer Ctr., dir. Bullous Disease Clinic and Immunofluorescence Lab. Med. Sch. Served to lt. comdr. USPHS, 1964-66. Recipient Husik Prize, N.Y. U. Sch. Medicine, 1968; Irma T. Hirschl research career award; Ford. Found. fellow, 1954-58; NIH grantee, 1970—. Diplomate Am. Bd. Dermatology, Am. Bd. Immunodermatopathology. Mem. Am. Dermatology Assn., Internat. Soc. Tropical Dermatology, Am. Acad. Dermatology Am. Assn. Immunologists, Am. Assn. Cancer Research, Soc. Investigative Dermatology, N.Y. Dermatol. Soc., Am. Soc. Cell Biology, N.Y. Dermatol. Soc. Contbr. articles to profl. jours. Office: 530 1st Ave New York NY 10016

BYWATER, ROBERT JAMES, veterinary pharmacologist; b. Bedstone, Salop, England, June 16, 1941; s. Caleb James and Doris (Watkins) B.; m. Elizabeth May Scott, Feb. 9, 1967; children: Owen, Simon. BS in Veterinary Med. Sci., Edinburgh (Scotland) U., 1964, MS, 1966, PhD, 1971. Lectr. Edinburgh U., 1964-74; veterinary surgeon Beecham Pharm., Tadworth, Eng., 1974-78, head veterinary pharmacology, 1978—. Author: (book) Introduction to Veterinary Pharmacology, 1933; patentee in field. Office: Beecham Pharms Research Div, Walton Oaks, Tadsworth England

CABALLE, MONTSERRAT, opera singer, soprano; b. Barcelona, Spain, Apr. 12, 1933; ed. Conservatorio del Liceo; m. Bernabe Marti; 2 children. Am. debut in Donizetti's Lucrezia Borgia with Carnegie Hall, N.Y.C., 1965; also appeared with La Scala Opera, Milan, Vienna Staatsoper, Glydebourne Festival, Met. Opera; appeared with Chgo. Symphony Orch., Orch. Hall, 1966; recorded by RCA Victor; performed in works of Richard Strauss, Mozart, de Falla, Luigi Nono; also appearences on radio and TV. Decorated Cross of Lazo de Damas, Order of Isabel the Catholic (Spain). Address: care Columbia Artists Mgmt Inc 165 W 57th St New York NY 10019 *

CABANIS, JOSÉ, writer; b. Toulouse, France, Mar. 24, 1922; s. Gaston and Franç oise (Bellomayre) C.; ed. U. Toulouse. Books: L'age ingat, 1952, Juliette Bonviolle, 1954, Les mariages de raison, 1958, Le bonheur du jour (Prix des Critiques), 1961, Les cartes du temps (Prix des Libraires), 1962, Les jeux de la nuit, 1964, La Bataille de Toulouse (Prix Thé ophraste Renaudot), 1966, Les jardins de la nuit, 1973, Michelet, le prê tre et la femme, 1978; criticism: Un essai sur Marcel Jounandeau, 1960, Plaisir et lectures, 1964, Plaisir et lectures II, 1968, Des jardins en Espagne, 1969, Le sacre de Napoleon, 1970, Charles X roi ultra (Prix des Ambassadeurs), 1972, Saint-Simon l'Admirable (Grand Prix de la Critique), 1975, Les profondes anné es (Grand Prix de Litterature de l'Acad. Franç aise), 1976; Michelet, le prê tre et la femme, 1978; Lacordaire et quelques autres, 1983; Le Musé e espagnol de Louis-Philippe-Goya, 1985. Home: Nollet, 31130 Balma France Address: 5 rue Darquie, 31000 Toulouse France *

CABASSOL, PHILIPPE CHARLES, manufacturing executive; b. Paris, Feb. 23, 1952; s. Jean Cabassol; m. Joelle L. Dedeurwaerder, July 4, 1981; children: Michael Charles, Melanie Caroline. MBA, U. Cordoba, Argentina, 1976. Tech. sec. Renault Corp., Douai, France, 1977-79, mgr. planning and supply, 1979-81; mgr. prodn. control Am. Motors Corp., Kenosha, Wis., 1981-82, mgr. prodn. planning, 1982-83; plant mgr. Coleman (Wis.) Products, 1983-85; dir. ops. Am. Motors Co. Jeep div., Toledo, 1985-86; dir. ops., project mgr. Chrysler Corp. (formerly Am. Motors Corp.), Brampton, Ont., Can., 1986-87; dir. of liaison Chrysler Corp. (formerly Am. Motors Corp.), Detroit, 1988—. Office: Chrysler Corp Chrysler Center Highland Park MI 48203

CABLE, CHARLES ALLEN, mathematician; b. Akeley, Pa., Jan. 15, 1932; s. Elton Thomas and Margaret (Fox) C.; m. Mabel Elizabeth Yeck, Dec. 19, 1955; children: Christopher A., Carolyn E. B.S., Edinboro State Coll., 1954; M.Ed., U. N.C., 1959; Ph.D. in Math., Pa. State U., 1969. Instr. math. Interlaken High Sch., N.Y., 1954-55, Tidioute High Sch., Pa., 1957-58; asst. prof. math Juniata Coll., Huntingdon, Pa., 1959-67; prof., chmn. dept. math Allegheny Coll., Meadville, Pa., 1969—. Editorial reviewer: Math. Mag., 1975-80; assoc. editor: Focus, 1981-85. Served with AUS, 1955-57. Gen. Elec. fellow, 1958; NSF fellow, 1959, 61, 68, 73; NDEA fellow, 1969. Mem. Am. Math. Soc., Math. Assn. Am. (chmn. Allegheny Mountain sect. 1973-75, bd. govs. 1981-84, mem. newletter editorial com. 1981-85, ad hoc com. on student chpts., publications com., 1983-86), AAUP. Republican. Presbyterian. Home: 199 Jefferson St Meadville PA 16335 Office: Allegheny Coll N Main St Meadville PA 16335

CABLE, THOMAS HAMILTON, JR., chemical company executive; b. Pitts., Nov. 22, 1935; came to Switzerland, 1977; s. Thomas Hamilton and Margaret Ruth (Cadwallader) C.; m. Beverly Wallace, Nov. 24, 1962; children—Thomas Graham, Susan Wallace. B.S. in Chem. Engring., Bucknell U., 1957. Sales engr. Union Carbide Corp., Pitts., 1957-64, mgr. sales engring., 1964-68, sales mgr., Houston, 1968-72, mktg. mgr., N.Y.C., 1972-74; product dir. Union Carbide Eastern, Tokyo, Japan, 1974-77; v.p., gen. mgr. indsl. gases Union Carbide Europe, Geneva, 1980—; chmn. UCAR Indsl. Gases NV, antwerp, Belgium, 1988—, chmn., mng. dir. Union Carbide Deutschland, Dusseldorf, Fed. Republic Germany, 1983—; chmn. Indugas N.V., Schoten, Belgium, 1980—, UCAR Splty. Gases NV, Belgium, 1980; dir. Argon S.A., Madrid, 1977—, Union Carbide U.K. Ltd., London, 1980—; chmn., dir. Unigas Spa, 1985—; v.p., dir. IGI, Milan, 1985; dir. Gas & Equipment Ltd., Rugby, 1986—, Union Carbide Europe, Geneva, 1987—, SIAD, Bergamo, Italy, 1987—, Union Carbide Iberica, Madrid, Spain, 1977—. Inventor use of oxygen in glass melting. Sr. warden Am. Ch. Geneva, 1981-83; dir. Am. Internat. Club Geneva, 1981, pres., 1982-83; bd. dirs. Found. Internat. Sch., Geneva. Served with C.E., U.S. Army, 1958-60, ETO. Mem. Indsl. Gases Com. (v.p.), Comite Permanent Industriel, Swiss Am. C. of C. Republican. Clubs: Fox Chapel Golf, University (Pitts.); Tennis (Geneva); Mirador Country (Vevey); Chevalier Confrerie du Tastevin; Golf (Geneve). Office: Union Carbide Europe SA, 15 Chemin Louis Dunant, 1211 Geneva 20 Switzerland

CABOT, HUGH, III, painter-sculptor; b. Boston, Mar. 22, 1930; s. Hugh and Louise (Melanson) C.; m. Olivia P. Taylor, Sept. 8, 1967; student Boston Museum, 1948, Ashmolean Mus., Oxford, Eng., 1960, Coll. Ams., Mexico City, 1956, San Carlos Acad., Mexico City. Portrait, landscape painter; sculptor in bronze; one-man shows: U.S. Navy Hist. and Recreation Dept., U.S. Navy Art Gallery, The Pentagon, Nat. War Mus., Washington, La Muse de la Marine, Paris; group shows include: Tex. Tri-state, 1969 (1st, 2d, 3d prizes). Served as ofcl. artist USN, Korean War. Named Artist of Yr., Scottsdale, Ariz., 1978. Clubs: Salmagundi (N.Y.C.). Author, illustrator: Korea I (Globe).

CABOT, LEWIS PICKERING, materials handling machinery manufacturing company executive, art consultant; b. Hague, Netherlands, Sept. 6, 1937; s. John Moors and Elizabeth (Lewis) C.; m. Judith Ogden, July 1, 1960 (div. 1974); children: Elizabeth Lewis, Edward Ogden, Timothy Pickering; m. Susan Knight, July 15, 1978; children: James Eliot, Alexander Lee. AB, Harvard U., 1961, MBA, 1964. Trainee F.S. Moseley & Co., Boston, 1961-62; analyst John P. Chase, Inc., Boston, 1964-68; prin. Gardner & Preston Moss, Boston, 1968-73; chmn., pres. Artcounsel, Inc., Portland, Maine, 1973—; chmn. ZY-AX Corp. (name formerly Southworth Corp.), Portland, 1977—, Shellback Corp., Portland, 1984—; dir. Arneson Corp. 1985—, San Francisco, Hov-air Internat., Ltd., Newbury, Eng. 1988—, Infra-Pak Corp., Dallas 1988—; trustee NE Pooled Common Fund, Princeton, N.J., 1972—. Trustee Mus. Fine Arts, Boston, 1966—; mem. MIT Arts Council, Cambridge, 1969—; trustee Portland Sch. Art, 1982—; vis. com. Harvard U. Art Mus., Cambridge, 1982—. Clubs: Met. (Washington); Somerset (Boston); Manchester Yacht (Mass.); N.Y. Yacht (N.Y.C.). Office: ZY-AX Corp PO Box 1980 2331 Congress St Portland ME 04104

CABOT, LOUIS WELLINGTON, chemical manufacturing company executive; b. Boston, Aug. 3, 1921; s. Thomas Dudley and Virginia (Wellington) C.; m. Mary Ellen Flynn de Pena Vera, Oct. 19, 1974; children by previous marriage: James Bass, Anne Louise, Godfrey Lowell, Amanda Cabot Kjellerup, Helen Reuter. A.B., Harvard U., 1943, M.B.A., 1948; LL.D. (hon.), Norwich U., 1961. With Cabot Corp., 1948—, pres., 1960-69, chmn. bd., 1969-86, also bd. dirs.; chmn. Brookings Instn., Washington, 1986—; dir. Owens-Corning Fiberglas Corp., R.R. Donnelley & Sons Co., Wang Labs Inc., New Eng. Tel. & Tel., 1965-82, Fed. Res. Bank Boston, 1970-78, chmn., 1975-78; U.S. rep. 15th Plenary Session UN Econ. Commn. for Europe, 1960; mem. bus. ethics adv. council Dept. Commerce, 1961-63; dir., New Eng. chmn. Nat. Alliance Businessmen, 1970-72, Boston chmn., 1968-69; chmn. Sloan Commn. on Govt. and Higher Edn., 1977-80; mem. Pres.'s Blue Ribbon Commn. on Def. Mgmt., 1985-86; def. sec.'s commn. on base realignment and closure. Overseer Harvard U., 1970-76; chmn. Harvard Coll. Fund Council, 1963-65; pres. Beverly (Mass.) Hosp., 1958-61; chmn. Com. Corp. Support Pvt. Univs., 1977-83; trustee Norwich U., 1952-77, Mus. of Sci., Boston; corp. mem. MIT; trustee Northeastern U., Nat. Humanities Ctr.; assoc. Governing Bds. Univs. and Colls. Fellow Am. Acad. Arts and Scis.; mem. Assn. Governing Bds. of Universities and Colls., C. of C. of U.S. (dir., exec. com. 1978-83), Nat. Council for U.S.-China Trade (dir. 1978-82), Bus. Council, Conf. Bd., Mass. Bus. Roundtable, Council Fgn. Relations, Phi Beta Kappa, Sigma Xi. Clubs: Somerset (Boston), Commercial (Boston) (pres. 1970-72), Harvard (Boston); Metropolitan (Washington); Wianno (Osterville, Mass.); N.Y. Yacht, River. Office: Cabot Corp 950 Winter St PO Box 9073 Waltham MA 02254-9073 also: The Brookings Instn 1775 Massachusetts Ave NW Washington DC 20036

CABRERA, CLARO D., microbiologist; b. San Pablo, Laguna, Philippines, Aug. 18, 1928; s. Angel R. and Loreto (Daya) C.; m. Beatrice Abarcar; children: Eric Anthony, Cheryl May. BS in Chemistry, U. Philippines, Quezon City, 1951, MD, 1956; postgrad., U. N.C., 1987—. Asst. instr. Far Eastern U. Med. Sch., Manila, 1956-66, instr., 1967-68, asst. prof., acting head dept. microbiology, 1968, assoc. prof., head dept. microbiology, 1969-72, prof., head dept. microbiology, 1972—; prof., head dept. microbiology and parasitology Fatima Coll. Medicine, Valenzuela, Philippines, 1979—; cons. Far Eastern U. Hosp., Manila, 1967—. Author: Laboratory Workbook and Guide in Microbiology Series, 1967, 72, 77, 79, 84. AID fellow, 1965-67; recipient Cert. Achievement U.S. Dept. State, 1967. Fellow Philippine Soc. Microbiology and Infectious Diseases (bd. dirs. 1981-84), Philippine Soc. Pathologists (gov. 1976-79); mem. Am. Soc. Microbiology, Am. Acad. Microbiology (specialist 1969—), Philippine Assn. of Schs. Med. Tech. (pres.), N.Y. Acad. Scis., Philippine Soc. Allergy and Immunology . Roman Catholic. Home: 24 Bignay St, Quezon City 3006, Philippines Office: Far Eastern Univ, Nicanor Reyes Ave, Manila 2806, Philippines

CABRERA HIDALGO, LUIS ALFONSO, Guatemalan government official; b. July 2, 1942. Student, U. Catolica de Chile, U. San Carlos de Guatemala, U. Rafael Landivar, Guatemala. Sec. propoganda Christian Dem. Party Guatemala, 1964, 70, 77, sec. fin., 1976, adj. sec. gen., 1979, 85—; asst. del. Congress of the Republic, 1974, titular del., 1976, elected del., 1982, 86, pres., 1986; del., 1st pres. Nat. Constitutional Assembly; minister specific matters to the pres. Guatemala, 1987; now minister fgn. relations. Address: Ministry Fgn Relations, Guatemala City Guatemala *

CABRINETY, PATRICIA BUTLER, software company executive; b. Earlville, N.Y., Sept. 4, 1932; d. Eugene Thomas and Helen Sylvester (Fulmer) Butler; m. Lawrence Paul Cabrinety, Aug. 20, 1955; children: Linda Anne, Margaret Marie, Stephen Michael. BS in Elem. Edn. and Music, SUNY, Potsdam, 1954. Cert. tchr. N.Y., Pa., Minn., Mass. Asst. tchr. music Hamilton (N.Y.) Cen. Sch., 1948-50; tchr. Cherry Lane Sch., Suffern, N.Y., 1954-56; instr. music, Towanda, Pa., 1960-63, Sayre, Pa., 1963-79; pres. Superior Software Inc., Mpls., 1981—; poet and illustrator, Edina, Minn., 1981—; cons. in field. Composer, artist numerous compositions; inventor: Musical for Computer, 1981; author monthly column on Boy Scouts, 1975-78, also more than 70 pub. poems and 35 pub. illustrations. Recipient Golden Poet award World of Poetry, 1985-87, Poet of Month award All Season's Poetry, 1986, Vantage Press Invitational award, 1985-88, Poet of Month award Editor's Desk, 1986, Internat. Poet award, 1986. Mem. Nat. Assn. Female Execs., Am. Soc. Profl. and Exec. Women, Nat. Assn. Bus. and Profl. Women, Nat. Writers Assn., Am. Mgmt. Assn., DAR, AAUW, Pioneers, Legion of Mary, Third Order Carmelite, Mpls. Music Tchrs. Forum, Edina C. of C., Worcester County Music Assn., Worcester

County Poetry Assn. Avocations: philately, art, needlecraft, photography, outdoor activities. Home: 925 Pearl Hill Rd Fitchburg MA 01420

CABROL, CHRISTIAN EMILE, cardiovascular surgeon, educator; b. Chezy sur Marne, France, Sept. 16, 1925; s. Roger and Lucien (Gratiot) C.; m. Annik Claude Piriou, Oct. 10, 1955. Cert. of Biology, U. Paris, 1944. Intern Parisian Hosp., 1950, asst. surgeon, 1956-61, surgeon, 1961-65; sci. dir. Sch. Surgery, Paris, 1973—; assoc. prof. anatomy U. Paris, 1955-65, prof., 1965—, chief dept., 1965—; chief surg. outpatient clinic Hopital Tenon, Paris, 1967-72; prof. cardiovascular surgery Hopital Pitie, Paris, 1971—, chief dept., 1972—. Decorated officier Ordre du Merite, chevalier Legion of Honor; recipient Claude Bernard prize City of Paris, 1986, Medaille of Vermeil, 1986. Mem. Am. Assn. Thoracic Surgery, European Soc. for Exptl. Surgery, European Soc. Transplantation (hon. pres. 1986), Internat. Soc. for Cardiac Transplantation (councillor 1983-87, sec. 1988), Mediterranean Soc. Cardiology and Cardiac Surgery (founder, pres. 1986), Internat. Assn. for Cardiac Biol. Implant (pres. 1985-87), France-Transplant Assn. (v.p.). Roman Catholic. Home: 15 rue Buffon, 75005 Paris France Office: Hopital Pitie, 47-83 Blvd de L'Hopital, 75651 Paris Cedex 13 France

CABUGAO, ANTONIO DE LA PENA, physician; b. Dagupan, Pangasinan, The Philippines, Feb. 13, 1940; s. Jorge Claveria and Rosita (De la Pena) C.; m. Glenda Barreras Bigornia, Dec. 18, 1969; children: Desiree Daphne, Stephanie, Lord Byron. BS, Far Eastern U., 1965; MD, Southwestern U., Cebu City, 1971. Adj. resident physician San Carlos Gen. Hosp., The Philippines, 1971; resident physician Luzon Med. Ctr., Dagupan City, 1972-73, Villaflor Clinic & Hosp., Dagupan City, 1973-74; med. officer Philippine Air Force Med. Services Group, Nichols AFB, 1974; officer-in-charge Philippine Air Force Med. Dispensary, Puerto Princesa, 1974, Philippine Air Force Out Patient Dept. and Med. Ward, 1974; officer-in-charge Philippine Air Force Med. Dispensary, 1975, sta. comdr., 1976-77; wing med. dir. Base Air Base Hosp., Pampanga, 1975-76, aviation med. examiner Philippine Air Force, flight surgeon, 1975-78, officer in charge, 1977-78; resident Ramos Children's Clinic, Dagupan City, 1979; co. physician Pantranco North Express Inc., Dagupan City, 1978-79, 86—, Fiafi Trading Med. Dispensary, Basrah, Iraq, 1981-82; resident physician Nazareth Gen. Hosp., Dagupan City, 1982—, Dagupan Drs. Villaflor Hosp., 1982-85; practice medicine Cabugao Med. Clinic, Dagupan City, 1985—; laparoscopist Johns Hopkins Program for Internat. Edn. in Ob/Gyn, 1984. Recipient citation Commn. on Nat. Integration, Republic of Philippines, 1975, award of recognition Health Mission for Bataan, 1976, commendation Philippine Air Force, 1976, others. Mem. Philippine Med. Assn., Pangasinan Med. Soc. (sec. 1985-86, Most Outstanding Officer award 1985-86), Philippine Assn. Mil. Surgeons. Address: 210 Fernandez Subd, Caranglaan Dist, Dagupan City, Pangasinan 0701, The Philippines

CACACE, MICHAEL JOSEPH, lawyer; b. Mt. Vernon, N.Y., Apr. 20, 1952; s. Jerry F. and Margaret F. (Pesditsch) C.; m. Maureen R. Brown, May 24, 1975; children—Joseph M., Christine M. B.A., Fordham U., 1974; J.D., N.Y. Law Sch., 1978. Bar: Conn. 1978, N.Y. 1979, U.S. Dist. Ct. Conn. 1979, U.S. Ct. Appeals (2nd cir.) 1981, U.S. Dist. Ct. (so. dist.) N.Y. 1982. Law clk. Saxe, Bacon & Bolan, N.Y.C., 1976-78, atty., 1978-79; atty. Abate, Fox & Farrell, Stamford, Conn., 1979-82, sole practice, Stamford, 1982-87; ptnr., D'Andrea & Cacace, 1988—; bd. dirs. The Vol. Ctr., Stamford, 1980—, pres. 1984-86; co.-chmn. 13th Charter Revision Com., Stamford, 1982-83; v.p. Gateway Communities, Inc., Stamford, 1981—; bd. dirs. Stamford Commn. on Aging, 1975-80, chmn. 1978-80; instr. adminstrv. law Norwalk Community Coll., Conn., 1980-82. Author book chpt. Age Discrimination Law, 1981. Bd. dirs. Vis. Nurses Assn., Stamford, 1982-87, Shippan Point Assn., Stamford, 1980-83, Stamford Ctr. for the Arts, 1986—, Stamford United Way, 1988—; mem. Conn. Com. Regional Plan, 1987—. Named Outstanding Young Man of Am., 1977, Community Leader of Yr., The Stamford Adv., 1986; recipient Dr. Max Reich award N.Y. Law Sch., Humanitarian award Southwestern Conn. Assn. Life Underwriters, 1987-88. Alumni Assn., 1978, Lawyers Co-op Book award Lawyers Co-op Book Co., 1977. Mem. Stamford/Darien Bar Assn. (mem. exec. com. 1980—, treas. 1986-87, sec. 1987-87, 1st v.p. 1988-89), Conn. Bar Assn., N.Y. Bar Assn., Conn. Trial Lawyers Assn., Am. Trial Lawyers Assn., State St. Debating Soc. Democrat. Roman Catholic. Club: Roasters (Stamford). Home: 316 Scofieldtown Rd Stamford CT 06903 Office: 1887 Summer St Stamford CT 06905

CACCAMISE, GENEVRA LOUISE BALL (MRS. ALFRED E. CACCAMISE), retired librarian; b. Mayville, N.Y., July 22, 1934; d. Herbert Oscar and Genevra (Green) Ball; B.A., Stetson U., DeLand, Fla., 1956; M.S. in L.S., Syracuse U., 1967; m. Alfred E. Caccamise, July 7, 1974. Tchr. grammar sch., Sanford, Fla., 1956-57, elem. sch., Longwood, Fla., 1957-58; tchr., librarian Enterprise (Fla.) Sch., 1958-63; librarian, media specialist Boston Ave. Sch., DeLand, 1963-82; head media specialist Blue Lake Sch., DeLand, 1982-87; ret., 1987. Charter mem. West Volusia Meml. Hosp. aux., DeLand, 1962—; Girl Scout leader, 1955-56, area dir. Fla. Edn. Assn., Volusia county, 1963-65; bd. dirs. Alhambra Villas Home Owners Assn., 1972-75; trustee, pres., DeLand Pub. Library, v.p. Friends of DeLand Pub. Library, 1987. Mem. AAUW (2d v.p. chpt. 1965-67, rec. sec. 1961-65, 78-80, pres. 1980-82, parliamentarian 1982-84), Assn. Childhood Edn. (1st v.p. 1965-66, corr. sec. 1963-65), DAR (chpt. registrar 1969—; asst. chief page Continental Congress, Washington 1962-65), Bus. and Profl. Women's Club (corr. sec. DeLand 1968-71, 2d v.p. 1969-70), Stetson U. Alumni Assn. (class chmn. for ann. fund drive 1968), Volusia County Assn. Media in Edn. (treas.), Volusia County Retired Educators Assn. (pres. Unit II 1988—), Soc. of Mayflower Descendants (lt. gov. Francis Cook Colony, 1988), Pilgrim John Howland Soc., Colonial Dames XVII Century, Magna Charta Dames, Delta Kappa Gamma (pres. Beta Psi chpt.). Democrat. Episcopalian. Club: Hibiscus Garden cirlce (treas. 1988—). An author Volusia County manual Instructing the Library Assistant, 1965. Address: PO Box 241 De Land FL 32721

CACCIATORE, EDOARDO, poet; b. Palermo, Italy, Nov. 18, 1912; s. Gaetano and Spoto Maria Cacciatore. Author: L'identificazione Intera, 1951, La Restituzione, 1955, Lo Specchio e la Trottola, 1960, Dal Dire al Fare, 1967, Ma chi è qui il Responsabile?, 1974, La Puntura dell 'Assillo, 1986, Graduali, 1986. Recipient Premio Arcangeli, Bologna, Italy, 1987. Home: Largo Cristina Di Svezia 12, 00765 Rome Italy

CACHA, ARNALDO ARCHIMEDES-MEDRANO, agricultural engineer; b. Manila, Mar. 3, 1950; s. Antonio Balan and Leticia Santos (Medrano) C.; m. Leonisa Tiongco Uy, Mar. 1, 1987; 1 child, Isabelle. B.S. in Agrl. Engring., U. of the Philippines, 1971, M. in Agri-Bus. Mgmt., 1976. Registered profl. agrl. engr. Research asst. Coll. Agr., U. Philippines, Los Banos, Laguna, Philippines, 1971-73; asst. mgr. ABC Ricemill, Calapan, Oriental Mindoro, Philippines, 1973-74, agrl. engr., 1973-76; gen. mgr., v.p. ABCD Milling Corp., Calapan, 1976—. Chmn. Calapan chpt. Nat. Citizens Movement for Free Elections, 1986-87. Mem. First Oriental Mindoro Integrated Rice and Corn Assn. (sec. 1978—), Oriental Mindoro Truckers Assn. (auditor 1983). Roman Catholic. Lodges: Rotary (pres. 1987-88), Masons (worshipful master 1984, sec. 1980-87, named knight comdr. of Ct. of Honor 1984, De Molay Cross of Honor, 1986). Avocation: reading. Home: Sto Nino, Masipit Oriental Mindoro Philippines Office: ABCD Milling Corp, Sto Nino, Calapan Oriental Mindoro Philippines

CACOYANNIS, MICHAEL, film and stage director, producer, actor; b. Limassol, Cyprus, June 11, 1922; s. Panayotis C. Barrister-at-law, Gray's Inn, U. London, 1942; acting diploma Central Sch. Dramatic Art, London, 1944; student Old Vic Sch., 1946; hon. degree Columbia Coll., Chgo., 1981. Producer, Overseas Service, BBC, 1941-50; screen and stage producer, 1950—; appeared in plays: (as Herod) Salome, 1947, Caligula, 1949, Two Dozen Red Roses, 1949; dir. films: Windfall in Athens, 1953; Stella, 1955; A Girl in Black, 1957; A Matter of Dignity, 1958; Our Last Spring, 1959; The Wastrel, 1960; Electra, 1961; Zorba the Greek, 1964; The Day the Fish Came Out, 1967; The Trojan Women, 1971; The Story of Jacob and Joseph, 1974; Attila 74, 1975; Iphigenia, 1976; Sweet Country, 1986; dir. plays: The Trojan Women, Paris, 1956; The Devils, N.Y.C., 1966; Mourning Becomes Electra, Met. Opera, N.Y.C., 1967; Romeo and Juliet, Paris, 1968; Iphigenia in Aulis, N.Y.C., 1968; La Bohè me, N.Y.C., 1972; King Oedipus, Dublin, 1973; The Bacchae, Comé die Franç aise, Paris, 1977; Anthony and Cleopatra, Athens, 1979; The Bacchae, N.Y.C., 1980; (musical) Zorba, U.S., 1983; Iphigenia in Aulis and in Tauris Frankfurt State Opera, 1987, La Clemenza Di Tito, Music Festival Aix-En-Provence, 1988; translator: Antony and Cleopatra, 1980; The Bacchae, 1982; Hamlet (into Greek), 1985. Decorated Order of Phoenix (Greece); commandeur des Arts et des Lettres (France).

CADAHIA, JOSE RAMON, chief of documentation service; b. Villa De Don Fadrique, Spain, Nov. 24, 1925; s. Jesus and Maria (Cicuendez) C.; m. Purificacion Casla, April 20, 1954; children: Gloria, Purificacion, Isabel, Paloma, Ramon, Antonio, Mar, Fatima, Natalia, Marta. M, Sch. Agronomic Engring., Madrid, 1953, D, 1960. Cert. agronomic engr. Researcher Inst. Nacional De Investigaciones Agrarias, Madrid, 1955-61, sect. head, 1961-79, chief documentation service, 1979—; prof. Escuela De Ingenieros Agronomos, Madrid, 1959-73; assessor Koipesol, Sevilla, Spain, 1969-73. V.p. Confederacion Sindical Independiente De Funcionarios, Madrid, 1980-85; treas. Colegio Oficial De Ingenieros Agronomos, Madrid, 1981—. Served to 2d. lt. with Spanish mil., 1953. Eisenhower fellow, 1964; recipient Merito Agricola Cross. Roman Catholic. Home: Paseo De La Castellana 217, 28046 Madrid Spain Office: Inst Nacional De Investigaciones, Agrarias, Jose Abascal 56, 28003 Madrid Spain

CADBURY, (GEORGE) ADRIAN (HAYHURST), manufacturing company executive; b. Birmingham, Eng., Apr. 15, 1929; s. Laurence John and Joyce (Mathews) C.; m. Gillian Mary Skepper, June 16, 1956; 3 children. M.A., Kings Coll., Cambridge U., 1952; D.Sc. (hon.), Aston U., Birmingham, 1973. Personnel dir. Cadbury Bros. Ltd., Birmingham, 1958-65; chmn. Cadbury Group, Birmingham, 1965-69; dep. chmn., mng. dir. Cadbury Schweppes PLC., London, 1969-74, chmn., 1975—; dir. Bank of Eng., London, IBM UK Ltd., London, Promotion of Non-Exec. Dirs., London; mem. Covent Garden Market Authority, London, 1974—; Nuffield Meml. lectr. 1969; lectr. Inst. Personnel Mgmt., 1970; Stockton lectr., 1974; Blackett Meml. lectr., 1983. Chancellor Aston U., Birmingham, 1979. Knight Bachelor, 1977; named freeman of City of Birmingham, 1982. Fellow Inst. Mktg. (hon.), Inst. Personnel Mgmt.; mem. Brit. Inst. Mgmt. (companion), Grocery Mfrs. Am. (dir.). Clubs: Boodles (London); Hawks (Cambridge, Eng.); Leander (Henley, Eng.). Office: Cadbury Schweppes PLC, 1-4 Connaught Pl, London W2 2EX, England also: Cadbury Schwepps Pk, 1-4 Connaught Pl, Bournville B30 2LU, England

CADDELL, FOSTER, artist; b. Pawtucket, R.I., Aug. 2, 1921; s. Foster and Clara (Bamford) C.; student R.I. Sch. Design, 1940-43; pvt. study with Peter Helck, Robert Brackman, Guy Wiggins; m. June A. Kaufmann, Apr. 10, 1943. Artist, Providence Lithograph Co. (R.I.), 1939-52; free-lance illustrator, 1951-65; owner, instr. Foster Caddell's Art Sch., Voluntown, Conn., 1958—; one-man shows Providence Art Club, 1948, 63, South County (R.I.) Art Assn., 1967, Slater Mus., Norwich Acad., 1976, Heritage Plantations of Sandwich, 1985; group shows include Springfield Mus. Fine Arts, 1962-77, Am. Watercolor Soc., 1973, NAD, 1973, Am. Artists Profl. League (awards 1953, 71, 72), Acad. Artists Am. (awards 1968, 73, 75), Slater Mus., Norwich Acad., 1975-80, Providence Art Club (award 1978, 79), Nat. Arts Club, 1978, Internat. Soc. Artists (award 1978), Societe Des Pastellists De France, 1987, others; specialist in portraiture, 1965—. Served as artist USAAC, World War II. Recipient awards Norwich Acad., 1947, Ogunquit Art Center, 1949, Conservative Painters R.I., 1962, Salmagundi Club, 1973, 80. Mem. Providence Art Club, Am. Artists Profl. League, Acad. Artists Am., Am. Portrait Soc., Salmagundi Club, Pastel Soc. Am., Internat. Soc. Artists. Author: Keys to Successful Landscape Painting, 1976; Keys to Successful Color, 1979; Keys to Painting Better Portraits, 1982, Oil Painting Techniques, 1983, Landscape Painting Techniques, 1984. Address: Northlight RFD 1 Rt 49 Voluntown CT 06384

CADDELL, HAROLD LEWIS, business educator, retired career military officer; b. Effingham, Ill., Mar. 15, 1934; s. Harold Lavergne and Mary Lou (Winkelman) C.; m. Wauneta Ann Hazlett, May 29, 1959; children: Harold Lynn, David Paul. BS in Aero. Engring., Okla. State U., 1957, MS in Aero. Engring., 1966; PhD in Leadership and Human Behavior, U.S. Internat. U., 1979. Ordained to ministry Bapt. Ch., 1982. Design engr. Goodyear (Ariz.) Aircraft, 1957-58; commd. aircraft maintenance officer USAF, Ellsworth AFB, S.D., 1958; adv. through grades to lt. col. USAF, 1974; project engr. Gemini Target Vehicle Program Office USAF, Los Angeles, 1964-68, project engr. Titan III Manned Orbiting Lab. program, 1968-72; with 6595th Aero. Test Wing USAF, Vandenberg AFB, Calif., 1974; commdr. site activation task force USAF, Wake Island, Calif., 1972-74; from chief maintenance to dep. commdr. and dir. 6595th Instrumentation Squadron USAF, Vandenberg AFB, Calif., 1974-78, shuttle liaison officer satellite control facility, 1979, from chief devel. test div., 1st Strategic Aero. div. to dir. test programs, 1978-79, dir. ops. 6595th Aero. Test Group, Western Space and Missile Ctr., 1982-83, retired, 1983; assoc. prof. bus. adminstrn. Calif. Bapt. Coll., Riverside, 1983—; speaker leadership and motivation seminars, Riverside, 1974-78. Fellow Nat. Assn. Ch. Bus. Adminstrn. (dir. West coast tng. ctr. 1984—); mem. Am. Mgmt. Assn., Christian Ministries Mgmt. Assn., U.S. Tennis Club. Club: Toastmasters (Vandenberg AFB chpt.). Home: 7885 Big Rock Dr Riverside CA 92509 Office: Calif Bapt Coll 8431 Magnolia Ave Riverside CA 92504

CADE, VICTOR ROSCOE, osteopathic surgeon; b. Larned, Kans., Apr. 7, 1911; s. Albert Benton and Minnie H. (Goodman) C.; m. Helen G. Shore, 1933; children—Sonya Marie Cade Steiner, Steven Ray Cade. D.O., U. Health Scis., Kansas City, Mo., 1934; diploma Am. Inst. Hypnosis, 1977; Postgrad. in surgery U. Vienna, Diplomate Am. Osteo. Bd. Surgery, Kans. State Bd. Healing Arts. Gen. practice osteo. medicine, Larned, 1934—, also Corpus Christi, Tex.; mem. staff St. Joseph Meml. Hosp., Larned, Corpus Christi Osteo. Hosp.; mem. faculty U. Health Scis. Mem. Coll. Osteo. Surgeons, ACS, Kans. Assn. Osteo. Medicine (hon. life mem.), Am. Osteopathy Assn., Am. Med. Soc. Vienna. Lodge: Masons. Office: Cade Bldg 820 Broadway Larned KS 67550

CADIER, ERIC YVES, endocrinologist; b. St. Germain en Laye, France, Oct. 31, 1950; s. Rene Albert and Odile Charlotte (Keller) C.; m. Martine Anne Jacquin; children: Emmanuel, Elsa. MD, U. Paris, 1978, diploma in aero. medicine, 1979, diploma in endocrinology and metabolic disease, 1981, diploma in phys. damage evaluation, 1982. Cert. in endocrinology and metabolic disease. Resident Henri Mondor Hosp. U. Paris, 1976-78, Berthelot Clinic for Cardiology, 1977; resident endocrinology dept. Hosp. St. Antoine Hosp., Cochin, 1980-81; gen. practice medicine and acupuncture Paris, 1980-84, practice medicine specializing in endocrinology and metabolic disease, 1984—; tchr. acupanucture Amenab Assocs., Paris, 1980-83. Active Assn. for Travel and Holidays for Mentally Handicapped Adults, 1986—. Mem. Societe Medicine Aeronautique et Spatiale, Societe Francaise Osteopathie. Home: 16 rue St Simon, 75887 Paris France Office: 203 bis bd St Germain, 75007 Paris France

CADWELL, DAVID ROBERT, lawyer; b. Hartford, Conn., June 7, 1934; s. Robert M. and Esther (Pinsky) C.; m. Carolle Cramer, 1964 (div. 1970); children—David, Kimberly; m. Sumiko Hashigiwa, Dec. 28, 1974; children—Kenneth, Daniel. B.A. magna cum laude, U. Minn., 1956; J.D., UCLA, 1959. Bar: Calif. 1960, U.S. Dist. Ct. (cen. and so. dists.) Calif. 1960, U.S. Supreme Ct. 1968. Dep. atty. gen. Calif. Atty. Gen., Los Angeles, 1960-61; sole practice, Santa Ana, Calif., 1961-70; adminstr. Jacoby & Meyers, Los Angeles, 1972-74, assoc., 1974-82; sole practice, Los Angeles, 1982-84; mng. ptnr. Cadwell & Glenn, Los Angeles, 1984—; lectr. Practical Law Course, Los Angeles, 1975-80. Author: How to Take a Case to Court, 1975; How to Handle Personal Injury Cases, 1976; How to Evaluate a Personal Injury Case, 1978, 80. Nat. committeeman Calif. Young Democrats, Los Angeles, 1959-60; mem. host com. Dem. Nat. Conv., Los Angeles, 1960, county com. Dem. Party, Orange County, Calif., 1962-64; exec. com. Fox Hills Dem. Club, Los Angeles, 1973-78. Recipient Outstanding Legal Services award NAACP, 1963. Mem. Assn. Trial Lawyers Am. Calif. Trial Lawyers Assn., Los Angeles Trial Lawyers Assn. Jewish. Home: 3575 Green Vista Dr Encino CA 91436 Office: Cadwell & Glenn 9744 Wilshire Blvd Suite 440 Beverly Hills CA 90212

CADY, DAVID CHRISTIAN, structural engineer; b. Birmingham, Mich., May 7, 1931; s. Leonard A. and Alma C. Cady; m. Barbara Lee Brown, Nov. 20, 1950; children—Charlene, David Christian, Rosanna Lyn, Phillip Lee, Brenda Jean. B.S., Mich. Technol. U., 1957. Sr. design engr. Gen. Dynamics, San Diego, 1961-68; design engr. LTV Aerospace Corp., Dallas, 1968-70; systems engr. McDonnel Aircraft Co., St. Louis, 1971-73; machine operator, product engr. Gardner Denver, Reed City, Mich., 1973-75; mine supt., chief engr. Gold Bond Bldg. Products (Va.), 1976-78; structural design contract engr., Brunswick, Marion, Va., 1978-79, Nordam, Tulsa, Okla., 1979; aircraft structural design contract engr. Swearingon Aircraft Co., San Antonio, 1979-80, Mooney Aircraft Co., Kerrville, Tex., 1980-82, Fairchild Aircraft Co., San Antonio, 1982-83, Gulfstream Aerospace Co., Bethany, Okla., 1983-85, E-Systems, Greenville, Tex., 1985, LTV Co., Grand Prairie, Tex., 1985-87, Dee Howard Co., San Antonio, 1987—. Safety officer 4th group Tex. Wing, CAP, Grand Prairie. Served with USAF, 1951-52. Club: Toastmasters Internat. (past pres.). Home: 16402 Spruce Cove San Antonio TX 78247

CADY, EDWIN HARRISON, English language educator, author; b. Old Tappan, N.J., Nov. 9, 1917; s. Edwin Laird and Ethel Sprague (Harrison) C.; m. Norma Woodard, Aug. 31, 1939; children: Frances (Mrs. Edward Hitchcock), Elizabeth (Mrs. Larry Saler). A.B., Ohio Wesleyan U., 1939, Litt.D., 1964; M.A., U. Cin., 1940; Ph.D., U. Wis., 1943; Litt.D., Oklahoma City U., 1967. Instr. English U. Wis., 1945, Ohio State U., 1946; from asst. prof. to prof. Syracuse U., 1946-59; Rudy prof. English Ind. U., 1959-73; prof. English Duke U., 1973—, Andrew W. Mellon prof. humanities, 1975—, prof. emeritus, 1987—; vis. prof. Am. lit., Uppsala and Stockholm, Sweden, 1951-52. Author: The Gentleman in America, 1949, The Road to Realism, The Early Years, 1837-1885, of William Dean Howells, 1956, The Realist at War: The Mature Years, 1885-1920, of William Dean Howells, 1958, Stephen Crane, 1962, rev. edit., 1980, John Woolman: The Mind of the Quaker Saint, 1965, The Light of Common Day, 1971, The Big Game: College Sports and American Life, 1979, Young Howells and John Brown, 1985. Editor: (with H.H. Clark) Whittier on Writers and Writing, 1950, Literature of the Early Republic, 1950, rev. edit, 1969, (with L. Ahnebrink) An Anthology of American Literature, 1953, (with L.G. Wells) Stephen Crane's Love Letters to Nellie Crouse, 1954, (with F.J. Hoffman and R.H. Pearce) The Growth of American Literature, 1956, W.D. Howells, The Rise of Silas Lapham, 1957, Corwin K. Linson, My Stephen Crane, 1958, (with D.L. Frazier) The War of the Critics Over William Dean Howells, 1962, W.D. Howells, The Shadow of a Dream and An Imperative Duty, 1962, William Cooper Howells, Recollections of Life in Ohio, 1963, The American Poets, 1800-1900, 1966, (with D.F. Hiatt) W.D. Howells, Literary Friends and Acquaintance, 1968, Nathaniel Hawthorne, The Scarlet Letter, 1969, W.D. Howells as Critic, 1973, (with C. Anderson and L. Budd) Toward a New American Literary History: Essays in Honor of Arlin Turner, 1980, (with N.W. Cady) Critical Essays on W.D. Howells, 1766-1920, 1983, A Modern Instance, 1984; (with Louis J. Budd) On Whitman: The Best from American Literature, On Mark Twain: The Best from American Literature, 1987; gen. editor: A Selected Edition of W.D. Howells, 1966-68; assoc. editor: Am. Lit. mag, 1973—; chmn. bd. editors, 1979-86, mng. editor, 1986-87. Mem. exec. com. Center Am. Editions, 1964-68; mem. U.S. Nat. Commn. for UNESCO, 1969-71. Served with Am. Field Service, 1943-44, Italy; with USNR, 1945. Guggenheim fellow, 1953-54, 75-76. Mem. MLA (chmn. Am. lit. sect. 1979), Guild Scholars, Am. Antiquarian Soc., Phi Beta Kappa, Omicron Delta Kappa, Phi Gamma Delta. Episcopalian.

CADY, WALLACE MARTIN, research geologist; b. Middlebury, Vt.; s. Frank William and Alice Marian (Kingsbury) C.; m. Helen Johanna Raitanen, Jan. 1, 1942; children—John Wallace, Nancy Helen, Norma Louise. B.S., Middlebury Coll., Vt., 1934; M.S., Northwestern U., 1936; Ph.D., Columbia U., 1944. Registered geologist, Colo., Vt., D.C. Research geologist U.S. Geol. Survey, Washington, 1939-45, Montpelier, Vt., 1945-61, Denver, 1961-85. Author: New England and Quebec, 1969; (with others) geol. maps. Fulbright lectureship, USSR, 1975; recipient Meritorious award U.S. Dept. Interior. Fellow Geol. Soc. Am.; Am. Geophys. Union; mem. Colo. Sci. Soc., (pres. 1975), Soc. Econ. Geologists, Vt. Geol. Soc. Home: 348 S Moore St Lakewood CO 80226 Office: US Geol Survey Fed Ctr Box 25046 Denver CO 80225

CAEN, JACQUES PHILIPPE, pathology educator; b. Metz, France, Mar. 11, 1927; s. Lucien and Renee (Levy) C.; m. Genevieve Francou, Feb. 2, 1951; children: Remi, Anne-Sophie. MD, U. Paris, 1951. Resident U. Paris, 1949-50; chief of lab. faculty medicine U. Paris VII, 1956-65, from assoc. prof. medicine to prof., 1966—; chief dept. hemostasis and thrombosis, U. Paris, 1971; m. faculty Caius and Gonville Coll., Cambridge U., Eng., 1976-77; assoc. prof. U. Sydney, 1983. Contbr. articles to profl. jours. Decorated chevalier Legion of Honor, Officer of Merit, 1984, Honoris Causa Suzhou, 1985, Maastricht, 1986; recipient Robert P. Grant medal, 1979. Fellow Royal Coll. Pathologists London; mem. Internat. Soc. Thrombosis and Hemostasis (sec.-gen. 1976), European Thrombosis Research Organ. (pres. 1972), Internat. Soc. Hematology, Inst. "Vaisseaux et Sang" Hosp. Lariboisière (bd. dirs.), French Acad. Sci. (corr.). Club: Racketts. Home: 32 Ch Flouquet, 75007 Paris France Office: 2A Pare, 75010 Paris France

CAGNAT, ROLAND, pediatrician; b. Lainsecq, Yonne, France, Sept. 7, 1926; s. Maurice Cagnat and Octavie Bourgoin; m. Helene Michel, June 29, 1948; 1 child, Geraldine. MD, U. Paris, 1955. Intern Hosp. Perpetual Secours, Levallois Perrett, France, 1951-56; pediatric asst. Hosp. Perpetual Secours, Levallois Perrett, 1956-86; medicin de maternal and infantile protection D.A.S.S., Hauts de Seine, France, 1963-86; cabinet liberal Levallois Perret, 1955—. Contbr. articles to profl. jours. Served to lt. French Armed Forces, 1943-44. Decorated Croix de Guerre, French Army, 1947; recipient Medal of Honor, Ville de Levallois, 1987. Mem. French Soc. Pediatrics, Soc. Medicine Paris. Roman Catholic. Home and Office: 5 Rue Voltaire, 92300 Levallois Perret France

CAHIER, PHILLIPPE, educator; b. Paris, Mar. 31, 1932; s. Fernand and Miriam (Faraforni) C.; m. Gabriella Buccelli, Dec. 7, 1960; 1 dau., Marie Laure. Lic. en droit Law Sch. Paris, 1953; diploma etudes superieures in econs. Law Sch. Lyon, 1956; Ph.D. in Poli t. Scis., Grad. Inst. Internat. Studies, Geneva, 1959. Ofcl., ILO, Geneva, 1957-60; asst. prof. Grad. Inst. Internat. Studies, Geneva, 1962-64, assoc. prof., 1964-66, prof. internat. law, 1966—; prof. Law Sch. Geneva, 1986; lectr. in field; counsel Spanish Govt. in Barcelona Traction Case, Internat. Ct. Justice, 1969; registrar Beagle Channel Ct. Arbitration, 1973-77; pres. Dubai-Sharjah Boundary Ct. Arbitration, 1978-81; counsel Guinea Govt. Arbitration, 1984-85; pres. adminstrv. tribunal Internat. Inst. Pvt. Law, Rome, 1978, pres. Internat. Comml. Indsl. Arbitration Ct., 1986. Mem. French Soc. Internat. Law, Swiss Soc. Internat. Law, Internat. Law Assn. Author: Etude des accords de siege conclus entre les Organisations Internationales et les Etats ou elles resident, Milan, 1959; Le droit diplomatique contemporain, 1962; Les Traites Et Les Etats Tiers, 1979. Home: 10 Rue Pedro Meylan, Geneva 1208, Switzerland Office: Grad Inst Internat Studies, 132 Rue de Lausanne, Geneva 1211, Switzerland

CAHILL, LINDA AMY ANN, publishing executive; b. Passaic, N.J., May 21, 1945; d. James F. and Doris G. (Mess) C. B.A., Pa. State U., 1967; J.D., Vanderbilt U., 1973; postgrad. Fla. Atlantic U., 1980—. Bar: Fla., 1974, U.S. Dist. Ct. (so. dist.) Fla., 1980. Continuity dir. sta. KDKA-TV, Pitts., 1967; comml. prodn. staff N.W. Ayer & Son, Phila., 1967-68; sole practice Ft. Lauderdale, Fla., 1976-84; asst. supr. research dept. The National Enquirer, Lantana, Fla., 1977-80; pub. relations cons., So. Fla., 1980-84; asst., editor The News, Mexico City, 1984-87; atty. immigration Mexico City, 1987-88; editor Traveller's Guide to Mex., 1988—; pres., founder Ancient America, Inc., Boynton Beach, 1983—; newsletter editor Univ. Club Mexico, 1985-86. Author: Collaborator: The HAB Theory, 1975. Contbr. articles to newspapers and mags. Vol. Guide H.M. Flagler Mus., Palm Beach, Fla., 1980-83; mem. Republicans Abroad, Mexico City, 1984—. Mem. Inst. Maya Studies, Am. Soc. Mex., Asociacion de Amigos del Museo Nacional de Antropologia A.C., Lambda Alpha. Avocations: private pilot, amateur archaeologist. Office: Admin Correos #1, Apdo M-10385, 06200 Mexico City Mexico

CAHN, RICHARD CALEB, lawyer; b. Bklyn., June 11, 1932; s. Irving and Pearl (Abel) C.; m. Vivian Isabel Meksin, Dec. 24, 1961; children—Michael, Lisa, Daniel, Sara. AB, Dartmouth Coll., 1953; LLB, Yale U., 1956; U. London, 1959. Bar: N.Y. 1956, Fla. 1966, U.S. Supreme Ct. 1960. Student asst. U.S. atty. So. Dist. N.Y., N.Y.C., 1955; atty. U.S. Dept. Justice, Washington 1956-57; ptnr. Cahn Wishod Wishod & Lamb, Melville, N.Y.; prin.

asst. dist. atty. Suffolk County (N.Y.), 1965-66; dep. atty. Town of Huntington (N.Y.), 1966-68; spl. counsel towns of Smithtown, Islip, Brookhaven, Babylon (N.Y.), 1967-68, Islip, N.Y., 1976-83, Huntington, N.Y., 1981—; counsel Brentwood Sch. Dist., 1977-82, 86—; spl. counsel Amityville Sch. Dist., 1978-79, Village of North Hills, 1978-79, Merrick Pub. Library; adj. prof. Touro Coll., Sch. Law, 1986—; hearing officer N.Y. State Edn. Dept., Nassau and Suffolk Counties, 1971-77; spl. dist. atty. Suffolk County, 1972; participant World Peace Through Law Conf., 1967, Malpractice Mediation Panel, 2d dept., 1974-84, Gov.'s Jud. Nominating Com. 2d dept., 1975-81; mem. screening com. bankruptcy judges U.S. Dist. Ct. Dist. N.Y., 1976-81, mem. screening com. U.S. magistrates, 1977-81; regional counsel SUNY-Stony Brook, 1972—. Bd. dirs. Stony Brook Found., 1974-86, Ea. Dist. Civil Litigation Fund, 1982-86. Fellow Soc. Values in Higher Edn., 1984—; mem. ABA, N.Y. Bar Assn. (ho. of dels. 1981-83), Suffolk County Bar Assn. (pres. 1981-82), Fed. Bar Assn., Am. Judicature Soc., Fed. Bar Council (v.p. 1982-84, trustee 1984—), Huntington Lawyers Club. Contbr. articles to profl. jours.; bd. editors Yale Law Jour., 1954. Office: 534 Broadhollow Rd CS 179 Melville NY 11747

CAHOON, STUART NEWTON, retired state health administrator, psychiatrist; b. Avalon, Pa., Dec. 9, 1916; s. Reno McCune and Belle Elizabeth (Newton) C.; m. Myrtle Katherine Opdyke, Sept. 19, 1942; children: Elizabeth Cahoon Knickerbocker, Sandra Cahoon Anderson. B.A., Oberlin Coll., 1939; M.D., Temple U., 1943; postgrad. psychoanalysis, William Alanson White Inst., N.Y.C., 1946-53. Intern Wilmington (Del.) Gen. Hosp., 1943-44; resident in psychiatry N.J. State Hosp., Greystone Park, 1944-47; clin. dir. N.J. State Hosp., Skillman, 1949-50; practice medicine specializing in psychoanalysis Newark, 1950-56, Miami, Fla., 1957-60; mem. staff Jackson Meml. Hosp., Miami, 1957-60; chief mental health clinics Honolulu; also mem. staff Leahi Hosp., 1961-64; clin. dir. Community Mental Health Center; also mem. staff Halifax Dist. Hosp., Daytone Beach, Fla., 1964-68; assoc. prof. psychiatry U. Fla. Med. Sch., Gainesville, 1968-73; clin. prof. U. Fla. Med. Sch., from 1974; dir. community mental health, State of Fla., 1971-74; dir. Fla. Div. Mental Health, Tallahassee, 1974-77; regional dir. mental health, Fort Myers, Fla., 1977-85; adv. com. lit. service State Instns. Fla., 1974-85. Contbr. profl. jours. Fellow Royal Soc. Health; mem. Mental Health Assn. Fla., Hawaii Psychiat. Soc. (past pres.), Am., Fla. psychiat. assns., Am. Acad. Psychotherapists, AAAS, Am., Fla. med. assns. Home: 75-5719 Alii Dr Kailua-Kona HI 96740

CAHOUET, FRANK VONDELL, banker; b. Cohasset, Mass., May 25, 1932; s. Ralph Hubert and Mary Claire (Jordan) C.; m. Ann Pleasonton Walsh, July 14, 1956; children: Ann P., Mary G., Frank V., David R. BA, Harvard U., 1954; MBA, U. Pa., 1959. Corp. loan asst. Security Pacific Nat. Bank, Los Angeles, 1960-66, v.p., 1966-69; sr. loan adminstr. Security Pacific Nat. Bank, Europe/Middle East/Africa, 1969-73; exec. v.p. Security Pacific Nat. Bank, 1978-80, vice chmn., 1980-84; exec. v.p. Security Pacific Corp., Los Angeles, 1973-80, vice chmn., 1980-84; chmn., pres. and chief exec. officer Crocker Nat. Bank, San Francisco, 1984-86; pres., chief operating officer Fed. Nat. Mortgage Assn., 1986-87; chmn., chief exec. officer Mellon Bank Corp., Pitts., 1987—; bd. dirs. Avery Internat. Corp., Los Angeles. Trustee Carnegie Inst., Pitts., Carnegie-Mellon U., Pitts., U. Pitts., Pa's. SW Assn., Pitts.; mem. Allegheny Conf. on Community Dvel.; bd. overseers Wharton Sch. U. Pa. Mem. Newcomen Soc. Clubs: Duquesne (Pitts.); California (Los Angeles). Home: 615 East Dr Sewickley PA 15143 Office: Mellon Bank Corp One Mellon Bank Ctr Pittsburgh PA 15258-0001

CAILLÉ, YVES, physician; b. Bordeaux, France, May 16, 1942; s. Maurice and Simone (Toulet) C.; children: Benedicte, Gregory. MD, Med. U., Bordeaux, 1971. Intern, then resident Boardeaux, 1966-69, faculté de medicine, 1969-85; faculté de medicine for corporal dammage splty. work Paris, 1985-86; gen. practice medicine Billere, France, 1971—; cons. Med. Group, Billere, France, 1971. Club: Royal Golf. Office: Groupe Med, 9 Pl de la Mairie, 64140 Billère France

CAIN, FRANCIS MICHAEL, historian, educator; b. Warracknabeal, Victoria, Australia, May 14, 1931; s. Francis Michael and Beatrice Monica (Dolley) C.; m. Elaine Beryl Lokan, Aug. 13, 1960; children: Penelope, Felicity. BA, U. Adelaide, South Australia, 1961, BA with honors, 1964, MA, 1972; PhD, Monash U., Victoria, 1980. Lectr. Australian Air Force Acad., Point Cook, Victoria, 1966-73, sr. lectr., 1973-80; vis. fellow U. New South Wales, Sydney, Australia, 1981-82; sr. lectr. dept. history, 1983—. Author: Origins of Political Surveillance in Australia, 1983; contbr. articles on Australian polit. history to profl. publs. Home: 8 Goldsworthy Pl, 2617 South Bruce Australia Office: U New South Wales, 2600 Campbell Australia

CAIN, MARCENA JEAN BEESLEY, retail store executive; b. Kingman, Kans., May 1, 1935; d. Albert Eugene and Stella Wanda (Ruthowski) Beesley; m. Kenneth B. Cain, Aug. 4, 1951; children—Kenneth Thomas, David Raymond. With AMVETS Thrift Stores, D.C., 1971—, asst. dir., 1971-87, exec. adminstr., 1987—, asst. dir. Amvets Value Village Thrift Stores, Balt.; ptnr. Bank St. Joint Venture Realty, Del-Mar Realty, Oakland Ctr. Partnership Ltd., 1987; pres. Family Thrift Ctr., Inc.; v.p. 4 corps. Mem. Bus. and Profl. Women's Club, Highlandtown Businessmen Assn., DAV Aux. (past nat. historian), PTA Valley Forge Mil. Acad. (D.C. area rep.), Highlandtown Mchts. Assn. (pres. 1983-84), Govanstown Mchts. Assn. (rec. sec.), Affiliated Mchts. Assn. Balt. (pres.). Republican. Christian Scientist. Office: 3424 Eastern Ave Baltimore MD 21224

CAINE, STEPHEN HOWARD, data process executive.; b. Washington, Feb. 11, 1941; s. Walter E. and Jeanette (Wenborne) C.; student Calif. Inst. Tech., 1958-62. Sr. programmer Calif. Inst. Tech., Pasadena, 1962-65, mgr. systems programming, 1965-69, mgr. programming, 1969-70; pres. Caine, Farber & Gordon, Inc., Pasadena, 1970—; lectr. applied sci. Calif. Inst. Tech., Pasadena, 1965-71, vis. asso. elec. engring., 1976, vis. asso. computer sci., 1976-84. Mem. Pasadena Tournament of Roses Assn., 1976—. Mem. Assn. Computing Machinery, Nat. Assn. Corrosion Engrs., AAAS, Am. Ordnance Assn. Clubs: Athenaeum (Pasadena); Engrs. (N.Y.C.). Home: 77 Patrician Way Pasadena CA 91105

CAIRNCROSS, ALEXANDER KIRKLAND, economist, university chancellor; b. Lesmahagow, Scotland, Feb. 11, 1911; s. Alexander Kirkland and Elizabeth Andrew (Wishart) C.; m. Mary Frances Glynn, May 29, 1943; children: Frances Anne, Philip Wishart, Alexander Messent, David John, Elizabeth Mary. Grad., Hamilton Acad., 1928; M.A., U. Glasgow, 1933; Ph.D., Cambridge U., 1936; LL.D., Mt. Allison U., 1962, Glasgow U., 1966, Exeter U., 1969; D.Litt., Reading U., 1968, Heriot Watt U., 1969; D.Sc., Univ. Coll., Swansea, 1971, Queen's U., Belfast, 1972; D. Univ., Stirling U., 1973. Lectr. U. Glasgow, 1935-39, prof. applied econs., dir. dept. social and econ. research, 1951-61; econ. adviser to Her Majesty's Govt., 1961-64; head of Her Majesty's Govt. Econ. Service, 1964-69; master St. Peters Coll., Oxford, Eng., 1969-78; chancellor U. Glasgow, 1972—; War Cabinet offices, Bd. Trade, Ministry Aircraft Prodn., 1939-45; econ. adviser Bd. Trade, 1946-49; head econ. adv. panel, Berlin, 1945-46; staff London Economist, 1946; econ. adviser OEEC, 1949-50; dir. Econ. Devel. Inst., Washington, 1955-56. Author: Introduction to Economics, 1944, Home and Foreign Investment, 1870-1913, 1953, Monetary Policy in a Mixed Economy, 1960, Factors in Economic Development, 1962, Essays in Economic Management, 1971, Control of Long-term International Capital Movements, 1973, Inflation, Growth and International Finance, 1975, Snatches, 1980, (with B. Eichengreen) Sterling in Decline, 1983, Years of Recovery, 1985, The Price of War, 1986, Economics and Economic Policy, 1986, A Country to Play With, 1987; editor: The Scottish Economy, 1954, Scottish Jour. Polit. Economy, 1954-61, The Managed Economy, 1970, Planning and Economic Management, 1970, Britain's Economic Prospects Reconsidered, 1971, others. Bd. govs. London Sch. Econs.; pres. Girls Public Day Sch. Trust, 1972—. Decorated comdr. Order St. Michael and St. George, 1950, knight comdr., 1966; hon fellow St. Peter's Coll., Oxford U., 1978; supernumerary fellow St. Antony's Coll., 1978; hon. fellow London Sch. Econs., 1981. Fellow Brit. Acad.; mem. Royal Econ. Soc. (v.p.), Scottish Econ. Soc. (v.p.), Am. Acad. Arts and Scis. (fgn. hon.), Brit. Assn. Advancement Sci. (pres. 1971), Nat. Inst. Econ. and Social Research of London (bd. govs.). Home: 14 Staverton Rd, Oxford England

CAIRNDUFF, IAN BRUCE, business consultant, accountant; b. Dublin, Nov. 11, 1935; s. Andrew and Doreen Dawson (Fitzpatrick) C.; m. Maureen Alice Bouchier-Hayes, Mar. 27, 1965; children: Robert, Bruce, David. Educated pvt. schs., Dublin. Sr. audit asst. Graig Gardner and Co., Dublin, 1959-60; chief acct. Gilbey's of Ireland Ltd., Dublin, 1960-61, joint mng. dir., 1961-68; mgmt. cons. Urwick Orr and Ptnrs. Ltd., London, 1968-72; mng. dir. Smyths of the Green Distbn. Ltd., Dublin, 1972-75, exec. chmn., 1975-82; nominee dir. Foir Teoranta, Waterford and Dublin, 1982-85; bus. cons. Inbucon Ireland Ltd., Dublin, 1985—; lectr., tutor Inbucon Devel. and Tng. Ltd., Dublin, 1986—; bd. dirs. Marble City Enterprises Ltd., Kilkenny, Ireland. Peace commr. Irish Cts. Justice, 1980. Fellow Inst. Chartered Accts. Ireland; mem. Commanderie Bontemps de Medoc et Graves (hon comdr.). Presbyterian. Clubs: Fitzwilliam, Old Wesley (Dublin). Home: 56 Waterloo Rd, Dublin 4, Ireland Office: Inbucon Ireland Ltd, 28 Lower Leeson St, Dublin 4, Ireland

CALAIS-AULOY, JEAN, educator; b. Sete, France, Feb. 5, 1933; s. Philibert and Genevieve (Laures) C.; m. Jacqueline Temple-Boyer, Jan 23, 1962; 1 child, Pauline. License en Droit, Faculte de Droit, Montpellier, 1953, Doctorat en Droit, 1959; Agregation de Droit Prive, Faculte de Droit, 1961. Prof. U. D'Abidjan, Cote D'Ivoire, 1961-64, U. Montpellier (France), 1964—; pres. Commn. le Refonte de la Consommation, Paris, 1982-85. Author: Essai Sur la Notion d'Apparence, 1959, Ventes Maritimes, 1983, Propositions pour un Nouveau Droit de la Consommations, 1985, Droit de la Consommation, 1986. Served to lt. French Army, 1955-57. Decorated Chevalier de la Legion d'Honneur, Grande Chancellerie, Paris, 1982. Mem. Centre du Doit de la Consommation d l'Universite de Montpellier (pres. 1975). Office: Faculte de Droit, Rue de l'Universite, 34000 Montpellier France

CALAMARAS, LOUIS BASIL, lawyer, association executive; b. Peabody, Mass., Jan. 6, 1908; s. Basil James and Margo (Papalexaton) C.; m. Pauline Spirrison, May 2, 1937; children—Margo, Basil, Georgia. Prep., L'école-Metaxa, Athens, Greece; B.A., Columbia U., 1931; LL.D., Georgetown U., 1934; postgrad. student law and commerce, Northwestern U. Dept. commr. Ind. Securities Commn., 1935-37; supr. Ill. Labor Dept., 1937-40; counsellor Labor Indsl. Relations, 1940-44; exec. sec. Nat. Electronic Distbrs. Assn., 1944-51, exec. v.p., 1951—; mng. dir. Midwest Elec. Distbrs. Assn.; bd. dirs., mem. exec. com. Electric Assn.; dir. Montclare Theatre Corp., Elm Theatre Corp., Geo. A. Davis Co.; trustee Nat. Assn. Wholesalers; mgmt. cons. Lawn and Garden Assn., Suburban Restaurant Assn.; Mem. Wholesalers Adv. Com. to Sec. of Commerce; chmn. Radio-TV Industry FTC Trade Practice Conf.; mem. Electronic Coordinating Com. Editor, pub.: Nat. Electronic Distbrs. Assn. Jour; contbr. articles to profl. jours. Chmn. Park-Recreation Bd., Planning Commn., Zoning Bd., Village of Lincolnwood. Recipient Disting. Service award Nat. Elec. Mfrs. Reps. Assn., 1985; named Man of Yr., Radio Electronic Industry, 1955, Man of Yr., Elec. Industry, 1975, Man of Yr., Elec. Industry Golf Club. Mem. Chgo. Exchange, Electric Assn., Am. Acad. Polit. Sci., Phi Delta Theta. Clubs: Variety, Tam O'Shanter Country, Lake Shore Athletic (Chgo.); Ridgemore Country (v.p., dir.), Columbia University, Lake Michigan (exec. dir.), Electric Golf, Tower, Countryside Country. Lodges: Rotary, Masons, KP (Chgo.). Home: 6712 N Leroy St Lincolnwood IL 60645 Office: 5901 N Cicero Ave Chicago IL 60646

CALASSO, ROBERTO, writer, publisher; b. Florence, Italy, May 30, 1941; s. Francescoand Melisenda (Codignola) C.; m. Fleur Jaeggy. D.Litt, U. Rome, 1966. Editorial dir. Adelphi Edizioni Pub. Co., Milan, Italy, 1968—. Author: L'Impuro Folle, 1974, La Rovina di Kasch, 1983; contbr. articles to profl. jours. Recipient Ehrenkreuz Litteris et Artibus award, Austria, 1981. Office: Adelphi Edizioni, Via S Giovanni sul Muro 14, 20121 Milan Italy

CALBOLI, GUALTIERO FEDERICO, linguistics educator, b. Bologna, Italy, Jan. 3, 1932; s. Primo Ettore and Anita Rita (Pignatti) C.; m. Lucia Montefusco, May 10, 1969; children: Irene, Federico, Francesco. BA, U. Bologna, 1955, PhD, 1955. Asst. prof. Latin lang. and lit. U. Tübingen, W. Germany, 1962-63; asst. prof. U. Bologna, 1964-69, prof., 1970—, chmn. Dipartimento di Filologia Classica e Medioevale, 1982—, mem. and chmn. faculty bds. Author books including: M. Porci Catonis, Oratio pro Rhodiensibus, with Historical Survey and Commentary, 1978; Papers on Grammar I, 1980, Problemi di Grammatica Latina, 1983, Papers on Grammar II, 1986, Latin Subordination, 1988. Contbr. articles, revs. to Italian, German, French profl. jours. Author studies on Latin grammar, Roman rhetoric and lit. Mem. Centro di Studi Ciceroniani, Centro di Studi Varroniani, Linguistic Soc. Am. Roman Catholic. Home: Via Riccoboni 12, 40127 Bologna Italy Office: Via Zamboni 34, 40126 Bologna Italy

CALBRIS, GENEVIEVE, research engineer; b. Hué, Vietnam, Jan. 25, 1941; arrived in France, 1959; d. Joël and Suzanne (Ammann) C. BS, Diploma in Psychology, Psychology Inst., Paris, 1962; D in Phonetics, U. Paris, 1973, LHD, 1983. Contract employee Ecole Normale Supérieure St. Cloud, France, 1963-86; research engr. Ecole Normale Supérieure, Fontenay-St. Cloud, France, 1988—. Author: Gestures and Verbal Communication, 1983, Semiotics of French Gestures, 198. Oh là là; co-author: Oh Pà Pà; Vocal and Gestural Expression, 1980, Saying it with Gestures and Words, 1986, Gestures and Communication, 198. Home: 30 rue des Favorites, 75015 Paris France Office: ENS de Fontenay-St Cloud, 31 Ave Lombard, 92266 Fontenay aux Roses France

CALCAGNO, ALBERTO, media executive; b. Paris, Sept. 22, 1919; arrived in Italy, 1937; s. Ettore and Isabelle (Liard) C.; m. Odette Lemmi, Feb. 11, 1946; children: Claudia, Carlo Ettore. Pub. Italy in the World mag., Genoa, Italy, 1938-42; pub., editor Italian Tourist Yearbook, Rome, 1948-52, advt. agt. tourism, 1952-60; mng. dir. Publimondial spa, Milan, 1961-62, owner, chief exec. officer, 1962-65; journalist Rome, 1966-69; owner, chief exec. officer Studio Calcagno Srl, Milan, 1970—. Contbr. articles to profl. jours. Office: Studio Calcagno Srl, Via Copernico 22, I-20125 Milan Italy

CALDEIRA, WINSTON RAMON, economist, agricultural consultant; b. Paramaribo, Suriname, June 4, 1941; s. Frank Rupert and Elsje Elenora (Karg) C.; m. Ellen Chrisje Comvalius, Oct. 19, 1967; children: Boni, Ebun. BSc, State U. Wageningen, The Netherlands, 1968, MSc in Agrl. Econs., 1971. Project economist Ministry of Agr., Suriname, 1971-74, chief agrl. devel. div., 1975-80; dir. Nat. Planning Office, Suriname, 1980-83, minister fin. and planning, 1983-84; cons. Orgn. Am. States, Washington, 1984-86, project coordinator, 1987—; chmn. Suriname Bauxite com., Paramaribo, 1981-83; gov. World Bank, IMF, 1983-84, nat. ordonnateur European Devel. Fund, 1981-84, mem. Dutch-Suriname Council, 1981-83. Mem. Internat. Assn. Agrl. Econs., Surinam Assn. Econs. (founding mem.), Progressive Union of Farmers and Workers (exec. sec. 1977-87), Trade Union Fedn. (bd. dirs. 1976-77). Lutheran. Club: Internat. Student. Home: 9129 Bridgewater St College Park MD 20740

CALDER, GEORGE ALEXANDER, educator; b. Detroit, Oct. 1, 1937; s. Alexander and Janette (Wolcott) C. B.A., Wayne State U., 1959, M.Ed., 1960. Cert. tchr., Mich. Math. tchr. Emerson Jr. High Sch., Livonia, Mich., 1960-79; tchr. Franklin High Sch., Livonia, 1979—, chmn. math. dept., 1980—. Recipient Outstanding Service award Livonia Edn. Assn., 1965, 1976, 1978; Outstanding Young Educator award Livonia Jaycees, 1969. Mem. NEA, Livonia Edn. Assn., Mich. Edn. Assn., Nat. Council Tchrs. Math., Detroit Council Tchrs. Math., Mich. Council Tchrs. Math., Hist. Soc. Livonia, Detroit Soc. for Geneal. Research, SAR (membership chmn. Detroit 1976-83, Nat. Membership award 1979, 81, 82). Methodist. Author: (with others) Discoveries in Modern Mathematics, Courses 1, 2, 1968, 1972; Daily Thoughts for the Classroom, 1974. Office: Franklin High Sch 31000 Joy Rd Livonia MI 48150

CALDER, ROBERT MAC, aerospace engineer; b. Vernal, Utah, Oct. 16, 1932; s. Edwin Harold and Sydney (Goodrich) C.; m. Yoshiko Iemura, Feb. 14, 1959; children—Suzanne, Alex, Irene, John. B.S. in Chem. Engring., U. Utah, 1956, M.S. in Math. and Geology (NSF grantee), 1967; postgrad. U. Wash., 1964, Utah State U., 1965, U. Iowa, 1966. Cert. secondary tchr., Utah. Tchr. Utah Pub. Schs., 1958-79; v.p. Sydney Corp., Bountiful, Utah, 1958-82; sr. engr. aero. div., Hercules Inc., Magna, Utah, 1979—; owner RMC Enterprises, Nations Imports; cons. in field, 1960—; cultural exchange participant to Israel, Egypt, 1982, 87. Active Boy Scouts Am., 1945-75, instr., Philmont Scout Ranch, 1972, asst. scoutmaster Nat. Jamboree Troop, 1973; instr. hunter safety and survival, Utah Dept. Fish and Game, 1964-74; state advisor U.S. Congl. Adv. Bd., 1982—. Served to capt. USAF, 1956-70. Mem. AIAA, Nat. Rifle Assn. (life), Am. Quarter Horse Assn., Internat. Platform Assn., Oratorio Soc. Utah, Republican Nat. Com. Mormon. Club: Hercules Toastmasters (treas. 1980, v.p. edn. 1981, pres. 1982). Home: 594 Calder Ct Kaysville UT 84037 Office: PO Box 98 Magna UT 84044

CALDERON, NISSIM, literary critic, Hebrew literature educator; b. Tel Aviv, Mar. 23, 1947; s. Meshulam and Esther (Ben-Uzio) C.; m. Hannah Sne, 1970 (div. 1974); m. Dorit Shahar, July 31, 1985 (div. 1988). BA, Tel Aviv U., 1972, PhD, 1980. Asst. editor Siman Kria Lit. Quarterly, TelAviv, 1973-76, 1980-84; lectr. Hebrew lit. Tel-Aviv U., 1972—; dramaturg The Haifa (Israel) Mcpl. Theater, 1980-81; mem. drama dept. The Israeli T.V., Tel-Aviv, 1982. Author: In a Political Context, 1980, On the Second Year of the War, 1984, A Previous Chapter, 1985. Served with Israeli Army, 1965-68. Fellow Nat. Bd. for Culture and Art. Office: Tel Aviv U, Ramat Aviv, Tel Aviv 69978, Israel

CALDERONE, JAMES JOSEPH, dentist; b. Conneaut, Ohio, Aug. 1, 1934; s. James Paul and August Cecilia (Polito) C.; m. Mary Louise Halbruegger, Dec. 28, 1957; children: Dominic J., James J., Theresa M., Martina M., Gina M., Camille M., Christina M., Anthony J. D.D.S., St. Louis U., 1959; M.P.H., U. Mich., 1974, DrPH, 1979. Diplomate Am. Bd. Dental Pub. Health. Pvt. practice dentistry, Belen, N.M., 1961-63, Albuquerque, 1963-73, Westland, Mich., 1974-75; pub. health dentist State of N.Mex., Santa Fe, 1975—; chmn. dental staff Bernalillo County Hosp., 1968-71; mem. N.Mex. Bd. Dentistry, 1972-74, v.p., 1974; cons. U.S. Indian Health Service, N.Mex. and Ariz., 1974—, Head Start, N.Mex., 1975—; adj. prof. U. N.Mex., Albuquerque, 1980—; bur. chief N.Mex. Health Dept., Santa Fe, 1980-84. Contbr. articles to profl. publs. Weblows leader Boy Scouts Am., Albuquerque, 1972; bd. dirs. St. Pius High Sch., Albuquerque, 1979-82. Served to lt. Dental Corps, USNR, 1959-61. Recipient Exemplary Performance award N.Mex. Health and Environ. Dept., 1981. Fellow Internat. Coll. Dentists; mem. Pierre Fauchard Acad., N.Mex. Pub. Health Assn. (pres.1988), N.Mex. Dental Assn. (legis. chmn. 1972), Albuquerque Dist. Dental Soc. (bd. dirs. 1969-72). Roman Catholic. Home: 7613 Comanche Rd NE Albuquerque NM 87110 Office: NMex Health and Environment Dept PO Box 968 Santa Fe NM 87504

CALDERWOOD, JAMES ALBERT, lawyer; b. Washington, Dec. 4, 1941; s. Charles Howard and Hilda Pauline (Dull) C.; m. Joyce M. Johnson, 1987; B.S., U. Md., 1964; J.D. cum laude, George Washington U., 1970; postgrad. Oxford Center Mgmt. Studies, Oxford U., 1977. Bar: Md. 1970, D.C. 1973, U.S. Supreme Ct. 1974. Trial atty. antitrust div. U.S. Dept. Justice, Washington, 1970-73, spl. asst. U.S. atty., Washington, 1973, trial atty. antitrust div., 1973-79; ptnr. Grove, Jaskiewicz, Gilliam & Cobert, Washington, 1979—; mem. faculty Transp. Law Inst. U. Denver; adj. prof. Washington Coll. Law, Am. U., 1983, 86; gen. counsel Soc. Govt. Economists. Served to capt. USAF, 1964-68. George Washington U. Law Ctr. scholar, 1969. Mem. ABA (Achievement award 1973), Fed. Bar Assn. (nat. co chmn. council young lawyers 1972-73, chmn. regulated industries com. 1976-79), Fed. Energy Bar Assn. (chmn. antitrust com. 1985-86), Md. Bar Assn., D.C. Bar Assn., U. Md. Alumni Assn. (pres. elect 1984-85, pres. 1985-86), Coll. Bus. Alumni Club (pres. 1980-81), Nat. Press Club, Pi Sigma Alpha, Delta Sigma Pi, Delta Theta Phi, English Speaking Union. Lutheran. Contbr. articles to profl. jours. Home: 5518 Western Ave Chevy Chase MD 20815 Office: 1730 M St NW Suite 501 Washington DC 20036

CALDICOTT, (CLIVE) EDRIC, French educator; b. Brecon, Wales, June 1, 1939; s. John David and Lucy Mabel (Jones) C.; m. Elizabeth Anne Kennedy, Sept. 9, 1967; children: David, Andrew, Katherine. BA, Trinity Coll., Dublin, 1963; MA, U. Aix/Marseille, 1964; PhD, Trinity Coll., 1968. Asst. U. Glasgow, Scotland, 1965-70; asst., then assoc. prof. Trent U., Peterborough, Ont., Can., 1970-78; prof., head French dept. U. Coll., Dublin, 1978—; external examiner New U. Ulster, Belfast, Ireland, 1973-75, Trinity Coll., Dublin, 1975—. Author: Marcel Pagnol, 1977; editor: Bouscal-Sanche Pansa, 1981 (prix de Graulhet 1982), Huguenots and Ireland, 1987. Recipient Ordre des Palmes Acads., 1980, Ordre Nat. du Merite, 1987, Medaille du Tarn, 1987, all from Govt of France. Mem. Modern Humanities Research Assn., Soc. Study Dix-Septieme Siecle. Clubs: Irish Ramblers, Leprechauns Cricket. Office: U Coll, Dept French, Belfield Dublin 4 Ireland

CALDWELL, BILLY RAY, geologist; b. Newellton, La., Apr. 20, 1932; s. Leslie Richardson and Helen Merle (Clark) C.; m. Carolyn Marie Heath, May 9, 1979; children—Caryn, Jeana, Craig. BA, Tex. Christian U., 1954, MA, 1970; Cert. petroleum geologist, Tex. Geologist, Geol. Engring. Service Co., Ft. Worth, Tex., 1954-60; sci. tchr. Ft. Worth and Lake Worth Sch. Dists., 1960-63; mgr. Outdoor Living, 1963-71; instr. geology Tarrant County Jr. Coll., Ft. Worth, 1971—; petroleum geologist cons., Ft. Worth, 1971—. Bd. dirs. Ft. Worth and Tarrant County Homebuilders Assn., 1973. Named Dir. of Yr., Ft. Worth Jaycees, 1966-67. Mem. Am. Inst. Profl. Geologists (cert.), Ft. Worth Geol. Soc., Am. Assn. Petroleum Geologists, Soc. Profl. Well Log Analysts, Geol. Soc. Am. Republican. Baptist. Avocations: traveling, gardening, ch. work. Home: 305 Bodart Ln Fort Worth TX 76108 Office: 101 Jim Wright Freeway Suite 402 Fort Worth TX 76108

CALDWELL, HAROLD LEROY, petroleum engineer; b. Pawnee, Okla., Aug. 14, 1925; s. Harold Ralph and Eula P. (Buckner) C.; B.S. in Petroleum Engring., U. Tulsa, 1951; m. Patricia T. Poorman, Dec. 24, 1948; children—Michael Alan and Douglas Owen. Exploitation engr. Sunray Oil Co., 1951-55; chief engr. Keener Oil Co., Tulsa, 1955-59, gen. supt. prodn., 1959-63; engr. Fenix & Scisson, Inc., 1963-65; gen. supt. prodn. KWB Oil Property Mgmt., Inc., Tulsa, 1965-67; tech. asst. to chmn. bd. Resource Scis. Corp., Tulsa, 1967-74; v.p.-mgr. Perrault-Caldwell, Inc., Tulsa, 1974-76; engr. Keplinger & Assos., Tulsa, 1976-79; pres. Caldwell & Assos., Inc., cons. engrs., Tulsa, 1979—. Served with AUS, 1943-46. Registered profl. engr., Okla. Mem. Am. Inst. Mining Engrs., Am. Petroleum Inst., Okla. Soc. Profl. Engrs. Republican. Mem. Reorganized Ch. of Jesus Christ of Latter-day Saints. Home: 5129 S Richmond Tulsa OK 74135 Office: 320 S Boston Suite 1118 Tulsa OK 74103

CALDWELL, JOHN BERNARD, naval architect, educator; b. Sept. 26, 1926; s. John Revie and Doris (Bolland) C.; m. Jean Muriel Frances Duddridge, 1955; 2 sons. B. Engring., Liverpool (Eng.) U.; PhD, Bristol (Eng.) U.; DSc (hon.), Gdansk (Poland) Tech. U., 1985. Research fellow civil engring. Bristol U., 1953; sr. sci. officer Royal Naval Sci. Service, 1955, prin. sci. officer, 1958; asst. prof. applied mechanics RNC, Greenwich, Eng., 1960-66; hd. dept. naval architecture Newcastle-upon-Tyne (Eng.) U., 1966-83, dean faculty engring., 1983-86, head Sch. Marine Tech., 1986—; bd. dirs. Nat. Maritime Inst. Ltd., Marine Design Cons. Ltd., Newcastle Tech. Ctr.; vis. prof. naval architecture MIT, 1962-63; pres. N.E. Coast Instn. Engrs. and Shipbuilders, 1976-78, RINA, 1984—. Contbr. articles to profl. jours. Decorated OBE, 1979; recipient David Taylor medal, 1987. Club: Nat. Liberal. Office: The White House, Cadehill Rd, Stocksfield, Northumberland NE43 7PT, England *

CALDWELL, MARY PERI, educator, counseling psychologist; b. Cleve., Aug. 21, 1935; d. Francesco and Gerlanda (Gagliano) Peri; m. Robert Joseph Caldwell, 1956 (div. 1962); children: Deborah Ann, Thomas Robert. BS in Edn., Kent State U., Ohio, 1961; MA in Counseling Psychology, Alfred Adler Inst., Chgo., 1981. Cert. clin. mental health counselor; lic. mental health counselor, Fla. Tchr. various sch. systems in Cleve. area, 1957-85; pvt. practice as counseling psychologist, Brunswick, Ohio, 1980-87; mem. faculty, dir. Cleve. Inst. Adlerian Studies, 1983—, exec. sec., 1978-82, pres., 1982-84; pvt. practice psychology, Coral Springs, Fla., 1987—; mem. med. staff Care Unit, Coral Springs; lectr. U.S. and Can. Author: Stress/Distress/Burnout: Resolving the Puzzle of Stress, 1983; editor: Adlerian Psychology Bull., 1983-86; contbr. articles to profl. jours. Leader various parent edn. groups, 1981—. Jennings Found. grantee, 1979; recipient Disting. Service award N.E. Ohio Tchrs. Assn., 1983. Mem. N.Am. Soc. Adlerian Psychology (clin. mem., assembly del., Outstanding Woman award 1980), Am. Assn. Counseling and Devel., Am. Mental Health Counselors Assn., Fla. Assn. Counseling and Devel., Broward County Mental Health Assn., Exec. Women Coral Springs, Am. Bus. Women's Assn., Gamma Phi Beta (pres. 1967-70). Avocations: tennis, travel, piano, watercolor painting. Home:

8208 NW 100th Way Tamarac FL 33321 Office: 3300 University Dr Suite 615 Coral Springs FL 33321

CALDWELL, OLIVER JOHNSON, educator, former government official; b. Foochow, China, Nov. 16, 1904; s. Harry Russell and Mary Belle (Cope) C.; m. Eda Joslin Holcombe, June 29, 1935; children: Eda Joslyn (Mrs. Edmund Becker), Gail Edna (Mrs. Warren Robinson). Student, U. Wash., 1922-23; A.B., Oberlin Coll., 1926, M.A., 1927; student music, aesthetics, 1927-29; student, Army Civil Affairs Tng. Sch., U. Chgo., 1943; L.H.D., Baldwin-Wallace Coll.; LL.D., Ithaca U., Albright Coll. Head social scis. Harvey Sch., Hawthorne, N.Y., 1929-35; assoc. prof. English U. Amoy, China, 1935-36; prof. English U. Nanking, China, 1936-37; acting head dept. fgn. langs. U. Nanking, 1937-38; pub. relations officer Asso. Bds. Christian Colls. in China, 1938-43; chief student br., fed. programs br., div. exchange of persons Dept. State, 1947-51; chief program devel. staff ednl. exchange service U.S. Internat. Information Adminstrn., 1951-52; asst. commr. internat. edn., dir. div. internat. edn. U.S. Office Edn., later acting asso. commr., 1952- 64; vis. prof. comparative edn. U. Md., 1964-65; dean internat. services So. Ill. U., Carbondale, 1965-69; prof. higher edn. So. Ill. U., 1969-73, prof. emeritus, 1973—; author, cons., 1973—. Author: A Secret War-Americans in China 1944-45, 1972; Collaborator: The Task of the Universities in a Changing World; Contbr. 250 articles to profl. and popular jours., also symposium. Mem. sch. bd., Falls Church, 1952-56. Served from capt. to maj., OSS, AUS, 1943-45. Mem. various profl. assns. Methodist. Club: Rotarian. Home: Rural Route 2 Box 657 Cobden IL 62920

CALDWELL, THOMAS JONES, JR., lawyer; b. New Orleans, Oct. 17, 1923; s. Thomas Jones and Ethel Marie (Lee) C.; B.S. in Mech. Engring., U. Tex., 1944, J.D., 1949; B.S. in Econs., U. Houston, 1969, M.A. in Philosophy, 1976. Admitted to Tex. bar, 1949, since practiced in Houston; asso. firm George Red, 1949-50; asso. firm Fouts & Moore and predecessor firm, 1950-52, mem. firm, 1952-76, counsel, 1976-86; sec., dir. Delta Engring. Corp., Houston, 1954-69. Treas., Houston Com. on Fgn. Relations, 1965-70, chmn., 1970-71; bd. dirs. Tex. Assn. Mental Health, 1969-77, v.p., 1970-73, pres., 1973-75; bd. dirs. Child Guidance Center, Houston, 1960-68, 69-72, sec., 1963-65, pres., 1965-67; bd. dirs. Mental Health Assn. Houston, 1969-75, v.p., 1970-71; bd. dirs. Nat. Assn. Mental Health, 1974-77. Served with USNR, 1943-46. Mem. Am., Tex., Houston Bar Assns., Am. Judicature Soc., Kappa Sigma, Phi Delta Phi, Tau Beta Pi, Pi Tau Sigma, Phi Kappa Phi. Home: 7506 Shoal Creek Austin TX 78757

CALDWELL, WILLIAM EDWARD, educational administration educator, arbitrator; b. Providence, Aug. 18, 1928; s. James E. and Eva E. (Barker) C.; m. Doris E. Parlee, June 17, 1950; children—William E., Donna E., Allen E. B.A. in Math., Eastern Nazarene Coll., 1950; M.Ed. in Secondary Edn., U. N.H., 1956; Ph.D. in Ednl. Adminstrn., NYU, 1968. Cert. prin., supt., arbitrator. Tchr. math., dir. music, coach pub. schs., Berwick, Maine, 1950-54; tchr. math., supr. pub. schs., Valley Stream, N.Y., 1954-61; guidance counselor, prin. pub. schs., Manchester, Conn., 1961-67; dir. secondary tchr. tng. U. Hartford, Conn., 1967-69; exec. dir. Pa. Sch. Study Council, University Park, 1970-78; prof. ednl. adminstrn. Pa. State U., University Park, 1969—, chmn. edn. adminstrn. program, 1987—, pres. faculty council, 1985-86, ombudsman Coll. Edn., 1986—; state dir. mediation Commonwealth of Pa., Harrisburg, 1979-80; conciliator, fact finder Pa. Labor Relations Bd., Harrisburg, 1971—; arbitrator AAA, FMCS, Pa. Labor Relations Bd., 1971—. Author: Collective Negotiation in Public Education, 1970; Agreement, Policy for Principal/Supervisor, 1983; contbr. articles to profl. jours., chpts. to books; author reports. Served to lt. col. USMCR. Nat. del. Am. Assn. Sch. Adminstrs., Washington, 1976, 77, 79; bd. dirs. Fed. Credit Union, Manchester, Conn., 1963-67, Appalachian Ednl. Lab., Charleston, W.Va., 1970-78; examiner Pa. Civil Service Commn., Harrisburg, 1972-79. Recipient Commendation award Pa. Sch. Bds. Assn., 1980, Acad. Achievement award Ea. Nazarene Coll., 1950, NYU, 1969, Outstanding Service Commonwealth of Pa., 1973, Outstanding Service award Pa. Dept. Labor, 1987. Mem. Am. Ednl. Research Assn. (presenter), Pa. Assn. Secondary Sch. Prins. (research chmn., Commendation award 1983, Edn. Excellence award 1986). Office: Pa State U 316 Rackley Bldg University Park PA 16802

CALDWELL, WILLIAM MACKAY, III, business executive; b. Los Angeles Apr. 6, 1922; s. William Mackay II and Edith Ann (Richards) C.; B.S., U. So. Calif., 1943; M.B.A., Harvard U., 1948; m. Mary Louise Edwards, Jan. 16, 1946 (dec. 1980); children—William Mackay IV, Craig Ed wards, Candace Louise; m. Jean Bledsoe, Apr. 27, 1985. Sec.-treas., dir. Drewry Photocolor Corp., 1957-60, Adcolor Photo Corp., 1957-60; treas., dir. Drewry Bennetts Corp., 1959-60; sr. v.p., chief fin. officer Am. Cement Corp., 1960-67; sr. v.p. corp., 1966-70, pres. cement and concrete group, 1967-70; pres., chmn. bd., chief exec. officer Van Vorst Industries, 1969; pres. Van Vorst Corp., Washington, 1969-77; chmn. bd., pres. So. Cross Industries, U.S. Bedding Co., 1979-84, St. Croix Mfg. Co., 1979-81, Hawaiian Cement Corp.; pres. Englander Co., 1979-84; v.p., dir. Am. Cement Internat. Corp., Am. Cement Properties; chmn. Kyco Industries Inc., 1982—; pres. BHI Inc., 1984—; cons. prof. U. So. Calif. Mem. men's com. Los Angeles Med. Center; bd. dirs. Commerce Assos., Calif. Mus. Sci. and Industry, U. So. Calif. Assos., bd. dirs. Pres.'s Circle; bd. dirs. Am. Cement Found. Served to lt. USNR, 1943-46. Mem. Newcomen Soc., Friends Huntington Library, Kappa Alpha (student pres. U. So. Calif. 1943-44), Alpha Delta Sigma, Alpha Pi Omega. Presbyterian. Clubs: Harvard Bus. Sch. of So. Calif. (dir. 1960-63); Los Angeles Country, Town Hall, Calif. (Los Angeles); Trojan; Annandale Golf; Eldorado Country; Marrakesh Golf. Office: PO Box 726 Pasadena CA 91102

CALDWELL, WILLIAM STUART, journalist, educator; b. Alexandria, S.D., Feb. 4, 1921; s. Leslie Omar and Margaret (Macauley) C.; B.A., U. Minn., 1943, M.A. (Regent's scholar), 1954, Ph.D., 1960; m. Marjorie Louise Searing, Jan. 31, 1944 (div. June 1968); children—Linda M. Caldwell Harper, Bonnie J. Caldwell Stroock, Angela M. Caldwell Reiner, Ralph W., Stephen L.; m. 2d, Therezinha A. Leony, May 29, 1970 (div. July 1974); 1 son, William Stuart; m. 3d, Mildred L. Murry, Apr. 21, 1979 (div. Sept. 1983). Fgn. service officer, Rome and Palermo, Italy, 1946-49; pub. relations dir. U. Minn., Duluth, 1949-50; journalist Mpls. Star and Tribune, 1950-55, 58-60; mem. faculties U. N.C., 1955-58, UCLA, 1960-62; assoc. prof., head pub. relations sequence U. So. Calif. Sch. Journalism, Los Angeles, 1962-73; assoc. prof. Ball State U., Muncie, Ind., 1973-75; sr. lectr. Calif. Poly. U., Pomona, 1977—; adj. prof. Am. Pacific U., 1984—; sr. lectr. U.S. Navy, 1985—; v.p. pub. relations AMSTRO Enterprises and Dudley Prodns. Ltd., Los Angeles, 1975-83; dir. Ctr. Geopolit. Studies, 1982-88; cons. edn. Los Angeles Times, 1961, Los Angeles Unified Sch. Dist., 1979, Orange County Acad. Decathlon, 1981-84; cons. on communication Calif. and Ind. agys., 1970—. Mem. Los Angeles Mayor's Com. on Internat. Visitors and Sister Cities, 1966-73, 75-87; vice chmn. Los Angeles Sister City Exec. Com., 1977-82; mem. adv. bd. Intercultural Found. Beverly Hills, 1982-86; mem. assembly Orange County Health Planning Council, 1980-86; Calif. state rep. Sister Cities Internat., 1977-1979; So. Calif. chmn. Educators for Ford, 1976; mem. Irvine Edn. Found., 1982-84. Served to lt. AUS, 1943-46. Recipient honors St. Andrews U., Scotland, 1981, Superior Performance USN, 1986; Nat. Endowment for Humanities fellow. Fellow Pub. Relations Soc. Am.; mem. Assn. Edn. in Journalism (nat. chmn. pub. relations div. 1969-71, mem. nat. com. affiliates 1976-78), Pub. Relations Student Soc. Am. (founder U. So. Calif. chpt.), Travel Research Assn., Am. Polit. Sci. Assn., AAUP, Los Angeles World Affairs Council, Kappa Tau Alpha, Theta Chi, Sigma Delta Chi, Alpha Delta Sigma. Contbr. articles to profl. publs., chpts. to books. Home: PO Box 202 El Toro CA 92630 Office: Am Pacific U 17526 Von Karman Irvine CA 92716

CALFEE, WILLIAM LEWIS, lawyer; b. Cleveland Heights, Ohio, July 12, 1917; s. Robert Martin and Alwine (Haas) C.; m. Eleanor Elizabeth Bliss, Dec. 6, 1941; children: William R., Bruce K., Cynthia B. B.A., Harvard Coll., 1939; LL.D., Yale U., 1946. Bar: Ohio 1946. Assoc. Baker & Hostetler, Cleve., 1946-56, ptnr., 1957—. Bd. dirs. Growth Assn. Greater Cleve., 1979—; trustee Greater Cleve. United Appeal; pres. Health Fund Greater Cleve. Served to lt. col. M.I. U.S. Army, 1941-45. Decorated Legion of Merit; decorated Order of Brit. Empire. Mem. ABA (ho. dels. 1980—, standing com. bar activities), Ohio Bar Assn., Bar Assn. Greater Cleve. (trustee, pres. 1979-80), Nat. Conf. Bar Pres. (exec. council 1982-85), Ohio C. of C. (dir. 1983). Republican. Episcopalian. Clubs: Mayfield Country (pres.), Union, Pepper Pike; Fiddlesticks (Ft. Myers, Fla.). Home: 21200 Claythorne Rd Shaker Heights OH 44122 Office: Baker & Hostetler 3200 Nat City Ctr Cleveland OH 44114

CALHOUN, EVELYN WILLIAMS, social worker; b. Tyler, Tex., Sept. 12, 1921; d. James Stanley and Norma (Skelton) Williams; B.A., Baylor U., 1941; M.S.W., Worden Sch. Social Work, 1960; postgrad. U. Chgo., 1955-56; m. William Benjamin Calhoun, Jr., Mar. 15, 1942 (div. Mar. 1949); children—William Benjamin III, Anne Stanley (Mrs. Donald Elliot Loyd). Field worker Tex. Dept. Pub. Welfare, Tyler, 1953-55; field placement Salvation Army Family Service, Chgo., 1955-56; child welfare worker Tyler-Smith County Child Welfare Unit, 1957-59; field placement Tex. Inst. Rehab. and Research, Baylor U., Houston, 1959-60, med. social worker, 1960-64; research social worker pre-natal research project dept. obstetrics and gynecology U. Tex. Med. Br. at Galveston, 1964-66, supr. social service dept. obstetrics and gynecology, 1966-74, cons. satellite clinics, 1967-74, cons. family planning project, 1969-74, cons., supr. head and neck cancer service, ear, nose and throat, chest surgery and neurosurgery, 1974-78, cons., supr. plastic surgery and oral surgery service, 1975-78, supr. internal medicine services, otolaryngology, ophthalmology and dermatology, 1978-81; field instr. U. Houston Grad. Sch. Social Work, 1968-81. Bd. dirs. Galveston County Community Action Council, 1966-68, Galveston chpt. Am. Cancer Soc., 1974-81; trustee Houston Intergroup Assn., 1974-76. Lic. social psychotherapist, Tex.; cert. social worker, advanced clin. practitioner, Tex. Mem. Nat. Assn. Social Workers (chmn. research council San Jacinto chpt. 1963-64, dir. chpt. 1964-67, chmn. Galveston br. 1964-67, sec. 1967-68; group leader so. regional inst. 1966, alt. Tex. del. 1969-71, Tex. del. 1971-73, dir. 1969-73; alt. del. Tex. state council 1967), Acad. Cert. Social Workers, Galveston County Soc. Social Service Dirs. (sec. 1979-80), AAUW, Baylor Alumnae Assn., Daus. King (pres. 1976-78), Order De Moley, Delta Alpha Pi. Episcopalian. Toastmistress. Home: PO Box 893 Galveston TX 77550

CALHOUN, JOHN COZART, fin. and mktg. exec.; b. Ft. Oglethorpe, Ga., Aug. 6, 1937; s. James Paul and Geneva F. (Fortson) C.; LL.B., Blackstone Sch. Law, 1970; B.A., Eastern Nebr. Coll., 1972; LL.D. (hon.), Edward Waters Coll., 1975, Morris Brown Coll., 1976, Daniel Payne Coll., 1976; Ph.D. (hon.), Va. Coll., 1976, Clayton U., 1977, postgrad. U. East Asia, Macau. Intelligence analyst NATO, Izmir, Turkey, 1959; corr. Stars and Stripes, Dept. Def., 1959-60; newspaper editor, Ft. Myer, Va., 1961-63; news editor Sta. VUNC, Okinawa, 1963-64; public affairs rep. Dept. Def., Maine-N.H.-Vt., 1964-67; Tokyo public affairs rep. UN, 1967-68; chief community relations Mil. Dist. Washington, 1969-70; dir. public affairs Nat. Farmers Union, 1970-71; dir. minority communications Peace Corps, 1971-73; staff asst., dep. spl. asst. to Pres. for minority affairs, 1973-74; spl. asst. to Pres., also dir. for media relations The White House, Washington, 1975-76; chmn. bd. Aaken Calhoun Group; pres. Calhoun Assocs., Counselors, Internat. Law, Bus. and Internat. Relations; dir. Am.-Asian Trading Co., Am. Bionics Enterprises. Bd. dirs. Bel-Pre Civic Assn., 1973-76; communications adv. Republican Nat. Com.; mem. Nat. Adv. Council on Edn. for Disadvantaged Children, World Affairs Council Washington D.C. Served with U.S. Army, 1955-59. Decorated Army Commendation ribbon; recipient award Middle Atlantic Assn. Indsl. Editors, 1961; Clio award Am. TV and Radio Comml. Festival Group, 1971; Andy award Advt. Club N.Y., 1971; Nat. Man of Yr. award Nat. Inst. Rural Agrarian Life, 1976; Disting. Public Service award Prairie View A&M U., 1976. Mem. Internat. Communication Assn., Am. Mgmt. Assn., Acad. Polit. Sci., DAV (life), Am. Legion, Am. Assn. Retired People, Assn. Internat. Practical Tng. (bd. dirs. U.S. affiliate), Nat. Press Club, Capital Press Club (dir. 1969—), Rep. Nat. Com. Assos. Republican. Club: Capital Office: Box 70620 SW Sta Washington DC 20024

CALHOUN, LILLIAN SCOTT, public relations company executive; b. Savannah, Ga.; d. Walter Sanford and Laura (McDowell) Scott; m. Harold William Calhoun, Sept. 20, 1950; children: Laura, Harold, Walter, Karen. BA, Ohio State U., 1944. Columnist, feature editor Chgo. Defender, 1963-65; assoc. editor Jet, Ebony, mags., 1961-63; reporter Chgo. Sun-Times, 1965-68; mng. editor Integrated Edn. mag., 1968-71; info. officer, acting info. dir. Dept. Labor, 1971-73; co-editor Chgo. Reporter, 1973-76; pres., founder Calmar Communications, Inc., Chgo., 1978—; columnist Crain's Chgo. Bus., 1978-80, Chgo. Journalism Rev., 1969-74. Vice-chairperson Ill. Commn. on Human Relations, 1973-75; mem. Gov.'s Commn. on Status of Women, 1965-67, Gov.'s Adv. Council on Manpower, 1973-75. Recipient YWCA Leader award, 1984. Mem. Soc. Midland Authors, Chgo. Network, Alpha Gamma Pi. Episcopalian. Clubs: Chgo. Press, Publicity, Arts. Office: 500 N Dearborn St Suite 910-912 Chicago IL 60610

CALICA, JOVENCIO CAYABYAB, municipal health officer; b. Bauang, Philippines, Feb. 8, 1943; s. Luis Carlos and Maria (Cayabyab) C.; m. Millionita Remorozo, Dec. 28, 1973; children: Dymphna, Gertrude, Jovencio. BS, U. Santo Tomas, Philippines, 1966, MD, 1970. Intern J.R. Reyes Meml. Hosp., Manila, 1969-70; asst. resident Nat. Orthopedic Hosp., Quezon City, Philippines, 1970-71; adj. resident Ospital NG Alaynila, Pasay City, Philippines, 1971-72; sr. resident San Mieguel Emergency Hosp., Bulacan Providence, Philippines, 1972-73; mcpl. health officer Ministry of Health, Manila, 1973—; med. cons. San Pedro, Philippines, 1980—. Bd. dirs. Elvinda Village Assn., 1980-81; adviser Pag-iribang Bikolnon, Inc., 1985-86. Mem. San Pedro Laguna Med. Soc. (asst. treas. 1987—, v.p.). Home: Cadena de Amor St, Elvinda Village San Pedro 4023, Philippines

CALIRI, JOSEPH LOUIS, lawyer; b. Rochester, N.Y., Mar. 16, 1916; s. Salvatore and Maria Teresa (Bottazzi) C.; A.B., U. Rochester, 1938; LL.B., Cornell, 1941; m. Dorothy Ann McGrath, Aug. 19, 1944; children—Robert Redmond, Barbara Jane. Admitted to N.Y. bar, 1941, Ill. bar, 1974; law dept. Kraft, Inc. (formerly Nat. Dairy Products Corp.), N.Y.C., 1941-51, asst. sec., 1951-52, sec., 1952-71, v.p., 1971—, dir., 1980—; v.p., sec. Dart & Kraft, Inc., 1980-81; ret., 1981. Past pres. Bd. Edn., Union Free Sch. Dist. No. 9, West Islip, L.I. Mem. Am. Judicature Soc., Am. Soc. Corp. Secs., Am., Ill., Chgo. bar assns., Cornell Law Assn., Phi Beta Kappa, Alpha Phi Delta. Clubs: Cornell (N.Y.); Mich. Shores, Westmoreland Country (Wilmette, Ill.). Home: 1500 Sheridan Rd Wilmette IL 60091

CALKINS, EVAN, physician, educator; b. Newton, Mass., July 15, 1920; s. Grosvenor and Patty (Phillips) C.; m. Virginia McC. Brady, Sept. 9, 1946; children: Sarah Calkins Oxnard, Stephen, Lucy McCormick, Joan Calkins Bender, Benjamin, Hugh, Ellen Rountree, Geoffrey, Timothy. Grad., Milton Acad., 1939; A.B., Harvard U., 1942, M.D., 1945. Intern, asst. resident medicine Johns Hopkins, 1946-47, 48-50; chief resident physician Mass. Gen. Hosp., 1951-52, mem. arthritis unit, 1952-61; NRC fellow med. scis. Harvard, 1950-51, instr., asst. prof. medicine, 1952-61; practice medicine, specializing in rheumatology Boston, 1951-61, Buffalo, 1961—; prof. medicine SUNY, Buffalo, 1961—; chmn. dept. SUNY, 1965-77, head div. geriatrics and gerontology, 1978—; head dept. medicine Buffalo Gen. Hosp., 1961-68; dir. medicine E.J. Meyer Meml. Hosp., 1968-78; head gerontology sect. Buffalo VA Med. Center, 1978—; head div. geriatrics/gerontology SUNY-Buffalo, 1978—; founder, pres. Network in Aging of Western N.Y., Inc., 1980-83; cons. Nat. Inst. Arthritis and Metabolic Diseases Tng. Grants Com., 1958-62, Program Project Com., 1964-68, Nat. Insts. Spl. Study Sect. for Health Manpower, 1969-77, for Behavioral Medicine, 1978-79; mem. acad. awards com. Nat. Inst. on Aging, 1979-80, mem. nat. adv. council, 1985—; dir. Western N.Y. Geriatric Edn. Center, 1983—. Editor: Handbook of Medical Emergencies, 1945, Geriatric Medicine, 1983, Practice of Geriatrics, 1986. Contbr. articles to profl. jours. Served to capt., M.C. AUS, 1943-45, 46-48. Recipient Presdl. citation for Community Service, 1983. Fellow A.C.P., Am. Rheumatism Assn. (founder, pres. 1967-68, master 1986); mem. Gerontol. Assn., Am. Geriatrics Soc. (Milo D. Leavitt award 1986), Am. Clin. and Climatological Assn. (v.p. 1987), Am. Soc. Clin. Investigation, Assn. Am. Physicians, Central Soc. for Clin. Research, Soc. Medicine Argentina (hon.), Alpha Omega Alpha. Home: 3799 Windover Hamburg NY 14075 Office: VA Med Center 3495 Bailey Ave Buffalo NY 14215

CALKINS, GARY NATHAN, lawyer; b. N.Y.C., Mar. 1, 1911; s. Gary Nathan and Helen R. (Williston) C.; m. Constantia H. Hommann, June 22, 1940 (div. Dec. 1948); m. Susannah Eby, Nov. 19, 1949; children: Helen (dec.), Margaret Calkins Van Auken, Sarah, Abigail. Student, Ecole Internationale, Geneva, Switzerland, 1926-27, Storm King Sch., 1927-29; A.B., Columbia U., 1933; LL.B., Harvard U., 1936. Bar: N.Y. 1936, D.C. 1955, U.S. Supreme Ct. 1965, Va. 1982. Assoc. Beekman & Bogue, N.Y.C., 1936-41; staff CAB, 1941-56, chief internat. and rules div., 1947-56; mem. Galland, Kharasch, Calkins & Morse, P.C. (and predecessor firms), Washington, 1956-81; mng. ptnr. Galland, Kharasch, Calkins & Morse, P.C. (and predecessor firms), N.Y.C., 1969-80, pres., 1980-81, of counsel, 1981-85; sole practice Washington, 1981-86; of counsel to county atty. Fairfax County (Va.), 1982-87, with Fairfax County Juvenile Ct., 1987—; mem. U.S. sect. Comité Internat. Tecnique d' Experts Juridiques Aériens, 1946-47. Mem. U.S. dels. legal com. Internat. Civil Aviation Orgn., 1947-55; delegation chmn. 1st, 3d, 5th, 9th and 10th meetings; chief U.S. negotiator and draftsman Mortgage Conv., Geneva, Switzerland, 1948, mem. drafting com. Rome Conv. on Surface Damage, 1952; chmn. U.S. delegation internat. Diplomatic Conf. for Revision of Warsaw Conv., The Hague, 1955; chmn. legal div. U.S. Air Coordinating Com., 1955-56; industry observer U.S.-U.K. bilateral air transport talks, London, 1956; asst. sec. Philippine Airlines, 1974-86.; vol. atty. Legal Counsel for the Elderly AARP, Washington, 1988—. Asso. editor: United States and Canadian Aviation Reports, 1956-61; asso. editor: Jour. Air Law and Commerce, 1956-58; editor-in-chief, 1958-63; Contbr. articles to profl. jours. Served as lt. USNR, 1943-45. Mem. ABA, D.C., Va., Fairfax County Bar Assns., Am. Judicature Soc., Internat. Platform Assn., Soc. Quiet Birdmen, Lincoln;s Inn Soc., Psi Upsilon. Clubs: Cosmos, Georgetown (Washington), Nacoms (Columbia U.). Home and Office: 6504 Dearborn Dr Falls Church VA 22044

CALKINS, JOANN RUBY, nursing administrator; b. Mich., June 28, 1934; d. William Russell and Imajean (Dunkle) Armentrout; A.S., Delta Coll., 1964; B.S., Central Mich. U., 1972, M.A., 1977; m. James W. Calkins, 1952; children—Russell, Jill, Cindy; m. W. Arthur Brindle, May 7, 1983. Staff nurse, L.P.N. clin. instr., asst. dir. Sch. Nursing, Midland (Mich.) Hosp., 1964-71; dir. nursing, dir. substance abuse unit Gladwin (Mich.) Hosp., 1972-76; prin. Calkins Profl. Counseling & Cons., Harrison, Mich., 1976-78, part-time, 1978-83; dir. nursing service Central Mich. Community Hosp., Mt. Pleasant, 1978-83; dir. nursing Oaklawn Hosp., Marshall, Mich., 1983-87; dir. nursing Betsy Johnson Meml. Hosp., Dunn, N.C., 1987—; part-time prin. W. Arthur and Assocs. Cons.; conducted workshops Mich. Dept. Public Health; Mich. Hosp. Assn.; exec. dir. Holistic Health Agy., 1977-82. Trustee, Mid-Mich. Community Coll. Recipient Murial A. Grimmason Nursing Scholarship award, 1962; Cert. nursing adminstr. Mem. Mich. Soc. Hosp. Nursing Adminstrs. (mem. steering com. 1979-80, dir., 14 county rep. 1980-83, pres. 1983-84, chmn. devel. com.), Mich. Nurses Assn., Am. Nurses Assn., Am. Orgn. Nurse Execs., Nat. Assn. Female Execs. Methodist. Lodge: Lioness Internat. (3d v.p. 1985). Home: 513 Argyll Dr Sanford NC 27330 Office: 800 Tilghman Dr Dunn NC 28334

CALLAGAN, DWIGHT A., naval medical officer; b. Sheridan, Ill., Sept. 26, 1917; s. Ralph J. and Amine (Hapeman) C.; m. Anne King, Sept. 26, 1943; children: Sharon Anne, Dwight Allen, Brian King, Wayne Reed. B.S. in Medicine, U. Ill., 1942, M.D., 1942. Diplomate Am. Bd. Obstetrics and Gynecology. Commd. lt. (j.g.) U.S. Navy, 1942, advanced through grades to capt., 1957; intern U.S. Naval Hosp., Mare Island, 1943; resident in gen. surgery U.S. Naval Hosp., Nat. Naval Med. Ctr., Bethesda, Md., 1945-46; resident in obstetrics and gynecology U.S. Naval Hosp., Nat. Naval Med. Ctr., 1945-50, chief obstetrics and gynecology service, 1962-65; chief obstet. and gynecol. service U.S. Naval Hosp., Camp LeJeune, N.C., 1950-51, Guantanamo Bay, Cuba, 1951-53, Bremerton, Wash., 1953-55, Portsmouth, Va., 1955-62; exec. officer, chief profl. services U.S. Naval Hosp., Great Lakes, Ill., 1966-67; comdg. officers U.S. Naval Hosp., Subic Bay, 1968-69; with Naval Dispensary, Treasure Island, Calif., 1969-72; asst. clin. prof. obstetrics and gynecology George Washington U. Med. Sch., 1962-65. Contbr. numerous articles on diagnosis and mgmt. of multiple pregnancies, smoking during pregnancy, effect of drugs in pregnancy and ultrasonic doppler diagnostic use. Decorated Bronze Star medal with combat V. Mem. AMA, Am. Coll. Obstetricians and Gynecologists, Alpha Omega Pi, Phi Rho Sigma. Home: 6385 W Evans Creek Rd PO Box 14 Rogue River OR 97537

CALLAGHAN, MORLEY EDWARD, author; b. Toronto, Ont., Can., 1903; s. Thomas and Mary (Dewan) C.; m. Lorrete Florence, 1929; 2 children. Student St. Michael's Coll.; B.A., U. Toronto, 1925, LL.D., 1966, U. Western Ont., 1965; Litt.D. (hon.), U. Windsor, 1973. Author: (novels) Strange Fugitive, 1928; Native Argosy, 1929; It's Never Over, 1930; No Man's Meat, 1931; Broken Journey, 1932; Such is My Beloved, 1934; They Shall Inherit the Earth, 1935; More Joy in Heaven, 1936; Now that April's Here, 1937; Jake Baldwin's Vow (for children), 1948; The Varsity Story, 1948; The Loved and the Lost, 1955; The Man with the Coat, 1955; A Many Coloured Coat, 1960; A Passion in Rome, 1961; That Summer in Paris, 1963; Morley Callaghan Vols. I and II, 1964; A Fine and Private Place, 1975; Close to the Sun Again, 1975; No Man's Meat and the Enchanted Pimp, 1978. Recipient Canadian Council medal, 1966; Royal Bank Can. award, 1970; decorated companion Order of Can., 1983. Roman Catholic. Address: 20 Dale Ave, Toronto, ON Canada M4W 1K4 *

CALLAHAN, ALSTON, physician, author, publisher; b. Vicksburg, Miss., Mar. 16, 1911; s. Neil and Effie (Alston) C.; m. Eivor Holst, Feb. 23, 1941; children—Kristina Alice, Patrick Alston, Michael Alston, Timothy Alston, Karin Eivor, Kevin (dec. 1961). A.B., Miss. Coll., 1929; M.D., Tulane U., 1933, M.S. in Ophthalmology, 1936. Diplomate Am. Bd. Ophthalmology. Intern Charity Hosp., New Orleans, 1933-35, resident in ophthalmology, 1936-37; staff mem. Eye Found. Univ. Hosps., Birmingham, Ala., 1959—; also pres. Eye Found. Hosp., Birmingham, Ala.; pres. Aesculapius Pub. Co. Author: Surgery of the Eye, Injuries, 1950, Surgery of the Eye, Diseases, 1956, Reconstructive Surgery of the Eyelids and Ocular Adnexa, 1966, (with M. Callahan) Ophthalmic Plastic Surgery, 1979; contbr. articles to profl. jours. Served to capt. M.C., AUS, 1944-46. Fellow ACS; mem. Am. Acad. Ophthalmology, So. Med. Assn. (emeritus), Am. Soc. Ophthal. Plastic Surgery, Alpha Omega Alpha, Sigma Alpha Epsilon. Clubs: Mountain Brook, The Club, Metropolitan, Explorers. Home: 2020 Warwick Dr Birmingham AL 35209 Office: 700 18th St S Birmingham AL 35233

CALLAHAN, DANIEL JOHN, institute director; b. Washington, July 19, 1930; s. Vincent Francis and Anita (Hawkins) C.; m. Sidney Cornelia de Shazo, June 5, 1954; children: Mark Sidney, Stephen Daniel, John Vincent, Peter Thorn, Sarah Elisabeth, David Lee. B.A., Yale U., 1952; M.A., Georgetown U., 1957; Ph.D., Harvard U., 1965; D.Sc. (hon.), U. Medicine and Dentistry of N.J., 1981. Exec. editor The Commonweal, N.Y.C., 1961-68; staff asso. Population Council, 1969-70; founder, dir. Inst. Soc. Ethics and the Life Scis., The Hastings Center, 1969—; resident scholar Aspen Inst. Humanistic Studies, 1975; vis. asst. prof. religion Temple U., 1964; vis. asst. prof. religious studies Brown U., 1965; vis. prof. theology Marymount Coll., 1966; vis. prof. U. Pa., 1970; cons. med. ethics, jud. council AMA, 1972-82, A.C.P., 1979—; spl. cons. Commn. on Population Growth and Am. Future, 1970-71, Nat. Endowment for Humanities, 1979. Author: The Mind of the Catholic Layman, 1963, Honesty in the Church, 1965, The New Church, 1966, Abortion: Law, Choice and Morality, 1970, Ethics and Population Limitation, 1971, The Tyranny of Survival, 1973, The Teaching of Ethics in the Military, 1982, Setting Limits: Medical Goals in an Aging Society, 1987; also essays, articles; co-editor: Christianity Divided: Protestant and Roman Catholic Theological Issues, 1961, Ethical Issues in Human Genetics, 1973; Editor: Federal Aid and Catholic Schools, 1964, Secular City Debate, 1966, The Catholic Case for Contraception, 1969, The American Population Debate, 1971, Science, Ethics and Medicine, 1976, Knowledge, Value and Belief, 1977, Morals, Science and Sociality, 1978, Knowing and Valuing, 1979, Ethics Teaching in Higher Edn, 1980, Ethical Issues in Population Aid, 1980, The Roots of Ethics, 1981; editor: Ethics in Hard Times, 1981, Ethics, the Social Sciences and Policy Analysis, 1983, Abortion: Understanding Differences, 1984, Applying the Humanities, 1985, Representation and Responsibility, 1985; Setting Limits, 1987; mem. editorial adv. bd. Tech. in Soc, 1981—; mem. adv. bd. Ency. of Life Scis., 1982, Sci., Tech. and Human Values, 1979—, Bus. and Profl. Ethics, 1981, Criminal Justice Ethics, 1982, Environ. Ethics, 1982, Jour. Bioethics, 1985—. Mem. N.Y. Council for Humanities, 1975-79; mem. Nat. Book Award Com., 1975, N.Y. State Health Adv. Council, 1975-76; selection com. Ford-Rockefeller Program in Population Policy, 1975-78, Rockefeller Found. Program in Humanities, 1980; elector Nat. Medal for Lit., 1979—; pub. mem. Am. Bd. Med. Specialties, 1982—, N.Y. Sci. Policy Assn., 1985—; mem. N.Y. Task Force on Life and Law, 1985-87; mem. nat. adv. bd. Health Promotion Program, Henry J. Kaiser Family Found., 1987—, N.Y. Panel and HIV Screening, 1987; trustee U. Pa. Med. Ctr., 1987—. Served with CIC AUS, 1952-55.

Recipient Thomas More medal, 1970, Daryl J. Mase Disting. Leadership award, 1987; named one of 200 Outstanding Young Am. Leaders, Time mag., 1974; Tekolste scholar Ind. Hosp. Assn., 1986; Shattuck lectr. Mass. Med. Soc., 1980. Fellow AAAS; mem. Am. Assn. Advancement Humanities, Inst. of Medicine of Nat. Acad. Scis., Am. for Generational Equity (adv. com. 1987—), Soc. for Study of Social Biology (bd. dirs. 1987—). Home: Box 7146 Ardsley-on-Hudson NY 10503 Office: The Hastings Ctr 255 Elm Rd Briarcliff Manor NY 10510

CALLAHAN, HARRY MOREY, photographer; b. Detroit, Oct. 22, 1912; s. Harry Arthur and Hazel (Mills) C.; m. Eleanor Knapp, Nov., 1936; children: Barbara, Mary. D.F.A. (hon.), R.I. Sch. Design, 1979. Mem. faculty Inst. Design, Ill. Inst. Tech., Chgo., 1946-61, head dept. photography, 1949-61; prof., head dept. R.I. Sch. Design, 1971-76. (one-man exhbns.) Mus. Modern Art, N.Y.C., 1976, Seibu Mus. of Art, Japan, 1983, Art Inst. Chgo., 1984, San Francisco Mus. Modern Art, 1984, Nat. Gallery of Victoria, Australia, 1986, Centre Georges Pompidou, France, 1989; U.S. rep., Venice Biennial, 1978. Fellow Graham Found., 1956; fellow Guggenheim Found., 1972; grantee Nat. Endowment Arts, 1976; recipient award Gov. R.I., 1969, Citation NASA, 1972. Office: 153 Benefit St Providence RI 02903 also: 145th ST NE #421 Atlanta GA 30361

CALLAHAN, MARILYN JOY, social worker; b. Portland, Oreg., Oct. 11, 1934; d. Douglas Quinlin and Anona Helen (Bergemann) Maynard; m. Lynn James Callahan, Feb. 27, 1960 (dec. June 1979); children: Barbara Erin, Susan Dana and Jeffrey Lynn (twins). BA, Mills Coll., 1955; degree secondary teaching, Portland State U., 1963, MSW, 1971. Cert. secondary tchr., Oreg.; registered clin. social worker, Oreg. Child welfare counselor Clackamas County Pub. Welfare, Oregon City, Oreg., 1955-58; med. social worker U. Oreg. Med. Sch., Portland, 1958-59; counselor Multnomah County Juvenile Ct., Portland, 1959-62, Marion County Juvenile Ct., Salem, Oreg., 1965-69; devel., adminstrn. 1st ednl. program Oreg. Women's Correctional Ctr., Salem, 1966-67; mental health counselor Benton County Mental Health Clinic, Corvallis, Oreg., 1970-71; tchr. inst. Hillcrest Sch., Salem, 1975-81; social worker Mid Will Valley Sr. Service Agy., Salem, 1981—; bd. dirs. Vols. for Srs., Tri County Area Conservator-Guardian Program, Statewide Seminar on Age Discrimination, 1985. Mem. exec. bd. South Salem Neighborhood Assn., 1982—, sch. bd. Sacred Heart Acad., 1977-81, Boys and Girls Aid Soc., past dist. v.p.; bd. dirs. Camp Fire Girls, 1971-81. Mem. Nat. Assn. Social Workers (cert. clin. social worker, acad. cert. social worker, diplomate), Acad. Cert. Social Workers, AAUW (past v.p., past bd. dirs., directed study on family ct. bill 1967), Salem City Club (directed and published research study), U.S. Power Squadron, Catalina 22 Nat. Sailing Assn. Republican. Methodist. Club: Eugene Yacht (Oreg.). Home: 2880 Mountain View Dr S Salem OR 97302 Office: Mid Willamette Valley Sr Services Agy 410 Senator Bldg 220 High St NE Salem OR 97301

CALLAHAN, ROBERT JOHN, JR., lawyer, arbitrator; b. St. Louis, July 3, 1923; s. Robert John and Elizabeth Mae Deck (Gentner) C.; m. Dorothy Foley, Apr. 18, 1958 (dec. Nov. 1980); m. Barbara Kelsall Couture, May 22, 1982. Grad. Chaminade Coll., 1941; B.S. in Bus. Adminstrn., Washington U., 1944; J.D. cum laude, Notre Dame U., 1948. Bar: Mo. 1948, U.S. Ct. Appeals (fed. cir.) 1951, U.S. Supreme Ct. 1955, U.S. Ct. Mil. Appeals. Ptnr. Callahan and Callahan, St. Louis, 1948-56; sole practice, St. Louis, 1956—. Contbr. articles to legal jours. Candidate for judge St. Louis County Cir. Ct., 1960. Coro fellow. Served with FBI and USCGR, 1944-45; former liaison officer USAF Acad. Served to capt. JAGC, USAFR. Mem. ABA, Lawyers Assn. of St. Louis, St. Louis Bar Assn., Am. Assn. Trial Lawyers Notre Dame U. Law Assn., U. Notre Dame Alumni Assn., Nat. Panel Consumer Arbitrators, Ret. Air Force Officers Assn. Phi Delta Theta. Republican. Roman Catholic. Office: 161 W Jefferson Saint Louis MO 63122

CALLAHAN, ROY HANEY, transportation facilities consultant, lawyer, naval officer, business executive; b. Marceline, Mo., July 7, 1904; s. William Paxton and Malvina (Haney) P.; A.B., U. Mich., 1926; J.D., 1929; LL.M., So. Meth. U.; children—Roy Haney, Michael C., Monita. Librarian, 1924-29; naval aviator, 1929-31, 40-46 as aircraft carrier exec. officer, task group ops. officer, task group chief of staff, asst. to dept. chief Bur. Aeros, asst. to asst. sec. navy for air, also asst. to sec. navy; exec. dir. N.Y.C. Airport Authority, also asst. commr. Marine and Aviation for N.Y.C., 1946; admitted to N.Y. state bar, 1931, Mich. bar, 1931, Tex. bar, 1949; asso. firm White & Case, N.Y.C., 1931-40; mem. Callahan & Durant, Ft. Worth, 1949-55, Kilgore & Kilgore, Dallas, 1955-56; v.p., gen. mgr. Airlines Terminal Corp., also Airlines Nat. Terminal Service Co., 1946-48; exec. dir. Greater Fort Worth Internat. Air Terminal Corp., 1950-51; lectr. U. Mich. Law Inst., 1940; pres. Simpson Grain Co., Inc., 1956—; pres. Swan Finch Oil Corp., pres., dir. Keta Oil & Gas Co., Olean Industries, Inc., Doeskin Products, Inc. 1956-57; v.p. Epsco, Inc., 1959; pres., gen mgr. Round Hill Limousine Service, Inc., 1960; exec. asst. to v.p. Eastern Air Lines, 1961-69; exec. v.p. Airlines Facilities Corp. Am., 1969—, AFCOA Inc., 1969—; dir. Bradley Facilities, Inc., Airlines Terminal Corp., Airlines Nat. Terminal Service Co. Trustee Southwestern Inst. for Alcohol Research. Res. officer with U.S. Army, 1926-29, reserve enlisted man or officer, 1929—, capt. USNR, 1945-55, rear adm., 1955—. Mem. Navy Roper Bd., 1948; occasional spl. asst. to sec. of navy, 1948. Mem. Bur. Aeros. Naval Res. Advisory Council, 1946—. Decorated Bronze Star medal, Air medal, Reserve medal Pacific. Life mem. Southwestern Legal Found.; mem. Com. of 100 on behalf of U. Mich. Phoenix Project for Atomic Research; mem. Am., City of N.Y., Tex., Fort Worth, Dallas bar assns. Clubs: University, New York Athletic; Cipango (Dallas). Lodge: Masons. Author: The Corporate Mortgage under Texas Law; Rescue and Slavage in the Everglades; A Neglected Air Market; Wall Street Lawyer and Naval Reserve Aviator; The Robinson Patman Act; Impact of the Next Two Aircraft Generations on Airport Design; Airport Role in the Community; Air Terminal Facilities: Cost Break-through; co-author: National Policy for Aviation, 1946; Airports for Future Aircraft-A Planning Guide.

CALLAHAN, SIDNEY, psychology educator; b. Washington, Mar. 6, 1933; d. George Sidney and Lethama Sarah (Jones) deShazo; m. Daniel J. Callahan, June 5, 1954; children: Mark Sidney, Stephen Daniel, John Vincent, Thomas Hawkins (dec.), Peter Thorne, Sarah Elisabeth, David Lee. BA magna cum laude, Bryn Mawr Coll., 1955; MA, Sarah Lawrence Coll., 1971; PhD, CUNY, 1980; LittD (hon.), Regis Coll., Weston, Mass., 1966, St. Mary's Coll., 1970. Staff psychologist Echo Hills Mental Health Clinic, Dobbs Ferry, N.Y., 1973-75; asst. prof. Fairfield (Conn.) U., 1977-80; assoc. prof. psychology Mercy Coll., Dobbs Ferry, 1980—. Author 6 books; contbr. articles to profl. jours. Fellow Soc. for Values in Higher Edn.; mem. Am. Psychol. Assn. Democrat. Roman Catholic. Home: Hudson House Ardsley-on-Hudson NY 10503 Office: Mercy Coll Dobbs Ferry NY 10522

CALLANAN, KATHLEEN JOAN, electrical engineer, airplane company executive; b. Detroit, Feb. 10, 1940; d. John Michael and Grace Marie (Kleehammer) C. BSE in Physics, U. Mich., 1963; postgrad. in physics Northeastern U., 1963-65; MSEE, U. Hawaii, 1971; diploma in Japanese lang. St. Joseph Inst. Japanese Studies, Tokyo, 1973; cert. in mgmt. Boeing Mil. Airplane Co. Employee Devel., 1985. Vis. scholar Sophia U., Tokyo, 1976-79; elec.-electronic components engr. Boeing Mil. Airplane Co., Wichita, Kans., 1979-83, instrumentation design engr., 1983-85, strategic planner for tech., 1985-86, research and engring. tech. supr., 1986-87 ; electromagnetic effects Avionics mgr., 1987—. Contbr. articles to profl. jours. Mem. Rose Hill Planning Commn., Kans., 1982-85; coordinator Boeing Employees Amateur Radio Soc., Wichita, 1982-83. Mem. Soc. Women Engrs. (sr. mem., sect. rep. 1981-83, sec. treas. 1985-86, regional bd. dirs. 1983-85, sect. pres. 1987-88), AIAA, Bus. and Profl. Women, Quarter Century Wireless Assn. (communications com. 1985-86). Lodge: Toastmasters (local pres. 1985-86, competent toastmaster 1985). Avocations: amateur radio, singing, bowling. Home: 1201 N West St Rose Hill KS 67133 Office: PO Box 7730 Wichita KS 67277-7730

CALLANDER, KAY EILEEN PAISLEY, educator; b. Coshocton, Ohio, Oct. 15, 1938; d. Dalton Olas and Dorothy Pauline (Davis) Paisley; m. Don Larry Callander, Nov. 18, 1977. BSE, Muskingum Coll., 1960; MA in Speech Edn., Ohio State U., 1964, postgrad., 1964-84. Cert. elem., gifted, drama, theater tchr., Ohio. Tchr. Columbus (Ohio) Pub. Schs., 1960-70, 80-88, drama specialist, 1970-80, classroom, gifted/talented tchr., 1986—; coordinator Artists-in-the-Schs., 1977-88; cons., presenter numerous ednl. confs. and sems., 1971—. Producer-dir., Shady Lane Music Festival, 1980-88; dir., tchr. (nat. distbr. video) The Trial of Gold E. Locks, 1983-84; rep., media pub. relations liason Sch. News., 1983-88. Benefactor, Columbus Jazz Arts Group; v.p., bd. dirs. Neoteric Dance and Theater Co., Columbus, 1985-87; tchr., participant Future Stars sculpture exhibt, Ft. Hayes Ctr., Columbus Pub. Schs., 1988; tchr. advisor Columbus Council PTA's, 1983-86, ch-chmn. reflections com., 1984-87; mem. Humane Soc. of U.S., Statue of Liberty-Ellis Island Found., Inc., Columbus Mus. Art; mem. call and worship coms. Old Trinity Luth. Ch., Columbus; supt.'s adv. council, Columbus Pub. Schs., 1967-68; presenter Young Author Sem., Ohio Dept. Edn., 1988; cons. and workshop leader for sem./workshop Teaching about the Constitution in Elem. Schs., Franklin County Ednl. Council, 1988; presenter for Illustrating Methods for Young Authors' Books, 1986-87; mem. Call and Worship Com. Trinity Luth. Ch., Columbus. Named Educator of Yr., Shady Lane PT, 1982; Sch. Excellence grantee Columbus Pub. Schs.; Commendation Columbus Bd. Edn. and Ohio Ho. of Reps. for Child Assault Prevention project, 1986-87. Mem. NEA, Ohio Edn. Assn., Ohio PTA, Columbus Edn. Assn., Capital Area Humane Soc., Cen. Ohio Tchrs. Assn., Ohio State U. Alumni Assn., Friends of Sta. WOSU-TV Ohio State U., NOW, Nat. Trust for Hist. Preservation, U.S. Army Officers' Club (def. constr. supply ctr., Columbus), The Navy League, Liturgical Art Guild Ohio, Columbus Jazz Arts Group, Columbus Mus. of Art, Humane Soc. of U.S., Internat. Platform Assn. Republican. Home: 570 Conestoga Dr Columbus OH 43213 Office: Columbus Pub Schs Shady Lane Elem Sch 1488 Shady Ln Rd Columbus OH 43227

CALLANDER, ROBERT JOHN, banker; b. Newark, Feb. 3, 1931; s. George and Mary (Law) C.; m. Marilyn Berg, June 11, 1955; children: Pamela Anne, Robert John Jr., David Webb. AB magna cum laude, Dartmouth Coll., 1952; BD magna cum laude, Yale U., 1955; postgrad., Dartmouth Grad. Sch. Credit and Fin., 1961-62, Harvard Bus. Sch., 1968. Sr. trainee Chem. Bank, N.Y.C., 1957-67, v.p., 1967-72, sr. v.p., 1972-78, sr. v.p., dep. head internat. div., 1978-79, exec. v.p., head internat. div., 1979-81, sr. exec. v.p., head World Banking Group, 1981-83, pres. World Banking Group, 1983-87, vice chmn., 1987—, also bd. dirs.; vice chmn., bd. dirs. Chem. N.Y. Corp., N.Y.C.; bd. dirs. ARA Services, Inc. Trustee Drew U., YMCA of Greater N.Y., Tomas Rivera Ctr.; adv. dir. Met. Opera Assn. Mem. Council Fgn. Relations, Assn. Res. City Bankers, Japan Soc. Clubs: Univ. (N.Y.C.); Baltusrol (Springfield, N.J.); Somerset Hills Country (Bernardsville, N.J.). Office: Chem NY Corp 277 Park Ave New York NY 10172 *

CALLAWAY, RICHARD EARL, dentist; b. Des Moines, Aug. 9, 1951; s. Grover Earl and Geraldine Anna (Dageforde) C.; m. Nancy Jean Clark, May 2, 1981; children: Scott, Jessica, Lindsey, Rachel. BA, Mo. Western State Coll., 1974; DDS, U. Mo., Kansas City, 1978. Gen. practice dentistry Fremont, Nebr., 1978—. Bd. dirs. Fremont Big Bros./Big Sisters, 1981-87. Named one of Outstanding Young Men of Am., Fremont Jaycees, 1985. Mem. ADA, Nebr. Dental Assn., Omaha Dist. Dental Assn., Tri Valley Dental Soc. (treas. 1980, v.p. 1981), Fremont Jaycees (bd. dirs. 1979-85, v.p. 1985-86, pres. 1986-87), Fremont Tennis Assn. Republican. Lutheran. Lodge: Optimists. Home: 545 N Platte Fremont NE 68025 Office: 1835 E Military Fremont NE 68025

CALLEJA, JOHN M., ship brokerage corporation executive; b. Sliema, Malta, July 29, 1931; s. Joseph Henry and Maria Assunta (Pace) C.; m. Winifred Joan Smith, Apr. 30, 1955; 1 dau., Stephanie Joan. Student, Stella Maris Coll., Gzira, Malta, 1936-45, Sundridge Park Mgmt. Ctr., Kent, Eng., 1960-61; cert., His Majesty's Dockyard Tech. Coll., Malta, 1949. Tech. estimator His Majesty's Dockyard Tech. Coll., Cospicula, 1953-56, leading estimator, 1956-58; asst. prodn. controller Bailey Ltd., Cospicula, 1959-60, prodn. controller, 1960-61, ship repair mgr., 1962-63; marine sales mgr. Malta Drydocks Corp., Cospicula, 1963-66, chief exec. comml. and sales div., 1966-69, gen. mgr., 1971-81; gen. mgr. Malta Overseas Trading Co., Ltd., Valletta, 1970-71; mng. dir. Calmarine Services Ltd., Valletta, 1981—; bd. dirs. Malta Shipbldg. Co., Ltd., Med. Underwriter Services Ltd., Cotor Services Ltd., Calprint Ltd. Fellow Brit. Inst. Mgmt.; mem. Assn. Cost. Engrs., Inst. of Petroleum, Malta C. of C., Fedn. Industries Malta (chmn. mgmt. com. 1969-73), Maritime Assn., Assn. Ship Agts., Friends of Japan (v.p.). Roman Catholic. Clubs: Dockyard Sports and Social (life pres. 1971—), Union, Marsa Sports. Lodge: Lions. Home: Stefania Upper Gardens, Saint Julians Malta Office: Calmarine Services Ltd, 27/28 Pinto Wharf, Valletta Malta

CALLEN, JEFFREY LAWRENCE, economist, educator; b. Schwab-Shall, Germany, June 14, 1947; s. Charles and Ethel (Rubenstein) C.; m. Mindy Morel, Sept. 23, 1950; children: David, Yehuda, Nathaniel, Miriam, Ayelet. BA, York U., Toronto, Ont., Can., 1976-79; MBA, U. Toronto, 1971, PhD, 1976. Asst. prof. U. Man., Winnipeg, 1973-76; from asst. prof. to assoc. prof. McMaster U., Hamilton, Ont., 1976-79; sr. lectr. econs. Hebrew U., Jerusalem, 1982—; assoc. prof. Hebrew U., 1986; adj. prof. McMaster U., 1986—. Contbr. articles to profl. jours. Fellow U. Toronto, 1969-73, Social Scis. and Humanities Research Council Can., 1982-83. Mem. Am. Econs. Assn., Am. Acctg. Assn., Am. Fin. Assn. Jewish. Office: Jerusalem Sch Bus Adminstrn, The Hebrew U, Mount Scopus, Jerusalem Israel

CALLEN, JEFFREY PHILLIP, dermatologist, educator; b. Chgo., May 30, 1947; s. Irwin R. and Rose P. (Cohen) C.; m. Susan B. Manis, Dec. 21, 1968; children: Amy, David. BS, U. Wis., 1969; MD, U. Mich., 1972. Diplomate Am. Bd. Internal Medicine, 1975, Am. Bd. Dermatology, 1977. Intern/resident in internal medicine U. Mich., 1972-75, in dermatology, 1975-77; asst. clin. prof. U. Louisville Sch. Medicine, 1977-81, assoc. clin. prof., 1982-84, assoc. prof., dir. residency tng. program, 1984-88; chief dermatology service Louisville VA Hosp., 1984—; prof., chief div. of dermatology, 1988—. Author: Manual of Dermatology, 1980, Cutaneous Aspects of Internal Disease, 1981; Neurology Clinics North America, 1987, Dermatologic Signs of Systemic Disease, 1988; editor: Clinics in Rheumatic Disease, 1982, Dermatologic Clinics, 1985, Med. Clinics of N.Am., 1982, 84, 86; editor-in-chief Dermavision video program; mem. editorial bd. Internat. Jour. Dermatology, 1980-87, Cutis; editor spl. issues of jours. in field. Bd. dirs. Actor's Theatre of Louisville, sec., 1986-87. Fellow ACP, Am. Acad. Dermatology (chmn. audio/visual edn. com., task force therapeutic agts., internal medicine symposium 1978-83, chmn. sci. and tech. exhibits 1986—, dir. symposium on cutaneous oncology 1984—), Am. Rheumatism Assn. (founder); mem. Am. Fedn. Clin. Research, AMA, Am. Dermatol. Assn. Dermatology Found. (bd. trustees 1984—). Research on condition in which systemic disease has cutaneous manifestations, lupus erythematosus, psoriasis, dermatomyositis. Office: U Louisville Dept Dermatology 310 E Broadway Suite 20 Louisville KY 40202

CALLEN, LON EDWARD, county ofcl.; b. Kingman, Kans., Mar. 31, 1929; s. Cleo Paul and Josephine Nell (Mease) C.; B.A. in Math. and Physics, U. Wichita (Kans.), 1951; m. Barbara Jean Sallee, Oct. 12, 1954; children—Lon Edward, Lynnette J. Commd. 2d lt. USAF, 1951, advanced through grades to lt. col., 1968; comdr. Tuslog Detachment 93, Erhac, Turkey, 1966-67; sr. scientist Def. Atomic Support Agy., Washington, 1967-71; ret., 1971; dir. emergency preparedness City-County of Boulder, Colo., 1976—; bd. dirs. Boulder County Emergency Med. Services Council, 1977, Boulder County Amateur Radio Emergency Services, 1978—. Mem. hon. awards com. Nat. Capital Area council Boy Scouts Am., 1971; chmn. Boulder County United Fund, 1976-82; mem. asst. staff Indian Princesses and Trailblazer programs Boulder YMCA, 1974-78. Decorated Joint Service Commendation medal; recipient cert. achievement Def. Atomic Support Agy., 1970. Mem. AAAS, Am. Ordnance Soc., Am. Soc. Cybernetics, Planetary Soc., Math. Assn. Am., N.Y. Acad. Scis., Fedn. Am. Scientists, Nat. Assn. Atomic Vets., Union Concerned Scientists, Boulder County Fire Fighters Assn., Colo. Emergency Mgmt. Assn., Ret. Officers Assn., Colo. Front Range Protective Assn., Mensa, Sigma Xi, Pi Alpha Pi. Clubs: Boulder Knife and Fork, Boulder Gunbarrel Optimists, Denver Matrix, U. Colo. Ski, U. Wichita. Author articles in field. Home: 4739 Berkshire Ct Boulder CO 80301 Office: Box 471 County Courthouse Boulder CO 80306

CALLENDER, NORMA ANNE, educator; b. Huntsville, Tex., May 10, 1933; d. Cleburn William Carswell and Nell Ruth (Collard) Hughes Bost; m. Billy Gene Callender, July 13, 1951 (div. Mar. 1964); children: Teresa Elizabeth, Leslie Gemey, Shannah Hughes, Kelly Mari. BS in Edn., U. Houston, 1969; MA, U. Houston at Clear Lake, 1977; postgrad. Lamar U., 1972-73, Tex. So. U., 1971, St. Thomas U., 1985, 86, U. Houston-Clear Lake, 1979, 87, 88, San Jacinto Coll., 1988. Aerospace Inst., NASA, Johnson Space Ctr., 1986. Cert. reading specialist, Tex. Tchr., Houston Ind. Schs., 1969-70; co-counselor and instr. Ellington AFB, Houston, 1971; tchr. Clear Creek Schs., Seabrook, Tex., 1970-75; part-time instr. San Jacinto Coll., Pasadena, Tex., 1980-81; tchr. Clear Creek Schs., Webster, Tex., 1975-86; adj. instr., 1986, supr. student tchrs., 1986—, U. Houston, Clear Lake, Tex., 1986; supr. student tchrs.1986—; owner, dir. Bay Area Tutoring and Reading Clinic, Clear Lake City, Tex., 1970—; owner Bay Area Tng. Assocs., Houston, 1981—; mem. adv. bd. Clear Creek Ednl. Resource Ctr. Publ., League City, 1976-77; mem. Prin's Council of Excellence, 1985-86; owner Bay Area Tng. Assocs., Webster, 1981-87. Editor: A Prism of Prose and Poetry, 1983. Mem. Bay Area Rep. Women's Fedn., 1987-88, Republican Presdl. Task Force (charter), 1982; state advisor U.S. Congl. Adv. Bd., 1985-87; charter mem. Clear Creek Assn. Retarded Citizens, Houston, 1982; mem. Assn. Children with Learning Disabilities, Novato, Calif., 1973; bd. dirs. Ballet San Jacinto, 1985-87. Recipient Franklin award U. Houston, 1965-67; Delta Kappa Gamma/Beta Omicron scholar, 1967-68; PTA scholar, 1973; Berwin scholar, 1976; Mary Gibbs Jones scholar, 1976-77; Found. Econ. Edn. scholar, 1976; Insts. Achievement Human Potential scholar, Phila., 1987-88. Mem. Clear Creek Educators Assn. (honorarium 1976, 77, 85), Internat. Reading Assn. (research com. chpt. 1976-77), U. Houston at Clear Lake Alumni Assn. (charter), Gulf Coast Council Fgn. Affairs, Leadership Clear Lake Alumni Assn. (charter, program and projects com mem. 1986-87, edn. com. 1985), Tex. Soc. Coll. Tchrs. Edn., Kappa Delta Pi, Phi Delta Kappa, Phi Kappa Phi. Mem. Life Tabernacle Ch. Club: Toastmasters (Johnson Space Ctr.). Home: 963 Seagate Ln Houston TX 77062 Office: PO Box 890932 Houston TX 77289-0932

CALLETON, THEODORE EDWARD, lawyer; b. Newark, Dec. 13, 1934; s. Edward James and Dorothy (Dewey) C.; m. Elizabeth Bennett Brown, Feb. 4, 1961; children: Susan Bennett, Pamela Barritt, Christopher Dewey.; m. Kathy E'Beth Conkle, Feb. 22, 1983; 1 child, James Frederick. B.A., Yale U., 1956; LL.B., Columbia U., 1962. Bar: Calif. 1963, U.S. Dist. Ct. (so. dist.) Calif. 1963, U.S. Tax Ct. 1977. Asso. firm O'Melveny & Myers, Los Angeles, 1962-69, Agnew, Miller & Carlson, Los Angeles, 1969; ptnr. Agnew, Miller & Carlson, 1970-79; individual practice law Los Angeles, 1979-83; ptnr. Kindel & Anderson, 1983—; academician Internat. Acad. Estate and Trust Law, 1974—; lectr. Calif. Continuing Edn. bar, 1970—, U. So. Calif. Tax Inst., 1972—, Calif. State U., Los Angeles, 1975—, Practising Law Inst., 1976—, Am. Law Inst., 1985—; bd. dirs. UCLA/CEB Continuing Edn. of Bar Estate Planning Inst. Author: The Short Term Trust, 1977, A Life Insurance Primer, 1978; co-author: California Will Drafting Practice, 1982, Tax Planning for Professionals, 1985; contbr. articles to legal jours. Chmn. Arroyo Seco Master Planning Commn., Pasadena, Calif., 1970-71; bd. dirs. Montessori Sch., Inc., 1964-68, chmn., 1966-68; bd. dirs. Am. Montessori Soc., N.Y.C., 1967-72, chmn., 1969-72; trustee Walden Sch. of Calif., 1970-86, chmn., 1980-86; trustee Episcopal Children's Home of Los Angeles, 1971-75. Served as lt. USMC, 1956-59. Fellow Am. Coll. Probate Counsel; mem. ABA, Los Angeles County Bar Assn. (chmn. taxation sect. 1980-81, chmn. probate and trust law sect. 1981-82), Aurelian Honor Soc., Beta Theta Pi, Phi Delta Phi. Unitarian. Clubs: Elihu, University. Home: 301 Churchill Rd Sierra Madre CA 91024 Office: 555 S Flower St Suite 2600 Los Angeles CA 90071 also: 1301 Dove St Suite 1050 Newport Beach CA 92660

CALLIES, DAVID LEE, lawyer, educator; b. Chgo., Apr. 21, 1943; s. Gustav E. and Ann D. C.; 1 child, Sarah Anne; m. Jane Ryburn Starn, June 7, 1987. AB, DePauw U., 1965; JD, U. Mich., 1968. Bar: Ill. 1969, Hawaii 1978. Spl. asst. states atty. McHenry County, Ill., 1969; assoc. firm Ross, Hardies, O'Keefe, Babcock & Parsons, Chgo., 1969-75; partner Ross, Hardies, O'Keefe, Babcock & Parsons, 1975-78; prof. law Sch. Law, U. Hawaii, Honolulu, 1978—; mem. adv. com. on planning and growth mgmt. City and County of Honolulu Council, 1978—, citizens adv. com. on State Functional Plan for Conservation Lands, 1979—. Author: (with Fred P. Bosselman) The Quiet Revolution in Land Use Control, 1971, (with Fred P. Bosselman and John S. Banta) The Taking Issue, 1973, Regulating Paradise: Land Use Controls in Hawaii, 1984; (with Robert Freilich) Cases and Materials on Land Use, 1986. Mich. Ford Found. fellow U. Nottingham, Eng., 1969. Mem. ABA (chmn. com. on land use, planning and zoning 1980-82, council, sect. on urban, state and local govt. 1981-85, exec. com. 1986—, sec. 1986-87, vice chmn., 1987-88, chair-elect 1988—), Am. Inst. Cert. Planners, Am. Planning Assn., Hawaii State Bar Assn., Ill. Bar Assn., Internat. Bar Assn., Nat. Trust Hist. Preservation, Royal Oak Soc., Sierra Club. Home: 4621 Aukai Ave Honolulu HI 96816 Office: Richardson Sch Law 2515 Dole St Honolulu HI 96822

CALLIHAN, HARRIET K., medical society executive; b. Chgo., Feb. 8, 1930; d. Harry Louis and Josephine (Olstad) Kohlman; m. Clair Clifton Callihan, Dec. 17, 1955; 1 child, Barbara Clair Callihan. BA, U. Chgo., 1951, MBA, 1953. Personnel dir. Leo Burnett Co., Chgo., 1953-57, John Plain & Co., 1957-62, Follett Pub. Co., 1962-64, Needham, Harper & Steers, N.Y.C., 1966-68, Bell, Boyd, Lloyd, Haddad & Burns, 1964-66, Hume, Clement, Hume & Lee, 1968-70; owner, operator PersD, 1970-75; exec. dir. Inst. Medicine Chgo., 1975—, mng. editor ofcl. med. publ. Proceedings, 1975—. Sec./treas. Interagy. Council on Smoking and Disease. Mem. Chgo. Soc. Assn. Execs., Conf. Med. Soc. Execs. Greater Chgo. (pres.), Am. Med. Writers Assn. (pres., v.p. publicity club), Nat. Sci. Writer's Assn., Lincoln Park Zool. Soc., Field Mus. Soc. Natural History, Nat. Soc. Fund Raising Exec. Profl. Conv. Mgrs. Assn., Chgo. Council Fgn. Relations, Chgo. Connection, Met. Chgo. Coalition Aging, Midwest Pharm. Advt. Club. Clubs: Westmoreland Country, Michigan Shores, Cliffdwellers. Office: Inst Medicine of Chgo 332 S Michigan Ave Chicago IL 60604

CALLINICOS, ALEXANDER THEODORE, political philosopher, educator; b. Harare, Zimbabwe, July 24, 1950; s. John Alexander and Aedgyth Bertha (Lyon-Dalberg-Acton) C. BA in Philosophy, Politics and Econs. with honors, U. Oxford, Eng., 1973, DPhil, 1979. Jr. research fellow St. Peter's Coll., U. Oxford, 1979-81; lectr. politics U. York, Eng., 1981-85, lectr. philosophy, 1985-86, lectr. politics, 1986—. Author: Althusser's Marxism, 1976, (with John Rogers) Southern Africa After Soweto, 1977, Southern Africa After Zimbabwe, 1981, Is There a Future for Marxism?, 1982, Marxism and Philosophy, 1983, The Revolutionary Ideas of Karl Marx, 1983, (with Mike Simons) The Great Strike, 1985, Making History, 1987, (with Chris Harman) The Changing Working Class, 1987. Mem. Assn. Univ. Tchrs. Office: U York Dept Politics, Heslington, York Y01 5DD, England

CALLISON, NANCY FOWLER, nurse; b. Milw., July 16, 1931; d. George Fenwick and Irma Esther (Wenzel) Fowler; m. B.G. Callison, Sept. 25, 1954 (dec. Feb. 1964); children: Robert, Leslie, Linda. Diploma, Evanston Hosp. Sch. Nursing, 1952; BS, Northwestern U., 1954. RN, Calif. Staff nurse, psychiat. dept. Downey VA Hosp., 1954-55; staff nurse Camp Lejeune Naval Hosp., 1955, 59-61; obstet. supr. Tri-City Hosp., Oceanside, Calif., 1961-62; pub. health nurse San Diego County, 1962-66; sch. nurse Rich-Mar Union Sch. Dist., San Marcos, Calif., 1966-68; head nurse San Diego County Community Mental Health, 1968-73; dir. patient care services Southwood Mental Health Ctr., Chula Vista, Calif., 1973-75; program cons. Comprehensive Care Corp., Newport Beach, Calif., 1975-79; dir. Manpower Health Care, Culver City, Calif., 1979-80; dir. nursing services Peninsula Rehab. Ctr., Lomita, Calif., 1980-81; clinic supr., coordinator utilization and authorizations, acting dir. provider relations Hawthorne (Calif.) Community Med. Group, 1981-86; mgr. Health Care Delivery Physicians of Greater Long Beach, Calif., 1986-87; clinic coordinator, translator Flying Samaritans, 1965—, mem. internat. bd. dirs., 1975-77, 79-86, pres. South Bay chpt., 1975-81. Mem. Am. Nurses Assn., Nat. Assn. Female Execs., Aircraft Owners and Pilots Assn., U.S.-Mex. Border Health Assn., Calif. Assn. of Quality Assurance Profls., Cruz Roja Mexicana (Delegacion Rosarito 1986—).

CALLMEYER, FERENC, architect; b. Miskolc, Hungary, Apr. 3, 1928; s. Ferenc and Ilona (Zachar) C.; m. Eva Szep, Jan. 30, 1953; children—Judith, Laszlo. Architect, Poly. U. Budapest, 1951; M.Arch., Hungarian Assn. Architects, 1953. Architect-designer Mezoterv, Budapest, 1951-55; head dept. Iparterv, Budapest, 1955-63; architect-designer Sheppard, Robson Pts.,

London, 1963-65; head office TTI, Budapest, 1965—; chmn. Archtl. Examining Bd., Budapest, 1978—, chmn. Creative Council, 1986. Author: Holyday Homes, 1972; Family Houses (award 1978), 1974. Recipient prize Council of Ministers, Budapest, 1957, Silver medal of Labor, 1981; Best Bldg. Yr. award Minister of Bldg., Budapest, 1978; U.S. Govt. grantee, 1984. Fellow Hungarian Assn. Architects (v.p. 1986—), AIA (hon.); mem. Internat. Solar Energy Soc.-Hungary. Office: Inst Archtl Tech, Asboth 9-11, 1075 Budapest Hungary

CALLOW, SIMON PHILLIP HUGH, actor; b. June 15, 1949; s. Neil and Yvonne Mary Callow. Student, Queen's U., Belfast, Ireland. Performances include: (plays) Schippel, 1975, A Mad World My Masters, 1977, Arturo Ui, Mary Barnes, 1978, The Beastly Beatitudes of Balthazar B, 1981, Total Eclipse, 1981, Restoration, 1981, The Relapse, 1983, On the Spot, 1984, Kiss of the Spider Woman, 1985, As You Like It, 1979, Amadeus, 1979; (films) Amadeus, 1983, A Room With A View, 1986, The Good Father, 1986, Maurice, 1987; (TV series) chance in a Million, 1983, 85-86, David Copperfield, 1986; director Loving Reno, 1984, Bush, 1984, The Passport, 1985, Nicolson Fights, 1986, Croydon, 1986; author: Being an Actor, 1984, A Difficult Actor: Charles Laughton, 1987; translator Jacques it son Maître by Kundera, 1986, The Infernal Machine by Jean Cocteau, 1987. Office: care Marina Martin, 7 Windmill St, London W1, England *

CALLOWAY, D. WAYNE, food and beverage products company executive. Exec. v.p., chief fin. officer Pepsico, Inc., Purchase, N.Y., 1983-85, pres., chief operating officer, 1985-86, chmn., chief exec. officer, 1986—; former chmn., pres., chief exec. and operating officer Frito-Lay, Inc. (subs. Pepsico, Inc.), Dallas. Office: Pepsico Inc Purchase NY 10577 *

CALMESE, LINDA, computer training center executive, consultant; b. East St. Louis, Ill., June 3, 1947; d. Lonnie Daniel and Louise (Anderson) C. BS, So. Ill. U., 1969, MS, 1972, specialist degree counselor edn., 1978. Tchr. bus. edn. St. Teresa Acad., East St. Louis, 1969-73, DODDS, Madrid, Spain, 1973-84; computer cons. Scott AFB, Ill., 1984-87, Norton AFB, Calif., 1986, Navy Fin. Ctr., Cleve., 1987, Billy Mitchell Air Field, Milw., 1987, Richards Gebaur AFB, Kansas City, Mo., 1988, NASA, Cleve., 1988, Army Corps Engrs., St. Louis, 1988, Nat. U. San Diego, 1988; pres. Bits and Bytes Computer Tng. Ctr., Belleville, Ill., 1985—; instr. State Community Coll., East St. Louis, 1986-87, Office Personnel Mgmt. San Diego, San Francisco, Los Angeles; computer cons. Army Aviation Systems Command, St. Louis, 1986-87, Ohio Army N.G., Worthington, Ohio, 1986, 88, Mil. Personnel Records Ctr., St. Louis, 1986, City of San Francisco, 1988, City of San Diego, 1988. Contbr. chpt. to book: Business Education for the 70's, 1969. Clk. Mt. Zion Baptist Mission East Ch., East St. Louis, 1987—. Mem. Nat. Assn. Female Execs., Delta Pi Epsilon, Pi Omega Pi. Baptist. Avocations: travel, computing, reading, aerobics. Office: Bits and Bytes Computer Tng Ctr 7705 West Main St Suite 7 Belleville IL 62223

CALORI, ROLAND GEORGES, business policy educator; b. Marseilles, France, Aug. 17, 1951; s. Jean Pierre and Suzanne Emilie (Jaume) C.; m. Maria Helena Tollikko, Mar. 26, 1975; children: Marc Adrien, Paul Oliver. PhD, I.A.E., Aix, France, 1983. Prof. Marseilles Bus. Sch., 1974-78; prof. Lyon Grad. Sch. Bus., France, 1982-84, head dept. bus. policy, 1985—; cons. in field. Contbr. articles to profl. jours. Sec. Assn. Pour la Recherche en Formation, Aix, France, 1981—. Mem. Strategic Mgmt. Soc., Hautes Etudes Commls., Assn. Francaise de Planification. Home: 29 Cours Vitton, 69006 Lyon France Office: Lyon Grad Sch Bus, 23 Ave Guy de Collongue, 69132 Ecully France

CALTABIANO, NERINA JANE, research psychologist, educator; b. Innisfail, Australia, July 2, 1956; d. Alfio and Rosa (Finocchiaro) C. BA with honors, James Cook U., 1979, PhD, 1988. Research asst. James Cook U., Townsville, Australia, 1980-86; tutor in behavioral scis. James Cook U., 1982—; cons. Catholic Family Welfare Bur., Townsville, 1982—, Migrant Resource Ctr., Townsville, 1984—, Pregnancy Help, Townsville, 1985—. Contbr. articles to profl. jours. Mem. Amnesty Internat., Queensland Right to Life, Townsville Mus. Inc., Nat. Trust Queensland, Australian Psychol. Soc., Australian Fedn. U. Women, Nat. Assn. Interdisciplinary Ethnic Studies, Soc. Dante Alighieri. Mem. Labour Party. Roman Catholic. Office: James Cook U, Townsville 4811, Australia

CALVERT, BRUCE DONALD, math educator; b. New Plymouth, New Zealand, Feb. 3, 1945; s. Eric Charles C.; m. Celia M. Wood; children: Rohan, Joel. PhD, U. Chgo., 1969. Asst. prof. U. Colo., Boulder, 1970; borsista Consiglio Nazionale delle Ricerche, Rome, 1970-71; lectr. U. Auckland, N. Zealand, 1971—. Contbr. articles to profl. jours. Mem. Am. Math. Soc., N. Zealand Math. Soc. Office: U Auckland, Auckland New Zealand

CALVERT, JACK GEORGE, atmospheric chemist, educator; b. Inglewood, Calif., May 9, 1923; s. John George and Emma (Eschstruth) C.; m. Doris Arlene Breimon, Nov. 8, 1946; children: Richard John, Mark Steven. B.S. in Chemistry, UCLA, 1944, Ph.D., 1949. Mem. faculty Ohio State U., 1950-81, prof. chemistry, 1960-81, Kimberly prof. chemistry, 1974-81, prof. emeritus, 1981—, chmn. dept., 1964-68; sr. scientist Nat. Center Atmospheric Research, Boulder, Colo., 1982—; Cons. air pollution tng. com. USPHS, 1964-66; mem. Nat. Air Pollution Control Manpower Devel. Com., 1966-69, chmn., 1968-69; bd. dirs. Gordon Research Confs., 1969-71; mem. air pollution control research grants com. EPA, 1970-72, chmn., 1971-72, mem. chemistry and physics adv. com., 1973-75; chmn. air pollution com. Conservation Found., 1968-70; mem. air conservation comm. Am. Lung Assn., 1973-75; chmn. EPA environ. chemistry/physics grants rev. panel, 1979-83; mem. State of Colo. Air Quality Control Commn., 1987;. Author: (with J. N. Pitts, Jr.) Photochemistry, 1966, Graduate School in the Sciences, 1972; also articles. Served to ensign USNR, 1944-46. Named Honor Prof. of Year Coll. Arts and Scis., Ohio State U., 1957; recipient Alumni award for disting. teaching, 1961, Disting. Research award, 1981; Fellow NRC Can., 1949; Guggenheim fellow, 1977-78. Fellow Ohio Acad. Sci., Am. Inst. Chemists; mem. Am. Chem. Soc. (award for creative research in environ. sci. and tech. 1981, Columbus sect. award 1981), AAUP, Air Pollution Control Assn. (Chambers award 1986), Phi Beta Kappa, Sigma Xi, Pi Mu Epsilon, Phi Lambda Upsilon, Alpha Chi Sigma. Office: NCAR Atmospheric Chemistry Div PO Box 3000 Boulder CO 80307

CALVERT, PETER ANTHONY RICHARD, political science educator; b. Islandmagee, Ireland, Nov. 19, 1936; s. Raymond and Irene (Earls) C.; m. Sue Ann Milbank, 1987. BA, U. Cambridge, Eng., 1960, MA, PhD, 1964; AM, U. Mich., 1961. Vis. lectr. U. Calif., Santa Barbara, 1966; research fellow Harvard U., Cambridge, 1969-70; lectr. U. Southampton, Eng., 1964-71, sr. lectr., 1971-74; reader U. Southhampton, Eng., 1974-83; prof. comparative and internat. politics U. Southampton, Eng., 1984—. Author: The Mexican Revolution, 1910-1914; The Diplomacy of Anglo-American Conflict, 1968, Latin America: Internal Conflict and International Peace, 1969, A Study of Revolution, 1970, The Mexicans: How They Live and Work, 1975, Emiliano Zapata, 1979, The Concept of Class, 1982, The Falklands Crisis: The Rights and The Wrongs, 1982, Politics Power and Revolution: An Introduction to Comparative Politics, 1983, Boundary Disputes in Latin America, 1983, Revolution and International Politics, 1984, Guatemalan Insurgency and American Security, 1984, Guatemala, A Nation in Turmoil, 1985, The Foreign Policy of New States, 1986, The Process of Political Succession, 1987; editor: The Central American Security System, 1988. Mem. Cambridge City Council, 1962-64, Dorset (Eng.) edn. com., 1985—. Ford Found. grantee, Southampton, 1984-88. Fellow Royal Hist. Soc.; mem. Polit. Studies Assn., Soc. Latin Am. Studies. Office: U Southampton, Southampton England SO9 5NH

CALVERT, WILLIAM PRESTON, radiologist; b. Warrensburg, Mo., July 2, 1934; s. William Geery and Elizabeth (Spaulding) C.; B.S., Mass. Inst. Tech., 1956; M.D., U. Pa., 1960; m. Mary Kay Kersh, Apr. 4, 1976. Intern, Pa. Hosp., Phila., 1960-61, resident in medicine, 1961-62, 64-66, chief med. resident, chief resident physician, 1965-66; resident in gastroenterology Jackson Meml. Hosp., U. Miami (Fla.), 1966-67, NIH fellow in gastroenterology, 1967-68, resident in radiology, 1968-71; radiologist Meml. Hosp., Hollywood, Fla., 1971-72; chief dept. radiology Larkin Gen. Hosp., South Miami, Fla., 1972-80, radiologist, 1980—; clin. instr. radiology U. Miami Sch. Medicine, 1971-76, now asst. clin. prof. dept. family practice, clin. asst. prof. radiology, 1984—. Bd. dirs. Wediko Farms Children's Services, Carbondale, Ill. Served with M.C., USAF, 1962-64. Diplomate Am. Bd. Nuclear Medicine, Am. Bd. Radiology. Mem. AMA, Fla. Med. Assn., Fla., Greater Miami radiol. socs., Soc. Nuclear Medicine, Radiol. Soc. N.Am., Explorers Club.

CALVIN, ALLEN DAVID, psychologist, educator; b. St. Paul, Feb. 17, 1928; s. Carl and Zelda (Engelson) C.; m. Dorothy VerStrate, Oct. 5, 1953; children—Jamie, Kris, David, Scott. B.A. in Psychology cum laude, U. Minn., 1950; M.A. in Psychology, U. Tex., 1951, Ph.D. in Exptl. Psychology, 1953. Instr. Mich. State U., East Lansing, 1953-55; asst. prof. Hollins Coll., 1955-59, assoc. prof., 1959-61; dir. Britannica Center for Studies in Learning and Motivation, Menlo Park, Calif., 1961; prin. investigator grant for automated teaching fgn. langs. Carnegie Found., 1960; USPHS grantee, 1960; pres. Behavioral Research Labs., 1962-74; prof., dean Sch. Edn., U. San Francisco, 1974-78; Henry Clay Hall prof. Orgn. and leadership, 1978—; pres. Pacific Grad. Sch. Psychology, 1984—. Author textbooks. Served with USNR, 1946-47. Mem. Am. Psychol. Assn., AAAS, Sigma Xi, Psi Chi. Home: 1645 15th Ave San Francisco CA 94122 Office: U San Francisco San Francisco CA 94117

CALVIN, DOROTHY VER STRATE, computer company executive; b. Grand Rapids, Mich., Dec. 22, 1929; d. Herman and Christina (Plakmyer) Ver Strate; m. Allen D. Calvin, Oct. 5, 1953; children—Jamie, Kris, Bufo, Scott. BS magna cum laude, Mich. State U., 1951; MA, U. San Francisco, 1988. Mgr. data processing. Behavioral Research Labs., Menlo Park, Calif., 1972-75; dir. Mgmt. Info. Systems Inst. for Prof. Devel., San Jose, Calif. 1975-76; systems analyst, programmer Pacific Bell Info. Systems, San Francisco, 1976-81; staff mgr., 1981-84; mgr. applications devel. Data Architects Inc., San Francisco, 1984-86; pres. Ver Strate Press, San Francisco, 1986—. Instr., Downtown Community Coll., San Francisco, 1980-84, Cañada Community Coll., 1986—; mem. computer curriculum adv. council San Francisco City Coll., 1982-84. Vice pres. LWV, Roanoke, Va., 1956-58; pres. Bulliss Purissima Parents Group, Los Altos, Calif., 1962-64; bd. dirs. Vols. for Israel, 1986-87. Mem. Nat. Assn. Female Execs., Assn. Systems Mgmt., Assn. Women in Computing. Democrat. Avocations: computing; gardening; jogging; reading. Office: Ver Strate Press 1645 15th Ave San Francisco CA 94122

CALVIN, JERRY GENE, industrial executive; b. Creston, Iowa, Dec. 28, 1938; s. Walter Robert and Cora Elizabeth (McNeil) C.; m. Sarah Mary Stellern, July, 1961 (div. May 1976); children: Deborah Lynn, James Michael, Kimberly Ann, Scott Allen; m. Gail Sue Shaffner, Oct. 10, 1976; 1 child, Shaun Michael. Student, Burlington Jr. Coll., 1962-63, U. Wis., Whitewater, 1965-66, LaSalle Coll., 1967-68, Ohio State U., 1970-72. Trainee mfg. engr. Gen. Electric Co., Burlington, Iowa, 1961-65; foreman Colt Industries, Beloit, Wis., 1965-66; supr., adv. mfg. engr. Eaton, Phila., 1966-67; mgr. prodn. control ITE Imperial, Phila., 1967-68, mgr. mfg., 1968-69; dir. shop ops. Cummins Engine Co., Columbus, Ohio, 1969-72; works mgr. FMC Corp., Indpls., 1972-76; dir. mfg. Bendix Corp., East Providence, R.I., 1976-80; v.p. mfg. N.H. Ball Bearings Inc., Peterborough, 1980-85, pres., chief exec. officer, 1986—, bd. dirs.; pres. Heim-Incom Internat., Fairfield, Conn., 1985-86; chmn. Planetics Engring. Inc., Paramont, Calif., chief exec. officer, 1986—; pres., chief exec. officer, bd. dirs. NMB-USA, Inc.; bd. dirs. NMB Techs., Inc., NMB Automotive, Inc., NMB Corp., IMC Magnetics, Inc. Served with USN, 1956-60. Mem. Anti-friction Bearing Mfg. Assn., Mfrs. Assn. (bd. dirs. Conn. 1985-86), Bus. and Industry Assn., Peterborough C. of C., Burlington Jaycess (v.p. 1962-65). Republican. Clubs: Rolling Hills Country (Wilton, Conn.); Keene (N.H.) Country; Peterborough Tennis; Hampshire Hills (Milford, N.H.). Home: 255 Old Dublin Rd Peterborough NH 03458 Office: NH Ball Bearings Inc US Rt 202 S Peterborough NH 03458

CALVIN, MELVIN, chemist, educator; b. St. Paul, Apr. 8, 1911; s. Elias and Rose I. (Hervitz) C.; m. Genevieve Jemtegaard, 1942; children: Elin, Karole, Noel. B.S., Mich. Coll. Mining and Tech., 1931, D.Sc., 1955; Ph.D., U. Minn., 1935, D.Sc., 1969; hon research fellow, U. Manchester, Eng., 1935-37; Guggenheim fellow, 1967; D.Sc., Nottingham U., 1958, Oxford (Eng.) U., 1959, Northwestern U., 1961, Wayne State U., 1962, Gustavus Adolphus Coll., 1963, Poly. Inst. Bklyn., 1962, U. Notre Dame, 1965, U. Gent, Belgium, 1970, Whittier Coll., 1971, Clarkson Coll., 1976, U. Paris Val-de-Marne, 1977, Columbia U., 1979, Grand Valley U., 1986. With U. Calif., Berkeley, 1937—; successively instr. chemistry, asst. prof., prof., Univ. prof., dir. Lab. Chem. Biodynamics U. Calif., 1963-80, assoc. dir. Lawrence Berkeley Lab., 1967-80; Peter Reilly lectr. U. Notre Dame, 1949; Harvey lectr. N.Y. Acad. Medicine, 1951; Harrison Howe lectr. Rochester sect. Am. Chem. Soc., 1954; Falk-Plaut lectr. Columbia U., 1954; Edgar Fahs Smith Meml. lectr. U. Pa. and Phila. sect. Am. Chem. Soc., 1955; Donegani Found. lectr. Italian Nat. Acad. Sci., 1955; Max Tishler lectr. Harvard U., 1956; Karl Folkers lectr. U. Wis., 1956; Baker lectr. Cornell U., 1958; London lectr., 1961, Willard lectr., 1982; Vanuxem lectr. Princeton U., 1969; Disting. lectr. Mich. State U., 1977; Prather lectr. Harvard U., 1980; Dreyfus lectr. Grinnell Coll., 1981, Berea Coll., 1982; Barnes lectr. Colo. Coll., 1982; Nobel lectr. U. Md., 1982; Abbott lectr. U. N.D., 1983; Gunning lectr. U. Alta., 1983; O'Leary disting. lectr. Gonzaga U., 1984; Danforth lectr. Dartmouth Coll., 1984, Grinnell Coll., 1984; R.P. Scherer lectr. U. S. Fla., 1984; Imperial Oil lectr. U. Western Ont., Can., 1985; disting. lectr. dept. chemistry U. Calgary, Can., 1986; Melvin Calvin lectr. Mich. Tech. U., 1986; Eastman prof. Oxford (Eng.) U., 1967-68. Author: (with G. E. K. Branch) The Theory of Organic Chemistry, 1940, Isotopic Carbon, (with others), 1949, Chemistry of Metal Chelate Compounds, (with Martell), 1952, Path of Carbon in Photosynthesis, (with Bassham), 1957, (with Bassham) Photosynthesis of Carbon Compounds, 1962, Chemical Evolution, 1969; contbr. articles to chem. and sci. jours. Recipient prize Sugar Research Found., 1950, Flintoff medal prize Brit. Chem. Soc., 1953, Stephen Hales award Am. Soc. Plant Physiologists, 1956, Nobel prize in chemistry, 1961; Davy medal Royal Soc., 1964; Virtanen medal, 1975; Priestley medal, 1978; Am. Inst. Chemists medal, 1979; Feodor Lynen medal, 1983; Sterling B. Hendricks medal, 1983, Melvin Calvin Medal of Distinction Mich. Tech. U., 1985. Mem. Britain's Royal Soc. London (fgn. mem.), Am. Chem. Soc. (Richards medal N.E. sect. 1956, Chem. Soc. Nichols medal N.Y. sect. 1958, award for nuclear applications in chemistry, pres. 1971, Gibbs medal Chgo. sect. 1977, Priestley medal 1978, Oesper award Cin. sect., 1981), Am. Acad. Arts and Scis., Nat. Acad. Scis., Royal Dutch Acad. Scis., Japan Acad., Am. Philos. Soc., Sigma Xi, Tau Beta Pi, Phi Lambda Upsilon. Office: Univ of Calif Dept of Chemistry Berkeley CA 94720

CALVIN, ROBERT JOSEPH, management consultant; b. Chgo., Dec. 28, 1936; s. Joseph K. and Pauline (Harris) C.; m. Jane L. Levy, Apr. 27, 1940; children—Susan D., Amy E. B.A., Conn. Wesleyan U., 1956; M.B.A., Columbia U., 1957. Salesman, acct., prodn. mgr. Cryovac div. W.R. Grace Co., Boston, 1958-60; asst. to pres. Lab. for Electronics, Boston, 1960-62; gen. mgr. Mid Continent Leasing, Chgo., 1963-65; pres. Hayward Marum Inc., Lawrence, Mass., 1970-80, Mgmt. Dimensions Inc., Chgo., 1962—, Hartmarx Furnishings Group, 1986-87. Lectr. Grad. Sch. Bus., U. Chgo., 1968—. Pres. bd. dirs. Jane Addams Ctr., Chgo.; bd. dirs. Hull House Assocs., Author: Profitable Sales Management and Marketing for Growing Businesses, 1983.

CALVO DE DIOS, JUAN JOSE, pulp and paper manufacturing executive; b. Havana, Cuba, Nov. 19, 1942; s. Juan Antonio and Francis America (De Dios) Calvo Gonzalez del Campillo; B.Sc.E.E., MIT, 1963, B.Sc. in Indsl. Mgmt., 1962, postgrad. Sloan Sch., 1963; Advanced Mgmt. Program, Harvard U., 1986; m. Mariá Valentina Perez Rami rez, Feb. 10, 1984; children: Juan Antonio, José; children by previous marriage—Gilda Maria, Maria Helena. Systems engr. IBM, Atlanta, 1963; with IBM Venezuela, 1963-73, br. mgr. govt. and petroleum accounts, 1968-73; ops. support mgr. IBM Latin Am.-Western region, 1974-75; v.p. NCR-Summa Sistemas, Caracas, Venezuela, 1976-77; gen. mgr. Moldeados Andinos, C.A., Caracas, 1981-88, dir., 1984—, exec. v.p., 1988— ; gen. mgr. Venepal, Caracas, 1981—, dir., 1984—; v.p. Chilena de Moldeados, Santiago, 1978-82; asst. prof. info. systems U. Simon Bolivar, Caracas, 1976-84; treas. Inmobiliaria Carpuente, Caracas, 1977—. Recipient Top Performer's Mktg. award IBM, 1969, 72, Orden al Merito enez Trabajo, 1987. Mem. Assn. Venezolana de Exportadores (dir.), Assn. Venezolana de Ejecutivos, Venezuelan-Am. C. of C., Camara Venezolana del Envase, China Inst. N. Am. Clubs: Lagunita Country, Harvard of Boston. Roman Catholic. Contbr. articles to profl. jours. Office: Apartado Postal 2075, Caracas Venezuela

CALVO SOTELO, LEOPOLDO, former prime minister Spain; b. Madrid, Apr. 14, 1926; s. Leopoldo Calvo-Sotelo and Mercedes Bustelo; D.C.E., U. Madrid, 1951; m. Pilar IbáñezMarti n, Apr. 26, 1954; children: Leopoldo, Juan, Pilar, Pedro, Victor, Jose María, Pablo y Andrés. Dir. gen. Perlofil, S.A., Madrid, 1954, Union Española de Explosivos S.A., Madrid, 1963-67; chmn. Spanish Rys., Madrid, 1967-68; procurador Spanish Court System, 1972-75; dir. Urquijo Bank, Madrid, 1974-75; minister of commerce Spain, 1975-76, minister of public works, 1976-77; dep. Congress of Deps., from 1977; minister for relations with European Communities, 1978-80; v.p. for econ. affairs Spain, 1980-81, prime minister, 1981-82; mem. European Parl., 1986—. Served as 2d lt., C.E., Spanish Army Res., 1947-52. Mem. Unión de Centro Democrático. Roman Catholic. Address: care Las Cortes Generales, Madrid Spain *

CALZADILLA-DAGUERRE, JESUS FRANCISCO, office systems manager; b. Madrid, July 22, 1954; s. Jose Calzadilla and Pilar Daguerre; m. Elizabeth Gough, Aug. 18, 1982. Ph.D. in Engring., Poly. U., Madrid, 1976; M.B.A., Instituto Estudios Superiores Empresariales, Madrid, 1984. Lectr. in computer sci. Poly. U., Madrid, 1976-79; office systems tech. mgr. Rank Xerox, Madrid, 1979-82; product mktg. mgr. I.C.L. Ltd. Computers, Madrid and London, 1982-84; office systems mgr., cons. Sperry Computers, Madrid, 1984-87; nat. dir. bus. services Wang Lab. España, Madrid, 1987-88; mktg. mgr. ECAI-Unisys, Madrid, 1988—. Author: AREA, A Relational View, 1979; author conf. book Personal Computers: The Uncertain Future, 1985. Mem. IEEE (bd. dirs. students br. 1977-80), Euromicro (bd. dirs. Netherlands 1979-85), Instituto Ingenieros Civiles. Avocations: riding; writing; reading. Home: Vereda de las Penas 51, 28100 Madrid Spain

CAMAGAY, ILUMINADA, physician; b. Manila, Philippines, Jan. 4, 1947; d. Alejandro and Iluminada (Tabora) C. BS, U. Philippines, Manila, 1967; MD, U. Philippines, 1972, diploma in anethesiology, 1974. Lic. to practice med., Philippine Bd. Med. Examiners, 1972, diplomate anesthesiology, Anesthesiology Ctr. Western Pacific, 1977. Resident Philippine Gen. Hosp., Manila, 1972-75; Danida fellow Rigshospitalet, Copenhagen, 1976-77; asst. prof. anesthesiology U. Philippines, Manila, 1978—; cons. Philippine Children's Med. Ctr., 1979—, Manila Drs. Hosp., 1985—, Philippine Gen. Hosp., 1978—; vice chmn. Anesthesiology dept. Philippine Gen. Hosp., 1985—, U. Philippines Coll. Med., 1985. Editor: Philippine Journal of Anesthesiology, 1987—; contbr. numerous articles to profl. jours. Mem. Philippine Bd. Anesthesiology (sec. 1982-83, chmn. 1983-84), Philippine Soc. Anesthesiology, Western Pacific Soc. Critical Care Med. Roman Catholic. Home: 6 Kew Garden, St Ignatius Village, Quezon City Metro Manila, Philippines Office: Philippine Gen Hosp, Dept Anesthesiology, Taft Ave, Manila Philippines

CAMARENA, VICENTE, mathematician, educator; b. Xativa, Valencia, Spain, Aug. 26, 1941; s. Vicente and Victoria Camarena; m. Carmen Grau; children: Victoria, Carmen, Rosa, Eva, Vicente. MA in Physics, U. Zaragoza, Spain, 1966, PhD in Math., 1972. Asst. prof. of math. U. Zaragoza, 1969-81, prof., 1981—, dep. dir., 1981-84, vice chancellor, 1984—. Author: Applied Mathematics; contbr. articles (with others) to profl. jours. Grantee French Nat. Aero. Research Office, European Spatial Research Orgn., 1970-71. Mem. Spanish Royal Soc. of Math., Spanish Assn. of Math., Spanish Soc. of Gen. Systems, Am. Math. Soc., Soc. for Indsl. and Applied Math., Internat. Astronomical Union, N.Y. Acad. Sci. Home: Latassa 17, Zaragoza Spain Office: Univ Rector, Plaza San Francisco s/n, Zaragoza Spain 50071

CAMBEL, ALI BULENT, engineer, educator; b. Merano, Italy, Apr. 9, 1923; came to U.S., 1943, naturalized, 1951; s. H. Cemil and Remziye (Hakki) C.; m. Marion dePaar, Dec. 20, 1946; children—Metin, Emel, Leyla, Sarah. BS, Robert Coll., Istanbul, Turkey, 1942; postgrad., U. Istanbul, 1942-43, MIT, 1943-45; MS, Calif. Inst. Tech., 1946; PhD, U. Iowa, 1950. Registered profl. engr. Instr. State U. Iowa, 1947-50, asst. prof., 1950-53; assoc. prof. mech. engring. Northwestern U., 1953-56, prof. mech. engring., 1956-61, Walter P. Murphy disting. prof., 1961-68, dir. gas dynamics lab., 1955-66, chmn. dept. mech. engring. and astronautical scis., 1957-66; dir. research and engring. support div. IDA, 1966-67, v.p. for research, 1967-68; dean Coll. Engring., Wayne State U., Detroit, 1968-70; exec. v.p. for acad. affairs Wayne State U., 1970-72; v.p., dir. System Research div. Gen. Research Corp., 1972-74; dep. asst. dir. for sci. and tech. NSF, 1974-75; prof. emeritus of engring. and applied sci. George Washington U., Washington, 1975-88; chmn. dept. civil, mech. and environ. engring. George Washington U., 1978-80, dir. energy programs, 1976-88; tech. cons. govt. agys., various firms; staff dir. Pres.'s Interdeptl. Energy Study, 1963; engring. scis. adv. com. USAF Office Sci. Research, 1961-63; mem. Commn. Engring. Edn., 1966-68, Army Sci. Advisory Panel, 1966-72; nat. lectr. Sigma Xi, 1961-62. Author: Plasma Physics and Magnetofluidmechanics, 1963; co-author: Gas Dynamics, 1958, Real Gases, 1963, Plasma Physics, 1965; co-editor: Transport Properties in Gases, 1958, The Dynamics of Conducting Gases, 1960, Second Law Analysis of Energy Devices and Processes, 1980, Magnetohydrodynamics, 1962, ACTA Astronautica, 1974-76; assoc. editor: Am. Inst. Aeros. and Astronautics jour., Jet Propulsion, 1955-60, Energy, The Internat. Jour., 1975—; contbr. numerous papers in field. Bd. dirs. YMCA. Recipient leadership award YMCA, 1953; citation for solar satellite power system evaluation Dept. Energy/NASA, 1981; cert. for patriotic service Sec. of Army; award for excellence NSF/RANN; award for contbns. to sci. and edn. U.S. Immigrants League.; Washburn scholar, 1938. Fellow AIAA (J. Edward Pendray award 1959, nat. dir.); mem. Am. Soc. Engring. Edn. (Curtiss McGraw award 1960, George Westinghouse award 1966, chmn. engring. & pub. policy div. 1986-87), ASME (founding chmn. energy systems analysis tech. com. 1980-82), Sigma Xi, Pi Tau Sigma, Tau Beta Pi.; Mem. Soc. of Friends. Club: Cosmos (Washington). Home: 6155 Kellogg Dr McLean VA 22101 Office: George Washington U Sch Engring and Applied Sci Office Energy Programs Washington DC 20052

CAMBRICE, ROBERT LOUIS, lawyer; b. Houston, Nov. 23, 1947; s. Eugene and Edna Bertha (Jackson) C.; m. Christine Jackson, Jan. 7, 1972; children—Bryan, Graham. B.A. cum laude, Tex. So. U., 1969; J.D., U. Tex.-Austin, 1972. Bar: Tex. 1973, U.S. Dist. Ct. (so. dist.) Tex. 1975, U.S. Ct. Apls. (5th cir.) 1975, U.S. Ct. Apls. (11th cir.) 1981, U.S. Sup. Ct. 1981. Asst. atty. City of Houston, 1974-76; sole practice, Houston, 1976-81; asst. atty. Harris County, Tex., 1981-85, City of Houston, 1986—; trial atty. City of Houston Legal Dept., 1986—. Earl Warren fellow, 1969-72. Mem. Nat. Bar Assn., ABA, NAACP, Alpha Kappa Mu. Democrat. Roman Catholic.

CAMERON, GORDON MURRAY, chemical engineer; b. New Liskeard, Ont., Can., Apr. 9, 1932; s. Murray and Vera Alice (Strader) C.; m. Marie Therese Skutezky, Feb. 2, 1963; children: Barbara, Ian, Vera, Ewen. Diploma, Royal Mil. Coll. Can., Kingston, Ont., 1953; BS with honors, Queen's U., Kingston, 1954; PhD in Chem. Engring., U. Del., 1962. Registered prof. engr. With CIL Inc., 1960-73, Chemetics Internat. Ltd., 1960-73; tech. mgr. Chemetics Internat. Ltd., Montreal, Que., Can., 1974-87; tech. mgr. Chemetics Internat. Ltd., Toronto, Ont., 1975-87, dir. tech., 1987; v.p. technology Chemetics Internat. Ltd., Toronto, 1987-88; pres. Cecebe Technologies Inc., North York, On., Can., 1988—; chmn. heat transfer com. Nat. Research Council of Can., Ottawa, Ont., 1966-70; bd. dirs. Chem. Inst. Can., Ottawa. Contbr. 20 tech. articles to profl. jours.; inventor, patentee in field. Mem. Can. Soc. Chem. Engring., Am. Inst. Chem. Engrs., Am. Chem. Soc., The Metall. Soc. Presbyterian. Home: 4 Wellesbourne Crescent, North York, Toronto, ON Canada M2H 1Y7 Office: Cecebe Technologies Inc, 4 Wellesbourne Crescent, North York, ON Canada M2H 1Y7

CAMERON, JOANNA, actress, director; b. Greeley, Colo.; d. Harold and Erna (Borgens) C.; m. Grant D. Conroy, July 4, 1980. Student, U. Calif., 1967-68, Pasadena Playhouse, 1968. media cons. to Cath. Bishops on Papal Visit of Pope John Paul II, Calif., 1987. Starred in: weekly TV series The Shazam-ISIS hour, CBS, 1976-78; host, dir.: for TV equipped ships USN Closed Circuit Network Program, 1977, 78, 79, 80; guest star: numerous network TV shows, including Merv Griffin Show, The Survivors, Love American Style, Mission Impossible, The Tonight Show; appeared in numerous commls.; network prime time shows including Name of the Game, Medical Center, The Bold Ones, Marcus Welby, Columbo, High Risk,

Switch; motion picture debut in How to Commit Marriage, 1969; other film appearances include The Amazing Spiderman; dir. various commls., CBS Preview Spl.; producer, dir. documentaries include Razor Sharp, 1981, El Camino Real, 1987. Mem. Dirs. Guild Am., Acad. TV Arts and Scis., AFTRA, Screen Actors Guild, Delta Delta Delta. Club: Los Angeles Athletic. Office: Cameron Prodns PO Box 1400 Pebble Beach CA 93953

CAMERON, JOHN ROBINSON, educator; b. Glasgow, Scotland, June 24, 1936; s. George Gordon Cameron; m. Mary Elizabeth Ranson, Aug. 19, 1959 (dec. 1984); children: Margaret Anne, Catherine Mary, Ian Charles; m. Barbara Elizabeth Moncur, June 25, 1987. MA in Pure and Applied Math. with honors, U. St. Andrews, Scotland, 1958, PhB, 1961. Asst. in philosophy Queen's Coll., Dundee, Scotland, 1962-63; lectr. in philosophy U. Dundee, 1963-73, sr. lectr., 1973-78; regius prof. of logic U. Aberdeen, Scotland, 1979—. Contbr. articles to profl. jours. Harkness fellow U. Calif., Cornell U., 1959-61. Mem. Ch. Scotland. Home: 70 Cornhill Rd, Aberdeen AB2 5DH, Scotland Office: U Aberdeen Dept Philosophy, Kings Coll, Old Aberdeen AB9 2UB, Scotland

CAMERON, JOHN STUART, nurse, educator; b. Glasgow, Scotland, Jan. 3, 1951; s. John and Grace (McLaren) C.; m. Helen Maloy. Grad. in Bus./Indsl. Relations, Gordonstoun, Scotland, 1969. Registered gen. nurse; registered psychiat. nurse. Charge nurse Acorn St. Day Hosp., Greater Glasgow Health Bd., 1980—; clin. lectr. in field; cons. various substance and drug agencies. Author: Solvent Abuse-A Guide for the Carer, 1988; contbr. chpts. to books and articles to profl. jours. Churchill Trust scholar. Home: 59 Meldrum Mains Glenmavis, Airdrie, Strathclyde Scotland Office: Acorn St Day Hosp, 23 Acorn St, Glasgow Scotland

CAMERON, JUDITH ELAINE MOELLERING, marketing and public relations company executive; b. Eagle Grove, Iowa, May 26, 1943; d. Albert Edwin and Marion (Trask) Moellering; m. William Ewen Cameron, Aug. 13, 1966 (div. 1970). BA, Drake U., 1965. Intern, Washington; model Younkers, Des Moines, 1962-65, asst. to columnist Harlan Miller, 1962-65, asst. buyer, copywriter, 1965-66; dir. personnel 4th Northwestern Nat. Bank, Mpls., 1966; head copywriter SPF Advt., Mpls., 1966-68; dir. spl. projects program U. Minn., Mpls., 1968-70; cons. pub. relations Fed. Republic of Germany, Italy, Spain, 1970-71; mgr. Jetset Sportswear, Footville, Wis., 1971-72; artist Almunecar, Spain, 1972-74; dir. pub. relations Topspin, Totalplan Sports Internat., A.G., Madrid, 1974-76, mng. dir., Madrid and London, 1976-80; European mgr. Siam Internat. Amalgamated Mfrs. Ltd., London, 1977-80; European rep. Siam Cement Trading Co., London, 1979-80; European mgr. Third Wave Electronics Co., Inc., London, 1980-82; exec. v.p., dir. Electronic Specialty Products, Inc., N.Y.C., 1983-84; pres. Comml. Brain, Inc., N.Y.C. and N.Mex., 1984—, Rennert and Cameron, Inc., N.Y.C., 1984-86. Six one-woman shows, Spain; 4 group exhbns., Europe. Mem. Republicans Abroad, Women Bus. Owners of N.Y., Nat. Assn. Female Execs., Iowa Soc. N.Y. (founding mem., pres.), Council on Internat. Relations, bd. dirs. N.Mex. Repertory Theater, Spotlighters, N.Mex. 1st Task Force, Alpha Phi.

CAMERON, NICHOLAS ALLEN, diversified corporation executive; b. Phila., Jan. 6, 1939; s. Nicholas Guyot and Katherine (Rogers) C.; m. Leslie Wood, Dec. 14, 1974; children: Christopher Wilson, Pamela Wilson. B.S., Yale U., 1960. Treas. Allied Corp., Morristown, N.J., 1979-81, v.p. and treas., 1981-82, v.p. fin., 1982-83, v.p. planning and devel., 1983-85; sr. v.p. planning, devel. and adminstrn. Allied-Signal Inc., Morristown, N.J., 1985-86; sr. v.p. tech. and bus. devel. Bendix Aerospace-Allied-Signal, Inc., Arlington, Va., 1986-87; group pres. Allied-Signal Aerospace, 1988; sr. v.p. ops. services Allied-Signal, Inc., Morristown, N.J., 1988—. Treas., bd. dirs. United Way of Morris County, Morristown, N.J., 1980-86. Mem. Morris County C. of C. (bd. dirs. 1975-86), Tau Beta Pi. Republican. Episcopalian. Clubs: St. Elmo Soc. (New Haven); Morris County Golf. Home: Five Noe Ave Madison NJ 07940 Office: Allied Signal Inc Morristown NJ 07960

CAMERON, RONDO, economic history educator; b. Linden, Tex., Feb. 20, 1925; s. Burr S. and Annie Mae (Dalrymple) C.; m. Claydean Zumbrunnen, July 26, 1946; children: Alan, Cindia. A.B., Yale U., 1948, A.M., 1949; Ph.D., U. Chgo., 1952. Instr. Yale, 1951-52; asst. prof. U. Wis. at Madison, 1952-56, assoc. prof., 1957-61, prof. econs. and history, dir. grad. program econ. history, 1961-69; William Rand Kenan Univ. prof. Emory U., 1969—; vis. prof. U. Chgo., 1956-57; spl. field rep. Rockefeller Found., S.A., 1965-67. Author: France and the Economic Development of Europe, rev. edit, 1966 (transl. into French and Spanish 1971), Banking in the Early Stages of Industrialization, 1967 (transl. into Japanese 1973, Spanish 1974, Italian 1975), The European World, 2d edit, 1970, Civilization: Western and World, 1975; Editor: Essays in French Economic History, 1970, Civilization Since Waterloo, 1971, Banking and Economic Development, 1972; Am. rev. editor of: Econ. History Rev, 1960-65; rev. editor: Jour. Econ. History, 1968-69; editor, 1975-81; Contbr. articles to profl. jours. Chmn. Council Research Econ. History, 1967-69; bd. dirs. Albert Schweitzer Fellowship. Fulbright scholar France, 1950-51; Guggenheim fellow Europe, 1954-55, 70-71; fellow Center Advanced Study Behavioral Scis., 1958-59; Fulbright prof. U. Glasgow, 1962-63; Fellow Woodrow Wilson Internat. Center for Scholars, 1974-75. Mem. Am. Hist. Assn. (co-chmn. program com. 1983), Internat. Econ. Hist. Assn. (exec. com., v.p.), Am. Econ. Hist. Assn. (pres. 1974-75), Brit. Econ. Hist. Assn., French Econ. Hist. Assn. Home: 1088 Clifton Rd NE Atlanta GA 30307

CAMERON, ROY EUGENE, scientist; b. Denver, July 16, 1929; s. Guy Francis and Ilda Annora (Horn) C.; m. Margot Elizabeth Hoagland, May 5, 1956 (div. July 1977); children: Susan Lynn, Catherine Ann; m 2d Carolyn Mary Light, Sept. 22, 1978. B.S., Wash. State U., 1953, 54; M.S., U. Ariz., 1958, Ph.D., 1961; D.D. (hon.), Ministry of Christ Ch., Delavan, Wis., 1975. Research scientist Hughes Aircraft Corp., Tucson, 1955-56; sr. scientist Jet Propulsion Lab., Pasadena, Calif., 1961-68, mem. tech. staff, 1969-74; dir. research Darwin Research Inst., Dana Point, Calif., 1974-75; dep. dir. Land Reclamation Lab. Argonne Ill. Nat. Lab., 1975-77, dir. energy resources tng. and devel., 1977-85; staff scientist Lockheed Engrng. & Mgmt. Services Co., Las Vegas, Nev., 1986—; cons. Lunar Recieving Lab. Baylor U., 1966-68, Ecology Ctr. Utah State U., Desert Biome, 1970-72, U. Alaska Tundra Biome, 1973-74, U. Maine, 1973-76, numerous others; mem. Nat. Agriculture Research and Extension Users Adv. Bd., 1986—. Contrb. articles to sci. books; participated in 7 Antarctic expdns. Served with U.S. Army, 1950-52, Korea, Japan. Recipient 3 NASA awards for tech. briefs; Paul Steere Burgess fellow U. Ariz., 1959; grantee NSF, 1970-74; Dept. Interior, 1978-80. Mem. AAAS, Soil Sci. Soc. Am., Am. Chem. Soc., Am. Soc. Microbiology, Am. Soc. Agronomy, Antarctican Soc., Polar Soc. Am., Am. Scientist Affiliation, World Future Soc., Internat. Soc. Soil. Sci., Council Agrl. Sci. and Tech., Am. Inst. Biol. Sci., Am. Geophys. Union, Sigma Xi. Mem. Christian Ch.

CAMERON, WILLIAM DUNCAN, plastic company executive; b. Harrell, N.C., June 14, 1925; s. Paul Archiebald and Atwood (Herring) C.; m. Betty Gibson, Oct. 3, 1953; children—Phillip McDonald, Colleen Kay. Student Duke U., 1945-49. Chmn. Reef Industries Inc., Houston, 1958—. Pres. bd. trustees Trinity Episcopal Sch., Galveston, Tex., 1981-82; trustee William Temple Found., 1987—. Served with U.S. Army, 1943-45. Mem. World Bus. Council, Houston C. of C. (chmn. mfg. com. 1967). Clubs: Rotary, Galveston Artillery, Bob Smith Yacht. Home: 2868 Dominique Dr Galveston TX 77551 Office: Reef Industries Inc 9209 Almeda-Genoa Rd Houston TX 77075

CAMMA, ALBERT JOHN, neurosurgeon; b. Cleve., Dec. 27, 1940; s. August and Amelia (Catalioti) C.; B.S. cum laude, John Carroll U., 1963; M.D., Western Res. U., 1967; m. Sheryl Virginia Doptis, Aug. 27, 1966 (div. Jan. 1986); children—August Leon, Albert David. Intern, surg. resident U. Pitts., 1967-69, resident in neurosurgery, 1971-75; practice medicine specializing in neurosurgery, Zanesville, Ohio, 1975—. Trustee Zanesville YMCA, 1976-82. Served with M.C., USN, 1969-71. Diplomate Am. Bd. Neurol. Surgeons, Nat. Bd. Med. Examiners. Mem. AMA, Ohio State Med. Assn., Muskingum County Acad. Medicine, Congress Neurol. Surgeons, Am. Acad. Thermology, Midwest Pain Soc., Soc. Behavioral Medicine, ACS, Am. Assn. Neurol. Surgeons, Ohio State Neurosurg. Soc. (bd. dirs. 1985-87, treas. 1987—), Mid-Atlantic Neurosurg. Soc., Am. Pain Soc., Am. Acad. Scis., AAAS, Am. Coll. Neurology, Am. Neurol. Soc. Office: 855 Bethesda Dr Zanesville OH 43701

CAMMA, PHILIP, accountant; b. Phila., May 22, 1923; s. Anthony and Rose (LaSpada) C.; m. Anna Ruth Karg, July 21, 1956 (dec. Aug. 1960); 1 child, Anthony Philip. BS, U. Pa., 1952. CPA, Ohio, Ky. Acct., Main and Co., CPA's, Phila., 1952-53; in-charge acct. Haskins & Sells, CPA's, Phila., St. Louis, Cin. and Columbus, Ohio, 1953-60; controller Marvin Warner Co., Cin., 1960-61, Leshner Corp., 1961-63; mng. ptnr. Camma & Patrick, CPA's, 1963-66; founder Philip Camma Co., CPA's, Cin., 1966—. Served with USAAF, 1942-45, ETO. Mem. Am. Inst. CPA's, Ohio Soc. CPA's, Ky. Soc. CPA's, Am. Acctg. Assn., Nat. Assn. Accts. Republican. Clubs: Cincinnati; University Pa.; Hamilton City. Home: Phelps Townhouse 506 E 4th St Cincinnati OH 45202 Office: 700 Walnut St Suite 603 Cincinnati OH 45202

CAMMACK, WILLIAM FREDERICK JAMES, physician; b. Sydney, New South Wales, Australia, Mar. 7, 1916; s. James and Mabel Elizabeth (Blakey) C.; m. Eileen Scott-Young, Oct. 5, 1944; children—Mary Elizabeth, Reginald John, William James. M.B., B.S., Sydney U., 1940. Resident med. officer St. George Dist. Hosp., Sydney, 1941-42, Concord Mil. Hosp., 1942-44; gen. practice medicine, Penrith, New South Wales, 1947—, Lismore, New South Wales, 1946-47; hon. med. officer Nepean Dist. Hosp., Penrith, 1947-84, Gov. Phillip Hosp., Penrith, 1956-84, Lismore Base and St. Vincent Hosps., Lismore, 1946-47; dir., vis. med. officer Jamison Pvt. Hosp., Penrith, 1965—; chmn. med. bd. Nepean Dist. Hosp., 1966, Gov. Phillip Spl. Hosp., 1978; mng. dir. Mountain Mists Pty. Ltd., 1970—. Author: S. Woodward-Smith, Australian Artist, 1974; several books on local history and sailing ships, 1984, 85. Editor: Emu Plains and Thereabouts, 1979. Pres. Nepean Dist. Hist. Soc., Penrith, 1982-83, v.p., 1984—; consort to mayor Penrith City Council 1975-78; found. sec. community Arts Council, Penrith, 1976. Served to capt. Australian Army Med Corps, Australia Imperial Force, 1942-46. Mem. Gen. Practitioner Soc. in Australia, AMA (found. pres. Nepean-Hawkesbury br. 1970-76). Liberal. Methodist. Club: Panther's Leagues (Penrith). Avocation: appreciation of art. Office: 30 Mulgoa Rd, Penrith New South Wales 2750, Australia also: 304 High St, Penrith New South Wales 2750, Australia

CAMOUGIS, GEORGE, research center director; b. Concord, Mass., May 10, 1930; s. Charles George and Angeliki (Georgekopoulou) C.; B.S. magna cum laude (Olmstead fellow), Tufts U., 1952; M.A., Harvard U., 1957, Ph.D., 1958; m. Irene Andreson, Nov. 18, 1961; children—Caroline A., Elizabeth M., Sarah A. Asst. prof. physiology Clark U., 1958-62, assoc. prof., 1962-64, affiliate prof., 1964-79; sr. neurophysiologist Astra Pharm. Products, Inc., Worcester, Mass., 1964-66, head sect. neuropharmacology, 1966-68; pres., research dir., dir. New Eng. Research, Inc., Worcester, 1968—; cons. numerous state and fed. agys. including Army C.E., Fed. Hwy. Adminstrn., U.S. Dept. Interior, EPA; affiliate prof. Worcester Poly. Inst., 1970-82; adj. prof. toxicology Tufts U. Sch. Vet. Medicine, 1981-84; panelist NSF; mem. corp. Bermuda Biol. Sta. for Research, 1968—; lectr. in field, U.S., Can.; mem. Worcester Sci. Center Planning Com., 1963. Bd. dirs. Worcester Children's Friend Soc., 1968—, v.p., 1978-84, pres., 1984-87. Served with USNR, 1952-54; Korea. Virginia B. Gibbs scholar, 1954-55; E.L. Mark fellow, 1956; USPHS fellow, 1957-58; NIH grantee, 1962-64; Office Naval Research grantee, 1963-64; recipient Sci. Achievement award Worcester Engrng. Soc., 1985 . Mem. AAAS, Biophys. Soc., Am. Physiol. Soc., N.Y. Acad. Scis., ASTM, Soc. Environ. Toxicology and Chemistry, Phi Beta Kappa, Sigma Xi. Republican. Greek Orthodox. Clubs: Tatnuck Country (Worcester); Chemists (N.Y.C.); Harvard (Boston). Author: Nerves, Muscles and Electricity, 1970; Environmental Biology for Engineers, 1981; contbr. numerous articles to profl. jours., 1959—; patentee drug; cons. editor Acad. Press, Inc., 1978; mem. editorial adv. bd. Hazardous Materials and Waste Mgmt., 1983—. Home: 7 Wheeler Ave Worcester MA 01609 Office: 15 Sagamore Rd Worcester MA 01605

CAMP, EHNEY ADDISON, III, mortgage banker; b. Birmingham, Ala., June 28, 1942; s. Ehney Addison and Mildred Fletcher (Tillman) C.; BA, Dartmouth Coll., 1964; m. Patricia Jane Hough, Sept. 17, 1966; children: Ehney Addison IV, Margaret Strader. Sr. v.p. Cobbs, Allen & Hall Mortgage Co., Inc., Birmingham, 1965-72; v.p., gen. mgr. The Rime Cos., Birmingham, 1972-75; pres. Camp & Co., Birmingham, 1975—; bd. dirs. AmSouth Corp., Birmingham. Bd. dirs. Community Chest/United Way Jefferson, Walker and Shelby Counties, Better Bus. Bur. of Gt. Birmingham; pres., trustee Civic Club Found, Inc.; bd. dirs. All Am. Bowl. Served with USAF, 1965, Ala. Air N.G., 1966. Mem. Am. Mortgage Bankers Assn. (income property com.), Ala. Mortgage Bankers Assn. (treas. 1985, sec. 1986, v.p. 1987, pres. 1988). Methodist. Clubs: Kiwanis (dir. 1977-78, 82-83, sec. 1983-84, v.p. 1985-86, pres. 1986-87); Mountain Brook (bd. govs. 1976-77); Birmingham Country; The Club (bd. dirs., fin. chmn. 1987-88), Wade Hampton Golf (Cashiers, N.C.); Downtown; Shoal Creek (bd. govs. 1983—). Home: 3510 Victoria Rd Birmingham AL 35223 Office: 3300 Cahaba Rd Suite 300 Birmingham AL 35223

CAMP, HAZEL LEE BURT, artist; b. Gainesville, Ga., Nov. 28, 1922; d. William Ernest and Annie Mae (Ramsey) Burt; student Md. Inst. Art, 1957-58, 62-63; m. William Oliver Camp, Jan. 24, 1942; children—William Oliver, David Byron. One-woman shows at Ga. Mus. Art, Rockville Art Mus., Coll. Notre Dame (Balt.), U. Md., Balt. Vertical Gallery, Cleveland Meml. Gallery (Balt.), Unicorn Gallery, 1982, Hampton Ctr. for Arts and Humanities (Va.), 1985, others; exhibited in juried shows at Peale Mus., Balt., Wilmington (Del.) Fine Arts Center, Smithsonian Instn., Turner Gallery, Balt., City Hall Balt., Bendann Art Gallery, Balt., 1980, City Hall Gallery, Balt., 1982, Balt. Watercolor Soc., 1983, others; represented in permanent collections: Ga. Mus. Art, Peabody Inst. (Balt.), Rehoboth Art League, numerous pvt. collections. Recipient 1st prize Md. chpt. Artists' Equity, 1967; St. Marys County Art Assn., 1964, 67, 1st prize still life Cape May, N.J., 1969, Catonsville (Md.) Community Coll., 1969, St. John's Coll., 1969, Best in Show York (Pa.) Art Assn. Gallery, 1972, 2d award Md. Inst. Alumni Founding Chpt., Balt., 1976, Best in Show Three Arts Club, 1978, Watercolor award State Art Exhbt., Nat. League Am. Pen Women, 1979, also 3d prize oil, Tulsa biennial, 1966, Honorable Mention, Rehoboth Art League, 1983; Purchase award Old Point Nat. Bank, Hampton, Va., 1985, Merit award Hampton (Va.) City Hall, 1986, Juror's Choice award Twentieth Century Gallery, Williamsburg, Va., 1987. Mem. Nat. League Am. Pen Women (pres. Carroll br. 1968-70, editor The Quill 1975-76, editor for Carroll br. 1982-83; rec. sec. nat. exec. bd. 1979-80; nat. nominating com. 1982; Md. art chmn. 1982), Artists' Equity, Rehoboth Art League, Va. Watercolor Soc., Md. Fedn. Art, Md. Inst. Alumni Assn., Balt. Watercolor Soc. (hon. mention 1982, sec. 1978-80), Peninsula Fine Arts Ctr. Democrat. Methodist. Contbr. illustrations to mags., booklets. Home: 2 Bayberry Dr Newport News VA 23601

CAMPANA, ANA ISABEL, architect; b. Banes, Oriente, Cuba, Jan. 16, 1934; came to U.S., 1967, naturalized, 1974; d. Abelardo Joaquin and Amparo (Cabrera) C. B.S., Instituto del Vedado, Havana, 1953; postgrad., Havana U., 1962, Albany (N.Y.) Inst. History and Art, 1970. Architect, Havana U., 1962, Ministry of Pub. Works, Havana, 1962-67; architect designer various firms, N.Y., 1967-74; sr. architect Gen. Electric Co., Schenectady, 1974—. Recipient 1st nat. award Nat. Mus. Com., Havana, 1948, 1st Province award, 1948, several international archtl. performance awards. Mem. AIA (assoc.). Roman Catholic. Home: 10 Mill Ln Apt 109 Schenectady NY 12305 Office: Gen Electric Co 1 River Rd Bldg 23 Room 301-A Schenectady NY 12345

CAMPBELL, BRIAN THOMAS, judge; b. Denver, May 15, 1948; s. Leonard Martin and Dot Jo (Baker) C.; m. Patricia Sue Adams, May 8, 1982; children: Rebecca Mae, Robert Michael. BA, Knox Coll., 1970; JD, U. Colo., 1972. Bar: Colo. 1973, U.S. Dist. Ct. Colo. 1973, U.S. Ct. Appeals (10th cir.) 1976. Law clk. U.S. Dist. Ct. Colo., Denver, 1973; assoc. Gorsuch, Kirgis, Denver, 1974-80; judge Denver County Ct., 1980—. Mem. Colo. Bar Assn. (bd. govs), Denver Bar Assn. (young lawyers exec. council), Colo. Women's Bar Assn., Catholic Lawyers Guild, State Trial Judges Council (sec. treas. 1987-88) County Ct. Judges Assn. (exec. council). Democrat. Roman Catholic. Home: 2986 S Whiting Way Denver CO 80231 Office: City and County Court 1437 Bannock St Denver CO 80202

CAMPBELL, CALVIN ARTHUR, JR., mining and plastics molding equipment manufacturing company executive; b. Detroit, Sept. 1, 1934; s. Calvin Arthur and Alta Christine (Koch) C.; m. Rosemary Phoenix, June 6, 1959; 1 dau., Georgia Alta. AB in Econs, Williams Coll., 1956; SB in Chem. Engring., M.I.T., 1959; J.D., U. Mich., 1961. With Exxon Chem. Co., N.Y.C., 1961-69; chmn. bd., treas. John B. Adt Co., York, Pa., N.Y.C., 1969-70; pres., chief exec. officer Goodman Equipment Corp., Chgo., 1971—; chmn. Improved Blow Molding Equipment Co. Inc., Hudson, N.H.; pres. Improved Parts and Service (subs. Goodman Equipment Corp.), Chgo., 1979—; founder, chmn. Goodman Conveyor Co. Inc., Belton, S.C., 1984—; mem. exec. com. Econ. Devel. Commn., City of Chgo., 1980-86; co-chmn. labor mgmt. com. Ill. Devel. Bd., 1982-86; bd. dirs., mem. compensation and benefits com. Cyprus Minerals Co. Inc. Trustee Ill. Inst. Tech., 1986—; mem. Gov's. Commn. on Sci. and Tech., Pres.'s council Mus. Sci. and Industry, Build Ill. Com.; mem. Chgo. adv. bd. The Salvation Army; dir. Chgo. unit Am. Cancer Soc., chmn. Chgo. Trades and Industry, 1978; pres. 1320 North State St. Coop. Apts. Inc., 1984-86. Mem. ABA, N.Y. Bar Assn., Am. Mining Congress (gov. 1972—, chmn. bd. govs. mfrs. div. 1980-83, dir. 1980—, chmn. product liability com.), Ill. Mfrs. Assn. (dir. 1978-84, exec. and fin. coms., chmn. long range planning com. 1984, succession com. 1983), Am. Inst Chem. Engrs., Chief Execs. Orgn. Inc., World Bus. Council, Newcomen Soc. U.S., Chgo. Pres.'s Orgn. (bd. dirs. 1987—), Psi Upsilon, Phi Delta Phi. Clubs: Racquet, Chicago, Commonwealth, Economic, Commercial (Chgo.); Glen View (Ill.). Home: 1320 N State Pkwy Chicago IL 60610 Office: Goodman Equipment Corp 4834 S Halsted St Chicago IL 60609

CAMPBELL, CARLOS BOYD GODFREY, neurobiology educator, army officer; b. Chgo., July 27, 1934; s. Joseph Gattaz Bumzahem and Ruby Viola Brown Campbell; B.S., U. Ill., 1955, M.S., 1957, M.D., 1963, Ph.D., 1965; m. Deborah Ellen Stephens, June 28, 1958 (div. July 1971); m. 2d, Nydia Haydee Gonzalez, Feb. 3, 1979; children—Ellen, Gowan, Kenneth, Christopher; 1 stepdau., Zinnia. Surg. intern Presbyn.-St. Luke's Hosp., Chgo., 1963-64; resident in neurology U. So. Calif. Med. Center, Los Angeles, 1973-74; resident in radiology U. Va., Charlottesville, 1974-75, U. Calif., Irvine, 1975-77; commd. 2d lt. U.S. Army, 1962, advanced through grades to capt., 1967, reentered in 1979, commd. lt. col., 1979, advanced to col., 1984; neuroanatomist Walter Reed Army Inst. Research, Washington, 1964-67, research neurologist div. neuropsychiatry, 1979—; staff neurologist Walter Reed Gen. Hosp., 1983—; asst. prof. neural scis. Ind. U., 1967-70, asso. prof., 1970-74; asso. clin. prof. anatomy U. Calif., Irvine, 1975-77; adj. prof. anatomy Georgetown U., Washington, 1980—; vis. asso. in biology Calif. Inst. Tech., 1976-77; prof. anatomy, chmn. dept. anatomy U. P.R., Rio Piedras, 1977-79; research prof. neurology Uniformed Services U. Health Scis., 1983—; collaborator div. mammals Smithsonian Inst., 1966-67. Decorated Sovereign Order Knights of St. John of Jerusalem Knights of Malta; USPHS fellow, 1959-61; NIH grantee, 1968-72; NSF grantee, 1969-70. Mem. AAAS, Soc. Neurosci., Am. Assn. Anatomists, Am. Soc. Primatologists, Internat. Primatol. Soc. Cajal Club, Am. Soc. Zoologists, Assn. Mil. Surgeons U.S., Washington Soc. for History of Medicine, J.B. Johnston Club, Phi Rho Sigma. Episcopalian. Club: Mermaid Tavern. Home: 6003 McKinley St Bethesda MD 20817 Office: Walter Reed Army Inst Research Div Neuropsychiatry Washington DC 20307

CAMPBELL, CARROLL ASHMORE, JR., governor of South Carolina, former congressman; b. Greenville, S.C., July 24, 1940; s. Carroll Ashmore and Anne (Williams) C.; m. Iris Rhodes, Sept. 5, 1959; children: Carroll Ashmore, III, Richard Michael. Ed., McCallie Sch., U. S.C.; M.A., Am. U.; LL.D. (hon.), Central Wesleyan Coll.; Hum.D., Sherman Coll. Pres. Handy Park Co., 1960-78; mem. S.C. Ho. of Reps., 1970-74, S.C. Senate, 1976; exec. asst. to Gov. S.C., 1975; mem. 96th-99th Congresses from S.C. 4th Dist., 1979-87; gov. S.C., 1987—; mem. banking, fin. and urban affairs com., com. on House adminstrn., appropriations com., ways and means com., asst. regional whip, Tenn., S.C., Ga. and Fla. Del. Republican Conv., 1976, 80, 84; mem. Nat. Republican Congl. Com., Textile Caucus, S.C. Gov.'s Com. on Employment of Handicapped; mem. adv. council White House Conf. on Handicapped Individuals; chmn. March of Dimes; hon. chmn. Arthritis Found. Dr. Recipient Disting. Service award Jaycees; Citizenship award Woodmen of World; K.C. award; Rehab. Assn. Citizenship award; Guardian of Small Bus. award Nat. Fedn. Inst. Bus.; Disting. Service award Ams. for Constl. Action; Watchdog of Treasury award Nat. Associated Businessmen; Humanitarian Service award Rutledge Coll., Leadership award Am. Security Council; Spirit of Am. award Nat. Grocers Assn.; Order of Palmetto, Gov. S.C.; Outstanding Freshman award 96th Club, numerous others. Episcopalian. Clubs: Sertoma (Citizenship award), Chowder and Marching. Lodge: Masons. Office: Office of Gov PO Box 11450 Columbia SC 29211 *

CAMPBELL, CLIFTON PAUL, JR., vocational training educator; b. Johnstown, Pa., July 5, 1938; s. Clifton Paul and Kathleen Marie (Calhoun) C.; BS, Calif. State Coll., 1964; MEd, U. Md., 1968, EdD, 1971; postgrad. U. Md., U. Del., 1973-75; m. Linda Lee Reavis, Apr. 30, 1971; children—Scott Alan, Douglas Eric. Instr. James Madison High Sch., Vienna, Va., 1964-66; asst. prof., coordinator drafting and design U. Md., College Park and Far East div., 1966-73; coordinator undergrad. occupational tchr. edn. U. Del., Newark, 1973-75; dean instrn. Del. Tech. and Community Coll., Stanton, 1975-76; vocat. tng. adv. Ministry of Labor and Social Affairs, Riyadh, Saudi Arabia, 1976-78; adv., tng. and contract adminstrn. Royal Saudi Naval Forces, Dammam, Saudi Arabia, 1978-83; prof. technol. and adult edn. U. Tenn.-Knoxville, 1983—; v.p. DTA, Ltd., Wilmington, Del., 1983—; adviser West Lake Indsl. Vocat. Sch., Taipei, Taiwan, 1971-72, Kuwait Pub. Authority for Applied Edn. and Tng., 1985; mem. Tech. Assistance Corps, U.S. Dept. Labor, 1976—; cons. Va. Peninsula Vocat. & Tech. Schs., 1983-84, U.S. Mil. Tng. Mission, Saudi Arabia, 1983, 86, Chattanooga State Tech. Community Coll., 1984-87, Internat. Labor Orgn., Geneva and Turin, Italy, 1986-88; judge Vocat. Indsl. Clubs Am., 1983—, Health Occupational Students Am., Tenn., 1983—. Served to comdr. USNR, 1955—. Recipient Outstanding Research award, 1975, Cert. Appreciation, 1981 Am. Indsl. Arts Assn., Cert. Appreciation Ala. State Dept. Edn., 1985; grantee U. Md., 1968, NEH, 1971, Tenn. Div. Vocat. Edn., 1984, 85, TVA, 1986, 87. Mem. Am. Vocat. Assn. (speaker confs. 1979—, resolutions com. 1983—), Am. Soc. Tng. and Devel., Am. Council on Indsl. Arts Tchr. Edn. (chmn. plant and facility com. 1984), Nat. Assn. Indsl. and Tech. Tchr. Educators (chmn. auditing com. 1984-86), Nat. Assn. Trade and Indsl. Edn. (com. to recognize excellence 1984, bd. dirs. 1988), Res. Officers Assn., Naval Res. Assn., Fleet Res. Assn., Navy League U.S., Omicron Tau Theta, Iota Lambda Sigma, Epsilon Pi Tau (Laureate Citation 1988). Republican. Presbyterian. Clubs: Nat. Sojourners (Wilmington, Del.); Naval (London). Lodge: Masons, Shriners. Author: Job Performance Analysis for Educators and Trainers, 1976; A Digest on Instructional Systems Development, 1984, Job Analysis, 1985, (with Mary C. Muller) Non-Formal Vacational Training Programmes as a Means of Developing Occupational Skills, 1986, Task Performance Tests, 1987, Instructional Systems Development Methodology, 1987, Adapting Instructional Materials, 1988; also monographs; contbr. numerous articles on vocat. and tech. edn. to profl. jours.; researcher in field. Avocations: writing, travel. Home: 1420 Moorgate Dr Knoxville TN 37922 Office: U Tenn Technol and Adult Edn Dept Knoxville TN 37996 also: DTA Ltd 702 Severn Rd Wilmington DE 19803

CAMPBELL, COLIN HERALD, mayor, former management consultant; b. Winnipeg, Man., Can., Jan. 18, 1911; s. Colin Charles and Aimee Florence (Herald) C.; B.A., Reed Coll., 1933; m. Virginia Paris, July 20, 1935; children—Susanna Herald, Corinna Buford, Virginia Wallace. Exec. sec. City Club of Portland, 1934-39; alumni sec., dir. endowment adminstrn. Reed Coll., 1939-42, exec. sec. N.W. Inst. Internat. Relations. 1940-42, instr. photography, 1941-42; contract engr. Kaiser Co., Inc., 1942-45; asst. personnel dir. Portland Gas & Coke Co., 1945-48; dir. indsl. relations Pacific Power & Light Co., Portland, 1948-76. Mem. Oreg. Advisory Com. on Fair Employment Practices Act, 1949-55; trustee, chmn., pres. Portland Symphonic Choir, 1950-54; trustee Portland Civic Theater, 1951-54; bd. dirs. Portland Symphony Soc., 1957-60, Community Child Guidance Clinic, 1966-68; active United Way, 1945-75; bd. dirs. Contemporary Crafts Assn., 1972-76, treas., 1975-76; bd. dirs. Lake Oswego Corp., 1961-65, 71-73, 74-76, corporate sec., 1964, pres., 1973-74, treas., 1975-76; mem. com. on Citizen Involvement, City of Lake Oswego, 1975-77; chmn. Bicentennial Com., Lake Oswego; sec.-treas. Met. Area Communications Commn., 1980-85; treas. Clackamas County Community Action Agy., 1980-82, chmn., 1982-85; mem. fin. adv. com. W. Clackamas County LWV, 1974-76, 78-80; councilman City of Lake Oswego, 1977-78, mayor, 1979-85; chmn. energy adv. com. League Oreg. Cities, 1982-84. Mem. Edison Electric Inst. (exec. com.), NW Electric Light and Power Assn., Lake Oswego C. of C. (v.p. 1986-87), Portland Art Assn., Pacific NW Personnel Mgmt. Assn. (past regional v.p.), St. Andrews Soc., Oreg. Hist. Soc. Republican. Presbyterian. Lodge: Rotary. Home: 1219 Maple St Lake Oswego OR 97034

CAMPBELL, COLIN KYDD, electrical and computer engineering educator, researcher; b. St. Andrews, Fife, Scotland, May 3, 1927; s. David Walker and Jean (Hutchison) C.; m. Vivian Gwyn Norval, Apr. 17, 1954; children—Barry, Gwyn, Ian. B.Sc. in Engring. with honors, St. Andrews U., 1952; S.M., MIT, 1953; Ph.D., St. Andrews U., 1960; D.Sc., U. Dundee, 1984. Registered profl. engr., Ont. Communications engr. Fgn. Office and Diplomatic Wireless Service, London, Eng., 1946-47; communications engr. Brit. Embassy, Washington, 1947-48; electronics engr. Atomic Instrument Co., Cambridge, Mass., 1954-57; asst. prof. elec. and computer engring. McMaster U., Hamilton, Ont., Can., 1960-63, assoc. prof. elec. and computer engring., 1963-67, prof. elec. and computer engring., 1967—. Author: Surface Acoustic Wave Devices and Their Signal Processing Applications, 1989; contbr. numerous articles to profl. jours. Served with Brit. Army, 1944-46. Recipient The Inventor insignia Canadian Patents and Devel. Ltd., 1973; Mass. Golf Assn. scholar, 1952. Fellow Royal Soc. Can. (Thomas Eadie medal 1983), Engring. Inst. Can., Royal Soc. Arts London, IEEE; mem. Sigma Xi. Mem. Ch. of England. Club: Royal Canadian Mil. Inst. (Toronto). Home: 160 Parkview Dr, Ancaster, ON Canada L9G 1Z5 Office: McMaster U, Dept Elec and Computer Engring, 1280 Main St W, Hamilton, ON Canada L8S 4L7

CAMPBELL, DAVID GWYNNE, petroleum executive, geologist; b. Oklahoma City, May 2, 1930; s. Lois Raymond Henager and La Vada (Ray) Henager Campbell; B.S., Tulsa U., 1953; M.S., U. Okla., 1957; m. Janet Gay Newland, Mar. 1, 1958; 1 son, Carl David. Geologist, Lone Star Producing Co., Oklahoma City, 1957-65; dist. geologist and geol. cons. Mid-Continent div. Tenneco Oil Co., Oklahoma City, 1965-77; exploration mgr. Leede Exploration, Oklahoma City, 1977-80; pres. Earth Hawk Exploration, Oklahoma City, 1980—; div. exploration mgr. PetroCorp., Oklahoma City, 1983—. Active Last Frontier council Boys Scouts Am., 1960-73, chmn. edn. com. Eagle dist., 1963-67, asst. scoutmaster Wiley Post dist., 1971-73, Oklahoma County rep. to Cherokee Nation, 1976-78, YMCA., Okla. City. Served with USNR, 1948-53, U.S. Army, 1953-55. Recipient cert. of recognition Okla.-Kans. Oil and Gas Assn., 1982. Mem. Am. Petroleum Inst., Am. Assn. Petroleum Geologists (infor. com. 1968 nat. convention, field trip chmn. 1978 conv., Ho. of Dels. 1980-83, 83-86, del. at large, 1987—, nat. chmn. Ho. of Dels. 1981-82, exec. com. 1981-82, found. trustee assoc. 1983—, mem. adv. council 1984-87, councillor mid-continent sect. 1984-87, nominating com. 1984-85, 86-87, astrogeology com. 1984—, chmn. liason subcom. astrogeology com. 1984, honors and awards com. 1984-85, 1985-86, adv. bd. Treatise of Petroleum Geology 1986—, Nat. Membership Adv. council 1987—, membership com., chmn. mid-continent sect., 1987-90, public relations chmn. Speakers bur. 1963-64, chmn. stratigraphic code com. 1967-68, presdl. appointee 1969-70, advt. mgr. Shale Shaker 1969-71, rep. to AAPG Ho. of Dels. 1980-86, bylaws and incorp. rev. com. 1986), Ind. Petroleum Assn. Am., Okla. Ind. Petroleum Assn., Tulsa Geol. Soc., Oklahoma City Assn. Petroleum Landmen, Oklahoma City Geol. Discussion Group (pres. 1975-76), Oklahoma City Petroleum Club (bd. dirs. 1988-91), Internat. Assn. Energy Economists, Soc. Ind. Profl. Earth Scientists (pres. Okla. chpt. 1988), Soc. Profl. Well Log Analysts, AAAS, N.Y. Acad. Scis., U. Okla. Search Com., 1984—, U. Okla. Alumni Adv. Council, U.S. C. of C., Oklahoma City C. of C., Okla. Hist. Soc., Cherokee Nat. Hist. Soc. (chmn. solicitation com. of heritage council, mem. search com. 1987-88, devel. com. 1987—, bd. dirs. nat. soc. 1983—), Mus. of Cherokee Indian Assn., Thomas Gilcrease Mus. Assn., Okla. Aircraft Owners and Pilots Assn., Sigma Xi, Pi Kappa Alpha. Contbr. articles to Jour. Cherokee Studies. Home: 6109 Woodbridge Rd Oklahoma City OK 73132 Office: 210 W Park Ave First Okla Tower Suite 3131 Oklahoma City OK 73102

CAMPBELL, DOUGLASS, banker; b. N.Y.C., Aug. 31, 1919; s. William Lyman and Helene (Underwood) C.; m. Marion Danielson Strachan, Jan. 13, 1962; step-children: Richard and Stephen Strachan. A.B., Yale U., 1941. With N.Y. Central System, 1939-67, timekeeper, traveling car agt., asst. train master, train master, asst. supt. asst. to freight traffic mgr., asst. to pres., supt. exec. rep., 1939-58; v.p. N.Y.C. R.R. (and subs.), 1958-67; also in charge pub. relations and advt. dept. N.Y.C. R.R. (and subsidiaries), 1960-67; also dir. N.Y.C. R.R. (affiliates and subsidiaries), chmn. pres. Bowater Paper Co., Inc., 1967-68; pres. Argyle Research Corp. (consultants), N.Y.C., 1968-83; v.p. Hambro Am., Inc., 1983-85; sr. v.p. Resource Holdings Ltd., N.Y.C., 1986—. Served as maj. AUS, 1942-46. Episcopalian. Clubs: Down Town Assn., River, Yale (N.Y.C.); Chagrin Valley Hunt (Cleve.); Saturn (Buffalo); Chgo. Racquet (Chgo.). Home: 3 E 71st St New York NY 10021 Office: 10 E 53d St New York NY 10022

CAMPBELL, EDWARD ADOLPH, judge, electrical engineer; b. Boonville, Ind., Jan. 16, 1936; s. Revis Allen and Sarah Gertrude (Hunsaker) C.; m. Nancy Colleen Keys, July 26, 1957; children—Susan Elizabeth Campbell Frisse, Stephen Edward, Sara Lynne. B.S. in Elec. Engring., U. Evansville, 1959; J.D. Ind. U. Sch. Law, 1965; grad. Nat. Coll. Dist. Attys., U. Houston, 1972, Nat. Jud. Coll. U. Nev., 1978, Am. Acad. Jud. Edn., U. Va., 1979. Bar: Ind. 1965, U.S. Dist. Ct. (so. dist.) Ind. 1965, U.S. Ct. Customs and Patent Appeals 1967, U.S. Supreme Ct. 1973, U.S. Ct. Appeals (fed. cir.) 1982. Patent examiner U.S. Patent Office, Washington, 1959-60; patent adv. U.S. Naval Avionics, Indpls., 1960-65; patent atty. Gen. Elec. Co., Fort Wayne, Ind., 1965-66; ptnr. Weyerbacher & Campbell, attys., Boonville, Ind., 1966-71; pros. atty. 2nd Jud. Cir., Warrick County, Ind., 1971-77; judge Warrick Superior Ct., 1977—. Mem. Ind. State Bar Assn., Ind. Judges Assn., Nat. Council Juvenile and Family Ct. Judges, Ind. Council of Juvenile and Family Ct. Judges, Warrick County C. of C. (bd. dirs. 1978-84), Sigma Pi Sigma, Phi Delta Phi. Democrat. Methodist. Club: Rolling Hills Country (Newburgh, Ind.). Lodges: Lions, Kiwanis. Home: 911 Julian Dr Boonville IN 47601 Office: Warrick Superior Ct PO Box 428 Boonville IN 47601

CAMPBELL, EDWARD FRANCIS, consulting psychologist; b. Kalgoorlie, Western Australia, Jan. 7, 1908; s. E.M. and Ethel Beatrice (Fletcher) C.; B.A., Dip.Ed., U. Western Australia; B.Ed., U. Melbourne; m. Ruby R.J. Scarborough, Dec. 21, 1936; children—Stuart, Heather. Commd. lt. Australian Army, 1937, advanced through grades to brig., 1967; served S.W. Pacific, 1944-45; dir. psychology Army Hdqrs., 1946-67; ret., 1967; cons. psychologist, 1967—; tutor clin. practice U. Melbourne, 1947-58; cons. clin. psychology Dept. Repatriation, 1947-49, other commonwealth depts., 1957—; hon. psychologist Melbourne Hosp., 1947-67, Austin Hosp., 1967-70. Mem. Commonwealth Govt. Expert Group on rd. Safety, 1970-76; mem. adv. panel applied psychology U. New South Wales, 1958-68. Decorated officer Order Brit. Empire. Fellow Brit., Australian (chmn. membership com. 1973-83, 86-87) psychol. socs., Cairhmilla Inst. (hon.), Aus. Soc. (hon.); mem. Australian Coll. Edn. Clubs: Naval and Mil. Author: Morale, 1947; also articles. Address: 589A Nepean Hwy Carrum, Victoria 3197 Australia Office: 80 Park Rd, Middle Park 3206, Australia

CAMPBELL, F(ENTON) GREGORY, college administrator, historian; b. Columbia, Tenn., Dec. 16, 1939; s. Fenton G. and Ruth (Hayes) C.; m. Barbara D. Kuhn, Aug. 29, 1970; children: Fenton H., Matthew W., Charles H. AB, Baylor U., 1960; postgrad., Philipps U., Marburg/Lahn, Fed. Republic of Germany, 1960-61; MA, Emory U., 1962; postgrad., Charles U., Prague, Czechoslovakia, 1965-66; PhD, Yale U., 1967; postgrad. in ednl. mgmt., Harvard U., 1981. Research staff historian Yale U., New Haven, 1966-68, spl. asst. to acting pres., 1977-78; asst. prof. history U. Wis., Milw., 1968-69; asst. prof. European history U. Chgo., 1969-76, spl. asst. to pres., 1978-87, sec. bd. trustees, 1979-87, sr. lectr., 1985-87; pres., prof. history Carthage Coll., 1987—; fellow Woodrow Wilson Internat. Ctr. for Scholars, Smithsonian Instn., Washington, 1976-77; mem. East European selection com. Internat. Research and Exchanges Bd., 1975-78; rev. panelist NEH, 1983-84, 86; participant Japan Study Program for Internat. Execs., 1987; mem. Regional Council, Boy Scouts Am. Author: Confrontation in Central Europe, 1975; joint editor: Akten zur deutschen auswartigen Politik, 1918-1945, 1966—; contbr. articles and revs. to profl. jours. Bd. dirs. Prairie Sch., Racine, Wis. Fulbright grantee, 1960-61, 1973-74; Woodrow Wilson fellow, 1961-62, U.S.A.-Czechoslovakia exchange fellow, 1965-66, 73-74, 85. Mem. Am. Hist. Assn., Am. Assn. for Advancement Slavic Studies, Czechoslovak History Conf. (pres. 1980-82), Conf. Group on Cen. European History (sec.-treas. 1980-83), Chgo. Council on Fgn. Relations (com. on fgn. affairs 1979—, exec. com. 1984—), Phi Beta Kappa. Club: Mid-Day (Chgo.). Home: 623 17th Pl Kenosha WI 53140 Office: Carthage Coll Kenosha WI 53141

CAMPBELL, FRANCES HARVELL, member congressional staff; b. Goldston, N.C.; d. George Henry and Evelyn (Meggs) Harvell; m. John T. Campbell, Jr., Apr. 27, 1968 (div. Aug. 1973). BS magna cum laude, U. Md., 1982. Asst. to Congressman Claude Pepper, U.S. Ho. of Reps., 1968-80, staff dir., 1980—; exec. dir., curator Mildred and Claude Pepper Library; 1st v.p. Pepper Found. Author: Young America Speaks, 1957. V.p. Dem. Women of Capitol Hill, 1982-83. Mem. Nat. Assn. Female Execs., Women in Govt. Relations, Adminstrv. Assts. Assn. Capitol Hill, Nat. Dem. Club, Internat. Platform Assn., Fla. State Soc. (bd. dirs. 1982—), Phi Kappa Phi, Alpha Sigma Lambda. Avocations: orchid culture, gourmet food preparation, gardening. Home: 6222 Hardy Dr McLean VA 22101 Office: 2239 Rayburn House Office Bldg Washington DC 20515

CAMPBELL, JAMES FROMHART, coal company executive, former ambassador; b. Lonacoming, Md., May 14, 1912; s. George Dowery and and Eleanor Stirling (Jones) C.; m. Mary Frances Cotton, Sept. 14, 1946; children—Mary Eleanor, James Russell, Margaret Ann. B.A., St. John's Coll., Annapolis, Md., 1932; postgrad. law studies, George Washington U., 1933-34; grad., Naval War Coll., Newport, R.I., 1946. Mem. sales devel. staff Griffith Consumers Co., Washington, 1934-35; mktg. and mgmt. tng. positions Esso Standard Oil Co., Washington, 1935-42; mktg. and mgmt. tng. coordinator Esso Tng. Center, N.Y.C., 1946-49; dir., sales mgr. Esso Standard Oil Co., San Juan, P.R., 1949-52, pres., dir., 1954-55; asst. regional mgr. Central Am. Esso Standard Oil Co., Panama City, Panama, 1952-53; asst. regional mgr. Caribbean area Esso Standard of South Am., Ciudad Trujillo, Dominican Republic, 1953-54; regional mgr. Esso Standard of South Am., Havana, Cuba, 1955-57; v.p., dir., mgr. Esso Standard Chile, Santiago, 1958-63; chmn. bd., mng. dir. Esso Standard South Africa, Johannesburg, 1963-70; vice chmn., dir. Triomf Fertilizer and Chem. Co., 1963-70; resident dir. Esso Exploration and Prodn. Co., South Africa, 1963-70; cons. Esso Africa, Inc., London, 1970-71; dep. asst. adminstr. for adminstrn. AID, Washington, 1971; asst. adminstr. for program and mgmt. services adminstrn. AID, 1971-74; ambassador to Republic of El Salvador, 1974-76; pres., dir. Campbell Coal Co., Cumberland, Md., 1976—; Pres. Am. Soc., Santiago, 1960-61, Johannesburg, 1966-67; pres. Am. Men's Luncheon Club, Johannesburg, 1965-66; bd. dirs. Am. C. of C., Santiago, 1961-63, Johannesburg, 1965-70; bd. dirs. Rehoboth Beach (Del.) Art League; mem. Ctr. for Arts, Vero Beach, Council Am. Ambassadors, Republican Presdl. Task Force. Served to lt. comdr. USN, 1942-46, MTO, PTO. Decorated Order José Matías Delgado, Order José Govt. El Salvador; recipient medallion Internat. House, New Orleans, 1975. Republican. Episcopalian. Clubs: Columbia Country (Chevy Chase, Md.); Rehoboth Beach Country (Rehoboth Beach), Henlopen Acres Beach (Rehoboth Beach); John's Island (Vero Beach, Fla.). Home: 500 Beach Rd Apt 105 John's Island Vero Beach FL 32963 also: 80 Oak Ave Rehoboth Beach DE 18971

CAMPBELL, JOHN ALEXANDER, management consultant; b. Stocksbridge, Yorkshire, England, Jan. 15, 1927; arrived N.Z., 1963; s. Alexander and Elsie Mayborne (Jackson) C.; m. Mollie Beecroft, July 23, 1955; children—Roderic, Fiona, Margaret. B.Sc. in Metallurgy, Sheffield U., Eng., 1952; Metallurgist, Firth-Vickers, Sheffield, Eng., 1952-57, prodn. mgr., 1957-60; mgmt. cons. Assoc. Indsl. Consultants, London, 1960-63, Auckland, N.Z., 1963-65, sr. cons., 1965-67; div. mgr. Alex Harvey Industries, Auckland, N.Z., 1967-74; chief exec. officer East Coast Fertiliser Co. Ltd., Napier, N.Z., 1974-85; prin. mgmt. cons. John Campbell & Assocs., 1985—; dir. NZ Phosphate Co. Ltd., Ammo-Phos NZ Ltd., N.Z. Fertiliser Mfrs., Internat. Fertilizer Assn., Paris (mem. council). Contbr. articles to profl. jours. Chmn., Epsom Community Com., Auckland, N.Z., 1973-74. Served with Royal Navy, 1946-49. Fellow N.Z. Inst. Mgmt. Cons.; mem. Inst. Mgmt., Sheffield Metallurgist Assn., Napier C. of C. (pres. 1983-85), Wellington Region Employers Assn. (v.p. 1983-84, pres. 1984-85). Methodist. Club: Hawke's Bay. Home and Office: Cranfield RD 5, Hastings, Hawke's Bay New Zealand

CAMPBELL, JOHN TIMOTHY, oil co. exec., lawyer, petroleum and indsl. cons.; b. Lake Charles, La., July 8, 1945; s. Aubrey Dorriss and Helen Teresa (Wilson) C.; m. Pamela A. Johnston, Apr. 18, 1987. B.A. in Econs., B.A. in Polit. Sci., Principia Coll., 1967; J.D., So. Meth. U., 1970. Bar: Tex. 1970. Landman, Amoco Prodn. Co., Houston, 1970; internat. negotiator Amoco Internat. Oil Co., Chgo., 1971; v.p. Amoco Tunisia Oil Co., 1972; pres. Campbell Energy Corp., Santa Barbara, Calif. and Dallas, 1975—; chmn. Alaska Pacific Refining Anchorage, Alaska, 1986—. Mem. ABA (Silver Key Award law student div. 1970), Am. Soc. Internat. Law, Inter-Am. Bar Assn., State Bar Tex., Phi Alpha Delta. Republican. Christian Scientist. Club: Birnam Wood Golf (Montecito, Calif.).

CAMPBELL, JONATHAN WESLEY, physicist, aerospace engineer; b. Alexander City, Ala., Sept. 1, 1950; s. Harry Underwood and Sarah Ruth Campbell; m. Mary Magdalene Sanders, Dec. 11, 1974; 1 son, Jason Jonathan. B.S. distinguished grad., Auburn U., 1972, M.S., 1974; M.S., U. Ala., 1980. Cert. filght instr. Coop. engr. Pratt & Whitney Aircraft, West Palm Beach, Fla., 1968-70; instr. physics Auburn U., 1972-74; physicist, aerospace engr. Missile Intelligence Agy., Huntsville, Ala., 1978-80; physicist, supervisory aerospace engr. propulsion, exec. asst. to dir., lead engr. space telescope fine guidance sensor NASA/Marshall Space Flight Ctr., Huntsville, Ala., 1980—; cons. Starflight Assocs. Served to capt. AUS, 1975-78. Recipient Eagle Scout award. Mem. AIAA, Air Force Assn., Res. Officer Assn., Aircraft Owners and Pilots Assn., Scabbard and Blade, Tau Beta Pi, Sigma Gamma Tau, Sigma Pi Sigma. Methodist. Home: PO Box 37 Harvest AL 35749 Office: E51 NASA Marshall Space Flight Ctr Huntsville AL 35812

CAMPBELL, LUCY BARNES, librarian; b. Windsor, N.C., Oct. 30; d. Eley and Frankie Elizabeth (Carter) Barnes; B.A., N.C. Central U., 1941, B.L.S., 1942, M.L.S., 1960; m. Alfonso L. Campbell, Sr., May 4, 1946; children—Alfonso L., Sharon I. Librarian, Darden High Sch., Wilson, N.C., 1942-45; asst. librarian Ala. State U., Montgomery, 1945-63; circulation librarian Hampton Inst., Huntington Library, Hampton, Va., 1963, acting dir., coordinator student activities, 1964, asst. reference librarian, 1964-65, asst. prof./head periodicals dept., 1966-84, coordinator residence hall reading rooms, 1967-73; participant Inst. Black Studies Librarianship, Fisk U., summer 1970. Solicitor, United Negro Coll. Fund, 1964-70, Hampton Inst. Peninsula Ann. Fund Campaign, 1972-78. Recipient citation for service and leadership Ala. State U., 1962; cert. of merit Women's Senate, 1965, named Mother of Yr., 1965, Mother of Men of Hampton, 1968 (all Hampton Inst.). Mem. ALA, Assn. Coll. and Research Libraries, Southeastern, Va. library assns., Assn. Study of Afro-Am. Life and History, YWCA, Black Caucus, NAACP (life), Alpha Kappa Alpha (life). Baptist. Club: Women's Service League. Lodge: Order Eastern Star. Author: Black Librarians in Virginia, 1976; The Story of the Hampton Institute Library School, 1925-39, 1976.

CAMPBELL, PETER NELSON, biochemist; b. Dartford, England, Nov. 5, 1921; s. Alan and Nora Campbell; m. Mollie Winifred Manklow, Jan. 3, 1946; children: Alastair, Julia. BSc, U. London, 1943, PhD, 1949, DSc, 1960. Production chemist Standard Telephones and Cables, London, 1942-46; asst. lectr. Univ. Coll. London, 1947-49; mem. staff Nat. Inst. for Med. Research, Hampstead and Mill Hill, 1949-54; with Courtauld Inst. Biochemistry Middlesex Hosp. Med. Sch., 1954-57, sr. lectr., 1957-64; reader in biochemistry U. of London, 1964-67; prof., biochemistry dept. head Leeds U., Eng., 1967-75. Author: Biochemistry Illustrated; editor-in-chief, Biotechnology and Applied Biochemistry. Fellow, Inst. Biology, U. Coll. London; mem., Biochem. Soc., Fed. European Biochem. Socs. (diplome d'honneur), Assn. Researchers in Medicine and Sci. (chmn.), Biological Council (trustee). Home: 1 Hillside Gardens, Highgate, London N65 SU, England Office: Univ Coll London, Dept Biochemistry, Gower St, London WC1E 6BT, England

CAMPBELL, REGINALD LAWRENCE, industrial hygienist, educator; b. Hartford, Conn., Apr. 8, 1943; s. Reginald L. and Etta M. (Ashton) C.; student Amherst Coll., 1961, Yale U. Sch. Medicine, 1965-67; Asso. Sci., Hahnemann Med. Coll., 1975; B.A., Fairmont State Coll., 1977; M.S., Marshall U., 1980. Propr., dir. Campbell Clin. Lab., Amherst, Mass., 1963-65; staff therapist St. Joseph's Hosp., Stamford, Conn., 1966-67; staff therapist Yale-New Haven Hosp., 1967-70; asst. research cardiothoracic surgery Yale U. Sch. Medicine, 1967-70; guest lectr. Royal Melbourne (Australia) Hosp., Monash U., 1968, Royal North Shore Hosp., U. Sydney (Australia), 1968; chief anesthetic technologist Montreal (Que.) Gen. Hosp., McGill U. Sch. Medicine, 1970; tech. dir. sect. respiratory disease services Danbury (Conn.) Hosp., 1970-72; dir. respiratory program adj. faculty Western Conn. State Coll., Danbury, 1970-72; sr. instr. medicine Sch. Respiratory Therapy, Hahnemann Med. Coll., Phila., 1972-75, asst. prof. dept. medicine Coll. Allied Health Professions, 1974-75; adminstr. So. W.Va. Lung Center, Inc., Beckley, 1975-77; cons. respiratory therapy program Fairmont (W.Va.) State Coll., 1975-76, Bluefield (W.Va.) State Coll., 1975-76; tech. cons. W.Va. Gov.'s Coal Worker's Respiratory Disease Control Program, 1975-78; indsl. hygienist Nat. Mine Health and Safety Acad., U.S. Dept. Interior, Beckley, W.Va., 1978-79; instr. occupational lung diseases and occupational health Nat. Mine Health and Safety Acad., U.S. Dept. Labor, Beckley, 1979-87; indsl. hygienist dept. def. Preventive Medicine Meddac, Ft. Huachuca, Ariz., 1987—; guest lectr. mil. history and firearms various mil. instns., 1965-69. Squadron comdr. CAP, Beckley, 1978-80, Lewisburg, 1980-83, wing staff, 1983—; mem. Pa. Gov.'s Task Force on Black Lung, 1974-75. Mem. Am. Public Health Assn., Am. Assn. Indsl. Hygiene, Am. Assn. Safety Engrs., Am. Assn. for Respiratory Therapy, Can. Soc. Respiratory Technologists, Am. Thoracic Soc. (asso. mem.), W.Va. Soc. Respiratory Therapy, Mil. Hist. Soc. S. Africa, Mil. Hist. Soc. Australia, Wheelchair Pilots Assn., Kappa Delta Pi, Yale Sch. Respiratory Therapy Alumni Assn. (pres. 1966-71). Democrat. Presbyterian. Clubs: Lions, Masons, Ruritan. Contbr. articles to profl. publs. Home: 553 Suffolk Dr Sierra Vista AZ 85635 Office: Preventive Medicine MEDDAC Fort Huachuca AZ 85613

CAMPBELL, ROBERT CHARLES, clergyman, religious organization administrator; b. Chandler, Ariz., Mar. 9, 1924; s. Alexander Joshua and Florence (Betzner) C.; m. Lotus Idamae Graham, July 12, 1945; children: Robin Carl, Cherry Colleen. A.B., Westmont Coll., 1944; B.D., Eastern Baptist Theol. Sem., 1947, Th.M., 1949, Th.D., 1951, D.D., 1974; M.A., U. So. Calif., 1959; postgrad., Dropsie U., 1949-51, U. Pa., 1951-52, N.Y. U., 1960-62, U. Cambridge, Eng., 1969; D.Lit., Calif. Bapt. Theol. Sem., 1972; Hum.D., Alderson-Broaddus Coll., 1979; L.H.D., Linfield Coll., 1982; L.L.D., Franklin Coll., 1986. Ordained to ministry Am. Bapt. Ch., 1947; pastor 34th St. Bapt. Ch., Phila., 1945-49; instr. Eastern Bapt. Theol. Sem., Phila., 1949-51; asst. prof. Eastern Coll., St. Davids, Pa., 1951-53; assoc. prof. N.T. Am. Bapt. Sem. of West, Covina, Cal., 1953-54, dean, prof., 1954-72; gen. sec. Am. Bapt. Chs. in U.S.A., Valley Forge, Pa., 1972-87; pres. Eastern Bapt. Theol. Sem., Phila., 1987—; Vis. lectr. Sch. Theology at Claremont, Calif., 1961-63, U. Redlands, Calif., 1959-60, 66-67; Bd. mgrs. Am. Bapt. Bd. of Edn. and Publ., 1956-59, 65-69; v.p. So. Calif. Bapt. Conv., 1967-68; pres. Am. Bapt. Chs. of Pacific S.W., 1970-71; Pres. N.Am. Bapt. Fellowship, 1974-76; mem. exec. com. Bapt. World Alliance, 1972—, v.p., 1975-80; mem. exec. com., gov. bd. Nat. Council Chs. of Christ in U.S.A., 1972-87; del. to World Council of Chs., 1975, 83, mem. central com., 1975—. Author: Great Words of the Faith, 1965, The Gospel of Paul, 1973, Evangelistic Emphases in Ephesians, Jesus Still Has Something To Say, 1987. Home: 970 Sproul Rd Bryn Mawr PA 19010 Office: Ea Bapt Theol Sem Lancaster and City Aves Philadelphia PA 19151

CAMPBELL, ROBERT DALE, geographer, educator; b. Omaha, Dec. 2, 1914; s. Robert Ward and Emma Mary Augusta (Klempnauer) C.; m. Ann Elizabeth Abel, Sept. 4, 1941; 1 child, Robert William Duncan. BA, U. Colo., 1938, MA, 1940; PhD, Clark U., 1949. Prof. geography, chmn. dept. geography George Washington U., Washington, 1947-66; Fulbright lectr. Alexandria (Egypt) U., 1952-53; prin. investigator hist. records project George Washington U.-C.E., U.S. Army, Washington, 1953-57; Fulbright lectr. U. Peshawer, Pakistan, 1957-58; prin. investigator Q.M.C. Intelligence Research Project, 1958-60, Outdoor Recreation Resources Rev. Commn., Shoreline and Beach Recreation Resources Study, 1960, Urban Planning Data Systems Project, Md. Nat. Capital Park and Planning Commission, 1961; pres. AREA, Inc., Arlington, Va.; v.p. Matrix Corp., Arlington, 1966-70; prof. geography U. N.Mex., Albuquerque, 1970-80, prof. emeritus, 1980—; lectr. Conf. Am. Studies Oxford (Eng.) U., 1955; chmn. theory group Army Logistics Research Project, 1955-56; cons. Office Q.M. Gen., 1947-49, George Washington U.-Office Naval Research Logistics Research Project, 1949-51, Spl. Ops. Research Office of Am. U., Washington, 1959-62, Arctic Inst., 1960-61; regional planning cons. Ford Found.; mem. adv. planning group Calcutta (India) Met. Planning Orgn., 1964-65; mem. adv. bd. Internat. Orgn. for Human Ecology, Vienna, Austria, 1986—. Author: Pakistan, Emerging Democracy, 1963, (with Fisher and Miller) A Question of Place, 1967; also articles and papers. Served with USNR, 1943-46. Mem. Phi Beta Kappa, Sigma Xi, Pi Gamma Mu, Kappa Delta Pi. Office: Dept Geography U New Mexico Albuquerque NM 87131

CAMPBELL, ROBERT HEDGCOCK, brokerage executive, lawyer; b. Ann Arbor, Mich., Jan. 16, 1948; s. Robert Miller and Ruth Adele (Hedgcock) C.; m. Katherine Dean Kettering, June 17, 1972; children—Mollie DuPlan, Katherine Elizabeth, Anne Kettering. B.A., U. Wash., 1970, J.D., 1973. Bar: Wash. 1973, U.S. Dist. Ct. (we. dist.) Wash. 1973, U.S. Ct. Appeals (9th cir.) 1981. Assoc., Roberts & Shefelman, Seattle, 1973-79, ptnr., 1979-85; sr. v.p. Shearson Lehman Hutton Inc., 1985-87, mng. dir., 1987—. Author: The Deficit Reduction Act of 1984 and Other Recent Developments Affecting Municipal Borrowing, 1984; also articles in profl. jours. Mem. financing com. U. Wash. Swim Team, 1982—; trustee Wash. Phikeia Found., 1983—; nation chief YMCA Indian Princesses, Bellevue, Wash., 1983—. Mem. Fed. Energy Bar Assn., Seattle-King County Bar Assn. (chmn. com. 1974-75), Wash. State Soc. Hosp. Attys. (pres. 1982-84), Northwest Small Hydroelectric Assn. (dir. 1980-85), Nat. Assn. Bond Lawyers (vice chmn. com. 1981-82, treas. 1982-84, bd. dirs. 1982-85), ABA (vice chmn. com. 1981-82), Phi Delta Theta. Republican. Clubs: Seattle Tennis (membership com.), Bellevue Athletic, Columbia Tower (Wash.). Home: 8604 NE 10th St Bellevue WA 98004 Office: Shearson Lehman Hutton Inc 999 3d Ave Suite 4000 Seattle WA 98104

CAMPBELL, ROBERT W., transportation executive; b. Valentine, Nebr., Oct. 22, 1922; s. Harry Lee and Margaret (Haley) C. Grad., Creighton U., 1948, grad. in law, 1950. Chmn. Can. Pacific Enterprises, Calgary, Alta., Can. Pacific Ltd., Calgary, 1986—; bd. dirs. Algoma Steel Corp. Ltd., AMCA Internat. Ltd., Can. Pacific Ltd., Can. Pacific Enterprises Ltd., Great Lakes Forest Products Ltd., Westinghouse Electronic Corp., Royal Bank Can., Pan Can. Petroleum Ltd. (also chmn.), Westinghouse Electric Corp. Served to capt. U.S. Army, World War II. Roman Catholic. Office: Can Pacific Enterprises, 125 9th Ave SE Suite 2300, Calgary, AB Canada T2G 0P6 also: Can Pacific Ltd, PO Box 6042, Station A, Montreal, PQ Canada H3C 3E4 *

CAMPBELL, RUTH, psychologist; b. Sheffield, Yorkshire, Eng., June 10, 1944; d. Hugo and Balbina (Lurié) Droller; m. Kenneth George; children: Sarah Ruth, Esther May. BA, U. Reading, 1970; PhD, U. London, 1979; MA (hon.), Oxford (Eng.) U., 1985. Research assoc. Birkbeck Coll., London, 1977-79; lectr. psychology U. Reading, 1979-80; traveling fellow Med. Research Council, Toronto, Ont., Can., 1980-81; research fellow Univ. Coll. Med. Research Council, London, 1981-85; lectr., fellow Oxford U., 1985—. Author: Hearing by Eye, 1987; contbr. articles to profl. jours. Grantee Tragaskis Found., London, 1986, Econ. and Social Sci. Research Council, 1986-87. Mem. European Soc. Cognitive Sci., Internat. Neurol. Soc., Exptl. Psychology Soc. (com. 1986-88). Office: Oxford U Exptl Psychology Dept, South Parks Rd, Oxford OX1 3VD, England

CAMPBELL, SALLY WORTHINGTON, publication and information officer; b. Pitts., Jan. 3, 1947; d. Aubrey Walter and Marie Ruth (Henningsen) Worthington; BA in Journalism, Auburn U., 1968; m. John Jette Campbell, Aug. 31, 1968; children—Ashley, Heather, John Jette, Jr. Reporter-intern Montgomery, Ala. Jour., 1968; asst. editor Auburn (Ala.) Extension Service, 1968-69; tchr. lang. arts Nichols Jr. High Sch., Tuskegee, Ala., 1969-70; editor Where Mag., Houston, 1971-79, southwestern editorial supr., 1979; dir. public relations Austin (Tex.) Civic Ballet, 1980-82, v.p. Ballet Austin, 1983-84, also bd. dirs.; publs. and info. officer St. Edward's U., Austin,

1987—; cons. public relations Retinitis Pigmentosa Found., Houston, 1979. Vice pres. Austin Jr. Forum, 1980-82; mem. Laguna Gloria Mus. Women's Art Guild, 1980—; writer for KTBC-TV 1st place award Region II public service announcement competition, Tex. Broadcasters Assn., 1981, Leadership Austin, 1983-84. Mem. Women in Communications, Alpha Omicron Pi. Republican. Presbyterian. Home: 6103 End of the Trail Austin TX 78734 Office: 3001 S Congress Ave Austin TX 78704

CAMPBELL, SHEPHERD SAUNDERS, magazine editor; b. N.Y.C., Oct. 20, 1931; s. Morgan Seaman and Cornelia Elizabeth (Shepherd) C.; m. Jennifer Anne Sherriff, May 26, 1962; children—Catherine Suzanne, Victoria Sarah, Malcolm Samuel. B.A., Oberlin Coll., 1954; M.S. in Journalism, Columbia U., 1955. Staff reporter Wall Street Jour., N.Y.C., 1955-58; staff writer AP, N.Y.C., 1958-60; assoc. editor USA 1 Mag., N.Y.C., 1960-62, Newsweek, N.Y.C., 1962-68; editor Newsweek Feature Service, N.Y.C., 1968-73, Tennis Mag., Trumbull, Conn., 1973-86, So. Travel, Trumbull, 1986—; v.p. Golf Digest, Tennis Inc., Trumbull, 1979—; broadcaster Tennis Spot, CBS Radio, 1973-86; commentator U.S. Open and Wimbledon, 1979-82. Author: The CBS Tennis Spot, 1981; editor: Tennis: How to Play, How to Win, 1978, Instant Tennis Lessons, 1978, Tennis Strokes and Strategies, 1975. Mem. Am. Soc. Mag. Editors, Am. Assn. Travel Editors. Clubs: Silver Spring (Ridgefield, Conn.); St. George's Hill (Weybridge, Eng.). Home: 124 Spectacle Ln Ridgefield CT 06877

CAMPBELL, VERNON DEENE, wire products company executive; b. Ft. Smith, Ark., June 24, 1944; s. Johnnie Vernon and Effie Tabitha (Dean) C.; m. Susan Kay Griffin, June 14, 1964; children—Eric Dean, Aaron David, Sean Allen. Student U. Ark., 1962-63; degree in advanced electricity O.T. Autry Vocat.-Tech. Sch., Enid, Okla., 1966; degree in emergency med. tech. Ark. Valley Vocat.-Tech. Sch., Ozark, Ark., 1982. Ordained to ministry Assemblies of God Ch., 1971. Technician, Okla. Gas & Electric Co., Enid, 1963-68, Serv-Air Inc., Vance AFB, Enid, 1968-69; mgr. die cast div. Gen. Electric Co., Ft. Smith, Ark., 1969; plant engr. Spalding Inc., Ft. Smith, 1970-75; plant engr. So. Steel & Wire Co., Ft. Smith, 1975-82, plant mgr., 1982—; pastor Assembly of God Ch., Van Buren, Ark., 1977—; owner, operator Barling Vol. Rescue Service, 1986—. Mem. pretreatment com. City of Ft. Smith; mem. adv. trustee bd. Sparks Regional Med. Ctr.; chmn. bd. dirs. Sebastian County chpt. ARC, 1979—, dist. chmn., 1976—; instr. first aid and CPR, ARC, 1972—, instr., trainer CPR, 1985—. Recipient gold medal award Nat. Sports Found., 1974; Outstanding Service award Polk County chpt. ARC, 1980, Sebastian County chpt., 1980; Clara Barton Honor award ARC, 1984, Loaned Exec. of 1986 award United Way, Ft. Smith, Ark. Govs.' award for excellency in volunteerism, 1988; perpetual outstanding service award established in his name by United Way Ft. Smith, 1986 . Mem. Ark. Fedn. Water and Air Users (bd. dirs., mem. hazardous waste mgmt. task force), West Ark. Pilots Assn. Republican. Home: PO Box 384 1108 22d St Barling AR 72923 Office: PO Box 6537 3501 S Tulsa St Fort Smith AR 72906

CAMPBELL, WALLACE JUSTIN, aid organization executive, economist; b. Three Forks, Mont., Jan. 25, 1910; s. Alvin Douglas and Julia Etta (MacDonald) C.; m. Helen Marie Gordon, Apr. 11, 1936; children—Bruce Gordon, Gale Ellen Campbell Martin. B.S., U. Oreg., 1932, M.S., 1934. Asst. sec. Coop. League U.S.A., N.Y.C., 1934-48, dir. Washington office, 1948-60; dir. public affairs, asst. to pres. and v.p. Nationwide Ins., Columbus, Ohio, 1960-64; pres. Found. for Coop. Housing, Washington, 1964-75; founder CARE, U.S.A., 1945, pres., 1978-86; chmn. CARE Internat., 1987—; cons. D.C. Nat. Bank, 1976-80; permanent rep. Internat. Coop. Alliance to Econ. and Social Council of UN, 1976-88; pres. Internat. Coop. Housing Devel. Assn., Washington, London, 1966-80; dir. Nat. Bur. Econ. Research, N.Y.C., 1956-78; treas., pres., chmn. Internat. Devel. Conf., Washington, 1952-78; mem. Nat. Commn. for UNESCO, 1955-58; adj. prof. Am. U., 1975; mem. Commn. on Internat. Econ. and Security Assistance, 1983-84; founder, vice chmn. Citizens Network for Fgn. Affairs. Author: (with J. Voorhis) The Morale of Democracy, 1946; Editor Coop. News Service, 1934-42, Consumer Cooperation, 1934-40. Recipient Presdl. End Hunger award, 1983, Internat. Humanitarian award MEDICO, 1984, Medal of City of Paris, 1986, Comdrs. Cross of Order Merit, Fed. Republic Germany, 1986; named Alumni of Yr., U. Oreg., 1980. Mem. Nat. Coop. Bus. Assn. (dir.). Democrat. Congregationalist. Home: 560 N St SW Washington DC 20024 Office: Suite 666 777 14 St NW Washington DC 20005

CAMPBELL, WILBUR HAROLD, research plant biochemist, educator; b. Santa Ana, Calif., Apr. 23, 1945; s. Russell Carton and Vivian (Yates) C.; m. Ellen Roth, June 6, 1981. AA, Santa Ana Coll., 1965; BA, Pomona Coll., 1967; PhD, U. Wis., 1972. Postdoctoral U. Ga., Athens, 1972-73, Mayo Clinic, Rochester, Minn., 1973-74, Mich. State U., East Lansing, 1974-75; asst. prof. Coll. Environ. Sci. and Forestry. SUNY, Syracuse, 1975-80, assoc. prof., 1980-85; assoc. prof. Mich. Technol. U., Houghton, 1985-86, prof., 1986—. Mem. editorial bd. Plant Physiology, 1982-88. Contbr. numerous articles to profl. jours. Guest prof. Botanisches Inst., U. Bayreuth, Fed. Republic Germany, 1982. Mem. Am. Chem. Soc., Am. Soc. of Plant Physiologists, AAAS, Am. Soc. Agronomy/Crop Sci. Soc. Am., Japanese Soc. Plant Physiologists, Plant Growth Regulator Soc. Am., N.Y. Acad. Sci., Internat. Soc. for Plant Molecular Biology, Scandinavian Soc. Plant Physiology, France Soc. Vegetable Physiology, Sigma Xi. Home: 334 Hecla St Lake Linden MI 49945

CAMPBELL, WILLIAM J., judge; b. Chgo., Mar. 19, 1905; s. John and Christina (Larsen) C.; m. Marie Agnes Cloherty, 1937; children—Marie Agnes (Mrs. Walter J. Cummings), Karen Christina (Mrs. James T. Reid), Heather Therese (Mrs. Patrick Henry), Patti Ann (Mrs. Peter V. Fazio, Jr.), Roxane (Mrs. Wesley Sedlacek), William J., Christian Larsen, Thomas John. J.D., Loyola U., 1926, LL.M., 1928, LL.D., 1955; LL.D., Lincoln Coll., 1960; Litt.D., Duchesne Coll., 1965; J.C.D., Barat Coll., 1966. Bar: Ill. 1927. Partner Campbell and Burns, Chgo., 1927-40; Ill. adminstr. Nat. Youth Adminstrn., 1935-39; U.S. dist atty. No. Dist. Ill., 1938-40; judge U.S. Dist. Ct., 1940—; chief judge No. Dist. Ill., 1959-70; Mem. Jud. Conf. U.S., 1958-62; chmn. Jud. Conf. Commn. Budget, 1960-70; asst. dir., chmn. seminars Fed. Jud. Center, 1971—. Mem. nat. exec. bd. Boy Scouts Am., 1934—, mem. regional exec. com., 1937—; mem. exec. bd. Chgo. council, 1930—; Trustee Barat Coll., Lake Forest, Ill.; mem. citizens bd. U. Chgo., Loyola U., Chgo.; bd. dirs. Catholic Charities Chgo. Recipient award of merit Citizens of Greater Chgo., 1966; named Chicagoan of Year, 1965; Lincoln laureate in law State of Ill., 1970; Devitt Disting. Service to Justice award, 1986. Clubs: Ill. Athletic (Chgo.), Union League (Chgo.), Standard (Chgo.), Mid-America (Chgo.); La Coquille (Palm Beach, Fla.). Home: 400 S Ocean Blvd Manalapan FL 33462 Office: US Dist Ct 401 Fed Bldg 701 Clematis St West Palm Beach FL 33401

CAMPBELL, WILLIAM STEEN, magazine publisher; b. New Cumberland, W.Va., June 27, 1919; s. Robert N. and Ethel (Steen) C.; m. Rosemary J. Bingham, Apr. 21, 1945; children: Diana J., Sarah A., Paul C., John W. Grad., Steubenville (Ohio) Bus. Coll., 1938. Cost accountant Hancock Mfg. Co., New Cumberland, 1938-39; cashier, statistician Weirton Steel Co., W.Va., 1939-42; travel exec. Am. Express Co., N.Y.C., 1946-47; adminstr., account exec. Good Housekeeping mag., 1947-55; pub. Cosmopolitan mag., 1955-57; asst. dir. circulation Hearst Mags., N.Y.C., 1957-61; gen. mgr. Motor Boating mag., 1961-62; v.p., dir. circulation Hearst Mags., 1962-85; pres. Internat. Circulation Distbrs., 1978-81, Mags., Meetings, Messages, Ltd., 1986—; with Periodical Pubs. Service Bur. subs. Hearst Corp., Sandusky, Ohio, 1964-85, pres. Periodical Pubs. Service Bur., 1970-85; dir. Audit Bur. Circulations, Periodical Pubs. Service Bur., 1974-86, Nat. Mag. Co., Ltd., London, Randolph Jamaica Ltd., Omega Pub. Corp. Fla., Hearst Can. Ltd., 1964-86; former chmn. Central Registry, Mag. Pubs. Assn.; Chmn. bd. trustees Hearst Employees Retirement Plan, 1971-85; mem. president's council Brandeis U., 1974—; chmn. nat. corp. and found. com. U. Miami, 1979-85; dir. Broadway Assn., 1985—, v.p. 1988—. Served to lt. col. USAF, 1942-46, ETO. Recipient Lee C. Williams award Mag. Fulfillment Mgrs. Assn.; Torch of Liberty award Anti-Defamation League, 1979. Lodge: Masons. Office: Mags Meetings Messages Ltd 240 Central Park S New York NY 10019

CAMPBELL BROWN, BEATRICE MARY, physician, researcher; b. Newcastle upon Tyne, Eng., Jan. 21, 1934; d. John and Lizzie Gillespie (Davison) Catto; m. Robert Colin Campbell Brown, May 2, 1959; children—Donald Colin, Catriona Mary, Brenda Elizabeth. M.B., Ch.B., U. St. Andrews, Scotland, 1958. Intern, Arbroath Infirmary, Scotland, 1958-59, Dundee Royal Infirmary, Scotland, 1959-60; asst. gynecologist Govt. Abudhabi, United Arab Emirates, 1969-72; research fellow Inst. Human Nutrition, Columbia U., N.Y.C., 1973-75; research asst. dept. ob-gyn Aberdeen U., Scotland, 1975-78; hon. vis. sci. worker Clin. Research Ctr., Northwick Park Hosp., Harrow, Eng., 1979—; hon. vis. research worker Qatar Women's Hosp., Dola, Qatar, Arabian Gulf. Councillor Parish Council, Chobham Woking, Surrey, 1979—. Mem. Brit. Med. Assn., Nutrition Soc., Devel. Pathology Soc., Med. Campaign Against Nuclear Weapons, Brit. Soc. Colposcopy and Cervical Pathology. Anglican. Avocations: hill walking; gardening; novels of the Victorian era. Home: Pepperstitch Bagshot Rd, Chobham Woking, Surrey 9U 248DE, United Kingdom Office: Sect Perinatal and Child Health Clin Research Ctr, Northwick Park Hosp, Watford Rd, Harrow, Middlesex HAI 3UJ, England

CAMPBELL-CAPEN, NANCY ANN, human service administrator; b. Toms River, N.J., Sept. 18, 1950; d. Clifford William and Ann Christine (Ashenfelter) C.; m. John M. Capen, May 16, 1982. B.A. with honors in German, Muskingum Coll., New Concord, Ohio, 1972; M.A. in German Lit., NYU, 1976; M.S. in Human Devel., U. Maine, Orono, 1979. Cert. counselor. Prodn. editor, bilingual sec. Springer-Verlag N.Y., Inc., 1972-75; substitute tchr. Denver Public Schs., 1975-76; adminstrv. asst. Teacher Corps, U. Maine, Orono, 1976-79, resident dir., 1979-80, resident dir., acad. programmer Living Learning Program, 1980-82, resident dir. high sch. jrs. program, summer 1981, coordinator New Student Welcome Program, summer 1981; coordinator Learning Resource Center, Regional Army Continuing Edn. System, Grafenwoehr, W.Ger., 1982-83, dir. child devel. services, 1983-84, army community services dir., Grafenwoehr, 1984-86, army family action program coordinator, Grafenwoehr, 1984-87, family support div. dir., Grafenwoehr, 1986-87; adminstrv. support services supr. USN, Bath, Maine, 1987—; coordinator for cooperating with profl. community Maine State Alanon; instr. seminars in human sexuality, 1978-82, instr. life mgmt. skills, 1980-81, army family programs class, sexual harassment prevention course, 1983—, co. comdr. and 1st sgt. course, Vilsech, Fed. Republic Germany, 1984-87; leader group counseling Devel. Studies Center, Bangor Community Coll., 1981; facilitator effective parenting groups, Old Town and Bangor, Maine, 1977-79. Contbr. articles to profl. jours. Mem. Am. Assn. Counseling and Devel., Mil. Educators and Counselors Assn., Maine Assn. Counseling and Devel., Maine Mental Health Counselors Assn., Am. Running and Fitness Assn., Omicron Nu.

CAMPBELL-SMITH, ROSEMARY GILLES, dental science educator; b. Rapid City, S.D., Mar. 16, 1939; d. Albert Peter and Anna (Schmitz) Gilles; m. Richard Lee Smith, Aug. 6, 1978; 1 dau. by previous marriage, Christina Lynn Campbell. Cert., Eastman Sch. Dental Hygiene, 1960; B.S.H.E. with high honors, U. Fla., 1964; M.S., U. Miami, 1968, Dr.Arts, 1976. Registered dental hygienist, Fla. Dental hygienist in pvt. practice, Palm Beach County, Fla., 1960-63; chief lab. technician dept. physiology U. Fla., Gainesville, 1965-66; instr. dept. biology U. Miami, Coral Gables, 1968-70; asst. prof. dept. dental hygiene Miami-Dade Community Coll., 1974-77; lead instr. Dental Aux. Programs, Santa Fe Community Coll., 1977-81; cons. Campbell-Smith Cons., Gainesville, 1982—. Author: Head and Neck: What's It All About, 1976. Recipient Albert E. Sevenson award for art. sci. and service N.Y. Dental Soc., 1960; Sci. award Eastman Sch. Dental Hygiene, 1960; J. Hillis Miller award U. Fla., 1964; Cancer Assn. award, 1964; Merit Citation Am. Dental Assn. Commn. on Accreditation Report, 1979. Mem. Am. Dental Hygienists Assn. (Profl. Excellence in Dental Hygiene award 1988, student liaison Dist. IV 1981-84, sec.-treas. 1984-88, Dist. IV trustee 1988—), Fla. Dental Hygienists Assn. (student advisor 1978-81), Internat. Assn. Dental Research, AAAS, Sigma Xi, Phi Kappa Phi, Phi Lambda Pi. Democrat. Roman Catholic. Office: 3609 NW 30 Blvd Gainesville FL 32605

CAMPEAU, JEAN, investment fund executive; b. Montréal, Qué., Can., July 6, 1931; m. Réjeanne Rouleau; 3 children. BA, St.-Ignace and Ste.-Marie Coll., 1952; license, École des Hautes Études Commerciales, 1955. Investment broker 1955-63, mfg. co. exec., 1963-71; head debt mgmt. Dept. Fin., Qué., 1971, asst. dep. minister, 1977-80; chmn., gen. mgr. Caisse de dépôt et placement du Qué., Montréal, 1980—. Office: Caisse de depot et placement Que, 1981 av McGill College, Montreal, PQ Canada H3A 3C7

CAMPEAU, ROBERT, real estate development company executive; b. Sudbury, Ont., Can., Aug. 3, 1924; m. Ilse Luebbert; 6 children. Machinist Inco Ltd., Sudbury, Ont.; homebuilder from 1948; chmn., chief exec. officer, dir. Campeau Corp., Toronto, Ont., until 1969, then 1972—; chmn., chief exec. officer Allied Stores Corp., N.Y.C., 1987—; mem. adv. bd. Can. Bus. Health Research Inst., Guaranty Trust Co. Can.; bd. dirs. Great West Life Ins. Co. Bd. govs. Ashbury Coll., Ottawa, Ont. Clubs: Lambton Golf and Country, Donalda, Rideau, Ottawa Hunt and Golf; Mt. Royal; Rivermead Golf, Aylmer Country; Laval sur-le-lac, Jupiter Hills, Metropolitan, Granite. Office: Campeau Corp, 320 Bay St, Toronto, ON Canada M5H 2P2 Office: Allied Stores Corp 1114 Ave of the Americas New York NY 10036 *

CAMPION, ROBERT THOMAS, manufacturing company executive; b. Mpls., June 23, 1921; s. Leo P. and Naomi (Revord) C.; m. Wilhelmina Knapp, June 8, 1946; 1 son, Michael. Student, Loyola U., Chgo., 1939-41, 46-48. C.P.A., Ill. With Alexander Grant & Co., Chgo., 1946-57; ptnr. Alexander Grant & Co., 1954-57; with Lear Siegler, Inc., Santa Monica, Calif., 1957—; pres. Lear Siegler, Inc., 1971-85, chief exec. officer, dir., 1971-86, chmn., 1974-86; pvt. investor 1987—. Served with AUS, 1942-46. Mem. Am. Inst. C.P.A.s, Ill. Soc. C.P.A.s. Republican. Clubs: Bel Air (Cal.) Country; Metropolitan (N.Y.C.); Jonathan (Los Angeles); Burning Tree (Md.). Office: 4188 High Valley Rd Encino CA 91436

CAMPO, J. M., mechanical engineer; b. Oct. 14, 1943; m. Vicky R. Herran, Dec. 2, 1971; children: Vanessa, Gunnar, Ingrid. MS in Mech. Engring., ETSIIB, Barcelona, Spain, 1964; PhD in Mech. Engring., ETSIIB, 1967; MBA, IESE, Barcelona, 1968. Sr. instrument engr. Davy-McKee, Cleve., 1968-73; prin. instrument engr. Parsons Co., Pasadena, Calif., 1973-77; resident engr. Alcan, 1977-80; project mgr. Aramco Oversea Co., The Hague, Holland, 1980-81; gen. mgr. Enertec Engring., Mex. City, 1981-83; sr. project mgr. Dragados Indsl. Div., Madrid, 1983—; dir. Trans Star Tech., Intertek Engring. Patentee in field. Mem. Orgn. for Devel. of Mgmt. Sci. Fellow Assn. Indsl. Engrs. Home: Ebro 44, Mayflower, Penascales, 28291 Torrelodones, Madrid Spain Office: Dragados Indsl Div, Felix Boix 8, 28036 Madrid Spain

CAMPODONICO, ANGELO, philosopher, researcher; b. Rosario, Argentina, May 29, 1949; arrived in Italy, 1963; s. Giovanni Angelo and Annetta (Perasso) C.; m. Giulia Ramo, May 3, 1981; children: Francesca, Rolando. Dr. degree, U. Genoa, Italy, 1972, M in Philosophy, 1975. Researcher dept. philosophy U. Genoa, 1980—; headmaster Cultural Assn. Charles Peguy, Genoa, 1980—; mem. Milan Research Inst., 1984—. Author: Filosofia dell'esperienza in R. Boyle, 1978, Metafisica e Antropologia in T. Hobbes, 1982, Alla scoperta dell'essere. Saggio su Tommaso d'Aquino, 1986; contbr. articles to profl. publs. Served to lt. Italian armed forces, 1973-74. Mem. Assn. Filosofica Italiana. Roman Catholic. Club: Cai (Chiavari). Home: Via Fiume 1, 16043 Chiavari, Genova Italy Office: U Genoa Dept Philosophy, Via Balbi 4, 16128 Genoa Italy

CAMPOS, LUÍS MANUEL BRAGA DA COSTA, applied mathematics, theoretical physics, acoustics and aeronautics educator; b. Lisbon, Portugal, Mar. 28, 1950; s. Elmano Neves and Francelina (dos Reis Braga) da Costa Campos; m. Maria Isabel Carreira de Vila-Santa, Aug. 8, 1978; 1 child, Nuno Luis. Diploma Mech. Engring., Inst. Superior Tecnico, Lisbon Tech. U., 1972, Sc.D., 1982; Ph.D., Cambridge U., 1977. Lectr. applied mechanics and math. Inst. Superior Tecnico, Lisbon Tech. U., 1972-78, aux. prof., 1978-80, assoc. prof., 1980-85, prof., 1985—. Counsellor Nat. Inst. Sci. Research, 1985—. Contbr. articles to profl. jours. Fellow Cambridge Philos. Soc.; mem. Am. Math. Soc., ASME, London Math. Soc., Soc. Indsl. and Applied Math., Internat. Astron. Union, Adv. Group for Aerospace Research and Devel., Acoustic Soc. Am., European Sci. Found. (mem. space sci. com.), NSF (liaison mem. space sci. bd.), Societe Francaise d'Acoustique. Avocations: classical music; plastic arts; photography; swimming. Office: Inst Superior Tech, Av Rovisco Pais, Lisbon Portugal 2670

CAMRE, MOGENS NIELS JUEL, telecommunications executive; b. Randers, Denmark, Mar. 29, 1936; s. Sigfred Niels Juel and Carna (Petersen) C.; m. Marianne Dybdahl, May 1, 1971 (div. 1980); children: Andreas, Alexander, Daniel; m. Vita Andersen, Aug. 26, 1981; children: Natasha, Tatiana, David. BA in Econs., Niels Brock U., Copehhagen, 1958; MA In Econs., Copenhagen Sch. Econs., 1961; PhD in Econs., U. Copenhagen, 1967. Co. planner Danish Unilever Ltd., Copenhagen, 1960-66; sec. Ministry of Fin., Copenhagen, 1967-68; head sect. Ministry of Fin., 1987—; mem. Danish Parliament, Copenhagen, 1968-87; judge Nat. Tax Ct., Copenhagen, 1974—; pres. Danish Telecom K.T.A.S., Copenhagen, 1982—; bd. dirs. Danish Mortgage Bank, Copenhagen, Danish Telecom Internat. Ltd., Arhus, Denmark; mem. bd. reps. Danish Cen. Bank, 1985-87. Author: Greek History 1821-1967, 1967; author, editor: Beyond The Future, 1965; contbr. articles to profl. jours. Chmn. Danish Com. for Democracy in Greece, Copenhagen, 1968-74. Served with infantry Danish Armed Forces, 1954-55. Mem. Royal Soc. Fgn. Affairs, Social Dem. Students and Grads. (chmn. 1962-66, pres. 1967-68. Social Democrat. Club: Danish Veteran Car. Office: House Parliament, Christianborg Castle, 1240 Copenhagen Denmark

CANARDO, HERNANDO VICENTE, import and export company executive, lawyer; b. Buenos Aires, Argentina, Jan. 26, 1957; s. Vicente and Maria Dolores (Espina) C. Abogado, U. Catolica Argentina, Buenos Aires, 1981, JD, 1982. Bar: Corte Suprema de Justicia de la Nación, 1982, Colegio Póblico de Abogados Buenos Aires, 1986. Asst. prof. internat. law U. Catolica Argentina, 1982-84, asst. prof. legal ethics, 1985-87; mgr. Union Olivarera Canardo and Co., Buenos Aires, 1981—, Importadora and Exportadora Indian, Buenos Aires, 1986—; adj. prof. internat. law U. Catolica Argentina, 1978-82, 85—. Official rep. to Second Argentine Congress of Internat. Law, 1985. Mem. Am. Soc. Internat. Law, ABA (internat. assoc.), Coll. Pub. Abogados Buenos Aires. Roman Catholic. Avocations: golf, swimming. Home: Paraguay 2421 7th Floor, Buenos Aires 1121, Argentina Office: Union Olivarera Canardo and Co, Sarmiento 3239, Buenos Aires 1196, Argentina

CANARINA, OPAL JEAN, nurse, administrator, educator, consultant, lecturer; b. Geneva County, Ala., Mar. 21, 1936; d. O. Lee and L. Ellen (Box) Peacock; m. Miles Steven Bajcar, June 27, 1953 (div.); children—Debra Lynn-Wilson; Wayne Steven; m. Arnold R. Canarina, June 19, 1965; children—Catherine Mary, Christopher John, Charles Benjamin. B.S.N. summa cum laude, George Mason U., Fairfax, Va., 1976, M.S.N., Vanderbilt U., 1981. R.N., Va., Tenn., Ky., Okla., Utah, Miss. Staff and charge nurse Georgetown U. Hosp., Washington, 1976; charge nurse ob-gyn Vanderbilt U. Hosp., Nashville, 1976-77; charge nurse labor and delivery service Baptist Hosp., Nashville, 1977-80; asst. prof. dept. baccalaureate nursing Austin Peay State U., Clarksville, Tenn., 1981-83; dir. nursing services Meml. Hosp., Guymon, Okla., 1983-85; dir. Women's Ctr./Maternal-Child Nursing, McKay-Dee Hosp. Ctr., Ogden, Utah, 1985-87; dir. nursing Jeff Anderson Regional Med. ctr., Meridian, Miss., 1987—; cons. to middle Tenn. and No. Utah areas health and nursing issues. Recipient cert. of excellence R.N.s on campus George Mason U., 1976. Mem. Nat. Assn. Female Execs., Am. Mgmt. Assn., Tenn. Nurses Assn. (legis. chmn. dist. 13, 1982-83, pres. 1982), Va. Nurses Assn. (Student Nurse of Yr. award 1975), Am. Nurses Assn., Am. Nurses Found., Miss. Nurses Assn., Nurses Assn. Coll. Ob-Gyn, Sigma Theta Tau, Alpha Chi.

CAÑAS-CRUCHAGA, RAUL, agriculture engineering educator; b. Santiago, Chile, Oct. 23, 1941; s. Raul Cañas-Zaldivar and Virginia Cruchaga-Santa Maria; m. Francisca Soffia Garcia de la Huerta, May 8, 1965; children—Francisca, Raul, Maria Ignacia. Agrl. Engr., U. Catolica de Chile, Santiago, 1965; Magister, Interam. Inst. Agrl. Scis., Estanzuela, Uruguay, 1967; Ph.D., U. Calif.-Davis, 1974. Cert. in agrl. engring. Animal sci. chmn. U. Catolica, Santiago, 1967-71, dir. research, 1975-81, acad. gen. dir. affairs, 1979-81, prof. animal sci., 1975—, chmn. dept., 1984—; research asst. U. Calif., Davis, 1971-74; prof. U. Coahuila, Mexico, 1974; cons. Sec. Agr. Embrapa, Brasilia, Brazil, 1976, Sec. Agr. Inta, Santa Fe, Argentina, 1982, U. Costa Rica, San Jose, 1979-83, Convenio Andres Bello, Bogota, Colombia, 1980, INIAP, Ecuador, 1987—, prof. U. Cojamarca, Peru. bd. dirs. Puchegin Agr. Co., 1985—, AASA Agr. Industry Corp., 1987—. Author: Research Administration, 1979. Contbr. articles to profl. jours., chpt. to book. Named Prof. Correspondiente, U. Mayor de San Simon, Cochabamba, Bolivia, 1968; recipient research prizes Latin Am. Assn. Animal Prodn., 1971, 83, Assn. Agr. Engring., Santiago, 1980. Mem. N.Y. Acad. Scis., Latin Am. Acad. Animal Sci., Chilean Assn. Animal Sci., Sigma Xi. Home: Francisco de Ginebra 4611, Santiago Chile Office: Univ Catolica de Chile, Facultad de Agronomia, Ave Vicuna Mackenna 4860, 114-D Santiago Chile

CANAVAGGIO, JEAN, educator; b. Paris, July 23, 1936; s. Dominique Canavaggio and Madeleine De Morati Gentile; m. Perrine Ramin, Feb. 19, 1977; children; Laure, FranÇois, Emmanuel. Grad., Ecole Normale Supérieure, 1956, Sorbonne, Paris, 1960; postgrad., Casa Vélasquez, Madrid, 1963-66, DLitt, 1975. Asst. prof. Sorbonne, Paris, 1966-69; chargé d'ens U. Caen, France, 1969-75, prof, chmn. Spanish dept., 1975-82; vis. prof. U. Va., Charlottesvillle, 1983. Author: Cervantes, 1986 (B. Goncourt award); autor books and articles in field. Mem. Soc. des Hispanistes FranÇais, Hispanic Soc. Am. (corresponding), Cervantes Soc. Am. Roman Catholic. Home: 4 Square Monceau, 75017 Paris France Office: U Caen, Esplanade de la Paix, 14032 Caen France

CANCELIER, LAURENT, physician; b. Neuilly sur Seine, France, Nov. 7, 1955; s. Andre and Irene (Mattrel) C.; m. Pascale Bettray, Sept. 21, 1985; children: Julia, Martin. MD, Xavier Bichat Coll. Univ. Paris, 1982. Vacataire medecine legale Hosp. Hōtel-Dieu, Paris, 1984-85; medecin generaliste et legiste Sannois, France, 1983—. Mem. Soc. de Medecine Legale et de Criminologie de France. Home: 9 Ave Andre le Goas, 95110 Sannois France Office: Cabinet Med, 35 Boulevard Charles de Gaulle, 95110 Sannois France

CANDEE, RICHARD ALEXANDER, JR., manufacturing corporation executive; b. Milw., Dec. 13, 1947; s. Richard Alexander and Vi (Egan) C.; m. Mary Linda Brown, May 26, 1979; 1 child, Alexander Darcy. BA magna cum laude, Lawrence U., 1970; MBA, Harvard U., 1978; student Mich. State U./Barcelona, Spain, 1968. Sales coordinator, asst. plant mgr. Barton Mfg., Inc., Wis. and P.R., 1970-72; v.p., treas. Cormac, S.A., Panama and Wis., 1972-73; export sales mgr. Latin Am., Gehl Co., West Bend, Wis., 1973-76; mktg. analyst Deere & Co., Moline, Ill., summer 1977; mktg. assoc. Eaton Corp., Cleve., 1978-88, planner, sales mgr., mktg. mgr., Brussels and Aurora, Ohio, 1982-86, dir. mktg. durable med. products div., Invacare Corp., Elyria, Ohio, 1986-87; pres. Vintage Motorpress, Inc., Shaker Heights, Ohio, 1982—; dir. Bill's Sporting Goods Inc., Lomira, Wis., Wolf's Galleries, Cleve. Author, pub.: Aston Martin in America (Davis award 1983), 1982; Facel Vega-The Glory That Was France..., 1975. Exec. producer video tape Austin Healeys-On the Road, 1985, Chicago Historic Races - The International Challenge, 1986. Capt. fund raising Cleve. Orch., 1978-85, Cleve. Ballet, 1980-82; trustee Friends of Shaker Square, Cleve., 1983—; jud. candidate rev. com. Citizens League, 1984, 85. Recipient Conn./Pa. driver Aston Martin Owners Club, Lakeville, Conn., 1982, S.C.H. Davis Publs. award, London, 1983, Elisha Walker Trophy, 1985. Mem. Phi Delta Theta. Clubs: Harvard Bus. Sch. (v.p. 1980-85), Skating (Cleve.). Avocation: vintage automobile racing. Home: 13623 Larchmere Blvd Shaker Heights OH 44120 Office: Vintage Motorpress Inc One Cleveland Ctr Suite 2130 Cleveland OH 44114

CANDEIAS, NELLY MARTINS FERREIRA, public health educator; b. São Paulo, Brazil, Apr. 11, 1930; d. Daniel Martins and Ermelinda (De Moraes Serrão) Martins F.; m. José Alberto Neves Candeias, July 12, 1949. BS, Sch. of Philosophy, Scis., and Langs., São Paulo, 1969, PhD, 1982; MPH, U. Calif., Berkeley, 1972; DrPH, U. Calif., 1979. Instr. Sch. Pub. Health, São Paulo, 1973-79, asst. prof., assoc. prof., 1982-87, prof., 1988—; cons. Pan Am Health Orgn./World Health Orgn., Washington, 1974, 75, 79, São Paulo, Santiago, Montevideo, 1985, UNESCO, Ann Arbor, Mich., 1974, Ministry of Health, Belem, 1982, Western Consortium Health Profls./PAHO, São Paulo, 1986; prin. investigator Pan Am. Health Orgn./World Health Orgn., São Paulo, 1986-88. Research grantee Ford Found., Brazil, 1974, Pan Am. Health Orgn./World Health Orgn., São Paulo, 1986-88, Conselho Nac. Desenvolvimento Científico e Technologico, Brazil, 1979; ellogg Found. fellow, Chapel Hill, N.C., 1983; recipeint Literary award

Fundação Emílio Oderbrecht, Brazil, 1985. Mem. Brazil Assn. Helath Edn., São Paulo Assn. Pub. Health, São Paulo Assn. Sociology, Ctr. Studies Rural and Urban Areas, Brazilian Assn. Grad Courses Collective Health, São Paulo Hosp. Assn., Internat. Union Health Edn., N.Am. Soc. Pub. Health Edn. Roman Catholic. Office: Faculdade de Sáude, Pública Ave Dr Arnaldo, 01255 São Paulo Brazil

CANDELL-RIERA, JAUME, cardiologist; b. Barcelona, Spain, Jan. 22, 1949; s. Francesc Candell-Espona and Montserrat Riera-Obre; M.D., U. Barcelona, 1971, specialist in internal medicine and cardiology, 1976; m. Montserrat Vilardaga-Ventosa, Nov. 12, 1972; children—Arianna, Berta. Resident in internal medicine, then resident in cardiology Ciudad Sanitaria Vall d' Hebron, Barcelona, 1972-77, mem. staff CCU, 1977—, cardiology service, 1980—. Mem. Soc. Catalana Cardiologia, Acad. Ciencies Mediques Catalunya i Balears, Soc. Española Cardiologia. Clubs: Galens V.H. Football, Sant Gervasi Tennis. Author: Ecocardiografia clinica; Atlas de Cardiologia Nuclear. Contbr. articles to med jours. Home: Cardedeu 53, 08023 Barcelona Spain Office: Servicio de Cardiologia Dept Medicina, Cuidad Sanitaria Vall d'Hebron, 08035 Barcelona Spain

CANDIB, MURRAY A., business executive, retail management consultant; b. Mass., Sept. 16, 1915; m. Claudette Aggie, Oct. 8, 1972; children—Nancy, Francesca, Rachel, David, Caroline. B.A., Boston U., 1950. Founder King's Dept. Store Inc., 1949; Pres. Canco Enterprises, Worcester, Mass.; dir. Canco Enterprises Holding Co. Subject of articles in Fortune Mag., Harvard Bus. Rev. and profl. jours. Founder, life trustee Mt. Sinai Hosp., Miami Beach, Fla., v.p. adv. bd.; bd. dirs. Miami Heart Inst.; bd. dirs. Temple Emanuel El, Fla., Visitors and Conv. Authority, Miami Beach; charter mem. Republican Presdl. Task Force, 1981—, U.S. Senatorial Club, 1981—, Nat. Rep. Senatorial Com., Fine Arts of Fla.; mem. Fla. Victory Com. Brandeis U. fellow, 1966; recipient Human Relations award Am. Jewish Com., Nat. Community Service award Jewish Theol. Sem. of Am., 1965, Man of Yr. award Mental Health Clinic, Mt. Sinai Hosp., N.Y.C., Man of Yr. award Boys Wear Industry of N.Y., Hall of Fame award U. Mass. Mem. Am. Heart Assn. Clubs: Westview Country, Palm Bay, Turnberry Isle (Miami); Ocean Reef (Key Largo); Le Club (N.Y.C.). Lodges: Shriners, Masons. Office: 306 Main St Worcester MA 01608

CANDILIS, GEORGES, architect, engineer; b. Bakou, Russia, Apr. 11, 1913; s. Panayotis and Vera (Skanavi) C.; Architecte-engenieur diplome, Nat. Poly. Sch., Athens, Greece; m. Christiane Richard, 1951; children—Alexis, Alexandrine Vera, Panayotis. Architect, Greek Ministry of Aviation, 1937-40; prof. Ecole nationale Sivitanivios, 1937-40, also architect specializing in homes and hosps.; asst. to Le Corbusier, 1946-51; dir. soc. Atbat-Afrique, Casablanca, 1951-54; prof. architecture Ecole nationale superieure des beaux-arts, Paris, France, 1963—; in assn. with Alexis Josie and Shadrach Woods, from 1956. Mem. Council for Cultural Devel., 1971-73. Decorated Greek Croix de Guerre Order of St. George, chevalier Legion d'Honneur; recipient numerous archtl. awards. Hon. fellow AIA. Designer residences in many countries; developer, designer urban places, comml. centers, hotels. Office: 18 rue Dauphine, 75006 Paris France *

CANDLAND, DOUGLAS KEITH, psychology educator; b. Long Beach, Calif., July 9, 1934; s. Horace George and Erma Louise (Downing) C.; m. Mary Homrighausen, June 18, 1959; children: Kevin, Christopher, Ian. A.B., Pomona Coll., 1956; Ph.D., Princeton U., 1959. Research fellow U. Va., 1959-60, Delta Primate Center, 1967-68, Pa. State U., 1968-69, U. Stirling, Scotland, 1972-73, Cambridge (Eng.) U., 1977-78, U. Mysore (India), 1983; asst. prof. psychology Bucknell U., 1960-64, assoc. prof., 1964-67, prof., 1967—, prof. animal behavior, 1985—, Presdl. prof., 1973-80, head program in animal behavior, 1968—, pres. div. teaching of psychology, 1976-77, head dept. psychology, 1970-75, Class of 1956 lectr., 1971; mem. adv. bd. psychology Princeton U., 1970-86. Author: Exploring Behavior, 1961, Psychology: the experimental approach, 1968, 2d rev. edit., 1978, Emotion, bodily change, 1961, Emotion, 1979; contbr. chpts. to profl. books; editor: The Primates, 1968-78, Animal Behavior, 1979—; assoc. editor: Animal Learning and Behavior, 1976-84, Teaching of Psychology, 1976-84, Am. Jour. Primatology, 1980-84; cons. editor Jour. Comparative Psychology, 1988—. Bd. dirs. Wildlife Preservation Trust Internat., Pa. Cinema Register. Recipient award Lindback Found., 1971; Harriman award Bucknell U., 1979. Fellow Am. Psychol. Assn. (award for disting. contbn. to edn. 1978); mem. Brit. Psychol. Assn., Psychonomic Soc., Internat. Soc. Primatologists, Animal Behavior Soc. (chmn. policy and planning). Home: 125 Stein Ln Lewisburg PA 17837 Office: Bucknell U Lewisburg PA 17837

CANDLER, JOHN SLAUGHTER, II, lawyer; b. Atlanta, Nov. 30, 1908; s. Asa Warren and Harriet Lee (West) C.; m. Dorothy Bruce Warthen, June 13, 1933; children: Dorothy Warthen (Mrs. Joseph W. Hamilton, Jr.), John Slaughter, Jr. A.B. magna cum laude, U. Ga., 1929; J.D., Emory U., 1931. Bar: Ga. bar 1931. Ptnr. Candler, Cox & Andrews and predecessor firms, Atlanta, 1931—; dep. asst. atty. gen. State of Ga., 1951-68; chmn. sect. fiduciary law State Bar Ga., 1964-65. Trustee Ga. Student Ednl. Fund, 1950—; trustee Kappa Alpha Scholarship Fund, 1955-86, pres., 1970-72; trustee Lovett Sch., 1953-59; mem. USO Council Greater Atlanta, 1969—, pres., 1974-75; sr. warden Episc. Ch, 1955, cathedral trustee, 1957-67, lay reader, 1971—; trustee St. Philip's Cathedral, 1957-67; sr. warden, 1955, lay reader, 1971—. Served to col. USAR, 1941-46. Decorated Army Commendation Ribbon. Fellow Am. Coll. Probate Counsel (bd. regents 1968-74), Ga. Bar Found., Internat. Acad. Law and Sci.; mem. ABA, Atlanta Bar Assn., Lawyers Club Atlanta, Nat. Tax Assn.-Tax Inst. Am. (adv. council Tax Inst. Am. 1969-72), Atlanta Estate Planning Council (pres. 1963-64), Am. Legion (post comdr. 1949-50), Res. Officers Assn. U.S. (state pres. 1946), Am. Judicature Soc., Newcomen Soc., Internat. Platform Assn., Mil. Order World Wars, English Speaking Union, U.S. Power Squadrons, Phi Beta Kappa, Phi Kappa Phi, Phi Delta Phi, Kappa Alpha Order, Sigma Delta Chi. Clubs: Atlanta Touchdown, Piedmont Driving, Capital City, Commerce, Peachtree Racket, Ft. McPherson Officers, Oglethorpe (Savannah), Army-Navy (Washington). Lodges: Kiwanis, Masons. Home: 413 Manor Ridge Dr NW Altanta GA 30305 Office: Candler Cox & Andrews 610 Eight Piedmont Ctr Atlanta GA 30305

CANE, ROY DOUGLAS, anesthesiology educator, researcher; b. Johannesburg, South Africa, Jan. 29, 1945; s. Francis John and Ruby (Nicholas) C. M.B.B.Ch., U. Witwatersrand, South Africa, 1969. Registered specialist anesthetist. Intern, Coronation Hosp., Johannesburg, 1970; registrar in anesthesia Baragwanath Hosp. and U. Witwatersrand Med. Sch., Johannesburg, 1971-73, sr. med. officer, 1974, anesthetist, dir. intensive care, 1975, prin. anesthetitist, dir. intensive care, 1976-77; resident in anesthesia Northwestern U., Chgo., 1974, asst. prof. clin. anesthesia, 1978-81, assoc. prof., asst. dir. respiratory/critical care, 1981-86 , pres. med. faculty senate, 1983-84; prof. clin. anesthesia, 1986—. mem. assoc. attending staff Northwestern Meml. Hosp., 1979-84, attending staff, 1984—, asst. med. dir. dept. respiratory therapy, 1978-84, assoc. med. dir. dept. respiratory therapy, 1985—; mem. attending staff Rehab. Ctr. Chgo., 1986—, Columbus Hosp., 1988—; lectr. Cook County Grad. Sch. Medicine, 1980—. Fellow Faculty Anesthetists of Coll. Medicine South Africa, 1973. Fellow Am. Coll. Chest Physicians; mem. Am. Assn. Respiratory Therapy, Ill. Soc. Respiratory Therapy (med. adviser 1980-83), Nat. Assn. Med. Dirs. of Respiratory Care, Soc. Critical Care Medicine, Am. Soc. Anesthesiologists, South African Critical Care Medicine Soc. (founder), South African Soc. Anesthetists (Atherstone prize 1972), South African Med. and Dental Council, Assn. Univ. Anesthetists, Med. Grads. Assn. Johannesburg, Chgo. Thoracic Soc., Ill. Soc. Anesthesiology, Sigma Xi. Co-author: Case Studies in Critical Care Medicine, Clinical Application of Respiratory Care, 3d edit., Clinical Application of Blood Gases, 4th edit.; reviewer for Jour. AMA, Critical Care Medicine, Chest and Respiratory Care, Am. Inst. Biol. Scis., 1982—, NIH, 1983—; editorial cons. Yr. Book Med. Pubs., Aspen Pubs.; mem. editorial bd. Critical Care Medicine, 1985—, Chest, 1988—; editor Year Book of Anesthesia, 1981, Anesthesiology Clinics, 1987; contbr. articles, abstracts to profl. jours., chpts. in books. Office: 250 E Superior St Suite 678 Chicago IL 60611

CAÑETE, ALFREDO, diplomate; b. Mar. 14, 1942; married, 1 son. Student, Nat. U., Asunción, Paraguay. With Ministry of Fgn. Affairs, Paraguay, 1960; assigned to internat. dept. orgns. and treaties Ministry of Fgn. Affairs; sec. Permanent Mission to UN, N.Y.C.; counselor, alternative rep. Latinamerican Free Trade Assn., Montevideo, Uruguay; consul gen. London; counselor and charge d'affairs Eng.; minister at Embassy Washington; dir. or fgn. trade Ministry of Fgn. Affairs; dep. dir. econ. affairs, sec. gen. Nat. Council for Fgn. Trade and Integration; ambassador to kingdom Belgium, the kingdom of the Netherlands and the Grand Duchy of Luxembourg 1981-82; head Paraguayan Mission to European Community, 1982-83; rep. Paraguay to UN, 1983—. Decorated Cross of Knight, Order of Civil Merit, Spain. Office: Perm Mission of Paraguay to UN 211 East 43d St Room 1202 New York NY 10017

CANETTI, ELIAS, author; b. Russe, Bulgaria, July 25, 1905; s. Jacques and Mathilda Arditi C.; Ph.D., U. Vienna; m. Venetia Toubner-Calderon, 1934 (dec. 1963); now remarried. Author: Hochzeit (play), 1932; Die Blendung (fiction), 1935; Fritz Wotruba (criticism), 1955; Masse und Macht, 1960; Welt im Kopf, 1962; Komoedie der Eitelkeit (play), 1964; Die Befristeten, 1964; Aufzeichnungen, 1942-48 (notebooks), 1965; Die Stimmen von Marrakesck, 1968; Die Andere Prozess, 1969; Diebespaltene Kukuuft, 1972; Macht und Veberleben (essays), 1972; Die Proving des Menschen, 1973; Der Ohrenzeuge, 1974; Das Oewissen der Wrote (essays), 1975; The Human Province, 1978; Earwitness, 1979; The Conscience of Words, 1979; The Tongue Set Free (autobiography), 1981; The Torch in My Ear (autobiography), 1982; Crowds & Power, 1982; Kafka's Other Trial, 1982; Comedy of Vanity and Life-Terms, 1983; Auto-da-Fe, 1984; The Voices of Marrakesh, 1984; The Play of the Eyes, 1985. Recipient Nobel prize for lit., 1981; numerous French and German lit. awards. Office: care C & J Wolfers Ltd, 3 Regent Sq, London WC1 England Address: Nobel Found, Stutegatan 14, S-11436 Stockholm Sweden *

CANFIELD, GRANT WELLINGTON, JR., organization executive; b. Los Angeles, Nov. 28, 1923; s. Grant Wellington and Phyllis Marie (Westland) C.; m. Virginia Louise Bellinger, June 17, 1945; 1 child, Julie Marie. BS, U. So. Calif., 1949, MBA, 1958. Personnel and indsl. relations exec., Los Angeles, 1949-55; employee relations cons., regional mgr. Mchts. and Mfrs. Assn. Los Angeles, 1955-60; v.p., orgnl. devel. cons. Hawaii Employers Council, Honolulu, 1960-75; pres., dir. Hawaiian Ednl. Council, 1969—; exec. v.p. Hawaii Garment Mfrs. Assn., 1965-75, Assn. Hawaii Restaurant Employers, 1966-75; exec. dir. Hawaii League Savs. Assns., 1971-78; exec. dir. Pan-Pacific Surg. Assn., 1980-81, exec. v.p., 1982-83; exec. dir. Hawaii Bus. Roundtable, 1983—; sec., treas. Econ. Devel. Corp. Honolulu, 1984-85; sec., treas. Hawaii Conv. Park Council, Inc., 1984-86, hon. dir., 1986—. Co-author: Resource Manual for Public Collective Bargaining, 1973. Bd. dirs. Hawaii Restaurant Assn., 1974-76, bd. dirs. Hawaii chpt. Nat. Assn. Accts., 1963-67, nat. dir., 1965-66; bd. dirs. Vol. Service Bur. Honolulu, 1965-66, pres., 1966-68; bd. dirs. Vol. Info. and Referral Service Honolulu, 1972-75, Goodwill Vocat. Tng. Ctrs. of Hawaii, 1973-81, Girl Scout council Pacific, 1961-65, 71-72; bd. dirs. Hawaii Com. Alcoholism, 1962-71, co-chmn., 1964-68; pres., dir. Friends of Punahou Sch., 1972-75; mem. community adv. bd. Jr. League Hawaii, 1968-70; exec. bd. Aloha council Boys Scouts Am., 1962-65; bd. regents Chaminade U., 1983-85. Served to 1st lt. inf. AUS, 1943-46. Decorated Bronze Star, Purple Heart, Combat Inf. badge. Mem. Am. Soc. Assn. Execs. (cert. assn. exec.), Am. Soc. Tng. and Devel., Am. Soc. Personnel Adminstrn. Clubs: Pacific Kaneohe Yacht, Plaza (Honolulu). Lodges: Rotary, Masons. Home: 1950 W Dry Creek Rd Healdsburg CA 95448 Office: PO Box 4145 Honolulu HI 96812-4145

CANGIALOSI, CHARLES PHILIP, podiatric surgeon; b. Passaic, N.J., Dec. 3, 1948; s. Charles Philip and Veronica Margaret (Jacobs) C.; B.S. magna cum laude, John Carroll U., 1970; D. Podiatric Medicine with honors, Ohio Coll. Podiatric Medicine, 1975; m. Debra Mae Mayer, June 5, 1976; 1 son, Thomas George. Resident Foot Clinic of Youngstown (Ohio) in conjunction with Community Hosp. Warren (Ohio) and Bashline Meml. Hosp., Grove City, Pa., 1975-76; practice gen. and surg. podiatry, Waldwick, N.J., 1976—; former mem. staff Bergen Pines Hosp., Ridgewood, N.J., Saddle Brook (N.J.) Gen. Hosp.; former staff mem. South Bergen Community Hosp., Hasbrouck Heights, N.J.; mem. dept. orthopedics The Valley Hosp., Ridgewood, N.J., dir. dept. podiatric surgery The Valley Hosp.; instr. dept. med. scis. Cuyahoga Community Coll. and Ohio Coll. Podiatric Medicine, 1973-75; adj. clin. prof. podiatric medicine, clin. externship program Osteo. Coll. Medicine and Health Scis., Des Moines; field researcher Innovative Products, Spenco Med. Corp., Waco, Tex., 1980-81. Merit badge counselor Bergen council Boy Scouts Am. Lic. podiatrist, Ohio, Pa., N.J.; diplomate Am. Bd. Podiatric Surgery, Internat. Podiatric Laser Soc. Fellow Acad. Ambulatory Foot Surgery, Am. Soc. Podiatric Medicine (sci. co-chmn. 1981-82; sec. treas. 1982-84), Am. Assn. Hosp. Podiatrists, Am. Soc. Podiatric Dermatology, Alpha Epsilon Delta; mem. N.J. Acad. Sci., Ohio Acad. Sci., AAAS, Am. Soc. Podiatric Microsurgery (diplomate; charter mem.), Am. Med. Writers Assn., Aircraft Owners and Pilots Assn., Nat. Assn. Flight Instrs., U.S. Seaplane Pilots Assn., N.J. Podiatry Assn., Am. Soc. Podopediatrics, Alpha Gamma Kappa, Pi Delta (pres. 1974-75). Contbr. articles to profl. jours.; contbg. editor dept. podiatric medicine Current Podiatry Jour., 1976-79, contbg. editor dept. podiatric neurology, 1979-81, editor-at-large, 1982—; gen. rev. editor Jour. Am. Podiatry Assn., 1981-83; editor-in-chief Jour. Acad. Ambulatory Foot Surgery, 1982, Current Podiatry, 1983. Office: 168 Franklin Turnpike Waldwick NJ 07463

CANIVELL, VICTOR FRANCISCO, computer company executive; b. Barcelona, Spain, Dec. 21, 1951; s. Francisco and Evelyn (Cretchley) C.; m. Rosario Fuste, Jan. 27, 1979; 1 child, Silvia. M.B.A., Escuela Superior Administració n Empresas, Spain, 1978; Ph.D. in Physics, U. Barcelona (Spain), 1978. Mem. field mktg. bus. computer group Hewlett Packard, Barcelona, 1979, sales devel. So. Europe, Boeblingen, Germany, 1979-81, European HP-3000 product mgr., Cupertino, Calif., 1981-82, area software mgr., Geneva, 1983-84; Southern Eurpope SVS computer mktg. mgr., Geneva, 1984-85; European software mgr., Geneva, 1986—. Author: Software: Crisis y Oportunidades, 1983; contbr. papers in field. Served to 2d lt. Inf., Spanish Army, 1971. Recipient Research scholarship Spanish Council of Edn., 1974-78. Mem. IEEE, Am. Phys. Soc., Nat. Geog. Soc. Club: de Esquí de Catalunya (Barcelona). Office: Hewlett-Packard SA, 7 route du Nant d'Avrie, CH 1217 Meyrin Geneva Switzerland

CANLAS, EDWIN ACOSTA, surgeon; b. Bataan, Philippines, Dec. 7, 1949; s. Adriano Mallari and Rufina Sison (Acosta) C.; m. Irene Compañero Domingo, June 10, 1979; 1 child, Filadrian. BS in Medicine, U. Santo Tomas, Manila, 1965-69, MD, 1969-73. Intern Rizal (Philippines) Med. Ctr., 1973-74; resident Ramon Magsaysay Med. Ctr., Zambales, Philippines, 1975-77, surgeon, 1977-80; chief of hosp. Dinalupihan Dist. Hosp., Bataan, 1980-85; gen. practice med. Canlas Clinic, Zambales, 1985—; cons. San Marcelino Dist. Hosp., 1985—. Mem. Bataan Med. Soc., Philippine Med. Soc., U. Santo Tomas Alumni Orgn., Mu Epsilon Delta, Dinalupihan Jaycees (bd. dirs. 1983-86). Roman Catholic. Lodge: Lions (project dir. San Marcelino chpt.). Home: Gen Luna St, Brgy Rizal, San Marcelino, Zambales Philippines Office: Canlas Clinic, Cen, San Marcelino, Zambales Philippines

CANN, SHARON LEE, health science librarian; b. Ft. Riley, Kans., Aug. 14, 1935; d. Roman S. and Cora Elon (George) Foote; m. Donald Clair Cann, May 16, 1964. Student Sophia U., Tokyo, 1955-57; B.A., Sacramento State U., 1959; M.S.L.S., Atlanta U., 1977. Cert. health scis. librarian. Recreation worker ARC, Korea, Morocco, France, 1960-64; shelflister Library Congress Washington, 1967-69; tchr. Lang. Ctr., Taipei, Taiwan, 1971-73; library tech. asst. Emory U., Atlanta, 1974-76; health sci. librarian Northside Hosp., Atlanta, 1977-85; library cons., 1985-86; librarian area health edn. ctr., learning resource ctr. Morehouse Sch. Medicine, 1985-86; edn. librarian Ga. State U., 1986—. Editor Update, publ. Ga. Health Scis. Library Assn., 1981; contbr. articles to publs. Chmn. Calif. Christian Youth in Govt Seminar, 1958. Named Alumni Top Twenty, Sacramento State U., 1959. Mem. ALA, Med. Library Assn., Spl. Library Assn. (dir. South Atlantic chpt. 1985-87), Ga. Library Assn. (spl. library div. chmn. 1983-85), Ga. Health Scis. Library Assn. (chmn. 1981-82), Atlanta Health Sci. Library (chmn. 1979), Am. Numis. Assn., Am. Overseas Assn. Club: Toastmasters (Atlanta) sec.-treas. 1983-84). Home: 5520 Morning Creek Circle College Park GA 30349

CANNADY, WILLIAM TILLMAN, architect, educator; b. Houston, Oct. 12, 1937; s. Henry Hilliard and Mary Elizabeth (Cummins) C.; m. Mollie Rehmet, Sept. 10, 1966; children—Sarah Katherine, Lucinda O'Neill. B.Arch., U. Calif.-Berkeley, 1961; M.Arch., Harvard U., 1962; postgrad., U. London, 1970. Registered architect, Tex., La., Mo. Designer various archtl. firms with experience on large-scale planning, urban design, and major bldg. projects, Tex., Calif., Mass. and London, 1962-72; pres. Wm. T. Cannady & Assocs., Inc., Houston, 1972-85; pres. Cannady, Jackson & Ryan, Architects, Inc., Houston, 1985—; mem. faculty Rice U. Sch. Architecture, Houston, 1963—; vis. lectr., critic in architecture to numerous univs. Served with USMC Res., 1955-62. Recipient of numerous local, state and nat. awards for excellence in architecture. Fellow AIA; mem. Houston Philos. Soc. (treas. 1981-82, v.p., 1982-83), The Shepherd Soc., Rice Design Alliance. Republican. Episcopalian. Clubs: Rice U. Faculty, Harvard of Houston, Houston City. Contbr. articles to profl. jours. and lectures to profl. confs. Home: 2246 Quenby Houston TX 77005 Office: Cannady Jackson & Ryan 2370 Rice Blvd Suite 208 Houston TX 77005

CANNALIATO, VINCENT, JR., investment banker, mathematician; b. Bklyn., July 12, 1941; s. Vincent and Margaret (Mancuso) C.; B.S. in Math., Fordham U., 1963; M.A. in Math., City U. N.Y., 1964; grad. cert. in system design U. Pa. Sch. Bus., 1970; m. June A. Marino, Apr. 8, 1967; children—Amy June, Kimberly Dawn, Douglas Vincent. Systems analyst N.Y. Telephone Co., N.Y.C., 1969-70; account exec. CIT Leasing Corp., N.Y.C., 1970-72; v.p. Kidder Peabody & Co., Inc., N.Y.C., 1972-80, head leasing and project financing group corp. fin. dept., 1977-80; sr. v.p., mng. dir., Smith Barney, Harris Upham & Co., Inc., dept. head leasing and project fin., corp. fin., 1980—; vis. instr. Southwestern Grad. Sch. Banking, 1976-77; speaker law jour. seminars equipment learning industry, 1986-87; adv. bd. U.S. Mcht. Marine Acad., 1974—, chmn., 1977—; instr. math. U. Md., 1966-69; mem. maritime adv. com. Dept. Transp., 1982-84, chmn. fin. subcom. 1983-84. Exec. bd., curriculum chmn. Gifted Child Soc., 1975-82; nation chief Rampo Indian Guides and Princesses, Western Hills YMCA, 1980-83; mem. parish council St. Elizabeth Roman Cath. Ch., 1986-88, pres., 1987-88. Served to capt. AUS, 1963-69. Decorated Bronze Star. Mem. Am. Assn. Equipment Lessors (bd dirs. exec. and nominating coms., fed. legis. com. 1975-84, chmn. keyman com. 1978-83, chmn. membership com. 1982-83, chmn. academia awareness task force), Acad. Magical Arts, Inc. Roman Catholic. Clubs: Metropolitan (N.Y.C.); Indian Trail (Franklin Lakes, N.J.); Ocean City (N.J.) Yacht. Contbg. author: U.S. Taxation of International Operations, 1975, 77, 87; Oil and Gas Taxes/Natural Resources Service, 1979; World Leasing Yearbook, 1980, 81. Home: 501 Alexis Ct Franklin Lakes NJ 07417 Office: Smith Barney 1345 Ave of the Americas New York NY 10105

CANNON, DANIEL WILLARD, lawyer; b. Pitts., Sept. 3, 1920; s. Edgar Carl and Violet Jessie (Burke) C.; m. Ann Marshall Price, Sept. 30, 1942; children—Susan Melchior, David, Judith Lillie, Barbara, Ann Finch. A.B., U. Pitts., 1941, J.D., 1968. Bar: Pa. 1948, D.C. 1952, U.S. Supreme Ct. 1952. Atty., U.S. Steel Corp., Pitts., 1947-50; sec., gen. counsel Bituminous Coal Operators Assn., Washington, 1951-58; dir. Indsl. Devel. and Natural Resources, NAM, N.Y.C., 1958-74, dir. environ. affairs, Washington, 1974-84, dir. program devel., 1984—; lectr. in field. Served to 1st lt. USAAF, 1942-46. Recipient Moot Ct. award, U. Pitts. Law Sch., 1947; Award of Appreciation, Water Quality Research Council, 1974. Mem. ABA, Fed. Bar Assn., Bar Assn. D.C., Allegheny County Bar Assn., Air Pollution Control Assn., Water Pollution Control Fedn., Order of the Coif. Republican. Episcopalian. Clubs: Univ., Army and Navy, Pa. Soc., Masons. Editorial adv. bd. Indsl. Wastes Mag., Air Quality Control, 1975; editor, Hazardous Waste Mgmt. Under RCRA: A Primer for Small Business, 1980; A Pollution Tax Won't Help Control Pollution, 1977; National Strength and the National Environmental Policy Act, 1972; Staying Out of Trouble: What You Should Know About the New Hazardous Waste Law, 1985; Preparing for Emergency Planning, 1987, Retroactive Emission Controls, 1987. Home: 637 E Capitol St SE Washington DC 20003 Office: 1331 Pennsylvania Ave NW Suite 1500 N Washington DC 20004-1703

CANNON, ELAINE WINIFRED ANDERSON, author, lecturer; b. Salt Lake City, Apr. 9, 1922; d. Aldon Joseph and Minnie (Egan) Anderson; B.S., U. Utah, 1943; m. Donald James Cannon, Mar. 25, 1943; children—James Quayle, Carla, Christine (Mrs. Bradford E. Knickerbocker), Su (Mrs. Bryant McOmber), Holly (Mrs. Richard Metcalf), Anthony Joseph. With Deseret News, Salt Lake City, 1943-69, feature writer, columnist, 1944-47, editor teen dept., 1947-69; assoc. editor New Era mag., Salt Lake City, 1970-73; assoc. editor Era of Youth mag., 1960-70; moderator It's a Date, Sta. KSL-TV, Salt Lake City, 1952-55, Focus on Youth, Sta. KUTV, 1961-65, 67-69, Public Pulse for Youth, Sta. KSL, 1966-67; v.p. Spicer's Internat. Instr. continuing edn. Brigham Young U., Provo, Utah, 1958—, U. Utah, Salt Lake City, 1964, Utah State U., Logan, 1968-70; Emeritus bd. U. Utah, 1984—; adv. bd. Dixie State Coll., St. George, Utah, 1987—. Del. White House Conf. on Children and Youth, 1950-51; mem. adv. bd. Juvenile Ct., Salt Lake City, 1970-71, Boy's Ranch Utah, Salt Lake City, 1966—; mem. spl. program com. Am. Cancer Soc., Salt Lake City, 1965-66. Bd. dirs. Women Unlimited Conv. Program Bur., Salt Lake City; internat. pres. Young Women Ch. Jesus Christ of Latter-day Saints, also mem. coordinating council; bd. dirs. Deseret Gymnasium, Promised Valley Theatre. Recipient 1st prize writing youth div. Nat. Press Women Assn., 1958, service to youth citation Seventeen mag., 1955; named Woman Year, Ricks Coll., 1965, Weber State Coll., 1971, Idaho State U., 1972; recipient Nat. Religious Heritage of Am. award, 1983, others. Mem. Authors Club, Am. Press Women Assn., Nat. Council Women of U.S.A. (exec. bd. 1979—, v.p.), Mortar Bd., Internat. Platform Assn., Internat. Council of Women (standing com. 1981—), Alpha Lambda Delta, Beta Sigma Phi, Chi Omega. Republican. Mem. Ch. Jesus Christ Latter-day Saints (All-Ch. Honored Woman 1967). Author: It's Great to Be Eight; Baptized & Confirmed; Adversity; Bedtime Stories for Grown Ups; Merry Merry Christmas; Summer of My Content, 1976; The Mighty Change, 1981; Putting Life in Your Life Story, 1981; The Seasoning, 1981. Life One to a Customer, 1982; The Girls Book, 1983; Heart to Heart, 1984. Weekly radio show You and Your World; voice, scriptwriter (cassettes) Elaine Cannon Speaks to Women, Heart to Heart, Mothers and other Mothers. Home: 1283 E South Temple Salt Lake City UT 84102 Office: 1450 W Canyon View Dr Saint George UT 84770

CANNON, HUGH, lawyer; b. Albemarle, N.C., Oct. 11, 1931; s. Hubert Napoleon and Nettie (Harris) C.; A.B., Davidson Coll., 1953; B.A. (Rhodes scholar) Oxford U., 1955, M.A., 1960; LL.B., Harvard U., 1958; m. Lorrie Clark, July 17, 1979; children by previous marriage—John Stuart, Marshall, Martha Janet. Admitted to N.C. bar, 1958, D.C. bar, 1978, S.C. bar, 1979; mem. staff U. N.C. Inst. Govt., Chapel Hill, 1959; mem. firm Sanford, Phillips, McCoy & Weaver, Fayetteville, 1960; asst. to Gov. of N.C., Raleigh, 1961; dir. adminstrn. State of N.C., 1962-65, state budget officer, 1963; mem. firm Sanford, Cannon, Adams & McCullough, Raleigh, 1965-79; individual practice law, Charleston, S.C., 1979—. Parliamentarian NEA, 1965—; lectr. N.C. State U., Raleigh, part-time, 1965, 66. State dir. N.C. Emergency Resources Planning Com., 1962-65; pres. Friends of Coll., Raleigh, 1963; alt. del. Democratic Nat. Conv., 1964; chief parliamentarian, 1976, 80, 84, 88; bd. govs. U. N.C., 1972-81; trustee Davidson Coll., 1966-74. Mem. Phi Beta Kappa, Omicron Delta Kappa, Phi Gamma Delta. Democrat. Episcopalian. Home: 32 Murray Blvd Charleston SC 29401 Office: 1625 Savannah Hwy Charleston SC 29407

CANNON, JOHN, III, lawyer; b. Phila., Mar. 19, 1954; s. John and Edythe (Grebe) C. BA, Denison U., 1976; JD, Dickinson Sch. Law, 1983. Bar: Pa. 1983, Hawaii 1986, U.S. Dist. Ct. (ea. dist.) Pa. 1983, U.S. Ct. Appeals (3d cir.) 1985. Account exec. PRO services, Inc., Flourtown, Pa., 1976-79, br. officer mgr., Pitts., 1979-80; law clk. Montgomery County Ct. of Common Pleas, Norristown, Pa., 1983-84; assoc. Rawle & Henderson, Phila., 1984-88; atty. CIGNA Corp., Phila., 1988— . Comments editor Dickinson Internat. Law Ann., 1983. Mem. Pa. Bar Assn., Phila. Bar Assn., Montgomery Bar Assn., ABA, Hawaii State Bar Assn., Kappa Sigma (pres. 1975-76), Gamma Xi (v.p., trustee 1982-86). Republican. Episcopalian. Office: CIGNA Corp 1600 Arch St Philadelphia PA 19103

CANNON, TOM, sociologist, educator; b. Liverpool, Eng., Nov. 20, 1946; s. Albert Edward and Bridget (Ryan) C.; m. Frances Mary Constable, 1971; children: Robin, Rowan. BA in Sociology, U. London, 1968. Research assoc. Warwick U., Coventry, Eng., 1968-71; lectr. Middlesex Poly. Inst., London, 1971-72, Durham U., U.K., 1975-81; brand mgr. Imperial group, Nottingham, Eng., 1972-75; prof. dept. bus. and mgmt. Stirling (Scotland) U., 1981—; bd. dirs. Mktg. Devel. and Export Services, Stirling, Scottish

Vocat. Edn. Council, Glasgow, Stirling Enterprise Park. Author: Advertising, 1976, Basic Marketing, 1981, How to Win Profitable Business, 1983, Building Business Overseas, 1984. Fellow Royal Soc. Arts, Inst. Export, Inst. Phys. Distbn. Mgmt. Address: 2 Westerton Dr, Bridge of Alan Stirling Scotland Office: Stirling U, FK9 4LA Stirling Scotland

CANNON, WILLIAM RAGSDALE, bishop; b. Chattanooga, Apr. 5, 1916; s. William Ragsdale and Emma (McAfee) C. A.B., U. Ga., 1937; B.D. summa cum laude, Yale U., 1940, Ph.D., 1942; D.D., Asbury Coll., 1950; LL.D., Temple U., 1955; L.H.D., Emory U., 1962; S.T.D. (hon.), Wesleyan Coll., 1980; Litt.D. (hon.), La Grange Coll., 1980, Duke U., 1983; D.C.L. (hon.), N.C. Wesleyan Coll., 1982; D.H., Meth. Coll., 1984. Ordained to ministry Methodist Ch., 1940; pastor Allen Meml. Methodist Ch., Oxford, Ga., 1942-43; prof. ch. history and hist. theology Candler Sch. Theology, Emory U., 1943-68, dean sch. theology, 1953-68; bishop Raleigh area United Meth. Ch., 1968-72, 80-84, Richmond area, 1970-72, Atlanta area, 1972-80; lectr. Fondren Found. So. Meth. U., 1948; vis. prof. Garrett Bibl. Inst., summer 1949, Richmond Coll., U. London, 1930; Mem. commn. on ritual and worship Meth. Ch., 1948-64; chmn. bd. ministerial tng. North Ga. Conf., Meth. Ch., 1948-64; del. to gen. and jurisdictional confs. Meth. Ch., 1948, 52, 56, 60, 64, 68; also mem. commn. on worship, commn. ecumenical affairs; del. Ecumenical Conf. Methodism, Oxford, Eng., 1951, World Meth. Conf., Lake Junalaska, N.C., 1956; fraternal del. from World Meth. Council to World Conf. on Faith and Order, Lund, Sweden, 1952, Nairobi, Kenya, 1975; chmn. exec. com. World Meth. Council; pres. World Meth. Conf., 1980—; hon. pres. World Meth. Council, 1986—; accredited visitor World Council Chs., Evanston, Ill., 1954; Meth. ch. del. 3d assembly World Council of Chs., New Delhi, 1961, Lund, Sweden, 1968, Nairobi, Kenya, 1976; del. World Meth. Conf., Oslo, Norway, 1961; Meth. Ch. del. Conf. on Faith and Order, Montreal, Can., 1963; pres. N. Am. sect., chmn. exec. com. World Methodist Council; mem. presidium; pres. World Meth. Conf.; ofcl. protestant observer from council to II Vatican Council of Roman Catholic Church; co-chmn. Conversations of Methodists and Roman Catholics at Internat. Level; deliverer Episcopal address Bicentennial Gen. Conf. United Meth. Ch., 1984; one of ten observers to Extraordinary Synod of Roman Cath. Ch., 1985; gave prayer at Inauguration of Jimmy Carter as Pres., 1977 and opening of Carter Presdl. Ctr., 1986. Author: A Faith for These Times, 1944, The Christian Church, 1945, The Theology of John Wesley, 1946, Accomplishments to Wesley's Death in Methodism, (edited by W. K. Anderson), 1947, Our Protestant Faith, 1949, The Redeemer, 1931, History of Christianity in the Middle Ages, 1960, journeys after St. Paul, 1963, Evangelism in a Contemporary Context, 1973, A Disciple's Profile of Jesus: On the Gospel of Luke, Jesus the Servant from the Gospel of Mark, 1978, The Gospel of Matthew, 1983, The Gospel of John, 1985. Editor: Selections from Augustine, Table Talk (Martin Luther), 1950. Trustee La Grange (Ga.) Coll., Asbury Coll.; trustee, vice chmn. bd. Emory U.; chmn. trustees Protestant Radio and TV Center, 1953-63. Mem. Oxford Inst. Wesleyan Studies, Phi Beta Kappa, Phi Beta Kappa Assos. (exec. com.), Theta Phi, Phi Kappa Phi. Address: The Plaza Towers 12F 2575 Peachtree Rd NE Atlanta GA 30305

CANTACUZENE, JEAN MICHEL, oil company executive; b. Bucharest, Roumania, Dec. 15, 1933; arrived France, 1947; s. Alexandre Jean and Marianne Manon (Labeyrie) C.; m. Anne Marie Szekely, July 25, 1956 (div. 1970); children—Marianne, Pierre; m. 2d, Daniele Amelie Ricard, July 17, 1971; 1 son, Nicolas. Chem. engr. Ecole Supérieure de Chimie Industrielle, 1957; Agrégé Physique, Ecole Normale Supérieure, Paris, 1960; Sc.D., Ecol. Normale Supérieure, 1960. Asst. prof. chemistry U. Paris, 1960-62; sci. attaché French Embassy, Moscow, USSR, 1962-64; dep. dir. Chem. Lab., Ecole Normale Supérieure, Paris, 1964-71; prof. chemistry U. Paris, 1972-82; sci. dir. CNRS, Paris, 1974-77; sci. counselor French Embassy, Washington, 1977-80; sci. dir. Total Cie Française des Petroles, 1980—; chmn. bd. Solems, Paris, 1983-86; sci. counselor French Ministry of Fgn. Affairs, Paris, 1971-77; mem. sci. adv. commn. French Govt., Paris, 1971-75; mem. bd. dirs. French Nuclear Safety Commn., 1982—; chmn. adv. com. on indsl. research and devel. Commn. of European Communities, Brussels, 1983. Co-author: Chimie Organique, 1971-75; America, Science and Technology in the 80's, 2 vols., 1981; contbr. articles to profl. jours. Recipient Le Bel award, French Chem. Soc., 1968; decorated French Ordre Nationale du Merite, chevalier, 1973, officer, 1988, Ordre Legion d'Honneur, 1982. Mem. Société Chimique de France, N.Y. Acad. Scis., Am. Chem. Soc., Assn. Franç aise des Techniciens du Petrole, Assn. Nationale Recherche Technique, Assn. pour la Va Porisation des Relations Internationales Scientifiques et Techniques. Office: Compagnie Française des Petroles, 5 rue Michel-Ange, Paris 16 France

CANTILLI, EDMUND JOSEPH, engineer, planner, educator, author, safety expert; b. Yonkers, N.Y., Feb. 12, 1927; s. Ettore and Maria (deRubeis) C.; m. Nella Franco, May 15, 1948; children—Robert, John, Teresa. A.B., Columbia U., 1954, B.S., 1955; cert., Yale Bur. Hwy. Traffic, 1957; Ph.D. in Transp. Planning, Poly. Inst. Bklyn., 1972; postgrad. in urban planning and pub. safety, NYU. Registered profl. engr., N.Y., N.J., Calif.; cert. safety profl. Transp. engr. Port of N.Y. Authority, N.Y.C., 1955-59; project planner Port of N.Y. Authority, 1958-60, terminals analyst, 1960-62, engr. safety research and studies, 1962-67, supervising engr., 1967-69; research assoc. div. transp. planning Poly. Inst. Bklyn., 1969-72; assoc. prof. transp. engring. Poly U., 1972-77, prof., 1977—; tchr. Italian, algebra, traffic engring., urban planning, transp. planning, urban and transp. geography, land use planning, aesthetics, environment, indsl., traffic and transp. safety engring., human factors engring., 1965—; prin. Impetus Services Inc., 1985—; pres. Urbitran Assocs., 1973-81; cons. community planning, traffic engring., transp. planning, transp. safety, accident reconstrn., environ. impacts, 1969—; pres., chmn. bd. Inst. for Safety in Transp., Inc., 1977—. Author: Programming Environmental Improvements in Public Transportation, 1974, Transportation and the Disadvantaged, 1974, Transportation System Safety, 1979; editor: Transportation and Aging, 1971, Pedestrian Planning and Design, 1971, Traffic Engineering Theory and Control, 1973; editor and calligrapher There is No Death That is Not Ennobled by So Great A Cause, 1976; contbr. over 200 articles to profl. jours. and trade jours.; developer methods of severity evaluation of accidents, identification and priority-setting of roadside hazards, transp. system safety; introduced diagrammatic traffic signs, collision energy-absorption devices. Served with U.S. Army, 1945-49, 50-51. Fellow ASCE, Inst. Transp. Engrs.; mem. Am. Planning Assn., Am. Inst. Cert. Planners (cert.), Am. Soc. Safety Engrs., System Safety Soc., Human Factors Soc., Mensa, Sigma Xi. Home: 134 Euston Rd S West Hempstead NY 11552 Office: Poly U 333 Jay St Brooklyn NY 11201

CANTILO, PATRICK HERRERA, lawyer; b. Santiago, Chile, Mar. 19, 1954; came to U.S., 1965; s. Luis M. and Yvonne (Cantilo) Herrera-Cantilo; m. Kathryn Gail Goltra, June 18, 1977; 1 child, Michael. BA, U. Tex., 1977, JD, 1980. Bar: Tex. 1980, U.S. Dist. Ct. (we. dist.) Tex. 1983, U.S. Dist. (no. dist.) Tex. 1988. Counsel to receiver Tex. Bd. Ins., Austin, 1980-83; assoc. Davis & Davis P.C., Austin, 1983-85; ptnr. Davis, Cantilo, Welch & Ewbank, Austin, 1985-86; of counsel Freytag, Perry, LaForce, Rubinstein & Teofan, Austin, 1986-87; ptnr. Rubinstein & Perry, Austin, 1987—. Contbr. articles to profl. jours. Mem. Tex. State Bd. Ins. Mem. ABA (litigation sect., tort and ins. sect.), Tex. Bar Assn. (litigation sect.), Travis County Bar Assn. (litigation sect.), Austin Young Lawyers Assn., Nat. Assn. Ins. Commrs. (liquidators task force 1982-83, adv. com. 1985—, chmn. fin. subcom., adv. com. health maintenance orgn. 1986), Nat. Assn. Health Maintanence Orgn. Regulators-Nat. Assn. Ins. Commrs. Democrat. Roman Catholic. Home: 7213 Hartnell Austin TX 78723 Office: Rubinstein & Perry 100 Congress Suite 900 Austin TX 78701

CANTLAY, GEORGE GORDON, retired army officer; b. Honolulu, Aug. 2, 1920; s. George Gordon and Helen (Reid) C.; m. Wilhelmina Shannon Davison, Apr. 27, 1946; children: George Gordon III, Donald Davison, Carolyn Reid. Student, U. Hawaii, 1938-39; B.S., U.S. Mil. Acad., 1943; grad., Armor Sch., 1952, Command and Gen. Staff Coll., 1955, Army War Coll., 1962; M.A., George Washington U., 1963. Commd. 2d lt. U.S. Army, 1943, advanced through grades to lt. gen., 1977; mem. faculty Army War Coll., 1962-65; brigade comdr. 2d Inf. Div. Korea, 1965-66; chief congl. activities div. Office Chief of Staff of Army, 1966-68; asst. div. comdr. 1st Inf. Div., Vietnam, 1968-69; dep. comdg. gen. Delta Mil. Assistance Command, Vietnam, 1969-70; comdg. gen. U.S. Army Armor Tng. Center, 1970; dep. comdg. gen. U.S. Army Armor Center, Fort Knox, Ky., 1970-71; comdg. gen. 2d Armored Div., Ft. Hood, Tex., 1971-73; dep. U.S. rep. NATO Mil. Com., Brussels, Belgium, 1973-77; dep. chmn. NATO Mil. Com., 1977-79. Decorated Def. Disting. Service medal, D.S.M., Silver Star medal, Legion of Merit with three oak leaf clusters, D.F.C. with oak leaf cluster, Bronze Star with V device and oak leaf cluster, Air medal with 16 oak leaf clusters, Army Commendation medal with oak leaf cluster, Purple Heart; RVN Army Distinguished Service Order 1st Class; RVN Gallantry Cross with palm; RVN Armed Forces Honor medal 1st Class Republic Vietnam). Mem. Armor Assn., Assn. U.S. Army, Assn. Grads. U.S. Mil. Acad. Episcopalian. Clubs: Army and Navy (Washington), Army Navy Country (Washington). Home: 501 Thomas Bransby Kingsmill on the James Williamsburg VA 23185-0071

CANTOR, ALAN BRUCE, management consultant, conputer software developer; b. Mt. Vernon, N.Y., Apr. 30, 1948; s. Howard and Muriel Anita Cantor; m. Judith Jolanda Szarka, Mar. 1, 1987; BS in Social Scis., Cornell U., 1970; MBA, U. Pa., 1973. Mgmt. cons. M & M Risk Mgmt. Services, N.Y.C., 1974-78, nat. services officer, spl. projects div. Marsh & McLennan, Inc., 1978-80, asst. v.p., mgr. Marsh & McLennan Risk Mgmt. Services, Los Angeles, 1980-81; sr. v.p. sr. cons. prin. Warren, McVeigh & Griffin, Inc., 1981-82, sr. v.p., prin., 1982; founder, pres. Cantor & Co., 1982—; co-mgr. Air Travel Research Group, N.Y.C., 1977-79; instr. risk mgmt. program Am. Mgmt. Assn.; lectr. Risk and Ins. Mgmt. Soc. Conf., 1980-87; seminar How to Use Spreadsheets in Risk Mgmt., 1986. Cons., Vol. Urban Cons. Group, N.Y.C. Mem. Cornell Alumni Assn. N.Y.C. (bd. govs., program chmn.), Cornell Alumni Assn. So. Calif. Clubs: Wharton Bus. Sch. (N.Y.C.); Los Angeles, Wharton of Los Angeles (chmn.) Los Angeles Athletic (Los Angeles). Copyright airline industry model, 1975. Contbr. articles to profl. jours.; creator, developer, copyright RISKMAP risk mgmt. software products, 1982, 83, 84, 85, 86, 87, 88; copyright airline industry model, 1975, Exposure Base Mgmt. System (EBMS), 1985, 86, patient care monitoring system, 1985,86, 87, 88, COLTS, corp. overall legal tracking system, 1983, hosp. risk info. mgmt. system, 1984. Office: 9348 Civic Ctr Dr Beverly Hills CA 90210

CANTOR, MURIEL G., sociologist, educator; b. Mpls., Mar. 2, 1923; d. Leo and Bess Goldsman; m. Joel M. Cantor, Aug. 6, 1944; children: Murray Robert, Jane Cantor Shefler, James Leo. B.A., UCLA, 1964, M.A., 1966, Ph.D., 1969. Lectr. dept. econs. and sociology Immaculate Heart Coll., Los Angeles, 1966-68; faculty Am. U., Washington, 1968—; instr. Am. U., 1968-69, asst. prof. sociology, 1969-72, assoc. prof., 1972-76, dept. chmn., 1973-75, 77-79, prof., 1976—; vis. prof. communication studies UCLA, 1982; cons. agencies including NIMH; cons. Corp. for Public Broadcasting, 1974-75, 80-81. Author: The Hollywood TV Producer: His Work and His Audience, 1971, 2d edit. with new intro., 1987, Prime Time Television: Content and Control, 1980, (with Phyllis L. Stewart) Varieties of Work Experience, 1974, (with Phyllis L. Stewart) Varieties of Work, 1982, (with Suzanne Pingree) The Soap Opera, 1983 (with Sandra Ball-Rokeach, Premio Diego Fabbri award 1988) Media, Audiences, and Social Structure (Premio Diego Fabbri award 1988), 1986; editor Nat. SWS newsletter, 1977-78. Bd. dirs. Population Inst., 1978-80; trustee WETA, 1972-76. NIMH grantee, 1979-81; recipient Premio Diego Fabbri for Soap Opera in Rome, 1988. Mem. Am. Sociol. Assn., D.C. Sociol. Soc. (pres. 1977-78, Stewart A. RIce Merit award 1987), Sociologists for Women in Society, Eastern Sociol. Soc. (exec. council 1981-84). Home: 8408 Whitman Dr Bethesda MD 20817 Office: Am U Dept Sociology Washington DC 20016

CANTOR, SAMUEL C., lawyer; b. Phila., Mar. 11, 1919; s. Joseph and Miryl (Ginzberg) C.; m. Dorothy Van Brink, Apr. 9, 1943; children: Judith Ann Stone, Barbara Ann Palm. B.S.S., CCNY, 1940; J.D., Columbia, 1943. Bar: N.Y. 1943, U.S. Dist. Ct. (so. and ea. dists.) N.Y. 1951, U.S. Supreme Ct 1969, D.C. 1971. Asst. dist. atty. N.Y.C., 1943-48; legislative counsel N.Y. State Senate; counsel N.Y.C. Affairs Com. N.Y. State Senate, 1949-59; mem. firm Newcomb, Woolsey & Cantor, Newcomb & Cantor, N.Y.C., 1951-59; 1st dep. supt. ins. State of N.Y., 1959-64, acting supt. ins., 1963-64; 2d v.p., gen. solicitor Mut. Life Ins. Co. N.Y., 1964-66, v.p., gen. counsel, 1967-72, sr. v.p., gen. counsel, 1973-74, sr. v.p. law and external affairs, 1974-75, sr. v.p. law and corporate affairs, 1975-78, exec. v.p. law and corp. affairs, 1978-84; counsel Rogers & Wells, 1984—; dir. Mut. Life Ins. Co N.Y., Mony Reins. Corp., Monyco, Inc., Key Resources, Inc., Mony Advisors, Inc., Mony Sales, Inc.; chmn. exec. com. N.Y. Life Ins. Guaranty Corp., 1974-84; Mem. spl. com. on ins. holding holding cos. N.Y. Supt. Ins., 1967, N.Y. State select com. pub. employee pensions, 1973. Contbr. to various legal and ins. publs. Fellow Am. Bar Found.; mem. Ins. Fedn. N.Y. (pres. 1967-68), Am. Bar Assn., N.Y. State Bar Assn., Am. Life Conv. (v.p. N.Y. State 1965-70), Am. Council Life Ins. (chmn. legal sect. 1977, chmn. legis. com. 1977-78, N.Y. State v.p. 1977-84), Health Ins. Assn. Am. (chmn. govt. relations com. 1975, chmn. health care com. N.Y. State 1974-80), Assn. Life Ins. Counsel (dir.), Am. Judicature Soc., Bar Assn. City N.Y., N.Y. Law Inst., Nat., N.Y. State dist. attys. assns., Union Internationale des Avocats, Columbia Law Sch. Alumni Assn. (dir.). Clubs: Mason. (N.Y.C.), University (N.Y.C.); Metropolitan, University (Washington); Fort Orange (Albany, N.Y.); Sawgrass Country, Marsh Landing, Ponte Vedra (Fla.); La Costa Country (Carlsbad, Calif.); Confrérie des Chevaliers du Tastevin; Fairview Country (Greenwich, Conn.); Royal Dornoch (Scotland) Golf. Home: Audubon Ln Greenwich CT 06830 Office: care Rogers & Wells 200 Park Ave New York NY 10166

CANTRELL, CYRUS DUNCAN, III, physics educator; b. Bartlesville, Okla., Oct. 4, 1940; s. Cyrus Duncan and Janet Ewing (Robinson) C.; m. Carol Louise Chandler, June 9, 1962 (div. 1971); m. Mary Lynn Marple, Nov. 18, 1972; 1 child, Katherine Anne. B.A. cum laude, Harvard U., 1962; M.A., Princeton U., 1964, Ph.D., 1968. From asst. to assoc. prof. Swarthmore Coll., Pa., 1967-73; staff mem. Los Alamos Sci. Lab., 1973-76, assoc. group leader, 1976-78, staff mem., 1978-79, cons., 1980—; assoc. prof. U. Paris-Nord, Villetaneuse, France, 1980; prof. physics U. Tex.-Dallas, Richardson, 1980—, dir. Ctr. for Applied Optics. Editor: Laser Induced Fusion and X-Ray Laser Studies, 1976, Multiple-Photon Excitation and Dissociation of Polyatomic Molecules, 1986; contbr. articles to profl. jours.; patentee infrared laser system, 1982, method and apparatus for laser isotope separation, 1987. Winner Nat. Westinghouse Sci. Talent Search, Washington, 1958; Nat. scholar Gen. Motors Corp., 1958-62; Woodrow Wilson Found. fellow, Princeton U., 1962-63; NSF fellow, Princeton, 1965-66. Fellow IEEE (chpt. chmn. 1978-82), Am. Phys. Soc., Optical Soc. Am. Home: 2409 Lawnmeadow Dr Richardson TX 75080 Office: U Tex 2601 N Floyd Rd Richardson TX 75083-0688

CANTWELL, JOHN DALZELL, JR., management consultant; b. Davenport, Iowa, July 17, 1909; s. John D. and Mary Edna (Taylor) C.; m. Margaret Jean Simpson, Apr. 30, 1938; children: Cynthia Jean, John Dalzell III. B.S. in Mech. Engring., U. Iowa, 1932; M.B.A., Wharton Sch., U. Pa., 1934. Registered profl. engr., Ill. Planner, Caterpillar Tractor Co., 1935; plants engr. Bettendorf Co. (Iowa), 1936-40; asst. to v.p. Thilmany Pulp & Paper Co., Kaukauna, Wis., 1941-42; div. engr. U.S. Gypsum Co., Chgo., 1943-48; mgr. home appliance div. Murray Corp. Am., 1949-53; v.p. mfg. Trane Co., 1954-61; v.p. Carrier Corp., 1961-74; exec. v.p. Carrier Air Conditioning Co., 1962-74; sr. asso. McCormick & Co., Tarrytown, N.Y. Pres., Cantwell-Conteville Family Assn. Served to lt. (s.g.) USNR, World War II. Mem. Am. Legion, Phi Delta Theta. Republican. Presbyterian. Clubs: Masons, Onondaga Golf and Country. Office: 606 Kimry Moor Fayetteville NY 13066

CAPASSO, VINCENZO, mathematics educator; b. Bari, Italy, Aug. 30, 1945; m. Rossana Casamassina, Oct. 25, 1969; children: Andrea, Marco. Laurea, Physics U., Bari, 1968; Diploma, Advanced Sch. Physics, 1972. Researcher CSATA, Bari, 1971; lectr. U. Bari, 1971-80, prof. math., 1980—; vis. prof. Pomona Coll., Claremont, Calif., 1982, U. Md., College Park, 1983, U. Graz, Austria, 1973; dir. IRMA Nat. Research Council, Bari, 1985—, Sasia, Sch. for Advanced Studies in Indsl. Math., Italy, 1985—. Editor: Mathematics in Biology and Medicine, 1985, Math Models in Environmental and Ecological Systems, 1987. Office: U Degli Studi, Dept Math Campus, 70125 Bari Italy

CAPE, RONALD DUNCAN THOMSON, medical educator; b. Edinburgh, Scotland, Feb. 9, 1921; s. John and Susan Mathieson (Aitkenhead) C.; m. Patricia Georgina Smallwood, Dec. 15, 1946; children—Randall, Jeremy. B.Sc.,M.B.,Ch.B., U. Edinburgh, 1944, BSc. with honors in Pathology, 1948, M.D., 1954. Med. registrar Perth Royal Infirmary, Scotland, 1949-50; research fellow Vancouver Gen. Hosp., B.C., Can., 1951-52; sr. med. registrar Selly Oak Hosp., Birmingham, Eng., 1952-55; cons. physician in geriatric medicine South Birmingham Group, Eng., 1957-75, United Birmingham Hosps., 1962-75; clin. lectr. U. Birmingham, 1967-73, part-time lectr., 1973-75; assoc. prof. U. Western Ont., London, Can., 1975-77, prof. and coordinator geriatric medicine, 1977-86; chief geriatric medicine Parkwood Hosp., London, 1975-86; acting dir. Nat. Research Inst. Gerontology and Geriatric Medicine, Mt. Royal Hosp., Melbourne, Australia, 1986-87; dir. West Midlands Inst. Geriatrics and Gerontology, Birmingham, 1971-75; chair Regional Adv. Com. on Geriatric Services, Birmingham, 1964-70, 73-75; mem. council Brit. Geriatrics Soc., 1969-72; mem. regional adv. panel Mental Health Services, 1970-75; mem. med. adv. bd. Osteoporosis Soc. Can., 1982-86; mem. Drug Quality and Therapeutics Com., Ont. Ministry of Health, 1985-86. Author: Aging: Its Complex Management, 1978; Geriatrica, 1982. Contbr. chpts. to books, articles to profl. jours. Editorial bd. 5 jours. Served as squadron leader RAF, 1945-47; NATOUSA. Fellow Royal Coll. Physicians and Surgeons Can., ACP, Royal Coll. Physicians Edinburgh; mem. Can. Assn. Gerontology, Can. Geriatrics Research Soc. (med. adv. bd. 1978-86), Can. Med. Assn., Can. Soc. Clin. Pharmacology, Can. Soc. Geriatric Medicine (chr exec. com. 1981-82), Gerontol. Soc., Ont. Psychogeriat. Assn., Am. Geriatric Soc., Brit. Soc. Research into Aging, Brit. Soc. Social and Behavioral Gerontology, others. Avocations: walking, swimming, golf, theater, ballet. Home: PO Box 109, Port Fairy, Victoria 3284, Australia Office: Geriatric Advisors Pty, 189 Victoria Parade, Fitzroy, Victoria 3065, Australia

CAPEHART, BARNEY LEE, industrial and systems engineer; b. Galena, Kans., Aug. 20, 1940; s. Samuel Alfred and Mary Jane (Bliss) C.; m. Lynne Carol Fowler, Sept. 2, 1961; children: Thomas David, Jeffrey Donald, Cynthia Diane. B.S.E.E., U. Okla., Norman, 1961, M.E.E., 1962, Ph.D., 1967. Instr. elec. engring. U. Okla., 1965-67; mem. tech. staff Aerospace Corp., San Bernardino, Calif., 1967-68; asst. prof. indsl. and systems engring. U. Fla., Gainesville, 1968-72; assoc. prof. indsl. engring. U. Tenn., 1972-73; assoc. prof. indsl. and systems engring. U. Fla., 1973-79, prof., 1979—; cons. Martin Marietta Corp., U.S. Naval Tng. Device Ctr.; expert witness in energy and safety cases; chmn. Regional Energy Action Com., 1977-79; Region IV adv. group on appropriate tech. Dept. of Energy, 1978-80; mem. Local Energy Action Program, 1980-81. Author books in field; editor Internat. Jour. Energy Systems, 1985—; contbr. articles to profl. jours. Pres. Fla. League Conservation Voters, 1984-86. Served with USAF, 1963-65. Decorated Air Force Commendation medal; Barney Capehart Day proclaimed by Alachua County, Fla., May 26, 1987, City of Gainesville, Dec. 21, 1987; recipient Palladium medal Am. Assn. Engring. Socs., 1988. Fellow AAAS; sr. mem. Am. Inst. Indsl. Engrs. (dir. energy mgmt. div. 1986-87), IEEE; mem. Soc. Computer Simulation, Audubon Soc. (Fla. chpt. Conservationist of Yr. 1987), Fla. Defenders of Environment, Fla. Conservation Found., Sierra Club, Sigma Xi, Sigma Tau, Alpha Pi Mu, Tau Beta Pi. Home: 1601 NW 35th Way Gainesville FL 32605 Office: Industrial and Systems Engineering Dept University of Florida 303 Weil Hall Gainesville FL 32611

CAPISTRANO, FRANCISCO VICTORINO, physician, hospital administrator; b. Manila, Philippines, Dec. 1, 1932; s. Gerardo Cruz Capistrano and Valeria Villamayor Victorino; m. Maxima Cipriano Maniquiz, Dec. 1, 1959; children: Armando, Nelson, Maria Lourdes, Josephine, Paul. AA, Letran Coll., Manila, 1951; Dr. Medicine, Manila Cen. U., 1959. Med. observer San Lazaro Hosp., Manila, 1959; adj. resident physician Bulacan Provincial Hosp., Malolos, Bulacan, Philippines, 1959-60, jr. resident physician, 1960-64, resident physician, 1964-67; resident physician San Miguel (Bulacan) Emergency Hosp., 1967-69, chief hosp., 1969—; dist. health officer San Miguel Health Dist., 1982—. Co-chmn. Primary Health Care Council, San Miguel, 1984—; adviser San Miguel Health Assn., 1987; active Goodwill Industries Philippines, Rehab. for Disabled Found. and Kapwa Ko, Mahal Ko, Manila, 1977—. Recipient Cert. Appreciation Regional Health Office #3, 1971, Cert. of Recognition Nat. Hosp. Week Exec. Com., 1973, Cert. Appreciation R.P.-Can. World Youth Exchange Program, 1975, Plaque for Outstanding Achievement Philippine Media Practitioners Assn., 1984, Plaque for Being Outstanding Govt. Employee Province of Bulacan, 1985; named Outstanding Physician and Socio-Civic leader, Operation Task Force Pagmamahal Inc., 1984, Outstanding Chief Hosp., Profl. Community Leader Service Inc., 1987, Outstanding Dr. Yr., Internat. Pub. Assistance Civic Orgn. Inc., 1987. Mem. Bulacan Med. Soc. Inc. (Cleanest Govt. Hosp. award 1980, 1st pl. in cleanliness and beautification contest 1981), Philippine Hosp. Assn., Assn. Med. Health Adminstrs. Roman Catholic. Home: 409 Pablo Pablo St, 10th Ave, Caloocan Philippines

CAPLAN, ALBERT JOSEPH, university dean; b. Phila., June 2, 1908; s. Joseph and Frances (Belber) C.; m. Sylvia Fay Bayuk, Mar. 13, 1932; children: Judith Ann Caplan Gould, Jerome Albert, Stephen Bayuk. B.S. in Edn, Temple U., 1929; LL.B., 1933. Account exec. Bayuk Bros. (brokerage firm), Phila., 1929-44; partner Bayuk Bros. (brokerage firm), 1944-51; pub. South Jersey News, Collingswood, N.J., 1934-40; partner Albert J. Caplan & Co. (brokerage firm), Phila., 1951-60; pres. Charles A. Taggart & Co. Inc. (brokerage firm), Phila., 1960-65; dean Charles Morris Price Sch. of Advt. and Journalism, Phila., 1966-75; dean emeritus Charles Morris Price Sch. of Advt. and Journalism, 1975—. Author: For You and Other Poems, 1925, Manuscript Making in the Middle Ages, 1927, A Bibliography of Sir Walter Scott, Bart, 1929; contbr. to newspapers and mags. Bd. dirs. Friends of Music, U. Pa.; hon. life bd. dirs. Cheltenham Twp. Art Center, Congregation Adath Jeshurun; chpt. membership chmn. ARC, 1975-77. Served with USNR, 1944-45. Fellow Library Co. Phila., Royal Soc. Arts (London) (life), AIM (pres.'s council 1967), Am. Philos. Soc. (library fellow), Phila. Mus. Art (life); life mem. Acad. Polit. Sci. of Columbia U., Am. Acad. Polit. and Social Scis. (del.), Am. Def. Preparedness Assn., Cruiser Olympia Assn., Franklin Inst. Pa., Hist. Soc. Pa., Navy League U.S., Pa. Assn. Adult Edn., Phila. Orch. Pension Fund Soc., Phila. Public Relations Assn. (hon.), Settlement Sch. Music Alumni, Temple U. Gen. Alumni Assn. (dir., com. chmn. Diamond Asso.), U. Pa. Alumni Assn., Chapel Four Chaplains (legion of honor 1966, 77, 81), Am. Legion (adj. Benjamin Franklin Post 405, past comdr. Louis N. Porter Post 224), Beta Sigma Rho (past trustee grand chpt.), Phila. Flag Day Assn. (dir.), Advt. Hall Fame (bd. judges 1964-74), Am. Inst. Graphic Arts (past v.p., dir.), Curtis Inst. Music (patron), Friends of Drama Guild (patron), Friends of Free Library (sponsor), Friends of Independence Nat. Hist. Park (patron), Internat. Graphic Arts Assn. (dir. 1955-70), Charles Willson Peale Soc. of Pa., Acad. Fine Arts, Am. Legion Press Assn., Phila. Orch. Assn. (pres.'s council), Rosenbach Found. Mus. (assoc.), So. Profl. Journalists, Law Alumni Temple U., Zoological Soc. Phila., Pi Lambda Phi, Lambda Sigma Kappa (past trustee). Clubs: Downtown of Temple U. (past pres.), Faculty of U. Pa, Diamond Temple U. Faculty, Franklin Inn, Poor Richard (sch. trustee, past officer, silver medal), Peale, Print (life), Varsity of Temple U. (life), Union League (chmn. bd. trustees, scholarship fund), B'nai B'rith. Home: The Wellington 135 S 19th St Philadelphia PA 19103

CAPLAN, DAVID LARRY, art dealer; b. N.Y.C., Dec. 20, 1934; arrived in Japan, 1962; s. Harry and Sarah (Levy) C.; m. Rie Tomita, July 28, 1967; children: Lawrence Tomi, Ken. Grad. jr. high. sch., Sydney, New South Wales, Australia. Mgr. Artisan Trading Co., Sydney, 1949-62; mng. dir. Opal Trading Co., Tokyo, 1962—, Mita Arts Co., Ltd., Tokyo, 1977—. Co-pub.: Understanding Japanese Prints, 1981. Mem. Japan Ukiyo-e Dealers Assn. (bd. dirs. 1981—). Clubs: Tokyo Am., Internat. House. Office: Itopia Roppongi Room 607, 2-2-2 Roppongi Minato-Ku, Tokyo 106, Japan

CAPLIN, MORTIMER MAXWELL, lawyer, educator; b. N.Y.C., July 11, 1916; s. Daniel and Lillian (Epstein) C.; m. Ruth Sacks, Oct. 18, 1942; children: Lee Evan, Michael Andrew, Jeremy Owen, Catherine Jean. BS, U. Va., 1937, LLB, 1940; JSD, NYU, 1953; LLD (hon.), St. Michael's Coll., 1964. Bar: Va. 1941, N.Y. 1942, D.C. 1964. Law clk. to judge U.S. Ct. Appeals (4th cir.), Richmond, 1940-41; assoc. Paul, Weiss, Rifkind, Wharton & Garrison, N.Y.C., 1941-50; prof. law U. Va., Charlottesville, 1950-61, vis. prof. law, 1964-87; prof. emeritus 1988—; ptnr. Perkins, Battle & Minor, Charlottesville, 1952-61; U.S. commr. IRS, Washington, 1961-64; ptnr. Caplin & Drysdale, Washington, 1964—; mem. Pres.' Task Force on Taxation, 1960; bd. dirs. Fairchild Industries Inc., Chantilly, Va., Presdl. Realty Corp., White Plains, N.Y., Easco Hand Tools Inc., Washington; mem. pub. rev. bd. Arthur Andersen & Co., Chgo., 1980—. Author: Proxies, Annual

Meetings and Corporate Democracy, 1953, Doing Business in Other States, 1959; editor-in-chief Va. Law Rev., 1939-40; contbr. numerous articles on tax and corp. matters to profl. jours. Former chmn. bd. dirs. Nat. Civil Service League, Am. Council on Internat. Sports; mem., former chmn. nat. citizens adv. com. Assn. Am. Med. Colls.; trustee George Washington U., Washington, 1964—, U. Va. Law Sch. Found., 1982—, Arena Stage, Washington; bd. overseers Coll. of V.I., 1964—; former pres. Atlantic Coast Conf. Served to lt. USNR, 1942-45, ETO. Cited as mem. of initial landing force Normandy Invasion, USN; recipient Alexander Hamilton award U.S. Treasury Dept., 1964, Achievement award Tax Soc. of NYU, 1962, Judge Learned Hand Human Relations award Am. Jewish Com., 1963, Disting. Service award Tax Execs. Inst., 1964. Fellow Am. Bar Found., Am. Coll. Tax Counsel; mem. Am. Law Inst. (life), ABA (ho. of dels. 1980—), N.Y. State Bar Assn., Va. Bar Assn., D.C. Bar Assn., Nat. Lawyers Club, Order of Coif, Phi Beta Kappa, Omicron Delta Kappa. Democrat. Jewish. Clubs: University (N.Y.C.) (Washington) (fin. com.); Fed. City, Nat. Lawyers (Washington). Home: 4536 29th St NW Washington DC 20008 Office: Caplin & Drysdale One Thomas Circle NW Washington DC 20005

CAPONE, LUCIEN, JR., management consultant, former naval officer; b. Fall River, Mass.; s. Lucien and Louise Dolores (Malafronte) C.; m. Charlotte Loretta Lammers, July 22, 1950; children: Lucien, Judith Ann. B.S., U.S. Naval Acad., 1949; grad., Naval Postgrad. Sch., 1955, Indsl. Coll. Armed Forces, 1967; M.S. in Bus. Adminstrn, George Washington U., 1967, postgrad., 1970-71. Commd. ensign U.S. Navy, 1949; advanced through grades to rear adm.; served on destroyers U.S. Navy (Atlantic Fleet), 1949-54; mem. staff (Office of Chief of Naval Ops., Dept. Navy), 1955-57; exec. officer (U.S.S. Huse), 1957-59; staff, comdr. (Middle East Force), Persian Gulf, 1959-61; head plans, programs, and requirements br. (Naval Communications System Hdqrs.), Washington, 1961-63; comdg. officer (U.S.S. Hammerberg), 1963-64; dep. chief of staff (Def. Communications Agy.), Washington, 1964-66; comdg. officer (U.S.S. Dahlgren), 1967-69; asst. comdr. plans, programs, requirements (Naval Communications Command), Washington, 1969-72; comdg. officer (U.S.S. Richmond K. Turner), 1972-73; dep. dir. nat. mil. command system tech. support (Def. Communications Agy.), Washington, 1974-76; dir. command and control tech. center (Def. Communications Agy.), 1976-78, dep. dir. command and control, 1976-78; dir. (Inter-Am. Def. Coll.), Washington, 1978-79; exec. Booz, Allen & Hamilton, Inc., Bethesda, Md., 1979—, v.p., 1983—. Decorated Legion of Merit, Def. Superior Service medal with oak leaf cluster. Mem. IEEE, Armed Forces Communications and Electronics Assn. (pres. D.C. chpt.), Nat. Assn. for Uniformed Services (chmn., bd. dirs.). Roman Catholic. Home: Bristol RI 02809 Office: Booz Allen & Hamilton Inc East West Towers 4330 East West Hwy Bethesda MD 20814

CAPPELLETTI, VINCENZO, science historian, administrator; b. Rome, Aug. 2, 1930; s. Camillo and Maria (Maresca) C.; m. Alippi Maurizia, Oct. 4, 1956; children—Claudia, Andrea. M.D., U. Rome, 1954, Ph.D., 1964. dir. gen. Inst. della Enciclopedia Italiana, Rome, 1970—; pres. Domus Galilaeana, Pisa, Italy, 1970—; prof. history of sci. U. Rome and Milano Cattolica. Author: Entelechia, 1966; Helmholtz, 1968; Freud, 1974; Scienza tra storia e società , 1978, Origini della Philosophia Anthropologica, 1985; editor: Studium, Il Veltro, 1958—. Mem. Soc. European of Culture (v.p. 1982—), Acad. Int. Hist. d. Scis. (v.p. 1985—). Roman Catholic. Home: 42 Via G Arrivabene, Rome 00191 Italy Office: Enciclopedia Italiana, P Paganica 4, Rome Italy

CAPPS, GEORGE DWAYNE, public relations executive; b. Grove, Okla., Oct. 22, 1942; s. William George and Phyllis Eva (Turpin) C.; m. Lee Ngoc. A.A., Los Angeles City Coll., 1962; student Calif. State U.-Northridge, 1963-65; B.A., Calif. State U., 1965. Interpreter, Thai lang. escort officer Dept. State, Washington, 1968-70; fgn. news editor Daily News, Bangkok, Thailand, 1970-73; cons. Burson-Marstieller (Thailand) Ltd., Bangkok, 1973-77, mng. dir., 1977—; chmn. pubs. com. Am. C. of C., Bangkok, 1978—. Editor, Collegian, 1962, Nite News, 1962. Vol., Peace Corps., Thailand, 1966-68, Princess Mother's Flying Doctors Found., Thailand, 1979-83. Mem. Armed Forces Communications and Electronics Assn., Am. C. of C. Bangkok (bd. govs. 1987—), Internat. Pub. Relations Assn., Sigma Delta Chi, Beta Phi Gamma. Republican. Buddhist. Clubs: Fgn. Corrs. of Thailand (pres. 1975-76) (Bangkok), Royal Bangkok Sports. Home: 219/1 Sukumvit 4 Rd, Bangkok 10110, Thailand

CAPPUCIO, RONALD JOSEPH, lawyer; b. Phila., Mar. 3, 1954; s. Anthony R. and Marie A. (Rigolizzo) C.; m. Sondra J. Lippl, Aug. 2, 1980; 1 child, Sondra Nicole. B.S.F.S. in Internat. Econs., Georgetown U., 1974, LL.M. in Taxation, 1977; J.D., U. Kans., 1976. Bar: N.J. 1976, U.S. Dist. Ct. N.J. 1976, D.C. 1977, U.S. Tax Ct. 1977. Chief law clk. to judge, 1977-78; assoc. Lario & Nardi, Haddonfield, N.J., 1978-80; sole practice 1980—; solicitor Gloucester Twp. Planning Bd., 1981-82, Evesham Twp Planning Bd., 1982-83; adj. instr. dept. govtl. services Rutgers U., 1977-80. Mem. ABA, N.J. Bar Assn., Camden County Bar Assn. Address: 1409 Kings Hwy N Cherry Hill NJ 08034

CAPPY, JOSEPH E., automobile company executive; b. 1934; married. BBA, U. Wis., 1956. With Ford Motor Co., 1956-80, mktg. plans mgr., custom cars and light trucks, 1969-71, gen. field sales mgr. Detroit dist., 1971-72, spl. projects mgr. recreational vehicles, 1972-73, recreational products sales mgr., 1973-74, dir. mktg. staff, sales planning office, 1974-77; dist. sales mgr. Ford Motor Co., Louisville, 1977-78; mktg. plans mgr. Lincoln-Mercury div. Ford Motor Co., 1978-80, gen. mktg. mgr. Lincoln-Mercury div., 1980; v.p. mktg. Am. Motors Corp., Southfield, Mich., 1982-84, group v.p. sales and mktg., 1984-85, exec. v.p., chief operating officer, 1985, chief exec. officer, 1986-87; pres., bd. dirs. Am. Motor Sales Corp. (subs. Am. Motors Corp.), 1985-87; group v.p. Jeep/Eagle mktg. Chrysler Motors, Southfield, 1987—. Office: Chrysler Motors 27777 Franklin Rd Southfield MI 48034

CAPRA, PIERRE JENS FREDERIC, history educator; b. Bordeaux, France, Sept. 22, 1915; s. Pierre Onesime and Marie Charlotte Dagmar (Dorph-Petersen) C.; licencie Sorbonne and U. Bordeaux, 1939; agrege, 1947; doctor, Sorbonne, 1972; m. Suzanne Labat, July 27, 1939; children—Pierre Bernard, Marguerite (Mrs. J.P. Ré gnier). High sch. tchr. in Bayonne, Perigueux, Libourne and Bordeaux, 1943-57; mem. Nat. Center Sci. Research, 1958-60; mem. faculty U. Bordeaux, 1960-83, prof., 1974-83, prof. medieval history, 1978-83, hon. prof., 1983—; hon. res. officer French Infanterie de Marine. Paul Harris fellow Rotary Internat., 1977; recipient History award Acad. Bordeaux, 1945, award Town of Bordeaux, 1960; Officer Pub. Edn. medal, 1966. Mem. French Soc. Numismatics, Soc. Medievalists for Higher Edn., Assn. Sorbonne Former Students, Inst. Nat. Def. High Studies (hon. local pres.), Scotch Whiskey Tasters (local dir.). Lodge: Rotary (past local pres., dir. gov. 1976-77); Bordeaux-Students (past rugby pres.). Contbr. numerous articles, particularly on Anglo-Gascon adminstrn. and 14th century coinage, to profl. publs. Home: 5 rue Charles Laterrade, 33400 Talence France

CAPRINO, LUCIANO, pharmocologist, toxicologist; b. Rome, Aug. 11, 1934; s. Giovani and Matilde (Alessndrello) C.; m. Donatella De Andreis, Oct. 19, 1966; children: Claudia, Carlo. Asst. prof. pharmacology med. sch. U. Rome, 1959-62, dir. IV chair of pharmacology La Sapienza med. sch., 1986—; asst. prof. U. Perugia, Italy, 1962-68; assoc. prof. toxicology sch. med. U. Cattolica del Sacro Cuore, Rome, 1969-86, prof. several postgrad. schs., 1968—; mem. expert panel ecology Ministry Justice, 1972—. Coeditor: Platelet Aggregation and Drugs, 1974; contbr. articles to profl. jours, 6 chpts. in books; patentee in field; research on platelet aggregation and thrombosis. Mem. Internat. Soc. Thrombosis and Haemostasis, European Soc. Study Drug Toxicity, Italian Soc. Pharmacology, Acad. Medica Roma, Assn. Argentina Farmacologia y Terapeutica Exptl., N.Y. Acad. Sci., Italian Soc. Toxicology. Home: 129 Via Trionfale, 00136 Rome Italy Office: U Rome, Inst Pharmocology, Piaz Aldo Moro 5, 00185 Rome Italy

CAPRIO, JOSEPH GIUSEPPE CARDINAL, clergyman; b. Lapio, Italy, Nov. 15, 1914. Ordained priest Roman Catholic Ch., 1938. Served in diplomatic missions, China, 1947-51, Belgium, 1951-54, South Vietnam, 1954-56; internuncio in China with residence at Taiwan, 1959-67; ordained titular archbishop of Apollonia, 1961; pro-nuncio in India, 1967-69; sec. Adminstrn. of Patrimony of Holy See, 1969-77, pres., 1979-81; substitute sec. of state, 1977-79; elevated to Sacred Coll. of Cardinals, 1979; deacon St. Mary Auxiliatrix in Via Tuscolana; pres. Prefecture of Econ. Affairs of Holy See, 1981—; mem. Congregation Evangelization of Peoples; mem. commn. Revision Code of Canon Law. Office: The Vatican Vatican City *

CAPSHAW, TOM DEAN, administrative law judge; b. Oklahoma City, Sept. 20, 1936; m. Dian Shipp; 1 child, Charles W. BS in Bus., Oklahoma City U., 1958; student U. Ark. Coll. Law, Fayetteville, 1958-59; JD, U. Okla.-Norman, 1961. Bar: Okla. 1961, Wyo. 1971, Ind. 1975. Assoc. Looney, Watts, Looney, Nichols and Johnson, Oklahoma City, 1961-63, Pierce, Duncan, Couch and Hendrickson, Oklahoma City, 1963-70; trial atty., v.p. Capshaw Well Service Co., Liberty Pipe and Supply Co., Casper, Wyo., judge HUD, adminstrv. law judge, Evansville, Ind., 1973-75, judge in charge, 1975—; acting regional chief adminstrv. law judge, Chgo., 1977-78; acting appeals council mem., Arlington, Va., 1980, acting chief adminstrv. law judge, 1984; mem. faculty U. Evansville, 1977; lectr. in field. Author: A Manual for Continuing Judicial Education, 1981, Practical Aspects of Handling Social Security Disability Claims, 1982; contbr. numerous articles to profl. jours., chpts. to textbooks. Mem. exec. council Boy Scouts Am., scoutmaster, den leader, 1969—; bd. dirs. Casper Symphony, 1972-73, Casper United Fund, 1972-73, Midget Football Assn., Casper, 1972-73, German Twp. Water Dist., 1982; pres. Unitarian Universalist Ch., 1984-86. Recipient Kappa Alpha Order Ct. of Honor award, 1962, Silver Beaver award Boy Scouts Am., 1980; named Ky. Col., 1984; Unitarian Universalist fellowship. Mem. ABA (chmn. edn. com. Conf. Adminstrv. law judges 1979-81), Okla. Bar Assn., Okla. County Bar Assn. (v.p. 1967),81), Wyo. Bar Assn., Evansville Bar Assn. (jud. rep. 1986-87, James Behtel Greshaw Freedom award, 1988), Young Lawyers Conf. of Okla. County (pres. 1966), Okla. Assn. Def. Council, Okla. City Trial Lawyers Assn., Assn. Adminstrv. Law Judges HHS (bd. dirs. 1979-82), Fed. Adminstrv. Law Judges Assn., Nat. Jud. Coll. U. Nev., Oklahoma City U. Alumni Assn. (bd. dirs. 1965). Home: 6105 School Rd #6 Evansville IN 47712

CAPUTO, DANTE, minister of foreign affairs of Argentina; b. Nov. 25, 1943; m. Anne Morel; 3 sons. Ed. U. Buenos Aires, Harvard U., Tufts U.; D.Polit. Sociology, U. Paris. Adj. prof. polit. sociology Salvador U., Buenos Aires; adj. prof. pub. services and state enterprises U. Buenos Aires; dir. Ctr. for Social Investigations on State and Adminstrn., 1976; adj. investigations on State and Administrn., 1976; adj. investigator Nat. Ctr. for Sci. Investigation, France; minister of fgn. affairs of Argentina, 1983—; pres. 43rd Gen. Assembly, UN, 1988—. Mem. La Union Civica Radical. Address: Ministro de Relaciones Exteriores, Buenos Aires Argentina *

CAPUTO, LUCIO, trade company executive; b. Monreale, Italy, May 22, 1935; s. Giuseppe and Gioacchina (Spinnato) C.; came to U.S., 1967; Law Degree, Palermo U., 1957, Journalism Degree, 1958, Degree in Polit. Sci., 1960, postgrad. economics, 1961; m. Maria Luisa Mayr, Oct. 5, 1967; 1 son, Giorgio. Journalist, Italy, 1950-65; admitted to Italian bar, 1961; asso. firm Studio Legale Caputo-Orlando, Palermo, Sicily, 1960-62; ofcl. Italian Fgn. Trade Inst., 1962-82, mkt. researcher, Libya, Cyprus, 1963, dep., London, 1964-67, dir. study mission SE Asia, 1967, Italian trade commr., Phila., 1967-71, N.Y.C., 1972-82; founder Italian Wine Promotion Center, N.Y.C., 1975—, Italian Tile Center, 1979—, Italian Fashion Center, 1980—, Italian Shoe Center, 1981—, Italian Trade Center, N.Y.C., 1981—; pres. Ital Trade USA Corp., 1982-86 ; pres. Italian Wine and Food Inst., 1984—; organizer ann. Italian Week on 5th Ave., N.Y.C.; exec. v.p., exec. com. Gruppo Esponenti Italiani, 1974—; adv. bd. Italy-Am. C. of C., 1972—; chmn. Internat. Trade Ctr., Inc., 1987—. Served to lt. Italian Air Force, 1959-61. Named Cavaliere Ufficiale all' Ordine del Merito della Repubblica Italiana, 1972, Commendatore, 1981. Mem. Italian Bar Assn., Italian Journalist Assn., Fgn. Consular Assn. Phila., Soc. Fgn. Consuls N.Y. Roman Catholic. Club: World Trade Center. Signer agreement between Italy and Peoples' Republic of China, 1967; editor trade mags.: Italy Presents, Quality (English, French, Spanish, German), 1962-64; contbr. articles to Italian mags. and newspapers. Office: 1 World Trade Ctr Suite 1513 New York NY 10019

CARAFOLI, ERNESTO, biochemistry educator; b. Sedegliano, Italy, Oct. 14, 1932; arrived Switzerland, 1973; s. Umberto and Margherita (Alzetta) C.; m. Annamria Benucci, July 14, 1963; children—Umberto, Federico. M.D., U. Modena, 1957; P.D. in gen. Pathology, 1965, P.D. in Biochemistry, 1968. Intern, Univ. Hosp., Modena, 1957-58; postdoctoral fellow Johns Hopkins U., Balt., 1963-65, vis. lectr., 1968-69; asst. prof. gen. pathology U. Modena, Italy, 1961-73; prof. U. Padova, 1973; prof. biochemistry Swiss Fed. Inst. Tech., Zurich, 1973—. Contbr. numerous articles to sci. jours.; editor books on membrane biochemistry and calcium metabolism. Grantee NATO, NIH, Swiss NSF, Italian Nat. Research Council. Hon. mem. Soc. Gen. Physiology; mem. Biochem. Soc., Am. Soc. Cell Biology, Biophys. Soc., European Molecular Biology Orgn., Swiss Biochem. Soc., Am. Soc. Biol. Chem. and Molecular Biol., Johns Hopkins Soc. Scholars. Home: Tennmoostrasse 40a, 8044 Gockhausen Switzerland Office: Labor of Biochemistry-ETH, Universitatstrasse 16, 8092 Zurich Switzerland

CARAMEL, JEAN-PIERRE-DANIEL-EDMOND, ophthalmologist; b. Montpellier, France, Sept. 9, 1953; s. Robert and Mireille (Gayraud) C.; m. Jocelyne Galea, July 18, 1975; children: Laurent, Audrey. Cert. kinesiologist superior, U. Montpellier, 1980, MD, 1981; ophthalmologist, U. Paris, 1981. Monitor U. Montpellier, 1972-76, asst., 1973-77, chief anatomy, 1973-82; resident Regional Hosp., Montpellier, 1973-82; practice medicine specializing in pediatric-ophthalmology Montpellier, 1982—. Mem. French Ophthalmology Soc., European Strobologic Soc., French Strobologic Soc., Strobological Research Students. Roman Catholic. Office: 18 Rue Henri Dunant, 34000 Montpellier France

CARANO, JOHN JOSEPH, JR, foundry products sales manager; b. Warren, Ohio, Oct. 19, 1954; s. John Joseph and Theresa Rose (Mattinat) C.; m. Teresa Helen Scott, Oct. 4, 1980. BS in Edn., Youngstown State U., 1979. Sales trainee Nat. Castings div. Midland Ross Corp., Sharon, Pa., 1979-80, coordinator mktg. services , sales rep. RR products, Chgo., 1980-81, sales rep. indsl. castings, Sharon, 1981-82, dist. sales mgr. mining and mill sales, Columbus, Ohio, 1982-86, regional sales mgr. Midwest sales, Nat. Castings, Inc., Columbus, 1986-87; dist. mgr. Columbia Steel Casting Co., Inc., Columbus, 1987—. Mem. Hubbard Vol. Fire Dept., Ohio, 1975-79; active Ohio Hist. Soc., Columbus, 1984—, Cat Welfare Assn., Misty Meadows Civic Assn., Northwest Civic Assn. Mem. Am. Foundrymen's Soc., Am. Acad. Polit. and Social Sci., Youngstown State U. Alumni Assn. Democrat. Roman Catholic. Clubs: Columbus Italian, Unity, Toastmasters (Columbus) (v.p. local chpt. 1984, pres. 1987—, Best Pub. Speaker award 1984-85, Pub. Debate speaker award 1984, Best Speaker Evaluator award 1985, Able Toastmaster award 1987). Avocations: running, book collecting, home repair and restoration. Home: 2667 Delcane Dr Columbus OH 43220-1712 Office: Columbia Steel Casting Co Inc 4663 Executive Dr Columbus OH 43220-3627

CARAPETYAN, ARMEN, editor, musicologist; b. Oct. 11, 1908; came to U.S., 1928, naturalized, 1942; s. Mackertoum and Miriam (Khazarian) C.; m. Harriette Esther Norris, Nov. 4, 1937; children—Francelle, Peter Anthony. Diploma, Am. Coll., Teheran, 1927; student in, Paris, France, then N.Y.C.; M.A., Harvard U., 1940, Ph.D., 1945. Founder 1945; since dir. Am. Inst. Musicology (specializing Medieval and Renaissance music), Cambridge, Mass.; spl. work in fostering research and publs. in field, directing project. Dir. Corpus Scriptorum de Musica, Corpus of Early Keyboard Music, Corpus Mensurabilis Musicae, Musicological Studies and Documents; editor, pub.: Musica Disciplina (yearbook); dir. Renaissance Manuscript Studies, Miscellanea. Hon. mem. Am., Internat. musicol. socs. Home: Monte de los Almendros, 18680 Solobreña Granada Spain Office: Hänssler Verlag, Postfach 1220, 7303 Neuhausen-Stuttgart Federal Republic of Germany

CARASSO, ALFRED SAM, mathematician; b. Alexandria, Egypt, Apr. 9, 1939; came to U.S., 1962; s. Samuel and Renee (Ades) C.; m. Beatrice Kozak, June 12, 1964; children—Adam, Rachel. B.S. in Physics, U. Adelaide (Australia), 1960; M.S. in Meteorology U. Wis., 1964, Ph.D. in Math, 1968. Asst. prof. math. Mich. State U., East Lansing, 1968-69; asst prof. math. U. N.Mex., Albuquerque, 1969-72, assoc. prof., 1972-76, prof., 1976-81; mathematician Nat. Bur. Standards, math. analysis div. Ctr. for Applied Math., Washington, 1982—; cons. Los Alamos Nat. Lab., 1972-81. Mem. Soc. for Indsl. and Applied Math. Jewish. Research on math. and computational analysis of inverse problems and their application in heat conduction, seismology, acoustics, image processing, and electromagnetics. Office: Nat Bur Standards, Adminstrn A-302 Gaithersburg MD 20899

CARAVATT, PAUL JOSEPH, JR., communications company executive; b. New Britain, Conn., Dec. 13, 1922; s. Paul Joseph and Bessie (Avery) C.; m. B. Laura Bennett, June 22, 1946; children—Cynthia Diane, Suzanne Laura. AB, Dartmouth, 1945, MBA, 1947. With Nat. Dairy Assn., 1947-49, Young & Rubicam, 1949-50; advt. mgr. Hunting and Fishing mag., 1950-52, Biow Co., 1952-56; v.p. Ogilvy, Benson & Mather, 1956-59; sr. v.p. Foote, Cone & Belding, 1960-64, LaRoche, McCaffrey & McCall (advt. agy.), N.Y.C., 1964-66; pres. Carl Ally, Ind. (advt. agy.), N.Y.C., 1966-67; chmn. bd., chief exec. officer Marschalk Co., Inc. (mem. Interpublic Group of Cos.), N.Y.C., 1967-69; sr. v.p., dir. Interpub. Group Cos., N.Y.C., 1970-72; pres., chief exec. officer, dir. Caravatt Communications, Newtel World Communications, N.Y.C., 1971—. Mem. Newcomen Soc., S.A.R., Zeta Psi. Republican. Conglist. Club: University (N.Y.C.). Home: 274 Westport Rd Wilton CT 06897 Office: 49 Riverside Ave Westport CT 06880 also: Caravatt Communications Video Disc Pub Inc 381 Park Ave S New York NY 10022

CARAZO ZELEDON, MARIO, lawyer, accountant; b. San José, Costa Rica, June 15, 1949; s. Rodrigo Carazo Odio and Estrella Zeledón Lizano; m. Melania Ortiz Volio, Oct. 10, 1971; children: Pia, Felipe, Rodrigo, Mariana. Lic. derecho and adminstrn. negocios, U. Costa Rica, 1971; diploma advanced studies in econ. devel., U. Manchester, Eng., 1972. Asst. gen. mgr. Fin. Co. London, Ltd., San José, 1972-73; sr. ptnr. Carazo, Montero & Fernández Law Office, San José, 1973—; prof. law U. Costa Rica, 1972—. Author: The Process of Industrial Growth in Central America, 1972. Advisor to pres., ambassador-at-large Republic of Costa Rica, 1978-82. Mem. Christian Social Unity Party. Roman Catholic. Office: Carazo Montero & Fernandez, Ave 8 Calle 9 and 11 #963, 1000 San Jose Costa Rica

CARBAJAL, ULYSSES MEJIA, ophthalmologist; b. San Nicolas, Pang., Philippines, Aug. 10, 1922; s. Crisanto Cabato and Candida Quinto (Mejia) C.; M.D., Manila Central U., 1952; M.Div., Philippine Union Coll., 1977; M.Th., Andrews U., Mich., 1980; m. Jovita Mercado de la Cruz, Dec. 6, 1952; children—Dwight, Ritchie, Jan, Eugene. Intern, Manila Sanitarium and Hosp., 1951-52; resident in ophthalmology Eye and Ear Hosp., Los Angeles, 1953-54, Los Angeles Children's Hosp., 1954-55, U. Calif., 1955-56; staff surgeon Santa Fe Coast Lines Hosp., Los Angeles, 1957-60; head eye, ear, nose and throat dept. Manila Sanitarium and Hosp., 1960—; propr. Carbajal Clinic Orthoptic Center, 1960—; med. dir. Nueva Vizcaya Doctors Hosp., 1972-76; pres. Nueva Vizcaya Doctors Hosp., Inc., 1972—; asst. clin. prof. ophthalmology Loma Linda (Calif.) U., 1957-60; assoc. dean Bicol Christian Coll. of Med., Philippines, 1982—; pres. Philippine Bd. Med. Specialists, 1972—; adviser Assn. Philippine Ophthalmologists in Am., 1979—. Named Most Outstanding Alumnus, Philippine Union Coll., 1961, 67, Manila Central U., 1966, 72. Named Most Outstanding Physician Philippine Med. Soc. So. Calif. Diplomate Am. Bd. Ophthalmology. Fellow A.C.S.; mem. Am., Philippine (pres. 1970-71), Pan Am. med. assns., Nueva Vizcaya Med. Soc., Philippine Soc. Ophthalmology, Philippine Coll. Surgeons, Internat. Assn. Ocular Surgeons (charter), Am. Assn. Ry. Surgeons, Philippine Hosp. Assn. (sec. 1974-76), World Strabismus Assn., Philippine Council Against Smoking, Alcohol and Drug Dependency, Philippine Assn. Colls. Nursing, Philippine Soc. for Music Edn., Philippine Assn. Geriatrics. Seventh-day Adventist. Club: Philippine Choral Condrs. Assn. (pres. 1973-77). Author: My Beloved Country First, 1975; The PMA Story, 1977; PMA Protocal and Procedures, 1965. Composer numerous songs, including theme song for Philippine Hosp. Assn. Contbr. sci. articles to med. jours. Address: 1502 E Chevy Chase Dr Glendale CA 91206

CARBERRY, JAMES JOHN, chemical engineer, educator; b. Bklyn., Sept. 13, 1925; s. James Thomas and Alice (McConnin) C.; B.S., U. Notre Dame, 1950, M.S., 1951; D.Eng., Yale U., 1957; m. Judith Ann Bower, Sept. 12, 1959 (div.); children—Alison Ann, Maura O'Malley; m. 2d, Margaret V. Bruggner, Sept. 24, 1974. Process engr. E.I. duPont de Nemours & Co., Gibbstown, N.J., 1951-53, sr. research engr., Wilmington, Del., 1957-61; teaching and research fellow Yale U., 1953-57; prof. chem. engring. U. Notre Dame (Ind.), 1961—; mem. U.S.-Soviet working com. chem. catalysis. cons. in field. Mem. adv. council chem. engring. dept. Princeton U., 1980—. Served with USNR, 1944-46. Recipient award for advancement pure and applied sci. Yale Engring. Assn., 1968. NSF fellow Cambridge U. (Eng.), 1965-66; Fulbright-Hays sr. scholar, Italy, 1973-74; Kelley lectr. Purdue U., 1978; Richard King Mellon fellow, Sir Winston Churchill fellow Cambridge U., 1979-82; vis. fellow Clare Hall Coll., Cambridge U., 1987; vis. chaired prof. Politecnico di Milano, Italy, 1987; life fellow Clare Hall, Cambridge U., 1988; gruppo attivitá Verdiane, Roncole Verdi, 1987—. Fellow Royal Soc. Arts (London), N.Y. Acad. Scis.; mem. Am. Chem. Soc., Am. Inst. Chem. Engrs. (R.H. Wilhelm award in chem. reaction engring. 1976), Yale Alumni Assn. (rep.), Yale Engring. Assn., Lucrezia Borgia Soc., Sigma Xi. Roman Catholic. Club: Yale (N.Y.C.). Author: Chemical and Catalytic Reaction Engineering, 1976; editor: Catalysis Revs. Office: Dept Chem Engring U Notre Dame Notre Dame IN 46556

CARBERRY, JOHN J. CARDINAL, former archbishop of St. Louis; b. Bklyn., July 31, 1904. Recipient D.D., S.T.D., Ph.D., J.C.D., LL.D. degrees. Ordained priest Roman Catholic Ch., 1929; apptd. titular bishop of Elis and coadjutor cum Jure successionis Lafayette, Ind., 1956; consecrated 1956; succeeded to See Lafayette, 1957-65; bishop of Columbus, Ohio, 1965-68; archbishop of St. Louis, 1968-79; named to Coll. Cardinals, 1969—; apptd. apostolic adminstr. 1979; Pres. Center Applied Research in the Apostolate, from 1970. Office: Archdiecese of St Louis 4445 Lindell Blvd Saint Louis MO 63108 *

CARBINE, SHARON, lawyer, coporation executive; b. Bryn Mawr, Pa., Feb. 14, 1950; d. Thomas Joseph and Mary Teresa (Loftus) Carbine. B.A., Temple U., 1972, J.D., 1974, LL.M. in Taxation, 1977. Bar: Pa. 1974, Tex. 1981; C.P.A., Tex., Pa. Atty., Altemose Cos., Center Square, Pa., 1973-75; law clk. presiding justice Ct. Common Pleas, Phila., summer, 1975; tax atty. Provident Mut. Life Ins. Co., Phila., 1975-77, Emhart Corp., Farmington, Conn., 1977-78; tax sr. Peat Marwick Mitchell & Co., Phila., 1978-79; legal counsel to gov.'s chief energy advisor Tex. Energy and Natural Resources Adv. Council, Austin, 1979-80; tax atty. Sun Co., Inc., Dallas, 1980-82; sole practice, Haverford, Pa., 1983-84; tax atty. Ebasco Services Inc., N.Y.C., 1983-84; sole practice law, King of Prussia, Pa., 1985-88; asst. treas., mgr. corp. taxation PQ Corp., Valley Forge, Pa., 1988—; dir. Quaker City Japanning and Enameling Co., Inc., Phila., Vol., Republican Party, 1964—; mem. Jaycees, Phila., 1978-79, Austin, Tex., 1979-80; bd. dirs. Republican Women of the Main Line, Bryn Mawr, Pa., 1983. Mem. Pa. Bar Assn., Montgomery Bar Assn., Delaware County Bar Assn., Phila. Bar Assn., Delaware County Atty.-C.P.A. Forum, Brehon Law Soc. Roman Catholic. Lodge: Rotary (King of Prussia). Home: 275 Bryn Mawr Ave #H28 Bryn Mawr PA 19010 Office: Valley Forge Exec Mall PO Box 840 Valley Forge PA 19482-0840

CARCAILLET, DANIEL LOUIS, physician; b. Brest, France, Oct. 3, 1944; s. Louis and Suzanne (Pouliquen) C.; m. Monique Lesaux, Feb. 22, 1965; children: Christopher, Astrid, Julien. MD, U. Rennes, 1972. Gen. practice medicine Quimper, France, 1972—; chief med. physician Brittany Ferries, Roscoff, France, 1977—, Securite Civile Dept. Finistere, Quimper, 1986—; maritime medicine research project leader ECC/CEE, Luxembourg, 1987; researcher Inst. Tech., Lorient, France, 1987. Contbr. articles to profl. jours. Served as physician with French Navy, 1971-72. Fellow French Soc. Emergency Medicine, Am. Occupational Med. Assn. Home: Tymenhir Plomelin, 29700 Finistere France Office: Brittany Ferries, PO Box 72, 29211 Roscoff France

CARCANI, ADIL, Prime Minister, chairman Council of Ministers of Albania; b. Shkoder, Scutari, May 4, 1922. Asst. commr. of 5th Assault Brigade during nat. war of liberation; various positions in several govt. ministries as asst. minister of commerce, 1948, minister of industry, 1951, asst. minister of the merged ministry of industry and constrn., 1953; minister of industry and mines, 1955; leading mem. of Tirana Communist Party Orgn., 1948, candidate mem. of the Central Com., 1952, full mem., 1956; candidate mem. of Politburo, 1956, full mem., 1961; dep. premier, 1965, 1st dep. premier, 1974-82; mem. parliament, 1946—; mem. gen. council of Albanian Democratic Front, 1967—; chmn., Council of Ministers and Prime Minister, 1982—; chmn. Central Electrification Commn., 1970; head Albanian Econ. Delegations to China, 1968, 75; mem. com. drafting new constrn., 1975. Decorated Order of Freedom First Class, 1962. Office: Council of Ministers, Tirana Albania *

CARDEN, ROBERT CLINTON, III, electrical engineer; b. Phila., Mar. 26, 1933; s. Robert Clinton and Mary Alice (Blanton) C.; B.E.E., Ga. Inst. Tech., 1955, M.S. in Elec. Engring., Ga. Inst. Tech., 1959; postgrad. UCLA, 1961-74, U. Calif.-Irvine, 1980-81; m. Mary Eleanore Clapp, Aug. 15, 1959; children—Robert Clinton IV, Linda Warren. Project engr. Bendix Radio div. Bendix Aviation, Towson, Md., 1950-57; mem. tech. staff Space Tech. Labs. TRW, 1959-62, El Segundo, Calif.; mem. tech. staff Marshall Labs., Torrance, Calif., 1962-68; founder, dir. Time Zero Corp., Torrance, 1968-71; founder, dir., mgr. engring. Comtec Data Systems div. Am. Micro Systems, Cupertino, Calif., 1971-75; engring. mgr., prin. engr. Ball Corp., Gardena, Calif., 1975-80, staff cons. Ball Corp., Huntington Beach, Calif., 1980-83; sr. staff engr. TRW Inc., Redondo Beach, Calif., 1983—; cons. engr. digital systems, 1980—; instr. in field. Served with AUS, 1957. Mem. Am. Rocket Soc., IEEE, Computer Soc., Ga. Tech. Alumni Assn., Tau Beta Pi, Eta Kappa Nu, Scabbard and Blade, Chi Phi. Republican. Presbyterian. Research in digital space systems. Author, producer: Space for the Everday Man, 1978; contbr. articles to profl. jours. Home: 1217 N Kennymead St Orange CA 92669 Office: TRW Inc 1 Space Park 105/2810 Redondo Beach CA 90278

CÁRDENAS, JUAN PABLO-SQUELLA, editor-in-chief; b. Santiago, Chile, Dec. 1, 1949; s. Augusto Cárdenas and María Squella; m. Patricia Urrutia Castro; children: Patricia, Juan Pablo, Cristobal, José Manuel, Alvaro, Francisco. Student, Cath. U. Chile, Santiago, 1971. Editor in chief Debate Univ., Santiago, 1971-73; prof. journalism dept. Cath. U. Chile, 1971-73; dir. journalism dept. Univ. of the North, Antofagasta, Chile, 1974-75; editor in chief Análisis, Santiago, 1977—; bd. dirs. Emisión Limitada, Santiago, Editorial Terranova, Santiago; v.p. Cen. Estudios Polit. Latin Am., Santiago, 1987—. Author: Por un Chile Libre, 1984, No a Pinochet, 1986. Mem. natural direction Intransigencia Dem., 1986. Recipient Wladimir Herzog award Brazil, 1985, Internat. Fedn. Newspaper Pubs. Golden Pen Freedom, 1987. Mem. Nat. Assn. Journalists, Fedn. Latin Am. Periodistas, Soc. Bilivariana, Soc. Escritores Chile. Office: Analisis, Manuel Montt 425, Santiago Chile

CARDIN, PIERRE, fashion designer; b. San Biagio di Callalta, Italy, July 2, 1922. Ed., St. Etienne, France. Tailor with Manby (men's tailor), Vichy, France, 1939-40; adminstr. with French Red Cross, World War II. Designer with Paquin, Paris, 1945-47, House of Dior, Paris, 1947-50, propr. own design house, Paris, 1950—; owner Maxim's Restaurants; founder, dir. Théatre des Ambassadeurs-Pierre Cardin, 1970, renamed Espace Cardin, 1971; designer costumes for films including La Belle et la bête, 1946, A New Kind of Love, 1963, The V.I.P.s, 1963, Eva, 1964, The Yellow Rolls Royce, 1965, Mata Hari, Agent H-21, 1967, A Dandy in Aspic, 1968, The Immortal Story, 1969, You Only Love Once, 1969, Little Fauss and Big Halsy, 1970. Decorated chevalier Legion d'Honneur, les insignes de Comdr. de l'Ordre du Méite de la République Italienne, 1976, ; recipient Basilica Palladiana prize, 1973, le prix de l'EUR (Italian theatre Oscar), 1974, Gold Thimble awards for most creative high fashion collections, 1977, 79, 82, Career Achievement award, Cutty Sark Men's Fashion Awards, 1984. Address: 59 rue de Fauborgh-Saint Honoré, 75008 Paris France *

CARDINAL, AGNES ELISABETH, Swiss-German educator; b. Zurich, Switzerland, Nov. 27, 1942; d. Josef and Agnes (Oswald) Meyer; m. Roger Cardinal, July 21, 1965; children: Daniel, Felix. BA with honors U. Kent, Canterbury, Eng., 1974; MA, U. Kent, 1978. Sec. Oppenheimer & Co., Zurich, 1964-65; tchr. French and German Kelvin High Sch., Winnipeg, Can., 1965-67; asst. in French and German Warwick (Eng.) High Sch. for Girls, 1967-68; sec. U. Kent, 1968-71, lectr. German, 1978—, research fellow in German, 1986—. Author: The Figure of Paradox in the Work of Robert Walser, 1982; editor: Christa Wolf: Der Geteilte Himmel, 1987. Rotary Club research grantee, London, 1974-75. Home: Heathfield Primrose Hill, Chartham Hatch, Canterbury CT4 7NS, England Office: U Kent, Canterbury CT2 7NP, England

CARDINALE, CLAUDIA, actress; b. Tunis, Tunisia, Apr. 15, 1939; d. Franco and Yolanda Cardinale; student Centro Sperimentale di Cinematografica, Rome, Italy; m. Franco Cristaldi, 1966; 1 son. Motion picture appearances include I soliti ignoti, 1958, Girl with a Suitcase, 1961, Persons Unknown, Upstairs and Downstairs, 1961, Rocco and his Brothers, 1961, Eight and a Half, 1963, Cantouche, 1964, Circus World, 1964, Of a Thousand Delights, The Pink Panther, 1964, Blindfold, 1966, The Centurion, 1961, Running World, Last Command, 1966, The Professionals, 1966, Don't Make Waves, 1967, Day of the Owl, 1968, The Queens, 1968, A Fine Pair, 1969, Once Upon a Time in the West, 1969, The Red Tent, 1971, Conversation Piece, La Scoumone, 1972, Days of Fury, 1973, Libera, Amore Mio, 1973, Escape to Athena, 1979, The Leopard, 1982, Le Ruffian, 1982, Fitzcarraldo, 1982, Burden of Dreams (documentary), 1982. Office: Vides Piazza, Pitagora 9, Rome Italy *

CARDMAN, CECILIA, artist; b. Soveria Mannelli, Italy; d. Samuel and Maria (Mendicino) Cardman. B.F.A., U. Colo., 1934, B.A., 1934; student Instituto dei Belli Arte, Naples, Italy, 1921-23, Denver Art Mus., 1930-31, studied with Leon Kroll, Nat. Acad., 1945-46, others. Head dept. painting Mesa Coll., Grand Junction, Colo., 1930-40; one-man shows: Naples, Italy, Grist Mill Gallery, Chester, Vt., Bergdorf-Goodman, 1978, Jarvis Gallery, Sandwich, Mass., 1975, Elliott Mus., Stuart, Fla., Grand Junction, Colo., 1981; group shows include: Nat. Arts Club, 1975-76, Nat. Acad., 1945, Knickerbocker Artists, 1979, Nelson Gallery, 1937-38, Denver Art Mus., 1924-25, Nat. League Am. Pen Women, 1979, Grand Central Art Gallery, 1977, Am. Artist Profl. League, 1979-80; one-woman show Elliott Mus., Stuart, Fla., 1988. Recipient numerous awards. Mem. Jackson Heights Art Club (1st prize 1982, 2d prize 1983), Pen & Brush (dir. admissions, Emily Nichols Hatch award 1982, 1st prize 1983, pres. 1987-88), Coll. Women's Club, Salmagundi Club (Lay Jury prize 1979), Nat. League Am. Pen Women (dir.; 1st br. v.p.), Sumi-e Soc. (prize 1982, recipient soc. award 1987), Ky. Watercolor Soc., Artist Fellowship, Inc., Knickerbocker Artists, Catherine Lorillard Wolfe Art Club (pres., dir., Best in Show award 1980, named Woman of the Year 1987), Am. Artists Profl. League (nat. dir.), Allied Artists Am. (dir. publicity, bd. dirs. 1983-86), Nat. Cowboy Hall of Fame, Western Heritage Ctr. Roman Catholic. Home: 34-06 81st St Penthouse Jackson Heights NY 11372

CARDOSO, ANTHONY ANTONIO, artist, educator; b. Tampa, Fla., Sept. 13, 1930; s. Frank T. and Nancy (Messina) C.; m. Martha Rodriguez, 1954; children: Michele Denise, Toni Lynn. BS in Art Edn., U. Tampa, 1954; BFA, Minn. Art Inst., 1965; MA, U. So. Fla., 1975; PhD. Art instr., head fine arts dept. Jefferson High Sch., Tampa, 1952-67, Leto High Sch., Tampa, 1967—, instr. adult art edn., 1965—; dir. , supr. Hillsboro County Schs.; rep. Tampa Art Council; artist, 1952-87; one-man shows include Warren's Gallery, Tampa, 1974, 75, 76, Tampa Realist Gallery, Tampa, 1975; group shows include Rotunda Gallery, London, Eng., 1973, Raymon Duncan Galleries, Paris, France, 1973, Brussells (Belgium) Internat., 1973; represented in permanent collections Minn. Mus., St. Paul, Tampa (Fla.) Sports Authority Art Collection, 1971—, Tampa Arts' Council, 1978-86. Recipient Prix de Paris Art award Raymon Duncan Galleries, 1970, Salon of 50 States award Ligoa Duncan Gallery, N.Y.C., 1970, Latham Found. Internat. Art award, 1964, XXII Bienniel Traveling award Smithsonian Instn., 1968-69, Purchase award Minn. Mus., 1971, 1st award Fla. State Fair, 1967, Accademia Italia Gold Medal, 1981-82, Medallion Merit, Internat. Parliament, Italy, 1984. Mem. Rho Nu Delta. Democrat. Roman Catholic. Executed murals at Suncoast Credit Union Bldg., Tampa, 1975, Tampa Sports Authority Stadium, 1972. Home: 3208 Nassau St Tampa FL 33607 Office: 901 E Kennedy Blvd Tampa FL 33601

CARDUCCI, BERNARDO JOSEPH, psychology educator, consultant; b. Detroit, May 20, 1952; s. Edward and Mary (Bosco) C.; 1 child, Rozana. AA, Mt. San Antonio Coll., 1972; BA, Calif. State U., Fullerton, 1974, MA, 1976; PhD, Kans. State U., 1981. Assoc. prof. psychology Ind. U.-S.E., New Albany, 1979—; textbook mktg. cons.; stress workshop dir.; research supr., tchr. Author: Instructor's Manual to Accompany Mehr's Abnormal Psychology, 1983; mem. editorial bd. Jour. Bus. and Psychology; contbr. numerous articles to profl. jours. Recipient Most Cert. of Merit award Mt. San Antonio Coll. Associated Men Students, 1971; Service award Ingleside Mental Health Ctr., 1976; Outstanding Faculty Contbn. award Ind. U.-S.E., 1981; named Psychology Alumnus of Yr. Calif. State U.-Fullerton, 1987. Mem. Am. Psychol. Assn., Soc. for Personality and Social Psychology, Midwestern Psychol. Assn., Council Undergrad. Psychology Depts. (pres. 1985-87), Southeastern Psychol. Assn., Soc. for Psychol. Study Social Issues, Psi Chi (recipient cert. recognition for outstanding research 1974). Home: 4002 Summer Pl New Albany IN 47150 Office: Dept Psychology Ind U SE New Albany IN 47150

CARDWELL, SUE POOLE, reclamation services company executive; b. Clearfield, Pa., Oct. 31, 1952; d. Robert Thomas Poole and Mary B. (Edwards) (stepmother) and Patricia Alice (Coleman) (stepmother) P.; m. Charles Howard Cardwell, Nov. 24, 1979; children—Jonathon Aaron, Jacqueline Leigh. Clk.-typist Ky. Dept. Mines and Minerals, 1974; sr. reclamation insp. div. reclamation Ky. Dept. Natural Resources, Madisonville, 1974-77; pres. Reclamation Services Unltd., Inc., Madisonville, 1977—; chmn. West Ky. adv. group Office Surface Mining, Dept. Interior, 1979—; adv. bd. U. Ky. Symposium on Surface Mining Reclamation and Hydrology, also mem. exec. adv. com.; mem. Ky. Adv. Com. on Strip Mine Regulation, 1979—; mem. exec. bd. Ky. Task Force on Exploited and Missing Children; bd. dirs., sec. Ky. Alliance for Missing and Exploited Children; mem. Rep. Senatorial Inner Circle, 1984—. Served with WAC, 1972-73. Named hon. Ky. col.; named to W.Va. Ship of State. Mem. West Ky. Coal Operators Assn. (dir.), West Ky. Assn. Gen. Contractors, Hazardous Materials Control Research Inst., Mining and Reclamation Council Am. (chmn. reclamation subcom.), Profl. Reclamation Assn. Am. (bd. dirs., charter), World Safety Assn., W.Va. Surface Mine Assn., Nat. Reclamation Assn. West Ky., West Ky. Constrn. Assn. of Associated Gen. Contractors, West Ky. Sonstrn. Assn. (bd, dirs.); contbg. editor Ky. Coal Jour. Office: 12 Hartland Ave Madisonville KY 42431

CARE, RAFAEL STOERK, epidemiologist, educator; b. Tiberias, Israel, Apr. 2, 1938; s. Carl and Henrietta (Stoerk) C.; m. Cynthia Albala, Feb. 10, 1966; children: Jordan, Evy, Sari. MD, Hebrew U., 1967; MS, Drexel U., 1969; PhD in Pub. Health, Johns Hopkins U., 1986. Intern Hadassah Hosp., Jerusalem, 1966, resident, 1967; resident Meir Hosp., Kfar Saba, Israel, 1972-75; med. dir. MOR Inst. Med. Data, Bnei-Brak, Israel, 1975—; adj. assoc. prof. community medicine Ben Gurion U., Beer Sheva, Israel, 1987—; head dept. occupational medicine Soroka Med. Ctr., Beer Sheva, 1987—. Mem. Am. Coll. Preventive Medicine, Am. Occupational Med. Assn., Internat. Epidemiol. Assn., Am. Pub. Health Assn. Office: Soroka Med Ctr, Beert Seva 84101, Israel

CARELLA, EUGENE JOHN, lawyer; b. Stamford, Conn., Apr. 27, 1943; s. Richard L. and Theresa (Uva) C.; m. Paula E. Pfister, 1988. BA in Polit. Sci., Denison U., 1965; JD, U. Toledo, 1968. Bar: Colo. 1968, U.S. Dist. Ct. Colo. 1968, U.S. Ct. Appeals (5th and D.C. cirs.) 1977, U.S. Supreme Ct. 1977. Cons. advanced underwriting Mut. Life Ins. Co. N.Y., N.Y.C., 1968-69; fin. planner U.S. Trust Co., N.Y.C., 1969-70; sr. v.p. corp. div. Groesbeck Fin. Advisors Inc., Century City, Calif., 1970-73; dir. mktg. Edward N. Hay Assocs., Phila., 1973-74; v.p. Inverness Planning Corp., N.Y.C., 1974-75; sole practice Century City, 1975—. Active support groups Boy's Club, Los Angeles, 1960-85. Fellow Assn. Trial Lawyers Am., Am. Mgmt. Assn.; mem. ABA (corp. banking and bus. sect.), Internat. Platform Assn., Am. Compensation Assn. (hon., award of distinction 1970), Smithsonian Inst., Phi Gamma Delta. Roman Catholic. Office: PO Box 67292 Century City Los Angeles CA 90067

CARETTI, RICHARD LOUIS, lawyer; b. Grosse Pointe, Mich., Dec. 17, 1953; s. Richard John and Doris Eleanor (Evans) C.; m. Nancy Louise Matouk, Oct. 14, 1983; 1 child, Katherine Lynn. BA, Wayne State U., 1975; JD magna cum laude, Detroit Coll. Law, 1980. Bar: Mich. 1980, U.S. Dist. Ct. (ea dist.) Mich. 1980, U.S. Ct. Appeals (6th cir.) 1982. Assoc. Dickinson, Wright, Moon, Van Dusen & Freeman, Detroit, 1979-84, ptnr., 1985—. Mem. ABA, Detroit Bar Assn., Mich. Def. Trial Counsel, Assn. Def. Trial Counsel. Delta Theta Phi. Roman Catholic. Club: Detroit Athletic (club open raquetball champion). Home: 1380 Devonshire Grosse Pointe Park MI 48230 Office: Dickinson Wright Moon et al 800 First Nat Bldg Detroit MI 48226

CAREY, BRENDAN PATRICK, advertising executive; b. Tipperary, Ireland, June 6, 1945; s. John Christopher and Shela (O'Brien) C.; m. Louisa Brendan; children: Nicola, Nadine, Preston. Artist Young Advt., Dublin, Ireland, 1965; finished artist, art dir. Wilson Hartnell Advt., Dublin, 1965-73; creative dir. Bell Advt., Dublin, 1974-88; joint mng. dir. Imagebank Group of Cos., Dublin, 1988—. Recipient various nat. and internat. artistic awards. Mem. Inst. Creative Advt. and Design. Roman Catholic. Home: Hadleigh Killiney Rd, Killiney, Dublin Ireland

CAREY, DEAN LAVERE, fruit canning company executive; b. Biglerville, Pa., Nov. 29, 1925; s. Earl E. and Ann Olivia (Newman) C.; m. Doris M. Dugan, July 21, 1949; children—Philip D., Juanita Ann. B.S., U. Pitts., 1949. With Knouse Foods Corp., Inc., Peach Glen, Pa., 1949—; controller Knouse Foods Corp., Inc., 1955-59, asst. gen. mgr., 1960-62, gen. mgr., 1963-65, pres., 1966—, also dir. Dir. Blue Cross, Harrisburg, Pa.; vice-chmn. Capital Blue Cross, Harrisburg. Served with USNR, 1944-46. Mem. Pa. Chamber Bus. and Industry (bd. dirs.). Lutheran. Clubs: Am. Legion, Masons, Shriners. Office: Knouse Foods Coop Inc Peach Glen PA 17306

CAREY, ERNESTINE GILBRETH (MRS. CHARLES E. CAREY), writer, educator; b. N.Y.C., Apr. 5, 1908; d. Frank Bunker and Lillian (Moller) Gilbreth; m. Charles Everett Carey, Sept. 13, 1930; children: Lillian Carey Clark), Charles Everett. B.A., Smith Coll., 1929. Buyer R. H. Macy & Co., N.Y.C., 1930-44, James McCreery, N.Y.C., 1947-49; lectr., book reviews, syndicated newspaper articles, 1951. Co-recipient (with Frank B. Gilbreth, Jr.) (Prix Scarron French Internat. humor award for Cheaper by the Dozen 1951), (with Lillian Moller Gilbreth) (McElligott medallion Assn. Marquette U. Women 1966); Author: Jumping Jupiter, 1952, Rings Around Us, 1956, Giddy Moment, 1958, (with Frank B. Gilbreth, Jr.) Cheaper by the Dozen, 1949, Belles on Their Toes, 1951; also mag. articles and book revs. Bd. dirs. Right to Read, Inc., 1968—, co-chmn., 1967; lay adv. com. Manhasset (N.Y.) Bd. Edn.; trustee Manhasset Pub. Library, 1953-59, v.p., 1956-59; trustee Smith Coll., 1967-72. Montgomery award Friends of Phoenix Public Library, 1981. Mem. Authors Guild Am. (life mem., mem. guild council 1955-60), P.E.N. Republican. Conglist. Clubs: North Shore, Smith College (L.I.) (asst. chmn. scholarship com. 1950-59); Smith Coll. (N.Y.); Smith College Phoenix (Phoenix) (vice chmn. scholarship com. 1967), 7 College Conf. Council (Phoenix). Home: 6148 E Lincoln Dr Paradise Valley AZ 85253

CAREY, KATHRYN ANN, corporate philanthropy, advertising and public relations executive, editor, consultant; b. Los Angeles, Oct. 18, 1949; d. Frank Randall and Evelyn Mae (Walmsley) C.; m. Richard Kenneth Sundt, Dec. 28, 1980. BA in Am. Studies with honors, Calif. State U.-Los Angeles, 1971. Tutor Calif. Dept. Vocat. Rehab., Los Angeles, 1970; teaching asst. U. So. Calif., 1974-75, UCLA, 1974-75; claims adjuster Auto Club So. Calif., San Gabriel, 1971-73; corp. pub. relations cons. Carnation Co., Los Angeles, 1973-78; cons., adminstr. Carnation Community Service Award Program, 1973-78; pub. relations cons. Vivitar Corp.; sr. advt. asst. Am. Honda Motor Co., Gardena, Calif., 1978-84; exec. dir. Am. Honda Found., 1984—; mgr. Honda Dealer Advt. Assns.; cons. advt., pub. relations, promotions. Editor: Vivitar Voice, Santa Monica, Calif., 1978, Honda Views, 1978-84, Found. Focus, 1984—; asst. editor Friskies Research Digest; contbg. editor Newsbriefs, Am. Honda Motor Co., Inc. employees mag.; Calif. Life Scholarship Found. scholar, 1967. Mem. Advt. Club Los Angeles, Pub. Relations Soc. Am., So. Calif. Assn. Philanthropy, Council Founds. of Washington, Airline Owners and Pilots Assn., Am. Quarter Horse Assn., Los Angeles Soc. for Prevention Cruelty to Animals, Greenpeace, German Shepherd Dog Club Am., Ocicats Internat., Am. Humane Assn., Elsa Wild Animal Appeal. Democrat. Methodist. Office: PO Box 2205 Torrance CA 90509-2205

CAREY, MARTIN CONRAD, gastroenterologist, molecular biophysicist, educator; b. Clonmel, County Tipperary, Ireland, June 18, 1939; came to U.S., 1967; s. John Joseph and Alice (Broderick) C.; m. Gracia Antonieta Ferná ndez, July 1, 1972 (div. 1987); children—Julian Albert, Dermot Martin. M.B., B.Ch., B.A.O. with 1st class honors, Nat. U. Ireland, 1962, M.D., 1981, D.Sc., 1984. Intern, St. Vincent's Hosp., Dublin, Ireland, 1962-63, resident, 1965-67; resident Nat. Maternity Hosp., Dublin, 1963, St. Luke's Hosp., Dublin, 1964, Queen Charlotte's Hosp., London, 1964; postdoctoral fellow, research assoc. Boston U. Sch. Medicine, 1968-73, asst. prof. medicine, 1973-75; asst. prof. medicine Harvard U. Med. Sch., Boston, 1975-79, assoc. prof., 1979-88 , Lawrence J. Henderson assoc. prof. health sci. and tech., 1979-88 ; faculty mem. Grad. Sch. of Arts and Scis., assoc. mem. Dept. of Cellular and Molecular Physiology, Harvard U. Med. Sch., Boston, 1983—, prof. medicine 1988—, Lawrence J. Henderson prof. health sci. and tech., 1988—. mem. staff Brigham and Women's Hosp., Boston, 1975—; cons. West Roxbury VA Hosp., Boston, 1975—, Calif. Biotech. Inc., Palo Alto, 1983—Dow Chem. Co., Midland, Mich., 1984—. Author: Bile Salts and Gallstones, 1974; Hepatic Excretory Function, 1975; contbr. numerous articles to med. and sci. jours.; assoc. editor Jour. Lipid Research, 1978-81; mem. editorial bds. Am. Jour. Physiology, 1976-81, Gastroenterology, 1983-88 , Hepatology, 1981-84. Recipient Acad. Career Devel. award NIH, 1976, also MERIT award, 1986; Adolf Windaus prize Falk Found., 1984; Guggenheim Found. fellow, 1974; Fogarty internat. fellow NIH, 1968; McIgrath guest prof., Royal Prince Alfred Hosp., U. Sydney, Australia, 1987. Fellow Royal Coll. Physicians Ireland; mem. Gastroenterology Research Group (vice chmn., steering coms.), Am. Soc. Clin. Investigation, Am. Gastroent. Assn., Am. Oil Chemists Soc., Biophys. Soc. Democrat. Roman Catholic. Club: Babson (Wellesley, Mass.). Current work: Phase transitions and equilibria in biologically relevant and classical lipid systems; physical-chemistry and pathophysiology of bile; biochemistry and biophysics of gallstone formation and dissolution and of lipid absorption and malabsorption; lipid-protein interactions; chemistry and physics of micelles, liquid crystals and emulsions. Subspecialties: Gastroenterology; Biophysics (physics).

CAREY, WILLIAM JOSEPH, retired controller; b. N.Y.C., May 15, 1922; s. Cornelius Montague and Ellen Katherine (Gannon) C.; m. Barbara L. Garrison, Aug. 24,7 1946; children: Kathleen, Eileen, Christine, Robert. B.S., Rider Coll., 1949; postgrad., NYU, 1952-53. C.P.A., N.Y. Mgr. Ernst and Ernst, N.Y.C., 1949-59; controller Reynolds and Co., N.Y.C., 1959-61; exec. v.p. Bache and Co., N.Y.C., 1961-69; exec. ptnr. Goodbody and Co., N.Y.C., 1970-71; v.p. Paine Webber, N.Y.C., 1971-73; controller, treas., and chief fin. officer J. Henry Schroder Bank and Trust Co., Franklin Lakes, N.J., 1973-84; arbitration panel mem. Nat. Assn. Securities Dealers, N.Y.C. Trustee emeritus Rider Coll. Served with USN, 1942-45, PTO. Decorated Purple Heart. Mem. N.Y. State Soc. C.P.A.s, Am. Inst. C.P.A.s, Fin. Execs. Inst. (ops. com., internat. com). Clubs: Franklin Lakes, Indian Trail. Home: 237 Mountainview Terr Mahwah NJ 07430

CAREY, WILLIAM POLK, investment banker; b. Balt., May 11, 1930; s. Francis J. and Marjorie A. (Armstrong) C. Grad., Pomfret Sch., 1948; student, Princeton, 1948-50; B.S. in Econs., Wharton Sch. of U. Pa., 1953. Vice pres., gen. mgr. A. J. Orbach Co., Plainfield, N.J., 1955-58; prin. W. P. Carey & Co., Bloomfield, N.J., 1958-63; pres., dir. Internat. Leasing Corp., N.Y.C., 1959—; prin. Carey Internat., N.Y.C., 1960—; chmn. bd. Carey Internat. (Australia) Pty. Ltd., 1962—; chmn. exec. com., dir. Hubbard, Westervelt & Mottelay, Inc. (now Merrill Lynch, Hubbard, Inc.), N.Y.C., 1964-67; dept. head Loeb, Rhoades & Co. (now Shearson Lehman Hutton Inc.), N.Y.C., 1967-71; vice chmn. investment banking bd., dir. corporate finance duPont Glore Forgan Inc., 1971-73; dir. W.P. Carey & Co., Inc. and affiliates, N.Y.C., 1973-83, chmn., 1983—; gen. ptnr. Corp. Property Assos., 1978—; bd. dirs. various financing corps.; ptnr. various partnerships owning property leased to major corps., 1964—. Mem. Com. for the Preservation of the U.S. Treasury Bldg.; trustee, mem. exec. com. Rensselaerville (N.Y.) Inst., 1979—, Anglo-Am. Contemporary Dance Found.; trustee Gilman Sch., Balt., Pomfret Sch., Conn.; chmn. bd. trustees Oxford Mgmt. Ctr. Assocs. Council; mem. council of mgmt. Oxford Ctr. for Mgmt. Studies, Templeton Coll., Oxford U.; chmn. St. Elmo Found. Served to 1st lt. USAF, 1953-55. Mem. Soc. Mayflower Descs. (gov. N.Y. chpt.), Delta Phi. Episcopalian. Clubs: Racquet and Tennis, Brook, University, Pilgrims (N.Y.C.); St. Elmo (Phila.). Home: 525 Park Ave New York NY 10021 also: The Manse Rensselaerville NY 12147 Office: WP Carey & Co Inc 689 Fifth Ave New York NY 10022

CARFORA, JOHN MICHAEL, economics, political science educator; b. New Haven, Conn., July 24, 1950; s. John Michael and Rose Mary (Mitro) C.; m. Linda Louise Palmer, July 22, 1972; 1 child, Rachel Ellen. BS, U. New Haven (Conn.), 1973, M in Pub. Adminstrn., 1975; MS in Econs. and Polit. Sci., London Sch. Econs. and Polit. Sci., 1978; AM, Dartmouth Coll., 1985. Vis. asst. prof. dept. def. Troy State U., 1979-80; vis. sr. lectr. Poly. of Central London, 1980; research asst. London Sch. Econs. and Polit. Sci., 1980-81; vis. asst. prof. internat. relations So. Conn. State U., New Haven, 1982; lectr. dept. polit. sci. Albertus Magnus Coll., New Haven, 1982-83; lectr. dept. econs. and quantitative analysis U. New Haven, 1982-83; program cons. Dartmouth Coll., 1984-85; asst. prof. internat. econ. Sch. Internat. Tng., 1985—; lectr. in field. Author book reviews; contbr. articles to profl. jours. Served with USAR, 1970-76. Recipient Roy E. Jenkins award, 1972; fellow Radio Free Europe-Radio Liberty, 1979, Internat. Research and Exchanges Bd., 1981-84. Mem. Am. Acad. Polit. Sci., AAAS, Am. Econ. Assn., Am. Polit. Sci. Assn., Acad. Polit. Sci., NE Slavic Assn., Royal Acad. Pub. Adminstrn. (eng.), Atlantic Econ. Soc., Am. Friends of the London Sch. Econs. (Conn. program chmn. 1981-85, N.H.-Vt. program chmn. 1985—). Democrat. Roman Catholic. Home: PO Box 964 Northampton MA 01060 Office: Sch Internat Tng Kipling Rd Brattleboro VT 10676

CARIDDI, ALAN FRANCIS, lawyer; b. Cairo, Egypt, Apr. 25, 1949; s. Charles A. and Andrée (Rathlé) C.; m. Marylise Odette Le Caignec, Oct. 22, 1977; children: Mélanie-Anne, Alan Jr. BA magna cum laude, Georgetown U., 1970; JD, Columbia U., 1973. Bar: N.Y. 1974, U.S. Dist. Ct. (so. dist.) N.Y. 1975, U.S. Ct. Appeals (D.C. cir.) 1983; registered Conseil Juridique, France 1977. Assoc. atty. Dewey, Ballantine, Bushby, Palmer & Wood, N.Y.C., 1973-75, Paris, 1976-80; assoc. atty. Mudge, Rose, Guthrie, Alexander & Ferdon, N.Y.C., 1981, resident ptnr.-in-charge Paris office, 1982—; mem. adv. bd. Am. Tax Inst. Europe, Paris, 1985—. Served with 1st lt. USAR, 1973—. Harlan Fiske Stone scholar Columbia U. Law Sch. Mem. ABA (sects. internat. law, corp., banking, and bus. law), Internat. Bar Assn., N.Y. State Bar Assn., D.C. Bar Assn. Clubs: Racing Club de France, Am. Club of Paris. Home: 1 rue du Marechal Harispe, 75007 Paris France Office: Mudge Rose Guthrie Alexander & Ferdon, 12 rue de la Paix, 75002 Paris France

CARLBERG, MICHAEL, economist, professor; b. Hamburg, Fed. Republic of Germany, Sept. 26, 1945; s. Siegfried and Christa (Breckwoldt) C.; m. Aloysia Wanstrath, July 21, 1972; children: Ruth, Esther. Diploma, U. Hamburg, 1971, PhD, 1974, habilitation, 1977. Asst. prof. econ. U. Hamburg, 1971-80, prof., 1980—. Author: Urban Economics, 1978, Input-Output Growth Model, 1979, Public Debt, Taxation ..., 1987. Office: U Hamburg, Holstenhofweg 85, D 2000 Hamburg Federal Republic of Germany

CARLESON, ROBERT BAZIL, corporation executive; b. Long Beach, Calif., Feb. 21, 1931; s. Bazil Upton and Grace Reynolds (Wilhite) C.; m. Betty Jane Nichols, Jan. 31, 1954 (div.); children: Eric Robert, Mark Andrew, Susan Lynn Carleson Zausch; m. Susan A. Dower, Feb. 11, 1984. Student, U. Utah, 1949-51; B.S., U. So. Calif., 1953, postgrad., 1956-58. Adminstrv. asst. City of Beverly Hills, Calif., 1956-57; asst. to city mgr. City of Claremont, Calif., 1957-58; sr. adminstrv. asst. to city mgr. City of Torrance, Calif., 1958-60; city mgr. City of San Dimas, Calif., 1960-64, Pico Rivera, Calif., 1964-68; chief dep. dir. Calif. Dept. Public Works, 1968-71; dir. Calif. Dept. Social Welfare, 1971-73; U.S. commr. welfare Washington, 1973-75; pres. Robert B. Carleson & Assocs., Sacramento, Calif. and Washington, 1975-81; chmn. Robert B. Carleson & Assocs., Washington, 1987—; spl. asst. to U.S. pres. for policy devel. Washington, 1981-84; prin., dir. govt. relations Main Hurdman KMG, Washington, 1984-87; Dir. transition team Dept. Health & Human Services, Office of Pres.-Elect, 1980-81; spl. adviser

Office of Policy Coordination; sr. policy advisor, chmn. welfare task force Reagan Campaign, 1980; dir. Fed. Home Loan Bank of Atlanta, 1987—; adv. com. Fed. Home Loan Mortgage Corp., 1985-87. Served with USN, 1953-56. Mem. Internat. City Mgmt. Assn. Republican. Clubs: Masons, Rotary (pres. 1964), City (Washington) Army & Navy (Washington), Capitol Hill, Fairfax Hunt. Office: Robert B Carleson and Assoc Box 2205 Crystal City Arlington VA 22202

CARLETON, BUKK G., III, real estate executive; A.B. cum laude (Nat. Merit scholar), Harvard U., 1961; M.B.A. (Stanford fellow), Stanford U., 1964; m. Mary Oliver Lee, July 8, 1967; children—Samantha Lee, Heather Tucker. Investment analyst First Nat. City Bank, N.Y.C., 1961-62, Capital Research and Mgmt. Co., Los Angeles, 1963; fin. project mgr. Am. Friends Service Com., Phila., 1964-66; cons., 1966-68; partner Investment Assos., Washington, 1965-74; founder, v.p. Landtect Corp., Phila., 1966-74, pres., 1974—, also dir.; pres. Landtect New Eng., 1976—, Waterville Valley Gateway, Inc., 1978-82, Northeast Comml., 1979—; treas., dir. Benefit Systems, Inc., Balt., 1970-76; cons. Stanford Research Inst., 1968-69; pres. BMM Inc., 1983—. Mem. Soc. Indsl. Realtors, Am. Mgmt. Assn., Delta Upsilon. Clubs: Harvard, Racquet, Merion Cricket (Phila.); Hasty Pudding Inst. (Cambridge). Home: Beaver Meadow Rd Norwich VT 05055 Office: Box A-247 Hanover NH 03755

CARLETON, BUKK GRIFFITH, lawyer, investment counsel; b. N.Y.C., May 30, 1909; s. Bukk G. and Clarice (Griffith) C.; A.B. magna cum laude, Harvard U., 1931, LL.B., 1934; m. Mary Elizabeth Tucker, June 16, 1934; children—Elizabeth Holland, Bukk Griffith. Bar: N.Y. 1935. Assoc. Larkin, Rathbone & Perry, N.Y.C., 1934-36; asst. counsel, asst. sec. Gen. Chem. Co., 1936-41; v.p., sec., dir. Perma-Bilt Homes, Inc., 1941-42; counsel RFC, 1942-44; head N.Y. law office Montgomery Ward & Co. 1944-46; mem. legal dept. Sinclair Refining Co., 1946-56; owner, investment counsel Griffith Carleton, 1946—. Pres., trustee Hicks-Stearns Mus. Mem. ABA, N.Y. Bar Assn., New Eng. Soc., Phi Beta Kappa. Quaker (com. nat. legis. 1957-58). Clubs: Met., Sleepy Hollow, Harvard (N.Y.C.); Woodway Country (Conn.); Quinnatisset Country (Conn.); R.I. Country; New Canaan Country, Harvard (New Canaan). Home: 61 Parade Hill Ln New Canaan CT 06840 Office: Bukkskin East Killingly CT 06243

CARLIE, KEVIN STUART, accountant; b. St. Louis, Feb. 26, 1955; s. Carl Jay Antoniette Rose (Gorczyca) C.; m. Robin Stoliar, June 1, 1980. AB in Econs., Dartmouth Coll., 1976; MBA in Taxation, NYU, 1982. CPA, Mo., Ill., N.Y.; cert. fin. planner. Assoc. Stone, Carlie and Co., St. Louis, 1979-84, ptnr., 1984—; mem. exec. roundtable Mark Twain Bank, Fenton, 1988—; mem. adv. council Fontbonne Coll. Bus., 1987—; speaker in field. Contbr. articles to profl. jours. Mem. Mo. Soc. CPA's (sub-com. chmn. pub. relations, charter mem. personal fin. planning com.), Ill. Soc. CPA's, N.Y. Soc. CPA's, Am. Inst. CPA's, Inst. Cert. Fin. Planners (internat. bd. standards and practices), Internat. Assn. Fin. Planners, Am. Assn. of Individual Investors. Clubs: Dartmouth (St. Louis) (pres. 1987-88), Sons of Bosses (St. Louis), St. Louis Breakfast (bd. dirs.). Home: 14061 Deltona Chesterfield MO 63017 Office: Stone Carlie and Co 7710 Carondelet Ave Suite 200 Saint Louis MO 63105

CARLIER, JEAN JOACHIM, cardiologist, educator, administrator; b. Jemeppe-sur-Sambre, Belgium, July 31, 1926; s. Edouard-Georges and Hermance (Doucet) C.; m. Marie-Louise Barbier, Aug. 17, 1954; children—Pierre, Philippe. Specialist in internal medicine, U. Liège (Belgium), 1958, specialist in cardiology, 1961, Agrégé de l'Enseignement Supérieur, 1967, specialist in cardiac rehab., 1981. Asst., U. Liège, 1953-60, chef de travaux, 1960-67, agrégé de Facheté, 1967-68, chargé de cours associé, 1968-73, associated prof., 1973—, founder Unities of Cardiac Pharmacology and Cardiac Rehab. Contbr. numerous articles to med. jours. Recipient prix Masius U. Liège, 1958, prix Amis, 1968; pres.'s Commn. Agregation Cardiologistes de Langue Française, Ministry of Pub. Health, 1972. Fellow Internat. Coll. Angiology; mem. Societies of Belgian, European, French cardiology, N.Y. Acad. Sci. Home: Rue Maghin 13, B-4000 Liège Belgium

CARLILE, ROBERT TOY, lawyer; b. Phila., July 27, 1926; s. Robert and Eva (MacQueen) C.; children—Robert A., Regan J. B.B.A., U. Miami, 1949; J.D., U. Fla., 1958. Bar: Fla. 1958. Assoc., Grimditch & Smith, Deerfield Beach, Fla., 1958-60; sole practice Deerfield Beach, 1960-65, 73—; ptnr. Carlile & Pulskamp, Deerfield Beach, 1965-69, Carlile, Pulskamp & Fletcher, 1969-72, Carlile & Fletcher, 1972-73; city atty., Deerfield Beach, 1963-68; mcpl. judge, 1971-77. Served with U.S. Army, 1944-46, USAF, 1951-53. Mem. Fla. Bar Assn., North Broward County Bar Assn. (pres. 1966), Broward County Bar Assn., Broward County Mcpl. Judges Assn. (v.p. 1975), Deerfield Beach C. of C. (pres. 1966), Phi Alpha Delta. Democrat. Clubs: Kiwanis (pres.), Billiken (pres.), Gold Coast Shriners, Jesters. Office: 1215 E Hillsboro Blvd Deerfield Beach FL 33441

CARLIN, CLAIR MYRON, lawyer; b. Sharon, Pa., Apr. 20, 1947; s. Charles William and Carolyn L. (Vukasich) C.; m. Cecilia Julia Reis, Sept. 21, 1971 (div. Mar. 1982); children—Elizabeth Marie, Alexander Myron; m. Pamela Ann Roshon, Sept. 30, 1982; 1 son, Eric Richard. B.S. in Econs., Ohio State U., 1969, J.D., 1972. Bar: Ohio 1973, Pa. 1973, U.S. Dist. Ct. (so. dist.) Ohio 1973, U.S. Dist. Ct. (no. dist.) Ohio 1975, U.S. Supreme Ct. 1976, U.S. Ct. Claims 1983, U.S. Ct. Appeals (6th cir.) 1983, U.S. Tax Ct. 1985. Staff atty. Ohio Dept. Taxation, Columbus, 1972-73; asst. city atty. City of Warren, Ohio, 1973-75; assoc. McLaughlin, DiBlasio & Harshman, Youngstown, Ohio, 1975-80; ptnr. McLaughlin, McNally & Carlin, Youngstown, 1980—. Mem. Trumbull County Bicentennial Commn., Ohio, 1976; v.p. Services for the Aging, Trumbull County, 1976-77; mem. Pres.' Club Ohio State U.Served to maj. Ohio NG, 1972-82. Mem. ABA, Ohio State Bar Assn., Ohio State Bar Coll., Mahoning County Bar Assn. (chmn. legal edn. com. 1985-86, counsel 1986-87), Assn. Trial Lawyers Am., Ohio Acad. Trial Lawyers (trustee 1988—), Ohio State U. Alumni Assn. (pres. Trumbull County chpt. 1985—), Cath. War Vets. (Ohio state commdr.). Democrat. Roman Catholic. Club: Tippecanoe Country (Canfield, Ohio). Lodge: Rotary. Home: 5510 W Boulevard Youngstown OH 44512 Office: McLaughlin McNally & Carlin 500 City Centre One Youngstown OH 44503

CARLIN, GABRIEL S., corporate executive; b. N.Y.C., Mar. 19, 1921; s. Samuel and Lena (Franco) C.; m. Rosalind Goldberg, Apr. 17, 1943; children: Donald B., Beverly J. B.S., N.Y. U., 1951, M.B.A., 1954. Army-Navy purchasing coordinator Dept. Def., 1946-49; gen. sales mgr. Old Town Corp., Bklyn., 1949-60; div. gen. mgr., mem. world planning group Xerox Corp., Rochester, N.Y., 1960-64; exec. v.p. Savin Corp., Valhalla, N.Y., 1964-83; also dir. Savin Corp.; chmn. Columbia Bus. Systems, Inc., Elmsford, N.Y., 1983—. Author: The Power of Enthusiastic Selling, 1962, How to Persuade and Motivate People, 1964. Served to 1st lt. U.S. Army, 1942-46. Home: 1807 Long Ridge Rd Stamford CT 06903 Office: Columbia Bus Systems Inc 2 Westchester Plaza Elmsford NY 10523

CARLIN, JOHN WILLIAM, former governor of Kansas; b. Salina, Kans., Aug. 3, 1940; s. Jack W. and Hazel L. (Johnson) C.; m. Ramona Hawkinson, 1962 (div. 1980); children: John David, Lisa Marie; m. Diana Bartelli Prentice, 1987. BS in Agr., Kans. State U., 1962, PhD (hon.), 1987. Farmer, dairyman Smolan, Kans., 1962—; mem. Kans. Ho. of Reps., 1971-79, speaker of ho., 1977-79; gov. State of Kans., Topeka, 1979-87; vis. prof. pub. adminstrn. and internat. trade Wichita State U.; vis. program prof. fellow U. Kans., 1987-88; chmn. Nat. Govs. Assn., 1984-85, Midwestern Govs. Conf., 1982-83. Mem. Econ. Devel. Assocs. (pres.). Democrat. Lutheran. Home: 3226 Skyline Pkwy Topeka KS 66614

CARLISLE, ANTHONY EDWIN CHARLES GLEN, marketing, managing executive; b. London, Mar. 10, 1947; s. George Geddes and Dorothy Louise C.; m. Nancy Susan Hayward, June 13, 1968. BA in Econs. with honors, Sussex U., 1968. Exec. Lintas Ltd., London, 1968-70; exec. Dewe Rogerson Ltd., London, 1970-72, also bd. dirs., dep. chmn., 1985—, mng. dir., 1987—; bd. dirs. Livery Co., Glovers Co., London. Contbr. articles on mktg. to profl. publs. Mem. Inst. Pub. Relations, Inst. Practitioners in Advt. Conservative. Anglican.

CARLISLE, JAY CHARLES, II, lawyer, educator; b. Washington, Apr. 8, 1942; s. Jay C. and Opal Fiske C.; m. Frances Bell, Nov. 22, 1970 (div.); 1 child, Marie Bell; m. Janessa C. Nisley, June 22, 1984. AB, UCLA, 1965; JD, U. Calif., Davis, 1969; postgrad. Columbia U., 1969-70. Bar: N.Y. 1970, N.Mex. 1972, U.S. Dist. Ct. (so., ea. and we. dists.) N.Y. 1971, U.S. Ct. Appeals (2d cir.) 1975, U.S. Supreme Ct. 1975. Asst. trial counsel ITT, Hartford, 1970-71; assoc. Bigbee, Bryd, Carpenter & Crout, Santa Fe, 1971-73; sole practice, 1973-75; asst. dean SUNY, AB Law Sch., 1975-78; counsel Nierenberg, Zeif & Weinstein, 1977-80, Olsen & Sorrentino, 1981-83; sole practice, N.Y.C., 1980—; lectr. Pace U., 1978-80, prof. civil procedure, N.Y. practice, criminal procedure and ethics, 1983—; adj. prof. Fordham U. Law Sch., 1987-88; commr. N.Y. Task Force on Women and Cts., 1984-86. Author: (with others) Weinstien Korn & Miller) New York Civil Practice; contbr. articles to profl. jours. Recipient SUNY-Buffalo Law Sch. Alumni award, 1978, Erie County Bar Assn. Commendation award 1978, cert. of Appreciation N.Y. Sup. Ct. for Spl. Master Service 1982. Mem. N.Y. State Bar Assn., Assn. Bar City N.Y. Republican. Episcopalian. Home: Stevens Pl Hartsdale NY 10530 Office: Pace U Sch Law 78 N Broadway White Plains NY 10603

CARLISLE, WILLIAM AIKEN, architect; b. West Point, Ga., July 11, 1918; s. Aiken Rast and Sara Allen (Lane) C.; m. Ruth Davidson, Feb. 17, 1945; children: Mettauer Lee, Carolyn Lane, Thomas Aiken, James Timmerman, Margaret Elizabeth. B.S. in Architecture, Clemson U., 1939. Draftsman E.R. Markley, Architect, Durham, N.C.; architect Durham, 1939-40; chief draftsman, area engr. Fort Jackson, S.C., 1940-42; v.p. LBC & W, Inc., Columbia, S.C., 1946-77; chmn. Carlisle Assos. (Architects-Engrs.), Columbia, 1977—; sec.-treas. State Bd. Archtl. Examiners, 1968-78; chmn. advisory com. to State Fire Marshal, 1966-79; pres. Nat. Archtl. Accreditation Bd., 1983; dir. Nat. Council Archtl. Registration Bds., 1974-77; mem. exec. com. Gov.'s Mgmt. Review Com., 1972. Served with U.S. Army, 1942-45. Fellow AIA (dir. 1972-74, S.C. pres. 1953); mem. Clemson Archtl. Found. (pres. 1964), Columbia C. of C. (past v.p.). Methodist. Clubs: Forest Lake Country (past pres.), Wildewood, Summit, Sertoma (past pres.). Home: 5645 Lake Shore Dr Columbia SC 29206 Office: PO Box 11528 Columbia SC 29211

CARLO, JAIME RAFAEL, immunologist, editor; b. Utuado, P.R., Sept. 15, 1943; s. Rafael and Carmen Aida (Casellas) C.; children—Judson Dupree, Tyler Bragg. B.S., Med. Coll. Ga., 1967; M.S., U. Ga., 1968; Ph.D., U. Md., 1976. Research immunologist Becton-Dickinson, Cockeysville, Md., 1972-73; pres. Immunodiagnostics, Inc., Houston, 1973-74; asst. prof. pathology U. Md., Balt., 1973-76; asst. prof. pathology/medicine Med. Coll. Va., Richmond, 1976-82; asst. prof. med. lab. sci. Northeastern U., Boston, 1982-84; dir. blood research U. Mass. Med. Ctr., Worcester, 1984-85; dir. CC Sci. Editorial Service, Framingham, Mass., 1984—. Contbr. articles to profl. jours. Advisor AIDS (Aquired Immune Deficiency Syndrome) Action Com., Boston, 1982-83. Served to lt. comdr. USN, 1968-72. Med. Coll. Va. grantee-in-aid, 1977; HHS grantee, 1977-79; NIH grantee, 1982; recipient Research and Scholarship Devel. award Northeastern U., 1983. Fellow Arthritis Found.; mem. Am. Assn. Immunologists, Am. Soc. Microbiology (pres. Va. br. 1979-81), Am. Soc. Clin. Pathologists, Am. Fedn. Clin. Research, N.Y. Acad. Scis. Democrat. Roman Catholic. Home and Office: 55 Dinsmore Ave-102 Framingham MA 01701

CARLOCK, MAHLON WALDO, financial consultant, former high school administrator; b. Plymouth, Ind., Sept. 17, 1926; s. Thorstine Clifford and Katheryn G. (Gephart) C.; m. Betty L. Dobbs, Aug. 24, 1954; children: Mahlon W. II, Rhena M., Shawn R., Steve. BS, Ind. U., 1951, MS, 1956. Tchr. jr. high Martinsville Schs. Corp., Brooklyn, Ind., 1952-53; tchr. high sch. Indpls. Pub. Schs., 1953-63, asst. to dean of boys, 1963-73, asst. dean of boys, 1973-75, bus. mgr., 1976-87; fin. cons. Indpls., 1987—; property builder, owner Ind. and Fla.; lectr. in fin. and real estate. Served as sgt. U.S. Army, 1945-47. Mem. NEA (life), Indpls. Adminstrs., Ind. Bus. Edn. Assn., Indpls. Edn. Assn. (rep. 1958-63). Republican. Baptist. Lodge: Masons. Home and Office: 9705 East Michigan St Indianapolis IN 46229

CARLON, GRAZIANO CARLO, anesthesiologist, educator; b. Padua, Veneto, Italy, Dec. 18, 1945; came to U.S., 1973; s. Carlo and Irene (Zadra) C.; m. Anne Teresa Corsa, Sept. 7, 1985. M.D., U. Padova, 1969. Resident in anesthesiology U. Padua (Italy), 1969-72, N.Y. Hosp., N.Y.C., 1975-78; attending physician Meml. Hosp., N.Y.C., 1978—, chief dept. critical care, 1978—; chief critical care service, 1986; assoc. prof. anesthesiology Cornell U., 1982—. Contbr. articles to profl. jours.; editorial bd. Critical Care Medicine, Internat. Jour. Computing, Critical Care Monitor. Brian Piccolo Found. grantee, 1978-81; NIH grantee, 1981—; Bear Med. Indsl. grantee, 1981-84. Fellow Am. Coll. Anesthesiologists, Am. Coll. Chest Physicians; me. N.Y. Soc. Critical Care Medicine (pres.). Republican. Home: 425 E 58 St 39A New York NY 10022 Office: Meml Hosp 1275 York Ave New York NY 10021

CARLSON, DALE BICK, author; b. N.Y.C., May 24, 1935; d. Edgar M. and Estelle (Cohen) Bick; B.A., Wellesley Coll., 1957; children—Daniel Carlson, Hannah Carlson. Author children's books, adult books 1961—, including: Perkins the Brain, 1964; The House of Perkins, 1965; Miss Maloo, 1966; The Brainstormers; 1966; Frankenstein, 1968; Counting is Easy, 1969; Your Country, 1969; Arithmetic 1, 2, 3, 1969; The Electronic Teabowl, 1969; Warlord of the Genji, 1970; The Beggar King of China, 1971; The Mountain of Truth (Spring Festival Honor book, named Am. Library Assn. Notable Book), 1972; Good Morning Danny, 1972; Good Morning, Hannah, 1972; The Human Apes, 1973 (named Am. Library Assn. Notable Book; Girls Are Equal Too, 1973 (named Am. Library Assn. Notable Book); Baby Needs Shoes, 1974; Triple Boy, 1976; Where's Your Head?, 1977; The Plant People, 1977; The Wild Heart, 1977; The Shining Pool, 1979; Lovingsex for Both Sexes, 1979; Boys Have Feelings Too, 1980; Call Me Amanda, 1981; Manners that Matter, 1982; The Frog People, 1982; Charlie the Hero, 1983; 1984-85: The Jenny Dean Science Fiction Mysteries, The Mystery of the Shining Children; The Mystery of the Hidden Trap; The Secret of the Third Eye; The James Budd Mysteries; The Mystery of Galaxy Games; The Mystery of Operation Brain, 1984-85, Miss Mary's Husbands, 1988; others. Vice pres. Parents League of N.Y., editor-in-chief Parents League Bull., 1967-72. Mem. Authors League Am., Authors Guild, Nature Connection. Address: 307 Neck Rd Madison CT 06443

CARLSON, GARY LEE, public relations executive, director, producer; b. Yakima, Wash., Oct. 15, 1954; s. Glenn Elmer and Helen Mary (McLean) Carlson. AA, Yakima Community Coll., 1975; BA in Communications, U. Wash., 1977. Dir. pub. affairs Sta. KCMU, Seattle, 1976-77; dir. programming and promotions Sta. KAPP-TV, Yakima, 1978-80; dir. promotions Sta. WBZ-TV, Boston, 1980-84; producer Sta. KCBS-TV, Los Angeles, 1985; dir. creative services Metromedia Producers, Los Angeles, 1985-86; dir. promotion publicity 20th Century Fox, Los Angeles, 1986—. Producer, dir.: M*A*S*H* 15th Ann. Campaign, 1987 (Internat. Film and TV Festival N.Y. award), The Fox Tradition, 1988 (Internat. Film and TV Festival N.Y. award, Clio Finalist award, 1988, Telly award, 1988, B.P.M.E. award, 1988); producer, writer, dir. Consumer Reports, 1983 (Internat. Film and TV Festival N.Y. award, Houston Internat. Film and TV award). Recipient Internat. Film and TV N.Y. award, Houston Internat. Film and TV award. Mem. Broadcast Promotion and Mktg. Execs., Nat. Assn. TV Program Execs., Beta Theta Pi. Home: 1510 Rockglen Ave Glendale CA 91205 Office: 20th Century Fox Film Corp 10201 W Pico Blvd Century City CA 90035

CARLSON, JEFFERY JOHN, lawyer; b. Mpls., May 23, 1947; s. John Joseph and Sylvia Lorraine (Sandberg) C.; children: Erik John, Bryan Jeffery, Kimberly Anne. Student Augsburg Coll., 1965-66; B.A. summa cum laude, U. Minn., 1969, postgrad., 1970-71; J.D., UCLA, 1974. Bar: Calif. 1974, U.S. Dist. Ct. (cen. dist.) Calif. 1974, U.S. Ct. Appeals (9th cir.) 1976. Teaching asst., research asst. U. Minn., Mpls., 1970-71; assoc. Harwood & Adkinson, Newport Beach, Calif., 1974-77; assoc. Haight, Dickson, Brown & Bonesteel, Santa Monica, Calif., 1977-81, ptnr., 1981-88; sr. ptnr. Dickson, Carlson & Campillo, Santa Monica, 1988—; judge pro tem West Los Angeles Mcpl. Ct., 1981-83; arbitrator Panel of Arbitrators, Los Angeles, Orange, and Ventura counties, 1980—; lectr. bus. law Calif. State U., Northridge, 1978; lectr. Calif. Author: Continuing Edn. of the Bar, 1984—, (supplement) California Continuing Education of the Bar, California Tort Guide; cons. Punitive Damages and 15, Restrictions on Recovery, of California Tort Damages Guide; contbr. articles to profl. jours. Mem. nominating com. Am. Soc. Pharmacy Law, pres. adv. com.; vice-chmn. Com. on Toxic and Hazardous Substances and Environ. Law. Mem. So. Clif. Def. Counsel, Def. Research and Trial Lawyers Assn., Phi Beta Kappa (James Harley Beal award 1987). Lutheran. Office: Haight Dickson Brown & Bonesteel 201 Santa Monica Blvd Santa Monica CA 90401

CARLSON, J(OHN) PHILIP, lawyer; b. Shickley, Nebr., Apr. 16, 1915; s. Christopher Theodore and Klara Louise (Blomquist) C.; m. Maryjo Suverkrup, Oct. 14, 1950. Student Luther Coll., 1931-33; A.B., Wayne State Coll., 1935; M.A., Columbia U., 1967; J.D., Georgetown U., 1951. Bar: D.C. 1952, U.S. Dist. Ct. D.C. 1952, U.S. Ct. Appeals D.C. cir. 1952, U.S. Supreme Ct. 1957, U.S. Ct. Mil. Appeals 1970, D.C. Ct. Appeals 1972. Tchr., athletic coach high schs. of Bristow, Nebr., 1935-37, Carroll, Nebr., 1937-38, Ashland, Nebr., 1938-42; vets. relations advisor OPA, Washington, 1946-47; tng. specialist Dept. Navy, 1947-56; minority counsel House Com. on Govt. Ops., 1956-80; sole practice law, Washington, 1980—. Bd. dirs. Fellowship Sq. Found., Reston, Va., 1961-86, Peter Muehlenberg Meml. Assn., 1972-86. Served to capt. USAAF, 1942-45; ETO. Congl. Staff fellow Am. Polit. Sci. Assn., 1964-65, 66-67; Decorated D.F.C., Air medal with oak leaf cluster; recipient Meritorious Service award Am. Nat. Standards Inst., 1980, Meritorious Service award Fellowship Square Found., 1986. Mem. ABA, Fed. Bar Assn., D.C. Bar Assn., Am. Econ. Assn., Air Force Assn., Res. Officers Assn. Republican. Lutheran. Clubs: Metropolitan, Capitol Hill, George Town, Nat. Econs. (Washington); Belle Haven Country (Alexandria, Va.). Home: 2206 Belle Haven Rd Alexandria VA 22307

CARLSON, PAUL EDWIN, real estate developer, writer; b. San Francisco, June 29, 1944; s. Carl John and Marguerite Eutha (Kovatch) C.; m. Sharon Raye Hammond, Nov. 14, 1964; children: Kimberley, Davin, Christina. AA, Yosemite Coll., 1964; BA, Calif. State U., Long Beach, 1971; cert. shopping ctr. mgr., Internat. Council of Shopping Ctrs. Mgmt. Sch., 1981. Vice and narcotics officer Modesto and Los Angeles Police Depts., Calif., 1964-69; owner Universal Prodns., N.Y.C. and Modesto, 1963-73; gen. mgr. City Investing Co., N.C.Y. and Beverly Hills, Calif., 1973-75; v.p. The Koll Co., Newport Beach, Calif., 1975-79, Irvine Co., Newport Beach, 1979-80; owner Willows Shopping Ctr., Concord, Calif., 1980-83; sr. v.p. Lee Sammis Co., Irvine, 1983-85; pres. Am. Devel. Co., Costa Mesa, Calif., 1985-86; chmn. bd. The Carlson Co., Huntington Beach, Calif., 1986—; guest lectr. U. So. Cal., U. Calif., Los Angeles, Orange Coast Coll.; real estate cons. Bank of Am., Union Bank, Chevron U.S.A., Aetna Life Ins. Co., James Lang Wooten, Eng., Peoples Republic of China. Author three screen plays for Police Story; comedy contbr. to The Tonight Show, Sat. Night Live, Late Night with David Letterman; pub. Property Mgrs. Handbook. mem. Calif. State Juvenile Justice Commn., Rep. Senatorial Inner circle, Washington; past chmn. City of Newport Beach Traffic Commn.; pres. bd. trustees Mt. Diablo Hosp.; v.p., bd. dirs. City of Concord Pavillion; bd. dirs. Concord Visitors and Conv. Bur. Mem. Am. Cancer Soc. (bd. dirs. Contra Costa Co.). Republican. Home: 1830 Port Barmouth Pl Newport Beach CA 92660 Office: The Carlson Co 19900 Beach Blvd Suite C Huntington Beach CA 92646

CARLSON, RANDY EUGENE, insurance executive; b. Central City, Nebr., Jan. 5, 1948; s. Ned Conrad and Bonnie Lee (Norgard) C.; m. Lorraine Marie Cordsen, Sept. 16, 1967; children: Lance, Brent. BA in Edn., Wayne State Coll., 1970. Tchr., coach Elgin (Nebr.) Pub. Schs., 1970-72, Lewiston (Nebr.) Consol. Schs., 1972-74, North Platte (Nebr.) Pub. Schs., 1974-78; sales assoc. Franklin Life Ins. Co., North Platte, 1977-79; mng. gen. agt. Life Investors Ins. Co., North Platte, 1979—; trustee Fortunaires Found., Davenport, Iowa, 1980—; bd. dirs. Life Investors Ownership Trust, Cedar Rapids, Iowa. Contbr. articles to profl. jours. Mem. North Platte Buffalo Bills, 1980—, North Platte Booster Club, 1983—; adv. bd. Communication for Agr., 1986—; designed plan for the Nebr. High Sch. football playoff system, 1973. Mem. Nat. Assn. Life Underwriters (local pres. 1985-86, state membership chmn. 1986-87), Nebr. State Life Underwriters Assn. (regional v.p. 1988—), Gen. Agts. and Mgrs. Assn. (1985—), North Platte C. of C. (bd. dirs. 1986-88, vice chmn. 1988—). Republican. Lutheran. Club: North Platte Country. Lodge: Elks. Home: 3301 West F St North Platte NE 69101 Office: Carlson and Assocs Inc 717 S Willow North Platte NE 69103

CARLSON, RIA MARIE, public relations executive, writer; b. Los Angeles, Apr. 8, 1961; d. Erick Gustaf and Roberta Rae (Bandelin) C.; m. James Bradley Gerdts, May 19, 1985. BA cum laude, U. So. Calif., 1983. Assoc. producer NBC, Burbank, Calif., 1982-85; account exec. Kerr & Assocs. Pub. Relations, Huntington Beach, Calif., 1985-86; pub. relations mgr. Orange County Performing Arts Ctr., Costa Mesa, Calif., 1986-88; dir. pub. relations and mktg. Bowers Mus., Santa Ana, Calif., 1988—; free lance writer, 1985—. Scriptwriter award ceremony Latin Bus. Assn., 1985; author, editor newsletter Am. Sch. Food Service Assn. Bus. Report, 1985-86; assoc. editor Revue mag., 1987; contbr. articles to publs; cast mem. Disneyland, Anaheim, Calif. Prodn. asst. Profiles in Pride, Black History Month, Burbank, 1985. Named one of Outstanding Young Women in Am., 1985. Mem. AAUW (dir. pub. relations, br. officer), Women in Communications, Nat. Assn. Female Execs., Am. Film Inst., U. So. Calif. Alumni Assn., Blackstonians Pre-Law Hon. Soc. (life), Calif. Scholarship Fedn. (sealbearer, life). Republican. Roman Catholic. Avocations: writing short stories, reading, skiing, softball, travel. Office: Bowers Museum 2002 N Main St Santa Ana CA 92706

CARLSON, ROBERT OSCAR, business educator; b. Erie, Pa., Dec. 23, 1921; s. Oscar Edward and Mary Gertrude (Wintroath) C.; m. Eileen E. Evers, Oct. 29, 1966. A.B. summa cum laude, U. Pitts., 1943; Ph.D., Columbia U., 1952. Research study dir. USPHS and Miss. Bd. Health, 1948-51; Middle East studies dir. Columbia U. Bur. Applied Social Research, 1951-53; overseas pub. relations adviser Standard Oil Co., N.J., 1953-71; pres. Pub. Relations Soc. Am., N.Y.C., 1971-72; v.p., dir. Internat. Research Assos., Inc., N.Y.C., 1972-74; dean Sch. Bus. Adminstrn., Adelphi U., Garden City, N.Y., 1974-82; prof. mgmt. and bus. policy Sch. Bus. Adminstrn., Adelphi U., Garden City; exec. v.p. Arthur J. Evers Corp., 1983—; Mem. men's com. Am. Mus. Natural History; mem. Market Research Council, J.F. Kennedy's Task Force USIA; mem. adv. com. Grad. Sch. Corp. and Polit. Communications, Fairfield U. Chmn. editorial bd.: Public Opinion Quarterly; editor: Communications and Public Opinion, 1975; Contbr. articles to profl. jours. Served to 1st lt. AUS, 1943-46. Mem. Am. Sociol. Assn. (exec. officer), Am. Assn. for Pub. Opinion Research (pres.), China Inst., Am. Petroleum Inst. (chmn. opinion research com.), Inst. for Religious and Social Studies, Jewish Theol. Sem., U.S. Ct. Tennis Assn. Clubs: University, Tuxedo, Watch Hill Yacht, Explorers, Shinnecock Hills Golf, Metropolitan; Desert Forest Golf (Carefree, Ariz.). Home: West Lake Dr Tuxedo Park NY 10987 Office: Sch Bus Adminstrn Adelphi U Garden City NY 11530

CARLSON, ROGER ALLAN, manufacturing company executive, accountant; b. Mpls., Dec. 12, 1932; s. Carl Albert and Borghild Amanda (Anderson) C.; m. Lois Roberta Lehman, Aug. 20, 1955; children: Gene, Bradley. BBA, U. Minn., 1954. CPA, Minn. Investment mgr. Mayo Found., Rochester, Minn., 1963-83; controller Luth. Hosp. and Homes Soc., Fargo, N.D., 1983-84; v.p., treas. Crenlo Inc., Rochester, 1984—, also bd. dirs.; instr. seminars, 1971, 82. Pres. Ability Bldg. Ctr., Rochester, 1974-75, United Way, Olmsted County, Minn., 1980; trustee Minn. Charities Rev. Council, Mpls., 1981-83. Served to capt. U.S. Army, 1955-57. Mem. Am. Inst. CPA's, Minn. Soc. CPA's, Nat. Assn. Accts. (pres. So. Minn. chpt. 1969). Methodist. Home: 1208 19th Ave NE Oakcliff Rochester MN 55904 Office: Crenlo Inc 1600 4th Ave NW Rochester MN 55901

CARLSON, THEODORE JOSHUA, lawyer, utility executive; b. Hartford, Conn., Jan. 4, 1919; s. John and Hulda (Larson) C.; m. Jacqueline L. Coburn, Apr. 25, 1953; children: Stephanie, Christopher J., Victoria, Antoinette. A.B., Montclair State Coll., 1940; J.D., Columbia U., 1948, A.M., 1951; postgrad., U. Chgo., 1942. Bar: N.Y. 1948. Assoc. Gould & Wilkie, N.Y.C., 1948-54, partner, 1954—, sr. partner, 1970—; dir. Central Hudson Gas & Electric Corp., Poughkeepsie, N.Y., 1968—, chmn., 1975—, prin. officer, 1975-86; mem., chmn. fin. and audit com. N.Y. State Energy Research Devel. Authority, 1980-88; dir. Empire State Electric Energy Research Corp., Edison Electric Inst., 1976-79; chmn. exec. com. Energy Assn. N.Y. State, 1976-77, 82-83, N.Y. Power Pool, 1977-78; dir., mem. exec. com. Mid-Hudson Pattern, Inc., Poughkeepsie, N.Y. Author: A

Design For Freedom. Pres. United Fund Rockville Centre, N.Y., 1966; chmn. Westchester County (N.Y.) advisory bd. Salvation Army, 1977-80, N.Y. State Advisory Bd., 1977-83; chmn. bd. trustees King's Coll. Served to capt. USAAF, 1942-46. Mem. Edison Electric Inst., Am., N.Y. bar assns., Bar Assn. City N.Y. (chmn. pub. utility sect. com. on post admissions-legal edn. 1970-73). Lodge: Rotary (hon.). Office: Cen Hudson Gas & Electric Corp 284 South Ave Poughkeepsie NY 12601 also: Gould & Wilkie 1 Wall St New York NY 10005

CARLSON, WILDA MAY, real estate sales agent; b. Rome, N.Y., Dec. 10, 1920; d. Percy Lloyd and Pearl Jessie (Huey) Bucklin; R.N., Buffalo Deaconess Hosp. Sch. Nursing, 1942; Public Health Nurse, SUNY, Buffalo, 1961; m. LeRoy E. Carlson, June 14, 1947; children—Nancy Carlson Stone, Carol Carlson Yannie. Admissions, supr. nurse W.C.A. Hosp., Jamestown, N.Y., 1942-45; indsl. nurse Proto Tool Co., Jamestown, 1963-65, 70-72, Marlin Rockwell div. TRW Corp., Falconer, N.Y., 1969-70; real estates saleswoman, 1973-74, 77—; pvt. investigator unclaimed property, 1986—; dir. Fenton Park Nursing Home, 1965-67; nurse Chautauqua County Resource Center, Jamestown, 1981-82. Pres., Kiantone Mothers Club, Stillwater Ch.; Republican com. woman Kiantone Twp., 1950. Jamestown Vis. Nurse Assn. grantee, 1960-61. Mem. Chautauqua County Grad. Nurses Assn. Club: Women's Bus. and Profl. (Marvin) House. Home: 512 Barr St Jamestown NY 14701

CARLSSON, HANS LENNART, paper company executive; b. Karlskoga, Sweden, Aug. 23, 1932; s. Sigurd V. and Dagmar L. (Helsing) C.; m. Borit L. Odmark, Aug. 15, 1959; children—Borit, Sigurd, Christina. M. Engring, KTH, 1957. Product supt. SCA, Sundsvall, Sweden, 1957-65, resident mgr., 1965-72; pres. Obbola, Umea, 1972-77; exec. v.p. ASSI, Stockholm, 1977-83, pres., 1983—; dir. Domanverket, Falun, Sweden, 1977—, Tumba Paper, Stockholm, 1983—, Swedish Pulp and Paper Assn., Stockholm, 1983—, Pulp and Paper Research Inst., Stockholm, 1985—. Served to capt. Air Force, 1954. Mem. TAPPI, Swedish Pulp and Paper Tech. Assn. Office: Assi Statens Skogsindustrier AB, Sveavagen 59, S 10522 Stockholm Sweden

CARLSSON, INGVAR GÖSTA, prime minister of Sweden; b. Boras, Sweden, Nov. 9, 1934; m. Ingrid Melander, July 10, 1957; children: Ingela, Pia. Degree in Polit. Sci. and Econs., Lund U., 1958; postgrad. Northwestern U., 1961. Sec., Prime Minister's Office, 1958-60; pres. Social Dem. Youth League, 1961-67; M.P., 1964—; undersec. of state, Statsradsberedningen, 1967-69; minister of edn. and cultural affairs, 1969-73; minister of housing and phys. planning, 1973-76; dep. prime minister, from 1982; minister for the environment, 1985-86; prime minister, 1986—. Mem. Social Dem. Party (exec. com. 1972—, chmn. exec. com. 1986—). Address: Statsradsberedningen, Office of the Prime Minister, S 103 33 Stockholm Sweden *

CARLSSON, ROINE, Swedish minister of defense; b. Hallstavik, Sweden, Dec. 10, 1937; m. Eva Birgersson. Mem., study organizer br. 68 Swedish Pulp and Paper Workers' Union, 1954-62, chmn., 1962-65, negotiating sec., 1965-70, chmn. from, 1970; nat. exec. Swedish Trade Union Confedn., 1971-82, mem. bd. Internat. Fedn. Chem., Energy and Gen. Workers Union, 1971-82, vice chmn., 1973-82; mem. joint devel. assistance com. and internat. com. Swedish Trade Union Confedn., Swedish Central Orgn. of Salaried Employees, until 1982; mem. Swedish Council on Trade Policy, bd. Third Pension Fund, sub. mem. Labour Ct., until 1982; active local politics, mem. Mcpl. Council, Central Bd. Adminstrn., Hall-tavik, Sweden, 1971-82; minister with spl. responsibility for state enterprises, Sweden, 1982-85, minister of transport and communications, 1985, minister of defense, 1985—. Address: Ministry of Def, Stockholm Sweden *

CARLUCCI, FRANK CHARLES, III, secretary of defense; b. Scranton, Pa., Oct. 18, 1930; s. Frank Charles, Jr. and Roxanne (Bacon) C.; m. Marcia Myers, Apr. 15, 1976; children: Karen, Frank, Kristin. A.B., Princeton U., 1952; postgrad., Sch. Bus. Adminstrn., Harvard U., 1956; postgrad. hon. dr. degree, Wilkes Coll., Kings Coll., 1973. With Jantzen Co., Portland, Ore., 1955-56; fgn. service officer Dept. State, 1956; vice consul, econ. officer Dept. State, Johannesburg, S. Africa, 1957-59; second sec., polit. officer Dept. State, Kanshasa, Congo, 1960-62; officer in charge Congolese polit. affairs Dept. State, 1962-64; consul gen. Dept. State, Zanzibar, 1964-65; counselor for polit. affairs Dept. State, Rio de Janeiro, Brazil, 1965-69; asst. dir. for ops. Office Econ. Opportunity, Washington, 1969, dir., 1970; assoc. dir. Office Mgmt. and Budget, 1971, dep. dir., 1972; undersec. HEW, 1972-74; ambassador to Portugal, 1975-78; dep. dir. CIA, Washington, 1978-81; dep. sec. Dept. Def., Washington, 1981-82; pres. Sears World Trade, Inc., Washington, 1983-84, chmn., chief exec. officer, 1984-86; asst. to the Pres. Nat. Security Affairs, Washington, 1986-87; sec. Dept. of Def., Washington, 1987—. Served as lt. (j.g.) USNR, 1952-54. Recipient Superior Service award Dept. State, 1972, Superior Honor award, 1969, HEW Disting. Civilian Service award, 1975, Def. Dept. Disting. Civilian award, 1977, Disting. Intelligence medal, 1981, Nat. Intelligence Disting. Service medal, 1981, Presdl. Citizens award, 1983. Office: Dept Def Office Sec The Pentagon Washington DC 20301 *

CARL XVI GUSTAF, HIS MAJESTY, King of Sweden; b. Apr. 30, 1946; s. Prince Gustaf Adolf and Princess Sibylla (Princess Saxe-Coburg-Gotha); ed. Royal Naval Acad., Royal Nat. Def. Coll., U. Uppsala, Stockholm U.; m. Silvia Renate Sommerlath, June 19, 1976; children: Victoria, Carl Philip, Madeleine. King of Sweden, 1973—, chmn. Swedish br. World Wildlife Fund; hon. pres. World Scout Found. Address: Royal Palace, Stockholm Sweden

CARMACK, COMER ASTON, JR., steel co. exec.; b. Phenix City, Ala., June 26, 1932; s. Comer Aston and Mary Kate (Mills) C.; A.S., Marion Mil. Inst., 1951; B.S., Ala. Poly. Inst., 1954; m. Blanche Yarbrough, Nov. 30, 1957; children—Comer Aston, Mary Kate. Project mgr. Muscogee Iron Works, Columbus, Ga., 1956-58, v.p. engring., 1958-73, pres., 1973—; pres. Universal Drives & Services; pres. M.K. Realty, Columbus, 1985—. Past bd. dirs. Better Bus. Bur. Served with USAF, 1954-56. Registered profl. engr., Calif. Mem. ASTM, Nat. Soc. Profl. Engrs., Ga. Soc. Profl. Engrs., Ga. Archtl. and Engring. Soc. (past pres., dir. Columbus chpt.), Order of Engr., Chattahooche Valley Safety Soc. Methodist. Club: Columbus Country. Office: Muscogee Iron Works 1324 11th Ave Columbus GA 31902

CARMALT, SAMUEL WOOLSEY, business consultant; b. Tarrytown, N.Y., May 21, 1944; arrived in Switzerland, 1981; s. Woolsey and Sarah Louise (Robbins) C.; m. Susan Platt, Apr. 4, 1970 (div. 1977); 1 child, Jean Marguerite; m. Linda Stuart Richards, Apr. 14, 1978; 1 child, Candice Churchill. AB, Yale U., 1966; MA, Harvard U., 1970. Exploration geologist, strategic planner Cities Service Corp., Houston and Tulsa, 1974-81; asst. to pres. Petrocons., S.A., Geneva, 1981-83; cons. SW Cons., S.A., Geneva, 1983-86; pres. Chambesy, Switzerland, 1986—. Author: Giant Oil and Gas Fields of the World, 1984. Treas. Holy Trinity Anglican Ch., Geneva, 1987—. Mem. Am. Assn. Petroleum Geologists, Geol. Soc. Am., Geneva Bus. Economists. Clubs: Am. Internat., Yale U. (N.Y.C.). Office: SW Consulting SA, 1 chemin du Jura, 1292 Chambesy Switzerland

CARMAN, GEORGE HENRY, physician; b. Albany, N.Y., Sept. 23, 1928; s. Simon Peter and Mary (Whish) C. B.A., Cornell U., 1948, M.D., 1951. Diplomate: Am. Bd. Internal Medicine, Am. Bd. Cardiovascular Disease. Intern, then asst. resident in medicine Barnes Hosp., St. Louis, 1951-53; asst. resident in medicine Salt Lake County Gen. Hosp., 1955-56; chief resident VA Hosp., Salt Lake City, 1956-57; fellow cardiovascular diseases U. Utah Coll. Medicine, 1957-60; practice medicine specializing in cardiology and internal medicine Dallas, 1960—; attending physician Baylor U. Med. Center; mem. faculty U. Tex. Southwestern Med. Sch., Dallas, 1960—; clin. prof. internal medicine U. Tex. Southwestern Med. Sch., 1972—. Served to 1st lt. M.C. AUS, 1953-55. Fellow A.C.P.; mem. AAAS, Am. Fedn. Clin. Research, AMA, Tex. Acad. Internal Medicine, Am. Heart Assn. (fellow council clin. cardiology), Tex. Heart Assn. (dir.), Dallas Heart Assn. (past pres.), Dallas Acad. Internal Medicine, Confrerie de Chaine des Rotisseurs (comdr.), L'Alliance Française, Phi Beta Kappa, Alpha Omega Alpha. Episcopalian. Club: Gun (Dallas). Office: 3600 Gaston Ave Dallas TX 75246

CARMEL, FRANK JOSEPH, lawyer; b. Hampton, Va., May 11, 1954; s. Melvin M. and Sylvia G. (Garfinkel) C.; m. Debra Ellen Chertok, Sept. 15, 1984. BS in Econs., Va. Polytech. Inst., 1976; JD, U. Va., 1979. Bar: D.C. 1979, Va. 1980, U.S. Ct. Appeals (4th and D.C. cirs.) 1980. Ptnr. Carmel & Carmel, Washington, 1984—; bd. dirs. Met. Builders Mortgage Corp. Named one of Outstanding Young Men of Am., 1980. Mem. ABA, D.C. Bar Assn., Fed. Bar Assn. (sustaining), Va. Bar Assn., Am. Resort Assn., Am. Resort and Residential Devel. Assn., Nat. Assn. Mortgage Brokers (cons. 1985-86). Jewish. Home: 4111 Emery Place NW Washington DC 20016 Office: Carmel & Carmel 1924 N Street NW Washington DC 20036

CARMICHAEL, CHARLES WESLEY, plant engr.; b. Marshall, Ind., Jan 18, 1919; s. Charles Wesley and Clella Ann (Grubb) C.; B.S., Purdue U., 1941; m. Eleanor Lee Johnson, July 2, 1948 (dec. 1984); 1 dau., Ann Bromley Carmichael Biada; m. Bernadine P. Carlson, Dec. 21, 1985. Owner, operator retail stores, West Lafayette, Ind., 1946-48, Franklin, Ind., 1950-53; mem. staff time study Chevrolet Co., Indpls., 1953-55; indsl. engr. Mallory Capacitor Co., Indpls., 1955-60, Greencastle, Ind., 1960-70, plant engr., 1970-81; contract cons. Northwood Assocs., 1981—; lectr. in field. Chmn. Greencastle br. ARC, 1962-63; bd. dirs. United Way Greencastle, 1976-79, 84-86. Served to capt., F.A., U.S. Army, 1941-46; ETO. Decorated Bronze Star, Purple Heart with oak leaf cluster. Mem. Greencastle C. of C. (dir. 1962-64), Am. Inst. Plant Engrs., Ind. Bd. Realtors (dir. 1983-85), Putnam County Bd. Realtors (pres. 1983-84), Ind. Hist. Soc, Am. Legion. Republican. Methodist. Clubs: John Purdue, Soc. Ind. Pioneers, Windy Hill Country. Lodges: Masons, Shriners, Kiwanis (past pres.). Home: 3628 Woodcliff Dr Kalamazoo MI 49008-2513

CARMICHAEL, JOHN LESLIE, retired surgeon; b. Goodwater, Ala., May 22, 1897; s. Daniel Monroe and Amanda (Lessley) C.; A.B., U. Ala., 1916; M.D., Tulane U., 1924; m. Grace Donald, Apr. 28, 1928; children—John L., Jr., Daniel Erskine, James Donald, Robert Glenn, Grace Amanda Carmichael Finkel. Attending surgeon Birmingham Baptist Hosp., from 1927, St. Vincent's Hosp., from 1934, now ret. prof. clin. surgery, Med. Coll., U. Ala., Birmingham, 1955—. Chmn. city council, Fairfield, Ala., 1932-36; mem. Jefferson County Bd. Health, 1947-57, pres., 1957; mem. steering com. Reynolds Library Assocs., U. Ala.-Birmingham, 1983—. Diplomate Am. Bd. Surgery. Fellow ACS, Southeastern Surg. Congress; mem. Birmingham Clin. Club, Birmingham Surg. Soc., Jefferson County Med. Soc. (archives com.), Ala. State Med. Assn., So., Am. med. assns., Phi Beta Kappa (life), Alpha Omega Alpha. Clubs: The Country, Birmingham, the Club. Contbr. numerous articles to med. lit. Home: 3803 Glencoe Dr Birmingham AL 35213

CARMICHAEL, VIRGIL WESLY, mining, civil and geological engineer, former coal company executive; b. Pickering, Mo., Apr. 26, 1919; s. Ava Abraham and Rosevelt (Murphy) C.; m. Emma Margaret Freeman, Apr. 1, 1939 (dec.); m. Colleen Fern Wadsworth, Oct. 29, 1951; children: Bonnie Rae, Peggy Ellen, Jacki Ann. BS, U. Idaho, 1951, M.S., 1956; Ph.D., Columbia Pacific U., San Rafael, Calif., 1980. Registered geol., mining and civil engr., geologist, land surveyor. Asst. geologist Day Mines, Wallace, Idaho, 1950; mining engr. De Anza Engring. Co., 1950-52; hwy. engring. asst. N.Mex. Hwy. Dept., Santa Fe, 1952-53; asst. engr. U. Idaho, 1953-56; minerals analyst Idaho Bur. Mines, 1953-56; mining engr. No. Pacific Ry. Co., St. Paul, 1956-67; geologist N.Am. Coal Corp., Cleve., 1967-69, asst. v.p. engring., 1969-74, v.p., head exploration dept., 1974-84; travel host Satrom Travel and Tour, 1988—. Asst. chief distbn. CD Emergency Mgmt. Fuel Resources for N.D., 1968—; bd. dirs., chmn. fund drive Bismarck-Mandan Orch. Assn., 1979-83; 1st v.p., bd. dirs., chmn. fund drive Bismarck Arts and Galleries Assn., 1982-86; mem. and spl. adivsor Nat. Def. Exec. Res., 1983—; mem. Fed. Emergency Mgmt. Agy., 1983—; mem. adv. bd. Bismarck Salvation Army, 1988—; mem. sci. research bd. N.D. Acad. of Sci., 1986—, N.D. Masonic Found. Bd., 1987—. Served with USNR, 1944-46. Recipient award A for Sci. writing Sigma Gamma Epsilon. Mem. Am. Inst. Profl. Geologists (past pres. local chpt.), Rocky Mountain Coal Mining Inst. (past v.p.), N.D. Geol. Soc. (past pres.), AIME (past chmn. local sect.), Am. Mining Congress (bd. govs. western div. 1973-84), N.Y. Acad. Sci., N.D. Acad. Sci., Sigma Xi. Republican. Clubs: Breezy Shores Resort and Beach (bd. dirs. 1987—), Service. Lodges: Kiwanis (past club pres., dist. lt. gov.), Masons (past master, trustee 1987—), Elks. Home: 1013 N Anderson St Bismarck ND 58501

CARMO, JOSÉ MILHEIRO, mining company executive; b. Grijó, V.N. Gaia Porto, Portugal, Sept. 1, 1947; s. António Pereira Balona Carmo and Margarida Milheiro Oliveira; m. Ana Fernanda Pereira, July 29, 1975; children: José Miguel, Ana Sofia. G in Econs., Oporto (Portugal) U., 1972; postgrad. in European studies, Coimbra (Portugal) U., 1986. Economist Gabinate Planeamento Algarve, Faro, Portugal, 1975-77; dir. personnel Soc. Constrn. William Graham, Porto, 1977-79; asst. dir. personnel Fábrica Cerâmica Valadares, V.N. Gaia, 1979-80, dir. fin., 1980-81, asst. gen. dir., 1982-84; adminstr. Empresa Carbonífera Douro, Porto, 1984—; cons. in human resources mgmt.; tchr. Inst. Superior Adminstr. Gestão, Oporto, 1982-86. Contbr. articles to profl. jours. Mgr. Portuguese Institut of Finance, 1987—. Served to 2d lt. Portuguese Army, 1973-75. Mem. Portuguese Mgmt. Assn. (mem. consultive council 1982-87). Roman Catholic. Home: R 20 nr 1436- r/c E, 4500 Espinho Porto Portugal Office: Empresa Carbonifera Do Douro SA, Pc D-joao I, N-25 5, 4000 Espinho Porto Portugal

CARMODY, ARTHUR RODERICK, JR., lawyer; b. Shreveport, La., Feb. 19, 1928; s. Arthur R. and Caroline (Gaughan) C.; m. Renee Aubry, Jan. 26, 1952; children: Helen Bragg, Renee, Arthur Roderick, Patrick, Timothy, Mary, Virginia, Joseph. BS, Fordham U., 1949; LLB, La. State U., 1952. Bar: La. 1952. Mem. firm Wilkinson & Carmody, Shreveport, 1952—; dir. Kansas City So. Transport Co., Kansas City, Shreveport and Gulf Terminal Co., Shreveport Captains Baseball Club. Chmn. Met. Shreveport Zoning Bd. Appeals, 1959-72; bd. dirs. Caddo Dem. Assn., Shreveport, 1966-72; pres. bd. trustees Jesuit High Sch., 1976-82; trustee Schumpert Med. Ctr.; bd. dirs. La. State U. Found., Baton Rouge, Agnew Day Sch., Shreveport, 1970-82 Ridgewood Montessori Sch.; nat. bd. dirs. N.Mex. Mil. Inst., Roswell, 1967-68; mem. adv. council La. State U. at Shreveport, 1982-86. Served to 1st lt. U.S. Army, 1948-50. Fellow Am. Coll. Trial Lawyers, La. Bar Assn; mem. ABA, Fed. Bar Assn., Shreveport Bar Assn., Fifth Fed. Cir. Bar Assn., North La. Hist. Soc., Nat. Soc. Sons of Am. Revolution, Univ. Assocs. of La. State U., Am. Judicature Soc., La. Law Inst., Nat. Assn. R.R. Trial Counsel, Internat. Assn. Def. Counsel, La. Assn. Def. Counsel, Nat. Acad. Law and Medicine, Mid-Continent Oil and Gas Assn. (exec. com. 1984—), Safari Soc., La. Assn. Bus. and Industry, Shreveport C. of C. (dir. 1968-70), Soc. Hosp. Council, La. Civil Service League, La. Bar Found., Res. Officers Assn., North La. Civil War Round Table (bd. dirs.), U.S. Horse Cavalry Assn., Phi Delta Phi, Kappa Alpha. Roman Catholic. Clubs: Shreveport, Petroleum (Shreveport); University, Pierremont Oaks Tennis, Cambridge. Home: 255 Forest Ave Shreveport LA 71104 Office: Wilkinson & Carmody 1700 Beck Bldg Shreveport LA 71166

CARMODY, JAMES ALBERT, lawyer; b. St. Louis, Nov. 21, 1945; s. Lawrence C. and Anna Louise (Hanes) C.; m. Helen "Tippy" Valin, Mar. 22, 1969; children: Paul Valin, Leigh Christin. BA, Vanderbilt U., 1967; JD, U. Ark., 1973. Bar: Tex. 1974, U.S. Dist. Ct. (so. dist.) Tex. 1974, U.S. Ct. Appeals (5th and 10th cirs.) 1975. Assoc. Mabry & Gunn, Texas City, Tex., 1974-75; mcpl. ct. judge Texas City, Tex., 1975; assoc. Chamberlain & Hrdlicka, Houston, 1975-78, ptnr., 1978—. Assoc. editor U. Ark. Law Rev., 1973. Incorporator, Gulf Coast Big Bros. and Sisters, Inc., Galveston County, Tex., 1975; mem. St. Maximillian Cath. Community Bldg. Com., Houston, 1985—. Served to lt. USN, 1967-71. Mem. Fed. Bar Assn., Galveston County Jr. Bar Assn. (pres. 1975, Outstanding Young Lawyer, 1985), Delta Theta Phi (master inspector 1983-85, dep. chancellor 1985—, dean Houston alumni senate, 1988). Republican. Roman Catholic. Club: Houston Met. Racquet Club. Home: 15910 Congo Houston TX 77040 Office: Chamberlain Hrdlicka et al 1400 Citicorp Ctr 1200 Smith St Houston TX 77002

CARMODY, ROBERT EDWARD, human resource information systems professional; b. N.Y.C., Dec. 13, 1942; s. Henry Adrian and Lucille Dorothy (Dorsey) C.; m. Sara Jane Morris, Oct. 4, 1969; children: Jon Andrew, Heather Brooke. BA in Psychology, U. Va., 1964. CLU. Personnel systems supt. State Farm Ins. Co., Bloomington, Ill., 1966-78; exec. project dir. Info. Sci. Inc., Chgo., 1978-79; dir. human resources systems CIGNA Corp., Phila., 1979-88, asst. v.p., human resources info. services, 1988—; founding mem. Ins. Personnel Systems Group, 1987—. Contbr. articles to profl. jours. Fire commr. Dade County, 1988—. Served with USNG, 1964-70. Mem. Am. Soc. Personnel Adminstrs., Am. Mgmt. Assn., Soc. Human Resource System Profls., Conf. Bd., Info. Industry Assn., Ins. Personnel Systems Group (founding mem. 1987). Home: 118 Oak Ave Haddonfield NJ 08033 Office: CIGNA Corp 1600 Arch St 12 Pennwalt Philadelphia PA 19103

CARMOUZE, PHILLIPE PIERRE, physician; b. Bordeaux, Gironde, France, Sept. 21, 1944; s. Pierre Emile Louis and Genevieve (Chavane de Dalmassy) C.; m. Marie-Francoise Grenié, Mar. 15, 1974; children Aurelie, Louis-Charles, Emilie. CES in Med., U. Bordeaux, 1973, U. Bordeaux, 1974; MD, U. Bordeaux, 1974. Physician Port Autonome de Bordeaux, 1974—; physician Soc. Nat. des Chemins de Fer Francais, Bordeaux, 1975—, Cellulose du Pin, St.Gobain, Usine de Facture, Biganos, France, 1986—. Home and Office: 3 Rue de Soissons, 33000 Bordeaux, Gironde France

CARNE, MARCEL ALBERT, film director; b. Aug. 18, 1906; s. Paul and Maria (Racouet) C.; Asst. operator Les Nouveaux Messieurs, 1928; asst. to dir. Cagliostro, 1929; mem. editorial staff Cinemagazine; asst. dir. René Clair in Sous les Toits de Paris, 1930; asst. dir. Le Grand Jeu, Pension Minosa, La Kermesse Heroique; dir. films: Jenny, 1936, Drô le de drame, 1937, Quai des brumes, 1938, Le jour se lève, 1939, Les visiteurs du soir, 1941, les enfants du Paradis, 1943, Les portes de la nuit, 1946, La Marie du port, 1949, Juliette ou la clé des songes, 1950, Thérèse Raquin, 1953, L'air de Paris, 1954, Le pays d'où je viens, 1956, Les tricheurs, 1958, Terrain vague, 1960, Du mouron pour les petits oiseaux, 1963, Trois chambres à Manhattan, 1965, Les jeunes loups, 1968, Les assassins de l'ordre, 1970, La merveilleuse visite, 1974, La Bible, 1976, César des Césars, 1979. Decorated commandeur Légion d'honneur; grand officier Ordre des Arts et des Lettres; commdr. Ordre National du Mérite; Grand Prix de Cinéma, 1958; Mé daille de Vermeil, 1972; Grand Prix Oecuménique, Cannes, 1977; Biennale de Suisse 1938-53, 1982. Author: La vie à belles dents, 1975; contbr. criticisms to profl. jours. Address: 16 rue de L'abbaye, Paris 75006 France *

CARNEIRO, MARIA CRISTINA, poet, translator; b. Montevideo, Uruguay, Oct. 31, 1948; arrived in Eng., 1980; d. Manuel Francisco and Marina Josefa (Miguélez) C.; m. David Jerome Stuart Legge, Dec. 16, 1978; 1 child, Simon. B in Law, Inst. Alfredo Vázquez Acevedo, Montevideo, 1968; diploma in drama, Escuela Mcpl. Arte Dramático, Montevideo, 1972. Free-lance journalist and translator Montevideo, 1968-75; internat. sec. UN Devel. Program, Luanda, Angola, 1976-78; personal asst. to chief exec. Camden Com. for Community Relations, London, 1980-82; asst. regional officer London Assn. Community Relations Councils, 1983; translator Amnesty Internat., London, 1987—. Author: Zafarrancho Solo, 1968 (1st prize Nat. Book Fair 1968), Libro de Imprecaciones, 1975. Mem. Nat. Council for Civil Liberties, Anti-Apartheid Movement, Campaign for Nuclear Disarmament. Mem. Labour Party (Eng.). Mem. Socialist Party (Uruguay). Home: 201 Ewell Rd, Surbiton KT6 6BE, England

CARNER, WILLIAM JOHN, banker; b. Springfield, Mo., Aug. 9, 1948; s. John Wilson and Willie Marie (Moore) C.; m. Dorothy Jean Edwards, June 12, 1976; children: Kimberly Jean, John Edwards Carner. AB, Drury Coll., 1970; MBA, U. Mo., 1972. Mktg. rep. 1st Nat. Bank Memphis, 1972-73; asst. br. mgr. Bank of Am., Los Angeles, 1973-74; dir. mktg. Commerce Bank, Springfield, Mo., 1974-76; affiliate mktg. mgr. 1st Union Bancorp., St. Louis, 1976-78; pres. Carner & Assocs., Springfield, Mo., 1977—; instr. Drury Coll., 1975, 84-86, U. Mo., Columbia, 1986-88; dir. Ozark Pub. Telecommunications, Inc. 1982—, sec., 1984-85, treas., 1985-86, vice chmn. 1986-87, chmn., 1987-88; asst. prof. SW Mo. State U., 1988—. Bd. dirs. Am. Cancer Soc., Greene County, Mo., 1974-82, crusade chmn., 1982-83, publicity chmn., 1974-78; bd. dirs. Springfield (Mo.) Muscular Dystrophy Assn., 1975-76, Greater Ozarks council Camp Fire Girls, 1980-81, Chameleon Puppet Theatre. Mem. Bank Mktg. Assn. (service mem. council 1985—), Mo. Banker's Assn. (instr. Gen. Banking sch.), Fin. Instns. Mktg. Assn. (chmn. service mem. com.), Assn. MBA Execs., Drury Coll. Alumni Assn. (v.p. 1985-86, pres. 1986-87). Democrat. Mem. Christian Ch. (Disciples of Christ). Club: Hickory Hills Country. Lodges: Masons, Shriners. Home: 1500 S Fairway Ave Springfield MO 65804 Office: PO Box 50005 Springfield MO 65805

CARNES, LAMAR, lawyer; b. Beaumont, Tex., Aug. 19, 1923; s. Garland and Hattie (Butler) C. B.A., Cornell U., 1941, M.B.A., 1942; J.D., So. Meth. U., 1948. Bar: Tex. 1948, U.S. Supreme Ct. 1954, U.S. Dist. Ct. (so. dist.) Tex. 1954, U.S. Dist. Ct. (no. dist.) Tex. 1971, U.S. Ct. Appeals (5th cir) 1954. Sole practice, Houston, 1948-53; v.p., gen. counsel ADA Oil Co., Houston, 1953-58; sole practice, Houston, 1958-68, Dallas, 1969—. Served to lt. col. USAF, 1942-46, ETO. Mem. ABA, Tex. Bar Assn., Dallas Bar Assn., Delta Theta Phi. Republican. Office: 401 Capital Bank Bldg Dallas TX 75206

CARNEY, PATRICIA, Canadian legislator, president treasury board; b. Shanghai, China, May 26, 1935; d. John James and Dora (Sanders) C.; two children. B.A. in Econs. and Polit. Sci., U. B.C., Can., 1960, M.A. in Comml. and Regional Planning, 1977. Econ. journalist various publs. 1955-70; owner, cons. Gemini North Ltd., Vancouver, B.C., Can., 1970-80, Yellowknife, N.W.T., Can., 1971, Alta., Can., 1971; mem. Can. Ho. of Commons, Ottawa, Ont., 1980—, minister of state, 1981, minister fin., 1983, minister energy, mines and resources, 1984-86, minister for internat. trade, 1986-88, pres. Treas. Bd., 1988—; mem. planning and priorities com.; mem. fgn. def. cabinet com. Recipient Can. Women's Press award, 1968, 3 MacMillan Bloedel Ltd. awards. Mem. Assn. Profl. Economists B.C., Can. Inst. Planners. Office: House of Commons, Parliament Bldgs, Ottawa, ON Canada K1A 0A6 *

CARNEY, ROBERT ARTHUR, restaurant executive; b. Haddonfield, N.J., Aug. 20, 1937; s. George Albert and Margret (Hollworth) C.; B.A., Ursinus Coll., 1963; m. Patricia Louise Igo, July 15, 1983; children—Lynn Ann, Jeffrey Todd, Jill Christine, Jason Michael, Justin David, Jennifer Lynn. Procurement agt. Campbell Soup Co., Paris, Tex., 1963-69, mgr. procurement, Salisbury, Md., 1969-72, dir. procurement, Camden, N.J., 1972-78; v.p. procurement Burger King Corp., Miami, Fla., 1978-82; v.p. purchasing Pizza Hut Inc., Wichita, 1978—. Served to capt. U.S. Army, 1958-60. Mem. Nat. Restaurant Assn. Republican. Roman Catholic. Home: 412 Lauber Ln Derby KS 67037 Office: 9111 E Douglas Wichita KS 67201

CARO, ANTHONY (ALFRED CARO), sculptor; b. London, Mar. 8, 1924; s. Alfred and Mary (Haldinstein) C.; m. Sheila May Girling, Dec. 17, 1949; children: Timothy Martin, Paul Gideon. M.A., Christ's Coll., Cambridge U., Eng., 1943; grad., Royal Acad. Schs., London, 1952; D.Litt. (hon.), East Anglia U., York U., Toronto, Ont., Can., Brandeis U. Asst. to Henry Moore, 1951-53; part-time tchr. sculpture St. Martin's Sch. Art, London, 1953-79; tchr. sculpture Bennington Coll., Vt., 1963, 65. Sculpture commd. by Nat. Gallery Art, Washington, 1977; one-man shows include, Galleria del Naviglio, Milan, Italy, 1956, Gimpel Fils Gallery, London, 1957, Whitechapel Art Gallery, London, 1963, Andre Emmerich Gallery, N.Y.C., 1964, 66, 68, 70, 72, 74, 77, 78, 79, 81, 82, 84, 86, Washington Gallery Modern Art, 1965, Kasmin Ltd., London, 1965, 67, 71, 72, David Mirvish Gallery, Toronto, Ont., Can., 1966, 71, 74, Galerie Bischofberger, Zurich, Switzerland, 1966, Kroller-Muller Mus., Netherlands, 1967, Hayward Gallery, London, 1969, Kenwood House, Hampstead, Eng., 1974, 81, Galleria dell'Ariete, Milan, 1974, Richard Gray Gallery, Chgo., 1975, 86, Watson/de Nagy Gallery, Houston, 1975, Mus. Modern Art, N.Y.C., 1975, Lefevre Gallery, London, 1976, Everson Mus., Syracuse, N.Y., 1976, Tel Aviv Mus., 1977, Piltzer-Rheims, Paris, 1977, Waddington & Tooth, London, 1977, Emmerich Gallery, Zurich, 1978, Harkus Krackow Gallery, Boston, 1978, 81, Knoedler, London, 1978, 82, 83, 84, Wentzel, Hamburg, 1978, Ace, Venice, Calif., 1978, Kahsahara, Japan, 1979, Glasgow, 1980, Acquavella Galleries, N.Y., 1980, Galerie Andre, Berlin, 1980, Downstairs Gallery, Edmonton, Alta, Can., 1981, Galerie Wentzel, Cologne, Ger., 1982, 84, 85, Gallery One, Toronto, 1982, 85, Knoedler & Waddington Galleries, London, 1983, Galerie de France, Paris, 1983, Acquavella Galleries, N.Y.C., 1984, 86, Brit. Council touring exhbn., Tel Aviv, N.Z., Australia, Germany, 1977-79,

Madrid, Barcelona, Bilbao, Valencia, Spain, 1986, Mus. Fine Arts, Boston, 1980, Constantine Grimaldis Gallery, Balt., 1987, numerous others; exhibited in group shows at 1st Paris Biennale, 1959 (sculpture prize), Battersea Park Open Air Exhbn., 1960, 63, 66, Gulbenkian Exhbn., London, 1964, Documenta III Kassel, 1965, Jewish Mus., N.Y.C., 1966 (David Bright prize), Venice Biennale, 1958, 66, Pitts. Internat., 1967, 68, Met. Mus. Art, 1968, Sao Paulo, 1969 (sculpture prize), U. Pa., 1969, Everson Mus., Mus. Modern Art, N.Y.C., 1975; represented in permanent collections Walker Art Gallery, Minn., Mus. Fine Arts, Houston, Boston, Dallas, Mus. Modern Art, N.Y.C., Phila. Mus. Art, Cleve. Mus. Art, Detroit Inst. Arts, Solomon R. Guggenheim Mus., N.Y.C., Yale U. Art Gallery, New Haven, numerous others. Trustee Tate Gallery, London, 1982, Fitzwilliam Mus., Cambridge, 1984. Decorated comdr. Order Brit. Empire; presented key to city N.Y.C., 1976; hon. fellow Christ's Coll., Cambridge, Royal Coll. Art, London, 1986, U. Surrey, England, 1987. Mem. Am. Acad. and Inst. Arts and Letters (hon.).

CARO, CHARLES CRAWFORD, microcomputer company executive, international consultant; b. Champaign, Ill., Feb. 15, 1946; s. William Crawford and Marian Dell (Heischmidt) C.; m. Sallye Simons, Dec. 18, 1977 (div. 1987); 1 son, Mark Christopher. BA, U. South Fla., 1973, MA, 1976. Program support specialist Bendix/Siyanco, Riyadh, Saudi Arabia, 1973-74; chmn., chief exec. officer Caro Internat. Trade and Relations Corp. (Citar), Tampa, Fla. and Jeddah, 1976-79, dir., 1976-79; mng. dir. Architect Lee Scarfone Assocs. (ALSA), Al-Khobar, Saudi Arabia, 1979-80; exec. dir. Caro Research Assocs., Tampa and New Orleans, 1980—; pres., chief exec. officer C3DS, Inc., Tampa, 1987—, Microfine, Inc., Tampa, 1983-84, also dir.; dir. Action Cons. Services, Inc., Brandon, Fla., 1986. Contbr. articles to publs. in field. Mem. Hillsborough Democratic Exec. Com., Tampa, 1982—; pres. Drug Abuse Awareness Group, 1987; mem. Communities Against Substance Abuse Inc., 1988—; assoc. editor Internat. Round Table, 1987—; pres. Communities Against Substance Abuse, Inc., 1988— . Served with U.S. Army Security Agy., 1967-71. Mem. World Inst. Achievement (life), Assn. Computing Machinery (computers and soc. spl. interest group), Internat. Platform Assn., Phi Kappa Phi, Pi Sigma Alpha. Episcopalian. Club: Tiger Bay of Tampa Bay.

CARPENTER, CLIVE DAVID, banker; b. Dartford, Kent, Eng., Dec. 25, 1951; s. Charles John and Hazel Jean (Prichard) C. Officer, Barclays Bank Plc, Kent, 1969-74; sr. officer Arbuthnot Latham & Co., Ltd., London, 1974-77; gen. mgr. East African Acceptances, Nairobi, Kenya, 1977-82; mng. dir. Jimba Credit Corp., Nairobi, 1982-86; mng. dir. Credit Kenya Ltd., Vipan Carpenter & Co., London, Credit Kent Ltd., London. Fellow Kenya Inst. Bankers (hon. sec., mem. exec. com. 1985—), Kenya Inst. Mgmt., Chartered Inst. Bankers, British Inst. Mgmt., Inst. Fin. Accts., Inst. Profl. Mgrs. Mem. Brit. Conservative Party. Mem. Ch. of England. Avocations: horticulture; meteorology. Office: Credit Kenya Ltd, Box 61064, Nairobi Kenya

CARPENTER, DONALD ALFRED, senior judge; b. Greeley, Colo., Jan. 2, 1907. J.D., George Washington U., 1931. Bar: Tex. 1931, Colo. 1949. Sole practice, El Paso, 1931-34; dir. Colo. Use Tax Div., Denver, 1938-40; adminstrv. asst. to Hon. William S. Hill, mem. U.S. Congress, 1940-43; judge Weld County (Colo.) Ct., 1946-52, Colo. Dist. Ct. 8th Jud. Dist., 1952-64; chief judge 19th Jud. Dist., 1964-79; adminstrv. judge No. Colo. Water Conservancy Dist., Greeley, 1965-79, Central Colo. Water Conservancy Dist., Greeley, 1965-79; water judge South Platte River System, 1969-79; master Colo. Supreme Ct., 1960-61; mem. Gov.'s Jud. Conf. Colo., 1957, 58, Colo. Jud. Council, 1958, chmn. com. appellate practice, 1958; mem. jud. council Chief Justice Colo. Supreme Ct., 1973-79. Mem. ABA, Colo. Bar Assn., Tex. Bar Assn., Weld County Bar Assn., Colo. Dist. Judges Assn., Nat. Coll. Probate Judges, Am. Judicature Soc., Nat. Conf. State Trial Judges, World Assn. Judges, Am. Acad. Polit. and Social Scis. Home and Office: 14953 Weld County Rd 70 Greeley CO 80631

CARPENTER, DONALD BLODGETT, real estate appraiser; b. New Haven, Aug. 20, 1916; s. Fred Donald and Gwendolen (Blodgett) C.; Ph.B., U. Vt., 1938; m. Barbara Marvin Adams, June 28, 1941 (dec. Aug. 1978); m. 2d, Lee Burker McGough, Dec. 28, 1980 (div. Apr. 1987); children—Edward G., John D., William V., Andrew J., Dorothy J. and James J. McGough. Reporter Burlington (Vt.) Daily News, 1938-39; guide chair operator Am. Express Co., N.Y. World's Fair, 1939; underwriter G.E.I. Corp., Newark, 1939-40; Sales corr. J. Dixon Crucible Co., Jersey City, 1940-41, asst. office mgr., priorities specialist, 1941-42, sales rep., San Francisco, 1946-52, field supr. Travelers Ins. Co., San Francisco, 1952-58; gen. agt. Gen. Am. Life Ins. Co., San Francisco, 1958-59; Western Supr. Provident Life & Accident Ins. Co., San Francisco, 1959-60; brokerage supr. Aetna Life Ins. Co., San Francisco, 1960-61, maintenance cons. J.I. Holcomb Mfg. Co., Mill Valley, Calif., 1961-68; ednl. service rep. Marquis Who's Who, Inc., Mill Valley, 1963-68; sales rep. Onox, Inc., Mendocino, Calif., 1965-68; tchr., coach Mendocino Jr.-Sr. High Sch., 1968; real property appraiser, Mendocino County, Calif., 1968-81; instr. Coll. of Redwoods, 1985-87 . Active numerous civic orgns.; co-chmn. Citizens for Sewers, 1971-72; mem. Mendocino County Safety Council, 1981. Served with USNR, 1942-46; lt. comdr., comdg. officer res. unit, 1967-68, now ret. Recipient Community Sportsman-of-Year award, 1971; Sec. of Navy Commendation with ribbon, 1946, other awards, certificates; companion Mil. Order World Wars. Mem. Internat. Orgn. Real Estate Appraisers (Life), Manufactured Housing Appraisal Inst., Internat. Inst. Valuers, Nat. Assn. Rev. Appraisers, Reserve Officers Assn. U.S. (life; chpt. pres. 1954, 56, state v.p. 1958-61), Ret. Officers Assn. (life; chpt. survivors assistance area counselor 1979—, chpt. scholarship com. 1986-87), Mendocino Art Center (sponsor mem.), Save-The-Redwoods League, Marines Meml. Assn., Mendocino County Employees Assn. (dir. 1981), Mendocino County Hist. Soc., Mendocino Hist. Research Inc. (docent), Nat. Assn. Uniformed Services (life), Nat. Ret. Tchrs. Assn., Calif. Ret. Tchrs. Assn., Naval Order of U.S. (life), Naval Res. Assn. (life), Navy League of U.S. (life), U.S. Naval Inst. (life), Am. Diabetes Assn., Alumni Assn. U. Vt. (founding pres. San Francisco Alumni Club 1964), Mendocino Coast Stamp Club (charter; dir. 1983—), Kappa Sigma (scholarship leadership award 1937-38). Republican. Congregationalist. Clubs: Rotary Internat. (club pres. 1975-76, dist. gov. area rep. 1977-78, Dist. Gov. awards 1974, 76, dist. ednl. awards com. 1978-81; dist. group study exchange com. 1981-88; Paul Harris fellow 1979—, Rotarian of the Yrs. 1969-88), Am. Legion (post comdr. 1972-73, state citation for outstanding community service 1972), Am. Legion Past Comdrs. Calif. (life), Mendocino Cardinal Booster (charter, life mem.; club pres. 1971), U. Vt. Catamount (charter), Old Mill. Home: Box 87 Mendocino CA 95460-0087

CARPENTER, EDMUND NELSON, II, lawyer; b. Phila., Jan. 27, 1921; s. Walter S. and Mary (Wootten) C.; m. Carroll Morgan, July 18, 1970; children: Mary W., Edmund Nelson III, Katherine R.R., Elizabeth Lea; stepchildren: John D. Gates, Ashley du Pont Gates. A.B., Princeton U., 1943; LL.B., Harvard U., 1948. Bar: Del. 1949, U.S. Supreme Ct. 1957. Assoc. firm Richards, Layton & Finger, Wilmington, Del., 1949-53; partner Richards, Layton & Finger, 1953-78, dir., 1978—, pres., 1982-85; dep. atty. gen. State of Del., 1953-54, spl. dep. atty., 1960-62; chmn. Del. Superior Ct. Jury Study Com., 1963-66, Del. Supreme Ct. Cts. Consolidation Com., 1985-87; mem. Del. Gov.'s Commn. Law Enforcement and Adminstrn. Justice, 1969; chmn. Del. Agy. to Reduce Crime, 1970-71, chmn. Del. Supreme Ct. Adv. Com. on Profl. Fin. Accountability, 1974-75; mem. Long Range Cts. Planning Com., 1976—. Trustee Wilmington Med. Center, 1965-82, U. Del., 1971-77, Princeton U., 1965—, World Affairs Council of Wilmington, 1968-80, Woodrow Wilson Found., 1985—; trustee Lawrenceville Sch., 1953-74, trustee emeritus, 1974—; bd. dirs. Good Samaritan Inc., 1973—; chmn. lawyers adv. com. U.S. Ct. Appeals 3d Circuit, 1975-77; mem. Del Health Care Injury Ins. Study Commn., 1976—. Fellow Am. Coll. Trial Lawyers, Am. Bar Found.; mem. ABA (ho. of dels. 1979-86), Del. State Bar Assn., Am. Judicature Soc. (dir. 1974—, exec. com. 1978-80, v.p. 1980-81, pres. 1981-83), Am. Trial Lawyers Assn. Home: 600 Center Mill Rd Wilmington DE 19807 Office: PO Box 551 One Rodney Sq Wilmington DE 19899

CARPENTER, HOYLE DAMERON, music educator emeritus; b. Stockton, Calif., Aug. 8, 1909; s. William Horace and Mabel (Hanna) C.; Mus.B., U. Pacific, 1930; Mus.M., U. Rochester, 1932; Ph.D., U. Chgo., 1951-57; postgrad. U. Calif. at Berkeley, 1949-50; m. Rose Mick, Feb. 24, 1968. Instr. Ft. Hays (Kans.) State Coll., 1942-44; asst. prof. Grinnell Coll., 1944-57; faculty Glassboro (N.J.) State Coll., 1957—, asst. prof., 1957-60, assoc. prof., 1960-61, prof., 1961-76, prof. emeritus, 1976—. Treas. Gloucester County Mental Health Assn., 1963-68. Committeeman Glassboro Democratic Com., 1964; v.p. Glassboro Dem. Club, 1964-66. Mem. Am., Internat. musicological socs., Music Tchrs. Nat. Assn. (sec. Eastern div. 1962-64), Music Educators Nat. Conf., Renaissance Soc. Am., Am. Guild Organists, AAUP, N.J. Music Tchrs. Assn. (pres. 1961-63), Pi Kappa Lambda. Author: Teaching Elementary Music without a Supervisor, 1959; also edits. Holyoke's Instrumental Assistant, 1959, Crequillon Pisne me peult venir, 1962; also several poster sets on music, 1970, also articles; writer program notes for Hollybush Festival, Lenape Chamber Players, Craftsbury Chamber Players, 1980-88. Home: 512 S Woodbury Rd Pitman NJ 08071

CARPENTER, LESLIE ARTHUR, publishing executive; b. June 26, 1927; s. William and Rose Carpenter. Student, Hackney Tech. Coll., Eng. Dir. Country Life, Eng., 1965, George Newnes, Eng., 1966; mng. dir. Odhams Press Ltd., Eng., 1968, Internat. Pub. Corp., Eng., 1972, Reed Internat. Ltd., Eng., 1974, IPC (Am.) Inc., 1975; chmn. Reed Holdings Inc., 1977, Reed Pub. Holdings Ltd., 1981; chief exec. pub. and printing Reed Internat. Inc., 1979; chief exec. Reed Internat. plc, 1982-86, chmn., 1986—. Office: Reed Internat plc, Reed House, Piccadilly, London W1A 1EJ, England *

CARPENTER-MASON, BEVERLY NADINE, executive health care quality assurance nurse; b. Pitts., May 23, 1933; d. Frank Carpenter and Thelma Deresa (Williams) Smith; m. Sherman Robert Robinson Jr., Dec. 26, 1953 (div. Jan. 1959); 1 child, Keith Michael; m. David Solomon Mason Jr., Sept. 10, 1960; 1 child, Tamara Nadina. RN, St. Joseph's Hosp., Pitts. BS, St. Joseph's Coll., North Windham, Maine, 1979; MS, So. Ill. U., 1981. Staff nurse med. surgery, ob-gyn neontology and pediatrics, Pa., N.Y., Wyo., Colo. and Washington, 1954-68; mgr. clinician dermatol. services Malcolm Grow Med. Ctr., Camp Spring, Md., 1968-71; pediatric nurse practitioner Dept. Human Resources, Washington, 1971-73; asst. dir. nursing Glenn Dale Hosp., Md., 1973-81; nursing coordinator medicaid div. Forest Haven Ctr., Laurel, Md., 1981-83, spl. asst. to supr. for med. services, 1983-84; spl. asst. to supt. for quality assurance Burr. Habilitation Services, Laurel, 1984—; asst. treas. ABQAURP, Inc., Sarasota, Fla., 1988—, also bd. dirs.; cons. and lectr. in field. Contbr. articles to profl. jours. Mem., star donor ARC Blood Drive, Washington, Md., 1975—; chair nominations com. Prince Georges Nat. Council Negro Women, Md., 1984-85. Recipient awards Dept. Air Force and D.C. Govt., 1966—, Della Robbia Gold medallion Am. Acad. Pediatrics, 1972, John P. Lamb Jr. Meml. Lectureship award East Tenn. State U., Johnson City, 1988. Mem. Am. Assn. Mental Retardation (conf. lectr. 1988), Am. Coll. Utilization Rev. Physicians, Am. Bd. Quality Assurance and Utilization Rev. (case study editor, mem. jour. editorial bd. 1985—, chmn. publs. com. 1987—), Assn. Retarded Citizens, Nat. Assn. Female Execs., Top Ladies of Distinction, Inc. (1st v.p. 1986—), Internat. Platform Assn., Chi Eta Phi. Democrat. Baptist. Avocations: studying languages, travel, reading, writing, collecting antiques. Home: 11109 Winsford Ave Upper Marlboro MD 20772 Office: Bur Habilitation Services 3360 Center Ave Laurel MD 20707

CARPINO, FRANCESCO CARDINAL, former archbishop of Palermo; b. Palazzolo Acreide, Italy, May 18, 1905; Ordained priest Roman Catholic Ch., 1927; ordained titular archbishop of Nicomedia and coadjutor archbishop of Monreale, 1951, archbishop of Monreale, 1951-61; titular archbishop of Sardica, 1961; assessor Sacred Consistorial Congregation, 1961; pro-prefect of Sacred Congregation of the Council, 1967; elevated to Sacred Coll. of Cardinals, 1967; archbishop of Palermo, 1967-70; entered order of cardinal bishops as titular bishop of Albano, 1978. Referendary of the Congregation of Bishops, 1970. Mem. Council for Public Affairs of the Ch., Congregation, Tribunal, Causes of Saints, Apostolic Signatura. Office: Piazza St Calisto 16, 1-001 53 Rome Italy *

CARPIO NICOLLE, ROBERTO, vice president of Guatemala; b. Guatemala City, Guatemala, July 16, 1930; m. Mercedes Blanco; 4 children. Licentiate in Polit. Scis., Rafael Landivar U. 1976. Pres. Agrl. Commn., 1976; dep. in Nat. Congress, 1974-78; pres. Nat. Constituent Assembly, 1984-85; v.p. of Guatemala, 1986—. Founding mem. Christian Democratic party. Office: Oficina de Vice Presidente, de la Republica, Guatemala City Guatemala *

CARR, ADRIAN WALTER, film director, editor; b. Melbourne, Australia, Oct. 2, 1952; s. Walter Hugo and Marie (McCarthy) C.; m. Joyce Singh, 1975 (div. 1976), m. Ann Lyons, 1976; 1 child, Anthony James Lyons. Student, Royal Melbourne Inst. Tech., 1970-71. Asst. film editor Australian Broadcasting Commn., Melbourne, 1970-73; editor Crawford Film Prodns., Melbourne, 1973-77, Film House P/L, Melbourne, 1977-82; free-lance editor, director 1982—. Dir. for feature film Now and Forever; short film Spiders; editor for films Dark Age, Prisoners, The Lighthorsemen, D.A.R.Y.L., The Aviator, The Man for Snowy River 1, Harlequin; for TV movies Mr. B Says No, Stopover; for mini-series The Far Country; automatic dialogue replacement editor: Crocodile Dundee, Sky Pirates; effects editor: Anzacs; dir. additional scenes (feature) 13th Floor, 1987. Mem. Melbourne Screen and Theatre Guild, Australian Theatrical and Amusement Employees Assn. Roman Catholic.

CARR, ARTHUR, electronic mfg. co. exec.; b. Newark, July 9, 1931; s. Michael Thomas and Gertrude A. (Levy) C.; grad. pub. schs.; m. Virginia Lea Merry, July 11, 1953; children—Karen, Vickie, William. Field tech. specialist Remington Rand Univac, Boston, 1955-61; dir. mktg. Computer Control div. Honeywell, Framingham, Mass., 1961-68; v.p. mktg. Codex Corp., Mansfield, Mass., 1968-70, pres., chief exec., 1970-82; also dir.; v.p. Motorola Inc., 1979-82, exec. v.p., gen. mgr. info. systems group, 1982-86, pres. Stellar Computer, Inc., Newton, Mass., 1986—; dir. Prime Computer Inc., 1972-82, Zymark Corp., 1984-87, StorageTech., 1984, Wellfleet Communications, 1987—. Mem. Recreation Com., Ashland, Mass., 1969, Federated Ch. (dir. 1964-69, 74-77), Dover Ch., 1984—; bd. dirs. Mass. Tech. Council, 1974—. Served with USN, 1951-55. Mem. Ind. Data Communications Mfrs. Assn. (v.p., dir. 1971-82). Home: 44 Donnelly Dr Dover MA 02030 Office: 100 Wells Ave Newton MA 02159

CARR, BESSIE, retired educator; b. Nathalie, Va., Oct. 10, 1920; d. Henry C. and Sirlena (Ewell) C. BS, Elizabeth City Coll., N.C., 1942; MA, Columbia U. Tchrs. Coll., 1948, PhD, 1950, EdD, 1952. Cert. adminstr., supr., tchr. Prin. pub. sch., Halifax, Va., 1942-47, Nathalie-Halifax County, Va., 1947-51; prof. edn. So. U., Baton Rouge, 1952-53; supr. schs. Lackland Schs., Cin., 1953-54; prof. edn. Wilberforce U., Ohio, 1954-55; tchr. Leland Sch., Pittsfield, Mass., 1956-60; chair math. dept., tchr. Lakeland Mid. Sch., N.Y., 1961-83. Founder, organizer, sponsor 1st Math Bowl and Math Forum in area, 1970-76; founder Dr. Bessie Carr award Halifax County Sr. High Sch., 1962. Mem. AAUW (auditor 1970-85), Delta Kappa Gamma (auditor internat. 1970-76), Assn. Suprs. of Math. (chair coordinating council 1976-80), Ret. Tchrs. Assn., Black Women Bus. and Profl. Assn. (charter mem. Senegal, Africa chpt.). Democrat. Avocations: travel, photography, souvenirs.

CARR, CAROLYN KEHLOR, educational administrator; b. St. Louis, July 23, 1948; d. James Kehlor Jr. and Jean Wheatly (Costen) C. BA in Art History, U. Mo., 1970, MEd in Learning Disabilities, 1971; Cert. in Spl. Edn. Adminstrn. and Supervision, U. Toledo, 1978—; postgrad., Cen. Mo. State U., 1986—. Learning lab. tchr. Jefferson County Pub. Schs., Lakewood, Colo., 1971-72; resource tchr. Littleton (Colo.) Pub. Schs., 1972-75; learning disabilities/behavior disorder spur. Lucas County Sch. Bd., Toledo, 1975-78; spl. edn. cons. Mo. Dept. Elem. and Secondary Edn., Jefferson City, 1978-80, interagy. supr., 1980—; mem. steering com. Mo. Gov's. Conf. on Health Edn. for Children, 1986; also presider working session for decision making profls. Bd. dirs. Jefferson City Community Concert Assn., Very Spl. Arts, Mo. Recipient Profl. Contbn. award Div. Youth Services, St. Louis region, 1988. Mem. Nat. Assn. State Dirs. Spl. Edn. (life), Council Adminstrs. Spl. Edn., Capital Kappans (steering com. chmn. 1980-81), Phi Delta Kappa Club (pres. 1981-82). Episcopalian. Office: Mo Dept Elem and Secondary Edn PO Box 480 Jefferson City MO 65102

CARR, DANIEL BARRY, anesthesiologist, endocrinologist, medical researcher; b. N.Y.C., Apr. 6, 1948; s. Andrew Joseph and Florence (Glassman) C.; m. Justine M. Meehan, Nov. 11, 1978; children—Nora, Rebecca, Andrew. B.A., Columbia U., 1968, M.A., 1970, M.D., 1976. Diplomate Am. Bd. Internal Medicine (subsplty. bd. Endocrinology and Metabolism). Intern Columbia-Presbyn. Med. Ctr., N.Y.C., 1976-78; resident med. service Mass. Gen. Hosp., Boston, 1978-79, endocrine fellow, 1979-82, staff physician endocrine unit, 1982—, clin. assoc. physician, clin. research ctr., 1982-84, fellow in anesthesiology, 1984-86; dir. analgesic peptide research unit, 1986—, staff physician anesthesia service and assoc. dir. anesthesia pain unit, 1986—; clin. asst. in medicine, 1983—; cons. internal medicine Mass. Eye and Ear Infirmary, 1980-82; instr. medicine Harvard U. Med. Sch., 1982-84, asst. prof., 1984-88; assoc. prof., 1988—; research staff Shriners Burns Inst., Boston, 1986—. Contbr. articles, research reports, essays, revs. to profl. lit. Daland fellow Am. Philos. Soc., 1980-83. Mem. AAAS, Am. Pain Soc., Am. Soc. Anesthesiologists, Am. Burn Assn., Am. Fedn. for Clin. Research, Endocrine Soc., Soc. for Neurosci., Internat. Anesthesia Research Soc., Alpha Omega Alpha. Clubs: Columbia (Boston); Corinthians. Research on neuroendocrinology of opioid peptides. Office: Mass Gen Hosp Dept Anesthesia Fruit St Boston MA 02114

CARR, DAVIC J., sales executive; b. Gillingham, Kent, Eng., June 16, 1938; s. Leonard Charles and Iris May (Grover) C.; m. Kirstine Janet Gerguson; children: Helen Elizabeth, Ashley David. Certificate, Kent Coll. Tech., 1972. Technician cryptographic MOD (N), Chatham, Eng., 1959-61; field mgr. MOD (N), Singapore, 1961-64; field mgr. MOD (N), Chatham, 1964-74, mgr. quality assurance, 1974-76, mgr. project, 1976-79, dir. refuelling, 1979-80; mgr. project Procurement Exec. MOD, London, 1980-81; mgr. project Babcock Power, London, 1981-86, mgr. export sales, 1986—. Mem. Inst. Nuclear Engrs. Conservative. Anglican. Office: Babcock Power, 165 Great Dover St, London England SE1 4YA

CARR, HUBERT FRANKLIN, lawyer; b. Pitts., Nov. 20, 1920; s. Peter John and Grace Marie (Franklin) C.; m. Barbara Patricia Madory, Aug. 23, 1980; children: John Peter, Peter John. BS, NYU, 1946; LLB, Bklyn. Law Sch., 1952. Bar: N.Y. 1953, U.S. Dist. Ct. (ea. and so. dists.) N.Y. 1956. Clk. L.C. Smith Typewriter Co., Newark, 1939-40, Mason-Dixon Lines, Newark, 1940-41; v.p., sec., gen. counsel Moore McCormack Lines Inc., N.Y.C., 1941-83; counsel U.S. Lines Inc., Cranford, N.J., 1983—; mem. U.S. del. to UN Conf. of Carriage of Goods by Sea UN Council Internat. Trade Law, Hamburg, Fed. Republic Germany, 1978; mem. adv. com. law of sea U.S. Dept. State, 1979-82; bd. dirs. Marine Index Bur., N.Y.C. Pres. Pearl River (N.Y.) Civic Assn., 1952. Mem. N.Y. County Lawyers Assn., Maritime Law Assn. (bill of lading com.). Republican. Roman Catholic. Club: Propellor N.Y. (bd. dirs. 1968—). Home: 116 Matthews Rd Colts Neck NJ 07722 Office: US Lines Inc 660 Madison Ave New York NY 10021

CARR, OSCAR CLARK, III, lawyer; b. Memphis, Apr. 9, 1951; s. Oscar Clark Carr Jr. and Billie (Fisher) Carr Houghton; m. Mary Leatherman, Aug. 4, 1973; children—Camilla Fisher, Oscar Clark V. B.A. in English with distinction, U. Va., 1973; J.D. with distinction, Emory U., 1976. Bar: Tenn. 1976, U.S. Dist. Ct. (we. dist.) Tenn. 1977, U.S. Dist. Ct. (no. dist.) Miss. 1977, U.S. Ct. Appeals (6th cir.) 1985. Assoc. firm Glankler, Brown, Gilliland, Chase, Robinson & Raines, Memphis, 1976-82, ptnr., 1982—. Bd. dirs. Memphis Ballet Soc., 1980, Memphis-Shelby County Unit Am. Cancer Soc., 1985—, Memphis Oral Sch. for the Deaf, 1988. Mem. ABA, Tenn. Bar Assn., Memphis and Shelby County Bar Assn. (bd. dirs. 1985-87), U. Va. Alumni Assn. Episcopalian. Clubs: Memphis Country, Memphis Hunt and Polo. Office: Glankler Brown et al 1700 One Commerce Sq Memphis TN 38103

CARR, ROBERT ALLEN, finance educator; b. Los Angeles, Sept. 28, 1917; s. Harry Newton and Elvaretta (Wilson) C.; m. Ruth Eleanor Holland, Dec. 7, 1946; children: Nancy Ellen, David Allen. A.B., San Francisco State Coll., 1951, M.A., 1953; Ph.D., U. So. Calif., 1959. Orgn. and methods examiner VA, San Francisco, 1946-48; instr. Golden Gate Coll., 1952; lectr. U. So. Calif., 1956-57; coordinator econ. edn. project Calif. State U., Fresno, 1952-56, asst. prof., 1957-61; asso. prof. Calif. State U., 1961-66, prof., 1966-83, asst. head div. bus., 1964-65, chmn. dept. fin. and industry, 1965-76, prof. emeritus, 1983—, coordinator Somali project, 1983—; cons. economist Fresno Planning Dept., 1962-63; cons. Somali Inst. Devel. Adminstrn. and Mgmt., 1982-83; trustee Fresno Meml. Gardens, 1977-86, chmn., 1978-80. Contbr. articles to profl. jours. Mem. Fresno County Econ. Devel. Adv. Council, 1977 80, vice chmn., 1978, chmn., 1979-80. Served to staff sgt. USAAF, 1941-45. Ford Faculty fellow, 1962; E.L. Phillips intern, 1963-64. Mem. Am. Western econ. assns., Am. Fin. Assn., Western Fin. Assn. (exec. com., v.p. 1966-67, pres. 1967-68), Fin. Mgmt. Assn. (dir. 1970-72, v.p. 1973-74), Soc. Internat. Devel., Am. Statis. Assn. (pres. San Joaquin Valley chpt. 1975-77), Regional Sci. Assn., AAUP. Home: 5734 N Bond St Fresno CA 93710

CARRE, ANDRE DANIEL, airport administrator; b. Paris, Feb. 3, 1941; s. Raymond Paul and Simone Marie (Broc) C.; m. Christian Moelle, July 20, 1963; children: Martine, Jean-Francois. Degree in acctg., HEC, 1964, degree in psychology, 1966. Asst. ops. mgr. Nice (France) Airport, 1967-73, ops. mgr., 1973-75, gen. mgr., 1975-82; gen. mgr. Cannes (France) Airport, 1975-82; gen. mgr. transports field Nice C. of C., 1982—; prof. Air Transport Inst., Aix en Provence, 1979—. Chevalier, Order Merit, 1987. Mem. Internat. Civil Airports Assn. (pres. French speaking region 1982—). Lodge: Rotary. Home: 104 bd Edouard Herriot, 06200 Nice France Office: Chambre de Commerce, Aeroport de Nice, 06056 Nice France

CARRÉ, PHILIPPE GUY, diplomat; b. Dakar, Senegal, Nov. 2, 1954; s. Guy Jean and Jacqueline Filippi (Philippine) C.; m. Marie-Valentine Rudiger, June 25, 1984; 1 child, Ariane. Diplome, Institut d'Etudes Politiques, Paris, 1976; Licence en Droit, U. Paris, 1977; Ancien Eleve, Ecole Nat. d'Adminstrn., Paris, 1980. 1st sec. French Embassy, Moscow, 1980-84; officer at planning staff Ministry of Foreign Affairs, Paris, 1984-85; officer French Sec.'s Office, Paris, 1985-86; consellor French Embassy, Bonn, Fed. Republic Germany, 1986—. Roman Catholic. Home: AM Buechel 43, 5300 Bonn Federal Republic of Germany

CARRELL, TERRY EUGENE, heat exchanger co. exec.; b. Monmouth, Ill., July 1, 1938; s. Roy Edwin and Caroline Hilma (Fillman) C.; AB, Monmouth Coll., 1961; MBA, Calif. State U., Los Angeles, 1967; D of Bus. Adminstrn., U. So. Calif., 1970; m. Bonnie Lee Clements, July 11, 1964; children—Philip Edwin, Andrew David. Prin. engr. reconnaissance and communications N.Am. Aviation, 1963-67; mgr. avionics analysis and techs. B-1 div. Rockwell Internat., 1967-73, dir. engring. Morse Controls div., 1973-74; gen. mgr. Morse Controls div. Incom Internat. Inc., 1974-78, pres. indsl. div. Morse Controls, 1978-80, pres. Morse Controls, 1980-82; pres. Heim Bearings, 1982-85;gen. mgr. Stewart-Warner Corp., 1985-88; pres. Stewart-Warner South Wind Corp., 1988—; cons.; lectr. U. So. Calif., 1967-70. Mem. Hudson (Ohio) Econ. Devel. Com., 1979-82; bd. dirs., council commr. Boy Scouts Am., 1980-85, mem. nat. council, 1980-85; mem. service rev. panel United Way of Summit County, 1980. NDEA fellow, 1961-63. Mem. Hudson C. of C. (trustee 1976-78), Boating Industry Assn. (chmn. steering task force 1974-85), Am. Boat and Yacht Council (dir. 1980-88). Contbr. articles to profl. jours. Patentee in field. Club: Columbia. Lodge: Kiwanis.

CARRERAS, JOSE, tenor; b. Barcelona, Spain, Dec. 5, 1947; s. Jose and Antonio C.; (married); children—Alberto, Julia. Profl. opera debut as Gennaro in Lucrezia Borgia, Liceo Opera House, Barcelona, 1970-71 season; appeared in La Bohème, Un Ballo In Maschera and I Lombardi alla Prima Crociata in Teatro Regio, Parma, Italy, 1972 season; Am. debut as Pinkerton in Madame Butterfly with N.Y.C. Opera, 1972; Met. Opera debut as Cavaradossi, 1974, La Scala debut as Riccardo in Un Ballo In Maschera, 1975; appeared in film Don Carlos, 1980, TV Great Performances: West Side Story, 1985; other appearances throughout the world include Teatro Colón, Buenos Aires, Argentina, Covent Garden, London, Vienna Staatsoper, Easter Festival, Summer Festival, Salzburg, Austria, Lyric Opera of Chgo.; recs. include Otello (Rossini), Un Ballo in Maschera, La Battaglia di Legnano, Il Corsaro, Un Giorno, I Due Fuscari, Simone Boccanegra, Macbeth, Don Carlo, Tosca, Thais, Aida, Cavalleria, Turandot, Pagliacci, Lucia di Lammermoor, Elisabetta d'Inghilterra. Office: care Columbia Artists Mgmt 165 W 57th St New York NY 10019 *

CARRERE, CHARLES SCOTT, judge; b. Dublin, Ga., Sept. 26, 1937; 1 son, Daniel Austin. B.A., U. Ga., 1959; LL.B., Stetson U., 1961. Bar: Fla. 1961, Ga. 1960. Law clk. U.S. Dist. Judge, Orlando, Fla., 1962-63; asst. U.S. atty. Middle Dist. Fla., 1963-66, 68-69, chief trial atty., 1965-66, 68-69; ptnr. Harrison, Greene, Mann, Rowe & Stanton, 1970-80; judge Pinellas County, Fla., 1980—. Mem. State Bar Ga., Fla. Bar, Phi Beta Kappa. Presbyterian. Address: PO Box 22034 Gateway Mall Station Saint Petersburg FL 33742 Office: 150 Fifth St N 305 County Bldg Saint Petersburg FL 33701

CARREY, NEIL, lawyer, educator; b. Bronx, N.Y., Nov. 19, 1942; s. David L. and Betty (Kurtzburg) C.; m. Karen Krysher, Apr. 9, 1980; children—Jana, Christopher; children by previous marriage—Scott, Douglas, Dana. B.S. in Econs., U. Pa., 1964; J.D., Stanford U., 1967. Bar: Calif. 1968. Mem. firm, v.p. corp. DeCastro, West, Chodorow & Burns, Inc., Los Angeles, 1967—; instr. program for legal paraprofls. U. So. Calif., 1977—. Author: Nonqualified Deffered Compensation Plans-The Wave of the Future, 1985. Officer, Vista Del Mar Child Care Center, Los Angeles, 1968-84; treas. Nat. Little League of Santa Monica, 1984-85, pres., 1985-86, coach Bobby Sox Team, Santa Monica, 1987—, bd. dirs. 1988; curriculum com. Santa Monica Sch. Dist., 1983-84, community health adv. com. Mem. U. Pa. Alumni Soc. So. Calif. (pres. 1971-79, dir. 1979-87), The Group, Alpha Kappa Psi (disting. life). Republican. Jewish. Club: Mountaingate Tennis Los Angeles). Home: 616 23d St Santa Monica CA 90402 Office: 10960 Wilshire Blvd Suite 1800 Los Angeles CA 90024

CARRIERE, JEAN PROSPER, banker; b. Chalon, France, Nov. 7, 1925; s. Julien Eugene and Anne Louise (Daubard) C.; m. Francoise Emery, Aug. 1, 1953; children: Anne-Sophie, Jean Philippe. D in Law, U. Dijon, France, 1949; Degree, Ecole Nat. d'Administration, Paris, 1957. Civil servant French Treasury, France, 1957-68; exec. dir. World Bank, Washington, 1968-72, dir. European office, Paris, 1972-78; pres. SEITA, Paris, 1978-81; pres. Soc. Lyonnaise de Banque, Lyon, France, 1982-87; gen. mgr. Banque Eurofin, Paris, 1987—; bd. dirs. Banque Pasche, Switzerland, Banque de L'Union Europeenne, France. Contbr. articles to profl. jours. Decorated Legion d'Honneur, Ordre du Merite France, Ordre du Cedre Lebanon. Mem. Assn. Francaise des Banques (treas. 1982). Home: 15 Quai General Sarrail, 69006 Lyon France Office: Banque Eurofin, 41 rue de la Bienfaisance, 75008 Paris France

CARRINGTON, LORD PETER ALEXANDER RUPERT, former secretary-general of NATO; b. London, June 6, 1919; s. 5th Baron Carrington and Sybil Marion Colville; ed. Eton Coll., Royal Mil. Coll., Sandhurst; LL.D., Cambridge U., 1981, Leeds U., 1981, U. Philippines, 1982; D., U. Essex, 1983; m. Iona McClean; 3 children. Joined Grenadier Guards, 1939, served in N.W. Europe; parliamentary sec. to Minister of Agr., 1951-54, Ministry of Def., 1954-56; high commr. in Australia, 1956-59; First Lord of the Admiralty, 1959-63; minister without portfolio, leader House of Lords, 1963-64, leader opposition, 1964-70; sec. of state for def., 1970-74, also minister aviation supply, 1971-74; sec. of state for energy, 1974, for fgn. and commonwealth affairs, 1979-82, minister overseas devel., 1979-82; leader opposition House of Lords, 1974-79; chmn. Gen. Electric Co., London, 1983-84; sec.-gen. NATO, Brussels, 1984-88; chmn. Conservative Party, 1972-74; chmn. Australia and N.Z. Bank Ltd., 1969-70. Sec. for fgn. corr., hon. mem. Royal Acad. Arts, 1982—; chmn. bd. trustees Victoria and Albert Mus., London, 1983—; chmn. Christie's Internat., 1988—. Decorated Knight Grand Cross of the Order of St. Michael and Saint George. Clubs: Pratt's, White's. *

CARRIOL, MICHEL-HENRI, import company executive; b. Paris, Apr. 11, 1940; s. Rene Carriol and Lucette Marot; m. Julie-Ann Zerky, Dec. 16, 1967; children—Jean-Marc, Jean-Philippe. Degree in Polit. Sci., Inst. Polit. Sci., France; degree in econs. U. Brussels. Diplomat, comml. attaché French Embassy, Australia, 1966-72; mng. dir. Trimex Pty., Ltd., Waterloo, New South Wales, Sydney, Australia, 1973—. Adviser to French govt. on fgn. trade. Mem. French C. of C. (pres. 1981—). Clubs: Maxims Bus. Cercle Interalliee (Paris); Nat. Am., Royal Sydney (Sydney). Avocations: skiing; stamp collecting; tennis. Office: Trimex Pty Ltd, 213 Botany Rd, Waterloo, Sydney 2017, Australia

CARRO, JORGE LUIS, law educator, consultant; b. Havana, Cuba, Nov. 27, 1924; came to U.S., 1967, naturalized, 1973; s. Luis and Maria G. (Gonzalez) C.; m. Edy Jimenez; 1 dau., Edy C. B.A., Havana Inst., 1945; J.D., U. Havana, 1950; M.L.S., Kans. State Tchrs. Coll., 1969. Bar: Havana, Cuba 1950. Practice, Havana, 1950-67; legal cons. Swiss embassy, Havana and legal adv. Apostolic Nuncio, Havana, 1963-67; asst. librarian U. Wis.-Milw., 1969; asst. librarian, instr. U. Wis.-Whitewater, 1969-72; librarian, asst. prof. Ohio No. U., 1972-75, assoc. prof., 1975-76; assoc. prof. law, librarian U. Cin., 1976-78, acting dean, 1978-79, prof., librarian 1979-86, prof., 1986—; Mem. ABA, Cin. Bar Assn. Republican. Roman Catholic. Author: Government Regulation of Business Ethics, 3 vols., 1981-82; contbr. articles, books revs. to profl. jours.; reviewer Law Books in Rev. Office: U Cin College of Law Cincinnati OH 45221

CARROL, WILFRED, internist; b. Russia, Mar. 18, 1909; s. Israel and Jennie C.; came to U.S., 1910, naturalized, 1932; A.B., Columbia U., 1929, M.D., 1933; postgrad. Mt. Sinai Med. Sch., 1944, NYU, 1948, Seton Hall Med. Coll. (now N.J. Coll. Medicine), 1947-49; m. Ruth Gluck, Feb. 11, 1938; children—Laura Carrol Guthart, Edward N. Intern, Clara Maass Meml. Hosp., Newark, 1933-34; practice internal medicine, Newark and Maplewood, N.J., 1935—; asso. attending physician Newark-Beth Israel Med. Center, 1954-75, emeritus, 1975—; clin. asso. prof. medicine Coll. Medicine and Dentistry N.J., 1969—; draft bd. physician, Newark, 1941-45. Recipient cert. of appreciation Pres. F.D. Roosevelt, 1944; Golden Merit award Med. Soc. N.J., 1983. Diplomate Am. Bd. Internal Medicine. Fellow ACP; mem. AMA. Home: 74 Parker Ave Maplewood NJ 07040

CARROLL, CHARLES LEMUEL, JR., mathematician; b. Whitsett, N.C., Sept. 16, 1916; s. Charles Lemuel and Erma Ruth (Greeson) C.; m. Geraldine Budd, June 8, 1938; children: Geraldine Wright, Charlda Sizemore, Charles Lemuel III. B.S., Guilford Coll., 1936; A.M., U. N.C., 1937, Ph.D., 1945. Instr. math. Ga. Inst. Tech., Atlanta, 1939-42; assoc. prof. math. N.C. State U., Raleigh, 1946-55; research adminstr. Air Force Office Sci. Research, Balt., 1955-56; mgr. systems analysis RCA Service Co., Patrick AFB, Fla., 1956-61; asst. dir. Aerospace Corp., Atlantic Missile Range, Fla., 1961-62; mgr. tech. staff Pan Am World Airways, Patrick AFB, 1962-72; mgr. Japanese Tech. Assistance project Pan Am, 1972-82; mgr. info. systems Pan Am World Services, Cocoa Beach, Fla., 1972-86; cins. 1986—. Elder, Eastminster Presbyn. Ch., Indialantic, Fla., 1962—; bd. dirs. South Brevard YMCA, Melbourne, Fla., 1959-65, v.p., 1962-63. Served to lt. comdr. USNR, 1943-57. Assoc. fellow AIAA; mem. Am. Math. Soc., Inst. Math. Stats. Sigma Xi. Democrat. Home: PO Box 3343 109 Michigan Ave Indialantic FL 32903

CARROLL, CHARLES MICHAEL, educator; b. Otterbein, Ind., Mar. 5, 1921; s. James William and Catherine Doretta (Bohan) C.; B.M., Ind. U. at Bloomington, 1949; M.M., Fla. State U., Tallahassee, 1951, Ph.D., 1960; m. Mary Lipford Rosenbush, Sept. 4, 1951; children—Charles Michael, Mary Catherine, Theresa Jane, William Rosenbush. Asst. coordinator music services Ind. U., 1949-50; instr. music Fla. State U., 1950-53; concert mgr. symphony orchs. Toledo, Washington, Savannah, Ga., 1953-58; prof. music Pensacola (Fla.) Jr. Coll., 1960-64; prof. St. Petersburg (Fla.) Jr. Coll., 1964—, chmn. communications dept., music critic Tallahassee Democrat, 1950-53, St. Petersburg Evening Independent, 1976-86. Served to capt., AUS, 1942-46, ETO. Mem. Am. Symphony Orch. League (v.p. 1955-56), Am. Musicol. Soc. (nat. council 1974-77, chmn. chpt. 1974-76), Am. Soc. Eighteenth-Century Studies (exec. bd. region 1974-82, regional pres. 1979-80), Coll. Music Soc. (editor 1979-83, nat. council 1978-81, chmn. chpt. 1979-80), Société d'Etudes Philidoriennes (conseiller bibliographique 1988—). Author: The Great Chess Automaton, 1975; contbr. articles to profl. jours. Home: 1701 80th St N Saint Petersburg FL 33710

CARROLL, GEORGE JOSEPH, pathologist, educator; b. Gardner, Mass., Oct. 14, 1917; s. George Joseph and Kathryn (O'Hearn) C. B.A., Clark U., Worcester, Mass., 1939; M.D., George Washington U., 1944. Diplomate: Am. Bd. Pathology. Intern Worchester City Hosp., 1944-45; resident in medicine Doctors Hosp., Washington, 1945-46; resident in pathology Sibley Hosp., Washington, 1948-49, VA Hosp., Washington, 1949-50; asst. pathologist D.C. Gen. Hosp., 1950-51, assoc. pathologist, 1951-52; pathologist Louise Obici Meml. Hosp., Suffolk, Va., 1952—; sec. med. staff Louise Obici Meml. Hosp., 1956-59, chief of staff, 1959-60, 67-69; pathologist Chowan Hosp., Edenton, N.C., 1952-71, Southampton Meml. Hosp., Franklin, Va., 1952—, Greensville Meml. Hosp., Emporia, Va., 1961—; instr. pathology Georgetown U. Sch. Medicine, 1950-52; instr. bacteriology Am. U., Washington, 1950-51; assoc. clin. prof. pathology Med. Coll. Va., Richmond, 1968-70; clin. prof. pathology Va. Commonwealth U., 1970—; prof. dept. pathology Eastern Va. Med. Sch., Norfolk, 1974—; sec.-treas. Va. Bd. Medicine, 1970-86. Contbr. articles to med. jours. Served with U.S. Army, 1946-48. Fellow Am. Soc. Clin. Pathologists (dir. 1969—, pres. 1977—), Coll. Am. Pathologists, Am. Coll. Physicians, Am. Soc. Clin. Pathologists (dir. 1969—, pres. 1977—), Internat. Acad. Pathology; mem. AMA, So. Med. Assn. (councilor from Va. 1965-70, pres. 1973-74), Med. Soc. Va. (pres. 4th Dist. 1968-70, del. 1960—), Med. Soc. D.C. (asso.), Seaboard (pres. 1957), George Washington, Tri-County (pres. 1971-73), med. socs), Am. Soc. Clin. Pharmacy Therapeutics, Va. Soc. Pathology (pres. 1973-74), Soc. Nuclear Medicine, Am. Assn. Blood Banks, Am. Cancer Soc. (dir. Va. div. 1955-62), Va. Med. Service Assn. (dir. 1960-71). Club: Rotary (Suffolk). Home: 219 Northbrooke Ave Suffolk VA 23434 Office: Louise Obici Meml Hosp 1900 N Main St PO Box 1100 Suffolk VA 23434

CARROLL, NORMAN EDWARD, college dean, educator; b. Chgo., Oct. 17, 1929; s. Ralph Thomas and Edith (Fay) C.; m. Ruth Carlton, July 26, 1960; children—Rebecca, Mark, John. B.S., Loyola U.-Chgo., 1956; M.S.A., Rosary Coll., 1983; M.A., DePaul U., 1965; Ph.D., Ill. Inst. Tech., 1971. Prin. Carroll Assocs., River Forest, Ill., 1956-65; prof. bus. and econs. Rosary Coll., River Forest, 1968-70, dean Grad. Sch. Bus., 1977—, v.p., dean faculty, 1970—. Contbr. articles to profl. publs. Bd. dirs. Oak Park Human Relations Com., Ill., 1965; mem. selection com. Chgo. Archdiocesan Sch. Bd., 1970; mem. adv. com. River Forest Sch. Bd., 1975. Served to cpl. U.S. Army, 1951-53. Mem. Acad. Mgmt., Am. Econ. Assn., Associated Colls. Chgo. Area (pres. 1973-75, treas. 1982—), Indsl. Relations Research Assn., Ill. Tng. and Devel. Assn. (chmn. membership 1983-84). Lodge: Rotary. Office: Rosary Coll 7900 Division River Forest IL 60305

CARROLL, PATRICIA WHITEHEAD, computer company executive; b. Tallahassee, Fla., Oct. 20, 1954; d. Albert and Lucinda (Brown) Whitehead; m. Napoleon A. Carroll, May 28, 1979 (div. 1985). BS cum laude in Psychology, Bethune-Cookman Coll., 1977. Records supr. State Farm Ins. Co., Winter Haven, Fla., 1977-79; ins. agt. Pat Carroll Ins. Agy., Orlando, Fla., 1979-82; dir. mktg. Systems Support Corp., Washington, 1982-85, v.p., 1985—. Recipient Youth Day Appreciation award City of Titusville, 1976, Millionaire Club award State Farm Ins. Co., 1981, Million Dollar Round Table award State Farm Ins. Co., 1979, others. Mem. Nat. Assn. Female Execs., Am. Mgmt. Assn., Delta Sigma Theta. Democrat. Avocations: reading, coin and stamp collecting, outdoor sports. Office: Systems Support Corp 1140 Connecticut Ave NW Suite 120 Washington DC 20036

CARROLL, RAOUL LORD, lawyer; b. Washington, Mar. 16, 1950; s. John Thomas and Gertrude Barbara (Jenkins) C.; m. Elizabeth Jane Coleman, Mar. 22, 1980; children: Alexandria Nicole, Christina Elizabeth. B.S., Morgan State U., 1972; J.D., St. Johns U., Jamaica, N.Y., 1975; postgrad. Georgetown U., 1980-81. Bar: N.Y. 1976, D.C. 1979, U.S. Dist. Ct. D.C. 1979, U.S. Supreme Ct. 1979, U.S. Dist. Ct. (so. and ea. dist.) N.Y. 1982. Asst. U.S. atty. Office U.S. Atty., Dept. Justice, Washington, 1979-80; assoc. mem. U.S. Bd. Vets. Appeals, Washington, 1980-81; ptnr. Hart, Carroll & Chavers, Washington, 1981-85, Bishop, Cook, Purcell & Reynolds, Washington, 1986—; dir., treas. Conwest-USA, Washington; chmn. Am. Ctr. for Internat. Leadership, Columbus, Ind. Pres. Black Asst. U.S. Attys. Assn., Washington, 1980-83; gen. counsel Md./D.C. Minority Supplier Devel. Council, Columbia, Md., 1984-86. Served to capt. U.S. Army, 1975-79. Decorated Joint Service Commendation medal, Army Commendation medal; named Outstanding Young Man Am., U.S. Jaycees, 1979. Mem. D.C. Bar Assn., Washington Bar Assn., Nat. Assn. Bond Lawyers, Omega Psi Phi. Baptist. Home: 7821 Morningside Dr NW Washington DC 20012 Office: Cook Purcell & Reynolds 1400 L St NW Washington DC 20005

CARROW, HARVEY HILL, JR., lawyer; b. Washington, Jan. 3, 1955; s. Harvey Hill Sr. and Senora Wilson (Lindsey) C.; m. Susan Champion Swindell, Aug. 8, 1981. AB, U. N.C., 1977; JD, Columbia U., 1980. Bar: N.C. 1980, U.S. Dist. Ct. (ea. dist.) N.C. 1980. Assoc. Manning, Fulton & Skinner, Raleigh, N.C., 1980-82; atty. Carolina Power and Light Co., Raleigh, 1982-85; exec. dir., pres. N.C. Amateur Sports/U.S. Olympic Festival, Research Triangle Park, 1985-88; also bd. dirs., pres. N.C. Amateur Sports/U.S. Olympic Festival, 1985—; pres., chief exec. officer Trace Corp., Raleigh, 1988—; bd. dirs. Buildecon Assocs., Inc., Raleigh. Mem. exec. com. Coliseum com. City of Raleigh, 1984—; vice chmn. Raleigh Transit Authority, 1984-86; bd. advisors McCallie Sch., Chattanooga, 1987—, Olympic Festival Com. of U.S. Olympic Com. , Colorado Springs, 1988—; founder, bd. dirs. N.C. Swimming Hall of Fame, 1985—; founder State Games of N.C.; bd. dirs. Boys and Girls Clubs of Wake County, Raleigh, 1985—, Greater Triangle Community Found., Durham, 1988—; chmn. Gov.'s Adv. Bd. on Athletes Against Crime, Raleigh, 1988—. Recipient Gov. Hunt's Vol. award State of N.C., 1985, Gov. Martin's Vol. award State of N.C., 1985, Disting. Service award Raleigh Jaycees, 1987, Leadership award Triangle J. Council of Govts., 1987, Spl. Recognition award Wake County 1987, Tribute of Appreciation award Boys and Girls Clubs, 1988, Raleigh Conv. and Visitors Industry award, 1988; named to Order of the Long Leaf Pine State of N.C., 1988; Raleigh Conv. and Visitors Industry award, 1988. Mem. ABA, N.C. Bar Assn., Wake County Bar Assn., Assn. Trial Lawyers Am., N.C. Acad. Trial Lawyers. Club: Raleigh Area Masters (v.p. 1984-85). Home: 1720 Canterbury Rd Raleigh NC 27608 Office: Trace Corp PO Box 19324 Raleigh NC 27619

CARROW, ROBERT DUANE, lawyer, barrister; b. Marshall, Minn., Feb. 5, 1934; s. Meddie Joseph and Estelle Marie (Kough) C.; m. Jacqueline Mary Givens, Sept. 3, 1960; children: Leslie, Tamara, Amelia, Vanessa, Creighton, Jessica, Ramsey. Student, U. Colo., 1952; BA, U. Minn., 1956; JD, Stanford U., 1958. Bar: Calif. 1959, N.Y. 1983; barrister: Eng. 1981. Sole practice Calif., 1959—; barrister London, 1981—; counsel Goldstein & Phillips, San Francisco, 1988—. Mayor City of Novato, Calif., 1962-64. Mem. ABA, Assn. Trial Lawyers Am., Calif. Bar Assn., San Francisco Bar Assns., Internat. Bar Assn., Honourable Soc. Middle Temple, Honourable Soc. Gray's Inn, Nat. Assn. Criminal Def. Lawyers. Office: 495 Miller Ave Mill Valley CA 94941 Chambers: 3 Gray's Inn Sq, London England WC1 also: Goldstein & Phillips 1 Embarcadero Ctr 8th Floor San Francisco CA 94111

CARRUTH, ALLEN HIGGINS, insurance company executive; b. Houston, Sept. 7, 1919; s. B.F. and Frances (Headly) C.; m. Ethel Mae Greasley, Feb. 28, 1943; children—Carolyn Carruth Rizza, J. Allen, Brady F. Student U. Tex., 1937-38; B.S. in Econs., U. Pa., 1942; LL.D. (hon.), Austin Coll. With firm John L. Wortham & Son, Houston, 1946—, ptnr., 1950—, mng. ptnr., 1965-85, chmn. exec. com., 1978—; dir., mem. exec. com., chmn. audit com. Am. Gen. Corp.; Pennzoil Co. (mem. Compensation Com., chmn. Stock Option Com., bd. dirs.) Pres. bd. dirs. Wortham Found.; bd. dirs. Houston Grand Opera; mem. exec. com., bd. dirs. Houston Soc. for Prevention Cruelty to Animals, 1950—; past trustee Austin Presbyn. Theol. sem.; trustee South Tex. Coll. Law; past elder, clk. of session 1st Presbyn. Ch.; chmn. bd., past pres. Houston Livestock Show and Rodeo, 1979-81. Served to maj. USAAF, 1941-46. Named Westerner of Yr., Houston Farm and Ranch Club, 1982; Humanitarian of Yr., Houston Soc. for Prevention Cruelty to Animals, 1980; Breath of Life award Cystic Fibrosis Found., 1983. Mem. Nat. Assn. Casualty and Surety Agts. (dir., past pres., mem. exec. com.), Houston C. of C. (past dir.), Santa Gertrudis Breeders Internat. (past officer and dir.). Presbyterian. Home: 5545 Candlewood Dr Houston TX 77056 Office: PO Box 1388 Houston TX 77251

CARRUTH, DAVID BARROW, landscape architect; b. Woodbury, Conn., June 28, 1926; s. Gorton Veeder and Margery Barrow (Dibb) C.; m. Enid Fran Levin, Aug. 11, 1979; children by previous marriage—Kathryn Paige, Todd David, Peter Richmond. Grad., U.S. Mcht. Marine Acad., 1946; B.S. in Land Planning, Cornell U., 1951; M. in Landscape Architecture, 1952. Lic. landscape architect, N.Y., Conn., Pa., Fla., Mass. nat. cert. as landscape architect. Landscape architect, assoc. Clarke & Rapuano, Inc. (cons. engrs., landscape architects), N.Y.C., 1952-70; pres. Kane and Carruth, landscape architects, Pleasantville, N.Y., 1970-83; founder DE Assocs., site design, environ. planning, 1983—; mem. N.Y. State Bd. Landscape Architecture, 1970-80; pres. Council Landscape Archtl. Registration Bds., 1975, Interprofl. Council on Registration, 1975, Landscape Archtl. Registration Bds. Found., 1976; Trustee Bayard Cutting Arboretum. Mem. Katonah-Lewisboro Sch. Bd., 1963-73; bd. dirs. Clark Garden. Served with USNR, 1944-46. Fellow Am. Soc. Landscape Architects. Office: 7 Seminary Hill Rd Carmel NY 10512

CARRUTHERS, GARREY EDWARD, governor of New Mexico; b. Alamosa, Colo., Aug. 29, 1939; s. William Core and Frankie Jane (Shoults) C.; m. Katherine Thomas, May 13, 1961; children: Deborah Ann Carruthers Joyce, Carol Lynn, Stephen Edward. BS in Agr., N.Mex. State U., 1964, MS in Agrl. Econs., 1965; PhD in Econs., Iowa State U., 1968. From asst. prof. to assoc. prof. dept. agrl. econs. and agrl. bus. N.Mex. State U., Las Cruces, 1968-76, 78-79, prof. agrl. econs. and agrl. bus., 1979-81, 84-87; spl. asst. U.S. Sec. of Agr., Washington, 1974-75; acting dir. N.Mex. Water Resources Research Inst., 1976-78; asst. sec. interior for land and water resources Dept. Interior, Washington, 1981-83, asst. sec. interior for land and minerals mgmt., 1983-84; Gov. State of N.Mex., 1987—; pres. Garrey Carruthers Assocs., Inc., 1979—; while serving on Pres. Ford's campaign com., coordinator N.Mex.'s 2d Congrl. Dist., 1976, co-chmn. Dona Ana County; Dallas panel commn. White House Fellowships, 1976. Contbr. articles to profl. jours. Mem. Am. Agrl. Econs. Assn., Western Agrl. Econs. Assn., Am. Acad. Polit. and Social Services, Univ. Golf Assn. (former v.p., pres.), Sigma Xi, Omicron Delta Kappa. Lodge: Optimist of Las Cruces (former v.p., pres.). Office: State Capitol Office of Gov 4th Floor Santa Fe NM 87503 *

CARRUTHERS, JOHN ALFRED, import company executive; b. London, Ont., Can., July 1, 1934; s. William Norman and Gladys F (Mills) C.; m. Emma Lillian Stacey, June 15, 1957; children: Jeffrey Allen, Susan Marie. Sales mgr. G.L. Griffith & Sons Ltd., Stratford, Ont., 1957-59, Fed. Mogul Bower Can. Ltd., Stratford, 1959-66; sales agt. Stratford, 1966-67; gen. mgr. Griffith Saddlery & Leather Ltd., Stratford, 1967-75; pres. Cavalier Equestrian Supply Ltd., Stratford, 1975—. The Progressive Conservative Party. United. Clubs: Stratford Country (bd. dirs. 1982-83, pres. 1984); Kinsmen (Stratford) (pres. 1966-67, dist. coordinator 1969-70, nat. coordinator 1973-74). Home: 16 Baker St, Stratford, ON Canada N5A 7A3 Office: Cavalier Equestrian Supply Ltd, 649 Ontario St, Stratford, ON Canada N5A 6S8

CARRY, L. RAY, mathematics educator, researcher; b. Ector, Tex., Aug. 27, 1932; s. O.R. and Oleta (Ramey) C.; m. Mary Joyce Cobern, May 6, 1951; children—Rodney Lynn, Lisa Carry Barbour, Susan. B.A., North Tex. State U., 1952, M.S., 1960; M.S., Stanford U., 1964, Ph.D., 1968. Elec. engr. S.W. Bell Telephone Co., Dallas, 1952-58; math. instr. North Tex. State U., Denton, 1958-61; instrumentation engr. Lockheed, Sunnyvale, Calif., 1961-62; math. instr. Foothill Coll., Los Altos Hills, Calif., 1964-65; research assoc. Sch. Math. Study Group, Stanford, Calif., 1965-68, cons., 1968-72; prof. U. Tex., Austin, 1968—; cons. Project Math. Devel. Children, Tallahassee, Fla., 1974-76. Co-author: Field Mathematics Program, 1973; contbr. articles to profl. jours. NSF grantee, 1978-80. Mem. Math. Assn. Am., Nat. Council Tchrs. Math (chmn. research jour., editorial bd. 1976-77), Am. Ednl. Research Assn. (steering com. 1970, 80). Republican. Avocation: house restoration. Office: Dept Math U Tex-Austin Austin TX 78712

CARS, HADAR H., Swedish politician; b. Stockholm, June 14, 1933; m. Jane Casten Carlberg; children: Hadar, Greger, Christine. M. Polit. Sci., U. Stockholm, 1959; postgrad. Columbia U., 1961-62, Geneva, Paris, 1963. Asst. sec. Swedish UNESCO Council, 1958-59, acting sec. gen., 1962; asst. Stockholm U., Inst. Polit. Sci., 1959-61, 62-63, lectr., 1964-67; project adminstr. Polit. Research Inst., 1967-68; dep. sec. gen. Swedish Nat. Com. Internat. C. of C., 1969-70, sec. gen., 1971-76, dir. 1977-78; sec. Stockholm C. of C., 1969-71, dep. mng. dir., head dept. econ. policy and fgn. trade, 1971-78; cabinet minister commerce Swedish Govt., 1978-79; mem. Swedish Parliament, 1980-82, 85—, mem. econ. com., 1980-82, dep. chmn. 1988—; alt. mem. fgn. affairs com., 1985—; chmn. Swedish Fund Substitution of Oil, 1981-83. Co-editor: Svensk statsforvaltning i omdaning, 1965, 68; contbr. to books and profl. jours. Chmn. Swedish Students United Nations Assn., 1957-58, Swedish Liberal Students Assn., 1960-61; dep. chmn. Swedish Liberal Youth, 1963-64; mem. Stockholm City Council and City Bd. Dirs., 1966-76, Bd. Marubeni Scandinavia AB, 1973-78, SGS Ates Scandinavia AB, 1974-78, AB Familjbostader, 1974-78; chmn. Swedish del. UNCTAD V, Manila, 1979, Govt. Com. Info. Promote Trade, 1979-80, Govt. Com. Use Electricity, 1980, Govt. Com. Energy Prices and Tariffs, 1980-81, Govt. Com. Swedish Radio Internat., 1985-86, Conf. W. European Parliamentarians Sanctions against S. Africa, The Hague, 1982. Served to capt. Royal Swedish Life Guards, 1953-74. Home: Odengatan 15, 114 24 Stockholm Sweden Office: Swedish Parliament, 100 12 Stockholm Sweden

CARSANIGA, GIOVANNI, Italian studies educator; b. Milano, Italy, Feb. 5, 1934; Arrived in Australia, 1982; s. Arnaldo Camillo and Annamaria (Visco-Gilardi) C.; m. Anne-Marie Girolami, 1959 (div. 1974); m. Pamela Helen Joyce Risbey, 1975. Laurea in lettere, U. Pisa, Italy, 1956; diploma di licenza, Sch. Normale Superiore, Italy, 1956. Lectr. U. Aberdeen, Scotland, 1957-58, U. Cambridge, Eng., 1958-59; asst. lectr. U. Birmingham, Eng., 1959-61, lectr., 1961-71; lectr. U. Sussex, Eng., 1966-71, reader, 1971-82; prof. U. We. Australia, Perth, 1975-77, La Trobe U., Melbourne, Australia, 1982—. Author: Geschichte der Italienischen Literatur, 1970, Giacomo Leopardi, 1977, Italiano Espresso, 1981. Mem. U. Sussex Assn. U. Tchrs. (pres. 1980-81), Assn. Tchrs. Italian (pres. 1971, hon. pres. 1980-81), Soc. for Italian Studies (mem. com. 1974-75, 79—), Assn. Internat. Studi Lingua e Lettra Italiana, Australian Coll. for Edn., Frederick May Found., Vaccari Hist. Trust (trustee). Office: La Trobe Univ, Bundoora 3083, Australia

CARSON, GORDON BLOOM, research institute executive; b. High Bridge, N.J., Aug. 1, 1911; s. Whitfield R. and Emily (Bloom) C.; m. Beth Lacy, June 19, 1937; children—Richard Whitfield, Emily Elizabeth (Mrs. Lee A. Duffus), Alice Lacy (Mrs. William P. Allman), Jean Helen (Mrs. Michael J. Gable). B.S. in Mech. Engring, Case Inst. Tech., 1931, D.Eng., 1957; M.S., Yale U., 1932, M.E., 1938; LL.D., Rio Grande Coll., 1973. With Western Electric Co., 1930; instr. mech. engring. Case Inst. Tech., 1932-37, asst. prof., 1937-40, asso. prof. indsl. engring. charge indsl. div., 1940-44; with Am. Shipbldg. Co., 1936; patent litigation 1937; research engr., dir. research Cleve. Automatic Machine Co., 1939-44; asst. to gen. mgr. Selby Shoe Co., 1944, mgr. engring., 1945-49, sec. of corp., 1949-53; sec., dir. Pyrrole Products Co., 1948-53; dean engring. Ohio State U., Columbus, 1953-58; v.p. bus. and finance, treas. Ohio State U., 1958-71; dir. Engring. Exptl. Sta., 1953-58; exec. v.p. Albion (Mich.) Coll., 1971-76, exec. cons., 1976-77; asst. to chancellor, dir. fin. Northwood Inst., 1977-82; v.p. Mich. Molecular Inst., 1982-88; prin. Whitfield Robert Assocs., 1988—. Editor: The Production Handbook, 1958; cons. editor, 1972—; Author of tech. papers engring. subjects. Trustee White Cross Hosp. Assn., 1960-71; bd. dirs. Cardinal Funds, 1966—; bd. dirs. Goodwill Industries, 1959-67, 1st v.p., 1963-64; bd. dirs. Orton Found., 1953-58; v.p. Ohio State U. Research Found., 1958-71; v.p., chmn. adv. council Center for Automation and Soc., U. Ga., 1969-71; Chmn. tool and die com. 5th Regional War Labor Bd., 1943-45; chmn. Ohio State adv. com. for sci., tech. and specialized personnel SSS, 1965-70. Fellow ASME, AAAS, Am. Inst. Indsl. Engrs. (pres. 1957-58); mem. Columbus Soc. Fin. Analysts (pres. 1964-65), Fin. Analysts Fedn. (dir. 1964-65), C. of C. (dir., treas. 1952-53), Am. Soc. Engring. Edn., Asso. U. for Research in Astronomy (dir. 1968-71), Midwestern Univs. Research Assn. (dir. 1958-71), U.S. Naval Inst., Nat. Soc. Profl. Engrs., Romophos, Sphinx, Sigma Xi (fin. com. 1975—, nat. treas. 1979—), Tau Beta Pi, Zeta Psi, Phi Eta Sigma, Alpha Pi Mu, Omicron Delta Epsilon. Lodge: Mason (32 deg.). Home: 5413 Gardenbrook Dr Midland MI 48640 Office: Whitfield Robert Assocs 121 Gordon St Midland MI 48640

CARSTEN, HUGO CHRISTIAAN GEORG, diplomat; b. Stockholm, June 2, 1926; s. Lambert and Edith E.M. (Strokirk) C.; m. Brita Magaretha Ekström, Sept. 18, 1927; children: Gabrielle, Lambert, Madeleine. M of Law, Leiden U., The Netherlands, 1954. Polit. attaché Ministry Fgn. Affairs, The Haugue, The Netherlands, 1957-58, Netherlands Embassy, Belgrade, Yugoslavia, 1958-60; 1st sec. Netherlands Embassy, Bonn, Fed. Rep.

Germany, 1964-67; counsellor Netherlands Embassy, Nairobi, Kenya, 1967-71; ambassador Netherlands Embassy, Addis Ababa, Ethiopia, 1976-80, Ankara, Turkey, 1980-84, Pretoria, Rep. South Africa, 1984-88, Helsinki, Finland, 1988—; vice-consul Netherlands Consulate-Gen., Bombay, 1960-63; def. counsellor Netherlands Permanent Del. to NATO, Brussels, 1971-76. Served to 1st lt. cav., Dutch Army, 1954-56. Decorated officer Order Orange-Nassau (Netherlands); Order of Merit (Fed. Republic Germany); recipient Coronation Medal (Netherlands) 1948. Lutheran. Office: Royal Netherlands Embassy, Raatimiehenkatu 2A1, 00140 Helsinki Finland

CARSTENS, HAROLD HENRY, publisher; b. Ft. Lee, N.J., June 20, 1925; s. Henry G. and Johanna L. (Wolf) C.; m. Phyllis M. Merkle, Apr. 25, 1959; children: Rebecca, Heidi, Henry, Harold. Student, Wagner Coll., 1946-48; B.S., Fairleigh Dickinson U., 1951. Asso. editor Model Craftsman Pub. Corps., Penn Publs., Inc. (became Carstens Publs., Inc., 1973), Fredon, N.J., 1951-54; mng. editor Penn Publs., Inc. (became Carstens Publs., Inc., 1973), 1954-57, v.p., 1957-63, pres., pub., 1963—; editor Railroad Model Craftsman mag., Carstens Hobby Books, 1952—; staff photographer N.Y. Lumber Trade Jour., 1954; mng. editor Toy Trains mag., 1954; pub. Flying Models mag., 1969—, Creative Crafts mag., Railfan and R.R. mag., 1974—, The Miniature mag., 1977. Chmn. Fredon Bicentennial Com., 1975-77; mem. Sussex County Overall Econ. Devel. Planning Commn., 1977-79; trustee Wagner Coll., 1977-88; mem. exec. com. Wagner Coll., 1981-88, sec. bd. trustees, 1985-88. Served with AUS, 1943-46. Recipient Alumni Achievement award Wagner Coll., 1976; Paul Harris fellow. Mem. Acad. Model Aeros., Ramsey C. of C. (dir.), Train Collectors Assn., Inc. (pres. 1964-65), Photog. Soc. Am. (asso. editor jour. 1960-62), Hobby Industry Assn. Am. (dir. 1965-68, 70-76, 77-80, pres. 1971-72, chmn. model r.r. div. 1967-70, 78, chmn. planning com. 1976-78, chmn. awards com. 1985-86, Meritorious award of Honor 1979, Big Wheel award 1987), Nat. Model R.R. Assn., Model R.R. Industry Assn. (pres. 1977-79, dir. 1975-83), Mag. Pubs. Assn., Phi Sigma Kappa., Sigma Delta Chi. Lutheran. Club: Rotary. Office: PO Box 700 Newton NJ 07860

CARTER, AARON LOUIS, aerospace company executive; b. Center, Tex., Dec. 6, 1944; s. John Robert and Mary (Dupree) C.; m. Mary Alice Jones, Aug. 20, 1967; children: Carol, Cheryl, Candice. BSME, Calif. State U., Fullerton, 1968, MSME, 1971; EDCE, U. So. Calif., 1978, PhDME, 1981. Mem. tech. staff Rockwell Internat. Inc., Anaheim, Calif., 1968-72; mgr. engring. div. Holmes & Narver Inc., Orange, Calif., 1972-83; lctr. UCLA, 1981-83, Calif. State U., Fullerton, 1982—. Mem. ASME. Office: Hughes Aircraft Co 1610 Forbes Way Long Beach CA 90810

CARTER, ARNOLD NICK, cassette learning systems company executive; b. Phila., Mar. 25, 1929; s. Arnold and Margaret (Richter) C.; A.A., Keystone Jr. Coll., 1949; B.S. in Speech and Dramatic Art, Syracuse U., 1951; postgrad. Syracuse U., 1951-52; M.A. in Communications, Am. Univ., 1959; m. Virginia Lucille Polsgrove, Oct. 14, 1955; children—Victoria Lynne, Andrea Joy. Actor Rome (N.Y.) Little Theater, summers, 1951-52; mgr. customer relations Martin Marietta, Orlando, Fla., 1959-70; v.p. communications research Nightingale-Conant Corp., Chgo., 1970—. Served with USNR, 1953-59; Korea. Recipient Continuare Professus Articulatus Excellare award, Nat. Speakers Assn., 1978. Mem. Sales and Mktg. Execs. Chgo. (v.p. 1979-81), Nat. Speakers Assn., Am. Soc. Tng. and Devel., Internat. Platform Assn. Republican. Presbyn. Author: Communicate Effectively, 1978; The Amazing Results-Full World of Cassette Learning, 1980; Sales Boosters, 1981. Home: 1315 Elmwood Ave Deerfield IL 60015 Office: Nightingale-Conant Corp 7300 N Lehigh Chicago IL 60648

CARTER, BARRY EDWARD, lawyer, educator; b. Los Angeles, Oct. 14, 1942; s. Byron Edward and Ethel Catherine (Turner) C.; m. Kathleen Anne Ambrose, May 17, 1987; 1 child, Gregory Ambrose. A.B. with great distinction, Stanford U., 1964; M.P.A., Princeton U., 1966; J.D., Yale U., 1969. Bar: Calif. 1970, D.C. 1972. Program analyst Office of Sec. Def., Washington, 1969-70; mem. staff NSC, Washington, 1970-72; research fellow Kennedy Sch., Harvard U., Cambridge, Mass., 1972; internat. affairs fellow Council on Fgn. Relations, 1972; pvt. practice law Washington, 1973-75; sr. counsel Select Com. on Intelligence Activities, U.S. Senate, Washington, 1975; assoc. Morrison & Foerster, San Francisco, 1976-79; assoc. prof. law Georgetown U. Law Ctr., Washington, 1979—; bd. dirs. Arms Control Assn., 1973—; mem. UN Assn. Soviet-Am. Parallel Studies Project; trustee No. Calif. World Affairs Council, 1978-80; sr. fgn. policy adviser Mondale-Ferraro presdl. campaign, Washington, 1984. Author: International Economic Sanctions: Improving the Haphazard U.S. Legal Regime, 1988; contbr. articles to profl. jours. Served with AUS, 1969-71. Mem. Council on Fgn. Relations, Am., Calif., D.C. bar assns., Phi Beta Kappa. Democrat. Roman Catholic. Home: 2922 45th St NW Washington DC 20016 Office: Georgetown U Sch Law 600 New Jersey Ave NW Washington DC 20001

CARTER, DONALD CLAYTON, psychiatrist; b. Blair, Nebr., July 30, 1922; s. Earl Dion and Josephine Emma (Romanowski) C.; pre-med. student S.E. Mo. State Tchrs. Coll., Cape Girardeau, 1943-45; M.D., U. Nebr., 1950; m. Selma Louise Smith, July 21, 1946; children—Gregory, Donna, Jeffrey, Theodore. Rotating intern Lincoln (Nebr.) Gen. Hosp., 1953-54; resident in internal medicine Riverside Hosp., Newport News, Va., 1950-51, in psychiatry Duke U. Med. Center, 1957-60; practice medicine specializing in family medicine, Beaver City, Nebr., 1954-57; asst. div. chief psychiatry VA Hosp., Durham, N.C., 1960-62; med. dir. Central Minn. Mental Health Center, St. Cloud, 1962-67; asst. prof. psychiatry U. Mo. Med. Sch., Columbia, 1967-68; practice medicine specializing in psychiatry, Morgantown, W.Va., 1968-87; mem. staff and faculty W.Va. Univ. Hosp. and Med. Sch., 1968-87, chief psychiatry outpatient dept., 1968-73, prof., chief psychosomatic consultative service, 1973-74, prof., dir. undergrad. edn. in psychiatry, 1974-82, chief of residency supervision, 1982-87, med. dir. AMHC, Elkins, W.Va., 1987—. Served to lt. (j.g.), USNR, 1942-46; as capt. M.C., U.S. Army, 1951-53. Decorated Bronze Star; recipient Outstanding Tchr. award W.Va. U., 1973-74, MacLachlin award, 1980, Psychiatry Resident Teaching award, 1986; diplomate Am. Bd. Psychiatry and Neurology. Fellow Am. Psychiat. Assn. (pres. W.Va. dist. br. 1977-78; assembly rep. 1977-87); mem. AMA, Tygert Valley County Med. Soc., W.Va. Med. Assn., Am. Acad. Psychiatry and Law, Am. Soc. Psychoanalytic Physicians. Republican. Presbyterian. Lodge: Masons. Address: Rt 3 Box 600 Elkins WV 26241

CARTER, EDWARD WILLIAM, retail executive. m. Hannah Locke Caldwell, 1963; children: William Dailey, Ann Carter Huneke. AB, UCLA, 1932; MBA cum laude, Harvard, 1937; LLD (hon.), Occidental Coll., 1962. Chmn. emeritus bd. dirs. Carter Hawley Hale Stores, Inc., Los Angeles. Trustee Occidental Coll., Brookings Instn., Los Angeles County Mus. Art, Nat. Humanities Ctr. Com. Econ. Devel.; bd. dirs. Assocs. Harvard Grad. Sch. Bus., Stanford Research Inst., James Irvine Found., Santa Anita Found., Los Angeles Philharm. Assn.; mem. vis. com. UCLA Grad. Sch. Mgmt.; mem. Woodrow Wilson Internat. Center Council, Harvard Bd. Overseers Com. Depts. Econs., Art Mus. and Univ. Resources, Council on Fgn. Relations. Mem. Bus. Council, Conf. Bd., Council on Fgn. Relations. Clubs: Calif. (Los Angeles), Los Angeles Country; Pacific Union, Bohemian, Burlingame Country (San Francisco); Cypress Point (Pebble Beach). Office: Carter Hawley Hale Stores 550 S Flower St Los Angeles CA 90071

CARTER, GERALD EMMETT, archbishop; b. Montreal, Que., Can., Mar. 1, 1912; s. Thomas Joseph and Mary (Kelty) C. B.Th., Grand Sem. Montreal, 1936; B.A., U. Montreal, 1933, M.A., 1940, Ph.D., 1947, L.Th., 1950; D.H.L., Duquesne U., 1963; LL.D. (hon.), U. Western Ont., 1966, Concordia U., 1976, U. Windsor, 1977, McGill U., Montreal, 1980, Notre Dame (Ind.) U., 1981; Litt.D., St. Mary's U., Halifax, 1980. Ordained priest Roman Cath. Ch., 1937; founder, prin., prof. St. Joseph Tchrs. Coll., Montreal, 1939-61; chaplain Newman Club, McGill U., 1941-56; charter mem., 1st pres. Thomas More Inst. Adult Edn., Montreal, 1945-61; mem. Montreal Cath. Sch. Commn., 1948-61; hon. canon Cathedral Basilica Montreal, 1952-61; aux. bishop London and titular bishop Altiburo 1961; bishop of London, Ont., 1964-78; archbishop of Toronto, 1978—; elevated to cardinal 1979; Chmn. Episcopal Commn. Liturgy Can., 1966-73; mem. Consilium of Liturgy, Rome, 1965, Sacred Congregation for Divine Worship, 1970; chmn. Internat. Com. for English in the Liturgy, 1971; appointee Econ. Affairs Council of Holy See, 1981; vice pres. Can. Cath. Conf., 1973, Cath. Conf. of Ont., 1971-73; pres. Canadian Conf. Cath. Bishops, 1975; mem. council Synod of Bishops, 1977. Author: The Catholic Public Schools of Quebec, 1957, Psychology and the Cross, 1959, The Modern Challange to Religious Education, 1961. Decorated companion Order of Can. Office: Chancery Office, 355 Church St, Toronto, ON Canada M5B 1Z8

CARTER, JAINE MARIE, human resources development company executive; b. Chgo., Oct. 29, 1946; d. Bruno and Louise (Cunningham) Kucinski; m. James Dudley Carter, Apr. 8, 1970; children: Paul, Todd. BS, Northwestern U., 1968; PhD, Walden U., 1978. Mgmt. cons. to bus. 1964-69; chmn. bd. Personnel Devel., Inc., Palatine, Ill., 1969—; dir. women's div. Lake Forest (Ill.) Coll. Advanced Mgmt. Inst., 1970—; writer, lectr., tchr., cons. mgmt. devel. programs; faculty AMA, AMR Internat., Penton Learning Systems. Author: How to Train for Supervisors, 1969, Career Planning Workshop for Women, 1975, Training Techniques that Bring About Positive Behavioral Change, 1976, Assertive Management Role Plays, 1976, Understanding the Female Employee, 1976, Rx for Women in Business, 1976, New Directions Needed in Management Training Programs, 1980, The Burnout of Retirement, 1983, Successfully Working with People, 1984, Assertiveness Training for Supervisors, 1985, Successfully Managing People, 1986, The New Success, 1986, Employee Assistance Program Handbook, 1988; author, narrator TV series Seminars by Satellite, 1987-88, Premier Video Conferences, 1988-89. Mem. Internat. Transactional Analysis Assn., Nat. Speakers Assn., Am. Soc. Tng. and Devel., Screen Actors Guild, AFTRA, AGVA, Exec. Club Am., Am. Mgmt. Assn. (pres.'s assn.). Address: 921 Scott Dr Marco Island FL 33937

CARTER, JAMES EARL, JR., former President of U.S.; b. Plains, Ga., Oct. 1, 1924; s. James Earl and Lillian (Gordy) C.; m. Rosalynn Smith, July 7, 1946; children: John William, James Earl III, Donnel Jeffrey, Amy Lynn. Student, Ga. Southwestern Coll., 1941-42, Ga. Inst. Tech., 1942-43; B.S., U.S. Naval Acad., 1946 (class of 1947); postgrad., Union Coll., 1952-53; LL.D. (hon.), Morris Brown Coll., 1972, Morehouse Coll., 1972, U. Notre Dame, 1977, Emory U., 1979, Kwansei Gakuin U., Japan, 1981, Ga. Southwestern Coll., 1981; D.E. (hon.), Ga. Inst. Tech., 1979; Ph.D. (hon.), Weizmann Inst. Sci., 1980, Tel Aviv U., 1983; LLD (hon.), N.Y. Law Sch., 1985, Bates Coll., 1985, Centre Coll., 1987, Creighton U., 1987; PhD (hon.), Haifa U., 1987; DHL (hon.), Cen. Conn. State U., 1985. Farmer, warehouseman Plains, Ga., 1953-77; mem. Ga. Senate, 1963-67; gov. of Ga. Atlanta, 1971-75; Pres. of U.S. 1977-81; Disting. prof. Emory U., 1982—. Author: Why Not the Best?, 1975, A Government as Good as Its People, 1977, Keeping Faith/Memoirs of a President, 1982, Negotiation: The Alternative to Hostility, 1984, The Blood of Abraham, 1985, (with Rosalynn Carter) Everything to Gain: Making the Most of the Rest of Your Life, 1987, An Outdoor Journal, 1988. Mem. Sumter County (Ga.) Sch. Bd., 1955-62, chmn., 1960-62; mem. Americus and Sumter County Hosp. Authority, 1956-70; bd. dirs. Ga. Crop Improvement Assn., 1957-63, pres., 1961; mem. Sumter County (Ga.) Library Bd., 1961; pres. Plains Devel. Corp., 1963; chmn. West Central Ga. Area Planning and Devel. Commn., 1964; pres. Ga. Planning Assn., 1968; chmn. congl. campaign com. Democratic Nat. Com., 1974; founder Carter Ctr. Emory U., 1982; bd. dirs. Habitat for Humanity, 1984-87; chmn. bd. trustees Carter Ctr., Inc., 1986—, Carter-Menil Human Rights Found., 1986—, Global 2000 Inc., 1986—. Served to lt. USN, 1946-53. Recipient Gold medal Internat. Inst. Human Rights, 1979; Internat. Mediation medal Am. Arbitration Assn., 1979; Martin Luther King Jr. Nonviolent Peace prize, 1979, Albert Schweitzer Prize for Humanitarianism, 1987. Democrat. Club: Lions (dist. gov. 1968-69). Office: The Carter Ctr One Copenhill Atlanta GA 30307

CARTER, JAMES EDWARD, JR., retired dentist, association official; b. Augusta, Ga., July 1, 1906; s. James Edward and Emma (Barnett) C.; D.D.S., Howard U., 1930; postgrad. Haines Normal and Indsl. Inst., 1920-24; m. Marjorie Butler, Jan. 7, 1928; 1 son, James Edward III. Pvt. practice dentistry, Augusta, 1930-81. Mem. Nat. Council YMCA, 1958-64, 67-69; chmn. 9th St. YMCA, Augusta, 1950-57; active United Coll. Fund, Cancer Dr., United Chest Fund, Boy Scouts Am. Del. Republican Nat., Conv., 1960. Bd. dirs. Augusta-Richmond County Library. Recipient Achievement award in pub. service Upsilon Sigma chpt. Omega Psi Phi, 1949, Whitney M. Young Jr. Service award Boy Scouts Am., 60 Year award Omega Psi Phi, 1986, Eastern Dist. Dental Soc. Service award, 1986, 50 Year and Hon. Fellowship award Ga. Dental Assn., 1980, Dentist of Yr. award Ga. Dental Soc., 1980, Achievement award Stoney Med. Dental & Pharm. Soc., 1980; award of merit Georgia Dental Soc., 1961; 55 Year award Thankful Bapt. Ch., 1973; Howard U. Alumni Dental Achievement award, 1982; Spl. award Stoney Med., Dental and Pharm. Soc., 1983. Fellow Internat. Coll. Dentists, Am. Coll. Dentists, Royal Soc. Health, Acad. Gen. Dentistry, World Wide Acad. Scholars, Acad. Dentistry Internat.; mem. Nat. (life; past pres.; mem. exec. bd. 1940-52), Am. (life), Ga. (life, pres. 1940-41, 35-year service plaque) dental assns., Stoney-Med. and Dental Soc. (pres. 1961-63), Ga. Dental Soc. (life mem. 1987—), Acad. Gen. Dentistry, John A. Andrew Clin. Soc. (pres. dental sect. 1947), Fedn. Dentaire Internationale, Pierre Fauchard Acad., Omega Psi Phi (past basilius Psi Omega chpt. 1936-37, treas. 7th dist. 1943-75; recipient achievement award human relations Psi Omega chpt. 1963, 50 Year Pin), Sigma Pi Phi, Omicron Kappa Upsilon. Republican. Baptist (chmn. bd. trustees 1937-77, chmn. emeritus, deacon 1961—). Clubs: Frontiers (Augusta, Ga.); Optimist Internat. Home: 2347 Fitten St Augusta GA 30904

CARTER, JAY BOYD, economic development executive; b. Turlock, Calif., Apr. 12, 1925; s. Arthur Wesley and Gail Bernice (Jaderberg) C.; m. Mary Louise Cross, Apr. 12, 1946; children—Jay Boyd, Kathleen Susanne, Brian Douglas, Annette Marie, Daniel Edward, Mary Beth, Jeannette Marie, Lawrence Scott. Student, U. N.Mex., 1944-45; B.S. in Elec. Engring, U. So. Calif., 1946, B.S. in Civil Engring, 1951; M.A. in Internat. Pub. Policy, Sch. Advanced Internat. Studies, Johns Hopkins, 1974. Engr. City of Los Angeles Dept. Water and Power, 1946-51; engr., supt. various engring., cons. and constrn. firms 1951-55; with State Dept./AID; power engr., Thailand, 1955-58; gen. engr., Taiwan, 1958-63; power engr., India, 1963-66; gen. engr., Washington, 1966-68; chief engr., Brazil, 1968-73; dir. infrastructure dept. Asian Devel. Bank, Manila, Philippines, 1974-79; mgr. internat. Asia ops. Stanley Cons., Inc., 1979-82; pres. Jay B. Carter & Assocs., Islamabad, Pakistan, 1982—; energy cons. Internat. Sci. and Tech. Inst., Govt. Sudan, 1983-88. Served with USNR, 1943-46. Mem. IEEE, Am. Pub. Works Assn., Mgmt. Assn. of Philippines, Soc. Am. Mil. Engrs. Home and Office: 9017 Hamilton Dr Fairfax VA 22030

CARTER, JOHN DALE, organizational development executive; b. Tuskegee, Ala., Apr. 9, 1944; s. Arthur L. and Ann (Bargyh) C.; AB, Ind. U., 1965, MS, 1967; PhD (NDEA fellow), Case Western Res. U., 1974; m. Veronica Louise Hopper, Oct. 12, 1986. Dir. student affairs Dental Sch., Case Western Res. U., Cleve., 1974-75, asst. prof. applied behavioral sci., 1974—, asst. dean orgn. devel. and student affairs, 1975-78; pres. John D. Carter and Assocs., Inc., Cleve., 1985—; ptnr. Portsmouth Cons. Group, 1984—; chmn. bd. Gestalt Inst. Cleve., 1974-80, program dir., fin. dir. 1981-86; mem. exec. bd. Nat. Tng. Labs., 1975-78; faculty Am. U., 1980—; bd. dirs. Behavioral Sci. Found., Cleve.; exec. bd. Fielding Inst., 1987—. Mem. Internat. Assn. Applied Social Scientists, (cert. cons. Internat.), Kappa Alpha Psi (pres. alpha chpt. 1964-65), Alpha Phi Omega. Author: Counselling the Helping Relationship, 1975, Managing the Merger Integration Process, 1986. Home: 2995 Scarborough Rd Cleveland Heights OH 44118 Office: PO Box 1822 Cleveland OH 44106

CARTER, LEIGH, tire and rubber company executive; b. San Francisco, 1925. Pres. Tremco Co., Cleve., 1949-82, now. chmn., dir.; exec. v.p., pres. engring. products group B.F. Goodrich Co., Akron, Ohio, 1982, vice chmn., now pres., chief operating officer, dir.; bd. dirs. Pultrusions, Cleve. Illuminating Co., Adams Express, Sherwin Williams; trustee First Union Real Estate Investment. Served as 2d lt. USAF, 1943-45. Office: The B F Goodrich Co 3925 Embassy Pkwy Akron OH 44313 *

CARTER, MAE RIEDY, retired college official, consultant; b. Berkeley, Calif., May 20, 1921; d. Carl Joseph and Avis Blanche (Rhodehaver) Riedy; B.S., U. Calif., Berkeley, 1943; m. Robert C. Carter, Aug. 19, 1944; children—Catherine, Christin Ann. Ednl. adv., then program specialist div. continuing edn. U. Del., Newark, 1968-78, asst. provost for women's affairs, exec. dir. commn. status women Office Women's Affairs, 1978-86; adv. bd. Rockefeller Family grant project, 1979-83. Regional v.p. Del. PTA, 1960-62; pres. Friends Newark Free Library, 1968-69; mem. fiscal planning com. Newark Spl. Sch. Dist., 1972. Recipient Outstanding Service award Women's Coordinating Council, 1977, 79; Spl. Recognition award, Nat. U. Extension Assn., 1977, award for credit programs, 1971, Creative Programming award, 1971; AAUW grantee, 1968; Fulbright grantee, 1976. Mem. AAUW (past br. pres.), Women's Equity Action League, Nat. Assn. Women Deans, Adminstrs. and Counselors, NOW, Women's Legal Def. Fund, Nat. Women's Polit. Caucus. Republican. Author: (with Geis and Butler) Seeing and Evaluating People, 1982, revised, 1986, Research on Seeing and Evaluating People; also papers, reports in field. Home: 604 Dallam Rd Newark DE 19711

CARTER, MARTHA ELIZABETH, educator; b. Fayetteville, N.C., Nov. 20, 1935; d. Charlie David and Emma (Dawson) Spell; m. Donald Claython Fuller, Apr. 4, 1954 (div. Apr. 1972); children: Deborah Johnson, Sharon Holmes, Donald C., Anthony Craig; m. Ronald A. Carter, June 14, 1974. BS in Sci. Edn., SUNY, Old Westbury, 1975; MS, Calif. State U., Fullerton, 1979; postgrad., U.S. Internat. U. Cert. community coll. tchr., ednl. adminstr., Calif. Tchr. Willard Intermediate Sch., Santa Ana, 1976—, coordinator Univ. Calif. at Irvine Partnership Program, 1980-81, adminstrv. asst., 1981-82; adminstrv. intern Valley High Sch., 1978-79; panel mem. Fulbright Tchr. Exchange Interviewing Com., Santa Ana Unified Sch. Dist. Reading Com., supt. forum; v.p. sch. improvement program Willard Intermediate Sch.; coordinator coop. teaching for thinking adv. council Orange County Dept. Edn. representing Santa Ana (Calif.) Unified Sch., 1984. Produced profl. devel. video, 1984. Contestant Mrs. Calif. Beauty Pagent, 1985. Mem. Assn. Supervision and Curriculum Devel., Santa Ana Educator Assn., Irvine C. of C., Black Cultural Council of Bowers Mus., Calif. Teaching Assn. Democrat.

CARTER, MEDORA ABBOTT, project administrator; b. Washington, July 18, 1953; d. Jackson Miles and Frances Elizabeth (Dowdle) A.; m. Donald Lynwood Carter, May 14, 1983. Student Chowan Jr. Coll., 1971-72, J. Sargeant Reynolds and Va. Commonwealth U., 1973-76; grad. with honors Am. Inst. Banking, 1981. Asst. cashier, br. mgr. Dominion Nat. Bank, Vienna, Va., 1977-82; fin. analyst McDonnell Douglas/TYMNET, Inc., Vienna, 1984-87; project adminstr. McDonnell, 1987—. Mem. Colonial chpt. Rep. Women's Club, Alexandria, Va., 1985—; del. to county and state Rep. convs., 1988; mem. membership drive com. Fairfax County C. of C., 1981, 82; treas. Kings Park Shopping Ctr. Mcht.'s Assn., Springfield, Va., 1981; page DAR 1976 Va. State Conv., also active mem.; mem. Alexandria Assn. Recipient Outstanding Achievement award Nat. Assn. Banking Women No. Va., 1981. Episcopalian. Office: McDonnell Douglas/TYMNET Inc 2070 Chain Bridge Rd Vienna VA 22180

CARTER, RICHARD DUANE, business educator. s. Herbert Duane and Edith Irene (Richardson) C.; m. Nancy Jean Cannell, Sept. 3, 1955; 1 son, Erich Richardson. A.B., Coll. William and Mary; M.B.A., Columbia U.; Ph.D., UCLA, 1968. Sr. advisor, dir. Taiwan Metal Industries Devel. Center (under auspices of ILO), 1966-67; dir. UNDP cons. services, Taiwan, 1966-67; chief exec. officer Human Resources Inst., Baton Rouge, La., 1968-70; liaison advisor Internat. Inst. Applied Systems Analysis, Vienna, Austria, 1975; U.S. rep., dir. indsl. mgmt. and cons. services program UN Indsl. Devel. Orgn., Vienna, 1970-75; mem. East-West Trade and Mgmt. Commn., 1973-75; sr. advisor, dir. Korean Inst. Sci. and Tech. (under auspices of UN), Seoul, 1974-75; dean Sch. Bus., Quinnipiac Coll., Hamden, Conn., 1977-80; chmn. bd. TCG Industries, Inc., N.Y.C., 1980—; prof. mgmt., program coordinator Fairfield (Conn.) U., 1980-84; founder, mng. dir. Internat. Mgmt. Consortium, Vienna, Westport and Millerton, N.Y., 1975—; asso. mem. Columbia U. Seminar on Orgn. and Mgmt., 1976—, vice-chmn., 1983—, chmn. research and publ. com., 1976—; mng. dir. Wainwright & Ramsey Securities, Inc., N.Y.C., 1985—. Editorial bd.: Indian Adminstrv. and Mgmt. Rev, New Delhi, 1974—; Author: Management: In Perspective and Practice, 1970, The Future Challenges of Management Education, 1981; also numerous articles and revs. Trustee Dingletown Community Ch., Greenwich, Conn., 1978—; mem. adv. council Calif. Coll. Tech., Los Angeles, 1978—. Fellow Internat. Acad. Mgmt.; mem. Acad. Mgmt., Am. Mgmt. Assns. (pres.'s council, dir. 1976-77), N.Am. Soc. Corp. Planning, N.Am. Mgmt. Council (bd. dirs.1983-87), Soc. Internat. Orgn. Devel., Mensa, Beta Gamma Sigma.

CARTER, THOMAS SMITH, JR., railroad executive; b. Dallas, June 6, 1921; s. Thomas S. and Mattie (Dowell) C.; m. Janet R. Hostetter, July 3, 1946; children: Diane Carter Petersen, Susan Jean, Charles T., Carol Ruth. B.S. in Civil Engring., So. Meth. U., 1944. Registered profl. engr., Mo., Kans., Okla., Tex., La., Ark. Various positions Mo. Kans. Tex. R.R., 1941-44, 46-54, chief engr., 1954-61, v.p. ops., 1961-66; v.p. Kansas City So. Ry. Co., La. and Ark. Ry. Co., 1966—; pres. Kansas City So. Ry. Co., 1973-86, also bd. dirs., chmn. bd., 1981—; pres. La. and Ark. Ry. Co., 1974-86, also bd. dirs., chmn. bd., 1981—, chief exec. officer, 1981—; dir. Kansas City So. Industries. Served with C.E. AUS, 1944-46. Fellow ASCE; mem. Am. Ry. Engring. Assn., Assn. Am. Railroads (dir. 1978—), Nat. Soc. Profl. Engrs. Clubs: Chgo, Kansas City, Shreveport. Home: 9319 W 92d Terr Overland Park KS 66212 Office: Kansas City So Ry 114 W 11th St Kansas City MO 64105

CARTER, WILLIAM CLARENCE, insurance agent; b. Mayodan, N.C., Mar. 29, 1928; s. William Comer and Lucy Pearl (Barrow) C.; B.A., Randolph-Macon Coll., 1950; m. Phyllis Jane Stephenson, Apr. 28, 1951; children—Anne Carter Marrin, Mary Claire. Chartered Fin. Cons. With Fidelity Mut. Life Ins. Co., Richmond, Va., 1953-56; gen. agt. Fidelity Bankers Life Ins. Co., Richmond, 1956—; adj. faculty Va. Commonwealth U., Million DollarRound Table. Served as capt. USMC, 1951-53. C.L.U., Chartered Fin. Cons. Mem. Am. Soc. C.L.U., Estate Planning Council. Episcopalian. Clubs: Bull and Bear, Hermitage Country (Richmond). Home and Office: 103 Rose Hill Rd Richmond VA 23229

CARTIER-BRESSON, HENRI, photographer; b. Chanteloup, France, Aug. 22, 1908; m. Martine Franck, 1970. Student painting of André Lhote, 1927-28; ed. Ecole Fénelon, Lycé e Condorcet, Paris; Dr. honoris causa, Oxford U., 1975. Asst. dir. to Jean Renoir, 1936-39; co-founder, assoc. Magnum Photos, 1947—. Photographs exhibited at Mus. Modern Art, N.Y.C., 1947, 68, Louvre, Paris, 1955, 67, Victoria and Albert Mus., London, 1969, Grand-Palais, Paris, 1970, Manege, Moscow, 1972, Edinburgh Festival, Hayward Gallery, London, 1978, Mus. Modern Art, Paris, 1982, Mus. Modern Art, N.Y.C., 1987, also in major museums Mexico, Japan and other locations; drawings and paintings exhibited Carlton Gallery, N.Y.C., 1975, Bischofberger Gallery, Zurich, 1976, P.A.C. of Milan (Italy), 1983, U. Rome, 1983, Mus. Modern Art, Oxford, 1984, Palais Liechtenstein, Vienna, 1985, Arnold Herstand Gallery, N.Y.C., 1987. Recipient award for story death of Gandhi, U.S. Camera, 1948; Best Photographic Reporting from Abroad award Overseas Press Club Am., 1949, for Russia, 1954, for Red China, 1960, for Cuba, 1964; Most Contbns. Progress for Mag. Photography award, Am. Soc. Mag. Photography, 1953; Internat. Understanding through Photography award, Photography Soc. Am., 1958; Hasselbladt award, 1983; Culture prize German Photography Soc., Am. Acad. Arts Scis.; Novocento award Jorge Luis Borges, Palermo, 1986. Documentary films: on hosps., Spanish Republic, 1937; (with Jacques Lemare) Le Retour, 1945; (with Jean Boffety) Impressions of California (CBS) 1969; Southern Exposures (with W. Donbrow) (CBS), 1970. Author: The Decisive Moment (also French editor), 1952; (with Franç ois Nourissier) Vive la France, 1970 (with Etiemble) L'Homme et la Machine (IBM), 1972; The Face of Asia, 1972; A Propos de l'U.R.S.S., 1973; HCB Photographer (text by Yves Bonneloy), 1979; Fotoportraits 1932-1982, (text by A. de Mandiarques) 1982; Coll. Livre de Poche, 1983. Office: care Magnum Photos, 20 rue des Grands Augustins, 75006 Paris France Other: care Helen Wright 135 E 74th St New York NY 10021 Other: care John Hillelson, 145 Fleet St, London England

CARTLAND, BARBARA, author; b. Eng., July 9, 1901; d. Bertram and Polly (Scobell) C.; m. Alexander George McCorquodale, 1927 (div. 1933); m. Hugh McCorquodale, Dec. 28, 1936 (dec. 1963); children: Raine (Countess Spencer), Ian, Glen. Student pvt. girls' schs. in, Eng. Lectr., polit. speaker; TV personality (2 lecture tours), Can., 1940. Author hist. novels; hist. biographer, writer on health and phys. fitness; autobiographer, playwright books include; history The Private Life of Elizabeth, Empress of Austria, 1959, Josephine, Empress of France, 1961, Diane de Poitiers, 1962; biography Ronald Cartland, 1942, Polly, My Wonderful Mother, 1956;

autobiography The Isthmus Years, 1943, The Years of Opportunity, 1948, I Search for Rainbows, 1967, We Danced All Night, 1971, I Seek the Miraculous, 1978; non-fiction Be Vivid, Be Vital, 1956, Etiquette, 1963, The Many Facets of Love, 1963, Sex and the Teenager, 1964; novels Jigsaw, 1925, Debt of Honour, 1970, The Queen's Messenger, 1971, No Darkness for Love, 1974, The Castle of Fear, 1975, Sweet Adventure, 1976, Rainbow to Heaven, 1976, The Mysterious Maid-Servant, 1977, Love in Hiding, 1977, The Disgraceful Duke, 1977, A Fugitive from Love, 1978, The Explosion of Love, 1979, From Hell to Heaven, 1980, Dreams Do Come True, 1981, From Hate to Love, 1982, Love and Lucia, 1983, A Duke in Danger, 1983, The Unbreakable Spell, 1983, Secrets, 1983, Bride of Brigand, 1983, A Very Unusual Wife, 1984, Terror for a Teacher, 1984, Helga in Hiding, 1984, Alone and Afraid, 1985, Look With Love, 1985, Love Is a Gamble, 1985, Love Is Heaven, 1985, Miracle for a Madonna, 1985, Crowned With Love, Forced Into Marriage, Little Tongues of Fire, Revenge is Sweet, Real Love or Fake, The Marquis Wins, Love is the Key, Love at First Sight, The Secret Princess, Heaven in Hong Kong, Paradise in Penang, A Game of Love, many others. County councillor, Hertfordshire, 9 years, hon. services welfare officer, Bedfordshire, 1941-45. Decorated Dames of Grace of St. John Jerusalem; recipient Bishop Wright Air Industry award for contbn. to devel. aviation, 1984. Mem. Nat. Assn. Health (Eng.) (pres.). Office: care Berkley Pubs Inc 200 Madison Ave New York NY 10016 *

CARTLEDGE, SIR BRYAN GEORGE, college principal; b. Bromley, Kent, Eng., June 10, 1931; s. Eric Montague George and Phyllis (Shaw) C.; m. Ruth Hylton Gass, Mar. 26, 1960; children: Fiona Jane, Charles Anthony Bryan. MA, St. John's Coll., 1955. Commonwealth Fund fellow Stanford, Harvard Univs., 1956-58; research fellow St. Anthony's Coll., Oxford, Eng., 1958-60; 2d sec. London Fgn. Office, 1960-61, Brit. Embassy, Stockholm, 1961-63; 1st sec. Moscow, 1963-65, Tehran, Iran, 1968-70; counsellor Moscow, 1972-75; 1st sec. London Fgn. and Commonwealth Office, 1965-68, head East European and Soviet dept., 1975-77, asst. undersec., 1983-84; fellow Ctr. for Internat. Affairs, Harvard U., Cambridge, Mass., 1971-72; pvt. sec. to prime minister Office of Prime Minister, London, 1977-79; Brit. ambassador to Budapest, 1980-83; dep. sec. Office of Cabinet, London, 1984-85; Brit. ambassador to Moscow, 1985-88; prin. Linacre Coll, Oxford U., 1988—. Served with Brit. Army, 1950-51. Recipient Companion Order St. Michael and St. George, Queen of Eng., 1980, 1985; hon. fellow St. John's Coll., 1986, St. Antony's Coll., Oxford, Eng., 1987. Mem. Ch. of Eng. Club: United Oxford and Cambridge U. (London). Office: Linacre Coll, Oxford OX1 3JA, England

CARTLEDGE, PAUL ANTHONY, ancient history educator; b. London, Mar. 24, 1947; s. Marcus Raymond and Margaret Christobel (Oakley) C.; m. Judith Susan Portrait, July 21, 1976; 1 child, Gabrielle. BA 1st class, Oxford U., Eng., 1969, PhD, 1975. Craven fellow Oxford U., 1969-70; Harold Salvesen jr. fellow Univ. Coll., 1970-72; lectr. classics New U. Ulster, Coleraine, No. Ireland, 1972-73, Trinity Coll., Dublin, Ireland, 1973-78; lectr. classical civilization U. Warwick, Eng., 1978-79; lectr. ancient history Cambridge U., Eng., 1979—, fellow, dir. studies in classics Clare Coll., 1981—. Author: Sparta and Lakonia, A Regional History 1300-362 B.C., 1979, Agesilaos and the Crisis of Sparta, 1987; co-editor: Crux. Essays in Greek History, 1985. Leverhulme Research Trustee grantee, Greece, 1982. Fellow Soc. Antiquaries London; mem. Soc. for Promotion Hellenic Studies. Office: Clare Coll, Cambridge CB2 1TL, England

CARTLIDGE, EDWARD SUTTERLEY, mechanical engineer; b. Trenton, N.J., Feb. 5, 1945; s. Leon James and Agnes Jean (Cinkay) C.; m. Marilyn Spinuzza, July 21, 1979. BS in Marine Engring, U.S. Mcht. Marine Acad., 1968; MS in M.E., N.J. Inst. Tech., 1971; MBA, Temple U., 1982. Registered profl. engr., Pa., Ill., Wis., Minn., Calif. Marine engr. Seatrain Lines, 1968-69; performance engr. Foster Wheeler Corp., Livingston, N.J., 1969-71; cons. engr. Fluor, Sargent & Lundy, and Kuljian Corp., 1971-75; chief engr. Gimpel Corp., Langhorne, Pa., 1976-79; sr. research and devel. engr. Yarway Corp., Bluebell, Pa., 1976-79; power utilities supr. Merck, Sharp & Dohme, West Point, Pa., 1982—; fin. cons. Served to comdr. USNR, 1968—. Mem. Nat. Soc. Profl. Engrs. (chpt. pres.), Pa. Soc. Profl. Engrs. (Young Engr. of Yr. 1980), ASME, Instruments Soc. Am., Soc. Mfg. Engrs., Am. Soc. Metals, Soc. Naval Architects and Marine Engrs., Naval Reserve Assn. Home: 680 Valley Rd Blue Bell PA 19422

CARTNER, JOHN A., investor; b. Jacksonville, N.C., Nov. 6, 1947; s. John Alexander and Anna G. (Hardison) C.; m. Tanya L. Morris, Feb. 18, 1978; children: Christian W.J., Natalie O.V. BS, U.S. Mcht. Marine Acad., 1969; MSc, U. Ga., 1974, PhD, 1975; MBA, Ga. State U., 1978; postdoctoral tng., U.S. Army Research Inst., 1976-78. Dir. marine transp. Grumman Corp., Bethpage, N.Y., 1980-81; v.p. IMA Resources, Washington, D.C., 1981; pres. Phillips Cartner & Co., Inc., Alexandria, Va., 1981-84, chmn., chief exec. officer, 1985-87; chmn. Windsor Holdings, Inc., Alexandria, Va. Contbr. numerous articles to profl. jours.; patentee in field. Bd. dirs. U.S. Mcht. Marine Acad. Found., Kings Point, N.Y., 1982-85, Alexandria Seaport Found., 1985—; vestryman Grace Episcopal Ch., Alexandria, 1986. Served to lt. USNR, 1969-73, master U.S. mcht. marine, 1966-82. Mem. Soc. Naval Architects and Marine Engrs., U.S. Mcht. Marine Acad. (Supt.'s Trophy award 1982, Outstanding Profl. Achievement award 1984), Sigma Xi. Democrat. Episcopalian. Club: Downtown Athletic. Office: Phillips Cartner & Co 700 N Fairfax St Alexandria VA 22314

CARTON, EDWIN BECK, plastics manufacturing company executive; b. Balt., Apr. 27, 1927; s. Jacob G. and Gertrude (Beck) C.; B.A. in Chemistry, Johns Hopkins U., 1949; M.S. in Organic Chemistry, U. Md., 1952; Ph.D. in Organic Chemistry, Pa. State U., 1955; m. Lonnie Frances Caming, June 19, 1949; children—Evan Bruce, Deborah Ann, Paula Bette. Research chemist Scott Paper Co., Chester, Pa., 1955-57, project leader, 1957-60; dispersions research and devel. mgr. Cabot Corp., Phila. office, 1960-64, head corp. applications research and devel., Billerica, Mass., 1964-66, mgr. mktg. oxides div., 1966-68; mgr. applications engring. dept. Chomerics Inc., Woburn, Mass., 1968-69; asst. dir. research and devel. U.S. M. Chem. Co., Middleton, Mass., 1969-76; pres., dir. Sharpe Plastic Products Inc., Concord, Mass., 1976-80; pres., dir. RIM Xinde Internat., Inc., Boston, 1978—; instr. Pa. State U., 1952-55. Founder, dir. Suburban Jewish Sch., Phila., 1957-64; chmn. United Fund, Chestnut Hill, Mass., 1966. Served with USAAF, 1945-46. Fellow Am. Inst. Chemists, AAAS; mem. Am. Chem. Soc. (chmn. Phila. sect. budget and audit com. 1961-63, mem. investment bd. trustees 1963-64), ASTM, Soc. Plastics Industry, N.Y. Acad. Scis., Am. Optical Soc., Soc. Plastics Engrs. (chmn. thermoplastic and foams div. 1968-69, dir. 1969—), Phi Lambda Upsilon. Contbr. articles on plastics and organic chemistry to sci. jours. and encys. Patentee in field. Home: 25 Sheffield Rd Newtonville MA 02160 Office: 29 Germania St Boston MA 02130

CARTWRIGHT, ALTON STUART, electrical manufacturing company executive; b. Casper, Wyo., Oct. 7, 1922; s. Alton Stuart and Blanche Susan (Harper) C.; m. Adelaide Frances Igoe, Dec. 22, 1951; children: Stuart Andrew, Matthew Alton, David Francis, Patrick Harper. B.S. in Elec. Engring, Oreg. State U., 1944; grad., Advanced Mgmt. Program, Harvard U., 1969. Registered profl. engr., Mass. With Gen. Electric Co., 1946-85; with Can. Gen. Electric Co. Ltd., 1970-85; exec. v.p. Can. Gen. Electric Co. Ltd., Toronto, Ont., 1972; pres. Can. Gen. Electric Co. Ltd., 1972-77, chmn. bd., chief exec. officer, 1977-85, also dir.; dir. Can. Imperial Bank Commerce, Toronto, Zurn Industries Inc., Erie, Pa., Co-Steel Inc., Toronto, Xerox Can. Inc., Xerox Can. Fin. Inc., Xerox Can. Holdings Inc., Toronto; sr. mem. Conf. Bd. Served to 1st lt. AUS, 1942-46. Mem. Newcomen Soc., Sigma Alpha Epsilon. Clubs: Toronto, Canadian, Empire, No. Lake George Yacht; John's Island (Vero Beach, Fla.). Home: 676 Ocean Rd Vero Beach FL 32963 also: Friend's Point Hague NY 12836

CARTWRIGHT, MYRON ROGER, accountant, mayor; b. Shevlin, Minn., Apr. 15, 1919; s. Clayton Samuel and Esther Seamuela (Rydeen) C.; m. Winona June Mattson, Oct. 24, 1942 (dec. July 1979); children—Lynn Priscilla, Karen Colette, Tracy April; m. Inez Patricia Solberg, Jan. 30, 1982. Grad. French's Bus. Coll., Bemidji, Minn., 1937; B.A. in Acctg. magna cum laude, Coll. of St. Thomas, St. Paul, 1942. C.P.A., Minn., 1952. Instr. acctg. Coll. of St. Thomas, 1946-53; pvt. practice pub. acctg., St. Paul, 1946-52, as C.P.A., 1952-88. Mayor of Bagley, Minn., 1985-88; bd. dirs. Bagley Indsl. Devel. Corp. Served to capt. USMCR, 1942-45; maj. Res. Mem. Am. Inst. C.P.A.s, Minn. Soc. C.P.A.s, Am. Legion, Minn. Golf Assn. (dir. 1965-66), Minn. Pub. Golf Assn. (sec. 1965-66), North Country Detachment, Marine Corps League. Democrat. Lutheran. Club: Twin Pines Golf (Bagley, Minn.). Home: 422 Lakeview St NW Rt 3 Box 74 Bagley MN 56621 Office: City Hall Bagley MN 56621

CARTWRIGHT, WILLIAM HOLMAN, teacher educator emeritus; b. Pine Island, Minn., Sept. 12, 1915; s. William Holman and Ada Caroline (Frisbie) C.; m. Elaine Mary McGladrey, Sept. 3, 1934; children: John Morris, Mary Elaine, Margaret Ann. B.S., U. Minn., 1937, M.A., 1942, Ph.D., 1950. Dairy farmer 1934-36; tchr. pub. sch. Mabel, Minn., 1937-40, Rochester, Minn., 1940-43; tchr. Univ. High Sch., Mpls., 1943-45; instr. U. Minn., 1943-45, Macalester Coll., 1944; historian Mil. Dist., Washington, 1945-46; asst. prof. edn. Boston U., 1946-50, asso. prof., 1950-51; prof. edn. Duke, 1951-82, prof. emeritus, 1982—, chmn. dept. edn., 1951-65, 67-70, chmn. acad. council, 1969-71; vis. prof. summers U. Calif., 1950, U. Colo., 1957; pres. So. Council on Tchr. Edn., 1959; curriculum cons.; staff James B. Conant Study of Edn. Am. Tchrs., 1961-63. Author: A History of Newburg Township and the Village of Mabel, 1943, The Military District of Washington during the War Years, 1946, (with Arthur C. Bining) The Teaching of History in the United States, 1950, (with Miriam E. Mason) Trailblazers of American History, 1961, rev. 1966, (with Oscar O. Winther) The Story of Our Heritage, 1962, last rev. edit., 1971, (with Edgar B. Wesley) Teaching Social Studies in Elementary Schools, 1968; also chpts. in yearbooks The National Council Social Studies; numerous articles, revs. ednl., hist. publs.; Editor: (with Richard L. Watson, Jr.) Interpeting and Teaching American History, 1961, The Reinterpretation of American History and Culture, 1973. Recipient Army Commendation Ribbon for hist. writing, 1946; Outstanding Achievement award U. Minn., 1959. Mem. Nat. Council Social Studies (pres. 1957), Am. Hist. Assn., NEA, N.E. History Tchrs. Assn. (pres. 1949-50), N.C. Council Social Studies (Distinguished Service award 1976), Phi Delta Kappa, Phi Alpha Theta, Pi Gamma Mu, Kappa Delta Pi. Unitarian. Home: Box 705 Seven Lakes West End NC 27376

CARVALHO, JULIE ANN, psychologist; b. Washington, Apr. 11, 1940; d. Daniel H. and Elizabeth Cecilia (Gardiner) Schmidt; B.A. with high honors, U. Md., 1962, postgrad., 1973; M.A., George Washington U., 1966; postgrad. Va. Poly. Inst., 1979—; children—Alan R., Dennis M., Melanie D., Celeste A., Joshua E. Social sci. research analyst Mental Health Study Center, NIMH, 1963-67; edn. and tng. analyst Computer Applications, Inc., 1967-68; edn. program specialist Nat. Center for Ednl. Research and Devel., U.S. Office of Edn., Washington, 1969-70, program analyst, 1970-73; equal opportunity specialist Office of Sec., HEW, Washington, 1973-77; legis. program, civil rights analyst Office for Civil Rights Dept. Health and Human Services, 1977-85, indep. cons., 1986—. Mem. steering com. Alliance for Child Care, 1975-80; bd. dirs. Child Care Centers, 1970-76, HEW Employees Assn., 1973-78. Mem. Am. Psychol. Assn. (panel conductor 1969—, presenter interagy. com. research and devel. children and adolescents, 1986—), Soc. for Psychol. Study of Social Issues, Am. Soc. Public Adminstrn., (condr. panels), Capitol Area Social Psychologists Assn. (conf. chmn. 1985). Federally Employed Women (nat. editor 1975-79), Fairfax County Assn. for the Gifted (pres. 1980), Psi Chi, Phi Alpha Theta. Contbr. articles on ednl. programs to profl. publs. Home and Office: 11668 Mediterranean Ct Reston VA 22090

CARVEL, ELBERT NOSTRAND, former governor Delaware, fertilizer company executive; b. Shelter Island Heights, N.Y., Feb. 9, 1910; s. Arnold Wrightson and Elizabeth (Nostrand) C.; engring. course, Balt. Poly. Inst., 1924-28; J.D., U. Balt., 1931; LL.D. (hon.), Del. State Coll., 1964; L.H.D. (hon.), U. Del., 1986; m. Ann Hall Valliant, Dec. 17, 1932; children—Elizabeth Nostrand Carvel Palmer, Edwin Valliant, Ann Hall Carvel House, Barbara Jean Carvel Krahn. Sales engr. Consol. Gas and Electric Power and Light Co., Balt., 1931-36; gen. mgr. and dir. Valliant Fertilizer Co., Laurel, Del., 1936-45, pres., 1945-72, chmn. bd., 1972-82, chmn. emeritus, 1982-85; dir. Milford Fertilizer Co., Del., 1937—, v.p., 1941-59, chmn. bd., 1959-82, chmn. emeritus, 1982—; chmn. Fischer Enterprises, 1969-75; v.p. Laurel Grain Co., 1965-75; dir. Peoples Bank and Trust Co., chmn., 1975-82; chmn. bd., dir. Beneficial Nat. Bank, Wilmington, 1983—; dir. Beneficial Corp., Wilmington, Del., 1975-85, emeritus dir., 1985—; dir. Beneficial Nat. Bank (USA), Central Grain Co., Laurel, Western Auto Supply Co., 1983-85; lt. gov. State of Del., 1945-49, gov., 1949-53, 61-65. Vice pres. Del. Safety Council; dir. Del. Motor Club, 1978, v.p., 1979; adv. bd. Delmarva council Boy Scouts Am.; mem. Del. Bicentennial Commn., 1968-70; pres. Del. Bd. Pardons, 1945-49; chmn. Delmarva Ecumenical Council, 1970-72, mem. exec. com., 1970-76, mem. adminstrv. bd., 1970—; co-chmn. Delawareans for Orderly Devel., 1971—; mem. BiCentennial Medal Commn. of Del., 1972; chmn. Del. Democratic Com., 1946-47, 54-56; del. Dem. Nat. Conv., 1948, 52, 56, 60, 64; jointly nominated Adlai Stevenson Dem. candidate for pres. nat. conv., 1952; chmn. Del. Dem. Renewal Commn., 1970; chmn. Del. Tax Study Commn., 1973; mem. Del. Jud. Nominating Com., 1977—; Dem. candidate U.S. Senate, Del., 1958, 64; chmn. Del. Const. Revision Commn., 1968-70; lay mem. Del. Com. on Judiciary, 1980—. Trustee U. Del., 1945-85, vice chmn. bd. trustees, 1972-85; trustee U. Balt., 1968-74; mem. U. Balt. Ednl. Found., 1980—; chmn. March of Dimes of Del., 1952-62; hon. chmn. Del. div. Am. Cancer Soc. 1984, 85 crusades; bd. dirs. Del. Wild Lands; mem. exec. com. Govs.' Conf., 1950-51, 62-63; chmn. Del. del. Del. Panama Partners, 1965-68; co-chmn. Delawareans for Panama Canal Treaties, 1977-78; hon. co-chmn. Del. Humanities Forum, 1978; co-chmn. Delawareans Ratification SALT II Treaty, 1978-80. Decorated comdr. Order Orange Nassau (Netherlands); recipient Good Govt. award Com. of 39, Wilmington, Good Citizenship medal Nat. Soc. SAR, 1967, Vrooman award Prisoners Aid Soc. Del., 1965, Silver Beaver award Boy Scouts Am., 1970; Ann. award NCCJ, 1979; Alumnus of Yr. award Balt. Poly. Inst., 1979; named Law Alumnus of Yr., U. Balt., 1981; Liberty award Del. Bar Assn., 1982. Mem. Del. Hist. Soc. (dir. 1983—), Del. Ducks Unlimited, Swedish Colonial Soc., Del., Lewes, Laurel, Milford hist. socs., Kent Island Heritage Soc., Sussex County Archaeol. and Hist. Soc., Sigma Delta Kappa, Alpha Zeta. Episcopalian (del. gen. conv. 1946, 52). Clubs: Tall Cedars of Lebanon, Antique Automobile of America, Lincoln of Del., Masons (33 deg.), Shriners, Lions. Address: PO Box 111 Laurel DE 19956

CARVER, BARBARA ANN, temporary help service executive; b. Niagara Falls, Ont., Can.; came to U.S., 1955; d. Robert Leroy Housser and Rosemary (Waloshuk) Murdoch; m. John Rudy Carver, Nov. 21, 1964; children: Kevin, Christopher. Student Tarrant County Jr. Coll., Ft. Worth, 1969-71. Nurse various hosps., Tex., 1971-79; staff supr. Norrell Service, Houston, 1979-80, office mgr., 1980-81, ter. mgr., 1981-82, mgr. major accounts, 1982-83, br. mgr., 1983-84; br. mgr. Temps & Co., 1984-88, area mgr., 1988—. Recipient Robert Gibson award Norrell Services, 1981, others; named Tex. Profit Ctr. of Yr., 1987-88. Office: Temps & Co 3707 FM 1960 W S-260 Houston TX 77068

CARVER, KENDALL LYNN, insurance company executive; b. Spencer, Iowa, Nov. 4, 1936; s. Marion and Letha G.; m. Carol Lee Spiers, July 1, 1961; children: Merrian, Kendra, Lee, Christine. B.S., U. Iowa, 1958. Rep. field sales Washington Nat. Ins. Co., Evanston, Ill., 1958-73; regional dir. Washington Nat. Ins. Co., 1974-77; pres. Washington Nat. Ins. Co., N.Y.C., 1977—; chief exec. officer Washington Nat. Ins. Co., 1978—; also mem. exec. com., chmn. fin. com., dir. C.L.U.; chmn. com. seminars Ins. Council N.Y.; bd. dirs. Life Ins. Council N.Y. Fellow Life Mgmt. Inst.; mem. Nat. Assn. Life Underwriters, Am. Coll. Life Underwriters, Life Ins. Council N.Y. (dir. 1979-82, 86—). Republican. Home: 5 Tanglewood Trail Darien CT 06820 Office: Washington Nat Life Ins Co NY 500 Fifth Ave New York NY 10036

CARWARDINE, RICHARD JOHN, historian, educator; b. Cardiff, Eng., Jan. 12, 1947; s. John Francis and Beryl (Jones) C.; m. Linda Margaret Kirk, May 17, 1975. MA, PhD, Oxford U., Eng., 1975. Lectr. in Am. History U. Sheffield, Yorks, Eng., 1971—. Author: Transatlantic Revivalism, 1978. Fellow Royal Hist. Soc.; mem. Orgn. of Am. Historians, British Assn. Am. Studies (treas.). Mem. Social and Liberal Democratic Party. Mem. Ch. of Eng. Office: U Sheffield, Dept History, Sheffield S10 2TN, England

CARY, ARLENE D., hotel company sales executive; b. Chgo., Dec. 19, 1930; d. Seymour S. and Shirley L. (Land) C.; student U. Wis., 1949-52; U. Miami, 1953; m. Elliot D. Hagle, Dec. 30, 1972 (div.). Public relations account exec. Robert Howe & Co., 1953-55; sales mgr. Martin B. Iger & Co., 1955-57; sales mgr., gen. mgr. Sorrento Hotel, Miami Beach, Fla., 1957-59; gen. mgr. Mayflower Hotel, Manomet, Mass., 1959-60; various positions Aristocrat Inns of Am., 1960-72; v.p. sales, McCormick Center Hotel, Chgo., 1972—. Active Nat. Women's Polit. Caucus, Internat. Orgn. Women Execs., membership promotion chmn., 1979-80, bd. dirs., 1980-81. Recipient disting. salesman award Sales and Mktg. Execs. Internat., 1977. Mem. Profl. Conv. Mgmt. Assn., Nat. Assn. Exposition Mgrs., Hotel Sales Mgmt. Assn., Meeting Planners Internat., Am. Soc. Assn. Execs., N.Y. Soc. Assn. Execs., Chgo. Soc. Assn. Execs., Ind. Hotel Alliance (sec. 1986—). Jewish. Home: 1130 S Michigan Ave Apt 3203 Chicago IL 60605 Office: McCormick Ctr Hotel 23d and Lakeshore Dr Chicago IL 60616

CASABONNE, PETER GIRARD, textile executive; b. Cohoes, N.Y., Apr. 21, 1932; s. Germain and Rhea (Girard) C.; B.S., Rensselaer Poly. Inst., 1959; m. Carol A. Pendell, June 20, 1954; children—Peter, Maribeth, Kenneth, John, David, Daniel. With Star Textile and Research, Inc., Albany, N.Y., 1949—, exec. v.p., 1969, chmn. bd., 1973—; v.p., dir. Casabonne Bros. Inc.; mng. ptnr. Fuller Realty; chmn. bd. Star Plastics Inc., Texstar Inc.; trustee Cohoes Savs. Bank. Bd. dirs. Cohoes Community Center, 1972—; mem. U.S. Senatorial Bus. Adv. Bd., Washington. Mem. ASTM, Internat. Textile Club (Zurich, Switzerland), Albany C. of C., U.S. C. of C., Bus. Council N.Y. State, Am. Mgmt. Assn. Clubs: Adirondack Mountain; Fort Orange (Albany, N.Y.). Home: 18 Innisbrook Dr Clifton Park NY 12065 Office: 136 Fuler Rd Albany NY 12205

CASADO, FERNANDO, marketing executive; b. Barcelona, Spain, July 13, 1943; s. Alfonso and Adelina (Juan) C.; m. Salome Caneque, Oct. 23, 1969; children—Cristina, Fernando, Ines, Alfonso. Grad. in Econs., U. Barcelona, 1967, Grad. in Tech. Ins., 1967, Diploma in Bus. Adminstrn., 1967; Diploma in Mktg. Research, Associazione Italiana per gliu Studi di Mercato, Rome, 1968; Dr. in Econs. cum laude, U. Barcelona, 1976. Tech. mgr. Instituto Dymsa, Barcelona, 1968-70; sales dir. Busquets Gruart S.A., Barcelona, 1970-72; cons. Profl. Bur., Barcelona, 1972—; gen. mgr. Consava S.S.A., Barcelona, 1982—; asst. prof. U. Barcelona, 1971-74, commd. prof., 1974-76, prof., 1976-83, full prof., 1984—; dean L'Escuela Adminstrn. Empresas de Barcelona, 1988—. Author: El Marketing en la Banca, 1980; Marketing Estrategico para los 80, 1982. Recipient Prat Gaballi award for books in mgmt. and bus. adminstrn., Barcelona, 1981. Mem. Ci rculo de Economiá , Asociació n Españ ola de Contabilidad y Administració n de Empresas, Colegio Economistas. Roman Catholic. Clubs: Real Club Tenis, Club Golf del Prat. Home: Sor Eulalia Anzizu 53, 08034 Barcelona Spain Office: Consava 5SA A Prat de la Riba 92-96, Hospitalet, Barcelona Spain

CASAL, DANIEL ALBERTO, bank executive; b. San Pedro, Buenos Aires, Argentina, Sept. 25, 1953; arrived in Eng., 1985; s. Alberto Luis and Diana Hilda (DaPonte) C.; m. Maria Liliana Montaldo; children: Julian, Agustina, Patricio. ESC, Carlos Pellegrini U., 1973; MBA, U. Buenos Aires, 1978. Credit officer Bank of Am., Buenos Aires, 1972-78; assets and liabilities officer Banco de la Nacion Argentina, N.Y.C., 1979-82; internat. treasury mgr. Banco de la Nacion Argentina, Buenos Aires, 1983-85; gen. mgr. Banco de la Nacion Argentina, London, 1985—. Mem. Anglo-Argentine Soc., Argentine C. of C., Fgn. Banks Assn., British Bankers Assn., Overseas Bankers Club. Club: Argentine. Office: Banco de la Nacion Argentina, Longbrow House, 14-20 Chiswell St, London England EC1Y 4TD

CÁSARES, J. RAMÓN, airline executive; b. Guadalajara, Mexico, June 5, 1924; s. José J. and Francisca (Ponce) C.; m. Beatriz Gil; children: Mercedes, Enrique, Hermelinda. Degree in graphic arts, Escuela Técnica, Guadalajara, 1945. With Mexicana Airlines, Mexico City, 1946—, comml. v.p., 1981; regional dir. Mex. P.R. Tourism Co., 1976—. Roman Catholic. Home: San Francisco 326-301, 03100 Mexico City Mexico Office: Mexicana Airlines, Xola 535 Piso 15, 03100 Mexico City Mexico

CASAROLI, CARDINAL AGOSTINO, Vatican secretary of state; b. Castel San Giovanni, Nov. 24, 1914. Ordained priest Roman Cath. Ch., 1938, titular archbishop, Cartagina, 1967; elevated to Sacred Coll. of Cardinals, 1979. Entered service of Vatican secretariat 1940, undersec., 1961-67; sec. Congregation for Extraordinary Ecclesiastical Affairs, 1967-79; sec. of state and prefect of Council for Pub. Affairs of the Ch. 1979—. Address: The Vatican Vatican City *

CASE, DAVID KNOWLTON, museum director, lecturer, consultant; b. Worcester, Mass., Mar. 26, 1938; s. Frederic Howard and Frances Mary (Knowlton) C.; m. Caroline Porter Richards, Feb. 3, 1974; children—Elizabeth, Sarah. B.A., Yale U., 1961; grad., Harvard Bus. Sch. Mktg. Mgmt. Program, 1973. Pub. relations rep. U.S. Steel Corp., Pitts., 1962-66; communications dir. John Hancock Ins. Co., Boston, Pitts., 1966-70; asst. v.p. Shawmut Bank, Boston, 1970-76; devel. dir. Boston Ctr. for the Arts, 1977; dir. Plimoth Plantation, Plymouth, Mass., 1977—. Trustee Arts-Boston, 1980—, exec. com. Mass. Cultural Alliance, Boston, 1983-86; pres. English-Speaking Union, Boston, 1984—; alumni rep. Gunnery Sch., Washington, Conn., 1984—; trustee Pilgrim Soc., Plymouth, Mass., 1984—; bd. dirs. Plymouth County Devel. Council, 1988—; adv. bd. Mass. Am. Automobile Assn., 1988—. Recipient Golden Coin award Bank Mktg. Assn., 1973; Nat. award Bus. Com. Arts, N.Y., 1975. Mem. Am. Assn. Museums, Colonial Soc., New Eng. Museums Assn. Republican. Episcopalian. Clubs: Yale, Harvard. Home: 378 River St Norwell MA 02061 Office: Plimoth Plantation Box 1620 Plymouth MA 02360

CASE, DOUGLAS MANNING, lawyer; b. Cleve., Jan. 3, 1947; s. Manning Eugene and Ernestine (Bryan) C.; m. Marilyn Cooper, Aug. 23, 1969. BA, U. Pa., 1969; JD, MBA, Columbia U., 1973. Bar: N.Y. 1974, N.J. 1975, Calif. 1980. Assoc. Brown & Wood, N.Y.C., 1973-77; corp. counsel PepsiCo Inc., Purchase, N.Y. and Irvine, Calif., 1977-83, Nabisco Brands Inc., N.Y.C., East Hanover, N.J. and London, 1983—. Chmn. Olde Colonial Dist.; active Morris-Sussex Area Council Boy Scouts Am., 1986—; sec., trustee Marble Scholarship Com., N.Y.C., 1983-88. Mem. ABA, N.Y. State Bar Assn. Clubs: Morris County Golf (Convent Station, N.J.); Columbia Bus. Sch. (N.Y.C.) (pres. and bd. dirs. 1974-79). Office: Internat Nabisco Brands Ltd, 26 Mount Row, Mayfair, London W1Y 5DA, England

CASE, HADLEY, oil company executive; b. N.Y.C., Mar. 28, 1909; s. Walter Summerhayes and Mary Soule (Hadley) C.; m. Julie Marguerite Ill, June 8, 1935 (dec. Mar. 1975); children: Mary C. Durham, Julie Anne, Rosalie C. Clark, Deborah Joan; m. Elizabeth M. McCabe, Nov. 8, 1975. Student, Kent (Conn.) Sch., 1924-29, Antioch Coll., 1929-33. Geol. field work Australia, 1933-34, Tex., 1935-36; with geol. dept. Case, Pomeroy & Co., Inc., 1936-39, v.p., 1939-41, pres., chief exec. officer, dir., 1941-83, chmn. bd., chief exec. officer, 1983—; pres. chief exec. officer Felmont Oil Corp., 1952-72; chmn. bd., chief exec. officer Felmont Oil Corp. (merger Felmont and Homestake Mining Co.), 1972-84; dir. Homestake Mining Co., 1984—, Brown Bros. Harriman Trust Co. Fla., 1986—; bd. dirs. N.W. Airlines, Inc., 1957-78, Copper Range Co., 1966-77, Nashua Corp., 1965-81, Numac Oil & Gas Ltd., 1963-88; trustee Antioch U., 1987—. Trustee Kent Sch., 1959-75, Brewster Acad., 1956-63, Boys' and Girls' Camps, Inc., Boston, 1971-76; trustee Hosp. St. Barnabas, Newark, 1942-59, pres. bd. trustees, 1949-52; bd. dirs. Greenwich Boys Club Assn., 1957-73, hon. mem., 1974—; trustee Naples (Fla.) Community Hosp., 1985—; dir. of The Conservancy, Naples, 1985—; chancellor Kent Sch., 1982—, trustee, 1986—. Mem. Am. Inst. Mining and Metall. Engrs., Am. Petroleum Inst., Ind. Petroleum Assn. Am. (past v.p., dir.). Office: Case Pomeroy & Co Inc 6 E 43d St New York NY 10017

CASE, KAREN ANN, lawyer; b. Milw., Apr. 7, 1944; d. Alfred F. and Hilda M. (Tomich) Case. B.S., Marquette U., 1963, J.D. 1966; LL.M., N.Y.U., 1973. Bar: Wis. 1966, U.S. Ct. Claims, 1973, U.S. Tax Ct. 1973. Ptnr. Meldman, Case & Weine, Milw., 1973-85; ptnr. Meldman, Case & Weine div. Mulcahy & Wherry, S.C., 1985-87; Sec. of Revenue Stateof Wis., 1987-88; ptnr. Case and Drinka, S.C., Milw., 1988—; lectr. U. Wis., Milw., 1974-78; guest lectr. Marquette U. Law Sch., 1975-78. Mem. Pres.'s council Alverno Coll., 1988—. Fellow Wis. Bar Found. (dir. 1977—, treas. 1980—); mem. Milw. Assn. Women Lawyers (bd. dirs. 1975-78, 81-82), Milw. Bar Assn. (bd. dirs. 1985-87), State Bar Wis. (bd. govs. 1981-85, 87—, dir. taxation sect. 1981-87, vice chmn. 1986-87), Am. Acad. Matrimonial Lawyers, Nat. Assn. Women Lawyers (Wis. del. 1982-83), Milw. Rose Soc. (pres. 1981, dir. 1981-83), Friends of Boerner Bat. Gardens (pres. 1984—), Clubs: Professional Dimensions (dir. 1985-87), Tempo (sec. 1984-85).

Contbr. articles to legal jours. Home: 9803 W Meadow Park Dr Hales Corners WI 53130 Office: 125 S Webster Madison WI 53708

CASE, MANNING EUGENE, JR., food company executive; b. Sioux City, Iowa, Mar. 19, 1916; s. Manning Eugene and Loretta (Seims) C.; m. Ernestine Bryan, July 26, 1941; children: Douglas Manning, Randall Bryan. A.B., Western Res. U., 1938, J.D., 1941. Bar: Ohio 1941. Asst. counsel B.F. Goodrich Co., Akron, 1941-52; sec., treas., gen counsel, dir. Perfection Industries, 1952-55; sec. Hupp Corp., 1955-57; v.p. service and fin. M&M Candies div. Mars Inc., 1957-60; asst. treas. Standard Brands Inc., N.Y.C., 1961-62, treas., 1962-68, v.p., treas., 1968-77, v.p., chief fin. officer, 1977-78, sr. v.p., chief fin. officer, 1978-80, sr. v.p. personnel, 1980-81; sr. v.p. personnel Nabisco Brands, Inc., Parsippany, N.J., 1981-82, sr. v.p., 1983-84; dir. Excelsior Income Shares, Inc. Active Boy Scouts Am. Served to col., JAGC U.S. Army, 1942-46. Mem. ABA, Phi Beta Kappa, Delta Sigma Rho, Omicron Delta Kappa, Beta Theta Pi, Phi Delta Phi. Clubs: Metropolitan (gov.), Morris County Golf, N.Y. Athletic, Royal Palm Yacht and Golf, New Zealand Golf, Econ. of N.Y. Home: 25 Lake End Pl Mountain Lakes NJ 07046 Office: 205 Cherry Hill Rd Parsippany NJ 07054

CASELLA, PETER F(IORE), patent and licensing executive; b. N.Y.C., June 5, 1922; s. Fiore Peter and Lucy (Grimaldi) C.; m. Marjorie Eloise Enos, Mar. 9, 1946; children—William Peter, Susan Elaine, Richard Mark. B.Ch.E., Poly. Inst. Bklyn. (Now Poly. U. N.Y.), 1943; student in chemistry St. John's U., N.Y.C., 1940. Registered to practice by U.S. Patent and Trademark Office, Can. Patent and Trade Mark Offices. Head patent sect. Hooker Electrochem. Co., Niagara Falls, N.Y., 1943-54; mgr. patent dept. Hooker Chem. Corp. (named changed to Occidental Chem. Corp. 1981), Niagara Falls, 1954-64, dir. patents and licensing, 1964-81, asst. sec., 1966-81, ret., 1981; pres., chief exec. officer Intra Gene Internat., Inc., Lewiston, N.Y., 1981—; chmn. bd., chief exec. officer In Vitro Internat., Inc., Linthicum, Md., 1983—; cons. patents and licensing, Lewiston, N.Y., 1981—; Dept. Commerce del. on patents and licensing exchange, USSR, 1973, Poland and German Democratic Republic, 1976. Editor: Drafting the Patent Application, 1957. Mem. Lewiston Bd. Edn., 1968-70. Served with AUS, 1944-46; MTO. Recipient Centennial citation Poly. Inst. Bklyn., 1955. Mem. Assn. Corp. Patent Counsel (emeritus, mem. exec. com. 1974-77, charter mem.), N.Y. Patent Law Assn., Niagara Frontier Patent Law Assn. (pres. 1973-74, Founder award 1974), Licensing Execs. Soc. (v.p. 1976-77, Trustees award 1977), Chartered Inst. Patent Agts. Gt. Britain, Patent and Trademark Inst. Can., Internat. Patent and Trademark Assn., U.S. Trademark Assn., Nat. Assn. Mfrs. (patent com.), Mfg. Chemists Assn., Pacific Indsl. Property Assn., U.S. Patent Office Soc. (assoc.), U.S. Trade Mark Office Soc. (assoc.), Am. Chem. Soc., Am. Inst. Chem. Engrs. Clubs: Chemists (N.Y.C.); Niagara (pres. 1973-74) (Niagara Falls).

CASEY, ETHEL LAUGHLIN, concert and opera singer; b. Tarboro, N.C., Jan. 14, 1926; d. Maurice Lee and Mary Irene (Williams) Laughlin; m. Willis Robert Casey, May 23, 1946; children: Willis Robert, Walker Laughlin. Student, Va. Intermont Coll., 1944-45; BA, Greensboro Coll., 1946-47; postgrad., U. N.C., 1948, 62, Meredith Coll., 1949, Northwestern U., 1961. Founder, owner Carolina Records Co.; founder concert series N.C. State Art Mus. Performed at numerous convs. and festivals; oratorio soloist, conv. and mus. comedy performer; author: Claude de France, 1963, Psalms (160 pslam poems), 1987; composer Christmas Night, 1971, America Will Endure, 1972, U.S.A., 1972; N.Y. debut Town Hall, 1961; concert singer performing at Carnegie Hall, all-Debussy concert, 1961, Tribute to Galli-Curci, 1965, Composer's Showcase, N.Y., 1965, Electronic Concert, Ann Arbor, Mich., 1966, Webern World Premieres Internat. Webern Festivals, Seattle, Buffalo, 1962-66, World Premieres of Graphic Music, 1965, command performance, Greek Royal Princess, 1966, New Vistas, World Premieres of Am. Music, 1968; command performance, electronic concert Philomel, 1968; Gov.'s concerts, Judson Hall, N.Y., 1969, 1970, Nat. Congress, Constn. Hall, Washington, 1970; world premieres Webern and Earls music, Carnegie Hall, 1971, world premieres own music and Webern, Lincoln Center, N.Y.C., 1971, Internat. Platform Assn., Washington, 1972, performed in Leningrad, USSR, 1975; TV and radio performer, 1936—. Founder, God's Ministry, Christian Broadcast Network, 1981-82. Named Alumna of Year, Va. Intermont Coll., 1967, Singer of Year, Nat. Assn. Tchrs. Singing, 1963; honored as singer All-Am. City Celebrations, Tarboro, N.C., 1978; recipient award Greensboro Coll. Concert, 1980. Mem. N.C. State Music Soc. (founder). Home and Office: 1605 Park Dr Raleigh NC 27605

CASEY, MAURICE FRANCIS, air force officer; b. Chgo., June 3, 1920; s. Maurice Francis and Marie (Rowan) C.; m. Dora Belle Neubert, Oct. 12, 1946; children—Faith Maureen, Shirley Marie, M.F. Timothy, Georgeanne, Michael Joseph. Student, U. Chgo., 1939-40, U. Miami, 1948-50, Nat. War Coll., 1962. Commd. 2d lt. USAAF, 1943; advanced through grades to lt. gen. USAF, 1975; leader heavy bomber air armada (8th Air Force), World War II, troop wing comdr. Far East, 1952-54; chief air traffic control USAF; also mem. tech. div. USAF (U.S. Air Coordinating Com.), 1954-55; mil. adviser Royal Danish Air Force; also chief air force MAAG, 1958-61; dep. dir. air force information 1955-58, 62-65; comdr. 60th Mil. Airlift Wing, Travis AFB, 1965-68; dir. transp. Hdqrs. USAF, 1968-73, J-4 dir. strategic mobility, 1977—, also dir. logistics; exec. v.p. Wayne A. Coloney Co. Inc., Tallahassee; pres. Howden Coloney, Inc. Schedule airline insp. CAA, 1947-50. Vice pres. McLean (Va.) Civic Assn., 1961-65; pres. St. John's Men's Council, 1962-65. Decorated D.S.M. (3), Legion of Merit (5), Bronze star, D.F.C. (3), Air medal (5); Croix de Guerre France; D.F.C. U.K.; Commendation of Honor Greece). Mem. S.E. Air Res. Assn. (v.p. 1950), Nat. Def. Transp. Assn. (pres.), Quiet Birdmen, Aviation Space Writers Assn., Greater Eastern Appaloosa Region (pres.), Nat. War Coll. Alumni (pres. 1977-79). Club: Lions. Home: Rt 2 5 Box 489-12 Marianna FL 32446 Office: Hdqrs USAF Washington DC 20333

CASEY, MICHAEL KIRKLAND, business executive, lawyer; b. Wheeling, W.Va., Jan. 24, 1940; s. Clyde Thomas and Joan Ferrell (McLure) C.; m. Mary Ann McCarten, Jan. 29, 1969; children—Michael Kirkland II, Mary Larkin, Colin McCarten. Student U. Notre Dame, 1957-58; B.S., W.Va. U., 1964; J.D., George Washington U., 1967. Bar: D.C. 1974, U.S. Dist. Ct. D.C., U.S. Ct. Appeals (D.C. cir.). Cons. to White House, Washington, 1977-81, handled overseas Presdl. missions in India, Western Europe, Brazil and Middle East; dir. White House Conf. on Small Bus., Washington, 1979-80; assoc. adminstr. for investment SBA, Washington, 1980-81; chmn. bd. MCW Internat. Ltd., Alexandria, Va., 1981—; nat. adminstr. fringe benefits program U.S. Conf. Mayors, 1984—. Advance man Kennedy for Pres. Com., 1968, spl. asst. Muskie for Pres. Com., 1972, asst. campaign mgr. Jackson for Pres. Com., 1976, campaign mgr. Carter-Mondale Reelection Com. in Mo. and Ill., 1980. Served with USMC, 1958-61, Mediterranean. Recipient Presdl. Cert., Pres. of U.S., 1977, 78, 79, plaque White House Commn. on Small Bus., 1980, Disting. Service award SBA, 1980. Mem. ABA, D.C. Bar Assn., Nat. Democratic Club, Nat. Conf. Democratic Mayors (founding). Roman Catholic. Club: Belle Haven Country (Alexandria). Home: 7105 Fort Hunt Rd Alexandria VA 22307 Office: MCW Internat Ltd 301 N Fairfax St Suite 110 Alexandria VA 22320

CASEY, MURRAY JOSEPH, physician, educator; b. Armour, S.D., May 1, 1936; s. Meryl Joseph and Gladice (Murray) C.; m. Virginia Anne Fletcher; children: Murray Joseph, Theresa Marie, Anne Franklin, Francix X., Peter Colum, Matthew Padraic. Student Chanute Jr. Coll., 1954-55, Rockhurst Coll., 1955-56; AB, U. Kans., 1958; MD, Georgetown U., 1962; postgrad. Suffolk U. Law Sch., 1963-64, Howard U., 1965, U. Conn., 1977; MS in Mgmt., Cardinal Stritch Coll., 1984; MBA Marquette U., 1983-88. Intern, USPHS Hosp.-Univ. Hosp., Balt., 1962-63; staff physician USPHS Hosp., Boston, 1963-64; staff asso. Lab Infectious Diseases, Nat. Inst. Allergy and Infectious Diseases, NIH, Bethesda, Md., 1964-66; virologist, resident physician Columbia-Presbyn. Med. Ctr., also Francis Delafield Hosp., N.Y.C., 1966-69; USPHS sr. clin. trainee, 1969-70; fellow gynecol. oncology, resident dept. surgery Meml. Hosp. Cancer and Allied Diseases, Meml. Sloan-Kettering Cancer Ctr., N.Y.C., 1969-71, Am. Cancer Soc. fellow, 1969-71; ofcl. observer in radiotherapy U. Tex. M.D. Anderson Hosp. and Tumor Inst., Houston, 1971; vis. scientist Radiumhemmet Karolinska Sjukhuset and Inst., Stockholm, 1971; asst. prof. ob-gyn U. Conn. Sch. Medicine, 1971-75, asso. prof., 1975-80, dir. gynecologic oncology, 1971-80, also mem. med. bd.; prof., asso. chmn. dept. ob-gyn U. Wis. Med. Sch., 1980—; chief ob-gyn Mt. Sinai Med. Ctr., Milw., 1980-82, dir. gynecologic oncology, 1980—, also mem. med. exec. com.; chmn. research adv. com., mem. council Conn. Cancer Epidemiology Unit; bd. dirs., mem. exec. com., chmn. profl. edn. com. Hartford unit. Am. Cancer Soc., dir. Wis. div., exec. com. 1985-87, v.p., 1985-86, pres.-elect, 1986-87, v.p. exec. com.. bd. dirs., chmn. profl. edn. com., 1987; mem. med. services 1980 Winter Olympic Games, Lake Placid, N.Y.; mem. med. supervisory team U.S. Nordic Ski Team. Diplomate Am. Bd. Med. Examiners, Am. Bd. Ob-Gyn. Fellow Am. Coll. Obstetricians and Gynecologists, ACS; mem. AAAS, Internat. Gynecol. Cancer Soc., Am. Coll. Sprts Medicine, N.Y. Acad. Scis., Am. Soc. Colposcopy, Am. Fertility Soc., Soc. Gynecologic Oncologists, New Eng. Assn. Gynecologic Oncologists (pres. 1980-81), Am. Radium Soc., Am. Soc. Clin. Oncology, Internat. Menopause Soc., Soc. Meml. Gynecologic Oncologists (exec. bd. 1979-84; pres. 1982-83), Lake Placid Sports Medicine Soc. (v.p. 1981-84, pres. 1984-86), Cedarburg C. of C. (Ambassadors com. 1983—, dir. 1983-85), St. George Soc. Contbr. articles to profl. jours., chpts. to books. Research in oncogenesis and tumor immunology. Office: PO Box 342 Dept Ob-Gyn U Wis Med Sch Milw Clin Campus Milwaukee WI 53201

CASEY, ROBERT P., governor of Pennsylvania; b. Jan. 9, 1932; m. Ellen Theresa Harding. BA cum laude, Holy Cross Coll.; JD, George Washington U. Gov. State of Pa., Harrisburg, 1987—. Office: Office of the Gov Main Capitol Bldg Rm 225 Harrisburg PA 17120 *

CASEY, WILLIAM ROSSITER, tool company and international transport executive; b. Los Angeles, June 15, 1922; s. William Rossiter and Clare (Gordon) C.; student Phillips Acad, Andover, Amherst Coll., 1940-42; B.S., U.S. Naval Acad., 1945; m. Carlyn Marie Temple, June 7, 1945; 1 son, Richard T. Successively treas., exec. v.p., pres. The Myers Group, Inc., Rouses Point, N.Y. and N.Y.C., 1953-76, chmn. bd., chief exec. officer, 1977—; mem. industry sector adv. com. U.S. Trade Rep. and Sec. of Commerce, 1981-88 . Bd. dirs. Champlain Valley Physicians Hosp., Plattsburgh, N.Y., 1966-71; trustee SUNY, Plattsburgh, 1970-72; mem. Thousand Island Park Commn., Alexandria Bay, N.Y., 1971-77. Served to lt. with USN, 1942-47. Mem. Nat. Customs Brokers and Forwarders Assn. Am. (pres. 1979-82, now chmn.), Customs Brokers Assn. No. U.S. Border (past pres.), Assn. Internat. Border Agys. (past Importers (dir. 1983—), Am. Assn. Exporters and Importers Inc. (bd. dirs. 1984—), Nat. Council Internat. Trade Documentation (bd. dirs. 1984—). Republican. Clubs: Downtown Athletic (N.Y.C.); Los Angeles Athletic. Contbr. articles to trade publs. Home: 310 Lake St Rouses Point NY 12979 Office: The Myers Group Inc Myers Bldg Rouses Point NY 12979 also: One World Trade Center New York NY 10048

CASH, FRANCIS WINFORD, hotel and restaurant executive; b. Buena Vista, Va., Mar. 16, 1942; s. Winsford McKinley and Elsie E. (Yates) C.; m. Judith R. Robey, Dec. 27, 1962; children: Jeri Cash Colton, Lori, Robin, David, Kristine. B.S. in Acctg, Brigham Young U., Provo, Utah, 1965. C.P.A., D.C. With Arthur Andersen & Co. (C.P.A.s), Washington, 1965-74; v.p., corp. controller Marriott Corp., Washington, 1974-79; sr. v.p. corp. services Marriott Corp., exec. v.p. Roy Rogers, 1980-84, group v.p. food service mgmt. and Courtyard, 1983, exec. v.p., 1984; exec. v.p. Host Internat. and Lifecare divs., 1984, all Marriott restaurants, 1986-88; pres. Marriott Service Group, 1988—; dir. Sailors and Mchts. Bank and Trust. Pres. Hayfield Elem. Sch. PTA, Fairfax, Va., 1973-74; chmn. Washington area Boy Scouts Am. show, 1978; bd. advisers Sch. Accountancy, Brigham Young U., 1978-84; mem. Presdl. Commn. on White House fellowships, 1985. Recipient Service award Boy Scouts Am., 1978, Beta Alpha Psi Outstanding Alumnus award Brigham Young U., 1984. Mem. Fin. Execs. Inst. Mormon. Office: Marriott Corp 1 Marriott Dr Washington DC 20058 also: 10400 Fernwood Rd Bethesda MD 20058

CASH, GERALD C., former governor-general Bahamas; b. Nassau, Bahamas, May 28, 1917; s. Wilfred Gladstone and Lillian Louise C.; m. Dorothy E. Long; children: Sharon, Gordon, Gerald Jr.; grad. Govt. High Sch., Nassau, Hon. Soc. Middle Temple, London. Called to Bahamas bar as counsel and atty. Supreme Ct. Bahamas, 1940; pvt. practice law, to 1945, from 1948; called to English bar as barrister-at-law, 1948; sr. rep. Western Dist. of New Providence, Hon. House of Assembly, Bahamas, from 1949, jr. rep., from 1956; mem. Her Majesty's Exec. Council, 1958-62; justice of peace Bahamas, 1940—; from mem. to pres. Senate of Bahamas, 1969-72; dep. to gov. gen. Bahamas, Nassau, 1973-76, acting gov. gen., 1976, gov. gen., 1979-88; former hon. vice consul Republic of Haiti. Mem. Bd. of Edn., Bahamas, 1950-62; chmn. Labour Bd., 1950-52; chmn. vis. com. Boys Indsl. Sch., 1952-62; chmn. bd. govs. Govt. High Sch., Nassau, 1949-63, 65-76; mem. Police Service Commn., 1964-69, Immigration Com., 1958-62, Rd. Traffic Com., 1958-62, Air Transport Licencing Authority, 1958-62; chmn. nat. com. United World Colls., 1977-81; vice chancellor Anglican Diocese of Bahamas and mem. diocesan council; treas. YMCA; chmn. exec. council Boy Scouts, Bahamas, v.p.; bd. dirs. Bahamas Assn. Mentally Retarded. Decorated Coronation medal, 1953, officer Order Brit. Empire, Silver Jubilee medal, 1977, knight comdr. Royal Victorian Order, 1977, knight grand cross Order St. Michael and St. George, 1980, Silver Medal of Olympic Order. Mem. Fla. Tennis Assn., Bahamas Lawn Tennis Assn. (pres.), Bahamas Table Tennis Assn. (pres.), Caribbean Lawn Tennis Assn. (v.p.), Bahamas Olympic Assn. (v.p.), Bahamas Swimming Assn. (v.p.), Bahamas Football Assn. (v.p.), Bahamas Cricket Assn. (treas.). Clubs: Gym Tennis (pres.), Rotary (pres.). Address: Govt House, PO Box 8301, Nassau The Bahamas *

CASH, PAUL THALBERT, physician; b. Lenox, Iowa, July 11, 1911; s. William Henry and Helen (Phalen) C.; m. Reva Lamb, Aug. 16, 1958; 1 stepchild, Peter Goodwin. Student, Creston Jr. Coll., 1929-31; M.D., U. Iowa, 1935. Diplomate: Am. Bd. Psychiatry and Neurology. Intern St. Vincents Hosp., Portland, Oreg., 1935-36; resident psychiatry Clarkson Meml. Hosp., Omaha, 1936-37, Albany (N.Y.) Hosp., 1937-38; vol. asst. internal medicine U. Iowa Hosps., Iowa City, 1938; resident neurology Neurol. Inst. N.Y., 1939; practice medicine specializing in psychiatry, neurology Omaha, 1940-48, Des Moines, 1948-82; instr. neurology, psychiatry U. Nebr. Coll. Medicine, 1946-48; chief service neurology and psychiatry Iowa Meth. Hosp., 1953-81; hon. staff Iowa Meth. Med. Ctr.; cons. VA Hosp. Contbr. articles to profl. jours. Served to maj. M.C. AUS, 1942-46. Fellow Am. Psychiat. Assn. (life), A.M.A.; mem. Central Neurophysciat. Assn., Iowa Neuropsychiat. Assn., Am. Acad. Neurology, Assn. for Research in Nervous and Mental Diseases, Am. EEG Soc. Home: 3315 Waco Ct Des Moines IA 50321

CASHEN, JOSEPH LAWRENCE, real estate broker; b. Kansas City, Mo., May 10, 1931; s. John Lawrence and Anna May (Sutcliffe) C.; m. Michele Ann Hayes, June 15, 1960; children: Michael, Patricia, Kelly. Student real estate U. Calif., Los Angeles, 1965-66. Sales cons. chems. Economics Lab., Los Angeles, 1954-64; broker Forest E. Olsen Realtors, Canoga Park, Calif., 1964-67; pres. Property World, Inc., Woodland Hills, Calif., 1967-71; pres. Century 21 Real Estate #1, Inc., Woodland Hills, 1971—; mem. Calif. State Senate Commn. on Franchises. Inventor in field. Pres. Police Activity League, Woodland Hills, 1975-80; dir., mem. adv. council Pierce Coll. Rotoract, 1974-75. Served with USMC, 1950-54. Mem. San Fernando Valley Bd. Realtors, Calif. Assn. Realtors, Nat. Assn. Realtors, Nat. Inst. Farm and Land Brokers, Nat. Assn. Home Builders, Aircraft Owners and Pilots Assn., Woodland Hills C. of C. (pres. 1976). Lodges: K.C., Rotary (pres. 1974-75). Office: 5959 Topanga Canyon Woodland Hills CA 91367

CASKEY, MIRIAM ERVIN, archaeologist; b. Phila., May 5, 1923; d. Spencer and Miriam Williams (Roberts) Ervin; m. John Langdon Caskey, June 24, 1967 (dec. Dec. 1981); 1 dau., Helen Clark. B.A., Bryn Mawr Coll. (Pa.), 1952, M.A., 1954, Ph.D., 1972; postgrad. Am. Sch. Classical Studies, Athens, 1955-56. Staff mem. Agora Excavations, Athens, 1956-58; tchr. Am. Community Schs., Athens, 1959-61; mem. faculty coll. yr., Athens, 1962-64, 75-76, 83; lectr. archaeology U. Cin., 1965-66; asst. to dir. Keos Excavations, Cin., 1968-81, research staff mem., 1964—. Co-author: Corpus der Minoffschen und Mykenischen Siegel, V, 1975; author: Keos II, 1. The Terracotta Statues, 1986; contbr. articles in field to profl. jours.; editor newsletter from Greece Am. Jour. Archaeology, 1967-81. Ella Riegel fellow, 1955-56. Mem. Hellenic Soc. London, Am. Inst. Archaeology, Am. Sch. Classical Studies. Office: Am Sch Classical Studies, 54 Souidias St, 10676 Athens Greece

CASO, ANTONIO DOMENICO, manufacturing company executive; b. Naples, Italy, July 16, 1950; m. Rita Ferrari; children: Matteo, Daniele. BBA, Genoa U., Italy, 1972. Product mgr. Johnson Wax, Milan, 1973-80; client dir. McCann Erickson, Milan, 1980-83; internat. market dir. Crinos Italy - Crinos USA, Como, Italy and U.S., 1984-86; gen. mgr. Serono OTC, Milan, 1986—; corp. gen. mgr. The Ares Serono Group, Geneva, 1987—. Served as sgt. cavallery Italian Army, 1970-71. Roman Catholic. Office: Serono OTC Spa, Piazzetta Bossi 3, I-20121 Milan Italy

CASON, DICK KENDALL, physician; b. Beaumont, Tex., June 27, 1922; s. Dick Kendall and Maurine (Mills) C.; B.A., Rice U., 1945; M.D., U. Tex., 1945; m. Maxine Skocdopole, Apr. 4, 1946; children—Dick Mills, Alma Christine. Intern, Kings County Hosp. Bklyn., 1945-46; med. resident Meth. Hosp., Dallas, 1948-49; gen. practice medicine, Hillsboro, Tex., 1949—; staff mem. Grant-Buie Hosp.; charter mem. Am. Bd. Family Practice. Pres. Hillsboro Indsl. Devel. Found., 1955-60, 79—; past mem. regional adv. com. Dallas Civic Opera Co., Served from 1st lt. to capt., AUS, 1946-48. Fellow Royal Soc. Health (Eng.); mem. Hill County Med. Soc. (pres. 1951), Tex. Med. Assn. (alt. del. to AMA 1980-84, del. 1984—), Am. Acad. Gen. Practice, N.Y. Acad. Sci.,Internat. Horn Soc., C. of C., Hill County Soc. Crippled Children, Royal Soc. Medicine (affiliate). Presbyterian (elder). Clubs: Hillsboro Country, Rotary (pres. Hillsboro 1955). Contbr. articles to profl. jours. Home: 1303 Park Dr Hillsboro TX 76645 Office: 150 Circle Dr Hillsboro TX 76645

CASORIA, GIUSEPPE CARDINAL, Italian ecclesiastic; b. Acerra, Italy, Oct. 1, 1908. Ordained priest Roman Catholic Ch., 1930; jurist, ofcl. Roman Curia, 1937—; under-sec. Congregation for Sacraments, 1959-69, sec., 1969-73, pro-prefect, 1981-83, prefect, 1983; consecrated titular archbishop of Vescovia, 1972; elevated to Sacred Coll. of Cardinals, 1983; deacon St. Joseph of Via Trionfale. Mem. Congregation for Doctrine of Faith, Congregation for Causes of Saints, Commn. for Interpretation of Canonical Directives. Correggere e confrontare con l'annesso foglio aggiornato. Address: Via Pancrazio Pfeiffer 10, Rome Italy

CASPARD, JEAN FRANÇOIS, obstetrician, gynecologist; b. Chambery, Savoy, France, Oct. 13, 1947; s. Paul and Marie (Meyer) C.; m. Barbara Friedrich, Oct. 17, 1964; children: Virginie, Dorothee. MD, U. Nancy, France, 1971. Practice medicine specializing in ob-gyn. Metz, France, 1971—. Mem. Nat. Soc. French Gynecologists and Obstetricians, Nat. Soc. Ultrasound Applications. Club: Lyons (pres. 1984-85). Office: 8 Rue Chatillon, 57000 Metz France

CASPARI, FRITZ, retired foreign service officer, educator; b. Baden, Switzerland, Mar. 21, 1914; s. Eduard and Elli (Klussmann) C.; m. Elita Galdós Walker, Feb. 3, 1944; children—Hans Michael (dec.), Conrad, Elisabeth, Andrea. Student Heidelberg U., 1932-33; Diploma in Econs. and Polit. Sci., Oxford U., 1934, MLitt, 1936; PhD, Hamburg U., 1939. Instr. Southwestern U., Memphis, Tenn., 1936-37, Scripps Coll., Claremont, Calif., 1939-42; reference librarian Newberry Library, Chgo., 1943-46; asst. prof. U. Chgo., 1946-54; hon. prof. English intellectual history U. Cologne, Fed. Republic of Germany, 1954—; with German Fgn. Service, 1954-69, 74-79, counselor Embassy, London, 1958-63, counselor, minister Mission to UN, N.Y.C., 1963-68, ambassador, Lisbon, Portugal, 1974-79; dep. chief, dir. Fed. Pres.'s Office, Bonn, 1969-74; hon. fellow St. John's Coll., Oxford U., 1972—. Author: Humanism and the Social Order in Tudor England, 1954; contbr. articles to profl. jours. Decorated Grand Cross of Merit, Fed. Republic of Germany; knight grand cross Order of Christ, Portugal; knight comdr. Royal Victorian Order, U.K., others; Rhodes scholar, 1933-36. Mem. Renaissance Soc. Am., German Fgn. Policy Assn., others. Clubs: Gremio Literario (Lisbon); Boodle's (London); American Embassy (Bonn.); Swiss Alpine Home: Casa das Nogueiras, Malveira da Serra, 2750 Cascais Portugal

CASPERSEN, BARBARA MORRIS, food company executive; b. Phila., Feb. 27, 1945; d. Samuel Wheeler and Eleanor May (Jones) Morris; B.A., Wellesley Coll., 1967, M.A., Drew U., 1983, M.P.H., 1986; m. Finn M.W. Caspersen, June 17, 1967. Treas., dir. Westby Corp., Wilmington, Del., 1971—, Westby Mgmt. Inc., Andover, N.J., 1967—, Tri-Farms, Inc., Andover, 1967—; pres., dir. Clark Hill Sugary Inc., Canaan, N.H., 1971-86. Bd. dirs. v.p. O.W. Caspersen Found., 1967—; trustee Hoosac Sch., 1968-76, Shipley Sch., 1980-84, Peck Sch., 1981—; bd. dirs. Drew U., 1984—, Groton Sch., 1984—, Gladstone Equestrian Assn.; trustee Hilltop Sch., 1974-83, pres., 1976-80, prin., 1980-81. Mem. English-Speaking Union U.S. (dir. 1972-73, dir. N.Y. chpt. 1970-75). Episcopalian. Club: Colony (N.Y.C.). Office: Westby Corp PO Box 800 Andover NJ 07821

CASPERSEN, FINN MICHAEL WESTBY, financial company executive; b. N.Y.C., Oct. 27, 1941; s. Olaus Westby and Freda Caspersen; m. Barbara Caspersen, June 17, 1967. B.A. With honors in Econs., Brown U., 1963; LL.B. cum laude, Harvard U., 1966; LL.D., Hood Coll.; H.H.D., Washington Coll., Chestertown, Md. Bar: Fla. 1966, N.Y. 1967. Assoc. Dewey, Ballantine, Bushby, Palmer & Wood, N.Y.C., 1969-72; assoc. counsel Beneficial Mgmt. Corp., Wilmington, Del, 1972-75; v.p., dir., mem. exec. com. Beneficial Corp., 1975, vice chmn., mem. exec., fin. coms., 1975, chmn. bd., chief exec. officer, mem. exec. com., 1976—; bd. dirs., mem. exec. com. Beneficial Nat. Bank; chmn., bd. dirs. Beneficial Trust Co. Ltd.; bd. dirs. Beneficial Found., Inc. Wilmington, Westby Corp., Westby Mgmt. Corp., Harbour Island, Inc.; bd. dirs., pres. Tri-Farms Inc.; chmn. 35th Ann. N.J. Bus. Conf., Rutgers U. Grad. Sch. Mgmt. and Sales Execs. Club N.J., 1983; mem. adv. bd. Nat. Ctr. Fin. Services, U. Calif., Earl Warren Inst., Inferential Focus, N.Y.C.; bd. advisors Inst. Law and Econs. U. Pa., John M. Olin speaker. Former trustee N.J. Coll. Fund Assn.; emeritus trustee Brown U.; trustee Camp Nejeda Found. for Diabetic Children, N.J. State Police Meml. Library & Mus. Assn.; mem. nominating com. Morristown Meml. Hosp.; past trustee Com. Econ. Devel.; mem. bd. govs. Winterthur Mus. Corp. Council; former mem. N.J. Bd. Higher Edn.; bd. dirs. Shelter Harbor Fire Dist.; bd. dirs., v.p. O.W. Caspersen Found.; chmn. bd. trustees, mem. exec. com. Peddie Sch., Hightstown, N.J.; past chmn. bd. Drumthwacket Found.; chmn. Waterloo Found. for Arts. Inc.; charter mem. Ptnrship for N.J., New Brunswick; trustee James S. Brady Presdl. Found., The Savings Forum; pres. Coalition of Service Industries,Inc., Washington; chmn. bd. trustees Gladstone Equestrian Assn. Inc.; mem. adv. com. to exec. bd. Morris-Sussex Area Council Boy Scouts Am.; mem. driving com. Am. Horse Shows Inc.; mem. corp. Cardigan Mountain Sch.; mem. bd. advisors Inst. for Law and Econs. U. Pa. Served to lt. USCG, 1966-69. Recipient President's medal Johns Hopkins U.; named Civic Leader of Yr. YMCA, 1982. Mem. Am. Fin. Services Assn. (trustee, chmn. govt. affairs com., chmn. membership com., adminstrn. com., vice chmn.), ABA, Fla. Bar Assn., N.Y. Bar Assn., Conf. Bd. (reg.), Harbour Island Inc. (chmn.). Clubs: Harvard; Knickerbocker (N.Y.C.); Univ. (Sarasota and Tampa, Fla.); Wilmington (Del.). Office: Beneficial Corp 1100 Carr Rd Wilmington DE 19899

CASS, ROBERT MICHAEL, lawyer, consultant; b. Carlisle, Pa., July 5, 1945; s. Robert Lau and Norma Jean (McCaleb) C.; BA, Pa. State U., 1967; JD, Temple U., 1971; m. Patricia Ann Garber, Aug. 12, 1967; children: Charles McCaleb, David Lau. Benefit examiner Social Security Adminstrn., Phila., 1967-68; mktg. rep. Employers Comml. Union Ins. Co., Phila., 1968-70; asst. sec. Nat. Reins. Corp., N.Y.C., 1970-77; admitted to N.Y. bar, 1974; asst. v.p. Skandia Am. Reins. Corp., N.Y.C., 1977-80; mgr. Allstate Reins. div., South Barrington, Ill., 1980-86; mgr. R.K. Carvill, Inc., Chgo., 1986-87; pres. R. M. Cass Assocs., Barrington, Ill., 1987—; lectr. Ins. Sch. Chgo. Mem. Am. Bar Assn. (com. on internat. ins. law, self ins. and risk mgrs., ins. law, excess, surplus lines and reins. law, vice chmn., newsletter editor), N.Y. State Bar Assn., Soc. CPCU's, Soc. Ins. Research. Home: 325 Old Mill Rd Barrington IL 60010 Office: PO Box 1362 Barrington IL 60011

CASSAK, ALBERT LOEB, publishing company executive; b. N.Y.C., Sept. 12, 1917; s. Michael and Lena (Pincus) C.; BS, NYU, 1940, MBA, 1953; m. Dorothy Mildred Reinke, Feb. 28, 1943; children—Laurie Nan, David James, Lance Douglas. Account exec. Ernest W. Greenfield Advt., Phila., 1946-47; salesman Surg. Bus. Mag., N.Y.C., 1947-53, v.p., 1953-68; pres. Cassak Publs., Inc., Springfield, N.J., 1968—; pub. Health Industry Today, J. B. Lippincott publ. div. Harper& Row, N.Y.C., 1985—; industry tech. rep. U.S. Med. Equipment Catalog Exhbn., Johannesburg and Capetown, South Africa, 1976, India, 1979, Zurich, 1982; co-sponsor Am. pavilion IFAS, 1984-86, 88, Zurich, with Am. Embassy, Bern.; industry tech. rep. Dept. Commerce, Australia and N.Z., 1985. Served to maj. U.S. Army, 1941-46. Health Industry Mfrs. Assn., Pharm. Advt. Club, Smithsonian

Assocs., Nat. Hist. Soc. Jewish. Lodge: Masons. Avocations: stamp and coin collection, woodworking. Home: 16 Notch Hill Dr Livingston NJ 07039 Office: Health Industry Today 454 Morris Ave Springfield NJ 07081

CASSEL, JOHN ELDEN, accountant; b. Verden, Okla., Apr. 24, 1934; s. Elbert Emry and Erma Ruth (McDowell) C.; m. Mary Lou Malcom, June 3, 1953; children—John Elden, James Edward, Jerald Eugene. Plant mgr., also asst. gen. mgr. Baker and Taylor Co., Oklahoma City, 1966-71; paymaster, office mgr. Robberson Steel Co., Oklahoma City, 1971-76; pvt. investor, 1976—. Democrat. Methodist. Home: 2332 NW 118th St Oklahoma City OK 73120

CASSERLY, ALVARO ALONSO, utility company executive; b. Ocho Rios, Jamaica, June 4, 1932; s. Patrick Owen and Rachael (Smith) C.; m. Jean Allison Mair, Jan. 28, 1961; children: Marie, Bruce, Patrick, Robert. Student in edn., Excelsior Coll., Kingston, 1947-51; student, U. Colo., 1969, U. Mich., 1975, IMI, Geneva, 1981. Exec. sec. Electricity Frequency Standardization Commn., Kingston, 1957-63; sec., mgr. Electricity Authority, Kingston, 1963-67; sec. Pub. Utility Commn., Kingston, 1967-70; asst. to pres. Jamaica Pub. Service Co. Ltd., Kingston, 1970-72, treas., 1972-78, dir. fin., 1978—; chmn. Bd. Electricians Examiners, 1968-70, Jamaica United Trust Services, 1978—, chmn. bd. dirs. Pres., UN Assn., Jamaica, 1964-69; chmn. Jamaica Council for Handicapped, 1973-76, Council of Voluntary Social Services, 1971-73. Mem. World Fedn. U.N. Assns. (v.p. 1966-69). Club: Constant Spring Golf, Jamaica. Lodges: Collegium Fabrorum (past master), Rotary (dist. gov. 1989—). Home: 5 Paddington Terr, Kingston 6 Jamaica Office: Jamaica Pub Service Co Ltd, 6 Knutsford Blvd, Kingston 10 Jamaica

CASSIDY, JACK, educator; b. Phila., Mar. 12, 1941; B.A. in English, Gettysburg Coll., Phila., 1962; M.Ed. in Secondary Edn., Temple U., Phila., 1965, Ph.D. in Ednl. Psychology, 1975; married; 2 children. Tchr., Hawaii Dept. Public Instrn., Island Kauai, Lihue, 1965-69; instr. Temple U., 1970-71; reading supr. Newark (Del.) Sch. Dist., 1972-78; asso. prof. reading and gifted edn. Millersville (Pa.) U. 1978-81, prof., 1981—; spl. cons. Ednl. Testing Service, 1977—. Coach Community Swim Teams, Kapaa, Hawaii, 1967-68. Mem. Internat. Reading Assn. (mem. legis. com. 1975-76, dir. 1976-79, pres. 1982-83), Diamond State Reading Assn. (pres. 1974-75), Nat. Council Tchrs. English, Council Exceptional Children, Assn. Gifted, Nat. Assn. Gifted, Nat. Council Accreditation Tchr. Edn. (exec. bd. 1986—, chmn. 1988—), Phi Delta Kappa. Sr. author: Basic Life Skills Read-Reason-Write, Scribner Ednl. Pubs. Reading Series; contbr. articles to profl. jours. Home: PO Box 55 Kemblesville PA 19347 Office: Millersville U Millersville PA 17551

CASSIDY, JAMES JOSEPH, public relations counsel; b. Norwood, Ohio, Dec. 31, 1916; s. Martin D. and Helen (Johnston) C.; m. Rita Hackett, Oct. 18, 1941; children: Claudia, James. Student, U. Cin., 1934-38. Dir. spl. events, internat. broadcasts Crosley Broadcasting Corp., 1939-44, war corr., 1944-45, dir. pub. relations, 1946-50; war corr. NBC, 1944-45; account exec. Hill & Knowlton, Inc., N.Y.C., 1950-53; v.p. Hill & Knowlton, Inc., 1953-61, sr. v.p., 1961-66, exec. v.p., 1966-71, pres., chief operating officer, 1971-74, vice chmn., 1974-75; vice chmn. Burson-Marsteller, Washington, 1975-81. Trustee Cabrini Health Care Center and Columbus Hosp., N.Y.C. Recipient Variety award 1944; citation for reporting in combat areas Sec. War, 1945. Mem. Pub. Relations Soc. Am. (past pres. N.Y. chpt.), Aviation Writers Assn., Ohio Soc., Internat. Assn. Bus. Communicators, Profit Sharing Council Am. (past chmn. bd.). Clubs: George Town, 1925 F St, Nat. Press, Sky, Overseas Press; International (Washington). Home: 826 Heritage Village Southbury CT 06488

CASSIDY, RICHARD ARTHUR, environmental engineer, governmental water resources specialist; b. Manchester, N.H., Nov. 15, 1944; s. Arthur Joseph and Alice Ethuliette (Gregoire) C.; m. Judith Diane Maine, Aug. 14, 1971; children—Matthew, Amanda, Michael. B.A., St. Anselm Coll., 1966; M.S., U. N.H., 1969, Tufts U., 1972. Field biologist Pub. Service Co. of N.H., Manchester, 1968; jr. san. engr. Mass. Div. Water Pollution Control, Boston, 1968-69; aquatic biologist Normandeau Assocs., Bedford, N.H., 1969-70; hydraulic engr. New Eng. div. U.S. Army C.E., Waltham, Mass., 1972-77, environ. engr., Portland Dist., Oreg., 1977-81, supr. environ. engring., 1981—. Contbr. articles to profl. jours. Den leader Pack 164 Columbia Pacific council Cub Scouts Am., Beaverton, Oreg., 1982-83, Webelos leader, 1984-85, troop 764 committeeman, 1985-87, Columbia Pacific council Boy Scouts Am., 1985-87; mem. Planning Commn. Hudson, N.H., 1976-77. Recipient commendation for exemplary performance Mo.-Miss. flood, 1973, commendation for litigation defense, 1986, commendation for mgmt. activities, 1987. Mem. Am. Inst. Hydrology (cert., profl. ethics com. 1986, v.p. Oreg. chpt. 1987), Am. Soc. Limnology and Oceanography. Democrat. Roman Catholic. Home: 7655 SW Belmont Dr Beaverton OR 97005 Office: Portland Dist COE Chief Reservoir Reg & Water Quality Sect PO Box 2946 Portland OR 82946

CASSIGNOL, PIERRE BRICE, plastic surgeon; b. Villemeuve-Corbieres, France, May 1, 1940; s. Jean and Gisele (Hermitte) C.; m. Anne Marie Franceschi, 1962 (div. 1976); children: Jean-Phillipe, Marie Pierre, Cecile; m. Marie-France Delporto, Feb. 1982; 1 child, Arnaud. MD, Faculte Medecine, Toulouse, France, 1964; postgrad., Ednl. Council Fgn. Med. Grads., 1969. Med. diplomate, cert. plastic surgeon. Resident Toulouse U. Hosp., 1963-69, chief resident, 1969-71, attending plastic surgeon, 1972-75; fellow, instr. plastic surgery NYU Inst. Reconstructive and Plastic Surgery, N.Y.C., 1971-72; practice medicine specializing in plastic surgery Toulouse, 1973—. Contbr. articles to med. jours. Served as capt. French Med. Corps. Fellow Inst. Plastic and Reconstructive Surgery; mem. Converse's Soc., French Soc. Aesthetic Surgery. Roman Catholic. Address: 8 Allee Paul Sabatier, Toulouse 31000, France

CASSIMATIS, EMANUEL ANDREW, county court judge; b. Pottsville, Pa., Dec. 2, 1926; s. Andrew Emanuel and Mary H. (Calopedis) C.; m. Thecla Karambelas, June 2, 1952; children—Mary Ann Maza, John E., Gregory E. B.A., Dickinson Coll., 1949, LL.B., 1951. Bar: Pa. 1951. Sole practice law, York, Pa., 1951-53, 55-57; assoc. Kain, Kain & Kain, York, Pa., 1953-55; ptnr. Stock & Leader, York, 1957-78; judge Ct. Common Pleas, York, Pa., 1978—; solicitor Springettsbury Twp., York, Pa., 1960-66, Sewer Authority, 1965-66; solicitor Wrightsville Borough, Pa., 1966-71, Municipal Authority, 1968-78, York Suburban Sch. Dist., 1970-77; faculty Pa. Coll. Judiciary, 1981, 82, 83; 1st v.p. Pa. Conf. State Trial Judges, 1987—. Pres. United Way of York County, 1964-65; co-chmn. steering com. York Community Audit for Human Rights, 1959; pres. Children's Growth and Devel. Clinic, 1974; trustee Meml. Osteopathic Hosp., 1963-80; bd. dirs. Capital Blue Cross, Harrisburg, Pa., 1970-79, Historic York, 1977-82. Served with U.S. Army, 1945-46. Named Young Man of Yr., York Jr. C. of C., 1960; Vol. of Yr., Pilot Club, 1965; Mem. Hall of Fame, William Penn Sr. High Sch., York, 1981. Mem. Pa. Conf. State Trial Judges (chmn. spl. projects com. 1980-82, ann. meeting com. 1984-85, pres. elect Juvenile Ct. sect. 1987—. Republican. Greek Orthodox. Lodges: Masons (hon. mem. supreme council), K.T., Tall Cedars of Lebanon, Shriners, Royal Order Jesters. Home: 176 Rathton Rd York PA 17403

CASSIN, WILLIAM BOURKE, lawyer; b. Mexico City, Sept. 11, 1931; s. William Michael and Elouise (Hall) C.; m. Kristi Shipnes, July 15, 1961; children: Clay Brian, Michael Bourke, Macy Armstrong. A.B., Princeton U., 1953; J.D., U. Tex., 1959. Bar: Tex. 1959. Law clk. Judge Warren L. Jones, Fifth Circuit U.S., 1959-60; atty. Baker & Botts, Houston, 1960-70; v.p., gen. atty. United Gas Pipe Line Co., Houston, 1970-73; sr. v.p., gen. atty. United Gas Pipe Line Co., 1973, group v.p., gen. counsel, dir., mem. exec. com., 1974-76; exec. v.p., gen. counsel, mem. exec. com. United Energy Resources, Inc., Houston, 1976-84, dir., 1976-86; of counsel Mayer, Brown & Platt, Houston, 1985-87; chmn., pres., chief exec. officer D2 Software, Inc., 1984—; gen. counsel Houston Grand Opera Assn., 1961-70, mem. governing council, 1977—, also bd. dirs.; adj. prof. U. Houston, 1988. Contbr. articles to profl. jours.; editor-in-chief Tex. Law Rev, 1959. Gen. counsel Harris County Republican Exec. Com., 1963-64, 67-68; exec. vp. Tex. Bill Rights Found., 1967-68; mem. exec. com. Associated Reps. of Tex., 1976—, Landmark Legal Found., 1985—, Armand Bayou Nature Ctr., 1986—; mem. Pub. Utility Commn. Tex., 1988—; bd. dirs. Houston Ballet Found., Legal Found. Am.; trustee Tex. Mil. Inst., Atwill Meml. Chapel; mem. vestry Christ Ch. Cathedral, 1970-72, 80-82, lay reader. Served to lt. Airborne Arty. AUS, 1953-57; capt. Res. ret. Fellow Tex. Bar Found. (life); mem. Am., Tex., Houston, Fed. Energy, Fed. bar assns., Order of Coif, Phi Delta Phi. Republican. Episcopalian. Clubs: Houston Country, Houston Met. Racquet, Bayou, Ramada, Allegro, Garwood Hunting; Argyle (San Antonio); Army and Navy (Washington); Northport Point (Mich.); Princeton (N.Y.C.); Princeton Terrace. Home: 1 S Wynden Dr Houston TX 77056 Office: Pub Utility Commn Tex 7800 Shoal Creek Blvd Suite 400 Austin TX 78757

CASSON, RICHARD FREDERICK, travel bureau executive; b. Boston, Apr. 11, 1939; s. Louis H. and Beatrix S. C. A.B., Colby Coll., 1960; J.D., U. Chgo., 1963. Bar: Ill. 1963, Mass. 1964. Ptnr., Casson & Casson, Boston, 1967-68; assoc. counsel, corporate sec. Bankers Leasing Corp., 1968-75; asst. gen. counsel, corporate sec. Commonwealth Planning Corp., 1975-76; assoc. gen. counsel, asst. sec. Pru Capital, Inc., 1976—; ptnr. Cities of Sea Cruise Cen., Travel Agency . Bd. dirs. Children's Speech and Hearing Found., Temple Ahavath Achim, Gloucester, Mass. Served to capt. JAGC U.S. Army, 1964-67. Decorated Bronze Star. Jewish. Club: B'nai B'rith (Gloucester) (v.p.). Address: Off Lowe Dr Magnolia MA 01930

CASTANO, ELVIRA PALMERIO, art historian, gallery director; b. Cin., July 23, 1929; d. John and Josephine Castano; BLI, Emerson Coll., Boston, 1950; postgrad. (Cardinal Spellman scholar), Pius XII Inst., Florence, Italy, 1954-55; m. Carlo Palmerio (dec.), June 1, 1958; 1 dau., Marina. Curator, Castano Art Gallery, Boston, 1965-78; dir. Castano Art Gallery, Needham, Mass., 1978—; Vatican translator; interpreter Italian art, specialist in Macchiaioli art; Italian lang. translator. Mem. Dante Alighieri Soc., Boston, Boston Mus. Fine Arts, Brockton (Mass.) Art Mus. (adv. bd.), Fogg Art Mus. of Harvard U., Friends of Needham Library, Needham Historical Soc. Roman Catholic. Address: 245 Hunnewell St Needham MA 02194

CASTE, JEAN F., financial executive; b. Paris, Mar. 19, 1929; came to U.S., 1971; s. Gaston A. and Valentine M. (Gellie) C.; m. Danielle Y. Feron, Dec. 5, 1953; children: Françoise, Philippe, Nathalie. Diploma, Ecole des Hautes Etudes Commerciales, Paris, 1951; Licence en Droit, U. Paris, 1952. Dir. market research, gen. mgr. Nestlé Group, SOPAD, Paris, 1954-63; dir. mktg. and acquisitions, dir. fin., dir. planning and control L'Oreal, Paris, 1963-71; pres., chief exec. officer Cosmair, Inc., N.Y.C., 1971-80; chmn., pres. The Nestlé Co., Inc., White Plains, N.Y., 1981-83; dir. gen. Nestlé, S.A., Vevey, Switzerland, 1983-85; chmn. Nestlé Enterprises, Inc., N.Y.C., 1983-85, Nestlé Enterprises, Ltd., Can., 1983-85; chmn., chief exec. officer Citicorp Corp. Adv. Services, Lausanne, Switzerland, 1986—. Served as lt. French Army, 1951-52. Decorated chevalier de la Légion d'Honneur and de l'Ordre National du Mérite. Mem. Cercle Interallié (Paris), France-Am. Soc. Club: Paris-Am. (N.Y.C.). Office: Citicorp Corp Adv Services, 22 ave Mon Repos, 1002 Lausanne Switzerland

CASTEL, GÉRARD JOSEPH, physician; b. Gardanne, France, Nov. 16, 1934; s. Roger Alphonse and Marguerite Henriette (Bossy) C.; m. Maryse Tartaise (div. 1965); 1 child, Gilles; m. Charlotte Elisabeth Gaglio; 1 child, David. MD, U. Marseille, France, 1961; D of History, U. Aix en Provence, France, 1978. Extern, then resident Conception Hosp., Marseille, 1956-57, Timone Hosp., Marseille, 1957-58, Salvator Hosp., Marseille, 1958-59, Sainte-Marguerite Hosp., Marseille, 1959-60; gen. practice medicine Rognac, France, 1961—; historian, conferenceer history Faculty Letters, Aix en Provence, 1978—, associated researcher, 1988; physician French Soc. Rys., 1966—; instr. physician French Red Cross, 1966—. Author: Contribution a l'Etude Historique de Rognac, 1969, Rognac Depuis 3000 Ans, 1976, Raymond des Baux, Premier Seigneur de Berre, 1983, Histoire de la Paroisse de Rognac du XIo au XXo siècle, 1984, Histoire de Berre, Vol. 1, 1985, Histoire de la Grande-Bastide de Rognac, 1986, Histoire de Berre, Vol. 2, 1987, Dictionnaire Archeologique de la Commune de Rognac, 1987, Musical Memories, 1987; contbr. articles to profl. jours.; composer romantic piano works, also several records by internat. pianists. Recipient French League Instrn. medal, 1978. Mem. History Soc. Rognac (chmn. 1965—), Sci. and Culture Assn. Berre, Authors, Composers and Editors Music, Chopin Soc. Paris. Office: 4 Rue Lamartine, 13340 Rognac France

CASTELA, JEAN DENIS, rheumatologist; b. Marseilles, France, June 16, 1955; s. René and Marie-Françoise (Festa) C.; m. Nicole Aubet, July 17, 1982; children: Emeline, Solene. M of Human Biology, Med. Univ. Marseilles, 1982; MD, Med. Univ. Nice, France, 1983. Interne Univ. Hosp., Nice, 1980-84, resident in rheumatology, 1984—; practice rheumatology Nice, 1984—. Contbr. articles to profl. jours. Served to capt. Med. Corps., French Army Reserve, 1983—. Mem. French Soc. Hemapheres, French Nat. Soc. Internal Medicine. Roman Catholic. Office: 11 Rue de la Liberte, 06000 Nice France

CASTELAIN, PIERRE-YVES, dermatologist; b. Raismes, France, Feb. 23, 1927; s. Michel Auguste and Laure (Freville) C.; m. Agnes Marie Gueit, July 17, 1951; children: Genevieve, Marie-Helene, Michel. MD, Med. U., Marseille, 1951, MS, 1952. Practice medicine specializing in dermatology Marseille, 1953—; cons. dermatologist Hotel Dieu Hosp., Marseille, 1953-73, Michel Levy Hosp., Marseille, 1973-86, St. Marguerite Hosp., 1987—; lectr. Med. U. Marseille, 1977—. Contbr. articles to profl. jours. Served to capt. French Army, 1954-55. Mem. European Acad. Dermatology and Clin. Immunology, European Contact Dermatitis Soc., Soc. Française d'Allergie, Soc. Française de Dermatologie et Syphiligraphie, Groupe d'Etudes et de Recherches en Dermato-Allergie (pres. 1983-86). Roman Catholic. Lodge: Rotary (pres. 1984-85). Home and Office: 13 Avenue de Montredon, 13008 Marseille France

CASTELE, THEODORE JOHN, radiologist; b. New Castle, Pa., Feb. 1, 1928; s. Theodore Robert and Anne Mercedes (McNavish) C.; m. Jean Marie Willse, Oct. 20, 1951; children: Robert, Ann Marie, Richard, Mary Kathryn, Thomas, Daniel, John. BS, Case Western Res. U., 1951, MD, 1957. Diplomate Am. Bd. Radiology, 1962. Intern then resident U. Hosps. Cleve., 1957-61, fellow, 1961-62; dir. of radiology Luth. Med. Ctr., Cleve., 1968-75, 77—; chief of staff Luth. Med. Ctr., 1975-81; pres. Med. Ctr. Radiologists, Inc., Cleve., 1978—; med. editor sta. WEWS-TV, Cleve., 1975—; chmn. bd. Med. Cons. Imaging Co., Cleve., 1981—; asst. clin. prof. radiology Case Western Res. U. Chmn. Southwestern dist. Greater Cleve. Council Boy Scouts Am., 1969, 73; mem. bd. med. cons. Cleve. Police Dept.; trustee Community Dialysis Ctr., Cleve. Health Edn. Mus., Luth. Med. Ctr. Found., chmn. bd. trustees 1969-75, Case Western Res. U., Blue Cross/Blue Shield Ohio, Greater Cleve. Hosp. Assn., Health Cleve., Luth. Med. Ctr., Fairview Hosp. Found., No. Ohio Lung Assn. Served with USN, 1946-47. Recipient Order of Merit award Boy Scouts Am. 1971, Silver Beaver award 1972, Nat. Disting. Eagle Scout award, 1984. Fellow Am. Coll. Radiology; mem. AMA (Physician Speaker Gold award 1978, 80, Silver 1979, Bronze 1978, chmn. Ohio del. 1987—), Ohio State Med. Assn. (5th dist. councilor, 1977-79, Spl. award 1979), Cleve. Radiol. Soc. (pres. 1969-70), Case Western Res. U. Med. Alumni Assn. (pres. 1971-72), Cleve. Acad. Medicine (pres. 1974-75). Home: 18869 Canyon Rd Fairview Park OH 44126 Office: Luth Med Ctr 2609 Franklin Ave Cleveland OH 44113

CASTELO, CARLOS ALBERTO MONTEIRO, journalist; b. Gouveia, Portugal, June 6, 1943; came to Belgium, 1959; s. Manuel Castelo and Maria Monteiro; m. Nelly Van Noorick, Aug. 23, 1969; children—Teresa, Bruno. Lic. Economy, U. Louvain, Belgium, 1970; Baccalaureat in Philosophy, 1961. Editor L'Echo des Bois, Brussels, 1969—, dir., 1974—.Mem. Union Internat. de Physique Pure et Appliquee, Internat. Assn. of the Furniture Trade Press. Office: L'Echo des Bois Rue De l'Abattoir 29,, B-1000 Brussels Belgium

CASTENSCHIOLD, RENE, engineering company executive; b. Mt. Kisco, N.Y., Feb. 7, 1923; s. Tage and Juno (Hagemeister) C.; m. Martha Naomi Stinson, Dec. 14, 1947; children—Gail F., Frederick T., Lynn Castenschiold Jones. BEE, Pratt Inst., 1944. Registered profl. engr. N.Y., N.J.; registered profl. planner, N.J. Test engr. (Manhattan Project) Gen. Electric Co., Schenectady, N.Y., 1944-45, design engr., 1946-47; sr. product engr. Am. Transformer Co., Newark, 1947-50; design engr. Automatic Switch Co., Florham Park, N.J., 1951-57, chief customer engr., 1957-74, exec. engring. mgr., 1974-85; pres. LCR Cons. Engrs. P.A., Green Village, N.J., 1986—; lectr. N.J. Inst. Tech., Newark, 1967-79; adviser Underwriter Labs. Inc., Melville, N.Y., 1973-85; chmn. U.S. Tech. Adv. Group and U.S. del. Internat. Electrotech. Commn., Geneva, 1981—. Contbr. chpts. to books, articles to profl. jours.; 9 patents in transfomer design, relays and controls. Chmn. Bd. of Adjustment, Harding Twp., 1975-77, chmn. Planning Bd., 1982-85, dir. Civil Def., 1966-70; trustee Wash. Assn. of N.J., Morristown, 1984—, sec., 1985-88. Named to disting. alumni bd. visitors Pratt Inst., 1979; recipient The James H. McGraw award, 1986. Fellow IEEE (standards bd. 1983-85, recipient IEEE Achievement award, 1988), Instrument Soc. Am., Nat. Soc. Profl. Engrs., Nat. Elec. Mfrs. Assn. (chmn. automatic transfer switch com. 1982-88), Internat. Assn. Elec. Insps., Nat. Acad. Forensic Scientists, Am. Cons. Engrs. Council, Nat. Fire Protection Assn., N.J. Christmas Tree Growers' Assn., Can. Standards Assn. Republican. Episcopalian. Clubs: Skytop (Pa.); Morristown (N.J.). Home: Lee's Hill Rd New Vernon NJ 07976 Office: LCR Cons Engrs PA PO Box 2 Green Village NJ 07935

CASTER, BERNARD HARRY, artist; b. Wolcott, N.Y., May 27, 1921; s. Edward Everett and Effie Armenia (Reed) C.; A.A., Syracuse U., 1956, B.A., 1960; m. Katherine Jane Capron, Nov. 29, 1941; children—Carol Sue (Mrs. Karl Schantz III), Cyril Everett, Allan David. One-man shows at Galerie Paula Insel, N.Y.C., Univ. Coll. Syracuse (N.Y.) U., Edinborough (Pa.) State Tchrs. Coll.; exhibited in group shows at Syracuse Mus. Fine Arts, Rochester (N.Y.) Meml. Art Gallery, Albright Art Gallery, Buffalo; represented in permanent collections at St. Lawrence U., Canton, N.Y., Newark Pub. Library, Newark, Savannah Elem. Sch., Comstock Foods Corp., Rochester. Served with USAAF, 1942-45; PTO. Recipient Wilner award Cayuga Mus. History and Art, Auburn, 1962, Ceramic award, 1966, Crafts prize, 1972. Mem. Am. Crafts Council. Home: PO Box 154 House # 13083 South Butler NY 13154

CASTILLO CLARAMOUNT, RODOLFO ANTONIO, El Salvador government official. V.p. El Salvador, San Salvador. Address: Office Vice President, San Salvador El Salvador *

CASTLE, MICHAEL N., governor of Delaware, lawyer; b. Wilmington, Del., July 2, 1939; s. J. Manderson and Louisa B. C. B.A., Hamilton Coll., 1961; J.D., Georgetown U., 1964. Bar: Del. 1964, D.C. 1964. Asso. firm Connolly Bove and Lodge, Wilmington, 1964-73; partner firm Connolly Bove and Lodge, 1973-75; dept. atty. gen. State of Del., 1965-66; partner firm Schnee and Castle (P.A.), 1975-80; lt. gov. State of Del., Wilmington, 1981-85; prin. Michael N. Castle (P.A.), 1981—; gov. State of Del., 1985—; mem. Del. Ho. of Reps., 1966-67, Del. State Senate, 1968-76, minority leader, 1976. Bd. dirs. Geriatric Service of Wilmington, Boys Club of Wilmington. Mem. Del. State Bar Assn., ABA, Council State Govts., Nat. Gov.'s Assn., Rep. Gov.'s Assn., Southern Gov.'s Assn. Republican. Roman Catholic. Office: Legislative Hall Dover DE 19901 *

CASTLE, RAYMOND NIELSON, chemist, educator; b. Boise, Idaho, June 24, 1916; s. Ray Newell and Lula (Nielson) C.; m. Ada Necia Van Orden, June 16, 1937; children: Raymond Norman, Dean Lowell, David Elliott, George Leonard, Elizabeth Anne, Edith Eilene, Christian Daniel, Lyle William. Student, Boise Jr. Coll., 1934-35; B.S., Idaho State U., 1939; M.A., U. Colo., 1941, Ph.D., 1944. Instr. chemistry U. Idaho, 1942-43, U. Colo., 1943-44; research chemist Battelle Meml. Inst., Columbus, Ohio, 1944-46; faculty U. N.M., 1946-70, prof. chemistry, 1956-70, chmn. dept., 1963-70; prof. chemistry Brigham Young U., Provo, Utah, 1970-81; grad. research prof. chemistry U. South Fla., 1981—; research fellow U. Va., 1952-53; vis. research scholar Tech. U. Denmark, Copenhagen, 1962; pres. First Internat. Congress Heterocyclic Chemistry, N.M., 1967; sec. Internat. Congress Heterocyclic Chemistry (2d congress), France, 1969; v.p. Internat. Congress Heterocyclic Chemistry (3d congress), Japan, 1971, Internat. Congress Heterocyclic Chemistry (4th congress), Utah, 1973, Internat. Congress Heterocyclic Chemistry (5th congress), Yugoslavia, 1975, Internat. Congress Heterocyclic Chemistry (6th congress), Iran, 1977. Contbr. research articles to profl. jours.; Editor, co-author: Chemistry of Heterocyclic Compounds, Vols. 27, 28, 1973; Editor: Jour. Heterocyclic Chemistry, 1964—, Topics in Heterocyclic Chemistry, 1969, Lectures in Heterocyclic Chemistry, Vol. I, 1972, Vol. II, 1974, Vol. III, 1975, Vol. IV, 1977, Vol. V, 1980, Vol. VI, 1982, Vol. VII, 1984, Vol. VIII, 1985, Vol. IX, 1987; adv. editor: English transl. Russian Jour. Heterocyclic Compounds. Fellow Chem. Soc. London (Eng.); mem. Am. Chem. Soc., Internat. Soc. Heterocyclic Chemistry (pres. 1973-75, past pres. 1976-77 Biennial award, 2d award 1983), Sigma Xi. Mem. Ch. of Jesus Christ of Latter-day Saints (bishop 1957-61). Home: 4337 Honey Vista Circle Tampa FL 33624

CASTLEBERRY, JAMES NEWTON, JR., legal educator; b. Chatom, Ala., Dec. 28, 1921; s. James Newton and Nellie (Robbins) C.; m. Mary Ann Blocker, Feb. 12, 1944; children: Jean, Nancy, James III (dec.), Elizabeth, Cynthia, Robert, Mary Ann. J.D. magna cum laude, St. Mary's U., 1952. Bar: Tex. 1952. Asst. atty. gen. State of Tex., 1953-55; prof. law St. Mary's U., San Antonio, 1955—, dean, 1978—; bd. dirs. M Bank North, N.A.; dir. St. Mary's U. Summer Program in Internat. and Comparative Law, Innsbruck, Austria, 1986—. Co-author: Water & Water Rights, 1970; contbr. articles to law jours. Mem. ABA, Tex. Bar Assn., Tex. State Bar (com. on historic preservation 1978—Phi Delta Phi (internat. pres. 1977-79). Home: 7727 Woodridge San Antonio TX 78209 Office: 1 Camino Santa Maria San Antonio TX 78284

CASTOR, WILBUR WRIGHT, corporate marketing executive; b. Harrison Twp., Pa., Feb. 3, 1932; s. Wilbur Wright and Margaret (Grubbs) C.; m. Donna Ruth Schwartz, Feb. 9, 1963; children: Amy, Julia, Marnie. BA, St. Vincent Studies, 1959; postgrad., Calif. U. Advanced Studies, 1986—. Sales rep. IBM, Pitts. and Cleve., 1959-62; v.p. data processing ops. Honeywell, Waltham, Mass., 1962-80; pres., chief exec. officer Aviation Simulation Tech., Lexington, Mass., 1980-82; sr. v.p. Xerox Corp., El Segundo, Calif., 1982—. Author: (play) Un Certaine Soirire, 1958, (mus. comedy) Breaking Up, 1960; contbr. articles to profl. jours. Mem. Presdl. Rep. Task Force; trustee Info. Inst., Santa Barbara, Calif.; pres. bd. dirs. Internat. Acad., Santa Barbara; active Town Hall Calif. Served to capt. USN, 1953-58, with USAFR, 1958-76. Mem. Internat. Platform Assn., World Future Soc., Aircraft Owners and Pilots Assn. Clubs: Manhattan Country (Manhattan Beach, Calif.); Caballeros, Rolling Hills (Calif.) Tennis; U.S. Senator's. Home: 19 Georgeff Rd Rolling Hills CA 90274 Office: Xerox Corp ES XC15-B 101 Continental Blvd El Segundo CA 90245

CASTORIADIS, CORNELIUS, psychoanalyst, writer; b. Constantinople, Greece, Mar. 11, 1922; arrived in France, 1945; s. Cesar and Sophia (Papachela) C.; m. Piera Aulagnier, Apr. 11, 1967 (div. 1978); m. Zoe Christophides, June 3, 1980; children: Sparta-Sonia, Cybele. MS in Law, Econ., Polit. Sci., U. Athens, 1942. Economist then dir. stats. Orgn. for Econ. Cooperation and Devel., Paris, 1948-70; pvt. practice psychoanalysis Paris, 1974—; dir. studies social scis. Ecole Hautes Etudes, Paris, 1980—. Author: The Imaginary Institution of Society, 1975, Eng. edit., 1987, Crossroads in the Labyrinth, 1978, Eng. edit., 1983; founder, contbr.: Socialism or Barbarism jour., 1949-66. Home: 1 Rue de l'Alboni, 75016 Paris France Office: Ecole Hautes Etudes, 54 Blvd Raspail, 75006 Paris France

CASTRO, ALBERT, medical educator, scientist; b. San Salvador, El Salvador, Nov. 15, 1933; came to U.S., 1952; s. Alberto Lemus and Maria Emma (de la Cotera) C.; m. Jeris Adelle Goldsmith, Oct. 19, 1956; children: Stewart, Sandra, Alberto, Juan, Richard. B.S., U. Houston, 1958; postgrad., Baylor U., 1958; Ph.D., U. El Salvador, 1962; M.D., Dominican Republic, 1982. Asst. prof. microbiology and biochemistry U. El Salvador, San Salvador, 1958-60, assoc. prof. Dental and Med. schs., 1960-63, prof., head dept. basic sci., 1965-68, dir. rsearch in basic sci. Dental Sch., 1964-68, co-dir. grad. research, 1965-66, bd. dirs. dental sch., 1961-66, mem. research and scholarship com., 1964-65; asst. prof. pediatrics, co-dir. pediatrics metabolic lab. U. Oreg., Portland, 1969-73; dir. endocrinol. dept. and research unit United Med. Lab., Portland, 1970-73; sr. scientist Papanicolauou Cancer Research Inst., Miami, Fla., 1973-75; assoc. prof. pathology and medicine U. Miami, 1973-77, prof. pathology, medicine and microbiology, 1977—, coordinator Inter Am. Tech. Transfer and Tng. Program, 1976—, dir. Hormone Research Lab., 1974-82. Contbr. over 200 publs. to nat. and internat. sci. jours. NIH postdoctoral fellow, 1966-70; Northwest Pediatric Research fellow, 1971; U. Oreg. Med. Sch. grantee, 1966-69. Fellow Am. Inst. Chemists, Royal Soc. Tropical Medicine and Hygiene; mem. Acad. Clin. Lab. Physicians and Scientists, N.Y. Acad. Scis., Am. Chem. Assn., Am. Assn. Microbiology, AAAS, Nat. Acad. Clin. Biochemists (charter), Tooth and Bone Research Soc., Acad. Sci. El Salvador. Roman Catholic. Home: 6275 SW 123d Terr Miami FL 33156 Office: U Miami Sch Medicine Dept Pathology South Campus 12500 SW 152 St Miami FL 33177

CASTRO, AMADO ALEJANDRO, economist, educator; b. Manila, May 29, 1924; s. Melquiades Madrid and Victoria (Yusi) Bundalian; B.Sc. in Bus. Adminstrn., U. Philippines, 1948; A.M., Harvard U., 1952, Ph.D., 1954. Instr. econs. Univ. Philippines, Quezon City, 1948-53, asst. prof., 1954-56, assoc. prof., 1956-62, head dept. econs., 1956-58, prof. econs., 1962—, acting dean Coll. of Bus. Adminstrn., 1958, dean Sch. Econs., 1965-73, Central Bank of Philippines prof. monetary econs., 1972—; econ. affairs officer Econ. Commn. Asia and Far East, 1957, 61; gov. and acting chmn. Devel. Bank of Philippines, 1962-66; dir. Inst. Econ. Devel. and Research, 1958-66, Econ. Bur. ASEAN Secretariat, 1977-80; cons. in field. Contbr. articles to profl. jours. Mem. Am. Econ. Assn., Social Economy Assn., Philippine Statis. Assn., Royal Econ. Soc., Philippine Econ. Soc. (pres. 1961-62), Pan Xenia (assoc.). Address: Sch of Economics, Univ of the Philippines, Quezon City Philippines 3004 also: 67 Valenzuela, San Juan Metro Manila 3134, Philippines *

CASTRO, FIDEL (FIDEL CASTRO RUZ), president and first secretary of Cuba; b. Mayari, Oriente Province, Cuba, Aug. 13, 1927; s. Angel Castro and Lina Ruz; grad. with degree of bachelor, Colegio Belen, Havana, Cuba, 1945; received law degree and doctorate U. Havana, 1950; m. Mirta Diaz Balart, Oct. 12, 1948 (div. 1955); 1 son, Fidel. Practiced law, 1950-52; took part in revolutionary movement expdn. against govt. Dominican Republic, 1947; leader of armed forces attacking Batista govt. in Cuba, 1953-58; unsuccessfully attacked Moncada Barracks, Santiago de Cuba, July 1953; captured, imprisoned, 1953-55; in exile, Mexico and N.Y., 1955-56; returned to Cuba, 1956, and led armed attacks against Batista govt., using Oriente Province as hdqrs. for armed forces; following successful campaign these forces entered Havana, Jan. 1, 1959; designated Manuel Urrutia provisional pres., and was named by Pres. Urrutia comdr.-in-chief of Cuban armed forces, Jan. 2, 1959; became prime minister, Feb. 1959; head state, pres. Council of State, 1976—; pres. Council of Ministers, 1976—; 1st sec. Partido Unido de la Revolucion Socialista, 1963-65; 1st sec. Partido Comunista, 1965—, mem. polit. bur., 1976—. Chmn. Agrarian Reform Inst., 1965—. Recipient Lenin Peace prize, 1961; Dimitrov prize, 1980; decorated Gold Star (Vietnam), 1982; Order of Lenin, Order of Oct. Revolution; Hero of Soviet Union, Somali Order (1st class), Order of Jamaica. Author: Ten Years of Revolution, 1964; History Will Absolve Me, 1968. Address: Office of Pres, Palacio del Gobierno, Havana Cuba *

CASTRO, LEONARD EDWARD, lawyer; b. Los Angeles, Mar. 18, 1934; s. Emil Galvez and Lily (Meyers) C.; 1 son, Stephen Paul. A.B., UCLA, 1959, J.D., 1962. Bar: Calif. 1963, U.S. Supreme Ct. 1970. Assoc. Musick, Peeler & Garrett, Los Angeles, 1962-68, ptnr., 1968—. Mem. ABA, Internat. Bar Assn., Los Angeles County Bar Assn. Office: Musick Peeler & Garrett 1 Wilshire Blvd Suite 2000 Los Angeles CA 90017

CASTRO, RAUL (RAUL CASTRO RUZ), Cuban first vice president; ed. Jesuit schs. Sentenced with brother Fidel Castro to 15 years imprisonment for insurrection, 1953; amnestied, 1954; assisted brother's movement in Mexico, later in Cuba after 1956; chief Armed Forces, 1959; head Ministry Revolutionary Armed Forces, 1960—; vice prime minister Cuba, 1960-76; 1st v.p. Council of State, 1976—, Council of Ministers, 1976—. Decorated medal for Strengthening of Brotherhood in Arms, 1977; Order of Lenin 1979; Order of Oct. Revolution 1981. Address: Office 1st Vice Pres, Palacio del Gobierno, Havana Cuba *

CASTRO, SALVADOR PICCIO, JR., civil engineer; b. Iloilo, The Philippines, Sept. 23, 1942; s. Salvador Quisumbing and Zenaida (Piccio) C.; m. Nora Demonteverde, May 21, 1967; children: Nora Zenaida, Pia, Pamela, Paula Melissa (dec.). BS in Civil Engring., Mapua Inst. Tech., Manila, 1964. Mgr. Tropical Homes Inc., The Philippines, 1969-75; sr. v.p. Alta Tierra Resources, Inc., The Philippines, 1975-78; v.p. Ayala Realty Devel. Corp., The Philippines, 1978-79; sr. v.p. Makati Devel. Corp., The Philippines, 1978-81; project dir. New Istana Project (Sultan's Palace), Brunei, 1980-85; gen. mgr., dir. Ayala Internat. Borneo SDN BHD, Dar'l Salam, Brunei, 1983-85, Ayala Internat. (Thailand) Ltd., Bangkok, 1985-86; mng. dir. SP Castro and Assocs., SDN BHD, Brunei and The Philippines, 1986—; project mgmt. cons. Ministry Devel., Brunei; cons. U.N. Devel. Programme, Chmn. Man and his Environment Com. (presdl. award), Manila Jaycees, 1978; sec., dir. Chamber of Real Estate and Brokers Assn., 1978. Recipient Testimonial of Proficiency Manila Bd. Realtors, 1970. Mem. Assn. Project Mgrs., U.K., Project Mgmt. Inst., USA, Am. Inst. Mgmt., Philippine Inst. Civil Engrs., Ea. Regional Orgn. Planning and Housing. Office: Suite 4-06 Badi'ah Complex, Mile 1 Jalan Tutong, Bandar Seri Begawan 2862, Brunei

CASTRO E COSTA, JORGE MANUEL MARTINS DE, communications and public relations executive; b. Lisbon, Portugal, Apr. 2, 1947; s. José Eduardo and Fernanda C.R.M. C.; m. Maria Emilia Neves Rapozo, Mar. 17, 1972; 1 child, Eduardo Rapozo. Grad. high sch., Lisbon, 1965. Sales engr. Rank Xerox Ltd., Lisbon, 1972-74; gen. mgrs. attaché Regisconta Group, Sari, Lisbon, 1974-77, mgr., 1977-78, publicity and pub. relation dep., 1978-79, tng. mgr., 1979-81, group mktg. coordinator, 1981-82; communications and pub. relations mgr. Atlas Copco Portugal, Lisbon, 1982—, communications, pub. relations and sales promotion mgr., 1986—; cons., area mgr., project leader, gen. mgr. and bd. dirs. Forma 3 Hortipor, LDA, Lisbon; dir. Ar Comprimido Mag., Lisbon. Served with Portuguese Army, 1969-72. Partido Social Decocrata. Roman Catholic. Clubs: Bananas, Automobile Portugal, Stone's. Home: Rua Bartolomeu Perestrelo 8, 1400 Lisbon Portugal

CASWELL, PAULETTE REVA, lawyer; b. Chgo., June 8, 1951; d. Ben and Lillian (Cohen) Watstein; m. Michael Evidson, May 15, 1975 (div. Mar. 1979); 1 child, David Allan Philip; m. Charles Frank Caswell, III, Jan. 8, 1983. A.A., West Los Angeles Community Coll., 1971; B.A., Calif. State U.-Los Angeles, 1975; J.D., Whittier Coll., 1982; D.D. (hon.), St. Alban's Coll., San Francisco, 1974. Bar: Calif. 1982, U.S. Dist. Ct. (cen. dist.) Calif., 1983. Dir., Mensa of Los Angeles, 1977-83; sole practice, Los Angeles, 1982—; dir., founder Amicus, Los Angeles Area Ctr. Law and the Deaf; cons. Editor: Consumer Rights, 1982; author legal articles pamphlets, booklets. Legal adv. Ind. Living Ctrs.; adv. for deaf and visually-impaired. Mem. ABA, Los Angeles County Bar Assn., Legal Assistance Assn. Calif., State Bar Calif., Arts. Democrat. Jewish. Home: 645 N Gardner St Los Angeles CA 90036-5712

CATABELLE, JEAN-MARIE HENRI, industrial firm executive; b. Mamers, Sarthe, France, Dec. 10, 1941; s. Christian Aristide and Annette Marie (Lemonnier) C.; children by previous marriage: Laurent, Christine, Diane; m. Michèle Archambaud, Sept. 1, 1987. Engr., Ecole Centrale des Arts et Manufactures, Paris, 1963-66; M.S. with honors, Yale U., 1967; M.B.A. with distinction, Harvard Bus. Sch., 1974. Dept. mgr. IBM France, Paris, 1969-72; asst. to controller IBM Am. Far East, White Plains, N.Y., 1973; ops. mgr. Raychem S.A., Pontoise, France, 1974-78; mktg. mgr. Europe Raychem, Pontoise, 1978-81; gen. mgr. Compagnie Franç aise des Isolants, France, 1981-82; mng. dir., chief operating officer DAV, Annemasse, France, 1982—; dir. ETUDOC, Annecy, France; chmn. bd. examiners LEP Profl. Sch., Annemasse, 1983—; dir. ASDTN, Annecy, 1983—; bd. dirs. French Nat. Edn. Com. Grenoble Acad., 1986—; chmn. edn. com. Employers Union (Haute Savoie). . Patentee in field. Contbr. articles to profl. jours. Trustee, LEP Profl. Sch., 1982; v.p. export sect. C. of C., Amiens, France, 1981. Served to lt. French Army, 1967-69. Fulbright fellow, 1966, 72; French Govt. fellow, 1972; Alliance Franç aise fellow, 1966. Mem. French Assn. for Tech. and Econ. Cybernetics, Ingenieurs and Scientifiques de France, Association Franç aise de l'Enseignement Technique (dir.), Ecole Centrale Alumni Assn. Roman Catholic. Clubs: Golf, Tennis. Lodge: Rotary. Avocation: travel. Home: 5 Impasse Des Champais, 74290 Veyrier Du Lac, Haute-Savoie France Office: DAV, Rue Jules Verne, Vetraz Monthoux, 74101 Annemasse France

CATAHIER, SERGE, surgeon, researcher; b. Aleppo, Syria, Nov. 14, 1930; arrived in France, 1948, naturalized, 1981; s. Izzat Catahier and Rakia Soufi; m. Mona Trefi, Aug. 10, 1967 (div. May 1986); children: Yazane, Chady, Syrine. Dr. en Médecine, Faculté de Paris, 1956, diploma in oto-rhino-laryngologie, 1965. Assoc. prof. U. Aleppo, 1966-72, prof. agrégé à la Faculté de Médecine, 1972-79, prof., 1979-82, prof. ear, nose and throat surgery, 1972-80, prof. history medicine, research Inst. for Sci. Heritage, 1975-80; pvt. practice in surgery Colombes, France, 1982—; attaché oto-rhino-laryngologie service Aulnay s/bois Hosp.; prof. recherche à l'Inst. du Patrimoine Sci. Arabe; participant various confs. Author 17 books; conseiller au rédaction Jour. History Arabic Scis., Islamic Monography, La Revue du Praticien; contbr. articles to profl. jours. Mem. Soc. Française des Médecins Oto-Rhino-Laryngology, Soc. Syrienne des Médecins Oto-Rhino-Laryngology, Union des Ecrivains Arabes, Soc. Internat. de l'Histoire de la Médecine (v.p.), Soc. Française d'Histoire de la Médecine, Soc. Arabe d'Histoire de la Pharmacie, Soc. Syrienne de l'Histoire des Scis. (sec.). Home: Domaine de Riviere Bat B2, 91290 Arpajon France

CATALDO, BERNARD FRANCIS, law educator; b. Phila., Jan. 5, 1907; s. Michael Angelo and Giuseppina (Polcari) C.; A.B. summa cum laude with first honors, U. Pa., 1929, LL.B. summa cum laude with first honors (Gowen law fellow), 1933, LL.M., 1936; Penfield law fellow Harvard, 1933-34; m. Sylvia La Monaca, Jan. 1, 1936; 1 dau., Marlene Annette. Admitted to Pa. bar, 1935; spl. atty. antitrust div. Dept. of Justice, 1935-36; tchr. Wharton sch. U. Pa., Phila., 1936—, prof., 1947-77, prof. emeritus, 1977—, chmn. dept. bus. law, 1947-61, chmn. dean's adv. com. faculty personel, 1961-65; chief price atty. Phila. regional office OPA, 1943-45; arbitrator Am. Arbitration Assn., 1946-47; cons. Am. Coll. Life Underwriters, Am. Inst. Property and Casualty Underwriters. Recipient Lindback award for distinguished teaching, 1964. Mem. Am. Assn. U. Profs., Order of Coif, Phi Beta Kappa, Beta Gamma Sigma, Eta Sigma Phi. Co-author: Introduction to Law and The Legal Process, 1965; Introductory Cases on Law and the Legal Process, 1967. Contbr. legal jours. Home: 2532 Hillcrest Rd Drexel Hill PA 19026 Office: 3620 Locust St Philadelphia PA 19104

CATALFO, ALFRED (ALFIO), JR., lawyer; b. Lawrence, Mass., Jan. 31, 1920; s. Alfio and Viencenza (Amato) C.; m. Caroline Joanne Mosca (dec. Apr. 1968); children—Alfred Thomas, Carol Joanne, Gina Marie. B.A., U. N.H., 1945, M.A. in History, 1952; LL.B., Boston U., 1947, J.D. (hon.), 1969; postgrad., Suffolk U. Sch. Law, 1955-56, Am. Law Inst., N.Y.C., 1959. Bar: N.H. 1947, U.S. Dist. Ct. 1948, U.S. Ct. Appeals 1978, U.S. Supreme Ct. 1979. Sole practice law Dover, N.H., 1948—; county atty. Strafford County, Dover, N.H., 1949-50, 55-56; mem. Bd. Immigration Appeals, U.S. Dept. Justice, 1953—; football coach Berwick Acad., South Berwick, Maine, 1944, Mission Catholic High Sch., Roxbury, Mass., 1945-46. Author: Laws of Divorces, Marriages, and Separations in New Hampshire, 1962, History of the Town of Rollinsford, 1623-1973, 1973. Pres. Young Democrats of Dover, 1953-55; 1st vice-chmn. Young Dems., N.H., 1954-56; mem. Strafford County Dem. com., 1948-75; vice chmn. N.H. Dem. com., 1954-56, 1st chmn., 1956-58, chmn. spl. activities, 1958-60; del. Dem. Nat. Conv., 1956, 60, 76; chmn. N.H. Dem. Conv., 1958, conv. dir., 1960; mem. Dem. state exec. com., 1960-70; Dem. nominee for U.S. Senate, 1962; vice chmn. Dover Cath. Sch. Com., 1969-71; mem. Dover Bd. Adjustment, 1960-65. Served as pilot AC, USN, 1942-44; lt. comdr. USNR. Recipient keys to cities of Dover, Somersworth, Concord, Berlin and Manchester, N.H.; 5 nat. plaques DAV; 3 disting. service awards Am. Legion; Am. Legion Life Membership award; spl. recognition award Berwick Acad., 1985. Mem. ABA, N.H. Bar Assn., Strafford County Bar Assn. (v.p. 1966-69, pres. 1968-69), Assn. Trial Lawyers Am., N.Y. State Trial Lawyers Assn., Mass. Trial Lawyers Assn., N.H. Trial Lawyers Assn., Tex. Trial Lawyers Assn., Nat. Assn. Criminal Def. Lawyers, Am. Judicature Soc., Phi Delta Phi, DAV (judge adv. N.H. dept. 1950-56, 57-68, 72—; comdr. chpt. 1953-54, comdr. N.H. 1956-57), Am. Legion (chmn. state conv. 1967, 77, 84), Navy League, N.H. Hist. Soc., Dover Hist. Soc., Rollinsford Hist. Soc. Clubs: Eagles (Somersworth, N.H.), Sons of Italy (Portsmouth, N.H.). Lodges: Lions, Elks, K.C. (grand knight 1975-77), Moose, Lebanese (Dover). Home: 20 Arch St Dover NH 03820 Office: 450 Central Ave Dover NH 03820

CATALLO, CLARENCE GUERRINO, JR., financial services company executive; b. Detroit, Feb. 1, 1940; s. Clarence Guerrino and Christine (Mi-ozzi) C.; m. Sharron Ann Teschendorf, Apr. 24, 1965; children—Curt Gregory, Cara Lynn. A.A., Long Beach City Coll., 1961; B.A., U. Detroit, 1963; postgrad., U. Toledo, 1963, Wayne State U., 1964. Account exec., asst. mgr. E.F. Hutton, Detroit, 1965-67, regional commodity mgr., 1967-70; br. mgr. E.F. Hutton, Southfield, Mich., 1970-80; dist. mgr., sr. v.p. E.F. Hutton, Birmingham, Mich., 1979-85; sr. v.p., regional v.p. Gt. Lakes region E.F. Hutton, 1986-87, exec. v.p. dir., regional v.p. Gt. Lakes region, 1987-88; sr. v.p., dir. North Cen. Div., including state of Mich., Ohio, Ind., Ill., Wis., Minn., N.D. and S.D. PaineWebber Inc., Farmington Hills, Mich., 1988—. Trustee Mich. Opera Theatre, Detroit, 1984-85. Republican. Roman Catholic. Club: Renaissance (LaSalle). Home: 29 Buffalo Clarkston MI 48016 Office: PaineWebber Inc North Cen Div 210 S Woodward #250 Birmingham MI 48009

CATE, WIRT ARMISTEAD, author; b. Hopkinsville, Ky., Nov. 16, 1900; s. James Henry and Mary Lou (Armistead) C. AB, Emory U., 1923, AM (fellow), 1925; postgrad. (Edward Austin fellow), Harvard, 1926-27, 28-29. Instr. Baylor Sch., Chattanooga, 1923-24, Ga. Sch. Tech., 1925-26, 27-28; lectr. English Emory U., summers 1926, 28; Julius Rosenwald fellow Am. history 1937-38; fellow Colonial Williamsburg, Inc., 1940-43; now engaged in biog., hist. research, writing. Author: Lucius Q.C. Lamar, Secession and Reunion, 1935, 3d edit., 1978; (with Margaret R. Cate) The Armistead Family and Collaterals, 1971; History of Richmond Virginia: 1607-1861; editor: Two Soldiers, The Campaign Diaries of Thomas J. Key, C.S.A. and Robert J. Campbell, U.S.A, 1938; Contbr. to: hist., philol. and coll. jours. Ency. Brit. Mem. Modern Lang. Assn. Am., So. Hist. Assn., Phi Beta Kappa, Sigma Upsilon, Sigma Chi. Democrat. Methodist. Home: 713 Lynnbrook Road Nashville TN 37215

CATECHIS, SPYROS CONSTANTINE, retired tourism executive, consultant; b. Aswan, Egypt, Nov. 20, 1919; came to Greece, 1923; s. Constantine and Angela (Tzala) C.; m. Theano Yamali, Oct. 26, 1944 (dec. 1955); children: Angela Catechis Watts-Keynes, Kostaki Panteli; m. Norma Cummings Murdoch, Apr. 30, 1960; children: Kimon Paul, Byron Philip. Grad., Coll. Tourism, Athens, Greece, 1938; degree in Econs., Greek Nat. Tourism Orgn. U., Athens, Greece, 1940. Mgr. M.O.I. Rhodes (Greece), Brit. Armed Forces, 1946-47; chief clk. Brit. Consulate, Rhodes, 1947-50; mem. info. staff Brit. Embassy, Athens, 1947-50; mng. dir. Trading Co., Rhodesia, 1950-66; dir. Greek Nat. Tourism Orgn., Rhodes, 1966-86; advisor Barclay's Bank, PLC, Rhodes, 1987—; lectr. tourism. V.p. Rhodes Boy Scouts Com., 1972—; mem. Greek Underground, 1942-43. Served to maj. Brit. Armed Forces, 1943-46. Decorated King's medal for Courage (Eng.); Disting. Service medal, Mil. Gross (C class) (Greece); Vieux Combatant (France); Paul Harris fellow Rhodes Rotary. Home: G Papanikolaou and Iroon, Polytechniou Sts, 85100 Rodos Greece Office: Barclays Bank PLC, PO Box 309, 85100 Rhodes Greece

CATER, JAMES THOMAS, financial and investment planner; b. Beatrice, Ala., Oct. 30, 1948; s. LaFayette Sigler and Lula Dell (Knight) C.; m. Sarah Frances Crisman, Apr. 12, 1975 (div. Sept. 1980); 1 child, Elizabeth Anne. MusB, U. Ala., 1971; MusM, U. Mich., 1974. Ind. paino and organ salesman 1974-80; fin. planner John Hancock Fin. Services, Houston, 1981—. Dir. music, organist, St. Luke's Presbyn. Ch., Houston, 1983—. Recipient numerous ins. awards, John Hancock Fin. Service. Mem. Houston Assn. Life Underwriters, Nat. Assn. Health Underwriters (leading producers round table 1984), Profl. Music. Fraternity, Phi Mu Alpha Sinfonia. Republican. Office: John Hancock Fin Services 720 N Post Oak Rd Suite 328 Houston TX 77024

CATES, JOHN MARTIN, JR., lawyer; b. Denver, Jan. 20, 1912; s. John Martin and Mary Arden (Randall) C.; m. Mary Perkins Raymond, July 4, 1942 (div. 1973); 1 son, John Martin III; m. Nelia Barletta, Nov. 19, 1976; 1 dau., Nelia M. Barletta Anselin. Grad., Phillips Andover Acad., 1932; B.A., Yale, 1936, J.D., 1939. Bar: Calif. bar 1940, D.C. bar 1946, N.Y. State bar 1976. With McCutchen, Olney, Mannon & Greene, San Francisco, 1939-41; labor relations San Francisco Warehousemen's Assn., 1941-42; with U.S. Maritime Commn. and War Shipping Adminstrn., Washington, 1942-47; fgn. affairs specialist on UN and specialized agencies U.S. Dept. State, 1947-53; with Nat. War Coll., 1952-53; legal adviser Am. embassy U.S. Dept. State, Bonn; also mem. War Criminal Parole Bd., 1953-55; legal advisor, 1st sec., negotiator compensation for agrl. land confiscated from U.S. citizens Am. Embassy, Mexico, 1955-57; chief polit. officer Am. embassy Venezuela, 1957-61; alternate U.S. rep. Council OAS, Washington, 1961-63; counsellor, adviser on Latin Am. Affairs and Liason U.S. Mission to UN, 1963-70; counsellor U.S. Mission to Geneva, 1970-71; pres., dir. Center for Inter-Am. Relations, 1971-75; cons., atty. 1976—; London counsel firm Pettit & Martin, San Francisco; adj. prof. Fairleigh Dickinson U. Contbr. articles to profl. jours. Mem. Latin Am. adv. council State Dept.; Committeeman Boy Scouts Am., N.Y.C., also Mexico, Venezuela, 1963—; mem. Am. Ch. Council, Bad Godesburg, Germany, 1953-55; mem. council Yale U., 1968-77; bd. dirs. Youth for Understanding, Incon Internat. Inc., Americas' Found., Programme for New World Anthropology, Ecuador; trustee Am. Aid Soc., London; asso.-cons. Phillips Acad. Bicentennial, 1978. Recipient medal of merit Venezuela Boy Scouts, 1960, superior honor award Dept. of State, 1967, gran cruz Vasco Nuñ ez de Balboa Panama, 1975; Order Francisco de Miranda Venezuela, 1976, Order St. John of Jerusalem (U.K.). Mem. Council Fgn. Relations, Am., Inter-Am., Calif. D.C., bar assns., Bar City N.Y., London Law Soc., Bolivian Soc. (dir. 1971—), Pan Am. Soc. (dir. 1974—), Cercle de la Presse et Amitie Etrangere (Geneva), Am. Polit. Sci. Assn., English Speaking Union (London), S.R., Soc. Colonial Wars (exec. com.), Pilgrims, St. Nicholas Soc. (exec. com. 1969), Phelps Assn. Wolfs Head (exec. com.), Am. Arbitration Assn., Phi Delta Phi. Clubs: Mason (N.Y.C.), Union (N.Y.C.), Century (N.Y.C.); Bucks (London), Am. (London), The Pilgrims (London); Met. (Washington); Bohemian (San Francsico); Lyford Cay (Nassau); Travellers (Paris), Circle de l'Union Interalliée (Paris).

CATES, NELIA BARLETTA DE, diplomat of Dominican Republic; b. Santo Domingo, Dominican Republic, Dec. 21, 1932; d. Amadeo and Nelia (Ricart) Barletta; m. Miguel Morales Abreu, Oct. 29, 1953 (div. 1961); m. John Martin Cates, Nov. 19, 1976. Ed. in Argentina, Cuba and U.S.A.; diploma Duchesne Coll., 1950. Cultural attache, embassy of Dominican Republic, London, 1975-85, ambassador, permanent rep. to Internat. Maritime Orgn., 1985—. Com. mem. Nat. Soc. Prevention Cruelty to Children, London; bd. dirs. Girls and Boys Service League, N.Y.C., Soc. of Meml. Sloan Kettering Cancer Ctr., N.Y.C.; mem. European Atlantic Group. Address: PO Box N-7776, Nassau The Bahamas

CATHEY, WILLIAM BLAIR, geologist, oil and gas exploration consultant; b. Columbia, Tenn., Nov. 30, 1954; s. Cecil Blair and Mary Lou (Sawyer) C.; m. Victoria Ann Russell, Oct. 18, 1974. BA in Geology, U. Tenn., 1977, MS in Geology, 1980; postgrad. Tulane U., 1982-83; MS in Indsl. Engring., U. Tenn., 1988. Cert. profl. geologist. Coop geologist Union Carbide, Oak Ridge, Tenn., 1975-77; assoc. geologist Exxon Minerals, Denver, 1978; prodn. geologist Conoco, Inc., New Orleans, 1980-81; exploration geologist Shell Oil Co., New Orleans, 1981-83; supr. phosphate-aquisition Occidental Petroleum, Columbia, Tenn., 1984-87; pres. Tnread, Inc., Knoxville, Tenn., 1983-84; grad. asst. in geology U. Tenn., Knoxville, 1978; grad. research fellow Oak Ridge Assoc. Univs., Tenn., 1979. Recipient Tarr award U. Tenn., 1977. Mem. Am. Inst. Profl. Geologists, Am. Assn. Petroleum Geologists, Geol. Soc. Am., New Orleans Geol. Soc., Phi Kappa Phi, Sigma Gamma Epsilon (v.p. 1979-80). Methodist. Lodge: Kiwanis. Avocations: hiking, camping, hunting, fishing. Home: 460 Bear Creek Ln Knoxville TN 37922

CATLING, DARREL CHARLES, film director, writer; b. London, Jan. 10, 1909; s. Frank and Clare Ethel Kate (Smith) C.; ed. pvt. tutors; m. Agatha Helen Cowie, Oct. 10, 1936; children—Psyche Patricia, Fiona Helen, Glen Boyd, Briony. Film dir. Gaumont Brit. Films, London, 1935-52, Elstree, 1953-55; film dir. Realist Film Unit, London, 1952-53, Impact Telefilms, London, 1955-60, Linfilms, London, 1960-61, Royalty House Prodns., London, 1962-67, Eothen Films, Elstree, 1967-68, Stewart Films, London, 1969-70; freelance film dir., London, 1970—; films include: Into the Blue; Colour in Clay; Morning Paper; Trouble at Townsend; Dusty Bates; Under the Frozen Falls; The Cat Gang; Material Evidence; Winged Citadel. Served with Home Guard, 1943-45. Fellow Royal Photog. Soc.; mem. Brit. Acad. Film and TV Arts (hon.), Brit. Film Inst., Cinema and TV Vets., Dirs. Guild Gt. Brit. Assoc. editor Cine-Technician, 1941-44. Contbr. articles to various publs. Home: Travellers Rest, Church St, Old Hatfield, Hertfordshire AL9 5AW England

CATO, ROBERT GEORGE, fin. co. mgr.; b. Portland, Oreg., Mar. 30, 1933; s. Archie Barnes and Etta Marie (Yager) C.; BA, U. Portland, 1954; postgrad. Portland State Coll., 1959-60, U. Portland, 1959-60, Johns Hopkins U., 1983; m. Nancy Louise Foord, Sept. 18, 1954; children—Cheryl, Sandra, Sharon. With Eastman Kodak Co., Portland, 1950-55; field rep. Gen. Motors Acceptance Corp., Portland, 1957-62, credit rep., Boise, Idaho, 1962-65, dist. rep., The Dalles, Oreg., 1965-66, credit supr., Seattle, 1966-69, credit mgr., 1969-72, sales mgr., 1972-74, staff asst., N.Y.C., 1974-77, asst. br. mgr., Norfolk, Va., 1977-79, control br. mgr., Balt., 1979-85, Buffalo, 1985-86, Pitts., 1986—. Served with U.S. Army, 1955-57. Mem. Carnegie Mus. Republican. Lodges: Elks, Masons, Shriners. Home: 4165 Pape Clement Ct Allison Park PA 15101 Office: 115 Gamma Dr Pittsburgh PA 15238

CATOLICO, ISAAC CAMELLO, surgeon; b. Narvacan, Ilocos Sur, Philippines, June 5, 1926; s. Mauricio Ramirez and Maria (Camello) C.; m. Maximina Sanidad Cheng, Apr. 26, 1950; children: Catherine, Emylyn. BA, Manila Cen. U., 1950, MD, 1954. Intern Tucson Med. Ctr., 1955-56, Pima County Gen. Hosp., Tucson, 1956-57; resident gen. medicine and surgery Manila Sanitarium and Hosp., 1958-59; practice medicine specializing in surgery Narvacan, 1959—; physician Philippine Union Coll., Manila, 1957-59; dir. health, home and family services Northern Legion Mission Seventh-Day Adventist, Philippines, 1988. Chief exec. Sta. Lucia Narvacan Barangay Barrio Council, 1971-74; mem. Seventh-day Adventist Ch. Fedn., Ilocos Sur, 1976-80, pres. dist adv. council, treas. calamity fund, 1986-87. Fellow Philippine Med. Assn.; mem. Ilocos Med. Soc. of Philippine Med. Assn. (councilor). Home: Narvacan, Ilocos Sur 0423, Philippines

CATON, HIRAM PENDLETON III, humanities educator; b. Concord, N.C., Aug. 16, 1936; s. Hiram Pendleton Jr. and Dorothy Virginia (Carl) C.; m. Sophia Margarete Richter (div. 1981); children: Sonia Luise, Claudia Ingeborg; m. Angela Helen Arthington, 1984. BA in Arabic, U. Chgo., 1960, MA in Arabic, 1962; MA in Philosophy, Yale U., 1965, PhD in Philosophy, 1966. Asst. prof. Bucknell U., Lewisburg, Pa., 1966-67; with dept. philosophy Pa. State U., State College, 1967-71; sr. research fellow Research Sch. Social Scis. Australian Nat. U., Canberra, 1971-76; prof. Sch. Humanities Griffith U., Brisbane, Queensland, Australia, 1976—; commentator radio, TV, documentary films. Author: The Origin of Subjectivity: An Essay on Descartes, 1973, The Humanist Experiment, 1986, The Politics of Progress, 1988; contbr. articles to profl. jours. Served with U.S. Army, 1955-58. Vis. scholar Harvard U., 1979; Nat. Humanities fellow, 1982-83. Mem. Polit. and Life Scis. Assn., Behavioral and Brain Scis. Assn., Australian and N.Z. Assn. Advancement of Sci., Australian Family Assn., Ams. United for Life. Mem. Nat. Party. Office: Sch Humanities, Griffith U, Brisbane 4111, Australia

CATROGA, EDUARDO DE ALMEIDA, agricultural products company executive; b. Abrantes, Portugal, Nov. 14, 1942; s. José Domingos and Joaquina Maria (de Almeida) C.; m. Maria Arlete Ribeiro Miranda; children: Clara Isabel, Teresa Margarida Ribeiro Miranda de Almeida. M in Fin. and Bus. Adminstrn., Lisbon Econs. Inst., Portugal, 1966. Cons. econs. and fin. Ministry of Fin., Portugal, 1966-67; with C.U.F., Portugal, 1966-78; exec. v.p. Quimigal, Portugal, 1978-81; chief exec. officer Produits et Engrais Chimiques du Portugal, Portugal, 1981—, also bd. dirs., 1981—. Named one of Key Mgrs. Portuguese Economy, Expresso, 1980, Top Ten Bus. Mgrs. Portugal, Semanàrio, 1985. Mem. Assn. Portuguesa Empresas Industriais Produtos Quimicos (pres.). Club: Gréio Literàrio Club Negócios (Lisbon). Home: Rua Açores 84-9th E, 1000 Lisbon Portugal Office: SAPEC, Rua Vitor Cordon 19, 1200 Lisbon Portugal

CATTANEO, FRANCO GIUSEPPE, manufacturing company executive; b. Trieste, Italy, July 11, 1939; s. Donato and Anita (Altarass) C.; m. Carla Luisa Ucelli, Nov. 26, 1964; children: Dino, Niccolò. PhD in Mech. Engring., U. Milan, Italy, 1963; program for mgmt. devel., Harvard U., 1970.

Mgr. service Nebiolo SPA, Turin, Italy, 1966-68; asst. to gen. mgr. Riva Calzoni SPA, Milan, 1968-72, gen. mgr., 1973-76; mng. dir. Jucker SPA, Milan, 1977-86, Pomini Farrel SPA, Castellanza, Italy, 1986—; exec. v.p. Morgan Pomini Co., Pitts.; sr. v.p. Morgan Pomini Co., Pitts.; pres. Pomini Inc., Akron; bd. dirs. Pivano SPA, Alessandra, Italy, Redaelli Techna SPA, Milan, Mezzera SPA, Milan; mng. bd. dirs. Giustina Internat. SPA, Turin, 1986. Mem. Assn. Sudden Infant Death Syndrome (bd. dirs. 1986). Clubs: Harvard Bus. Sch. Italy (chmn. 1987—). Office: Pomini Farrel SPA, 20 Via Leonardo Da Vinci, 21053 Castellanza Italy

CATZ, BORIS, physician; b. Troyanov, Russia, Feb. 15, 1923; s. Jacobo and Esther (Galbmilion) C.; came to U.S., 1950, naturalized, 1955; B.S., Nat. U. Mexico, 1941, M.D., 1947; M.S. in Medicine, U. So. Calif., 1951; m. Rebecca Schechter; children—Judith, Dinah, Sarah Lea, Robert. Intern, Gen. Hosp., Mexico City, 1945-46; prof. adj., sch. medicine U. Mexico, 1947-48; research fellow medicine U. So. Calif., 1949-51, instr. medicine, 1952-54, asst. clin. prof., 1954-59, assoc. clin. prof., 1959-83, clin. prof., 1983—; pvt. practice, Los Angeles, 1951-55, Beverly Hills, Calif., 1957—; chief Thyroid Clinic Los Angeles County Gen. Hosp., 1955-70; sr. cons. thyroid clin. U. So. Calif.-Los Angeles Med. Center, 1970—; clin. chief endocrinology Cedars-Sinai Med. Ctr., 1983-87. Served to capt. U.S. Army, 1955-57. Boris Catz lectureship named in his honor Thyroid Research Endowment Fund, Cedars Sinai Med. Ctr., 1985. Fellow ACP, Am. Coll. Nuclear Medicine (pres. elect 1982); mem. AMA, Cedars Sinai Med. Ctr. Soc. for History of Medicine (chmn.), Los Angeles County Med. Soc., Calif. Med. Assn., Endocrine Soc., Am. Thyroid Assn., Soc. Exptl. Biology and Medicine, Western Soc. Clin. Research, Am. Fedn. Clin. Research, Soc. Nuclear Medicine, So. Calif. Soc. Nuclear Medicine, AAAS, N.Y. Acad. Scis., Los Angeles Soc. Internal Medicine, Am. Soc. Internal Medicine, Calif. Soc. Internal Medicine, The Royal Soc. Medicine (affiliate), Collegium Salerni, Cedar Sinai Soc. of History of Medicine, Beverly Hills C. of C., Phi Lambda Kappa. Jewish. Mem. B'nai B'rith. Club: The Profl. Man's (past pres.). Author: Thyroid Case Studies, 1975, 2d edit., 1981. Contbr. numerous articles on thyroidology to med. jours. Home: 300 El Camino Dr Beverly Hills CA 90212 Office: 435 N Roxbury Dr Beverly Hills CA 90210

CAU, JEAN, writer, journalist; b. Bram, Aude, France, July 8, 1925; s. Etienne and Rose (Olivier) C. Licencie Philosophie, Sorbonne, U. Paris. Sec. to Jean-Paul Sartre, 1947-56; editor Les Tempes Modernes, 1949-54; journalist L'Express, Le Figaro litteraire, Candide, France-Observateur, Paris-Match, also others; writer Figaro-Dimanche, 1978—. Author novels: Le coup de barre; Les paroissiens; La pitie de Dieu; Les enfants, 1975; stories: Mon village; chronicle: Les oreilles et la queue, L'incendie de Rome, 1964; plays: Les parachutistes; Le maitre du monde; Dans un nuage de poussiere, 1967; Les yeux creves, 1968; Pauvre France, 1972; transl.: Who's Afraid of Virginia Woolf; Lettre ouverte aux tetes de chiens de l'Occident, 1967; L'agonie de la vieille, 1969; Tropicanas, 1970; Le tempes des esclaves, Les entrailles du taureau, 1971; Traite de moralel: les ecuries de l'occident, 1973, II: la grande prostituee, 1974; Toros, 1973; Pourquoi la France, 1975; Les otrages, 1976; Le chevalier; la mort et le diable; Une nuit a Saint-Germaine des pres; La conquete de Zanzibar et Nouvelles du Paradis, 1980; Le grand soleil, 1981; Une rose à lamer, 1983; film scripts: La curee, 1966; Don Juan, 1973. Decorated chevalier Legion d'honneur; recipient prix Goncourt, 1961. *

CAUAS, JORGE, economist; b. San Felipe, Chile, Aug. 13, 1934; s. Nuncio and Elena (Lama) C.; Civil Engr., U. Chile, 1958; M.A. in Econs., Columbia U., 1961; m. Rosario Montero, Oct. 7, 1972. Vice pres. Central Bank Chile, 1967-70; dir. Inst. Econs., Catholic U. Chile, 1970-72; dir. Devel. Research Center, World Bank, 1972-74; minister of finance of Chile, 1974-76; ambassador to U.S., 1977-78; dir. various corps.; prof. econs. U. Chile, 1965—, Cath. U. Chile, 1965—; mem. devel. com. World Bank-IMF, 1974-78. Decorated Gt. Cross Order Liberator San Martin (Argentina). Mem. Am. Econ. Assn. Roman Catholic. Contbr. to profl. publs. Address: Hernando de Aguirre 600, Apt 112, Santiago Chile

CAUPIN, GILLES MARIE, nuclear engineering company executive, consultant; b. La Madeleine, Nord, France, Sept. 21, 1943; s. Jean-Henri and Edith (de Wazieres) C.; m. Damienne Toulemonde, June 22, 1967; children—Arnaud, Vincent, Matthieu. Engr., Institut Industriel du Nord, Lille, france, 1967. Asst. to chmn. Ets Fenet, Bergueneuse, France, 1967-70; project and cnstrn. group mgr. Procter & Gamble, Brussels, 1970-78; cons. Booz Allen & Hamilton Internat., Paris, 1978-80, Cegos, Paris, 1980-84, project control mgr. Framatome, Paris, 1984—. Contbr. articles on project control to profl. publs. Served to lt. C.E., French Army, 1967-69. Mem. Project Mgmt. Inst., Am. Assn. Cost Engrs. (bd. dirs. French sect. 1982—), Assn. Project Mgrs. (U.K.), Assn. Francaise des Ingenieurs et Techniciens d'Estimation et de Planification (bd. dirs. 1982—), Assn. Francaise de Management de Projet (bd. dirs. 1985—). Avocation: hunting. Office: Framatome Tour Fiat, 92084 Paris-La Defense France

CAUST, COLIN DOUGLAS, market research executive; b. Toowoomba, Queensland, Australia, Sept. 25, 1958; s. Colin James and Gloria May (Sowden) C. BA with distinction, Darling Downs Inst. Advanced Edn., Toowoomba, 1983. Project dir. Australian Sales Research Bur., Melbourne, 1983-84, Roy Morgan Research Ctr., Melbourne, 1984-85; gen. mgr. Roy Morgan Research Ctr., Brisbane, Queensland, 1985—. Author: Segmentation Analysis in Research, 1986; contbr. articles to profl. jours. Mem. Australian Statis. Soc., Australian Market Research Soc., Australian Social Research Assn. Mem. Ch. of Eng. Home: 598 Waterworks Rd Ashgrove, Brisbane 4060, Australia Office: Roy Morgan Research Ctr Suite 1, 96 Lytton Rd, East Brisbane 4169, Australia

CAUTHEN, CHARLES EDWARD, JR., retail food and department store executive; b. Columbia, S.C., Oct. 26, 1931; s. Charles Edward and Rachel (Macaulay) C.; BA, Wofford Coll., 1952; cert. Charlotte Meml. Hosp. Sch. Hosp. Adminstrn., 1956; MS in Bus. Adminstrn. and Labor Mgmt., Kennedy-Western U., 1986, PhD in Bus. Adminstrn., 1986; m. Hazel Electa Peery, June 13, 1959; children—Portia Cauthen White, Sara Rohrer, Rachel Macaulay, Sidney Peery. Asst. adminstr. Union Meml. Hosp., Monroe, N.C., 1956-58; adminstr. Lowrance Hosp., Inc., Mooresville, N.C., 1958-61; v.p., mgr. Va. Acme Market, Bluefield, W.Va., 1961-68; v.p. Acme Markets and A-Mart Stores, (name now Acme Markets of Tazewell, Va., Inc.), North Tazewell, Va., 1965—, exec. v.p., 1968-71, pres., 1971-87, also dir., provost King Coll., Bristol, Tenn., 1987—; dir. Bluefield Supply Co., W.Va., 1968-85; pres. Doran Devel. Corp., 1971-87, Big A Market, Inc., 1981-87. Author: Evaluation of the Small Company For Strategic Planning, Merger or Acquisition, 1987. Deacon, elder, trustee Westminster Presbyn. Ch., Bluefield, W.Va.; provost King Coll., Bristol, Tenn. Served to 1st lt. AUS, 1952-54. Decorated Army Commendation medal, Combat Med. badge. Mem. W.Va. Assn. Retail Grocers (v.p., dir. 1968-82), Va. Food Dealers Assn. (dir. 1978), Bluefield Sales Exec. Club (dir. 1965-67). Republican. Lodge: Rotary (dir. 1966). Home: 1626 King College Rd Bristol TN 37620 Office: King Coll Bristol TN 37620

CAVACO SILVA, ANIBAL, Portuguese prime minister, educator; b. Loule, Portugal, July 15, 1939; s. Teodoro Silva and Maria do Nascimento Cavaco; m. Maria Alves, 1963; children: Patricia, Bruno. BA in Fin., Superior Inst. Econs. and Fin. Scis., Lisbon; grad. Tech. Inst. of Lisbon, 1964; PhD, York U., U.K., 1973. Tchr. pub. econs. and polit. economy Inst. Econ. and Fin. Studies, 1965-67, Cath. U., 1975—, New U. of Lisbon, 1977—; research fellow Calouste Gulbenkian Found., 1967-77; dir. research and statis. dept. Bank of Portugal, 1977-79, 81-85; Minister of Fin. and Planning, 1980-81; pres. Council for Nat. Planning, 1981-84; Prime Minister of Portugal, 1985—; dir. Economia. Author: Budgetary Policy and Economic Stabilization, 1976, Economic Effects of Public Debt, 1977, Public Finance and Macroeconomic Policy, 1982, The Economic Policy of Sa Carneiro's Government, 1982. Contbr. articles on fin. markets, pub. economies and Portuguese econ. policy to profl. jours. Pres. Civic Inst. Algarve. Social Democrat. Address: Partido Social Democrata, Rua Buenos Aires 39, 1269 Lisbon Portugal *

CAVALIERE, ANTONIO, business analyst; b. Naples, Italy, Apr. 25, 1960; s. Tiberio and Matilde (Destefano) C. Degree in econs., Naples U., 1983; MBA, NYU, 1985—. Fin. analyst Eli Lilly and Co., Indpls., 1985-86; bus. analyst Eli Lilly Gesellschaft mit Beschräkter Haftung, Bad Homburg, Fed. Republic Germany, 1986—. Home: 38 Dorotheen Strasse, D-6380 Bad Homburg Federal Republic of Germany Office: Eli Lilly GMBH, 153 Saalburgstrasse, D-6380 Bad Homburg Federal Republic of Germany

CAVANAGH, MICHAEL JAMES, advertising executive; b. Kampala, Uganda, Sept. 22, 1952; arrived in Eng., 1960; s. Desmond Michael and Lesley Anne (Higson) C.; m. Suzanne José Camp, Sept. 22, 1984. Grad. secondary sch., Harpenden, Eng. Traffic controller, asst. to chmn. Howard Panton/Warren Seymour, London, 1969-73; exec. producer Planned Presentations Ltd., London, 1973-77; mng. dir. D. Cavanagh Assocs. Ltd., Harpenden, 1977—. Producer: (directory) Intercoiffure Maison des Nations, 1987. Mem. Inst. Mktg. (social sec. local br. 1987). Mem. Conservative Party. Roman Catholic. Club: Rotoract (pres. 1980-82), Round Table (Harpenden). Home: 2 Giles Close Church End, AL4 9DR Sandridge England Office: Cavanagh Assocs, 10 Vaughan Rd, AL5 4ED Harpenden England

CAVANAGH, PAUL AUGUSTINE, bakery executive; b. Providence, May 27, 1922; s. John Francis and Agnes Louise (Turbitt) C.; m. Helena E. Nadeau, Oct. 5, 1946; children: Denise, Brian, Steven, Peter, Mark, Paula, Jane, Claire. PhB, Providence Coll., 1946; student Biarritz Am. U., 1945, R.I. Sch. Design, 1947. Founder, owner, pres. Cavanagh Co., Smithfield, R.I., 1947—; owner, v.p. Rallypoint Tennis Club; treas. No. Realty, artist, sculptor. Commns. include: bronze portrait bust Bishop McVinney, 1975, design and constrn. of mace, Georgetown U., U. N.H. Coll. St. Rose, and St. Norbert Coll.; numerous figures in silver, bronze and wood; patentee cutting equipment. Mem. Liturg. Commn., Diocese of Providence; bd. trustees Coll. St. Rose (Albany), St. Phillip Ch. Served with AUS, 1943-46. Recipient Personal Achievement award Providence Coll. Roman Catholic. Office: 610 Putnam Ave Greenville RI 02828

CAVANAGH, RICHARD EDWARD, academic administrator, consultant, writer; b. Buffalo, June 15, 1946; s. Joseph John and Mary Celeste (Stack) C. AB, Wesleyan U., Conn., 1968; MBA, Harvard U., 1970. Assoc. McKinsey & Co., Inc., Washington, 1970-77, sr. cons., 1979, ptnr., 1980-87; exec. dir. fed. cash mgmt. U.S. Office Mgmt. and Budget, Washington, 1977-79; exec. dean John F. Kennedy Sch. Govt., Harvard U., Cambridge, Mass., 1987—; mem. staff Carter-Mondale Policy Planning, 1976; cons. Carter-Mondale Presdl. Transition, 1976-77; domestic coordinator Pres.'s Reorgn. Project, The White House, Washington, 1978-79; mem. exec. com. Pres.'s Pvt. Sector Survey on Cost Control, Grace Commn., 1982-83; mem. bus. adv. com. advanced study program Brookings Instn., 1983—; adviser to nat. govts., EEC, N.Y.C. Partnership, Am. Bus. Conf.; quoted on pub. issues in Time, Bus. Week, Nation's Bus., Inc., Fortune, Venture, AP, UPI. Co-author: (with Donald K. Clifford, Jr.) The Winning Performance, 1985; contbr. articles to Wall Street Jour., Mgmt. Rev., Fin. World., Planning Rev., N.Y. Times. Bd. judges Dively Award, Harvard U., 1984—; bd. visitors Georgetown U. Sch. Bus., 1985—; trustee Ctr. for Excellence in Govt., 1985. Served with U.S. Army, 1968. Recipient Presdl. commendation, 1979, 80, 83; John Reilly Knox fellow, 1979, Clark fellow, 1979. Mem. Am. Soc. Pub. Adminstrn., Acad. Polit. Sci., Raimond Duy Baird Assn., Beta Theta Pi. Democrat. Roman Catholic. Club: Harvard (N.Y.C.). Office: Harvard U John F Kennedy Sch Govt 79 John F Kennedy St Cambridge MA 02138

CAVANAH, GARY LYNN, technical services company executive, engineer; b. Kansas City, Mo., Feb. 1, 1941; s. Zillman Gail and Betty Brooke (Burchett) C.; m. Patricia Jane Armbrecht, May 1, 1976. BSEE, Finlay Engring. Coll., 1966. Registered profl. engr., Calif., Kans., Ill., Ohio. Elec. engr. Bailey Controls Co., Wickliffe, Ohio, 1966-73; cons. Fisher Controls Co., Marshalltown, Iowa, 1973-78; pres. SEGA, Inc., Stanley, Kans., 1973—. Mem. Instrument Soc. Am., Nat. Soc. Profl. Engrs. Office: Sega Inc 15238 Cherry St Stanley KS 66223

CAVAZOS, LAURO FRED, university president; b. King Ranch, Tex., Jan. 4, 1927; s. Lauro Fred and Tomasa (Quintanilla) C.; m. Peggy Ann Murdock, Dec. 28, 1954; children—Lauro, Sarita, Ricardo, Alicia, Victoria, Roberto, Rachel, Veronica, Tomas, Daniel. B.A., Tex. Tech U., 1949, M.A., 1951; Ph.D., Iowa State U., 1954. Teaching asst. Tex. Tech U., Lubbock, 1949-51, pres. health scis. ctr., 1980—, prof. biol. sci., 1980—, prof. anatomy health scis. ctr., 1980—; instr. anatomy Med. Coll. Va., asst. prof. anatomy, 1956-60, assoc. prof., 1960-64; prof. anatomy Tufts U. Sch. Medicine, Boston, 1964-80, chmn. dept., 1964-72, assoc. dean, 1972-73, acting dean, 1973-75, dean, 1975-80; spl. and sci. staff New Eng. Med. Ctr. Hosp., Boston, 1974-80; sec. U.S. Dept. Edn., Washington, 1988—; mem. adv. com. fellows program, Nat. Bd. Med. Examiners, 1978; project site visitor Nat. Library of Medicine, 1978, mem. biomed. library rev. com., 1981-85; cons. council med. edn., Tex. Med. Assn., 1980—; active Pan Am. Health Orgn., bd. regents Uniformed Services U. Health Scis., 1980-85; bd. dirs. Diamond Shamrock R&M Inc., 1987—. Mem. editorial bds. Anat. Record, 1970-73, Med. Coll. Va. Quar., 1964—, Tufts Health Sci. Rev., 1972—, Jour. Med. Edn., 1980-85; contbr. articles to profl. jours., chpts. to books. Bd. dirs., campaign chmn. Tex. Tech U. United Way, 1980; mem. Tex. Gov.'s Task Force on Higher Edn., 1980-82; mem. Tex. Gov.'s Higher Edn. Mgmt. Effectiveness Council, 1980-82, chmn., 1981-82; trustee Southwest Research Inst., 1982—; chmn. Lubbock Boy Scout Campaign, 1981, SW Athletic Conf. Council Pres., 1987—. Served with U.S. Army, 1945-46. Elected Disting. Grad., Tex. Tech U., 1977, edn. and teaching awards from graduating med. class, 5 years; recipient Alumni Achievement awards Iowa State U., 1979, Lauro F. Cavazos award Tex. Tech U., 1987; named to Hispanic Hall of Fame League of United Latin American Citizens, 1987, Hispanic Hall of Fame, Hispanic Bus. mag., 1987. Mem. Am. Assn. Anatomists, Endocrine Soc., Histochem. Soc., AAAS, Assn. Am. Med. Colls., Pan Am. Assn. Anatomy (founding, councilor from U.S., rep. Am. Assn. Anatomy, 1974—); Philos. Soc. Tex., Tex. Sci. and Tech. Council (chmn. edn. com. 1984-85), Lubbock C. of C. (bd. dirs.), Tufts Med. Alumni Assn. (hon.), Sigma Xi. Roman Catholic. Office: Dept of Education Office of the Secretary 400 Maryland Ave SW Washington DC 20202 *

CAVAZZA, FABIO LUCA, publishing executive; b. Bologna, Italy, May 24, 1927; s. Giulio and Marina M. (Rossi) C.; m. Adriana Cassarini, July 1, 1961; children: Federico, Marianna. JD, U. Bologna, 1950. Gen. mgr. Il Mulino Publishing House, Bologna, 1951-64, dir., 1964—; dir. La Stampa, Torino, Italy, 1969-71; mng. dir. Il Sole-24 Ore, Milan, 1972-78, editor-in-chief, 1978-80, dep. chmn., 1980-82; dir. Il Corriere della Sera, Milan, 1984—; chmn., chief exec. officer Studi & Servizi Internazionale, Milan, 1986—. Bd. dirs. Inst. per gli Studi Storici Croce, Naples, 1986—. Mem. Océ Italia S.p.A. (chmn.). Roman Catholic. Home: 4 Via Tommaso Salvini, 20122 Milan Italy Office: C & C Co, Via Rossini 5, 20122 Milan Italy

CAVE, RICHARD LESTER, psychologist; b. Wilmington, Del., Dec. 25, 1934; s. Isaac Lester and Nellie Gray (Miller) C.; m. Iva Loretta Efaw, May 14, 1966; children—Carolyn, Richard Alyn, Daniel. Student Maryville Coll., 1952-53, U. Del., 1953-54; B.A., Harding Coll., 1961; postgrad. U. Miss., 1957; LL.B., U. Memphis, 1961; Ph.D., U. Tenn., 1967. Advt. account exec. advt. Memphis Pub. Co., 1958-61; admitted to Tenn. bar, 1961; tech. writer Mallory AFB, Memphis, 1961-62; psychology asst. VA, N.C., Tenn., Md., 1963-65, psychology technician, Washington, 1965-66; instr. in psychology U. Tenn., Knoxville, 1966-67; asst. prof. psychology Okla. Christian Coll., 1967-72; missionary for Church of Christ, Belo Horizonte, Brazil, 1972-76; prof. behavioral scis., chmn. dept. behavioral scis. Freed-Hardeman Coll., 1975-76. Pres. North Chester Elem. Sch. PTA, Henderson, Tenn., 1981-82. Served with USMC, 1954-56. Mem. Psychol. Assn. Founder psychology program Okla. Christian Coll., 1967, Freed-Hardeman Coll., 1978; devel. computer techniques for psychology, 1977—. Home: 623 Barham Ave Henderson TN 38340 Office: Freed-Hardeman Coll Henderson TN 38340

CAVENEY, WILLIAM JOHN, pharmaceutical company executive, lawyer; b. Wheeling, W.Va., Aug. 5, 1944; s. James Joseph and Esther Virginia (Ackermann) C.; AB cum laude, W.Va. U., 1966; JD, Vanderbilt U., 1969; LLM in Taxation, NYU, 1977, Advanced Profl. Cert. in Fin., Grad. Sch. Bus. Adminstrn., 1979; m. Margaret Carol Serota, Sept. 18, 1971; children: Ryan Benjamin, Christine Joanna. Bar: N.Y. 1972, U.S. Supreme Ct. 1976. Tax mgr. Arthur Andersen & Co., N.Y.C., 1969-73; tax atty. Texaco, Inc., N.Y.C., 1973-76; mgr. tax planning Norton Simon, Inc., N.Y.C., 1976-78; dir. tax planning Warner-Lambert Co., Morris Plains, N.J., 1978-79, tax counsel, mem. tax planning com., 1979—; mem. Township Com., Millburn, N.J., Bd. Health , Millburn; lectr. Taxation and internat. fin. CPA, N.Y. Council mem., auditor The Short Hills Assn. Mem. N.Y. State Bar Assn. (mem. exec. com. tax sect.), ABA (com. fgn. activities of U.S. taxpayers), Am. Inst. CPA's, N.Y. State Soc. CPA's, Canadian Tax Found., Tax Execs. Inst., (chmn. internat. tax steering com.), World Trade Inst. Contbr. articles to profl. jours. Club: Beacon Hill (Summit, N.J.). Home: 88 Stewart Rd Short Hills NJ 07078 Office: 201 Tabor Rd Morris Plains NJ 07950

CAVNAR, MARGARET MARY (PEGGY), business executive, former state legislator, nurse; b. Buffalo, July 29, 1945; d. James John and Margaret Mary Murtha Nightengale; B.S. in Nursing, D'Youville Coll., 1967; m. Samuel M. Cavnar, 1977; children—Heather Anne, Heide Lynn, Dona Cavnar Hambly, Judy Cavnar Bentrim. Utilization rev. coordinator South Nev. Meml. Hosp., Las Vegas, 1975-77; v.p. Ranvac Publs., Las Vegas, 1976—; ptnr. Cavnar & Assocs., Reseda, Calif., 1976—, C & A Mgmt., Las Vegas, 1977—; pres. PS Computer Service, Las Vegas, 1978—. Mem. Clark County Republican Central Com., 1977-87, Nev. Rep. Central Com., 1978-80; mem. Nev. Assembly, 1979-81; Rep. nominee for Nev. Senate, 1980; Rep. nominee for Congress from Nev. 1st dist., 1982, 84; bd. dirs., treas. Nev. Med. Fed. Credit Union; v.p. Community Youth Activities Found., Inc., Civic Assn. Am.; mem. utilization rev. bd. Easter Seals; trustee Nev. Sch. Arts, 1980-87; nat. adviser Project Prayer, 1978—; co-chmn. P.R.I.D.E. Com., 1983—; co-chmn. Tax Limitation Com., 1983, Personal Property Tax Elimination Com., 1979-82, Self-Help Against Food Tax Elimination Denial Com., 1980; mem. Nev. Profl. Standards Rev. Orgn., 1984; co-chmn. People Against Tax Hikes, 1983-84; bd. dirs. Nev. Eye Bank, 1988—. Mem. Nev. Order Women Legislators (charter, parliamentarian 1980—), Sigma Theta Tau. Club: Cosmopolitanly Hers Info. (pres.). Office: PO Box 26073 Las Vegas NV 89126

CAVNAR, SAMUEL MELMON, author, publisher, activist; Denver, Nov. 10, 1925; s. Samuel Edward and Helen Anita (Johnston) C.; m. Peggy Nightengale, Aug. 14, 1977; children by previous marriage—Dona Cavnar Hambly, Judy Cavnar Bentrim; children—Heather Anne, Heide Lynn. Student pub. schs., Denver. Dist. mgr. U.S. C. of C., various locations, 1953-58; owner Cavnar & Assocs., mgmt. cons., Washington, Las Vegas, Nev., Denver and Reseda, Calif., 1958—; v.p. Lenz Asso. Advt., Inc., Van Nuys, Calif., 1960—; dist. mgr. Western States Nu-Orm Plans, Inc., Los Angeles, 1947-52; cons. to architect and contractor 1st U.S. Missile Site, Wyo., 1957-58; prin. organizer Westway Corp. and subsidiaries, So. Calif. Devel. Co., 1958—; chmn. bd. Boy Sponsors, Inc., Denver, 1957-59; pres. Continental Am. Video Network Assn. Registry, Inc., Hollywood, Calif., 1967—; pres. United Sales Am., Las Vegas and Denver, 1969—; sr. mgmt. cons. Broadcast Mgmt. Cons. Service, Hollywood, Las Vegas, Denver, Washington, 1970—; pres., dir., exec. com. Am. Ctr. for Edn., 1968—; pub. Nat. Ind., Washington, 1970—, Nat. Rep. Statesman, Washington, 1969—, Nat. Labor Reform Leader, 1970—, Nat. Conservative Statesman, 1975—; owner Ran Vac Pub., Las Vegas and Los Angeles, 1976—; ptnr. P.S. Computer Services, Las Vegas, 1978—, C & A Mgmt., Las Vegas, 1978—, Westway Internat., 1983—; lectr. in field; spl. cons. various U.S. senators, congressmen, 1952—. Author: Run, Big Sam, Run, 1976, The Girls on Top, 1978, Big Brother Bureaucracy, The Cause and Cure, 1979, Kiddieland West, 1980, Games Politicians Play: How to Clean Up Their Act, 1981, A Very C.H.I.C. President, 1981, How to Clean Up Our Act, 1982, Assassination By Suicide, 1984, How to Get Limited Government, Limited Taxes, 1985, Tax Reform or Bust, 1985, At Last: Real Tax Reform, 1986. Nat. gen. chmn. Operation Houseclean, 1966-81; nat. candidate chmn. Citizens Com. To Elect Rep. Legislators, 1966, 68, 70, 72-74, 85—; mem. Calif. and Los Angeles County Rep. Cen. Coms., 1964-70; nat. gen. chmn. Project Prayer, 1962—; exec. dir. Project Alert, 1961—; nat. chmn. Nat. Labor Reform Com., 1969—; sustaining mem. Rep. Nat. Com., 1964—; Western states chmn. and nat. co-chmn. Am. Taxpayers Army, 1959—; area II chmn. Calif. Gov.'s Welfare Reform Com., 1970; chmn. Com. Law and Order in Am., 1975; mem. Nev. State Rep. Com., 1972—; mem. Clark County Rep. Com., 1972—; bd. dirs. Conservative Caucus, Las Vegas, 1980—; Rep. candidate for U.S. Senate from Nev., 1976, 82; Rep. candidate for U.S. Congress from 30th dist. Calif., 1968, 70; nat. chmn. Return Pueblo Crew, 1968, Citizens League for Labor Reform, 1984—; nat. co-chmn. U.S. Taxpayers Forces, 1985—; pres., trustee Community Youth Activities Found., 1977—; nat. chmn. Operation Bus Stop, 1970—, P.R.I.D.E. Com., 1981—, Positivics Program, 1982—; co-chmn. Question 8 Com., 1980-82, S.H.A.F.T.E.D. Tax Repeal Com., 1982 C.H.I.C. Polit. Edn. Com., 1977—, People Against Tax Hikes Com., 1983—. Served with USN, 1942-45, USAF, 1950-53, Korea; comdr. USCG Aux., 1959-60. Recipient Silver medal SAR. Mem. Am. Legion (comdr. 1947-48, mem. nat. conv. disting. guest com. 1947-52), DAV, VFW, Am. Security Council (nat. adviser 1966—). Home: 301A Misty Isle Ln Las Vegas NV 89107 Office: PO Box 26073 Las Vegas NV 89126

CAVONIUS, CARL RICHARD, physiology educator; b. Santa Barbara, Calif., Dec. 23, 1932; came to W. Ger., 1977; s. Carl Volmar and Lillie (Vertti) C.; m. Rita Catherine Euerle, July 11, 1981; 1 dau., Lillie. B.A., Wesleyan U., 1953; M.S., Brown U., 1960, Ph.D., 1961. Sr. research scientist Human Scis. Research, McLean, Va., 1962-64; dir. Eye Research Found., Bethesda, Md., 1965-70; prof. U. Munich, Fed. Republic Germany, 1971-72; Cattell fellow U. Cambridge, Eng., 1972-73; sr. sci. officer U. Amsterdam, Netherlands, 1974-76; prof. physiology Inst. Arbeitsphysiologie, U. Dortmund, Fed. Republic Germany, 1977—; fgn. corr. Nat. Acad. Sci., Washington, 1977—; dir. Inst. Pedestrian Res., Grantchester, U.K., 1974—; ad hoc reviewer NIH, Bethesda, NSF, Washington. Contbr. numerous articles to sci. jours. Served to lt. comdr. 1954-59. USPHS fellow, 1961, Humboldt fellow, 1971, Cattell fellow, 1973; European Sci. Found. grantee, 1983. Fellow Optical Soc. Am.; mem. Exptl. Psychology Soc., European Brain and Behavior Soc., European Vision Conf. (chmn. 1986), Res. Officers Assn. (v.p. Europe 1983). Home: Am Paternoster, D-4600 Dortmund-Somborn Federal Republic of Germany Office: Inst Arbeitsphysiologie, Ardeystrasse 67, D-4600 Dortmund 1 Federal Republic of Germany

CAYETANO, DAVID MATA, safety engineer, consultant; b. Laoag, Philippines, Dec. 22, 1909; came to U.S., 1930; s. Pascual Hernando (Cayetano) and Teodora (Cid) Mata; m. Felipa Kihano, Nov. 23, 1933; children: Gloriana Cayetano Castillo, Lorna, Fay Cayetano Vazquez, Esther Cayetano Bieda. Diploma in engring., Internat. Correspondence Sch., Scranton, Pa., 1944; diploma, Real Estate Inst., Honolulu, 1975; student, Cen. Mich. U., 1978; BA in Pub. Adminstrn. and Polit. Sci., U. Hawaii, 1981. Registered profl. engr., Calif. Safety dir., engr. Oahu Sugar Co., Waipahu, Hawaii, 1956-72; cons. Honolulu, 1972—; liquor commr. City of Honolulu, 1964-72; bd. dirs. Internat. Cooperation Ctr. hawaii, 1958. Active Gov.'s Commn. Fgn. Aid, Honolulu, 1956. Named Engr. of Yr., Hawaii Dept. Labor, 1961, Man of Week, Honolulu C. of C., 1949, Father of Yr., Honolulu Star Bull., 1961; recipient War Service award Office of Price Adminstrn., 1945, Honor award Hawaii chpt. ARC, 1962. Mem. NSPE, Hawaii Soc. of NSPE, Am. Soc. Safety Engrs. Home: 91-623C Pohakupuna Rd Ewa Beach HI 96706

CAZALAS, MARY REBECCA WILLIAMS, lawyer, nurse; b. Atlanta, Nov. 11, 1927; d. George Edgar and Mary Annie (Slappey) Williams; m. Albert Joseph Cazalas (dec.). R.N., St. Joseph's Infirmary Sch. Nursing, Atlanta, 1948; B.S. in Pre-medicine, Oglethorpe U., 1954; M.S. in Anatomy, Emory U., 1960; J.D., Loyola U., 1967. Gen. duty nurse, 1948-68; instr. maternity nursing St. Joseph's Infirmary Sch. Nursing, 1954-59; med. researcher in urology Tulane U. Sch. Medicine, 1961-65; legal researcher for presiding judge La. Ct. Appeals (4th cir.), 1965-71; sole practice, 1967-71; asst. U.S. atty., New Orleans, 1971-79; sr. trial atty. EEOC, New Orleans, 1979-84; owner Cazalas Apts., New Orleans, 1962—; lectr. in field. Contbr. articles to med. and legal publs. Bd. advisors Loyola U. Sch. Law, New Orleans, 1974, v.p. adv. bd., 1975; mem. New Orleans Drug Abuse Adv. Com., 1976-80, task force Area Agy. on Aging, 1976-80, pres.'s council Loyola U., 1978—, adv. bd. Odyssey House, Inc., New Orleans, 1973; chmn. women's com. Fed. Exec. Bd., 1974; bd. dirs. Bethlehem House of Bread, 1975-79. Named Hon. La. State Senator, 1974; recipient Superior Performance award U.S. Dept. Justice, 1974, Cert. Appreciation Fed. Exec. Bd., 1975, 76, 77, 78, Rev. E.A. Doyle award, 1976, commendation for teaching Guam Legislature, 1977. Mem. Am. Judicature Soc., La. State Bar Assn., Fed. Bus. Assn. (v.p. 1976—, pres. 1976-78, bd. dirs. 1972-75), Fed. Bar Assn. (1st v.p. 1973, pres. New Orleans chpt. 1974-75, nat. council 1974-79), Assn. Women Lawyers, Nat. Health Lawyers Assn., DAR, Bus. and

Profl. Women's Club, Am. Heart Assn., Emory Alumni Assn., Oglethorpe U. Alumni Assn., Loyola U. Alumni Assn. (bd. dirs. 1974-75, 1977, v.p. 1976), Jefferson Parish Hist. Soc., Phi Delta Delta (merged with Phi Alpha Delta, pres. 1970-72, bd. dirs., vice justice 1974-75), Sierra Club, Alpha Epsilon Delta, Phi Sigma, Leconte Hon. Sci. Soc. Democrat.

CAZAN, MATTHEW JOHN, educator; b. Beclean, Romania, Mar. 10, 1912; s. John and Marie (Sipos) C.; student U. Bucharest Law Sch., Youngstown Coll., Georgetown U. Sch. Fgn. Service; m. Sylvia Marie Buday, July 14, 1935; 1 son, Matthew John George. Lectr. Georgetown U., 1942-44; spl. lectr. Indsl. Coll. of the Armed Forces, 1947; asso. in Romanian Georgetown U. Inst. Langs. and Linguistics, 1949—, lectr. polit. sci. and econs. Sch. Fgn. Service, 1943-57; lectr. The Inst. Fgn. Service Officer Preparation, 1953—; lectr. polit. sci. George Washington U., 1963—; spl. employee U.S. Dept. of Justice, 1947-60, 63—; internat. claims analyst fgn. claims settlement commn., 1960-63. Chmn. Lobarca youth guidance com. Va. Gov.'s Conf. Youth. Mem. Am. Assn. U. Profs., Am. Polit. Sci. Assn., Am. Soc. Internat. Law, Conf. Democratic Theory, Pi Gamma Mu. Home: 6369 Lakeview Dr Lake Barcroft Estates Falls Church VA 22041 Office: George Washington U Washington DC 20052 also: Dept Justice Washington DC 20530

CAZAN, SYLVIA MARIE BUDAY (MRS. MATTHEW JOHN CAZAN), realtor; b. Youngstown, Ohio, Nov. 17, 1915; d. John J. and Sylvia (Grama) Buday; student U. Bucharest, (Rumania), 1933-35. Youngstown Coll., 1936-38, Georgetown U. Inst. Langs. and Linguistics, 1950; m. Matthew John Cazan, July 14, 1935; 1 son, Matthew John G. Adminstrv. asst. statistics U.S. Dept. Def., 1941-52; spl. employee Dept. Justice, 1956-58; mgr. James L. Dixon & Co. Realtors, Falls Church, Va., 1959-70; mgr. Lewis & Silverman Inc., Chevy Chase, Md., 1970—. Mem. bd. Examiners Georgetown U., 1950. Bd. dirs. Magnolia Internat. Debutante Ball. Recipient Commendation and Meritorious award Dept. Justice, 1958. Mem. Gen. Fedn. Women's Clubs (pres. 1955-56), Interscholastic Debating Soc., Md. Bd. Realtors, Washington, No. Va. real estate bds. Mem. Rumanian Orthodox Ch. Home: 6369 Lakeview Dr Lake Barcroft Estates Falls Church VA 22041 Office: 8401 Connecticut Ave Chevy Chase MD 20015

CAZEAU, BERNARD JEAN-FRANÇOIS, physician; b. Bordeaux, Aquitaine, France, Apr. 27, 1939; s. Jean Cazeau; m. Danielle Jeanne Poumares, Apr. 1958 (div. 1980); children: Jean Francois, Cèline; m. Claude Lechêne, Mar. 2, 1986. Dr. en Medecine, Faculté de Medecine, Bordeaux, 1968. Diplomate in Gènèraliste Medecin. Maire Riberac, France, 1971—; conseiller gèneral De la Dordogne, Ríberac, 1976—; conseiller regional D'Aquitaine, Ríberac, 1977—; v.p. Conseil Regional, 1981-85; 1st v.p. Conseil Gen. de Dordogne, 1982—. Served as medecin aspirant French Marines, 1967-68. Mem. Parli Socialiste. Home: La Crouzille, 24600 Riberac France Office: Maison Medicale, 36 rue du 26 Mars, 24600 Riberac France

CAZENAVE, ROBERT, lawyer; b. Orthez, France, Feb. 28, 1913; s. Georges and Marie (Vieira) C.; Baccalaureat in Latin-Greek, Phil., Math., U. Bordeaux, 1931; Licence en Droit, U. Toulouse, 1935, diplomes d'Etudes Superieures Droit Prive, Droit Romain and Histoire du Droit, Sc. Pénales, 1936, Dr.Droit, 1937; m. Simonne Pepin, Sept. 15, 1936; children—Raymond (dec.), Bertrand. Admitted to bar, 1935; advocate, Toulouse, 1935-50, Yaounde, Cameroons, 1951-68; patent and trade mark atty., Yaounde, 1964—; mem. Commn. Reform Législative Cameroons, pres. subcommn. civil procedures, 1958-62; prof. indsl. property Ecole Nat. d'Adminstrn. et de Magistrature Cameroons, 1967-78; lectr. in field. Pres. Conseil Dept. Resistance, Toulouse, 1944-50; v.p. Office Dept. War Vets, 1944-50. Union Dept. Assns. Familiales, 1948-50; mem. French abroad council Ministry Fgn. Affairs France, 1970-75. Served with French Army and Resistance (staff underground Region 4), 1940-45. Decorated Medaille de la Resistance, Croix du Combattant, Croix du Combattant Volontaire de la Resistance, chevalier Legion of Honor; chevalier and officer Ordre de la Valeur (Cameroons). Fellow Internat. Inst. Community Service; mem. Internat. Assn. Protection Indsl. Property (v.p. 1966—), World Assn. Lawyers (a founder), Assn. Protection Indsl. Property in French-Speaking Africa (pres. 1966—), Ligue Camerounaise des Droits de l'Homme (pres. 1956-60), Ligue Camerounaise de l'Enseignement (pres. 1956-60), Académie Européenne des Scis., Lettres et des Arts (corr.). Clubs: Yaounde Rotary (past pres.), Yaounde Golf (pres. bd. dirs. 1960-80). Author: La Procedure en Justice, 1959; contbr. to various books, including: Patents Throughout the World, 1980; Trademarks throughout the World, 1980; Katzarov's International Manual on Industrial Property, 1980; La Fontaine Salee de Salies-de-Bearn, une forme de Propriete en marge du Code Civil 1937; contbr. numerous articles to newspapers, jud. and indsl. property jours. Home: Quartier Stade Omnisports, Yaounde BP 500, Cameroons also: 21 Blvd Jean Sarrailh, 64000 Pau France Office: Quartier Stade Omnisports, PO Box 500, Yaounde Cameroon

CAZES, BERNARD, long-term planner; b. Hanoi, North Vietnam, Feb. 14, 1927; s. Antoine and Yvonne (Charrier) C.; m. Georgette Beros, Feb. 2, 1952; children: Jerome, Vincent (dec.). BA in History, U.Bordeaux, France, 1948; Grad., Nat. Sch. Adminstrn, Paris, 1955. Jr. civil servant French Treasury, Paris, 1956-59; staff mem. Commissariat Gen. du Plan, Paris, 1960-78, head div. long-term studies, 1978—. Author: La Vie Economique, 1966, L'Histoire des Futurs, 1986; editor Turgot's Economic Writings. Comdr. order Alfonso X the Wise, officer Legion D'Honneur. Mem. Agorametrie Survey Assn. (pres.). Home: 60B rue Benoit Malon, 92130 Issy France Office: Commissariat du Plan, 18 rue de Martignac, 75007 Paris France

CÉ, MARCO CARDINAL, patriarch of Venice, former bishop of Bologna; b. Izano, Italy, July 8, 1925. Ordained priest Roman Catholic Ch., 1948; tchr. sacred scripture and dogmatic theology at sem. in Diocese of Crema (Italy); rector seminary, 1957; presided over diocesan liturgical commn., preached youth retreats; ordained titular bishop of Vulturia, 1970; aux. bishop of Bologna (Italy), 1970-76; gen. eccles. asst. of Italian Cath. Action, 1976-78; patriarch of Venice, 1978—, elevated to Sacred Coll. of Cardinals, 1979; titular ch., St. Mark. Mem. congregations Clergy, Cath. Edn. Office: Curia Patriarcale, S Marco, 320-A, Venice 30124 Italy *

CEADEL, MARTIN ERIC, politics educator; b. Cambridge, Eng., Jan. 28, 1948; s. Eric Bertrand and Pamela Mary (Perkins) C.; m. Deborah Jane Stockton, July 27, 1974; children: Jack, Jemima, Dickon. BA, Oxford U., 1969, MA, PhD, 1977. Lectr. Sussex U., Eng., 1973-74, Imperial Coll., London, 1974-79; fellow, tutor New Coll., Oxford, Eng., 1979—. Author: Pacifism in Britain 1914-45, 1980, Thinking About Peace and War, 1987; contbr. articles to profl. jours. Home: 47 Bainton Rd, Oxford OX2 7AG, England Office: New Coll, Oxford OX1 3BN, England

CEAUSESCU, ELENA, Romanian government official; b. Jan. 7, 1919; ed. Coll. Indsl. Chemistry Poly. Inst., Bucharest; Dr. (hon.), U. Buenos Aires, 1974, U. Malta, 1983, U. Islamabad, 1984, others; m. Nicolae Ceausescu. Active, Union Communist Youth; mem. Romanian Communist Party, 1937—, mem. central com., 1972—, mem. exec. com., 1973—, mem. polit. exec. com., 1974—, mem. standing bur., 1979—; mem. Grand Nat. Assembly, 1975—; 1st dept. prime minister Govt. of Romania, 1980—; prof. extraordinary Nat. Autonomous U. Mex., 1978. Dir., Inst. of Chemistry, 1964-65; gen. dir. Central Inst. Chemistry, 1975-80; dep. chair Supreme Council of Socio-Econ. Devel., 1982—; Decorated Hero Socialist Labour, Order Victory of Socialism, Star Socialist Republic of Romania, Hero of Socialist Republic of Romania. Fellow Royal Inst. Chemistry; mem. Nat. Council Front of Socialist Democracy and Unity, 1980—, Central Inst. Chem. Research, Nat. Council Sci. and Tech. (mem. exec. bur. 1972—, chmn., 1979—), Romanian Acad., N.Y. Acad. Scis., Inst. Egypt, Athens Acad., Internat. Inst. Indsl. Chemistry, Internat. Soc. Indsl. Chemistry France, Royal Inst. Chemistry (U.K.), Acad. of Sci. (Ill.), Chem. Soc. Méx., Acad. Scis. III. Author: Research on the Synthesis and Description of Macromolecular Compounds, 1974; Stereospecific Polymerization of Isopreme, 1979; New Research Work on Macromolecular Compounds, 1981; Studies on Chemistry and Technology of Polymers, 1983; Encyclopedia of Chemistry, vol. 1, 1983; contbr. articles to profl. jours. Office: Comitetul Cen, Partidul Comunist Roman, Str Academiei 34, Bucharest Romania *

CEAUSESCU, NICOLAE, president of Romania; b. Scornicesti-Olt, Romania, Jan. 26, 1918; state diploma econs. Acad. Econ. Studies, Bucharest; D. Polit. Sci. and D.Econs. Acad. Socialist Republic of Romania, 1978; PhD (hon.), univs. Bucharest, 1973, Bogotá, 1973, Quito, 1973, Lima, 1974, Beirut, 1974, Buenos Aires, 1974, Bahia Blanca, 1974, Nice, 1975, Quezon City, 1975, Yucatán, 1975, Teheran, 1975, Liberia, 1988; m. Elena Ceausescu; children: Valentin, Elena, Nicolae. Participant in working revolutionary movement, 1931—; mem. Union Communist Youth, 1930, sec. central com., 1939-40, sec.-gen., 44-46; mem. Romanian Communist Party, 1933—, mem. central com., 1945—, sec. cen. com., 1954-65, party, 1965-69; sec.-gen. party, 1969—, mem. polit. exec. com., 1974—; dep. minister of agr., 1948-50, of armed forces, 1950-54; dep. Grand Nat. Assembly, 1946—; pres. Council of State of Socialist Republic of Romania, 1967—, pres. republic, 1974—; pres. Nat. Council Socialist Unity Front, 1968—, Def. Council, 1969—; supreme comdr. Armed Forces, 1969—; chmn. Supreme Council Social and Econ. Devel., Nat. Council Working People. Hon. pres. Acad. Social and Polit. Scis. Socialist Republic of Rumania, 1970—; hon. pres. Acad. Socialist Republic of Romania, 1985—. Named Hero of Socialist Republic of Romania, 1971, 78, 81; decorated orders and distinction of 64 states, including Order Karl Marx (E.Ger.); Order Lenin (USSR); Gold Medal Frederic Joliot-Curie Peace award, 1977; named hon. mem. Anversane Acad., 1983—; Author: Romania on the Way to Building Up the Multilaterally Developed Society, 30 vols., 1969-87; Selected Works, vols. 1-5, 1965-87, Interviews, Statements and Press Conferences, vols. 1-4, 1966-85. Address: Office of Pres, Bucharest Romania

CEBRIÁN ECHARRI, JUAN LUIS, editor; b. Madrid, Spain, Oct. 30, 1944; s. Vicente Cebriá n Carabias and Carmen Echarri; grad. in journalism EOP, Madrid, 1963; divorced; children—Daniel, Eva, Juan, Rebecca. Founding mem. Cuadernos para el Dialogo, Madrid, 1963; sr. editor Pueblo, Madrid, 1962-67; sr. editor Informaciones, Madrid, 1968, dep. editor, 1969-75; dir. news programming Spanish TV, Madrid, 1974; editor-in-chief El País newspaper, Madrid, 1976—. Recipient first prize Control to dir. of an info. medium, 1976-77, 77-78, 78-79, 79-80, 80-81; Blanco y Negro (best journalist), 1979; Pantera (award Arca de Noe), best journalist, 1979; Editor-of-Yr. award World Press Rev., 1980; Spanish Nat. Journalism prize, 1983. Mem. Internat. Press Inst. (exec. bd. 1978—, working com. 1980, v.p. 1982-86, chmn., 1986—), Nueva Generación, Sociedad Económica Madritense, Asociación de la Prensa. Contbr. articles to profl. jours. Office: Miguel Yuste 40, 28037 Madrid Spain *

CEBRIK, MELVIN LAWRENCE, banker; b. Newark, Mar. 19, 1947; s. Michael and Melvina Helen (Nemo) C.; A.B., Colgate U., 1968; M.B.A., N.Y.U., 1970, advanced profl. cert., 1975; m. Elizabeth Ann Recchione, Aug. 16, 1970; children—Kimberly, Kristta. Asst. sec. Chemical Bank, N.Y.C., 1970-76; dir. planning Bradford Nat. Corp., N.Y.C., 1976-78; v.p. Chase Manhattan Bank, N.A., N.Y.C., 1978—; exec. v.p., dir. Western Hemisphere Life Ins. Co., affiliate Chase Manhattan Bank, N.Y.C., 1982—; v.p., dir. Chase Agy. Services, Inc., 1983—. Mem. Kappa Mu Epsilon, Beta Gamma Sigma. Home: 43 Gloria Dr Allendale NJ 07401

CECCARELLI, JEAN GABRIEL, airline executive; b. Tunis, Tunisia, July 29, 1941; s. Albert and Helene (Aicardo) C.; m. Yanick Guiteau, Oct. 15, 1971; children: Aude, Diane. Mcht. marine, Naval Acad., Le Havre, FRance, 1962; degree in mgmt., Coll. Social and Econ. Scis., Nat. Coll. Arts and Trades, Paris, 1969. Commd. 2d lt. French Navy; advanced through grades to lt. comdr; gen. mgr., v.p. Sodetair, Paris, 1981-85; gen. mgr. cargo for Japan Air France, Tokyo, 1985—. Roman Catholic. Home: Homat Orient ichi Bancho, Chiyoda-ku, Tokyo Japan Office: Air France, New Aoyama Bldg, West 15 F, Minato-ku, Tokyo 107, Japan

CECCHETTI, GIOVANNI, poet, educator, literary critic; b. Pescia, Italy, July 12, 1922; came to U.S., 1948, naturalized, 1954; s. Agostino and Adorna (Fattorini) C.; m. Ruth Elizabeth Schwabacher, Dec. 27, 1953; children: Stephen G., Margaret F. Liceo Machiavelli, Lucca, 1939-40; Liceo Dante, Florence, Italy, 1940-41, Maturità classica, 1941; Lit.D., U. Florence, 1947. Lectr. to asst. prof. U. Calif. at Berkeley, 1948-57; assoc. prof., prof. Tulane U., 1957-65; prof. Stanford U., 1965-69, charge Italian program, 1965-69; prof. UCLA, 1969—, disting. prof., 1985—, chmn. dept. Italian, 1969-77; cons. U. Colo., U. Iowa, 1957; disting. vis. internat. lectr. Author: La poesia del Pascoli, 1954, G. Verga, The She-Wolf and other stories, 1958, rev., 1973, Leopardi e Verga, 1962, Diario nomade, 1967, Il Verga maggiore, 1968, 73, 75, Impossible scendere, 1978, Giovanni Verga, a critical monograph, 1978, Le Operette morali, Tre studi con un poscritto sui Canti, 1979, G. Verga, Mastró -don Gesualdo, 1979, Il villaggio degli inutili, 1980, Nel cammino dei monti, 1980, G. Leopardi, Operette morali/Essays and Dialogues, 1982, Spuntature e intermezzi, 1983, Danza nel deserto, 1985, Favole spente, 1988; assoc. editor: Forum Italicum; contbr. essays and poems to European and Am. jours. Served with Italian Liberation Army, 1943-45. Decorated Star of Solidarity Italian Govt., knight and cavaliere ufficiale, Presdl. gold medal for spl. cultural and artistic merits Republic of Italy, Targa d'Oro Regione Puglia; honored with a Festschrift, 1988. Mem. MLA, Am., Am. Assn. Tchrs. Italian, Dante Soc. Am., Leonardo Da Vinci Soc., Patrons of Italian Culture. Home: 1191 Lachman Ln Pacific Palisades CA 90272 Office: Dept Italian U Calif Los Angeles CA 90024

CEDAR, PAUL ARNOLD, minister; b. Mpls., Nov. 4, 1938; s. C. Benjamin and Bernice P. Cedar; m. Jean Helen Lier; children: Daniel Paul, Mark John, Deborah Jean. BS, No. State Coll., S.D., 1960; postgrad., Trinity Div. Sch., 1962, Wheaton Grad. Sch., 1962, U. Iowa Grad. Sch. of Religion, 1965; M Div., No. Baptist Theol. Sem., 1968; postgrad., Calif. State U., Fullerton, 1971; D Ministry, Am. Baptist Sem., 1973. Ordained to ministry, 1966. Crusade dir. Leighton Ford Team, 1967-69; sr. pastor Evang. Free Ch. of Yorba Linda, Calif., 1969-73; exec. pastor of evangelism 1st Presbyn. Ch. of Hollywood, Calif., 1975-80; sr. pastor Lake Ave. Congl. Ch., Pasadena, Calif., 1981—; pres. Dynamic Communications, Pasadena, Calif., 1973—; mem. adv. bd. World Wide Pictures, Mpls., 1982-86; guest dean Billy Graham Sch. Evangelism, Mpls., 1983—; adj. prof. Fuller Theol. Sem., Pasadena, 1978—, Talbot Theol. Sem., LaHabra, Calif., 1978—. Author: Seven Keys to Maximum Communication, 1980, Servant Leadership in The Church, 1986. Vice chmn. Billy Graham So. Calif. Crusade, 1984-85. Mem. Lausanne Com. for World Evangelization, Phi Kappa Delta (life). Club: University. Home: 848 W Huntington Dr Arcadia CA 91006 Office: Lake Ave Congl Ch 393 North Lake Ave Pasadena CA 91101

CEDENO, GEORGE LUIS, architect; b. N.Y.C., June 8, 1936; s. George Luis and Odile (Ramirez) C.; m. Diana M. Gambaro, Dec. 26, 1959; children—Karen, Anthony, Debra. B.Arch., Rensselaer Poly. Inst., 1960. Registered architect N.J. Jr. architect Alfonso Alvarez, Montclair, N.J., 1960-62; assoc. W.O. Biernacki-Poray, Montclair, 1962-67, The Grad Partnership, Newark, 1967-74; prin. The Hillier Group, Princeton, N.J., 1974—; works include: Eastern Airlines Reservation Ctr., 1971 (Concrete Design award N.J. Soc. Architects 1971); Jersey City Health Ctr. (award 1978), 1977. Archtl. advisor Boy Scouts Am., Montclair, 1972; bd. trustees Assn. Advancement Mental Health, Princeton, 1982-87; bd. dirs. Internat. Assn. of Conf. Ctrs., 1987—; pres. Greater Princeton Youth Orch., Princeton, 1984—. Mem. N.J. Soc. Architects (N.J. conv. chmn. 1978), AIA. Home: 1201 Stuart Rd Princeton NJ 08540 Office: The Hillier Group 500 Alexander Park Princeton NJ 08543-0023

CEDERVALL, GOESTA HUGO, metallurgical company executive; b. Vaestanfors, Sweden, Feb. 7, 1925; arrived in W.Ger., 1968; s. Carl Gustaf and Aina Maria (Goerling) C.; m. Viveka Margareta Huitfeldt, Jan. 4, 1963; children—Camilla, Christina, Patrik. Degree in Mining and Metall. Engring., Royal Inst. Tech., Stockholm, 1949. Asst. to mgr. R-N Process Agy, Brussels, Belgium, 1958-61; tech. adviser Ferrox SA, G Geneva, 1961-65; metall. engr. Stora Kopparberg, Falun, Sweden, 1965-68; mgr. tech. services QIT-Fer et Titane GmbH, Frankfurt, W.Ger., 1968-69, mng. dir., 1969—; chmn. ductile iron com. Internat. Pig Iron Secretariat, Duesseldorf, W.Ger., 1970-72, chmn. tech. devel. com., 1987—. Patentee in steel casting; contbr. articles to profl. jours. Chmn. Alliance Française, Falun, Sweden, 1965-68; bd. dirs. Swedish Ch., Frankfurt. Recipient Dropsy medal, 1968. Mem. Iron and Steel Inst., Metals Soc., Verein Deutscher Eisenhuettenleute, Svenska Bergsmannafoereningen, Svenska Metallograffoerbundet. Lodge: Sancte Oerjens Gille (Stockholm). Office: QIT-Fer et Titane GmbH, Westendstrasse 8, D-6000 Frankfurt am Main 1 Federal Republic of Germany

CELA, CAMILO JOSE, author; b. May 11, 1916; student U. Madrid. Dir., pub. Jour. Papeles de Son Armadans; mem. Real Acad. Espanola, 1957, Premio de la critica, 1955—, Premio Nacional de Literatura, 1984—; Premio Principe de Asturias, 1987—; author: La Familia de Pascual Duarte, 1942; Pabellon de reposo, 1943; Nuevas andanzas y desventuras de Lazarillo de Tormes, 1944-55; Pisando la dudosa luz del dia, 1945; Mesa revuelta, 1945, 57; Viaje a la Alcarria, 1948; La Colmena, 1951; Del Mino al Bidasoa, 1952; Mrs. Caldwell habla con su hijo, 1953; La Catira, 1955, Judios, moros y cristianos, 1956; El molino de viento, 1956; Nuevo retablo de don Cristobita, 1957; Tobogan de hambrientos, 1962; Viaje al Pirineo de Lerida, 1965; Diccionario Secreto, 1968; Maria Sabina, 1968; San Camilo 1936, 1969; Oficio de tinieblas, 1973; A vueltas con Espana, 1973; Rol de cornudos, 1976; Vuelta de hoja, 1981; Mazurca para dos muertos, 1983; El asno de Buridan, 1986; Nuevo viaje a la Alcarria, 1986. Address: La Bonanova, 07015 Palma de Mallorca Spain

CELEDON, HERNANDO, petrochemical company executive; b. Barranquilla, Colombia, Jan. 27, 1936; s. Martin and Priscila (Manotas) C.; m. Yasmina Moreno, Sept. 17, 1960; children: Beatriz, Marjorie, Hernando. Degree in Chem. Engring., U. Tulsa, 1959. Process and design engr. Internat. Petroleum Co., Cartagena, Bolivia, 1959-62; tech.-prodn. supt. Amocar Corp., Cartagena, 1962-67; v.p. ops. Monómeros Colombo Venezolanos S.A., Barranquilla, 1968-81, pres., 1981—; bd. dirs. Banco Cafetero/Promotora del Atlántico, ADIFAL. Patentee system for crystallization of ammonium sulfate. Chmn. Prodevel. Inc., Barranquilla, 1979-80; founder Social Crusade, 1987; bd. dirs. Barranquilla C. of C., Mcpl. Water Works, Mcpl. Telephone Co., State Electric Co., 1970-78. Recipient Medal of Profl. Merit Colombian Assn. Chem. Engrs., 1982. Mem. Presidents Assn. AMA, Assn. Petroquimica del Atlántico. Mem. Partido Conservative. Roman Catholic. Clubs: Executives, Barranquilla, Barranquilla Country. Office: Monomeros Colombo Venezolanos SA, Via 40 Las Flores, Barranquilla 044310, Colombia

CELESTE, RICHARD F., governor of Ohio; b. Cleve., Nov. 11, 1937; s. Frank C.; m. Dagmar Braun, 1962; children: Eric, Christopher, Gabriella, Noelle, Natalie, Stephen. B.A. in History magna cum laude, Yale U., 1959; Ph.B. in Politics, Oxford U., 1962. Staff liaison officer Peace Corps, 1963; dir. Peace Corps, Washington, 1979-81; spl. asst. to U.S. ambassador to India, 1963-67; mem. Ohio Ho. of Reps., Columbus, 1970-74, majority whip, 1972-74; lt. gov. State of Ohio, Columbus, 1974-79, gov., 1983—. Mem. Ohio Democratic Exec. Com. Rhodes scholar Oxford U., Eng. Mem. Am. Soc. Pub. Adminstrn., Italian Sons and Daus. Am. Methodist. Office: Office of Gov State Capitol Columbus OH 43215 *

CELESTIN, MARTIAL, former prime minister of Haiti; b. Ganthier, Haiti, Oct. 4, 1913. 1st sec. to ambassador from Haiti Paris, 1950-53; chargé d'affaires Haiti, 1950-51, prin. asst. to minister fgn. affairs, 1953-56, sec. gen., 1956; prof. law Faculty of Law, Port-Au-Prince, Haiti, 1982-86; prime minister, minister of justice Haiti, Port-Au-Prince, 1988. Address: Office Prime Minister, Port-au-Prince Haiti *

CELEYRETTE, NICOLE PIETRI, French literature educator; b. Nice, France, Apr. 29, 1931; d. Antoine Salle and Julie Martin (Tallon) Pietri; m. Charles Hesse Schön, Dec. 27, 1955 (div. 1971); children: Walter, Wilfrid; m. Jean Deillias Celeyrette, Dec. 29, 1972; 1 child, Agathe. Docteur d'Etat in French Lit., U. Paris Sorbonne, 1977. Tchr. Lycée Marcelin Berthelot, St. Maur, France, 1956-68; fellow asst. U. Paris X, Nanterre, France, 1969-71; asst. U. Paris XII, Créteil, France, 1972-82, prof. French lit., 1983—. Author: Valéry et le Moi, 1979, Les Dictionnaires des Poétes, 1985; editor: P. Valéry Cahiers I., 1987; contbr. articles to profl. jours. and dictionaries. Home: 7 Bis Ave du Rocher, 94100 Saint Maur France Office: U Paris XII, Ave Gal de Gaulle, 94000 Creteil France

CELIO, NELLO, lawyer, political official; b. Feb. 12, 1914. Ed., U. Basel, U. Berne. Sec. Cantonal Dept. Interior, Switzerland, 1941-45; Public Procurator Switzerland, 1945-46, mem. Council of States, 1946-49; mem. Swiss Nat. Council 1963—, mem. Swiss Fed. Council, 1967-73, v.p. Swiss Fed. Council, 1971, pres., 1972, head Fed. Def. Dept., 1967-68, Head Fin. and Customs Dept., 1968-73; chmn. Swiss Aluminum, Ltd., 1987—, also bd. dirs.; former pres. Swiss Radical Dem. Party; chmn. Interfood, Banco Rasini of Milan, 1984—. Home: Via Ronchi 13, Lugano Switzerland *

CELLI, ROBERTO, science administrator; b. Milan, Oct. 4, 1937; s. Aldo and Osvalda (Macchetta) C.; m. Gianna Bellei, Sept. 9, 1965; children: Giulia B., Pierfrancesco B. BA, U. Wis., 1962; postgrad., Johns Hopkins U., 1962-64. Editor, supr. Library of Congress, Washington, 1964-68, subject cataloger, 1968-70; plant dir. Imexals Co., Trieste, Italy, 1970-74; mgr. Villa Serbelloni, Bellagio, Italy, 1974-78; dir. Bellagio (Italy) Study and Conf. Ctr. Rockefeller Found., 1979—. Home and Office: Villa Serbelloni, 22021 Bellagio Italy

CELLIERS, PETER JOUBERT, public relations specialist; b. Vogelfontein, S. Africa; s. Bartilimy and Elsie Blanche (Goldberg) C.; ed. Eng., Continent; m. Helen Rassaby, Sept. 10, 1949; children—Gordon A.J., Jennefer A.J. Editor, to 1959; cons. to fgn. govts., internat. corps. Peter J. Celliers Co., N.Y.C., 1958-68; chief fgn. press services Olympic Organizing Com., Mexico, 1968; dir. for N.Am., Mexican Nat. Tourist Council, 1962-72; owner Ellis Assos., N.Y.C., 1969—; tech. adviser internat. market devel. to UN, hotels, carriers, govts. Mem. Soc. Am. Travel Writers (past pres.), N.Y. Assn. Travel Writers, Am. Soc. Journalists and Authors. Clubs: Nat. Press (Washington); Overseas Press, Dutch Treat (N.Y.C.). Home: 240 Garth Rd Scarsdale NY 10583 Office: 41 Union Sq West Suite 420 New York NY 10003

CEMPEL, CZESLAW, vibroacoustics engineer, educator; b. Biskupice, Poland, July 22, 1938; s. Jan and Pelagia (Paz) C.; m. Krystyna Dominiak, Nov. 7, 1963. MS in Acoustics, Mickiewicz U., Poland, 1962, PhD, 1968, DSc, 1971. Faculty mem. Applied Mechanics Inst. Tech. U. Poznan, Poland, 1964—, assoc. prof. acoustics, 1977—, head noise and vibration lab., 1970—, vice-dir. Inst., 1974-81, head vibroacoustic machinery research group, 1974—, dir. Inst., 1987—; cons. in field. Author: Reduction of Machinery Vibration, 1976, Applied Vibroacoustics, 1978, THe Fundamentals of Vibroacoustical Diagnosis of Machinery, 1982, Mechanical Vibrations, 1982, Vibroacoustical Diagnostics of Machinery, 1985; contbr. numerous articles to profl. jours. Recipient several awards from sci. orgns. Mem. Diagnostic Engring. Inst., Gesellschaft für Andegour, Mathematic und Mechanic Germany, Instn. Maintenance Engring. Eire, Polish. Soc. Applied Mechanics (past pres. Poznan br.), Polish Acoustical Soc., Polish Acad. Scis. (acoustical com., pres. machinery condition-monitoring group of mech. engring. com.). Home: Os Piastowskie 40-m-5, 61152 Poznan Poland Office: Tech U Poznan, Piotrowo 3, 60965 Poznan Poland

CENAC, CHRISTIAN LOUIS, physician; b. Paris, July 1, 1943; s. Jean Philippe and Jeannine (Micheau) C.; m. Sophie Deglaire, Aug. 6, 1969 (div. 1982). MD, Toulouse U., France, 1970, cert. in Stomatology, 1971, cert. in Geriatry, 1988. Pres. Externe Toulouse Hosps., 1966-67; practice medicine specializing in stomatology Toulouse; adminstr. Inst. Transport, Tourism and Communication, Toulouse, 1985. Author: Railroad Models, 1985. V.p. Customers Assn. Popluar Bank Mid-Pyrenees, Toulouse, 1986. Club: Railroad Modeler of Toulouse (pres. 1982). Address: 23 rue Martyrs de la Liberation, 31400 Toulouse France

CENCIARINI, RENZO ALCESTE, finance company executive; b. Milan, Italy, July 28, 1948; s. Enrico and Illia (d'Aragona) C.; m. Elena Cristina Carli, July 5, 1975; children: Cristina, Laura. Dr. Econs., Bocconi U., Milan, 1974; M.B.A., Harvard U., 1978. Asst. prof. Bocconi U., 1974-76; officer Chase Manhattan Bank, N.Y.C., 1975-76; mgmt. cons. Boston Cons. Group, Munich, W.Ger., 1978-81; dir. corp. devel. Fidinam Group, Lugano, Switzerland, 1981-86, exec. asst. to pres., 1981-86; area gen. mgr. Adv. Services Citicorp Corp., Lausanne, Switzerland, 1987—. Assolombarda fellow, Milan, 1975, 76. Club: Harvard Business School (Milan). Home: Il Ronco, 6933 Muzzano Switzerland Office: Citicorp Corp Adv Services, 22 Ave Mon Repos, 1002 Lausanne Switzerland

CENTNER, CHARLES WILLIAM, lawyer; b. Battle Creek, Mich., July 4, 1915; s. Charles William and Lucy Irene (Patterson); m. Evi Rohr, Dec. 22, 1956; children—Charles Patterson, David William, Geoffrey Christopher. A.B., U. Chgo., 1936, A.M., 1936, A.M., 1939, Ph.D., 1941; J.D., Detroit Coll. Law, 1970; LL.B., LaSalle Extension U., 1965. Bar: Mich. 1970. Asst. prof. U. N.D., 1940-41, Tulane U., New Orleans, 1941-42; liaison officer for Latin Am., Lend-Lease Adminstrn., 1942; assoc. dir. Western Hemisphere div. Nat. Fgn Trade Council, 1946-52; exec. Ford Motor Co., Detroit, 1952-57, Chrysler Corp. and Chrysler Internat. S.A., Detroit and Geneva, Switzerland, 1957-70; adj. prof. Wayne State U., U. Detroit, Wayne County Community Coll., 1970—. Served to lt. comdr. USNR, 1942-45. Mem. State Bar of Mich., ABA, Detroit Bar Assn., Oakland County Bar Assn. Republican. Episcopalian. Club: Masons. Author: Great Britain and Chile, 1810-

1914, 1941. Home: 936 Harcourt Rd Grosse Pointe Park MI 48230 Office: 100 Renaissance Ctr Suite 1575 Detroit MI 48243-1075

CEREZO, VINICIO, president of Guatemala; b. Guatemala City, Guatemala, Dec. 26, 1942; s. Marco Vinicio Cerezo Cierra; m. Raquel Blandon, 1965; 4 children. LLB, San Carlos Nat. U., 1968. Pres. Christian Democratic Student Orgn., 1964-66; sec. for Orgn. of Christian Democratic party, 1968-74, sec. gen., after 1974; mem. Nat. Congress, 1974-78; pres. of Guatemala, 1986—. Office: Oficina del Presidente de, la Republica, Guatemala City Guatemala *

CERMAK, JOSEF RUDOLF CENEK, lawyer; b. Skury, Czechoslovakia, Nov. 15, 1924; s. Rudolf and Rosalie (Zahalkova) C.; JUC, Charles U., Prague, Czechoslovakia, 1945-48; LLB, U. Toronto (Ont., Can.), 1958. Called to Ont. bar, 1960, created Queen's counsel, 1975; mem. firm Borden, Elliot, Kelley & Palmer, Toronto, 1960-61; mem. firm Wahn, Mayer, Smith, Creber, Lyons, Torrance & Stevenson (name now Smith, Lyons, Torrance, Stevenson & Mayer), Toronto, 1962—, ptnr., 1967—; bd. dirs. Wright Line Can. Ltd., Belfield Steel Warehouse Ltd., Westminster Devel. Corp. Ltd., Galahad Investments Ltd., Carleton Homes (Lincoln) Ltd., D.W. Naylor Realty Ventures Ltd., Lecadon Internat. Ltd., 68 Pubs., Inc. Actor, New Theatre, Toronto, Snizek Theatre, N.Y.C., CBC Radio; mem. Exec. Pro Arte Orch. Assn., 1963-66; bd. dirs. Can. Ethnic Heritage Found., Pro Arte Orch. Soc. Recipient Panhellenic prize, Epstein award Univ. Coll., U. Toronto. Mem. Can., Ont. bar assns., Czechoslovak Soc. Arts and Scis. Am. (pres. Toronto chpt. 1970-79), Czechoslovak Nat. Assn. Can. (mem. exec. 1958-70). Clubs: Sokol Gymnastic Assn.; Lawyers. Author: Pokorne Navraty, 1955; Going Home, 1963; MY Toronto, 1984; editor: Zpravy News, 1965-67; chmn. editorial bd. Nase Hlasy, Toronto Czech Weekly, 1960-68; contbr. articles to various Czechlovakian newspapers in Can. and U.S. Office: Exchange Tower Suite 3400, 2 First Canadian Pl PO Box 420, Toronto, ON Canada M5X 1J3

CERNAT, MANUELA GHEORGHIU, film historian; b. Paris, Apr. 23, 1945; arrived in Romania, 1947; s. Mihnea and Esmeralda (Boldur) Gheorghiu; m. Cernat Răzvan, Jan. 26, 1979; children: Răzvana, Emanuel. MA, Inst. Art, Bucharest, Romania, 1968; PhD in Cinematography, U. Bucharest, 1974. Researcher Inst. Art History, Bucharest, 1968-82, sr. researcher, 1982-84, dep. dir., 1984—; chair dept. film history U. Cultural Sci., Bucharest, 1968. Author: Arms and the Film, 1983, A Concise History of Romanian Film, 1983; editor: Contemporary Romanian Cinematography, 1975. Mem. Romanian Filmmakers Assn. (mem. exec. bd. 1974—, Film Criticism prize 1980). Home: 141 Aurel Vlaicu, 2 Bucharest Romania Office: Inst Art History, 196 Calea Victoriei, 1 Bucharest Romania

CERNUDA, CHARLES EVELIO, physician; b. Tampa, Fla., June 19, 1941; s. Evelio Perez and Angelina (Leto) C.; B.A., Emory U., 1963, M.D., 1968; m. Mary Margaret McElory, Nov. 24, 1967; children—Mary Robin and Meredith Lynley (twins), Lindsey Elizabeth. Intern, Emory U. Affiliated Hosps., Atlanta, 1968-69, resident in internal medicine, 1969-70, fellow in pulmonary disease, 1970-72; practice medicine specializing in internal medicine and pulmonary disease, Tampa, 1974—; med. dir. ICU, pulmonary lab. and respiratory therapy depts. St. Joseph's Hosp., 1974—, sec. treas., 1977-81, pres.-elect med. staff, 1982, pres. med. staff, 1982-85; med. dir. pulmonary lab. and respiratory therapy depts. Centro Asturiano Hosp., 1974-87, vice chief med. staff, 1975-78; bd. dirs. Commerce Bank Tampa, 1985-87. Trustee Berkeley Prep. Sch., Tampa, 1985—. Served with M.C., USAF, 1972-73. Diplomate Am. Bd. Internal Medicine, also Sub-Bd. Pulmonary Disease. Fellow Am. Coll. Chest Physicians, ACP; mem. Nat. Assn. Med. Dirs. Respiratory Care, So. Med. Assn., Fla. Med. Assn., AMA, Am., Fla. thoracic socs., Fla. Soc. Internal Medicine, Hillsborough County Med. Assn. (chmn. bd. censors 1981-82), West Coast Acad. Medicine (sec.-treas. 1981-83), Am. Soc. Internal Medicine. Democrat. Episcopalian. Clubs: Univ. Tampa Yacht and Country, Rotary of Ybor City (Tampa). Home: 4930 Andros Dr Tampa FL 33609 Office: 4900 N Habana Ave Tampa FL 33614

CERNUSCHI-FRIAS, BRUNO, electrical engineer; b. Montevideo, Uruguay, Apr. 7, 1952; became citizen of Argentina, 1978; s. Felix and Zulema (Frias) Cernuschi. B.E.E., U. Buenos Aires, 1976; M.E.E., Brown U., Providence, R.I., 1983, Ph. D. in Elec. Engring., 1984. Asst. faculty engring. U. Buenos Aires, Argentina, 1976-78, chief asst., 1979-83, asst. prof., 1984-85. Contbr. articles to profl. publs. Recipient 1st Prize for ship engine control design, Secretaria de Estado de Intereses Maritimos, Buenos Aires, 1978, Bernardo Houssay prize Consejo Nacional de Investigaciones Cientificas y Tecnicas, 1987. Mem. IEEE, Assn. Computing Machinery, AAAS, Am. Math. Soc., Sigma Xi. Roman Catholic. Home: Larrea 1065-8B, 1117 Buenos Aires Argentina Office: Facultad Ingenieria U Buenos Aires, Paseo Colon 850, Buenos Aires Argentina

CERNY, JIRI, control systems designer; b. Prague, Czechoslovakia, Mar. 30, 1940; s. Vaclav and Marie (Napravnikova) C.; m. Dagmar Povrova, May 30, 1972 (div. Feb. 1988); children: Barbara, David, Jiri. MSc in Engring., U. Tech., Prague, 1966. Advance designer Research and Devel. Ctr. for Control Systems in Industry, Prague, 1969—; tech. mgr. Art Centrum-Studio Shape, Prague, 1975-86; mgr. Art Centrum-Studio Artechnic, 1987—. Contbr. articles to profl. jours.; patentee in field. Home: 20 Makarenkova, Prague 120 00, Czechoslovakia Office: Artechnic-Art Centrum, 2 Pod Dvorem, Prague 162 00, Czechoslovakia

CERNY, JOSEPH CHARLES, urologist, educator; b. Oak Park, Ill., Apr. 20, 1930; s. Joseph James and Mary (Turek) C.; m. Patti Bobette Pickens, Nov. 10, 1962; children—Joseph Charles, Rebecca Anne. BA, Knox Coll., 1952; MD, Yale U., 1956. Diplomate Am. Bd. Urology. Intern U. Mich. Hosp., Ann Arbor, 1956-57, resident, 1957-62; practice medicine specializing in urology, Ann Arbor, and Detroit since 1962—; inst. surgery (urology) U. Mich., Ann Arbor, 1962-64, asst. prof., 1964-66, assoc. prof., 1966-71, clin. prof., 1971—; chmn. dept. urology Henry Ford Hosp., Detroit, 1971—; pres. Resistors, Inc., Chgo., 1960—; cons. St. Joseph Hosp., Ann Arbor, 1973—. Contbr. articles to profl. jours., chpts. in books. Bd. dirs., trustee Nat. Kidney Found. Mich., Ann Arbor, 1980—, chmn. urology council 1987—, exec. com. 1987—, pres. 1987—; bd. dirs. Ann Arbor Amateur Hockey Assn., 1980-83; pres. PTO, Ann Arbor Pub. Schs., 1980. Served to lt. USNR, 1956-76. Recipient Disting. Service award Transplantation Soc. Mich., 1982. Fellow ACS (pres.-elect Mich. br. 1984-85, pres. 1985—); mem. Internat. Soc. Urology, Am. Urol. Assn. (pres. North Cen. sec. 1985-86, Manpower com. 1987-88, Jud. Rev. com. 1987-91, tech. exhibits 1987-88, Best Sci. Exhibit award 1978, Best Sci. Films award 1980, 82), Transplantation Soc. Mich. (pres. 1983-84), ACS (pres. Mich. chpt. 1985-86), Am. Assn. Transplant Surgeons, Endocrine Surgeons, Soc. Univ. Urologists, Am. Assn. Urologic Oncology, Am. Fertility Soc. Republican. Methodist. Clubs: Barton Hills Country; Ann Arbor Raquet (Ann Arbor). Avocations: tennis; fishing; Civil War. Home: 2800 Fairlane Dr Ann Arbor MI 48104 Office: Dept Urology Henry Ford Hosp 2799 W Grand Blvd Detroit MI 48202

CERRITO, ORATIO ALFONSO, real estate investor, financial advisor; b. Cleve., Mar. 10, 1911; s. Carl and Lillian (DiVita) C.; m. Rita McCue, Oct. 9, 1931 (div. 1946); children: Lillian, Rita-Diane; m. Maria Capri, Dec. 18, 1947; children: Miriam, Linda, Claudia. BA, John Carroll U., 1935; LLB, Cleve. Law Sch., 1940. Bar: Ohio, 1941, U.S. Dist. Ct. (no. dist.) Ohio, 1950. Foreman Chase Brass and Copper Co., Euclid, Ohio, 1931-41; assoc. Sindell & Sindell, Cleve., 1941-42; law violations investigator Wage-Hour div. U.S. Dept. Labor, Cleve., 1942-44; price officer Allied Control Commn. of Allied Mil. Govt., Rome, 1944-45; hdqs. distbn. officer UNRRA, Athens, 1945-46; pres., gen. mgr. U.S. Store Fixture Co., Cleve., 1946-52; account exec. Research Inst. Am., Cleve., 1952-54, So. Calif., 1954-60; regional mgr. indsl. div. Marlin, So. Calif., 1960-81; fin. advisor, mgr. O.A. Cerrito Family Trust, Fountian Valley, Calif., 1981—. Home and Office: 18173 Santa Cecilia Circle Fountain Valley CA 92708

CERTO, SIR DOMINIC NICHOLAS, sales executive; b. New Brunswick, N.J., Mar. 14, 1950; s. Pasquale A. and Concetta (D'Angolini) C.; A. in Bus., N.W. Mo. U., 1976; m. Joan Linke, Apr. 6, 1969; children—Dominic Jason, Laurann Marie. Spl. agt. Prudential Ins. Co., Edison, N.J., 1970-73; sales mgr. N.Y. Life Ins. Co., Edison, 1973-77; dir. sales ARA Food Services, White Plains, N.Y., 1977-81, Macke Services, Phila., 1981—; pres. Hillside Pubs.; v.p. worldwide dir. Pro-Bodybuilding; coll. lectr. on bus. Adv. bd. Middlesex Coll., Edison, N.J.; Democratic county committeeman, 1977. Served with USMC, 1968-70. Recipient Pres.'s award and blue ribbon N.Y. Life Ins. Co., 1975; named Writer of Month, Vega Mag., 1978; decorated Knight Royal Order St. John, Knights of Malta (Netherlands). Mem. Am. Writers Assn., Authors Guild, Internat. Fedn. Body Bldg. (past pres. N.J., bd. dirs.), Profl. Sports Com. (nat. judge), VFW. Author: The Valor of Francesco D'Amini (novel), 1979; Future Shape, Success—Pure and Simple or How To Make It in Business, Sports, and the Arts. Finalist Mr. North America contest, 1976. Home: PO Box 385 Keasbey NJ 08832

CERVINI, CLAUDIO, rheumatology educator; b. Rome, Aug. 14, 1925; s. Angelo Maria and Lina (Sabatini) C.; m. Arianna Tribaudino, Feb. 5, 1978; children—Rossella, Monica. Degree, U. Rome, 1947. Asst. prof. U. Rome, 1951-69, assoc. prof., 1969-80; full prof. Rheumatology Faculty of Medicine, Ancona, 1980—, chmn. ednl. com., 1980-84; gen. sec. World Conf. on Rheumatism, Rome, 1961; head dept. rheumatology Ancona U., 1983—. Author: numerous books in field; contbr. articles to profl. jours. Recipient Gold medal Fedn. Medico-Sportiva Italiana, 1964. Mem. Nat. League Against Rheumatic Diseases. Lodge: Rotary. Home: Via Arbia 52, Rome Italy 00199 Office: Univ Med Sch, V P Ranieri, Ancona 60131, Italy

CESARMAN, EDUARDO VITIS, cardiologist; b. Santiago, Chile, S. Am., Oct. 19, 1931; Mexican citizen; s. Carlos M. and Esther (Vitis) C.; B.Sc., Centro U. Mex., 1948; M.D., U. Nacional Autonoma de Mex., 1955; m. Esther T. Kolteniuk, June 24, 1961; children—Carlos, Laura, Andrea, Paola. Intern, Univ. Hosp., U. Md., College Park, 1955-56; resident Mt. Sinai Hosp., N.Y.C., 1956-57, N.Y. Hosp.-Cornell U., 1957-59; fellow Instituto Nacional de Cardiologia de Mex., 1960-62, medico adjunto, 1962-73, chief dept. epidemiology, 1976-78; chief med. services Comision Federal de Electricdad, 1976-77; dir. gen. Higiene Escolar y Programas de Salud, Secretaria de Educacion Publica, 1978-80; chief supervision and control med. services Inst. Mexicano Seguro Social, 1980-83; asso. prof. cardiology Facultad de Medicina, Universidad Nacional Autonoma de Mexico, 1961-74, prof. nosology, 1968-74, dir. gen. Servicios Escolares, U. Mex., 1965-67; pres. Mexican sci. council Weisman Inst., 1967-69; adv. Secretaria de Salubridad y Asistencia, 1967-70, U. Mex., 1973-76, Instituto Mexicano del Seguro Social, 1977-85, Fondo de Cultura Economica, 1973; dir. Colegio de Ciencias y Humanidades, U. Mex., 1970. Mem. steering com. Internat. Exec. Corps, 1976-85. Recipient Justo Sierra, U. Mex., 1955. Mem. Sociedad Mexicana de Cardiologia (sci. com. 1976-78), Am. Coll. Cardiology (chpt. gov. 1966-69), N.Y. Acad. Sci., Internat. Coll. Angiology, Am. Coll. Angiology, Israel Med. Assn., Am. Coll. Chest Physicians (chpt. gov. 1985—), Asociacion de Investigacion Pediatrica, Council on Epidemiology and Prevention of Internat. Soc. Cardiology, Sociedad Mexicana de Educacion para la Salud, Asociacion Mexicana de Periodismo Cientifico, Asociacion de Escritores Mexicanos. Author: Parametros Cardiologicos, 1968; Aforismos Farmacologicos y Terapeuticos en Cardiologia, 1970; Hombre y Entropia, 1974; A Redefinition of the Resting State of the Myocardial Cell, 1976; La Vida es Riesgo, 1978; Orden y Caos, 1982; Fuera de Contexto, 1983; Cuarto Menguante, 1985; Dicho en Mé xico, 1986; Con alguna Intención, 1987; co-editor Fundamentos del Diagnó stico, 1976; contbr. articles to profl. jours. Home: 825 Sierra Ventana, 11000 Mexico City Mexico Office: 172-9 Hamburgo, 06600 Mexico City Mexico

CESKA, FRANZ, diplomat; b. Vienna, Austria, Jan. 31, 1936; s. Paul and Emma (Koenig) C.; m. Ceska Veronique Moyret, Feb. 1, 1960; children: Christophe, Caroline, Stephanie. D in Law, U. Vienna, 1958; Diploma, Coll. Europe, Brussels, 1959. Attaché Ministry Fgn. Affairs, Vienna, 1959-61, 1st sec., 1961-65, dir., 1965-69; counsellor permanent mission of Austria to the UN, Geneva, 1969-75, Ministry Gov. Orgns., Geneva, 1969-75; counsel gen. Permanent Ministry Justice, Berlin, 1975-77; dir. for sec. Affairs and Disarmament Ministry for Fgn. Affairs, Vienna, 1977-82; ambassador Austrian Embassy, Brussels, 1982—; Austrian ambassador UN, 1988—; spl. agt. Geneva, 1988—. Contbr. articles on internat. affairs to profl. jours. Decorated Merite Nat. Officier (France); Isabella La Catolica Cmndr. (Spain); Grande Croix de l'O.d.l. Couronne (Belgium), Gross. Silb.EZ f.Verdienste u.RÖ (Austria). Office: Ballhausplatz 2, A-1016 Vienna Austria

CESKA, ZDENEK, civil procedure educator; b. Prague, Feb. 6, 1929; s. Jaroslav and Marie (Ceskova) C.; m. Vera Tropperova, Aug. 14, 1952; 1 child: Richard. M.Law, Charles U., Prague, 1952. Sub dean faculty of law Charles U., Prague, 1964-66, dean, 1970-73, vice rector, 1973-76, dir. Inst. State and Law, Czecoslovak Acad. Scis., 1973-78, rector, 1976—. Contbr. articles to profl. jours. Mem. central com. Communist Party, Czechoslovakia, chmn. legal council Ho. of the People, 1981—. Holder of the Order of Labour, 1979; recipient Gold medal Charles U., 1979; Hon. medal Bulgarian Acad. Scis., 1980, Hon. doctor U. Moscow, U. Vilnjus, Humboldt U. Berlin. Mem. World Peace Council, Internat. Assn. Univs. (v.p. 1985), Czechoslovak Soc. Internat. Relations (v.p. 1976), Czechoslovak Acad. Scis. (presidium). Avocation: tennis. Home: Lukesova 40, 14200 Prague Czechoslovakia Office: Charles U, Ovocny trh 5, 11636 Prague Czechoslovakia

CESZKOWSKI, DANIEL DAVID, financial analyst; b. Geneva, Dec. 9, 1954; s. Ignaz Ceszkowski and Veronika Noemi (Goldstein) Blanc. Lic. Sci. Commerce & Industry, U. Geneva, 1977; MBA, Internat. Mgmt. Devel. Inst., Lausanne, Switzerland, 1985. Systems engr. Honeywell Bull, Geneva, 1977-80; dir. Corinfo S.A., Geneva, 1980-81; systems analyst Hewlett Packard, Meyrin, Switzerland, 1981-84; fin. cons. Merrill Lynch Internat., Inc., Geneva, 1986-87; pvt. practice in fin., investment advising Geneva, 1988—; bd. dirs. Mievda S.A., Geneva, 1974—.

CEVC, TONE, ethnologist, researcher; b. Kamnik, Yugoslavia, May 31, 1932; s. Emil and Pavla (Klampfer) C.; m. Vladimira Južina, June 29, 1960 (dec. Mar. 1962); 1 child, Barbara; m. Veronika Peterlin, May 18, 1968; children: Monika, Marjeta, Ambrož. B of Ethnology, B of History Arts, U. Ljubljana, 1957, D of Ethnology, 1969. Librarian Slovenija Project, Ljubljana, Yugoslavia, 1959-71; sci. collaborator Inst. for Slovenian Folk Studies, Ljubljana, 1971-75, sr. sci. collaborator, 1975-84, sci. advisor, 1984—. Author: Velika Planina, 1972, 87, Arhitekturno izročilo pastirjev drvarjev in oglarjev na Slovenskem (The Architectural Tradition of Shepherds and Woodsmen in Slovenia), 1984 (Kidrič award 1985). Mem. Slovenian Ethnol. Soc. Roman Catholic. Office: Inst for Slovenian Folk Studies, Novi Trg 3, 6100 Ljubljana Yugoslavia

CHA, SE DO, physician; b. Seoul, Korea, Dec. 17, 1942; came to U.S., 1966, naturalized, 1977; s. Young Sun and Hee Joo (Chang) C.; m. Elsa Jane Greene, Dec. 21, 1974. M.D., Yon Sei U., 1966. Diplomate Am. Bd. Internal Medicine. Intern Presbyn.-U. Pa. Med. Ctr., Phila., 1966-67; resident in medicine Harrisburg Hosp., Pa., 1967-70; chief resident in medicine Roger Williams Gen. Hosp., Providence, 1970-71, cardiologist, 1973-75; fellow in cardiology Deborah Heart and Lung Center, Browns Mills, N.J., 1971-73, cardiologist, 1975—, asst. dir. adult cardiac catheterization lab., 1975-86, dir. 1987—; clin. asst. prof. U. Medicine and Dentistry N.J., 1987; instr. Brown U., Providence, 1973-75. Contbr. articles to profl. jours. Fellow Am. Coll. Angiology, Soc. for Cardiac Angiography, ACP; mem. AMA, Fedn. Clin. Research, Internat. Soc. Heart Transplantation, Am. Heart Assn. Office: Deborah Heart and Lung Center Trenton Rd Browns Mill NJ 08015

CHABRIER, JEAN-CLAUDE C., musicologist, researcher; b. Neuilly, France, Nov. 10, 1931; s. Jules Marcel Francis and Marcelle Marie (Brun) Charbonnier; children: Carine- Ann-Véronique, Cyrille-Louis-Cyriaque. D of Medicine, Faculte de Medecine, Paris, 1959; Ecole Nat. des langues Orientales, Nat. Sch. Oriental Langs., Paris, 1967; D of Musicology, U. Sorbonne, 1976. Gen. practice medicine France, 1955-71; export exec. Pharm. Labs., East Europe, 1960-62; sci. relations Roche Labs., Paris, 1963-67; space perception researcher Centre Scientifique et Technique Bâtiment, Paris, 1968-72; musicology researcher Centre National Recherche Scientifique, Paris, 1976-88—; charge de cours Universite Sorbonne Nouvelle, Paris, 1985—; charge de conferences Conservatoire Superieur Region Boulogne, 1986. Editor Arabesques-Recitalbum Anthologie Phonographique du Recital Oriental, 1974. Recipient Grand Prix de l'Acad. du Disque, 1975, Grand Prix de l'Acad.Charles Cros, 1980. Mem. Ordre National des Medecin, Societe Asiatique, Societe des Explorateurs et Voyageurs Francais, Societe Francais de Musicologie, Internat. Council Traditional Music, Inst. de la Maison de Bourbon. Home: 3 Rue Fresnel, 75116 Paris France Office: Centre National Recherche Scientifique, Paris France

CHABROW, PENN BENJAMIN, lawyer; b. Phila., Feb. 16, 1939; s. Benjamin Penn and Annette (Shapiro) C.; m. Sheila Sue Steinberg, June 18, 1961; children—Michael Penn, Carolyn Debra, Frederick Penn. B.S., Muhlenberg Coll., Allentown, Pa., 1960; J.D., George Washington U., 1962, LL.M. in Taxation, 1968; postgrad. in econs. Harvard U. Bar: Va. 1963, D.C. 1964, U.S. Ct. Appeals (D.C. cir.) 1964, U.S. Tax Ct. 1964, U.S. Supreme Ct. 1966, Fla. 1972, U.S. Ct. Claims 1974, U.S. Ct. Appeals (5th and 11th cirs.) 1981; bd. cert. tax atty., Fla. Tax law specialist IRS, Washington, 1961-67; tax counsel C. of C. U.S., Washington, 1967-74; sole practice, Miami, Fla., 1974—; pres. Forum Realty Co., Phila.; lectr. fed. taxation Barry U. Grad. Sch. of Bus., 1977-81. Mem. ABA, Fla. Bar Assn., Fed. Bar Assn., Va. Bar Assn., D.C. Bar Assn., Greater Miami Estate Planning Council, Collier County Estate Planning Council, Phi Alpha Delta, Phi Sigma Tau. Contbr. articles profl. jours. Office: 2222 Ponce De Leon Blvd Suite 300 Coral Gables FL 33134

CHACKO, GEORGE KUTTICKAL, systems science educator, consultant; b. Trivandrum, India, July 1, 1930; came to U.S., 1953.; s. Geevarghese Kuttickal and Thankamma (Mathew) C.; m. Yo Yee, Aug. 10, 1957; children: Rajah Yee, Ashia Yo. MA in Econs. and Polit. Philosophy, Madras (India) U., 1950; postgrad. (Coll. scholar), St. Xavier's Coll., Calcutta, India, 1950-52; B in Commerce, Calcutta U., 1952; cert. postgrad. tng. (Inst. fellow), Indian Stat. Inst., Calcutta, 1951; postgrad. (SE Asia Club fellow), Princeton U., 1953-54; PhD in Econometrics, New Sch. for Social Research, 1959; postgrad. (Univ. fellow), UCLA, 1961. Asst. editor Indian Fin., Calcutta, 1951-53; comml. corr. Times of India, 1953; dir. mktg. and mgmt. research Royal Metal Mfg. Co., N.Y.C., 1958-60; mgr. dept. ops. research Hughes Semicondr. div. Calif., 1960-61; ops. research staff cons. Union Carbide Corp., N.Y.C., 1962-63; mem. tech. staff Research Analysis Corp., McLean, Va., 1963-65, MITRE Corp., Arlington, Va., 1965-67; sr. staff scientist TRW Systems Group, Washington, 1967-70; cons. def. systems, computer, space, tech. systems and internat. devel. systems; assoc. in math. test devel. Ednl. Testing Service, Princeton, N.J., 1955-57; asst. prof. bus. adminstrn. UCLA, 1961-62; lectr. Dept. Agr. Grad. Sch., 1965-67; asst. professorial lectr. George Washington U., 1965-68; professorial lectr. Am. U., 1967-70, adj. prof., 1970; vis. prof. def. systems Mgmt. Coll., Ft. Belvoir, Va., 1972-73; vis. prof. U. So. Calif., 1970-71, prof. systems mgmt., 1971-83, prof. systems sci., 1983—; sr. Fulbright prof. Nat. Chengchi U., Taipei, 1983-84, sr. Fulbright research prof., 1984-85; prin. investigator and program dir. Tech. Transfer Project/Taiwan Nat. Sci. Council, 1984-85; disting. fgn. expert lectr. Taiwan Ministry Econ. Affairs, 1986; sr. vis. research prof. for Taiwan Nat. Sci. Council Nat. Chengchi U., Taipei, 1988-89; v.p. program devel. Systems and Telecommunications Corp., Potomac, Md., 1987—. Author: 18 books in field, including Applied Statistics in Decision-Making, 1971, Computer-aided Decision-Making, 1972, Systems Approach to Public and Private Sector Problems, 1976, Operations Research Approach to Problem Formulation and Solution, 1976, Management Information Systems, 1979, Robotics/Artificial Intelligence/Productivity - U.S.-Japan Concomitant Coalitions, 1986, Technology Management for Missions and Markets - Corporate and Country Concommitant Coalitions, 1988, Dynamic Program Management - Experience, Diverse Applications, 1988, The Systems Approach from Corporate Markets to National Missions, 1989; contbr. articles to profl. publs.; editor, contbr.: 17 books, including The Recognition of Systems in Health Services, 1969, Reducing the Cost of Space Transportation, 1969, Systems Approach to Environmental Pollution, 1972, National Organization of Health Services—U.S., USSR, China, Europe, 1979, Educational Innovation in Health Services-U.S., Europe, Middle East, Africa, 1979; guest editor Jour. Research Communication Studies, 1978-79; assoc. editor Internat. Jour. of Forecasting, 1982-85. Active Nat. Presbyn. Ch., Washington, 1967-84, mem. ch. council, 1969-71, mem. chancel choir, 1967-84; chmn. worship com. Taipei Internat. Ch., 1984, chmn. membership com., 1985, chmn. Stewardship com., 1985; co-dean Ch. Family Camp, 1977; coordinator Life Abundant Discovery Group, 1979; adult Sunday Sch. leader 4th Presbyn. Ch., Bethesda, Md., 1986—, mem. Sanctuary choir, 1985—, mem. Men's Ensemble, 1986—. Recipient awards, including Gold medal Inter-Collegiate Extempore Debate in Malayalam U. Travancore, Trivandrum, India, 1945, 1st Pl. Yogic Exercises Competition U. Travancore, 1946, 1st prize Inter-Varsity Debating Team Madras, 1949, NSF internat. sci. lectures award, 1982; USIA sponsored U.S. Sci. emissary to Egypt, Burma, India, Singapore, 1987. Fellow AAAS (mem. nat. council 1968-73, chmn. or co-chmn. symposia 1971, 72, 74, 76, 77, 78), Am. Astronautical Soc. (v.p. publs. 1969-71, eitor Tech. Newsletter 1968-72, mng. editor Jour. Astronautical Scis. 1969-75); mem. Ops. Research Soc. Am. (vice chmn. com. of representation on AAAS 1972-78, mem. nat. council tech. sect. on health 1966-68, editor Tech. Newsletter on Health 1966-73), Washington Ops. Research Council (trustee 1967-69, chmn. tech. colloquia 1967-68, editor Tech. Newsletter 1967-68), Inst. Mgmt. Scis. (rep. to Internat. Inst. for Applied Systems Analysis in Vienna, Austria 1976-77, session chmn. Athens, Greece 1977, Atlanta 1977), World Future Soc. (editorial bd. publs. 1970-71), N.Y. Acad. Scis. Democrat. Club: Kiwanis (Capital Dist. Div. One Internat. Disting. Service award 1968, 70, Friendship Heights Club Outstanding Service award 1972-73, 1st disting. dir. Taipei-Keystone Club 1978, spl. rep. of internat. pres. and counselor to dist. of Republic of China 1983—, pioneer premier project award Asia-Pacific Conf. 1986, Legion of Honor 1985, chmn. citizenship services, chmn. fund raising Bethesda Club 1986-87). Office: U So Calif Office 5510 Columbia Pike Arlington VA 22204

CHADHA, OM PARKASH, physician; b. Kuala Lumpur, Malaysia, Nov. 30, 1936; s. Kanshi Ram and Parmeshiri Devi C.; m. Veena Chadha, Mar. 9, 1969; children: Dheeraj, Sujata. MBBS, U. Punjab, Amritsar, India, 1962. Gen. practice medicine Kuala Lumpur, Malaysia, 1963—. Mem. Malaysian Med. Assn. Club: Royal Selangor. Home: 42 Pesiaran Bruas, 50490 Kuala Lumpur Malaysia Office: Kelink Parkash, K19 Jalan Ipoh, 51200 Kuala Lumpur Malaysia

CHADHA, SUJAN SINGH, small business owner; b. Warwal, Panjab, India, Oct. 15, 1923; came to U.S., 1974; s. Grad. in Panjabi lang. and lit. with honors, U. Panjab Lahore, Pakistan, 1943; BA, U. Panjab Lahore, Pakistan, 1946. Clerical cadre controller mil. accts. N.W. Army, Rawalpindi, Pakistan, 1942-66; acct. SAS Def. Accounts, India, 1967-73; owner Chadha Imports-Exports, Wis., 1974—; ptnr. R. A. Bazar, Meerut, India, 1948-55, R.A. Bazar, Lucknow, India, 1957-60; part owner fleet of taxis, India, 1970-73. Mem. Metro Milw. Assn. of Commerce, Credit Bur. Milw. Inc., Better Bus. Bur. Greater Milw., Internat. Inst. Wis., All India Def. Accts. Employees Assn. Republican. Lodge: Rotary. Home: 9308 S 35th St Franklin WI 53132 Office: Chadha Imports-Exports 9661 S 20th St Oak Creek WI 53154

CHADIRJI, RIFAT KAMIL, architect, educator; b. Baghdad, Iraq, Dec. 6, 1926; s. Kamil Rifat and Muniba Asif (Aga) C.; m. Balkis Mohammed Sharara, 1954. Diploma in Arch., Hammersmith Sch. of Arts and Crafts, London, 1952. Founder, dir., chmn. Iraq Consult, 1952-78, chmn., 1978—; sect. head Baghdad Bldg. Dept. Waqaf Orgn., 1954-57; dir. gen. Housing Ministry of Planning, Baghdad, 1958-59; vis. scholar Grad Sch. Design Harvard U., Cambridge, Mass., 1984-86, Philosophy of Edn. Research Ctr. Harvard U., 1986-88, Aga Khan Program Islamic Architecture MIT, Cambridge, 1986—. Designer numerous pvt. houses, indsl. and govt. bldgs., Iraq; major works include Scientific Acad., Baghdad, 1965, Fedn. Industries Bldg., Baghdad, 1966, Council of Ministers Bldg. (architect's award), Baghdad, 1975, Nat. Theatre (award), Abu Dhabi, United Arab Emirates, 1977; author: A Collection of Twelve Etchings, 1984, Portrait of a Father (Arabic), 1985, Taha Street and Hammersmith (Arabic), 1985, Eight Etchings from Photographs by Kamil Chadirji, 1985, Concepts and Influences Toward a Regionalized International Architecture, 1986; contbr. numerous articles to profl. jours. Mem. Mayor's Council, Baghdad, 1958-61, Iraqi Tourist Bd., Baghdad, 1970-75; counselor to Mayorality of Baghdad, 1980-82. Loeb fellow, 1983-84; recipient chmn.'s award Aga Khan Award for Architecture, 1986. Fellow Am. Inst. Architects (hon.), Royal Inst. Brit. Architects (hon.); mem. Iraqi Architects Assn., Iraqi Artists Assn. (hon.). Office: The Architects Collaborative 46 Brattle St Cambridge MA 02138

CHADWICK, GEORGE ALBERT, JR., retired lawyer; b. Alexandria, Va., Nov. 20, 1911; s. George Albert and Asenath Moore (Graves) C.; m. Eleanor

Worthington Margerum, Aug. 10, 1934; children: George Albert III, Charles M.; m. Avaleen Seamans Gazaway, June 14, 1960; stepchildren: Tarillis Jane (Mrs. T. Paul Adams), Dan Lee Seamans. A.B., Princeton, 1932; LL.B., Georgetown U., 1937. Bar: D.C. 1936, Md. 1944. Practiced in Washington, 1936-75, Rockville, Md., 1975; of counsel firm Chadwick & Whaley, 1975; engaged in farming 1957—; owner Chadwick Bar Rev. Sch., 1937-43; pres., dir. York & Frederick Ry., 1975-76; dir. Prodelin, Inc., Hightstown, N.J., 1953-64, So. Oxygen Co., Bladensburg, Md., 1955-62; dir., gen. counsel Horsemen's Benevolent and Protective Assn., 1959-75; pres., dir. Md. Midland Ry., 1978-81, chmn. bd., dir., 1981-87, chmn. bd. emeritus, v.p. plant rationalization, 1987—; pres. Boyds (Md.) Fed. Credit Union, 1962-67, dir., 1962-80. Author articles. Pres. Washington Grove (Md.) PTA, 1947-50, Edward U. Taylor Sch. P.T.A., Boyds, 1961-63; life mem. Md. PTA. Served to capt. AUS, 1943-46. Named to Horsemen's Benevolent and Protective Assn. Hall of Fame, 1976. Mem. Am., Md., D.C., Montgomery County (Md.) bar assns., Phi Alpha Delta. Democrat. Episcopalian (jr. warden, vestryman 1965-68). Clubs: Barristers (Washington), Princeton (Washington), Army and Navy (Washington); Princeton (N.Y.C.). Home: Huckleberry Hill Boyds MD 20841 Office: 41 N Main St Union Bridge MD 21791

CHADWICK, OWEN, educator, historian; b. Bromley, Kent, Eng., May 20, 1916; s. John and Edith (Horrocks) C.; m. Ruth Hallward, Dec. 28, 1949; children: Charles, Stephen, Helen, Andre. BA, Cambridge U., 1939; LittD (hon.), Bristol U., 1939, London U., Columbia U.; DD (hon.), Oxford U., St. Andrews U.; Litt.D., Cambridge U., U. East Angola, U. Kent, Leeds U.; LLD, Aberdeen U. Ordained priest to Ch. of Eng. Prof. ecclesiastical history Cambridge U., 1958-68, Regius prof. modern history, 1968-83, master of Selwyn Coll., 1956-83, vice chancellor, 1969-71; pres. Brit. Acad., London, 1981-85. Author: The Victorian Church (2 vols), 1966-70; The Popes and European Revolution, 1981, Created Knight; author 16 books on church history. Decorated knight Order of Merit (England); recipient Wolfson prize for historical writing, 1981. Office: Univ of Cambridge, Cambridge CB21 England

CHAFEE, JOHN HUBBARD, senator; b. Providence, Oct. 22, 1922; s. John S. and Janet (Hunter) C.; m. Virginia Coates, Nov. 4, 1950; children: Zechariah, Lincoln, John, Georgia, Quentin. B.A., Yale U., 1947; LL.B., Harvard U., 1950; LLD (hon.), Brown U., 1964, Providence Coll., 1965, U. R.I., 1965, Jacksonville U., 1970, Bryant Coll., 1979. Bar: R.I. 1950. Practice law Providence, 1952-62, 73-76; mem. R.I. Ho. of Reps. 3d Dist. Warwick, 1957-62, minority leader, 1959-62; gov. R.I., 1963-69; sec. Navy, 1969-72; mem. U.S. Senate from R.I., 1977—. Chmn. Republican Gov.'s Assn., 1967; Mem. corp. Yale, 1972-78; trustee Deerfield Acad., 1970-79. Served to capt. USMCR, 1942-45, 51-52. Chubb fellow Yale, 1965. Mem. R.I. Bar, Fed. Bar Assn. Office: 567 Dirksen Senate Bldg Washington DC 20510

CHAFFIN, DOUGLAS GEORGE, investment company executive; b. Springfield, Mass., Dec. 13, 1943; s. Maurice Marshall and Laura (Lidgertwood) C.; m. Ramona Maria Kuzniar, Apr. 11, 1981; s. Christopher, Timothy, Marybeth. Student Wentworth Inst., Boston, Western New England Coll., Engr., Gen. Instrument Co., Chicopee, Mass., 1961-65, Anderson Labs., Bloomfield, Conn., 1965-69; registered rep. Spain & Starkel, Vernon, Conn., 1969-71; v.p. Denton & Co., Hartford, Conn., 1971-80; v.p., dir. N.Am. Investment Corp., East Hartford, Conn., 1980-88; assoc. v.p. 1st Albany Corp., Hartford, 1988—; pres. Evergreen Ventures, Inc., Norfolk, Conn., 1982-86; adv. dir. Sci. Measurement Systems Inc., Austin, Tex. Mem. Am. Stock Exchange Club, Security Traders Assn. of Conn., Security Traders Assn. of North Am., Hartford Stockbrokers Assn. Office: N Am Investment Corp 333 East River Dr East Hartford CT 06108

CHAGHAGHI, FRANCOIS SOHRAB, statistician, educator; b. Lausanne, Vaud, Switzerland, Aug. 31, 1950; s. Syavoush Georges Valdimir and Simone Renee (Dutoit) C. BBA, U. Lausanne, 1974, PhD in Econs., 1986; MS in Stats., Stanford U., 1976; postgrad. in stats., Swiss Fed. Inst. Tech., Lausanne, 1976, postgrad. in bus. adminstrn., 1985. Trainee Swiss Bank Corp., Geneva, 1976-77; statistician Nestle, Inc., Vevey, Switzerland, 1977-78; teaching asst. U. Lausanne, 1978-81, research asst., 1981-83, lectr. stats. dept. psychology, 1983—; 1st research asst. Fed. Fund for Sci. Research, Lausanne, 1983-84; sr. lectr. dept. psychology and computer scis. U. Geneva, 1987—, pres. bd. trustees RM Techniques de Pointe S.A., Lausanne, 1983-86. Author: TS Pack: Time Series Package, 1985, L'Analyse Chronologique au Sein de L'Entreprise Industrielle, 1986. Mem. Inst. Statisticians, Internat. Assn. Applied Psychology. Club: XIII Siecle (Lausanne). Home: Cesar Roux 20, 1005 Lausanne, Vaud Switzerland Office: U Lausanne Faculty Polit. and Social Scis BFSH-2, 1015 Lausanne Switzerland

CHAI, WINBERG, political science educator, foundation official; b. Shanghai, China, Oct. 16, 1932; came to U.S., 1951, naturalized, 1973; s. Ch'u and Mei-en (Tsao) C.; m. Carolyn Everett, Mar. 17, 1966; children: Maria May-lee, Jeffrey Tien-yu. Student, Hartwick Coll., 1951-53; B.A., Wittenberg U., 1955; M.A., New Sch. Social Research, 1958; Ph.D., N.Y. U., 1968. Lectr. New Sch. Social Research, 1957-61; vis. asst. prof. Drew U., 1961-62; asst. prof. Fairleigh Dickinson U., 1962-65; asst. prof. U. Redlands, 1965-68, assoc. prof., 1969-73, chmn. dept., 1970-73; prof., chmn. Asian studies CCNY, 1973-79; disting. prof. polit. sci., v.p. acad. affairs, spl. asst. to pres. U. S.D., Vermillion, 1979-82; prof. polit. sci. U. Wyo., Laramie, 1988—; chmn. Third World Conf. Found., Inc., Chgo.; vice chmn. U.S.-Asia Research Inst., N.Y.C. Author: (with Ch'u Chai) The Story of Chinese Philosophy, 1961, The Changing Society of China, 1962, rev. edit., 1969, The New Politics of Communist China, 1972, The Search for a New China, 1975; editor: Essential Works of Chinese Communism, 1969, (with James C. Hsiung) Asia in the U.S. Foreign Policy, 1981; co-editor: (with James C. Hsiung) U.S. Asian Relations: The National Security Paradox, 1983; co-editor (with Cal Clark) Political Stability and Economic Growth, 1988; co-translator: (with Ch'u Chai) A Treasury of Chinese Literature, 1965. Ford Found. humanities grantee, 1968, 69; Haynes Found. fellow, 1967, 68; Pacific Cultural Found. grantee, 1978, 86; NSF grantee, 1970; Hubert Eaton Meml. Fund grantee, 1972-73; Field Found. grantee, 1973, 75; Henry Luce Found. grantee, 1978, 80; S.D. Humanities Com. grantee, 1980; Asian Pacific Fund grantee, 1987. Mem. Am. Assn. Chinese Studies (pres. 1978-80), AAAS, AAUP, Am. Polit. Sci. Assn., N.Y. Acad. Scis., Internat. Studies Assn., NAACP. Democrat. Home: 1071 Granite Dr Laramie WY 82070 Office: University Sta Box 4098 Laramie WY 82071

CHAILLY, RICCARDO, conductor; b. Milan, Feb. 20, 1953; s. Luciano and Anna Maria (Motta) C.; ed. conservatories Giuseppe Verdi, Milan, Perugia. Asst. to condr. La Scala, Milan, 1972-74; debut as condr. with Chgo. Opera, 1974, at La Scala, 1978; Brit. operatic debut at Covent Garden, 1979; Brit. concert debut London Symphony Orch., Edinburgh Festival, 1979; Met. Opera debut, 1982; engagements with major orchs. including Vienna and Berlin philharm. orchs., Concertgebouw, Orch. de Paris, Israel Philharm., London Symphony, Royal Philharm.; condr. Salzburg Festival, 1984-86; prin. guest condr. London Philharm., 1982-85; chief condr. Teatro Comunale, Bologna, Italy, 1986; chief condr. Berlin Radio Symphony Orch., 1982—; prin. condr. Concertgebouw Orch., Amsterdam, 1988—; recs. for Decca Philips records. Address: care Harrison Parrott Ltd, 12 Penzance Pl, London W11 England also: Radio-Symphonie Orchester, Kaiserdamm 26, D-1000 Berlin 19 Federal Republic of Germany

CHAIN, BOBBY LEE, electrical contractor, former mayor; b. Hattiesburg, Miss., Sept. 19, 1929; s. Zollie Lee and Grace (Sellers) C.; BS, U. So. Miss., Hattiesburg, 1974; DBA (hon.), William Carey Coll., Hattiesburg; m. Betty Sue Green, June 30, 1967; children: Robin Ann, Laura Grace, Bobby Lee, John Webster. Chief electrician Miss. Power & Light Co., Natchez, 1950-53; asst. to gen. supt. atomic energy plant Allegany Electric Co., Oak Ridge, 1954-55; owner, chmn. bd. Chain Electric Co., Hattiesburg, 1957—, Chain Lighting & Appliance Co., Hattiesburg, 1957—; owner, pres. Chainco, Inc., oil properties, Hattiesburg, 1974—; dir. Deposit Guaranty Nat. Bank, Jackson, Deposit Guaranty Corp., Jackson; adv. dir. Deposit Guaranty Nat. Bank, Hattiesburg; mem. Interstate Oil Compact Commn., 1972—; nat. adv. council SBA, 1966-67; dir. Miss. Econ. Council, 1982—; mayor City of Hattiesburg, 1980-85. Mem. Council for Support Higher Edn. in Miss., Miss. Junior Coll. Economic Devel. Found.; past mem., past pres. Miss. Trustees Instns. Higher Learning; past mem. So. Regional Edn. Bd., Postsecondary Edn. Bd.; alt. del. Dem. Nat. Conv., 1964. Served with AUS, 1950. Recipient Albert Gallatin award Zurich Am. Ins. Co., 1975; Disting. Service award U. So. Miss., 1976; Compatriot in Edn. award Kappa Delta Pi, 1976; 1961-68; Hub award, 1979; Continuous Outstanding Service award U. So. Miss., 1980; Liberty Bell award, 1980; Service to Edn. award Phi Delta Kappa, 1980; Bobby L. Chain Tech. Ctr. named in his honor; Bobby L. Chain Mcpl. Airport named in his honor. Mem. Newcomen Soc. N.Am., U. So. Miss. Alumni Assn. (Outstanding Service award 1972; Sales and Mktg. Man of Yr. award 1981), Hattiesburg C. of C. (past dir.), Omicron Delta Kappa, Beta Gamma Sigma. Baptist. Clubs: Kiwanis, Hattiesburg Country, U. So. Miss. Century, Shriners; University. Home: 312 6th Ave Hattiesburg MS 39401 Office: PO Box 2058 Hattiesburg MS 39401

CHAKRABARTY, ANANDA MOHAN, microbiologist; b. Sainthia, India, Apr. 4, 1938; s. Satya Dos and Sasthi Bala (Mukherjee) C.; m. Krishna Chakraverty, May 26, 1965; children—Kaberi, Asit. B.Sc., St. Xavier's Coll., 1958; M.Sc., U. Calcutta, 1960, Ph.D., 1965. Sr. research officer U. Calcutta, 1964-65; research asso. in biochemistry U. Ill., Urbana, 1965-71; mem. staff Gen. Electric Research and Devel. Center, Schenectady, 1971-79; prof. dept. microbiology U. Ill. Med. Center, 1979—. Editor: Genetic Engineering, 1977, Biodegradation and Detoxification of Environmental Pollutants, 1982. Named Scientist of Year Indsl. Research Mag., 1975; recipient Inventor of the Yr. award Patent Lawyers' Assn., 1982, Pub. Affairs award Am. Chem. Soc., 1984, Disting. Scientist award U.S. Environ. Protection Agy., 1985, Merit award Nat. Inst. Health, 1986. Mem. Am. Soc. Microbiology, Soc. Indsl. Microbiology, Am. Soc. Biol. Chemists. Home: 206 Julia Dr Villa Park IL 60181 Office: Dept Microbiology U Ill Med Center 835 S Wolcott St Chicago IL 60612

CHAKRAVARTY, SATYA RANJAN, economics educator; b. Noakhali, Bangladesh, June 1, 1954; arrived in India, 1969; s. Prafulla Ranjan and Basanti (Chatterjee) C.; m. Sumita Ray, July 5, 1987. B Stats. with honors, Indian Statis. Inst., Calcutta, 1976, M Stats., 1977, PhD, 1981. Research fellow Indian Statis. Inst., Calcutta, 1977-82, research assoc., 1982-84, asst. prof., 1984-88; assoc. prof. U. Karlsruhe, Fed. Republic of Germany, 1988—; asst. prof. U. B.C., Vancouver, Can., 1984-85. Expert referee Internat. Econ. Rev., Math. Social Scis., Social Choice and Welfare, Sankhya, Indian Jour. of Pure and Applied Maths.; contbr. articles to profl. jours. Ford Found. grantee, 1980. Office: Universitate Karlsruhe, Institut Fur Wirtschaftstheorie, Kaiserstrasse 12, D-7500 Karlsruhe Federal Republic of Germany

CHAKRAVARTY, SUGOTO, scientist; b. New Delhi, India, June 17, 1957; s. Manindra Chandra and Joyshree (Bhattacharya) C. BSc with honors in physics, Delhi U., 1977; MSc in Physics, Bhabha Atomic Research Ctr., 1981. Sci. officer Bhabha Atomic Research Ctr., Bombay, India, 1981-85; sci. officer/SD Bhabha Atomic Research Ctr., Bombay, 1985—. Contbr. articles to profl. jours. Mem. Indian Physics Assn. (life). Office: Bhabha Atomic Research Ctr, Bombay 400 085, India

CHALFI, RAQUEL, poet, film-maker; b. Tel Aviv; d. Shimshon and Miriam C.; 1 child, Daniel. M.A., Hebrew U., 1971. Radio producer, writer Israel Broadcasting Authority, 1960—; documentary film dir., 1969-71; lectr. film and TV dept. Tel Aviv U., 1973—; ind. film-maker, Tel Aviv, 1979—. Author: Submarine and Others, 1975; Free Fall, 1979; Chameleon or The Principle of Uncertainty, 1986; (plays) Ha'agunnah, 1966 (original play award 1966), Photosynthesis, 1971 (Shubert Playwriting award U. Calif.-Berkeley 1971-72); (film script) Kobby, What the Hell is He Looking For, 1978 (Film Script award 1978). Dir., writer, editor film: Possibilities/or: Bluebeard & Me, 1983 (Internat. Ondas award), Her Dream, 1987. Radio producer, presenter: Shai and His Friends, 1974 (Internat. Documentary Ondas award 1977). Jewish. Home: 23 Mane St, 64363 Tel Aviv Israel

CHALHOUB, ANTHONY, retail executive; b. Damascus, Syria, July 25, 1955; arrived in Kuwait, 1975; s. Michel and Widad Mireille Marie (Mazloum) C.; m. Katia Louise Marie El Kayem. BA in Econs., St. Joseph U., Beirut, 1975. Statistician Burinspro, Inc., Beirut, 1973; hotels shop supr. G.D.M., Beirut, 1974-75; sales supr. Habchi & Chalhoub W.L.L., Kuwait, 1974-77; new projects mgr. Habchi & Chalhoub W.L.L., 1978-79; gen. mgr. Tanagra, Kuwait, 1979-80, Habchi & Chalhoub W.L.L., 1980—; pres., gen. mgr. Al Rajaan Trading Co., Kuwait, 1984—; trustee Chalhoub Inc.; pres. Anthony Chalhoub Inc., Kuwait, 1976—; v.p. Burinspro Inc., 1976—; sec. gen. Michel Chalhoub Inc., Kuwait, 1975—. Office: Habchi & Chalhoub WLL, PO Box 21074 Safat, Kuwait 13071, Kuwait

CHALINE, JEAN-PIERRE, historian, educator; b. Orleans, Loiret, France, Dec. 18, 1939; s. Roger and Madeleine Chaline; m. Nadine-Josette Pelletier, Mar. 31, 1964; children: Olivier, Pascale, Emmanuelle. Degree in edn., Sorbonne U., Paris, 1963, D d'État es Lettres, 1979. Prof. agrégé Lycée Corneille, Rouen, France, 1965-68; researcher Centre National Recherche Scientifique, Paris, 1969-71; asst. U. Caen, France, 1971-73; asst. U. Rouen, 1974-78, maitre-asst., 1978-80, prof., 1981—. Author: Histoire de Rouen, 1979, Les Bourgeois de Rouen, 1982 (Prix de l'Académie Française 1984), Histoire du Havre, 1983, L'Affaire Noiret, 1986 (Prix de l'Académie Française 1987). Recipient Palmes Académiques Nat. Edn. Bd., France, 1980. Mem. Soc. de l'Histoire de Normandie (pres. 1977—), Conseil Supérieur des Univs. Office: U Rouen, UER Lettres, Lavoisier, 76130 Mont-St-Aignan France

CHALMERS, DAVID B., petroleum executive; b. Denver, Nov. 17, 1924; s. David Twiggs and Dorit (Bay) C.; 1 child, David B. B.A., Dartmouth Coll., 1947; A.M.P., Harvard U., 1966. Various positions Bay Petroleum Co., Denver, 1951-55; various positions Tenneco Oil Co., Houston, 1955-57; v.p. Occidental Petroleum Corp., Houston, 1957-68; pres. Can. Occidental Petroleum Ltd., 1968-73; pres., chief exec. officer Petrogas Processing Ltd., 1968-73; officer Cansulex Ltd., 1968-73; chmn., chief exec. officer, dir. Coral Petroleum, Inc. and subs., Houston, 1973—; dir. Leeward Petroleum Co., Hamilton, Bermuda. Served to lt. USMC, 1943-45, 49-50, Korea. Mem. Am. Petroleum Inst. Republican. Episcopalian. Clubs: Lakeside Country, Houston. Home: 908 Town & Country Blvd Apt 600 Houston TX 77024 Office: Coral Petroleum Inc PO Box 19666 Houston TX 77224

CHALOUPEK, GUENTHER KARL, economist; b. Zwentendorf, Austria, June 5, 1947; s. Ferdinand and Maria Adele (Hoechtl) C.; m. Gertrude Maria Kotzmanek, Feb. 13, 1976; children: Ralph Alexander, Iris Simone. JD, Vienna U., Austria, 1969; MA in Econs., Kansas U., 1971. Mem. staff Inst. Regional Planning, Vienna, 1971-72; mem. staff econ. research dept. Chamber of Labour, Vienna, 1972-86, head econ. research dept., 1986—; exec. sec. Econ. and Social Adv. Bd. Joint Commn. on Prices and Wages, Vienna, 1976—; v.p. survey bd. Postal Sav. Bank, Vienna, 1982—. Author: Die zweifelnde Gesellschaft, 1983, Gesamtwirtschaftli che Planung in Westeuropa, 1987; editor jour. Wirtschaft und Gesellschaft, 1978—; contbr. articles to profl. jours. Sec., mem. com. Austrian Socialist Party, 1976. Mem. Kautsky-Kreis, Austrian Econ. Soc. Roman Catholic. Home: Linzer Strasse 227 RH8, A 1140 Vienna Austria Office: Chamber of Labour, Prinz Eugen-Strasse 20, A 1040 Vienna Austria

CHAMBERLAIN, JOHN ANGUS, sculptor; b. Rochester, Ind., Apr. 16, 1927; s. Claude Chester and Mary Francis (Waller) C.; m. Lorraine Belcher, Dec. 31, 1977 (div.); children: Angus, Jesse, Duncan. Student, Art Inst. Chgo., 1950-52, U. Ill., Black Mountain Coll., 1955-56. One-man shows include Cleve. Mus. Art, 1967, New HemisFair, 1968, York U., Toronto, Ont., Can., 1969, Guggenheim Mus., 1971, Indpl. Mus. Art, 1972, Pratt Inst., 1974, Josechoff Gallery U. Hartford, 1977, Flint (Mich.) Inst. Art, 1978, Whitney Mus. Am. Art, 1979, Leo Castelli Gallery, 1982, U. Calif.-Santa Barbara, Xavier Fourcade, 1984, Pace Gallery, 1988, numerous others; two-man shows include Taft Mus., Cin., 1972, Newport Art Festival, 1976, U. Calif. Art Mus., Santa Barbara, 1984; group shows include Galerie Rive Droit, Paris, 1960, Sao Paolo (Brazil) Mus. Modern Art, Art Inst. Chgo., 1961, Tate Gallery, 1964, Carnegie Inst., 1967, Nova Scotia Coll. Art, Palais de Beaux-Arts, Brussels, 1970, Louisiana Mus., Copenhagen, 1972, Inst. Contemporary Art, Phila., 1975, Fitzwilliam Mus., Cambridge, Eng., 1977, Grace Borgenicht Gallery, 1982, Nat. Gallery Art, Washington, Ecole Nat. Superior des Beaux-Arts, Paris 1985, Weatherspoon Art Gallery, 1984, numerous others; films include Wedding Night, 1967, The Secret Life of Hernando Cortez, 1968, Wide Point, 1968, Thumbsuck, 1971. Served with USN, 1943-46. Recipient Brandeis award, Creative Arts award, 1984. Republican. Taoist. Club: Sarasota Sailing Squadron. Office: care of Pace Gallery 32 E 57th St New York NY 10022

CHAMBERLAIN, JOHN HAROLD, JR., county official; b. Omaha, Oct. 20, 1929; s. John Harold and Geneva Mildred (Roland) C.; m. Mary Elizabeth Mendietta, July 3, 1950; children—Cecilia Marie, John Nicholas, Mary Francis. Student in acctg. Ranger Jr. Coll., Tex., 1953-57; student in criminal justice Los Medanos Coll., 1978; student in math. San Diego Jr. Coll., 1950. Cert. disaster planner. Vice pres. Geneva Petroleum Co., Eastland, Tex., 1953-59, Chamberlain Lithographing & Direct Advt., Oakland, Calif., 1959-71; mgr. dispatching services Alameda County Sheriff's Dept., San Leandro, Calif., 1971—; mem. disaster planning com. Oakland Internat. Airport, 1977—; mem. prehosp. ops. com. Alameda County Health Care, Oakland, 1983—. Regional campaign dir. Eastland March of Dimes, 1957. Served with USN, 1948-53. Recipient award for lithographic excellence Crown Zellerback Corp., Oakland, 1969. Fellow Am. Biographical Inst. (Medal of Honor 1987); mem. Assn. Pub. Safety Communications Officers, Dublin Fire Fighters Assn. (pres. 1974-75, award for outstanding accomplishments 1975), Nat. Acad. TV Arts and Scis. Democrat. Roman Catholic. Club: Lone Cedar Country (pres. 1957-58) (Eastland). Lodge: K.C. (3d degree). Office: OES Consol Dispatch 2000 150th Ave San Leandro CA 94578

CHAMBERLAIN, OWEN, nuclear physicist; b. San Francisco, July 10, 1920; divorced 1978; 4 children; m. June Steingart, 1980. AB (Cramer fellow), Dartmouth Coll., 1941; PhD, U. Chgo., 1949. Instr. physics U. Calif., Berkeley, 1948-50; asst. prof. U. Calif., 1950-54, assoc. prof., 1954-58, prof., 1958—; civilian physicist Manhattan Dist., Berkeley, Los Alamos, 1942-46. Guggenheim fellow, 1957-58; Loeb lectr. at Harvard U., 1959; Recipient Nobel prize (with Emilio Segré) for physics, for discovery anti-proton, 1959. Fellow Am. Phys. Soc., Am. Acad. Arts and Scis.; mem. Nat. Acad. Scis. Office: Univ of Calif Physics Dept Berkeley CA 94720 •

CHAMBERLIN, JOHN STEPHEN, cosmetics company executive; b. Boston, July 29, 1928; s. Stephen Henry and Olive Helen (McGrath) C.; m. Mary Katherine Leahy, Oct. 9, 1954; children—Mary Katherine, Patricia Ann, Carol Lynn, John Stephen, Liane Helen, Mark Joseph. A.B. cum laude, Harvard U., 1950, M.B.A., 1953. Lamp salesman Gen. Electric Co., N.Y.C., 1954-57, mgmt. cons., 1957-60; mgr. product planning TV receiver dept. Gen. Electric Co., Syracuse, N.Y., 1960-63; mgr. mktg., gen. mgr. radio receiver dept. Gen. Electric Co., Utica, N.Y., 1963-70; exec. v.p., dir. Lenox Inc., Trenton, N.J., 1970-71; v.p., gen. mgr. housewares div. Gen. Electric Co., Bridgeport, Conn., 1971-74, v.p., gen. mgr. housewares and audio div., 1974-76; pres., chief exec. officer, dir. Lenox Inc., Lawrenceville, N.J., 1976-81, chmn., chief exec. officer, 1981-85; pres., chief operating officer Avon Products, Inc., N.Y.C., 1985-88; pvt. investor N.Y.C., 1988—; bd. dirs. Travelers Companies; mem. Industry Policy Adv. Com. for U.S. Trade Policy Matters. Trustee Med. Ctr. at Princeton, Woodrow Wilson Nat. Fellowship Found.; bd. overseers Parson Sch. Design; bd. dirs. Jr. Achievement of N.Y. Mem. N.J. C. of C. (bd. dirs.). Clubs: Bedens Brook; Harvard (N.Y.C.), Union League (N.Y.C.). Home: 182 Fairway Dr Princeton NJ 08540 Office: Avon Products Inc 9 W 57th St New York NY 10019

CHAMBERS, BETTE, humanist association executive; b. Seattle, July 31, 1930; d. Ralph George and Edda (Sommers) Johnson; m. Charles M. Chambers, Sept. 19, 1949; children—Janice E. Chambers Sharar, Martha J., Patrice L. Chambers. Student, U. Wash., 1952, Humboldt State U., 1957, Sacramento State U., 1960, Eastern Wash. State U., 1967. Pres. Minn. Humanist Assn., Mpls., 1961-64; dir. Am. Humanist Assn., Amherst, N.Y., 1968-82, pres., 1973-79, pres. emeritus, 1979—, exec. dir., 1978-79, 81-84, asst. to the pres., Dr. Isaac Asimov, 1984—. Co-founder, fellow Com. for the Sci. Investigation of Claims of the Paranormal, Buffalo, 1976—. Mem. editorial bd. The Humanist Mag., 1973—; editor, Free Mind Newsletter, 1975—; contbr. articles to profl. jours. Assoc. trustee The Churchman Mag., 1983—. Mem. AAAS, ACLU, N.Y. Acad. Scis. Democrat. Unitarian. Home: 4116 Candlewood Dr SE Lacey WA 98503 Office: Am Humanist Assn 7 Harwood Dr Amherst NY 14226

CHAMBERS, BEVERLY ZIVITSKI, graphics company manager, tax consultant; b. Middletown, Conn., July 31, 1952; d. Paul and Anne (Kost) Zivitski. AA, Daytona Beach Community Coll., 1977, AS in Tech. Illustration, 1978; BS in Art Adminstrn., U. Tampa, 1985. Artist Eastern Graphics, Old Saybrook, Conn., 1973-74; sch. artist Inex, Daytona Beach, Fla., 1978; art dir. Daytona pub. and pvt. schs., Daytona Beach, 1979-80; artist Pearson & Clark, Lakeland, Fla., 1980-83; ops. mgr. Imperial Graphic, Largo, Fla., 1985-87, chief exec. officer, 1987—; tax preparer H & R Block, 1979-85. Recipient 1st prize Fla. Advt. Council, 1979. Mem. Suncoast Archel. Soc., Nat. Audubon Soc. Home: 1455 Corey Way S South Pasadena FL 33707 Office: Imperial Graphics 9075 B 130th Ave N Largo FL 33543

CHAMBERS, WALTER R., investment banker; b. Lancaster, Ohio, May 2, 1931; s. Walter R. and Martha Blanche (Notestone) C.; m. Sue Hartley, Aug. 8, 1953; children—James R., Mark R. B.S., Ohio State U., 1952. With Ohio Co., Columbus, 1961—, adminstr. pub. fin., fixed income and equity trading depts., 1968—, dir., exec. v.p., 1972—; dir. Ohio Equities Inc., Ins. Ohio Co. Agy.; sr. exec. v.p., dir. The Ohio Co.,pres., dir. Midwest Parking Inc. Treas., bd. dirs. Health Services Found.; trustee Coll. of Wooster; treas. Upper Arlington Civic Assn., 1966-67; cabinet mem. Franklin County United Way, 1982-83; adv. bd. Goodwill CORC. Served with U.S. Army, 1956-58. Mem. Pub. Securities Assn. (chmn., dir.), Securities Industry Assn. (dir., exec. com.), Mcpl. Fin. Forum Washington, Mcpl. Fin. Forum N.Y., Nat. Press Club. Republican. Episcopalian. Clubs: Muirfield Village Golf, Scioto Country, University (Columbus). Lodge: Masons. Contbr. articles to profl. jours. Office: 155 E Broad St Columbus OH 43215

CHAMBERS, WILLIAM DOUGLAS, dentist; b. Madison, W.Va., Sept. 23, 1945; s. Arlie and Emma Jean (Chandler) C.; m. Sheryl Lynn Leatherman, May 25, 1966; children: Jeffery Douglas, Terin Raphe, Tory Lynn, Lindsey Paige, Cody Lane. BA, Emporia (Kans.) State U., 1973; DDS, U. Mo., Kansas City, 1978. Midwest customer service mgr. Standard Brands Foods, Kansas City, 1973-74; gen. practice dentistry Andover, Kans., 1978—; comml. developer Cloud City Devel., Andover, 1982—; cons. Midwest Dental Consultation, Andover, 1986—. Contbr. articles to Andover Jour. and Kans. Dental Assn. Jour. Coach Andover Little League Baseball Program, 1979—; v.p. South Cen. Little League Baseball, 1987; deacon Cen. Ch. of Christ, Wichita, 1980—; mem. adv. bd. Christ Villa Nursing Home, Wichita, 1980—; fund raiser Citizens for Alcohol-Drug Abuse Awareness, Andover, 1985-86; chmn., sponsor First Ann. Tooth Fair, Andover, 1988. Served with USAF, 1963-67. Mem. 7th Dist. Dental Soc. (sec., treas. 1981-83, pres. 1984-85, del. 1986—), Kans. Dental Assn. (co-chmn. com. on dental practice, 1985-86, chmn. 1986—, recipient Harry M. Klenda award for Outstanding Dental Practice 1987-88), Andover C. of C., Tri Bete. Home: 314 Pineview Andover KS 67002 Office: 310 W Central Suite B Box 246 Andover KS 67002

CHAMBERS (GREENMAN), ANTONIA MARGUERITE, lawyer; b. Niagara Falls, N.Y., Aug. 10, 1955; d. Morgan Andrew and Gloria Irene Greenman; m. William L. Chambers, June 6, 1987. B.A. summa cum laude, Niagara U., 1977; J.D., U. Notre Dame, 1980; cert. London Sch. Econs., 1979. Bar: D.C. 1981. Bar: D.C. 1981. Assoc. dir. Am. Family Inst., Washington, 1980-81; legis. asst. Senator Al D'Amato, Washington, 1981; exec. dir. Hale Found., Washington, 1982-83; fgn. affairs specialist Republican Study Com., Ho. of Reps., Washington, 1983-84; spl. asst. Office Pub. Diplomacy, Dept. State, Washington, 1984-87; dep. counsel asylum policy and review unit, Dept. Justice, Washington, 1987—. Editor-in-chief U. Niagara Yearbook, 1976-77; research editor Jour. Legislation, 1978-79; contbr. govt. and fgn. affairs articles to jours. Recipient Sr. medal Niagara U., 1977, Fr. Duggan medal, 1977; Niagara U. scholar, 1974-77, U. Notre Dame scholar, 1978-80. Mem. ABA (internat. law sect.), Bar Assn. D.C., Phi Alpha Delta. Roman Catholic. Club: Capitol Hill. Office: Office Asylum Policy & Rev Unit Dept Justice Washington DC 20530

CHAMIS, CHRISTOS CONSTANTINOS, aerospace engineer, educator; b. Sotira, Greece, May 16, 1930; came to U.S., 1948; s. Constantinos and Anastasia (Kyriakos) C.; m. Alice Yanosko, Aug. 20, 1966; children—Chrysantie, Anna-Lisa, Constantinos. B.S. in Civil Engring., Cleve. State U., 1960; M.S., Case Western Res. U., 1962, Ph.D., 1967. Draftsman, designer Cons. Engring., Cleve., 1955-60; research asst. Case Western Res. U., Cleve., 1960-62, research assoc., 1964-68, lectr., 1984—; research mathematician B. F. Goodrich, Brecksville, Ohio, 1962-64; aerospace engr. Lewis Research Ctr., NASA, Cleve., 1968-84, sr. research engr., 1984—; cons. Lawrence Livermore Labs., Calif., 1974-79; adj. prof. Cleve. State U., 1968—, Akron U., 1980—, Case Western Reserve U., 1984—. Editor: Composites Analysis/Design, 1975; mem. editorial bd. Jour. Composites Research and Tech., Reinforced Plastics and Composites, Nonlinear Computational Mechanics. Contbr. numerous articles to sci. jours. Patentee in field. Served with USMCR, 1953-54. Fellow AIAA (assoc., editor); mem. ASCE, ASME, ASTM, Soc. Experimental Mechanics, Soc. Aerospace Processing and Materials Engring., Soc. Plastics Industry, Sigma Xi. Clubs: Dodoni, Hellenic U. Home: 24534 Framingham Dr Westlake OH 44145

CHAMMAS, JACQUES, construction company executive; b. Aleppo, Syria, May 16, 1950; s. Simon and Farida C.; m. Agnes Pellerin, Oct. 9, 1981; children: Anne-Sophie, Simon. B of Engring., Am. U. of Beirut, 1972; grad. in hydraulics engring., Ecole Nat. SUperieure d'Hydraulique, Grenoble, France, 1974. Dep. project mgr. Bandar Shahpour Port Constrn. Dumez Co., Iran, 1975-78; mgr. Saudi constrn. projects Nanterre, France, 1979-80; dir. Khashm-Al-Aan Twp. constrn. Riyadh, Saudi Arabia, 1981-86; dep. sec. gen. Nanterre, 1987—; Bd. dirs. Comex Services SA, Marseille, France, Doris Engring. Co., Paris. Home: 54 Ave Sainte Foy, 92200 Neuilly Sur Seine France Office: Dumez Co, 345 Ave Georges Clemenceau, 92000 Nanterre France

CHAMPIE, ELLMORE ALFRED, historian, writer; b. Eden, Tex., Sept. 11, 1916; s. Sam Houston and Nora Louise (Sorrell) C.; student Tex. Coll. Mines and Metallurgy, 1941-42; B.A. with highest honors, U. Tex, Austin, 1947, M.A. (Univ. Scholar), 1948; Ph.D. in History (Bayard Cutting Scholar), Harvard U., 1967; m. Rosemary Erter, Sept. 7, 1947 (dec. Nov. 1962); children—Ellmore Alfred, Nora Beatrice; m. 2d, Miriam Helene Boysen Mann, Aug. 28, 1971 (div. Oct. 1974). Archivist, Nat. Archives, 1952-55; historian U.S. Marine Corps Hdqrs., 1955-56, Joint Chiefs of Staff, U.S. Dept. Def., 1956-61; asso. agy. historian Fed. Aviation Agy., 1961-67; agy. historian FAA, Dept. of Transp., 1967-72; hist. researcher and writer, 1972—; mem. tech. com. on history U.S. Inst. of Aeros. and Astronautics, 1970-72; editorial cons. history of FAA and predecessor agys., 4 vols. Served with U.S. Navy, 1936-40; served to 1st lt. USAAF, 1942-45. Mem. Am. Hist. Assn., Am. Acad. Polit. and Social Sci., Am. Soc. for Eighteenth-Century Studies, Am. Soc. for Pub. Adminstrn., Phi Beta Kappa. Democrat. Clubs: Masons, Harvard (So. Ariz.). Author: The Federal Turnaround on Aid to Airports, 1926-38, 1973. Home: 7480 E Rio Verde Dr Tucson AZ 85715

CHAMPION, PIERRE DHEILLY, surgeon, researcher; b. Chatou, Ile de France, France, Nov. 26, 1936; s. Julien Joseph and Raymonde (Dheilly) C.; m. Genevieve Massonnet, June 25, 1964; children: Marie-Blandine, Herve, Christian. MD, U. Paris, 1964. Asst. surgeon Argenteuil Hosp., France, 1969-73; oral surgeon Beaumont, France, 1973-75; mgr. Centre Med., Bourg la Reine, France, 1975—. Mem. Soc. Stomatologie Chirurgie Maxillo Faciale (sec. 1966). Roman Catholic. Office: Ctr Med, 73 Bd Marechal Joffre, 92340 Bourg la Reine France

CHAMPION DE CRESPIGNY, (RICHARD) RAFE, Asian studies educator; b. Adelaide, Australia, Mar. 16, 1936; s. Richard Geoffrey and Kathleen Cavenagh (Cudmore) Champion de Crespigny; m. Christa Charlotte Boltz, May 17, 1959; children: Christine Anne, Richard Mark. MA, Cambridge (Eng.) U., 1961; BA, Australian Nat. U., Canberra, 1962, MA in Oriental Studies, 1964, PhD, 1968. Mem. faculty Australian Nat. U., 1965—, reader in Chinese, 1974—, dean faculty of Asian studies, 1979-82, head. China Ctr., 1982-85; sec. gen. Internat. Congress Orientalists, Canberra, 1971; v.p. Australian Inst. Internal Affairs, 1973-76. Author: The Last of the Han, 1969, China: The Land and its People, 1971, China This Century, 1975, Northern Frontier, 1984. Fellow Australian Acad. Humanities, Oriental Soc. Australia; mem. Asian Studies Assn. Australia, Royal Geog. Soc. Australiasia. Anglican. Clubs: Adelaide; Commonwealth (Canberra). Office: Australian Nat U Faculty Asian, Studies PO Box 4, 2601 Canberra Australia

CHAMPNEY, RAYMOND JOSEPH, advertising agency executive; b. N.Y.C., Aug. 6, 1940; s. Raymond Joseph and Florence (McConnell) C.; m. Anne Kelly, Jan. 10, 1976. Student CCNY, 1961-63; B.S. in Mktg., NYU, 1965. With BBDO Advt., N.Y.C., 1964-66, McCann Erickson Advt., 1966-68, Clinton E. Frank Advt., 1968-71, Norman Craig & Kummel Advt., 1971-73, Doyle Dane Bernbach Advt., 1973-74, Guest Pub. Co., 1974-77, Bozell & Jacobs Advt., 1977-79; pres. Weekley & Champney Advt., Dallas, 1979-86; pres., chief exec. officer Champney and Assoc. Advt., Dallas, 1986—. Served with U.S. Army, 1959-61. Mem. Sales Mktg. Execs., Dallas Ad League, Mex. Am. C. of C. Home: 3302 St Albans Circle Colleyville TX 76034 Office: Champney & Assoc Advt 1440 W Mockingbird Ln Suite 300 Dallas TX 75247

CHAN, CHAK-FU, hotel executive, real estate investment company executive; b. Hong Kong, Apr. 18, 1918; s. Kwan-Tung and Kwei-Heung (Cheng) C.; m. Esther Chi-Lan Wong, Oct. 22, 1953; children—Lawrence M. Y., Charles M. W., Joseph M.C. Civil engring. degree, Lingnam U., 1937. Mng. dir. Fu Investment Co. Ltd., Hong Kong, 1961—, Internat. Hoteliers Ltd., Hong Kong, 1972—; chmn., pres. Fu Investment Co., Ltd., Los Angeles, 1973—, Pearl City Investment Corp., Los Angeles, 1974—; chmn. Pacific Renaissance Assocs., San Francisco, 1986—, Park Lane Hotels Internat., Hong Kong and N.Y.C., 1986—; mng. gen. ptnr. U.S. Hotelier Assn., San Francisco, 1981—; dir. Real Estate Developers Assn., Hong Kong, 1974—. Mem. Am. Soc. Travel Agts., Australian Fedn. Travel Agts., Pacific Area Travel Assn. Clubs: Country, Jockey (Hong Kong). Office: Park Lane Hotel, Room 135, 310 Gloucester Rd, Causeway Bay Hong Kong

CHAN, CHIU SUCK, anesthesiologist; b. Hong Kong, Sept. 5, 1939; s. Hak Tan and Ching Yuen (Lam) C.; m. Agnes Yeung, June 8, 1966; children: Elaine, Arthur, Carol. B in Medicine and Surgery, Hong Kong U., 1964; D in Anesthesiology, Royal Coll. Surgeons, London, 1968. Med. officer Queen Mary Hosp., Hong Kong, 1965-67; hon. registrar Hammersmith Hosp., London, 1968; med. officer Queen Mary Hosp., Hong Kong, 1969-72, cons., 1972-82, sr. cons., 1982—; hon. lectr. Hong Kong U., 1969—. Contbr. articles to profl. jours. Grantham scholar, 1957-59; Commonwealth Scholar Assn. Commonwealth Univs., London, 1968; fellow Royal Coll. of Surgeons Eng., 1968; fellow Royal Australian Coll. Surgeons, 1983. Mem. Soc. Anesthetists Hong Kong (council mem. 1969—, pres. 1987—). Office: Queen Mary Hosp, Pokfulam Rd, Hong Kong Hong Kong

CHAN, CHIU-HUNG, banker; b. Swatow, Kwangtung, China, Oct. 12, 1932; came to Hong Kong, 1948; s. Hak Tan and Ching-Yuen (Lam) C.; m. Cecilia Ling-Kuen, Nov. 28, 1966; children—Patrick Chung-Pak, Henrietta Yuen Kar Ling Ying Coll., 1950; M.S. in Mgmt., U. Beverly Hills, 1984. Mgr. bills Kar Cheung Chong Bank, Hong Kong, 1950-55; dep. gen. mgr. The Hongkong Chinese Bank Ltd., 1955-81; mng. dir. Allied Capital Resources Ltd., Hong Kong, 1981; lectr. The Hong Kong Productivity Centre, 1973—, Hong Kong Mgmt. Assn., 1985—; mng. dir. Allied Capital Resources Ltd., Hong Kong, 1981—; dir. ACR Nominees Ltd., Hong Kong, 1981—, Corporate Fin. DTC Ltd., Hong Kong, 1982—. Author: Practices for Executives, Vol. I, 1976, 2nd edit. 1984, Vol. II, 1977. Fellow Internat. Rd. Safety Assn., Inst. Bankers; mem. Hong Kong Chiu Chow C. of C., Hong Kong History Soc., South China Athletic Assn., Chi Tung Assn., Am. Mgmt. Assn. (internat. mem. banking tng. bd. 1987-88). Clubs: Overseas Bankers, Pacific. Office: Ice House St 32-38, Allied Capital Resources Ltd, Edko Tower Hong Kong

CHAN, EDWIN YUK LEUNG, manufacturing executive; b. Canton, Peoples Republic China, Aug. 17, 1946; s. To Sang and Shui Ying (Lo) C.; m. So Kwai Shuen; children: Chan Wai Mum, Chan Fook Shing. Grad. high sch., Hong Kong. Sales exec. Dreyer & Co. Ltd., Hong Kong, 1966-71; mgr. Tak Cheong Ltd., Hong Kong, 1971-75; chmn. Waly Decorative Products Ltd., Hong Kong, 1967—. Home: 1 Fontana Garden, 4/F Ka Ning Path, Causeway Hill Hong Kong Office: Waly Decorative Products Ltd, 39 Gloucester Rd, Harcourt House Hong Kong

CHAN, JULIUS, government official; b. Tanga, New Ireland, Papua New Guinea, Aug. 29, 1939; m. Stella Ahmat, 1966; 4 children. Student, Maurist Bros. Coll., Ashgrove, Queensland; grad., U. Queensland, Australia; D. of Econ. (hon.), Dankook U., Seoul, 1978; D. of Tech. (hon.), U. Tech., Papua New Guinea, 1983. Cooperative officer Papua New Guinea Adminstrn., 1960-62; mng. dir. Coastal Shipping Co. Pty. Ltd.; mem. House of Assembly, Papua New Guinea, 1968-75, 1982—, dep. speaker, vice chmn. pub. accounts com., 1968-72; parliamentary leader People's Progress Party, Papua New Guinea, from 1970; minister fin., parliamentary leader govt. bus. Papua New Guinea, 1972-77, dep. prime minister, minister primary industry, 1977-78, prime minister, 1980-82, dep. prime minister, 1986-88, minister trade and industry, 1986-88; Gov. Papua New Guinea, vice chair Asian Devt. Bank 1975-77. Fellow Internat. Banker's Assn. (U.S.). Address: Office Dep Prime Minister, Port Moresby Papua New Guinea *

CHAN, KAM LUN TONY, obstetrician, gynecologist; b. Hong Kong, Aug. 29, 1951; s. Kwai Ming and Tit San (Leung) C.; m. Heng Yook Lee, July 8, 1976; children: Adrian Kin-Shing, Karen Ka-Yan. MBChB, Liverpool (Eng.) Med. Sch., 1976; DRCOG, Royal Coll. Ob-Gyn, Eng., 1980, MRCOG, 1981. Registrar Cuckfield Hosp., West Sussex, Eng., 1979-82; sr. med. officer Caritas Med. Centre, Hong Kong, 1982-86; cons., head dept ob-gyn Evangel Hosp., Hong Kong, 1986—; hon. clin. lectr. U. Hong Kong, 1982-86; examiner Hong Kong Midwives Bd., 1984—; hon. cons. Family Planning Assn., Hong Kong, 1986—; clin. supr. Coll. Gen. Practitioners, Hong Kong, 1986—. Mem. Royal Coll. Ob-Gyn, Hong Kong Med. Assn. Office: Tung Ying Bldg, Room 203, 100 Nathan Rd, Kowloon Hong Kong

CHAN, LIEN, Republic of China government official; b. Tainan City, Taiwan, Republic China, Aug. 27, 1936; m. Fang Yui; 2 sons, 2 daughters. BA, Nat. Taiwan U.; MA, U. Chgo., PhD. Asst. prof. U. Wis., 1965-66, U. Conn., 1966-68; prof. Nat. Taiwan U., 1968-69; ambassador to El Salvador 1975-76; minister communications Republic China, 1981-88, minister fgn. affairs, 1988—. Home: 2d Floor 5, Lane 464 Tunhua S Rd, Taipei Taiwan, Republic of China Office: Ministry Fgn Affairs, Taipei Taiwan, Republic of China *

CHAN, MILAGROS ABESAMIS, obstetrician, gynecologist, educator; b. Tacloban, Leyte, Philippines, Nov. 22, 1940; d. Manuel Bernardo and Marcelina (Say) Abesamis; m. Cesar D. Chan, Aug. 21, 1962; children: Maria Cynthia Hortelano, Cesar Jr., Marinela. BSin Pre-Med, St. Paul's Coll., Tacloban, Philippines, 1958; MD, Cebu Inst. Medicine, Philippines, 1963. Diplomate Am. Bd. Ob-Gyn, Philippines Bd. Ob-Gyn. Instr. pathology Cebu Inst. Medicine, 1963-64; resident physician U. Ill Hosps., Chgo., 1965-70; asst. prof. ob-gyn Cebu Inst. Medicine, 1970-77; asst. prof. Cebu Doctors' Coll. Medicine, 1977-81, assoc. prof., chmn. dept. ob-gyn, 1981-85, prof., chmn. dept. ob-gyn, 1985—; cons. Cebu City Med. Ctr., 1980-85, So. Islands Med. Ctr., 1985-87. Bd. dirs. Inner Wheel Club Cebu, 1980; mem. Family Planning Organization Philippines, Cebu City, 1985. Fellow Philippine Ob-Gyn Soc. (bd. dirs. 1983—, pres. Cebu chpt. 1984—), Philippine Coll. Surgeons, Am. Coll. Ob-Gyn (affiliate), Am. Coll. Surgeons. Roman Catholic. Home: Maria Luisa Estate Park, Cebu Philippines Office: Cebu Doctors Hosp, Dept Ob-Gyn, Osmena Blvd, Cebu City Philippines

CHAN, MING KONG, manufacturing company executive, consultant; b. Canton, Kwang Tung, Peoples Republic China, June 6, 1937; s. P. Chun and S. Wah (Chou) C.; m. Eunice Yim; children: Timothy, Sarah, Joyce. BS, U. Ohio, 1961; cert., Japan Productivity Ctr., 1967. Jr. engr. Coleman Inc., Wichita, Kans., 1961-62; equipment designer Warren Corp., Pitts., 1962-63; from mgr. factory to exec. dir. Chung Mei Mfg. Ltd., Kowloon, Hong Kong, 1963—; cons. U.N. Econ. Social Commn. Asia and Pacific, N.Y.C., 1983; bd. dirs. Chung Mei Mfg. Ltd., Chung Mei Metal Plastic Factory Ltd. Patentee various lighting, heating equipment; design patentee in U.S., Eng., Australia, Sweden, Fed. Republic Germany, 1980-87. Recipient Good Design award, 1979, Design Spl. Products award, 1980, Metal Products award, 1981, Gov. award Good Design Products, 1986, Fedn. Hong Kong Industries. Mem. ASME, ASHRAE, Hong Kong Engrs. Soc. Club: Chinese (Hong Kong). Office: Chung Mei Mfg Ltd, 58 Hung To Rd, Kwun Tong Hong Kong

CHAN, ROBIN YAU-HING, banker; b. Swatow, China, Nov. 6, 1932; s. Chin and Kwai Ying (Lau) Sophonpanich; grad. Ling Ying Coll., Hong Kong, 1950; grad. Inst. of Banking, N.Y.C., 1954; m. Lily Sim See Hoon; children—Stephen, Maryann, Donna, Bernard. Exec. trainee Asia Trust Bank, Bangkok, Thailand, 1950-52, Bangkok Bank, 1952-53, Mfrs. Trust Co. N.Y., Irving Trust Co. N.Y., Guarantee Trust Co. N.Y.C., 1953-54; with Comml. Bank of Hong Kong Ltd., 1955—, chmn., mng. dir., 1965—; chmn. Bangkok Merc. (HK) Co. Ltd., United Asia Co. Ltd., chmn. exec. com. Asia Ins. Co., Ltd.; dir. Liu Chong Hing Bank Ltd., Sun Hung Kai Securities Ltd., Pioneer Industries (Holdings) Ltd. Exec. dir. Tung Wah Group of Hosps., 1965-66; pres. Chiu Yang Residents Assn., Hong Kong, 1973-79. Fellow Internat. Bankers Assn.; mem. Hong Kong Chiu Chow C. of C. (chmn.). Clubs: Am., Country, Royal Hong Kong Jockey (Hong Kong). Office: Comml Bank of Hong Kong Bldg, 120-122 Des Voeux Rd, Hong Kong Hong Kong

CHAN, SHIH HUNG, mechanical engineering educator, consultant; b. Chang Hwa, Taiwan, Nov. 8, 1943; came to U.S., 1964; s. Ping and Fu Zon (Liao) C.; m. Shirley Shih-Lin Wang, June 14, 1969; children: Bryan, Erick. Diploma Taipei Inst. Tech., Taiwan, 1963; MS, U. N.H., 1966; PhD, U. Calif.-Berkeley, 1969. Registered profl. engr., Wis. Asst. to assoc. prof. NYU, N.Y.C., 1969-73; assoc. prof. Poly. Inst. N.Y., N.Y.C., 1973-74; research staff mem. Argonne Nat. Lab., Ill., 1974-75; assoc. prof. U. Wis., Milw., 1975-78, prof. mech. engring., 1978—, chmn. dept., 1979—; cons. Argonne Nat. Lab., Ill., 1975—, Allen-Bradley Co., Milw., 1984, Gen. Electric Co., Schenectady, 1980, Teltech Resource Network, 1986—, Eclipse, Inc., 1988. Contbr. articles to profl. jours. Bd. dirs. Orgn. Chinese Americans, State of Wis., 1983—; v.p. Civic Club, Milw., 1984—, pres., 1985—. Served to 2d lt. Taiwan M.C., 1963-64. Recipient Outstanding Research award U. Wis.-Milw. Research Found., 1983, Research citation Assembly State of Wis., Madison, 1984, 1st Coll. Research award, 1987, Coll. Outstanding Research award, 1987; grantee NSF, Dept. Energy, Argonne Nat. Lab., Office of Naval Research, 1969—. Mem. Am. Nuclear Soc. (pres. Wis. 1982-83), Profl. Ergrs. State of Wis., ASME. Avocations: fishing, Tae-Kwon-do. Home: 3416 W Meadowview Ct Mequon WI 53092 Office: U Wis-Milw Dept of Mech Engring Milwaukee WI 53201

CHAN, SIU-HUNG, urologist; b. Hong Kong, Feb. 19, 1944; s. Chi-Man and Yun-(Lan) C.; m. Theresa K. K. Kwan (div. Dec. 1979); children: Charmaine S. Y., Charleen S. C. MBBS HK, U. Hong Kong, 1969; clin. fellow in urology, Harvard U. Med. Sch., 1975. Intern Queen Elizabeth Hosp., Hong Kong, 1969, intern in surgery, 1970, resident med. officer in orthopaedics, 1970, resident med. officer in surgery, 1970-76; practice medicine specializing in urology St. Teresa's Hosp., Hong Kong, 1976—; lectr. Chinese art, Melbourne, Auckland. Co-editor: Treatise of Urology, 1987; exhibited in group shows City Hall, Hong Kong, 1981, 84, 86, Sejong Cultural Centre, Republic of Korea, 1982, 1st Internt. Seal-Carving Exhbn., Seoul, Republic of Korea, 1984, Macau, 1985, Guangzhou, Peoples Republic of China, 1st Internat. Calligraphy and Seal competition, 1985, Hong Kong Biennial Arts Exhbn., 1985, Union Book Store, Hong Kong, 1985, Artist's Gallery, Xian, Peoples Republic of China, 1986, Mus. de Limo, Macau, 1986, Beijing ShouDu Mus., 1986, TianJin Mus., 1986, Wu Chang Shi Meml. Mus., 1987; calligraphy inscribed in stone Wu Hon Meml. Pavillion, Hunan Province, Peoples Republic of China, 1985, Henan Kai Fong Hon-Yuen Pavillion, 1986, Adelaide, 1988, Xinin, People's Republic China, 1988. Fellow Royal Coll. Surgeons; mem. Royal Photographic Soc. (assoc.), Leisurly Study Art Assn. (founder 1986). Home: 5D Block 6, Beverly Villa, 16A La Salle Rd, Hong Kong Hong Kong

CHAN, SOH HA, microbiology educator, immunologist; b. Batu Pahat, Johor, Malaysia, Apr. 5, 1942; s. Low Cheong and Cheun Moi (Wong) C.; m. Holey Chan; children: Kheong Sann, Yiu Lin. MBBS, Monash U., 1966; PhD, Melbourne U., 1972, FRCPA, 1986. Med. officer Alfred Hosp., Melbourne, Australia, 1967-69; research scientist dept. pathology Nat. U. Singapore, 1972-75, lectr., sr. lectr., assoc. prof. dept. microbiology, 1976-84, prof. microbiology, 1985—; vis. scientist Nat. Cancer Inst., Washington, 1975-76, Internat. Agy. for Research on Cancer, 1972, Lyon, France, 1982-83; bd. dirs. WHO Immunology Ctr., Singapore, 1976—. Research scholar Walter & Elisa Hall Inst., Melbourne, 1969-72. Mem. Singapore Med. Assn. Soc. Immunology and Rheumatology (v.p. 1984-86), Australian Tissue Typing Assn., Asian Pacific Assn. Study of Liver. Office: WHO Immunology Ctr, Faculty Medicine Nat U Singapore, Lower Kent Ridge Rd, 0511 Singapore Singapore

CHAN, W. Y., pharmacologist, educator; b. Shanghai, China, Dec. 1, 1932; came to U.S., 1952, naturalized, 1968; m. Beatrice Ho Chan, June 11, 1961; children—Mina, Jennifer. B.A., U. Wis., 1956; Ph.D. in Pharmacology, Columbia, U., 1961. Research assoc. to asst. prof. biochemistry Cornell U. Med. Coll., N.Y.C., 1960-67, asst. prof. to assoc. prof. pharmacology, 1966-76, prof., 1976—, acting chmn., 1982—; mem. basic pharmacology adv. com. Pharm. Mfrs. Assn. Found., 1973-80; mem. study sect. NIH, 1977, cons., 1981. Contbr. articles to profl. jours. Recipient NIH research career devel. award, 1968-73; Irma T. Hirschl Career Scientist award 1973-77; NIH grantee, 1965—. Mem. Am. Soc. Pharmacology and Exptl. Therapeutics, Soc. for Study of Reprodn., Soc. Exptl. Biology and Medicine, Harvey Soc., N.Y. Acad. Scis., AAAS. Research on pharmacology of neurohypophys hormones and polypeptides, uterine and renal actions of oxytocin and prostaglandins, pathophysiology and pharmacology of dysmenorrhea. Office: Cornell U Med Coll 1300 York Ave New York NY 10021

CHAN, WAI-YEE, molecular geneticist; b. Canton, China, Apr. 28, 1950; came to U.S., 1974; s. Kui and Fung-Hing (Wong) C.; B.Sc. with first class honors, Chinese U. of Hong Kong, 1974; Ph.D., U. Fla., 1977; m. May-Fong Sheung, Sept. 3, 1976; children—Connie Hai-Yee, Joanne Hai-Wei, Victor Hai-Yue. Teaching asst. dept. biochemistry and molecular biology U. Fla., Gainesville, 1974-77; research asso. U. Okla., Oklahoma City, 1978-79, asst. prof. dept. pediatrics, 1979-82, asst. prof. dept. biochemistry and molecular biology, 1979-82, asso. prof., 1982—, asso. prof. dept. pediatrics, 1982—; staff affiliate Pediatric Endocrine Metabolism & Genetic Service, Okla. Children's Meml. Hosp., Oklahoma City, 1979—, dir. Clin. Trace Metal Diagnostic Lab., 1979-85, asst. sci. dir. Biochem. Genetics and Metabolic Screening Lab., 1980-87; cons. VA Med. Center, Oklahoma City, 1981-87; co-sci. dir. State of Okla. Teaching Hosp., 1982-87. Chinese U. Hong Kong scholar, 1972-74, 73-74; NATO fellow, 1979. Mem. Okla. Med. Research Found. (assoc., Merrick award 1988), Am. Inst. Nutrition, Am. Soc. Biol. Chemistry, Nutrition Soc. (U.K.), Am. Soc. Human Genetics, Am. Fedn. Clin. Research, Am. Chem. Soc., Assn. of Clin. Scientists, Biochem. Soc. (U.K.), Internat. Assn. BioInorganic Scientists, N.Y. Acad. Sci., Soc. Exptl. Biology and Medicine Am. Soc. Cell Biology Soc. Pediatric Research, Central Okla. Pediatric Soc., So. Soc. Pediatric Research, Tissue Culture Assn., Am. Genetic Assn., Am. Coll. Nutrition, Sigma Xi. Editor 2 books; editor Jour. of Am. Coll. Nutrition; contbr. articles to profl. jours. Home: 8725 Raven Ave Oklahoma City OK 73132 Office: PO Box 26901 Oklahoma City OK 73190

CHAN, WAN CHOON, mining company executive; b. Batu Gajah, Perak, Malaysia, Aug. 6, 1937; s. Tong Thye and Seow Ying (Ng) C.; m. Nguk Lan Wong, June 5, 1965; children—Mayee, Mayin. A.C.S.M., Camborne Sch. of Mines, 1960. Mining engr. Malayan Tin Dredging Ltd., Batu Gajah, Perak, Malaysia, 1960-64; chief planning dept. Anglo Oriental (M) Ltd., Batu Gajah, 1964-66; asst. supt. Selangor Dredging Bhd., Kuala Lumpur, Malaysia, 1966-67, supt., 1967-79, gen. mgr., 1979—. Chmn. mining Standards and Indsl. Research Inst., Malaysia, 1980—; mem. employers panel Indsl. Ct., 1984—. Recipient Pingat Jasa Kebaktian, His Royal Highness the Sultan of Selangor, 1983. Fellow Instn. Mining and Metallurgy (overseas council mem. 1977—), Inst. Mineral Engring. (council mem. 1973-74); mem. Council Engring. Instns., Malayan Mining Employers Assn. (council 1973—, pres. 1977-78, 80-82), Malaysian Employers Fedn. (council 1986—). Home: 88 Lorong Buluh Perindu 1, Damansara Heights, Kuala Lumpur 59000, Malaysia Office: Selangor Dredging, 142-C Jalan Ampang, Kuala Lumpur 50450, Malaysia

CHAN, WAN HOR, physician; b. Batu Gajah, Malaysia, Dec. 13, 1939; came to U.S., 1971, naturalized, 1979; s. Tong Thye and Seow Ying (Ng) C.; M.B.B.S., U. Singapore, 1964; m. Amy Chan, June 29, 1967; children—Evelyn, Jennifer, Donald. Intern, Loma Linda U., 1971; resident Royal Maternity Hosp., Belfast, No. Ireland, 1967-70; asst. lectr. ob-gyn U. Singapore, 1966; tutor, fellow ob-gyn Queen's U. Belfast, 1967-71; asst. prof. ob-gyn U. So. Calif., 1972-74, Charles Drew Postgrad. Med. Sch., 1972-74; practice medicine specializing in ob-gyn, Los Banos, Calif., 1974—; asst. clin. prof. family practice U. Calif., Davis, 1976-80. William Blair Bell Meml. Research fellow, 1970. Fellow Royal Coll. Surgeons Can., Am. Coll. Obstetricians and Gynecologists, Royal Coll. Obstetricians and Gynecologists (Eng.), Methodist. Club: Rotary. Author: Outline of Obstetrics and Gynecology, 1971. Internat. Coll. Surgeons, Am. Soc. Abdominal Surgeons; mem. Am. Fertility Soc., AMA, N.Y. Acad. Scis. Office: 600 West I St Los Banos CA 93635

CHAN, YUN LAI, medical educator, physiologist; b. Taichung, Taiwan, China, Dec. 3, 1941; came to U.S. 1968, naturalized, 1977; s. Yunn-Perng and Tsai-Mei C.; m. Vicky Chiu, June 18, 1968; children—Jason, Grace. B.S., Kaohsiung Med. Coll., 1965; M.S., Nat. Taiwan U., 1967; Ph.D., U. Louisville, 1971. Instr. U. Louisville, 1971, 73; fellow Max Planck Inst., Frankfurt, Germany, 1972-73; instr. Yale U., New Haven, 1974-76; asst. prof. U. Ill.-Chgo., 1976-81, assoc. prof., 1981-88, prof. 1988—; vis. prof. Nat. Yang Ming Med. Coll., Taipei, Taiwan, 1982, 84; vis. specialist Nat. Sci. Council, Taipei, 1982-84; prin. investigator NIH, Bethesda, Md., 1981—. Contbr. articles to profl. jours. Active Chgo. Heart Assn. Recipient Golden Apple award U. Ill., 1980; grantee Pharm. Mfrs. Assn., 1972, Am. and Chgo. Heart Assn., 1977. Mem. Am. Physiol. Soc., Am. Soc. Nephrology, Internat. Soc. Nephrology, Am. Fedn. Clin. Research, Am. Heart Assn. (mem. council).

CHANCE, LEO ALPHONS IGNATIUS, Netherlands Antilles government official; b. Saba, Netherlands, Nov. 8, 1932; m. Eulalie Mingo; 4 children. Adminstrv. positions Lago Oil & Transport Co., Aruba; capt. Esso San Nicolas, Esso Oranjestad, Arikok; harbour master St. Maarten; co-founder Windward Islands sect. Aruban Patriotic Party; mem. Island Council Aruba, 1959-63, 63-67, 67-69; mem. Netherlands Antilles Parliament Aruba, 1966-69, 73-76, 77; mem. Netherlands Antilles Parliament from Windward Islands, 1979-82; minister communications and transport, 1969-73; minister justice and vice prime minister, 1976-79, minister for devel. cooperation, 1982-84, minister labor and social affairs, 1984-85, minister justice, minister communications and transport, vice prime minister, 1986-88. Decorated Orden Francisco de Miranda, Companionship of Order of Nederlandse Leeuw; named Hon. Citizen of City of Medellin, Colombia, 1972, Hon. Citizen of Louisville, 1979. Roman Catholic. Home: Upper Prince's Quarter z/n, PO Box 478, Saint Maarten Netherlands Antilles Office: Raad van Ministers, Fort Amsterdam 17, Curacao Netherlands Antilles *

CHANCEL, PIERRE JEAN, former paper company executive; b. Calanas, Spain, Nov. 9, 1924; s. Paul P. and Louise C. (Garnaud) C.; m. Nicole J. Sauzède, Aug. 9, 1947; children—Dominique (Mrs. Michel Bourgeois), Karine. C.E., U. Strasbourg (France), 1946, D.-è s-Sci., 1949; postgrad. MIT, 1952-53. Dir. S.Am. chem. div. St. Gobain Corp., Sao Paulo, Brazil, 1958-60, dir. flat glass div., Sao Paulo, 1960-66, gen. mgr. in Brazil, Sao Paulo, 1966-70, gen. mgr. Spain and Portugal, Madrid, 1970-80, chmn. Paper div., chief exec. officer, Paris, 1980-83. Decorated chevalier Legion of Honor (France); 1st comdr. Isabel la Cató lica (Spain); Medalha Cultural Jose Bonifacio de Andrade (Brazil). Mem. Ctr. d'Etudes Iberiques et Latino Americaines, Paris U., Sorbonne. Mem. French C. of C. in Spain (chmn. 1977-79), French-Spanish C. of C. in France (chmn. 1984—). Club: Automobile de France. Home: 31 Cino del Duca, 75017 Paris France Office: 97 Blvd Haussmann, 75008 Paris France

CHANCELLOR, JOHN WILLIAM, news correspondent; b. Chgo., July 14, 1927; s. Estil Marion and Mollie (Barrett) C.; m. Constance Herbert; 1 child, Mary; m. Barbara Upshaw, Jan. 25, 1958; children: Laura, Barnaby. Student, DePaul Acad., Chgo., U. Ill. Reporter Chgo. Sun-Times; staff NBC News, 1950-65, newswriter, gen. assignment reporter U.S., 1953-

58, Vienna corr., 1958, with London bur., 1959-60, Moscow corr., 1960-61, staff N.Y.C. office, 1961-63, Brussels corr., 1963-65; communicator TV program Today, 1961-62, staff corr., 1962-65; dir. Voice of Am., Washington, 1966-67; network nat. affairs corr. NBC, 1967—; anchorman NBC Nightly News, 1970-82; commentator NBC News, 1982—. Address: care NBC 30 Rockefeller Plaza New York NY 10020

CHANDHOKE, SATISH KUMAR, sociologist; b. Sargodha, Punjab, India, Aug. 23, 1936; s. Tara Chand and Sushila Chandhoke; m. Hira Mani, Oct. 12, 1967; children: Gautam, Gayatri. BA, T.N.J. Coll., Bhagalpur, India, 1957; MA in Sociology, Patna U., 1960; MLitt in Sociology, U. Delhi, 1976. Research officer Intensive Agrl. Dist. Programme, Ludhiana, Punjab, India, 1961-63; spl. tech. asst. to group leader Ohio State U. Team U.S. AID, Ludhiana, Punjab, 1963; research asst. Centre for Study of Developing Socs., 1964-65; lectr. in Socio-Econs., extension officer Sch. Planning and Architecture, New Delhi, 1965-82, asst. prof., reader of Sociology, 1983—; lectr. Punjab Engring. Coll., Chandigarn, Haryana Agrl. U., Hissar, Lady Irwin Coll., New Delhi, Cen. Tng. Orgn., Cen. Pub. Works Dept., Govt. of India, Inst. Town Planners of India, New Delhi. Author: Nature and Structure of Rural Habitations, 1988; contbr. articles to profl. jours. Mem. Indian Sociol. Soc. (life), Indian Anthropol. Assn. (life), Delhi Sociol. Assn. (hon. treas. 1976-79), Indian Inst. Pub. Adminstrn. (life), Indian Environ. Congress, World Soc. for Ekistics, Eastern Regional Orgn. Planning and Housing (council mem.), Internat. Tech. Coop. Centre (exec. com. 1977-79), Indian Sci. Congress Assn. Clubs: Bhartiya Navyug Samiti (Bhagalpur) (v.p. 1955-57); Delhi Yog Sabha (Delhi). Home: 145 Saini Enclave, Vikas Marg, Delhi 110 092, India Office: Sch Planning and Architecture, Block 4-B, Indraprastra Estate, New Delhi 110 002, India

CHANDLER, ARTHUR BLEAKLEY, pathologist, educator; b. Augusta, Ga., Sept. 11, 1926; s. Clemmons Quillian and Mary Isabella (Bleakley) C.; m. Jane Stoughton Downing, Sept. 2, 1953; children—Arthur Bleakley, John Downing. Student, U. Ga., 1943-44; M.D., Med. Coll. Ga., Augusta, 1948. Diplomate: Am. Bd. Pathology. Intern Baylor U. Hosp., Dallas, 1948-49; resident in pathology, trainee in cancer, dept. pathology Med. Coll. Ga., 1949-51, asst. in pathology, 1949-50, mem. faculty, 1949—, prof. pathology, 1962—, chmn. dept., 1975—; attending physician Augusta VA Hosp., 1957—; cons. Eisenhower Army Med. Center, Augusta, 1977—; mem. coms. Nat. Heart, Lung and Blood Inst., 1969-85. Author papers in field, chpts. in books; mem. editorial bd.: Haemostasis, 1975-83, Pathology Research and Practice, 1987—. Trustee Young Mens Library Assn. Fund, 1962-72, Historic Augusta, Inc., 1966-69; Trustee Augusta-Richmond County Mus., 1965-87, Dan Printup Meml. Trust, 1985—, trustee Acad. Richmond County, 1984—. Served as officer M.C. AUS, 1951-53. Commonwealth Fund fellow Norway, 1963-64. Mem. Internat. Acad. Pathology, Internat. Soc. Thrombosis and Haemostasis; mem. Am. Assn. History Medicine, Coll. Am. Pathologists, Am. Assn. Pathologists, Am. Soc. Hematology, Am. Heart Assn. (fellow council arteriosclerosis, chmn. council on thrombosis, chmn. 1979-80, chmn. com. on coronary lesions and myocardial infarctions 1980-82), Ga. Assn. Pathologists (pres. 1984-85), AMA, Ga. Heart Assn., Med. Assn. Ga., Richmond County Med. Soc. (trustee 1984—, sec. 1987, v.p. 1988), Alpha Omega Alpha. Episcopalian. Home: 803 Milledge Rd Augusta GA 30904 Office: Dept Pathology Med Coll Ga Augusta GA 30912

CHANDLER, COLBY H., photographic equipment and materials manufacturing executive. married. B.S., U. Maine, 1950; postgrad., MIT. With Eastman Kodak Co., Rochester, N.Y., 1950—, mem. sales estimating council, then corp. asst. v.p., until 1972, exec. v.p., 1972-77, pres., 1977-83, chmn. chief exec. officer, 1983—, also dir.; exec. dir. Lincoln 1st Bank, Rochester.; dir. Continental Group, Inc., Ford Motor Co., J.C. Penney Co. Bd. dirs. Indsl. Mgmt. Council Rochester; bd. dirs. Congl. Award Com.; Bd. dirs. United Way of Greater Rochester; bd. dirs. Rochester-Monroe County Conv. and Visitors Bur., Nat. Orgn. on Disability; exec. dir. Rochester Civic Music Assn.; trustee Rochester Inst. Tech., Colgate Rochester Div. Sch., U. Rochester, Nat. 4-H Council, Internat. Mus. Photography at George Eastman House; mem. MIT Corp. Mem. Soc. Sloan Fellows (bd. govs. 1964, pres. 1966-68), Tau Beta Pi, Sigma Pi Sigma, Phi Kappa Phi, Beta Gama Sigma. Office: Eastman Kodak Co 343 State St Rochester NY 14650 *

CHANDLER, JOHN BRANDON, JR., lawyer; b. Boston, Sept. 25, 1939; s. John Brandon and Juliette (Blackburn) C.; m. Helen Elizabeth Demski, Mar. 22, 1986; 1 son, John Brandon III. B.A., Vanderbilt U., 1961, J.D., 1964. Bar: Tenn. 1964, Fla. 1967, U.S. Supreme Ct. 1971. Assoc. Rogers Towers Bailey Jones & Gay, Jacksonville, Fla., 1967-72, ptnr., 1973—. Served to capt. U.S. Army, 1964-66. Mem. ABA (regional chmn. discovery com., litigation sect.), Fla. Bar, Am. Arbitration Assn. (mem. panel), Jacksonville Bar Assn. (bd. govs. 1975-80), Phi Delta Phi. Clubs: Fla. Yacht, Ponte Vedra, Ye Mystic Revellers, Friars, Sawgrass, University, Jacksonville Vanderbilt (pres. 1973-84). Contbr. articles to legal jours. Home: 2025 Oceanfront Atlantic Beach FL 32233 Office: 1300 Gulf Life Dr Jacksonville FL 32207

CHANDLER, LAWRENCE BRADFORD, JR., lawyer; b. New Bedford, Mass., June 20, 1942; s. Lawrence Bradford and Anne (Crane) C.; m. Madeleine Bibeau, Sept. 7, 1963 (div. June 1984); children: Dawn, Colleen, Brad; m. Cynthia Korn Howe, May 11, 1985. BS in Bus. Adminstrn., Boston Coll., 1963; LLB, U. Va., 1966, JD, 1970. Bar: Mass. 1966, U.S. Supreme Ct. 1967, Va. 1970. Ptnr. Chandler, Franklin & O'Bryan, Charlottesville, Va., 1971—. Served to cpt. U.S. Army, 1967-71. Mem. ABA, Charlottesville Bar Assn., Assn. Trial Lawyers Am., Va. Trial Lawyers Assn. (pres. 1985-86), Assn. U.S. Army. Roman Catholic. Lodges: Elks, K.C. Home: 1445 Old Ballard Rd Charlottesville VA 22901 Office: Chandler Franklin & O'Bryan PO Box 6747 Charlottesville VA 22906

CHANDLER, MARGUERITE NELLA, real estate corporation executive; b. New Brunswick, N.J., May 16, 1943; d. Edward A. and Marguerite (Moore) C.; m. Ronald Wilson, May 30, 1964 (div. Nov. 1973); children: Mark, Adam; m. Richmond Shreve, Nov. 22, 1979; 1 child, Laura. BS in Acctg., Syracuse U., 1964; postgrad., Grad. Sch. Polit. Mgmt., 1987-88. Tax acct. Peat Marwick Mitchell, Providence, 1964; grant adminstr., psychology dept. Brown U., Providence, 1965; intern in devel. cons., Washington, 1973-75; prin., tng. cons. M. Chandler Assocs., 1975-76; mgmt. cons. Edmar Corp., Bound Brook, N.J., 1976-78, pres., chief exec. officer, 1978—. Peace Corps vol., 1966-68; established Food Bank Network of Somerset County, 1982-85, Worldworks, 1983; founder PeopleCare Ctr., 1984, pres., 1984-86; bd. dirs. N.J. Council for Arts, 1986-87; treas. Somerset Community Devel. Group, 1986-87; pres. bd. trustees N.J. Council of Chs., 1985—; v.p. mktg. United Way Somerset Valley, 1985-88; recorder Blue Ribbon Com. on Ending Hunger in N.J., 1984-86; vol. Somerset Community Action Program, 1969-71, Missionaries of Charity, Calcutta, India, 1981; treas. Somerset County Day Care Assn., 1969-71; mem. adv. bd. US-USSR Youth Exchange, Ptnrs. in Peacemaking, The Giraffe Project; chairperson numerous fund-raising events to combat world hunger. Named Woman of Yr., Women's Resource Ctr. Somerset County, 1983, Citizen of Yr., Somerset County C. of C., 1985, N.J. Chpt. Nat. Assn. Soc. Workers, 1986, Bus. and Profl. Women's Club, 1987; recipient People's Champion award Somerset Family Planning Service, 1985, Disting. Service award N.J. Speech-Language-Hearing Assn., 1986, N.J. Women of Achievement award Douglass Coll. and N.J. Fedn. Women's Clubs, 1986, Brotherhood award Central Jersey chpt. Nat. Conf. Christians and Jews, 1986, Presdl. End Hunger award, 1987. Mem. Somerset C. of C. (housing com. 1985—, transp. com. 1985-86), N.J. Gov.'s Task Force on Pub./Pvt. Sector Initiatives. Mem. Soc. of Friends. Home: 6 Lisa Terr Somerville NJ 08876 Office: Edmar Corp 9 Easy St PO Box 149 Bound Brook NJ 08805-0149

CHANDLER, MURIEL JANE, artist; b. Caney, Kans., June 21, 1927; d. Jesse James and Rose Esther (Vincent) Barger; m. Keith Arthur Chandler, Sept. 26, 1955. BFA, Sch. of Art Inst. of Chgo., 1968. Exec. asst. Charles James, Designer, Chgo., 1957-58; mgr., wire chief B&O RR Communications, Chgo., 1958-68; chmn. bd. dirs. Caribatik, Ltd., Falmouth, Jamaica, 1970—. Represented in permanent collections; prin. works include Batik paintings. Mem. Artists Equity, Alumni Assn. of Sch. of Art Inst. of Chgo., Western Jamaica Soc. Fine Artists. Home and Office: Rock Wharf PO Box 2, Falmouth Jamaica

CHANDLER, REUBEN CARL, packaging company executive; b. Lawrenceville, Ga., Oct. 25, 1917; s. Reuben C. and Florine (Doster) C.; m. Sarah Megee, Oct. 27, 1940; children: Carla Evalynee, Robert Megee, David Pratt, Craig D. Grad., Marist Coll., Atlanta, 1935; student, Ga. Inst. Tech., 1935-37; A.B., Emory U., 1941; student, Atlanta Law Sch., 1946-48; D.Sc. in Bus. Adminstrn. (hon.), Detroit Inst. Tech., 1960. Sales rep. Gen. Motors Acceptance Corp., Atlanta, 1941-42; asst. dir. tng. Southeastern Shipbldg. Corp., Savannah, Ga., 1942-43; prodn. mgr. Mead-Atlanta Paper Co., 1946-49; salesman Union Camp Corp. (formerly Union Bag & Paper Corp.), 1949-50; dist. sales mgr. Union Camp Corp. (formerly Union Bag & Camp Paper Corp.), Trenton, N.J., 1950-51; Eastern div. sales mgr. Union Camp Corp. (formerly Union Bag & Camp Paper Corp.), 1951-52; dir. corrugated container and bd. sales Union Camp Corp. (formerly Union Bag & Camp Paper Corp.), N.Y.C., 1952; v.p. sales Union Camp Corp. (formerly Union Bag & Camp Paper Corp.), 1952-55; chmn., chief exec. officer, chmn. exec., finance coms. Standard Packaging Co., N.Y.C., 1955-66; chmn. bd. Crowell-Collier Pub. Co., N.Y.C., 1957; ltd. partner Elliott & Co. (investment bankers), N.Y.C., 1960-62; chmn bd. J.D. Jewell, Inc., Gainesville, Ga., 1962-72; pres. J.D. Jewell, Inc., 1969—; also chmn. exec. com., dir.; pres. Identiseal Systems, Atlanta, 1972—, Perkins-Goodwin Mgmt. Services Co., N.Y.C., 1973—, Am. Resources Corp., 1973-75; chmn. bd. Lanier Mortgage Corp., Gainesville, Ga., 1973-75; pres., chief exec. officer Duncan & Copeland, Inc., 1976-79, Va. Packaging Supply Co., McLean, 1979-84; dir. Am. Agy. Life Ins. Co., Atlanta, Berry Steel Corp., Edison, N.J., Jones & Presnell, Charlotte, N.C. Trustee Detroit Inst. Tech., 1960—, Christ Ch. Sch., Short Hills, N.J., 1963—, Brenau Coll., 1968—, Emory U., Atlanta, 1972—, Ga. Found. for Ind. Colls., 1969—; bd. dirs. Am. Soc. Indsl. Security Found. Served as lt. (s.g.) USNR, 1943-46; Lt. col. aide de camp Gov.'s staff Ga. 1951-52, 70-72. Recipient Man of Year award Am. Jewish Com., 1964; Horatio Alger award, 1965; Achievement award Delta Tau Delta, 1966; Disting. Alumni award Marist Coll., 1985. Mem. Savannah Jr. C. of C. (v.p. 1942-43), Gainesville C. of C., Navy League (life), Def. Orientation Conf. Assn., Am. Pulp and Paper Mill Supts. Assn. (life), Emory U. Alumni Assn. (pres. 1965, Honor award 1968), Ga. Tech. Nat. Alumni Assn. (nat. adv. bd. 1964 —), Ga. Poultry Fedn. (mem. round table 1970—), Tenn. Wesleyan Coll. Parents Assn., U.S. Navy Supply Corps Assn. (trustee 1972—), Delta Tau Delta (life), Alpha Delta Sigma, Omicron Delta Kappa. Episcopalian. Clubs: Atlanta, Athletic (Atlanta); N.Y. Area Emory (pres. 1964), University, Economic (N.Y.C.). Home: 4101 Dunwoody Club Dr Apt 25 Dunwoody GA 30338

CHANDLER, ROBERT FLINT, JR., consultant international agriculture; b. Columbus, Ohio, June 22, 1907; s. Robert F. and Harriet Clark (Loring) C.; m. Eunice Copeland, May 22, 1931 (div. 1955); children: David, Ralph Hewitt, Sara Eunice; m. Muriel Boyd, Oct. 4, 1957. BS, U. Maine, 1929, LLD, 1951; PhD, U. Md., 1934; postgrad (NRC fellow), U. Calif., 1935; LLD, Notre Dame U., 1971; LittD, U. Singapore, 1971; LHD, Cen. Luzon (Philippines) State U., 1971; ScD, Punjab (India) Agrl. U., 1971, U. Philippines, 1972, U. N.H., 1972, U. Md., 1975. State horticulturist Maine Dept. Agr., 1929-31; grad. asst. U. Md., 1931-34; asst. prof. forest soils Cornell U., 1935-41, asso. prof., 1941-46, prof., 1946-47; dean coll. agr. U. N.H., 1947-50, pres., 1950-54; asst. dir. div. natural scis. and agr. Rockefeller Found., N.Y.C., 1954-57; assoc. dir. agrl. scis. Rockefeller Found., 1957; dir. Internat. Rice Research Inst., Manila, Philippines, 1959-72, Asian Vegetable Research and Devel. Center, Taiwan, 1972-75; cons. internat. agr. 1972—; Vis. prof. agronomy Tex. A&M Coll., summer 1940; soil sci. Rockefeller Found., Mexico, 1946-47. Author: Rice in the Tropics, 1979, An Adventure in Applied Science—The Early History of the International Rice Research Institute, 1982. Trustee Internat. Council for Research in Agroforestry, Kenya, 1976-79; bd. dirs. Near East Found., N.Y.C. Decorated Star of Merit Indonesia; recipient Gold medal award Govt. India, 1966, Sitara-I-Imtiaz award Govt. Pakistan, 1968, Golden Heart award Govt. Philippines, 1972, Internat. Agronomy award, 1972, Presdl. End Hunger award US Agy. for Internatl Devel., 1986, World Food prize Gen. Foods Corp., 1988. Fellow Am. Acad. Arts and Scis.; mem. Crop Sci. Soc. Am., Soc. for Internat. Devel., Royal Agrl. Soc. (hon.). Home: 421 E Minnehaha Ave Clermont FL 32711

CHANDLER, STEPHEN L., insurance company executive; b. Milw., Dec. 14, 1926; s. Harold George and Sarah (Goodsen) K.; m. Dorothy S. Collins, Jan. 10, 1948; 1 child, Carolyn. BA, Drake U., 1947. With Prudential Insurance Co. Am., Chgo., 1948—, v.p., 1949-58, sr. v.p., 1958-78, exec. v.p. Mid-Am. ops., 1978—; dir. Am. Cyanamid Corp., Eagle Picher Industries, Inc., Central Bancorp., Ohio Nat. Life Ins. Co. Bd. dirs. Chgo. area chpt. ARC; trustee U. Ill.; commr. Kane County Park Dist. Mem. Am. Insurance Assn., Life Office Mgmt. Assn. (past pres.). Clubs: Glenview Country; Cliff dwellers (Chgo.), Tavern (Chgo.). Office: Werik Bldg 24 N Wabash Ave Suite 823 Chicago IL 60602

CHANDRA, HERMANTO, manufacturing company executive; b. Medan, Sumut, Indonesia, Nov. 21, 1959; s. Husin Tjandra and Ailannie C. BA in Engring., McGill U., Montreal, Can., 1982; M. in Engring. and Mgmt., McGill U., 1984, MBA, 1985. Registered profl. engr. Gen. mgr. P.T. Gunung Harapan Sentana, Medan, Indonesia, 1982-83; chief exec. officer P.T. Gunung Harapan Sentana, Medan, 1985—; teaching asst. McGill U., Montreal, 1983-84; mng. dir P.T. Daya Guhara Perkasa, Medan, 1986—; chmn. P.T. First Mujur Plantation, Medan, 1986—; dir. P.T. Cahaya Pelita Andhika, Medan, 1986—, P.T. Gunung Bangau, Medan, 1986—, P.T. Inti Mina Utama, Medan, 1986—. Patentee in field. Mem. Assn. Indonesian Engrs. Club: Medan.

CHANDRASEKARA, MAGUNDI PUTTAPPA, civil engineer; b. Bangarapet, Karnataka, India, Mar. 2, 1943; s. Puttappa and Nagamma C.; m. Vimalamma Sekara, June 9, 1972; children—M. C. Girish, M.C. Nandeesh. Diploma in C.E., Govt. Poly. Chinthamani, Karnataka, 1967; Diploma in Personnel Mgmt., French Acad., New Delhi, 1978; MA in Polit. Sci., U. Mysore, 1987. Engring. supr. Karnataka Power Corp. Ltd., Ganeshgudi, Karnataka, 1973—. Contbr. articles on constrn. industry and forestry to profl. jours. Mem. Karnataka Power Corp. Recreation Assn. Lodge: Jaycees. Avocations: table tennis; swimming; reading and writing; collecting classic books and articles. Home: Type VI-24/1 2nd Cross Rd, Ganeshgudi Karnataka 581 365 India Office: Chief Engr's Office, Karnataka Power Corp Ltd, Ganeshgudi Karnataka 581 365 India

CHANDRASEKHAR, SUBRAHMANYAN, theoretical astrophysicist, educator; b. Lahore, India, Oct. 19, 1910; came to U.S., 1936, naturalized, 1953; m. Lalitha Doraiswamy, Sept. 1936. M.A., Presidency Coll., Madras, 1930; Ph.D., Trinity Coll., Cambridge, 1933, Sc.D., 1942; Sc.D., U. Mysore, India, 1961, Northwestern U., 1962, U. Newcastle Upon Tyne, Eng., 1965, Ind. Inst. Tech., 1966, U. Mich., 1967, U. Liege, Belgium, 1967, Oxford (Eng.) U., 1972, U. Delhi, 1973, Carleton U., Can., 1978, Harvard U., 1979. Govt. India scholar in theoretical physics Cambridge, 1930-34; fellow Trinity Coll., Cambridge, 1933-37; research asso. Yerkes Obs., Williams Bay and U. Chgo., 1937, asst. prof., 1938-41, assoc. prof., 1942-43, prof., 1944-47, Disting. Service prof., 1947-52, Morton D. Hull Disting. Service prof., 1952-86, prof. emeritus, 1986—; Nehru Meml. lectr., Padma Vibhushan, India, 1968. Author: An Introduction to the Study of Stellar Structure, 1939, Principles of Stellar Dynamics, 1942, Radiative Transfer, 1950, Hydrodynamic and Hydromagnetic Stability, 1961, Ellipsoidal Figures of Equilibrium, 1969, The Mathematical Theory of Black Holes, 1983, Eddington: The Most Distinguished Astrophysicist of His Time, 1983, Truth and Beauty: Aesthetics and Motivations in Science, 1987; mng. editor: The Astrophysical Jour., 1952-71; contbr. various sci. periodicals. Recipient Bruce medal Astron. Soc. Pacific, 1952, gold medal Royal Astron. Soc., London, 1953; Rumford medal Am. Acad. Arts and Scis., 1957; Nat. Medal of Sci., 1966; Nobel prize in physics, 1983; Dr. Tomalla prize Eidgenössiches Technische Hochschule, Zurich, 1984. Fellow Royal Soc. (London) (Royal medal 1962, Copley medal 1984); mem. Nat. Acad. Scis. (Henry Draper medal 1971), Am. Phys. Soc. (Dannie Heineman prize 1974), Am. Philos. Soc., Cambridge Philos. Soc., Am. Astron. Soc., Royal Astron. Soc. Club: Quadrangle (U. Chgo.). Office: Lab for Astrophys & Space Research 933 E 56th St Chicago IL 60637

CHANDRU, G. A. See ADVANI, CHANDERBAN GHANSHAMDAS

CHANG, B(YUNG) JIN, electrical engineer, optical systems executive; b. Danyang, Korea, Sept. 26, 1941; came to U.S., 1968, naturalized, 1974; s. Yung S. and Ahzie (Chon) C.; m. Sharon O. Hong, Dec. 27, 1969; children—Jane Y., Michael. Ph.D. in Elec. Engring., U. Mich., 1974. Research engr. ERIM, Ann Arbor, Mich., 1971-79; v.p., chief scientist Kaiser Optical Systems, Inc. subs. Kaiser Aerospace & Electronics Corp., Ann Arbor, 1979—. Contbr. articles to profl. jours. Mem. IEEE, Optical Soc. Am., Soc. Info. Display, Soc. Photo-optical Instrumentation Engrs. Methodist. Lodge: Ann Arbor Rotary. Patentee in field. Home: 1495 Folkstone Ann Arbor MI 48105 Office: 371 Parkland Plaza PO Box 983 Ann Arbor MI 48106

CHANG, C. YUL, bank executive; b. Seoul, Korea, Feb. 21, 1934; came to U.S., 1958, naturalized, 1972; s. Insuk and Insook Chang; children: Edward W., Leonard W., Mira W. BS, Naval Acad., Korea, 1953; MA in Fin., U. Miami, 1961; postgrad., Columbia U., 1962; DD (hon.), Calif. Missionary Coll., 1984. Sr. fin. cons. Mobil Oil Corp., N.Y.C., 1963-74; gen. mgr. Chem. Bank, N.Y.C., 1974-86; chmn., chief exec. officer Hanam Capital Corp./SBIC, N.Y.C., 1986—; chmn. adv. bd. Capital Nat. Bank, N.Y.C., 1986-87; advisor Korean Businessmen's Assn., N.Y.C., 1982, Korean-Am. Credit Union, N.Y.C., 1985. Author: Automated Banking, 1968; also articles. Recipient cert. of Commendation Korean Consulate Gen., 1982, Korean Assn. of N.Y., 1982, Korean Ch.'s Fedn., 1985. Mem. Nat. Assn. Investment Cos. Republican. Methodist. Lodge: Rotary (pres. Riverdale, N.Y. club 1987—). Home: 5900 Arling Ave #20 K Riverdale NY 10471 Office: Hanam Capital Corp One Penn Plaza Suite 3330 New York NY 10119

CHANG, CHI-CHENG, central bank governor; b. Hwayang, Szechwan, Republic of China, Dec. 7, 1918; married; 2 children:. BA, Nat. Tung-Chi U.; MA, Cornell U., 1942, PhD, 1944. Chief gen. div. Council U.S. Aid, 1958-60, chief 2d div., 1960-63; sec.-gen. Council Internat. Econ. and Devel., 1963-65, 69; vice minister Ministry Econ. Affairs, 1965-69; minister Ministry of Communications, 1969-72; vice chmn., sec.-gen. Council Internat. Econ. Cooperation & Devel., 1972-73; chmn. Econ. Planning Council Exec. Yuan, 1973-76; sec.-gen. Exec. Yuan, 1976-78; minister Ministry of Fin., 1978-81; nat. policy advisor to pres., chmn. bd. govs. Cen Bank of China, 1984—. Office: Cen Bank of China, 2 Roosevelt Rd, Section 1, Taipei Republic of China

CHANG, DARWIN RAY, civil engineer; b. Jukao, Kiangsu, China, Aug. 1, 1917; s. Wey and Susan (Hsiong) C.; came to U.S., 1945, naturalized, 1962; B.S., Chiao Tung U., Shanghai, China, 1940; M.C.E., Cornell U., 1946;; m. Yen Ma, Dec. 23, 1961; children—Gordon, Susan, Martha, Leslie. Structural engr. Borsari Tank Corp., N.Y.C., 1951; project engr. Ebasco Internat. Corp., N.Y.C. 1956-60; prin. engr. Public Service Electric and Gas Co., Newark, 1960-81; mktg. mgr. Lehigh Utility Assos., Inc., South Plainfield, N.J., 1981—; pres. D and Y Chang Enterprises Inc.; 1980—. Mem. utilities adv. com. Downtown Devel. Commn. Madison, N.J. Mem. N.J. Soc. Profl. Engrs., IEEE, Chinese Inst. Engrs. Presbyterian. Club: Masons. Contbr. articles on esthetic transmission structures to trade mags. Club: Rotary. Home: 108 Green Ave Madison NJ 07940 Office: 1 Central Ave Madison NJ 07940

CHANG, GENGZHE, mathematics educator, researcher; b. Changsha, Hunan, Peoples Republic of China, Aug. 17, 1936; s. Chengren and Tangshi Chang; m. Huidi Wang, Aug. 1, 1965; children: Yiqun, Qing. Grad., Nankai U., Tianjin, 1958. Mathematical diplomate. Teaching asst. U. Sci. and Tech. of China, Beijing, 1958-60; instr. Beijing, Hefei, 1960-78; assoc. prof. Hefei, 1978-85, prof., 1985—, vice dir. Math. Research Inst., 1985—; vis. scholar U. Utah, Salt Lake City, 1980-81, Wilfrid Laurier U., Waterloo, Ont., Can., 1982; research assoc. Brown U., Providence, 1982; vis. prof. Technische Hochschule, Darmstadt, Fed. Republic Germany, 1984, 87, Tech. U., Berlin, 1985, 87, Internat. Ctr. for Theoretical Physics, Trieste, Italy, 1985, U. Duisburg, Fed. Republic Germany, 1987, U. Linköping, Sweden, 1988; participant and speaker several internat. confs. on computer aided geometric design and multivariate approximation theory, U.S., Fed. Republic Germany, Peoples Republic of China; invited speaker numerous univs. and instns. in China and other countries; leader Chinese team 29th Internat. Math. Olympiad, Canberra, Australia. Author: Pigeonhole Principles and Others, 1978, Complex Number Computations and Proving Geometric Problems, 1980, Nice Problems from Mathematical Olympiads and Their Solutions, 1987; (with Wu) Complex Numbers and Geometry, 1964, (with Xu) Mathematical Basis for Computing Airplane Shape, 1977, (with Su) Odd and Even Integers, 1986; translator Chinese monograph: Computational Geometry; contbr. articles to profl. jours.; assoc. editor numerous Chinese and foreign jours. ; editor-in-chief Chinese jour. The Math. Olympiads; co-editor: Lectures for Math. Olympiads, 1987, Lectures on Math. Olympiads for Senior High School Students, 1987. Grantee, Academica Sinica, Beijing, 1983-85, Nat. Edn. Com., Beijing, 1985-88. Mem. Chinese Math. Soc. (edn. com., popularity com.), Am. Math. Soc., Internat. Ctr. Theoretical Physics (assoc.). Office: Univ Sci and Tech of China, Math Dept, Hefei Peoples Republic of China

CHANG, HENRY CHUNG-LIEN, library administrator; b. Canton, China, Sept. 15, 1941; came to U.S., 1964, naturalized, 1973; s. Ih-ming and Lily (Lin) C.; m. Marjorie Li, Oct. 29, 1966; 1 dau., Michelle. LL.B., Nat. Chengchi U., 1962; M.A., U. Mo., 1966; M.A. in L.S, U. Minn., 1968; Ph.D., 1974. Book selector Braille Inst. Am., Los Angeles, 1965-67; reference librarian U. Minn., Mpls., 1968-70; instr., librarian U. Minn., 1970-72, asst. head govt. document div., 1972-74; asst. head library div., lectr. social scis. Coll. of the V.I., St. Croix, 1974-75; dir. div. libraries, museums and archeol. services V.I. Dept. Conservation and Cultural Affairs, 1975—; dir. V.I. Library Tng. Inst., 1975-76; coordinator, chmn. V.I. State Hist. Records Adv. Bd., 1976—; chmn. microfilm com. ACURIL, 1977—; coordinator V.I. Gov.'s Library Adv. Council, 1975—; mem. V.I. Bicentennial Commn., 1975-77, Ft. Frederik Commn., 1975-76; mem. adv. com. on research tng. Caribbean Research Inst., 1974-75; coordinator Library Conf., 1977—; project dir. cultural heritage project Nat. Endowment for Humanities, 1979-83. Author: A Bibliography of Presidential Commissions, Committees, Councils, Panels and Task Forces, 1961-72, 1973, Taiwan Democraphy, 1964-71: A Selected Annotated Bibliography of Government Documents, 1973, A Selected Annotated Bibliography of Caribbean Bibliographies in English, 1975, A Survey of the Use of Microfilms in the Caribbean, 1978, Long-Range Program for Library Development, 1978, Institute for Training in Library Management and Communications Skill, 1979; also needs assessments and reports; contbr. numerous articles and book revs. on library sci. to profl. jours. Served to 2d lt. Taiwan Army, 1962-63. Recipient Library Adminstrs. Devel. Program fellowship award, 1972, cert. of appreciation Govt. V.I., 1985; named Mem. Staff of Year Coll. V.I., 1974-75; Nat. Commn. on Libraries and Info. Sci. grantee. Mem. ALA (counselor 1980-84), AAUP, Population Assn. Am., Am. Sociol. Assn., Assn. Carribean Univ. and Research Libraries, V.I. Library Assn. Club: Rotary. Home: PO Box 818 Kingshill Saint Croix VI 00850 Office: PO Box 390 Saint Thomas VI 00801

CHANG, JAE CHAN, physician, educator; b. Chong An, Korea, Aug. 29, 1941; s. Tae Whan and Kap Hee (Lee) C.; came to U.S., 1965, naturalized, 1976; M.D., Seoul (Korea) Nat. U., 1965; m. Sue Young Chung, Dec. 4, 1965; children—Sung-Jin, Sung-Ju, Sung-Hoon. Intern, Ellis Hosp., Schenectady, 1965-66; resident in medicine Harrisburg (Pa.) Hosp., 1966-69, fellow in nuclear medicine, 1969-70; instr. in medicine U. Rochester, N.Y., 1970-72; chief hematology sect. VA Hosp., Dayton, Ohio, 1972-75; hematopathologist Good Samaritan Hosp., Dayton, 1975—, dir. oncology unit, 1976—, coordinator of med. edn., 1976-77, chief oncology-hematology sect., 1976—; asst. clin. prof. medicine Ohio State U., Columbus, 1972-75; assoc. clin. prof. medicine Wright State U., Dayton, 1975-80, clin. prof., 1980—; staff St. Elizabeth Med. Center, Dayton, Miami Valley Hosp., Dayton; cons. in hematology VA Hosp. Mem. med. adv. com. Greater Dayton Area chpt. Leukemia Soc. Am., 1977; trustee Montgomery County Soc. for Cancer Control, Dayton, 1976-85, Dayton Area Cancer Assn., 1985—, Community Blood Ctr., 1982-86. Nat. Cancer Inst. fellow in hematology and oncology, 1970-72; diplomate Am. Bd. Internal Medicine, Am. Bd. Pathology. Fellow A.C.P.; mem. Am. Soc. Hematology, Am. Fedn. Clin. Research, Am. Soc. Clin. Oncologists, Am. Assn. Cancer Research, AAAS, Dayton Oncology Club, Dayton Soc. Internal Medicine. Contbr. articles to profl. med. jours., essays to newspaper columns. Home: 1122

Wycliffe Pl Dayton OH 45459 Office: Good Samaritan Hosp and Health Center 2222 Philadelphia Dr Dayton OH 45406 also: 2200 Philadelphia Dr Dayton OH 45406

CHANG, JOHN C. H., chemist; b. Taiwan, China, Sept. 29, 1936; came to U.S., 1964, naturalized, 1976; s. Chin Fu and Lien Kwei (Chen) C.; Ph.D., Ill. Inst. Tech., 1969; m. Shirley H. L. Chen, Dec. 17, 1966; children—Patricia, Julita. Group leader Champion Internat. Corp., Chgo., 1971-77, sect. leader, Hamilton, Ohio, 1977; corp. dir. research Wallace Computer Services, Inc., Hillside, Ill., 1977—. Prin. Coop. Chinese Lang. Sch., 1982-84. Mem. Am. Chem. Soc. Patentee in microencapsulation, coating, dyes, ink. Home: 636 Edward Rd Naperville IL 60540 Office: Wallace Computer Services Inc 4600 W Roosevelt Rd Hillside IL 60162

CHANG, SHIRLEY (HSIU-CHU) LIN, librarian; b. Chia-yi, Taiwan, June 22, 1937; came to U.S., 1962, naturalized, 1977; d. Tzu-kun and Ying (Chang) Lin; m. Parris H. Chang, Aug. 3, 1963; children: Yvette Y., Elaine Y., Bohdan P. BA, Nat. Taiwan U., Taipei, 1960; postgrad. U. Wash., 1962-63, 1982—, Pa. State U., 1976-77 MLS, MA in EDTHP, 1985-88, Columbia U., 1967. Library asst. Yale U., New Haven, 1964, Columbia U., N.Y.C., 1964-67; asst. reference librarian Pa. State U., University Park, 1971-75; cataloguer Australian Nat. U., Canberra, 1978; catalog and reference librarian Lock Haven U. Pa., 1979—, asst. prof., 1982-88, assoc. prof., 1988—. Mem. ALA, Chinese-Am. Librarians Assn. (chmn. awards com. 1982-83), Asian/Pacific Am. Librarians Assn. Home: 1221 Edward St State College PA 16801 Office: Lock Haven U Pa Stevenson Library Lock Haven PA 17745

CHANG, SHOU-SHIAN, diversified companies executive; b. Tsing Tao, China, Sept. 18, 1929; arrived Hong Kong, 1949; s. Mong-Kiu and Ying Ying (Tsui) C.; m. Pak-Joen Yang, June 5, 1938; children: Hsian-Shing (Caroline), Hsian-Sang (Cecil). BME, Nat. Taiwan U., 1960. Mgr. engring. Aero Tech. Corp., Hong Kong, 1963-65; project engr. Standard Oil Co. (N.J.), Singapore, Hong Kong, 1965-68; mgr. Indsl. Engrs. Ltd., Hong Kong, 1968-74, mng. dir., 1974—; mng. dir. Asia Petroleum Co. Ltd, Hong Kong, 1975—, Yang's Taxi Co. Ltd., Hong Kong, 1972—. Home: 6A Cumberland Rd, Kowloon Hong Kong Office: Indsl Engrs Ltd, 6 Tung Fong St, Kowloon Hong Kong

CHANG, STEPHEN S., food scientist, educator; b. Beijing, China, Aug. 15, 1918; came to U.S., 1957, naturalized, 1962; s. Zie K. and Hui F. (Yuang) C.; m. Luch Ding, June 2, 1952. B.S., Nat. Chi-nan U., 1941; M.S., Kans. State U., 1949; Ph.D., U. Ill., 1952. Research chemist Swift & Co., Chgo., 1955-57; sr. research chemist A.E. Staley Co., Decatur, Ill., 1957-60; assoc. prof. Rutgers U., New Brunswick, N.J., 1960—, prof. food chemistry, 1977-86, chmn. food sci. dept., 1987—; cons. to industry; convenor adv. com. to Taiwan Food Industry; chmn. bd. dirs. Cathay Food Cons. Co., Inc. Contbr. articles to profl. jours. Patentee in field. Named hon. prof. Wuxi Inst. Light Industry, Peoples Republic China, 1984, spl. invited prof. Jinan U., Peoples Republic China, 1987; recipient award for excellence in research, bd. trustees Rutgers U. Mem. Am. Oil Chemists Soc. (pres. 1970-71; lipid chemistry award 1979, A.E. Bailey award 1974), Inst. Food Technologists (Disting. Food Scientist award 1970, Nicholas Appert award 1983). Methodist. Office: Rutgers U Dept Food Sci New Brunswick NJ 08903

CHANG, TONG-YING (KATHY), academic administrator, translator, journalist; b. Hsin-chu, Republic of China, Apr. 9, 1958; d. Ching-ting and Hsiu-yen (Yao) C. BA, Nat. Taiwan U., Taipei, 1980; MA in Journalism, U. Mo., 1982. Writer Govt. Info. Office, Taipei, Republic of China, 1983-84; reporter AP, Taipei, Republic of China, 1984-87; spokesman asst. Am. Inst. in Taiwan, Taipei, Republic of China, 1987—; lectr. Chinese Culture U., 1984—, Nat. Chengchi U., Taipei, 1986—. Grantee U. Mo., 1982. Home: #21 Floor 3 Ln 256 Ray-An St, Taipei Republic of China

CHANG, Y. C., transportation company executive; b. China, Aug. 27, 1918. Chmn., mng. dir. Pacific Internat. Lines Pte. Ltd., Singapore, 1967—; chmn. bd. Maya Group of Cos., Singapore and Malaysia, bd. dirs. Far East Levingston Shipbuilding Ltd., Singapore, Smit Tak Towage and Salvage (S) Pte. Ltd., Singapore. Mem. Singapore Chinese C. of C. and Industries. Club: Singapore Island Country. Office: Pacific Internat Lines Pte Ltd, 140 Cecil St, 03-00 PIL Bldg, Singapore 0106 Singapore

CHANG-MOTA, ROBERTO, electrical engineer; b. Caracas, Venezuela, Dec. 28, 1935; s. Roberto W. and Mary C. (Mota) Chang; D.E.E., U. Central Venezuela, 1960; M.S., U. Ill., 1962; A.R., Harvard U., 1970; m. Alicia Santamaria-Gonzales, May 4, 1968; children—Roberto Ignacio, Roxana Ivette, Ricardo Ignacio. Dir. Sch. Elec. Engring., also prof. Central U., 1964-69; prof., dean Schs. Engring., Architecture and Sci., Simon Bolivar U., 1971-77; pres. Colegio de Ingenieros de Venezuela, 1974-79; dir. Venezuelan Power Co., 1974-79; pres. Latin Am. Orgn. Engring., 1977-79, Corporoil, 1981—, Audio Interface Corp., 1983—; cons. in field. Spl. cons. Venezuelan Navy and Army, 1971-75; mem. tech. com. Venezuelan Supreme Election Council, 1971-81, exec. dir., 1981-82, gen. dir., 1982-88; trustee Simon Bolivar U., 1985-88. Mem. Venezuelan Soc. Elec. and Mech. Engring. (pres. 1972-73), IEEE, Am. Soc. Engring. Edn., Instn. Elec. Engrs. Roman Catholic. Clubs: Puerto Azul, Playa Pintada, Caracas Racquet. Home: Quinta Cumana Calle Colon, Prados de Este Estado, Miranda Venezuela Office: Torres Centro Simon Bolivar, Consejo Supremo Electoral, Esq Pajarito, Caracas Venezuela

CHANG-WAILING, KASION JOSEPH, ombudsman, auditor; b. Vacoas, Mauritius, Sept. 13, 1930; came to Switzerland, 1960; s. Andre and Suimui (Cheng) Chang-Wailing; m. Marie Mathilde Vincent, Apr. 27, 1963; children—Catherine, Alexia. Baccalaureat, Kings Coll., Mauritius, 1952; Expert comptable, postgrad. diploma mgmt. Poly. Sr. Coll. Commerce, 1957. Cert. info. systems auditor, CPA ; corporate pub. acct.; chartered sec. Co. adminstr. Trafalgar Travel Ltd., London, 1958-60; acct. Nat. Relief Services, Geneva, Switzerland, 1961; pub. acct., audit Peat, Marwick & Fides, Geneva, 1962-63; auditor WHO, Geneva, 1963-82, ombudsman, 1983—, Internat. Agy. Research on Cancer, Lyon, France, 1983—. Fellow Soc. Co. Accts.; mem. Inst. Chartered Adminstrs. (assoc.), Inst. Internal Auditors, Assn. C.P.A.s, Assn. Systems Mgmt., Brit. Inst. Mgmt., Am. Acctg. Assn., EDP Auditors Assn. Home: 61 Rue de Moillebeau, Geneva 1209, Switzerland Office: WHO, Ave Appia 1211, Geneva 27, Geneva Switzerland

CHANNELL, DAVID FRANCIS, history educator; b. Cleve., Dec. 8, 1945; s. William Francis and Helen Stone (Aldous) C.; B.S., Case Inst. Tech., 1967; M.S., Case Western Res. U., 1969, Ph.D., 1975; m. Carolyn Jean Eilmann, Aug. 3, 1968. Fellow dept. physics Case Western Res. U., Cleve., 1967-69, teaching asst., 1974-75; asst. prof. history U. Tex., Dallas, 1975-80, asso. prof., 1980—; Nat. Humanities Inst. fellow U. Chgo., 1978-79. NRC grantee, 1977; NEH grantee, 1981-82; NSF grantee, 1981-83; Am. Council Learned Socs. grantee, 1985. Mem. AAAS, Soc. History Tech., History Sci. Soc., Soc. for Social Studies of Sci., Hastings Ctr. (Inst. Social Ethics and Life Scis., Soc. for Lit. and Sci., N.Y. Acad. Scis. Author: Scottish Men of Science—W.J.M. Rankine, 1986, The History of Engineering Schience, 1988; contbr. articles to profl. jours. Home: 513 Lawnmeadow Dr Richardson TX 75080 Office: University of Texas at Dallas Richardson TX 75083

CHANNER, HAROLD HUDSON, television producer, interviewer; b. Detroit, Mar. 14, 1935; s. Harold Hudson and Grace (Sprunk) C.; m. Eileen McLanhagan, June 11, 1960 (div. 1974); children—Lisa Eileen, David Donald. B.A., Wayne State U., 1959, M.A., 1961; Ph.D., Ind. U., 1963. Instr. So. Ill. U., Edwardsville, Ill., 1963-64, Wayne State U., Detroit, 1965-66; asst. prof. Utah State U., Logan, 1966-67, Calif. State U., Long Beach, 1967-68, N.Y. State U., New Paltz, 1968-71; pres., chief exec. officer Conversations, Inc., New Paltz, 1973—, producer and host TV interview series. Served with U.S. Army, 1954-56. Mem. Acad. TV Arts and Scis. Avocations: reading; swimming; dancing. Office: Conversations with Channer PO Box 65 New Paltz NY 12561

CHANNIN, GEORGE HARVIE, manufacturing company executive; b. N.Y.C., Aug. 15, 1944; arrived in Taiwan, 1984; s. Harvie Emmett George Channin and Eleanor (Hutchins) Michelsen. AB, Rutgers U., 1966; MBA, Harvard U., 1968. Sr. systems engr. Norton Co., Worcester, Mass., 1968-73; fin. and adminstrn. mgr. Norton East Asia Inc., Tokyo, 1974-77; asst. to v.p. Pacific Ops. div. Otis Elevator Co., Tokyo, 1978-81; dir. strategic planning Otis Elevator Co., Singapore, 1982-83; pres., gen. mgr. Tatung Otis Elevator Co., Taipei, Taiwan, 1984—. Mem. Chaine des Rotisseurs (chevalier). Republican. Office: Tatung Otis Elevator Co, 22 Chung Shan N Rd Sect 3, Taipei Republic of China

CHANNON, (HENRY) PAUL (GUINNESS), secretary of state for transport; b. England, Oct. 9, 1935; s. Sir Henry and Lady Honor Svejdar Guinness C.; m. Ingrid Olivia Georgia Wyndham, 1963; one s., one d. (one d. dec.). Grad., Lockers Park, Hemel Hempstead, Eton Coll., Christ Ch., Oxford. Parliamentary pvt. sec. to minister of power Parliament, London, 1959-60, Parliamentary pvt. sec. to home sec., 1960-62, Parliamentary pvt. sec. to first sec. of state, 1962-63, Parliamentary pvt. sec. to fgn. sec., 1963-64, opposition spokesman on arts and amenities, 1967-70, Parliamentary sec. min. of housing and local govt., 1970, Parliamentary under sec. of state Dept. Environment, 1970-72, minister of state No. Ireland Office, 1972, minister for housing and constrn. Dept. Environment, 1972-74, opposition spokesman on prices and consumer protection, 1974, opposition spokesman on environ. affairs, 1974-75, minister of state CSD, 1979-81, minister for the arts, 1981-83, minister for trade, 1983-86, sec. of state for trade and industry, 1986-87, sec. of transport, 1987—; dep. leader Conservation Del. to WEU and Council of Europe, 1976-79; mem. gen. Adv. council to ITA, 1964-66. Served to 2d lt. Royal Horse Guards (The Blues), 1955-56. Address: House of Commons, London SW1 England *

CHANON, CHARLES, civil engineer; b. Baghdad, Irak, May 16, 1934; came to U.K., 1965; s. Simon and Zelda (Behar) Shamoon; m. Marina Nepomiachty, July 22, 1964 (div. 1986); children—Robert, Sophie, Nathalie. B.Sc. in Civil Engring., Technion U., Haifa, Israel, 1956. Design engr. Schwartz Hautmont, Paris, 1957-60, chief engr. Oth, Paris and London, 1960-69, assoc. ptnr. Lowe, Rodin & Oth, London, 1969-71, mng. dir. Oth U.K., London, 1971-73; pres. Charles Chanon & Ptnrs., London, Paris, 1973—. Author: (handbook) Construction in the Common Market, 1974. Contbr. articles to profl. jours. Fellow Brit. Inst. Mktg.; mem. Instn. Civil Engrs., Inst. Mktg. Chartered Engrs. Jewish. Avocations: swimming; shooting; music. Home: 70 Alleyn Rd, London SE21 8AH, England Office: Charles Chanon & Ptnrs, 9 Belgrave Rd, London SW1V 1QB, England

CHANT, ANTHONY DAVID, vascular surgeon, educator; b. Eng., Feb. 21, 1938; s. Percival James and Ethel Helen (Quick) C.; m. Ann Nadia Venning, Mar. 21, 1959; children—Ben, Harvey, Thomas. B.Sc. in Physiology with honors, U. London, 1961, M.B., 1964, M.S., 1971. House surgeon St. Bartholomew Hosp., London, 1965-66; research asst. Welsh Nat. Sch. Medicine, Cardiff, 1968-69; lectr. U. Soton, Southampton, Eng., 1971-74; cons. vascular surgeon Royal South Hants Hosp., Southampton, 1975—; hon. clin. tchr. U. Southampton, 1975—. Contbr. articles to profl. jours. Mem. Anmesty Internat. Fellow Royal Coll. Surgeons (Eng.), Royal Soc. Medicine; mem. Royal Inst. Philosophy. Avocation: fishing. Office: Royal Hants Hosp, Dept Surgery, Graham Rd, Southampton SO9 4PE, England

CHAO, CHEN KUO, cosmetics executive; b. Shanghai, Peoples Republic China, Mar. 18, 1946; s. Kung Lin and Wong Pei Fun C.; m. Reiko Sato. BS in Hair Bus., Tokyo Inst. Tech., 1972. Mng. dir. CK Chao & Co., LTD., Artistic Hair Products Co., Ltd., Hong Kong, 1988—. Chmn. Asian Hair and Make-Up Competition, 1978. Recipient Cert. Appreciation Prime Minister Nakosone, 1985. Mem. Hopeh and Shantung Native Assn. Office: Artistic Hair Products Co Ltd, 152 Kwong Fuk Rd, 15/F Tai Po Comml Ctr, Tai Po New Ters Hong Kong

CHAO, DANIEL PAO-HSI, UN official; b. Wushing, Chekiang Province, China, Jan. 24, 1932; s. Po-chi and Shai-chu (Chung) C.; BA in Econs., Defiance (Ohio) Coll., 1959; MBA in Mktg., City U. N.Y., 1968; postgrad. N.Y. U., 1969-71; m. Lydia Yui-cheng Yu, Nov. 15, 1953; 1 child, Victor Tzu-ping. Adminstrv. officer Office of Tech. Cooperation, UN, N.Y.C., 1967-70, program mgmt. officer, 1970-83, econ. affairs officer dept. tech. cooperation for devel., 1983-87; prof. Pub. Adminstrn., Tunghai U. Taichung, Taiwan, 1987—; tchr. N.Y. U., 1969-71. Recipient Alumni Achievement award Defiance Coll., 1980. Lutheran. Home: 4 Pasadena Pl Mount Vernon NY 10552 Office: UN New York NY 10017

CHAO, JAMES MIN-TZU, architect; b. Dairen, China, Feb. 27, 1940; s. T. C. and Lin Fan (Wong) C.; came to U.S., 1949, naturalized, 1962; m. Kirsti Helena Lehtonen, May 15, 1968. BArch, U. Calif., Berkeley, 1965. Cert. architect, Calif.; cert. instr. real estate, Calif. Intermediate draftsman Spencer, Lee & Busse, Architects, San Francisco, 1966-67; asst. to pres. Import Plus Inc., Santa Clara, Calif., 1967-69; job capt. Hammaberg and Herman, Architects, Oakland, Calif., 1969-71; project mgr. B A Premises Corp., San Francisco, 1971-79; constrn. mgr. The Straw Hat Restaurant Corp., 1979-81, mem. sr. mgmt., dir. real estate and constrn., 1981-87; sole practice architect, Berkeley, Calif., 1987—; pres. Food Service Cons., Inc., 1987—; pres., chief exec. officer Stratsac, Inc., 1987—; lectr. comml. real estate site analysis and selection for profl. real estate seminars; coordinator minority vending program, solar application program Bank of Am.; guest faculty mem. Northwest Ctr. for Profl. Edn. Patentee tidal electric generating system; author first comprehensive consumer orientated performance specification for remote banking transaction. Recipient honorable mention Future Scientists Am., 1955. Mem. AIA. Republican. Clubs: Encinal Yacht (dir. 1977-78).

CHAO, JOHN TUNG, metallurgist; b. Taipei, Republic of China, Mar. 17, 1950; arrived in Can., 1975; s. Yung-Ming and Mei-Chu (Liu) C.; m. Lily Li-Fu Chu, Dec. 15, 1976; children: Esther, Aaron. BS, Tunghai U., Taichung, Republic of China, 1972; ME, U. N.B., Can., 1977, PhD, 1981. Asst. tchr. Tunghai U., 1974-75; research asst. U. N.B., 1975-80; research engr. QIT-Fer et Titane, Inc., Sorel, Que., Can., 1980-85, sr. research engr., 1985—. Recipient Hofmann Prize Spl. award Internat. Consortium Lead Devel. Assn., London, 1981. mem. The Metall. Soc.-Am. Inst. Metall. Engrs. (Extractive Metallurgy Tech. award 1981). Home: 7855 Trinidad, Brossard, PQ Canada J4W 1N6

CHAO, YUNG-FA, medical association administrator, dermatologist; b. Tainan, Taiwan, Republic of China, Apr. 25, 1925; s. Tu-Sheng and Hsu-Yeh Chao; m. Shu-Foa F.; children: Phyllis, Elena, Pin-Hising, Ye-Ling. MD, Taiwan U., Taipei, Republic of China, 1950. Diplomate Nat. Bd. Physicians, Dermatologists. Bd. dirs. Chinese Dermatol. Soc, Taipei, Republic of China, 1974-87; pres. China Christian Med. Assn., Taipei; pres., trustee Happy Mount Colony for Handicapped Children, 1984—. V.p. Internat. Assn. Y's Men's Club, Geneva, Switzerland, 1978; pres. Taipei YMCA, 1986; elder Presbyn. Ch., Taipei, 1966—. Mem. Internat. Leprosy Assn., Internat. Soc. of Dermatology, Internat. Soc. of Dermatologic Surgery, Am. Acad. of Dermatology, Chinese Dermatol. Soc. Home: 112 Minsheng E Rd, Taipei 10443, Republic of China Office: Mackay Meml Hosp, 92 sec 2 Chung-san North Rd, Taipei 10449, Republic of China

CHAPANIS, ALPHONSE, human factors consultant, educator; b. Meriden, Conn., Mar. 17, 1917; s. Anicatas and Mary (Barkevich) C.; m. Marion Rowe, Aug. 23, 1941 (div. 1960); children: Linda and Roger (twins); m. Natalia Potanin, Mar. 25, 1960 (div. 1987). B.A., U. Conn., 1937; M.A., Yale U., 1942; Ph.D., Yale, 1943. Psychologist Tenn. Dept. Pub. Health, 1939-40; asst. psychologist Aero. Med. Lab., Wright Air Devel. Center, 1942-43; asst. prof., research fellow Johns Hopkins, 1946-49, assoc. prof., 1949-56, research contract dir., 1952-53, 55-83, prof. psychology, indsl. engring., 1956-63, prof. psychology, 1963-83; pres. Alphonse Chapanis, Ph.D., P.A., 1974—; mem. tech. staff Bell Telephone Labs., 1953-54; Cons. exec. council Joint Services Human Engring. Guide to Equipment Design, 1953-60; mem. panel on tng., com. on undersea warfare NRC, 1953-57; adv. panel behavioral scis. research Air Force Office Sci. Research, 1956-59; sci. liaison officer Am. embassy Office Naval Research Br. Office, London, 1960-61; mem. com. on human factors Nat. Research Council, 1980-85. Author: (with W.R. Garner, C.T. Morgan) Applied Experimental Psychology: Human Factors in Engineering Design, 1949, The Design and Conduct of Human Engineering Studies, 1956, Research Techniques in Human Engineering, 1959, Man-Machine Engineering, 1965; Editor: Ethnic Variables in Human Factors Engineering, 1975; corr. editor: Jour. Applied Psychology, 1955-60; co-editor: (with C.T. Morgan, J.S. Cook, M.W. Lund) Human Engineering Guide to Equipment Design, 1963; editorial adv. bd.: Jour. Systems Engring, 1969-70; mem. editorial bd.: Behaviour and Info. Tech, 1980—; Contbr. articles to profl. jours. Mem. NRC, 1971-74, mem. com. on human factors, 1980-85. Served from 2d lt. to capt. USAAF, 1943-46. Recipient Franklin V. Taylor award, 1963, Paul M. Fitts award, 1973, Distinguished Contbn. for Applications in Psychology award, 1978, Outstanding Sci. Contbns. to Psychology award, 1981, Polish Ergonomics Soc. award, 1982. Fellow AAAS, Am. Psychol. Assn., Human Factors Soc. (pres. 1963-64), Soc. Engring. Psychologists (pres. 1959-60), Soc. Exptl. Psychologists; mem. Ergonomics Soc. (hon.), Internat. Assn. Applied Psychology, Eastern Psychol. Assn., Systems Safety Soc., Internat. Ergonomics Assn. (mem. council 1967-73, pres. 1976-79, award 1982, Pres.'s Disting. Service award 1987), Phi Beta Kappa, Sigma Xi. Address: Suite 210 Ruxton Towers 8415 Bellona Ln Baltimore MD 21204

CHAPIN, HORACE BEECHER, allergist; b. Batavia, N.Y., Dec. 22, 1917; s. Horace Heal and Desdamona (Baldwin) C.; m. Deirdre Jane Frances O'Brien, Apr. 23, 1954. AB, Dartmouth Coll., N.H., 1939; MD, McGill U., Can., 1942. Rotating intern Abington (Pa.) Meml. Hosp., 1942-43; intern Yonkers (N.Y.) Gen. Hosp., 1943; internist Bellevue Hosp., N.Y.C., 1947; resident in internal medicine Ft. Howard Hosp., Balt., 1948-49; succesively resident in allergy, fellow in allergy, fellow in allergy research, asst. attending physician in medicine, also allergy Roosevelt Hosp., N.Y.C., 1949-54; assoc. Drs. R.A. Cooke and W.B. Sherman, N.Y.C., 1950-54, Drs. Carlisle Boyd and Vansel Johnson, N.Y.C., 1954-55, Dr. Horace S. Baldwin, N.Y.C., 1955-68; chief allergy clinic, assoc. attending allergist, dir. allergy research lab. Manhattan Eye, Ear and Throat Hosp., N.Y.C., 1957-78; cons. allergy Consol. Edison Co., N.Y.C., 1955—. Contbr. articles to profl. jours. Served to capt. MC, AUS, 1943-46. Fellow Am. Acad. Allergy; mem. AMA, N.Y. State Med. Assn., N.Y. Allergy Soc., N.Y. Acad. Medicine. Home: Mizzentop 47 Harbour Rd, Warwick Bermuda

CHAPLIN, GEORGE, editor; b. Columbia, S.C., Apr. 28, 1914; s. Morris and Netty (Brown) C.; m. Esta Lillian Solomon, Jan. 26, 1937; children—Stephen Michael, Jerry Gay. B.S., Clemson Coll., 1935; Nieman fellow, Harvard U., 1940-41. Reporter, later city editor Greenville (S.C.) Piedmont, 1935-42; mng. editor Camden (N.J.) Courier-Post, 1946-47, San Diego Jour., 1948-49; mng. editor, then editor New Orleans Item, 1949-58; asso. editor Honolulu Advertiser, 1958-59, editor, 1959-86, editor at large, 1986—; Pulitzer prize juror, 1969, 83; mem. selection com. Jefferson fellowships East-West Ctr.; Chmn. Gov.'s Conf. on Year 2000, 1970; chmn. Hawaii Commn. on Year 2000, 1971-74; co-chmn. Conf. on Alt. Econ. Future for Hawaii, 1973-75; charter mem. Goals for Hawaii, 1979—; alt. U.S. rep. South Pacific Commn., 1978-81; chmn. search com. for pres. U. Hawaii, 1983; chmn. Hawaii Gov.'s Adv. Council on Fgn. Lang. and Internat. Studies, 1983—; rep. of World Press Freedom Com. on missions to Sri Lanka, Hong Kong, Singapore, 1987. Editor, officer-in-charge: Mid-Pacific edit. Stars and Stripes World War II; Editor: (with Glenn Paige) Hawaii 2000, 1973. Bd. dirs. U. Hawaii Research Corp., 1970-72, Inst. for Religion and Social Change, Hawaii Jewish Welfare Fund; bd. govs. East-West Ctr., Honolulu, 1980—, chmn., 1983—, Pacific Health Research Inst., 1984—, Hawaii Pub. Schs. Found., 1986-87—; Am. media chmn. U.S.-Japan Conf. on Cultural and Ednl. Interchange, 1978-86; co-founder, v.p. Coalition for A Drug-Free Hawaii, 1987—. Served as capt. AUS, 1942-46. Decorated Star Solidarity (Italy), Order Rising Sun (Japan), Prime Minister's medal (Israel); recipient citations Overseas Press Club, 1961, 72, Headliners award, 1962, John Hancock award, 1972, 74, Distinguished Alumni award Clemson U., 1974, E.W. Scripps award Scripps-Howard Found., 1976, Champion Media award for Econ. Understanding, 1981, Judah Magnes Gold medal Hebrew U. Jerusalem, 1987; inducted Honolulu Press Club Hall of Fame, 1987. Mem. Soc. Nieman Fellows, Honolulu Symphony Soc., Pacific and Asian Affairs Council (dir.), Internat. Press Inst., World Future Soc., Am. Soc. Newspaper Editors (dir., treas. 1973, sec. 1974, v.p. 1975, pres. 1976), Friends of East-West Center, Sigma Delta Chi. Clubs: Pacific, Waialae Country. Home: 4437 Kolohala St Honolulu HI 96816 Office: care Honolulu Advertiser PO Box 3110 Honolulu HI 96802

CHAPMAN, CHRISTINE MURIEL, nurse, educator; b. Birmingham, Eng., Oct. 15, 1927; d. Richard F. and Doris M. (Hulbert) C. BS with honors, U. London, 1969, MPhil, 1974. RN, cert. midwife. Staff nurse Gen. Hosp., Birmingham, 1949-50, night sister, 1950-51; ward sister Royal Salop Infirmary, Shrewsbury, Eng., 1952-55, nurse tutor, 1955-56; nurse tutor Middlesex Hosp., London, 1959-69; lectr. York (Eng.) U., 1969-72; dir. nursing studies U. Wales, Cardiff, 1972-84, prof. nursing edn., dean nurse studies, 1984—; cons. Council Europe, Strasbourg, France, 1979-84, Brunei Govt., 1985—; mem. U.K. Gen. Council Nurses, 1987—, Welsh Nat. Bd. Nursing, Cardiff, 1979—, chmn., 1986. Author: Medical Nursing, 3 edits., 1968-80, Sociology for Nurses, 3 edits., 1979-86, Theory of Nursing: Practical Application, 1985. Named officer Order Brit. Empire, 1984. Fellow Royal Coll. Nursing (council 1974-79). Office: Coll Medicine U Wales, Health Park, Cardiff Wales CF4 4XW

CHAPMAN, CONRAD DANIEL, lawyer; b. Detroit, July 31, 1933; s. Conrad F. and Alexandrine C. (Baranski) C.; m. Carol Lynn DeBash, Sept. 1, 1956; children: Stephen Daniel, Richard Thomas, Suzanne Marie. BA, U. Detroit, 1954, JD summa cum laude, 1957; LLM in Taxation, Wayne State U., 1964. Bar: Mich. 1957, U.S. Dist. Ct. (so. dist.) Mich. 1957. Ptnr. Powers, Chapman, DeAgostino, Meyers & Milia and predecessor firms, Troy, Mich., 1964—. Mem. ABA, Detroit Bar Assn., Oakland Bar Assn., Am. Arbitration Assn., Detroit Estate Planning Council, Oakland Estate Planning Council. Clubs: Detroit Athletic, Detroit Golf. Lodge: Elks. Office: Powers Chapman DeAgostino Meyers & Milia 3001 W Big Beaver Rd Suite 704 Troy MI 48084

CHAPMAN, JAMES WILLIAM, educator, researcher; b. Lower Hutt, New Zealand, Apr. 10, 1948; s. Thomas James and Margaret Howard (Young) C.; m. Jennifer Mhairi Hooker, May 9, 1970; children—Mathew James, Joanna Mhairi. BA, Victoria U., Wellington, New Zealand, 1970, MA, 1973; PhD, U. Alta., Edmonton, Can., 1979. Instr. Horowhenua Coll., Levin, New Zealand, 1973-74; research assoc. U. Alta., 1975-79; sr. lectr. Massey U., Palmerston North, New Zealand, 1980—; vis. prof. dept. family studiesU. Guelph, Ontario, Can. 1986-87. Author: Affective Correlates of Learning Disabilities, 1980, (psychol. scale) Students Perception of Ability Scale, 1977; contbr. articles to profl. jours. Claude McCarthy fellow, 1984. Fellow Internat. Assn. for Research in Learning Disabilities; mem. Am. Ednl. Research Assn., New Zealand Psychol. Soc. Avocations: photography, home brewing. Office: Massey U, Palmerston North New Zealand

CHAPMAN, JEFFREY IAN, educator; b. Milw., Jan. 16, 1946; s. Philip and Sophia (Shachnov) C.; m. Elaine Jonas, June 22, 1969; children—Michael Aaron, Allison Beth. A.B., Occidental Coll., 1967; M.A., U. Calif.-Berkeley, 1968, Ph.D., 1971. Research economist Inst. of Govt. and Pub. Affairs, UCLA, 1971-73; prof. U. So. Calif., Los Angeles, 1973-79, assoc. prof. sch. pub. adminstrn., 1979-86, prof. 1986—, dir. grad. ednl. instn., 1983—; cons. HR&A, Inc., Los Angeles, 1981-83, Kirlin & Assocs., 1982-83. Author: Proposition 13 and Land Use, 1981, Long Term Fin. Planning, 1987; contbr. articles to profl. jours. Lincoln Inst. grantee, 1979; HUD grantee, 1978; NSF grantee, 1983. Mem. Am. Soc. Pub. Adminstrn. (regional bd.), Am. Econ. Assn., Nat. Tax Assn. Democrat. Jewish. Club: Comstock. Lodge: Rotary. Home: 4841 Sherlock Way Carmichael CA 95608 Office: U So Calif Sch Pub Adminstrn Los Angeles CA 90007

CHAPMAN, JOSEPH DUDLEY, gynecologist, sexologist, author; b. Moline, Ill., Apr. 29, 1928; s. Joseph Dudley and Lillian Caroline (Pruder) C.; m. Mary Kay Sartini, June, 1949 (div.); children—Mary Jo Tucker, Nancy Jo Robinson; m. 2d, Virginia Helene Milius, June, 1958 (div.). B.S., U. Ill. and Roosevelt Coll., Chgo., 1950; D.O., Coll. Osteo. Medicine and Surgery, 1953; D.Sc., 1963; M.D., Calif. Coll. Medicine, 1962, PhD Inst. Advanced Study Human Sexualtiy, 1986. Cert. Am. Osteo. Bd. Ob-Gyn. Intern, resident in ob-gyn Still Coll. Hosp., Des Moines; practice medicine specializing in ob-gyn, North Madison, Ohio, 1973—; clin. prof. ob-gyn Ohio U., 1979—; mem. faculty, acad. bd. Inst. Advanced Study Human Sexuality, San Francisco, 1979—; TV appearances on Phil Donahue Show, Good Morning Am., The Last Word, and others; med. examiner FAA, comml. pilot. Active Boy Scouts Am. Mem. Am. Fertility Soc., Am. Assn. Gynocol. Laparoscopists, Am. Coll. Osteo. Ob-Gyn (Purdue Frederick awards, editor),

Acad. Psychosomatic Medicine (bd. govs.), Am. Med. Writers Assn. Lutheran. Author: The Feminine Mind and Body, 1966; The Sexual Equation, 1977; editor-in-chief O.P., 1968-77; editorial cons. Penthouse Forum, J.A.O.A.: Psychosomatic Medicine; contbr. chpts. to books, articles to profl. jours. Home: Box 340 North Madison OH 44057

CHAPMAN, LORING, psychologist, neuroscientist; b. Los Angeles, Oct. 4, 1929; s. Lee E. and Elinore E. (Gundry) Scott; children: Robert, Antony, Pandora. B.S., U. Nev., 1950; Ph.D., U. Chgo., 1955. Lic. psychologist, Oreg., N.Y., Calif. Research fellow U. Chgo., 1952-54; research asso., asst. prof. Cornell U. Med. Coll., N.Y.C., 1955-61; asso. prof. in residence, mem. Neuropsychiat. Inst., UCLA, 1961-65; research prof. U. Oreg., Portland, 1965; br. chief NIH, Bethesda, Md., 1966-67; prof., chmn. dept. behavioral biology Sch. Medicine U. Calif., Davis, 1967-81; prof. psychiatry Sch. Medicine U. Calif., 1977—, prof. neurology, 1977-81, prof. human physiology, 1977-81; vice chmn. div. of sci. basic to medicine 1976-79; vis. prof. U. Sao Paulo, Brazil, 1959, 77, Univ. Coll., London, 1969-70, U. Florence, Italy, 1979-80; clin. prof. Georgetown U., 1966-67; mem. Calif. Primate Research Center, 1967—; dir. research Fairview Hosp., 1965-66; cons. Nat. Inst. Neurol. Disease and Stroke, 1961—, Nat. Cancer Inst., 1977—, Nat. Inst. Child Health Devel., 1967—, mem. research and tng. com., 1968-72. Author: Pain and Suffering, 3 vols, 1967, Head and Brain 3 vols, 1971, (with E.A. Dunlap) The Eye, 1981; contbr. sci. articles to publs. Recipient Thornton Wilson prize, 1958, Career award USPHS, 1964, Commonwealth Fund award, 1970; grantee NASA, 1969—; grantee NIH, 1956—; grantee Nat. Inst. Drug Abuse, 1971—; Forgarty Sr. Internat. fellow, 1980. Mem. Am. Acad. Neurology, Am. Physiol. Soc., Am. Psychol. Assn., Royal Soc. Medicine (London)., Am. Neurol. Assn., Am. Assn. Mental Deficiency, Aerospace Med. Assn., Soc. for Neurosci. Home: 205 Country Place Sacramento CA 95831 Office: Dept Psychiatry U Calif Med Ctr 2315 Stockton Blvd Sacramento CA 95817

CHAPMAN, RICHARD LEROY, public policy researcher; b. Yankton, S.D., Feb. 4, 1932; s. Raymond Young and Vera Everette (Trimble) C.; m. Marilyn Jean Nicholson, Aug. 14, 1955; children: Catherine Ruth, Robert Matthew, Michael David, Stephen Raymond, Amy Jean. BS, S.D. State U., 1954; postgrad., Cambridge (Eng.) U., 1954-55; MPA, Syracuse U., 1958, PhD, 1967. Profl. staff mem. com. govt. ops. U.S. Ho. Reps., Sec. of Def., Executive Office of Pres. (Bur. of Budget), Washington, 1966-67; program dir. NIH, Bethesda, Md., 1967-68; sr. research assoc. Nat. Acad. Pub. Adminstrn., Washington, 1968-72, dep. exec. dir., 1973-76, v.p., dir. research, 1976-81; sr. research scientist Denver Research Inst., 1982-86; mem. adv. com. Denver Research Inst. U. Denver, 1984-86; ptnr. Milliken Chapman Research Group Inc., Denver, 1986—; cons. U.S. Office Personnel Mgmt., Washington, 1977-81, Denver, 1986; cons. CIA, Washington, 1979, 80, 81, Arthur S. Fleming Awards, Washington, 1977-81. Contbr. articles to profl. jours. Mem. aerospace com. Colo. Commn. Higher Edn., Denver, 1982-83; chmn. rules com. U. Denver Senate, 1984-85; bd. dirs. S.E. Englewood Water Dist., Littleton, 1984-88, pres. 1986-88. Served to capt. U.S. Army, 1955-57, Korea. Brookings fellow, 1964-65. Mem. Tech. Transfer Soc., Am. Soc. Pub. Adminstrn., AAAS, IEEE, Engring. Mgmt. Soc., Futures Soc. Republican. Lodges: Masons, Commandery, Order of DeMoley (Cross of Honor 1982). Office: Milliken Chapman Research Group 6631 S University Blvd Suite 212 Littleton CO 80121

CHAPMAN, ROBERT BRECKINRIDGE, III, high technology company executive; b. Balt., May 12, 1917; s. Robert B. and Mary (McCord) C.; m. Audrey Lee Frank, Apr. 5, 1941; children: Linda Lee (Mrs. Russell W. Fabiszak), Robert B. IV. B.Engring. with honors, Johns Hopkins, 1938. Registered profl. engr., Md. Structural engr. John E. Greiner Co., Balt., 1938-41; structural engr., missile project mgr., bus. mgr. spl. weapons sales Glenn L. Martin Co., Balt., 1941-50; chief contracts AAI Corp., Balt., 1950-52, dir., 1952-75, exec. v.p., 1956-67, pres., chief exec. officer, 1967-75; prof., v.p. institutional planning and devel. Coppin State Coll., Balt., 1975-82; sr. v.p. ops. AMAF Industries, Inc., 1982-86; contracts mgr. Integral Techs. Inc., Hunt Valley, Md., 1987—; dir. adminstrn. PAI Inc., Vienna, Va., 1987—. Past chmn. Vol. Council for Equal Opportunity; past mem. exec. bd. Balt. area council Boy Scouts Am.; past chmn. Md. Commn. on Dyslexia; past chmn. indsl. adv. council Opportunities Industrialization Center Balt.; past chmn. Met. Balt. Nat. Alliance Businessmen. Served to lt. col. USAAF, 1941-46. Assoc. fellow AIAA; mem. Nat. Security Indsl. Assn. (exec. com., past chmn. bd. trustees, trustee emeritus, hon. life mem.), Nat. Contracts Mgmt. Assn. (cert. profl. contracts mgr.), Orton Dyslexia Soc. (past nat. treas., past nat. dir.), World Future Soc., Alpha Tau Omega (past pres. Johns Hopkins Psi chpt., also Balt. alumni chpt.). Presbyn. (ordained elder). Home: 1505 Cranwell Rd Lutherville MD 21093

CHAPMAN, WALTER HOWARD, artist, educator; b. Toledo, Dec. 7, 1912; s. Ralph Martin and Lillian Minor (Seagrave) C.; m. Marie Louise Repasz, Aug. 29, 1943 (div. Nov., 1962); children—Anne Marie, Patricia Lee; m. Jean Clarice Sayre, Jan. 29, 1963. Pvt. study Cleve. Sch. Art., 1930-34, John Huntington Poly., Cleve., 1933, Art Students League N.Y.C., 1939. Artist-in-residence Toledo Blade, 1937-38; freelance illustrator, N.Y.C., 1938-39; artist-in-residence Jack Binder Studio, N.Y.C., 1943-44; creative dir., Phillips Assocs., Toledo, 1946-79; tchr. Toledo Mus. Sch. of Design, 1952-60, 1978—, Chapman-Kohn Art Seminars, Toledo and Columbus 1978-85; owner, operator Chapman Art Gallery, Sylvania, Ohio, 1969—. Contbr. watercolor paintings and illustrations to books and magazines; exhibited in group shows: Springfield Art Mus., Mo., Mainstream Internat., Marietta, Ohio, Salmagundi Club, N.Y.C., Grumbacher Corp., N.Y.C.; one-man show Toledo Mus. Art, 1988. Served to sgt. U.S. Army, 1942-45, ETO. Decorated Bronze Star. Mem. Illustrators Club Toledo (pres. 1964), Allied Artists of Am., Watercolor U.S.A., Ohio Watercolor Soc. (bd. dirs. 1979), Northwest Ohio Watercolor Soc. (pres. 1968), Toledo Fedn. Art Socs. (pres. 1961) Toledo Artists Club (bd. dirs. 1962-64, 85). Republican. Clubs: Toledo Advt.; Salmagundi (N.Y.C.). Lodge: Rotary (Toledo). Avocations: landscape painting; portrait painting. Home: 6001 Gregory Dr Sylvania OH 43560 Office: Chapman Art Gallery 5151 S Main St Sylvania OH 43560

CHAPPELL, DUNCAN, criminology educator; b. Blandford, Dorset, Eng., Aug. 1, 1939; came to Can., 1980; s. Francis Roy and Dorothy M. (Lardner) C.; m. Susan Fenn Parsons, Apr. 29, 1962 (div. Sept. 1976); children—Hamish, Kirstin; m. Rhonda Dorothea Moore, Apr. 9, 1982. B.A., U. Tasmania, 1962, LL.B. with 1st class honors, 1962; Ph.D., U. Cambridge, 1965. Barrister and solicitor, Tasmania. Sr. lectr. Faculty of Law, U. Sydney, Australia, 1966-70; assoc. prof. Sch. Criminal Justice, SUNY-Albany, 1971-73; dir. Law and Justice Study Ctr., Battelle Meml. Inst., Seattle, 1973-77; vis. prof. legal studies La Trobe U., Melbourne, Australia, 1977-78; mem. Australian Law Reform Commn., Sydney, 1978-79; prof. Sch. Criminology Simon Fraser U., Burnaby, B.C., Can., 1980-87, chair dept., 1982-84; dir. Australian Inst. Criminology, Canberra, Australia, 1987—; adv. criminal procedure project Law Reform Commn. Can., sentencing reform project Ministry of Justice Can., Ottawa, 1983; cons. B.C. Law Found., 1982, U.S. Senate Select Com. on Small Bus., 1973-74; mem. working group Australian Criminal Scis. Com., 1979. Editorial cons. Jour. Criminal Law and Criminology, 1973—; author: From Sawdust to Toxic Blobs: A Consideration of Sanctioning Strategies to Combat Pollution in Canada, 1987; co-author: The Police and the Public in Australia and New Zealand, 1969, The Police Use of Deadly Force: Canadian Perspectives, 1985; co-editor: The Australian Criminal Justice System, 1972, 77, 87—; Violence and Criminal Justice, 1975; Forcible Rape: The Crime, the Victim and the Offender, 1977; contbr. chpts. to books, articles to profl. jours., encys. Bd. mgmt. No. Conf., Vancouver, 1983-84; mem. rape edn. com. Premier's Dept., Melbourne, Australia, 1978. Brit. Commonwealth scholar, 1962-65; Harkness fellow, 1969. Mem. Am. Soc. Criminology (exec. com. 1976-78, 83-84), Australian Acad. Forensic Sci., Australian Assn. Cultural Freedom. Home: 28 Black St #16, Yarralumla Australia Office: Australian Inst Criminology, PO Box 28, Woden 2606, Australia

CHAPPELL, GARY ALAN, software designer; b. Independence, Mo., Jan. 24, 1954; s. Jesse Earl and Eunice Mildred (Ralston) C. B.S. in Computer Sci., B.S. in Chemistry, U. Mo.-Rolla, 1976. Grad. teaching asst. Stanford U., 1976-77; graphics programmer Lawrence Livermore Lab., Calif., 1977-79; prin. investigator research and devel. Def. and Space Systems Group TRW, Redondo Beach, Calif., 1979; product mgr. Comtal Image Processing, Inc., Pasadena, Calif., 1979-80; mgr. user interface devel. Tymshare, Inc., Cupertino, Calif., 1980-82; software mgr.-graphics Qubix Graphic Systems, Saratoga, Calif., 1982-84; sr. software engr. Suntek Tech. Internat., Sunnyvale, Calif., 1984-86; mgr. software applications Atherton Tech., Sunnyvale, 1986-88; user interface designer Make Systems Inc., Mountain View, Calif., 1988—. Mem. Assn. Computing Machinery (mem. Special Interest Group on Computer Graphics, Special Interest Group on Computer and Human Interaction), Soc. Info. Display, Am. Chem. Soc., Mensa. Subspecialities: Research in design and implementation of interactive, graphics-oriented human-computer interfaces for non-technical computer system users; research into software and hardware components of highly interactive graphics systems. Home: 421 Fernando Ave Palo Altos CA 94306 Office: 201 San Antonio Circle #225 Mountain View CA 94040

CHAPPELL, WALTER, photographer, artist; b. Portland, Oreg., June 8, 1925; s. Elmer and Margaret Louise (Willis) C.; children: Dharma, Theo, Aryan, Piki, Robin, Riversong. Student of Minor White. Curator exhbns. and prints George Eastman House of Internat. Mus. Photography, Rochester, N.Y., 1957-61; founder, dir. Assn. of Heliographers Gallery Archives, N.Y.C., 1962-65. One-man shows include George Eastman House of Internat. Mus. Photography, 1957, Smithsonian Instn., Washington, 1959, Musee d'Art Moderne de la Ville de Paris, 1973, Visual Studies Workshop, 1973, 76, Volcano Art Ctr., Hilo, Hawaii, 1976, Vision Gallery, Boston, 1978, Phila. Mus. Art, 1978, Santa Fe Gallery Photography, 1979, Nicholas Potter Gallery, Santa Fe, 1980, Colo. Photog. Art Ctr., Denver, 1981, Ctr. for Media Art of Am. Ctr., Paris, 1981, Grapestake Gallery, San Francisco, 1981, Photography Gallery, La Jolla, Calif., Am. Ctr., Cairo, 1982, New Gallery, Taos, N.Mex., 1982, Scheinbaum and Russek Gallery Photography, Santa Fe, 1983, DVS Gallery, Taos, 1984, The Art Mus. U. N.Mex., Albuquerque, 1985, Neikrug Photographica, N.Y.C., 1986, Afterimage Gallery, Dallas, 1987, Gov.'s Gallery, Santa Fe, 1987, Workspace, U. Colo., Boulder, 1987, Infinity Gallery governors State Univ., Park Forest, Ill., 1988, The New Gallery, Houston PhotoFest, 1988, numerous others; 25 yr. retrospective, Colo. Ctr. for Photog. Art, Denver, 1980, exhibited in group shows George Eastman House Mus., 1959, 86, Mus. Modern Art, N.Y.C., 1960, 79-81, Whitney Mus. Am. Art, 1974, San Francisco Art Inst., 1977 Mus. Fine Arts Houston, 1977, U. Nebr., Lincoln, U. N.C., Chapel Hill, 1981, Phila. Mus. Art, 1981, Mus. Art and Sci., San Francisco, 1983, Stables Gallery, Taos, 1984, Sonoma County Photographers, Santa Rosa, Calif., 1986, Mus. Fine Arts, Mus. N. Mex., San Jose Mus. Art, San Jose, Calif., Philip Bareiss Fine Arts, Taos, Andrew Smith Gallery Santa Fe, Armory of Arts, 1986, Los Angeles County Mus., 1987, numerous others; travelling exhbn., Europe, 1981-84; represented in permanent collections Smithsonian Instn., George Eastman House Internat. Mus. Photography, Mus. Modern Art, N.Y.C., U. Los Angeles, MIT, Polaroid Corp., Cambridge, Mass., Exchange Nat. Bank of Chgo., Ind. U., Whitney Mus. Am. Art, U. Nebr., Houston Mus. Fine Arts, Fogg Mus., Harvard U., Cambridge, Stanford Mus. Art, U. Ariz., Princeton U., New Orleans Mus. Art, Wight Gallery at UCLA, Visual Studies Workshop, Rochester, N.Y., others; author: Logue and Glyphs 1943-49, 1951; author-designer: Gestures of Infinity, 1957, Under the Sun, 1960; author-artist: Aperture Quar., 1957-81, Metaflora Portfolio, 1980, Solar Incarnate Portfolio, 1981. Served with U.S. Army, 1943-47. Frank Lloyd Wright Taliesin fellow Ariz., 1953-54; Nat. Endowment for Art photographers fellow Hawaii, 1977, N.Mex., 1980, 85. Address: PO Box 8736 Santa Fe NM 87504 also: El Rito NM 87504

CHAPPELL, WARREN, artist, writer; b. Richmond, Va., July 9, 1904; s. Samuel Michael and Mary Lillian (Hardie) C.; m. Lydia Anne Hatfield, Aug. 28, 1928. B.A., U. Richmond, 1926, D.F.A. (hon.), 1968; student, Art Students League, N.Y.C., 1926-30, Offenbacher Werkstatt, Ger., 1931-32. Tchr. Art Students League, 1932-35, mem. bd. control, 1927-30; instr. Colorado Springs Fine Arts Center, 1935-36; artist-in-residence U. Va., 1979—. Typographic and decorative designer for mags., 1926-35, book designer and illustrator, 1936—; prin. works illus. include: Adventures of Don Quixote, 1939, The Temptation of St. Anthony, 1943, A History of Tom Jones, 1982, Shakespeare: Tragedies, 1944, The Complete Novels of Jane Austen, 1950, Moby Dick, 1976, Gulliver's Travels, 1977, The Complete Adventures of Tom Sawyer and Huckleberry Finn, 1979, The Magic Flute, 1962, Bottom's Dream, 1969, Anatomy of Lettering, 1934, A Short History of the Printed Word, 1970, The Living Alphabet, 1975, They Say Stories, 1960, Miracle at Philadelphia, 1986; designer of typefaces: Lydian, 1938, Trajanus, 1940. Recipient Goudy award Rochester Inst. Tech., N.Y., 1970. Mem. Master Drawings Assn., Lawn Soc. of U. Va., Chilmark Assos. (Mass.), Phi Beta Kappa. Home: 500 Court Sq Charlottesville VA 22901 Studio: Alderman Library U Va Charlottesville VA 22903

CHARBIT, MICHEL, gastroenterologist; b. Sidi Bel Abbes, Algeria, Mar. 5, 1953; arrived in France, 1962; s. Andre and Nelly (Korchia) C.; m. Dominique Benarrosh, Dec. 7, 1975; children: Candice, Stephane. MD, U. Paris, 1978. cert. in gastroenterology, 1980, digestive endoscopy, 1981, surgical coloproctology, 1981, U. Paris. Cons. Hosp., Paris, 1978-83; cons. Hertford Brit. Hosp., Levallois, France, 1981-83, head dept. digestive disease, 1983—; cons., researcher Inst. G. Roussy, Villejuif, France, 1981—. Contbr. articles to profl. jours. Home: 53 Blvd Victor Hugo, 92200 Neuilly sur Seine France Office: 37 rue Louis Rouquier, 92300 Levallois France

CHAREST, JEAN J., parliamentary member; b. June 24, 1958. JD, U. Sherbrooke, 1980. Bar: Que., 1981. Assoc. Sherbrooke Legal Aid Office; ptnr. Beauchemin, Dussault; mem. parliament Sherbrooke-Lennoxville, 1984—; asst. dep. chmn. coms. Whole House of Commons, 1984; vice chmn. Can.-U.S. Inter-Parliamentary Group, 1984—; minister State for Youth, 1986—, State for Fitness and Amateur Sport, 1988—. Appointed mem. Cabinet Com. on Communications, Fed.-Provincial Relations, Social Devel., Legis. and House Planning, Treasury Bd., and the Priority Planning's Subcom. on Trade, 1986—. Mem. Que. Bar Assn., Can. Bar Assn. Office: House of the Commons, Parliament Bldg, Ottawa, ON Canada K1A 0A6

CHARIL, JEAN-PIERRE GEORGES, electronics firm executive; b. L'etang la ville, France, July 12, 1940; s. Pierre Louis and Simonne Andree (Hoisnard) C.; m. Josette Claire Leroy, June 5, 1965; children—Pascale, Laurence. 1st degree Bachelor, Lycee Carnot, Paris, 1959; 2d degree Bachelor, Lycee Janson de Sailly, Paris, 1961; Engr. Diplomate, Ecole Speciale Mecanique et Electricité , Paris, 1965. Electronic engr. Intertechnique, Plaisir, Yvelines, France, 1967-69; engring. mgr. Thomson Med. Telco, Paris, 1969-71; system and tech. mgr. for telecommunications Association des Ouvriers en Instruments de Precision, Paris, 1971-79; telecommunications mktg. mgr. Matra Harris Semicondrs., Paris, 1979-81; mktg. mgr. Cit Alcatel, Arcueil, France, 1981-85; sales mgr. Telecom, Mostek France, Fresnes, 1985-86; ASIC system partitioning mgr. Thomson Semicondrs., Velizy, France, 1986—; cons. Bur. Info. et Previsious Economiques, Paris, 1977—, Groupement Industries Electroniques, 1983—. Patentee in field. Mem. bd. Vivre a Clamart, 1976-79. Mem. Ingenieurs et Scientifiques de France (mem. bd. 1982—), Internat. Soc. Hybrid Microelectronics. Club: Cercle du Fusil de Chasse (Plaisir). Lodge: Saint Nom la Bretèche Lions (sec. 1985, pres. 1987). Office: SGS-Thomson, 7 Ave Galliéni, 94253 Gentilly Ceoex France

CHARITY, NEIL MITCHELL, management counsel, educator; b. Canandaigua, N.Y., Jan. 16, 1915; s. James Henry and Blanche Cordelia (Mitchell) C.; B.Chem. Engring., Cornell U., 1938; M.B.A., Harvard U., 1940; m. Lillian Santacreu, Oct. 1964; children—Mitchell, Andrew. Asst. plant mgr. Seagram Distillers Corp., N.Y.C., 1941-42, purchasing agt., 1946-49, asst. plant mgr. ops., 1950-52; asst. to pres. Coty, Inc., N.Y.C., 1953-64; internal cons. Pfizer, Inc., N.Y.C., 1965, div. controller 1966-67, long range planner, 1968-72; mgmt. counsel Econ. Devel. Council, N.Y.C., 1973-74, N.Y. State Ct. System, N.Y.C., 1975-85; adj. asst. prof. NYU, 1975-82, adj. asso. prof., 1982—; pres. Orgn. Devel. Council, N.Y.C., 1978-88. Served to lt. USNR, 1942-46. Mem. Met. N.Y. Assn. Applied Psychology, Internat. Personnel Mgrs. Assn., Internat. Personnel Mgrs. Assn. Assessment Council, Am. Soc. Macro-Engring., Japan Soc., N.Y. Acad. Scis., Am. Soc. Public Adminstrn., AAAS, World Future Soc., Human Resource Planning Soc. Clubs: Harvard (N.Y.C.); Harvard Business School New York. Home: 315 E 56th St New York NY 10022

CHARLES, PRINCE (PHILIP ARTHUR GEORGE), Prince of Wales, Earl of Chester, Duke of Cornwall and Rothesay, Baron of Renfrew, Earl of Carrick, Lord of Isles, Great Steward Scotland, b. Nov. 14, 1948; s. Prince Philip, Duke of Edinburgh and Queen Elizabeth II; B.A., Trinity Coll., Cambridge, 1970, M.A., 1975; barrister Gray's Inn, 1974, hon. bencher, 1975; student U. Wales; m. Lady Diana Spencer, July 29, 1981; children: William Arthur Philip Louis (Prince William of Wales), Henry Charles Albert David (Prince Henry of Wales). Became Duke of Cornwall and Rothesay, Earl of Carrick, Baron of Renfrew, Lord of the Isles and Gt. Steward of Scotland, 1952; created Prince of Wales and Earl of Chester, 1958, invested, 1969; created knight Order of Garter, 1958, invested, 1968; col.-in-chief Royal Regiment Wales, 1969—, Cheshire Regiment, 1977—, Gordon Highlanders, 1977—, Lord Strathcona's Horse Regiment, 1977—, Parachute Regiment, 1977—, Royal Australian Armoured Corps, 1977—, Royal Regiment Canada, 1977—, 2d King Edward VII Own Goorkhas, 1977—, Royal Winnepeg Rifles, 1977—, others; col. Welsh Guards, 1974—; comdr. Royal Navy, 1976—; chmn. Prince of Wales Comm. for Wales, 1971—; high steward Borough Windsor and Maidenhead, 1974—; pres. Prince's Trust, 1975—; chancellor U. Wales, 1976—; chmn. Queen's Silver Jubilee Trust, 1978—; pres. United World Colls., 1978—; dir. Commonwealth Devel. Corp., 1979—. Served in RAF, 1971; to comdr. Royal Navy, 1971. Created knight Grand Cross of Mil. Div. of Order of the Bath, 1975; privy councillor, 1977; knight Order of Thistle, 1977; decorated grand cross White Rose (Finland); grand cordon Supreme of Chrysanthemun (Japan); grand cross House of Orange (Netherlands); grand cross Order of Oak Crown (Luxembourg); knight Order of Elephant (Denmark); grand cross Order Ojasvi Rajanya (Nepal); grand cross So. Cross (Brazil). Hon. fellow Royal Coll. Surgeons, Royal Aero. Soc., Inst. Mech. Engrs.; royal fellow Australian Acad. Sci. Club: Royal Navy. Address: Buckingham Palace, London SW 1 England *

CHARLES, MARGOT GRATZ, nurse; b. Phila., June 23, 1938; d. Earl Jay and Margaret Greil (Gerstley) Gratz; B.S.N., Cornell U., 1961; m. David Jay Charles, Aug. 29, 1965; children—Daniel Jay, Margery Gratz. Staff nurse Hosp. U. Pa., Phila., 1961-62; head nurse cardiopulmonary renal research unit Einstein No. Div., Phila., 1962-64; instr. Hosp. Sch. Nursing Temple U., 1964-65; part time positions, 1965-72; instr. Miami Dade Community Coll., 1972-74; nurse epidemiologist Coral Reef Gen. Hosp., Miami, Fla., 1974-77; instr. Jackson Meml. Hosp. Sch. Nursing, Miami, 1977-78; nurse epidemiologist AMI Kendall Regional Med. Ctr., Miami, 1978-84. Treas., mem. Nat. Cert. Bd. Infection Control, 1985; pres. The Charles Connection Inc., . Unit leader LWV, 1971-72, tel. chmn. Dade County, 1972; active Boy Scouts, Girl Scouts. Mem. Assn. Practitioners Infection Control (chmn. ways and means Dade County 1977, dir. Dade County chpt. 1982-83), Fla. Practitioners Infection Control (treas. 1981-85, bd. dirs. 1986-87), Beta Sigma Phi, Republican. Jewish. Home: 7701 Palmetto Ct Miami FL 33156

CHARLES, MARY EUGENIA, lawyer, prime minister Commonwealth of Dominica; b. Pointe Michel, Dominica, May 15, 1919; d. John Baptiste and Josephine (Delauney) C.; student U. Toronto (Ont., Can.), 1942-46, Inns. of Ct., London, 1946-47, London Sch. Econs., 1947-50. Barrister-at-law, Dominica, 1950-80; prime minister Commonwealth of Dominica, 1980—. M.P., Dominica, 1970-75, leader opposition, 1975-79, now also minister of external affairs, fin., def. and econs. Mem. Internat. Fedn. Univ. Women, Internat. Fedn. Women Lawyers, Dominica Bar Assn., Orgn. Caribbean Commonwealth Bar Assn., Royal Commonwealth Soc. Mem. Freedom Party. Roman Catholic. Home: Wall House Commonwealth of Dominica Office: Office of Prime Minister, PO Box 121, 28 Old St, Roseau Commonwealth of Dominica *

CHARLES, REID SHAVER, municipal official; b. Wichita, Kans., Sept. 16, 1940; s. Harry Lytton and Margaret Virginia (Shaver) C.; m. Mary Elizabeth Rouland, June 1, 1963; children—Reid Shaver II, Rouland Shannon. B.A., U. Wichita, 1964, postgrad., 1964-65; postgrad. Tulane U., 1968-69; M.A., Wichita State U., 1970. Grad. fellow Wichita State U., 1965; asminstrv. asst. to city mgr. Newton (Kans.), 1965-66; planning assoc., New Orleans, 1966-69; adminstrv. asst. to exec. sec. devel. Town of Brookline (Mass.), 1969-73; chief systems planning City of Kansas City (Mo.), 1973-74, acting. dep. dir. city devel., 1974-75; prin. CHJ Assocs., Kansas City, Mo., 1975-78; adminstrv. dir. City of Lincoln (Nebr.), 1976-79; chief adminstrv. officer City of Shreveport (La.), 1979; mgmt. cons., Shreveport, 1980-83; city mgr. City of Ankeny (Iowa), 1983-84; town mgr. Town of Agawam, Mass., 1985—; lectr.in field; participant Nat. Urban Policy Roundtable IV, 1977; mem. tech. adv. group Urban Econ. Policy and Mgmt. Group, U.S. Conf. Mayors-Nat. League Cities, 1977-82. Author mcpl. budgeting manuals. Served with USAAF, 1961. Mem. Am. Polit. Sci. Assn., Am. Inst. Cert. Planners, Am. Acad. Polit. and Social Scis., Internat. City Mgmt. Assn., Am. Planning Assn., Am. Soc. Pub. Adminstrn., Pi Sigma Alpha. Quaker. Home: 2B Castle Hills Agawam MA 01001 Office: 36 Main St Agawam MA 01001

CHARLTON, JOHN FRASER, publisher; b. Sussex, Eng., Apr. 23, 1940; s. Paul Henry and Margaret (Smith) C.; m. Susan Ann Allan, Apr. 30, 1966; children: Anna, David, Lisa. Student, Winchester Coll., Hampshire, Eng., 1953-59; BA in History, Magdalene Coll., Cambridge, Eng., 1962. Trainee Longmans Green and Co. Ltd., London, 1964-65; jr. editor Chatto and Windus Ltd., London, 1965-67, dir., 1967—, chmn., 1985—; jr. editor The Hogarth Press Ltd., London, 1965-67, dir., 1970—; dir. Random House U.K. Ltd. (formerly Chatto, Bodley Head & Jonathan Cape Ltd.), London, 1977—; chmn. Gt. Gardens of Eng. Investments Ltd., Brentford, Middlesex, Eng. Clubs: Garrick, Groucho (London). Office: Chatto & Windus Ltd, 30 Bedford Sq, London WC1B 3SG, England

CHARLTON, MARGARET ELLEN JONSSON, civic worker; b. Dallas, Aug. 7, 1938, d. John Erik and Margaret Elizabeth (Fonde) Jonsson; ed. Skidmore Coll., 1956-57, So. Methodist U., 1957-60; children: Emily, Erik. Civic worker, Dallas; dir. KRLD radio, Dallas, 1970-74; dir. 1st Nat. Bank, Dallas, 1976-85, vice-chmn. dirs. trust com.; trustee Meth. Hosps., 1972-82, mem. exec. com., 1977-82; dir., chmn. exec. com. Lamplighter Sch., 1967—; mem. vis. com. dept. psychology M.I.T.; mem. vis. com. Stanford U. Libraries, 1984—; bd. dirs. Winston Sch., 1973-85; bd. dirs., mem. exec. com. Episcopal Sch., 1976-83; bd. dirs. Callier Center Communication Disorders, 1967—, v.p., 1974—; chmn. Crystal Charity Ball; active Stanford Centennial Campaign (co-chmn. nat. major gifts com.), bd. dirs. Children's Med. Center, Hope Cottage Childrens' Bur., Baylor Dental Sch., Dallas Health and Sci. Mus., Dallas YWCA, Day Nursery Assn.; trustee Dallas Mus. Art; mem. collectors com. Nat. Gallery Art. Margaret Jonsson Charlton Hosp. of Dallas named in her honor, 1973. Mem. Internat. Council Mus. of Modern Art., Ctr. for Strategic and Internat. Studies. (exec. com. of adv. bd.), mem. steering com. Stanford Centennial Campaign, 1986—, co-chmn. major gifts com., 1986—; pres. MJC Fund, Jonsson Found., Susan G. Komen Found, 1988— (mem. steering com.); trustee Southern Meth. U., U. Tex., Dallas; mem. adv. bd. Tiffany & Co., Dallas, 1987, Dallas Breakfast Group. Republican. Club: Dallas Women's, Tower, Crescent, Brook Hollow Golf, Dallas County.

CHARLU, SREENIVASAPURAM SESHA, physician, writer; b. Gudiyatham, Taluk, Tamil Nadu, India, Sept. 1, 1921; s. S. Krishnama and S. (Adilakshmamma) C.; MDH, MAMS, Old Indian Med. Coll., 1945; m. S. Rukmini Devi, Dec. 13, 1944; 8 children. Intern, Gen. Council and State Faculty of Ayurvedic Medicine W. Bengal, Calcutta, 1950; resident Jyothi Clinic, Punganuru; practice medicine specializing in chronic diseases, 1950-67; kulapathi and founder sec. Navyandhra Bharathi, Punganuru, India, 1967—; sr. mem. med. staff Jyothi Clinic, Punganuru, Andhra Pradesh, India, 1950—; hon. personal Ayurvedic physician to M.A. Ayyangar, Gov. Bihar (India), 1965-67; sec. Bharateeya Vaidya Samaj, Chittoor, 1977—. Recipient awards, including Ponna award Zamindar of Punganuru, 1965. Mem. Ayurvedic Drs. Assn. India (pres. 1952—), Acad. Gen. Practice (founder mem.), Liga Medicorum Homoepathica Internationalis (asso.), Royal Soc. Health (London) (affiliate), PEN All India Centre, Andhra Pradesh Telugu Small Newspapers Assn. (v.p. 1984—). Mem. Chattada Sri Vaishnava Semajam. Author: South Indian History on Vijayanagar Empire: 1224-1656 A.D.; (with others) Sreenivasapuram Sodarulu, 19 vols. in Telugu, 1960-68; editor, pub. Naveena monthly, 1954—. Home: Jyothi Clinic, Punganuru 517247/Andhra Pradesh India Office: Postal Ramacharlu House, Lakshmi Nagar Palmaner 517408, Andhra Pradesh India

CHARPENET, REMY LOUIS JEAN, orthopedic surgeon; b. Villemurlin, France, Dec. 20, 1948; s. Louis and Paulette (Hofer) C.; m. Chantael Charpenet, Dec. 21, 1974; children: Vinciane, Eudes, Aloïs. Biomed.

diploma, U. Nancy, France, 1978. Intern, Nancy, 1972-78; head of clinic U. Hosp. Nancy, 1978-80; practice medicine specializing in orthopedic surgery, Clinic St. Jean, Epinal, France, 1981—; Instr. Coll. Francais, Paris, 1980. Contbr. articles to med. jours. Mem. Soc. Française d'Orthopédie, Soc. d'Orthopédie de l'Est, Coll. Français des Chirurgiens Orthopédiques. Club: Round Table. Home: 5 Ave Cederlin, 88150 Thaon les Vosges France Office: Clinique St Jean, 31 rue Thiers, 88000 Epinal France

CHARTERIS, RICHARD, musicologist, writer, editor; b. Chatham Islands, New Zealand, June 24, 1948; s. Desmond Suttcliffe Charteris and Joyce (Signal) Whitty. BA, Victoria U., Wellington, 1970; MA with honors, U. Canterbury, New Zealand, 1972; PhD, U. Canterbury, U. London, 1976—. Rothmans postdoctoral fellow U. Sydney, Australia, 1976-78; postdoctoral research fellow U. Queensland, Australia, 1979-80; chief investigator Australian Research Grant Scheme U. Sydney, Australia, 1981—. Author: John Coprario: A Thematic Catalogue of his Music with a Biographical Introduction, 1977, A Catalogue of the Printed Books on Music, Printed Music and Music Manuscripts in Archbishop Marsh's Library, Dublin, 1982, Critical Commentary and Additional Material for Volumes I, II, III of Corpus Mensurabilis Musicae no. 96: the opera omnia of Alfonso Ferrabosco the Elder, 1984, Alfonso Ferrabosco the Elder (1543-1588): A Thematic Catalogue of his Music with a Biographical Calendar, 1984; editor numerous volumes of music; contbr. articles to profl. jours. Sr. scholar U. Canterbury, 1970-71; recipient Louise Dyer award Royal Musical Assn. of Gt. Britian, 1975; Mary Duncan scholar N.Z.U.G.C., 1975; Australian Acad. of Humanities traveling fellow, 1979-80. Mem. Internat. Musicological Soc. (life), Nat. Early Music Assn. Great Britain Royal Musical Assn. of Gt. Britain (life), Am. Musicological Soc. (life), Dolmetsch Found. of Gt. Britain (life), Australian Musicological Soc. (life), Viola da Gamba Socs. of Gt. Britain and Am. Office: Univ of Sydney, Dept Music, 2006 Sydney Australia

CHARTIER, ROGER ANDRÉ, social science educator; b. Lyon, Rône, France, Dec. 9, 1945; s. Georges and Laurence (Fonvielle) C.; m. Anne Marie Trépier, July 17, 1967; children: Pierre, Isabelle. Agregation d'Histoire, École Normale SupÉrieure de Saint-Cloud, France, 1969. Prof. Lycée Louis-Le Grand, Paris, 1959-70; asst. U. Paris I-Sorbonne, 1970-76; maître asst. Ecole des Hautes Etudes Scis. Sociales, Paris, 1976-83, dir. etudes, 1983—; vis. prof. Newberry Library, Chgo., 1985, Yale U., New Haven, 1985, U. Calif.-Berkeley, 1987, Cornell U., 1988. Homeor: The Cultural Uses of Print in Early Modern France, 1988, Cultural History Between Practices and Representations, 1988. Home: 51 Ave du Gen Leclerc, 76220 Viroflay France Office: Ecole des Hautes Etudes Scis Sociales, 54 Blvd Raspail, 76006 Paris France

CHARTIER, VERNON LEE, electrical engineer; b. Ft. Morgan, Colo., Feb. 14, 1939; s. Raymond Earl and Margaret Clara (Winegar) C.; m. Lois Marie Schwartz, May 20, 1967; 1 child, Neal Raymond. B.S. in Elec. Engring., U. Colo., 1963, B.S. Bus., 1963. Registered profl. engr., Pa. Research engr., cons. Westinghouse Electric Co., East Pittsburgh, Pa., 1963-75; chief high voltage engr. Bonneville Power Adminstrn., Vancouver, Wash., 1975—. Contbr. articles to profl. jours. Fellow IEEE (chmn. transmission and distbn. com.); mem. Internat. Conf. Large High Voltage Electric Systems, Acoustical Soc. Am., Internat. Electrotech. Commn., Club: Chartier Family Assn. Baptist. Home: 5190 SW Dover Ln Portland OR 97225 Office: Bonneville Power Adminstrn PO Box 491 Vancouver WA 98666

CHARUE, JEAN L., university educator; b. Paris, July 20, 1930; s. Charles J. and Marie T. (Ferret) C.; m. Jeanine M. Ferrucci, Aug. 28, 1957. Lic., Ecole Normale Superieure, Paris, 1954, Agregation, 1956, Doctorat d'Etat, 1976. Prof. secondary sch. Belfort, France, 1959, Dijon, France, 1959-62; asst. U. Burgundy, Dijon, France, 1962-67; maitré asst. U. Paris, 1967-68; chargé d'enseignement U. Burgundy, Dijon, France, 1969-79, instr., 1979—. Editor: Ferdinand V. Saar, 1976, Correspondence Saar/Altmann, 1984; contbr. articles to profl. jours. Served with French Army, 1957-59. Recipient Palmes Academiques award, 1976. Mem. Internat. Vereinigung, Germanischer Sprach Und Literaturwissenschaft, Assn. des Germanistes de d'Enseignement Superieur, Grillparzer Gesellschaft, Internat. Lenau Gesellschaft. Roman Catholic. Clubs: Police Shooting (Dijon); Ordre Internat. (des Anysetiers). Office: Univ de Bourgogne, 2 Blvd Gabriel, F 21000 Dijon France

CHASE, ALLEN, investment banker; b. Los Angeles, Sept. 11, 1911; s. Edward Tilden and Lenna (Prather) C.; B.S., U. Calif. at Los Angeles, 1933; postgrad. London Sch. Econs., U. London (Eng.), 1934; children—Charlene, Diane Chase Randolph. Salesman, Chase Securities Co., Los Angeles, 1934-39; pres. Standardized Aircraft Co., Los Angeles, 1939—; chmn. bd. dirs. Esperence Plains Pty. Ltd., Australia, 1956—, Agra Paraguay, 1967—; pres. Allen Chase & Co., 1964—; dir. Allied Pastoral Enterprises, Pty. Ltd., Australia, Australian Ocean Products, Bank of Scottsdale, Trans World Bank, Pacific Basin Industries, Pty. Ltd. Clubs: University, Riviera Country, Bel Air Country, Beverly Hills Wine and Food Soc., Coronado Yacht, Kaneoe Yacht. Conceived establishment over one million virgin acres to agr. in single area by pvt. enterprise. Home: Marina City Club Marina City Dr Marina del Rey CA 90291 Other: Wandollan Sta, No Ter Australia Office: Marina City Club 4216 Marina City Dr #204-G Marina del Rey CA 90292

CHASE, FRANCIS MICHAEL, manufacturing executive; b. Canton, Mass., Feb. 27, 1920; s. Francis G. and Mary A. (Griffin) C.; m. Barbara Ann Sullivan, Apr. 19, 1952; children—Francis G., Michael C., Anne L. B.S. in Civil Engring., U. N.H., 1941. Pres., chmn. bd. Chase & Sons, Inc., Randolph, Mass., 1947—; chmn., chief exec. officer Columbia Chase Corp., Braintree, Mass., 1971—; chmn. bd. Royston Labs., Inc., Pitts., 1973—; bd. dirs. Internat. Contacts Inc., Cohasset, Mass. Bd. dirs. Family Counseling and Guidance Ctrs., Braintree, World Affairs Council, Boston. Served as capt. U.S. Army, 1941-46, ETO. Decorated Bronze Star medal. Mem. World Bus. Council (founding), Chief Execs. Orgn. Republican. Roman Catholic. Clubs: Metropolitan (N.Y.C.); Orleans (Mass.) Yacht; Cohasset Golf. Office: Columbia Chase Corp 220 Forbes Rd Braintree MA 02184

CHASE, LORIENE ECK, psychologist; b. Sacramento; d. Walter and Genevieve (Bennetts) Eck; A.B., U. So. Calif., 1948, M.A., 1949, Ph.D., 1953; m. Leo Goodman-Malamuth, 1946 (div. 1951); 1 son, Leo; m. 2d, Allen Chase, Mar. 4, 1960 (div.); m. 3d, Clifton W. King, 1974. Psychologist, Spastic Children's Found., Los Angeles, 1952-55, Inst. Group Psychotherapy, Beverly Hills, Calif., 1957-59; pvt. practice, 1953—; v.p. VSP Exec. Relocation Consultants. Condr., Dr. Loriene Chase Show, ABC-TV, Hollywood, Calif. 1966—. Cons., Camarillo State Hosp.; bd. dirs., pres.'s circle U. So. Calif.; founding mem. Achievement Rewards for Coll. Scientists; bd. dirs. Chase-King Personal Devel. Center, Los Angeles; v.p. Chase-King Prodns. Inc., Los Angeles, Shell Beach, Calif.; exec. bd. Cancer Research Center, Los Angeles. Writer syndicated newspaper column Casebook of Dr. Chase. Served with Waves World War II. Recipient Woman of Year in Psychology award Am. Mothers Com. Mem. Diadames, Assn. Media Psychologists, Les Dames de Champagne, Dame de Rotisseur, Nat. Art Assn., AFTRA, Screen Actors Guild, Internat. Platform Assn. Clubs: Regency, Lakeside Country, Santa Maria Country. Author: The Human Miracle; columnist Westways mag. Address: 375 Palomar Shell Beach CA 93449

CHASE, MORRIS, international management consultant; b. N.Y.C., May 19, 1918; s. Samuel and Bessie (Rabinowitz) Cherkasky; m. Claire Pernitz, Mar. 14, 1942; children—Sylvia, Viviane. B.B.A., Coll. City N.Y., 1939; student econ. sci., U. Paris, 1959. C.P.A., N.Y. State. Mem. staff several C.P.A. firms 1939-42; asst. to dir. finance and accounting Am. Joint Distbn. Com., 1946-48; dep. controller Marshall Plan mission to France, 1949; controller, finance officer U.S. spl. econ. mission to Cambodia, Laos and Vietnam, 1950; controller U.S. spl. econ. mission to Yugoslavia, 1951; economist Office U.S. Rep. in Europe, Paris, 1952-53; chmn. Internat. Bd. Auditors for Infrastructure, NATO., Paris, 1954-60; dir. infrastructure program Internat. Bd. Auditors for Infrastructure, NATO., 1961-68, chmn. def. installations com., 1966-68, chmn. payments and progress com; cons. NATO Air Def. Ground Environment Consortium, 1968—. Served to capt. USAAF, 1942-46; maj. Res. Mem. Am. Inst. C.P.A.'s, N.Y. State Soc. C.P.A.'s, Fed. Accountants Assn. (pres. Paris 1961-62), Fed. Govt. Accountants Assn. Paris (pres. 1964-65), Beta Gamma Sigma. Home: Flaminia C, Crans-sur-Sierre, Valais Switzerland also: 163 Ave Winston Churchill, 1180 Brussels Belgium

CHASTEL, ANDRÉ ADRIEN, art historian, educator; b. Paris, Nov. 15, 1912; s. Adrien Marie and Marie Isabelle (Morin) C.; student Ecole Normale Supé rieure, 1933; Agregation des lettres, 1937, Doctorat è s lettres, 1951; m. Paule-Marie Grand de Saint-Avit, 1942; children—Louis, Arnaud (dec.), Laurent. Prof., Lycéte Rollin, Henry IV, Carnot; asst. Inst. Art and Archaeology, Paris, 1945-48; dir. d'Etudes, Ecole pratique des Haute Etudes (IV sect.), Paris, 1951-81; prof. Sorbonne, 1955-70; prof. College de France, Paris, 1970-84; art critic newspaper Le Monde, Paris, 1950—; v.p. Internat. Com. Art History, 1969—; pres. French Com. Art History, 1970-77; Andrew Mellon lectr. Nat. Gallery, Washington, 1977. Served with French Army, 1939-40. Decorated Croix de Guerre, Légion d'Honneur, Palmes Acadé miques, Com. Repubblica Italiana. Mem. L'Institut Acadé mie des Inscriptions et Belles-Lettres, Am. Acad. Arts and Scis. Club: Racing of France. Author: L'art italien, 1947, 83, English edit., 1963; Art et Humanisme à Florence, 1949, 82; Marsile Ficin et l'Art, 1954, 75; La Renaissance Méridionale, le Grand Atelier, 1965; La crise de la Renaissance, le mythe de la Renaissance, 1967; Fables, 1988, Formes Figures, 2 vols., 1978, Italian edit., 1988; L'Image dans le Miroir, 1980; The Sack of Rome, 1983, French edit., 1984; Chronique de la peinture italienne, 1983; Musca Depicta, 1984; Cardinal Louis d'Aragon, 1986, Italin edit., 1987; L'illustre incomprise (Mona Lisa), 1988; La grotesque, 1988; editor Revue de l'Art, 1969-88. Home: 30 rue de Lubeck, 75116 Paris France Office: Coll de France, 11 Place Marcelin Berthelot, 75005 Paris France

CHATEAU, GEORGES MICHEL, petroleum engineer; b. St. Leonard de Noblat, France, May 13, 1934; came to U.S., 1981; s. Jean Roger and Marcelle M. (Lachaise) C.; m. Ruth M. Loeffler, June 12, 1964. Engr., Ecole Nationale Superieure de Mecanique de Nantes, France, 1957, Ecole Nationale Superieure des Petroles, Rueil-Malmaison, France, 1959. Drilling engr. S.N. Repal, Algiers, Algeria, 1962-65; offshore engr. Elf Aquitaine, Pau-Paris-Bordeaux, France, 1965-81, Port-Gentil, Gabon, 1968; frontiers arctic and offshore studies and ops. staff Elf Aquitaine Petroleum, Houston, 1981—. Contbr. articles to profl. publs. Patentee in field. Served with French Armed Forces, 1959-62. Mem. Soc. Petroleum Engrs., ASME, Assn. Francaise des Techniciens du Petrole. Current work: Deep sea and Arctic engineering for oil and gas production facilities, design and on-site full scale live tests. Subspecialties: Petroleum engineering; Mechanical engineering. Home: 5000 Montrose Blvd Apt 13B Houston TX 77006

CHATELIN, FRANÇOISE HELENE, mathematics educator, industrial engineer; b. Grenoble, France, Sept. 21, 1941; d. Jean Marcel and Marguerite (Bosson) Laborde; divorced; children: Laurent, Isabelle. Maitrise in math., U. Paris, 1962; agrégé in math., Ecole Normale Superieure, Paris, 1963; PhD in Math., U. Grenoble, 1971. Teaching asst. U. Grenoble, 1963-64, asst. prof., 1964-71, prof., 1976-81, 82-84; research fellow IBM, San Jose, Calif., 1974-75; sr. scientist IBM, Yorktown Heights, N.Y., 1981-82; engr. IBM Sci. Ctr., Paris, 1984—; prof. U. Paris Dauphine, 1984—. Author: Spectral Approximation of Linear Operators, 1983, PSE in Scientific Computing North Holland, 1987, Valeurs propes de matrices Masson, 1988. Mem. Soc. Indsl. Math. Applications, Soc. Math. France, Soc. Math. Applications and Indsl. Home: 18 Rue Pierre Anoux, 92190 Meudon France Office: IBM Sci Ctr, 5 Place Vendôme, 75021 Paris Cedex 01 France

CHATROO, ARTHUR JAY, lawyer; b. N.Y.C., July 1, 1946; s. George and Lillian (Leibowitz) C. BChemE, CCNY, 1968; JD cum laude, New York Law Sch., 1979; MBA with distinction, NYU, 1982. Bar: N.Y. 1980. Process engr. Standard Oil Co. of Ohio, various locations, 1968-73; process specialist BP Oil, Inc., Marcus Hook, Pa., 1974-75; sr. process engr. Sci. Design Co., Inc., N.Y.C., 1975-78; mgr. spl. projects The Halcon SD Group, N.Y.C., 1978-82; corp. counsel, tax and fin. The Lubrizol Corp., Wickliffe, Ohio, 1982-85; gen. counsel Lubrizol Enterprises, Inc., Wickliffe, 1985. Mem. Met. Parks Adv. com., Allen County, Ohio, 1973. Mem. ABA, Am. Chem. Soc., Am. Inst. Chem. Engrs., N.Y. State Bar Assn., Cleve. Bar Assn., Jaycees (personnel dir. Lima, Ohio chpt. 1972-73), Omega Chi Epsilon, Beta Gamma Sigma. Club: Toastmasters. Home: 1 Bratenahl Pl Suite 705 Bratenahl OH 44108 Office: Lubrizol Enterprises Inc 29400 Lakeland Blvd Wickliffe OH 29400

CHATTERJEE, RAMDAS, biochemist; b. Barrackpur, West Bengal, India, Jan. 15, 1947. BS, St. Xavier's Coll., Calcutta, India, 1966; MS, U. Calcutta, 1968, PhD in Biochemistry, 1978. Jr. research fellow Indian Inst. Chem. Biology, Calcutta, 1969-72, sr. research fellow, 1972-74; research assoc. U. Baroda, India, 1975-76; biochemist Baroda Med. Coll., 1976-78; jr. scientific officer Chittaranajan Nat. Cancer Ctr., Calcutta, 1978—, sr. sci. officer, 1986—, head dept. tumor virology; with Research Ctr., Calcutta, 1978-83; research assoc. U. Pa., 1983-85, U. Pitts., 1985-86; mem. bd. examiners for biochem. U. Calcutta. Contbr. articles to profl. jours. Jr. and sr. research fellow Council Sci. Indsl. Research Ctr., New Delhi, 1969-74. Mem. Soc. Biol. Chemists India, Tissue Culture Assn. India (sec. 1988). Club: Milan Mitali (pres. 1986—). Home: SN Banerjee Rd, Barrackpore, West Bengal 743101, India Office: Chittaranjan Nat Cancer Research Ctr, 37 S P Mukherjee Rd, Calcutta, West Bengal 700026, India

CHATTERJEE, SATYA NARAYAN, medical educator, surgeon; b. Calcutta, India, Dec. 31, 1934; came to U.S., 1973; s. R. N. and J. C.; m. Patricia Sheppard, Sept. 26, 1964; children—Sharmila, Shalini, Arun. Inter.Sci., Scottish Ch. Coll., Calcutta, 1951; M.B.B.S., R.G. Kar Med. Coll., Calcutta, 1957. Diplomate: Brit. Bd. Surgery. Registrar dept. surgery North Staff Royal Infirmary, Stoke, Eng., 1963-64; med. supt. A.R.T. Co., Margherita, India, 1965-69; registrar transplant unit U. Edinburgh, Scotland, 1970-73; clin. and research fellow U. So. Calif. Med. Sch., Los Angeles, 1973-75; asst. prof. surgery UCLA, 1975-77; assoc. prof. surgery U. Calif.-Davis, Sacramento, 1977-84, prof. surgery, 1984-88; cons. surgeon Martin Luther King Gen. Hosp., Los Angeles, 1975-77; dir. renal transplant unit No. Calif. Tissue Bank, San Jose, 1977-78. Editor: Surgical Clinics of North America, 1978; author: Manual of Renal Transplantation, 1979, Renal Transplanation: A Multidisciplinary Approach, 1980, Organ Transplantation, 1982. R.G. Kar Med. Coll. scholar, 1954. Fellow ACS; mem. Am. Soc. Transplant Surgeons, Assn. Acad. Surgery, Transplantation Soc., Royal Soc. Medicine, Western Assn. Transplant Surgeons (pres. 1979-80). Hindu. Club: Tennis (Davis). Home: PO Box 3102 El Macero CA 95618 Office: 4301 X St Sacramento CA 95817

CHATTOPADHYAY, SUKUMAR, technical consultant; b. Calcutta, India, Aug. 30, 1950; s. Sudhansu and Menaka (Bandopadhyay) C.; m. Anindita Mukherjee, June, 1986. B.S. in Metallurgy and Materials Sci., U. Calcutta, 1970; M.S., U. Sheffield, 1972, Ph.D., 1975. Chartered engr., U.K. Quality control metallurgist Metal Box Co. of India Ltd., 1970-71; research and devel. metallurgist Tata Iron & Steel Co. Ltd., India, 1971-72; process metallurgist Brit. Steel Corp., 1975-76; postdoctoral research fellow Imperial Coll. Sci. and Tech., London, 1976-80; vis. prof. Universidad Autó noma Metropolitana, Mexico City, 1979; project mgr., magnetic and elec. materials Instituto de Investigaciones Elé ctricas, Cuernavaca, Morelos, Mexico, 1980—, now coordinator magnetic and elec. materials; mem. com. for import Substitution Govt. of Mex. Contbr. articles to profl. jours. Calcutta U. merit scholar, 1965-70; Brit. Council scholar, 1972-73; Robert Styring scholar, 1973-75; Research Council U.K. fellow, 1976-80; Nat. Research Scientist awardee Mex. Sci. Research Council and Dept. Edn. Mem. Instn. Metallurgists London, Instn. Chartered Engrs. London, Metall. Soc. of AIME, Am. Soc. Metals, Am. Ceramic Soc., ASTM, IEEE, Japan Inst. Metals. Home: Apartado Postal 564, Admon 3, 62271 Cuernavaca Morelos Mexico Office: Dept Materiales Inst de Investigaciones Elé ct, Apartado Postal 475 Interior Internado P, almira, 62000 Cuern Mexico

CHATTOPADHYAYA, HARINDRANATH AGORNATH, poet, film actor; b. Hyderabad, India, Apr. 2, 1898; s. Agornath Mathuranath and Varada Sundari C.; m. Kamila Dhareshwar (div.) ; 1 child, Ram; m. Sundarvali Achari, Aug. 15, 1947; 1 child, Lakshman. LittD (hon.), Andhra U., Hyderabad, 1980; D B.C. (hon.) Royal Nat. award for lit., Delhi, India, 1982. Producer emritus Doordarshan India, TV and Radio of India, Bombay, 1975-78. Author: (poems) Feast of Youth, 1916, Perfume of Earth, 1920, Magic Tree, 1925, Feast of Thirsts, Iconoclast, A Bird Sang on a Bough, Reflections, 1988. Mem. Parliament, Vijaywada, Andhra Pradesh, India, 1950-55. Recipient Padmabhushan Govt. of India, 1972, Dr. B.C. Roy Nat. Lit. award, New Delhi, 1982. Home and Office: 10 Kismet Carter Rd, Bandra, 400050 Bombay India

CHATWANI, VIDYADHAR POPATLAL, international agency executive; b. Zanzibar, Tanzania, May 11, 1929; s. Popatlal Jadavji and Devkunver C.; m. Chandrika, Feb. 15, 1962; children—Sheila, Neha, Rupesh. B. Commerce, Sydenham Coll., Bombay, India, 1952; mem. Inst. Chartered Accts, Eng., 1957. Pvt. practice acctg., Daressalaam, Tanzamia, 1957-62; internal auditor Williamson Diamonds Ltd., Mwadui, Tanzania, 1962-68; auditor UNRWA, 1968-75, sr. auditor, 1975-78, chief audit div. hdqrs., Vienna, 1983—. Fellow Inst. Chartered Accts. in England and Wales; mem. Inst. Internal Auditors. Hindu. Home: 15/2 Naaffgasse, A-1180 Vienna Austria Office: Vienna Internat Ctr, PO Box 800, A-1400 Vienna Austria

CHAU, WING FAN THOMAS, pharmacist; b. Tsuen Wan, Hong Kong, Nov. 24, 1957; s. Tik-Hin Chau and Yuet-Chun Wong. BS in Pharmacy, U. Wyoming, 1981; cert. in hosp. and nursing adminstrn., Chinese U. Hong Kong, 1985, diploma in nursing adminstrn., 1986-87; cert. in 2d aseptic dispensing course, Nat. U. Hosp., Singapore, 1988. Registered pharmacist, Hong Kong. Teaching asst. pharm. preparation U. Wyoming, Laramie, 1980, asst. in Chemistry, 1981; pharmacy intern County Hosp. Cheyenne (Wyoming), 1981, Gibson's Discount Pharmacy, Cheyenne, 1981; dispenser Our Lady of Maryknoll Hosp., Kowloon, Hong Kong, 1982-83, pharmacist, 1987—; dispenser Hong Kong Med. and Health Dept., 1983-87. Author: Trouble in a Hospital, 1984; mem. edit. staff Jour. Practicing Pharmacists, 1987—. Mem. Govt. Dispenser Assn. (exec. com. 1984-87), Wong Tai Sin Health Promotion Assn. (exec. com. 1987—), Hong Kong Nursing Mgmt. Soc. (sec. 1986—), Pharm. Soc. Hong Kong (editorial subcom. 1987—, exec. com. 1988), Hong Kong Practicing Pharmacists Assn., Rho Chi (treas. 1980-81). Home: 78C 5F Kwan Mun Hau St, Sha Tsui Rd, Tsuen Wan Hong Kong Office: Our Lady of Maryknoll Hosp, Sha Tin Pass Road, Wong Tai Sin, Kowloon Hong Kong

CHAUDHRY, JAWADE OSMAN, metal processing company executive, farmer; b. Nairobi, Kenya, Feb. 13, 1957; s. Abdul Ghafar Chaudhry and Zubeda Begum; m. Frah Tabasum Mauladad, Mar. 29, 1985; 1 child, Nadir Jawade. BS, U.S. Internat. U., Nairobi, 1984. Gen. mgr. Cherangani Farms, Ltd., Kitale, Kenya, 1976-77; mng. dir. River Hardware Stores, Ltd., Nairobi, 1978-81; trustee, adminstr. Group of Companies, Nairobi, 1980-84; mng. dir. Kenya Marifarms, Ltd., Nairobi, 1982-86, Ghafar, Ltd., Nairobi, 1980-87; chmn. Precision Casting, Ltd., Nairobi, 1986—; bd. dirs. Cloverdale Farm Ltd., Old Mark Soap Factory Ltd. Moslem. Club: Royal Nairobi Golf. Lodge: Fidelity. Office: Precision Castings Ltd, Mogadishu Rd, PO Box 46102, Nairobi Kenya

CHAUDHRY, TALIB HUSSAIN, physician, surgeon; b. Shorkot, Punjab, Pakistan, Dec. 22, 1951; s. Shah Mohammed and Daulat Begum Chaudry.; m. Simi Habib, Sept. 26, 1986. BS in Medicine, Sind Med. Coll., Karachi, Pakistan, 1980. House surgeon Sarfaraz Rafiqui Shaheed Hosp. div. Karachi Met. Corp., Karachi, 1980-81; resident med. officer Karachi Port Trust Hosp., 1981—, casualty med. officer, 1981, incharge med. ward, 1982-84, asst. to chief med. officer, 1984-86, adminstrn., cons., male out patient dept., 1987—; cons. in gen. practice. Assoc. editor: Quick Index of Medical Preparations Quarterly, 1980—. Mem. Pakistan Med. Assn. (mem. exec. com. 1983-87, mem. W.H.O. com. XVI biennial med. conf., 1984), Pakistan Soc. Physicians (mem. audiovisual com. Karachi chpt. 1987), First All Pakistan Annual Congress Gastroenterology and Endoscopy (mem. organizing com., 1984).

CHAUDRY, IRSHAD HUSSAIN, medical biochemist; b. Jalander-Musaibpur, Punjab, India, May 2, 1945; came to U.S., 1971; s. Noor Mohammed and Anayat (Bagam) C.; m. Micheline Denise Laperle, Mar. 22, 1974; children: Khalil, Jameel, Sabiha. BS, Sind U., Pakistan, 1965, MS, 1966; PhD, Monash U., Clayton, Australia, 1970. Asst. prof. Washington U., St. Louis, 1971-75; assoc. prof. Yale U., New Haven, 1976-83, prof., 1983-86; prof. surgery and physiology, dir. surg. research labs. Mich. State U., East Lansing, 1986—; research cons. U. Toronto, Ont., Can., 1971-72, Monash U., 1978; ad hoc cons. NIH, Bethesda, Md., 1982-85, mem. site visit team, 1983-85, surgery, anesthesiology & trauma study sect., 1986—; mem. VA surgery study sect., 1987—. Mem. editorial bd. Am. Jour. Physiology, 1982—, Circulatory shock, 1981—, Jour. Critical Care, 1987—; contbr. chpts. to books. Mem. Shock Soc. (founding mem.; exec. council 1984-86, chmn. publ. com.; session chmn. 1983-85), Am. Physiol. Soc., Am. Coll. Nutrition, Am. Soc. Mgrs. Research, Surg. Infection Soc., Reticuloendothelial Soc., Soc. Critical Care Medicine, Soc. Exptl. Biology and Medicine, Sigma Xi. Republican. Muslim.

CHAUNU, PIERRE RENE, history educator; b. Belleville, Verdun, France, Aug. 17, 1923; s. Jean and Heloise (Charles) C.; m. Huguette Catella, Sept. 13, 1947; 6 children, (1 dec.). Mem. faculty Sch. Advanced Hispanic Studies, Madrid, 1948-51; with CNRS, 1956-59, now mem. directorate, mem. sci. com., history sec., 1980—; with U. Caen (France), 1959-70; prof. history Sorbonne, U. Paris, 1970—; assoc. prof. Faculte de Theologie Reformee, Aix-en-Provence, France, 1974; mem. sect. Conseil Econ. et Social, 1976-77; pres. Conseil Superieur des Corps Universitaires, 1977. Author numerous books, the most recent being: Le sursis, 1979; Histoire et foi, Histoire et imagination, 1980; Reforme et contre-reforme; Eglise, Culture et Societe, Histoire et Decadence, 1981 (Premier prix Gobert 1982); La France, 1982; Ce que Je Crois, 1982; Le Chemin des Mages, 1983; Combats Pour L'Histoire, 1983; L'Historien dans tous les états, 1984; L'Historien en Cet Instant, 1985; contbr. numerous articles to profl. jours. Decorated chevalier Legion d'honneur. Mem. Acad. des Sciences morales et politiques. Office: Universite Paris-Sorbonne, 1 Rue V Cousin, 75005 Paris France *

CHAUVIN, MARCEL JEAN CLAUDE, anesthesiology educator, researcher; b. Paris, Jan. 2, 1950; s. George and Jeanne (Duperron) C.; m. Hélène Sophie Costes, June 1988. Student, Hôpitaux de Paris, 1977-81; diploma of cardiology, U. Paris, 1981, diploma of anesthesia, 1983. Asst. in pharmacology U. Paris, 1975-78, chef de clinique, asst. des hôpitaux, 1981-83, asst. prof. anesthesiology, 1983—, prof., 1988—. Contbr. articles to profl. jours. Home: 7 Rue de Saint Cloud, Suresnes 92150, France Office: Hopital Ambroise Pare, Dept d'Anesthesie, 9 Ave Charles de Gaulle, Boulogne 92100, France

CHAUVIN, RICHARD LUCIEN, software company executive; b. Manchester N.H., Apr. 6, 1949; s. Lucien F. and Violette G. (LeMay) C.; m. Theresa Ann Pachtner, June 20, 1977; children—Christopher Scott, Michael Andrew. Computer supr. Nat. CSS, San Francsico 1974-76, tech. rep., 1976-77, computer systems programmer, 1977-78, sr. systems programmer, 1978-79; with Fireman's Fund Ins. Co., San Rafael, Calif., 1979-80; with Magnuson Computer Systems, San Jose, Calif., 1979-80, systems software specialist, 1980, mgr. systems software, 1980-82; owner Chauvin Cons., 1982—; chmn. bd., chief fin. officer, sr. exec. v.p. Dovetail Systems, Inc., Sunnyvale, Calif., 1982-85; pres. Software Assistance, Sunnyvale, 1984-85; founder Virtual Techs. Inc., San Carlos, Calif., 1988—. Served with U.S. Air Force, 1968-74. Mem. Assn. Computing Machinery, Aircraft Owners and Pilots Assn. Home and Office: 418 Ridge Rd San Carlos CA 94070

CHAVES, EDUARDO BELTRÃO, medicinal herbs company executive; b. Rio de Janeiro, Brazil, Aug. 31, 1951; s. Rubem Baptista and Iêda (Beltrão) C. Diploma in publicity advt. and pub. relations, Fed. U. Rio de Janeiro, 1977. Advt. copywriter CM Publicidade, Rio de Janeiro, 1972-75; publicity cons. Franco's Sch., Rio de Janeiro, 1975-78; audio visual writer A.P.C. Skills do Brasil, São Paulo, 1978-79, audio visual test cons., 1979; jr. mgr. Florasil, Rio de Janeiro, 1979-81, sr. mgr., 1981-84, gen. mgr., 1984-85, exec., 1985—. Author: Mensagem dos Deuses, 1976; also articles. Awarded 1st prize for writing contest on importance of aviation in present world Brazilian Assn. Propaganda, 1973. Hon. mem. Ancient Astronaut Soc. (pres. com. for orgn. of 4th world conf. 1976-77). Mem. Green Party. Club: Sheraton Internat. (Cin.). Office: Florasil, Rua Silva Rego 34, 20970 Rio de Janeiro Brazil

CHAVES, JOSÉ MARÍA, educator, lawyer, diplomat; b. Bogotá, Colombia, Aug. 19, 1922; s. Carlos Chaves and María García de C.; m.

Elena Gómez y Samperio; children—Cristina María, Tomás José. Bachiller, Bogotá, 1939, certificate in anthropology, 1942, J.D., 1945; D.Sc. (hon.), U. Antióquia, 1948; M.A., Columbia, 1951, Ph.D., 1953; LL.D., U. Popayán, Colombia, 1957. Editor-in-chief Revista Colegio del Rosario (arts and letters mag.), Colombia; gen. legal duties specializing in public adminstrn.; asst. atty. gen. Colombia, Bogotá, 1942-45; instr. Romance langs. Columbia U., N.Y.C., 1945-48, 50-51; founder, 1st dean faculty U. Andes, Bogotá, 1948-49; head area studies Queens Coll., N.Y. U., 1951-53; counselor Colombian Embassy, Washington, 1953-55; prof. internat. law U. Colombia, 1955-58, U. Paris, 1957; guest prof. internat. law and relations Brit. Council, various univs. Eng., Scotland, 1957; dir., chief exec. Am. Found. for Cultural Popular Action, Inc. (pvt. internat. orgn. for mass edn. by radio), N.Y.C., 1958—; dir. Center Latin Am. Studies, City U. N.Y.; chmn. Hispanic Am. editorial bd. Grolier, Inc., 1971—; ambassador extraordinary, permanent del. Iberoam. Bur. Edn. to UN; A.E. and P., permanent rep. Grenada to OAS; permanent rep. orgn. Iberoam. Countries to UN and OAS, 1986—; alt. gov. World Bank and Internat. Monetary Fund, 1974-77; chmn. C.I.P., 1972—; Organizer, dir. tech. assistance mission Unitarian Service Com. in Latin Am.; dir. gen. Nat. Univ. Fund, Colombia, 1955-58. Editor-in-chief: Grolier Spanish Universal Ency; author: Chaves Plan for settlement religious conflict between Caths. and Protestants in Latin Am; Author: Francisco de Vitoria. Founder International Law, 1945, Intergroup relations in the Spain of Cervantes, 1953, University Reform in Colombia, 1957. Decorated Legion of Honor, France; gran cruz Order of St. Constantine the Gt.; comdr., knight comdr. Grand Order Isabel La Católica (Spain); knight comdr. Alfonso El Sabio; recipient medaglia universitaria U. Pro Deo. Rome, 1957; medalla de los Andes U. Andes, 1958; grand cross Vasco Núnez de Balboa Panama, 1970; grand cross Juan P. Duarte Sanchez y Mella Dominican Republic, 1970; Medal of Jerusalem Israel, 1972; grand cross Order of Malta, 1976; grand cross Order Justice Law and Peace of Mex., 1977; grand cross Order Latin Am. Unity, 1986. Mem. Internat. Law Assn., Inter-Am. Bar Assn., Acad. Polit. Sci., MLA, Academia Hispano Americana, Assn. for Latin Am. Unity (founder, pres. 1984), Summit Council for World Peace (dir. 1987), Phi Delta Kappa. Clubs: Metropolitan, Columbia U. (N.Y.C.); Quill of U.S.A. (pres.). Home: 118 E 60th St New York NY 10022 Office: 393 Fifth Ave New York NY 10016

CHAVEZ, JOSE GUADALUPE, aerospace company executive; b. Chihuahua, Mex., Dec. 14, 1950; s. Alfredo and Petra (Flores) C.; m. Lilia Irene Mena, June 4, 1976; children: Miguel Alberto, Laura Irene. BSEE, U. Tex.; MA in Mgmt., Redlands U.; postgrad., Western State U. Sr. staff engr. Hughes Aircraft Corp., Fullerton, Calif., 1978-80, head acctg. sect., 1980-81; pres., chief engr. Guaranteed Energy Mgmt. Corp., Fullerton, 1981-83; cons. Tech. Devel. Systems, Fullerton, 1983-84, pres., 1985—; cons. U.S. Energy Mgmt. Corp., Encino, Calif., 1984-85; pres. Facilities Automation, Orange, Calif., 1985—; cons. Hughes Aircraft, 1982-83, IBM, Tucson, 1982, Power Efficiency Mgmt. Cor., 1983-84, Infotec, Costa Mesa, Calif., 1984-86. State Dem. rep., El Paso, Tex., 1972; mem. YMCA, Orange County Indian Guides. Recipient Outstanding Performance award Enlog of Calif., 1985, Achievement award U.S. Energy Corp. of Nev., 1986. Mem. IEEE, Assn. Energy Engring., ASHRAE, Orange County C. of C. Libertarian. Roman Catholic. Home: 161 La Paz Anaheim Hills CA 92807

CHAWLA, MAN MOHAN, mathematician, educator; b. Lahore, Punjab, West Pakistan, Sept. 1, 1939; s. Gian Chand and Tarawati C.; m. Anju, Aug. 9, 1969; children: Dhruv, Ritika. BSc (Hons.) Math., U. Delhi, India, 1960, MSc Math., 1962; PhD in Numerical Analysis, Indian Inst. Tech., New Delhi, 1968. Lectr., Indian Inst. Tech., 1963-68, asst. prof., 1971-78, prof., 1978—, head dept. math., 1986—; vis. asst. prof. U. Ill., Urbana, 1969-71; vis. prof. State U. N.Mex., Las Cruces, 1980-81, computing lab. U. Oxford, Eng., 1975-76; reviewer Am. Math. Soc., Assn. for Computing Machinery; referee various internat. jours. Edit. rev. bd. Internat. Jour. Computer Math., Eng., 1986—; contbr. research articles to internat. sci. jours. Fellow Inst. Math. and Its Applications U.K., Soc. for Indsl. and Applied Math. Avocations: reading general scientific literature and history of science. Home: III/III/B-1, I I T Campus, Hauz Khas, New Delhi 110 016, India Office: Indian Inst Tech, Dept Math, Hauz Khas 100 016, India

CHAWLA, NRIPJIT SINGH, hotel executive; b. Simla, India, Dec. 25, 1949; s. Bhagat Singh and Prakash Kaur (Dang) C.; m. Nilima Bhalla, May 4, 1975; children: Simran, Shabad. BA, Punjab U., Chandigarh, India, 1967; MBA, Indian Inst. Mgmt., Calcutta, India, 1970. Summer trainee Hindustan Lever Ltd., Bombay, 1969; publicity officer India Tourism Devel. Corp., New Delhi, 1971-74; sales mgr. Welcomgroup ITC Hotels, Madras, Indi, 1974-76, gen. mgr. Presidency Kid Leather Ltd., Madras, 1976-78; regional sales mgr. Welcomgroup Hotels ITC Ltd., New Delhi, 1978-79, gen. mgr. mktg. WG Mughal Sheraton, 1985-87, dir. mktg. devel. Welcomgroup, 1987—; bd. dirs. Internat. Travel House Ltd., New Delhi. Mem. Duke Edinburgh's Award Com., New Delhi, 1987. Mem. All India Mgmt. Assn. (mem. research com., 1987—), Pacific Asia Travel Assn. (mem. exec. com. India chpt., chmn. publicity and promotion com. 1986—), Indian Assn. Tour Operators (exec. com.). Sikh. Club: Skal of Delhi. Office: Welcomgroup Hotels Hdqrs, Chanakyapuri, New Delhi 110021, India

CHAZOV, YEVGENY, cardiologist; b. Gorky, USSR, June 10, 1929. M.D., Ph.D., Kiev Med. Inst., 1958. Sr. sci. worker Inst. Therapy, 1959-63; dep. dir. Inst. Therapy, USSR Acad. Med. Sci., 1963-65, dir. Inst. Cardiology, 1965-67; dep. minister pub. health, 1967-87; minister pub. health USSR Ministry, 1987—; mem. Supreme Soviet, 1974-84; dir. Cardiology Research Centre, Acad. Med. Sci., 1975-82. Author: (with others) Myocardial Infarcation, 1971; Cardiac Rhythm Disorders, 1972; Anti-Coagulants and Fibrinolytics, 1977. Contbr. articles to profl. publs. Recipient Hero of Socialist Labour State prize, 1969, 76; Lenin prize, 1982; UNESCO Peace prize, 1984. Mem. USSR Soc. Cardiology (pres.), Internat. Physicians for Prevention of Nuclear War (co-pres. 1980). Office: USSR Cardiology Research Ctr, Rachmanovsky per 3, Moscow 101431, USSR Address: Communist Party Central Com, Moscow USSR

CHEAH, CHIN TEIK, electronics and computer company executive; b. Georgetown, Penang, Malaysia, Oct. 10, 1956; s. Leong Swee and Phaik Suan (Yeap) C.; m. Swee Peng Chang, Feb. 10, 1983; 1 child, Wei-Sern. BS in Social Sci. with honors, U. Sains Malaysia, Penang, 1978. Area supr. Malaysia SDB BHD div. Intel Corp., Penang, 1978-80, gen. foreman, 1980-82, personnel officer, 1982-83, tng. officer, 1983-84, mgr. tng. sect., 1984-86, mgr. tng. dept., 1986—; cong. Ins. Orgn., Penang. Mem. Malaysian Inst. Tng. and Devel., Am. Soc. Tng. and Devel. Club: Penang Sports. Lodge: Rotary. Home: 106 Jalan Tembaga Island Park, Georgetown 11600, Malaysia Office: Intel Malaysia SDN BHD, Free Trade Zone Bayan Lepas, Penang 11900, Malaysia

CHEBAN, ION KONSTANTINOVICI, writer, educator; b. Booday, Moldavia, USSR, Oct. 27, 1927; s. Konstantin Georgievici and Ecaterina Fiodoro (Borsh) C.; m. Ariadna Nicolaevna Tholari; children: Konstantin Ivanovici. Headmaster Teleneshty Sch., Moldavia, 1944-46; sec. Regional Young Communist League Com., Teleneshty, Moldavia, 1946-47, Orgeev, Moldavia, 1947; headmaster Sch. for Young Pioneer Leaders, Bendery, Moldavia, 1953; head lit. and arts dept. The Youth of Moldavia Sch., Kishinev; editor-in-chief Soviet Sch. Pub. House, Kishinev, State Pub. House, Kishinev. Author: (novels) Kodry, Bridges (State prize), Kukoara, The Podgorjanje (named by State as Best Book about working class and collective farmers); (collections of short stories) Meeting a Hero, Blackthorn, Voices Above the Water; (essays) The Strength of the Artistic Word, Echoes, Artistic Modelling; novels and short stories pub. in Bulgarian, Moldavian, Lithuanian, Lettish, Ukranian, and Estonian; short stories pub. in Russian, English, Spanish, French, German, and Japanese. Decorated Order of the Red Banner, Order of Friendship Between Nations, Order of the Great Oct. Socialist Revolution, medal for Disting. Labor during Great Patriotic War of 1941-45, others. Mem. Moldavian Writers Union (chmn. bd. dirs., editor-in-chief Neestru mag.). Home: Lenin St, bldg 6 apt 135, 277001 Kishinev Moldavia USSR Office: Union of Writers of, Moldavian SSR, Kievskaiya 98, Kishinev Moldavia USSR

CHEBRIKOV, VIKTOR MIKHAILOVICH, Soviet state security officer; b. Ukraine, 1923. Student Dnepropetrovsk Metall. Inst., 1950. Mem. Communist Party Soviet Union, 1944—, party posts, 1951—; mem. auditing com. of Ukraine Communist Party, 1956-61, cand. mem. of Central Com., 1961-71, sec., 1963-65; 2d sec. of Dnepropetrovak Dist. Com. 1965-67; 2d sec. of Dnepropetrovak City Com. of Ukraine, 1958-59, 1st sec., 1961-63; head of personnel dept., 1967-68; dep. chmn. of USSR State Security Com. (KGB), 1968-82, 1st dep. chmn., 1982, chmn. with rank of marshal; 1982—cand.; mem. Central Com. of USSR, 1971-81, full mem., 1981—; mem. Politburo, 1985—. Address: State Secuirity Com, The Kremlin, Moscow USSR *

CHEDID, ANTONIO, pathologist, educator, researcher; b. Barranquilla, Colombia, May 5, 1939; came to U.S., 1966; s. Aziz Antonio and Maria (Turbay) C.; m. Hoda Abi-Rached, Sept. 14, 1974; children—Anthony John, Marie-Claude, Erica Houda. B.S., Coll. of Barranquilla, 1954; M.D., U. Madrid, 1962. Diplomate Am. Bd. Pathology. Intern Columbus Hosp., Chgo., 1967-68; resident in pathology Michael Reese Hosp., Chgo., 1968-72; instr. pathology Pritzker Sch. Medicine, U. Chgo., 1972-73; asst. prof. pathology U. Cin. Coll. Medicine, 1973-76; assoc. prof. pathology Chgo. Med. Sch., North Chicago, Ill., 1976-84, prof. pathology, 1985—; core pathologist coop. study of alcoholic hepatitis VA, 1979-85, 87—; ECOG primary reviewer liver cancer. Am. Cancer Soc. grantee, 1974; NIH grantee, 1985—. Mem. Am. Assn. Pathology, Am. Assn. for Study Liver Diseases, Am. Soc. for Cell Biology, Fedn. Am. Socs. Exptl. Biology, Internat. Acad. Pathology. Current work: Cell markers of neoplasia, alcoholic liver disease. Subspecialties: Pathology (medicine); hepatology. Home: 650 Rockefeller Rd Lake Forest IL 60045 Office: 3333 Green Bay Rd North Chicago IL 60064

CHEE, PERCIVAL HON YIN, ophthalmologist; b. Honolulu, Aug. 29, 1936; s. Young Sing and Den Kyau (Ching) C.; B.A., U. Hawaii, 1958; M.D., U. Rochester, 1962; m. Carolyn Siu Lin Tong, Jan. 27, 1966; children—Lara Wai Lung, Shera Wai Sum. Intern, Travis AFB Hosp., Fairfield, Calif., 1962-63; resident Bascom Palmer Eye Inst., Miami, Fla., 1965-68, Jackson Meml. Hosp., Miami, 1965-68; partner Straub Clinic, Inc., Honolulu, 1968-71; practice medicine specializing in ophthalmology, Honolulu, 1972—; mem. staffs Queen's Med. Center, St. Francis Hosp., Kapiolani Children's Med. Center, Honolulu; clin. assoc. prof. surgery U. Hawaii Sch. Medicine, 1971—; cons. Tripler Army Med. Center. Mem. adv. bd. Services to Blind; bd. dirs. Lions Eye Bank and Makana Found. (organ bank), Multiple Sclerosis Soc. Served to capt. USAF, 1962-65. Fellow Am. Acad. Ophthalmology, ACS; mem. AMA, Pan Am. Med. Assn., Pan Pacific Surg. Assn., Am. Assn. Ophthalmology, Soc. Eye Surgeons, Hawaii Ophthal. Soc. Pacific Coast Ophthal. Soc., Am. Assn. for Study Headache, Pan Am. Ophthal. Found. Contbr. articles to profl. pubs. Home: 3755 Poka Pl Honolulu HI 96816 Office: Kukui Plaza 50 S Beretania St Honolulu HI 96513

CHEEK, JAMES RICHARD, foreign service officer; b. Decatur, Ga., Apr. 27, 1936; s. Woodrow Wilson and Dorothy (Webb) C.; m. Carol Ruth Rozzell, Sept. 1, 1957; children—Leesa Lynn, Forrest Craig, Surya Tamang. B.A., Ark. State Tchrs. Coll., 1959; M. Internat. Service, Am. U., 1961. Dep. chief mission Am. Embassy, Montevideo, Uruguay, 1977-79; dep. asst. sec. state U.S. Dept. State, D.C., 1979-81; dep. chief mission Am. Embassy, Kathmandu, Nepal, 1982-85; charge d'affaires, chief mission Am. Embassy, Addis Ababa, Ethiopia, 1985—. Served to capt. U.S. Army, 1954-56. Spl. Commendation award Women's Orgn. Dept. State, 1979, Group Valor award U.S. Dept. State, 1973. Mem. Am. Fgn. Service Assn. (William R. Rivkin award 1974). Home: 5 Valley Ct Little Rock AR 72204 Office: Dept State Addis Ababa Washington DC 20520 also: US Embassy, Entoto St, POB 1014, Addis Ababa Ethiopia

CHEEK, MALCOLM, electrical engineering consulting company executive; b. Boston, Apr. 12, 1950; s. Bruce M. and Alison M. (Western) C.; m. Stephanie A. Howard, Sept. 9, 1967; children: Malcolm A., Benjamin A. Student, U. Va., 1968-75; BSBA, SUNY, Albany, 1979; postgrad., U. Alaska, 1979-81, Webster Coll., 1982. Pub. utilities specialist USDA Rural Elec. Adminstrn., Washington, 1972-78; gen. mgr. Matanuska Electric Assn., Palmer, Alaska, 1978-81; sr. v.p., chief fin. officer The L.E. Myers Co. Group, Chgo., 1981-84; v.p. corp. devel. Burnup and Sims, Inc., Ft. Lauderdale, Fla., 1984-85; pres., chief exec. officer D. Ralph Young and Assocs., St. Louis, 1985—, also bd. dirs.; chmn. credit com. Rural Elec. Adminstrn., Washington, 1974-76, safety com. Alaska Rural Elec. Assn., Anchorage, 1979-81. Mem. Nat. Investor Relations Inst., Am. Mgmt. Assn., Nat. Assn. Over the Counter Cos. Episcopalian. Club: The Chgo. Office: D Ralph Young and Assocs Inc 16301 Fontaine Rd #230 Chesterfield MO 63017

CHEH, HUK YUK, electrochemist, engineering educator; b. Shanghai, China, Oct. 27, 1939; s. Tze Sang and Sue Lang (Che) C.; m. An-li, July 26, 1969; children: Emily, Evelyn. B.A.Sc. in Chem. Enging, U. Ottawa, Can., 1962; Ph.D., U. Calif.-Berkeley, 1967. Mem. tech. staff AT&T Bell Labs., N.J., 1967-70; asst. prof. chem. enging. Columbia U., N.Y.C., 1970-73; assoc. prof. Columbia U., 1973-79, prof., 1979—, Ruben-Viele prof., 1982—, chmn. dept., 1980-86; program dir. NSF, 1978-79; vis. research prof. Nat. Tsinghua U., Taiwan, 1977. Contbr. articles to sci. jours. Recipient Harold C. Urey award, 1980, Research award The Electrochem. Soc., 1988. Mem. Am. Inst. Chem. Engrs., N.Y. Acad. Scis., Electrochem. Soc., Am. Electroplaters Soc., Sigma Xi. Office: Columbia U New York NY 10027

CHEHVAL, MICHAEL JOHN, surgeon; b. Racine, Wis., June 30, 1941; s. Michael K. and Iva Alma (Makovsky) C.; m. Marijane S. Jakaitis, Sept. 2, 1967; children—Kelley, Michael, Benjamin, Vincent. B.S., Northeast Mo. State U., 1963; M.D., St. Louis U., 1967. Diplomate Am. Bd. Urology. Intern St. Louis U. Hosp., 1967-68; resident U. Iowa Hosps., Iowa City, 1970-75; fellow Am. Cancer Soc., 1973-74; assoc. clin. prof. urology St. Louis U. Sch. Medicine, 1985—; chmn. div. urology St. John's Mercy Med. Ctr., St. Louis, 1983—; sec. med. staff Cardinal Glennon Hosp. for Children, St. Louis, 1985-86, chmn. dept. of surgery, 1988—; pres. Central Eastern Mo. Peer Rev. Orgn., St. Louis, 1984-86; chmn. med. adv. com. Vis. Nurses St. Louis, 1984-86; staff St. John's Hosp., St. Louis U. Hosp.; staff, chmn. dept. of surgery St. Mary's Health Ctr. Contbr. articles to med. publs. Served with USN, 1968-70. Mem. ACS, Am. Urologic Assn., Soc. Pediatric Urology, AMA, Mo. State Med. Assn., Am. Fertility Soc., St. Louis Med. Soc., St. Louis Urol. Soc. (pres. 1986—), St. Louis Surg. Soc. Lutheran. Home: 1260 Glenvista Pl Saint Louis MO 63122 Office: Michael J Chehval Inc 621 S New Ballas Rd Saint Louis MO 63141

CHELAZZI, GIOVANNI, hematologist; b. Milan, Italy, Sept. 27, 1936; s. Bruno and Maria Irma (Tamburini) C.; M.D., U. Milan, 1963; m. Gabriella Colombo, Dec. 7, 1968; children—Barbara, Stefano, Paolo. Resident in internal medicine U. Parma (Italy), 1963-66; resident in hematology U. Modena, 1966-69; asst. in immunohematology E.S. Macchi Found. Hosp. of Varese, 1966-69, asst. in medicine, 1969-80; prof. gen. pathology Generic Nurses Sch., Varese, 1973-80; prof. hematology Profl. Nurses Sch., Varese, 1977-86, prof. immunohematology, 1980-81; instr. med. pathology Pavia Faculty of Medicine, 1976-78; sr. asst. Del Ponte Hosp. of Varese, 1980-87; chief immunohematology service, Regional Hosp. of Varese, 1987—; cons. in hematology. Mem. Italian Assn. Med. Oncology, Italian Soc. Hematology, Italian Soc. Immunohematology, Blood Center's Italian Assn., Italian Soc. Rheumatology. Roman Catholic. Contbr. articles to profl. jours.; editor: (with R. Crespi Porro) La linfografia nella pratica ospedaliera, 1979; Protocolli diagnostici e terapeutici dei tumori maligni, 1979. Home: 1 Buonarroti, Varese 21100 Italy Office: 57 Borri, Varese 21100, Italy

CHEMLA, MARIUS, physical chemist, educator; b. Tunis, Tunisia, Nov. 6, 1927; s. Victor and Julie (Samama) C.; m. Laure Valensi, Dec. 29, 1956; children—Florence, Franç oise, Corrine. Chem. Engr., Ecole National Superieure de Chimie, Paris, 1949; D.Sc., U. Paris. Research assoc. C.N.R.S., Paris, 1949-58; dep. dir. Coll. de France, Paris, 1958-63; prof. phys. chemistry U. Paris, 1963—, dir. dept. phys. chemistry, 1972—. Author: Separation of Isotopes, 1976; Traite Delectricite, 1977; contbr. Ency. of Electrochemistry, 1983; contbr. articles to profl. jours. Mem. Am. Electrochem. Soc., Internat. Soc. Electrochemistry, Société Française de Chimie (high prize), French Acad. Scis. (laureate). Home: Boulevard Arago 25, 73 Paris France Office: Univ Paris, Place Jussieu4, 75005 Paris 5 France

CHEN, CHAO-WU JOSEPH, architect; b. Tainan, Taiwan, Feb. 14, 1942; s. Bai-Hai and Wan (Sun) C.; B.S., Nat. Cheng Kung U., 1964; m. Lee-Yah Ho, May 10, 1969; children—Wan-Ching, Jun-Ting, Jun-Yu. Designer, What Thai Architect & Assocs., Taipei, Taiwan, 1965-68; partner Tsai & Chen & Assocs., Taipei, 1968-77; architect Chen & Assocs., Taipei, 1977—; instr. Shin Po Jr. Coll. Tech., 1973-74. Recipient Chin-Din prize Universal Constrn. Service, 1975, Art Exhbn. prize Nat. Art Gallery, 1980, Architecture Design prize Taipei City Govt., 1980; Chinese Architect award, 1985; Architecture Design prize Taipei City Govt., 1985. Served as 2d lt. Architecture Engring. Troops, Taiwan Navy, 1964-65. Recipient citation Chinese Architect Monthly, 1985, Architect Design prize Taipei City Govt., 1985. Charter mem. Republic of China Architects Assn., Taiwan Architects Assn., Taipei Architects Assn. Buddhist. Club: Shihlin Rotary (charter). Prin. works include: Mackay Meml. Hosp., 1971, Brother Hotel, 1980. Home: No 8 Jen Ming Rd, Yang Ming Shan, Taipei Republic of China Office: Chen & Assocs, No 8B Jen Ming Rd, Yang Ming Sham Taipei Republic of China

CHEN, CHI, artist; b. Wusih, China, May 2, 1912; s. Shih-Pei and Shih (Tsai) C.; m. Alice Zu Min Huang, Oct. 5, 1962. Mem. faculty St. John's U., Shanghai, China, 1942-46; mem. faculty Pa. State U., summers 1959-60; artist in residence Ogden, Utah, 1967, Utah State U., 1971; Pres. Chen Chi Found. First one-man exhbn. Shanghai, China, 1940; others at various U.S. museums and art galleries in N.Y.C., Boston, N.H., R.I., Conn., Vt., Maine, R.I., Fla., Ariz., Phila., Allentown, Washington, Chgo., New Orleans, Iowa, Houston, Dallas, Fort Worth, San Antonio, Denver, Boulder, Seattle, San Francisco, Los Angeles, San Diego, Columbus, Ga., Anchorage, Alaska, Okla., Kans., Mo., S.C., W.Va., Santa Fe, N.Mex., Youngstown, Ohio, Ogedn, Utah, Logan, Utah, Wusih, Peking, Shanghai, Taipei, Tai-chung, China; group exhbns. include Met. Art Mus., Nat. Acad. N.Y.C., Springfield, Art Mus., Mo., Bklyn. Mus., Contemporary Chinese Am. Artists, San Diego, Whitney Mus. Am. Art, Corcoran Gallery, Washington, Butler Inst., Am. Acad. Arts and Letters, numerous others; painter series Am. city scenes, Colliers, Olympic Winter Games, Squaw Valley, Sports Illustrated, also other publs.; works represented in permanent collections Met. Mus. Art, Pa. Acad., Nat. Acad., Butler Inst., Cleve., Allentown Mus., IBM Corp., Ford Motor Co., Gen. Mills, numerous museums, univs., pvt. collections: jury selection and awards Butler Inst. Am. Art, Frye Mus., Seattle, Am. Watercolor Soc., Allied Artists, Audubon Artists, sole judge ann. N.W. Coast Art Exhibit, Seattle, Washington, Pitts., Birmingham, Ala., San Diego, Columbia, S.C., Wilmington, Del., Detroit, Anchorage, also others. Author: Watercolors by Chen Chi, 1942,China, Chen Chi Paintings, Switzerland, 1965, Two or Three Lines from Sketchbooks of Chen Chi, 1969, China from the Sketchbooks of Chen Chi, 1974, Chen Chi Watercolors, Drawings, Sketches, 1980, Chen Chi Watercolors, China, Heaven and Water-Chen Chi, 1983. Recipient numerous awards, gold medals NAD, Am. Watercolor Soc., Nat. Arts Club, Salmagundi Club, Knickerbocker Artists, Audobon Artists, Phila. Watercolor Club; gold medal ann. watercolor exhbn. Nat. Arts Club, 1954, gold medal oil, 1954, Adolph and Clara Obrig prize NAD, 1955, Spl. $1000 award for watercolor 88th Exhbn. Am. Watercolor Soc., 1955; 1st watercolor prize, Butler Inst. Art, 1955, also Chautauqua Art Assn., 1955; Gold medal for Watercolor, 14th ann. Audobon Artists, 1956, spl. $1000 award 21st ann. exhbn.; $1500 grant Nat. Inst. Arts and Letters; gold medal honor, 47th ann. Allied Artists Am., 1960; Samuel Finley Breese Morse medal NAD, 1961; spl. award and medal Audbon Artists, 1963; John Singer Sargent Meml. award Springfield Art Mus.; medal honor Nat. Arts Club, 1966; 99th Ann. $600 Grand award and gold medal of honor Am. Watercolor Soc.; Winslow Homer Meml. award Watercolor U.S.A., Springfield Art Mus.; Gold Medal Honor, Nat. Arts Club, 1967, Audubnon Artists, 1968; Thomas Hart Benton award, 1968, Saltus Gold medal or merit NAD, 1969, Silver medal Nat. Arts Club, 1970, High Winds award Am. Watercolor Soc., 1972, 74, Pres.'s award Audubon Artists, 1974, Am. Watercolor Soc. Bicentennial Gold medal, 1976, Benjamin West Clinedinst meml. medal, 1976, others. Mem. Internat. Inst. Arts and Letters, NAD, Am. Watercolor Soc. (hon.), Nat. Arts Club, Audubon Artists, Allied Artists. Clubs: Century, Dutch Treat, Salmagundi, Nat. Arts. Home: 23 Washington Square N New York NY 10011 Studio: 15 Gramercy Park S New York NY 10003

CHEN, CHIA-MING, resin chemist, wood scientist, educator; b. Chia-Yi, Taiwan, July 20, 1935; came to U.S., 1967, naturalized, 1974; s. Pi-Ching and Jong (Huang) C.; m. Shu-Hsien Lai, Sept. 27, 1963; children—Edward Po-Chung, Frederick Yen-Ching. B.S., Chung-Hsing U., Taichung, Taiwan, 1958; M.S., U. Tokyo, 1963, Ph.D., 1966. Research assoc. Yale U. Sch. Forestry, New Haven, 1967-68; products devel. engr. Champion Bldg Products, Seattle, 1968-69; wood scientist, resin chemist chem. div. Ga.-Pacific Corp., Decatur, Ga., 1969-71; sr. wood scientist, assoc. prof. U. Ga. Sch. Forest Resources, Athens, 1971—, mem. grad. faculty; cons. in field to various cos. Mem. Athens Internat. Council. Registered forester, Ga.; U.S. Dept. Agr. grantee, 1982-85. Fellow Am. Inst. Chemists; mem. Am. Chem. Soc., Forest Products Research Soc., N.Am. Taiwanese Profs.' Assn., Adhesion Soc., Formosan Assn. for Pub. Affairs (pres. Ga. chpt. 1986—). Club: Formosan (pres. and faculty adviser Athens chpt.). Contbr. numerous articles on resin and adhesive chemistry, wood sci. and tech. to profl. jours.; patentee in field. Home: 205 Dove Valley Dr Athens GA 30606

CHEN, CONCORDIA CHAO, mathematician; b. Peiping, China; came to U.S., 1955, naturalized, 1969; d. Chun-fu and Kwie Hwa (Wong) Chao; B.A. in Bus. Adminstrn., Nat. Taiwan U., 1954; M.S. in Math., Marquette U., 1958; postgrad. Purdue U., 1958-60, M.I.T., 1961-62; m. Chin Chen, July 2, 1960; children—Marie Hui-mei, Albert Chao. Teaching asst. Purdue U., Lafayette, Ind., 1958-60; system analysis engr. electronic data processing div. Mpls.-Honeywell, Newton Highlands, Mass., 1960-63; mgmt. planning asst. Lederle Labs., Am. Cyanamid Co., Pearl River, N.Y., 1964, computer applications specialist, 1967, ops. analyst, 1967; staff programmer IBM, Sterling Forest, N.Y., 1968-73, adv. programmer Data Processing Mktg. Group, Poughkeepsie, 1973-80, mgr. systems programming and systems architecture, Princeton, N.J., 1980-82, sr. systems analyst, 1982-83, data processing mktg. cons., Beijing, 1983-88, Poughkeepsie, 1988—. Mem. edml. council MIT. Mem. Am. Math. Soc., Soc. Indsl. and Applied Maths. Home: 12 Mountain Pass Rd Hopewell Junction NY 12533 Office: IBM Corp DSD Myers Corners Lab Dept Y27 Bldg 920 PO Box 950 Poughkeepsie NY 12602

CHEN, HO-HONG H. H., industrial engineer, educator; b. Taiwan, Apr. 11, 1933; s. Shui-Cheng and Mei (Lin) C.; m. Yuki-Lihua Jenny, Mar. 10, 1959; children—Benjamin Kuen-Tsai, Carl Joseph Chao-Kuang, Charles Chao-Yu, Eric Chao-Ying, Charmine Tsuey-Ling, Dolly Hsiao-Ying, Edith Yi-Wen, Yvonne Yi-Fang, Grace Yi-Sin, Julia Yi-Jiun. Owner, Tai Chang Indsl. Supplies Co., Ltd., 1967—; pres. Pan Pacific Indsl. Supplies, Inc., Ont., Can., 1975—, Maker Group Inc., Md., 1986—, Wako Internat. Co., Ltd., Md., 1986—. prof. First Econ. U., Japan. Clubs: Internat. (Washington); Kenwood Golf and Country (Bethesda, Md.). Author: 500 Creative Designs for Future Business, 1961; A Summary of Suggestions for the Economic Development in Central America Countries, 1979; Access and Utilize the Potential Fund in Asia, 1980. Office: PO Box 5674 Friendship Sta Washington DC 20016

CHEN, HUIYI, internal medicine educator; b. Wuhu, Anhui, People's Republic of China, Mar. 11, 1926; s. Choulin Chen and Tsiojin Diao; m. Liu Shinchen, Apr. 12, 1952; children: Chen Qianshun, Chen Qianfeng, Chen Qianfang, Chen Qianjin. Grad., Nat. Jiangsu Med. Coll., Zhenjiang, Jiangsu, 1952. Resident The Huai-Harnessing Com. Hosp., Bengbu, Anhui, 1952-58; vis. doctor Hosp. of Bengbu Med. Coll., 1958-64; dir. dept. respiratory medicine Bengbu Med. Coll., 1964-78, dep. dir. dept. internal medicine, 1978-83, head dept. internal medicine, 1983—, head Inst. Respiratory Diseases, 1984—; postgrad. advisor Bengbu Med. Coll., 1984—; cons. Rehab. Ctr. Cancer Chinese Cancer Research Fund, Bengbu, 1987—. Author: Pulmonary Emergency, 1984; chief editor: Handbook of OPD of Internal Medicine, 1981; editor: Acta Academiae Medicinae Bengbu, 1978—; invited editor Jour. Continuing Edn. of Physicians, 1984—; contbr. over 60 articles to profl. jours. Mem. Chinese People's Polit. Consultative Conf. of Bengbu City, 1980—, Anhui Province, 1988—. Recipient Sci. Advanced prize Anhui Sci. Assn., Hofei, 1986, Outstanding Tchr. award Anhui People's Govt., Hofei, 1985. Mem. Anhui Acad. Respiratory Diseases (chmn.), China Acad. Respiratory Diseases of Combining Traditional Chinese and Western medicine (council mem.), Chinese Anti-Tuberculosis Assn. (council mem. Anhui br.), Anhui Acad. Internal Medicine (vice chmn. 1985—). Home and Office: Bengbu Med Coll, Bengbu Anhui, People's Republic China

CHEN, JIAHUANG, petroleum geologist; b. Malaysia, Sept. 6, 1938. B.S., Beijing Petroleum Inst., 1960. Chief div. acquisitions and overseas ops., dep. mgr. Info. Service Dept. Chinese Petroleum Soc., Beijing, 1979—. Mem. Chinese Petroleum Soc. Office: PO Box 1411,, Info Service, Dept Chinese Petroleum Soc, Hepingli 7Qu 16 Lou,, Beijing, China

CHEN, KOK-CHOO, lawyer, educator; b. Hong Kong, Oct. 24, 1947; d. Chin Poo and Kim Suan (Lin) Tan; children: Shahn Y., Mei-Mei. Barrister-at-law, Inns of Ct., Eng., 1968. Bar: Calif., 1974. Assoc. Law Offices of Tan, Rajah and Cheah, Singapore, 1969-70; lectr. Nanyang U., Singapore, 1970-71; law clk. Sullivan and Cromwell, N.Y.C., 1971-74; assoc. Heller, Ehrman, White and McAuliffe, Calif., 1974-75; founding ptnr. Ding and Ding, Taipei, Taiwan, 1975-88, Ding, Ding and Chan, Calif., 1983-88; prin. Chen & Assocs., Taipei, Republic of China, 1988—; assoc. prof. Soochow U., Taipei, 1981—. Author: Licensing Technology to Chinese Enterprise (Chia Hsin Found. award), 1986. Named One of Ten Most Outstanding Women of Yr., Taiwan, 1982. Mem. Honorable Soc. of Inner Temple, Calif. Bar Assn., Zonta Internat. Office: Chen & Assocs, 602 Minchuan Rd E, Suite #824, Taipei Taiwan

CHEN, KUAN, mechanical engineering educator; b. Tai Chung, Taiwan, Mar. 1, 1953; s. James T.R. and Jye-Fen (Han) C. B.S., Chung Yuan U., 1974; M.S., Nat. Taiwan U., 1976; Ph.D., U. Ill., 1981. Design engr. 202d Arsenal, Nankong, Taiwan, 1977-78; asst. prof. mech. engring. U. Utah, Salt Lake City, 1981—. Contbr. articles to profl. jours. Mem. ASME (assoc.), Am. Soc. for Metals, Sigma Xi, Phi Kappa Phi. Home: 1415 E 4045 S Salt Lake City UT 84124 Office: Dept Mech Engring Univ Utah Salt Lake City UT 84112

CHEN, KURT CHIEN LUN, manufacturing executive; b. Pan-Yu, Kwang-Tung, China, Jan. 2, 1920; came to Taiwan, 1946; s. Lam Cheung and Lai-Kiu (Cheung) C.; m. Pheobe Shou-ling Sun, June 2, 1962; children—Hsiung-Kang, Geoffrey Hsiung-Chieh, Hsiung-Wan. Acctg. Diploma, Canton U., 1943; postgrad. Wayne State U., 1967. Cost acct. Tse Yu Steel & Iron Works, Chungking, China, 1945-46; div. chief dep. dir. Taiwan Power Co., Taipei, Taiwan, 1946-73; fin. and adminstrn. mgr. Petwood Internat. Ltd., Taipei, 1973-74; purchasing mgr. China Steel Corp., Kaohsiung, Taiwan, 1974-78; v.p. Walsin Lihwa Electric Wire & Cable Corp., Taipei, 1978—; pres. Kolin Constrn. & Devel. Corp., Taipei, 1983-86. Contbr. articles to profl. jours. Recipient Citation for outstanding achievements, Ministry of Econ. Affairs, 1956, Taiwan Power Co., 1962, 67; medal for outstanding achievement, China Steel Corp., 1978. Mem. Taiwan Electric Appliance Mfrs. Assn. (rep.), Sino-Arabian Cultural & Econ. Assn., Chinese Mgmt. Assn., Liability Ins. Research Found. (research fellow), Chinese Nat. Standards Certification Mark Assn. (dir.). Avocations: hiking; swimming; reading; bridge. Home: 96 Chao Chow St, Taipei Republic of China Office: Walsin Lihwa Electric Wire & Cable, 221 Chung Hsiao E Rd 12th Floor, 10646 Taipei Republic of China

CHEN, MAY JANE, psychology educator; b. Taipei, Republic of China, Jan. 3, 1940; arrived in Australia, 1968; d. Kwong Yei and Mei Jau (Kao) Wang; m. Jaw-yaw Chen, Dec. 20, 1962; children: Grace, Wayne. BSc, Nat. Taiwan U., Taipei, 1962, MSc, 1964; PhD, Sydney (Australia) U., 1973. Lectr. Nat. Taiwan U., 1964-68; tutor Sydney U., 1968-71; lectr. Australian Nat. U., Canberra, 1971-83, sr. lectr. psychology, 1984—; dir. honors program Australia Nat. U., 1981-84; grant assessor Nat. Health and Med. Research Council, Canberra, 1982—; vis. scholar Chinese U. Hong Kong, 1985-86, 87—; chief investigator revision of Thematic Apperception Test for use in Taiwan, 1967. Research grantee Asian Founds., 1967. Mem. Internat. Council Psychologists, Internat. Assn. for Cross-Cultural Psychology, Internat. Soc. of Study of Behavioral Devel. Home: Chinese U of Hong Kong, 2A Residence 1, Shatin, NT Hong Kong Hong Kong Office: Australian Nat U, Action PO Box 4, 2601 Canberra Australia

CHEN, MICHAEL SHIH-TA, diversified company executive; b. India, Sept. 30, 1945; s. Chih-Ping and Lilleo Yung-Chieh (Wong) C.; A.B. with honors, U. Calif., 1966; M.A., Cornell U., 1969, Ph.D., 1973; M.B.A., Harvard U., 1972; m. Lilian Hsiao-Mei Oung, Dec. 11, 1976; children—Te-kuang, Te-Ming. Staff officer Citibank N.A., N.Y.C., 1973-76, mgr., Hong Kong, 1976-78, asst. v.p., Hong Kong, 1979-80, v.p., Hong Kong, 1980-86; chmn. Chen Group Internat. Ltd., Hong Kong, 1986—; mem. coordinating com. of mgmt. for exec. devel. program, Chinese U. Hong Kong; vis. lectr. M.B.A. programs; mem. adv. com. for mgmt. edn. Hong Kong Council Social Service; mem. social work com. Caritas, Hong Kong. Mem. Harvard Bus. Sch. Assn. Hong Kong (pres., dir., chmn. 1980-86), Asia Soc. Clubs: Harvard (pres. 1979-80), Royal Hong Kong Jockey, Fgn. Corrs., American, Ladies' Recreation (Hong Kong); Taipei Bankers. Contbr. articles to profl. publs. Home: 9A 4/F Borrett Mansion, Bowen Rd, Hong Kong Hong Kong Office: Chen Group Internat Ltd, 2202 Fung House, 20 Connaught Rd Central, Hong Kong Hong Kong

CHEN, MING, physiological biochemist; b. Hubei, People's Republic China, June 8, 1934; s. Xing Zhou and Chun Zhi (Shi) C.; m. Ai Yuan Li, Aug. 14, 1964; children: Xiao Min and Xiao Dong. Bachelors degree, Beijing U., People's Republic China, 1957; PhD, Shanghai Inst. Physiology, Chinese Acad. Scis., 1961. Research assoc. Shanghai Inst. Physiology, Chinese Acad. Scis., 1961-84, assoc. prof., 1985—; vis. assoc. prof. U. Arizona. Editor: Physiology of Cardiac Muscle; contbr. articles and research papers to profl. jours. Mem. Chinese Soc. Physiology, Chinese Soc. Biophysics, Chinese Soc. Biochemistry; bd. dirs. Shanghai Soc. Biochemistry. Office: Shanghai Inst of Physiology, 320 Yo-yang Rd, Shanghai 200031, Peoples Republic of China

CHEN, PING-FAN, geologist; b. Kiangyin, Kiangsu, China, May 13, 1917; s. Mou-Chu and Lan-yin (Men) C.; B.S., Nat. Central U. China, 1938; M.S., U. Cin. (fellow), 1956; Ph.D. (fellow), Va. Poly. Inst. and State U., 1959; m. Tsing-fang Tsao, Jan. 1, 1947 (dec.); children—Jane, June, Julia; m. 2d, Esther Fu-Mei Yang, Aug. 10, 1979; came to U.S., 1956, naturalized, 1969. Petroleum geologist Nat. Geol. Survey China, 1938-46; sr. petroleum geologist Chinese Petroleum Corp., Taiwan, 1946-55; stratigrapher W.Va. Geol. Survey, Morgantown, 1960—; pres. E & W United Corp.; adj. prof. W.Va. U., 1975—. Adviser W.Va. U. Chinese Student Assn., 1962-81. Mem. Geol. Soc. China, Chinese Engrs. Assn., Chinese Assn. Advancement Scis., Sigma Xi, Sigma Gamma Epsilon. Author: Mineral Resources of China, 1954; New Outlook for the Oil Fields of Taiwan, 1949; Tectonic Analogies and Antitheses between Taiwan and the Appalachians, 1976; Lower Paleozoic Stratigraphy in the Central Appalachians, 1978. Home: 1277 Dogwood Ave Morgantown WV 26505 Office: PO Box 879 Morgantown WV 26505

CHEN, ROGER KO-CHUNG, electronics executive; b. Tainan, Republic of China, Apr. 16, 1951; arrived in U.S., 1980; s. Ja-bing and Chi-ping (Tsui) C.; m. Shu-chen Kao, May 25, 1980; 1 child, Wickham. BS, Nat. Taiwan Normal U., Taipei, Rep. China, 1974; MS, U. Tex., 1982. Tchr. Tainan 1st High Sch., 1976-80; teaching asst. U. Tex., Dallas, 1980-82; jr. applications engr. Internat. Power Machines, Dallas, 1982-83, sr. applications engr., 1983-85, regional mgr., 1985, Pacific dir., 1985-86; gen. mgr. Liegert Hong Kong Ops., 1987—. Served to lt., infantry Republic China armed forces, 1974-76. Mem. IEEE. Lodge: Masons. Office: Liebert Internat 1050 Dearborn Dr Columbus OH 43229 also: Liebert Hong Kong, 1106 E Point Ctr, 555 Hennessy Rd, Causeway Bay Hong Kong

CHEN, TAR TIMOTHY, biostatistician; b. Fuching, China, June 23, 1945; came to U.S., 1967, naturalized, 1979; s. Lin-Tsang and Ai-Ying (Chang) C.; m. Meei-Ming Li, Aug. 9, 1969; children—Stephen, Daniel. B.S., Nat. Taiwan U., 1966; M.S., U. Chgo., 1969, Ph.D., 1972. Statistician, Ill. Bell Telephone, Chgo., 1971-73; asst. prof. Calif. State U.-Hayward, 1973-74; vis. assoc. prof. Chung-Hsing U., Taichung Taiwan, 1974-75; biostatistician The Upjohn Co., Kalamazoo, 1975-79; asst. prof. biometrics U. Tex. System Cancer Ctr., Houston, 1979-84; sr. biostatistician Alcon Labs., Fort Worth, 1984—. Contbr. articles to profl. jours. Treas. Chinese for Christ Chgo. Fellowship Ch., 1972-73; deacon, Houston Chinese Ch., 1981-83, McKinney Meml. Bible Ch., Ft. Worth, 1988—. Served to 2d lt. Republic of China Army, 1966-67. Mem. Am. Statis. Assn., Biometric Soc., Soc. Clin. Trials, Sigma Xi. Office: Alcon Labs 6201 S Freeway Fort Worth TX 76134

CHEN, WAI-KAI, electrical engineering and computer science educator, consultant; b. Nanking, China, Dec. 23, 1936; came to U.S., 1959; s. You-Chao and Shui-Tan (Shen) C.; m. Shirley Shiao-Ling, Jan. 13, 1939; children—Jerome, Melissa. B.S., Ohio U., 1960, M.S., 1961; Ph.D., U. Ill.-Urbana, 1964. Asst. prof. Ohio U., 1964-67, assoc. prof., 1967-71, prof., 1971-78, disting. prof., 1978-81; prof., head dept. elec. engring. and computer sci. U. Ill.-Chgo., 1981—; vis. assoc. prof. Purdue U., 1970-71. Author: Applied Graph Theory, 1970, Theory and Design of Broadband Matching Networks, 1976, Applied Graph Theory: Graphs and Electrical Networks, 1976, Active Network and Feedback Amplifier Theory, 1980, Linear Networks and Systems, 1983, Passive and Active Filters: Theory and Implementations, 1986, The Collected apaers of Professor Wai-Kai Chen, 1987, Modern Network Analysis, 1988, Broadband Matching: Theory & Implementations, 1988; editor: Brooks/Cole Series in Electrical Engineering, 1982-84, Advanced Series in Electrical and Computer Engineering, 1984-86; editor-in-chief Advanced Series in Elec. and Computer Engring., World Sci. Pub. Co., Singapore, 1986—; assoc. editor: Jour. Circuits, Systems and Signal Processing, 1981—. Recipient Lester R. Ford award Math. Assn. Am., 1967, Baker Fund award Ohio U., 1974, 78, Disting. Accomplishment award Chinese Acad. & Profl. Assn. in Mid-Am. , 1985, disting. Guest Prof. award Chuo U., Tokyo, 1987, Outstanding Service award Chinese Acad. & Profl. assn. in Mid-Am., 1988, Outstanding Achievement award Mid-Am. Chinese Sci. & Tech. Assn, 1988, disting. alumnus award Electrical and Computer Engring. Dept. Alumni Assn. U. Ill. Urbana-Champaign, 1988, Alexander von Humboldt award Alexander von Humboldt Stiftung, Fed. Republic of Germany, 1985, hon. prof. award Nanjing Inst. of Technology and Zhejing U., Peoples Republic of China, 1985, The Northeast U. Tech., East. China Inst. Tech., Nanjing Inst. of Posts & Telecommunications, AnHui U., Chengdu Inst. Radio Engring.; Research Inst. fellow Ohio U., 1972, Japan Soc. for Promotion of Sci., 1986, Sr. U. Scholar award U. Ill., 1986, Ohio U. Alumni Medal Merit for Disting. Achievement in Engring. Edn., 1987. Fellow IEEE (adminstrv. com. Circuits and Systems Soc. 1985-87, exec. v.p. 1987, assoc. editor transactions on circuits and systems, 1977-79), AAAS; mem. Nat. Soc. Profl. Engrs., Mid-Am. Chinese Sci. & Tech. Assn. (bd. dirs. 1984-88), Chinese Acad. and Profl. Assn. of Mid-Am. (adv. to bd. dirs. 1984—, pres. 1986-87), Soc. Indsl. and Applied Math., Assn. Computing Machinery, Tensor Soc. Gt. Britain, Sigma Xi (sec.-treas. Ohio U. chpt. 1981), Phi Kappa Phi, Pi Mu Epsilon, Eta Kappa Nu. Office: U Illinois Dept Electrical Engineering and Computer Science PO Box 4348 Chicago IL 60680

CHEN, WANYONG, paleontologist; b. Anshan, Liaoning, Republic of China, Aug. 28, 1935; parents: Ximing Chen and Guirong Qiao; m. Yuying Li, July 15, 1978. Grad., Geol. Inst. Chang Chun, Republic of China. Research asst. commn. comprehensive survey natural resources Chinese Acad. Scis., Beijing, 1959-72; research assoc. Inst. Vertebrate Paleontology and Paleoanthropology, Acad. Sinica, Beijing, 1972-85; assoc. research prof. Inst. Vertebrate Paleontology and Paleoanthropology, Acad. Sinica, 1985—; invited researcher Commn. Comprehensive Survey NAtural Resources, Chinese Acad. Scis., Beijing, 1985-87. Recipient award sci. and tech. progress Acad. Sinica, 1986. Home: PO Box 643 (28), Beijing Peoples Republic of China

CHEN, WAN-YU, physician, educator; b. Taipei, Taiwan, Republic of China, Dec. 10, 1916; s. Han-Ren and Shi (Lee) C.; m. Lin Hui-Fan, Aug. 8, 1922, 1945; children: Tien-Yi, Chi-Pen, Hen-Lie. MD, Nat. Taiwan U., 1942; D in Med. Sci., Kumamoto U., Japan, 1949. Asst. dept. internal medicine Nat. Taiwan U. Hosp., Taipei, 1942-46, instr., 1946-50, assoc. prof., 1954-56, prof., 1956-86, prof. emeritus, 1986—, acting chmn. dept., 1962-63, acting vice supt., 1964-65, head toxicology lab., 1966-72; cons. Cathay Gen. Hosp., Taipei, 1985—; chief cons. Nephrology Patients Assn., Taipei, 1984—. Served as lt. Med. Service Corps Chinese Army, 1959. Kidney Research grantee Tatung Corp., Taipei, 1960, 65, Sci. Research grantee Chuan Sou Ken Fund, Taipei, 1981, 86. Mem. Formosan Med. Assn. Republic of China (officer 1971—), Soc. Nephrology Republic of China (pres. 1983—), Transplantation Assn. Republic of China (officer 1985—), Chinese Soc. Internat. Medicine (officer 1987—), Internat. Soc. Nephrology, European Dialysis Assn., Asian Colloquium Nephrology, Asian-Pacific Soc. Nephrology (Plaque award). Buddhist. Home: No 124 Ta-Tung Rd, Shi-Lin, Taipei 10016, Republic of China Office: NTUH Dept Internal Medicine, Chang-Te St, Taipei 10016, Republic of China

CHEN, YUH-CHING, mathematician, educator; b. Fujien, China, May 20, 1930; came to U.S., 1962; s. Jinlan and Chigui (Lin) C.; m. Jane Yan Huang, July 16, 1955; children—Shwu-ming, Yie-ming, Tse-ming. B.S., Taiwan Normal U., 1953; M.S., U. Ill., 1963; Ph.D., CUNY, 1966. Asst. prof. math. Wesleyan U., Middletown, Conn., 1966-70; assoc. prof. math. Fordham U., Bronx, N.Y., 1971—, chmn. dept., 1974-78, 87—; math./econs. advisor, 1979—. vis. scholar U. Paris, 1971; vis. prof. Beijing Normal U. and Nankai U., People's Republic of China, 1978-79, tchr. mgmt. sci. Huanghe U., People's Republic of China, 1987. Author: (with X.C. Li) General Topology, 1983. Contbr. articles to profl. jours. Mem. Math. Assn. Am., N.Y. Acad. of Scis., Sigma Xi. Home: 79 Chestnut Ave Park Ridge NJ 07656 Office: Fordham U Math Dept Fordham Rd Bronx NY 10458

CHEN, ZHIHUA, mathematician, educator; b. Shanghai, People's Republic of China, Jan. 24, 1939; s. Jishi Chen and Zhifang Miao; m. Yin Chen, Apr. 30, 1968, 1 child, Jing. BS, Beijing U., 1962. Research asst. Acad. Sinica, Inst. Math., Beijing, 1962-78, asst. researcher, 1978-80, assoc. researcher, 1980-85; prof. math. Shanghai Jiao Tong U., 1985—, chmn. dept. math., 1985—. Author: Compact Riemann Surface, 1981, Complex Analysis, 1987; contbr. articles to profl. jours. Chinese Acad. Scis. grantee, 1986—. Mem. Shanghai Math. Soc., Am. Math. Soc. Office: Shanghai Jiao Tong U, Dept Math, 1954 Hua Shan Rd, 200030 Shanghai People's Republic of China

CHENAUX, ROBERT GEORGES, food products executive; b. Hato Rey, P.R., Nov. 29, 1943; arrived in Canada, 1975; s. Georges Emile and Jean Watson (Knight) C.; m. Ellen Sherry Gutman, Aug. 1968; children: Eric Steven, Peter Reid. BS, Rutgers U., 1966; MBA, Internat. Mgmt. Devel. Inst., Lausanne, Switzerland, 1973-74. Product mgr. Nestle Co. Inc., White Plains, N.Y., 1970-72; asst. regional mgr. Nestle Alimentana SA, Vevey, Switzerland, 1972-75; dir. non food div. Loblaw Cos. Ltd., Toronto, Can., 1975-78; dir. corp. brands div. Loblaw Cos. Ltd., Toronto, 1978-82, v.p. internat. trade, 1982-86, sr. v.p., 1986—. Pres. Bayview Ratepayers Assn., Thornhill, Ont., 1984; mem. Swiss Olympic Team, 1960, 64. Served to capt. USAF, 1966-70, Vietnam. Mem. Can. Coffee and Tea Assn., Can. Importers Assn. (bd. dirs. 1987—). Club: Bayview Tennis. Office: Loblaw Cos Ltd, 22 St Clair Ave E, Toronto, ON Canada M4T 2S8

CHÊNEAU, JACQUES PIERRE JOSEPH, orthopedist; b. Tunis, Tunesia, May 14, 1927; s. Maurice Charles and Appoline Marie (Isanove) C.; m. Giraud Gisèle, Sept. 6, 1952 (dec. Jan. 1986); 1 child, Françoise. MD, Faculty of Medicine, Toulouse, France, 1953. Pvt. practice medicine Toulouse, France, 1955-63, pvt. practice medicine specializing in rehab., 1965-85; pvt. practice medicine specializing in rehab. Werner Wicker Clinic, Bad Wildungen, Fed. Republic Germany, 1986; pvt. practice specializing in orthotist Midi Oxygene Orthoses, Marseille, France, 1987—. Author: C.T.M. Korzet, 1953, Handbuch zur Herstellung des C.T.M. Korsetts, 1986. Served as lt. with French army, 1952, Vietnam. Fellow Soc. Physical Medicine, Soc. Osteopathy (adminstr.), Skoliose Selbsthilfe Verband. Club: Canoeing Fedn. (Toulouse). Home: Chemin du Château de l'Hers, 31500 Toulouse France Office: Midi Oxygene Ortheses, 70 rue d'Italie, 13006 Marseille France

CHENETIER, MARC, literature educator; b. Blois, France, Nov. 1, 1946; s. Jean-Yves and Claire Marguerite (Villéger) C.; m. Odile Genevieve Antoine, Aug. 29, 1969; children: Marion, Chloe. Degree in English, U. Tours, 1967, M Degree, 1968, D Degree, 1979. Lectr. in French Stanford U., Calif., 1970-72, vis. profl. English, 1981; asst. profl. in English Sorbonne-Nouvelle, Paris, 1972-79; vis. prof. U. East Anglia, Norwich, Eng., 1979-80, U. Va., 1983-84, Princeton U., N.J., 1987; prof. Am. lit. U. Orleans, France, 1980—; chmn. Groupe René Tadlov, Paris. 1981—. Author: The Aesthetics of Vachel Lindsay, 1979, Richard Brautigar, 1983; co-author: Textuellement, 1973; editor: Selected Letters of Vachel Lindsay, 1979, Critical Angles, 1986. Am. Council Learned Socs. fellow, 1975; Fulbright scholar, 1983, 87. Mem. French Assn. Am. Studies, Vachel Lindsay Assn. Friends of Tor House, Ste. Anglicistes Enst Superieur. Office: U Orleans, Domaine de la Source, 45072 Orleans France

CHENEY, LYNNE ANN, national cultural organization administrator, writer; b. Casper, Wyo., Aug. 14, 1941; d. Wayne and Edna (Lybyer) Vincent; m. Richard Bruce Cheney, Aug. 29, 1964; children: Elizabeth, Mary. BA, Colo. Coll., 1963; MA, U. Colo., 1964; PhD, U. Wis., 1970. Freelance writer 1970-83; lectr. George Washington U., Washington, 1972-77, U. Wyo., Casper, 1977-78; researcher, writer Md. Pub. Broadcasting, Owing Mills, 1982-83; sr. editor Washingtonian Mag., Washington, 1983-86; chmn. NEH, Washington, 1986—; commr. U.S. Constitution Bicentennial Commn., Washington, 1985—. Author: Executive Privilege, 1978, Sisters, 1981, Kings of the Hill, 1983; contbr. articles to periodicals including Smithsonian, Am. Heritage, Washingtonian mag. Republican. Methodist. Office: Nat Endowment Humanities 1100 Pennsylvania Ave NW Washington DC 20506

CHENG, CHO HONG, pharmacist; b. Chungsen, Kwung Tung, China, Jan. 9, 1932; children: Anthony, Bernard, Clement. Diploma in Pharmacy, U. Hong Kong, 1959, BSc, 1960. Sr. pharmacist Tung Wah Group Hosps., Hong Kong, 1959—. Mem. Pharm. Soc. Hong Kong, Inst. Pharmacy Mgmt. Internat. Home: 60 Cloud View Rd, Hilltop Apt Block, I 3d Fl Hong Kong Office: Tung Wah Group Hosps, Waterloo Rd Hong Kong Mailing: GPO Box 2379 Hong Kong

CHENG, CHU YUAN, educator; b. Kwangtung Province, China, Apr. 8, 1927; came to U.S., 1959, naturalized, 1964; s. Hung Shan and Shu Chen (Yang) C.; B.A. in Econs., Nat. Chengchi U., Nanking, China, 1947; M.A., Georgetown U., Washington, 1962, Ph.D., 1964; m. Alice Hua Liang, Aug. 15, 1964; children—Anita Tung I, Andrew Y.S. Research prof. Seton Hall U., 1960-64; vis. prof. George Washington U., Washington, 1963; sr. research economist U. Mich., Ann Arbor, 1964-69; assoc. prof. Lawrence U., Appleton, Wis., 1970-71; assoc. prof. econs., chmn. Asian studies com. Ball State U., Muncie, Ind., 1971-73, prof. econs., 1974—; cons. NSF, Washington, 1964—. Bd. dirs., pres. Dr. Sun Yat-sen Inst., Chgo., 1978—. Grantee, NSF, 1960-64, Social Sci. Research Council, 1965-67, 74; recipient Outstanding Research award Ball State U., 1976; Outstanding Educator in Econs., Ball State U., 1981-82. Mem. Am. Econ. Assn., Assn. Asian Studies, Assn. Comparative Econ. Studies, Am. Acad. Polit. and Social Sci., Assn. Chinese Social Scientists in N.Am. (bd. dirs. 1986—), Am. Assn. Chinese Studies, Chinese Acad. and Profl. Assn. Mid-Am. (pres. 1983-84), Ind. Acad. Social Sci., Omicron Delta Epsilon. Author: Scientific and Engineering Manpower in Communist China, 1966; The Machine-Building Industry in Communist China, 1971; China's Petroleum Industry: Output Growth and Export Potential, 1976; China's Economic Development: Growth and Structural Change, 1981; The Demand and Supply of Primary Energy in Mainland China, 1984; Taiwan as a Model for China's Modernization, 1986; Sun Yat-sen's Doctrine in Modern World, 1988; mem. adv. com. Chinese Econ. Studies Quar., 1966—. Home: 1211 Greenbriar Rd Muncie IN 47304 Office: Ball State U Coll Bus Room 123 Muncie IN 47306

CHENG, DAVID GEE, real estate developer; b. Shanghai, China, Sept. 1, 1915; came to U.S., 1966, naturalized, 1972; s. Tsi Fei and Wai Wen (Liang) C.; B.S. in Civil Engring., St. John's U., Shanghai, 1939; postgrad. Grad. Sch. of Design, Harvard U., 1966-67; children—David, Vida, Anthony. Pres., Nat. Housing Devel. Corp., Jakarta, Indonesia, 1956-66; minister of city planning and constrn. Republic of Indonesia, 1964-66; devel. dir. Hawaii Council of Housing Action, Honolulu, 1968-70; pres. DGC Devel. Corp., Honolulu, 1971—. Mem. transp. com. Oahu Devel. Conf., 1975-81. Recipient Devel. Achievement medal Republic of Indonesia, 1964. Mem. Nat. Assn. Realtors, Honolulu Bd. Realtors. Roman Catholic. Club: Plaza (charter mem.). Office: 700 Bishop St Suite 1928 Honolulu HI 96813

CHENG, HONG KOK, petroleum corporation executive; b. Georgetown, Penang, Malaysia, June 29, 1942; s. Yeng Cheong and Swee Peng (Lai) C.; m. Chan Yeok Fay, May 7, 1966; children—Peter, Gwendoline, Jacqueline. B.Sc. in Chem. Engring., U. London, 1964; Advanced Exec. Mgmt. Cert., J.L. Kellogg Grad. Sch. Mgmt., Northwestern U., 1981. Projects officer Econ. Devel. Bd., Singapore, 1964-65, prin. projects officer, 1966-68, chief project div., econ. research div., 1968-70; pres., chief exec. Singapore Petroleum Co. Pte. Ltd., Singapore, 1981—; chmn. Singapore Petroleum Trading Co. Ltd., Hong Kong, 1981—, Singapore Oil Transp. Co. Ltd., Hong Kong, 1983—; dir. Singapore Carbon Dioxide Co. Pte. Ltd. Singapore Govt. State scholar, 1961, U.K. Govt. Colonial Welfare and Devel. scholar, 1961, U. Malaya scholar, 1961; U Cambridge fellow, 1964; Eisenhower Exchange fellow, 1979. Mem. Eisenhower Exchange Fellowships. Clubs: Jurong Country, Tanah Merah Country (Singapore). Office: Singapore Petroleum Co Pte Ltd, 42-01 DBS Bldg, 6 Shenton Way 42-01, Singapore 0106, Singapore

CHENG, KUANG LU, chemist; b. Yangchow, China, Sept. 14, 1919; came to U.S., 1947, naturalized, 1955; s. Fong Wu and Yi Ming (Chiang) C.; children: Meiling, Chiling, Hans Christian. Ph.D., U. Ill., 1951. Microchemist Comml. Solvents Corp., Terre Haute, Ind., 1952-53; instr. U. Conn., Storrs, 1953-55; engr. Westinghouse Electric Corp., Pitts., 1955-57; assoc. dir. research metals div. Kelsey Hayes Co., New Hartford, N.Y., 1957-59; mem. tech. staff RCA Labs., Princeton, N.J., 1959-66; prof. chemistry U. Mo., Kansas City, 1966—. Recipient Achievement award RCA, 1963; N.T. Veatch award for disting. research and creative activity U. Mo., Kansas City, 1979; cert. of recognition U.S. office of Naval Research, 1979; cert. of recognition Coll. Engring., Tex. A&M U., 1981; Bd. Trustees fellow U. Kansas City, 1984. Fellow AAAS, Chem. Soc. London; mem. Am. Chem. Soc., Electrochem. Soc., Soc. Applied Spectroscopy, Am. Inst. Physics. Home: 34 E 56th Terr Kansas City MO 64113 Office: Dept Chemistry U Mo Kansas City MO 64110

CHENG, LESLIE YU-LIN, neurologist, psychiatrist, educator; b. Soochow, China, May 27, 1905; s. James H. and Mary Chung (Chou) C.; came to U.S., 1950, naturalized, 1956; student Soochow U., 1920-22; M.D., Peking Union Med. Coll., 1928; postgrad. SUNY, 1928; m. Mary M. Chan, June 2, 1945; children: Alfred K., Barbara Jane Cheng Neunes, Clara Joan Cheng Mok, Joyce Cheng Schlessinger, Elaine Cheng Lin, Marian Leslie; m. 2d, Elissa C. Chin, Oct. 25, 1980. Intern, Peking Union Med. Coll. Hosp., 1927-28, resident, 1928-30; resident in neurology and psychiatry Deutsche Forschungsanstalt fur Psychiatrie, Munich, Germany, 1932, Boston Psychopathic Hosp., 1932-33; practice medicine specializing in neurology and psychiatry, 1933—; chmn. dept. neuro-psychiatry United Univs., Chengtu, Szechuan, China, 1938-46, Central Hosp., Canton, China, 1946-47; dir. Nat. Neuropsychiatry Inst., Nanking, China, 1947-49; supt. Taiwan Provincial Mental Hosp., 1949-50; staff psychiatrist, chief neurology service Topeka State Hosp., 1950-58; clin. dir. No. State Hosp., Sedro Wooley, Wash., 1958-59; clin. dir. Kans. Neurol. Inst., Topeka, 1960-65; founder, supt. med. dir. Broadview Center, Cleve., 1966-72; undergrad. chmn., chmn. dept. psychiatry Mich. State U., 1973-75; med. dir. Gen. County Community Mental Health Services, Flint, Mich., 1975-76; staff psychiatrist family practice residency tng. St. Joseph Hosp., Flint., 1977-78; prof. neuropsychiatry Nat. Central U., Nanking and Chengtu, China, 1938-46; prof. neuro-psychiatry Lingnan U. Med. Sch., 1946-47, Nat. Taiwan U., 1949-50; clin. asst. prof. psychiatry U. Wash., 1959; clin. prof. Mich. State U., 1971-73, prof., 1973-75; med. cons. Vets. Gen. Hosp., vis. prof. Nat. Def. Med. Center and Nat. Yangming Med. Coll., after 1978. Diplomate Am. Bd. Psychiatry and Neurology. Fellow Am. Psychiat. Assn. (life), Am. Acad. Neurology; mem AMA, Chinese Med. Assn., Chinese Mental Hygiene Assn., Am. Child Neurology Soc. Methodist. Lodges: Masons, Rotary. Author: Textbook of Neurology (Chinese), 1983; Textbook of Psychiatry (Chinese), 1983; Medical Aspects of Mental Retardation (Chinese), 1988. Home: 9129 Bonny Brook San Antonio TX 78239

CHENG, LUNG, mechanical engineer; b. Shaoxing, Zhejiang, China, Mar. 13, 1920; s. Ren Ching and Chi Wan (Chen) C.; came to U.S., 1964, naturalized, 1972; B.M.E., Nat. Chekiang U., 1945; M.Engring., McGill U., 1961; Ph.D., U. Ill., 1969; m. Carol Dzwen-hua Dju, June 23, 1962; 1 dau., Lilie. Instr. mech. engring. Nat. Taiwan U., 1954-59; engr. Combustion Engring. Incorp., Montreal, Que., Can., 1962-64; asst. prof. mech. engring. Christian Bros. Coll., Memphis, 1969-70; supervisory mech. engr. dust control and project leader dust explosion suppression U.S. Dept. Interior, Bur. Mines, Pitts., 1970—. Mem. ASME, AAAS. Contbr. articles to profl. publs. on nature, behavior of dusts, suppression methods. Home: 140 E Highland Dr McMurray PA 15317 Office: Bur Mines US Dept Interior Cochrans Mill Rd Pittsburgh PA 15236

CHENG, SAMSON, architect; b. Wu Chow, Kwong Si, China, Mar. 15, 1934; emigrated to Can., 1958; s. Wai Shun and Fong (Wong) C.; children—Colleen, Caron. B.Sc. in Architecture, Cheng Kung U., Tainan, Taiwan, 1957; B.Arch., U. Man., Winnipeg, Can., 1960, M.Arch., 1962. Planner Central Mortgage and Housing Corp., Ottawa, Ont., 1962-63; architect John B. Parkin Assoc., Bregman & Hammann, Toronto, Ont., 1963-67, Toronto Bd. Edn., 1967-73; self-employed architect, planner, 1973—; archtl. cons. cement industry, hotel industry, Venezuela, U.K., Far East and Can., 1974-77; cons. Ky. Fried Chicken internat. image design, 1978—. Recipient Nat. House Design award Expo '67, Montreal, 1967. Mem. Ont. Archtl. Assn., Illuminating Engring. Soc. N.Am., Urban Design Internat. Avocations: tennis, skiing, badminton, photography, writing poetry, painting.

CHENG, TSUNG O., cardiologist, educator; b. Shanghai, China, Mar. 30, 1925; came to U.S., 1950, naturalized, 1960; s. Keith S. and Fanny (Wang) C.; m. Marie Ellen Roe, June 18, 1955; children: Mark Dudley, Yvonne Joyce. B.S., St. John's U., China, 1945; M.D., U. Pa., 1950, M.S. in Medicine, 1956. Diplomate: Am. Bd. Internal Medicine (subsplty. cardiovascular disease), Nat. Bd. Examiners. Intern St. Barnabas Hosp., Newark, 1950-51; resident Cook County Hosp., Chgo., 1952-55; fellow in cardiovascular disease George Washington U., D.C. Gen. Hosp., Washington, 1955-56; instr. cardiology Harvard Med. Sch. Mass. Gen. Hosp., Boston, 1956-57; fellow in cardiorespiratory physiology Johns Hopkins U. Sch. Medicine and Hosp., 1957-59; practice medicine specializing in cardiology Washington, 1970—; asst. prof. medicine SUNY Downstate, 1959-70; asso. prof. medicine George Washington U., 1970-72, prof., 1972—; chief cardiology D.C. Gen. Hosp., 1971-72; dir. cardiac catheterization lab. George Washington U. Med. Center, 1972-78, assoc. dir. cardiology, 1972-75; asst. physician Cardiac Clinic, Johns Hopkins Hosp., 1957-59, mem. staff cardiac catheterization lab., 1957-59; dir. cardiopulmonary lab. Bklyn. Hosp., 1959-66; co-chief Pediatric Cardiac Clinic, 1959-66; chief Adolescent Cardiac Clinic, 1961-66; attending physician Adult Cardiac Clinic, 1959-66; chief pediatric cardiac clinic Cumberland Hosp., Bkly., 1963-66; asst. chief cardiology VA Hosp., Bklyn., 1966-69; chief Cardiovascular Lab., 1966-70, chief cardiology, 1969-70; asst. vis. physician Kings County Hosp. Med. Center, Bklyn., 1964-70; attending physician Univ. Hosp., SUNY, Bklyn., 1967-70; cons. Beth Israel Med. Center, N.Y.C., 1970-82; guest lectr. Chinese Med. Assn., China, 1972, 73, 75, 77, 79, 83, 86; hon. prof. Shanghai Second Med. Univ. 1986—; vis. prof. Peking Union Med. Coll., 1986—; adv. Guangdong Provincial Cardiovascular Inst., 1986—. Sr. editor Vascular Medicine, 1983—; assoc. editor Angiology; editor The International Textbook of Cardiology, 1986; contbr. numerous articles to sci., med. jours. Fellow ACP, Am. Coll. Chest Physicians, Am. Coll. Cardiology (ofcl. rep. to standards com. on catheters Assn. Advancement Med. Instrumentation 1971—), Am. Heart Assn., Council Clin. Cardiology, Soc. Cardiac Angiography, Internat. Coll. Angiology, Am. Coll. Angiology; mem. AAAS, Am. Fedn. Clin. Research, Am. Heart Assn., Washington Heart Assn. Home: 7508 Cayuga Ave Bethesda MD 20817 Office: George Washington U Med Ctr 2150 Pennsylvania Ave NW Washington DC 20037

CHENG, WEI-YUAN, government official; b. Anhwei, Republic China, Jan. 20, 1913; m. Hui-Lin Tsao. Grad., Infantry Sch., Italy, 1938, Armed Forces Staff Coll., Republic China, 1953, U.S. Army Command & Staff Coll., 1956; LLD (hon.), Dankook U., Republic Korea, 1982; DSc (hon.), Fla. Inst. Tech., 1984. Army attache Embassy Republic China, Italy, 1948-49; commandant Marine Corps, Taipei, Republic China, 1961-63; dep. comdr.-in-chief Army Gen. Hdqrs., Taipei, 1967-69; exec. vice chief gen. staff Ministry Nat. Def., Taipei, 1969-72; comdr.-in-chief Combined Service Force, Taipei, 1972-75, Taiwan Garrison Gen. Hdqrs., Taipei, 1975-78; vice minister Ministry Nat. Def., Taipei, 1978-81; chmn. Vocat. Assistance Commn. for Ret. Servicemen, Taipei, 1981-87; def. minister Ministry Nat. Def., 1987—; v.p. Soc. for Strategic Studies, Republic China, 1982—. Pres. Republic China Amateur Sports Fedn., Taipei, 1982—, Chinese Taipei Olympic Com., Taipei, 1982-88; v.p. Sino-Thai Cultural and Econ. Assn., Taipei, 1982—. Served to gen. Republic China Army, 1933-81. Mem. Kuomintang Party. Home: 115 Fu Hsing Rd, Sect 2, Taipei Republic China

CHENG, YANAN, sculptor, educator; b. Huang Gu Tun, Shen Yang, People's Republic of China, Jan. 5, 1936; s. Guo Liang Cheng and Shi Jing Liu; m. Zuo Ming Zhang, Apr. 28, 1962; children: Zhang Xiao-lei, Zhang Yann. Student, U. Nationalities, Beijing, 1956-61. Prof. sculpture Cen. Inst. Fine Arts, 1961—. Works include wood sculptures Summer, 1979, Evening Wind, 1983; stone sculpturesFlower Bud, 1980, Chinese Soul, 1985. Mem. China Art Assn., Beijing Art Assn; cons. China Young Art Assn, 1985—. Recipient awards for Encouragement of Arts and Arts produced Govt. of Beijing, 1981, 85, Govt. of China, 1983, 87. Mem. Chinese Dem. Party. Home: 452 New Bldg, No 3 Shuaifuyah Ln, East Dist, Beijing 100005, Peoples Republic of China Office: Cen Inst of Fine Arts, He Bei, Beijing Peoples Republic of China

CHENG, YUK-BUN DEREK, electrical engineer; b. Swatow, Kwangtung, China, Aug. 7, 1950; s. Leung-Wing and Wai-Shan (Ma) C.; m. Susanna Wai-Hing Yuen, Aug. 6, 1983. Student E. Tex. State U., 1970-71; B.S.E.E., W.Va. Inst. Tech., 1974; M.S.E.E., W.Va. U., 1976. Grad. research asst. dept. elec. engring. W.Va. U., Morgantown, 1974-77; antenna research engr. Andrew Corp., Orland Park, Ill., 1977-82, sr. antenna research engr., 1982-84, sect. leader antenna analysis, 1984—. Recipient William E. Jackson award Radio Tech. Commn. for Aeronautics, 1976. Mem. IEEE, IEEE Antennas and Propagation Soc., IEEE Microwave Theory Tech. Soc., IEEE Chgo. joint chpt. Antennas and Propagation Soc. and Microwave Theory and Techniques Soc. (sec.-treas. 1984-85, chmn. 1985-86), Sigma Xi, Eta Kappa Nu, Tau Beta Pi, Phi Kappa Phi. Mem. Chinese Christian Union Ch. Contbr. articles to profl. jours.; patentee in field. Home: 13905 Cherokee Trail Lockport IL 60441 Office: 10500 W 153d St Orland Park IL 60462

CHENG-GUI, HUANG, mathematician, educator; b. Shaoyang, Hunan, People's Republic of China, Nov. 2, 1935; s. Jun Heang and De-Yuan (Li) H.; m. Su-Hua Chen; 1 child, Yu-Heng Huang. Student, Biejing (China) U., 1953-63. Asst. Beijing U., 1965-75; asst. Tianjin (China) Normal U., 1976-79, lectr., 1979-83, assoc. prof. math., 1983-88, prof. math., 1988—; Rep. Chinese Math. Congress, 1978, 83. Author: Twophase Calculus, 1979, 84, The New Theory of the Delta Function, 1987, The Computation Principles of Math. Physics, 1988; editor: Chinese Quarterly Jours. Math., 1986—. Mem. Tianjin Math. Soc., Tianjin Logical Soc., Am. Math. Soc. Home: 9 Tuanjielou Apt 203-204, Shida Beiyuan, Tianjin Peoples Republic of China Office: Tianjin Normal U Dept Math, Balitai, Tianjin Peoples Republic of China

CHENHALLS, ANNE MARIE, nurse, educator; b. Detroit, May 26, 1929; d. Peter and Beatrice Mary (Elliston) McLeod; m. Horacio Chenhalls, 1953 (dec.); children—Mark, Anne Marie Chenhalls Delamater. Student Detroit Conservatory Music, 1946-47; B. Vocat. Edn., Calif. State U.-Los Angeles, 1967, B.S. in Nursing, 1968; M.A., Calif. State U.-Long Beach, 1985. R.N., Calif. Nurse, Grace Hosp., Detroit, 1951-52; pvt. duty nurse, Mexico City, 1953-54; nurse St. Francis Hosp., Lynwood, Calif., 1957-63; assoc. prof. nursing Compton Coll. (Calif.), 1964-72; health educator, sch. nurse Santa Ana Unified Sch. Dist. (Calif.), 1972-76, 79—; med. coordinator, internat. health cons. Agape Movement, San Bernardino, Calif., 1976-79; instr. community health, Uganda, 1982; med. evaluator Athletes in Action, 1979. Assoc. staff mem. Campus Crusade for Christ. Solo vocalist, Santa Ana, Orange, Seal Beach, Calif. U.S. govt. grantee, 1968. Mem. Calif. Sch. Nurses Assn., Nat. Educators Assn., Calif. Assn. Vocat. Educators, Internat. Platform Assn. Democrat. Home: 12092-69 Sylvan River Fountain Valley CA 92708 Office: Santa Ana Unified Sch Dist 1405 French St Santa Ana CA 92701

CHEN JUNSHENG, government official; b. 1927. Mem. Standing Com., sec. gen. Heilongjiang Province Communist Party, 1979; sec. Qiqihar City Communist Party, 1980; sec. Heilongjiang Province Communist Party, 1982-84, dep. sec., 1983-84; dep. chmn. exec. com., sec. Fedn. Trade Unions, 1984-85, v.p., 1985; sec.-gen. State Council, 1985-88; state councilor 1988—; dep. for Heilongjiang Province to 6th Nat. People's Congress, 1983. Address: Office of Sec Gen, Beijing Peoples Republic of China *

CHEN MUHUA, People's Republic of China government official; b. Qingtian County, Zhejiang Province, China, 1921; married; 2 children. Student Jiaotong U., Shanghai, People's Republic of China. Dep. dir. Bur. Integrated Indsl. Equipment, 1962-70; vice minister Commn. Econ. Relations with Fgn. Countries, 1970-77; mem. 10th Cen. Com. Chinese Communist Party, 1973, alt. mem. Politburo, 11th Cen. Com., 1977, mem. presidium 12th Cen. Com., 1982; minister for econ. relations with fgn. countries, 1977-82; dep. Zhejiang Province, Nat. People's Congress, 1978-83; vice premier, 1978-82; minister commn. family planning, 1981-82; minister fgn. econ. relations and trade, 1982-85; state councilor, 1982-88; vice chmn. standing com. 19th Nat. People's Congress, 1988—; pres. People's Bank 1985; chmn. Council of People's Bank, 1985; head numerous world dels., 1978—. Address: Nat People's Congress, Standing Com, Beijing People's Republic of China Other: People's Bank of China, San Li He, West City, Beijing People's Republic of China *

CHENNAULT, ANNA CHAN, aviation executive, author, lecturer; b. Peking, China, June 23, 1925; came to U.S., 1948, naturalized, 1950; d. P.Y. and Isabel (Liao) Chan; m. Claire Lee Chennault, Dec. 21, 1947 (dec. July 1958); children: Claire Anna, Cynthia Louise. BA in Journalism, Lingnan U., Hong Kong, 1944; LittD, Chungang, Seoul, Korea, 1967; LLD (hon.), Lincoln U., 1970; HHD (hon.), Manahath Ednl. Center, 1970, St. Johns U., 1982, Am. U. of Caribbean, 1982; D Bus. Admin. (hon.), John Dewey U. Consortium, 1983. War corr. Central News Agy., 1944-48, spl. Washington corr., 1965—; with Civil Air Transp., Taipei, Taiwan, 1946-57, editor bull., 1946-57, pub. relations officer, 1947-57; chief Chinese Sect. Machine Translation Research, Georgetown U., 1958-63; broadcaster Voice of Am., 1963-66; U.S. corr. Hsin Shen Daily News, Washington, 1958—; v.p. internat. affairs Flying Tiger Line, Inc., Washington, 1968-76; pres. TAC Internat., 1976—; cons. various airlines and aerospace corps.; lectr., writer, fashion designer U.S. and Asia; bd. dirs. Sovran, D.C. Nat. Bank. Feature writer: Hsin Ming Daily News, Shanghai, 1944-49; Author: Chennault and the Flying Tigers: Way of a Fighter, 1963; best seller A Thousand Springs, 1962; Education of Anna, 1980; also numerous books in Chinese including Song of Yesterday, 1961, M.E.E, 1963, My Two Worlds, 1965, The Other Half, 1966, Letters from U.S.A, 1967, Journey Among Friends and Strangers, Chinese edit. 1978, China Times, Chinese-English Dictionaries. Mem. Pres.'s adv. com. arts John F. Kennedy Center Performing Arts, 1970—; Pres. Nixon's spl. rep. Philippine Aviation Week Celebration, 1973; mem. women's adv. com. on aviation to sec. transp.; v.p. Air and Space Bicentennial Organizing Com.; spl. asst. to chmn. Asian-Pacific council AmChams, mem. spl. com. transp. to sec. transp., 1972, chmn. com. for spl. transp. activities, 1972; mem. U.S. nat. com. for UNESCO, 1970—; mem. adv. council Am. Revolution Bicentennial Adminstrn., 1975-77, also mem. ethnic racial council; advisor Nat. League Families of Am. Prisoners and Missing in S.E. Asia; presdl. appointee Pres.'s Export Council, 1981, vice chmn., 1981-85; pres. Chinese Refugee Relief, Washington, 1962-70, Gen. Claire Chennault Found., 1960—; hon. chmn. Chinese-Am. Nat. Fedn., 1974—; committeewoman Washington Republican Party, 1960—; mem. Nat. Rep. Finance Com., 1969—; cons. heritage groups, nationalites div. Asian affairs Rep. Nat. Com., 1969—; chmn. Nat. Rep. Heritage Council, 1979, 87; bd. govs. Am. Acad. Achievement, Dallas; trustee Center Study Presidency, Library Presdl. Papers, 1970—, Helping Hand Found.; bd. visitors Civil Air Patrol; presdl. appointee Presdl. Scholars Commn., 1985—; bd. dirs. People to People Internat; founder Nat. Rep. Asian Assembly. Recipient Woman of Distinction award Tex. Tech. Coll., Lubbock, 1966; Freedom award Order Lafayette Washington, 1966; Freedom award Free-China Assn., Taipei, 1966; Golden Plate award as champion of democracy and freedom Am. Acad. Achievement, 1967; Lady of Mercy award, 1972; Republican of Yr. award D.C. Rep. Fedn., 1974; award of honor Chinese-Am. Citizens Alliance, 1972; Mother Gerard Phelan award, Marymount Coll., 1985, Ams. by Choice award, 1981, Capital Presswomen's award, Women of Achievement Internationally award. Fellow Aerospace Med. Assn. (hon.); mem. Nat. Aero. Assn. (bd. dirs.), Nat. League Am. Pen Women, Writers Assn., Free China Writers Assn., 14th Air Force Assn. (chmn. awards com. 1969—), U.S. Air Force Wives Club, Flying Tiger Assn., U.S. C. of C. (dir. internat. policy com., council on trends and perspective), Am. Newspaper Women's Club Washington, Nat. Mil. Families Assn. (founder, chmn.), Theta Sigma Phi, others. Clubs: Overseas Press (N.Y.C.); Pisces, 1925 F Street, International, Capitol Hill, National Press, Aero, George Town, Army-Navy (Washington). Home: 2510 Virginia Ave NW Washington DC 20037 Office: TAC Internat 1511 K St NW Washington DC 20005

CHEN XITONG, mayor, government official; b. Anyue County, Sichuan, People's Republic of China. Student, Beijing U., 1948. Dep. head police substation, chief of sec. sect. after 1949; sec. to 2d sec. Beijing Mcpl. Com., Communist Party of China, after 1963; former sec. People's Commune Party Com., County Party Com.; former chmn. County Revolutionary Com.; dep. mayor City of Beijing, 1979-83; sec. Beijing Mcpl. Party Com., after 1979; mayor City of Beijing, 1983—; dir. Beijing Planning and Cons. Com., from 1983; state councilor 1988—; mem. 12th and 13th Chinese Communist Party Central Coms. Office: State Council, Beijing Peoples Republic of China *

CHERCHI USAI, PAOLO, editor, film historian; b. Rossiglione, Genoa, Italy, Nov. 8, 1957; s. Licinio and Anita (Piccardo) C. U. MD, Genoa U., 1980. Reviewer book sect. Il Lavoro, Genoa, 1982—; editor Segnocinema, Vicenza, Italy, 1985—; correspondent Filmographic Analysis Project, Québec, Can., 1985—; lectr. Laval U., Québec, 1986, Utrecht (The Netherlands) U., 1986; dep. curator Friuli Film Archive, Gemona, Italy, 1987—. Author: Georges Méliès, 1983, Giovanni Pastrone, 1986; editor: Cinema Under the Vitagraph Flag (1896-1925), 1987; (with others) Thomas H. Ince, 1984. Fellow Italian Assn. for Film History; mem. Domitor Film Assn., Soc. for Cinema Studies. Home: 90/3 via Gandin, 16142 Genoa Italy Office: Friuli Film Archive, 26 via Osoppo, 33014 Gemona, Udine Italy

CHÉREAU, PATRICE, theater, opera and film director; b. Lézigné, France, Nov. 2, 1944; s. Jean-Baptiste and Marguerite (Pélicier) C. Ed. Lycée Louis-le-Grand and Faculté de Lettres, Paris, 1958-62. Co-dir. Théatre National Populaire, 1972-81; dir. Théatre des Amandiers, Nanterre, 1982—. Theater prodns. include: L'Intervention, 1964, L'Affaire de la rue de Lourcine, 1966, Les Soldats, 1967, La Révolte au Marché noir, 1968, Don Juan, L'Italienne a Alger, 1969, Richard II, Splendeur et Morte de Joaquin Murieta, 1970, La Finta Serva, 1971, Massacre à Paris, 1972, Toller, 1973; La Dispute, 1973, Lear, 1975, Peer Gynt, 1981, Les Paravents, 1983, Combat de Nègre et de Chiens, 1983; operas include: The Tales of Hoffmann, 1974, Der Ring des Nibelungen, Bayreuth, 1976-80, Lulu, 1979; films include: La Chair de l'Orchidée, 1974, Judith Therpauve, 1978, L'Homme blessé, 1982. Decorated officier des Arts et des Lettres. Office: Nanterre-Amandiers, 7 ave Pablo Picasso, 92000 Nanterre France *

CHERENKOV, PAVEL ALEXEYEVICH, physicist; b. Novaya Chigla, Voronezh, July 28, 1904; ed. Voronezh U. Prof., Moscow Engring. Phys. Inst.; mem. Inst. Physics USSR Acad. Scis.; mem. CPSU, 1946; corr. mem. Acad. Scis., 1964-70, academician, 1970—. Recipient Nobel prize for physics (with Tamm and Frank), 1958, State Prize (3), Order of Lenin (2), Order of Red Banner of Labor (2), Badge of Honor, other decorations. Discoverer of Cherenkov Effect. Mem. Nat. Acad. Scis. (fgn. assoc.). Office: Lebedev Physics Inst, USSR Academy of Sciences, Leninsky Prospekt 53, Moscow USSR *

CHERFAN, GEORGE CAMILLE, pharmaceutical executive; b. Beirut, Sept. 16, 1943; s. Camille Khalil and Julnar (Dib) C.; m. Sana Jeha, Aug. 29, 1970; children: Hisham, Maher, Naji. BA, St. Joseph's U., Beirut, 1965. Med. sales rep. Ayerst Lab., Beirut, 1965-67; sales rep. E.R. Squibb and Sons, Beirut, 1967-70, supr., 1970-74; regional sales and mktg. mgr. Mid. East Region, 1974-79; mng. dir. CCM Mid East, Athens, Greece, 1979-85, sr. cons., pres., mktg. dir., 1985—; bd. dirs. Am. Cynamid, Abbott, others. Author, editor: Middle East Medical Index, 1982. Active Red Cross, Lebanon, 1975-78, S.O.S., Lebanon, 1980-83, Beirut Univ. Coll., 1986. Fellow Tack Internat.; mem. Internat. Advt. Assn. Lodge: Lions. Home: 7 Essopou St Politia, 145 63 Athens Greece Office: CCM Mid East, 15-17 Tsoha St Ampelokipi, 115 10 GR Athens Greece

CHERMANN, JEAN CLAUDE, virologist; b. Paris, Mar. 23, 1939; s. Camille Andre and Benbeneda (Montoya) C.; m. Pearron Daniele, Dec. 22, 1962; children—Jean Francois, Olivier. Bachelor, Michelet, 1959; Maitrise Biochemistry, Paris U., 1963, Ph.D., 1967. Research asst. Pasteur Inst., Paris, 1963-77, head lab., 1977-87; chief viral oncology lab., Pasteur Inst., Paris; research dir. Insti. Nat. de le Recherche Medicale, Marseille, France, 1988—; vis. scientist Nat. Cancer Inst., Bethesda, Md., 1971. Decorated Ordre Nat. du Merite Pres. de la Republique (France). Office: Campus Universitaire de Luminy Bt INSERM, Laboratoire de Recherches INSERM, sur les Retrovirus et Maladies Associeęs, F-13273, Cedex 9 Marseille France

CHERRY, CHARLES LEWIS, petroleum exploration company executive; b. Platteville, Colo., Mar. 5, 1926; s. Ernest Joseph and Mildred Helen (Hall) C.; m. Eleanor Marie Rasmussen, Dec. 22, 1946; children: Bryan Alan, Jilleen Marie Cherry Day. Student Colo. State Coll. Edn., 1946-47; BS, U. Wyo., 1950. Regional geologist Royal Resources Corp., Denver, 1969-71; pvt. practice cons. geologist, Littleton, Colo., 1971-78; staff geologist Natural Resources Corp., Denver, 1972-73; pres. Charles L. Cherry and Assocs., Inc., Fayette, Ala., 1978—. Author: (with others) Geology of the Paradox Basin, 1953. Mem. bd. dirs. Assn. for Retarded Citizens, 1987—. Served with USMC, 1943-45, PTO. Decorated Bronze Star, Purple Heart. Mem. Am. Assn. Petroleum Geologists, Rocky Mountain Assn. Geologists, Am. Petroleum Inst. (Warrior Basin chpt. bd. dirs. 1984), Fayette C. of C. (bd. dirs. 1985-86), Ala. Sight Conservation Assn. (bd. dirs. 1985-86), Internat. Platform Assn. Republican. Lodges: Lions (pres. 1981-82), Exchange Club. Avocations: fishing, hunting. Home: 1136 11th Ave NW Fayette AL 35555 Office: Charles L Cherry and Assocs 1600 Temple Ave N Fayette AL 35555

CHERRY, GORDON EMANUEL, educator; b. Barnsley, Yorkshire, Eng., Feb. 6, 1931; s. Emanuel and Nora (Goddard) C.; m. Margaret Mary Loudon Cox, June 8, 1957; children: Shona Margaret, Shelagh Louise, Iain Gordon. BA, U. London, 1953; DSc (hon.), Heriot Watt U., 1984. Cert. town planner; chartered surveyor. Town planner various towns in Eng., 1956-68; latterly research officer City of Newcastle Upon Tyne, 1963-68; sr. lectr. Centre for Urban and Region Studies U. Birmingham, 1968—, prof. urban and region planning, 1976, dean faculty of commerce and social sci., 1981-86, head dept. geography, 1987—. Author: Cities and Plans, 1988, The Politics of Town Planning, 1982, Pioneers in British Planning, 1981, Shaping an Urban World, 1980, Environmental Planning, 1985, Town Planning in its Social Context, 1970, 2d edit., 1973, Urban Change and Planning, 1972; (with J.L. Penny) Holford: a study in architecture, planning and civic design, 1986, (with Anthony Sutcliffe) Planning Perspectives: an internat. jour. of history, planning and the environment, 1986—; others. Ch. warden Hampton in Arden; trustee Bournville Villlage Trust; mem. Local Govt. Boundary Commn. for Eng., Landscape Adv. Com., Ministry of Transport. Mem. Fellow Royal Town Planning Inst. (pres. 1978-79), Royal Instn. of Chartered Surveyors; mem. Planning History Group (chmn. 1974—). Home: 66 Meriden Rd, Hampton in Arden, Solihull, West Midlands B92 OBT, England Office: U Birmingham, Sch Geography, Birmingham B15 2TT, England

CHERVENAK, FRANCIS ANTHONY, obstetrician and gynecologist; b. Newark, Dec. 20, 1953; s. Francis and Jody (DiGiacomo) C.; B.S. with highest distinction, Pa. State U., 1974; M.D., Jefferson Med. Coll., 1976. Intern, N.Y. Med. Coll., 1976-77; resident ob-gyn N.Y. Med. Coll., 1977-79, St. Luke's Med. Center, N.Y.C., 1979-81; fellow maternal-fetal medicine Yale U., 1981-83, also instr. ob-gyn Yale-New Haven Hosp., 1981-83; asst. prof. Mt. Sinai Sch. Medicine, N.Y.C., 1983-86; assoc. prof. Cornell Med. Ctr., 1987—. Fellow Am. Coll. Obstetricians and Gynecologists (jr.); mem. AMA, Soc. Perinatal Obstetricians (asso.), Am. Inst. Ultrasound in Medicine, Alpha Omega Alpha. Roman Catholic. Contbr. articles and abstracts to profl. jours., including New Eng. Jour. Medicine, Lancet. Home: 82 Park Pl South Orange NJ 07079 Office: NY Hosp Cornell Med Ctr 525 E 68th St New York NY 10021

CHESAREK, FERDINAND JOSEPH, business executive, former army officer; b. Calumet, Mich., Feb. 18, 1914; s. Joseph and Mary (Pontello) C.; m. Martha Jayne Rullman, Sept. 1, 1938 (dec. 1979); 1 child, John Laymon; m. Joan Tepe. B.S., U.S. Mil. Acad., 1938; M.B.A., Stanford, 1950; M.B.A. grad, Nat. War Coll., 1956, Advanced Mgmt. Program, Harvard U., 1958. Commd. 2d lt. U.S. Army, 1938, advanced through grades to gen., 1968; comdg. officer 28th F.A. Bn., 8th Inf. Div., ETO, World War II, 5th Arty. Group, Korean War; comdg. gen. 4th Logistical Command, Europe, 1959-62; asst. dep. chief staff logistics Dept. Army, 1962-66; comptroller of army 1966; asst. vice chief staff Army, 1967-68; comdg. gen. U.S. Army Materiel Command, 1968-70; ret. 1970; now owner Chesarek Industries, Inc.; pres. Consol. Investment & Devel. Corp., Luxembourg.; chmn. bd. dirs. Proximity Systems, Inc. Decorated Silver Star, Legion of Merit, Bronze Star, Commendation medal, Air medal, Purple Heart, D.S.M.; Legion of Honor; Croix de Guerre (France), Croix de Guerre (Luxembourg), Order Ulchi (Korea), Order of Republic (Italy). Home: 25706 Elena Rd Los Altos Hills CA 94022

CHESHIRE, JENNIFER LILIAN, linguist, educator, writer; b. London, Feb. 26, 1946; d. Sydney Harold and Elsie Millicent (Bassett) Russell; m. Paul Charles Cheshire, May 1, 1970; children: Jack Nathaniel, Sarah Margaret. BA in French and Linguistics with honors, U. London, 1971; PhD in Linguistics, U. Reading, Eng., 1979. Lectr. U. Reading, 1979-80, U. Bath, Eng., 1980-83, U. London, 1983—; cons. Open U., Eng., 1986-87; research dir. Econ. and Social Research Council, London, 1986—. Author: Variation in an English Dialect, 1982, (with others) Describing Language, 1987, (with others) Dialect and Educations: Some European Perspectives; contbr. articles to profl. jours. Recipient Postgrad. Research award Social Sci. Research Council, U.K., 1972-75, U. Reading, 1975-76, Research Project Fin. award Econ. and Social Research Council, U.K., London, 1986—, Linked Studentship award, 1985-88. Mem. Linguistics Assn. Gt. Britain, Brit. Assn. Applied Linguistics. Office: U London, Birkbeck Coll, 43 Gordon Square, London WC1 0PD, England

CHESNI, YVES GÉRARD ALEXANDRE, psychiatrist; b. Paris, Feb. 4, 1920; s. Alexandre Victor Marie and Rachel (Solinski) C.; m. Jeanne Marie Victoria Vergne, June 24, 1951. Student in medicine and neuropsychiatry, U. Geneva, 1948-56; student, Inst. Pasteur, Paris, 1949-50; degree in neurology and psychiat., U. Geneva, 1956. Asst. various hosps. Paris and Geneva, 1950-54; cons. dept. psychiatry U. Geneva, 1954-58; dir. Service Médico-Pédagogique, Geneva, 1954-58; pvt. practice neuropsychiatry Geneva, 1958-79, St. Philbert, France, 1979—; lectr. in field. Author: Dialectical Realism, Towards a Philosophy of Growth, 1973, On the Development of Consciousness, 1983, (with others) Neurological Examination of The Infant, 1955; contbr. articles to profl. jours. Physician Civil Def. Corps, Geneva, 1970-79. Mem. Swiss Soc. Neurology, Swiss Soc. Psychiatry, Swiss Soc. Philosophy, French Soc. Neurology (hon.), Internat. Stress and Tension Control Soc. (v.p. 1984), Inst. for Stress Mgmt. (advisor 1985). Home and Office: 8 Rue de l'Hôtel Ville, 44310 Saint Philbert Grand Lieu France

CHESNUTT, CAROLYN CRAWFORD, engineering consortium executive; b. Maryville, Tenn., Sept. 16, 1933; d. John Calvin Jr. and America Arey (Moore) Crawford; m. John Calvin Chesnutt, Sept. 7, 1955 (div. Feb. 1981); children—John Calvin, Thomas Walter, Margaret America, Carolyn Christian; m. H. Thomas Thorsen, Apr. 25, 1987. B.A., Agnes Scott Coll., Decatur, Ga., 1955; M.Ed., U. S.C., 1972; M.S., Ga. Inst. Tech., 1979. Asst. librarian Hartsville Meml. Library, S.C., 1964-65; tchr. music Darlington Sch. System, S.C., 1965-68, tchr. math. and psychology, Hartsville, 1968-73; tchr. math. DeKalb County Sch. System, Clarkston, Ga., 1973-75; asst. to dean engring. Ga. Inst. Tech., Atlanta, 1975-77; exec. dir. Southeastern Consortium for Minorities in Engring., Inc., Atlanta, 1977—. Vice pres. Hartsville Arts Council, 1968-72; campaign chairperson Community Concert Assn., Hartsville, 1968-70, pres., 1970-72; pres. PTA, Hartsville, 1973, Class of 1955, Agnes Scott Coll., 1985—; mem. Atlanta Symphony Orch. Chorus, 1985-87; mem. com. to restructure bds. and agys. Presbyterian Ch. U.S., 1968-71, mem. gen. exec. bd., 1971-72. Grantee Alfred P. Sloan Found., 1977-81, NASA, 1982-86, Carnegie Corp., 1985-88, NSF, 1985-88; recipient Reginald H. Jones Disting. Service award Nat. Action Council for Minorities in Engring. Mem. Nat. Assn. Precoll. Dirs. (charter, chairperson 1984-85), Soc. Women Engrs., Am. Soc. Engring. Edn., Am. Guild Organists, NEA,

S.C. Edn. Assn. Avocations: playing organ; travel; jogging. Home: 1054 Robin Ln Atlanta GA 30306 Office: Southeastern Consortium for Minorities in Engring Inc care Ga Inst Tech Atlanta GA 30332-0270

CHESNUTT, EDWIN LEE, JR., marketing executive; b. Atlanta, Mar. 4, 1940; s. Edwin Lee and Mary Ellen (Bell) C.; B.S. in Engring., Duke U., 1963; M.B.A., U. N.C., 1964; grad. advanced mgmt. program Harvard Bus. Sch., 1982; m. Ann Tanner, Nov. 17, 1977; 1 son, Edwin Lee III; 1 stepson, James Harold Mason III. With Cryovac div. W.R. Grace Co., Duncan, S.C., 1964—, dir. mktg., 1975-77, v.p. mktg., planning, and new bus. devel., 1977—. Mem. Greenville County (S.C.) Devel. Bd., 1971-74, chmn., 1974; trustee United Way of Greenville, 1969-76; pres. Jr. Achievement of Greenville, 1975-76, v.p., 1974-75, sec.-treas., 1973-74; mem. Greenville County Planning Commn., 1976-82, vice chmn., 1977, 81, 82; bd. dirs. Am. Cancer Soc., Greenville, 1975, Greenville Housing Found., 1971-73; v.p. Community Council of Social and Welfare Agys., 1973-74. Named Boss of Yr., Nat. Secs. Assn., Greenville, 1974, Young Man of Yr., Greenville Jaycees, 1973; S.C. Young Man of Yr., S.C. Jaycees, 1974, one of Outstanding Young Men of Am., Jaycees, 1976. Mem. Soc. Plastics Engrs., Am. Mgmt. Assn., Soc. Profl. Planners, Greenville C. of C. (v.p. 1973-74). Republican. Episcopalian. Office: PO Box 464 Duncan SC 29334

CHESTERFIELD, RHYDONIA RUTH EPPERSON, financial company executive; b. Dallas, Tex., Apr. 23, 1919; d. Leonard Lee and Sally E. (Stevenson) Griswold; m. Chad Chesterfield, Apr. 21, 1979. BS Southwestern U., 1952; BS, N. Tex. U., 1954, ME, 1956; PhD, Bernardean U., 1974, Calif. Christian U., 1974, LLD (hon.), 1974. Evangelist with Griswold Trio, 1940-58; tchr., counselor Dallas public schs., 1952-58, Los Angeles public schs., 1958-74; pres. Griswold-Epperson Fin. Enterprise, Los Angeles, 1974—; pres. GEC Enterprises, 1979—; guest speaker various schs., chs. and civic orgns. in U.S. and Can. Author: Little Citizens series, Cathedral Films; contbr. articles on bus. to profl. publs. Fellow Internat. Naturopathic Assn.; mem. Los Angeles Inst. Fine Arts, Assn. of Women in Edn. (hon.), Internat. Bus. and Profl. Women, Calif. C. of C., Los Angeles C. of C., Pi Lambda Theta (hon.), Kappa Delta Pi (hon.). Office: 10790 Wilshire Blvd 202 Los Angeles CA 90024

CHEUNG, FAN-BILL, mechanical engineer; b. Canton, China, Mar. 6, 1949; s. Kong-Kwan and Yu-Mui (Kong) C.; m. Pattie P. Hsieh, Feb. 4, 1975; children—Lily, Simon, Jennifer. BS in Chem. Engring., Nat. Taiwan U., Taipei, 1969; Ph.D. in Mech. Engring., U. Notre Dame, 1974. Grad. research asst. U. Notre Dame, Ind., 1970-74; asst. mech. engr. Argonne Nat. Lab., Ill., 1974-78, mech. engr., 1978-82, group leader, 1982-85; assoc. prof. Pa. State U., University Park, 1985—. Contbg. author Annual Review of Fluid Mechanics, 1983, Advances in Transport Processes, 1984, Annual Review of Numerical Fluid Mechanics and Heat Transfer, 1987, mem. adv. bd. Grantee NSF, Gen. Electric Co., San Jose, FMC Corp., Mpls. Mem. Am. Soc. Mech. Engrs. (mem. K-13 com. on nucleonics heat transfer), Am. Phys. Soc. Home: 100 Cherry Ridge Rd State College PA 16803 Office: Dept Mech Engring Pa State U University Park PA 16802

CHEUNG, FLORENCE MAN-FUNG, pathologist; b. Hong Kong, July 18, 1953; d. Hon Kit and Lai Lan (Chan) C.; m. Alwin Siu-Wah Pang, Mar. 6, 1983; children: Clement Ho-Yan Pang, Christie Hong-Yee Pang. MB BS, U. Hong Kong, 1977. Med. officer United Christian Hosp., Kwun Tong, Hong Kong, 1978-79; lectr. dept. pathology U. Hong Kong, 1979-86, part-time lectr. dept. pathology, 1986—; sr. tutor Lady Ho-Tung Hall, U. Hong Kong, 1979-82. Contbr. articles to profl. jours. Mem. Royal Coll. Pathologists U.K. Mem. Evang. Free Ch. of China. Office: United Christian Hosp, Dept Pathology, Kwun Tong Hong Kong

CHEUNG, YAU KAY TONY, consumer products executive; b. Hong Kong, Dec. 17, 1952; s. Chak and Siu Chuen (Chan) C.; m. Priscilla Chung Han Mo, Sept. 30, 1987; children: Hiu Yan, Hiu Sze. Diploma in Bus. Studies, Hong Kong Poly., 1974; postgrad. in bus., U. Hong Kong. With Jardine Matheson and Co., Ltd., Hong Kong, 1977—; gen. mgr. Jardine Consumer Products, Hong Kong. Mem. Inst. Chartered Secs. and Adminstrs. (assoc.), Inst. Mktg., British Inst. Mgmt. Home: 64-68 Pokfulam Rd Block B 15/F, Kingsfield Tower Room 1, Hong Kong Hong Kong Office: Jardine Consumer Products, World Trade Ctr 34th Floor, Causeway Bay, Hong Kong Hong Kong

CHEVAILLIER, GERARD, ear, nose and throat specialist; b. Saintes, France, July 19, 1951; s. Gilbert and Huguette (Rondolat) C. BS, U. Paris, 1971, MD, 1979. Specialty in voice therapy and otorhionolaryngology, 1982. Practice medicine specializing in voice therapy and surgery Paris, 1982—; mem. staff Hosp. de la Pitié-Salpêtrière, Paris; cons. in communication Temps Pub., Paris, 1987; counselor voice students Studio des Variétes, Paris, 1986—. Mem. Phoniatric Soc. Roman Catholic. Avocations: singing, tennis. Office: 34 Blvd de L'Hôpital, 75005 Paris France

CHEVALIER, JEAN-PIERRE, management consultant; b. Saigon, Vietnam, Aug. 26, 1935; s. Maxime and Madeleine (Rossignol) C.; m. Monique, Oct. 30, 1960; 1 child, Christophe. M.B.A., European Inst. Bus. Adminstrn., INSEAD, Fontainebleau, France, 1972; Grad. with Honors, Brit. C. of C., Paris, 1962. Area sales mgr. CGE, France, 1962-66; mktg. dir. Quaker Oats Corp., Paris, 1966-68; acctg. dir. Havas-Conseil, Paris, 1970-73; bus. mgr. Arts et Metiers de l'Industrie, Paris, 1973—; lectr. mktg. mgmt., Casablanca, Morocco, 1974, various other confs. Named Leader in Mktg. Mgmt. Thought, Ministry Post and Telecommunications Patronage. Fellow Alexander Hamilton Inst. (cert. of recognition 1979). Clubs: Diners Internat., F.F. Golf. Office: Arts Metier Ind AETMI, 77 Ave Des Champs Elysees, 75008 Paris France

CHEVALIER, ROGER EMILE, engineering executive; b. Marseille, France, May 3, 1922; s. Louis and Marie Louise (Assaud) C.; m. Monique Marie Rose Blin, Aug. 12, 1947; children: Alain, Philippe. Student, Ecole Poly., Paris, 1944, Ecole Nat. Superieure Aeronautique, Paris, 1948. Engr. Arsenal Aeronautique, Paris, 1948-53, Nord Aviation, Paris, 1953-59; dir. tech. Sereb, Paris, 1960-66, dir. gen., 1966-70; dir. gen. Aeruspatiale, Paris, 1970-83, vice chmn., 1973-87; chmn. Serat, Paris, 1987—. Named commdr. Legion d'Honneur, 1983. Fellow AIAA; mem. Acad. Internat. Astronautique (v.p., pres. 1973-82). Home: 4 rue Edouard Detaille, 75017 Paris France Office: Serat, 20 rue de la Baume, 8 Paris France

CHEVENEMENT, JEAN-PIERRE, French government official; b. Belfort, France, Mar. 9, 1939; s. Pierre Chevènement and Juliette Garessus; m. Nisa Grünberg, 1970; 2 sons. Ed., U. Paris, Ecole Nat. Adminstrn. Dep. to Nat. Assembly, Paris, 1973-81, 86—; v.p. Deptl. Assembly Franche-Comté; minister state, minister research and tech. France, Paris, 1981-82, minister industry, 1982-83, minister nat. edn., 1984-86, minister def., 1988—. Mem. Socialist Party. Home: 22 rue Descartes, 75005 Paris France Office: 69 rue de Varenne, 75700 Paris France *

CHEVERS, WILDA ANITA YARDE (MRS. KENNETH CHEVERS), educator; b. N.Y.C.,; d. Wilsey Ivan and Herbertlee (Perry) Yarde; B.A., Hunter Coll., 1947; M.S.W., Columbia, 1959; Ph.D., N.Y.U., 1981; m. Kenneth Chevers, May 14, 1950; 1 dau., Pamela Anita. Probation officer, 1947-55; supr. probation officer, 1955-65; br. chief Office Probation for Cts. N.Y.C., 1965-72, asst. dir. probation, 1972-77, dep. commr. dept. probation, 1978-86; prof. pub. adminstrn. John Jay Coll., 1986—; conf. faculty mem. Nat. Council Juvenile and Family Ct. Judges; mem. faculty N.Y.C. Tech. Coll., Nat. Coll. Juvenile Justice; mem. adv. com. Family Ct., First Dept. Sec. Susan E. Wagner Adv. Bd., 1966-70. Sec., bd. dirs. Allen Community Day Care Center, 1971-75; bd. dirs. Allen Sr. Citizens Housing, Allen Christian Sch., Queensboro Soc. for Prevention Cruelty to Children. Named to Hunter Coll. Hall of Fame, 1983. Mem. ABA (assoc. criminal justice com.), N.Y. Bar Assn. (juvenile justice com.), Nat. Council on Crime and Delinquency, Nat. Assn. Social Workers, Acad. Cert. Social Workers. Middle Atlantic States Conf. Correction, Alumni Assn. Columbia Sch. Social Work, NAACP, Am. Soc. Pub. Adminstrn. (dir.), Counseliers, Delta Sigma Theta. Club: Hansel and Gretel (pres. 1967-69) (Queens, N.Y.). Home: 105-62 132d St Richmond Hill Queens NY 11419

CHEVES, HARRY LANGDON, JR., physician; b. Birmingham, Ala., Oct. 17, 1924; s. Harry Langdon and Myrtle (Churchill) C.; A.B., Mercer U., 1949; M.D., Med. Coll. Ga., 1953; m. Lois Rebecca Corry, Dec. 25, 1949; children—Rebecca Churchill, Harry Langdon III; m. 2d, Mary Agnes Moon; 1 son, Harry Michael. Intern, Univ. Hosp., Augusta, Ga., 1953-54; practice medicine, East Point, Ga.; mem. staff S. Fulton Hosp., chief of staff, 1980-81. Served with USAAF, 1942-46. Fellow Internat., Am. colls. angiology; mem. Royal Soc. Health, AMA, So. Med. Assn., Med. Assn. Atlanta, Atlanta, So. Dist. (past pres.) med. socs., Am. Geriatric Soc., Med. Assn. Ga., Ga. Heart Assn., Phi Delta Theta. Clubs: Am. Antique Automobile, Classic Car Club Am., Packard Automobile Classics, Rolls-Royce Am., Rolls-Royce Owners, Model A, Chrysler Restorers. Home: 333 Plantation Circle Riverdale GA 30296 Office: 2726 Felton Dr East Point GA 30344

CHEVRAY, RENE, physics educator; b. Paris, Feb. 6, 1937; came to U.S., 1962; s. Robert and Marie-Louise (Fracher) C.; m. Keiko Uesawa, Aug. 9, 1964; children: Pierre-Yves Masaki, Veronique Mie. B.S., U. Toulouse, France, 1962; Dipl. Ing. (French Govt. Highest scholar), Ecole Nationale Supé rieure d'Électronique, d'Electrotechnique et d'Hydraulique de Toulouse, 1962; MS (Alliance Française of N.Y. fellow), U. Iowa, 1963, Ph.D., 1967; D.Sc., U. Claude Bernard, Lyon, France, 1978. Product and mfg. engr. Centrifugal Pumps Worthington, Paris, 1963-64; research assoc. Iowa Inst. Hydraulic Research, Iowa City, 1964-67; postdoctoral fellow, lectr. aeronautics Johns Hopkins U., 1967-69; asst. prof. SUNY, Stony Brook, 1969-72; assoc. prof. SUNY, 1972-79, prof., 1979-82; prof. dept. mech. engring. Columbia U., N.Y.C., 1982-87, chmn. dept. mech. engring., 1987—; cons. physics of fluids and instrumentation; vis. prof. Japan Soc. for Promotion Sci., 1975; vis. prof., von. Humboldt fellow U. Karlsruhe, 1975-76. Fulbright scholar, 1962-63; NSF grantee, 1970-73, 1973—; Research Found. State U. N.Y. Faculty Research fellow, 1970-71; Dept. Energy grantee, 1979—; Office of Naval Research grantee, 1985—. Mem. Internat. Assn. Hydraulic Research, Am. Phys. Soc., N.Y. Acad. Scis., Sigma Xi. Home: 445 Riverside Dr New York NY 10027 Office: Mech Enging Columbia U New York NY 10027

CHEVRETTE, FRANCOIS, law school dean. Dean Sch. Law, U. Montreal, Que. Office: U Montreal, Faculte de Droit, CP 6128 Succursale A, Montreal, PQ Canada H3C 3J7 *

CHEVRILLON, OLIVIER, government official; b. Paris, Jan. 28, 1929; s. Louis and Hedwige C.; m. Marie France Renaud; 1 child, Melisande. Student, d'Etude Politique de Paris, 1946-49, Ecole Naheuole d'Adminstn., 1949-52. With French Conseil of State, Paris, 1953-68; v.p. L'Express, Paris, 1968-70, chmn. bd., editor, 1970-71; chmn., columnist Le Point, Paris, 1972-86; dir. French museums Ministry Culture, Paris, 1987—. Vice chmn. French-Am. Found., Paris, 1978—. Served to lt. French Air Force, 1952-53. Club: Le Siecle. Home: 4 Quoi des Juileries, 75001 Paris France Office: Direction des Musees de France, Palais du Louvre, 75001 Paris France

CHEW, LIM KIAN, productivity consultant; b. Singapore, June 5, 1949; s. Boh Goh and Ee Thoi (Yap) Lim; m. Doreen Quek, Dec. 24, 1977; 1 son, Lionel. H.S.C., Hua Yi Govt. Sch., Singapore, 1968. Supr., N.S. Electronics, Singapore, 1969-72; sect. supr. Siemens Components, Singapore, 1972-74; factory mgr. Eastronics Pte. Ltd., Singapore, 1975-77; mfg. mgr. Neston Electronics, Singapore, 1977-79; gen. mgr. Kempthorne Lighting Co., Singapore, 1979-81; factory mgr. Luxor (S) Pte. Ltd., Singapore, 1981-83; ops. mgr. Otrona (S) Pte. Ltd., Singapore, from 1981-84, productivity cons., 1984-85, materials mgr., 1986—. Editor: Materials and Purchasing Management Manual, 1982. Singapore Nat. Productivity Bd. fellow, 1987—. Mem. Nat. Productivity Assn., Singapore Quality and Reliability Assn. Address: 1 Pearl Bank, Apt 26-03, Singapore 0316 Singapore

CHEYSSON, CLAUDE, French politician; b. Paris, Apr. 13, 1920; s. Pierre and Sophie (Funck-Brentano) C.; Engr., Ecole Polytechnique, 1942; grad. Ecole Nat. d'Adminstrn., 1948; Dr. Social Scis. (hon.), U. Louvain (Belgium); m. Daniele Schwarz, Oct. 18, 1969; children—Bettina, Jean-Christian, Christophe, Thomas, Amelie, Carole. Liaison officer to German Fed. authorities, Bonn, 1948-52; polit. adviser to prime minister Vietnam, 1952-53; personal adviser to prime minister France, 1954-55, to French minister for Morocco and Tunisia, 1956; sec.-gen. Commn. Coop. in Africa, Lagos, Nigeria, 1957-62; dir. gen. Sahara Authority, Algiers, 1962-66; French ambassador to Indonesia, 1966-70; pres. Entreprise miniere et chimique, Paris, 1970-73; mem. European Commn. for Budget, 1973-77, European Commn. for 3d World, 1973-81, European Commn. North South, 1985—; pres. Congo Potash Co., 1970-73; mem. bd. Le Monde, daily, 1969-81, 85—; minister external relations Govt. France, 1981-85. Served with Free French Forces, 1943-45. Decorated French War Cross (5), comdr. Legion of Honor; grand cross nat. orders Saudi Arabia, Austria, Denmark, Egypt, Germany, Guinea, Iceland, Italy, Japan, Liberia, Malta, Morocco, Netherlands, Portugal, Spain, Sweden, Syria, Tunisia, United Kingdom; grand officer nat. orders Belgium, Benin, Cameroun, Chad, Gabon, Ivory Coast, Lebanon, Niger, Senegal, Togo, Upper Volta; comdr. nat. orders Centrafrica, Indonesia, Mali; recipient Joseph Bech prize, 1978. Socialist. Roman Catholic. Author articles, booklets. Home: Samudra, 40150 Hossegor, France Office: care Commn of the European Communs, 200 rue de la Loi, Brussels 1049 Belgium

CHHATWAL, SUBIR JIT SINGH, diplomat; b. Bannu, India, Oct. 1, 1931; s. Datar Singh and Rattan (Kaur) C.; m. Neelam Singh, May 13, 1962; children: Ritu, Param Jit Singh. M of Polit. Sci., Agra (India) U., 1954. In tng. Ministry of External Affairs New Delhi and Cambridge U., India and Eng., 1955-58; 3d sec. Indian Embassy, Madrid, 1958-60; undersec. Ministry External Affairs, New Delhi, 1960-62; 1st sec. Indian Embassy, Cuba, 1962-64; dep. sec. Ministry External Affairs Office, New Delhi, 1964-66; 1st sec. high commn. Ottawa, Ont., Can., 1966-68; 1st. consul gen. Seoul, Korea, 1968-71; dir. Ministry of Fgn. Trade, New Delhi, 1971-73; chief protocol, joint sec. Govt. of India, New Delhi, 1973-75; High Commr. India Kuala Lumpur, Malaysia, 1975-79; Indian ambassador Kuwait, 1979-82; High Commr. India Colombo, Sri Lanka, 1982-85, Ottawa, Can., 1985—. Sikh. Clubs: Delhi Gymkhana, Delhi Golf, Delhi Panch Shila, India Internat. Center; Ottawa Athletic. Home: 585 Acacia Ave, Rockcliffe, Ottawa, ON Canada K1M 0M5 Office: High Commn India, 10 Springfield Rd, Ottawa, ON Canada K1M 1C9

CHIA, JACK TEHTSAO, producer, director; b. Chongqing, Sichwan, People's Republic China, June 5, 1924; came to U.S., 1949; s. Peiyong Chia and Wenyu Chen; m. Linda Lou Jeffers, Aug. 25, 1979; children: Christopher, Clint, Cynthia. BA, Nat. U. Polit. Sci., Nanking, People's Republic China, 1947; MA, Fordham U., 1952; BA, Columbia Coll., Chgo., 1970. Asst. to chmn. dept. diplomacy Nat. U. Polit. Sci., Nanking, 1947-48; writer Voice of Am., N.Y.C., 1952-54; pres. Good Time Pub. Co., Chgo., 1962-66; writer Encyclopaedia Britannica, Chgo., 1966-68; producer, dir. Chia's Prodns., Inc., Chgo., 1970—. Author plays include The Egg, 1964, Girl-a-Week, 1965; writer film documentary Teen Scene, 1971 (5 awards 1972); columnist internat. relations Social Welfare Daily; patentee in field. Recipient 1st. prize Nat. Essay Contest Peace Daily, 1947, Golden award Toastmasters Internat., 1964, Bronze award Internat. Film and TV Festival N.Y., 1972, Silver award Internat. Film and TV Festival N.Y., 1977. Mem. Dramatists Guild, Inventors Council. Office: Chia's Prodns Inc 1247 W Wellington Ave Chicago IL 60657-4227

CHIANG, BENJAMIN BI-NIN, health science facility administrator, educator; b. Republic of China, July 18, 1929; m. Annie Ying-Wha Shai, Aug. 23, 1958; children: Jane, Lily. MD, Nat. Def. Med. Ctr., Taipei, Republic of China, 1954. Chief cardiology div. Vets. Gen. Hosp., Taipei, 1966-80, chmn. dept. of medicine, 1980-85, dir. clin. research ctr., 1982—, dep. dir., 1985—; prof., chmn. dept. of medicine Nat. Yang Ming Med. Coll., Taipei, 1980-85, dir. inst. clin. medicine, 1986—, dean sch. of medicine, 1985—. Author: Clinical Echocardiography, 1979, Clinical Electrocardiography, 1983; editor Jour. Echocardiography, 1984, Jour. AMA (Southeast Asia div.), 1984, Jour. Medicine Digest, 1984. Named one of 10 Most Outstanding Young Men Jr. Chamber of Commerce, Taipei, 1966, one of 10 Most Outstanding Vets. Vocat. Aaaistance Commn. of Retired Servicemen, Taipei, 1979; research fellow U. London, 1962-64, U. Mich, 1967-69. Fellow Royal Coll. Physicians, Am. Coll. Cardiology, Am. Coll. Chest Physicians; mem. Republic of China Soc. Cardiology (pres. 1987—), Chinese Med. Assn. (exec. bd. 1969—). Home: 128-9B Sect 4 Chung Hsiao E Rd, Taipei 10646, Republic of China Office: Vets Gen Hosp, 210 Sect 2 Shih-Pei Rd, Taipei 11217, Republic of China

CHIANG, FU-PEN, mechanical engineering educator, researcher; b. Checkiang, China, Oct. 10, 1936; s. Chien-lo and Lien-yin (Mao) C.; m. Charlotte Chen-yi Chen, June 1, 1963; children—Brian (dec.), Ted, Michelle. BS in Civil Engring. Nat. Taiwan U., 1953-57; MS U. Fla., 1963; PhD in Engring. Sci. and Mechanics, 1966. Civil engr., 1958-62; asst. prof. mech. engring. SUNY-Stony Brook, 1967-70, assoc. prof., 1970-73, prof., 1974-87, lead prof., 1987—, dir. Lab. for Exptl. Mechanics Research, 1984—; vis. prof. Swiss Fed. Inst. Tech., Lausanne, 1973-74; sr. vis. fellow dept. physics Cavendish Lab., U. Cambridge, Eng., 1980-81; cons. Army Material and Mechanics Research Ctr., Army Missile Command, Grumann Aerospace Corp., and others. Editor Internat. Jour. Optics and Lasers in Engring.; contbr. articles to profl. jours. Postdoctoral fellow Cath. U. Am.; NSF grantee, 1968-73, 76-87; Office Naval Research grantee, 1982—; Army Research Office grantee, 1988—; Dept. Def. grantee, 1984-85, 87-88. Fellow Soc. Exptl. Mechanics, Optical Soc. Am.; mem. Soc. Photo-Optical Instrumentation Engrs., Am. Acad. Mechanics, AAAS, ASME, N.Y. Acad. Scis. Research on devel. of optical stress analysis techniques such as laser speckles techniques, holographic interferometry, white light speckle techniques, moire methods, photoelasticity, electron speckle and acoustic speckle techniques. Office: SUNY Dept Mech Stony Brook NY 11794-2300

CHIANG, JOHN YOUNG LING, biochemistry educator, researcher; b. Hangchew, CheKiang, China, July 29, 1947; came to U.S., 1970, naturalized, 1980; s. Ming-ming and Ya-Jung (Huang) C.; m. Lisa H. Kang, Aug. 3, 1973; children—Eric, David. B.S., Chung-Hsing U., Taichung, Taiwan, 1969; M.S., SUNY-Albany, 1973, Ph.D., 1976. Postdoctoral scholar U. Mich. Med. Sch., Ann Arbor, 1976-78; asst. prof. biochemistry and molecular pathology Northeastern Ohio U. Coll. Medicine, Rootstown, 1978-83, assoc. prof., 1983-88, prof., 1988—. Contbr. articles to profl. jours. NIH fellow, 1977-78; Pharm. Mfrs. Assn. Found. grantee, 1982-83; Am. Heart Assn. grantee, 1980-82; NIH grantee, 1983—. Mem. AAAS, Am. Soc. Biol. Chemists. Subspecialty: Biochemistry (medicine), Molecular biology. Current work: Biochemical research in studying the induction and regulation of enzymes involved in cholesterol and bile acid metabolism and liver detoxication enzymes. Home: 3020 Fox Burrow Dr Stow OH 44224 Office: Northeastern Ohio University College of Medicine 4209 State Route 44 Rootstown OH 44272

CHIANG CHU-CHIEN, educator, college dean; b. Fu Chien, China, Sept. 8, 1918; s. Yu Lang Chiang and Chang Ying Teng; B.A., Nat. U. Amoy, 1945; m. Yang Shu-Hui, July 22, 1953; children—Chiang Hui-Wen, Chiang Hui-Ming. Mem. faculty Tunghai U., Taichung, Taiwan, 1955—, prof., chmn. Chinese lit., 1964-71, dir. Humanity Center, 1971-73, dir. Chinese Grad. Sch., 1975-79, dean Arts Coll., 1978—; spl. chair prof. Nat. Chung Hsin U., 1970-72, Providence Coll., Taichung, 1972-78; spl. chair prof. Kookmin U. Korea, 1980-81, dir. Tunghai Lit. Quar., 1981—; doctoral examiner in Chinese lit.; mem. com. on scholarship evaluation Ministry of Edn. Republic of China, mem. com. on scholarship evaluation Ministry Edn. Served to 2d lt. Army, 1945. Harvard Yenching Inst. fellow; recipient Chungchien Cultural award Chia Hsin Cultural and Lit. Found. award. Mem. Fei Tao Fei. Chinese Nationalist. Author: A Rhyming Dictionary of Shih Ching, 1964; Synthetic Studies of Shuo Wen Chieh Tzu, 1968; Theories of Liu Shu, 1974; A Study on the Kuo-Feng of Shih Ching, 1978; The Phonetic Reconstruction of the Ancient Chinese of the Kuang Yun (I) (II); Study on Ancient Tones; A Commentary on the Introduction to Shuo Wen; An Analysis of Tonal Changes of Archaic Chinese through the Study of Occlusive Sound Markers in Shuo-Wen Chieh-tzu; An Analysis of the Irregular Rhyme in Shih-Ching; The Characteristic of the Han Language; Relations and Sources of Chou and Chuan in Shou Wen; Introduction of Structure Principles and Changes of Han Language; Correction of the Ping Sound of Chiang Yu-Kao T'ang Yun Four Tones; Correction of the Shang Sound of Chiang Yu-Kuo T'ang Yun Four Tones; Correction of the Chu Sound of Chiang Yu-Kao T'ang Yun Four Tones; The Explanation of Further Seeing off to South from Shih-Ching Yen-Yen; Comprehensions—the Characteristic of Chinese Culture from Han Characters; Study of Ku-Wen of Shou Wen; The Healthy Spirit of Kuo-Feng Shih-Ching Jen-Tao of Confucianism; Traditional Chinese Attitude of Scholar and Idea of Being Official; Principles of Chuan-Chu; The Rosource of Development of Chinese Modern Poetry; Comprehension of Confucian Great Education from Lun-Yu; Discussion of Humanistic Cultivation of Confucian; Chinese Character and Chinese Literature; Self-examination of Chinese Filial Piety; The Beauty of Chinese Characters; A Study on Chia-Chieh in Liu Shu (in Chinese); A Study on Hsing-Shenf in Liu Shu.

CHIANG KAI-SHEK, MADAME (MAYLING SOONG CHIANG), sociologist; b. Shanghai, China, 1899; d. C. J. Soong; ed. Wellesley Coll.; L.H.D. (hon.), John B. Stetson U., Bryant Coll., Hobart and William Smith Coll., Nebr. Wesleyan U.; LL.D. (hon.), Rutgers U., Loyola U., Los Angeles, Goucher, Wellesley, Russell Sage, Hahnemann Med., Wesleyan (Macon, Ga.) Colls., U. Mich., Bob Jones U., U. Hawaii; m. Chiang Kai-shek, 1927 (dec. 1975). Engaged in social service work in China; first women mem. Child Labor Commn.; inaugurated Moral Endeavor Assn.; established schs. in Nanking for orphans of Revolutionary Soldiers; former mem. Legis. Yuan; served as sec.-gen. Chinese Commn. on Aero. Affairs; dir.-gen. and chmn. women's Adv. council New Life Movement; founder, dir. Nat. Chinese Women's Assn. for War Relief, Nat. Assn. for Refugee Children, Chinese Women's Dept. of Kuomintang; founder, chmn. Cheng-Hsia Med. Rehab. Ctr. First Chinese woman to be decorated by Nat. Govt. of China, recipient highest mil. and civil decorations: Medal of Honor, N.Y.C. Fedn. Women's Clubs; YWCA Emblem; Gold medal N.Y. So. Soc.; Chi Omega nat. achievement award for 1943; Gold medal for dist. services Nat. Inst. Social Scis.; Dist. Service award Altrusa Internat. Assn.; Churchman 5th ann. award, 1943. Hon. pres. Am. Bur. Med. Aid to China; patroness Internat. Red Cross Com.; hon. pres. Com. for Promotion of Welfare of Blind, U. Seven Seas, Whittier, Calif.; hon. pres. bd. trustees Wego Orphange; chmn. bd. trustees Huashing Children's Home, Fujen Cath. U., Taipei, Taiwan. Hon. pres. Nurse's Assn. of China, Am. U. Club, Anti-Tb Assn. of China. Life mem. San Francisco Press Club, Associated Country Women of World; mem. Catherine Lorillard Wolf Club (hon.), Phi Beta Kappa (hon. Eta chpt.), Tau Zeta Epsilon, Phi Delta Gamma (hon.). Author: Sian: A coup d'Etat, 1937; China in Peace and War, 1939; China Shall Rise Again, 1939; This is Our China, 1940; We Chinese Women, 1941; Little Sister Su, 1943; Album of Reproduction of Paintings, Vol. I, 1952, Vol. II, 1962; The Sure Victory, 1955; Madame Chiang Kai-shek Selected Speeches, Vol. 1, 1959, Vol. 2, 1966; Album of Chinese Orchid Paintings, 1971; Album of Chinese Bamboo Paintings, 1972; Album of Chinese Landscape Paintings, 1973; Album of Chinese Floral Paintings, 1974; Conversations with Mikhail Borodin, 1977; religious writings, 1934-63. Address: Lattingtown Long Island NY Other: The President's Residence, Taipei Republic of China *

CHIAPPELLI, FREDI, literary critic, educator; b. Florence, Italy, Jan. 24, 1921; came to U.S., 1969; s. Francesco and Maria (Von Zdekauer) C.; m. Aymerica Bollati, Dec. 1 1945 (div. Aug. 1970); children: Marina, Francesco; m. Gabriella R. Carboneschi, June 10, 1980. LittD, U. Florence, 1945; postdoctoral, U. Zurich, Switzerland, 1948; LittD (hon.), McGill U., Montreal, Can., 1978, Ariz. State U., 1982. Asst. prof. U. Florence, 1945-46; lectr. U. Zurich, 1946-49; prof. Italian U. Lausanne and Neuchatel, Switzerland, 1950-59; prof. Italian, dean Coll. Letters U. Lausanne, 1959-69; prof. Italian UCLA, 1969—, dir. Ctr. Medieval and Renaissance Studies, 1972-87, spl. adv. for quincentenary programs, 1987—. Author: Niccoló Machiavelli: Legazioni Commissarie, 1971, 73, 84, 1985, Il Legame Musaico, 1984. Served as 2d lt. Italian Army, WWII. Decorated Grand Officer Order of Merit (Italy), Comdr. Palmes Académiques (France), Officer Order of Orange-Nassau (The Netherlands), Officer Order of Merit (Germany), Order of Alfonso el Sabio (Spain); Guggenheim fellow, 1972. Fellow Accademia della Crusca (Italy), Real Academia de Buenas Letras (Barcelona, Spain), Academia das Ciencias (Lisbon, Portugal), Accademia Ligure di Scienze e Lettere (hon., Italy). Roman Catholic. Home: 600 N Kenter Ave Los Angeles CA 90049 Office: UCLA 1100 Glendon Ave Suite 1548 Los Angeles CA 90024

CHIARAMONTE, JOSEPH SALVATORE, allergist, educator; b. Bklyn., Mar. 30, 1938; s. Joseph I. and Concetta (Tuttolomondo) C.; B.S., L.I. U., 1960; M.D., U. Padua, Italy, 1965; m. Lucy Conte, Sept. 3, 1961; children—Joseph Vincent, Andrea Concetta. Intern, Bklyn.-Cumberland Med. Center, Bklyn., 1966; resident Brookdale Hosp. and Med. Center, 1967-68; fellow in allergy and clin. immunology L.I. Coll. Hosp., Bklyn., 1970-71; practice medicine specializing in allergy and clin. immunology, Bay Shore, N.Y., 1971—; mem. staff Good Samaritan, also assoc. dir. Cystic Fibrosis Ctr., dir. Chronic Childhood Asthma Ctr.; mem. staff Southside Hosp.; asst. prof. clin. pediatrics Stony Brook U., N.Y.C., 1975—. Served to capt. USAF, 1969-70. Diplomate Am. Bd. Pediatrics, Am. Bd. Allergy and Immunology. Fellow Am. Assn. Cert. Allergists, Am. Acad. Allergy, Am. Acad. Pediatrics, Am. Coll. Chest Physicians; Am. Coll. Allergists; mem. AMA, Suffolk County, Nassau-Suffolk County med. socs., Nassau-Suffolk Allergy Soc., Suffolk County Pediatric Soc., N.Y. Trudeau Soc., Phi Sigma. Home: 2 Southwood Ct Bayshore NY 11706 Office: 649 Montauk Hwy Bay Shore NY 11706

CHIARELLI, BRUNETTO ANTONIO, anthropologist, educator; b. Florence, Tuscany, Italy, July 7, 1934; s. Raffaele and Masini Anna Chiarelli; m. Sorti Matilde; children: Ilaria, Cosimo, Francesca. PhD in Natural History, U. Florence, 1958, PhD in Biology, 1960. Docent in anthropology Ministry of Edn., Rome, 1962, docent in gen. biology, 1963; asst. prof. primatology U. Turin, Italy, 1961-68, prof., 1968-79; prof. anthropology U. Florence, 1979—; vis. prof. anthropology U. Toronto, Ont., Can., 1972-76. Chief editor, founder: Jour. Human Evolution, 1969-85, Human Evolution Internat. Jour. Anthropology, 1986—. Lodge: Rotary. Office: U Florence Inst Anthropology, Via del Proconsolo 12, 50123 Florence Italy

CHIARELLI, JOSEPH, accountant, banker; b. N.Y.C., Sept. 23, 1946; s. Biagio John and Mary Teresa (Cancellieri) C.; m. Eileen Mary Cook, Sept. 7, 1968; children: Claire Marie, Matthew Joseph, Christopher Joseph. BBA, Manhattan Coll., 1968; MBA, U. Hawaii, 1973. CPA, N.Y., Mont. Auditor Coopers & Lybrand, N.Y.C., 1973-77, audit mgr., 1977-81; asst. comptroller Morgan Guaranty Trust Co., N.Y.C., 1981-82, dep. comptroller, 1982-83; v.p., comptroller Morgan Bank Del., Wilmington, 1983-86, Morgan Securities Services Corp., N.Y.C., 1986—; chmn. adv. bd. acctg. dept. U. Del., Newark, 1985-87. Served to capt. USAF, 1968-73, maj. res. Named Outstanding Res. Officer of Yr., Air Force Audit Agy., 1980. Mem. Am. Inst. CPA's, N.Y. Soc. CPA's, Fin. Execs. Inst. (founding dir. Del. chpt. 1985-87. Roman Catholic. Home: 510 Farview Ave Wyckoff NJ 07481 Office: Morgan Securities Services Corp 37 Wall St New York NY 10015

CHIBA, KIYOSHI, chemist; b. Muroran, Hokkaido, Japan, Nov. 6, 1946; s. Jiro and Kaoru C.; m. Chikako Tajima, May 27, 1978; children: Yu, Atuko. BS, U. Tokyo, 1969, MS, 1971, DEng, 1988. Cert. engr. Sr. chemist Cen. Research Labs., Teijin Ltd., Tokyo and Hino, Japan, 1971—; research assoc., MIT, Boston, 1974-75, U. Tokyo, 1979-80. Contbr. articles to profl. jours.; patentee in field. Mem. Optical Soc. Am., Soc. Photo-Optical Instrumentation Engrs. Home: C-204, 2-8-3 Somechi, Chyofu, Tokyo 182, Japan Office: Teijin Ltd, 4-3-2 Asahigaoka, Hino Tokyo 191, Japan

CHIBA, TANETAKA, pathologist, consultant; b. Kyoto, Japan, Mar. 24, 1922; s. Matsutaro and Mitsuko Chiba; m. Ikeda Hiroko, May 22, 1949 (div. 1950); m. Seiko Chiba, May 10, 1966. DVM, Hokkaido Imperial U., 1944; MD, Nagoya U., 1953. Asst. pathologist Nagoya U. Sch. Medicine, 1952-55, pathologist, lectr. pathology div. environ. medicine, 1955-70, asst. prof., 1970-71; research dir. Research and Devel. div. Eisai Co., Tokyo, 1971-82; prof. Chukyo Women's U., Ohbu, Japan, 1982-83, Ichinomiya Women's Jr. Coll., Japan, 1983—; advisor Aichi Vet. Med. Assn., Nagoya, 1970—. Author: Oncoloby, 1965, revised edit., 1973, Avian Tumor, 1966, Pathology of Zoo Animals, 1988. Served with Japanese mil., 1944-45. Recipient Honor award Japanese Clin. Vet. Assn., Tokyo, 1965; grantee Tokai Cancer Soc., 1963-69. Mem. Japanese Path. Assn. (councilor 1955—), Japanese Toxocological Assn. (councilor 1980—), Aichi Vet. Assn. (v.p. 1968-70), Internat. Acad. Pathology. Home: 280 Imojiya, Seki, Gifu t501-32, Japan Office: 6 Nikko Cho, Ichinomiya, Aichi t491, Japan

CHIBUCOS, THOMAS ROBERT, family and child studies educator, researcher, writer; b. Chgo., Apr. 14, 1946; s. Gus and Jennie (Lalla) C.; m. Pamela Elizabeth Perry; children—Thomas, Marcus, Elise, Elizabeth. B.A. in Psychology, No. Ill. U., 1969, M.A., 1970; Ph.D. in Developmental Psychology, Mich. State U., 1974. Research assoc. Nat. Inst. Edn., Washington, 1973-75; asst. prof. psychology No. Ill. U., 1975-76, asst. prof. child devel., 1976-80, assoc. prof., coordinator div. family and child studies, 1981-83; cons. Akm. Council Edn., 1985-86; day care cons. Growing Place Day Care, DeKalb, 1979-81; expert witness Kane County States Atty., Wheaton, Ill., 1982. Guest editor: spl. issue Infant Mental Health Jour, 1980; contbr. chpt. to book, articles to profl. jours. Coach Am. Youth Socer Orgn., DeKalb, Little Leauge, DeKalb; mem. DeKalb Human Relations Commn., 1982. Mich. Office Edn. grantee, 1972-83; Ill. Office Edn. grantee, 1977; Am. Council Edn. fellow, 1983-84. Mem. Am. Psychol. Assn., Soc. Research in Child Devel., Ill. Assn. Infant Mental Health (co-founder, dir. 1981—), Internat. Assn. Infant Mental Health Subspecialties: Developmental psychology; Child development and family studies. Current work: Social policy, children and families, child mistreatment, fathers and infants life span development, family violence, research methodology. Office: No Ill Univ Dept Human and Family Resources DeKalb IL 60115

CHICK, EDWARD WILLIAM GEORGE, insurance executive; b. London, June 12, 1932; arrived in Can., 1956; s. Edward William George and E. May (Mattock) C.; m. Elfreda Shirley Littlejohn , Aug. 14, 1953; children: Edward William George III, Janet Rosemarie. With litigation dept. Sir William Charles Crocker, London, 1953-56, Beaumont & Sons Solicitors, London, 1956; with Royal Ins. Can., Toronto, Ont., Can., 1956—, v.p., 1980—; lectr., moderator Ont. Ins. Agts. Assn., Toronto, 1967-69; pres. Can. Fedn. Ins. Claimsmen, Toronto, 1969-70. Mem. Kinsmen Orgn., Toronto, 1961-65; mem. adv. councils on internat. arbitration and tort reform Atty. Gen., Toronto, 1987—. Fellow Ins. Inst. Can.; mem. Arbitrators Inst. Can. (v.p. 1987—), Ont. Ins. Adjusters Assn., Can. Ins. Claims Mgrs. Assn. (v.p. 1987-88, pres. 1988—). Mem. Ch. of England. Club: Donalda. Home: 89A Gloucester St, Toronto, ON Canada M4T 1M2 Office: Royal Ins Can, 10 Wellington St E, Toronto, ON Canada M5E 1L5

CHICKLIS, BARBARA KAREN BURAK, data processing company executive; b. Woonsocket, R.I., July 1, 1942; d. Steven and Stella Burak; B.S. in Math., Suffolk U., 1964; M.S.E.E. in Computer Sci., Northeastern U., 1974; m. William A. Gianopoulos, Apr. 3, 1981; children—Karen Barbara, Paul Steven. Systems programmer Raytheon Corp., Lexington, Mass., 1965-68, ITEK Corp., Lexington, 1968-71; project and staff leader Computation Center, Northeastern U., Boston, 1971-74; staff cons. Control Data Corp., Waltham, Mass., 1974—. Recipient award Internat. Profl. Services Analyst Symposium, 1977. Mem. Assn. Computing Machinery. Republican. Office: 60 Hickory Dr Waltham MA 02154

CHIEN, FREDRICK FOO, diplomat of Taiwan b. Peiping, China, Feb. 17, 1935; s. Shih-liang and Wan-tu (Chang) C.; m. Julie Tien, Sept. 22, 1963; children—Carl, Carol. B.A., Nat. Taiwan U., 1956; M.A., Yale U., 1959, Ph.D., 1962; LL.D., Sung Kyun Kwan U., Korea, 1972. Sec., Exec. Yuan, 1962-63; vis. assoc. prof. Nat. Chengchi U., 1962-64; chief 1st sect. N.Am. Affairs dept. Ministry Fgn. Affairs, 1964-67; dep. dir. N.Am. Affairs dept., 1967-69; vis. prof. Nat. Taiwan U., 1970-72; dir. N.Am. Affairs Dept., 1969-72; dir. gen. Govt. Info. Office, 1972-75; vice minister Ministry of Fgn. Affairs, 1975-82; rep. Coordination Council for N.Am. Affairs, Washington, 1983—. Author: The Opening of Korea: A Study of Chinese Diplomacy 1876-1885, 1967; Speaking as a Friend, 1975; More Views of a Friend, 1976. Mem. central com. Nationalist Party Republic of China, 1976—. Decorated Order Diplomatic Service Merit, Heung-In medal (Republic Korea), Order of Kim-Khanh (Republic of Vietnam); Order of Brilliant Star with Grand Cordon (Republic China); grand cruz Orden Nacional del Mérito (Paraguay); gran oficial and gran cruz Orden del Mérito de Duarte, Sánchez y Mella (Dominican Republic); gran cruz Orden Civil José Cecilio de Valle (Honduras); gran cruz Orden Nacional Jose Matias Delgado (El Salvador); grand officier Ordre National Honneur et Mérite (Haiti); grand cross Order of Good Hope (Republic S.Africa); gran cruz Orden de Vasco Nuñez de Balboa (Panama); gran cruz, Orden de Cristobal Colón (Dominican Republic). Clubs: Chevy Chase (Md.); Kenwood Country (Bethesda, Md.); Cosmos (Washington). Home: 3828 Cathedral Ave NW Washington DC 20016 Office: Coordination Council N Am Affairs Office USA Bldg 1 5161 River Rd Bethesda MD 20816

CHIEN, ROBERT CHUN, Republic of China government official; b. Peiping, China, Feb. 8, 1929; m. Ruth Cheng, June 18, 1955; children: Debra Liu, Kathy Chou. BA, Nat. Taiwan U., 1951; MA, U. Minn., 1957. Dir. econ. research dept. Bank of China, 1963-68; exec. sec. Commn. on Taxation Reform, Exec. Yuan, 1969-70; dir. secretariat Central Bank of China, Taipei, Taiwan, 1970-73, gen. mgr. banking dept., 1973-77, dep. gov., after 1972; minister fin., Taipei, Republic of China, until 1988. Contbr. articles to profl. jours. Eisenhower fellow, 1970. Office: Ministry of Fin, 2 Ai-Kuo West Rd, 10729 Taipei Taiwan *

CHIEPE, GAOSITWE KEAGAKWA TIBE, Botswana minister external affairs; b. Serowe, Botswana, Oct. 20, 1922; d. Tibe and Sefalana (Sebina) C.; B.Sc., U. Ft. Hare, 1947; M.A., U. Bristol (Eng.), 1957. With Botswana Dept. Edn., 1948-68, dir. edn., 1968-69; ambassador, high commr., 1970-74; cabinet minister, after 1971, then minister of mineral resources and water affairs; minister of external affairs, 1984—. Decorated Order Brit. Empire; recipient Presdl. Hon. award for meritorious service. Fellow Royal Soc. Arts. Democrat. Office: Ministry External Affairs, Gaborone Botswana *

CHIERI, PERICLE ADRIANO C., retired educator, consulting mechanical and aeronautical engineer, naval architect; b. Mokanshan, Chekiang, China, Sept. 6, 1905; came to U.S., 1938, naturalized, 1952; s. Virginio and Luisa (Fabbri) C.; m. Helen Etheredge, Aug. 1, 1938. Dr Engring., U. Genoa, Italy, 1927; ME, U. Naples, Italy, 1927; Dr Aero. Engring., U. Rome, 1928. Registered profl. engr., Italy, N.J., La., S.C. chartered engr., U.K. Naval architect. mech. engr. research and exptl. divs., submarines and internal combustion engines Italian Navy, Spezia, 1929-31; naval architect, marine supt. Navigazione Libera Triestina Shipping Corp., Libera Lines, Trieste, Italy, 1931-32, Genoa, 1933-35; aero. engr., tech. adviser Chinese Govt. commn. aero. affairs Nat. Govt. Republic of China, Nanchang and Loyang, 1935-37; engring. exec., dir. aircraft materials test lab., supt. factory's tech. vocational instrn. SINAW Nat. Aircraft Works, Nanchang, Kiangsi, China, 1937-39; aero. engr. FIAT aircraft factory, Turin, Italy, 1939; aero. engr. and tech. sec. Office: Air Attache, Italian Embassy, Washington, 1939-41; prof. aero. engring. Tri-State Coll., Angola, Ind., 1942; aero. engr., helicopter design Aero. Products, Inc., Detroit, 1943-44; sr. aero. engr. ERCO Engring. & Research Corp., Riverdale, Md., 1944-46; assoc. prof. mech. engring. U. Toledo, 1946-47; assoc. prof. mech. engring., faculty grad div. Newark (N.J.) Coll. Engring., 1947-52; prof., head dept. mech. engring. U. Southwestern La., Lafayette, La., 1952-72; cons. engr. Lafayette, 1972—; research engr., adv. devel. sect., aviation gas turbine div. Westinghouse Electric Corp., South Philadelphia, Pa., 1953; exec. dir. Council on Environment, Lafayette, 1975—. Instr. water safety ARC Nat. Aquatic Schs., summers 1958-67; Bd. dirs. Lafayette Parish chpt. ARC. Fellow Royal Instn. Naval Architects London (life); asso. fellow Am. Inst. Aeronautics and Astronautics; mem. Soc. Naval Architects and Marine Engrs. (life mem.), AAAS, AAUP (emeritus), Am. Soc. Engring. Edn. (life), Am. Soc. M.E., Soc. Automotive Engrs., Instrument Soc. Am., Soc. Exptl. Stress Analysis, Nat. Soc. Profl. Engrs., N.Y. Acad. Scis., La. Engring. Soc., La. Tchrs. Assn., AAHPER, La. Acad. Scis., Commodore Longfellow Soc., Cons. Engrs. Council La., Phi Kappa Phi., Pi Tau Sigma (hon.). Home: 142 Oak Crest Dr Lafayette LA 70503 Office: PO Box 52923 Lafayette LA 70505

CHIERICI, GIAN LUIGI, petroleum engineer, educator; b. Parma, Italy, Dec. 1, 1926; s. Giuseppe and Anna (Ferrari) C.; D.Chemistry, U. Parma, 1949; D.Chem. Engring., U. Padua, 1955; D.Physics, U. Parma, 1965; Ph.D. in Petroleum Engring., U. Bologna, 1963; m. Graziella Antonioli, Jan. 7, 1956; 1 son, Marcello. Research chemist Carlo Erba, 1949-51; head thermodynamics lab. AGIP SpA, 1951-55, head reservoir physics dept., 1955-70, head phys. chemistry dept., 1970-78, v.p. fields devel. and prodn., 1978-82, v.p. petroleum engring., 1982-87, chmn. research and devel. com., 1984—; assoc. prof. petroleum engring. U. Bologna, 1961-85, prof. petroleum reservoir mechanics, 1987—; hon. prof. U. Patagonia (Argentina), 1962—; mem. adv. com. mgmt. projects on geothermal energy EEC, Brussels, 1976-83, cons. to dirs. gen., 1987—; mem. Italian nat. com. for World Petroleum Congresses, 1980—; mem. permanent council World Petroleum Congresses, 1982—, mem. sci. program com., 1983—; chmn. com. for tech. and sci. cooperation Ministry of Oil Industry of USSR and Agip S.p.A., 1980—; chmn. steering com. for research on petroleum recovery Norsk Agip/Statoil/IKU, 1980-85; mem. sci. program com. European Symposium on Enhanced Oil Recovery 1982—; mem. sci. com. Rogalandsforskning U., Stavanger, Norway, 1987—. Mem. Soc. Petroleum Engrs., AIME. Author: Volumetric and Phase Behaviour of Hydrocarbon Reservoir Fluids, 1962; Enhanced Oil Recovery-A State-of-the-Art Review, 1980. Contbr. articles to internat. tech. mags. Home: Via Triulziana 36/A, San Donato, I-20097 Milan Italy Office: AGIP SpA, PO Box 12069, Milan I-20120, Italy

CHIGAS, VICTOR, brokerage firm executive; b. Peekskill, N.Y., Aug. 1, 1927; s. Christopher Ernest and Ethel (Irwin) C.; children—Christopher R., William J., Victor J. B.S.B.A., Denver U., 1956. Gen. mgr. Rolling Green Country Club, Arlington Heights, Ill., 1958-61; gen. mgr. No. Shore Country Club, Glenview, Ill., 1961-67; acct. exec. Walston & Comp., Chgo., 1967-69; option coordinator, account exec. Shearson, Hammill & Co., Chgo., 1969-74; 1st v.p. Drexel Burnham Lambert, Chgo., 1974-83; sr. v.p. Drexel Trust Co. of Midwest, 1983—, bd. dirs., 1983-86, investment mgr. income mut. fund asset, 1986—; bd. dirs. Harbor Trust Co., Hoboken, N.J. Pres. Greater Chgo. Denver Alumni Assn., Chgo., 1971; dir. Parent's Bd. Drake U., Des Moines, 1980-82; mem. Ill. Cemetary Advisory Commn., Chgo., 1980-81. Served to sgt. USAF, 1950-52. Mem. Greater Chgo. Club Mgrs. Assn. (pres. 1965). Republican. Office: Drexel Burnham Lambert 1 South Wacker Dr Chicago IL 60606

CHIGOS, DAVID, university president; b. Scranton, Pa., Mar. 29, 1933; s. Andrew D. and Emma (Kossmann) C.; m. Ruth Elizabeth Chamberlain, May 22, 1954; children: Catherine Mary Chigos Bradley, Carla Jane Chigos Sotelo, Lisa Anne, Laura Elizabeth. B.S. in Chemistry, W.Va. Wesleyan Coll., 1954, LL.D., 1980; M.A. in Counseling and Guidance, U.S. Internat. U., 1968, Ph.D., 1972. Teaching asst. U. Tex., 1954-56; commd. ensign USN, 1957, advanced through grades to capt., 1967, Res., 1983; indsl. relations Convair Aerospace div. Gen. Dynamics Corp., San Diego, 1967-70; faculty U. Calif. Extension at San Diego, 1967-83, San Diego State U. Extension, 1968-71, San Diego Evening Coll., 1967-71; pres. Nat. U., San Diego, 1971—. Bd. dirs. Nat. Def. U. Found., San Diego council Boy Scouts Am. Mem. Nat. Mgmt. Assn. (exec. adv. com., Golden Knight award 1979), Convair Nat. Mgmt. Assn. (hon. life), Am. Assn. of Presidents of Ind. Colls. and Univs., Naval Res. Assn. (life), Navy League U.S. (life, nat. dir.; Scroll of Honor 1979), Res. Officers Assn. (life, mem. pvt. sector council Washington). Clubs: San Diego Yacht, Kona Kai, Cuyamaca, University (San Diego); Army-Navy , Capitol Hill (Washington). Office: Nat Univ University Park San Diego CA 92108-4194

CHIH, CHUNG-YING, physicist, consultant; b. Yuki, Fukien, China, Dec. 11, 1916; s. Lai Sui and Sung-Yee (Lin) C.; B.Sc., Nat. Tsing Hua U., Peking, China, 1937; Ph.D., U. Calif., Berkeley, 1954; m. Alice Yuen, Aug. 15, 1955; came to U.S., 1948, naturalized, 1962. Instr. physics Fukien Med. Coll., 1937-40; instr., then asso. prof. Fukien Tchrs. Coll., 1940-44; asso. prof., then prof. physics Nat. Chi-Nan U., 1944-45; prof. physics Kiang-su Coll., 1945-48; physicist Radiation Lab., U. Calif., Berkeley, 1948-54, summer 1956; mem. faculty Middlebury (Vt.) Coll., 1954-68, prof. physics, 1966-68; sci. cons., Bridgeport, Conn., 1968—. NSF grantee, 1957-60. Mem. Am. Phys. Soc., AAUP, Sigma Xi. Address: PO Box 2556 Noble Station Bridgeport CT 06608

CHIHOREK, JOHN PAUL, electronics company executive; b. Wilkes-Barre, Pa., June 22, 1943; s. Stanley Jospeh and Caroline Mary C.; m. Christina Maria Marroquin, Dec. 28, 1968; children: Jonathan, David, Crista, Daniel. BSEE, Pa. State U., 1965; postgrad., Calif. State U., San Diego, 1970-71; MBA, Calif. State U., Sacramento, 1972. Officer program Hdqrs. Air Force Logistic Command, Dayton, Ohio, 1972-75; sr. engr. Hdqrs. Air Force Space Div., Los Angeles, 1975-78; mgr. software systems dept. Logicon Inc., San Pedro, Calif., 1978; mgr. software product assurance dept. Ford Aeronutronic, New Port Beach, Calif., 1978-85; mgr. software engring. Ford Aeronutronic, New Port Beach, 1985—; owner CMC Systems. Mem. Congl. Adv. Bd., 1980; active PTA, mem. Republican Nat. com. Served with USN, 1965-70, Vietnam. Decorated Bronze Star. Mem. IEEE, Air Force Assn., AAAS, Internat. Platform Assn. Roman Catholic. Clubs: Lions, Odd Fellows. Office: Ford Aeronutronic Ford Rd Newport Beach CA 92633

CHILA, ANTHONY GEORGE, osteopathic educator; b. Youngstown, Ohio, Dec. 14, 1937; s. Paul and Anne (Jurenko) C.; m. Helen Paulick, Oct. 9, 1965; 1 child, Anne Elizabeth. BA, Youngstown State U., 1960; DO, Kansas City Coll. Osteopathy and Surgery, 1965. Assoc. prof. family medicine Mich. State U. Coll. Medicine, East Lansing, 1977-78; assoc. prof. family medicine Ohio U. Coll. Medicine, Athens, 1978-83, prof. family medicine, 1983, chief clin. research, 1982; chmn. instl. rev. bd. Ohio U., Athens, 1986-88; George C. Kozma Meml. lectr. Cleve. Acad. Osteo. Medicine, 1979. Contbr. numerous articles to profl. jours. Trustee Saint Vladimir's Orthodox Theol. Sem., Tuckahoe, N.Y., 1975—; active Kootaga Area council Boy Scouts Am. Mem. AAAS, Am. Osteo. Assn. (Louisa M. Burns lectr. Clearwater, Fla. 1987), Am. Coll. Gen. Practitioners, Am. Acad. Osteopathy (pres. 1983-84, 85-87, Scott Meml. lectr. Kirksville, Mo. 1984, Thomas L. Northup lectr. Las Vegas, Nev. 1986), Cranial Acad., N.Y. Acad. Scis., N.Am. Acad. Manipulative Medicine, Gen. Charles Grosvenor Civil War Round Table. Republican. Office: Ohio U Coll Osteo Medicine Grosvenor Hall Athens OH 45701

CHILCOTE, SAMUEL DAY, JR., association executive; b. Casper, Wyo., Aug. 24, 1937; s. Sam D. and Juanita C. (Cornelison) C.; m. Ellen Sheridan Spear, Nov. 11, 1966. B.S., Idaho State U., 1959. Adminstrv. asst. Continental Oil Co., Glenrock, Wyo., 1960-63; asst. supt. public instrn., dir. Wyo. Surplus Property Agy., Wyo. Sch. Lunch Program, Cheyenne Wyo. Dept. Edn., 1963-67; supr. N. Central region Distilled Spirits Inst., Denver, 1967-71; exec. dir., chief operating officer N. Central region Distilled Spirits Inst., Washington, 1971-73; exec. v.p., chief operating officer Distilled Spirits Council, Inc., Washington, 1973-77, pres., chief exec. officer, 1978-81; pres. Tobacco Inst., Washington, 1981—; mem. industry sect. adv. council consumer goods, Dept. Commerce. Pres. Sky Ranch Found. for Boys, 1975-81, pres. emeritus, 1981—; treas. Ford's Theatre, 1984-88, vice-chmn., bd. trustees, 1988—; bd. dirs., exec. com. Art Barn. Served to capt., U.S. Army, 1959-60. Recipient Profl. Achievement award, Idaho State U. Coll. Bus., 1986, Man of Yr. award, Anti-Defamation League, 1986. Mem. U.S. C. of C. Clubs: George Town, Congressional Country (past pres., exec. com., bd. govs.), Burning Tree; Nat. Press, Capitol Hill, City, F Street, TPC Avenel (Washington). Lodges: Masons, Elks, Shriners, Rotary. Office: 1875 Eye St Washington DC 20006

CHILD, JOHN SOWDEN, JR., lawyer; b. Lansdale, Pa., July 22, 1944; s. John Sowden and Beatrice Thelma (Landes) C. B.S. in Polit. Sci., MIT, 1967; B.S. in Chem. Engring., 1967; J.D., U. Pa., 1973; B.Lit. in Politics, Oxford U., 1974. Bar: Pa. 1974, N.Y. 1977, U.S. Dist. Ct. (ea. dist.) Pa. 1978, U.S. Dist. Ct. (ea. dist.) N.Y. 1978, U.S. Patent and Trademark Office 1978, U.S. Ct. Appeals (2d cir.) 1978, U.S. Ct. Appeals (fed. cir.) 1981, U.S. Ct.Appeals (3d cir.) 1986. Assoc. Davis Hoxie Faithfull & Hapgood, N.Y.C., 1974-78; assoc. Synnestvedt & Lechner, Phila., 1978-88; of counsel Dann, Dorfman, Herrell and Skillman, Phila., 1988— ; arbitrator Pa. Ct. Common Pleas, Phila., 1979—, U.S. Dist. Ct., Ea. Dist.) Pa., Phila., 1983-88. Firm coordinator United Way Southeastern Pa., 1983—. Mem. Am. Intellectual Property Law Assn., N.Y. Patent, Trademark and Copyright Law Assn., Phila. Bar Assn., Phila. Patent Law Assn. (chmn. program com. 1981-85, editor, co-editor newsletter 1980—, gov. 1985-87, sec. 1987—), Mil. Order Fgn. Wars, Com. of Seventy, Soc. Colonial Wars, English Speaking Union, Colonial Soc. Pa., Phila. Oxford and Cambridge Soc. (sec. 1985—). Republican. Mem. Soc. of Friends. Clubs: Union League, Cricket (Phila.). Home: 8221 Seminole Ave Philadelphia PA 19118 Office: Dann Dorfman Herrell & Skillman Three Millon Ctr Suite 900 Philadelphia PA 19102-2440

CHILD, PAUL LORIN, dentist; b. Clinton, Utah, Sept. 14, 1940; s. John Theodore and A. Katherine Child; m. Mary Margaret Ginn, June 7, 1963; children: Michael D., John T., David S., Mark B., Melissia A., Paul Lorin, Cassandra, Jennifer, Thomas. Cert. completion Weber Jr. Coll., 1960; BS, Brigham Young U., 1966; DDS, Northwestern U., 1967. Gen. practice dentistry, Ogden, Utah, 1970—; dental health rep. Weber County Dental Assn., Ogden, 1975-77; lectr. continuing edn. U. Utah, Salt Lake City, 1972, Ogden City Schs., 1970—, civic groups, 1970—. Author: John L. Child, 1978, Childe and Bradshaw Genealogy, 1986, Child at Bedford, England, 1986-87, Childe Maternal Lines, 1987, Childe of England, 1988; co-author: Genealogy of Child, Childe, Childs, 1980. Contbr. articles to profl. jours. Explorer chmn. Boy Scouts Am.; voting dist. chmn., county del., state del., 1974—; presdl. elector Utah, mem. Utah Rep. Com. 1974—, Rep. Nat. Com., 1980—. Served to capt. U.S. Army, 1967-70. Recipient Scouters Key, Scouters Tng. award, Explorers Tng. award, Explorers Key, Commrs. Arrowhead award, 30 Yrs. Vets. award, award of merit. Mem. ADA, Acad. Gen. Dentistry (continuing edn. com. 1973—), Am. Profl. Practice Assn., Am. Preventive Dentistry Assn., Weber Dist. Dental Soc., Utah Dental Assn. (ho. of dels. 1978-83), Am. Coll. of Arms (Child Arms registered in name), Internat. Platform Assn., The Order of the Holy Cross of Jerusalem (invited to be knighted, 1988). Mormon. Home: 3787 Jackson Ave Ogden UT 84403 Office: 3785 Harrison Blvd Suite 1 Ogden UT 84403

CHILDERS, JOHN HENRY, talent company executive, personality representative; b. Hoopston, Ill., July 26, 1930; s. Leroy Kendal and Marie Ann (Sova) C.; m. JoAnn Uhlar, July 27, 1956; children—Michael John, Mark Joseph. Sales rep. Universal Match Corp., Chgo., 1956-59; v.p. sales to pres. Sales Merchandising, Inc., Chgo., 1959-63; chmn. bd., chief exec. officer Talent Services, Inc. and Talent Network, Inc., Skokie, Ill., 1963—. Served as pilot USAF, 1950-56. Mem. Assn. Reps. of Profl. Athletes (v.p.); Internat. Wine and Food Soc., Chaine des Rotisseurs, Les Amis du Vin, Wine finders, Classic Car Club Am., Auburn-Cord-Dusenberg Club. Republican. Roman Catholic. Clubs: Knollwood Country; Big Foot Country; Lake Geneva Country, PGA Country. Home: Apt 4G North-of-Nell Aspen CO 81611 also: 219 Club Cottages Palm Beach Gardens FL 33410 Office: 5200 W Main St Skokie IL 60077

CHILDERS, VILDIZ GUNDUZ, manufacturing company executive; b. Gevas, Turkey, Nov. 28, 1939; came to U.S., 1960; naturalized, 1967; d. Yosuf Ziya and Sadiye (Buzkaya) Gunduz; m. William L. Childers, 1967 (dec. 1972). BA, Istanbul Kiz Lisesi, Turkey, 1958. Pres. Childers Mfg. Co., Inc., Albuquerque, 1967—. Mem. Nat. Pavement Assn., Assn. Equipment Distbrs., Ladies Aux. of Nat. Asphalt Pavement Assn., Can. Assn. Equipment Distbrs., Asphalt Recycling and Reclaiming Assn., Assn. Gen. Contractors Am. Republican. Moslem. Club: Four Hills Country. Lodge: Elks. Home: 1004 Cuatro Cerros SE Albuquerque NM 87123 Office: 2010 6th St NW Albuquerque NM 87197

CHILDS, CLINTON LANGWITH, real estate investment consulatant; b. Honolulu, Sept. 14, 1922; s. Clinton Stibbs and Eleanor (Langwith) C.; m. Frances A. Johnston, Jan. 6, 1944; children: Candis L., Patrick J., Cristy S. BBA, U. Oreg., 1947. With Bishop Nat. Bank, 1946-51; asst. to v.p. Lihue Plantation Co., 1951-65; Kauai mgr. comml. land devel. Amfac Corp., 1965-68; pres. Kauai Helicopters, Inc., 1966-76, Clint Childs, Inc., Realtors, Hanamaulu, Hawaii, 1974-88; real estate investment cons., 1988; mng. dir. Alii Travel, Inc., 1977-81, SRI & Assoc., 1980—. Mem. Hist. Hawaii Found. Served to capt. U.S. Army, 1944-46. Mem. Hawaii State C. of C. (pres. 1965), Kauai Bd. Realtors (pres. 1970-73), Kauai Hist. Soc., Acad. of Arts, Punahou Alumni Assn. (dir.), Sigma Alpha Epsilon. Republican. Episcopalian. Office: PO Box 431 Lihue HI 96766

CHILDS, ERIN THERESE, psychotherapist; b. Redlands, Calif., Apr. 2, 1958; d. C. Russell and Maryann (Carpenter) C. B.A. cum laude, Loyola Marymount U., Los Angeles, 1979, M.A. magna cum laude, 1980; postgrad. Calif. Grad. Inst., 1982—. Lic. marriage, family and child therapist, Calif. Youth counselor II, Chino Youth Services (Calif.), 1979-81; counselor chem. dependency Behavioral Health Services, Gardena, Calif., 1981-83; pvt. practice psychotherapy, West Los Angeles, Calif., 1982—; psychotherapist, part-time cons. Thomas Aquinas Psychotherapy Clinic, Encino, Calif., 1982-84;

clin. dir. Emergency Crisis Counseling, West Los Angeles, 1983; unit supr., dir. driving under the influence program Southbay unit. Behavioral Health Services, Gardena, Calif., 1984-86; treatment coordinator New Beginnings, Century City Hosp., Los Angeles, 1986-87, staff psychotherapist, 1987—; instr. community services Pierce Jr. Coll., Woodland Hills, Calif., 1983, Santa Monica City Coll. (Calif.), 1984, West Los Angeles Community Coll., Culver City, Calif., 1984. Mem. Calif. Womens' Commn. on Alcoholism. Mem. Calif. Assn. Marriage and Family Therapists, ACLU, Psychologists for Social Responsibility, Psi Chi, Alpha Sigma Nu. Democrat. Roman Catholic. Office: 2080 Century Park East Suite 1405 Los Angeles CA 90067

CHILDS, GAYLE BERNARD, educator; b. Redfield, S.D., Oct. 17, 1907; s. Alva Eugene and Dora Amelia (Larsen) C.; A.B., Nebr. State Tchrs. Coll., Wayne, 1931; M.A., U. Nebr., 1936, Ph.D., 1949; M.Ed., Harvard, 1938; m. Doris Wilma Hoskinson, Dec. 22, 1930; children—Richard Arlen, George William, Patricia Ann (Mrs. Ronald Bauers). Tchr. sci. Wynot (Nebr.) High Sch., 1928-30; tchr. sci. Wayne (Nebr.) High Sch., 1931-38, prin., 1938-41; supt. Wakefield (Nebr.) pub. schs., 1941-44, West Point (Nebr.) pub. schs., 1944-46; curriculum specialist U. Nebr. extension div., Lincoln, 1946-49, instr. secondary edn. Tchrs. Coll., also curriculum specialist extension div., 1949-51, asst. prof., 1951-53, asso. prof., 1953-56, prof., head class and corr. instrn., 1956-63, prof., asso. dir. extension div., 1963-66, prof., dir. extension div., 1966-74. Nebr. del. White House Conf. on Aging, 1981; Congl. sr. intern First dist. Congl. Office, Washington, 1981; mem. state curriculum com. Nebr. State Dept. Edn., 1951-55. Sr. Fulbright-Hays scholar Haile Sellassie I U., Addis Ababa, Ethiopia, 1974. Mem. Capitol City Edn. Assn. (pres. 1949-50), Nebr. Edn. Assn. (dist. III sec. 1941-42), Nat. U. Extension Assn. (mem. adminstrv. com., div. corr. study 1952-68, chmn. 1963-65, chmn. research com. 1952-63, assn. dir. 1963-65, mem. joint com. minimum data and definitions 1965-70, chmn. 1970-73; Walton S. Bittner award 1971; establishment Gayle B. Childs award div. ind. study 1969; Gayle B. Childs award 1973), Internat. Council on Corr. Edn. (chmn. com. on research 1961-69, program com. 9th internat. conf. 1971-72), Assn. Univ. Evening Colls. (program com. 1971-72, membership com. 1971-73), Nebr. Schoolmasters Club, Phi Delta Kappa (dist. rep. 1957-63, dir., 1963-69, mem. commn. on edn. and human rights and responsibilities 1963-74, mem. adv. panel on commns. 1970-72; Disting. Service award 1970), North Central Assn. Colls. and Secondary Schs. (cons. def. com. 1953-55, mem. panel vis. scholars 1971-73), Fulbright Alumni Assn., U. Nebr. Emeriti Assn. (pres. 1979-80). Club: Kiwanis (bd. dirs. 1978-81). Contbr. articles to profl. jours. Home: 4530 Van Dorn St Lincoln NE 68506 Office: Nebr Ctr for Continuing Edn 33d and Holdrege Sts Lincoln NE 68503

CHILDS, JOHN DAVID, computer hardware and services company executive; b. Washington, Apr. 26, 1939; s. Edwin Carlton and Catherine Dorothea (Angerman) C.; m. Margaret Rae Olsen, Mar. 4, 1966 (div.); 1 child, John-David. Student Principia Coll., 1957-58, 59-60; BA, Am. U., 1963. Jr. adminstr. Page Communications, Washington, 1962-65; account rep. Friden Inc., Washington, 1965-67; Western sales dir. Data Inc., Arlington, Va., 1967-70; v.p. mktg. Rayda, Inc., Los Angeles, 1970-73, pres., 1973-76, chmn. bd., 1976-84; sr. v.p. sales Exec. Bus. Systems, Encino, Calif., 1981—; sr. assoc. World Trade Assocs., Inc., 1976—. Pres. Coll. Youth for Nixon-Lodge, 1959-60, dir. state fedn.; mem. OHSHA policy formulation com. Dept. Labor, 1967. Served with USAFR, 1960-66. Mem. Assn. Data Ctr. Owners and Mgrs. (chmn. privacy com. 1975, sec. 1972-74, v.p. 1974). Democrat. Christian Scientist. Office: 15760 Ventura Blvd #700 Encino CA 91436

CHILDS, JULIAN BRUCE, financial information services executive; b. Bedford, Eng., July 31, 1949; s. Basil Ernest and Georgette Estelle (Mossé) C. BA in Oriental Studies, Cambridge (Eng.) U., 1972, MA, 1974. Articled clk. Ernst and Whinney, London, 1973-74; broker Astley and Pearce, London, 1974-77; mgr. Astley and Pearce, Manila, Philippines, 1977-78, Tokyo, 1978-79; mng. dir. Astley and Pearce, Hong Kong, 1979-82, Tokyo, 1982-83; mng. dir. Asia/Pacific region Telerate, Hong Kong, 1984—, also bd. dirs. Conservative. Clubs: United Oxford and Cambridge Univs., Hong Kong. Home: 5 Repulse Bay Rd, Hong Kong Hong Kong Office: Telerate II Exchange Sq, 8 Connaught Pl, Hong Kong Hong Kong

CHILDS, MARQUIS WILLIAM, journalist; b. Clinton, Iowa, Mar. 17, 1903; s. William Henry and Lilian Malissa (Marquis) C.; m. Lue Prentiss, Aug. 26, 1926 (dec.); children: Prentiss, Malissa Elliott (dec.); m. Jane Neylan McBaine. A.B., U. Wis., 1923, Litt.D., 1966; A.M., U. Iowa, 1935, Litt.D., 1969; LL.D., Upsala Coll., 1943. With UPI, 1923, 25-26; with St. Louis Post-Dispatch, 1926-44, spl. corr., 1954-62; chief St. Louis Post-Dispatch (Washington corr.), 1962-68; columnist United Feature Syndicate, 1944-54; made 3 month tour battlefronts, 1943; lectr. Columbia Sch. Journalism; Eric W. Allen Meml. lectr. U. Oreg., 1950. Author: Sweden The Middle Way, 1936, They Hate Roosevelt, 1936, Washington Calling, 1937, This Is Democracy, 1938, This Is Your War, 1942, I Write From Washington, 1942, The Cabin, 1944; Editor, writer: evaluation new edit. Brooks Adams' America's Economic Supremacy, 1947, The Farmer Takes a Hand, 1952, Ethics in Business Society, (with Douglass Cater), 1954, The Ragged Edge, 1955, Eisenhower, Captive Hero, 1958, The Peacemakers, 1961, Taint of Innocence, 1967, Witness to Power, 1975, Sweden The Middle Way on Trial, 1980; Co-editor: Walter Lippmann and His Times, 1959, Mighty Mississippi: Biography of a River. Decorated Order of North Star Sweden; Order of Merit Fed. Republic of Germany; Order of Aztec Eagle Mex.; recipient Sigma Delta Chi award for best Washington corr., 1944; award for journalism U. Mo.; Pulitzer prize for commentary, 1969. Mem. Kappa Sigma, Sigma Delta Chi. Clubs: Overseas Writers (pres. 1943-45); Century (N.Y.C.); Washington Press (Washington), Gridiron (Washington) (pres. 1957), Metropolitan (Washington), Cosmos (Washington). Office: 1701 Pennsylvania Ave NW Washington DC 20036

CHILDS, MICHAEL STANLEY, airline executive; b. Leicester, Eng., May 2, 1940; arrived in Australia, 1970; s. Stanley Ernest and Edith Linda (Boulds) C.; m. Rosemary Leong, Aug. 25, 1968. Grad. high sch., Rhodesia, 1957. With Cen. African Airways Corp., Salisbury, Rhodesia, 1959-65; sales mgr. Air Botswana, Gaberones, 1966-70; regional mgr. Connair Airlines, Darwin, Australia, 1970-74; asst. br. mgr. Air Niugini, Lae, Papua New Guinea, 1974-75; regional mgr. Air Niugini, Kieta, Papua New Guinea, 1975-77; airport mgr. Air Queensland, Brisbane, Australia, 1977-84; ops. mgr. Codair Airlines, Brisbane, 1984-85; gen. mgr. Norfolk Airlines, Brisbane, 1985—. Mem. Chartered Inst. Transport. Office: Norfolk Airlines, Creek & Adelaide Sts, Brisbane Queensland 4000, Australia

CHILDS, RAND HAMPTON, data processing executive; b. Charlotte, N.C., Oct. 20, 1949; s. Wade Hampton and Francis Marion (Rand) C.; m. Anne Elizabeth Turner, Jan. 4, 1986. B.S. in Chemistry, Ga. Inst. Tech., 1971, M.S. in Chemistry, 1977; postgrad. Eidgenossische Technische Hochschule, Zurich, Switzerland, 1971-72. Systems analyst Ga. Inst. Tech., Atlanta, 1974-80; assoc. dir. office of computing services, 1983-87 ; v.p. Software Devel., Sirsi Corp., 1987—; cons. in field. World Student Fund Scholar Ga. Inst. Tech. and Swiss Govt., 1971-72. Compiler: (with Naugle and Sherry) A Concordance to the Poems of Samuel Johnson. Mem. AAAS, Am. Chem. Soc., Assn. Computing Machinery, Info. Industry Assn., VIM (Control Data Corp. User Group), Sigma Xi, Alpha Iota Delta of Chi Psi, Atlanta. Contbr. articles to profl. jours. Home: 189 Newcomb Rd Owens Crossroads AL 35763-9752 Office: SIRSI Corp 2904 Westcorp Blvd Suite 209 Huntsville AL 35805

CHILES, LAWTON MAINOR, U.S. senator; b. Lakeland, Fla., Apr. 3, 1930; s. Lawton Mainor and Margaret (Patterson) C.; m. Rhea May Grafton, Jan. 27, 1951; children: Tandy M., Lawton Mainor III, Edward G., Rhea Gay. B.S., U. Fla., 1952; LL.B., 1955; LL.B. hon. degrees, Fla. So. Coll., Lakeland, 1971, Jacksonville U., 1971. Bar: Fla. 1955. Practiced in Lakeland 1955-70, U.S. senator from Fla., 1971—; Mem. Fla. Ho. of Reps., 1958-66, Fla. Senate, 1966-70. Trustee U. Fla. Law Center, 1968—, Fla. So. Coll., from 1971, Eckerd Coll., St. Petersburg, Fla., from 1971. Served as 1st lt. AUS, 1952-54. Mem. Phi Delta Phi, Alpha Tau Omega. Presbyterian. Office: Office of the Senate 250 Russell Senate Bldg Washington DC 20510 *

CHILLIDA JUANTEGUI, EDUARDO, sculptor; b. San Sebastian, Spain, Jan. 10, 1924; Student Colegio Marianistas, San Sebastian, Univ. Madrid. Sculptor, 1947—; one man show, Madrid, 1954; numerous one-man and group exhbns., Europe, Japan and U.S.; illustrator several books; vis. prof. Carpenter Centre, Harvard Univ., 1971. Recipient Gran Premio Internat. de Escultura Venice Biennale, 1958; Prix Kandinsky, 1960; Carnegie Prize Pitts. Internat., 1964, 1979; North Rhine Westphalian prize for Sculpture, 1965; Wilhelm Lehmbruck prize, Duisburg, 1966; Premio Rembrandt, Basel, 1975; numerous other prizes. Mem. Hispanic Soc. Am. N.Y. (hon.), Bayerische Akademic der Schonen Kunst (corr.). Address: Villa Paz, Alto de Maracruz, San Sebastian Spain

CHILTON, ALICE PLEASANCE HUNTER (MRS. ST. JOHN POINDEXTER CHILTON), former state ofcl., vocat. counselor; b. Boyce, La., Apr. 16, 1911; d. Albert Eugene and Maggie (Texada) Hunter; B.A., La. Coll., 1930; M.S., La. State U., 1934, Ph.D., 1982, Guidance Counselor certificate, 1954; m. St. John Poindexter Chilton, Mar. 2, 1935. Tchr. secondary sch., Glenmora, La., 1931-35; with La. Div. Employment Security and USES, Baton Rouge, 1937-74, employment interviewer and supr., 1937-43, personnel officer, 1943-46, ops. analyst, 1946-55, supr. counseling and tech. services, 1955-74. Vice pres., dir. LaPlace Enterprises, Inc., Belle Pointe Enterprises, Inc. Mem. curriculum study com. East Baton Rouge, Parish Sch. Bd., 1968; rec. sec. Quota Internat., Baton Rouge, 1961-62, 2d v.p., 1963-64. Bd. dirs. YWCO. Recipient certificate of merit La. Acad. Sci., 1960. Mem. Internat. Assn. Personnel in Employment Security, Nat. Trust Historic Preservation, La. Geneal. and Hist. Soc. (pres. 1957), La. Landmarks Soc., Found. for Hist. La., Kent Plantation House, Inc. (sec.1979-81), Preservation Resource Ctr., La. Preservation Alliance (dir. 1984-86), Hist. Assn. of Cen. La. (bd. dirs. 1980-86), Alexandria Hist. and Geneal. Library and Mus. (bd. dirs. 1986—), Phi Kappa Phi. Clubs: Campus La. State U. Faculty Wives). Methodist. Address: 431 Belgard Bend Boyce LA 71409

CHILTON, ST. JOHN POINDEXTER, former plant pathology educator, farm owner; b. Phila., Feb. 3, 1909; s. St. John P. and Helen Frances (McGloin) C.; m. Alice Pleasance Hunter, Mar. 2, 1935. B.S., La. State U., 1935, M.S., 1936; Ph.D., U. Minn., 1938. Agt. plant pathology U.S. Dept. Agr., 1938-40; faculty La. State U., 1940—, prof., 1948—, chmn. dept. botany and plant pathology, 1950-70; plant pathologist, head dept. plant pathology La. Agr. Expt. Sta., 1950-76; rep. div. biology and agr. NRC, 1952-57; pres., dir. LaPlace Enterprises, Inc.; pres., mgr. Esperanza Farms, 1974-83; cons. Nicaraque Sugar Estates, Ingenio San Antonio. Fellow AAAS; mem. Am. Phytopath. Soc. (ex-counselor), Internat. Soc. Sugarcane Technologists (vice chmn. 10th congress), Am. Soc. Sugarcane Technologists (past pres.), SAR (past pres. Phil Thomas chpt.), La. Acad. Sci. (past pres.), La. Geneal. and Hist. Soc. (pres. 1972-76), Hist. Assn. Central La. (pres. 1980-82), Am. Sugarcane League U.S. (life). Club: Rotarian. Home: 431 Belgard Bend Boyce LA 71409

CHIN, HONG WOO, physician, educator, researcher; b. Seoul, Korea, May 14, 1935; came to U.S., 1974; s. Jik H. and Woon K. (Park) C.; m. Soo J. Cheung, Dec. 27, 1965; children—Richard, Helen, Ki. M.D., Seoul Nat. U., 1962, Ph.D., 1974. Diplomate: Am. Bd. Radiology. Radiation oncologist, asst. prof. dept. radiation medicine U. Ky. Med. Ctr., Lexington, 1979-86; clin. prof. radiology, U. Mo., Kans. City; physician-in-charge sect. neuro-radiation oncology; assoc. dir. The Radiarium; chief radiation oneology VA Med. Ctr., Shreveport, La., 1988—. Contbr. articles, monographs and abstracts to med. lit. Mem. AMA, Am. Coll. Radiology, Am. Soc. Therapeutic Radiologists, AAAS, Can. Assn. Radiologists, N.Y. Acad. Scis., Radiation Research Soc., Radiol. Soc. N.Am., Pan Am Med. Assn. (mem. council), Sigma Xi. Subspecialties: Oncology; Cancer research (medicine). Current work: Researcher in cancer treatment, especially brain tumors.

CHIN, HSIAO-YI, museum director; b. Hunan Province, Hengshan County, Republic of China, Feb. 11, 1921; m. Hsu Hai-ping. LLB, Shanghai Law Coll., Republic of China, 1946; LHD (hon.), Oklahoma City U., 1984. Sec. to Pres. Chiang Kai-shek Republic of China, 1941-74; tenure prof. Chinese Culture U., Republic of China, 1963—; prof. Nat. Taiwan U., Republic of China, 1974—; chmn. history com. Kuomintang Cen. Com., 1976—. Author: Basic Course in Sun Yat-sen Thought, President Chiang Kai-shek's Thorough Understanding and Forthrightness, Application of Dr. Sun Yat-sen's Thought, 1965, The Spring of Advancing Virtue, 1961. Pres. Chinese Hist. Assn., 1984; dir. Nat. Palace Mus. Republic of China, 1983—. Recipient Order of Brilliant Star with Grand Cordon Pres. Office Republic of China, Order of Resplendent Banner Pres. Office Republic of China, award Ministry Edn. Republic of China. Office: Nat Palace Mus, Wai-shuang-hsi, Taipei Republic of China

CHIN, KIM HOCK, public relations consultant; b. Singapore, Mar. 25, 1957; came to U.S., 1979; s. Richard K.H. and Bobbie J.E. (Ou) C.; m. Virginia Marie Rentschler, June 19, 1984. BJ, U. Oreg., 1983. Account exec. Cawood Communications, Eugene, Oreg., 1983; gen. mgr. King Design Inc., Eugene, 1983-85; dir. devel. Clark County Pub. Transp. Benesti Area Authority (formerlyl C-Tran), Vancouver, Wash., 1986—; cons. mktg. communications, Portland, Oreg., 1985—. Author: Singaporean Literature in Perspective, 1980. Vol. fundraiser Tualatin (Oreg.) Valley Bod Ctr., 1986; chmn. community relations com. Health and Welfare Planning Council. Mem. Internat. Trade and Communications Inst. (chmn. pub. relations com. 1985—), Internat. Assn. Bus. Communicators, Chartered Inst. Secs. and Adminstrs. (assoc.), Pub. Relations Soc. Am., Ad 2, Portland Advt. Fedn., Met. Ethnic Minority Execs. Coalition, Chinese C. of C., Wash. State Transit Assn. Club: Singapore Island Country. Home and Office: 3434 NW Vaughn Portland OR 97210

CHIN, MICHAEL KUO-HSING, agricultural products company executive; b. Singapore, Sept. 19, 1921; s. Chin-cho and Wen-chih (Chang) C.; m. Edith Tzu-lin Fang; children: Lucy Wei-Tzu, May An-Tzu, Peggy Hsien-Tzu, Judy Pei-Tzu. BS, Yen Ching U., Cheng-tu, People's Republic of China, 1945. Asst. proctor's office Yenching U., Cheng-tu, People's Republic of China, 1945-46; asst. bur. of relief Chinese Nat. Rural Rehab., Nanking, People's Republic of China, 1946-48; statistician-in-charge, personnel-in-charge Nanking Phys. Rehab. Ctr., People's Republic of China, 1948-50; technician soil analysis Pub. Health Research Inst., Taipei, Republic of China, 1950-51; asst., jr. adminstrv. asst., adminstrv. asst. Sino-Am. Joint Commn. on Rural Reconstrn., Taipei, Republic of China, 1960-71; exec. officer Asian Vegetable Research and Devel. Ctr., Shanhua, Tainan, Republic of China, 1971-83, dir. adminstrn., 1983—. Baptist. Home: #60 Yi-Min-Lao Shanhua, Tainan Hsien 74103, Republic of China Office: AVRDC, PO Box 42 Shanhua, Tainan Hsien 74199, Republic of China

CHIN, SUE S. (SUCHIN), artist, photographer, community affairs activist; b. San Francisco; d. William W. and Soo-Up (Swebe) Chin; grad. Calif. Coll. Art, Mpls. Art Inst., (scholar) Schaeffer Design Ctr.; student Yasuo Kuniyoshi, Louis Hamon, Rico LeBrun. Photojournalist, All Together Now show, 1973, East-West News, Third World Newscasting, 1975-78, KNBC Sunday Show, Los Angeles, 1975, 76, Live on 4, 1981, Bay Area Scene, 1981; graphics printer, exhbns. include Kaiser Ctr., Zellerbach Plaza, Chinese Culture Ctr. Galleries, Capricorn Asunder Art Commn. Gallery (all San Francisco), Newspace Galleries, New Coll. of Calif., Los Angeles County Mus. Art, Peace Plaza Japan Ctr., Calif. Mus. Sci. and Industry, Lucien Labaudt Gallery, Salon de Medici, Madrid, Salon Renacimento, Madrid, Sacramento State Fair, AFL-CIO Labor Studies Ctr., Washington, Asian Women Artists (1st prize for conceptual painting, 1st prize photography), 1978; represented in permanent collections Los Angeles County Fedn. Labor, Calif. Mus. Sci. and Industry, AFL-CIO Labor Studies Ctr., Australian Trades Council, Hazeland and Co., also pvt. collections. Del. nat., state convs. Nat. Women's Polit. Caucus, 1977-83, San Francisco chpt. affirmative action chairperson, 1978-82, nat. conv. del., 1978-81, Calif. del., 1976-81. Recipient Honorarium AFL-CIO Labor Studies Ctr., Washington, 1975-76; award Centro Studi Ricerche delle Nazioni, Italy, 1985; bd. advisors Psycho Neurology Found. Bicentennial award Los Angeles County Mus. Art, 1976, 77, 78. Mem. Asian Women Artists (founding v.p., award 1978-79, 1st award in photography of Orient 1978-79), Calif. Chinese Artists (sec.-treas. 1978-81), Japanese Am. Art Council (chairperson 1978-84, dir.), San Francisco Women Artists, San Francisco Graphics Guild, Pacific/Asian Women Coalition Bay Area, Chinatown Council Performing and Visual Arts. Chmn., Full Moon Products; pres., dir. Aumni Oracle Inc. Featured in Calif. Living Mag., 1981. Address: PO Box 1415 San Francisco CA 94101

CHINAI, MAHESH RASIKLAL, chemical company executive; b. Ahmedabad, Gujarat, India, May 5, 1933; s. Rasiklal Jivanlal and Urmila Rasiklal C.; m. Damayanti; children: Darshana Ogale, Samir, Kishore. Diploma, Riverdale Country Sch., N.Y.C., 1951; student, Va. Poly. Inst., 1952-53, Adminstrv. Staff Coll. India, Hyderabad, 1962. Mng. dir., chief exec. adminstrv.-comml. Nat. Art Silk Mills Pvt. Ltd., Bombay, 1954; atty. in charge purchase dept. and gen. adminstrn., dir. mng. agy. Nat. Rayon Corp. Ltd., Bombay, 1955-70; ptnr. Nagindas Foolchand Chinai, Bombay, 1968-79; dir. Chinai & Co. Pvt. Ltd., Bombay, 1968-79; chief exec. Catalyst (India) Pvt. Ltd., Bombay, 1979, joint mng. dir., 1980—; chmn. Everest Shipping Co. Pvt. Ltd., Bombay, 1976-83, dir. 1988; dir. Splty. Chems. Ltd., Bombay. Club: Cricket Club of India (Bombay). Home: Saahil 8th Floor, 14 Altamount Rd, Bombay 400026, India Office: Catalyst (India) Pvt Ltd, Embassy Ctr, Mariman Point, Bombay 400021, India

CHING, ANTHONY BARTHOLOMEW, lawyer, educator, consultant; b. Shanghai, China, Nov. 18, 1935; came to U.S., 1956; s. William L.K. and Christina Ching; m. Nancy Ann Prigge, Apr. 10, 1961; children—Anthony, Alice, Alexander, Andrew, Ann, Audrey, Anastasia, Albert. Student Universite Catholique de L'ouest, 1953-54, Cambridgeshire Tech. Coll., 1954-55; matriculated Cambridge U., 1955, St. John's Coll., 1956; B.S. in Geology, U. Ariz., 1959, postgrad., 1959-60, LL.B., 1965; LL.M., Harvard U., 1971. Bar: Ariz. 1965, U.S. Dist. Ct. Ariz. 1965, U.S. Ct. Appeals (9th cir.) 1969, U.S. Supreme Ct. 1969, U.S. Ct. Appeals (5th cir.) 1972. Geologist, Duval Sulphur and Potash, Kingman, Ariz. and Tucson, 1959-60, Am. Smelting and Refining Co., Tucson, part-time 1960-61; engr. Marum and Marum Cons. Engrs., Tucson, 1961-65; sole practice, Tucson, 1965-66; atty., chief trial counsel Pima County Legal Aid Soc., Tucson, 1966-70; fellow clin. legal edn. Harvard Law Sch., Cambridge, Mass., 1970-71, acting prof. Law Sch., Loyola U., Los Angeles, 1971-73, 74-75, adj. prof., 1982; dir. litigation, acting project dir. Hawaii Legal Aid Soc., Honolulu, 1973-74; chief counsel Econ. Protection div. Atty. Gen.'s Office, State of Ariz., Phoenix, 1975-79; solicitor gen. Ariz. Dept. Law, Phoenix, 1979—; chmn. Western Attys. Gen. Litigation Action Com., 1983-86; pres. Nat. Consumer Law Ctr., Boston, 1979—; judge pro tem Maricopa County Superior Ct., 1984—. Mem. Pima County Democratic Com., 1966-70, Tucson Community Council, 1968-70, Pio Decimo Ctr., 1968-70; bd. dirs. Ariz. Consumer Council, 1968-70; pres. Young Dems. Greater Tucson, 1969-70. Mem. ABA, State Bar Ariz., Maricopa County Bar Assn., Nat. Legal Aid and Defender Assn. (treas. 1973-74, Reginald Heber Smith award 1969), Harvard Law Sch. Assn. Ariz. (pres. 1980-83). Roman Catholic. Home: 2632 S Fairfield St Tempe AZ 85282 Office: 1275 W Washington Phoenix AZ 85007

CHING, GEORGE TA-MIN, banking executive; b. Berkeley, Calif., Nov. 25, 1914; s. Tin Ku and Yuk Yim (lee) C.; m. Tsui Lin Chan; children: Toni Fu-I, Nannette Fuchai, Deborah Fu-Yuen. BA, Lingnan U., Canton, China, 1937; MA, Stanford U., 1939. Research fellow U. So. Calif., Los Angeles, 1940; asst. mgr. The China State Bank Ltd., Hong Kong, 1949-52; specialist Farmer & Mcht. Nat. Bank, Los Angeles, 1954-59; treas., gen. mgr. Jordan Internat., Inc., San Francisco, 1959-62; founder, dir., pres. Cathay Bank, Los Angeles, 1962-85, vice chmn. bd. dirs. Bd. dirs. Vols. Am. Los Angeles, 1975-77; advisor Mayor's Community Adv. Com., Los Angeles, 1970; active Calif. Student Aid Commn., Los Angeles, 1978-82. Recipient Good Scout award Boy Scouts Am., 1980, Spirit of Enterprise award Chinese Am. Council of Hist. & Cultural Found., 1987. Banker Credit Men's Assn. (gov. 1964-65), Ind. Banker Assn. So. Calif. (bd. dirs. 1967-69, 73-75), Calif. Bankers Assn. (bd. dirs. 1974-77). Club: Town Hall. Lodge: Masons. Office: Cathay Bank of Los Angeles 777 North Broadway Los Angeles CA 90012

CHING, LARRY FONG CHOW, construction company executive; b. Honolulu, Mar. 15, 1912; s. Dung Sen and Dai (Chong) C.; m. Beatrice Jook Yee Fong, Aug. 6, 1944; children: Randall Ming-Yu, Thalia Ping-Hsia. BCE, U. Hawaii, 1935; postgrad. in mining engring., U. Utah, 1938-39. Registered profl. engr., Hawaii. Instr. math. and engring. U. Yunan, Kunming, Peoples Republic of China, 1935-37; engr. Moses Akiona, Contractor, 1939-42, 45; supr. roads and airport constrn. U.S. Corps Engrs., 1942-44; mgr. Universal Contracting Co., 1945-47; supt. constrn. Associated Builders, 1948-49; pres., gen. mgr. Hwy. Constrn. Co., Ltd., Honolulu, 1949—; bd. dirs. Hawaii Franchise No-Joint Concrete Pipe, Hawaii Contractor's License Bd., 1960-63; pres., bd. dirs. Constrn. Industry Legis. Orgn., 1977-78; sub-chmn. design constrn. and maintenance Hawaii Hwy. Safety Council. Pres. Larry and Beatrice Ching Found; pres., dir. Hawaii Chinese History Ctr., 1971; pres. Hawaii Heritage Ctr., 1982-83. Mem. Assn. Gen. Contractors Am. (bd. dirs., treas. 1983), Gen. Contractors Assn. Hawaii (pres. 1968, bd. dirs.), Hawaii C. of C. (bd. dirs.), Chinese C. of C. (bd. dirs., pres. 1971-72), Honolulu Better Bus. Bur., Friends of East-West Ctr., United Chinese Soc. (pres. 1980—), Tu Chiang Sheh (pres.). Home: 18 Kimo Dr Honolulu HI 96817 Office: 720 Umi St Honolulu HI 96819

CHIOCCA, FRANCO, engineer; b. Naples, Italy, Aug. 27, 1941; s. Renato and Irma (Perullo) C.; m. Cecilia De Leoni, Oct. 14, 1970; children: Simona, Renato. Degree in elec., Naples State U., 1968. Quality and REL mgr. Gen. Inst. Europe, Naples, 1969-73; mfg. mgr. semiconductor div. Tex. Instruments Italy, Rieti, Italy, 1973-76, mktg. research mgr., 1976-77; mfg. mgr. Autovox-Motorola, Rome, 1977-79; plant mgr. VoxsonùEMI, Rome, 1979-82; gen mgr. Soc. Agrl. Molisana-ARENA, Campobasso, Italy, 1982-83; mng. dir. All-Zoo, Campobasso, 1982-83; gen. mgr. Nuova Mistral, Sermoneta, Italy, 1983; mng. dir. Comp El Italia MIAL, Sabaudia, Italy, 1985—; bd. dirs. Soc. Tech. Avanz, Frosinone, Italy. Home: Via Nino Bixio 65, 04100 Latina Italy Office: Nuova MISTRAL, Via Le Pastine 32, 04010 Sermoneta Italy

CHIOGIOJI, MELVIN HIROAKI, government official; b. Hiroshima, Japan, Aug. 21, 1939; came to U.S., 1939; s. Yutaka and Harumi (Yamasaki) C.; m. Eleanor Nobuko Oura, June 4, 1960; children: Wendy A., Alan K. B.S. in Elec. Engring., Purdue U., 1961; M.B.A., U. Hawaii, 1968; D.Bus. Adminstrn., George Washington U., 1972. Registered profl. engr., Hawaii. Head weapons gen. component div. Quality Evaluation Lab., Oahu, Hawaii, 1965-69; dir. weapons evaluation and engring. div. Naval Ordinance Systems Command, Washington, 1969-73; dir. Office Indsl. Analysis Fed. Energy Adminstrn., Washington, 1973-75; asst. dir., div. bldg. and community systems Dept. Energy, Washington, 1975-79, dir. fed. program div., 1980—, dep. asst. sec. state and local assistance program, 1980-85, dir. office of transp. systems, 1985—; prof. mgmt. sci. George Washington U., 1972—. Author: Industrial Energy Conservation, 1979, Energy Conservation in Commercial and Residental Buildings, 1982; contbr. articles to profl. jours. Mem. Md. State Adv. Com. on Civil Rights, 1976—; mem. Nat. Naval Res. Policy Bd., 1977—; vestryman Grace Episcopal Ch., Silver Spring, Md., 1982—. Served with USN, 1961-65. Decorated Navy Commendation medal, Meritorious Service medal. Mem. IEEE (sr.), Nat. Soc. Profl. Engrs., Acad. Mgmt., Naval Res. Assn., Assn. for Sci., Tech. and Innovation (pres. 1979-81), Soc. Am. Mil. Engrs., Armed Forces Mgmt. Assn., Purdue U. Alumni Assn. Home: 15113 Middlegate Rd Silver Spring MD 20904 Office: 1000 Independence Ave SW Washington DC 20585

CHIPOT, MICHEL MARIE, mathematics educator; b. Gérardmer, Vosges, France, May 23, 1949; s. Lucien and Anne Marie (Raty) C.; m. Yveline M. Miclot; children: Alexis, Thibaut. BA, U. Nancy I, France, 1971; These d'État, U. Paris VI, 1981. Agrégé de Math. Asst. U. Nancy I, 1971-81, maitre asst., 1982-83; prof. U. Metz, France, 1985—; vis. asst. prof. Brown U., Providence, 1981-82; vis. assoc. prof. U. Md., College Park, 1983-84; research fellow U. Minn., Mpls., 1984-85, 87; vis. prof. Carnegie Mellon U., Pitts., 1987. Author: Variational Inequalities and Fluid Flow in Porous Media, 1984; contbr. articles to math. jours. Mem. Am. Math. Soc., Soc. Math. France. Office: U De Metz, Ile Du Saulcy, 57045 Metz France

CHIRURG, JAMES THOMAS, JR., investment company executive; b. Wellesley, Mass., May 21, 1944; s. James Thomas and Virginia Burtt (Low) C.; A.B. in Oriental Studies, Cornell U., 1964; M.B.A. in Internat. Business, Harvard U., 1969; B.Litt. in Internat. Economics, U. of Oxford (Knox fellow), 1972; postgrad. U. Calif., Berkeley; m. Lynne Louise Robertson Day, Sept. 15, 1983. Asst. mktg. mgr. Gen. Mills Inc., Tokyo, 1968; mem. corp. fin. dept. First Boston Corp., N.Y.C., 1969-70; gen. mgr. Protasis Trust, Ltd., London, 1971-72, lead partner, Berkeley, 1973—; dir. Protasis Holdings (S.A.R.L.), Luxembourg, 1980—; fin. adv. AID investment mission,

Tanzania, 1980; fellow Salzburg Seminar (Austria), 1980; alumnus, Harvard U., JFK School of Govt., Program for Senior Execs. in Nat. and Internat. Econ. Security, 1985; participant, The Ditchley Found. Confs. (U.K.), 1986; lectr. internat. fin. U. Calif. Trustee, Adelphic Cornell Ednl. Fund, 1987—. Bd. dirs. World Affairs Council No. Calif., 1973-75. Served to lt. (j.g.) USN, 1964-67. Decorated Bronze Star with combat V. Served to Comdr., USNR, 1968-80. Decorated Navy Commendation Medal. Fellow Inst. Dirs. (U.K.), Royal Asiatic Soc. (U.K.); mem. Acad. Internat. Bus., Brit. Inst. Mgmt., Royal Econ. Soc., Am. Econ. Assn., Fin. Mgmt. Assn., Fin. Execs. Inst., Asia Soc., Chinese Culture Found., Soc. Asian Art, Navy League U.S. (Commodore Club), Naval Order U.S., Fraternal Order UDT/SEAL, Internat. Wine and Food Soc. Clubs: Commonwealth (San Francisco); Union League (N.Y.C.); Harvard (Boston); United Oxford and Cambridge, Royal Naval (London); Internat. House of Japan (Tokyo). Home: 2115 Bush San Francisco CA 94115 Office: Protasis Trust Ltd PO Box 4000 Berkeley CA 94704

CHISHOLM, MARGARET ELIZABETH, library school director; b. Grey Eagle, Minn., July 25, 1921; d. Henry D. and Alice (Thomas) Bergman; children: Nancy Diane, Janice Marie Lane. BA, U. Washington, 1957, MLS, 1958, PhD, 1966. Librarian Everett (Wash.) Community Coll., 1961-63; asst. and assoc. prof. edn. U. Oreg., Eugene, 1963-67; assoc. prof. edn. U. N.Mex., Albuquerque, 1967-69; prof., dean Coll. Library and Info. Sci. U. Md., College Park, 1969-75; v.p. univ. relations and devel. U. Washington, Seattle, 1975-81; Commr. Western Interstate Commn. Higher Edn., Colo., 1981-85. Served as civilian aide U.S. Army, 1978-88. Recipient Ruth Worden award U. Wash., Seattle, 1957, Disting. Alumni award St. Cloud (Minn.) U., 1977, Disting. Alumni award U. Wash., 1979, John Brubaker award Cath. Library Assn., 1987. Mem. Am. Library Assn. (v.p. 1986-87, pres. 1987-88), Nat. Assn. Pub. TV Stations (trustee 1975-84, 87). Home: 5892 NE Parkpoint Pl Seattle WA 98115 Office: U Washington Grad Sch Library & Info Sci 133 Suzzallo Library FM-30 Seattle WA 98195

CHISHOLM, TOMMY, utlity company executive; b. Baldwyn, Miss., Apr. 14, 1941; s. Thomas Vaniver and Rube (Duncan) C.; m. Janice McClanahan, June 20, 1964; children: Mark Alan (dec.), Andrea, Stephen Thomas, Patrick Ervin. B.S.C.E., Tenn. Tech. U., 1963; J.D., Samford U., 1969; M.B.A., Ga. State U., 1984. Bar: Ala. 1969; Registered profl. engr., Ala., Fla., Ga., Miss., Del., N.C., S.C., Tenn., La., W. Va., Va., Ky., P.R., N.H., Pa., Tex., Ark. Civil engr. TVA, Knoxville, Tenn., 1963-64; design engr. So. Co. Services, Birmingham, Ala., 1964-69; coordinator spl. projects So. Co. Services, Atlanta, 1969-73; sec., house counsel So. Co. Services, 1977-82, v.p., sec., house counsel, 1982—; asst. to pres. So. Co., Atlanta, 1973-74; sec., asst. treas. So. Co., 1977—; mgr. adminstrv. services Gulf Power Co., Pensacola, Fla., 1975-77; sec. So. Electric Internat., Atlanta, 1981-82, v.p., sec., 1982—; sec. The So. Investment Group, 1985—. Mem. Am. Bar Assn., State Bar Ala., ASCE, Am. Soc. Corp. Secs., Am. Corporate Counsel Assn., Phi Alpha Delta, Beta Gamma Sigma. Home: 1611 Bryn Mawr Circle Marietta GA 30068 Office: The Southern Co 64 Perimeter Ctr E Atlanta GA 30346

CHISM, JAMES ARTHUR, data processor; b. Oak Park, Ill., Mar. 6, 1933; s. William Thompson and Arema Eloise (Chadwick) C.; A.B., DePauw U., 1957; M.B.A., Ind. U., 1959; postgrad. exec. program Wharton Sch. Bus., U. Pa., 1984; postgrad. sr. exec. devel. program Sch. Bus. U. Notre Dame, 1988. Mgmt. engr. consumer and indsl. products div. Uniroyal, Inc., Mishawaka, Ind., 1959-61, sr. mgmt. engr., 1961-63; systems analyst Miles, Inc., Elkhart, Ind., 1963-64, sr. systems analyst, 1965-69, project supr., distbn. systems, 1969-71, mgr. systems and programming for corporate finance and adminstrv. depts., 1971-73, mgr. adminstrv. systems and corp. staff services, 1973-75, group mgr. consumer products group systems and programming, 1975-79; dir. adminstrn. and staff services Cutter/Miles, 1979-81, dir. advanced office systems and corp. adminstrn. 1982-84; dir. advanced office systems Internat. MIS and Adminstrn., 1984-85, dir. advanced office systems, tng. and adminstrn., 1985-87; exec. dir. Advanced Office Systems, Fin. and Adminstrn., 1987—. Bd. dirs. United Way Elkhart County, 1974-75. Served with AUS, 1954-56. Mem. Assn. Systems Mgmt. (chpt. pres. 1969-70, div. dir. 1972-77, recipient Merit award 1975, Achievement award 1977, cert. systems profl. 1984, disting. service award 1986), Dean's Assocs. of Ind. U. Sch. Bus.-Bloomington (mem. adv. council), Assn. Internal Mgmt. Cons., Fin. Execs. Inst., Office Automation Soc. Internat., Nat. Assn. Bus. Economists, DePauw U. Alumni Assn., Ind. U. Alumni Assn., Delta Kappa Epsilon, Sigma Delta Chi, Sigma Iota Epsilon, Beta Gamma Sigma. Republican. Episcopalian. Clubs: Morris Park Country (South Bend, Ind.); Delta Kappa Epsilon Club (N.Y.C.), Yale of N.Y.C., Vero Beach Country (Fla.); Coast (Melbourne, Fla.); Ind. Soc. of Chgo. Home: 504 Cedar Crest Ln Mishawaka IN 46545 Office: Miles Labs Inc PO Box 40 1127 Myrtle St Elkhart IN 46515

CHISSANO, JOAQUIM ALBERTO, president of Mozambique; b. Chibuto, Gaza Province, Mozambique, Oct. 22, 1939; ed. Lourenco Marques Sec., minister def. Frente de Libertacao de Mozambique, 1964-74, mem. cen. com., also charge conduct and coordination of war against Portuguese Army; prime minister Transitional Govt. Mozambique, 1974-75; minister fgn. affairs Mozambique, 1975-86, pres., comdr.-in-chief armed forces, 1986—. Address: Office of President, Maputo Mozambique *

CHITTY, ARTHUR BENJAMIN, JR., educational consultant; b. Jacksonville, Fla., June 15, 1914; s. Arthur Benjamin and Hazel T. (Brown) C.; m. Elizabeth Nickinson, June 16, 1946; children: Arthur Benjamin III, John Abercrombie Merritt, Em Turner, Nathan Harsh Brown. B.A., U. of South, 1935; M.A., Tulane U., 1952; L.H.D., Canaan (N.H.) Coll., 1969; LL.D., Cuttington (West Africa) Coll., 1974, St. Paul's Coll., 1984. Vice pres., sales mgr. Chitty & Co., Jacksonville, 1935-45; chmn. bd. Chitty & Co., 1962-67; pres. Assn. Episcopal Colls., N.Y.C., 1965-70, 74-79, pres. emeritus, 1979—; dir. pub. relations U. of South, 1946-65, 70-73, historiographer, 1954—; Am. coordinator Oxford scholar program Keble Coll., Eng., 1969-79; bd. dirs. N.Am. Alliance for Keble Coll. Author: Reconstruction at Sewanee, 1954, Sewanee Sampler, 1978, Eli and Ruth Lilly, 1979, (with Moultrie Guerry) Men Who Made Sewanee, 1980; editor: Sewanee News, 1946-65, Ely: Too Black Too White, 1969; Contbr. articles to profl. jours.; Iconographer hist. windows, All Saints Chapel, Sewanee, 1957; dir.: documentary film Education in West Africa, 1974. Pres. Sewanee (Tenn.) Civic Assn., 1948-49; historian, Franklin County, Tenn., 1965-69; sr. warden Episc. Ch., 1956-65; trustee U. South, 1944-45, St. Andrews Sch., Tenn., 1970-72, St. Augustine's Coll., N.C., 1971-80; trustee St. Paul's Coll., Va., 1974-82, chmn. bd. assocs., 1983—; cons. Trinity Coll., Quezon City, 1974-79, Voorhees Coll., S.C., 1979-83, St. Dunstan's Sch., St. Croix, 1987—; bd. advisors St. Andrew's-Sewanee Sch., 1984—; Am. sec. Friends of St. James Am. Ch. Florence, Italy, 1984-87; trustee The Anglican Digest, 1960—; editorial adv. bd. St. Luke's Jour. of Theology, 1975—. Served with USNR, 1942-45. Named hon. paramount chief Kpelle Tribe, Liberia, 1974. Mem. Ch. Hist. Soc. (dir. 1964—), English-Speaking Union (pres. Hudson Stuck chpt. 1972-73, mem. nat. bd. 1973-82), N.Y. Acad. Scis., Newcomen Soc., Nat. Inst. Social Scis., Brotherhood St. Andrew (nat. v.p. 1969-74), Sigma Nu (pres. Ednl. Found. 1969-79, Nat. Hall of Honor 1974), Phi Beta Kappa, Pi Gamma Mu, Sigma Upsilon, Phi Alpha Theta. Episcopalian. Clubs: Century (N.Y.C.); E.Q.B. (Sewanee). Home: 100 South Carolina Ave Sewanee TN 37375 Office: 815 2d Ave New York NY 10017

CHIU, PETER YEE-CHEW, physician; b. Republic of China, May 12, 1948; came to U.S., 1965; naturalized, 1973; s. Man Chee and Yiu Ying (Cheng) C. BS, U. Calif., Berkeley, 1969, MPH, 1970, DrPH, 1975; MD, Stanford U., 1983. Diplomate Am. Bd. Family Practice; registered profl. engr., Calif.; registered sanitarian, Calif. Asst. civil engr. City of Oakland, Calif., 1970-72; assoc. water quality engr. Bay Area Sewage Services Agy., Berkeley, 1974-76; prin. environ. engr. Assn. Bay Area Govts., Berkeley, 1976-79; resident physician San Jose (Calif.) Hosp., 1983-86; ptnr. Chiu and Crawford, San Jose, 1986—; adj. prof. U. San Francisco, 1979—; clin. prof. Stanford U. Med. Sch., 1987—. Contbr. articles to profl. publs.; co-authored one of the first comprehensive regional environ. mgmt. plans in U.S.; composer, publisher various popular songs Southeast Asia, U.S. Mem. Chinese for Affirmative Action, San Francisco, 1975—; bd. dirs. Calif. Regional Water Quality Control Bd., Oakland, 1979-84, Bay Area Comprehensive Health Planning Council, San Francisco, 1972-76; mem. Santa Clara County Cen. Dem. Com., 1987—. Recipient Resident Tchr. award Soc. Tchrs. Family Medicine, 1986, Resolution of Appreciation award Calif. Regional Water Quality Control Bd., 1985. Mem. Am. Acad. Family Physicians, Am. Pub. Health Assn., Chi Epsilon, Tau Beta Pi. Democrat. Office: Chiu and Crawford 1610 Westwood Dr San Jose CA 95125

CHIURA, ENOS DZENGEDZA, holding company executive; b. Harare, Zimbabwe, Feb. 12, 1933; s. Ezekiel Tawodzera and Elinah Tarupiwa (Chadehumbe) C.; m. Faith Mary Chirisa, Dec. 22, 1962; children: Allen, Michael. BSc. in Econs., U. Zimbabwe, Harare, 1967; MSc. in Mgmt., Salford U., U.K., 1969. Mktg. researcher Rhodesian Breweries Ltd., Harare, 1968-69, cons., 1969-76, mgr. mktg. services, 1977-78; mgr. mktg. Nat. Breweries Ltd., Harare, 1978-79; exec. chmn. OK Bazaars, United Bottlers Ltd., Harare, 1980-82; mgr. manpower resources Delta Corp. Ltd., Harare, 1979-80, dep. chmn., 1985-86, exec. chmn., 1986—; chmn. Zimbabwe Electricity Supply Authority, Harare, 1986—, Bank of Credit and Commerce Zimbabwe Ltd., 1981—; dir. AFrican Distillers Ltd., Harare, 1986—. Advisory mem. Internat. Exec. Service Corps., Harare, 1985—; mem. Cambridge Livingstone Trust, Harare, 1979—, Zimbabwe Cambridge Trust, 1987—. Fellow Inst. of Dirs. Mem. Zanu Party. Methodist. Lodge: Rotary. Office: Delta Corp Ltd, PO Box BW294, Borrowdale, Harare Zimbabwe

CHIZICK, JERRY LAWRENCE, marketing and sales executive; b. Toronto, Ont., Can., Sept. 24, 1948; s. Nathan and Fay (Katz) Chizick; m. Sarah Politzer, Jan. 13, 1974; children: Jayson, Michelle. Degree in elec. engring., Ryerson Poly. Inst., Toronto, 1969. Inventory control clk. Faberge of Can. Ltd., Concord, Ont., 1969, purchasing agt., 1970-71, corp. product mgr., 1971-72; mktg. coordinator Wampole Pharms., Toronto, 1972-76; sales mgr. Holway Packaging, Scarborough, Ont., 1976-77; dir. mktg. Max Factor Can. Ltd., Scarborough, Ont., 1977-80; mktg. mgr. Corp. Foods Ltd., Etobicoke, Ont., 1980-81, dir. mktg., 1981-86, v.p. sales and mktg., 1986—; bd. dirs., chmn. steering and membership coms. Bakery Council Can., Toronto. Conservative. Jewish. Office: Corp Foods Ltd, 10 Four Seasons Pl, Etobicoke, ON Canada M9B 6H7

CHIZMADIA, STEPHEN MARK, lawyer; b. Perth Amboy, N.J., June 19, 1950; s. Stephen Thomas and Madeline Cecilia (Vojack) C. BA in Econs., U. Pa., 1971; MS in Mgmt., N.J. Inst. Tech., 1975; JD with honors, N.Y. Law Sch., 1977. Bar: N.J. 1977, Fla. 1978, N.Y. 1980, U.S. dist. ct. (so. and ea. dists.) N.Y. 1981, U.S. dist. ct. N.J. 1977. Assoc., Hampson & Millet, P.C., Somerset, N.J., 1978, sole practice, New Brunswick, N.J., 1979-80; counsel Home Ins. Co., Short Hills, N.J., 1980-81; assoc. John M. Downing, P.C., N.Y.C., 1981-84, Schneider, Kleinick & Weitz, P.C., N.Y.C., 1984—; arbitrator Small Claims, N.Y.C. Civil Ct., 1986—, arbitrator U.S. Dist. Ct. (ea. dist.) N.Y., 1987—, U.S. Dist. Ct. (east dist.), N.Y., 1987—; lectr. legal topics profl. seminars; adj. instr. law and bus. mgmt. Middlesex County Coll., 1978-80. Dir. Raritan Bay (N.J.) Area YMCA, 1980-86, N.J. Inst. Tech. Alumni Council, 1987—. Recipient Am. Jurisprudence award, 1977, several community service awards. Mem. N.J. Bar Assn., N.Y. State Bar Assn., Fla. Bar Assn., Am. Judicature Soc., Internat. Platform Assn., N.J. Inst. Tech. Alumni Council. Home: 125 Sun Dance Rd Stamford CT 06905 Office: 11 Park Pl New York NY 10007

CHMELEV, VSEVOLOD, engineer; b. Czechoslovakia, Feb. 5, 1932; s. Vsevolod Ivanovich and Anna Maria (Janish) C.; m. Antaram Nina Nerses, June 17, 1956; children: Marianna, Alexander. B. Mech. Engring., Poly. Inst. Bklyn., 1957, M. Mech. Engring., 1958, PhD., 1978. Registered profl. engr., N.Y.; lic. pilot. Engr., Ford Instrument Co., Long Island City, N.Y., 1957-60; sr. engr. Fairchild Astrionics, Wyandanch, N.Y., 1960-61; sr. engr. Sperry Corp., Great Neck, N.Y., 1961—; cons. engr. Chmelev Cons. Engrs., Huntington, N.Y., 1964—, pres. Pvt. Tchrs. and Cons. Registry, Huntington, 1982—. Author study guide Scientific Russian, 1966, also Articles. Inventor Doppler Velocimeter, 1970, Hybrid velocity system, 1972. Served USAF. Fellow Poly. Inst. Bklyn., 1968. Mem. IEEE; founder Internat. Inst. Info. Interchange (pres. 1980—), Pi Tau Sigma. Home: 4 Royal Oak Dr Huntington NY 11743 Office: Sperry Corp Great Neck NY 11020

CHMIELINSKI, EDWARD ALEXANDER, electronics company executive; b. Waterbury, Conn., Mar. 25, 1925; s. Stanley and Helen C.; m. Elizabeth Carew, May 30, 1946; children: Nancy, Elizabeth, Susan Jean. BS, Tulane U., 1950; postgrad. Colo. U., 1965. V.p., gen. mgr. Clifton Products, Litton Industries, Colorado Springs, Colo., 1965-67; pres. Memory Products div. Litton Industries, Beverly Hills, Calif., 1967-69, Bowmar Instruments, Can., Ottawa, Ont., 1969-73; gen. mgr. Leigh Instruments, Carleton Pl., Ont., 1973-75; pres., dir. Lewis Engring. Co., Naugatuck, Conn., 1975-85; pres., dir. Liquidometer Corp., Tampa, Fla., 1975-85; pres. Lewis div. Colt Industries, 1985—. Pres., Acad. Water Bd., 1963-65; bd. dirs. United Way, Colorado Springs, 1965-67; fellow Tulane U. Pres.'s Council. Served with USN, 1943-46. Mem. Am. Mgmt. Assn., C. of C., Pres.'s Council, Pres.'s Assn., Nat. Mfrs. Assn., IEEE, Air Force Assn., Navy League, Nat. Aero. Assn., Am. Helicopter Soc., Nat. Bus. Aircraft Assn. Club: Sales Execs. of N.Y.

CHMURA, GABRIEL, music director; b. Wroclaw, Poland, May 7, 1946; s. Jechiel and Zlata (Litwak) C.; m. Mareile Hinterholzinger, Dec. 16, 1977; 1 child, Natalie. Diploma, Ecole Normale, Paris, 1969, Wiener Acad., Vienna, 1971; MA, Tel Aviv Acad. Music, 1968; student, Ecole Normale, 1968-69, Vienna Music Acad., 1969-71. Gen. music dir. Opernhaus, Aachen, Fed. Republic of Germany, 1974-82, Bochumer Symfoniker, Bochum, Fed. Republic of Germany, 1981-86; music dir. Nat. Arts Centre Orch. of Can., Ottawa, Ont., 1987—; guest conducting throughout world. Recipient 1st prize Von Karajan Conducting Competition, Berlin, 1971, Golden medal Cantelli Competition, La Scala Milan, 1971. Office: care Susan Loignon, Nat Arts Ctr Orch, Ottawa, ON Canada K1P 5W1

CHNOUPEK, BOHUSLAV, minister of foreign affairs Czechoslovakia; b. Bratislava, Czechoslovakia, Aug. 10, 1925; ed. Coll. Econ. Scis., Bratislava. Sec., then reporter newspaper Smena, Presov, Czechoslovakia, 1950-58; Presov reporter Pravda, 1958-60, Moscow corr., 1960-65; editor-in-chief Predvoj, Bratislava, 1965-67; vice minister of culture, 1967-69; gen. dir. Czechoslovak Radio, 1969-70; Czechoslovak ambassador to USSR, 1970-71; minister of Fgn. Affairs, 1971—; alt. mem. Central Com., Communist Party of Czechoslovakia, 1967-69, mem., 1969—; dep. Ho. of People of the Fed. Assembly, 1972—. Recipient Klement Gottwald State prize, 1966; decorated Order of Labor, 1970, 75. Author: Dunaj konci v Izmaile (The Danube Ends in Ismailia), 1957; Dobyvatel vesmiru (Conqueror of the Universe), 1961; General s levom (General with a Lion), 1973; Milniky (Milestones), 1974. Office: Ministry Fgn Affairs, Loretanske nam 5, Prague 1 Czechoslovakia *

CHO, DAVID DONG-JIN, missiologist; b. Pyung Buk, Republic of Korea, Dec. 19, 1924; s. Sang Hang Cho; married; children: Eung Chun, Eung Soon, Eung Oak, Eung Sun, Eun Hea. BD, Presbyn. Sem., Seoul, Republic of Korea, 1949; ThM, Asbury Sem., Wilmore, Ky., 1960; DD (hon.), Belhaven Coll., 1979, Asbury Sem., 1981. Chief editor Christian Weekly News, Seoul, Republic of Korea, 1951-54; gen. sec. Korean Evang. Fellowship, Seoul, Republic of Korea, 1953-57; pres. Korea Internat. Mission, Seoul, Republic of Korea, 1968—; gen. dir. East-West Ctr. Missions, Seoul, Republic of Korea, 1973—; gen. sec. Asia Missions Assn., Seoul, Republic of Korea, 1973-86; coordinating dir. Billy Graham Seoul Crusade, Seoul, Republic of Korea, 1973; pres. Cen. Coll. Social Industries, Dae-Jeoun, Republic of Korea, 1984—; chmn. Joint Council Third World Missions Advance, Pasadena, Calif., 1986—. Author: Church Administrations, 1963, New Forces in Mission, 1976, The Third Forces, 1986; editor jour. Asia Missions Advance, 1977—. Home: CPO Box 2732, Seoul 100, Republic of Korea Office: Korea Internat Mission, CPO Box 3476, Seoul 100, Republic of Korea also: PO Box 40288 Pasadena CA 91104

CHO, TAI YONG, lawyer; b. Seoul, Republic of Korea, May 27, 1943; came to U.S., 1966; s. Nam Suck and Sun Yeo (Yoon) C; m. Hea Sun Cho, July 14, 1973; children: Robert, Richard, Susan. BS, Seoul U., 1965; MS, Cooper Union, 1971; CE, Columbia U., 1971; JD, Fordham U., 1981. Bar: N.Y. 1982; registered profl. engr., N.Y. Engr. Ministry of Constrn., Seoul, 1965-66, Andrews & Clark, N.Y.C., 1967-68, Parsons, Brinckerhoff, Quade & Douglas, N.Y.C., 1969-71; v.p. John R. McCarthy Corp., N.Y.C., 1972-80; owner, pres.. Tai CPM Corp., N.Y.C., 1980—; sole practice N.Y.C., 1982—; owner Tai Han Broadcasting Corp., N.Y.C., 1988—. Mem. ASCE, ABA, N.Y. State Bar Assn., Am. Arbitration Assn. (panel of arbitrators), Am.-Korean Lawyers Assn. of N.Y. (pres. 1988). Home: 56 Tuttle Rd Briarcliff Manor NY 10510 Office: 1 Penn Plaza New York NY 10001

CHO, YUK-KEI CARLOS, architect; b. Hong Kong, July 15, 1940; s. Kam-Cheung and Lum-Chun C.; m. Ruby Myao-Che Chang, Nov. 17, 1968; children—Vincent Woon-Ming, Wilson Wah-Kit. B.Arch., U. Hong Kong, 1967. Asst. architect Av Alvares & Assocs., Hong Kong, 1967-68; architect Samuel Tak Lee & Ptnrs., Hong Kong, 1969-70; assoc. ptnr. Kho Kiem An Assocs., Hong Kong, 1971-76; prin. ptnr. Kho & Cho Assocs., Hong Kong, 1976—; chmn. Daric Investments Ltd., Hong Kong, 1980—; permanent dir. Wide Project Holdings Ltd., Hong Kong, 1981—; dir. Above Board Co. Ltd., Hong Kong, Wing Mou Oil Co. Ltd., Hong Kong, Wings Metalworks Ltd., Hong Kong. Bd. dirs. Pok Oi Hosp., New Territories, Hong Kong, 1975-76. Fellow Royal Soc. Health, Inst. Dirs., Royal Australian Inst. Architects; mem. Hong Kong Inst. Architects, Chinese Gen. C. of C. of Hong Kong. Clubs: Royal Hong Kong Jockey, Royal Hong Kong Golf, Chinese Recreation. Home: 11 Penwood Crescent, Toronto, ON Canada M3B 3B1 Office: Kho & Cho Assocs,, 258 Hennessy Rd 18/F,, Hong Kong Hong Kong

CHOAIN, JEAN GEORGES, physician, acupuncturist; b. West Cappel, France, Dec. 8, 1917; s. Felix Auguste and Marguerite Marie (Van Der Schooten) C.; m. Christiane Marie Maurin, Apr. 21, 1954; 1 child, Françoise-Marie. MD, Faculty of Medicine, Lille, France, 1945. Cons. physician in acupuncture Lille, 1953—; tchr. acupuncture Faculty of Medicine, Lille, 1979—; physician Centre Hospitalier Regional, Lille, 1979—. Author: La Voie Rationelle de la Medecine Chinoise, 1957, Introduction au Yi-king, 1983; contbr. articles to profl. jours. Mem. Assn. Scientifique des Medecins Acuponcteurs France (v.p. 1980—), Soc. Gens de Lettres. Home: 83 Rue Reine Astrid, Marcq En Baroeul 59700, France

CHOATE, ROGER NYE, advertising executive; b. N.Y.C., Dec. 30, 1940; s. Stuart King and Joyce Winnefred (Nye) C.; m. Lisa Wilhelmina Wendelius, June 18, 1968; 1 child, Abigail Lisa. BA, Pomona Coll., 1962; M in Internat. Affairs, Columbia U., 1965; postgrad., Stockholms U., 1971. Procurement officer Afghanistan-India Projects Tchrs. Coll., Columbia U., 1963-64; reporter Staten Island (N.Y.) Advance, 1964-66; staff writer AP, Atlanta, 1966-68; desk editor Reuters, London, 1968-70; Stockholm corr. The Times, London, 1970-80, Stockholm corr. ednl. supplement, 1971-74; pub., editor Marketplace Sweden Mag., Stockholm, 1979-83; prin. Apprentice Alliance, San Francisco, 1980-85, The Plum Co., Stockholm, 1984—. Contbr. articles to Reader's Digest, N.Y. Times, Encyclopaedia Brittanica, others, 1971-83; free-lance scriptwriter radio and TV, BBC, 1971-80; editor: War and Peace Book, 1976. Fundraiser The Albany Settlement House, London, 1969-70; advisor No to Nuclear Power Com., Stockholm, 1975-79, pub. TV series, Fla., 1983-85; cons. Swedish Challenge for the America's Cup, 1977, 80. Fellow Columbia U. Sch. Internat. Affairs, N.Y.C., 1962-64; grantee Writers Fedn., Stockholm, 1976. Mem. Fgn. Press Assn. of Sweden. Home: Allévägen 8G, 191 77 Sollentuna Sweden Office: Plum Co AB, Wallingatan 18ög, 11124 Stockholm Sweden

CHOBOT, JOHN CHARLES, lawyer; b. N.Y.C., Feb. 14, 1948; s. Arthur E. and Eleanore L. (Lotito) C.; m. Catherine Anne Moran, Aug. 24, 1974; children: Christine, Keith. BA, Cornell U., 1969; MS in Edn., CCNY, 1971; JD, Fordham U., 1975. Bar: N.Y. 1976, U.S. Dist. Ct. (we. dist.) N.Y. 1976, N.J. 1985, U.S. Dist. Ct. N.J. 1985. Assoc. Phillips, Lytle, Hitchcock, Blaine & Huber, Buffalo, 1975-85; v.p., atty. The CIT Group/Sales Financing, Inc., Livingston, N.J., 1985—. Contbr. articles on bankruptcy and secured transactions to legal jours. Mem. ABA,. Kappa Alpha Soc. Home: 53 Ann Rd Long Valley NJ 07853 Office: The CIT Group 650 CIT Dr Livingston NJ 07039

CHOCK, ALVIN KEALI'I, botanist; b. Honolulu, June 18, 1931; s. Hon and Eleanor Kam Hoon (Au) C.; AA, Hannibal-LaGrange Coll. (Mo.), 1949; BA, U. Hawaii at Manoa, 1951, MS in Botany, 1953; postgrad. U. Mich., 1953-55, U.S. Dept. Agr. Grad. Sch., 1959; m. Yona Nahenahe Bielefeldt, June 18, 1962; children: T. Makana, D. 'Alana, D. Malama. Tech. adminstrv. asst. European Exchange Service, Katterbach bei Ansbach/Mfr., Fed. Republic Ger., 1958-59; plant quarantine insp. Agrl. Research Service, U.S. Dept. Agr., N.Y.C., 1959-60, Honolulu, 1961-67, supervisory insp., Balt., 1967-70; program specialist Office of Pesticide Programs, EPA, Washington, 1970-71, supervisory program specialist, 1971-74, supervisory biologist, 1975; agrl. officer (plant quarantine) FAO, Rome, 1975-78, also tech. sec. Near East Plant Protection Commn. and Caribbean Plant Protection Commn., 1976; supervisory biologist, registration div. Office of Pesticide Programs, EPA, Washington, 1978-81; acting coordinator internat. programs Plant Protection and Quarantine, Animal and Plant Health Inspection Service Dept. Agr., Hyattsville, Md., 1981-82, dir. Region II (Europe, Near East and Africa), 1981-82, The Hague, Netherlands, 1982-88; dir. region III (Asia, Pacific), Hyattsville, Md., 1988—; lectr. botany U. Hawaii, Manoa, 1961-67, 69, 72, 79, 84, 86, 88; asst. botanist B.P. Bishop Mus., Honolulu, 1961-65; botanist Kokee Natural History Mus., Hawaii, 1953-55; bot. cons. Nat. Park Service, 1962-63; mem. work panels European and Mediterranean Plant Protection Orgn., Paris, 1976-78. Mem. governing bd. Nat. Conf. State Socs., Washington, 1972-75, dep. dir. gen., 1973-74, 2d v.p., 1974-75; governing bd. Asian Pacific Am. Heritage Council, Inc., 1979-81; sec. PTA, Overseas Sch. Rome, 1976-77. Served with inf. U.S. Army, 1955-57. Plant species Cyanea chockii named in his honor; recipient other awards in field. Mem. Hawaiian Acad. Sci. (dir. jr. acad. 1963-64), Assn. Tropical Biology (charter), Hawaiian Bot. Soc. (sec. 1962, dir. 1963, 65, pres. 1964), Internat. Assn. Plant Taxonomists, Pacific Sci. Assn., Soc. Econ. Botany, FAO Assn. Profl. Staff (appeals and procedures com. 1976-77, standing com. career devel. 1976-78), Nat. Capital Area Square Dance Leaders Assn. (editor newsletter 1980-81, Callerlab traditional dance com., contra com. 1981—), Mediterranean Area Callers and Tchrs. Assn. (founder; publicity dir. 1977-78), European Callers and Tchrs. Assn., Hawaii State Soc. of D.C. (dir. 1968-69, 1st v.p. 1969-71, pres. 1971-72, adv. 1978-79, 2d v.p. 1979-80), Am. Square Dance Soc., Folklore Soc. Greater Washington, Consumers Union, Bishop Mus. Assn., Bairich und Steirisch, Sigma Xi. Club: Ramblin' Romans Sq. Dance (founder). Founding editor Hawaii Bot. Soc. newsletter, 1962-63, 66; editor Fed. Plant Quarantine Insps. Nat. Assn. newsletter, 1963-65, Ka Nupepa, 1968-71; chmn. editorial com. FAO Plant Protection Bull., 1976-78; contbg. author books; editor: (with G. L. Addicott) Favorite Songs of the Hawaii State Society, 1973; contbr. articles to profl. jours. Home: 11801 Danville Dr Luxmanor Rockville MD 20852 Office: PPQ-APHIS-USDA Am Embassy APO New York NY 09159

CHÔE, KIL SŎNG, anthropology educator; b. Kyunggi Province, Korea, June 17, 1940; m. Sachiko Sugawara, Aug. 6, 1977. BA, Seoul Nat. U., 1963; MA, Korea U., 1965; PhD, Tsukuba U., 1985. Instr. Korean Mil. Acad., Seoul, Republic Korea, 1966-69; cons. Ministry Culture and Info., Seoul, Republic of Korea, 1969-72; instr. Kyungnam U., Masan, Republic of Korea, 1977-79; asst. vice prof. then prof. Keimyung U., Taegu, Republic of Korea, 1979—; researcher Tokyo U., 1976-77. Author: Study of Korean Shamanism, 1978, Essays on Korean Shamenism, 1981, Korean Shamans, 1981, Introduction to Japanology, 1980, Korean Ancestor Worship, 1986. Served to capt. Korean Mil., 1966-69. Mem. Korean Soc. Cultural Anthropology (com. mem.). Home: Samick New Town 206-303, Taegu 703, Republic of Korea Office: Keimyung U, 2139 Daemyung-dong, Taegu 037, Republic of Korea

CHOI, CHONG WHAN, construction company executive; b. Seoul, Korea, May 10, 1925; s. Sang Lim and Lim Ja (Kim) C.; m. Kwang Young Chai, Feb. 7, 1949; children—Yong Kwon, Yong Ju. B.A. in Econs., Kun Kuk U., 1958; Founder, pres. Samwhan Corp., 1946—; chmn. Woosung Devel. Co., Ltd., 1967—, Woosung Food Stuff Industry Co., Ltd., 1969—, Samwhan Engring. Co., Ltd., 1976—, Sun Travel Co., Ltd., 1977—, Samwhan Corp., 1978—, Shinmin Mut. Savs. & Fin. Co., Ltd., 1978—, Hoehyon Co., Ltd., 1978—, Samwhan Camus Co., Ltd., 1978—, Samwhan Platt Co., Ltd., 1979—, Samsam Investment & Fin. Corp., 1982—; hon. consul-gen. in Korea for Kingdom of Swaziland, 1971—. Chmn., Korea-Saudi Arabia Econ. Cooperation Council, 1979—; vice-chmn. Korea-U.S. Econ. Council, 1980—; mem. Adv. Council Peaceful Unification Policy, Republic of Korea, 1981—; dean Corps Hon. Consuls in Korea, 1982—; v.p. Korea-Arab Friendship Soc., 1976-82. Decorated Order of Indsl. Service Merit, 1967, 70,

72, 74, 75, 76, Silver Tower, 79, Gold Tower, 84; Royal Order of Sobhuza II (Swaziland), 1981; Order Indsl. Service Merit; Silver Tower, 1979, Gold Tower, 1984; others. Mem. Korea Mil. Constrn. Contractors Assn. (chmn. 1966), Internat. Fedn. Asian and Western Pacific Contractors Assns. (pres. 1974-75), Constrn. Assn. Korea (pres. 1975-81; hon. pres. 1981—), Korea C. of C. and Industry (v.p. 1976-82), Fedn. Korean Industries (dep. chmn. 1983—), Confederation of Internat. Contractors Assn. (pres. 1983-85). Home: 1-216 Gahoe-Dong, Chongro-ku, Seoul 110, Republic of Korea Office: Samwham Corp, 98-20 Wooni-dongChongro-ku, Seoul 110, Republic of Korea

CHOI, JAE HOON, retired university president, legal educator; b. San Cheong, Korea, Apr. 8, 1929; s. Ki Seop and Bok Cho (Jeong) C.; m. So Hee Kim, Apr. 15, 1952; children: Shi Hyuen, Jang Hyuen, Jee Hee. LLB, Seoul Nat. U., 1953, LLM, 1955; PhD, Pusan Nat. U., 1971; researcher The Hague (Netherlands) Acad. Internat. Law, 1971; LL.D. (hon.), Nat. Chengchi U., Republic of China, 1984; LL.D. (hon.), U. S.C., 1987. Prof. law Pusan Nat. U., 1956-83, dean Coll. Law and Polit. Sci., 1971-73, dir. Inst. Problem of Korean Unification, 1974-77, dean Grad. Sch. Public Adminstrn., 1981-83, pres., 1983-87; prof. law Kyushu Nat. U., Japan, 1988—. Mem. Korean Assn. Internat. Law (v.p. 1974-77, pres. 1983-84), Am. Soc. Internat. Law, Japanese Assn. Internat. Law. Author: International Law, 1984; contbr. articles to profl. jours.

CHOI, JIN-HAK, internist, educator; b. Sachon, Gyeong-nam, Republic of Korea, Nov. 15, 1928; s. Moon-Kyoung and Kyoung-Ee (Lee) C.; m. Sun-Young Kim. BA in Medicine, Seoul Nat. U., Republic of Korea, 1955, PhD in Medicine, 1955. Chmn. internal medicine Korean Electric Co. Hanil Hosp., Seoul, 1962-74, dir., 1974-78; attending prof. Seoul Nat. U., 1963-84, Korea U., Seoul, 1969-86; dir. Inchon (Republic of Korea) Gil Hosp., 1978-79, Korea Vets. Hosp., Seoul, 1981-84. Mem. Korean Med. Assn. (v.p. 1980-81, 85-86), Korean Hosp. Assn. (v.p. 1976-78), Korean Soc. Gastroenterology (pres. 1984-85). Home: 442-40 Seokyo Dong, Ma Po Gu, Seoul 121, Republic of Korea

CHOI, MICHAEL KAMWAH, mechanical engineer, researcher; b. Baoan, Quangdong, China, Aug. 16, 1952; came to U.S., 1972, naturalized, 1987; s. Ying-Loi and Kan-Hau (Yuen) C. Sc.B. with honors, magna cum laude, Brown U., 1976; M.S.M.E., MIT, 1978, Engr., 1979. Registered profl. engr., Va. Research asst. MIT, Cambridge, Mass., 1977-79; sr. research engr. Sci. Applications Internat. Corp., McLean, Va., 1979-87; sr. engr. spacecraft systems Fairchild Space Co., Germantown, Md., 1987—; project leader, mgr. numerous projects for govt., industry and utilities. Contbr. articles to profl. jours. Reviewer Solar Energy Jour., ASME Solar Energy Div., 1983—. Mem. ASME, NSPE, Va. Soc. Profl. Engrs., Am. Solar Energy Soc., Sigma Xi, Tau Beta Pi. Home: 2237 Halter Ln Reston VA 22071

CHOI KWANG SOO, government official; b. Seoul, Republic of Korea, Feb. 24, 1935. Grad., Seoul Nat. U. Coll. of Law, 1957; student, Georgetown U. Sch. Fgn. Service, 1958-59. With Ministry of Fgn. Affairs, 1956; third sec. Korean Embassy, Washington, 1958; sec. sec. Korean Diplomatic Mission, Japan, 1962; dir. Northeast Asia Div. Asian Affairs Bur., 1965; counsellor Korean Embassy, Washington, 1967; research commr. Inst. of Fgn. Affairs, 1970; dir.-gen. Trade Promotion, 1970, Asian Affairs Bur., 1971; asst. minister of nat. def. for logistics and def. industries Ministry of Nat. Def., 1972, vice minister, 1973; chief of protocol Pres. of Republic of Korea, 1974, sec.-gen., 1979; mem. Standing Com. for Emergency Nat. Security Measures, 1980; first minister 1980; minister of communications Govt. of Republic of Korea, 1981; ambassador extraordinary and plenipotentiary Govt. of Republic of Korea, Kingdom of Saudi Arabia, 1983; ambassador extraordinary and plenipotentiary, permanent observer to the U.N. Govt. of Republic of Korea, N.Y.C., 1985; minister fgn. affairs Govt. of Republic of Korea, 1986—. Decorated Order of Service Merit (Red Stripes), 1972, Order of Service (Yellow Stripes), 1978, Order of Diplomatic Service Merit (Gwanghwa medal), 1980, Order of Service Merit (Blue Stripes), 1982. Home: San 8 Hannam-dong, Yongsan-ku, Seoul Republic of Korea Office: Office of Minister of Fgn Affairs, Seoul Republic of Korea *

CHOMIAK, ROSS LEO, journalist; b. Lviv, Ukraine, Jan. 2, 1936; came to U.S., 1963, naturalized, 1967; s. Alexander and Catherine Anastasia (Federchuk) C.; m. Martha Ingrid Bohachevsky, Dec. 29, 1962; children—Tania B., Theodora B. B.A., McMaster U., Hamilton, Ont., Can., 1960; B.Journalism, Carleton U., Ottawa, Ont., 1962. Editor, Ukranian Weekly, Jersey City, N.J., 1960-61, Radio Liberty, N.Y.C., 1967-72; reporter Calgary Herald, Alta, Can., 1962-63; assoc. editor Prolog Research, N.Y.C., 1963-67; broadcaster Voice of Am., Washington, 1972-74; mng. editor USIA Press. Service, Washington, 1974—. Contbr. articles to mags. and newspapers. Mem. council Holy Family Shrine, Washington, 1974—. Reader's Digest fellow, 1962. Mem. Nat. Press Club, Ukranian Assn. Washington (v.p. 1983-85), Washington Group (dir. 1985—). Democrat. Ukranian Catholic. Avocations: photography; travel. Home: 1802 Rupert St McLean VA 22101 Office: USIA 400 C St SW Washington DC 20547

CHOMSKY, AVRAM NOAM, educator; b. Phila., Dec. 7, 1928; s. William and Elsie (Simonofsky) C.; m. Carol Doris Schatz, Dec. 24, 1949; children: Aviva, Diane, Harry Alan. B.A., U. Pa., 1949, M.A., 1951, Ph.D., 1955, D.H.L. (hon.), 1984; D.H.L., U. Chgo., 1967, Loyola U. Chgo., 1970, Swarthmore Coll., 1970, Bard Coll., 1971, U. Mass., 1973; D.Litt., U. London, Eng., 1967, Delhi (India) U., 1972, Visva-Bharati U., Santiniketan, West Bengal, 1980. Faculty MIT, 1955—, prof. modern langs., 1961—, Ferrari P. Ward prof. modern lang. and linguistics, 1966—, Inst. prof., 1976—; vis. prof., Columbia, 1957-58; mem. Inst. Advanced Study, Princeton, 1958-59; Linguistic Soc. Am. prof. UCLA, summer 1966; Beckman prof. U. Calif.-Berkeley, 1966-67; John Locke lectr., Oxford, 1969; Bertrand Russell Meml. lectr. Cambridge, 1971; Nehru Meml. lectr. New Delhi, 1972; Huizinga lectr. Leiden, 1977; Woodbridge lectr. Columbia U., 1978; Kant lectr. Stanford U., 1979; Jeanette K. Watson disting. vis. prof. Syracuse U., 1982. Author: Syntactic Structures, 1957, Current Issues in Linguistic Theory, 1964, Aspects of the Theory of Syntax, 1965, Cartesian Linguistics, 1966, Topics in the Theory of Generative Grammar, 1966, (with Morris Halle) Sound Pattern of English, 1968, Language and Mind, 1968, American Power and the New Mandarins, 1969, At War with Asia, 1970, Problems of Knowledge and Freedom, 1971, Studies on Semantics in Generative Grammar, 1972, For Reasons of State, 1973, (with Edward Herman) Counterrevolutionary Violence, 1973, Peace in The Middle East, 1974, Logical Structure of Linguistic Theory, 1975, Reflections on Language, 1975, Essays on Form and Interpretation, 1977, Human Rights and American Foreign Policy, 1978, (with Edward Herman) The Political Economy of Human Rights, 2 vols, 1979, Rules and Representations, 1980, Lectures on Government and Binding, 1981, Concepts and Consequences of the Theory of Government and Binding, 1982, Towards a New Cold War, 1982, Fateful Triangle, 1983, Turning the Tide, 1985, Barriers, 1986, Knowledge of Language, 1986, Pirates and Emperors, 1986, On Power and Ideology, 1987, Language and Problems of Knowledge, 1987, Language in a Psychological Setting, 1987, Generative Grammar, 1987, Culture of Terrorism, 1988, (with Edward Herman) Manufacturing Consent, 1988. Recipient disting. sci. contbn. award Am. Psychol. Assn., 1984, Kyoto prize, 1988; Jr. fellow Soc. Fellows, Harvard, 1951-55; research fellow Harvard Cognitive Studies Center, 1964-67. Fellow AAAS, fellow Brit. Acad. (corr.), Brit. Psychol. Soc. (hon.); mem. Nat. Acad. Scis., Am. Acad. Arts and Scis., Linguistic Soc. Am., Deutsche Akademie der Naturforscher Leopoldina, Am. Philos. Assn., Utrecht Soc. Arts and Scis. Home: 15 Suzanne Rd Lexington MA 02173 Office: MIT 77 Massachusetts Ave Cambridge MA 02139

CHONG, ANDRÉS, minerals and metals company executive, consultant; b. Lima, Perú, Dec. 17, 1945; arrived People's Republic of China, 1981; s. Andrés and Lucía (Geng) C.; m. Nury Ordóñez; children: Roxana, Andrés, Waldo. Grad., U. Villarreal, Lima, 1966; MS, U. Agraria La Molina, Lima, 1967; postgrad., Fundación Getulio Vargas, Rio de Janeiro, 1967-68. Economist SIPA Ministerio Agricultura, Lima, 1967-68; advisor Ministerio Agricultura/BID, Lima, 1867-68; dean Universidad Católica Ayacucho (Perú), 1968-69; economist Ministerio Transporte, Lima, 1970-73; chief planning Minpeco SA, Lima, 1974-80; prof. U. Federico Villareal, Lima, 1970-80, U. Garcilaso de la Vega, Lima, 1970-80; comml. counsellor Embajada del Perú, Beijing, People's Republic of China, 1981—; bd. dirs. Minpeco SA, Beijing, 1981—; co. rep. various metals and minerals orgns., rep. govtl. and internat. orgns., parcicipant profl. confs. Author numerous tech. studies and reports. 0em. Colegio de Economistas de Lima, Instituto de Investigaciones Económicas Y Sociales (pres. 1981), Organización del Instituto de Investigaciones de la Universidad Particular Inca Garcilaso de la Vega, Asociación de Graduados Fundación Getulio Vargas, Touring Automóvil Club del Perú. Home: San Li Tun 9-12, Beijing Peoples Republic of China Office: MINPECO SA, San Li Tun 2-71, Beijing Peoples Republic of China

CHONG, DOROTHY BIERMA, trading and consulting company executive; b. Detroit, Mar. 27, 1925; d. Charles Allen and Jessica (Griffiths) Bierma; student Los Angeles City Coll., 1942-43, U. Mich., 1946-47; m. Richard Seng-Hoon Chong, Jan. 9, 1980; step-children—David C.S., Stephen C.L., Daniel C.Y. Adminstrv. asst. to plant mgr. Monsanto Co., Trenton, Mich., 1952-65; adminstrv. asst. to pres. Adache Assocs., Inc., Engrs., Cleve., 1965-69; credit mgr. Hawaiian Crane & Rigging, Ltd., Honolulu, 1969-70; adminstrv. mgr. East Central region Booz, Allen & Hamilton, Inc., Cleve., 1970-73; v.p. Amer-Asia Trading Co., Inc., Orlando, Fla., 1973—; broker, co-owner Sungold Realty Internat., Inc., Orlando, 1979—, Sungold Decor, Inc.; dir. Crown Savs. Assn. Mem. Chinese-Am. Assn. Central Fla. (sec., dir. 1980-81), World Trade Council for Central Fla., Nat. Assn. Realtors, Fla. Assn. Realtors, Orlando Area Bd. Realtors. Presbyterian. Club: Citrus. Home: 9652 Woodmont Pl Windermere FL 32786 Office: Amer-Asia Trading Co Inc 7201 Lake Ellenor Dr Suite 112 Orlando FL 32809

CHONG, JUAN, infosystems entreperneur; b. Tapachula, Chiapas, Mex., Jan. 11, 1950; s. Juan and Rosa Angelica Chong; m. Leticia Loo, July 30, 1977; children:, Heidy, Alexander. BA in Acctg. with honors, Tec. De Monterrey, 1974, MBA, 1978, MSC in Info. Systems, 1984. Chief budgeting control Fundidora Monterrey, S.A., 1975-77, chief budgeting planning, 1977-79, acct., 1979, staff info. systems of v.p. finance, 1981-85; bd. dirs Exportadora de Esmaltados, S.A., 1973-85; ind. computer software developer, 1984—; cons. in fin. and infosystems, 1984—; chmn. bd. Distribuidora del Hogar de Tapachula, Chiapas, 1985—; pres., bd. chmn. Sistemas De Informacion Aplicados, S.A. de C.V., Tapachula, Chiapas, 1986—.

CHONG, MARY DRUZILLEA, nurse; b. Fairview, Okla., Mar. 8, 1930; d. Charles Dewey and Viola Haddie (Ford) Crawford; A.A. (Bells scholarship), El Camino Jr. Coll., 1950; R.N., Los Angeles County Hosp. Sch. Nursing, 1953; B.S. in Nursing, Calif. State U., 1968; m. Nyuk Choy Chong, Aug. 24, 1952 (div. 1968); children—Anthony, Dorlinda. Staff nurse neurosurgery Los Angeles County Gen. Hosp., Los Angeles, 1957-58; staff nurse Harbor Gen. Hosp., Torrance, Calif., 1958-59, emergency room staff nurse, 1959-61, asst. head nurse, 1963-64, supr. neurosurgery intensive care unit, 1964-67, part-time relief nurse, 1967-69, head nurse chest medicine, 1969-72; instr. Licensed Vocat. Nursing program Los Angeles YWCA Job Corps., 1972-74; emergency room staff nurse mobile intensive care nurse Victor Valley Hosp., Victorville, Calif., 1974-79; dir. nursing San Vicente Hosp., Los Angeles, 1980-82, Upjohn Healthcare Services, Los Angeles, 1983-85; dir. home health services Bear Valley Community Hosp. Home Health Agy., Big Bear Lake, Calif., 1986-87; dir. nursing Helen evans Home for Developmentally disahled Children, 1987—, Adon Care, West Palm Springs, 1988; asst. dir. nursing Care West Palm Springs (Calif.) Nursing Ctr., 1988—. Leader, South Bay council Girl Scouts Am., 1968; tchr. YWCA Job Corps, 1972-74; dir. nursing Helen Evans Home for Developmentally Disabled Children, 1987—. Mem. AAUW, Nat. Assn. Female Execs., Calif. State U. Los Angeles Alumni Assn., Internat. Platform Assn. Home: PO Box 697 Lucerne Valley CA 92356 Office: 15125 E Gale Ave Hacienda Heights CA 91745

CHONG, SHUI-FONG, graphic designer; b. Canton, China, Dec. 19, 1954; came to U.S., 1971; s. Muk-Wing and Kau-Mui C. B.A., CUNY-N.Y.C., 1978; postgrad. Sch. Visual Art, N.Y.C., 1978-79, Parsons Sch. Design, N.Y.C., 1979-82. Asst. art dir. Schein/Blattstein Advt., Inc., N.Y.C., 1978-79; asst. art dir. Creative Decisions, Inc., N.Y.C., 1979-81, H/T Graphic Design, Inc., N.Y.C., 1981-82; graphic designer Kwasha Lipton, N.J., 1982-87; prin., graphic designer Shui-Fong Chong Design, N.Y.C., 1982—. Recipient Excellence award N.Y. Internat. Assn. Bus. Communication, N.Y.C., 1985, Best of Sch. winner Visual Art Competition, N.Y.C., 1973. Mem. Art Dirs. Club, Graphic Artists Guild, Am. Inst. Graphic Arts, Chinese Am. Designers Assn. Avocations: art; music; sport; travel.

CHOO, YEOW MING, lawyer; b. Johore Bahru, Malaysia, Aug. 1, 1953; s. Far Tong and Kim Fong (Wong) C.; LLB with honors (1st in class), U. Malaya, 1977; LLM, Harvard U., 1979; JD, Chgo.-Kent Coll., 1980. Admitted to Malaysia bar, 1977, Ill. bar, 1980; lectr. law U. Malaya Law Sch., Kuala Lumpur, Malaysia, 1977-78, Monash U. Law Sch., Melbourne, Australia, 1978; internat. atty. Standard Oil Co. (Ind.), Chgo., 1979-82; partner firm Anderson, Liu and Choo, Chgo., 1982-84; ptnr. Baer Marks and Upham, N.Y.C., 1984-85; ptnr. Winston and Strawn, Chgo., 1985-87; ptnr. Dorsey and Whitney, N.Y.C., 1987—; dir. Harvard Bros. Internat. Corp.; Boston; chmn. tax subcom. Nat. Council for US-China Trade, 1980-84. Mem. Am. Mining Congress (alt. mem. com. on law of sea 1980-82), ABA, Ill. Bar Assn., Chgo. Bar Assn., Malayan Bar Council, U.S. Chess Fedn., Harvard Law Sch. Alumni Assn. Club: Harvard. Office: Dorsey & Whitney 350 Park Ave New York NY 10022

CHOOI, WENG KWONG, physician; b. Ipoh, Perak, West Malaysia, Malaysia, July 9, 1951; s. Loon Sui Chooi and Lai Nhoh Leong; m. Dolly Kwah, Aug. 11, 1976; children: Jo Lyn, Yew Vern. MBBChir, Med. Faculty U. Malaysia, Kuala Lumpur, 1976. Intern Med. Faculty U. Hosp., Kuala Lumpur, 1976-77; med. officer Gen. Hosp. Kuala Lumpur, 1977-80; ptnr. City Polyklinik and Surgeri, Petaling Jaya, Selangor, Klang, 1980—; bd. dirs. Citi Med. Edn. Bd., Petaling Jaya, Selangor, 1983—. Mem. Malaysian Med. Assn., U. Malaya Med. Alumni Assn. Club: Sultan Alam Shah. Home: No 22 Jalan 17/33, Petaling Jaya, Selangor West Malaysia 46400, Malaysia

CHOON, LEE FOOK, insurance surveyor; b. Singapore, Feb. 12, 1950; s. Lee Yan and Lai Siew (Lee) Kuen; m. Lee yeo Wee Tsan, July 5, 1975; 1 child, Mabel Li Yimei. Cert. master mariner, Singapore. Marine surveyor Singapore Adjusters & Surveyors, 1978-80; gen. mgr. Overseas Pacific Pte Ltd., Singapore, 1981-84; prin. surveyor Integral Marine Cons., P.C., Singapore, 1984—. Fellow Inst. Petroleum (U.K.); mem. Nautical Inst. (U.K.), Singapore Ins. Inst., Inst. Arbitrators, Singapore Nautical Inst. Office: Integral Marine Cons, 29 Binjai Park, Singapore 2158, Singapore

CHOONHAVAN, CHATICHAI, prime minister, minister of defense; b. Bangkok, Apr. 5, 1922. Student, Chulachomklao Royal Mil. Acad., Cavalry Sch., Royal Thai Army. Troop commdr. First Royal Cavalry Guards, Bangkok; asst. mil. attaché Thai Embassy, Washington; commandant Armour Sch., Bangkok; ambassador to Argentina, Austria, Turkey, Switzerland, Yugoslavia and UN Thai govt.; with Erawan Trust Co. Ltd., Erawan Internat. Co. Ltd.; dep. fgn. minister Thai govt., Bangkok, 1972, fgn. minister, 1975, industry minister, 1976; dep. leader Chat Thai Part; dep. prime minister Thai govt., Bangkok, 1986-88, prime minister, minister of def., 1988—. Office: Office of the Prime Minister, Govt House, Nakhon Pathom Rd, Bangkok Thailand *

CHOPRA, KULDIP PRAKASH, physicist; b. Srinagar, India, Mar. 25, 1932; s. Madan Gopal and Shanti Devi (Handa) C.; B.S. with honors, U. Delhi, 1951, M.S., 1953, Ph.D., 1960; came to U.S., 1957, naturalized, 1968; m. Phyllis Shirley McGrath, July 15, 1968 (dec. 1979); m. 2d, Gail Catherine Forger, June 11, 1983; 1 son, Andrew Paul. Research assoc. physics U. Md., 1957-58; vis. asst. prof. physics, research scientist U. So. Calif., 1958-60; research asst. prof. astronautics Poly. Inst. Bklyn., 1960-63; sr. scientist, head space sci. lab. Melpar, Inc., Falls Church, Va., 1963-65, cons., 1965-66; asso. prof. atmospheric and space scis., dir. Summer Sch. Environ. and Planetary Scis., U. Miami (Fla.), 1965-67; prof. applied physics Nova U., Ft. Lauderdale, Fla., 1967-69; prof. physics Old Dominion U., Norfolk, Va., 1969—; vis. prof. physics U. Md. Eastern Shore, 1985-86, author, cons., lectr., 1986—; vis. prof. Va. Inst. Marine Scis., Gloucester Point, 1972-77; mem. adv. bd. Sci. Spectrum, 1970; cons. NASA Wallops Flight Center; sci. advisor to Gov. of Va., 1976-78; tech. adv. com. Air Pollution Control Bd., 1979-80. Recipient Melpar Author-of-Yr. award, 1965, J. Shelton Horsely Research award Va. Acad. Sci., 1974. Fellow Am. Phys. Soc.; mem. Am. Geophys. Union (life), AAAS, AIAA, AAUP, Am. Meterol. Soc. Editor Va. Jour. Sci., 1977-79; contbr. profl. jours. Office: Univ of Md Eastern Shore Princess Anne MD 21853

CHOQUET, GUSTAVE, mathematics professor, researcher; b. Solesmes, Nord, France, Mar. 1, 1915; s. Gustave and Marie (Fosse) C.; m. Marie Pihan, Jan. 23, 1941 (div. 1961); children: Bernard, Christian, Claire; m. Yvonne Bruhat, May 16, 1961; children: Daniel, Genevieve. Licence and agrégation, Ecole Normale Supérience, Paris, 1937; Doctorat en Scis., Centre Nat. de la Recherche Sci., Paris, 1946. Prof. Grenoble U., France, 1947-49; prof. Paris U., 1949-84, prof. emeritus, 1985—. Author several books on math., plus articles. Served with French Army, 1939-40. Elected mem. Acad. des Scis., Paris, 1976. Mem. Soc. Math. de France, Am. Math. Soc. Home: 16 ave d'Alembert, 92160 Antony France

CHOROT, PALOMA, psychotherapist, educator; b. Madrid, June 4, 1958; s. Jose Luis Chorot and Carmen Raso. PhD in Psychology, U. Nacional Edn. Distancia, Madrid, 1986. Investigator U. Nat. Edn., Madrid, 1981-83, prof. psychodiagnostics, 1983—, prof. psychopathology, 1986—. Author: Investigations on Skin and Salivary pH and its Relationship with Anxiety and Phobic Fear, 1982, Experimental Studies About the Conditioning Model of Fear, 1983, Theorists Work at Psychological Assessment, 1983; cons. Internat. Jour. Psychosomatics, Phila., 1984. Mem. Internat. Psychosomatics Inst., Soc. Española de Psicologia, Assn, Española de Terapia de Conducta. Home: C/Bailen #33, 28005 Madrid Spain Office: U Nacional Edn Distancia, PO Box 60148, 28040 Madrid Spain

CHOTINER, KENNETH LEE, judge; b. Los Angeles, Aug. 14, 1937; s. Murray M. and Phyllis Sylvia (Levenson) C.; m. Florence Helene Penney, May 29, 1964; children—Dana Lynne, Cara Lee. BA in Polit. Sci. with honors, UCLA, 1959; JD with honors, Loyola U., Los Angeles, 1969; grad. Hastings Coll. Law Coll. Criminal Advocacy, San Francisco, 1980, Calif. Jud. Coll., U. Calif., Berkeley, 1981. Bar: Calif. 1970, U.S. Ct. Customs and Patent Appeals 1971, U.S. Ct. Mil. Appeals 1974, U.S. Sup. Ct. 1975. Instr. Am. govt. U. Alaska, 1962; dep. city atty., Los Angeles, 1970-71; sole practice, Santa Monica, Calif., 1971-81; spl. counsel City of Hawthorne (Calif.), 1973-80; judge pro tem Los Angeles Mcpl. Ct., 1975-81, Santa Monica Mcpl. Ct., 1977-81; judge Los Angeles Mcpl. Ct., 1981—, supervising judge valley div., 1983, Van Nuys-Encino br., 1983-84; justice pro tem Calif. Ct. Appeal, 1982; adj. prof. U. West Los Angeles Sch. Law, 1981-82; faculty Calif. Jud. Coll., Earl Warren Legal Inst., U. Calif., Berkeley, 1982, Calif. Ctr. Jud. Edn. and Research, Berkeley, 1982—, Media Workshop on Calif. Cts., 1982—; chmn. Media Conf. on Calif. Cts., 1986; conf. del. State Bar Calif., 1972, 73, 76-80. Author: Restricting Handguns, 1979; contbr. articles to legal jours. Mem. exec. com. Los Angeles Mcpl. Ct., 1985, 88. Bd. dirs. So. Calif. ACLU, 1972-81, v.p., 1978-81; dir. ex-officio Legal Aid Soc. Santa Monica, 1979-80; bd. dirs. Friends of the Santa Monica Mountains, Parks and Seashore, 1979-81; mem. dean's council UCLA Coll. Letters and Sci.; mem. wildlife adv. com. Los Angeles County Fish and Game Commn., 1973-75, chmn., 1974; mem. Los Angeles County Interdepartmental Drinking Driver Program, task force, 1985-87; mem. PTA, 1973-81, Los Angeles Olympic Organizing Com. Criminal Justice System Subcom., 1983-84. Served to capt. USAF, 1961-66. Recipient recognition awards Calif. Trial Lawyers Assn. (trial lawyer and criminal def.), 1980, U. W. Los Angeles Sch. Law award for Outstanding Service, 1984, Nat. Council on Alcoholism award of Appreciation, 1984, Eagle Scout award Boy Scouts Am., Order of the Arrow. Mem. Nat. Conf. State Trial Judges, Nat. Conf. Spl. Ct. Judges (del. 1985), Calif. Judges Assn., Nat. Conf. Bar Pres., ABA (presdl. showcase program, Washington 1985), Nat. Eagle Scout Assn., Mcpl. Ct. Judges Assn. Los Angeles County, Irish Am. Bar Assn., Am. Arbitration Assn. (panel 1970-81), Santa Monica Bay Dist. Bar Assn. (pres. 1979), Assn. Trial Lawyers Am., Women's Lawyers Assn. Los Angeles, Criminal Ct. Bar Assn., Los Angeles County Bar Assn., St. Thomas More Law Soc., UCLA Alumni Assn., UCLA Blue and Gold Circle, U. Calif. Santa Cruz Fiat Lux Soc., Am. Judicature Soc., Ephebian Soc., Quill and Scroll Soc., Santa Monica C. of C., Sealbearer Soc., Phi Alpha Delta. Lodge: Lions (zone chmn. 1975-76). Office: Los Angeles Mcpl Ct 110 N Grand Ave Los Angeles CA 90012-3055

CHOU, SHYAN-YIH, nephrologist, internist, researcher; b. Taipei, Taiwan, Aug. 7, 1941; came to U.S., 1968, naturalized, 1980; s. En-Truen and Lin-Oh (Lin) C.; m. Wanda Louie, Dec. 7, 1974; children—Janet, Denise. M.D., Nat. Taiwan U., Taipei, 1966. Diplomate Am. Bd. Internal Medicine. Intern Brookdale Hosp. Med. Ctr., Bklyn., 1968-69, resident in medicine, 1969-70; Nat. Kidney Found. fellow, 1970-73, asst. attending physician, 1973-74, assoc. attending physician, 1974-77, attending physician, 1977—, physician-in-charge, 1977—; asst. prof. medicine SUNY Health Sci. Ctr. at Bklyn., 1978-84, assoc. prof., 1984—. Contbr. sci. articles to profl. publs. N.Y. State Health Research Council grantee; NIH grantee. Fellow ACP, Am. Coll. Clin. Pharmacology; mem. Am. Soc. Nephrology, Internat. Soc. Nephrology, Am. Fedn. Clin. Research, Am. Heart Assn., AAAS, Am. Physiol. Soc. Research on hormonal factors regulating medullary blood flow; role of medullary hemodynamics in regulating renal sodium excretion. Office: Brookdale Hosp Med Center Nephrology-Hypertension Div Linden Blvd Brooklyn NY 11212

CHOU, TING-CHAO, pharmacology educator; b. Taiwan, Sept. 9, 1938, came to U.S., 1965, naturalized, 1976; s. Chao-Yun and Sheng-Mei (Chen) C.; B.S., Kaohsiung Med. Coll., Taiwan, 1961; M.S., Nat. Taiwan U., 1965; Ph.D., Yale U., 1970; m. Dorothy Tsui-chin Tseng, June 26, 1965; children—Joseph Hsin-I, Julia Hsin-Ya. Teaching asst. pharmacology Nat. Taiwan U., 1964-65; research asst. pharmacology Yale U., 1969; postdoctoral fellow Johns Hopkins U., Balt., 1969-72; asso. Sloan-Kettering Inst. Cancer Research, N.Y.C., 1972-78, asso. mem., 1978-88, mem., 1988—, head lab. pharmacology, 1988—; asst. prof. Cornell U., 1972-78, asso. prof., 1978-88, prof. pharmacology, 1988—. Research grantee Nat. Cancer Inst. and Am. Cancer Soc., 1975—. Mem. AAAS, Am. Assn. Cancer Research, Am. Soc. Pharmacology and Exptl. Therapeutics, Am. Soc. Preventive Oncology (founding mem.), Am. Soc. for Biochem. and Molecular Biol., Kaohsiung Med. Coll. Alumni Assn. Am. (dir. 1968-81, pres. 1972), Sigma Xi. Author (with J. Chou) Dose Effect Analysis with Microcomputers, 1986; mem. edit. adv. bd. Cancer Biochemistry Biophysics, 1984—, Jour. of the Nat. Cancer Inst., 1988—; contbr. articles and abstracts on cancer chemotherapy and theoretical biology to profl. jours. Office: 1275 York Ave New York NY 10021

CHOUDHRY, GHULAM HUSSAIN, controller; b. Rahimyarkhan, Punjab, Pakistan, Mar. 6, 1942; s. Mohammad Sharif and Nazeer Choudhry; m. Tasawar Choudhry, Feb. 3, 1969; children: Moneeza, Sameera, Mahira, Aman. BA with honors, Emerson Coll., Pakistan, 1959. Chartered acct., Eng., Wales. Audit mgr. J.H. Champness, Cordroy Beesly & Co-Chared Accts., London, 1965-66; with Lever Bros. Pakistan Ltd., 1966—; cen. acct. Lever Bros. Pakistan Ltd., Karachi, 1981-84, accounts controller, 1985-86, accounts controller Levers/Liptons subs.,, 1987—. Fellow Inst. Chartered Accts. in Pakistan, Inst. Chartered Accts. in U.K. Club: Gymkhana (Karachi). Home: 74 5th Commercial St Phase IV, Comml Def Housing Authority, Karachi Pakistan Office: Lever Bros Pakistan Ltd, PO Box 220, Avari Plaza, Fatima Jinnah Rd, Karachi Pakistan

CHOUDHURY, DEO CHAND, physicist; b. Darbhanga, India, Feb. 1, 1926; came to U.S., 1955; s. Kapleshwar and Gutainya Choudhury; B.Sc., U. Calcutta, 1944, M.Sc., 1946; Ph.D., UCLA, 1959; m. Annette Patricia DuBois, Aug. 3, 1963; 1 son, Raj. Research fellow Niels Bohr Inst., Cophenhagen, 1952-55; research asst. physics U. Rochester, N.Y., 1955-56; research, teaching asst. physics UCLA, 1956-59; asst. prof. physics U. Conn., Storrs, 1959-62; assoc. prof. Poly. Inst. of N.Y., Bklyn., 1962-67, prof. physics, 1967—; vis. asst. physicist Brookhaven Nat. Lab., summer 1960; vis. physicist Oak Ridge Nat. Lab., summer 1962, Niels Bohr Inst., 1978-79. Govt. India Council Sci. and Indsl. Research scholar U. Calcutta Coll. Sci., 1947-52. Mem. Am. Phys. Soc., N.Y. Acad. Scis., AAAS, Indian Phys. Soc., Sigma Xi, Sigma Pi Sigma. Contbr. chpt. to book, articles on nuclear models, structure and reactions to profl. publs. Home: 90 Gold St New York NY 10038 Office: Poly U Dept Physics 333 Jay St Brooklyn NY 11201

CHOUDHURY, HUMAYUN RASHEED, ambassador of Bangladesh to U.S.; b. Sylhet, Bangladesh, Nov. 11, 1928; s. Abdur Rasheed and Begum A. (Rasheed) C.; m. Mehjabeen Choudhury, Oct. 23, 1947; children: Nasrine

Karim, Nauman Rasheed. B.A. with 1st class honors, Cambridge U., 1944; postgrad. Dacca U.; B.S. in Geology, Chemistry, Geography, Muslim U., India; Diploma in Internat. Affairs, U. London; grad. cert. honor Fletcher Sch. Law and Diplomacy. Third sec. Pakistan Embassy, Rome, 1956-59, Baghdad, Iraq, 1959-61; 2d sec., Paris; dir. personnel Ministry Fgn. Affairs, 1964-67; minister of fgn. affairs, 1985—; charge d'affaires Pakistan embassy, Lisbon, 1967-69; dep. chief, counsellor Pakistan embassy, Djakarta, 1969-71; chief Bangladesh diplomatic mission, New Delhi, India, counsellor Pakistan High Commn., 1971-72; permanent rep. of Bangladesh to UN Indsl. Devel. Orgn., to Internat. AEC; ambassador of Bangladesh to W.Ger., until 1975; ambassador to Saudi Arabia, 1976-81; permanent rep. to Orgn. Islamic Conf.; fgn. sec. Govt. Bangladesh, 1981-82; ambassador to U.S., Washington, from 1982. Pres. gen. assembly UN, N.Y.C., 1987. M.P., 1886—. Office: Ministry Fgn Affairs, Dhaka 20007, Bangladesh *

CHOULIKA, VLADIMIR THEODORE, electrical engineer, consultant; b. Beirut, Sept. 21, 1928; s. Theodore David and Maria (Gavalof) C.; m. June 4, 1959; 2 children. Diploma in Civil Engring., Ecole Superieure d'Ingenieurs, Beirut, 1950; Lic. es-Scis, Faculte de Lyon, 1950; Diploma Elec. Engring., Ecole Superieure d'Electricite, Paris, 1952. Registered profl. elec. engr., Lebanon; Eng. Asst. chief engr. Kadischa Elec. Power Co., Tripoli, Lebanon, 1953-60; site engr. Dar Al Handasah, Cons., Beirut, Cairo, London, 1961-62; design engr. Dar Al Handasah, Cons., 1962-65; then chief elec. engr. Dar Al Handasah, Cons., Tripoli, 1966-69, ptnr., dir. elec. and telecom. dept., 1970-86; free-lance cons. Paris, 1987—. Fellow Inst. Elec. Engrs. (Gt. Britain); mem. Lebanese Order Engrs., IEEE (sr., U.S.A.), Soc. Elec. and Electronic (France). Home: 361 Rue Lecourbe, 75015 Paris France

CHOURAKI, LUCIEN, rheumatologist; b. Tunis, Tunisia, Mar. 2, 1931; s. Joseph and Rachel (Aidan) C.; m. Monique Bessudo, Mar. 19, 1966; children: Olivier, Laurent, Heloise. MD, Faculte de Medicine, Paris, 1962. Extern Paris hosps., 1950-55, intern, 1956-62; practice medicine specializing in rheumatology Paris, 1964—; cons. Hopital Cochin, Paris, 1964—, Hopital Rothschild, Paris, 1964—. Served as lt. French Air Force Med. Service, 1957-59. Jewish. Home and Office: 37 Ave de Lowendal, 75015 Paris France

CHOUTEAU, CHRISTIAN, physician; b. Paris, France, Jan. 24, 1929; s. Ernest and Alice (Durinck) C.; m. Nichole Richard, July 28, 1954; children: Dominique, Philippe, Didier, Anne, Cecile. MD, U. Paris, 1956. Interne Hosp. de St. Brueuc, France, 1954-57; practice medicine Penvenan, France, 1958—; medecin attache Hosp. de St. Breux anexe de Trestel, Trevou, France, 1965—; pres. various med. assns. Served to capt. French mil., 1957-58. Mem. Assn. Formation Médicale Continue de Lannion (founder, pres. 1967), Fedn. Régionale Assns. Enseignement Médicale Continu de Bretagne (founder, sec. gen. 1979, pres. 1982—), Cunseil Régional de Formation Médicale Coninue de Bretagne (founder, pres. 1982—, pres. fundraising com.), Bd. Observatoire Régional de Santé de Bretagne (past v.p.), Commn. Études Médicales de Bretagne, Conseil Adminstrn. Union Nat. Formation Médicale Continue (del. de la Bretagne à Paris), Syndicat Mèdecins (v.p.), Conf. Syndicats Médicaux Français (regional del.).

CHOW, BRENDA KAM-WAH, tobacco company executive; b. Guangzhou, Guangdong, Republic China, Jan. 23, 1945; arrived in Hong Kong, 1950; d. Kam Cheong and Ping Hoi (Ho) C. BA, U. Calif., Berkeley, 1971. Personnel mgr. Hyatt Regency Hong Kong, 1973-76; area ops. mgr. Chase Manhattan Bank, Hong Kong, 1977-81; mgmt. cons. Coopers & Lybrand, Hong Kong, 1981-83; pub. affairs mgr. Brit.-Am. Tobacco Co. Ltd., Hong Kong, 1983—; bd. dirs. Tobacco Inst. Hong Kong. Editor Ying Mei mag. Pub. relations com. Soc. Homes for the Handicapped, Hong Kong, 1985; friends com. Asian Cultural Council, 1987; vice chmn. Maryknoll Hosp. Med. and Welfare Assn., Hong Kong, 1985—. Mem. Internat. Assn. Bus. Communicators, So. Dist. Indslists. Assn. Ltd. of Hong Kong. Roman Catholic. Clubs: Royal Hong Kong Jockey, Aberdeen Boat, Pacific of Hong Kong, Foreign Correspondents'. Lodge: Zonta (2d v.p. Hong Kong 1987). Home: 6 Miramar Villa #4-F, 2B Shiu Fai Terr, Stubbs Rd, Hong Kong Hong Kong Office: Brit-Am Tobacco Co Ltd, 2 Heung Yip Rd, Aberdeen Hong Kong

CHOW, CHI-MING, mathematics educator; b. Tai-Yuan, Shansi, Republic of China, Nov. 15, 1931; came to U.S., 1959; s. Wei-Han Chow and Lu-Tsen Hsu. Cert. tech. officer, Chinese Air Force Tech. Inst., Republic of China, 1954; BS in Math., Ch. Coll. Hawaii, 1962; MS in Math., Oreg. State U., 1965. Tech. officer Chinese Air Force, Republic of China, 1954-59; prof. math Oakland Community Coll., Farmington Hills, Mich., 1965—; student advisor Oakland Community Coll., Union Lake, Mich., 1968; mem. scholar com. Oakland Community Coll., Farmington Hills, 1985—. Contbr. articles to prof. jours. Donor United Fund, Mich., and others. Served to 1st lt. Air Force of Republic of China, 1954-59. Mem. NEA, Mich. Edn. Assn., Oakland Community Coll. Faculty Assn., Pi Mu Epsilon. Home: PO Box 903 Novi MI 48050 Office: Oakland Community Coll Math Dept 27055 Orchard Lake Rd Farmington Hills MI 48018

CHOW, FRANKLIN SZU-CHIEN, physician; b. Hong Kong, Apr. 15, 1956; came to U.S., 1967; s. Walter Wen-Tsao and Jane Ju-Hsien (Tang) C. BS, CCNY, 1977; MD, U. Rochester, 1979. Diplomate Am. Bd. Ob-Gyn. Intern Wilmington (Del.) Med. Ctr., 1979-80, resident in ob-gyn, 1980-83; practice medicine specializing in ob-gyn Vail (Colo.) Valley Med. Ctr., 1983—, chmn. obstetrics com., 1984-85, 86-87, chmn. surg. com., 1987—. Named to Athletic Hall of Fame, CCNY, 1983. Fellow Am. Coll. Ob-Gyn's; mem. AMA, Colo. Med. Soc., Intermountain Med. Soc. (pres. 1985-86), Internat. Fedn. Gynecol. Endoscopists, Am. Assn. Gynecol. Laparoscopists, Gynecologic Laser Soc. Home: 0746 N Deer Blvd PO Box 3257 Vail CO 81658 Office: Vail Valley Med Ctr 181 W Meadow Dr Suite 600 Vail CO 81657

CHOW, KWOK-CHUEN, architect; b. Hong Kong, Feb. 10, 1943; s. Cho-Poon and Grace C.; m. Amy Fung yee-ling, Oct. 9, 1976; 1 child, Jolene Chow Wei-Man. BArch with 1st honors, Nat. U. Ireland, Dublin, 1967; MS, Ill. Inst. Tech., 1969; MBA, U. Chgo., 1971. Assoc. ptnr. Skidmore Owings & Merrill, Chgo., 1974-79; mng. dir. SOM H.K., Hong Kong, 1976-79; chief architect, designer Profl. Assocs., world-wide, 1980—; hon. chmn. S. China Athletic Assn., 1980, hon. cons. C. of C. & Industry fro Four Provinces, 1976; dir. Tung Wah Group Hosps., 1976, Pok Oi Hosp. 1975. Mem. panel assessors Dept. Jud., Hong Kong, 1979. Mem. AIA, Am. Soc. Interior Design, Royal Inst. Architects of Ireland, Royal Inst. British Architects, Royal Australian Inst. Architects, Singapore Inst. Architects, Hong Kong Inst. Architects. Clubs: Royal Island, Royal Hong Kong Jockey. Home: Penthouse 11 Fontana Gardens 1/F, Causeway Bay, Hong Kong BCC Office: Chow House, 140-142 Robinson Rd, Singapore 0106, Singapore also: Suite 804, 66 King St, New South Wales 2000, Australia also: 420 W Wrightwood Chicago IL 60614

CHOW, SHEW PING, orthopedic surgeon; b. Shewhing, Republic of China, Oct. 29, 1944; s. Kowk On and Wing Han (Yeung) C.; m. Grace Man Yuen Chan, Sept. 3, 1973; children: Yan Yee, Oi Yee. MB BS, U. Hong Kong, 1968. House officer Govt. Hosps., Hong Kong, 1968-69; intern St. Joseph's Hosp., London, Ont., Can., 1969-70; med. officer Queen Mary Hosp., Hong Kong, 1970-73; lectr. U. Hong Kong, 1973-80, sr. lectr., 1980-84, reader, 1984—; vol. vis. specialist CARE-MEDICO program, Bangladesh, 1982; bd. dirs. Physically Handicapped and Able Bodied Assn., Hong Kong, 1984—. Contbr. articles to profl. jours. Fellow Royal Coll. Surgeons Edinburgh, Am. Coll. Surgeons, Brit. Orthopedic Assn., Hong Kong Orthopedic Assn.; mem. Brit. Soc. Surgery of Hand, Western Pacific Orthopedic Assn. (sec. gen. hand sect. 1982-85), Internat. Fedn. Surgery of Hand (mem. research com. 1986—), Brit. Med. Assn. (mem. council Hong Kong br. 1984—), Supplementary Med. Professions Council (mem. council 1986—). Office: Queen Mary Hosp, Dept Orthopedic Surgery, Hong Kong Hong Kong

CHOW, STEPHEN HEUNG WING, physician; b. Hong Kong, Nov. 26, 1954; s. Hon Wing Chow and Kam Wah Choi; m. Clare Chau Fung Sin, Mar. 10, 1986; children: Tin Yee, Tin Yan. MBBS, Hong Kong U., 1979. House officer Queen Elizabeth Hosp., Hong Kong, 1979, Nethersole Hosp., Hong Kong, 1980; gen. practice medicine Hong Kong, 1981—. U.S. Bicentennial Scholar, 1978. Mem. Hong Kong Med. Assn. Home: B1 240 Prince Edward Rd, Kowloon Hong Kong Office: 235 Ground Floor, Nam Cheong Street, Kowloon Hong Kong

CHOW, TONY, restauranteur; b. Hong Kong, Dec. 3, 1953; arrived in Eng., 1971; s. Yuen-nien and Bong-Kung (Cheung) C.; m. Ellen Au; children: Jocelyn, Justin. Student, Imperial Coll. for Computer Studies, 1973. Ptnr. Maxim Chinese Restaurant, London, 1973—, Maxie's Wine Bar, London, 1984—, 1986—. Home: 23 Gunnersbury Ave, London W5, England Office: Maxie's Wine Bar, 143 Knightsbridge, London SW1, England

CHOW, WINSTON, chemical engineer; b. San Francisco, Dec. 21, 1946; s. Raymond and Pearl C.; m. Lilly Fah, Aug. 15, 1971; children: Stephen, Kathryn. BSChemE, U. Calif., Berkeley, 1968; MSChemE, Calif. State U., San Jose, 1972; MBA with honors, Calif. State U., San Francisco, 1985. Registered profl. chem. and mech. engr.; instr.'s credential Calif. Community Coll. Chem. engr. Sondell Sci. Instruments, Inc., Mountain View, Calif., 1971; mem. research and devel. staff Raychem Corp., Menlo Park, Calif., 1971-72; with Bechtel Power Corp., San Francisco, 1972-79, engr., 1972-76, sr. engr., 1976-77, engring. mech. supr., 1977-79; sr. project mgr. water quality and toxic substances control program Electric Power Research Inst., Palo Alto, Calif., 1979—. Contbr. author Water Chlorination, vol. 4; contbr. articles to profl. publs. Pres., chief exec. officer Directions, Inc., San Francisco, 1985-86, bd. dirs. 1984-87, chmn. strategic planning com., 1984-85. Recipient Grad. Disting. Achievement award, 1985; Calif. Gov.'s Exec. fellow. Mem. Am. Inst. Chem. Engrs. (Profl. Devel. Recognition cert.), NSPE, Calif. Soc. Profl. Engrs. (pres. Golden Gate chpt. 1983-84, v.p. 1982-83, state dir.), Water Pollution Control Fedn., Calif. Water Pollution Control Assn., ASME, Calif. Alumni Assn., Beta Gamma Sigma. Democrat. Presbyterian. Office: Electric Power Research Inst 3412 Hillview Ave Palo Alto CA 94303

CHOWDHURI, PRITINDRA, electrical engineering educator; b. Calcutta, July 12, 1927; came to U.S., 1949, naturalized, 1962; s. Ahindra and Sudhira (Mitra) C.; m. Sharon Elsie Hackebeil, Dec. 28, 1962; children—Naomi, Leslie, Robindro, Rajendro. B.Sc. in Physics with honors, Calcutta U., 1945, M.Sc., 1948; M.S., Ill. Inst. Tech., 1951; D.Eng., Rensselaer Poly. Inst., 1966. Jr. engr. lightning arresters sect. Westinghouse Electric Corp., East Pittsburgh, Pa., 1951-52; elec. engr. high voltage lab. Maschinenfabrik Oerlikon, Zurich, 1952-53; research engr. High Voltage Research Commn., Daeniken, Switzerland, 1953-56; devel. engr. high voltage lab. Gen. Electric Co., Pittsfield, Mass., 1956-59; elec. engr. research and devel. ctr. Gen. Electric Co., Schenectady, N.Y., 1959-62; engr. elec. investigations transp. systems div. Gen. Electric Co., Erie, Pa., 1962-75; staff mem. Los Alamos Nat. Lab., N.Mex., 1975-86; prof. elec. engring. Ctr. Elec. Power Tenn. Tech. U., Cookeville, 1986—; lectr. Pa. State U. Behrend Grad. Ctr., Erie, 1969-75. Patentee in field. Fellow Instn. Elec. Engrs. (Eng.), AAAS, N.Y. Acad. Scis.; sr. mem. IEEE. Democrat. Unitarian. Home: 690 Valley Forge Rd Cookeville TN 38501 Office: Tenn Tech U Ctr Elec Power PO Box 5032 Cookeville TN 38505

CHOWDHURY, MIZANUR RAHMAN, government official; b. Bangladesh, Oct. 19, 1928; married, 1955. Student, Feni Coll., Bangladesh. Head master Bamoni High Sch., Bangladesh, 1952; tchr. Chandpur Nuria High Sch., Bangladesh, 1956; elected mem. Nat. Assembly, Bangladesh, 1962, 65, 70; organising sec. E. Pakistan wing Awami League, Bangladesh, 1966; acting gen. sec. Awami League, 1966, joint convenor, 1976; minister of info. and broadcasting People's Republic Bangladesh, 1972-73, minister of posts and telecommunications, 1985-88, prime minister, 1986-88, minister of state for communications, 1988—; sr. vice-chmn. Janadal, 1984, sec.-gen., 1985; mem. steering com. Jatiyo (Nat.) Front, 1985. M.P. 1972, 79. Office: Ministry for Communications, Sher-e-Bangla Nagar, Dhaka Bangladesh *

CHOWDHURY, MUNIBUR RAHMAN, mathematics educator; b. Faridpur, Banlgadesh, Jan. 17, 1941; s. Hashmat Ali and Ayatun Nessa (Khan) C.; m. Fatema Khatun, Apr. 7, 1963; children: Sabina, Samina, Sajedur Rahman. BSc, U. Dhaka, 1960; Vordiplom, U. Hamburg, 1963; Dipl Math, U. Göttingen, 1966, Dr rer Nat, 1967. Tchrg. asst. U. Göttingen, Fed. Republic Germany, 1966-67; reader Islamabad U., Pakistan, 1968-69; research fellow, lectr. U. Del., Newark, 1969-70; sr. lectr. math. U. Duaka, Bangladesh, 1970-71, prof., 1984—, chmn. dept., 1984-87; assoc. prof. math. Jahangirnagar U., Savar, Bangladesh, 1971-78; prof. Jahangirnagar U., Savar, 1981-84; acting dean Jahangirnagar U., Savar, 1973, chmn. dept. math., 1973, 77-78; assoc. prof. King Abdulaziz U., Jeddah, Saudi Arabia, 1979-81; assoc. mem. Internat. Ctr. for Theoretical Physics, Trieste, Italy, 1982-87. Author: Elementary Trigonometry, 1972, Algebra, 2 vols., 1984. Named Staff Fellow U.K. Commonwealth Scholarship and Fellowship Commn., 1974-75. Mem. Bangladesh Math. Soc. (v.p. 1975-76, exec. editor jour. 1987—), Am. Math. Soc., London Math. Soc., Deutsche Mathematiker-Vereinigung, Alumni Assn. German Univs. in Bangladesh (sec. 1984—). Sunni Muslim. Club: Dhaka U. Home: 3/6 Block G, Lamatia Housing Estate, Dhaka 1207, Bangladesh Office: Dhaka U Dept Math, Dhaka 1000, Bangladesh

CHOYKE, ARTHUR DAVIS, JR., manufacturing company executive; b. N.Y.C., Mar. 13, 1919; s. Arthur Davis and Lillian (Bauer) C.; A.B., Columbia, 1939, B.S., 1940; m. Phyllis May Ford, Aug. 18, 1945; children—Christopher Ford, Tyler Van. With indsl. engring. dept. Procter & Gamble Co., S.I., N.Y., 1940-43; instr. Pratt Inst., Bklyn., 1942-45; chief indsl. engr. M & M, Ltd., Newark, 1943-47; ptnr. Ford Distbg. Co., Chgo., 1947-57; incorporator, pres., treas., dir. Artcrest Products Co., Inc., Chgo., 1951—; dir. Gallery Series, Harper Sq. Press. Mem. pres.' com. Landamrk Preservation Council Ill., Hist. Alliance Chgo. Hist. Soc. Clubs: Chgo. Farmers, Arts (Chgo.); John Evans Northwestern U. Lodge: Rotary. Home: 29 E Division St Chicago IL 60610 Office: 500 W Cermak Rd Chicago IL 60616

CHOYKE, PHYLLIS MAY FORD (MRS. ARTHUR DAVIS CHOYKE, JR.), ceiling systems company executive, editor, poet; b. Buffalo, Oct. 25, 1921; d. Thomas Cecil and Vera (Buchanan) Ford; m. Arthur Davis Choyke Jr., Aug. 18, 1945; children: Christopher Ford, Tyler Van. BS summa cum laude, Northwestern U., 1942. Reporter City News Bur., Chgo., 1942-43, Met. sect. Chgo. Tribune, 1943-44; feature writer OWI, N.Y.C., 1944-45; sec. corp. Artcrest Products Co., Inc., Chgo., 1958—, v.p., 1964—, founder, dir. Harper Sq. Press div., 1966—. Bonbright scholar, 1942. Mem. Soc. Midland Authors (treas. 1988), Mystery Writers Am. (assoc.), Chgo. Press Vets. Assn., Hist. Alliance of Chgo. Hist. Soc., Phi Beta Kappa. Clubs: Arts (Chgo.); John Evans (Northwestern U.). Author: (under name Phyllis Ford) (with others) (poetry) Apertures to Anywhere, 1979; editor: Gallery Series One, Poets, 1967, Gallery Series Two, Poets—Poems of the Inner World, 1968, Gallery Series Three—Poets: Levitations and Observations, 1970, Gallery Series Four, Poets—I am Talking About Revolution, 1973, Gallery Series Five/Poets—To An Aging Nation (with occult overtones), 1977; (manuscripts and papers in Brown U. Library). Home: 29 E Division St Chicago IL 60610 Office: 500 W Cermak Rd Chicago IL 60616

CHRIST, DUANE MARLAND, computer systems engineer; b. Lakota, Iowa, Jan. 5, 1932; s. George Andrew and Esther Gertrude (Franke) C.; m. Lily Esther Shih, Sept. 14, 1963; 1 son, Wesley Anzo. B.S., Iowa State U., 1953; M.A., U. Minn., 1960. Sci. programmer United Aircraft Corp., Hartford, Conn., 1960-63; computer systems analyst IBM, N.Y.C., 1963-68, staff instr., 1968-76, adv. systems engr., 1976-82, sr. systems engr., 1982-87, prin., 1987—. Served to 1st lt. USAF, 1953-56. IBM Resident Study fellow, 1966-68, S.E. Regional Dir. award, 1983; named Area Specialist of Yr., 1986. Mem. Assn. Computing Machinery, Soc. Indsl. and Applied Math., Math. Assn. Am. Lutheran.

CHRISTELOW, ALASTAIR DONAL, public relations executive; b. Harrogate, Yorkshire, Eng., Apr. 13, 1933; s. Donald McKenzie and Carrie (Crammond) C.; m. Sheila Sinton, May 28, 1955; children: Mark Mckenzie, Jean Elizabeth, Ian James. Student, pub. schs., York, England. Publicity mgr. English Electric Valve Co., Chelmsford, Essex, Eng., 1980—. Mem. Assn. Inst. Co. Accts. Home: 120 Beehive Ln, Chelmsford, Essex CM2 9SH, England Office: English Electric Valve Co, Waterhouse Ln, Chelmsford, Essex CM1 2QU, England

CHRISTENSEN, ALLEN CLARE, agricultural educator, university dean, administrator, consultant; b. Lehi, Utah, Apr. 14, 1935; s. Clare Bernard and Relia Sarah (Allen) C.; m. Kathleen Ruth Atwater, Dec. 19, 1958; children—Ann Marie, Allen Clare Jr., James Lynn, Niel Daniel, Eric Wayne. B.S. with Honors, Brigham Young U., 1957; M.S., U. Calif.-Davis, 1960; Ph.D., Utah State U., 1979. Cert. Am. Registry Profl. Animal Scientists. Vocat. agr. tchr. White Pine County Schs., Lund, Nev., 1961-64; from asst. to assoc. prof. agr. Calif. State Poly. U., Pomona, 1964-73, prof., 1973—, dean coll. agr., 1980-85, 87—; acting provost and acad. v.p., 1985-87; cons. Agrl. Edn. Found., Davis, Calif., 1971-85, AID, Washington, 1983—, W.K. Kellogg Found., Battle Creek, Mich., 1984; trustee Consortium for Internat. Devel., Tucson, Ariz., 1980—, vice chair of bd., 1988—; mem. deans' council Calif. Agr. Leadership Program, Davis, 1980-85, 87—; mem. joint com. on agr. research and devel., AID, 1982-87, chmn. strengthening grant panel bd. internat. food and agrl. devel., 1983-87; chair BIFAD panel Humane Capital Devel., 1985-87. Author: (with others) Working in Animal Science, 1978. Contbr. articles to profl. jours. Pres. Chino, Calif Latter-day Saint Stake, 1979—, mem. exec. bd. Old Baldy Council Boy Scouts Am., 1988—. Recipient Hon. State Farmer Degree, Calif. Assn. Future Farmers Am., 1983. Mem. Am. Soc. Animal Scis., Poultry Sci. Assn., Golden Key Nat. Honor Soc. (hon.), Phi Beta Delta, Phi Kappa Phi, Gamma Sigma Delta (Outstanding Faculty award of Merit, 1976, pres. 1969-70), Alpha Zeta. Republican. Mormon. Office: Calif State Poly U Coll Agr 3801 W Temple Ave Pomona CA 91768

CHRISTENSEN, C. LEWIS, real estate developer; b. Laramie, Wyo., June 3, 1936; s. Raymond H. and Elizabeth C. (Cady) C.; m. Sandra Stadheim, June 11, 1960; children: Kim, Brett. BS in Indsl. Engring., U. Wyo., 1959. Mgmt. trainee Gen. Mills, Chgo., 1959, Mountain Bell, Helena, Mont., 1962-63; data communications mgr. Mountain Bell, Phoenix, 1964-66, dist. mktg. mgr., So. Colo., 1970-73; seminar leader AT&T Co., Chgo., 1966-68, mktg. supr., N.Y.C., 1968-70; land planner and developer Village Assocs., Colorado Springs, Colo., 1973, exec. v.p., 1975-77; v.p. Cimarron Corp., Colorado Springs, 1974-75; pres. Lew Christensen & Assocs., Inc.; ptnr., gen. mgr. Briargate Devel. Group, 1977—. bd. dirs. Pikes Peak council Boy Scouts Am., Citizens Goals, Colo. Council on Econ. Edn., Cheyenne Mountain Zoo. Served with USAF, 1959-62. Mem. Colorado Springs Home Builders Assn. (bd. dirs.), Urban Land Inst., Colorado Springs C. of C. (bd. dirs. chmn. bd.). Republican. Presbyterian. Clubs: Broadmoor Golf, Colorado Springs Country (bd. dirs.). Developer of 10,000-acre New Town area, east of USAF Acad., Colorado. Home: 2948 Country Club Dr Colorado Springs CO 80909 Office: Lew Christensen & Assocs Inc 7710 N Union Blvd Colorado Springs CO 80920

CHRISTENSEN, CHERRYL JUNE, physician; b. Muscatine, Iowa, June 7, 1948; d. Wildon Wayne and Lillian June (Hurlburt) H.; m. Doran Michael Christensen, Feb. 14, 1975; children—Julia Anna, Vasthi. B.S. in Pharmacy, U. Iowa, 1971; D.O., Coll. Osteo. Medicine and Surgery, 1975. Head health evaluation occupational medicine service Navy Environ. Health Ctr., Norfolk, Va., 1979-82; occupational and environ. medicine physician U. Cin., 1982—, assoc. dir. Med. Ctr. Health Services, U. Cin., dir. clin. outreach Occupational and Environ. Medicine Dept., asst. clin. prof. occupational medicine, environ. health, Coll. Medicine; pres. Occupational and Environ. Medicine Cons., Cin. Contbr. articles to profl. jours. Mem. AMA, Am. Occupational Med. Assn., Am. Pub. Health Assn., Am. Osteo. Assn. Lutheran. Home: 2736 Grandin Rd Cincinnati OH 45208 Office: Univ Cin Med Ctr ML 705 Cincinnati OH 45267

CHRISTENSEN, DON M., general contractor, realtor; b. Hinckley, Utah, Jan. 3, 1929; s. Joseph M. and Lula (Payne) C.; m. Arda Jean Warnock, Oct. 8, 1953; children—Jean Larie, Jolene, Mary Kaye, Martin Don, Evan Warnock, Rachel, Glenn Leroy, Ruth Angela. Student agr. Utah State U., 1951-53, student bldg. Brigham Young U., 1955-56. Ptnr. Christensen Bros. Constrn. Co., Salt Lake City, 1956-59; pres. Constrn. Realty, Inc., Salt Lake City, 1959—, Don M. Christensen Constrn. Co., Salt Lake City, 1965—, Bountiful Constrn. Co., Salt Lake City, 1960-65, Advanced Reprodns., Inc., Salt Lake City, 1960-61, Land Investors, Inc., Salt Lake City, 1960-63. Co-author: Yours Can Be a Happy Marriage, 1983. Co-editor: Precious Testimonies, 1976. Bishop's counselor Ch. of Jesus Christ of Latter Day Saints, Salt Lake City, 1960-66, bishop, 1966-76, high councilman, 1976-85, counselor to stake pres., 1985—. Served with U.S. Army, 1954-55. Named Missionary of Yr., Mormon Finland Mission, 1951. Mem. Home Builders Assn. Republican. Home: 1630 Olive Dr Salt Lake City UT 84124 Office: Constrn Realty Inc 345 E 33d S Salt Lake City UT 84115

CHRISTENSEN, KAI, architect; b. Copenhagen, Denmark, Dec. 28, 1916; s. J.C. and Jenny Christensen; m. Kirsten Vittrup Andersen, 1941; two daus. Grad., Royal Acad. of Fine Arts, Copenhagen, 1943. Dir. tech. dept. Fedn. Danish Architects, 1947-52; mng. dir. Danish Bldg. Centre, 1952-61; attached to Danish Ministry of Housing, 1961—, graphic adviser to ministry, 1981—; chief Scandinavian Design Cavalcade, 1962-69; mem. Fedn. Danish Architects, 1943, The Archtl. Assn., London, 1955, Danish Com. for Bldg. Documentation, 1950-79; mem. Danish Soc. History, Lit. and Art, 1969, com. mem., 1979, pres., 1985; sec.-gen. Nordisk Byggedag (Scandinavian Bldg. Conf.) VIII, 1961, XIII, 1977; pres. Internat. Conf. Building Centres, 1960, Danish Ministries Soc. Art, 1982—; mem. Scandinavian Liaison Com., concerning Govt. Bldg., 1963-72. Associated Edn. Building Research and Practice/Batiment Internat. mag., 1968-85. Works include designs for arts and crafts, graphic designs for Danish govt. depts., exhbns., furniture for Copenhagen Cabinet Makers' Exhbns.; contbr. feature articles and articles to profl. publs. Recipient awards and prizes in pub. competition. Fellow Royal Soc. Arts, London. Address: 100 Vester Voldgade, DK-1552 Copenhagen V Denmark Other: Ministry of Housing, 12 Slotsholmsgade, DK-1216 Copenhagen K Denmark *

CHRISTENSEN, MARY LUCAS, virologist, laboratory administrator, researcher; b. St. Louis, Oct. 18, 1937; d. Kermit and Margaret Isabelle (Lucas) C. B.A. in Bacteriology, U. Iowa, 1959, M.S. in Bacteriology, 1961, Ph.D. in Microbiology, Northwestern U., 1974. Research virologist Wyeth Labs., Phila., 1961-65, Abbott Labs., North Chicago, Ill., 1965-68; chief clin. virology lab. Northwestern U., 1969-71; research fellow Nat. Cancer Inst., Northwestern U., 1974-78, asst. prof. pathology and pediatrics, 1978-87, assoc. prof., 1987—; dir. virology lab. Children's Meml. Hosp., 1978—; guest lectr. in field. Author: Basic Laboratory Procedures in Diagnostic Virology, 1977, Microbiology for Nursing and Allied Health Students, 1982; contbr. articles to profl. jours. Mem. Am. Soc. Microbiology, Ill. Soc. Microbiology (pres.), AAAS, N.Y. Acad. Sci., Am. Pub. Health Assn., U. Iowa Alumni Assn., Northwestern U. Alumni Assn., Iota Sigma Pi, Gamma Phi Beta. Episcopalian. Home: 900 N Lake Shore Dr Apt 1905 Chicago IL 60611 Office: 2300 Children's Plaza Chicago IL 60614

CHRISTENSON, GORDON A., legal educator; b. Salt Lake City, June 22, 1932; s. Gordon B. and Ruth Arzella (Anderson) C.; m. Katherine Joy deMik, Nov. 2, 1951 (div. 1977); children: Gordon Scott, Marjorie Lynne, Ruth Ann, Nanette; m. Fabienne Fadeley, Sept. 16, 1979. B.S. in Law, U. Utah, 1955, J.D., 1956; S.J.D., George Washington U., 1961. Bar: Utah 1956, U.S. Supreme Ct. 1971, D.C. 1978. Practiced in Salt Lake City, 1957-58; law clk. to chief justice Utah Supreme Ct., 1956-57; assoc. firm Christenson & Callister, Salt Lake City, 1956-58; atty. Dept. of Army, Nat. Guard Bur., Washington, 1957-58; atty., acting asst. legal adviser Office of Legal Adviser, U.S. Dept. State, Washington, 1958-62; asst. gen. counsel for sci. and tech. U.S. Dept. Commerce, 1962-67, spl. asst. to undersec. of commerce, 1967, counsel to commerce tech. adv. bd., 1962-67, chmn. task force on telecommunications missions and orgn., 1967, counsel to panel on engring. and commodity standards, tech. adv. bd., 1963-65; assoc. prof. law U. Okla., Norman, 1967-70; exec. asst. to pres. U. Okla., 1967-70; univ. dean for edn. devel., central adminstrn. State U. N.Y., Albany, 1970-71; prof. law Am. U. Law Sch., Washington, 1971-79; dean Am. U. Law Sch., 1971-77; on leave 1977-79; Charles H. Stockton prof. internat. law U.S. Naval War Coll., Newport, R.I., 1977-79; dean, Nippert prof. law U. Cin. Coll. Law, 1979-85, univ. prof. law, 1985—; assoc. professorial lectr. in internat. affairs George Washington U., 1961-67; vis. scholar Harvard U. Law Sch., 1977-78; vis. scholar Yale Law Sch., 1985-86; participant summer confs. on internat. law Cornell Law Sch., Ithaca, N.Y., 1962, 64; cons. in internat. law U.S. Naval War Coll., Newport, R.I., 1969; faculty mem., reporter seminars for experienced fed. dist. judges Fed. Jud. Center, Washington, 1972-77. Author:

(with Richard B. Lillich) International Claims: Their Preparation and Presentation, 1962, The Future of the University, 1969; Contbr. articles to legal jours. Cons. to Center for Policy Alternatives Mass. Inst. Tech., Cambridge, 1970-81; mem. intergovtl. com. on Internat. Policy on Weather Modification, 1967; Vice pres. Procedural Aspects of Internat. Law Inst., N.Y.C., 1962—. Served with intelligence sect. USAF, 1951-52, Japan. Recipient Silver Medal award Dept. Commerce, 1967; fellow Grad. Sch. U. Cin. Mem. Am. Soc. Internat. Law (mem. panel on state responsibility), D.C. Bar Assn., Am. Bar Assn., Utah Bar Assn., Cin. Bar Assn., Order of Coif, Phi Delta Phi, Kappa Sigma. Clubs: Literary (Cin.); Cosmos (Washington). Home: 3465 Principio Ave Cincinnati OH 45208 Office: U Cin Coll Law Cincinnati OH 45221

CHRISTENSON, WILLIAM NEWCOME, physician; b. Biltmore Forest, N.C., Dec. 2, 1925; s. William Lambert and Beth (Newcome) C.; B.S., U. N.C., 1949; M.D., Johns Hopkins U., 1948; m. Elizabeth Chandler White, Aug. 9, 1957; children—Lisa Ann, Laurie E., Susan. Intern, asst. resident Mass. Gen. Hosp., Boston, 1948-50; asst. resident N.Y. Hosp., N.Y.C., 1953-55; dir. personnel health service, 1960-85, asst. attending physician, 1961-64, assoc. attending physician, 1964-85; attending physician Westchester County Med. Ctr., 1985—, physician Employee Health Service, 1985—; postgrad. research fellow USPHS; Postgrad. Med. Sch. London, 1955-56; instr. medicine Cornell U. Med. Coll., N.Y.C., 1956-59, asst. prof. medicine, 1959-65, clin. assoc. prof. medicine, 1965-79, assoc. prof. clin. medicine, 1979-85; dir. Office Grad. Med. Advising, N.Y. Med. Coll., 1985-88, assoc. dean, 1988—, prof. clin. medicine, 1986-88, assoc. dean, 1988—; cons. N.Y. Blood Center, 1976—; practice medicine specializing in internal medicine and occupational medicine, N.Y.C., 1960-85. Served with USNR, 1950-52. Fellow ACP, Am. Occupational Med. Assn.; mem. Am. Fedn. Clin. Research, Am. Soc. Hematology, Am. Occupational Med. Assn., Am. Pub. Health Assn., Phi Beta Kappa, Alpha Omega Alpha, Delta Kappa Epsilon. Research in hematology and human ecology. Home: 4 Legget Rd Bronxville NY 10708 Office: NY Med Coll Sunshine Cottage Valhalla NY 10595

CHRISTIAN, JOHN CATLETT, JR., lawyer; b. Springfield, Mo., Sept. 12, 1929; s. John Catlett and Alice Odelle (Milling) C.; m. Peggy Jeanne Cain, Apr. 12, 1953; children: Cathleen Marie, John Catlett, Alice Cain. A.B., Drury Coll., 1951; LL.B., Tulane U., 1956. Bar: La. 1956, Mo. 1956, U.S. Supreme Ct. bar 1975. Asso. firm Porter & Stewart, Lake Charles, La., 1956-58, Wilkinson, Lewis, Wilkinson & Madison, Shreveport, La., 1958-62; partner Wilkinson, Lewis, Wilkinson & Madison, 1962-64; partner firm Milling, Benson, Woodward, Hillyer, Pierson & Miller, New Orleans, 1964—; pres. Sherburne Land Co., 1974-83; dir. Emerald Land Corp. Pres. Kathleen Elizabeth O'Brien Found., 1963—. Served with USMCR, 1951-53. Fellow Am. Coll. Trial Lawyers; mem. Am. Bar Assn., Am. Judicature Soc., Mo. Bar Assn., Fed. Bar Assn., La. Bar Assn., La. Landowners Assn. (bd. dirs. 1983—), Kappa Alpha Order, Omicron Delta Kappa, Phi Delta Phi. Clubs: Boston, Plimsoll, Petroleum (New Orleans); Beau Chene Country. Home: 807 Tete L'Ours Dr Mandeville LA 70448 Office: Milling Benson Woodward et al LL&E Tower Suite 2300 909 Poydras St New Orleans LA 70112

CHRISTIAN, RICHARD CARLTON, educator, former advertising agency executive; b. Dayton, Ohio, Nov. 29, 1924; s. Raymond A. and Louise (Gamber) C.; m. Audrey Bongartz, Sept. 10, 1949; children: Ann Christian Carra, Richard Carlton. B.S. in Bus. Adminstrn, Miami U., Oxford, Ohio, 1948; MBA, Northwestern U., 1949; LLD (hon.), Nat. Coll. Edn., 1986; postgrad., Denison U., The Citadel, Biarritz Am. U. Mktg. analyst Rockwell Mfg. Co., Pitts., 1949-50; exec. v.p. Marsteller Inc., Chgo., 1951-60; pres. Marsteller Inc., 1960-75; bd. dirs., exec. com. Young and Rubicam, Inc., 1979-84; chmn. bd. Marsteller Inc., 1975-84, chmn. emeritus, 1984—; assoc. dean Kellogg Grad. Sch. Mgmt. Northwestern U., 1984—; dir., chmn. Bus. Pubis. Audit Circulation, Inc., 1969-75; Speaker, author marketing, sales mgmt., marketing research and advt. Trustee Northwestern U., 1970-74, Nat. Coll. Edn., Evanston, Ill., 1970—, James Webb Young Fund for Edn., U. Ill., 1962—; pres. Nat. Advt. Rev. Council, 1976-77; bd. adv. council mem. Miami U.; mem. adv. council J. L. Kellogg Grad. Sch. Mgmt., Northwestern U.; v.p., dir. Mus. Broadcast Communications. Served with inf. AUS, 1942-46, ETO. Decorated Bronze Star, Purple Heart; recipient Ohio Gov.'s award, 1977, Alumni medal, Alumni Merit and Service awards Northwestern U. Mem. Am. Mktg. Assn., Indsl. Marketing Assn. (founder, chmn. 1951), Bus./Profl. Advt. Assn. (life mem. Chgo., pres. Chgo. 1954-55, nat. v.p. 1955-58, G.D. Crain award 1977), U. Ill. Found., Northwestern U. Bus. Sch. Alumni Assn. (founder, pres.), Am. Assn. Advt. Agys. (dir., chmn. 1976-77), Am. Acad. Advt. (1st disting. service award 1978), Northwestern U. Alumni Assn. (nat. pres. 1968-70), Council Better Bus. Burs. Chgo. (dir.), Council Fgn. Relations, Bus. Press Ednl. Fedn. (bd. dirs.), Alpha Delta Sigma, Beta Gamma Sigma, Delta Sigma Pi, Phi Gamma Delta. Baptist (trustee). Clubs: Mid-America, Commercial, Chicago, Executives, Economic (Chgo.); Kenilworth; Westmoreland Country (Wilmette, Ill.); Pine Valley Golf (Clementon, N.J.). Office: J L Kellogg Grad Sch Mgmt Northwestern U Leverone Hall Evanston IL 60208

CHRISTIAN, THOMAS FRANKLIN, JR., aerospace engineer, educator; b. Macon, Ga., Mar. 2, 1946; s. Thomas Franklin and Lucille Vanessa (Solomon) C.; B.A.E., Ga. Inst. Tech., 1968, M.S.A.E., 1970, Ph.D., 1974; M.S. in Engring. Adminstrn., U. Tenn., 1976; m. Jan McGarity, Apr. 30, 1983; children: Ellen Caroline, Thomas Franklin III. Sr. design engr. nuclear analytical engring. Combustion Engring., Inc., Chattanooga, 1973-77; team mgr. IF-1 pilot plant Procter & Gamble, Macon, 1977-80; program mgr. durability and damage tolerance assessment, Warner Robins Air Logistics Center, Robins AFB, Ga., 1980-85, chief engr., 1985—; adj. prof. math. Cleveland State Community Coll., 1976-77; adj. prof. engring. Mercer U., 1986—; continuing engr. edn., DTA short course coordinator, instr. George Washington U. Registered profl. engr., Ga., Tenn. Adminstrn. br. mem., ednl. chmn. Perry United Meth. Ch. Assoc. fellow AIAA (nat. tech com. on aerospace maintenance 1982-86, structures 1985—); mem. N.Y. Acad. Scis., ASME, Soc. for History Tech., Soc. for Exptl. Stress Analysis, AAAS, Soc. Logistics Engrs. (Ga. state dir. 1983—, Schoenberg award 1985), ASTM, Air Force Assn., Am. Acad. Mechanics, Ga. Inst. Tech. Alumni Assn., Macon Little Theater, Order of Engr., Sigma Xi, Pi Tau Chi. Home: 101 Chadwick Dr Warner Robins GA 31093 Office: WR ALC/MMSR Robins AFB GA 31098

CHRISTIANS, F. WILHELM, banker; b. Germany, May 1, 1922. Mem. supervisory bd. Deutsche Bank AG, Frankfurt, Fed. Republic of Germany; chmn., dep. chmn., mem. supervisory bd. numerous major companies. Address: Konigsallee 51, D-4000 Dusseldorf Federal Republic of Germany Office: Deutsche Bank, Generalsekretariat, Postfach 10 06 01, D-6000 Frankfurt 1, Federal Republic of Germany

CHRISTIANSEN, DONALD DAVID, editor, publisher, electrical engineer; b. Plainfield, N.J., June 23, 1927; s. David Carsten and Rita (Holmes) C.; m. Joyce Ifill, Jan. 1, 1951; children: Jacqueline, Jill. B.E.E., Cornell U., Ithaca, N.Y., 1950; postgrad., Mass. Inst. Tech., 1951, 54, U. Wis.-Madison, 1966, 68, 71. Registered profl. engr., Mass. Engr. Philco Corp., Phila., 1948-50, CBS, Danvers, Lowell and Newburyport, Mass., 1950-62; solid-state editor Electronic Design, Hayden Pub. Co., N.Y.C., 1962-63; sr. editor EEE-Circuit Design Engring. Mactier Pub. Co., N.Y.C., 1963-66; sr. assoc. editor Electronics McGraw-Hill Pub. Co., N.Y.C., 1966, sr. editor, 1966-67, assoc. mng. editor, 1967-68, editor-in-chief, 1968-70, mgr. planning, devel. electronics publs., 1970-71; gen. mgr. Electronics in Medicine, 1971; editor and pub. Spectrum jour. of IEEE, N.Y.C., 1971—, chmn. editorial bd., 1972—; IEEE rep. to UN, 1974-87; lectr. Newark Coll. Engring., 1967, U. Mich., Ann Arbor, 1973, Walla Walla (Wash.) Coll., 1973, Ga. Inst. Tech., 1976, NASA Goddard Space Flight Center, 1981, Cornell U., 1982; Disting. lectr. Purdue U., 1986; cons. Bur. of Census, Dept. Commerce, NSF; mem. NRC Com. on Edn. and Utilization of the Engr.; mem. elec. engring. adv. com. Worcester Poly. Inst. Editor: Electronic Engineers' Handbook, 2d edit. 1981, Engineering Excellence, 1987; mem. publ. com. Cornell Alumni News mag., 1986-87; contbr. articles to profl. jours. Bd. dirs. YMCA, Newburyport, Mass., 1962, Broadband Info. Services, N.Y.C., 1970-87. Served with USNR, 1945-46. Recipient medal and citation for advancement of culture Flanders Acad. Art, Sci., and Lit. Fellow IEEE (Centennial medal), World Acad. Art and Sci., Radio Club of Am.; mem. N.Y. Acad. Sci., Cornell Soc. Engrs., Council Engring. and Sci. Soc. Execs., Am. Soc. Assn. Execs., Am. Soc. Mag. Editors, Soc. Nat. Assn. Publs. (dir. 1976-79, chmn. editorial com. 1976-79, pres. 1981-83), N.Y. Bus. Press Editors (dir. 1978-79), Cornell Engring. Alumni Council, Delta Club, Union Internationale de la Presse Radiotechnique et Electronique, Deadline Club, Nat. Conf. Electronics in Medicine (chmn. 1971), IEEE (co-founder, charter exec. com. chpt. 1958), Soc. for History Tech., Jovians, Antique Wireless Assn., Franklin Inst., Royal Instn., Eta Kappa Nu (chmn., outstanding elec. engr. award 1976-78, dir. 1982-84, eminent mem.), Mu Sigma Tau, Sigma Delta Chi. Clubs: Cornell, Nat. Press. Office: Spectrum Magazine 345 E 47th St New York NY 10017

CHRISTIANSEN, ERIK, scientist; b. Oslo, July 31, 1938; s. Olaf Kristian and Bergliot (Berger) C.; m. Tove Emilie Pettersen, Feb. 21, 1964; children: Mi Hanne, Kim Dag, Geir. BS, Agrl. U. Norway, 1966, DSc in Forest Entomology, 1971. Tech. asst. Norwegian Inst. Wood Tech., Oslo, 1962-63; sci. asst. Norwegian Forest Research Inst., Ås, 1966-70, research assoc., 1971-77, project leader, 1978—; vis. scholar U. Calif., Davis, 1975-76; vis. prof. Oreg. State U., Corvallis, 1986. Served as pvt. Norwegian Corps. Engrs., 1957-58. Mem. Norwegian Human-Ethical Assn. (bd. dirs. 1983-87). Office: Norwegian Forest, Research Inst, PO Box 61, N-1432, Ås-NLH Norway

CHRISTIANSEN, JOHN, surgeon, consultant; b. Jvderup, Denmark, Nov. 17, 1934; s. Einar and Grethe (Jensen) C.; m. Inge Brydensholt, Sept. 5, 1959; children—Merete, Anette. M.D., U. Copenhagen, 1961, Ph.D., 1972. Sr. resident Glostrup Hosp., Copenhagen, 1970-72, chief surgeon, 1976—; sr. resident Bispebjerg Hosp., Copenhagen, 1972-76; sr. lectr. U. Copenhagen, 1985—; cons. in surgery Danish Nat. Bd. Health, Copenhagen, 1979—; gen. sec. Danish Surg. Soc., Copenhagen, 1980—. Editor Danish Med. Jour., 1980—; corr. editorial mem. Annales de Chirurgie, Paris, 1987—. Fellow Royal Soc. Medicine (London), Soc. Surgery Alimentary Tract, U.S.A., Am. Soc. Colon and Rectal Surgeons; mem. Internat. Soc. Colon and Rectal Surgeons (v.p. northern Europe 1988). Home: 24 Bregentved Alle, 2820 Gentofte, Copenhagen Denmark Office: Glostrup Hosp, 2600 Glostrup, Copenhagen Denmark

CHRISTIANSON, RICHARD LINDBERGH, mortgage banker; b. Des Moines, May 21, 1927; s. Marion Sanford and Grace Alverda (Alleman) C.; m. Jeanne Lee Carpenter, Sept. 4, 1953; children: Nancy, Deborah, Thomas. B.S., U. Oreg., 1951; postgrad., U. Colo., 1952-53. Exec. v.p. M.S. Christianson Mortgage & Investment Co., Eugene, Oreg., 1953-68; v.p., div. mgr. 1st Nat. Bank of Oreg., Portland, 1968-72; sr. v.p., div. mgr. Pacific Nat. Bank of Wash., Seattle, 1972-79; pres., chief exec. officer Western Bancorp Mortgage Co., Denver, 1979-80; chmn., chief exec. officer 1st Interstate Bank of Idaho, Boise, 1980-83; pres., chief exec. officer, chmn. CalFed Mortgage Co. subs. Calif. Fed. Savs. & Loan, Los Angeles, 1983-85; chmn. Am. Diversified Capital Corp., Costa Mesa, Calif., 1986—, Am. Diversified Investment Corp., Costa Mesa, Calif., 1986—; bd. dirs. Security Savs. and Loan, Phoenix, Land Resources Corp., Phoenix. Served with U.S. Army, 1945-46. Mem. Kappa Sigma. Republican. Clubs: Rotary, Multnomah Athletic. Office: 3200 Park Center Dr Costa Mesa CA 92626

CHRISTIE, GEORGE NICHOLAS, economist; b. Wilmington, N.C., Nov. 2, 1924; s. Nicholas and Helen (Lymberis) C.; B.B.A., U. Miami, 1948; M.B.A., N.Y. U., 1956, Ph.D., 1963; m. Mary Danatos, July 22, 1951; children—Sultana Helen, Stephanie Hope, Susan Adrianne, Sandra Alicia, Gregory Nicholas. With Dun and Bradstreet, Inc., N.Y.C., 1949-61, staff bus. writer, 1959-61; asso. dir. Credit Research Found., asst. dir. edn. Nat. Assn. Credit Mgmt., N.Y.C., 1961-63; asst. sec. credit policy com., small bus. credit com. Am. Bankers Assn., N.Y.C., 1963-64, sec., 1964-67; v.p., dir. research Credit Research Found., 1967-80, sr. v.p., 1980-82, exec. v.p., 1983—; assoc. dir. Grad. Sch. Credit and Financial Mgmt., 1967-86, exec. dir., 1986-87; dir. Nat. Inst. of Credit, 1967-84. Instr. N.Y. Inst. Credit; lectr. Dartmouth, Stanford U.; asso. prof. L.I. U.; adminstr. 2d year banking course Stonier Grad. Sch. Banking, Rutgers U. Served with AUS, 1943-46. Mem. Am. Econ. Assn., Am. Fin. Assn., Fin. Mgmt. Assn. Contbr. articles to profl. publs. Home: 65 Nassau Rd Great Neck NY 11021 Office: Credit Research Found 3000 Marcus Ave Lake Success NY 11042

CHRISTIE, IAN RALPH, historian, educator; b. Preston, Eng., May 11, 1919; s. John Reid and Gladys Lillian (Whatley) C. BA, U. Oxford, Eng., 1948, MA, 1948. Asst. lectr. U. Coll. London, 1948-51, lectr., 1951-60, reader, 1960-66, prof., 1966-84, Astor chair Brit. history, 1979-84, hon. research fellow, 1984—. Contbr. articles to profl. jours.; mem. editorial bd. History of Parliament Trust, 1973—. Served with RAF, 1940-46. Fellow Brit. Acad., Royal Hist. Soc.; mem. Hist. Assn. Mem. Conservative Party. Home: 10 Green Ln, Croxley Green, Hertfordshire WD3 3HR, England

CHRISTIE, JULIE, actress; b. Chukua, India, Apr. 14, 1940; d. Frank St. John and Rosemary Ramsden C. Student, Central Sch. Dramatic Art, London, Brighton Coll. Tech. Profl. Debut in: Brit. television series A is for Andromeda, 1962; films include: Crooks Anonymous, 1962, The Fast Lady, 1963, Billy Liar, 1963, Young Cassidy, 1964, Darling, 1965, Dr. Zhivago, 1965, Farenheit 451, 1966, Far From the Madding Crowd, 1967, Petulia, 1968, In Search of Gregory, 1969, The Go-Between, 1971, McCabe and Mrs. Miller, 1971, Don't Look Now, 1974, Shampoo, 1975, Demon Seed, 1977, Heaven Can Wait, 1978, The Return of the Soldier, 1981, Heat and Dust, 1983, Power, 1986, Miss Mary; appeared with Birmingham Repertory Co., 1963, Royal Shakespeare Co., 1964. Recipient Academy award for best actress in Darling, 1965; N.Y. Film Critics Circle award, 1965; Best Dramatic Actress Laurel award and Herald award, 1967. Office: care Internat Creative Mgmt 40 W 57th St New York NY 10019 also: care Internat Creative Mgmt, 388-396 Oxford St, London W1 England *

CHRISTIE, TIMOTHY JOHN, engineering executive; b. Oxford, Eng., June 2, 1943; s. Michael Alexander Hunter and Pamala Mary (Du Sautoy) C.; m. Annabelle Bronson Albery, Jan. 27, 1966; children: Oliver, Nicholas, William. Student pvt. schs., Abingdon, Eng. Mktg. exec. L.P.E. Ltd., London, 1963-65, 66-69, Honda U.K. Ltd., London, 1965-66; account exec. J. Walter Thompson Ltd., London, 1969-71; mktg. mgr. Alexander Engring. Co. Ltd., Haddenham, Eng., 1971-76, mktg. dir., 1976-81, mng. dir., 1981—. Mem. London Bus. Sch. Assn. Mem. Ch. of England. Office: Alexander Engring Co Ltd, Haddenham Aylesbury, Bucks HP17 8BZ, England

CHRISTIE, WALTER SCOTT, state official; b. Indpls., 1922; s. Walter Scott and Nina Lilian (Warfel) C. BS in Bus. Adminstrn., Butler U., 1948. CPA, Ind.; cert. fin. examiner. With Roy J. Pile & Co., CPAs, Indpls., 1948-56, Howard E. Nyhart Co., Inc., actuarial consultants, Indpls., 1956-62; with Ind. Dept. Ins., Indpls., 1962—, dep. commr., 1966-74, adminstrv. officer, 1974-79, sr. examiner, 1979-81, adminstrv. asst., 1981-82, chief auditor, 1982—; bd. dirs. Sr. Enterprises. Bd. dirs. Delt House Corp., Butler U. Served with AUS, 1942-45. Named Ky. Col. Mem. Ind. Assn. CPAs, Soc. Fin. Examiners (state chmn.), Indpls. Acturarial Club, Nat. Assn. Ins. Commrs. (chmn. zone IV life and health com. 1970-75), Internat. Platform Assn. Episcopalian (assoc. vestryman 1948-60). Club: Optimist (dir.). Home: 620 E 53d St Indianapolis IN 46220 Office: Indiana Dept Ins 311 W Washington St Suite 300 Indianapolis IN 46204

CHRISTMAN, HENRY MAX, author; b. Kansas City, Mo., Jan. 21, 1932; s. Henry Max and Irene Blanche (McBride) C. B.A. in History and Govt, U. Mo. at Kansas City, 1953; Ph.D., U. Belgrade, 1971. Pub. info. cons. Fund for Republic, 1956-62; past dir. city record City N.Y., 1966-74; adj. prof. polit. sci. L.I. U., 1971-74; mem. Worker's Compensation Bd., State of N.Y., 1977-84; Mem. com. candidates Citizens Union, City N.Y., 1961-66; vice-chmn. N.Y. County, Liberal Party, 1974—. Author: The Public Papers of Chief Justice Earl Warren, 1959, The Mind and Spirit of John Peter Altgeld, 1960, A View of the Nation, 1960, Walter P. Reuther-Selected Papers, 1961, This is our Strength-Selected Papers of Golda Meir, 1962, Walt Whitman's New York, 1963, Peace and Arms-Reports from the Nation, 1964, The South As It Is, 1965, One Hundred Years of the Nation, 1965, The Essential Works of Lenin, 1966, The American Journalism of Marx and Engels, 1966, Communism in Practice: A Documentary History, 1969, The State Papers of Levi Eshkol, 1969, The Essential Tito, 1970, Neither East Nor West: The Basic Documents of Non-alignment, 1973, Indira Gandhi Speaks: On Democracy, Socialism, and Third World Nonalignment, 1975, Mahout, 1982, Kingfish to America: Share Our Wealth, 1986; editor: (Myers) The History of Bigotry in the United States, 1960, (La Guardia) The Making of an Insurgent, 1961, (Garland) A Son of the Middle Border, 1962, (Qaddafi) Qaddafi's Green Book: An Unauthorized Edition, 1988; also contbr. articles to profl. jours., mags. Decorated Star Yugoslavia 1st class, 1970; recipient gold medal City of Athens, 1976. Mem. Am. Ethical Union, Soc. Am. Historians, League Indsl. Democracy (past dir., nat. council), Ams. for Democratic Action (N.Y. State vice chmn. 1963-67, dir., chmn. Greenwich Village chpt. 1965-66), A.A.U.P., Am. Polit. Sci. Assn., Phi Alpha Theta, Pi Gamma Mu, Sigma Delta Chi. Home: 453 Franklin D Roosevelt Dr New York NY 10002

CHRISTMANN, HANS HELMUT, philology and linguistics educator; b. Mainz, Rheinland, Fed. Republic of Germany, Aug. 28, 1929; s. Robert and Marie Luise (Schwöbel) C.; m. Ursula Dietze Christmann, Dec. 18, 1930. PhD, Staatsexamen, U. Mainz, 1955, Habilitation, 1965. Wissenschatl. asst. U. Mainz, Fed. Republic of Germany, 1956-61, privatdozent, 1965; ord. prof. U. Saarbrücken, Fed. Republic of Germany, 1965-74, U. Tübingen, Fed. Republic of Germany, 1965-71, 76—. Author: Elise Richter, 1980, Filología idealista, 1985, Ernst Robert Curtius, 1987. Named Officier des Palmes Académiques Govt. France, 1972. Mem. Akademie der Wissenschaften und der Literatur Mainz (corr. mem.). Home: Erlenweg 50, D-7400 Tübingen Federal Republic of Germany Office: Univ Tübingen, Wilhelmstrasse 50, D-7400 Tübingen Federal Republic of Germany

CHRISTO (CHRISTO VLADIMIROV JAVACHEFF), artist; b. Gabrovo, Bulgaria, June 13, 1935; came to U.S., 1964; s. Vladimir Ivan and Tzveta (Dimitrova) C.; m. Jeanne-Claude de Guillebon; 1 child, Cyril. Student, Fine Arts Acad., Sofia Bulgaria, 1952-56, Vienna (Austria) Fine Arts Acad., 1957. Stacked Oil Drums, Cologne Harbor (Germany), 1961, Paris, 1962, Phila. Mus. Contemporary Art, 1968, Air Package and Wrapped Tree, Stedelijk van Abbemuseum, Eindhoven, Netherlands, 1966, Air Packages, Walker Art Ctr., Mpls. Sch. Art, 1966, Kassel, Germany, 1968; wrapped fountain and tower, Spoleto, Italy, 1968; packaged pub. bldgs., Kunsthalle, Bern, Switzerland, 1968, Mus. Contemporary Art, Chgo., 1969; Stacked Hay, Phila. Inst. Contemporary Art, 1969; wrapped monuments to Vitorio Emanuele and Leonardo da Vinci, Milan, Italy, 1970; Wrapped Coast, Little Bay, Sydney, Australia, 1969, Valley Curtain Grand Hogback, Rifle, Colo., 1970-72; wrapped Roman Wall Porta Pinciana, Rome; Ocean Front, Newport, R.I., 1974, Running Fence, Sonoma and Marin Counties, Calif., 1972-76; wrapped Walk Ways, Kansas City, Mo., 1977-78; Surrounded Islands, Biscayne Bay, Miami, Fla., 1980-83; Pont Neuf wrapped, Paris, 1975-85. Address: 48 Howard St New York NY 10013

CHRISTODOULIDIS, THEODOSIUS, chemical company manager; b. Athens, Greece, July 3, 1942; s. Christos and Helen C.; m. Marcella, Dec. 27, 1978; children—Helen, Marina. Pharmacy Diploma, U. Athens, 1965; Ph.D. in Chemistry, Mich. State U., 1972. Teaching asst. Mich. State U., East Lansing, 1968-72; research assoc. Syracuse U., N.Y., 1972-73; mgr. prodn. Pfizer Hellas A E, Athens, 1974-79, mgr. quality control, 1979—. Mem. Am. Chem. Soc., Greek Chemists Assn. Greek Orthodox. Avocation: photography. Home: 26 Periandrou St, 15771 Athens Greece Office: Pfizer Hellas AE, 5 Alketou St, 11633 Athens Greece

CHRISTODOULOU, RENOS JOHN, trading company executive; b. Nicosia, Cyprus, Sept. 8, 1935; s. John and Helen (Efthymiadou) C.; m. Elli Philippidou, Oct. 9, 1965; children: John, Stephanie. BA in Econs., Durham U., Newcastle-upon-Tyne, Eng., 1960. Inventory control and statistics officer N.P. Lanitis Co., Ltd., Limassol, Cyprus, 1960-61; asst. mgr. Limassol br. N.P. Lanitis Co., Ltd., 1962-63, mgr. Limassol br., 1964-77; dir., gen. mgr., chief exec. officer N.P. Lanitis Co., Ltd., Limassol, 1977—; chmn. R.J. Christodoulou Enterprises Ltd., Limassol, 1981—; bd. dirs. Star Mfg. & Exporting Co., Ltd., Toxon, Ltd., KEX Ltd., all Limassol. Greek Orthodox. Clubs: Limassol Marine, Limassol Sporting. Home: 11 Panayioti Symeou, Limassol Cyprus Office: NP Lanitis Co Ltd, Lanitis Building, Limassol Cyprus

CHRISTOPHER, CHRIS CONSTANTINE, internist; b. Akaki, Cyprus, Jan. 20, 1921; s. Costas and Maria (Pitsilli) Papachristophorou; m. Erma Kyriou, Oct. 5, 1939; children: Chris., Deborah, Steven. MD, U. Athens, Greece, 1952. Rotating intern Luth. Med. Ctr., Bklyn., 1953; resident in pediatrics Harlem Hosp., N.Y.C., 1954-57, resident in internal medicine, 1957-59; resident in psychiatry Trenton (N.J.) State Hosp., 1957-59, staff physician in psychiat., 1960-62; practice medicine specializing in internal medicine Nicosia, Cyprus, 1962-64; mem. staff for pulmonary diseases Downey Vet. Hosp., North Chicago, Ill., 1964-66; practice medicine specializing in internal medicine Milw., 1967-78, Nicosia, 1978—. Mem. Cyprus Med. Assn., Cyprus Internat. Med. Assn., Internat. Med. Assn. Home: 1 Georghios Markides St, Ayii Omoloyitae Nicosia 150,, Nicosia Cyprus Office: 5 Mycenae St, 136 Nicosia Cyprus

CHRISTOPHERSEN, HENNING, government official; b. Copenhagen, Nov. 8, 1939; m. Jytte Christophersen; three children. Degree in Econs., Copenhagen U., 1965. Head econ. div. Danish Fedn. Crafts and Smaller Industries, 1965-70; econs. reporter NB periodical, 1970-71, Weekendavisen, 1971-78; M.P. Denmark, 1971-85; v.p. Commn. European Communities, Brussels, Belgium, 1985—. Author various books; contbr. articles to profl. jours. Polit. spokesman Liberal M.P.'s, 1973-78; pres. Liberal Party parliamentary group, 1979-82; mem. parliamentary fin. and budget com., 1972-76, vice-chmn., 1975; nat. auditor, 1976-78; chmn. parliamentary fgn. affairs com., 1979-81; mem. Nordic Council, 1981-82; dep. leader Danish Liberal Party, Venstre, 1972-77, acting leader, 1977, leader, 1978-84. Office: care Commn European Communities, 200 rue de la Loi, 1049 Brussels Belgium

CHRISTOV, DRAGAN SPIROV, international executive, engineering consultant; b. Koutouguertzi, Bulgaria, Aug. 18, 1934; s. Spiro Stoyev and Jordanka (Angelova) C.; m. Euterpe-Terezingha Correia, Aug. 18, 1967; children: Virginia, Marco, Stefan, Daniel. Diploma technician, Technicum Ch. Botev, Sofia, Bulgaria, 1953; cert. in engring., Sofia High Sch. Engring., 1963; diploma engring., Inst. Bldg. and Constrn., Paris, 1964; cert. in gen. mgmt., La Sorbonne, Paris, 1966. Unit chief Regional Municipality of Kustindil, Bulgaria, 1953-55; regional supr. Governorat, Sofia, 1957-59; project engr. Ponts et Chaussees, Paris, 1964-66; chief engr. Ministry Constrn., Sofia, 1966-67; expert Internat. Labour Office ONU/ILO, Tunis, 1967-68; tng. mgr. Internat. Labour Office ONU/ILO, Geneva, 1968-74; dir. Internat. Labor Office, Dacca, Bangladesh, 1975-78; chief indsl. tng. Internat. Labor Office, Geneva, 1979—. Co-author: Training of Foreman in Building Industry, 1981. Mem. Bldg. and Constrn. Assn. Club: Diplomatic (Geneva).

CHRISTY, ARTHUR HILL, lawyer; b. Bklyn., July 25, 1923; s. Francis Taggart and Catherine Virginia (Damon) C.; m. Gloria Garvin Osborne, Feb. 14, 1980; children by previous marriage: Duncan Hill, Alexandra. A.B., Yale U., 1945; LL.B., Columbia U., 1949. Bar: N.Y. 1950. Assoc. firm Baldwin, Todd & Lefferts, N.Y.C., 1950-52; spl. asst. atty. gen. Saratoga Investigation, N.Y., 1952-53; asst. U.S. atty. So. Dist. N.Y., 1953-54; chief prosecutor spl. asst. atty. gen. Saratoga and Columbia County Investigations, 1954-55; asst. atty. gen. N.Y., 1955; chief criminal div. U.S. atty.'s Office, So. Dist. N.Y., 1955-57; chief asst. U.S. atty. 1957-58, U.S. atty., 1958-59; partner firm Christy & Viener (and predecessors), N.Y.C., 1959—; spl. asst. to Gov. Rockefeller, 1959-61; apptd. 1st spl. prosecutor Under Ethics in Govt. Act of 1978 to investigate charges against White House Chief of Staff, 1979-80; dir. CrossLand Savs. Bank. Artist in scrimshaw. Trustee, v.p. Bklyn. Hosp., Community Service Soc.; mem. council N.Y. Heart Assn. Served as lt. USNR, 1944-46. Mem. Am., N.Y. State, Fed. bar assns., Assn. Bar City N.Y. (chmn. exec. com. 1966-67), Am. Coll. Trial Lawyers. Republican. Episcopalian. Clubs: Century Assn., Rockefeller Luncheon, Univ., Netherland, Town Tennis (N.Y.C.); Mastigouche Fish and Game (Que., Can.). Home: 430 E 57th St New York NY 10022 Office: 620 Fifth Ave New York NY 10020

CHRISTY, AUDREY MEYER, public relations consultant; b. N.Y.C., Mar. 11, 1933; d. Mathias J. and Harriet Meyer; B.A., U. Buffalo, 1967; m. James R. Christy, Apr. 19, 1952; children—James R., III, Kathryn M. Smith, John T., Alysia A. Coleman, William J. Public relations officer Turgeon Bros., Buffalo, 1968-69; mem. public relations staff Sch. Fine Arts, U. Nebr., Omaha, 1972; public relations exec. Mathews & Clark Advt., Sarasota, Fla., 1974-75; profiles editor Tampa Bay mag., Tampa, Fla., 1972;

public relations cons. Bildex Corp., 1973-79; owner, operator Christy & Assocs., Venice, Fla., 1976—. Vice chmn. Erie County March of Dimes, 1970; bd. dirs. Sarasota chpt. Am. Cancer Soc., Manasota (Pvt.) Industry Council, 1987—; mem. S.W. Fla. Ambulance Adv. Com., 1981; pres. Community Health Edn. Council. Recipient various advt. awards. Mem. Pub. Relations Soc. Am. (Outstanding Pub. Service award 1984), Fla. Hosp. Assn., Sarasota County C. of C. (v.p., bd. dirs., vice chmn. mktg. 1984-85, vice chmn. 1988-89), Sarasota Manatee Press Club, LWV (editor Sarasota publ. 1978-79). Home: 216 Bayshore Circle Venice FL 33595 Office: Christy & Assoc 100 W Venice Ave #L Venice FL 33595-2240

CHRUNEY, JOHN, food company executive, systems developer-operational controller; b. Wilkes-Barre, Pa., Dec. 20, 1930; s. George and Mary (Watlack) C.; m. Marian Agnes Walsh, June 30, 1956; children—George, James, John, Jr., Jeffrey, Colleen. B.S. in Bus. Edn., Bloomsburg State Coll., 1956; postgrad. U. Pitts., 1956-57, Lehigh U., 1958, Syracuse U., 1959-62. Cert. tchr. bus. Mass., 1974, systems profl., 1985. Field auditor Liberty Mut. Ins., Syracuse, N.Y., 1956-62, sr. methods analyst, Boston, 1962-68; cons., project engr. Auerbach Corp., Phila., 1968-72; div. controller Dunkin Donuts, Inc., Randolph, Mass., 1972-76, dir. systems devel., 1976-86 ; lectr. mgmt. Northeastern U., Boston, 1970-81. Bd. dirs. Yorkshire Terr. Civic Assn., 1960-62; chmn. Indsl. Devel. Commn., Norfolk, Mass., 1965-68; chmn. Capital Budget Com., Norfolk, 1972-76; pres. Norfolk Youth Football Program, 1974-77; mem. Gov's. Mgmt. Engring. Task Force, 1965. Served to 1st lt. U.S. Army, 1951-54, Korea. Recipient Outstanding Service award Gov. Mass., 1965; Merit award Systems and Procedures Assn., 1968. Mem. Assn. for Systems Mgmt. (pres. chpt. 1966-67, Outstanding Service award 1966, Achievement award 1973, Distinguished Service award,1988), Am. Mgmt. Assn., Pi Omega Pi. Roman Catholic. Club: King Phillip Sports (v.p. 1974-75). Avocation: antique auto restoration. Home: 283 Pleasant St Pembroke MA 02359 Office: Dunkin Donuts Inc Pacella Park Dr Randolph MA 02368

CHRYSOULAKIS, HIS GRACE BISHOP GENNADIOS See GENNADIOS, HIS GRACE BISHOP

CHRYSSIDES, GEORGE DAVID, philosopher, lecturer; b. Glasgow, Scotland, July 4, 1945; s. Andrew George and Elizabeth (Watson) C.; m. Fiona Low, Aug. 16, 1972; children: David, Alison. MA in Philosophy with honors, U. Glasgow, 1967, B in Divinity in Systematic Theology with honors, 1970; PhD, Oxford U., 1974. Tutorial asst. U. Glasgow, 1969-70; lectr. philosophy Plymouth (Eng.) Poly., 1972-74, sr. lectr., 1974—; tutor philosophy and religion courses Open U., Buckinghamshire, Eng., 1973—; cons. new religious movements United Reformed Ch., 1983-87; mem. adv. bd. Ctr. for New Religious Movements, Selly Oak Coll., Birmingham, Eng., 1985—; participant various internat. confs. Internat. Religious Found., 1985—; mem. social policy group Brit. Council Chs., 1987—; convenor Working Party on Religious Freedom, 1988—. Author: Advertising: Myth and Message, 1985, The Path of Buddhism, 1988; contbr. articles to religious jours. Mem. Royal Inst. Philosophy, Philosophy of Edn. Soc. Great Britain. Mem. Labour Party. Mem. United Reformed Ch. Office: Plymouth Poly, Drake Circus, Plymouth PL4 8AA, England

CHRYSSIS, GEORGE CHRISTOPHER, business executive; b. Crete, Greece, May 21, 1947; came to U.S., 1966; naturalized U.S. citizen; s. Christopher and Ourania (Kamisakis) C.; m. Margo Sayegh, May 21, 1978; children: Rania, Lilian, Alexander. AS in Elec. Engring., Wentworth Inst., 1969; BEE, Northeastern U., 1972, MEE, 1977. Electronic engr. Orion Research, Boston, 1977-78; sr. engr. Datel Systems Co., Mansfield, Mass., 1978-79; co-founder, v.p. ops. and engring. Power Gen. Corp., Canton, Mass., 1979-85; pres., founder Intelco Corp., Acton, Mass., 1985—, also chmn. bd. dirs.; dir. nat. council Northeastern U. (mem. Pres. Club, 500 Club), Wentworth Inst. (mem. Pres. Council, chmn. membership com.); mem. BSSC Boston U. Author: Switching Power Supplies, 1984; contbr. articles to profl. jours. Active bus. adv. bd. U.S. Senate; bd. dirs. St. Demetrios Ch., Weston, Mass. Served to 2d lt. Greek Army, 1973-75. Fellow Orth. Stuart Boston Diocese. Mem. Pancretan Assn. Am (pres. Boston chpt. 1987-89, co-chmn. 30th ann. conv. 1988, chmn. publicity com.). Greek Orthodox. Office: Intelco Corp 8 Craig Rd Acton MA 01720

CHRZAVZEZ, GEORGES LADISLAS, surgeon; b. Marseille, France, Mar. 17, 1963; s. Pierre and Yvonne (Miard) C.; m. Liliane Lemoine, Oct. 12, 1987; children: Valerie, Emmanuelle, Elodie. Grad. Stomathology, U. Nancy, France, 1969, MD, 1970, D Maxillo Facial Surgery, 1979; D Mountain Medicine, U. Paris, 1985. Diplomate French Bd. Surgery. Intern U. Hosp., Nancy, 1963-66; cons. Belair Hosp., Thionville, France, 1970-71, head dept. stomatologie, 1975—, clin. tchr. dept. stomatologie, 1972, head dept. stomatologie, 1975—; clin. tchr. Nancy Med. Coll., 1971-79. Author: Functional Conception of Nasal Surgery: Cottle's Septorhine Plasty, 1970. Served to lt. French M.C., 1966-67. Mem. French Soc. Stomatology and Maxillo Facial Surgery, Internat. Assn. Oral Surgery, French Soc. Aesthetic Surgery, Internat. Assn. Maxillo Facial Surgery, European Soc. Rhinology. Roman Catholic. Home: 3 Rue Gambetta, 57100 Thionville France Office: Belair Hosp, 57100 Thionville France

CHU, CHO-HO, mathematics educator; b. Hong Kong, Oct. 31, 1947; came to U.K., 1970; s. Yu-Sang and Mo-Yuen (Lau) C.; m. Hsiao-Yen Sze, Dec. 23, 1982; 1 child, Clio Poppia. B.S., Chinese U., Hong Kong, 1970; Ph.D., U. Wales, U.K., 1973. Research fellow U. Reading, U.K., 1973-76; asst. prof. U. Tripoli, Libya, 1976-77; lectr. U. Benin, Nigeria, 1977-78, U. London Goldsmiths Coll., 1979-82; sr. lectr., 1982—. Contbr. articles to profl. jours. Shell scholarship, 1970-73. Mem. London Math. Soc. Avocations: music; painting; travel. Home: 51 Hassendean Rd, London SE3 8TR England Office: U London Goldsmiths Coll, Lewisham Way, London SE14 6NW England

CHU, ERNEST DAVID, high tech and biomedical instrument company executive; b. N.Y.C., Sept. 15, 1946; s. Philip Mei Bao and Esther M. (Tang) C.; student U. Delhi (India), 1966-67; B.A. cum laude, Amherst Coll., 1968; postgrad. Columbia U., 1968-69; m. Rosalind M. Hale, Feb. 13, 1972 (div.); children—Christopher James, Jonathan Peter; m. Diane Hom, May 28, 1983. Staff writer Wall St. Jour., Dow Jones News Service, N.Y.C., 1968-69; account exec. Carter, Berlind & Weill, N.Y.C., 1969-71; spl. asst. to exec. com. Walters, Yeckes & Gallant Co., 1971-72, v.p., 1972-73; allied mem. N.Y. Stock Exchange, 1972-73; sr. v.p., dir. Danes Cooke & Keleher, Inc., N.Y.C., 1973-76; v.p., mem. exec. com. Roussel Capital Corp., N.Y.C., 1976-77; chmn. bd., pres. Ernest Chu & Co., Inc., 1976—; v.p. fin., treas. Haber Inc., Towaco, N.J., 1979, chief fin. officer, dir., 1981, sr. v.p. 1985, exec. v.p. 1986; v.p., dir. Life Signs Inc., Towaco, 1979—; sec., dir. Silvertech Mines Inc.; dir. various cos.; cons. in field. Bd. dirs. Nat. Com. Am. Fgn. Policy, 1979-82 ; mem. alumni scholarship com. Amherst Coll.; bd. dirs. Orgn. Chinese Ams., Inc., 1976-79, v.p., 1977-79. Mem. Am. Profl. Platform Tennis Assn. (pro adv. bd. 1977-79), Asia Soc., Asian Mgmt. Bus. Assn. (chmn., chief exec. officer 1979-80), Amherst Alumni Assn. (dir. 1975-80). Congregationalist. Lodges: Masons, Shriners. Contbg. author: Guide to Venture Capital Sources, 4th edit.; author: (with others) Winning Platform Tennis, Contemporary Platform Tennis, Understanding Tax Shelters; also articles; co-editor Valley Review of Books, 1968. Office: Haber 470 Main Rd Towaco NJ 07082

CHU, JOHNSON CHIN SHENG, physician; b. Peiping, China, Sept. 26, 1918; came to U.S., 1948, naturalized, 1957; s. Harry S.P. and Florence (Young) C.; m. Sylvia Cheng, June 11, 1949; children—Stephen, Timothy. M.D., St. John's U., 1945. Intern Univ. Hosp., Shanghai, 1944-45; resident, research fellow NYU Hosp., 1948-50; resident physician in charge State Hosp. and Med. Ctr., Weston, W.Va., 1951-56; chief services, clin. dir. State Hosp., Logansport, Ind., 1957-84; active mem. Meml. Hosp., Logansport, Ind., 1968—. Research in cardiology and pharmacology; contbr. articles to profl. jours. Fellow Am. Psychiat. Assn., Am. Coll. Chest Physicians; mem. AMA, Ind. Med. Assn., Cass County Med. Soc., AAAS. Home: E 36 Lake Shafer Monticello IN 47960 Office: Southeastern Med Ctr Walton IN 46994

CHU, JOSEPH QUANG, mechanical engineer; b. Phanrang, Ninhthuan, Vietnam, May 27, 1955; came to U.S., 1973, naturalized, 1981; s. Thuc Nang and Cuoi Thi (Pham) C. BA, William Jennings Bryan Coll., 1977; MS, U. Tenn., 1979, PhD, 1982. Lab. asst. William Jennings Bryan Coll., Dayton, Tenn., 1975-77; sr. project engr. Allison Gas Turbine Div. Gen. Motors Corp., Indpls., 1982-87; devel. engr., 1987—. Contbr. articles to profl. jours. Mem. AIAA, ASME (assoc.), Phi Kappa Phi. Republican. Roman Catholic. Avocations: canoeing, soccer, photography, hiking, sailing. Home: 8175 Pascal Ct Indianapolis IN 46268 Office: PO Box 420 Speed Code T20A Indianapolis IN 46206-0420

CHU, RICHARD CHAO-FAN, mechanical engineer; b. Beijing, Hopei, Peoples' Republic China, May 28, 1933; came to U.S., 1958, naturalized, 1968; s. Liang Hsi and Yun Hwa (Wang) C.; m. Theresa Sou-Chin Lee, Aug. 24, 1963; children: Banjamin, Benson, Benedict, Bonita. BSME, Nat. Cheng-Keng U., Tainan, Taiwan, 1958; MSME, Purdue U., 1960. Jr. assoc. engr. IBM Corp., Poughkeepsie, N.Y., 1960-64, sr. assoc. engr., 1964-65, project engr., mgr., 1965-67, devel. engr., mgr., 1967-69, sr. engr., mgr., 1969-75, program mgr., product technology, 1975-79, program mgr., engring. lab., 1979-83, fellow, 1983—. Author 2 books; patentee in field; contbr. articles to profl. jours. Pres. Mid-Hudson Chinese-Am. Civic Assn., Poughkeepsie, 1969. Recipient Disting. Alumnus award Purdue U., 1984, Outstanding Alumni award Nat. Cheng-Kung U., 1986. Fellow ASME (Heat Transfer Meml. award 1986), AAAS; mem. N.Y. Acad. Sci., Nat. Acad. Engring. Republican. Roman Catholic. Home: 4 Sun Ln Poughkeepsie NY 12601 Office: IBM Corporation BO2/701 Poughkeepsie NY 12602

CHU, ROBERT CHAO YUN, air transport company executive; b. Shanghai, China, July 3, 1928; m. Jennifer Yeh Chu, June 19, 1983; 1 child, Jason; children by previous marriage—Jesse, Jerry, Jeffery. B.A., St. John's U., Shanghai, 1948. With China Nat. Aviation Co., Taipei, Taiwan, 1949-50; mgr. Eurasia Travel Service, Taipei, 1951-54; mgr. passenger, cargo sales Civil Air Transport, Taipei, 1954-62; pres. Sita World Travel, Taipei, 1962—, World Express, Inc., Taipei, 1962—. Mem. Am. Soc. Travel Agts., Taiwan Soc. Travel Agts. Home: 620 Tun Hua S Rd, Taipei Republic of China Office: World Express Co, 90 Chien Kuo N Rd Sec 2, Taipei Republic of China

CHU, VALENTIN YUAN-LING, author; b. Shanghai, China, Feb. 14, 1919; s. Thomas V.D. and Rowena S.N. (Zee) Tsu; B.A., St. John's U. (Shanghai), 1940; m. Victoria Chao-yu Tsao, Sept. 25, 1954; 1 son, Douglas Chi-hua. Came to U.S., 1956, naturalized, 1961. Asst., Shanghai Mcpl. Council, 1940-42; asst. mgr. Thomas Chu & Sons, pub., printer, Shanghai, 1943-45; chief reporter China Press, Shanghai, 1945-49; pub. relations officer Central Air Transport Corp., Shanghai, Hong Kong, 1949; Hong Kong corr. Time & Life mags., 1949-56, with Time Inc., N.Y.C., 1956-76, writer, asst. editor Time-Life Books, 1968-76; assoc. editor Reader's Digest Gen. Books, N.Y.C., 1978-83; lectr. on China. Recipient spl. award UN Internat. Essay Contest, 1948. Mem. Authors League Am., Authors Guild, China Inst. in Am. Presbyterian. Author: Ta Ta, Tan Tan—Fight Fight, Talk Talk, 1963. Thailand Today, 1968; (with others) U.S.A., A Visitor's Handbook, 1969; contbr. articles to popular mags. Home: 10 O'Connor Ct Montrose NY 10548

CHUA, PRIMITIVO D., physician, pharmaceutical company executive; b. Manila, Nov. 27, 1935; s. Vincente and Segundina Vivas (Dy) C.; m. Maria Lurline D. Aparri, Feb. 17, 1965; children: Marie Lynn Louella, Lynette, Marie Lyle, Marie Lizette. AA, U. Santo Tomas, Manila, 1956; MD, Manila Cen. U., 1962. Diplomate Philippine Bd. Family Medicine, Philippine Bd. Pharm. Medicine; clin. research cert., Coventry, Eng. Intern Armed Forces Philippines Med. Ctr., Quezon City, 1961-62; surg. resident Marian Gen. Hosp., Manila, 1962-63; chief resident Riverside Med. Ctr., Bacolod City, Philippines, 1963-64; lectr. Sch. Nursing and Sch. Midwifery, 1963-64, Concordia Coll. Nursing, Manila, 1965-66; practice family medicine Met. Hosp., Manila, 1965—; guest lectr. Manila Cen. U., Caloocan City, 1968-73; med. dir. Boehringer Ingelheim, Inc., Makati, Philippines, 1979-86,Rubicon Med. Clinic and Diagnostic Lab., Manila, 1965—; med. services cons. Boehringer Ingelheim Internat., Hong Kong, 1980-86; v.p. med. Meridien Pharma, Inc., Makati, 1987—. Mem. editorial adv. bd. Asian Med. Jour., Japan, 1983—; contbr. articles to profl. jours. Chmn. Philippine Nat. Red Cross, 1981—, Anti-TB Ednl. and Fund Campaign, 1971-78; v.p., bd. dirs. Philippine Found. for Rehab. Disabled, 1983—; active Nat. Movement for Free Elections, 1986—. Recipient numerous internat. and nat. awards including Gov.'s award Lions Clubs Internat., 1976. Fellow Philippine Acad. Family Physicians (pres. 1978-82), Philippine Bd. Pharm. Medicine; mem. Philippine Med. Assn., (life; gov. 1987—), Manila Med. Soc. (life, pres. 1987—), Confedn. Med. Assns. in Asia and Oceania (sec., treas. 1973-87). Roman Catholic. Lodges: KC (4th degree), Lions (chp. pres. 1973-74), Rotary (com. chmn. 1980-87), Elks. Home: 4 Jaime Velasquez, BF Homes Paranaque Metro, Manila Philippines Office: Confedn Med Assns in, Asia and Oceania, 864 Guillermo Masangkay St, Manila 2085, Philippines

CHUAH, MENG INN, anatomist, educator; b. Ayer Itam, Penang, Malaysia, Mar. 24, 1956; arrived in Hong Kong, 1983; d. Kim Hye and Soon May (Tan) C.; m. David Wai Lun Yick, May 28, 1983; 1 child, Lee. BA in Biology cum laude, U. Rochester, 1979; PhD in Cell Biology and Anatomy, Northwestern U., 1983. Lectr. Dept. Anatomy Chinese U. Hongkong, Shatin, 1983—; vis. scientist Neurosci. Unit Montreal Gen. Hosp., Crouche Found., 1988. Co-author: A Lab Manual of Neuroanatomy, 1986; contbr. articles in neurosci. jours. Genesee scholar U. Rochester, 1975-79; fellow Northwestern U., 1979-83, Croucher Found., 1988-89. Mem. Soc. for Neurosci., Internat. Brain Research Orgn., Internat. Soc. Developmental Biologists, Hong Kong Soc. Neuroscis. (council mem. 1986). Home: Chinese U, 2A Residence 7, Shatin Hong Kong Office: Chinese U Hong Kong, Dept Anatomy, Shatin Hong Kong

CHUANG, HANSON YII-KUAN, biochemist, experimental pathologist; b. Nanking, China, Sept. 24, 1935; came to U.S., 1963; s. Wei-Ching and Yei-Feng (Chang) C.; m. Lucy W. Tai, Apr. 2, 1966; children—Philip Duen-Ho, Helen Duen-Feng. BS, Nat. Taiwan U., 1958; PhD, U. N.C., 1968. Research asst. Academia Sinica, Taipei, Taiwan, 1960-63; instr. to asst. prof. U. N.C., Chapel Hill, 1971-75; asst. prof. Brown U., Providence, 1975-77; asst. prof. U. S. Fla., Tampa, 1977-79; research assoc. prof. U. Utah, Salt Lake City, 1979—. Author: (with R.G. Mason, S.F. Mohammad) Hemostasis & Thrombosis, 1982, Replacement of Renal Function by Dialysis, 1983; (with R.G. Mason, S.F. Mohammad, H.I. Saba) The Thromboembolic Disorders, 1983; Blood Compatibility, 1987; contbr. articles to profl. jours. NIH grantee, 1979—, 1978—; NIH postdoctoral fellow, 1968-71. Mem. Am. Chem. Soc., Am. Assn. Pathologists, Am. Assn. Blood Banks, Internat. Soc. Artificial Organs, N.Y. Acad. Sci. Republican. Home: 3427 E Brockbank Dr Salt Lake City UT 84124 Office: U Utah Dept Bioengring & Pathology 2059 MEB Salt Lake City UT 84112

CHUAQUI, ROLANDO BASIM, mathematics educator; b. Santiago, Chile, Dec. 30, 1935; s. Basim and Georgina (Kettlun) C.; m. Kathleen Ellen Henderson, Aug. 17, 1963; children—Miguel Basim, Benjamin Elias, Tomas Agustin, John David (dec.), Maria Jose. M.D., U. Chile, 1960; Ph.D., U. Calif.-Berkeley, 1965. Asst. in medicine U. Chile, Santiago, 1960-62, prof. math., 1965-69; prof. math. Cath. U. Chile, Santiago, 1969-79, titular prof. math., 1979—, dean area of exact scis., 1969-72, dir. Inst. of Math., 1978-82, dean Faculty of Math., 1982-83; vis. asst. prof. UCLA, 1967-68; mem. Inst. Advanced Study, Princeton, 1969-70; vis. prof. U. Sã o Paulo, Brazil, 1971-82; vis. assoc. prof. U. Calif.-Berkeley, 1973, vis. assoc. research mathematician, 1973-74; vis. prof. State U. Campinas, Brasil, 1976, 77, 78; vis. scholar Stanford U., Calif., 1984; mem. math. adv. com. NSF, Santiago, 1985; vis. prof. San Jose State U., 1986—. Author: Axiomatic Set Theory: Impredicative Theories of Classes, 1981. Editor: Non-Classical Logics, Model Theory, and Computability, 1977; Math. Logic: Procs. of 1st Brazilian Conf., 1978; Mathematical Logic in Latin America, 1980; Analysis Geometry, and Probability, 1985. Contbr. articles on math. and philosophy to profl. jours. John Simon Guggenheim fellow, 1983-84. Mem. Chilean Acad. Scis. (titularmem., treas. 1983, pro-sec. 1985-86), Latin Am. Acad. Scis. (titular academician), Acad. Scis. of State of Sao Paulo (Fgn. corr.), Assn. Symbolic Logic (mem. council 1973-76), Soc. Math. Chile (pres. 1975-78, 80-82), Brazilian Soc. Logic, Chilean Soc. Philosophy, Bernouilli Soc. Math. Stats. and Probability. Roman Catholic. Home: 2434 Benjamin Dr Mountain View CA 94043

CHUBB, JAMES GILBERT, accountant, data processing designer; b. London, Jan. 26, 1960; s. Richard Morley and Joanna (Baverstock) C.; m. Caroline Jane Dean; 1 child, Edward Wilfred. Asst. mgmt. acct. Coca-Cola So. Bottlers Ltd., Sunburyon Thames-Middx, Eng., 1981-85; mgmt. acct., mgr. data processing Rosser and Russell Bldg. Services Ltd., London, 1985—; dir. mng. Designer Software Ltd., Brighton, Sussex, 1987—. Designer: (program) Management Accounting System, 1987, Sales and Marketing System, 1987, Heat Loss/Gain Engineering System, 1987. Mem. Inst. Cost and Mgmt. Accts. Anglican. Home: 64 Regency Sq, Brighton England BN1 2FF

CHUCK, WALTER G(OONSUN), lawyer; b. Wailuku, Maui, Hawaii, Sept. 10, 1920; s. Hong Yee and Aoe (Ting) C.; m. Marian Chun, Sept. 11, 1943; children: Jamie Allison, Walter Gregory, Meredith Jayne. Ed.B., U. Hawaii, 1941; J.D., Harvard U., 1948. Bar: Hawaii 1948. Navy auditor Pearl Harbor, 1941; field agt. Social Security Bd., 1942; labor law insp. Terr. Dept. Labor, 1943; law clk. firm Ropes, Gray, Best, Coolidge & Rugg, 1948; asst. pub. prosecutor City and County of Honolulu, 1949; with Fong, Miho & Choy, 1950-53; ptnr. Fong, Miho, Choy & Chuck, 1953-58; pvt. practice law Honolulu, 1958-65; ptnr. Chuck & Fujiyama, Honolulu, 1965-74; ptnr. firm Chuck, Wong & Tonaki, Honolulu, 1974-76, Chuck & Pai, Honolulu, 1976-78; sole practice Honolulu, 1978-80; pres. Walter G. Chuck Law Corp., Honolulu, 1980—; dist. magistrate Dist. Ct. Honolulu, 1956-63; treas., dir. M & W, Inc.; gen. ptnr. Tripler Warehousing Co., Kapalama Investment Co.; dir. Pacific Resources, Inc., Gasco, Inc., Aloha Airlines, Inc., Hawaiian Ind. Refinery, Inc., Honolulu Painting Co., Ltd., Enerco, Inc., Negov Inc. subs. Volkswagen of Am. Inc.s. Chmn. Hawaii Employment Relations Bd., 1955-59; bd. dirs. Nat. Assn. State Labor Relations Bd., 1957-58, Honolulu Theatre for Youth, 1977-80; chief clk. Ho. of Reps., 1951, 53; chief clk. Hawaii senate, 1959-61; govt. appeal agt. SSS, 1953-72; mem. jud. council, State of Hawaii; exec. com. Hawaiian Open; dir. Friends of Judiciary History Ctr. Inc., 1983—; former bd. dirs. YMCA. Served as capt. inf. Hawaii Territorial Guard. Fellow Internat. Acad. Trial Lawyers (dir.); mem. ABA (chmn. Hawaii sr. lawyers div.), Hawaii Bar Assn. (pres. 1963), Am. Trial Lawyers Assn. (editor), U. Hawaii Alumni Assn. (Distinguished Service award 1967, dir., bd. govs.), Law Sci. Inst. (pres.), Assoc. Students U. Hawaii, Am. Judicature Soc., Internat. Soc. Barristers, Am. Inst. Banking, Chinese C. of C. Republican. Clubs: Harvard of Hawaii, Waialae Country (pres. 1975), Pacific, Oahu Country. Home: 2691 Aaliamanu Pl Honolulu HI 96813 Office: Suite 1814 745 Fort St Honolulu HI 96813

CHUDOBIAK, WALTER JAMES, electronics company executive, electronics engineer; b. Gliechen, Alta., Can., Apr. 2, 1942; s. John and Clara (Suchy) C.; m. Mary Annetta Budarick, Oct. 11, 1969; children—Michael, Anne. B.Sc. in Elec. Engring., U. Alta., Edmonton, 1964; M.Eng. in Electronic Engring., Carleton U., Ottawa, Ont., Can., 1965, Ph.D. in Electronic Engring., 1969. Research officer Def. Research Bd., Ottawa, 1965-69; group leader, research scientist Communications Research Centre, Dept. Communications, Ottawa, 1969-75; assoc. prof. Carleton U., 1975-81; pres., founder Avtech Electrosystems Ltd., Ottawa, 1975—, also dir. U. Alta. scholar, 1960-64; Carleton U. scholar, 1964-65. Mem. IEEE, Assn. Profl. Engrs. (Ont.). Conservative. Contbr. numerous articles to profl. jours.; patentee in field; inventor nanosecond pulse circuits. Home: 12 Timbercrest Ridge, Nepean, ON Canada K2H 7V2 Office: 15 Grenfell Crescent, Suite 205, Nepean, ON Canada K2G 0G3

CHUE KUANG, CHUA, hotel and resort executive; b. Kuantan, Pahang Darul Makmur, Malaysia, May 27, 1948; s. Tsai Nan Chien and Lee Su Gor; m. Nyam San Ngo, May 31, 1978. Accounts controller Merlin Inn Resort, Kuantan, 1972-87, Cameron Highlands, Pahang Darul Makmur, 1987—; risck cons. Arab-Malaysian Eagle Ins., Berhad, Kuantan, 1988—. Treas. Teo Chew Assn., Kuantan, 1984-87. Mem. Malaysian Investors' Assn. Home: PO Box 15, 25700 Kuantan Malaysia Office: Arab-Malaysian Eagle Assurance, Berhad 76 1st Floor, Jalan Telok Sisek, 25000 Kuantan Malaysia

CHUI, CHUN WING, lighting company executive; b. Canton, People's Republic of China, Dec. 1, 1944; m. Yuk Yiae Lely; children: Chui Yuk Chee, Chui Chi Wei. Student, Progressive Coll., Hong Kong. Mng. dir. William Artists Advt. Co., Ltd., Hong Kong, 1969-73; mng. dir., lighting cons. Archtl. Lighting, Ltd., Hong Kong, 1973—. Lodge: Rotary (Hong Kong). Office: Archtl Lighting HK Ltd, 37th Floor Hennessey Ctr, East Wing, Hong Kong Hong Kong

CHUJO, SHIMOBU, university educator; b. Yokohama, Japan, Jan. 2, 1936; s. Shinpei and Mitsuko (Mochizuki) C.; m. Nobu Tonozaki, April 27, 1962; children: Osumu, Motoi. BA, Tokyo U., 1959, MA, 1962. Lectr. U. Aoyama Gakuin, Tokyo, 1967-70, asst. prof., 1970-82; prof. U. Aoyama Gakuin, 1983—; mgr. Soc. de Langue et Lit. Françaises, Tokyo, 1977-79, mem. editorial staff, 1979-82. Author: Bibliographie des études de Littérature Française au Japan, 1984; contbr. articles to profl. jours. Home: 3-19-18, Minami-Oizumi Nerima-ku, 178 Tokyo Japan Office: Univ Aoyama Gakuin, 4-4-25 Shibuya Shibuya-ku, 150 Tokyo Japan

CHUKS-ORJI, AUSTIN OGONNA, automotive executive; b. Enugu, Anambra, Nigeria, May 29, 1943; came to U.S., 1964; s. Arum Okosisi and Maria NNeze (Ogbuonye) C.; m. Mabel Ekenma Nwatu, Feb. 12, 1972 (div. 1978); children: Loretta, Leslie, Austin Jr.; m. Gloria Nnenna Nkwonta; children: Nancy, Brenda, Michael, Robert. AA, Coll. of Marin, Kentfield, Calif.; BA, San Francisco State U.; MBA, U. San Francisco; PhD, Oxford (Calif.) U. Franchise owner McDonald's, Oakland, Calif., 1971-85; founder Martins Fast Foods, Enugu and Lagos, Nigeria, 1979-84; chmn. Macon's, Lagos, Nigeria, 1979-86; pres. Real Co., San Francisco, 1973—; chmn. Am. Investrade, Oakland, Calif., 1984—; pres. Mission Blvd Lincoln-Mercury, Hayward, Calif., 1985—. Author: Names from Africa, 1972, African Wise Sayings, 1973. Senatorial chmn. Nat. Polit. Party, Enugu, 1979, deputy chmn. Anambra state br. 1980, v.p., nat. chmn. 1979-83; mem. YMCA-Oakland; chmn. Housing Corp., Enugu, 1979-83; bd. dirs. Royal Exchange Assuyana, Lagos. Named one of Top 100 Black-owned Bus. in USA Black Enterprise mag., N.Y.C., 1986, 87. Named one of Top 2 Black-owned Bus. in San Francisco, 1986, 87. Mem. Black Auto Dealers Assn., Nat. Auto Dealers Assn., Lincoln-Mercury Dealers Assn., Ford Dealers Assn., NAACP. Democrat. Baptist. Office: Mission Blvd Lincoln-Mercury 24644 Mission Blvd Hayward CA 94544

CHUKS-ORJI, CHARLES EJIMOFOR, business executive; b. Enugu, Nigeria, Nov. 21, 1940; s. Orji and Maria (Nneze) (Nwachukwu); B.A., U. San Francisco, 1964, M.B.A., 1968; Ph.D., Calif. Christian U., Los Angeles, 1978. Came to U.S., 1960, naturalized, 1968. Ins. staff Golden State Mut. Ins. Co., Los Angeles, 1968-69, staff mgr., 1969-71; owner, operator franchise McDonald's, Oakland, Calif., 1971—; founder, owner Milanco Export Corp., Oakland, 1976—; dir. McDonald's Operators of Oakland, Unux Exco Co.; pres. Chuks-Orji Consol. Services, Oakland, 1977—; chmn., mng. dir. C.C. Macon's Group, 1987; founder Chuks-Orji Ednl. Projects, Ozalla, Nigeria, 1988; group dir. Macon's Group (U.K.) Ltd., 1979—; pub. Oakland First mag., 1982; exec. producer Total Entertainment Networks. Mem. Am.-Nigerian C. of C. (founder). Republican. Roman Catholic. Rotarian. Home: 919 45th St PO Box 3001 Oakland CA 94609

CHUKWU, ETHELBERT NWAKUCHE, math educator; b. Mbano, Imo, Nigeria, Nov. 22, 1940; s. Nwachukwu Chukwu Uwaezeoke and Ihejere Theresa; B.Sc., Brown U., 1965; M.Sc., Nsukka U., Nigeria, 1973; Ph.D. (Univ. fellow), Case Western Res. U., 1972; m. Regina Chukwu Nyere, Dec. 26, 1966; children—Chika, Eze, Emeka, Uche, Obioma, Ndubise. Asst. lectr. U. Nigeria, Nsukka, 1970; asst. prof. math. Cleve. State U., 1972-76, asso. prof., 1976-78; prof. U. Jos (Nigeria), 1978-81, dean Postgrad. Studies, 1977-81; vice chancellor Fed. U. Tech., Yola, Nigeria, 1981-86; prof. math. N.C. State U., Raleigh, 1987—; mem. Nat. UN Commn. on African Scholarship Program for Am. Univs. fellow, 1962-65. Mem. Nigerian Math. Soc. (v.p. 1980-82), Math. Assn. Nigeria (pres. 1981-82), Am. Math. Soc., Soc. Indsl. and Applied Math. Roman Catholic. Research, publs. in field. Address: NC State U Mathematics Dept, Raleigh NC 27695

CHUN, DAI HO, educational consultant; b. Waipio, Hamakua, Hawaii, Jan. 8, 1905; s. Hin and Shee (Kwock) C.; B.A. with honors, U. Hawaii, 1930, M.A., 1937; Ph.D., Ohio State U., 1947. Tchr. pub. schs., Hawaii, 1930-41; dir. placement and ednl. vocat. guidance, 1941-42; asst. prof. edn., supr. practice teaching U. Hawaii, Honolulu, 1945-51, assoc. prof. edn., 1951-58, prof., 1958-70, prof. emeritus, 1970—; dir. Internat. Coop. Center Hawaii, 1956-61; exec. dir. Inst. Tech. Interchage, East-West Center, 1961-69, dir. Tech. and Devel. Inst., 1969-70; internat. ednl., mgmt. and devel. cons., Honolulu, 1970—; adviser Hawaii Tng. Council, 1968-70, Utah State U. East-West Inst., 1972-75, Taiwan Bur. Tourism, 1971—; cons. to Pacific Investment Fund, 1957-58, Pacific Mgmt., Ltd., 1957-58; dir. Security Assos. Ltd., Honolulu, 1956-60; trustee Norco Corp. Mem. Gov.'s Commn. on Pub. Edn., 1950-70, on East-West Ctr., 1959-61, on Internat. Visitors, 1961-64; on Peace Corps,, 1962-65, on Tourism, 1969-70; mem. pres.'s club Ohio State U.; mem. Friends of East-West Ctr.; state chmn. 11th Anniversary UN, 1956; bd. mgrs. Mid-Pacific Inst., 1946-47, sec., 1946; mem. Community Chest Steering Com., Honolulu, 1960-61. Served to lt. col. USAAF, 1942-45. Recipient Disting. Service award U. Hawaii Alumni Assn., 1959; Disting. leadership award U. Hawaii Found., 1982; fellow Ohio State U., 1951; research fellow Joint Council on Econ. Edn., 1952. Fellow Progressive Edn. Assn., Internat. Inst. Arts and Letters.; mem. Mensa, AAUP (v.p. Hawaii chpt.1955-56), Internat. Platform Assn., John Dewey Soc., Soc. Internat. Devel., Air Force Assn., Hawaii Union (pres. 1929-30), Phi Beta Kappa (counselor 1953-55), Phi Kappa Phi, Pi Gamma Mu (sec.-treas. 1947), Delta Sigma Rho, Phi Delta Kappa. Lodge: Rotary (dir. 1960-62). Author: Mooneys Problem Check List, 1942; Personal Problems of Adolescent Youth (script and film strip), 1952; Meeting the Manpower Needs of Taiwan's Tourism Industry, 1974; others; editor: Hawaii Plan for Teacher Education, 1949; University High School Curriculum Guide, 1955; Hawaii-U.S.A.: Resources for Technical Assistance, 1958; Hawaii's Training Resources, 1959. Home and Office: 1588 Laukahi St Honolulu HI 96821

CHUN, SE-CHOONG, trading company executive; b. Mokpo, Chonnam, Republic of Korea, June 10, 1929; s. Chung-Pyo Chun and Yang-Duk Ko; m. Anita Kim; children: Josefine, Johan. B in Polit. Sci., Korea U., Seoul, 1971; diploma in social welfare, Stockholm U., 1974; PhD in Indsl. Mgmt., Pacific States U., Los Angeles, 1981. Acting mgr. Logistics Auto Works, Pusan, Republic of Korea, 1967; mgr. Logistics Machine Works, Pusan, Republic of Korea, 1968-72; vice advisor Logistics Hdqrs., Republic of Korea, 1972-73; owner Birkan Trading, Stockholm, 1977—; lectr. Stockholm U., 1983-84; researcher Tokyo U., 1985-86. Author: Social Welfare System, 1986 (pub. in Republic of Korea). Pres. Korean Residents Soc. in Sweden, 1975-76, advisor, 1981-84; dir. Korea Ctr. in Sweden, 1984—. Served to lt. Q.M. Korean Army, 1953-56. Recipient UN medal, 1955. Social Democrat. Home: Lummergangen 39, 13535 Tyreso Sweden Office: Birkan, PO Box 168, 13523 Tyreso Sweden

CHUN, WENDY SAU WAN, investment company executive; b. China, Oct. 17, 1951; came to U.S., 1975; d. Siu Kee and Lai Ching (Wong) C.; m. Wing Chiu Ng, Aug. 12, 1976. B.S., Hong Kong Bapt. Coll., 1973; postgrad. U. Hawaii-Manoa, 1975-77. Real estate saleswoman Tropic Shores Realty Co., Honolulu, 1977-80; pres., prin., broker Advance Realty Investment Co., Honolulu, 1980—; owner Video Fun Centre, Honolulu, 1981-83; pres, Asia-Am. Bus Cons., Inc., Canada, 1986—; co-owner, dir. H & N Tax, Honolulu, 1983—; bd. dirs. B.P.D. Internat., Ltd., Hong Kong. Mem. Nat. Assn. Realtors. Avocations: singing; dancing; swimming; dramatic performances. Home: Apt 3302 2333 Kapiolani Blvd Honolulu HI 96826

CHUN DOO HWAN, former president Republic of Korea; b. Kyongsangnamdo Province, Korea, Jan. 18, 1931; s. Chun San Woo and Kim Jun Mun; grad. Mil. Acad., 1955, U.S. Army Inf. Sch., 1960, Army Coll., 1965; m. Soon ja Lee, 1958; children: Chun Jae Kook, Chun Hyo Seon, Chun Jae Yong, Chun Jae Mahn. Commd. 2d lt. Republic of Korea Army, 1955, advanced through grades to gen., 1980; chief personnel adminstrn. dept., 1963; exec. officer 1st Airborne Spl. Forces Group; comdr. 30th Bn., Capital Garrison Command, 1967-69; sr. aide to chief of staff of Army, 1969-70; comdr. 29th Regiment, 9th Army Inf. Div., Vietnam, 1970-71; comdr. 1st Airborne Spl. Forces Group, 1971; comdg. gen. 1st Army Inf. Div., 1978; comdg. gen. Def. Security Command, 1979; acting dir. ., 1980; chmn. Standing Com. of Spl. Com. for Nat. Security Measures, 1980; ret., 1980; pres. Republic of Korea, 1980-88; founder, past pres. and hon. chmn. Dem. Justice Party. Decorated Grand Order of Mugunghwa, Order of Mil. Merit, Taeguk, May 16th Nat. award, Order of Nat. Security Merit, Chonsu; Bronze Star (U.S.); recipient Presdl. Citation for Meritorious Service, 1976. Office: Office of the Pres, Seoul Republic of Korea *

CHUNG, CHAI-SIK, sociologist, educator; b. Wonju, Korea, July 14, 1930; s. Young-hun and Aedok (Hahn) C.; M.Th., Yonsei U., 1957; B.D., Harvard U., 1959; Ph.D. in Social Ethics and Sociology, Boston U., 1964; m. Soon Ria Paik, June 10, 1937; children—Eugene, Warren Euwon. Instr. social studies Emory U., Oxford, Ga., 1962-63; asst. prof. sociology Bethany Coll., W.Va., 1963-65; asst. prof. sociology Fla. Atlantic U., Boca Raton, 1965-66; asst. prof. social sci. Boston U., 1966-69; assoc. prof., chmn. dept. sociology Heidelberg Coll., Tiffin, Ohio, 1969-72, prof., chmn. dept., 1972-80; prof. sociology Yonsei U., Seoul, 1980—, chmn. dept., 1984-86, dir. Inst. for Humanities, 1983-87; vis. scholar Ctr. Japanese and Korean Studies, U. Calif., Berkeley, 1974, Koret vis. prof. dept. sociology, 1986-87. Vis. prof. Yonsei U. and Meth. Theol. Sem., Seoul, 1979; evaluator div. public program Nat. Endowment Humanities, 1978-80. Boston U. faculty research grantee, 1967-69; Joint Com. on Korean Studies of Am. Council Learned Socs. and Social Sci. Research Council faculty research grantee, 1974. Mem. Assn. Asian Studies, Soc. Sci. Study of Religion, Am. Sociol. Assn. Methodist. Author: Religion and Social Change, 1982; contbr. numerous articles to profl. jours. Research on Korean and Asian religions and society. Home: 17-4 Chung Dong, Choong-ku, Seoul 100 Republic of Korea Office: Dept of Sociology, Yonsei Univ, Shinchon, Seoul 120 Republic of Korea

CHUNG, CHARLES C.K., corporate executive; b. Hong Kong, Mar. 30, 1956; s. Chung Yuen Ching and Ng Ah Lui. Chmn. bd., chief exec. officer Cevin Investments Ltd., Hong Kong. Office: Cevin Investments Ltd, 31 Tonkin St 9/F Hong Kong

CHUNG, CHI YUNG, college administrator; b. Changsha, Hunan, China, July 29, 1920; d. Ling and Chan (Shi) C.; m. Henry H. L. Hu, Nov. 12, 1945; children—Y.S. Hu, F.C. Hu. LL.B., Hu-Han U. (China), 1944; Ph.D., U. Paris, 1953. Judge, Dist. Ct., Chung King, China, 1943-45; dean arts faculty Bapt. Coll., Hongkong, 1968-70; sr. lectr. Chung Chi Coll., Chinese U., Hong Kong, 1960-67; founder, v.p. Hong Kong Shue Yan Coll., 1971—. Hon. pres. Hong Kong Children's Arts Edn. Assn.; mem. consultative com. for basic law Hong Kong Spl. Adminstrv. Region, People's Republic of China, Release Under Supervision Bd. Hong Kong. Author: Ta Tsing Lu Li in Hong Kong, 1957; Human Rights and Questions of Nationality, 1957; A Study of Social Legislation, 1963; Chinese Law and Custom, 1963; Problem of Juvenile Delinquency in Hong Kong, 1965; Youth Problem and Education in Hong Kong, 1966. Home: Flat 404, 114 Macdonnell Rd, Hong Kong Hong Kong Office: Shue Yan Coll, 10 Wai Tsui Crescent, Braemar Hill Rd, North Point Hong Kong

CHUNG, CHIEH, acupuncturist, educator; b. Chiao-Ling, Republic China, June 11, 1924; s. Fon-Sin Chung and Tsui-Ying Lai; m. Fong-Tz'u, Apr. 7, 1965; children: Wei-Wen, Wie-Yu, An-Chia. MD, Nat. Taiwan U., 1964. Resident Vets. Gen. Hosp., Taipei, Republic China, 1964-68, chief resident, 1969-70, vis. physician, 1970, dir. acupuncture dept., 1977—; flight surgeon Aviation Med. Ctr., Taipei, 1970-74, dep. dir., 1975-77; trainee FAA U.S., Taipei, 1973-74; research fellow Chinese Acupuncture Sci. Research Found., Taipei, 1974; clin. prof. acupuncure Nat. Yang-Ming Med. Coll., Taipei, 1981—, Taipei Med. Coll., 1987—. Author: Golden Points, 1984, Handbook of Acupuncture Prescription, 1985, Ah-Shih Points, 1986; chief editor Acupuncture Research Quar., 1973; inventor disposable acupuncture needle. Served with Republic China Army, 1965-66. Recipinet Chin Ting award Taiwan Info. Bur., 1980, Silver medal, Brussels, 1982, Bronze medal, Geneva, 1982. Fellow Aerospace Med. Assn. (assoc.); mem. Taiwan Med. Assn. (Chen-Hsing award 1978), Taipei Physicians Assn., Chinese Soc. Neurology and Psychiatry. Mem. Kuomintang Party. Home: 2F No 312 Sect 2 Shih-Pai Rd, Taipei 11217, Republic of China Office: Vets Gen Hosp # 201, Sect 2 Shih-Pai Rd, Taipei 11217, Republic of China

CHUNG, DAE HYUN, geophysicist; b. Jeongup, Korea, Dec. 6, 1934; came to U.S., 1956, naturalized, 1974; s. Mynn and Mockdaan (Rhee) C.; m. Inhan Choi, Oct. 19, 1963; children: Henry H., Gene H. A.B., Alfred U., 1959, M.Sc., 1961; Ph.D., Pa. State U., 1966. Postgrad. research fellow MIT, Cambridge, 1967-68; research asso. geophysics MIT, 1968-74; prof. geophysics, dir. Weston (Mass.) Obs., 1972-74; geophysicist, coordinator geophysics progams, dept. applied sci. U. Calif. and Lawrence Livermore Nat. Lab., 1974-80; staff geophysicist Lawrence Livermore Nat. Lab., 1980—; pres. Livermore Associated Research Group, 1982—; sr. fellow and Inst. prof. Internat. Ctr. Peace Studies, Internat. Assn. Univ. Pres., 1980—; bd. dirs. Am. Inst. of Ednl. Leadership and Devel., 1987—; instr., researcher Pa. State U., MIT, U. Calif.; cons. MIT Lincoln Lab.; staff councillor to Minister Sci. and Tech. Republic of Korea, 1969-70; mem. seismic expert panel IAEA, Vienna, 1982—; mem. field mission to Turkish Govt., Ankara and Istanbul, 1982; cons. Atomic Energy Bd., Pretoria, South Africa, 1982; seismic cons. Korea Advanced Energy Research Inst., Seoul, 1984—, others. Contbr. articles to profl. jours. and chpts. to textbooks. Recipient Maj. Edward Holmes award SUNY-Alfred, 1959; recipient achievement citation Geol. Survey, Korea, 1970; decorated Order of Confrerie des Vignerons de St. Vincent, 1977. Mem. AAAS, Am. Geophys. Union, Am. Acad. Mechanics, N.Y. Acad. Scis., Sigma Xi. Club: M.I.T. Faculty. Home: 4150 Colgate Way Livermore CA 94550 Office: Mail Code L-196 U Calif PO Box 808 Livermore CA 94550

CHUNG, HWAN YUNG, neurosurgeon; b. Seoul, June 16, 1927; s. Yoon Sik and Bok Hyun (Bak) Chung; M.D., Junnam U., 1949; Ph.D., Korea U., 1966; m. Jong Sun Kim; children—Hyo Min, Hyo Sook, Hyo Sun, Tchun Gi, Hyo Gyung, Soon Gi. Commd. lt. Republic of Korea Army, 1951, advanced through grades to col., 1965, discharged, 1965; neurosurgeon Korea U. Hosp., Seoul, 1956-60, 121st Evacuation Hosp., U.S. Army in Korea, 1960-61, Letterman Gen. Hosp., San Francisco, 1961-62; chief neurosurgeon 1st Korean Army Hosp., Daegu; clin. asst. prof. Gyungbook U., Daegu, 1963-65; asst. prof. Korea U., 1965-66; asst. prof. Yonsei U., Seoul, 1966-69, assoc. prof., 1969-72, prof., 1972; prof., chmn. neurosurgery Hanyang U., Seoul, 1972—; dir. Hanyang U. Hosp., 1986-87. Decorated Bronze Star (U.S.A.), Hwarang Medal of Hon., Korea, 1952; Recipient Citation of Merit, Ministry Def., Republic of Korea, 1964, Citation of Merit, Ministry Health and Welfare, 1987. Diplomate Korean Neurosurgery Splty. and Korean Gen. Surgery Splty. Bd. Mem. Korean Neurosurg. Soc. (pres. 1978-79), Korean Microsurg. Soc. (pres. 1984-85), Korean Vascular Surg. Soc. (adviser 1984—), Pan-Pacific Surg. Assn. (pres. Korean chpt. 1984—, v.p. hdqrs. 1984—), Spinal Neurosurgery Research Soc. (pres. 1987—). Home: 80-102 Hyundai-Apt, Abgoojung Gangnam, Seoul 135-110 Republic of Korea

CHUNG, IN YOUNG, government official; b. Pyungyang, Republic South Korea, Nov. 29, 1934; s. Min Jo and Gi Bock (Yui) C.; m. Hae Yul Kim; children: Joon Mo, Jung Ha, Eum Ha, Ryung Ha. BA in Law, Seoul Nat. U., Republic South Korea, 1957, MA in Pub. Adminstrn., 1961. Asst. minister Ministry Fin., Seoul, 1977-80, vice minister, 1980-82, minister fin., 1986-87; vice minister Econ. Planning Bd., Seoul, 1982-83, minister econ. planning, dep. prime minister, 1987—; pres. Korea Exchange Bank, Seoul, 1983-85; supt. Bank Korea, Seoul, 1985. Recipient Order of Service Merit, 1969, 76. Roman Catholic. Home: 477-8 Pyungchang-Dong, Chongro-Ku, Seoul Republic of Korea Office: Econ Planning Bd, Joonang-Dong, Kwacheon-Shi Republic of Korea

CHUNG, KYOO-BYUNG, physician, educator; b. Kyungnam, Korea, Jan. 30, 1947; s. Tae-Hong and Soon-Hee (Park) C.; m. Hae-Sun Park, June 25, 1973; children: Soo-Jin, Ye-Joo, Jinkyung, Jinhee, Jinwon. MD, Seoul Nat. U., 1971, PhD, 1981. Instr. Korea U., Seoul, 1979-83, asst. prof., 1983-85, assoc. prof., 1985—; fellow Cornell Med. Ctr., N.Y.C., 1982-83. Author: (with others) Textbook of Radiology, 1981; editor Korean Radiol. Soc. Jour., 1980; contbr. numerous articles to profl. jours. Served as lt. Korean Navy, 1971-74. Mem. Korean Med. Assn., Korean Radiol. Soc., Korean Soc. of Ultrasound, Radiol. Soc. of North Am., Am. Inst. of Ultrasound in Medicine. Home: 26-804 Eunma Apt, Kangnam-ku Seoul Republic of Korea Office: Korea U Dept Radiology, Guro Hosp, Guro-ku, 152-050 Seoul Republic of Korea

CHUNG, KYU HO, foreign language educator; b. Seoul, Republic of Korea, Apr. 9, 1938; s. Su Man and Ju Yun (Kim) C.; m. Yoon Sook Kim, Mar. 25, 1972; children: Won Suk, Da Won. MS, Escola Post-Grad. de Sociologia e Politica de Sao Paulo, Brazil, 1970. Prof. Portugese Hankuk U. Fgn. Studies, Seoul, 1971—, chmn. dept. Portugese, 1971-82; dir. Research Inst. for Overseas Koreans, 1967. Author: Portugese-Korean Dictioary, 1975, Modern Portugese Lecture, 1975. Recipient Ana Neri Cultural medal Govt. Brazil, 1977. Mem. Korea-Brazil Assn. (chmn. 1980-87), Hankuk U. Fgn. Studies Alumni Assn. (vice-chmn. 1987). Presbyterian. Office: 270 Imundong Dongdaemunku, 132 Seoul Republic of Korea

CHUNG, KYUNG-WHA, violinist; b. Seoul, Mar. 26, 1948; s. Chun Chai and Won Sook (Lee) C.; pvt. study Juilliard Sch. Music with Galamian, from 1960. European debut in violin with Previn and London Symphony, 1970; violinist with various London orchs., Chgo. Symphony, Boston Symphony, N.Y. Philharm., Cleve., Phila., Los Angeles, Berlin, Vienna Philharm. Orchs., Israel Philharm., Orch. de Paris; played under numerous condrs. including Barenboim, Davis, Dorati, Dutoit, Giulini, Haitink Jochum, Kempe, Levine, Solti, Previn; frequent tours of Am., Japan, Europe with above orchs.; rec. artist for Decca Records. Office: care Columbia Artists Mgmt Inc 165 W 57th St New York NY 10019 *

CHUNGBONG, JUN, marketing research institute executive, consultant; b. Seoul, Korea, Nov. 25, 1947; m. Youngim Lee, Apr. 3, 1977; children—Inpyung Jun, Soomi Jun. B.B.A., Seoul Nat. U., 1974, M.B.A., 1976. Mgr. secretariat Korea Heavy Machinery Industry Ltd., Seoul, 1976-80; pres. Korea Mktg. Research Inst., Seoul, 1981—; cons. mktg. Author: The Great Small Talk, 1978; The Bankruptcy of the Big Business, 1983. Active Korea-Am. Friendship Assn., Seoul. Mem. Am. Mktg. Assn., Advt. research Found. Buddhist. Avocations: skin diving; skiing; photographer. Office: Korea Mktg Research Inst, 14-33 Yoido-dong Yongdungpo-gu, Shinwa BLD 9th Fl, Seoul Korea

CHURCH, MERVYN ROBERT, manufacturing company executive; b. Sydney, Australia, Oct. 18, 1934; s. William Edward and Josephine Ada (Fryer) C.; m. Linda Gwendoline Adney, Jan. 9, 1960; children—Andrew, Lianne, Matthew. B.Tech., Adelaide U., Australia, 1966. Design engr., Hawker Siddeley, Adelaide, 1964-66; chief engr. Hawker De Havilland, Adelaide, 1967-71, comml. mgr., 1971; chief engr. Hawker Siddeley Electronics, Sydney, 1972-74, gen. mgr., 1974-76; comml. dir. Hawker Pacific, Sydney, 1978—; dir. Australian Aerospace, Sydney, Astro Pacific, Hawker Pacific Inc. Patentee Data transmission system, 1967, machinery protection system, 1969. Justice of Peace, New South Wales, Australia, 1982. Mem. Inst. Dirs. Pentecostal. Clubs: Royal Aero (Bankstown, Australia); Royal Sydney Yacht Squadron. Home: 40 Laitoki Rd, Terrey Hills, New South Wales Australia 2084 Office: Hawker Pacific Pty Ltd, 4-8 Harley Crescent, Condell Park 2200, Australia

CHURCH, RICHARD DWIGHT, electrical engineer; b. Ogdensburg, N.Y., June 27, 1936; s. Dwight Perry and Carmeta Elizabeth (Walters) C.; B.E.E., Clarkson Coll. Tech., 1963; m. Vernice Naomi Ives, Aug. 26, 1961; children—Joel, Benjamin. Electronic design engr. IBM, Owego, N.Y., 1963-69; prin. engr., pres. ASL Systems, Inc., Afton, N.Y., 1969—, chmn. bd., dir.; sr. electronic design engr. Magnetic Labs., Inc., Apalachin, N.Y., 1980-82; power supply engring. cons., 1982—. Treas., trustee Candor Congregational Ch., 1972-84; vice chmn. Town Planning Bd. Candor, 1975-82; rep., mem. Candor Fire Co., 1972-87; bd. dirs., treas. Candor Community Club, 1970-72. Served with USAF, 1955-59. Recipient Dr. Carl Michel award Clarkson Coll. Tech., 1960. Mem. N.Y. Assn. Fire Chiefs. Republican. Club: Candor Coin (pres. 1978-81). Patentee in field. Home: RD 1 Box 702 Long Hill Rd Afton NY 13730 Office: PO Box 110 Afton NY 13730

CHURG, JACOB, physician; b. Dolhinow, Poland, July 16, 1910; came to U.S., 1936, naturalized, 1943; s. Wolf and Gita (Ravich) C.; m. Vivian Gelb, Oct. 18, 1942; children: Andrew Marc, Warren Bernard. M.D., U. Wilno, Poland, 1933; M.D. in pathology, 1936. Diplomate: Am. Bd. Pathology. Intern City Hosp., Wilno and State Hosp., Wilejka, Poland, 1933-34; asst. in gen. and exptl. pathology U. Wilno, 1934-36; asst. in bacteriology Mt. Sinai Hosp., N.Y.C., 1938; fellow in pathology Mt. Sinai Hosp., 1941-43, research asso., 1946—, attending physician, 1962-81, cons., 1982—; resident in pathology Beth Israel Hosp., Newark, 1939-40; pathologist Barnert Meml. Hosp., Paterson, N.J., 1946—; prof. pathology and community med. Mt. Sinai Sch. Med., N.Y.C., 1966-81, prof. emeritus, 1982—; cons. pathologist VA Hosp., Bronx, N.Y., Nassau County Med. Center, East Meadow, N.Y., St. Barnabas Med. Center, Livingston, N.J., Valley Hosp., Ridgewood, N.J., St. Joseph's Hosp., Paterson, Englewood Hosp.; chmn. mesothelioma reference panel Internat. Union Against Cancer, 1965-81, mem., 1982—; chmn. com. for histologic classification renal diseases WHO, 1975—; Lady Davis vis. prof. pathology, Jerusalem, 1975; former mem. sci. adv. group NIH, Bethesda, Md.; mem. Internat. Union Against Cancer, 1982—; clin. prof. pathology U. Medicine and Dentistry N.J. Author: Histological Classification of Renal Diseases, Renal Disease—Present Status, Glomerular Diseases, Tubulo-Interstitial Diseases, Tumors of Serosal Surfaces, Vascular Diseases of the Kidney, Developmental and Hereditary Diseases of the Kidney, Infections and Tropical Diseases of the Kidney; also numerous articles in sci. jours. Served to capt., M.C. AUS, 1943-46. Fellow Coll. Am. Pathologists; mem. AMA, Am. Assn. Pathologists, Am. Soc. Nephrology (John P. Peters award 1987), N.Y. Acad. Medicine, Internat. Acad. Pathology, Harvey Soc., Internat. Soc. Nephrology, Alpha Omega Alpha. Address: 711 Ogden Ave Teaneck NJ 07666

CHYNOWETH, ALAN G., communications executive; b. Harrow, Eng., Nov. 18, 1927; came to U.S. 1952; s. James Charles and Marjorie (Fairhurst) C.; m. Betty Freda Edith Boyce, Nov. 22, 1950; children: Trevor Alan, Kevin Ray. BS in physics, U. London Kings Coll., 1948, PhD, 1950. Post doctoral fellow Nat. Research Council, Ottawa, Can., 1950-52; mem. tech. staff Bell Labs., Murray Hill, N.J., 1953-60, dept. head, 1960-65, dir., 1965-76, exec. dir., 1976-83; v.p. Bell Communications Research, Morristown,, N.J., 1984—; cons. advanced study inst. and research workshops com. NATO, Brussels, 1982—; alt. dir. Microelectronics and Computer Technology Corp., 1985; lectr. Electrochem. Soc., 1983. Assoc. editor Solid State Communications, 1975-83; co-editor: Optical Fiber Telecommunications, 1979; contbr. articles to profl. jours.; patentee in field. Mem. vis. com. Cornell U. Materials Sci. Ctr., 1973-76. Fellow Am. Phys. Soc., Inst. Physics and Phys. Soc. (London), IEEE (W.R.G. Baker prize 1967); mem. The Metall. Soc. of AIME, Matls. Research Soc., Nat. Research Council (survey dir. com. on survey of materials sci. and engring, 1970-74, panel chmn. com. on mineral resources and the environment 1973-75, panel chmn. materials sci. engring. study com. 1986—), Nat. Matls. Adv. Bd. Home: 6 Londonderry Way Summit NJ 07901 Office: Applied Research Bell Communications Research 435 South St Morristown NJ 07960-1961

CHYUNG, CHI HAN, management consultant; b. Seoul, Korea, Jan. 27, 1933; s. Do Soon and Boksoon (Kim) C.; came to U.S., 1954, naturalized, 1963, B.S., Kans. Wesleyan U., 1958; M.B.A., Mich. State U., 1960; postgrad. Mass. Inst. Tech.; m. Alice Yvonne Whorley, Dec. 23, 1961; children—Eric, Diana. Ops. analyst Chevrolet div. Gen. Motors Corp., Detroit and Flint, Mich., 1959-61; economist Internat. Harvester Co., Chgo., 1961-63; sr. analyst market div. Internat. Minerals & Chem. Corp., Skokie, Ill., 1963-66; mgr. market info. and planning Gulf & Western Industries, N.Y.C., 1966-68; dir. market planning and devel. Am. Standard, Inc., N.Y.C., 1968-71; pres. Oxytech Corp.; mgmt. cons., internat. market devel., Darien, Conn., 1971—; dir. Korea Hapsum Co.; cons. Govt. of Korea, Taisei Constrn. Co., Tokyo. Served with Korean Army, 1951-53. Mem. Inst. Mgmt. Scis., Am. Mktg. Assn., Ops. Research Soc., Am. Chem., N.Am. Corp. Planning Soc., Beta Gamma Sigma. Contbr. papers to profl. lit. Office: 433 Post Rd Darien CT 06820

CIAPPI, MARIO LUIGI CARDINAL, ecclesiastic; b. Florence, Italy, Oct. 6, 1909. Ordained Roman Catholic priest, 1932, bishop, 1977. Papal theologian, 1955—; bishop of Misenum, 1977, elected Sacred Coll. Cardinals, 1977; deacon Our Lady of Sacred Heart. Mem. Causes of Saint Congregation, Apostolic Signatura Tribunal. Address: 00120 Città del Vaticano, Rome Italy *

CIATTEO, CARMEN THOMAS, psychiatrist; b. Clifton Heights, Pa., May 25, 1921; s. Ralph and Grace (Manette) C.; A.B. in Chemistry, U. Pa., 1947; M.D., Loyola U., Chgo., 1951; m. Lucille Dolores Ranum, Nov. 1, 1957; children—William, Jane, Thomas. Intern, Mercy Hosp., Chgo.; resident Fitzsimons Army Hosp., Denver, 1952-53, Hines (Ill.) VA Hosp., 1957-59; practice medicine specializing in psychiatry, Joliet, Ill., 1959-72; correctional and forensic psychiatrist, 1966, 77—; psychiatrist VA hosps., 1959; cons. Dept. Vocat. Rehab., 1959-72, Matrimonial Tribunal Diocese Joliet, 1959-76, Cath. Archdiocese Ft. Wayne and South Bend, Ind., Assn. Retarded Citizens, Wells and Adams Counties, Ind.; cons. Fed. Prison System, U.S. Dept. Justice, Chgo., 1975-76, 77-82; tchr. nursing tng. Hines VA Hosp., 1957-59; med. dir. Community Counseling Service, Inc., Ft. Wayne, Adams County Meml. Hosp. Psychiatric unit, Decatur, Ind. Served with USAF, 1942-46, 51-56. Diplomate Am. Bd. Psychiatry and Neurology. Mem. Ill. Psychiat. Soc., Am. Psychiat. Assn., Am. Acad. Psychiatry and Law, Am. Correctional Assn. Democrat. Roman Catholic. Home: Route 2 135 Little Creek Lockport IL 60441 Office: 815 High St Ste D Decatur IN 46733

CICET, DONALD JAMES, lawyer; b. New Orleans, May 24, 1940; s. Arthur Alphonse and Myrtle (Ress) C. B.A., Nicholls State U., 1963; J.D., Loyola U., New Orleans, 1969. Bar: La. 1969, U.S. Dist. Ct. (ea. dist.) La. 1972, U.S. Ct. Appeals (5th cir.) 1972, U.S. Supreme Ct. 1972, U.S. Dist. Ct. (mid. dist.) La. 1978, U.S. Dist. Ct. (we. dist.) La. 1979. Sole practice, Reserve, La., 1969-88, LaPlace, La., 1988—; staff atty. La. Legis. Council, 1972-73; legal counsel Nicholls State U. Alumni Fedn., 1974-76, 78-80; spl. counsel Pontchartrain Levee Dist., 1976—; administrv. law judge La. Dept. Civil Service, 1981—. Mem. St. John the Baptist Parish Emergency Planning Com., 1987—; bd. dirs. Boys' State of La. Inc., 1988—. Served with AUS, 1964, USNG, 1964-70. Recipient Am. Jurisprudence award Loyola U., 1968. Mem. 40th Jud. Dist. Bar Assn., (pres. 1985-87), La. Bar Assn. (ho. dels. 1973-77, 79-85), ABA, La. Trial Lawyers Assn., Assn. Trial Lawyers Am., Nicholls State U. Alumni Fedn. (exec. council 1972-76, 77-85, pres. 1982, James Lynn Powell award 1980), Am. Judicature Soc., Am. Legion (post comdr. 1976-77, dist. judge advocate, 1975—, mem. La. dept. comn. on nat. security and govtl. affairs, 1974—, chmn. 1977-78, 79-81, 85—, M.C. "Mike" Gehr Blue Cap award 1983). Roman Catholic. Lodge: K.C. Home: 124 W 1st St Reserve LA 70084 Office: 176 Belle Terre Blvd PO Box 461 La Place LA 70069-0461

CICOLANI, ANGELO GEORGE, research company executive, operating engineer; b. Norwood, Mass., Mar. 4, 1933; s. Luigi and Maria (Fossa) C.; m. Marilyn Adell Griffith, June 4, 1955 (div. 1968); children—George, Susanne, Diana; m. Reda Jeanne McWhorter, July 9, 1969 (div. 1978); children—Julie Pingree, Jennifer. Student Northeastern U., 1950; B.S., U.S. Naval Acad., Annapolis, Md., 1955; Profl. Cert., Advanced Nuclear Powwer Sch., 1960; B.S., Naval Postgrad. Sch., 1969. Commd. ensign U.S. Navy, 1955, advanced through grades to lt. comdr., 1975, chief reactor operator, 1958-62, exec. officer, 1963-67, systems analyst, Arlington, Va., 1969-75; cons. Arlington, 1975-77; sr. reseacher R&D Assocs., Arlington, 1977-82, program mgr., 1977-88, sr. scientist, 1982-87, dir. research, 1988—. Author: The Role of Systems Analysis, 1974. Author, editor Mineral Minutes Jour., 1972 (best newsletter 1974); designer Low Speed Ram-Jet, 1954 (Inst. Aeronautical Scis. 1st Place award). Pres. emeritus bd. dirs. Dumbarton Concert Series, Washington, 1982—. Mem. Ops. Research Soc. Am., Naval Inst., Mineral Soc. D.C. (pres. 1972-77), Ret. Officers Am., Nature Conservancy. Office: 2100 Washington Blvd Arlington VA 22204-5706

CIELINSKI, AUDREY ANN, communications specialist, free-lance writer, editor; b. Cleve., Sept. 10, 1957; d. Joseph and Dorothy Antoinette (Hanna) Cielinski. B.J. with high honors, U. Tex. at Austin, 1979. Reporter, writer Med. World News mag., N.Y.C., 1979, asst. copy chief, Houston, 1983-84; free-lance writer, editor, 1984—; editorial asst. Jour Health and Social Behavior, Houston, 1980-81; sec. dept. psychiatry Baylor Coll. Medicine, Houston, 1980-81; procedures analyst, tech. writer, tech. librarian Harris County Data Processing Dept., Houston, 1981-83; communications specialist III, Wang systems adminstr., Office of Planning and Research, Houston Police Dept., tchr. tech. writing class. Contbr. stories and articles to newspapers and mags. Recipient Commendation award, Chief of Police, Houston. Vol. writer, graphic designer, office religious edn. St. Ambrose Roman Cath. Ch., Houston, 1983—; vol. editor newsletters Greater Houston area

Am. Cancer Soc. and VGS, Inc. Mem. Women in Communications, Women Profls. in Govt., Am. Med. Writers Assn., Soc. for Tech. Communication, Soc. Children's Book Writers (assoc.), Austin Writer's League, Sigma Delta Chi, Phi Kappa Phi, Alpha Lambda Delta. Home: 4250 W 34th St Apt 84 Houston TX 77092 Office: Houston Police Dept Office of Planning and Research 33 Artesian Houston TX 77002

CILIBERTO, CARLO, mathematics educator; b. Ercolano, Italy, Oct. 8, 1923; s. Ciro Ciliberto and Concetta Corcione; children: Ciro, Gennaro. Laurea scienze mat., U. Naples, Italy, 1945. Assistente ordin. Facolta' Scienze U., Naples, 1953, libero docente, 1956; prof. ordin. Bari, Italy, 1958; preside Naples, 1968-76; direttore Istituto Analisi Mat. U., Bari, 1961-62; pres. Centro Calcolo Elettron. Int., Naples, 1975-81; rettore Universita' Degli Studi, Naples, 1981—; pres. comitato C.N.R. Scienze Matematiche, 1977. Home: Via Maurizio Piscicielli, n 29, 80128 Naples Italy Office: Universita' Degli Studi, Corso Umberto I, 80138 Naples Italy

CILLIE, PETRUS JOHANNES, publishing company executive, journalism educator; b. Stellenbosch, South Africa, Jan. 18, 1917; s. Gabriel Gideon and Maria Elizabeth (Van Niekerk) C.; m. Elizabeth Frederika Bester, Aug. 13, 1936; children: Maria Elizabeth Cillie De Vries, Angelique Maryn Cillie Faber. BSc, Stellenbosch U., 1935, DLitt (hon.), 1975. Reporter Die Burger, Afrikaans daily, Cape Town, South Africa, 1935-38, subeditor, 1938-44, asst. editor, 1944-54, editor, 1954-77; prof. journalism Stellenbosch U., 1977-83, lectr. extraordinary, 1983-85, mem. univ. council, 1984— ; chmn. Nasionale Pers, Cape Town, 1977—. Author books of essays. Recipient Markus Viljoen medal Akademie Vir Wetenskap En Kuns, 1979, D.F. Malan medal, 1985; decorated Order for Meritorious Service (Gold), 1988. Mem. National Party. Mem. Dutch Reformed Ch. Club: Here XVII (Cape Town). Office: Nasionale Pers, 40 Heerengracht, Cape Town 8001 Republic of South Africa

CIMINERO, GARY LOUIS, economist; b. Youngstown, Ohio, Dec. 16, 1943; s. Felix Louis and Rosalind Janet (Carano) C.; m. Anita Cecile Turgeon, Sept. 3, 1966; children: Steven, Sabina. BS, Case Inst. Tech., Cleve., 1965; MS, MIT Sloan Sch. Mgmt., 1972; postgrad., Harvard U., 1972. Sr. analyst Booz, Allen & Hamilton, Bethesda, Md., 1967-70; sr. research officer The Boston Co., Mass., 1970-75; dir. industry fin. service Data Resources, Inc., Lexington, Mass., 1975; sr. v.p., mgr. macro forecasting Merrill Lynch Econs., Inc., N.Y.C., 1975-82; sr. v.p. , chief economist Fleet/Northstar Fin. Group, Providence, 1982—; mgr. R.I. econ. forecast New Eng. Econ. Project, Boston, 1982—, pres. New Eng. Econ. Project,1986—, appointed to exec. com. of gov.'s R.I. Workforce 2000 Council, 1988—. Designed (with others) Merrill Lynch Econs. Macroecon. Forecasting Model, 1979; Contbr. econ. forecasts to profl. jours. Mem. tax study com. of R.I. Pub. Expenditure Council, Providence, 1985—; appointed to govs. R.I. Workforce 2000 Council, 1988—. Sloan Found. scholar Case Inst. Tech., Cleve. 1962-65, Inst. scholar MIT-Sloan Sch. Mgmt., Cambridge, 1966-67. Mem. Nat. Assn. Bus. Economists, Eastern Econ. Assn., Am. Bankers Assn. (mem. econ. adv. com. 1985—). Home: 2 Bay Vista Pl Warwick RI 02886 Office: Fleet Nat Bank 111 Westminster St Providence RI 02903

CINEAS, FRITZ N(ERVAL), diplomat; b. Port-Au-Prince, Haiti, June 15, 1932; s. Nerval and Emilia (Eveillard) C.; m. Gladys Magloire, Dec. 1, 1963; children: Regine, Sybil. Student, Ecole De Medecine, Port-Au-Prince, 1953-57; MD, U. Mexico, 1960. Sec. embassy of Haiti, Mexico City, 1960-62; pvt. sec. to Pres. Francois Duvalier of Haiti, 1962-64; undersec. of state for commerce and industry Govt. Haiti, 1964-65, undersec. of state for labor and social welfare, 1965-67, minister of coordination and info., 1971-73; head Haitian Mission to Chile, 1967-68; consul-gen. Haitian Consulate, San Juan, P.R., 1968-69; Haitian ambassador to Mexico, 1969-71, to Italy, 1973-76, to Argentina, Uruguay, and Paraguay, 1976-79, to the Dominican Republic, 1979-81; Haitian ambassador and permanent rep. to UN, 1981-83; Haitian ambassador to U.S. and OAS, 1983-85; Haitian Ambassador to Spain, Madrid, 1985-87; leader Haitian del. InterAm. Com. of Alliance for Progress, Washington, 1964; leader Haitian Ofcl. Mission to France, W.Ger., Israel, Lebanon, 1972; mem. Haitian del. X and XI Extraordinary Session of OAS, 1980, 81. Decorated grand croix Order of Honour and Merit (Haiti); grand crois Aguila Azteca (Mexico); grand croix Merito della Republica (Italy); grand croix De Mayo (Argentina); grand croix Duarte, Sanchez y Mella (Dominican Republic); grand croix Star of Africa (Liberia); grand croix Republic of China; grand croix Libertador San Martin (Argentina). Mem. Mexican Acad. Internat. Law. Roman Catholic.

CINGOLANI, PATRICK ANGELO, sociologist, researcher; b. Villepinte, Seine St. Denis, France, Nov. 24, 1954; s. Parise Cingolani and Blanche (Le Corvic) Vouillot. MA, U. Paris V, 1977; PhD, U. Paris VII, 1983. Sociology researcher Groupe d'Etudes sur les Representations du Social, Paris, 1982—; lectr. Coll. Internat. de Philosophie, Paris, 1988. Author: L'Exil du Precaire, 1986; also articles. Served with French mil., 1977-78. Office: U Paris VIII 2 rue de la, Liberté, Groupe d'Etudes sur les, Representations du Social, Saint Denis 93526, France

CINTRON, CARMEN DELIA, religious organization administrator; b. Las Piedres, P.R., Feb. 6, 1939; d. Bernardo and Juanita (Fernandez) C.; divorced; children: Mario Ramirez, Humberto Jose Ramirez. AA, Boricua Coll., 1983; postgrad. Baruch Coll., 1984. Sec. labor dept.-unemployment div. Office of Gov. P.R., Santurce, 1958-60; posting-machine operator Corona Brewer Corp., Santurce, 1960-62; consumer service rep. II Aqueduct and Sewer Authority, Rio Piedras, P.R., 1962-71; exec. sec. First Spanish Presbyn. Ch., Bklyn., 1975—; colloquim rep. Boricua Coll., Bklyn., 1983-84. Helper Presbyn. Sr. Citizens, Bklyn., 1975—; mem. Puerto Rican Traveling Theatre, 1983—, N.Y. Mus. Natural History, 1985. Mem. Am. Hort. Soc., Nature Conservancy, Citizens for Decency through Law, Am. Film Inst., NOW, Smithsonian Inst., Postal Commemorative Soc., Nat. Trust for Historic Preservation, People's Med. Soc., Nat. Health Fedn. Republican. Avocations: reading, bicycling, walking. Home: 84-25 Elmhurst Ave Apt 1-I Queens NY 11373

CIOLLI, ANTOINETTE, librarian, retired educator; b. N.Y.C., Aug. 20, 1915; d. Pietro and Mary (Palumbo) C.; A.B., Bklyn. Coll., 1937, M.A., 1940; B.S. in L.S., Columbia U., 1943. Tchr. history and civics Bklyn. high schs., 1943-44; circulation librarian Bklyn. Coll. Library, 1944-46; instr. history Sch. Gen. Studies, Bklyn. Coll., 1944-50, asst. prof. library dept., 1965-73, assoc. prof., 1973-81, prof. emerita, 1981—; reference librarian Bklyn. Coll. Library, 1947-59, chief sci. librarian, 1959-70, chief spl. collections div., 1970-81, hon. archivist, 1981—. Mem. ALA, Am. Hist. Assn., Spl. Libraries Assn. (museum group chpt. sec. 1950-51, 52-54), N.Y. Library Club, Beta Phi Mu. Author: (with Alexander S. Preminger and Lillian Lester) Urban Educator: Harry D. Gideonse, Brooklyn College and the City University of New York, 1970; contbr. articles to profl. jours. Home: 1129 Bay Ridge Pkwy Brooklyn NY 11228

CIORAN, EMIL W., writer; b. Rasinari, Romania, Apr. 8, 1911; arrived in France, 1937; s. Emilian and Elvira (Comanicin) C. Student in philosophy, U. Bucharest, Romania, 1929-33. Author: The Temptation to Exist, The Fall into Time, The New Gods, A Short History of Decay, Drawn and Quartered, History and Utopia, The Trouble with Being Born. Greek Orthodox.

CIPRIANO, PATRICIA ANN, educator, consultant; b. San Francisco, Apr. 24, 1946; d. Ernest Peter and Claire Patricia (Croak) C. B.A. in English, Holy Names Coll., Oakland, Calif., 1967; M.A. in Edn. of Gifted, Calif. State U.-Los Angeles, 1980. Cert. tchr., tchr. spl. edn., adminstrv. service, Calif. Tchr. English, math. and bus. Bancroft Jr. High Sch., San Leandro, Calif., 1968-79, 83-85, coordinator gifted edn., 1971-79; tchr. English, math. computers San Leandro High Sch., 1979-83, 85—, coordinator gifted and talented edn., 1981-83; cons. Calif. State Dept. Edn., various Calif. sch. dists. Recipient Hon. Service award Tchr. of Yr., Bancroft Jr. High Sch. PTA, 1973. Mem. Calif. Assn. for Gifted (rep. Region 3 tchr. com.), Assn. for Gifted, Nat. Assn. for Gifted, World Council Gifted and Talented, Central Calif. Council of Tchrs. English (past pres.), Calif. Assn. Tchrs. English (bd. dirs., treas.), Nat. Council Tchr. English, San Leandro Tchrs. Assn., Calif. Tchrs. Assn., NEA, Delta Kappa Gamma. Roman Catholic. Avocations: reading, piano, calligraphy, tennis, racquetball. Contbr. articles to profl. jours. Office: San Leandro High Sch 2200 Bancroft Ave San Leandro CA 94577

CIRESI, MICHAEL VINCENT, lawyer; b. St. Paul, Apr. 18, 1946; s. Samuel Vincent and Selena Marie (Bloom) C.; m. Nathalia Catherine Faribault, June 21, 1969; children: Dominic, Adam. BBA, St. Thomas Coll.; JD, U. Minn. Bar: Minn. 1971, U.S. Dist. Ct. Minn. 1971, U.S. Ct. Appeals (8th cir.) 1971, U.S. Supreme Ct. 1981, U.S. Ct. Appeals (2d cir.) 1986, U.S. Ct. Appeals (9th cir.) 1987. Assoc. Robins, Zelle, Larson & Kaplan, Mpls., 1971-78, ptnr., 1978—, also exec. council, 1983—. Mem. ABA, Hennepin County Bar Assn., Ramsey County Bar Assn., Assn. Trial Lawyers Am., Minn. Trial Lawyers Assn. Roman Catholic. Home: 1654 Pinehurst Ave Saint Paul MN 55116 Office: Robins Zelle Larson & Kaplan 900 2d Ave S Minneapolis MN 55402

CIRILO, AMELIA MEDINA, chemistry educator, educational consultant; b. Parks, Tex., May 23, 1925; d. Constancio and Guadalupe (Guerra) C.; m. Arturo Medina, May 31, 1953 (div. June 1979); children—Dennis Glenn, Keith Allen, Sheryl Amelia, Jacqueline Kim. B.S. in Chemistry, North Tex. State U., 1950; M.Ed., U. Houston, 1954; Ph.D. in Edn. and Nuclear Engring., Tex. A&M U., 1975; cert. in radioisotope tech. Tex. Woman's U., Denton, 1962. Cert. in supervision, bilingual Spanish, Tex.; cert. permanent profl. tchr., Tex. Tchr. sci., dept. head Starr County Schs., Rio Grande City, Tex., 1950-53; elem. tchr. San Benito-Brownsville, Tex., 1953-54, Kingsville (Tex.) Schs., 1954-56; tchr. sci., head dept. chem. physics LaJoya (Tex.) Pub. Schs., 1956-70; teaching asst. Tex. A&M U., College Station, 1970-74; instr. fire chemistry Del Mar Jr. Coll., Corpus Christi, Tex., 1974-75; exec. dir Hispanic Ednl. Research Mgmt. Analysis Nat. Assn., Inc., Corpus Christi, 1975-79; head dept. chem. physics San Isidro (Tex.) High Sch., 1979-82; tchr. chemistry W.H. Adamson High Sch., Dallas, 1979-82, Skyline High Sch. 1988—; chmn. faculty adv. com., 1983-84; tchr. high intensity lang. sci. Skyline High Sch., Dallas, 1984—; mem. core faculty Union Grad. Coll., Cin., P.R., Ft. Lauderdale, and San Diego, 1975-79; mathematician Well Instrument Devel. Co., Houston, summers 1950-54; panelist, program evaluator Dept. of Edn., Washington, 1977-79; program evaluator, Robstown, Tex., 1975-79; tchr. trainer Edn. 20 and 2 Region Ctrs., Corpus Christi and San Antonio, 1975-79; researcher, writer Coll. Edn. and Urban Studies, Harvard U., Cambridge, Mass., 1978-80; vis. prof. bilingual dept. East Tex. State Coll., Commerce, 1978; conf. presenter program evaluation, 1977-79. Author: Comparative Evaluation of Bilingual Programs (named one of best U.S. books), 1978; Reflections (poetry), 1983; contbr. chpt. to book. NSF grantee, 1963-65; bd. dirs. Meth. Home for Elderly, Weslaco, Tex., 1968, Am. Cancer Soc. fund drive, College Station, 1971-74; Brazos County advisor Tex. Constl. Revision Commn., 1973-74; sec. Goals for Corpus Christi Com. of 100; Corpus Christi rep. Southwestern Ednl. Authority, Edinburg, Tex., 1977-79; co-founder, dir. Women's Shelter, Corpus Christi, 1977-78; exec. bd. Nat. Com. Domestic Violence, 1978-80; pres. Elem. PTA, 1972-75; mem. Women's Polit. Caucus, Mex. Am. Democrats; Mem. Tex. Tchrs. Assn., NEA, Tex. Assn. Bilingual Educators, AAUW, Chem. Soc., Pan Am. Round Table, So. Sociol. Assn., Rocky Mountain Sociol. Assn., Metroplex Educators Sci. Assn., League United Latin Am. Citizens (pres. College Station 1973-74, past dist. dir. Corpus Christi). Home: 4959 Lomax Dr Dallas TX 75227 Office: Skyline High Sch 7777 Forney Dallas TX 75227

CIRONE, WILLIAM JOSEPH, educational administrator; b. Bklyn., Dec. 27, 1937; s. Joseph Nicholas and Marie Ann (Basile) C.; m. Barbara Jane Skirkie, Dec. 22, 1962; 1 son, Peter Craig. B.A., Providence Coll., 1959; M.A., NYU, 1960; adminstrv. cert. U. Calif.-Santa Barbara, 1977. Tchr., N.Y.C. Pub. Schs., 1960-68; dir. product devel. ednl. div. Mead Corp., Atlanta, 1968-70, dir. mktg., 1970-73; founder/dir. Ctr. Community Edn. and Citizen Participation, Santa Barbara, Calif., 1973-82; supt. schs. Santa Barbara County, 1983—; vis. fellow Chisholm Inst. Technology, Melbourne, Australia, 1986; vis. scholar Ctr. for Excellence Tenn. State U., 1986. Contbg. editor New Designs for Youth Development, 1984—. Bd. dirs. Community Action Commn., 1973-81, Community Resource Info Service, 1978-82, Community Housing Corp., 1980-82; bd. dirs., sec. Pvt. Industry Council, Santa Barbara, 1983—; bd. dirs. Industry Edn. Council, Santa Barbara, 1983—, Santa Barbara Lung Assn., 1983—, Community Devel. Assistance Corp., 1980—; hon. bd. dirs. So. Coast Spl. Olympics; mem. Gov.'s Commn. on Earthquake Hazards, 1981; mem. state bd. Common Cause, 1974-77, organizer and 1st state chmn., Ga., 1970-73; mem. voter accessibility adv. bd. Santa Barbara County, 1986—; mem. adv. bd. CALM, Peace Resource Ctr., Marymount Sch., Women's Community Bldg., Jodi House, commdrs. community liasion com. Vandenburg AFB. Recipient Smallheiser award United Fedn. Tchrs., 1968; Meritorious Service award Community Action Com., Santa Barbara, 1981, Ind. Living Resource Ctr., 1985; named Calif. Community Educator Yr., Calif. Community Edn. Assn., 1984, Pub. Servant of Yr., Santa Barbara County, 1987; Hon. Service award 15th Dist. PTA, 1979. Mem. World Future Soc. (life), Am. Assn. Sch. Adminstrs., Assn. Calif. Sch. Adminstrs., So. Coast Coordinating Council (past chmn., past exec. com.), Nat. Soc. Fundraising Execs., Phi Delta Kappa. Democrat. Unitarian. Home: 953 Elk Grove Ln Solvang CA 93463-9608 Office: PO Box 6307 Santa Barbara CA 93160

CITRIN, WALTER JOSEPH, business executive; b. Kiev, Russia, June 2, 1913; s. Joseph Victor and Helen (Golenpolsky) C.; m. Judith Zirinsky, Aug. 9, 1938; children—Jacob, David, Daniel Alan. B.Sc., U. Hong Kong, 1936. Designer S.E. Faber, F.I.C.E., Hong Kong, 1936-40; dir. United Paper Co., Ltd., Shanghai, 1940-42, 45—; mng. dir. Internat. Textiles Inc., Tokyo, 1953—, Associated Agys. Ltd., Tokyo, 1953—; dir. United Agys. Ltd., Hong Kong, Sabre Time Ltd., Hong Kong. Pres. Shanghai Jewish Club, 1948-50; pres. Jewish Community Japan, Tokyo, 1969-81, chmn., 1981—; chmn. United Jewish Appeal, Japan, 1959-80. Club: American (Tokyo).

CIVARDI, ERNESTO CARDINAL, titular archbishop of Sardica; b. Fossarmato, Italy, Oct. 21, 1906. Ordained priest Roman Catholic Ch., 1930; asst. rector Pontifical Lombard Sem., Rome; held various curial offices; undersec., 1953-67, sec. Congregation for Bishops (known as the Consistorial Congregation until 1967), 1967-79; consecrated titular archbishop of Sardica, 1967, elevated to Sacred Coll. of Cardinals, 1979; deacon St. Theodore; sec. Coll. of Cardinals, 1967-79; filled office of sec. at 1978 conclaves which elected Popes John Paul I and John Paul II. Mem. Congregations: Causes of Saints, Evangelization of Peoples. Office: Piazza del S Uffizio II Vatican City 00913 *

CIVASAQUI, JOSE (SOSUKE SHIBASAKI), poet; b. Saitama Prefecture, Japan, Jan. 2, 1916; s. Namitaro and Sato (Izawa) Shibasaki; m. Setsuko Hirose, Sept. 18, 1940; children: Takashi, Seishi, Sonoe. Grad., Saitama County Sch., 1935, studied writing with Edmund Blunden, 1947-50; LHD (hon.), L'Univ. Libre D'Asie, Karachi, Pakistan, 1977; HHD, World U., Tucson, 1977; PhD (hon.), Nat. Acad. Mgmt., Tapiei, 1987. Adviser liaison dept. Hakodate Dock Co. Ltd., Tokyo, 1948-51; mgr. liaison sect. Watanabe Confectionary Co., Ltd., Tokyo, 1951-54; mem. lit. staff Toshiba EMI Co., Ltd., Tokyo, 1955-76; lectr. Japan Transl. Acad., Tokyo, 1978-84, Sunshine Coll., Tokyo, 1985—. Author: In His Bosom, 1950, In Thy Grace, 1971, Beyond Seeing, 1977, Living Water, 1984, Invitation to the World of Haiku, 1985; translator: Dos hin Shien (R.L. Stevenson's A Child's Garden of Verse), 1973, Kusa no Tsuyu (Novin Afrouz's Dew of Grass), 1987; also numerous songs. Recipient World Poetry award 3d World Cong. Poets, 1976, 4th World Cong. Poets, 1979, 8th Cong., 1985, Gerald L.K. Smith award, 1985, Platformers USA, 1985, Italia '85 indetto del Centro Nazionale Culturale, 1985, Amando M. Yuzon Meml. award 10th World Cong. Poets, 1987. Fellow Internat. Soc. Lit. (Eng.), Internat. Acad. Poets (Eng.); mem. United Poets Laureate Internat. (hon. pres.), Japan Guild Authors and Composers (mng. dir.), Japan League Poets (mng. dir.), Japan Song Translators Soc. (pres.), Shakespeare Soc. Japan, Internat. Shakespeare Assn., World Jnana Sadahk Soc. (India), Poetry Soc. Japan (pres.), Acad. Mentis, Tagore Inst. Creative Writing Internat. (India), Poetry Soc. (London), PEN. Address: 2-12-11 Honcho Ikebukuro, Toshima-ku, Tokyo 170 Japan

CIVIT, JOSEP MARIA, filmmaker; b. Barcelona, Spain, June 24, 1954; s. Antoni and Maria (Fons) C. BA in Theory of Contemporary Arts, U. Barcelona, 1977. Mag. press photographer Cambio 16, Triunfo, Mundo, Interviu, Barcelona, 1974-78; newspaper press photographer Tele-Xprés, Mundo Diario, Barcelona, 1976-78; camera asst. for feature films various prodn. cos., 1978-83; dir. photography various TV series, feature films, 1983—. Films include Lola, 1985, Anguish, 1986, La Iguana, 1987, Lights and Shadows, 1988. Recipient Best Technician of Yr. award, Prix of Cinematography Generalitat de Catalunya, 1985, 88, Spl. Mention of Jury Avoriaz Film Festival, 1988. Mem. Inst. del Cinema Catala. Home and Office: Mare de Deu del Carmel, 23 Prim-Seg, 08022 Barcelona Spain

CLABAUGH, ELMER EUGENE, JR., lawyer; b. Anaheim, Calif., Sept. 18, 1927; s. Elmer Eugene and Eleanor Margaret (Heitshusen) C.; m. Donna Marie Organ, Dec. 19, 1960 (div.); children—Christopher C., Matthew M. B.B.A. cum laude, Woodbury U.; B.A. Summa Cum Laude, Claremont McKenna Coll., 1958; J.D., Stanford U., 1961. Bar: Calif. 1961, U.S. Dist. Ct. (cen. dist.) Calif., U.S. Ct. Apls. (9th cir.) 1961, U.S. Sup. Ct. 1971. Fgn. service staff U.S. Dept. State, Jerusalem and Tel Aviv, 1951-53; field staff Pub. Adminstrn. Service, El Salvador, Ethiopia, U.S., 1953-57; dep. dist. atty. Ventura County, Calif., 1961-62; practiced in Ventura, Calif., 1962—; mem. Hathaway, Clabaugh, Perrett and Webster and predecessors, 1962-79, Clabaugh & Perloff, Ventura, 1979—; state inheritance tax referee, 1968-78. Bd. dirs. San Antonio Water Conservation Dist., Ventura Community Meml. Hosp., 1964-80; trustee Ojai Unified Sch. Dist., 1974-79; mem. pres.'s adv. council Claremont Mckenna Coll.; mem. Ventura County Found. for Parks & Harbors. Served with USCGR, 1944-46, USMCR, 1946-48. Mem. Calif. Bar Assn., Am. Arbitration Assn., NRA, Safari Club Internat., Phi Alpha Delta. Republican. Methodist. Clubs: Masons, Shriners. Home: 241 Highland Dr Channel Island Harbor CA 93035 Office: 1st Nationwide Savs Bldg 1190 S Victoria Rd Suite 305 Ventura CA 93003

CLAES, DANIEL JOHN, physician; b. Glendale, Calif., Dec. 3, 1931; s. John Vernon and Claribel (Fleming) C.; A.B. magna cum laude, Harvard U., 1953, M.D. cum laude, 1957; m. Gayla Christine Blasdel, Jan. 19, 1974. Intern, UCLA, 1957-58; Bowyer Found. fellow for research in medicine, Los Angeles, 1958-61; practice medicine specializing in internal medicine, Los Angeles, 1962—; v.p. Am. Eye Bank Found., 1978-83, pres., 1983—, dir. research, 1980—; pres. Heuristic Corp., 1981—. Mem. Los Angeles Mus. Art, 1960—. Mem. AMA, Calif. Med. Assn., Los Angeles County Med. Assn., Am. Diabetes Assn., Internat. Diabetes Fedn. Clubs: Harvard and Harvard Med. Sch. of So. Calif.; Royal Commonwealth (London). Contbr. papers on diabetes mellitus, computers in medicine to profl. lit. Office: 845 Via de la Paz Suite A236 Pacific Palisades CA 90272

CLAES, WILLY, politician; b. Hasselt, Belgium, Nov. 24, 1938; m. Suzanne Meynen, 1965; 2 children. Student, U. Libre de Bruxelles. Mem. Limbourg Council, 1964, Chamber of Deputies, 1968—; minister of edn. (Flemish) 1972-73, minister of econ. affairs, 1973-74, 77-81; mem. exec. com., joint pres. Belgian Socialist Party, 1975-77; dep. prime minister 1979-81, 88—. Office: Berkenlaan 23, B3500 Hasselt Belgium *

CLAGETT, ARTHUR F(RANK), JR., consulting sociologist, social psychologist, criminologist; b. Little Rock, Dec. 3, 1916; s. A.F. and Mary Gertrude (Bell) C.; m. Dorothy Ruth Pinckard, Dec. 23, 1954. BA in Chemistry, Baylor U., 1943; MA in Psychology, U. Ark., 1957; PhD in Sociology, La. State U., 1968. Shift chemist Celanese Corp., Cumberland, Md., 1942-44; shift supr. penicillin prodn. Comml. Solvents Corp., Terre Haute, Ind., 1944-45; research supr. streptomycin pilot plant Schenley Labs., Lawrenceburg, Ind., 1945-48; asst. mgr. Clagett's Feed and Seed Store, Donna, Tex., 1948-50; med. service rep. Blue Line Chem. Co., St. Louis, 1952-56; prison classification officer La. State Penitentiary, 1956-59, classification supr. new admissions, 1959-60; counseling psychologist, Baker, La., 1960-64; asst. prof. sociology Lamar State Coll. Tech., Beaumont, Tex., 1964-66; assoc. prof. sociology Stephen F. Austin State U., Nacogdoches, Tex., 1968-83, prof., 1983-85, prof. emeritus, 1986—; cons. in field, Nacogdoches, 1986—. Named Outstanding Educator in Am., 1974-75. Mem. univ. research council, 1973-75, Sch. Liberal Arts council, 1970-71, 78-79. Mem. editorial bd. Quar. Jour. Ideology, 1982—. Contbr. numerous articles to profl. jours. Mem. So. Sociol. Soc., Mid-South Sociol. Assn., Am. Soc. Criminology, Am. Acad. Criminal Justice Scis., Am. Sociol. Assn., Inst. Criminal Justice Ethics, ACLU (chaired annual meetings, presented 23 papers). Methodist. Avocations: reading, fishing. Home and Office: 609 Egret Dr Nacogdoches TX 75961

CLAIBORNE, C. CLAIR, polymer materials scientist; b. Fredonia, Kans., May 30, 1952; s. Sylvester Oty and Edna Claire (Cummings) C. B.A., U. Kans., 1973, Ph.D., Northwestern U., 1984. Chemotechnician Sued Chemie A.G., Moosburg, W.Ger., 1973-75; engr. Janes Mfg. Inc., Fort Scott, Kans., 1975-76; research asst. Northwestern U., 1976-80; research chemist Phillips Petroleum, Bartlesville, Okla., 1980-84; sr. materials engr. Westinghouse Electric, Sharon, Pa., 1984—. Author: Working with Metals, 1981; Working with Non-Metals, 1981. Contbr. articles to profl. jours. Achievement Rewards for Coll. Scientists Found. fellow, 1980. Mem. Am. Chem. Soc., Soc. Plastics Engrs., Alpha Kappa Lambda. Home: 44 S 6th St Sharpsville PA 16150

CLAIR, CAROLYN GREEN, civic worker; b. Boston, Sept. 18, 1909; d. James Maddocks and Marietta Cecelia (Foeley) Green; m. Miles Nelson Clair, June 16, 1928 (dec. 1981); children: Cynthia York Clair Norkin, Valerie DeLuce Clair Stelling, Ardith Monroe Clair Houghton. BS, Boston U., 1930, postgrad., 1933. Clk. of corp., dir. Thompson & Lichtner Co., Inc., 1951-77; treas. MNCC, Inc., 1977—; translator Am. Concrete Inst., Chgo., 1930-37. Regent Mass. Soc. DAR, 1933-35, page, 1932-36; pres. Mass. Soc. Children Am. Revolution, 1936-38, historian, 1937-39; dir., clk. The Thompson & Lichtner Co., Inc., 1951-78; v.p. Mass. chpt. Daus. Colonial Wars, 1969-71; active Salvation Army Aux., 1970-86; active Assn. Country Women World, 1968—, lectr., 1972—, alt. to UN, 1974-80, del. to Conf. U.S. Norway, Kenya, U.N., 1974-80; bd. dirs., mem. service league Boston Hosp. Women, 1966-76, officer, 1969-76; bd. overseers, 1974-82 , chmn. patient care adv. com., 1977—; pres. New Eng. Farm & Garden Assn., 1968-71, chmn. fellowship Woods Hole Oceanographic Instn.; mem. Cataument Civic Assn., Bourne Preservation Open Spaces; assoc. Woods Hole Oceanographic Instn.; trustee Brigham & Women's Hosp. Boston, 1982-87, mem. pathology com.; mem. Women's Rep. Club of N.Y.C., English-Speaking Union; Friend of Libraries of Boston U.; bd. dirs. Boston Morning Musicales, Tufts U., 1966-80; mem. council Boston Symphony Orch., 1969—; pres. Women's Nat. Farm Assn., 1972-74, chmn. adv. bd., 1974—; mem. corp. Affiliated Hosps. Ctr., Boston, 1975-76; mem. adv. bd. Nat. Arboretum, Washington, 1974-78; exec. bd. Country Women's Council, 1972-74; v.p. Mass. Hort. Soc., 1970—; lectr. environ. concerns. Recipient Brit. War Relief award, 1945. Mem. New Eng. Hist. Soc. (life), Mass. Hist. Soc., Pan Am. Soc., Internat. Platform Assn., People to People (translator), Boston Mus. Fine Arts, Internat. Womens Ednl. and Indsl. Union, Assn. Country Women of World (life, council mem.), Audubon Soc., Nat. Wildlife Fedn., Nat. Trust Historic Preservation, Bostonian Soc., Arnold Arboretum (mem. adv. bd. 1972-78). Republican. Episcopalian. Home: Clair de Loon Box 63 Cataumet MA 02543 also: North Hill 865 Central Ave Apt F401 Needham MA 02192

CLAIRMONT, WILLIAM EDWARD, contractor, banker, rancher; b. Walhalla, N.D., Jan. 2, 1926; s. Emil O. and Mae E. (Bisenius) C.; student N.D. State U., 1948-49; m. Patricia Ann Filben, Oct. 7, 1950; children—Stephen, Julie, Cynthia, Nancy. Founder, William Clairmont, Inc., Bismarck, N.D., 1949, owner, 1949—; chmn. bd. First Southwest Bank (N.D.), 1975—, Grant County State Bank, Carson, N.D., 1981-85; land developer, Bismarck; owner farm, N.D. Mem. City Council, Walhalla, 1955-56; owner ranch irrigation farm, Costa Rica, 1975-83; mem. exec. com. bd. regents U. Mary, Bismarck, chmn. bd., 1980-81; trustee YMCA, Bismarck. Served with USMCR, 1944-46. Mem. N.D. Assoc. Gen. Contractors (dir. 1964-67, pres. 1971). Club: Apple Creek Country. Home: 1938 Santa Gertrudis Dr Bismarck ND 58501 Office: 1720 Burnt Boat Rd Bismarck ND 58501

CLAMAR, APHRODITE J., psychologist; b. Hartford, Conn., Sept. 26, 1933; d. James John and Georgia (Panas) Clamar; B.A., CCNY, 1953; M.A., Columbia U., 1955; Ph.D., N.Y.U., 1978; m. Richard Cohen, June 24, 1973. Mgmt. cons., psychologist Milla Alihan Assos., N.Y.C., 1957-62; research psychologist coordinator Inst. Devel. Studies, N.Y. Med. Coll., N.Y.C., 1964; intern psychologist Bellevue Psychiat. Hosp., N.Y.C., 1964-66; asso. prof. Fashion Inst. Tech., N.Y.C., 1966-69; supervising psychologist Lifeline Center Child Devel., N.Y.C., 1966-67; chief psychologist Beth Israel Med.

Center, I Spy Health Program, N.Y.C., 1967-70; dir. community-sch. mental health programs Soundview Community Services, Albert Einstein Coll. Medicine, Yeshiva U., N.Y.C., 1970-73; dir. treatment program court-related children, dept. child psychiatry Harlem Hosp.; mem. faculty dept. Psychiatry Columbia U. Coll. Physicians and Surgeons, N.Y.C., 1973-76; pvt. practice psychotherapy, N.Y.C., 1976—; cons. to public health and mental health agys., N.Y.C., 1976—; mem. faculty Lenox Hill Hosp. Psychoanalytic and Psychotherapy Tng. Program, 1982—. Fellow AAAS; mem. Soc. Clin. and Exptl. Hypnosis, Am. Psychol. Assn. (chairperson com. for women div. psychotherapy 1980-82), Soc. for Psychoanalytic Psychotherapy. Democrat. Greek Orthodox. Author: (with Budd Hopkins) Missing Time, 1981; contbr. articles in field to profl. jours. Home: 162 E 80th St New York NY 10021 Office: 30 E 60th St New York NY 10022

CLAPP, ALLEN LINVILLE, electric supply and communications consultant; b. Raleigh, N.C., Oct. 8, 1943; s. Byron Siler and Alene Linville (Hester) C.; m. Anne Stuart Calvert, Dec. 18, 1966. BS in Engring. Ops., N.C. State U., 1967, M in Econs., 1973. Registered profl. engr., N.C., N.J. Asst. engr. Booth-Jones and Assocs., Raleigh, 1965-67; assoc., 1969-71; chief ops. analysis N.C. Utilities Commn., Raleigh, 1971-77, engring. and econs. advisor to commrs., hearing examiner, 1977-82; dir. tech. assessment N.C. Alternative Energy Corp., Research Triangle Park, 1982-85; mng. dir. Clapp Research Assocs., 1985—; pvt. practice electric safety cons., Raleigh, 1971—; chmn. Nat. Elec. Safety Code Com., 1984—; lectr. in field. Author: National Electrical Safety Code Handbook, 1984, 87, Assembly and Testing of Aerial Mines, 1968; contbr. to McGraw-Hill Standard Handbook for Electrical Engineers; contbr. articles to profl. jours. Co-chmn. Brookhaven/Deblyn Park Action Com., Raleigh. Served with U.S. Army, 1967-69. Recipient cert. of Recognition and Appreciation Aerial Mine Lab., 1969. Mem. NSPE, Profl. Engrs. N.C. (pres. 1980; Disting. Service award cen. Carolina chapt. 1978), N.C. Assn. Professions (pres. 1981), IEEE, Power Engring. Soc., Nat. Safety Council, Am. Soc. Safety Engrs., Indsl. Applications Soc., Am. Nat. Standards Inst. Republican. Baptist. Avocations: competitive target shooting, photography, raising orchids. Home: 3206 Queens Rd Raleigh NC 27612 Office: Clapp Research Assocs PO Box 30189 Raleigh NC 27622-0189

CLAPPER, JAMES MICHAEL, management educator, consultant; b. Boston, July 25, 1946; s. John Clarence and Joan Ruth (McCarthy) C.; m. Deborah Musgrove, June 14, 1969; children: Sasha McCarthy, Evan Howes. BS in Mgmt., Rensselaer Poly. Inst., 1968, MS, 1970; PhD in Bus. Adminstrn., U. Mass.-Amherst, 1974. Instr. bus. adminstrn. U. Mass., 1969-73; asst. prof. mktg. U. S.C., Columbia, 1973-75; asst. prof. mgmt. Wake Forest U., Winston-Salem, 1975-79, assoc. prof. Babcock Grad. Sch., 1980—, dir. MBA exec. program, 1980-83, assoc. dean, 1982-87; commodity industry specialist U.S. Dept. Commerce, Washington, 1979, assoc. dir. Office of Bus. Liaison, 1980; mem. White House Task Force on Energy Conservation Outreach, 1980. Bd. dirs., treas. Greenspring Food Coop., Winston-Salem, 1980-82; mem. mktg. adv. com. Winston-Salem/Forsyth County Arts Council, 1982-85; mem. communications com. United Way, 1984—; bd. dirs. Salvation Army Boys Club, Winston-Salem, 1986—. Served with USAR, 1970-76. Am. Assembly Collegiate Schs. of Bus. fellow, 1979-80. Mem. Decision Scis. Inst. (book rev. editor for Decision Line 1976-79, v.p. 1982-84, pres. 1987-88), Am. Mktg. Assn., So. Mktg. Assn., Acad. Mktg. Sci., Epsilon Delta Sigma, Alpha Iota Delta. Lodge: Rotary (pres. local chpt. 1988-89). Contbr. articles to profl. jours. Office: PO Box 7659 Winston-Salem NC 27109

CLARE, DAVID ROSS, pharmaceutical executive; b. Perth Amboy, N.J., July 21, 1925; s. Robert Linn and Helen M. (Walsh) C.; m. Margaret Mary Corcoran, July 5, 1947; children: Lynne Clare Ferree, Carol Clare Brown, David Ross, Christopher E. B.S. in Mech. Engring., MIT, 1945. With Johnson & Johnson, New Brunswick, N.J., 1946—, pres. domestic operating co., 1970, corp. pres., 1976—, dir., 1971—, mem. exec. com., 1971—, chmn. exec. com., 1976—. Mem. corp. Mass. Inst. Tech.; bd. dirs. Overlook Hosp. Served as lt. (j.g.) USNR, 1944-46. Roman Catholic. Clubs: Echo Lake Country (Westfield, N.J.); Lost Tree (North Palm Beach, Fla.). Office: Johnson & Johnson One Johnson & Johnson Plaza New Brunswick NJ 08933 *

CLARE, GEORGE, safety engineer; b. N.Y.C., Apr. 8, 1930; s. George Washington and Hildegard Marie (Sommer) C.; student U. So. Calif., 1961, U. Tex., Arlington, 1963-71, U. Wash., 1980; m. Catherine Saidee Hamel, Jan. 12, 1956; 1 son, George Christopher. Enlisted man U.S. Navy, 1948, advanced through grades to comdr., 1968; naval aviator, 1951-70; served in Korea; comdr. Res., 1963-70; ret., 1970; mgr. system safety LTV Missiles and Electronics Group, Missiles div., Dallas, 1963—. Mem. Nat. Republican Com., Rep. Senatorial Com., Rep. Congl. Com., Tex. Rep. Com., Citizens for Republic. Decorated Air medal with gold star, others; cert. product safety mgr. Mem. AIAA, Am. Security Council, Internat. Soc. Air Safety Investigators, System Safety Soc., Am. Def. Preparedness Assn., Assn. Naval Aviation, Ret. Officers Assn., Air Group 7 Assn. (pres.). Roman Catholic. Home: 817 N Bowen Rd Arlington TX 76012 Office: LTV Missiles and Electronics Group Missiles Div PO Box 650003 Dallas TX 75265-0003

CLARE, STEWART, research biologist, educator; b. nr. Montgomery City, Mo., Jan. 31, 1913; s. William Gilmore and Wardie (Stewart) C.; m. Lena Glenn Kaster, Aug. 4, 1936. B.A. (William Volker scholar), U. Kans., 1935; M.S. (Rockefeller Research fellow, teaching fellow), Iowa State U., 1937; Ph.D. (Univ. fellow), U. Chgo., 1949. Dist. survey supr. entomology bur. entomology and plant quarantine CSC, 1937-40, tech. cons., 1941-42; instr. meteorology USAAF Weather Sch., 1942-43; research biologist Midwest Research Inst., Kansas City, Mo., 1945-46; spl. study, research Kansas City Art Inst., U. Mo., 1946-49; instr. zoology U. Alta., 1949-50, asst. prof. zoology, lectr.-instr. sci. color, dept. fine arts, 1950-53; interim asst. prof. physiology Kansas City Coll. Osteopathy and Surgery, 1953; lectr. zoology U. Adelaide, S. Australia, 1954-55; sr. research officer and cons. entomology Sudan Govt. Ministry Agr., Khartoum, Sudan and Gezira Research Sta., Wad Medani, Sudan, N.Africa, 1955-56; sr. entomologist and cons. Klipfontein Organic Products Corp., Johannesburg, Union S.Africa, 1957; prof., head dept. biology Union Coll., 1958-59, chmn. sci. div., prof., head biology, 1959-61, spl. study grantee, 1960; prof., head dept. biology Mo. Valley Coll., Marshall, 1961-62; research grantee Mo. Valley Coll., 1961-62; lectr., instr. biology, meteorology, sci. of color Adirondack Sci. Camp and Field Research Sta. at Twin Valleys, SUNY, Plattsburgh, 1962-66; dir. acad. program SUNY, 1963-66, research facilities grantee, 1963-66; Buckbee Found. prof. biology Rockford (Ill.) Coll., lectr. biology evening coll., 1962-63, spl. research grantee, 1962-63; prof., chmn. dept. biochemistry, mem. research div. Kansas City (Mo.) Coll. Osteopathy and Surgery, U. Health Scis., 1963-67; also NIH basic research grantee, 1963-67; prof. biology Coll. of Emporia, Kans., 1967-74; dir. biol. research Coll. of Emporia, 1972-74, prof. emeritus, 1974—; research biologist, cons. 1974—; research study grantee, 1967-74, spl. research grantee study in, Arctic, 1970, 72, C. Am. and Mexico, 1973; cons. VITA, 1962—, Adirondack Research Sta., 1962-66, Nat. Referral Center for Sci. and Tech., other orgns. Contbr. over 100 papers and monographs on capillary movement in porous materials, physiology and biochemistry of arthropoda; numerous local, nat., internat. exhbns. on color, also articles to profl. jours. Mem. adv. bd. Fine Art Registry Soc. N.Am. Artists. Served with USNR, 1943-45. Recipient Certificate of Service Vols. Internat. Tech. Assistance, 1970; Creativity Recognition award Internat. Personnel Research, 1972; Distinguished Achievement and Service awards for edn. and research in biology; Certificate of Merit in Art Internat. Biog. Centre, Cambridge, 1968, 72, 73, 76; Outstanding Service to Community award Am. Biog. Inst., 1975, 76, 77, 79-80; Notable Ams. of Bicentennial Era award, 1976; Book of Honor award, 1978; named Outstanding Educator Coll. of Emporia, 1973; research grantee Alta. Research Council, 1951-53; research facilities grantee U. Alaska, 1970; research facilities grantee No. Research Survey Arctic Inst. N.Am., 1970, 72. Fellow Internat. Biog. Assn. (life), Am. Biog. Inst., Explorers Club, Anglo-Am. Acad. (hon.); mem. N.Y. Acad. Scis. (life), Brit. Assn. Adv. Sci. (life), Am. Entomol. Soc. (life), Nat. Assn. Biology Tchrs., AAUP, Arctic Inst. N.Am., Am. Polar Soc., Inter-Soc. Color Council, Sigma Xi, Phi Sigma, Psi Chi, numerous others. Home: 405 NW Woodland Rd Indian Hills in Riverside Kansas City MO 64150

CLARK, ALICIA GARCIA, political party official; b. Vera Cruz, Mex., Jan. 13; came to U.S., 1970; d. Rafael Aully and Maria Luisa (Cobos) Garcia; m. Edward E. Clark, Oct. 20, 1970; 1 son, Edward E. M.S. in Chem. Engring., Nat. U. Mex., Mexico City, 1951. Chemist, Celanese Mexicana, Mexico City, 1951-53, lab. mgr., 1951-53, sales promotion mgr., 1958-65, sales promotion and advt. mgr., 1965-70. Nat. chmn. Libertarian Party, Houston, 1981-83; pres. San Marino (Calif.) Guild of Huntington Hosps., 1981-82, chmn. Celebrity Series, 1979—; Pres. Multiple Sclerosis Soc., San Gabriel Valley, Calif., 1977-78. Recipient award La Mujer de Hoy mag., 1969. Mem. Fashion Group (treas. 1969-70), Mex. Advt. Assn. (dir. 1969-70, award 1970). Club: San Marino Woman's (ways and means chmn. 1980, 87).

CLARK, ARTHUR BRODIE, electrical equipment manufacturing company executive; b. Exeter, N.H., July 11, 1935; s. Leslie Clinton and Eva Jane (Proctor) C.; B.S., U. N.H., 1959; M.B.A., Lynchburg Coll., 1973; M of Engring. George Washington U., 1987; m. Mary Ann Maddox, June 15, 1974; children—Melanie, Belinda. With Gen. Electric Co., 1959—, sr. project/tech. unit leader mobile communications mfg. dept., sr. engr. U.S. mobile radio dept., Lynchburg, Va., 1973—. Mem. Am. Soc. Mech. Engrs. (past chmn., Cert.), Pi Kappa Alpha. Methodist. Club: Elks. Home: 2312 Heron Hill Pl Lynchburg VA 24503 Office: Gen Electric Co Mountain View Rd Room 1614 Lynchburg VA 24502

CLARK, ARTHUR JOSEPH, JR., mechanical and electrical engineer; b. West Orange, N.J., June 10, 1921; s. Arthur Joseph and Marjorie May (Courter) C.; B.S. in Mech. Engring., Cornell U., 1943; M.S., Poly. Inst. Bklyn., 1948; M.S. in Elec. Engring., U. N.Mex., 1955; m. Caroline Katherine Badgley, June 12, 1943; children—Arthur Joseph, III, Durward S., David P. Design engr. Ranger Aircraft Engines Co., Farmingdale, N.Y., 1943-46; sr. structures engr. propeller div. Curtis Wright Co., Caldwell, N.J., 1946-51; mgr. space isotope power dept., also aerospace nuclear safety dept. Sandia Labs., Albuquerque, 1951-71, mgr. environ. systems test lab., 1971-79, mgr. mil. liaison dept., 1979—; mem. faculty U. N.Mex., 1971-75; invited lectr. Am. Mgmt. Assn. Pres. Sandia Base Sch. PTA, 1960-61; chmn. finance com. Albuquerque chpt. Am. Field Service, 1964-66; chmn. Sandia Labs. div. U.S. Savs. Bond drive, 1972-74, chmn. employee contbn. drive, 1973-75; active local Boy Scouts Am., 1958-66. Recipient Order Arrow, Boy Scouts Am., 1961, Order St. Andrew, 1962, Scouters Key award, 1964; cert. outstanding service Sandia Base, 1964. Fellow ASME (nat. v.p. 1975-79, past chmn. N.Mex. sect.); mem. IEEE (sr.), Cornell Engring. Soc., Theta Xi. Clubs: Kirtland Officers, Four Hills Country. Home: 905 Warm Sands Trail Albuquerque NM 87123 Office: Sandia Labs Dept 7210 Albuquerque NM 87185

CLARK, BILLY PAT, physicist; b. Bartlesville, Okla., May 15, 1939; s. Lloyd A. and Ruby Laura (Holcomb) C. BS, Okla. State U., 1961, MS, 1964; PhD, 1968. Grad. asst. dept. physics Okla. State U., 1961-68; postdoctoral research fellow dept. theoretical physics U. Warwick, Coventry, Eng., 1968-69; sr. mem. tech. staff Booz-Allen Applied Research, 1969-70; sr. mem. tech. staff field services div. Computer Scis. Corp., Leavenworth, Kans., 1970-73, sr. mem. tech. staff, field services div., Hampton, Va., 1973-76, head quality assurance engring. Landsat project Goddard Space Flight Center, NASA, Greenbelt, Md., 1976-77, quality assurance sect. mgr., 1977-79, sr. staff scientist engring. dept., 1979-80, sr. staff scientist image processing ops., 1980-82, sr. prin. engr./scientist GSFC sci. and application operation, system scis. div., 1982-83, sr. adv. staff CSC/NOAA Landsat Operation, 1983—; tech. rep. internat. Landsat Tech. Working Group (representing USA Landsat operation). Author tech. publs. Recipient undergrad. scholarships Phillips Petroleum Co., 1957-61, Am. Legion, 1957-58, Okla. State U., 1957-58. Mem. Am. Acad. Polit. and Social Sci., Internat. Platform Assn., Am. Phys. Soc., AAAS, N.Y. Acad. Scis., Soc. Photo Optical Instrumentation Engrs., Internat. Soc. for Photogrammetry and Remote Sensing, Am. Soc. for Photogrammetry and Remote Sensing, IEEE, Pi Mu Epsilon, Sigma Pi Sigma. Club: Victory Hills Golf and Country (Kansas City, Kans.). Home: 5811 Barnwood Pl Columbia MD 21044

CLARK, BRADLEY LINTHICUM, program manager, publications editor; b. Rockville, Md., Jan. 4, 1926; s. William Dorsey and Carrie (England) C. B.B.A., U. N.Mex., 1951; postgrad. Georgetown U., 1952, George Washington U., 1970. Dir. advt. Fox Amusement Corp., Denver, 1954-55; mgmt. cons. Govt. of Montgomery County, Rockville, Md., 1955; legal editor E.N. Raymond Assocs., San Francisco, 1959-62; editor Goodway, Arlington, Va., 1962-69; tech. pubs. editor Hdqrs., U.S. Coast Guard, Washington, 1969-79; program mgr., publs. editor Naval Facilities Engring. Command, Alexandria, Va., 1979—; instr. U.S. Coast Guard, Washington, 1970-78; seminar leader, program coordinator Govt. Communicators, Washington, 1980-82. Author: Yankee Doodle Poodle, 1987; contbr. articles to profl. jours. Librettist, lyricist, composer (musical comedy) The Shopper, 1986. Patentee: Line drawer for typewriter; numerous inventions, several in photography. Served to 1st lt. USAF, 1951-53. Democrat. Episcopalian. Clubs: Naval Officers (Bethesda); Andrews Officers (Camp Spring Md.); Toastmasters (Washington) (pres. 1978, area gov. 1979). Avocations: travel; home movies; cycling. Home: 5480 Wisconsin Ave Chevy Chase MD 20815

CLARK, CARL ARTHUR, psychology educator, research, writer; b. Oak Park, Ill., Sept. 20, 1911; s. Alfred Houghton and Mary (Geist) C.; m. Janet Picquet, 1946; 1 child, Peter Picquet. BA cum laude, Colo. Coll., 1948, MA, 1951; PhD, State U. Iowa, 1954. Mem. faculty Colorado Springs High Sch., 1948-50; research asst. State U. Iowa, Iowa City, 1951-53; research assoc. U. Chgo., 1953-54; prof. psychology Chgo. State U., 1954-76, prof. emeritus, 1976—; adj. prof. U. Mo.-Rolla, 1976-77; research evaluator Ford Found. projects, Chgo., 1963-66. Mem. editorial bd. Ill. Schs. Jour., 1966-76. Contbr. articles and revs. to profl. jours. Served with U.S. Army, 1942-45. Recipient Outstanding Achievement award Black Students Psychology Assn., 1973. Mem. N.Y. Acad. Scis., Am. Psychol. Assn., AAAS, Sigma Xi. Avocations: portrait painting, classical guitar, chess. Home: 616 W Washington Kirkwood MO 63122

CLARK, CAROLYN ARCHER, technologist, scientist; b. Leon County, Tex., Feb. 16, 1941; d. Ray Brooks and Dena Mae (Green) Archer; m. Frank Ray Clark, Nov. 20, 1960 (div. Oct. 1979); children: Frank Ray, Valerie Lynn, Bruce Layne. BA, Sam Houston State U., 1961; MS, Tex. A&M U., 1973, PhD, 1977. Supr., bookkeeper Republic Sewing Machine Distbrs., Dallas, 1961-65; door-to-door sales Avon Products, Inc. Bryan, Tex., 1965-72; lectr. Tex. A&M Univ., College Station, Tex., 1977, research assoc., 1977-79; sr. sci. Lockheed Emsco, Houston, 1979-82, prin. scientist 1983-85; aerospace technologist phys. scientist NASA Stennis Space Ctr., Miss., 1986-88—; sr. project mgr. Ctr. for Space and Advanced Tech., Houston, 1988—; staff scientist Lockheed EMSCO, Houston, 1986—; cons. in field. Contbr. articles to profl. publs. Recipient Commendation for Outstanding Contbns. Lockheed, 1979-80, Commendation for Excellence, 1984; Cert. of Merit U.S. Dept. Agr. 1980; Grad. Research Fellow Tex. A&M, 1975-76; NSF co-grantee Tex. A&M, 1976-77. Mem. Am. Soc. Plant Taxonomists, Bot. Soc. Am., Am. Soc. Photogrammetry, Nat. Mgmt. Assn., Sigma Xi, Phi Sigma, Alpha Chi, Kappa Delta Pi. Republican. Avocations: sailing, scuba diving, tennis, piano. Office: Ctr for Space and Advanced Tech 17629 El Camino Real Houston TX 77059

CLARK, DAYLE MERITT, civil engineer; b. Lubbock, Tex., Sept. 5, 1933; s. Frank Meritt and Mamie Jewel (Huff) C.; B.S., Tex. Tech. U., 1955; M.S., So. Meth. U., 1967; m. Betty Ann Maples, Apr. 11, 1968; 1 dau., Alison. Registered profl. engr., pub. surveyor. Field engr. Chgo. Bridge & Iron Co., 1955; mgr. L.K. Long Constrn. Co., 1958-64; faculty U. Tex., Arlington, 1964—; cons. AID, 1966, NSF, 1967-68; expert witness in court cases. Served to capt. USAF, 1955-57. Mem. ASCE (pres. Dallas br. 1987). Club: Rotary (pres. Arlington-West 1986). Editor Tex. Civil Engr., 1967-71. Contbr. papers, reports to profl. jours. Office: Box 185 Arlington TX 76004

CLARK, DONALD OTIS, lawyer; b. Charlotte, N.C., May 30, 1934; s. Otis and Ruby Lee (Church) C.; m. Jo Ann Hager, June 15, 1957 (div. 1980); children: Deborah Elise, Stephen Merritt; m. Anja Maria Smith, Nov. 5, 1983. A.B., U. S.C., 1956, J.D. cum laude, 1963; M.A., U. Ill., 1957. Bar: S.C. 1963, Ga. 1964. Practice law Atlanta, 1963-83; mem. Candler, Cox, McClain & Andrews, 1968-70, McClain, Mellen, Bowling & Hickman, 1970-75; ptnr. King & Spalding, 1975-78; sr. ptnr. Hurt, Richardson, Garner, Todd & Cadenhead, 1978-83; ptnr. Bishop, Liberman, Cook, Purcell & Reynolds, Washington, 1983-86, Kaplan Russin & Vecchi, Washington, 1986—; mem. dist. export council U.S. Dept Commerce, 1974—; adj. prof. law Emory U., 1970—, U.S.C., 1974; lectr. Ga. State U., 1972; lectr. numerous internat. trade seminars and workshops. Author: German govt. study on doing bus. in Southeastern U.S., 1974; editor-in-chief: S.C. Law Rev., 1963; contbr. articles to profl. jours. Served to capt. USAF, 1957-60. Decorated knight Order St. John of Jerusalem, Knights of Malta, knight and minister of justice Order of New Aragon, Sungrye medal Korea; recipient Nat. Leadership medal Air Force Assn., 1956, Coll. award Am. Legion, Outstanding Sr. award U. S.C., 1956, hon. consul Republic of Korea, 1972—. Mem. Atlanta Bar Assn., ABA, S.C. Bar Assn., Ga. Bar Assn., Lawyers Club Atlanta, Am. Judicature Soc., Am. Soc. Internat. Law, Atlanta C. of C., Ga. C. of C. (exec. com. Internat. Councils), Inst. Internat. Edn. (chmn. Southeastern regional adv. bd. 1974—, nat. trustee), So. Consortium Internat. Edn. Inc. (dir.), Wig & Robe, Sigma Chi (pres. 1956 Province Balfour award), Omicron Delta Kappa, Kappa Sigma Kappa, Phi Delta Phi (pres. 1963 Province Grad. of Yr. award).

CLARK, DUNCAN WILLIAM, physician, educator; b. N.Y.C., Aug. 31, 1910; s. William H. and Lillian (Keating) C.; m. Carol Dooley, Jan. 30, 1943 (dec. 1971); children: Carol Ann, Duncan William, James Fenton (dec.).; m. Ida O'Grady, June 10, 1972. A.B., Fordham U., 1932. Diplomate: Am. Bd. Internal Medicine, Am. Bd. Preventive Medicine. Intern Bklyn. Hosp., 1936-38; resident in medicine coll. div. Kings County (N.Y.) Hosp., 1938-40; fellow in medicine Yale U., 1940-41; dir. student health L.I. Coll. Medicine, 1941-49, dean, 1948-50, asst. prof. medicine, 1948-50; prof., chmn. dept. environ. medicine and community health State U. Coll. Medicine at N.Y.C., 1951-78, prof. preventive medicine, 1978-82, prof. emeritus, 1982—; cons. USPHS, 1961-81; cons. NIH, 1961-65, NRC, 1965-68; chmn. health services research tng. com. USPHS, 1965-69, mem. health services research study sect., 1961-65, 73-77; WHO traveling fellow, 1952; vis. prof. Med. Sch., U. Birmingham, Eng., 1961. Co-editor, co-author: Textbook of Preventive Medicine, 1967, 2d edit., 1981; Contbr. articles on med. edn., pub. health and medicine. Bd. dirs. Health Ins. Plan of N.Y.C., 1953-71; chmn. N.Y. Study Com. Research Accident Prevention in Children, 1958-60, Assn. Aid Crippled Children; Bd. dirs. Health Systems Agy., N.Y.C., 1980—, Kings County Health Care Rev. Orgn., 1980-84; mem. Gov.'s Adv. Council on AIDS to N.Y. State Health Dept., 1984—; chmn. Nat. Adv. Com. on Local Health Depts., 1960-61; mem. N.Y. State Commn. on Grad. Med. Edn., 1985; mem. distbn. com. N.Y. Community Trust, 1983-85. Recipient Fordham Alumni award, 1958, Fordham Coll. Encaenia award, 1962; Frank L. Babbott award Downstate Med. Center Alumni Assn., 1974; 1st Duncan W. Clark award Assn. Tchrs. Preventive Medicine, 1974; medallion for disting. service to Am. medicine SUNY Coll. at N.Y.C., 1982. Fellow Am. Pub. Health Assn., N.Y. Acad. Medicine (trustee 1975, 85—, v.p. 1976-78, council 1979—, pres. 1983-84, Disting. Service plaque 1986), ACP, Am. Coll. Preventive Medicine; mem. N.Y. Pub. Health Assn. (bd. dirs. 1951-55, 86-88, pres. 1954-55), Conf. Profs. Preventive Medicine (chmn. 1953-54), Assn. Tchrs. Preventive Medicine (pres. 1954-56, editor Newsletter 1959-70), Com. to Protect Our Children's Teeth (pres. 1957-60), AAAS, Am. Arbitration Assn., AMA (alt. del. 1983—), N.Y. State Med. Soc. (del. 1978—), Kings County Med. Soc. (chmn. community medicine com. 1975-83, pres. 1983-84, trustee 1978—, v.p. 1981-82), Harvey Soc., N.Y. Acad. Sci., Internat. Epidemiological Assn., Alpha Omega Alpha (faculty councillor 1948-76). Roman Catholic. Home: 35 Prospect Park W Brooklyn NY 11215 Office: 450 Clarkson Ave Brooklyn NY 11203

CLARK, EDGAR SANDERFORD, insurance broker, consultant; b. N.Y.C., Nov. 17, 1933; s. Edgar Edmund, Jr., and Katharine Lee (Jarman) C.; student U. Pa., 1952-54; B.S., Georgetown U., 1956, J.D., 1958; postgrad. INSEAD, Fountainbleau, France, 1969, Golden Gate Coll., 1973, U. Calif., Berkeley, 1974; m. Nancy E. Hill, Sept. 13, 1975; 1 dau., Schuyler; children by previous marriages—Colin, Alexandra, Pamela. Staff asst. U.S. Senate select com. to investigate improper activities in labor and mgmt. field, Washington, 1958-59; underwriter Ocean Marine Dept., Fireman's Fund Ins. Co., San Francisco, 1959-62; mgr. Am. Fgn. Ins. Assn., San Francisco, 1962-66; with Marsh & McLennan, 1966-72, mgr. for Europe, resident dir. Brussels, Belgium, 1966-70, asst. v.p., mgr. captive and internat. div., San Francisco, 1970-72; v.p., dir. Risk Planning Group, Inc., San Francisco, 1972-75; v.p. Alexander & Alexander Inc., San Francisco, 1975—; lectr. profl. orgns.; guest lectr. U. Calif., Berkeley, 1973, Am. Grad. Sch. Internat. Mgmt., 1981, 82. Served with USAF, 1956-58. Mem. Am. Mgmt. Assn., Am. Risk and Ins. Assn., Chartered Ins. Inst., Am. Soc. Internat. Law, Pub. Risk & Ins. Mgmt. Assn., Nat. League of Cities, Nat. Inst. Mcpl. Law Officers, Govt. Fin. Officers Assn., Internat. City Mgrs. Assn. Episcopalian. Clubs: Meadow (Fairfax, Calif.); World Trade (San Francisco). Editorial adv. bd. Risk Mgmt. Reports, 1973-76. Home: 72 Millay Pl Mill Valley CA 94941 Office: Alexander & Alexander Inc Suite 1280 Two Embarcadero Ctr San Francisco CA 94111

CLARK, ELLERY HARDING, JR., historian, educator; b. Cohasset, Mass., Aug. 6, 1909; s. Ellery Harding and Victoria Mary (Maddalena) C.; A.B. cum laude in English, Harvard U., 1933; A.M. in History, Boston U., 1950; m. Grace Marion Gelinas, Oct. 24, 1934; children—Grace Victoria, William Ellery, Susan Elizabeth. Commd. ensign U.S. Navy, 1933, advanced through grades to capt., 1957; ret., 1964; mem. sec. navy's com. on reorgn. Navy, 1945-46; from asst. prof. to prof. dept. history U.S. Naval Acad., Annapolis, Md., 1946-78, head coach cross country and track teams, 1946-78. Bd. dirs. World Series Room, Northeastern U., Boston; trustee Boston Sports Mus. Inc.; mem., contbr. Cohasset Hist. Soc.; mem. Bo Sox Club; active numerous charity drives; treas. Annapolis Civic Ballet Co., Inc. Decorated Navy Commendation with Combat V, numerous others. Mem. U.S. Naval Inst., N.Am. Soc. Sport History, Soc. Am. Baseball Research (Salute award 1984), Cohasset Hist. Soc., Charitable Irish Soc. Boston, SAR Democrat. Episcopalian. Club: Army and Navy (Washington). Author: Boston Red Sox, 1975; Red Sox Forever, 1977; Red Sox Fever, 1979; (with others) Sea Power, 2d edit., 1981; author on Am. antique working duck decoys; advisor film on 1st Am. Olympic team, 1896. Contbr. to Scribner's Dictionary of American History, Collier's Ency., Brassey's Ann. (London), Jour. United Services Inst. Def. Studies (London); founder, contbr. Ann. Rev., U.S. Naval Inst.; contbr. Biographical Dictionary of American Sport, Boston Red Sox Scorebook, 1985, 86, Yankee mag., 1988, The Baseball Encyclopedia. Home: 25 Franklin St Annapolis MD 21401 also: 262 Jerusalem Rd Cohasset MA 02025 Office: USN Acad Dept History Annapolis MD 21402

CLARK, FRANK RINKER, JR., retired pipe line executive; b. Washington, May 4, 1912; s. Frank Rinker and Theresa Louise (Burton) C.; m. Evelyn Crews, June 27, 1943 (dec. July 1972); children: Theresa Lynn, Frank Robert; m. Annelle Macon Beaty, June 3, 1973. Student, Northwestern U., 1930-33, U. Tulsa, 1933-35, Harvard Law Sch., 1935-36, U. Okla. Law Sch., 1936-38, U. Tulsa, 1939-42, 45-47. Bar: Okla. 1938, U.S. Supreme Ct. 1938. Claims adjuster Travelers Ins. Co., 1938; trainee Helmerich & Payne, Tulsa, 1938-39; law clk. Settle, Monnet & Clammer, Tulsa, 1939-42; prodn. planning Douglas Aircraft Co., 1942-45; tax acct. Exxon Pipeline Co. (formerly Interstate Oil Pipe Line, later Humble Pipe Line Co.), 1945-50, tax atty., 1950-63, sec., 1955-77, treas., 1958-61, 63-77; past treas. Dixie Pipeline Co., 1966-76, sec., 1972-76. Mem. Am., Okla. bar assns., Am. Soc. Corp. Secs., Houston Soc. Fin. Analysts, Sigma Chi. Republican. Presbyterian (elder). Club: East Ridge Country (Shreveport, La.). Home: 125 Harpeth Trace Dr Nashville TN 37221

CLARK, FRANKLIN JACOB, JR., architect; b. Anderson, S.C., Dec. 7, 1937; s. Franklin Jacob and Corrie Elizabeth (Watson) C.; m. Beverly Thornton Bowie, Nov. 19, 1960; 1 child, Franklin Jacob. BArch, Clemson U., 1962. Registered architect, S.C., Ga., N.C., Tenn.; cert. Nat. Council Archtl. Registration Bds. Designer, A.G. Odell, Jr. & Assocs., 1966, Ledbetter & Earle Architects, 1966-67; dir., assoc. architect, v.p. Odell Assos., Inc., Charlotte, N.C., 1967-73; co-founder, pres., dir. Clark Tribble Harris & Li, Architects, Charlotte, 1973-78; pres., chmn. bd. FJ Clark Inc., Anderson, 1977—; bd. dirs. Anderson Heritage, Inc., 1986—; gen. ptnr. Group Three and Group Four Ltd. Partnerships, 1985—; assoc. prof. Clemson U. Coll. Architecture, 1984. Works include Cedar Forest Racquet Club, Charlotte, N.C. State Govt. Office Bldg., Raleigh, Mecklenburg County Parking Facility, Charlotte, U. N.C. Phys. Plant Bldg., Charlotte, New Prospect Sch., Anderson, Clemson U. Bookstore. Vice chmn. Anderson Devel. Corp., 1983-84, chmn., 1985. Served to lt. USAF, 1962-66. Recipient design honor awards. Mem. AIA Anderson C. of C. Presbyterian. Clubs: Charlotte City, Anderson Country, Cobb's Glen Country. Home:

1004 E Calhoun St Anderson SC 29621 Office: 201 S Murray Ave Anderson SC 29624

CLARK, FREDRIC HALLIE, electrical engineer; b. Marmaduke, Ark., Mar. 30, 1944; s. Clines Ben and Bernice Arneda C.; student Ark. State U., 1962-64; m. Judith Rayanna Hill, June 5, 1966 (div. 1981); children—Kimberly Ann, Sheri Lyn. B.S.E.E., U. Ark., Fayetteville, 1967; M.S.E.E., U. Ala., Huntsville, 1970, Ph.D. in E.E., 1980. Analyst guidance and control Saturn-Apollo program IBM, Huntsville, 1967-71, charge design, devel. and verification control laws Skylab program, 1971-72, mgr. Systems Engring. group IBM, 1972-79; owner, mgr. CAS, Inc., Huntsville, 1979—. Mem. IEEE, Assn. U.S. Army, Am. Def. Preparedness Assn., Assn. Old Crows (past pres.), Eta Kappa Nu, Tau Beta Pi. Methodist. Home: 3454 Charity Ln Toney AL 35773 Office: 555 Sparkman Dr Suite 1022 Huntsville AL 35805

CLARK, HALLIDAY, marketing company executive; b. Bklyn., May 15, 1918; s. David Hatfield and Elizabeth C.H. (Halliday) C.; m. Hazel J. Frost, June 28, 1941; children—Halliday Clark, Jr., Elizabeth F. Kubie, Deborah G. Reinhart. Student NYU, 1938-41; LL.B., LaSalle Law Sch., Chgo., 1966; M.B.A., Calif. Coast U., Santa Ana, 1982, Ph.D., 1983. Assoc. editor Variety Store Merchandiser Publs., N.Y.C., 1945-48; nat. accounts mgr. Best Foods Inc., N.Y.C., 1948-55; gen. sales mgr. Yale & Towne Mfg. Co., White Plains, N.Y., 1955-63; gen. mgr. Towne Hardware div., N.Y.C., 1963-68; v.p. sales Arrow Fastener Corp., Saddle Brook, N.J., 1968-72; pres., chmn. What to Do County Publs., Chappaqua, N.Y., 1972-78; pres. Halliday Clark & Assoc., Chadds Ford, Penn., 1978—; pres., dir. Westchester Sales Execs., White Plains, N.Y., 1955-57; v.p. Sales, Mktg. Execs. Internat., N.Y.C., 1964-67; chmn. bd. UCP of Westchester, Harrison, N.Y., 1965-74. Author, publisher: What to do in Connecticut, 1973; What to do on Long Island, 1975; What to do in New Jersey, 1976. Pres. bd. visitors Wassaic Devel. Ctr. (N.Y.), 1966-78; mem. U.S. Olympic Adv. Com., 1967-68. Served as capt. USAF, 1942-45, ETO. Recipient Civic Virtue award, UCP of Westchester, 1964. Republican. Episcopalian (lic. lay reader).

CLARK, HARRY EDGAR, pharmacist; b. Canton, N.Y., Apr. 12, 1925; s. Harold Safford and Edgarita (Blankman) C.; B.S., Union U., 1949. Pharmacist, Brooks Pharmacy, Ithaca, N.Y., 1949-51; partner, pharmacist Clark Pharmacy, Waverly, N.Y., 1951-71, owner, sr. pharmacist, 1971—; staff pharmacist VA Outpatient Clinic, Sayre, Pa., 1984—. Bd. dirs. Tioga County unit Am. Cancer Soc., 1970—, pres., 1973-74. Served with USNR, 1943-46. Am. Cancer Soc. fellow, Strong Meml. Hosp., Rochester, N.Y., 1980. Mem. Nat. Assn. Retail Druggists, Am. Pharm. Assn., N.Y. State Pharm. Soc., Acad. Gen. Practice, Am. Legion, VFW. Mem. Ch. of Jesus Christ of Latter-day Saints. Clubs: Masons (32 deg.), Rotary (dir. 1963-79, pres. 1967-68, sec. 1964-79). Home: 444 Clark St Waverly NY 14892 Office: 330 Broad St Waverly NY 14892

CLARK, SIR JOHN A., British diversified business executive; b. Feb. 14, 1926; s. Sir Allen and Lady Jocelyn (Culverhouse) Clark; m. Deidre Waterhouse, 1952 (div. 1962); 2 children; m. Olivia Pratt, 1970; 3 children. Ed. Harrow and Cambridge. Royal Naval vol. Res., Second World War; formerly with Met. Vickers and Ford Motor Co.; asst. to gen. mgr. Plessey Internat. Ltd., 1949; dir., gen. mgr. Plessey (Ireland) Ltd. and Wireless Telephone Co. Ltd., 1950; mem. bd. dirs. Plessey Co. Ltd., 1953—, gen. mgr. Components Group, 1957, mng. dir. and chief exec., 1962-70, dep. chmn., 1967-70, chmn. and chief exec., 1970—; dir. ICL Ltd., 1968-79, Banque Nationale de Paris, 1976—; pres. Telecommunication Engring. and Mfg. Assn., 1964-66, 72-74; v.p. Inst. of Works Mgrs., Engring. Employers Fedn.; mem. council and pres.'s com. CBI Nat. Def. Industries Council; past mem. Rev. Body on Top Salaries. Fellow Inst. Mgrs. Companion IEE; Order of Henry the Navigator, Portugal, 1973. Avocations: shooting; swimming; riding. Address: The Plessey Co PLC, Millbank Tower, London SW1P 4QP, England *

CLARK, JOYCE NAOMI JOHNSON, nurse; b. Corpus Christi, Oct. 4, 1936; d. Chester Fletcher and Ermal Olita (Bailey) Johnson; m. William Boyd Clark, Jan. 4, 1958; (div. 1967); 1 child, Sherene Joyce. Student, Corpus Christi State U., 1975-77. RN; cert. instrument flight instr. Staff nurse Van Nuys (Calif.) Community Hosp., 1963-64, U.S. Naval Hosp., Corpus Christi, 1964-68, asst. clin. mgr. surgery Meml. Med. Ctr., Corpus Christi, 1968—. Leader Paisano Council Girl Scouts U.S.A., Corpus Christi, 1968-74. Recipient Charles A. Mella award Meml. Med. Ctr., 1981, Paul E. Garber award CAP, 1986, cert. of appreciation in recognition of Support Child Guard Missing Children Edn. Program Nat. Assn. Chiefs of Police, Washington, 1987, Grover Loenig Aerospace award, 1986, Cert. of World Leadership Internat. Biographical Ctr., Cambridge, Eng., 1987. Mem. Am. Assn. Operating Room Nurses (v.p. 1969), Aircraft Owners and Pilots Assn., USAF Aux. CAP Air Search and Rescue (past comdr. 3d group, wing chief pilot, Sr. Mem. of Yr. 1985), Am. Fed. Police, Smithsonian Instn. Avocation: flying. Home: 1001 Carmel Pkwy #15 Corpus Christi TX 78411 Office: Meml Med Ctr Operating Room 4606 Hospital Blvd Corpus Christi TX 78405

CLARK, MELVIN EUGENE, chemical company executive; b. Ord, Nebr., Oct. 2, 1916; s. Ansel B. and Ruth Joy (Bullock) C.; m. Virginia May Hiller, Sept. 16, 1938; children—John Robert, Walter Clayton, Dale Eugene, Merry Sue. B.S. in Chem. Engring. cum laude, U. Colo., 1937; grad. exec. program, Columbia U., 1952; grad., Advanced Mgmt. Program Harvard U., 1961. Asst. editor Chem. Engring., McGraw-Hill, N.Y.C., 1937-41; mktg. staff Wyandotte Chem. Corp., Mich., 1941-53; chief program br. War Prodn. Bd., Washington, 1942-44; v.p. mktg. Frontier Chem. Co., Wichita, 1953-69; exec. v.p. chems. div. Vulcan Materials Co., Birmingham, Ala., 1969-81; v.p. planning, chems. and metals group Vulcan Materials Co., 1981-82; cons. 1982—; pres. Chlorine Inst., 1977-80. Contbr. numerous articles to profl. jours. Recipient U. Colo. Alumni Recognition award, 1962; named Chem. Market Research Assn. Man of Year, 1963; Disting. Engring. Alumnus, U. Colo., 1985. Mem. Am. Inst. Chem. Engrs., Chem. Mktg. Research Assn., Am. Chem. Soc., Tau Beta Pi, Pi Mu Epsilon. Republican. Mem. Christian Disciples. Clubs: Inverness Country (Birmingham), Relay House (Birmingham), Shoal Creek Country (Birmingham). Home: 3200 Kiltie Ln Birmingham AL 35242 Office: PO Box 7497 Birmingham AL 35253

CLARK, MONTAGUE GRAHAM, JR., former college president; b. Charlotte, N.C., Feb. 25, 1909; s. Montague G. and Alice C. (Graham) C.; m. Elizabeth Hoyt, May 2, 1933; children: Elizabeth (Mrs. Joe Embser), Alice (Mrs. Harold Davis), Margaret (Mrs. William Miller), Julia (Mrs. Cecil Hampton). Student, Ga. Tech. Sch. Engring.; LL.D., Drury Coll., 1957; Ed.D., S.W. Bapt. Coll., 1972; Litt.D., Sch. of the Ozarks, 1975, D.Sc., 1986; D.D., Mo. Valley Coll., 1977; DSc, Sch. Ozarks, 1986. Ordained to ministry Presbyn. Ch., 1950. V.p. W.R. Hoyt & Co., Atlanta, 1934-46; v.p. Sch. of Ozarks, Point Lookout, Mo., 1946-52, pres., 1952-81, sec. bd. trustees, 1957-71, pres. emeritus, chmn. bd. emeritus, 1981—; past dir. Bank of Taney County.; Past mem. Commn. on Colls. and Univs., North Central Assn. Colls. and Secondary Schs.; former moderator Lafayette Presbetery and Synod of Mo., Presbyn. Ch. of U.S.; Past mem. nat. adv. council on health professions edn. NIH; dir. Empire Gas Corp. Mem. Nat. council Boy Scouts Am., Mo. Com. on Pub. Schs., Thomas Hart Benton Nat. Com. for Exhibition; also mem. adv. bd. Ozarks Empire Area council; mem. Wilson's Creek Battlefield Nat. Commn., 1961—; mem. bd., exec. com., sec. Blue Cross; hon. mem. Mo. Am. Revolution Bicentennial Commn.; former v.p., dir. Am. Heart Assn., mem. exec. com., chmn. fund raising adv. and policy com., Gt. Plains regional chmn.; chmn. Mo. Heart Fund; past chmn. bd. Mo. Heart Assn.; mem. adv. council Council on Am. Affairs.; founding pres. of Sch. of Ozarks; mem. security panel Aircraft War Prodn. Council, N.Y., Mo. Com. Pub. Schs., Thomas Hart Benton Nat. Com. for Exhibition, Grand Cross; v.p., vice chmn. Thomas Hart Benton Homestead Meml. Commn.; bd. dirs. St. Louis Scottish Towers Residence Found.; chmn. burns prevention com. Shrine of N.Am.; hon. chmn. So. Mo. div. Am. Cancer Soc.; pres. Youth Council Atlanta; mem. exec. com. Atlanta Christian Council; mem. Park and Recreation Commn. Fulton County; chmn. planned giving and legacies Mo. div. Am. Cancer Soc., hon. edn. chmn. So. Mo. div., chmn. planned giving and legacy Mo. div.; bd. trustees Patriotic Edn., Inc. Served to maj. Internal Security, World War II. Named Ark. traveler, 1962; recipient Silver Beaver award Boy Scouts Am., Gold Heart award Am. Heart Assn., George Washington certificate Freedoms Found., 1974, 78, In God We Trust award Family Found., Red Cross of Constantine York Rite, Disting . Service award Am. Legion Dept. of Mo., numerous other awards; named to Ozark Hall of Fame. Mem. Royal Order Scotland; Mem. S.A.R. (past pres. gen. nat. soc., hon. v.p. Mo. Soc., patriotic com., Nat. Soc. Good Citizenship medal, Patriot medal, Minute Man award, Va. Soc. medal), Acad. Mo. Squires, Navy League U.S., Mo. C. of C., Assn. Grand Jurors of Fulton County, Atlanta Sunday Sch. Supts. Assn. (pres., treas.), Mo. Pilots Assn. (1st chmn. bd.), Civil Air Patrol (dir. adv. bd.), White River Valley Hist. Soc. (past pres.), Soc. Colonial Wars, Order Founders and Patriots Am., Air Force Assn., Assn. U.S. Army, Mo. Assn. State Troopers Emergency Relief Soc., Internat. Assn. Chiefs of Police, Nat. Gavel Soc., Red Cross Constantine, Patriotic Edn., Inc. Clubs: Masons (33 deg., awards, grand chaplain 1980-81, chmn. Americanism Com., others), Shriners (past imperial chaplain, others, Civic Service award), K.T, Rotary (past local pres., dist. gov. 1966-67), DeMolay, Imperial Council, Nobles of Mystic Shrine of N.A. Office: Sch of the Ozarks Point Lookout MO 65726

CLARK, PAUL, airline analyst; b. London, Mar. 16, 1954; arrived in France, 1984; m. Judith Ann Holt, July 15, 1978. MSc, Poly. Inst. Cen. London, 1983. Various positions Brit. Railways Bd., London, 1972-84; sr. airline analyst Airbus Industrie, Toulouse, France, 1984—. Author: Railways of Devil's Dyke, 1976, Chichester and Midhurst Railway, 1980; producer film Devil's Dyke-A Victorian Pastime, 1980. Mem. Chartered Inst. Transport. Home: Bellis, Beaupuy, 82600 Verdun sur Garonne France Office: Airbus Industrie, 31700 Blagnac France

CLARK, RICHARD LEFORS, systems research scientist; b. Aberdeen, S.D., Oct. 29, 1936; s. Robert Montgomery and Marion (Shook) C.; m. Barbara Louise Battersby, Mar. 28, 1980; 1 child, Robert James. BA, Pacific Western U., 1974, MS, 1975, PhD, 1978; BS in Engring. and Applied Sci., Jackson State Coll., 1968, MA in Bus. Mgmt., 1972. Technician Honeywell Co., 1957-58; quality assurance Martin Co., 1958-59, Remington Rand, 1959; engr. Gen. Dynamics/Electronics, 1959-68; supr. Graco, Inc., 1971-74; with Internat. Harvester, 1975-81, Caterpiller Tractor Co., 1981—, Solar Turbines subs. Caterpiller Tractor Co.; systems research in fusion power, parapsychology and physics, over unity elec. generators, archeol. research and gravity research, San Diego, 1975—; lectr. gravity/Maxwell-Faraday physics systems and devices. Inventor vortex fusion engine; author tech. papers. Served with U.S. Army, 1954-57.

CLARK, SIR ROBERT (ANTHONY), financial services company executive; b. Jan. 6, 1924; s. John and Gladys (Dyer) C.; m. Andolyn Marjorie Lewis, 1949; 3 children. Student, U. Cambridge. Ptnr. Slaughter and May, Solicitors, Eng., 1953; dir. Alfred McAlpine plc, 1957—; with Hill Samuel and Co. Ltd., 1961—, chmn., 1974-87; chief exec. Hill Samuel Group, 1976-80, chmn., 1980—; bd. dirs. Rover, Shell Transport and Trading Co. plc, Eagle Star Holdings Ltd.; chmn. Indsl. Devel. Adv. Bd., 1973-80, Rev. Body on Doctors' and Dentists' Remuneration, 1979-86. Mem. council Charing Cross and Westminster Med. Sch., 1982—; bd. dirs. ENO, 1983—. Served with Royal Navy, World War II. Decorated Knight, 1976. Home: Munstead Wood, Godalming, Surrey England Office: Hill Samuel and Co Ltd, 100 Wood St, London EC1P 2AJ, England *

CLARK, ROBERT HENRY, JR., construction equipment executive; b. Springfield, Mass., July 31, 1955; s. Robert Henry and Elizabeth (Reed) C.; m. Ann Marie Kalagher, May 21, 1977; children: Robert Henry III, Kathryn Ann. BS, St. Anselm's Coll., 1977; cert. in criminal justice, Police Acad., Holyoke, Mass., 1977; postgrad., Western New Eng. Coll., 1979-80. Patrolman Police Dept., West Springfield, Mass., 1976-77; salesman Tri-County Contractors Supply, Inc., West Springfield, 1977-80, v.p. sales, 1980-83, exec. v.p., 1983—, sec., 1984; bd. dirs. Equip-Lease, Inc., Tri-R Mcpl. Equipment, Inc. Fin. com. mem. Our Lady of the Lake Ch., Southwick, Mass., 1981-82; chmn. Southwick Park and Recreation Com., 1982; mem. Southwick Bd. Appeals, 1986—; mem. Lower Pioneer Valley Planning Com., West Springfield, 1982; coach and dir. Southwick Recreation Ctr., 1983—; chmn. Southwick Beach Commn., 1985—. Mem. Am. Pub. Works Assn., Nat. Truck Equipment Assn., Conn. Assn. Street and Hwy. Officials, Associated Equipment Distbrs., New Eng. Equipment Distbrs. Assn., St. Anselm's Alumni Assn. Roman Catholic. Clubs: Springfield Country (West Springfield), European Health (Agawam, Mass.); St. Anselm's Varsity. Office: Tri-County Contractors Supply 154-81 Wayside Ave West Springfield MA 01089

CLARK, R(UFUS) BRADBURY, lawyer; b. Des Moines, May 11, 1924; s. Rufus Bradbury and Gertrude Martha (Burns) C.; m. Polly Ann King, Sept. 6, 1949; children: Cynthia Clark Maxwell, Rufus Bradbury, John Atherton. BA, Harvard U., 1948, JD, 1951; diploma in law, Oxford U., Eng., 1952; D.H.L., Ch. Div. Sch. Pacific, San Francisco, 1983. Bar: Calif. Assoc. firm O'Melveny & Myers, Los Angeles, 1952-62, sr. ptnr., 1961—, mem. mgmt. com., 1983—; dir. So. Calif. Water Co., Econ. Resources Corp., Brown Internat. Corp., Automatic Machinery & Electronics Corp., John Tracy Clinic, also pres. 1982-88. Editor: California Corporation Laws, 6 vols, 1976—. Chancellor Prot. Episcopal Ch. in the Diocese of Los Angeles, 1967—, hon. canon, 1983—. Served to capt. U.S. Army, 1943-46. Decorated Bronze star with oak leaf cluster; decorated Purple Heart with oak leaf cluster; Fulbright grantee, 1952. Mem. ABA (subcom. on audit letter responses, com. on law and acctg., task force on legal opinion), State Bar Calif. (chmn. drafting com. on gen. corp. law 1973-81, chmn. drafting com. on nonprofit corp. law 1980-84, mem. exec. com. bus. law sect., 1977-78, 84-87, sec. 1986-87), Los Angeles County Bar Assn. Republican. Clubs: California (Los Angeles), Harvard (Los Angeles), Chancery (Los Angeles); Alamitos Bay Yacht (Long Beach). Office: O'Melveny & Myers 400 S Hope St Los Angeles CA 90071-2899

CLARK, STEPHEN PETER, insurance company executive; b. Bremerton, Wash., May 22, 1943; s. Gerald Robert and Ruth M. (Barth) C.; B.C.S., Seattle U., 1967; postgrad. Atlanta Law Sch., 1979-82; m. Evelyn Ann Wilson, Dec. 17, 1966; children—Jennifer D., Peter Haynes, Merydith Hamilton. Acct., Arthur Andersen & Co., C.P.A.s, 1967-69; controller No. Life Ins. Co., 1969-73; asst. to trustee in bankruptcy Equity Fund Corp. Am., Los Angeles, 1973-74; v.p., treas. Sun Life Group of Am., Inc., Atlanta, 1974-82; exec. v.p., chief operating officer Blue Cross of Wash. and Alaska, Seattle, 1982-83; pres. States West Life Ins. Co., 1983—; pres. N.C.A.S. Northwest, Inc., 1986—; founder, chmn. Southeastern Ins. Tax Forum; dir. HealthPlus, States West Life. Trustee Paideia Sch., Atlanta, 1982; mem. adv. council Ga. State U. Sch. Accountancy; mem. Wash. Gov.-Elect Transition Team, 1985. C.P.A., Wash. Mem. Am. Inst. C.P.A.s, Wash. Soc. C.P.A.s, Ga. Soc. C.P.A.s. Clubs: Sand Point Country; Wash. Athletic. Home: 5824 Vassar Ave NE Seattle WA 98105 Office: Blue Cross of Wash and Alaska 15700 Dayton Ave N Seattle WA 98111

CLARK, WARREN, diplomat; b. Bronxville, N.Y., Nov. 7, 1936; Three children. BA, Williams Coll., 1958; MA, Johns Hopkins U., 1964, Georgetown U., 1972; MPA, Harvard U. Joined Fgn. Service, 1963; vice consul U.S. Consulate in Aleppo, Syria, 1964-66; econ. officer U.S. Embassy in Luxembourg, 1966-68; economist Dept. of State, 1968-71, Libyan desk officer, 1974-76; Treasury rep. U.S. Embassy in Ottawa, Ont., Can., 1977-81; dep. rep. U.S. Econ. and Social Council United Nations, 1981-82; minister-counselor U.S. Mission to United Nations, 1982-85; econ. counselor U.S. Embassy in Lagos, Nigeria, 1985-86; dep. chief of mission Lagos, 1986-87; U.S. Ambassador to Gabon, Sao Tome, Principe 1987—. Served with USN, 1958-62. Office: Dept of State US Ambassador to Gabon Washington DC 20520 *

CLARKE, ARTHUR CHARLES, author; b. Dec. 16, 1917; s. Charles Wright and Norah (Willis) C.; m. Marilyn Mayfield, June 15, 1953 (div. 1964). B.Sc. with 1st class honors, King's Coll., London, 1948. Auditor Exchequer and Audit Dept., 1936-41; asst. editor Physics Abstracts, 1949-50; lectr., author 1951—; chancellor U. Moratuwa, Sri Lanka, 1979—; Vikram Sarabhai prof. Phys. Research Lab., Ahmedabad, 1980; engaged in underwater photography on Great Barrier Reef of Australia and coast of Ceylon, 1955—; numerous TV, radio appearances; fgn. assoc. Nat. Acad. Engring. (U.S.). Author: (non fiction) Interplanetary Flight, 1950; the Exploration of Space, 1951; Going Into Space, 1954; (with R.A. Smith) The Exploration of the Moon, 1955; The Coast of Coral, 1956; The Making of a Moon, 1957; The Reefs of Taprobane, 1957; Voice Across the Sea, 1958; The Challenge of the Spaceship, 1959; The Challenge of the Sea, 1960; (with Mike Wilson) The First Five Fathoms, 1960; Boy Beneath the Sea, 1958; Indian Ocean Adventure, 1961; The Treasure of the Great Reef, Indian Ocean Treasure, 1964; Profiles of the Future, 1962, rev. 1982; (with editors of Life mag.), Man and Space, 1964; Voices from the Sky, 1965, The Promise of Space, 1968; (with astronauts) First on the Moon, 1970; Report on Planet Three, 1972; (with Chesley Bonestell) Beyond Jupiter, 1973; The View from Serendip, 1977; 1984; Spring, 1984; Ascent to Orbit, 1984; (fiction) Islands in the Sky, 1952; Against the Fall of Night, 1953; The Sands of Mars, 1953; Childhood's End, 1953; Prelude to Space, 1954; Expedition to Earth, 1953; Earthlight, 1955; Reach for Tomorrow, 1956; The City and the Star, 1956; Tales from the White Hart, 1957; The Deep Range, 1957; The Other Side of the Sky, 1958; Across the Sea of Star, 1959; A Fall of Moondust, 1961; From the Ocean, From the Star, 1962; Tales of Ten Worlds, 1962; Dophin Island, 1962; Glide Path, 1963; Prelude to Mar, 1965; (with Stanley Kubrick) 2001: A Space Odyssey (novel and screenplay), 1968; The Nine Billion Names of God, 1967; The Wind from the Sun, 1972; Of Time and Stars, 1972; The Lost Worlds of 2001, 1972; Rendezvous with Rama, 1973; The Best of Arthur C. Clarke, 1973; Imperial Earth, 1975; The Fountains of Paradise, 1979; 2010-Odyssey Two, 1982; The Sentinel, 1983; The Songs of Distant Earth, 1987; 2061: Odyssey Three, 1987. Served to flight lt. RAF, 1941-46. Recipient Kalinga prize UNESCO, 1961; Stuart Ballantine medal Franklin Inst., 1963; nominee Acad. Motion Picture Arts and Scis. award, 1968; AAAS-Westinghouse Sci. Writing award, 1969; Nebula award, 1973, 74, 79; John Campbell Sci. Fiction award, 1974; Hugo award, 1974, 80; Galaxy award, 1979; Engring. award Nat. Acad. TV Arts and Scis., 1981; Centennial medal IEEE, 1984; fellow King's Coll., London, 1977; Marconi Internat. fellow, 1982; Bradford Washburn award, 1977, Charles A. Lindbergh award, 1987. Fellow Brit. Interplanetary Soc. (past chmn.), AIAA (hon.), Inst. Robotics of Carnegie-Mellon U., Instn. Engrs. Sri Lanka (hon.), Royal Sri. Lanka (pres. 1960—) Astrn. Soc., Internat. Acad. Astronautics, World Acad. Art and Sci., Nat. Space Inst. (dir.), Brit. Sci. Writers, Brit. Sub-Aqua Club, Brit. Astorn. Assn., H.G. Wells Soc. (hon. v.p.), Sci. Fiction Writers Am., Internat. Sci. Writers Assn., Sci. Fiction Found., Soc. Authors (council), Am. Astronautical Assn. Address: 25 Barnes Pl, Colombo 7, Sri Lanka also: care Scott Meredith 845 3d Ave New York NY 10022 *

CLARKE, CYRIL ASTLEY, physician, educator; b. Leicester, Eng., Aug. 22, 1907; s. Astley Vavasour and Ethel Mary (Gee) C.; student Caius Coll., Cambridge, 1926-29, M.D., 1937; Guys Hosp. Med. Sch., London, 1929-32, Sc.D., 1963 (hon.); D.Sc., U. Edinburgh, 1971, U. Leicester, 1971, U. East Anglia, 1973, U. Birmingham, 1974, U. Liverpool, 1974, U. Sussex, 1974, Hull U., 1977, U. Wales, 1978, U. London, 1980; m. Frieda Margaret Mary Hart, Dec. 27, 1935; children—Miles David Astley, John Stephen Astley, Charles Richard Astley. Jr. staff appointments Guy's Hosp., 1932-36; life ins. practice, London, 1936-39; med. registrar Queen Elizabeth Hosp., Birmingham, 1946; cons. physician United Liverpool Hosps. and Liverpool Regional Hosp. Bd., 1946-72; reader in medicine U. Liverpool, 1958-65, prof. medicine, 1965-72, dir. Nuffield Unit Med. Genetics, 1963-72, Nuffield research fellow dept. genetics, 1972—. Served with Royal Naval Vol. Res., 1939-45. Decorated comdr. Brit. Empire, Knight Brit. Empire; recipient Gold medal in therapeutics Worshipful Soc. Apothecaries, 1970; James Spence medal Brit. Pediatric Assn., 1973; John Scott award, Phila., 1976; Gairdner award, 1977; Artois Baillet Latour Health prize, Linnaean Gold medal in zoology, 1981; Gold medal Royal Soc. Medicine, 1985-86. Fellow Royal Soc., Royal Entomol. Soc. London, Royal Coll. Physicians London (pres. 1972-77, dir. med. services study group 1977-83, dir. research unit 1983-88); research fellow U. Liverpool, 1987—; recipient Lasker award, 1980. mem. Liverpool Med. Instn. (past pres.), British Soc. for Research on Ageing (chmn.), Oxford and Cambridge Sailing Soc. (pres. 1975). Clubs: Athenaeum; West Kirby Sailing; Royal Mersey Yacht. Author: Genetics for the Clinician, 1962; Selected Topics in Medical Genetics, 1970; Human Genetics and Medicine, 1987 (3rd edit.); Rhesus Hemolytic Disease, 1975. Contbr. articles profl. jours. Office: care Royal Soc, 6 Carlton House Tce, London SW1Y 5AG England

CLARKE, EDWARD OWEN, JR., lawyer; b. Balt., Dec. 19, 1929; s. Edward Owen and Agnes Oakford C.; m. P. Rhea Parker, Dec. 18, 1954; children—Deborah Jeanne, Catherine Ann, Carolyn Agnes, Edward Owen III. AB magna cum laude, Loyola Coll., Balt., 1950; LLB with honors, U. Md., 1956. Bar: Md. 1956, U.S. Dist. Ct. Md. 1956. Law clk. U.S. Dist. Ct. Md., 1956-57; assoc. Smith, Somerville & Case, Balt., 1957-62; ptnr. Smith, Somerville & Case, Balt., 1962-71; ptnr. Piper & Marbury, Balt., 1971—, mem. policy and mgmt. com. 1981—, mng. ptnr., 1987—; mem. Gov.'s Com. to Study Blue Sky Law, 1961; mem. Md. Commn. on Revision Corp. Law, 1965-66. Bd. dirs. Bon Secours Hosp., 1964-73, sec., 1968-73; bd. dirs. Hosp. Cost Analysis Service, 1966-81; bd. pres. mem. exec. council Md. Hosp. Assn., 1968-74, chmn. com. on legislation, 1971-73, treas., 1973; trustee St. Mary's Coll. Md., 1983—, chmn. bd. 1988—; trustee St. Mary's Sem., U. Balt., 1986—, Loyola High Sch., Balt., 1984—. Served with USNR, 1952-55. Mem. ABA, Md. State Bar Assn. (mem. sect. council corp., banking and bus. law sect. 1968-71, chmn. 1970-71), Balt. City Bar Assn., Alpha Sigma Nu, Tau Kappa Alpha, Order of Coif. Clubs: Wednesday Law (sec., treas. 1987-88), Center (Balt.). Office: 1100 Charles Ctr S 36 S Charles St Baltimore MD 21201

CLARKE, ELLIS EMMANUEL INNOCENT, former president Trinidad-Tobago; b. Trinidad, Dec. 28, 1917; s. Cecil E. and Elma D. (Pollard) C.; student St. Mary's Coll., Trinidad; LL.B., London U., 1940; m. Eyrmyntrude Hagley, June 28, 1952; children—Peter, Margaret-Ann. Barrister-at-law, 1940; pvt. practice law, Trinidad, 1941-54; solicitor-gen. Trinidad and Tobago, 1954-56; dep. colonial sec., 1956-57, also gov.'s dep.; atty. gen. Legal Dept., 1957-60; gov. Trinidad and Tobago, 1960-61; chief justice designate Trinidad and Tobago, 1961; constl. adviser Cabinet of Trinidad and Tobago, 1961-62; ambassador to U.S., permanent rep. to UN, 1962-66; ambassador to Mexico, 1966-73; ambassador to U.S., 1962-73; rep. to OAS, Washington, 1967-73; gov.-gen., comdr.-in-chief Trinidad and Tobago, 1973-76, pres., 1976-87. Created knight, 1963; decorated Trinity Cross, 1969; companion Order St. Michael and St. George, created knight grand cross, 1972; recipient Jerningham Silver medal, 1933, Book prize, 1954, Gold medal, 1936; hon. master of bench Gray's Inn, 1980. Roman Catholic. Clubs: Tobago Golf, Arima Race, Trinidad Turf, Queen's Park Cricket. Office: Office of Pres, Port of Spain Trinidad and Tobago *

CLARKE, GRAHAM THOMAS, mathematics educator, researcher; b. Melbourne, Victoria, Australia, Sept. 30, 1955; s. Edmond Henry and Josephine Mary (Emery) C.; B.A. with honors, Monash U., Victoria, Australia, 1977, Ph.D., 1982. Tutor Monash U., Victoria, 1981, Chisholm Inst. Tech., Victoria, 1982; asst. prof. U. Ark., Fayetteville, 1982-83; lectr. Swinburne Inst. Tech., Victoria, 1984-87; lectr. Royal Melbourne Inst. Tech., Victoria, 1987—. Contbg. author: Semigroups, 1980; also articles. Mem. Amnesty Internat., Melbourne, 1974—. Mem. Am. Math. Soc. Australian Labor Party. Roman Catholic. Avocation: music. Office: Royal Melbourne Inst Tech, Math Dept, Melbourne 3000, Australia

CLARKE, KENNETH (HARRY), government cabinet minister; b. Nottingham, England, July 2, 1940; s. Kenneth C.; m. Gillian Mary Edwards, 1964; 1 son, 1 dau. Student, Nottingham High Sch., England; BA, Gonville and Caius Coll.; LLB, Cambridge U. Bar: Nottingham 1963. Mem. Parliament Rushcliffe, Nottinghamshire, 1970—; parliamentary pvt. sec. Solicitor Gen., 1971-72; asst. govt. whip 1972-74; lord commnr. HM Treasury, 1974; mem. parliamentary del. to Council of Europe and WEU, 1973-74; opposition spokesman social services, 1974-76, industry, 1976-79; parliamentary under-sec. of state dept. of transport, 1979-82; minister of state health, 1982-85; paymaster gen. 1985-87, chancellor of the Duchy of Lancaster, 1987—, minister of trade and industry, 1987—. Author: New Hope for the Regions, 1979, The Free Market and the Inner Cities, 1987. Address: House of Commons, London SW1 England *

CLARKE, MICHAEL JOHN, sociology educator; b. London, July 13, 1945; s. Neville George Steele and Jean (Fleming) C.; children: Imogen, Cedric, Clive. BA with honors, U. E. Anglia, Norwich, Eng., 1967; MA in Econs., U. Manchester, Eng., 1969; PhD, U. Durham, Eng., 1972. Lectr. in sociology U. Birmingham (Eng.), 1971—. Author: Fallen Idols, 1981, Politics of Pop Festivals, 1982, Regulating the City, 1986; editor: Corruptido, 1983; contbr. over 20 articles to acad. jours. Home: 7 White House Rd,

Oxford OX1 4PA, England Office: U Birmingham, Dept Social Adminstrn, Birmingham B15 2TT, England

CLARKE, (JOHN) NEIL, financial company executive; b. Aug. 7, 1934; s. George Philip and Norah Marie (Bailey) C.; m. Sonia Heather Beckett, 1959; 3 sons. LLB, U. London. Ptnr. Rowley, Pemberton, Roberts and Co., Eng., 1960-69; ptnr. Charter Consolidated, 1969—, dep. chmn., chief exec., 1982—; chmn. Johnson Matthey, 1984—, Anderson Strathclyde, 1987—; bd. dirs. Consolidated Gold Fields, 1982—. Clubs: MCC, Royal West Norfolk Golf, Addington Golf. Office: High Willows, 18 Park Ave, Farnborough Park, Orpington, Kent BR6 8LL, England *

CLARKE, NEIL (JACKSON), SR., lawyer; b. Ava, Mo., Oct. 16, 1905; s. Joshua S. and Lucinda (Hayes) C.; m. Gertrude McCollom, May 10, 1961; children: Neil Jackson, Elizabeth Hall. Student, State Coll., Springfield, Mo., 1924-28, U. Mo., 1929-31. Bar: Mo. 1931, Calif. 1949. Prin. grade sch. Ava, 1926-27; city atty. Town of Ava, 1931-35, sole practice, 1931-40; referee Mo. Compensation Bd., Ava, 1940-43; assoc. Blackinton, Reid & Clarke, St. Louis, 1943-48; sole practice Pasadena, Calif., 1949—; atty. Ink Makers, Inc., Oriental Contractors, Inc., Welsh Printing Co., Inc., Tulleners Enterprises, Inc., Tie-Man, Inc., CCDM, Inc., Denny Sheet Metal, Inc., John L. Richardson Prodns., Inc., Bubble and Squeak, Inc., H.E. Witt Co., Inc., J.C. Naylor Co., Inc., Axco Ins. Assocs., Inc., Witcon Mgmt., Inc., Ahead With Houses, Inc.; adjuster Assoc. Indemnity, 1946-49. Mem. ABA, Mo. Bar Assn., Calif. Bar Assn., Pasadena Bar Assn., Delta Theta Phi. Republican. Presbyterian. Club: Los Angeles Lawyers. Home: 9148 S View Rd San Gabriel CA 91775 Office: 3820 E Colorado Blvd Suite 102 Pasadena CA 91107

CLARKE, OSCAR WITHERS, physician; b. Petersburg, Va., Jan. 29, 1919; s. Oscar Withers and Mary (Reese) C.; m. Susan Frances King, June 18, 1949; children—Susan Frances, Mary Elizabeth, Jennifer Ann. B.S., Randolph Macon Coll., 1941; M.D., Med. Coll. Va., 1944. Intern Boston City Hosp., 1944-45; resident internal medicine Med. Coll. Va., 1945-46, 48-49, fellow in cardiology, 1949-50; practice medicine specializing in internal medicine and cardiology Gallipolis Holzer Med. Ctr., Ohio, 1950—; dir. Ohio Valley Devel. Co., Gallipolis, Community Improvement Corp.; pres. Ohio State Med. Bd.; chmn. Ohio Med. Edn. and Research Found.; pres. Gallipolis City Bd. Health, 1955—, Gallia County Heart Council, 1955—. Contbr. articles to med. jours. Vice pres. Tri-State Regional council Boy Scouts Am., 1957; pres. Tri-State Community Concert Assn., 1957-59; trustee Med. Meml. Found., Holzer Hosp. Found. Served as capt. M.C., AUS, 1946-48, ETO. Recipient John Stewart Bryant pathology award Med. Coll. Va., 1943, Disting. Service award Ohio State Med. Assn., 1988. Fellow ACP, Royal Soc. Medicine; mem. Gallia County Med. Soc. (pres. 1953), AMA (council on ethical and jud. affairs), Am. Heart Assn., Central Ohio Heart Assn. (Merit medal 1960, trustee), Ohio Med. Assn. (pres. 1973-74), Am. Soc. Internal Medicine, Ohio Soc. Internal Medicine, Alpha Omega Alpha, Sigma Zeta, Chi Beta Phi. Presbyterian. Club: Rotary (pres. 1953-54). Home: Spruce Knoll Gallipolis OH 45631 Office: Box 344 Holzer Med Clinic Gallipolis OH 45631

CLARKE, RICHARD ALAN, lawyer, electric and gas utility company executive; b. San Francisco, May 18, 1930; s. Chauncey Frederick and Carolyn (Shannon) C.; m. Mary Dell Fisher, Feb. 5, 1955; children: Suzanne, Nancy C. Stephen, Douglas Alan. AB cum laude, U. Calif.-Berkeley, 1952, JD, 1955. Bar: Calif. 1955. Atty. Pacific Gas and Electric Co., San Francisco, 1955-60, 69, sr. counsel, 1970-74, asst. gen. counsel, 1974-79, v.p., asst. to chmn., 1979-82, exec. v.p., gen. mgr. utility ops., 1982-85, exec. v.p., pres., 1985-86, chmn. bd., chief exec. officer, 1986—; ptnr. Rockwell, Fulkerson and Clarke, San Rafael, Calif., 1960-69; bd. dirs. Potlach Corp. Trustee Com. for Econ. Devel; mem. exec. com. San Francisco Edn. Fund-Permanent Fund; active United Way of Bay Area, Campaign Cabinet, 1988; bd. dirs. Ind. Colls. No. Calif., San Francisco, 1980—, Invest-in-Am., 1986—, Bay Area Council. Mem. Calif. Bar Assn., Pacific Coast Elec. Assn., Pacific Coast Gas Assn., Edison Electric Inst. (bd. dirs. 1986—), Calif. Bus. Roundtable (bd. dirs. 1986—), Calif. C. of C. (bd. dirs. 1986—), San Francisco C. of C. (bd. dirs., econ. devel. v.p.). Clubs: Marin Tennis (San Rafael); Pacific Union (San Francisco). Office: Pacific Gas & Electric Co 77 Beale St San Francisco CA 94106

CLARKE, ROBERT EMMETT, writer, poet; b. Cleve., May 28, 1906; s. Robert Emmett and Mary Bernadette (Paquette) C. Student schs. Lakewood, Ohio. Reporter, Cleve. Times, 1925; asst. mgr. UP, Cleve., 1925-26; police reporter Canton Daily News (Ohio), 1926-27; courthouse and police reporter, asst. sports editor Akron Times-Press (Ohio), 1927-30; with Thompson Products, 1943-45, Erie R.R., 1945-46; hotel cashier, 1937-38; with Grant Photo Products, 1946-55. Author: polit. satire: Charley Horse, 1944, 4 line poetry: Rhyming Robert, 1966, Violets, Tulips, Rosebuds, Buttercups, 1971; works included in World of Poetry Anthology, 1984, Am. Poetry Anthology, Vol. III, No. 3-4, 1984, Ashes to Ashes, Vol. V, 1985, The Art of Poetry, 1985, The National Poetry Anthology, 1985, Masterpieces of Modern Verse, 1985, Our Wold's Most Beloved Poems, 1984, Our Western World's Most Beautiful Poems, 1985, Moods and Mysteries (Poetry Press vol. 3), Pauses in Time, 1986, American Poetry Anthology, 1986, 87, numerous editions of Am. Poetry Assn. and Poetry Press, 1986, Words of Praise Vol. II, 1986, Peace on Earth Poetry Anthology, 1986, World of Poetry--American Poetry Anthology, vol. 6, no. 1, 1986, Pleasant Journeys, 1986, Riders of the Rainbow, 1986, The New York Poetry Foundation Anthology, 1986, The World's Most Cherished Poems, 1986, Celebrations of Life, 1987, The Poet's Hand, 1987, Words of Praise III, 1987, American Poetry Anthology Vol. VI, No. 5 (Golden Poet award, 1986, 87), World of Poetry Anthology, 1986, numerous others. Precinct committeeman Democratic Party, Ohio, Cuyahoga County, 1944-48; candidate Ohio Senate Primary, 1944. Recipient Golden Poetry award World of Poetry, 1986. Roman Catholic. Home: 212 S 6th St Apt B Alhambra CA 91801

CLARKE, ROBERT FRANCIS, metallic ore processing research executive; b. Mpls., Mar. 20, 1915: s. Charles Patrick and Maurine Elizabeth (Clark) C.; B.S. with honors, U. Fla., 1948; M.S., U. Ariz., 1971; m. Charlotte Adele Radwill, July 24, 1966; children—Robert, Carol, David. Meteorologist, U.S. Weather Bur., 1940-42, 48-50, 52-55; supervisory electronics engr., chief navigation br. aviation dept. U.S. Army Electronics Proving Ground, 1956-58, nuclear physicist, chief scientist nuclear surveillance div., 1958-62; aerospace engr. NASA, Lewis Research Ctr., 1962-66; physicist Hughes Aircraft Co., 1966-68; instr. Math. Pima Community Coll., 1969-74, and San Juan campus N.Mex. State U., 1974-75; instr. math. Am. Internat. Sch., Kabul, Afghanistan, 1976-78; dir. Polaris Internat. Metals Corp., Tucson. Radiol. def. officer Fed. Emergency Mgmt. Agy., CAP. Trustee Rep. Presdl. Task Force; mem. mayor's com. Celebration of Bicentennial of Constn., 1987. Served with U.S. Army, 1942-46, USAF, 1950-52; res. ret. as col., 1975. Recipient nat. award for best articles in Officer Rev.; honor cert. for excellence in published works Freedoms Found. of Valley Forge; recipient Presdl. Medal of Merit. Sr. mem. IEEE (plasma physics and computer sects.), AIAA; mem. Am. Nuclear Soc. (fusion power and reactor physics sect.), Space Studies Inst., Internat. Platform Assn., Fusion Power Assocs., Soc. Photo-Optical Instrumentation Engrs., Am. Meteorol. Soc., Am. Optical Soc., Soc. Unmanned Vehicle Systems, Arctic Inst. N.Am., AAUP, Assn. Former Intelligence Officers, Am. Def. Preparedness Assn., Scientists and Engrs. for Secure Energy, N.Y. Acad. Scis., Ariz.-Nev. Acad. Scis., Navy League, Am. Legion, VFW, (pres. 1986, honor degree), AMVETS, Ret. Officers Assn. (pres. Tucsonchpt. 1986), U.S. Naval Inst., Assn. U.S. Army (chpt. pres. 1982-83), Air Force Assn., Mil. Order World Wars (chpt. commdr. 1987—), Am. Security Council, Vets. Affairs Tucson (com. chmn. 1986), Inst. Polit. Sci. Club: Army and Navy. Lodges: Odd Fellows, Kiwanis, Elks. Contbr. articles in aerospace and nat. def. to mags., jours. Home: 5846 E South Wilshire Dr Tucson AZ 85711 Office: 1745 E Factory Ave Tucson AZ 85719

CLARKE, URANA, musician, writer, educator; b. Wickliffe-on-the-Lake, Ohio, Sept. 8, 1902; d. Graham Warren and Grace Urana (Olsaver) C.; artists and tchrs. diploma Mannes Music Sch., N.Y.C., 1925; certificate Dalcroze Sch. Music, N.Y.C., 1950; student Pembroke Coll., Brown U.; B.S., Mont. State U., 1967, M.Applied Sci., 1970. Mem. faculty Mannes Music Sch., 1922-49, Dalcroze Sch. Music, 1949-54; adv. editor in music The Book of Knowledge, 1949-65; v.p., dir. Saugatuck Circle Housing Devel.; guest lectr. Hayden Planetarium, 1945; guest lectr., bd. dirs. Roger Williams Park Planetarium, Providence; radio show New Eng. Skies, Providence, 1961-64, Skies Over the Big Sky Country, Livingston, Mont., 1964-79, Birds of the Big Sky Country, 1972-79, Great Music of Religion, 1974-79; mem. adv. com. Nat. Rivers and Harbors Congress, 1947-58; instr. continuing edn. Mont. State U. Chmn., Park County chpt. ARC, co-chmn. county blood program, first aid instr. trainer, 1941—; instr. ARC cardio-pulmonary resuscitation, 1976—; mem. Mont. Commn. Nursing and Nursing Edn., 1974-76; mem. Park County Local Govt. Study Commn., 1974-76, chmn., 1984-86; mem. Greater Yellowstone Coalition. Mem. Am. Acad. Polit. Sci., Am. Musicol. Soc., Royal Astron. Soc. Can., Inst. Nav., Maria Mitchell Soc. Nantucket, N.Am. Yacht Racing Union, AAAS, Meteoritical Soc., Internat. Soc. Mus. Research, Skyscrapers (sec.-treas. 1960-63), Am. Guild Organists, Park County Wilderness Assn. (treas.), Trout Unlimited, Nature Conservancy, Big Sky Astron. Soc. (dir. 1965—), Sierra Club, Greater Yellowstone Coalition. Lutheran. Club: Cedar Point Yacht. Author: The Heavens are Telling (astronomy), 1951; Skies Over the Big Sky Country, 1965; also astron. news-letter, View It Yourself, weekly column Big Skies; contbr. to mags. on music, nav. and astronomy. Pub. Five Chorale Preludes for Organ, 1975; also elem. two-piano pieces. Inventor, builder of Clarke Adjustable Piano Stool. Address: Log-A-Rhythm 9th St Island Livingston MT 59047

CLARKSON, JULIAN DERIEUX, lawyer; b. Coral Gables, Fla., Mar. 12, 1929; s. Julian Livingston and Hazel (Lamar) C.; m. Joan Combs, Dec. 24, 1950, children—James L., Julian L., Joanna D., Melinda C.; m. 2d, Shirley Lazonby, Nov. 8, 1979; children—George Allen, Shirley Lamar. B.A., U. Fla., 1950, LL.B., 1955, J.D., 1967. Bar: Fla. 1955, U.S. Ct. Appeals (5th cir.) 1961, U.S. Supreme Ct. 1964, U.S. Ct. Appeals (11th cir.) 1981, D.C. 1983. Ptnr., Henderson, Franklin, Starnes & Holt, Ft. Myers, Fla., 1955-76; sole practice, Ft. Myers, 1976-77; ptnr. Holland & Knight, Ft. Myers, 1977-79, Tampa, 1979-82, Tallahassee, 1982—; lectr. in field. Chmn. Fla. Supreme Ct. Jud. Nominating Commn., 1976-78. Served to 1st lt. U.S. Army, 1950-53. Decorated Purple Heart, 1951; named Outstanding Grad. Province V Phi Delta Phi, 1955. Mem. Am. Coll. Trial Lawyers, Am. Law Inst., Fla. Blue Key, Order of Coif, Phi Beta Kappa. Democrat. Episcopalian. Author: Let No Man Put Asunder—Story of a Football Rivalry, 1968. Address: 821 Lake Ridge Rd Tallahassee FL 32312

CLARKSON, KENNETH WRIGHT, economics educator; b. Downey, Calif., June 30, 1942; s. William Wright and Constance (Patch) C.; m. Mary Jane Purdy, June 20, 1965; children: Steven Wright, Thomas David. A.B., Calif. State U., 1964; M.A., UCLA, 1966, Ph.D., 1971. Economist Office Mgmt. and Budget, Washington, 1971-72, assoc. dir., 1982-83; asst. prof. econs. U. Va., 1969-75; prof. econs. U. Miami, Coral Gables, Fla., 1975—, dir. Law & Econs. Ctr., 1981—; cons. in field; mem. Pres.'s Task Force on Food Assistance, 1983-84; mem. governing bd. Credit Research Ctr., Purdue U., 1981—; mem. research com. Fla. C. of C. Found., 1985—; mem. nat. adv. bd. Nat. Ctr. for Privatization, 1985—, Washington Legal Found., 1985—; mem. Fla. adv. com. U.S. Commn. Civil Rights, 1985—. Author: Food Stamps and Nutrition, 1975, Intangible Capital and Rates of Return, 1975; co-author: Correcting Taxes for Inflation, 1975, Distortions in Official Unemployment Statistics, 1979, Industrial Organization: Theory, Evidence and Public Policy, 1982, West's Business Law, 1980, 3d edit., 1986, The Federal Trade Commission Since 1970, 1981, Economics Sourcebook of Government Statistics, 1983, The Role of Privatization in Florida's Growth, 1987, Using Private Management to Foster Florida's Growth: Initial Steps, 1987, A Proposal for Medical Malpractice Insurance in Florida, 1987; contbr. numerous articles to profl. jours. Mem. Regan-Bush Transition Team, Washington, 1980; mem. econ. adv. panel Fla. State Comprehensive Plan Com., 1986—; bd. dirs. Econs. Inst. for Fed. Adminstrv. Law Judges, 1982—. NSF grantee, 1972-74; Heritage Found. adj. scholar, 1977—. Mem. Am. Econ. Assn., Am. Bus. Law Assn., Western Econ. Assn., Mont Pelerin Soc., Phil. Soc., Sigma Xi. Home: 15925 SW 77th Ct Miami FL 33157 Office: 1541 Brescia Ave Coral Gables FL 33146

CLARY, RICHARD WAYLAND, lawyer; b. Tarboro, N.C., Oct. 10, 1953; s. S. Grayson and Jean (Beazley) C.; m. Claudia Anne Stone, Oct. 18, 1980. BA magna cum laude, Amherst Coll., 1975; JD magna cum laude, Harvard U., 1978. Bar: N.Y. 1981, U.S. Dist. Ct. (so. and ea. dists.) N.Y. 1981, U.S. Tax. Ct. 1981, U.S. Dist. Ct. (no. dist.) Calif. 1982, U.S. Ct. Appeals (9th cir.) 1983. Law clk. to judge U.S. Ct. Appeals (2d cir.), N.Y.C., 1978-79; law clk. to Justice Thurgood Marshall U.S. Supreme Ct., Washington, 1979-80; assoc. Cravath, Swaine & Moore, N.Y.C., 1980-85, ptnr., 1985—. John Woodruff Simpson fellow Amherst Coll., 1975-76. Mem. ABA, N.Y. State Bar Assn., Assn. of Bar of City of N.Y., Phi Beta Kappa. Episcopalian. Clubs: Harvard, Wall St. (N.Y.C.). Office: Cravath Swaine & Moore 1 Chase Manhattan Plaza New York NY 10005

CLARY, ROSALIE BRANDON STANTON, timber farm executive, civic worker; b. Evanston, Ill., Aug. 3, 1928; d. Frederick Charles Hite-Smith and Rose Cecile (Liebich) Stanton; B.S., Northwestern U., 1950, M.A., 1954; m. Virgil Vincent Clary, Oct. 17, 1959; children—Rosalie Marian, Frederick Stanton, Virgil Vincent, Kathleen Elizabeth. Tchr., Chgo. Public Schs., 1951-55, adjustment tchr., 1956-61; faculty Loyola U., Chgo., 1963; v.p. Stanton Enterprises, Inc., Adams County, Miss., 1971—; author Family History Record, genealogy record book, Kenilworth, Ill., 1977—; also lectr. Leader, Girl Scouts, Winnetka, Ill., 1969-71, 78-86, Cub Scouts, 1972-77; badge counselor Boy Scouts Am., 1978-87 ; election judge Republican party, 1977—. Mem. Nat. Soc. DAR (Ill. rec. sec. 1979-81, nat. vice chmn. program com. 1980-83, state vice regent 1986-88), Am. Forestry Assn., Forest Farmers Assn., North Suburban Geneal. Soc. (governing bd. 1979—), Winnetka Hist. Soc. (governing bd. 1978—), Internat. Platform Assn., Delta Gamma (mem. nat. cabinet 1985—). Roman Catholic. Home: 509 Elder Ln Winnetka IL 60093 Office: PO Box 401 Kenilworth IL 60043

CLASSEN, CARL JOACHIM, university professor; b. Hamburg, Fed. Republic of Germany, Aug. 15, 1928; s. Erwin and Erika (Petersen) C.; m. Roswitha née Rabl; children: Claus Dieter, Carl Friedrich, Hans Christoph. PhD, U. Hamburg, 1952; BLitt, U. Oxford, Eng., 1957; DLitt, U. Oxford, 1988; habilitation, U. Göttingen, Fed. Republic of Germany, 1961. Assessor Christianeum, Hamburg, 1956; lectr. classics U. Coll. Ibadan, Nigeria, 1956-59; lectr. U. Göttingen, 1960-63, dozent, 1961-66; prof. Technische Univ., Berlin, Fed. Republic of Germany, 1966-69, U. Würzburg, Fed. Republic of Germany, 1969-73, U. Göttingen, 1973—; vis. prof. U. Tübingen, 1964-65, U. Tex., Austin, 1967-68; mem. Inst. Advanced Study, Princeton, 1975; vis. fellow All Souls Coll., Oxford, 1980. Author: Sprachliche Deutung, 1959, Laudes Urbium, 1980, Recht Rhetorik Politik, 1985, Ansätze, 1986. Mem. Mommsen Gesellschaft (pres. 1983-87), Internat. Soc. Hist. Rhetoric (pres. 1987—), Akademie der Wissenschaften Göttingen. Home: 7 Am Brachfelde, D34 Göttingen Federal Republic of Germany Office: U Göttingen, Nikolausbergerweg 9 c, D 34 Göttingen Federal Republic of Germany

CLASSON, ROLF ALLAN, pharmaceutical company executive; b. Nassjo, Sweden, Aug. 20, 1945; s. Allan K.E. and May Britt (Lagerquist) C.; m. Birgitta Larsson, Feb. 3, 1968; children—Peter, Karin, Erik. M. in Bus. Econs., Gothenburg U., 1969. Personnel mgr. Pharmacia, Uppsala, Sweden, 1969-74; mgmt. cons. Asbjorn Habberstad, Stockholm, 1974-77; mktg. mgr. Pharmacia, Uppsala, 1977-80; div. gen. mgr. Tarkett, Ronneby, 1980; pres. Pharmacia Infusion, Uppsala, 1981-84, Pharmacia Devel. Co. Inc., Piscataway, N.J., 1984—; bd. dirs. Electronucleonics, Inc., 1986—, Pharmacia Deltec, Inc., 1986—, Pharmacia Genetic Engring., Inc., 1986—, Pharmacia/LKB Biotech., Inc., 1987—. Office: Pharmacia Devel Co Inc 800 Centennial Ave Piscataway NJ 08854

CLAUSEN, ALDEN WINSHIP, banker; b. Hamilton, Ill., Feb. 17, 1923; s. Morton and Elsie (Kroll) C.; m. Mary Margaret Crassweller, Feb. 11, 1950; children: Eric David, Mark Winship. B.A., Carthage Coll., 1944, LL.D., 1970; LL.B., U. Minn., 1949; grad., Advanced Mgmt. Program, Harvard U., 1966. Bar: Minn. 1949, Calif. 1950. With Bank Am. (NT & SA), San Francisco, 1949-81, 1986—; v.p. Bank Am. (NT & SA), 1961-65, sr. v.p., 1965-68, exec. v.p., 1968-69, vice chmn. bd., 1969, pres., chief exec. officer, 1970-81, chmn., chief exec. officer, 1986—; pres. World Bank, 1981-86; past pres. Internat. Monetary Conf., San Francisco; Clearing House Assn. Past pres. Fed. Adv. Council, 1972; past chmn. Bay Area Council; past bd. govs. United Way of Am.; past chmn. United Way of Bay Area; past mem. Bus. Roundtable; mem. Bus. Council; past mem. Japan-U.S. Adv. Council; past bd. dirs. Conf. Bd., San Francisco Opera; past bd. dirs., mem. adv. council SRI Internat.; mem. adv. council Stanford U. Grad. Sch. Bus.; bd. dirs. Harvard Bus. Sch.; trustee Carthage Coll., Brookings Instn. Mem. Res. City Bankers Assn. (hon.), Calif. Bar Assn. Clubs: Bankers of San Francisco, Pacific Union, Burlingame Country; Bohemian, Links (N.Y.C.); Metropolitan (Washington); Chevy Chase (Md.). Office: BankAmerica Corp Bank of America Ctr 555 California St San Francisco CA 94104 *

CLAUSEN, HENRY CHRISTIAN, fraternal organization executive, lawyer; b. San Francisco, June 30, 1905; s. Louis and Lena (Clausen); m. Virginia Palmer, Aug. 17, 1935; children—Henry Christian, Florian Clausen Elliot, Donald, Karen Clausen Freeman. J.D., U. San Francisco, 1927; postgrad., U. Calif., San Francisco, 1927-32, U. Mich., 1942-43. Bar: Calif. bar 1927. Since practiced in San Francisco; asst. U.S. atty. for No. Dist. Calif.; chief counsel for chief engr. Joseph B. Strauss during constrn. Golden Gate Bridge, 1931-33; law asso. Judge George E. Crothers, Thomas G. Crothers, Francis V. Keesling and his sons, 1947-67. Author: Emergence of the Mystical, Clausen's Commentaries on Morals and Dogma, Masons Who Helped Shape Our Nation, Messages for A Mission, Authentics of Fundamental Law for Scottish Rite, Beyond the Ordinary, Your Amazing Mystic Powers, Stabiltity Strength and Serenity, Stanford's Judge Crothers; contbr. articles to publs. Pres. San Francisco YMCA; trustee George Washington U. Served to lt. col., JAGC AUS, 1942-45. Decorated Legion of Merit. Mem. Calif. Jr. C. of C. (pres.). Congregationalist. Clubs: Masons, K.T, Shriners (pres. Scottish Supreme Rite Councils of World; sovereign grand comdr. Supreme Council Ancient and Accepted Scottish Rite of Freemasonry, So. Jurisdiction U.S.A. 1949-86, editor in chief monthly mag. The New Age during term), Bohemian, San Francisco Golf. Office: 234 Van Ness San Francisco CA 94102

CLAUSEN, HUGH DAVID, retail executive; b. Beckenham, Kent, Eng., Mar. 1, 1938; arrived in South Africa, 1966; s. Carl Eugen and Agnes Eva (MacBean) C.; m. Pamela Rosemary Constance, Sept. 14, 1963; children: Duncan, Barry, Jacqueline. Diploma in agr., Shuttleworth Coll., Bedfordshire, Eng., 1960. Salesman, mgr. T. Parker & Sons Sports Ground Maintenance, Surrey, Eng., 1961-66; asst. to mng. dir. Quinton Hazel Superite, Johannesburg, Republic of South Africa, 1967-69; owner Oakvale Cane and Dairy Farm, Natal, Republic of South Africa, 1969-85; retailer and mfr. cane furniture Cane Assocs. Natal Ltd., 1987—, also bd. dirs.; bd. dirs. Mediterranean Cane Export Co., New Germany, Natal. Mem. Illovo Planters Assn. (sec. Eston, Natal chpt. 1974-85). Methodist. Club: Eston Farmers (chmn. 1979-81). Home: 44 Oakleigh Ave, Pietermaritzburg, Natal 3201, Republic of South Africa Office: Cane Assocs Natal Ltd, 6 Otto Volek Rd, New Germany, Natal 3610, Republic of South Africa

CLAUSON, SHARYN FERNE, consulting company executive, educator; b. Phila., Oct. 4, 1946; d. Eugene and Gertrud Jayn (Besser) C. BA in English, Temple U., 1968; MEd in Psychology, Beaver Coll., 1979; MBA, Drexel U., 1982; postgrad in law, Temple U. Market analyst Epstein Research, Bala, Pa., 1967-69; cons. Ednl. Testing Service, Princeton, N.J., 1979-80; chief exec. officer CCX, Narberth, Pa., 1978-79; tchr. Cheltenham Twp. Sch. Dist., Elkins Park, Pa., 1969-86; dir. Sharyn Clauson Bus. Communications, Narberth, Pa., 1975-85; pres. S. Clauson & Assocs., Inc., 1985—; dir. Executwriter, 1985—; mem. adj. faculty Drexel U., Phila., 1979—, Phila. Coll. Textiles & Sci., Phila, 1985—, St. Joseph's U., Phila., 1986—, Phila. Ctr. of Great Lakes Coll. Assn., 1988—; talk show host Sta. WDVT-AM, Phila., 1985—; mem. governing bd. Site Selex, Inc., Jenkintown, Pa., dir. communications/pub. relations, 1988—; communications cons., 1975—. Editor: Curriculum for Optacon Music Reading, 1984; mem. editorial adv. bd. Bus. Communications and Concepts, 2d edit., 1985. Mem. com. Women's Polit. Caucus, Phila., 1982—; mem. exec. bd., arts and scis. alumni bd. Temple U. Women's Law Caucus, 1987—. Mem. Am. Mktg. Assn., Internat. Platform Assn., Nat. Speakers Assn. (chair 1985), Nat. Assn. Profl. Saleswomen, (honoree 1982—), Nat. Council Tchrs. English, Del. Valley Writing Council, Wallenberg Communicators, Phi Delta Kappa. Home: 308 Oak Hill E Narberth PA 19072

CLAUSS, PETER OTTO, lawyer; b. Knoxville, Tenn., Sept. 23, 1936; s. Alfred and Jane (West) C.; m. Elizabeth Mary Lou Percival, Apr. 28, 1962; children—Andrew Bradford, Victoria Johns. AB, U. Chgo., 1955; LLB, Yale U., 1958. Bar: Pa. 1959, U.S. Dist. Ct. (ea. dist.) Pa. 1959, U.S. Tax Ct. 1959, U.S. Ct. Appeals (3d cir.) 1959, U.S. Supreme Ct. 1963, U.S. Ct. Claims 1960, U.S. Ct. Customs 1962. Assoc. Clark, Ladner, Fortenbaugh & Young, Phila., 1958-65, ptnr., 1966—, mem. exec. com., 1967-76, mng. ptnr., 1968-72, sr. ptnr., chmn. corp. and bus. dept., 1983—; past dir. Norcross, Inc., Nutrion Corp., Helicrane Constrn. Corp., Mannion Co., Henry Cantor, Inc.; dir. Keystone Helicopter Corp., Interactive Graphics, Inc.; asst. sec. C.H. Masland, 1974-86. Past sec., mem. vestry Christ Ch., mem. Outreach Com., stewardship com.; past coach Little League Baseball; past treas. Ithan Sch. PTA; past treas. Boy Scouts Am., Ithan, Pa. Ford Found. fellow, 1952-55. Served with Army N.G., 1959-67. Mem. ABA (past chmn. sales, exchanges and basis com. tax sect.), Phila. Bar Assn. (past chmn. unpopular causes com., past vice chmn. pub. service com.). Pa. Bar Assn., Juristic Soc. of Phila. (past bd. govs.), Yale Law Sch. Assn. for Eastern Pa. (pres. 1974-82), Assn. Yale Alumni (Phila. del. 1982-84), Phi Gamma Delta (nat. sec., bd. dirs., past gen. counsel), Phi Delta Phi. Republican. Episcopalian. Clubs: Yale of Phila. (past pres.), Racquet of Phila., First Troop Phila. City Calvary, University Barge; Merion Cricket, Orpheus; First Monday (past pres.); Ocean Point Golf (Fripp Island, S.C.) Contbr. articles to legal jours. Home: 758 Darby-Paoli Rd Newtown Square PA 19073 Office: 1818 Market St 32d Floor Philadelphia PA 19103

CLAUSSEN, HOWARD BOYD, recruiting company executive; b. Kansas City, Mo., May 12, 1946; s. Harry Ben and Mary Loraine (Shipley) C.; m. Virginia Ione Nehf, July 21, 1973; children: Paul, Rebecca, Debora, Arienne, John, Jennifer. BA in Econs., Yale U., 1968. Systems engr. IBM Corp., 1969-70; salesman Sperry Corp., Kansas City, 1970-72; sr. salesman Honeywell Inc., Kansas City, 1972-73; dist. mgr. Singer Bus. Machines, Kansas City, 1973-75; pres. 'C' Cons., Inc., Kansas City and Terre Haute, Ind., 1975-80, 82—; nat. sales mgr. Delta Systems, Seattle, 1980-82; cons. CBS, Inc., N.Y.C., 1976-80, Southwestern Bell Telephone Co. subs. AT&T, St. Louis, 1978-80, Convergent Tech., San Jose, Calif., 1983—, Multiflow Computer, Branford, Conn., 1986—. Mem. instructional adv. com. Vigo County Sch. Bd., 1984-87; v.p. Yale Club of Western Washington, 1983-84; coach Terre Haute Baseball Little League, 1986—, YWCA Basketball. Mem. AAAS, Nat. Trust Hist. Preservation. Republican. Methodist. Club: Yale of Ind. Home and Office: 4519 Park Ln Ct Terre Haute IN 47803

CLAVANO, NATIVIDAD RELUCIO, pediatrician, consultant; b. Cabiao, Philippines, Oct. 1, 1932; d. Francisco Roque and Mercedes Garcia (Nunez) Relucio; m. Graciano Diaz Clavano, 1956; children: Gregory, Graciano III, Guido Glenn. D Medicine and Surgery, U. St. Tomas, Manila, 1957. Intern local hosps., Manila, 1956-57; resident Children's Med. Ctr., Manila, 1957-58; adj. resident physician Maternity and Children's Hosp., Manila, 1960; resident Baguio Gen. Hosp., Baguio City, Philippines, 1961-64, sr. resident, 1965-69, med. specialist I, 1969-73, head dept. pediatrics, 1973-83; chief, founder Under Six Clinic, Philippines, 1975—; program coordinator region I Under Six Clinic, 1975-82; nat. cons. dept. health, 1979—; cons. Dept. Health, Philippines, 1979—, Nursing Mother's Assn. Philippines, 1985—, World Health Orgn., UNICEF. Author: The Promotion of Breastfeeding, 1984, pamphlets on maternity and child care; contbr. to Standards of Child Health Care, 1982, also profl. jours., tng. materials in field. Scholar Brit. Council Columbo Plan, 1974-75; Misereor grantee, 1975; Brit. Council visitor, 1982. Mem. Philippine Med. Assn. (Child Welfare Service award 1980, Dr. Carmelita Belmonte-Cuyugan award 1983), Philippine Pediatric Soc., Baguio-Benguet Med. Soc., Maternal and Child Health Assn. of Philippines, Philippine Med. Women's Assn. Club: Pines City Lioness. Lodge: Rotary Anns of Bagio. Home: Europa Condominium, Baguio City Philippines Office: Baguio's Under Six Clinic, DECMMC, Baguio City Philippines

CLAVEL, BERNARD CHARLES HENRI, writer; b. Lons-le-Saunier, France, May 29, 1923; s. Henri and Heloise (Dubois) C.; m. Andrée David, 1945 (div. 1982); 3 sons; m. 2d Josette Pratte, 1982. Author: L'ouvrier de la nuit, 1956, Pirates du Rhône, 1957, Qui m'emporte, 1958, Paul Gauguin,

1958, L'espagnol, 1959, Malataverne, 1960, La célébration du bois, 1962, Le voyage du père, 1965, L'Hercule sur la place, 1966, Leonard de Vinci, 1967, L'Arbre qui chante, 1967, La maison des autres, 1962, Celui qui voulait voir la mer, 1963, Le coeur des vivants, 1964, Les fruits de l'hiver, 1968, Victoire au Mans, 1968, L'espion aux yeux verts, 1969, Le tambour du bief, 1970, Le massacre des innocents, 1970, Le seigneur du fleuve, 1972, Le silence des armes, 1974, Lettre à képi képi blanc, 1975, La boule de neige, 1975, La saison des loups, 1976, La lumière du lac, 1977, Ecrit sur la neige, 1977, La fleur de sel, 1977, La femme de guerre, 1978, le Rhône ou la métamorphose d'un dieu, 1979, Le chien des laurentides, 1979, L'Iroquoise, 1979, Marie Bon Pain, 1980, La bourrelle, 1980; (with Josette Pratte) Felicien le fantôme, 1980; Compagnons du Nouveau-Monde, 1981; Terres de mémoire, 1981; Arbres, 1981; Poèmes et Comptines, 1981; Le hibou qui avait avalé la lune, 1981; Odile et le vent du large, 1981; Rouge Pomme, 1982; l'Homme du Labrador, 1982; Harricana, 1983; l'or de la terre, 1984; Le roi des poissons, 1984; Le mouton noir et le loup blanc, 1984; miserere, 1985; L'oie equiarait perdu le nord, 1985; author numerous plays for radio and TV; contbr. revs. for jours. Recipient Prix Eugene Leroy, 1956, Prix populiste, 1962, Prix Jean Mace, 1968, Prix Goncourt, 1968, Grand Prix litteraire de la Ville de Paris, 1968, Prix Albert Olivier, 1968. Address: care Doon House, Maam, County Galway Ireland Other: care Robert Laffont, 6 Place St-Sulpice, 75006 Paris France *

CLAWSON, JOHN ADDISON, financier, investor; b. Monaco, Pa., June 4, 1922; s. Ralph S. and Elsie (Winnett) C.; m. Patricia Harmon, July 5, 1947; children: Christine (Mrs. Jan Brandwie), Hunter Winnett. B.S. Miami U, 1943, LL.D., 1979; postgrad., Harvard U., 1968. Vice pres., nat. mgr. bus. and labor reports div. Prentice-Hall, N.Y.C., 1948-55; with DuBois Chems. div. Chemed Corp., Cin., 1955-78; dist. mgr. DuBois Chems. div. Chemed Corp., N.Y.C., 1955-60; regional mgr. Eastern div. DuBois Chems. div. Chemed Corp., 1960-64, divisional mgrs. v.p., 1964-66, exec. v.p., dir. sales, 1966-70, gen. mgr., 1968-70, pres., chief exec. officer, 1970-79, group exec., 1975-79; v.p. Chemed Corp., 1971-77, exec. v.p., 1978-79, ret., 1979; chmn. Whitehall Mgmt. Corp., Cin., Triple T Enterprises, Palm Beach Gardens, Fla. Dir. Suburban Fed. Savs. & Loan Assn., Cin.; Trustee Providence Hosp., 1974-76; dean's assoc. Miami U., 1973—. Served to lt. (j.g.) USNR, 1943-46. Mem. Cin. C. of C. (city and county planning com. 1971-74), Soap and Detergent Assn. (vice chmn. bd. 1971-73, chmn. bd., chief exec. officer 1974-75, mem. exec. com., bd. dirs. 1976-79), Delta Sigma Phi, Sigma Alpha Epsilon. Presbyterian. Clubs: Queen City (Cin.), Kenwood Country (Cin.); John's Island (Fla.), Riomary Bay Yacht (Fla.); Caty Cay, Ltd., Commodore (Bahamas). Home: Rio Mar Bay Yacht Club PO Box 3028 Vero Beach FL 32963 Office: Triple T Enterprises 10335 Ironwood Rd Palm Beach Gardens FL 33410

CLAWSON, RAYMOND WALDEN, independent oil producer; b. San Jose, Calif.; s. Benjamin B. and Mae Belle (Names) C.; LL.B., Am. U., 1936; m. Barbara M. Robbins, 1965. Ind. operator, exploration and devel. oil properties, 1936—; pub. Los Angeles Mirror, 1945-47; pres. Ariz. Securities, Phoenix, 1947-50, Transcontinental Oil Co., Los Angeles, 1947-49; geophys. cons. in offshore drilling ops. Gulf of Mexico, 1963—, North Sea, 1970—; chmn., chief exec. officer Clawco Petroleum Corp., Newport Beach, Calif., 1979—. Clubs: Balboa Bay, Acapulco Yacht. Office: PO Box 2102 Newport Beach CA 92663

CLAY, HARRIS AUBREY, chemical engineer; b. Hartley, Tex., Dec. 28, 1911; s. John David and Alberta (Harris) C.; B.S., U. Tulsa, 1933; Ch.E., Columbia U., 1939; m. Violette Frances Mills, June 19, 1948 (dec. June 1972); m. 2d, Garvice Stuart Shotwell, Apr. 28, 1973. Pilot plant operator Phillips Petroleum Co., Burbank, Okla., 1939-42, resident supr. Burbank pilot plants, 1942-44, process design engr., Bartlesville, Okla., 1944-45, process engring. supr. Philtex Plant, Phillips, Tex., 1946-56, tech. adviser to pilot plant mgr., Bartlesville, 1957-61, chem. engring. assoc., 1961-74; cons. engr., 1974—; chmn. tech. com. Fractionation Research, Inc., 1966-71, mem. tech. com., 1972-73. Mem. dist. commn. Boy Scouts Am. Fellow Am. Inst. Chem. Engrs.; mem. Am. Chem. Soc., Electrochem. Soc. Presbyterian. Clubs: Elks, Lions. Contbr. articles to profl. jours. Patentee in field. Home: 1723 Church Ct Bartlesville OK 74006

CLAY, LORI LEE GARBER, retailer; b. Gary, Ind., Mar. 19, 1957; d. Robert Samuel and Vivian May (Bray) Garber; m. Terry Dean Clay, Jan. 2, 1982; 1 child, Melisa B. BBA with honors, N.Mex. State U., 1980; MBA, Columbus Coll., Ga., 1985. Mgr. Army and Air Force Exchange Service, Ft. Bragg, N.C., 1980-81, Eglin AFB, Fla., 1981-82, Pope AFB, N.C., 1982-83, mgr. retail ops., Ft. Benning, Ga., 1983-84, mgr. retail sales and mdse., 1985-87, retail store mgr., Munich, 1988—; referral agt. Coldwell Bankers-Kennon Realtors, Columbus, Ga. Mem. Nat. Assn. Female Execs. Republican. Methodist. Avocations: water and snow skiing, aerobics, poetry, reading. Home: Perlacher Forst, 306 A-4, D8000 Munich Federal Republic of Germany Office: Perlacher Forst, Cincinnatistrasse 472, D8000 Munich 90, Federal Republic of Germany

CLAY, MICHELLE MARY, physiologist; b. Reading, Berkshire, Eng., May 19, 1955; d. Harold Henry and Mary Josephine (Goodrich) C. BSc with honors, U. Coll. Wales, Aberystwyth, 1976; postgrad., U. London, 1981—. Technician dept. surgery Hammersmith Hosp., London, 1976-77, tech. officer dept. medicine, 1977-81, research officer dept. pediatrics, 1987—; research officer dept. thoracic medicine Royal Free Hosp., London, 1981-86. Author numerous journals in field, 1981—; illustrator: Use of Aerosols, 1984. Mem. Med. Research Soc., Assn. Inhalation Toxicologists, Breathing Club. Club: London Corinthian (hon. treas. 1985—). Office: Hammersmith Hosp Dept Pediatrics, Du Cane Rd, London W12 OHA, England

CLAYTON, ANTHONY HUGH LE QUESNE, historian, educator; b. Upavon, Wiltshire, Eng., Sept. 3, 1928; s. Emilius and Irene (Strong) C.; m. Judith Mary Blackstone, Apr. 28, 1973; children: Robert Anthony Emilius, Penelope Fleur. Diploma in French, U. Paris, 1947; MA in History, U. St. Andrews, Fife, Scotland, 1951, PhD in History, 1970. Edn. officer Dept. of Edn., Nairobi, Kenya, 1952-65; sr. history lectr. Royal Mil. Acad. Sandhurst, Camberley, Eng., 1965—; cons., vis. lectr. Ctr. for Internat. Briefing, Farnham, Surrey, 1976—. Author: The Zanzibar Revolution and its Aftermath, 1981, The British Empire as a Superpower, 1986, France, Soldiers and Africa, 1988; (with others) Government and Labour in Kenya, 1973. Served to col. Intelligence Corps, 1948-82. Mem. Inst. Hist. Research, African Studies Assn. Mem. Church of England.

CLAYTON, HERBERT KENNETH, musician; b. Rushden, Northamptonshire, Eng., Jan. 29, 1920; s. Herbert and Edith (Pettitt) C.; Exhbn. scholar, Trinity Coll. Music, Lond, 1931-34; lic. pianoforte teaching, Royal Acad. Music, 1940; asso. pianoforte performing, Royal Coll. Music, London, 1945; diploma edn. with distinction, U. London, 1970; pupil of Greville Cooke, Gilbert Thomas, Norman Sprankling; m. Joan Paget, Sept. 4, 1959. Local govt. officer Rushden Urban Dist. Council, 1935-40; music master Windley Sch., also William Crane Boys Sch., Nottingham, 1946-52; music master, dep. head Forster Boys Sch., Nottingham, 1953-54; music dir. Cranley Girls Operatic Soc., Nottingham, 1950-54; headmaster Worcestershire County Council, 1954-57, Essex County Council, 1957-65, London Borough Havering, 1965-75; freelance musician and educationalist, 1976—; sec. Nottingham Music Festival Soc., 1950-54; adjudicator music festivals, lectr. tchrs. inservice tng. Served with Brit. Army, 1940-46. Life fellow Royal Soc. Arts; asso. Coll. Preceptors; life mem. Nat. Assn Head Tchrs., Assn. Therapeutic Edn., Nat. Union Tchrs.; mem. Incorporated Soc. Musicians. Methodist. Club: Masons. Composer: (operetta) Bows and Belles, 1951, Sonatine for pianoforte, 1946, Tangita for 2 pianos, 1951, Shepherd's Tune for pianoforte and recorders, 1950, Evening for pianoforte and recorders, 1951. Address: 62 Mimosa Ave, Merley Wimborne, Dorset BH21 1TT England

CLAYTON, HUGH NEWTON, lawyer; b. Ripley, Miss., Aug. 22, 1907; s. Ira L. and Nancy (McCord) C.; m. Cathryn Rose Carter, June 26, 1939; children: Rose Clayton Cochran, Hugh Carter. A.B., U. Miss., 1929, J.D., 1931. Bar: Miss. 1931, Tenn. 1931. Practiced in Memphis, 1931-33; practiced in Ripley, 1933-36, city atty., 1933-36; city atty. New Albany, Miss., 1937-75, 76-82; atty. New Albany Sch. Bd., 1937-85; dir. Bank of New Albany. Editor: Miss. Law Jour, 1931; asso. editor: New Orleans Christian Advocate, 1941-42; contbr. articles to profl. jours. Chmn. Union County chpt. ARC, 1945-51, nat. com. on internat. ops., 1946-47, chmn. nat. conv., 1959, mem. nat. exec. com. and chmn. nat. chpt. relations com., 1954-56, vice chmn. and parliamentarian, 1948; nat. conv.; chmn. area adv. com. Southeastern U.S., 1949-51, nat. bd. govs., 1950-56, vol. field cons., 1956—, chmn. nat. conv., 1959, chmn. state conv., 1961, mem. state div. council, 1979—; mem. exec. bd. Yocona Area council Boy Scouts Am., 1955—, pres., 1963-65, chmn. com. on advancements, 1956-57, chmn. com. on orgn. and extension, 1958-60; chmn. com. on trust fund promotion Region 5, 1968-72, chmn. fin. com., 1972-73, mem. nat. council, 1959-81, mem. regional exec. com., 1966—, mem. nat. ann. meeting com., 1970-72, mem. nat. com. on local council fin., 1973—, chmn. trust fund com. S.E. region, 1974-80, vice chmn. adminstrn. com. S.E. region, 1973-75; chmn. adminstrn. com. 1975-77; pres. Union County Tb Assn., 1937-40, New Albany Planning Com., 1945-49; mem. nat. conf. Commrs. on Uniform State Laws, 1956—; mem. Miss. Democratic Exec. Com., 1952-56; mem. Nat. Dem. Com., 1956-60, mem. exec. com., 1958-60; mem. Dem. Nat. Adv. Council, 1959-60; Founder, 1st pres. Miss. Jr. Bar, 1936. Served from lt. to lt. comdr. USNR, 1942-45; served as acting comdg. officer Naval Air Sta., 1945, New Orleans. Recipient Silver Beaver award Boy Scouts Am., 1962, Silver Antelope award, 1968; Paul Harris award Rotary Internat., 1976; Disting. Alumnus award U. Miss., 1983; named Outstanding Law Alumnus U. Miss., 1977-78. Fellow Am. Coll. Trial Lawyers, Miss. Bar Found. (trustee), Am. Bar Found. (State chmn. fellows 1980—), Am. Coll. Probate Counsel, Internat. Acad. Law and Sci.; mem. Am. Judicature Soc. (dir. 1962-65), Internat. Platform Assn., Internat. Bar Assn. (patron), Fed. Bar Assn., Am. Counsel Assn. (bd. dirs. 1980-83), ABA (mem. various coms., mem. ho. dels. 1966-86, state del. 1974-80, chmn. communications com. 1967-68, chmn. standing com. on membership 1973-78, chmn. standing com. on jurisprudence, tenure and compensation 1980-81, gov. 1981-84, bd. govs. fin. com. 1981-84, chmn. bd. govs. fin. com. 1983-84, bd. coms. long range fin. planning, planning and mgmt. systems, relocation 1983-84, mem. exec. com. 1983-84, mem. standing com. on scope and correlation of work 1984—, sec. 1986, chmn. 1987-88), Miss. Bar Found. (trustee 1963-65, pres. 1965-66), Miss. Def. Lawyers Assn. (bd. dirs. 1980-83), Miss. State Bar (1st v.p. 1958-59, pres. 1959-60), Miss. Law Jour. Assn. (bd. dirs. 1978-84), 3d Miss. Circuit Bar Assn. (pres. 1963-68), Jud. Conf. U.S. 5th Circuit, U. Miss. Alumni Assn. (dir. 1962-65, founder, 1st pres. law alumni chpt. 1964-65), Am. Acad. Polit. and Social Sci., Miss. Assn. Meth. Ministers and Laymen (pres. 1958), Am. Bar Retirement Assn. (bd. dirs. 1981-82), Inst. Jud. Adminstrn., Am. Legion, Scribes (dir. 1969-73), Omicron Delta Kappa, Phi Delta Theta, Phi Alpha Delta, Tau Kappa Alpha, Sigma Upsilon. Methodist (treas. North Miss. Conf. bd. missions 1938-60, trustee North Miss. Conf. 1960—, chmn. bd. trustees Miss. Conf. 1973—, treas. Lewis Meml. Hosp. Fund Miss. 1938-49, nat. emergency com. 1940). Clubs: Masons (New Albany, Miss.), Rotary (New Albany, Miss.) (dist. gov. 1965-66), Oaks Country (New Albany, Miss.). Office: Clayton Bldg PO Box 157 New Albany MS 38652

CLAYTON, JACK, film director; b. Brighton, Sussex, Eng., Mar. 1, 1921; m. Christine Norden; m. 2d, Katherine Kath. Prodn. mgr. (film) An Ideal Husband; assoc. producer Queen of Spades, Flesh and Blood, Moulin Rouge, Beat the Devil, The Good Die Young, I am a Camera; producer, dir. The Bespoke Overcoat, 1955; dir. Room at the Top, 1958; producer, dir. The Innocents, 1961, Our Mother's House, 1967; dir. The Pumpkin Eater, 1964, The Great Gatsby, 1974, Something Wicked This Way Comes, 1983, The Lonely Passion of Judith Hearne, 1987. Served to flight lt. RAF, 1940-45.

CLEARY, JAMES CHARLES, JR., audio-visual producer; b. N.Y.C., Mar. 15, 1921; s. James Charles and Elizabeth Adelaide (Anglin) C.; grad. Scarsdale (N.Y.) High Sch., 1940; m. Adele Lillian Coe, Nov. 28, 1954. Lithographer, cameraman Advt. Lit. Inc., N.Y.C., 1940-41; advt. copy writer Grosset & Dunlap, book pubs., N.Y.C., 1942-44; advt. copy writer, editor Baker & Taylor, book wholesalers, N.Y.C., 1945-46; asst. mgr. sales Camera Craft Inc., retail photog. sales, White Plains, N.Y., 1946-50, Colortone Camera Inc., White Plains, 1950-57; producer, lectr. Ansco div. Gen. Aniline & Film Corp., Binghamton, N.Y., 1959-61; lab. photographer Nevis Lab. Nuclear Research, Columbia U., 1959-75; audio-visual specialist Edgemont Sch. Dist., Scarsdale, 1975-83; owner-producer Cleary Sound-Slides, New Rochelle, N.Y., 1950—. Mem. Scarsdale Camera Club (pres. 1948-49), Color Camera Club Westchester N.Y. (dir. 1958-59), Am. Security Council (advisory bd. 1970—), U.S. Air Force Assn., Am. Def. Preparedness Assn., Westchester County Grand Jurors Assn., The Baker Street Irregulars, Three Garridebs, Sherlock Holmes Socs., Thomas Wolfe Soc. Patentee of complete sound-synchronized, dissolving slide projection control system, 1966; pioneer in use of dissolve projection and synchronized sound in presentation of color slide continuities. Address: Cleary Sound-Slides 28 Pengilly Dr New Rochelle NY 10804

CLEARY, MANON CATHERINE, artist, educator; b. St. Louis, Nov. 14, 1942; d. Frank and Crystal (Maret) Cleary. B.F.A., Washington U., St. Louis, 1964; M.F.A., Tyler Sch. Art, Temple U., 1968. Instr. fine arts SUNY-Oswego, 1968-70; from instr. to assoc. prof. D.C. Tchrs. Coll., Washington, 1970-78; from assoc. prof. to prof. art U. D.C., 1978-85, acting chmn. dept. art, 1985-86; one woman shows at Mus. Modern Art Gulbenkian Found., Lisbon, Portugal, 1985, Iolas/Jackson Gallery, N.Y.C., 1982, Osuna Gallery, Washington, 1974, 77, 80, 84, U. D.C., 1987, Tyler Gallery SUNY at Oswego, 1987, others; group exhibits include Twentieth Century Am. Drawings: The Figure in Context, Traveled Nat. Acad. Design, 1984-85, others. Artist-in-residence Herning Hojskole, Denmark, 1980, Ucross Found., Wyo., 1984; recipient faculty research award, U. D.C., 1983. Mem. Coll. Art Assn., NEA, Pi Beta Phi. Democrat. Presbyterian. Home: 1736 Columbia Rd NW Apt 402 Washington DC 20009 Office: U DC Art Dept 916 G St NW Washington DC 20001

CLEARY, RICHARD JAMES, publishing company owner and executive; b. Sydney, Australia, July 2, 1942; s. James William and Joan Eileen (Dineen) C. Secondary teaching diploma. Secondary sch. tchr. New South Wales Edn. dept., 1960-69; mng. dir., pub. R.J. Cleary Pubs. Ltd., Sydney, 1970-78, exec. chmn., owner, 1979—. Author: Success Mathematics (series), 1969—. Home: 86/77 Riley St, East Sydney Australia 2010 Office: Cleary Pub Group, PO Box 939, Darlinghurst NSW 2010, Australia

CLEARY, ROBERT EMMET, gynecologist, infertility specialist; b. Evanston, Ill., July 17, 1937; s. John J. and Brigid (O'Grady) C.; M.D., U. Ill., 1962; m. June 10, 1961; children—William Joseph, Theresa Marie, John Thomas. Intern, St. Francis Hosp., Evanston, 1962-63, resident, 1963-66; practice medicine specializing in gynecology and infertility, Indpls., 1970—; head Sect. of Reproductive Endocrinology and Infertility, Chgo. Lying-In Hosp., U. Chgo., 1968-70; head Sect. of Reproductive Endocrinology and Infertility, Ind. U. Med. Center, Indpls., 1970-80; prof. ob-gyn Ind. U., Indpls., 1976-80, clin. prof. ob-gyn, 1980—. Recipient Meml. award Pacific Coast Obstetrical and Gynecol. Soc., 1968; diplomate Am. Bd. Ob-Gyn, Am. Bd. Reproductive Endocrinology and Infertility. Fellow Am. Coll. Ob-Gyn, Am. Fertility Soc.; mem. Endocrine Soc.,Soc. Gynecol. Investigation, Pacific Coast Fertility Soc., Soc. Reproductive Endocrinologists, Soc. Reproductive Surgeons, N.Y. Acad. Scis., Sigma Xi. Roman Catholic. Contbr. articles in field to med. jours. Home: 7036 Dubonnet Ct Indianapolis IN 46278 Office: 8091 Township Line Rd Indianapolis IN 46260

CLEARY, WILLIAM RICHARD, superintendent of schools; b. Wagoner, Okla., Sept. 24, 1933; s. William R. and Tressie (Bird) C.; m. Barbara J. Berry, June 2, 1956; 1 child, Richard Bryant. BA, Cen. State U., Edmond, Okla., 1959, ThM, 1963; PhD, Nat. Christian U., 1974. Tchr. Unified Sch. Dist. 259, Wichita, Kans., 1966-68; supt. Unified Sch. Dist. 462, Burden, Kans., 1968-75, Unified Sch. Dist. 402, Augusta, Kans., 1975-79, Unified Sch. Dist. 368, Paola, Kans., 1979—; Chmn. East Cen. Kans. Spl. Coop., Paola, 1979—; joint commn. Law Related Edn., Topeka, Kans., 1985—; mem. Council of Supts., Topeka, 1985—. Served to sgt. U.S. Army, 1952-55. Mem. Am. Assn. Sch. Adminstrs., Kans. Assn. Sch. Adminstrs. (bd. dirs. 1973-75), Kans. Assn. Supervision and Curriculum Devel. Republican. Methodist. Lodge: Lions (pres. 1985-86). Home: 602 E Miami Paola KS 66071 Office: Unified Sch Dist 368 202 E Wea Paola KS 66071

CLEAVE, STEWART WESLEY, architect; b. Morristown, N.J., Oct. 17, 1947; s. Kingdon and Catherine (Johnson) C.; m. Judith Morey, June 6, 1972; children— Shawn Michael, Jennifer Michelle, Christopher James, Richard K. Student SUNY, 1967, BArch, Mont. State U., 1971. Assoc. architect Steimer & Assocs., Downingtown, Pa., 1971-73, Sakellar & Assocs., Tucson, 1973-75; pres. Cleave-Lundgren, Benson, Ariz., 1975—. Recipient Energy Efficient Bldg. award Electric League Ariz., 1983. Mem. AIA. Avocation: collecting Lionel trains. Office: Cleave-Lundgren & Assocs 196 E 5th St Benson AZ 85602

CLEESE, JOHN MARWOOD, writer, actor, comedian; b. Weston-super-Mare, Eng., Oct. 27, 1939; s. Reginald and Muriel Cleese; m. Connie Booth, 1968 (div. 1978); m. 2d Barbara Trentham, 1981; children: Cynthia, Camilla. Student Clifton Coll., Bristol, Eng.; M.A., Downing Coll., Cambridge U. (Eng.); LL.D., St. Andrews U. Profl. writer, comedian, 1963—; 1st appearance on Brit. TV as writer, performer on The Frost Report, 1966; other TV series include At Last the 48 Show; co-author, actor Monty Python's Flying Circus, from 1969, Fawlty Towers; appeared in BBC prodn. of The Taming of the Shrew, 1981; film appearances include: Interlude, 1968; The Magic Christian, 1970; The Rise and Rise of Michael Rimmer, 1970; And Now for Something Completely Different, 1972; Monty Python and the Holy Grail, 1975; Romance with a Double Bass, 1975; Life of Brian, 1979; The Secret Policeman's Ball, 1979; Time Bandits, 1981; Monty Python Live at the Hollywood Bowl, 1982; The Secret Policeman's Other Ball, 1982; Privates on Parade; Yellowbeard, 1983; The Meaning of Life, 1983; Silverado, 1984; Clockwise, 1986; A Fish Called Wanda (author screenplay), 1988; founder, dir. Video Arts Ltd., London, 1979—; also created series of radio commls. for products advertised internationally. Co-author: Monty Python's Big Red Book, 1975; The Strange Case of The End of Civilizations as We Know It, 1977; Families and How to Survive Them, 1983. Recipient Queen's award for Exports (awarded to Video Arts Ltd.), 1982. Address: care Video Arts Ltd, 68 Oxford St, London W1, England also: care David Wilkinson, 6-8 Haymarket St, London SW1, England *

CLEGHORN, GEORGE EDWARD, apartment management executive; b. Terre Haute, Ind., Sept. 15, 1950; s. Edward Melle and Dorothy Pearl (Jones) C.; m. Laura Maureen Boyke, Dec. 18, 1971; children—Kathleen Mary, Corey Bruce. A.A.S. in Electronics Engring., SAMS Tech. Inst., 1970; A.A.S. in Mid Mgmt., Coll. Lake County, 1981, A.A.S. in Indsl. Supervision, 1983; Supr. Imperial Towers, Waukegan, Ill., 1976-84, gen. mgr., 1984-88 ; v.p. Imperial Renla Corp., Vernon Hills, Ill., 1988—. Served with USN, 1970-76. Mem. Waukegan/Lake County C. of C. (investing mem. 1985), Phi Theta Kappa. Republican. Home: 560 Forest View Dr Lindenhurst IL 60046 Office: Imperial Renla Corp 10 Phillips Rd Suite 107 Vernon Hills IL 60061

CLEGHORN, JOHN EDWARD, banker; b. Montreal, Que., Can., July 7, 1941; m. Pattie E. Hart; children: Charles, Ian, Andrea. B.Comm., McGill U., Montreal, 1962. Articled with Clarkson Gordon, chartered Accts., Montreal, 1964, St. Lawrence Sugar Ltd., Montreal, 1964-66; with Merc. Bank of Can., 1966-74; asst. gen. mgr. project financing Royal Bank of Can., 1975-76, dep. gen. mgr. corp. lending, 1976-78, v.p. nat. accounts, 1978-79, sr. v.p. planning and mktg. internat. div., 1979-80; sr. v.p. and gen. mgr. B.C. Royal Bank of Can., Vancouver, 1980-83; exec. v.p. Internat. Banking div. Royal Bank of Can., Toronto, 1983-86; pres. Royal Bank of Can., Montreal, 1986—; bd. dirs. Royal Bank Can. Dir. MacDonald Stewart Found., Montreal Gen. Hosp. Research Inst., Can. Club Montreal; mem. adv. council faculty of Commerce and Bus. Adminstrn., U. B.C.; bd. govs. Montreal com. Ludwig Inst. for Cancer Research, Olympic Trust Can; chmn. capital campaign Bishop's U.; council mem., v.p. Montreal Bd. Trade. Mem. Can., Quebec and B.C. Inst. Chartered Accts. Clubs: Vancouver, Royal Canadian Yacht (Toronto); Mount Royal, Hillside Tennis, Forest and Stream, Montreal Indoor Tennis. Office: The Royal Bank Can, 1 Place Ville Marie, Box 6001, Montreal, PQ Canada H3C 3A9

CLELAND, RONALD JAMES, financial executive; b. No. Ireland, May 22, 1934; s. John and Anne (Burns) C.; m. Rhoda McVeigh, Sept. 21, 1956 (div. 1963); children—Linda, Paul; m. Suzanne A. Georges, July 18, 1964; children—Richard, Robin. Gen. mgr., dir. Bailey's (Elect) Ltd., Middle East and Africa, Malta, 1965-81; exec. v.p. Mepa Group Holding, Middle East, Europe and Africa, Cyprus, 1981—, chmn. Mepa Ins. Consultants Ltd., Mepa Underwriting Mgmt. Ltd., Mepa Agys. Ltd., Allied Assurance & Reins. Co. Ltd., Apem Surveyors & Adjusters Ltd., Cyprus, Mepa Ins. Agys. Ltd., Protection Ins. Agys. Ltd.; dir. Pancyprian Ins. Co. Ltd., Pancyprian Fin. Corp. Ltd., Transmepa Can. Inc., Mekran Enterprises Ltd., Jersey. Cert. internal auditor: Fellow Brit. Inst. Mgmt., Inst. Dirs., Inst. Indsl. Mgrs.; mem. Inst. Internal Auditors. Mem. Ch. of Ireland. Clubs: Marsa Sports; South Kensington Squash; Royal Overseas League. Home: 14 Torregiani Gardens High Ridge, Saint Andrews Malta also: 4A Tenarou St, Ayios Dometios, Nicosia Cyprus also: Apt 3/5 Sloane Ct, East Chelsea, London SW3, England Office: 65 Ave d'Iena, 75116 Paris France also: PO Box 5509, Nicosia Cyprus

CLEMENS, T. PAT, manufacturing company executive; b. Hibbing, Minn., July 26, 1944; s. Jack LeRoy and Mildred (Coss) C.; m. Marianne Paznar, Oct. 1, 1966; children: Patrick Michael, Heather Kristen. BS in Econs. and Mgmt., St. Cloud State U., 1968, student, Coll. St. Thomas, 1985-87. Sales adminstr. Transistor Electronics Co., Eden Prarie, Minn., 1969; head instnl. sales Chiquita Brands, Edina, Minn., 1970; dist. sales mgr. Menley & James Labs., Phila., 1971-75; owner, pres. T.P. Clemens Labs., Eagan, Minn., 1975—; instr community edn. Rosemount, Minn., 1979—; bd. dirs. Rosemount Hockey, 1977-78; v.p. Sch. Dist. #196 Booster Club, 1984-85; lectr. econs. to corps., high schs. and colls. in U.S., Scotland, Ireland, and Jamaica, 1979—. Author, editor: How Prejudice and Narcissism Control Economics of the United States and the World, 1979. Recipient letter recognition Dakota County Atty.'s Dept. Mem. Rosemount Community Edn. Bd., 1985, chmn. 1986-87; chmn. speakers bur. Citizens Steering Com., 1984-85; little League coach, 1970-82; high sch. weight lifting coach, 1975—; vol. worker with comatose children. Mem. Internat. Platform Assn. Home and Office: 1276 Vildmark Dr Eagan MN 55123

CLEMENT, JOHN, food products company executive; b. May 18, 1932; s. Frederick and Alice Eleanor Clement; m. Elisabeth Anne Emery, 1956; 3 children. Student, Bishop's Stortford Coll., Eng. With Howards Dairies, Westcliff on Sea, Eng., 1949-64, United Dairies London Ltd., 1964-69; asst. mng. dir. Rank Leisure Services Ltd., 1969-73; chmn. Unigate Foods Div., 1973; chief exec. Unigate Group, 1976, chmn., 1977—; non-exec. chmn. The Littlewoods Orgn., 1982—. Mem. Securities and Investments Bd. Clubs: Farmers', London Welsh Rugby Football, Cumberland Lawn Tennis, Royal Yarwich Yacht. Office: Tuddenham Hall, Tuddenham, Ipswich, Suffolk IP6 9DD, England *

CLEMENT, PAUL PLATTS, JR., educational development consultant; b. Geneva, Ill., Aug. 30, 1935; s. Paul P. and Vera Elizabeth (Dahlquist) C.; BA in Math., Coe Coll., 1957; m. Susan Alice Aikins, June 7, 1958; children: Paul P. IV, Kathleen Elizabeth. Sales tech. rep. Burroughs Corp., Chgo., 1960-63; mgr. EDP, Harding-Williams Corp., Chgo., 1963-65; edn. coordinator Standard Oil Co., Chgo., 1965-69; mgr. product planning Edutronics Systems Internat., Chgo., 1969-71; interactive video instrn. specialist Advanced Systems Inc., Chgo., 1971-88; ind. cons. in tng., media use (animated film, videotape, interactive videodiscs), computers, Downer Grove, Ill., 1988—; part-time data processing faculty Coll. of DuPage and Coll. extension, Harper Coll., Ill.; invited speaker numerous computer and tng. confs., nat. and internat. assns.; developer, presenter workshops in field; mem. adv. bd. Northeastern Ill. U., Chgo. Served to capt. USAF, 1958-60. Developer and pub. 12 animated films with supplementary texts, 81 videotapes, 17 interactive videodiscs and over 5000 pages of expository texts; collaborator 100 other videotapes with supplementary texts; prin. developer micro-computer based People Compatability System, 1983; developer Decision Table Algorithms,1986, 94th Inf. Div. Assn. Info. System, 1977, Basic Computer Programmer Tng. Curriculum for Eng. Govt., 1979, Computerized Data Processing Curricula Devel. System, 1973, Early COBOL Lang. Compiler, 1967;contbr. articles to Datamation mag., Data Training Mag. Mem. Nat. Soc. Performance & Instrn. (contbr. to jour.). Home and Office: 4942 Linscott Ave Downers Grove IL 60515

CLEMENT, RICHARD FRANCIS, business executive; b. Chgo., Nov. 29, 1906; s. Robert Fawne and Jennie (Halvorson) C.; m. Margaret Buchanan, Aug. 11, 1934 (dec. Apr. 1986); children—Richard Bradley, Jane Elizabeth (Mrs. David L. Wilemon), Charles Frederic; m. Julia Vandivort Stein, Jan. 29, 1988. B.S., U. Wis., 1928. Men's furnishings merchandiser Wilson

Bros., Chgo., 1935-39; sportswear merchandiser Ely & Walker, St. Louis, 1939-47; v.p., dir. Ely & Walker, 1949-65, dir. sales, 1954-63, dir. marketing and planning, 1963-65; partner Yates & Co. (investments), St. Louis, 1965-69; v.p. Newhard, Cook & Co. (investments), St. Louis, 1970—; chmn. C & B Investment Assocs., Inc., Los Alamos, Precious Metals, Inc., Webster Groves, Mo., 1979—; operator Rippling River Ranch, Steelville, Mo.; chmn. Champion Springs Ranch, Annapolis, Mo. Chmn. adv. bd. Midland div. Salvation Army, 1979-80, gen. chmn. Tree of Lights, 1970; moderator First Congl. Ch., Webster Groves, Mo., 1972-73. Recipient William Booth award Salvation Army, 1984. Mem. Sales and Mktg. Execs. of Met. St. Louis (pres. 1965-66), Alpha Tau Omega. Club: Algonquin. Lodge: Kiwanis (pres. Downtown St. Louis chpt. 1968). Home: 524 N Kirkwood Rd Kirkwood MO 63122 Office: 1600 S Brentwood Blvd PO Box 6717 Saint Louis MO 63144

CLEMENTE, JOSE ZULUETA, insurance executive; b. Manila, Philippines, May 14, 1930; s. Clemente Enrique Bayot and Manolita Da Costa (Zulueta) C.; m. Emma Mercado Salvatierra, Feb. 17, 1967; children—Jose S., Louis S. B.S. in Commerce, De La Salle U., Manila, cum laude, 1954. Sect. chief FGU Ins. Corp., Manila, 1951-63; asst. dist. mgr. N.Z. Ins. Corp., Manila, 1963-64; ins. mgr. Imperial Ins. Corp., Manila, 1964-68; asst. v.p. Malayan Ins. Co., Inc., Manila, 1968-72, v.p., 1972-78, sr. v.p., 1978-85, sr. v.p. mktg., 1985; pres., dir. Malayan Zurich Ins. Co., Inc.; dir. 1st Nationwide Assurance Corp.; chmn. Finman Gen. Assurance Corp.; bd. dirs. Finman Fin. & Investment Corp., Finman Lending Investors, Inc. Mem. Ins. and Surety Assn. Philippines (v.p. 1980-81), Philippine Ins. Rating Assn. (vice chmn. 1982, dir. 1983, chmn. 1984), DBP Pool of Accredited Cos. (vice chmn. 1981-82). Roman Catholic. Clubs: Philippine Insurers (pres.), Lodge: Makati West Rotary Office: Pioneer Ins & Surety Corp, Pioneer House, 108 Paseo de Roxas 5th Floor, Makati Philippines

CLEMENTS, JAMES DAVID, medical educator, physician; b. Pineview, Ga., May 7, 1931; s. Marcus Monroe and Dewey Thelma (Gammage) C.; m. Janet Collier Swan, Aug. 25, 1952; children—Leiliar Ann, David Marcus. B.A., Emory U., 1952; M.D., Med. Coll. Ga., 1956. Intern Temple U., Phila., 1956-57; resident in pediatrics Temple U., 1957-59; fellow mental retardation Sch. Medicine, Yale U., 1959-60; med. dir. Gracewood (Ga.) State Sch. Hosp., 1960-62, asst. supt., 1963-64; dir. planning mental retardation Ga. Dept. Pub. Health, Atlanta, 1964-65; dir. Ga. Retardation Center, Atlanta, 1964-79; med. cons. mental retardation Ga. Dept. Human Resources, 1979-81; clin. asst. prof. pediatrics and psychiatry Emory U. Sch. Medicine, Atlanta, from 1964, now asst. prof. psychiatry; assoc. clin. prof. neurology, asst. clin. prof. pediatrics Med. Coll. Ga., Augusta, 1970—; spl. cons. neurology mental retardation dept. pediatrics Ga. Bapt. Hosp., 1965—; mem. adv. com. program exceptional children Ga. Dept. Edn., 1968-70; mem. adv. bd. Sch. Allied Health Sci., Ga. State U., 1971-76; mem. accreditation council mental retardation council Joint Commn. on Accreditation Hosps., Chgo., 1975-79; del. White House conf. Ga. com. children youth, 1970; mem. Pres.'s Com. on Mental Retardation, 1975-78; chmn. Willowbrook rev. panel Fed. Ct. Eastern Dist. N.Y.; reviewer NSF; cons. Inst. Society, Ethics and Life Scis., Hastings Center; commr. Am. Bar Assn., 1976—. Contbr. articles to profl. jours., anthologies, seminars. Mem. adv. bd. Arbor Acad., DeKalb County (Ga.) Dept. Edn., 1973-75; mem. bd. founders, adv. com. Ashdun Hall, 1965-70; trustee Gatchell Sch., Mental Health Law Project; adv. com. Kennedy Center, Johns Hopkins U. Recipient Leadership award Am. Assn. Mental Deficiency, 1980. Fellow Am. Acad. Pediatrics (cons. head start med. cons. service), Am. Assn. Mental Deficiency (pres. 1974-75), Pan Am. Med. Assn., Am. Geriatrics Soc.; mem. Ga. Pediatric Soc., Nat. Assn. Supts. Pub. Residential Facilities Mentally Retarded, Nat. Assn. Retarded Citizens (legal advocacy adv. com. 1975), Internat. Assn. Sci. Study Mental Deficiency (chmn. local organizing com. 4th internat. congress, mem. council 1976—). Home: 475 Grant St SE Atlanta GA 30312 Office: Willie M Revie Panel Albemarle Bldg Room 406 325 N Salisbury St Raleigh NC 27611

CLENDINEN, JAMES AUGUSTUS, retired newspaper editor; b. Eufaula, Ala., Dec. 1, 1910; s. Thomas A. and Katherine M. (Powell) C.; m. Barbara Harrison, May 22, 1943; children: James Dudley, Melissa Louise. Student, U. Fla., 1929-30. Reporter, then mng. editor Clearwater (Fla.) Evening Sun, 1930-35; mem. staff Tampa Tribune, Fla., 1935-42, 46—; editor Tampa Tribune, 1958-85, chmn. editorial bd., 1974-85; ret. 1985; pres. Nat. Conf. Editorial Writers, 1966; mem. Pulitzer Prize Jury, 1967, 68. Mem. Gov.'s Commn. on Edn., 1971-73; mem. Fla. Jud. Commn., 1975—. Served with USAAF, 1942-45. Recipient 1st prize for editorial writing Fla. Daily Newspaper Assn., 1953, 57, 58, 60, 64, 66, 68, 70, 71, 76, 78, 83, 84; traveling fellow to study conditions in Spain So. Assn. Nieman Fellows, 1957; Freedoms Found. award for editorial writing, 1961, 62; Fla. Edn. Assn. award, 1963; Nat. Headliners Club award, 1964; Pub. Service award Fla. Bar, 1965; Distinguished Service award U. Fla. Coll. Journalism, 1974; Pub. Service award ABA, 1977; Pub. Service award Fla. Legislature, 1965; named Outstanding Citizen, Tampa Civitan Club, 1985. Mem. Am. Soc. Newspaper Editors (mem. del. to Red China 1972, dir.), Fla. Soc. Editors (founder, 1st pres. 1955), Sigma Delta Chi (award editorial writing 1962), Phi Kappa Tau. Episcopalian. Clubs: Tampa Yacht and Country, University, Exchange (Tampa); Gasparilla Krewe.

CLERGUE, LUCIEN GEORGE, photographer; b. Arles, France, Aug. 14, 1934; s. Etienne and Jeanne (Grangeon) C.; m. Yolande Wartel, Jan. 10, 1963; children: Anne, Olivia. Dr. es Letters in Photography, U. Provence, 1979. tchr. workshops New Sch., N.Y.C., Art Ctr., Pasadena, other U.S. univs. and colls. Freelance photographer, 1959—; artistic dir. Arles Festival, 1971-75, 86-88; founder, Rencontres Internationales de la Photographie, Arles, 1969; dir. C.R.E.A.L.T.A. Arles, 1986—; one-man exhbns. include, Kunstgewerbe Mus., Zurich, 1958, 63, Mus. Modern Art, N.Y.C., 1961—, Musée d'Arts Decoratifs, Paris, 1962—, Moderna Museet, Stockholm, 1969—, Art Inst. Chgo., 1970—, Kunsthalle, Düsseldorf, Fed. Republic Germany, 1970—, Gallery Witkin, N.Y.C., 1972-79, Bruxelles Musee d'Ixelles, 1974—, Israel Mus., Jerusalem, 1974—, Centre Pompidou, Paris, 1980—, Musée d'Art Moderne Paris, 1984, George Eastman House, Rochester, 1985, ICP, N.Y., 1986, Amos Anderson Mus., Helsinki, 1987; works rep. books, movies. Decorated chevalier Nat. Order Merit, 1980; recipient Louis Lumière prize, 1966; Grand Prix of Higashigawa Photo Fest, 1986. Mem. Assn. Nat. Photographers Createurs, Parc Regional Camargue, Ste. des Amis Jean Cocteau, Rencontres Internat. de la Photographie Arles, ENP Nat. Sch. of Photography. Roman Catholic. Address: 17 A Briand BP84, 13632 Arles France

CLERJEAUD, GEORGES PAUL, technology company executive; b. Saintes, France, Oct. 23, 1934; s. Georges Jean Louis and Paule Marie (Ferrand) C.; m. July 8, 1960 (div. 1984); children: Eric, Karine; m. Ping-Huei Chow, May 11, 1985. MA in Civil Engring., U. Paris, 1960. Various positions Ingersoll-Rand, France and U.S., 1962-66; — S.Am., 1967-71; pres. Kirwan, Paris, 1972-79; mgr. internat. mktg. Alsthom/Diesel, Paris, 1980-85; founder, mng. dir. SINTECO, 1985—. Contbr. articles on elec. power plants to profl. jours. Served with French Air Force, 1960-62. Roman Catholic. Club: Internat. Bus. (Paris). Home and Office: 8 rue Charles d'Orléans, 78540 Vernouillet France

CLEVELAND, HELEN BARTH, teaching consultant, civic worker; b. Alliance, Ohio, Aug. 28, 1904; d. Luther Martin and Ella Mae (Forest) Barth; A.B., Mt. Union Coll., 1927; postgrad. Kent State U., 1929-32, Akron U., 1946-48, N.Y. U., 1950-53; M.A., Syracuse U., 1955, Ph.D., 1958; postgrad. London Acad. Arts, 1970, U. San Juan, 1972, Acad. Arts Honolulu, 1973; m. Harold J. Cleveland, Oct. 26, 1946; children—Carol, Ronald, Marilyn, George, Donald. Tchr., cons. Alliance Public Schs., 1927-74; instr. crafts Syracuse U., 1953-60; instr. art, Sierra Leone, 1963-64; pres., dir. Chautauqua (N.Y.) Art Gallery, 1963-76, pres. emeritus, bd. dirs., 1977—; bd. dirs., cons. adminstr. Mabel Hartzel Mus., Alliance, 1974—; bd. dirs. Lighthouse Gallery, Tequesta, Fla., 1970-72, Canton (Ohio) Culture Center, 1970—; trustee Alliance Art Center; mem. Keating (Mich.) Antique Village. Recipient Bronze plaque Community Alliance Bi-Centennial Com., 1976, Community Service award Am. Legion Aux., 1975. Mem. Am. Assn. Ret. Persons (pres. 1980-82), Am. Fedn. Art, Ohio Fedn. Art; life mem. NEA, Ohio Edn. Assn. Republican. Methodist. Clubs: Mt. Union College Women, Alliance Woman, Chautauqua Woman, Univ. Women, Order Eastern Star, K.T. Ladies, Shrine Ladies, DeMolay-Rainbow (Mom of Year 1959). Author: Arts and Crafts, 1955; Art in Poetry, 1959; Creativity in Elementary Schools, 1963. Home: 1192 Parkside Dr Alliance OH 44601

CLEVELAND, PAUL MATTHEWS, diplomat; b. Boston, Aug. 25, 1931; m. Carter Sellwood; children—James, Peter, Robin, Sandra. B., Yale U., 1953; M., Fletcher U., 1965. Mgmt. analyst Naval Office Mgmt., 1956-57; staff aide, dep. asst. sec. for ops. Dept. State, 1957-59; econ. officer, then polit. officer Am. Embassy, Canberra, Australia, 1959-62; aide to U.S. ambassador Am. Embassy, Bonn, Fed. Republic Germany, 1963-64; econ. officer Am. Embassy, Jakarta, Indonesia, 1965-69, Office Fuels and Energy, 1968-70; spl. asst. to asst. sec. for East Asian affairs Dept. State, 1970-73; polit.-mil. officer, then polit. counselor Am. Embassy, Seoul, Republic of Korea, 1973-77; dep. dir., dir. regional affairs Bur. East Asian and Pacific Affairs, 1977-80, dir. Thai office, 1980-81, dir. Korean affairs, 1981-82; dep. chief of mission Am. Embassy, Seoul, Republic of Korea, 1982-85; U.S. ambassador to New Zealand and Western Samoa Am. Embassy, Wellington, New Zealand, 1985—. Served as pilot USAF, 1953-56. Mem. Am. Fgn. Service Assn. Office: US Ambassador to New Zealand US Dept State Washington DC 20520

CLIBURN, VAN (HARVEY LAVAN CLIBURN, JR.), concert pianist; b. Shreveport, La., July 12, 1934; s. Harvey Lavan and Rildia Bee (O'Bryan) C. Studied music with, mother, 1937-51; studied with, Mme. Rosina Lhevinne; grad. with highest honors; grad. (Frank Damrosch scholar), Julliard Sch. Music, 1954; HHD (hon.), Baylor U., 1958. Pub. appearances, Shreveport, 1940, debut, Houston Symphony Orch., 1947; appeared with Dallas Symphony Orch., 1952, N.Y. Philharm. Orch., Carnegie Hall, 1954, 58; concert pianist on tour, U.S., 1955-56, Soviet Union, 1958, recs. RCA Victor; guest TV shows, concert with Symphony of the Air, Carnegie Hall, 1958, concert Brussels Fair, Belgium, 1958, other appearances: Phila., Chgo., Hollywood, Denver, London, Amsterdam, Paris; nation-wide tour U.S., 1958—; composer classical music. Recipient Tex. State prize, 1947; Nat. Music Festival award, 1948; G.B. Dealy award Dallas, 1952; Kosciuszko Found. Chopin award, 1952; Grand Olga Samaroff Found., 1953; 1st place Julliard Concerto concert, 1953; Edgar M. Leventritt Found. award, 1954; Carl M. Rosder Meml. award Julliard Sch. Music, 1954; 1st prize Internat. Tschaikovsky Piano Competition Moscow, 1958; citation Am. Assn. Sch. Adminstrs., 1959; named number in classical field Top Artists on Campus Poll (album sales), 1968. Mem. Am. Guild Mus. Artists. Baptist. Clubs: Thespian (Kilgore, Tex.) (pres.); Rotary (hon.), Lotus (life). Home: 455 Wilder Pl Shreveport LA 71104 Office: care Van Cliburn Found 2525 Ridgmar Blvd Suite 307 Fort Worth TX 76116 *

CLIFF, BARRY LEE, financial planner; b. Reading, Pa., Mar. 31, 1943; s. James Denton and Virginia Mae (Kelly) C. AAS, Capitol Inst. Tech., 1964; student in engring. econs., Iowa State U., 1967-68. Cert. in fin. planning. Dist. mgr. Equity Funding Securities Corp., Washington, 1969-73; br. mgr. Investors Fin. Services, Rockville, Md., 1973-74; co-founder, chief exec. officer, pres. Am. Fin. Cons., Silver Spring, Md., 1974—; mem. adj. faculty Coll. Fin. Planning. Served with USN, 1961-63. Named to Coll. Fin. Planning Hall of Fame, 1978; fellow Captitol Inst. Tech., 1987. Fellow Capitol Coll.; mem. Inst. Cert. Fin. Planners, Fin. Products Standards Bd. (chmn.), Internat. Assn. Fin. Planners, Registry of Fin. Planning Practitioners. Home: 10112 Kensington Pkwy Kensington MD 20895 Office: 8555 16th St Suite 701 Silver Spring MD 20910

CLIFFORD, CLARK MCADAMS, lawyer; b. Fort Scott, Kans., Dec. 25, 1906; s. Frank Andrew and Georgia (McAdams) C.; m. Margery Pepperell Kimball, Oct. 3, 1931; children: Margery Pepperell Clifford Lanagan, Joyce Carter Clifford Burland, Randall Clifford Wight. LL.B., Washington U., St. Louis, 1928. Assoc. Holland, Lashly & Donnell, St. Louis, 1928-33; assoc. Holland, Lashly & Lashly, 1933-37; ptnr. Lashly, Lashly, Miller & Clifford, 1938-43; sr. ptnr. Clifford & Miller, Washington, 1950-68; sec. Dept. Def., Washington, 1968-69; sr. ptnr. Clifford & Warnke, Washington, 1969—; Chmn. bd. First Am. Bankshares, Inc., Washington, 1982—; dir. Knight-Ridder Newspapers; spl. counsel to Pres. U.S., 1946-50. Served to capt. USNR, 1944-46; naval aide to Pres. U.S. 1946. Recipient Medal of Freedom from Pres. U.S. Mem. ABA, Mo. Bar Assn., D.C. Bar Assn., St. Louis Bar Assn., Kappa Alpha. Clubs: Burning Tree (Washington), Metropolitan (Washington), Chevy Chase (Washington). Home: 9421 Rockville Pike Bethesda MD 20814 Office: Clifford & Warnke 815 Connecticut Ave NW Washington DC 20006 also: 1st Am Bankshares Inc 15th & H Sts NW Washington DC 20005

CLIFFORD, H. CURTIS, business executive; b. Lincoln Park, Mich., July 22, 1935; s. Harry Benjamin and Terressa Belle (Huff) C.; student mech. engring. Ohio State U., 1953-57; B.S., SUNY, 1980; m. Sandra Jean Lamberson, Mar. 30, 1968; children—Daniel, Mark, James. Asst. chief draftsman Seagrave Fire Apparatus (div. FWD 1962), Columbus, Ohio, 1954-63, chief engr., Clintonville, Wis., 1963-66; chief engr. Ward LaFrance Truck Corp., Elmira, N.Y., 1966-68, sales mgr., 1968-71, sales mgr. Am. LaFrance, 1971-78, dir. customer services, 1978-80, v.p. mktg., 1980-84; pres. Clifford Enterprises, 1984—; exec. v.p. Wayne Metal Products, 1985-87. Bd. dirs. Capabilities; coach Bantam Boys Bowling League, Kiwanis Boys Baseball. Served with C.E., U.S. Army, 1955. Mem. N.Y. State Assn. Retarded Children, Adminstrv. Mgmt. Soc., Nat. Fire Protection Assn. Methodist. Office: 400 E Logan St Markle IN 46770

CLIFFORD, PAUL INGRAHAM, psychologist, association executive; b. Martinsburg, W.Va., Jan. 22, 1914; s. J. Paul and Mabel (Douglass) C.; B.S., State Tchrs. Coll., Shippensburg, Pa., 1938; A.M., Atlanta U., 1948; Ph.D., U. Chgo., 1953; m. Elizabeth Edith Sterrs, Jan. 21, 1950 (dec.); m. 2d, Margaret E. Washington, Nov. 26, 1975. Civilian administrv. asst. USAAF, 1941-46; prof. chemistry Paine Coll., Augusta, Ga., 1947-48; instr. in edn. Atlanta U., 1948-51, asst. prof., 1952-54, asso. prof., 1954-57, prof., 1957-68, registrar, 1954-66, dir. admissions, 1954-66, dir. summer sch., 1957-68; staff psychologist Am. Mgmt. Psychologists, Inc., 1966—, v.p., dir., 1969—, nat. dir. profl. services, 1969-71; prof., chmn. dept. psychology S.C. State Coll., 1971-76; psychologist Career Mgmt. Atlanta, Inc., 1976—; dir. Summer Sch. Atlanta U., 1982—. Cons. U.S. Office Edn., 1961—; vis. prof. edn. U. Calif. at Berkeley, 1968-69; cons. psychologist various indsl. orgns. Bd. dirs. So. Fellowships Fund, Nat. Fellowships Fund; trustee Zale Found., Dallas. Lic. psychologist, Ga., Ill. Fellow AAAS, Ga., Pa. psychol. assns.; mem. Am., Southeastern, S.C., Ill. psychol. assns., Soc. for Psychol. Study Social Issues, Nat. Soc. Study Edn., AAUP, Assn. Higher Edn., NEA, Am. Ednl. Research Assn., Assn. Counseling and Devel., Nat. Vocational Guidance Assn., Nat. Assn. Guidance Suprs., Assn. Counselor Edn. and Supervision, Assn. Measurement Edn. and Guidance, Nat. Council on Measurement in Edn., Am. Acad. Polit. and Social Scis., N.Y. Acad. Scis., Internat. Platform Assn., Phi Delta Kappa, Omega Psi Phi. Episcopalian. Author monograph, articles for ednl. and psychol. jours. Home and Office: 859 Woodmere Dr NW Atlanta GA 30318

CLIFFORD, STEWART BURNETT, banker; b. Boston, Feb. 17, 1929; s. Stewart Hilton and Ellinor (Burnett) C.; m. Cornelia Park Woolley, Apr. 26, 1952; children—Cornelia Lee Wareham, Rebecca Lyn Mailer-Howat, Jennifer Leggett Danner, Stewart Burnett. A.B., Harvard U., 1951, M.B.A., 1956. Asst. cashier Citibank, N.A., N.Y.C., 1958-60, asst. v.p., 1960-63; exec. v.p., gen. mgr. Merc. Bank, Montreal, Que., Can., 1963-67; v.p. planning Overseas div. Citibank, N.A., N.Y.C., 1967-68, v.p., adminstr. comml. banking group, 1969-72; v.p. head world corp. dept. Citibank, N.A., London, 1973-75; sr. v.p. domestic energy Citibank, N.A., N.Y.C., 1975-80, sr. v.p., head pvt. banking and investment div., 1981-87; div. exec., dir. Pvt. Banking Group-Investment div. Cititrust Ltd., Bahamas, 1988—; dir. Monumental Corp., Balt. Pres., 120 East End Ave. Corp., Woolley-Clifford Found.; trustee Spence Sch.; bd. dirs. Horizon Concerts, Inc., James Lenox House; mem. Neighborhood Com. for Asphalt Green; elder, trustee Brick Presbyterian Ch.; trustee YWCA, N.Y.C. Served to 1st lt. arty. U.S. Army, 1951-54. Republican. Clubs: Pilgrims, Union, University (N.Y.C.); Duxbury Yacht (Mass.). Home: 120 East End Ave New York NY 10028 Office: Citibank NA 153 E 53d St New York NY 10043

CLIFTON, RUSSELL B., financial executive; b. Maroa, Ill., Jan. 16, 1930; s. Russell Thomas and Clara Leoda (Luckenbill) C.; m. Mary Joyce Hartline, Oct. 10, 1948; 1 son, Steven Shawn. B.S., Mich. State U., 1957. Bank auditor Arthur Andersen & Co., Detroit, 1957-59; v.p. Mich. Nat. Bank, Lansing, 1959-65; sr. v.p. Assoc. Mortgages Co., Kansas City, Mo., 1965-69; v.p. Fed. Nat. Mortgage Assn., Washington, 1969-85; pres., chief exec. officer First Chesapeake Mortgage, Inc., Beltsville, Md., 1985-86, now bd. dirs.; mem. adv. com. Home Owner's Warranty Corp., Washington, 1978-81; bd. dirs., mem. exec. com. Nat. Acad. Conciliators, Washington, 1979—; bd. dirs. Lincoln Savs. & Loan; cons. mortgage bankning, Washington, 1987—. Served with U.S. Army, 1952-54. Named disting. fellow Nat. Assn. Cert. Mortgages Bankers, 1975. Assoc. mem. Mortgage Bankers Assn., Nat. Savs. and Loan League, Nat. Assn. Home Builders, U.S. League Savs. Assn., Nat. Assn. Mut. Savs. Banks, Am. Bankers Assn., Nat. Assn. Realtors, Am. Savs. and Loan League, Community Assn. Inst.; mem. Phi Kappa Phi, Beta Alpha Psi, Beta Gamma Sigma, Tau Sigma. Methodist.

CLIFTON, YERGER HUNT, English literature educator; b. Jackson, Miss., July 26, 1930; s. Yerger Hunt and Sudie Cocke (Wilson) C. B.A., Duke U., 1952; student law Washington and Lee U., 1952-53; M.A., U. Va., 1958; Ph.D., Trinity Coll., Dublin, Ireland, 1962; postgrad. Oxford U., U. Munich. Instr., Coll. William and Mary, Williamsburg, Va., 1958-59, U. Ky., Lexington, 1962-65; vis. lectr. Youngstown U. (Ohio), 1964-65; lectr. humanities Memphis Coll. Arts, 1966-69; asst. prof. English lit. Rhodes Coll., Memphis, 1965-70, assoc. prof., 1970-77, prof., 1977—; dean Brit. studies Univ. Coll. of Oxford U., 1970-79, St. John's Coll., 1980—, So. Coll. Univ. Union, dir. Rhodes in Europe, 1987—, pres. 26th So. Lit. Festival, 1967, trustee, 1967-70. Served to lt. USNR, 1953-56. Menkenmeller fellow, 1952-53. Mem. AAUP, MLA, Oxford Soc., Green Ribbon Soc., Phi Kappa Sigma. Republican. Episcopalian. Clubs: Athenaeum, Oxford and Cambridge Univs. (London); Monteagle (Tenn.) Assembly. Author: Angelic Knowledge in Paradise Lost, 1958; Milton and the Fall of Man, 1962. Home: 2907 Iroquois Rd Memphis TN 38111 Office: 2000 North Pkwy Memphis TN 38112

CLINE, ANN, artist, designer; b. Greensboro, N.C., Apr. 7, 1933; d. Grady Alton and Mae Josephine (Karsten) Merriman; scholar Cooper Union, N.Y.C., 1954, Fashion Inst. Tech., 1957, Arts Students League, 1961-62, Fine Arts Acad., 1962-63, Joachim Simon Atelier, Tel Aviv, 1962; A.B., N.E. La. U., Monroe, 1971; m. S.C. Johananoff, Mar. 9, 1959 (div. 1973); 1 child, Pamela; m. Francis X. Cline, Feb. 14, 1973. Asst. designer Adele Simpson Couture, 1959; pres. Johananoff Designs, 1967-70, Ann Cline Art Objects, Monroe, La., 1975—; pres. 165 North Properties; artist; works exhibited in group shows Haifa Mus., 1961, Am. Watercolor Soc., 1962; one person shows include: Barzansky Gallery, 1962, La. Polytech. U. Art Gallery, 1967, Mittel's Art Gallery, 1969, N.E. La. U., 1973, 71, Am. Consulate, Tel Aviv, 1962, Contemporary Gallery, Dallas, 1970, Brooks Gallery, Memphis, 1971, 14th Ann. Delta Art Exhbn. Nat. Found. Arts, 1971, Jackson Arts Ctr. Ann. Exhbn., Miss., (prize award 1971), 22d Ann. Delta Exhbn., Ark. Arts Ctr., 1972, 79, Mayor's Show, Monroe, 1979, Wesley Found. Award Show, 1979, 80, 81, Roundtree Gallery, Monroe, 1985-87, others. Bd. dirs. La. Council Performing Arts, 1974; rep. Gov.'s Conf. Arts; bd. adjustments Monroe Zoning Commn.; trustee Masur Mus., 1974-75; bd. dirs. Little Theater of Monroe, 1975-76; bd. dirs. Women of the Ch., Episcopal Ch., 1977-78, mem. Daus. of the King, 1979-82, chmn. meml. com. Recipient Young Designer competition award Fontana of Rome, 1957, 1st prize Fashion Inst. Tech., 1957, Young Designer's award Women's Wear Daily, 1960, 1st prize, Arts Students League, 1961, 2d prize, 1963, 2d prize Fine Arts Acad., 1962, 1st prize, Woodstock Gallery, 1962, 1st prize, La. Folk Art Festival, 1966, 68, 72, prize awards Temple Emmanuel Ann., Dallas, 1969, 71, 74. Mem. Butler Soc. Clubs: Bayou Desiard Country, Lotus, Illustrator: Jessie Strikes Louisiana Gold, 1969, Rhet, the Egret. Home and Office: 503 Speed Ave Monroe LA 71201

CLINE, CAROLYN JOAN, plastic and reconstructive surgeon; b. Boston; d. Paul S. and Elizabeth (Flom) Cline. B.A., Wellesley Coll., 1962; M.A., U. Cin., 1966; Ph.D., Washington U., 1970; diploma Washington Sch. Psychiatry, 1972; M.D., U. Miami (Fla.) 1975. Diplomate Am. Bd. Plastic and Reconstructive Surgery. Research asst. Harvard Dental Sch., Boston, 1962-64; research asst. physiology Laser Lab., Children's Hosp. Research Found., Cin., 1964, psychology dept. U. Cin., 1964-65; intern in clin. psychology St. Elizabeth's Hosp., Washington, 1966-67; psychologist Alexandria (Va.) Community Mental Health Ctr., 1967-68; research fellow NIH, Washington, 1968-69; chief psychologist Kingsbury Ctr. for Children, Washington, 1969-73; sole practice clin. psychology, Washington, 1970-73; intern internal medicine U. Wis. Hosps., Ctr. for Health Sci., Madison, 1975-76; resident in surgery Stanford U. Med. Ctr., 1976-78; fellow microvascular surgery dept. surgery U. Calif.-San Francisco, 1978-79; resident in plastic surgery St. Francis Hosp., San Francisco, 1979-82; practice medicine, specializing in plastic and reconstructive surgery, San Francisco, 1982—; cons. VA Hosp. Stanford U., Palo Alto. Contbr. articles to profl. jours. Mem. Am. Bd. Plastic and Reconstructive Surgery (cert. 1986). Address: 450 Sutter St Suite 2433 San Francisco CA 94108

CLINE, KERMIT RUSSELL, farm supply cooperative executive; b. Mt. Solon, Va., Apr. 19, 1918; s. Cyrus H. and Edith K. (Showalter) C.; B.S. in Agrl. Engring., Va. Poly. Inst., 1940; m. Betty Jean Pendergrass, Apr. 22, 1967; 1 son, Charles. Field engr. REA, Washington, 1940-41; product mgr. farm and home equipment So. State Coop., Richmond, Va., 1947-59, mgr. farm supply procurement, 1959-73, v.p. seed and farm supply div., 1973-84, exec. v.p. ocean shipping and trading, 1984—; bd. dirs. Universal Coops., Mpls., 1972-82, vice chmn. bd., 1980-81, chmn. bd., 1981-82; bd. dirs. FFR Coop., West Lafayette, Ind., 1973-83, pres. bd. dirs., 1979-81. Served to maj. U.S.Army, 1941-47, lt. col. Res. Mem. Richmond C. of C., West Richmond Businessmen's Assn., Alpha Zeta, Phi Kappa Phi. Clubs: Richmond Export-Import (pres. 1966-67); Kiwanis of Tuchahoe (Va.); Westwood Racquet; Salisbury Country. Home: 3831 Victoria Ln Midlothian VA 23113 Office: PO Box 26234 Richmond VA 23260

CLINE, MICHAEL ROBERT, lawyer; b. Parkersburg, W.Va., Oct. 13, 1949; s. Robert Rader and Hazel Mae (Boice) C.; m. Carole R. Davis, Aug. 28, 1972. A.B., Morris Harvey Coll., 1972; J.D., Wake Forest U., 1975. Project coordinator Gov.'s Office Fed.-State Relations, Charleston, W.Va., 1970-72; spl. asst. W.Va. Office Econ. Opportunity, 1973; spl. asst. W.Va.-Dept. Labor, Charleston, 1974; staff asst., hearing officer, 1975-77; sole practice, Charleston, 1977—. Mem. ABA, Assn. Trial Lawyers Am., Comml. Law League Am., Nat. Assn. Criminal Defense Lawyers, W.Va. Trial Lawyers Assn. (treas. 1984, v.p. 1985-86, outstanding mem. 1983), W.Va. Bar Assn. (chmn. com. on econs. of law practice 1986), Pi Kappa Delta, Phi Alpha Delta. Republican. Methodist. Lodge: Kiwanis, Elks, Rotary. Home: 1531 Dixie St Charleston WV 25301 Office: 323 Morrison Bldg Charleston WV 25301

CLINE, RAY STEINER, world affairs educator; b. Anderson, Ill., June 4, 1918; s. Charles and Ina May (Steiner) C.; m. Marjorie Wilson, June 4, 1941; children: Judith, Sibyl. A.B., Harvard U., 1939, M.A., 1941, Ph.D., 1949; Ph.D. (Henry prize fellow), Balliol Coll., Oxford (Eng.) U., 1939-40. Jr. fellow Harvard U., 1941-42; with OSS, 1943-46, Office Chief Mil. History, Dept. Army, 1946-49, CIA, 1949-51; attaché Am. embassy, London, 1951-53; with CIA, 1954-58; dir. U.S. Naval Aux. Communications Center, Taipei, 1958-62; dep. dir. for intelligence CIA, 1962-66; spl. adviser Am. embassy, Bonn, Germany, 1966-69; dir. Bur. Intelligence and Research, Dept. State, 1969-73; dir. world power studies Georgetown U. Center Strategic and Internat. Studies, Washington, 1973-86; chmn. U.S. Global Strategy Council, Washington, 1986—; pres. Nat. Intelligence Study Center, Washington, Com. for Free China, Washington; adj. prof. Georgetown U., 1974—. Author: Washington Command Post, 1951, World Power Assessment, 1975, Secrets, Spies and Scholars, 1976, World Power Assessment-1977, 1977, World Power Trends and U.S. Foreign Policy for the 1980's, 1980, The CIA: Reality vs. Myth, 1982, (with Herbert Block) The Planetary Product in 1982, 1983, (with Yonah Alexander) Terrorism: the Soviet Connection, 1984, Terrorism as State-Sponsored Covert Warfare, 1986; editor: Asia in Soviet Global Strategy, 1987, Western Europe in Soviet Global Strategy, 1987; contbr. articles to publs. Mem. Oxford Soc., Council Fgn. Relations, Washington Inst. Fgn. Affairs, Phi Beta Kappa. Clubs: Internat., DACOR (Washington); Harvard of N.Y.C. Home: 3027 N Pollard St Arlington VA 22207 Office: 1800 K St NW Internat Club Bldg Suite 1102 Washington DC 20006

CLINE, WILSON ETTASON, retired judge; b. Newkirk, Okla., Aug. 26, 1914; s. William Sherman and Etta Blanche (Roach) C.; student U. Ill.,

1932-33; A.B., U. Okla., 1935, B.S. in Bus. Adminstrn., 1936; J.D., U. Calif., Berkeley, 1939; LL.M., Harvard U., 1941; m. G. Barbara Verne Pentecost, Nov. 1, 1939 (div. Nov. 1960); children—William, Catherine Cline MacDonald, Thomas; m. Gina Lana Ludwig, Oct. 5, 1969; children—David Ludwig, Kenneth Ludwig. Admitted to Calif. bar, 1940; atty. Kaiser Richmond Shipyards, 1941-44; pvt. practice, Oakland, 1945-49; atty., hearing officer, asst. chief adminstrv. law judge, acting chief adminstrv. law judge Calif. Pub. Utilities Commn., San Francisco, 1949-80, ret., 1981, dir. gen. welfare Calif. State Employees Assn., 1966-67, chmn. retirement com., 1965-66, mem. member benefit com., 1980-81, mem. ret. employees div. council dist. C, 1981-82. Trustee Cline Ranch Trust, various family trusts. Mem. ABA, State Bar Calif., Conf. Calif. Pub. Utility Counsel (steering com. 1967-71), Am. Judicature Soc., Boalt Hall Alumni Assn., Phi Beta Kappa (pres. No. Calif. assn. 1969-70), Beta Gamma Sigma, Delta Sigma Pi (Key award, 1936), Phi Kappa Psi, Phi Delta Phi, Pi Sigma Alpha. Republican. Mem. United Ch. Christ. Clubs: Harvard, Commonwealth (San Francisco); Sleepy Hollow Swim and Tennis (Orinda, Calif.); Masons, Sirs (Peralta chpt. 12). Home: 110 St Albans Rd Kensington CA 94708 Office: 1400 Webster St Suite 212 PO Box 526 Alameda CA 94501

CLINGERMAN, THOMAS BURDETTE, avionics manufacturing company executive; b. Beech Grove, Ind., Feb. 26, 1948; s. Cleo Burdette and Ruth Veronica (Beach) C.; m. Karen Marie Slanika, May 22, 1976; children: Michael Thomas, John Anthony. BA, Va. Mil. Inst., 1970; MPA, Boise State U., 1980; postgrad. in mgmt. USAF Air Command and Staff Coll., 1975-79. Commd. 2d lt. U.S. Air Force, 1970; advanced through grades to maj., 1984; assigned Del Rio, Tex., 1970-74, Nellis AFB, Las Vegas, 1974-76, Mt. Home, Idaho, 1977-80; resign, 1980; with USAFR, 1980—; indsl. engr. Rockwell Internat. Collins div., Cedar Rapids, Iowa, 1980, mgr. process engring., 1980-82, mgr. flight control, 1983, program mgr. Peoples Republic of China, 1984, program mgr. railroad system, 1984—; advisor CAP, 1982—. Mem. Robotics Internat. (sr.), Exptl. Aircraft Assn., Nat. Assn. for Search and Rescue, Iowa Sled Dog Drivers (pres. 1982-87). Republican. Roman Catholic. Avocations: flying, scuba diving, sailing, skiing, dog sled racing. Home: RR 1 Box 269C Solon IA 52333 Office: Rockwell Internat Collins Div 400 Collins Rd 108-157 Cedar Rapids IA 52498

CLINGMAN, WILLIAM HERBERT, JR., mgmt. cons.; b. Grand Rapids, Mich., May 5, 1929; s. William Herbert and Elizabeth (Davis) C.; BS with distinction and honors in Chemistry, U. Mich., 1951; MA, Princeton U., 1954, PhD, 1954; m. Mary Jane Wheeler, Feb. 6, 1951; children—Mary Constance, James Wheeler. Chemist, Am. Oil Co., Texas City, Tex., 1954-57, group leader, 1957-59; head thermoelectric sect. Tex. Instruments, Inc., Dallas, 1959-61, dir. energy research lab., 1961-62, mgr. corp. research and devel. mktg. dept., 1962-67; pres. W.H. Clingman Co., Inc., Dallas, 1967—; v.p., bd. dirs. Precision Measurement Inc., Dallas; speaker, cons. SBA, 1967-70; mem. adv. com. on sci., tech. and economy Nat. Planning Assn., 1966-67. Mem. Am. Chem. Soc., IEEE, Assn. Computing Machinery, Sigma Xi. Club: Brook Hollow Golf (Dallas). Mem. editorial adv. bd. Jour. Advanced Energy Conversion, 1961-66. Home: 4416 McFarlin St Dallas TX 75205 Office: 700 N Pearl St Suite 300 Dallas TX 75201

CLINTON, BILL, governor of Arkansas, lawyer; b. Hope, Ark., Aug. 19, 1946; married; 1 child. BS in Internat. Affairs, Georgetown U., 1968; postgrad. Rhodes scholar, U. Coll., Oxford (Eng.) U., 1968-70; JD, Yale U., 1973. Prof. law U. Ark. Sch. Law at Fayetteville and ltd. individual practice law, 1973-76; atty. gen. Ark., 1977-79; gov. State of Ark., 1979-81, 83—; of counsel firm Wright, Lindsey & Jennings, Little Rock, 1981-82; chmn. So. Growth Policies Bd., 1985-86. Chmn. Edn. Commn. of the States, 1986-87, mem. steering com.; mem. Task Force on Adolescent Edn. Carnegie Found.; vice chmn. Dem. Gov.'s Assn., 1987-88. Mem. ABA, Ark. Bar Assn., Nat. Govs.' Assn. (vice chmn. 1986, chmn. 1986-87, exec. com., fin. com., com. on human resources, com. on internat. trade and fgn. relations, task force on rural devel.). Office: Office of the Gov 250 State Capitol Little Rock AR 72201

CLINTON, LAWRENCE PAUL, psychiatrist; b. Lubbock, Tex., Apr. 27, 1945; s. Lewis Paul Clinton and Dorothy E. (Higgins) Clinton-Billingslea; m. Bonnie Gail Orenstein, June 22, 1969; children—Kerry Elizabeth, Andrew James, Alexander Geoffrey, Kaylin Lee. B.A., with honors, So. Conn. State Coll., 1966; postgrad. Ohio State U., 1966-68; M.D., Hahnemann U., 1972. Diplomate Am. Bd. Psychiatry and Neurology. Teaching asst. Ohio State U., Columbus, 1966-68, research fellow, 1966-68; clin. instr. psychiatry Hahnemann U., Phila., 1975-82, asst. clin. prof., 1982—; chief exec. officer Bldg. Mgmt. Group, Vinelaw, N.J., 1986-87; psychiat. dir. James Guiffre Med. Ctr., Phila., 1976-79; cons. Superior Ct. N.J., 1975—. Contbr. articles to profl. jours. Mem. Am. Security Council, 1975—, Rep. Senatorial Com., 1978—, Rep. Nat. Com., 1978. Recipient award Am. Security Council, 1982, Buena Regional Sch. Dist., N.J., 1983. Mem. AMA, Am. Psychiat. Assn., Internat. Assn. Group Psychotherapy, N.J. Psychiat. Soc., Phila. Coll. Physicians and Surgeons, Med. Club Phila., World Fedn. Mental Health, Internat. Coll. Physicians and Surgeons, Phi Lambda Kappa (v.p. 1972), Societe d'Chemie (pres. 1965-66). Club: SPQR (pres. 1961-62) (Milford, Conn.). Avocations: gardening; art collecting; book collecting; historical biography. Office: 1138 E Chestnut Ave Bldg 6 Vineland NJ 08360

CLOONAN, JAMES BRIAN, investment executive; b. Chgo., Jan. 28, 1931; s. Bernard V. and Lauretta D. (Maloney) C.; student Northwestern U., 1949-52, B.A., 1957, Ph.D., 1972; M.B.A., U. Chgo., 1964; m. Edythe Adrianne Ratner, Mar. 26, 1970; children—Michele, Christine, Mia; stepchildren—Carrie Madorin, Harry Madorin. Prof., Sch. Bus., Loyola U., Chgo., 1966-71; pres. Quantitative Decision Systems, Inc., Chgo., 1972-73; chmn. bd. Heinold Securities, Inc., Chgo., 1974-77; prof. Grad. Sch. Bus., DePaul U., Chgo., 1978-82; chmn. Investment Info. Services, 1981-86; pres. Mktg. Systems Internat., Inc., 1985—, Analytics Systems, Inc., 1987—. Served with U.S. Army, 1951-54. Mem. Ops. Research Soc., Inst. for Mgmt. Sci., Am. Fin. Assn., Am. Mktg. Assn. Author: Estimates of the Impact of Sign and Billboard Removal Under the Highway Beautification Act of 1965, 1966; Stock Options - The Application of Decision Theory to Basic and Advanced Strategies, 1973; An Introduction to Decision-Making for the Individual Investor, 1980; Expanding Your Investment Horizons, 1983. Home: 950 N Michigan Ave Chicago IL 60611 Office: 625 N Michigan Ave Chicago IL 60611

CLOPINE, GORDON ALAN, consulting geologist, educator; b. Los Angeles, Nov. 28, 1936; s. Walter Gordon and Sara Elizabeth (Donahue) C.; m. Sara Rose Lapinski, Mar. 2, 1979; children—William, Susan, Russell, Cynthia. B.S., U. Redlands, Calif., 1958; M.S., U. Houston, 1960. Registered geologist, Calif.; cert. profl. geol. scientist, Calif. Pres. Clopine Geol. Services, cons. geologists, Redlands, 1961—; prof. San Bernardino Valley Coll., San Bernardino, Calif., 1961-84, dean instrn., 1978-81; lectr. U. Redlands, 1961—; mem. extension faculty U. Calif.-Riverside, 1965—, field leader geol. field studies and natural environ. series. Author numerous reports and studies on geol. hazards in So. Calif. and San Andreas Fault Zone. Pres. San Bernardino County Mus. Assn., 1972. Fellow Geol. Soc. Am.; mem. Am. Inst. Profl. Geologists (cert. profl. geol. scientist). Republican. Research on geologic field studies; lecturer and researcher on San Andreas fault zone in So. Calif.; geologic hazards investigation. Home and Office: Clopine Geol Services 13093 Burns Ln Redlands CA 92373

CLOSEN, MICHAEL LEE, law educator, lawyer; b. Peoria, Ill., Jan. 25, 1949; s. Stanley Paul and Dorothy Mae (Kendall) C.; B.S., Bradley U., 1971, M.A., 1971; J.D., U. Ill., 1974. Bar: Ill. 1974. Instr. U. Ill., Champaign, 1974; jud. clk. Ill. Appellate Ct., Springfield, 1974-76, 77-78; asst. states atty. Cook County, Chgo., 1978; prof. law John Marshall Law Sch., Chgo., 1976—vis. prof. No. Ill. U., 1985-86; reporter Ill. Jud. Conf., Chgo., 1981—; arbitrator Am. Arbitration Assn., Chgo., 1981—; lectr. Ill. Inst. Continuing Legal Edn., Chgo., 1981—. Author casebook Agency, Employment and Partnership Law, 1984; (with others) Contracts, 1984; co-author: The Shopping Bag: Portable Art, 1986; contbr. articles to profl. jours. Recipient Service award Am. Arbitration Assn. 1984; named one of Outstanding Young Men in Am., 1981. Mem. ABA, Ill. Bar Assn., Appellate Lawyers Assn. Home: 1247 N State #204 Chicago IL 60610 Office: John Marshall Law Sch 315 S Plymouth Ct Chicago IL 60604

CLOSSE, WILLIAM DENIS, trading company executive, consultant; b. Liege, Belgium, Mar. 24, 1940; s. Closse Alexandre and Juliette (Gardedieu) C.; m. Francine Rossius; 1 child, Carine. Licencie en Scis. Economiques, U. Liege (Belgium), 1963; MBA, Institut Européen d'Adminstrn. des Affaires, Fontainbleau, France, 1973. Attache de direction Westminster Fgn. Bank Ltd., Brussels and London, 1965-67; chef de service Soc. Generale des Minerais, Brussels, 1967-72; corporate banker Banque Bruxelles Lambert, Brussels, 1972-77; adminstr., fin. dir. Robinetterie Close, Sclessin, Belgium, 1978-80; pres., chief exec. officer Dispo ETS, Liege, 1982—; cons., Liege, 1978—. Contbr. articles to profl. jours. Mem. State Bur. Young Liberals, Liege, 1968-70, Nat. Bur., Brussels, 1970-72; dir. Jaycee, Liege, 1977-80. Recipient Scholarship, Am. Field Service Internat., 1958. Club: RTCL. Office: Dispo ETS, Av Du Memorial 2, 4200 Liege Belgium

CLOSSER, PATRICK DENTON, artist, radio evangelist; b. San Diego, Apr. 27, 1945; s. Edward and Helen Thompson. Diploma Am. Schs. of Cinema, 1970; hon. doctorate cinema arts World U., Tucson, 1985. Artist, Sta. KBFI-TV, Dallas, 1972-73; with Stas. KVTT and KDTX, Dallas, 1976-81, Stas. KTER and KTXO, 1980-83; worked on TV commls. for Dr. Pepper, Am. Chiropractic Assn., feature movies, show Comment on Our Times, Bible's Forecast; evangelist Stas. KDTX-FM, KVTT-FM; worked on theatre trailers, network TV shows, Nelson Golf Classic, Operation Entertainment; radio evangelist Sta. Radio Africa, KXVI, WINB-shortwave; contbr. articles on evangelism to various mags. Mem. coalition for Better Television CBTV, Tupelo, Miss. Named to Life History Center, Conroe, Tex., Internat. Hall of Leaders, 1988; recipient First 500 award Internat. Biog. Assn., Bronze and Silver medals Am. Biog. Inst. Fellow Internat. Platform Assn., Internat. Biog. Assn. (life); mem. Anglo-Am. Acad., Internat. Christian Broadcasters Assn., Am. Biog. Assn. Religious Broadcasters, Soc. Motion Picture and TV Engrs., Nat. Fedn. Decency, Internat. Hall of Leaders. Home: PO Box 540881 Dallas TX 75220

CLOUD, PRESTON, geologist, author, consultant; b. West Upton, Mass., Sept. 26, 1912; s. Preston E. and Pauline L. (Wiedemann) C.; m. Janice Gibson, 1972; children by previous marriage: Karen, Lisa, Kevin. B.S., George Washington U., 1938; Ph.D., Yale U., 1940. Instr. Mo. Sch. Mines and Metallurgy, 1940-41; research fellow Yale U., 1941-42; geologist U.S. Geol. Survey, 1942-46, 48-61, 74-79, chief paleontology and stratigraphy br., 1949-59; research geologist 1959-61, 74-79; asst. prof., curator invertebrate paleontology Harvard U., 1946-48; prof. dept. geology and geophysics U. Minn., 1961-65, chmn., 1961-63; prof. geology UCLA, 1965-68; prof. biogeology and environ. studies dept. geol. scis. U. Calif., Santa Barbara, 1968-74, prof. emeritus, 1974—; vis. prof. U. Tex., 1962, 78; H.R. Luce prof. cosmology Mt. Holyoke Coll., 1979-80; Sr. Queens fellow Baas-Becking Geobiology Lab., Canberra, Australia, 1981; internat exchange scholar Nat. Sci. and Engring. Research Council Can., 1982; hon. vis. prof. U. Ottawa (Ont. Can.), 1982; Nat. Sigma Xi lectr., 1967; Emmons lectr. Colo. Sci. Soc.; Bownocker lectr. Ohio State U.; French lectr. Pomona Coll.; Dumaresq-Smith lectr. Acadia Coll., N.B., Can.; A.L. DuToit Meml. lectr. Royal Soc. and Geol. Soc. of South Africa; mem. governing bd. NRC, 1972-75; mem. Pacific Sci. Bd., 1952-56, 62-65; del. internat. sci. congresses; cons. to govt., industry, founds. and agys. Author: Terebratuloid Brachiopoda of the Silurian and Devonian, 1942; (with Virgil E. Barnes) The Ellenburger Group of Central Texas, 1948; (with others) Geology of Saipan, Mariana Islands, 1957; Environment of Calcium Carbonate Deposition West of Andros Island, Bahamas, 1962, Cosmos, Earth and Man, 1978, Oasis in Space, 1988; editor and co-author: (with others) Resources and Man, 1969, Adventures in Earth History, 1970; Author articles. Recipient A. Cressey Morrison prize natural history, 1941, Rockefeller Pub. Service award, 1956, U.S. Dept. Interior Distinguished Service award and gold medal, 1959, Medal, Paleontol Soc. Am., 1971, Lucius W. Cross medal Yale U., 1973, Penrose medal Geol. Soc. Am., 1976, C.D. Walcott medal Nat. Acad. Scis., 1977, R.C. Moore medal Soc. Econ. Paleontologists and Mineralogists, 1986; J.S. Guggenheim fellow, 1982-83. Fellow Am. Acad. Arts and Scis. (com. on membership 1978-80, council 1980-83); mem. Am. Philos. Soc., Nat. Acad. Scis. (com. on sci. and pub. policy 1965-69, mem. council 1972-75, exec. com. 1973-75, chmn. com. on resources and man 1965-69, chmn. ad hoc com. nat. materials policy 1972, chmn. study group on uses of underground space 1972, chmn. com. mineral resources and environment 1972-73, chmn. com. geology and climate 1977, chmn. sect. geology 1976-79, mem. assembly math. and phys. scis. 1976-79), Polish Acad. Scis. (fgn. assoc.), Geol. Soc. Am. (council 1972-75), Paleontol. Soc. Am., Paleontol. Soc. India (hon.), AAAS, Geol. Soc. Belgium (hon. fgn. corr.), Paläont. Soc. Deutschland (hon., corresponding mem.), Phi Beta Kappa, Sigma Xi, Sigma Gamma Epsilon. Home: 400 Mountain Dr Santa Barbara CA 93103 Office: U Calif Dept Geol Scis Santa Barbara CA 93106

CLOUDT, FLORENCE RICKER, architectural products company executive; b. Houston, July 12, 1925; d. Norman Hurd and Sallie Lee (St. Louis) Ricker; m. William Sandford Pottinger, Dec. 28, 1946 (div. Jan. 1975); children—Norman Sandford, Margaret Halliday; m. Frank Winfield Cloudt, Aug. 12, 1977 (div. May 1982). B.F.A., Tulane U., 1946. Founder, pres. Florence Pottinger Nursery Sch., Atlanta, 1955-56; tchr. Montgomery County Schs., Md., 1956-60; master tchr. The Nat. Cathedral Sch., Washington, 1960-62; founder, pres. Florence Pottinger Interiors, Atlanta, 1962-78; co-founder, v.p. Focal Point, Inc., Atlanta, 1970-78, pres., 1978—; mem. decorative arts adv. bd. Nat. Trust for Hist. Preservation, Washington, 1985-87; mem. adv. bd. family bus. forum Kennesaw Coll., 1987—. Producer pub. service TV program for Jr. League of Washington, 1957-62. Bd. dirs. Atlanta Landmarks, 1972—, Atlanta Preservation Council, 1988; sec. Roswell Hist. Soc., Ga., 1972-74; bd. advisors Atlanta Preservation Ctr., 1979, trustee, 1980—; mem. adv. bd. Family Bus. Forum, 1988. Recipient Industry Found. award Am. Soc. Interior Designers, 1982; Outstanding Service award Atlanta Preservation Soc., 1983, Acorn award Designews mag., 1988. Mem. Women Bus. Owners, CEO Exec. Forum (charter). Republican. Episcopalian. Club: Women Commerce (Atlanta). Avocations: painting; writing. Office: Focal Point Inc 2005 Marietta Rd NW Atlanta GA 30318

CLOULAS, IVAN, archivist; b. St. Junien, France, Dec. 26, 1932; s. Adrien and Lucie (Boutet) C.; m. Annie Brousseau, July 16, 1962; children: Catherine, Sophie, Silvain, Cecile. Diploma archivist paleograph, Ecole des Chartes, Paris, 1957; D in History, U. Paris Sorbonne, 1968. Conservator Archives Nationales, Paris, 1957, conservator of modern series, 1965, chief automated data processing, 1972-85, chief history dept., 1985—; researcher Ecole Francaise de Rome, 1957-59, Casa de Velazquez, Madrid, 1965-68; chief departmental archives Evreux, France, 1968=72; gen. sec. Reg. Com. for Automation, UNESCO, 1972-84. Author: Catherine de Medecis, 1979, Laurent le Magnifique, 1982, Vie Quotidiene in Renaissance, 1983, Henri II, 1985, Charles VIII, 1986, Les Borgia, 1987; contbr. articles to profl. jours. Arts and letters officer, Paris, Merite officer, Paris. Recipient grand prize Ville de Paris, 1982, Histoire de L'Academie Francaise, 1986. Fellow Soc. de l'Ecole des Chartes, Soc. de L'Histoire de France, Soc. Libre de l"Eure (gen. sec.), Acad. de Rouen, Soc. Archeologique et Historique du Limousin. Office: Archives Nationale, 60 rue des Frances Bourgeois, Paris 75141, France

CLOUSE, JOHN DANIEL, lawyer; b. Evansville, Ind., Sept. 4, 1925; s. Frank Paul and Anna Lucille (Frank) C.; m. Georgia L. Ross, Dec. 7, 1978; 1 child, George Chauncey. AB, U. Evansville, 1950; JD, Ind. U., 1952. Bar: Ind. 1952, U.S. Supreme Ct. 1962, U.S. Ct. Appeals (7th cir.) 1965. Assoc. firm James D. Lopp, Evansville, 1952-56; pvt. practice law, Evansville, 1956—; guest editorialist Viewpoint, Evansville Courier, 1978-86, Evansville Press, 1986—, Focus, Radio Sta. WGBF, 1978-84; 2d asst. city atty. Evansville, 1954-55; mem. appellate rules sub-com. Ind. Supreme Ct. Com. on Rules of Practice and Procedure, 1980. Pres. Civil Service Commn. of Evansville Police Dept., 1961-62, active 1988—; pres. Ind. War Memls. Com., 1963-69; mem. jud. nominating com. Vanderburgh County, Ind., 1976-80. Served with inf. U.S. Army, 1943-46. Decorated Bronze Star. Fellow Ind. Bar Found.; mem. Evansville Bar Assn. (v.p. 1972), Ind. Bar Assn., Selden Soc., Pi Gamma Mu. Republican. Methodist. Club: Travelers Century (Los Angeles). Home: 819 S Hebron Ave Evansville IN 47715 Office: 1010 Hulman Bldg Evansville IN 47708

CLOUSER, NANCY JANE, governmental personnel adminstrator; b. Los Angeles; d. Glen Rich and Emily Esther (Kirk) Price; m. Robert E. Clouser, Apr. 26, 1961. BS, S.W. Tex. State U., 1977; M in Mgmt. and Human Relations, Webster U., St. Louis, 1978; postgrad., Nova U., 1978, Fielding Inst., Santa Barbara, Calif., 1979-84; PhD, Columbia Pacific U., 1985. Classification specialist Lackland AFB, San Antonio, Tex., 1977-80; employee relations specialist Kelly AFB, San Antonio, 1980-82, personnel mgmt. specialist Hdqrs. Air Force Commissary Service, 1982-85; dir. civilian personnel Air Force Commissary Service European region, 1985-87; civilian personnel officer Hellenikon AFB, Athens, 1987—; keynote speaker Fed. Womens Program, 1987. Recipient Dan Berkant award Air Force Assn., 1983. Mem. Am. Soc. for Tng. and Devel., Internat. Personnel Mgmt. Assn., Am. Soc. for Personnel Adminstrn., Am. Soc. for Personnel Mgmt. Episcopalian. Office: Hellenikon AFB Greece 7206 Air Base Group/DPC APO New York NY 09223-5000

CLUBB, BRUCE EDWIN, lawyer; b. Blackduck, Minn., Feb. 6, 1931; s. Ernest and Abigail (Gordy) C.; m. Martha Lucia Trapp, Dec. 19, 1954; children: Bruce Allen, Christopher Wade. B.B.A., U. Minn., 1955, LL.B. cum laude, 1958. Bar: D.C. 1959. Atty. Covington & Burling, 1958-61, Devel. Loan Fund, 1961-62, Chapman, DiSalle and Friedman, 1962-67; commr. U.S. Tariff Commn., 1967-71; ptnr. firm Baker & McKenzie, Washington, 1971—; disting. lawyer in residence U. Minn. Law Sch., 1981-82. Contbr. law revs. Served with AUS, 1952-54. Mem. D.C. Bar Assn., Am. Judicature Soc., Order of Coif. Republican. Clubs: Cosmos (pres. 1986), Metropolitan, Army Navy. Home: 100 Quay St Alexandria VA 22314 Office: Baker & McKenzie 815 Connecticut Ave NW Washington DC 20006

CLUMP, CARL CYRIL, oil executive; b. Calcutta, India, Feb. 11, 1953; s. Herwin Augustine and Rita Josephine (Wemyss) C.; m. Brenda Kathryn Stevens, July 16, 1977; children: Philip James, Angela Louise, Nicola Marie. BSc in Physics, London External, 1975; MBA, Cranfield Sch. Mgmt., 1980. Systems analyst Post Office D.P. Exec., London, 1975-79; bus. analyst Texaco Ltd., London, 1980-82, planning coordinator, 1982-84; area mgr. Star Service Stas. Ltd., London, 1984-85; European coordinator Texaco Services Europe Ltd., Brussels, 1985—; speaker on electronic funds transfer. Recipient Bursary Cranfield Inst. Tech., Bedfordshire, 1979. Mem. Bus. Grads. Assn. Roman Catholic. Home: 19 Church Ave, Pinner England Office: Texaco Services Europe Ltd, Ave Louis 149, B-1050 Brussels Belgium

CLURMAN, RICHARD MICHAEL, business executive; b. N.Y.C., Mar. 10, 1924; s. Will N. and Emma (Herzberg) C.; divorced; children: Susan Emma, Carol Mae; m. Shirley Potash, Apr. 13, 1957; 1 child, Richard Michael. PhB, U. Chgo., 1946, postgrad., 1946-48. Asst. editor Commentary mag., 1946-49; press editor Time mag., 1949-55; editorial dir. Newsday, 1955-58; dep. chief corr. Time and Life mag., N.Y.C., 1958-60; chief Time and Life mag., 1960-69; v.p. Time Inc., 1969-72; chmn. bd. Time-Life Broadcast, 1971-72; adminstr. Parks, Recreation and Cultural Affairs Adminstrn. and Commn. Parks, City N.Y., 1973-74; cons. Am. Revolution Bicentennial Adminstrn., 1974; dir. E.M. Warburg, Pincus & Co., Inc., 1976-81; pres. Richard M. Clurman Assocs., Inc., 1975—; pub. policy advisor Office of Chmn., Joseph E. Seagram & Sons, Inc., 1980-84. Author: Beyond Malice: The Media's Years of Reckoning, 1988. Chmn. bd. N.Y.C. Ctr. Music and Drama, Inc., 1968-75; pres. N.Y. Found. for Arts, Inc., 1971-72; bd. dirs. Lincoln Ctr. for Performing Arts, 1968-75, Sch. Am. Ballet, 1970-76, Parks Council, 1975-77; chmn. Gov.'s Task Force on Arts and Cultural Life, 1975; mem. adv. council NYU Sch. of Arts, 1974—; chmn. adv. com. WNCN, chmn., 1975-76; bd. dirs. Citizens Com. N.Y.C., 1976—; chmn. bd. govs. Columbia U. Grad. Sch. Journalism media and society seminars, 1981—. Served with AUS, 1942-46. Mem. Council Fgn. Relations. Clubs: Federal, City (Washington); Century Assn. (N.Y.C.). Office: Suite 4328 Time & Life Bldg Rockefeller Ctr New York NY 10020

CLUTTERBUCK, DAVID ASHLEY, small business owner, editor; b. London, June 4, 1947; s. Leslie Herbert and Doris Violet (Maylett) C.; m. Pauline Sandra Neudegg, Oct. 20, 1949; children: Simon, Alan, Daniel, Jonathan. BA in English with honors, London U., 1968. Editor Jour. Brit. Nuclear Energy Inst. Civil Engrs., London, 1969-70; news editor tech. New Scientist, London, 1970-73; assoc. editor Internat. Mgmt., London, 1973-80, mng. editor, 1980-83; chmn. The Item Group, Burnham, Eng., 1983—; sr. ptnr. Clutterbuck Assocs., Maiderhead, 1984—; hon. reader bus. policy Stirling u. Author: How To Be A Good Corporate Citizen, 1981, The Tales of Gribble the Goblin, 1983; co-author: The Remaking of Work, 1981, The Winning Streak, 1983, The Winning Streak Check Book, 1985, Everyone Needs A Mentor, 1985, Clore: The Man and His Millions, 1987, Management Buyouts, 1987; co-editor: Businesswoman, 1987, The Marketing Edge, 1987; editor Strategic Direction, Tech. Strategies, Issues, 1984—. Mem. Assn. Brit. Sci. Writers, Inst. Journalists, Brit. Assn. Indsl. Editors. Liberal. Office: The Item Group, Burnham House High St, Burnham SL1 7JZ, England

CLUVER, MICHAEL ALBERT, paleontologist, museum director; b. Caledon, Cape Province, Republic South Africa, Dec. 20, 1942; s. Ralph Paul and Anne Magdalene (Mossop) C.; m. Estelle Laäs, May 28, 1966; children: Anthony Charles, Penelope Anne, Michelle Elizabeth. BSc, U. Stellenbosch, Republic South Africa, 1964, BSc with honors, 1964; MSc cum laude, U. Stellenbosch (Republic S. Africa), 1966, PhD in Zoology, 1970. Research officer S. African Mus., Capetown, 1966-73; head dept. paleontology South African Mus., Capetown, 1973-77, asst. dir., 1977-85; dir. S. African Mus., Capetown, 1985—; hon. prof. U. Cape Town, 1987. Author: Fossil Reptiles of South Africa, 1979; contbr. articles to profl. jours. Fellow Royal Soc. South Africa; mem. Paleontol. Soc. South Africa, South Africa Assn., South African Mus. Assn. Clubs: Owl (Cape Town), City Civil Service (Cape Town). Home: 2 Reitz St, Parow North, Cape Town 8000, Republic of South Africa Office: S African Mus, Queen Victoria St, Cape Town 8001, Republic of South Africa

CLYBURN, LUTHER LINN, real estate broker; b. Evansville, Ind., May 17, 1942; s. Luther and Robbie (Cobb) C.; children: Lisa Michelle Clyburn Swain, Luther Brent. Grad., Am. Savs. and Loan Inst., 1970; ABA, Pontiac (Mich.) Bus. Inst., 1972; BS, Detroit Coll. Bus., 1972; M of Bus. Mgmt., Cen. Mich. U., 1983. Chief loan officer First Fed. Savs. and Loan Assn. Oakland, Pontiac, 1964-74; assoc. broker Bateman Real Estate Corp., Pontiac, 1975-77; regional rep. United Guaranty Residential Ins., Troy, Mich., 1977-83; sr. account mgr. Investors Mortgage Ins. Co., Boston, 1983-87; real estate broker, appraiser Pontiac, 1977—, Clyburn Appraisal Services, Pontiac, 1987—. Project dir., capt.: (documentary film) Angels of the Sea, 1982 (N.Y. Film Festival award 1983). Capt., comdr. "Noble Odyssey" Tng. Ship, Mt. Clemens, Mich., 1977—; dir., comdr. U.S. Naval Sea Cadet Corps Great Lakes div., Southfield, Mich., 1973—; project dir. Interseas Inc., Pontiac, 1982; ship capt. Great Lakes Botanical Island research project for Cranbrook Inst. Sci. (Thunder Bay Islands, Lake Huron), 1987. Recipient Cert. Appreciation award Southfield Bicentennial Commn., 1976, Letter of Commendation award Sec. of Navy, 1983. Mem. Internat. Ship Masters Assn., Navy League of U.S., Am. Soc. Appraisers, Mich. Assn. Real Estate Appraisers. Club: Detroit Econs. Home and Office: 9000 Gale Rd Pontiac MI 48054

COAKER, JAMES WHITFIELD, mechanical engineer; b. Boston, Nov. 12, 1946; s. George W. and Margaret N. Coaker; m. Ruth Johnson, May 17, 1969; children—James W., John A., Stephen D. B.S.M.E., Lafayette Coll., 1968; M.S.B., Va. Commonwealth U., 1976. Registered profl. engr., Va. Application engr., pump and condenser div. Ingersoll-Rand Co., Richmond, Va., 1972-76; project mgr. Reco Industries, Inc., Richmond, 1976-77, asst. mgr. engring., 1977-79, mgr. engring., 1979-83; systems engr., program mgr. Advanced Tech., Inc., Arlington, Va., 1983-87, program mgr. Boiler and Elevator Safety, U.S.Postal Service, Washington, 1987—; lectr. and educator in field. Served with USN, 1969-72; to comdr. USNR. Mem. ASME (nat. chnm. plant engr. and maintenance div.), Elevator Inspection Com., Nat. Soc. Profl. Engrs., Nat. Council Engring. Examiners (affiliate). Home: 11675 Captain Rhett Ln Fairfax Station VA 22039-1236

COATES, KENNETH SIDNEY, reader in adult education, author, editor; b. Leek, Stafford, Eng., Sept. 16, 1930; s. Eric Coates and Mary (Griffiths) C.; m. Betty Marina, 1949 (div. 1959); children: Dylan, Lawrence, Michael; m. Tamara Tura, Aug. 21, 1969; children: Deborah, Francesca, Helena. BA in Sociology, U. Nottingham, 1959. Tutor in sociology then reader U. Nottingham, 1960—. Author: Work-Ins, Sit-Ins and Industrial Democracy, 1981, Heresies, 1983, The Most Dangerous Decade, 1984; co-author: Poverty-The Forgotten Englishmen, 1971; Industrial Democracy in Great

Britain, 1967, Trade Unions in Britain, 1980, Trade Unions and Politics, 1986. Joint sec. internat. liaison com. European Nuclear Disarmament, Brussels and Nottingham, 1981—; mem., editor-in-chief Russell Found. Labour. Office: Bertrand Russell House, Gamble St, Nottingham England

COATS, SIR WILLIAM DAVID, financial executive; b. July 25, 1924; s. Thomas Heywood Coats and Olivia Violet Pitman; m. Elizabeth Lilian Graham MacAndrew, 1950; 3 children. Student, Eton Coll.; LLD (hon.), U. Strathclyde, 1977; DL, U. Ayr and Arran, 1986. With Coats Patons plc, 1948—, dep. chmn., 1979-81, chmn., 1981-86; dep. chmn. Clydesdale Bank, 1985—, bd. dirs., 1962—; past bd. dirs. The Cen. Agy. Ltd., Coats Patons plc, Murray Caledonian Trust Co. Ltd., Weir Group Ltd., Murray Investment Trusts. Mem. S. of Scotland Electricity Bd., 1972-81. Club: Western (Glasgow). Home: The Cottage, Symington, Ayrshire KA1 5QG, England *

COBB, DANIEL W., JR., editor, media consultant; b. Hartford, Ala., Aug. 12, 1921; m. Stella Morris, Nov. 19, 1944 (dec. 1975); 1 child, David Childs. City editor Birmingham News, Ala., 1951-53; asst. city editor Houston Chronicle, Tex., 1953-57, city editor, 1957-62, news editor, 1962-77, news editor, asst. mng. editor, 1970-77, exec. mng. editor news, 1977-86; proprietor The Cobb Co., Media Cons. of Houston, 1986—. Episcopalian. Office: The Cobb Co 3209 W Lamar Houston TX 77019

COBB, DAVID BILSLAND, oil company executive; b. Glasgow, Scotland, Jan. 14, 1936; s. John Alexander and Ellen Elizabeth (Moore) C.; m. Johanna Craig, Mar. 31, 1958 (div. 1983); children: David B., Hilary P., Alison L.; m. Audrey Kathryn Connell, Apr. 5, 1983. BS in Naval Architecture, Royal Tech. Coll., Glasgow, Scotland, 1956; LLD (hon.), Strathclyde U., Glasgow, Scotland, 1985. Mng. dir. Ross Group Subs., Selby, Eng., 1964-69; chmn. Rowbotham Tankships, London, 1970-85; chmn., mng. dir. Richard Dunston Industries, Hull, Eng., 1971-85; dir. Ingram Corp., New Orleans, 1974-85; pres. Ingram Internat. S.A., Monaco, 1982-85; chmn. Helsman Ins. Brokers Lloyds, London, 1982-85; dir. London Steamship, 1974-85; mng. dir. Belgravia Internat. Trading , Ltd., London, 1986—; cons. Zodiac Maritime, Ltd., London and Hong Kong, 1986—. Fellow Royal Inst. Naval Architects, Inst. Marine Engrs.; mem. Worshipful Co. of Shipwrights, Worshipful Co. Painter Stainers, Waterman and Lightermen of River Thames. Methodist. Clubs: Caledonian, Annabels (London); Royal and Ancient, Golf St. Andrews, Sunningdale Golf, Ganton Golf. Home: West Lea Cadsden, Aylesbury, Bucks HP17 0NA, England Office: Belgravia Internat Trading Ltd, 29 Chesham Pl, London SW1, England

COBB, HENRY STEPHEN, archivist; b. Wallasey, Cheshire, Eng., Nov. 17, 1926; s. Ernest and Violet Kate (Sleath) C.; m. Eileen Margaret Downer, Apr. 5, 1969. BA, London Sch. Econs., 1950, MA, 1957. Asst. archivist House of Lords, London, 1953-59; asst. clk. of records House of Lords, 1959-73, dep. clk., 1973-81, clk. of records, 1981—; examiner London U. Archive Diploma, 1981—, U. Coll. North Wales Archive Diploma, 1986—. Editor: The Local Port Book of Southampton, 1439-40, 1961; contbr. articles to profl. jours. Fellow Soc. Antiquaries, Royal Hist. Soc.; mem. Soc. Archivists, London Record Soc. Office: House of Lords Record Office, London SW1A, England

COBB, SHIRLEY ANN, public relations specialist, journalist; b. Oklahoma City, Jan. 1, 1936; d. William Ray and Irene (Fewell) Dodson; m. Roy Lampkin Cobb, Jr., June 21, 1958; children: Kendra Leigh, Cary William, Paul Alan. BA in Journalism with distinction, U. Okla., 1958, postgrad., 1972; postgrad., Jacksonville U., 1962. Info. specialist Pacific Missle Test Ctr., Pt. Mugu, Calif., 1975-76; corr. Religious News Service, N.Y.C., 1979-81; splty. editor fashion and religion Thousand Oaks (Calif.) News Chronicle, 1977-81; pub. relations cons., Camarillo, Calif., 1977—; sr. mgmt. analyst pub. info City of Thousand Oaks, 1983—. Contbr. articles to profl. jours. Trustee Ocean View Sch. Bd., 1976-79; pres. Pt. Mugu Officers' Wives Club, 1975-76; bd. dirs. Camarillo Hospice, 1983-85. Recipient Spot News award San Fernando Valley Press Club, 1979. Mem. Pub. Relations Soc. Am., Sigma Delta Chi, Phi Beta Kappa. Republican. Clubs: Las Posas Country, Town Hall of Calif. Home: 2481 Brookhill Dr Camarillo CA 93010 Office: 2150 W Hillcrest Dr Thousand Oaks CA 91360

COBB, WILLIAM MONTAGUE, anatomist, physical anthropologist, medical editor, emeritus educator; b. Washington, Oct. 12, 1904; s. William Elmer and Alexzine E. (Montague) C.; m. Hilda B. Smith, June 26, 1929 (dec. June 1976); children: Carolyn Cobb Wilkinson, Hilda Amelia Cobb Gray. A.B. (Blodgett scholar), Amherst Coll., 1925, Sc.D. (hon.), 1955; M.D., Howard U., 1929, D.H.L. (hon.), 1980; Ph.D., Western Res. U., 1932; Sc.D. (hon.), Colby Coll., 1984; D.H.L. (hon.), Med. Coll. Pa., 1986; cert. in embryology, Marine Biol. Lab., Woods Hole, Mass.; student, U.S. Nat. Museum, Washington U.; LL.D., Morgan State Coll., 1964, U. Witwatersrand, South Africa, 1977; Sc.D., Georgetown U., 1978, Med. Coll. Wis., 1979, U. Ark., 1983; D.Med. Sci., Brown U., 1983. Intern Freedmen's Hosp., Washington, 1929-30; instr. embryology Howard U., 1928-29, asst. prof. anatomy, 1932-34, assoc. prof., 1934-42, prof. anatomy, 1942-69, head dept., 1947-69, distinguished prof. anatomy, 1969-73, prof. emeritus, 1973—; vis. prof. anatomy Stanford U., 1972, U. Md., 1974, W.Va. U., 1980; Disting. Univ. prof. U. Ark. Med. Scis. Center, 1979; vis. prof., Danz lectr. U. Wash., 1978; vis. prof. orthopaedic surgery Harvard U., 1981; vis. prof. anatomy Med. Coll. Wis., 1982; dir. Disting. Sr. Scholars Lecture Series U. D.C., 1983; jr. med. officer U.S. Dept. Agr., 1935; mem. Pub. Health Advisory Council of D.C., 1953-61, chmn., 1956-58; chief med. examiner Freedmen's Hosp. Bd., D.C. SSS, 1941; civilian cons. to surgeon gen. U.S. Army, 1945; mem. exec. com. White House Conf. on Health, 1965; Fellow in anatomy Western Res. U., 1933-39, asso. anatomy, 1942-44. Founder: Bull. of Medico-Chirurg. Soc. D.C, 1941; editor, 1945-54, Jour. Nat. Med. Assn, 1949-77; author monographs, articles. Rosenwald fellow, 1941-42; recipient citations from Opportunity mag., 1947, citations from Chgo. Defender, 1948, citations from Washington Afro-Am., 1948; Distinguished Service award Medico-Chirurg. Soc. D.C., 1952; D.S.M. Nat. Med. Assn., 1955; Meritorious Service award Med. Soc. of D.C., 1968; Meritorious Pub. Service award Govt. of D.C., 1972; Disting. Public Service award U.S. Navy, 1978, 82; recognized with inaguration of W. Montague Cobb Collection Moorland-Springarn Research Ctr., Los Angeles, 1979, dedication of W. Montague Cobb Med. Edn. Bldg., King-Drew Med. Ctr., ;os Angeles, 1984, dedication of A Century of Black Surgeons-The U.S.A. Experience (book) to W. Montague Cobb, Howard U. Hosp., 1987. Fellow Am. Anthrop. Assn., Gerontol. Soc., AAAS (mem. 1957-59), Assn. Anatomists (Henry Gray award 1980), Am. Assn. Phys. Anthropologists (v.p. 1948-50, pres. 1957-59), Am. Eugenics Soc. (dir. 1957-68), Anat. Soc. Gt. Brit. and Ireland, Nat. Med. Assn. (state v.p. 1943, editor 1949-77, chmn. council on med. edn. and hosps. 1949-63, nat. pres. 1964-65), Nat. Urban League (health specialist 1945-47), NAACP (chmn. nat. med. com. 1950, dir. 1949—, pres. 1976-82), Am. Soc. Mammalogists, Am. Assn. History of Medicine, Washington Soc. History of Medicine (pres. 1972), Assn. Study of Negro Life and History, Anthrop. Soc. Washington (pres. 1949-51), Medica-Chirurgical Soc. D.C. (rec. sec. 1935-41, pres. 1945-47, 54-56), Omega Psi Phi (chmn. scholarship com. 1939-48), Sigma Xi, Alpha Omega Alpha. Presbyterian. Club: Cosmos (Washington). Home: 1219 Girard St NW Washington DC 20009 Office: Howard U Washington DC 20059

COBBETT, EDWARD LAKE, oil and gas company executive; b. Hamilton, Ont., Can., June 25, 1941; s. Harold Frank and Gladys (Mathews) C.; m. Carolyn Ann Davidson; children: Jacqueline Ann, Edward Lake II. Student, U. McMaster, 1960-63; BA, U. Fla., Orlando, 1971; degree in mgmt., Fla. Tech. U., 1972; postgrad. in civil engring., U. McMaster, Hamilton. Designer McCargar, Filer, Hachborn, Engrs., Hamilton, 1963-67; design engr. Pointer, Briel, Rhame-NASA Cape Kennedy, Titesville, Fla., 1967-69; project mgr. Walt Disney World, Orlando, 1969-72; gen. mgr. Chatham Assoc. Contractor/Engr., Hamilton, 1972-74; mgr. contracts, adminstrn. Fluor Can. Ltd., Calgary, Alta., Can., 1974-75; chmn., chief exec. officer Egypt Can. Corp. div. of E.L. Cobbett Inc., Toronto, Cairo, Switzerland, 1975-80; pres., chief exec. officer Non Destructive Testings Inc. div. of E.L. Cobbett Inc., Toronto, 1975-80; mng. ptnr., chief exec. officer Cobbett, Wasylow, Nester Ltd. div. of E.L. Cobbett Inc., Toronto, 1975-80; mng. dir. Spencer Stuart, Calgary, 1980-85; v.p. corp. affairs Oakwood Petroleums Ltd., Calgary, 1985—; bd. dirs. Lake Syndicates, Calgary/Toronto, 1985—. Contbr. articles to profl. jours. Bd. dirs. Alta. Ballet, Calgary, 1984-86, Jr. Achievement, Calgary, 1985—; bd. govs. Calgary Bd. Edn., 1986—. Club: Bow Valley (Calgary). Home: 64 Edgewood Rd NW, Calgary, AB Canada T3A 2T5 Office: Oakwood Petroleums Ltd, 1800-311-6th Ave SW, Calgary, AB Canada T2P3H2

COBERLY, WILLIAM BAYLEY, JR., cotton oil corporation executive; b. Tucson, May 8, 1908; s. William Bayley and Winifred (Wheeler) C.; m. Aileen Dorsey, Dec. 10, 1934 (dec. Nov. 1948); children: Sheryl (Mrs. Griffith), Aileen (Mrs. Hadley), William 3d; m. Victoria Nebeker Mudd, Sept. 16, 1969. A.B., Stanford, 1930. Asso. Calif. Cotton Oil Corp. (predecessor firms), 1930—, dir., asst. gen. mgr., 1945-51, v.p., gen. mgr., 1951—, pres., 1956—, chmn., 1983—; chmn. now Coberly-West Co., 1983—; v.p., dir. Coberly-West Co., Bakersfield, Calif., 1951-57; pres., dir. Coberly-West Co., 1957—; chmn., dir. Coberly Ford, Inc., 1957-82; dir. So. Calif. Edison Co., 1953-81. Trustee Found. Econ. Edn., Irvington, N.Y., 1951-76, Harvey Mudd Coll., Claremont, Calif.; bd. overseers Hoover Instn. on War, Revolution and Peace, Stanford, Calif. Mem. Nat. Cottonseed Products Assn. (pres. 1952-53, dir., hon. mem.), Chi Psi. Republican. Conglist. Clubs: California (Los Angeles), Beach (Los Angeles), Sunset (Los Angeles), Lincoln (Los Angeles). Home: 247 Muirfield Rd Los Angeles CA 90004 Office: 606 N Larchmont Blvd Los Angeles CA 90004

COBEY, JAMES ALEXANDER, law educator; b. Frostburg, Md., Oct. 3, 1913; s. James Carpinter and Elizabeth Kownslar (Earle) C; m. Virginia Joy Branum, Aug. 1, 1942; children—Hope Batey, Christopher E., Lisa. A.B., Princeton U., 1934; J.D., Yale U., 1938; cert. Harvard Grad. Sch. Bus. Adminstrn., 1938. Bar: D.C. 1939, U.S. Supreme Ct. 1946, Calif. 1947. Atty. review, NLRB, Washington, 1938-39, field, Los Angeles, 1940-41, 1946; chief research atty. Calif. Ct. Appeal, Los Angeles, 1946-48; dep. county counsel Los Angeles County, 1948; assoc. C. Ray Robinson, Merced, Calif., 1949-60; ptnr. Cobey & Adams, Merced, 1961-66; prof. law Southwestern U., Los Angeles, 1982—; mem. Calif. State Senate from Merced-Madena Counties, 1955-66; assoc. justice Calif. Ct. Appeal, Los Angeles, 1966-81. Dist. commdr. Am. Legion, Merced, 1952; pres. Constl. Rights Found., Los Angeles, 1976-78; trustee Westridge Sch., Pasadena, 1972-82. Served to lt. USNR, 1942-46. Recipient Golden Gavel award Nat. Assn. Legis. Leaders, 1962, Disting. Alumnus award Mercersburg Acad., 1982. Justice James A Cobey Day proclaimed by Mayor Los Angeles, 1981. Mem. ABA, Democrat. Episcopalian. Club: Valley Hunt (Pasadena). Home: 645 Westbridge Pl Pasadena CA 91105 Office: Southwestern U Sch Law 675 S Westmoreland Ave Los Angeles CA 90005

COBIELLA, ROBERT MARIO, mechanical engineer; b. St. Louis, June 12, 1930; s. Angel Jose and Jean Miller (Brown) C.; BSME, U. P.R., Mayaguez, 1954; m. Yvette Rosello, Sept. 22, 1960; children: Grace M., Robert S., Angel M., Jeannette. Sr. design engr. N.Am. Aviation, Calif., Ala., and Miss., 1962-66; sr. research engr. Boeing Co., Cocoa, Fla., 1966-68, research, Orlando, Fla., 1968-70; project mgr. Rexco Industries, Inc., San Juan, P.R., 1970-72; dir. tech. Las Colinas Devel. Corp., San Juan, 1972-75; on-scene coordinator Region II Site Mitigation Sect., EPA, Edison, N.J., 1975—Dir. Precinct Computation and Data Analysis Office, 1976; mem. Precinct Central Com., San Juan, 1976. Recipient Outstanding Performance cert. Fed. Disaster Assistance Adminstrn., 1975, 79, Outstanding Service award Boeing Co., Cape Canaveral, Fla., 1968, EPA, 1981-87, Disting. Achievement award, 1985, 87; Letters of Commendation various govt. agys.; Disting. Achievement award EPA, 1985. Registered profl. engr., P.R. Mem. P.R. Coll. Engrs., P.R. Mech. Engrs. Assn., Am. Security Council (nat. adv. bd. 1980-87). Patentee in field. Home: 5 Gudz Rd Lakewood NJ 08701 Office: Emergency Response Section EPA Region II Edison NJ 08817

COBLENTZ, GASTON, stockbroker; b. N.Y.C., June 8, 1918; s. Gaston and Lillian (Lashanska) C.; m. Zoubida Bentaieb, Jan. 22, 1982; m. Milosava Mikich, Jan. 16, 1952 (div. 1981); children—Andrea, Marina. Grad. cum laude Hotchkiss Sch., 1936; B.A. cum laude, Harvard Coll., 1939. Fgn. corr. N.Y. Herald Tribune, N.Y.C., 1946-63; ptnr., dir. Mitchell Hutchins & Co., Inc., N.Y.C., 1963-77; sr. v.p., dir. Paine Webber Mitchell Hutchins Internat., Inc., Paris, 1977-79; dir. Gaston Coblentz & Co. Ltd., St. Helier, Jersey, C.I., 1979-81, U.K. rep., 1982—; cons. Golden Eagle Investments SA, 1983—, Lula 10100 Gold Mining N.V., 1985—. Co-author: Duel on the Brink, 1960. Served as maj. USAAF, 1941-45. Decorated D.F.C.; Croix de Guerre avec etoile de bronze (France); recipient Disting. Service in Journalism award Sigma Delta Chi, 1961. Clubs: Harvard, Overseas Press (N.Y.C.); Cercle de l'Union Interallie (Paris). Home: Morley Old Hall, Morley St Peter, Wymondham Norfolk NR18 9TT England

COBURN, HERBERT DIGHTMAN, JR., mechanical engineer; b. N.Y.C., Nov. 5, 1919; s. Herbert Dightman and Miriam (Ware) C.; m. Julia Mae Ledbetter, July 29, 1944; children—Herbert Bryant, Randall Nye. Student, Friends Sem., N.Y.C., 1936-39, Newark Coll. Engring., 1939-42; B.S.M.E., So. Meth. U., 1947. Chem. lab. asst. Philip Stroughton & Co., N.Y.C., 1936-39; plate grainer Photoplate Co., Newark, 1939-42; results engr. Southwestern Electric Service Co., Jacksonville, Tex., 1947-50, Tex. Electric Service Co., Monahans, 1950-52; mech. design engr., geophys. exploration equipment Tex. Instruments Inc., Dallas, 1952—. Active Circle Ten council Boy Scouts Am., 1958-75; active Southwood Meth. Ch., Dallas, 1958-82, including chmn. bd., 1959-60. Served with U.S. Army, 1942-45. Recipient Order of Arrow award Boy Scouts Am., 1962. Mem. ASME. Patentee in field. Home: 3427 S Ravinia Dallas TX 75233 Office: PO Box 225621 M/S 3904 Dallas TX 75265

COBURN, MARJORIE FOSTER, psychologist, educator; b. Salt Lake City, Feb. 28, 1939; d. Harlan A. and Alma (Ballinger) Polk; m. Robert Byron Coburn, July 2, 1977; children—Robert Scott Coburn, Kelly Anne Coburn, Polly Klea Foster, Matthew Ryan Foster. B.A. in Sociology, UCLA, 1960; Montessori Internat. Diploma honor grad. Washington Montessori Inst., 1968; M.A. in Psychology, U. No. Colo., 1979; Ph.D. in Counseling Psychology, U. Denver, 1983. Licensed clin. psychologist. Probation officer Alameda County (Calif.), Oakland, 1960-62, Contra Costa County (Calif.), El Cerrito, 1966, Fairfax County (Va.), Fairfax, 1967; dir. Friendship Club, Orlando, Fla., 1963-65; tchr. Va. Montessori Sch., Fairfax, 1968-70; spl. edn. tchr. Leary Sch., Falls Church, Va., 1970-72, sch. adminstr., 1973-76; tchr. Aseltine Sch., San Diego, 1976-77, Coburn Montessori Sch., Colorado Springs, Colo., 1977-79; pvt. practice psychotherapy, Colorado Springs, 1979-82, San Diego, 1982—; cons. spl. edn., agoraphobia, women in transition. Mem. Am. Psychol. Assn., Am. Orthopsychiat. Assn., Phobia Soc., Council Exceptional Children, El Paso Psychol. Assn., Calif. Psychol. Assn., Acad. San Diego Psychologists, AAUW, NOW, Mensa. Episcopalian. Lodge: Rotary. Contbr. articles to profl. jours.; author: (with R.C. Orem) Montessori: Prescription for Children with Learning Disabilities, 1977. Office: 826 Prospect Suite 201 La Jolla CA 92037

COCANOWER, DAVID LEHMAN, lawyer; b. Elkhart, Ind., Dec. 3, 1939; s. Glen Merl and Augusta Mae (Lehman) C.; m. Liana Cheryl Miller, Sept. 21, 1983; 1 child, Emily Elizabeth; children by previous marriage: Michael Whitten, Joseph Charles. BS with high distinction, Ind. U., 1967, JD magna cum laude, 1970. Bar: Ariz. 1970, U.S. Dist. Ct. Ariz. 1970, U.S. Ct. Appeals (9th cir.) 1970. Assoc., Lewis and Roca, Phoenix, 1970-73, ptnr., 1973-87; mgr. Laventhol & Horvath, Phoenix.; chmn. sect. corp. banking and bus. law State Bar Ariz., 1978-79. Articles editor Ind. U. Law Jour., 1969-70. Bd. dirs. Ariz. Kidney Found., 1978-82, Hospice of the Valley, Phoenix, 1977-82, Neighborhood Housing Services of Phoenix, 1976-78, Phoenix Integrated Surgical Residency Program Found., Inc., 1980—. Served with USN, 1961-65. Mem. ABA (Ariz. liaison com. corp. laws 1979-87), Maricopa County Bar Assn., Nat. Assn. Bond Lawyers, Indiana U. Alumni Club of Phoenix (pres. 1976-77), Order of Coif, Beta Gamma Sigma, Beta Alpha Psi, Phi Delta Phi, Delta Sigma Pi, Tau Kappa Epsilon. Republican. Presbyterian. Clubs: Plaza, Mansion. Lodge: Rotary (pres. Phoenix East 1981-82, dir. 1979-84, dist. 549 gov. 1987-88). Office: 3200 N Central Ave 16th Floor Phoenix AZ 85012

COCCIOLI, LUIGI, banker; b. Naples, Italy, Oct. 20, 1931; s. Cosimo and Bianca (Ferrari) C.; m. Vanda Lancieri; children: Lamberto, Giancarlo, Riccardo. Degree in Agrl. Scis., U. Naples, 1953. Prof. econ. statistics U. Naples, 1953—; chmn. San Paolo di Torino (Italy) Banking Inst., 1979-83, Finban-Merchant Bank Banco di Napoli Internat., Naples and Luxembourg, 1983—. Office: Banco di Napoli, Via Toledo 177, 80132 Naples Italy

COCHRAN, CAROLYN, librarian; b. Tyler, Tex., July 13, 1934; d. Sidney Allen and Eudelle (Frazier) C.; m. Guy Milford Eley, June 1, 1963 (div.). B.A., Beaver Coll., 1956; M.A., U. Tex., 1960; M.L.S., Tex. Woman's U., 1970. Librarian, Canadian (Tex.) High Sch., 1970-71; rep. United Food Co., Amarillo, Tex., 1971-72; librarian Bishop Coll., Dallas, 1972-74; interviewer Tex. Employment Commn., Dallas, 1975-76; librarian St. Mary's Dominican, New Orleans, 1976-77; librarian DeVry Inst. Tech., Irving, Tex., 1978—; with Database Searching Handicapped Individuals, Irving, 1983—; vol. bibliographer Assn. Individuals with Disabilities, Dallas, 1982-85. Mem. Am. Coalition of Citizens with Disabilities, 1982—, Assn. Individuals with Disabilities, 1982-86, Vols. in Tech. Assistance, 1985—, Radio Amateur Satellite Corp., 1985-86. HEW fellow, 1967; honored Black History Collection, Dallas Morning News, Bishop Coll., Dallas, 1973. Mem. ALA, Spl. Library Assn. Club: Toastmistress (pres. 1982-83) (Irving). Reviewer Library Jour., 1974, Dallas Morning News, 1972-74, Amarillo Globe-News, 1970-71. Office: DeVry Inst Tech 4250 N Beltline Rd Irving TX 75038-4299

COCHRAN, GEORGE CALLOWAY, III, banker; b. Dallas, Aug. 29, 1932; s. George Calloway and Miriam (Welty) C.; m. Jerry Bywaters, Dec. 9, 1961; children—Mary, Robert. B.A., So. Meth. U., 1954; J.D., Harvard U., 1957; cert., Sch. Banking, La. State U., 1969. Bar: Tex. 1957. Assoc. Leachman, Gardere, Akin and Porter, Dallas, 1960-62; various positions Fed. Res. Bank of Dallas, 1962-76, sr. v.p., 1976—; mem. adv. com. Bank Ops. Inst., East Tex. State U., Commerce, 1982—; mem. task force on truth in lending regulation Bd. Govs. of FRS, Washington, 1968-69; bd. dirs. Dallas chpt. Am. Inst. of Banking, 1986—. Mem. hist. landmark survey task force City of Dallas, 1974-78. Served to capt. USAF, 1958-60. Mem. ABA, State Bar Tex., Dallas Bar Assn., Phi Beta Kappa. Methodist. Club: Harvard (Dallas). Home: 3541 Villanova Dallas TX 75225 Office: Fed Res Bank of Dallas 400 S Akard St Dallas TX 75222

COCHRAN, THAD, senator; b. Pontotoc, Miss., Dec. 7, 1937; s. William Holmes and Emma Grace (Berry) C.; m. Rose Clayton, June 6, 1964; children: Thaddeus Clayton, Katherine Holmes. B.A., U. Miss., 1959, J.D. cum laude, 1965; postgrad. (Rotary Found. fellow), U. Dublin, Ireland, 1963-64. Bar: Miss. 1965. Practiced in Jackson 1965-72; assoc. firm Watkins & Eager, 1965-72; mem. 93d-95th congresses from Miss., 1973-79, U.S. Senate from Miss., 1979—. Mem. exec. bd. Andrew Jackson council Boy Scouts Am., from 1973. Served to lt. USNR, 1959-61. Named Outstanding Young Man of Jackson, 1971, One of Three Outstanding Young Men of Miss., 1971. Mem. ABA, Miss. Bar Assn. (pres. young lawyers sect. 1972-73), Omicron Delta Kappa, Phi Kappa Phi, Pi Kappa Alpha. Republican. Baptist. Club: Rotarian. *

COCHRANE, JAMES LOUIS, economist; b. Nyack, N.Y., Aug. 31, 1942; s. Thomas and Anna (Yaroscak) C.; m. Katherine Prince Schirmer, Mar. 24, 1984; 1 child, Katherine Anne. BA, Wittenberg U., 1964; PhD, Tulane U., 1968. Instr. Tulane U., New Orleans, 1967-68; asst. prof. U. S.C., Columbia, 1968-70, assoc. prof., 1970-72, prof., 1972-77; sr. staff mem. NSC, Washington, 1978-79; directorate of intelligence CIA, Washington, 1980-83; sr. v.p., chief economist Tex. Commerce Bancshares, Inc., Houston, 1984—; assoc. staff mem. Brookings Instn., Washington, D.C., 1972-74, 76-78; editorial bd. History of Polit. Economy Duke U., 1974-80, So. Econ. Jour. U. N.C., 1976-79; 1st v.p. So. Econ. Assn. U. N.C., 1976-77. Author: Macroeconomics Before Keynes, 1970, Macroeconomics Analysis and Policy, 1974, Industrialism and Industrial Man in Retrospect, 1977; editor: Multiple Criteria Decision Making, 1975. Mem. History of Econs. Soc. (treas. 1974-80), Asia Soc. (adv. dir. 1986). Home: 2019 Dunstan Houston TX 77005 Office: Texas Commerce Bancshares Inc 600 Travis St PO Box 2558 Houston TX 77252

COCHRANE, PEGGY, architect, writer; b. Alhambra, Calif., July 9, 1926; d. E. Elliott and Gladys (Moran) C.; B.A., Scripps Coll., 1945; postgrad., U. So. Calif., 1951-52, Columbia U., 1954; m. Hugh Bowman, Nov. 24, 1954 (div.). Job capt. Kahn and Jacobs, N.Y.C., 1954-55; project architect Litchfield, Whiting, Panero & Severud, Teheran, Iran, 1956; archtl. designer Daniel, Mann, Johnson and Mendenhall, Los Angeles, 1956-59; individual practice architecture, Sherman Oaks, Calif., 1966—. Recipient Architecture prize Scripps Coll., 1945. Mem. Assn. Women in Architecture (life), Union Internationale des Femmes Architects. Republican. Episcopalian. Club: Dionysians (S. Pasadena). Author (musical) Mayaland, 1979; (play) I Gave at the Office, 1980; The Witch Doctor's Manual, 1984; The Witch Doctors' Cookbook, 1984; mem. editorial bd. Los Angeles Architect, 1978—; contbr. to Contemporary Architects. Office: 14755 Ventura Blvd Suite 1-626 Sherman Oaks CA 91403

COCHRANE, ROBERT LOWE, biologist; b. Morgantown, W.Va., Feb. 10, 1931; s. Thomas Joseph and Isabelle Durston (Lowe) C. B.A., W.Va. U., 1953; M.S., U. Wis., 1954, Ph.D., 1961. Research asst. genetics U. Wis., Madison, 1953-55, research asst. zoology, 1957-60; agt. in animal husbandry U.S. Dept. Agr., Madison, Wis., 1955-61; biologist FDA, Washington, 1961-62; sr. research fellow dept. anatomy U. Birmingham (Eng.), 1962-65; project assoc. dept. physiology U. Pitts., 1965-66; sr. endocrinologist Eli Lilly & Co., Indpls., 1966-80; research assoc. G.D. Searle & Co., Skokie, Ill., 1980-81; with Short's Fur Farm, Granton, Wis., 1981-83; research assoc. Marshfield (Wis.) Med. Found., 1983-84; biologist Northwood Fur Farms, Inc., Cary, Ill., 1984; cons. for FAO to Wildlife Inst. India, Dehra Dun, 1985; adj. prof. div. animal and vet. sci., W.Va. U., Morgantown, 1987—; ad hoc reviewer various sci. jours. Contbr. numerous research articles and abstracts on reproduction to profl. jours.; participant Internat. Mink Show, Madison, Wis., 1976-88. Recipient Knight of Golden Horse Shoe award W.Va. Pub. Sch. System, 1945; U. Birmingham (Eng.) sr. research fellow, 1962-65. Mem. AAAS, Am. Inst. Biol. Scis., Soc. Exptl. Biology and Medicine, Soc. for Study of Fertility, Soc. Study of Reproduction, Am. Soc. Animal Sci., Endocrine Soc., N.Y. Acad. Sci., Soc. Endocrinology, Council Agrl. Sci. and Tech., Internat. Platform Assn., Nat. Rifle Assn. (life), Sigma Xi, Pi Kappa Alpha. Presbyterian. Home: 404 Junior Ave Morgantown WV 26505

COCHRANE, WILLIAM HENRY, business executive; b. Norfolk, Va., Apr. 3, 1912; s. William F. and Gretchen (Schneider) C.; m. Elizabeth J. Ballantine, Aug. 3, 1935 (dec. July 1977); children: William Henry, Elizabeth J., Susan B., Peter B.; m. Deborah E. Collyer, June 14, 1978. Student, Princeton, 1931-32. Successively chemist, salesman, dist. mgr., mgr. market and sales analysis, mgr. detergent project U.S. Indsl. Chems. Co., 1932- 52; gen. mgr. indsl. div. Lever Bros. Co., 1952-57; exec. v.p. Neptune Internat. Corp., 1957-58, pres., 1958-69, chmn., 1966-72; also dir.; dir. Los Angeles Soap Co.; v.p. Mountain Lake Corp., 1975-77, pres., 1978-81. Mem. Vero Beach (Fla.) City Council, 1980—, vice mayor, 1980-82, mayor, 1982—; Bd. dirs. Lake Wales Hosp., Vero Beach Civic Assn.; trustee Vero Beach Ctr. Arts, 1983—, pres., 1984—. Served from lt. (j.g.) to lt. USNR, 1944-46. Mem. Am. Waterworks Assn. Nat. Planning Assn., Soc. Chem. Industry, Newcomen Soc., UN Assn., Fla. Columbia Alliance. Clubs: Princeton (N.Y.C.); Nassau; Riomar Bay Yacht (Fla.), Mountain Lake (Fla.); Riomar Country. Home: 2320 Club Dr Vero Beach FL 32963 Office: City Hall Vero Beach FL 32960

COCKE, WILLIAM MARVIN, JR., surgeon; b. Balt., Aug. 2, 1934; s. William M. and Clara E. (Bosley) C.; m. Sue Ann Harris, Apr. 25, 1981; children: Gregory William, Laura Marie; children by previous marriage: William Marvin III, Catherine Lynn, Deborah Kay, Brian Thomas. B.S. with honors in Biology, Tex. A&M U., 1956; M.D., Baylor U., 1960. Diplomate: Am. Bd. Plastic Surgery (guest examiner 1978). Intern surgery Vanderbilt U. Hosp., Nashville, 1960-61; fellow gen. surgery Ochsner Clinic and Found. Hosp., New Orleans, 1961-64; chief resident surgery Monroe (La.) Charity Hosp., 1963-64; resident reconstructive surgery Roswell Park Meml. Inst., Buffalo, 1965-66; chief resident plastic surgery VA Hosp., Bronx, N.Y., 1966; practice medicine specializing in plastic surgery Nashville, 1968-75, Sacramento, 1976-79, Bryan, Tex., 1980—; mem. staff St. Joseph's Hosp., Bryan, Bryan Hosp.; asst. prof. plastic surgery Vanderbilt U. Sch. Medicine, Nashville, 1968-69, asst. clin. prof. plastic surgery, 1969-75; assoc. prof. plastic surgery Ind. U. Sch. Medicine, Indpls., 1975-76; chief plastic surgery service Wishard Meml. Hosp., Ind. U., 1975-76; assoc. prof. surgery U. Calif. Sch. Medicine, Davis, 1976-79, chmn. dept. plastic surgery, 1976-79; prof. surgery, chief div. plastic surgery Tex. Tech. U. Sch. Medicine, Lubbock, 1979-80, dir. Microsurg. Research Lab., 1979-80; clin. prof. surgery Tex. A&M U. Sch. Medicine, 1980-86, prof. surgery, 1986—.

Author textbooks on plastic surgery; contbr. articles to profl. jours. Served with M.C. USAF, 1966-68. Recipient Dean Echols award Ochsner Hosp. Found., 1963. Mem. AMA, ACS, Am. Soc. Plastic and Reconstructive Surgery (award 1966), Am. Assn. Plastic Surgeons, Soc. Head and Neck Surgeons, Assn. for Acad. Surgery, Internat. Soc. Aesthetic Plastic Surgery, Alton Ochsner Surg. Soc., Brazos-Robertson County Med. Soc. Republican. Episcopalian. Home: 306 Crescent Dr Bryan TX 77802 Office: Scott-White Clinic Div Plastic Surgery 1600 University Dr College Station TX 77840

COCKERHAM, LORRIS G., toxicologist; b. Denham Springs, La., Sept. 27, 1935; s. Warren Conrad and Leda Frances (Scivicque) C.; BA, La. Coll., 1957; MS, Colo. State U., 1973, PhD, 1979; m. Patricia Ann Stagg, Aug. 16, 1957; children—Michael B., Richard L., Ann E., Joseph D. Commd. 2d lt. U.S. Air Force, 1961, advanced through grades to lt. col., 1977; instr. James Connelly AFB, Tex., 1963-66; Squadron electronic warfare officer Fairchild AFB, Wash., 1966-71; asst. prof. dept. chemistry and biology U.S. Air Force Acad., Colo., 1973-77; wing electronic warfare officer Griffiss AFB, N.Y., 1977-78, comdr. 416 Munitions Maintenance Squadron, 1978-80, Armed Forces Radiobiology Research Inst., Def. Nuclear Agy., Bethesda, Md., 1980-86; Air Force Office of Scientific Research, Bolling AFB, D.C., 1986-87; exec. dir. NCTR-Associated Univs., Little Rock, 1988—; asst. prof. physiology Sch. Medicine, Uniformed Services U. Health Scis., 1981-87; assoc. prof. U. Ark. for Med. Scis., 1988—. Troop com. chmn. Iroquois council Boy Scouts Am., 1978-80. Decorated D.F.C. (2), Airman's medal, Air medal (12), Meritorious Service Medal, Air Force Commendation medal; Air Force Logistics Command Dioxin Research grantee, 1974-79; recipient Order of Arrow, Boy Scouts Am. Mem. N.Y. Acad. Sci., Soc. Neurosci., Radiation Research Soc., Internat. Brain Research Orgn., World Fedn. Neuroscientists, Soc. Toxicology, Aerospace Med. Assn., Am. Physiol. Soc., Am. Coll. Toxicology, Am. Physiol. Soc., Soc. Environ. Toxicology Chem., Sigma Xi, Phi Kappa Phi. Republican. Southern Baptist.

COCKMAN, ANTHONY GEORGE, pre-retirement counsellor; b. Manchester, Lancashire, Eng., Apr. 23, 1939; came to S. Africa, 1980; s. Lloyd George and Lillian (Hibbert) C.; m. Cynthia Hildred Jane King, Mar. 15, 1961; children—Alan V.G., Christopher J.A., Ruth Louise. Student Open U., 1968-70; student bus. adminstrn. Cranfield Sch., 1972-73. Chief steward/purser Merchant Navy, U.K., 1956-62; co. mgr. Fiffes Group, London, 1962-71; mgr. Vestric, Runcorn, 1971-75; co. mgr. Ferrant Group, Hastings, Eng., 1975-80; cons., self-employed counsellor, Durban, Natal, S. Africa, 1980-82; counsellor Nat. Fund Raising, Natal, 1983-84; exec. dir. Pre-Retirement Council, Natal, 1984—. Author: Management/Marketing Positions, 1979; Pre-Retirement Planning, 1985; Controlling Stress, 1986; Mid-Life Crisis or the Male in Middle Age-Progression, Crisis or Benefit, 1986; contbr. articles to profl. jours. Served with RAF, 1954-56. Fellow Brit. Soc. Commerce; Inst. Sales and Mktg. Mgmt.; mem. Inst. Data Processing Mgmt., Inst. Mktg., Inst. Factory Mgmt., Inst. Personnel Mgmt., S. African Bd. for Personnel Practice. Conservative. Methodist. Club: Wildlife Soc. Home: 61 Brandwell, 60 Cromwell Rd, Glenwood Durban Republic of South Africa Office: Retirement Council, PO Box 2983, Durban, Natal 3600, Republic of South Africa

COCKRELL, CLAUDE O'FLYNN, JR., container company executive; b. Memphis, May 10, 1937; s. Claude O'Flynn and Audrey (Roberts) C.; student Memphis State U., 1955, U. Miami, 1955-57; div.; children: Cana Lynn, Claude O'Flynn III. Pres., Shelby Paper Box Co., Memphis, 1952-56; pres.-owner Memphis Corrugated Container Co., 1956-61; owner Cockrell Container Co., Memphis, 1961—; pres. West Corp., Memphis, 1971—, Great Am. Container Corp., 1975—, Nashville Corrugated Box Inc., 1975—, West Prodns., 1977—, Photo Finish, Inc., 1978—, Cockrell Communication Corp., World Racing Network, 1982—; pres., owner Am. Divers, 1972—; pres. Cockrell Export Ltd., Nassau, Bahamas, 1979, Gt. Atlantic Seafood Corp., Halifax, N.S. and Goose Bay, Nfld., Can., Secret Charters, Ft. Lauderdale, Fla., 1977, Cockrell Oil Corp., 1985—, Cockrell Oil Ltd., 1985—. State marshall Freedom Trail Found. Tenn., 1973—. Head campaign George Wallace for Pres., Memphis and Tri-state area, 1968. Mem. Tenn. Breeders and Racing Assn. (pres.), Pi Kappa Alpha. Presbyterian. Club: Moose. Office: PO Box 2589 Murfreesboro TN 37133-2589

COCKRUM, WILLIAM MONROE, III, investment banker, consultant, educator; b. Indpls., July 18, 1937; s. William Monroe II C. and Katherine J. (Jaqua) Moore; m. Andrea Lee Deering, Mar. 8, 1975; children: Catherine Anne, William Monroe, IV. A.B. with distinction, DePauw U., Greencastle, Ind., 1959; M.B.A. with distinction, Harvard U., 1961. With A.G. Becker Paribas Inc., 1961-84, mgr. nat. corp. fin. div., 1968-71; mgr. pvt. investments A.G. Becker Paribas Inc., Los Angeles, 1971-84; fin. and adminstrv. officer A.G. Becker Paribas Inc., 1974-80, sr. v.p., 1975-78, vice chmn., 1978-84, also dir.; mem. faculty Northwestern U., 1961-63; UCLA Grad. Sch. Mgmt., 1984—; dir. Knapp Communications Corp., Cinema Capital Mgmt., Inc. ; trustee Bruin-Trojan Superstar Classic; vis. lectr. UCLA Grad. Sch. Mgmt., 1984—. Mem. Delta Kappa Epsilon. Clubs: University (Chgo.); Monterey (Palm Desert, Calif); Deke (N.Y.C.); Alisal Golf (Solvang, Calif.).

COCRON, RONALD ROBERT, food distbn. co. exec.; b. Phila., Oct. 31, 1937; s. Nick Peter and Naomi Ruth (Hagy) C.; student U. Del., 1968; m. Gloria Jean MacLennan, Feb. 8, 1964; children—Lisa Ann, Cheryl Ann; m. 2d, Noreen Ryan, Apr. 5, 1984. Clk., Penn Fruit Co., Phila., 1955-60; salesman Samuel Zukerman & Co., Pennsuaken, N.J., 1963-65; supermarket mgr. Supermarkets Gen. Corp., Woodbridge, N.J., 1965-69; v.p. sales Progressive Brokerage Co., King of Prussia, Pa., 1975-78; sr. v.p. Samuel Zukerman & Co., Bensalem, Pa., 1969-85, pres., 1985—; pres. Meadow Lane Packing Corp., Bensalem, 1981-85; exec. v.p. Bulk Food Concepts, Bensalem., 1986—; sec.-treas. ICN, Bensalem/Antwerp, Belgium, 1986—. Served with AUS, 1960-63. Presbyterian. Home: 5100 Valley Park Rd Doylestown PA 18901 Office: I-95 Industrial Park Bensalem PA 19020

CODELLI, LORENZO, film journalist; b. Trieste, Italy, Jan. 29, 1946; s. Laura (Buda) C. Organizer Centro Univ. Cinematografico, Padua, Italy, 1968-71; co-dir. Cappella Underground Film Assn., Trieste, 1970—; co-founder, organizer Silent Film Festival, Pordenone, Italy, 1982—; organizer Prix Sergio Amidei, Gorizia, Italy, 1981—; cons. Sci.-Fiction Internat. Film Festival, Trieste, 1973-80. Co-author: Dictionnaire Larousse du Cinema, 1986; editor: L'Arte della Commedia (Mario Monicelli), 1986; contbr. The International Film Guide, 1981—, Postif monthly, Paris, 1971—. Home: Via Romagna 44, 34134 Trieste Italy Office: Cappella Underground, Via Franca 17, 34100 Trieste Italy

CODEN, MICHAEL HENRI, fiber optics and electronics manufacturing company executive; b. N.Y.C., Mar. 6, 1947; s. William and Ruth (Carmel) C.; m. Leslie Carol Sachs, Apr. 19, 1975 (div. Aug. 1978). B.S. in Elec. Engring., MIT, 1967; M.S. in Bus., Columbia U., 1975; M.S. in Math, NYU, 1979. Engr., Hewlett Packard Co., Palo Alto, Calif., 1967-69; mktg. mgr. Digital Equipment Corp., Maynard, Mass., 1969-72; v.p. data processing Maher Terminals Co., Jersey City, 1972-75; div. mgr. Exxon Enterprises, Inc., N.Y.C., 1975-79; pres., chief exec. officer Codenoll Tech., Yonkers, N.Y., 1979—, also chmn. bd. Patentee compound semiconductor and communications equipment, computer local network equipment; contbr. articles to profl. jours. Recipient Distinction cert. Laser Inst. Am., Am. Chem. Soc. Mem. IEEE, Optical Soc. Am., N.Y. Acad. Sci., AAAS, Inst. Mgmt. Sci., Beta Gamma Sigma. Jewish. Club: Columbia. Home: 750 Kappock St Riverdale NY 10463 Office: Codenoll Tech Corp 1086 N Broadway Yonkers NY 10701

CODOBAN, AUREL-TEODOR, philosopher, educator; b. Cluj, Romania, Dec. 1, 1948; s. Petru and Ana (Ilea) C.; m. Zorica Letitia Banaduc, Sept. 4, 1976; children: Mihai-Andrei, Ioana-Andrea. Degree in Philosophy, U. Cluj-Napoca, 1972, PhD, 1984. From asst. prof. to prof. philosophy and sociology of art and culture U. Cluj-Napoca, Romania, 1972—. Author: Coordinates and Prefigurations, 1982, Semiotic Structure of Structuralism, 1984; co-author 3 books; editor-in-chief Echinox, 1983—; contbr. articles to profl. jours. Recipient youth orgn. award, 1983. Home: Mehedinti 78 Block G 8, Apt 33, Cluj-Napoca Romania Office: U Cluj-Napoca, M Kogalniceanu 1, Cluj-Napoca Romania

CODRON, MICHAEL VICTOR, theatrical producer; b. June 8, 1930; s. I.A. and Lily (Morganstern) C.; ed. St. Paul's Sch.; B.A., Worcester Coll., Oxford U. Dir. Hampstead Theatre; adminstr. Aldwych and Adelphi Theatres; co-proprietor Vaudeville theatre; prodns. include: Breath of Spring, 1957; The Birthday Party, 1958; Pieces of Eight, 1959; The Caretaker, 1960; The Tenth Man, 1961; Rattle of a Simple Man, 1962; Next Time I'll Sing to You, Private Lives, The Lovers and the Dwarfs, Cockade, 1963; Poor Bitos, Windows, The Formation Dancers, Entertaining Mr. Sloane, 1964; Loot, The Killing of Sister George, Ride a Cock Horse, 1965; Little Malcolm and His Struggle Against the Eunuchs, The Anniversary, There's a Girl in My Soup, Big Bad Mouse, 1966; The Judge, The Flip Side, Wise Child, The Boy Friend, 1967; Not Now Darling, The Real Inspector Hound, 1968; The Contractor, Slag, The Two of Us, The Philanthropist, 1970; The Foursome, Butley, A Voyage Round My Father, The Changing Room, 1971; Veterans, Time and Time Again, Crown Matrimonial, My Fat Friend, 1972; Collaborators, Savages, Habeas Corpus, Absurd Person Singular, 1973; Knuckle, Flowers, Golden Pathway Annual, The Norman Conquests, John Paul George Ringo...and Bert, 1974; A Family and A Fortune, Alphabetical Order, A Far Better Husband, Ashes, Absent Friends, Otherwise Engaged, Stripwell, 1975; Funny Peculiar, Treats, Donkey's Years, Confusions, Teeth n' Smiles, Yahoo, 1976; Dusa Stas, Fish & Vi, Just Between Ourselves, Oh, Mr. Porter, Breezeblock Park, The Bells of Hell, The Old Country, 1977; The Rear Column, Ten Times Table, The Unvarnished Truth, The Homecoming, Alice's Boys, Night and Day, 1978; Joking Apart, Tishoo, Stage Struck, 1979; Dr. Faustus, Make and Break, The Dresser, Taking Steps, Enjoy, 1980; Hinge & Bracket, Rowan Atkinson in Revue, House Guest, Quartermaine's Terms, 1981; Season's Greetings, Noises Off, Funny Turns, 1982, The Real Thing, 1982; The Hard Shoulder, 1983; Look, No Hans!, Benefactors, 1984; Jumpers, Who Plays Wins, Clockwise (film), 1985, Made in Bangkok, 1986, Woman in Mind, 1986; Hapgood, Uncle Vanya, Re:Joyce!, The Sneeze, Henceforward, 1988. Club: Garrick. Office: Aldwych Theatre Offices, Aldwych, London WC2 England

CODY, ALAN MORROW, management consultant; b. Huntington, W. Va., June 7, 1947; s. Peer John and Nancy (Speer) C.; m. Elisabeth Anne Allen, Nov. 29, 1969; 1 child, David Miles. AB, Cornell U., 1969; SM, MIT, 1974. Economist, Data Resources Inc., Lexington, Mass., 1974-76, dir. indsl. mktg., 1976-78, v.p., 1978-79; v.p. The Planning Economics Group, Woburn, Mass., 1979-81; sr. mgr. Mitchell and Co., Cambridge, Mass., 1982-84; sr. staff Arthur D. Little, Inc., Cambridge, Mass., 1984—; editor Sloan Mgmt Rev. Cambridge, 1973-74. Active, Ripon Soc., Boston, 1982—; dir. bd. investment First Unitarian Soc. Newton (Mass.), 1984; bd. dirs. Fgn. Film Soc. of Montgomery (Ala.), 1971-72, Newton Conservators, 1988—. Served to 1st lt. USAF, 1969-72. Mem. Am. Mktg. Assn., N. Am. Soc. Corp. Planning (Boston chpt. dir. 1981—, v.p.). Republican. Unitarian. Club: Cornell (Boston). Office: Arthur D Little Inc Acorn Park Cambridge MA 02140

CODY, HIRAM SEDGWICK, JR., retired telephone company executive; b. Evanston, Ill., Nov. 1, 1915; s. Hiram Sedgwick and Harriett Mary (Collins) C.; B.S. cum laude, Yale U., 1937, LL.B., 1940; m. Mary Vaughn Jacoby, Oct. 4, 1941; children—Margaret Vaughn, Harriett Mary, Hiram Sedgwick, Henry Jacoby, William Collins. Admitted to N.C. bar, 1940; with Western Electric Co., Inc., 1946-71, regional mgr. engring. and installation, Chgo., 1961-64, dir. orgn. planning, N.Y.C., 1964-65, sec., treas., 1965-71; asst. treas. AT&T, N.Y.C., 1971-80. Vice pres. Morris-Sussex council Boy Scouts Am., 1970-80; vice chmn. Zoning Bd. Adjustment Mountain Lakes, 1968-80; boro councilman, Mountain Lakes, N.J., 1960-61; trustee, treas. Asheville (N.C.) Sch., 1974-84; trustee Asheville Symphony Orch., 1981—, Asheville Community Concert Assn., 1981—; bd. advisors Warren Wilson Coll., 1983—, chmn. 1987—. Served to comdr. USNR, 1941-46. Mem. N.C. State Bar, Telephone Pioneers Am. (v.p. 1969-71, treas. 1971-78), Tau Beta Pi. Home: 64 Wagon Trail Black Mountain NC 28711-2533

COE, ILSE G., lawyer; b. Koenigsberg, Germany, May 28, 1911; came to U.S., 1938, naturalized, 1946. Referendar, U. Koenigsberg, 1935, JSD, 1936; LLB, Bklyn. Law Sch., 1946. Bar: N.Y. 1946. Dir. econ. research Internat. Gen. Electric Co., Berlin, 1936-38; asst. to sales promotion and advt. mgr. Ralph C. Coxhead Corp., N.Y.C., 1940-44; law clk. Mendes & Mount, N.Y.C., 1944-46; assoc. Hill, Rivkins & Middleton, N.Y.C., 1946-50, McNutt, Longcope & Proctor, N.Y.C., 1950-52, Chadbourne, Hunt, Jaeckel & Brown, N.Y.C., 1952-54; asst. v.p., asst. trust officer Schroder Trust Co. and J. Henry Schroder Banking Corp., N.Y.C., 1954-76; dir., sec., editor Fgn. Tax Law Assn., Inc., L.I., 1945-55; tchr. Drakes Bus. Sch., N.Y.C., 1946-49; lectr. on estate planning to ch., women's and bar assn. groups, 1947—; tutor literacy vols., 1977-79; lectr. wills trusts and estates and photography Pace U., St. Francis Coll. Life mem. exec. bd. Active Retirement Ctr., Pace U., v.p., 1980-81, pres., 1982-85; Rep. county com. woman, 1948-50; former deacon, now ruling elder, chmn. investment com. 1st Presbyn. Ch., Bklyn.; v.p., chair house com. Florence Ct. Corp. Coop. Recipient Human Relations award NCCJ, 1979. Mem. Bklyn. Women's Bar Assn. (past treas., sec., bd. dirs. 1960—), Protestant Lawyers Assn. of N.Y. Inc. (sec. 1960-75, 1st v.p. 1976-77, pres. 1978-88, lifetime pres. emeritus 1988—), Internat. Fedn. Women Lawyers, Bklyn. Heights Assn., Bklyn. Hist. Soc. (investment com.), N.Y. Color Slide Club (by-laws chmn. 1983—, bd. dirs. 1973-74), Bklyn. Mus., Bklyn. Botanic Garden, others. Home: 187 Hicks St Brooklyn Heights NY 11201

COE, JACK MARTIN, lawyer; b. Orange, N.J., Mar. 25, 1945; s. Irving and Evelyn (Phillips) C.; m. Diana Jean Martino, Oct. 24, 1981. B.A., U. Va., 1967; A.M., Brown U., 1969; J.D., U. Fla., 1975; postgrad. law, Oxford U., Eng., 1973. Bar: Fla. 1975, U.S. Ct. Appeals (5th cir.) 1976, U.S. Dist. Ct. (so. dist.) Fla. 1976, D.C. 1978, U.S. Supreme Ct. 1978, U.S. Ct. Appeals (11th cir.) 1981. Assoc. Adams, George, Lee & Schulte, Miami, Fla., 1975-77, Thomas E. Lee Jr., P.A., Miami, 1977-78; ptnr. Lee, Schulte, Murphy & Coe, P.A., Miami, 1978—; alumni dir. Sta. WUVA, U. Va., Charlottesville, 1977—. Active in Tiger Bay Polit. Club, Miami, 1978-87; mem. Elephant Forum. Served to 1st lt. USAF, 1969-72. Mem. ABA, Assn. Trial Lawyers Am., Acad. Fla. Trial Lawyers (rules com. 1985—), Pa. Trial Lawyers Assn., Dade County Bar Assn., Palm Beach County Bar Assn. Republican. Lodge: Kiwanis (vice-chmn Key Club Coral Gables, Fla.).

COE, JOHN EMMONS, research immunologist; b. Evanston, Ill., Sept. 1, 1931; s. Emmons S. and Lillian E. (Beckman) C.; m. Nancy Rowland, June 18, 1954; children—Kristine Wing Coe-Sutton, Anne Lindstrom, Paul Rowland. B.A., Oberlin Coll., 1953; M.D., Hahnemann Med. Coll., 1957. Intern, U. Ill. Research and Ednl. Hosp., Chgo., 1957-58; resident in medicine U. Colo. Med. Ctr., Denver, 1958-60; surgeon USPHS, NIH, Hamilton, Mont., 1960-63; fellow dept. pathology Scripps Clinic and Research Found., La Jolla, Calif., 1963-65; med. officer Nat. Inst. Allergy and Infectious Diseases, NIH Rocky Mountain Lab., Hamilton, 1965—; affiliated prof. dept microbiology U. Mont., Missoula, 1966—. Contbr. articles to sci. jours. Pres. bd. dirs. Mill Lake Irrigation Dist., 1982—. Mem. Am. Assn. Immunologists, Hamster Soc. (pres. 1983-84), Soc. to Preserve Mauser, Alpha Omega Alpha. Clubs: Lacrosse (pres. 1965—), Handball (Hamilton). Home: NW 986 Orchard Dr Hamilton MT 59840 Office: Rocky Mountain Lab NIH Hamilton MT 59840

COEBERGH, JAN WILLEM, epidemiologist; b. Bussum, The Netherlands, July 8, 1946; s. Jan and Claar (Kuypers) C.; m. Christiane E. Surie, Nov. 27, 1971; children: Willemyn, Jan Adriaan. Degree in French, U. Fribourg, Switzerland, 1965; MD, U. Leiden, The Netherlands, 1974; Degree in Pub. Health Adminstrn., Nat. Inst. Preventive Medicine, Leiden, 1979. Staff asst. to mgmt. Univ. Hosp., Leiden, 1974-79; house officer Dept. of Internal Medicine Elisabeth Hosp., Leiderdorp, The Netherlands, 1980-81; researcher Dept. Epidemiology, Rotterdam, The Netherlands, 1981—; asst. prof. social medicine Dept. Health Care Adminstrn., Rotterdam, 1984—; cons. Sooz Cancer Registry, 1984—, Dutch Childhood Leukemia Study Group, 1984—. Bd. dirs. Rheuma Nursing Home, Rotterdam, 1983—, Anna Orthopaedic Clinic, Leiden, 1979—, Netherlands Student Travel Bur., Leiden, 1967-74. Mem. Royal Dutch Med. Soc. Club: Leiden Mixed Hockey. Home: Van Ledenberghstraat 6, Leiden 2334 AT, The Netherlands Office: Erasmus Univ, PO Box 1738, Rotterdam 3000 DR, The Netherlands

COELHO, CARLOS ALBERTO DA SILVA, computer company executive; b. Lisbon, Portugal, Nov. 25, 1937; s. Antonio Dias and Maria Dos Anjos (Silva) C.; m. Maria Margarida Vidal C. Da Cunha, Dec. 30, 1961; children—Maria Joao, Eunice Maria, Joao Nuno. Student Liceu Camoes, Lisbon, 1949-54, Northwestern U., Chgo. Trainee Nat. Broadcasting Co., Lisbon, 1954-57, tabulator equipment operator, 1957-58, EDP mgr., 1959-64; service bur. mgr. Univac Distbrs., Lisbon, 1965-67, sales mgr., 1967-70; mktg. dir. Sperry Univac, Lisbon, 1971-75, gen. mgr., 1976—; mktg. research cons. Mensor/Ciesa WCK, Lisbon, 1964-68; dir. Gabimec, Lisbon, 1965-71. Active Sch. Parents Com. Lodge: Rotary. Home: Rua Vieira Lusitano 68, 2825 Charneca Da Caparica, Lisbon Portugal

COEN, SALVATORE, mathematics educator; b. Mendrisio, Switzerland, May 16, 1944; s. Giordano and Clara (Levi) C. Laureate in Math., U. Pisa, Italy, 1967. Asst. prof. math. U. Pisa, 1967-76; prof. U. Bologna, Italy, 1976—; vis. prof. Johns Hopkins U., Balt., 1986-87. Author: (textbook) Domini di Riemann, 1980; editor: Seminari di Geometria, 1981, 82, 83, 84, 85. Mem. Am. Math. Assn., Unione Mat. Italiana, Soc. Math. de France. Office: U Bologna Dept Math, Piazza di Porta San Donaio 5, I 40127 Bologna Italy

COENEN, ROBERT GERARDUS, publisher; b. Nijmegen, Holland, Aug. 22, 1941; came to Switzerland, 1976; m. Gerardus Wilhelmus and Johanna Theodora (Willemse) C.; m. Gabriele Susanne Zelenka, June 5, 1980. HBS-A, Canisius Coll., Nijmegen, Holland, 1958; Ph.D., Am. Internat. U., 1979. Mgr. internat. affairs De Nederlanden van 18701 Aetna Life/Assicurazione Generali, 1964-72; mng. dir. PDC-Flair, Baar, Switzerland, 1972-77; chief exec. officer Clyancourt Corp., Cham, Switzerland, 1977—; TNCB Ag, Cham, Meducation Verlages m.b.H., Vienna; editor Medipress. Served with Royal Dutch Navy 1958-64. Decorated New Guinea Cross; recipient cert. of appreciation AMA, 1985.

COETZEE, JOHN M., educator and writer; b. South Africa, Feb. 9, 1940. Ed. U. Cape Town, 1957-61, U. Tex., 1965-68. Asst. prof. English, SUNY-Buffalo, 1968-71; lectr. U. Cape Town, 1972-76, sr. lectr., 1977-80, assoc. prof., 1981-83, prof. gen. lit., 1984—. Recipient CNA Lit. award, 1977, 80, 83; Geoffrey Faber Prize, 1980; James Tait Black Meml. Prize, 1980, Jerusalem Prize, 1987. Author: Dusklands, 1974; In the Heart of the Country, 1977; Waiting for the Barbarians, 1980; Life and Times of Michael K (Booker-McConnell prize, 1983); Prix Feminina Etranger, 1985), 1983; Foe, 1986; White Writing, 1988. Editor: (with André Brink) A Land Apart, 1986. Address: PO Box 92, Rondebosch Cape Province 7700, Republic of South Africa

COFFEE, JAMES FREDERICK, retired lawyer; b. Decatur, Ind., Mar. 6, 1918; s. Claude M. and Frances N. (Butler) C.; m. Jeanmarie Hackman, Dec. 29, 1945 (dec. 1978); children: James, Carolyn, Susan, Sheila, Kevin, Richard, Elizabeth, Thomas, Claudia; m. Marjorie E. Masterson, Oct. 4, 1980. B.C.E., Purdue U., 1939; J.D., Ind. U., 1947. Bar: Wis. 1947, Ill. 1952. Patent atty. Allis Chalmers Mfg. Co., Milw., 1947-51; mem. firm Anderson, Luedeka, Fitch, Even & Tabin (and predecessors), Chgo., 1951-64; partner Anderson, Luedeka, Fitch, Even & Tabin (and predecessors), 1956-64; individual practice law Chgo., 1964-71; partner law firm Coffee & Sweeney, Chgo., 1971-76; partner, gen. counsel design firm Marvin Glass & Assos., Chgo., from 1973, now ret. Served to capt. AUS, 1941-46, Japanese prisoner of war, 1942-45. Mem. ABA, Ill. Bar Assn., Chgo. Bar Assn. (chmn. com. patents, trademark and unfair trade practices 1967), Am. Patent Law Assn., Patent Law Assn. Chgo. (chmn. com. copyrights 1969), Am. Judicature Soc. Club: Tower of Chgo. (bd. govs. 1978—, sec. 1982-83, treas. 1983-85). Home: 320 Earls Ct Deerfield IL 60015

COFFEY, GEORGE HAROLD, utilities company executive; b. New Haven, Apr. 27, 1943; s. Robert John and Marian L. (Taylor) C.; student Eli Whitney Tech., 1962-63, Bullard Havens Tech., 1963-64, U. Bridgeport, 1964-70; m. Diane Lee Eastman, Oct. 30, 1976 (div. Jan. 1980); children: Donald Robert, David Francis, Stephanie Angelica. Electrician, Avco Lycoming, Stratford, Conn., 1962-66, computer technologist, 1966-69; tech. asst. to mgr. sales Data Products, Stamford, Conn., 1969, quality assurance design engr., 1969-71; pres., owner G.H. Coffey Co., Inc., Internat., Gaysville, Vt., 1972-85, dir., 1975—; pres., dir. C. & D Realty & Devel. Co., Gaysville, 1976-79; v.p., dir. Bridgewater Constrn. Co., Randolph, Vt., 1977-78; founder, past pres. North Country Electric, Rochester, Vt.; pres. Energy Spltys. and Navigational Aids Co., 1979-80; pres., treas. Central Vt. Systems, 1979-83; owner George H. Coffey & Assos., property devel. co., Vt.; developer, v.p., sec. Wintergreen at Killington Inc., 1981-84; pres., treas. Elcom Sci. Corp., Bethel, Vt., 1984 ; tech. advisor Assoc. Gen. Contractors Vt., 1977—; concert accordionist. Mem. Internat. Illumination Engring. Soc., Am. Soc. Quality Control, Assoc. Builders and Contractors Assn., Assoc. Gen. Contractors Vt. Patentee (2). Republican. Roman Catholic. Home: PO Box 162 Gaysville VT 05746 Office: PO Box 92 Route 107 Gaysville VT 05746

COFFILL, MARJORIE LOUISE, civic leader; b. Sonora, Calif., June 11, 1917; d. Eric J. and Pearl (Needham) Segerstrom; A.B. with distinction in Social Sci., Stanford U., 1938, M.A. in Edn., 1941; m. William Charles Coffill, Jan. 25, 1948; children—William James, Eric John. Asst. mgr. Sonora Abstract & Title Co. (Calif.), 1938-39; mem. dean of women's staff Stanford, 1939-41; social dir. women's campus Pomona Coll., 1941-43, instr. psychology, 1941-43; asst. to field dir. ARC, Lee Moore AFB, Calif., 1944-46; partner Riverbank Water Co., Riverbank and Hughson, Calif., 1950-68. Mem. Tuolumne County Mental Health Adv. Com., 1963-70; mem. central advisory council Supplementary Edn. Center, Stockton, Calif., 1966-70; mem. advisory com. Columbia Jr. Coll., 1972—, pres., 1980—; pres. Columbia Found., 1972-74, bd. dirs., 1974-77; mem. Tuolumne County Bicentennial Com., 1974—; active PTA, ARC. Pres., Tuolumne County Republican Women, 1952—, asso. mem. Calif. Rep. Central Com., 1950. Trustee Sonora Union High Sch., 1969-73, Salvation Army Tuolumne County, 1973—; bd. dirs. Lung Assn. Valley Lode Counties, 1974—. Recipient Pi Lambda Theta award, 1940; Outstanding Citizen award C. of C., 1974, Citizen of Yr. award, 1987. Mem. AAUW (charter mem. Tuolumne County br., pres. Sonora br. 1965-66). Episcopalian (mem. vestry 1968, 75). Home: 376 E Summit Ave Sonora CA 95370

COFFILL, WILLIAM CHARLES, lawyer; b. Sonora, Calif., Jan. 19, 1908; s. Harris James and Olive Moore (Hampton) C.; m. Marjorie Louise Segerstrom, Jan. 25, 1948; children—William James, Eric John. A.B., U. Calif.-Berkeley, 1933; J.D., Hastings Coll. Law, 1937. Bar: Calif. 1938, U.S. Dist. Ct. (no. dist.) Calif. 1938, U.S. Dist. Ct. (so. dist.) Calif. 1938, U.S. Ct. Appeals (9th cir.) 1938, U.S. Supreme Ct. 1941, U.S. Dist. Ct. (ea. dist.) 1967. Gen. Mgr. Riverbank Water Co., Riverbank and Hughson, Calif., 1948-68; sole practice, Sonora, 1938-41, 45-76; ptnr. Coffill & Coffill, Sonora, 1976—; city atty. City of Sonora, 1952-75. Past mem., chmn. Tuolumne County Republican Central Com., Calif. Served to lt. comdr. USNR, 1941-46. Mem. Tuolumne County Bar Assn. (past pres.), Am. Legion, VFW. Lodges: Lions, Masons (32 degree), Elks. Office: Coffill and Coffill 23 N Washington St PO Box 1117 Sonora CA 95370

COFFIN, ROBERT PARKER, architect; b. Chgo., Aug. 6, 1917; s. Charles Howells and Irene (Parker) C.; m. Emily Elizabeth Magie, Jan. 2, 1944; children: Betsy, Robert Jr., Barbara John. BEngring., Yale U., 1939. Registered architect, Ill., Wis., Minn., Mo., Ind., Mich.; registered engr., Ill. Field engr. Commonwealth Edison, Chgo., 1939-50; architect Shaw Metz and Dolio, Chgo., 1950-56; ptnr. Coffin and Scherschel, Barrington, Ill., 1956—. Pres., sec. Long Grove (Ill.) Sch. Bd., 1950-56; trustee Long Grove Village, 1956-59, pres., 1959-81, chmn. plan commn., 1981—. Served to (j.g.) USN Air Corps, 1942-46. Recipient 3 Gold Key awards Nat. Home Builders Assn. Mem. AIA, ASCE (life), Am. Soc. Archtl. Historians, Interfaith Forum on Ch. Architecture. Office: Coffin and Scherschel 119 North Ave Barrington IL 60010

COFFMAN, KENNETH MORROW, mechanical contractor; b. Ann Arbor, Mich., Aug 3, 1921; s. Harold Coe and Aletha (Morrow) C.; B.S., Lawrence U., 1943; m. Barbara Ann Porth, Dec. 30, 1943 (dec. 1983); children: Gregory, Deborah Coffman Greene, Jenifer Coffman Dillon; m. Robin Sanders Gibbs, Dec. 28, 1986. Exec. v.p. Stanley Carter Co. Ohio, Toledo, 1957-59; v.p. sales Wenzel & Henoch Co., Milw., 1959-64; exec. v.p. Milw. W & H Inc., 1964-70; exec. v.p. Downey Inc., Milw., 1970-76, pres., 1977-85, chmn. bd. dirs., 1986—. Bd. dirs. YMCA, Milw., 1965-87, Tri County, 1973-78; chmn. bd. mgrs. Camp Minikani, 1965-82; chmn. Am. Cancer Soc. Council, 1987. Served with USMC 1943-46. Named Layman of year, Tri County YMCA, 1973, Disting. Service award Milwaukee YMCA,

1979. Mem. Nat. Cert. Pipe Welders Bur. Wis. (bd. dirs. 1973-86), Mech. Contractors Assn. South East Wis. (dir. 1970-80, pres. 1974-75), Mech. Contractors Devel. Fund. (bd. dirs. 1972-87, pres. 1972-73), Wis. Constrn. Employers Council (bd. dirs. 1973-87), Mech. Contractors Assn. of Wis. (bd. dirs. 1977-86, pres. 1983-84), Nat. Fire Protection Assn., Nat. Assn. Plumbing, Heating, Cooling Contractors, Mech. Contractors Assn. Am. (bd. dirs. 1982-86, pres. 1988), Nat. Mech. Equipment Service and Maintenance Bur. (bd. dirs. 1982-87), Sheet Metal and Air Conditioning Contractors Nat. Assn. Congregationalist. Home: 925 E Wells St Milwaukee WI 53202 Office: Box 1155 Milwaukee WI 53201

COGBURN, MAX OLIVER, lawyer; b. Canton, N.C., Mar. 21, 1927; s. Chester Amberg and Ruby Elizabeth (Davis) C.; m. Mary Heidt, Oct. 15, 1949; children: Max O. Jr., Michael David, Steven Douglas, Cynthia Diane. AB, U. N.C., 1948, LLB, 1950; LLM, Harvard U., 1951. Bar: N.C. 1950, U.S. Dist. Ct. (we. dist.) N.C. 1953, U.S. Ct. Appeals (4th cir.) 1984. Asst. dir. Inst. Govt., Chapel-Hill, N.C., 1951-52; staff mem. Atty. Gen. N.C., Raleigh, 1952-54; adminstr. asst. Chief Justice N.C., Raleigh, 1954-55; judge Gen. County Ct. Buncombe County, Asheville, N.C., 1968-70; sole practice Canton, Asheville, N.C., 1968, 1971—; ptnr. Roberts, Stevens & Cogburn, P.A., Asheville, 1986—. Chmn. Buncombe County Dem. Exec. Com., Asheville, 1974-76; mem. State Dem. Exec. Com., Raleigh, 1974-76. Mem. ABA, N.C. State Bar Assn., N.C. Bar Assn., 28th Judicial Dist. Bar State of N.C., Buncombe County Bar Assn. (past pres.). Roman Catholic. Home: Rt 1 Pisgah View Ranch Candler NC 28715 Office: Roberts Stevens et al PO Box 7647 Asheville NC 28807

COGGESHALL, NORMAN DAVID, former oil company executive; b. Ridge Farm, Ill., May 15, 1916; s. Lester B. and Grace (Blaisdell) C.; m. Margaret Josephine Danner, Aug. 22, 1940; children: Nancy Ellen Von der Ohe, David M., M. Gwen Calabretta, Phillip A. BA, U. Ill., 1937, MS, 1938, PhD, 1942. Tcrh. physics U. Ill., 1942-43; scientist Gulf Oil Research, Pitts., 1943-50, asst. dir. physics div., 1950-55, dir. analytical sci. div., 1955-61, dir. phys. scis. div., 1961-67, v.p. process scis., 1967-70, v.p. exploration and prodn., 1970-76, v.p. tech. govt. coodination, 1976-81; pvt. investor and pvt. cons., Lynn Haven, Fla., 1981—. Contbg. author: Colloid Chemistry, 1946, Physical Chemistry of Hydrocarbons, 1950, Organic Analysis, 1953, Advances in Mass Spectrometry, 1963; contbr. articles to tech. jours.; patentee in field. Recipient Resolution of Appreciation, Am. Petroleum Inst., 1970. Fellow Am. Phys. Soc.; mem. Am. Chem. Soc. (award in chem. instrumentation 1970), Spectroscopy Soc. Pitts., Bay County C. of C. (mil. affairs com.). Republican. Clubs: St. Andrews Bay, Yacht (Panama City, Fla.). Lodge: Rotary. Home and Office: 701 Driftwood Dr Lynn Haven FL 32444

COGGESHALL, ROBERT WALDEN, ret. govt. ofcl.; b. Darlington, S.C., Sept. 11, 1912; s. Robert Werner and Beulah (Walden) C.; B.S., U. S.C., 1932; M.A., George Washington U., 1964; postgrad. Am. U., 1964-69; m. Ellie Mason Thomas, Sept. 3, 1934; children—Peter Collin V., John Pennington. Administrv. analyst Home Owners Loan Corp., Washington, 1934-41; budget analyst Fed. Works Agy., 1941-43; asst. dep. adminstr. for rent control OPA, 1943-46; chief systems and procedures Bur. Reclamation, 1946-53; editor Postal Manual, Office Postmaster Gen., 1954; chief mgmt. analysis Bur. Indian Affairs, 1954-57; chief div. mgmt. sci. Office of Sec., Dept. Interior, 1957-68; fellow Brookings Instn., 1968-69; mem. faculty U.S. Dept. Agr. Grad. Sch., 1959-65. S.C. chmn. Common Cause, 1974-75. Mem. Alpha Tau Omega. Episcopalian. Author: Administrative Functions of the Fish and Wildlife Service, 1958; Coordination of Federal Oceanography, 1963, Ancestors and Kin, 1988. Home: Shaggy Acres Ballentine SC 29002

COHEN, ABRAHAM J. (AL COHEN), educational administrator; b. Chelsea, Mass., Mar. 19, 1932; s. Samuel and Sarah (Lisofsky) C.; m. Isabel M. Reardon, Aug. 23, 1959; children: David Joseph, Jonathan William, Jennifer Eve. B.S., Salem State Coll., 1959; M.Edn., Boston U., 1960; postgrad., U. Calif. at Santa Barbara, 1968, Fordham U., 1965; Ed.D., Columbia U., 1974; grad., U.S. Army Command and Gen. Staff Coll., 1975, Indsl. Coll. Armed Forces, 1976, Air Force War Coll., 1977. Tchr. social studies Chelsea jr. high schs., 1959-61; coordinator instructional materials and service North Reading (Mass.) Pub. Schs., 1961-64; supr. instructional materials and sch. libraries White Plains (N.Y.) Pub. Schs., 1964—, coordinator health edn., 1974—; pres. Ednl. Film Library Assn. and Am. Film Festival, N.Y.C., 1971-73; Lectr. sch. continuing edn. NYU, 1965-68, Sch. Library Service Columbia U., 1972—; dir. audio visual center Salem (Mass.) State Coll., 1961-62; mem. adv. bd. Ednl. Products Information Exchange Inst., N.Y.C., 1972—; instr. U.S. Army Command Gen. Staff Coll.; comdt. 1150th USARF Sch., Ft. Hamilton, N.Y., 1983-87; dir. Sta. 36-TV, White Plains, N.Y., 1982—. Contbr. articles to profl. jours. Scoutmaster, instl. rep. Muscoot-Westchester council Boy Scouts Am., 1971-72; pres. Westchester Library Assn., 1972-74; mem. expansion com. J.C. Hart Library, Yorktown, N.Y., 1969-71; pres. Westchester County Ednl. Communications Assn., 1968-69; Chmn. bd. dirs., pres. Yorktown Jewish Center, 1969-70; bd. dirs. Westchester div. Am. Cancer Soc., chmn. pub. edn., 1981-83. Served with AUS, 1952-54; col. Res. ret., apptd. mem. of U.S. Army Disting. Med. Regiemnt Hall of Fame, 1987, apptd. to N.Y. State Employer Guard and Res. Com., 1987. Recipient Gen. John J. Pershing award U.S. Army Command and Gen. Staff Coll., 1975, Educator of Yr. award Am. Cancer Soc., 1983, Legion of Merit award, Col. Cohen Day proclaimed by the County of Westchester and the township of Yorktown. Mem. Mass. Audio Visual Assn. (dir. 1962-64), Ednl. Media Council (dir. 1971-73, exec. com. 1972-73), N.Y. State Edn. Communications Assn. (dir. 1968-69), Assn. Edn. Communications and Tech., Phi Delta Kappa. Club: Mason. Home: 2601 Darnley Pl Yorktown Heights NY 10598 Office: Education House 5 Homeside Lane White Plains NY 10605

COHEN, BURTON JEROME, business executive; b. Phila., Dec. 8, 1933; s. Alexander David and Esther (Mirrow) C.; m. Jane McDowell, Mar. 16, 1968; children: Paul, Joshua, Douglas, Glen. B.S. in Acctg. Temple U., 1955; student, c. Program, Harvard U. Ops. v.p. Cakemasters, Inc., Phila., 1957-61; mgr. IBM, Phila., White Plains, N.Y., N.Y.C., 1961-70; ptnr. Touche & Ross & Co., N.Y.C., 1970-77; ptnr., nat. dir. fin. and adminstrn. Coopers & Lybrand, N.Y.C., 1977-82; exec.-chief adminstrv. officer Paul, Weiss, Rifkind, Wharton & Garrison, N.Y.C., 1982—; adj. prof. Columbia U. Grad. Sch. Bus.; lectr. Am. Mgmt. Assn. seminars.; Mem. adv. bd. Borough Manhattan Community Coll. Author: Cost Effective Information Systems, 1971; contbr. to: Info. Systems Handbook, 1975. Served with Fin. Corps U.S. Army, 1955-57. Mem. Fin. Execs. Inst. Club: Masons. Home: 63 Adams Ln New Canaan CT 06840 Office: Paul Weiss Rifkind Wharton & Garrison 1285 Ave of Americas New York NY 10019

COHEN, BURTON MARCUS, physician, clinical investigator; b. Elizabeth, N.J., Dec. 13, 1925; s. Philip and Beatrice (Kaufman) C.; AB, Columbia U., 1945; MD, U. Rochester, 1948; m. Elaine N. Mohr, Dec. 24, 1950; children: Elizabeth, Hugh, Claire Cohen Lerner, Suzanne. Intern, resident Maimonides Hosp., Bklyn., 1948-51; resident physician Strong Meml. Hosp., also asst. medicine U. Rochester, 1950-51; research fellow Columbia U. Research Service, Goldwater Meml. Hosp., asst. medicine Columbia Coll. Phys. and Surg., 1954-58; asst. prof. clin. medicine and clin. preventive medicine N.J. Coll. Medicine, 1959-61, clin. asst. prof. medicine, 1961-63; assoc. prof. clin. medicine, 1963-82, clin. prof. medicine, 1982—; gov's task force on phys. edn. dept. environmental and community medicine Robert Wood Johnson Med. Sch., Piscataway, N.J., 1986—; mem. Clean Air commn., N.J., 1988; pres. Burton M. Cohen, M.D.; attending physician Jersey City Med. Center; assoc. dir. White Cardiopulmonary Inst., Pollak Hosp., Jersey City, 1959-63; sr. attending physician Elizabeth Gen. Hosp., chmn. dept. medicine, 1975-77; med. bd. Deborah Hosp., Browns Mills; assoc. U. Rochester. Dir. Clodagh Assos., Ltd., Ireland; active Clean Air Council, Dept. Environ. Protection, State of N.J. Served as midshipman USNR, 1943-44, lt comdr., USPHS, 1952-55; comdr. (sr. surgeon) Res., 1968-79, capt. (med. dir.), 1979—. Fellow Am. Coll. Cardiology. Am. Coll. Chest Physicians, Acad. Medicine N.J., ACP, Royal Soc. Medicine (London), Royal Soc. Health, Internat. Acad. Sci. and Medicine, Am. Coll. Clin. Pharmacology and Chemotherapy (a founding fellow), Am. Soc. Clin. Radiology; mem. Union County Heart Assn. (past pres.), Am. Fedn. Clin. Research. Internat. Soc. Internal Medicine, Internat. Cardiovascular Soc., European Soc. Clin. Respiratory Physiology, AAAS, Am. Therapeutic Soc., AAUP, Mil. Surgeons U.S. Soc. Automotive Historians, Res. Officers U.S., N.J. Acad. Sci., John Jay Soc., George Hoyt Whipple Soc. (charter), Soc. Older Grads. Columbia U. Club: Columbia University (N.Y.C.); Rolls-Royce Owners (U.S.), Rolls-Royce Enthusiast, Rolls-Royce and Bentley Drivers (Eng.). Cardiology editor Medecine et Hygiene (Switzerland), 1961—; editor-in-chief Current Concepts in Pacing. Contbr. articles to profl. jours. Home: 15 Roberts Rd Warren Township NJ 07060 Office: 425 Westfield Ave Elizabeth NJ 07208

COHEN, DANIEL ISAAC ARYEH, mathematician, computer science educator; b. Reading, Pa., Dec. 26, 1946; s. Samuel Philip and Marjorie (Mendelsohn) C.; m. Sandra Kopit, May 7, 1978. A.B. summa cum laude, Princeton U., 1967; M.A., Harvard U., 1970, Ph.D., 1975; J.D., Columbia U., 1987. Bar: N.Y. 1988. Asst. prof. Northeastern U., Boston, 1975-78; vis. assoc. prof. Rockefeller U., N.Y.C., 1978-81; prof. computer sci. Hunter Coll., N.Y.C., 1980—, chmn. dept. computer sci., 1986—; vis. scholar Yale U. Law Sch., 1987-88; exchange scholar to USSR, Nat. Acad. Sci., Washington, 1978; faculty IBM Research Ctr., Yorktown Heights, N.Y., 1979; adj. assoc. prof. biostats. of psychiatry, Cornell U. Med. Coll., N.Y.C., 1980—. Author: Basic Techniques of Combinatorial Theory, 1978; Introduction to Computer Theory, 1986; (with others) National Academy of Science: Outlook for Science and Technology, 1982. Univ. scholar Princeton U., 1963-66. Mem. Math. Assn. Am., Am. Math. Soc., N.Y. Acad. Sci., Assn. for Computing Machinery, ABA, N.Y. State Bar Assn. Jewish. Clubs: Harvard, Princeton. Home: 420 E 54th St Apt 10B New York NY 10022 Office: Hunter Coll CUNY Dept Computer Sci 685 Park Ave New York NY 10021

COHEN, EDWARD, civil engineer; b. Glastonbury, Conn., Jan. 6, 1921; s. Samuel and Ida (Tanewitz) C.; m. Elizabeth Belle Cohen, Dec. 19, 1948 (dec. June 1979); children: Samuel, Libby M. Wallace, James; m. Carol Simon Kalb, Jan. 11, 1981; stepchildren: Anne Kalb Bronner, Paul Kalb. BS in Engring., Columbia U., 1945, MS in Civil Engring., 1954. Registered profl. engr., N.Y., Conn., Fla., Ga., Md., N.J., La., Mass., Mich., Pa., D.C., Okla., Va., Wis., Del., Nat. Council Engring. Examiners; chartered civil engr., Gt. Britain; lic. land surveyor, N.Y., Conn., Mass., N.J. Engring. aide Conn. Hwy. Dept., 1940-42; asst. engr. East Hartford Dept. Pub. Works, 1942-44; structural engr. Hardesty & Hanover, N.Y.C., 1945-47, Sanderson & Porter, N.Y.C., 1947-49; lectr. architecture Columbia U., 1948-51; with Ammann & Whitney, N.Y.C., 1949—; ptnr. Ammann & Whitney, 1963-74, sr. ptnr., 1974-77, mng. ptnr., 1977—, dir. co. work as engrs. of record restoration of Statue of Liberty, West Face of U.S. Capitol Bldg. and Roebling Del. Canal Bridge; exec. v.p. Ammann & Whitney, Inc., 1974, in charge bldg., transp., communications, mil. and hist. preservation projects, chmn., chief exec. officer, 1977—; v.p. Ammann & Whitney Internat. Ltd., 1963-73; pres. Safeguard Constrn. Mgmt. Corp., 1973-77, chmn., chief exec. officer, 1977—; cons. RAND Corp., Santa Monica, Calif., 1958-72, Dept. Def., 1962-63, Hudson Inst., Croton-on-Hudson, N.Y., 1967-71, World Bank, 1984, TVA, 1987; Stanton Walker lectr. U. Md., 1973, Henry M. Shaw lectr. N. Carolina State U., 1987; deptl. adv. com. Urban and Civil Engring. U. Pa., 1978-84, Rutgers U., 1984—; mem. engring. council Columbia U., 1975—, vice chmn., 1985-86; mem. adv. bd. Dept. Civil Engring. and Engring. Mechs. Ctr. for Infrastructure Studies, 1987—; chmn. engring com. first presdl. awards for design excellence Nat. Endowment for Arts, 1985. Mem. adv. bd. Jour. Resource Mgmt. and Tech., 1981—; co-editor: Handbook of Structural Concrete, 1983; contbr. more than 100 articles to profl. jours. and govt. manuals on structural, seismic, hardened design, wind forces, dynamic analysis, ultimate strength and plastic design guyed towers and shell structures. Commr. Bklyn. Bridge Centennial Commn., 1981-83; spl. adv. N.Y. State Statue of Liberty Centennial Commn., 1985; bd. dirs. Cejwin Youth Camps, 1972—, Com. of 100 Trailblazer Summer Camp for Underprivileged Children, 1985—; trustee Hall of Sci., N.Y.C., 1976—; mem. exec. com. March of Dimes Transp. Award Luncheon, 1983—; mentor in engring. N.Y. Alliance for Pub. Schs., 1986—; N.Y. area chmn. engring. sect. Orgn. for Rehabilitation through Tng., 1983— (Sci. and Tech. award 1987). Recipient Illig medal in Applied Sci. Columbia U., 1946, Egleston medal Columbia U., 1981, Goethals medal for Engring. Achievement Soc. Am. Mil. Engrs., 1985, Mayor's Award of Honor for Sci. and Tech., N.Y., 1988; Patriotic Civilian Service award Dept. of Army, 1973. Hon. mem. ASCE (chmn. com. design loads for bldgs. and other structures A58, 1968—, chmn. reinforced concrete research council 1980—, met. sect. v.p. 1978-79, pres. 1980, Ridgeway award 1946, Civil Engring. State-of-the-Art award 1974, Raymond Reese award 1976, Ernest Howard Gold Medal 1983, Met. Civil Engr. of Yr. award 1986, Service to People award 1987); fellow Am. Cons. Engr. Council (Grand award for Engring. Excellence 1986), Inst. Civil Engrs. (Gt. Britain); mem. N.Y. Assn. Cons. Engrs. (bldg. code adv. com., bd. dirs. 1981-82, 85—), N.Y. Acad. Scis. (hon. life, Laskowitz Aerospace research gold medal 1970, chmn. 1977-79), Am. Concrete Inst. (hon. mem., dir. 1966-76, v.p. 1970-72, pres. 1972-73, chmn. com. bldg. code requirements for reinforced concrete 1963-71, Wason medal 1956, Delmar Bloem award 1973), N.Y. Concrete Industry Bd. (dir. 1976—, pres. 1978-79), Columbia U. Sch. Engring. Alumni Assn. (bd. dirs. 1985-86), N.Y. Concrete Constrn. Design Inst. (pres. tall bldgs. council 1975-80), NSPE (Outstanding Engring. ement award 1987), N.Y. State Soc. Profl. Engrs. (Engr. of Yr. 1987, Nassau chpt. Engr. of Yr. 1987), Internat. Bridge and Turnpike Assn., Internat. Assn. Bridge and Structural Engrs., Am. Welding Soc., comite European de Beton (specialist mem.), Moles, Century Assn., Sigma Xi, Chi Epsilon, Tau Beta Pi. Clubs: Engrs. N.Y.C. (dir. 1974-75), Wings, Club at World Trade Ctr. Lodge: B'nai Brith. Home: 56 Chestnut Hill Roslyn NY 11576 Office: Ammann & Whitney 96 Morton St New York NY 10014

COHEN, EDWARD LAWRENCE, architect, consultant; b. Bronx, N.Y., Nov. 1, 1947; s. Solomon and Matilda (Russo) C.; m. Lena Garofalo, Dec. 21, 1975; children—Karen Ann, Jessica Ann. B.Arch., Pratt Inst., 1970, M.Arch., 1973. Registered architect, N.Y. VISTA assoc., Bklyn., 1969-70; vol. Peace Corps, Venezuela, 1970-72; grad. instr. architecture, Pratt Inst., Bklyn., 1973-79; dep. dir. City Planning Dept., N.Y.C., 1973-79; pres. Total Design Group P.C., N.Y.C., 1979-86; prin. Total Design Concepts, 1987—; cons. Gruzen Partnership, N.Y.C., 1979-82, Urbahn Assocs., N.Y.C., 1981—, Dattner Assocs., N.Y.C., 1983—, Daniel Frankfurt Engrs., N.Y.C., 1983—, Deleuw Cather Engrs., 1987—. Project dir. st. revitalization, 1976 (NEA award 1978); author: New Town in Town, 1979 (Paris prize 1976); contbr. article to mag. Bd. mem. Ditmas Park Assn., Bklyn., 1979-84, Family Crisis Ctr., Bklyn., 1983-84; mem. Mcpl. Arts Soc., N.Y.C., 1982-84, Flatbush Devel. Corp., Bklyn., 1978-84. Recipient Urban Design award Urban Design Mag., 1978; Design Excellence award Downtown Sts. Nat. Endowment Arts, Washington, 1978, Design Excellence award N.Y.C. Arts Commn., 1985. Mem. AIA (chmn. transp. com. 1984), Nat. Inst. Archtl. Edn. (program com. 1983). Democrat. Jewish. Home: 484 E 17th St Brooklyn NY 11226 Office: Total Design Group PC 84 Mercer St New York NY 10012

COHEN, EDWIN SAMUEL, lawyer, educator; b. Richmond, Va., Sept. 27, 1914; s. LeRoy S. Cohen and Mirian (Rosenheim) C.; m. Helen Herz, Aug. 31, 1944; children: Edwin C., Roger, Wendy. B.A., U. Richmond, 1933; J.D., U. Va., 1936. Bar: Va. 1935, N.Y. 1937, D.C. 1973. Assoc. firm Sullivan & Cromwell, N.Y.C., 1936-49; partner Root, Barrett, Cohen, Knapp & Smith and (predecessor firm), N.Y.C., 1949-65; counsel Root, Barrett, Cohen, Knapp & Smith and (predecessor firm), 1965-69; prof. law U. Va., Charlottesville, 1965-68, Joseph M. Hartfield Prof., 1968-69, 73-85, prof. emeritus, 1985—; asst. sec. treasury for tax policy 1969-72, under sec. treasury, 1972-73; counsel Covington & Burling, Washington, 1973-77; ptnr. Covington & Burling, 1977-86, sr. counsel, 1986—; mem. and counsel adv. group on corporate taxes Ways and Means Com. Ho. of Reps., 1956-58; spl. cons. on corps. Am. Law Inst. Fed. Income Tax Project, 1949-54; mem. adv. group Fed. Estate and Gift Tax Project, 1964-68; mem. Va. Income Tax Conformity Study Commn., 1970-71; cons. Va. Income Tax Study Commn., 1966-68; mem. adv. group Commr. Internal Revenue, 1967-68. Recipient Alexander Hamilton award Treasury Dept. Mem. Am. Judicature Soc., ABA (chmn. com. on corporate stockholder relationships 1956-58, mem. council 1958-61, chmn. spl. com. on substantive tax reform 1962-63, chmn. spl. com. on formation tax policy 1977-80), Va. Bar Assn., D.C. Bar Assn., N.Y. State Bar Assn., Va. Tax Conf. (planning com. 1965-68, 85—), C. of C. of U.S. (bd. dirs., chmn. taxation com. 1979-84), Assn. Bar City N.Y., N.Y. County Lawyers Assn., Am. Law Inst., Am. Coll. Tax Counsel, Order Coif, Raven Soc., U. Va., Phi Beta Kappa, Omicron Delta Kappa, Pi Delta Epsilon, Phi Epsilon Pi (Nat. Achievement award). Clubs: Broad Street, Colonnade, Boar's Head, Farmington; International (Washington); Capitol Hill, City. Home: 104 Stuart Pl Ednam Forest Charlottesville VA 22901

COHEN, EUGENE ERWIN, university health institute administrator, accounting educator emeritus; b. Johnstown, Pa., Nov. 1, 1917; s. Leroy Samuel and Ann (Aronson) C.; m. Lee Woodard Edmundson, Dec. 31, 1944; children: William Palmer, Margaret Gene, Ann Woodard. B.B.A., U. Miami, Fla., 1941, M.B.A., 1951; postgrad., Wayne State U., 1944-45, U. N.C., 1951-52. Mem. faculty U. Miami, 1945—, asso. prof. accounting, 1954-67, prof. accounting, 1967-79, prof. emeritus, 1979—, treas., 1957-79, v.p., 1958-79, v.p. emeritus, 1979—; also treas. Univ. Research Found.; treas. Howard Hughes Med. Inst., 1979—; v.p., dir. Dormitory Housing Assn., Inc.; chmn., pres. Laurel Corp., 1971-73; dir., chmn. Fed. Res. br. Bank, Miami, Fla., Am. Laser Corp., Garrett & Co., Fla. Fed. Savs. & Loan Assn.; dir. Am. Bankers Ins. Co., Fla.; mem. adv. bd. Tech. Systems, Inc.; cons. Greyhound Corp., Plastetics, Inc., Reynolds & Co., NSF, NIH; U.S. Office Edn., So. Assn. Colls. and Schs., J.L. Mailman Found., A.L. Mailman Family Found.; stockholders agt. Garrett Trust; rep. Univ. Corp. for Atmospheric Research, 1969-73; mem. com. taxation Am. Council Edn. Cons. editor Coll. and Univ. Bus. Mag, 1963-68; author articles in field. Bd. dirs. Miami Goodwill Industries, Dade County Citizens Safety Council, Greater Miami Indsl. Commn., Heart Learning Resource Center; vice chmn. bd. Nat. Children's Cardiac Hosp.; pres. Orange Bowl Com., mem., 1950—; chmn. Dade County Higher Edn. Facilities Authority, 1969-81, Jackson Found., 1972—; v.p., dir. Nat. Childrens Cardiac Hosp.; trustee United Way Dade County, White Belt Found., J. Parker Mickle Research Found., Robert Z. Greene Found.; asso. mem. Internat. Center Coral Gables, 1973—, New World Center, Miami; mem. Health Systems Agy., South Fla.; bd. dirs. Family Services, Miami, 1968-74; mem. Miami Mayor's Spl. Adv. Com. on Interama, 1969-72. Served to maj. U.S. Army, 1941-45. Recipient Distinguished Alumni award U. Miami, 1961, Distinguished Grad. Alumnus award, 1963. Mem. Dade County C. of C., Am. Mgmt. Assn., The Miamians, Nat. Assn. Coll. and Univ. Bus. Officers (dir.), So. Assn. Coll. and Univ. Bus. Officers (pres. 1963), Coll. and Univ. Personnel Assn., Coll. and Univ. Housing Officers Assn., Nat. Assn. Cost Accts., Fin. Execs. Inst. (founder mem. Fla. chpt., chpt. pres. 1963), Fin. Analysts Soc. Miami, Econ. Soc. South Fla., Miami Beach Com. of 100, Hist. Assn. So. Fla. (dir.), Coral Gables Com. of 21, Friends of Univ. Library, Newcomen Soc., Iron Arrow, Omicron Delta Kappa, Alpha Phi Omega, Phi Mu Alpha, Beta Gamma Sigma, Alpha Kappa Psi. Clubs: Univ. Yacht, Miami; Ocean Reef Yacht and Country (Key Largo, Fla.). Home: 6700 SW 117th St Miami FL 33156 Office: Howard Hughes Med Inst PO Box 330837 Coconut Grove FL 33133

COHEN, EUGENE JOSEPH, rabbi; b. N.Y.C., Aug. 22, 1918; s. Philip J. and Rose (Cohen) C.; Rabbi, Yeshiva U., 1942; Ph.D., Boston U., 1954; m. Ada Twersky, Dec. 1, 1948; children: Burton, Bethsheva Michael, Leeber. Rabbi, Congregation Derech Emunoh, Arverne, N.Y., 1948-66, Internat. Synagogue, Queens, N.Y., 1967-85, Brith Milah Bd. Am., N.Y.C., 1960—; chief chaplains VA Hosp., Bklyn., 1969—. Active Bricha underground rescue movement, World War II. Served to capt. AUS, 1945-47. Recipient award Fedn. Jewish Philanthropists, 1964. Mem. Religious Zionists Am. (v.p.), Jewish Chaplains U.S. (past pres.), Rabbinical Council (sec. 1984), Rabbinical Alumni, N.Y. Bd. Rabbis, Brith Milah Am., Fedn. Jewish Philanthropies (mem. med. ethics com.). Lodge: B'nai B'rith (pres. Milah bd. of world). Author: Jewish Concepts of the Servant, 1954; Ritual Circumcision and Redemption of the First-Born Son, Presentation and Analysis of Routine Circumcision (40 vols. in print), Hope for Humanity; also articles; editor: Pediatrics and Urology and Their Relationship to Brith Milah; Medical Dilemmas and the Practise of Milah; Brith Milah and Medicine; speaker radio and tv. Home: 258 Riverside Dr New York NY 10025 Office: 800 Poly Pl Brooklyn NY 11209

COHEN, GERARD DENIS, mathematician, educator; b. Paris, Aug. 25, 1951; s. Maurice and Clairette (Hassid) C. Degree in engring., U. Paris, 1973, D of Math., 1980. Asst. prof. math. Sch. Nat. Super Telecommunications, U. Paris, 1976-82, prof., 1982—, researcher, 1984—. Editor: Three Days on Coding Theory, 1987; referee and contbr. to sci. jours. Mem. IEEE, Am. Math. Soc., French Math. Soc. Home: 22 Rue Dussoubs, 75002 Paris France Office: U Paris Sch Telecommunications, 46 Rue Barrault, 75013 Paris France

COHEN, GLORIA ERNESTINE, educator; b. Bklyn., July 6, 1942; d. Victor George and Marion Theodosia (Roberts) C. B.S. in Edn., Wilberforce U., 1965; M.A. in Elem. Edn., Adelphi U., 1975; Profl. Diploma in Ednl. Adminstrn., L.I. U., 1984; M.S. in Edn., Bklyn. Coll., 1986. Tchr. Bd. Edn., Bklyn., 1965—; case worker Dept. Welfare, Bklyn., 1965—. Mem. Northwest Civic Assn., Freeport, N.Y., 1973—, Roosevelt-Freeport Civic Assn., Freeport, 1984—. Mem. NOW, Assn. for Supervision and Curriculum Devel., Nat. Alliance of Black Sch. Educators, Inc., Bklyn. Reading Council of Internat. Reading Assn., N.Y. State Reading Assn., Assn. Black Educators of N.Y., Nat. Assn. Female Execs., Inc., NOW, Zeta Phi Beta, Kappa Delta Pi. Democrat. Roman Catholic. Clubs: FSO Internat. (Jamaica, N.Y.); Freeport Indoor Tennis. Avocations: tennis; skiing; swimming. Home: 4 Sterling Pl Freeport NY 11520 Office: Bd Ed PS 149 700 Sutter Ave Brooklyn NY 11207

COHEN, HARTOG, retired economist; b. Venlo, The Netherlands, Dec. 17, 1917; s. Philip and Sophie (Kleermaker) C.; m. Jose Ann Spearing, July 9, 1937. Doctorandus Econ., U. Amsterdam, 1955; CPA, N.I.V.A. Sch., 1960; Diploma in A.M.B.I., N.O.V.I. Sch., 1966. Acct. Meyer & Horcher, CPA's, Amsterdam, The Netherlands, 1955-57; economist UN, Geneva, 1958-61; translator Commn. European Communities, Brussels, 1962-81; ret. 1981. Co-author: The Black Economy, 1981; contbr. articles on econs. and linguistics to profl. publs. Home: Ave des Nerviens 51, 1040 Brussels Belgium

COHEN, IDA BOGIN (MRS. SAVIN COHEN), export-import executive; b. Bklyn.; d. Joseph and Yetta (Harris) Bogin; student St. Johns U.; B.S., N.Y.U.; m. Barnet Gaster, June 26, 1941 (div. May 1955); m. 2d, Savin Cohen, Aug. 30, 1964. Sec.-treas. J. Gerber & Co., Inc., N.Y.C., 1942-54, v.p., dir., 1954-73; pres., dir. Austracan U.S.A., Inc., N.Y.C., 1960-73; v.p. Parts Warehouse, Inc., Woodside, N.Y., 1970-72, sec.-treas., 1972-83; also engaged in pvt. investments. Contbr. articles to South African Outspan, newspapers. Home: 12 Shorewood Dr Sands Point NY 11050

COHEN, IRVING DAVID, science administrator; b. Bklyn., May 12, 1945; s. Harry and Fay (Michenberg) C.; B.E. in Chem. Engring., CCNY, 1967; M.E., N.Y.U., 1970, postgrad. in environ. safety and health, 1970—; m. Dorothy Ann Joseph, Aug. 21, 1966; children—Miriam Susan, Esther Heidi, Daniel Marc, Aaron Michael. Sr. process engr. Crawford & Russell, Inc., Stamford, Conn., 1967-71; asso. chem. emgr. Hoffmann-LaRoche, Nutley, N.J., 1971-72; sr. project mgr. Woodward-Envicon, Inc., Clifton, N.J., 1972-75; pres. Enviro-Scis., Inc., Mt. Arlington, N.J., 1975—, Aero Instrumentation Resources, Inc., 1978—; pres., tech. dir. Environ. Title Inc., 1984—; pres. Ecra Labs, Inc., 1986—; cons. Environ. Defense Fund, Rockaway Twp. Environ. Commn. Cert. environ. profl. Mem. Am. Inst. Chem. Engrs., Am. Indsl. Hygiene Assn., Internat. Assn. for Pollution Control, Scientists Com. for Public Info., Air Pollution Control Assn., Nat. Assn. Environ. Profls., N.Y. Acad. Sci. Jewish. Author environ. impact reports for energy related projects. Home: 19 Copeland Rd Denville NJ 07834 Office: Enviro-Scis Inc 111 Howard Blvd Suite 108 Mount Arlington NJ 07856

COHEN, IRWIN, economist; b. Bronx, N.Y., Feb. 29, 1936; s. Samuel and Gertrude (Levy) C.; B.S. in Accounting, N.Y. U., 1956, M.B.A. in Finance, 1964, M.A. in Econs., 1969; B.S. in Math., CCNY, 1970. Financial analyst U.S. SEC, N.Y.C., 1965-67, Fed. Res. Bank N.Y., N.Y.C., 1967-72, Prudential Ins. Co. Am., 1973-74, SEC, N.Y.C., 1974—. Life Fellow Internat. Biog. Assn., Am. Biog. Inst. Research Assn. (dep. gov.), World Acad. Scholars, World Literary Acad., World Inst. Achievement; mem. Internat. Biographical Ctr. (dep. dir. gen.), Internat. Platform Assn (life), Math. Assn. Am., Am. Finance Assn., Econ. History Assn. Home: 372 Central Park Ave Apt 2K Scarsdale NY 10583

COHEN, JAY LORING, lawyer; b. Erie, Pa., Oct. 26, 1953; s. Harold H. and Adelle (Stein) C.; m. Martha Kaepplein, June 20, 1976; children—Natanel M., Katrielle Z. B.A. cum laude, U. Rochester, 1974; J.D., Georgetown U., 1977. Bar: Pa. 1977, U.S. Claims Ct. 1978, U.S. Ct. Appeals (D.C. cir.) 1978, D.C. 1979, U.S. Supreme Ct. 1981, U.S. Ct. Appeals (fed. cir.) 1982, Md. 1986. Mem. firm Israel, Raley & Cohen, Chartered (formerly Israel & Raley), Washington, 1977-87; sole practice, Washington, 1988—.

Editor Am. Criminal Law Rev., 1977. Vice-chmn. Montgomery County Ethics Commn., 1986—; bd. dirs. Hebrew Day Inst., 1984—, v.p., 1987-88, treas. 1988—. Mem. Assn. Trial Lawyers Am. (comml. litigation sect.), ABA (pub. contract law sect.), Fed. Bar Assn. (fed. litigation sect.), Fed. Cir. Bar Assn. (gov. contract appeals sect.). Office: 2000 L St NW Suite 200 Washington DC 20036

COHEN, JEFFREY ALAN, management consultant; b. Atlantic, N.J., Apr. 7, 1953; s. Jack W. and Ethel (Adams) C.; m. Patricia Hetzel Cohen, Sept. 25, 1983; children: Lisa Beth, Debra Lynne. BS, Fairleigh Dickinson U., 1975; MS, Pace U., 1982; cert. for advanced grad. study, Yale U., 1983. CPA, N.J. Tax and audit staff Touche Ross & Co., Gateway I, Newark, 1975-78, sr. mgmt. cons., 1986—; sr. fin. analyst N.J. Casino Control Commn., Trenton, N.J., 1978-80, supr., 1980-82, mgr. fin. evaluation and control, 1982-83, dep. dir. fin., 1983-86; mem. faculty Sch. Bus., Rutgers U., part-time 1985—; staff mem. Atlantic City Conv. Hall Blue Ribbon Panel, 1982. Yale U. fellow, 1983. Fellow N.J. Soc. CPA's (gaming conf. com.); mem. Am. Mgmt. Assn., Am. Inst. CPA's, Nat. Assn. Govt. Accts., Nat. Assn. Accts., Am. Acctg. Assn., Govt. Fin. Officers Assn., Tau Epsilon Phi. Jewish. Home: 273 Maple Point Dr Langhorne PA 19047 Office: Touche Ross & Co Gateway I Newark NJ 07102

COHEN, JEFFREY M., physicist; b. Elizabeth, N.J., Aug. 30, 1940; s. Isadore M. and Hilda (Pollack) C.; m. Marion Deutsche, Aug. 9, 1964; children: Marielle, Arin, Bret, Devin. BS, N.J. Inst. Tech., 1962; MS, Yale U., 1963, PhD, 1966. Am. Math. Soc. fellow Cornell U., 1965; postdoctoral fellow Yale U., New Haven, 1965-67; Nat. Acad. Scis. postdoctoral research assoc. Goddard Inst. Space Studies, N.Y.C., 1967-69; mem. staff Inst. Advanced Study, Princeton, N.J., 1969-71; prof. physics U. Pa., Phila., 1971—; vis. scientist Max-Planck Institut fur Physik und Astrophysik, Munich, 1972; cons. Naval Research Lab., Washington, 1974-77; communications specialist N.J. Recipient Nat. Prize Paper award IEEE, 1962; AEC fellow, 1966-67; grantee Nat. Acad. Scis., 1967-68, 72-73, Office Naval Research, 1973-74, Advanced Project Research Agy., 1977, Air Force Office Sci. Research, 1977-79, NSF, 1977—. Fellow N.Y. Acad. Scis., Am. Phys. Soc.; mem. Am. Astron. Soc., Internat. Astron. Union, Sigma Xi, Tau Beta Pi. Research, numerous publs. in field, especially gen. relativity, astrophysics; developed theory of rotating bodies using Einstein's gen. theory of relativity; predicted Vela-X remnant expansion rate. Office: U Pa Physics Dept Philadelphia PA 19104

COHEN, JUDITH W., ednl. adminstr.; b. N.Y.C., May 14, 1937; d. Meyer F. and Edith Beatrice (Elman) Wiles; B.A., Bklyn. Coll., 1957, M.A., 1960; cert. advanced studies Hofstra U., 1978; MA Columbia U., 1986, postgrad. 1986—. m. Joseph Cohen, Oct. 19, 1957; children—Amy Beth, Lisa Carrie, Adam Scott Frank. Tchr. N.Y.C. Public Schs., Bklyn., 1957-60; tchr. Middle Country Sch. Dist., Centereach, N.Y., 1970—, Title IX compliance officer, 1980-86, team leader 1987—. Bus. adv. Women's Equal Rights Congress, Suffolk County Human Rights; chmn. bd. edn., Temple Beth David, trustee, 1975-79; pres. CHUMS, 1979—; Tchr. of Gifted Post-L.I. U. Saturday Program; L.I. Writing Project fellow, Dowling Coll., 1979—; cert. sch. dist. adminstr., supr., adminstr., N.Y. State. Mem. Nassau Suffolk Council Adminstrv. Women in Edn. (pres. 1979—), Assn. for Supervision and Curriculum Devel., Assn. Gifted/Talented Edn., Women's Equal Rights Congress Com. (exec. bd.), Suffolk County Coordinating Council Gifted and Talented, Phi Delta Kappa, Delta Kappa Pi. Author: Arts in Education Curriculum in Social Studies and Language Arts, 1981. Home: 35 Gaymor Ln Commack NY 11725 Office: Middle Country Sch Dist Adminstrn 43rd St Centereach NY 11720

COHEN, LOUIS ALEXANDER, civil engineer, AID official; b. San Antonio, Apr. 1, 1923; s. Sultan Gabriel and Bernice (Alexander) C.; B.S. in Civil Engring., Purdue U., 1948; postgrad. Am. U., 1966-70; m. Barbara B. Zucrow, June 11, 1948; 1 son, Marc Jacob. Project engr., Ind. Hwy. Dept., 1948-51; chief engr. S&L Excavating Co., Inc., Indpls., 1951-55; assoc., cons. engring. firms, Poughkeepsie, N.Y. and Englewood, N.J., 1955-59; hwy. engr. ICA/Saigon, 1959-61; with AID, various locations, 1961—, chief engr. UN/Mekong Com., Bangkok, 1970-74, dep. dir. RED, Bangkok, 1974-76, dir. REDSO, Nairobi, 1976-79, dir. AID, Gaborone, Botswana, 1979-82, Mogadishu, Somalia, 1983—. Registered profl. engr., Ind., N.Y.; registered profl. land surveyor, Ind. recipient Meritorious Service award Ministry Public Works Vietnam, 1973. Served with AUS, 1943-46. Mem. Nat. Soc. Profl. Engrs., ASCE, Am. Fgn. Service Assn., Soc. Am. Mil. Engrs., Am. Water Resources Assn., Internat. Water Resources Assn., U.S. Com. Large Dams, African Studies Assn., Am. Assn. Asian Studies, Soc. Internat. Devel., Fgn. Policy Assn., Botswana Soc. Democrat. Jewish. Clubs: Rotary (Gaborone); Notwane Tennis. Home: 2939 Van Ness St NW Apt 414 Washington DC 20520 Office: USAID, Am Embassy, Mogadishu Somalia

COHEN, MARK N., business executive; b. Camden, N.J., July 14, 1947; s. Morris and Esther (Sobel) C.; m. Rhoda Posner, Dec. 19, 1971; children—Michele Rebecca, Gregory Leighton. B.S., U. Mo.-Kansas City, 1969; postgrad. N.Y. Med. Coll., 1969-70; M.S., Am. Western U., Tulsa, 1972, Ph.D., 1976. Cert. state advisor U.S. Congl. Adv. Bd. Founder, pres., chmn. Nat. Recall Alert Ctr., Marlton, N.J., 1973—, Acad. Guidance Services, Marlton, 1975—, Nat. Corp. Services, Marlton, 1977—, Nat. Pub. Corp., Marlton, 1979—. Pres. Am. Bus. Opportunity Commn., N.J., 1975; bd. dirs., chmn. Health Sytems Agy., Bellmawr, N.J., 1982; treas., bd. dirs. Perinatal Coop./South N.J., Camden, 1983; mem. bd. advisors Free Enterprise, Marlton, 1985; pres. Cohenterprises, Inc., Marlton, 1986, Am. Profl. Copy-Quick Printing Corp., Marlton, 1985, Nationwide Wats Telephone Answering Service, Inc., Marlton, 1985. Mem. exec. com. Deborah Hosp.; bd. dirs. Beth Israel Synangogue. Recipient Young Exec. of Yr. award Jim Walter Corp., Tampa, Fla., 1972, Disting. Leadership award Am. Security Council Found., 1984, Annual Register award Esquire mag.; named one of 50 Bus. People to Watch, N.J. Bus. Jour. Mem. C. of C., Am. Assn. Fin. Profls., Nat. Council on Patient Info. and Edn., Nat. Health Lawyers Assn., N.J. Assn. Commerce and Industry (chmn. 1974), Am. Assn. Sch. Adminstrs., Am. Assn. Univ. Adminstrs., Am. Assn. Indiv. Investors, Mensa. Republican. Jewish. Home: 6 Alluvium Lakes Dr West Berlin NJ 08091 Office: Acad Guidance Services Inc PO Box 609 Marlton NJ 08052

COHEN, MARTIN HARVEY, architect; b. Bklyn., Apr. 17, 1932; s. Benjamin and Beatrice (Wexler) C.; m. Arline Sitner, Sept. 30, 1956; children: Bruce, Paul, Adam. Cert. in architecture, Cooper Union Art Sch., 1952; BArch, MIT, 1954. Registered architect, N.Y., N.J., Conn., Pa. Designer Studio Architetti BBPR, Milan, Italy, 1955; designer Anderson, Beckwith & Haible, architects, Boston, 1955-56; architect Skidmore, Owings & Merrill, Architects, N.Y.C., 1956-81, assoc., 1963-73, assoc. ptnr., 1973-81; pres., dir. health facilities planning and design SMP Architects, P.C., N.Y.C., 1981-83; v.p. Ellerbe Assocs., Inc., N.Y.C., 1983-84; prin. Martin H. Cohen FAIA, Armonk, N.Y., 1984—, Payette/Cohen Joint Venture, 1985—; mem. N.Y.C. Landmarks Preservation Commn., 1968-73. Works include: 1st Nat. Bank, Fort Worth, 1961, IBM Corp. Hdqrs., Armonk, N.Y., 1961-64, Yale Computer Ctr., New Haven, 1961, N.Y.C. Terminal Markets, Hunts Point, 1960-66, Beekman-Downtown Hosp., N.Y.C., 1963-66, NYU Med. Ctr., N.Y.C., 1965—, Kiewit Computation Ctr., Dartmouth Coll., Hanover, N.H., 1966, Otis Elevator Co., Yonkers, N.Y., 1973-76, N.Y. Hosp., 1977-78, Wausau Hosp., Wis., 1975-79, Mass. Gen. Hosp., 1978-81, Bally Park Pl Casino Hotel, Atlantic City, 1979-80, Stevens Inst. Engring. Ctr., Hoboken, N.J., 1980-81, 84—, Hosp. Santo Tomas, Panama City, Panama, 1981, 780 Third Ave Office Bldg., N.Y.C., 1980-81, Mfrs. Hanover Trust Co. Hdqrs., N.Y.C., 1980-81, Presbyn. Hosp., N.Y.C., 1981, Augustana Luth. Home for Aged, Bklyn., 1981-87, Manchester Health Park, N.J., 1982, Chest Diseases Hosp., Taif, Saudi Arabia, 1981-83, Mt. Sinai Med. Ctr., N.Y.C., 1983-84, N.Y. Hosp./Cornell Med. Ctr., N.Y.C., 1984-85, Lenox Hill Hosp., N.Y.C., 1984. Mem. adv. council Cooper Union Sch. Art and Architecture, 1967-75, admission com., 1975-78, adminstrn. com., 1979-80; mem. adv. council hist. Am. bldgs. survey Nat. Parks Service, 1973; active Hebrew Rehab. Ctr. for Aged, Boston, 1988—. Recipient Profl. Achievement citation Cooper Union, 1971; Fulbright scholar, Italy, 1954-55. Fellow AIA (N.Y. chpt. awards com., chmn. hist. bldgs. com. 1966-68, hosps. and health com. 1971—, vice chmn. 1973-76, urban design commn. 1967-68, ethics com. 1978-80, nat. hist. resources com. 1971-74, chmn. 1973, nat. com. architecture for health 1975—, steering group 1982-86, vice chmn. 1984, chmn. 1985, chmn. nat. task force on design for aging 1983-85), Archtl. League N.Y., N.Y. Soc. Architects, N.Y. State Assn. Architects (com. architecture for health 1975—, chmn. 1976-79, Mathew W. Del Gaudio award 1978), Mcpl. Arts Soc. (adv. com. 1973-74), Tau Beta Pi. Home and Office: 40 Green Valley Rd Armonk NY 10504

COHEN, MAX, retired government official; b. Bklyn., May 19, 1918; s. Harry and Jennie (Friedlander) C.; Widowed; 1 child, Jay Stuart. B.B.A., Baruch Coll., 1946. Registered pub. acct., N.Y. Agt. IRS, U.S. Treasury, N.Y., 1945-73; tax cons., N.Y., 1973—. Advisor Levittown Sch. Bd., N.Y., 1975—; tax aide Nassau County Sr. Citizens, Hempstead, N.Y., 1975—. Served with inf. U.S. Army, 1941-45. Decorated Bronze Star. Democrat. Jewish. Avocations: golf; reading; baseball fan. Home: 1 Short Ln Levittown NY 11756

COHEN, MELANIE ROVNER, lawyer; b. Chgo., Aug. 9, 1944; d. Millard Jack and Sheila (Fox) Rovner; m. Arthur Wieber Cohen, Feb. 17, 1968; children—Mitchell Jay, Jennifer Sue. A.B., Brandeis U., 1965; J.D., DePaul U., 1977. Bar: Ill. 1977, U.S. Dist. Ct. (no. dist.) Ill., U.S. Ct. Appeals (7th cir.). Law clk. to justice U.S. Bankruptcy Ct., 1976-77; instr. secured and consumer transactions creditor-debtor law DePaul U., Chgo., 1980—; ptnr. Antonow & Fink, Chgo., 1977—. Mem. Supreme Ct. of Ill. Atty. Registration and Disciplinary Commn. Inquiry Bd., 1982-86, hearing bd., 1986—. Panelist, speaker. Bd. dirs., v.p. Brandeis U. Nat. Alumni Assn., 1981—; life mem. Nat. Women's Com., 1975—, pres. Chgo. Chpt., 1975-82; mem. Glencoe Caucus (Ill.), 1977-80. Mem. ABA, Ill. State Bar Assn., Chgo. Bar Assn. (chmn. bankruptcy reorganization com. 1983-85), Commenal Law League, Ill. Trial Lawyers Assn. Contbr. articles to profl. jours. Home: 167 Park Ave Glencoe IL 60022 Office: Antonow & Fink 111 E Wacker Dr Chicago IL 60601

COHEN, MYRON LESLIE, business executive; mechanical engineer; b. N.Y.C., Mar. 7, 1934; s. Henry and Minnie (Pechenik) C.; B.S.M.E., Purdue U., 1955; M.S.E., U. Ala., 1958; Ph.D., Poly. Inst. Bklyn., 1966; m. Sally Claire Gilman, June 19, 1955; children—Amy Beth, David Lawrence, Hilary Ann. Research engr. Allegany Ballistics Lab., Hercules, Inc., Cumberland, Md., 1955-56; sr. thermodynamics engr. Republic Aviation Corp., Farmingdale, N.Y., 1958-60; instr. mech. engring. Poly. Inst. Bklyn., 1960-66; asst. prof. mech. engring. Stevens Inst. Tech., 1966-69, assoc. prof., 1969-77, prof., 1977-78, dir. Med. Engring. Lab., 1975-78; prof. Institut fur Biokybernetik und Biomedizinische Technik, Universitat Karlsruhe (W.Ger.), 1974-75; dir. research and devel. hosp. products, Chesebrough-Ponds's Inc., Trumbull, Conn., 1978-83; pres. CAS Med. Systems, Inc., Branford, Conn., 1983—; v.p. Freshet Press, Rockville Centre, N.Y., 1970-78; pres. C.A.S., Inc., Upper Montclair, N.J., 1975-78; adj. assoc. prof. surgery Coll. Medicine and Dentistry N.J., Newark, 1978—; bd. dirs. Conn. River Salmon Assn., 1987—. Vice pres. Temple Beth Tikvah, Madison, Conn., 1980-82. Served to lt. U.S. Army, 1956-58. Recipient Humboldt prize, Sr. U.S. Scientist award Govt. W.Ger., 1974; registered profl. engr., N.J. Fellow N.Y. Acad. Medicine (assoc.); mem. ASME (chmn. standards com. on med. devices 1982), Assn. Advancement Med. Instrumentation, AAUP, Soc. Biomaterials, Cardiovascular System Dynamics Soc., AIAA (chmn. N.Y. sect. 1971-72), N.Y. Acad. Sci. Sigma Xi, Pi Tau Sigma. Club: Theodore Gordon Flyfishers. Contbr. articles on heat transfer, thermodynamics, tech. applied to medicine, phys. properties human skin, biomed. engring. to profl. jours.; research in rocket propulsion, biomed. engring. Home: 401 Three Corners Rd Guilford CT 06437 Office: 29 Business Park Dr Branford CT 06405

COHEN, PHILIP FRANCIS, publishing company executive; b. Manchester, England, July 16, 1911; came to U.S. 1928; s. Reuben and Frances (Kneeter) C.; m. Fay Roytman, Dec. 5, 1943; children—David, Anne, Karen. Cert. Library Sch., Columbia U. Acquisitions librarian internat. law Columbia U. Law Library, N.Y.C., 1928-42; founder, pres. The Oceana Group Pubs., Dobbs Ferry, N.Y., 1946—, Inst. for Continuing Edn. In Law and Librarianship, 1982—; chmn. bd. Harvey House Inc., Dobbs Ferry, N.Y., 1982—. Author: (under name of Philip Francis) How to Serve On A Jury, 1953, Legal Status of Women, 1963, Protection Through the Law, 1964. Mem. Dobbs Ferry Bicentennial Com. Served with USAAF, 1942-46. Mem. Am. Soc. Internat. Law, Brit. Inst. Internat. Comparative Law, Am. Assn. Law Libraries, Vanderbilt Assocs. NYU Law Sch. Clubs: Commonwealth (London); Ardsley Country. Home: Shalford—Cricket Ln Dobbs Ferry NY 10522 Office: Oceana Publs Inc 75 Main St Dobbs Ferry NY 10522

COHEN, PHILIP HERMAN, accountant; b. Bklyn., Dec. 4, 1936; s. David J. and Toby (Jaeger) C.; m. Susan Rudd; children: Davina Ellen, Tobias Samuel Dory. B.S., NYU, 1957. Acct. Touche Ross & Co., N.Y.C., 1957-64, supr., 1965, mgr., 1966-69, ptnr., 1969-81; exec. v.p. fin., chief fin. officer Integrated Resources, Inc., N.Y.C., 1981-86, sr. exec. v.p. fin., chief fin. officer, 1986—; dir. W.J. Schafer & Assocs., ALI Equipment Mgmt. Corp., ALI Capitol Corp., ALI Leasing Service; lectr. in field. Bd. dirs. Alpha Epsilon Pi Found., Inc., Nat. Interfrat. Conf., 1975-86, Jewish Bd. Family and Children's Service; bd. dirs., fin. sec. Sutton Pl. Synagogue; bd. dirs. joint purchasing com. Fedn. Jewish Philanthropies, 1977-78; N.Y. bd. govs. State of Israel Bonds. Recipient State of Israel Bond Peace award 1983, Accts. Bankers and Fin. award Am. Jewish Congress. Mem. Found. Acctg. Edn., Am. Inst. C.P.A.s (real estate com. 1987—), N.Y. State Soc. C.P.A.s (admissions com. 1968-69, chmn. fin. and leasing com. 1972-74, com. on relations with the bar 1974-76, com. on real estate acctg. 1976-79, com. ins. 1980-81, fin. acctg. standards com. 1983-86, chmn. mem.-in-industry com. 1981-83, chief fin. officers com. 1984-86, furtherance com. 1986, annual conf. com. 1985-87, com. on ops. 1987—, bd. dirs. 1983-86, v.p. 1985-86, Outstanding CPA in Industry award 1986), Fin. Execs. Inst., Am. Acctg. Assn., Nat. Assn. Accts., Soc. Ins. Accts., Alpha Epsilon Pi (supreme gov. 1966-73, nat. pres. 1974-76, mem. fiscal control bd. 1977-81, vice chmn. 1981—), Beta Alpha Psi, Areopagus. Jewish. Club: N.Y. Alumni of Alpha Epsilon Pi. Lodge: Masons. Home: 30 Beekman Pl New York NY 10022 Office: Integrated Resources Inc 666 3d Ave New York NY 10017

COHEN, ROBERT (AVRAM), lawyer; b. Pitts., July 23, 1929; s. Max R. and Mollie (Segal) C.; m. Frances H. Steiner, Dec. 24, 1951 (div. Feb. 1974); children: Deborah E., David R.; m. Mary E. Connors, Mar. 11, 1974; children: Deborah A., Charles E., Chrisann. AB magna cum laude, Harvard U., 1951, JD, 1954. Bar: Pa. 1955, U.S. Dist. Ct. (we. dist.) Pa. 1955, U.S. Ct. Appeals (3d cir.) 1961, U.S. Supreme Ct. 1962, Fla. 1974, U.S. Dist. Ct. (so. dist.) Fla. 1974, U.S. Tax Ct. 1983. Assoc. Goldstock, Schwartz, Teitelbaum & Schwartz, Pitts., 1955-60; ptnr. Goldstock, Schwartz, Cohen & Schwartz, Pitts., 1960-67, Fine, Perlow, Stone & Cohen, Pitts., 1967-70, Cohen & Goldstock, Pitts., 1970-73; assoc. Herring, Evans & Fulton, West Palm Beach, Fla., 1974; from assoc. to ptnr. Rothman, Gordon, Foreman and Groudine, P.A., Pitts., 1974-86; sole practice Pitts., 1986—. Mem. ABA, Pa. Bar Assn., Allegheny County Bar Assn. (mem. civil litigation council 1988—), Acad. Trial Lawyers Allegheny County, Am. Judicature Soc., Assn. Trial Lawyers Am. (pres. Western Pa. chpt. 1972-73), Pa. Trial Lawyers Assn., Fla. Bar Assn., Fla. Trial Lawyers Assn. Democrat. Jewish. Lodges: Golden Triangle (v.p. 1966-69), B'nai B'rith. Home: 205 Oak Heights Dr Oakdale PA 15071 Office: 819 Frick Bldg Pittsburgh PA 15219

COHEN, ROBERT SONNÉ, physicist, philosopher, educator; b. N.Y.C., Feb. 18, 1923; m. Robin Gertrude Hirshhorn, June 18, 1944; children: Michael, Daniel, Deborah. B.A., Wesleyan U., Middletown, Conn., 1943; M.S., Yale U., 1943, Ph.D. (NRC fellow), 1948; LHD, Wesleyan U., 1986. Instr. physics Yale U., 1943-44, instr. philosophy, 1949-51; sci. staff, war research div. Columbia U. and Communications Bd., U.S. Joint Chiefs Staff, 1944-46; asst. prof. physics and philosophy Wesleyan U., 1949-57; assoc. prof. physics Boston U., 1957-59, prof. physics and philosophy, 1959—, chmn. dept. physics, 1959-73, chmn. dept. philosophy, 1986—; acting dean Coll. Liberal Arts, 1971-72; chmn. faculty Senate, 1975-76; chmn. Boston U. Center for Philos. and History Sci., 1970—; vis. lectr. humanities and philosophy of sci. Mass. Inst. Tech., 1958-59, 61-62; vis. prof. history of ideas Brandeis U., 1959-60; lectr. history and philosophy of sci. Am. U., Washington, summers 1958-68; vis. fellow Polish and Yugoslav Acad. Sci., 1963, Hungarian Acad. Sci., 1964; vis. prof. philosophy U. Calif. at, San Diego, 1969, Yale U., 1973; research fellow history of sci. Harvard, 1974; Mem., chmn. U.S. Nat. Com. for Internat. Union History and Philosophy of Sci., 1969-75; Trustee Wesleyan U., 1968-84, Tufts U., 1984—. Author, editor articles, books and jours. in field.; Editor: Boston Studies in Philosophy of Sci., Vienna Circle Collection, Sci. in Context Jour. Trustee Bill of Rights Found. Am. Council Learned Soc. fellow philosophy and sci., 1948-49; Ford faculty fellow Cambridge, Eng., 1955-56; fellow Wissenschafts Kolleg zu Berlin, 1983-84. Fellow AAAS (chmn. sect. L history and philos. sci. 1978-79); mem. Am. Phys. Soc., Am. Assn. Physics Tchrs., Am. Philos. Assn., History Sci. Soc., Philosophy Sci. Assn. (v.p. 1972-75, pres. 1982-84), AAUP, Nat. Emergency Civil Liberties Com. (mem. nat. council), Am. Inst. Marxist Studies (chmn. 1964-82), Fedn. Am. Scientists (nat. council 1967-70), Inst. for Unity of Sci. (exec. com. 1960-74). Home: 44 Adams Ave Watertown MA 02172 Office: Dept Philosophy Boston U Boston MA 02215

COHEN, ROBERT STEPHAN, lawyer; b. N.Y.C., Jan. 14, 1939; s. Abraham and Florence C.; m. Margery H. Cohen, Jan. 17, 1968; children—Christopher, Ian, Nicholas. B.A., Alfred U., 1959; LL.B., Fordham U., 1962. Bar: N.Y. 1963, U.S. Dist. Ct. (so. and ea. dists.) N.Y. 1964, U.S. Ct. Appeals (2d cir.) 1965. Assoc. Saxe, Bacon & O'Shea, N.Y.C., 1963-68; ptnr. Morrison, Cohen & Singer, and predecessor firms, N.Y.C., 1968—; lectr. in field; faculty Am Acad. Psychiatry and the Law, 1984—. Bd. dirs. N.Y. Council Alcoholism, N.Y.C., 1980—, N.Y. Pops, 1982—; trustee Alfred U., 1984—. Served to 1st lt. JAG, USAR, 1965-67. Mem. ABA, Fed. Bar Assn., N.Y. State Bar Assn., N.Y.C. Bar Assn., Assn. Trial Lawyers Am., N.Y. Acad. Matrimonial Lawyers. Club: Univ. (N.Y.C.). Contbr. to legal jours. Home: 1107 Fifth Ave New York NY 10028 Office: 110 E 59th St New York NY 10022

COHEN, SAMUEL ISRAEL, clergyman, organization executive; b. Asbury Park, N.J., Apr. 17, 1933; s. Meyer and Henrietta (Gershman) C.; B.A., Bklyn. Coll., 1955; M.R.E., Yeshiva U., 1959, Ed.D., 1967; m. Mira Hager, Sept. 5, 1960; children—Baruch Chaim, Michael Nachum, Miriam Rachel. Rabbi, 1956; exec. dir. L.I. Zionist Youth Commn., Queens, N.Y., 1957-61; regional dir. Supreme Lodge B'nai B'rith, Queens, 1961-66, dir. membership dept. dist. 1, N.Y.C., 1966-72; nat. dir. orgn. Am. Jewish Congress, N.Y.C. 1972-74; exec. dir. Am. Zionist Fedn., 1974-77; exec. v.p. Jewish Nat. Fund, 1977—; adj. asst. prof. sociology L.I. U., 1967; lectr. sociology Queensborough Community Coll., 1968, adj. asst. prof., 1971-74; lectr. Borough of Manhattan Community Coll., 1968, adj. asst. prof., 1970-72; adj. asst. prof. John Jay Coll. Criminal Justice, 1973—; lectr. Herzl Inst., N.Y.C., 1974-78. Contbr. articles to nat. publs. Chmn. edn. adv. bd. Yeshiva Toras Chaim, Woodmere, N.Y., 1971-74; mem. Religious Zionists Am., 1960—, Zionist Orgn. Am., 1960—, Nat. Council Jewish Edn., 1970—; mem. Conf. Jewish Communal Service, 1970—; mem. Congregation Shaarei Tephila, Lawrence, N.Y., 1983-87, Congregation Kneseth Israel, 1983—; sec Olam Chadash, 1980—. Bd. dirs. Union Orthodox Jewish Congregations Am., 1973—, United Israel Appeal, 1984—. Mem. Adult Edn. Assn. (nat. com. on goals and objectives religious edn. sect. 1967-68), Educators Council Am., Young Israel of Wavecrest and Bayswater (v.p. 1973-75), Assn. Jewish Community Orgn. Profls., Nat. Council for Adult Jewish Edn., Nat. Soc. Fund Raising Execs. Lodge: B'nai B'rith (v.p. Briarwood Lodge, 1964). Home: 112 Rand Pl Lawrence NY 11559 Office: 42 E 69th St New York NY 10029

COHEN, SANFORD IRWIN, physician, educator; b. N.Y.C., Sept. 5, 1928; s. George A. and Gertrude (Slater) C.; m. Jean Steinbruecker, Nov. 30, 1952; children—Jeffrey, Debra, John, Robert. A.B. magna cum laude, N.Y. U., 1948; M.B., M.D., Chgo. Med. Sch., 1952. Intern Jackson Meml. Hosp., Miami, Fla., 1952-53; resident psychiatry U. Colo. Med. Center, 1953-54; resident Duke Med. Center, 1954-55, 57-58, mem. faculty, 1956-68, prof. psychiatry, 1964-68, head div. psychosomatic medicine and psychophysiol. research, 1964-68, lectr. psychology, 1960-68; instr. Washington Psychoanalytic Inst., 1964-68; cons. VA Hosp., Durham, N.C., 1957-65, NIMH, 1963-66; prof. psychiatry Boston U. Med. Sch., 1970-86, chmn. dept., 1970-86; vis. research scientist health and behavior br., div. basic scis. NIMH, 1986-88; prof. psychiatry U. Miami (Fla.) Med. Sch., 1988—; Markle scholar med. sci., 1957-62. Contbr. articles to profl. jours., chpts. to books. Recipient Robert Morse award excellence in sci. writing, 1965. Fellow Am. Psychiat. Assn., Am. Coll. Clin. Pharmacology; mem. A.A.A.S., Am. Psychosomatic Soc. Home: 6844 Sunrise Ct Coral Gables FL 33133

COHEN, SEYMOUR MARTIN, hematologist, educator; b. N.Y.C., Dec. 19, 1936; s. Harry and Rose (Ehrlich) C.; B.A., Bklyn. Coll., 1957; B.Med. Sci., U. Geneva, 1959; M.D., U. Pitts., 1962; m. Carole J. Pomerantz, Aug. 16, 1976; children Roger, Michael. Intern Montefiore Hosp. N.Y.C., 1962-63, asst. resident in medicine, 1963-64; resident in medicine Mt. Sinai Hosp., N.Y.C., 1964-65, Am. Cancer Soc. fellow in hematology, 1965-66, mem. staff, 1969—; fellow in hematology L.I. Jewish Hosp., 1968-69; pvt. practice medicine specializing in med. oncology and hematology, N.Y.C., 1969—; clin. asso. in medicine Mt. Sinai Med. Sch., 1969-73, sr. clin. asso. physician in medicine, 1969-73, asst. clin. prof. medicine, 1973-78, asso. clin. prof. medicine, 1979—; mem. Cancer and Leukemia B Group. Mem. exec. com. Jewish Am. Polit. Action Com., 1975-79, v.p., 1979-81, pres., 1981-83; bd. govs. State of Israel Bonds, 1979—. Served as capt. M.C., USAF, 1966-68. Diplomate Am. Bd. Internal Medicine and subsplty. in med. oncology. Fellow A.C.P.; mem. Am. Soc. Clin. Oncology, Internat., Am. Socs. Hematology, AAUP, N.Y. Cancer Soc. (sec. 1983-86, v.p. 1987, pres. elect 1988), AMA, New York County Med. Soc. Contbr. articles to profl. publs.; research on malignant melanoma. Office: 1045 Fifth Ave New York NY 10028

COHEN, STANLEY, biochemistry educator; b. Bklyn., Nov. 17, 1922; s. Louis and Fannie (Feitel) C.; m. Olivia Larson, 1951 (div.); children: Burt Bishop, Kenneth Larson, Cary; m. Jan Elizabeth Jordan, 1981. BA, Bklyn. Coll., 1943; MS, Oberlin Coll., 1945; PhD in Biochemistry, U. Mich., 1948; PhD, U. Chgo., 1985. Instr. dept. biochemistry and pediatrics U. Colo., Denver, 1948-52; Am. Cancer Soc. fellow in radiology Washington U., St. Louis, 1952-53, assoc. prof. dept. zoology, 1953-59; asst. prof. biochemistry, sch. medicine Vanderbilt U., Nashville, 1959-62, assoc. prof., 1962-67, prof. biochemistry, 1967-86, disting. prof., 1986—; research prof. biochemistry Am. Cancer Soc., Nashville, 1976—; Charles B. Smith vis. research prof. Sloan Kettering, 1984; Feodor Lynen lectr. U. Miami, 1986, Steenbock lectr. U. Wis., 1986. Mem. editorial bd. Abstracts of Human Developmental Biology, Jour. of Cellular Physiology. Cons. Minority Research Ctr. for Excellence. Recipient Research Career Devel. award NIH, 1959-69, William Thomson Wakeman award Nat. Paraplegia Found., Earl Sutherland Research Prize Vanderbilt U., 1977, Albion O. Bernstein MD award Med. Soc. State N.Y., 1978, H.P. Robertson Meml. award Nat. Acad. Sci., 1981, Lewis S. Rosentiel award Brandeis U., 1982, Alfred P. Sloan award Gen. Motors Cancer Research Found., 1982, Louisa Gross Horwitz prize Columbia U., 1983, Disting. Achievement award UCLA Lab. Biomed. and Environ. Scis., 1983, Lila Gruber Meml. Cancer Research award Am. Acad. Dermatology, 1983, Bertner award MD Anderson Hosp. U. Tex., 1983, Gairdner Found. Internat. award, 1985, Fred Conrad Koch award Endocrine Soc., 1986, Nat. Medal Sci., 1986, Albert and Mary Lasker Found. Basic Med. Research award, 1986, Nobel Prize in physiology medicine, 1986, Tennessean of Yr. award Tenn. Sports Hall of Fame, 1987, Franklin Medal, 1987, Albert A. Michaelson award Mus. Sci. and Industry, 1987. Fellow Jewish Acad. Arts and Sci.; mem. Nat. Acad. Sci., Am. Soc. Biol. Chemists, Am. Chem. Soc., AAAS, Internat. Inst. Embryology, Internat. Acad. Sci. (hon. internat. council for sci. devel.). Office: Vanderbilt U Sch Medicine Dept Biochemistry Nashville TN 37203 *

COHEN, WALLACE M., lawyer; b. Norton, Va., July 11, 1908; s. Jacob Edward and Annie (Hyman) C.; m. Sylvia J. Stone, Sept. 7, 1932; children: Anne E. (Mrs. Steven A. Winkelman), Edward S., David W. Grad., Lake Forest Acad., 1925; SB, Harvard U., 1929; postgrad., Law Sch., 1930-31; LLB, Cornell U., 1932. Bar: Mass. 1932, Md. 1952, D.C. 1946, U.S. Supreme Ct 1946. Sole practice Boston, 1932-38; mem. staff NLRB, Dept. Labor, Shipbldg. Stablzn. Commn., Adv. Commn. Council Nat. Def., OPA, Lend Lease Adminstrn., Fgn. Econ. Adminstrn., 1938-45; dep. adminstrv. asst. to Pres.; partner Landis, Cohen, Rauh & Zelenko, Washington, 1951—; Former mem. adv. bd. Clinch Valley Coll. of U. Va.; Fellow Brandeis U. Served with USCGR, 1943-45. Mem. Am., Fed., Fed. Communications, D.C., Mass., Md. bar assns. Clubs: Harvard (Boston and Washington) (former dir. Washington); Lonesome Pine Country (Norton, Va.); Federal City (Washington), International, Nat. Press (Washington); Federal Bar. Home: 2444 Massachusetts Ave NW Washington DC 20008 Office: Landis Cohen Rauh & Zelenko 1019 19th St NW Washington DC 20036

COHEN, WILLIAM SEBASTIAN, U.S. senator; b. Bangor, Maine, Aug. 28, 1940; s. Reuben and Clara (Hartley) C.; children: Kevin, Christopher. BA cum laude, Bowdoin Coll., 1962; LLB cum laude, Boston U., 1965; LL.D., St. Joseph's Coll., Windham, Maine, 1974, U. Maine, 1975, Western New Eng. Coll., 1975, Bowdoin Coll., 1975, Nasson Coll., 1975; postgrad., Thomas Coll., 1988, Colby Coll., 1988. Bar: Maine, Mass., D.C. Ptnr. Paine, Cohen, Lynch, Weatherbee & Kobritz, Bangor, 1966-72; instr. U. Maine, 1968-72; asst. county atty. Penobscot County, Maine, 1968-70; mem. 93d-95th congresses from, Maine; U.S. Senator from Maine, 1979—; Mem. Bangor Sch. Com., 1970-71, Bangor City Council, 1969-72, mayor, Bangor, 1972; Trustee Unity Coll.; bd. overseers Bowdoin Coll., 1973-85. Author: Of Sons and Seasons, 1978, Roll Call, 1981, Getting the Most Out of Washington, 1982, A Baker's Nickel, 1986; author: (with Gary Hart) The Double Man, 1985. Recipient Alumni award for disting. pub. service Boston U., 1976; named to N.E. Hall of Fame Basketball Team, 1962, Silver Anniversary award Nat. Collegiate Athletic Assn., 1987; Outstanding Young Man of Yr. Nat. Jaycees, 1975; James Bowdoin scholar, 1961-62; Alumni Fund scholar, 1962, selected for Balfour Silver Anniversary All-Am. Team, Nat. Assn. Basketball Coaches U.S., 1987. Office: 322 Hart Senate Office Bldg Washington DC 20510

COHEN-TANUGI, PIERRE-NESSIM, sales executive, advertising executive; b. Tunis, Tunisia, Feb. 26, 1938; arrived in France, 1956; s. David and Henriette (Berrebi) C.; m. Anne Marie Levy, Feb. 1, 1973; children: Stéphane, Deborah, Léa, Judith. PhB, Lycée Carnot, Tunis, 1955; Cert. in modern lit., Sorbonne, Paris, 1956; Grad. Bus. Sch., HEC, Paris, 1960. Exec. Galeries Lafayette, Paris, 1961-64; sec. gen. Compagnie Immobilière de Courtage et d'Administration, Paris, 1964-68; mgr. mktg. Societe Alsacienne de Magasins, Paris, 1968-72; mgr. div. Sapac-Prisunic, Paris, 1972-74; gen. mgr. Communication Sur Les Lieux De Vente, Paris, 1974-76; pres. Cohen-Tanugi, Lemoine Associés, Paris, 1976—; v.p. Images Et Promotion, Paris, 1983—; pres. Communicance, Issy les Moulineaux, France, 1988. Mem. Counsel of Comml. Devel., Council of Sales Promotion Agys. (v.p. European chpt.). Jewish. Clubs: Cercle Foch, Racing Club de France. Office: Cohen-Tanugi Lemoine Assoc, 115 quai Pres Roosevelt, 92136 Issy Les Moulineaux France

COHLER, JONAS, psychoanalyst; b. Chgo., July 15, 1934; s. Jonas Robert and Therese Isabell C.; B.A. with honors cum laude, U. Mich., 1956; Ph.D. in Clin. Psychology, Harvard U., 1962; certificate in psychoanalysis William Alanson White Inst. Psychiatry and Psychoanalysis, N.Y.C., 1969; m. Lisa Selsby; children—Eric, Jennifer, Matthew, Luke. Lectr. dept. social relations Harvard U., 1961-64; research asso. Mass. Mental Health Center, 1961-64; instr. psychiatry Columbia U., 1964-65; cons. mental health Luth. Ch. Am., N.Y.C., 1964-71; cons. ITT Corp., N.Y.C., 1964—, Gen. Instrument Corp., 1980—; gen. practice psychoanalysis, N.Y.C., 1969—; clin. asst. prof. psychiatry Cornell Med. Coll., 1977—; clin. assoc. Columbia U. Tchrs. Coll., 1977-80; supr. low cost clin. services William Alanson White Psychoanalytic Inst., 1978—, supervising and tng. analyst, 1980—; dir. group therapy program Payne Whitney Clinic. Fellow Social Sci. Research Council, 1955, USPHS, 1956-57, 65-66. Mem. Am. Group Psychotherapy Assn., Am. Psychol. Assn., William Alanson White Psychanalytic Soc., Harvard Grad. Soc. for Advanced Study and Research (council). Clubs: Harvard of N.Y., N.Y. Corinthians, Castine Maine Yacht. Contbr. articles to profl. jours. Address: 795 West Rd PO Box 1265 New Canaan CT 06840

COHN, DAVID V(ALOR), oral biology and biochemistry educator; b. N.Y.C., Nov. 11, 1926; s. Ralph and Clara (Schenkman) C.; m. Evelyn Turner, 1947; children—Robert Warren, Emily. BS, CCNY, 1948; PhD, Duke U., 1952; postgrad., Western Res. U., 1953. Faculty U. Kans. Sch. Medicine, Kansas City, 1953-84, prof. biochemistry, assoc. dean research, 1974-82; assoc. chief staff for research devel. VA Med. Ctr., Kansas City, Mo., 1953-82; prof. biochemistry U. Mo., Kansas City, 1971-82; v.p. research and devel. Immuno Nuclear Corp., Stillwater, Minn., 1982, sci. cons., 1983; research prof. oral biology and biochemistry U. Louisville Sch. Medicine, Sch. Dentistry 1984—; pres. Internat. Conf. on Calcium Regulating Hormones 1980-86, exec. sec. 1986—; mem. bd. sci. counselors Nat. Inst. Dental Research, Bethesda, Md., 1980-84; chmn. bd. sci. advisors Endotronics, Inc., 1983-85; bd. dirs. Cambridge Med. Tech. Inc., 1985-86. Editor: Hormonal Control of Calcium Metabolism, 1981, Endocrine Control of Bone and Calcium Metabolism, 1984, Calcium Regulation and Bone Metabolism: Basic and Clinical Aspects, 1987; editor-in-chief Bone and Mineral, 1986—; contbr. articles to profl. jours. Served with USN, 1945-46. USPHS grantee 1957—, VA grantee, 1975-82, Am. Cancer Soc. grantee, 1959-60. Mem. Am. Soc. Biol. Chemists Am. Chem. Soc., AAAS, Gordon Research Conf. Chem. and Biol. of Bones and Teeth (chmn. 1974). Jewish. Research on calcium metabolism, parathyroid gland biosynthesis and secretion, bone cell growth, differentiation and hormone responsivity. Home: 5709 Apache Rd Louisville KY 40207 Office: U Louisville Health Scis Ctr Dept Oral Health Louisville KY 40292

COHN, HARRY, mathematics educator, probabilist; b. Bucharest, Rumania, July 27, 1940; arrived in Australia, 1975; s. Ionel and Perla (Zissu) C.; m. Mariana Littman, June 4, 1966; children: Viviana, Yael, Diploma U. Bucharest, 1963; PhD, Rumania Acad. Scis., 1966. Researcher Rumanian Acad. Sci., 1963-66, chief researcher, 1966-70; sr. lectr. Technion, Haifa, Israel, 1971-75; sr. research fellow Australian Nat. U., Canberra, 1975-77; reader Melbourne U., Australia, 1978—. Fellow Inst. Math. Statis., 1988. Contbr. articles to profl. jours. Recipient Gauss Professorship Gottingen Acad. Sci., 1984. Avocations: music; reading; table tennis (university champion 1960). Home: 84 Tunstall Rd, Victoria 3111, Australia Office: Melbourne U, Swanston St, Melbourne Victoria 3052, Australia

COHN, MICHAEL, public relations consultant; b. Amsterdam, The Netherlands, June 13, 1936; s. Adolph and Elfriede (Strauss) C.; m. Rosa Louise Van West, May 11, 1971; children: Itamar, Ilan. PhD in Econs., U. Amsterdam, 1962. Sr. economist Amsterdam-Rotterdam Bank, 1963-69; editor Folkertsma Bus. Publs., Amsterdam, 1969-70; research economist Boekman Found. for Culture, Amsterdam, 1971-72; pub. relations officer Berenschot Mgmt. Cons., Utrecht, The Netherlands, 1972-77; pub. relations cons. Cohn Pub. Relations, The Hague, The Netherlands, 1977—. Contbr. articles to periodicals; editor books and reference works in field; translator works on various topics. Bd. dirs. Middeloo Inst. Advanced Studies Creative Therapy, Amersfoort, The Netherlands, 1980-87. Mem. Internat. Pub. Relations Assn., Pub. Relations Associon. The Netherlands, Assn. Pub. Relations Consultancies The Netherlands.

COHN, NATHAN, engineer, consultant; b. Hartford, Conn., Jan. 2, 1907; s. Harris and Dora Leah (Levin) C.; m. Marjorie Kurtzon, June 30, 1940; children: Theodore Elliot, David Leslie, Anne Harris, Amy Elizabeth, Julie Archer. S.B., M.I.T., 1927; D.Eng. (hon.), Rennsalear Poly. Inst., 1976. With Leeds & Northrup Co., Phila., 1927-72; mgr. market devel. div. Leeds & Northrup Co., 1955-58, v.p. tech. affairs, 1958-65, sr. v.p. tech. affair, 1965-67, exec. v.p. research and corp. devel., 1967-72, dir., 1963-75; cons. mgmt. and tech. of measurement and control Jenkintown, Pa., 1972—; dir. AEL Industries Inc., Alkco Mfg. Co., Weinschel Engring. Co.; dir. Milton Roy Co., Modular Comptar Systems, Parlex Corp.; gen. partner Network Systems Devel. Assos.; pres. Nat. Electronics Conf., 1950; mem. NRC; exec. bd. Found. Instrumentation, Edn. and Research, 1962-64; del. congress Internat. Fedn. Automatic Control, 1960, 63, 66, 69, 72, 75, 78, 81, 84, 87; chmn. tech. com. on applications, 1969-72; chmn. U.S. organizgin com. 1975 World Congress, mem. tech. coms. on computers, systems, mem. com. on social effects of automation, 1975—, lifetime advisor, 1984—; mem. vis. com. libraries M.I.T., 1964-69, mem. vis. com. philosophy, 1972-74. Contbr. articles to profl. jours., chpts. to books, textbook. Bd. dirs., v.p. Eagleville (Pa.) Hosp. and Rehab. Center. Fellow IEEE (life, Lamme medal 1968, Edison medal 1982, Centennial medal 1984 chmn. fellow com. 1974-76, chmn. awards bd. 1977-78, mem. Centennial com. 1979-84); chmn. Intersoc. Hoover Medal (Bd. of Award 1978-81); mem. Instrument Soc. Am. (v.p. industries and scis. 1960-61, sec. 1962, pres. 1963, Sperry medalist 1968, hon. mem. award 1976), AAAS, Franklin Inst. (life, Wetherill medalist 1968, mem. bd. mgrs. 1971—, chmn. bd. mgrs. 1971-75), Nat. Acad. Engring., Engrs. Joint Council (exec. bd. 1975-78, commn. on internat. relations 1978-79), Am. Assn. Engring. Socs. (council for internat. affairs 1980-81), Indsl. Research Inst., Engrs. Council Profl. Devel. (vis. com. curriculum accreditation), Sci. Apparatus Makers Assn. (exec. bd. 1961-62, 66-73, pres. 1969-71, SAMA award 1978), Nat. Soc. Profl. Engrs. (Engr. of Yr. Delaware Valley 1968, State of Pa. 1969), Sigma Xi, Tau Beta Pi, Eta Kappa Nu, Pi Lambda Phi. Jewish. Club: Rydal (Phila.).

COHN, NATHAN, lawyer; b. Charleston, S.C., Jan. 20, 1918; s. Samuel and Rose (Baron) C.; 1 son, Norman; m. Carolyn Venturini, May 18, 1970. J.D., San Francisco Law Sch., 1947. Bar: Calif. 1947, U.S. Supreme Ct. 1957. Sole practice, San Francisco, 1947—;judge pro tem Mcpl. Ct., Superior Ct. Mem. Calif. State Recreation Commn., 1965-68; former mem. Democratic State Central Com. Served to 1st lt. USAF, 1950-55. Fellow Am. Bd. Criminal Lawyers (past pres.), Am. Acad. Matrimonial Lawyers; mem. Am. Bd. Trial Advs. (diplomate, chpt. pres. 1984), Assn. Trial Lawyers Am., Calif. Trial Lawyers Assn., San Francisco Trial Lawyers Assn. (past pres.). Jewish. Columnist San Francisco Progress, 1982-86; condr. and author seminars in field. Office: 1255 Post St San Francisco CA 94109

COHN, SANFORD JAY, educator; b. Hanover, Pa., Nov. 29, 1945; s. Benjamin Kahanovitz and Rose Hilda (Goldman) C.; married. B.A., Johns Hopkins U., 1967, M.Ed., 1976, M.A., 1978, Ph.D., 1980. Project assoc. intellectually gifted child study group Johns Hopkins U., Balt., 1974-76, project assoc. study of mathematically precocious youth, 1976, asst. dir. study, 1977-79, editor Intellectually Talented Youth Bull., 1977-79; asst. prof. dept. spl. edn. and dir. project for study of acad. precocity Ariz. State U., 1979-84, assoc. prof., 1984—; cons. Nat. Interagency Task Force on Gifted and Talented Youth, 1978; mem. adv. com. on educating the gifted State of Ariz., lectr. in field. Author: Educating the Gifted: Acceleration and Enrichment, 1979. Contbr. articles to profl. jours. Mem. Am. Psychol. Assn., Am. Ednl. Research Assn., Ariz. Assn. for Gifted and Talented, Sigma Xi, Phi Delta Kappa, Phi Beta Kappa, Omicron Delta Kappa, Phi Lambda Upsilon, Delta Phi Alpha.

COHN-SHERBOK, DANIEL MARK, clergyman, university center administrator, educator; b. Denver, Feb. 1, 1945; s. Bernard and Ruth (Goldstein) S.; m. Lavinia Charlotte Heath, Dec. 19, 1976. B.A., Williams Coll., 1966; B.H.L., Hebrew Union Coll.-Cin., 1968, M.A. in Hebrew Letters, 1971; M.Litt., Cambridge (Eng.) U., 1974. Ordained rabbi, 1971. Assoc. rabbi West London Synagogue, 1972-74; lectr. in theology U. Kent.-Canterbury, Eng., 1975-79, chmn. theology dept., 1979-81, dir. Ctr. for Study of Religion and Soc., 1981—; vis. scholar Oxford (Eng.) Center for Postgrad. Hebrew Studies, 1983. Author: The Jews of Canterbury, 1983, Christian, Muslim and Jew, 1983; (monograph): Law in Reform Judaism, 1983; Jews, Christians and Liberation Theology, 1986; Exploring Reality, 1987; Jewish Petitionary Prayer, 1988; The Jewish Heritage, 1988; contbr. theol. articles to profl. publs. Chaplain, Colo. Ho. of Reps., 1971-72. Hebrew U. Coll. grad. fellow 1972-73. Fellow Royal Soc. Arts, Acad. Jewish Philosophy; mem. Royal Soc. Asian Affairs, Central Conf. Am. Rabbis, Am. Acad. Religion, Soc. Old Testament Studies, Brit. Assn. Jewish Studies, Soc. for Study of Theology, London Soc. Study of Religion, 's Religions (exec. com. 1985—). Clubs: Athenaeum (gen. com.), Lansdowne (London). Home: 62 Saint Peter's Grove, CT1 2DJ Canterbury Kent, England also: 11 Orme Ct Flat 11, London W2 England Office: U Kent Rutherford Coll, Faculty of Humanities, C71 2DJ Canterbury Kent, England

COHRSSEN, JOHN JOSEPH, lawyer, consultant; b. N.Y.C., Nov. 4, 1939; s. Hans and Alice (Natt) C.; m. Roberta Gross, Aug. 27, 1964; children—James, Noah. B.S. with honors, CCNY, 1961; M.Sc., McGill U., Montreal, Que., Can., 1963; J.D., George Washington U., 1967. Bar: Va. 1968, D.C. 1972, U.S. Dist. Ct. D.C., U.S. Ct. Appeals (D.C. cir.), U.S. Supreme Ct. Sr. asso. Pres.'s Adv. Council Exec. Orgn., 1970; exec. dir. White House Conf. Youth, Drug Task Force, 1971; counsel U.S. Nat. Commn. Diabetes, 1976, White House Conf. Libraries and Info. Services, 1979, U.S. Regulatory Council, 1979-81, office of sci. and tech. policy Exec. office Pres., 1985-86, atty. advisor council on environ. quality, 1986—; exec. office pres., sr. advisor Nat. Sci. Found., 1986—; mem. drug abuse adv. com. FDA, 1978-80; of counsel Boasberg, Klores, Feldsman & Tucker, Washington, 1977-85; pres. John J. Cohrssen, P.C., Washington and Arlington, Va., 1972-86; cons. to various White House and govt. agencies on adminstrv. regulatory and health law, info. systems, 1972—; sr. policy advisor NSF, 1986—; cons. Bur. Justice Statistics, Bur. Narcotics and Dangerous Drugs, Can. Commn. Inquiry into Non-Med. Use of Drugs, Drug Abuse Council, EPA, FDA, Nat. Ctr. Health Statistics, Nat. Commn. Marihuana and Drug Abuse, NIMH, Nat. Inst. Alcohol Abuse and Alcoholism, Nat. Inst. Drug Abuse, Office Mgmt. and Budget, Exec. Office of Pres., White House Office of Planning and Eval., White House Spl. Action Office for Drug Abuse Prevention; mem. drug abuse adv. com. FDA, 1978-80. Served to maj. USPHS, 1967-70. Mem. ABA, Va. Bar Assn., D.C. Bar Assn., Arlington County Bar Assn. Contbr. articles to profl. jours. Office: 722 Jackson Pl Washington DC 20503

COIL, LOWELL MICHAEL, pharmacist; b. Iowa, June 11, 1929; s. Michael Moses and Ethel Mae (Lindsey) C.; m. Janelle Kay Seidel, June 16, 1962; children: Lowell Michael II, Melissa Kay. BS in Pharmacy, BS in Edn., Drake U., 1961. Prin., owner Mike's Pharmacy, Omaha, 1962-74, Des Moines, 1977—; owner Janelle's Maternity, Omaha, 1965—, Des Moines, 1980—. Leader Boy Scouts Am. Omaha council, 1971-75; coach football, softball, track, basketball YMCA, Omaha, 1974-77, football, Little All-Am. League, Des Moines, 1977-80; founder/coach West Des Moines Track Club, 1978—; founder, charter mem. Iowa Athletic Congress, 1979; pres. Iowa Youth Athletics Jr. Olympics, 1979-85, exec. dir., 1979—; official Athletic Congree Nat. level Track and Field. Named Hon. Football Coach of Yr. Omaha YMCA, 1976. Mem. Nat. Assn. Retail Druggists, Polk County Pharmacy Assn., Pi Kappa Alpha. Republican. Methodist. Home: 1716 Plaza Circle Des Moines IA 50322 Office: Mikes Pharmacy 3510 University Ave Des Moines IA 50311

COKE, C(HAUNCEY) EUGENE, consulting company executive, scientist, educator, author; b. Toronto, Ont., Can; s. Chauncey Eugene and Edith May (Redman) C.; m. Sally B. Tolmie, June 12, 1941. B.Sc. with honors, U. Man., M.Sc. magna cum laude; M.A., U. Toronto; postgrad., Yale U.; Ph.D., U. Leeds, Eng., 1938. Dir. research Courtaulds (Can.) Ltd., 1939-42; dir. research and devel. Guaranty Dyeing & Finishing Co., 1946-48; various exec. research and devel. positions Courtaulds (Can.) Ltd., Montreal, 1948-59, dir. research and devel.; mem. exec. com. Hart-Fibres Co., 1959-62; tech. dir. textile chem. Drew Chem. Corp., 1962-63; dir. new products fibers div. Am. Cynamid Co., 1963-68, dir. applications devel., 1968-70; pres. Coke & Assoc., Cons., Ormond Beach, Fla., 1970-78, chmn., 1978—; pres. Aqua Vista Corp. Inc., 1971-74; vis. research prof. Stetson U., 1979—; internat. authority on man-made fibers; guest lectr. Sir George Williams Coll., Montreal, 1949-59; chmn. Can. adv. com. on Internat. Standards Orgn. Tech. Com. 38, 1951-58; mem. Can. Standards Assn., 1958-59; del. Textile Tech. Fedn. Can., 1948-57, bd. dirs., 1957-59. Contbr. articles to profl. jours. Vice chmn. North Peninsula adv. bd. Volusia County Council, 1975-78; mem. Halifax Area Study Commn., 1972-74, Volusia County Elections Bd., 1974—; bd. dirs. Council of Assns. N. Peninsula, 1972-74, 76-77. Served from 2d lt. to maj. RCAF, 1942-46. Recipient Bronze medal Can. Assn. Textile Colourists and Chemists, 1963. Fellow Royal Soc. Chemistry (Gt. Britain life), Textile Inst. (Gt. Britain), Soc. Dyers and Colourists (Gt. Britain), Inst. Textile Sci. (co-founder, 3d pres.), Chem. Inst. Can. (life, mem. council 1958-61), AAAS, N.J. Acad. Sci., Am. Inst. Chemists; mem. Am. Assn. Textile Tech. (life, past pres. Bronze medal), Can. Assn. Textile Colourists and Chemists (hon. life, past pres.), N.Y. Acad. Scis. (life), Fla. Acad. Scis., U.S. Metric Assn. (life). Clubs: Greater Daytona Beach Republican Men's (pres. 1972-75), Rep. Pres.'s Forum (pres. 1976-78, v.p. 1978-81), The Chemist's. Home: 26 Aqua Vista Dr Ormond Beach FL 32074 Office: Coke & Assoc Cons Ormond by the Sea Ormond Beach FL 32074

COKER, DAVID ABIODUN, civil engineer; b. Abeokuta, Nigeria, Dec. 22, 1925; s. Solomon Oyeneye and Christianah Moweade C.; m. Victoria Abosede Aina, Sept. 30, 1961; children: Olufemi, Olufunke, Adebayo, Oyeneye, Abiodun, Olutayo. Diploma in Engring., Hammersmith Coll., London, 1964; postgrad. in Civil Engring., U. Strathclyde, Glasglow, Scotland, 1967; postgrad. in Mgmt., Cranfield Coll., Bedford, England, 1974. Registered engr. COREN. Contract engr. Nigerian Rds. & Dredging Ltd., Gusau, 1964-66; sr. engr. T.A. Oni & Sons Ltd., Ibadan, Nigeria, 1967-70; contract mgr. T.A. Oni & Sons Ltd., Ibadan, 1970-72; tech. mgr. Harboni Ltd., Ibadan, 1972-74, tech. dir., 1974-75; joint mng. dir. Caaso Constructional Works Ltd., Lagos, Nigeria, 1975—. Tech. officer Boys Brigade of Nigeria; elder Christ Apostolic Ch., Yaba, Nigeria. Commonwealth scholar, 1972, Federal scholar, Indsl. scholar. Fellow Nigerian Soc. Engrs., Inst. Hwys. & Transp., Brit. Inst. Mgmt.; mem. ASCE. Home: 5 Seidu Ajibowo St, Ikeja Nigeria Office: Caaso Constructional Works Ltd, PO Box 611, Lagos Nigeria

COKER, ELIZABETH BOATWRIGHT (MRS. JAMES LIDE COKER), writer; b. Darlington, S.C., Apr. 21, 1909; d. Purves Jenkins and Bessie (Heard) Boatwright; m. James Lide Coker, Sept. 27, 1930; children: Penelope, James Lide. A.B., Converse Coll., 1929; postgrad., Middlebury Coll., 1938. Asso. prof. English Appalachian State U., Boone, N.C., 1971-72. Author: Daughter of Strangers, 1950, The Day of the Peacock, 1952, India Allan, 1953, The Big Drum, 1957, La Belle, 1959, Lady Rich, 1963, The Bees, 1968, Blood Red Roses, 1977, The Grasshopper King, 1981; Contbr. mag. articles, poems. Mem. Hartsville Sch. Bd., 1939-49; sec., dir. Blowing Rock Horse Show Assn., 1943-49; dir. United Cerebral Palsy of S.C.; mem. nat. bd. Med. Coll. Pa.; trustee Converse Coll.; nat. adv. council I.S.S. Mem. Poetry Soc. Ga., AAUW, P.E.N., S.C. Poetry Soc., Authors Guild, Acad. Am. Poets, S.C. Hist. Soc., Garden Club Am., Caroliniana Soc. (exec. council 1983—). Republican. Episcopalian. Clubs: Springdale Hall (Camden, S.C.); Hound Ears (Blowing Rock, N.C.). Home: 620 W Home Ave Hartsville SC 29550

COLAHAN, PATRICK TIMOTHY, veterinary surgeon; b. Klamath Falls, Oreg., May 31, 1948; s. Robert Martin and Maggie A. (Lovelady) C.; m. Carlye Ann Baker, July 28, 1973. B.S., U. Calif.-Davis, 1970, D.V.M., 1974. Diplomate Am. Coll. Vet. Surgeons. Intern N.Y. Vet. Coll., Ithaca, 1974-75; resident U. Calif. Sch. Vet. Medicine, Davis, 1975-77, lectr., 1977-78; asst. prof. vet. surgery U. Fla. Coll. Vet. Medicine, Gainesville, 1978-84, assoc. prof. large animal clin. scis., 1984—, chief large animal surgery service, 1979-84, chief Large Animal Hosp., 1984-86. Mem. League Conservation Voters, Gainesville, 1982—. Recipient award for proficiency in vet. clin. medicine Upjohn Co., 1974. Mem. Am. Assn. Equine Practitioners, Vet. Orthopedic Soc., AVMA, Am. Forestry Assn., Phi Zeta. Democrat. Roman Catholic. Club: Commonwealth of Calif. (San Francisco). Home: 7716 SW 53d Pl Gainesville FL 32608 Office: U. Fla Coll Vet Med Large Animal Clin Scis Box J 136 HJMHC Gainesville FL 32610

COLANGELO, DOMENICK ANTHONY, mental health and child guidance center executive; b. N.Y.C., Sept. 11, 1911; s. Michael and Giulia (Menna) C.; B.A. cum laude, Coll. City N.Y., 1944; M.S.S., Fordham U., 1947; m. Pauline C. Filloramo, Jan. 25, 1942; children—Juliette Nadler, Annita, Gloria. Diplomate in clin. social work. Asst. chmn. social welfare dept. Ben Franklin High Sch., N.Y.C., 1935-38; supr. Dept. Welfare, N.Y.C., 1938-44; caseworker Cath. Guardian Soc., N.Y.C., 1944-47; psychiat. casework cons., supr. Cath. Charities Guidance Inst., N.Y.C., 1947-52; exec. dir. Child Guidance Center of Mercer County, Trenton and Princeton, N.J., 1952-75; pvt. practice, 1975—; dir. devel. Cath. Welfare Bur., Trenton; exec. dir. N.J. Assn. Mental Health Agys.; cons. parent-child relations; lectr. family problems, child guidance; mem. adv. bd. program for adolescents mothers St. Vincent de Paul Soc., 1969-79; mem. steering com. N.J. Mental Health Planning Com., 1965; bd. dirs. Bucks County Dept. Child Welfare, Doylestown, Pa., 1963—, v.p., 1966, pres., 1966-68, 77-78, 84-86; profl. adv. com. Mercer County Mental Health Bd.; mem. Bucks County Crime Commn.; mem. Trenton Diocese Com. on Edn. in Human Sexuality. Founder and pres. Valley Day Sch., Morrisville., 1958-62, bd. mem., 1958—; pres. Friends of Valley Day Sch., 1975-78; bd. dirs. Fallsington Pub. Library, Pa. Lic. marriage counselor, N.J. Mem. Am. Assn. Psychiat. Clinics for Children (treas. 1965-67, liaison officer com. on regions 1965-67, evaluations visitor membership com. 1962—, chmn. membership com. 1970-72), N.J. Assn. Mental Hygiene Clinics (legis. com. chmn. 1957-61), Mercer County Assn. Mental Health (dir. 1958-70), Nat. Assn. Social Workers (registered clin. social worker, diplomate in clin. socal work, Social Worker of Year award N.J. chpt. 1970, N.J. del. 1972-75), Acad. Certified Social Workers, N.J. Assn. Mental Health Agys. (v.p. 1969-70, pres. 1971-72, exec. dir., editor Newsletter 1970-71), Conf. Agy. Execs. Mercer County (chmn. 1962-64). Democrat. Clubs: Mercer County Social Welfare (Trenton, N.J.). Editor newsletter Am. Assn. Psychiat. Clinics for Children, 1962-65; contbr. articles to various newspapers and mags. Home: 430 W Palmer St Morrisville PA 19067

COLBERG, MARSHALL RUDOLPH, economist; b. Chgo., June 11, 1913; s. Rudolph E. and Elvira (Wester) C.; m. Peggy Lou Dean, Nov. 25, 1942 (dec. 1964); children: Marsha, Daniel; m. Grace G. Metz, June 6, 1976; stepchildren: Judith, Barbara, Paul Metz. A.B., U. Chgo., 1934, A.M., 1938; Ph.D., U. Mich., 1950. Economist WPB, 1940-43, Civilian Prodn. Adminstrn., 1945-46; analyst USAF, 1946-50; mem. faculty Fla. State U., 1950-84, prof. econs., 1953-84, chmn. dept., 1956-67, dir. Ctr. Econ. Edn., 1979-81; assoc. dir. Center for Yugoslav-Am. Studies, Research and Exchanges, 1960—; guest lectr. U. Belgrade, 1965-76. Author: (with Clark Allen and James M. Buchanan) Prices, Income and Public Policy, 2d edit, 1959, (with Forbush and Whitaker) Business Economics, 6th edit., 1981, 7th edit. (with Forbush), 1986, (with M. Greenhut) Factors in the Location of Florida Industry, 1962, Human Capital in Southern Development, 1939-1963, 1965, Consumer Impact of Repeal of 14-B, 1978, The Social Security Retirement Test: Right or Wrong?, 1978. Served with USAF , 1943-45. Mem. Am. Econ. Assn. (com. econ. edn.), So. Econ. Assn. (pres. 1962, chmn. nominating com. 1964), Mont Pelerin Soc. Home: 4509 Andrew Jackson Way Tallahassee FL 32303

COLBURN, GENE LEWIS, insurance consultant; b. Bismarck, N.D., July 12, 1932; s. Lewis William and Olga Alma (Feland) C.; Ph.D., UCLA, 1982. Pres., gen. mgr. Multiple Lines Ins. Agy., Auburn, Wash., 1953-79; ins. and risk mgmt. cons., Auburn, Wash., 1980—; pres. Feland Safe Deposit Corp.; bd. dirs. Century Service Corp. sub. Capital Savs. Bank, Olympia, Wash.; mem. exec. com. Great Republic Life Ins. Co., Portland, Oreg., 1971-75; mem. Wash. State Ins. Commrs. Test Devel. Com., 1986—. cons. indsl. risk mgmt. and psychology. Councilperson Auburn City, 1982-85; Mayor-pro tem, City of Auburn, 1984; co-incorporator, chmn. bd. SE Community Alcohol Center, 1971-75; mem. Wash. State Disaster Assistance Council, 1981—, founding mem.; pres. Valley Cities Mental Health Center, 1980; mem. instn. rev. com. Auburn Gen. Hosp., 1978—; prin. trustee Dr. R. B. Bramble Med. Research Found., 1980—; bd. dirs. Wash. Assn. Chs. (Luth. Ch. in Am.), Asian Refugee Resettlement Mgmt. div., 1981-83, Columbia Luth. Home, Seattle, 1985—, Wash. Law Enforcement Officers and Fire Fighter's Pension Disability Bd., Auburn, 1980-84. Cert. ins. counselor, 1978. Recipient Disting. Alumni award Green River Community Coll., 1982. Fellow Acad. Producer Ins. Studies (charter); mem. Internat. Platform Assn. Lodge: Auburn Lions (past pres.). Office: 201 A St NW Auburn WA 98002

COLBURN, RICHARD DUNTON, business executive; b. Carpentersville, Ill., June 24, 1911; s. Cary R. and Daisy (Dunton) C.; children—Richard Whiting, Carol Dunton, Keith Whiting, Christine Isabel, David Dunton, McKee Dunton; m. Tara Glynn, Aug., 1984. Student, Antioch Coll., 1929-33. Pres. Consol. Foundries Mfg. Corp. (and predecessors), 1944-64; chmn. U.S. Rentals Inc.; Decco/Stern Osmat, Edmundson Elec. Ltd., UK Plant; dir. Consol. Elec. Distbrs., Inc., Edmundson Internat. Inc., Hajoca Corp., Rolled Alloys, Inc.; underwriting mem. Lloyds of London. Home: 1120 La Collina Beverly Hills CA 90210 Office: 30 Chester Sq, London England SW1W 9HT

COLDSTREAM, JOHN NICOLAS, archaeologist, educator; b. Mar. 30, 1927; s. Sir John and Phyllis Mary (Hambly) C.; Class. Tripos, B.A., King's Coll., Cambridge (Eng.) U., 1951, M.A., 1956; m. Imogen Nicola Carr, 1970. Nat. Service, Buffs and HLI (Egypt and Palestine), 1945-48; asst. master Shrewsbury Sch., 1952-56; temporary asst. keeper dept. Greek and Roman antiquities Brit. Mus., 1956-57; Macmillan student Brit. Sch. at Athens, 1957-60, mem. mng. com., 1966—, editor Ann., 1968-73; lectr. Bedford Coll., U. London, 1960-66, reader, 1966-75, prof. Aegean archaeology, 1975-83; Yates prof. classical archeology Univ. Coll., London 1983—; Geddes-Harrower vis. prof. classical archeology U. Aberdeen, 1983; chmn. Nat. Organizing Com., XI Internat. Congress Classical Archaeology, London, 1978. Fellow Soc. Antiquaries, Brit. Acad., Archaeol. Soc. Athens (hon.); mem. Deutsches Archaologisches Inst. Publs.: Greek Geometric Pottery, 1968; (with G. L. Huxley) Kythera: Excavations and Studies, 1972; Knossos:

The Sanctuary of Demeter, 1973; Geometric Greece, 1977; contbr. articles to Brit., fgn. classical and archaeol. jours.

COLE, CAROLYN JO, brokerage company executive; b. Carmel, Calif.; d. Joseph Michael, Jr., and Dorothea Wagner (James) C.; A.B., Vassar Coll., 1965. Mgr. tech. services Aims Group, N.Y.C., 1965-67; editor Standard & Poor's Corp., N.Y.C., 1968-74; sr. v.p. PaineWebber, Inc., N.Y.C., 1975—; guest lectr. Harvard U. Bus. Sch. Mem. N.Y.C. Commn. on Status of Women. Named to YWCA Acad. Women Achievers. Mem. N.Y. Soc. Security Analysts (bd. dirs.), Fin. Analysts Fedn., Soc. Fgn. Analysts, Aspen Inst. Humanistic Studies, Fin. Women's Assn., Women's Econ. Roundtable, Econ. Club N.Y., Women in Need (chmn. fin. com.), NOW, DAR. Democrat. Episcopalian. Club: Vassar (N.Y.C.). Contbr. to Ency. Americana. Office: Paine Webber Inc 1285 Ave of the Americas New York NY 10019

COLE, DIANE JACKSON, textile manufacturing company executive; b. Amesbury, Mass., Sept. 14, 1952; d. Robert Keith and Lois Elizabeth (Fogg) Jackson. B.F.A. cum laude, U. N.H., 1974; student U. London, Sir John Cass Coll. Art, London, Richmond Coll., Surrey, Eng. Owner Diane Jackson Cole Handweaving, Kennebunk, Maine, 1974—; pres. Kennebunk Weavers, Inc., 1981—. Contbr. articles to profl. jours., mags. Exhbns. include: Fiber Invitational, Milw., 1977, Currier Gallery Art, N.H., 1981, League N.H. Craftsmen, 1983. Mem. Profl. Crafts Orgn. Maine (newsletter editor 1978, sec. 1979, v.p. 1980), League N.H. Craftsmen, Nat. Bath, Bed and Linen Assn. Republican. Avocations: swimming, sailing, skiing, reading. Home: 9 Grove St Kennebunk ME 04043 Office: Kennebunk Weavers Inc Box A Canal St Suncook NH 03275

COLE, DONALD POWELL, anthropology educator; b. Bryan, Tex., Mar. 21, 1941; s. Donald Putnam and Edna Lee (Powell) C. BA, U. Tex., 1963; MA, U. Calif., Berkeley, 1968, PhD, 1971. Asst. prof. Am. U. Cairo, 1971-75, assoc. prof., 1975-86, prof., 1986—, dept. chmn., 1987—; vis. asst. prof. U. Calif., Berkeley, 1973-74; vis. assoc. prof. U. Chgo., 1976, U. Tex., 1983; cons. World Bank, Washington, 1977—. Author: Nomads of Nomads; contbr. numerous articles to profl. jours. Recipient Middle East Research award Population Council, Cairo, 1986; Ford Found. grantee 1987. Democrat. Presbyterian. Office: Am U Cairo, 113 Kasr El-Aini, Cairo Arab Republic of Egypt

COLE, DONALD WILLARD, clergyman, consulting psychologist; b. San Diego, Jan. 12, 1920; s. Rolland Ames and Genevieve (Bender) C.; m. Ann Bradford, Sept. 18, 1942; 1 son, Timothy Bradford. Student, U. Redlands; A.B., Stanford, 1942; B.D., Eastern Bapt. Theol. Sem., 1945; Ed.D., Southwestern Bapt. Theol. Sem., 1952; Ph.D., U. London, 1962. Ordained to ministry Bapt. Ch., 1945; pastor Linden Bapt. Ch., Camden, N.J., 1944-46; asso. pastor First Bapt. Ch., San Diego, 1946-48; univ. pastor, dir. Bapt. student work So. Calif., 1948-52, dean, dir. Bapt. confs., camps, coll. and univ. students, 1948-52; pres. Calif. Bapt. Theol. Sem. and Coll., 1952-59; Brit. Nat. Health Service fellow, 1959-61; dean students, prof. psychology Fuller Theol. Sem., Pasadena, Calif., 1962-70; pvt. practice cons. clin. psychology, psychotherapy, religion Monrovia, Calif., 1970-74; pastor S. Shores Bapt. Ch., Laguna Niguel, Calif., 1974—. Author: The Role of Religion In The Development of Personality; Contbr. articles to religious publs. Fellow Royal Geog. Soc. London; mem. NEA, Religious Edn. Assn., Am. Group Psychotherapy Assn., Nat. Assn. Mental Health, Acad. Religion and Mental Health, Am. Psychol. Assn., Am. Assn. Schs. Religious Edn., Western, Cal. State, Los Angeles County psychol. assns., Nat. Council Family Relations, Am. Soc. Psychical Research, Am. Acad. Polit. and Social Sci., U.S. Air Force Assn., Alpha Gamma Nu, Alpha Phi Omega. Republican. Home: 245 Via Ballena San Clemente CA 92672 Office: 32712 Crown Valley Pkwy Laguna Niguel CA 92677

COLE, ELMA PHILLIPSON (MRS. JOHN STRICKLER COLE), social welfare executive; b. Piqua, Ohio, Aug. 9, 1909; d. Brice Leroy and Mabel (Gale) Phillipson; m. John Strickler Cole, Oct. 3, 1959. AB, Berea Coll., 1930; MA, U. Chgo., 1938. Various positions in social work, 1930-42; dir. dept. social service Children's Hosp. D.C., Washington, 1942-49; cons. pub. cooperation Midcentury White House Conf. on Children and Youth, Washington, 1949-51; exec. sec. Nat. Midcentury Com. on Children and Youth, Washington, 1951-53, cons. recruitment Am. Assn. Med. Social Workers, 1953; assoc. dir. Nat. Legal Aid and Defender Assn., 1953-56; exec. sec. Marshall Field Awards, Inc., 1956-57; dir. assoc. orgns. Nat. Assembly Social Policy and Devel., 1957-73; assoc. exec. dir. Nat. Assembly Nat. Vol. Health and Social Welfare Orgns., 1974; dir. edn. parenthood project Salvation Army, 1974-76, asst. sec. dept. women's and children's social services, 1976-78, dir. research project devel. bur., 1978—, mem. Manhattan adv. bd., 1975—, sec., 1984—, mem. hist. commn., 1978—, mem. exec. com., 1988—; cons. nat. orgns. Golden Anniversary White House Conf. on Children and Youth, 1959-60; mem. adv. council pub. service Nat. Assn. Life Underwriters and Inst. Life Ins.; mem. judges com. Louis I. Dublin Pub. Service awards, 1961-74; v.p. Blue Ridge Inst. So. Community Service Execs., 1977-79, mem. exec. com., 1979-81; mem. awards jury Girls Clubs of Am., 1981—; mem. adv. bd. Nat. Family Life Edn. Network, 1982—. Mem. com. public relations and fund raising Am. Found. for Blind Commn. on Accreditation, 1964-67; mem. task force on vol. accreditation Council Nat. Orgns. for Adult Edn., 1974-78; mem. adv. bd. sexuality edn. project Ctr. for Population Options, 1977—; sec., bd. dirs. James Lenox House and James Lenox House Assn., 1985—; bd. dirs. Values and Human Sexuality Inst., 1980—. Mem. Pub. Relations Soc. Am. (cert.), Nat. Assn. Social Workers (cert.), Nat. Conf. Social Welfare (mem. pub. relations com. 1961-66, 69-82, chair adminstrn. sect. 1966-67), Jr. League N.Y., Pi Gamma Mu, Phi Kappa Phi. Club: Women's of N.Y. Home: 19 Washington Sq N New York NY 10011 Office: 120 W 14th St New York NY 10011

COLE, EUGENE ROGER, clergyman, author; b. Cleve., Nov. 14, 1930; s. Bernard James and Mary Louise (Rogers) C.; B.A., St. Edward Sem., 1954; student John Carroll U., 1957; M.Div., Sulpician Sem. N.W., 1958; A.B., Central Wash. U., Ellensburg, 1960; M.A., Seattle U., 1970; Litt.D. (hon.), 1983. Ordained priest Roman Catholic Ch., 1958; Newman moderator and cons. Central Wash. U., Ellensburg, 1958-59; bus. mgr. Experiment Press, Seattle, 1959-60; chaplain St. Elizabeth Hosp., Yakima, Wash., 1959-61; chmn. English dept. Yakima Central Cath. High Sch., 1959-66, Marquette High Sch., Yakima, 1966-68; poetry critic Nat. Writers Club, Denver, 1969-72; poet in service Poets & Writers Inc., N.Y.C., 1974—; founder Godspeople, Inc., 1985, dir. 1985—, originator, anapoem, 1985; instr. contract bridge, Ind., 1975-79; freelance writer, editor, researcher, 1958—; researcher Harvard, 1970; religious counselor; owner, pres. Grand Slam softball team, 1985—. Recipient Poetry Broadcast award, 1968, Musical Expertise award, 1970, Lorraine Harr Haiku award, 1974, Ann. Mentor Poetry award, 1974, Pro Mundi Beneficio award, 1975, Readers Union award, 1976, Diploma di Merito, 1982, Marathon award Cleve. Orchestra, 1983. Authors Guild, Poetry Soc. Am. (judge 1970), Western World Haiku Soc., Acad. Am. Poets, World Acad. Poets, World-Wide Acad. Scholars, Internat. Poetry Soc., Soc. for Scholarly Pub., Internat. Platform Assn., Eighteen Nineties Soc. (London), Friends of the Lilly Library, Expt. Group, Soc. for Study of Midwestern Lit., Nat. Fedn. State Poetry Socs., Poetry Soc. (London), Sir Thomas Beecham Soc., Chgo. Symphony Orch. Assn., Cleve. Mus. Art, Ohioana Library Assn., No. Ohio Bibliophilic Soc., Century Club of Cleve. State Univ., Poets' League Greater Cleve., Am. Contract Bridge League, Kappa Delta Pi. Composer: Werther: Tone Poem for Piano, 1948; Chronicle for Tape, 1960. Author: Which End, the Empyrean?, 1959; April Is the Cruelest Month, 1970; Falling Up: Haiku & Senryu, 1979; Act & Potency (poems), 1980; Ding an sich: anapoems, 1985; Uneasy Camber: Early Poems & Diversions 1943-50, 1986; A Key to Ding an sich, 1986; Godspeople: Not a Church but a People, 1987; (under pseudonym Peter E. Locré) Songpoems/poemsongs: new lyrics, 1988; lyrics for male prodn. Finian's Rainbow, 1958; 3 hymns on Bach melodies, 1958; editor: Grand Slam: 13 Great Short Stories about Bridge, 1975; In the Beginning, 1978; assoc. editor: The Harvester, 1955; guest editor Experiment: An Internat. Rev., 1961; editorial staff This Is My Best, 1970; contbr. Your Literary I.Q. Saturday Rev., 1970-72; author religious monograph, also contbr. articles, poetry and drama to numerous lit. jours. and anthologies. Home: 9810 Cove Dr North Royalton OH 44133 Office: PO Box 91277 Cleveland OH 44101

COLE, IRAD DEAN, computer systems specialist; b. Blair, Nebr., Mar. 14, 1930; s. Oliver and Mabel Louise (Reel) C.; m. Patricia Ann DeWitt, Nov. 12, 1950; 1 child, Steven Robert. B.A. in Math. and Physics, Omaha U., 1959; M.A. in Econs., U. Nebr.-Omaha, 1970. Computer programmer Lawrence Radiation Lab., Livermore, Calif., 1959-60; statistician Dow Chem. Co., Denver, 1960-61; programmer analyst System Devel. Corp., Santa Monica, Calif., 1961-71, project head, McLean, Va., 1973-86; computer systems specialist UNISYS Corp., McLean, 1986—; computer systems analyst U.S. Govt., Omaha, 1971-73. Author: DEMOCRAN. 88. Contbr. papers on rhetoric and systems to profl. confs. Co-chmn. Citizens for Goldwater Com., Sarpy County, Nebr., 1964. Served with U.S. Army, 1954-56. Mem. IEEE, Computer Soc. of IEEE, Systems, Man and Cybernetics Soc. of IEEE, Assn. for Computers and Humanities, Austrian Soc. for Cybernetic Studies (fgn. affiliate). Lutheran. Home: 9014 Jersey Dr Fairfax VA 22031

COLE, JACK ELI, physician; b. Matamoras, Pa., Jan. 7, 1915; s. Eli Martin and Louise (Henneberg) C.; B.S., Pa. State U., 1937; M.D., U. Pa., 1941; m. Evelyn Gaston Darragh, Apr. 26, 1941; children—Jack Eli, Thomas, Beverly, Martin, Robert, Leslie, Christopher, Candace, Champa. Intern, Wilkes-Barre (Pa.) Gen. Hosp., 1941-42; practice medicine, specializing in family practice, Matamoras, Pa., 1946-47, Bethlehem, Pa., 1952-68, 1973—; staff St. Luke's Hosp., Bethlehem, 1948—, sec. dept. family practice, 1973—; incorporator, mem. staff Muhlenberg Med. Ctr., Bethlehem, 1960—, pres. med. staff, 1961-62; student health physician Lehigh U., Bethlehem, Pa., 1948-52; Peace Corps physician Afghanistan, Swaziland, India, 1968-73; leader mission med. team, Honduras, 1987; preceptor Temple U. Med. Sch., Phila., 1978-86. Charter mem. mission partnership com. N.E. Pa. conf. United Ch. of Christ, 1984. Served with U.S. Army, 1942-45. Decorated Purple Heart, Combat Medic badge; recipient Recognition award Temple U. Med. Sch., 1979; Boss of Yr. award Allentown Bus. Womens Assn., 1975; diplomate Am. Bd. Family Practice. Fellow Am. Acad. Family Physicians; mem. Northampton County Med. Soc., Pa. Med. Soc., Lehigh Valley Acad. Family Physicians (v.p. 1979-81, pres. 1981-83), Pa. Acad. Family Physicians, Am. Acad. Family Physicians. Republican. Clubs: Met. Opera Guild, Masons. Home: 782 Barrymore Ln Bethlehem PA 18017 Office: 65 E Elizabeth Ave Bethlehem PA 18018

COLE, JAMES RANDOLPH, II, oral and maxillofacial surgeon; b. Albuquerque, May 19, 1941; s. James Randolph and Orrel (Brooks) C.; m. Carol Williams, Nov. 1985; children—Kristin, Kimberly. BS, U. N.Mex., 1963; DDS, U. Mo.-Kansas City, 1967; cert. in oral maxillofacial surgery, U. Okla., 1973. Diplomate Am. Bd. Oral and Maxillofacial Surgeons. Practice oral and maxillofacial surgery, Albuquerque, 1973—. Served to capt. USAF, 1967-73. Fellow Am. Soc. Oral Maxillofacial Surgeons, Internat. Coll. Dentists; mem. Rocky Mt. Soc. Oral Surgeons (pres. 1985-86), Albuquerque Dist. Dental Soc. (pres. 1985-86), Coll. Dentists, N.Mex. Dental Assn., N.Mex. State Bd. of Dentistry. Republican. Episcopalian. Lodge: Rotary. Avocations: skiing, woodworking. Office: Oral Maxillofacial Surgery Assocs 6800-A Montgomery St NE Albuquerque NM 87109

COLE, JOAN HAYS, social worker, clinical psychologist; b. Pitts., Sept. 4, 1929; d. Frank L. Wertheimer and Edith H. Einstein; BA, Western Res. U., 1951; MSSA in Social Work, Case Western Res. U., 1962; PhD, Wright Inst., 1975; m. Robert M. Wendlinger, June 1984; children: Geoffrey F. Cole, Douglas R. Cole, Peter Hays Cole. Social group worker Alta House Settlement House, Cleve., 1958-59; housing dir. Cleve. Urban League, 1961-62; dir. Citizens for Safe Housing, Cleve., 1963; housing dir. United Planning Orgn., Washington, 1963-68; asst. prof. community orgn. U. Md., Balt., 1968-72; asso. prof. Lone Mountain Coll., San Francisco, 1975-78; psychotherapist, supr., organizational cons., Berkeley, Calif., 1977—; cons. various public and vol. social welfare, health and housing agys., 1969—; mem. adj. faculty Union Grad. Sch. and Antioch West Coll., 1978-80; lectr. U. Calif. Sch. Social Welfare, Berkeley, 1980-84; mem. faculty Berkeley Psychotherapy Inst., 1981—, pres., 1983-85. NIMH grantee, 1971-72, Sr. Social Work Career Devel. grantee, 1973-75. Fellow Soc. Clin. Social Work, Am. Orthopsychiat. Assn.; mem. Nat. Assn. Social Workers, Soc. Study of Social Issues, ACLU, NOW, Acad. Cert. Social Workers, Nat. Conf. on Social Welfare and Psychotherapists for Social Responsibility. Home: 1377 Campus Dr Berkeley CA 94708 Office: 1905 Berkeley Way Berkeley CA 94704

COLE, JOHN L., JR., city official; b. Johnstown, Pa., Nov. 8, 1928; s. John L. and Susie L. (Stamper) C.; div.; 1 dau., Keia D. Student U. Buffalo, 1956-58; diploma Bryant and Stratton Bus. Inst., Buffalo, 1960. Exec. asst. City of Cleve., 1966-69, compliance officer, 1969-72; asst. to gen. mgr. for equal employment opportunity Met. Atlanta Rapid Transit Authority, Atlanta, 1972—. Bd. dirs. Cleve. Urban League, 1971 (Outstanding Service award 1971). Served with U.S. Army, 1951-53; Korea. Recipient Meritorious Pub. Service award NAACP, 1971; Cleve. City Council resolution, 1973; Berkely G. Burrell pvt. Sector award Nat. Bus. League, 1983. Mem. Am. Pub. Transit Assn. (chmn. minority affairs com. 1975-80), Com. To Increase Minority Profls. Engring. and Architecture, Greater Cleve. Growth Assn. (dir.), Conf. Minority Transp. Ofcls. (Ann. Sibling award 1980). Home: 2691 Laurens Circle Atlanta GA 30311

COLE, JONATHAN RICHARD, sociologist, educator; b. N.Y.C., Aug. 27, 1942; s. Richard and Sylvia (Dym) C.; B.A., Columbia U., 1964, Ph.D., 1969; m. Joanna Miller Lewis, June 5, 1968; children—Daniel Lewis, Susanna Dora. Asst. prof. sociology Columbia U., N.Y.C., 1969-73, assoc. prof., 1973-76, prof., 1976—, dir. Center for Social Scis., 1979-87, v.p. Arts and Scis., 1987—; adj. prof. Rockefeller U., 1983-85 ; cons. Ford Found., NSF, Nat. Acad. Scis., Russell Sage Found., AT&T. Guggenheim fellow, 1975-76, Center for Advanced Study in Behavioral Scis. fellow, 1975-76. Mem. Am., Internat., Eastern sociol. assns., AAAS, Soc. Research Assn. (hon.). Author: Social Stratification in Science, 1973; Fair Science: Women in the Scientific Community, 1979; Peer Review in the National Science Foundation, Vol. 1, 1978, Vol. 2, 1981; The Wages of Writing: Per Word, Per Price, or Perhaps, 1986; The Sociological Analysis of Science, 1988; Women in the Pursuit of Science, 1988; editor Am. Jour. Sociology; contbr. articles to profl. jours. Home: 404 Riverside Dr New York NY 10025 Office: Columbia U Dept Sociology New York NY 10027

COLE, KAREN LORRAINE, operating engineer; b. Norco, Calif., Apr. 12, 1954; d. William G. Willis and Lorraine Ruth (Buratti) Willis-Beisner; children: Cirdon Brion, Vanna Alia. Apprentice, Trade Tech. Coll., Los Angeles, 1980-84, Journeyman Grad., 1984. Apprentice engr. Cushman & Wakefield, Los Angeles, 1980-83, Bank of Calif., 1983-84, chief operating engr., 1984—. Active Boy Scouts Am. Mem. Nat. Assn. Female Execs., Bldg. Owners and Mgrs. Assn., Local 501 Internat. Union Operating Engrs. (Apprentice of Yr. award 1984). Avocations: design and construction of stained-glass windows, scuba diving, off-road driving. Office: Cushman & Wakefield Calif Inc 515 S Flower St Suite 2200 Los Angeles CA 90071

COLE, MALVIN, physician, educator; b. N.Y.C., Mar. 21, 1933; s. Harry and Sylvia (Firman) C.; A.B. cum laude, Amherst Coll., 1953; M.D. cum laude, Georgetown U. Med. Sch., 1957; m. Susan Kugel, June 20, 1954; children: Andrew James, Douglas Gowers. Intern, Seton Hall Coll. Medicine, Jersey City Med. Ctr., 1957-58; resident Boston City Hosps., 1958-60; practice medicine specializing in neurology, Montclair and Glen Ridge, N.J., Montville, N.J., 1963-72, Casper, Wyo., 1972—; teaching fellow Harvard Med. Sch., 1958-60; Research fellow Nat. Hosp. for Nervous Diseases, St. Thomas Hosp., London, Eng., 1960-61; instr. Georgetown U. Med. Sch., 1961-63; clin. assoc. prof. neurology N.J. Coll. Medicine, Newark, 1963-72, acting dir. neurology, 1965-72; clin. prof. neurology U. Colo. Med. Sch., 1973—; mem. staff Martland Hosp., Newark, Wyo. Med. Ctr., Casper, U. Hosp., Denver. Served to capt. M.C., AUS, 1961-63. Licensed physician, Mass., N.Y., Calif., N.J., Colo., Wyo.; diplomate Am. Bd. Psychiatry and Neurology, Nat. Bd. Med. Examiners. Fellow ACP, Am. Acad. Neurology, Royal Soc. Medicine; mem. Assn. Research Nervous and Mental Disease, Acad. Aphasia, Am. Soc. Neuroimaging, Internat. Soc. Neuropsychology, Harveian Soc. London, Epilepsy Found. Am., Am. Epilepsy Soc., Am. EEG Soc., N.Y. Acad. Sci., Osler Soc. London, Alpha Omega Alpha. Contbr. articles to profl. jours. Office: 246 S Washington St Casper WY 82601

COLEIRO, CHARLES, ink mill manager; b. Rabat, Malta, Nov. 8, 1949; s. Vincent and Maryrose (Buhagiar) C.; m. Eleonora Scicluna, May 2, 1976; children: Peter Paul, Andrew Thomas. Diploma in religious studies, U. Malta, 1982. Monk Missionary Soc. St. Paul, Rabat, 1964-74; ink mill mgr. Thomas de La Rue, Zejtun, Malta, 1976—. Contbr. articles on history to ency.; chmn. edit. bd. Il Hsieb, 1988. Mem. mgmt. Manoel Theatre, Valletta, 1982-87; sec. Malta Labour Party Club, St. Julian's, 1982—. Home: 85 Lapsi St, Saint Julians Malta Office: Thomas de La Rue, PO Box 304, Valletta Malta

COLEMAN, BRUCE FREDERICK, economist, municipal bond trader; b. Pontiac, Mich., Aug. 13, 1944; s. Frederick George and Edith Maud (Eley) C.; B.S., U. Mich., 1967; m. Diane Marie Base, May 18, 1968; children—Christine, Carrie, Christopher, Craig, Amanda. With Mfrs. Nat. Bank of Detroit, 1975-76; asst. v.p. Ann Arbor Bank and Trust (Mich.), 1976-78; exec. v.p. Mich. Mcpl. Bond Corp., Ann Arbor, 1978-80; gen. partner Roney & Co., Detroit, 1980-87, 1st v.p. Mich. Nat. Bank, Farmington Hills, Mich., 1987—. Mem. Fin. Analysts Soc. Detroit, Bond Club Detroit, Nat. Security Traders Assn., Basis Club Detroit. Office: c/o Mich Nat Bank PO Box 9065 Farmington Hills MI 48333

COLEMAN, BRYAN DOUGLAS, lawyer, corporate executive, educator; b. Texarkana, Tex., Aug. 16, 1948; s. William Bryan and Armeda (Crawford) C.; m. Tommye Lou Bettis, Jan. 31, 1984; children: Douglas Patrick, Sarah Elizabeth. AS, Texarkana Coll., 1968; BS in Bus. Admistrn., Stephen F. Austin U., 1970; postgrad. Rice U., 1971-73; JD (E.E. Townes award, Am. Jurisprudence award), South Tex. Coll. Law, 1973; grad. JAG Sch., U.S. Army, 1978. Bar: Tex. 1973, U.S. Dist. Ct. (so. dist.) Tex. 1974, U.S. Tax Ct., 1987, U.S. Ct. Appeals (11th cir.) 1982, U.S. Ct. Appeals (5th cir.) 1975; cert. Fellow Life Mgmt. Inst. Quality control insp. Lone Star Ammunition Plant, Texarkana, 1966-68; law clk. Fulbright & Jaworski, Houston, 1970-71, Boswell, O'Toole, Davis & Pickering, Houston, 1971-72, Helm, Pletcher & Hogan, Houston, 1972-73; assoc. Law Office Gus Zgourides, Houston, 1973-76, Ray & Coleman, P.C., Houston, 1976—; dir. Med. Assurance Group, Houston, 1978—; counsel Gt. SW Life Ins. Co., Houston, 1983—, First Columbia Life Ins. Co., Dallas, 1987—; instr. U. Houston, 1979-81. Mem. Republican Nat. Com., 1983—. Served to comdr. Army ROTC, 1972-73, to 1st lt. U.S. Army, 1973-79. Mem. ABA, State Bar Tex. (founder law student div. 1973, chmn. grievance com. 1979-81), Am. Judicature Soc., Houston Bar Found., Houston Bar Assn., Alpha Kappa Psi (sec. 1969-70), Alpha Phi Omega (pledge trainer 1970) Delta Theta Phi. Home: 3510 Saratoga Ln Houston TX 77088 Office: Ray & Coleman PC 1314 Tex Ave 500 Great SW Bldg Houston TX 77002

COLEMAN, CARLA SWAN, clinical psychologist; b. Denver, Apr. 5, 1908; d. Henry and Carla (Denison) Swan; m. Albert Jones Coleman, Oct. 11, 1952. A.B., Bryn Mawr Coll., 1929; M.A., Yale U., 1936, Ph.D., 1938. Cert. psychologist Am. Bd. Psychologists in Pvt. Practice. Psychol. tester Denver Pub. Schs., 1929-32, tchr. parent edn. and pre-sch. program, 1938-45; research asst. Guidance Nursery, Yale Inst. Human Relations, 1932-38; pvt. practice clin. psychology, Denver, 1945-72, part-time, 1972—; dir., psychol. cons. Innsmont Ctr. for Children, Denver, 1967-72; vol. counselor with pediatricians, psychiatrists, psychologists, 1945—. Bd. dirs. Colo. State Children's Home, 1947-60. Mem. Am. Psychol. Assn., Colo. Psychol. Assn. (Disting. Service award 1970), AAAS, Assn. Gifted and Talented, Colo. Ednl. Assn., Colo. Women Psychologists, Mental Health Assn. Colo., Colo. Assn. Mental Hygiene, Colo. Assn. Children with Learning Difficulties, Colonial Dames Am., Sigma Xi. Republican. Episcopalian. Clubs: University, Fortnightly, Garden of Denver. Address: 475 Humboldt St Denver CO 80218

COLEMAN, CLARENCE WILLIAM, banker; b. Wichita, Kans., Mar. 24, 1909; s. William Coffin and Fanny Lucinda (Sheldon) C.; m. Emry Regester Ingham, Oct. 2, 1935; children—Rochelle, Pamela, Kathryn Sheldon. Student, U. Kans., 1928-32; LL.D., Ottawa U., 1973; D.H.L., Friends U.; D. Laws, Ottawa U. bd. dirs. Union Blvd. Nat. Bank, 1987—. With Coleman Co., Inc., Wichita, 1932—; v.p. charge mfg. Coleman Co., Inc., 1944, dir., 1935—, asst. gen. mgr., 1951-54; pres. Union Nat. Bank, Wichita, 1957-72; vice chmn. bd. Union Nat. Bank, 1972—; chmn. bd. dir. Cherry Creek Inn, Inc., Denver, 1961-69, Kans. Devel. Credit Corp.; bd. dirs. Union Blvd. Nat. Bank, 1987—. Bd. dirs. Inst. Logopedics, 1940-74, chmn. bd., 1947-48; bd. dirs. Wichita Symphony Soc.; trustee Wichita Symphony Soc. Found.; bd. dirs. Found. for Study of Cycles, Pitts., Wichita Mental Health Assn., 1956-74, United Fund Wichita and Sedgewick County, 1957-74, Friends U., 1956-74; bd. dirs. Wichita Crime Commn., 1953-74, pres., 1958; mem. Nat. Budget Com., 1952; chmn. State Mental Health Fund Kans., 1953; Trustee Peddie Sch., Hightstown, N.J., chmn. bd. trustees, 1972-76, chmn. emeritus, 1981. Mem. Mid-Ark. Valley Devel. Assn. (treas.), Wichita C. of C. (pres. 1956, dir. 1947-74), Phi Kappa Psi. Club: Rotarian. Office: Union Nat Bank 1005 Union Ctr Wichita KS 67202 also: Coleman Co Inc 250 N St Francis Ave Wichita KS 67202

COLEMAN, EARL MAXWELL, publishing company executive; b. N.Y.C., Jan. 9, 1916; s. Samuel Sidney and Rose (Ensleman) C.; m. Frances Louise Allan, Mar. 23, 1942 (div. Mar. 15, 1965); children: Allan Douglass, Dennis Scott; m. Ellen Schneid, Aug. 19, 1973. Student, NYU, 1933-34, CCNY, 1934-35, Columbia U., 1946. Founder, pres. Plenum Pub. Corp. (and predecessors), N.Y.C., 1946-77; chmn. bd. dirs. Plenum Pub. Corp. (and predecessors), 1960-77, cons., 1977—; founder Earl M. Coleman Enterprises, Inc. (Pubs.), 1977—; pres. Nat. Pubs. The Black Hills Inc., 1984—. Contbr. poems, short stories to mags. Served with USAAF, 1941-45. Mem. Info. Industry Assn. (dir. 1971—), Assn. Am. Publishers (exec. com. tech.-sci.-med. div. 1970—), Sci. Tech. Med. Publishers (Holland). Home: 125 Mount Airy Rd S Croton-on-Hudson NY 10520 Office: PO Box T Crugers NY 10521

COLEMAN, FRANCIS XAVIER, JR, investment banker; b. N.Y.C., Dec. 9, 1930; s. Francis Xavier and Cecilia Estelle (Campion) C.; m. Agnes Catherine Lyons, June 20, 1953; children—Neil, Janice, Ellen, Denys, Francis X. III. B.S., N.Y.U., 1955. Ptnr. Goldman Sachs & Co., N.Y.C., 1975-86, ltd. ptnr., 1986—; bd. dirs. FGIC Corp. Trustee, Friends Acad., Locust Valley, N.Y., 1980—; mem. Cardinal's Com. of the Laity, Roman Catholic Ch., N.Y.C., 1982—; trustee Fordham Prep. Sch., N.Y.C., 1983—. Named Man of Yr., Nat. Housing Conf., N.Y.C., 1983; decorated Knight of Malta, 1984. Mem. Mcpl. Bond Club N.Y., N.Y. Mcpl. Forum, Washington Mcpl. Forum. Republican Roman Catholic. Home: 70 High Farm Rd Glen Head NY 11545 Office: Goldman Sachs & Co 85 Broad St New York NY 10004

COLEMAN, GERALD CHRISTOPHER, business executive; b. Boston, Sept. 27, 1939; s. Gerald Christopher and Anna Rose (Dubanevich) C.; m. Kathleen Louise Dolan, June 3, 1967; children—Lisa, Emily, Craig, Mary. A.B., Boston Coll., 1964; M.B.A., Dartmouth Coll., 1966. Asst. nat. retail sales mgr. photog. products Sears Roebuck & Co., Chgo., 1966-68, asst. nat. buyer calculators, 1968-69, staff asst. to v.p., 1969-70, nat. buyer, product mgr. bedding products, 1970-72, nat. retail sales mgr. toy products, 1972-73, nat. retail mktg. mgr. furniture products, 1973-74; v.p. Wilson, Haight & Welch, Inc., Boston, 1974-77; sr. v.p. N.W. Ayer, Inc., Chgo., 1977-83, N.Y.C., 1983-87; also dir. N.W. Ayer Midwest, Chgo., 1982-83; corp. v.p. New Eng. Devel. & Mgmt., Inc., Newton, Mass., 1987—; dir. Allied Fin. Instns. Inc., Boston, Ayer Midwest, Inc., 1982-83. Rep.-at-large Kenilworth Citizens Adv. Com., Ill., 1982. Mem. Am. Mktg. Assn. (officer, chpt. bd. dirs. 1983-84). Roman Catholic. Clubs: Economic of Chgo.; Dartmouth, N.Y. Athletic (N.Y.C.); Middlesex (Darien, Conn.). Home: 9 Sherry Ln Darien CT 06820 Office: New Eng Devel & Mgmt Inc 1 Wells Ave Newton MA 02159

COLEMAN, HOWARD S., engineer, physicist; b. Everett, Pa., Jan. 10, 1917; s. Howard Solomon and Amy (Ritchey) C.; children: Michael Howard, Madeline Frances, Thomas Robert, Carl William, Stephen Mitchell Rosenberg; m. Jeannette Eve Dresher, Dec. 27, 1969. B.S., Pa. State U., 1938, M.S. in Physics, 1939, Ph.D., 1942. Registered profl. engr., Va., Ariz., Tex. Faculty Pa. State U., 1934-47, dir. optical inspection lab., 1941-47; dir. optical research lab., asso. prof. physics U. Tex., 1947-51; with Bausch & Lomb, Inc., 1951-62, mgr., v.p. research and engring., 1954-62; head physics research dept., tech. asst. to v.p. charge research Melpar, Inc., Falls Church,

Va., 1962-64; dean U. Ariz. Coll. Engring., prof. elec. engring., 1964-68; dir. Spl. Projects Center, Schellenger Research Labs., U. Tex., El Paso, 1968-75, Howard S. Coleman and Assos., El Paso, 1975—; dep. dir. solar energy div. ERDA, 1976-77; dep. dir. div. solar energy tech. U.S. Dept. Energy, 1977-78, dir. central solar tech. div., 1978-80, dir. tech. and utilization alcohol fuels, 1980-81, prin. dep. asst. sec. for conservation and renewable energy, 1981-84, dir. Div. Solar Thermal Tech., 1984—; cons. to industry, govt., 1941—; spl. research optical inspection devices; mem. Ariz. Bd. Tech. Registration.; Mem. adv. vis. com. electronics U. Rochester, 1952; chmn. vis. com. math. Clarkson Coll. Tech., 1953-63. Recipient Joint Service award, 1952. Fellow Optical Soc. Am.; mem. Am. Phys. Soc., Meteorol. Soc., Inst. Aero. Scis., Am. Assn. Physics Tchrs., Am. Soc. Metals, Internat. Commn. Optics, Am. Geophys. Union, Am. Inst. Physics, Am. Soc. Engring. Edn., Nat. Soc. Profl. Engrs., N.Y. Acad. Scis., Illuminating Engring. Soc., Soc. Photo-Optical Instrumentation Engrs. Home: PO Box 26368 El Paso TX 79926

COLEMAN, JOHN HARROD, municipal bond specialist; b. Jacksonville, Fla., May 2, 1926; s. John H. and Mary Ellen (Joseph) C.; student The Citadel, 1943; B.A. with honors, U. Fla., 1949; postgrad. Goethe U. (Germany), 1956; cert. Sorbonne, Paris, 1957, others. With Marine Midland Trust Co., N.Y.C., 1960-66; fin. advisor Roosevelt & Son, N.Y.C., 1966-72; v.p. First Equity Corp. Fla., Tampa, 1972-75, Shearson Loeb Rhoades, Miami, Fla., 1975-79, NCNB Nat. Bank of Fla., Boca Raton, 1979-85, First Nat. Bank in Palm Beach, Boca Raton, 1985—. Served with USNR, 1944-46, 51-52. Mem. Soc. Colonial Wars, St. Nicholas Soc., English Speaking Union, SR, Order of Crown of Charlemagne, Baronial Order of Magna Charta, Nat. Soc. Ams. of Royal Descent, St. Andreas Soc. Democrat. Presbyterian. Clubs: Municipal Bond N.Y., Municipal Forum N.Y., Union, Selva Marina Country, St. Andrews Soc. Home: 1542 Park Terrace West Atlantic Beach FL 32233 Office: 76 Royal Palm Plaza Boca Raton FL 33432

COLEMAN, JOHN JOSEPH, telephone company executive; b. Boston, Aug. 2, 1937; s. Martin Joseph and Anna Veronica (Leonard) C.; B.S. cum laude in Bus. Adminstrn., Boston Coll., 1964; postgrad. Harvard U. Bus. Sch., 1970; m. Carol Ann Holmes, May 6, 1961; children—Mark Christopher, Cara Romaine. With New Eng. Telephone Co., 1955—, various supervisory positions in plant and acctg. depts., Mass., R.I., now v.p., Boston; dir. Merchants Nat. Bank, Manchester. Bd. dirs. United Way of Greater Manchester, chmn., 1980; chmn. Gov.'s Mgmt. Rev., 1981; chmn. fundraising campaign, Manchester Crimeline, Inc., 1982; bd. dirs. Boston Mcpl. Research Bur., 1984-86, Mass. Taxpayers Found. Inc., 1984-86; mem. New Spirit in Boston Com., 1984-85. Served with USN, 1956-58. Mem. Bus. and Industry Assn. of N.H. (dir.), N.H. Safety Council (adv. bd.), Am. Automobile Assn. Mass. (mem. adv. bd.), Greater Boston C. of C. (chmn. pub. safety com. 1985-86). Office: 101 Huntington Ave Suite 2100 Boston MA 02199

COLEMAN, KENNETH WILLIAM, publishing company executive; b. Phila., Apr. 22, 1930; s. George Craig Coleman and Catherine Estelle (Irwin) Cohen; m. Seraphine Elizabeth Rinaudo, Aug.9, 1952; 1 child, Catherine Elizabeth Coleman Chambers. BA in History, Calif. State U., Los Angeles, 1957; MS in Ednl. Psychology, Calif. State U., Long Beach, 1975. Cert. tchr., Calif. Tchr. Los Angeles city schs., 1957-75; chief exec. officer Seraphim Press, Carlsbad, Calif., 1978—. Author and pub.: The Misdirection Conspiracy, 1982, 2d rev. ed. 1983, U.S. Financial Institutions in Crisis, 1982, 4th rev. ed. 1986, America's Endangered Banks, 1984, 2d rev. ed. 1986, Reality Theory, 1982—, The Fed Tracker, 1984—, dir. Am. Monetary Found., 1987—, fin. editor Mobilehome News, Santa Ana, Calif., 1983-84; regular contbr. Am. Assn. Fin. Profls. mag., Orange County Bus. Jour., Smart Money Investor mag. Bus. and fin. adv. com., Chet Wray for Calif. Assembly, Cerritos, Calif., 1978-84; consumer affairs com., Richard Robinson for Calif. Assemby, Garden Grove, Calif., 1986—; pres. Chansall Mut. Water Co., Bell, Calif. 1961-65. Served with U.S. Army, 1945-47. Lodge: Elks. Home and Office: 4805 Courageous Ln Carlsbad CA 92008

COLEMAN, MORTON, oncologist, hematologist; b. Norfolk, Va., Sept. 15, 1939; s. Isadore and Bessie (Levin) C.; AA, Coll. William and Mary, 1958; BA, Johns Hopkins U., 1959; MD, Med. Coll. Va., 1963; m. Joyce Goodman, May 26, 1968; children—Ingrid Alexandra, Benjamin Lee, Abigail Rachael. Intern, Grady Meml. Hosp.-Emory U., Atlanta, 1963-64, resident, 1964-65; resident N.Y. Hosp.-Cornell U. Med. Center, N.Y.C., 1967-68; NIH fellow in hematology Cornell U. Med. Coll., 1968-70, asst. prof. medicine, 1970-74, assoc. prof., 1974-85, clin. prof., 1986—; asst. attending N.Y. Hosp., N.Y.C., 1970-74, assoc. attending, 1974-85, attending, 1986—, assoc. dir. oncology service, 1974-84; attending staff Manhattan Eye, Ear and Nose Hosp., 1972—, Doctors Hosp., 1973—. chmn. new agts. com. Cancer and Leukemia Group B, 1975-82; chmn. bd. dirs. Fund for Blood and Cancer Research, 1975—; mem. sci. adv. bd. United Leukemia Fund, 1976-82; cons. New Rochelle Med. Ctr., N.Y., 1986—; assoc. editor Cancer Research. Served to lt. comdr. USN, 1965-67. Diplomate Am. Bd. Internal Medicine. Fellow ACP; mem. AAAS, Am. Assn. Cancer Research, Am. Fedn. Clin. Research, AMA, Am. Radium Soc., Am. Soc. Clin. Oncology, Am. Soc. Hematology, Am. Heart Assn., Harvey Soc., Internat. Soc. Hematology, Internat. Soc. Thrombosis and Hemostasis, N.Y. Acad. Sci., N.Y. Cancer Soc., Soc. Study of Blood, Alpha Omega Alpha, Sigma Zeta. Research, publs. on blood, cancer. Office: 407 E 70th St New York NY 10021

COLEMAN, NORMAN ARTHUR, insurance company executive; b. New Philadelphia, Ohio, Mar. 4, 1923; s. Harrison Arthur and Margaret Ersman (Campbell) C.; B.S., Northwestern U., 1947; postgrad. U. Ky., 1947-48; m. Yvonne Lou Cotterman, Apr. 7, 1956; 1 son, Matt Arthur. Salesman, Youngen Ins. Agy., New Philadelphia, 1949-59; pres. CBS Ins., Colorado Springs, Colo., 1959—; dir. Air Acad. Nat. Bank. Trustee U.S. Naval Acad. Found. Served to rear adm. USNR. Mem. Soc. Chartered Property Casualty Underwriters, Ret. Officers Assn. Clubs: Army and Navy, Broadmoor Golf, Garden of the Gods. Home: 14-2 Miramar Dr Colorado Springs CO 80906 Office: PO Box 1900 Colorado Springs CO 80901

COLEMAN, REXFORD LEE, lawyer, educator; b. Hollywood, Calif., June 2, 1930; s. Henry Eugene and Antoinette Christine (Dobry) C.; m. Aiko Takahashi, Aug. 28, 1953 (div.); children: Christine Eugenie, Douglass Craig; m. Sucha Park, June 15, 1978. Student, Claremont McKenna Coll., 1947-49; A.B., Stanford U., 1951, J.D., 1955; M. in Jurisprudence, Tokyo U., 1960. Bar: Calif. 1955, Mass. 1969. Mem. faculty Harvard U., 1959-69; mem. firm Baker & McKenzie, 1969-83, income ptnr., 1971-73, capital ptnr., 1973-83, mng. ptnr. Tokyo office, 1971-78; sr. ptnr. Pacific Law Group, Los Angeles, 1983—; cons. U.S. Treasury Dept., 1961-70; counselor Japanese-Am. Soc. for Legal Studies, 1964—; guest lectr. Ford Seminar on Comparative History, MIT, 1968; lectr. Legal Tng. and Research Inst., Supreme Ct., Japan, 1970-73; chmn. fgn. bus. customs consultative com. Bur. Customs, Ministry of Fin., Govt. of Japan, 1971-72; chmn. fgn. bus. consulatative commn. Japanese Ministry of Internat. Trade and Industry, 1973-76. Author: Am. Index to Japanese Law, 1961, Standard Citation of Japanese Legal Materials, 1963, The Legal Aspects Under Japanese Law of an Accident Involving a Nuclear Installation in Japan, 1963, An Index to Japanese Law, 1975. Editor: Taxation in Japan, World Tax Series, 1959—, Japanese Ann. of Internat. Law, 1970—; Chmn. bd. editors: Law in Japan: An Ann., 1964-67; bd. editors Stanford Law Rev., 1954-55. Participant in Japanese-Am. Program for Cooperation in Legal Studies, 1956-60; co-chmn. Conf. on Internat. Legal Protection Computer Software, Stanford Law Sch., 1986, Tokyo, Japan, 1987. Served to 1st lt., Inf. AUS, 1951-53; now lt. col. Res. Ford Found. grantee, 1956-60. Mem. Japanese-Am. Soc. for Legal Studies, Assn. Asian Studies, Am. Polit. Sci. Assn., Internat. Studies Assn., Internat. Fiscal Assn. U.S. and Japan, Acad. Polit. Sci., Am. Acad. Polit. and Social Sci., Am. Soc. Internat. Law, Am. Fgn. Law Assn., ABA, State Bar Calif., Mass. Bar Assn., Mil. Govt. Assn., Res. Officers Assn. (v.p. army dept. Far East 1974-75), U.S. Army Judge Adv. Gen.'s Sch. Alumni Assn., Internat. House Japan (Tokyo), Stanford U. Alumni Assn., Gakushi Kai, Internat. Law Assn. Japan, Japan-Western Assn., Pacific Basin Econ. Council, (U.S. exec. com. 1985-87), Am. C. of C. in Japan, Nihon Shihō Gakkai, Nihon Kokusai Hō Gakkai, Nihon Kokusai Shihō Gakkai, Sozei Hō Gakkai, Phi Alpha Delta. Episcopalian (vestryman 1966-69; del. Conv. Episcopal Diocese Mass. 1968, Bishop's com. 1983-87). Clubs: Tokyo Am; Harvard (N.Y.C.); Los Angeles Marina City, North Ranch Country. Home: 32314 Blue Rock Ridge Westlake Village CA 91361 Office: Pacific Law Group 1875 Century Park E Los Angeles CA 90067

COLEMAN, ROBERT LEE, lawyer; b. Kansas City, Mo., June 14, 1929; s. William Houston and Edna Fay (Smith) C. B.Mus. Edn., Drake U., 1951, LL.B., U. Mo., 1959. Bar: Mo. 1959, Fla. 1973. Law clk. to judge U.S. dist. ct. (we. dist.) Mo., Kansas City, 1959-60; assoc. Watson, Ess, Marshall & Enggas, Kansas City, 1960-66; asst. gen. counsel Gas Service Co., Kansas City, 1966-74; corp. counsel H & R Block, Inc., Kansas City, 1974—. Served with U.S. Army, 1955-57. Mem. ABA, Kansas City Bar Assn., Lawyers Assn. Kansas City.

COLEMAN, ROGER DIXON, bacteriologist; b. Rockwell, Iowa, Jan. 18, 1915; s. Major C. and Hazel Ruth Coleman; A.B., UCLA, 1937; postgrad. Balliol Coll., Oxford (Eng.) U., 1944; M.S., U. So. Calif., 1952, Ph.D., 1957; m. Lee Aden Skov, Jan. 1, 1978. Sr. laboratorian Napa (Calif.) State Hosp., 1937-42; dir. Long Beach (Calif.) Clin. Lab., 1946—, pres., 1980—; mem. Calif. State Clin. Lab. Commn., 1953-57. Served as officer AUS, 1942-46. Diplomate Am. Bd. Bioanalysts. Mem. Am. Assn. Bioanalysts, Am. Assn. Clin. Chemists, Am. Soc. Microbiologists, Am. Chem. Soc., Am. Venereal Disease Assn., AAAS (life), Calif. Assn. Bioanalysts (past officer), Med. Research Assn. Calif., Bacteriology Club So. Calif., Sigma Xi, Phi Sigma (past chpt. pres.). Author papers in field. Home: 30041 Running Deer Ln Laguna Beach CA 92677 Office: Cen Diagnostic Lab 3500 W Lomita #104 Torrance CA 90505

COLER, MYRON A(BRAHAM), chemical engineer, educator; b. N.Y.C., Mar. 30, 1913; s. Marcus and Bertha (Bebarfald) C.; m. Viola Ethel Buchbinder, Nov. 15, 1942; children: Mark D., Sandra Coler Carson. A.B., Columbia U., 1933, B.S., 1934, Ch.E., 1935, Ph.D., 1937; postgrad., N.Y. U., Bklyn. Poly. Inst. With N.Y. U., 1941-75, prof., dir. surface tech. program dir. creative sci. program; supr., research scientist Manhattan Project, 1943-45; cons. numerous cos. and govt. agys.; founder, pres., dir. chmn. bd. Markite Co., Markite Corp., Markite Engring. Co., 1948-67, Coler Engring. Co., 1967—; sponsor-in-residence Franklin Inst. Research Labs., 1975-81. Contbr. numerous articles to profl. jours.; author: Aircraft Engine Finishes, 1941; editor, contbg. author: essays on Creativity in the Sciences, 1963; Contbg. author: essays on Invention and Education, 1977; hon. editor Leonardo, 1984. Bd. dirs. Van Weazel Found., Woodward Envicon, Marcus and Bertha Coler Found.; mem. advisory com. Dept. Phys. and Engring. Metallurgy, Polytechnic Inst. N.Y.; mem. pres.'s com. for Sch. Continuing Edn. N.Y. U.; appointee Nat. Inventors Council, 1966-74; mem. state tech. service com. Dept. Commerce; with div. cultural studies UNESCO-Dept. State, 1982; hon. advisor family issues and substance abuse program San Francisco State U. Named hon. prof. Polytechnic Inst. N.Y.; Weston fellow Electrochem. Mem. Am. Math. Soc., AAAS, N.Y. Acad. Sci., Electrochem. Soc., Am. Ceramic Soc., Am. Chem. Soc., Am. Soc. for Metals, Am. Def. Preparedness Assn., Internat. Precious Metals Inst., Sigma Xi, Phi Beta Kappa, Phi Lambda Upsilon, Tau Beta Pi, Epsilon Chi. Clubs: Princeton, Kona Kai. Home: 56 Secor Rd Scarsdale NY 10583 Office: NY Univ One Washington Square Village New York NY 10012

COLEY, ROBERT BERNARD, software company executive, management consultant; b. Bethesda, Md., Aug. 10, 1951; s. Robert L. and Anne M. (Antrum) C.; m. Denise Elena Bolden, July 4, 1976; children: Robert Jr., Elena. AB, Harvard U., 1973; JD and MBA, Stanford U., 1977. Mgmt. cons. McKinsey and Co., N.Y.C., 1976, Am. Mgmt. Systems, Foster City, Calif., 1977-79; adminstrv. mgr. ISD ADPAC Corp., San Francisco, 1979-80; pres., chief exec., fin. officer Avalanche Prodns., Inc., Palo Alto, Calif., 1980-83, PRIMS, Inc., Redwood City, Calif., 1984-86, PSMG, Inc., Palo Alto, 1986—; prin. RBC and Assocs., 1974—; bd. dirs., chief exec. officer RBC Acquisitions Corp., 1982—, Palo Alto. Dir. St. Elizabeth Seton Sch. bd., Palo Alto, 1984-87, chmn. fin., 1985-88; bd. dirs. Palo Alto YMCA, 1988—; asst. coach Palo Alto Little League, 1986—, 87, 88; coach Little League Basketball, 1987-88; fundraiser YMCA, 1988. Phillip Morris fellow Stanford Grad. Sch. Bus., 1975; recipient numerous other acad. awards. Mem. Nat. Assn. Corp. Dirs., Stanford Bus. Sch. Alumni Assn., Nat. Tech. Assn. (Achievement award for Excellence in Tech. Mgmt. 1987), Fundraising Exhibitors Assn. (steering com. 1987-88). Democrat. Baptist. Office: PSMG Inc 2124 Clarke Ave Palo Alto CA 94303

COLGIN, RUSSELL WEYMOUNT, clinical psychologist, consultant screenwriter, producer; b. Ontonagon, Mich., May 10, 1925; s. Russell W. and Signe E. (Peterson) C.; divorced; children—Dennis, Russell, Marc, Kevin, Sean, Siobhan. B.S., Lake Forest Coll., 1949, M.A., 1950; Ph.D., Northwestern U., 1953. Cert. clin. psychologist, Calif. Psychologist VA Hosp., Downey, Ill., 1949; asst. prof. Lake Forest Coll. (Ill.), 1950-53; asst. prof. North Park Coll., Chgo., 1951-53; pvt. practice clin. psychology, 1953—; cons. to Big Bros. of Los Angeles 1965-78, Midtown Sch., Los Angeles, 1968-78; instr. Los Angeles State U., Northridge, 1965-66; producer, chmn. bd. Star Cinema Prodns., Hollywood, Calif., 1980—; screenwriter, co-producer, dir., second unit, Nightforce. Served with USN, 1942-45. Mem. Am. Psychol. Assn., Los Angeles County Psychol. Assn., AAUP, Los Angeles World Affairs Council, Sigma Xi. Club: Rotary of Los Angeles. Contbr. articles to profl. jours.; screenwriter Young Warriors, 1982. Office: 648 N Doheny Dr Los Angeles CA 90069

COLIN, GEORGIA TALMEY, interior designer; b. Boston; d. George Nathan and Rose (Broad) Talmey; m. Ralph Frederick Colin, June 2, 1931 (dec.); children—Ralph Frederick, Pamela Talmey Colin Harlech. Student Smith Coll., 1928, U. Genoble (France), 1927. Co-ptnr., Talmey Inc., Interior Designers, N.Y.C., 1928-54, pres., 1954—. Sec. Young Peoples Concert Com. of N.Y. Philharmonic Soc., 1940-49; mem. vis. com. Smith Coll. Mus. Art, 1951-70, chmn., 1954-57; bd. counselors Smith Coll., 1954-57. Mem. Am. Inst. Interior Designers, Decorators Club, Nat. Soc. Interior Designers, Am. Soc. Interior Designers. Home and Office: 941 Park Ave New York NY 10028

COLLADO, EMILIO GABRIEL, energy company executive, consultant; b. Cranford, N.J., Dec. 20, 1910; s. Emilio Gabriel and Carrie (Hansee) C.; m. Janet Gilbert, June 30, 1932 (dec.); children: Emilio Gabriel, Lisa; m. Maria Elvira Tanco, Oct. 6, 1972. Student, Phillips Acad., Andover, Mass., 1925-27; S.B., Mass. Inst. Tech., 1931; A.M., Harvard, 1934, Ph.D., 1936. With printing and pub. firm 1931; econ. analyst U.S. Treasury Dept., 1934-36; economist Fed. Res. Bank N.Y., 1936-38; with Dept. State, 1938-46; asst. chief div. Am. Republics, 1940, spl. asst. to under sec. state, 1941-44; exec. sec. Bd. Econ. Operations, 1941-43, asso. adviser internat. econ. affairs, 1943-44, chief div. financial and monetary affairs, 1944-45; dir. Office Fin. and Devel. Policy, also dep. to asst. sec. for econ. affairs, 1945-46; U.S. exec. dir. Internat. Bank for Reconstrn. and Devel., 1946-47; trustee Export-Import Bank, Washington, 1944-45; with Exxon Corp., 1947-75, asst. treas., 1949-54, treas., 1954-60, dir., 1960-75, v.p., 1962-66, exec. v.p., 1966-75; pres., chief exec. officer Adela Investment Co. S.A., 1976-79; also dir.; chmn., chief exec. officer, dir. Grace Geothermal Corp., 1981-84, dir., cons., 1984—; chmn., dir. Internat. Planning Corp., 1981-84; mem. adv. council Morgan Guaranty Trust Co. N.Y.; U.S. alt. mem. Inter-Am. Fin. and Econ. Adv. Com., 1939-46; bd. dirs. Collado Assocs. Former chmn. vis. com. Sch. Pub. Health, Harvard U.; bd. visitors Fletcher Sch. Internat. Diplomacy; trustee, chmn. Com. Econ. Devel., 1972-75; trustee Hispanic Soc.; past chmn. Ctr. for Inter-Am. Relations; bd. dirs. emeritus Ams. Soc., Work in Am. Inst.; bd. govs., exec. com. Atlantic Inst. Internat. Affairs. Mem. USA/BIAC, bus. and industry adv. com., OECD (former chmn.), Am. Acad. Arts and Scis., Am. Econ. Assn., Internat. C. of C. (mem. exec. com. U.S. council internat. bus.), Atlantic Council U.S. (past vice chmn.), Acad. Polit. Sci. (past chmn.), Council Fgn. Relations, Phi Mu Delta. Clubs: Met. (Washington); Piping Rock, Racquet and Tennis, River. Home: 130 Shu Swamp Rd Locust Valley NY 11560 Office: 1 Rockefeller Plaza New York NY 10020

COLLARD, EUGENE ALBERT, clergyman, publisher; b. Liège, Belgium, July 1, 1915; s. Jules Marie and Eugenie Marie (Deronchêne) C. Student philosophy and theology Diocesan Sem., Tournai, Belgium, 1933-40; D.C.L., Université Catholique de Louvain (Belgium), 1942, diploma in Social and Polit. Scis., 1943. Ordained priest Roman Catholic Ch., 1940. Curator, Our Lady Parish, Farciennes, Belgium, 1942-44; dir. media orgn. Diocese of Tournai, Mons, Belgium, 1945—; pub. weekley Dimanche, Mons, 1946—; lectr. sociology of religion Université Catholique de Louvain, 1951-80; dir. Instituto Pastoral Conf. dos Bispos do Northeast Brazil, Natal, 1964-65. Mem. M.N.B. (resistance orgn.), occupied Belgium, 1943-44. Served with Belgian Health Service, 1937, 39-40. Decorated chevalier de l'Ordre de Leopold, Belgium, 1956; hon. canon Diocese of Tournai, 1965. Mem. Union des Editeurs de la Presse Périodique Belge (adminstr., pres. 1974-75). Roman Catholic. Home: Place de Vannes 19, B 7000 Mons, Hainaut Belgium Office: Dimanche, Place de Vannes 20, B 7000 Mons, Hainaut Belgium

COLLAS, JUAN GARDUÑO, JR., lawyer; b. Manila, Apr. 25, 1932; s. Juan D. and Soledad (Garduño) C.; m. Maria L. Moreira, Aug. 1, 1959; children: Juan Jose, Elias Lopes, Cristina Maria, Daniel Benjamin. LL.B., U. of Philippines, Quezon City, 1955; LL.M., Yale U., 1958, J.S.D., 1959. Bar: Philippines 1956, Ill. 1960, Calif. 1971, U.S. Supreme Ct. 1967. Assoc., Sy Cip, Salazar & Assocs., Manila, 1956-57; atty. N.Y., N.H. & H. R.R., New Haven, 1959-60; assoc. Baker & McKenzie, Chgo., 1960-63, ptnr., Manila, 1963-70, San Francisco, 1970—. Contbr. articles to profl. jours. Trustee, sec. Friends of U. of Philippines Found. in Am., San Francisco, 1982; co-chmn. San Francisco Lawyers for Better Govt., 1982—; chmn. San Francisco-Manila Sister City Com., 1986—. Recipient Outstanding Filipino Overseas in Law award, Philippine Ministry Tourism Philippines Jaycees, 1979. Mem. ABA, Am. Arbitration Assn. (panelist), Ill. Bar Assn., State Bar Calif., Integrated Bar of Philippines, Filipino-Am. C. of C. (bd. dirs. 1974—, pres. 1985-87, chmn. bd. dirs. 1987—). Republican. Roman Catholic. Clubs: World Trade, Commercial (San Francisco). Office: Baker & McKenzie Two Embarcadero Ctr Suite 2400 San Francisco CA 94111

COLLEN, DÉSIRÉ J., medical educator; b. Sint-Truiden, Belgium, June 21, 1943; s. Frans Collen and Maria Hoebrechs; m. Louisa Reniers, July 14, 1966; children: Ann, Peter, Christine. MD, U. Leuven, Belgium, 1968, PhD in Chemistry, 1974; Doctor honoris causa, Erasmus U., Rotterdam, The Netherlands, 1988. Resident in internal medicine U. Leuven, Belgium, 1968-71, docent, 1976-81, prof. medicine, 1982—; investigator Nat. Fund for Scientific Research, Leuven, Belgium, 1968-75; prof. biochemistry and medicine U. Vermont, 1985—; vis. prof. medicine Harvard U., 1987—; dir. research team Ctr. for Thrombosis and Vascular Research U. Leuven, 1975—. Contbr. articles, research papers and revs. to profl. jours. Recipient Francqui Found. award, Brussels, 1984, Louis Jeantet de Medecine Found. prize, Geneva, 1986. Mem. Internat. Soc. on Thrombosis and Haemostasis. Office: Univ of Leuven, Oude Markt 13, B-3000 Leuven Belgium

COLLER, GARY HAYES, osteopathic physician, surgical specialist; b. Detroit, June 5, 1952; s. Eldon Hayes and Shirley Elaine (Makima) C.; m. Mary Elaine Irrer, Oct. 15, 1977; children—Christopher, Michael, Kimberly, Jonathon. B.S. with honors, Mich. State U., 1974, D.O., 1978. Diplomate Nat. Bd. Examiners for Osteopathic Medicine. Gen. practice osteopathic medicine, Montague, Mich., 1979—; mem. staff Muskegon (Mich.) Gen. Hosp.; trainee in preventive medicine Farmington (Mich.) Med. Center. Mem. Nat. Republican Com., 1975-83. Mem. Am. Osteo. Assn., W. Mich. Osteo. Assn., Mich. Osteo. Assn., Am. Acad. Med. Preventics, Internat. Acad. Preventive Medicine, Northwest Acad. Preventive Medicine, Am. Soc. Gen. Laser Surgeons, N.Y. Acad. Scis., Christian Med. Soc., Nat. Health Service Corp., U.S. C. of C. Contbr. articles on osteopathy to profl. jours. Home: 1424 Waukazoo Holland MI 49424 Office: 9883 US 31 N Montague MI 49437

COLLET, BERNT JOHAN, government official, economist; b. Copenhagen, Denmark, Nov. 23, 1941; s. Harald Collet. Student, various agrl. insts., Denmark. Mem. Folketing, Denmark, 1981—; minister of def. Denmark, 1987-88. Office: care Ministry of Def, Copenhagen Denmark *

COLLETT, BARRY, historian, educator; b. Melbourne, Australia, June 11, 1934; s. Leonard Frederick and Ruth (Binns) C.; m. Pauline Simpson, Dec. 16, 1960; children: Katrina, Gabrielle, Naomi, Christopher, Danielle. BA with honors, Melbourne U., 1956, MA, 1963; TSTC, Melbourne State Coll., 1969; DPhil, U. Oxford, 1985. Cons. UNESCO, Australia, 1956-61; freelance bus. agt. Eng., 1961-64; tchr. Reading (Eng.) Edn. Authority, 1964-69; lectr. history Melbourne Coll. Advanced Edn., 1970—; dep. chmn. history examiner Victorian Inst. Secondary Edn., Melbourne, 1984—. Author: Pictorial History of Australia, 1975, Italian Benedictine Scholars and the Reformation, 1985. Research grantee Gladys Delmas Krieble Found., 1980, Australian Research Grants Council, 1986, 87, 88. Office: Melbourne Coll Advanced Edn, 757 Swanston St, 3053 Carlton Australia

COLLIER, BOYD DEAN, finance educator, management consultant; b. Waco, Tex., Jan. 16, 1938; s. Denis Lee and Anne Alice (Berry) C.; m. Barbara Nell Joseph, June 20, 1966; children: Diedra Michelle, Christopher Boyd. BBA, Baylor U., Waco, 1963, MS, 1965; PhD, U. Tex., 1970. CPA, Tex. Asst. prof. Sch. Bus. and Econs., U. N.C., Greensboro, 1969-72, asst. dean, 1970-72; assoc. prof. Coll. Bus. Adminstrn., U. Houston, 1972-73; chief ops. auditor Glastron Boat Co., Austin, Tex., 1973; prof. bus. econs., dean Ctr. for Bus. Adminstrn., St. Edward's U., Austin, 1974-83; prof. fin., head dept. acctg. and fin. Tarleton State U., Stephenville, Tex., 1983—; co-owner Vranich, Collier Co., CPA's, Austin, 1974-83; v.p. fin. Execucom Systems, Austin, 1979; sr. lectr. U. Tex., Austin, 1980-83; bd. dirs. Acctg. Info. Systems, Houston, 1974-78; advisor Office of Atty. Gen., State of Tex., Austin, 1986, Office of Comptroller, State of Tex., Austin, 1986. Author: Measurement and Environmental Deterioration, 1971; editorial advisor Jour. Accountancy, N.Y.C., 1982-87; contbr. articles to profl. jours. Faculty advisor Coll. Reps. of Tex., Stephenville, 1984—. Served with USN, 1955-59. Fellow Earhart Found., Ann Arbor, Mich., 1963, 68, NSF, Washington, 1966. Mem. Nat. Acctg. Assn. (v.p. 1978-83, Outstanding Service award 1983), Am. Acctg. Assn., Am. Inst. CPA's, Tex. Soc. CPA's, Southwestern Fin. Assn., U. Tex. at Austin Ex-Students Assn. (life). Baptist. Avocations: tennis, hiking, collecting coins, collecting walking canes. Home: 930 Charlotte St Stephenville TX 76401 Office: Tarleton State U 1603 W Washington Stephenville TX 76402

COLLIER, FELTON MORELAND, architect; b. Bessemer, Ala., Mar. 20, 1924; s. Felton and Grace (Moreland) C.; m. Elizabeth Pettus Buck, Oct. 22, 1955 (dec. June 1966); children: Felton Moreland, Marcus Ashby Moreland. Student, Birmingham-So. Coll., 1942-43, Howard Coll. (now Samford U.), 1943; B.A., U. N.C., 1945; postgrad., N.C. State U., 1948-50; B.Arch., Auburn U., 1954; certificate, Nat. War Coll., 1963, Naval War Coll., 1964, Armed Forces Staff Coll., 1966. Archtl. experience with firms in Birmingham, Ala. and Durham, N.C., 1949-51, 54-57; architect Felton Moreland Collier, Birmingham, 1958—, Felton Moreland Collier and Carroll C. Harmon (Asso. Architects), Birmingham, 1965—; chmn. bd. Harmon, Collier, Bondurant Assos., Inc., Architects/Planners/Designers, 1977-84, Harmon, Collier Assocs., Inc., 1984—; dir. Stereo Components, Inc., Birmingham, chmn. bd., 1974-84; dir., sec.-treas. Bourgeois, Collier, Harmon & Co., Inc., 1974-84; chmn. bd. Regent Townhomes, Inc., 1979-84; ptnr. Collier-Traylor Properties, 1985-87, proprietor, 1987—; chief lectr. Naval Res. Officers Sch. Birmingham, 1957-69; mem. U.S. Cultural exchange del. architects to, USSR, 1973. Prin. works include McAlpine Community Center; new campus, Daniel Payne Coll., Spain Park, Birmingham Zoo 10 year master plan, entrance bldg. and children's zoo, Magnolia Park, Episc. Cathedral Ch. of Advent Parish House, U. Ala. Diabetes Hosp. (asso. with Carroll C. Harmon), all Birmingham, other recreational, ednl., med. and comml. projects; lit. editor Ala. Architect, 1969-70; editor: AIA/DATA, 1976-79; contbr. articles to recreational and archtl. jours.; surveyor Caribbean recreational facilities, 1969, 72, 79; photographer ancient Greek monuments, architecture, Agean Islands, Crete, Malta, 1974. Democratic primary candidate Ala. Ho. Reps., 1970; bd. dirs. Ala. Zool. Soc., 1975-78, Advent Episcopal Day Sch., 1977-86; pub. mem. U.ALA.-Birmingham Univ. Coll. Senate, 1977-78, 79-80; v.p. Redmont Neighborhood Assn., Birmingham, 1984-86; mem. Birmingham Zoning Bd. Adjustment, 1977—. Served with USNR, 1945-46, PTO, ETO; to lt. 1951-53, Korea; lt. comdr. Res. Recipient Regional Merit award A.I.A., 1962, Honor award Birmingham chpt. A.I.A., 1965, 81. Mem. A.I.A. (founding mem., sec. Birmingham chpt. 1963-64, v.p. 1966), Explorers Club, Alpha Tau Omega. Episcopalian (lay reader, vestryman 1969-71, 75-77, 81-83, parish architect 1977-85). Home: 2223 20th Ave S Birmingham AL 35223 Office: 1623 S 21st St Birmingham AL 35205

COLLIER, HELEN VANDIVORT, counseling psychologist; b. Nagpur, India; d. William Boardley and Stephena Ruth (Hecker) C.; children—Keith Vandivort, Daniel Vandivort . AB Ohio Wesleyan U., 1950; MEd U. Toledo, 1968, EdD 1974; post grad. San Diego Gestalt Tng. Ctr. Lic. psychologist, Ohio, marriage and family therapist, Nev. tchr. elem. schs., Itasca, Ill., 1950-53; ednl. cons. Toledo Bd. Edn., 1960-67; elem. counselor Toledo Pub. Schs., 1968; counseling psychologist, asst. prof. U. Toledo, 1968-74; pvt. practice psychotherapy and counseling cons., Bloomington, Ind., 1974—; asst. dir. adult counseling project Sch. Continuing Studies Ind. U., Bloomington, 1975-76, Ctr. for Study of Human Mobility; research assoc. Ctr. for Human of Human Mobility, Ind. U., 1974-75, cons., adj. faculty, 1976-80; dir. HVC Assocs.; ptnr. Nat. Ct. Services, Inc., Reno; adj. faculty Nat. Jud. Coll., Reno; cons. orgnl. devel. Author: Free Ourselves: Removing Internal Barriers to Equality, 1979, Counseling Women: A Guide for Therapists, 1982; Co-editor: Meeting the Educational and Occupational Planning Needs of Adults, 1975. Contbr. articles to jours. Women's Ednl. Equity Act Office of Edn. grantee, 1977—. Mem. Am. Psychol. Assn., Am. Assn. Marriage and Family Therapists.

COLLIER, MICHAEL THOMAS, news agency executive; b. N.Y.C., Oct. 17, 1950; s. Patrick and Eileen (Casey) C. BA, Hunter Coll., 1975. Dir. Riverdale Protection Group, N.Y.C., 1975-77; supr. cen. services B'nai Jeshurun Community Ctr., N.Y.C., 1975-76; pres. M.T.C.'s News Agy., Phila., 1976—; chief exec. officer M.T.C., 1978—; chmn. Grams Unltd., Inc., 1982. Active Nationalities Service Ctr., ednl. services, Phila., 1979; mem. Mus. Nat. History. Mem. AAAS, N.Y. Acad. Sci., Geog. Soc. Phila. Club: Vanderbilt Athletic. Address: PO Box 1733 Murray Hill Sta New York NY 10156

COLLIER, NATHAN MORRIS, musician, music educator; b. Clinton, Okla., July 23, 1924; s. Lotan Morris and Annie Carlletta (Willsey) C.; m. Frances Aleta Snell, June 24, 1955; children—Susan Aleta Kowalski, Ray Morris. Mus.B., U. Okla., 1949; Mus.M., Eastman Sch. Music, U. Rochester, 1951. String music cons. Lincoln (Nebr.) Pub. Schs., 1951-68; asst. concertmaster Lincoln Symphony Orch., 1953—; assoc. concertmaster Omaha (Nebr.) Symphony, 1977-78, first violin, 1956-79; first violinist Lincoln String Quartet, 1951—; concertmaster Lincoln Symphony, Lincoln Little Symphony, 1977-78; asst. prof. violin and theory Nebr. Weslyan U., Lincoln, 1968-84; now string tchr. St. John Luth. Sch., Seward, Nebr., vis. instr. music Concordia Tchrs. Coll., Seward, 1985; asst. concertmaster Nebr. Chamber Orch., 1973—, acting concertmaster on occasion; guest prin. violinist Des Moines Symphony, 1979, 87, guest violinist, violist, 1985—; with the Met. String Quartet, Omaha, 1988—; asst. prof. music Kans. State U., Manhattan, 1980-81, condr. symphony orch., 1980-81; pvt. tchr. and ensemble coach, Lincoln, 1951—; cons., lectr. in field, arranger of numerous compositions for string quartet 1980—; mem. adv. bd. Rocky Ridge Music Ctr., 1972—. Tchr., co-organizer Brownville (Nebr.) Summer Music Festival, 1972-77. Served with USN, 1943-46. U.S. Govt. grantee 1966-67. Mem. Am. String Tchrs. Assn., Music Tchrs. Nat. Assn., Music Educators Nat. Conf., Violin Soc. Am., Lincoln Music Tchrs. Assn., Nat. Sch. Orch. Assn., NEA, Nebr. State Edn. Assn., Lincoln Musicians Assn., Omaha Musicians Assn., Internat. Soc. of Bassists. Democrat. Methodist. Composer various musical pieces. Home: 4544 Mohawk Lincoln NE 68510

COLLIER, WILLIAM JEWELL, physician; b. Albany, Mo., Apr. 25, 1925; s. Ora and Mabel (Adkisson) C.; B.S., Tulane U., 1947; M.D., Bowman Gray Sch. Medicine, Wake Forest U., 1949; m. Mary Evelyn Fisher, Mar. 29, 1952; children—William Jewell II, Sherry Lynn, Terri Lee, Linda Lorraine. Intern, U.S. Naval Hosp., Great Lakes, Ill., 1949-50; resident internal medicine VA Hosp., Wadsworth, Kans., 1950-51, resident gen. surgery, 1951-52, 54-57; asst. chief surgery VA Hosp., Wichita, Kans., 1957-58; pvt. practice gen. and thoracic surgery, McPherson, Kans., 1958—. Dir. Home State Bank & Trust. Former mem. aviation adv. bd. McPherson City-County Airport. Served from lt. (j.g.) to lt. M.C., USNR, 1952-54. Diplomate Am. Bd. Surgery. Fellow Southwestern Surg. Congress, ACS, Internat. Coll. Surgeons; mem. C. of C. Mem. Christian Ch. Rotarian. Home: 302 S Walnut St McPherson KS 67460 Office: 400 W 4th St McPherson KS 67460

COLLINGE, NEVILLE EDGAR, linguist, educator; b. Manchester, Eng., Dec. 18, 1921; s. Edgar Thomas and Constance Mabel (Vallintine) C.; m. Mildred Elizabeth Owen, Aug. 31, 1949; children: Thomas, Anna. BA, U. Manchester, 1942, MA, Cambridge U., Eng., 1952, PhD, 1967. Lectr. to sr. lectr. classics U. Durham, Eng., 1947-69; prof. classics, linguistics U. Toronto, Ont., Can., 1969-74; prof. linguistics U. Birmingham, Eng., 1974-79; prof. comparative philology U. Manchester, 1980-87, prof. emeritus, 1987—. Author: The Structure of Horace's Odes, 1961, Collectanea Linguistica, 1970, The Laws of Indo-European, 1985; contbr. numerous articles to linguistic jours. Served to capt. Brit. Army, 1941-45. Decorated Mil. Cross. Mem. Linguistic Soc. Am., Can. Linguistic Assn., Linguistics Assn. Gt. Britain (chmn. 1962-65), Philol. Soc., Societas Linguistica Europaea (pres. 1984-85). Office: U Manchester, Manchester M13 9PL, England

COLLINS, CHARLES EDWARD, real estate appraising company executive; b. Lancaster, Pa., Dec. 27, 1906; s. Hugh R. and Catherine (Edwards) C.; 1 child, Shirley Collins Rutz. B.S. in Edn., Temple U.; student Wagner Inst. Sci. With S.S. Kresge Co., N.Y.C., 1930-46; sec. YMCA, Orange, N.J. and Lancaster, Pa., 1946-50; owner-operator Coll. Real Estate Sch., Las Vegas, Nev.; pres. Bond Realty, Las Vegas, 1957—. Chmn., North Las Vegas Planning Commn., 1965; pres. Citizens Adv. Com. for Las Vegas Transp. Mem. Internat. Inst. Valuers (sr.), Internat. Orgn. Real Estate Appraisers, Nat. Assn. Rev. Appraisers, Am. Assn. Cert. Appraisers, Am. Soc. Appraisers (pres. Las Vegas chpt. 1964-65), Am. Coll. Real Estate Cons., Las Vegas Bd. Realtors (pres. 1956-57). Republican. Presbyterian. Club: Las Vegas University (pres. 1985). Home: 1921 Canosa Ave Las Vegas NV 89104 Office: Bond Realty 522 E Saint Louis St Las Vegas NV 89104

COLLINS, HARKER, economist, publisher, financial and business consultant; b. Denver, Nov. 24, 1924; s. Clem Wetzel and Marie (Harker) C.; m. Emily Harvey, Aug. 23, 1957; children: Catherine Emily, Cynthia Lee, Constance Marie. B.S., U.S. Naval Acad., 1945. Asst. buyer Montgomery Ward & Co., N.Y.C., 1947-51; prodn. mgr. Diamond Hosiery Mills, High Point, N.C., 1953-55; v.p. Vanette Hosiery Mills, Dallas, 1955-59; v.p., dir. Grote Mfg. Co., Madison, Ind., 1959-71; group v.p., gen. mgr. Bendix Corp., South Bend, Ind., 1971-73; pres., dir. Bandag, Inc., Muscatine, Iowa, 1973-78; chief exec. officer Bandag, Inc., 1974-78; pres., chief exec. officer Harker Collins & Co., 1978—, also dir.; dir. Mid-Am. Industries, Inc.; pub. newsletter The Economy and You, Update, 1978—; dir. CEO Internat. Inc., 1986-87; instr. U. Denver, 1948; Bd. dirs. Hwy. Users Fedn., 1970-86; chmn. automotive industry liaison com. with Dept. Transp., 1968-86, automotive industry excise tax com., 1964-70, automotive industry tariff com., 1964-70, joint operating com. for automotive trade shows, 1969-77. Mem. Pres.'s Com. Hwy. Safety, 1966-68; Bd. dirs. Iowa Ind. Coll. Found., 1976-86; bd. fellows Northwood Inst., 1974—; alderman City of Rancho Viejo, Tex., 1980-87. Served to ensign USN, 1945-47; to lt. USNR, 1951-53. Recipient Automotive Industry Leadership award, 1965, 74; Fin. World award as chief exec. of yr., 1975, 77. Mem. Automotive Service Industry Assn. (v.p. 1966-67, pres. 1968-69, dir. heavy duty exec. com. 1969-71, chmn. safety and environ. protection com. 1962-67, 70-78), Automotive Sales Council (dir. 1966-67, sec. 1971-72, v.p. 1972-73, pres. 1973-74), Am. Nat. Standards Inst. (chmn. task force on used vehicle standards 1966-74), Home Products Safety Council (pres. 1960-63), Medicine Cabinet Mfg. Council (pres. 1960-63, dir. 1960-68), Truck Safety Equipment Inst. (pres. 1960-63, dir. 1960-68), Internat. Platform Assn., Muscatine C. of C. (dir. 1975-78). Clubs: Rotary, 33 Club (treas. 1977-78). Office: Tex Commerce Tower Suite 200 545 E Carpenter Freeway Irving TX 75062

COLLINS, HARRY DAVID, mechanical engineer, consultant, retired army officer; b. Brownsville, Pa., Nov. 18, 1931; s. Harry Alonzo and Cecelia Victoria (Morris) C.; B.S. in Mech. Engring., Carnegie Mellon U., 1954; M.S., U.S. Naval Postgrad. Sch., 1961; postgrad. George Washington U., 1971-72; m. Suzanne Dylong, May 11, 1956; children—Cynthia L., Gerard P. Commd. 2d lt. C.E., U.S. Army, 1954, advanced through grades to lt. col. 1969; comdr. 802d Heavy Engr. Constrn. Bn., Korea, 1972-73; dep. dist. engr. and acting dist. engr. Army Engr. Dist., New Orleans, 1973-75; ret., 1975; v.p. deLaureal Engrs., Inc., New Orleans, 1975-78; v.p. Near East mktg. Kidde Cons., Inc., 1978-82; dir. new bus. devel. for Middle East, Am. Middle East Co., Inc., 1982-84; sr. cons. Wagner, Hohns, Inglis, Inc., 1984—. Decorated Legion of Merit, Bronze Star, Meritorious Service medal; registered profl. engr., Miss., La. Mem. ASME, Am. Soc. Mil. Engrs., La. Engring. Soc., N.Y. Acad. Sics., NSPE, Am. Nuclear Soc., AAA, Internat. Platform Assn., Sigma Xi. Home: 2024 Audubon St New Orleans LA 70118

COLLINS, JAMES WILLIAM, lawyer; b. Chgo., Dec. 10, 1942; s. Martin Joseph and Elen (Boyle) C.; m. Laura Ann Geraty, June 29, 1968; children: James R., Martin R. AB, Marquette U., 1964; JD, Loyola U., Chgo., 1967. Bar: Ill. 1968, U.S. Supreme Ct. 1972. Assoc. Boodell, Sears, Chgo., 1969-73, ptnr., 1973-87; ptnr. Bell, Boyd & Lloyd, Chgo., 1987—; bd. dirs. Frantz Mfg. Co., Sterling, Ill.; asst. spl. state atty. State of Ill., Chgo., 1971-72. Sec., Terra Mus. Am. Art, Chgo., 1982—. Served to sgt. USMC, 1967-70. Mem. ABA, Chgo. Bar Assn., Econ. Club, Legal Club. Roman Catholic. Club: Union League (Chgo.). Home: 9345 N Hamlin Evanston IL 60203 Office: Bell Boyd & Lloyd 70 W Madison St Chicago IL 60602

COLLINS, JOAN HENRIETTA, actress; b. London, May 3, 1933; came to U.S., 1954; d. Joseph William and Elsa (Bessant) C.; m. Ronald S. Kass, Mar., 1972 (div.); 1 child, Katie; m. Anthony Newley (div.); children: Cynara, Sacha; m. Peter Holm, 1985 (div.). Films include: I Believe in You, Girl in the Red Velvet Swing, Rally Round the Flag Boys, Island in the Sun, Seven Thieves, Road to Hong Kong, Sunburn, The Stud, Game for Vultures, The Bitch, The Big Sleep, The Good Die Young, 1954, Land of the Pharoahs, 1955, The Bravados, 1958, Esther and the King, 1960, Warning Shot, 1967, The Executioner, 1970, Tales from the Crypt, The Bawdy Adventures of Tom Jones, 1975; theater appearance in The Last of Mrs. Cheyney; TV films include: The Man Who Came to Dinner, The Moneychanger, Paper Dolls, The Wild Women of Chastity Gulch, The Cartier Affair, The Making of a Male Model, Her Life as a Man; miniseries: Sins, Monte Carlo; star TV series: Dynasty, 1981—; author: Past Imperfect (autobiography), 1978, Katy, A Fight for Life, Joan Collins Beauty Book, Spare Time. Recipient Emmy award, Golden Globe award. *

COLLINS, JOANNE ANITA, accounting educator; b. Chgo., Aug. 2, 1946; d. Elmer and Lucille Ann (Dombrowski) C. BS in Math., Ill. Inst. Tech., 1968, MBA, 1970; PhD in Acctg., Northwestern U., 1976. CPA, Ill.; cert. mgmt. acct.; cert. cost analyst; cert. tax acct. Mem. staff EDP ops. Internat. Harvester, 1965-70; instr. Ill. Inst. Tech., Chgo., 1969-73; fin. analyst Continental Can Co., 1970-73; econ. analyst Sargent & Lundy, 1973; asst. prof. acctg. Wharton Sch., U. Pa., Phila., 1976-82; prof. acctg. Calif. State U., Los Angeles, 1982—; cons. in field. Contbr. articles to profl. jours. Recipient Alumni award Ill. Inst. Tech., 1968; Legion of Honor, Chapel of Four Chaplains, 1980. Mem. Am. Acctg. Assn., Am. Inst. CPA's, Nat. Assn. Accts. (Author of Yr. Los Angeles chpt. 1983-85), Inst. Mgmt. Acctg., Am. Women's Soc. of CPA's (charter mem. Los Angeles chpt.), Am. Soc. Women Accts., ACLU, Calif. Soc. CPA's, Mensa, Beta Alpha Psi, Phi Eta Sigma, Sigma Iota Epsilon, Beta Gamma Sigma. Democrat. Unitarian-Universalist. Home: 8328 Rush St Rosemead CA 91770 Office: Calif State U 5151 State University Dt Los Angeles CA 90032

COLLINS, JOHN JOSEPH, telecommunications executive; b. Syracuse, N.Y., Dec. 9, 1921; s. Joseph John and Mildred Catherine (Hummel) C.; student Syracuse U., 1940-41; B.S., U.S. Naval Acad., 1945; m. Phyllis Duran Reed, July 5, 1947 (dec. July 1985); children—Cynthia Collins Peters, Priscilla Collins O'Hara. With N.Y. Telephone Co., 1947-60, asst. v.p. personnel, to 1960; plant ext. engr. AT&T, 1960-62; gen. plant mgr. N.Y. Telephone Co., L.I., 1962-64, chief engr.-L.I., 1964-66, asst. v.p.-bldgs., 1966-78, gen. mgr. bldg. mgmt. and constrn., 1978-84; gen. mgr. bldg. mgmt. NYNEX-N.Y. Telephone Co., 1984-85, gen. mgr. corp. support services, 1985, ret., 1985; v.p. Cushman & Wakefield, Inc., 1986—; mem. L.I. adv. bd. Bank of N.Y., 1981—; life mem. N.Y. Bldg. Congress. Mayor, Village of Roslyn Harbor (N.Y.), 1976—; mem., pres. North Shore Sch. Bd., Glen Head, N.Y., 1960-69. Served with USN, 1945-47. Named Man of Year, Talbot Perkins Children's Services, 1972; recipient Pyramid award N.Y.C. chpt. Soc. Mktg. Profl. Services, 1982; D. Russel Harlow award Building Contractors Assn., 1983; named Master of Ceremonies Flag Day Parade-S.R., Downtown Lower Manhattan Assn., N.Y.C., 1987. Mem. IEEE, Real Estate Bd. N.Y., N.Y. Building Congress Council of Pres. (chmn. 1976-83), Council of Bus. and Labor for Econ. Devel. (chmn. 1984-86), N.Y.C. Con strn. Users Council, Building Industry Employers of N.Y. State (dir., chmn. assoc. membership com. 1972), Downtown Lower Manhattan Assn. (dir., exec. com. 1977—), Assn. for Better N.Y. (mem. exec. com. 1972—). Republican. Episcopalian. Clubs: Club at World Trade Ctr. (N.Y.C.); North Hempstead Country (Port Washington, N.Y.) (bd. dirs. 1986—). Home: 6 Fairway Rd Roslyn Harbor NY 11576

COLLINS, JOHN PATRICK, oil company executive, lawyer; b. Evanston, Ill., July 5, 1942; s. John Allen and Rosalie Elizabeth (Grossenkemper) C.; m. Gretta O'Connell, June 4, 1974; 1 child, Courtney Ellen. A.B., Marquette U., 1966; J.D., Georgetown U., 1970; LL.M., Harvard U., 1972. Bar: D.C. 1970, Mass. 1972, N.Y. 1975. Vis. prof. Law Sch., Ind. U., Indpls., 1970-71; assoc. Debevoise & Plimpton, N.Y.C., 1973-79; pres., chief exec. officer Plains Resources Inc., Oklahoma City, 1979—. Editor-in-chief Law and Policy in Internat. Bus., 1969-70. Nat. Commn. on Marijuana and Drug Abuse grantee, 1972. Mem. Assn. Bar City N.Y., D.C. Bar Assn. Roman Catholic. Clubs: Union of City N.Y., Racquet and Tennis, Harvard of N.Y.C. (N.Y.C.). Home: 423 Hunterwood Houston TX 77024 Office: Plains Resources Inc 1600 Smith St #1500 Houston TX 77002

COLLINS, KATHLEEN, author; b. Lowell, Mass., Nov. 10, 1953; d. John Joseph and Barbara Ann (McCarthy) Collins. BA, Mich. State U., 1975. Sr. researcher Central States, SE and SW Areas Health and Welfare Fund, Chgo., 1976-79; steward Teamster Local 743, Chgo., 1978-79; tchr. religious edn. Roman Cath. Ch., 1976-77, 81, eucharistic minister, 1985-88; data and info. coordinator, Schooley's Mt., N.J., 1980-84; English lang. tutor for fgn. students Mich. State U., East Lansing, 1971-74, entertainment and movie coordinator, 1972-74. Author: (with Mary E. Collins) A People Worth Saving, 1981, Treasures, 1983, Israel--Destroyed?, 1986, NOW, 1987; co-author, editor booklets. Election judge Democratic Party, Washington Twp., N.J., 1985, election clk., 1984, 85, 86, 87, election inspector 1988; advisor to bd. trustees Mich. State U., 1975. Mem. Internat. Platform Assn. Avocations: ceramic painting, real estate. Home: 57 Nestling Wood Dr Long Valley NJ 07853

COLLINS, MARTHA LAYNE, former governor; b. Shelby County, Ky., Dec. 7, 1936; d. Everett Larkin and Mary Lorena (Taylor) Hall; m. Bill Collins, July 3, 1959; children: Stephen Louis, Marla Ann. Student, Lindenwood Coll.; B.S., U. Ky., 1959. Formerly tchr. Fairdale High Sch., Louisville, Seneca High Sch., Louisville, Woodford County Jr. High Sch., Versailles; former lt. gov. State of Ky., 1979-83, gov., 1983-87; exec. in residence U. Louisville Sch. of Bus., 1988—; pres. Martha Layne Collins & Assocs., Lexington, 1988—; sec. Ky. Edn. and Humanities Cabinet; chmn. Nat. Conf. Lt. Govs., 1982-83, So. Growth Policies Bd., 1986-87, So. Regional Edn. Bd., 1985, Nat. Govs.' Task Force on Drug and Substance Abuse, 1986, So. Growth Policies Bd., 1987; bd. dirs. Eastman-Kodak Co., Inc., Rochester, N.Y., R.R. Donnelley & Sons, Chgo., Bank of Louisville. Mem. Woodford County (Ky.) Democratic Exec. Com.; mem. Dem. Nat. Com., 1972-76; chmn. Dem. Nat. Conv., San Francisco, 1984; former coordinator Women's Activities for State Dem. Hdqrs.; del. Dem. Nat. Conv., Miami, 1972, Mid-term charter Conf., Kansas City, 1974; mem. credentials com. Dem. Nat. Com. Vice Presdl. Selection Process Commn., co-chair credentials com. Dem. Nat. Conv., Atlanta, 1988; Ky. chairwoman 51.3 Com. for Carter, 1976; mem. Ky. Dem. Central Exec. Com.; sec. Ky. Dem. Party; elected clk. Ct. of Appeals, 1975; clk. Supreme Ct. Ky., 1975; past tchr. Sunday sch.; mem. Ky. Commn. on Women; exec. dir. Ky. Friendship Force; mem. Dem. Nat. Com. Policy Commn. and Fairness Commn.; hon. chmn. bd. USO of Ky. Inc.; hon. co-chmn. Parents Against Child Exploitation; mem. adv. bd. Lexington Child Abuse Council; bd. govs. Dream Factory. Mem. So. Gov.'s Assn. (chmn. 1987), Woodford County Jaycee-ettes (past pres.), U. Ky. Alumni Assn., Women's Missionary Union (past pres.), Nat. Conf. Appellate Ct. Clks., Psi Omega Dental Aux. (past pres.). Baptist. Clubs: Bus. and Profl. Women's, Order Eastern Star. Office: PO Box 11890 Lexington KY 40578-1890

COLLINS, MICHAEL, aerospace consultant, former astronaut; b. Rome, Oct. 31, 1930; s. James L. and Virginia (Stewart) C. (parents Am. citizens); m. Patricia M. Finnegan, Apr. 28, 1957; children: Kathleen, Ann Stewart, Michael Lawton. B.S., U.S. Mil. Acad., 1952; grad., Advanced Mgmt. Program, Harvard U., 1974; D.Sc., Northeastern U., 1970, Stonehill Coll., 1970; LL.D., St. Michael's Coll., 1970, Southeastern U., 1975. Commd. officer U.S. Air Force, advanced through grades to col., 1970; fighter pilot, flight comdr. U.S., Europe; exptl. flight test officer (Edwards AFB), Calif.; named astronaut NASA, 1963; astronaut NASA (Gemini 10, 1966); astronaut, space walker, comdr., Command Module pilot NASA (Apollo 11), 1963-69; apptd. asst. sec. state for pub. affairs Washington, 1970-71; dir. Nat. Air and Space Mus., Smithsonian Instn., Washington, 1971-78; undersec. Smithsonian Instn., 1978-80; v.p. LTV Aerospace & Def. Co., 1980-85; pres. Michael Collins Assocs., 1985—; bd. dirs. Rand Corp., Avemco Corp. Author: Carrying the Fire, 1974, Flying to the Moon and Other Strange Places, 1976, Liftoff, 1988. Trustee Nat. Geog. Soc. Decorated D.S.M., D.F.C.; recipient Presdl. Medal of Freedom, NASA Distinguished Service and Exceptional Service medals, Hubbard medal, Collier trophy, Goddard Meml. trophy, Harmon trophy, Gen. Thomas D. White USAF Space trophy, gold space medal Fedn. Aeronautique Internat. Fellow Am. Inst. Aeros. and Astronautics, Am. Astronautical Soc.; mem. Washington Inst. Fgn. Affairs, Soc. Exptl. Test Pilots, Order of Daedalians, Washington Nat. Monument Soc. Clubs: Metropolitan, Alfalfa, Alibi. Office: 4206 48th Place NW Washington DC 20016

COLLINS, MOIRA ANN, graphics and communications company executive, calligrapher; b. Washington, Dec. 16, 1942; d. Peter William and Louise (Carroll) Collins; m. Andrew Joseph Griffin, Aug. 21, 1965; children—Andrew Fitzgerald, Timothy. BA, U. Toronto (Ont., Can.), 1964; MA in Teaching, Northwestern U., 1965; MEd in Urban Studies, Northeastern U., Chgo., 1968. Tchr., Chgo. Bd. Edn., 1965-68; studied with profl. calligraphers, scribes and illuminators, Haystack Mountain Sch., Deer Isle, Maine, 1973, U. Calif. Santa Cruz, 1973-74; freelance calligrapher, 1974-78; mem. publicity and promotional staff Swallow Press, Chgo., 1978-79; owner Letters, Chgo., 1979—; pres. Astrogram, Chgo. 1986. HEW fellow Northeastern U., 1967-68. Author, contbr.; Celebration: Anais Nin, 1975; contbr. to Goodfellow Rev. of Crafts, 1979. Calligrapher: Erotica, 1976, Chgo. Rev., 1978. Chmn. fund-raising Van Gorder Walden Sch., Chgo., 1979-80. Mem. Chgo. Calligraphy Collective (co-founder, chmn. 1976-77, pres. 1978-79, hon. mem.), Soc. Scribes N.Y., Soc. Calligraphers, Soc. Scribes and Illuminators (Eng.), Friends Calligraphy Calif. Democrat. Roman Catholic. Home: 3920 N Lake Shore Dr Apt #9-N Chicago IL 60613 Office: 3600 N Lake Shore Dr Suite 1817 Chicago IL 60613

COLLINS, RALPH EARL, III, fire protection engineering consultant, educator; b. Washington, Dec. 27, 1939; s. Ralph Earl and Marguerite Mary (Scruggs) C.; m. Joan M. Bielaski, Sept. 3, 1960. BS in Engring. Fire Protection, U. Md., 1964. Sr. field engr. Factory Ins. Assn., Phila., 1964-67; asst. mgr., sr. engr. fire protection TWA, Kennedy Space Ctr., Fla., 1967-71; v.p. property loss control Johnson & Higgins, Richmond, Va., 1971-85; exec. v.p., chief operating officer FirePro Inc., Wellesley Hills, Mass., 1985-86; pres. RE Collins Assocs., Needham, Mass., 1987—; adj. faculty fire sci. Valentin Jr. Coll., Orlando, Fla., Brevard Jr. Coll., Cocoa, Fla., John Tyler Community Coll., Chester, Va., J. Sargeant Reynolds Community Coll., Henrico, Va. Sec. Landover Hills, Md. vol. fire dept., Brentwood, Md. vol. fire dept.; pres. Crestwood PTA, 1973; v.p. Chesterfield County Council PTA's; pres. Southham Civic Assn., 1974. Mem. Soc. Fire Protection Engrs. (pres. 1985-87), Am. Soc. Safety Engrs., System Safety Soc., Bldg. Officials and Code Adminstrs., Nat. Fire Protection Assn., Richmond Joint Engrs. Council, Am. Assn. Engring Soc., Va. Fire Prevention Assn., Am. Soc. for Testing Materials. Roman Catholic. Club: Engrs. of Richmond.

COLLINS, THOMAS WILLIAM, caterer, consultant; b. Lewiston, Idaho, Nov. 4, 1926; s. William James and Mary (Egan) C.; m. Mary Charlene Tracy, Aug. 1, 1947 (dec. Apr. 1984); children: Kathleen, William, Charles. Grad. high sch., Staples, Minn., 1944. Owner Collins Cafe, Park Rapids, Minn., 1947-63, Tom Collins Restaurant, Walker, Minn., 1963-83, Tom Collins Catering, Walker, 1983—. Author: Collins Cooking Secrets, 1981. Fundraiser DFL, 1976-83; adv. bd. Lake Country Food Bank, Mpls., 1981-86. Served with USN, 1945-46, 51-52. Tom Collins Day proclaimed Minn. Gov. Rudy Perpich, 1977; recipient Recognition award Mont. Gov. Ted Schwinden, 1978. Mem. Assn. Great Lakes Outdoor Writers, Am. Legion. Lodge: Masons (sr. warden 1958), Shriners. Home and Office: PO Box 33 Walker MN 56484

COLLINS, WILLIAM LEROY, telecommunications engineer; b. Laurel, Miss., June 17, 1942; s. Henry L. and Christene E. (Finnegan) C. Student, La Salle U., 1969; BS in Computer Sci., U. Beverly Hills, 1984. Sr. computer operator Dept. Pub. Safety, Phoenix, 1975-78, data communications specialist, 1978-79, supr. computer ops., 1981-82; mgr. network control Valley Nat. Bank, Phoenix, 1979-81; mgr. data communications Ariz. Lottery, Phoenix, 1982-85; mgr. telecommunications Calif. Lottery, Sacramento, 1985—. Served as sgt. USAF, 1964-68. Mem. Soc. Mfg. Engrs., Data Processing Mgmt. Assn., Am. Mgmt. Assn., Assn. Computing Machinery. Roman Catholic. Lodge: K.C. Home: 610 Howe Ave #44 Sacramento CA 95825 Office: Calif State Lottery 600 N 10th St Sacramento CA 95814

COLLISCHON, ROBERT DAVID, publisher; b. Ilford, Essex, Eng., July 19, 1937; s. Robert Frederick and Vera May (Pilbeam) C.; m. Lesley Elizabeth Chard, Apr. 3, 1965; children: Lois Anne, Hayley Claire, Adrian Robert. Promotion mgr. Collins Pubs., London, 1960-64; sales dir. Studio Vista, London, 1964-69, Collier MacMillan, London, 1969-72; mktg. dir. Gower Press, Epping Essex, 1972-78; chmn., mng. dir. Bowker Pub. Co., Epping Essex, 1978-85, Norman & Hill Ltd., Ilford, Essex, 1980-86, Filofox p.l.c. Illford, 1986—. Author: Furniture Making, 1967. Served with Army, 1956-57. Fellow Inst. Dirs. (London); mem. Inst. Mktg., Worshipful Co. Marketors. Ch. Eng. Clubs: Fairlop Sailing Assn., Groucho (London). Avocations: sailing, gardening, music. Office: Filofax plc, Filofax House Forest Rd, Ilford 1G6 3HP, England

COLLMER, RUSSELL CRAVENER, data processing executive, educator; b. Guatemala, Jan. 2, 1924; s. G. Russell and Constance (Cravener) C.; B.S., U. N.M., 1951; postgrad. Calif. Inst. Tech., 1943-44; M.S., State U. Iowa, 1955; m. Ruth Hannah Adams, Mar. 4, 1950; 1 son, Reed Alan. Staff mem. Mass. Inst. Tech., Lincoln Lab., Lexington, 1955-57; mgr. systems modeling, computer dept. Gen. Electric, Phoenix, 1957-59; mgr. ARCAS Thompson Ramo Wooldridge, Inc., Canoga Park, Cal., 1959-62; asso. mgr. tech. dir. CCIS-70 Bunker-Ramo Corp., 1962-64; sr. asso. Planning Research Corp., Los Angeles, 1964-65; pres. R. Collmer Assos., Benson, Ariz., 1965—; pres. Benson Econ. Enterprises Corp., 1968-69. Lectr. computer scis. Pima Community Coll., Tucson, 1970—. Served with USAAC, 1942-46, to capt. USAF, 1951-53. Mem. IEEE, Am. Meteorol. Soc., Assn. for Computing Machinery, Phi Delta Theta, Kappa Mu Epsilon. Republican. Baptist. Office: PO Box 864 Benson AZ 85602

COLMAN, SIR MICHAEL (JEREMIAH), manufacturing executive; b. July 7, 1928; s. Sir Jeremiah Colman and Edith Gwendolyn Tritton; m. Judith Jean Wallop, 1955; 5 children. Student, Eton Coll., Eng. Bd. dirs. Reckitt and Colman plc, chmn., 1986—; bd. dirs. Trinity House Lighthouse; mem. council Royal Warrant Holders, 1977—, pres., 1984-85; bd. dirs. U.K. Ctr. for Econ. and Environmental Devel., 1985—. Mem. council Scout Assn., 1985—. Served with Brit. mil., 1967. Mem. Chemical Industries Assn. (mem. council 1982-84). Club: Cavalry and Guards. Office: 40 Chester Sq, London SW1, England also: Tarvie, Bridge of Cally, Blairgowrie, Perthshire England *

COLMANT, ANDREW ROBERT, lawyer; b. Bklyn., Oct. 10, 1931; s. Edward J. and Mary Elizabeth (Byrne) C.; m. Anselma DeLuca, Sept. 19, 1959; children: Stephen, Robert, Elizabeth, Carolyn. BBA, St. Johns U., 1957, LLB, 1959. Bar: N.Y. 1959, U.S. Dist. Ct. N.Y. 1959. Assoc. Hill, Rivkins, Carey, Loesberg, O'Brien & Mulroy and predecessor firms, 1959-73, ptnr., 1973—; of counsel Vincent, Berg & Russo, N.Y.C., 1987, McDonald & Hagen, 1987-88, Jerrold E. Hyams, 1988—. Served as cpl. USMC, 1952-54. Mem. ABA, N.Y. State Bar Assn., N.Y. County Lawyers Assn., Maritime Law Assn. Home: 15 Rosemary Dr Hazlet NJ 07730 Office: 90 John St New York NY 10006

COLMER, JOHN ANTHONY, English educator; b. Plymouth, Eng., Oct. 2, 1921; s. Vyvyan and Jessie (Paton) C.; m. Dorothy Mildred Penson, Mar. 2, 1951; children: Rosemary Margaret, Vivienne Mary. MA, Oxford U., 1951; PhD, U. London, 1955. Lectr., sr. lectr. English U. Khartoum (Sudan), 1949-60; research fellow Birmingham (Eng.) U., 1960-61; sr. lectr. English U. Adelaide (Australia), 1961-64, reader, 1964, prof., 1964-86, prof. emeritus, 1986—. Author: Coleridge: Critic of Society, 1959, Coleridge to Catch-22: Images of Society, 1978, E.M. Forster: The Personal Voice, 1975, Patrick White, 1984, The Penguin Book of Australian Autobiography, 1987. Served with Brit. Army, 1941-46, NATOUSA, MTO. Fellow Australian Acad. Humanities; mem. Australasian Univs. Lang. and Lit. Assn., Internat. Assn. Profs. English, English Assn. Club: Royal Commonwealth (London). Home: 4 Everard St, Glen Osmond 5064, Australia

COLMET DAAGE, DIDIER FRANCIS, advertising agency executive; b. Paris, Dec. 14, 1943; s. Jean Pierre and Jeanine (Gastaldi) C.D.; m. Marie Noelle Moulin-Roussel, Sept. 4, 1971; children: Olivia, Laura. MBA, Hautes Études Commercialles, Paris, 1968. With DuPuy-Compton, Neuilly, France, 1969-82; mktg. dir. DuPuy-Compton, Neuilly, 1975-78, dep. mng. dir., 1978-80, mng. dir., 1980-82; chmn., chief exec. officer DuPuy-Saatchi, Neuilly, 1982—; bd. dirs. Saatchi and Saatchi Compton W., Neuilly. Office: DuPuy Saatchii, 30 Blvd Vital Bouhot, 92200 Neuilly France

COLODNY, EDWIN IRVING, airline executive; b. Burlington, Vt., June 7, 1926; s. Myer and Lena (Yett) C.; m. Nancy Dessoff, Dec. 11, 1965; children: Elizabeth, Mark, David. AB, U. Rochester, 1948; LLB, Harvard, 1951. Bar: N.Y. 1951, D.C. 1958. With Office Gen. Counsel, GSA, 1951-52, CAB, 1954-57; with Allegheny Airlines, Inc. (now USAir, Inc.), 1957—, exec. v.p. mktg. and legal affairs, 1969-75; pres., chief exec. officer Allegheny Airlines, Inc. (now USAir Inc.), 1975—, chmn. bd. dirs., 1978—; bd. dirs. PNC Fin. Corp., Martin Marietta Corp. dir. Martin Marietta Corp; mem. bd. trustees U. Rochester. Served to 1st lt. AUS, 1952-54. Recipient James D. McGill Meml. award U. Rochester. Mem. ABA, U.S. C. of C. (bd. dirs.), U. Rochester (bd. trustees).

COLOMBO, FREDERICK J., lawyer; b. Detroit, Dec. 7, 1916; s. Louis J. and Irene Elizabeth (McKinney) C.; m. Frances Elizabeth Fisher, June 12, 1947; children—William, Joan, Richard, John. A.B., U. Mich., 1938, J.D., 1940. Bar: Mich. 1940, U.S. Dist. Ct. (ea. dist.) Mich. 1940, U.S. Ct. Appeals (6th cir.) 1940, U.S. Supreme Ct. 1940. Ptnr., Colombo and Colombo, P.C., Birmingham, Mich., 1945-86, ret. 1986; of counsel, Birmingham, 1987—. Trustee emeritus Harper Grace Hosp., Detroit; chmn. spl. gifts com. United Found.; mem. exec. com. Mich. Republican Party. Mem. ABA, Mich. State Bar Assn., Am. Judicature Soc., Detroit Bar Assn., Oakland County Bar Assn. Roman Catholic. Club: Cardinal (past pres.) (Detroit). Office: Colombo & Colombo 1500 N Woodward Ave Birmingham MI 48009

COLOMBO, GIOVANNI CARDINAL, cardinal, bishop; b. Milan, Dec. 6, 1902. Ordained to priesthood, 1926. Consecrated Titular Bishop of Philli-popolis in Arabia 1960, Archbishop of Milan, 1963-79, created Cardinal, 1965; mem. Com. of the Ecumenical Council on Cath. Sems. and Edn. Address: Corso Venezia 11, 20121 Milan Italy *

COLOMBO, UMBERTO PAOLO, Italian government official; Energy Commn.; b. Livorno, Italy, Dec. 20, 1927; s. Eugenio and Maria (Eminente) C.; Sc.Dr. in Phys. Chemistry, U. Pavia, 1950; Prof. Indsl. Chemistry, U. Genoa, 1964; m. Milena Piperno, July 5, 1951; children—Carla, Claudia. Scientist in phys. chemistry Montecatini's G. Donegani Research Inst., Novara, Italy, 1951-66, dir., 1967-78; Fulbright fellow MIT, Cambridge, 1953; gen. mgr. research and devel. div. Montedison's, Milan, Italy, 1973-78; chmn. Italian Commn. Atomic and Alt. Energy Sources, Rome, 1979—. Chmn. European Econ. Commn. Com. for Sci. and Tech., 1983—; UN Com. Sci. and Tech. for Devel., 1984-86; mem. internat. council UN U. Trustee Aspen Inst. for Humanistic Studies; gov. Internat. Devel. Research Centre, Can.; vice chmn. Council UN U. Mem. Italian Chem. Soc., Am. Chem. Soc., AAAS, N.Y. Acad. Scis., Sci. Policy Found. London (mem. internat. adv. bd. 1975—). Club: Chemist (N.Y.C.). Author: WAES Report-Italy, 1977; Beyond the Age of Waste, 1978; Il Secondo Pianeta, 1983; contbr. articles to profl. jours. Home: 26 bis Via San Martino ai Monti, 00184 Rome Italy Office: ENEA, 125 Via Regina Margherita, 00198 Rome Italy

COLÓN, LYDIA M., banker, small business owner, financial consultant; b. Santurce, P.R., June 2, 1947; d. Angel Luis and Lydia Maria (Pagán) Colón. BA magna cum laude, Marymount Manhattan Coll., 1978. Admissions office supr. NYU, N.Y.C., 1965-70; asst. v.p. Chem. Bank, N.Y.C., 1971-85; sr. assoc. First Washington Assocs., Arlington, Va., 1985-87; owner LMC Internat., 1987—. Co-author: Innovations in Industrial Competitiveness at the State Level, 1985, Guide to State Capital Formation, 1984. Vice chmn. N.Y. State Adv. Council for Minority and Women-Owned Bus. Enterprise, 1984-87; mem. ARC Minorities Initiative Task Force, 1985-87, N.Y. Bus. Devel. Corp. Gov.'s Task Force N.Y., 1985; trustee Community Service Soc., N.Y., 1985-87; mem. Gov.'s Task Force on Work and the Family, 1988—; co-founder Nat. P.R. Women's Caucus, Inc. Recipient Woman of the 80's award U.S. Dept. of Housing & Urban Devel., 1985, Polit. Sci. Gold medal Marymount Manhattan Coll., N.Y., 1978. Mem. Nat. Assn. Bank Women, Nat. Conf. Puerto Rican Women, 100 Hispanic Women of N.Y.C.

COLONEY, WAYNE HERNDON, civil engineer; b. Bradenton, Fla., Mar. 15, 1925; s. Herndon Percival and Mary Adore (Cramer) C.; m. Anne Elizabeth Benedict, June 21, 1950; 1 child, Mary Adore. B.C.E. summa cum laude, Ga. Inst. Tech., 1950. Registered profl. engr. and surveyor, Fla., Ga., Ala., N.C., also Nat. Council Engring. Examiners. Project engr. Constructora Gen., Venezuela, 1948-49, Fla. Rd. Dept., 1950-55; hwy. engr. Gibbs & Hill, Inc., Guatemala, 1955-57; project mgr. Gibbs & Hill, Inc., Tampa, Fla., 1957-59; project engr., then assoc. J.E. Greiner Co., Tampa, 1959-63; ptnr. Barrett, Daffin & Coloney, Tallahassee, 1963-70; pres. Wayne H. Coloney Co., Inc., Tallahassee, 1970-78, chmn., bd. chief exec. officer, 1978-85; pres., sec. Tesseract Corp., 1975-85; chmn. bd., chief exec. officer Coloney Co. Cons. Engrs., Inc., 1978—; dep. chmn. Howden Airdynamics Am., Tallahassee, 1985—; v.p. Howden Coloney Inc., Tallahassee, 1985—; chmn. adv. com. Area Vocat. Tech. Sch., 1965-78. Patentee roof framing system, dense packing external aircraft fuel tank, tile mounting structure, curler rotating device, bracket system for roof framing; contbr. articles to profl. jours. Pres. United Fund Leon County, 1971-72; bd. dirs. Springtime Tallahassee, 1970-72, pres., 1981-82; bd. dirs. Heritage Found., 1965-71, pres., 1967; mem. Pres.'s Adv. Council on Indsl. Innovation, 1978-79; bd. dirs. LeMoyne Art Found., 1973, v.p., 1974-75; bd. dirs. Goodwill Industries, 1972-73, Tallahassee-Popoyan Friendship Commn., 1968-73; mem. Adv. Com. for Hist. and Cultural Preservation, 1969-71, Better Bus. Bur. Served with AUS, 1943-46. Fellow ASCE; mem. NSPE, Fla. Engring. Soc. (sr.), Nat. Acad. Forensic Engrs. (diplomate), Fla. Inst. Cons. Engrs., Fla. Soc. Profl. Land Surveyors, Tallahassee C. of C., Anak, Koseme Soc., Am. Arbitration Assn., Phi Kappa Phi, Omicron Delta Kappa, Sigma Alpha Epsilon, Tau Beta Pi. Episcopalian. Clubs: Governor's, Killearn Golf and Country, Met. Dinner (past pres.). Home: 3219 Thomasville Rd Apt 1-D Tallahassee FL 32312 Office: PO Box 668 Tallahassee FL 32302

COLOT, PAUL-BRUNO, physician; b. Hue, Vietnam, Mar. 21, 1945. MD, U. Saigon, Vietnam. Médecin résident L'Hosp. Grall, Saigon, 1972-73; chirurgen l'Hosp civil Taynimh, Vietnam, 1974-75; médecin attaché CHR di Reims (France), 1978, omnipraticien (gen. medicine), 1979—. Home: 55 Rue Mazarin, 51100 Reims France Office: Cabinet Medical, Rue Vauban, 51100 Reims France

COLOTKA, PETER, deputy prime minister of Slovak Republic of Czechoslovakia; legal educator; b. Sedliacka Dubova, Jan. 10, 1925; ed. Comenius U., Bratislava, Czechoslovakia. Asst. lectr. faculty of law Comenius U., 1950-56, asst. prof., 1956-64, prof., 1964—, vice dean, 1956-57, dean, 1957-58, pro-rector, 1958-61; commr. for justice Slovak Nat. Council, 1963-68, dep. prime minister, 1963—, mem. presidium, 1963-68, dep. premier, 1968; dep. premier Fed. Govt., 1969—; mem. central com. Communist Party of Czechoslovakia, 1966—, mem. presidium, 1969—; dep. House of Nations Fed. Assembly, 1968—, pres., 1969; premier Slovak Socialist Republic, 1969—. Mem. Internat. Ct. of Arbitration, The Hague, 1962-70. Decorated Distinction for Merit in Constrn., 1965, Order of Labour, 1969, Gold medal of J.A. Comenius U., Order of Victorious, 1973, Order of the Republic, 1975. Author: Personal Property, 1956; Our Socialist Constitution, 1961. Office: Office of Dep Premier, Prague Czechoslovakia *

COLQUHOUN, JOHN ALEXANDER, dental researcher; b. Palmerston North, New Zealand, Jan. 4, 1924; s. John Alexander and Lurline Emmaline (Scully) C.; m. Pauline Joyce Child, Dec. 21, 1949; children: David Alister, Sara, Rachel. B in Dental Sci., U. Otago, 1948; diploma in edn., U. Sydney, 1970; MPhil, U. Auckland, 1975, PhD, 1987. Registered dentist, New Zealand. Pvt. practice dental surgeon Auckland, 1955-66; dental officer New Zealand Dept. Health, Hokianga, 1949-51, Wellington, 1951-52; sr. dental officer New Zealand Dept. Health, Auckland, 1952-55, Auckland and Sydney, 1967-70; prin. dental officer New Zealand Dept. Health, Auckland, 1971-84, world study tour, 1980; researcher, tutor U. Auckland, 1984-87, tutor, 1987—. Contbr. articles to profl. jours. Chmn. library com. Glen Eden Borough Council, Auckland, 1955-58; dep. chmn. bd. govs. Kelston High Sch., Auckland, 1956-60; sec. Auckland Council on Vietnam, 1968-69; mem. Campaign for Nuclear Disarmament, 1950—. Mem. New Zealand Dental Assn., New Zealand Soc. Dentistry for Children (exec. com, pres. 1982-84), Internat. Soc. for Fluoride Research, Pub. Health Assn. of Australia and New Zealand, New Zealand Assn. for Research in Edn., New Zealand Assn. for Community Edn. (v.p. 1974-76), Auckland Workers Edn. Assn. (pres. 1964-82). Mem. Labour Party. Home: 216 Atkinson Rd, Titirangi, Auckland New Zealand

COLTER, ELIZABETH ANN, nurse; b. Norristown, Pa., Jan. 26, 1931; d. Lewis J. and Nancy (Hardy) Coffey; diploma Sacred Heart Hosp., Allentown, Pa., 1951; A.A.S., Meramec Community Coll., St. Louis, 1976; B.S. in Mgmt. Maryville Coll.; M.A. in Mgmt., Central Mich. U., 1983; m. Norman C. Colter, July 4, 1952 (div. Sept. 1979); children—Gregory, Marianne. Nurse, Mercy Hosp., Jackson, Mich., 1954-56, Madigan Meml. Hosp., Houlton, Maine, 1956-59; staff nurse to asst. head nurse operating room Mercy Hosp., Jackson, 1959-69; staff nurse St. Lawrence Hosp., Lansing, Mich., 1969-70; nurse Barnes Hosp., St. Louis, 1970-80, head nurse operating room, 1971-74, asst. dir. operating room, 1974-80; dir. operating rooms U. Mich., Ann Arbor, 1980-87; mgr. critical care Aga Khan U. Hosp., Karacki, Pakistan, 1987— . Mem. Assn. Operating Room Nurses (pres. St. Louis 1973-74), Am. Coll. Hosp. Adminstrs. (nominee), Sigma Theta Tau, Phi Theta Kappa. Democrat. Lutheran. Home: 290 Mohican Florri Sant MO 63033 Office: Aga Khan U Hosp, Stadium Rd PO Box 3500, Karachi 5, Pakistan

COLTER, MEL A., systems educator, consultant; b. Conway, Iowa, June 11, 1947; s. Archie B. and Jessie E. (Brown) C.; B.S. in Physics, Iowa State U., 1969; Ph.D. in Mgmt. Sci., U. Iowa, 1975. Lab. asst. Ames Lab., Iowa State U., Ames, 1966-69; teaching asst. Coll. Bus., U. Iowa, Iowa City, 1970-75, vis. asst. prof., 1976-79; project dir. Computer Cons. Service, Dubuque, Iowa, 1975-76; assoc. prof. bus. U. Colo., Colorado Springs, 1979-86; pres. Colter Enterprises, Inc., 1982—, mem. univ. computing policy com.; cons. and lectr. in field. Mem. ACM, IEEE (mem. program com., keynote speaker numerous confs.). Co-author: (with J.D. Couger & R. Knapp) Advanced System Development/Feasibility Techniques, 1982; (with J. Daniel Couger) Motivation of the Maintenance Programmer, 1983; contbr. research reports and articles to profl. jours. Office: 19520 Indian Summer Ln Monument CO 80132

COLTON, CLARK KENNETH, chemical engineering educator; b. N.Y.C., July 20, 1941; s. Sidney and Goldie (Chases) C.; m. Ellen Ruth Brandner, June 20, 1965; children: Jill Erin, Jason Adam, Michael Ross, Brian Scott. B of Chem. Engring., Cornell U., 1964; PhD, MIT, 1969. Asst. prof. chem. engring. MIT, Cambridge, 1969-73, assoc. prof., 1973-76, prof., 1976—, Bayer prof. chem. engring., 1980-85, dep. head dept. chem. engring., 1977, chmn. centennial chem. engring. edn., 1988; cons. to NIH, FDA, various indsl. orgns.; mem. adv. bd. mil. personnel supplies NRC, 1971-75. Mem. editorial bd.: Jour. Membrane Sci, 1975-81, Jour. Bioengring, 1976-79, Med. Engring. and Biotech. jour.; contbr. articles to sci. jours. Ford found. fellow, 1969-70; recipient Tchr./Scholar award Camille and Henry Dreyfus Found., 1972. Mem. N.Y. Acad. Scis., Am. Inst. Chem. Engrs. (dir. food, pharm. and bioengring. div. 1978-81, Allan P. Colburn award 1977), Am. Soc. Artificial Internal Organs (editorial bd. Jour. 1978-84), Am. Diabetes Assn., Am. Soc. for Engring. Edn. (Curtis W. McGraw research award 1980), N.Am. Membrane Soc., Internat. Soc. on Oxygen Transport to Tissue, Am. Chem. Soc., Internat. Soc. Artificial Organs, Internat. Soc. Blood Purification (Gambro award 1986), Biomed. Engring. Soc., AAAS, Sigma Xi, Tau Beta Pi, Phi Lambda Upsilon. Club: Cornell (Boston). Home: 279 Commonwealth Ave Newton MA 02167 Office: Dept Chem Engring Mass Inst Tech Cambridge MA 02139

COLTON, ROY CHARLES, management consultant; b. Phila., Feb. 26, 1941; s. Nathan Hale and Ruth Janis (Baylinson) C.; B.A., Knox Coll., 1962; M.Ed., Temple U., 1963. With Sch. Dist. of Phila., 1963-64; systems analyst Wilmington Trust Co., 1967-69; exec. recruiter Atwood Consultants Inc., Phila., 1969-71; pres. Colton Bernard Inc., San Francisco, 1971—; occasional lectr. Fashion Inst. Tech., Phila. Coll. Textiles and Scis. Served with AUS, 1964-66. Mem. San Francisco Fashion Industries, San Francisco C. of C., Calif. Exec. Recruiter Assn., Nat. Assn. Exec. Recruiters, Am. Apparel Mfrs. Assn., Am. Arbitration Assn. (panel arbitrators), Am. Mgmt. Assn. Office: Colton Bernard Inc 417 Spruce St San Francisco CA 94118

COLTRIN, STEPHEN HUGH, public relations, advertising and marketing executive; b. Rupert, Idaho, June 7, 1945; s. Ira Hugh and Beverly (Luke) C.; m. Gwen Moore; children—Stephanie Ann, Jennifer Lynn and Susan Michelle Coltrin, Joel, Bryce and Gretel Cundick. B.S. in Psychology, Brigham Young U., 1970. Sales and mktg. rep. Burroughs Wellcome, Tucson, 1970-73, spl. rep. to med. ctrs., Salt Lake City, 1973-76, product mgr., spokesman Pharm. Mfrs. Assn., Raleigh, N.C. and Washington, 1976-78; dir. eastern pub. relations Ch. of Jesus Christ of Latter-day Saints, N.Y.C., 1978-82; chmn. Coltrin & Assocs., N.Y.C., 1982—; dir. Internat. Radio and TV Found., N.Y.C; v.p. Internat. Radio and TV Soc. Named Pharm. Industry Spokesman of Yr., Pharm. Mfrs. Assn., 1974, Outstanding Young Man, Jaycees, 1982. Republican. Mormon. Avocations: skiing, tennis. Office: Coltrin & Assocs 17 E 45th St at Madison Suite 608 New York NY 10017

COLUSSY, DAN ALFRED, service executive; b. Pitts., June 3, 1931; s. Dan and Viola E. (Andreis) C.; m. Helene Graham, June 6, 1953; children: Deborah, Jennifer. B.S. U.S. Coast Guard Acad., 1953; M.B.A., Harvard U., 1965. Applications engr. Jet Propulsion div. Gen. Electric Co., 1956-63; dir. ops. Am. Airlines, N.Y.C., 1965-66; v.p. mktg. N.E. Airlines, Boston, 1966-69; v.p. Wells, Rich, Green Advt. Agy., N.Y.C., 1969-70; v.p. mktg. devel. Pan Am. World Airways, N.Y.C., 1970-72, v.p. passenger mktg., 1972-74, sr. v.p. passenger mktg., 1974, sr. v.p. field ops., 1974-75, sr. v.p. mktg. and services, 1975-76, exec. v.p. mktg. and services, dir., 1976-78, pres., chief operating officer, mem. exec. com., 1978-80; chmn., chief exec. officer Columbia Air, Balt., 1980-82; pres., chief exec. officer, mem. exec. com. Can. Pacific Air, Vancouver, B.C., 1982-84, chmn., 1985-86, now bd. dirs.; mem. exec. com. Can. Pacific Hotels, 1983-84; pres., chief exec. officer, chmn. exec. com. UNC Inc., Annapolis, Md., 1985—, also bd. dirs.; mem. Anne Arundel County Exec.'s Bus. Roundtable. Mem. bd. visitors Coll. of Bus. and Mgmt. U. Md., bd. dirs. Nat. Aquarium in Balt., Hist. Annapolis, Inc. Served to lt. USCG, 1953-56. Mem. Md. C. of C. (bd. dirs.), Md. Econ. Growth Assocs. (bd. dirs.), Campaign Cabinet, U.S. Naval Inst., Am. Bus. Conf. Clubs: Royal Vancouver Yacht, Larchmont Yacht, Annapolis Yacht, Harvard. Lodge: Order of St. John. Office: UNC Inc 175 Admiral Cochrane Dr Annapolis MD 21401

COLVIN, EUTA MILLER, surgeon, educator; b. Chester, S.C., Nov. 13, 1918; s. D. Euta and Havilene (O'Donnell) C.; m. Dorothy Eugenia Horner, Dec. 22, 1942; children—William Euta, Ronald Horner Colvin. B.S., Furman U., 1936-40; M.D., Med. U. S.C., 1943. Diplomate Am. Bd. Surgery. Intern Roper Hosp., Charleston, S.C., 1944, Greenville (S.C.) Gen. Hosp., 1946; surg. preceptorship with pvt. physician, Spartanburg, S.C., 1946-50; resident Lawson VA Hosp, Emory U. group, Atlanta, 1950-52; practice surgery, Spartanburg, 1952—; established Surg. Assoc. of Spartanburg, P.A. 1957; attending surgeon Spartanburg Regional Med. Ctr., 1952—, former chief staff, chief surgery, dir. surg. edn.; attending surgeon Mary Black Meml. Hosp., 1953—; courtesy surg. staff. Dr. Meml. Hosp., 1975—; clin. prof. surgery Med. U. S.C., 1976—. Bd. dirs., treas. S.C. Polit. Action Com., 1974—; gov.'s appointee bd. dirs. S.C. Dept. Health and Environ. Control; gov.'s appointee adv. com. S.C. HHS Fin. Commn.; mem. session 1st Presbyn Ch., Spartanburg, pres. 1982. Fellow ACS (S.C. gov.-at-large 1978—, chmn. state adv. com. 1976-78); mem. S.C. Med. Assn. (chmn. council 1979-81, pres. 1982-83) AMA (alt. del. from S.C. 1984—), Spartanburg County Med. Assn. (pres. 1955), So. Med. Assn., Southeastern Surg. Congress, S.C. Surg. Soc. (pres. 1978-79), Am. Trauma Soc., S.C. Inst. Med. Edn., Research (bd. dirs., pres.), Alpha Omega Alpha. Contbr. articles to profl. publs. Home: 102 Rosewood Ln Spartanburg SC 29302 Office: 711 N Church St Spartanburg SC 29303

COLWELL, JAMES LEE, humanities educator; b. Brush, Colo., Aug. 31, 1926; s. Francis Joseph and Alice (Bleasdale) C.; BA, U. Denver, 1949; MA, U. No. Colo., 1951; cert. Sorbonne, Paris, 1956; diploma U. Heidelberg (Ger.), 1957; A.M. (Univ. fellow), Yale U., 1959, PhD (Hale-Kilborn fellow), 1961; m. Claudia Alsleben, Dec. 27, 1957; children—John Francis, Alice Anne. Tchr. high sch., Snyder and Sterling, Colo., 1948-52; civilian edn. adviser U.S. Air Force, Japan, 1952-56; assoc. dir. Yale Fgn. Student Inst., summers 1959-60; asst. dir. European div. U. Md., Heidelberg, 1961-65; dir. Office Internat. Edn., assoc. prof. Am. lit. U. Colo., Boulder, 1965-72; prof. Am. studies, chmn. lit. U. Tex. Permian Basin, Odessa, 1977-82, dean Coll. Arts and Edn., 1972-77, 82-84, K.C. Dunagan prof. humanities, 1984-87, prof. emeritus, 1988—. Mem. nat. adv. council Inst. Internat. Edn., 1969-75. Vice pres. Ector County chpt. ARC, 1974-76; mem. Ector County Hist. Commn., 1973-75. Served with USAAF, 1945; brig. gen. USAF Res. Ret. Mem. AAUP, Am. Studies Assn., Western Social Sci. Assn. (life; pres. 1974-75), MLA, NEA (life), Orgn. Am. Historians (life), South Central MLA, Permian Basin Hist. Soc. (life; pres. 1980-81), Air Force Assn. (life), Air Force Hist. Found. (life), Res. Officers Assn. (life), Ret. Officers Assn. (life), Phi Beta Kappa. Unitarian-Universalist. Contbr. articles to learned jours. Home: 4675 Gordon Dr Boulder CO 80303-6747

COMBE, BERNARD MARIE-JOËL, physician; b. Avignon, France, May 24, 1947; s. John and Alberte (Vernède) C.; m. Annie Genevieve Bartoccioni, June 30, 1973; children: Guillaume. Bachelor's degree, Lycee Carnot, Cannes, 1968; MD, Sci. and Med. U. Grenoble, France, 1975. Intern CHU Grenoble, 1971-74, asst. instr., 1972-74, practice med., 1975; staff pvt. gerontological hosp., 1977-81, Civil Soc. Coberome, LeCannet, 1982—; pres. Hosp. staff, 1973-74; med. creative staff S.O.S., Cannes, 1977-78. Served with the French mil., 1974-1975. Mem. Geriatric and Gerontologic Mediterranean Soc. Roman Catholic. Home: Gen de Gaulle Ave 1291, 06250 Mougins Alpes Maritimes France

COMBE, IVAN DEBLOIS, drug company executive; b. Fremont, Iowa, Apr. 21, 1911; s. Louis Abel and Elsie (Mange) C.; m. Mary Elizabeth Deming, Dec. 10, 1938; children—Diana M. Combe McDermott, Juliette M. Combe Larson, Christopher Bryan. BS, Northwestern U., 1933, postgrad. Law Sch., 1933-35. Salesman, pub. relations exec. Nat. Dairy Products, Chgo., 1935-36; div. sales mgr. Wilbert Products Co., N.Y.C., 1936-40; merchandising account exec. Young & Rubicam, Inc., N.Y.C., 1940-43; v.p. sales and advt. Pharmacraft Corp. (subs. Seagram Distillers), N.Y.C., 1944-49; pres., founder Combe Inc., White Plains, N.Y., 1949-70; chmn., 1970—. Chmn. Council on Family Health, N.Y.C., 1972-79; bd. dirs. White Plains Hosp. Med. Ctr., 1962—; trustee Northwestern U., 1968—, life trustee, 1979—, life regent. Recipient Alumni Service award Northwestern U., 1962, Merit award, 1971. Mem. U.S. Proprietary Drug Mfrs. Assn. (bd. dirs., exec. com. 1958—, chmn. 1964-66), World Fedn. Proprietary Medicine Mfrs. (bd. dirs., exec. com. 1977—, chmn. 1977-79), Alpha Delta Phi. Clubs: Metropolitan (N.Y.C); Blind Brook (Purchase, N.Y.); Country of Fla. (Delray); Ekwanok Country (Manchester, Vt.). Lodge: Rotary. Home: 25 Wilshire Rd Greenwich CT 06830

COMBES, RICHARD WILLARD, anesthesiologist; b. Cleve., July 2, 1926; s. Willard Wetmore and Vivian C. (Kepler) C.; A.B., Oberlin Coll., 1947; M.D., Case Western Res. U., 1951; m. Angela Katryn Wright, Aug. 26, 1949; children—Carol Combes Lanier, Holly Combes Dorst, Willard Wright, Pamela. Intern, St. Lukes Hosp., Cleve., 1951-52; resident, research asst. in neuroanatomy Case Western Res. U., 1952; gen. practice medicine, Oberlin, Ohio, 1954-57; resident in anesthesiology St. Luke's Hosp., Cleve., 1957-59, mem. med. staff, 1959-60; dir. anesthesiology services Booth Meml. Hosp., Salvation Army, Cleve., 1961-70; practice medicine specializing in anesthesiology, Rock Island, Ill., 1970-73, Rutland, Vt., 1973-88; owner, dir. Oak Research Labs., histochemistry solvent systems, azeotropy, design and synthesis of sterospecific fluorescent and reactive stains, testing in histological and cytological use, Rutland, 1961—. Bd. dirs. Birthright of Rock Island County, 1972-73; mem. Laymen's & Retreat Project. Served to lt. USNR, 1944-45, 52-54. Invited visitor designate to Ch. of Scotland Gen. Assembly from United Presbyn. Ch. U.S.A., 1973; recipient cert. profl. chemist Nat. Cert. Commn. in Chemistry and Chem. Engring., 1985 Fellow Royal Microscopic Soc., Am. Inst. Chemists; mem. Royal Soc. Chemistry, AAAS, Am. Chem. Soc., N.Y. Acad. Scis., Am. Soc. Anesthesiologists, Internat. Union Pure and Applied Chemistry, S.A.R., Brit. Pteridological Soc., Assn. Ofcl. Analytical Chemists. Home and Office: 3 Robinwood Ln Rutland VT 05701

COMBIER, MARC ROBERT, publisher; b. St. Fons, France, Mar. 15, 1951; s. Jean-Marie and Fernande (Lacharme) C.; m. Catherine Maisonnier, Oct. 6, 1978; children: Martin, Pauline. Diploma in graphic arts, Ecole Estienne, Paris, 1970. Dir. art Combier Printers, Macon, France, 1970-76, dir. editorial, 1977-84; gen. mgr. Images et Loisirs, Macon, 1976—; pres. Club du Temps Gourmand, Macon, 1986—; v.p. Percom, Inc., N.Y.C. Editor: (postcards) Cim, Asphodele, 1970-87, (fichecards) Les Fiches de M. Cinéma, 1976—. V.p. Syndicat d'Initiative de Macon, 1974-87. Served with French mil., 1971-72. Mem. Rencontres Internat. de Lure (v.p. 1976—), Gens d'Images. Lodge: Kiwanis (pres. 1985-86). Home: Agut 4, 71000 Macon France Office: Images et Loisirs, Route de Lyon 81, 71000 Macon France

COMBS, AUSTIN OLIN, real estate and insurance broker; b. Harr, Tenn., Aug. 5, 1917; s. Clyde Harmon and Bess (Widner) C.; 1 child by previous marriage, Hope; m. Marjorie Thayer Mason, Dec. 28, 1947; 1 child, Carolyn; adopted children: Dianne, Marjorie, Duncan Dowling III. Student Stetson Bus. Coll. V.p. Kipp & Combs, Inc., 1952-54; ptnr. Combs-Sibley, 1954; pres. Austin O. Combs, Inc., Daytona Beach, Fla., 1954—; airplane pilot. Trustee Volusia County Heart Assn., 1955-56, pres., 1965; trustee, chmn. bd. visitors Embry-Riddle Aero. U.; bd. dirs. YMCA; bd. dirs., pres. Fla. Internat. Festival Com. Served with USAAF, 1944-46, Air Def. Command, Air Res. Adv. Bd., 1946-47. Mem. Flying Realtors, Fla. Aero Club, Aircraft Owners and Pilots Assn., Daytona Beach C. of C., Tomoka Gems and Minerals Soc. (past pres.), Internat. Platform Assn., Quiet Birdmen, UN Assn. U.S., Internat. Order Characters, Silver Wings, Soc. for the Preservation and Enrichment of Barber Shop Quartet Singing in Am. (past judge, bd. dirs. Daytona Beach chpt.). Clubs: Elinor Village Country (past pres., bd. dirs.), Dayton Beach Yacht; Miami Springs Exec.; Oceanside Country, Pelican Bay Country. Lodges: Masons, Shriners, Jesters, Elks, Moose, Rotary (past pres.). Home: 3756 Cardinal Blvd Daytona Beach FL 32019 Office: 2008 S Atlantic Ave Daytona Beach FL 32018

COMEGYS, WALKER BROCKTON, lawyer; b. Oklahoma City, July 30, 1929; s. Walker B. and Dorcas (McConnell) C.; m. Adelaide M. Eicks, June 19, 1954; children: Elizabeth Lee Comegys Chafee, Catherine. B.A. with honors, U. Tex., 1951; LL.B., Harvard U., 1954. Bar: Mass. 1955, D.C. 1972, U.S. Supreme Ct. 1970. Assoc. Goodwin, Procter & Hoar, Boston, 1954-64; ptnr. Goodwin, Procter & Hoar, 1964-69; dep. asst. atty. gen. antitrust Dept. Justice, Washington, 1969-72; asst. atty. gen. antitrust Dept. Justice, 1972; ptnr. Powers & Hall, Boston, 1975-79; dir. Powers & Hall, 1979-84; practice law offices Walker B. Comegys P.C., Boston, 1984—; lectr. Boston U. Sch. Law, 1984-85; U.S. del. OECD, Paris, 1970, 72; chmn. New Eng. Antitrust Conf., 1967, 68, co-chmn., 1983, 84, 85. Adv. bd. editors: Antitrust Bull., 1967-69; contbr.: ABA Antitrust Section Antitrust Law Developments, 2d edit., 1984; author: "Antitrust Compliance Manual, A Guide for Counsel, Management and Public Officials", Practicing Law Institute, 1986. Mem. Bd. Zoning Appeals, Town of Wenham (Mass.), 1972-87; bd. overseers Met. Center Performing Arts, Boston, 1981-84, Wang Center Performing Arts, 1984—. Mem. ABA (chmn. Sherman act com. antitrust sect. 1966-69, mem. council antitrust sect. 1972-76), Internat. Bar Assn. (com. 1984—), Boston Bar Assn. (chmn. antitrust com. 1968-69), N.Y. State Bar Assn., Fed. Bar Assn. Home: 202 Main St Wenham MA 01984 Office: 28 State St 18th Floor Boston MA 02109

COMERFORD, WALTER THOMPSON, JR., lawyer; b. Bristol, Va., May 27, 1949; s. Walter Thompson, and Mary Lou (Phetteplace) C.; m. Joyce Faye Call; children—Callison Taylor, Erin Elizabeth, Kristen Nicole. Student, U. Tenn., 1968-70; B.A. magna cum laude, Wake Forest U., 1972, J.D. cum laude, 1974. Bar: N.C. 1974, U.S. Dist. Ct. (mid. and we. dists.) N.C. 1974, U.S. Ct. Appeals (4th cir.) 1977. Ptnr., Petree, Stockton, Robinson, Vaughn, Glaze & Maready, Winston-Salem, N.C., 1980—. Contbr. articles to profl. jours. Chmn. profl. div. Forsyth County Arts Council Fund Drive, Winston-Salem, 1977, Wake Forest Law Fund Campaign, 1980. Recipient Disting. Achievement award Intenat. Acad. Trial Lawyers, 1974. Mem. Internat. Assn. Def. Counsel, N.C. Assn. Def. Attys., ABA (vice chmn. property ins. com.), N.C. Bar Assn., N.C. State Bar, Forsyth County Bar Assn., Aviation Ins. Assn. Home: 461 Heritage Dr Lewisville NC 27023 Office: Petree Stockton Robinson Vaughn Glaze & Maready 1001 W 4th St Winston-Salem NC 27101

COMISSIONA, SERGIU, conductor; b. Bucharest, Romania, June 16, 1928; came to U.S., 1969; s. Isaac and Jean L. (Haufrecht) C.; m. Robinne Florin, July 16, 1949. Ed. music conservatoire, Bucharest; Mus.D. (hon.), Peabody Conservatory Music, 1972; L.H.D. (hon.), Towson State U., 1980; D.F.A. (hon.), Washington Coll., Chestertown, Md., 1980, Western Md. Coll., 1977, U. Md., 1981, Johns Hopkins U., 1982. Mus. dir. Rumanian State Ensemble Orch., 1950-55; prin. condr. Rumanian State Opera, 1955-59; mus. dir. Haifa (Israel) Symphony, 1959, Israel Chamber Orch., 1960-65; Am. debut with Phil. Orch., 1965; mus. dir. Goteburg (Sweden) Symphony Orch., 1966-69; mus. adviser, condr. Ulster Orch., Belfast, No. Ireland, 1967-69; mus. dir. Balt. Symphony Orch., 1969-84; mus. adviser Temple U. Music Festival, 1975-76, artistic dir. 1976-80; music dir., prin. condr. Chautauqua Symphony Orch. Summer Festival, 1976-78; music adviser Am. Symphony Orch., 1978-82; artistic advisor Houston Symphony Orch., 1983-88; music dir. Houston Symphony Orch.; mus. dir., N.Y.C. Opera, 1987—; permanent guest condr. Radio Philharm. Orch. of Netherlands, 1982-83, chief condr., 1983—. Decorated Order Merit 2d Class Rumania; winner internat. competition for young condrs. Besancon, France, 1956; recipient Gold medal award City of Goteborg, 1973, Ditson Condr.'s award Columbia U., 1979. Mem. Royal Swedish Acad. Music (hon.). Office: ICM Artist Ltd 40 W 57th St New York NY 10019 also: care NYC Opera NY State Theater Lincoln Center New York NY 10023

COMMITO, RICHARD WILLIAM, podiatrist; b. Chgo., May 2, 1951; s. Mario Fiore and Aileen Margaret (Stang) C. B.S., U. Ill.-Chgo., 1972; D.P.M., Ill. Coll. Podiatric Medicine, 1976. Diplomate Nat. Bd. Podiatry Examiners, Am. Bd. Ambulatory Foot Surgery; cert. Internat. Inst. Reflexology, Am. Bd. Podiatric Surgery. Podiatrist, Chgo., 1976—; dir. Podiatry Services Community Hosp., Evanston, Ill., 1978-80; cons. staff podiatry Ridgeway Hosp., Chgo., 1981—; owner Foot Doc Products, New Foot Pharmical; dir. podiatry service Lawndale Plaza Surgicenter, Chgo.; ind. examiner of counsel R.S. Connors Assocs., Chgo. Bd. dirs. Little Village unit Chgo. Boys' Clubs, 1981—, mem. One hundred Club, 1982, mem. 400 Club, Marshall Sq. unit, 1981-82; mem. Art Inst. Chgo., 1980-85, Lincoln Park Zool. Soc., Chgo., 1980-85. Fellow Acad. Ambulatory Foot Surgery; mem. Soaring Soc. Am., Ill. Podiatry Edn. Group, Am. Podiatric Med. Assn., Ill. Podiatry Soc., Am. Med. Soc. of Vienna (life), Nat. Assn. Professions, Nat. Assn. of the Self-Employed. Roman Catholic.

COMMON, FRANK BREADON, JR., lawyer; b. Montreal, Can., Apr. 16, 1920; s. Frank Breadon and Ruth Louise (Lang) C.; m. Katharine Ruth Laws, Sept. 7, 1946; children: Katharine Ruth, Anne Elizabeth, Frank Breadon (dec.), Diana Melanie, Ruth Elizabeth, Jane Laws, James Lang. Diploma in engring, Royal Mil. Coll., 1940; B.Civil Law, McGill U., 1948; LLD, St. Francis Xavier U., 1980. Admitted to Can. bar, 1948; created Queen's Counsel, 1958. Assoc., now sr. ptnr. Montgomery, McMichael, Common, Howard, Forsyth & Kerr (and successor firms), 1948—; counsel Ogilvy & Renault, 1948—; chmn. bd. Can. Corps., Ltd., NOMMOC, Cadbury Schweppes Can., Inc., Acadia Life Ins. Co., others; bd. dirs. Sun Alliance Ins. Co., Royal Bank Can., Ciba-Geigy Can., Cadbury Schweppes Ltd.-U.S., others; pres. Brown Boveri Realty Corp.; founder, chmn. dir. World Intellectual Properties, Ltd., Bermuda, Atwater Inst. The World Info. Economy Ctr., Montreal; lectr. in law McGill U., 1953-59 Past pres., bd. dirs. Que. div. Can. Red Cross; alderman, commr. fin. and pub. works City of Westmont, Can., 1959-62, acting mayor, 1961-62; chmn. 1st Montreal Combined Appeal, 1962; past bd. govs. Montreal Gen. Hosp., Montreal Symphony Orch.; past. chmn., gov. Douglas Hosp.; founder 1st pres., gov. Can. Found. Endl. Devel.; founder, chmn. Common Cents Ltd. Served as officer Royal Can. Engrs., 1940-45. Mentioned in dispatches. Mem. Can. Bar Assn. (council 1956-58), Can. Tax Found., Mil. Engrs. Assn. Can. (past pres. Montreal br.), Grad. Soc. of McGill U. (bd. dirs.), McGill Alma Mater (faculty chmn.). Mem. United Ch. Can. (com. steward). Clubs: Mount Royal; Mount Bruno Country; Brook (N.Y.C.); Bayou (La.); Seigniory (past pres.), others. Home: 3940 Cote des Neiges Rd, Apt B-101, Montreal, PQ Canada H3H 1W2 Office: Ogilvy & Renault, 1981 McGill College Ave, Suite 1100, Montreal, PQ Canada H3A 3C1

COMPAORÉ, BLAISE, head of government. Chmn. Popular Front; head of state Burkina Faso, 1987—. Office: Office of Head of State, Ouagadougou Burkina Faso *

COMPTON, JOHN GEORGE, Prime Minister of St. Lucia; b. Canouan, St. Vincent, Granandines, Apr. 29, 1926; s. Ethel Compton; m. Janice Clark, June 28, 1968; children: Jean, Jeannine, Maya, Nina, Fiona. B.Sc., London Sch. Econs., 1950, LL.B., 1951. Bar: St. Lucia. Sole practice law, St. Lucia, 1951—; ind. mem. St. Lucia Legis. Council, 1954; minister for trade and prodn., St. Lucia, 1957; chief minister St. Lucia, 1964, premier, 1967-69, prime minister, 1979, 1982—, minister fgn. affairs and fin., 1982—, now also minister planning and devel. and home affairs. Joined Labour Party, St. Lucia, 1954, dep. leader, 1957-61; formed Nat. Labour Movement, 1961 (later became United Workers Party), now leader. Address: Office of the Prime Minister, Castries Saint Lucia *

COMPTON, WILLIAM THOMAS, computer consulting firm owner; b. Bedford, Ind., Dec. 1, 1945; s. Thomas Franklin and Dorothy Jane (Smith) C.; m. Nancy Marie Radocchia, Sept. 13, 1969; children: Kimberly Dawn, Lindsay Ann. BS in Mgmt., MIT, 1968, Postgrad., 1968-70. Cert. data. processing. Sr. systems analyst First Nat. Bank Boston, 1970-73; systems analyst Gen. Computer Systems, Wellesley, Mass., 1973-76; bus. systems analyst Fram Corp., East Providence, R.I., 1976-78; v.p. Span Mgmt. Systems, East Providence, 1978; project leader Prime Computer Inc., Natick, Mass., 1979-81; owner Computer Software Solutions, Tiverton, R.I., 1981—. Author several computer software programs, 1982-85. Loaned officer United Fund Boston, 1970. Mem. Data Processing Mgmt. Assn. (cert. data processing instr. 1985-86). Republican. Methodist. Lodge: Kiwanis (local v.p. 1985, pres. 1985-86). Home and Office: Compton Software Solutions 23 Jennifer Ln Tiverton RI 02878

CONABLE, BARBER B., JR., international agency administrator; b. Warsaw, N.Y., Nov. 2, 1922; s. Barber B. and Agnes G. (Gouinlock) C.; m. Charlotte Williams, Sept. 13, 1952; 4 children. AB, Cornell U., 1942, LLB, 1948. Bar: N.Y. 1948. Sole practice Buffalo, 1948-50, Batavia, N.Y., 1952-64; U.S. senator from N.Y. 1963-64; mem. 89th-98th congresses from 30th N.Y. dist., 1965-85, Pres. Reagan's Commn. on Defense Mgmt., from 1985; prof. U. Rochester, N.Y., 1985-86; pres. Internat. Bank for Reconstrn. and Devel., Washington, 1986—; sr. fellow, Am. Enterprise Inst., 1985. Editor: Cornell U. Law Quar., 1947-48. Mem. sr. adv. com. Kennedy Inst. Politics; trustee U.S. Capitol Hist. Soc., Mus. Am. Indian. Served with USMCR, 1942-46, 50-51. Republican. Lodge: Rotary (pres. Batavia chpt.). Office: Internat Bank for Reconstrn and Devel 1818 H St NW Washington DC 20433 *

CONANT, STEVEN GEORGE, psychiatrist; b. Elkhart, Ind., July 8, 1949; s. Hubert Eugene and Ruth (Weaver) C. BA in Zoology with distinction, DePauw U., 1971; MD, Ind. U., 1975. Diplomate Am. Bd. Psychiatry and Neurology. Intern Ind. U. Med. Ctr., Indpls., 1975-76, resident in psychiatry, 1976-78; asst. prof. psychiatry Ind. U., Indpls., 1978-80; cons. psychiatry Gallahue Mental Health Ctr., Indpls., 1979-85; staff psychiatrist Metro Health, Indpls., 1983—; staff privileges at Community Hosp., Indpls., 1979—; cons. psychiatrist Ind. Prison Systems, 1986, social security div. Ft. Benjamin Harrison Army Hosp. Mem. Conductor's Circle of the Indpls. Symphony, 1984—, Indpls. Symphonic Choir Orch., 1976-83, Ensemble Music Soc., 1983—; trustee Indpls. Mus. Art, 1988—. Mem. Am. Psychiat. Assn., Ind. Psychiat. Soc., Am. Acad. Clin. Psychiatrists, Mensa, The Hoosier Group. Republican. Presbyterian. Home: 3651 Totem Ln Indianapolis IN 46208 Office: Metro Health 3266 N Meridian 9th Floor Indianapolis IN 46208

CONARY, DAVID ARLAN, investment company executive; b. South Paris, Maine, Mar. 3, 1937; s. Wilfred Grindle and Arline (Whitney) C.; m. Frances Jane Harrison, June 8, 1957; children: Lee Harrison, Neil Whitney. AB, Bowdoin Coll., 1959; postgrad. Northeastern U., 1965-66, Mass. Inst. Tech., 1966-67; Boston U., 1967. Securities trader H.C. Wainwright & Co., Boston, 1959-60; securities trader May & Gannon, Boston, 1960-65, v.p., 1968-71; securities analyst, adminstr. The Boston Co., Boston, 1965-68; mgr. instl. trading Fahnestock & Co., Boston, 1971-72; resident mgr. G.A. Saxton & Co., Boston, 1972-75; instl. trader Baker, Weeks & Co., N.Y.C., 1975; equities trader State St. Research & Mgmt. Co., Boston, 1976-87; v.p. Howard, Weil, Inc., 1987—; dir. Astra Corp., Security 1 Specialists, Inc.; pres., chmn. Granite Solid State, Inc.; lectr. in field. Dist. dir. Mass. Bay United Fund, 1966. Mem. Nat. Security Traders Assn., Boston Securities Traders Assn. (gov. 1972-73, 81-82), Boston Investment Club (pres. 1985-86), Bowdoin Club of Boston (dir. 1965-66, dir. 175th anniversary campaign 1973-74), Mensa, Theta Delta Chi. Club: Weymouth Sportsmen's (sec. 1965-66, 71-72). Republican. Home: 79 Atlantic Ave North Hampton NH 03862 Office: 225 Franklin St Boston MA 02110

CONCHON, GEORGES, author; b. Saint-Avit, France, May 9, 1925; s. Eugene and Marcelle (Gancille) C.; m. Yvonne Message, Aug. 8, 1946; 1 dau., Catherine. Licence de philosohie, Sorbonne, U. Paris, 1946, Diplom etudes superieures de philosophie, 1947. Div. head Assemblee de L'Union Francaise, Paris, 1947-58; sec.-gen. Assemblee Nationale Bangui, 1959; journalist France-Soir, Paris, 1960; div. head Senat, Paris, 1960-80; producer Antenne 2, Paris, 1981-84; author novels, screenplays, 1953—. Author: (novels) L'Etat Sauvage (prix Goncourt 1964), 1964; Le Bel Avenir, 1984, Colette/Stern, 1987; (films) Black and White in Color (Oscar for best fgn. film 1978), 1977; La Banquiere, 1980; Mon Beau-frere a tué ma soeur, 1986. Named officer des Arts et Lettres, officier Ordre National du Merite; chevalier de la légion d'honneur.

CONDICT, EDGAR RHODES, medical electronics, aviation instrument manufacturing executive, medical health care executive, inventor; b. Boston, Apr. 27, 1940; s. Clinton Adams and Elizabeth May (Lane) C.; BS, Bucknell U., 1962; m. Judith Pond, June 9, 1962; children: Edgar Rhodes, Robert Adams, Carolyn Helen. Chmn. bd., pres. Bio-Tronics Research, Inc., 1962—, Kearsarge Healthcare, Inc., 1978—, Kearsarge Rehab. Hosp., Inc., Condict Instruments, Inc., 1985—; pres. Medel Corp., patent devel. investment, 1965—; cons. U. Tex. Med. Sch., 1968-70; cons. in med. electronics, electronics, biophysics, biofeedback, telecommunications, environ. health and welfare. Chmn., Mantowa dist., exec. bd. Daniel Webster council Boy Scouts Am., 1979-84. Recipient various grants in neuro-brain scis.; numerous med. awards from fgn. countries. Mem. Sigma Chi. Baptist. Author: A Theory of Anesthesia, Feedback Anesthesia, Electronic Pain-Killing Devices, others. Patentee in med. electronics, telecommunications fields. Address: Rural Rt 2 Box 475 Main St New London NH 03257

CONDOM, PIERRE PHILIPPE, periodical editor and publisher; b. Toulouse, France, Nov. 30, 1941; s. Joseph and Gabrielle (Brochon) C.; m. Mariele Nicaud, Apr. 2, 1971; children: Raphael, Chloe. Speciales in Math., Lycée Chaptal, Paris, 1963. Avionics editor Aviation Mag. Internat., Paris, 1967-75, def. editor, 1969-75, editor-in-chief, 1975-81; editor-in-chief Interavia Aerospace Rev., Geneva, 1982—; dir. aerospace pubs. Interavia S.A., Geneva, 1982—, pub. dir., 1988—. Active Nat. French Fencing Team. Served with French army, 1965-66. Mem. Assn. des Journalists, Profls. de l'Aeronautique et de l'Espace, Aviation Space Writers Assn., Inernat. Found. Airline Passengers Assns. Home: 288 Les Mannessières, Collonges/Saleve France 74160 Office: Interavia, 86 Ave Louis Casai, Geneva Switzerland 1216

CONDOS, MARIOS JOHN, plastics manufacturing executive; b. Famagusta, Cyprus, Nov. 13, 1924; s. John Charalambous and Joan George (Papadopoulos) C.; m. Dhora Michalaki Epaminonda, Apr. 27, 1958; children: Katherine, Maria. Grad., Famagusta Gymnasium. Acct. Controller of Transport and Mktg., Famagusta, 1943; mgr. KEO Ltd., Famagusta, 1951, N. P. Lanitis Co. Ltd., Famagusta, 1960; mng. dir. Cyprus Vineyards Ltd., Famagusta, 1964-74; mgr. Hadjikyriacos & Sons (Famagusta) Ltd., 1970; dep. mng. dir. Regis Group of Cos., Nicosia, Cyprus, 1976; mng. dir. Fooditems Trading Co. Ltd., Nicosia, 1979—; also bd. dirs. Home: Ayias Ekaterinis 6, Flat 11, Nicosia 164, Cyprus also: PO Box 1398, Nicosia Cyprus Office: Fooditems Trading Co Ltd, Synergasias 1 Kaimakli, PO Box 1398, Nicosia 127, Cyprus

CONDRELL, WILLIAM KENNETH, lawyer; b. Buffalo, N.Y., Sept. 19, 1926; s. Paul Kenneth and Celia Olga (Schinas) C.; m. Constance A. Katsaros, June 22, 1958 (div. 1978); children—Paul, William, Alexander. B.S., Yale U., 1946; S.M., MIT, 1947; JD, Harvard U., 1950. Bar: N.Y. 1951, D.C. 1964, U.S. Ct. Appeals (4th cir.) 1974, U.S. Ct. Appeals (Fed. cir.) 1982, U.S. Ct. Appeals (D.C. cir.) 1984, U.S. Supreme Ct. 1965. Assoc. econ. adv. Exec. Office Pres., D.C., 1951-54; mgmt. cons. McKinsey and Co., Chgo., 1954-55; mgr. budgets Hotpoint div. Gen. Electric Co., Chgo., 1955-59; sole practice 1959-68; ptnr. Steptoe & Johnson, D.C., 1968—; adj. prof. Duke U., dir. Duke Ctr. Forestry Investment; gen. counsel Coalition for Uniform Product Liability Law, Am. Geophys. Union. Editor: Timber Tax Journal, 1965—. Served to lt.j.g. USNR, 1944-46. Mem. ABA, Am. Inst. C.P.A.s, National Press Club. Clubs: Metropolitan (D.C.); Congressional Country (Bethesda, Md.). Home: 6601 Michaels Dr Bethesda MD 20817 Office: Steptoe & Johnson 1330 Connecticut Ave Washington DC 20036

CONDRILL, JO ELLARESA, logistician, speaker; b. Hull, Tex., Oct. 25, 1935; d. Freddie and Ida (Donatto) Founteno; m. Edwin Leon Ellis, Jan. 9, 1955 (div. 1979); children—Michael Edwin, James Alcia, Resa Ann, Thomas Matthew; m. Donald Richard Condrill, Sept. 21, 1980 (div. 1985). BS in Bus. Adminstrn., Our Lady of the Lake U., 1982; grad. Logistics Exec. Devel. Course, Army Logistics Mgmt. Ctr., 1985; MS in Pub. Adminstrn., Cen. Mich. U., 1987. Cert. seminar coordinator. Sec. USAF, Wiesbaden, Fed. Republic Germany, 1968-73; sec. mil. tng. ctr. USAF, San Antonio, 1973-77; editorial asst. Airman Mag., San Antonio, 1978; mgmt. analyst San Antonio Air Logistics Ctr., San Antonio, 1979-82; inventory mgr. ground fuels Detachment 29, Alexandria, Va., 1982-83; logistics plans officer Mil. Dist. Washington, 1983-85, chief logistics plans ops. and mgmt., 1985-88, hdqrs. dept. of the army staff, 1988—; owner Seminars by Jo, Alexandria, Va., 1984-86; specialist logistics mgmt. Dep. Chief Staff Logistics Info. Mgmt. Div. Hdqrs. Dept. Army, 1988—; field instr. Golden State U., Los Angeles, 1985-86, field instr. Fairfax County Adult Edn., Springfield, Va., 1984; vol. aide ARC Wilford Hall Hosp., San Antonio, 1978; constn. drafter KC Women's Aux., San Antonio, 1977; den mother Boy Scouts Am., San Antonio, 1967; docent Nat. Mus. Am. History, 1988. Recipient Cert. of Achievement, Dept. Army, 1984; Best Speaker award Def. Logistics Agy. Mem. Soc. Logistics Engrs., Federally Employed Women (Pentagon I chpt. treas. 1987-88), Assn. U.S. Army, Internat. Platform Assn., Am. Soc. Pub. Adminstrn., Nat. Assn. Female Execs. Republican. Roman Catholic. Club: Toastmasters (disting., area gov. 1984-85, div. lt.-gov. 1988—). Home: 5904 Mount Eagle Dr #317 Alexandria VA 22303

CONGCO-MACAPINLAC, EVANGELINE GOZUN, internist, endocrinologist; b. Bacolor, Philippines; came to U.S., 1972; naturalized, 1980; d. Engracio D. and Rosario (Gozun) Congco; m. Efren L. Macapinlac, June 19, 1976; 1 child, Elaine Congco-Macapinlac. B.S. magna cum laude, U. Santo Tomas, Manila, 1966, M.D. cum laude, 1971. Intern in internal medicine U.Wis.-Milw., 1972-73; resident in internal medicine Wayne State U., Detroit, 1973-76; fellow in endocrinology U. Calif.-San Francisco, 1976-77; practice medicine specializing in internal medicine and endocrinology, Daly City, Calif., 19—; mem. staff Seton Med. Ctr., Daly City, 1980—, lectr. endocrinology, 1981—; acting med. dir. Guadalupe Health Ctr., Daly City, 1977-81; preceptor for lic. nurse practitioners San Francisco State U., 1978-81. Contbr. articles to med. jours. Recipient Am. Humanitarian award No. San Mateo County, Cindy Smallwood Found., 1980. Mem. AMA, World Med. Assn., Nat. Assn. Female Execs. Avocations: hybrid tea roses; writing poems; travelling. Office: Westlake Med Bldg 48 Park Plaza Suite 306 Daly City CA 94015

CONIGLIO, FAITH BOULT, social worker; b. Sault Ste. Marie, Mich., Apr. 19, 1926; d. James Ben and Grace Anne (Corrigan) Boult; A.B., U. Mich., 1948; M.S.W., U. Denver, 1952; m. Gioacchino Charles Coniglio, Sept. 1, 1951; children—Gina Mari, Giuli Anna. Social worker Sedgwick County Welfare Bd., Wichita, Kans., 1949-50; psychiat. social worker Topeka (Kans.) State Hosp., 1952-56; social worker Youth Center at Topeka, 1973-78, social work supr., 1978-82; sr. psychiat. social worker Sedgwick County North Mental Health Ctr., 1982-88 . Kans. Bd. Social Welfare grad. scholar, 1950-51; NIMH grantee, 1951-52. Mem. Nat. Assn. Social Workers (charter), Am. Assn. Partial Hospitalization, Inc. Office: 1801 E 10th St Wichita KS 67214

CONINE, THOMAS EDMUND, JR., educator; b. Bridgeport, Conn., June 16, 1951; s. Thomas Edmund and Isabelle (Johnson) C.; m. Mary Ann Lee, May 20, 1979; children—Thomas E. III, Tara Elizabeth. B.S., U. Conn., 1973; M.B.A., NYU, 1975, M.Phil., 1978, Ph.D., 1979. Instr. Pace U., N.Y.C., 1976-78; asst. prof. U. Conn., Storrs, 1978-80; assoc. prof. then prof., assoc. dean Fairfield U., Conn., 1980—; corp. teaching GE, ATT, Texaco, United Techs., and numerous other cos. Contbr. articles to profl. jours. Recipient Wall St. Jour. award U. Conn., 1973; Thesis of Yr. award NYU, 1975. Mem. Fin. Mgmt. Assn., Am. Fin. Assn., Eastern Fin. Assn. Club: Brooklawn Country. Avocations: golf; travel. Home: 63 Rolling Wood Dr Trumbull CT 06611 Office: Fairfield U Sch Bus North Benson Rd Fairfield CT 06430

CONKEL, ROBERT DALE, pension consultant, lawyer; b. Martins Ferry, Ohio, Oct. 13, 1936; s. Chester William and Marian Matilda (Ashton) C.; m. Elizabeth A. Cargill, June 15, 1958; children—Debra Lynn Conkel McGlone, Dale William, Douglas Alan; m. 2d, Brenda Jo Myers, Aug. 2, 1980. B.A., Mt. Union Coll., 1958; J.D. cum laude, Cleve. Marshall Law Sch., 1965; LL.M., Case Western Res. U., 1972. Bar: Ohio 1965, U.S. Tax Ct. 1974, U.S. Supreme Ct. 1974, Tex. 1978, U.S. Ct. Appeals (5th cir.) 1979. Supr., Social Security Adminstrn., Cleve., 1958-65; trust officer Harter Bank & Trust Co., Canton, Ohio, 1965-70; exec. v.p. Am. Actuaries, Inc., Grand Rapids, Mich., 1970-73, pension cons., southwest regional dir., Dallas, 1974—; mgr. plans and research A.S. Hansen, Inc., Dallas, 1973-74; sole practice, Dallas, 1973—; mem. devel. bd. Met. Nat. Bank, Richardson, Tex.; instr. Am. Mgmt. Assn., 1975, Am. Coll. Advanced Pension Planning, 1975-76. Sustaining mem. Republican Nat. Com., 1980—. Enrolled actuary, Joint Bd. Enrollment U.S. Depts. Labor and Treasury. Mem. ABA (employee benefit com. sect. taxation), Ohio State Bar Assn., Tex. Bar Assn., Dallas Bar Assn., Am. Soc. Pension Actuaries (dir. 1973-81), Am. Acad. Actuaries. Contbr. articles to legal publs.; editorial adv. bd. Jour. Pension Planning and Compliance, 1974-83. Office: PO Box 31481 Dallas TX 75231

CONLON, THOMAS JAMES, marketing executive; b. N.Y.C., July 30, 1935; s. Kenneth Charles and Catherine (Gavaghan) C.; m. Joan Anna Erickson, Jan. 19, 1957; children—Brian T., Michael K. Keith J.K. Ed. Art Students' League, N.Y.C., 1951-53, St. Peter's Coll., Jersey City, 1953-56. Staff artist N.Y. News, N.Y.C., 1953-57; spl. features writer-reporter, 1957-59; mktg. mgr. Tricolator Inc., Wantagh, N.Y., 1959-64; assoc. dir. promotion Benton & Bowles, N.Y.C., 1964-68; chmn. bd. D.L. Blair Corp., Garden City, N.Y., 1968—; chmn. PMI, Inc., Atlanta, 1986—; bd. dirs. Conlon & Nye Advt., Inc., N.Y.C.; chmn. DLB/W, Beverly Hills, Calif., 1987—; illustrator for various mags., 1952-53. Contbr. articles to Advt. Age, other publs. Mem. Promotion Mktg. Assn. Am. (treas. 1982-85), Direct Mktg. Assn. (assoc. ethics com. 1983-86, chmn. ethics com. 1986-87). Roman Catholic. Clubs: Brookville; Cherry Valley Country. Avocations: Joycean literature; fencing; art collecting. Home: Wolver Hollow Rd Upper Brookville NY 11771 Office: D L Blair Corp 1051 Franklin Ave Garden City NY 11530

CONN, BERNARD, sales director; b. London, June 26, 1930; s. David and Maisie (Stevens) C.; m. Pamela Park, Oct. 3, 1959 (div. Aug. 1979); children: Judith, Stephanic. Degree, City of London Coll., 1952. Sec. Duprez Etcie Ltd., London, 1946-52; ops. and mgmt. officer Ford Motor co., Dagenham, Eng., 1954-55; mgr. br. Burroughs Corp., London, 1955-78, sr. cons. sales and mktg., 1978-79; mgr. sales Systime Computers Ltd., London, 1980-85; dir. sales Autofile Ltd., Slough, Eng., 1985—. Served as lt. Brit. Army, 1952-54. Mem. Chartered Inst. Secs. (assoc.). Office: Autofile Ltd, Weston Rd, Slough, Bershire SL1 4HR, England

CONN, HADLEY LEWIS, JR., physician, educator; b. Danville, Ind., May 6, 1921; s. Hadley L. and Fyrne (Holtsclaw) C.; m. Betty Jean Aubertin, Sept. 18, 1946; children: Eric Hadley, Jeffrey Wood, Thomas Brian, Andrew Randall, Lisabeth Ann. B.A., U. Ind., 1942, M.D., 1944; M.S. (hon.), U. Pa., 1972. Assoc. scientist Brookhaven Nat. Lab., N.Y., 1953-55; asst. prof. U. Pa. Sch. Medicine, Phila., 1956-59; assoc. prof. U. Pa. Sch. Medicine, 1959-64, prof. medicine, 1964-72; dir. Clin. Research Center Hosp. of U. Pa. Sch. Medicine, 1970-72; chmn. dept. medicine Presbyn.-U. Pa. Med. Center, Phila., 1964-69; vis. prof. medicine Am. U. Beirut, 1969-70; chmn. dept. medicine Univ. Medicine and Dentistry N.J.-Rutgers Med. Sch., Piscataway, N.J., 1972-83, dir. Cardiovascular Inst., 1982—. Author: Myocardial Cell, 1966, Cardiac and Vascular Disease, 1971, Platelets, Prostaglandins and Lipids, 1980, Health and Obesity, 1983. Sec. Nat. Bd. Med. Examiners, 1962-65; bd. govs. Am. Heart Assn., 1969-72; pres. Heart Assn. S.E. Pa., 1967, Detweiler Found., 1973-85. Served to capt. M.C., AUS, 1946-48. Mem. ACP, Am. Coll. Cardiology (trustee 1963-69), AMA, Am. Soc. Clin. Investigation, Am. Clin. and Climatological Soc., Assn. Univ. Cardiologists, Am. Phys. Soc., Assn. Profs. Medicine, Phi Beta Kappa, Alpha Omega Alpha. Republican. Clubs: Rittenhouse; Merion Cricket (Phila.). Home: 253 Wendover St Princeton NJ 08540

CONN, HAROLD O., physician, educator; b. Newark, Nov. 16, 1925; s. Joseph H. and Dora (Kobrin) C.; m. Marilyn Barr, May 2, 1951; children: Chrysanne, Steven A., Dorianne. BS, U. Mich., 1946, MD, 1950; MS, Yale U., 1972. Diplomate: Am. Bd. Internal Medicine. Intern Johns Hopkins Hosp., 1950-51; asst. resident Grace New Haven Community Hosp., 1951-52, chief resident, 1955-56; James Hudson Browne research fellow 1952-53; dir. med. edn. Middlesex Meml. Hosp., 1956-57; clin. investigator VA, 1957-61; chief med. service VA Hosp., West Haven, Conn., 1959-60; chief hepatic research lab. VA Hosp., 1961—; instr. Yale Sch. Medicine, 1955-58, asst. prof., 1958-66, asso. prof., 1966-71, prof., 1971—; vis. asso. prof. Washington U. Sch. Medicine, 1968; vis. prof. Stanford U. Sch. Medicine, 1975-76, UCLA Sch. Medicine, 1982-83; dir. continuing med. edn. program Yale U., 1988—. Author: The Hepatic Coma Syndromes and Lactulose, 1979; editor: Cyanidanol in Diseases of the Liver, 1981; mem. editorial bd.: Viewpoints on Digestive Disease, 1968-73; editorial bd.: Gastroenterology, 1970-80, editor for Liver Disease and Physiology, 1973-77; editorial bd.: Jour. Clin. Trials, Italian Jour. Gastroenterology, 1977-87; assoc. editor: Hepatology, 1980-85; book editor: Hepatology, 1985—; editor: Hepatology Elsewhere, 1985—. Bd. dirs. Am. Liver Found., 1977-80. Served to ensign USNR, 1943-44. Recipient Rorer award Am. Jour. Gastroenterology, 1973, William Beaumont award clin. research, 1974; Conn. paddle tennis mixed doubles champion (asphalt), 1963. Fellow ACP; mem. Assn. Am. Physicians, Am. Soc. Clin. Investigation, Internat. Assn. Study Liver, Sydenham Soc. (sec. 1968—, mem. med. adv. bd. Seminars and Symposia 1974-80), Hepatic Perfusion Soc. (pres. St. Louis chpt.), Am. Assn. Study Liver Disease (v.p. 1971, pres. 1972, dir. postgrad. course on portal hypertension), Am. Fedn. Clin. Research, Am. Gasteroenterol. Assn. (councillor 1974-77), Viral Hepatitis Venereal Transmission Soc. (pres. 1976), Soc. for Clin. Trials (dir. 1978-83), Ascites Internat. Diagnostic Soc. (pres. protem 1983-86), Nat. Assn. Va. Physicians (bd. dirs. 1986—, chmn. continuing med. edn. com. 1987—), Am. Acad. Postgrad. Medicine (bd. dirs. 1986—); hon. mem. Australian Soc. Gastroenterology, Brazilian Assn. for Study of Liver, China Med. Assn. (Shanghai br.). Clubs: Conn. Sunfish (commodore 1967), Westwood Cinema and Sun Soc. (chmn. 1982-83). Home: 160 Morgan Ave East Haven CT

06512 Office: VA Hosp W Spring St West Haven CT 06516 Other: 333 Cedar St New Haven CT 06608

CONNALLY, ERNEST ALLEN, federal agency administrator; b. Groesbeck, Tex., Nov. 15, 1921; s. Ernest Lackey and Eleanor Pauline (Allen) C.; m. Janice Muriel Wegner, Aug. 28, 1951; children—Mary Allen, John Arnold. Student, Rice U., 1939-40, U. Tex., 1940-42; BArch, U. Tex., 1950; student, U. Florence, Italy, 1947; MA, Harvard U., 1952, PhD, 1955. Asst. prof. architecture Miami U., Oxford, Ohio, 1952-55; assoc. prof. Washington U., St. Louis, 1955-57; vis. prof. Washington U., 1962; assoc. prof. U. Ill., Urbana, 1957-61; prof. U. Ill., 1961-67; assoc. Ctr. for Advanced Study, 1966-67; asst. dir. Nat. Park Service, Dept. Interior, Washington, 1967-72, assoc. dir., 1972-78, chief appeals officer, 1982—; assoc. dir. Heritage Conservation and Recreation Service, 1978-79; cons. restoration hist. bldgs., 1952—; UNESCO cons. Govt. of Nepal, 1968, Govt. of Thailand, 1982—; sec.-treas, U.S. com. Internat. Council on Monuments and Sites, 1969-73, chmn., 1973-75, sec.-gen. Internat. Council on Monuments and Sites, 1975-81; Fulbright lectr. U. Melbourne, Australia, 1963; U.S. del. UNESCO Conf. on Cultural Property, 1968; U.S. rep. Internat. Conf. on Rec. Hist. Monuments, Prague, Czechoslovakia, 1969; U.S. del. v.p. Gen. Assembly, Internat. Centre for Study of Preservation of Cultural Property, Rome, 1971, 77; mem. U.S.-USSR Joint Working Group on Urban Environment, 1973-81; bd. dirs. Pa. Ave. Devel. Corp., 1974-78. Author: Printed Books on Architecture, 1485-1805, 1960; also articles in jours., encys.; mem. editorial bd. Monumentum, 1967-75; important works include restoration of Louis Bolduc house, 1956-57, Bolduc-LeMeilleur house, St. Genevieve, Mo., 1967. Served to maj. USAAF, 1942-46, lt. col. Res., ret. Decorated Officier Ordre des Arts et des Lettres, France, 1987; recipient Research award Am. Philos. Soc., 1957, Disting. Service award Dept. Interior, 1978, Crowninshield award Nat. Trust Hist. Preservation, 1980; named membre d'Honneur, ICOMOS, 1981, Trustee of Am., 1986. Mem. Coll. Art Assn. Am., Soc. Archtl. Historians (past bd. dirs.), AIA (hon.), Assn. for Preservation Tech., Nat. Trust for Hist. Preservation (past bd. trustees), Am. Assn. State and Local History, Nat. Parks and Conservation Assn., Gargoyle, SAR, Alpha Rho Chi, Tau Sigma Delta, Phi Kappa Phi. Episcopalian. Club: Cosmos (Washington). Home: 1601 Ruffner Rd Alexandria VA 22302 Office: Nat Park Service PO Box 37127 Washington DC 20013

CONNELL-SMITH, GORDON EDWARD, history educator, author, broadcaster; b. London, Nov. 23, 1917; s. George Frederick and Margaret (Woolerton) Smith; m. Wendy Ann Tomlinson, Mar. 27, 1954; children—Sarah, Nicholas. B.A. with honors in History, Univ. Coll., Exeter, 1939; Ph.D. in History, U. London, 1950. Faculty, U. Hull, Eng., 1952—, lectr., 1952-63, sr. lectr., 1963-69, reader, 1969-73, prof., 1973-85, prof. emeritus, 1985—, chmn. contemporary history, 1973-85; chmn. Latin Am. Newsletters Ltd., London, 1969-72; broadcaster BBC, London, 1959—. Author: Forerunners of Drake, 1954; Pattern of the Post-War World, 1957; The Inter-American System, 1966 (Spanish 1971); The United States and Latin America, 1974 (Spanish 1977); co-author: The Relevance of History, 1972; contbr. articles to jours., writings to anthologies. Served to maj. Brit. Army, 1940-46. Recipient Julian Corbett Prize, Inst. Hist. Research, 1949. Fellow Royal Hist. Soc.; mem. Royal Inst. Internat. Affairs, Brit. Assn. for Am. Studies, Soc. for Latin Am. Studies. Home: 7 Braids Walk, Kirkella, Hull HU10 7PA, North Humberside England

CONNELLY, WILLIAM JOSEPH, marketing and public relations executive; b. Pottsville, Pa., Sept. 29, 1931; s. Joseph Thomas and Marie Cecelia (Ryan) C.; m. Margaret Ann Scanlan Carl, Oct. 6, 1951; children: Margaret Marie, William Joseph, Colleen; m. 2d, Ellen Marie Bufe, May 20, 1972; 1 son, Sean Ryan. AB, King's Coll., Wilkes-Barre, Pa., 1966; postgrad. U. Scranton, 1965-66, St. Louis U., 1968-71. Profl. broadcaster and journalist, 1949-66; corp. communications specialist Mgmt. Cons., Kingston, Pa., 1958-63; cons. to pres. ednl. radio/TV King's Coll. Wilkes-Barre, Pa., 1963-66; dir. pub. relations St. Louis U. Med. Ctr., 1967-71; dir. pub. affairs Chgo. State U., 1971-74; dir. pub. relations Schwab Rehab. Hosp., Chgo., 1974-76; dir. mktg. pub. relations Bankers Life and Casualty Co., Chgo., 1976-80; dir. mktg. communications and pub. relations Underwriters Labs. Inc., Northbrook, Ill., 1980-83; sr. cons. JN Co., 1983-85; prin. Bufe, Connelly & Ryan, Mktg. & Pub. Relations, 1985—; adj. prof. journalism Chgo. State U., 1973-74. Active Boy Scouts Am., 1951-62, Suburban Cook County-Du Page County Health (Planning) Systems Agy., 1984—. Served with USAF, 1950-51. Mem. Pub. Relations Soc. Am. Democrat. Roman Catholic.

CONNER, WILLIAM BOUDINOT, retired Romance educator, parascience researcher; b. Portland, Oreg., Apr. 25, 1913; s. William Boudinot and Boeske (Ruh) C. B.A., Oberlin Coll., 1937; M.A., U. Ill., 1939. Instr. State Coll. Wash., Pullman, 1946-47; assoc. prof. Huron Coll., S.D., 1958-61, St. Cloud State Coll., Minn., 1961-63; instr. Temple U., Phila., 1963-66; assoc. prof. French and Spanish, Kutztown U., Pa., 1966-77, prof. emeritus Romance langs., 1977—; now parasci. researcher. Author: Harmonic Mathematics, 1982, Math's Metasonics, 1983, Music's Metasonics, 1983, The Attunergy Crystal, 1984, Mathematical Heaven and Timebound Earth: An Interpenetration, 1985, Time in a New Key, 1987, The Crystals of Spirituality, 1987. Contbr. articles to profl. jours. Patentee tonalingua chordmaster set, keyboard actuated lighting instrument. Served to cpl. U.S. Army, 1942-44. World U. fellow 1975. Mem. Borderland Scis. Research Found., U.S. Psychotronics Assn., Soc. Investigation of Unexplained. Democrat. Unitarian Univeralist. Avocations: poetry; history; improvising at piano; tennis. Home: 117 S 4th St Apt 507 Allentown PA 18102

CONNOLLY, GEORGE CHARLES, JR., civil district judge; b. New Orleans, La., July 20, 1928; s. George Charles and Clare (Walsh) C.; m. Elinor C. Van Geffen, Apr. 19, 1958. BA, Loyola U.-New Orleans, 1947, JD, 1950, BBA, 1952. Bar: La. 1950, U.S. Dist. Ct. (ea. dist.) La. 1952, U.S. Supreme Ct. 1968. Pvt. practice, New Orleans, 1950-70; commr. and judge ad hoc Civil Dist. Ct., Parish of Orleans, 1960-70, judge, 1970—; chief judge Civil Dist. Ct., 1981-82; judge pro tem U.S. Ct. Appeals (4th cir.), 1973. Pres. Met. Safety Council, New Orleans, 1981-82; Cystic Fibrosis Found. New Orleans, 1975-76. Served to col. USNG, 1948-84. Recipient Disting. Service award New Orleans Jaycees, 1962-63, Exceptional Service and Meritorious Service medal Selective Service System. Mem. 4th & 5th Cir. Judges Assn. (pres. 1980), Young Men's Bus. Club (pres. 1961-62, hon. life mem.), Loyola U. Law Alumni (pres. 1968-69), New Orleans Bar Assn. (hon. mem.), Blue Key Nat. Hon. Soc. (hon. mem.), La. Bar Assn. (hon. mem.). Democrat. Roman Catholic. Clubs: La. Nat. Guard Officers (New Orleans) (pres. 1957-68), Tulane-Newman Alumni (New Orleans) (pres. 1956-57-58). Office: Civil Dist Ct Div J 421 Loyola Ave New Orleans LA 70112

CONNOLLY, JOHN EARLE, surgeon, educator; b. Omaha, May 21, 1923; s. Earl A. and Gertrude (Eckerman) C.; m. Virginia Hartman, Aug. 12, 1967; children: Peter Hart, John Earle, Sarah. A.B., Harvard U., 1945, M.D., 1948. Diplomate: Am. Bd. Surgery (bd. dirs. 1976-82), Am. Bd. Thoracic and Cardiovascular Surgery, Am. Bd. Vascular Surgery. Intern. in surgery Stanford U. Hosps., San Francisco, 1948-49, surg. research fellow, 1949-50, asst. resident surgeon, 1950-52, chief resident surgeon, 1953-54, surg. pathology fellow, 1954, instr. surgery, 1957-60, John and Mary Markle Scholar in med. scis., 1957-62; surg. registrar professional unit St. Bartholomew's Hosp., London, 1952-53; resident in thoracic surgery Bellevue Hosp., N.Y.C., 1955; resident in thoracic and cardiovascular surgery Columbia-Presbyn. Med. Ctr., N.Y.C., 1956; from asst. prof. to assoc. prof. surgery Stanford U., 1960-65; prof., chmn. dept. surgery U. Calif.-Irvine, 1965-78; attending surgeon Stanford Med. Ctr., Palo Alto, Calif., 1959-65; chmn. cardiovascular and thoracic surgery U. Calif.-Irvine Med. Ctr., 1968—; attending surgeon St. Joseph's Children's Hosp., Orange, Calif., 1968—, Anaheim Meml. Hosp. (Calif.), 1970—; A.H. Duncan vis. prof. U. Edinburgh, 1984; Hunterian prof. Royal Coll. Surgeons Eng., 1985-86; Kinmonth lectr. Royal Coll. Surgeons, Eng., 1987; mem. adv. council Nat. Heart, Lung, and Blood Inst.-NIH, 1981—; cons. Long Beach VA Hosp., Calif., 1965—, Long Beach Naval Hosp., Calif. Contbr. articles to profl. jours.; editorial bd.: Jour. Cardiovascular Surgery, 1974—, chief editor, 1985—; editorial bd. Western Jour. Medicine, 1975—, Jour. Stroke, 1979—, Jour. Vascular Surgery, 1983—. Bd. dirs. Audio-Digest Found., 1974—; bd. dirs. Franklin Martin Found., 1975-80. Served with AUS, 1943-44. Recipient Cert. of Merit, Japanese Surg. Soc., 1979. Fellow ACS (gov. 1964-70, regent 1972-82, vice chmn. bd. regents 1980-82, v.p. 1984-85), Royal Coll. Surgeons Eng. (hon.), Royal Coll. Surgeons Ireland (hon.); mem. Am. Surg. Assn., Soc. Univ. Surgeons, Am. Assn. Thoracic Surgery (council 1974-78), Pacific Coast Surg. Assn. (pres. 1985-86), San Francisco Surg. Soc., Los Angeles Surg. Soc., Soc. Vascular Surgery, Western Surg. Assn., Internat. Cardiovascular Soc. (pres. 1977), Soc. Internat. Chirurgie, Soc. Thoracic Surgeons, Western Thoracic Surg. Soc. (pres. 1978), Orange County Surg. Soc. (pres. 1984-85), James IV Assn. Surgeons (councillor 1983—). Clubs: California (Los Angeles); San Francisco Golf, Pacific Union, Bohemian (San Francisco); Cypress Point (Pebble Beach, Calif.); Harvard (N.Y.C.); Big Canyon (Newport Beach). Home: 7 Deerwood Ln Newport Beach CA 92660 Office: U Calif Dept Surgery Irvine CA 92717

CONNOLLY, THOMAS EDWARD, lawyer; b. Boston, Nov. 7, 1942; s. Thomas Francis and Catherine Elizabeth (Skehill) C.; A.B., St. John's Sem., Brighton, Mass., 1964; J.D., Boston Coll., 1969. Admitted to Mass. bar, 1969; assoc. Schneider & Reilly, Boston, 1969-73; ptnr. Schneider, Reilly, Zabin, Connolly & Costello, P.C., Boston, 1973-85, Connolly & Leavis, Boston, 1986—; instr. law Northeastern Law Sch., Boston, 1975-76. Mem. governing council Boston Coll. Law Sch. Alumni Council, 1980—. Mem. ABA (vice chmn. products liability sect. 1978—), Am. Trial Lawyers Assn. (nat. gov. 1977-80), Mass. Acad. Trial Lawyers (gov. 1976—), Am. Coll. of Trial Lawyers. Democrat. Roman Catholic. Club: Univ. (Boston). Home: 15 Vincent Rd Roslindale MA 02131 Office: Connolly & Leavis 168 Milk St Boston MA 02109

CONNOLLY-O'NEILL, BARRIE JANE, interior designer; b. San Francisco, Dec. 22, 1943; d. Harry Jr. and Jane Isabelle (Barr) Wallach; m. Peter Smith O'Neill, Nov. 27, 1983. Cert. of design, N.Y. Sch. Interior Design, 1975; BAF in Environ. Design, Calif. Coll. Arts and Crafts, 1978. Profl. model Brebner Agy., San Francisco, 1963-72; TV personality KGO TV, San Francisco, 1969-72; interior designer Barrie Connolly & Assocs., Boise, Idaho, 1978—. Best Interior Design award Mktg. and Merchandising Excellence, No. Calif., 1981, 1984;, Sales and Mktg. Council, San Diego, 1985, 86; Best Residential Design award Boise Design Revue Com., 1983;, Grand award Best in Am. Living, Nat. Assn. Homebuilders, River Run, Boise, 1986. Mem. Mannequin League of Marin. Home: 2188 Bluestem Ln Boise ID 83706

CONNOR, JAMES RUSSELL, automobile executive; b. Lima, Ohio, Oct. 30, 1940; s. Russell Thurman and Esther Mae (Rowe) C.; student Bowling Green State U., 1969-71; B.S. in Bus., Defiance Coll., 1972; M.B.A. in Prodn. Mgmt., Ind. U., 1974; m. Beryl Anna Dixon, Aug. 25, 1973; children—Steven Eric, Jeffrey Allen. Corp. responsibility mgr. Cummins Engine Co., Columbus, Ind., 1975-76; gen. supr. Ford Motor Co., Lima, Ohio, 1976-78, shift supt., 1978-79, area supt., 1979-80, quality control supt., 1980-81; mfg. mgr. Kelsey-Hayes Co., Marlette, Mich., 1981-82, plant mgr., 1982-83; dir. quality assurance Gen. Motors Corp., 1984-88; dir. engine and powertrain systems, 1988— . Chmn. Urban Bus. Assn., 1980—; mem. Human Rights Commn., 1976; minority placement advisor, 1973-74; active Jr. Achievement, 1976; trustee, mem. fin., profl. relations and safety coms. Good Samaritan Hosp., 1984—; active Sandusky LEADS Program, 1984-85; co-chmn. Erie County United Way, 1985; trustee Community Action Com., 1985. Served with USMC, 1961-66. Consortium Grad. Study in Mgmt. fellow, 1973-74; Ednl. Opportunity fellow, 1974. Mem. NAACP, Sandusky C. of C., Am. Soc. Quality Control, Am. Mgmt. Assn., Assn. M.B.A. Execs., Beta Gamma Sigma. Baptist. Club: Ind. U. Varsity. Home: 4608 Venice Heights Blvd Sandusky OH 44870 Office: New Departure-Hyatt Div 2509 Hayes Ave Sandusky OH 44870

CONNOR, JOHN THOMAS, JR., lawyer; b. N.Y.C., June 16, 1941; s. John Thomas and Mary (O'Boyle) C.; m. Susan Scholle Connor, Dec. 18, 1965; children: Seanna, Marin, John. BA cum laude, Williams Coll., 1963; JD, Harvard U., 1967. Bar: N.Y. 1968, D.C. 1980. Assoc. Cravath, Swaine & Moore, N.Y.C., 1967-71; dep. dir. Office Econ. Policy and Case Analysis, Pay Bd., Washington, 1971-72; dep. dir. Bur. E.-W. Trade, U.S. Dept. Commerce, Washington, 1972-73; sr. v.p. U.S.-USSR Trade and Econ. Council, Moscow, 1973-76; assoc. Milbank, Tweed, Hadley & McCloy, N.Y.C., 1976-79; ptnr. Curtis, Mallet-Prevost, Colt and Mosle, Washington, 1980-82; v.p., gen. counsel, sec. PHH Group, Inc., 1982—; bd. dirs., mem. mgmt. com., mem. credit com., chmn. Employee Benefits Union Micros Systems, Inc.; chmn. audit com. Nat. Assn. Securities Dealers. Exec. dir. Dem. party N.J., 1969-70; trustee Council for Religion in Ind. Schs.; trustee St. Mary's Coll., Council Nat. Security. Fulbright tutor Ferguson Coll., Poona, India, 1963-64. Mem. ABA, N.Y. State Bar Assn., D.C. Bar Assn., Council Fgn. Relations, Am. Law Inst., Phi Beta Kappa. Clubs: Met. (Washington); Union (N.Y.C.); Chevy Chase (Md.). Home: 12 Primrose St Chevy Chase MD 20815 Office: PHH Group Inc 11333 McCormick Rd Hunt Valley MD 21031

CONNOR, PAUL EUGENE, social worker; b. Atchison, Kans., Aug. 11, 1921; s. Samuel Walters and Juanita Marie (Fry) C.; BS. with honors in History, Columbia U., 1962; M.A., 1963; grad. cert. in social work, Fordham U., 1973; m. Louise Dorothy Schiddel, June 28, 1959 (div. 1964). Lectr. Am. History Rutgers State U., 1966-67; lectr. S.E. Asian history New Sch. Social Research, 1967-68; caseworker Bergen Center, South Bronx, N.Y., 1970-73; caseworker Protective Services, Bur. of Child Welfare, Bronx, 1973-75; caseworker Preventive Services Spl. Services for Children, N.Y.C., 1975-83; supr. I family program Crisis Intervention Services, 1983-87; tchr. The Internat. Center, 1977-86. Rec. sec. Bronx Council for Environ. Quality, 1981-83, bd. dirs., 1983—; docent Mus. of City of N.Y., 1988—. Served with USN, 1941-42. Mem. Internat. Council Social Welfare, Asia Soc., Am. Hist. Assn., S.C. Hist. Soc., N.C. Lit. and Hist. Assn., Soc. of Boonesborough. Democrat. Home: 2755 Reservoir Ave #5A Bronx NY 10468 Office: Fifth Ave at 103d St New York NY 10029

CONNOR, SEYMOUR VAUGHAN, historian, writer; b. Paris, Tex., Mar. 4, 1923; s. Aikin Beard and Gladys (Vaughan) C.; 1 son, Charles Seymour. B.A., U. Tex., 1948, M.A., 1949, Ph.D., 1952. Archivist W.Tex. State U., 1952-53, Tex. State Library, 1953-55; prof. history, dir. S.W. collection Tex. Tech. U., Lubbock, 1955-63; prof. history Tex. Tech. U., 1965-79, prof. emeritus, 1979—; vis. prof. Angelo State Coll., 1964-65. Author: Preliminary Guide to Texas Archives, 1956, Peters Colony of Texas, 1959, A Biggers Chronicle, 1961, Adventure in Glory, 1965, (with others) The Battle of Texas, 1967, The Capitols of Texas, 1970, Texas: A History, 1971, (with Odie Faulk) North America Divided: The Mexican War, 1846-48, 1971, (with W.C. Pool) Texas, the 28th State, 1971, (with Odie Faulk) La Guerra de Intervencion, 1846-1848, 1975, Texas in 1776, 1975, (with J.M. Skaggs) Broadcloth and Britches: The Santa Fe Trade, 1976; Editor: Texas Treasury Papers (3 vols.), 1955, The West Is for Us, 1957, Builders of the Southwest, 1959, Saga of Texas (6 vols.), 1965, Dear America, 1971; Contbr. articles to profl. jours. Served with AUS, 1943-45, ETO; Served with USAR, 1946-52. Fellow Tex. State Hist. Assn. (exec. council 1957-70, pres. 1967-68); mem. Phi Kappa Tau, Phi Kappa Psi, Phi Alpha Theta. Home: 3503 45th St Lubbock TX 79413

CONNORS, JAMES SCOTT (JIMMY CONNORS), professional tennis player; b. East St. Louis, Ill., Sept. 2, 1952; s. James and Gloria (Thompson) C.; m. Patti McGuire; 1 son, Brett David. Student, UCLA. Joined World Championship Tennis, Inc., 1972. Recipient Player of Year award, 1974; named All-Am., 1971; ranked no. 1 male tennis player in U.S., 1974, 1976; ranked no. 1 in world, 1978. Office: Pro Serv Inc 888 17th St NW Washington DC 20006 also: care US Tennis Assn Membership Dept PO Box 1726 Hickville NY 11802 •

CONNORS, JIMMY See CONNORS, JAMES SCOTT

CONNORS, JOHN JOSEPH HAYWARD, health services consultant; b. Manchester, Eng., June 27, 1918; s. John Joseph and Nora (Hayward) C.; student Regiopolis Coll., 1932-34, Balliol Coll., Oxford U., 1945; LL.B., LaSalle U., 1958; M. Hosp. Adminstrn., Baylor U., 1960; m. Doreen Mary Goodall, Jan. 27, 1940; children—John J.G., Michael A., M. Anne T. Entered Can. Regular Army, 1935, advanced through grades to maj., 1966, ret., 1966; chief hosp. cons. Man. Hosp. Commn., 1966, asst. dir. hosp. services, 1966-68; exec. dir. Misericordia Gen. Hosp., Winnipeg, 1968-76; health services cons., 1976—; chmn. Man. Medico-Moral Com., 1970-76, Man. Com. on Human Experimentation; tchr. med. jurisprudence and human relation in med. and para-med. fields. Mem. adv. com. Red River Community Coll.; bd. dirs. Can. Council Christians and Jews; chmn. bd. dirs. Sisters of Providence of Kingston in Man. Decorated 1939-45 Star, France and Ger. Star, Def. medal, Can. Vol. Service medal with clasp; War medal 1939-45, Can. Forces Decoration with clasp; Mentioned in Despatches. Fellow Royal Soc. Health; mem. Can. Coll. Health Service Execs., Winnipeg Regional Hosp. Council, Royal Can. Legion, United Services Inst., Cath. Hosp. Assn. Can. (pres. 1972-73), Cath. Health Conf. Man. (pres. 1969-73), Def. Med. Assn. (pres. 1978), Cath. Hosp. Assn. (U.S.), Man. Medico-Legal Soc. Contbr. to publs. in field. Home and Office: 7-A Harness Ln, Ottawa, ON Canada K2M 1E1

CONNORS, JOSEPH ALOYSIUS, III, lawyer; b. Washington, June 24, 1946; s. Joseph Aloysius Jr. and Charlotte Rita (Fox) C.; m. Mary Louise Bucklin, June 14, 1969. BBA, U. Southwestern La., 1970; JD, U. Tex., 1973. Bar: Tex. 1973, U.S. Dist. Ct. (so. dist.) Tex. 1975, U.S. Supreme Ct. 1976, U.S. Ct. Appeals (5th cir.) 1976, U.S. Dist. Ct. (ea., we. and no. dists.) Tex. 1981, U.S. Ct. Appeals (11th cir.) 1981, U.S. Ct. Appeals (3d, 4th, 6th, 7th, 8th, 9th, 10th and D.C. cirs.) 1986. Law clk. to assoc. justice Tex. Ct. Civil Appeals, Amarillo, 1973-74; assoc. Rankin & Kern, McAllen, Tex., 1974-76; asst. criminal dist. atty. Hidalgo County, Tex., 1976-78; sole practice McAllen, 1978—; faculty mem. Criminal Trial Advocacy Inst., Huntsville, Tex., 1981-84; speaker State Bar of Tex. seminars, 1980-81, 84. Contbg. editor Criminal Trial Manual, Tex., 1984—; contbr. articles to legal pubs. Served with USMCR, 1966-71. Mem. Hidalgo County Bar Assn. (bd. dirs. 1981-83), Nat. Assn. Criminal Def. Lawyers, Tex. Assn. Criminal Def. Lawyers (bd. dirs. 1982—, award of excellence 1983, 84, medal of honor, 1987), Am. Soc. Writers on Legal Subjects, Tex. Bd. Legal Specialization (bd. cert., criminal law). Democrat. Roman Catholic. Office: 804 Pecan St PO Box 5838 McAllen TX 78502-5838

CONNORS, STEPHEN WILFRED, lawyer; b. Monroe, Wis., Mar. 11, 1918; s. Patrick J. and Alice (Norder) C.; student U. Wis., 1937-41, U. Minn., 1951; B. Sci. Law, St. Paul Coll. Law, 1950, LL.B. cum laude, 1952; J.D., William Mitchell Coll. Law, 1969; m. Louise Pharr, Feb. 4, 1946; children—Maureen, Patricia, Constance, Mary, Michele, Kelly. Bar: Minn. 1952, Ariz. 1954, U.S. Dist. Ct., 1954, U.S. Ct. Appeals (9th cir.) 1963, U.S. Supreme Ct., 1960; practice Phoenix, 1953—; pres. Olympia Realty, Inc.; dir. Truten Investment Corp. Mem. Ariz. State Athletic Commn., 1961; founding mem. Ariz. State U. Law Sch.; mem. adv. council Am. Security Council; precinct committeeman Democratic Party, 1954-59, 61-72, 84—; mem. Dem. State Central Com., 1954-59, 61-72. Served as sr. pilot USAF, 1943-53, disch. capt. Mem. Am., Ariz., Maricopa County, Minn., Ramsey County bar assns., VFW (life), Am. Legion, Amvets, Hump Pilots Assn. (life), Mil. Flight Service (life dir., legal officer, past pres.), Air Force Assn., Fraternal Order of Police, Friendly Sons of St. Patrick, Am. Trial Lawyers Assn., Internat. Assn. Jewish Lawyers and Jurists, Internat. Acad. Law and Sci., Am. Judicature Soc., Academia Internationali Lex et Scientia. Roman Catholic. Moose. Clubs: Phoenix Execs., Prescott Mountain, Phoenix Press, Terrace, Arizona, Thunderbird Country (founding mem.), Statesman's, Westerner. Home: 8650 E Sandalwood Dr Scottsdale AZ 85253 Office: 810 Clubhouse Dr Prescott AZ 86301

CONNORS, TRACY DANIEL, business executive, editor, writer; b. Jacksonville, Fla., Sept. 30, 1939; s. Woodrow Daniel and Miriam (Morris) C.; m. Faith Cottrell Raymond, Dec. 22, 1961; children: Karen Connors Henson, Miriam Faith. BA, U. Fla., 1962; MA, U. R.I., 1968. Dir. community relations Bicycle Inst. Am., N.Y.C., 1970; dir. Community Devel. Act Plan Agy., Stamford, Conn., 1971; dir. pub. relations and mktg. F.D. Rich Co., Stamford, 1972-75; exec. dir. Arts Assembly, Jacksonville, 1975-77; dir. One-Stop Jobs/Edn. Ctr., Jacksonville, 1977-79; v.p. Taft Corp., Washington, 1979-82; congl. exec. asst. U.S. Ho. of Reps., Washington, 1982-83; area mgr. bus., dir. corp. communications sect. def. bus. Gould, Inc., Glen Burnie, Md., 1983-86; sr. analyst Kapos Assocs., Inc., Washington, 1987-88; pub. Brit. Bus. Today, Crofton, Md.; cons. in field govt. relations and mgmt. nonprofit orgns. Editor-in-chief: Nonprofit Organization Handbook, 1980, 2d edit., 1988, Longman Dictionary of Mass Media and Communication, 1982, Financial Management for Nonprofit Organizations, 1982; also articles. Pres., bd. dirs. Stamford Jaycees, 1970-71; trustee 1st Congl. Ch. Stamford, 1972-74; founder, 1st pres. Stamford Ambulance Corps, 1972-73, Stamford Council Arts, 1973-74; founder, bd. dirs. Stamford Art Assn., 1973-74; mem. Jacksonville U. Council, 1975-76, Am. Bicentennial Commn. of Jacksonville, 1975-77; bd. dirs. Opera Co. Jacksonville, 1970, Bold Cityfest of Jacksonville, 1975-77. Served as lt. USN, 1961-69, now comdr. USNR. Recipient various serivce and profl. awards. Mem. Surface Navy Assn. (life, founder, bd. dirs. Greater Washington chpt.), Res. Officers Assn., Naval Res. Assn., Nat. Eagle Scout Assn. Home: 2705 Birdseye Ln Bowie MD 20715 Office: Brit Bus Today Box 3310 Crofton MD 21114

CONOBY, JOSEPH FRANCIS, chemist; b. Albany, June 12, 1930; s. Joseph Francis and Helen Emma (Brucker) C.; B.S., Union Coll., 1952; m. Mary Joan A. Ryan, June 21, 1958; children—James Francis, Mark Joseph. Sr. tech. service engr. Allied Chem. Corp., Syracuse, N.Y., 1956-66; research chemist Conversion Chem. Corp., Rockville, Conn., 1966-69; environ. engr., indsl. hygienist, mgr. environ. and health engring. Honeywell Bull, Billerica, Mass., 1969-87, mgr. environ. engring. Boston products div., 1987—; mem. adv. bd. Mass. Water Resources Authority Sewer Use (rules and regulations, policy and procedures, and facilities planning task forces); cons. exptl. project course Mass. Inst. Tech., 1977-78. Served to lt. USN, 1952-56. Mem. Am. Electroplaters Soc. (chmn. project com.), Am. Inst. Plant Engrs., Am. Indsl. Hygiene Assn. Patentee in field, U.S., Germany. Contbr. articles to profl. jours. Home: 5 Samuel Parlin Dr Acton MA 01720 Office: Honeywell Bull Inc Billerica MA 01821

CONOLE, CLEMENT VINCENT, corporate executive; b. Binghamton, N.Y., Sept. 29, 1908; s. P.J. and Briget (Holleran) C.; m. Marjorie Anable, Sept. 26, 1931; children—Barbara (Mrs. Francis B. McElroy), Marjorie (Mrs. Marjorie A. Hargrave), Richard, Jacalyn (Mrs. John N. Harman III). B.S.C.E., Clarkson Coll. Tech., Potsdam, N.Y., 1931; postgrad., Cornell U., N.Y. U., Yale U.; M.B.A., Fla. Atlantic U. Licensed profl engr. and land surveyor, N.Y., Pa. Engr. City of Binghamton, also N.Y. State, 1930-32; ptnr. Richmeyer, Harding and Conole, 1932-33; engr. Dept. of Interior, 1933-35; dist. dir. Fed. Works Adminstrn.; dist. supt. N.Y. Unemployment Ins. Div., 1936-37; asst. state indsl. commr. N.Y., 1937-39; dep. indsl. commr. 1939-43; dir. indsl. bur. C. of C. Bd. of Trade of Phila., 1943-44, operating mgr., 1945-46, exec. v.p., 1946-52; also editor, pub. Greater Phila. mag., 1945-50; v.p. Bankers Securities corp., 1952-55; pres. Municipal Pubs., Inc., 1947-50; pub. relations cons. Phila.-Balt. Stock Exchange, 1947-52; chmn. bd., pres., dir. Hearn Dept. Stores, Inc., N.Y.C., 1952-54; dir., chmn. bd. James McCutcheon & Co., 1956-57; chmn. bd., dir. Bus. Supplies Corp. Am., Skytop, Pa., 1962-65; chmn. bd. dir., pres. Tabulating Card Co., Inc., Princeton, N.J., 1955-62; chmn. bd. dir. Am. Bus. Mgmt. Co., 1955-62, Whiting Paper Co., Inc., 1959-62, Sky Meadow Farms, Inc., 1965-68, Am. Bus. Machines Co., 1958-65, Data Processing Supplies Co., 1959-65, Am. Bus. Execs. Co., 1960-65, Am. Bus. Investment Co., 1958-62, Gen. Bus. Supplies Corp., 1965-70; prof. adminstrn. Fla. Atlantic U., 1972-74; now chmn. bd. trustees, pres. Am. Coll. Adminstrs. Execs. Mgrs., Laguna Hills, Calif.; dean Sch. Adminstrn., Coll. Boca Raton; exec. head. mgmt. engring. div. S.D. Leidesdorf & Co., 1954-55; dir. City Stores Corp., City Stores Merc. Co., Inc., City Splty. Stores Co., Inc., Oppenheim Collins & Co., Franklin Simon Co., N.Y.C., R.H. White Co., Boston, Wise Smith & Co., Hartford, Conn. Mem. Broome County Planning Commn., 1936-38, Pa. War Manpower Commn.; chmn. War. Emergency Bd. N.Y. State, 1941; industry mem. appeals com. Nat. War Labor Bd., 1943-45; cons. HOLC and FHA, 1936-39; chmn. Armed Forces Regional Council, Pa. and Del., 1950-52; mem. adv. com. 2d Army, 4th Naval Dist.; pres. 175th Anniversary of the Signing of the Declaration of Independence, 1951, Phila. Conv. and Visitors Bur., 1953; chmn. United Com. Fund, Princeton; apptd. mem. State Commn. to reorgn. Govt. City N.Y., 1953; apptd. mem. Mayor's Adv. Council, chmn. com. on city mgmt. and adminstrn., 1954; Citizens Com. to Keep N.Y. Clean, 1955, Citizens Com. on Cts., 1955; pres. Quiet City Campaign, 1956; vice chmn., sec. Phila. Parking Authority.; Trustee William Shelton Harrison Found., Hun School, Princeton, N.J., Clarkson Coll. of Tech. Mem. Am. Mgmt. Assn., A.I.M. (president's council, charter mem. adv. bd.), Nat. Retail Research Inst. (dir.), Bronx Bd. Trade (dir. 1954-64), Ave. of Americas Assn. (dir. 1952-55), Soc. for Advancement Mgmt., Nat. Assn. Cost Accountants, Commerce and Industry Assn. N.Y. (treas., dir., mem. exec. com. 1954-58), Lambda Iota (pres.), Delta Upsilon (trustee), Phi Beta Lambda. Clubs: Midday (Phila.), Philadelphia Country (Phila.), Lake

Placid (N.Y.) Skytop (Pa.), Merion Cricket, Racquet, Poor Richard, Pen and Pencil (Phila.); Economic (N.Y.C.), Union League (N.Y.C.); Nat. Golf Links of Am. (Southampton, L.I.); Uptown; Springdale Golf (Princeton, N.J.), Rotary (Princeton, N.J.), Nassau (Princeton, N.J.); Laguna Hills (Calif.) Golf, Boca Raton, Pinehurst Country, Royal Palm Yacht and Country (gov.), Mission Viejo Country, El Niguel Country (Calif.), P.G.A. National Golf, Calif. Office: Executive Center PO Box 2704 Laguna Hills CA 92653

CONOLE, RICHARD CLEMENT, business executive; b. Binghamton, N.Y., Dec. 7, 1936; s. Clement V. and Marjorie E. (Anable) C.; student U. Pa., 1955, 1960, Clarkson Coll., 1956-57; children—Margaret Ann, Linda Elizabeth Fandel; m. Sharyn Stafford, Apr. 18, 1969; 1 dau., Samantha Erin. Data processing dept. Campbell Soup Co., Inc., Camden, N.J., 1954; draftsman Gannett, Fleming, Corddry & Carpenter, Inc., Ardmore, Pa., 1955-56; plant mgr., office mgr. Tabulating Card Co., Inc., Princeton, N.J., 1957-59, asst. to pres., asst. sec.-treas., sec. 1959; pres., dir. Data Processing Supplies Co., Inc., Princeton, 1959; sec., dir. Whiting Paper Co., Inc., Princeton, 1959, pres. 1961-62; pres., dir. Mercer-Princeton Realty Co., Inc., Princeton, 1959-61; pres. Am. Bus. Investment Co., Inc., Princeton, 1960; pres., dir. Business Supplies Corp. Am., Skytop, Pa., 1962-65, Gen. Bus. Supplies Corp., Ardmore, 1965-71; chmn. bd. Nat. Productive Machines, Inc., Elkridge, Md., 1965-71; v.p., chmn. finance com., dir. Pocono Internat. Raceway Inc., 1964-74; pres. Gen. Automotive Supplies Co., 1971-72; pres., dir. Autoberfest, Inc., 1973—, Promotional Printing Ltd., 1973; pres. The World Series of Auto Racing Corp., 1973-78, Tex. World Speedway Inc., 1976—, Speedway Mgmt. Corp., 1978—; pres., chief exec. officer Gt. Tex. Truckstop, Tex. World Affordable Homes; sales cons. Hess & Barker, 1972-76; mem. competition com. U.S. Auto Club, 1976—; treas., chmn. fin. com. Tex. Pvt. Sch. Found., Inc.; trustee Allen Acad. Founder Tex. 500, Tex. Grand Prix, Tex. Race of Champions. Mem. Am. Mgmt. Assn., Tex. Manufactured Housing Assn., Phila. Dist. Squash Racquets Assn. (life), U.S. Squash Racquets Assn., Nat. Greyhound Assn., Tex. Greyhound Assn., Tex. Horse Race Assn., Texas Thoroughbred Breeders Assn. Clubs: Skytop (Skytop, Pa.); Phila. Country, Merion Cricket (Haverford, Pa.); Manor (Pocono Manor, Pa.). Patentee magnetic printing cylinder. Home: Box 9191 College Station TX 77840 Office: Box AJ College Station TX 77840

CONOLEY, JOANN SHIPMAN, educational administrator; b. Bartlesville, Okla., July 19, 1931; d. Joe and Frances Loomis (Wall) Shipman; B.S. in English and Edn., Midwestern State U., Wichita Falls, Tex., 1968, M.S. in English and Edn., 1971; postgrad. Tex. A&M U., 1978—; m. Travis A. Conoley, Oct. 29, 1976; children by previous marriage—James F. Lane, Joe Scott Lane, Kimberly Diane Lane. Tchr. 3d grade Queen of Peace Sch., Wichita Falls, 1968-69; lang. arts team leader, jr. high sch. Wichita Falls Public Schs., 1969-74; fed. programs dir., reading coordinator Rockdale (Tex.) Public Schs., 1974-78, adminstrv. asst. to supt., 1978-79, asst. supt. adminstrn. and instrn., 1979—; reading cons. ALCOA, 1977—; cons. U.S. Dept. Edn. Secondary Sch. Recognition Program, 1987. Bd. dirs. Rockdale Public Library, 1975-79, pres., 1976-77; bd. dirs. Am. Cancer Soc. Cert. elem. and high sch. tchr., reading/lang. arts coordinator, reading cons., adminstr., Tex. Mem. NEA, Tex. State Tchrs. Assn., Nat. Council Tchrs. English, Internat. Reading Assn., Assn. Compensatory Edn. Tex. (exec. bd. 1977-83), Assn. Supervision and Curriculum Devel., Alpha Chi, Delta Kappa Gamma, Kappa Delta Pi. Home: 405 Bounds St Rockdale TX 76567 Office: Box 632 Rockdale TX 76567

CONOVER, ARTHUR VERNER, III, finance company executive; b. Washington, June 25, 1942; s. Arthur Verner and Alma Irene (Van Sciver) C.; m. Joan P. Hughes. Student, Strayer Bus. Coll., 1960-62, U.S. Dept. Agr. Grad. Sch., 1963-64. Cost acct. County of Fairfax, Va., 1961-65; acctg. mgr. ARIES Corp., McLean, Va., 1965-67; controller Williams Enterprises, Inc., Merrifield, Va., 1967-73; v.p. Sonny Hylton Cos., Woodbridge, Va., 1973; chief fin. officer Williams Industries, Inc., Merrifield, 1973—, also bd. dirs., mem. exec. com.; bd. dirs. Williams Steel Erection Co., Inc., Creative Iron, Inc., Indsl. Alloy Fabricators, Greenway Corp., Comml. Mfg. and Repair Co., Inc., Dominion Caisson Corp., Concrete Structures, Inc., others. Mem. Washington Bd. Trade, 1974—, task force on workmen's compensation, 1974-78, task force on unemployment compensation, 1974-78. Served with USAF, 1960-61. Mem. Am. Mgmt. Assn., Nat. Assn. Accts., Nat. Assn. Purchasing Mgmt., Nat. Fedn. Ind. Bus. (guardian adv. council), Nat. Fedn. Ind. Bus. Lodge: Lions. Home: PO Box 156 Linden VA 22642 Office: 2849 Meadow View Rd Falls Church VA 22042

CONRAD, HAROLD THEODORE, psychiatrist; b. Milw., Jan. 25, 1934; s. Theodore Herman and Alyce Barbara (Kolb) C.; A.B., U. Chgo., 1954, B.S., 1955, M.D., 1958; m. Elaine Marie Blaine, Sept. 1, 1962; children—Blaine, Carl, David, Erich, Rachel. Intern USPHS Hosp., San Francisco, 1958-59; commd. sr. asst. surgeon USPHS, 1958, advanced through grades to med. dir., 1967; resident in psychiatry USPHS Hosp., Lexington, Ky., 1959-61, Charity Hosp., New Orleans, 1961-62; chief of psychiatry USPHS Hosp., New Orleans, 1962-67, clin. dir., 1967; dep. dir. div. field investigations NIMH, Chevy Chase, Md., 1968; chief NIMH Clin. Research Center, Lexington, 1969-73; cons. psychiatry, region IX, USPHS, HEW, San Francisco, 1973-79; dir. adolescent unit Alaska Psychiat. Inst., Anchorage, 1979-81, supt., 1981-85 ; clin. assoc. prof. psychiatry U. Wash. Med. Sch., 1981-85; med. dir. Bayou Oaks Hosp., Houma, La., 1985—. Decorated Commendation medal; recipient various community awards for contbns. in field of drug abuse and equal employment opportunity for minorities. Diplomate Am. Bd. Psychiatry. Fellow Royal Soc. Health, Am. Psychiat. Assn.; mem. AMA, Alpha Omega Alpha, Alpha Delta Phi. Contbr. to publs. in field. Office: 855 Belanger St Houma LA 70360

CONRAD, KENT, U.S. senator; b. Bismarck, N.D., Mar. 12, 1948; m. Lucy Calantti, Feb. 1987; 1 child, Jessamyn Abigail. Student, U. Mo., 1967; BA, Stanford U., 1971; MBA, George Washington U., 1975. Asst. to tax commr. State of N.D. Tax Dept., Bismarck, 1974-80, tax commr., 1981-86; U.S. senator from N.D. Washington, 1987—. Office: Office of Senate Members 361 Dirksen Senate Bldg Washington DC 20510 *

CONRADI, PETER JOHN, literature educator; b. London, May 8, 1945; s. Gordon Henry and Dulcie Phoebe (Cohen) C. BA in English Studies, U. East Anglia, Eng., 1967; MA in English and Am. Lit., U. Sussex, Eng., 1969; PhD, U. London, 1984. Lectr. South Bank Poly., London, 1971-73, sr. lectr., 1973-80; vis. prof. U. Colo., Boulder, 1978-80; vis. lectr. U. East Anglia, 1981; sr. lectr. Kingston Poly., London, 1981-85; reader Kingston Polytechnic, London, 1985—. Author: John Fowles, 1982, Iris Murdoch: The Saint and the Artist, 1985, Dostoevsky, 1988. Office: Kingston Polytechnic, Arts Dept, Penrhyn Rd, London KT1 2EE, England

CONROY, DAVID JEROME, lawyer; b. New Orleans, Dec. 27, 1929; s. George E. and Lilyon (Bowling) C.; B.A., Tulane U., 1950, J.D., 1952; m. Ann Kathryn Gunderson, May 15, 1954; children—Kathryn Ann, David Michael, Elizabeth Helen, Mary Daire, Peter George Edward, Patrick Frank. Bar: La. 1952. Ptnr. Milling, Benson, Woodward, Hillyer, Pierson & Miller, New Orleans, 1956—, mng. ptnr., 1974-84; sec. Jahncke Service Inc., New Orleans, 1961-69, Public Grain Elevator New Orleans, 1964-83; sec., dir. C.B. Fox Co., New Orleans, 1965—. Mem. planning com. Tulane Tax Inst., 1975-79; del. La. Constl. Conv., 1973; bd. dirs. New Orleans Speech and Hearing Center, 1968-74, pres., 1970-72; bd. dirs. Louise S. McGehee Sch., 1970-77, pres., 1975-77; trustee Public Affairs Research Council La., 1974-80; bd. dirs. Family Service Soc., 1972-77, United Way Greater New Orleans, 1974-80; bd. dirs. Human Services on Cable, Inc., 1982-87, v.p., 1985-87; bd. dirs., exec. com., pres. Council for A Better La.; bd. dirs. Greater New Orleans Ednl. TV Found., 1986—; bd. dirs., exec. com. Greater New Orleans Found.; bd. supres. La. State U., 1988—. Served with AUS, 1952-54. Fellow Am. Bar Found., La. Bar Found; mem. ABA, La. Bar Assn. (chmn. sect. corp. law 1968-69, chmn. com. law reform 1977-78), New Orleans Bar Assn. (chmn. com. on profl. ethics and grievances 1985—), Am. Law Inst., World Trade Ctr. (dir. 1978-81), St. Thomas More Cath. Lawyers Assn. (bd. govs. 1969-72, 78-80, 1st v.p. 1971-72). Roman Catholic. Clubs: Pickwick (bd. dirs. 1985—, v.p. 1987—), New Orleans Country, City (New Orleans). Home: 437 Dorrington Dr Metairie LA 70005 Office: 909 Poydras St Suite 2300 New Orleans LA 70112

CONSAGRA, PIETRO, sculptor; b. Mazara, Italy, Oct. 4, 1920; 4 children. Student Acad. Fine Arts, Palermo. One-man shows: Rome, 1947, 1949, 1951, 1959, 1961; Milan, 1958, 1961; Venice, 1948; Brussels, 1958; Paris, 1959; Zurich, 1961; Sao Paulo Bienal, 1955, 1959; Venice Biennale, 1956, 1960, N.Y.C., 1962; Buenos Aires, 1962; Boston, 1962; represented in permanent collections: Tate Gallery, London; Nat. Mus. and Middleheim Park, Antwerp; Mus. Modern Art, Sao Paulo; Paris, Rome, N.Y.C., Buenos Aires, Caracas, Zagreb, Helsinki; Guggenheim Mus., N.Y.C.; Art Inst., Chgo.; Carnegie Inst., Pitts.; Inst. Fine Arts, Mpls. Recipient Grand Prize for Sculpture Venice Biennale, 1960. Address: Via Cassia 1162, Rome Italy *

CONSALVI, SIMON ALBERTO, former minister of foreign affairs for Venezuela; b. July 7, 1929; m. Maria Eugenia Bigott de Consalvi; 1 son. Ed., U. Central de Venezuela. Mem., Nat. Congress, Venezuela, 1959-64, 1974—; ambassador to Yugoslavia, 1961-64; dir. Central Office of Info. for the Presidency, 1964-67; pres., Nat. Inst. Culture and Art, 1967-69; dir. Nat. Magazine of Culture, internat. editor El Nacional newspaper, 1971-74, minister of state for info., 1974, permanent rep. to UN, 1974-77, minister of fgn. affairs, 1977-79, 1985-88; former Sec-Gen. of Presidency; mem. Nat. Congress Fgn. Relations Com.; senator for Merida State, Venezuela. Contbr. numerous essays on nat. and fgn. affairs to profl. jours. *

CONSTABLE, ELINOR GREER, diplomat; b. San Diego, Feb. 8, 1934; d. Marshall Raymond and Katherine (French) Greer; m. Peter Dalton Constable, Mar. 8, 1958; children: Robert, Philip, Julia. B.A., Wellesley Coll., 1955. Mem. staff Dept. Interior, 1955-71, Dept. State, 1955-71, OEO, 1955-71; sr. assoc. Transcentury Corp., Washington, 1971-72; with Dept. State, Washington, 1973-80, 83—, dir. investment affairs, 1978-80; dep. asst. sec. Internat. Fin. and Devel., 1980-83; dep. asst. sec. for econ. and bus. affairs Dept. State, 1983—; Ambassador to Kenya, 1986—; capital devel. officer US AID, Pakistan, 1977-78. Office: Am Embassy APO New York NY 09675-8900 *

CONSTANT, CLINTON, chemical engineer; b. Nelson, B.C., Can., Mar. 20, 1912; came to U.S., 1936, naturalized, 1942; s. Vasile and Annie (Hunt) C.; m. Margie Robbel, Dec. 5, 1965. B.Sc. with honors, U. Alta., 1935, postgrad., 1935-36; Ph.D., Western Res. U., 1939. Registered profl. engr. Devel. engr. Harshaw Chem. Co., Cleve., 1936-38, mfg. foreman, 1938-43, sr. engr. semi-works dept., 1948-50; supt. hydrofluoric acid dept. Nyotex Chems., Inc., Houston, 1943-47, chief devel. engr., 1947-48; mgr. engring. Ferro Chem. Co., Bedford, Ohio, 1950-52; tech. asst. mfg. dept. Armour Agrl. Chem. Co. (name formerly Armour Fertilizer Works), Bartow, Fla., 1952-61, mfg. research and devel. div., 1961-63, mgr. spl. projects Research div. (co. name changed to USS Agri-Chems 1968), 1963-65, project mgr., 1965-70; chem. adviser Robert & Co. Assocs., Atlanta, 1970-79; chief engr. Almon & Assocs., Inc., Atlanta, 1979-80; project mgr. Engring. Service Assocs., Atlanta, 1980-81; v.p. engring. ACI Inc., Hesperia, Calif., 1981-83; sr. v.p., chief engr. MTI (acquisition of ACI), Hesperia, 1983-86; engring. cons. San Bernardino County APCD, Victorville, Calif., 1986—. Fellow AAAS, Am. Inst. Chemists, Am. Inst. Chem. Engrs., N.Y. Acad. Scis., AIAA (assoc.); mem. Am. Chem. Soc., Am. Astron. Soc., Astron. Soc. Pacific, Royal Astron. Soc. Can., NSPE, Am. Water Works Assn., Calif. Water and Pollution Control Assn., Air Pollution Control Assn., Soc. Mfg. Engrs., Calif. Soc. Profl. Engrs. Author tech. reports, sci. fiction; patentee in field.

CONSTANTINE, STEPHEN, educator; b. Salford, Lancashire, Eng., June 13, 1947; s. William Bernard and Bertha (Gleave) C.; m. Wendy Jane Taylor, Sept. 27, 1969; children: Matthew, Emily Jane. BA with honors, U. Oxford, Eng., 1968, postgrad., 1968-71, PhD, 1974. Lectr. in history U. Lancaster, Eng., 1971-86, sr. lectr., 1986. Author: Unemployment in Britain between the wars, 1980, Social Conditions in Britain 1918-1939, 1983, The Making of British Colonial Development Policy 1914-1940, 1984, Buy and Build: The Advertising Posters of the Empire Marketing Board, 1986. Sch. gov. primary and secondary schs., Lancaster, 1981—. Fellow Royal Hist. Soc.; mem. Econ. History Soc., Social History Soc. of the U.K., Hist. Assn. Mem. Labour Party. Office: U Lancaster, Dept History, Bailrigg, Lancaster, Lancashire LA1 4YG, England

CONSTANTINESCU, CORNELIU, mathematician; b. Buzau, Romania, Feb. 9, 1929; arrived in Switzerland, 1972, naturalized, 1987; s. Octav and Clara (Widmer) C. M in Math., U. Bucharest, 1954, D Docent in Sci., 1968; diploma in engring., Inst. Constn., Bucharest, Romania, 1954; PhD in Physics and Math., Inst. Math., Bucharest, 1958. Research fellow Math. Inst. Romanian Acad., Bucharest, 1954-72; vis. prof. math. Swiss Fed. Inst. Tech., Lausanne, 1972-73; vis. prof. math. Swiss Fed. Inst. Tech., Zurich, Switzerland, 1973-76, prof., 1978—; prof. Techische U., Hannover, Fed. Republic of Germany, 1976-78. Author: (with A. Cornea) Ideale Raender Riemannscher Flaechen, 1963, Potential Theory on Harmonic Spaces, 1972; (with A. Sontag and K. Weber) Integration Theory, vol. I, 1985; author: Duality in Measure Theory, 1980, Spaces of Measures, 1984. Recipient Gheorghe Lazar prize Romanian Acad., 1963. Mem. Deutsche Mathematiker Vereinigung, Schweizerische Mathematische Gesellschaft, Am. Math. Soc. Home: Bodenacherstrasse 53, CH-8121 Benglen Switzerland Office: Eidgenossische Technische, Hochschule Ramistrasse 101, CH-8092 Zurich Switzerland

CONTAMINE, PHILIPPE, educator; b. Metz, France, May 7, 1932; s. Henry and Marie-Therese (Dufays) C.; m. Genevieve Bernard, 1956; 3 children. Student Lycee Malherbe, Caen, Lycee Louis-le-Grand, Paris, Sorbonne. Tchr. history and geography Lycee, Sens, 1957-60, Lycee Carnot, Paris, 1960-61; asst. prof. medieval history Sorbonne, 1962-65; asst. lectr., lectr., prof. medieval history U. Nancy, 1965-73; prof. U. Paris (Nanterre), 1973—, dir. dept. history, 1976-79; dir. Centre Jeanne d'Arc, Orleans. Author: La Guerre de cent ans, 1968; Guerre, Etat et Societe a la fin du Moyen Age, 1972; La Vie quotidienne en France et en Angleterre pendant la guerre de cent ans, 1976; La guerre au Moyen Age, 1980; La France aux XIVe et XVe siecles, 1981; La France de la fin du XVe siecle, 1985. Recipient Premier Prix Gobert de l'Academie des Inscriptions et Belles-Lettres, Inst. de France, 1972. Address: 12 villa Croix-Nivert, 75015 Paris France *

CONTARD, SERGE PIERRE, nephrologist; b. La Mure, France, Aug. 10, 1951; s. Rene Charles and Honerine (Panerio) C.; m. Marie Claire Hourdou, July 19, 1975; children: Christophe, Amandine. MD, U. Grenoble, 1976, degree in Nephrology, 1980. Practice medicine specializing in nephrology Mont St. Martin, France, 1980—; chief nephrologist Hotel Dieu, Mont St. Martin, 1976—; cons. Extracorporeal Lab., France, 1982-84. Contbr. articles to profl. publs. Mem. European Dialysis and Transplant Assn., French Soc. Nephrology. Roman Catholic. Home: BP 17, 54920 Villers la Montagne France Office: Hotel Dieu, 4 rue A Labbe, 54350 Mont Saint Martin France

CONTE, JEAN JACQUES, medical educator, nephrologist; b. Tours, France, Nov. 6, 1938; s. Rene G. and Anne J. (Grangier) C.; m. Anne Y. Viatge, June 4, 1970; 1 dau., Stephanie C. M.D., Faculte de Medecine, Toulouse, France, 1966. Cert. nephrologist Comité Consultatif des Universités. Prof. medicine Universite P. Sabatier, Toulouse, France, 1971—, cons. Mission de la Recherche, 1983—; chief nephrology dept. Centre Hospitalo-Universitaire Purpan, Toulouse, 1974—; vice doyen Faculte de Medecine Purpan, Toulouse, 1980—; dir. Research Unit in Renal Immunopathology and Immunopharmacology, 1984—; expert in medicine Toulouse Ct. Appeals, 1984—; pres. U. Paul Sabatier, Toulouse III, 1986—; v.p. de la Conf. des Pres. Univ., 1987, Assn. des Univs. Partiellement ou Entièrement de Langue Française, 1987. Co-author: Glomerulonephritis, 1973; Advanced in Nephrology, 1974, 76; Plasmapheresis, 1983. Mem. European Soc. for Clin. Investigation, Internat. Soc. Nephrology, French Soc. Immunology, French Soc. of Plasma Exchange (founding mem.). Roman Catholic. Clubs: Compagnie des Mousquetaires d'Armagnac (Auch, France); Golf of Vieille-Toulouse (Toulouse). Office: Université Paul Sabatier, 118 route de Narbonne, 3162 Toulouse France

CONTÉ, LANSANA, president of Republic of Guinea; b. 1944. Army officer, former comdr. Boké Region; pres. of Republic of Guinea, 1984—, prime minister, from 1984, former minister of def., security, planning, cooperation and info.; chmn. Comité militaire de redressement nat., 1984—. Office: Office of Pres, Conakry Guinea *

CONTI, THOMAS ANTONIO, actor, writer, director; b. Paisley, Scotland, Nov. 22, 1941; s. Alfonso and Mary (McGoldrick) C.; m. Kara Drummond Wilson, July 2, 1967; 1 child, Nina. Appeared in plays on London's West End; Savages, Other People, The Black and White Minstrels, Don Juan; Broadway debut in: Whose Life Is It Anyway, 1979 (Tony award); appeared in: They're Playing Our Song, 1980; dir.: Before the Party, 1980; appeared in films, including: Galileo, Eclipse, Merry Christmas Mr. Lawrence, Reuben, Reuben, 1983, American Dreamer, 1984, Saving Grace, Miracles, Heavenly Pursuits, Beyond Therapy, The Dumb Waiter; appeared in TV plays including The Beaux Stratagem; appeared in American TV prodns. Glittering Prizes, Princess and the Pea, Faerie Tale Theatre, The Beate Klarsfeld Story, The Quick and the Dead, Fatal Dosage. Club: Garrick (London). Office: care John Gaines APA 9000 Sunset Blvd Los Angeles CA 90069

CONTNEY, JOHN J., association executive; b. Milw., Oct. 15, 1932; s. Francis Anthony and Rose (Nowicki) C.; m. Dawn Georgette Wintz, Sept. 7, 1963; children: Wade Anthony, Ross Joseph. B.S., Marquette U., 1954, M.B.A., 1965; M.S., Barry U., 1975. Asst. to v.p. Boston Store, Milw., 1950-56; exec. v.p., sales mgr. Records Unlimited, Inc., Milw., 1956-59; exec. v.p. Columbia S.E., Miami, Fla., 1959-63; sales controller Color Corp., Tampa, Fla., 1964-65; mgr. mktg. Textile Rental Services Assn. Am. (formerly Linen Supply Assn. Am.), Miami, 1965-72; asst. exec. dir. Textile Rental Services Assn. Am. (formerly Linen Supply Assn. Am.), 1973, gen. mgr., 1974-75, exec. dir., 1975—; Lectr. various groups.; chmn. Clean '83 Edn. com., sponsor, World Ednl. Congress for Laundering & Dry Cleaning. Contbr. articles to profl. jours. Served with AUS, 1954-56. Mem. Am. Soc. Assn. Execs., Fla. Soc. Assn. Execs. (past pres., Exec. of Year 1982), Laundry Cleaning Council (chmn.), South Fla. Soc. Assn. Execs. (bd. dirs.), Found. for Internat. Meetings (bd. dirs.). Home: 601 Grand Concourse Miami Shores FL 33138 Office: Textile Rental Services Assn Am 1130 E Hallandale Beach Blvd Hallandale FL 33009

CONTRERAS, MICHAEL ANTONIO, banker; b. L.I., N.Y., Dec. 7, 1953; s. Antonio Manuel and Emily (Rico) C.; m. Milagros Concepcion Meaux, Mar. 14, 1981; children: Michael A., Manuel A. BBA, Berry Coll., 1976; MBA, Interam. U., San Juan, P.R., 1980. With Citibank N.A., various locations, 1976—; v.p., area mgr. Citibank N.A., Valencia, Venezuela, 1982-84; v.p., product mgr. Citibank N.A., Caracas, Venezuela, 1984-85; v.p., gen. mgr. Citibank N.A., Santo Domingo, Dominican Republic, 1985—; dir. Econ. Found. Dominican Republic; mem. eocn. adv. group Cen. Bank Dominican Republic. Mem. Am. C. of C. (bd. dirs.), Dominican Republic Bankers Assn. (v.p.), Dominican Republic C. of C. (bd. dirs.), Assn. Fgn. Investors (treas.), Nat. Businessman Council. Office: Citibank NA, Apartado 1492, Santo Domingo Dominican Republic

CONWAY, CASEY ANTHONY, petroleum company executive; b. Portland, Oreg., Mar. 11, 1953; s. James William and Wanna Donna (Caspers) C. AA, Orange Coast Coll., 1974; BA in Bus. Adminstrn., Calif. State U.-Fullerton, 1976; MS in Safety, U. So. Calif., 1978. Cert. instr./trainer in surface/underground mine safety; cert. mine foreman surface uranuim; cert. Colo. audiometric technician; lic. amateur redio operator (extra class). Safety and environ. technician energy mining div. Union Oil Co. Calif., 1979, Rawlins, Wyo., safety trainer, 1979-80, safety supr., 1980-82, regulatory compliance coordinator oil shale ops., Parachute, Colo., 1983-85; safety supr. UNOCAL Los Angeles Refinery, Wilmington, Calif., 1986; supr. regulatory compliance, refining and mktg. div. UNOCAL, Los Angeles, 1986—; vol. examiner FCC amateur radio lics. Mem. Am. Soc. Safety Engrs. (membership chmn. Wyo. chpt. 1981-82, Wyo. safety congress com. 1982, sec. 1982-83, Western Slope chmn. 1983-86), Am. Petroleum Inst. (hazard communication and labeling issues group), Western Oil and Gas Assn. (chmn. occupational health and safety subcom.), Nat. Safety Mgmt. Soc., Am. Mgmt. Assn., Am. Radio Relay League (asst. dir. SW Div. 1986—) Soc. Advancement Mgmt. (Outstanding mem. 1975; v.p. membership 1976), Carbon County Amateur Radio Assn. (pres. 1980), Grand Mesa Contesters (sec.-treas. 1985), South Orange Amateur Radio Assn., So. Calif. Contest, Cactus Radio.Roman Catholic. Lodge: Elks. Home: 310 Driftwood Rd Corona Del Mar CA 92625 Office: Unocal Refining and Mktg Div PO Box 7600 911 Bldg Los Angeles CA 90051

CONWAY, FRANK HARRISON, lawyer, government official; b. Providence, May 2, 1913; s. Frank Harrison and Margaret Mary (Cannon) C.; m. Jean Arthur Watt, Apr. 6, 1940; m. Elizabeth Hoppin Chafee, Feb. 7, 1973; stepchildren—Arthur, William, Sherrill, Henry. Ph.B., Providence Coll., 1935; J.D., Boston U., 1952; spl. student Harvard U. Law Sch., 1952-53. Bar: Mass. 1952, U.S. Dist. Ct. Mass. 1954, U.S. Supreme Ct. 1962. Mgmt. ofcl. New Eng. Tel.&Tel., Boston, 1935-77; pvt. practice law, Boston, 1977-80; mem. Jameson, Locke & Fullerton, Wellesley, Mass., 1980-87; mem. Fgn. Claims Settlement Commn., Washington, 1981—; treas., dir. Young Orchard Co., Providence, 1975-81; trustee Young Orchard Trust. Mem. Mass. Republican State Com., 1974-80, treas., 1976-80; del. Nat. Rep. Conv., 1976, 80, 84, also mem. rules com.; mem. bd. Selectmen Wellesley, 1979-82. Served to maj. Signal Corps, U.S. Army, 1942-46. Mem. Norfolk Bar Assn., Mass. Bar Assn. Republican. Roman Catholic. Clubs: Harvard of Boston, Wellesley Country; University (Washington). Home: 37 Longmeadow Rd Wellesley MA 02181

CONWAY, FRENCH HOGE, lawyer; b. Danville, Va., June 11, 1918; s. Lysander Broadus and Mildred (Hoge) C.; BS, U. Va., 1942, JD, 1946; m. Louise Throckmorton, Feb. 3, 1961; children—French Hoge, William Chenery, Helen (Mrs. Carlton Bedsole), Donna L. Starnes. Bar: Va. 1942. sole practice, Danville, 1942—; mem. firm Clement, Conway & Winston, 1950-60. Sec., Danville City Bd. Rev., 1985—; v.p. Va. Election Bd. Assn., 1974. Served with USNR, 1942-46. Mem. Am., Va., Danville (pres. 1985-86) bar assns., Am. Trial Lawyers Assn., Va. Trial Lawyers Assn., Soc. Cincinnati in State of Va., Ret. Officers Assn., Boat Owners Assn. U.S. Lodges: Kiwanis, Masons. Home: 912 Main St Danville VA 24541 Office: 105 S Union St Danville VA 24541

CONWELL, HALFORD ROGER, physician; b. Cin., Jan. 28, 1924; s. Halford Fredrick and Erma Pearl (Cornelius) C.; B.A., U. Wooster, 1948; M.A., U. Louisville, 1950; M.D., U. Cin., 1955; diplomate crew coordination tng. Continental Airlines; m. Margaret Ann King, Dec. 15, 1965; children—Mark A., Sherri L. Intern, Christ Hosp., Cin., 1955-56; resident Maumee Valley Hosp., Toledo, 1956-57, Baylor U. Hosp., Houston, 1957-58; gen. practice medicine and aviation medicine, Huntsville, Tex., 1959—; mem. staff Huntsville (Tex.) Meml. Hosp., chief of staff, 1974-75, chief medicine, 1976-80; cons. Tex. Dept. Corrections, 1970-80; sr. U.S. med. officer Brit. Caledonian Airways; cons. Aeromexico, Brit. Airways; mem. Walker County Hosp. Dist., 1975-79, chmn., 1976-79; med. dir. Planned Parenthood Assn., Huntsville, 1975-77; asst. dean of men, instr. psychology Heidelberg U., Tiffin, Ohio, 1950-51; instr. psychology Cin. Coll.; sr. med. examiner FAA; examiner C.A.A. (U.K.). Trustee Biol. Analysis and Research Found.; mem. adv. council liberal arts Sam Houston State U. capt. (hon.) Tex. Internat. Airline. Served to lt. USNR, 1942-46. Recipient safe pilot award Nat. Pilots Assn. Fellow Am. Soc. Abdominal Surgeons, Airline Med. Dirs. Assn.; asso. fellow Aerospace Med. Assn., Brit. Assn. Aerospace Medicine, Latin Am. Aviation Med. Assn.; mem. Tex. Med. Assn., Walker-Madison-Trinity Med. Soc. (pres. 1974-75), Civil Aviation Med. Assn. (v.p. 1968-80, dir. 1968—, pres. 1980-81), Mitchell Pediatric Soc., Academie Internationale de Medicine Aeronatque et Spatiale, Confederate Air Force, Friends of RAF Mus., Amigos de Guadalajara, Order Ky. Cols., Proud Birdmen (hon.), Psi Chi. Club: Drs. Lodge: Masons. Home: 825 Cherry Hills Elkins Lake TX 77340 Office: 2800 Lake Rd Huntsville TX 77340

COOGAN, EDWARD RICHARD, psychotherapist; b. Archbald, Pa., Sept. 1, 1931; s. John Edward and Dora Marie (McHale) C.; m. Patricia Ann Hardwick, Dec. 19, 1955 (div. May 1975); children—Christine, Lynne, Cynthia; m. Kathryn Theresa Stevens, June 4, 1977. B.A., Chapman Coll., 1974; M.S. with distinction, Calif. State Coll.-Stanislaus, 1983. Lic. marriage, family and child counselor, Calif.; lic. hypno-analyst, Calif. Commd. 2d lt. U.S. Air Force, 1953, advanced through grades to col., 1975; ret., 1977; psychotherapist Family Service Agy., Turlock, Calif., 1978-83; pvt. practice psychotherapy, Modesto, Calif., 1983—; child custody mediator Stanislaus County, Modesto, 1983—; cons. Eastern Wash. U., Cheney, 1979—. Mem. adv. bd. Salvation Army, Turlock, 1982-84. Decorated Silver Star. Mem. Calif. Assn. Marriage, Family and Child Therapists, Phobia Soc. Am. (therapist 1984), Ret. Officers Assn. (bd. dirs. Merced, Calif. 1984), Mensa. Democrat. Roman Catholic. Home: 1150 La Rosa Ct Turlock CA 95380 Office: Coogan Counseling Services 1400 K St Suite C Modesto CA 95354

COOK, ALBERT THOMAS THORNTON, JR., financial advisor; b. Cleve., Apr. 24, 1940; s. Albert Thomas Thornton and Tyra Esther (Morehouse) C.; m. Mary Jane Blackburn, June 1, 1963; children: Lara, Thomas, Timothy. BA, Dartmouth Coll., 1962; MA, U. Chgo., 1966. Asst. sec. Dartmouth Coll., Hanover, N.H., 1972-77; exec. dir. Big Brothers, Inc., N.Y.C., 1977-78; underwriter Boettcher & Co., Denver, 1978-81; asst. v.p. Dain Bosworth Inc., Denver, 1981-82, Colo. Nat. Bank, Denver, 1982-84; pres. The Albert T.T. Cook Co., Denver, 1984—; arbitrator Nat. Assn. Securities Dealers, N.Y.C., 1985-87, Mcpl. Securities Rulemaking Bd., Washington, 1987—. Pres. Etna-Hanover Ctr. Community Assn., Hanover, N.H., 1974-76; mem. Mayor's Task Force, Denver, 1984; dir. Rude Park Community Nursery, Denver, 1985-87; trustee The Iliff Sch. Theol., Denver, 1986—. Mem. Dartmouth Alumni Council (exec. com., mem. nominating and trustee search coms. 1987-88), Delta Upsilon. Presbyterian. Clubs: University, Cactus (Denver); Dartmouth of N.Y.C., Yale. Lodge: Lions (bd. dirs. Denver chpt. 1983-85, treas. 1986—, pres. Denver Found., 1987-88). Home: 7099 E Hinsdale Pl Englewood CO 80112 Office: 1225 Seventeenth St 23rd Floor Denver CO 80202

COOK, ALEXANDER BURNS, educator, museum curator; b. Grand Rapids, Mich., Apr. 16, 1924; s. Gorell Alexander and Harriette Florence (Hinze) C.; B.A., Ohio Wesleyan U., 1949; M.S., Case Western Res. U., 1967. Editorial cartoonist, artist Cleve. Plain Dealer, 1949-55; account exec. Edward Howard & Co., Cleve., 1955-61; spl. art tchr. Cleve. Pub. Schs., 1964—; curator exhibits Gt. Lakes Mus., Vermilion, Ohio, 1970-78, curator, 1978—, chmn. mus. operating com., 1977—. Trustee, Berkshire Condominium Owners Assn., 1981-83, pres., 1982-83. Served with AUS, 1943-45. Recipient award of honor Ohio Wesleyan U., 1955; Distinguished Achievement award Gt. Lakes Hist. Soc., 1973; 1st pl. award for editorial cartoons Union Tchr. Communications Assn., 1980, 81, 82, 87. Mem. Gt. Lakes Hist. Soc. (exec. v.p. 1959-64, v.p. 1964—, trustee, mem. exec. com. 1959—), Ohioana Library Assn., Akron Art Mus., Cleve. Mus. Art, Am. Soc. Marine Artists, Delta Tau Delta, Pi Delta Epsilon, Pi Sigma Alpha. Republican. Episcopalian. Contbr. editorial cartoons to Reid Cartoon Collection, U. Kans. Jour. Hist. Center, The Critique, 1975—; editorial adviser, numerous articles to Inland Seas, 1957—, The Chadburn, 1976—; cover illustrations for Ohioana Quar., 1979—; book cover illustrations Dodd, Mead & Co., 1984. Paintings represented in pvt. collections, 1960—; executed mural depicting Gt. Lakes shipping Gt. Lakes Mus., 1969. Mem. The English Speaking Union. Home: 11820 Edgewater Dr Lakewood OH 44107

COOK, AUGUST JOSEPH, lawyer, accountant; b. Devine, Tex., Sept. 25, 1926; s. August E. and Mary H. (Schmidt) C.; m. Matie M. Brangan, July 12, 1952; children—Lisa Ann, Mary Beth, John J. B.S., Trinity U., 1949; B.B.A., U. Tex., 1954; J.D., St. Mary's U., 1960. Bar: Tex. 1960, Tenn. 1975. Bus. mgr., corp. sec. Life Enterprises, Inc. and affiliated cos., San Antonio, 1950-58, also dir.; mgr. Ernst and Whinney, San Antonio, 1960-69, ptnr. Memphis, 1970-84; ptnr. Wildman, Harrold, Allen, Dixon, and McDonnel, Memphis, 1984—. Author newspaper column A.J.'s Tax Fables, 1983—. Author: A.J. $ Tax Court, 1987; contbr. articles to profl. jours. Alderman City of Castle Hills, Tex., 1961-63, mayor, 1963-69; chmn. Bexar County Council Mayors, 1967-69; v.p. Tex Mcpl. League, 1968-69; bd. dirs. San Antonio Met. YMCA. Served with U.S. Army, 1945-46, PTO. Mem. Tex. Soc. CPA's, Tex. Bar Assn., Am. Inst. CPA's, Estate Planning Council San Antonio (pres. 1967), Tenn. Soc. CPA's, Tenn. Bar Assn., Estate Planning Council Memphis (pres. 1983-84), Toastmasters (pres. 1963), Delta Theta Phi, Kappa Pi Sigma. Roman Catholic. Clubs: University (Memphis); Canyon Creek Country (San Antonio) (bd. dirs.). Lodges: Optimists (bd. dirs.), Rotary (treas. bd. dirs. 1978-79). Home: 6785 Slash Pine Cove Memphis TN 38119 Office: Wildman Harrold Allen Dixon and McDonnell 6060 Primary Pkwy Memphis TN 38119

COOK, BENJAMIN HOPSON, manufacturing company executive; b. Shreveport, La., Apr. 7, 1926; s. Tom and Eva (Hopson) C.; m. Irene Owen, Aug. 20, 1948; children: Lura Haden Cook Norman, Terry Ellen Cook Slater, Paul Stuart. B.S. in Bus. Adminstrn, La. State U., 1948. Co-founder Stemco Mfg. Co., Longview, Tex., 1951; (merged into Garlock Inc, Rochester, N.Y. 1964), v.p. oil seal group, 1969-72, pres., parent co., 1972-76, chmn., chief exec. officer, 1976—, also dir.; group v.p. Colt Industries, N.Y.C., 1976-82; sr. v.p. Colt Industries, 1982-83, exec. v.p., 1983—; dir. Tex. Commerce Bank-Longview, Schlegel Corp., Rochester. Bd. dirs. Tex. Mfrs. Assn., 1969-71, Longview YMCA, 1966-69, United Fund, Longview, 1970-72. Mem. Indsl. Mgmt. Council (dir. 1976—), Soc. Automotive Engrs., La. State U. Alumni Assn. Methodist. Home: Rt 2 Box 209N Longview TX 75605 Office: PO Box 8090 Longview TX 75601 also: Colt Industries Inc 430 Park Ave New York NY 10022

COOK, CHARLES DAVID, international lawyer, arbitrator, consultant; b. Saginaw, Mich., Apr. 5, 1924; s. Charles Christian and Grace (Robins) C.; m. Bobette Ringland, Oct. 30, 1947 (dec. 1984); children: Ian Ainsworth, Kendra. A.B., U. Mich., 1947; LL.B., Columbia U., 1950, M.A. in Internat. Affairs, 1950. Bar: N.Y. 1951, D.C. 1965, Fed. Dist. Ct. So. N.Y 1965, Supreme Ct. U.S 1967. Assoc. dir. Inst. World Affairs seminar, Twin Lakes, Conn., summer 1950; mem. U.S. Mission to UN, 1950-62, dep. counselor, chief polit. sect., 1956-60, counselor, 1960-62; ptnr. Barco, Cook, Patton & Blow, 1962-67; sr. counsel Gen. Tel. & Electronics Internat., 1967-72; v.p., gen. counsel, sec., dir. GTE Internat., 1972-78; gen. counsel, cons. Copadco Ltd., 1978-81, 85—; of counsel Patton, Boggs & Blow, Washington, 1981—; resident Law Office of Ismail S. Nazer, 1981-85; affiliate Law Offices Ismail S. Nazer, Al-Khobar, Saudi Arabia, 1981—; adj. prof. internat. bus. transactions Bklyn. Law Sch., 1980; lectr. in field. Counselor U.S. delegations UN Gen. Assemblies, 1958-61; accompanied Ambassador Adlai Stevenson on Presdl. mission to S.Am., 1961; mem. U.S. delegation disarmament com., Geneva, Switzerland, 1962; adviser U.S. delegation WHO, Geneva, 1962; spl. cons. Pres. Nixon's Commn. for Observance of 25th Anniversary of UN. Mem. adv. bd. Westchester-Putnam council Boy Scouts Am.; pres. bd. dirs. the Maxwell Inst., Inc., Bronxville and Tuckahoe, N.Y.; v.p. bd. dirs. Family Consultation Service of Bronxville, Eastchester, Tuckahoe; chmn. Bronxville Littile Forum, 1987—. Served to ensign USNR, 1943-46. Univ. seminar assoc. Columbia U., N.Y.C., 1961-73, 86—. Mem. ABA, Assn. Bar City N.Y. (past com. on lawyers role in search for peace), Internat. Law Assn. (Am. br.), Am. Soc. Internat. Law, Westchester-Fairfield Counties Corporate Counsel Assn. (1st chmn. internat. com.), Am. Arbitration Assn. (internat. arbitrator). Clubs: Bronxville Field Club; American (London); Faculty House of Columbia U. Home: One Legget Rd Bronxville NY 10708 Office: PO Box 188 Bronxville NY 10708

COOK, CLAYTON HENRY, rancher; b. Moundridge, Kans., Apr. 21, 1912; s. Herbert and Bertha (Wilkening) C.; student public schs., Moundridge; m. Margery Maxine Manning, Apr. 13, 1941; children—Larry Clayton, Ronald Leigh, Michael Craig, Melanie Beth. Engaged in ranching, Vega, Tex. Mem. Tex. Econ. Commn., 1950-57-59, 62-—; mem. Gov.'s Com. on Aging, Tex. Constn. Revision Com.; profl. actor; play critic, judge Tex. U. Interscholastic League; past mem. governing bd. Amarillo Little Theatre; mem. governing bd. High Plains Center Performing Arts; bd. dirs. Friends of Fine Arts West Tex. State U., Amarillo Symphony; chmn. Oldham County Democratic Exec. Com. Mem. Internat. Platform Assn. (chmn.). Methodist. Clubs: Masons, Kiwanis (lt. gov. Tex.-Okla. dist. 1959, chmn. new club bldg. 1960, chmn. past lt. govs. 1967); Amarillo Knife and Fork (dir.). Home: Box 57 Vega TX 79092

COOK, DORIS MARIE, accountant, educator; b. Fayetteville, Ark., June 11, 1924; d. Ira and Mettie Jewel (Dorman) C. BS in Bus. Adminstrn., U. Ark., 1946, MS, 1949; PhD, U. Tex., 1969. CPA, Okla., Ark. Jr. acct. Haskins & Sells, Tulsa, 1946-47; instr. acctg. U. Ark., Fayetteville, 1947-52, asst. prof., 1952-62, assoc. prof., 1962-69, prof., 1969-88, univ. prof. and Nolan E. Williams lectr. in acctg., 1988—; mem. Ark. State Bd. Pub. Accountancy, 1987—; apptd. Nolan E. Williams lectrship in acctg., 1988—. Contbr. articles to profl. jours. Mem. Ark. Bus. Assn. (editor newsletter 1982-85), Am. Acctg. Assn. (chair nat. membership 1982-83, chair Arthur Carter Scholarship com. 1984-85, chair membership Ark. 1985-87), Am. Inst. CPA's, Am. Women's Soc. CPA's, Ark. Soc. CPA's (v.p. 1975-76, pres. NW Ark. chpt. 1980-81, sec. Student Loan Found. 1981-84, treas. Student Loan Found. 1984—, chair pub. relations 1984-88), Acad. Acctg. Historians (trustee 1985-87, mem. review bd. 1984—), Ark. Fedn. Bus. and Profl. Women's Clubs (treas. 1979-80), Mortar Bd., Beta Gamma Sigma, Beta Alpha Psi (editor nat. newsletter 1973-77, nat. pres. 1977-78), Phi Gamma Nu, Alpha Lambda Delta, Delta Kappa Gamma (sec. 1976-78, pres. 1978-80), Phi Kappa Phi. Club: Fayetteville Bus. and Profl. Women's (pres. 1973-74, 75-76, Woman of Yr. 1977). Home: 1115 Leverett St Fayetteville AR 72703 Office: U Ark Dept Acctg Fayetteville AR 72701

COOK, EDWARD WILLINGHAM, diversified industry executive; b. Memphis, June 19, 1922; s. Everett Richard and Phoebe (Willingham) C.; m. Patricia Long, Mar. 17, 1973; children: Patricia Kendall, Mark W.; children by previous marriage: Edward Willingham, Jr., Everett Richard II, Barbera Moore Cook Brooks. A.B., Yale U., 1944. Chief exec. officer Cook Internat., Palm Beach, Fla.; dir. First Tenn. Corp., Memphis, 1969-88; chmn. Mid-South Internat. Agricenter, Memphis, 1979-82 (chmn.); mem. Cotton Adv. Com., 1964-68; mem. exec. com. Nat. Council for U.S.-China Trade, 1973-78; mem. President's Export Council, 1973-79; dir. Chgo. Bd. Trade, 1974-76. Chmn. Memphis-Shelby County Airport Authority, 1968-81, to Squire, Shelby County Ct., 1948-66; bd. dirs. Planned Parenthood of Palm Beach Area, 1983—, Palm Beach Civic Assn., 1984—, Hospice Guild of Palm Beach, Palm Beach County Devel. Bd., Econ. Council Palm Beach County, Brandywine River Mus., Chadds Ford, Pa. Served to maj. USAAF, 1943-45, MTO. Decorated D.F.C., Bronze Star, Air medal with six oak leaf clusters. Mem. So. Cotton Assn. (past pres.), Cotton Council Am. (bd. dirs. 1962-65), Cotton Council Internat. (bd. dirs. 1964-65), Am. Cotton Shippers Assn. (past pres.). Episcopalian. Clubs: Memphis Country, Memphis Hunt and Polo; Links (N.Y.C.); Palm Beach Polo, Everglades, Govs., Bath and Tennis (Palm Beach, Fla.). Address: 205 Royal Palm Way Palm Beach FL 33480

COOK, EUGENE AUGUSTUS, lawyer; b. Houston, May 2, 1938; s. Eugene A. and Estelle Mary (Stiner) C.; m. Sondra Attaway, Aug. 27, 1968; children—Laurie Ann, Eugene A. B.B.A., U. Houston, 1961, J.D., 1966. Bar: Tex. 1966, U.S. Dist. Ct. (so. dist.) Tex. 1967, U.S. Ct. Appeals (5th cir.) 1969, U.S. Supreme Ct. 1971, U.S. Ct. Claims 1972, U.S. Tax Ct. 1974, U.S. Ct. Appeals (11th cir.) 1982, U.S. Dist. Ct. (no., we. and ea. dists.) Tex. 1983. Ptnr. Butler & Binion, Houston, 1966-85; founding ptnr. Cook, Davis & McFall, 1985—. adj. asst. prof. law U. Houston, 1971-72, 74; editor-in-chief, contbg. author: Creditors' Rights in Texas, 2d edit., 1982. Bd. dirs. U. Houston Law Rev., 1978-79; contbr. articles to law jours. Fellow Am. Coll. Trial Lawyers, Am. Acad. Matrimonial Lawyers, Internat. Acad. Matrimonial Lawyers, Am. Bar Found., Tex. Bar Found.; mem. ABA, Houston Bar Found., State Bar of Tex. (chmn. grievance com. 1971-72, bd. dirs. 1975-80, vice chmn. consumer law sect. 1976-77, chmn. consumer law sect. 1979-80, Presdl. Citation 1979, dir. family law sect. 1984-88, Outstanding Atty. 1983, 84, 86, bd. dirs. 1981-85, chmn. pubs. com. 1981-82, Achievement award 1982, chmn. litigation sect. 1982-84, legal edn. com. 1988-89), Houston Bar Assn. (seminar com. 1976-77, Chmn. of Yr. award, 1976-77, chmn. insts. com. 1977-78, Outstanding Service award 1977-78, chmn. continuing legal edn. com. 1978-79, Pres.'s award 1978-79, chmn. consumer law sect. 1978-79, vice chmn. family law sect. 1981-82, chmn. family law sect. 1982-83, Officers award 1983, chmn. staff and staffing com. 1985-86, dir. 1984-86, 2d v.p. 1986-87, 1st v.p. 1987-88, pres. 1988—), Tex. Bd. Legal Specialization (cert.), Civil Trial and Family Law, Tex. Assn. Cert. Civil Trial Law Lawyers, Gulf Coast Family Law Specialists Assn., Tex. Acad. Family Law Specialists, ABA, State Bar Tex., Phi Kappa Phi, Phi Theta Kappa, Omicron Chi Epsilon, Omicron Delta Kappa, Phi Rho Pi. Home: 8316 Winningham St Houston TX 77055 Office: Cook Davis & McFall 2600 Two Houston Ctr 909 Fanin Houston TX 77010-1003

COOK, FRANCES D., diplomat; b. Charleston, W.Va., Sept. 7, 1945; d. Nash and Vivian Cook. B.A., Mary Washington Coll. of U. Va., 1967; M.P.A., Harvard U., 1978. Certificats d'Etudes, Université d'Aix-Marseille (France), 1966. Commd. fgn. service officer Dept. State, 1967; spl. asst. to R.S. Shriver, ambassador to France, 1968-69; mem. U.S. Del. Paris Peace Talks on Viet-Nam, 1970-71; cultural affairs officer, consul Am. Consul Gen., Sydney, Australia, 1971-73; cultural affairs officer, first sec. Am. Embassy, Dakar, Senegal, 1973-75; personnel officer for Africa USIA, Washington, 1975-77; dir. office public affairs African Bur. Dept. State, Washington, 1978-80; ambassador to Republic of Burundi, 1980-83; consul gen. Alexandria, Egypt, 1983-86; dep. asst. sec. of state Dept. State, Washington, 1986-87, dir. Office of West African Affairs, 1987—. Recipient various honor awards Dept. State. Mem. Am. Fgn. Service Assn., Council on Fgn. Relations, Washington Alumni Council Kennedy Sch. Harvard U. Club: Harvard of N.Y.C. Office: Office West African Affairs Dept State Room 4250 Washington DC 20520

COOK, FRANK ROBERT, JR., business chance, real estate, and insurance broker, builder, developer, accountant, management consultant, lawyer; b. Washington, Aug. 19, 1923. B.S. in Psychology, Howard U., 1945, postgrad. in psychology, 1946, J.D., 1949; LL.M., Georgetown U., B.C.S. Southeastern U., 1963, M.C.S., 1964; Ph.D., Western U., 1951 Bar: U.S. Ct. Appeals 1949, U.S. Supreme Ct. 1954, D.C. 1967, U.S. Dist. Ct. Md. 1976. Bus. chance broker, Washington, 1944—; real estate broker, Washington, 1945—; ins. broker, Washington, 1946—; pvt. practice acctg., Washington, 1944—; prin. Frank R. Cook, Jr. and Assocs., mgmt. cons., Seat Pleasant, Md. Minister, Ministry of Salvation, Washington. Mem. Washington Bar Assn., D.C. Unified Bar, Nat. Soc. Pub. Accts., Am. Assn. Sex Educators and Counselors, Nat. Assn. Real Estate Appraisers (cert.), Cert. Bus. Opportunity Appraisers. Office: 1715 11th St NW Washington DC 20001-5099

COOK, HAROLD RODNEY, army medical center administrator; b. Sterling, Colo., Feb. 13, 1944; s. Harold E. Cook and Adelaide Cook; m. Shirley Carnel; children: Dawn, Danae, Kevin (dec.). BS in Bus., Psychology and Sociology, Kearney State Coll., 1973, MA in Psychology, 1974; MHA, Baylor U., 1985. Commd. 2d lt. U.S. Army, 1974, advanced through grades to maj., 1986; med. adminstr. U.S. Gen. Hosp., Nürnberg, Germany, 1975-78; comdr. 560th Ambulance Co., Korea; chief ops. med. med./surg. div. Acad. of Health Sci., Ft. Sam Houston, Tex., 1980-83; with health care adminstrn. Baylor U., Waco, Tex., 1983-85; surgery adminstr. Fitzsimons Army Med. Ctr., Aurora, Colo., 1985—; exec. dir., pres. Colo. Petrolon Inc; asst. regional dir. Petrolon Inc. Mem. Am. Coll. Hosp. Adminstrs., Am. Soc. Mgmt., Nat. Assn. Collegiate Vets. (exec. bd.). Clubs: Fitz Alpine (pres. 1985-87), Pantera. Home: 722 Bruns Ave Suite B Aurora CO 80045 Office: Fitzsimons Army Med Ctr PO Box 6065 Aurora CO 80045

COOK, HARRY CLAYTON, JR., lawyer; b. Washington, Mar. 25, 1935; s. Harry Clayton and Lillian June (A'harrah) C.; children—Christianne, Nicole, Harry Clayton III. BS in Chem. Engring, Princeton U., 1956; LLB, U. Va., 1960. Bar: Colo. 1960, N.Y. 1961, Pa. 1966, D.C. 1973. Assoc. firm Sullivan & Cromwell, N.Y.C., 1960-63, Holme Roberts & Owen, Denver, 1964, Pepper Hamilton & Scheetz, Phila., 1965-69; ptnr. Pepper Hamilton & Scheetz, 1969-70, 73; on assignment as sr. tax counsel Sun Oil Co., Phila., 1970; ptnr. Cadwalader Wickersham & Taft, Washington, 1974-87, Bishop, Cook, Purcell & Reynolds, Washington, 1988—; page to U.S. Sen. E.D. Milliken, Colo., 1950-52; gen. counsel Maritime Adminstrn.; mem. Maritime Subs. Bd., U.S. Dept. Commerce, Washington, 1970-73; U.S. del. to Soviet Union for Maritime Agreement between U.S. and USSR, 1971-73; mem. Adminstrv. Conf. U.S., 1980—, chmn. com. on jud. rev., 1982-86; mem. Nat. Def. Exec. Res., U.S. Mil. Sealift Command, 1983—, U.S. Office of Tech. Assessment; mem. citizens' adv. panel on U.S. Maritime Industry, 1982-85, cargo policy workshop participant, 1984-85; presdl. transition team Fed. Maritime Commn., 1980-81. Contbr. articles to profl. jours. Bd. dirs. Inst. for Fgn. Policy Analysis, Inc., 1980—, Com. on the Present Danger, 1981—, Inst. for Sustainable Devel., 1988—. Served to 1st lt. USAR JAGC, 1957-65. Mem. ABA (standing com. on law and nat. security 1987, tax sect. 1965—, adminstr. practice sect. 1974—, chmn. maritime law and nat. security workgroup), D.C. Bar Assn., Fed. Bar Assn. (com. gen. counsels 1970—), Am. Law Inst., Maritime Law Assn. U.S. (marine fin. com. 1981—), Order of Coif, Phi Delta Phi. Clubs: Racquet of Phila; University (N.Y.C.), University (D.C.). Home: 1011 Langley Hill Dr Langley VA 22101 also: Pinery Farm Cornwell Farm Rd Great Falls VA 22066 Office: Bishop Cook Purcell & Reynolds 1400 L St NW Washington DC 20005-3502

COOK, HELGA GISELA, executive assistant, management holding company executive; b. Koenigsberg, East Prussia, Germany, June 12, 1941; came to U.S., 1963, naturalized, 1974; d. Albert and Maria (Wunderlich) Woelk; bi-lingual bus. grad. in English and French, Vorbeck Lang. Inst., W.Ger., 1959; 1 son, Raymond J. Sec. EDP div. U.S. Army, Pirmasens, 1959-62, Internat. Leather Exhbn., Pirmasens, 1962-63; with comml. div. Honeywell, Pitts., 1966-70; with Mobay Chem. Corp., Pitts., 1970—, pricing clk., mktg., 1970-71, bilingual exec. sec., polyurethane div., 1971-74, exec. asst. to pres. and chief exec. officer, 1974-81, to chmn. and pres., 1981-86; exec. asst. to pres., chief exec. officer Bayer USA Inc., 1986—. Assoc. Merrick Art Gallery, New Brighton. Mem. Am. Soc. Profl. and Exec. Women, Pitts. NAFE Network (pres.), LWV of Beaver County (2d v.p.). Office: Bayer USA Inc One Mellon Ctr Pittsburgh PA 15219-2502

COOK, LODWRICK MONROE, petroleum company executive; b. Grand Cane, La., June 17, 1928; married. B.S., La. State U., 1950, B.S. in Petroleum Engring., 1955; M.B.A., So. Meth. U., 1965. Petroleum engr. Union Producing Co., 1955-56; with Atlantic Richfield Co., Los Angeles, 1956—; engring. trainee Atlantic Richfield Co., Inc., Los Angeles, 1956-61, adminstrv. asst., 1961-64, sr. personnel dept., then personnel mgr., 1964-67, labor reins. con., 1967-69, mgr. labor reins. dept., 1969-70, v.p., gen. mgr. product div. Western area, 1970-72, v.p. mktg. products div., 1972-73, v.p. corp. planning div., 1973-74, v.p. products div., 1974-75, v.p. transp. div., 1975-77, sr. v.p. transp. div., 1977-80, exec. v.p., dir., 1980-85, pres., chief exec. officer, 1985, chmn., chief exec. officer, 1986—. Chmn. bd. dirs. Nat. Jr. Achievement; bd. regents Pepperdine U., La. State U. Found; bd. govs. Music Ctr. Los Angeles. Served to 1st lt. U.S. Army, 1950-53. Mem. Bus. Roundtable, Nat. Petroleum Council, Am. Petroleum Inst. (dir.), U.S. C. of C. (dir.). Office: Atlantic Richfield Co 515 S Flower St Los Angeles CA 90071

COOK, M(ELVIN) GARFIELD, chemical company executive; b. Woodbury, N.J., June 17, 1940; s. Melvin Alonzo and Wanda (Garfield) C.; m. Margo Dawn Taylor, Aug. 24, 1965; children: Dawn Ann, Melvin, Katherine, JoAnn, Carol, Mary, Taylor, Stephen, Michael. B.S. in Physics, U. Utah, 1966. Research assoc. IRECO Chems., Salt Lake City, 1966-67; gen. mgr. Mesabi Blasting, Inc., Biwabik, Minn., 1967-69; v.p. ops. IRECO Chems., 1969-71, exec. v.p., 1971-72, pres., chief exec. officer, 1972—; dir. Def. Systems, Inc., Salt Lake City, Nobel Ins. Ltd.; advisor on explosives and propellants Dept. Def., Washington, 1979—; chmn. bd. govs. Inst. of Makers of Explosives, Washington, 1972—; chmn. Non-Evasive Med. Tech. Corp., 1988—. Author: Everlasting Burnings, 1981, Ency. Modern Explosives, 1972—, (with M.A. Cook) Science and Mormonism, 1967. Vice pres. N.E. Bench Region Council, Salt Lake City, 1974; chmn. voting dist. Republican Party, 1973; vice-chmn. Utah Symphony, 1988—. Served with USAR, 1958-66. Mem. Mayflower Soc. Republican. Mormon. Lodge: Rotary. Office: IRECO Incorporated 11th Floor Crossroads Tower 50 S Main St Salt Lake City UT 84144

COOK, NOEL ROBERT, manufacturing company executive; b. Houston, Mar. 19, 1937; s. Horace Berwick and Leda Estelle (Houghton) C.; student Iowa State U., 1955-57; B.S. in Indsl. Engring., U. Mich., 1960; children—Laurel Jane, David Robert. Engr. in tng. Eaton Mfg., Saginaw, Mich., 1960-61; mgr. mfg. and contracting J. N. Fauver Co., Madison Heights, Mich., 1961-65; pres. Newton Mfg., Royal Oak, Mich., 1965—; soc. Indsl. Piping Contractors, Birmingham, Mich., 1969-75; pres. RNR Metal Fabricators, Inc., Royal Oak, Mich., 1974-78; chmn. bd. Kim Internat. Sales Co., 1978—; pres. Newton Sales Co., Royal Oak, 1978—, Power Package Windsor Ltd., Windsor, Ont., Can., 1981—. Served with U.S. Army, 1960-61. Registered profl. engr., Mich. Mem. Fluid Power Soc., Nat. Fluid Power Assn., Birmingham Jr. C. of C. (past bd. dirs.). Patentee in field. Home: 4481 W Cherry Hill Dr Orchard Lake MI 48033 Office: 4249 Delemere Blvd Royal Oak MI 48073

COOK, ROBERT NEVIN, educator, consultant; b. Vicksburg, Pa., Dec. 11, 1912; s. Ralph B. and Mabel Grace (Maurer) C.; m. Frances Katherine Murphy, Mar. 18, 1939; children—Katherine Cook Leith, Robert N., Ann Cook Krebs. A.B. cum laude, Bucknell U., 1933; J.D., Duke U., 1936. Bar: Pa. 1937. Assoc. firm Knight & Kivko, Sunbury, Pa., 1936-37; instr. Mercer U. Sch. Law, 1937-38 asst. prof., law librarian Vanderbilt U., 1938-39; asst. prof. U. Louisville Sch. Law, 1939-41; atty. NLRB, 1941, office Gen. Counsel, Treas. Dept., 1941-45, office Alien Property, 1945, office Small Bus., 1946; assoc. prof. Western Res. U. Sch. Law, 1946-50, prof. 1950-63; prof. U. Cin. Coll. Law, 1963-81, prof. emeritus, 1982—, cons., researcher Nat. Research Council, Nat. Acad. Sci.; prin. organizer N. Am. Inst. for Modernization of Land Data Systems, 1974, dir., 1974-79, cons., 1979—, hon. life dir., 1984—; procs. organizer, participant, editor Tri-State Conf. on Comprehensive Unified Land Data System, Coll. Law U. Cin., 1966. Mem. ABA (chmn. land title records improvement com. Real Property, Probate and Trust Law Sect., 1964-69), Pa. Bar Assn., Cin. Bar Assn., Am. Coll. Real Estate Lawyers, Order of Coif. Democrat. Methodist. Author: Legal Drafting, 1950; contbr. articles in field to law jours.; prin. developer of Comprehensive Unified Land Data System (CULDATA) now known as Compatible Multi-Purpose Land Info. System. Home: 62 Rawson Woods Circle Cincinnati OH 45220 Office: Cin Coll Law Cincinnati OH 45221

COOK, SAMUEL DUBOIS, university president, political scientist; b. Griffin, Ga., Nov. 21, 1928; s. Manuel and Mary Beatrice (Daniel) C.; m. Sylvia Merelene Fields, Mar. 18, 1960; children: Samuel DuBois, Karen Jarcelyn. A.B., Morehouse Coll., 1948, LL.D., 1972; M.A., Ohio State U., 1950, Ph.D., 1954, L.H.D. (hon.), 1977; LL.D. (hon.), Duke U., 1979, Ill. Coll., 1979, Chgo. Theol. Sem., 1988. Assoc. prof. polit. sci. So. U., 1955-56; prof., chmn. dept. polit. sci. Atlanta U., 1956-66; assoc. prof. Duke U., Durham, N.C., 1966-71; prof. Duke U., 1971-74; pres. Dillard U., New Orleans, 1975—; vis. prof. U. Ill., 1962-63, UCLA, summer 1966; program officer higher edn. and research Ford Found., 1969-71; cons. in field. Contbr. articles to profl. jours. and anthologies. Mem. So. Growth Policies Bd., 1972-73, N.C. Council on Goals and Policies, 1971-74; mem. exec. com. So. Regional Council, 1967-69; trustee Martin Luther King Jr. Center for Social Change, 1968—; bd. dirs. Council for Library Resources, 1976—; mem. advisory council Jt. Center for Polit. Studies, 1972-75; chmn. council of presidents Am. Missionary Assn. Colls., 1988—, United Meth.-Related Black Colls., 1987—; chmn. of presidents United Negro Coll. Fund, 1988—; chair Council Higher Edn. United Ch. Christ, 1985-87; trustee Duke U. Served with U.S. Army, 1953-55. Fellow Rockefeller Found., Ford Found., Social Sci. Research Council, So. Edn. Found., Omega Psi Phi Nat.; Mem. Am. Polit. Sci. Assn. (past mem. exec. council, v.p. 1978-79), Conf. Black Polit. Scientists, Assn. for Study Afro-Am. Life and History (mem. exec. council), So. Polit. Sci. Assn. (past pres.), Nat. Council for Humanities, Pi Sigma Alpha, Phi Beta Kappa, Omicron Delta Phi, Omega Psi Phi, Sigma Pi Phi. Democrat. Baptist. Office: Dillard U 2601 Gentilly Blvd New Orleans LA 70122

COOK, SHARON EVONNE, academic administrator, educator; b. Pocatello, Idaho, July 16, 1941; d. Willard Robert and Marian (Bartlett) Leisy; m. John Fred Cook, June 19, 1971 (div. Nov. 1980). BEd, No. Mont. Coll., 1970; M in Secondary Edn., U. Alaska, Juneau, 1980; EdD, U. San Francisco, 1987. Cert. secondary sch. tchr., Alaska. Loan officer 1st Nat. Bank, Havre, Mont., 1964-68; adminstrv. asst. Alaska State Legis., Juneau, 1970-71; tchr. Juneau Dist. High Sch., 1971-75; instr. Juneau Dist. Community Coll., 1975-79; assoc. prof. U. Alaska, Juneau, 1979—, dean Sch. Bus. and Pub. Adminstrn.,, 1986—; editor in chief office tech. McGraw Hill Book Gregg Div., N.Y.C., 1983-84; mem. exec. bd. statewide assembly U. Region V Vocat. Assn., 1978-80, del. 1982. Treas. Alaska State Vocat. Assn., 1980-82, pres.-elect, 1986, pres., 1987; pres. U. Alaska Juneau Assembly, 1978-80, v.p., 1980-82. No. Mont. Coll. scholar, Havre, 1968-70; named Outstanding Tchr., U. Alaska, 1976. Republican. Home: 2400 Douglas Hwy #5 Juneau AK 99801 Office: U Alaska Sch Bus & Pub Adminstrn 1108 F St Juneau AK 99801

COOK, VICTOR JOSEPH, JR., marketing educator, consultant; b. Durant, Okla., June 25, 1938; s. Victor Joseph and Athelene Ann (Arduser) C.; m. Linda Lee Potter, June 6, 1960 (div. 1971); children: Victor Joseph III, William Randall, Christopher Phelps. B.A., Fla. State U., 1960; M.S., La. State U., 1962; Ph.D., U. Mich., 1965. Research assoc. Mktg. Sci. Inst., Phila., 1965-68, assoc. research dir., Boston, 1968-69; asst. prof. U. Chgo.,

1969-75; pres., dir. Mgmt. & Design, New Orleans, 1975-78; prof. Freeman Sch. Bus., Tulane U., 1978—; cons. Ford Motor Co., Dearborn, Mich., 1964-67, IBM, N.Y.C., 1968-72, Sears, Roebuck & Co., Chgo., 1975-77, STC/ICL, London, 1981—. Author: Brand Policy Determination, 1967; designer, patentee furniture, Sud Möbel, 1976. Mem. Republican Presdl. Task Force, Washington, 1981—. Mem. Am. Mktg. Assn., Am. Econ. Assn., Inst. Mgmt. Scis., Assn. for Consumer Research, Beta Gamma Sigma, Phi Beta Kappa. Republican. Methodist. Avocations: golf; drawing; art collecting; travel. Office: Tulane U AB Freeman Sch Bus New Orleans LA 70118

COOK, WARREN AYER, industrial hygienist; b. Conway, Mass., July 22, 1900; s. Charles Lincoln and Anna Marean (Wiswall) C.; A.B., Dartmouth Coll., 1923; postgrad. Yale U. Grad. Schs. 1923-24; m. Marion Allen Chase, Sept. 8, 1928; 1 dau., Marion Allen Cook Huff. With engring. and inspection div. Travelers Ins. Co., Hartford, Conn., 1925-28; chief indsl. hygienist Conn. State Dept. Health, Bur. Occupational Diseases, Hartford, 1928-37; dir. indsl. hygiene and engring. research Zurich-Am. Ins. Cos., Chgo., 1937-53; assoc. prof. U. Mich. Sch. Public Health dept. indsl. health, Ann Arbor, 1953-56, prof., 1956-70, prof. emeritus, 1970—, research assoc. Inst. Indsl. Health, 1953-70; adj. prof. U. N.C. dept. environ. scis. and engring., Chapel Hill, 1971—; lectr. on occupational exposure limits, U.S., Denmark, Spain, West Germany, Czechoslovakia; cons. in field. Fellow Am. Public Health Assn. (chmn. occupational health sect. 1953-54, governing council 1955-57), Am. Indsl. Hygiene Assn. (pres. 1940-41, dir. 1941-43, hon. mem. 1968—, pres. Chgo. Sect. 1945-46, recipient Borden award 1979, Donald E. Cummins award 1953), Carolinas sect. Am. Indsl. Hygiene Assn. (pres. 1972-74, recipient awards 1981, 87), Mich. Indsl. Hygiene Soc. (pres. 1958-59), Am. Conf. of Govtl. Indsl. Hygienists (recipient meritorious achievement award 1973), Am. Acad. Indsl. Hygiene (diplomate), Am. Acad. Occupational Medicine (hon. mem.), Am. Soc. Safety Engrs. (exec. com. 1955-57), Greater Detroit chpt. Am. Soc. Safety Engrs. (pres. 1955-56), Am. Chem. Soc., Alpha Chi Sigma, Delta Omega (pres. Delta chpt. 1967-68). Republican. Methodist. Author: (monograph) Occupational Exposure Limits—Worldwide, 1987, American Industrial Hygiene Association Occupational Exposure and Work Practice Guidelines for Formaldehyde, 1988; contbr. numerous articles on indsl. hygiene to profl. jours., also Ency. Occupational Health and Safety, 1983, Alkylating Agents and Ethers, Ency. Chemistry, 1973; assoc. editor Jour. Indsl Hygiene and Toxicology, 1947-49; editor Am. Indsl. Hygiene Assn. Quar., 1940-50; assoc. editor Indsl. Medicine and Surgery, 1950-68. Home: 713 Emory Dr Chapel Hill NC 27514

COOK, WILLIAM WILBER, advertising agency executive; b. Evansville, Ind., Apr. 23, 1921; s. Wilburn Frederick and Mabel (Brookins) C.; student UCLA, 1940-42; B.A. in Bus., Evansville Coll., 1947; LL.D. (hon.), Bethune-Cookman Coll., 1976; m. Mary Andross Brewster, Nov. 2, 1963; children—William F., Constance C., Betty B., Jane R., Robert B. Sales rep. Sta. WIKY, Evansville, 1947-49, WMBR Radio and TV, Jacksonville, Fla., 1949-55; v.p. Dennis, Parsons & Cook Advt. Agy., Jacksonville, 1955-65; pres. William Cook Advt., Inc., Jacksonville, 1965-77, chmn. bd., 1977—. Former chmn. United Negro Coll. Fund; mem. lay adv. com. St. Vincent's Med. Center; trustee Jacksonville U.; former vestryman Episcopal Ch. Served as aviator USNR, 1942-46. Recipient CHIEF award Fla. Pvt. Higher Edn. Assn., 1977. Mem. Jacksonville C. of C. (gov.), Com. of 100), Am. Assn. Advt. Agencies (past chmn. S.E. Council), Am. Advt. Fedn. (Silver medal), Fla. Public Relations Assn., Sales and Mktg. Execs. Assn. (Top Mgmt. award). Clubs: River, Univ., Selva Marina Country, Waynesville (N.C.) Country, Ponte Vedra Country, Tournement Players; Laurel Ridge Country (Waynesville, N.C.). Lodges: Rotary (dir.), Masons, Shriners. Avocations: golf, reading, travel. Home: 1325 Beach Ave Atlantic Beach FL 32233

COOK, WINFIELD CLINTON, sales and marketing company executive; b. Camden, N.J., Nov. 23, 1908; s. Clinton and Loretta (Florence) C.; m. Isabelle Killian, Oct. 28, 1933; children—Nancy, Thomas, Barbara, Roger. A.B., Dickinson Coll., 1932; postgrad. U. Pa., 1942, U. Md., 1943; D.H.L. (hon.), Combs Coll., 1973. Supr. Wear Ever Aluminum Co., New Kensington, Pa., 1932-39; pres. Vitacraft Pa. Sales Inc., Williamsport, 1939-59, Homec Inc., Williamsport, 1959-73. Bd. dirs. Pop Warner Little Scholars, Phila., 1974-88; Island Players, Long Boat Key Hist. Soc.; bd. dirs. emeritus Suburban Gen. Hosp., Norristown, Pa., 1959—; trustee Dickinson Coll., Carlisle, Pa., 1956-64; cons. U.S. Jaycees Found.; pres. Nixon Clubs, Montgomery County, Pa., 1960, Island Republican Club, Manatee, Fla., 1982, pres. bd. trustees Presbyterian Ch., Ambler, Pa., 1956-60, chmn. Manatee Exec. Com., 1963-66. Mem. Sales and Mktg. Execs. Assn. (bd. dirs. 1956-57), Nat. Assn. Direct Selling Cos. (past pres., chmn. bd.), Am. Hotel and Motel Assn., Longboat Key C. of C., (bd. dirs. 1974—). Clubs: Union League (Phila.); Seaview Country (Absecon, N.J.); Ocean City Yacht. Lodges: Masons, Shriners. Home: 4235 Gulf of Mexico Longboat Key FL 33548

COOKE, GERALD EDWARD, management consultant, foundation executive, retired air force officer; b. West Jefferson, Ohio, Aug. 13, 1925; s. Dexter Hoag and Mary Catherine (Burtis) C.; B.S., U. Md., 1959, Ph.D. in Govt., 1969; M.A., San Francisco State Coll., 1963; postgrad. Air War Coll., 1967-68; m. Margie L. Hall, Dec. 24, 1945; children—Cindy Lou, Melanie Sue. Comml. and test pilot, flight instr., 1945-51; commd. 1st lt. USAF, 1951, advanced through grades to maj. gen., 1977, ret., 1980; comdt. Air Force Inst. Tech., comdt. Def. Inst. Security Assistance Mgmt., Wright-Patterson AFB, Ohio, 1978-80; pvt. mgmt. cons. on edn. and tech., San Antonio, 1980—; pres. Tex. Research and Tech. Found., 1984—; adj. prof. bus. law George Washington U., 1970-78. Trustee Aerospace Edn. Found., 1983—. Served with USAAF, 1943-45. Decorated D.F.C., Bronze Star, Air medal with 4 oak leaf clusters, others. Mem. Am. Polit. Sci. Assn., Am. Soc. for Engring. Edn., Soc. Logistics Engring., Am. Def. Preparedness Assn., Air Force Assn., U. Md. Alumni Assn.

COOKE, LAWRENCE HENRY, lawyer, former judge; b. Monticello, N.Y., Oct. 15, 1914; s. George L. and Mary (Pond) C.; m. Alice McCormack, Nov. 25, 1939; children—Edward M., George L., II, Mary L. Cooke Opie. BS cum laude, Georgetown U., 1935; LLB, Union U., 1938, LLD (hon.), 1975; LLD (hon.), Siena Coll., 1964, N.Y. Law Sch., 1979, Bklyn. Law Sch., 1980, Pace U., 1980, Syracuse U., 1985. Bar: N.Y. 1939. Individual practice law Monticello, 1939-53, Sullivan County judge, 1954-61; Supreme Ct. justice 3d Jud. Dist., 1962-68; assoc. justice Appellate div. 3d Dept., Albany, 1969-74; assoc. judge N.Y. State Ct. Appeals, Albany, 1975-78; chief judge N.Y. State Ct. Appeals, 1979-84; sr. counsel Hall, Dickler, Lawler, Kent & Friedman, N.Y.C., 1985-87; counsel White, Brenner & Feigenbaum, Albany, N.Y., 1987—; arbitrator internat. law cases, 1986—; chmn. Conf. Chief Justices, 1982-83; pres. Nat. Center for State Cts., 1982-83; chmn. N.Y. Fair Trial, Free Press Conf., 1979-84; chmn. adv. council Nat. Symposium on Civil Justice Issues, 1986; chmn. assocs. com. Nat. Ctr. for State Cts., 1985-86; lectr. Brookings Inst., 1984, 86; John F. Sonnett Meml. lectr. Fordham U. Law Sch., 1981; Charles Evans Hughes Meml. lectr. New York County Lawyers Assn., 1981; keynote speaker Internat. Jewish Jurists and Lawyers Conv., Jerusalem, 1981; mem. Senator Daniel P. Moynihan Jud. Screening Com., 1985—. Supr. Town of Thompson, N.Y., 1946-49; chmn. Sullivan County Bd. Suprs., 1947-48; bd. visitors Sch. Law Fordham U., 1987—; bd. dirs. State Justice Inst. Recipient Torch of Liberty award B'nai B'rith, 1967, Friend of Press award N.Y. State Soc. Newspaper Editors, 1985, 1st Amendment award Deadline Club, 1985, Seymour medal Am. Arbitration Assn., 1985, Toney Rivers Watson award Jud. Friends of Nat. Bar Assn., 1984, award of merit Am. Judges Assn., 1983, Law Day award N.Y. State Trial Laywers' Assn., 1983, John Carroll award Georgetown U. Alumni Assn., 1982, Golda Meir Meml. award Jewish Lawyers Guild, 1983. Fellow Am. Bar Assn. Found.; mem. ABA, N.Y. State Bar Assn. (past chmn. young lawyers sect., Gold medal 1985), Assn. Bar of City of N.Y., Am. Law Inst., Sullivan County Bar Assn. (pres.), Am. Judicature Soc. (bd. dirs. 1987—), N.Y. State Women's Bar Assn. (hon.), Nat. Ctr. for State Cts. (Disting. Service award 1987), Rockland County Magistrates' Assn. (Disting. Service award 1987). Democrat. Roman Catholic. Home: 415 Broadway Monticello NY 12701

COOKE, ROBERT JOHN, emeritus history and law educator; b. Kingston, N.Y., Apr. 12, 1923; s. Harry and Anna (Hyland) C.; children: Kathleen Anne, Christian Seán, Kevin Michaél, Deirdre Gobnait, Brian Patrick, Siobhán Brighid; m. Margaret Mary McGowan (dec. 1984). B.S. in Social Sci., SUNY, 1949; A.M. in History, Columbia U., 1950; Ph.D. in Am. Studies, Maxwell Grad. Sch. Pub. Affairs, Syracuse U., 1964. Asst. in Am. civilization Columbia U., 1949-50; tchr. social studies and English Goshen (N.Y.) High Sch., 1950-54; staff Citizens Edn. Project, Carnegie Found., 1950-54; asst. prof. social sci. Ball State U., Muncie, Ind., 1954-59; instr. Am. studies Maxwell Grad. Sch. Pub. Affairs, Syracuse U., 1960-65, dir. Chautauqua Center, 1960-62; assoc. Inter-Univ. Project I, Ford Found., 1962-65; prof. Am. studies and history Southampton Coll., L.I. U., 1965-83, prof. emeritus, 1983—, chmn. history dept., 1966-70, 73-83, chmn. Am. studies program, 1968-83, dir. humanities div., 1970-73, chmn. exec. com. faculty council, 1977-79, dir. pre-law program, 1975-83; vis. lectr. Trinity Coll., Dublin, Ireland, 1974. Contbr. articles to profl. jours., chpts. to books. Mem. legis. affairs com. N.Y. State Democratic Com., 1973-75. Served to lt. USMC(Air), 1942-46, PTO. Mem. Am. Hist. Assn., Am. Studies Assn. (chmn. and editor bibliography com. 1964-65), Nat. Council for Social Studies (book rev. editor jour. 1964-68, chmn. standing com. on research 1961-63, bd. dirs. 1966-69), Am.-Irish Hist. Soc., Am. Com. for Irish Studies, Irish Nat. Caucus, Orgn. Am. Historians, Sinn Féin (provo). Home: PO Box 265 Quogue NY 11959

COOKEY, SAMUEL JOSEPH, educational consultant; b. Opobo, Nigeria, Jan. 25, 1918; s. Joseph George and Rosanna Taba C.; student Achimota Coll., Ghana, Wycliffe Hall, Oxford, 1944-46; BA, U. London, 1944, postgrad. cert. in edn., 1953; HDL, Silliman U., Philippines, 1965, LLD, U. Sci. & Tech., Port Harcourt, Nigeria, 1986; m. Virginia Oboaya Emuchay, Feb. 18, 1950; children: Atowarifagha Donald, Alaibi Samuel, Ibelema Patricia, Taba Adela. Prin. secondary sch., Okrika, 1946-52, Onitsha, 1954-59; chief fed. adviser on edn. to Fed. Govt. Nigeria, 1967-71; dir. edn. Commonwealth Secretariat, London, 1972-77; ednl. cons. UNESCO, 1972—; chmn. Pan African Bank Ltd., Nigeria, 1978-79; chmn. Evans Ednl. Pubs., Nigeria, 1980—; dir. Mentor Ednl. Cons.; mem. exec. bd. UNESCO, 1962-70. Internat. commr. for Scouts, 1962-66; chmn. Nigeria Ednl. Research Council, 1967-71, Adv. Council Edn., Rivers State, Nigeria; mem. West African Exam. Council, 1962-71, Nigerian Acad. Edn., 1984, Constituent Assmebly, 1988; chmn. Presdl. Commn. on Nigerian Univs., 1980-81; pro-chancellor, chmn. council U. Ibadan, 1984-85, U. Benin, 1985-86; chmn. Fed. Govr. Polit. Bureau, 1986-87. Decorated officer Order of Niger. Fellow Coll. Preceptors (London). Clubs: Rotary, Ikoyi. Home: 12 Degema Close, Rumuibekwe Estate, PO Box 3396, Port Harcourt Rivers State, Nigeria

COOKSON, LILLIAN SYBIL, humanitarian worker; b. Stroud, England, 1902; d. Ulric Norman and Lydia (Bidlake) Holborow; m. C.E. Cookson, Nov. 5, 1931 (dec.); children: Brian Danvers, Robert Ulric, Bridget Jane. nat. chmn. Brit. sect. Women's Internat. League for Peace and Freedom, 1968-72, internat. rep., 1972-77, vice chmn. Brit. sect., 1979—. Chair local UN Assn., mem. regional council. Mem. World Federalist, Anti-Apartheid Movement, Conservation, World Wildlife, Green Party Green Peace, Labour Action for Peace, Oxford Com. Famine Relief. Christian Socialist. Home: Trelawny's, Sompting, Sussex BN15 OAX, England

COOKSON, PETER WILLIS, JR., sociologist, writer; b. N.Y.C., Nov. 17, 1942; s. Peter Willis and Maureen (Grey) C.; m. Susan Stern, Sept. 16, 1968; children: Alexandra Genvieve, Aram Nathaniel. BA, NYU, 1966, MA, 1968, PhD, 1981. Asst. headmaster Berkshire County Day Sch., Lenox, Mass., 1973-74, dean of students, 1974-75; instr. NYU, N.Y.C., 1975-82, research assoc., 1982—; ptnr. Cookson Prodns., Inc., N.Y.C., 1978—; pres. Sashari Prodns., Ltd., N.Y.C., 1982—; pres. 362 W. Broadway Corp., N.Y.C., 1982—; cons. Soho Alliance, N.Y.C., 1983; vis. assoc. prof. Manhattan Coll. Author: Preparing for Power: America's Elite Boarding Schools, 1985; contbr. articles to profl. jours. Mem. Fin. Com., West Stockbridge, Mass., 1974-75. Served with USAR, 1963-69. Research grantee Nat. Inst. Edn., 1983, NYU, 1983; travel grantee Elmgrant Trust, Devon, Eng., 1983, Tel Aviv U., 1983. Mem. N.Y. Acad. Scis., Am. Sociol. Assn., AAAS, Acad. Polit. Sci., Am. Ednl. Research Assn. Democrat. Roman Catholic. Home: 32 Norfolk Rd Southfield MA 01259 Office: Sashari Prodns Ltd 362 W Broadway New York NY 10013

COOLAHAN, JOHN MICHAEL, education educator; b. County Kerry, Ireland, June 9, 1941; s. William and Jane (Murphy) C.; m. Mary T. Ellis; children: Marie-Louise, Iseult, Deirdre, William. BA, Univ. Coll., Dublin, 1964, diploma higher edn., 1965, MA, 1967; PhD, Trinity Coll., Dublin, 1971, MEd, 1973. Tchr. 1961-70; lectr. edn. Carysfort Coll. Edn., Dublin, 1971-74, Univ. Coll., 1974-87; prof. edn. St. Patrick's Coll. Maynooth, County Kildare, Ireland, 1987—. Author: Irish Education, History and Structure, 1981, Asti and Post-Primary Education in Ireland, 1984; contbr. numerous articles to profl. jours.; editor Irish Ednl. Studies, 1979-84. Mem. Pub. Com. Edn. Mem. Ednl. Studies Assn. (pres. 1983-84), Reading Assn. Ireland, Hist. Assn. Office: St Patrick's Coll, Maynooth County Kildare Ireland

COOLEY, RICHARD PIERCE, banker; b. Dallas, Nov. 25, 1923; s. Victor E. and Helen (Pierce) C. B.S., Yale, 1944. With Wells Fargo Bank, San Francisco, 1949-82; exec. v.p. Wells Fargo Bank, 1965-66, pres., chief exec. officer, 1966-79, chmn. bd., chief exec. officer, 1979-82, also dir.; chmn., chief exec. officer, pres. Seattle-1st Nat. Bank (now Seafirst Corp.),, 1983-86, chmn., chief exec. officer, 1986—; chmn. bd., chief exec. officer, dir. Wells Fargo & Co., 1968-83; dir. UAL, Inc., Howmett Turbine Components Corp., Pechiney Ugine Kuhlmann Corp. Trustee Children's Hosp., San Francisco, Rand Corp., Calif. Inst. Tech., Pasadena. Served to 1st lt. Armed Services. Decorated Air medal. Mem. Assn. Res. City Bankers, Smithsonian Instn. Nat. Assn. (bd. dirs.), Calif. C. of C. (bd. dirs.). Office: Seafirst Corp PO Box 3977 Seattle WA 98124 also: Bank of Amer Nat Trust & Savs Bank of America Ctr San Francisco CA 94104 *

COOLIDGE, THOMAS RICHARDS, finance executive; b. Boston, Jan. 29, 1934; s. Harold Jefferson and Helen Carpenter (Isaacs) C.; m. Susan Lane Freiberg, May 8, 1965; children: Laura Jefferson, Anne Richards, Thomas Lawrence. A.B. cum laude, Harvard U., 1955, J.D., 1960. Bar: N.Y. 1963. Assoc. firm Carter, Ledyard & Milburn, N.Y.C., 1960-68; partner Carter, Ledyard & Milburn, 1968-74; pres. Diebold Group, Inc. (cons.), N.Y.C., 1974-75; sr. v.p. Parsons & Whittemore, Inc., N.Y.C., 1975-82; v.p., dir. Stenbeck Reassurance Co., Inc., N.Y.C., 1982—; pres. Coolidge & Co., Inc., 1982—; dir. Millidyne Inc., Sandvik, Inc., 1972-82. Founder, bd. dirs., vice chmn. Neighborhood Com. on Asphalt Green, 1969—; trustee Vincent Astor Found., 1972—, Sala, Inc., 1974-77. Served as lt. Armored F.A. U.S. Army, 1955-57. Mem. Am. Bar Assn., N.Y. State Bar Assn., Assn. Bar City N.Y. Republican. Episcopalian. Clubs: Brook, River. Office: Coolidge & Co Inc Beebe Hill Rd Falls Village CT 06031

COOMBE, JOHN RAYMOND, engineering executive; b. Trenton, N.J., Sept. 26, 1926; s. John Raymond and Elizabeth (Tholander) C.; m. Kathleen Marie Jennings, Feb. 22, 1958; children: John, Mary, Elizabeth, James. B.A., Washington and Jefferson U., 1951. Engr. Gen. Electric Co., Schenectady, 1951-59; physicist Tech. Ops., Burlington, Mass., 1959-60; supr. Alco Products, Schenectady, 1960-62; mgr. Westinghouse Co., Pitts., 1962-72; asst. chief licensing Stone & Webster, Boston, 1972—. Mem. Am. Nuclear Soc. (nat. program com., standards com.); gen. chmn. internat. meeting on severe accident eval., tech. program chmn. nat. meeting internat. meeting reactor safety, tech. program com. and session chmn. internat. meeting nuclear power plant op.). Patentee in field. Current Work: Power plant and advanced concept licensing activities. Subspecialties: Nuclear engineering; Cryogenics. Office: Stone & Webster 245 Summer St Boston MA 02107

COOMBS, C'CEAL PHELPS (MRS. BRUCE AVERY COOMBS), air company executive, civic worker; b. nr. Portland, Oreg.; d. Perry Edwin and Flora (Gowey) Phelps; B.S., U. Idaho, 1929; student Wash. State Coll., 1941; m. Bruce Avery Coombs, Nov. 28, 1929; children—Keith Avery, Glinda C'Ceal (Mrs. Nick E. Mason). Tchr. pub schs., Idaho, 1929-30; adminstrv. asst. Coombs West-Air Co. and Coombs Flying C Ranches, Yakima, Wash., 1945—; lobbyist for civic activities Wash. Legislature, 1947—; notary pub., Wash., 1960—. Del. White House Conf. on Children and Youth, 1960, Wash. State White House Conf. on Edn., 1955; mem. Wash. Citizens Council, Nat. Council on Crime and Delinquency, 1956—; bd. dirs., mem. exec. com. Wash. State Council Crime and Delinquency, 1956—, chmn., 1970-71, recipient Spl. State award, 1972, 76; mem. Allied Sch. Council Wash. 1951-53; mem. Western regional scholarship com. Ford Found., 1955-57; chmn. regional dist. Wash. Cities Legislation, 1960; chmn. Yakima County Sch. Bd., 1957-59; mem. Yakima County Health Dept., 1959-60; city councilwoman Yakima, 1959-61, asst. mayor, 1960; mem. Wash. Library Commn., 1960, 64-68, 72—, vice chmn., 1965-70, 75-76, recipient gov's. citation, 1976; del. UNESCO Conf. on Crime and Delinquency, Kyoto, Japan, 1970, Caracus, Venezuela, 1980; del. to Internat. Library Assn., Toronto, 1968, Washington, 1975, del. to worldwide seminar, Seoul, 1976, London, Brussels, 1977; del. Internat. Fedn. Libraries, Manila, 1980; trustee Wash. 4-H Found., 1960-79, chmn., 1969—, hon. trustee, 1979—; bd. mem. Wash. State Friends of Libraries, 1976, pres., 1977; mem. bd. Yakima County Law and Justice. Recipient Outstanding Citizen award Western Correctional Assn., 1974. Mem. Am. Library Trustee Assn. (regional dir. 1962—, pres. 1967-68), C. of C., Oreg., Idaho, Elmore County, Washington County, Calif. hist. socs., Windsor (Conn.) Hist. Assn. (life), Friends of Tewkesbury Abbey Eng. (life), Daus. Am. Colonists, Founders and Patriots, New Eng. Hist. Geneal. Soc., Conn. Hist. Soc., Dorchester (Mass.) Antiquarian and Hist. Soc., Conn. Soc. Genealogists, Ft. Simcoe Restoration Soc. (life), ALA (internat. trustee citation 1966, mem. bd. 1972—, council 1967-68, 71-72), Pacific N.W. (chmn. trustee sect. 1962-63), Wash. (chmn. 1960, trustee award 1967) library assns., Nat. Soc. Crown of Charlemagne, LWV, Allied Arts Council, Broadway Theatre League, Nat., Am., aviation assns., P.E.O., Federated Women, Colonial Dames (state rec. sec., pres. local chpt.), Altrusa, Nat. Soc. Magna Charta Dames, Descs. of Conqueror and His Companions, Friends of N.Y.C. Library. Home: 11430 Mieras Rd Yakima WA 98901

COONEY, DAVID FRANCIS, lawyer; b. Chgo., Sept. 21, 1954; s. John Thomas and Margaret (Bonner) C.; m. René Marie Struzzieri, June 20, 1987. BBA in Fin. magna cum laude, U. Notre Dame, 1975, JD, 1978. Bar: Fla., U.S. Dist. Ct. (so. dist.) Fla., U.S. Ct. Appeal (5th, 8th and 11th cirs.). Assoc. Grimmett, Scherer & James, Ft. Lauderdale, Fla., 1978-82; ptnr. Conrad, Scherer & James, Ft. Lauderdale, 1982—. Republican. Roman Catholic. Home: 1325 Ponce de Leon Dr Fort Lauderdale FL 33316 Office: Conrad Scherer & James 633 S Federal Hwy Fort Lauderdale FL 33301

COONEY, PATRICIA R., civic worker; b. Englewood, N.J.; d. Charles Aloysius and Ruth Jeannette (Foster) McEwen; m. J. Gordon Cooney, June 8, 1957; 1 child, J. Gordon, Jr. Grad. Katharine Gibbs Sch., 1948; student Fordham U., 1950-51. Blood bank chmn. Strafford Village Civic Assn., 1968-69, sec., 1970-71; vice chmn. Spl. Gifts Com. Cath. Charities Appeal of Archdiocese of Phila., 1980—, chmn. 1985; mem. Council of Mgrs. Archdiocese of Phila., 1982—, sec., exec. com., 1983—; bd. dirs. Cath. Charities of Archdiocese of Phila., 1984—, sec., exec. com., 1988—; bd. dirs. Village of Divine Providence, Phila., 1982—, sec., 1983-85; bd. dirs. St. Edmond's Home for Crippled Children, Phila., 1984—, Don Guanella Village of Archdiocese of Phila., 1984—; mem. Women's Com. Wills Eye Hosp., 1973—, mem.-at-large, 1st v.p.; mem. Women's Aux. St. Francis Country House, Darby, Pa., 1976—, treas., 1978-82; exec. com. United Way of Southeastern Pa., 1984—, sec., 1986—; bd. dirs. Chapel of Four Chaplains, 1984—. Decorated Cross Pro Ecclesia et Pontifice, 1982. Republican. Roman Catholic. Avocations: reading; tennis; sailing. Home: 320 Gatcombe Ln Bryn Mawr PA 19010

COONS, ELDO JESS, JR., manufacturing company executive; b. Corsicana, Tex., July 5, 1924; s. Eldo Jess and Ruby (Allison) C.; student engring. U. Calif., 1949-50; m. Beverly K. Robbins, Feb. 6, 1985; children by previous marriage—Roberta Ann, Valerie, Cheryl. Owner C & C Constrn. Co., Pomona, Calif., 1946-48; sgt. traffic div. Pomona Police Dept., 1948-54; nat. field dir. Nat. Hot Rod Assn., Los Angeles, 1954-57; pres. Coons Custom Mfg., Inc., Oswego, Kans., 1957-68; chmn. bd. Borg-Warner Corp., 1968-71; pres. Coons Mfg., Inc., Oswego, 1971-84; pres. E.B.C Mgmt. Cons., Grove, Okla., 1984—. Mem. Kans. Gov.'s Adv. Com. for State Architects Assn. Served with C.E., AUS, 1943-46. Named to Exec. and Profl. Hall Fame, Recreational Vehicle/Mobile Homes Hall of Fame; recipient Paul Abel award Recreation Vehicle Industry Assn., 1978, 1st Ann. New Product award Kans. Gov.'s Office and Kans. Engring. Soc. 1982-83. Mem. Oswego C. of C. (dir.), Nat. Juvenile Officers Assn., Municipal Motor Officers Assn., Am. Legion, AIM (fellow pres.'s council), Young Pres.'s Orgn. Mason (K.T., Shriner), Rotarian (pres. Oswego 1962-63). Originator 1st city sponsored police supervised dragstrip. Home and Office: Rt 4 Box 246 Grove OK 74344

COONTZ, ERIC JOHN, periodontist; b. Worcester, Mass., Mar. 22, 1949; s. Gustaf and Clare Elliot (McSheehy) C.. BA in Biology cum laude, Assumption Coll., Worcester, 1971; DDS, Loyola U., Maywood, Ill., 1976, MS in Oral Biology, 1981, Cert. in Periodontics, 1981. Practice dentistry specializing in periodontics Kankakee, Ill., 1982—; mem. staff Foster G. McGaw Hosp., Maywood, Riverside Med. Ctr., Kankakee, Ill., St. Mary's Hosp., Kankakee; from asst. prof. periodontics to clin. assoc. prof. periodontics Loyola U. Med. Ctr., Maywood, 1981—; primary researcher Interplak. Served to capt. U.S. Army, 1976-79. St. Louis U. anatomy fellow, 1971. Mem. ADA, Chgo. Dental Soc., Kankakee Dist. Dental Soc., Acad. Gen. Dentistry, Am. Acad. Periodontology, Am. Assn. Hosp. Dentists, Pierre Fauchard Acad., Midwest Soc. Periodontists, Ill. Soc. Periodontology, Am. Acad. Implant Dentistry, Delta Sigma Delta (Chgo. grad. chpt. officer). Republican. Roman Catholic. Home: 375 Yale Ct Bourbonnais IL 60914 Office: 555 W Court St Kankakee IL 60901

COOPER, CHARLES JASPER, lawyer, educator; b. Tampa, Fla., Mar. 20, 1929; s. Harry Alva and Ruth (Smith) C.; m. Sally Ann Hill, Sept. 8, 1951; children—Carol, Douglas, Charles, Elizabeth, Kate. A.B., Brown U., 1951; J.D., Harvard U., 1954; Ph.D., Bryn Mawr Coll., 1967. Bar: Pa. 1955, Va. 1985. Assoc. counsel Montgomery, McCracken, Walker & Rhoads, Phila., 1954-55; assoc. counsel Bellwoar, Rich & Mankas, Phila., 1956-60; lectr. polit. sci. Bryn Mawr Coll., Pa., 1961-63; lectr. polit. sci. U. Pa., Phila., 1964-67, asst. prof., 1967-68, vis. lectr., 1968-69; assoc. gen. counsel ARA Services, Inc., Phila., 1968-71; v.p., sec.-treas., dir. InterAx, Inc., Phila., 1971-72; sole practice Bryn Mawr, Pa., 1972-83; legal counsel for devel. Randolph-Macon Coll., Ashland, Va., 1984-87. Trustee, treas. Friends Cen. Sch., 1970-74, Ardmore Ave. Community Ctr., Soul Shack, 1975-81; chmn. Harold and Ida Hill Charitable Fund, 1969—; bd. mgrs., treas. Friends Pub. Corp., 1972-79; bd. dirs. Phoenix House, 1973-79, 80-83, Phila. Child Guidance Clinic, 1981-83, Va. League Planned Parenthood, 1988—; bd. dirs., treas. Family Support Ctr., 1976-79; treas. Friends Sch., Haverford, Pa., 1979-83; trustee Bryn Mawr Coll., 1978—; treas. Montgomery County Dem. Com., 1979-81; mem. agy evaluation com. United Way Greater Richmond, 1984—; bd. govs. William Byrd Community House, 1987—, Va. League of Planned Parenthood Inc. Mem. ABA, Pa. Bar Assn., Phila. Bar Assn., Va. Bar Assn., Am. Polit. Sci. Assn., Am. Acad. Polit. and Social Sci., Ams. for Dem. Action (bd. dirs. Southeast Pa. 1955-83, nat. bd. 1967-88), Phi Beta Kappa. Home: 1516 Park Ave Richmond VA 23220

COOPER, C(LYDE) JAMES, JR., lawyer; b. Denver, Mar. 5, 1931; s. Clyde James and Mary (Champie) C.; m. Rose Marie, Dec. 21, 1951 (div.); children—Jill A., Julie L., James P.; m. E. Michelle Fourroux, Aug. 24, 1984. Student Colo. Coll., 1948-50; B.A., U. Denver, 1952, LL.B., 1955. Bar: Colo. 1955. Assoc. Calkins, Rodden and Kramer, 1955-58, ptnr., 1958-60; gen. counsel corp. sec. Consol. Oil & Gas, Inc., 1960-64; ptnr. Rodden, Cooper, Woods & Mitchell, Denver, 1964-72; sole practice, Denver, 1972-82; pres. C. James Cooper, Jr., P.C. 1982—. Author articles. Recipient outstanding scholastic award Nat. Law Week, 1955. Mem. Am. Immigration Lawyers Assn. (chmn. Colo. chpt. 1980-81), Internat. Bar Assn., Colo. Bar Assn., Denver Bar Assn., Internat. Common Law Exchange Soc., Phi Delta Phi, Phi Gamma Delta. Republican. Episcopalian. Clubs: Masons, Shriners. Bds. editors, Transnational Immigration Law Reporter, Common Law Lawyer. Home: 461 Gilpin St Denver CO 80218 Office: 999 18th St Suite 3220 Denver CO 80202

COOPER, DORIS JEAN, market research executive; b. N.Y.C., Dec. 17, 1934; d. James N. and Georgina N. (Cassidy) Breslin; student Sch. of Commerce, N.Y. U., 1953-55, Hunter Coll., 1956-57; m. S. James Cooper, June 17, 1956; 1 son, David Austin. Asst. coding supr. Crossley S-D Surveys, N.Y.C., 1955-57; asst. field supr. Trendex, Inc., N.Y.C., 1957-59; coding dir. J. Walter Thompson Co., N.Y.C., 1960-63, Audits & Surveys, N.Y.C., 1964-65; pvt. practice cons., N.Y.C., 1965-73; pres. Cooper Services, Hastings-on-Hudson, N.Y., 1973—; cons. market research prodn. problems. Mem. Am.

Mktg. Assn. (N.Y. chpt.), Nat. Bus. Women Owners Assn., Am. Assn. Opinion Research (N.Y. chpt.), Hastings C. of C. Republican. Episcopalian. Office: Cooper Services 419 Warburton Ave Hastings on Hudson NY 10706

COOPER, EDWARD SAWYER, internal medicine educator, consultant; b. Columbia, S.C., Dec. 11, 1926; s. Henry Howard and Ada Crosland (Sawyer) C.; m. Jean Marie Wilder, Dec. 2, 1951; children—Lisa Marie Cooper Hudgins, Edward Sawyer, Jan Ada, Charles Wilder. A.B., Lincoln U., Pa., 1946; M.D., Meharry Med. Coll., Nashville, 1949; M.S., U. Pa., 1972. Diplomate Nat. Bd. Med. Examiners, Am. Bd. Internal Medicine. Intern Phila. Gen. Hosp., 1949-51, resident in medicine, 1951-54, NIH fellow in cardiology, 1956-57, pres. med. staff, 1969-71, co-dir. Stroke Research Ctr., 1968-74, chief med. service, 1973-76; prof. medicine U. Pa., Phila., 1973—; dir. Blue Cross of Greater Phila.; mem. adv. bd. Hypertension Detection and Followup Program, Phila., 1974—. Trustee Am. Found. Negro Affairs, 1969—. Served to capt. USAF, 1954-56. Fellow ACP (govs. adv. bd.), Phila. Coll. Physicians (council), Am. Coll. Chest Physicians; mem. Am. Heart Assn. (chmn., dir.), Alpha Omega Alpha. Democrat. Methodist. Research on stroke and hypertension. Home: 6710 Lincoln Dr Philadelphia PA 19119 Office: University of Pa Hosp 3400 Spruce St Philadelphia PA 19104

COOPER, HOWARD JONATHAN, psychotherapist, rabbi, lecturer; b. Manchester, Eng., Jan. 29, 1953; m. Sara Schraer, Oct. 5, 1975; 1 child, Raphael. BA in Religious Studies, U. Sussex, Eng., 1974; Rabbinical diploma, Leo Baeck Coll., London, 1980. Ordained rabbi, 1980. Dir. edn. Finchley Reform Synagogue, London, 1982-86; pvt. practice psychotherapy London, 1984—; lectr. Leo Baeck Coll., 1984—. Contbr. articles on psychol. understanding of Judaism and Bibl. texts to profl. jours. Fellow Leo Baeck Coll.; mem. Assn. for Group and Individual Psychotherapy (cert.). Home and Office: 37 Lansdowne Rd, London N3 1ET, England

COOPER, IVAN LEVESON, publisher, retired architect; b. Stoke-on-Trent, Staffordshire, Eng., July 25, 1925; s. John and Annie Eliza (Walker) C.; m. Peggy Reneta Murray Hinett, July 25, 1949; children: Susan Louise, Ella Rosamund, Margaret Olivia Lagina. Student, Christ Ch., Oxford, Eng., 1943, Liverpool U., Eng., 1947-52. Registered architect, N.J., Pa. Architect Keele (Eng.) U., 1962-67; sr. assoc. Kramer, Hirsch & Carchidi, AIA, Trenton, N.J., 1967-76; prin. Ivan L. Cooper, AIA, Morrisville, Pa., 1976-86; pres., chief exec. officer PC Research Services, Traverse City, Mich., 1986—; mem. archtl. adv. commn. Mercer County Coll., Trenton, 1973-86. Served as navigator RAF, 1944-47. Mem. Ch. of England.

COOPER, JOHN ALLEN DICKS, medical educator; b. El Paso, Tex., Dec. 22, 1918; s. John Allen Dicks and Cora (Walker) C.; m. Mary Jane Stratton, June 17, 1944; children—Margaret Ann, John Allen Dicks, Patricia Alison, Randolph Arend Stratton. B.S. in Chemistry, N.Mex.State U., 1939, LL.D. (hon.), 1971; Ph.D. in Biochemistry, Northwestern U., 1943, M.D., 1951, D.Sc. (hon.), 1972; D.Honoris Causa, U. Brasil, 1958; D.Sc. (hon.), Duke U., 1973, Med. Coll. Ohio, Toledo, 1974, Med. Coll. Wis., 1978, N.Y. Med. Coll., 1981, Wake Forest U., 1985, Georgetown U., 1986; D.Med. Sci (hon.), Med. Coll. Pa., 1973; DHL (hon.), Thomas Jefferson U., 1984. Intern Passavant Meml. Hosp., Chgo., 1951; mem. attending staff Passavant Meml. Hosp., 1955-69; mem. faculty Northwestern U., 1943-69, prof. biochemistry, 1957-69; asso. dean Northwestern U. (Med. Sch.), 1959-63, dean scis., 1963-69; mem. faculty Northwestern U. (Grad. Sch.), 1955-69, Georgetown U., 1970—; prof. practice of health policy Duke U., 1973-78; faculty Baylor Coll. Medicine, Houston, 1987—; disting. physician VA, 1988—; vis. prof. U. Brasil, 1956, U. Buenos Aires, 1958, Harvard Med. Sch., 1985; mem. policy adv. bd. Argonne Nat. Lab., 1957-63, mem. review com. divs. biol. and med. research and radiol. physics, 1958-63, chmn. review com., 1958-62; mem. com. on licensure AEC, 1956-69, cons. div. edn. and tng., 1963; mem. adv. council on health research facilities NIH, 1965-69; organizing com. Pan Am. Fedn. of Assn. Med. Colls., 1962-64, treas., 1963-76; adv. com. personnel for research Am. Cancer Soc., 1962-66; cons. commr. food and drugs FDA, 1965-70; spl. cons. to dir. NIH, 1968-70; cons. to div. physician and health professions edn. Bur. Health Manpower Edn. NIH, 1970-73; mem. adv. com. instnl. relations NSF, 1967-71; cons. edn. and tng. surgeon gen. U.S. Navy, 1972-73; mem. Inst. Medicine, Nat. Acad. Scis., 1972—; chmn. Fedn. Assns. Schs. Health Professions, 1972; mem. spl. med. adv. group VA, 1981—; Mem. alumni council Northwestern U.; Mem. bd. higher edn., Ill., 1964-69; chmn. Gov.'s Sci. Adv. Council, State Ill., 1967-69; mem. council Asso. Midwest Univs., 1963-68, v.p., bd. dirs., 1964-65, pres., bd. dirs., 1965-66; v.p., bd. trustees Argonne Univs. Assn., 1965-68; bd. dirs. Nat. Fund Med. Edn., 1970-79. Editor: Jour. Med. Edn, 1962-71. Trustee Georgetown U., 1986—. Served to 1st lt., San. Corps AUS, 1945-47. Recipient Outstanding Alumnus award N.Mex. State U., 1960; Alumni medal Northwestern U., 1976; Abraham Flexner award Assn. Am. Med. Colls., 1985; John and Mary R. Markle scholar in acad. medicine, 1951-56. Mem. Am. Soc. Biol. Chemists, Assn. Am. Med. Colls. (del. numerous confs., mem. various coms., pres. 1969-86, pres. emeritus 1986—), AMA, AAAS, Inst. Med. Nat. Acad. Scis., Am. Hosp. Assn. (hon.), Asociación Venezolana Para el Avance de la Ciencia (hon.), Sigma Xi, Alpha Omega Alpha. Club: Tavern (Chgo.). Home: 4118 N River St Arlington VA 22207 Office: No 1 DuPont Circle NW Washington DC 20036

COOPER, KENNETH CARLTON, training consultant; b. St. Louis, May 2, 1948; s. George Carlton and Mary Frances (Kavanaugh) C.; BS, U. Mo. Columbia, 1970, MS in Indsl. Engring., 1971; PhD in Adminstrn. and Mgmt., Columbia Pacific U., 1985; m. Susan Ann Bujnak, Sept. 6, 1969; children—Jeffrey Carlton, Daniel Stephen, Mara Elizabeth. Mktg. rep. IBM, St. Louis, 1971-76; account exec. Downtowner Newspaper, St. Louis, 1976; pres. Ken Cooper Communications, Chesterfield, Mo., 1976—; bd. dirs. Juvenile Shoe Corp.; adj. faculty St. Louis U., 1972-73, Columbia Coll., 1976-79, Webster Coll., 1977-79; speaker in field. Roy P. Hart Scholar-Athlete grantee, 1970-71; registered profl. engr., Mo.; cert. adminstrv. mgr.; cert. speaking profl. Mem. ASTD. Republican. Methodist. Author: Nonverbal Communication For Business Success, 1979, Spanish edit., 1982; (with Lance Humble) The World's Greatest Blackjack Book, 1980; Body Business, 1981; Kroppsspråket, 1981; Always Bear Left, 1982; Stop It Now, 1985. Home: 16457 Wilson Farms Chesterfield MO 63017 Office: 744 J Spirit of St Louis Blvd Chesterfield MO 63005

COOPER, KENNETH REGINALD, chief executive of the British Library; b. London, June 28, 1931; s. Reginald Frederick and Louisa May (Turner) C.; m. Olga Ruth Harvey; children: Sharon Julia, Richard Charles, Nicholas Kenneth, Caroline Jemina. MA, New Coll., Oxford, Eng., 1954. Asst. prin. Ministry of Labor, Eng., 1954-60; prin. Her Majesty Treasury, Eng., 1961-65; asst. sec. Dept. of Employment, 1966-70; chief exec. Employment Service Agy., 1971-75, Tng. Services Agy., 1975-79; dir. gen. Bldg. Employers Confedn., 1979-84; chief exec. The British Library, 1984—; vis. prof. U. Strathclyde, 1987—; bd. dirs. Confedn. Info. Communication Industries, London. Contbr. articles to profl. jours. Mem. Council Confedn. of British Industry, 1979-83; Library and Info. Services Council for Eng., London, 1984—. Fellow Inst. Personnel Mgmt., Inst. Tng. and Devel. (past pres.), Inst. Info. Scientists (pres. elect 1987—). Mem. Ch. of Eng. Office: The British Library, 2 Sheraton St, London W1V 4BH, England

COOPER, L. E., JR., merchant banking executive; b. Roanoke, Ala.; s. L.E. and Evelyn C.; BS, U. Ala., 1965, LLB, 1967; MBA, Harvard U., 1973; m. Mary Patricia A. Wood, Aug. 20, 1977; children—William E. Whitmel, Patricia E. Fitzsimons, Henry Elgin B. Bar: Ala. 1967. With Blyth Eastman Dillon & Co., Inc., N.Y.C., 1973-80, v.p., 1976, 1st v.p., 1977-79, sr. v.p., 1980; mng. dir., v.p. Dean Witter Reynolds, Inc., N.Y.C., 1980-83; mng. dir. Elmsmere Co., 1983—, Delapré Co., 1986—, E. Co. Leasing, 1985—. Trustee Copper Trust, Pa. Trust, Cooper Edn. Trust, Cooper Med. Trust; Served as capt. JAGC, USAF, 1968-71. Mem. Jasons, Omicron Delta Kappa, Kappa Alpha. Home: 210 Sasco Hill Rd Southport CT 06430 Office: 109 E 73d St 4A New York NY 10021 Other: Box 874 Southport CT 06490

COOPER, LEON N., physicist, educator; b. N.Y.C., Feb. 28, 1930; s. Irving and Anna (Zola) C.; m. Kay Anne Allard, May 18, 1969; children: Kathleen Ann, Coralie Lauren. A.B., Columbia U., 1951, A.M., 1953, Ph.D., 1954, D.Sc., 1973; D.Sc. hon. degrees; D.Sc., U. Sussex, Eng., 1973, U. Ill., 1974, Brown U., 1974, Gustavus Adolphus Coll., 1975, Ohio State U., 1976, U. Pierre et Marie Curie, Paris, 1977. NSF postdoctoral fellow, mem. Inst. for Advanced Study, 1954-55; research assoc. U. Ill., 1955-57; asst. prof. Ohio State U., 1957-58; assoc. prof. Brown U., Providence, 1958-62, prof., 1962-66, Henry Ledyard Goddard U. prof., 1966-74, Thomas J. Watson Sr. prof. sci., 1974—; co-dir. Center for Neural Sci.; lectr. pub. lectures, internat. conf. and symposia; vis. prof. various univs. and summer schs.; cons. indsl., ednl. orgns.; sponsor Fedn. Am. Scientists; mem. counseil superieur de la recherche U. Rene Descartes. Author: Introduction to The Meaning and Structure of Phsyics, 1968; Contbr. articles to profl. jours. Alfred P. Sloan Found. research fellow, 1959-66; John Simon Guggenheim Meml. Found. fellow, 1965-66; recipient Nobel prize (with J. Bardeen and J.R. Schrieffer), 1972; award of Excellence, Grad. Facilities Alumni of Columbia, U., 1974; Descartes medal Acad. de Paris, U. Rene Descartes, 1977; John Jay award Columbia Coll., 1985. Fellow Am. Phys. Soc., Am. Acad. Arts and Scis.; mem. Am. Philos. Soc., Nat. Acad. Scis. (Comstock prize with J.R. Schrieffer 1968), Soc. Neurosci, AAAS, Phi Beta Kappa, Sigma Xi. Office: Brown Univ Dept of Physics Providence RI 02912

COOPER, RICHARD ALAN, lawyer; b. Hattisburg, Miss., July 19, 1953; s. H. Douglas and Elaine (Reece) C.; m. Margaret Jeanne Luth, May 9, 1981. BA, BS, U. Ark.-Little Rock, 1976; JD, Washington U., St. Louis, 1979. Bar: Mo. 1979, Ill. 1980, U.S. Dist. Ct. (ea. dist.) Mo. 1980. Law clk. U.S. Dist. Ct., St. Louis, 1979-80; assoc. William R. Gartenberg, St. Louis, 1980-81, Danis, Reid, Murphy, Tobben & Cooper, St. Louis, 1983-87, ptnr. 1987-88, law office Terry Sharp, P.C., 1988— ; liaison to Washington U. Sch. Law, Mo. Assn. Trial Attys., St. Louis, 1983-85 . Bus. mgr. Urban Law Jour., 1978-79; editor Bankruptcy Law Reporter, 1983—, co-mgr., editor, 1984—. Recipient Milton F. Napier trial award Lawyers Assn. of St. Louis, 1979. Mem. ABA, Mo. Bar Assn., Am. Assn. Trial Attys., Nat. Orgn. Social Security Claimants Reps., Ill. State Bar Assn. Clubs: Clayton, Media (St. Louis). Avocation: basketball. Home: 982 Sonerfor Pl Saint Louis MO 63141 Office: Law Office Terry Sharp PC 1114 Harrison PO Box 906 Mount Vernon IL 62864

COOPER, RICHARD I., judge; b. Reed City, Mich., Dec. 28, 1940; s. Dic I. and Bette Kay (Zimmerman) C.; m. Carol Susan Schneider, Sept. 2, 1978; 1 child, Craig R. BA, Central Mich. U., 1963; MA, Ind. U., 1970; JD, Detroit Coll. Law, 1973. Bar: Mich. 1973. Lang. instr. Brit. Sch. Milan, Italy, 1963-64; tchr. high sch., Greenville, Mich., 1967-68; intern Internat. Affairs, NASA, Washington, summer 1969; city pros. atty. Reed City, 1973-76; probate judge Lake County, Baldwin, Mich., 1977-78; cir. judge 51st Cir., Ludington and Baldwin, Mich., 1979—; vis. judge Mich. Ct. Appeals; instr. bus. law Ferris State Coll., Big Rapids, Mich., 1974-75. Bd. dirs. Mental Health Clinic, Baldwin, 1975-77. Recipient Gideons Ann. Bible award 1983; Rotary fellow U. Vienna, Austria, 1965-66. Mem. Mich. Bar Assn., Mason/Lake Bar Assn., Mich. Judges Assn. Congregationalist. Home: PO Box 416 Ludington MI 49431

COOPER, ROGER MERLIN, government executive, educator; b. Scottsbluff, Nebr., Feb. 25, 1943; s. Dean P. and Bette Jane (Ward) C.; m. Erica Feuer; children: Gregory Joseph, Lisa Jane. BS, grad. Fed. Execs. Inst., 1950 U. Utah, 1964; MSA, George Washington U., 1970; MBA, U. So. Calif.; grad., Harvard U., 1984. Lic. ship capt. U.S. Coast Guard. Mgr. systems programming Larwin Group, Beverly Hills, Calif., 1973-74; chief teleprocessing sect. U.S. CSC, Washington, 1974-76, chief, info. tech. div., 1976-77, dir. Office Automated Systems Devel., Macon, Ga., 1977-78; asst. dir. U.S. Office Personnel Mgmt., Washington, 1979-82; dir. med. info. resources mgmt. office VA, Washington, 1982-85; dep. asst. sec. for info. systems Treasury Dept., Washington, 1985—; adj. prof. Am. U.; instr. U. D.C.; prin. Nat. Telecommunications Info. Systems Security Council, Council of Prins., Nat. Communications Systems. Officer Harvard Kennedy Sch. D.C. Alumni Council. Served to lt. USN, 1964-69, comdr. USNR. Recipient Ofcl. Commendation, U.S. Civil Service Commn., 1976, Spl. Achievement award VA, 1983; Dept. Deteme Joint Service Achievement medal, 1988. Mem. Am. Soc. Pub. Adminstrn., Data Processing Mgmt. Assn., Communications Data Panel, Interagy. Communication Mgt Council, FTS 2000 (adv. bd.). Home: 2002 Windmill Ln Alexandria VA 22307 Office: Dept of Treasury 15th and Pennsylvania Ave NW Washington DC 20220

COOPER, WILLIAM CLARK, physician; b. Manila, P.I., June 22, 1912 (father Am. citizen); s. Wibb Earl and Pearl (Herron) C.; M.D., U. Va., 1934; M.P.H. magna cum laude, Harvard U., 1958; m. Ethel Katherine Sicha, May 1, 1937; children—Jane Willoughby, William Clark, David Jeremy, Robert Lawrence. Intern, asst. resident U. Hosps., Cleve., 1934-37; commd. asst. surgeon USPHS, 1940, advanced through grades to med. dir., 1952; chief occupational health Field Hqrs., Cin., 1952-57; mem. staff div. occupational health USPHS, Washington, 1957-62, chief div. occupational health, 1962-63; ret., 1963; research physician, prof. occupational health in residence Sch. Pub. Health, U. Calif.-Berkeley, 1963-72; med. cons. AEC, 1964-73; sec.-treas. Tabershaw-Cooper Asso., Inc., 1972-73, v.p., sci. dir., 1973-74; v.p. Equitable Environ. Health Inc., 1974-77; cons. occupational medicine, 1977—. Served to 1st lt. M.C., U.S. Army, 1937-40. Diplomate Am. Bd. Internal Medicine, Am. Bd. Preventive Medicine, Am. Bd. Indsl. Hygiene. Fellow AAAS, Am. Pub. Health Assn., Am. Coll. Chest Physicians, Am. Occupational Medicine Assn., Am. Acad. Occupational Medicine, Royal Soc. Medicine (London); mem. Internat. Commn. on Occupational Health, Western Occupational Med. Assn., Am. Indsl. Hygiene Assn. Club: Cosmos (Washington). Contbr. articles to profl. jours. Home: 8315 Terrace Dr El Cerrito CA 94530 Office: 3687 Mt Diablo Blvd Suite 320 Lafayette CA 94549

COOPER, WILLIAM EDWARD, investment firm executive; b. Wichita, Kans., Oct. 16, 1921; s. Richard Percy and Natalie (Noel) C.; m. Suzanne Blessington, June 2, 1947; children: William Patrick, Madelyn Cooper Abercrombie, Catherine Cooper Wilson, Thomas Edward. BBA, Wichita State Coll., 1939-48. Regional mgr. Western Lithograph Co., Wichita, 1946-58; chmn., chief exec. officer Dallas Market Ctr. Co., 1958-1983; owner W.E. Cooper Investments, 1983—; bd. dirs. BMCFund, Inc., Dallas Market Ctr. Co., First City Bank Dallas, others. Bd. dirs. Dallas County Hosp. Dist. Bd., Theater Operating Co., Cen. Dallas Assn., Dallas Citizens Council, Aerospace Heritage Found., Better Bus. Bur. Met. Dallas, Greater Dallas Crime Commn., Inst. Aerobics Research, Dallas Council on World Affairs, Com. for a Qualified Judiciary, Dallas Ft Worth Internat. Airport Bd., Jesuit Coll. Prep. Sch. Found., Communities Found. Tex., Friends of Dallas Fire Dept.; co-chair bldg. com. Zale-Lipshy Univ. Hosp. Served to capt. USAF, 1942-46, PTO. Recipient Outstanding Citizen award S.W. Roadrunners, 1968, Shining Hours Pub. Relations Soc. of Am., 1973, Outstanding Alumni, Wichita State U., 1976, Brotherhood Citation Natl. Conf. of Christians and Jews, 1980, World Trade award Dallas Mkt. Ctr., 1981, Southwesterner of Yr. Southwestern Furniture Mfrs. Assn., 1982, Outstanding Leadership Award Natl. Home Fashion League, 1983, L. Storey Stemmons Dallas Urban League, 1984, Hon. Chief Dallas Fire Dept., 1985, Neil Mallon for Disting. Service Dallas Council on World Affairs, 1985; named Hon. Chief, Dallas Fire Dept., 1985. Mem. 315th Bomb Wing, Dallas C. of C. (vice chmn. exec. com., chmn. state govtl. affairs com.). Republican. Roman Catholic. Lodge: Rotary. Home: 5418 Preston Haven Dr Dallas TX 75229

COOPER, WILLIAM THOMAS, retired air force officer, writer, educator; b. Itta Bena, Miss., Feb. 3, 1938; s. Singleton Moore and Vera Ernestine (Bussell) C.; m. Janet Faye Johnston, Mar. 8, 1960 (div. 1984); children—William Thomas Jr., Teryl Catherine, Jonathan Gregory; m. Joan Ellen Schulhafer, Aug. 17, 1985. B.A., La. Tech. U., 1962; M.A. in Polit. Sci., U. Louisville, 1970. Commd. 2d lt., 1962, advanced through grades to colonel, 1983; chief internal info. Hdqrs. SAC, Offutt AFB, Nebraska, 1973-75, chief publ affairs 3902nd Air Base Wing, 1975-78; dir. pub. affairs Hdqrs. Eighth Air Force, Barksdale AFB, La., 1978-81; special asst. for B-1 Bomber Pub. Affairs U.S. Air Force, Pentagon, Washington, 1981-83, chief, media relations, 1983-84, dir. internal info., 1984-86. Author: Triad of Knives, 1984; Warmoon, 1985. Decorated Legion of Merit, Meritorious Service medal with 1 oak leaf cluster, Commendation medal with 1 oak leaf cluster. Baptist. Avocations: art; photography.

COOPERSMITH, BERNARD IRA, gynecologist, obstetrician; b. Chgo., Oct. 19, 1914; s. Morris and Anna (Shulder) C.; m. Beatrice Klass, May 26, 1940; children: Carol, Cathie. BS cum laude, U. Ill., 1936, MD cum laude, 1938. Diplomate Am. Bd. Ob-Gyn. Intern Michael Reese Hosp., Chgo., 1938-39, resident in ob-gyn, 1939-42; practice medicine specializing in ob-gyn Chgo., 1942—; mem. staff Prentice Women's Hosp. of Northwestern Meml. Hosp., Michael Reese Hosp., Mt. Sinai Hosp., Chgo. Maternity Ctr.; asst. prof. ob-gyn Northwestern U. Med. Sch., Chgo., 1948—. Contbr. articles to profl jours. Pres. Barren Found. Chgo., 1971-73. Fellow ACS; mem. AMA, Ill. Med. Soc., Chgo. Med. Soc., Chgo. Gynecol. Soc., Cen. Assn. Ob-Gyn, Am. Coll. Ob-Gyn, Alpha Omega Alpha. Jewish. Clubs: Bryn Mawr Country, Carleton. Home: 1110 N Lake Shore Dr Chicago IL 60611 Office: 333 E Superior St Suite 444 Chicago IL 60611

COORAY, THOMAS CARDINAL, clergyman; b. Negombo, Sri Lanka, Dec. 28, 1901; s. Jayalath Aratchige Jacob and Marguerita (Silva) C.; B.A., U. London, 1924; Degree in Philosophy, St. Bernard's Sem., Colombo, 1925-26; Ph.D., Acad. St. Thomas, Rome, 1928; Ph.D. in Div., Angelicum U., Rome, 1931. Ordained priest Roman Catholic Ch., 1929, archbishop, 1946, cardinal, 1965. Prof. botany St. Joseph's Coll., Colombo, Sri Lanka, 1931-37; warden Roman Cath. Hostel for Undergrads., Colombo, 1932-37; supr. Oblate Sem., Colombo, 1937-46; co-adjutor Archbishop of Colombo, 1946-47; archbishop of Colombo, 1947-76, archbishop emeritus, 1976—; pres. Roman Cath. Bishops Conf. Sri Lanka, 1947-76; planned Nat. Basilica/Sanctuary Our Lady of Lanka, 1948-75; established Aquinas U. Coll. Higher Edn., 1954, Nat. Seminary Ecclesiastical Studies in Sri Lanka, 1955, Cath. Radio Ctr., 1970; mem. ante prep. council Vatican Council, 1959-62, participant, 1962-65; mem. Sacred Congregations of Propaganda Fide and Oriental Chs., 1965-70; mem. Pontifical Commn. for Revision of Canon Law, 1968-83; founder, mem. Fedn. Asian Bishops Confs., 1970-76. Writer pamphlets on sanctity and family planning. Named Asst. at the Pontifical Throne, Holy Father Pope Pius XII, Rome, 1954. Address: Emmaus Cardinal's Residence, Tewatta Ragama Sri Lanka also: Vatican City Vatican

COOTER, DALE A., lawyer; b. Syracuse, N.Y., Aug. 28, 1948; s. Charles Henry and Mavis Elizabeth (Wagner) C.; m. Mary Kathryn Nolan, Oct. 8, 1977; children: John Andrew, Jessica Averie. BA cum laude, SUNY, Fredonia, 1970; JD, Georgetown U., 1975. Bar: Md. 1975, D.C. 1976, Va. 1984, U.S. Dist. Ct. Md. 1976, U.S. Dist. Ct. D.C. 1976, U.S. Ct. Appeals (4th and D.C. cirs.) 1976, U.S. Supreme Ct. 1979. Ptnr. Cooter & Gell, Washington, 1976—; adj. prof. law Georgetown U., Washington, 1985—. Editor Georgetown U. Law Jour., 1973-75. Served with N.G. Mem. ABA, Va. Bar Assn., Md. Bar Assn., D.C. Bar Assn. Home: 4675 Kenmore Dr NW Washington DC 20007 Office: Cooter & Gell 1333 H Street NW Washington DC 20005

COPE, ALFRED HAINES, political scientist, educator; b. Oakbourne, Pa., May 29, 1912; s. Joseph and Ellen (Fussell) C.; m. Ruth Balderston, Aug. 23, 1937; 1 child, Joan. AB, Earlham Coll., 1934; PhD, U. Pa., 1948. Agt. Equitable Life Ins. Co., 1934-36; dir. Am. Friends Service Co., Chgo., 1936-38, War Relief Adminstrn., Spain, 1938-39; adminstrv. asst. U. Pa. Inst. Local and State Govt., 1940-42, instr., 1946-48; sr. adminstrv. aid. U.S. CSC, Phila., 1942-43; asst. prof. Syracuse (N.Y.) U., 1948-51, assoc. prof., 1951-56; asst. dean Coll. Liberal Arts, 1960-70, prof. citizenship, 1965-75, prof. polit. sci., 1962-75, prof. emeritus, 1975—, registrar, mgr. student data systems, 1970-74; asst. dean, prof. citizenship Utica Coll., 1956-60. Author: Administration of Civil Service in Cities of the Third Class in Pennsylvania, 1948; (with Fred Krinsky) Franklin Roosevelt and the Supreme Court, 1952, rev. edit., 1969; Current Defense of the U.S., 1954; (with E.E. Palmer) The Dixon Yates Contract and the National Power Policy, 1955; The Basis for a New Legal System, 1973; Managing World Resources, 1975. Pres. bd. dirs. Child and Family Services, 1963-66; arbitrator Syracuse Better Bus. Bur.; trustee Oakwood Sch., Poughkeepsie, N.Y., 1974—, treas., 1977-84, chmn. fin. com., 1984—, pres. bd. mgrs., 1987—; chmn. fin. com. Friends World Com., 1976-81, mem. world fin. group, 1975-81, del. triennial meeting Gwatt, Switzerland, 1980; Friends Assn. for Higher Edn.; co-clerk Task Force on Peace Studies, 1985-88; mem. cen. com. Friends Gen. Conf., 1978-84; chmn. devel. com., mem. exec. personnel and advancement coms.; mem. gen. services com. N.Y. Yearly Meeting, Religious Soc. Friends, 1978-81, chmn. com. sharing of world resources, 1981-85; mem. gen. bd. Pendle Hill, Wallingford, Pa., 1982—; treas., trustee Syracuse Friends Meeting; trustee Lindley Murray Fund, 1984—. Served to capt. AUS, 1943-46. Fellow AAAS; mem. Am. Acad. Polit and Soc. Sci., Friends Assn. Higher Edn. (assoc.), Acad. Polit. Sci., Am. Judicature Soc., Friends Hist. Soc., Geneol. Soc. Pa., Chester County Hist. Soc. (life), Pi Gamma Mu, Phi Delta Kappa. Club: Torch (Syracuse) (pres. 1969-70). Home: 201 Houston Ave Syracuse NY 13224

COPELAND, EDWARD JEROME, lawyer; b. Chgo., Oct. 29, 1933; s. Harvey and Lilyan (Rubin) C.; m. Ruth Caminer, Sept. 2, 1962; children—Ellyn, Bradley. B.A., Carleton Coll., 1955; J.D., Northwestern U., 1958. Bar: Ill. 1959, N.Y. 1981. Mem. Ill. Legislature, Springfield, 1967-71; ptnr. Foss, Schuman, Drake & Barnard, Chgo., 1971-86, Wood,Lucksinger & Epstein, Chgo., 1986—; chmn. Bank of the North Shore, Northbrook, Ill., 1976-81. Mem. Ill. Bd. Edn., 1975-83, chmn., 1981-83. Mem. ABA, Ill. Bar Assn., Chgo. Bar Assn. Republican. Jewish. Home: 1431 Sherwood Rd Highland Park IL 60035 Office: Wood Lucksinger & Epstein 333 W Wacker Dr Chicago IL 60606

COPELAND, EUGENE LEROY, lawyer; b. Fairfield, Iowa, Mar. 5, 1939; BA, Parsons Coll., 1961; JD with distinction, U. Iowa, 1965. Admitted to Colo. bar, 1965, Iowa bar, 1965, U.S. Supreme Ct. bar, 1966; individual practice law, Denver, 1965-66; sr. v.p., gen. counsel, sec. Security Life of Denver, 1966—; gen. counsel Nationale Nederlanden U.S. Corp., 1986—; lectr., speaker at legal and industry convs., seminars, meetings; participant contemporary issue program Today show NBC, 1980. Bd. dirs. Buffalo Mountain Met. Dist., Summit County, Colo.; bd. dirs. Friends Found. of Denver Pub. Library; v.p. Denver Pub. Library Commn.; bd. dirs. Colo. Pub. Expedition Council. Served with U.S. Army. Fulbright scholar (alt.). Mem. ABA, Colo. Bar Assn., Denver Bar Assn., Iowa Bar Assn., Assn. Life Ins. Council, Am. Council Life Ins. (state v.p. 1973-83, legis. com., reins. com., policyholder tax com., v.p.), Colo. Life Conv. (v.p. 1987-88, legis. chmn. 1973-86), Colo. Assn. Corp. Counsel, Denver Estate Planning Council, Colo. Assn. Life Underwriters (co-author learning guide 1978), Law Club Denver, Phi Kappa Phi. Unitarian. Author: Preventive Law for Medical Directors and Underwriters, 1973; Underwriting in a New Age of Legal Accountability, 1978; Insurance Law, 1982; bd. editors Iowa Law Rev., 1965. Office: Security Life Ctr 1290 Broadway Denver CO 80203

COPENHAVER, ELMER RANDALL, consultant, real estate investment executive; b. Waco, Tex., Oct. 11, 1931; s. Elmer Randall and Margie Belle (Chadwick) C.; m. Maria DelRosario Chavarria, Nov. 12, 1959 (div. 1976); children: Edward, David, Janice; m. Marina Escalante Borges, Sept. 26, 1987. BA, Tex. A&I Coll., 1952; BS, MBA, UCLA, 1965; PhD, Polyglot Inst., Kuwait, 1982, U. Alta., Edmonton, Can., 1982. Registered chartered property and casualty underwriter. Surety underwriter Fidelity & Casualty Co., N.Y.C, Los Angeles, f1954-58; surety mgr. Continental Casualty Co., Los Angeles, 1958-62; v.p. Nat. Auto & Casualty Ins., Los Angeles, 1962-65; pres. Copenhaver Cons. Ltd., Edmonton, 1979-83, also bd. dirs.; bd. dirs. Copenhaver Cons. S.A., San Jose, Costa Rica; chmn. bd. dirs., chief exec. officer Copenhaver Cons. Inc., Montebello, Calif., 1965—; bd. dirs. Western Tech Labs., Ltd., Edmonton. Mem. Housing Mediation Bd., City of Montebello, 1985—. Served to sgt. USAF, 1952-54. Republican. Methodist. Home: Box 83 1345 Manzanita Way Lake Arrowhead CA 92352 also: 1545 So 7th Ave Hacienda Heights CA 91745 Office: Copenhaver Cons Inc PO Box 1300 Montebello CA 90640

COPES, MARVIN LEE, educational administrator; b. Connersville, Ind., Sept. 19, 1938; s. Kenneth Edward and Frances Gertrude (Bean) C.; B.S., Purdue U., 1961, M.S., 1962, Ph.D., 1975; postgrad. Ind. State U., 1967-68, Ind. U., 1967-68; m. Luretta Ann Grenard, Aug. 26, 1961; children—Bradley Alan, Brian Keith, Brent Lee. Grad. asst. agr. edn. Purdue U., 1961-62, grad. instr., 1968-69; tchr. vocat. agr. Tri-County Sch. Corp., Walcott, Ind., 1964-65; vocat. dir. Met. Sch. Dist. Vernon Twp., Crothersville, Ind., 1965-68, also dir. Ind. Vocat. Agr. Demonstration Center; asst. exec. sec. Kappa Delta Pi Hdqrs., West Lafayette, Ind., 1969-70; dir. Blue River Vocat.-Tech. Center, Shelbyville, Ind. 1970-79; nat. curriculum devel. coordinator ITT Ednl. Services, Indpls., 1979-80, nat. dir. edn., 1980-82, dir. ITT Tech. Inst., Ft. Wayne, Ind., 1982-83, Indpls., 1983-86, Am. Coll., Mobile, Ala., 1986—. Pres., Loper Parent Tchr. Orgn., 1974—; leader 4-H, 1964—; adviser Future Farmers Am., 1964—; cubmaster Cub Scouts Am.,

1976; scoutmaster, commr. Boy Scouts Am.; bd. dirs. Shelbyville Boys Club Am., 1976, Northeast India Christian Mission, 1974; chmn. tech. edn. com. Futuring Project, N.Y. State Dept. Edn.; chmn. Shelby County Youth for Christ; mem. vocat. tng. com. Corp. Sci. and Tech. Served to 1st lt., AUS, 1962-64. Mem. Am., Ind. vocat. assns., Ind., Nat. councils local adminstrs., Nat. Bus. Edn. Assn., Soc. Mfg. Engrs., Robotics Internat., Ind. Assn. Pvt. Career Schs. (bd. dirs.), Future Farmers Am. Alumni Assn., Shelby County C. of C., Pershing Rifles, Gideons Internat., Alpha Tau Alpha, Kappa Delta Pi, Phi Delta Kappa, Delta Pi Epsilon. Mem. So. Baptist Ch. Mason; mem. Order Eastern Star. Author: A Curriculum Guide for Training in Agricultural Supply, 1968, Student Handbook for Cooperative Progress in Agricultural Occupations, 1968, A Predictability of Career Choices of High School Seniors, 1975. Home: 6931 Rose Ching Dr Mobile AL 36618 Office: 424 S Wilson Ave Prichard AL 36610

COPLAND, AARON, composer; b. Bklyn., Nov. 14, 1900; s. Harris Morris and Sarah (Mittenthal) C. Grad., Boys High Sch. Bklyn., 1918; studied music privately; pupil piano, Victor Wittgenstein and Clarence Adler; composition, Rubin Goldmark and Nadia Boulanger; H.H.D., Brandeis U., 1957, Ill. Wesleyan U., 1958; Mus. D., Princeton U., 1956, Oberlin Coll., 1958, Temple U., 1959, U. Hartford, 1959, Harvard U., 1961, Syracuse U., U. R.I., U. Mich., 1964, Kalamazoo Coll., 1965, U. Utah, 1966, Jacksonville U., 1967, Rutgers U., 1967, Fairfield U., 1968, Ohio State U., 1970, N.Y. U., 1970, Columbia U., 1971, York U., Eng., 1971, U. Fla., 1972, L.I. U., 1974, Bklyn. Coll., 1975, U. Portland, Oreg., 1975, Ottawa (Kans.) U., 1976, U. Rochester, N.Y., 1976, U. Leeds, Eng., 1976, Tulane U., New Orleans, 1976. Lectr. music New Sch. for Social Research, N.Y.C., 1927-37, Harvard U., spring 1935, 44; instr., then asst. dir. Berkshire Music Center, 1940; Charles Eliot Norton prof. poetry Harvard U., 1951-52; dir. Am. Music Center; treas. Arrow Music Press.; dir. Koussevitsky Music Found.; v.p. Edward MacDowell Assn., Walter W. Naumberg Found. Founder (with Roger Sessions) Copland-Sessions Concerts, 1928-31, Am. Music Festivals at Yaddo, Saratoga Springs, N.Y., 1932; composer music, 1920—; works include Orchestral Variations, 1957, First Symphony, 1928, Music for the Theatre, 1925, A Dance Symphony, 1925, Concerto for Piano and Orchestra, 1926, Symphonic Ode, 1929, 55, Short Symphony, 1933, Statements, 1935, El Salon Mexico, 1936, Music for Radio, 1937, An Outdoor Overture, 1938, Quiet City, 1940, Lincoln Portrait, 1942; ballet Grohg, 1925, Hear Ye, Hear Ye, 1934, Billy the Kid, 1938, Rodeo, 1942, Appalachian Spring, 1944; opera for high schs. The Second Hurricane, 1937; music for motion pictures The City, 1939, Of Mice and Men, 1939, Our Town, 1940, North Star, 1943, The Red Pony, 1948, The Heiress, 1949, Something Wild, 1961; chamber music Two Pieces for String Quartet, 1928, Vitebsk, 1929, Piano Variations, 1930, Piano Sonata, 1941, Violin Sonata, 1943, Third Symphony, 1946, In the Beginning, mixed chorus, 1947, Clarinet Concerto, 1948, Twelve Poems of Emily Dickinson, 1950, Quartet for Piano and Strings, 1950, Music and Imagination, 1952, The Tender Land, opera, 1954, Piano Fantasy, 1957, Nonet for strings, 1960, Connotations for Orch., 1962, Music for a Great City, 1964, Emblems for Band, 1965, Inscape for orch., 1967, Duo for flute and piano, 1971, Three Latin America Sketches for orch, 1971, Night Thoughts for piano, 1972, Threnody I: Igor Stravinsky, In Memoriam, 1971, Threnody II: Beatrice Cunningham, In Memoriam; author: What to Listen For in Music, 1939, rev. ed., 1957, Our New Music, 1941, 1968, Copeland on Music, 1960; contbr. to: Modern Music. Guggenheim fellow, 1925-26; recipient RCA Victor award ('65,000), 1930, Pulitzer prize for music, 1944, N.Y. Music Critics Circle award for Appalachian Spring, 1945, Acad. Award for film score The Heiress, Acad. Motion Picture Arts and Sci., 1950, gold medal for music Am. Acad. Arts and Letters, 1956, Presdl. medal of Freedom, 1964, Howland Meml. prize Yale U., 1970, Nat. Medal of Arts, 1986; decorated comdr.'s cross Order Merit West Germany; hon. mem. Accademia Santa Cecilia, Rome, Academia Nacional de Bellas Arts, Buenos Aires, Argentina, Royal Philharmonic Soc., London, N.Y. Philharmonic Soc., Internat. Soc. for Contemporary Music, Royal Acad. Music, London. Mem. Am. Acad. Arts and Scis., League Composers (chmn. bd. dirs.), ASCAP, Nat. Inst. Arts and Letters, Am. Acad. Arts and Letters (past pres.), Royal Soc. Arts London, Academie de Beaux Arts of Academie Francaise. Address: care Boosey & Hawkes Inc 24 W 57th St New York NY 10019 *

COPLEY, JOHN (MICHAEL HAROLD), opera director, producer; b. June 12, 1933; s. Ernest Harold and Lilian (Forbes) C. Ed. Sadler's Wells Ballet Sch.; Diploma with honors in Theatre Design, Central Sch. Arts and Crafts, London. Stage mgr. for opera and ballet cos. at Sadler's Wells, in Rosebery Ave., 1953-57; also various musicals, plays, etc. in London's West End; joined Covent Garden Opera Co., London, dep. stage mgr., 1960-63, asst. resident producer, 1963-66, assoc. resident producer, 1966-72, resident producer, 1972-75, prin. resident producer, 1975—; prodns. include: Suor Angelica, 1965; Cosi fan Tutte, 1968, 81; Orpheo ed Euridice, 1969; Le Nozze di Figaro, 1971; Don Giovanni, 1973; La Boheme, 1974; Faust, 1974; L'elisir d'amore, 1975, 81; Benvenuto Cellini, 1976; Ariadne auf Naxos, 1976; Maria Stuarda; Royal Silver Jubilee Gala, 1977; Werther, 1979; La Traviata, Lucrezia Borgia, 1980; Alceste, 1981; Semele, 1982; prodns. at London Coliseum include: Carmen, Il Seraglio, Il Trovatore, La Traviata, Mary Stuart; Rosenkavalier, La Bell Helene, 1975; Werther, 1977; Manon, Aida, Julius Caesar, Les Mamelles de Tiresias, 1979; other prodns. include: Macbeth, Athens Festival; Lucia, Netherlands Opera; Lucia, Opera National de Belge; La Clemenza di Tito and L'Infedelta delusa, Wexford Festival; Lucia, Dallas Civic Opera, Chgo. Lyric Opera, Can. Opera, Toronto, Ont.; Madame Butterfly, Otello, Greek Nat. Opera; Fidelio, Nozze di Figaro, Rigoletto, Magic Flue, Jenufa, Ariadne aux Naxos, Madame Butterfly, Fra Diavolo, Macbeth, La Traviata; Manon Lescaut, Lucia di Lammermoor, Tosca, Adriana LeCouvreur, Peter Grimes, Manon, for Australian Opera; La Traviata, Falstaff, Peter Grimes, Tosca, for WNO; Les Mamelles de Tiresias for English Opera North; Madama Butterfly for Opera North; Lucia, Ballo in Maschera, Dido and Aeneas, for Scottish Opera; Acis and Galatea for English Opera Group in Stockholm, Paris, Aldeburgh Festival; Le Nozze di Figaro and Der Freischutz for N.Y.C. Opera; Midsummer Night's Dream, Eugene Onegin for Ottawa Festival; Carmen for Vancouver Opera; Falstaff, Lucia Di Lammermoor, La Boheme for Can. Opera; Julius Caeasar, Midsummer Marriage, Don Giovanni, Orlando for San Francisco Opera; Adriana LeCouvreur for Bavarian Staatsoper; La Boheme and Orlando for Chgo. Lyric; La Boheme, Don Carlos for Melbourne Opera Australia; London's West end prodns. include: The World of Paul Slickey; My Fair Lady; appeared as apprentice in Britten's Peter Grimes, Covent Garden Opera Co., 1950; soloist in Bach's St. John Passion, Bremen, Germany, 1965; appeared as Ferdy in A Patriot for Me, Royal Ct. Theatre, 1965; co-dir. (with Patrick Garland): Fanfare for Europe Gala, Covent Garden, 1973. Address: 9D Thistle Grove, London SW10 9RR, England *

COPMAN, LOUIS, naval officer, radiologist; b. Phila., Jan. 17, 1934; s. Jacob and Eve (Snyder) C.; m. Avera Schuster, June 8, 1958; children: Mark, Linda. BA, U. Pa., 1955, MD, 1959. Diplomate Am. Bd. Radiology; Nat. Bd. Med. Examiners. Commd. ensign Med. Corps USN, 1958; advanced through grades to capt. Naval Hosp., 1975; asst. chief radiology dept. Naval Hosp., Pensacola, Fla., 1966-69; chief radiology dept. Doctors Hosp., Phila., 1969-73; radiologist Mercer Hosp. Ctr., Trenton, N.J., 1973-75; chmn. radiology dept. Naval Hosp., Phila., 1975-84; chief. radiology dept. Naval Med. Clinic, Pearl Harbor, Hawaii, 1984—; cons. Radiology Services, Wilmington, Del., 1978-84, Yardley (Pa.) Radiology, 1979-84. Author: The Cuckold, 1974. Recipient Albert Einstein award in Medicine, U. Pa., 1959. Mem. AMA, Assn. Mil. Surgeons of the U.S., Royal Soc. Medicine, Radiol. Soc. N.Am., Am. Coll. Radiology, Photographic Soc. Am., Sherlock Holmes Soc., Phi Beta Kappa, Alpha Omega Alpha. Jewish. Home: 1774 Akaakaawa St Kailua HI 96734 Office: Naval Med Clinic PO Box 121 Pearl Harbor HI 96860

COPPIETERS, EMMANUEL, lawyer, economist, educator; b. Bruges, Belgium, Jan. 1, 1925; m. Agnés de Munter, 1982. D.Juris, Louvain U., 1947, D.Econ. Scis., 1955; M.Scis. in Econs., London U., 1952. Barrister 1947-57; prof. internat. econ. orgn. faculty econs. Nat. U. Antwerp, Belgium, 1954—; dir.-gen. Inst. Royal des RelationsInternationales, Brussels, 1954—; ofcl. auditor nanks Brussels, 1962—; bank auditor various internat. banks, Belgium; fgn. trade advisor Belgian Govt.; prof. Royal Mil. Acad., Brussels, 1963-66; consul gen. for Honduras in Belgium 1961—, minister charge d'affaires a.i. of Honduras to European Communities, 1973-77; Mem. Belgium nat. commn. UNESCO, 1955—; gov. Assn. pour l'Etude des problems of Europe, UNESCO, 1955—; gov. Assn. pour l'Etude des problemes of Europe, Paris—, European Cultural Found., 1973—; advisor on fgn. trade to Fgn. Ministry, 1960—. Author: English Bank Note Circulation 1994-1954, 1955, l'Accord Monetaire European en les Progres de la Convertibilte des Monnaies, 1959; Internationale Organizaties en Belgische Econ., 1960; La integratcion monetaria y fiscal europa, culminacion de la intergracion politica, 1963; co-editor Intermnat. Spectator, Tijaschrift voor Internat. Politiek, 1961—; contbr. articles in English, Dutch, French and Spanish to various publs. Mem. Belgium Nat. Commn. UNESCO, 1955—; gov. Assn. pour l'Etude Des Problemes of Eunrope, Paris, 1959—, European Communities, 1973—; adviser on Fgn. Trade to Fgn., 1960—. Decorated medals and recipient numerous honors. Mem. Royal Acad. Scis., Belgian Nat. Council Statistics, Mex. Acad. Internat. Law. Served with Belgium and British Armed Forces, 1944-45; now lt. col. Home: 88 avenue de la Couronne, 1050 Brussels Belgium also: Vijverskateel Loppem bij, Brugge Belgium

COPPOC, WILLIAM JOSEPH, chemist; b. Cumberland, Iowa, July 14, 1913; s. James Sunderland and Winifred (Fowler) C.; B.S., Ottawa U., 1935, D.Sc. (hon.), 1955; M.A., Rice Inst., 1937, Ph.D. in Phys. and Colloid Chemistry, 1939; m. Eleanor Louise Lister, July 2, 1939; children—Teresa Anne DeNies, William Edmund. With Texaco Inc., 1939—, successively chemist grease research, asst. to asst. chief chemist, Port Arthur, Tex., acting supr. grease research, asst. dir. research, Beacon, N.Y., assoc. dir. research, N.Y.C., 1939-53, dir. research, N.Y.C., 1953-54, mgr. research, N.Y.C. and Beacon, 1954-57, mgr. research and devel., Beacon, 1957-60, mgr. sci. planning and info., 1960-65, gen. mgr. research and tech. dept., 1965-68, v.p. research and tech. dept., 1968-71, v.p. environ. protection dept., 1971-78, cons., 1978—; former mem. environ. studies bd. NRC; mem. adv. bd. to environ. scis. div. Oak Ridge Nat. Labs., 1978-81; Woodrow Wilson vis. fellow, 1980—. Mem. investment com. Am. Baptist Chs. N.Y. State, 1979-88 ; trustee, past chmn. bd. Ottawa U. (Kans.), 1960—; trustee Cottey Coll., Nevada, Mo., 1984-87, Resource Recovery Agy. Dutchess County (N.Y.), 1983-88 ; trustee Vassar Bros. Hosp. , Poughkeepsie, N.Y., 1979-86, chmn. hosp. found., 1986-88; trustee Oakwood Sch. Found., 1984-88 ; trustee Area Fund Dutchess County, 1980-85 , pres., 1984. Fellow Am. Inst. Chemists; mem. Am. Chem. Soc., Soc. Automotive Engrs., Am. Petroleum Inst., AAAS, Sci. Research Soc. Am. (chmn. 1960-63), N.Y. Acad. Scis., Dirs. Indsl. Research (chmn. 1971-72), Gordon Research Confs. (chmn. bd. trustees 1970), Soc. Chem. Industry (hon. treas. Am. sect. 1972-76), Sigma Xi, Phi Lambda Upsilon. Home: 14 Kingwood Park Poughkeepsie NY 12601 Office: PO Box 509 Beacon NY 12508

COPPOCK, ROBERT A., social scientist, research consultant; b. Walla Walla, Wash., Jan. 25, 1946; s. William R. and Doris H. (Lieuallen) C.; m. Marilyn Cohen, Sept. 24, 1971 (dec. 1976); m. Arlette Marcelle Perruchas, Dec. 28, 1978; 1 child, Eric. B.S., Wash. State U., 1968; M.P.A., U. Wash., 1970; Dr. rer.oc., GHS Wuppertal (West Germany), 1984. Research asst. Battelle Meml. Inst., Seattle, 1969-73; research scientist Battelle Institut e.v., Frankfurt, W. Ger., 1973-76; research fellow Sci. Ctr. Berlin, West Berlin, 1976-84; fellow Nat. Research Council, Washington, 1985—, program officer, 1986—. Mem. editorial bd. Soc. Risk Analysis, 1981—. Author: Social Constraints on Technological Progress, 1984; Regulating Chemical Hazards in Japan, West Germany, France, The United Kingdom and the European Community: A Comparative Examination, 1986. Editor: (with others) Technological Risk: Its Perception and Handling in the European Community, 1980. Home: 6166 Leesburg Pike B115 Falls Church VA 22044 Office: Nat Acad Scis 2101 Constitution Ave NW Washington DC 20418

COPULSKY, WILLIAM, chemical company executive; b. Zhitomir, Russia, Apr. 4, 1922; s. Boris and Betty (Bruman) C.; came to U.S., 1923, naturalized, 1929; B.A., N.Y. U., 1942, Ph.D., 1957; m. Ruth B. Brody, Dec. 26, 1948; children—Stephen, Jonathan, Lewis. Chemist, Ammeco Chem. Co., Rochester, N.Y., 1942; asst. research dir. J.J. Berliner Co., N.Y.C., 1946-48; research dir. R. S. Aries and Assos., N.Y.C., 1948-51; comml. dir. W.R. Grace and Co., N.Y.C., 1951-74, v.p. operations services group, 1974-86; prof. mktg. Baruch Coll., City Univ., N.Y., 1987—. Served with AUS, 1942-46. Mem. Am. Chem. Soc., Chemists Club, Beta Gamma Sigma. Author: Marketing Chemical Products, 1948; Forecasting Chemical Commodity Demand, 1962; Practical Sales Forecasting, 1970; Entrepreneurship and the Corporation, 1974. Home: 23-35 Bell Blvd Bayside NY 11360 Office: Baruch Coll Mktg Dept 17 Lexington Ave New York NY 10010

COQUILLETTE, DANIEL ROBERT, lawyer, educator; b. Boston, May 23, 1944; s. Robert McTavish and Dagmar Alvida (Bistrup) C.; m. Judith Courtney Rogers, July 5, 1969; children: Anna, Sophia, Julia. A.B., Williams Coll., 1966; M.A. Juris., Univ. Coll., Oxford U., Eng., 1969; J.D., Harvard U., 1971. Bar: Mass. 1974, U.S. Dist. Ct. Mass. 1974, U.S. Ct. Appeals (1st cir.) 1974. Law clk. Mass. Supreme Ct., 1971-72; to Warren E. Burger, chief justice U.S. Supreme Ct., 1972-73; assoc. Palmer & Dodge, Boston, 1973-75, ptnr., 1980-85; assoc. prof. law Boston U., 1975-78; dean, prof. Boston Coll. Law, 1985—; vis. assoc. prof. law Cornell U., Ithaca, N.Y., 1977-78; vis. prof. law Harvard Law Sch., 1978-79, 83-85; reporter com. rules and procedures Jud. Conf. U.S.; vis. assoc. prof. law Cornell U., Ithaca, N.Y., 1977-78; vis. prof. law Harvard U., 1978-79, 83-85. Author: The Civilian Writers of Doctors, 1988; editor: Law in Colonial Massachusetts, 1985; bd. dirs. New England Quarterly, 1986—; contbr. articles to legal jours. Trustee, sec.-treas. Ames Found., Cambridge Friends Day Sch.; treas. Byron Meml Fund; trustee Boston Athenaeum. Recipient Kaufman prize in English Williams Coll., 1966; recipient Sentinel of the Republic prize in polit. sci. Williams Coll., 1965; Hutchins scholar, 1966-67; Fulbright scholar, 1966-68. Mem. Am. Law Inst., ABA, Mass Bar Assn. (task force on model rules of profl. conduct), Boston Bar Assn., Am. Soc. Legal History (bd. dirs. 1985—), Mass. Soc. Continuing Legal Edn. (dir.), Social Welfare Research Inst. (dir.), Selden Soc. (state corr.), Colonial Soc. Mass. (v.p.), Anglo-Am. Cathedral Soc. (dir.), Mass. Hist. Soc., Am. Antiquarian Soc., Phi Beta Kappa. Democrat. Quaker. Clubs: Curtis, Tavern, Country, Club of Old Volumes. Home: 12 Rutland St Cambridge MA 02138 Office: Boston Coll Law Sch 885 Centre St Newton Center MA 02159

CORAN, ARNOLD GERALD, pediatric surgeon, educator; b. Boston, Apr. 16, 1938; s. Charles and Anne (Cohen) C.; m. Susan Williams, Nov. 17, 1960; children: Michael, David, Randi Beth. B.A. cum laude, Harvard U., 1959, M.D. cum laude, 1963. Diplomate: Am. Bd. Surgery, Am. Bd. Thoracic Surgery. Intern Peter Bent Brigham Hosp., Boston, 1963-64; resident in surgery Peter Bent Brigham Hosp., 1964-68, chief surg. resident, 1969; resident in surgery Children's Hosp. Med. Center, Boston, 1965-66; sr. surg. resident Children's Hosp. Med. Center, 1966, chief surg. resident, 1968; instr. surgery Harvard, Cambridge, Mass., 1967-69; asst. clin. prof. surgery George Washington U., 1970-72; head physician pediatric surgery Los Angeles County-U. So. Calif. Med. Center, 1972-74; asst. prof. surgery U. So. Calif., 1972-73, assoc. prof., 1973-74; prof. surgery U. Mich., Ann Arbor, 1974—; head sect. pediatric surgery U. Mich. Hosp., 1974—; Surgeon-in-chief Mott Children's Hosp. Contbr. numerous articles in field to profl. jours. Served to lt. comdr. MC AUS. Fellow ACS; mem. Am. Acad. Pediatrics, Am. Surg. Assn., Soc. Univ. Surgeons, Am. Pediatric Surg. Assn., Western, Central surg. assns. Home: 3450 Vintage Valley Rd Ann Arbor MI 48105 Office: Mott Children's Hosp Room F7516 Box 0245 Ann Arbor MI 48109

CORBER, ROBERT JACK, I, lawyer; b. Topeka, June 29, 1926; s. Alva Forrest and Katherine (Salzer) C.; m. Joan Irene Tennal, July 16, 1949 (dec. July 1987); children: Janet, Suzanne, Wesley Sean, Robert Jack II. B.S. in Aero. Engring, U. Kans., 1946; J.D. cum laude, Washburn U., 1950; postgrad., U. Mich., 1950-51. Bar: Kans. bar 1950, D.C. bar 1951, U.S. Supreme Ct. bar 1964. Asso. firm Steptoe & Johnson, Washington, 1951-57; partner Steptoe & Johnson, 1957-75, 80—; commr. ICC, Washington, 1975-76; partner firm Conner, Moore & Corber, Washington, 1977-80. Author: Motor Carrier Leasing and Interchange Under the Interstate Commerce Act, 1977; contbr. legal and polit. articles to various publs. Chmn. Arlington (Va.) Republican Com., 1960-62; chmn. Va. 10th Congl. Dist. Rep. Com., 1962-64; state chmn. Rep. Party of Va., 1964-68. Served to lt. (j.g.) USNR, 1944-47. Mem. ABA (chmn. motor carrier com. pub. utility sect. 1983-86), Bar Assn. D.C. (chmn. adminstrv. law sect. 1978-79, chmn. continuing legal edn. com. 1979-83), Transp. Lawyers Assn., Assn. Trans. Practitioners. Methodist. Clubs: Met. (Washington), Capitol Hill (Washington), Washington Golf and Country (Washington).

CORBETT, MAURICE CLARK, orthodontist; b. Turlock, Calif., Feb. 4, 1935; s. Maurice Virgil and Opal (Clark) C.; student Fresno State Coll., 1954; A.A., Coll. Sequoias, 1955; D.D.S., U. Calif. at San Francisco, 1959; postgrad. U. Calif., 1971-73; children—Sandra Lea, Christin Ann, Maurice Virgil. Individual practice dentistry specializing in children, San Jose, Calif., 1962-73; practice dentistry, specializing in orthodontics, San Jose, 1973—; clin. instr., lectr. U. Calif. Dental Sch., San Francisco, 1963-67; mem. staff O'Connor Hosp., San Jose. Founder, exec. dir., treas. Found. for Advanced Continuing Edn. Served with USN, 1958-62. Mem. Calif. Soc. Dentistry for Children (pres.), Am. Acad. Pedodontics, Santa Clara Valley Pedodontic Acad. (pres. 1965-66), Am. Assn. Orthodontists. Home: 14 Aliso Rd Carmel CA 93924 Office: 100 O'Connor Dr San Jose CA 95128

CORBETT, MICHAEL DERRIK, accountant; b. Galway, Ireland, Sept. 17, 1929; s. John Patrick and Mary (O'Connor) C.; m. Margaret Veronica Pitcher, June 27, 1957; children: Margaret, Catherine. BA, Nat. Univ. Ireland, 1951; postgrad., Columbia U., 1961-62. Chartered acct. Controller Carroll Industries, Inc., Dublin, 1959-66, fin. dir., 1967-71, 75-87; chief exec. officer Brooks Watson Group, Ltd., Dublin, 1971-75; chmn. Norwich-Union Ins. Group, Ireland, 1981—; mem. Irish Govt. Decimal Currency Bd., Dublin, 1968-71, Dublin Port and Docks Bd., 1973-74. Mem. Inst. Chartered Accts. Ireland, Confedn. Irish Industry (nat. council 1968-80). Roman Catholic. Clubs: Royal Irish Yacht, Milltown Golf. Home: 5 Green Park, Dublin 14, Ireland

CORBIN, HERBERT LEONARD, public relations executive; b. Bklyn., Mar. 30, 1940; s. H. Dan and Lillian C.; m. Carol Heller, June 2, 1963; children: Jeffrey, Leslie Faith. BA, Rutgers U., 1961. Staff corr. Newark News, 1961-63; asst. dir. pub. relations Rutgers U. News Service, New Brunswick, N.J., 1963-65; account exec. A.A. Schechter Assocs., N.Y.C., 1965-66, Barkis & Shalit, Inc., N.Y.C., 1965-66; sr. account exec. Daniel J. Edelman, Inc., N.Y.C., 1967-69; founder, pres., mng. ptnr. Kanan, Corbin, Schupak & Aronow, Inc., N.Y.C., 1969—. Bd. dirs., sec. Altro Health and Rehab. Services; chmn. pub. relations com. White Plains Pub. Access Cable TV Commn. Mem. Pub. Relations Soc. Am., Pub. Relations Soc. N.Y., Sigma Delta Chi. Clubs: Williams Coll., Old Oaks Country. Home: 31 Hathaway Ln White Plains NY 10605 Office: KCS&A Pub Relations 820 2nd Ave New York NY 10017

CORBIN, KRESTINE MARGARET, author, fashion designer, columnist; b. Reno, Apr. 24, 1937; d. Lawrence Albert and Judie Ellen (Johnston) Dickinson; m. Lee D. Corbin, May 16, 1959 (div. 1982); children: Michelle Marie, Sheri Karin. BS, U. Calif., Davis, 1958. Asst. prof. Bauder Coll., Sacramento, 1974—; columnist Sacramento Bee, 1976-81; owner Creative Sewing Co., Sacramento, 1976—; pres., chief exec. officer Sierra Machinery Corp., Sparks, Nev., 1983—; nat. sales and promotion mgr. Westwood Retail Fabrics, N.Y.C., 1985—; bd. dirs. No. Internat. Bank, F.S.C. Mgmt. Services Ltd.; cons. in field. Author: Suede Fabric Sewing Guide, 1973, Creative Sewing Book, 1978, (audio-visual) Fashions in the Making, 1974; producer: (nat. buyers show) Cream of the Cream Collections, 1978—, Style is What You Make It!, 1978-83. Mem. Crocker Art Gallery Assn., 1960-78, Rep. Election Com., Sacramento, 1964, 68. Mem. Home Economists in Bus., Am. Home Econs. Assn., Internat. Fashion Group, Women's Fashion Fabrics Assn., Nat. Tool Builders Assn., Omicron Nu. Address: PO Box 435 Reno NV 89504 Office: Sierra Machinery Inc 1651 Glendale Rd Sparks NV 89431

CORBIN, RICHARD HENRY, business development consultant; b. Cleve., Dec. 21, 1936; s. Milford H. and Miriam (Eshner) C.; m. Eileen Richards; children—Philip, Caroline, Peter. B.A., Lehigh U., 1958. Project mgr. St. Regis Paper Co., N.Y.C., 1963-65; dir. New products Kayser Roth, N.Y.C., 1965-67; mem. sr. mgmt. staff Helena Rubinstein/Faberge, N.Y.C., 1967-75; cons. Richard Corbin Assocs., Westport, Conn., 1975-77; sr. v.p. Innotech Corp., Trumbull, Conn., 1977-82; v.p., ptnr. Glendinning Assocs., Westport, 1982-86; sr. v.p., ptnr. Westport Cons. Group Inc., Westport, 1986—; sr. cons. Advanced Mgmt. Research, N.Y.C., 1977-79; lectr. Am. Mgmt. Assn., N.Y.C., 1973-77, Bus. Week, N.Y.C., 1984—, Frost & Sullivan, Eng., 1986—. Contbr. articles to bus. jours. Served to lt. (j.g.) USNR, 1959-62. Home: 8 Indian Point Ln Westport CT 06880

CORBOY, JAMES MCNALLY, investment banker; b. Erie, Pa., Nov. 3, 1940; s. James Thomas and Dorothy Jane (Schluraff) C.; BA, Allegheny Coll., 1962; MBA, U. Colo., 1986. m. Suzanne Shaver, July 23, 1965; children: Shannon, James McNally. Sales staff Boettcher & Co., Denver, 1964-70; sales staff Blyth Eastman Dillon, Denver and Chgo., 1970-74; sales staff William Blair & Co., Chgo., 1974-77; mgr. corp. bond dept. Boettcher & Co., Denver, 1977-79; ptnr. in charge William Blair & Co., Denver, 1979-86; first v.p. Stifel, Nicolaus & Co., 1986—. Served with USMC, 1962-67. Mem. Securities Industry Assn., Nat. Assn. Securities Dealers (bd. arbitrators). Republican. Presbyterian. Clubs: The Attic (Chgo.), Glenmoor Country, Metropolitan. Home: 60 Meade Ln Englewood CO 80110-6024 Office: 5445 DTC Pkwy Suite 1025 Englewood CO 80111

CORCORAN, C. TIMOTHY, III, lawyer; b. Kansas City, Mo., Dec. 18, 1945; s. Clement T. and Bette Lou (Hohl) C. B.A., U. N.C.-Chapel Hill, 1967; J.D., U. Va., 1973. Bar: Fla. 1973, U.S. Dist. Ct. (mid. dist.) Fla. 1973, D.C. 1974, U.S. Dist. Ct. (no. and so. dists.) Fla. 1975, U.S. Ct. Appeals (5th cir.) 1979, U.S. Supreme Ct. 1979, U.S. Ct. Appeals (11th cir.) 1981. Law clk. U.S. Dist. Ct., Tampa, 1973-75; assoc., shareholder Carlton, Fields, Ward, Emmanuel, Smith & Cutler, P.A., Tampa, 1975—; dir. Bay Area Legal Services, Inc., Tampa, 1983—, v.p., 1987-88, pres., 1988—; bd. dirs. Fla. Council Bar Pres., 1982—, pres. 1986-87; arbitrator Ct. Annexed Arbitration Program, U.S. Dist. Ct. (mid. dist.) Fla., 1984—; counselor U. Tampa, 1981-86. Served to lt. USNR, 1967-70. Fellow U. Tampa, 1986—. Co-author: Conflicts of Interest, 1984; contbr. articles to legal jours. Mem. ABA (assoc. editor Litigations News 1982-87, mng. editor, 1987, editor-in-chief 1988—), Fla. Bar Assn. (chmn. voluntary bar liaison com. 1985-86, chmn. grievance com. 13-D 1986—, chmn. legal edn. com. 1981-82, Most Prodn. Young Lawyer award 1981), Am. Judicature Soc., Hillsborough County Bar Assn. (Red McEwen award 1980, pres. 1982-83). Democrat. Roman Catholic. Home: 2530-B Maryland Ave Tampa FL 33629 Office: PO Box 3239 Tampa FL 33601

CORCORAN, PAUL EDWARD, university senior lecturer, author; b. Fremont, Mich., Oct. 1, 1944; arrived in Australia, 1974; s. Arthur John and Flora Elsie (Holcomb) C.; m. Annie Homan Barlow, Dec. 31, 1970 (dec. June 1981); m. Suzanne Alexis Sheehan, Dec. 21, 1984. AB cum laude, Princeton U., 1966; AM, Duke U., 1968, PhD, 1970. Instr. in politics Washington and Lee U., Lexington, Va., 1969-70; asst. prof. Rider Coll., Lawrenceville, N.J., 1970-74; sr. lectr. U. Adelaide (Australia), 1974—; bd. dirs., bd. govs. State Theatre Co. of South Australia, Adelaide, 1986—. Author: Political Language and Rhetoric, 1979, Before Marx: Socialism and Communism in France, 1830-48, 1983. Recipient Younger Humanist award U.S. Nat. Endowment for Humanities, 1973. Mem. Am. Polit. Sci. Assn., Australasian Polit. Studies Assn., Internat. Communications Assn. Club: Elm (Princeton). Home: 16 Clifton St, 5082 Prospect Australia Office: U Adelaide, Dept of Politics, North Terrace, 5001 Adelaide Australia

CORCORAN, THOMAS JOSEPH, writer, consultant, former ambassador; b. N.Y.C., Sept. 6, 1920; s. John T. and Mary A. (Carroll) C. B.S.S., St. John's U., 1940; student S.E. Asia lang. and area, Georgetown U., 1953. Mem. U.S. Fgn. Service, 1948—; vice consul Barcelona, Spain, 1948-50, Hong Kong, 1950-51; sec. embassy Saigon, Viet-Nam, 1951-53; charge d'affaires ad interim Vientiane, Laos, 1951-52, Phnom Penh, Cambodia, 1952; consul Hanoi, N. Viet-Nam, 1954-55; officer in charge Viet-Nam affairs Dept. of State, 1956-58, Dept. of State (Laos affairs), 1958-59; assigned (Armed Forces Staff Coll.), 1959-60, dep. polit. adv. to comdr. in chief Pacific, 1960-62; dep. chief mission, counselor Ouagadougou, Upper Volta, 1962-64; dir. working group Vietnam, 1964-65; 1st sec. Saigon, 1965; consul gen. Danang, Vietnam, 1966; grad. Nat. War Coll., 1968; country dir. Laos and Cambodia, 1968-73; dep. chief mission, counselor Port-au-Prince, Haiti, from 1973; prin. officer Quebec, Que., Can., 1974-75; minister-counselor Am. embassy, Vientiane, Laos, 1975-77; ambassador to Burundi, 1977-80; now writer/cons. Served to lt. (s.g.) USNR, World War II. Home: 2725 29th St NW Washington DC 20008

CORCUERA, CEZAR FELIPE PILI, chemical manufacturing and leasing company executive, entrepreneur; b. Manila, Aug. 23, 1945; s. Vicente Alcantara and Natividad Anzures (Pili) C.; m. Nanette Buan King, Jan. 5, 1968; children—Stephannie, Patrick, Richard, Natasha, Philip, Natalie, Ma. Tanya, Ramon Miguel. B.S. in Commerce cum laude, San Beda Coll., Manila, 1965; M.B.A., U. Philippines, 1970. Mem. audit staff SyCip, Gorres, Velayo & Co., Philippines, 1965-67; instr. Coll. of Holy Spirit, Manila, 1968-82, St. Theresa's Coll., Quezon City, Philippines, 1968-82; v.p., dir. Mgmt. Dynamics, Inc., Philippines, 1970-74; pres., dir. Philippines Amusement Enterprises, Inc., 1974-86, chmn., chief exec. officer, 1986—; pres., vice chmn. Republic Chem. Industries, Inc., Philippines, 1977—; cons. to various bus. orgns., Manila, 1972—; lectr. Meralco Found., Inc., Manila, 1981-84; pres., dir. Ednl. Exponents Corp., 1984—; mem. exec. com. Dualtech Found., Inc., Manila, 1985—. Amado Araneta scholar U. Philippines, 1966-69. Mem. Mandaluyong Chamber Commerce and Industry (pres. 1986-88, 1st v.p., bd. dirs., President's award 1984), Sales and Mktg. Exec. Internat. (past pres. Philippines, Disting. Service award 1975-83), Philippine Inst. C.P.A.s, San Beda Alumni Assn. (v.p., bd. dirs. 1987—), DBP Entrepreneurs Forum (group coordinator 1987) Roman Catholic. Clubs: Alabang Country, Valley Golf (Manila). Home: 233 Ma Cristina St, Ayala Alabang Village, Muntinlupa, Manila 1702, Philippines Office: Philippine Amusement Enterprises Inc, 731 Aurora Blvd, Cubao, Quezon City, Manila Philippines

CORDEIRO, JOSEPH CARDINAL, archbishop of Karachi; b. Bombay, India, Jan. 19, 1918. BA, U. Bombay, 1939; MA, Oxford (Eng.) U., 1950. Ordained priest Roman Catholic Ch., 1946. Archbishop of Karachi Pakistan, 1958—, created cardinal, 1973. Mem. congregation Religious and Secular Insts.; mem. Secretariate Non-Christian Religions. Address: Archbishop's House, St Patrick's Cathedral, Karachi 3 Pakistan

CORDELL, ROBERT JAMES, geologist, research company executive; b. Quincy, Ill., Jan. 7, 1917; s. Vail R. and Gertrude (Robison) C.; m. Frances Regina Sparacio, Sept. 20, 1942; children—Victor V., David M., Margaret L. B.S., U. Ill., 1939, M.S., 1940; Ph.D, U. Mo., 1949. Instr. U. Mo., Columbia, 1946-47; from instr. to asst. prof. Colgate U., Hamilton, N.Y., 1947-51; research paleontologist, research geologist, sr. research geologist Sun Oil Co., Abilene, Tex., 1951-55; mgr. geol. research Sun Oil Co., Richardson, Tex., 1955-63; sr. sect. mgr., sr. research and profl. scientist Sun Co., Richardson, 1963-77; pres. Cordell Reports Inc., Richardson, 1977—; mem. exec. bd. Potential Gas com., Colorado Springs, 1976-82. Co-editor: Problems of Oil Migration, 1981; contbr. articles to profl. jours., treatises. Bd. dirs. Richardson Community Concerts Inc., Tex., 1958-70, pres., 1963-64; bd. dirs. Richardson Symphony Inc., 1962-82, pres., 1970-71, chmn. bd., 1971-72; area chmn. James Collins Campaign for U.S. Senate, Richardson, 1982. Fellow Geol. Soc. Am., AAAS; mem. Am. Assn. Petroleum Geologists (gen. chmn. nat. cov. 1975, Spl. Service award 1975, co-winner Spl. Pubs. award 1982), Dallas Geol. Soc. (hon. life, pres. 1977-78, Spl. Service award 1975, Research Publ. award 1980), Soc. Econ. Paleontologists and Mineralogists. Republican. Episcopalian. Home: 305 W Shore Dr Richardson TX 75080

CORDERO, LUIS ANGEL, geometry educator; b. Guitiriz, Galicia, Spain, Sept. 6, 1946; s. Domingo and Luisa (Rego) C.; m. Luisa Puentes Carballeira, Dec. 13, 1969; children—Luis-Angel. Santiago. Grad. in Math., U. Santiago, Spain, 1968, Ph.D. in Math., 1971. Asst. prof. U. Santiago, 1968-75; hon. research fellow dept. math. Harvard U., Cambridge, Mass., 1974; prof. U. Valladolid, Spain, 1975-76, U. La Laguna, Canary Islands, Spain, 1976-79; prof. dept. geometry U. Santiago, 1979—; reviewer Zentralblatt fur Mathematik, Springer-Verlag, Berlin, 1973—, Math. Revs., Am. Math. Soc., 1976—. Editor: Fourth International Colloquium on Differential Geometry, Proceedings, 1979, Differential Geometry, Proceedings of the Fifth International Colloquium on Differential Geometry, 1984, Research Notes in Mathematics, 1985. Contbr. research articles to profl. jours. Mem. Am. Math. Soc., Tensor Soc. (Japan), Acad. Scis. of Galicia (Spain), Sci. Cons. Commn. (Xunta of Galicia, Spain). Avocation: philately. Home: 19 Republica de El Salvador, Santiago de Compostela, Coruna Spain Office: U Santiago, Faculty Math, Santiago de Compostela, Coruna Spain

CORDES, LOVERNE CHRISTIAN, interior designer; b. Cleve., Feb. 13, 1927; d. Frank Andrew and Loverne Louise (Brown) Christian; m. William Peter Cordes, Nov. 14, 1959; children: Christian Peter, Carey Pomeroy. B.S., Purdue U., 1949. Owner, mgr. Loverne Christian Cordes, Chagrin Falls, Ohio, 1967—; tchr. John Carroll U., Cleve., 1976-77. Interior designer, Fred Epple Co., Cleve., 1949-67. Fellow Am. Soc. Interior Designers, AIA, Nat. Home Fashion League (past pres. Ohio chpt.), Am. Inst. Interior Designers (past pres. Ohio chpt., nat. bd. dirs. 1969-75, nat. v.p. East Central region 1972-75, nat. exec. bd. 1972-75, recipient 1st Presdl. citation 1973, 74, 75); mem. Soc. Collectors Dunham Tavern Mus. (bd. dirs. 1961-62), Dunham Dames (past pres.), Western Reserve Hist. Soc., Cleve. Mus. Art, Cleve. Garden Center, Chagrin Falls Hist. Soc., Nat. Trust for Historic Preservation, Internat. Platform Assn., Arcadian, Kappa Kappa Gamma. Republican. Congregationalist. Clubs: Chagrin Valley Country, Dogwood Garden. Address: 60 S Franklin St Chagrin Falls OH 44022

CORDIER, PIERRE, artist, educator; b. Brussels, Belgium, Jan. 28, 1933; s. Leon and Renee (Philippe) C. Student in Scis., Politics and Adminstrn., U. Libre de Bruxelles (Belgium), 1952-55. Tchr. Ecole Nat. Superieure des Arts Visuels, Brussels, 1965—; represented in permanent collections: Nationale, Paris, Mus. of Modern Art, N.Y., Internat. Mus. of Photography, George Eastman House, Rochester, N.Y., Fogg Art Mus., Harvard U., Cambridge, Mass., Gernsheim Collection, U. Tex.-Austin, Ctr. for Creative Photography, U. Ariz., Tucson; individual exhbns. include: A European Experiment, Mus. of Modern Art, N.Y., 1967; Pierre Cordier: Chimigrammi, Glaeria Spectrum, Barcelona, 1976; 20 Ans de Chimigrammes, Palais des Beaux-Arts, Brussels, 1976; 20 Years of Chemigrams, Neikrug Galleries, N.Y., 1977; Pierre Cordier: Chimigrammes, Bibliotheque Nationale, Paris, 1979; Benteler Galleries, Houston, 1983; Laurence Miller Gallery, N.Y.C., 1984, Shadai Gallery, Tokyo, 1985, Galerie Photo Art, Basel, Switzerland, Libreria Agora, Turin, Italy, 1986; group exhbns. include: Subjektive Fotografie III, Photokina, Cologne, 1958, Generative Fotografie, Kunsthaus, Bielefeld, West Germany, 1968, Vision and Expression, Internat. Mus. of Photography, George Eastman House, Rochester, N.Y., 1969, Contemporary Photographs I, Fogg Art Mus., Harvard U., 1971, Octave of Prayer, MIT, Cambridge, 1972, Centre George Pompidou, Paris, 1981, The Franklin Inst. Sci. Mus., 1983; patentee: Chemigram, 1956; Foto-Chemigram, 1963; author: Chimigrammes, 1974; 20 Years of Chemigrams, 1976; films include: Start, 1974; Antenne 2: Les Suaires de Veronique, 1980; lectr. Internat. Ctr. of Photography, N.Y., 1978; workshops Internat. Ctr. of Photography, N.Y. 1983. Served in Belgian army, Germany, 1955-57. Mem. Deutsche Gesellschaft fur Photographie, Europeam Soc. for History of Photography, Amina-World Assn. Inventors and Researchers. *

CORDOVA, ANGEL R., airline company executive; b. Quito, Pichincha, Ecuador, Nov. 21, 1937; s. Angel R. and Ana C. (Ricaurte) C.; m. Fanny E. Moscoso, Jan. 5, 1965; children: Angel R. Jr., Christian R. Diploma in nav., USAF Sch., Harlingen, Tex., 1959; grad., Ecuador Air Force Sch., Salinas, 1960. Commd. 2d lt. Ecuador Air Force, Quito-Guayaquil, 1960; advanced through grades to major Ecuador Air Force, resigned, 1968; mgr. airport Tame Airlines, Guayaquil, 1968-69; gen. mgr. Air Force Social Services, Quito, 1969-71; regional mgr. Ecuador Social Security, Guayaquil, 1972-74; gen. mgr. Corpa S.A., Guayaquil, 1974-78; regional mgr. Ecuatoriana Airlines, Guayaquil, 1977-78; gen. mgr. Ecuavia Oriente S.A., Quito, 1978-82, Saeta Airlines, Quito, 1982-86; v.p. Ecuatoriana Airlines, Quito, 1986—; chmn. bd. Perforec S.A., Quito, 1981-87; bd. dirs. Edimbactur, Quito, 1986-87. Author: Aviation History, 1975, Navigation for Pilots, 1977. chmn. Antique Societatis Jesu Alumni, Quito, 1981-82, bd. dirs., 1982-84; vice chmn. U. Tecnológica Equinoccial, Quito, 1981-82. Decorated Abdon Calderon Sec. of Def., 1965, 70, Servicios Militares Sec. of Def., 1967, 72. Fellow Dale Garnegie and Assocs. (instr. 1978-81, Outstanding Instr. award 1983); mem. Sociedad Bolivariana. Roman Catholic. Clubs: Air Force Officer, Skäl, Ret. Officers Air Force (Quito). Home: Mañosca, 200 Quito Ecuador Office: Ecuatoriana de Aviacion, Box 505, Quito Ecuador

CORDOVEZ, DOMINGO XAVIER, computer company executive; b. Quito, Pichincha, Ecuador, Apr. 9, 1953; s. Miguel Angel and Beba (Perez) C.; m. Maria del Carmen Dammer, May 15, 1976; children: Domingo Tadeo, Martin. Grad., U. Catolica, Quito, 1979. Various profl. positions IBM Ecuador, Quito, 1974-81, controller, 1982-83, mgr. fin., 1984, mgr. ops., 1985-86; adminstrv. undersec. Ministry Fin., Quito, 1986; Minister of Fin. Quito, 1986-87; assignee IBM World Trade Am. Far East Corp., Tarrytown, N.Y., 1985; gen. mgr. IBM Ecuador, 1988—; gov. Internat. Devel. Bank, Washington, 1986—, World Bank, Washington, 1986—; alt. pres. Monetary Bd., Quito, 1986-87; pres. Ecuadorian Devel. Bank, Quito, 1986—. Contbr. articles to profl. jours. Named Cavalier of Pichincha, Pichincha Provincial Council, Quito, 1987. Mem. Ecuadorian-Am. C. of C. Club: Agricultores (Quito). Office: IBM Ecuador, Casilla 642, Quito, Pichincha Ecuador

CORDUNEANU, CONSTANTIN C., mathematics educator, researcher; b. Iasi, Moladvia, Romania, July 26, 1928; came to U.S., 1978; s. Costache and Aglaia (Anitoaie) C.; m. Alice Olga Vultur, July 23, 1949. Diploma in Math, U. Iasi, 1951, D.Math., 1956. Instr. U. Iasi, Romania, 1949-55, asst. prof., 1955-62, assoc. prof., 1962-67, prof., 1968-78; prof. dept. math. U. Tex.-Arlington, 1979—; vis. prof. U. R.I.- Kingston, 1967-68, 73-74, 78, U. Tenn.-Knoxville, 1978-79. Author: Almost Periodic Functions, 1968, Principles of Differential and Integral Equations, 1971, 77, Integral Equations and Stability of Feedback Systems, 1973; assoc. editor: jours. including Math. System Theory, 1967-75, Revue Roumaine Pure Applied Math, 1973-78, Nonlinear Analysis, 1977-85, Jour. Integral Equations, 1979—, Libertas Mathematica, 1981—. Served with Romanian Army, 1952. Recipient research prizes Romanian Acad., Bucharest, 1963, research prizes Ministry of Edn., Bucharest, 1965; research fellow Inst. Math. Romanian Acad., Iasi, 1954-59, 63-67. Mem. Am. Math. Soc., Math. Assn. Am., Soc. Indsl. and Applied Math., Am. Romanian Acad. Arts and Scis. Christian Orthodox. Office: Univ Tex-Arlington S Cooper St Arlington TX 76019

CORE, MARY CAROLYN W. PARSONS, radiologic technologist; b. Valpariso, Fla., Dec. 8, 1949; d. Levi and Mary Etta (Elliott) Willey; m. Joel Kent Core, Aug. 3, 1979; 1 child, Candace W. Parsons. Student, Peninsula Gen. Hosp. Sch. Radiologic Tech., Salisbury, Md., 1969, U. Del. Extension, 1969-73, Del. Tech. Community Coll., 1973-79, St. Joseph's Coll., 1983-86, BSBA, 1987. Technologist, Peninsula Gen. Hosp., Salisbury, 1967-72, tech. dir. edn. Sch. Radiologic Tech., 1973-75; technologist Johns Hopkins Hosp., 1972-73, Nanticoke Meml. Hosp., Seaford, Del., 1975-79; adminstrv. chief technologist, imaging depts. Shady Grove Adventist Hosp., Rockville, Md., 1979-81; dir. dept. radiol. scis. Anne Arundel Diagnostics, Inc., then chief ops. officer Anne Arundel MRI (Magnetic Resonance Imaging), Annapolis, Md., 1981—. Recipient twin awards YWCA, 1988. Mem. Cen. Md. Council Girl Scouts U.S. Mem. Md. Soc. Radiologic Technologists (pres. 1980-81, sr. bd. mem. 1982-83, various awards including 1st Pl. Essay awards 1974, 76, 84, 87), Am. Hosp. Radiology Adminstrs. (v.p. 1984-85, chmn. by-laws com. 1984-85, statis. resources com. 1985-86), Am. Mgmt. Assn., Radiology Bus. Mgrs. Assn., Nat. Assn. Female Execs., Eastern Shore Dist. Radiologic Technologists (pres. 1976-78). Republican. Methodist. Home: 1907 Harcourt Ave Crofton MD 21114 Office: Franklin and Cathedral Sts Annapolis MD 21401

COREN, LANCE SCOTT, consulting firm executive; b. Inglewood, Calif., Dec. 19, 1949; s. Melville and Shirley Ann (Ehrlich) C.; m. Susan Hodges; 1 child, Amy Elizabeth. BBA, Calif. State U., Long Beach, 1972; JD, Los Angeles U. Sch. Law, 1974; cert. ins. law, UCLA, 1975; cert. comparative psychology, The Calif. Grad. Inst., 1975; MBA, Cal-Western U., 1976. Auto claims adjustor Gulf & Western Cos., Los Angeles, 1974-77; western region claims adjustor Lloyd's of London, Los Angeles, 1977-80; pres., chief exec. officer L.S.C. Enterprises, Inc., Torrance, Calif., 1980—; cons. Lloyd's of London, 1980-88, Ford Motor Co., Detroit, 1984-88, Automobile Assn. Am., Los Angeles, 1984-88, State Farm Ins. Co., Los Angeles, 1984-88, Farmers Ins. Co., Los Angeles, 1984-88; U.S.A. Ins. Co., Los Angeles, 1986-88, Ins. Inst. Hwy. Safety, 87-88; mem. govs. com. on ins. practices, 1987. Author: The International Firm, 1976, Exotic Automotive Investments, 1985. Fund Childrens' Hosp. Orange County, 1987, raiser Soroptimist Internat., Newport Beach, 1983, Children's Hosp. Soc. of Calif., Fresno, 1985; mem. govs. council Ins. Practices, 1987. Named One of Outstanding Young Men in Am., U.S. Jaycees, 1986; recipient Presdl. Sports award (skiing), Washington, 1973. Mem. Internat. Soc. Automotive Appraisers (pres. 1983-84), Am. Assn. Auto Appraisers (pres. 1984-85), Inter-Industry Conf. on Auto Collision Repair. Democrat. Jewish. Office: L S C Enterprises Group Inc 20545 Eastwood Ave Torrance CA 90503-3611

COREY, ELIAS JAMES, chemistry educator; b. Methuen, Mass., July 12, 1928; s. Elias and Tina (Hashem) C.; m. Claire highham, Sept. 14, 1961; children: David, John, Susan. BS, MIT, 1948, PhD, 1951; AM (hon.), Harvard U., 1959; DSc (hon.), U. Chgo., 1968, Hofstra U., 1974, Oxford U., 1982, U. Liege, 1985, U. Ill., 1985. From instr. to asst. prof. U. Ill., Champaign-Urbana, 1951-55, prof., 1955-59; prof. chemistry Harvard U., Cambridge, Mass., 1959—, Sheldon Emory prof., 1968—. Contbr. articles to profl. jours. Bd. dirs. phys. sci. Alfred P. Sloan Found., 1967-72; mem. sci. adv. bd. dirs. Robert A. Welch Found. Recipient Intrasci. Found. award, 1968; recipient Ernest Guenther award in chemistry of essentials oils and related products, 1968, Harrison Howe award, 1971, Ciba Found. medal, 1972, Evans award Ohio State U., 1972, Linus Pauling award, 1973, Dickson prize in sci. Carnegie Mellon U., 1973, George Ledlie prize in sci. Harvard U., 1973, Nichols medal, 1977, Buchman award Calif. Inst. Tech., 1978, Franklin medal in sci. Franklin Inst., 1978, Sci. Achievement award CCNY, 1979, J.G. Kirkwood award, Yale U., 1980, Chem. Pioneer award, Am. Inst. Chemists, 1981, Wolf prize (chem.), Wolf Found., 1986, numerous others; fellow Swiss-Am. exchange, 1957, Guggenheim Found., 1957-58, 68-69, Alfred P. Sloan Found., 1956-59. Mem. Am. Acad. Arts and Scis., AAAS, Am. Chem. Soc. (award in synthetic chemistry 1971, Pure Chemistry award 1960, Fritzche award 1968, Md. sect. Remsen award 1974, Arthur C. Cope award 1976), Nat. Acad. Sci., Sigma Xi. Office: Harvard Univ Dept of Chemistry Cambridge MA 02138

COREY, KENNETH EDWARD, geography and urban planning educator, researcher; b. Cin., Nov. 11, 1938; s. Kenneth and Helen Ann (Beckman) C.; m. Marie Joanne Fye, Aug. 26, 1961; children: Jeffrey Allen, Jennifer Marie. BA with honors, U. Cin., 1961, MA, 1962, M in City Planning, 1964, PhD, 1969. Instr. U. Cin., 1962-65, asst. prof. community planning, 1965-69, assoc. prof., 1969-74, prof., 1974-79, head grad. community planning and geography, 1969-78; assoc. prof. community planning and geography U. R.I., 1966-67; prof. geography, planning, chmn. dept. geography, dir. urban studies U. Md., 1979—; vis. prof. geography Univ. Coll. Wales, Aberystyth, 1974-75, Beijing U., 1986; chmn. Cin. Model Cities Bd., 1974; Fulbright research scholar Inst. S.E. Asian Studies, 1986, Fulbright study abroad, Sri Lanka, 1983; trustee Met. Washington Housing Planning Assn., 1980-82. Author: The Local Community, 1968, Community Internships for Undergraduate Geography Students, 1973, The Planning of Change, 3d edit., 1976. Bd. dirs. Potomac River Basin Consortium, Washington, 1982-85. Recipient Service award Community Chest and Council Cin., 1979; recipient Service award Planning Div., 1979, Service award Coalition of Neighborhoods, Cin., 1979, 83, medal of city Mayor of Seoul, South Korea, 1980. Fellow Royal Geog. Soc.; mem. Am. Inst. Cert. Planners, Am. Planning Assn., Assn. Am. Geographers (award spl. group on planning and regional devel. 1985), Assn. Asian Studies, Asia Soc., World Future Soc. Democrat. Office: U Md 1113 LeFrak Hall College Park MD 20742

CORI, GREGORY SALVATORE, management consultant; b. Bklyn., May 22, 1925; s. Domenick and Catherine (Ruggiero) Corigliano; m. Theresa M. Priolo, Oct. 29, 1949; children—Janice-Cathy, Joyce-Terri. Student, Juilliard Sch. Music, 1942; B.S., Columbia, 1949, M.S., 1950; postgrad., City Coll. N.Y., 1952-53, N.Y. U., 1954. Sales promotion work with Am. Tobacco Co., 1949-50; mktg. and mktg. research work Willmark Research Co., N.Y.C., 1950-51; advt. mgr. Miehle-Goss-Dexter Co., N.Y.C., 1951-55; mgr. mktg. div. Sel-Rex Corp., Nutley, N.J., 1955-62; founder, pres. Mktg. Communications, Inc., Wayne, N.J., 1962—; officer, dir. Summit Sci. Corp., Fairfield, N.J., 1974-84, Summit Sci. Internat., Milan, Italy, 1984—; adj. prof. mktg. and adminstrn. William Paterson Coll. N.J., 1987—; dir. Platronics, Inc., Linden, N.J., 1967—; asso. prof. mktg. studies Rutgers U., 1957—, Rutgers U. (Grad. Sch. Bus. Adminstrn.), 1974—; mktg. cons. Am. Motors Co., 1964-65, Battelle Research Inst., Geneva, 1968-69; guest speaker, lectr. in field. Contbr. profl. jours. Served with USMCR, 1943-46. Named Advt. Man of Yr. Nat. Indsl. Advertisers Assn., 1960. Mem. Nat. Assn. Indsl. Advertisers (pres. N.J. chpt. 1961-62). Home: 60 Pine Lake Dr NE Wayne NJ 07470 Office: 31 Dwight Pl Fairfield NJ 07006

CORLETT-THIELMANN, EMMA JEAN, social services administrator; b. Knox City, Tex., Aug. 4, 1926; d. LeRoy and Luella (Burns) Massey; B.A. in Secondary Edn. cum laude, N.W. Nazarene Coll., 1965; M.S.W. with honors, U. Utah, 1972; m. John Paul Corlett, Jan. 1, 1946 (dec. 1969); children—Jeanne Marie, Thomas Lee, Jan Louise. Feature writer Statesman Newspaper, Boise, Idaho, 1960-63; caseworker Idaho Dept. Pub. Assistance, Boise, 1965-68; mental health counselor Community. Inst. Human Resources, Boise, 1969-70; dir. patient and family counseling Mercy Med. Center, Nampa, Idaho, 1972-75; edn. counselor U.S. Army, Seoul, S. Korea, 1975-76; med. social worker Kern Med. Center, Bakersfield, Calif., 1976-78, dir. med. social services, 1978-79; dir. med. social services Santa Barbara (Calif.) Cottage Hosp., 1979—. Named Mrs. Idaho, 1959; licensed clin. social worker, Calif. Mem. Nat. Assn. Social Workers, Acad. Certified Social Workers, Internat. Register Clin. Social Workers, AAUW, Soc. Hosp. Social Worker Dirs., Am. Hosp. Assn., U.S. Postal Clks. Aux. (nat. v.p. 1959-63). Phi Delta Lambda. Office: Santa Barbara Cottage Hosp Pueblo at Bath St Santa Barbara CA 93109

CORMACK, ALLAN MACLEOD, physicist, educator; b. Johannesburg, South Africa, Feb. 23, 1924; came to U.S., 1957, naturalized, 1966; s. George and Amelia (MacLeod) C.; m. Barbara Jeanne Seavey, Jan. 6, 1950; children: Margaret, Jean, Robert. B.Sc., U. Cape Town, South Africa, 1944, M.Sc., 1945; research student, Cambridge (Eng.) U., 1947-50. Lectr. U. Cape Town, 1946-47, 1950-56; research fellow Harvard U., 1956-57; asst. prof. physics Tufts U., Medford, Mass., 1957-60; assoc. prof. Tufts U., 1960-64, prof., 1964-80, University prof., 1980—. Recipient Ballou medal Tufts U., 1978; Nobel prize in medicine and physiology, 1979; Medal of Merit U. Cape Town, 1980. Fellow AAAS, Am. Phys. Soc., Am. Acad. Arts and Sci., Royal Soc. South Africa (fgn.); mem. South African Phys. Soc., Nat. Acad. Scis., Sigma Xi. Office: Tufts U Physics Dept Medford MA 02155

CORMIE, DONALD MERCER, investment company executive; b. Edmonton, Alta., Can., July 24, 1922; s. George Mills and Mildred (Mercer) C.; m. Eivor Elisabeth Ekstrom, June 8, 1946; children: John Mills, Donald Robert, Allison Barbara, James Mercer, Neil Brian, Buce George, Eivor, Robert. BA, U. Alta., 1944, LLB, 1945; LLM, Harvard U., 1946. Bar: Can. 1947. With Queens counsel, 1964; sessional instr. faculty law U. Alta., 1947-53; sr. ptnr. Cormie & Kennedy, 1954-87; instr. real estate law Dept. of Extension, U. Alta., 1958-64; pres., bd. dirs. Collective Securities, Ltd., Cormie Ranch, Inc., Sea Investors Corp.; bd. dirs. Sea Mgmt., Inc. Served with Can. Mcht. Marine, 1943-44. Recipient Judge Green Silver medal in law. Mem. Law Soc. Alta., Dean's Council of 100 Ariz. State U., World Bus. Council, Chief Execs. Forum (bd. dirs. 1976-79), Can. Bar Assn. (mem. council 1961-76, chmn. adminstrv. law com. 1963-66, chmn. taxation 1972-82, v.p. Alta. 1968-69). Home: 6301 E Yucca Rd Paradise Valley AZ 85258 Office: 1800 Royal Le Page Tower, 10130-103 St, Edmonton, AB Canada T5J 3N9

CORNABY, KAY STERLING, lawyer, state senator; b. Spanish Fork, Utah, Jan. 14, 1936; s. Sterling A. and Hilda G. (Stoker) C.; m. Linda Rasmussen, July 23, 1965; children: Alyse, Derek, Tara, Heather, Brandon. AB, Brigham Young U., 1960; postgrad. law Heidelberg (W.Ger.), 1961-63; JD, Harvard U., 1966. Bar: N.Y. 1967, Utah 1969, U.S. Patent and Trademark Office 1967. Assoc. Brumbaugh, Graves, Donahue & Raymond, N.Y.C., 1966-69; ptnr. Mallinckrodt & Cornaby, Salt Lake City, 1969-72; sole practice, Salt Lake City, 1972-85; shareholder Jones, Waldo, Holbrook & McDonough, Salt Lake City, 1985—; mem. Utah State Senate, 1977—, majority leader, 1983-84. Chmn. 2d Congl. Dist., Utah Rep. Party, 1973-77; mem. council legal advisers Rep. Nat. Com., 1981—. chmn. North and East Regional Council of Neighborhoods, 1976-77, Nat. Commn. on Uniform State Laws, 1988; mem. Salt Lake County Commn. on Youth, 1988—; mem. Utah Health Cost Found., 1979-86, chmn., 1979-84; mem. Utah State Jud. Conduct Commn., 1983—, chmn. 1984-85; bd. dirs. KUED-KSER Pub. TV and Radio, 1982—, chmn. 1985-87; bd. dirs. Salt Lake Conv. and Visitors Bur., 1985—; mem. adv. council Salt Lake dist. Small Bus. Adminstrn.; pres. Utah Opera Co., 1985-86. Mem. Utah Bar Assn., Utah Harvard Alumni Assn. (pres. 1977-79), Harvard U. Law Sch. Alumni Assn. (v.p. 1979—). Mormon. Club: Alta (Salt Lake City). Office: Jones Waldo Holbrook & McDonough 1500 First Interstate Plaza 170 S Main St Salt Lake City UT 84101

CORNE, JOHN CHRISTOPHER, French educator; b. Auckland, N.Z., July 5, 1942; s. Charles Frederick and Marie Cynthia (Restall) C.; m. Michele Paule Boissery, 1964 (div. 1973); children—Philippe Paul Charles, Brigitte Marie; m. Daphne Wong Too, Dec. 20, 1978; children—Cecilia Jane Lei Kum, Chloe Lucinda Lei Yin, Nicholas Christopher. BA, U. Auckland, 1964, MA with honors, 1965, PhD, 1970. Lectr. in French, U. Auckland, 1968-71, sr. lectr., 1972-85, assoc. prof., 1986—; mem. Comite Internat. des Etudes Creoles, Aix-en-Provence, 1976-79. Author: Seychelles Creole Grammar, 1977, (with Philip Baker) Isle de France Creole: Affinities and Origin, 1982; editor jour. Te Reo, 1982-87; mem. editorial bd. Jour. of Pidgin and Creole Langs., Carrier Pidgin, Antipodes; contbr. articles to profl. publs. Mem. Linguistic Soc. Am., Linguistic Soc. N.Z. (editor 1982-87, sec. 1988—), Soc. for Caribbean Linguistics, Assn. Quebecoise de Linguistique. Club: University (Auckland). Avocations: brewing, cooking, gardening, golf. Office: U Aukland, Private Bag, Auckland New Zealand

CORNELISSEN, JOANNES ANTONIUS THOMAS, Netherlands board of tourism managing director; b. Nijmegen, Gelderland, The Netherlands, May 2, 1938; s. Antony Johannes Maria and Elisabeth Maria Emma (Van der Steen) C.; m. Gerarda Anna Mathilde Vrolijk, July 24, 1965; children: Patricia, Birgit, Erik. LLD, U. Leyde, The Netherlands, 1964. Mktg. mgr. Pharm. div. AKZO, 1965-70; sr. mktg. and mgmt. cons. MARKON, 1970-75; dep. dir. sales and mktg. Van Melle, 1975-78; mng. dir. Duyvis, 1978-80, Netherlands Bd. of Tourism, Leidschendam, 1980—; bd. dirs. Netherlands Research Inst. for Tourism, Breda, 1982—, Netherlands Conv. Bur., Amsterdam, 1983—. Served as lt. intelligence Army of the Netherlands, 1958-59. Fellow Strategic Mgmt. Soc. (chmn. bd. 1971-76), Soc. for Mgmt. Roman Catholic. Club: Forescate Hockey (Voorschoten, The Netherlands) (chmn. 1984—). Home: Von Weberlaan 2, 2253 BM Voorschoten The Netherlands Office: Netherlands Bd of Tourism, Vlietweg 15, 2266 KA Leidschendam The Netherlands

CORNELISSEN, MICHAEL ADRIAAN, trust company executive; b. Durban, Republic of South Africa, June 1, 1943; s. Marinus and Koos (Van der Hoeven) C.; m. Catriona Butcher, Jan. 1967; 2 children. C.A., U. Natal, 1965; M.B.A., U. Capetown, 1970. Audit supr. Touche Ross and Co., 1961-69; dir., v.p. fin. Rennies Consol. Holdings Ltd., 1971-75; v.p. Edper Investments Ltd., 1976; exec. v.p., chief operating officer Trizec Corp. Ltd., 1977-83, now dir.; pres., chief exec. officer, dir. Royal Trustco Ltd., Toronto, Ont., Can., 1983—; dir. Trilon Fin. Corp., Hees Internat. Corp. Inc., London Life Ins. Co., Royal LePage Ltd., Trizec Corp. Ltd. Chmn. United Way Greater Toronto, 1984; bd. govs. Appleby Coll., Oakville; chmn. capital campaign Nat. Ballet Sch.; chmn. Can.'s Challenge for Am.'s Cup; bd. dirs. The Chamber Players of Toronto, The Toronto symphony. Conservative. Clubs: Toronto, York, Royal Can. Yacht, Oakville Yacht Squadron. Office: Royal Trustco Ltd, PO Box 7500, Toronto, ON Canada M5W 1P9 *

CORNELL, GARY WARREN, state forestry official; b. Utica, N.Y., Sept. 4, 1951; s. William Fredrick and Marie (Detraglia) C.; m. Patricia Wright, July 1, 1976 (div. Oct. 1978); m. Jean C. Reddoor, Sept. 10, 1982; (div. Oct. 1984); children—Denise, Chris. B.S. in Forest Mgmt., No. Ariz. U., 1973. Firefighter, USDA Forest Service, Camelo, Ariz., 1967-70, 71-72, forestry tech. supr., Sierra Vista, Ariz., 1973-75; asst. area forester Utah State Lands and Forestry Dept., Heber City, 1976-77, area forester, 1977-78, fire mgmt. officer, Salt Lake City, 1978—. Developer, instr. basic wildland fire course, Utah. Tech. Coll., 1980. Recipient cert. Appreciation USDA Forest Service Nat. Forest, 1981, Park City Vol. Fire Dept., 1981. Mem. Soc. Am. Foresters, Am. Forestry Assn., Utah County Chief Fire Officers Assn., Forestry Conservation Communications Assn. (agy. rep. 1978—), Intermountain Fire Council (agy. rep. 1978—), Gt. Basin Incident Mgmt. Team, Western Fire Mgrs (co-founder, chmn.-elect 1987). Office: Utah State

Lands and Forestry 355 W North Temple 3 Triad Center Suite 400 Salt Lake City UT 84180

CORNELL, ROBERT WITHERSPOON, engineering consultant; b. Orange, N.J., Aug. 16, 1925; s. Edward Shelton and Helen Lauretta (Lawrence) C.; m. Patricia Delight Plummer, June 24, 1950; children—Richard W., Delight W. Cornell Dobby, Elizabeth Cornell Wilkin, Roberta Shelton. B. Mech. Engring., Yale U., 1945, M. Mech. Engring., 1947, D. Engring., 1950. Registered profl. engr., Conn., N.Y. Instr. math. New Haven Jr. Coll., 1947-48; analytical engr. Pratt & Whitney Aircraft, East Hartford, Conn., 1947; with Hamilton Standard, Windsor Locks, Conn., 1948-87, chief applied mechanics and aerodynamics, 1961-87; instr. engring. Hillyer Coll., Hartford, 1955; pres. Cornell Enterprises, West Hartford, 1984—; adj. prof. Yale U., 1985. Contbr. articles to profl. jours. Patentee in field. Bd. dirs., treas. Yale Sci. and Engring. Assn., 1969—; Conn. State Taxpayers Assn., Stratford, 1984-86; past pres., dir. West Hartford Taxpayers Assn., 1972—. Served with USN, 1943-46. Mem. ASME, Sigma Xi, Tau Beta Pi. Clubs: Yale (Hartford and N.Y.C.); Hartford Golf. Avocations: tennis; squash; jogging; swimming; gardening. Home: 40 Belknap Rd West Hartford CT 06117

CORNELSEN, PAUL FREDERICK, manufacturing and engineering company executive; b. Wellington, Kans., Dec. 23, 1923; s. John S. and Theresa Albertine (von Klatt) C.; m. Floy Lila Brown, Dec. 11, 1943; 1 son, John Floyd. Student, U. Wichita, 1939-41, 45-46; B.S. in Mech. Engring, U. Denver, 1949. With Boeing Airplane Co., 1940-41, Ralston Purina Co., St. Louis, 1946—; v.p. internat. div. Ralston Purina Co., 1961-63, adminstrv. v.p., gen. mgr. internat. div., 1963-64, v.p., 1964-68, dir., 1966—, exec. v.p., 1968-78, vice chmn. bd., chief operating officer, 1978-81, pres. internat. group, 1964-77; pres., chief exec. officer Moehlenpah Industries Inc., St. Louis, 1981-82, M.Tek Industries (formerly Moehlenpah), St. Louis, 1982—; bd. dirs. DeKalb (Ill.) Corp., Sunmark Cos., St. Louis, Petrolite Corp., St. Louis, Lindsey Mfg. Co., Omaha; founding mem. Latin Am. Agribus. Investment Corp., 1970—; founding mem. industry coop. program UN Agys., Rome, Italy. Mem. Nat. 4-H Council Adv. Com.; trustee Ill. Coll., Jacksonville. Served to 1st lt. AUS, World War II; Served to 1st lt. AUS, also Korean War. Decorated Silver Star. Home: 506 Fox Ridge Rd Saint Louis MO 63131 Office: 11710 Old Ballas Rd Creve Coeur MO 63141

CORNESS, COLIN ROSS, business executive; b. Chorlton, Eng., Oct. 9, 1931; s. Thomas and Mary Evlyne (Lovelace) C. M.A., Cambridge U., 1958; advanced mgmt. diploma Harvard U., 1970. Dir., Taylor Woodrow Constrn. Ltd., London, 1961-64; mng. dir. Redland Tiles Ltd., Reigate, Surrey, Eng., 1965-70; group mng. dir. Redland PLC, Reigate, 1967-82, chmn. bd., 1977—; dir. Bank of Eng., Gorden Russell plc (formerly Giroflex Ltd.), London, Courtaulds plc, London, S.G. Warburg plc, Unitech plc. Served to lt. 3d Dragoon Guards, Brit. Army, 1949-50. Clubs: Cavalry and Guards White's (London); Australian, Sydney. Office: Redland PLC, Redland House, Reigate, Surrey RH2 0SJ England

CORNEVIN, ROBERT, language professional, educator; b. Malesherbes, Loiret, France, Aug. 26, 1919; s. Maurice and Geneviéve (Chameaux) C.; m. Rau Marianne; children: François, Geneviéve, Bernard, Hubert, Etienne, Heléne. Student, Ecole Nat. France D'Outre Mer, Paris; Docteur es Lettres, U. Paris Sorbonne. Adminstr. France D'Outre Mer, successively Togo, Dahomey, Senegal, cambodgia, 1941-56; civl adminstr. Minister Nat. Edn., Paris, 1958-60; adminstr. Documentation Francaise, Paris, 1960-85; pres. Assn. Ecrivains Langue Francaise, Paris, 1974—; permanent sec. Acad. Sci. D'outre Mer, Paris, 1971—. Author: 30 books on history of Togo, Africa, Zaire, African Lit., theatre, others. Served to lt. French Infantry, 1940-47. Home: 10 rue Vandrezanne, 75013 Paris France Office: Assn Ecrivains Langue Francaise, 14 rue Broussais, 75014 Paris France also: Acad des Scis d'Outre Mer, 15 rue Laperouse, 75116 Paris France

CORNFORTH, JOHN WARCUP, chemist; b. Sydney, Australia, Sept. 7, 1917; s. John William and Hilda (Eipper) C.; B.Sc., U. Sydney, 1937, M.Sc., 1938; D.Phil., Oxford U., 1941, D.Sc. (hon.), 1976; D.Sc. (hon.), E.T.H. Zurich, 1975, Trinity Coll., Dublin, Univs. Liverpool, Warwick, Aberdeen, Hull, Sussex and Sydney; m. Rita H. Harradence, Sept. 27, 1941; children—Brenda (Mrs. David Osborne), John, Philippa. Mem. sci. staff Med. Research Council, London, 1946-62; dir. Milstead Lab. Chem. Enzymology, Shell Research Ltd., Sittingbourne, Kent, Eng., 1962-75; Royal Soc. research prof. Sch. Molecular Scis., U. Sussex, Brighton, Eng., 1975-82. Decorated comdr. Brit. Empire; knighted, 1977; recipient Stouffer prize, 1967; Prix Roussel, 1972; Nobel prize in chemistry, 1975. Fellow Royal Soc., 1953 (Davy medal 1968, Royal medal 1976, Copley medal 1982), Royal Soc. Chemistry (Corday-Morgan medal 1953, Flintoff medal 1966), Am. Chem. Soc. (Ernest Guenther award 1969); mem. Biochem. Soc. (CIBA medal 1966), Am. Soc. Biol. Chemists (hon.), Am. Acad. (hon. fgn. mem.), Australian Acad. Sci. (corr.), Netherlands Acad. Sci. (fgn.), Nat. Acad. Scis. (fgn. assoc.). Contbr. articles on chemistry of penicillin, total synthesis of steroids and other biol. active natural products, chemistry of heterocyclic compounds, biosynthesis of steroids, enzyme chemistry to profl. jours. Home: Saxon Down, Cuilfail, Lewes BN7 2BE, England Office: U Sussex, Sch Molecular Scis, Falmer, Brighton BN1 9QJ, England

CORNIC, JEAN-CLAUDE LOUIS-JACQUES, ophthalmologic surgeon; b. Brest, France, Jan. 30, 1946; s. Raymond and Denise C.; m. Pascale Chassagne, Sept. 12, 1981; 1 child, Jean-Baptiste. MD, U. Paris, 1977; diplome medicine, Santé Tropicales, 1973. Intern Hopitaux de Paris, 1971-76; chef de clinique La Faculté de Paris, 1977-81; asst. Hopitaux de Paris, 1977-81; surgical course dir. Hotel Dieu, Paris, 1981—; practice medicine specializing in ophthalmological surgery Clinique Bizet, Paris, 1981—; surg. cons. Hotel Dieu Hosp., Paris, 1981—; internat. med. adv. bd. Project Orbis, 1980—. Author: Precis D'Ophtalmologie, 1984, New Microsurgical Concepts, 1987; contbr. 50 articles to sci. jours. Mem. Société D'Ophtalmologie de Paris, SociétéFrancaise D'Ophtalmologie, Assn. Francaise des Implants et de la Chirurgie Refractive. Roman Catholic. Office: Clinique Bizet, 23 Rue Georges Bizet, 75116 Paris France

CORNISH, EDWARD SEYMOUR, editor; b. N.Y.C., Aug. 31, 1927; s. George Anthony and Elizabeth Furniss (McLeod) C.; m. Sally Woodhull, Oct. 12, 1957; children: George Anthony, Jefferson Richard Woodhull, Blake McLeod. Diplome d'etudes, U. Paris, France, 1948; A.B., Harvard U., 1950. Copy boy, cub reporter Evening Star, Washington, 1950-51; staff corr. U.P. Assn., Richmond, Va., 1951-52, Raleigh, N.C., 1952-53, London, 1953-54, Paris, 1954-55, Rome, 1956; staff writer Nat. Geog. Soc., 1957-69; founder, pres. World Future Soc., Washington, 1966—; creator, editor The Futurist Mag., 1966—; editor World Future Soc. Bull., 1967—; cons. to govt., bus. and ednl. orgns. Author: The Study of the Future, 1977; editor: Resources Directory for America's Third Century, 1977, The Future: A Guide to Information Sources, 1977, 1999: The World of Tomorrow, 1978, Communications Tomorrow, 1982, Careers Tomorrow, 1983, Global Solutions, 1984, The Computerized Society, 1985; editorial cons.: Nat. Goals Research Staff, 1970, White House report Toward Balanced Growth, 1970. Bd. dirs. World Watch Inst., 1974—; adv. bd. Inst. for Alternative Futures. Mem. Internat. Sci. Writers Assn. Home: 5501 Lincoln St Bethesda MD 20817 Office: World Future Soc 4916 St Elmo Ave Washington DC 20814

CORNISH, GRAHAM PETER, librarian; b. Croydon, Eng., Nov. 22, 1942; s. Leslie William and Winifred (Thorne) C.; m. Jennifer Mary Stokes, Dec. 27, 1968; 1 child, Emma Mary. BA, St. Chad's U., Eng., 1967; DTh, NE Ord Coll., 1969. Sci. asst. Nat. Lending Library, Boston Spa, Eng., 1968-72; sci. officer, welfare officer, then higher sci. officer Brit. Library Lending Div., Boston Spa, 1972—; asst. to dir. office internat. lending Internat. Fedn. Library Assns., Boston Spa, 1985—; sec. Nat. Audiovisual Archives Forum, London, 1985—. Author: Religious Periodicals Directory, 1986 (named Academic Book of Yr. 1987), Audiovisual Archives, 1986; contbr. articles to profl. jours. Hon. parish priest, St. Luke's Anglican Parish, Harrogate, 1984—. Mem. Library Assn., Am. Theol. Library Assn. Mem. Ch. of Eng. Clubs: Civil Service, Union Jack (London). Home: 33 Mayfield Grove, Harrogate HG1 5HD, England Office: Brit Library, Boston Spa, Wetherby LS23 7BG, England

CORNISH, RICHARD JOSEPH, international affairs consultant, retired diplomat; b. Omaha, Nov. 7, 1925; s. Lebbeus Morrison and Lydia Christine (Herrmann) C.; m. Beverly Anne Cormier, July 28, 1958; children—Pamela Anne, Allyson Juillette, Carolyn Lydia. B.A., Yale U., 1949; M.A., Am. U., 1965; diploma U.S. Air War Coll., 1976. Commd. fgn. service officer Dept. State, 1959; 2d sec., vice consul U.S. Embassy, Rangoon, Burma, 1959-62; 2d sec., consul U.S. Embassy, Lome, Togo, 1964-66; regional dir. AID, Savannakhet and Vientiane, Laos, 1967-71; polit. adviser Dept. Def., Frankfurt, Germany, 1973-75; dir. mil. assistance Dept. Def., Addis Ababa, Ethiopia, 1975-77; 1st sec. for polit. and econs. affairs U.S. embassy, Yaounde, Cameroon, 1979-81; 1st sec., polit., U.S. Embassy, London, 1981-85; ret., 1985; cons. London Diplomatic Assn., 1985-87, The Parvus Co., 1985—, Trefoil Partnership, Ltd., London, 1987—; bd. dirs. Cornish Assocs., 1987—. Author: The Development of Nationalism in Burma, 1966, The National Decision Making Process, 1975, Deployment of Military Forces, 1975. Served to lt. col. USAFR, 1949-77. Mem. Diplomatic and Consular Officers Ret., Am. Fgn. Service Assn., Assn. Diplomatic Studies, Assn. Asian Studies, Royal Commonwealth Soc., Kipling Soc. Clubs: Chevy Chase (Md.); Travellers, RAF (London); University (Washington); Yale (N.Y.C.). Lodges: Rotary (bd. dirs. 1976-77), Masons. Home: 25 Pireos St, GR-166 73, Voula, Athens Greece

CORNYN, JOHN EUGENE, accounting company executive; b. San Francisco, Apr. 30, 1906; s. John Eugene and Sara Agnes (Larkin) C.; B.S., St. Mary's Coll., 1934; M.B.A., U. Chgo., 1936; m. Virginia R. Shannahan, Sept. 10, 1938 (dec. May 1964); children—Virginia R., Kathleen R. Cornyn Arnold, John Eugene, Madeleine A. Cornyn Shanley, Carolyn G. Cornyn Clemons; m. 2d, Marian C. Fairfield, Aug. 21, 1965. Partner, John E. Cornyn & Co., C.P.A.s, Winnetka, Ill., 1951-73; pres. John E. Cornyn & Co. Ltd., 1973—. Exec. sec. North Shore Property Owners Assn., 1953—. C.P.A., Ill. Mem. Am. Inst. C.P.A.s, Ill. Soc. C.P.A.s, Am. Acctg. Assn., Am. Tax Assn., Fellowship Cath. Scholars. Catholic (Byzantine Rite). Home: 126 Bertling Ln Winnetka IL 60093-4299

CORONA, PETER, superintendent of schools; b. San Diego, Dec. 22, 1928; s. Joseph and Mary (Piranio) C.; A.B., U. Calif., Berkeley, 1953; M.A., San Francisco State U., 1957; postgrad. U. Calif., Berkeley, 1957-62, U. So. Calif., 1980; Ph.D., U.S. Internat. U., San Diego, 1969; m. Yolanda Della Zoppa, June 20, 1954; children—Joel David, Marvee Anne. Asst. varsity baseball coach U. Calif., Berkeley, 1952-53; tchr. Byron Schs., Calif., 1953-55, Walnut Creek Schs., 1955-59, adminstr., sch. prin., coordinator, 1960; supt. schs., Sunol, Calif., 1960-70, Benicia, Calif., 1970-73, Montebello, Calif., 1974-77, San Jose, Calif., 1977-78, Bellflower, Calif., 1978-79, Castaic, Calif., 1979-82, Emeryville, Calif., 1982—; vis. prof. Calif. State U.-Long Beach, 1981-82. Mem. Western Assn. Schs. and Colls. Evaluation Team for Accreditation of Secondary Schs., 1966—. Pres. Walnut Creek Parks and Recreation Commn.; pres. Amador-Livermore Valley Hist. Soc., 1965-66; mem. admissions and budget com. United Fund Solano and Napa Counties, U.S. Internat. U. Alumni Soc. (bd. dirs. 1987—, pres. 1988—); active Montebello-Iguala and Montebello-Ashiya sister city programs; bd. dirs. Lynnewood Found., cultural center Amador-Livermore Valley, Beverly Hosp., Montebello. Recipient citation City of Montebello, 1977; named Man of Yr., Emeryville, 1984. Mem. Am. Assn. Sch. Adminstrs. (chmn. nat. panels 1976-87), Calif. Assn. Sch. Adminstrs. (mem. instrn. com., resolution com., urban affairs com., polit. action com., equal edn. opportunity com.), Calif. Tchrs. Assn., Calif. Assn. Sch. Bus. Ofcls., Solano County Sch. Adminstrs. Assn. (pres. 1973-74), Alameda County Adminstrs. Assn., Montebello Sch. Adminstrs., Montebello C. of C. (dir.), Montebello Hist. Soc., Phi Delta Kappa. Clubs: Rotary (v.p. Pleasanton 1965-66, pres. 1966-67); Scottsdale Swim (Walnut Creek v.p. 1967), Commonwealth of Calif. Author: Role of the Superintendent as Perceived by Community Leaders and School Administrators, 1969. Toured schs. of U.S.S.R., Czechoslovakia, Poland, Denmark, Finland, Austria (sponsored by NEA and Am. Assn. Sch. Adminstrs.), 1966. Home: 98 Las Lomas Way Walnut Creek CA 94598 Office: 4727 San Pablo Ave Emeryville CA 94608

CORR, EDWIN GHARST, ambassador; b. Edmond, Okla., Aug. 6, 1934; s. E.L. and Rowena C.; m. Susanne Springer, Nov. 24, 1957; children: Michelle Ruth, Jennifer Jean, Phoebe Rowena. B.S., U. Okla., 1957, M.A., 1961; postgrad., U. Tex., 1968-69. Fgn. service officer Dept. State, Washington, 1961-62; assigned to Mex. 1962-66; Peace Corps dir. Cali, Colombia, 1966-68; Panama desk officer Dept. State, 1969-71; program officer Inter Am. Found., 1971; exec. asst. to ambassador Am. embassy, Bangkok, Thailand, 1972-75, counselor polit. affairs Am. embassy, Quito, Ecuador, 1976, dep. chief of mission, 1977-78; dep. asst. sec. internat. narcotics matters Dept. State, 1978-80; ambassador to Peru Dept. State, Lima, 1980-81; ambassador to Bolivia Dept. State, La Paz, 1981-85; ambassador to El Salvador San Salvador, 1985—. Author: The Political Process in Colombia, 1971. Served to capt. USMC, 1957-60. Mem. Am. Fgn. Service Assn. Home: 1617 Jenkins St Norman OK 73069 Office: US Ambassador to El Salvador care US Dept of State 2201 C St Washington DC 20520

CORREA, CHARLES M., architect; b. Hyderabad, India, Sept. 1, 1930; m. Monika Sequeira, 1961; 2 children. Grad. U. Mich., M.Arch., MIT. Pvt. practice architecture, 1958—; chief architect New Bombay, 1971-74; cons. Govt. of Karnataka, 1975-78; mem. Governing Council Nat. Inst. of Design, Ahmedabad, 1974-77; dir. Western Bd. Res. Bank of India, CIDCO, New Bombay, 1976—; chmn. Housing Urban Renewal and Ecology Bd. (BMRDA), 1975—; mem. Steering Com. Aga Khan award for Arch., 1977—; Padma Shri, Pres. of India, 1972. Works include: Mahatma Gandhi Meml. Mus., Sabarmati Ashram, Ahmedabad, Jeevan Bima twps., Kanchanjunga apts., Bombay, Tara group housing, Delhi, New India Centre, Delhi, Previ low-income housing, Peru, others. Fellow AIA (hon.). Mem. Indian Inst. Architects (R.I.B.A. Gold Medal 1984). Office: 9 Mathew Rd, Bombay 400004 India

CORREA DA COSTA, ZAZI ARANHA, Brazilian government official; b. Rio De Janeiro, Feb. 29, 1944; d. Sergio and Luiza Zilda (Aranha) Correa da C.; m. Carlos Eduardo Paes de Carvalho, Dec. 29, 1967 (div. 1979); children: Luiza, Anna, Pedro, Thereza. Student, Carleton U., Ottawa, Ont., Can., 1963-64; BA in Langs., Catholic U., Rio de Janeiro, 1965; Degree in Lit., U. Nancy, France, 1970. Cert. tchr. English and French. Asst. to dir. Nat. Book Inst. Ministry Edn., Brasilia, Brazil, 1974-75; coordinator internat. tech. cooperation Fin. Adminstrn. Sch., Brasilia, 1975-80; coordinator internat. affairs, cabinet chief spl. secretariat info. Nat. Security Council, Brasilia, 1980-85; cabinet chief Ministry Fin., Brasilia, 1985; coordinator internat. affairs Ministry Industry and Trade, Brasilia, 1985—; cons. for govt. relations and investment various cos., Brasilia, 1987—. editor, translator, supr. Ency. Delta Larousse, 1965. Named chevalier, Ordre des Palmes Academiques, Brasilia, 1980, ofcl. Order of Santos Dumont, Brasilia, 1985, Rio Branco, Brasilia, 1986. Home: SHIS QL 22-03-20, 71 600 Brasilia Brazil

CORREIA, JOSÉ BARATA, construction company executive; b. Tomar, Santarém, Portugal, Sept. 26, 1939; s. José Barata and Maria Ilda (Gameiro) C.; m. Maria Teresa Barata Correia, June 6, 1970; children: Inês, Rodrigo, Joana. MSCE, Inst. Superior Ténico, Lisbon, Portugal, 1964. Civil engr. Profabril, Lisbon, 1967-70; mgr. North dept. José Bento Pedroso, Lisbon, 1970-76, gen. mgr., 1976-78; tech. mgr. Latin Am. de Establecimientos de Estudyos y Construciones, Caracas, Venezuela, 1979-81; mgr. planning Edifer Sarl, Lisbon, 1981-83; prin., pres. G.B. Buccellato, Lisbon, 1984—; bd. dirs. Haus Habitação e Gestão B. Imobiliária, Lisbon, Urbiza Urbanização e G. Imobiliária, Lisbon; cons. Soc. de Destilação Lda., Tomar, 1985—, Co. Carris Ferro Lisboa SA, 1985—, Amadeu Gaudêncio SA, Lisbon, 1985—, Haus HabitaçãOo e G. Imobiliária, Lisbon, 1983-84. Served to lt. Portugese army, 1965-67. Mem. Coll. Engrs. Club: Sporting (Lisbon). Home: Rua Monte Olivete 39, 1200 Lisbon Portugal Office: GB Buccellato Construtores Lda, Empreendimento das Amoreiras, Torre 1-Piso 7, 1000 Lisbon Portugal

CORREIA-AFONSO, JOHN, priest, history institute executive; b. Goa, India, July 15, 1924; s. Francis and Luza (de Heredia) C.-A. BA, U. Bombay, 1943, MA, 1945, PhD, 1953; Licentiate in Sacred Theology (STL), Weston (Mass.) Coll., 1958. Ordained priest Roman Cath. Ch., 1957. Prof. history St. Xavier's Coll., Bombay, 1960-65, 75-84, prin., 1963-65, 80-84; dir. Heras Inst. Indian History and Culture, Bombay, 1960-67, 76—; sec.-gen. S.J., Rome, 1967-70, asst. to superior-gen., 1970-75; mem. Indian Hist. Records Commn., New Delhi. Author: Jesuit Letters and Indian History, 1955, The Soul of Modern India, 1960; editor: Letters from the Mughal Court, 1980. Fellow Royal Asiatic Soc., Portuguese Acad. History; mem. Assn. for Asian Studies. Home and Office: 5 Mahapalika Marg, Bombay 400 001, India

CORRELL, NOBLE OTTO, JR., thoracic surgeon; b. Robinson, Ill., July 16, 1920; s. Noble Otto and Margaret (Hull) C.; m. Violet Butler, June 25, 1944. BS, Ind. State U., 1942; MS, U. Ill., 1950, MD, 1950. Intern U.S. Naval Hosp., San Diego, 1951-52; surg. resident VA Hosp., Hines, Ill., 1953-54; thoracic resident and fellow Presbyn.-St. Lukes Hosp., Chgo., 1955-57; chief-of-surgery Community Meml. Gen. Hosp., LaGrange, Ill., 1962-64, Luth. Gen. Hosp., Park Ridge, Ill., 1965-67, pres. med. staff, 1970-72; assoc. clin. prof. U. Ill., 1973-75; dir. continuing med. edn. Cypress Community Hosp., Pompano Beach, Fla., 1975-78; chief surgery VA Med. Ctr., Salisbury, N.C., 1986—. Contbr. articles to profl. jours. Pres. Margaret H. Correll Meml. Research Found. Served as lt. USNR, 1942-46. Fellow Am. Coll. Chest Physicians; mem. Soc. Thoracic Surgeons, So. Thoracic Surg. Assn., Midwest Surg. Soc., Pvt. Drs. Am. Inc. (v.p. 1972-80, pres. 1980-81, pres. No. Ill. chpt. 1971-73), Am. Council Med. Staffs, Ill. Thoracic Surg. Soc. (founder, pres. 1970). Home: 659 SE Saint Lucie Blvd Stuart FL 34996 Office: VA Adminstrn Med Ctr 1601 Brenner Ave Salisbury NC 28144

CORRIGAN, PAUL JAMES, JR., health care administrator, management consultant; b. Cleve., Nov. 11, 1933; s. Paul James and Lucille (Ryan) C.; m. Dyann Robertson, Nov. 27, 1976; children by previous marriage: Michael Shaun, Patricia Colette. B.S., U. Nebr., 1962; M.H.A., Baylor U., 1969; J.D., Nashville Sch. Law, 1983. Entered USAF, 1952, advanced through grades to maj., 1972; adminstr. health services Med. Service Corps, Calif., Tex., Germany, 1952-72; hosp. adminstr. Western State Psychiat. Hosp., Bolivar, Tenn., 1972-76; asso. dir. Vanderbilt U. Hosp., Nashville, 1976-86; mem. faculty div. med. adminstrn. Vanderbilt U. Sch. Medicine, 1977-86; dir. Mid-south Med. Center Council; preceptor grad. program hosp. adminstrn. Med. Coll. Va. Decorated Meritorious Service medal.; recipient Service Testimonial Chief Chaplains USAF. Mem. Tenn. Hosp. Assn. (council on profl. practice and edn.), Assn. Mental Health Adminstrs., Am. Coll. Health Care Execs., Ret. Officers Assn., Assn. Mil. Surgeons U.S., VFW. Clubs: Masons (32 deg.), Shriners. Address: 806 Fountainhead Ct Brentwood TN 37027

CORRIGAN-MAGUIRE, MAIREAD, peace worker; b. Belfast, No. Ireland, Jan. 27, 1944; d. Andrew and Margaret C.; grad. Miss Gordon's Comml. Coll., 1967; LL.D. (hon.), Yale U., 1976; m. Jackie Maguire, Sept. 8, 1981; 1 child, John Francis; stepchildren—Mark, Joanne, Marie-Louise. Various secretarial positions in Belfast, 1959-76; co-founder Community of Peace People (No. Ireland Peace Movement), Belfast, 1976, chmn., 1980-81; now exec. mem. dir. Peace People Co. Ltd. Lay mem. Legion of Mary, Roman Catholic Ch., 1959—. Co-recipient Nobel prize for peace, 1976; recipient Carl von Ossietzky medal for courage, 1976. Address: care Peace People, 224 Lisburn Rd, Belfast BT9 6GE Northern Ireland *

CORRIPIO AHUMADA, ERNESTO CARDINAL, archbishop; b. Tampico, Mex., June 29, 1919. Ordained priest Roman Catholic Ch., 1942. Aux. bishop, Zapara, Mex. 1953; named bishop of Tampico, 1956, of Artequera, 1967, of Puebla de los Angeles, 1976; now archbishop of Mexico City, primate of Mex.; tchr. sem., Tampico, 1945-50. Address: Apartado Postal 24-433, Mexico City 06700, Mexico *

CORROTHERS, HELEN GLADYS, government criminal justice official; b. Montrose, Ark., Mar. 19, 1937; d. Thomas and Christene (Farley) Curl; m. Edward Corrothers, Dec. 17, 1968 (div. Sept. 1983); 1 child, Michael Edward. AA in Liberal Arts magna cum laude, Ark. Bapt. Coll., 1955; BS in Bus. Adminstrn. Mgmt., Roosevelt U., 1965; grad. officer leadership sch. WAC Sch., 1965; grad. Inst. Criminal Justice, Exec. Ctr. Continuing Edn., U. Chgo., 1973; postgrad. Calif. Coast U., 1981—. Enlisted U.S. Army, 1956, advanced through grades to capt., 1969; chief mil. personnel Hdqrs. and Hdqrs. Co., U.S. Army, Ft. Meyer, Va., 1965-67; dir. for housing Giessen Support Ctr., Fed. Republic Germany, 1967-69; resigned, 1969; social interviewer Ark. Dept. Corrections, Grady, 1970-71, supt. women's unit, Pine Bluff, 1971-83; chief commr. U.S. Parole Commn., Burlingame, Calif., 1983-85, U.S. Sentencing Commn., Washington, 1985—; instr. corrections U.Ark.-Pine Bluff, 1976-79; mem. bd. visitation Jefferson County Juvenile Ct., Pine Bluff, 1978-81; bd. dirs. Vols. in Cts., 1979-84, Vols. Am., 1985-88; mem. Am./Can. study team, Mexican penal system Am. Correctional Assn., Islas Marias, Mex., summer 1981; mem. Ark. Commn. on Crimes and Law Enforcement, 1975-78. Mem. Ark. Commn. on Status of Women, 1976-78; bd. dirs. Com. Against Spouse Abuse, 1982-84. Recipient Ark. Woman of Achievement award Ark. Press Women's Assn., 1980, Human Relations award Ark. Edn. Assn., 1980, Outstanding Woman of Achievement award Sta.-KATV-TV, Little Rock, 1981, Correctional Service award Vols. Am., 1984, William H. Hastie award Nat. Assn. Blacks in Criminal Justice, 1986. Mem. Am. Correctional Assn. (treas. 1980-86, v.p. 1986-88), U.S. Attorney Gen.'s Correctional Policy Study Team, 1987, N.Am. Assn. Wardens and Supts., Ark. Law Enforcement Assn., Nat. Assn. Female Execs., Nat. Council on Crime and Delinquency, Am. Soc. Criminology, Ark. Sheriff's Assn. (hon.), Delta Sigma Theta (local sec. 1976-79, local parliamentarian 1983-84). Baptist. Avocations: reading, music. Office: US Sentencing Commn 1331 Pennsylvania Ave NW Washington DC 20004

CORSELLO, LILY JOANN, minister, educator; b. Newark, Mar. 30, 1953; d. Joseph DiFalco and Antonietta (Gandolfo) C.; B.A., Fla. State U., 1974; M.Ed., Fla. Atlantic U., 1977. Media coordinator, sec. Church-by-the-Sea, Fort Lauderdale, Fla., 1968-71; student asst. Fla. State U., 1972-73; lang. arts tchr. Plantation (Fla.) High Sch., 1974-80; guidance counselor Boyd Anderson High Sch., Lauderdale Lakes, Fla., 1980-81, Lauderhill (Fla.) Middle Sch., 1981-83; guidance dir. B.F. James Adult Ctr., Hallandale, Fla., 1983-84; minister single adults Park Place Bapt. Ch., Houston, 1985-87; drama and communications tchr., coordinator John Robert Powers Sch. Modeling, 1978-80; mem. ops. com. Sta. WAFG, 1974-75. Writer, lectr. singles ministry and Christian Single mag. So. Baptist Conv., Nashville, 1979—. Mem. Nat. Council Tchrs. English, Am. Personnel and Guidance Assn., NEA, Nat. Educators Fellowship, Fla. Council Tchrs. English (lobbyist 1978), Fla. Adult Edn. Assn., Fla. Teaching Profession and Classroom Tchrs. Assn. (rep. 1975), Internat. Platform Assn., Lambda Iota Tau. Republican. Club: Ft. Lauderdale Pilot (Anchor coordinator Outreach com. 1982). Home and Office: 2801 Hamlett Ln Flower Mound TX 75028

CORSO, FRANK MITCHELL, lawyer; b. N.Y.C., July 28, 1928; s. Joseph and Jane (DeBenedetto) C.; m. Dorothy G. McVeety, Apr. 7, 1951; children: Frank, Elaine, Patricia, Dorothy. LL.B., St. John's U., 1952. Bar: N.Y. 1954, D.C. 1981, U.S. ct. mil. apls. 1954, U.S. Sup. Ct. 1960. Ptnr. Corso & Fertig, 1957-61, Corso & Petito, 1966-69, ptnr. Corso & Landa, Jericho, N.Y., 1971-73, Corso & Engelberg, 1973-82;sole practice, Westbury, N.Y., 1982—. Appointed bd. dirs. UN Devel. Corp. by former N.Y. Gov., N.Y. Mcpl. Bond Bank Agy.; trustee WLIW pub. TV channel. Served with U.S. Army 1951-53. Named Man of Yr., Am.-Italians of L.I., 1966. Mem. ABA, N.Y. State Bar Assn., Nassau Bar Assn., Assn. Trial Lawyers Am., Internat. Bar Assn., World Assn. Lawyers (founding mem.), Vatican Knight of Holy Sepulchre. Contbr. articles to legal jours.; TV commentator legal topics. Home: 5 Suncrest Dr Dix Hills NY 11746 Office: 999 Brush Hollow Rd Westbury NY 11590

CORSO, JOHN FIERMONTE, psychologist, consultant; b. Oswego, N.Y., Dec. 1, 1919; m. Josephine A. Solazzo, Feb. 8, 1943 (dec.); children—Gregory Michael, Douglas Jerome, Christine Ann. B.Ed., SUNY-Oswego, 1942; M.A., U. Iowa, 1948, Ph.D., 1950. Lic. psychologist, N.Y. Chief sound and vibration sect. psychology br. Army Med. Research Lab., Ft. Knox, Ky., 1950-51; chief human factors offfice Rome Air Devel. Ctr., Griffiss AFB, Rome, N.Y., 1951-52; prof., dir. human factors research program Pa. State U., 1952-62; prof., dir. dept. psychology St. Louis U., 1962-63; prof., chmn. dept. psychology SUNY-Cortland, 1963-80, Disting. prof., 1973-85, Disting. prof. emeritus, 1985—; staff psychologist U.S. Naval Tng. Device Ctr., Port Washington, N.Y., 1959; vis. research scientist SUNY Otolaryngol. Ctr., 1971—; vis. disting. prof. N.Mex. State U., 1982. Author: The Experimental Psychology of Sensory Behavior, 1967, Aging Sensory Systems and Perception, 1981; contbr. chpts. to books; editor Psychol. Scis., Jour. Gerontology, 1984-87. Served to capt. U.S. Army, 1942-46. Grantee NSF, 1955-58, Pa. State U., 1956-61, Nat. Inst. Neurol. Diseases and Blindness, 1960-63, SUNY, 1965-80; Nat. Inst. Child Health and Human Devel. fellow, 1969-70. Fellow Am. Psychol. Assn., AAAS, Human Factors Soc.; mem. Eastern Psychol. Assn., Acoustical Soc. Am., N.Y. Acad. Sci., Internat. Soc. Cybernetic Medicine, Internat. Soc. Audiology, Psychonomic Soc., Sigma Xi, Psi Chi. Roman Catholic. Office: Dept Psychology SUNY Cortland NY 13045

CORSON, THOMAS HAROLD, recreational vehicle manufacturing company executive; b. Elkhart, Ind., Oct. 15, 1927; s. Carl W. and Charlotte (Keyser) C.; m. Dorthy Claire Scheide, July 11, 1948; children: Benjamin Thomas, Claire Elaine. Student, Purdue U., 1945-46, Rennsselaer Poly. Inst., 1946-47, So. Meth. U., 1948-49. Chmn. bd. Coachmen Industries, Inc., Elkhart, Ind., 1965—; also chmn. bd. Coachmen Industries, Inc. (numerous subs. cons.); bd. dirs. First State Bank, Middlebury, Canton Drop Forge Co. (Ohio), Olofsson Corp., Lansing, Mich., R.C.R. Scientific Inc., Goshen, Ind.; chmn., sec. Greenfield Corp., Middlebury. Adv. council U. Notre Dame; Trustee Ball State U., Interlochen (Mich.) Arts Acad. and Nat. Music Camp. Served with USNR, 1945-47. Mem. Ind. Mfrs. Assn. (dir.), Elkhart C. of C. (past dir.). Methodist. Clubs: Masons, Shriners, Elcona (past dir.); Capitol Hill (Washington); Imperial Golf (Naples, Fla.). Home: PO Box 504 Middlebury IN 46540 Office: Coachmen Industries Inc 601 E Beardsley Ave Box 3300 Elkhart IN 46515

CORTES, FERNANDO DE LA PENA, surgeon, educator; b. Guadalajara, Jalisco, Mex., Dec. 6, 1920; s. Angle Maldonado Cortes and Rosa Hernandez De la Pena; m. Araceli Alcaraz Cardenas, Oct. 26, 1953; children: Fernando, Ricardo, Barbara. MD, U. Nacional Autonoma Mex., 1946. Intern Cooper Hosp., Camden, N.J., 1946-47; resident in pulmonary diseases Glen Dale (Md.) Tuberculosis Sanatorium, 1949-50; prof. chest diseases U. Autonoma, Guadalajara, 1951—; gen. practice medicine Guadalajara, 1953—; sub-chief med. officer Hosp. Regional Occidente, Zoquipan, Mex., 1951-56, chief med officer medicine and chest surgery, 1956-78; med. examiner, chief of staff Am. Consulate Gen., Guadalajara, 1952—; med. examiner Cerveceria Corona de Guadalajara, 1954-72, IBM, 1954-75; chief med. services film plant Kodak, Guadalajara, 1970—. Columnist: (sports) El Informador, 1952—. Recipient Disting. Citizen award Mayor of Guadalajara, 1964, Spl. Local Artist award President of Mex., 1964. Mem. Am. Trudeau Soc., Am. Coll. Chest Physicians, Mex. Soc. Chest Physicians, Pneumology Nat. Council (Cert.). Roman Catholic. Club: Mar-Caribe Country. Lodge: Rotary. Home: Asirios 484, Fraccionamiento Altamira, Zapopan Jalisco 45160, Mexico Office: 203 and 204 Diagnostic Clinic, Guadalajara Jalisco, Mexico

CORTES, WILLIAM PATRICK, telecommunications executive; b. Ellenville, N.Y., Apr. 23, 1955; s. Robert Paul and Joan Helen (Whitstock) C. AB, Stanford U., 1977; MBA, U. Wash., 1983, JD, 1984. Bar: Wash. 1984; CPA, Wash. Accts. payable mgr. Cen. Distbrs., Inc., Portland, Oreg., 1977-78; fin. instr. Sch. Bus. Adminstrn. U. Wash., Seattle, 1980-83; strategic planning analyst Burlington No., Inc., Seattle, 1982, 83; sr. cons. Ernst & Whinney Telecommunications Group, Tacoma, 1985-86; fin. mgr. spec. projects U S West NewVector Group Inc., Bellevue, Wash., 1986—. Treas. Erxleben for State Rep. Campaign, Bellevue, 1982. Mem. ABA, Wash. State Bar Assn., Fed. Communications Bar Assn., Wash. Soc. CPA's, Am. Inst. CPA's, U. Wash. Grad. Sch. Bus. Adminstrn. Alumni Assn. (bd. dirs. 1985-87). Democrat. Roman Catholic. Office: US West NewVector Group Inc 3350 161st Ave SE Bellevue WA 98008

CORTESE DE BOSIS, ALESSANDRO, diplomat; b. Rome, Apr. 23, 1926; s. Giannantonio and Caris (de Bosis) Cortese; m. Marina Boesch: children: Alessandra, Raffaella, Adriana. Law Doctorate, Rome, 1968. 2d sec. OEEC, Paris, 1956-60; sec. Ministry Fgn. Affairs, Rome, 1960-62, Italian Embassy, Moscow, 1962-66; counselor Italian Embassy, Washington, 1966-69; vice diplomatic adviser to Pres. of Italy Rome, 1969-76; consul gen. of Italy N.Y.C., 1976-82; ambassador to Hungary 1982-83; ambassador to Denmark Copenhagen, 1983—; dir. gen. cultural relations Ministry of Fgn. Affairs, Rome. Author essay European Unity (1st Place), 1952. Served to 2d lt. Italian Army, 1944-45. Decorated War Merit Cross. Mem. Scuola d'Italia in N.Y. (hon. chmn. bd. trustees), Dante Alighieri (hon. counselor). Office: Embassy of Italy, 2, Fredericiagade, Copenhagen Denmark

CORTES-LOBATO, ANTONIO ANSELMO, sales executive; b. La Coruna, Spain, Mar. 24, 1956; s. Antonio Ctenfuegos Cortes and Concepcion Alonso Lobato; m. Olga Fuertes Lacasta, Sept. 8, 1958; 1 child, Antonio Leon. BS in Econ., London Sch. Econs., U.K., 1977. Field rep. Pepsi-Cola Co., Valencia, Spain, 1978-80, field mgr., 1981; asst. mktg. mgr. Pepsi-Cola Co., Rome, Italy, 1982-83, mktg. mgr., 1984; franchise dir. Pepsi-Cola Co., Rome, 1985; sales dir. Scheppes S.A., Madrid, Spain, 1986—; bd. dirs. Hullas Del Coto Cortes, S.A., Video A. S.A., Edificio Cortes. Com. mem. Pantenee Pompeiane, Naples, Italy, 1985, Residencia Padre Rubonos, Spain, 1986—. Mem. United World Coll. Com. Roman Catholic. Clubs: Dirigentes Mktg., De Golf, De Campo. Office: Schweppes SA, C Sor Angela De La Cruz 3, 28020 Madrid Spain

CORTEZ, JOSE ONESIMO, college administrator, vocational educator, consultant; b. Laredo, Tex., Jan. 20, 1942; s. Onesimo and Herminia (Obregon) C.; m. Bonnie Jean Frampton, Jan. 4, 1964 (div.); children—Sonya, Mathew, Carl. BA cum laude, Calif. State U., Long Beach, 1976, MA, 1980. Tool and die maker Huck Mfg. Co., Carson, Calif., 1971-76; indsl. engr. ITT Cannon Electric, Santa Ana, Calif., 1976-78; asst. prof. metals tech. Los Angeles Trade Tech. Coll., 1978-83, asst. dean, 1983—, instr. tool and die making, numerical control, 1978—; cons. in field; mem. com. on gen. edn. Community Coll. State Chancellor, Sacramento, 1982, mem. task force on acad. quality, 1983. Los Angeles Trade Tech. Coll. Pres.'s grantee, 1981. Mem. Computer Assisted Systems Assn., Soc. Mfg. Engrs., Am. Vocat. Assn., Phi Kappa Phi, Epsilon Pi Tau. Democrat. Roman Catholic. Office: Los Angeles Trade Tech Coll 400 W Washington Blvd Los Angeles CA 90015

CORWIN, JOYCE ELIZABETH STEDMAN, construction company executive; b. Chgo.; d. Cresswell Edward and Elizabeth Josephine (Kimbell) Stedman; student Fla. State U., U. Miami; m. William Corwin, May 1, 1965; children—Robert Edmund Newman, Jillanne Elizabeth Newman. Pres. Am. Properties, Inc., Miami, Fla., 1966-72; v.p. Stedman Constrn. Co., Miami, 1971—; owner Joy-Win Horses, Gray lady ARC, 1969-70; guidance worker Youth Hall, 1969-70; sponsor Para Med. Group of Coral Park High Sch., 1969-70. Hostess, Rep. presdl. campaign, 1968; aide Rep. Nat. Conv., 1972. Salzburg fellow, 1988. Mem. Dade County Med. Aux. (chmn. directory com. 1970), Fla. Psychiat. Soc. Aux., Vizcayans, Fla. Morgan Horse Assn., Fla. Thoroughbred Breeders Assn. Clubs: Coral Gables Junior Women's (chmn. casework com. 1959-63), Golden Hills Golf and Turf, Royal Palm Tennis, Heritage, Golden Hills Golf & Turf, Royal Dames of Ocala. Home: 5780 SW 59 Ave Miami FL 33143 Other: Windrift Farm Rt 1 Box 239 F Reddick FL 32686

CORY, PAUL RUSSELL, insurance company executive; b. Chgo., Oct. 8, 1926; s. Victor E. and Bernice C. (Tucker) C.; m. Carol Ann Schmitt, Apr. 3, 1976; children by previous marriage: Barbara Ellen, Susan Elizabeth, Tucker Paul. A.B., Wheaton Coll., 1949; postgrad., Northwestern U., 1949-50. Pres., dir. Currency Services, Inc. (predecessor Travelers Express Co.), 1955-64; organizer, chmn. bd., chief exec. officer N.J. Life Ins. Co., Saddle Brook, 1964—; owner, chmn. bd., chief exec. officer N.J. Life Co., Saddle Brook, 1969—; chmn. bd., chief exec. officer NJL Services Corp., Saddle Brook, 1970—, NJL Data Corp., Saddle Brook, 1973—; mem. Lloyds of London, 1984—. Trustee Upsala Coll., East Orange, N.J., 1985-87. Served with USAAF, 1944-45. Mem. Nat. Assn. Life Cos. (pres. 1978-79, bd. dirs. 1979-84). Presbyterian. Clubs: Union League (Chgo.); Upper Montclair Country (Clifton, N.J.); Arcola Country (Paramus, N.J.); West Lake Country (Augusta, Ga.). Home: 6 Denison Dr E Saddle River NJ 07458 Office: NJ Life Ins Co E 15 Midland Ave PO Box 981 Paramus NJ 07652

COSAR, AHMET, accountant, telecommunications company executive; b. Mersin, Turkey, May 17, 1952; s. Ibrahim and Fatma Cosar; m. Ayla Yilmaz, July 19, 1977; children: Bala, Irem. Student, Toros Coll., Mersin, 1970; BS in Fin., Acad. Econs. and Comml. Sci., Istanbul, Turkey, 1977; MS in Bus. Adminstrn., Faculty Adminstrn. in Bus. Adminstrn., Istanbul, 1980. Cost acct. Elmet A.S., Inc., Istanbul, 1975-77; mgr. acctg. Kurtkaya Holding, Inc., Istanbul, 1977-80; acctg. controller Hisar Fgn. Trade Co., Istanbul, 1980-82; asst. gen. mgr. Delta Fgn. Trade Co., Istanbul, 1981-83; fin. and acctg. dir. Teletas Telecommunications Co., Istanbul, 1983—. Mem. Turkish Assn. Acct. Experts. Moslem. Lodge: Lions. Office: Teletas Telecommunications, AS, Alemdag Caddesi, Istanbul Turkey

COSCAS, GABRIEL JOSUE, ophthalmologist, educator; b. Tunis, Mar. 1, 1931; s. Jules Joseph and Gilda (Guez) C.; M.D., U. Paris, 1963; m. Gisele Nataf, Mar. 23, 1957; children—Florence, Brigitte. Chief ophthalmology clinic Hotel Dieu, Paris, 1963-70; maitre conf. agrege Univ. Paris-Val de Marne, 1970-79, prof. ophthalmology, chmn. dept. Univ. Eye Clinic de Creteil, 1979—; founder Conf. Angiographic de Creteil, 1972—. Served as med. lt. French Army, 1958-60. Decorated chevalier de l'Ordre de Palmes Academiques, 1984, chevalier de l'Ordre Nat. de la Legion d'Honneur, 1985. Mem. Internat. Orgn. Against Trachoma (pres. 1977), French Soc. Photocoagulation (Pres. 1988). Author books, articles in field. Home: 203 Vaugirard, 75015 Paris France Office: 40 Ave Verdun, 94010 Creteil France

COSGRIFF, STUART WORCESTER, internist; b. Pittsfield, Mass., May 8, 1917; s. Thomas F. and Frances Deford (Worcester) C.; m. Mary Shaw, Jan. 23, 1943; children: Mary, Thomas, Stuart, Richard, Robert. B.A. cum laude, Holy Cross Coll., 1938; M.D., Columbia U., 1942, D.Med. Sci., 1948. Diplomate: Am. Bd. Internal Medicine. Intern Presbyterian Hosp., N.Y.C., 1942-43; asst. resident in medicine 1943, 46-47, chief resident, 1947-48; instr. in medicine Columbia U., N.Y.C., 1948-50, clin. asst. prof. medicine, 1951-63, clin. assoc. prof., 1963-73, clin. prof. medicine, 1973-83, clin. prof. emeritus, 1983—; attending physician Presbyn. Hosp., N.Y.C., 1948-83; cons. emeritus Presbyn. Hosp., 1984—; individual practice medicine, specializing in internal medicine and vascular diseases 1948—; cons. internal medicine Dir. Selective Service, N.Y.C., 1957-73; dir. thrombo-embolic clinic Vanderbilt Clinic, N.Y.C., 1948-83. Contbr. articles to med. jours. Served to capt. M.C., U.S. Army, 1943-45, ETO. Fellow ACP, Pan Am. Med. Assn.; mem. Am. Heart Assn., N.Y. Heart Assn., Alpha Omega Alpha. Roman Catholic. Club: Knickerbocker Country (Tenafly, N.J.). Home and Office: 11 Park St Tenafly NJ 07670 Office: 161 Ft Washington Ave New York NY 10032

COSINDAS, MARIE, photographer; b. Boston, 1925; studied at Modern Sch. Fashion Design, Boston; studied painting at Boston Mus. Sch.; attended photography workshops, under Ansel Adams, 1961, Minor White, 1963, 64; D.F.A. (hon.), Moore Coll. Art, 1967. Worked as illustrator and designer, 1945-60; free-lance photographer, Boston, 1960—; instr. Colo. Coll. Summer Photo Workshops, Colorado Springs, 1972-78; vis. lectr. in visual and environ. studies Harvard U., Cambridge, Mass., 1977-78; artist-in-residence Dartmouth Coll., Hanover, N.H., 1976; one-woman shows: U. N.H., Durham, 1962, Harvard U., 1963, Arlington St. Ch., Boston, 1973, Nat. Shawmut Bank, Boston, 1964, (3-woman show) Internat. Mus. Photography at George Eastman House, Rochester, N.Y., 1964, Mus. Fine Arts, Boston, 1966, Mus. Modern Art, N.Y.C., 1966, Phila. Coll. Art, 1966, Gropper Galleries, Cambridge, 1966, U. N.C., Chapel Hill, 1967, Art Inst. Chgo., 1967, 80, 10th Festival of Two Worlds, Spoleto, Italy, 1967, Currier Gallery Art, Manchester, N.H., 1968, (3-woman show) Moor Coll. of Art, Phila., 1968, Kenyon and Eckhardt, N.Y.C., 1968, Louisburg Coll., N.C., 1969, Bi-Nat. Cultural Inst., Mexico City and Monterrey, Mexico, 1969, U. Wis.-Madison, 1969, Brockton Art Ctr. (Mass.), 1969, U. Conn., Storrs, 1971, Dartmouth Coll., 1976, Inst. Contemporary Art, Boston, 1976, Amsterdam Art Ctr., 1977, Carpenter Ctr., Harvard U., 1977, Kunstlerhaus, Vienna, Austria, 1977; group shows include: Sheldon Meml. Art Gallery, U. Nebr., Lincoln, 1966, Nat. Gallery Can., Ottawa, Ont. and on tour Can. and U.S., 1967-73, Friends of Photography, Carmel, Calif., 1968, Boston Ctr. for Arts, 1972, Internat. Ctr. Photography, N.Y.C., 1975, Boston Atheneum, 1977, Mus. Fine Arts, Boston, 1977, Het Sterckshof Mus., Antwerp, Belgium, 1978, Mus. Modern Art, N.Y.C., and on tour U.S., 1978-80, Corcoran Gallery, Washington, and on tour U.S., 1979; represented in permanent collections: Mus. Modern Art, N.Y.C., Met. Mus. Art, N.Y.C., Visual Studies Workshop, Rochester, Internat. Mus. Photography, Rochester, Addison Gallery Am. Art, Andover, Mass., Polaroid Corp., Cambridge, Art Inst. Chgo., Exchange Nat. Bnk, Chgo., U. Nebr., Lincoln, Nat. Gallery Can., Photographer book: (text by Tom Wolfe) Marie Cosindas: Color Photographs, 1978. Recipient Artist-in-TV award WGBH/Rockefeller Found., Boston, 1967, Nat. Acad. TV Arts and Scis. award, 1976; Guggenheim fellow, 1967.

COSSIGA, FRANCESCO, president Republic of Italy; b. Sassari, Sardinia, July 26, 1928; married; 2 children. Prof. constl. law U. Sassari, 1959-74; provincial sec. Christian Democratic Party, 1956-58; Chamber of Deps. from dist. Cagliari, Nuoro and Sassari, 1958-83; undersec. def., 1966-70; minister without portfolio for bureaucratic reform, 1974-75; minister of interior, 1976-78; pres. Council of Ministers, 1979-80; mem. Italian Senate, 1983-85, pres. Senate, 1983-85; pres. Republic of Italy, 1985—. Nat. counsellor Christian Dem. Party, until 1958; chmn. commn. fgn. affairs, mem. commn. constl. affairs, rules and regulations com. Ho. of Parliament. Address: Consiglio Superiore Magistratura, Office of the President, I-00185 Rome Italy

COSSONS, NEIL, museum director; b. Nottingham, Eng., Jan. 15, 1939; s. Arthur and Evelyn Edith (Bettle) C.; m. Veronica Edwards; children: Nigel, Elisabeth, Malcolm. BA in Geography with honours, U. Liverpool, Eng., 1961; MA in Geography, U. Liverpool, 1968; D in Social Scis., U. Birmingham, Eng., 1979. Curator of technology Bristol (Eng.) City Mus., 1964-69; dep. dir. City of Liverpool Museums, 1969-71; dir. Ironbridge Gorge Mus. Trust, Shropshire, Eng., 1971-73, Nat. Maritime Mus., London, 1983-86, Nat. Mus. Sci. and Industry, London, 1986—. Author: Industrial Archaeology, 1975,Ironbridge--Landscape of Industry, 1977; editor: (5 vols.) Rees's Manufacturing Industry, 1975. Decorated Order of British Empire, 1982. Fellow Soc. Antiquaries, Museums Assn. (pres. 1981-82), Tourism Soc.; mem. Assn. Ind. Museums (chmn. bd. dirs. 1978-83, pres. 1983—). Club: Athenaeum (London). Home: Church Hill, Ironbridge TF8 7PW, England Office: Sci Mus, Exhibition Rd, London SW7 2DD, United Kingdom

COSSOTTO, FIORENZA, mezzo-soprano; b. Crescentino, Italy, 1935; m. Ivo Vinco. Student, Turin (Italy) Conservatory, La Scala Sch., Milan, Italy. Opera debut as Sister Mathilde in world premier of Dialogue of Carmelites, La Scala Opera, 1957; played first major role at La Scala as Leonora in world premier of La Favorita, 1962; Covent Garden debut as Neris in world premier of Medea, 1959; Am. debut as Leonora in La Favorita at Chgo. Lyric Opera, 1964; Met. Opera debut as Amneris in world premier of La Gioconda, 1968; Paris Opera debut as Adalgisa in world premier of Samson et Dalila, 1965, other appearances include, Vienna Staatsoper, Teatro Colon, Easter and Salzburg festivals, numerous opera cos., Europe, Mex., U.S.; also recital and concert artist. Office: care ICM Artists Ltd 40 W 57th St New York NY 10019 *

COSTA, EMANUELE, diplomat; b. Rome, May 17, 1931; s. Enrico and Alberta Costa; m. Lucilla Durante, May 6, 1970; 1 child, Manuela. BS in Econs., U. Rome, 1955. Vice consul San Francisco, 1960-62; 1st comm. councilman Rio de Janeiro, 1971, Brasilia, Brazil, 1973; head. dept. econs. Ministry Fgn. Affairs for Latin Am., Rome, 1974, head dept. energy, sci., tech. and space, 1975-78; consul gen. Madrid, 1978-81; Italian ambassador to Seoul, Republic of Korea, 1981-85, Helsinki, Finland, 1985—. Decorated grand officer Order of Merit Italian Republic, comdr. Order Isabela la Catolica Spain, comdr. Order Nat. Cruzeiro do Sul Brazil; recipient Grand Cross for merit Order Diplomatic Service Republic of Korea. Home: Via di Filiomarino 13, 00199 Rome Italy Office: Ministry for Fgn Affairs, Piazzale della Farnesina 1, 00194 Rome Italy

COSTA, JOAQUIM JOSÉ SOARES, publishing company manager; b. Vila Nova de Gaia, Portugal, Mar. 28, 1938; s. Joaquim and Maria Augusta (Soares) C.; m. Ruth Magalhães, Mar. 25, 1972 (div. 1976); m. Ana Maria Guimarães, July 23, 1982. Grad. in comml. adminstrn. expertise Escola Comml. e Indsl., Vila Nova de Gaia, 1955. Dept. chief Livraria Divulgação, Lisbon, Portugal, 1963-65; mgr. Portugalia Editora, Lisbon, 1966-70; gen. mgr. Edições 70, Lisbon, 1970—. Mem. Assn. Portuguesa de Editores e Liveiros. Home: Rua da Bempostinha, 21-5 Esq, 1100 Lisbon Portugal Office: Avenida Elias Garcia 81, 1000 Lisbon Portugal

COSTA, KEITH ANTHONY, health and science company executive; b. Corning, N.Y., July 2, 1937; arrived in Eng., 1978, came to U.S., 1986; s. Anthony Patrick and Winifred Jeanette (Williams) C.; m. Beverly Ann Shaughnessy, Apr. 9, 1960; children—Kimberly Rose, Stephanie Jeanette, Christopher Keith. A.B., Harvard U., 1959; postgrad. MIT, 1977. Plant mgr. Corning Med., Medfield, Mass., 1970-74, mgr. mfg. devel., 1972-74; gen. mgr. Microbiology, Roslyn, L.I., N.Y., 1974-75, Corvac and Microbiology, Corning, N.Y., 1975-78, Corning Med. Europe, Halstead, Eng., 1978-82; pres. Corning Med. and Sci., Europe/Asia, London, 1982-85; sr. v.p., gen. mgr. Europe and Asia Ciba Corning Diagnostics Corp., 1986—, pres. Ciba Corning Diagnostics Internat. Corp., 1986—; bd. dirs. Ciba Corning Diagnostics Ltd Eng., Ciba Corning Diagnostic KK, Tokyo, Optimetrics Ltd., Leeds, Eng.; chmn. MetPath Europe, Ltd. Served to capt. USMC, 1959-63. Republican. Episcopalian. Home: 4 Edgehill Rd Wellesley MA 02181 Office: Ciba Corning Diagnostics Corp 63 North St Medfield MA 02052

COSTA, NICHOLAS, manufacturing and services company executive; b. London, Nov. 19, 1932; s. Georgis and Doris Evelyn (Johnston) C.; m. Monica Watkins, May 5, 1953 (div. 1972); children: Guy Nicholas, Kent Laramie; m. Barbara Ann Farfan, Apr. 7, 1977; 1 child, Jason Luke. Student pub. schs., Leicester, Margate, Eng. Chief engr. Pepsi Cola Bottling Co., East African Terrs., 1956-63, Coca Cola Bottling Plant, Trinidad, West Indies, 1963-74; chief exec. Mecalfab Group Cos., Port of Spain, West Indies, 1974—; bd. dirs. Cocorite/St. James Credit Union, Port of Spain. Served with RAF, 1953-56. Decorated AGSM with bar, RAF. Mem. ASHRAE. Anglican. Clubs: Union, Country (Port of Spain). Office: Mecalfab House, 92 Queen St, Port of Spain Trinidad

COSTA E SILVA, MANUEL FERNANDO, film director; b. Lisbon, Portugal, Mar. 19, 1938; s. Manuel Barreto and Maria (Ernestina) C.; m. Gabrielle Ekstrand, Dec. 28, 1962 (div. 1965); 1 child, Jacques. Grad., Inst. de Hauts Etudes, 1962. dir. of photography various feature films, including Uma Abelha na Cuva, 1969O Mal Amado, 1972, A Santa Aliança, 1977, Nós Por Ça Todos Bem, 1977, Amor de Perdição, 1978, Crónica dos Bons Malandros, 1984, Saudades Para D. Genciana, 1984, Reporter X, 1985, Relação Fiel e Verdadeira, 1986, Roman Holliday, 1987; dir. prodn. TV series episode Madigan, 1972, Love Boat, 1985, for films Lionheart, 1986, Il Giovani Toscanini, 1987; film critic for Portugese Film Revs. mag., Swedish mag.; cameraman for election of Portugese Pres. Ramalho Eanes, 1984. Recipient awards for Best Dir. Casa de Imprensa, 1970, Best Photography, Nat. Film Festival, 1971, Fedn. Cine Clube, 1986, Best Film Festa Trabalho e Pão em Grijo da Parada, 1974. Mem. Conservary Nat. Lisbon, Film Technicians of Republic of Angola. Home and Office: Avenida Almirante Reis, 89F-80-Dto, 1100 Lisbon Portugal

COSTA-GAVRAS, KOSTANTINOS, director, writer; b. Athens, Greece, Feb. 13, 1933; naturalized French citizen; m. Michele Ray, Sept. 12, 1968; children: Alexandre, Helene, Romain. Student, Hautes Etudes Cinematographiques, Sorbonne, Paris, Sorbonne U. Diplomate, Inst. Higher Cinematic Studies. Ballet dancer Greece; asst. to film dirs. Yves Allegret, Jacques Demy, Rene Clair, Rene Clement, Jean Giorno; pres. Cinematheque francaise, 1982—, Chevalier of Arts and Letters, France. Dir., screenwriter films The Sleeping Car Murders, 1964, Z, 1969 (Acad. award for best fgn. lang. film, 1970, Golden Palm award Cannes 1969, Raoul-Levy prize 1969, Golden Globe award 1970), Missing, 1982 (Golden Palm award Cannes 1982, Acad. Award for best screenplay 1982); dir. films Un Homme de Trop, 1966 (Moscow Film Festival prize), L'Aveu (The Confession), 1970, State of Siege, 1973 (Louis Delluc prize 1973), Special Section, 1975 (Cannes Film Festival award 1975), Madame Rosa (also actor), 1978, Clair de Femme, 1979, Hanna K, 1983, Conseil de Femme, 1986, Family Business, 1986, Betrayed, 1988. Named Best Dir., Cannes Film Festival 1975. Office: care William Morris Agy 151 El Camino Blvd Beverly Hills CA 90212 *

COSTAGLIOLA, FRANCESCO, former government official; b. Cranston, R.I., Aug. 24, 1917; s. Luigi and Rose (Lubrano) C.; student U. R.I., 1935-37; B.S. in Elec. Engring., U.S. Naval Acad., 1941; postgrad. Naval Postgrad. Sch., 1946-47, MIT, 1947-49, Cath. U. Am., 1967-71; M.B.A., Am. U., Washington, 1974; m. Agnes Mary Ross, June 14, 1952; children: Francesca Gensler, Marisa Consoli, Antonia Burns, Rose Ann. Commd. ensign U.S. Navy, 1941, advanced through grades to capt., 1960; served in U.S.S. Phoenix in 24 ops. PTO, 1941-46; comdg. officer U.S.S. Halsey Powell, Korea, 1951-52; various positions naval sea and shore assignments involving atomic energy, 1952-64; mil. asst. to asst. to Sec. Def., 1964-67; ret., 1968; commr. AEC, 1968-69; engr. RCA, 1974-76; staff mem. Joint Congressional Com. on Atomic Energy, Washington, 1967-68, 69-71, 76-77; staff mem. Office of Sec. of Senate, Washington, 1977-86; mem. Md. Radiation Control Adv. Bd., 1973-81. Decorated Legion of Merit, Bronze Star with Combat V. Mem. Am. Nuclear Soc., Ops. Research Soc. Am., U.S. Naval Inst., Pearl Harbor Survivors Assn., Naval Acad. Alumni Assn., MIT Alumni Assn., Mil. Order World Wars. Roman Catholic. Club: Army and Navy (Washington). Contbr. articles to profl. jours. Home: 307 Gibbon St Alexandria VA 22314

COSTANDI, WAHIB ASSAAD, accountant, educator; b. Cairo, Jan. 16, 1939; came to U.S., 1966; s. Assad and Alice (Aristidis) C.; m. Mireille Rothstein, July 3, 1969. BSc in Chemistry, Am. U., Cairo, 1964; MBA, U. San Francisco, 1974; PhD in Fin., U. Santa Clara, 1981. Sr. fin. analyst Memorex, Santa Clara, Calif., 1970-74; mgr. cost acctg. Precision Monolithic, Santa Clara, 1974-75; mgr. ops. acctg. IVC, Sunnyvale, Calif., 1975-78; real estate developer, gen. ptnr. R&W Costandi & Co., 1979-85; v.p. fin. 3H Industries, Sunnyvale, 1980-84; assoc. prof. bus. adminstrn. San Jose (Calif.) State U., 1984—; gen. ptnr. CR Development, Ltd., 1985—; pres. Acton Realty, Inc. Mem. Am. Acctg. Assn., Am. Fin. Assn., Nat. Acctg. Assn. Home: 22999 Voss Ave Cupertino CA 95014 Office: 1503 Grant Rd Mountain View CA 94040

COSTANZO, CHRISTOPHER DAVID, foreign service officer; b. N.Y.C., Oct. 7, 1941; s. Joseph Bruno and Helen Sloan (Gordon) C.; A.B., Harvard U., 1962; m. Margaret Elaine Lutz, May 2, 1970; 1 dau., Catherine. Historian, Dept. of Navy, Washington, 1962; office mgr. Guardian Indsl. Products, Roslindale, Mass., 1963-64; reports officer Dept. State, Washington, 1966-69; commd. fgn. service officer Dept. of State, 1969; 2d sec. Am. Embassy, Madrid, 1969-73, Rome, 1973-76, sr. reports officer, Washington, 1976-80, 1st sec. Am. Embassy, Yaounde, United Republic Cameroon, 1981-84; 1st sec., U.S. consul Am. Embassy, Somalia, 1984-87; sr. analyst, Washington, 1987-88; assigned Am. Embassy, Lima, Peru, 1988—. Served with USMC, 1964-66. Mem. Am. Fgn. Service Assn. Unitarian-Universalist. Club: Army and Navy (Washington). Office: US Embassy Lima APO Miami FL 34031

COSTA SANSEVERINO, HILARY MARY, writer, consultant Islamic arts and archeology; b. Hindhead, Surrey, England, June 24, 1937; d. Henry Smith and Vida Mary (Evans) Lindsay; m. Julian Edwin Cook (div. 1966); children: Nicholas, Katherine; m. Luigi Costa Sanseverino; children: Luca, Tommaso. Grad., Croft House, Eng., 1954; student, U. Paris, Sorbonne, 1956. Dir. Ancient & Modern Antiques, Eng., 1960-65; freelance journalist, archeology cons. Eng., Italy, U.S.A., 1966—, Nat. Acad. Arts and Scis., Magadishu, Somalia, 1981-84; writer Islamic affairs 1984—; pioneer survey of so. Somali coast for archeol. remains., organizer series archeol. stamps depicting these sites; stamp cons. Inst. Poligrafico e zecco eello Stato, Rome, 1984—. Contbr. articles to archeol. jours., Trans-Siberian guidebook, others. Club: Univ. Women's (London). Home and Office: Ambassade d'Italia, 18 Rue Finalteri, El Biar, Algiers Algeria

COSTEA, NICOLAS VINCENT, physician, researcher; b. Bucharest, Romania, Nov. 10, 1927; came to U.S., 1957; s. Nicolas and Florica (Ioncescu) C.; m. Ileana Paunescu, Apr. 20, 1973. B.A., Nat. Coll. Bucharest, 1946; M.S., U. Paris, 1949, M.D., 1956. Intern St. Francis Hosp., N.Y.C., 1956-57; resident L.I. Jewish Hosp., 1957-59; fellow in hematology Tufts U., 1959-62; dir. clinic Pratt Clinic, Boston, 1962-63; clin. investigator Va. West Side Med. Ctr., Chgo., 1963-68; chief hematology U. Ill., Chgo., 1968-70; prof. medicine U. Ill., 1970-72; chief hematology-oncology UCLA-VA Hosp., Sepulveda, 1972—; prof. UCLA, 1972—; vis. prof. Nat. Acad. Scis., 1972. Contbr. numerous chpts., articles to profl. publs. Recipient Lederle award Lederle Industries, 1966. Mem. Am. Soc. Hematology, Am. Soc. Immunology, N.Y. Acad. Scis., Western Soc. Clin. Research. Home: 3651 Terrace View Encino CA 91436 Office: VA Med Center-UCLA Sepulveda CA 91343

COSTELLO, JOHN ROBERT, linguistics educator; b. N.Y.C., Sept. 12, 1942; s. John and Helen (May) C. BA, Wagner Coll., 1964; MA, NYU, 1966, PhD, 1968. Instr. NYU, 1967, asst. prof., 1968-72, assoc. prof., 1973-85, prof., 1986—, chmn. dept. linguistics, 1986—; cons. Universe Pubs., N.Y.C., 1979-81, Lexik House Pubs., Cold Spring, N.Y., 1980—, NYU Press, 1982, Geers Gross Advt., N.Y.C., 1985, Kenyon & Kenyon Law Offices, N.Y.C., 1988. Author: A Generative Grammar of Old Frisian, 1977, Syntactic Change and Syntactic Reconstruction, 1983; editor: Pole Poppenspaeler, 1970, Word, 1977—, Studies Presented to Robert A. Fowkes, 1980; assoc. editor: Lang. Scis., 1984—; contbr. articles to profl. jours. Research grantee NYU, 1978, NEH grantee, 1981. Mem. Am. Soc. of Geolinguistics, Internat. Linguistic Assn. (v.p. 1979-81, pres. 1981-82), Linguistic Assn. of Can. and U.S., Linguistic Soc. Am., Soc. for German-Am. Studies, Seminar for Germanic Philosophy, Phi Beta Kappa (pres. Beta chpt. 1984). Mem. Christian Ch. Office: New York Univ Dept of Linguistics 719 Broadway New York NY 10003

COSTIGAN, EDWARD JOHN, investment banker; b. St. Louis, Oct. 31, 1914; s. Edward J. and Elizabeth Keane; m. Sara Guth, Mar. 30, 1940; children—Sally, Ed Jr., James, Betsy, Robert, David, Louise. A.B., St. Louis U., 1935; M.B.A., Stanford U., 1937. Analyst, v.p. Whitaker & Co., St. Louis, 1937-43; ptnr. Edward D. Jones & Co., 1943-72; sr. v.p. Stifel Nicolaus & Co. Inc., St. Louis, 1972-74, pres., 1974-79, vice chmn., 1979-83, emeritus, 1983; gov. Nat. Assn. Securities Dealers, 1967-70, Investment Bankers Assn., 1968-69, Midwest Stock Exchange, Chgo., 1962-64. Trustee Calvary Cemetery Assn., St. Louis, 1956—. Republican. Roman Catholic. Clubs: Bellerive, Mo. Athletic, Noonday. Office: 500 N Broadway Saint Louis MO 63102

CÔTÉ, PIERRE, petrochemical and fiber manufacturing company executive; b. Quebec, Que., Can., ; s. Jules H. and Andrée (Fortier) C.; chmn., Celanese Can. Inc., Montreal, Que.; chmn. Can. Devel. Corp., Toronto; bd. dir. Can. Tire Corp., CAE Industries, Ltd., Consolidated Bathurst, Inc., Polysar, Inc., Savin Corp., Guarantee Co. of North Am., Hoechst Can., Inc., Bank of Montreal, Bombardier, Inc., Canron Inc., Mut. Life Assurance Co. Can.; past pres. Que. C. of C. Office: Celanese Can Inc, 800 Boul Dorchester O, Montreal, PQ Canada H3B 1X9 also: Can Devel Corp, 444 Yonge St, Toronto CA M5B2H4 *

COTLAR, MORTON, organizational scientist, educator; b. Phila., Feb. 19, 1928; s. Joseph and Henrietta B. (Klaits) C.; m. Gayle Epstein, Aug. 20, 1954; children: Geri Lynda, Gary Michael. B.S. in Mech. Engring., Drexel U., 1950, M.S. in Aero. Engring., 1955; Ph.D., U. Ga., 1969. Registered profl. engr. Chief engr. Sunshine Sci. Instruments, Phila., 1953-56; sr. mgmt. engr. Sperry Rand, Great Neck, N.Y., 1956-67; adj. prof. systems mgmt. Poly. Inst. N.Y., N.Y.C., 1964-67; asst. prof. mgmt. U. Ga., Athens, 1967-70; prof. mgmt. U. Hawaii, Honolulu, 1970—; L. J. Buchan Disting. prof. Colo. State U., 1977-78; vis. prof. Colo. State U., Fort Collins, 1974-75, 77-78, Boston U., 1981-82, U. Colo., Boulder, 1985; founder, exec. dir. Videodocumentary Clearinghouse; cons. comml. and instl. orgns.; lectr. mgmt. devel. programs. Author books jour. articles, monographs, films, videotapes in field. Mem. Acad. of Mgmt. (nat. officer 1975-76), Acad. Ind. Scholars, Mensa, Beta Gamma Sigma (Nat. Disting. Prof. award), Phi Delta Kappa, Pi Tau Sigma. Home: Suite 2201 Harbor Sq 700 Richards St Honolulu HI 96813-4631 also: 753 Sugarloaf Rd Boulder CO 80302-9639

COTRUBAS, ILEANA, opera singer, lyric soprano; b. Galati, Romania; d. Vasile C. and Maria C. m. Manfred Ramin, 1972. Student, Scoala speciala de Musica, Bucharest, Ciprian Porumbescu Conservatory, Bucharest, Musikakademie, Vienna, Austria. Debut as Yniold in Pelleas et Melisande, Bucharest Opera, 1964; appeared with Frankfurt (W. Ger.) Opera, 1968-71, Staatsoper, Vienna, 1970—, Covent Garden, London, 1971—, Staatsoper, Munich, W. Ger., 1973—, Lyric Opera Chgo., 1973-75, 83—, Opera Paris, 1974—, La Scala, Milan, Italy, 1975—, Met. Opera, N.Y.C., 1977—, San Francisco Opera, 1978; major roles include: Zerlina in Don Giovanni, Norina in Don Pasquale, Mimi in La Boheme, also Susanna, Pamina, Gilda, Violetta, Tatyana, Micaela, Manon, Antonia, Melisande. Recipient 1st prize Internat. Singing Competition, Hertogenbosch, Netherlands, 1965; 1st prize Munich Radio Competition, 1966; Kammersängerin Vienna Staatsoper, 1981. Address: care Royal Opera House, Covent Garden, London WC2, England *

COTTEN-HUSTON, ANNIE LAURA, psychologist, educator; b. Oxford, N.C., Nov. 18, 1923; d. Leonard F. and Laura Estelle (Spencer) Cotten; diploma Hardbarger Bus. Coll., 1944; A.B., Duke U., 1945; M.Ed., U. Hartford, 1965; Ph.D., Union Grad. Sch., 1979; children—Hollis W., Rebecca Ann, Laura Cotten. Asst. to pres. So. Meth. U., 1953; research asst. Duke U., 1947-49; exec. sec. Ohio Wesleyan U., 1955-56, Conn. Council Chs., 1958-60; adj. prof. U. Hartford, 1976-78; clin. pastoral counselor Hartford Hosp., 1962-65; asst., then asso. dir. social services Hartford Conf. Chs., 1965-67; teaching fellow U. N.C., 1970-71; adj. prof. U. Hartford, 1976-78; asst. prof. Central Conn. State Coll., New Britain, 1967—; cons. Somers Correctional Center (Conn.), 1980-81, instr./researcher, 1980-81; cons. Life Ins. Mktg. Research, 1981—; ambassador to China, spring, 1986; presenter 3d Internat. Interdisciplinary Cong. on Women, 1987. Mem. Am. Personnel and Guidance Assn., Am. Assn. Marriage and Family Therapists (cert.), Am. Psychol. Assn. (presenter conf. 1987), AAUW, Nat. Council Family Relations, Am. Assn. Sex Educators, Counselors and Therapists (cert.), Conn. Psychol. Assn., Conn. Council Chs. (dir.), Hartford Women's Network. Contbr. articles to profl. jours. Home: 193 Westland Ave West Hartford CT 06107 Office: Cen Conn State Coll Dept Psychology New Britain CT 06050

COTTER, MAUREEN HELEN, executive search company executive; b. Lawrence, Mass., Jan. 25, 1943; d. John Joseph and Helen Theresa (Kavanagh) C.; B.A. in Theatre Arts, Pasadena Playhouse, 1963; B.A., Calif. State Coll., 1970. Chaplain's asst. Pacific State Hosp., Pomona, Calif., 1967-68; correctional counselor Calif. State Penintentiary for Women, Frontera, 1969-70; mgr. Forum, Los Angeles, 1971-72; exec. recruiter V.I.P., Los Angeles, 1972-74; owner, pres. Actuarial Search Assocs., Los Angeles, 1974—. Mem. NOW, Nat. Assn. Female Execs., Am. Entrepreneurs Assn., Women in Bus. Los Angeles. Home: 910 S Curson Los Angeles CA 90036 Office: 910 S Curson Los Angeles CA 90036

COTTERILL, DAVID LEE, banker; b. Rochester, N.Y., May 7, 1937; s. Henry John and Ethel May (Townsend) C.; m. Joan Elizabeth Royer, July 1, 1961; children—Jonathan David, Susan Elizabeth. B.S. in Indsl. Psychology, Pa. State U., 1960. Trainee Mellon Nat. Bank & Trust Co., Pitts., 1961-64; pres. First Wachovia Student Fin. Services, Inc. (formerly Wachovia Services, Inc.) subs. Wachovia Corp., Winston-Salem, 1964-68, 70-72, 78—; dir. electronic data processing Wachovia Bank & Trust Co. N.A., Winston-Salem, 1968-70, sr. v.p. ops., 1972-79, exec. v.p., head adminstrn. div., 1979—; exec. v.p., head operational services div. First Wachovia Corp., 1985—; organizer N.C. Payments System, Inc., 1973-74, dir., chmn. systems-ops. subcom., 1975, chmn. bd., 1975-77; mem. ops. adv. com. 5th Fed. Res. Dist., 1978-82; chmn. bd. dirs. Video-Fin. Services, Inc.; mem. bd. advisors Bankers Mag.; instr. Sch. Banking of South, also profl. courses. Contbr. articles to profl. jours. Bd. dirs. Child Guidance Ctr. of Forsyth County, Inc., Forsyth Country Day Sch., 1979-82; mem. citizens adv. group Oncology Research Ctr. Served with USNR, 1954-62. Mem. Bank Adminstrn. Inst. (industry systems commn. 1974—, chmn. 1977-78, mem. exec. com. 1979-80, chmn. banking services steering com. 1979-80, dir.-at-large 1986—), Am. Bankers Assn. (exec. com. ops./automation div. 1981-83), N.C. Bankers Assn., Am. Nat. Standards Inst., Internat. Standards Orgn., Sigma Nu. Lodge: Rotary. Home: Box 595 Bermuda Run NC 27006 Office: First Wachovia Corp PO Box 3099 Winston-Salem NC 27150

COTTI, FLAVIO, federal agency administrator; b. Muralto, Ticino, Switzerland, Oct. 18, 1939. Student of law, U. Freiburg, Uechtland. Sole practice Locarno, Switzerland, 1965-75; mem. state legislature Ticino, 1965-75, head depts. Econony, Justice, Mil. and Interior, 1975-77, pres. of govt., 1977-81; nat. councillor (mem. of Swiss Ho. of Reps.) Bern, 1983-86, fed. councillor, 1986, head Dept. Interior, 1986—. Office: Dept of Interior, Bern Switzerland *

COTTLE, ROBERT DUQUEMIN, otolaryngologist; b. Montreal, Que., Can., May 10, 1935; s. Melvin Wheeler and Lilian Louise (Butt) C.; m. Mildred Isabel Cave, 1960 (div. 1968); children—Stephen, Michael, Sean, Scott; m. Suzanne Kern, 1969; 1 child, Melanie Catherine. B.A. magna cum laude, Loyola Coll., Montreal, 1956; M.D., C.M., McGill U., Montreal, 1960. Diplomate Am. Bd. Otolaryngology. Intern, then resident in gen. surgery Henry Ford Hosp., Detroit, 1960-62; research fellow in otology Columbia U., N.Y.C., 1964; asst., resident surgeon in otolaryngology/head and neck surgery Columbia-Presbyn. Med. Ctr., N.Y.C., 1965-67; practice medicine specializing infacial plastic surgery, head and neck surgery, otolaryngology, Stamford, Conn., 1967—; pres., med. dir. Stamford Hearing and Speech Ctr., Stamford; pres. SKC AIR, Inc., White Plains, N.Y., 1972—; chmn. bd. dirs., chief exec. officer Maple Leaf Petroleum, Dallas, 1982-85, ; chief div. otolaryngology/head and neck surgery St. Joseph Hosp., Stamford, 1979—; mem. staff Stamford Hosp. Bd. dirs. United Way Stamford, PSRO Conn., Fairfield Health Plan (bd. chmn. IPA 1986-87), Physicians Health Services Conn. Recipient Gov.-Gen. of Can. medal, 1956. Fellow Am. Acad. Cosmetic Syrgery, Am. Acad. Otolaryngology/Head and Neck Surgery, Am. Acad. Facial Plastic Surgery, ACS; mem. Am. Soc. Cosmetic Surgeons, Am. Coll. of Surgeons (sec. Conn. state council 1987—), N.Y. Acad. Scis., Fairfield County Med. Assn. (trustee 1986—, chmn. bd. trustees 1988—), Internat. Platform Assn., Stamford Med. Soc. (pres. 1978-79). Republican. Club: Landmark. Office: 22 Long Ridge Rd Stamford CT 06905

COTTRELL, MALCOLM, engineering designer; b. Liverpool, Lancashire, Eng., May 13, 1945; s. Herbert and Lili (Yeo) C.; m. Margaret Christine Treacy, Nov. 21, 1970; children: Michael Joseph, Sarah Louise. Cert. in plant engring., Carlett Park Tech. Coll., Eastham, Cheshire, Eng., 1968. Mech. designer Moon Bros. Ltd., Birkenhead, Eng., 1968-70; pres. Co-Tech Services, Birkenhead, 1970-75, 78-79; piping designer Lummus Corp., Toronto, Ont., 1975-76, Polysar Corp., Sarnia, Ont., 1976-78; plant designer Simon Carves Can. Ltd., Toronto, 1979-80; lead plant designer Bechtel Can. Ltd., Edmonton, Alta., 1980-81; prin. piping designer SNC Group, Inc., Edmonton, 1981-87; pres. Co-Tech Services, Edmonton, 1987—; lectr. No. Alberta Inst. Tech., Edmonton, 1981-83. Author tech. manual Piping Design, 1981. Mem. Young Conservative Party, Birkenhead, 1967-68. Mem. Am. Mgmt. Assn., Alberta Aviation Council, Can. Owners and Pilots Assn. Clubs: Edmonton Flying, Edmonton Road and Track. Home and Office: 11310-57 St, Edmonton, AB Canada T5W 3V2

COTTRELL, MARY-PATRICIA TROSS, banker; b. Seattle, Apr. 24, 1934; d. Alfred Carl and Alice-Grace (O'Neal) Tross; m. Richard Smith Cottrell, May 17, 1969. BBA, U. Wash., 1955. Systems service rep. IBM, Seattle, also Endicott, N.Y., 1955-58, customer edn. instr., Endicott, 1958-60, 62-65, edn. planning rep., San Jose, Calif. and Endicott, N.Y., 1960-62; cons. data processing, Stamford, Conn., 1965-66; asst. treas. Union Trust Co., Stamford, 1967-68, asst. v.p., 1969-76, v.p., 1976-78, v.p., head corp. services, 1978-83; v.p. corp. fin. services Citytrust, Bridgeport, Conn., 1983—. Bd. dirs. Family and Children's Aid of Greater Norwalk (Conn.), chmn. 1986-87, Gaylord Hosp., 1986—, Bridgeport Housing Services, New Eng. Network, Inc., Bank Mktg. Assn., 1988—; trustee New Money Inst., Washington. Mem. Electronic Funds Transfer Assn. (vice chmn., bd. dirs., chmn. bd. dirs. 1983-84), Fairfield County Bankers Assn. (dir., pres. 1984-85), West Norwalk Assn. (bd. dirs.). Republican. Roman Catholic. Club: Grad. Office: Citytrust 961 Main St Bridgeport CT 06601

COUËT, BENOIT, oil services company executive; b. Québec City, Can., Mar. 15, 1952; s. André and Fernande (Gaudreau) C.; m. Marie-Christine Zolcinski, July 18, 1980; children: Marie-Laure, Nathalie. BSc in Math., Laval U., Que., 1974; MS in Math., NYU, 1976; MSEE, Stanford U., 1979, PhD in Computational Physics, 1979. Research assoc. Stanford U., Calif., 1979-81; research scientist Schlumberger, Ridgefield, Conn., 1981-86; sr. research scientist Schlumberger, Cambridge, Eng., 1986—. Contbr. articles to profl. jours. Mem. Am. Phys. Soc., Soc. Indsl. and Applied Math., AIAA. Office: Schlumberger Cambridge, High Cross, Madingley Rd, Cambridge CB3 0El, England

COUFAL, FRANZ ANTON, sculptor; b. Eichgraben, Austria, Aug. 21, 1927; s. Franz and Maria Coufal; ed. Vienna Acad. Art, 1953-59; m. Martha Hartl, 1959. One-man show Galerie Fuchs, Vienna, 1961, Hand Drawings, Austrian Cultural Inst., 1961, Rome, 1963, Austrian State Printing Office, 1964, Galerie Zentrum 107, Innsbruck, Austria, 1969, Galerie Vallombreuse, Biarritz, 1970, Galerie der N.O. Landesregierung, Vienna, 1971, 76, Gallery Sur Terrain: Hand Drawings, 1972, Paintings, 1973, K. a. V. Danubia, Vienna, 1976, Z Kassenhalle, Hauptgebä ude, Vienna, 1978, Plastik, Grafik, Beethovenhaus, Baden, N.O., 1978; group shows include Vienna Acad. Art, 1955, 57, Galeria Wurthle, Vienna, 1957, 59, Young Generation, 1959, El Salvador, 1960, Paris, 1961, Brussels, 1964, Provincial Mus. Lower Austria, 1964, Regensburg, Germany, 1964, Passau, 1965, Kü nstlerhaus, Vienna, 1976, 80, Mostviertler Kunstmarkt, 1979; founder studio, Vienna, 1968; works include busts, numerous statues. Mem. Internat. Artists Club, Austrian Art Center, Kü nstlerhaus (Vienna). Author: Jorg Lampe, 1961; Walter Zettel, 1961; Rupert Feuchtmuller, 1963, 64, 75; Alfred Focke, 1964, 69; Otto Breicha, 1964; J.J. Muschik, 1966; Alois Vogel, 1968, 76; Alfred Sammer, 1976; Elisabeth Koller-Glü ck, 1976; Maria Buchsbaum, 1978; W. Schmidt, 1980, 82. Home: Weyringergasse 21, 11, Vienna IV Austria Studio: Karolinengasse 21, Vienna IV, Austria

COUGHLIN, CORNELIUS EDWARD, accounting company executive; b. Boston, Sept. 9, 1927; s. Cornelius Stephen and Mabel Josephine (McMahon) C.; BBA with honors, Northeastern U., 1956; student Bentley Coll., 1948-50; m. Rosemarie Toppi, Sept. 5, 1954; children: William, Brian, Stephen, Christopher, Maureen, Michael. Office mgr. Trim Alloys, Inc., Boston, 1952-57; controller Form-A-Lite Inc., Northbridge, Mass., 1957-59; sales adminstr. Reiss Assos., Inc., Lowell, Mass., 1959-61; ops. mgr. GPS Instrument Co., Newton, Mass., 1961-65. Computer Products, Newton, 1965-67; partner McShane & Coughlin, Milton, Mass., 1967-74; owner, mgr. C.E. Coughlin & Co., Acton, Mass., 1974-78; pres. Coughlin, Sheff & Assocs., Acton, 1979—. Mem. auditcom. Town of Acton. Served with USN, 1945-48, 50-51. Mem. Mass. Soc. CPAs, Mass. Assn. Public Accts. (2d v.p. 1978-87, 1st v.p. 1978—), Am. Inst. CPAs, Nat. Soc. Public Accts., Nat. Assn. Accts., Small Business Assn. N.E. Democrat. Roman Catholic. Lodge: Rotary. Home: 98 Summer St Acton MA 01720 Office: 289 Great Rd Acton MA 01720

COUGHRAN, TOM BRISTOL, banker; b. Visalia, Calif., Mar. 18, 1906; s. William L. and Rose (Bristol) C.; m. Florence Montgomery, Mar. 29, 1930; 1 child, Jane N. AB, Stanford U., 1927. With Bank of Am. Nat. Trust & Savs., 1927-57, v.p. internat. banking, 1946-57; v.p. Bank of Am. (Internat.), N.Y.C., 1950-59, exec. v.p., chief exec. officer, 1959-70, vice chmn., 1970-71; mem. export adv. com. Dept. Commerce, 1953-57; asst. sec. for internat. affairs U.S. Treasury, 1957-58; U.S. exec. dir. IBRD, 1957-58, Internat. Fin. Corp., 1957-58; dir. U.S. Devel. Loan Fund, 1958; dir. Capitol Industries, EMI; chmn. bd. Wobaco Holding Co., Luxembourg, and its 5 banking, trust and fin. cos. in Luxembourg, Bahamas, Jersey, London, Cayman, 1971-75. Mem. presdl. commns. to NATO, Latin Am. and Colombo Conf., 1957, 58; chmn. U.S.A. bus. and industry adv. com. OECD, 1966-68. Served as lt. col. AUS, 1942-46, ETO. Mem. Council Fgn. Relations. Clubs: Internat., F Street, Metropolitan (Washington); Pacific Union, Bohemian (San Francisco); Links (N.Y.C.). Home: Tannery House 601 Wilkes St Alexandria VA 22314

COULOMBE, GUY, electric company executive; b. Que., Can., June 15, 1936. B.A., Jesuit Coll., Que., 1957; B.Sc., U. Laval, 1959, M.A. in Sociology, 1961; doctoral studies in sociology of econ. devel., U. Chgo., 1963. Planner, researcher mgr. Eastern Que. Planning Bur., Que., Can., 1963, chief planner, chmn., 1963-66; mgr. rep. planning studies Que. Orientation Bd., Que., Can., 1966-67; chief exec. officer Eastern Que. Devel. Bd., Que., Can., 1968-70; asst. dep. minister planning and fin. Dept. of Supply and Services, Ottawa, Ont., Can., 1970-73; asst. sec. Treasury Bd., 1971-73, sec., 1973-75; gen. sec. Exec. Council, Govt. of Que., 1975-78; pres., chief exec. officer Soc. Gen. de Financement, 1978-81; pres., chief exec. officer Hydro-Que., Montreal, 1982-88, also dir; bd. dirs. Churchill Falls Corp., Ltd., Domtar Inc. Woodrow Wilson Found. Scholar U. Chgo. Office: Hydro-Que, 505 De Maisonneuve Blvd W, Montreal, PQ Canada H3A 3E4 *

COULSON-THOMAS, COLIN JOSEPH, corporate professional; b. Mullion, Cornwall, Eng., Apr. 26, 1949; s. Joseph Coulson and Elsie (Cannicott) Thomas; m. Margaret Ann Grantham, 1977; children: Yvette May, Vivien Jane. MS, London Bus. Sch., 1975; Diploma in Pub. Adminstrn., 1976; MS in Econs., London U., 1980; MA, U. So. Calif., 1982; M of Pub. Adminstrn., U. South Africa, 1986; PhD, Aston U., 1988. Cons. Coopers & Lybrand Assocs., London, 1975-77; research exec. Inst. Dirs., London, 1977-78; editor profl. adminstrn., head publs., pub. relations Inst. Chartered Secs. and Adminstrs., London, 1978-81; pub. dir. Longman Group, Harlow, Essex, Eng., 1981-84; mgr. corp. affairs Rank Xerox U.K., Uxbridge, Eng., 1984-87, dir. corp. affairs, European bus., 1987—; head exec. programs U. So. Calif., Los Angeles, 1987—; chmn., chief exec. officer Adaptation Ltd., London, 1987—; mem. council Parliamentary Info. Tech. Com., 1987—, Found. Sci. and Tech. U.K., 1987—; mem. Council for Professions Supplementary to Medicine, Nat. Biol. Standards Bd., Eng., 1985—; corp. affairs advisor Brit. Inst. Mgmt., 1987—; bd. dirs. Centre for Study of Professions, Aston U. Author: Marketing Communications, 1983, Public Relations in Your Business, 1981, Public Relations: A Practical Guide, 1979, A Guide to Business Schools, 1975, Company Administration Made Simple, 1975, The New Professionals, 1988. Bd. govs. Moorfields Eye Hosp., London, 1978-88; dep. chmn. London Electricity Consultative Council, Eng., 1978-85; councillor London Borough Greenwich, Eng., 1971-82. Internat. scholar Govt. of Brazil, 1975-76. Mem. Crosshencher Programme (chmn. 1977-81), The Bow Group (chmn. 1982-83), The Focus Group (pres. 1983-86), Soc. Co. and Comml. Accts. (pres. 1984-85), Royal Commonwealth Soc. (past cen. council, exec. com.). Conservative. Club: Carlton (London). Lodge: Knight of the Order of St. Lazarus of Jerusalem (chevalier, sec., gen. grand priory Eng. and Wales). Home: Rathgar House, 237 Baring Rd, Grove Park, London SE12 OBE, England Office: Brit Inst Mmgt, Africa House 64-78 Kingsway, London WC2B GBL, England

COULTER, BORDEN MCKEE, JR., management consultant; b. Casper, Wyo., Feb. 9, 1917; s. Borden McKee and Josephine Helen (Grother) C.; B.S., UCLA, 1939, M.B.A., 1947; m. Emily Sawtelle, Aug. 23, 1950; children—Borden, Terry Lynn, Leigh, Richard. Research analyst Australian Nat. R.R., 1939-40; indsl. engr. Lockheed Aircraft, 1940-47, staff indsl. engr., 1948-50; with div. indsl. engring. U.S. Steel Corp., 1947; mgr. prodn. control Bakewell Products, 1947; supr. orgn. and procedures Norris Industries, 1950-53; gen. mgr. Roed Engring. Assos., 1943—; prin., sr. v.p., dir. The Emerson Cons., Inc., mgmt. cons., N.Y.C., 1954—; chmn. bd. Omega Cons. Inc., Atlanta, 1980—. Mem. Am. Inst. Indsl. Engrs. (pres. Los Angeles), Am. Mgmt. Assn. (Wall of Honor), Am. Inst. Plant Engrs., Nat. Assn. Accountants Am., Newcomen Soc., U.S. Naval Inst., Navy League U.S., Internat. Mgmt. Consultants, Nat. Petroleum Refiners Assn., Am. Arbitration Assn., Nat., Tex. Socs. Profl. Engrs., Assn. Mng. Cons., Houston Soc. Cons. Engrs. Blue Key, Kappa Kappa Psi, Alpha Kappa Psi, Tau Kappa Alpha, Phi Gamma Delta. Club: Petroleum (Houston). Contbr. articles to profl. jours. Home: 12351 Escala Dr San Diego CA 92128

COULTON, MARTHA JEAN GLASSCOE (MRS. MARTIN J. COULTON), librarian; b. Dayton, Ohio, Dec. 11, 1927; d. Lafayette Pierre and Gertrude Blanche (Miller) Glasscoe; student Dayton Art Inst., 1946-47; m. Martin J. Coulton, Sept. 6, 1947; children—Perry Jean, Martin John. Dir., Milton (Ohio) Union Public Library, 1968—. Active, West Milton (Ohio) Cable TV Com. Named Outstanding Woman Jaycees, 1978-1979. Mem. ALA, Ohio Library Assn., Miami Valley Library Orgn. (sec. 1981, v.p. 1982, pres. 1983), Internat. Platform Assn., Puppeteers of Am., West Milton C. of C., DAR. Home: 1910 N Mowry Rd Pleasant Hill OH 45359 Office: 560 S Main St West Milton OH 45383

COUNIO, GILBERT ALBERT, physician, educator; b. Avignon, France, June 23, 1942; s. Sabetay Saby and Ines Edmee (Delmer) C.; m. Françoise Jacqueline Leclerc, July 10, 1965; children: Nicolas, Guillaume. Diplomas in Physics, Chemistry, Biology, U. Scis., Marseille, France, 1960; MD, Med. U., Marseille, France, 1967, Cert. in Pediatrics, 1973, Cert. in Allergology, 1975, Cert. in Sports Traumatology, 1987, Cert. in Chiropractic, 1988. Intern Frejus Hosp., France, 1966-67; gen. practice medicine St. Jeoire in Faucigny, France, 1967-68, Marseille, France, 1968—; teaching staff in pediatrics Conception Hosp., Marseille, France, 1968-78, teaching staff internal medicine Michel Levy Hosp., Marseille, France, 1979-85, Concepcion Hosp., Marseille, France, 1986—; cons. physician ice hockey team, Villard de Lans, France, 1980—, The Winning Club; cins. anti-tobacco campaign, Paris and Marseille, 1986. Author: Treatment of Fracture of Femoral Neck, 1967, All Terrain Bike Traumatology, 1987. Mem. Com. for Prevention of Smoking, Assn. of Sports Traumatology Physicians (pres. bd. dirs.). Office: Consulting Room 99, Bld Sakakini, 13005 Marseille France

COUNSELMAN, CLARENCE JAMES, agricultural research corporation administrator; b. West Palm Beach, Fla., July 4, 1925; s. Clifford and Victoria C.; m. Marion Helseth, July 9, 1949; children—Michael, Jenine Talantis, Lynn C. Garriott, Steven. B.S., Auburn U., 1952, M.S., 1953. Prodn. mgr. Big Springs Hatchery, Albertville, Ala., 1953-55; project leader State of Fla., Vero Beach, 1955-57; asst. mgr. Mobay (then Vero Beach Labs.), Vero Beach, 1957-63; mgr. CIBA-GEIGY Corp., Vero Beach, 1963—. Contbr. to profl. confs. Served with USN, 1942-46. Decorated Purple Heart. Mem. Am. Inst. Biol. Sci., Am. Phytopath. Soc., Am. Soc. Photogrammetry, Entomol. Soc. Am., Fla. Hort. Soc., Internat. Platform Assn., N.Y. Acad. Scis., Soc. Nematology, Phi Kappa Phi. Democrat. Patentee chlordimeform with organophosphate compounds. Office: PO Box 1090 Vero Beach FL 32961

COURCOULAS, J. H., electric company executive. BSEE, U. Toronto, Ont., Can., 1952, MM, 1955. With Westinghouse Can., Ltd., 1956—; with Westinghouse Electric Corp., Pitts., 1956—, mgr. mfg. system control div., 1971-73, mgr. mktg. industry system div. (then zone dir. Europe industry products mktg.), 1976-86, v.p. Europe, Africa and Middle East divs., 1986, pres. Europe, Africa and Middle East divs., 1986—. Office: Westinghouse Electric Corp Gateway Ctr Westinghouse Bldg Pittsburgh PA 15222 *

COURGEAU, DANIEL GUSTAVE, engineer; b. Antananarivo, Democratic Madagascar, Jan. 12, 1937; arrived in France, 1948; s. Daniel and Marie-Marcelline (Ravaomalala) C.; m. Hella Constant, Dec. 11, 1964; children: Christophe, Cyril. Engr., Paris Poly., 1956; D of Demography, Inst. Demography, Paris, 1969. Engr. Seita, Paris, 1959-66; sr. researcher Ined, Paris, 1966—; prof. Nat. Inst. Study Demographics, Paris, 1969—. Author: Les Champs Migratoires en France, 1970, Analyse Quantitative des Migrations Humaines, 1980, Three Centuries of Spatial Mobility in France, 1982. Served as lt. Algerian Army, 1958-59. Mem. Internat. Union for Sci. Study Population, European Assn. for Population Studies. Office: Nat Inst Study Demographics, 27 Rue Commandeur, 75 675 Paris France

COURSHON, ARTHUR HOWARD, lawyer, banker; b. Chgo., Feb. 21, 1921; s. Aaron H. and Beatrice (Pollak) C.; BA, U. Fla., 1942; JD, U. Miami, Coral Gables, Fla., 1947; m. Carol Biel, Feb. 20, 1943; children: Barbara Courshon Mills, Deanne. Admitted to Fla. bar, 1947; ptnr. firm Courshon & Courshon, Miami Beach, 1948—; organizer, chmn. bd. dirs. Washington Savs. and Loan Assn. Fla., Miami Beach, 1952-81; chmn. bd. Jefferson Bancorp., Inc., holding co. for Jefferson Nat. Bank, Jefferson Nat. Bank, Sunny Isles; cons. savs. and loan system in Chile, ICA, 1958—; cons. housing loans to Latin Am., 1960—, Devel. Loan Fund, Inter-Am. Devel. Bank, 1961—; cons. Govt. of Peru, 1960—; mem. U.S. Govt. task force Fed. Home Loan Bank Bd., 1961-62; mem. savs. and loan adv. council Fed. Home Loan Bank Bd., 1969; housing finance cons. Latin Am. Affairs Subcom., Senate Fgn. Relations Com., 1960-69, State of Israel, 1977-80; mem. housing and urban devel. adv. com. AID, 1965-68; pub. mem. Adminstrv. Conf. of U.S., 1968-72. Mem. Met. Dade County Urban Renewal Agy., 1963-67; bd. dirs. South Fla. Housing Found., Miami Heart Inst.; trustee Pub. Health Trust of Dade County; chmn. Democratic Nat. Fin. Council, 1983-84, nat. trustee John F. Kennedy Library Found. Served with USAAF, 1942-46. Recipient citation for establishment savs. and loan system in Chile, ICA, 1960. Mem. Dade County Bar Assn., Fla. Bar (banking liaison com.), U.S. Savs. and Loan Inst., Nat. Savs. and Loan League (pres. 1969, exec. com., legis. com.), Internat. Union Bldg. Socs. (devel. com., council), Nu Beta

Epsilon, Pi Lambda Phi. Democrat. Jewish. Home: 3 Grove Isle Drive Apt 1702 Miami FL 33133 Office: Jefferson Bancorp Inc Jefferson Nat Bank Bldg 301 41st St Miami Beach FL 33140

COURT, ARNOLD, climatologist; b. Seattle, June 20, 1914; s. Nathan Altshiller and Sophie (Ravitch) C.; m. Corinne H. Feibelman, May 27, 1941 (dec. Feb. 1984); children: David, Lois, Ellen. BA, U. Okla., 1934; post-grad., U. Wash., 1938, MS, 1949; PhD, U. Calif., Berkeley, 1956. Reporter and city editor Duncan (Okla.) Banner, 1935-38; observer, meteorologist U.S. Weather Bur., Albuquerque, Washington, Little Am., Los Angeles, 1938-43; chief meteorologist U.S. Antarctic Service, 1939-41; climatologist office Q.M. Gen. U.S. Army, Washington, 1946-51; research meteorologist U. Calif., Berkeley, 1951-56; meteorologist U.S. Forest Service, Berkeley, 1956-60; chief applied climatology, Cambridge Research Labs. USAF, Bedford, Mass., 1960-62; sr. scientist Lockheed-Calif. Co., Burbank, 1962-65; prof. climatology San Fernando Valley State Coll. (now Calif. State U.), Northridge, 1962-85, chmn. dept. geography, 1970-72, prof. emeritus, 1985—; part-time prof. Calif. State U., Northridge, 1985—, UCLA, 1987—. Editor: Eclectic Climatology, 1968; assoc. editor Jour. Climate and Applied Meteorology, 1978—; chmn. editorial bd. Jour. Weather Modification, 1978-86; contbr. articles and revs. to profl. jours. Served to 1st lt. USAAF, 1943-46. Recipient Spl. Congl. medal, 1944. Fellow AAAS, Am. Meteorol. Soc., Royal Meteorol. Soc.; mem. Am. Geophys. Union, Am. Statis. Assn., Assn. Am. Geographers, Assn. Pacific Coast Geographers (pres. 1978-79), Calif. Geog. Soc., Weather Modification Assn. (trustee 1973-76), Western Snow Conf., Sigma Xi, Phi Beta Kappa. Home: 17168 Septo St Northridge CA 91325 Office: Calif State U Dept Geography Northridge CA 91330

COURT, LEONARD, lawyer, educator; b. Ardmore, Okla., Jan. 11, 1947; s. Leonard and Margaret Janet (Harvey) C.; m. JoAnn Dilleshaw, Sept. 2, 1967; children—Chris, Todd, Brooke. B.A., Okla. State U., 1969; J.D., Harvard U., 1972. Bar: Okla. 1973, U.S. Dist. Ct. (we. dist.) Okla. 1973, U.S. Dist. Ct. (no. dist.) Okla., 1978, U.S. Dist. Ct. (ea. dist.) Okla. 1983, U.S. Ct. Appeals (10th cir.) 1980, U.S. Ct. Mil. Appeals 1973., Assoc. Crowe & Dunlevy, Oklahoma City, Okla., 1977-81, ptnr., 1981—; adj. prof. Okla. U. Law Sch., Norman, 1984-85, 1988—; planning com. Annual Inst. Labor Law, S.W. Legal Found., Dallas, 1984—. Contbg. author: (supplement book) The Developing Labor Law, 1978, Corporate Counsel's Annual, 1974. Chmn. bd. elders Meml. Christian Ch., Oklahoma City, 1980; cubmaster Last Frontier council Boy Scouts Am., 1984. Served to capt. USAF, 1973-77. Mem. Okla. State Univ. Bar Assn. (bd. dirs. 1980—), Oklahoma City C. of C. (mem. sports and recreation com. 1982-85, indsl. devel. com. 1986), Okla. State U. Alumni Assn., Harvard Law Sch. Assn., ABA (labor and employment law sect. com. on devel. of law under Nat. Labor Relations Act, com. on EEO law, subcom. on substantive devels involving sex under Title VII, and subcom. of EEOC process Title VII coverage and multiple forums, litigation sect./employment and labor relations law com.), Okla. Bar Assn. (labor and employment law sect. council 1978-83, 85—, chmn. 1986), Okla. County Bar Assn., Fed. Bar Assn., Defence Research Inst. Okla. Assn. Defense Counsel. Office: Crowe & Dunlevy 20 N Broadway Oklahoma City OK 73102

COURTEL, ROBERT JACQUES, engineer; b. Rennes, Brittany, France, July 4, 1933; s. Gervais Courtel and Fernande Tricot; m. Annie Fontauzard, July 13, 1963; children: Nicolas, Laurent. Degree in engring., Ecole Polytechnique, Paris, 1955, Ecole Nationale Pont et Chaussées, Paris, 1961. Engr. Tunzini, Paris, 1963-68, sales engr., 1963-64, br. mgr., 1965-68; dir., mng. dir. TNAB, Paris, 1968-70; mng. dir. AB 21, Aix en Provence, France, 1971-82, mgr., 1968-82; mng. dir., gen. mgr. AB21-Mediteranée, Aix en Provence, France, 1982—; gen. mgr. Epure, 1988—. Served to capt. French Army, 1955-63, Algeria. Home: Les Hameaux de la Torse B2, 13100 Aix en Provence France Office: AB21 Mediterranee, Le Mansard C Ave du 8 Mai, 13090 Aix en Provence France

COUSINS, BERNICE BRIGANDO, educator, consultant; b. Flushing, N.Y., Nov. 2, 1937; d. August and Olympia (Tortora) Brigando; BFA in Interior Design, Pratt Inst., 1955, postgrad. 1959; postgrad. City U. N.Y., 1966; children—David Bruce, Jason Bruce. Asst. to dir., tchr., Mus. Modern Art, Dept. Edn., N.Y.C., 1963-72; tchr. N.Y.C. Bd. Edn., 1966-73; with Am. Map Corp., N.Y.C., 1975-84, dir cartographic services, dir. mktg. services, also dir., 1979-81; co-dir. CW Assocs., Flushing, N.Y., 1982—; lectr. in field. Curriculum Adv. Com., Pub. Sch. 85Q, 1976-77. Mem. Nat. Assn. Female Execs., Assn. for Research and Enlightment, Women Bus. Owners N.Y., Am. Space Found., High Frontier Soc., Am. Fedn. Astrologers. Contbr. articles to profl. jours.; researcher, compiler, editor: Nutritive Value of Common Foods, 1978; researcher, editor: Art Work: Schick-Colorprint Anatomy Charts, 1976-84. Office: PO Box 310 Flushing NY 11352

COUSTEAU, JACQUES-YVES, marine explorer, film producer, writer; b. St. Andre-de-Cubzac, France, June 11, 1910; s. Daniel P. and Elizabeth (Duranthon) C.; m. Simone Melchior, July 11, 1937; children: Jean-Michel, Philippe (dec.). Bachelier, Stanislas Acad., Paris, 1927; midshipman, Brest Naval Acad., 1930; D.Sc., U. Calif., Berkeley, 1970, Brandeis U., 1970. Founder Groupe d'etudes et de recherches sous-marines, Toulon, France, 1946; founder, pres. Campagnes oceanographiques francaises, Marseille, 1950, Centre d'etudes marines avancees (formerly Office Francais de recherche sous marine), Marseille, 1952; leader Calypso Oceanographic Expdns.; dir. Oceanographic Mus., Monaco, 1957—; promoted Conshelf saturation dive program 1962; gen. sec. I.C.S.E.M., 1966. Recipient numerous awards, including: Motion Picture Acad. Arts and Scis. award (Oscar) for best documentary feature, The Silent World, also for The World Without Sun, 1965, for best short film The Golden Fish 1960, Grand Prix, Gold Palm, Festival Cannes for The Silent World 1956; author and producer documentary films which received awards at Paris, Cannes and Venice film festivals; producer over 70 films for TV; TV series include The World of Jacques-Yves Cousteau, 1966-68, The Undersea World of Jacques-Yves Cousteau, 1968-76, Oasis in Space, 1977, The Cousteau Odyssey Series, 1977-81, The Cousteau/Amazon Series, 1984—; TV spls. include The Tragedy of the Red Salmon, The Desert Whales, Lagoon of Lost Ships, The Dragons of Galapagos, Secrets of the Southern Caves, The Unsinkable Sea Otter, A Sound of Sea Dolphins, South to Fire and Ice, The Flight of Penguins, Beneath the Frozen World, Blizzard of Hope Bay, Life at the End of the World; author: Par 18 metres de fonds, 1946, La Plongee en scaphandre, 1950, The Silent World, 1952, (editor with James Dugan) Captain Cousteau's Underwater Treasury, 1959, (with James Dugan) The Living Sea, 1963, World Without Sun, 1965, (with Philippe Cousteau) The Shark: Splendid Savage of the Sea, 1970, (with Philippe Cousteau) Life and Death in a Coral Sea, 1971, Diving for Sunken Treasure, 1971, The Whale: Mighty Monarch of the Sea, 1972, Octopus and Squid, 1973, Three Adventures: Galapagos-Titicaca- the Blue Holes, 1973, The Ocean World of Jacques Cousteau, 1973, Diving Companions, 1974, Dolphins, 1975, Jacques Cousteau: The Ocean World, 1979, A Bill of Rights for Future Generations, 1980, The Cousteau Almanac of the Environment, 1981, Jacques Cousteau's Calypso, 1983, Jacques Cousteau's Amazon Journey, 1984; contbr. articles to Nat. Geographic Mag. Served as lt. de vaisseau French Navy, World War II. Decorated comdr. Legion of Honor, Croix de Guerre with palm, Merite Agricole, Merite Maritime, officier des Arts et des Lettres; Potts medal Franklin Inst., 1970; Gold medal Grand Prix d'oceanographie Albert I, 1971; Presdl. medal of Freedom, 1985; Founders award Internat. Council Nat. Acad. Arts and Scis., 1987; inducte into TV Hall of Fame, 1987. Fgn. asso. Nat. Acad. Scis. U.S.A. Office: Fondation Cousteau, 25 Avenue Wagram, F 75017 Paris France also: care Cousteau Soc Inc 425 E 52d St New York NY 10022 also: 930 W 21st St Norfolk VA 23517 also: 8440 Santa Monica Blvd Los Angeles CA 90069-4221

COUTAGNE, DENIS, museum curator; b. Ugines, Savoie, France, May 5, 1947; s. Jean and Gabrielle (Tournier) C.; m. Marie-Jeanne Wathier, June 30, 1950; children: Pauline, Eugenie, Gabriel. Student, Sorbonne U., Paris, 1970-74. Curator Aix-en-Provence, France, 1974-80. Prin. works include Cezanne ou la Peinture en jeu, 1982, la mosaique de Demaeter, 1987. Decorated Chevalier de L'Orde Des Arts et Des Lettres, 1988. Office: Musee Granet, Pl St Jean de Malte, 13100 Aix-en-Provence France

COUTARD, CHRISTIAN EDMOND, physician; b. Azay le Rideau, Indre et Loire, France, June 27, 1945; s. Fernand Coutard and Jeannine Léontine (Halopé) Chaussepied; m. Dominique Lechapelier, Oct. 12, 1974 (div. Oct. 1985); children: Florence, Anne-Céline. MD, U. Paris, 1977. Gen. practice medicine Montlouis sur Loire, Indre et Loire, France, 1977—; cons. gen. medicine Montlouis sur Loire, 1977—. Home: 2 allee des Ralluères, Montlouis sur Loire, 37270 Indre et Loire France Office: Med Ctr, 2 allee des Acacias, 37270 Montlouis sur Loire France

COUTINHO-LOPES, JORGE MANUEL, automobile manufacturing company executive; b. Torres Novas, Portugal, Sept. 10, 1944; s. Antonio Jose and Maria Eugenia (Coutinho) L.; m. Manuela Carneiro, May 20, 1972; 1 child, Sofia Carneiro. Degree in engring., Inst. Superior Tecnico, Lisbon, Portugal, 1971. Leader comml. studies Industrias Lusitanas Renault, Lisbon, 1972-74, mgr. cen. comml. service, 1974-75, succursal dir., 1976-79; nat. sales mgr. Renault Portuguesa, Lisbon, 1980-87; gen. mgr. SAME Tractors Portugal, Évora, 1987—. Served to lt. Portuguese Army, 1971-74. Mem. Nat. Engrs. Assn. Home: R Sarmento Beires, Lote 45-4 ESQ, 1900 Lisbon Portugal Office: SAME Tractors Portugal, Zona Industrial, 7000 Evora Portugal

COUTO, MIA, playwright, journalist; b. Beira, Sofala, Mozambique, July 5, 1955; s. Fernando and Maria Couto; m. Patricia Silva. Student, U. Eduardo Mondlane. Dir. A.I.M., Maputo, Mozambique, 1977-79; dir. news mag. Tempo, Maputo, 1979-81; dir. daily newspaper Noticias, Maputo, 1981-85; dir. weekly mag. Domingo, Maputo, 1981-85; dramatist, playwright Mutumbela Gogo Group, Maputo, 1986—. Author (poetry) Raiz de Oryalho, 1983, stories Vozes Anottecidas, 1986. Frelim O. Office: Noticias, Rua Joaquim Lapa, CP 327, Maputo Mozambique

COUTO, ROBERT, industrial company executive; b. New Bedford, Mass., June 30, 1946; s. Manuel P. and Mary G. Couto; diploma in indsl. tech. NE Inst. Tech., 1965; gemologists diploma Gemological Inst. Am., 1979; B.S. in Orgnl. Behavior, Leslie Coll., 1983. Quality assurance/electronic technician Instrument Devel. Labs., Attleboro, Mass., 1966-69; broadcast journalist WBSM Radio, New Bedford, 1969-71; spl. asst. U.S. Rep. Hastings Keith of Mass., Washington, 1971-73; mgr. gemologist Karten's Jeweler's Inc., Nashua, N.H., 1973-78; mgr. mktg. communications Ferrofluidics Corp., Nashua, 1978-81, dir. corp. communications, asst. treas., asst. clk., adminstrv. asst. to pres., 1982—; pres. Spiritual Renewal Services, Inc., Diocese of Manchester, N.H., 1987—; vol. Spiritual Renewal Services. Mem. Republican City Com., New Bedford, 1971-72; chmn. bd. advs. Nashua Vocat. Tech. Coll.; mem. spl. task force to study promotional needs State of N.H.; dir. media presdl. candidates in N.H. primaries; bd. dirs. Nashua Girls Club, Granite State Cerebral Palsy, Suburbanettes Drum and Bugle Corps, Friends of the Library, Whaling City Festival, Whalers Drum and Bugle Corps, Whaling City 125th Anniversary, Greater New Bedford Immunization Program. Recipient award for Leadership SAR, 1964; Best News Story of Year award UPI Tom Phillips, 1970; cert. bus. communicator. Mem. Bus./Profl. Advt. Assn. (bd. dirs.), Am. Film Inst., Am. Tech. Edn. Assn., Nat. Acad. TV Arts and Scis., Bus. and Industry Assn. of N.H. (legis. affairs com.), Assn. for Bus. Communication, C. of C. (2 accreditation staff coms. So. N.H. Assn. Commerce and Industry), Nat. Investor Relations Inst., Securities Industry Assn. Contbr. articles to profl. jours. Home: 5 Little John Ct Merrimack NH 03054 Office: Ferrofluidics Corp 40 Simon St Nashua NH 03061

COUTURIER, RONALD LEE, services company executive, consultant; b. Toledo, Ohio, Mar. 18, 1949; s. James Carl and Caroline Betty (Chiles) C.; m. Rebecca Lohnas; children: Scott James, Aimee Colette, Renee Leigh. BBA cum laude, U. Toledo, 1972; MBA, U. N.H., 1981; postgrad., U. Toledo. Intern, Owens-Ill., Inc., Toledo, 1969-71, planning analyst, 1969-72; mgr. mgmt. info. systems div. McCord Corp., Cedar Rapids, Iowa, 1972-75; mgr. group mgmt. info. systems Carborundum Co. subs. Standard Oil of Ohio, Niagara Falls, N.Y., 1975-80; dir. mgmt. info. systems Kennecott Engineered Systems subs. Standard Oil of Ohio, Niagara Falls, 1980-82; dir. worldwide computer tech. Pfaudler div. Standard Oil of Ohio, Rochester, N.Y., 1982-86; v.p. New Tech. div. Meszaros Assocs., Inc., Buffalo, 1986-87; founder, pres. Amsys Inc., 1988—; bd. dirs. FP Techs., Ltd., Advanced Computer Techs.; mem. adv. council Applied Data Research Princeton, N.J., 1984-86; cons. Rod Williams Assocs., Rochester, 1984—, Coca-Cola Consol., 1985-88, Cordis Corp., Contel Corp., Ga. Fed. Bank, Duke Power Co., Touro Infirmary, Upstate Milk Coops., Buffalo, Moog Inc., 1986-87, Buffalo, Guilford County, N.C., Parmed Pharmaceuticals, Inc., 1986-87, Niagara Falls, N.Y., Rochester Telephone Co., 1986-87, Hanes Corp., Agway Data Services, Syracuse, N.Y., 1986-88, Citibank, N.Y.C., 1988, GTE, Tampa, Fla., 1988, Winston-Salem, Inc., 1987-88, Cordis Corp., 1988—, Ga. Fed. Bank, 1988—, Duke Power Co., 1988—, Citibank, 1988. Contbg. author to various profl. jours. Mem. Rochester Philharm. Orch. Assn., 1984-86, Geva Theatre, Rochester, 1984-86; dist. exec. Standard Oil of Ohio Polit. Action Com., Washington, 1984-85; mem. Republican Nat. Com., Washington, 1981—. Mem. Assn. for Systems Mgmt. (cert.), Charlotte C. of C., Assn. for Data Processing Service Cos., Assn. for Inst. for Cert. of Computer Profls., ASME, Beta Gamma Sigma. Roman Catholic. Avocations: theatre, electronics; skiing; woodworking.

COVAULT, LLOYD R., JR., hospital administrator, psychiatrist; b. Troy, Ohio, Feb. 3, 1928; s. Lloyd R. and Anne Marie (Grisez) C.; m. Janet Eileen Davidson, June 12, 1951; children: Sheryl Ann, Jane Helen, Michael Lee, Roger Ken. B.A., Miami U., Oxford, Ohio, 1950; M.D., Ohio State U., 1954. Extern Orient (Ohio) State Inst., 1953-54, staff physician, 1954-57, clin. dir., until 1966, asst. supt., 1968-70; psychiat. trainee Cen. Ohio Psychiat. Hosp., Columbus, 1966-68, psychiatrist, 1982-85; supt. Columbus State Inst., 1970-74; med. dir. North Cen. Community Mental Health Ctr., Columbus, 1974-79, cons. psychiatry, 1985—; dir. S.E. Mental Health Ctr., Columbus, 1979-82, med. dir., 1985-86, psychiatrist, 1986—; med. dir. Madison County Mental Health Ctr., London, Ohio, 1984-85; pvt. practice psychiatry Columbus, 1968-75; mem. Franklin County Mental Health and Retardardation Bd., 1970-74, Ohio Dept. Mental Health, ret. 1983. Fellow Am. Assn. Mental Deficiency; mem. Am. Psychiat. Assn., Ohio Psychiat. Assn. (mem. council 1975), Neuropsychiat. Soc. Cen. Ohio (pres. 1973-74), Mental Health Supts. Assn. (pres. Ohio dept. 1973-74). Home: 11096 Darby Creek Rd Orient OH 43146 Office: Southeast Mental Health Center 1455 S 4th St Columbus OH 43207 also: North Cen Mental Health 1301 N High St Columbus OH 43201

COVELLO, VINCENT THOMAS, foundation adminstrator; b. N.Y.C., June 23, 1946; s. Alfonso and Lillian (Picciotti) C.; B.A. with honors, Cambridge U., 1971, M.A., 1973; Ph.D., Columbia U., 1976. Prof. sociology Brown U., Providence, 1974-77; study dir. Nat. Acad. Scis., Washington, 1977-79; program dir. NSF, Washington, 1979—; dir. NATO Advanced Study Inst., 1983; mem. U.S. bd. dirs. UN Man in the Biosphere, 1983—; dir. UN Conf. on Risk Analysis in Developing Countries, 1985; dir., NATO Advanced Research Inst., 1987—; visiting prof., Columbia U., 1987—. Author: The Japanese Art of Stone Appreciation, 1984, Biotechnology Risk Assessment; editor: Poverty and Public Policy, 1980; The Analysis of Actual and Perceived Risk, 1983; Low Probability/High Consequence Risk Analysis, 1984; Risk Analysis in the Private Sector, 1985, Risk Evaluation and Management, 1986, Uncertainty in Risk Assessment and Management, 1986, The Social and Cultural Construction of Risk, 1987, Benefits Assessment, 1985; contbr. articles to profl. jours. Peace Corps vol., 1968-69; trustee, Japan-Am. Soc., 1982-84. Woodrow Wilson fellow, 1971; recipient Superior Performance award U.S. Govt., 1981, Quality of Service award, 1983, Outstanding Performance award Govt. of U.S., 1986. Mem. Soc. Risk Analysis (exec. com. 1981-84, pres.-elect 1986, pres., 1987, Disting. Service award 1986), Am. Sociol. Assn., Am. Soc. Pub. Adminstrn. Home: 39 Claremont Ave Apt 71 New York NY 10027 Office: NSF 1800 G St NW Washington DC 20550

COVI, LINO, psychiatrist; b. Trento, Italy, Mar. 19, 1926; came to U.S., 1956, naturalized, 1965; s. Giuseppe and Giuseppina (Mariotti) C.; student in philosophy U. Florence (Italy), 1945-47, Sch. Social Work Trento and Rome, 1949-51; M.D., U. Rome, 1955; m. Beverly A. Yeutsy, Dec. 30, 1958; children—Lisa Martina, Michelle Peppina, Gina Albina, Tina Maria. Asst., U. Rome Neuropsychiat. Clinic, 1955-56; intern Albert Einstein Med. Center, Phila., 1956-57; resident fellow psychiatry Johns Hopkins Hosp., 1957-60, dir. outpatient clin. research unit, 1968-83, dir. treatment assessment research unit, 1983—, dir. Cognitive Therapy Clinic, 1982—; assoc. clin. prof. U. Md. Med. Sch., Balt., 1986—; instr. psychiatry Johns Hopkins U., 1960-67, asst. prof., 1967-72, assoc. prof., 1972—; vis. psychiatrist Balt. City Hosp., 1960-80; vis. scientist Nat. Inst. Drug Abuse-Addiction Research Ctr., Balt. 1988—; psychiatrist Francis Scott Key Med. Ctr., Balt., 1988—; staff psychiatrist Patuxent Instn., Jessup, Md., 1960-62; chief out-patient-dept. Gundry Hosp., Balt., 1962-86, pres. bd. dirs., 1972-84, research dir., 1973-86; mem. bd. govts. Central Md. Health Systems Agy., 1978-83; research psychiatrist NIMH Collaborative Studies, 1962-64, co-prin. investigator, 1964-65, prin. investigator, 1965-83, prin. investigator clin. trials of new drugs for depression and anxiety, 1970—, studies of group cognitive therapy in depression, 1980—; profl. staff drug evaluation Council on Drugs, AMA, 1968-71; teaching assoc. Sheppard and E. Pratt Hosp., 1973-79; cons. Pharm. Research Labs., 1971—, Centro Psicologia Clinica, Milan, Italy, 1981—. Mem. human rights com. Coop. Studies Program, VA, 1981-84. Recipient Am. Psychiat. Assn. Newsletter award, 1977. Mem. Am. Assn. Psychoanalytic Physicians, Am. Coll. Neuropsychopharmacology (com. mem.), Md. Psychiat. Soc. (com. mem.), Am. Psychiat. Assn. (mem. nat. com., dep. rep. Md.), Am. Psychosomatic Soc., AAAS, World Fedn. Mental Health, Johns Hopkins Med. Soc., Am. Group Psychotherapy Assn., AMA, Assn. Advancement Behavior Therapy, Md. Med. Soc., Balt. Med. Soc. (mem. coms.) Collegium Internat. Neuropsychopharmacologicum, Italian-Am. Hist. Assn. Democrat. Roman Catholic. Editor: The Md. Psychiatrist, 1974-80, Today's Psychiatry , Md. Med. Jour., 1985—; contbr. articles to profl. jours. Home: 501 Columbia Ct Baltimore MD 21228 Office: 10 Church Ln Pikesville MD 21208-3760

COVINGTON, PATRICIA ANN, educator, university administrator, director, artist; b. Mount Vernon, Ill., June 21, 1946; d. Charles J. and Lois Ellen (Combs) C.; m. Burl Vance Beene, Aug. 10, 1968 (div. 1981). BA, U. N.Mex., 1968; MS in Ed., So. Ill. U., 1974, PhD, 1981. Lab dir. Anasazi Origins Project, Albuquerque, 1969; tchr. pub. schs., Albuquerque, 1969-70; teaching asst. So. Ill. U., Carbondale, 1971-74, prof. art, 1974-88, adminstr. in admissions, 1988—; dir. Artist of the Month for U.S. rep. Paul Simon, Washington, 1974-81; vis. curator Mitchell Mus., Mount Vernon, Ill., 1977-83, judge Mitchell Mus., Dept. Conservation; panel mem. Ill. Arts Council, Chgo., 1982; faculty advisor European Bus. Seminar, London, 1983; edn. cons. Ill. Dept. Aging, Springfield, 1978-81, Apple Computer, Cupertino, Calif., 1982-83. Exhibited papercastings in nat. and internat. shows in Chgo., Fla., Calif. Tenn. N.Y. and others, 1974—; author: Diary of a Workshop, 1979, History of the School of Art at Southern Ill. Univ. at Carbondale, 1981. Bd. dirs. Humanities Council John A. Logan Coll., Carterville, Ill., 1982-88. Grantee Kresge Found., 1978, Nat. Endowment for the Arts, 1977, 81; named Outstanding Young Woman of Yr. for Ill., 1981. Fellow Ill. Ozarks Craft Guild (bd. dirs. 1976-83); mem. Ill. Higher Edn. Art Assn. (chmn. bd. dirs. 1978-88), Nat. Assn. Female Execs., NOW, Sphinx Hon., Phi Kappa Phi. Presbyterian. Home: 352 Lake Dr Rt 6 Murphysboro IL 62966 Office: So Ill U Admissions and Records Carbondale IL 62966

COVVEY, HARRY DOMINIC JOSEPH, health infosystems specialist, consultant, medical educator; b. Phila., Mar. 14, 1944; arrived in Can., 1968; s. Harry Joseph and Florence V. (Miller) C.; m. Carol L.P. Thompson, Mar., 1973; children: Laura, Beth, Mark. BA, U. Wis., 1967; MS, U. Toronto, Ont., Can., 1971. Jr. physicist Toronto Gen. Hosp., 1968-71; profl. asst. Toronto Gen. Hosp, U. Toronto, 1971-74; coordinator of computer application Univ. Hosp., London, Ont., 1973-77; sr. research fellow U. Toronto, Ontario Heart Found., 1974-83; pres. Clinicom Internat., Winnipeg, Man., Can., 1984—; lectr. psychiatry U. Western Ont., London, 1973-77, lectr. preventive medicine, asst. prof. computer sci. U. Toronto, 1979-84, computer sci., 1979-84; lectr. preventitive medicine U. Toronto, 1975-82, asst. prof., 1982-84, lectr. medicine, 1978-84, Sch. Grad. Studies, Toronto, 1981-84; asst. prof. medicine U. Man., 1986—. Author: Computers in the Practice of Medicine, 1980, Computer Consciousness, 1980, Computer Choices, 1981, Concepts and Issues in Health Care Computing, 1985; editor Healthcare Computing Strategies, 1988. Grantee Ont. Heart Found., Toronto, 1974-83, Natural Sci. Engring. and Research Council, 1980-84. Fellow Acad. of Medicine; mem. IEEE (sr.), Assn. for Computing Machinery, Can. Info. Processing Soc., Am. Assn. for Med. Systems and Informatics, Canadian Coll. Health Service Execs., Health Care Info. and Mgmt. Systems Soc., Can. Cardiovascular Soc. Home: 103 Handsart Blvd, Winnipeg, MB Canada R3P 0C4 Office: Clinicom Internat Inc, 208-93 Lombard Ave E, Winnipeg, MB Canada R3B 3B1

COWAN, HENRY JACOB, architectural engineer, educator; b. Glogow, Poland, Aug. 21, 1919; s. Arthur and Erna (Salisch) C.; B.S. with honors, U. Manchester, 1939, M.S., 1940; Ph.D., U. Sheffield (Eng.), 1952, D.Eng., 1963; M.Arch., U. Sydney, 1984; DArch (hon.), U. Sydney, 1987; m. Renate Proskauer, June 22, 1952; children—Judith Anne, Esther Katherine. Mem. faculty dept. archlt. sci. U. Sydney (Australia), 1953—, prof., 1953—, head dept., 1953-84, dean architecture, 1966-67, pro-dean, 1968-84; vis. prof. Cornell U., 1962, Kumasi (Ghana) U., 1973, Trabzon (Turkey) U., 1976; pres. Bldg. Sci. Forum of Australia, 1969-71. Served with Royal Engrs., 1941-45. Decorated officer Order of Australia. Fellow Royal Australian Inst. Architects (hon.), Royal Soc. Arts (corr. mem. council), Inst. Structural Engrs., Instn. Engrs. Australia (recipient R.W. Chapman medal 1956), ASCE. Author 21 books including: The Master Builders, Structural Systems; editor Archtl. Sci. Rev., 1958—, Vestes, 1966-78. Home: 6 Hale Rd Apt 57, Mosman New South Wales Australia 2088 Office: U Sydney, Sydney New South Wales 2006, Australia

COWAN, JOHN, structural engineering educator; b. Glasgow, Strathclyde, Scotland, Mar. 19, 1932; s. James Allan and Effie (Stark) C.; m. Audrey Walker Henderson, June 15, 1957; children: David, Peter, Janet, Sandy. BS with 1st class honors, U. Edinburgh, Scotland, 1952; MS, Heriot-Watt U., Edinburgh, 1967, PhD, 1975, DEng, 1988. Sr. design engr. Blyth & Blyth, Edinburgh, 1954-64; lectr. Heriot-Watt Coll., 1964-66; lectr. Heriot-Watt U., 1966-67, sr. lectr., 1967-77, reader, 1977-82, prof. engring. edn., 1982-87; dir. Open U. in Scotland, Edinburgh, 1987—. Fellow Inst. Structural Engrs. (exams advisor 1982—, Murray Buxton diploma 1977), Inst. Civil Engrs. Presbyterian. Home: 34 Caiystane Ave, Edinburgh EH10 6SH, Scotland Office: Open U in Scotland, 60 Melville St, Edinburgh EH3 7HF, Scotland

COWAN, STUART MARSHALL, lawyer; b. Irvington, N.J., Mar. 20, 1932; s. Bernard Howard and Blanche (Hertz) C.; m. Marilyn R.C. Toepfer, Apr., 1961 (div. 1969); m. Jane Alison Averill, Feb. 24, 1974; children—Catherine R.L., Erika R.L., Bronwen P. B.S. in Econ., U. Pa., 1952; LL.B., Rutgers U., 1955. Bar: N.J. 1957, Hawaii 1962, U.S. Supreme Ct., 1966. Atty., Greenstein & Cowan, Honolulu, 1961-70, Cowan & Frey, Honolulu, 1970—; arbitration Fed. Mediation & Conciliation Service, Honolulu, 1972—, Am. Arbitation Assn., Honolulu, 1978—, Hawaii Pub. Employees. Relation Bd., 1972—. Served to lt. USN, 1956-61. Mem. Hawaii Bar Assn., ABA, Am. Judicature Soc., Trial Lawyers Assn. of Am. (state committeeman for Hawaii 1965-69, bd. govs. 1972-75), Hawaii Trial Lawyers Assn. (v.p. 1972-78), Japan-Hawaii Lawyers Assn., Soc. Profls. in Dispute Resolution. Jewish. Clubs: Waikiki Yacht (Honolulu), San Francisco Comml., Hawaii Scottish Assn. (chieftain 1983-88), Caledonian Soc. (vice chieftain 1983-85), St. Francis Yacht, Honolulu Club, Honolulu Pipes and Drums (sec.-treas. 1985-88). Lodges: Masons, Pearl Harbor (master 1971), Composite. Home: 47-339 Mapumapu Rd Kaneohe HI 96744 Office: Cowan & Frey 1600 Grosvenor Ctr Towers 733 Bishop St Honolulu HI 96813

COWART, T(HOMAS) DAVID, lawyer; b. San Benito, Tex., June 12, 1953; s. Thomas W. Jr. and Glenda Claire (Miller) C.; m. Marquita Rea Stearman, May 28, 1983; children: Thomas Kevin, Lauren Michelle, Megan Leigh. BBA, U. Miss., 1975, JD, 1978; LLM in Taxation, NYU, 1979. Bar: Miss. 1978, Tex. 1979; CPA Tex., Miss. Assoc. Dossett, Magruder and Montgomery, Jackson, Miss., 1978; assoc. Strasburger and Price, Dallas, 1979-84, ptnr., 1985-87; ptnr., shareholder Johnson & Swanson P.C., Dallas, 1988—; lectr. Tex. Soc. CPA's, 1985—, Am. Soc. Pension Actuaries, 1983-84, Tex. Soc. CLU's, 1985, Dallas Bar Assn., 1985, Ali-ABA, 1986—, Am. Banking Assn. Nat. Grad. Trust Sch., 1988—; adj. prof. law So. Meth. U. Sch. Law, 1988—. Mem. adv. com. Goals for Dallas, 1984-85; deacon Ch. of Christ. Mem. ABA (sect. taxation, employee benefits com., fiduciary responsibility subcom.), Tex. Bar Assn. (sect. taxation, com. compensation and employee benefits, fed. legis., regulations and revenue rulings subcom. 1986-87, chmn. fiduciary standards of trustees subcom. 1987—), S.W. Pension Conf., Phi Delta Phi, Omicron Delta Kappa. Office: Johnson & Swanson 900 Jackson St Founders Sq Suite 300 Dallas TX 75202

COWEN, DONALD EUGENE, physician; b. Ft. Morgan, Colo., Oct. 8, 1918; adopted s. Franklin and Mary Edith (Dalton) C.; B.A., U. Denver, 1940; M.D., U. Colo., 1943; m. Hulda Marie Helling, Dec. 24, 1942; children—David L., Marilyn Marie Cowen Dean, Theresa Kathleen Cowen Cunningham, Margaret Ann. Intern, U.S. Naval Hosp., Oakland, Calif., 1944; gen. practice medicine, Ft. Morgan, 1947-52; resident internal medicine U. Colo. Med. Center, Denver, 1952-54; practice medicine specializing in allergy, Denver, 1954—; mem. staff Presbyn. Med. Center, Denver, Porter, Swedish hosps., Englewood, Colo.; clin. asst. prof. medicine U. Colo. Med. Center, 1964—; postgrad. faculty U. Tenn. Coll. Medicine, Memphis, 1962-82; cons. Queen of Thailand, 1973, 75, 77. Pres. Community Arts Symphony Found., 1980-82. Served to lt. M.C., USN, 1943-47. Fellow ACP, Am. Coll. Chest Physicians (vice chmn. com. on allergy 1968-72, 75-87, sec.-treas. Colo. chpt. 1971-77, pres. 1978-80), Am. Coll. Allergy and Immunology, Acad. Internat. Medicine, West Coast Allergy Soc., Southwest Allergy Forum, Am. Acad. Otolaryngic Allergy; mem. Am., Colo. socs. internal medicine, Am. Thoracic Soc., Colo. Allergy Soc. (past pres.), Ill. Soc. Opthalmology and Otolaryngology (hon.), Denver Med. Soc. (chmn. library and bldg. com. 1963-73), Arapahoe Med. Soc. (life emeritus mem.). Presbyterian (ruling elder 1956—). Club: Lions. Contbr. numerous articles to profl. jours. Home: 1501 E Quincy Ave Cherry Hills Village Englewood CO 80110 Office: 3510 S Marion St Englewood CO 80110

COWEN, ZELMAN, college provost; b. St. Kilda, Victoria, Australia, Oct. 7, 1919; s. Bernard and Sara (Granat) C.; ed. Scotch Coll., Melbourne, Australia; B.A., 1939, LL.B., 1941, LL.M., 1942, LL.D. (hon.), U. Melbourne, 1973; M.A., 1947, B.C.L., 1947, D.C.L., 1968, D.Litt. (hon.), 1983, Oxford (Eng.) U.; LL.D. (hon.), U. Hong Kong, 1967, U. Queensland, 1972, U. Western Australia, 1981, U. Turin (Italy), 1981; D.Litt. (hon.), U. New Eng., 1979, U. Sydney, 1980, James Cook U. of North Queensland, 1982; D.H.L. (hon.), Hebrew Union Coll., Cin., 1980; D.Univ., U. Newcastle, 1980, Griffith U., 1981; D.Phil. (hon.), Hebrew U. Jerusalem, 1982; LLD (hon.) Australian Nat. U., 1985; D.H.L. (hon.), U. Redlands, 1986; m. Anna Wittner, June 7, 1945; children—Simon, Nicholas, Katherine, Benjamin. Hon. master of bench Gray's Inn; Queen's counsel of Queensland Bar; mem. Victorian bar; privy counsellor, 1981; fellow Oriel Coll., Oxford U., 1947-50, hon. fellow, 1977, now provost; hon. fellow New Coll., 1978; prof. public law, dean Faculty of Law, U. Melbourne, 1951-66, emeritus prof., 1967—; vice-chancellor U. New Eng., 1967-70, U. Queensland, 1970-77; gov. gen. Australia, Canberra, 1977-82; acad. gov. of bd. govs. Hebrew U., Jerusalem, 1969-77, 82, Tel Aviv U., 1987—; mem. council U. Lesotho, 1976-77; pres. Australian Inst. Urban Studies, 1973-77; law reform commr. Commonwealth of Australia, 1976-77; chmn. Australian Vice-Chancellor's Com., 1977; vis. prof. Harvard U. Law Sch., 1953-54, 63-64, also univs. Chgo., Ill., Utah, Wash., Fletcher Sch. Law and Diplomacy; Menzies scholar in residence U. Va., 1983. Bd. dirs. Australian Opera, 1969-77; chmn. bd. govs. Utah Found., 1975-77; chmn. Australian Studies Centre Com., London, 1982—; chmn. Press Council (U.K.), 1983-88; chmn. council Victoria League for Commonwealth Friendship, 1987—, chmn. trustees, Visnews, 1986—; chmn. bd., Van Leer Inst. Jerusalem, 1988. Decorated chancellor and prin. knight Order of Australia; knight grand cross Order St. Michael and St. George; knight bachelor Order St. John of Jerusalem, then asso. knight of justice; knight grand cross Royal Victorian Order; companion Order St. Michael and St. George; Rhodes scholar, 1940; Supreme Ct. fellow, Melbourne, 1941; Vinerian scholar, Oxford U., 1947. Fellow Royal Soc. Arts, Acad. Social Scis. in Australia (hon.), Australian Coll. Edn. (hon.), Australian Nat. U. (hon.), Univ.House of Australian Nat. U. (hon.), Royal Australian Inst. Architects (hon.), Australian Acad. Tech. Scis. (hon.), Inst. Chartered Accts. in Australia (hon.), Royal Australian Coll. Physicians (hon.), Royal Australian Coll. Med. Adminstrs. (hon.), Royal Australian Coll. Ob-Gyn (hon.), Australian Acad. Humanities (hon.), Australian Soc. Accts. (hon.), Australian Coll. Rehab. Medicine (hon.), Australian and N.Z. Assn. Advancement of Sci.; fgn. hon. mem. Am. Acad. Arts and Scis. Specialist editor: Dicey: Conflict of Laws, 1949; editor: Australia and the United States: Some Legal Comparisons, 1954; (with P.B. Carter) Essays on the Law of Evidence, 1956; American-Australian Private International Law, 1957; Federal Jurisdiction in Australia, 1959, (with Leslie Zines), 2d edit., 1978; (with D. Mendes da Costa) Matrimonial Causes Jurisdiction, 1961; The British Commonwealth of Nations in a Changing World, 1964; Sir John Latham and Other Papers, 1965; Sir Isaac Isaacs, 1967; Introduction to 2d edit., Evatt: The King and His Dominion Governors, 1967; author The Private Man (A.B.C. Boyer Lectures, 1969); Individual Liberty and The Law (Tagore Law Lectures, 1975); contbr. chpts., articles, essays on legal, polit., social and univ. subjects to Australian, U.K., U.S., Can. and European publs. Office: Oriel Coll, Oxford Univ, Oxford England OX1 4EW

COWLES, ROGER WILLIAM, government audit executive; b. Ft. Madison, Iowa, July 5, 1945; s. Arthur William and Enid Francis (Smith) C. B.B.A. cum laude, Tex. Wesleyan Coll., 1968; M.A., Central Mich. U., 1980. Cert. cost analyst, Va. Contract auditor Def. Contract Audit Agy., Ft. Worth, 1967-76, course mgr., Memphis, 1976-78, program mgr. hdqrs., Alexandria, Va., 1978-80, chief mgmt. info. branch, 1980-81, chief spl. audits, 1982-86, auditor dir. contract mgmt. Office of Asst. Sec. Def., 1986— ; mem. congl. staff U.S. Congress, Washington, 1981-82. Creator toothpick sculpture (Spl. Merit award 1975). Contbr. articles to profl. jours. Mem. Assn. Govt. Accts. (facilitator 1985-87, Tng. Program award 1981), Nat. Contract Mgmt. Assn., Inst. Cost Analysis, Mgmt. Devel. Program. Republican. Methodist. Avocations: bowling; golf; computer technology. Office: Office of Asst Sec Def The Pentagon Room 4B923 Washington DC 22304

COWPER, STEVEN CAMBRELENG, governor of Alaska, lawyer; b. Petersburg, Va., Aug. 21, 1938; s. Marion Cowper and Stephanie Smith; m. Michael Margaret Stewart; children: Katherine, Grace, Wade. BA, U. N.C., 1960, JD, 1963. Sole practice Norfolk, Va.; asst. dist. atty. State of Alaska, Fairbanks, 1968-70; ptnr. Cowper & Madson, Fairbanks, 1971-84; mem. legislature Alaska Ho. of Reps., Fairbanks and Juneau, 1974-78; Gov. State of Alaska, Juneau, 1986—. Columnist Alaska newspapers, 1979-80, 85; author: (documentary film) A Trail to Break-A History of Alaska Lands. Mem. Alaska Native Brotherhood Klawock Camp, Eielson Area Grange, Fairbanks. Served with U.S. Army, 1960. Democrat. Episcopalian. Club: Sundawgs Rugby. Office: Office Gov State Capitol PO Box A Juneau AK 99811

COX, BENJAMIN VINCENT, electrical engineer; b. Chgo., Jan. 25, 1934; s. Benjamin and Lorretta Deloris (Jozwiak) C.; BS in Elec. Engring., U. Utah, 1963, MS, 1969, PhD, 1979; m. Mary Patricia Mitchell, Apr. 18, 1959; children: Linda Marie, Stephen Martin. With Sperry Univac Co. (now UNISYS), 1963-73, 74—, staff engr., 1974-78, engring. mgr., advanced research and devel., dir. advanced tech., Salt Lake City, 1978—; engring. dir. Naval Civil Engring. Lab., Port Hueneme, Calif., 1973-74; adj. prof. U. Utah. Served with U.S. Army, 1954-57. Recipient Utah Gov.'s medal for Sci. and Tech., 1987, Unisys fellow award, 1988. Mem. AIAA (council Utah chpt. 1980-81), IEEE, Am. Def. Preparedness Assn., Air Force Assn., Assn. Old Crows. Author papers, reports in field. Home: 2760 E Blue Spruce Dr Salt Lake City UT 84117 Office: 640 N Sperry Way Salt Lake City UT 84116-2988

COX, BRIAN DOUGLAS, construction company executive, civil engineer; b. Johannesburg, South Africa, May 21, 1942; s. James Edwin and Lylie (Parks) C.; m. Susan Janet Hodges, Feb. 29, 1968 (div. 1978); children—Adam, Camilla; m. Sara Ann Milton, May 20, 1981; children—Murray. B.Sc. in Civil Engring., U. Capetown, 1965. Registered profl. engr., Republic of South Africa. Engr. in tng. G. Maunsell & Ptnrs., London, Eng., 1966-68; civil engr., mng. dir. Steeledale Systems, Johannesburg, 1968—; lectr. Brixton Sch. Bldg., London, Eng., 1966-68; dir. Steeledale Holding Co., Johannesburg, 1979—. Mem. Inst. Civil Engrs., South African Inst. Civil Engrs. Anglican. Clubs: Bryanston Country (Sandton, South Africa); Loch Vaal (Vereeniging, South Africa). Avocations: tennis; hockey; golf; boating. Home: 2 Hugo St, Randburg 2194, Republic of South Africa Office: Steeledale Systems (Pty) Ltd, 8 Nansen Pl, Johannesburg 2197, Republic of South Africa

COX, CLARK, journalist; b. Jefferson, N.C., Feb. 21, 1943; s. Scott Joseph and Jaunita Geneva (Weiss) C.; grad. high sch.; m. Brenda Sue Bowers, Oct. 30, 1971 (div.); m. 2d, Helen Jeanette Parks, June 9, 1979. Reporter, Watauga Democrat, Boone, N.C., 1963; editor Blowing Rocket, Blowing Rock, N.C., 1964, Marshville (N.C.) Home, 1965, Henry County Jour., Bassett, Va., 1966-67; reporter Messenger and Intelligencer, Wadesboro, N.C., 1969-71; sports editor Richmond County Daily Jour., Rockingham, N.C., 1971-73, investigative reporter, 1974-77, asst. editor, 1977-88, assoc. editor, 1988— ; freelance journalist, 1967-69, 73-74. Active Big Bros. Am. Recipient Sport reporting award N.C. Press Assn., 1971, 72, 1st place investigative reporting award, 1974, 1st place feature writing award, 1983, 1st place criticism award, 1985. Democrat. Baptist. Author: (play) The Justice of Our Cause, 1976; (biography) Gen. Henry William Harrington, 1979; (history) Rockingham: 1784-1984, 1984. Home: 326 Curtis Dr Rockingham NC 28379 Office: PO Box 1056 Rockingham NC 28379

COX, CLARK BURGESS, dentist; b. St. George, Utah, Feb. 23, 1929; s. Emerald Lane and Elsie (Burgess) C.; Asso. Sci., Dixie Jr. Coll., 1949; D.D.S., U. So. Calif., 1953; PhD in Environ Sci., K.W. U., 1986; m. Donna Anderson, July 15, 1949; children—David C., Craig E., Suzanne, Dianne, Gary L., Cynthia. Practice dentistry, Delta, Utah, 1955—; v.p. Habb Corp., Delta, 1962—, Cox Trucking Inc., Delta, 1976—; farmer, livestock rancher, 1960—; dir. Del-Tex Corp., Oasis Seed Corp.; partner Fransworth-Cox Real Estate, C&D Indsl. Minerals; environ. cons. R&C Environ. Services; vice chmn. W. Millard Soil Conservation Service, 1970-76. City councilman, Delta, 1968-76, mem. bd. adjustment, 1978—. Served with Dental Corps, AUS, 1953-55. Mem. Acad. Gen. Dentistry, Am., Utah, Provo Dist. dental assns., Brigham Young U. Acad. Dentists (charter), Alpha Tau Epsilon, Psi Omega. Mem. Ch. Jesus Christ of Latter-day Saints (Delta 2d ward bishopric 1962-65, high councilor Delta West stake). Home: RFD Delta PO Box 695 Delta UT 84624 Office: Hobb Bldg Main St Delta UT 84624

COX, EXUM MORRIS, investment manager; b. Santa Rosa, Calif., Feb. 5, 1903; s. Exum Morris and Mary Eleanor (Anderson) C.; m. Elsie Margaret Storke, Sept. 6, 1934; children—Cynthia Morris Huntting, Susana More (Mrs. James T. Fousekis), Thomas Storke. A.B., U. Calif., 1924; M.B.A., Harvard U., 1928. With Dodge & Cox, 1933—, ptnr., 1933-59, pres., 1959-72, chmn. bd., 1972-77, hon. chmn., 1977—; chmn. bd. Dodge & Cox Balanced Fund, 1933-79, trustee, 1979-88; dir. Dodge & Cox Stock Fund., 1965-85. Bd. dirs., v.p. San Francisco, Community Chest, 1946-48; bd. dirs. San Francisco Tb Assn., 1948-52, Bay Area Ednl. TV Assn., 1961-70; trustee San Francisco Mus. Modern Art, pres., 1955-60; trustee Katherine Branson Sch., 1950-57, Grace Cathedral, 1976; vice chmn. Citizens Adv. Com. to Atty. Gen. Calif. on Crime Prevention, 1954-58; mem. Calif. Delinquency Prevention Commn., 1963-67, San Francisco Library Commn., 1963-64; trustee U. Calif. at Berkeley Found., 1972—, v.p., 1974-77, pres., 1977-79. Mem. Investment Counsel Assn. Am. (gov. 1955-58, 61-67), Calif. Acad. Scis. (trustee, chmn. bd. trustees 1967-73, treas. 1963-67), Sigma Chi. Clubs: Anglers (N.Y.C.); Bankers, Pacific Union, Bohemian. Office: 1 Post St 35th Floor San Francisco CA 94104

COX, GLENN ANDREW, JR., petroleum company executive; b. Sedalia, Mo., Aug. 6, 1929; s. Glenn Andrew and Ruth Lonsdale (Atkinson) C.; m. Veronica Cecelia Martin, Jan. 3, 1953; children: Martin Stuart, Grant Andrew, Cecelia Ruth. B.B.A., So. Methodist U., 1951. With Phillips Petroleum Co., Bartlesville, Okla., 1956—; asst. to chmn. operating com. Phillips Petroleum Co., 1973-74, v.p. mgmt. info. and control, 1974-80, exec. v.p., 1980-85, dir., 1982—, pres., chief operating officer, 1985—. Pres. Cherokee Area council Boy Scouts Am., 1977-82, South Cen. Region, 1987; bd. curators Cen. Meth. Coll., Fayette, Mo., 1984—. Served as pilot USAF, 1951-55. Mem. Am. Petroleum Inst. (bd. dirs.), Nat. Assn. Mfrs. (bd. dirs.), Bartlesville Area C. of C. (pres. 1978). Methodist. Club: Hillcrest Country. Office: Phillips Petroleum Co 6A1 Phillips Bldg Bartlesville OK 74004

COX, JAMES CARL, JR., chemist, researcher, consultant; b. Wolf Summit, W.Va., June 17, 1919; s. James Carl and Maggie Lillian (Merrells) C.; m. Alma Lee Tenney, Sept. 8, 1945; children—James Carl III, Joseph Merrells, Alma Lee, Elizabeth Susan Cox Unger, Albert John. B.S. summa cum laude, W.Va. Wesleyan Coll., 1940; M.S. in Organic Chemistry, U. Del., 1947, Ph.D. in Phys. Organic Chemistry, 1949; postgrad. in law Am. U., summer 1953, George Washington U., summer 1954; J.D. with honors, U. Md., 1955. Bar: Md. 1955. Registered profl. sanitarian, Tex. Research chemist E.I. du Pont de Nemours Corp., Belle, W.Va., 1940-43; grad. instr. chemistry U. Del., Newark, 1946-49; prof. chemistry, head dept. chemistry Wesleyan Coll., Mason, Ga., 1949-51; prof. U.S. Naval Acad., Annapolis, Md., 1951-55; prof., research dir. Lamar U., Beaumont, Tex., 1955-65; prof., head dept. chemistry, dir. div. sci. and math. Oral Roberts U. Tulsa, 1965-68; prof., head dept. chemistry Wayland Baptist U., Plainview, Tex., 1968-76; v.p., research dir. Agrl. & Indsl. Devel., Inc., Plainview, 1976-79; environ. health expert Tex. Dept. Health, Plainview, 1979-84; cons. in field; vis. prof. organic chemistry Middle Tenn. State U., Murfreesboro, summer 1950, U. Baghdad, Iraq, 1956-57. Author books, the most recent being: Lives of Splendor, 1970; Patterson's German-English Chemical Dictionary, rev. edit., 1985, contbr. articles to profl. jours., also abstracts. Editor The Condenser, 1957-65. Hale County Republican precinct chmn., Plainview, 1983-84; bd. dirs. Plainview chpt. ARC, 1969-73, United Way, Plainview, 1972-75. Served to cpl. Combat Engrs., U.S. Army, 1943-45, ETO. Named Outstanding Prof., Lamar U., 1963-64, Wayland Bapt. U., 1971-74; fellow DuPont Endowment Found., 1947-49, Carnegie Found., 1949-51, State of Tex., 1957-59. Fellow Tex. Acad. Sci.; mem. Am. Chem. Soc., AAAS, AAUP, Tex. Pub. Health Assn., Tex. Environ. Health Assn. (governing council 1982-84). Methodist. Lodge: Rotary (pub. relations officer 1969-84). Current work: Novel fuels for industry; agricultural chemicals. Subspecialties: Organic chemistry; Polymer chemistry.

COX, JAMES DARRELL, lawyer; b. Wilmington, N.C., Nov. 11, 1950; s. Albert Darrell and Christine Elizabeth (Eubank) C.; m. Shearin Leigh Teague, Aug. 10, 1974; children—Amy Elizabeth, Amanda Leigh. B.A. with honors, N.C. State U., 1972; J.D. cum laude, Wake Forest U., 1975; LLM in Taxation, Georgetown U., 1978. Bar: N.C. 1975, U.S. Tax Ct. 1976, U.S. Ct. Claims 1976, U.S. Dist. Ct. (ea. dist.) N.C. 1981. Staff atty. IRS-Chief Counsel, Washington, 1975-78; assoc. Smith, Anderson, Raleigh, N.C., 1978-82; ptnr. Reynolds & Cox, P.A., Raleigh, 1983, Smith, Moore, Smith, Schell & Hunter, Raleigh, 1983-84; sole practice, Raleigh, 1984-86; ptnr. Cox, Carraway & Wilson, Raleigh, 1986-88; sole practice, Raleigh, 1988—. Author: Farming and Ranching-Tax Accounting-Tax Management Portfolio, 1981. Treas. Cary Jaycees, N.C., 1980-81. Mem. ABA (com. on agr., tax sect.), Wake County Bar Assn., N.C. Bar Assn. (tax sect.), Phi Kappa Phi.

COX, JIM DALE, general contracting company executive; b. Harris, Mo., Nov. 24, 1931; s. John Clarence and Helen LuVerna (Holiday) C.; A.A. in Indsl. Mgmt., Independence (Kans.) Jr. Coll., 1951; B.S. in Real Estate and Constrn., U. Denver, 1956, M.B.A. in Fin., 1970; m. Joan Gregerson Green, Mar. 14, 1980; children—Susan J., John H., Charles Green, Andrea Green. Gen. mgr. Hopkins Mfg. Co., 1951-53, Shepard Constrn. Co., 1957-60; pres. Cox Constrn. Co., Colorado Springs, Colo., 1960-70, Village Contractors, Inc., Colorado Springs, 1980—; ptnr. SCS Co., constrn. mgmt., Colorado Springs, 1970—, Village Cos., Colorado Springs, 1972—; dir. First Bank Colorado Springs, Colo. Western Properties, Denver; lectr. U. Denver, 1965—. Mem. El Paso County Courthouse Com., 1969-72, Colo. Small Bus. Council; vice chmn. Colorado Springs Contractors Bd., 1964-65; chmn. Colorado Springs Fire Bd., 1979-86; chmn. adv. bd. Regional Bldg. Dept., 1987—; vice chmn. Regional Bldg. Dept., 1984-87. Mem. Home Builders Assn. Met. Colorado Springs (pres. 1963-64), Colorado Springs C. of C. Republican. Episcopalian. Clubs: El Paso, Garden of Gods, Country of Colo., Jaguar Clubs N. Am., U. Denver Pikes Peak Alumni (pres.). Home: 52 Polo Dr Colorado Springs CO 80906 Office: 104 S Nevada Ave Suite 107 Colorado Springs CO 80903

COX, LARRY GLEN, manufacturing company executive; b. Pampa, Tex., Jan. 16, 1938; s. Odis and Dorothy Izela (Woods) C.; B.S., U.S. Naval Acad., 1960; children—Terri, David. Commd. ensign, U.S. Navy, 1960, advanced through grades to lt. comdr.; with Polaris Nuclear Submarine Service, 1960-69; engr., mgr. prodn. ops. Exxon Gas System, King Ranch Gas Plant, Gulf Coast, Tex., 1969-76; mem. mgmt. staff Prudhoe Bay Prodn. Facilities Project, Pasadena, Calif., div. supervising engr., 1976-79; v.p. ops. Williams Instrument Co., Inc. and partner U.S.A. Industries, Inc., Valencia, Calif., 1979-81; prin. project mgr. The Ralph M. Parsons Co., Pasadena, Calif., 1981-82; dep. program dir. Sohio Endicott Arctic Ocean Prodn. Facilities, Beaufort Sea, Alaska, 1983; offshore programs bus. devel. advisor, Parsons Co., 1984; project dir. Amerada Hess North Star Arctic Project, 1985; proposal mgr. office of civilian radioactive waste salt repository project Dept. Energy, 1986; project mgr. Advanced Solid Rocket Motor Mfg. Facilities, 1987—; chief exec. officer Precision Systems Internat., Port Hueneme, Calif., 1987—. Active Boy Scouts Am.; elder 1st Presbyterian Ch., Bel Air, Calif. Served to capt. USNR. Registered profl. engr., Tex. Mem. ASME (chmn. Arctic ops. com.), Calif. Export Mgrs. Assn., Soc. Petroleum Engrs., Pacific Energy Assn., Pacific Coast Gas Assn. Club: Rotary. Office: 23528 San Fernando Rd #5 Newhall CA 91321-3121

COX, MYRON KEITH, educator; b. Akron, May 6, 1926; s. Carney F. and Nina Castilla (Kenny) C.; B.S., Va. Poly. Inst., 1949; B.S., Pa. State Coll., 1952; M.S., M.I.T., 1957; D.Sc., London Coll., Eng., 1964; m. Emma A. Edwards, July 2, 1950; children—Carney K., Myron D., Eric L., Brett W. Commd. staff sgt. U.S. Air Force, 1950, advanced through grades maj., 1964; radar meteorology staff Hanscom AFB, Mass., 1964-66; electronic countermeasures Wright Patterson AFB, Ohio, 1966-69; ret., 1969; faculty Wright State U., Dayton, Ohio, 1969—, prof. mgmt. sci., quantitative bus. analysis, 1981—. Bd. govs. Fairborn (Ohio) YMCA, 1972-73. Served with USN, 1944-46. Registered profl. engr., Mass. Fellow Acad. Mktg. Sci.; mem. Inst. Mgmt. Sci., Am. Statis. Assn., Assn. Inst. Decision Sci., So. Mktg. Assn., Phi Kappa Phi, Tau Beta Pi, Sigma Xi, Eta Kappa Nu, Beta Gamma Sigma, Alpha Iota Delta. Club: Lions, Masons, Shriners. Patentee surface friction tester; contbr. mktg., mgmt., forecast modeling and simulation. Home: 2527 Grange Hall Rd Beavercreek OH 45431 Office: Wright State Univ Dayton OH 45435

COX, ROBERT GENE, consultant; b. Liberal, Kans., June 3, 1929; s. Clarice Elden and Margaret Verene (Jones) C.; m. Eileen Frances Hinshaw, July 10, 1953; children: Ann Rebecca, Allan Robert. B.A. with honors, U. N.Mex., 1951, J.D., 1955; grad., Fgn. Service Inst., 1956, Harvard Bus. Sch., 1978, 79. Joined fgn. service 1956; 3d to 2d sec. Am. embassy, Panama, 1956-58; Am. consul Caracas, Venezuela, 1959-61; Korea desk officer Dept. State, Washington, 1961-62; chief of staff mgmt. planning Dept. State, 1963-65; officer in charge mission to Dept. State, Israel, 1965; staff asst. to Pres., The White House, 1966-68; partner William H. Clark Assos., N.Y.C. and Chgo., 1968-71; sr. staff officer UN Secretariat, Vienna and N.Y.C., 1971-72; pres. Hennes & Cox, Inc., N.Y.C., Washington and Los Angeles, 1972-75; prin., nat. dir. human resource systems Ernst & Ernst, Cleve., 1975-78; ptnr., mng. dir. Arthur Young & Co., N.Y.C., 1979-83; pres. PA Exec. Search Group, N.Y.C., 1983-86; chmn. PA Computers and Telecommunications NA, N.Y.C., 1985-86; mng. dir. Kearney Exec. Search Group, 1987—; bd. dirs. The Alden Owners, Inc., Le Roy Industries Inc.; mem. history faculty Fla. State U., 1958; cons. Commn. U.S.-Latin Am. Relations, 1974; sr. advisor Commn. Orgn. of Govt. for Conduct of Fgn. Policy, 1974-75; expert witness on mil. value of Panama Canal U.S. Ho. of Reps., 1977; ITT lectr. Georgetown U., 1981. Author: Defense Department Diplomacy in Latin America, 1964, Choices for Partnership or Bloodshed in Panama, 1975, The Canal Zone: New Focal Point in U.S.-Latin American Relations, 1977, The Chief Executive, 1980, Planning for Immigration: A Business Perspective, 1981, Selection of the Chief Executive Officer, 1982. Bd. dirs. community drug control program, Glen Ridge, N.J., 1971-72, Unitarian-Universalist Christian Fellowship, 1987—; dep. to county chmn. Albuquerque Dem. Party, 1954; adviser on exec. selection to transition staff of Pres.-elect Carter, 1976-77; treas. Caribbeana Council, 1977-78; bd. advisors Georgetown U. Program in Bus. Diplomacy, 1981-84; bd. dirs. Council on Econ. Priorities; trustee Meadville Theol. Sch. U. Chgo., 1986—, Unitarian Ch. of All Souls, N.Y.C., 1981—, sec., 1979-80, pres., 1983-84, deacon, 1985—. Served to capt. USMC, 1951-55, Korea. Mem. Jonesville (Mich.) Heritage Assn., Council Fgn. Relations (chmn. study group on immigration and U.S. fgn. policy 1978), Royal Econ. Soc. (Eng.), Am. Soc. Internat. Law, Unitarian Hist. Soc. Eng., Internat. Assn. Religious Freedom, SAR. Unitarian. Club: Union League (N.Y.C.). Home: 225 Central Park W New York NY 10024 Office: 875 Third Ave New York NY 10022

COX, WILLIAM ANDREW, cardiovascular thoracic surgeon; b. Columbus, Ga., Aug. 3, 1925; s. Virgil Augustus and Dale Jackson C.; student Presbyn. Coll., 1942-43, Harvard U., 1944-45, Cornell U., 1945; BS, Emory U., 1950, MD, 1954; M.S. in Surgery, Baylor U., 1960; m. Nina Recelle Hobby, Jan. 1, 1948; children—Constance Lynn Cox Rogers, Patricia Ann Cox Brown, William Robert, Janet Elaine. Commd. 1st lt. M.C., U.S. Army, 1954, advanced through grades to col., 1969; intern Brooke Army Med. Ctr., San Antonio, 1954-55, resident in gen. surgery, 1956-60; resident in cardiovascular thoracic surgery Walter Reed Army Med. Ctr., Washington, 1960-62, staff cardiothoracic surgeon, 1962; asst. chief cardiothoracic surgery Letterman Gen. Hosp., 1962-65; chief dept. surgery and cardiothoracic surgery 121 Evacuation Hosp., Seoul, Korea, cons. cardiothoracic surgery Korean Theatre, 1965-66; asst. chief cardiothoracic surgery Brooke Army Med. Ctr., 1966-69, chief, 1969-73, bd. dirs. thoracic surgery residency programs, 1966-73, ret., 1973; clin. prof. cardio-thoracic surgery U. Tex. Sch. Medicine, San Antonio, 1971—; practice medicine specialized in cardiovascular thoracic surgery, Corpus Christi, Tex., 1973—; cons. cardio-thoracic surgery Brooke Army Med. Ctr., San Antonio, 1977—; chief staff Meml. Med. Ctr., 1980; dir. disaster med. care region 3A Tex. State Dept. Health, 1973—; mem. Coastal Bend council Gov.'s Emergency Med. Service Commn., 1979—; mem. adv. bd. on congenital heart disease Tex. Dept. Health, 1980—; participant joint confs. on cardiovascular surgery and thoracic surgery Am. People Ambassador Program, Leningrad, Moscow, Bucharest, Romania, Belgrade, Yugoslavia, Prague, Czechoslovakia, 1987; del. Vanderbilt U. joint conf. vascular surgery Dublin, Ireland, Edinburgh, Scotland, London, 1986. Served to lt. USN, 1945-48. Decorated Legion of Merit; recipient A Prefix award Surgeon Gen. Army; diplomate Am. Bd. Surgery, Am. Bd. Thoracic Surgery. Fellow Am. Coll. Chest Physicians; mem. AMA, Soc. Thoracic Surgeons, Denton A. Cooley Cardiovascular Surgery Soc., Tex. Med. Assn. (del. conf. infectious diseases Bankgkok, Hong Kong, Beijing, Shanghai, 1983, So. Thoracic Surgery Assn., Nueces County Med. Soc., Corpus Christi Surg. Soc., 38th Parallel Med. Soc. Republican. Presbyterian. Clubs: Yacht (past commodore presidio)(San Francisco); T-Bar-M Racquet Corpus Christi Country; Ft. Sam Houston Officer's (San Antonio). Contbr. numerous articles in field to profl. jours. Home: 5214 Wooldridge Rd Corpus Christi TX 78413 Office: Suite 302 Spohn Tower 613 Elizabeth Corpus Christi TX 78404

COX, WILLIAM MARTIN, lawyer, educator; b. Bernardsville, N.J., Dec. 26, 1922; s. Martin John and Nellie (Fotens) C.; m. Julia S., June 14, 1952; children—Janice Cox Walker, William Martin, Joann Cox Cahoon, Julieann. A.B., Syracuse U., 1947; J.D., Cornell U., 1950. Bar: N.J., U.S. Dist. Ct. Mem. Dolan & Dolan, Newton, N.J., 1950—; mem. faculty, tchr. zoning adminstrn. Rutgers U.; gen. counsel N.J. Fedn. Planning Ofcls.; bd. dirs. Newton Cemetery Assn.; pres. N.J. Inst. Mcpl. Attys., 1982-84; mem. Land Use Law Drafting Com., 1970—. Recipient Pres.'s Disting. Service award N.J. League Municipalities, 1981. Mem. ABA, N.J. Bar Assn., Sussex County Bar Assn., Am. Planning Assn. Baptist. Clubs: Rotary, Masons (Newton). Author: Zoning and Land Use Administration in New Jersey, rev. edit. 1987. Office: 1 Legal Ln Newton NJ 07860

COYLE, CHARLES A., business educator; b. Phila., June 13, 1931; s. Charles A. and Roseanne (McPeake) C.; m. Suzanne B. McCann, Sept. 28, 1963; children—Suzanne, Christopher, Kevin, Timothy. B.S.B.A., LaSalle U., 1955; M.B.A., Drexel U., 1967; Ed.D., Temple U., 1974. Sales rep. IBM, SCM, Diebold, Inc., R.E. Lamb, 1958-67; asst. prof. mktg. and mgmt. Community Coll. of Phila., 1967-70; asst. prof. mktg. Phila. Coll. Textiles and Sci., 1970-74; tchr., coordinator distributive edn. Middle Bucks (Pa.) AVTS, 1974-76; prof., chmn. mktg. Kutztown (Pa.) U., 1976—, dept. chmn.; chmn. mktg. adv. com. Lehigh Valley Vocat. Tech. Sch., 1984-87. Contbr. articles to profl. pubs. Resource leader Nat. Conf. on New Strategies for Learning, 1969; eucharistic minister, mem. parish adv. council Allentown Diocese; prefect minister St. Francis Order; mgr., coach Warminster Little League, 1973-79, Grandlawn Baseball Assn., 1987; treas. Deerfield Community Assn., 1983-85. Served with CIC, U.S. Army, 1956-58. Recipient outstanding service award Distributive Edn. Clubs Am., 1975-85. Mem. Sales and Mktg. Execs., Am. Mgmt. Assn., AAUP, Cross Keys, Alpha

Epsilon, Epsilon Delta Epsilon, Phi Delta Kappa. Club: Faculty and Adminstrn. (pres.) (Kutztown U.). Home: 1236 Buck Trail Rd Allentown PA 18104 Office: Kutztown U Kutztown PA 19530

COYLE, DAVID JOSEPH, municipal government administrator, recreation program administrator; b. Phila., June 19, 1949; s. Joseph Francis and Julia Adlin (Palmer) C.; m. Peggy Jean O'Neal, June 6, 1970; 1 child, Jaime. B.S., West Chester Coll., 1971; M.S., Temple U., 1981. Recreation dir. City of Milford, Del., 1976-81, dir. pub. works, 1981-86; commr. Parks and Urban Forestry City of Cleve., 1986-88; dep. dir. Parks, Recreation and Properties, Cleve., 1988—; regional coordinator Hershey Foods, Pa., 1982-86. Served to sgt. USAF, 1971-75. Recipient Press Assn. award Md.-Del.-D.C. Press Assn., 1982, Parks and Recreation award Milford Parks Commn., 1982. Mem. Del. Recreation and Park Soc. (pres. 1981-83), Nat. Recreation and Park Assn. (chmn. mid-Atlantic region 1983—), Am. Pub. Works Soc., Gov.'s Council Phys. Fitness, Amateur Softball Assn. (dist. commr. Milford 1976—), U.S. Flag Football Assn. (treas. 1978-83). Democrat. Roman Catholic.

COYNE, CHARLES COLE, lawyer; b. Abington, Pa., Dec. 3, 1948; s. James Kitchenman and Pearl (Black) C.; m. Paula J. Latta, May 15, 1976; 1 dau., Anna Elizabeth. B.S. in Econs., U. Pa., 1970; J.D., Temple U., 1973. Bar: Pa. 1973, U.S. Dist. Ct. (ea. dist.) Pa. 1974, U.S. Ct. Appeals (3d cir.) 1982, U.S. Supreme Ct. 1982, N.J. 1985. Assoc. Fell, Spalding, Goff & Rubin, Phila., 1973-78; mng. atty. Charles C. Coyne & Assocs., Phila., 1978-80; mng. ptnr. Coyne & Perry, and predecessor firm Coyne & Moore, Phila., 1980-86; ptnr. Fell & Spalding, Phila., 1987—; dir., sec., mem. mgmt. com. George S. Coyne Chem. Co., Inc., Croydon, Pa. Assoc. editor Temple Law Quar., 1972-73. Chester County (Pa.) rep. Del. Valley Regional Planning Commn., 1982—; bd. dirs. Chester County Hosp. Authority, 1982—, sec., 1984—; bd. suprs. East Fallowfield Twp., Chester County, 1982-83; mem. Chester County Rep. Com., 1980-82, Phila. Rep. City Com., 1974-76; bd. dirs. Pa. Young Reps., 1976-77; chmn. Greater Phila. Young Reps., 1975-76; trustee Doe Run Presbyn. Ch., Chester County, 1981-82. Recipient Disting. Young Rep. award Greater Phila. Young Reps., 1976. Mem. ABA, Pa. Bar Assn., Phila. Bar Assn. (chmn. sub-com. local bankruptcy rules 1974-75), Chester County Bar Assn., Temple Law Sch. Alumni Assn. (chmn. 10th reunion com.). Clubs: Union League (Phila.), Racquet, Right Angle (bd. control 1984-85). Lodge: Masons (master 1982). Home: Sycamore Run Farm Box 454 RD8 Coatesville PA 19320 Office: 211 S Broad St 8th Floor Philadelphia PA 19107

COYNE, RICHARD DAVID, architectural educator; b. Leek, Stafford, Eng., Dec. 30, 1952; arrived in Australia, 1957; s. John and Kathleen Carol (Sylvester) C. BArch with honors, U. Melbourne, Australia, 1976, M of Landscape Architecture, 1982; PhD, U. Sydney, Australia, 1986. Architect several practices Melbourne, 1976-80; archtl. researcher U. Sydney, 1981-87, lectr. architecture, 1987—. Contbr. articles to profl. jours. Mem. Royal Australian Inst. Architects. Mem. Church of England. Office: U Sydney, Dept Archtl Scis, Sydney Australia 2006

COZART, JOSEPH STEPHEN, business executive; b. Racine, Ohio, Sept. 22, 1937; s. Hubert Clinton and Rebecca Ruth (Hilton) C.; m. Kathlyn Marie Jones, Dec. 20, 1974; 1 son, Joseph Stephen; children by previous marriage—Velenna Jo, Veronica Ann. B.Acctg., Franklin U., 1969; postgrad. Central Mich. U., 1971. C.P.A., Ohio. Cost acct. Western Electric Co., Columbus, 1966-69; audit and tax staff Alexander Grant & Co., Columbus, 1969-72; comptroller, treas. Maxwell & Assocs., Inc., Lancaster, Ohio, 1972-75; treas. Constrn. Advisors, Inc., Columbus, 1975-79; pres. Nu-Tech Housing Services, Inc., Reynoldsberg, Ohio, 1979—; cons. real estate Hudson-Hanover Cos., Ohio, 1981-82, Amer. Cities, Inc., Columbus, 1982-83, Mid-American Housing Services, Inc. Youngstown, Ohio, 1979-84. Served to maj., U.S. Air Force, 1955-59, 68-69. Mem. Ohio Soc. C.P.A.'s Am. Inst. C.P.A.'s, Nat. Acctg. Assn., Ohio Home Builders Assn., Multi-Housing Builders Assn. Republican. Methodist. Home: 5605 Stouder Pl NW Pickerington OH 43147 Office: Nu-Tech Housing Services Inc 1676 Brice Rd Reynoldsburg OH 43068

CRABB, DARRELL WAYNE, motel owner; b. Osceola, Iowa, Oct. 24, 1935; s. Harold Wayne Crabb and Dorothy Mae (Winter) Rose; m. LaVonna Marie Leanord (div.); children—Harold Wayne (dec.), Lorrie Lee Collins; m. Patricia Diane Polson, Nov. 13, 1970; 1 stepchild, Kari Lynn Dodge. Designer, Independent Engring., Independence, Mo., 1960-65, Stearns Rodgers, Denver, 1965-68; design engr. LeHigh Design, Boulder, Colo., 1968-73, Denver Equipment, 1973-74; owner Resort Lodge, Cooke City, Mont., 1974—; heavy equipment operator, Iowa, Mo., Kans., 1954-60. Republican. Clubs: Snowmobile, Billings Trap. Lodge: Elks. Home: Hwy 212 PO Box 1130 Cooke City MT 59020 Office: All Seasons Inn Hwy 212 Cooke City MT 59020

CRADDOCK, PAUL TERENCE, archaeological scientist; b. Redditch, Worcestershire, Eng., May 2, 1945; s. William and Gwenneth (Melksham) C.; m. Brenda Rose Le Fevre. BS in Chemistry, U. Birmingham, 1966; Diploma in prehistory, Inst. of Archaeology, London, 1970, PhD in Roman Metallurgy, 1975. Scientist Brit. Mus. Research Lab., London, 1966—; lectr. London U., 1972—. Contbr. numerous articles to profl. jours. Fellow Soc. Antiquaries of London. Office: Research Lab, The British Museum, London WC1B 3DF, England

CRAEHN, SVEN OVE, commercial agency executive, marketing consultant; b. Linkoping, Sweden, Apr. 18, 1938; s. Sven Folke and Antonie Emilie (Schmidt) Krahn; m. Bibbi Eleonora Grundstrom, Jan. 1, 1961; children—Annika Birgitta, Conny Georg. Cert. in econs. Polhelmsskolan Sch., Stockholm, 1955; student in selling technique Stockholm Stads Handels Sch., 1956; student in trading technique Palmans Inst., Stockholm, 1957. Office clk. Charles Nilsson & Co., Stockholm, 1954-55, Heurlins Kaffe AB, Stockholm, 1955-58; purchaser Sv Maskin AB Greiff, Stockholm, 1958-59; purchasing dir. Toledo Svenska AB, Stockholm, 1959-63; sales mgr. Danwitt Ltd. AB, Stockholm, 1963-64; pres. Skandinavisk Elimport AB, Hallsberg, Sweden, 1964—, Sun Invest HB, Hallsberg, 1988—, IEM Indsl. Elmaterial HB, Hallsberg, 1977—, cons. ptnr., 1987—; cons. ptnr. Annikas Videohorna HB, Hallsberg, 1982-87. Served to cpl. FRA, 1957-58. Office: Skandinavisk Elimport AB, PO Box 43, S-694 01 Hallsberg Sweden

CRAFTON-MASTERSON, ADRIENNE, real estate executive; b. Providence, Mar. 6, 1926; d. John Harold and Adrienne (Fitzgerald) Crafton; m. Francis T. Masterson, May 31, 1947 (div. Jan. 1977); children: Mary Victoria Masterson Bush, Kathleen Joan, John Andrew, Barbara Lynn Wickes. Student, No. Va. Community Coll., 1971-74. Mem. staff Senator T.F. Green of R.I., Washington, 1944-47, 54-60, U.S. Senate Com. on Campaign Expenditures, 1944-45; asst. chief clk. Ho. Govt. Ops. Com., 1948-49, clk. Ho. Campaign Expenditures Com., 1950; asst. appointment sec. Office of Pres., 1951-53; with Hubbard Realty, Alexandria, Va., 1962-67; owner, mgr. Adrienne Investment Real Estate, Alexandria, 1968-73; pres. AIRE, Ltd., 1973—. Mem. adv. panel Fairfax County (Va.) Council on the Arts; founder, pres. Mt. Vernon/Lee Cultural Ctr. Found., Inc., 1984—. Mem. Nat. Assn. Realtors, No. Va. Bd. Realtors (chmn. comml. and indsl. com. 1981-82, community revitalization com. 1983-84), Va. Assn. Realtors, Internat. Orgn. Real Estate Appraisers (sr.), Alexandria C. of C., Mt. Vernon Lee C. of C., Friends of Kennedy Ctr. (founder). Democrat. Home: 1200 Olde Towne Rd Alexandria VA 22307 Office: 6911 Richmond Hwy #450 Alexandria VA 22306 also: PO Box 1271 Alexandria VA 22313

CRAGUN, RICHARD, ballet dancer; b. Sacramento, Calif., Oct. 5, 1944. Student, Banff Sch. Fine Arts, Can., Sch. Royal Ballet, London; studied with Vera Volkova, Royal Danish Ballet, Mrs. Briggs, Sacramento. Joined Stuttgart Ballet, 1962—, now prin.; created over 60 roles: John Cranko's Opus 1, Pré sence, Brouillards, Poeme de l'Extase, Traces, The Taming of the Shrew, Carmen, Initials R.B.M.E.; Kenneth Macmillan's Song of the Earth, Brother Sisters, Requiem; Glen Tetley's Voluntaries, Daphnis and Chloe; Maurice Béart's La Danse and Operatta. Recipient Dance Mag. award, 1985; named Kammertänzer, Fed. Republic of Germany, 1983. Office: Stuttgart Ballett, Oberer Schlossgarten 6, Pf 982, 7000 Stuttgart 1 Federal Republic of Germany

CRAIB, KENNETH BRYDEN, resource development executive, physicist, economist; b. Milford, Mass., Oct. 13, 1938; s. William Pirie and Virginia Louise (Bryden) C.; m. Gloria Faye Lisano, June 25, 1960; children—Kenneth Jr., Judith Diane, Lori Elaine, Melissa Suzanne. B.S. in Physics, U. Houston, 1967; M.A. in Econs., Calif. State U., 1982. Aerospace technologist NASA, Houston, 1962-68; staff physicist Mark Systems, Inc., Cupertino, Calif., 1968-69; v.p. World Resources Corp., Cupertino, 1969-71; dir. resources devel. div. Aero Service Corp., Phila., 1971-72; dir. ops. Resources Devel. Assocs., Los Altos, Calif., 1972-80, pres., chief exec. officer, Diamond Springs, Calif., 1980-85; owner Sand Ridge Arabians, 1980—; chmn., dir. Resources Devel. Assocs., Inc., 1982—, Devel. Support Internat. Inc., Placerville, Calif., 1981—; pres., chmn., dir. RDA Internat., Inc., 1986—; dir. Sierra Gen. Investments, 1985—. Contbr. articles to profl. jours. Served with USAF, 1957-61. Recipient Sustained Superior Performance award NASA, 1966. NASA grantee, 1968. Mem. Am. Soc. Photogrammetry, Soc. Internat. Devel., Agrl. Research Inst., Calif. Select Com. Remote Sensing, Internat. Assn. Natural Resources Pilots, Remote Sensing Soc. (council), Am. Soc. Oceanography (charter), Aircraft Owners and Pilots Assn., Gulf and Caribbean Fisheries Inst., Placerville C. of C. Republican. Universalist. Home: 6431 Mary Ann Ln Placerville CA 95667 Office: RDA Internat Inc 801 Morey Dr Placerville CA 95667

CRAIG, ASHLEY RON, psychology educator, clinical psychologist; b. Sydney, New South Wales, Australia, Nov. 11, 1952; s. Ronald John and Nola Irene (Blamey) C.; m. Magali Laurence Decrevel, Feb. 5, 1977; children: Daniel, Stephen, Rachel. BS in Psychology with honors, U. New South Wales, Sydney, 1978, PhD, 1985. Clin. psychologist, researcher Prince Henry Hosp. U. New South Wales, 1978-85, head dept. clin. psychology Prince Henry Hosp., Prince Wales Hosp., 1985-86; lectr. pyschology U. Tech., Sydney, 1986—; cons. clin. psychologist, researcher Royal North Shore Hosp. Univ. Sydney, 1987—. Contbr. articles to profl. jours. Mem. Australia Psychol. Soc., Bd. Clin. Psychologists, Australia Soc. Psychiat. Research. Home: Holden St, 2250 Gosford, New South Wales Australia Office: Univ Tech Sydney, PO Box 123, 2007 Broadway New South Wales, Australia

CRAIG, CHARLES SAMUEL, business educator; b. Atlantic City, May 6, 1943; s. Charles Hays and Catherine Sara (McMullen) C.; m. Elizabeth Anne Coyne, Aug. 10, 1985. B.A., Westminster Coll., 1965; M.S., U. R.I., 1967; Ph.D., Ohio State U., 1971. Mktg. rep. IBM, Providence, 1966-68; asst. dir. Mechanized Info. Center, Columbus, 1971-73; asst. prof. library adminstrn. Ohio State U., Columbus, 1971-73, asst. prof. mktg., 1972-74; asst. prof. mktg. Grad. Sch. Bus. and Public Adminstrn., Cornell U., Ithaca, N.Y., 1974-77, assoc. prof., 1977-79; vis. assoc. prof. mktg. Grad. Sch. Bus. Adminstrn., N.Y.U., 1979-81, assoc. prof. mktg., 1981-84, prof. mktg., 1984—, assoc. dean acad. affairs, 1984—; dir. Presbyterian and Reformed Pub. Co., Phila., 1973—; mem. exec. bd. Jour. Retailing, 1985—. NDEA fellow, 1969-71. Mem. Am. Mktg. Assn., Assn. Consumer Research, Phi Kappa Phi, Omicron Delta Epsilon, Psi Chi. Presbyterian. Co-author: Consumer Behavior: An Information Processing Perspective, 1982; International Marketing Research, 1983; co-editor: Personal Selling: Theory, Research and Practice, 1984; The Development of Media Models in Advertising; Repetition Effects over the Years; and the Relationship of Advertising Expenditures to Sales, 1986; mem. editorial bd. Jour. Mktg. Research, 1978-85, Jour Retailing, 1980-85. Contbr. articles to profl. jours. Home: 110 Bleecker St Apt 3-F New York NY 10012 Office: 100 Trinity Pl NYU New York NY 10006

CRAIG, JACK EUGENE, furniture designer; b. Cleveland, Okla., June 7, 1934; s. Carl Robert and Gladys Celesta (Brown) C.; m. Ginko Nishimura, June 1, 1961 (div.); 1 child, Mrs. Winter Kjeldsen Jr.; m. 2d, Sumiyati Muhanan, June 10, 1987. Student, Calif. Coll. Arts and Crafts, 1954, 56, San Jose (Calif.) State Coll., 1955, Chouinard Inst. of Art, 1957. Archtl. draftsman Menlo Research Lab., San Jose, 1957-58; tech. illustrator Lockheed Aircraft Corp., Sunnyvale, Calif., 1958-60; freelance designer textiles and home furnishings Kyoto and Osaka, Japan, 1960-62; tech. illustrator, comml. artist Lockheed Aircraft Corp., Sunnyvale, 1963-65; freelance designer textiles and home furnishings Tokyo, 1965-71; freelance designer, jobber rattan furniture items Penang, Malaysia, 1971-72; freelance designer rattan furniture, organizer various rattan factories Cebu, Philippines, 1972-82; freelance designer, jobber rattan furniture and decorator accessories Cirebon, West Java, Indonesia, 1982-83; freelance designer, jobber rattan items East Java, Indonesia, 1983—. Contbr. articles to profl. jours. Buddhist. Home and Office: Kampong Jalen Desa Jejalen Jaya, Kec Tambun Kabupaten DT II, Bekasi Jawa Barat Indonesia

CRAIG, LEXIE FERRELL, educator, career vocational and guidance counselor; b. Halls, Tenn., Dec. 12, 1921; d. Monroe Stancil and Hester May (Martin) Ferrell; m. Philip L. Craig, May 19, 1951; children: Douglas H., Laurie K., Barbara J. BS magna cum laude, George Peabody Coll., Vanderbilt U., 1944; MA with honors, Denver U., 1965; postgrad. Colo. U., 1972—, Colo. State U., 1964—, U. No. Colo., 1964—. Cert. local vocat. adminstr., vocat. guidance specialist, vocat. bus. specialist, vocat. home econs. specialist, reading specialist, nat. recreation dir. specialist. Danforth grad. fellow, counselor Mich. State U., East Lansing, 1944-46; nat. student counselor, field dir. student counseling dept. higher edn. Am. Bapt. Conv., summer service career projects dir. U.S. and Europe, 1946-51; coordinator religious and career activities counselor, Colo. U., 1951-52; tchr. home econs., phys. edn., counseling, dist. 96, Riverside, Ill., 1952-54; substitute tchr., psychometrist, reading specialist part time, Deerfield, Ill., 1956-59; substitute tchr. Littleton (Colo.) Dist. VI, 1961-63, guidance and career counselor Littleton Pub. Schs., 1963-67, 68-86, career devel. specialist, guidance counselor spl. assignments state and nat., Gov.'s Youth 2000 Task Force Com., 1988—, also mem. vocat. needs and assessment com., 1988—; dir., counselor YWCA Extension Program, Job Corps, Denver, 1967-68; tchr. adult edn. home econs. evenings, 1963-66; mem. Colo. State Career Task Force, 1973-77; vol. home econ. cons. Colo. State U extension office, 1987. Lay conf. rep. Meth. Ch. Pastor/Parish Commn.; vol. sr. citizens programs United Meth. Ch., Littleton Community Ctr., mem. nominating and personnel work area com.; chmn. membership com. St. Andrew United Meth. Ch., Colo. Ch. Women United; mem. Greater Denver Frienship Force; bd. dirs. Career Awareness Council Boy Scouts Am., Metro Denver; also mem. Colo. Career Awareness Council; mem. So. Suburban Recreation, Littleton Community Arts Ctr.; adv. council Powell PTO, 1981-84; adv. council SEMBCS area vocat. schs.; mem. local caucus com. Republican Party; mem. Dist. Environ. Sci. Council. Didcott scholar, 1942; mem. AVS adv. council Early Childhood Edn., Health Occupation, Restaurant Arts and Coop Career Devel., 1970—; Danforth home econs. and leadership scholar, 1943; Am. Leadership Camp Found. scholar, Shelby, Mich., 1942-45; Hildegarde Sweet Scholar, 1983; recipient Sullivan award and grant, named outstanding grad., 1944; named Littleton Mother of Year, 1977, Colo. Vocat. Counselor of Yr., 1978, Colo. Vocat. Guidance Assoc. Counselor of Yr., 1984; recipient plaque for recruiting and career guidance Navy and Air Force, 1980, Clifford G. Houston award, 1985, Outstanding award Boy Scouts of Am. Career Awareness Council, 1986, Recognition Gold Pin award United Meth. Ch. Women, 1988. Mem. NEA, AAUW, Colo. Edn. Assn., Littleton Edn. Assn., Am. Vocat. Assn., Colo. Vocat. Assn., Am. Assn. Counseling and Devel., Colo. Assn. for Counseling and Devel. (exec. bd.), Nat. Career Devel. Assn. (membership chmn.), Colo. Career Devel. Assn. (past pres., membership chmn.), Nat. Vocat. Guidance Assn. (Colo. rep.), Am. Assn. Retired Persons, Colo. Retired Sch. Employees Assn., Arapahoe County Retired Tchrs., Colo. Sch. Counselors Assn., Am. Field Service (pres. Littleton chpt.), Lit. Book Club Littleton Arts Ctr., Home Economists in Homemaking (Littleton and Bega, Australia clubs), Phi Delta Kappa, Delta Kappa Gamma Alpha Delta (past chpt. pres., Omega State DKG, state com. chmn. personal growth and services), Delta Pi Epsilon (past pres.), Pi Omega Pi (past pres.), Pi Gamma Mu (past pres.), Kappa Delta Pi (past pres.). Clubs: Order Eastern Star, Country Western Dance. Editor, pub. Join in a Song, 1949; editor The Church Follows Its Youth, 1950, curriculum units in consumer edn., home econs., careers, parenting classes.

CRAIG, ROBERT JOHN, civil engineer, educator; b. Columbus, Ohio, July 6, 1943; s. Robert Heckert and Mary Lou (Losey) C.; B.S. in Civil Engring., Purdue U., 1966, M.S. (NDEA asst.), 1969, Ph.D., 1973. Asst. prof. Pa. State U., Middletown, 1972-75; prof. civil and environ. engring. N.J. Inst. Tech., Newark, 1975—, asst. chmn. dept., 1978-80, dir. structural and concrete lab., 1975-82; cons. in field. Active local Boy Scouts Am. Mem. Am. Soc. Engring. Edn. (Dow award Middle Atlantic region 1978), ASCE (pres. N.J. br. 1980-81, sect. sec. 1981-83, sect. treas. 1984-86, sect. pres. 1987—, vice chmn. nat. com. on student services 1982-83, 85-87, chmn. com. 1987—), Am. Concrete Inst. (chmn. com. E801, 1979—), Soc. Exptl. Stress Analysis, ASTM, N.J. Soc. Profl. Engrs. (v.p. chpt. 1986-87), Sigma Xi (chpt. pres. 1979-84, nominating com. Nat.-Mid Atlantic Region), Order Engrs. (bd. dirs. N.J. chpt.), U.S. Canoe Assn., Chi Epsilon (hon.), Tau Beta Pi (hon., faculty adviser), Omicron Delta Kappa (hon., faculty sec.). Roman Catholic. Author articles in field. Home: 128 Newark Ave Apt 3 Belleville NJ 07109 Office: Civil and Environ Engring NJ Inst Tech Newark NJ 07102

CRAIGHEAD, WENDEL LEE, educational and business film producer, director; b. Burr Oak, Kans., May 30, 1936; s. Alfred and Eva May (Burton) C. Student, Kans. State U., 1954-55; BA, Bethany (Okla.) Nazarene Coll., 1959; postgrad., U. Mo., Kansas City, 1962-63. Film editor Calvin Prodns., Kansas City, 1959-63, film dir., 1963-68; v.p., mgr. producer services Calvin Communications, Kansas City, 1968-75, producer, 1975-80, producer, v.p. sales, 1980-82; owner Craighead Films, Prairie Village, Kans., 1982—. Dir. A Place in History, 1969 (Cine award 1970); producer, dir. 60 motion pictures. Mem. Smoky Hill. Ry. Hist. Soc., Kansas City. Mem. Assn. N.Am. Radio Clubs (nat. exec. sec. 1970-72), Greater Kansas City C. of C. Republican. Nazarene. Home and Office: 2110 W 74th Terr Prairie Village KS 66208

CRAIN, CHESTER RAY, statistician, consultant; b. St. Louis, Apr. 17, 1944; s. Chester Raymond and Mary Louise (Landers) C.; m. Barbara Hope Fagnan, Sept. 2, 1967; 1 child, Michelle Wigmore. A.B., Knox Coll., 1965; M.A., U. Calif.-Riverside, 1967; Ph.D., U. N.Mex., 1974. Research statistician Knoll Pharm. Co., Whippany, N.J., 1980; mgr. stats. McNeil Pharm., Spring House, Pa., 1980-81; sr. biostatistician Miles Pharms., West Haven, Conn., 1981-83; dir. statis. services Boots Pharms., Shreveport, La., 1983-84; mgr. biometrics Du Pont Co., Wilmington, Del., 1984-85, cons. dept. central research and devel., 1985—; dept. coordinator, Corporate Electronic Info. Security Com.; developer Scientific Computing Div. Enhanced Stats. Products Product Plan; departmental coordinator Electronic Info. Security Com. Author: Scientific Computing Division's Enhanced Statistical Products Product Plan; Cont S.c. Clinical Trialsssrticles to profl. jours. Mem. Am. Soc. Quality Control, Soc. for Clin. Trials, Am. Statis. Assn., Internat. Assn. for Statis. Computing, Computer Security Inst., Soc. Clin. Trials, Biometric Soc., Phi Beta Kappa, Sigma Xi. Democrat. Unitarian. Home: 14 Longview Dr Thornton PA 19373 Office: EI DuPont Co CR&D Dept E320-115 Wilmington DE 19898

CRALLEY, ELZA MONROE, agricultural educator; b. Carmi, Ill., Nov. 20, 1905; s. John W. and Martha (Jones) C.; B.S., McKendree Coll., 1928; Ph.D., U. Wis., 1931; m. Cleda Ann Renner, Feb. 5, 1930; children—Barbara Ann (Mrs. Roy Shaw), Patricia Sue (Mrs. Philip E. Duncan). Asst. dept. botany U. Wis., 1928-31; successively instr., asst. prof., asso. prof. dept. plant pathology U. Ark., 1931-46, prof., 1948-52, prof., 1953-72, prof. emeritus, 1973—, head dept., 1953-59; dir. Ark. Agrl. Expt. Sta., 1959-72; pathologist U.S. Mil. Govt., Korea, 1947, Point 4 Program, Panama, 1952; cons. pathologist, Cuba, 1955, Ford Found., India, 1959; exhibited landscapes in local and regional shows, 1973—; represented in pvt. permanent collections. Named Ark. Man of Yr., Progressive Farmer, 1970. Mem. Alpha Zeta, Gamma Sigma Delta. Episcopalian. Club: Rotary. Author: Distant Horizons, 1983; featured in book A Fine Age, Creativity as a Key to Successful Aging, 1984. Contbr. articles to sci. jours. Home: 1502 Cedar St Fayetteville AR 72703

CRAM, DONALD JAMES, chemistry educator; b. Chester, Vt., Apr. 22, 1919; s. William Moffet and Joanna (Shelley) C.; m. Jane Maxwell, Nov. 25, 1969. B.S., Rollins Coll., 1941; M.S., U. Nebr., 1942; Ph.D. (Nat. Research fellow), Harvard, 1947; Ph.D. (hon.), U. Uppsala, 1977; D.Sci. (hon.), U. So. Calif., 1983. Research chemist Merck and Co., 1942-45; asst. prof. chemistry UCLA, 1947-50, assoc. prof., 1950-56, prof., 1956—, S. Winstein prof., 1985—; chem. cons. Upjohn Co., 1952—, Union Carbide Co., 1960-81, Eastman Kodak Co., 1981—, Technicon Co., 1984—; State Dept. exchange fellow to Inst. de Quimica, Nat. U. Mex., summer 1956; guest prof. U. Heidelberg, Germany, summer 1958; guest lectr., South Africa, 1967; Centenary lectr. Chem. Soc. London, 1976. Author: (with S.H. Pine, J.B. Hendrickson and G.S. Hammond) Organic Chemistry, 1960, 4th edit., 1980, Fundamentals of Carbanion Chemistry, 1965, (with John H. Richards and G.S. Hammond) Elements of Organic Chemistry, 1967, (with J.M. Cram) Essence of Organic Chemistry, 1977; Contbr.: chpts. to Applications of Biochemical Systems in Organic Chemistry; also articles in field of host-guest complexation chemistry, carbanions, stereochemistry, mold metabolites, large ring chemistry. Named Young Man of Yr. Calif. Jr. C. of C., 1954, Calif. Scientist of Yr., 1974, Noble Laureate in Chemistry, 1987; recipient award for creative work in synthetic organic chemistry Am. Chem. Soc., 1965, Arthur C. Cope award, 1974, Richard Tolman medal, 1985, Willard Gibbs award, 1985, Roger Adams award, 1985; Herbert Newby McCoy award, 1965, 75; award for creative research organic chemistry Synthetic Organic Chem. Mfrs. Assn., 1965; Am. Chem. Soc. fellow, 1947-48; Guggenheim fellow, 1954-55. Mem. Am. Chem. Soc., Nat. Acad. Scis., Am. Acad. Arts and Scis., Royal Soc. Chemistry, Sigma Xi, Lambda Chi Alpha. Club: San Onofre Surfing. Home: 1250 Roscomare Rd Los Angeles CA 90077 Office: UCLA Dept of Chemistry Los Angeles CA 90024

CRAMAROSSA, FRANCESCO, chemist; b. Grassano, Italy, Sept. 17, 1933; s. Raffaele and Brigida (Carbone) C.; m. Annamaria Anatasi, July 2, 1963; 2 sons, Roberto, Sergio. Dottore in Chimica, U. Rome, 1958; postdoctoral fellow, U. Calif.-Berkeley, 1963-65. Research dir. Italian Nat. Council Research, Rome and Bari, 1961-75; asst. prof. chemistry U. Bari, 1966-75, prof., 1975-82, head dept. chemistry, 1982-85; dir. Centro Studio Chimica Plasmi CNR, 1970—. Contbr. articles to profl. jours. Served with Italian Air Force, 1959-61. Mem. Am. Chem. Soc., Combustion Inst., Internat. Union Pure and Applied Chemistry. Home: 239 Via Fanelli, 70125 Bari Italy Office: U Di Bari, Via Amendola, 173, Dept Chimica, Bari Italy

CRAMER, HANS MAX, art dealer; b. Cassel, Fed. Republic Germany, Jan. 7, 1920; s. Gustav and Gertrud V.A.M. (Reisewitz) C.; naturalized Dutch citizen, 1951; m. Ada N.Th. Deurvorst, June 17, 1954 (div. Apr. 1978); children—Catharina Helena, Anna-Paulina. Student Netherlands Inst. Art History, The Hague, 1940-45. Asst. curator Netherlands Inst. Art History, 1948-50; owner G. Cramer Oude Kunst, old master paintings, The Hague, 1961—. Mem. bd. Dutch Art Dealer's Fair, Prinsenhof Mus., Delft, 1959—, chmn., 1966, 71; del. Confedn. Internat. des négociants en Oeuvres d'art, 1962—, v.p., 1970; mem. bd. Soc. Friends Mcpl. Mus., The Hague, 1968-82. Decorated officer Order Orange Nassau, The Netherlands. Mem. Dutch Art Dealer's Assn. (dir. 1968—), Nieuwe of Littèraire Sociëteit de Witte. Author numerous articles, catalogues; contbr. WinklerPrins Ency., Art Ency. Address: 38 Javastraat, 2585 AP The Hague The Netherlands Address: Chesa Vuorcha, 7524 Zuoz Switzerland

CRAMER, HAROLD, lawyer; b. Phila., June 16, 1927; s. Aaron Harry and Blanche (Greenberg) C.; m. Geraldine Hassuk, July 14, 1957; 1 dau., Patricia Gail. A.B., Temple U., 1948; LL.B. cum laude, U. Pa., 1951. Bar: Pa. 1951. Law clk. to judge Common Pleas Ct. No. 2, 1953; mem. law faculty U. Pa., 1954; assoc. firm Shapiro, Rosenfeld, Stalberg & Cook, 1955-56, partner, 1956-67; partner firm Mesirov, Gelman, Jaffe & Cramer, Phila., 1974-77, Mesirov, Gelman, Jaffe, Cramer & Jamieson, 1977—; instr. Nat. Inst. Trial Advocacy, 1970—; pres. Jewish Exponent, Times. Co-author: Trial Advocacy, 1968; contbr. articles to profl. jours. Chmn. bd. Eastern Pa. Psychiat. Hosp., 1974-81, Grad. Hosp., 1975—; trustee Fedn. Jewish Agys., Jewish Publ. Soc. Served to 1st lt. U.S. Army, 1951-53. Decorated Bronze Star. Fellow Am. Bar Found.; mem. Phila. Bar Found. (pres. 1988, trustee, pres. elect), ABA, Pa. Bar Assn. (ho. of dels. 1966-75, 78—, bd. govs. 1975-78), Phila. Bar Assn. (bd. govs. 1967-69, chmn. 1969, vice chancellor 1970, chancellor 1972, editor The Shingle 1970—), Am. Law Inst., U. Pa. Law Alumni Soc. (bd. mgrs. 1959-64, pres. 1968-70), Order of Coif (past chpt. pres., nat. exec. com. 1973-76), Tau Epsilon Rho (chancellor Phila. grad. chpt. 1960-62). Clubs: Locust, Philmont Country. Home: 728 Pine St Philadelphia PA 19106 Office: Mesirov Gelman Jaffee Cramer & Jamieson Fidelity Bldg 123 S Broad St Philadelphia PA 19109

CRAMP, DONALD ARTHUR, hospital executive; b. Meaford, Ont., Can., Dec. 23, 1936; s. Reginald Graham and Sarah Agnus (Robinson) C.; m. Lynda Maria D'Acunto, Feb. 14, 1970; 1 son, Donald Arthur. B.A., U. Western Ont., 1960; M.Sc., Columbia U., 1962. With Bank of Am., San Francisco, 1962-64; with Gen. Motors Corp., Oshawa, Ont., 1964-66; asst. adminstr. South Nassau Communities Hosp., Oceanside, N.Y., 1966-70; dir. Highland View Hosp., Cleve., 1970-71; sr. v.p. Cuyahoga County Hosp. Systems, 1971-76; exec. dir. Univ. Hosp., U. Louisville, 1976-80; asst. v.p. Ohio State U. Hosps., Columbus, 1980-84; exec. dir. Univ. Hosps., Columbus, 1980-84; pres. U. Alta. Hosps., Edmonton, Can., 1984-87, U. Alta Hosp. Found., 1984-87; pres. and chief exec. officer Phila. Hosps. and Higher Edn. Authority, 1987—; asst. prof. Sch. Medicine, Case Western Res. U., Cleve., 1970-76, Sch. Allied Med. Professions, Ohio State U., 1981—; guest lectr. N.Y. Sch. Adminstrv. Medicine, Columbia U., 1966-70. Contbr. to profl. publs. Bd. dirs. Nassau Heart Assn., 1967-70. Fellow Am. Public Health Assn., Am. Coll. Hosp. Adminstrs.; mem. Am. Hosp. Assn. (chmn. research and publ., public gen. sect. 1971—), Phila. Health Mgmt. Corp. (bd. dirs. 1988), Beta Theta Pi. Club: Nat. Exchange (dir. 1967-70). Home: 9 Rex Ct Chestnut Hill Philadelphia PA 19118

CRANDALL, IRA CARLTON, consulting electrical engineer; b. South Amboy, N.J., Oct. 30, 1931; s. Carlton Francis and Claire Elizabeth (Harned) C.; m. Jane Leigh Ford, Jan. 29, 1954; children—Elizabeth Anne, Amy Leigh, Matthew Garrett. BS in Radio Engring., Ind. Inst. Tech., 1954, BS in Elec. Engring., 1958; BS in Electronics Engring., U.S. Naval Postgrad. Sch., 1962; PhD, U. Sussex, 1964; MA, Piedmont U., 1967, DSc (hon.), 1968; LLB, Blackstone Sch. Law, 1970; DLitt, St. Matthew U., 1970; EdD, Mt. Sinai U., 1972; Assoc. Bus., LaSalle U., 1975, B in Computer Sci., 1986. Tchr. Madison Twp. Pub. Schs., N.J., 1954-55; commd. ensign U.S. Navy, 1955, advanced through grades to lt. comdr., 1965, released to inactive duty, 1972; engring. cons. Concord, Calif., 1972—; pres. 7C's Enterprises, Concord, 1972—; v.p. Dickinson Enterprises, Concord, 1973-77, Williamson Engring., Inc., Walnut Creek, Calif., 1974-82; pres., chmn. bd. I.C. Crandall and Assocs., Inc., Concord and Westminster, Calif., Tigard, Oreg., 1976-82; pres. Internat. Research Assocs., Concord, 1982—; chief elec. engr. Gayner Engring. Inc., San Francisco, 1982—. Vice pres. PTA, Concord, 1969; tribal organizer Mt. Diablo YMCA Indian Guide Program, 1971-74; pres. Mt. Diablo Unified Schs. Interested Citizens. Decorated Vietnamese Cross of Valor. Fellow Am. Coll. Engrs.; mem. U.S. Naval Inst. Am. Naval Assn., Assn. Elec. Engrs., IEEE, Am. Inst. Tech. Mgmt. (sr.), Soc. Am. Mil. Engrs., Nat. Model Ry. Assn., Assn. Old Crows, Concord Homeowners Assn., Concord Chamber Singers, Concord Blue Devils, SAR, Pi Upsilon Eta, Gamma Chi Epsilon, Alpha Gamma Upsilon. Republican. Methodist (adminstrv. bd. ch. 1971-76). Clubs: Navy League, Century. Lodge: Optimists (pres.). Home: 5754 Pepperridge Pl Concord CA 94521 Office: PO Box 3268 Walnut Creek CA 94598

CRANDALL, NELSON DAVID, III, lawyer; b. Auburn, Calif., Aug. 8, 1954; s. Nelson David and Alice (Reimer) C.; m. Elizabeth L. Donovan, Aug. 25, 1984; 1 child, Darren. Student, U. Calif., Irvine, 1974-76; AB with high honors, U. Calif., Berkeley, 1976; JD, U. Calif., Davis, 1979. Bar: Calif. 1979, U.S. Dist. Ct. (no. dist.) Calif. 1979, U.S. Dist. Ct. (ea. dist.) Calif. 1980. Ptnr. Hopkins & Carley, San Jose, Calif., 1979—. Contbr. articles to profl. jours. Mediator, arbitrator Santa Clara County Neighborhood Small Claims Project, San Jose, 1980-82; active Santa Clara Valley chpt. ARC, San Jose, 1986—, sec. 1987-89; trustee Jr. Statesman Found., 1986—; bd. dirs. Hope Rehab. Services, San Jose, 1985-88. Mem. ABA, Calif. Bar Assn., Santa Clara County Bar Assn., Phi Beta Kappa. Republican. Club: San Jose Athletic. Lodge: Rotary. Office: Hopkins & Carley 150 Almaden Blvd Suite 1500 15th Floor San Jose CA 95113-2089

CRANDALL, RIEL STANTON, military engineer; b. Fairfax, Minn., Oct. 22, 1914; s. Arthur M. and Lydia (Miller) C.; B.S., U.S. Mil. Acad., 1939; M.S., Cornell U., 1947; grad. U.S. Command and Staff Coll., 1951; m. Beatrice M. Mayer, June 28, 1947; children—Adrienne M., Fern L. Commd. 2d lt. U.S. Army, 1939, advanced through grades to col., 1956; co. comdr., Co. B., 65th Engrs., Hawaii, Pearl Harbor, 1941-42; bn. comdr., 300th Combat Engring. Bn., Europe, 1943-45; asst. prof. mil. sci. and tactics City Coll. N.Y., 1947-50; installation ops. and planning, communications zone, France, 1951-54; post engr., Ft. Leavenworth, Kans., 1954-57; comdr. 1st tng. regiment, Ft. Leonard Wood, Mo., 1957-59; chief engring. div., engring. sect., Korea, 1959-60; post engr., Ft. Benning, Ga., 1960-63, U.S. Mil. Acad., West Point, N.Y., 1963-69; engr. Trinity Coll., Hartford, Conn., 1969-83. Mem. Wethersfield Flood and Erosion Control Com., 1974-79 Bd. dirs. Hartford Neighborhood Centers, 1971-85; mem. Cromwell Bldg. Com., 1981-86; mem. Cromwell Bd. Selectmen, 1985—. Decorated French Croix de Guerre, Legion of Merit. Registered profl. engr., Ga., N.Y. Mem. Nat. Soc. Profl. Engrs., Am. Soc. Engring. Edn., Assn. Phys. Plant Adminstrs., Soc. Am. Mil. Engrs. Club: Rotary. Home: 4 Riverside Dr Cromwell CT 06416

CRANDALL, ROBERT LLOYD, airline executive; b. Westerly, R.I., Dec. 6, 1935; s. Lloyd Evans and Virginia (Beard) C.; m. Margaret Jan Schmults, July 6, 1957; children: Mark William, Martha Conway, Stephen Michael. Student, Coll. William and Mary, 1953-55; B.S., U. R.I., 1957; M.B.A., Wharton Sch., U. Pa., 1960. With Eastman Kodak Co., Rochester, 1960-62, Hallmark Cards, Kansas City, Mo., 1962-66; asst. treas. TWA Inc., N.Y.C., 1966-70; v.p. systems and data services TWA Inc., 1970-71, v.p., controller, 1971-72; sr. v.p., treas. Bloomingdale Bros., N.Y.C., 1972-73; sr. v.p. fin. Am. Airlines, Inc., N.Y.C., 1973-74, sr. v.p. mktg., 1974-80, pres., 1980-85, chmn., 1985—, also dir.; bd. dirs. Republic Bank Corp., Halliburton Co., Recognition Equipment, Inc. Bd. dirs. Boy Scouts Am. Served with Inf. U.S. Army, 1957. Office: AMR Corp PO Box 619616 Dallas TX 75261

CRANDALL, VERN JAY, computer science educator, consultant; b. Logan, Utah, Mar. 18, 1939; s. Bliss Hansen and Mildred (Johnson) C.; m. Linda Rae Storms, Jan. 28, 1972; children: Lance Vernon, Shane Lewis, Scott David. BA, Brigham Young U., 1963; MS, Kans. State U., 1966; PhD, U. Wash., 1972. Machine operator, systems programmer DHI Computing Service, Provo, Utah, 1954-63, statistician, 1963-65, v.p. research and devel., 1965-79; asst. prof. computer sci. and stats. Brigham Young U., Provo, 1968-72, assoc. prof., 1972-79, prof., 1979—; pres., chmn. Vern J. Crandall & Assocs. Inc., Provo, 1982—; bd. dirs., treas. Innovation Enterprises, Inc., 1972-79; cons. Inst. Logopedics Wichita (Kans.) State U., 1963-65, IBM, Sperry Corp., IOMEGA Crop., Pacific Telesis, Novell Corp., others 1978—. Author: Problem Solving and Writing Commercial Grade Programs Using Pascal, 1986; also articles to profl. jours. Grantee NIH Kans. State U., 1963-65, U. Wash., Seattle, 1965-68, 72, NSF, 1971-72, others. 1982—. Mem. IEEE, Assn. Computing Machinery. Republican. Mormon. Lodge: Lions (officer Provo club 1968-74). Home: 1224 E 700 South Provo UT 84601 Office: Brigham Young U 236 TMCB Provo UT 84602

CRANE, GLENDA PAULETTE, educator; b. Orlando, Fla., June 29, 1946; d. James Author and Elizabeth Lorine (Johnson) C. AA in Edn., Orlando Jr. Coll., 1966; BA in Elem. Edn., U. S. Fla., 1967; postgrad. So. Bapt. Theol. Sem., 1970; MEd, Rollins Coll., 1985. Tchr., Orange County Schs., Orlando, 1967-70, 79-80, Lake Highland Prep. Sch., Orlando, 1981—; tchr. Belle Glade (Fla.) Christian Sch., 1970-79, asst. prin., 1970-74, prin., 1975-79. State treas. Fla. Rainbow Girls., 1964. Mem. NEA, Fla. Edn. Assn., Fla. Council Tchrs. English, Orange County Tchrs. Assn., Assn. Supervision and Curriculum Devel., Internat. Reading Assn., Orange County Reading Council of Internat. Reading Assn., Fla. Reading Assn., Nat. Council for the Social Studies, Alumni Assn. U. South Fla., Alumni Assn. So. Bapt. Theol. Sem., Kappa Delta Pi. Democrat. Baptist. Clubs: Winter Park Pilot, Eastern Star, Winter Park Rainbow Girls. Home: 2406 S Bumby St Orlando FL 32806 Office: 901 N Highland Ave Orlando FL 32803

CRANE, JAMES GORDON, artist, writer, visual arts educator; b. Hartsborne, Okla., May 21, 1927; s. Gordon Turner and Naomi (Harrison) C.; m. Jeanette Marie Forgie, June 23, 1951 (div.); children: Lise Crane Tuley, Catherine Crane Knorpel, James Carey; m. Heidemarie Dhom Albright, June 26, 1982. AA, Jackson Community Coll., Mich., 1949; BA, Albion Coll., 1951; MA, State U. Iowa, 1953; MFA, Mich. State U., 1962. Art tchr., Jackson, Mich., 1951-55; instr. art U. Wis., River Falls, 1955-57, St. Cloud State Coll., Minn., 1957-58; chmn. dept. art U. Wis., River Falls, 1958-63; coordinator art dept. Fla. Presbyn. Coll./Eckerd Coll., St. Petersburg, 1963-72, 75-85, chmn. collegium of creative arts Eckerd Coll., 1972-75, prof. visual arts, 1976—. Author: What Other Time, 1953, On Edge, 1965, GTM-The Great Teaching Machine, 1966, Inside Out, 1967, Parables, 1971; one-man show: Colombo Americano USIA, Cali, Colombia, 1983; exhibitor group shows: U.S. Embassy Art Collection, Katmandu, Nepal, 1967-75, Lima, Peru, 1975-80; painter collage: Valley of Dry Bones, Ford Found. Walker Art Ctr., 1962; contbg. artist Motive mag., 1950-70, mem. editorial adv. bd., 1966-68; feature cartoonist Ave Maria, 1964-69, United Ch. Herald, 1967-71, Circuit Rider, 1987. Founding bd. dirs. St. Petersburg Arts Commn., 1974-75; bd. dirs. The Arts Ctr., St. Petersburg, 1987—. Danforth Found. grantee, 1960; recipient Disting. Alumni award Albion Coll., 1972, Outstanding Alumni award, 1974, Staub Disting. Tchr. award, 1987. Office: Eckerd College Art Dept PO Box 12560 Saint Petersburg FL 33733

CRANE, KENT BRUCE, management services executive; b. North Hornell, N.Y., July 25, 1935; s. Willard L. and Elizabeth (Ewart) C.; BA cum laude, Dartmouth Coll., 1957; postgrad. in internat. econs. Am. U., 1958; divorced;children—Jeffrey Stuart, James Andrew. Third sec. polit. sect. U.S. Embassy, Jakarta, Indonesia, 1960-62; with U.S. Dept. State, Washington, 1963-64; vice consul in charge econ. sect. U.S. Consulate, Zanzibar, 1964-65; 2d. sec. polit. sect. U.S. Embassy, Accra, Ghana, 1965-67; sr. research asso. for fgn. affairs, sec. to task force on conduct of fgn. relations, Republican Nat. Com., 1967-68; spl. asst. to Senator George Murphy, 1968-69; nat. security affairs adv. to v.p. of U.S., 1969-72; asst. dir. for East Asia and Pacific, USIA, 1972-74; adminstrv. asst. to Rep. Peter H.B. Frelinghuysen, 1974-75; project dir. U.S. Commn. on Orgn. of Govt. for Conduct of Fgn. Policy, 1974-75; chmn. bd. Crane Pub. Co., Ridgewood, N.J., 1975-80; co-chmn. Africa subcom. Rep. Nat. Com., 1978-80; pres., mng. dir. Crane Group Ltd., Washington, 1978—; pres. Ranch Devel. and Mgmt., Inc., Tex., 1980—; officer, dir. various cos. U.S. and abroad including Corona Co., Harrow Corp., Belize-Orient Corp.; real estate joint ventures U.S., N.Z., Spain, Africa. Served to 1st lt. U.S. Army, 1957-59, to capt. USAR. Mem. Inst. Strategic Studies (London), Nat. Rifle Assn. (dir.), Explorers Club, Game Conservation Internat. Clubs: Met. (N.Y.C.); Internat., Capitol Hill (Washington); Internat. Economists, Mt. Kenya Safari, Safari Internat. Office: PO Box 25535 Washington DC 20007

CRANE, LEO STANLEY, railroad executive; b. Cin., Sept. 7, 1915; s. Leo Vincent and Blanche Gottlieb (Mitchell) C.; m. Joan McCoy, Sept. 3, 1976; children by previous marriage—Pamela Blanche, Penelope Ann. B.S.E., George Washington U., 1938. With So.Ry. Co., Washington, 1937-63, 65-80, engr. of tests, 1948-56, mech. research engr., 1956-59, v.p. engring. and research, 1965-70, exec. v.p. ops., 1970-76, pres., chief adminstrv. officer, 1976-77, pres., chief exec. officer, 1977-79, chmn., 1979-80; chmn., chief exec. officer, dir. Consolidated Rail Corp. (known as Conrail), Phila., 1981-88. Trustee George Washington U. Fellow ASTM (past pres.), ASME; mem. Nat. Acad. Engring., Soc. Automotive Engrs., Am. Ry. Engring. Assn., Am. Soc. Traffic and Transp. Clubs: Metropolitan, Burning Tree, Phila. Country, Union League (Phila.); Gulph Mills Golf (King of Prussia, Pa.). Office: Consol Rail Corp 6 Penn Center Plaza Philadelphia PA 19103-2959

CRANE, ROGER RYAN, management consulting executive; b. Hamilton, Mont., Sept. 17, 1921; s. Ralph Lane and Rose (Casserly) C.; m. Jeannette Hurlbut, June 9, 1945 (div. 1968); children: Roger Jr., Carolyn, Gregory; m. Licia Chini, June 5, 1968; 1 son, Matteo. BA, U. Toronto; MSc, MIT; PhD, Kennedy-Western U. Cert. mgmt. cons., U.S. Mem. ops. evaluation group MIT, Cambridge, 1948-51; dir. ops. research West Air Brake Co., Pitts., 1951-55; nat. dir. mgmt. services Touche Ross & Co., N.Y.C., 1955-68; sr. v.p. Sci. Mgmt. Corp. N.J., 1968-75; pres. Roger Crane Group Inc., Washington, 1975—; chmn. IBO Ltd., London, 1988—. Editor: Jour. Mgmt. Tech., 1961-66. Served to lt. USNR, 1943-46. Mem. Inst. Mgmt. Scis. (pres. 1957), Ops. Research Soc. Am. (mem. council 1967-69), Inst. Purchasing and Supply (U.K.), Sigma Xi. Home: Via Gignous 9, 20149 Milan Italy

CRANIN, ABRAHAM NORMAN, oral surgeon, researcher; b. Bklyn., June 17, 1927; s. Samuel Leonard and Henrietta C.; m. Marilyn Sunners, June 14, 1953; children: Jonathan, Andrew, Elizabeth. A.B., Swarthmore Coll., 1947; D.D.S., NYU, 1951; cert., Mt. Sinai Hosp., 1952, 53; DEng. (hon.) Rose-Hulman Inst. Tech., 1987. Assoc. attending oral surgeon Mt. Sinai Hosp., N.Y.C., 1961—; practice dentistry specializing in oral surgery; chief oral surgery Greenpoint Hosp., Bklyn., 1961-63; attending oral surgeon Community Hosp., Bklyn., 1962-72; assoc. clin. prof. Mt. Sinai Sch. Medicine, N.Y.C., 1974—; clin. prof. oral and maxillofacial surgery NYU, 1975—; dir. dental and oral surgery Brookdale Hosp. Med. Ctr., Bklyn., 1965—; cons. Nat. Patent Devel. Corp., N.Y.C., 1964-70; dir. Soc. for Biomaterials, San Antonio, 1973—, pres. 1988-89, recipient Clemson award 1976; chmn. study sect. NIH Oral Biology and Medicine, 1982—, mem. study sect. Clin. Scis. Rev. Group Div. Research Group; clin. prof. oral and maxillofacial surgery N.J. Dental Sch., 1987—, dir. dental implant ctr., 1987—; cons. oral surgeon Bklyn. Devel. Ctr., 1973—. Author 4 books; editor-in-chief: Jour. Oral Implantology Quar, 1973 (Gold Key 1974), 1987—. Jour. Biomed. Materials and Research, 1978-88 (cert. 1981, award Am. Assn. Pubs.). Pres. Informed Citizens Com. Hewlett Bay Park, N.Y., 1976. Served to ensign USN, 1950-51. Named Man of Yr. Fedn. of Jewish Philanthropies, Bklyn., 1973; honoree United Jewish Appeal, Brookdale Hosp., 1980; recipient award of honor Met. Conf. Hosp. Dentists, 1982. Fellow Am. Acad. Implant Dentistry (pres. 1972), Internat. Coll. Dentists, Am. Dental Soc. Anesthesiology, Royal Soc. Health, Internat. Coll. Dentistry, Brazilian Soc. Oral and Maxilofacial Surgery (hon., Rene Lefort medal 1980), Acad. Dental Materials, Japanese Soc. for Biomaterials; hon. mem. Japanese Soc. Implant Dentistry (medal and plaque 1980). Clubs: Woodmere Bay (Bay Park, N.Y.); Woodmere (N.Y.). Home: Copper Top Hewlett Bay Park NY 11557 Office: Brookdale Hosp Med Ctr Brookdale Plaza Brooklyn NY 11212

CRANN, GORDON PARKER, columnist; b. Toronto, Ont., Can., Feb. 20, 1952; s. Joseph Parker and Elsie (Bramwell) C. BA in Geography, U. Toronto, 1975, MA in Pub. Adminstrn., 1985. Alderman Borough Ea. York, Toronto, 1978-85; political columnist Toronto Star, 1986-87; chmn. Nuclear Weapons Legal Action, Toronto, 1988—; cons. Gordon Crann Assocs.; bd. dirs. Flemingdon Community Legal Services, World Federalists Can. Chmn. Ea. York Inter-Agy. Com., 1983; candidate New Dem. Party Ont., 1985, 86.; bd. dirs. Social Planning Council Met. Toronto, 1982-85. Recipient Laskin prize Constl. Law U. Toronto, 1987. Mem. Can. Bar Assn. (Ont. sect. sec. 1987—, Pitney Bowes Achievement award 1988), Can. Civil Liberties Assn., Inst. Pub. Adminstrn. Can., Bd. Trade Met. Toronto, Jaycees. Mem. United Ch. Can. Lodge: Ind. Order Foresters.

CRANSTON, ALAN, U.S. senator; b. Palo Alto, Calif., June 19, 1914; s. William MacGregor and Carol (Dixon) C.; m. Norma Weintraub, May 19, 1978; children: Robin MacGregor (dec.), Kim MacGregor. Student, Pomona Coll., 1932-33, U. Mexico, 1933; A.B., Stanford, 1936. Fgn. corr. Internat. News Service, Eng., Italy, Ethiopia, Germany, 1936-38; Washington rep. Common Council Am. Unity, Washington, 1940-41; chief fgn. lang. div. O.W.I., Washington, 1942-44; exec. sec. Council for Am.-Italian Affairs, Inc., Washington, 1945-46; partner bldg. and real estate firm Ames-Cranston Co., Palo Alto, Calif., 1947-58; controller State of Calif., 1959-67; pres. Homes for a Better America Inc., 1967-68; v.p. Carlsberg Financial Corp., Los Angeles, 1968; mem. U.S. Senate from Calif., 1969—; Democratic whip U.S. Senate, 1977—; mem. com. on banking, housing and urban affairs, chmn. subcom. housing and urban affair, mem. com. on fgn. relations, chmn. subcom. East Asia affairs, chmn. com. on vets. affairs, mem. Dem. steering com., Dem. policy com. and Select com. on Intelligence. Author: The Big Story, 1940, The Killing of the Peace, 1945. Mem. exec. com. Calif. Democratic Central Com., 1954-60; pres. Calif. Dem. Council, 1953-57. Served with AUS, 1944-45. Mem. United World Federalists (nat. pres. 1949-52). Club: Overseas Press Am. Office: 112 Hart Senate Bldg Washington DC 20510

CRANSTON, HOWARD STEPHEN, lawyer; b. Hartford, Conn., Oct. 20, 1937; s. Howard Samuel and Agnes (Corvo) C.; m. Karen Youngman, June 16, 1962; children: Margaret, Susan. BA cum laude, Pomona Coll., 1959; LLB, Harvard U., 1962. Bar: Calif. 1963, U.S. Dist. Ct. (cen. dist.) Calif. 1966, U.S. Dist. Ct. (no. dist.) Calif. 1973, U.S. Dist. Ct. (so. dist.) Calif. 1976, U.S. Supreme Ct. 1972. Assoc. MacDonald & Halsted, Los Angeles, 1964-68; ptnr. MacDonald, Halsted & Laybourne, Los Angeles, 1968-82, of counsel, 1982-86; pres. Knapp Communications, Los Angeles, 1982-87; pres. S.C. Cons. Corp., 1987—; dir. Wood Knapp & Co., Cambridge Mfg., St. Clair & Co. (mem. conf. bd.). Served to 1st lt. U.S. Army, 1962-64. Mem. Assn. Corp. Growth (mem. conf. bd.). Republican. Episcopalian. Club: San Gabriel Country, Harvard (N.Y.C.). Office: Knapp Communications Corp 1613 Chelsea Rd #252 San Marino CA 91108

CRANSTON, JOHN WELCH, historian; b. Utica, N.Y., Dec. 21, 1931; s. Earl and Mildred (Welch) C.; B.A., Pomona Coll., 1953; M.A., Columbia U., 1964; Ph.D., U. Wis., 1970. Asst. prof. history W. Tex. State U., 1970-74, U. Mo., Kansas City, 1970; asst. prof. Rust Coll., Holly Springs, Miss., 1974-80, asso. prof., 1980-83; historian U.S. Army Armor Ctr., Ft. Knox, Ky., 1983—. Served with U.S. Army, 1953-55. Nat. Endowment for Humanities fellow, summer 1976, summer 1981. Mem. Am. Hist. Assn., Phi Alpha Theta. Democrat. Episcopalian. Contbr. hist. articles to profl. lit. Home: PO Box 892 Radcliff KY 40160

CRANSTON, MAURICE (WILLIAM), political science educator, author; b. London, May 8, 1920; s. William and Catherine (Harris) C.; m. Helga May, July 20, 1940 (div. Oct. 1949); m. 2d Baroness Maximiliana von und zu Fraunberg, Nov. 11, 1958; children—Nicholas, Stephen. B.A., St. Catherine's Coll, Oxford U., 1948, M.A., 1951, B.Litt., 1951. Lectr. in polit. sci. London Sch. Econs., 1959-64, reader, 1964-68, prof., 1968-77, 82-86; head dept. polit. sci. European Univ. Inst., Florence, Italy, 1978-82; vis. prof. U. Calif., San Diego, 1986-88; lit. adviser Methuens, London, 1959-69. Author books, the most recent being: Philosophy and Language, 1969; La Quintessence de Sartre, 1970; The Mask of Politics, 1972; Jean-Jacques: the early life and work of J.J. Rousseau, 1983; Philosophers and Pamphleteers, 1986; editor books, the most recent being: (with R.S. Peters) Hobbes and Rousseau, 1972; (with Peter Mair) Ideologie et Politique, 1980, Langage et Politique, 1982; translator: (J.J. Rousseau) The Social Contract, 1964, Discourse on Inequality, 1983; (J. Hartnack) Wittgenstein and Modern Philosophy, 1965. Hon. fellow St. Catherine's Coll., Oxford U., 1984; named Commandeur Ordre des Palmes Académiques, Paris, 1987. Fellow Royal Soc. Lit; mem. Alliance Francaise (v.p. London chpt. 1964—), Internat. Inst. Polit. Philosophy (pres. 1978-81), Am. Acad. Arts and Scis. (hon. fgn.). Mem. Ch. of England. Clubs: Garrick, Internat. PEN (London). Office: London Sch Econs, London WC2A 2AE England

CRANSTON, WILBER CHARLES, engineering company executive; b. Wenatchee, Wash., Nov. 4, 1933; s. Wilber James and Dorothy June (Thompson) C.; m. Martha Elisabeth Nyqvist, Dec. 26, 1975; children: John Albert, Cinthia Carrol, Barbara June. Student pub. schs. Mech. draftsman Cranston Machinery Co., Inc., Portland, Oreg., 1950-52, supt. shop, 1954-60; indsl. engr. Norris Thermador Corp., Riverbank, Calif., 1952-54; mgr. dept. engring. C. Tennant, Sons & Co. of N.Y., Warren, Ohio, 1960-70; cons. A. Ahlstrom Osakeyhtio, Karhula Engring. Works, Finland, 1971-77; founder, mng. dir. Cranston Ky, Kotka, Finland, 1977—. Patentee automatic binding machines, semi-automatic hooks, one-trip load lifting straps. Mem. Internat. Cargo Handling Coordination Assn. Office: Cranston Ky, PO Box 14, 48400 Kotka Finland

CRANTON, ELMER MITCHELL, physician; b. Haverhill, Mass., Sept. 17, 1932; s. Watson Hallet and Laura Mae (Mitchell) C.; children—John Allen, Anne Elizabeth, Catherine Louise, Jennifer Lynn. M.D., Harvard U., 1964; student U. Colo., 1957-59, U. Erlangen (W. Ger.), 1959-60. Rotating intern U.S. Naval Hosp., Pensacola, Fla., 1964-65, gen. surg. staff, 1965; gen. practice medicine, Encinitas, Calif., 1969-72, Arcadia, Calif., 1972-75; chief of staff USPHS Indian Hosp., Talihina, Okla., 1975-76; practice medicine specializing in family practice and preventive medicine, Trout Dale, Va., 1976—; med. dir. Mt. Rogers Clinic, Trout Dale, 1977—. Tchr., med. adv. Vol. Rescue Squads, Mt. Rogers, 1977—. Served with USN, 1951-58, 64-69; USPHS, 75-76. Diplomate Am. Bd. Family Practice. Fellow Am. Acad. Family Physicians, Internat. Coll. Applied Nutrition; mem. Am. Holistic Med. Assn. (pres. 1980-82), Smyth County Med. Soc. (pres. 1980), AMA, Med. Soc. Va., S.W. Va. Med. Soc., Va. Acad. Family Physicians, Internat. Acad. Preventive Medicine, Internat. Acad. Parapsychology and Medicine, Am. Geriatrics Soc., Mensa, Alpha Epsilon Delta. Republican. Methodist (trustee 1979—). Home: Route 1 Box 13 Trout Dale VA 24378 Office: Mt Rogers Clinic Ripshin Rd PO Box 44 Trout Dale VA 24378

CRAPON DE CAPRONA, NOËL FRANÇOIS MARIE (COUNT), lawyer, historian; b. Chambery, Savoie, France, May 23, 1928; s. Denys and Eleanor Worthington (Mather) C. de C.; Baccalaureats, Coll. St. Martin, Pontoise, France, 1947; LL.B., U. Paris, 1952, Diploma, Inst. Comparative Law, 1951, postgrad. Sch. Polit. Scis., 1952-54; m. Barbro Sigrid Wenne, 1954; children—Guy, Yann. Asst. mgr. Sta. Catalina Estancias, Argentina, 1947-48; editor dept. gen. affairs and info. FAO, UN, Rome, 1954-57, liaison officer for UN and various orgns. FAO Office Dir. Gen., 1957-65, chief reports and records, 1966-72, chief conf. ops. br., 1972-74, sec. gen. FAO Conf. and Council, 1974-78, dir. FAO Conf., Council and Protocol Affairs, Rome, 1974-83. Served with French Army, 1944. Recipient 25 Years of Service award, Silver medal FAO, 1979. Mem. Alumni Assn. Coll. St. Martin, Alumni Assn. Ecole des Sciences Politiques; Soc. in France of SAR. Roman Catholic. Research on early medieval history, especially Longobards. Home: Lojovägen 73, S-18147 Lidingo Sweden

CRAPSE, LARRY MURDAUGH, educational administrator; b. Walterboro, S.C., Aug. 5, 1947; s. Murdaugh and Ida (Chisolm) C. BA, U. S.C., 1969; MAT, The Citadel, 1973; postgrad., Ind. U., 1975, Columbia U. Tchrs. Coll., 1978, Harvard U., summer 1981, Yale U., 1987; cert. in lit. NYU, 1978, in thinking, Havard U., 1987. English tchr. Southside High Sch., Florence, S.C., 1969-70; head English dept. Wilson High Sch., Florence, 1970-77; coordinator gifted programs Florence Dist. 1 Schs., 1977-79, coordinator secondary English, 1977—; instr. rhetoric U. Ill., 1983-84; instr. cert. courses for tchrs. Contbr. articles to profl. publs. Mem. NEA, S.C. Edn. Assn., Nat. Council Tchrs. of English, S.C. Council Tchrs. of English, Assn. Supervision and Curriculum Devel., Internat. Reading Assn. Mem. Christian Ch. (Disciples of Christ). Home: 803-F Cheraw Dr Florence SC 29501 Office: 319 S Dargan St Florence SC 29501

CRASILNECK, HAROLD BERNARD, clinical psychologist; b. San Antonio, Apr. 4, 1921; s. John and Kate (Wolfson) C.; m. Sherry Gold, Jan. 18, 1959; children—Rik, Candace, Jonathan. B.A., Trinity U., San Antonio, 1947; M.A., U. Houston, 1948, Ph.D., 1954. Diplomate Am. Bd. Examiners in Psychol. Hypnosis. Asst. prof. Trinity U., 1949-51; instr. U. Houston, 1951-53; intern in clin. psychology U. Tex. Southwestern Med. Sch., 1953-54, asst. prof., 1954-60, clin. prof. dept. anesthesiology, 1971—, dept. psychiatry, 1971—; pvt. practice clin. psychology and hypnotherapy, 1961—; staff Parkland Meml, Children's Med. Ctr., Baylor U. hosps. Served with USN, 1942-44. Recipient awards Soc. Clin. and Exptl. Hypnosis, 1958, 69, 71; Ben Raginsky award, 1965; Morton Prince award, 1968; Dorcus award, 1971, Best Book award, 1976, Milton Erickson award, 1979, 81; cert. merit Nat. Coll. Criminal Def. Lawyers. Fellow Am. Soc. Clin. Hypnosis (v.p. 1985, pres. 1986-87, editorial bd.); mem. Australian Soc. Clin. Hypnosis (hon.), Royal Soc. Physicians and Surgeons (hon.), Am. Psychol. Assn., Dallas Psychol. Assn. (pres. 1959-60), Southwestern Psychol. Assn., Soc. Clin. and Exptl. Hypnosis (pres. 1963-65, editorial bd.), Mensa, Sigma Xi, Phi Kappa Phi, Psi Chi. Author: Clinical Hypnosis: Principles and Applications, 2d edit., 1985. Contbr. articles to profl. jours. Home: 5635 Yolanda Circle Dallas TX 75229 Office: Medical City Dallas Suite C 606-7777 Forest Ln Dallas TX 75230

CRASSARIS, LEONIDAS G., pharmaceutical products executive, researcher; b. Alexandria, Egypt, Mar. 23, 1935; s. George P. and Helen (Vakirtzi) C.; m. Valentina-Victorovna Erascova, Aug. 4, 1962; children: George, Alexios-Victor. BS in Medicine, Faculty of Medicine, 1960, PhD in Pharmacology, 1978. Diplomate Am. Bd. Med. Examiners. Salesperson Squibb AEBE, Athens, Greece, 1961-63, mgr. sales, 1963-66, dir. mktg., 1966-79, chmn., chief exec. officer, 1979—. Contbr. articles to profl. jours. Mem. Med. Assn. Athens, N.Y. Acad. Sci., Am. Soc. Microbiology, Brit. Soc. for Venereal Diseases, Assn. Greek Pharm. Industry (bd. dirs. Athens chpt. 1982—), Greek Working Group Pharm Mfg. Assn. (chmn. 1982—), Greek-Am. C. of C. (bd. dirs. 1982—). Clubs: Propeller (Porto Piraeus); Athenian (Athens). Home: 52-54 Vas. Sophias Str, 153 41 Aghia Paraskevi

Greece Office: Squibb AEBE, Messohgion Ave, 67 Tzavela Str, 152 31 Halandri Greece

CRAVEN, DONALD NEIL, former finance company executive; b. Springfield, Mass., Aug. 18, 1924; s. C.S. and Edna B. (Blanchard) C.; m. Betty L. Rodda, July 16, 1947; 1 dau., Patricia Craven Matheson. Student, Williams Coll., 1942-43, Grad. Sch. Bus., Columbia U., 1967. Advt. sales staff Springfield Newspapers, 1946-51; fin. br. mgr. Assos. Investment Co., South Bend, Ind., 1951-62; br. mgr. Ford Motor Credit Co., Boston, 1962-64; br. mgr., then regional mgr. Chrysler Fin. Corp., 1964-69; v.p. Eastern U.S., 1969-80; dir. Indsl. Components Corp., Wilbraham, Mass. Mem. ARC (bd. dirs. fin. com. Springfield chpt., Northeast Regional Blood Services, dist. rep. for Mass.), S.C.O.R.E. Served with USMC, 1943-46, 50-51. Clubs: Landmark (Stamford, Conn.); Dennis (Mass.) Yacht. Lodges: Masons, Shriners. Home: 18 Manchester Terr Springfield MA 01108

CRAVEN, HOMER HENRY, JR., pilot, aviation consultant; b. Seattle, Jan. 31, 1925; s. Homer Henry and Juanita Normah (Briscoe) C.; student S.W. Tex. State Coll.; m. Mary Kathleen Weaver, May 3, 1945; children—James Michael, Scott Marshall, Anne Elizabeth Craven McDonald. With Boeing Airplane Co., Seattle, 1946-48, Smith Aviation, Renton, Wash., 1948-52; pilot Northwest Orient Airlines, Seattle, 1952-85, B-747 capt., 1976-85; aviation cons. 19—. Served with USAAF, 1943-45; PTO. Decorated Air medal. Mem. Am. Soc. Aerospace Edn., Nat. Aero. Assn., Exptl. Aircraft Assn., Aircraft Owners and Pilots Assn., 14th Air Force Assn., Northwest Captain's Club, Confederate Air Force. Episcopalian. Author research papers on fuel conservation. Home: 2005 180th Ct NE Redmond WA 98052 Office: Northwest Airlines Sea-Tac Airport Seattle WA 98001

CRAVEN, JOHN ANTHONY GEORGE, economics educator; b. London, June 17, 1949; s. George Marriot and Dorothy (Walford) C.; m. Laura Elizabeth Loftis, July 12, 1974; children: Matthew Thomas, Rebecca Mary. BA, King's Coll., Cambridge, Eng., 1970, MA, 1974. Lectr. U. Kent, Canterbury, Eng., 1971-76, sr. lectr., 1976-80, reader, 1980-86, prof. econs., 1986—, dean social scis., 1987—; cons. English govt., 1975—. Author: Distribution of the Product, 1979, Introduction to Economics, 1984. Kennedy Meml. scholar, 1970-71. Mem. Royal Econ. Soc., Econometric Soc., Electoral Reform Soc. Home: Old Lynch Cottage, Eastry Kent CT13 OHR, England Office: U Kent, Eliot Coll, Canterbury Kent CT2 7NS, England

CRAWFORD, EARL BOYD, former government official; b. Washington, Apr. 13, 1906; s. James Albert and Olla Lola (Nigh) C.; m. Gertrude Galloway, June 15, 1927; 1 son, Christopher Paul. Student, Strayer Bus. Coll., 1924; grad., Mt. Pleasant Sch. for Secs., 1929. Sec. to mem. of Congress, 1932-36; sec., chief staff to dir. gen. U.S. Constn. Sesquicentennial Commn., 1936-39; staff adminstr., clk. Com. Fgn. Affairs Ho. of Reps., 1939-70; mem. U.S. del. UN Conf. Internat. Orgn., San Francisco, 1945, UN Gen. Assembly, London, 1946, N.Y., 1946, 49, 50, 53, Paris, 1951; sec. UN com. UNRRA, 1946; mem. U.S. del. UN com. UNRRA (Fourth Council Meeting), 1946; staff mem. U.S. del. Consultative Assembly Europe, Strasbourg, France, 1965, 66, 67; Mem. adv. com. inst. position U.S. world affairs Am. U., lectr. U.S. fgn. policy, 1949, 50; served with spl. Congl. study mission, Alaska, 1947, Europe, 1951, Far East, South Asia, Middle East, 1954, Mediterranean, 1956, Guatemala, Mex., 1957, Japan, Vietnam, Thailand, 1965, Colombia, 1968; congl. del. 6th-8th NATO Parliamentarian's Conf., Paris; mem. del. Brit.-Am. Parliamentary Conf., Bermuda, 1961, 63, 64, 66, 68, staff mem., 1966, 68; U.S. del. Commonwealth Parliamentary Conf., Wellington, New Zealand, 1965, Consultative Assembly Council Europe, 1968; staff mem. U.S. del. North Atlantic Assembly, The Hague, Netherlands, 1970; ofcl. observer 22d ann. session North Atlantic Assembly, Colonial Williamsburg, Va., 1976. Author: ofcl. report U.S. Constn. Sesquicentennial Commn. contained in History of the Formation of the Union Under the Constitution, 1941. Mem. Am. Polit. Sci. Assn., Am. Acad. Polit. and Social Sci., Am. Soc. Internat. Law. Home: 8235 The Midway Annandale VA 22003

CRAWFORD, EDWARD E., psychologist; b. Lawton, Ky., July 31, 1929; s. Thurmon Ray and Hazel Mae (Johnson) C.; AB, W.Va. U., 1956, MA, 1958; postgrad. U. Pa., 1956-57; PhD, Cath. U. Am., 1969; m. Patricia Ann Dulin, Sept. 4, 1954; children—Scott, Susan. Clin. psychologist Rosewood State Hosp., Owings Mills, Md., 1957-67; sr. staff psychologist Montrose Sch. for Girls, Reisterstown, Md., 1967-71; psychol. cons. Md. Dept. Health and Mental Hygiene, Balt., 1971-74, dir. psychol. and developmental services Md. Preventive Medicine Adminstrn., 1974-76, chief psychology programs Dept. Health and Mental Hygiene, 1976-80; chief psychology services Md. Administrn. Chronically Ill and Aging, 1980-81, chief psychologist Henryton (Md.) Center, 1981-84; co-owner Psychol. Assessment & Therapy, 1984-86; pvt. practice psychology, 1984—; psychol. cons. Kernan Crippled Children's Hosp., 1972, Wicomico County (Md.) Health Dept., 1958-60, Anne Arundel County (Md.) Pub. Schs., 1965-66. Served with AUS, 1948-52. VA trainee, 1956-57. Fellow Md. Psychol. Assn.; mem. Am. Psychol. Assn., Psi Chi. Methodist (bd. stewards 1965-66). Club: Masons. Office: 1005 Timber Trail Rd Towson MD 21204

CRAWFORD, HOMER, retired lawyer, paper company executive; b. St. Louis, Nov. 28, 1916; s. Raymond S. and Mary (Homer) C.; m. Esther Wilkinson, Oct. 4, 1944 (div. 1949); 1 dau., Candace C.; m. Sara E. Twigg, May 3, 1952; children—Georgiana, William Twigg. A.B., Amherst Coll., 1938; LL.B., U. Va., 1941. Admitted to N.Y. bar, 1942; assoc. firm LeBoeuf, Lamb, Leiby & MacRae, 1942-54, partner, 1954-56, v.p., sec. St. Regis Paper Co., 1956-82, gen. counsel, 1981, now ret. Mem. Am., N.Y. State bar assns., Am. Soc. Corp. Secs. (dir. 1965-68), Theta Delta Chi. Republican. Presbyterian. Home: PO Box 1057 11 Laurel Heights Old Lyme CT 06371

CRAWFORD, JEAN ANDRE, counselor; b. Chgo., Apr. 12, 1941; d. William Moses and Geneva Mae (Lacy) Jones; student Shimer Coll., 1959-60; BA, Carthage Coll., 1966; MEd, Loyola U., Chgo., 1971; postgrad. Nat. Coll. Edn., Evanston, Ill., 1971-77, Northwestern U., 1976-83; m. John N. Crawford, Jr., June 28, 1969; cert. counselor Nat. Bd. Cert. Counselors, elem. edn., spl. edn. and pupil personnel services, Ill. Med. technologist, Chgo., 1960-62; primary and spl. edn. tchr. Chgo. Pub. Schs., 1966-71, counselor maladjusted children and their families, 1971-88; counselor juvenile first-offenders, 1968-88; post-secondary vocat. counselor, 1988—. Vol. Sta. WTTW-TV; vol. counselor deaf children and their families; counselor post-secondary students. Mem. Ill. Assn. Counseling and Devel., Am., Ill. sch. counselors assns., Council Exceptional Children, Am. Assn. Counseling Devel., Coordinating Council Handicapped Children, Shimer Coll. Alumni Assn. (sec. 1982-84), Phi Delta Kappa. Home: 601 E 32d St Chicago IL 60616 Office: 3233 W 31st St Chicago IL 60623

CRAWFORD, JOHN FORT, lawyer; b. N.Y.C., Sept. 23, 1937; s. Alfred Ross and Barbara (Fort) C.; m. Elisabeth Tjerneld, June 6, 1962 (div.); 1 child, Alexander Olaf. BA, Haverford Coll., 1958; MA, Fletcher Sch. Law and Diplomacy, Tufts U., 1959; postgrad. Institut d'Etudes Politiques, Paris, 1959-61; JD, Columbia U., 1964. Bar: D.C. 1965, U.S. Ct. Appeals D.C. 1965. Assoc., Surrey & Morse, Washington, 1964-68; spl. asst. to dir. gen. ILO, Geneva, 1968-70; assoc. Surrey & Morse, Paris, 1970-71, ptnr., 1971-85, Jones, Day, Reavis & Pogue, Paris, 1986— . Bd. govs. Am. Hosp. Paris, 1983—. L.J. Palmer scholar, 1957-58; Noble Found. fellow, 1958-60. Mem. Bar Assn. D.C., ABA, Assn. of Bar of City of N.Y., Internat. Bar Assn., Am. C. of C. in France (dir. 1976— pres. 1985-88), European Council Am. C. of C. (chmn. 1987—), Internat. C. of C. (council mem. 1976—), U.S. Council for Intetrnat. Bus. (trustee 1988—), Institut pour l'Arbitrage International (treas., dir. 1985—), Council Fgn. Relations. Democrat. Presbyterian. Club: Cercle de l'Union Interalliee (Bd. dirs.; Paris), Maxim's Bus. (decorated Chevalier Légion d'Honneur.

CRAWFORD, LEWIS CLEAVER, engineer; b. Salina, Kans., Dec. 7, 1925; s. Percival Wallace and Viva Estelle (Beichle) C.; m. Helen Alleyne Henry, May 28, 1950; children: Dorothy Caroline, Lewis Henry. B.Engring., Yale U., 1946. Registered profl. engr., Kans. Engr. Cemenstone Corp., Pitts., 1946-47; engr., then assoc. Wilson & Co. (engrs. and architects), Salina, 1947-67; ptnr. Wilson & Co. (engrs. and architects), 1967-87, cons., 1988—; dir. Saltec, Inc.; bd. dirs. Kans. Builders Forum, Kans. U. Center for Research; mem. adv. com. Am. Gas Assn. Served with USNR, 1943-46. Fellow ASCE; mem. Nat. Soc. Profl. Engrs., Am. Concrete Inst., Kans. Cons. Engrs. (chmn.), Kans. Engring. Soc. (dir.), SAR. Republican. Methodist. Club: Salina Country. Office: 631 E Crawford St Salina KS 67401

CRAWFORD, LINDA SIBERY, lawyer, educator; b. Ann Arbor, Mich., Apr. 27, 1947; d. Donald Eugene and Verla Lillian (Schneck) Sibery; m. Leland Allardice Crawford, Apr. 4, 1970; children: Christina, Lillian, Leland. Student, Keele U., 1969; BA, U. Mich., 1969; postgrad., SUNY, Potsdam, 1971; JD, U. Maine, 1977. Bar: Maine 1977, U.S. Dist. Ct. Maine 1982, U.S. Ct. Appeals (1st cir.) 1983. Tchr. Pub. Sch., Tupper Lake, N.Y., 1970-71; asst. dist. atty. State of Maine, Farmington, 1977—; asst. atty. gen. State of Maine, Augusta, Maine, 1979—; ptnr. The Forensic Cons. Group, Lexington, Mass., 1988—; legal advisor U. Maine, Farmington, 1975; legal counsel Fire Marshall's Office, Maine, 1980-83, Warden Service, Maine, 1981-83, Dept. Mental Health, 1983—; teaching team trial advocacy Harvard Law Sch., Cambridge, Mass., 1987—. Mem. Natural Resources Council, Maine, 1985—; bd. dirs. Diocesan Human Relations Council, Maine, 1977-78, Arthritis Found., Maine, 1983-88. Named one of Outstanding Young Women of Yr. Jaycees, 1981. Mem. ABA, Maine Bar Assn., Kennebec County Bar Assn., Assn. Trial Lawyers Am., Maine Trial Lawyers Assn., Nat. Health Lawyers Assn., Nat. Assn. State Mental Health Attys. (treas. 1984-86, vice chmn. 1987—), Bus. and Profl. Womens Club. Home: 25 Winthrop St Hallowell ME 04347 Office: State of Maine Dept of Atty Gen State House Sta #6 Augusta ME 04333

CRAWFORD, MARTHA JEANNE, architectural interior designer; b. Rockford, Ill., June 25, 1925; d. Woodruff Lynden and LaVerna (Means) C. Student Vassar Coll., 1943-45, Rockford Coll., 1945, Parsons Sch. Design, 1945-48, Columbia U. Sch. Architecture, 1951-53. Asst. interior designer Eleanor LeMaire Assocs., N.Y.C., 1948-49; head color dept. Amos Parrish & Co., N.Y.C., 1950-52; contract interior designer Beeston and Patterson, N.Y.C., 1952-53, Welton Becket & Assocs., N.Y.C., 1952-53; cons. interior designer, N.Y.C., 1953-58; owner Martha Crawford and Assocs., comml. design co., N.Y.C., 1958-66; cons. interior designer Joseph Maxwell Assocs., Ft. Lauderdale, Fla., 1969-70, VVKR Ptnrship., Alexandria, Va., 1972-74, Design for Bus. Interiors, Washington, 1973-74; archtl. interior designer, Waukesha, Wis., 1975—;cons. color coordinator Timbertone Corp., N.Y.C., 1958-61, R.C.A. Rubber Co., Akron, Ohio, 1954-59; brochure cons. Rockcote Paints, Rockford, 1960-61. Contbr. to profl. pubs. Vol. Inst. for Crippled and Disabled, N.Y.C., 1950-53; sec. Child Care Found., Ft. Lauderdale, 1968-69; co-founder, coordinator Job Hunter's Network, Waukesha, Wis., 1982-86. Recipient hon. mention award for outstanding interior of yr. S.M. Hexter Co., Cleve., 1959; 2d place award Dow Chem. Co., N.Y.C., 1960. Mem. Constrn. Specifications Inst. (D.C. bd. dirs. 1975, President's plaque 1975), N.Y.C. AIA (assoc.), Archtl. League N.Y. (co-chmn. current work 1959-60). Club: Altrusa (pres. 1969-70) (Ft. Lauderdale). Avocations: paint jazz pastels; listening to jazz; book discussion groups. Home and Office: W305 S4522 Brookhill Rd Waukesha WI 53188

CRAWFORD, MARY LOUISE PERRI, naval officer; b. Grand Haven, Mich.; d. Louis and Helen Marie (Buckley) Perri; m. Keith Eugene Crawford, Feb. 23, 1974 (dec. Oct. 1986); children—Matthew Perri, Michael Kirk. A.A., Muskegon County Community Coll., 1969; B.A., U. Mich., 1971. Commd. ensign U.S. Navy, 1972, advanced through grades to comdr., 1987; pub. affairs officer Naval Air Sta., Key West, Fla., 1974-77, adminstrv., personnel officer Naval Air Res. Detachment, Patuxent River, Md., 1977-78, adminstrn. br. head Strike Aircraft Test Directorate, Naval Air Test Ctr., Patuxent River, 1978-80, ops. watch officer Command Ctr., Comdr.-in-Chief Naval Forces Europe Staff, London, 1980-84, officer-in-charge Personnel Support Activity Detachment, Patuxent River, 1984-86; engring. officer Chief Test and Evaluation Div., Strategic C3 Systems Directorate, Ctr. for Command, Control, and Communications, Def. Communications Agy., Washington, 1986—. Mem. AAUW, Women's Overseas Service League, U. Mich. Alumni Assn. Roman Catholic. Avocation: painting, ballet. Office: Def Communications Agy Ctr Command Control Communications Test & Evaluation Div Washington DC 20305-2000

CRAWFORD, MURIEL LAURA, lawyer, author, educator; b. Bend, Oreg., Oct. 10, 1931; d. Mason Leland and Pauline Marie (Desllets) Henderson; m. Barrett Matson Crawford, May 10, 1959; children—Laura Joanne, Janet Muriel, Barbara Elizabeth. Student, U. Calif., Berkeley, 1958-60, 67-69; B.A. with honors, U. Ill., 1973; J.D. with honors, Ill. Inst. Tech./Chgo.-Kent Coll. Law, 1977. Bar: Ill. 1977; C.L.U.; Chartered Fin. Cons. Atty., Washington Nat. Ins. Co., Evanston, Ill., 1977-80, sr. atty., 1980-81, asst. counsel, 1982-83, asst. gen. counsel, 1984-87, assoc. gen. counsel, sec., 1987—. Author: (with Greider and Beadles) Law and the Life Insurance Contract, 1984, also articles. Recipient Am. Jurisprudence award Lawyer's Coop. Pub. Co., 1975; 2d prize Internat. LeTourneau Student Med.-Legal Article contest, 1976; Bar and Gavel Soc. award Ill. Inst. Tech./Chgo.-Kent Student Bar Assn., 1977. Mem. ABA, Ill. Bar Assn., Chgo. Bar Assn., Am. Corporate Counsels Assn., Ill. Inst. Tech./Chgo.-Kent Alumni Assn. (dir. 1981—) Republican. Congregationalist.

CRAWFORD, PRISCILLA RUTH, social psychologist; b. Ferndale, Mich., Oct. 13, 1941; d. Ernest Henry and Ethel Ruth (Huth) Thomas; m. Thomas Earl Crawford, June 10, 1963 (div.). B.A., Butler U., 1962; postgrad. (Fulbright scholar) Goethe U., Ger., 1963; M.A. in Sociology (fellow), Ohio State U., 1965, Ph.D. (NIMH fellow), 1970. Mem. faculty sociology dept. Bklyn. Coll., 1966-67, Ind. U., Indpls., 1967-70; adj. faculty Roosevelt U., Chgo., 1974-77, Ind. U./Purdue U., Indpls., 1978—; research assoc. Gary (Ind.) Income Maintenance Expt., Ind. U. Northwest, 1970-73; cons. human resource and orgn. devel., Chgo., 1973-77; dir. human resource devel Ind. State Dept. Mental Health, Indpls., 1978-84, dir. edn. and tng., 1984-86, dir. ops. research, policy analysis, 1986—; vol. cons. numerous womens's groups, 1977—; cons. to state agys., So. Regional Edn. Bd., Nat. Orgn. Human Service Educators, NIMH, 1978—; mem. tng. adv. com. Ind. State Personnel Dept., 1983—; mem. adv. com. M.S. in Nursing degree program Ind. U. Sch. Nursing, 1982—; adv. com. Lic. Practical Nursing Initiative, 1981. Bd. dirs. Ind. Conf. Social Concerns, 1979-81; mem. Gov.'s Spl. Grant Com., Ind. Employment Tng. Council, 1981-82; mem. adv. bd. Program in Ind. Living, 1980-82; mem. adv. com. Indpls. Preschs., Inc., 1982—; mem. planning com. Ind. U. Sch. Medicine Women's Health Research Inst., 1986—; mem. planning com. Women in the Year 2000; bd. dirs. Women's Agenda for Action, 1981-83. Mem. Am. Sociol. Assn., Midwest Sociol. Soc., North Central Sociol. Assn., Am. Mgmt. Assn., Nat. Assn. State Mental Health Program Dirs. (mem. human resources com. 1986—), N.Y. Acad. Sci., Ohio Acad. Sci., Ind. Acad. Social Scis. (dir. 1978-81, 84—), Inst. Noetic Scis., AAUP, Phi Kappa Phi, Alpha Lambda Delta. Home: 1653 E Kessler Indianapolis IN 46220

CRAWFORD, RONALD LYLE, microbiology educator, consultant; b. Santa Anna, Tex., Sept. 28, 1947; s. Lester Crawford and Doris Delores (Smith) Crawford Norman; m. Onie Ann Thompson, Dec. 30, 1967; 1 child, Lisa Brooks. B.A. in Biology cum laude, Oklahoma City U., 1970; M.S. in Bacteriology, U. Wis.-Madison, 1972, Ph.D. in Bacteriology, 1973. Research assoc. U. Minn. St. Paul, 1973-74; research scientist N.Y. State Dept. Health, Albany, 1974-75; asst. prof. microbiology U. Minn.-Twin Cities, 1975-79, assoc. prof., 1979-83, prof., 1983-86; head dept. bacteriology and biochemistry, U. Idaho, Moscow, 1987—; research dir. Chem Waste Control, Wayzata, Minn., 1984-85; cons. to industry, 1975—; adviser on environ. pollution to U.S. Senator David Durenberger, Mpls., 1983. Author: Lignin Biodegradation and Transformation, 1981; also book chpts., numerous articles. Editor: (with R.S. Hanson) Microbial Growth on C1 Compounds, 1984; Applied and Environ. Microbiology, 1982—. Weyerhauser fellow U. Wis.-Madison, 1970-73. Mem. Am. Soc. Microbiology, Blue Key, Sigma Xi, Beta Beta Beta. Democrat. Avocations: playing guitar and banjo, long distance running.

CRAWLEY, JANE CAROLYN, business educator; b. Campbellsville, Ky., Nov. 17, 1950; d. J.B. and Elizabeth (Perkins) C. BS, Ea. Ky. U., 1972, MA, 1974. Bus. educator Ky. Bus. Coll., Lexington, 1972-74, LaBelle High Sch., Fla., 1974-76, Cyesis Ctr., Ft. Lauderdale, Fla., 1979, Ft. Lauderdale Coll., 1979, Fla. Coll. Bus., Pompano Beach, 1979-83, Broward County Sch. Bd., Fla., 1983-84; instr. visually handicapped Broward County Sch. Bd., 1976-78; bus. and computer educator Businessland, Ft. Lauderdale, 1984—; dir. edn. Fla. Coll., 1981-83; ednl. cons. Hammel Coll., 1983. Recipient cert. of Recognition for outstanding service aiding in finding missing children Broward County Sheriff's Dept., 1985; commd. Ky. Col. Gov. of Ky., 1988. Mem. Am. Council of Blind, Visually Handicapped Transcribers Assn. Republican. Baptist. Home: 2389 NE 30th Ct Lighthouse Point FL 33064 Office: Businessland 830 E Oakland Park Blvd Fort Lauderdale FL 33334

CRAWLEY, PAUL F., nuclear engineer; b. Carthage, N.Y., Nov. 23, 1943; s. Richard F. and Alice M. (Franks) C.; m. Lorraine J. Campbell, Jan. 28, 1967; children—Kevin, Sean. J.T. A.B. cum laude, Kenyon Coll., 1965; M.S., Carnegie-Mellon U., 1967. Scientist, Bettis Atomic Power Lab., West Mifflin, Pa., 1967-72; nuclear engr. Middle South Services, New Orleans, 1972; scientist Bettis Atomic Power Lab., 1972-74; sr. nuclear engr. Boston Edison Co., 1974-78; nuclear supr. Ariz. Pub. Service, Phoenix, 1978-83, mgr. nuclear fuel mgmt., 1983—. Chmn. Litchfield Little League, 1981-82. Mem. Am. Nuclear Soc., N.Y. Acad. Scis. Republican. Roman Catholic. Home: 300 W Llano Dr Litchfield Park AZ 85340 Office: Ariz Pub Service Co PO Box 21666 Phoenix AZ 85036

CRAWSHAW, ALWYN, painter; b. Mirfield, Yorkshire, Eng., Sept. 20, 1934; s. Fred and Doris Letitia Gertrude (Brannon) C.; student Hastings Sch. Art, 1949-51; m. June Eileen Bridgman, Mar. 16, 1957; children—Natalie, Donna, Clinton. Founding partner Russell Artists Mcdg. Ltd., Kingston-upon-Thames, Surrey, 1958-80; lectr., demonstrator acrylic and watercolor painting for Daler-Rowney & Co. Ltd., Bracknell, Berkshire, Eng., 1972—; exhibited work at Royal Soc. Brit. Artists, 1981, 82, 83, 84, 85, 86; guest on BBC-TV, BBC radio, ind. radio. Fine art print Wet and Windy included in top 10 prints, 1975. Fellow Royal Soc. Arts; mem. Soc. Equestrian Artists, British Watercolour Soc. Mem. Ch. of Eng. Author: Painting with Acrylic Colours, 1974; Learn To Paint with Acrylic Colours, 1979; Learn To Paint with Watercolours, 1979; Learn To Paint Landscapes, 1981; Learn To Paint Boats and Harbours, 1982; Learn To Sketch, 1983; Learn to Paint Still Life, 1984; The Artist at Work: Alwyn Crawshaw, 1984; Learn to Paint Outdoors in Watercolour, 1986, Learn to Paint in Oils for the Beginner, 1987; (video) Learn to Paint with Watercolour, 1986, Learn to Paint with Watercoulor II, 1987; also articles. Home and Studio: Metcombe Vale House, Metcombe, Ottery St Mary, Devon EX11 1RS, England

CRAXI, BETTINO, government official of Italy; b. Milan, Italy, Feb. 24, 1934; m. Anna Maria Moncini; children: Vittorio, Stefania. LL.D., Brown U., 1983. Mem. cental com. Socialist Party, Rome, 1957—, mem. Chamber of Deps., Rome, 1968—; dep. sec. gen. Socialist Party, 1970-76; sec. gen. Italian Socialist Party, 1976—; prime minister Italian Republic, 1983-87. Address: Palazzo Chigi, Piazza Colonna, 00100 Rome Italy *

CREA, ENZO FRANCESCO SAVERIO, publisher; b. Cosenza, Calabria, Italy, Oct. 5, 1927; s. Nicola and Ada (Ferrari) C.; m. Maria Grazia Vascotto, Nov. 16, 1955 (div. 1978); children: Nicola, Alessio, Saverio; m. Benedetta Rosa Origo, May 14, 1980. Doctorate, U. Degli Studi, Bari, Italy, 1953. Picture editor Ency. Filosofica, Rome, 1955-56; dir. photographic archives Ency. World Art, N.Y.C., 1956-63, Ency. Universale Dell'Arte, Rome, 1956-63; picture editor Dizionario di Architettura e Urbanistica, Rome, 1964-67; pub., founder Edizioni Dell'Elefante, Rome, 1964—; editorial cons. Larousse, Paris, 1955-57, Sansoni, Florence, Italy, 1955-60, Laterza, Bari and Rome, 1964-75. Author, photographer: Images of Persons in Calabria, 1982; photographer: La Pittura Italiana al Prado, 1961, Le Ville Lucchesi, 1964. Named Chevalier des Arts et des Lettres, Ministère de la Culture, Paris, 1982. Office: Edizioni Dell'Elefante, Piazza dei Caprettari 70, 00186 Rome Italy

CREAGER, CLIFFORD RAYMOND, editor; b. N.Y.C., Oct. 8, 1937; s. Clifford Henry and Catherine (Raymond) C.; m. Dorothy Ann Carlson, Dec. 18, 1965; children: Christopher, Curtis. AB, U. Mich., 1960. Reporter, wire editor, photographer Grand Haven (Mich.) Daily Tribune, 1960-61; reporter, photographer, city editor, editor Covina (Calif.) Sentinel, weekly, 1963-72; mng. editor Car Craft mag., Los Angeles, 1972-75, Motor Trend mag., Los Angeles, 1975-81; free-lance writer, editor 1981-85; program dir. Safety Edn. Ctr., 1986—; editor, co-founder Profl. Counselor mag., 1986—; v.p. A/D Communications Corp., 1986—. Served with AUS, 1961-63. Mem. U. Mich. Alumni Assn., Calif. Assn. Alcoholism And Drug Abuse Counselors.

CRECINE, JOHN PATRICK, political science, sociology, economics educator; b. Detroit, Aug. 22, 1939; s. Jess and Janet K. (Hull) C.; m. Barbara Paltnavich, Aug. 17, 1968; children: Robert Patrick, Kathryn Alicia. BS in Indsl. Mgmt., Carnegie-Mellon U., 1961, MS, 1963, PhD, 1966. Asst. prof. polit. sci. and sociology U. Mich., 1965-67, prof., dir. Inst. Pub. Policy Studies, 1968-75; economist Rand Corp., Santa Monica, Calif., 1967-68; fellow Ctr. for Advanced Study Behavioral Scis., 1973-74; prof. polit. economy Carnegie-Mellon U., Pitts., 1976-87, pres., 1976-87, sr. v.p. for acad. affairs, 1983-87; pres. BPT, Inc., 1963—, Ga. Inst. Tech., Atlanta, 1987—; fellow commoner, vis. scholar Cambridge U., 1981-82; bd. dirs. NEXT, Inc., Liebert Corp., Arizona 386; chmn. adv. council Internat. Security Studies Program Wilson Ctr., 1987—. Author: A Dynamic Model of Urban Structure, 1968, Governmental Problem Solving: A Computer Simulation of Municipal Budgeting, 1969, Defense Budgeting: Organizational Adaptation of External Constraints, 1970, Research in Public Policy Analysis and Management: Basic Theory, Methods, and Perspectives, 1981, The New Educational Programs in Public Policy: The First Decade; editor: Financing the Metropolis: The Role of Public Policy in Urban Economics, 1970. Sec., commr. Ann Arbor Planning Commn., Mich., 1969-73. Mem. Am. Econ. Assn., Am. Soc. Pub. Adminstrs., Am. Polit. Sci. Assn., Inst. Mgmt. Scis., Am. Coll. Swimming Coaches Assn. Office: Ga Inst Tech Office of Pres Atlanta GA 30332

CREECH, RICHARD HEARNE, physician; b. Boston, Apr. 6, 1940; s. Hugh J. and E. Marie (Hearne) C.; m. Charlotte E. Goetz, Dec. 28, 1963; children—Susan Marie, Nancy Elizabeth. A.B., Johns Hopkins U., 1961; M.D., U. Pa., 1965. Diplomate: Am. Bd. Internal Medicine (Subspecialty in med. oncology, hematology). Intern, resident in medicine Hosp. of U. Pa., 1965-67; clin. assoc. lab. molecular pharmacology Nat. Cancer Inst., Bethesda, Md., 1967-70; fellow in hematology and immunology U. of Pa., 1970-71; chief med. oncology service Phila. Gen. Hosp., U. Pa. Service, 1971-72; assoc. attending physician Am. Oncologic Hosp., Fox Chase Cancer Ctr., Phila., 1972-84, Jeanes Hosp, 1984—. Contbr. articles to profl. jours. Served with USPHS, 1967-70. Fellow ACP; mem. Am. Soc. Clin. Oncology, Am. Assn. Cancer Research, AMA, Coll. Physicians Phila. Republican. Episcopalian. Office: 7500 Central Ave Suite 203 Philadelphia PA 19111

CREEDON, JOHN J., insurance company executive; b. N.Y.C., Aug. 1, 1924; s. Bartholomew and Emma (Glynn) C.; m. Vivian Elser, Aug. 17, 1947 (dec. 1981); children: Juliette, Michele, John, David; m. Diane Ardouin, 1983; children: Jean Philippe, Genevieve. B.S. magna cum laude, N.Y. U., 1952, LL.B. cum laude, 1955, LL.M., 1962. Bar: N.Y. State 1955, U.S. Supreme Ct. 1960. With Met. Life Ins. Co., N.Y.C., 1942—; v.p., asso. gen. counsel Met. Life Ins. Co., 1970-73, sr. v.p., gen. counsel, 1973-76, exec. v.p., 1976-80, pres., dir., 1980-83, pres., chief exec. officer, 1983—; chmn. bd. Met. Property & Liability Ins. Co., 1979-80, dir., 1986; adj. prof. law NYU Law Sch., 1962-72; bd. dirs., pres. Am. Bar Found., 1980-82; chmn. bd. Met. Life Found.; trustee Practicing Law Inst. NYU, 1968-81, NYU Law Ctr. Found.; mem. legal adv. com. N.Y. Stock Exchange, 1978-83; chmn. Life Ins. Council N.Y., 1977-78; chmn. Am. Council of Life Ins., 1986-87; bd. dirs. NYNEX Corp., Union Carbide Corp., Banco Santander, Albany Assurance Co., Ltd., Melville Corp., Rockwell Internat. Corp., Sonat Inc., State St. Research and Mgmt. Co., Met. Property and Liability Ins. Co. Editor: The Bus. Lawyer, 1973-74; contbr. articles to profl. jours. Served with USNR, 1943-46. Mem. ABA (assembly del. 1972-75, chmn. sect. corp. banking and bus. law 1975-76), N.Y. State Bar Assn., Assn. Bar City N.Y., Assn. Life Ins. Counsel (pres. 1977-78), Am. Law Inst., Bus. Council N.Y. State (chmn. 1987), N.Y. State C. of C. and Industry, Alliance for Free Enterprise. Office: Met Life Ins Co 1 Madison Ave New York NY 10010

CREEK, MALCOLM LARS, diplomat; b. Bradford, Yorkshire, Eng., Apr. 2, 1931; s. Edgar and Lily (Robertshaw) C.; m. Gillian Mary Bell, July 10, 1970; children: Alison, Sarah, Richard. BA with honors, London U., 1956. Diplomatic service officer London Fgn. Office, 1950-56; vice consul Mogadishu and Harar, London, 1956-58; 2d sec. Her Majesty's Fgn. Service,

Mexico City, Abidjan and Santiago, 1959-68; 1st sec. San Jose and Havana, Cuba, 1968-74, Tunis and Lima, Peru, 1978-85; high commr. Port Vila, Vanuato, 1985-88; Brit. consul gen. Auckland, New Zealand, 1988—. Decorated Lt. of Victorian Order, Officer of Order of Brit. Empire. Methodist. Office: Fgn and Commonwealth Office, King Charles St, London SW1, England

CREEL, JOE, lawyer; b. Guntersville Ala., Oct. 23, 1912; s. Elisha O. and Florence A. (Bynum) C.; A.B., U. Ala., 1932, J.D., 1934; m. Nellie Jo Morton, Sept. 21, 1935; children—Sallie R. (Mrs. Warren Quillian), Joe Morton. Admitted to Ala. bar 1934, Fla. bar, 1945; spl. asst. U.S. atty. No. Dist. Ala., 1943-44; regional litigation atty. OPA, Southeastern Area, 1944, chief enforcement officer, Miami, dist., 1945; city atty., Guntersville, 1941-43; pvt. practice, Miami 1945—; pres. Russell Aluminum Corp., 1955-56, sec.-treas., dir., 1956-70. Mem. Am. (ho. dels. 1968-70), Dade County bar assns. (pres. 1958-59), Phi Beta Kappa, Phi Delta Phi, Omicron Delta Kappa, Tau Kappa Alpha. Home: 4120 University Dr Coral Gables FL 33146 Office: 370 Minorca Ave Suite 19 Coral Gables FL 33134

CREEL, THOMAS LEONARD, lawyer; b. Kansas City, Mo., June 21, 1937; s. Thomas Howard and Elizabeth Alberta (Sharon) C.; m. Frances Ann Martin, Aug. 29, 1959; children—Charles, Andrew, Andrea, Thomas. B.S., U. Kans., 1960; LL.B., U. Mich., 1963. Bar: Mich. 1963, N.Y. 1967, D.C. 1983, U.S. Supreme Ct. 1973, Ct. Mil. Appeals 1964, U.S. Patent and Trademark Office 1965. Assoc. Kenyon and Kenyon, N.Y.C., 1966-74, ptnr., 1974—; faculty lectr. Columbia U., N.Y.C., 1984—. Editor: Guide to Patent Arbitration, 1987. Served to capt. U.S. Army, 1963-66. Mem. N.Y. Patent, Trademark and Copyright Law Assn. (chmn arbitration com. 1982—), Am. Intellectual Property Law Assn., Internat. Trade Commn. Trial Lawyers Assn. Clubs: Scarsdale Golf (gov. 1982-83) (Hartsdale, N.Y.); Graduates (New Haven). Home: 21 Clubway Hartsdale NY 10530 Office: Kenyon and Kenyon 1 Broadway New York NY 10004

CREEL SISNIEGA, SALVADOR JOSÉ, banker; b. Mexico City, Oct. 10, 1927; s. Salvador and Carolina (Sisniega) C.; m. Mari a Luisa Ryan, May 28, 1955; children—Ines Maria, Salvador, Ricardo, Maria Cristina. LL.D., U. Mex., 1951; postgrad. in money and banking Columbia U., 1952-53. Bar: Mex. 1951. Founder, head nat. law dept. Banco Commercial Mexicano, S.A., 1954-63; founder, sr. ptnr. Creel, Garcia and Cruz, Mexico, 1955—; prof. econs. U. Chihuahua, Mex., 1955-65; pres. Financiera y Fiduciaria de Chihuahua, S.A., 1955-68; chmn. bd. Grupo Econó mico Mexicano, S.A., Banco Cré dito Mexicano S.A., Cré dito Financiero S.A., Harinas S.A. de C.V., Fomento Indsl. y Bursatil, S.A. de C.V., Inversiones y Valores Mexicanos, S.A. de C.V., Auto Camoines de Chihuahua, S.A., Ganado del Norte, S.A., Impulsora de Restaurantes S.A., Albergues y Hoteles Mexicanos, S.A., Tecnica Hotelera del Norte, S.A., Parques Industriales Mexicanos, S.A., Planeacion Inmobiliaria de Chihuahua, S.A., Chihuahua Futuro, S.A., Hogares, Comercio e Industria, S.A. de C.V., Seguros La Republica, S.A., Union de Seguros, S.A.; dir. Seguros La Comercial de Chihuahua, S.A., Aceros de Chihuahua, S.A., Banco Capitalizador de Chihuahua, S.A., Mueblerias Villareal, S.A. Author: Hacia Una Suma Juri dica, 1951. Contbr. articles to profl. jours. Bd. dirs. Found. Educacion Chihuahuense, Found. Inmuebles Escolares de Chihuahua; pres. Hispanic Culture Inst., Chihuahua; founding mem., dir. Chihuahua Inst. Social Studies. Decorated knight Equestrian Order of Holy Sepulcher of Jerusalem, knight Hispanic-Am. chpt. Knights of Corpus Christi of Toledo; recipient award Inst. Hispano-Am. Culture; Disting. Exec. of Yr. award, Chihuahua, 1976. Mem. Numisatic Soc. Mex. Roman Catholic. Clubs: Casino de Chihuahua, Chihuahua Country. Home: Blas Caño de Los Rios 102, 31240 Chihuahua Mexico Office: Libertad 9, Desp 1406-10, 31000 Chihuahua Mexico

CREHAN, JOSEPH EDWARD, lawyer; b. Detroit, Dec. 8, 1938; s. Owen Thomas and Marguerite (Dunn) C.; m. Sheila Anderson, Nov. 6, 1965; children: Kerry Marie, Christa Ellen. A.B., Wayne State U., Detroit, 1961; J.D., Ind. U., 1965. Bar: Ind. 1965, Mich. 1966, U.S. Supreme Ct. 1984. Practice in Detroit 1966-68; assoc. Louisell & Barris (P.C.), 1968-73; ptnr. Fenton, Nederlander, Dodge, Barris & Crehan (P.C.), 1973-76, Barris & Crehan (P.C.), 1976-78; sole practice Bloomfield Hills, Mich. and Naples, Fla., 1977—. Mem. Am. Trial Lawyers Assn. Roman Catholic. Home and Office: 827 Bentwood Dr Naples FL 33963

CREIGH, THOMAS, JR., utility executive; b. Evanston, Ill., Jan. 3, 1912, s. Thomas and Frances (Connor) C.; m. Dorothy Claire Weyer, July 17, 1948; children: Mary Elizabeth, Thomas III, John, James. Grad., Mercersburg (Pa.) Acad., 1929; A.B., Wabash Coll., 1933. With No. Natural Gas Co., 1933-36; with KN Energy, Inc. (formerly Kans.-Nebr. Natural Gas Co., Inc.), 1936-86; v.p. KN Energy, Inc., 1951-61, pres., 1961-78, chmn. bd., 1978-85, chmn. emeritus, 1985—, also dir.; v.p., dir. Excelsior Oil Corp., 1955-68, pres., 1968-84; pres., dir. Western Gas Corp., 1967-84; v.p., dir. Helium, Inc., 1960-85; sec., dir. Western Plastics Corp., 1953-69; dir. Dunne Gardner Drilling Co., City Nat. Bank, Hastings, Western Alfalfa Corp., Cap-Con Internat Inc., Cape Constrn. Co., Energy Transmission System, Inc., Advanced Fuel Systems, Inc., Slurry Transport Assos.,. Mem. Nebr. Gov.'s Task Force for Govt. Improvement, 1980-82, Nebr. Bd. Ednl. Lands and Funds, 1987—; trustee Hastings Coll., Inst. Gas Tech., U. Nebr. Found., Nebr. State Hist. Soc. Found.; bd. dirs. Nebr. Art Collection. Mem. Am. Gas Assn. (dir. 1969-73), Midwest Gas Assn. (dir. 1965-68), Interstate Natural Gas Assn. (dir. 1967-71, 74-82), Nebr. Assn. Commerce and Industry (past pres.), Nebr. Council Econ. Edn. (chmn. 1967-70). Presbyterian (trustee). Office: KN Energy Inc Hastings NE 68901

CREITZ, JAMES PHILIP, violist; b. Madison, Wis., Apr. 7, 1957; s. Lowell Miller and Joan Margaret (Harrison) C.; m. Ina Meurer, June 21, 1985; children: Clara, Anna. Student, Hochschule, Detmold, Germany, 1977-79, Music Acad. Chigiana, Siena, Italy, summers 1977-80; BA in Music magna cum laude, Yale U., 1981; pvt. studies with Gerald Stanick, Milton Thomas, Broadus Erle, Bruno Giuranna, Walter Trampler, others. Prin. violist Victoria Symphony Orch., B.C., Can., 1974-75; violist-solo and ensemble Deutshes Kammeracademie, Neuss, Fed. Republic Germany, 1981—; violist Quartetto Academica, 1983—; judge several internat. competitions; tchr. master classes Internat. Festival CIPAM, Arezzo, Italy. Debut with Milw. Symphony Orch., 1974; solo or chamber music performances in Germany, Switzerland, Eng., Scotland, Italy, Mid East, Far East, Brazil, U.S., Can., others; appeared with S. Accardo, Bruno Giuranna, Franco Gulli, Gazelloni, Johan Goritski, Yo Yo Ma, others; recordings with Quartetto Academica for Dynamic Records. Recipient Certs. of Excellence Chigiana-Sienna, Italy, 1981, 82. Mem. Phi Beta Kappa. Home: 9238 Hwy 14 Black Earth WI 53515 Office: Quartetto Academica, Via Kennedy 332, 21040 Venegono Italy

CREMER, LEON E., federal agent, lawyer; b. Cin., Dec. 30, 1945; s. Walter H. and Beatrice (Campbell) C. BS, Calif. State U., 1973, MA, George Washington U., 1976, JD, Rutgers U., 1982. Bar: Pa. 1983. Officer, U.S. Secret Service, Washington, 1975-77; spl. agt. U.S. Bur. Alcohol Tobacco and Firearms, U.S. Dept. Treasury, Phila., 1977-83; spl. agt. FBI, U.S. Dept. Justice, N.Y.C., 1983—. Served with U.S. Army, 1968-69. Mem. FBI Agts. Assn., Phila. Bar Assn., Pa. Bar Assn., ABA, Am. Trial Lawyers Assn., Internat. Platform Assn., Am. Mensa Soc. Avocations: skiing, tennis, long distance running, aviation, travel. Office: FBI 26 Fed Plaza New York NY 10278

CRENSHAW, MARGARET PRICE, lawyer; b. Eugene, Oreg., Apr. 16, 1945; d. Warren Charles and Lillian Irene (Shidell) Price; B.A., Stanford U., 1967, M.A., 1968; J.D., Georgetown U., 1975; m. Albert Burford Crenshaw, Aug. 11, 1973; children—David Ollinger, Caroline Abbey. Bars: D.C. bar 1975, U.S. Ct. Appeals 1976, U.S. Ct. Claims 1976, U.S. Supreme Ct. 1983. Reporter Eugene Register-Guard, 1965, 66; press asst. Californians for Humphrey San Francisco, 1968; newswoman AP, New Haven, Conn., 1969; press asst. Rep. Jeffery Cohelan, Washington, 1969; research writer Congl. Quar., Washington, 1969-70; asst. editor Washington Post, 1970-72; law clerk firm Harrison, Lucey, Sagle & Solter, Washington, 1974-75; legis. counsel Senator Philip A. Hart, Washington, 1975-77; legis. counsel Senator Paul S. Sarbanes, Washington, 1977; asso. firm Brownstein, Zeidman & Schomer, Washington, 1977-79; counsel Senate Subcom. on Govt. Efficiency and the D.C., 1979-81, minority chief counsel, 1981-85, minority staff dir. Senate Com. on Govtl. Affairs, 1985-87; v.p. Govt. Retirement and Benefits, Inc., Alexandria, Va., 1987-88; pres. Employee Benefits Rev., Inc., Washington, 1988—; adj. prof. journalism U. Md., College Park, 1975. Trustee Capitol Hill Day Sch., Washington, 1984-87. Ford Found. fellow, 1967-68. Mem. ABA, D.C. Bar Assn., Women's Bar Assn. D.C. Democrat. Episcopalian.

CREPS, PHILIP LLOYD, chemist; b. Bowling Green, Ohio, Dec. 16, 1951; s. Wayne LeRoy and Elsie Marie (Frank) C.; m. Barbara Dawn Keller, Dec. 11, 1976; children: Jesse Jean, Sarah Marie. BS, Bowling Green (Ohio) State U., 1973; BA, U. Toledo, 1980, MS, 1988; AS, Aurora (Colo.) Community Coll., 1986. Research project dir. Mich. State U., East Lansing, 1984-85; instr. Lansing Community Coll., 1984-85; environ. scientist Ohio EPA, Bowling Green, 1985; research chemist Fitzsimmons Med. Ctr., Aurora, 1985-86. Youth dir. Assembly of God Ch., Fostoria, Ohio, 1969-71; music dir. 1st Assembly of God Ch., Toledo, 1977-79; sec. Citizen's Council #3, Lansing, 1980-83. Served with USN, 1980-83. Recipient Alfred award South Counties Council, Newport, R.I., 1981, Mayor's Commendation City of Toledo, 1980. Mem. Am. Chem. Soc., Alpha Epsilon Delta, Psi Chi, Beta Beta Beta. Libertarian.

CRESIMORE, JAMES LEONARD, food broker; b. Statesville, N.C., Jan. 24, 1928; s. Fred Clayton and Cleo (Edison) C.; B.S. in Bus. Adminstrn., High Point Coll., 1949; m. Mary Josephine Conrad, June 3, 1956; children—James Conrad, Jennifer Cheryl, Joel Clayton. Gen. mgr. Home Service Stores, Inc., High Point, N.C., 1948-50; co-founder, sec. Red Dot Food Stores, Inc., 1952-56; sec. Consol. Wholesale Corp., 1952-56; owner Village Super Market, High Point, 1953-56; co-owner Bunker Hill Packing Corp., Bedford, Va., 1964—; chmn. bd., co-owner Assoc. Brokers, Inc., Raleigh, N.C., 1956—; founding dir., chmn. bd. State Bank Raleigh; chmn. bd. Smithfield Cos. Inc., Va.; past chmn. United Carolina Bank, Raleigh; dir. United Carolina Bank N.C. Chmn. Mayor's Manpower Com., Raleigh. Chmn. Wake County Republican Com., 1963—, del. nat. conv. San Francisco, 1964; 4th Congl. dist.; mem. platform com. Rep. Nat. Convention, Miami, Fla., 1968. Mem. advisory bd. Salvation Army; trustee Pheiffer Coll.; bd. dirs. Raleigh Community Hosp., N.C. Citizens for Bus. and Industry, Bapt. Children's Homes of N.C. Served with U.S. Army, 1950-52. Mem. Sales and Marketing Execs. Internat. (mem. bd., pres. Raleigh now v.p.), Raleigh Food Brokers Assn. (past pres.), Nat. Food Brokers Assn. (regional rep.), (lt. regional dir.) food brokers assns., Raleigh C. of C. (dir. 1973-74). Lodge: Rotary. Home: 3720 Williamsborough Ct Raleigh NC 27609 Office: 3309 Drake Circle Raleigh NC 27609

CRESSLER, JOHN CHARLES, former army medical officer, medical administrator; b. Wilkes-Barre, Pa., June 17, 1915; s. John Webster and Cora Irene (Reimard) C.; B.S. in Biology, Lafayette Coll., 1937; M.D., Jefferson Med. Coll., 1941; M.H.A. with honors, Northwestern U., 1952; m. Kathleen Hutton Smith, Jan. 18, 1942; 1 son, John Webster II. Commd. 2d lt. U.S. Army, 1937, advanced through grades to col., 1959; rotating intern Walter Reed Gen. Hosp., Washington, 1941-42, gen. surgery tng., 1945-46; gen. surgery tng. Gorgas Gen. Hosp., Panama C.Z., 1946-49; instr. Med. Field Service Sch., Carlisle Barracks, Pa., 1942-43; adminstrv. surgeon, M.C. instr. Anti-Aircraft Sch., Camp Davis, N.C., 1943-44; med. instr. F.A. Sch., Ft. Sill, Okla., 1944; comdg. officer Armored Med. Co., Europe, 1944-45; comdg. officer, chief operating surgeon Sta. Hosp., Ft. Sheridan, Ill., 1949-50; dep. corps surgeon, Korea, 1950-51; comdg. officer Combined Hosp. Facilities, Korea, 1951; dep. comdr. William Beaumont Gen. Hosp., El Paso, Tex., 1952-54; chief M.C. assignment sect. Office Surgeon Gen., Washington, 1954-55, chief officer br. personnel div. OTSG, 1955-58; asst. Army attache U.S. embassy, London, Eng., 1958-61; chief ops. div. Surgeon's Office 2d U.S. Army, Ft. Meade, Md., 1961-62, Army surgeon, 1962-64; comdg. officer Walson Army Hosp., Ft. Dix, N.J., 1964-67, also post surgeon; staff dir. Def. Med. Materiel Bd., Potomac Annex, Washington, 1967-70; ret., 1970; asso. dir. Greater Delaware Valley Regional Med. Program, Haverford, Pa., 1970-74; cons., 1974—. Decorated Legion of Merit with oak leaf cluster. Fellow Am. Coll. Hosp. Adminstrs.; mem. AMA, Am. Hosp. Assn., Assn. Mil. Surgeons, Fed. Hosp. Inst. Assn., Assn. U.S. Army, Soc. Plastic Engrs., Royal Soc. Health (Eng.) Address: 6011 Bradley Blvd Bethesda MD 20817

CRETTIEN, CHARLES JEAN, diplomat; b. Nice, France, July 3, 1931; s. Jean and Jacqueline (Gastaud) C.; m. Micheline Gillet, July 29, 1953 (separated Mar. 1987); children: Jean-François, Helene, Philipps. MA in Lit., U. Sorbonne, Paris, 1953; diploma in Arabic, Persian, Inst. Oriental Studies, Paris, 1953. 2d sec. French Embassy, Rabat, Morocco, 1960-63, Cairo, 1963-65; 1st sec. Algiers, Algieria, 1967-70; counsellor Rabat, 1972-75, London, 1975-78; cultural counsellor Tunis, Tunisia, 1978-81; counsellor Washington, 1982-85; ambassador Abu Dhabi, United Arab Emirates, 1985-87, Mogachshu, Somalia, 1987—; counsul French Consulate, San Francisco, 1965-67; cousul gen. Chgo., 1981-82; counsellor Ministry Fgn. Affairs, Paris, 1971-72. Served to lt. French navy, 1958-60. Decorated officier Ordre du Monté, 1982; recipient Chevalier Legion d'Honneur, 1979. Socialist. Home: 22 Bd St Michel, 75006 Paris France Office: Foreign Affairs, 37 Quai d'Oway, 75007 Paris France

CREVELT, DWIGHT EUGENE, computer company executive; b. Kansas City, Mo., Jan. 16, 1957; s. James Robert and Louise Gwendolynn (Wolchek) C.; m. Jean Anne Cassens, Aug. 11, 1979; children: William Michael, Michelle Anne, Matthew Henry. Student U. Las Vegas, 1973-74, U.S. Naval Acad., 1975-77; BS in Computer Engring., Iowa State U., 1979. Computer engr., cons., Las Vegas, Nev., 1972-73; software engr. Gamex Industries, Las Vegas, 1973-74, United Audio Visual, Las Vegas, 1977; computer engr. Sircoma, Las Vegas, 1979-80; dir. research Mills-Jennings, Las Vegas, 1981; pres., chmn. Crevelt Computer, Las Vegas, 1977—. Corr. sec. Clark County Rep. Party; del. Rep. Nat. Conv., 1988. Author: (computer programs) CDC160/NCR310 Disassembler, 1971; Computer Networking, 1983; Telephone Access Control, 1984; Fiber Optic Network, 1984. Co-author: Slot Machine Mania. Mem. Nat. Eagle Scout Assn., U.S. Congl. Adv. Bd.; del. Rep. Nat. Conv., 1988. Mem. Soc. Naval Engrs., Sales Mktg. Execs. Assn., Am. Philatic Soc., U.S. Naval Acad. Alumni Assn. (sec.), USN League, U.S. Naval Inst., Las Vegas Exchange Club (bd. dirs.). Office: Crevelt Computer System Inc 3111 S Valley View E-103 Las Vegas NV 89102

CREW, LOUIE (LI MIN HUA), language professional, educator; b. Anniston, Ala., Dec. 9, 1936; s. Erman and Lula (Hagin) C. B.A., Baylor U., 1958; M.A., Auburn U., 1959; Ph.D., U. Ala., 1971. Teaching fellow Auburn U., 1958-59; master English and sacred studies Darlington Sch., 1959-62, St. Andrew's, Del., 1962-65; master of English and English history Penge Secondary Modern, London, Eng., 1965-66; instr. English U. Ala., 1966-70; dir. Independent Study Program of Experiment in Internat. Living, Eng., 1970-71; prof. English Claflin Coll., Orangeburg, S.C., 1971-73; assoc. prof. Fort Valley (Ga.) State Coll., 1973-79; asso. prof. U. Wis., Stevens Point, 1979-84 (on leave); fgn. expert in composition Beijing 2d Fgn. Lang. Inst., Peoples Republic China, 1983-84; dir. writing program Chinese U. Hong Kong, 1984-87; free lance writer, 1987—; cons. in field. Author: Sunspots, 1976, The Gay Academic, 1978; Guest editor: College English, 1974, Margins, 1975, Midnight Lessons, 1987; editorial bd.: Jour. Homosexuality, 1977—, Notes on Teaching English, 1973—, Progressive Composition Caucus, 1988—. Alt. del. Wis. Democratic Conv., 1983; Founder INTEGRITY Nat. Orgn. Gay Episcopalians, 1974; bd. dirs. Nat. Gay Task Force, 1976-78; mem. Wis. Gov.'s Council Lesbian and Gay Issues, 1983-85. Recipient INTEGRITY award for outstanding contbns. to Christian understanding of human sexuality, 1975, best article award Hong Kong Computer Soc., 1985; NEH fellow, 1974, 77, 81; Fulbright grantee, 1974; resident fellow Ragdale Found., 1988. Mem. Conf. Coll. Composition and Communication, Nat. Coalition Black and Third World Gays, Internat. Assn. Black and White Men Together, Gay Acad. Union, Nat. Council Tchrs. English (dir. 1976-80, co-chmn. com. on lesbians and gay males in the profession 1976-80), Assn. Tchrs. Advanced Composition, Inst. Study of Human Resources (nat. adv. trustee 1979—), Hong Kong Poetry Soc. (co-organizer), Phi Kappa Phi, Alpha Psi Omega, Sigma Tau Delta, Lambda Iota Tau. Democrat. Clubs: Campus Gay People's Union, Episcopal Peace Fellowship, Lambda Nat. Book (advisor), SAR.

CREWS, JOHN ERIC, rehabilitation administrator; b. Marion, Ind., Aug. 4, 1946; s. Odis Earl and Beatrice True (Wright) C.; m. Nancy J. Murphy, Aug. 9, 1975; 1 dau., Katherine. B.A. in English, Franklin Coll., 1969; M.A. in English, Ind. U., 1971; M.A. in Blind Rehab. with honors, Western Mich. U., 1977, postgrad in pub. administrn., 1983—. Mem. English faculty Ball State U., Muncie, Ind., 1971-73, S.W. Mo. State U., Springfield, 1973-76, Western Mich. U., Kalamazoo, 1976-77; rehab. tchr. Mich. Commn. for the Blind, Saginaw, 1977-80, program mgr. Sr. Blind Program, Saginaw, Southeastern Mich. Ctr. for Ind. Living, Detroit, 1980—; program mgr. Ind. Living Rehab. Program, 1986—; v.p. bd. Midland County Council on Aging, 1982-84; bd. dirs. Saginaw Valley Spl. Needs Vision Clinic, 1981—; mem. adv. bd. rehab. continuing edn. program So. Ill. U., Carbondale, 1985—; sec. Statewide Ind. Living Council, 1987—. Mem. editorial bd. Jour. Visual Impairment and Blindness, 1984—. Contbr. to book and profl. publs. Recipient Grant award Ind. Living Services for Older Blind Rehab. Services Adminstrn., 1986; grantee Ctr. Ind. Living U.S. Dept. Edn., 1980, 82, Ind. Living for Elderly Blind, 1986; All-Univ. grad. research and creative scholar Western Mich. U., 1988. Mem. Nat. Council Aging, Assn. Retarded Citizens (pres. Midland 1981-87; Ann. Appreciation award 1981). Methodist. Home: 5502 Whitehall Midland MI 48640 Office: Mich Commn for the Blind 411-G E Genesee Saginaw MI 48607

CREWS, RONALD KEITH, city official; b. Monroe, La., Sept. 1, 1938; s. Keith Brady and Julia Marguerite (Nix) C.; student N.E. La. State U., 1956-59; B.S., Ariz. State U., 1963; M.S. in Sch. Systems and Logistics, Air Force Inst. Tech., 1972; m. Barbara Bernell Wells, July 23, 1979; 1 child, Rebecca Rene. Enlisted U.S. Air Force, 1959, advanced through grades to lt. col., 1978; auditor, resident auditor, audit mgr. Air Force Audit Agy., 1963-75, audit mgr., 1978-79; asst. prof. Miss. State U., 1975-78; ret., 1979; internal auditor City of Shreveport (La.), 1979-86; asst. city auditor, Dallas, 1986—. C.P.A., La., Tex.; cert. internal auditor. Mem. Am. Inst. C.P.A.s, Inst. Internal Auditors (chpt. pres., internat. membership com.), Assn. Govt. Accts., Council on Mcpl. Performance, Mcpl. Fin. Officers Assn., Assn. Govtl. Accts. Contbr. article to publ. in field. Home: 12407 Montego Plaza Dallas TX 75230 Office: Office of City Auditor 3FS 1500 Marilla Dallas TX 75201

CRIARES, NICHOLAS JAMES, obstetrician and gynecologist; b. Bronx, N.Y., Apr. 2, 1934; s. James George and Christina (Brim) C.; M.D., St. Louis U., 1960; D.Sc., U. Pa., 1963; m. Helen Athos, July 3, 1966; 1 son, Peter. Commd. 2d lt. U.S. Air Force and U.S. Army, 1960, advanced through grades to col.; intern Meadowbrook Hosp., 1960-61; resident in ob-gyn Met. Hosp., N.Y.C., 1961-62, Misericordia Hosp., Phila., 1962-65, Johns Hopkins U., 1965-66; asst. attending staff Montefiore-Morrisania Affiliation, Bronx, N.Y., 1968-69; asst. prof. ob-gyn Upstate Med. Ctr., Syracuse, N.Y., 1969-72; pres. Nicholas J. Criares, M.D., P.C., Hartsdale, N.Y., 1972—; asst. attending staff Hosp. of Albert Einstein Coll. Medicine, Bronx Mcpl. Hosp. Ctr., Keller Army Hosp. of U.S. Mil. Acad.; clin. asst. prof. ob-gyn Albert Einstein Coll. Medicine. Mem. Soc. Urban Physicians, 1968-69, Doctors Council, 1978-80. Diplomate Am. Bd. Ob-Gyn. Fellow Am. Coll. Obstetricians and Gynecologists, Internat. Coll. Obstetricians and Gynecologists, Am. Coll. Quality Assurance and Utilization Rev. Physicians (cert.); mem. Bronx Ob-Gyn Soc., Assn. Mil. Surgeons U.S., AMA (Physicians Recognition award), Med. Soc. State N.Y., Westchester County Med. Soc., Am. Coll. Legal Medicine. Greek Orthodox. Club: West Point Officers. Contbr. articles profl. jours. Research on alkaline phosphatase during pregnancy, teratology, the Feto-Placental Unit, anomalies in gynecology. Office: 34 Andover Rd Hartsdale NY 10530

CRIBBET, JOHN EDWARD, legal educator, former university chancellor; b. Findlay, Ill., Feb. 21, 1918; s. Howard H. and Ruth (Wright) C.; m. Betty Jane Smith, Dec. 24, 1941; children: Carol Ann, Pamela Lee. B.A., Ill. Wesleyan U., 1940, LL.D., 1971; J.D., U. Ill., 1947. Bar: Ill. 1947. Practiced law Bloomington, Ill., 1947—; prof. law U. Ill., Urbana, 1947-67, dean. Coll. Law, 1967-79; chancellor Urbana-Champaign Campus, U. Ill., 1979-84, Corman prof. law, 1984—; dir. Champion Fed. Savs. & Loan Assn., State Farm Ins. Co. Author: Cases and Materials on Judicial Remedies, 1954, Cases on Property, 5th edit., 1984, Principles of the Law of Property, 1962, (2d edit.), 1975; editor: U. Ill. Law Forum, 1947-55; contbr. articles to legal jours. Chmn. com. on jud. ethics Il. Supreme Ct.; pres. United Fund Champaign County, (Ill.), 1962-63; trustee Ill. Wesleyan U.; mem. exec. com. Assn. Am. Law Schs., 1973-75, pres., 1979. Served to maj. AUS, 1941-45. Decorated Bronze Star; decorated Croix de Guerre. Mem. ABA, Ill. State Bar Assn., Champaign County Bar Assn., Order of Coif. Lodge: Rotary. Home: 23 Sherwin Circle Urbana IL 61820 Office: U Ill Coll of Law 504 E Pennsylvania Ave Champaign IL 61820

CRICHTON-BROWN, SIR ROBERT, financial company executive; b. Melbourne, Australia, Aug. 23, 1919; s. L. Crichton-Brown; m. Norah Isabelle Turnbull, 1941; 2 children. Student, Sydney (Australia) Grammar Sch. Chmn. Rothmans Internat. plc, 1985—; exec. chmn. Edward Lumley Ltd., 1974—, Security Life Assurances Ltd., 1961-85, Security and Gen. Ins. Co. Ltd., NEI Pacific Ltd., 1961-85, Rothmans of Pall Mall (Australia) ltd., 1981-85, Comml. Banking Co. of Sydney Ltd., 1976-82, Comml. and Gen. Acceptance Ltd., 1977-82, Westham Dredging Co. Pty. Ltd., 1975-85; vice-chmn. Nat. Australia Bank Ltd., 1982-85, Custom Credit Corp., 1982-85; bd. dirs. Daily Mail and Gen. Trust Ltd. (U.K.). Pres. Med. Found., Sydney U.; Australian nat. chmn. United World Colls. Trust, 1984-85; mem. fed. exec. and fed. hon. treas., Liberal Party of Australia, 1973-85; hon. life gov. Australian Postgrad. Fedn. in Medicine; mem. adv. bd. Girl Guides Assn. of Australia, 1973-85, Salvation Army, 1973-85; internat. forum and panel mem. Duke of Edinburgh's Award, nat. co-ordinator, 1979-84; bd. dirs. Royal Prince Alfred Hosp., 1970-84; nat. councillor Scout Assn. of Australia, 1980-85; council Imperial Soc. of Knights Bachelor; underwriting mem. Lloyd's, 1946—. Served with Australian mil., World War II. Hon. fellow, Sydney U., 1987; recipient Sydney-Hobart Yacht Race, 1970; team-recipient Admiral's Cup Team award, U.K., 1967. Mem. Inst. of Dirs. in Australia (fed. pres. 1967-80, chmn. NSW br. 1965-80). Clubs: White's Royal Cruising, Royal Yacht Squadron, Australian, Union (Sydney), Cruising Yacht of Australia, Royal Sydney Yacht Squadron, Royal Prince Alfred Yacht. Office: Rothmans Internat plc, 15 Hill St, London W1X 7FB, England *

CRICK, FRANCIS HARRY COMPTON, biologist, educator; b. June 8, 1916; s. Harry and Annie Elizabeth (Wilkins) C.; m. Ruth Doreen Dodd, 1940 (div. 1947); 1 son; m. Odile Speed, 1949; 2 daus. B.Sc., Univ. Coll., London; Ph.D, Cambridge U., Eng. Scientist Brit. Admiralty, 1940-47, Strangeways Lab., Cambridge, Eng., 1947-49; biologist Med. Research Council Lab. of Molecular Biology, Cambridge, 1949-77; Kieckhefer Disting. prof. Salk Inst. for Biol. Studies, San Diego, 1977—, non-resident fellow, 1962-73; adj. prof. psychology and chemistry, U. Calif.-San Diego; vis. lectr. Rockefeller Inst., N.Y.C., 1959; vis. prof. chemistry dept. Harvard U., 1959, vis. prof. biophysics, 1962; fellow Churchill Coll., Cambridge, 1960-61, Warren Triennial prize lectr. (with J.D. Watson), Boston, 1959; Korkes Meml. lectr. Duke U., 1960; Henry Sedgewick Meml. lectr. Cambridge U., 1963; Graham Young lectr., Glasgow, 1963; Robert Boyle lectr. Oxford U., 1963; Vanuxem lectr. Princeton U., 1964; William T. Sedgwick Meml. lectr. MIT, 1965; Cherwell-Simon Meml. lectr. Oxford U., 1966; Shell lectr. Stanford U., 1969; Paul Lund lectr. Northwestern U., 1977; Dupont lectr. Harvard U., 1979, numerous other invited, meml. lectrs. Author: Of Molecules and Men, 1966, Life Itself, 1981, What Mad Pursuit, 1988; contbr. papers and articles on molecular, cell biology and naurobiology to sci. jours. Recipient Prix Charles Leopold Mayer French Academies des Sciences, 1961; recipient (with J.D. Watson) Research Corp. award, 1961, (with J.D. Watson & Maurice Wilkins) Nobel Prize for medicine, 1962, Gairdner Found. award, 1962, Royal Medal Royal Soc., 1972, Copley Medal, 1976, Michelson-Morley award, 1981, Benjamin P. Cheney medal, Spokane, Wash., 1986, Golden Plate award, Phoenix, 1987, Albert medal Royal Soc. of Arts, 1987, Wright Prize VIII Harvey Mudd Coll., 1988. Fellow AAAS, Royal Soc.; mem. Am. Acad. Arts and Scis. (fgn hon.), Am. Soc. Biol. Chemistry (hon.), U.S. Nat. Acad. Scis. (fgn. assoc.), German Acad. Sci., Am. Philos. Soc. (fgn. mem.), French Acad. Scis. (assoc. fgn. mem.). Office: Salk Inst for Biol Studies PO Box 85800 San Diego CA 92138

CRIDER, ROBERT AGUSTINE, international financier, law enforcement official; b. Washington, Jan. 3, 1935; s. Rana Albert and Terasa Helen (Dampf) C.; student law enforcement U. Md., 1959-63; m. Debbie Ann Lee, Feb. 1960. Police officer Met. Police Dept., Washington, 1957-67; substitute tchr., bldg. trades instr. Maries R-1 Sch., Vienna, Mo., 1968-70; vets. constrn. tng. officer VA Dept. Edn., Mo., 1968-70; constrn. mgr. Tectonics Ltd., Vienna, 1970-79; owner, dir. R-A Crider & Assocs., St. Louis, 1979—; bd. dirs. TI-CO Investment Corp., Langcaster Corp. Served with USAF, 1952-56. Mem. Assn. Ret. Policemen, Internat. Conf. Police, Internat. Assn. Chiefs of Police, Nat. Police Assn., World Future Soc., Internat. Platform Assn., Mo. Police Chiefs Assn., Mo. Sheriff's Assn., Am. Correctional Assn., Law Enforcement Intelligence Assn., Internat. Drug Enforcement Assn., Nat. Assn. Fin. Cons., Internat. Soc. Financiers, Am. Legion, St. Louis Honor Guard. Roman Catholic. Clubs: Lions, K.C. (4th deg.). Home: PO Box 109 Vienna MO 65582 Office: R-A Crider & Assocs PO Box 3459 2644 Roseland Terr Saint Louis MO 63143

CRIGLER, TRUSTEN FRANK, ambassador; b. Phoenix, Oct. 17, 1935; s. Robert Rawlins and Elsie Merle (Crain) C.; m. Bettie Ann Morris, Dec. 26, 1954; children: Jeffrey, Lauren, Jeremy. BA magna cum laude, Harvard U., 1957. With U.S. Fgn. Service, Washington, 1961—; intelligence analyst Bur. Intelligence and Research, Washington, 1961-62; polit. officer Am. Consulate Gen., Guadalajara, Mex., 1963-64; consular officer U.S. Embassy, Mex., 1964-66; polit. officer U.S. Embassy, Kinshasa, Zaire, 1966-67; Am. consul resident U.S. Embassy, Bukavu, Zaire, 1967; Am. consul non-resident U.S. Embassy, Kisangani, Zaire, 1967-69; polit.-econ. officer U.S. Embassy, Libreville, Gabon, 1969-70; polit. advisor U.S. Mission to Orgn. of Am. States, Washington, 1970; polit. officer U.S. Embassy, Mex., 1974; ambassador U.S. Embassy, Kigali, Rwanda, 1976-78; dep. chief of mission U.S. Embassy, Bogotá, Colombia, 1979, chargé d'Affaires, 1979-81; dir. Office of Mexican Affairs, Washington, 1981-83; sr. insp. Office Insp. Gen. U.S. Dept. State, Washington, 1983-86; ambassador U.S. Embassy, Somalia, 1987—. Recipient Congl. fellowship, 1970. Mem. Am. Fgn. Service Assn. (Christian A. Herter award 1980). Office: US Ambassador to Somalia Care US Dept of State Ahogadishu Washington DC 20520-2360

CRISCI, VICTOR EUGENE, manufacturing company executive; b. Benevento, Italy, Sept. 11, 1919 (parents Am. citizens); s. Pietro Carmen and Anna (Lombardi) C.; student night sch.; m. Agnes Frole, June 1941 (div. 1957); children—Victor Peter, George Arthur, Susan Marie, Nancy Ellen, m. 2d, Maddalena Casale, Feb. 23, 1959; children—Daniel Joseph, Virginia Maddalena, David. Toolmaker, Burchell Products, N.Y.C., 1939-42; prodn. supr. Guy P. Harvey & Sons, Leominster, Mass., 1942-45, toolmaker instr. Standard Tool Co., Leominster, 1945-49; pres. Vic Sam Tool Co., Leominster, 1949-54; plant supt., engr., Acad. Plastics, Leominster, 1954-59; pres. Mammoth Plastics Inc., Wellsburg, W.Va., 1959-78; pres. N. Am. Container Corp., Leominster, 1978—. Chmn. Rehab. Advisory Com.; chmn. com. Boy Scouts Am. Mem. Wellburg C. of C. (dir.). Club: Lions. Patentee plastics. Office: 11 Jytek Park Leominster MA 01453

CRISCUOLO, WENDY LAURA, lawyer, interior design consultant; b. N.Y.C., Dec. 17, 1949; d. Joseph Andrew and Betty Jane (Jackson) C.; m. John Howard Price, Jr., Sept. 5, 1970 (div. Apr. 1981). AB with honors in Design, U. Calif., Berkeley, 1973; JD, U. San Francisco, 1982. Space planner GSA, San Francisco, 1973-79; sr. interior designer E. Lew & Assocs., San Francisco, 1979-80; design dir. Beier & Gunderson, Inc., Oakland, Calif., 1980-81; sr. interior designer Environ. Planning and Research, San Francisco, 1981-82; interior design cons., Mill Valley, 1982—; law clk. to Judge Spencer Williams, U.S. Dist. Ct., San Francisco, 1983-84; atty. Ciros Investments, Mill Valley, 1985—. Author: (with others) Guide to the Laws of Charitable Giving, 3d rev. edit., 1983; mem. U. San Francisco Law Rev., 1983. Bd. dirs., v.p. and treas. Marin Citizens for Energy Planning; bd. dirs., treas. The Wildlife Ctr. Mem. ABA, State Bar Calif., Queen's Bench (San Francisco), Calif. Women Lawyers. Republican. Episcopalian. Club: Commonwealth (San Francisco). Avocation: creative writing.

CRISMAN, MARY FRANCES BORDEN, librarian; b. Tacoma, Nov. 23, 1919; d. Lindon A. and Mary Cecelia (Donnelly) Borden; m. Fredric Lee Crisman, Apr. 12, 1975 (dec. Dec. 1975). BA in History, U. Wash., 1943, BA in Librarianship, 1944. Asst. br. librarian in charge work with children Mottet br. Tacoma Pub. Library, 1944-45, br. librarian, 1945-49, br. librarian Moore br., 1950-55, asst. dir., 1955-70, dir., 1970-74, dir. emeritus, 1975—; librarian co. Frank Russell Co., 1985—; chmn. Wash. Community Library Council, 1970-72. Hostess program Your Library and You, Sta. KTPS-TV, 1969-71. Mem. Highland Homeowners League, Tacoma, 1980—, incorporating dir. 1980, sec. and registered agt., 1980-82. Mem. ALA (chmn. mem. com. Wash. 1957-60, mem. nat. library week com. 1965, chmn. library adminstrn. div. nominating com. 1971, mem. ins. for libraries com. 1970-74, vice chmn. library adminstrn. div. personnel adminstrn. sect. 1972-73, chmn. 1973-74, mem. com. policy implementation 1973-74, mem. library orgn. and mgmt. sect. budgeting acctg. and costs com. 1974-75), Am. Library Trustee Assn. (legis. com. 1975-78, conf. program com. 1978-80, action devel. com. 1978-80), Pacific N.W. (trustee div. nominating com 1976-77), Wash. (exec. bd. 1957-59, state exec., dir. Nat. Library Week 1965, treas., exec. bd. 1969-71, 71-73), library assns., Urban Libraries Council (editorial sec. Newsletter 1972-73, exec. com. 1974-75), AAUW (2d v.p., mem. chmn. Tacoma 1958-59), Ladies Aux. to United Transp. Union (past pres. Tacoma), Friends Tacoma Pub. Library (registered agt. 1975-83, sec. 1975-78, pres. 1978-80, bd. dirs. 1980-83), Smithsonian Assocs., Nat. Railway Hist. Soc. Roman Catholic. Club: Quota (sec. 1957-58, 1st v.p. 1960-61, pres. 1961-62, treas. 1975-76, pres. 1979-80) (Tacoma). Home: 6501 Burning Tree Ln Tacoma WA 98406 Office: Frank Russell Co 1201 Pacific Ave Tacoma WA 98402

CRISPIN, JAMES HEWES, engineering and construction company executive; b. Rochester, Minn., July 23, 1915; s. Egerton Lafayette and Angela (Shipman) C.; A.B. in Mech. Engring., Stanford U., 1938; M.B.A., Harvard U., 1941; grad. Army Command and Gen. Staff Sch., 1943; m. Marjorie Holmes, Aug. 5, 1966. With C.F. Braun & Co., Alhambra, Calif., 1946-62; treas. Bechtel Corp., San Francisco, 1962-73, v.p., mem. fin. com., 1967-75, mgr. investment dept., 1973-75, ret.; personal investments, 1976—. Served to lt. col. Ordnance Corps, AUS, 1941-46. Registered profl. mech. engr., Calif. Mem. Mil. Order World Wars, S.R., Soc. Colonial Wars Calif., Baronial Order Magna Carta, Mil Order Crusades, Am. Def. Preparedness Assn., World Affairs Council No. Calif. (trustee 1968-75), Santa Barbara Mus. Art (trustee 1979—, pres. 1986—), Calif. Hist. Soc. (trustee 1979-86), Beta Theta Pi. Republican. Clubs: Valley of Montecito (Santa Barbara) (pres. 1987—, bd. dirs. 1981—); Calif. (Los Angeles); St. Francis Yacht, San Francisco Golf, Pacific-Union, World Trade (pres. 1977-78, dir. 1971-78) (San Francisco). Home: 1340 E Mountain Dr Santa Barbara CA 93108 Office: La Arcada Bldg 1114 State St Suite 220 Santa Barbara CA 93101

CRISTESCU, ROMULUS, mathematician, educator; b. Ploiesti, Romania, Aug. 4, 1928; s. Ioan and Ecaterina (Georgescu) C.; m. Eufrosina Barbu, May 20, 1957. D of Math., U. Bucharest, Romania, 1955. Asst. prof. math. U. Bucharest, 1950-55, lectr. math., 1955-60, assoc. prof., 1960-66, prof., 1966—, dir. Inst. Math., 1973-75. Author: Functional Analysis, 1965, 4th edit., 1983, Ordered Vector Spaces and Lin ear Operators, 1976, Topological Vector Spaces, 1977, others; contbr. articles to profl. jours. Mem. Am. Math. Soc., Romanian Math. Soc., Romanian Acad. (corr. mem., prize 1966). Home: Intrarea Dridu 2, 78416 Bucharest Romania Office: Faculty Math, Str Academiei 14, 70109 Bucharest Romania

CRISWELL, CHARLES HARRISON, analytical chemist, evironmental and forensic consultant and executive; b. Springfield, Mo., Jan. 9, 1943; s. John Philip and Elba Anne (Denton) C.; m. Joyce LaVonne Louth, Apr. 26, 1968; 1 child, Christina Rachel. AB in Chemistry and Biology, Drury Coll., 1967; postgrad., U. Mo., 1967-68. Cert. hazardous materials and waste specialist; registered profl. sanitarian. Dir. Water Pollution Control Labs City of Springfield, 1968-72, chief Water Pollution Sect., 1972-80; pres., chmn. bd. dirs. Consulting Analytical Services Internat., Springfield, 1979—; assoc. Environ. Planning Assocs., Inc., 1985—; appointed mem. Mo. Hazardous Waste Mgmt. Commn., 1978; mem. Mo. Joint Commn. on Hazardous Waste Mgmt. Legis., statewide Ad-hoc Com. on Regulations; speaker in field. Contbr. numerous articles to profl. jours. Active Springfield Employees Activities Club, ARC, Friends of Zoo; ruling elder First & Calvary Presby. Ch., elected for life 1974, bd. deacons, sr. high youth advisor, active numerous coms.; permanent judicial commn. John Calvin Presbytery, 1977-85, treas., 1975—, mem. spl. commns., Synod Gen. Assembly Inter-judicatory Consultation on Long Range Ch. Fin., various clerk positions and other offices. Fellow Am. Biog. Inst.; mem. Am. Inst. Biol. Scis., Am. Chem. Soc. (charter mem. Ozarks sect.), Mo. Acad. Sci., Mo. Water Pollution Control Assn. (pres. 1979, exec. com. 1977-83, chmn. 1979-80, newsletter editor, mem. numerous coms., chmn. confs.), Water Pollution Control Fedn. (chmn. ann. nat. conf. 1982, 83, asst. chmn. 1980, 81, 84, active numerous other coms. 1976—, Arthur Sidney Bedell award); mem. Am. Mensa , Ltd., Beta Beta Beta, Phi Mu Alpha. Republican. Office: Cons Analytical Services Internat 2804 E Battlefield Rd Springfield MO 65804

CRISWELL, ELEANOR CAMP, psychologist; b. Norfolk, Va., May 12, 1938; d. Norman Harold Camp and Eleanor (Talman) David; m. Thomas L. Hanna. B.A., U. Ky., 1961, M.A., 1962; Ed.D., U. Fla., 1969. Asst. prof. edn. Calif. State Coll., Hayward, 1969; prof. psychology Calif. State U., Sonoma, 1969—; faculty adviser Humanistic Psychology Inst., San Francisco, 1970-77; biofeedback trainer Novato Inst. Somatic Research and Tng.; mng. editor Somatics jour.; cons. Venturi, Inc., Autogenic Systems, Inc.; clin. dir. Biotherapeutics, Kentfield Med. Hosp., 1985—. Founder Humanistic Psychology Inst., 1970. Co-editor: Biofeedback and Family Practice Medicine, 1983, How Yoga Works, 1987. Mem. Am. Psychol. Assn., Biofeedback Soc. Calif. (dir.), Aerospace Med. Assn., Assn. for Transpersonal Psychology. Patentee optokinetic perceptual learning device. Office: Sonoma State U Psychology Dept Rohnert Park CA 94928

CRITCHLEY, IAN RANALD, electronic company executive; b. Sialkot, India, Feb. 7, 1926; s. Drury Ranald and Julia Olive (O'Brien) C.; m. Isobel Mary Hamilton, Jan. 6, 1951; children—Anna Collins, Bruce, Lady Julia Balgonie, Adrian. Grad., Wellington Coll., 1942, Staff Coll., 1959, Ecole Superieure de Guerre, Paris, France, 1971. Commd. 2d lt. Brit. Army, 1944, advanced through grades to col., 1971; regimental officer The Black Watch Regiment, U.K., Germany, Palestine, Egypt, India, Korea, Malaya, 1944-51; brigade maj. 152d Brigade U.K., 1960-62, command 51st Highand Vols. and staff officer, 1966-78; dep. comdr. 3d Brigade, 1974; chief of staff Brit. Mil. Govt., Berlin, 1977-78; ret., 1978; mktg. mgr. trainers and simulators Marconi Space and Def. Systems Ltd. and Marconi Instruments Ltd., Dunfermline, Scotland, 1978-82; mil. advisor, 1982-86; instr. Ecole Superieure de Guerre, 1970-71; mem. Queen's Body Guard for Scotland (Royal Co. Archers), 1976—; mem. Brit. Legion, 1978—; Chmn. Muthill br. Conservative and Unionist Party, 1978-83. Decorated officer Order Brit. Empire. Fellow Brit. Inst. Mgmt. Mem. Ch. of England. Clubs: Naval and Military (London); Puffins (Edinburgh); Highland Brigade. Home: Altina, Crieff, Perthshire Scotland Office: Marconi Instruments Ltd, Napier Bldg, Donibristle Inds Estate, Dunfermline KY11 5JE, Scotland

CRITCHLOW, ROBERT HOWARD, electronics company executive; b. Lichfield, Eng., Sept. 15, 1950; s. Norman Edwin and Audrey Emily (Dunstan) C.; m. Gigi Marie Delfosse, Jan. 14, 1984; children: Maxine Dominique, Carolyn Marie. MA/BA, Cambridge U., Eng., 1972; MBA, Harvard U., Cambridge, Mass., 1980. European mktg. mgr. Intel Corp., Belgium and Swindon, Eng., 1980-86; v.p. sales and mktg. European Mktg. and Sales Ltd., London, 1986—. Mem. Ch. of Eng. Office: European Mktg and Sales Ltd, Cardinal Point, Newall Rd, Heathrow England TW6 2EY

CRITES, RICHARD DON, lawyer; b. Ft. Worth, Sept. 3, 1943; s. Ewell Barnett Crites and Frances Loretta (Prichard) Castro; m. Annabel Lee Sheilds, June 17, 1964 (div. 1975); children—Amy Lee, Jonathon Peter; m. Judith Jean Gildig, May 30, 1976; children—Kimberly Ann, Kevin John. B.S., Ariz. State U., 1965; J.D., U. Ariz., 1968. Bar: Ariz. Assoc., Knez & Glatz, Tucson, 1968-73; ptnr. Knez, Glatz & Crites, Tucson, 1973-78; chief counsel City Utilities, Springfield, Mo., 1978-79; sole practice, Springfield, 1979—; referee Pima County Juvenile Ct., Tucson, 1972-76. Contbr. articles to law revs. Recipient Excellence in Ins. Law award Bancroft-Whitney Co., 1967, Excellence in Criminal Law award, 1968. Mem. Greene County Bar Assn., Mo. Bar Assn., ABA. Republican. Presbyterian. Lodges: Elks, Shriners, Optomists, Royal Order of Jesters. Home: 2268 Thompson Pl Springfield MO 65804 Office: 4139 S Fremont Springfield MO 65807

CRITIEN, FRANCIS EDWARD, business consultant; b. Valletta, Malta, Oct. 15, 1912; s. John and Carmela (Ellul) C.; m. May Crech, Jan. 21, 1943 (dec. 1986); children: Anton, John. Student, St. Aloysius Coll., 1925-28, Staff Coll., Sandhurst, Eng., 1945-46. Commd. maj. King's Own Malta Regiment, 1941, brigade staff officer, 1942-45, aide-de-camp to constl. commr., 1946; welfare officer H.M. Dockyard, Malta, 1949-64; married quars. officer H.M. Naval Base, Malta, 1964-70; ret. 1970; dir., cons. Joseph Cachia & Son Ltd. (M. Demajo Group of Cos.), Valletta, 1970—. Hon. treas. St. John Ambulance, Malta, 1952—; hon. sec.-treas. Friends of Cathedral Mus., Malta, 1985—. Recipient Efficiency decoration, 1958; named Knight of Grace Most Venerable Order St. John, 1986. Club: Casino (1852). Home: 7/1 Saint Mary St, Sliema Malta Office: Joseph Cachia & Son Demajo House, 103 Archbishop St, Valletta Malta

CRIVELLI, GIOCONDA MARIA CATHERINE, artist, jewelry designer; b. Florence, Italy, d. Lorenzo and Catherine Anderson (Lester) R.; student Istituto Santa Reparata, Istituto della Santissima Annunziata al Poggio Imperiale Florence; m. Eric Richards Rippel, Nov. 6, 1974; 1 child, Schoenly Shearer Alexandra. Mem. pub. relations staff S. Ferragamo, Florence, 1959-63; pub. relations fashion coordinator Irene Galitzine couture, Rome, 1963-67, Titti Brugnoli, 1967-69; owner, mgr. Gioconda, N.Y.C., 1969—; editor Harpers Bazaar, Italy, 1969-71. Mem. organizing com. Scuola d'Italia, N.Y.C., 1977; one-woman shows: Aaron Faber Gallery, N.Y.C., 1978, Martha, Park Ave, N.Y.C., 1985; painting exhbn. Essex Art Gallery, 1979; collage exhbn. Rizzoli Art Gallery, N.Y.C., 1980; collage and jewelry show Gallery Il Borro, Florence, Italy, 1981; jewelry exhbn. Am. Mus. Natural History, N.Y.C., 1980, coordinator Pompeii A.D. '79 Show, 1982, Art Students League, N.Y.C.; jewelry, sculpture exhbn. Dyansen Gallery, SoHo, N.Y., 1987; coordinator, pub. relations "Italy on Stage" art festival, 1987, N.Y.; bd. dirs. Compagnia Italiana Turismo, 1987—. Mem. Pres.'s Council Vis. Nurses, N.Y.C.; mem. coms. N.Y. Infirmary-Beekman Downtown Hosp., N.Y.C.; mem. com. Internat. Inst. Rural Reconstrn., N.Y.C.; bd. control Art Students League, 1984-87. Club: Circolo Nautico E Della Vela, Porto Ercole, Italy. Office: Art Students League 215 W 57th St New York NY 10019

CROCKER, MALCOLM JOHN, mechanical engineer, noise control engineer, educator; b. Portsmouth, Eng., Sept. 10, 1938; came to U.S., 1963, naturalized, 1975; s. William Edwin and Alice Dorothy (Mintram) C.; m. Ruth Catherine, July 25, 1964; children: Anne Catherine, Elizabeth Claire. B.Sc. in Aeros. with honors, Southampton (Eng.) U., 1961, M.Sc. in Noise and Vibration, 1963; Ph.D. in Acoustics, Liverpool (Eng.) U., 1969. Co-op. apprentice, Vickers scholar Brit. Aerospace Co., Weybridge, Surrey, Eng., 1957-62; research asst. Southampton U., 1962-63, vis. research fellow, 1976; scientist Wyle Labs. Research, Huntsville, Ala., 1963-66; research fellow U. Liverpool, 1967-69; assoc. prof. mech. engring. Purdue U., West Lafayette, Ind., 1969-73; prof. Purdue U., 1973-83; asst. dir. acoustics and noise control Herrick labs., 1977-83; prof., chmn. dept. mech. engring. Auburn U. (Ala.), 1983—; vis. prof. U. Sydney, Australia, 1976; cons. to industry, speaker in field; gen. chmn. acoustics confs. including Inter-Noise 72, Washington, 1972, Noise-Con 79 Nat. Conf. Noise Control Engring., West Lafayette, 1979; cons. and lectr. in field. Author: Noise and Noise Control, 2 vols, 1975, 82, Benchmark Papers in Acoustics: Noise Control, 1984; editor: Noise and Vibration Control Engineering, 1972, Reduction of Machinery Noise, 1974, rev. edit., 1975, others; editor-in-chief: Noise Control Engineering Jour., 1973—; mem. editorial bd.: Archives Acoustics, Warsaw, Poland, 1979—; contbr. numerous articles to profl. jours. Grantee NSF, 1972-74, 75-77, U.S. Dept. Transp., 1972-73, 79-81, EPA, 1976-80, NASA, 1980-83, 84—, Dept. Def., 1984—, others; Acoustical Soc. India hon. fellow, 1985. Fellow Acoustical Soc. Am.; mem. Inst. Noise Control Engring./ U.S.A. (dir., v.p. for communications, pres. 1981), Inst. Acoustics (London) (assoc.), Am. Soc. Engring. Edn., ASME, Am. Nat. Standards Inst. (com. chmn.). Home: 454 Pinedale Dr Auburn AL 36830 Office: Dept Mech Engring Auburn U Auburn AL 36849

CROCKETT, JAMES EDWIN, physician, educator; b. Kansas City, Kans., Oct. 20, 1924; s. John Edward and Orva Rose (Ramsey) C.; m. Martha Adam, June 8, 1949; children—Kevin, Brian, Cara. B.A., Park Coll., 1945; M.D., U. Kans., 1949. Diplomate Am. Bd. Internal Medicine and Cardiovascular Diseases. Intern U.S. Naval Hosp., Long Beach, Calif., 1949-50; resident U. Kans. Med. Ctr., Kansas City 1950-56; asst. prof. medicine U. Kans. Sch. Medicine, Kansas City, 1956-58, assoc. prof., 1958-63, dir. cardiology, 1960-63; clin. prof. medicine U. Mo.-Kansas City Sch. Medicine, 1972—; mem. adv. bd. Chinese Inst. Cardiology, Beijing, 1984—; co-founder, cons. cardiologist Mid-Am. Heart Inst., Kansas City; sr. cons. cardiology Scripps Clinic, LaJolla, Calif. Author: Your Heart, 1983; contbr. articles to profl. jours. Bd. dirs. St. Lukes Hosp. Research Found., 1973-75. Served to lt. USN, 1949-57. Fellow ACP, Am. Coll. Cardiology (bd. trustees 1965-67, 71-73, treas. 1966-67, sec. 1972-74, assoc. editor Accel. 1969-81, Cummings Internat. Teaching award, 1967). Republican. Episcopalian. Clubs: River, Carriage. Avocations: music; reading; tennis. Home: 1233 W 63 Terr Kansas City MO 64113 Office: Cardiovascular Cons Office Pres 4320 Wornall Kansas City MO 64111

CROFTON, FIONA STEPHANIE, human development consultant, educator; b. Vancouver, B.C., Can., Nov. 20, 1954; d. Kurt Wiencke and Edita (Moldenhauer) Whipple. B of Gen. Sci., Simon Fraser U., Burnaby, B.C., 1980, MA in Edn., 1984, postgrad., 1987—; postgrad., U. B.C., Vancouver. Cert. tchr., B.C. Coordinator data control systems Crown Zellerbach Paper, 1971-73; actuarial asst. Newco Fin., 1973-78; pvt. practice counselling therapy 1978—; instr., researcher Simon Fraser U., Burnaby, 1980-84; freelance cons. Vancouver, 1986—; bd. dirs. Human Devel. Services, Vancouver. Mem. Indsl. Relations Mgmt. Assn., Social Planning and Research Council.

CROGHAN, GARY ALAN, cancer research scientist; b. Ft. Wayne, Ind., Oct. 2, 1954; s. Robert Thomas and Catherine Marie (Krantz) C.; B.A., Wabash Coll., Crawfordsville, Ind., 1977; Ph.D., SUNY, Buffalo, 1982; postgrad., Buffalo Sch. Med., 1986—; m. Ivana Tallerico, July 3, 1982. Research asst. dept. diagnostic immunology research and biochemistry Nat. Breast Cancer Project Lab., Roswell Park Meml. Inst., SUNY, Buffalo, 1980-82, researcher, 1982-84, cancer research sci., 1984—, prin. investigator ovary and breast cancer lab, Diagnostic Immunology Research, 1985—, asst. research prof. pathology, 1986—; cons., lectr. in field. N.Y. State Cancer Predoctoral fellow, 1978-82, postdoctoral fellow, 1983-84, Cancer Immunology fellow Cancer Research Inst., 1984-86. Mem. AAAS, AMA, N.Y. Acad. Sci., Am. Assn. Clin. Chemists, Internat. Assn. Breast Cancer Research, Med. Soc. N.Y. State, Am. fertility Soc., Assn. Scientists RPMI, Union Concerned Scientists. Am. Soc. Microbiology, Sigma Xi. Democrat. Contbr. articles in field. Office: Roswell Park Meml Inst Dept Pathology 666 Elm St Buffalo NY 14263

CROLL, ROBERT FREDERICK, educator, economist; b. Evanston, Ill., Feb. 3, 1934; s. Frederick Warville and Florence (Campbell) C.; B.S. in Bus. Adminstrn., Northwestern U., 1954; M.B.A. (Burton A. French scholar) with high distinction, U. Mich., 1956; D.B.A., Ind. U., 1969; D.Litt., John F. Kennedy Coll., 1970; m. Sandra Elizebeth Bell, June 15, 1968; 1 son, Robert Frederick. Instr. Ind. U. Sch. Bus., Bloomington, 1956, researcher in bus. econs., 1960-62; mng. dir. Motor Vehicle Industry Research Assocs., Evanston, 1962-63; personal asst. to speaker Ill. Ho. of Reps., 1963-65; asst. prof. bus. adminstrn. Kans. State U., 1965-66; asst. prof. Inst. Indsl. Relations, Loyola U. Chgo., 1966-70; assoc. prof. Sch. Bus. Adminstrn., Central Mich. U., 1970-76, prof., 1976—. Mem. platform committee Ind. Republican Com., 1958; Ind. del. Young Rep. Nat. Conv., 1959; nat. chmn. Youth for Goldwater Orgn., 1960-61; chmn. coll. clubs Young Rep. Orgn. Ill., 1960-62, treas., 1963-65; asst. chief page Rep. Nat. Conv., 1964; mem. Mt. Pleasant City Charter Commn., 1973-76. Trustee estate of F.W. Croll, Chgo., 1959—; bd. govs. Clarke Hist. Library, 1986—. Recipient Grand prize Gov. of Ind., 1958. Accredited personnel diplomate Am. Soc. Personnel Adminstrn. Accreditation Inst. Mem. Soc. Automotive Engrs., Am. Inst. Mgmt., Soc. Advancement Mgmt., Am. Econ. Assn., Mt. Pleasant C. of C., Young Ams. for Freedom (founder 1960, vice chmn. 1962-63), Phila. Soc. (founder 1964), Beta Gamma Sigma, Delta Sigma Pi Key, Phi Delta Kappa, Phi Kappa Phi, Pi Sigma Alpha, Delta Mu Delta, Sigma Pi, Alpha Kappa Psi, Sigma Iota Epsilon, Phi Chi Theta, Pi Omega Pi. Episcopalian. Clubs: Little Harbor (Harbor Springs, Mich.); Mount Pleasant Country. Author: Fall of an Automotive Empire: A Business History of the Packard Motor Car Company, 1945-1958, others. Contbr. articles to profl. jours. Address: 1224 Glenwood Dr Mount Pleasant MI 48858

CROMBIE, WINIFRED HEATHER, linguist, educator; b. Edinburgh, Scotland, July 6, 1947; d. Alexander and Muriel Edith (Owens) C.; m. Michael Alan Carter. MA, U. Edinburgh, 1970; M in Philosophy, The Hatfield Poly., Eng., 1978; Phd, U. London, 1985. Lectr. in Linguistics The Hatfield Poly., Eng., 1973-87, prin. lectr., 1987—. Author: Discourse and Language Learning, 1985, Process and Relation in Discourse and Language Learning, 1985, Free Verse and Prose Style, 1987; contbr. articles to profl. jours. Mem. Labour Party. Office: The Hatfield Poly, College Ln, Hatfield AL10 9AB, England

CROMLEY, JON LOWELL, lawyer; b. Riverton, Ill., May 23, 1934; s. John Donald and Naomi M. (Mathews) C.; B.S., U. Ill., 1958; J.D., John Marshall Law Sch., 1966. Real estate title examiner Chgo. Title & Trust Co., 1966-70; admitted to Ill. bar, 1966; practiced in Genoa, Ill., 1970—; mem. firm O'Grady & Cromley, Genoa, 1970—; dir. Genoa State Bank, Kingston Mut. Ins. Co. Bd. dirs. Genoa Day Care Center, Inc. Mem. Am. Judicature Soc., Am., Ill., Chgo., DeKalb County bar assns. Home: 130 Homewood Dr Genoa IL 60135 Office: 213 W Main St Genoa IL 60135

CROMLEY, RAYMOND AVOLON, syndicated columnist; b. Tulare, Calif., Aug. 23, 1910; s. William James and Grace Violet (Bailey) C.; m. Masuyo Marjorie Suto (dec. Apr. 1946); m. Helen Sue Holcomb (dec. July 1967); children—Donald Stowe, Helen Sue Cromley Shisler, Jessica Lynn, Linda Grace, William Holcomb, Mary Ann, John Austin. BS in Physics, Calif. Inst. Tech., 1933; student, Japanese Lang. Inst., Tokyo, 1936-39, Strategic Intelligence Sch., Washington, 1954. Reporter Pasadena (Calif.) Post, 1928-34, Honolulu Advertiser, 1934-35, Flintridge Sch., Pasadena, 1935-36; reporter, then financial editor Japan Advertiser, Tokyo, 1936-40; editor Trans Pacific (econ. and financial weekly), 1938-40; with Wall St. Jour., 1938-55; far Eastern corr. 1938-47, Washington corr., 1947-55; sci. editor radio program Monitor, 1955-56; econ. and financial commentator NBC radio, 1956-57; asst. producer CBS Radio, 1957-58; mil. analyst Newspaper Enterprise Assn., 1958-64; pres. Cromley News-Features, 1976—; syndicated columnist 1964—; Asst. logic, freshman English Calif. Inst. Tech., 1928-30; lectr. Air War Coll., 1952, 54, Dept. State Fgn. Service Inst., 1955, 65-67; cons. guerilla war, Asian politics, 1952—. Author: Veterans Benefits, 1966, 2d edit., 1970, 3d edit., 1973, rev. edit., 1975, Educational Benefits, 1968. Chmn. dist. bds. charter rev. Boy Scouts Am., 1956-60; sec. bishop's com. pastoral benefits Va. Conf. Meth. Ch., 1967-68; organizer com. establishment Martha Washington Library, Mt. Vernon, Va., 1954; chmn. Inter-ch. Council Teen Activities and Teen Clubs, Mt. Vernon, 1955-57, World Council Youth, 1932-35. Served to col. AUS, 1943-46; comdg. officer U.S. Mil. and Dept. State Mission to Mao Tse-tung's hdqrs. 1944-45, Yenan) Communist China. Decorated Legion of Merit, Bronze Star medal. Mem. Nat. Trust for Historic Preservation, Asiatic Soc. Japan, State Dept. Corrs. Assn. (pres. 1954-55), White House Corrs. Assn., Ret. Officers Assn., Smithsonian Assos., Nat. Archives Assn., Am. Fgn. Service Assn., Assn. Corcoran Gallery Art, Sigma Delta Chi, Pi Kappa Delta. Republican. Methodist (lay speaker, Sunday sch. tchr.). Clubs: Tokyo Correspondents (exec. com. 1947); Overseas Writers (Washington). Home: 1912 Martha's Rd Hollin Hills Alexandria VA 22307 Office: PO Box 46989 Washington DC 20050-6989

CROMWELL, VALERIE, history educator; b. Bradford, Yorkshire, Eng.; m. Sir John Kingman; children: John, Charlotte. Grad., U. London, 1957. Asst. lectr. Bedford Coll., London, 1960-61; lectr., fellow Newnham Coll., Cambridge, Eng., 1961-64; lectr. U. Sussex, Brighton, Eng., 1964-75, reader, 1975—; sec.-gen. Internat. Commn. for the History of Rep. Parliamentary Instns., 1975-85, v.p., 1985—. Author: Revolution or Evolution: British Government in the Nineteenth Century, 1977. Grantee Econ. and Social Research Council, 1982. Fellow Royal Hist. Soc. (councilor, v.p. 1987, mem. lord chancellor's adv. com. on the pub. records 1987—). Office: U Sussex, Sch English Am Studies, Brighton BN1 9QN, England

CRONER, RICHARD, banker, farmer; b. Berlin, Pa., Apr. 3, 1919; s. Joe and Erma C.; m. Helen Schmucker, Jan. 4, 1941; 1 son, Tommy. B.S., Pa. State U., 1940. Engaged in farming Berlin, 1940—; chmn. Philson Nat.

Bank, Berlin, from 1971, T. Rich Inc., Berlin, from 1979; past chmn., dir. Curtice-Burns Inc., Rochester, N.Y., now dir.; chmn. bd. Agway Inc., Syracuse, N.Y., 1980—, dir., 1957—; dir. Pro-Fac Coop, Rochester, Telmark Inc., Agway Ins., Curlice Burns. Mem. Gamma Sigma Delta. Mem. United Ch. Christ. Club: Lions. Address: 310 Dimond St Berlin PA 15530 Office: AGWAY Inc Box 4933 Syracuse NY 13221 *

CRONE-RAWE, BERNARD GERHARD, textile mill executive; b. Berlin, Aug. 16, 1924; s. August and Elisabeth (Rawe) Crone-Munzebrock; m. Renate Diersch, June 11, 1958; children—Barbara (by previous marriage); Bernard F., Alexander (by present marriage). Textile Engr., Textile High Sch., 1948. Mng. dir. B. Rawe GmbH, & Co., Nordhorn, 1948-77, mem. supr. bd., 1978—; treas., dir. Gesamttextil Ev., Frankfurt, 1978—; dir. Bremen Cotton Exchange, 1958—; mem. Cotton Standard Com., U.S. Dept. Agr., Memphis, 1959—. Mem. Appeal Ct. of Justice, German Auto Sport, 1970—; mem. Sports Com. AvD, Frankfurt, 1956—; v.p. AvD Club Bremen E.V., 1977; bd. dirs. Textile Group of VDI, Dusseldorf, 1983—; pres. REFA Textile Commn., Darmstadt, 1963—. Served to lt., Germany Army, 1942-45. Decorated Iron Cross, Service Cross of Germany; Gold medal of Honor, Assn. Engrs. Mem. Textilburo Osnabruck, Eurocoton Brx., Bausie Nordhonr, GFA Nordhorn (pres.), Internat. Textile Mfrs. Fedn. (hon. life mem., past pres.), German Spinners Assn. (pres. 1973—). Clubs: Lions, VDI, AVD. Home: van Delden Strasse 34, D4460 Nordhorn Federal Republic of Germany Office: B Rawe GmbH and Co, PO Box 2249, D4460 Nordhorn Federal Republic of Germany

CRONIGER, JAMES DEWEY, electrical engineer; b. Cleve., Apr. 20, 1930; s. Wilbur and Elloree A. (Dewey) C.; m. Patricia A. O'Donnell, Sept. 3, 1960; children—Mary Eileen, Colleen, James. B.Sc., Case Inst. Tech., 1952. Registered profl. engr., Ohio. Control engr. Clark Controller, Cleve., 1952-60; systems engr. Reliance Electric, Cleve., 1961-68, supr. fed. marine dept., 1968-74, product mgr., 1974-80, project mgr., 1980—. Precinct committeeman Rep. Party, Euclid, Ohio, 1960-65. Served with U.S. Army, 1953-55. Mem. IEEE, Assn. of Iron and Steel Engrs. Republican. Roman Catholic. Club: Euclid Hockey Assn. (pres. 1979-80). Avocations: photography; skeet; ice skating; baseball; watercolor painting. Home: 75 E 217 St Euclid OH 44123 Office: Reliance Electric 24703 Euclid Ave Euclid OH 44117

CRONIN, JAMES WATSON, educator, physicist; b. Chgo., Sept. 29, 1931; s. James Farley and Dorothy (Watson) C.; m. Annette Martin, Sept. 11, 1954; children: Cathryn, Emily, Daniel Watson. A.B., So. Methodist U. (1951); Ph.D., U. Chgo. Asso. Brookhaven Nat. Lab., 1955-58; mem. faculty Princeton, 1958-71, prof. physics, 1965-71; prof. physics U. Chgo., 1971—; Loeb lectr. physics Harvard U., 1967. Recipient Research Corp. Am. award, 1967; John Price Wetherill medal Franklin Inst., 1976; E.O. Lawrence award ERDA, 1977; Nobel prize for physics, 1980; Sloan fellow, 1964-66; Guggenheim fellow, 1970-71, 82-83. Mem. Am. Acad. Arts and Scis., Nat. Acad. Sci. Home: 5825 S Dorchester St Chicago IL 60637 Office: Univ of Chgo Enrico Fermi Inst 5630 S Ellis Ave Chicago IL 60637 *

CRONJE, FRANS JOHANNES, ambassador; b. Delmas, Transvaal, Republic of South Africa, Mar. 16, 1927; s. Johannes Cristoffel and Dorothy Crafter (Fish) C.; m. Millicent Wagner, Nov. 28, 1953; children: Johannes, Carel, Frans. BA, U. Stellenbosch, Republic of South Africa, 1948. Cert. tchr., Transvaal. Vice consul Republic of South Africa Consulate, Elisabethville, Belgian Congo, 1949-50; 3d sec. Republic of South Africa Legation, Rio de Janeiro, 1956-58, Republic of South Africa High Commn., Salisbury, Rhodesia, 1958-61; 1st sec. Republic of South Africa Embassy, London, 1964-70; consul gen. Republic of South Africa Consulate Gen., Munich, 1973-75; head chancery Republic of South Africa Embassy, Bonn, Fed. Republic of Germany, 1975-76; ambassador to Greece Athens, 1985—. Nat. Party. Mem. Dutch Reformed Ch. Club: Yacht of Greece (Piraeus). Office: Embassy of South Africa, 124 Kifissias Ave, Athens Greece 115-26

CRONQUIST, ARTHUR JOHN (FRANKLIN ARTHUR BEERS), botanist; b. San Jose, Calif., Mar. 19, 1919; s. Frank and Edith Marguerite (Cronquist) Beers; m. Mabel Allred, Dec. 25, 1940; children: John, Elizabeth Lynne. Student, U. Idaho, 1934-36; BS, Utah State Coll., 1938, MS, 1940; PhD, U. Minn., 1944. Mem. staff N.Y. Bot. Garden, 1943-46, 52—, sr. scientist, 1974—; asst. prof. U. Ga., 1946-48; asst. prof. State Coll. Wash., 1948-51, research asso., 1953—; tech. adviser Belgian Govt., 1951-52. Author: Introductory Botany, 1961, 2d edit., 1971, The Evolution and Classification of Flowering Plants, 1968, 2d edit., 1988, Basic Botany, 1973, Asteraceae of Southeastern United States, 1980, An Integrated System of Classification of Flowering Plants, 1981; also numerous articles; co-author: Manual of the Vascular Plants of Northeastern U.S. and Adjacent Canada, 1963, Vascular Plants of the Pacific Northwest, 5 vols, 1955-69, Natural Geography of Plants, 1964, Intermountain Flora, 4 vols., 1972-88. Fellow Linnean Soc. London; mem. Internat. Assn. Plant Taxonomists, Bot. Soc. Am. (pres. 1973), Am. Soc. Plant Taxonomists (pres. 1962), Torrey Bot. Club, New Eng. Bot. Club, AAAS, Am. Inst. Biol. Scis., Ecol. Soc. Am., Calif. Bot. Soc. Home: 29 Dunderave Rd White Plains NY 10603 Office: NY Botanical Garden Bronx NY 10458

CROOKS, DONALD LAWRENCE, financial executive; b. Jersey City, Mar. 1, 1946; s. Vincent Lawrence and Dorothy (Blackburn) C.; B.S. in Edn., Wagner Coll., 1969, M.B.A. in Fin., 1972; Ph.D., Calif. Coast U., 1980; m. Carol Ann Caldwell, Aug. 26, 1967; children—Donald Edward, Allyson Caldwell, Casey Blackburn, Brady Brehensey, Tucker Davis, Michael. Sr. trader Shearson & Hammill, securities co., N.Y.C., 1969-71; sr. trader Oppenheimer & Co., N.Y.C., 1971-76, special partner, 1971-76; v.p., sr. trader, registered options prin., registered rep. Allen & Co., Inc., N.Y.C., 1976-81; mng. dir., prin. br. office mgr. Morgan Stanley, N.Y.C., 1981—; condr. industry seminars. Coach wrestling team Twp. Bernards, Basking Ridge, N.J., 1977—. Registered commodoties prin. Mem. Nat. Assn. Security Dealers, Zamma Taro (hon.). Lutheran. Lodge: Knights of Malta. Achieved rank of black belt in Okinawan Isshinryn Karate in record time of 8 mos.; instr. Karate; holder 4th degree black belt. Home: 96 Clark Rd Bernardsville NJ 07924 Office: 1251 Ave of the Americas New York NY 10022

CROS, EDMOND GEORGES, sociocriticism educator; b. Privas, Ardeche, France, Aug. 29, 1931; s. Marcel and Georgette (de Mars) C.; m. Christine Dongan; 1 child, Jean Manuel. Agregation d'Espagnol, Paris, 1956; Doctorat d'etat, U. Montpellier, 1967. Prof. agrege, Lycee, 1956-60; asst. agrege U. Paul Valery, Monpellier, 1960-63, maitre de conferences, 1963-67, prof., 1967—; Mellon prof. U. Pitts., 1984—, dir. Internat. Inst. Sociocriticism, 1985—. Author: Protee et le Gueux, 1967, Mateo Aleman, 1971, Ideologia y Genetica Textual, 1981; Theorie et Pratique Sociocritiques, 1983, Literatura, Ideologia y Sociedad, 1986, Theory and Practice of Sociocriticism, 1988; editor collections: Etudes Sociocritiques, 1975, Etudes critiques, 1982; editor jours. Imprevue, 1977—, Co-Textes, 1980—, Sociocriticism, 1985—. Served to lt. French Army, 1958-60. Mem. Association Internationale des Hispanistes, Centre d'Etudes et de Recherches Sociocritiques (bd. dirs., pres. 1975—). Home: 87 Rue de la Chênaie, 34090 Montpellier France Office: CERS, Univ Paul Valery, 34000 Montpellier France

CROS, GEORGES NOEL, rehabilitative medicine physician; b. Saint Flour, Cantal, France, Dec. 25, 1930; s. Louis and Jeanne Marie (Macary) C.; m. Marie Elizabeth Lefebvre, Dec. 21, 1963; children: Pascal, Stephane. MD, U. Clermont Ferrand, France, 1961. Cert. sport medicine rehabilitation, acupuncture. Intern Universitary Hosp., Clermont Ferrand, 1955-61, clinical chief, 1962-69; chief medicine Les Sources Rehabilitation Ctr., Vernet Les Bains, France, 1970-81; chief dir. medicine Beaumont Rehabilitation Ctr., Clermont Ferrand, 1981—; tech. councilor Physiotherapist Coll., Vichy, France, 1967-83; regional councilor Med. Order, Montpellier, France, 1973-81. Mem. rehabilitation French Nat. Soc., Hydrology French Nat. Soc. Roman Catholic. Home: 8 May St 13, 66500 Prades France Office: CRPA Michel Barbat, Montalembert St, 63110 Beaumont France

CROSBIE, JOHN CARNELL, Canadian government official; b. St. John's, Nfld., Can., Jan. 30, 1931; s. Chesley Arthur and Jessie (Carnell) C.; m. Jane Furneaux, Sept. 8, 1952; children: Chesley, Michael, Beth. B.A. in Polit. Sci. and Econs, Queen's U., Kingston, Ont.; LL.B., Dalhousie U.; postgrad., London Sch. Econs. Bar: Called to Nfld. 1957. Practice in St. John's, 1957-66; mem. St. John's City Council, 1965-66, dep. mayor, 1966; minister Nfld. Dept. Mcpl. Affairs and Housing, 1966-67, Dept. Health, 1967-68; rep. Nfld. Ho. of Assembly from St. John's West, as Liberal, 1966-68; as Progressive Conservative after 1971, govt. house leader, 1974-75; minister of fin., pres. Treasury Bd., also minister econ. devel. Nfld., 1972-74; minister fisheries 1974-75, minister intergovtl. affairs Nfld., 1974-76, minister mines and energy, 1975-76; mem. Canadian Ho. of Commons for St. John's West, 1976—, chmn. Progressive Conservative caucus on energy, after 1977, also parliamentary critic for industry, trade and commerce; minister of fin. for Can., 1979-80; minister of justice, atty. gen. Can., 1984-86, minister of transp., 1986-88, minister internat. trade, 1988—. Office: House of Commons, Ministry of Internat Trade, Ottawa, ON Canada K1A 0A6 *

CROSBY, PHILIP BAYARD, management consultant, author; b. Wheeling, W.Va., June 18, 1926; s. Edward Karg and Mary (Campbell) C.; Dr. Podiatry, C.P.M., 1950; m. Peggy Davis, Jan. 15, 1984; children—Phylis B., Philip Bayard. With AVCO, Richmond, Ind., 1953-55; reliability engr. Bendix-Mishawaka (Ind.), 1955-57; quality mgr. Martin Co., Orlando, Fla., 1957-65; v.p. quality ITT, N.Y.C., 1965-79; chief exec. officer Philip Crosby Assos., Winter Park, Fla., 1979—. Served with USMC, USNR, 1944-46, 51-52. Recipient Outstanding Civilian Service award for creating zero defects. Mem. Internat. Acad. Quality. Republican. Presbyterian. Clubs: Stanwich Country (Greenwich, Conn.); Interlachen Country (Winter Park, Fla.); Isleworth Country (Windemere, Fla.), N.Y. Athletic (N.Y.C.). Author: Cutting the Cost of Quality, 1967; Strategy of Situation Management, 1969; The Art of Getting your own Sweet Way, 1972; Quality is Free, 1978; Quality Without Tears, 1984; Running Things, 1986, The Eternally Successful Organization, 1988. Home: 115 Palmer Ave Winter Park FL 32789 Office: 807 Morse Blvd PO Box 2369 Winter Park FL 32789

CROSS, CHESTER JOSEPH, lawyer, acct.; b. Cicero, Ill., June 16, 1931; s. Chester Walter and Stephanie (Nowaczyk) Krzyzaniak. Student Northwestern U., 1950-56, DePaul U., 1958-59; LL.B., U. Ill., 1962. Bar: Ill. 1963, U.S. Dist. Ct. (no. dist.) Ill. 1963. Sr. acct. S.D. Leidesdorf & Co., Chgo. 1954-57, Hall, Penny, Jackson & Co., Chgo. 1957-58; controller Comml. Discount Corp., Chgo. 1958-59; sole practice law, Oak Park, Ill. and Chgo. 1963—. Mem. Ill. State Bar Assn., Chgo. Bar Assn., West Suburban Bar Assn., Am. Inst. C.P.A.s, Ill. C.P.A. Soc. Clubs: East Bank (Chgo.); Elks (Berwyn, Ill.). Office: 300 W Washington St Suite 907 Chicago IL 60606

CROSS, DENNIS WARD, insurance company executive; b. Santa Barbara, Calif., Sept. 22, 1943; s. Ward H. and Durith Ann (Stonner) C.; B.S., Ill. Wesleyan U., 1965; M.B.A., Ind. U., 1967; C.L.U., Am. Coll., 1972; m. Judith M. Marston, Feb. 5, 1967; 1 child, Kimberly. Dir. consultation projects Life Ins. Mktg. and Research Assn., Hartford, Conn., 1970-75; asst. v.p. sales USAA Life Ins. Co., San Antonio, 1975-78, v.p. sales, 1978-80, sr. v.p. sales, 1980-81, sr. v.p. mktg., 1981—, sr. v.p. fin. services mktg. div., 1986—, also dir.; pres. USAA Life Gen. Agy.; v.p. USAA Life Series Fund; sr. v.p. USAA Retirement Communities, bd. dirs. USAA Life Ins. Co.; instr., hon. faculty Army Logistics Mgmt. Center, Ft. Lee, Va., 1968-70; guest instr. U. Tex., San Antonio, 1970—, San Antonio Coll., 1978-81, St. Mary's U., 1981—. Mem. Cattle Barrons Steering com.; bd. dirs., v.p. Am. Cancer Soc.; bd. dirs., pres. Jr. Achievement of South Tex.; with mktg. task force, United Way of San Antonio. Served as capt. U.S. Army, 1967-70. Fellow Life Office Mgmt. Assn.; mem. Am. Soc. C.L.U.s, Life Advertisers Assn., Life Ins. Mktg. and Research Assn. (bd. dirs., nominating and market research coms., past chmn. direct response mktg. com., bd. dirs. 1986—), Direct Response Mktg. Ins. Council (Exec. of Yr. 1987), Am. Advt. Fedn., Army Res. Assn., No-Load Mut. Fund Assn. (bd. govs. 1987—). Club: Oak Hills Country. Office: USAA Life Ins Co 9800 Fredericksburg Rd San Antonio TX 78288

CROSS, DOROTHY ABIGAIL, librarian; b. Bangor, Mich., Sept. 9, 1924; d. John Laird and Alice Estelle (Wilcox) C.; B.A., Wayne State U., 1956; M.A. in Library Sci., U. Mich., 1957. Jr. librarian Detroit Public Library, 1957-59; adminstrv. librarian U.S. Army, Braconne, France, 1959-61, Poitiers, France, 1961-63; area library supr., 1963, asst. command librarian, Kaiserslautern, Germany, 1963-67, acquisitions librarian, Aschaffenburg, Germany, 1967, Munich, Germany, 1967-69, sr. staff library specialist, Munich, 1969-72, command librarian, Stuttgart, Germany, 1972-75, dep. staff librarian, Heidelberg, Germany, 1975-77; chief librarian 18th Airborne Corps and Ft. Bragg (N.C.), 1977-79; chief ADP sect. Pentagon Library, Washington, 1979-80, chief readers services br., 1980-83, dir., 1983—. Mem. ALA, U. Mich. Alumni assn., Delta Omicron. Methodist. Home: 6511 Delia Dr Alexandria VA 20310-6000 Office: Pentagon Library Rm 1A526 Pentagon Washington DC 06000

CROSS, HERSTLE LEE, JR., construction and engineering company executive, accountant; b. McAllen, Tex., Oct. 19, 1951; s. Herstle Lee and Leela (Byrd) C.; m. Sally Denise Mitchell, May 19, 1972; children: Katherine, Ryan, Laura, Nathan. BBA, Baylor U., 1973. CPA, Tex. Audit mgr. Arthur Andersen & Co., Houston, 1973-79, Guatemala, 1979-82, Mexico City, 1982-83; chief fin. officer Brown & Root, Inc., Mexico City, 1983-87; chief exec. officer Tex. Gulf Petroleum, Houston, 1987—. Treas. Am. Soc. Guatemala, Guatemala City, 1979-81, pres., 1981-82; bd. dirs. Am. Guatemalan Inst., Guatemala City, 1981-82; chmn. Republicans Abroad-Mex., Mexico City, 1985-86. Mem. Am. Inst. CPA's, Tex. Inst. CPA's, Investment Club of Am. Expatriates in Mex. Clubs: P.E.S.O. (sec. 1985—), Valle Escondido (Mexico City), Tomball Country. Office: Tex Gulf Petroleum 1980 S Post Oak Blvd Suite 1620 Houston TX 77056

CROSS, JEREMY LADD, aviation company executive; b. Lawrence, Mass., Mar. 23, 1939; s. Jerome Whitman and Margaret (Bain) C.; m. Beverly Brown, Sept. 12, 1964 (div. 1970); 1 child, Malcolm Tyler; m. Erlinda Kalinga, Sept. 14, 1970; children: Wynn, José, Kristine, Sarah. BSA, Bently Coll., 1965; MBA, Boston Coll., 1967. V.p. fin., controller Winthrop Sterns Co., Philippines and Japan, 1969-71; cons. Sarmiento Enterprises, Philippines, 1971-72; v.p. fin., controller Dynatics Inc., Philippines, 1972-76; v.p. fin. Systrol Mfg. Inc., Philippines, 1976-78; chmn. ATS Aviation Inc., Manila, 1978-80, also bd. dirs.; bd. dirs. Systrol Mfg. Inc. Cons. Christian Unity Helps Fellowship, 1981. Served with USMC, 1957-60. Clubs: Manila Polo, Manila Yacht; Alabang Country. Office: ATS Aviation Inc, PO Box 1803 MCC, Makati, Metro Manila Philippines

CROSS, JUDITH ANN, lawyer; b. Balt., Sept. 23, 1949; d. Joseph William and Ruth Marie (Pratt) Ortman; m. Kris Roger Cross, Nov. 15, 1969. A.A., Villa Julie, 1969; B.A. magna cum laude, U. Balt., 1980, J.D. magna cum laude, 1983. Bar: Md. 1983, U.S. Dist. Ct. Md. 1983, U.S. Ct. Appeals (4th cir.) 1983. Legal sec. various firms, Balt., 1970-72; pretrial release officer Dist. Ct. Md., Balt., 1972-78; fiscal officer, legal. asst. Office Atty. Gen., Balt., 1978-80; law clk. House Counsel Liberty Mut. Ins. Co., Balt., 1980-83; intern, student prosecutor State's Atty. Office, Balt., summer 1982; trial atty. Law Offices Eugene A. Edgett, Jr., Balt., 1983—. Contbr. articles to legal jours. Mem. jud. evaluation team Sheppard and Enoch Pratt Hosp., Balt., 1972-78; mem. Ednor Gardens Community Assn., 1975—. Mem. ABA, Md. Bar Assn., Balt. City Bar Assn., Women's Bar Assn. Home: 3627 Rexmere Rd Baltimore MD 21218 Office: Law Office of Eugene A Edgett Jr 250 West Pratt St Suite 900 Baltimore MD 21201

CROSS, LAURA ELIZABETH, lawyer; b. Lathrop, Mo.; d. Pross T. and Nina (Peel) C.; A.B., Lindenwood Coll., 1923; B.Litt., Columbia Sch. Journalism, 1925; J.D., George Washington U., 1939. Bibliog. research Library of Congress, Washington, 1931-42; admitted to D.C. bar, 1940; atty. Office Chief of Engrs., U.S. Army, 1942-73; practiced in Washington, 1973—. Mem. ABA, Fed., D.C. bar assns., Am. Judicature Soc., Women in Communications, Kappa Beta Pi, Theta Sigma Phi. Home: 2500 Wisconsin Ave NW Apt 709 Washington DC 20007

CROSS, LOUISE PORTLOCK, manufacturing company executive; b. Norfolk, Va., Jan. 20, 1907; d. William Seth and Mary Louise (Fanshow) Portlock; m. James Byron Cross, July 17, 1929; 1 child, Blanche Louise. Grad. high sch. With J.B. Cross Inc., Norfolk, 1952—, exec. pres., 1959-60, then pres., chief exec. officer, from 1960, now pres., treas., agt. Mem. Audeubon Soc., Nature Conservancy, Heritage Found., Va. Beach Maritime Hist. Mus. Lodges: Order Eastern Star, Ladies Oriental Shrine N.Am. Office: 3797 Progress Rd Norfolk VA 23502

CROSS, REX DEVERS, hardware manufacturing company executive; b. Syracuse, N.Y., Feb. 13, 1922; s. Clarence and Mildred (Ferguson) C.; m. Geneive Hinman, June 201, 1945 (div. 1955); children: Alexander, Melissa; m. Joy Thompson, Jan. 27, 1957 (div. 1967). V.p. Johnson Pump Co. div. Youngstown Sheet & Tube Co., 1951-53; pres., mgmt. cons. Rex D. Cross, Inc., 1953-55; v.p. H.K. Porter Co., Inc., 1955-57; pres. Pomeroy, Inc., Stamford, Conn., 1957—, chmn. bd., chief exec. officer, 1960—; bd. dirs mem. exec. com. Lone Star Industries, Ames Iron Works; bd. dirs. Fitzgibbons Boiler Co., Unique Sash Balance Co. Ltd., Unique Balance Co., Unique Balance Co. Eng., Unique Balance Co. Brazil, Equipment Leasing Co., Assocs. Research Co., Mchts. Bank & Trust. Served with USCGR, 1942-45. Clubs: Blind Brook (Purchase, N.Y.); Brook Hollow, Preston Trail (Dallas); Belair (Los Angeles); Seminole (Palm Beach, Fla.). Home: One Old Church Rd Greenwich CT 06830 Office: 64 Sunnyside Box 1377 Ave Stamford CT 06904

CROSS, RONALD, musicologist, educator; b. Fort Worth, Feb. 18, 1929; s. John Butler and Verna (Bailey) C.; B.A., Centenary Coll. La., 1950; M.A., N.Y.U., 1953, Ph.D., 1961; postgrad. Fulbright fellow U. Florence, Italy, U. Vienna Austria, 1955-57; S. I. Council on the Arts, 1986-88. Faculty, Notre Dame Coll. S.I., 1958-68; assoc. prof. music Wagner Coll., S.I., 1968-75, prof., 1975—, chmn. music dept., 1981-84, dir. Collegium Musicum, 1968—, Kurt and Auguste Reimann chair of music, 1984—. Organist, choirmaster various chs. Am. Council Learned Socs. grantee, 1954, recipient performance grants Staten Island Council on the Arts, 1986, 87,88; recipient Founders Day award N.Y.U., 1962, Alumni Achievement award. Mem. Am. Guild Organists (asso.), Internat., Am. musicol. socs., Coll. Music Soc., Soc. for Ethnomusicology, Am. Recorder Soc. Recorded and directed Songs and Dances of the Renaissance (Lieder and Tänze der Renaissance) Collegium Pro Musica FSM Pantheon, 1984. Author: Matthaeus Pipelare: Opera Omnia, 3 vols., 1966-67; reviewer Renaissance recs. for Music Quar., 1971-76; contbr. articles to profl. jours. Home: 221 Ward Ave Staten Island NY 10304

CROSS, SAMUEL S., lawyer; b. Detroit, Oct. 19, 1919; s. Samuel Stogden and Mildred Lurline (Hay) C.; m. Jodie E. Hecht, Jan. 3, 1947 (div. 1948); 1 child, Edward T.; m. Audrey Brauneck, Nov. 25, 1950; children—Stephen W., Lauren E., Robert A., Wendy A. B.S., Lehigh U., 1941; LL.B., U. Pa., 1949. Bar: N.Y. 1951, Conn. 1953, Pa. 1977. Test engr. Bethlehem Steel Co., Steelton, Pa., 1941-43; assoc. Watson, Johnson, Leavenworth & Blair, N.Y.C., 1949-52; gen. counsel, sec. Perkin-Elmer Corp., Norwalk, Conn., 1952-64; counsel Maguire, Cole & Bentley, Stamford, Conn., 1964-68; ptnr. Cross, Brodrick & Chipman, Stamford, Conn., 1969-79, Kelley Drye & Warren, N.Y.C., 1979—; gen. counsel Southwestern Area Commerce and Industry Assn. of Conn., Inc., Stamford, 1970—. Author: Corporation Law in Connecticut, 1972; editor-in-chief Conn. Bar Jour., 1982-85; contbr. articles to profl. jours. Mem. Legis. Commn. on Revision of Corp. Laws, Hartford, Conn., 1957-62; pres. The Ferguson Library, Stamford, Conn., 1977-78; trustee The Ferguson Library Found., 1987—, Engring. Edn. Found. Inc., 1969—; chmn. Forum for World Affairs Inc., 1987—. Served as lt. (j.g.), USNR, 1943-46. Mem. ABA, Am. Soc. Corp. Secs., Inc., Am. Soc. Internat. Law, Southwestern Legal Found. (adv. bd. Internat. and Comparative Law Ctr.), Tau Beta Pi. Republican. Congregationalist. Clubs: Union League (N.Y.C.); Metropolitan (Washington). Home: 1021 Ridgefield Rd Wilton CT 06897 Office: Kelley Drye & Warren 101 Park Ave New York NY 10178

CROSS, STEVEN JASPER, professor of finance; b. Hohenwald, Tenn., Apr. 19, 1954; s. Thomas Edward and Eula Mae (Mealer) C.; m. Martha Ellen Bradshaw, Aug. 23, 1974. B.S., Middle Tenn. State U., 1976, M.A.T., 1980, D.A., 1984. Sales rep. University Ford Inc., Murfreesboro, Tenn., 1976; ins. underwriter Continental Ins. Inc., Nashville, 1976-77; credit rep. SunAm., Inc., Murfreesboro, 1977-78; instr. mgmt. Dyersburg (Tenn.) State Community Coll., 1980-81; instr. Motlow State Community Coll., Tullahoma, Tenn., 1981-83, asst. prof. econs. 1983-85; assoc. prof. fin. Delta State U., 1985-88, prof., chmn. div. of econ. and fin., 1988—. Contbr. articles to profl. jours. Mem. Am. Econ. Assn., Nat. Assn. Bus. Economists, Am. Fin. Assn., Eastern Fin. Assn., So. Fin. Assn., Southwestern Fin. Assn., Midsouth Acad. Econs. and Fin., Midwest Econs. Assn., Sigma Rho, Phi Beta Lambda, Delta Mu Delta. Home: 25 Memorial Dr Boyle MS 38730 Office: Delta State U Sch Bus div Econs and Fin Cleveland MS 38733

CROSS, WILLIS JOLLIFF, JR., catalytic process consultant; b. Newport News, Va., Dec. 15, 1923; s. Willis J. and Sallie Gladis (Bateman) C.; m. Audrey Sheddan, June 28, 1947; children—Wendy, Mark, Janet. B.S., Va. Poly. Inst., 1945. Cat cracking research and devel. Atlantic Refining Co., Phila., 1945-46; mgr. tech. service Houndry Process Corp., Phila., 1960-64, mgr., v.p. sales and service, 1964-66, 67-68; gen. mgr. profit ctr. Air Products and Chems., Allentown, Pa., 1969-80; pres. TEK Assocs., Inc., Media, Pa., 1981—. Sec., Rose Tree-Media Sch. Authority, Media, Pa., 1974—. Patentee in field. Served with U.S. Army, 1944. Mem. Am. Petroleum Inst., Am. Inst. Chem. Engrs., Am. Chem. Soc., Chem. Industry Assn. Republican. Club: Catalyst (Delaware County, Pa.). Home: 61 Paxon Hollow Rd Media PA 19063 Office: TEK Assocs Inc 111 Veterans Sq PO Box 652 Media PA 19063

CROSSLAND, HARRIET KENT, portrait painter; b. Cleve., Sept. 8, 1902; d. Carl and Harriet Emily (Bacon) Dueringer; pupil of Margaret McDonald Phillips; m. Paul Marion Crossland, Sept. 20, 1959. Portrait painter, 1952—; freelance editor med. papers, 1953-70; represented in permanent collection John F. Kennedy Library, Boston. Mem. Santa Rosa Symphony League; mem. art mus. com. Luther Burbank Center for the Arts, Santa Rosa, 1982—. Recipient award of merit Am. Cancer Soc., 1979, 84. Mem. Sonoma County Med. Assn. Aux., Am. Med. Women's Assn. (friend), DAR, Stanford U. Alumni Assn. Clubs: Ret. Officers Wives, Sonoma County Press, Sat. Afternoon (Santa Rosa). Editor, illustrator: X-Rays and Radium in Treatment of Diseases of the Skin, 1967; included in The Fifty American Artists by Margaret McDonald Phillips, 1969. Prin. donor Crossland Lab. for Audiovisual Learning in Dermatology, Stanford U. Sch. Medicine. Address: 2247 Sunrise Dr Santa Rosa CA 95405

CROSSLAND, WILLIAM EDWARD, safety engineer; b. Detroit, July 13, 1932; s. Ernest Edward and Clara Gertrude (Davis) C.; m. Helen Charlene Thompson, July 23, 1976. B.S. in Safety Engring., U. Ala., 1960; postgrad. U. So. Calif., 1975. Registered profl. engr., Calif.; cert. safety profl., Ill.; lic. pvt. pilot; cert. police officer. Founder, chmn. bd. Internat. Safety Cons., Inc., 1969-81; dir. safety Handy Andy Corp., San Antonio, 1972-73; safety engr. Royal Globe Ins. Co., 1973-74; dir. safety U.S. Air Force, Oklahoma City, 1974-77; safety and health mgr. Dept. Labor, Kansas City, Mo., 1977-84; safety and health mgr. U.S. Air Force, Hawaii, 1984-86, San Antonio, 1986—; tchr. safety engring. Okla. State U.; cons. AF Community Coll.; mem. energy com. Fed. Exec. Bd., 1979-84. Composer: Never, 1958; Is It the Same, 1978. Contbr. articles to profl. jours. Vol. Kansas City chpt. ARC. Served with USAF, 1951-72. Decorated Commendation Medal with 3 oak leaf clusters, Meritorious Service Medal with 2 oak leaf clusters; named Top Civilian Safety Dir. in USAF, 1974; created the Safety and Health Hall of Fame, Warrensburg, Mo. Mem. Assn. Fed. Safety and Health Profls. (past pres.), Am. Soc. Safety Engrs., Vets. Safety Internat. (past pres.), Nat. Safety Mgmt. Soc., Fed. Safety and Health Council San Antonio (chmn. 1988—), System Safety Soc., Am. Legion. Baptist. Office: 5820 Royal Bend San Antonio TX 78239

CROTT, HELMUT WILHELM, psychologist, researcher; b. Aachen, Fed. Republic Germany, Aug. 19, 1938; s. Josef and Barbara (Birken) C. Degree in Psychology, State U. Hamburg, Fed. Republic Germany, 1964; Habilitation, State U. Mannheim, Fed. Republic Germany, 1975. Asst. prof. State U. Mannheim, Fed. Republic Germany, 1967-70, acad. cons., 1971-75; guest prof. State U. W. Va., Morgantown, 1970; prof. U. Freiburg, Fed. Republic Germany, 1975—. Author: Negotiations, 1977, Social Interaction and Group Processes, 1979; editor: Organizational and Social Psychology, 1978. Office: Psychologisches Inst, Niemensstr 10, Freiburg 7800, Federal Republic of Germany

CROTTY, PHILIP JOHN, bank executive; b. TeAwamutu, New Zealand, Apr. 16, 1955; s. Leonard John and Pamela Mary (Connop) C.; m. Elisa Pastoral Bulawan, June 20, 1987. B in Agrl. Commn., U. Canterbury, New

Zealand, 1977, M in Agrl. Commn., 1980; MBA, Intern. Mgmt. Inst., Geneva, 1986. Cons. economist Brown, Copeland & Co., Christchurch, New Zealand, 1979-81, Tate and Lyle Agribus., London, 1981-82; project economist Asian Devel. Bank, Manila, 1982-85; pres., gen. mgr. Crotty and Assocs., Manila, 1986—. mem. Nomad Rugby Football Club, Manila (capt. 1984-85), 1985—, Nomad Squash Club team, 1987—. Mem. Asian Inst. Tech., New Zealand Econs. Soc., Australian Agrl. Econ. Soc., New Zealand Inst. Agrl. Sci. Roman Catholic. Club: Manila. Office: Crotty and Assocs Ltd Suite 202, 168 Salcedo St, Legaspi Village, Makati Metro Manila Philippines

CROUCH, COLIN JOHN, social sciences educator; b. London, Mar. 1, 1944; s. Charles John and Doris Beatrice (Baker) C.; m. Joan Ann Freedman, June 10, 1970; children: Daniel James, Benjamin Thomas. BA in Sociology, London Sch. Econs., 1969; PhD, Nuffield Coll., Oxford, Eng., 1975. Editorial asst. Royal Soc. Prevention of Accidents, London, 1961-64; sub-editor Mcpl. Engring., London, 1964-65; temp. lectr. in Sociology London Sch. Econs., 1969-70, lectr. in Sociology, 1973-79, sr. lectr. in Sociology, 1979-80, reader in Sociology, 1980-85; lectr. in Sociology U. Bath, Eng., 1972-73; fellow and tutor in Polit. Sci. Trinity Coll., Oxford, 1985—; chmn. sub-faculty sociology dept., U. Oxford, 1987—; asst. organizer Ford Found. project on labour conflict in Western Europe, 1973-76; mem. Brookings Instn. project on polit. economy of global inflation and recession, 1977-80, EEC project on future of trade unions in Europe, 1986-88; joint editor Polit. Quar., 1985—. Author: The Student Revolt, 1970, Class Conflict and the Industrial Relations Crisis, 1977, The Politics of Industrial Relations, 1979, 2d edit., 1982, Trade Unions: The Logic of Collective Action, 1982; editor: (with L. Lindberg, others) Stress and Contradiction in Modern Capitalism, 1975, British Political Sociology Yearbook, Vol. III: Participation in Politics, 1977; (with A. Pizzorno) The Resurgence of Class Conflict in Western Europe Since 1968, 2 vols., 1978, State and Economy in Contemporary Capitalism, 1979; (with F. Heller) International Yearbook of Organizational Democracy, vol. I, 1983; contbr. numerous articles in profl. jours. Mem. exec. com. Fabian Soc., London, 1969-79, chmn., 1978. Mem. Internat. Sociol. Assn. Mem. Labour Party. Jewish. Home: 109 Southmoor Rd, Oxford OX2 6RE, England Office: Trinity Coll, Oxford OX1 3BH, England

CROUCH, HOWARD EARLE, health service organization executive; b. New Brunswick, N.J., Mar. 15, 1918; s. Louis S. and Sarah Maria (Buckelew) C.; cert. Washington and Lee U., 1944; B.S., Tchrs. Coll., Columbia U., 1948, M.A., 1954; M.S. in Adminstrv. Medicine, Columbia U. Sch. Public Health and Medicine, 1954. Adminstr., St. Peters Gen. Hosp., New Brunswick, N.J., 1954-58; instr. biol. scis. Kennedy Sch., Bellmore, N.Y., 1958-78; weekend adminstr. Meml. Sloan Kettering Cancer Center, N.Y.C., 1958-81; pres. Damien Dutton Soc. for Leprosy Aid Inc., Bellmore, N.Y., 1978—. Served with M.C., U.S. Army, 1941-45. Recipient Community Service award Nassau County, N.Y., 1987, Country award Cath. War Vets., 1959, Celtic Cross, 1960; Good Samaritan award Alexian Bros. Hosp. Center, 1975; Am. Leprosy Missions award, 1985. Mem. Internat. Leprosy Assn., N.Y. State Ret. Tchrs. Assn., Cath. Press Assn., Cath. Tchrs. Assn. (pres. 1962-64), Columbia U. Alumni Assn. Roman Catholic. Author: Brother Dutton of Molokai, 1968; After Damien-Dutton Yankee Soldier on Molokai, 1981; contbr. articles on health service adminstrn. to profl. publs.; contbg. editor Catholic Youth Ency. Home: 2572 Riverside Dr Wantagh NY 11793 Office: 616 Bedford Ave Bellmore NY 11710

CROUCHER, JOHN SYDNEY, statistician, educator; b. Sydney, NSW, Australia, Apr. 11, 1947; s. Sydney Ross and Phyllis May (Taylor) C.; m. Lynn Margaret Stevens, Dec. 4, 1970; children: Joanne, Amy. BA with hons., Macquarie U., NSW, Australia, 1970; MS, U. Minn., 1972, PhD, 1973. Actuarial clk. M.L.C. Life Assurance Co., Sydney, 1963-67; teaching assoc. U. Minn., Mpls., 1971-73; univ. lectr. stats. Macquarie U., Sydney, 1974—; cons. various cos., Sydney, 1975—, Totalisator Agy. Bd., Sydney, 1985—; sports journalist Fairfax Media Orgn., Sydney, 1984-86; TV presenter Channel 10 TV Network, Sydney, 1985—. Author Elementary Statistics for Business, 1977, Statistics: an Introduction, 1980, Operations Research: a First Course, 1982, Statistics: a Modern Introduction for Business and Management, 1986. Ruth Cumming scholar, English Speaking Union, 1970, travel scholar P&O Shipping Lines, Sydney, 1970; grantee NSW Dept. Sport and Recreation, 1986. Mem. Ops. Research Soc. Australia.

CROUZET, M-J. MICHEL, professor; b. Nantes, France, Jan. 7, 1928. Student, Ecole Normale Superieure, 1948. Prof. U. Sorbonne, 1983—. Contbr. numerous and books articles on Stendhal Modern French Lit.and critical Theory. Office: U Sorbonne, 1 rue Victor Cousin, 75005 Paris France

CROVITZ, LOUIS GORDON, journalist; b. Durham, N.C., Aug. 22, 1958; s. Herbert Floyd and Elaine Sandra (Kobrin) C. B.A., U. Chgo., 1980, M.A. Oxford U., 1982; J.D., Yale U., 1986. Editor, founder Chgo. Jour., 1976-79; research assoc. Lexecon, Inc., Chgo., 1979-80; editorial writer Wall St. Jour., N.Y.C., 1980-82, editorial page editor, Brussels, 1982-84, editorial writer, mem. editorial bd., N.Y.C., 1984-86, asst. editorial page editor, 1986—. Contbr. articles to profl. publs. Mem. Com. for Free World, N.Y. and London, 1982—. Rhodes scholar, 1980-82; recipient Disting. Alumni award Durham Acad., 1984. Mem. Federalist Soc., Phi Beta Kappa. Jewish. Office: Wall St Jour 200 Liberty St New York NY 10281

CROW, JOHN WILLIAM, banker; b. London, 1937; s. John Cornell and Mary Winifred (Weetch) C.; m. Ruth Kent, 1963; children—Rebecca, Jonathan. B.A., Oxford U., 1961. Economist Western Hemisphere dept. Internat. Monetary Fund, 1961-67, asst. chief Cen. Am. div., 1967-70, chief N.Am. div., 1970-73; dep. chief research dept. Bank of Can., Ottawa, 1973-74, chief research dept., 1974-79, adviser, 1979-81, dep. gov., 1981-84, sr. dep. gov., 1984-87, gov., 1987—. Office: Bank of Canada, 234 Wellington St, Ottawa, ON Canada K1A 0G9

CROWDER, BARBARA LYNN, lawyer; b. Mattoon, Ill., Feb. 3, 1956; d. Robert Dale and Martha Elizabeth (Harrison) C.; m. Lawrence Owen Taliana, Apr. 17, 1982; children: Paul Joseph, Robert Lawrence. BA, U. Ill., 1978, JD, 1981. Bar: Ill. 1981. Assoc., Louis E. Olivero, Peru, Ill., 1981-82; asst. state's atty. Madison County, Edwardsville, Ill., 1982-84; ptnr. Robbins & Crowder, Edwardsville, 1985-87; ptnr. Robbins, Crowder & Bader, Edwardsville, 1987-88; ptnr. Crowder & Italiana, 1988—. Chmn. City of Edwardsville Zoning Bd. Appeals, 1986-87; committee woman. Edwardsville Dem. Precinct 15, 1986—; mem. City of Edwardsville Planning Commn., 1985-87. Named Best Oral Advocate, Moot Ct. Bd., 1979, Outstanding Sr., Phi Alpha Delta, 1981, Young Career Woman, Dist. XIV. Ill. Bus. and Profl. Women, 1986; recipient Parliamentary Debate award U. Ill., 1978, Alice Paul award Alton-Edwardsville NOW, 1987, Jr. Service award Edwardsville Bus. and Profl. Women, 1987. Mem. ABA, Ill. Bar Assn., Assn. Trial Lawyers Am., Phi Alpha Delta, Women Lawyers Assn. Met. East (v.p. 1985, pres. 1986), LWV, Edwardsville Bus. and Profl. Women (Woman of Achievement 1985, Jr. Service award 1987). Democrat. Home: 982 Surrey Dr Edwardsville IL 62025 Office: PO Box 451 Edwardsville IL 62025

CROWE, DANIEL WALSTON, lawyer; b. Visalia, Calif., July 1, 1940; s. J. Thomas and Wanda (Walston) C.; m. Nancy V. Berard, May 10, 1969; children—Daniel W., Karyn Louise, Thomas Dwight. B.A., U. Santa Clara, 1962; J.D., U. Calif. Hastings Coll. Law, 1965. Bar: Calif. 1966, U.S. Dist. Ct. (ea. dist.) Calif. 1969, U.S. Dist. Ct. (cen. dist.) Calif. 1973, U.S. Ct. Appeals (9th cir.) 1973, U.S. Supreme Ct. 1973. Assoc. Crowe, Mitchell & Crowe, and predecessors, Visalia, Calif., 1968-74, ptnr., 1974-83; ptnr. Crowe & Williams, 1983—; sec., treas., dir. The Exeter Devel. Co.; dir., treas. Willson Ranch Co., 1983—. Founding mem., dir. Visalia Balloon Assn., Inc. Served to capt. U.S. Army, 1965-68. Decorated Bronze Star, Air medal, Purple Heart, Nat. Def. Service medal. Mem. ABA, Calif. Bar Assn., Tulare County Bar Assn. Republican. Roman Catholic. Clubs: Visalia Rotary, Elks, Moose, Am. Radio Relay League, DAV. Address: PO Box 1110 Visalia CA 93279

CROWE, DENNIS TIMOTHY, JR., veterinary surgeon, researcher, educator; b. Milw., Nov. 21, 1946; s. Dennis Timothy and Anna Mae (Persen) C.; m. Deborah Gene Coulson, Jan. 2, 1971; children—Michael, Kristin. D.V.M., Iowa State U., 1972. Diplomate: Am. Coll. Veterinary Surgeons. Intern Colo. State U., 1972-73; resident in surgery Ohio State U., 1973-76; chief surgery Westcott Hosp. and Animal Emergency Room, Detroit, 1976-78; asst. prof. surgery Kans. State U., Manhattan, 1978-80, now assoc. prof. surgery; asst. prof. surgery U. Ga., Athens, 1980-87, assoc. prof. surgery, chief emergency and critical care service, 1987—, dir. Shock Trauma team, 1981—, co-dir. intensive care unit, 1981—; instr., cons. paramedic program Athens Gen. Hosp. (name now Athens Regional Med. Ctr.) Emergency Med. Services; nat. and internat. lectr. on vet. emergency and critical care and traumatology; lectr. in field. Author 15 textbook chpts.; cons. editor Jour. Am. Animal Hosp. Assn., Vet. Surgery, also book; contbr. numerous articles to profl. jours. Vet. Med. Expt. Sta. grantee, 1981-83; recipient G.G. Graham award in clin. veterinary medicine Iowa State U., 1972. Mem. AVMA, Am. Coll. Vet. Surgeons, Am. Animal Hosp. Assn., Vet. Emergency and Critical Care Soc. (past pres.). Methodist. Research on shock (hemorrhagic, septic) abdominal counterpressure, gen. surgery subjects and CPR. Home: 630 Sandstone Dr Athens GA 30605 Office: U Ga, H316 Vet Teaching Hosp Dept Small Animal Medicine & Surgery Coll of Vet Medicine Athens GA 30602

CROWE, EUGENE BERTRAND, investment counselor; b. Wadley, Ala., Nov. 2, 1916; s. Will Mack and Eudoxie (Bonner) C.; children: Harold, Julie. B.S. in Pub. Adminstrn., Am. U., 1945. With SEC, 1938-40, VA, 1946-48; mgmt. and budget analyst CAA, 1948-50; analyst State Dept., 1950-51; budget examiner Exec. Office Pres., 1951-54; asst. controller Bur. Ordnance, 1954-58; prof. polit. sci. Bir Zeit (Jordan) Coll., 1960-61; pub. adminstrn. adviser to King Hussein of Jordan, 1959-61; dep. asst. postmaster gen., controller Post Office Dept., 1963-66, exec. asst. to dep. postmaster gen., 1967-68; mgmt. cons. Tallahassee, 1968-69; planning and program cons. Fla. Office State Planning, 1969-72; investment counselor Santa Cruz, Calif., 1972-78, Palm Beach, Fla., 1978-86, Sarasota, Fla., 1987—. Author: (with Sir Eric Franklin) Economic Development in Jordan, 1961. Served to maj. USAAF, 1942-46. Cited by King Hussein, 1961. Mem. Am. Soc. Pub. Adminstrn., Soc. Internat. Devel., Fed. Govt. Accountants Assn., Pi Kappa Alpha. Episcopalian. Home: 969 Citrus Ave Sarasota FL 34236

CROWE, WILLIAM JAMES, JR., naval officer; b. La Grange, Ky., Jan. 2, 1925; s. William James and Eula (Russell) C.; m. Shirley Mary Grennell, Feb. 14, 1954; children: William Blake, James Brent, Mary Russell. BS, U.S. Naval Acad., 1946; MA in Edn., Stanford U., 1956; PhD in Politics (Harold W. Dodds fellow), Princeton U., 1965. Commd. ensign U.S. Navy, 1946, advanced through grades to adm.; comdg. officer U.S.S. Trout, 1960-62; comdr. Submarine Div. 31 San Diego, 1966-67; sr. adviser Vietnamese Navy Riverine Force 1970-71, dep. to Pres.'s Spl. Rep. for Micronesian Status Negotiations, 1971-73; dir. East Asia and Pacific region Office of Sec. of Def. Washington, until 1976; comdr. Middle East Force Bahrain, 1976-77; dep. chief of naval ops. Dept. Navy Washington, 1977-80; comdr.-in-chief Allied Forces So. Europe 1980-83, comdr.-in-chief Pacific, 1983-85; chmn. Joint Chiefs of Staff, 1985—. Author supr. ops. plan for repatriation of U.S.S. Pueblo crew. Decorated D.S.M., D.D.S.M., Legion of Merit, Bronze Star, Air medal with 6 oak leaf clusters. Mem. U.S. Naval Inst., Am. Polit. Sci. Assn., Internat. Studies Assn., Phi Gamma Delta, Phi Delta Phi. Office: US Defense Dept Office Joint Chiefs of Staff The Pentagon Washington DC 20301 *

CROWLEY, JAMES MICHAEL, lawyer; b. Phila., Feb. 16, 1942; s. Joseph M. and Mary V. (McCall) C.; m. Beverly Ann Crystal, Mar. 28, 1987; children—David M., Benjamin T. Ph.B. magna cum laude, Lateran U., Rome, 1965, S.T.B. magna cum laude, 1967, S.T.L., 1969, J.C.B. magna cum laude, 1970, J.C.L. magna cum laude, 1973; J.D., Notre Dame U., 1972. Bar: N.Y. 1973, U.S. Dist. Ct. (so. dist.) N.Y. 1973, U.S. Supreme Ct. 1976. Assoc., Shearman & Sterling, N.Y.C., 1972-78, resident, Algiers, Algeria, 1976-78; sole practice, N.Y.C., 1978-80; sr. counsel CIGNA Corp., Phila., 1980-84; v.p. CIGNA Internat. Holdings Ltd., Wilmington, Del., 1982—; sr. v.p., chief counsel CIGNA Worldwide, Incorporated, Phila., 1984—; dir. CIGNA Worldwide Ins. Co., Wilmington. Mem. Archdiocesan Fin. Council, Phila., 1984-87; exec. bd. Phila. council Boy Scouts Am., 1983-86; pro bono publico litigation Matter of Karen Ann Quinlan, N.J., 1976. Recipient Cardinal Dougherty medal St. Charles Coll., Phila., 1963; Silver medal Pope Paul VI, Rome, 1967. Mem. Am. Soc. Internat. Law, ABA, Assn. Bar City N.Y., N.Y. State Bar Assn., N.Y. County Bar Assn. Roman Catholic. Club: University (N.Y.C.). Home: 2127 Brandywine St Philadelphia PA 19130 Office: CIGNA Corp 1600 Arch St Philadelphia PA 19103

CROWLEY, JOHN CRANE, real estate developer; b. Detroit, June 29, 1919; s. Edward John and Lean Helen (Crane) C.; m. Barbara Wenzel Gilfillan, Jan. 12, 1945; children: F. Alexander, Leonard, Philip, Eliot, Louise, Sylvia. BA, Swarthmore Coll., 1941; MS, U. Denver, 1943. Mem. staff Pub. Adminstrn. Service, Chgo., 1942-46; asst. dir. Mcpl. Finance Officers Assn., Chgo., 1946-48; So. Calif. mgr. League Calif. Cities, Los Angeles, 1948-53; mgr. City of Monterey Park, Calif., 1953-56; v.p. Community Facilities Corp., Los Angeles, 1956-59, DSI Corp., Beverly Hills, Calif., 1961—; founder, exec. v.p. Nat. Med. Enterprises, Los Angeles, 1968; pres. Ventura Towne House (Calif.), 1963—; mem. faculty U. So. Calif. Sch. Pub. Adminstrn., 1950-53. Contbr. articles to profl. jours. Mem. State Adv. Council on Retirement Housing, 1965-68, Los Angeles County Com. on Affairs of Aging, 1966—; Mayor City of Pasadena, 1986—; city dir. Pasadena, 1979—; bd. dirs. Nat. Mcpl. League, 1986—, Pacificulture Found. and Asia Mus., 1971-76, pres., 1972-74; bd. dirs. Pasadena Area Liberal Arts Ctr., 1962-72, pres., 1965-68; trustee Pacific Oaks Friends Sch. and Coll., Pasadena, 1954-57; chmn. Pasadena Cultural Heritage Commn., 1975-78; pres. Pasadena Civic Improvement Corp., 1985—; bd. mgrs. Swarthmore Coll., 1986—. Recipient Disting. Citizen award Nat. Mcpl. League, 1984; Sloan Found. fellow, 1941-43. Mem. Internat. City Mgmt. Assn., Nat. Mcpl. League (nat. bd. 1980—), Phi Delta Theta. Democrat. Unitarian. Home: 615 Linda Vista Ave Pasadena CA 91105 Office: PO Box 93223 Pasadena CA 91109

CROWN, DAVID ALLAN, criminologist, educator; b. Long Beach, N.Y., Sept. 13, 1928; s. John and Florence (Coe) C.; m. Maria Braml, Feb. 13, 1954; children: Ingrid, Eric. B.S., Union Coll., 1948; M.Criminology, U. Calif., 1960, D.Criminology, 1969. Spl. agt. CIC, 1951-53; asst. dir. San Francisco Indentification Lab., U.S. Postal Inspection Service, 1957-67; dir. Questioned Document Lab., Records Analysis Group, Dept. Army, Washington, 1967-72, Questioned Documents Staff, INR/DDC, U.S. Dept. State, Washington, 1972-77; chief Questioned Documents Lab., Office of Tech. Services, 1977-82; Lectr. Chabot Coll., Hayward, Calif., 1966-67, Georgetown U., Washington, 1973; adj. prof. Am. U., Washington, 1971-80; professorial lectr. George Washington U., 1973-77, Antioch Sch. Law, until 1981; pres. Crown Forensic Labs., Inc.; chmn. recert. com. Am. Bd. Forensic Document Examiners. Author: The Forensic Examination of Paints and Pigments, 1968; co-author: Forensic Science, 1982, Legal Medicine 1985, 1985; Contbr. articles to profl. pubs.; Editorial bd.: Jour. Forensic Scis, 1971-73; book rev. editor, 1973-74, assoc. editor, 1974-84. Mem. Am. Acad. Forensic Scis. (chmn. questioned document sect. 1969-70, exec. com. 1970-74, pres. 1974-75), Am. Soc. Questioned Document Examiners (chmn. accreditation com. 1969-70, sec.-treas. 1976-78, pres. 1980-82), ASTM (chmn. questioned document com. 1970-71, vice chmn. 1972), Forensic Sci. Found. (dir. 1971-72, trustee 1973-75), Am. Coll. Document Examiners (dir. 1970—). Club: Arlington Hall Officers. Home: 3103 Jessie Ct Fairfax VA 22030

CROWTHER, PAUL DAVID, educator, lecturer; b. Leeds, Yorkshire, Eng., Aug. 24, 1953; s. Henry and Joyce Freda (Marsden) C. BA with honors, Leeds U., 1975; MA, York (Eng.) U., 1977; cert. in edn., Cambridge (Eng.) U., 1978, postgrad., 1979-80; PhD, Oxford (Eng.) U., 1987. Lectr. art history Lancashire Poly., Preston, Eng., 1978-79; lectr. U. St. Andrews, Scotland, 1980-83, 1985—; researcher The Queen's Coll. Oxford U., 1983-85; lectr. philosophy, Balliol Coll. Oxford U., England, 1985; cons. Basil Blackwell Ltd., Oxford, 1987—. Book reviewer: Brit. Jour. Aesthetics, Brighton, Eng., 1982—, Radical Philosophy, London, 1984—, Am. Hist. Rev., Bloomington, Ind., 1985—, The Kantian Sublime: From Morality to Art; contbr. articles to profl. jours. visiting fellow Warwick U., 1988; Oxford U. Pirie-Read scholar, 1983. Mem. Brit. Soc. Aesthetics (mem. exec. com.), Scottish Phenomenology Soc. (mem. exec. com.), Brit. Soc. for Phenomenology, Assn. Art Historians. Office: U St Andrews Dept Art History, College Gate, Saint Andrews, Fife KY16 9AL, Scotland

CROZIER, RONALD DAVID, mineral processing and economics consultant; b. Antofagasta, Chile, Sept. 9, 1929; s. Hector McIvor and Marietta (Rendic) C.; m. Sabine L.M. Slotta, Feb. 2, 1951; children—Ralph Charles, Vanessa Louise, Susan Elaine, Janette Lynn. Student U. Glasgow, 1948-50; B.S.E. in Chem. and Metall. Engring., U. Mich., 1953, M.S.E., 1954, Ph.D., 1957. Chartered engr., U.K. Head process div. research dept. Dow Chem. Co., Williamsburg, Va., 1958-64; bus. devel. mgr. Dow Europe S.A., Zurich, Switzerland, 1965-68; v.p., chief operating officer Soquimich, Santiago, Chile, 1969-72; pres. Minerec Corp., N.Y.C., 1972-76; mng. dir. Tecnomin Ltda, Santiago, Chile, 1977-82; cons. Crozier Assocs., Santiago, 1982—. Patentee in field. Contbr. tech. articles to profl. publs. Fellow Inst. Mining and Metallurgy (council mem.); mem. Am. Chem. Soc., Am. Inst. Chem. Engrs. (co-chmn. research com. 1961-63), AIME. Clubs: Mining (N.Y.C.); Prince of Wales (Santiago); Royal Overseas League (London). Home: 4 Daisy Ln Ridgefield CT 06877 Office: Crozier Assocs, Casilla, 3284 Santiago 1 Chile

CROZIER, WILLIAM PATRICK, construction executive; b. Cambridge, Mass., Oct. 11, 1930; s. Patrick Joseph and Mary Veronica (Hallihan) C.; student, Boston Archtl. Center, 1955, univ. extension program Harvard U., M.I.T.; m. Gloria Ann Mancini, July 3, 1955; children—Judith Ann, Patrick William. With Hoyle, Doran & Berry, architects, Boston, 1958-69; assoc. Julian J. Borowko & Assocs., architects, Weymouth, Mass., 1969-73, Graham Gund & Assocs., architects, Cambridge, 1974-76; ind. cons., Boston, 1977; rep. Kennedy Library Corp. for constrn. of J.F.K. Presdl. Library, Boston, 1977-80; ind. cons. to Dr. Edwin H. Land/Rowland Found., Cambridge, 1980-81; chief site ops. for Copley Place, The Architects Collaborative, Boston, 1981-83; project mgr. hotel design Howard Johnson Co., North Quincy, Mass., 1984-86; dir. constrn. adminstrn. Graham Gund Architects, Inc., Cambridge, Mass., 1986—. Served with USMC, 1949-50, 50-52; Korea.

CRUICKSHANK, DON WILLIAM, Spanish literature educator; b. Kincardineshire, Scotland, Aug. 16, 1942; s. William and Mary Elizabeth (Duncan) C.; m. Margrit Rose Ritchie, Aug. 12, 1967; children: Catriona, Andrew, Kirsten. MA, U. Aberdeen, Scotland, 1965; PhD, U. Cambridge, Eng., 1969. Research fellow Emmanuel Coll., Cambridge, 1968-70; coll. lectr. Univ. Coll., Dublin, Ireland, 1970-79, statutory lectr., 1979-86, assoc. prof., 1986—. Author: Samuel Pepys' Spanish Plays, 1980; editor: The Comedias of Calderon, 1973; contbr. articles to profl. jours. Mem. Bibliog. Soc., Assn. Hispanists Great Britain and Ireland. Club: Delgany Golf. Office: Univ Coll, Belfield, Dublin 4 Ireland

CRUICKSHANK, STEVEN ALLAN, construction company executive; b. Winchester, Ont., Can., Nov. 11, 1960; s. Leslie Keith Cruickshank and Marlene Gladys Hanes. BSc in Civil Engring., Queen's U., Kingston, Ont., 1983; MBA, U. Western Ont., 1986. Cost engr. Peter Kiewit Sons Constrn. Co., Nipawin, Sask., Can., 1983-84; estimator Peter Kiewit Sons Constrn. Co., Nipawin, Sask., 1984; asst. to pres. Cruickshank Constrn. Ltd., Morrisburg, Ont., 1986, v.p., 1987. Mem. Morrisburg Tubie Orgn. (v.p. 1985-86). Mem. Progressive Conservative Party. Club: Flamingo's (Morrisburg) (pres. 1987—). Office: Cruickshank Constrn Ltd, PO Box 780, Morrisburg, ON Canada K0C 1X0

CRUIKSHANK, THOMAS HENRY, corporation executive; b. Lake Charles, La., Nov. 3, 1931; s. Louis James and Helene L. (Little) C.; m. Ann Coe, Nov. 17, 1955; children: Thomas Henry, Kate Martin, Stuart Coe. B.A., Rice U., 1952; postgrad., U. Tex. Law Sch., 1952-53, U. Houston Law Sch., 1953-55. Bar: Tex.; C.P.A., Tex. Accountant Arthur Andersen & Co., Houston, 1953-55, 58-60; mem. firm Vinson & Elkins, Houston, 1961-69; v.p. Halliburton Co., Dallas, 1969-72, sr. v.p., 1972-80, exec. v.p., 1980, pres., chief exec. officer subs. Otis Engring. Corp., 1980-81, pres., 1981-83, pres., chief exec. officer, 1983—, dir., 1977—; bd. dirs. Goodyear Tire & Rubber Co. Pres. Jr. Achievement, Dallas, 1974-76, chmn., 1976-78, mem. nat. bd., 1976—. Served to lt. (j.g.) USNR, 1955-58. Mem. Am., Tex. socs. C.P.A.s, Am., Tex. bar assns. Clubs: Dallas Petroleum, Dallas Country (gov. 1977-79, 86—); River Oaks Country (Houston); Pine Valley (N.J.) Golf. Home: 3508 Marquette Dallas TX 75205 Office: Halliburton Co 3600 Lincoln Plaza 500 N Akard St Dallas TX 75201-3391 *

CRUM, JAMES MERRILL, lawyer; b. Virginia, Ill., Oct. 14, 1912; s. Elton M. and Anna C. (Freitag) C.; m. Thelma Mae Williams, June 28, 1941; children—Suzanne, Deborah, James Frederick. A.B. with honors, Ind. U. (1937), J.D. with distinction, 1939. Bar: Ind. bar 1939, Fla. bar 1947. Practiced in Evansville, 1939-40, Indpls., 1941-47, Ft. Lauderdale, Fla., 1947—; assoc. firm Kahn & Dees, 1939-40; law clk. U.S. Dist. Ct., Indpls., 1941, 46; agt., acting agt. charge U.S. Secret Service, 1941-45; ptnr. firm McCune, Hiaasen, Crum, Ferris & Gardner, 1947—; city atty. Hallandale, Fla., 1949-53, 57-63, Plantation, Fla., 1953-59, Miramar, Fla., 1955-59; Supr. Old Plantation Water Control Dist., 1952-74; mem. Broward County Law Library Com., 1955-65. Mem. City Council, Miramar, 1955-59. Mem. Fedn. Ins. Counsel, Am., Fla., Broward County bar assns., Order of Coif. Clubs: The Drummers (Ft. Lauderdale), One Hundred of Broward County (Ft. Lauderdale). Home: 441 Holly Ln Plantation FL 33313 Office: PO Box 14636 Fort Lauderdale FL 33302

CRUMBAKER, MARY KATHRYN, business educator; b. Great Falls, Mont.; d. Calvin and Kathryn Elizabeth (Harbaugh) Crumbaker; student U. Mont., 1939, Southwestern U. at Memphis, 1942-43, Whitman Coll., 1939-41; B.S., U. Oreg., 1946; postgrad. Hochschule for Music, Vienna, Austria, 1947-48; M.Ed., Oreg. State U., 1966; Ph.D., Nat. Christian U. Dallas, 1974; m. William Goodman Williamson, Dec. 17, 1941 (dec. Oct. 1970); children—James Calvin, Albert Jerome, Kathryn Erilda. Sec., exec. sec. Granada (Miss.) Elem. Sch., also U.S. C.E., 1941-44; substitute sec. U. Oreg., 1944-46; head comml. studies Internat. Trade Coll., Chgo., 1948-51; tchr. Mich. Dept. Rehab., Am. Legion Tb Hosp., Battle Creek, 1952-53; tchr. U.S. Army, Kokura, Japan, 1954-56; tchr. Clark Bus. Coll., Topeka, 1956-58; charm sch. dir., dir. tng. Eugene (Oreg.) Bus. Coll. 1959-70, mgr., corp. sec.-treas., 1970-74, pres., 1974-85, pres. emerita, 1986—; prof. bus. Eugene Coll. Bus. and Tech., 1985-88; placement specialist with sr. profl. care, 1987—; curriculum cons. Eugene Ctr. Profl. Studies, 1988—; lectr., Am. econ. system and music Austro-Am. Soc., Vienna, 1946-48. Mem. exec. bd. S.W. Oreg. Mus. Sci. and Industry, 1972-75; den mother Oreg. Trail council Boy Scouts Am., 1959-69; chmn. West Univ. Neighborhood, 1981, 82; mem. Neighborhood Leaders Council, 1981; treas. Eugene WCTU, 1980-82, sec., 1987—; precinct committeeman Republican party, 1960—; pres. Central Lane Rep. Women, 1970; chmn. constn. and bylaws Lane County Council Orgns., 1985-86; pres. Lane County WCTU, 1985-88, named Sr. Woman of Yr. Lane County Council of Orgns., 1986, sr. v.p., 1987-88, pres. 1988—. Named Troop Mother of Yr. Boy Scouts Am., 1971. Mem. Nat. Fedn. Bus. and Profl. Women's Clubs, Oreg. Fedn. Bus. and Profl. Women (found. chmn. 1986-87), Am. Bus. Women, Am. Inst. Profl. Cons., Rubicon Soc., Eugene Bus. and Profl. Women's Club (pres. 1966, 79), DAR, Daus. of Nile, DAV Aux. #42, Am. Forestry Assn., Nat. Rifle Assn., PEO (treas. chpt. H, 1986-88, bd. dirs. 1987—), AAUW, Beta Gamma Sigma, Mu Phi Epsilon. Clubs: Eugene City, Zonta (pub. Newsletter 1984-88), Dial (pres. Eugene 1973-74, 86-87). Lodges: Order Eastern Star (musician, matron 1988—), White Shrine of Jerusalem (musician), Order of Amaranth (musician; condr. 1982-83, royal matron 1984-85). Kiwanis (hon.). Author: Typing with Less Than 2 Hands, 1962. Home: 760 Jefferson Eugene OR 97402-5204

CRUMLEY, LAURA LEE, literature educator; b. Pitts., Mar. 30, 1949; d. William Wolf and Laura Marie (Canning) C.; child from previous marriage, Stefan Gregory Perez-Crumley. BA, Indiana U. Pa., 1971; MA, U. Pitts., 1975, PhD, 1983. Tchr. Berlitz Sch. Langs., Pitts., 1971-73; educator U. San Buenaventura, Cali, Colombia, 1979-81; educator U. Valle, Cali, Colombia, 1980-82, asst. prof., chairperson dept. lit., 1982-85, assoc. prof. lit., 1985-87, prof., researcher, 1987—; free-lance translator, Pitts., 1971-77, Cali, 1977-81; speaker, lectr. ednl. instns., Cali, 1980—; participant poetry workshop with Leslie Ullman, Cali, 1984, Maya Hieroglyphic Seminars, U. Tex.-Austin, 1986, 87, 88. Contbr. articles to lit. jours.; co-editor lit. jour. Revista Poligramas, 1985. Grantee U. Valle, 1984-87, Colombian Inst. Higher Learning, 1987-88. Mem. Latin Am. Indian Lit. Assn., Inst. Internat. Lit. Iberoamericana, Am. Translators Assn., Latin Am. Studies Assn. Presbyterian. Home: Apartado Aereo 25493, Cra 79 6-57, Cali, Valle

Colombia Office: U del Valle Dept Letras, Apartado Aereo 25360, Cali, Valle Colombia

CRUMP, GERALD FRANKLIN, lawyer; b. Sacramento, Feb. 16, 1935; s. John Laurin and Ida May (Banta) C.; m. Glenda Roberts Glass, Nov. 21, 1959; children—Sara Elizabeth, Juliane Kathryn, Joseph Stephen. A.B., U. Calif.-Berkeley 1956, J.D., 1959; M.A., Baylor U., 1966. Bar: Calif. 1960. Dep. county counsel Los Angeles County, 1963—, legis. rep., 1970-73; chief pub. works div. Los Angeles County Counsel, 1973-84, sr. asst. county counsel, 1984-85, chief asst. county counsel, 1985—; lectr. Pepperdine U., 1978, U. Calif., 1982. Served to capt. USAF, 1960-63; to col. USAFR, 1963—, staff judge advocate USAFR Systems Command. Mem. ABA, State Bar of Calif. (del.), Los Angeles County Bar Assn. (chmn. govtl. law sect. 1983-84), Am. Judicature Soc., Am. Acad. Polit. and Social Sci., Res. Officers Assn., Air Force Assn., Phi Alpha Delta, Delta Sigma Phi. Home: 4020 Camino de la Cumbre Sherman Oaks CA 91423 Office: 648 Hall of Administration Los Angeles CA 90012

CRUMP, ROBERT JAMES, lawyer; b. Winnipeg, Man., Can., June 21, 1945; s. Robert Kipling and Helen Sinclair (Flett) C.; m. Lois Anne Cove, May 24, 1972 (div. 1985); children: Trafford, Kalynn; m. Dawn Marie Bisson, Jan. 12, 1986; children: Sean, Garrett. LLB, U. Manitoba, Winnipeg, 1970. Bar: Can. 1971. Article student Can. Dept. Justice, Winnipeg, 1970-71; solicitor Ottawa, 1971-73; tax counsel, mgr. ins. Mobil Oil Can., Ltd., Calgary, 1973-76; ptnr. Crump, Harasym, DuVal, Winnipeg, 1976-80; sr. assoc. Clark, Dymond, Crump, Calgary, 1980—; bd. dirs. Lift Air Internat. Leasing, Inc., Calgary; pres. R.J. Crump Profl. Corp., 1984-87. Chair 49th Scout Pack, Calgary, 1984-85; vestryman St. Peter's Ch., Calgary, 1985—; bd. dirs. Calgary Big Bros., 1984-86. Mem. Law Soc. Manitoba, Law Soc. Alta. Mem. Conservative Party. Anglican. Office: Clark Dymond Crump, 800 550-6th Ave SW, Calgary, AB Canada T2P 0S2

CRUMP, THOMAS RICHARD, lawyer; b. Seguin, Tex., Oct. 24, 1945; s. Tom and Helen Margaret (Smith) C.; m. Theresa Frazier, Dec. 24, 1979; children—Tony, Kim, Wade, Val, Jon. B.S. summa cum laude, St. Mary's U., 1969; J.D., 1971. Bar: Tex. 1972, U.S. Tax Ct. 1976. With Petty Geophys., San Antonio, 1966-73; instr. St. Mary's U., San Antonio, 1967-69; sole practice, Seguin, 1973—. Mem. State Bar Tex., San Antonio Bar Assn., Guadalupe County Bar Assn., South Central Tex. Bar Assn., ABA, Tex. Trial Lawyers Assn., Delta Theta Phi. Office: PO Box 1306 108 W Court St Seguin TX 78155

CRUSE, IRMA BELLE RUSSELL, writer; b. Hackneyville, Ala., May 3, 1911; d. Charles Henry and Nellie Dunn (Ledbetter) Russell; m. Jesse Clyde Cruse, Dec. 22, 1931; children: Allan Baird, Howard Russell. Student, Birmingham So. Coll., 1927-28; corr. student U. Chgo., U. Wis., U. Minn., intermittently 1958-68; AB, U. Ala., 1976; MA in English, Samford U., MA in History, 1984. With So. Bell and successor South Cen. Bell, Birmingham, Ala., 1928-44, 54-76, pub. relations supr., 1965-68, rate supr., 1968-76; free lance writer, 1956—. Bd. dirs. Festival of Arts, Birmingham, 1970-73, Birmingham Council Christian Edn.; v.p. Birmingham Council Clubs, 1973-74; pres. Jefferson County Radio and TV Council, 1971-72; mem. Gov.'s Commn. Employment of Handicapped; chmn. oral history program Ala. Bapt. Hist. Commn., 1985—; clk. Mt. Brook Bapt. Ch., 1986-87; chmn. Women's Work/Women's Worth for Birmingham br. AAUW, 1977-78. Editor: The Ala. Bapt. Historian, 1986—; contbr. articles to various publs. Recipient numerous awards including Freedoms Found., 1967-69, Reed Silver Bowl for Literature award Birmingham Festival of Arts, 1987; named Beautiful Activist, 1972, Woman of Achievement, Met. Bus. and Profl. Women's Club, 1970-71. Mem. Birmingham Bus. Communicators, Ala. Writers' Conclave (pres. 1973-74), Birmingham Bus. and Profl. Women (pres. 1970-71), Women in Communications (pres. 1970-71), Birmingham Bus. Communicators (pres. 1968-69), Telephone Pioneers Am. (editor newsletter 1970-74, pres. Birmingham South Life Mem. Club 1986-87, historian Ala. chpt. 1987-88), Ala. State Poetry Soc. (program chmn. 1972-74, editor newsletter 1976-78), Women's C. of C. (2d v.p. 1978—), Ala. Bapt. Hist. Commn., Freedoms Found. of Valley Forge, Birmingham Geneal. Soc., Salvation Army Women's Aux., Women's C. of C., Nat. Soc. Am. Pen Women, Sigma Tau Delta, Phi Kappa Phi, Phi Alpha Theta. Club: Quota of Birmingham (pres. 1976-77). Home: 136 Memory Ct Birmingham AL 35213

CRUSE, JULIUS MAJOR, JR., pathologist; b. New Albany, Miss., Feb. 15, 1937; s. Julius Major and Effie (Davis) C. B.A., B.S. with honors, U. Miss., 1958; D.Microbiology with honors (Fulbright fellow), U. Graz, Austria, 1960; M.D., U. Tenn., 1964, Ph.D. in Pathology (USPHS fellow), 1966, USPHS postdoctoral fellow, 1964-67. Mem. faculty U. Miss. Med. Sch., 1967—; prof. immunology Grad. Sch., 1967-74, prof. pathology, 1974—, asso. prof. microbiology, 1974—, dir. grad. studies program in pathology, 1974—, dir. clin. immunopathology, 1978—, dir. immunopathology sect., 1978—, dir. tissue typing lab., 1980—; lectr. pathology U. Tenn. Coll. Medicine, 1967-74; adj. prof. immunology Miss. Coll., 1977—. Author: Immunology Examination Review Book, rev. edit, 1975, Introduction to Immunology, 1977, Principles of Immuno-pathology, 1979; editor-in-chief-:Immunologic Research, Pathology and Immunopathology Research, Concepts in Immunopathology, The Year in Immunology, contbns. to Microbiology and Immunology; editor Immunomodulation of Neoplasia, Antigenic Variation: Molecular and Genetic Mechanisms of Relapsing Disease, Autoimmunoregulation and Autoimmune Disease: The Year in Immunology, vol.2, 1985-86, The Year in Immunology, vol. 3, 1987, The Year in Immunology, vols. 4,5, 1988, Genetic Basis of Autoimmune Disease, Cellular Aspects of Autoimmunity; also articles. Recipient Pathologists award in continuing edn. Coll. Am. Pathologists-Am. Soc. Clin. Pathologists, 1976; Julius M. Cruse collection in immunology established in his honor Middleton Med. Library U. Wis., Madison, 1979. Fellow AAAS, Royal Soc. Promotion Health, Am. Acad. Microbiology, Am. Soc. for Histocompatibility and Immunogenetics (chmn. pub. com.), Intercontinental Biog. Assn.; mem. Am. Assn. Pathologists, Am. Chem. Soc., Brit. Soc. Immunology, Canadian Soc. Immunology, Am. Soc. Microbiology, Internat. Acad. Pathology, Am. Assn. Immunologists, AMA (Physicians Recognition award 1969-75), Am. Inst. Biol. Scis., Am. Soc. Clin. Pathologists, Canadian Soc. Microbiologists, N.Y. Acad. Scis., Soc. Exptl. Biology and Medicine, Soc. Francaise d'Immunologie, Reticuloendothelial Soc., Transplantation Soc., Electron Microscopy Soc. Am., Am. Assn. History Medicine, Sigma Xi, Phi Kappa Phi, Phi Eta Sigma, Alpha Epsilon Delta, Gamma Sigma Epsilon, Beta Beta Beta. Episcopalian. Office: U Miss Med Ctr Dept Pathology 2500 N State St Jackson MS 39216

CRUTCHFIELD, WILLIAM GAYLE, JR., retailing executive; b. Charlottesville, Va., Oct. 14, 1942; s. William Gayle and Theresa F. (Saltzsieder) C.; B.S. in Commerce, U. Va., 1965; m. Jana Kay Heischman, Dec. 5, 1981; 1 dau., Jennifer Anne. Asst. to pres. Ridge Electronics Corp., Charlottesville, 1971-72; sec.-treas. Haight Engring. Co., Inc., Charlottesville, 1972-75; pres. Crutchfield Corp., Charlottesville, 1974—, Crutchfield Electronics, Inc., Jacksonville, Fla., 1980—; vis. lectr. Darden Grad. Bus. Sch., U. Va. Chmn. adv. bd. McIntire Sch. of Commerce, U. Va., 1981-85. Served to capt. USAF, 1966-70. Decorated Air Force Commendation medal; recipient award SBA, 1980; named Central Va. Marketer of Yr., Am. Mktg. Assn., 1983. Mem. Young Pres. Orgn., Charlottesville-Albemarle C. of C. (bd. dirs. 1984), Beta Gamma Sigma. Republican. Home: 448 Ednam Dr Charlottesville VA 22901 Office: 1 Crutchfield Park Charlottesville VA 22906

CRUTHIRD, ROBERT LEE, sociology educator; b. LeFlore County, Miss., Dec. 10, 1944; s. Harvie and Mary Florence (Black) C.; m. Julie Mae Boyd, Dec. 17, 1965; 1 son, Robert Lee. M.A., U. Ill.-Chgo., 1976. Correctional counselor Ill. Dept. Corrections, Joliet, 1977-78; instr. in sociology Kennedy-King Coll., Chgo., 1978-80, 81-84, asst. prof., 1984-87, assoc. prof., 1987—, dir. instl. research, 1980-81; cons. Ednl. Mgmt. Assocs., 1981-82; site coordinator MSYEP CCC, 1984-86; KKC Title III basic skills devel., 1985-86; coordinator acad. support services, 1986-87; CCC coordinator CCC Coll. Advisement Project, 1987, asst. dir. CCC MSYEP, 1987-88. Author: Black Rural-Urban Migration 1915-50, 1984, Remedial/Developmental Instructions in Classroom, 1987; with Chgo. State U., 1982, U. Chgo., 1986. Served with U.S. Army, 1965-67. Crime and delinquency research tng. fellow U. Ill.-Chgo., 1976-77; NEH fellow, summer 1983. Mem. Am. Sociol. Assn., Assn. Instl. Research, Nat. Assn. Devel. Edn., Assn. Study of Afro-Am. Life and History, U. Ill. Chgo. Alumni Assn. (life), Alpha Phi Alpha (life), Phi Theta Kappa (named to Ill. Hall of Honor 1984, 86, 88). Democrat. Baptist. Home: 5050 S Lake Shore Dr #3203S Chicago IL 60615 Office: 6800 S Wentworth Suite 326E Chicago IL 60621

CRÜWELL, BERNDT WILHELM, bank executive; b. Münster, Westfalia, Fed. Republic of Germany, Apr. 1, 1935; s. Ludwig and Hella (von Frankenberg) C.; m. Amélie von Klitzing, Oct. 18, 1986; children: Ludwig, Christoph, Ulrich. JD, U. Bonn. Exec. sec. Millupa Ac, Friedrichsdorf, Fed. Republic of Germany; dir. Industriekreditbank AG, Deutsche Industriebank, Frankfurt, Main, Fed. Republic of Germany; examiner for CPA's, Mainz, Fed. Republic of Germany. Mem. Wirtschaftsrat der CDU, Bonn, Fed. Republic of Germany. Lodge: Rotary. Office: Industriekreditbank AG, Zeppelinallee 38, D 6000 Frankfurt M 90 Federal Republic of Germany

CRUYPENYNCK, JEAN, match manufacturing company executive; b. Melun, France, June 8, 1939; came to Ghana, 1972; s. Maurice-Jules and Suzanne-Louise (Barbier) C.; m. Annette-Suzanne Dossi, Sept. 23, 1968; children—Francois, Julien, Henri. Engr. 1st class, Ecole Nationale de la Marine Marchande, Nantes, France, 1966; certificate d'aptitude a la profession de transporteur routier Assocation pour la Formation des Cadres dans Les Transports, Paris, 1968; Laureat Zellidja, Fondation Nationale des Bourses Zellidja, Paris, 1958. Marine engr. Compagnie Generale Transatlantique, Paris, 1959-67; mgr. road bldg. co., Melun, France, 1967-71; factory mgr. New Match Factory Ghana, Ltd., Accra., Ghana, 1971—; resident dir. Compagnie Internationale de Services, Accra, 1984—. Counsellor Comite Conseillers du Commerce Exterieur, Paris, 1980. Decorated chevalier du merite agricole French Ministry of Agr., 1982. Mem. Assn. Ghana Industries. Mem. Front National Party. Roman Catholic. Lodge: Rotary. Avocations: beach and water sports; reading. Home: Plot 39 Dadeban Rd, NIA, Accra Ghana Office: New Match Factory Ghana Ltd, PO Box 4332, Accra Ghana

CRUZ, CONRADO PATRICIO, accountant; b. Mandaluyong, Rizal, Philippines, Nov. 26, 1946; s. Antonio Domingo and Lourdes (Patricio) C.; m. Praxedes Guieb Antolin, July 28, 1974; children—Ruby Anthea, Rose Anne, Rey Alexander, Rex Anthony. A.Comml. Sci., Philippine Coll. Commerce, 1964, B.S. in Commerce, 1966. C.P.A., Philippines, N.Y. Sr. acct. Wolf & Co., N.Y.C., 1971-72; supr. Martin L. Buchbinder, N.Y.C., 1972-80; prin. Bennie L. Hadnott, N.Y.C., 1980-82; ptnr. Watson Rice & Co., N.Y.C., 1982—. Mem. Am. Inst. C.P.A.s, N.Y. Soc. C.P.A.s., Assn. of Filipino-Am. Accts. (exec. v.p.). Home: 560 Mabie St New Milford NJ 07646 Office: Watson Rice & Co 928 Broadway New York NY 10010

CRUZ, LUIS ECHEVARRÍA, public relations and marketing educator, consultant; b. Santurce, P.R., Sept. 11, 1952; s. Fernando Luis Cruz and Lydia Echevarria (Rodriguez) E. B.S., Cath. U., Ponce, P.R., 1973; M.A., Ball State U., 1976, M.B.A., 1977. Accredited pub. relations and mktg. educator. slaes mgr. CVC Prodn./Advt. Agency, Rio Piedras, P.R., 1973-75; asst. sales/mktg. mgr. U.S. div. Tourism Co., N.Y.C., 1977-79; exec. v.p. Communications Cons., Inc., Pueblo Viejo, P.R., 1979-86; v.p. Consultories Publicitarius, Puerto Nuevo, P.R., 1987—; dir. dept. communications Univ. Sacred Heart, Santurce, P.R., 1979-81; asst. prof. pub. relations U. Sacred Heart, Santurce, P.R., 1981—; cons. various cos. and hosps.; prof. mktg. Interamerican U., Rio Pierras, P.R., 1983—. Named Pub. Relations Educator of Yr., San Juan Civic Club, 1982. Mem. Pub. Relations Soc. Am. (accredited), Am. Mgmt. Assn., Internat. Assn. Bus. Communicators, Internat. Mktg. Assn., Assn. Relacionistas Profesionales, Kappa Tau Alpha. Clubs: Pan-American Gun (Bayamon, P.R.); Exchange (Hato Rey, P.R.). Home and Office: Cond Villa Caparra Exec Apt 10-F Guaynabo PR 00657

CRUZ, MARCELLANO SANTOS, dermatologist, consultant; b. Manila, Apr. 6, 1947; s. Pacifico Legaspi and Contancia (Santos) C.; m. Jocelyn Muhi Garcia, July 5, 1980; children: Mark Jay, Marc Jeremy, Mark Joseph. BS in Pre-Medicine, U. of East, 1967; BS in Medicine, Cebu Inst. of Medicine, 1973. Intern Rizal Provincial Hosp., Pasig, Philippines, 1973-74; resident in dermatology Ministry of Health, Manila, 1977-79; med. dir., adminstrv. cons., dermatologist Santo Nino Med. and Indsl. Clinic, Manila, 1980—; practice medicine specializing in dermatology Quezon City, Philippines, 1981—; cons. dermatologist San Pablo Doctors Hosp., San Pablo City, Philippines, 1983—, Quezon City Med. Ctr., 1987—. Named Most Outstanding Dermatologist Far East Social and Civic Orgn., 1983; recipient Bronze medal of Merit Boy Scouts Philippines, 1986. Mem. Philippine Med. Assn., Philippine Soc. Aesthetic Medicine, Philippine Leprosy Soc., Philippine Venereal Disease Assn., Am. Venereal Disease Assn., Internat. Soc. Tropical Dermatology, Res. Officers Legion Philippines (treas. Marikina chpt. 1981—). Lodges: Rotary (bd. dirs. Quezon City 1983-84); KC. Home: 16 MH del Pilar St, Calumpang Marikina, Manila Philippines Office: Marikina Santo Nino Med, and Indsl Clinic, 442 JP Rizal St Santo Nino, Manila Philippines

CRUZ-DIEZ, CARLOS, painter; b. Aug. 17, 1923; Student Sch. of Plastic and Applied Arts, Caracas. Dir. art Venezuelan subs. of McCann-Erickson Advt. Agy., 1946-51; tchr. history of applied arts Sch. of Arts, Caracas, 1953-55; worked on phys. qualities of colour now named Physichromies, 1955-56; owner, mgr. studio vis. arts and indsl. design, Caracas, 1957; prof., asst. dir. Sch. of Arts, Caracas, 1959-60; painter, Paris, 1960—. One-man shows: Caracas, 1947; Madrid, Genoa, Turin, London, Paris, Cologne, Oslo, Brussels, Ostwald Mus., Dortmund, N.Y.C., Bogota, Rome, Venice Essen, Munich, Mus. Quadrat, Albers Mus., Bottrop, Fed. Republic Germany. Represented in numerous group shows; represented in permanent collections at Mus. de Bellas Artes, Caracas, Victoria and Albert Mus., Tate Gallery, London, Casa de las Americas, Havana, Stadtisches Mus., Leverkusen, Germany, Mus. Modern Art, N.Y.C., Mus. Contemporary Art, Montreal, Mus. des 20, Jahrhunderts, Vienna, U. Dublin, Mus. Contemporary Art, Chgo., others. Recipient Grand Prix 3d Biennale, Cordoba, Argentina; Prix Internat. de Peinture a la IX Biennale de Sao Paulo. Address: 23 rue Pierre Semard, Paris 75009 France

CRYSTAL, JAMES WILLIAM, insurance company executive; b. N.Y.C., Oct. 9, 1937; s. I. Frank and Evelyn G. Crystal; B.S., Trinity Coll., 1958; m. Jean Crystal; children—James F., Sanford F., Jonathan F. With Royal Globe Ins. Group, N.Y.C., 1956; underwriter Home Ins. Co., N.Y.C., 1957, spl. agt., San Francisco, 1958-59; pres., chief exec. officer Frank Crystal & Co. Inc., N.Y.C., 1960—; dir. Gt. Am. Industries, Inc., F.F.H. Ins. Co., Northeast Ins. Co. Bd. dirs. Gar Reichman Found.; trustee Mt. Sinai Hosp., N.Y.C. Mem. Nat. Assn. Casualty and Surety Agts. Republican. Clubs: Harmonie, Century Country. Home: 33 E 70th St New York NY 10021 Office: 40 Broad St New York NY 10004

CSAPÓ, BENÖ, education educator; b. Szentgál, Hungary, Mar. 5, 1953; s. Benö Csapó and Jolán Csefkó; m. Vilma Tóth, Oct. 27, 1979; children: Gergely, Andräs. MS in Chemistry, Attila Jozsef U., Szeged, Hungary, 1977, PhD in Edn., 1979. Research asst. Attila József U., Szeged, Hungary, 1976-77, research fellow, 1977-79, asst. lectr., 1979-82, asst. prof., 1982-87, assoc. prof., 1987—, vice chair dept. edn., 1987—; chmn. Council for research funds of Ministry Edn., Budapest, Hungary, 1986—. Mem. Internat. Soc. Study of Behavioral Devel., World Assn. Ednl. Research, European Assn. Research on Learning and Instruction (nat. correspondent), Hungarian Psychol. Assn., Hungarian (chmn. research methodological working group ednl. com. 1986—). Home: Tapei U 41, H-6723 Szeged Hungary Office: Attila József Univ, Petöfi sgt 30-34, H-6722 Szeged Hungary

CSEHAK, JUDIT, minister of social welfare; b. Szekszard, Hungary, Jan. 16, 1940; d. Ferenc Csehak and Maria Kucsera; divorced; 2 children. MD, Budapest Semmelweis Med. U., Hungary, 1964. Gen. practice medicine Fadd, Hungary, 1964-72; chief med. officer Szekszard, 1972-75; sec. Trade Union for Med. Health Workers, Budapest, 1975-78, Nat. Council Hungarian Trade Unions, Budapest, 1978-84; mem. Hungarian Socialist Workers' Party, Budapest, 1967—, dep. prime minister, 1984-88, mem. cen. com., 1985, minister of social affairs and health, 1988—; mem. Politburo, 1987—. Mem. Hungarian Workers' Movement, 1954. Office: Ministry of Social Affairs, and Health, Budapest Hungary

CSENDES, ERNEST, chemist, corporate and financial executive; b. Satu-Mare, Romania, Mar. 2, 1926; s. Edward O. and Sidonia (Littman) C.; came to U.S., 1951, naturalized, 1955; m. Catharine Vera Tolnai, Feb. 7, 1953; children: Audrey Carol, Robert Alexander Edward. BA, Protestant Coll., Hungary, 1944; BS, U. Heidelberg (Ger.), 1948, MS, PhD, 1951. Research assoc. biochemistry Tulane U., New Orleans, 1952; fellow Harvard U., 1953; research chemist organic chems. dept. E. I. Du Pont de Nemours and Co., Wilmington, Del., 1953-56, elastomer chems. dept., 1956-61; dir. research and devel. agrl. chems. div. Armour & Co., Atlanta, 1961-63; v.p. corp. devel. Occidental Petroleum Corp., 1963-64, exec. v.p. research, engring. and devel., 1964-68, also mem. exec. com.; exec. v.p. Occidental Research and Engring. Corp., 1963-68; pres., chief exec. officer TRI Group, Bermuda and Amsterdam, 1968-84; chmn. TRI Internat., Ltd., Bermuda, 1971-84; mng. dir. TRI Capital N.V. (Netherlands), 1971—; chmn., chief exec. officer Micronic Techs., Inc., 1981-85; mng. ptnr. Inter-Consult Ltd., Pacific Palisades, Calif., 1984—. Contbr. articles to profl. jours.; patentee in field. Recipient Pro Mundi Beneficio medal Brazilian Acad. Humanities. Fellow AAAS, Am. Inst. Chemists, Royal Soc. Chemistry (London); mem. Am. Chem. Soc., German Chem. Soc., N.Y. Acad. Sci., Am. Inst. Chem. Engrs., Acad. Polit. Sci., Global Action Econ. Inst., Am. Mgmt. Assn., AIAA, Am. Def. Preparedness Assn., Sigma Xi. Research in area of elastomers, rubber chemicals, dyes and intermediates, organometallics, organic and biochemistry, high polymers, phosphates, plant nutrients, pesticides, process engring. and design of fertilizer plants, ammonia, urea, sulfur, iron, potash and phosphate ore mining and metallurgy, coal burning and acid rain, grinding processes for solids; also acquisitions, mergers, internat. fin. related to leasing, banking, trusts and ins.; regional devel. related to agr. and energy resources. Home: 514 Marquette St Pacific Palisades CA 90272

CSERMELY, THOMAS JOHN, computer engineer, physicist; b. Szombathely, Hungary, June 25, 1931; s. Janos and Maria (Szarvas) C.; diploma in engring. Poly. U. Budapest, 1953; Ph.D., Syracuse U., 1968; m. Tiiu Vaharu, June 17, 1962; 1 son, Erik Thomas. Instr., Inst. Theoretical Physics, Poly. U. Budapest (Hungary), 1953-56; nuclear engring. cons. Design Bur. Power Stas., Budapest, 1956; research engr. Carrier Corp., Syracuse, N.Y., 1957-67; research asso. physics Syracuse U., 1967-68, asso. prof. elec. and computer engring., 1976—; asst. prof. physiology SUNY Upstate Med. Center, Syracuse, 1968-76; asst. prof. physics LeMoyne Coll., Syracuse, 1976-77. Recipient Wolverine Diamond Key award ASHRAE, 1965. Mem. Am. Phys. Soc., IEEE, Biophys. Soc., N.Y. Acad. Scis., Am. Assn. Physics Tchrs., Am. Nuclear Soc., Soc. Computer Simulation, Am. Soc. Engring. Edn., AAAS, Sigma Xi. Club: Tech. Syracuse. Contbr. articles to profl. publs. and orgns. on control, heat exchange dynamics, quantum biochemistry, brain functions and computer simulation neuronal network dynamics, computer applications in medicine. Home: 149 Humbert Ave Syracuse NY 13224

CSIKÓS, REZSÖ, chemical engineer; b. Udvard, Hungary, Feb. 5, 1930; s. Ferenc and Mária (Németh) C.; Chem. Engr., Veszprém U., 1954; Engr.-Economist, Karl Marx U., Budapest, 1962, Ph.D., 1963, C.Sci., 1978; m. Alice Zentai, June 8, 1957; children—Alice, Dóra. Dept. head Kőolajipari Vállalat, oil refinery, Szöny, 1954-62; asst. mng. dir. Hungarian Oil and Gas Research Inst., Veszprém, 1962-70, mng. dir., 1970—; mng. dir. R & D Assn., 1980—; mem. com. tech. chemistry Hungarian Acad. Scis., 1972—; titular asst. prof. Veszprém U. Chem. Engring., 1984; lectr. in field. Councillor, Town of Veszprém, 1962—, mem. exec. com., 1962-73; councillor Veszprém County, 1973—. Recipient Gold medal Veszprém County, 1970; Gold medal for service to country, 1971; Silver degree Order Labour, 1972, Gold degree, 1980; Eötvös Lorá nd medal, 1975; Gold degree of excellent inventor, 1978; 4th of April medal, 1986; named Eminent Worker of Heavy Industry, 1960, 62, 73. Mem. Hungarian Chem. Soc. (mem. presidium petroleum div. 1965—, councillor), Am. Chem. Soc. Mem. Hungarian Socialist Workers Party. Club: Veszprém Acad. Club. Author: A fuvatott bitumen, 1965; Kőolajparaffinok, 1972; Paraffin Products, 1982; also articles. Office: 34 József Attila, H-8200 Veszprém Hungary

CUATREACASAS, JOSE, botanist; b. Camprodon, Catalonia, Spain, Mar. 19, 1903; came to U.S., 1947:; s. Jose and Carmen (Arumi) C.; m. Martha Nowack, July 27, 1933; children: Teresa, Gil, Pedro. Lic. Ph., U. Barcelona, 1923; PhD, U. Madrid, 1928. Asst. prof. botany U. Barcelona, Spain, 1924-31; full prof. U. Madrid, 1932-39; curator Bot. Garden, Madrid, 1933-39, dir., 1937-39; prof. Inst. Bot., Nat. U., Colombia, 1939-42; dir. bot. mission Valle Cauca Agrl. Sch., Calif., 1942-47; curator NSF Field Mus., Chgo., 1947-50; Guggenheim fellow 1950-52; prin. investigator Smithsonian, Washington, 1952-57, research assoc. botany, 1957—. Mem. Am. Soc. Plant Taxonomists, Ecol. Soc. Am., Internat. Assn. Plant Taxonomists, Soc. Study Evolution, Internat. Soc. Tropical Ecology, NSF. Home: 3707 34th St NW Washington DC 20008 Office: Smithsonian Inst Botany NHB 166 Washington DC 20008

CUATRECASAS, PEDRO MARTIN, research pharmacologist; b. Madrid, Sept. 27, 1936; came to U.S., 1947; s. Jose and Martha C.; m. Carol Zies, Aug. 15, 1959; children: Paul, Lisa, Diane, Julia. AB, Washington U., St. Louis, 1958, MD, 1962; DSc honoris causa, U. Barcelona, 1984, Mt. Sinai Sch. Medicine, 1985. Intern, then resident in internal medicine Osler Service, Johns Hopkins Hosp., 1962-64, asst. physician, 1972-75; clin. asso., clin. endocrinology br. Nat. Inst. Arthritis and Metabolic Diseases, NIH, 1964-66; spl. USPHS postdoctoral fellow Lab. Chem. Biology, 1966-67, med. officer, 1967-70; professorial lectr. biochemistry George Washington U. Med. Sch., 1967-70; assoc. prof. pharmacology and exptl. therapeutics, assoc. prof. medicine, dir. div. clin. pharmacology, Burroughs Wellcome prof. clin. pharmacology Johns Hopkins U. Med. Sch., 1970-72, prof. pharmacology and exptl. therapeutics, assoc. prof. medicine, 1972-75; v.p. research, devel. and med. Wellcome Research Labs.; dir. Burroughs Wellcome Co., Research Triangle Park, N.C., 1975-86; sr. v.p. research and devel. Glaxo Research Labs., Glaxo Inc., 1986—, also bd. dirs.; adj. prof. Duke U. Med. Sch., 1975—; adj. prof., mem. adv. com. cancer research program U. N.C. Med. Sch., 1975—; bd. dirs. Burroughs Wellcome Fund, 1975-86, Glaxo Internat. Research. Ltd., London. Editor: Receptors and Recognition Series, 1975, Jour. Solid-Phase Biochemistry, 1975-80; editorial bd.: Jour. Membrane Biology, 1973, Internat. Jour. Biochemistry, 1973, Molecular and Cellular Endocrinology, 1973-77, Biochimica Biophysica Acta, 1973-79, Life Scis., 1978—, Neuropeptides, 1979—, Jour. Applied Biochemistry, 1978—, Cancer Research, 1980-81, Jour. Applied Biochemistry and Biotech., 1980—, Toxin Revs., 1981—, Biochem. Biophys. Research Communications, 1981—; contbr. articles to profl. jours. Active Am. Diabetes Assn., PMA Commn. Drugs and Rare Diseases, N.C. Supercomputer Task Force. Recipient John Jacob Abel prize in pharmacology, 1972, Laude prize Pharm. World, 1975, Beerman award Soc. Investigative Dermatology, 1981, Isco award U. Nebr., 1985, Dupont Splty. Diagnostics award Clin. Ligand Assay Soc. 1986, Alumni Achievement award Washington U. Sch. Med., 1987. Mem. Am. Soc. Biol. Chemists, Nat. Acad. Scis., Inst. Medicine of Nat. Acad. Scis., Am. Soc. Pharmacology and Exptl. Therapeutics (Goodman and Gilman award 1982), Am. Soc. Clin. Investigation, Am. Soc. Clin. Research, Spanish Biochem. Soc., Md. Acad. Scis. (Outstanding Young Scientist of Year 1970), Am. Cancer Soc., Endocrine Soc., Am. Chem. Soc., Am. Diabetes Assn. (Eli Lilly award 1975), Am. Diabetes Assn., Sigma Xi. Home: 3803 Bluestone Ct Chapel Hill NC 27514-9648 Office: Glaxo Inc 5 Moore Dr Research Triangle Park NC 27709

CUBILLOS, HERNAN SALLATO, business executive; b. Viña del Mar, Chile, Feb. 25, 1936; s. Hernan and Maria Graciela (Sallato) C.; m. Marcela Sigall, Mar. 20, 1960; children: Luis Hernán, Felipe, Nicolas, Marcela. Cmmd. ensign Chilean Navy, 1953, advanced through grades to lt., ret., 1961; gen. sec. Empresas Industriales el Melon S.A., Santiago, Chile, 1961-62; exec. asst. to pres. Empresa el Mercurio S.A.P., Santiago, Chile, 1963-70, v.p., 1972-73, pres., 1973-74; pres. Compañia de Inversiones la Transandina S.A., Santiago, Chile, 1974—; minister fgn. affairs Chilean Govt., Santiago, Chile, 1978-80; v.p. Compañia Cervecerias Unidas S.A.; pres. Santillana del Pacifico S.A. de Ediciones, Editorial Portada Ltd.; chmn. Empresas CCT S.A.; chmn. bd. dirs. Ecom S.A.; vice chmn. Banco de Credito Inversiones. Decorated Presidente de la Republica de Chile, La Ilustre Municipalidad de Santiago of Chile, Abdon Calderon Republic of Equador, Antonio Nariño Republic of Colombia, Orden del Sol del Peru Republic of Peru, Servicios Meritorios a la Republica Govt. of Chile, Bicentenario del Libertador Bernardo O'Higgins Chile. Clubs: Los Leones Golf (Santiago), Yachting Marina de Algarrobo, Naval. Home: Candelaria Goyenechea 4241, PO Box 830, Santiago Chile Office: Compania de Inversiones la Transandina, Merced 22, 7th Floor, PO Box 830, Santiago Chile

CUCCINELLI, KENNETH THOMAS, utilities executive; b. Jersey City, Aug. 12, 1945; s. Dominick and Josephine (Policastro) C.; BSChemE, Cath. U. Am., 1967; MBA, Marymount Coll. of Va., 1981; m. Maribeth Reilly, Sept. 16, 1967; children: Kenneth Thomas, Kevin James, Kristopher Devin. Sales engr. Trane Co., La Crosse, Wis. and East Orange, N.J., 1967-70; project engr. Shefferman & Bigelson Cons. Engrs., Silver Spring, Md., 1970-71; mgr. energy systems research and devel. Am. Gas Assn., Arlington, Va., 1971-73, mgr. energy systems, mktg. services, 1973-79, dir. mktg. services, 1979-80, staff v.p. mktg. services, 1980-83, v.p. mktg., 1983-87; v.p. mktg. and tech. Consol. Natural Gas Service Co., Pitts., 1987—; guest lectr. Cath. U. Am., Washington, 1974-76, Duke U., Durham, N.C., 1978. Program chmn. McLean Youth, Inc., 1973-75, coach, 1973, mgr. football, basketball, soccer, 1974-80; bd. dirs. Nat. Energy Found.; team mgr. McLean Little League, 1976—. Recipient Leadership award Dartmouth Coll., 1965; NSF grantee, 1965. Mem. ASHRAE (chpt. pres. 1980-81; award of merit 1975), Sales and Mktg. Execs., Am. Mktg. Assn., Natural Gas Industry Soc. (named to Hall of Flame and Residential Hall of Honor), Delta Epsilon Sigma. Roman Catholic. Club: Chesterbrook Swim and Tennis (pres. 1984-86). Lodge: Rotary. Contbr. articles to profl. jours. Home: 1801 S Villa Dr Gibsonia PA 15044-0001 Office: Consol Natural Gas Service CNG Tower Pittsburgh PA 15222

CUCIN, ROBERT LOUIS, plastic surgeon, medical researcher; b. N.Y.C., Apr. 17, 1946; s.Robert and Julia C.; B.A. magna cum laude, Cornell U., 1967, M.D., 1971; J.D., Fordham U., 1985. Bar: N.J. State Supreme Ct., Washington Ct. of Appeals; bd. cert. legal medicine. Intern, Cornell-N.Y. Hosp., N.Y.C., 1971-72, resident in gen. surgery, 1972-76, resident in plastic surgery, 1977-79; fellow in surgery Meml.-Sloan Kettering Found., 1972-76, 77-79, J.D. Fordham Law Sch., 1985; practice medicine specializing in plastic surgery, N.Y.C., 1979—; instr. surgery Cornell U. Med. Coll., 1980—; asst. attending surgeon (plastic) Doctor's Hsop., N.Y. Infirmary-Beekman Downtown Hosp., 1979—, N.Y. Hosp., 1980—, Drs. Hosp., 1987—; pres. Esquire Cadillac Limousine Service Inc., 1977—, Beaux Arts Holdings, 1979—, Rocin Labs., Inc., 1981—. Mem. N.Y. County Health Service Rev. Orgn., 1976—; founder, dir. Rocin Found. for Plastic Surg. Research, 1979—; Served to maj. M.C., USAF, 1976-77; Japan. Diplomate Am. Bd. Surgery; Am. Bd. Plastic Surgery; licensed physician, N.J., N.Y. State, Calif., Va. Fellow Internat. Coll. Surgeons, Am. Soc. Abdominal Surgeons, Am. Coll. Legal Medicine; mem. Am. Soc. Plastic and Reconstructive Surgery, Royal Soc. Medicine, AMA (physicians recognition award 1978, 81), N.Y. State Med. Soc., N.Y. County Med. Soc. (health systems, public relations, peer rev. coms.), N.Y. Acad. Scis., Phi Beta Kappa. Republican. Clubs: Atrium, Platform, Vertical, N.Y. Athletic, Cornell. Author: The Kindest Cut; Keeping Face; contbr. articles to profl. publs. Home and Office: 8 E 62d St New York NY 10021

CUCKNEY, SIR JOHN GRAHAM, banker; b. India, July 12, 1925; s. E. J. Cuckney; m. 2d, Muriel Boyd, 1960. M.A., U. St. Andrews. Civil asst., gen. staff War Office, 1949-57; dir. various indsl. and fin. cos., 1957-72, including Lazard Bros. & Co., 1964-70, J. Bibby & Sons, 1970-72; chmn. Standard Indsl. Trust, 1966-70, Mersey Docks and Harbour Bd., 1970-72, Bldg. Econ. Devel. Com., 1976-79; ind. mem. Ry. Policy Rev. Com., 1966-67; spl. mem. Hops Mktg. Bd., 1971-72; chief exec., 2d permanent sec. Property Services Agy., 1972-74; sr. crown agt., chmn. Crown Agts. for Oversea Govts. and Adminstrns., 1974-78, chmn. Port of London Authority, 1977-79; chmn. Thomas Cook Group Ltd., 1978-87; chmn. Internat. Mil Services Ltd., 1974-85; dir. Midland Bank Ltd., Royal Ins. PLC, 1979—, dep. chmn. 1982-85, chmn., 1985—; dir. Brooke Bond Liebig Ltd., 1978-84; dir. John Brown PLC, 1981-86, chmn. 1983-86; Brixton Estate, PLC, Touche Remnant Holdings Ltd., chmn. Internat. Maritime Bur., 1981-85, Westland PLC, 1985—, Investors in Industry Group, PLC, 1987—. Elder brother Trinity House, 1980—. Office: care The Thomas Cook Group Ltd, 45 Berkeley St, London W1A 1EB England also: Brooke Bond Group PLC, Thames House, Queen Street Pl, London EC4R 1DH England

CUELLAR, DANN RAY, television journalist; b. Beeville, Tex., Apr. 12, 1954; s. Daniel Ray and Olga (Naranjo) C.; m. Marilyn Neal Blanton; children: Trinna Lee, Daniel Benjamin, Carley Marissa. Student, U. Houston, 1975, Victoria Coll., 1973. Radio personality Stas. KVIC and KTXN, Victoria, Tex., 1973-75; photographer, editor Sta. KXIX-TV, Victoria, 1975-78, anchorman, reporter, 1975-78; reporter, producer Sta. KHOU-TV, Houston, 1978-83, weekend anchor, 1980-83; news anchorman Sta. KMOL-TV, San Antonio, 1983-88; journalist Sta. WPVI-TV, Phila., 1988—. Producer: (documentary) Houston Warfare, 1980, (documentary) Lost Generation, 1984, (T.V. series) Hispanics: Dawn at New Hope, 1978. Bd. dirs. Greater San Antonio Credit Counseling, 1984-85; vol. Literacy Council, 1983-85; hon. chmn. Toys for Tots, 1984. Recipient Hispanic of Yr. award Lulac, 1979, Best News Story award Anti Defamation League, 1980, TV Reporting award Houston Firefighters Assn., 1981, Best Creative Work award Sigma Delta Chi, 1982, Merit award Bexar County Hist. Soc. Fellow Ctr. Latin Am. Studies; mem. Am. Film Inst., Smithsonian Instn. (assoc.), Nat. Trust Historic Preservation, Sigma Delta Chi. Roman Catholic. Avocations: film making, racquetball, photography. Home: 7 Fairhill Rd Morton PA 19070 Office: Sta WPVI-TV Channel 6 4100 City Line Ave Philadelphia PA 19131

CUELLO, AUGUSTO CLAUDIO GUILLERMO, medical research scientist, author; b. Buenos Aires, Argentina, Apr. 7, 1939; came to Can., 1985; s. Juan Andres and Rita Maria (Sagarra) Cuello-Freyre; m. Martha Maria J. Kaes, Mar. 10, 1967; children: Paula Marcela, Karina Rosa. MD, U. Buenos Aires, 1965; MA (hon.), Oxford (Eng.) U., 1978, DSc, 1986. Asst. prof. Sch. Biochemistry, U. Buenos Aires, 1974-75; scientist MRC Neurochem. Pharmacology, Cambridge, Eng., 1975-78; lectr. depts. pharmacology and human anatomy U. Oxford, 1978-85; med. tutor, E.P. Abraham sr. research fellow Lincoln Coll., Oxford, 1978-85; chmn., prof. pharmacology and therapeutics McGill Univ., Montreal, Que., Can., 1985—; cons. Seralab Ltd., Sussex, Eng., 1981-85, Sandoz Ltd., Basel, Switzerland, 1982-84, Medicorp, Montreal, 1985—, Synthelabo, Paris, 1977-78; internat. advisor Cajal Inst., Madrid, 1983—. Editor: Co-Transmission 1, 1982, Immunohistochemistry, 1983, Brain Microdissection Techniques, 1983, Jour. of Chem. Neuroanatomy; mem. editorial bd. profl. jours. Recipient Estela A. de Goytia prize Argentinian Assn. Advancement Sci., 1968, Prof. A. Rosenblueth award Grass Found., 1979, Robert Feulgen prize Gesselschaft für Histochemie, 1981; NIH Postdoctoral fellow, 1970-72. Mem. Brit. Pharm. Soc., Brain Research Assn., European Neurosci. Assn., Internat. Soc. Neuroendocrinology, Physiol. Soc., Soc. for Neurosci., Basal Ganglia Internat. Soc., Oxford Soc., Physiol. Soc. Gt. Britian, Pharm. Soc. of Can., Corr. Pharma. Soc. of Argentina. Avocations: tennis, reading, theatre, history, Spanish and Latin American literature. Office: McGill Univ, Dept Pharmacology & Therapeutics, 3655 Drummond St, Montreal, PQ Canada H3G 1Y6

CUETO, ARMANDO GERONIMO, pediatrician; b. Manila, Philippines, Nov. 27, 1931; s. Nemesio C. and Modesta (Geronimo) C. AA, U. Santo Tomas, Manila, 1951, MD, 1957. Observer, extern J. Fabella Meml. Govt. Hosp., Manila, 1958, adj. resident, 1958-59, clinic physician, 1960, jr. resident physician, 1960-63; pediatrician Sacred Heart Med. and Surgical Clinic, Manila, 1963-64, Dr. Jose Alvarez Barias Clinic, Manila, 1964-66, Family Medicine and Pediatric Clinic, Quezon City, Philippines, 1966-68; pediatrician, clinic physician L. Vazquez & Assocs., Manila, Makati, 1968-71; pediatrician, asst. med. dir. IBMS Clinic, Makati, Philippines, 1971-77; registrar pediatrics Ondo Gen. Hosp., Nigeria, 1977-80; prin. med. officer II Gongola Health Bd., Nigeria, 1980-84; pediatrician, med. officer IBMS Clinic, Manila, 1984—. Fellow Philippine Pediatric Soc., Inc. (assoc. 1961—, specialist 1964—). Roman Catholic. Home: 1368 Geliños, Santa Cruz, Manila 1003, Philippines

CUEVAS, JOSE LUIS, painter, illustrator; b. Mexico City, Feb. 26, 1934; s. Alberto and Maria Regia (Novelo) Cuevas Gomez; m. Bertha Riestra, Feb. 17, 1961; children: Mariana, Zimena, Maria-Jose. Student, Sch. Painting & Sculpture La Esmerelda Inst. Nat. Bellas Artes, Mexico City. Resident artist Phila. Mus. Sch. Art, 1957; lectr. artist San Jose State Coll., 1970, Fullerton Coll., 1975, Washington State U., 1975. Exhibited one-man shows, Prisse Gallery, Mexico City, 1953, Pam-Am. Union, Washington, 1954, N.Y.C., Paris, Rome, Los Angeles, Buenos Aires, numerous other cities; exhibited group exhbns. throughout N.Am., S.Am., Europe, India, Japan; represented in permanent collections Mus. Modern Art, N.Y.C., Solomon R. Guggenheim Mus., N.Y.C., Bklyn. Mus., Art Inst. Chgo., Phillips Collection, Washington; represented in other leading collections.; illustrator: The Worlds of Kafka and Cuevas, 1959, Recollections of Childhood, 1962, Cuevas-Charenton, 1965, Crime by Cuevas, 1968, Homage to Quevedo, 1969, Cuevas Comedies, 1971, Cuaderno de Paris, 1977; Author: Cuevas by Cuevas, 1964, Cuevario, 1973, Confesiones de Jose Luis Cuevas, 1975. Recipient 1st Internat. Drawing award Sao Paulo (Brazil) Bienal, 1959; 1st Internat. award Mostra Internazionale di Bianco e Nero de Lugano, Zurich, Switzerland, 1962; 1st prize Bienal de Grabado, Santiago, Chile, 1964; 1st Internat. award 1st Triennale New Delhi, India, 1968; 1st prize Bienal de Grabado, San Juan, P.R., 1974. Office: care Tasende Gallery 820 Prospect St La Jolla CA 92037 *

CUIL DE STRATCLUT, ALECSANDR (ALASTAIR KYLE), merchant banking consultant; b. London, Mar. 12, 1931; came to U.S., 1940, naturalized, 1951; s. Allan Granger and Dora Jessie Ellen (Taylor) Kyle; student St. John's Coll., Annapolis, Md., 1947-49; A.B., U. Michoacán (Mex.), 1951; postgrad. U. Havana (Cuba), 1951-52, U. Chgo., 1959; m. Corinne Lois Silverman, Aug. 28, 1959; children—Joshua Reis, Peredur Thomas, Julia Dora; m. 2d, Mary Carmela Giarrizzo, Mar. 3, 1969; children—Allan Salvatore, Kentigern Sigvard. Child actor, radio, stage, and TV, 1940-44; radio dir. Clyde de Mex., S.A., Acapulco, 1950; salesman Radiovision Internacional, S.A., Mexico City, 1951; mem. staff Atlantic Union Com., N.Y.C., 1953-54; with investment dept. Grace Internat. Devel. Co., N.Y.C., 1955-56; v.p., dir. Index & Retrieval Systems, Inc., N.Y.C. and Woodstock, Vt., 1957-62; prin. Alec Kyle & Co., N.Y.C., 1962-66; pres. Inst. Computer Assisted Instrn., Inc., Doylestown, Pa., 1967-70; mng. partner Corp. Fin. Cons., Phila. and Princeton, N.J., 1971-82; prin. Cromwell & Kyle, Fountainville, Pa. and Fairfield, Conn., 1982-85; prin. Kyle & Hayes-Morrison, Frazer, Pa., 1986—; chmn. Strathclyde Corp., Phila.; dir. Cia Minera Santa Domingo, S.A. de C.V., Chihuahua, Mex.; condr. seminars, lectr. in field. Co-founder, bd. dirs. Am. Council on NATO, 1954-57; sec., dir. No. New Eng. Passenger R.R. Conf., 1960-62; co-founder, sec. Fountainville Hist. Farm Assn. Bucks County (Pa.), 1972—; cons. preservation agrl. land Buckingham (Pa.) Twp., 1977-78; pres. New Britain (Pa.) Twp. Democratic Orgn., 1974-78; mem. exec. bd. Bucks County Dem. Com., 1974-78; chmn. Nat. Task Force on Religion and Animal Rights, 1981—; chmn. Internat. Network for Religion and Animals, 1985—; bd. dirs. Pa. Soc. Prevention of Cruelty to Animals, 1987—; lay reader, dep. convs., mem. coms. Episcopal Diocese Pa.; vestryman St. Paul's Ch., Doylestown, Pa., Anglican Ch. of Incarnation, Telford, Pa. Recipient Supervisors commendation Buckingham Twp., 1979. Mem. Newcomen Soc., Inst. Effective Mgmt. (v.p. 1978—), Assn. Corp. Growth, Am. Mgmt. Assn. (cons.), Family Assn. Cumbrian Dynasty (convenor), Welsh Soc. Phila. (steward 1982-84, 2d v.p. 1984-86, v.p. 1986—), Royal Stuart Soc., Cymdeithas Madog, Celtic League, Internat. Com. for the Def. of the Breton Lang., (dir. Am. br. 1984—), Phila. Vegetarian Soc., Mensa. Clubs: St. Andrew's, Athenaeum (Phila.); St. Andrew's (Mexico City); Cercle des Princes (Paris), Sloane (London). Office: 7 Frame Ave PO Box 925 Frazer PA 19355

CUILLIERE, MICHEL FRANCOIS, cardiologist; b. Pont-a-Mousson, Meurthe-et-Moselle, France, May 28, 1935; s. Lucien and Marguerite (Chardin) C.; m. Marie-Louise Chollot; children: Jean-Christophe, Benoît, Beatrice. Docteur en Medecine, Faculté de Medecine, Nancy, France, 1961, D.E.S. de Cardiologie, 1962. Practice medicine specializing in cardiology Nancy, 1964—; cons. C.H.U. de Nancy, 1964—. Contbr. articles to profl. jours. Mem. Soc. Française de Cardiologie. Roman Catholic. Home and Office: 15 Bis Rue de Saint-Lambert, 54000 Nancy France

CUISENIER, JEAN HENRI EUGENE, sociologist, educator; b. Paris, France, Feb. 9, 1927; s. André Lucien and Therese (Tostain) C.; Agregate in Phil., Sorbonne, U. Paris, 1954, D.Litt. and Human Scis., 1971; m. Solange, July 20, 1950; children—François, Isabelle, Laurent, Emmanuelle. Prof. philosophy Lycee de Caen (France), 1950-54, Lycee de Carthage (Tunisia), 1954-55; prof. sociology and ethnology Inst. des Hautes Etudes de Tunis, 1956-59; mem. staff Centre National de Recherche Scientifique, 1959—, research dir., 1971—; head Musée National des Arts et Traditions Populaires, Paris, 1968—; dir. Centre d'Ethnologie Française; prof. Ecole des Hautes Etudes en Sciences Sociales de Paris. Served with French Air Force, 1951-52. Mem. Société d'Ethnologie Française, Société Internationale d'Ethnologie Europé enne et de Folklore. Author: Economie et Parente, 1975; L'Art populaire en France, 1975, German transl., 1976, English transl., 1977; editor: Europe as a Cultural Area, 1978; The Family Life Cycle in European Society, 1977; Ethnologie de la France, 1986; dir. series: L'architecture rurale française, Le mobilier regional français, Recits et contes populaires; dir. jour.: Ethnologie franç aise. Office: Musee Nat des Arts et Traditions, 6 avenue du Mahatma Gandhi, 75116 Paris France

CUKOR, PETER, chemist; b. Szolnok, Hungary, Aug. 29, 1936; s. Andor and Lili C.; B.Chem. Engring., CCNY, 1961; M.S., St. Johns U., N.Y.C., 1963, Ph.D. in Chem., 1963, Ph.D., 1966; m. Adele Bieler, June 6, 1964; children—David, Jeffrey, Barry. Sr. technologist Mobil Oil Co., Bklyn., 1964-67; tech. staff Gen. Telephone and Electronics Inc. labs., Bayside, N.Y., 1967-72, sect. head organic analysis and organic materials, 1972-78, prin. investigator advance tech. lab., 1978-80, research mgr., Waltham, Mass., 1980-82, sr. tech. analyst specializing in materials Sci., chemistry and biology GTE Labs. Strategic Tech. Office, 1982-86; dir. research adminstrn., support, in charge of univ. interactions, materials analysis, library, engring. services and formulation of research related policies and procedures, 1986; vis. prof. chemistry Queens Coll. CUNY, 1967-72; adj. prof. chemistry Worcester Poly. Inst. (Mass.), 1982—. NIH grad. fellow, 1961-64. Mem. Am. Chem. Soc., AAAS, N.Y. Acad. Scis., Sigma Xi. Jewish. Contbr. chpt. to book, articles to profl. publs. on analytical chemistry, medicinal chemistry, material sci., particularly polymers. Patentee in field. Home: 39 Foxhill Dr Natick MA 01760 Office: 40 Sylvan Rd Waltham MA 02154

CULBERTSON, CHARLES RICHARD, electrical engineer; b. Marysville, Kans., Aug. 30, 1946; s. Charles Hubert and Phyllis Evelyn (Swan) C.; m. Vicki Lynn Goodson, July 9, 1970 (div. June 1979); children—Steven Richard; m. Carol Ann Furr, Mar. 20, 1986. B.S., Okla. State U., 1970. Registered profl. engr., Okla. Tex., Field engr., apprentice lineman Indian Electric Coop., Cleveland, Okla., 1965-70; elec. engr. Okla. Gas & Electric Co., Western div., Oklahoma City, 1970-73; field engr. REA, U.S. Dept. Agr., Crescent, Okla., 1973-80; system engr., dept. head Central Rural Electric Coop., Stillwater, 1980-83; div. distbn. engr. S.E. div., Tex.-N.Mex. Power Co., Texas City, 1983—; mem. Texas City Elec. Bd., 1984-87. Dep. comdr. cadets CAP, Stillwater, 1980-83; bd. dirs. Texas City Rebels Youth-Football, 1983-86; youth coach football, baseball, Stillwater, 1981-82, Texas City, 1984-86, wrestling and baseball, Crescent, 1977-80. Served to capt. USAR, 1970-80. Eugene Tuttle scholar C.H. Guernsey & Co., 1967. Mem. Okla. Assn. Elec. Coop. Engrs. (co-founder; pres. 1979-80, parliamentarian 1981-83), NSPE, IEEE, Profl. Photographers Okla., Profl. Photographers Guild Houston, Tex. Profl. Photographers Assn., Gulf Coast Baseball Umpires Assn. (sec./treas. 1988—), S.W. Baseball Umpires Assn. Republican. Lodge: Kiwanis (pres. 1979-80). Clubs: Crescent Takedown, Rebel Booster. Home: 2205 28th St N Texas City TX 77590 Office: 702 36th St N PO Box 2190 Texas City TX 77590

CULLEN, ANNE-MARIE, marketing professional; b. Hamilton, New Zealand, Nov. 21, 1953; d. Liston William and Betty Stella (Blake) Jones. Student, Sacred Heart Girls Coll., Hamilton. Sales sec. Radio Waikato, Hamilton, 1969-71; producer radio and TV Dormer Beck Advt., Auckland, New Zealand, 1971-74; stewardess Air New Zealand, Auckland, 1975-85, coordinator mktg. service standards, 1985—. Mem. Nat. Party. Roman Catholic. Office: Air New Zealand, 1 Queen St, Auckland New Zealand

CULLEN, BERNARD ANTHONY, philosopher, educator; b. Belfast, Northern Ireland, Jan. 11, 1950; s. Matthew and Mary (Darcy) C.; m. Jean Murray, June 22, 1970; children: Martin, Eleanor. BA first class, The Queen's U., Belfast, 1971; MA, U. Mich., 1972, PhD, 1975; BSc in Econs., The Queen's U., 1980. Lectr. Queen's U., Belfast, 1974-87, sr. lectr. philosophy, 1987—; guest lectr. U. Mich., U. S.C., Bochum U., Vanderbilt U., Boston Coll., U. Manchester and others. Author: Hegel's Social and Political Thought, 1979; editor: Hegel Today, 1987, Irish Philosophy Jour., 1984—; assoc. editor: Jour. British Soc. Phenomenology, 1985—; contbr. articles on med. philosophy, social and polit. philosophy to profl. books, jours. and dictionaries. Exec. mem. Belfast and Dist. Trades Union Council, 1977—, v.p. 1981. Alexander von Humboldt-Stiftung research fellow Hegel-Archives, Bochum, 1987-88. Mem. Hegel Soc. Great Britain (mem. council 1984—), Soc. Internat. l'Étude Philosophie Médiévale, Nat. Com. for Philosophy Royal Irish Acad. (sec. 1985—), Irish Philosophy Soc. (sec. 1983-86). Office: Queen's U Belfast, Belfast BT7 1NN, Northern Ireland

CULLIGAN, JOHN WILLIAM, corporate executive; b. Newark, Nov. 22, 1916; s. John J. and Elizabeth (Kearns) C.; m. Rita McBride, Feb. 19, 1944; children: Nancy, Mary Carol, Elizabeth, Sheila, Jack, Neil. Student, U. Utah, U. Chi, Philippine U. With Am. Home Products Corp., N.Y.C., 1937—, chmn. bd. dirs., 1981-86, chmn. exec. com., 1986—. Bd. dirs., v.p. Council on Family Health; bd. dirs. Am. Found. for Pharm. Edn., Valley Hosp. Found., Ridgewood, N.J.; adv. bd. St. Benedict's Prep. Sch., Newark; co-chmn. Archbishop's Com. of Laity, Newark. Served with AUS, 1943-46. Mem. Proprietary Assn. (v.p., bd. dirs.). Clubs: N.Y. Athletic, Sky, Union League (N.Y.C.), Hackensack Golf. Lodges: Knights of Malta, Knights of St. Gregory, Friendly Sons of St. Patrick. Office: Am Home Products Corp 685 3d Ave New York NY 10017

CULLINGFORD, HATICE S., chemical engineer; b. Konya, Turkey, June 10, 1945; came to U.S., 1966; d. Ahmet and Emine (Kadayifcioglu) Harmanci. Student, Mid. East Tech. U., 1962-66; BS in Engring. with high honors, N.C. State U., 1969, PhD, 1974. Registered profl. engr., Tex.; cert. mgr. Statis. clk. Research Triangle Park Inst., 1966; reactor engr. AEC, Washington, 1973-75; spl. asst. ERDA, Washington, 1975; mech. engr. Dept. Energy, Washington, 1975-78; staff mem. Los Alamos Nat. Lab., 1978-82; sci. cons., Houston, 1982-84; ECLSS test bed mgr. Johnson Space Ctr., NASA, Houston, 1984-85, sr. project engr. advanced tech. dept., 1985-86, sr. staff engr. div. solar system exploration, 1986-88, asst. div. advanced devel., 1988—; mem. internal adv. com. Ctr. for Nonlinear Studies Los Alamos Nat. Lab., 1981; organizer tech. workshops, sessions at soc. meetings; lectr. in field. Editor, author tech. reports; contbr. articles to profl. jours.; patentee in field. Mem. curriculum rev. com. U. N.Mex., Los Alamos, 1980. Recipient Woman's badge Tau Beta Pi, 1968, ERDA Spl. Achievement award, 1976, Inventor award Los Alamos Nat. Lab., 1982; Cities Service fellow, 1969-72. Mem. Am. Nuclear Soc. (sec.-treas. fusion energy div. 1982-84, vice chmn. South Tex. sect. 1984-86, mem. local sects. com. 1986—), Am. Inst. Chem. Engrs. (organizer, 1st chmn. No. N.Mex. club 1980-81, chmn. low-pressure processes and tech. 1981—), Am. Chem. Soc., Fusion Power Assocs., Internat. Assn. Hydrogen Energy, AIAA, NSPE, Soc. for Risk Analysis (organizer, sec. Lone Star chpt. 1986—), No. N.Mex. Chem. Engrs. Club, Engrs. Council Houston (councilor, sec. energy com.), Sierra Club, Phi Kappa Phi, Pi Mu Epsilon. Club: Houston Orienteering.

CULLISON, WILLIAM LESTER, association executive; b. Balt., Aug. 26, 1931; s. William Lester and Margaret Elizabeth (Quick) C.; m. Lorraine Stella Wirtz, Dec. 24, 1953; 1 child, Beth Lynn. BS, U.S. Merchant Marine Acad., 1953; LLB, LaSalle Extension U., Chgo., 1968; MBA, Fla. Atlantic U., 1975. 3d asst. engr. Am. Trading and Production Co., N.Y.C., 1953, 54-55; asst. dir. sci. and tech. Am. Petroleum Inst., N.Y.C., 1957-68; exec. dir. Tech. Assn. Pulp and Paper Ind., Atlanta, 1968—. Served as lt. USN, 1954-56. Mem. Am. Soc. Mechanical Engrs., Soc. Research Adminstrs. (charter), Ga. Soc. Assn. Execs. (pres. 1975-76, Cliff Clark award 1977), Am. Soc. Assn. Execs. (sec. treas. 1986-87, vice chmn. 1987-88, Key award 1985). Republican. Episcopal. Club: Peachtree Tennis (Norcross, Ga.). Lodge: Masons. Office: TAPPI 15 Technology Pkwy Norcross GA 30092

CULLOM, WILLIAM OTIS, organization executive; b. Huntsville, Ala., Mar. 20, 1932; s. Otis McKinley and Elna (Reese) C.; m. Caryl James, May 26, 1956; children—Cheryl Ann, Jennifer James. B.S., Fla. State U., 1958. Finger-print expert FBI, 1950-52; asst. bus. mgr. Fla. State U., 1954-64; with Ryder Truck Rental Inc., Miami, Fla., 1964-79; exec. v.p. mktg., to Ryder Truck Rental Inc., 1979; pres., chief operating officer Jartran, Inc., Coral Gables, Fla., 1979-85; pres. Greater Miami C. of C., 1985—. Mem. cabinet United Way, Miami, 1974-80; trustee Bethune-Cookman Coll., Daytona Beach, Fla.; past chmn. bd. trustees Fla. State U.; trustee Barry U.; mem. pres.'s adv. com. Fla. Meml. Coll., Miami; bd. dirs. Coconut Grove Playhouse, Goodwill Industries, Salvation Army; mem. Orange Bowl Com. Served with airborne inf. U.S. Army, 1952-54. Mem. Am. Trucking Assn., Truck Leasing and Renting Assn. (pres. Fla. chpt. 1972-73), Fla. State U. Nat. Alumni Assn. (pres.), Miami Hist. Assn. Democrat. Methodist. Clubs: University, Riviera Country, City, Bankers (Miami); Ocean Reef Yacht, Governor's (Tallahassee). Lodge: Rotary. Home: 8445 SW 151st St Miami FL 33158 Office: Greater Miami C of C 1601 Biscayne Blvd Omni Complex Miami FL 33132

CULP, FREDERICK L(YNN), physics educator; b. Duquesne, Pa., May 12, 1927; s. Elmer E. and Elizabeth M. (Rawlings) C.; m. Louise Zundell Overly, June 7, 1953; children—David Frederick, Diane Lynn. B.S., Carnegie-Mellon U., 1949, M.S., 1960; Ph.D., Vanderbilt U., 1966. Indsl. research U.S. Steel and Westinghouse Electric Corp., 1949-51, 53-55; research staff Carnegie-Mellon U., Pitts., 1956-59; mem. faculty Tenn. Tech. U., Cookeville, 1959—, prof. physics, 1965—, chmn. dept., 1965—, prof. emeritus, 1987—. Served to lt. (j.g.) USN, 1945-46, 51-53. Recipient Outstanding Faculty award Tenn. Tech. U., 1983. Fellow Tenn. Acad. Sci.; mem. Am. Phys. Soc., Am. Assn. Physics Tchrs., Sigma Xi, Sigma Pi Sigma, Kappa Mu Epsilon, Phi Kappa Phi, Omicron Delta Kappa. Democrat. Presbyterian. Lodge: Rotary. Contbr. numerous articles to profl. publs. Home: 516 E 4th St Cookeville TN 38501 Office: Tenn Tech Univ Physics Dept Cookeville TN 38505

CULP, GERARD HUBBARD, assets protection executive; b. Reno, Nev., Jan. 16, 1930; s. W. Ray and Ruth Lee (Hubbard) C.; m. Audrey Elizabeth Crompton, May 26, 1955 (div. Sept. 1977); children—Stephen Gerard, Heather Janeane; m. Sandra Lee Jaksina, Dec. 23, 1977. B.A., U. Redlands, 1958; postgrad. U. Maine, 1966. Cert. protection profl. Enlisted U.S. Air Force, 1951, advanced through grades to col., 1973; served in U.S., Can., Eng., Pakistan; dir. personnel investigations ctr. Dept. Def., Balt., 1975-76, ret., 1976; dir. corp. security Pa. Power & Light Co., Allentown, 1977-80; mgr. nuclear security Portland Gen. Electric Co., Oreg., 1980—. Contbr. articles to profl. jours. Decorated Air Force Commendation medal with one oak leaf cluster, Meritorious Service medal, Joint Service Commendation medal, Legion of Merit. Mem. Am. Soc. Indsl. Security (chpt. chmn.), Inst. Nuclear Materials Mgmt., Edison Electric Inst. Security Com., Geneal. Forum Oreg., Am. Assn. Individual Investors, Am. Mgmt. Assn., Phi Kappa Phi.

CULP, JAMES DAVID, lawyer; b. Montgomery, Ala., June 12, 1951; s. Delos Poe and Martha Edwardine (Street) C.; m. Gretchen Ina Greene, Aug. 4, 1974; children: James Delos, Sarah Diana. B.S., East Tenn. State U., 1973, M.A., 1978; J.D., U. Tenn., 1977. Bar: Tenn. 1978, U.S. Dist. Ct. (ea. dist.) Tenn. 1978. Sole practice, Johnson City, Tenn., 1978-79; ptnr. Culp and Fleming, Johnson City, 1979-81, Thornton, Culp and Fleming, Johnson City, 1981-83; sole practice, Jonesborough, Tenn., 1983-86; part-time instr. polit. sci. East Tenn. State U., 1980; part-time instr. bus. law Draughons Jr. Coll., 1983-85; city staff atty., Johnson City, 1987—. Active Johnson City Symphony Orch., 1969-74, Jr. Achievement, 1978-79; pres. Alcohol and Drug Counseling and Prevention Ctr., 1981-82; mem. East Tenn. State U. Wesley Found., 1979—, treas., 1981-82; mem. Upper East Tenn. Council on Alcoholism and Drug Dependence, 1981—; mem. East Tenn. State U. Friends of Music, 1981-82, pres., 1982; mem. Johnson City Bd. Dwelling Standards and Rev., 1983-87, Washington County Election Commn., 1986-87. Served with USNR, 1971-73. Mem. Washington County Bar Assn., Tenn. Trial Lawyers Assn., Mensa, Internat. Soc. for Philos. Enquiry, Am. Legion (judge adv. 1981-82), Johnson City Jaycees (state dir. 1979, named Spoke of Yr. 1978-79). Democrat. Methodist. Home: 913 Beech Dr Johnson City TN 37601 Office: 601 E Main St Municipal & Safety Bldg Johnson City TN 37601

CULP, MICHAEL, research director; b. N.Y.C., June 17, 1952; s. Robert Walter and Anna Lee (Filtzer) C.; B.A. in Econs. magna cum laude, City U. N.Y., 1973. Security analyst Standard & Poor's, N.Y.C., 1974-79; v.p., security analyst E. F. Hutton & Co., Inc., N.Y.C., 1979-82; v.p., sr. security analyst Prudential-Bache Securities, N.Y.C., 1982-86, sr. v.p., mng. dir.

research, 1986—, also bd. dirs. Chartered fin. analyst U. Va. Mem. N.Y. Soc. Security Analysts, Fin. Analysts Fedn., Inst. Chartered Fin. Analysts, Phi Beta Kappa. Home: 251 Central Park W New York NY 10024 also: Passing Rd East Hampton NY 11937 Office: 1 Seaport Plaza New York NY 10292

CULVER, DAVID M., aluminum company executive; b. Winnipeg, Man., Can., Dec. 5, 1924; s. Albert Ferguson and Fern Elizabeth (Smith) C.; m. Mary Cecile Powell, Sept. 20, 1949; children: Michael, Andrew, Mark, Diane. B.Sc., McGill U., 1947; M.B.A., Harvard U., 1949. With Alcan Internat. Ltd., 1949—; mem. staff Centre d'Études Industrielles Alcan Internat. Ltd., Geneva, 1950; mgr. sales office Alcan Internat. Ltd., N.Y.C.; v.p. internat. sales Alcan Internat. Ltd., Montreal, pres., 1962-68, also bd. dirs.; exec. v.p. fabricating and world-wide sales Alcan Aluminium Ltd., 1968-75, regional exec. v.p. Can., U.S. and Caribbean, 1975-77, pres., 1977-87, chief exec. officer, 1979—, chmn., 1987—, also bd. dirs.; pres., chief exec. officer Aluminum Co. Can. Ltd., 1975-87, chmn., 1978-79, 83-87; chmn. Alcan Pacific Ltd., 1984; bd. dirs. Am. Express Co., Shearson Lehman Hutton Holdings Inc., Am. Cyanamid Co., Seagram Co. Ltd. ; chmn. Internat. Primary Aluminium Inst., Can. Japan Businessmen's Cooperation Com., Bus. Council on Nat. Issues; mem. Morgan Guaranty Trust Internat. Council, N.Y. Bd. govs. Joseph H. Lauder Inst. Mgmt. and Internat. Studies, Phila.; bd. dirs. C.D. Howe Inst.; mem. adv. council Centre Can. Studies Johns Hopkins U. Sch. Advanced Internat. Studies, Washington. Served with Can. Inf. Corps, World War II. Mem. Order of Can. (officer), Alpha Delta Phi. Office: Alcan Aluminium Ltd, 1188 Sherbrooke St W, Montreal, PQ Canada H3A 3G2 *

CULVER, ROBERT ELROY, osteopathic physician; b. Toledo, Oct. 1, 1926; s. Elroy and Helen Mary C.; m. Sallie Jane Corder, June 10, 1972; children: Diana L., Galen R., Ronald A., Richard A., Patricia A., Robert B. B.S., U. Toledo, 1951; D.O., Chgo. Osteo. Medicine, 1959. Intern Sandusky Meml. Hosp., Ohio, 1960; practice medicine specializing in family practice and sports medicine Oregon, Ohio, 1960—; mem. City of Oregon Bd. of Health; mem. staff Parkview Hosp., Riverside Hosp., Toledo Hosp.; physician Oreg. Sch. System; Oregon police surgeon; chief dep. coroner, 1978-80; chmn. wrestling div. physicians Nat. AAU; U.S. med. rep. Federation Internationale Lute Amateur; physician U.S. World Wrestling Team; med. dir. World Cup of Wrestling; pres. Northwestern Ohio AAU; 3d v.p. Ohio AAU. Mem. Air Force Mus., Toledo Mus. Art; dir. Toledo Zoo; mem. Smithsonian Instn. Served with C.E., U.S. Army, 1944-46; col. Ohio Def. Service. Recipient commendation Ohio Ho. of Reps., 1983, honor award Oregon Sch. System, 1983; named Outstanding Team Physician, State of Ohio, 1984. Mem. Am. Osteo. Assn., Ohio Osteo. Assn., 1st Dist. Acad. Osteo. Medicine (state trustee, past pres.), Am. Coll. Gen. Practitioners in Osteo. Medicine and Surgery, Ohio Osteo. Assn. Physicians and Surgeons, Chgo. Coll. Osteo. Med. Alumni Assn., Nat. Rifle Assn. (life), U. Toledo Alumni Assn. (life), Air Force Assn., Aircraft Owners and Pilots Assn., Nat. Hist. Soc., Ohio Hist. Soc., Am. Legion. Methodist. Club: Atlas. Lodges: Masons, Elks, Shriners. Office: 5517 Corduroy Rd Oregon OH 43616

CULVER, ROBERT LONZO, JR., real estate executive, insurance broker; b. Hartselle, Ala., July 13, 1922; s. Robert Lonzo and Lelma Lee (Alford) C.; grad. Anderson Airplane Sch., 1942, Alverson Bus. Coll., 1948; student U. Ala., Birmingham, 1955-58; m. Imogene Webb, Apr. 11, 1959; 1 dau., Jeri Dawn. Assemblyman Glenn L. Martin Aircraft Corp., Middleriver, Md., 1942-44; sec. U.S. Steel Corp., Fairfield, Ala., 1948-71, with plant security, 1971-86; owner, propr. Westside Realty & Ins. Co., Birmingham, 1956-76; pres. Bob Culver Realty, Inc., Birmingham, 1976—. Served with U.S. Army, 1944-46, with USAF, 1951-52. Recipient award Ins. Women of Birmingham, 1960; named hon. lt. col. Ala. State Militia, 1965. Mem. Nat. Assn. Real Estate Appraisers, Nat. Assn. Realtors, Ala. Assn. Realtors, Birmingham Area Bd. Realtors, Forestdale C. of C. (charter), Internat. Platform Assn., VFW. Democrat. Baptist. Club: Masons (worshipful master Adamsville lodge, 1953-54). Developer, property owner Hardee's of Forestdale, Inc. and Quincy's Family Steak House of Forestdale, Inc. Home: 644 Forestwood Rd Birmingham AL 35214 Office: 2061 Forestdale Blvd Birmingham AL 35214

CUMMIN, ALFRED S(AMUEL), chemist; b. London, Sept. 5, 1924; came to U.S., 1940, naturalized, 1948; s. Jack and Lottie (Hainesdorff) C.; m. Sylvia E. Smolok, Mar. 24, 1945; 1 dau., Cynthia Katherine. B.S., Poly. Inst. Bklyn., 1943, Ph.D. in Chemistry, 1946; M.B.A., U. Buffalo, 1959. Research chemist S.A.M. labs, Manhattan Project, Columbia U., 1943-44; plant supr. Metal & Plastic Processing Co., Bklyn., 1946-51; research chemist Gen. Chem. div. Allied Chem. & Dye Corp., N.Y.C., 1951-53; sr. chemist Congoleum Nairn, Kearny, N.J., 1953-54; supr. dielecs-advance devel. Gen. Elec. Co., Hudson Falls, N.Y., 1954-56; mgr. indsl. products research dept. Spencer Kellogg & Sons, Inc. (Textron), Buffalo, 1956-59; mgr. plastics div. Trancoa Chem. Corp., Reading, Mass., 1959-62; asso. dir. product devel. service labs. chem. div. Merck & Co., Inc., Rahway, N.J., 1962-69; dir. product devel. Borden Chem. div. Borden Inc., N.Y.C., 1969-72; tech. dir. Borden Chem. div. Borden Inc., 1972-73; tech. dir. Borden Inc., 1973-78, v.p. product safety and quality, 1978-81, v.p. sci. and tech., 1981—; mem. exec. com. Food Safety Council, 1976-81, trustee, chmn. membership com., 1976-81; bd. dirs. Formaldehyde Inst., 1977-86, vice chmn., 1982—, mem. exec. com., 1981—, mem. med. com., 1977—, steering com., 1977—; bd. dirs. Internat. Life Scis. Inst., 1986—, Nutrition Found., 1986—; instr. Poly. Inst. Bklyn., 1946-47; asst. prof. Adelphi Coll., 1952-54; prof. math. sci. U.S. Merchant Marine Acad., 1954; seminar leader Am. Mgmt. Assn.; prof. mgmt. N.Y. U. Sch. Mgmt., 1968—. Contbr. articles to profl. jours. Recipient cert. award Fedn. Socs. Paint Tech., 1965. Mem. Am. Chem. Soc. Fedn. Coatings Tech., Inst. Food Tech., ASTM, Synthetic Organic Chems. Mfg. Assn. (dir. 1977-84), Paint Research Inst., Delta Sigma Pi, Gamma Sigma Epsilon, Beta Gamma Sigma, Phi Lamda Upsilon. also: 277 Park Ave New York NY 10017

CUMMIN, SYLVIA ESTHER, educator; b. N.Y.C., Mar. 15; d. Harry and Sarah (Josephson) Smolok; B.S., N.Y. U., 1946, M.A., 1947; m. Alfred S. Cummin, Mar. 24, 1946; 1 dau., Cynthia Katherine. Mktg. adminstr. Ayerst Labs. div. Am. Home Products, N.Y.C., 1946-55; tchr. Queensbury (N.Y.) High Sch., 1955-57, Corfu (N.Y.) Central Sch., 1957-59, Brookline (Mass.) High Sch., 1959-63; tchr. bus. Westfield (N.J.) Secondary Sch., 1963—. Active, Westfield PTA, 1963—, YWCA, 1966—; sponsor, committeewoman Nat. Debutante Assembly, N.Y.C., 1972—, Internat. Debutante Ball, N.Y.C., 1973—, Debutante Cotillion, Washington, 1973—, Ball of the Silver Rose, Vienna, Austria, 1973—; Cert. tchr., Mass., N.Y., N.J. Mem. NEA, N.J. Edn. Assn., Mass. Tchrs. Assn., N.Y. Educators Assn., Eastern Bus. Tchrs. Assn., Nat. Bus. Edn. Assn., N.Y. U. Alumni Assn., N.Y. U. Faculty Wives Assn., Am. Platform Assn. Clubs: Westfield Coll. Women's, Glens Falls Country, Garden. Contbr. articles to profl. jours. Home: 2 Naworth Pass Westfield NJ 07090 Office: Edison Jr High Sch Rahway Ave Westfield NJ 07090

CUMMINGS, ERWIN KARL, data processing executive; b. Toledo, Ohio, June 19, 1954; s. Idell and Mae Sue (Jones) C. AS in Electronic Engring., U. Toledo, 1976, BS in Bus. Services, 1981. Telecommunications analyst Owens-Ill. Inc., Toledo, 1975-78, ops. and planning analyst, 1978-81, software systems analyst, 1981-83, sr. data communications analyst, 1983-86, lead data communicatons analyst, 1986—. Mem. Christian Youth Fellowship, Phillips Temple, 1968-72, pres., 1971-72, young adult tchr., 1971-79, supt. Sunday sch., 1979-81, asst. supt., 1983—, asst. Ch.treas., 1985—, head coach basketball, 1986-87, asst. supt., 1983-87. Named one of Outstanding Young Men of Am., 1985, 86. Mem. NAACP, DAV (Commdrs. Club 1985-88). Democrat. Methodist. Home: 1323 Oak Hill Ct #153 Toledo OH 43614 Office: Owens-Ill Inc 1 Seagate Sq Toledo OH 43666

CUMMINGS, JOHN HUGH, college president; b. Glen White, W.Va., Apr. 14, 1923; s. Melville Homer and Mary Louise (Kacmar) C.; A.B., Marietta Coll., 1943; S.T.B., M.Div., Wesley Theol. Sem., 1946; Th.D., Iliff Sch. Theology, 1950; m. Elsa Maria Simons-Ebanks, Mar. 17, 1966; children—April Annette, Ian Hugh. Ordained to ministry United Meth. Ch., 1945; pastor chs., Va., W.Va., Colo., 1943-61; instr. Morris Harvey Coll., W.Va. Wesleyan Coll., 1961-64; coll. program sec. Am. Friends Service Com., 1964-68; instr. Lewis and Clark Coll., Portland State U., 1968-70; pres. Internat. Coll. of Cayman Islands (West Indies), 1970—. Mem. Caribbean Studies Assn. Home: Newlands, Grand Cayman West Indies Office: Internat Coll of the Cayman Islands, Newlands, Grand Cayman West Indies

CUMMINGS, KATHERINE FIONA, librarian, writer; b. Aberdeen, Scotland, Mar. 28, 1935; d. John Walter and Jeannie May (Whent) C.; children: Fiona, Philippa, Clare. BA, U. Sydney, Australia, 1956; BLS with hons., U. Toronto (Can.), 1963. Librarian U. Sydney, 1956-60, Nat. Library of Australia, Canberra, 1960-62; librarian reader services U. New South Wales, Sydney, 1963-67; librarian reader services, reference depts. State Library of Oreg., Salem, 1967-69; dir. library Upsala Coll., East Orange, N.J., 1969-73; dep. univ. librarian U. Queensland, Brisbane, Australia, 1973-76; head info. resources Sydney Coll. of the Arts, 1976—; mem. state and nat. com. adv. council on bibliog. services. Editor: Changes and Exchanges, 1987; critic book reviews; contbr. articles to profl. jours. Mem. Library Assn. of Australia (assoc., univ. coll. library section), Arts Libraries Soc. (chairperson Australia and New Zealand chpt.). Office: Univ Sydney, Box 231 Holme Bldg, Sydney 2006, Australia

CUMMINGS, NICHOLAS ANDREW, psychologist; b. Salinas, Calif., July 25, 1924; s. Andrew and Urania (Sims) C.; m. Dorothy Mills, Feb. 5, 1948; children—Janet Lynn, Andrew Mark. AB, U. Calif., Berkeley, 1948; MA, Claremont Grad. Sch., 1954; PhD, Adelphi U., 1958. Chief psychologist Kaiser Permanente No. Calif., San Francisco, 1959-76; clin. dir. Biodyne Inst., San Francisco, 1976—; chmn., chief exec. officer Am. Biodyne, Inc., San Francisco, 1985—; co-dir. Golden Gate Mental Health Ctr., San Francisco, 1959-75; pres. Calif. Sch. Profl. Psychology, Los Angeles, San Francisco, San Diego, Fresno campuses, 1969-76; chmn. bd. Calif. Community Mental Health Ctrs., Inc., Los Angeles, San Diego, San Francisco, 1975-77; pres. Blue Psi, Inc., San Francisco, 1972-80, Inst. for Psychosocial Interaction, 1980-84; mem. mental health adv. bd. City and County San Francisco, 1968-75; bd. dirs. San Francisco Assn. Mental Health, 1965-75; pres., chmn. bd. Psycho-Social Inst., 1972-80; dir. Mental Research Inst., Palo Alto, Calif., 1979-80; pres. Nat. Acads. of Practice, 1981—. Served with U.S. Army, 1944-46. Fellow Am. Psychol. Assn. (dir. 1975-81, pres. 1979); mem. Calif. Psychol. Assn. (pres. 1968). Office: Am Biodyne Inc 400 Oyster Point Blvd Suite 218 South San Francisco CA 94080

CUMMINS, ANDREW DOUGLAS, investment company executive; b. Melbourne, Australia, Aug. 24, 1949; s. Douglas Charles Verdun and Marjorie Pamela (Sturrock) C.; m. Jennifer Muriel Knight, Feb. 18, 1972; children: Alexia Patricia, Jonathan Andrew Knight. BE with honors, Monash U., Australia, 1970; postgrad. diploma in bus., U. Newcastle, Australia, 1974; MBA, Stanford U., 1976. Engr. BHP Co. Ltd., Newcastle, 1971-74; assoc. McKinsey & Co., Inc., Cleve. and Sydney, Australia, 1976-83; prin. Melbourne and Sydney, 1983-85; dir. group strategy Elders IXL Ltd., London and Melbourne, 1985—; chief exec. Elders Investments Ltd., Hong Kong, 1987—. Mem. Instn. Engrs. Australia. Mem. Ch. of Eng. Clubs: Union of Sydney; Athenaeum (Melbourne); St. James (London). Home: 4 Argyll Rd, Kensington W8 7DB, England Office: Elders IXL Ltd, 5 St James Sq, London SW 1, England

CUMMINS, DELMER DUANE, academic administrator, historian; b. Dawson, Nebr., June 4, 1935; s. Delmer H. and Ina Z. (Arnold) C.; m. Darla Sue Beard, Oct. 6, 1957; children: Stephen Duane, Cristi Sue, Caroline Renee. B.A., Phillips U., Enid, Okla., 1957; M.A., U. Denver, 1965; Ph.D., U. Okla., 1974; LL.D., Williams Woods Coll., 1979; Hum.D., Phillips U., 1983. Tchr., Jefferson County Pub. Schs., Denver, 1956-67; mem. faculty Oklahoma City U., 1967-77, Darbeth-Whitten prof. history, 1974-77, curator George Shirk Collection, 1977; chmn. dept. history Oklahoma City U., 1969-72; dir. Robert A. Taft Inst. Govt., 1970-77; pres. div. higher edn. Christian Ch., 1977-88; pres. Bethany (W.Va.) Coll., 1988—. Author: The American Frontier, 1968, Origins of the Civil War, 1971, The American Revolution, 1968, Contrasting Decades: 1920's and 1930's, 1972, Consensus and Turmoil, 1972, William R. Leigh: Biography of a Western Artist, 1980, A Handbook for Today's Disciples, 1981, (with D. Hohweiler) An Enlisted Soldier's View of the Civil War, 1981, (with others) Seeking God's Peace in a Nuclear Age, 1985, The Disciples Colleges: A History, 1987; editor The Disciples Theol. Digest, 1986—; contbr. articles to profl. jours. Trustee Culver-Stockton Coll., 1978—; trustee Tougaloo Coll., 1978—, vice chmn., 1986—; Danforth asso., 1976—. Mem. Okla. Council Humanities (grantee 1974), Phillips U. Alumni Assn. (pres. 1975-76), Nat. Assn. Ind. Colls. and Univs. (secretariat). Mem. Christian Ch. (multiple nat. bds. and task forces). Home and Office: Pendelton Heights Bethany Coll Bethany WV 26032

CUMMINS, EVELYN FREEMAN, social agency administrator; b. Beatrice, Nebr., Mar. 24, 1904; d. John Allen and Irene (Townsend) Freeman; student Nebr. Wesleyan, 1920-23; B.A., U. Nebr., 1928, postgrad. U. Chgo., 1934-36, 41; M.S., Columbia, 1946; m. Paul Otto Cummins, Oct. 8, 1927 (dec. Sept. 1943); 1 dau., Beverly Anne (Mrs. Cummins Spangler). Tchr. rural Gage County, Nebr., 1921-22, Wilber, Nebr., 1923-25, Lincoln, Nebr., 1925-27; sch. social worker Lincoln, 1930-36; supr. Fla. Dept. Pub. Welfare, Orlando, 1936-42, dist. dir., 1942-45; dir. Nebr. Gov.'s Com. to Study Services to Blind, Lincoln, 1946-47; field rep. Fla. Dept. Pub. Welfare, Jacksonville, 1948-51, appeals officer, 1950-51; exec. dir. Community Council Oklahoma City Area, 1952-61; exec. dir. spl. projects Chgo. Community Fund, 1962-63; exec. dir. Family Service Assn. La Porte County (Ind.), 1964—; lectr. social problems Purdue North Central; field supr. Valparaiso U., Loyola U., Jane Addams Sch. Social Work, Chgo. Del. Area II Adv. Council on Aging, 1976-80; mem. housing com. Mayor of Michigan City (Ind.), 1973; pres. Community Service Council Michigan City, 1966-68; chmn. residential campaign United Way Michigan City, 1966-68. Diplomate Conf. Advancement Pvt. Practice in Social Work. Mem. Nat. Assn. Social workers, Acad. Certified Social Workers, Council Social Work Edn., Ind. Council Family Service Assns., Ind. Home Service Agys. Assn., Ind. Conf. on Social Concerns, Internat. Platform Assn., LaPorte County Council on Aging (pres. 1978). Democrat. Methodist. Home: 1317 Washington St Michigan City IN 46360 Office: Suite 228 Warren Bldg Michigan City IN 46360

CUMMINS, JAMES MICHAEL, biology educator; b. Abbottabad, India, June 3, 1943; s. Patrick Henry and Christian Eileen (Somerville) C.; m. Erlene Siu Yoong Chun, Dec. 8, 1973; children: David, Philip. BSc, Portsmouth (Eng.) Coll. Tech., 1965; MSc, U. North Wales, Bangor, 1966; PhD, Liverpool (Eng.) U., 1967. Research assoc. Vanderbilt U., Nashville, 1970-71; Ford Found. fellow U. Hawaii, Honolulu, 1971-74; lectr., sr. lectr. Victoria U., Wellington, N.Z., 1974-77; sr. lectr., reader U Queensland, Brisbane, Australia, 1977-88; sci. dir. Pivet Med. Ctr., Leederville, Western Australia, 1988—; cons. Queensland Fertility Group, Brisbane, 1982—, PIVET Labs., Perth Australia, 1986—. Author, co-author numerous research papers, teaching manuals. Mem. Soc. Study Fertility, Soc. Study Reprodn., N.Z. Endocrine Soc., Australian Soc. Reproductive Biology (sec. 1974-76), Inst. Biology U.K., Inst. Biology Australia, Australian Soc. Human Biology. Office: PIVET Med Ctr, 166 Cambridge St, Leederville Western Australia, Australia

CUMMINS, NEIL JOSEPH, JR., land surveyor, lawyer; b. Oxnard, Calif., Sept. 14, 1945; s. Neil Joseph and Helen Louise (Porter) C.; student Claremont Men's Coll., 1962-64, Calif. State Poly. Coll., 1965-67; JD, Mid Valley Coll. Law, 1978; Bar: Calif. 1978. m. Lynn D. Mealer, Sept. 16, 1967. Designer, Ludwig Engring., San Bernardino, Calif., 1967-69; field supr. Sikand Engring., Van Nuys, Calif., 1969-77; land surveyor, Reseda, Calif., 1977—; lectr. civil engring. Calif. Poly. Coll., Pomona, 1979-80; admitted to Calif. bar, 1978. Registered profl. engr., Ariz., Calif., Nev.; registered land surveyor, Calif., Nev., Ariz. Fellow ASCE; mem. Am. Congress Surveying and Mapping (chmn. So. Calif. sect. 1984), Am. Water Works Assn., ABA, Los Angeles County Bar Assn., Calif. Land Surveyors Assn. Office: 7122 Reseda Blvd Reseda CA 91335-4210

CUNHA, GEORGE MARTIN, emeritus conservator; b. Providence, Dec. 25, 1911; s. Anthony Martin and Augusta Elizabeth (Dwyer) C.; m. Dorothy Bourne Grant, Dec. 31, 1938; 1 stepson, James H. Ryan; children: George Martin, Suzanne Elizabeth. Student MIT, 1930-32, Lowell Inst., 1935-36, USN Line Sch., 1946-47, Naval War Coll., 1958-59. Control chemist Phillips Baker Rubber Co., Providence, 1932-34; devel. chemist Vultex Chem. Co., Cambridge, Mass., 1935-37; apptd. aviation cadet USN, 1937, advanced through grades to capt., 1957; conservator rare books, documents and works of art on paper Library of Boston Athenaeum, 1963-73; dir. New Eng. Document Conservation Center, 1973-78, dir. emeritus, 1978—; adj. prof. of conservation, U. Ky. Coll. of Library Sci., 1982—; cons. in conservation, writer, lectr., 1963—. Author: The Conservation of Library Materials, 1967, rev. edit., 1971; Library and Archives Conservation, 1980s and Beyond, 1983, Mass Deacidification for Libraries, 1987; editor Procs. of Boston Athenaeum's 1971 Seminar on the Conservation of Library Materials, 1972, Seminar on Conservation Adminstrn., 1975. Mem. Ky. State Archives and Records Commn., 1981—; chmn. advancement com. Narragansett council Boy Scouts Am., 1956-59, pres. C.Z. council, 1960-61. Decorated D.F.C., Air medal with star; recipient Silver Beaver award Boy Scouts Am., 1958; cert. of merit Assn. de Scouts de Panamá, 1961. Fellow Soc. Am. Archivists, Royal Soc. Arts, Pilgrim Soc. (editorial com. 1972), Am. Inst. Conservation; mem. Internat. Inst. for Conservation Historic and Artistic Works, Guild of Book Workers (v.p.-at-large 1971-77), Colonial Soc. Mass. Republican. Club: Louisville Filson. Lodge: Masons. Home and Office: 4 Tanglewood Dr Lexington KY 40505

CUNHA, MARK GEOFFREY, lawyer; b. Lexington, Mass., Sept. 26, 1955; s. John Henry and Dolores (DeRosas) C. AB magna cum laude, Cornell U., 1977; JD, Stanford U., 1980. Bar: N.Y. 1981, U.S. Dist. Ct. (so. and ea. dists.) N.Y. 1981. Assoc. Simpson, Thacher & Bartlett, N.Y.C., 1980—. Mem. ABA, Assn. of Bar of City of N.Y., Phi Beta Kappa. Democrat. Home: 322 W 57th St #12S New York NY 10019 Office: Simpson Thacher & Bartlett 1 Battery Park Plaza New York NY 10004

CUNLIFFE, SYDNEY JOSEPH, civil engineer, consultant; b. Port Haney, B.C., Can., Oct. 28, 1919; s. Sydney Alred and Catherine Euphemia (Jones) C.; m. Doris Ethel Beaulne, Sept. 2, 1946; children: Robert, Douglas, Raymond, Edward. BASc, U. B.C., Vancouver, 1950, PEng, 1952; LLD, U. Victoria. Field engr. B.C. Dept. Hwys., Vancouver Island, 1950-51; asst. surfacing engr. B.C. Dept. Hwys., B.C., 1951-56; chmn. bd. Willis, Cunliffe, Tait and Co., Victoria, B.C., 1956-87, DeLeuw Cather (Can.) Ltd., 1979-87; mem. Victoria adv. bd. Royal Trust Co.; chmn. Constrn. Industry Devel. Council, 1980-87; chmn. Consultative Com. on Cons. Engring.; vice chmn. Victoria Art Gallery, 1963-67, Victoria Planning Commn., 1965-75, chmn., 1970-75. Pres. Victoria YM-YWCA, 1963-65; chmn. bd. U. Victoria Found. Served to capt. Royal Can. Arty., 1940-46. Recipient R.A. McLachlan award, 1966; named Hon. Citizen City of Victoria, 1971, Citizen of Year, 1978; decorated Order of Can., 1981. Fellow Engring. Inst. Can., Can. Soc. Civil Engring.; mem. Assn. Cons. Engrs. Can. (pres.), Victoria Downtown Bus. Assn. (v.p.), Can. Tech. Asphalt Assn. (pres. 1962), Assn. Profl. Engrs. B.C. (hon. life mem., pres. Victoria br. 1961-62, R.A. McLachlan award 1966), Rds. and Transp. Assn. Can., Asssn. of Physical Engrs. B.C. (hon. life). Clubs: Union of B.C. (pres. 1970-72), Rotary, Victoria Golf, Faculty of U. Victoria. Home: 1530 Despard Ave, Victoria, BC Canada V8S 1T3 Office: 827 Fort St, Victoria, BC Canada V8W 1H6

CUNNIFF, MARY TERESA, business executive; b. Boston, Nov. 16, 1950; d. John Patrick and Marie-Theresa (Riccelli) Rose; m. James Walter Cunniff, Nov. 21, 1971; children: Ann-Marie, Teresa Jean, Sean James. Treas., J.W. Cunniff Co., 1971-81; pres., treas. Berniff Industries, Inc., Stoughton, Mass., 1983—, chmn. bd., 1983—, also dir. Dir. vols.; pres., owner J.M.C. Enterprises, Inc., 1988—. Goddard Hosp., Stoughton, 1969-71. Mem. C. of C. (bd. dirs., pres.). Democrat. Roman Catholic. Home: 309 Morton St Stoughton MA 02072 also: JMC Enterprises Inc 25 Brock St Stoughton MA 02072

CUNNIFFE, CHARLES LAWRENCE, architect; b. Waltham, Mass., July 21, 1951; s. Charles Walen David and Jacqueline Louise (Reade) C.; BFA in Architecture, R.I. Sch. Design, 1974, B.Arch., 1975. Registered architect, Colo., R.I. Project architect, designer Keyes Assocs., Waltham, 1974-78; project architect Robinson, Green & Beretta, Providence, 1978-80, Thomas Wells & Assocs., Aspen, Colo., 1980-81; prin. Charles Cunniffe & Assocs., Aspen, 1981—. Mem. AIA, Nat. Historic Trust, City of Aspen Hist. Preservation Commn. Home: PO Box 3534 Aspen CO 81612

CUNNINGHAM, ATLEE MARION, JR., aeronautical engineer; b. Corpus Christi, Aug. 17, 1938; s. Atlee Marion and Carlos Dean (Shepherd) C.; B.S. in Mech. Engring., U. Tex., 1961, M.S. in Mech. Engring., 1963, Ph.D., 1966; m. Diana Wahl Bonelli, July 17, 1976; children by previous marriage—Christopher Atlee, Scott Patrick, Sean Michael. Research scientist Def. Research Lab., Austin, Tex., 1965; engring. specialist sr. Gen. Dynamics Corp., Fort Worth, 1965—; vis. indsl. prof. So. Meth. U. Inst. Tech., Dallas, 1969-70; vis. assoc. prof. aero. engring. U. Tex., 1978—; lectr. in aeroelasticity Nat. Cheng Kung U., Taiwan, 1984; cons. NASA, USAF, U. Tex. Vice pres. Tex. Fine Arts Assn., Fort Worth, 1972. Served with USN, 1962-64. Welding Research Assn. fellow, 1961-62; NATO fellow, 1964-65; recipient NASA Cert. of Recognition for tech. publ., 1980, Extraordinary Achievement award Gen. Dynamics, 1980, 83. Fellow AIAA (assoc.; tech. reviewer jours.); mem. Sigma Xi. Contbr. articles to profl. jours.; inovator in subsonic, transonic and supersonic steady and oscillatory aerodynamics method; developer new methods for predicting high angle of attack aerodynamics in subsonic and supersonic flows. Pioneer in new technology development for unsteady separated flows and buffeting on aircraft maneuvering at high angle of attack involving support of Air Force, Navy, NASA, National Aerospace Laboratory (Netherlands), General Dynamics and University of Texas at Austin. Home: 2221 Stanley Ave Fort Worth TX 76147

CUNNINGHAM, CLARENCE MARION, chemist, educator; b. Cooper, Tex., July 24, 1920; s. Willie Lee and Naomi Mae (Stokes) C.; B.S., Tex. A&M U., 1942; M.S., U. Calif., 1948; Ph.D., Ohio State U., 1954; m. Janet Ruth Kohl, Sept. 16, 1951; children—Elizabeth Jane, Daniel Marvin, Steven Charles, Margaret Helen. Asst. prof. Calif. Poly. State U., San Luis Obispo, 1948-49; cryogenic engr., cons. H.L. Johnston, Inc., Columbus, Ohio, 1951-53; vis. research prof. Ohio State U., Columbus, summer 1961; mem. faculty Okla. State U., Stillwater, 1954—, assoc. prof. chemistry, 1959-85, prof. emeritus, 1985—; cons. Arrow Machinery Inc., Oklahoma City, 1985—; cons. in field. Vice pres. Stillwater United Way, 1959-60, bd. dirs., 1958-62; v.p. Stillwater YMCA, 1958-61; bd. dirs. Payne Community Action Bd., 1965-69; bd. dirs., v.p. Stillwater Neighborhood Nursery, 1968-72, 78-85; sec. Payne County Dem. Central Com., 1964-67, 75-77. Served to capt. U.S. Army, 1942-46, to col. USAR, 1946-72. Recipient Silver Beaver award Boy Scouts Am., 1976; Research Corp. Am. grantee, 1955-56; NASA grantee, 1966-72. Mem. AAAS, Am. Phys. Soc., Am. Chem. Soc., AAUP (chpt. pres. 1964-65, state pres. 1965-67), Okla. Acad. Sci. Democrat. Quaker. Club: Kiwanis. Author: A Student's Guide for General Chemistry, 1977. Home: 924 Lakeridge Ave Stillwater OK 74075 Office: Okla State U Dept Chemistry Stillwater OK 74078

CUNNINGHAM, DAVID GRAHAM, government analyst, researcher; b. Cape Town, Republic of South Africa, Oct. 12, 1925; s. James Alexander and Marie-Louise (Feinauer) C.; m. Brenda Elisabeth Lockett, Jan. 19, 1978. BS, U. South Africa, Cape Town, 1950, BS (hon.), 1972; MS, U. Cape Town, 1974. Registered pharmacist; registered analyst. Mng. dir. W.R. Warner Pty. Ltd., Cape Town, 1950-59; prin. profl. officer State Pub. Service, Cape Town, 1961—; mem. old medicines com. Medicine Control Council, Cape Town, 1983—. Editor: (gazette) The South African Croquet Gazette, 1972-86. Recipient South African Sports Merit award Office of the State Pres., Cape Town, 1981, 82. Fellow Pharm. Soc. South Africa; mem. South African Assn. Hosp. Pharmacists (chmn. 1975, vice chmn. 1985), Ratepayers Assn. (sec. 1979, chmn. 1985). Mem. Anglican Ch. Club: Rondebosch Croquet (v.p. 1972-85). Home: 4 Bucksburn Rd, Cape Town 7700, Republic of South Africa

CUNNINGHAM, EARLENE BROWN, biochemistry educator; b. Cleve., Aug. 27, 1930. BS, U. Ill., 1949; MS, UCLA, 1951; PhD, U. So. Calif., 1954. Research assoc. Ind. U. Sch. Medicine, Indpls., 1954-59; asst. prof. Howard U. Coll. Medicine, Washington, 1959-63, assoc. prof., 1963-64; research assoc. U. Calif.-Berkeley, 1964-67; lectr. chemistry U. S.C., Columbia, 1968-71, assoc. prof. Med. U. S.C., Charleston, 1971-78; assoc. prof. U. Medicine and Dentistry N.J., N.J. Med. Sch., Newark, 1978—. Author: Biochemistry: Mechanisms of Metabolism, 1978; contbr. articles, abstracts to sci. publs.; conducted research, regulation cell devel. and proliferation. Recipient Lederle Med. Faculty award Howard U., 1961; spl. fellow NIH, 1964. Mem. Sigma Xi. Office: 100 Bergen St Newark NJ 07103

CUNNINGHAM, JAMES EVERETT, energy services company executive; b. Iowa, Apr. 14, 1923; s. James Franklin and Julia (Connors) C.; BS in Chem. Engring., U. Ala., 1946; m. Delores Ann Foytik, Jan. 31, 1959;

children: Sharon Lee, Sandra Dee, Matthew Joseph, Susan Elizabeth, Michael James, Marc David. With Fluor Corp., Houston, 1947-54; pvt. practice oil bus., 1955-58; with J. Ray McDermott & Co., Inc., New Orleans, 1958—, treas., 1964-67, exec. v.p., 1967-78, vice chmn. fin. and adminstrn., 1978, vice chmn., chief exec. officer, 1979, chmn., chief exec. officer, 1979—; dir. Reading & Bates Corp., The Greyhound Corp. Mem. president's council Loyola U.; vice chmn. Ctr. Internat. Bus.; bd. dirs. Bus. Task Force on Edn. Served with USNR, World War II. Mem. NAM (former vice chmn., so. div., mem. exec. com.), Conf. Bd. (policy com.), New Orleans C. of C. (econ. devel. council, dir.). Office: McDermott Internat Inc PO Box 61961 New Orleans LA 70161

CUNNINGHAM, KEITH ALLEN, mining and manufacturing company executive; b. Weaver, W.Va., Aug. 21, 1922; s. James Arthur and Blanche (Proudfoot) C.; B.S. in Bus. Adminstrn., W.Va. U., 1948, J.D., 1951; m. Jeanne Antoinette Viquesney, June 6, 1942; children—Keith Allen, Kathe Jan. Bldg. constrn. engr. Gibbs & Hills, Inc., N.Y.C., 1942-43; admitted to W.Va. bar, 1951, practiced law in Belington, 1952; asso. Touche, Niven, Bailey & Smart, C.P.A.'s, Detroit, 1952-60, partner-in-charge Dayton (Ohio) office Touche, Ross, Bailey & Smart, 1960-65, dir. adminstrn. and office ops., 1965-67, exec. adminstrv. partner, vice chmn. bd. dirs., 1967-70; pres. Energy Conversion Devices, Inc., Troy, Mich., 1969-72, dir., 1969-74; exec. v.p. United Nuclear Corp., Falls Church, Va., 1973-75, pres., chief exec. officer, 1975-84, chmn. bd., 1982-84, also dir.; chmn. bd., chief exec. officer Atlis Inc., 1984—; dir. Clevepak Corp.; chmn. bd. Atlis Corp.; lectr. W.Va. Tax Inst. Mem. Council for Reorgn. Ohio State Govt., 1963-64; treas. Mich. Employers Unemployment Compensation Bur., 1957-60; mem. advisory com. Mich. Security Commn., 1958-60. Served with USAAF, 1943-46. C.P.A., Mich., Ohio, N.Y., Ind., La. Mem. Am. Acctg. Assn., Nat. Assn. Accountants, Am. Inst. C.P.A.'s, Mich., Ohio (dir.), N.Y., N.J. socs. C.P.A.'s, Mich., W.Va. state bars, Detroit Bar Assn., Phi Beta Kappa, Phi Delta Phi. Methodist. Clubs: Mining (N.Y.C.); Detroit Athletic, Petroleum, Albuquerque Country; Congressional Country; Farmington Country (Charlottesville, Va.). Home: 12208 Meadow Creek Ct Potomac MD 20854 Office: 6011 Executive Blvd Rockville MD 20852

CUNNINGHAM, PATRICK JOSEPH, JR., addictions counselor; b. Chgo., Nov. 29, 1950; s. Patrick Joseph and Sally Mary (Kmiotek) C. BS, Western Ill. U., 1975; MA, Governors State U., 1979. Cert. tchr., Ill.; cert. addictions counselor; clin. cert. substance abuse counselor. Acad. advisor Triton Coll., 1975-80, biofeedback trainer, 1976-80, acting records evaluator, 1978-79, mem. faculty, 1980; alcoholism counselor The Abbey, Winfield, Ill., 1981, St. Joseph Hosp., Joliet, Ill., 1981-84; addictions counselor Pape and Assocs., Wheaton, Ill., 1984-87; instr. addiction counselor tng. Coll. of DuPage, Glen Ellyn, Ill., 1985-87; dir. addictions counselor tng. program Coll. of DuPage, Glen Ellyn, 1986-87; pvt. practice addictions counselor Lisle, Ill., 1987—; mem. staff REACH Found., Westmont, Ill., 1988—. Mem. staff REACH Found., Westmont, Ill., 1988. Mem. Nat. Assn. Alcoholism and Drug Abuse Counselors, Nat. Assn. for Children of Alcoholics (exec. service bd. Ill. chpt. 1988—), Assn. Labor-Mgmt. Adminstrs. and Cons. on Alcoholism. Office: 3060 Ogden Ave Suite 307 Lisle IL 60532

CUNNINGHAM, STANLEY VERNON, mathematics educator; b. Karlsruhe, W.Ger., Aug. 29, 1953; s. Stanley Vernon and Anna Josephine (Hoffmann) C.; m. Susan J. Wisdom, Mar. 22, 1985; children: Sara Ann, Crystal Marie; stepchildren: David Loren, Benjamin Robert, Erica Rachell. BS, Kearney State Coll., 1977, MS, 1979. Cert. tchr. in math., physics, Nebr. Grad. asst. Kearney State Coll. (Nebr.), 1977-78; mem. programming staff AT&T, Kansas City, Mo., 1979; instr. math. Three Rivers Community Coll., Poplar Bluff, Mo., 1980—. Mem. Am. Math. Assn Two Year Colls., Nat. Council Tchrs. Math., Mo. Assn. Community and Jr. Colls., Three Rivers Amateur Radio Assn., Kappa Mu Epsilon, Sigma Pi Sigma. Democrat. Lutheran. Home: 1102 White Oak Dr Poplar Bluff MO 63901 Office: Three Rivers Community Coll Dept Math Poplar Bluff MO 63901

CUNNINGHAM, TOM ALAN, lawyer; b. Houston, Nov. 5, 1946; s. Warren Peek and Ellen Ardelle (Benner) C.; m. Jeanne Adrienne Moran, July 21, 1972; 1 child, Christopher Alan. B.A., U. Tex., 1968, J.D., 1974. Bar: Tex. 1974, U.S. Ct. Appeals (5th and 11th cirs.) 1981, U.S. Dist. Ct. (so. dist.) Tex. 1976, U.S. Dist. Ct. (no. dist.) Tex. 1982, U.S. Dist. Ct. (we. dist.) Tex. 1984. Ptnr., Fulbright & Jaworski, Houston, 1974—. Bd. dirs. Childrens Charity Fund, Houston, 1983—. Served to lt. (j.g.) USNR, 1969-72. Mem. Houston Bar Assn. (chmn. constn. bicentennial com.), State Bar Tex. (Pres's. award 1983, chmn. dist. 4H grievance com. 1982—, chmn. spl. com. on lawyer advt. and solicitation 1982). Clubs: Houston, Houston Yacht. Lodge: Kiwanis. Home: 10811 Pine Bayou St Houston TX 77024

CUNNINGHAM, WILLIAM HENRY, food products executive; b. Oxnard, Calif., Dec. 2, 1930; s. William Henry and Carrie Edna (Wilson) C.; m. Carmen Nelson Alden, Jan. 19, 1957; children: Nelson, Clifford, Cynthia. BA, U. Calif., Santa Barbara, 1952; B of Foreign Trade, Am Grad. Sch. Internat. Mgmt., 1958. With Colgate-Palmolive Internat., N.Y., Columbia, San Salvador, El Salvador, 1958-63; mktg. cons. Anderson, Clayton Co., Mexico City and Buenos Aires, 1963-66; mgr. consumer div. Cynamid, S.Am., Buenos Aires, 1966-69; dir. mktg. and sales Alimentos Kraft, S.Am., Caracas, Venezuela, 1969-74; pres., mng. dir. Alimentos, S.Am., Caracas, Venezuela, 1980-85; regional mgr. Kraft Foods, S.Am., Panama City, Panama, 1974-80; v.p., dir. Kraft, Inc., Orlando, Fla., 1986—, The Land-Epcot Ctr., Walt Disney World, Orlando, 1986—. Served to sgt. U.S. Army, 1952-54. Recipient Tribute Appreciation award U.S. State Dept., 1980, Order of Vasco Nunez de Balboa, Govt. Panama, 1980, First Class Work Merit award Govt. Venezuela, 1985. Mem. Am. C. of C. (pres., founder Panama City chpt. 1979, sec. Caracas 1986), Am. Soc. (pres. Panama City chpt. 1977). Democrat. Methodist. Home: 3861 Winderlakes Dr Orlando FL 32811 Office: The Land Epcot Ctr PO Box 22261 Lake Buena Vista FL 32830

CUNNINGHAM, WILLIAM HUGHES, university president, marketing educator; b. Detroit, Jan. 5, 1944; married; 1 child. B.A., Mich. State U., 1966, M.B.A., 1967, Ph.D., 1971. Mem. faculty U. Tex., Austin, 1971—, assoc. prof. mktg., 1973-79, prof., 1979—, assoc. dean grad. programs, 1976-82, Foley/Sanger Harris prof. retail merchandising, 1982-83, acting dean Coll. Bus. Adminstrn. and Grad. Sch. Bus., 1982-83, dean, 1983-85, pres., 1985—, Centennial chmn. bus. edn. leadership, 1983-85; mem. econ. adv. com. U.S. Dept. Commerce, 1984—; regents chair Higher Edn. Leadership, U. Tex., 1985—; bd. govs., bd. electors Internat. Ins. Seminar, Inc., 1983—; bd. dirs. La Quinta Motor Inns, Inc., Jefferson-Pilot Corp., Criterion Group, Inc., Freeport-McMoRan, Inc.; regular mem. Corp. of the Conf. Bd. Author: (with W.J.E. Crissy and I.C.M. Cunningham) Selling: The Personal Force in Marketing, 1977, Effective Selling, 1977, Spanish edit., 1980; (with S. Lopreato) Consumers' Energy Attitudes and Behavior, 1977, (with Cunningham) Marketing: A Managerial Approach, 1981, (with R. Aldag and C. Swift) Intro. to Business, 1984, (with B. Verhage and Cunningham) Grondslagen van het Marketing Management, 1984, also monographs and articles; editor Jour. Mktg., 1981-84. Bd. dirs. Houston Area Research Council, 1984; mem. Mental Health/Mental Retardation Legis. Oversight Com., 1984; mem. adv. bd. Found. for Cultural Exchange/The Netherlands-USA; bd. dirs. Lyndon Baines Johnson Found.; mem. bd. visitors Air U. Recipient teaching excellence award Coll. Bus. Adminstrn., U. Tex., 1972, Alpha Kappa Psi, 1975, Hank and Mary Harkins Found., 1978; disting. scholastic contbn. award Coll. Bus. Adminstrn. Found. Adv. Council, 1982; disting. alumnus award Coll. and Grad. Sch. Bus., Mich. State U., 1983; named among top 20 profs. UTmost Mag., 1982; research grantee Univ. Research Inst., 1971, 72-73, Latin Am. Inst., 1972, So. Union Gas Energy, 1975-76, ERDA, 1976. Mem. Am. Inst. for Decision Scis., Am. Mktg. Assn., Assn. Consumer Research, So. Mktg. Assn., S.W. Social Sci. Assn., Phi Kappa Phi, Omicron Delta Kappa. Office: U Tex at Austin Office of Pres Austin TX 78712

CUNTZ, ECKART KARL HEINRICH, diplomat; b. Mannheim, Fed. Republic Germany, Apr. 3, 1950; arrived in Brunei, 1985; s. Heinrich and Elisabeth (Meister) C.; m. Ursula Adam, Sept. 16, 1983 ; children: Jochen, Charlotte. Student, U. Heidelberg and U. Freiburg, Fed. Republic Germany, 1968-73; JD, U. Hanover, Fed. Republic Germany, 1985. With German Embassy, Kabul, Afghanistan, 1977, Kuala Lumpur, Malaysia, 1977-80, Luanda, Angola, 1980-82; ambassador German Embassy, Bandar Seri Begawan, Brunei Darussalam, 1985—; with polit. div. Fed. Fgn. Office, Bonn, Fed. Republic Germany, 1983-85. Author: Verfassungstreue der Soldaten, 1985. Mem. Deutsche Gesellschaft fuer Auswaertige Polit., Deutsche Atlantische Gesellschaft. Clubs: Royal Brunei Polo, Jerudong, Pantai Mentiri Golf. Office: Embassy Fed Republic of Germany, PO Box 3050, Bandar Seri Begawan Brunei

CUNTZ, JOACHIM JOHANNES RICHARD, mathematics educator; b. Mannheim, Fed. Republic Germany, Sept. 28, 1948; arrived in France, 1983; Diploma math., U. Heidelberg, Fed. Republic Germany, 1974; PhD, U. Bielefeld, Fed. Republic Germany, 1975; habilitation, TU Berlin-U. Heidelberg, West Berlin, 1977; M. U. Pa., 1981. Asst. prof. Tech. U., Berlin, 1976-78; researcher U. Heidelberg, 1978-81; assoc. prof. U. Pa., Phila., 1982-83; prof. U. Aix-Marseille II, France, 1984-88, U. Heidelberg, 1988—; dir. Lab. de Math. Associe au CNRS de Marseille, 1986—. Author numerous articles to profl. jours. Office: U Heidelberg Math Inst, Im Neuenheimer Feld 288, 6900 Heidelberg Federal Republic of Germany

CUNY, BERNARD, cardiologist; b. Gisors, Eure, France, July 21, 1932; s. Andre Cuny and Louise Gillon; m. Lucie Aversang, Jan. 30, 1958; children: Charles, Claire. MD, Paris Med. Sch., 1964. Asst. in cardiology Troyes (France) Hosp., 1964-76, chief dept., 1976—; part-time lectr. Reims (France) Med. Sch., 1975—, mgmt. bd., 1982—. Mem. French Med. Assn. (regional sec.-gen. 1978—). Home: Chateau Barberey St Sulpice, La Chapelle St Luc, 10600 Aube France Office: Hopital Troyes, 2 Ave Marechal Joffre, 10000 Troyes France

CUOMO, MARIO MATTHEW, governor of New York; b. Queens County, N.Y., June 15, 1932; s. Andrea and Immaculata C.; m. Matilda Raffa; children: Margaret Cuomo Perpignano, Andrew, Maria Cole, Madeline, Christopher. B.A. summa cum laude, St. John's Coll., 1953; LL.B. cum laude, St. John's U., 1956. Bar: N.Y. 1956, U.S. Supreme Ct 1960. Confidential legal asst. to Hon. Adrian P. Burke, N.Y. State Ct. Appeals, 1956-58; assoc. Corner, Weisbrod, Froeb and Charles, Bklyn., 1958-63; ptnr. Corner, Cuomo & Charles, 1963-75; sec. of state State of N.Y., 1975-79, lt. gov., 1979-82, gov., 1983—; mem. faculty St. John's U. Sch. Law, 1963-73; counsel to community groups, including Corona Homeowners, 1966-72; charter mem. First Ecumenical Commn. of Christian and Jews for, Bklyn. and Queens, N.Y. Author: Forest Hills Diary: The Crisis of Low-Income Housing, 1974, Diaries of Mario M. Cuomo, Campaign for Governor, 1983; contbr. articles to legal publs. Speaker keynote address Dem. Nat. Conv., San Francisco, 1984. Recipient Rapallo award Columbia Lawyers Assn., 1976, Dante medal Italian Govt.-Am. Assn. Tchrs. Italian, 1976, Silver medallion Columbia Coalition, 1976, Pub. Adminstr. award C.W. Post Coll., 1977; Theodore Roosevelt award Internat. Platform Assn., 1984. Mem. Am., N.Y. State, Bklyn. Nassau and Queens County bar assns., Assn. Bar City N.Y., Am. Judicature Soc., St. John's U. Alumni Fedn. (chmn. bd. 1970-72), Cath. Lawyers Guild of Queens County (pres. 1966-67), Skull and Circle. Office: Office Gov State Capitol Albany NY 12224

CUPPINI, GIANNI CARLO, industrial engineer; b. Bologna, Italy, Mar. 21, 1933; s. Amedeo Cuppini and Cesarina Zanetti; m. Bassi Marisa, Aug. 4, 1963; children: Monica, Francesca, Elena. Degree in indsl. engring., U. Degli Studi Bologna, 1959. Orgn. mgr. Sasib SpA, Bologna, 1961-69; mgmt. cons. Orga Srl, Milan, 1969-86; pres. Cubo Srl, Bologna, 1987—. Contbr. articles to profl. jours. Roman Catholic. Lodge: Lions. Home: Via E Masi 9, 40137 Bologna Italy Office: Cubo Srl, Via Mazzini 51/2, 40137 Bologna Italy

CURATI, WALTER LUIGI, physician; b. Geneva, Switzerland, Nov. 8, 1943; s. Mario A. and Clotilde M. (Alasonatti) C. M.D., U. Geneva, 1970, P.D., 1980. Jr. research fellow McGill U., Montreal, 1974-76; jr. research fellow U. London, 1976-77, sr. research fellow, 1984-86; cons. radiologist 1987—. Contbr. chpts. to books, articles to profl. jours. Adminstr., S.I. Helvetique Scie., Geneva, 1963—. Fellow Swiss Soc. Radiology and Nuclear Medicine, Radiol. Soc. N.Am., Am. Inst. Ultrasound in Medicine. Club: Aeroclub of Switzerland. Home: Camoletti 4, CH 1207 Geneva Switzerland Office: Royal Postergrad Med Sch, Hammersmith Hosp X-ray Dept, London W12, England

CURATOLA, ANTHONY PAUL, JR., accounting educator; b. Phila., Aug. 3, 1948; s. Anthony Paul and Neafa Mary (Glaviano) C.; BS, Drexel U., 1975, MBA, 1977; MA, U. Pa., 1979; PhD, Tex. A&M U., 1981; m. Patricia A. Richner, July 11, 1970; children—Anthony, Amanda, Adam. Switchman, Bell Telephone Co. of Pa., Phila., 1966-77; adj. instr. fin. Drexel U., Phila., 1975-76, instr. acctg., 1976-77; instr. acctg. Wharton Sch. Bus., U. Pa., Phila., 1977-79, Tex. A&M U., College Station, 1979-81; asst. prof. acctg. La. State U., Baton Rouge, 1981-84, assoc. prof., 1984—. Researcher Internat. Found. Employee Benefit Plans, 1985-86, 87-88; dep. gov. Am. Biographical Inst. Served with U.S. Army, 1968-70. Decorated Army Commendation medal, Bronze Star medal; recipient Deloite, Haskins & Sells Found. award, 1978. Mem. Am. Acctg. Assn., Nat. Tax Assn., Tax Inst. Am., Nat. Assn. Accts., Am. Econ. Assn., Am. Statis. Assn., Beta Alpha Psi. Roman Catholic. Contbr. articles to profl. jours. Home: 10231 Azrok Ave Baton Rouge LA 70809 Office: Dept Acctg CEBA Bldg Baton Rouge LA 70803

CURFMAN, DAVID RALPH, neurological surgeon, musician; b. Bucyrus, Ohio, Jan. 2, 1942; s. Ralph Oliver and Agnes Mozelle (Schreck) C.; student Capital U., 1960-62; A.B., Columbia Union Coll., 1965; M.S., George Washington U., 1967, M.D., 1973; diplomate Nat. Bd. Med. Examiners; m. Blanche Lee Anderson, June 6, 1970. Asst. organist, choirmaster Peace Luth. Ch., Galion, Ohio, 1956-62; bus. mgr. Mansfield/Galion Ambulance Service, 1962-66; with news div. Sta. WTOP-TV, Washington, 1965; choirmaster, asso. organist Grace Luth. Ch., Washington, 1966-73, historian, curator, 1969—; teaching fellow in anatomy George Washington U., 1966-67, gen. surgery intern, 1973-74, resident in neurol. surgery, 1974-78; resident in neuropathology Armed Forces Inst. Pathology, 1975; resident in pediatric neurol. surgery Children's Hosp. Nat. Med. Center, 1976; teaching fellow in anatomy Georgetown U., 1967-69, clin. instr. neurol. surgery, 1978—; practice medicine specializing in neurol. surgery, Washington, 1978—. Mem. Assn. Am. Med. Colls. (nat. student chmn. rules and regulations com. 1971-73), Med. Soc. D.C. (chmn. medicine and religion com. 1981-83, chmn. medico-legal com. 1986—), Pan Am. Med. Soc., Congress Neurol. Surgeons, Am. Coll. Legal Medicine, Washington Acad. Neurosurgery, Galion Hist. Soc. (charter), Children Am. Revolution (pres. Ohio 1963-64, hon. pres.), SR, U.S. Capitol Hist. Soc. (founding supporting mem.), Nat. Cathedral Assn., Cathedral Choral Soc. (v.p. bd. trustees 1981-83, pres. 1984-86), Am. Guild Organists (dean D.C. chpt. 1974-76, publicity chmn. nat. conv. 1982, state chmn. 1984—), Internat. Congress Organists (Washington program chmn. 1977), Royal Sch. Ch. Music (Eng.), Am. Polit. Items Collectors Assn., English-Speaking Union, Luth. Laymen's Fellowship, Hymn Soc. Am., Sovereign Mil. Order Temple of Jerusalem, Sigma Xi (pres. chpt. 1981-82, Phi Delta Epsilon. Republican. Clubs: Crawford County (Ohio) Coin (Charter), George Washington U. Chmn., chief author: Physician's Reference Guide for Medicolegal Matters, 1982. Home: 4201 Massachusetts Ave NW Washington DC 20016 Office: 3301 New Mexico Ave NW Suite 210 Washington DC 20016

CURFMAN, LAWRENCE EVERETT, lawyer; b. Champaign, Ill., Apr. 13, 1909; s. Lawrence Everett and Winifred (Williams) C.; m. Margaret Sylvia Baldwin, May 1, 1937; children: Lawrence Everett III, Elizabeth Ann (Mrs. Peter Koch), John Edward. A.B., U. Mich., 1930, J.D., 1932. Bar: Kans. 1932. Since practiced in Wichita; ptnr. Curfman, Harris, Borniger & Rose, 1984—. Contbr. articles to legal jours. Pres. Wichita Pub. Library Bd., 1954, 57, 58; Trustee E.A. Watkins Found. Mem. ABA (chmn. sect. urban, state and local govt. law 1970- 71), Wichita Bar Assn. (pres. 1956), City Attys. Assn. Kan. (pres. 1953). Club: University (Wichita) (pres. 1965-66). Home: 7900 Donegal Wichita KS 67206 Office: 830 First Nat Bldg Wichita KS 67202

CURIE, EVE, author, lecturer; b. Paris, Dec. 6, 1904; d. Pierre (Nobel prize winner for work in radium 1903) and Marie (Sklodowska) (Nobel prize winner in radio-active substances, 1903, in chemistry 1911) Curie; B.S., Ph.B., Sevigne Coll.; D.H.L. (hon.), Mills Coll., 1939, Russell Sage Coll., 1941; Litt.D. (hon.), U. Rochester, 1941; Hartwick Coll., 1983; m. Henry Richardson Labouisse, Nov. 19, 1954. Took up study of music and gave first concert as pianist, Paris, 1925; later concerts in France and Belgium; mus. critic for Candide (weekly jour.) for several years; also wrote articles on motion pictures and the theater; made first visit to U.S. with mother, 1921; on 2d visit lectured in 10 U.S. cities (speaks English, French and Polish), 1939; witnessed fall of France, 1940, went to London to work for cause of Free France; came to U.S., 1941, lectured on war in France and Eng.; because of pro-ally activities deprived of French citizenship by Vichy Govt., 1941. Served in Europe with Fighting French as officer in Women's div. of army; one of pubs. Paris Presse (daily), resigned to return to ind. writing, 1949. Spl. adviser Sec. Gen., NATO, 1952-54. Decorated Chevalier Legion of Honor (France), 1939; Polonia Restituta (Poland), 1939; Croix de Guerre (France), 1944. Author: Madame Curie (selection of Lit. Guild, Jr. Guild, Book-of-the-Month Club, Scientific Book of the month; Nat. book award for non-fiction), 1937; Journey Among Warriors (Lit. Guild Selection), 1943. Home: 1 Sutton Pl S New York NY 10022

CURRAN, BILL, lawyer; b. Mpls., Feb. 27, 1946; s. William P. and Margaret (Killoren) C.; m. Jean Lorraine Stabenow, Jan. 1, 1978; children: Patrick, Lisa, John. B.A., U. Minn., 1969; J.D., U. Calif., 1972. Bar: Calif. 1972, Nev. 1974, D.C. 1982. Adminstr. Nev. State Ct., Carson City, 1973-74, clk. Nev. Supreme Ct., 1973-74; assoc. Wiener, Goldwater, Galatz & Waldman, Las Vegas, 1974-75; chief dep. atty. Clark County Dist. Atty.'s Office, Las Vegas, 1975—; mem. Clark County Jud. Task Force, Las Vegas, 1977—; county counsel Clark County, 1979—; head Civil Div., Clark County Dist. Atty.'s Office. Co-author: (manual) Nevada Judicial Orientation Manual, 1974. Mem. ABA, Nat. Dist. Attys. Assn., Am. Trial Lawyers Assn., Nat. Assn. County Civil Attys. (pres. 1984-85), Calif. Bar Assn., Nev. Bar Assn. (gov. 1978—, v.p. 1986-87, pres.-elect 1987-88, pres. 1988—), Nev. Dist. Attys. Assn., Nev. Judges Assn. (hon.). Democrat. Roman Catholic. Home: 3865 Alice Ln Las Vegas NV 89103 Office: Clark County Dist Atty's Office 200 S 3rd St Las Vegas NV 89155

CURRAN, JOHN JOSEPH, data processing company executive; b. Bellaire, Ohio, Mar. 16, 1946; s. John Francis and Mayme (DiMattia) C. B.S. in Chem. Engring., Ohio State U. Systems analyst Mobil Oil Co., Tripoli-Libya, Rome, N.Y.C., 1969-73; sr. cons. Computer Usage Co., Milan, Italy, 1973-74; dir. mktg. Computer Resource Mgmt., Milan, 1974-77; v.p., gen. mgr. Nat. Advanced Systems, div. Nat. Semiconductor, London, 1977-88; corp. v.p., gen. mgr. Control Data Corp., 1988—. Home: 69 Elm Bank Gardens, London SW13, England Office: Control Data Corp, 3 Roundwood Ave, Stockley Park Uxbridge UB11 1AG, United Kingdom

CURRAN, MAURICE FRANCIS, lawyer; b. Yonkers, N.Y., Feb. 20, 1931; s. James F. and Mary (O'Brien) C.; m. Deborah M., May 7, 1960; children—James, Maurice, Amy, Bridget, Ceara, Sara. Student Cathedral Coll., 1950; BA in Philosophy, St. Joseph Coll. and Sem., 1952; LLB, Fordham U., 1958. Bar: N.Y. 1958, U.S. Dist. Ct. (so. and ea. dists.) N.Y. 1960, U.S. Ct. Appeals (2d cir.) 1982, U.S. Supreme Ct. Assoc. Kelley, Drye, Newhall & Maginnes, N.Y.C., 1958-60; assoc. Wilson & Bave, Yonkers, 1960-65; div. counsel Merck & Co., Rahway, N.J., 1965-67; asst. gen. counsel E. R. Squibb & Sons, Inc., N.Y.C., 1967-70; corp. counsel, chief law dept. City of Yonkers, 1970-72; ptnr. Bleakley, Platt, Schmidt & Fritz, White Plains, N.Y., 1972-83, Anderson, Banks, Moore, Curran & Hollis, Mt. Kisco, N.Y., 1983—; counsel Yonkers Bd. Edn. Trustee, vice-chmn. Westchester Community Coll. Served to capt. USMC, 1952-58. Mem. ABA, N.Y. State Bar Assn., City Bar City N.Y. Democrat. Roman Catholic. Home: 388 Bronxville Rd Yonkers NY 10708 Office: 61 Smith Ave Mount Kisco NY 10549

CURRAN, SAMUEL CROWE, physicist; b. Ballymena, North Ireland, May 23, 1912; s. John Hamilton and Sarah (Crowe) C.; M.A., Glasgow (Scotland) U., 1933, B.Sc., 1934, Ph.D., 1937, D.Sc., 1950; Ph.D., Cambridge (Eng.) U., 1941; D.Eng. (hon.), Tech. U. N.S.; LL.D. (hon.), Glasgow, Aberdeen; Sc.D. (hon.), U. Lodz, U. Strathclyde; hon. fellow St. Johns Coll., Cambridge; m. Joan Elizabeth Strothers, Nov. 7, 1940; children—Sheena, John, Charles, James. Research fellow Cambridge U., 1937-39; research in radar Ministry Aircraft Prodn., 1940-44; research Manhattan Project, U.S.A., 1944-45; sr. lectr. Glasgow U., 1945-55; dep. chief scientist U.K. Atomic Energy Authority, 1955-58; chief scientist A.W.R.E., Aldermaston, Berkshire, Eng., 1958-59; prin. Royal Coll. Sci. and Tech., 1959-64; prin., vice chancellor U. Strathclyde, Glasgow, Scotland, 1964-80; vis. prof. energy studies U. Glasgow, 1980—; mem. Adv. Council on Tech., 1964-70; chmn. Adv. Com. on Med. Research, 1962-75, chmn. Adv. Bd. on Relations with Univs., 1966-70; chief sci. adviser for civil def. in Scotland, 1967-77; dep. lt. Glasgow, 1969—; mem. Oil Devel. Council for Scotland, 1973-78; dep. chmn. Electricity Council, 1977-80; chmn. Electricity Supply Research Council, 1978-82; dir. Scottish TV Ltd., 1963-82, Internat. Research and Devel. Co. Ltd., 1973-80, Hall-Thermotank Ltd., 1969-76, Cetec Systems Ltd., 1965-77, Nuclear Structures (Protection) Ltd., 1982—. Pres., Scottish Soc. for Mentally Handicapped; hon. pres. Scottish-Polish Cultural Assn., 1972—. Decorated comdr. Royal Order St. Olav; comdr. Polonia Restituta; freeman Burgh of Motherwell and Wishaw, City of Glasgow, 1980; knight bachelor; comdr. Order Polish People's Republic; St. Mungo prize City of Glasgow. Fellow Royal Soc. Edinburgh, Royal Soc., Phys. Soc., Royal Coll. Physicians and Surgeons Glasgow, St. Andrews Soc. (pres. Glasgow 1982—). Author: Counting Tubes, 1949; Scintillation Counter, 1953; Energy and Human Needs, 1979, Recollections and Reflections, 1988; also numerous articles. Research on nuclear transmutations, proximity fuse, centimetre radar, spectrum long-lived radioelements and work on ultra-sensitive radiation detection devices; discovered scintillation counter modern gas-filled proportional counter and spectrometer. Address: 93 Kelvin Ct, Glasgow G12 0AH Scotland Other: care Royal Soc, 6 Carlton House Tce, London SW1Y 5AG England

CURRIE, CATHERINE CECILIA, sociology educator, consultant; b. London, Sept. 18, 1942; d. Roben George and Helena Amelia (Davis) C.; divorced; 1 child, Yasmin Zenith Ashraf. BSc in sociology, London Sch. Econs., 1966, MSc in Econs., 1969. Research officer Research Services Ltd., London, 1966-67; tchr. econs. H.H. Aga Khan High Sch., Nairobi, Kenya, 1967-68; research officer U. Essex, Eng., 1969-70; lectr. dept. sociology U. Lancaster, Eng., 1970—; vis. prof. U. Colo., 1973, U. Delhi, U. Gujarat, U. Bangalore (all in India), 1974, U. Fla., 1978; examiner Oxford U., 1985; cons. World Devel. Movement, London, 1982-83; reviewer Econ. and Social Research Council, London, 1980—; mem. Sociology, Social Sci. and Medicine, London, 1980-84. Gov. Heysham High Sch., Morecambe, 1981-84. Brit. Council fellow, London, 1974, Brit. Acad. travel fellow, 1984, Govt. India travel fellow, 1987; World Devel. Movement grantee, 1982. Mem. Assn. Univ. Tchrs. (com. mem.), British Sociol. Assn. Mem. Brit. Labour Party. Humanist. Club: Royal Calcutta Turf. Home: 2 Brook St, Lancaster LA1 1SL, England Office: U Lancaster, Bailrigg, Lancaster SA1 4YL, England

CURRIE, CLIFFORD WILLIAM HERBERT, librarian, art historian; b. Ramsgate, Kent, Eng., Nov. 24, 1918; s. William Albert and Gladys Irene (Slingsby) C.; m. Inga-Britta Olsson, Oct. 14, 1972. B.A., Fitzwilliam Coll., Cambridge (Eng.) U., 1949; LL.M., Cambridge (Eng.) U., 1950, M.A., 1954; M.A., St. Edmund Hall, Oxford (Eng.) U., 1973, B.C.L., 1974. Asst. librarian Cambridge U., 1951-53; public library dir. London Borough of Bromley, Eng., 1953-59; librarian Imperial Coll. Sci. and Tech., London, 1959-68; exec. dir. Can. Library Assn., Ottawa, Ont., 1968-71; librarian Ashmolean Library, Oxford, Eng., 1972-78, Coll. William and Mary, Williamsburg, Va., 1978-86. Author: Prospects in Librarianship, 58, 63; editor: Can. Library Jour, 1968-71; adv. editor: Eighteenth Century Life, 1980—. Served with Brit. Army, 1939-45. Fellow Library Assn. Eng. (bd. advanced studies 1966-68); mem. Internat. Assn. Tech. Univ. Libraries (v.p. 1968, sec. 1962-67, dir.), Working Party Librarians and the Book Trade (founding mem.), Soc. Bookmen (exec. com. 1976—). Clubs: Athenaeum, Arts, Authors, London, Frewen, Oxford; Grolier (N.Y.C.). Home: 37 St Martins, Marlborough Wiltshire SN8 1AS, England

CURRIE, DAVID CAMERON, physician; b. Leeds, Yorkshire, Eng., May 16, 1956; s. James Irvine And Margaret Yvonne (Rogers) C.; m. Katherine Barbara Ashwell, Jan. 19, 1980; children: Susanna Kate, James Cameron. BA in Genetics, Cambridge (Eng.) U., 1977, MB, B in Surgery, 1979, MA, 1980; mem., Royal Coll. Physicians, London, 1982. Cert. med. practitioner. House officer Addenbrookes Hosp., Cambridge, 1980, Dist. Hosp., York, Eng., 1980; sr. house officer, registrar St. James U. Hosp., Seacroft Hosp., Killingbeck Hosp., Leeds, Eng., 1981-83; registrar North Staffordshire Hosp. Ctr., Stoke-on-Trent, Eng., 1983-84, chmn. jr. med. staff subcom., 1983-84; clin. lectr., hon. registrar Cardiothoracic Inst. and Brompton Hosp., London, 1984-87; registrar Brompton Hosp., 1987—. Contbr. articles to profl. jours. Mem. British Thoracic Soc. Mem. Anglican Ch. Office: Brompton Hosp, Fulham Rd, London SW3 6HP, England

CURRIE, HARRY MACLEOD, humanities educator; b. Glasgow, Scotland, Sept. 30, 1930; s. Harry and Mary (MacLeod) C.; m. Anne Hilary Pearson, Aug. 8, 1959; children: Robin, Gervais, Giles. MA, U. Glasgow, 1953; BA, St. John's Coll., Cambridge (Eng.) U., 1955. Asst. lectr. in Greek Bedford Coll., U. London, 1955-57; asst. lectr. in classics King's Coll., U. London, 1957-58; lectr. to sr. lectr. classics Queen Mary Coll., U. London, 1959-75; prof., head dept. humanities Teesside Poly. U., Middlesbrough, Cleveland, Eng., 1976—; external examiner U. Leicester, Eng., 1968-70, U. Southampton, Eng., 1978-81, U. London, 1986—. Author/editor several textbooks; contbr. numerous articles to profl. jours. Mem. Classical Assn., Roman Soc. (mem. Council 1987—), Virgil Soc. (hon. sec. 1962-68, editor proceedings 1962-74). Home: 25 West St, Yarm, Cleveland TS15 9B7, England

CURRIE, RICHARD JAMES, food store chain executive; b. St. John, N.B., Canada, Oct. 4, 1937; s. Hugh O'Donnell and Agnes Coltart (Johnstone) C.; m. Beverly Trites, Sept. 15, 1962; children: Jennifer Lee, Bryn Margaret, Elizabeth Gay. B in Engring., Tech. Univ. N.S., 1960; MBA, Harvard U., 1970. Process engr. Atlantic Sugar Refineries, 1960-63, refining supt., 1963-68; sr. assoc. McKinsey & Co., 1970; v.p. Loblaws Cos. Ltd., Toronto, Ont., Can., 1972-74, exec. v.p., 1974-76, pres., from 1976; food distbg. group parent co. George Weston Ltd., Toronto, to 1986, sr. v.p., 1986—, also bd. dirs.; chmn. Nat. Tea Co., from 1981. Mem. bd. regents Mt. Allison U.; bd. govs. Bishop Strachan Sch. Clubs: York, Rosedale Golf, Granite. *

CURRIER, ROBERT DAVID, neurologist; b. Grand Rapids, Mich., Feb. 19, 1925; s. Frederick Plummer and Margaret (Hoedemaker) C.; m. Marilyn Jane Johnson, Sept. 1, 1951; children—Mary Margaret, Angela Maria. A.B., U. Mich., Ann Arbor, 1948, M.D., 1952, M.S. in Neurology, 1956; postgrad., Nat. Hosp., U. London, 1955; postgrad. Medico-Social Research Bd, Dublin, Ireland, 1972. Intern, then resident in neurology Univ. Hosp., Ann Arbor, 1952-56; from instr. to asso. prof. U. Mich. Med. Sch., 1956-61; mem. faculty U. Miss. Med. Center, Jackson, 1961—; prof. neurology U. Miss. Med. Center, 1971—, chief div., 1961-77, chmn. dept., 1977—, H.F. McCarty prof., 1987—; med. adv. bd. Nat. Ataxia Found., research dir., 1985—; mem. clin. adv. council Amyotrophic Lateral Sclerosis Soc. Am., 1979—; mem. Ataxia com. World Fedn. Neurology, 1981—, co-sec., 1985—, sec. research group on heredoataxia, 1987—. Co-editor: Yearbook of Neurology and Neurosurgery, 1981—; (jour.) Key Quar. Neurology and Neurosurgery, 1986—; asst. editor for history: Archives of Neurology, 1983—; contbr. articles to med. jours. Served with USAAF, 1943-45, ETO. Decorated Air medal with 2 oak leaf clusters; NIH grantee, 1961-74. Fellow Am. Acad. Neurology (chmn. history com. 1980-82); mem. Am. Neurol. Assn., Central Soc. Neurol. Research (pres. 1971), Sigma Xi, Alpha Omega Alpha. Home: 5529 Marblehead Dr Jackson MS 39211 Office: 2500 N State St Jackson MS 39216

CURRIVAN, JOHN DANIEL, lawyer; b. Paris, Jan. 15, 1947. B.S. with distinction, Cornell U., 1968; M.S., U. Calif.-Berkeley, 1969, U. West Fla., 1971; J.D. summa cum laude, Cornell Law Sch., 1978. Bar: Ohio 1978. Mng. ptnr. Southwest Devel. Co., Kingsville, Tex., 1971-76; note editor Cornell Law Review, Ithaca, N.Y., 1977-78; prosecutor, Naval Legal Office, Norfolk, Va., 1978-79, chief prosecutor, 1979-81; sr. atty. USS Nimitz, 1981-83; trial judge Naval Base, Norfolk, 1983-84; tax atty. Jones, Day, Reavis & Pogue, Cleve., 1984—. Recipient Kerr prize Cornell Law Sch., 1977, Corpus Juris Secundum award West Pub. Co., 1978, Younger Fed. Lawyer award Fed. Bar Assn., 1981. Mem. ABA, Ohio State Bar Assn., Nat. Assn. Bond Lawyers, Order of Coif, Tau Beta Pi, Eta Kappa Nu. Home: 2842 Sedgewick Rd Shaker Heights OH 44120 Office: Jones Day Reavis & Pogue 901 Lakeside Ave Cleveland OH 44114

CURRY, ALPHA OMEGA, psychologist, lecturer, educator, consultant; b. Ft. Lauderdale, Fla.; s. George Matthew and Lessie Lee (Allen) C. B.A., Pepperdine U., Los Angeles, 1972, M.A., 1973; M.S., Pa. State U., 1977, Ph.D., 1981. Pvt. tutor Pepperdine U., 1970-73; counselor, tchr. asst. Los Angeles Unified Schs., 1972-73; acad. advisor Pa. State U., 1975-76, counselor, 1976-79; instr. Rockview State Correctional Inst., Bellefonte, Pa., 1978-79; psychology intern Dept. Justice Fed. Prison System, Lompoc, Calif., 1979-80, clin. psychologist, 1980-87, dir. drug abuse program, 1982-87; chief psycology services, clin. psychologist Fed. Prison System Dept. Justice, Safford, Ariz., 1987—; adminstr. Suicide prevention companion observer program, 1987—; dir. chem. abuse program for chem. dependency substance abuse addictive behaviors, 1987—; author, researcher, cons. Am. Forum for Internat. Study, West Africa 1977. Vocalist Inland Choraleers, Zurich, Switzerland, 1969; active Affirmative Action, Equal Employment Opportunity, 1968—. Recipient numerous awards, Dept. Justice/Fed. Prison System, 1980—; USPHS fellow, 1974. Mem. Am. Psychol. Assn., Nat. Assn. Blacks in Criminal Justice, Assn. Black Psychologists (western region rep.), Nat. Assn. Black Psychologists (acting treas. 1987-88), AAUW, Las Flores Assn. Christian Women (pres. 1986-87), Psi Chi. Adventist. Club: Los Flores Christian Women's (Lompoc) (v.p. 1985-86). Office: Fed Correctional Inst Safford AZ 85546

CURRY, ANNE ELIZABETH, history educator; b. Durham, Eng., May 27, 1954; d. Ralph and Jean Mary (Whittaker) C.; m. John Geoffrey Painter, July 14, 1979; 1 child, Thomas Ralph Painter. BA in History, U. Manchester, Eng., 1975, MA, 1977; PhD, Council for Nat. Acad. Awards, 1985. Research asst. Teesside Poly., Middlesbrough, Eng., 1976-78; lectr. history U. Reading, Eng., 1978—; sec. U. Reading Grad. Ctr. for Medieval Studies, 1985—. Editor: (annual) Reading Medieval Studies, 1985—; contbr. articles to profl. jours. Fellow Royal Hist. Soc.; mem. Soc. de l'Histoire de France. Anglican. Home: 5 Melrose Ave, Reading RG6 2BN, England

CURRY, DONALD ROBERT, lawyer; b. Pampa, Tex., Aug. 7, 1943; s. Robert Ward and Alleith Elizabeth (Elliston) C.; m. Carolyn Sue Boland, Apr. 17, 1965; 1 son, James Ward. B.S., West Tex. State U., 1965; J.D., U. Tex., 1968. Bar: Tex. 1968, U.S. Dist. Ct. (no. dist.) Tex. 1970, U.S. Tax Ct. 1973. Assoc., Day & Gandy, Ft. Worth, 1968-69, ptnr., 1970-72; sole practice, Ft. Worth, 1972—; lectr. in field. Bd. regents West Tex. State U., Canyon, 1969-77, sec., mem. exec. com., 1972-75; mem. exec. bd. Longhorn council Boy Scouts Am., 1970—, dist. chmn., 1970-75; precinct chmn. Tarrant County (Tex.) Democratic Party, 1982—, election judge, 1982—. Mem. State Bar Tex., ABA, Fort Worth-Tarrant County Bar Assn., Ft. Worth Bus. and Estate Council, Tex. Ind. Producers and Royalty Owners Assn., Phi Alpha Delta. Methodist. Clubs: Ft. Worth, Petroleum of Fort Worth. Home: 3800 Tulsa Way Fort Worth TX 76107 Office: 905 Ft Worth Club Bldg Fort Worth TX 76102

CURRY, FRANCIS JOHN, physician; b. San Francisco, July 19, 1911; s. William Martin and Madonna (Burke) C.; m. Beryl Marguerite Swannel, Apr. 10, 1948; children: Francis John, Joan F., Elizabeth Anne, Patrick F., Thomas F., Robert, William, James. B.S., U. San Francisco, 1936, Sc.D. (hon.), 1984; M.D., Stanford U., 1946; M.P.H., U. Calif., 1964. Diplomate Am. Bd. Preventive Medicine. Teaching asst., research asst. Stanford U., 1942-43; intern San Francisco Gen. Hosp., 1945-46; resident Fresno (Calif.) Gen. Hosp., 1946-47; resident, asst. dir. Ahwahnee Tri-county Hosp., Madera, Calif., 1947-50; resident Santa Clara County (Calif.) Hosp., 1951-53; practice medicine specializing in pulmonary diseases and internal medicine San Francisco, 1956—; chief Tb div. San Francisco Health Dept., 1960-74, dir. health, hosps. and mental health, 1970-76; prof., spl. lectr. U. Calif., Berkeley, 1966—; prof. health care adminstr. Golden Gate U., 1973—; mem. staff San Francisco Gen. Hosp., 1956—, dir. chest clinic, 1956-74; mem. staff U. Calif. Hosp.; asst. clin. prof. medicine Stanford U., 1957-70, clin. prof., 1970—; asst. clin. prof. U. Calif., San Francisco, 1958-68, asso. clin. prof., 1968-70, clin. prof., 1970—; clin. prof. community dentistry U. Pacific, 1970—; project dir. Tb Control Project for San Francisco, USPHS, 1962-76; vice chmn. med. advisory com. San Francisco Hosp. Service Study Project, 1962—; mem. U. Calif. at San Francisco Gen. Hosp. Planning Com., 1963-78; mem. adv. council Tb Control Surgeon Gen. USPHS, 1965-78; cons., lectr. in field. Contbr. articles to profl. jours. Served as capt. AUS, 1953-55. Fellow ACP, Am. Coll. Preventive Medicine, Am. Coll. Chest Physicians (pres. Calif. chpt. 1962-63, regent 1971-78), Am. Pub. Health Assn.; mem. AMA, Calif. Med. Assn., Sci. Research Soc. Am., Am. Thoracic Soc., Royal Soc. Health, Acad. Preventive Medicine, Internat. Coll. Chest Physicians (dir. 1972-78), Am. Legion, Sigma Xi. Home: 350 Arballo Dr 4K San Francisco CA 94132 Office: U Calif Med Ctr Div Ambulatory & Com Medicine 3d & Parnassus Ave San Francisco CA 94143

CURTEIS, IAN BAYLEY, television playwright; b. London, May 1, 1935; m. Dorothy Joan Macdonald, 1964 (div.); 2 children; m. Joanna Trollope, 1985; 2 stepchildren. Dir., actor in theatres throughout U.K., BBC-TV script reader, 1956-63; staff dir. drama BBC and ATV, 1963-67; chmn. com. on censorship Writers' Guild Great Britain. Plays for TV include: Beethoven, Sir Alexander Fleming (BBC entry, Prague Festival 1973), Mr. Rolls and Mr. Royce, Long Voyage Out of War (trilogy), The Folly, The Haunting, Second Time Round, A Distant Chill, The Portland Millions, Philby, Burgess and Maclean (Brit. entry Monte Carlo Festival 1978), Hess, The Atom Spies, Churchill and the Generals (Grand Prize Best Programme 1980 New York Internat. Film and TV Festival), Suez 1956, Miss Morison's Ghosts (Brit. entry Monte Carlo Festival), BB and Lord D., Lost Empires, The Trials of Lady Sackville, Stalin, The Nightmare Years; screenplays include: La condition humaine (Andre Malraux), Tom Paine (for Sir Richard Attenborough), A Personal Affair 1982, Graham Green's The Man Wilhin. Author: Long Voyage out of War (trilogy), 1971; Churchill and the Generals, 1980; Suez, 1956, 1980; The Falklands Play, 1987. Address: The Mill House, Coln St Aldwyns, Cirencester Gloucestershire, England

CURTIN, BRIAN JOSEPH, ophthalmologist; b. N.Y.C., July 25, 1921; s. James Joseph and Julia Margaret (Smith) C.; m. Claire Margaret Flood, June 18, 1955; children—Edward Brian, James Martin, Thomas Hayes, Deirdre Claire. B.S., Fordham U., 1942; M.D., NYU, 1945. Intern St. Vincent's Hosp., N.Y.C., 1945-46; resident surgeon Manhattan Eye, Ear and Throat Hosp., 1950-53, asst. attending surgeon, asso. attending surgeon, 1953-74, surgeon dir., 1974—, pres. med. bd., 1977-79, vice chmn. dept. ophthalmology, 1983—; attending ophthalmologist, chief service Misericordia-Lincoln Affiliated Hosps., 1958-79; attending ophthalmologist N.Y. Hosp., 1969-84; assoc. attending ophthalmologist Columbia Presbyn. Med. Ctr., 1985—; asst. prof. clin. ophthalmology NYU, 1954-70; assoc. prof. clin. ophthalmology Cornell Med. Coll., 1970-84, Columbia U. Coll. Physicians and Surgeons, 1985—; chmn. med. adv. bd. Eye Bank for Sight Restoration, N.Y.C., 1978—; attending ophthalmologist, chmn. dept. St. Clare's Hosp. and Health Center, 1978-81. Editorial bd. Cornea, 1981-85; author: The Myopias: Basic Science and Clinical Management, 1985; contbr. chpts. to textbooks, articles to med. jours. Served with U.S. Navy, 1946-48. Mem. ACS, Am. Ophthalmol. Soc., AMA, N.Y. State Med. Soc., N.Y. County Med. Soc., N.Y. Acad. Medicine, N.Y. Acad. Scis., AAAS, Am. Acad. Ophthalmology, N.Y. Ophthal. Soc. (v.p. 1981-82, pres. 1982-83), Am. Eye Study Club. Roman Catholic. Club: Siwanoy Country. Home: 2 Stoneleigh Plaza Bronxville NY 10708 Office: 133 E 58th St New York NY 10022

CURTIN, RICHARD DANIEL, management consultant, retired air force officer; b. Taunton, Mass., Apr. 2, 1915; s. Patrick Henry and Della (Hart) C.; m. Mary Shirley Ray, May 10, 1969. Student, Brown U., 1933-35; B.Sc., U.S. Mil. Acad., 1939; M.Sc., U. Mich., 1950. Commd. 2d lt. U.S. Army, 1939; advanced through grades to maj. gen. USAF, 1963; various assignments U.S., Panama, Eng., France, Germany, 1939-46; instr. Air U., Maxwell AFB, Ala., 1946-48; plans officer, war plans div. Hdqrs. USAF, Washington, 1950-54; dir. plans, later chief staff Hdqrs. 17th AF, N.Africa, 1954-56; exec. weapons systems Hdqrs. ARDC, Balt., 1956-58; asst. dep. comdr. tech. ops., dep. comdr. space programs AF Ballistic Missile Div., Inglewood, Calif., 1958-60; dir. systems devel., DCS/D, Hdqrs. USAF, Washington, 1960; dir. Office Space Programs, Office Sec. Air Force, Washington, 1960-62; dir. devel. plans DCS/R&D, Hdqrs. USAF, Washington, 1962-65; dep. U.S. def. advisor NATO, Paris, 1965-67; ret. NATO, 1967; dir. mgmt. engring. Bell Aerosystems Co., Buffalo, 1967-68; group v.p., dir. Southwestern Research Corp., Phoenix, 1968-70; pres. Dynamic System Electronics, Tempe, Ariz., 1968-70; v.p. Planning Research Corp., Chgo., 1970-73; gen. mgr. The Jacobs Co., Chgo., 1970-73; dir. tech. mgmt. Am. Def. Preparedness Assn., Washington, 1973-77; pres. Curtin Assos., Inc., Phoenix, 1977—, Petro Pure Corp., Palm Springs, 1981—. Mem. adv. bd. Heard Mus., Phoenix. Decorated Legion of Merit with clusters, Bronze Star with cluster; D.S.M.; Dept. Air Force; Croix de Guerre, etoile Vermeille. Asso. fellow AIAA; mem. Nat. Mcpl. League, Air Force Assn., Brown U. Alumni Assn., U. Mich. Alumni Assn., Assn. Grads. U.S. Mil. Acad. Club: Army-Navy. Home: 19434 Camino del Sol Sun City West AZ 85375

CURTIS, ALVA MARSH, artist; b. N.Y.C., June 15, 1911; d. Charles Johan and Elizabeth (Hagstrom) Berg; student Art Students League, N.Y.C., 1928-29, Grand Central Art Sch., 1934-36, N.Y. Sch. Fine Arts, 1930-31, Nat. Acad., N.Y.C., 1934-35, Columbia U., 1943-44, Yale U., 1969-70; m. Terrill Belknap Marsh, Nov. 3, 1932; children—Owen Thayer, Charles Ames, Ronald Belknap; m. Russell G. Curtis, Aug. 11, 1979; children—Russell G. Jr., William E. One woman shows: Scranton Meml. Library, Madison, Conn., 1969, Phippsburg (Maine) Library, 1964, Town and County Club, Hartford, Conn., 1976, Conn. Bank & Trust Co., Madison, 1977, 1st Fed. Savs. & Loan, Madison, 1977; group shows include: The Mariner's Mus., Newport News, Va., Va. Salmagundi Club, N.Y.C., Smithsonian Inst., Washington, 1964, 66, Internat. Maritime Art Award Show (Sculpture award), 1981, Nat. League Am. Penwomen Art Show (Sculpture award), Atlanta, 1982, Arnold Gallery, Newport, R.I., 1984, Copley Gallery, Boston, 1986, Candlewood Gallery (Sculpture award 1986), New Milford, Conn., 1986; represented in permanent collections: Swedish Club, Chgo., Conn. Bank & Trust Co., Windsor, Phippsburg Library, also pvt. collections; partner, art dir. Terrill Belknap Marsh, Assos., N.Y.C., 1934-69; lectr. in field. Vice chmn. Madison Inland Wetlands Agy., 1974-84. Mem. Am. Soc. Marine Artists, New Eng. Sculpture Assn., Nat. Arts Club, Nat. League Am. Penwomen (pres. 1978—, Greenwich br. 1958). Republican. Episcopalian. Clubs: Lyme Art Assn., Madison Winter, Garden Madison. Home: 12 Dogwood Ln Madison CT 06443

CURTIS, GREGORY DYER, investment and philanthropic company executive; b. Mechanicsburg, Ohio, Jan. 14, 1947; s. Vernon L. and Jean (Dyer) C.; m. Lynne Everett, June 29, 1968; children: Sarah E., Alice D. AB cum laude, Dartmouth Coll., 1969; JD cum laude, Harvard U., 1974. Bar: Pa. 1974, U.S. Dist. Ct. (we. dist.) Pa. 1974. Assoc. Reed, Smith, Shaw & McClay, Pitts., 1974-79; counsel Roldiva, Inc., Pitts., 1979-81, v.p., bd. dirs., 1981-83; fin. adv. C.S. May Family Interests, Pitts., 1983—; pres. Laurel Found., Pitts., 1983—; pres., bd. govs. Laurel Assets Group, Pitts., 1983—; bd. dirs. Clark Techs., Inc., Boulder, Enrecon, Inc., Golden, Colo., L.C. Holdings, Inc., Boulder, Phoenix Technologies, Inc., Denver, Water Resources Am., Tulsa, Western Water Reserves, Inc., Boulder, Sewickley Heights Estates, Inc., Pitts., Tenir, Inc., Pitts., Winding River Properties, Inc., St. George, Utah. Mem. legal com. ACLU, Pitts., 1974-78; bd. dirs. Neighborhood Legal Services Assn., Pitts., 1976-79, Grantmakers Western Pa., Pitts., 1986—, The Ellis Sch., 1987—. Served to sgt. U.S. Army, 1970-72. Mem. ABA, Allegheny County Bar Assn. Club: Duquesne (Pitts.), Rolling Rock (Ligonier). Home: No 8 Dunmoyle Pl Pittsburgh PA 15217 Office: Laurel Found 3 Gateway Ctr-6 N Pittsburgh PA 15222

CURTIS, JAMES RICHARD, flight engineer; b. Champaign, Ill., Feb. 2, 1930; s. John Wesley and Jessie May (Quackenbush) C.; m. Constance Ann Sticher, Jan. 10, 1954; children: Christie Lynn, James Richard Jr., Stephen Lawrence. Student, U. Ill., 1947-48. Profl. flight engr.; cert. airframe and power plant mechanic, commercial pilot. Plant mgr. Dean's Dairy, Champaign, 1947-50; draftsman C.S. Johnson Co., Champaign, 1955; aircraft mechanic Am. Airlines, Ft. Worth, 1955; flight engr. Chgo., 1956—; trained flight crews Spantax Airlines, Madrid, 1966-69, Middle East Airlines, Beirut, Lebanon, 1966-69; check airman, flight engring. instr. Am. Airlines, Chgo., 1964—; examiner designee, FAA, Chgo., 1966-67. Served as sgt. USAF, 1950-54. Mem. Flight Engrs. Internat. Assn.

CURTIS, JAMES THEODORE, lawyer; b. Lowell, Mass., July 8, 1923; s. Theodore D. and Maria (Souliotis) Koutras; B.A., U. Mich., 1948; J.D., Harvard, 1951; Sc.D. (hon.), U. Lowell, 1972; m. Kleanthe D. Dusopol June 25, 1950; children—Madelon Mary, Theodore James, Stephanie Diane, Gregory Theodosius, James Theodore. Admitted to Mass. State bar, 1951; asso. Adams & Blinn, Boston, 1951-52; legal asst., asst. atty. gen. Mass., 1952-53; pvt. practice law, Lowell, 1953-57; sr. partner firm Goldman & Curtis, and predecessors, Lowell and Boston, 1957—. Chmn. Lowell and Greater Lowell Heart Fund, 1967-68; mem. adv. bd. Salvation Army, sec., 1956-58; mem. Bd. Higher Edn. Mass., 1967-72; mem. Lowell Charter Commn., 1969-71; del. Democratic Party State Convs., 1956-60; trustee U. Lowell, 1963-72, chmn. bd., 1968-72; bd. dirs. U. Lowell Research Found., 1965-72, Merrimack Valley Health Planning Council, 1969-72. Served with AUS, 1943-46. Decorated Knight Order Orthodox Crusade Holy Sepulcher. Mem. Am., Mass., Middlesex County, Lowell bar assns., Am., Mass. trial lawyers assns., Mass. Acad. Trial Lawyers, Am. Judicature Soc., Harvard Law Sch., U. Mich. alumni assns., Lowell Hist. Soc., DAV, Delta Epsilon Pi. Democrat. Greek Orthodox. Clubs: Masons, Harvard of Lowell (pres. 1969-71, dir.). Home: 111 Rivercliff Rd Lowell MA 01852 Office: 144 Merrimack St Lowell MA 01852

CURTISS, THOMAS, JR., lawyer, educator; b. Buffalo, Nov. 4, 1941; s. Thomas and Hope (Middleton Plumb) C.; B.A., Yale U., 1963; J.D., Harvard U., 1970. Bar: Calif. 1971. Assoc., Musick, Peeler & Garrett, Los Angeles, 1970-72; assoc. Macdonald, Halsted & Laybourne, Los Angeles, 1972-76, ptnr., 1976-88; ptnr. Baker & McKenzie, Los Angeles, 1988—; adj. prof. Loyola U., Los Angeles Law Sch., 1982—. Mem. vestry Trinity Episcopal Ch., Los Angeles, sr. warden, 1982, 84-86; mem. Commn. on Ordained Ministry, Diocese of Los Angeles, 1983-88; mem. Music Center Found. Legal Com. Served to maj. USMCR, 1963-78. Mem. ABA (mem. sect. real property, probate and trust law), Los Angeles County Bar Assn. (exec. com., probate and trust law sect.). Contbr. articles to profl. jours. Home: 2250 Micheltorena St Los Angeles CA 90039 Office: Baker & McKenzie 725 S Figueroa St 36th Floor Los Angeles CA 90017

CUSACK, CYRIL JAMES, actor, writer; b. Durban, Nov. 26, 1910; s. James Walter and Alice Violet (Cole) C.; ed. Univ. Coll., Dublin, Nat. U.; m. Mary Margaret Kiely, 1945; 2 sons, 4 daus. Joined Abbey Theatre, Dublin, 1932; actor Nat. Theatre, Dublin, 1932, 45, 46, asso., shareholder, 1966—; producer Gaelic Players, 1935-36; mng. dir. Cyril Cusack Prodns., 1946-61; 1st London appearance in Ah Wilderness, 1936; leading roles in Ireland, U.K., Broadway, including Playboy of the Western World, The Moon for the Misbegotten, Julius Caesar, The Physicists, Andorra, The Cherry Orchard, Mr. O, Arms and the Man (Internat. Critics' award 1961), Krapp's Last Tape (Internat. Critics' award 1961), The Plow and the Stars, A life; films include: The Small Back Room, Odd Man Out, The Elusive Pimpernel, The Man Who Never Was, Ill Met by Moonlight, A Terrible Beauty, The Blue Veil, Johnny Nobody, The Waltz of the Toreadors, I Thank a Fool, 80,000 Suspects, One Spy Too Many, The Spy Who Came in from the Cold, The Taming of the Shrew, Oedipus Rex, Galileo Galilei, King Lear, David Copperfield, Country Dance, Day of the Jackal, Juggernaut, The Temptation of Mr. O; also TV appearances. Author: Timepieces (poems), 1970. Office: 2 Vincent Terr, London N1 England *

CUSHING, HARRY COOKE, IV, retired investment banker; b. N.Y.C.; s. Harry Cooke and Cathleen (Vanderbilt) C.; m. Ruth Swift Dunbar, Jan. 14, 1961 (div.); 1 son, Harry Cooke V.; m. Laura Alvarez, Jan. 23, 1976 (div.). Student, Cornell U., 1945. Adviser for European ops. to chmn. bd. Ventures Ltd., 1955-59; pvt. adviser individuals and corps. 1966; ltd. partner Hallgarten & Co., N.Y.C., 1966-74; bd. dirs. Biskra Realty, Inc., The Future Group, Inc. Chmn. polo com. People-to-People Sports Com., 1962—. Served with AUS, 1942-46. Decorated commendatore Order Crown of Italy. Mem. S.R. Clubs: Turf (London), White's (London); Travellers (Paris), Polo (Paris); Polo (Rome), Golf (Rome); Hurlingham (Buenos Aires, Argentina); Racquet and Tennis (N.Y.C.), Brook (N.Y.C.); Corviglia (St. Moritz, Switzerland); Palm Beach Polo and Country, Malta Polo. Address: Via Barnaba Oriani 36, Rome Italy

CUSHING, PETER WILTON, actor; b. Kenley, Surrey, Eng., May 26, 1913; s. George Henry and Nellie Maria (King) C.; ed. Purley County Schs.; m. Violet Helene Beck, Apr. 10, 1943. Actor in plays: War and Peace, 1943; Richard III, 1948; The School for Scandal, 1949; The Soldrier and the Lady, 1954; The Silver Whistle, 1956; The Heiress, 1975; films include The Man in the Iron Mask, 1939; Alexander the Great, 1933, The Curse of Frankenstein, 1957; The Hound of the Baskervilles, 1959; Dr. Terror's House of Horrors, 1964; Star Wars, 1976; Touch of the Sun, 1978; A Tale of Two Cities, 1980; She, 1984; others; also TV and radio. Author: Peter Cushing: An Autobiography, 1986, Past Forgetting—Memoirs of the Hammer Years, 1988. Recipient Daily Mail TV award, 1954; TV Guild award, 1955; award 2d Conv. Franç aise du Cinema Fantastique, 1973. Office: 16 Berners St, London W1P 3DD England Other: care John Redway, CMA Ltd, 22 Grafton St, London W1 England

CUSHING, STEVEN, computer science educator, consultant; b. Brookline, Mass., June 25, 1948; s. Alfred Edward and Evelyn (Kaufman) C. SB, MIT, 1970; MA, UCLA, 1972, PhD, 1976. Research asst. MIT, 1967-70, UCLA, 1973-74; instr. U. Mass., Boston, 1974-75; Roxbury Community Coll., Boston, 1975-77; research staff Higher Order Software Inc., Cambridge, Mass., 1976-82; research assoc. Rockefeller U., N.Y.C., 1979; lectr. Northeastern U., Boston, 1983-86; master lectr. Boston U., 1986—; research fellow NASA-Ames Research Ctr., Moffet Field, Calif., 1987-88, Stanford U., Palo Alto, Calif., 1987-88; asst. prof St. Anselm Coll., Manchester, N.H., 1983-85, Stonehill Coll., North Easton, Mass., 1985—; mem. bd. editorial commentators The Behavioral and Brain Scis., 1978—; chmn. software design Internat. Conf. System Scis., Honolulu, 1978; participant workshops. Author: Quantifier Meanings: A Study in the Dimensions of Semantic Competence, 1982; contbr. articles to profl. jours. Mem. nat. exec. council Nat. Ethical Youth Orgn., 1965-66; violist Brockton (Mass.) Symphony Orch. Recipient New Eng. Regional award Future Scientists of Am., 1965; NSF grantee, 1965, 70-71, NIMH grantee, 1970-71, NDEA grantee, 1970-73; Woodrow Wilson Found. fellow, 1970-71, NASA Summer Faculty fellow, 1987-88; research affiliate MIT, 1978-79; Boston U., 1986-88. Mem. AAAS, N.Y. Acad. Scis., Linguistic Soc. Am., Assn. Symbolic Logic, Assn. Computing Machinery, Am. Math. Soc., Am. Assn. for Applied Linguistics, Internat. Council Psychologists (profl. affiliate), Assn. for Computers and Humanities, Cognitive Sci. Soc., Math. Assn. Am., Assn. Computational Linguistics, Internat. Pragmatics Assn. Home: 90 Bynner St #4 Jamaica Plain MA 02130 Office: Stonehill Coll Dept Math and Computer Sci North Easton MA 02357

CUSTODIO, DEOGRACIAS BANABAN, oncologist; b. Cavite, Philippines, Aug. 29, 1935; s. Domingo Barrera and Encarnacion (Banaban) C.; m. Eleanor Palafox, Dec. 1, 1962; children: Deogracias Gerard, Paul Jerome. Dr. med., U. Philippines, 1960. Diplomate Philippine Bd. Oncology. Intern St. Peter's Hosp., Albany, N.Y., 1960-61; sr. resident Kingsbrook Jewish Med. Ctr., 1961-64; fellow oncology Maimonides Med. Ctr., Bklyn., 1965-67; sect. chief Up-PGH Med. Ctr., Manila, 1967-71; mem. staff Makat Med. Ctr., Manila, 1968, Manila Med. Ctr., 1967—; cons. in field. Contbr. articles to profl. jours. Fellow Philippine Soc. Oncologists; mem. Philippine Soc. Med. Oncology (chartered mem.), Philippine Columbian Assn., Philippine Med. Assn., Philippine Soc. Med. Oncology (pres. 1971-76), Am. Soc. Clin. Oncology, Soc. Gynecologic Oncologists (dir. 1985-87), Internat. Gynecologic Cancer Soc., N.Y. Acad. Sci. Clubs: Filipino, Valle Verde Country, Greenhill Tennis. Home: 19 Polk St Greenhills, San Juan, Metro Manila Philippines Office: Makati Med Ctr, Amorsolo St, Makati, Metro Manila Philippines

CUTHBERT, JACK AGNEW, architect; b. Winnipeg, Man., Can., June 30, 1929; s. Charles Leslie and Margaret (Agnew) C. BArch, U. Man., Winnipeg, 1951. Registered architect, Minn. Asst. architect Can. Nat. Railways, Montreal, Que., 1951-54; architect various firms, Winnipeg, 1954-65, Toltz, King, Duvall & Anderson, Architects Engrs., St. Paul, 1969-71, Gen. Housing Industries, State Coll., Pa., 1971-72, Giffels Assoc. Inc. Architects Engrs., Detroit, 1972-76, So. Calif. Edison, Rosemead, 1978-80; prin. J.A. Cuthbert, Architect, Surrey, B.C., Can., 1965-69, 82—. Prin. works include Delineations on exhibition to Architectural League N.Y. Mem. AIA. Club: Fairlane. Home and Office: 2550 142nd St, Surrey, BC Canada

CUTHBERTSON, ROBERT FRED, physician; b. Phoenix, Dec. 15, 1929; s. Fred A. and Mary Catherine (Crowell) C.; student Phoenix Jr. Coll., 1947-49, U. Calif.-Berkeley, 1949-50; M.D., U. So. Calif., 1954; m. Shirley June Hermann, June 27, 1953; children—Robert Fred, Karen Suzanne, Susan Lynn. Intern, Los Angeles County Gen. Hosp., 1954-55; resident U.S. Naval Sch. of Aviation Medicine, Pensacola, Fla., 1955-56; practice family medicine, Phoenix, 1958—; pres. Saguaro Med. Center, Phoenix, 1969—; chmn. com. designing health edn. State of Ariz., 1973—. Bus. project mgr. Jr. Achievement, 1981. Served as lt. comdr., flight surgeon M.C., USNR, 1955-60. Diplomate Am. Bd. Family Practice. Fellow Am. Acad. Family Physicians; mem. AMA, Soaring Soc. Am. Mem. Ch. Jesus Christ of Latter-day Saints. Club: Rotary (past pres., Phoenix camelback gov. dist. 549, 1985-86). Office: Saguaro Med Ctr Ltd 4426 E Indian Sch Rd Phoenix AZ 85018 also: 10250 N 92d St Scottsdale AZ 85258

CUTLER, ARNOLD R., lawyer; b. New Haven, Mar. 20, 1908; s. Max Nathan and Kate (Harder) C.; m. Hazel Lourie, Apr. 8, 1942; 1 son, David. B.A., Yale U., 1930, J.D., 1932. Bar: Conn. 1932, Mass. 1946. Mem. staff Office of Gen. Counsel, Pub. Works Adminstrn., Washington, 1933-36; chief counsel State of Wash., 1937-38; spl. asst. to chief counsel IRS, 1939-42, trial counsel New Eng. div., 1945-47; ptnr. Lourie & Cutler, Boston, 1947—; lectr. on taxation. Contbr. to books articles to legal jours. Trustee Beth Israel Hosp.; trustee Brandeis U.; trustee, past mem. exec. com. Combined Jewish Philanthropies Greater Boston; past. bd. dirs. Nat. Jewish Welfare Bd.; past pres. Brookline, Brighton and Newton Jewish Community Center; past. treas. Associated Jewish Community Centers of Greater Boston; past chmn. bd. Yale Law Sch. Fund; chmn. bequest com. Yale Law Sch. Lt. comdr. USCG, 1942-45. Fellow Am. Coll. Tax Counsel, Mass. Bar Found.; mem. ABA (com. on govt. submissions 1987—, past chmn. spl. adv. exempt orgns. com. tax sect.), Mass. Bar Assn., Boston Bar Assn. (past chmn. fed. tax com., past mem. council), Am. Law Inst. Clubs: New Century (past pres.), Greater Boston Brandeis (past pres.), Yale, Harvard, Wightman Tennis, Rotary (past bd. dirs.). Office: Lourie & Cutler 60 State St Boston MA 02109

CUTLER, RUTH ELLEN LEMON, publisher; b. York, Nebr., Feb. 26, 1928; d. Harry Oliver and Ruby Elizabeth (Hartgrave) Lemon; m. Harold Max Cutler, Nov. 17, 1944 (div. 1971); children—Sheryl, Harold Max, Pamela. Student Latter-day Saints Bus. Coll., 1946. Sec., photostat operator IRS, Salt Lake City, 1951-54; sec. Purdue U. Sch. Civil Engring., West Lafayette, Ind. and engring. firms, 1954-60; exec. sec. Rico Argentine Mining Co., Salt Lake City and Rico, Colo., 1960-63; exec., legal sec. Manpower, Inc., Salt Lake City, 1959-71; owner, operator Mountain View Motel and Country Club Motel, Salt Lake City, 1963-64; exec. sec., adminstrv. asst. to clin. psychologist in pvt. practice, Salt Lake City, 1964-70; legal sec., head office staff Watkins & Faber, attys., Salt Lake City, 1971-73; adminstrv. sec. F-15 Radar div. Hughes Aircraft Co., El Segundo, Calif., 1973—; dir., v.p., sec. Cutler Enterprises, Inc., Salt Lake City, 1963-71; founder, pres., pub., bd. dirs. Gallant House Inc., Heber City, Utah, 1983—. Utah Rep. del., 1967-69; active various community drives. Mem. League Utah Writers. Home: 8628 S 300 E Sandy UT 84070

CUTLER, WALTER LEON, diplomat; b. Boston, Nov. 25, 1931; s. Walter Leon and Esther Dewey (Bradley) C.; m. Sarah G. Beeson, Mar. 16, 1957 (div. 1981); children: Allen Bradley, Thomas Gerard.; m. Isabel K. Brookfield, Nov. 28, 1981. B.A., Wesleyan U., Middletown, Conn., 1953; M.A., Fletcher Sch. Law and Diplomacy, 1954. Joined U.S. Fgn. Service, 1956; vice consul Am. consulate Yaounde, Cameroon, 1957-59; fgn. affairs officer Dept. State, Washington, 1959-60; staff asst. to sec. of state Dept. State, 1960-62; 2d sec. Am. Embassy Algiers, Algeria, 1962-65; prin. officer Am. Consulate Tabriz, Iran, 1965-67; polit. officer, 1st sec. Am. Embassy Seoul, Korea, 1967-69, Saigon, Vietnam, 1969-71; fgn. affairs officer Dept. State, 1971-73; mem. Sr. Seminar in Fgn. Policy, 1973-74; dir. Office Central African Affairs, 1974-75; ambassador to Zaire 1975-79, ambassador-designate to Iran, 1979; dep. asst. sec. for congl. relations Dept. State, Washington, 1979-81; ambassador to Tunisia 1982-84, ambassador to Saudi Arabia, 1984-87, 1988—; research prof. diplomacy Georgetown U., Washington, 1987-88. Served with U.S. Army, 1954-56. Recipient Disting. Alumnus award Wesleyan U., 1983, King Abdul Aziz award, Saudi Arabia, 1986, Presdl. Performance award, 1986, 87; decorated Order of the Leopard, Zaire, 1979. Mem. Council Fgn. Relations, Am. Fgn. Service Assn. Club: Metropolitan (Washington). Office: Am Embassy, Riyadh 11143, Saudi Arabia *

CUTLIP, RANDALL BROWER, psychologist, college president emeritus; b. Clarksburg, W.Va., Oct. 1, 1916; s. M.N. and Mildred (Brower) C.; m. Virginia White, Apr. 21, 1951; children: Raymond Bennett, Catherine Baumgarten. A.B., Bethany Coll., 1940; student, So. Meth. U., 1944; M.A., East Tex. U., 1949; Ed.D., U. Houston, 1953; LL.D., Bethany Coll., 1965, Columbia Coll., 1980; L.H.D., Drury Coll., 1975; Sc.D., S.W. Bapt. Coll., 1978; Litt.D., William Woods Coll., 1981. Tchr., adminstr. Tex. pub. schs., 1947-50; dir. tchr. placement U. Houston, 1950-51, supr. counselling, 1951-53; dean students Atlantic Christian Coll., Wilson, N.C., 1953-56, dean, 1956-58; dean personnel, dir. grad. div. Chapman Coll., Orange, Calif., 1958-60; pres. William Woods Coll., Fulton, Mo., 1960-81, pres. emeritus, 1981—, trustee, 1981-85; chmn. bd. dirs. Mo. Colls. Fund, 1973-75; chmn. Mid-Mo. Assn. Colls., 1972-76; pres. bd. dirs. Marina del Sol, 1985-88. Bd. visitors Mo. Mil. Acad., 1966—, chmn. bd. visitors, 1968-73; trustee Schreiner Coll., Kerrville, Tex., 1983—, Amy McNutt Charitable Trust, 1983—; bd. dirs. U. of Ams., Puebla, Mex., 1984—, exec. v.p., 1985—; elder 1st Christina Ch., pres., bd. dirs. Marina del Sol, 1985—. Served with AUS, 1943-45. Recipient McCubbin award, 1968, Delta Beta Xi award, 1959. Mem. Am. Personnel and Guidance Assn., Alpha Sigma Phi, Phi Delta Kappa, Kappa Delta Pi, Alpha Chi. Address: 1400 Ocean Dr Corpus Christi TX 78404

CUTNAW (CUGNEAU), MARY-FRANCES, speech educator, writer; b. Dickinson, N.D., June 15, 1931; d. Delbert A. and Edith (Calhoun Pritchard) Cutnaw; B.S., U. Wis.-Mdison, 1953, M.S., 1957, doctoral candidate, 1959-60, 67-68. Tchr., Community Service Displaced Persons Vocat. Sch., Stevens Point, Wis., 1951-52, Pulaski High Sch., Milw., 1953-55; teaching asst. dept. speech U. Wis.-Madison, 1956-57, spl. asst. Sch. Edn., summer 1957; instr. speech and English, U. Wis.-Stout, Menomonie, 1957-58, dean of women, 1958-59, asst. prof. speech, 1959-64, assoc. prof., 1964-74, prof. emeritus, 1974—; hon. scholar, teaching asst. dept. speech U. Wis.-Madison, 1959-60, hon. scholar dept. speech, 1967-68. Organizer, past adviser Young Democratic Orgn., U. Wis.-Stout. Mem. Internat. Platform Assn., Progressive Round Table, U. Wis. Alumni Assn., Assn. U. Wis. Faculties, Wis. Acad. Scis., Arts and Letters, Wis. Women's Network, Am. Quarter Horse Assn., Nat. Soc. Prevention Cruelty to Animals, Nat. Anti-Vivisection Soc., Nat. Ret. Tchrs. Assn., Am. Personnel and Guidance Assn., Smithsonian Asso., Linus Pauling Inst., Center for Study Democratic Instns., ACLU, Common Cause, NOW, Walker Art Center, Phi Beta, Sigma Tau Delta, Pi Lambda Theta, Gamma Phi Beta. Roman Catholic. Clubs: University (St. Paul); Blaisdell Place (dir.), Calhoun Beach. Contbr. articles to profl. jours. Research in speech proficiency and teaching success, curricular speech for spl. occupational groups, speech as guidance tool. Founder, Edith and Kent P. Cutnaw Scholarship, U. Wis.-Stevens Point. Home: Red Cedar Farm Box 282 Menomonie WI 54751 also: Cedars on the St Croix Box 176 Lakeland MN 55043

CUTNER, ROLANDE REGAT, lawyer; b. Paris, Sept. 6, 1934; came to U.S., 1963, naturalized, 1970; d. Luis Felipe and Marguerite (Thibault) Ibarra; m. Charles Yves Regat, Feb. 4, 1960 (dec. 1971); m. David Alan Cutner, June 25, 1977 (div. 1985). Diploma in Polit. Sci., U. Paris, 1959; Lic. in Law, Paris Faculty of Law, 1971; grad. Inst. Jud. Studies, 1972. Bar: Paris 1976, N.Y. 1978, U.S. Dist. Ct. (so. dist.) N.Y. 1978. Atty. Compagnie General d'Electricite, Paris, 1972-76, Usinor Steel Corp., N.Y.C., 1976-77; mem. firm Griggs, Baldwin & Baldwin, 1978-79, Regat-Cutner, 1980—. Mem. Internat. Bar Assn., ABA, Am. Fgn. Law Assn., Fed. Bar Council, Ordre des Avocats a la Cour de Paris, N.Y. County Lawyer Assn. (com. on immigration, nationality, and naturalization), Asia-Pacific Lawyers Assn. (com. on Customs and Internat. Trade Law). Home: 67 Park Ave One Wall St New York NY 10016 Office: Regat-Cutner 67 Park Ave Suite 12 D New York NY 10006

CUTRONE, LUIGI CUTRONE, chemist; b. Ielsi, Italy, May 18, 1950; s. Pasquale and Giovanna (Passarelli) C.; m. Maria Teresa Maiorano, Aug. 8, 1976; children: Giovanna, Pasquale, Annarita. BSc in Chemistry, Loyola Coll., Montreal, Can., 1974; MS in Organic Chemistry, McGill U., Montreal, Can., 1980. Research and devel. chemist M.F. Paints 1972, Laval, Que., Can., 1977-81; application devel. Tioxide Can. Inc., Tracy, Que., 1981-85; section. mgr. Tioxide UK Ltd, Stockton-on-Tees, Eng., 1985-87; tech. service mgr. Tioxide Italia, Scarlino, 1987—. Contbr. articles to profl. jours. Fellow Oil and Colour Assn.; mem. Fedn. Coating Soc. Roman Catholic. Office: Tioxide Italia SPA, Contrada Casone CP 113, 58022 Follonica Italy

CUYPERS, JAN HENDRIK, dairy company executive, consultant; b. Heythuysen, Netherlands, Aug. 7, 1936; s. Frans Joseph and Nelly Henrica (Poels) C.; m. Marijke Johanna Kranendijk, Aug. 22, 1969; children—Jan-Mathijs, Henriette Anne, Floris-Jan. Grad., Episcopal Coll., Weert, Netherlands, 1956; M.Sc., Cath. U., Nijmegen, Netherlands, 1965; postgrad. Centre d'Etudes Industrielles, Geneva, 1970, INSEAD, Fontainebleau, France, 1972, Mgmt. Centre Europe/Am. Mgmt. Assn., Brussels, 1982-87. Product mgr., tng. officer, internat. mktg. mgr. Unilever NV, Rotterdam, Netherlands, 1966-73; mktg. mgr. Ahold NV, Zaandam, Netherlands, 1973-76; gen. mgr. Ahrend BV, Amsterdam, Netherlands, 1976-79; pres. NV Provinciale Gelderse Energie-Maatschappij, Arnhem, Netherlands, 1979-87 ; pres. Melkunie Holland BV, Woerden, Netherlands, 1988—; dir. Tyresoles Rubberindustrie BV, Naarden, Netherlands, 1982—; chmn. bd. Ossfloor Netherlands BV; dir. Coopra-Rotterdam BA, VEG-Gasinstituut NV, Apeldoorn, Netherlands, NV Dutch Nuclear Power Plant, Arnhem, Netherlands, Peinjnenburg's Koekfabrieken, Geldrop, Netherlands. Author: Handboek voor Managers, 1979; Handbook for Marketing Management, 1983. Editor: Handboek voor Commerciele Beleidsvraagstukken, 1980, Overheidsmgmt. 1987. Pres. local tourist, trade assns., Doetinchem, Netherlands, 1983-87. Served with Dutch Army, 1957-58. Mem. Netherlands Assn. Dirs. Electricity Cos. (bd. dirs.), Netherlands Mgmt. Assn. (pres. 1984—), Netherlands Mktg. Assn. (pres. 1974-78), Netherlands Inst. for Mgmt. Info. Studies, Netherlands Social-Econ. Council/Bus. Devel. Com. (adv. bd. 1979-85). Christian Democrat. Roman Catholic. Club: Hilversum Lions. Office: Melkunie Holland BV, PO Box 222, 3440 AE Woerden De Bleek 1, 3447 GV Woerden The Netherlands

CYBUL, MARTIN JAY, architect; b. Bklyn., May 6, 1951; s. David N. and Norma T. (Trugerman) C.; m. Miriam Karen Strickler, Mar. 27, 1982; children: Brandt J., Mathew S. BArch., Tulane U., 1974; MArch., MIT, 1976; student Nottingham U.-Eng., 1972-73. Registered architect, N.J., N.Y., Mass., Conn. Research asst. MIT, Cambridge, Mass., 1974-75, 75-76; designer/draftsman Khachadourian & Cahill, Bloomfield, N.J., 1973, 74, 75, 1976-77, Miele Assocs., Queens, N.Y., 1977, David N. Cybul, Edgewater, N.J., 1977-79; ptnr. Cybul & Cybul, Architects, Edgewater, 1980—; adj. prof. N.J. Inst. Tech., 1981-82, spl. lectr., 1982-86. MIT fellow, 1975, 76; Clarence Tabor scholar, 1976; NSF grantee, 1972. Mem. AIA, N.J. Soc. Architects, Architects League No. N.J., Nat. Council Archtl. Registration Bds., Tau Sigma Delta. Home: Warren Ln Alpine NJ 07620 Office: Cybul & Cybul Architects 1064 River Rd Edgewater NJ 07020

CYERT, RICHARD MICHAEL, economist, university president; b. Winona, Minn., July 22, 1921; s. Walter Michael and Anne Fostine (Brown) C.; m. Margaret Shadick, Sept. 8, 1946; children: Lynn Cyert Westbrook, Lucinda Carol Steffes, Martha Sue. B.S. in Econs., U. Minn., 1943; Ph.D., Columbia U., 1951; Ph.D. (hon.), U. Gothenburg, Sweden, 1972, U. Leuven, Belgium, 1973; LL.D. (hon.), Waynesburg Coll., 1979, Allegheny Coll., 1980; D.Sc. (hon.), Westminster Coll., 1979; Ed.D. (hon.), Bethany Coll., W.Va., 1984, La Roche Coll., 1986. Instr. U. Minn., 1946, CUNY, 1948; instr. econs. Carnegie Inst. Tech. (now Carnegie-Mellon U.), Pitts., 1948-49; asst. prof. econs. and indsl. adminstrn. Carnegie Inst. Tech. (now Carnegie-Mellon U.), 1949-55, assoc. prof. econs. and indsl. adminstr., head indsl. mgmt. dept., 1955-60, prof. econs. and indsl. adminstrn., 1960-62, dean Grad. Sch. Indsl. Adminstrn., 1962-72, pres., 1972—; dir. First Boston Corp., Inc., Allegheny Internat. Inc., Strategic Planning Assn., Copperweld Corp., H.J. Heinz Co., Regional Indsl. Devel. Corp. Author: (with R.M. Trueblood) Sampling Techniques in Accounting, 1957, (with H.J. Davidson) Sampling for Accounting Information, 1962, (with J.G. March) A Behavioral Theory of the Firm, 1963, (with K.J. Cohen) Theory of the Firm: Resource Allocation in a Market Economy, 1965; editor: (with L.A. Welsch) Management Decision Making, 1970; author: (with L.A. Welsch) Management of Non-Profit Organizations: With Emphasis on Universities, 1975, (with R.L. Ackoff and H.D. Wood) Decision Making Under Uncertainty and Managerial Leadership, 1977, (with C. Argyris) Leadership in the 80's: Essays on Higher Education, 1980, The American Economy 1960: 2000: A Retrospective and Prospective Look, 1983; (with M.H. DeGroot) Bayesian Analysis and Uncertainty in Economic Theory, 1987; bd. editors: Behavioral Sci; contbr. articles to profl. jours. Bd. dirs. Carnegie Inst. Served USNR, 1943-46. Recipient Hofstra Disting. Scholar award, 1973, Outstanding Achievement award U. Minn., 1975; Ford fellow, 1959-60; Guggenheim fellow, 1967-68. Fellow Am. Statis. Assn., AAAS, Econometric Soc.; mem. Am. Econ. Assn., Am. Statis. Assn., Econometric Soc., Inst. Mgmt. Scis., Phi Beta Kappa, Beta Gamma Sigma. Home: 12 Edgewood Rd Pittsburgh PA 15215 Office: Carnegie Mellon U 5000 Forbes Ave Pittsburgh PA 15213

CYN, T. G., writer; b. Hollywood, Calif., Feb. 29, 1948; d. Edwin Whitfield and Virginia Lou (Newcomb) McKinley; m. Gerald J. Harvey, June 26, 1970 (div. 1976); m. Stanley John Maleski Jr., Oct. 21, 1979 (div. 1984); m. Bruce B. McCulloch, Sept. 13, 1986. Student, Riverside City Coll., 1965-67, Orange Coast Coll., 1967-68. Editor Al buraag mag., 1979; freelance writer, editor Profl. Horseman, Equine Practitioner, Small Animal Practitioner, The Cons., Arabian Horse Mktg. and Bus. Rev., Washington, 1980-82; dir. publs. Am. Horse Council, Washington, 1982-84; cons. Haifa Arabians, Diamond Bar, Calif., 1983-86, Khemosabi Syndicate, Diamond Bar, 1983—; pres. T.G. Cyn & Co. Author: Tangled Mane, 1983, Gardner Bloodstock Consultant, 1980, Resilient Heart, 1985, Cowards, 1985, Tangled Mane, Vol. II, 1986, The Lonesome Pony, 1986, A New Wrinkle, 1988. Mem. Women in Communications, Internat. Arabian Horse Assn., Arabian Horse Registry Am., Am. Horse Shows Assn.

CYR, J. V. RAYMOND, telecommunications and management holding company executive; b. Montreal, Que., Can., Feb. 11, 1934; s. Armand and Yvonne (Lagace) C.; m. Marie Bourdon, Sept. 1, 1956; children: Helene, Paul Andre. Student, Ecole Poly.; B.A.Sc., U. Montreal, 1958; postgrad. studies in engring., Bell Labs., N.J., Nat. Def. Coll., 1972-73. With Bell Can., 1958—, engr., 1958-65; staff engr. Bell Can., Montreal, 1965-70; chief engr. Bell Can., Quebec City, 1970-73; v.p. ops. staff region Bell Can., Montreal, 1973-75, v.p., 1975; exec. v.p. Bell Can., Quebec, 1975-79, v.p. adminstrn., 1979-83; pres. Bell Can., Montreal, 1983-85, chmn., pres., chief exec. officer, 1985-87, chmn. bd., 1987-88, also bd. dirs.; pres., chief exec. officer BCE Inc. (formerly Bell Can. Enterprises), Montreal, 1988—, also bd. dirs.; bd. dirs. No. Telecom Ltd., Steinbergs Inc., Banque Nationale de Canada, Bell-No. Research Ltd., Confederation Life Assurance Co. of Can., Dominion Textiles, Centre de development technologique de l'Ecole Polytechnique, TransCanada PipeLines, No. Telecom Ltd. Dir. Quebec Arthritis Soc.; chmn. Mus. Contemporary Art of Montreal; chmn. Centre Inst. for Tech., Montreal; assoc. gov. U. Montreal; vice-chmn. Jr. Achievement of Can. Recipient Can. Engrs. Gold Medal award, 1987. Mem. C.D. Howe Inst. (Quebec com.), Ordre des Ingenieurs du Que., Can.-U.S. Com., U. Montreal (bd. govs.), Can. C. of C., Internat. Bus. Council of Can. Roman Catholic. Clubs: St. Denis; Mount Royal; St. James; Mt. Bruno Golf. Office: BCE Inc Suite 2100, 2000 McGill Coll Ave, Montreal, PQ Canada H3A 3H7

CYR, REGINALD JOHN, electronics engineering executive; b. Caribou, Maine, Dec. 24, 1933; s. Dennis Merchant and Regina Agnes (Trusty) C.; m. Clare Marie Tardif, Dec. 26, 1953; children—Roxanne M., Philip Dennis, Scott M., Krista M. B.S. in E.E. magna cum laude, U. Maine, 1959; postgrad., UCLA, 1962, 66. Design engr. Bendix Electrodynamics Div., Sylmar, Calif., 1959-63; v.p., dir. engring. Aquasonics Engrs., 1963-65; staff engr. to chief engr. Bendix Corp., Sylmar, 1966-68; dir. engring. EMS div. Marine Resources, Inc., Northridge, Calif., 1968-73; pres. Sonatech Inc., Goleta, Calif., 1973—, also dir. Served with USN, 1951-54. Recipient IR 100 award, 1971. Mem. Acoustical Soc. Am., Inst. Navy. Democrat. Roman Catholic. Subspecialties: Electronics; Acoustical engineering. Current work: Development of acoustic navigation systems, command and control, acoustic telemetry, acoustic sensors—for government, offshore petroleum and deep sea mining. Patentee in field. Home: 1442 Crestline Dr Santa Barbara CA 93105 Office: Sonatech Inc 879 Ward Dr Santa Barbara CA 93111

CYWINSKI, JOZEF KAZIMIERZ, medical instrumentation company executive; b. Warsaw, Poland, Mar. 13, 1936; came to U.S., 1967, naturalized, 1973; s. Kazimierz and Miroslawa (Niewiarowicz) C.; M.S. in E.E., Warsaw Inst. Tech., 1960, Sc.D., 1967; m. Hanna D. Zawistowska, Apr. 27, 1957; 1 son, L. Mark. Pres., Ridan Instruments Co., Warsaw, 1960-65; research asso. physiology U. Pa., Phila., 1967-69; asso. prof. radiology and elec. engring. U. Mo., Columbia, 1969-70; dir. med. engring. dept. Mass. Gen. Hosp., Boston, 1970-81; v.p. research and devel. Bio-Med. Research Ltd., Hartsdale, N.Y., 1981-82; exec. v.p. Medinet, Inc., Purchase, N.Y., 1982-86; lectr. M.I.T.; pres. Corsan Engring. Co., N.Y.C. Fellow Am. Coll. Cardiology; mem. IEEE (sr.), Assn. Advancement Med. Instrumentation, Bio-Med. Engring. Soc., Neuroelectric Soc. Republican. Author: Essentials in Blood Pressure Monitoring, 1980; mem. editorial bd. Pace, 1977-80; contbr. numerous articles to profl. jours.

CZAPLINSKI, WLADYSLAW ANDRZEJ, lawyer, educator; b. Gdansk, Poland, Nov. 25, 1954; s. Andrzej and Maria (Burghart) C.;m. Magdalena Procner-Czaplinska, Feb. 4, 1978; children: Maciej, Zofia. Mag. jur., U. Gdansk, 1973-77; D of Jur., U. Poznań, 1985. Research asst. Ministry of Justice Research Inst., Warsaw, Poland, 1980-81; asst. prof. West Inst., Poznan, Poland, 1982. Contbr. numerous articles in field of Internat. Law. Mem. Internat. Law Assn. (Polish chpt.). Home: Widawska 7/36, 01-494 Warsaw Poland

CZARNIECKI, WINCENTY MARIAN, cardiologist, educator; b. Wilno, Poland, Apr. 5, 1924; s. Ludwik and Maria (Baniewicz) C. MD, Acad. Medicine Warsaw, Poland, 1960, Dr. Medicine Habilitation, 1970. Intern in Medicine Warsaw Med. Sch., Poland, 1950, resident in Internal Diseases, 1952-59; asst., sr. asst. then asst. prof. Med. Sch., Warsaw, 1950-76; assoc. prof. dept. cardiology Ctr. Postgrad. Edn., Warsaw, 1976—; cons. cardiology dept. Univ. Hosp., Benghazi, Libya, 1987—. Contbr. numerous articles on cardiology, blood coagulation and nephrology to profl. jours. Served to maj. med. corps Polish armed forces, 1952-56. Rockefeller Found. fellow Harvard U. Sch. Medicine, Boston, 1961-62. Mem. European Biometerol. and Balnol. Assn. (mem. council), N.Y. Acad. Scis., European Assn. Blood Coagulation and Hemostasis. Roman Catholic. Club: Legia (Warsaw). Home: Nowotki 16 apt 11, 00-201 Warsaw Poland Office: Cardiology Dept, Soszczynskieso 1, Warsaw Poland

CZARNOWSKI, PIOTR ANDRZEJ, editor, journalist; b. Warsaw, Poland, Jan. 12, 1950; s. Jan Waclaw and Marie Czarnowski; m. Elzbieta Krystyna Trembinska, Apr. 2, 1972; 1 child, Aleksander-Pavel. MSc in Engring., Agr. U., Warsaw, 1972; MSc in Journalism, Warsaw U., 1974, Warsaw U., 1978. Editor Pubs. of Tech. Periodicals, Warsaw, 1972-79; editor-in-chief Ochrona Pracy, Warsaw, 1979-83; mng. editor Horyzonty Techniki/Mikroklan, Warsaw, 1983—; pub. relations cons. KLM, Warsaw, 1981—, Sulzer, Warsaw, 1986—, others. Mem. Polish Soc. Engrs., Polish Ergonomics Assn. (founding), Polish Journalist Assn., Interchange Editors Soc. (founding). Office: Horyzonty Techniki, Swietokrzyska 14A, 00-950 Warsaw Poland

CZERWINSKI, EDWARD JOSEPH, language educator; b. Erie, Pa., June 6, 1929; s. Joseph and Anna (Branecka) C. B.A., Grove City Coll., 1951; M.A. in Drama and English, Pa. State U., 1955; postgrad., Emory U., 1955-57, Ind. U., 1960-61; M.A. in Russian, U. Wis., Madison, 1964, Ph.D. in Russian and Polish, 1965. Instr. English Ga. Tech. Inst., Atlanta, 1957-59; asst. prof. English and drama McNeese State Coll., La., 1959-60; assoc. prof. Russian and Polish lits. U. Pitts., 1965-66, SUNY at Buffalo, 1966-67; assoc. prof. Russian and Polish U. Kans., Lawrence, 1967-70; prof. Russian and comparative lit. SUNY, Stony Brook, 1970—; ofcl. translator from Polish into English Interpress Pubs., Warsaw; founder, exec. and artistic dir. Slavic Cultural Center, Port Jefferson, N.Y., 1970—, pres. bd. trustees, 1970—. Editor: (with J. Piekalkiewicz) The Soviet Invasion of Czechoslovakia: The Effects on East Europe, 1972; editor, translator Pieces of Poland: Four Polish Dramatists, 1983, (with Mario Suško) Twenty Yugoslav Poets: the Meditative Generation, 1982, Bogdan Suchodolskies A History of Polish Culture, 1986; editor: Alternatives: An Anthology of Slavic and East European Drama, 1983, (with Mario Susko) The Mythmakers: An Anthology of Contemporary Yugoslav Short Stories, 1984, (with Nicholas Rzhevsky) The Dramaturg and Dramaturgy, 1986, Chekhov Reconstructed: New Translations of Chekhov's Plays, 1987, Satire Cum Poesis: Three Bulgarian Plays, 1987; author numerous articles and revs.; mem. editorial bd.: Books Abroad (now World Lit. Today), 1968—, Gradiva, 20th Century Lit, Comparative Drama, spl. editor, 1969-70; editor: Slavic and East European Arts Jour., 1982—, Polish lit. sect. Ency. Brit, 1975-78; area editor ea. Europe Theatre Companies of the World, 1986—. Served to 2d lt. USAF, 1951-53. Kosciuszko Found. grantee, 1962-64; Wanda Rohr Found. grantee, 1963; Internat. Dimensions grantee, 1966; Fulbright grantee Yugoslavia, 1968-69; Inter-Univ. travel grantee USSR, 1968-69; Inter-Univ. travel grantee Czechoslovakia, 1969; Internat. Research and Exchange Bd. fellow, Yugoslavia, 1983-84, summer seminar grantee, Bulgaria, 1985, Irex grantee, Poland, 1987; recipient Disting. Alumni award Grove City Coll., 1973; Chancellor's Excellence in Teaching award SUNY, 1973-74; Amicus Poloniae award Poland, 1974; Disting. Prof. award N.Y. State Tchrs. of Fgn. Langs., 1975; Man of Yr. in Culture and Arts, Am. Council Polish Cultural Clubs, 1986. Mem. MLA (exec. com. Slavic-Western lit. relations 1970-72), Polish Acad. Arts and Scis. Am., AAUP, Am. Assn. Tchrs. of Slavic and East European Langs., Am. Assn. Advancement of Slavic Studies. Home: Private Rd Box 127 Shoreham NY 11786 Office: SUNY Stony Brook NY 11794

DAAB-KRZYKOWSKI, ANDRE, pharmaceutical and nutritional manufacturing company administrator; b. Warsaw, Poland, May 16, 1949; came to U.S., 1973, naturalized, 1981; s. Aleksy Czeslaw crest Polkozic and Zofia (Dyszkiewicz crest Kudrys) Krzykowski; m. Susan Elizabeth Read, June 26, 1987. MSChemE, Tech. U. Warsaw, 1973; MBA, Memphis State U., 1979. Research chemist Schering-Plough, Memphis, 1974-77; process control mgr. Ralston Purina Co., Memphis, 1977-80; dir. Pharm. projects indsl. div. Bristol Myers, Bristol-Myers Co., Mayaguez, P.R., 1980—. Served to 2d lt. Polish Army Res. Mem. Am. Mgmt. Assn., Am. Chem. Soc. Republican. Lutheran. Club: Toastmasters (pres. local chpt. 1986). Avocations: sailing, scuba diving, karate. Office: Bristol Myers Indsl Div PO Box 897 Mayaguez PR 00709

DABINOVIC, TOMISLAVO ESTEBAN, lawyer; b. Zagreb, Yugoslavia, Sept. 20, 1930; s. Vladimiro and Margarita (Sauer) D.; m. Maureen O'Sullivan, Oct. 19, 1968. Asst. dir. Bur. Naturalization of Foreigners Dept. Interior, 1956-57; dir. dept. legal affairs State Dept. Province of Buenos Aires, 1957-58; legal advisor to Intergovt. Com. for European Migration, Buenos Aires, 1959-60; ptnr. Mayer, Lobos & Clusellas, Buenos Aires, 1965-77, Dabinovic & Assocs., Buenos Aires, 1977—; mem. hon. drafting com. new Argentine Fgn. Investment Law, 1976; sr. prof., lectr. polit. economy dept., law and social scis. Nat. U. Buenos Aires. Contbr. articles to profl. jours. Mem. Internat. Bar Assn. (council mem.), Am. Soc. Internat. Law, Corp. Lawyers Club, Argentine Assn. Comparative Law (past vice chmn.), Argentine Assn. Energy Law (chmn.), Argentine C. of C. (econ. advisor 1976), Soc. Internat. Devel., Argentine Petroleum Inst. Bar Assn. City of Buenos Aires (past vice chmn.), Buenos Aires Bar Assn. (bd. dirs., sec., vice chmn.). Roman Catholic. Office: Dabinovic & Assocs, 328 Cangallo St, 1038 Buenos Aires Argentina

DABKOWSKI, JOHN, electrical engineer, consultant, researcher; b. Chgo., Feb. 15, 1933; s. John and Harriet (Sierakowski) D.; m. Cecilia Klonowski, June 26, 1976. B.S.E.E., Ill. Inst. Tech., 1955, M.S.E.E., 1960, Ph.D. in Elec. Engring., 1969. Sr. research engr. Ill. Inst. Tech. Research Inst., Chgo., 1957-79; ops. mgr. Sci. Applications Internat. Corp., Hoffman Estates, Ill., 1979-85, dir. EM effects research, 1985-87, div. mgr., 1987-88; pres. Electro Scis., Inc., 1988—; instr. Grad. Sch., Ill. Inst. Tech., Chgo., 1962-79. Research, publs. in field. Served with U.S. Army, 1955-57. Mem. IEEE (sr. mem.), Nat. Assn. Corrosion Engrs., Am. Geophys. Union, Sigma Xi. Roman Catholic. Home: 7021 Foxfire Dr Crystal Lake IL 60012

DACHOWITZ, HENRY MOSES, investment research analyst; b. Jan. 22, 1956; s. Pincus and Seyma Anne (Sacksner) D.; m. Mary-Jane Moskowitz,

May 1, 1983. BS, Bklyn. Coll., 1977; MBA, Harvard U., 1980. CPA, Md., N.Y. Founder, owner, pres. Tutoring Referral Service, Bklyn., 1974-77; auditor Coopers & Lybrand, N.Y.C., 1977-78; trader and gen. mgr. Empire Steel Trading Co., N.Y.C., 1980-82; v.p. fin. IGI Biotech., Inc., Columbia, Md., 1982-84; sr. mgmt. cons. Touche Ross & Co., N.Y.C., 1984-87; investment research analyst Sanford C. Berstein & Co., Inc., N.Y.C., 1987—; tchg. fellow in acctg. Harvard Coll., Cambridge, Mass., 1979-80; bus. mgr. Kingsman Newspaper, Bklyn., 1976-77; speaker Md. Assn. CPA's, Columbia, 1982-84. Adv. Inst. Politics Harvard U., Cambridge, 1979-80. Recipient Innovation award Touche Ross Fin. Services Ctr., 1986; Louis P. Goldberg scholar, Bklyn. Coll., 1977, N.Y. State Regents scholar, 1973. Mem. Am. Inst. CPA's, N.Y. State Soc. CPA's (fin. planning and control com.), Am. Mgmt. Assn., Internat. Platform Assn., Mensa. Republican. Jewish. Club: Century Club (Harvard). Home: 2 Salem Ln Port Washington NY 11050 Office: Sanford C Bernstein & Co 767 Fifth Ave New York NY 10153

DA COSTA, OLAF ST. JOHN, consultant orthopedic surgeon; b. Nagpur, India, Dec. 27, 1936; came to U.S., 1962; s. Albert Francis and Emilia (Heredia) da C.; m. Jane Elizabeth Barker, Sept. 23, 1966; children—Anna-Marie, Sara. M.B.B.S., Grant Med. Coll., 1962. Intern, Royal Infirmary, Huddersfield, Yorkshire; resident Royal Orthopedic Hosp., Birmingham; cons. orthopedic surgeon Kiderminster Gen. Hosp., Worcestershire, Eng., 1974—, Droitwich Center for Rheumatic Diseases, Worcestershire, 1974—. Fellow Brit. Orthopedic Assn., Royal Coll. Surgeons. Home: Moorlands, 28 Whitehill Rd, Kidderminster Worcestershire DY11 6JJ, England

DA CUNHA, JACOB, advertising executive; b. Amsterdam, The Netherlands, Nov. 19, 1925; s. Ab and Grietje (de Leeuw) da C.; m. Grete Bekemeier, Dec. 8, 1948; 1 child, Ronald. Grad. high sch., Amsterdam. Salesman de Vries van Buuren, Amsterdam, 1946-47; mng. dir. Vaz Dias Advt., Amsterdam, 1947-53, Vaz Dias Clipping Service, Amsterdam, 1955—. Contbr. articles on internat. advt. to profl. jours., 1955-64. Recipient Clio award Clio Awards Bd., N.Y.C., 1975. Mem. Dutch Advt. Assn., Dutch Exporters Group (advisor, Export Promotion award 1985). Jewish. Lodge: Lions (pres. Amsterdam chpt. 1955-56, 70-71). Office: Vaz Dias Advt, Singel 91, 1012 VG Amsterdam The Netherlands

DADA, NAYYAR ALI, architect; b. Delhi, India, Nov. 11, 1943; s. S. Anwar Ali and Kaneez Fatima; children: Reza Ali, Amir Ali. Diploma in architecture, Nat. Coll. Arts, Lahore, Pakistan, 1963. Mng. ptnr. Nayyar Dada Assocs., Lahore, 1974—; owner pvt. art gallery Lahore; sr. lectr. Nat. Coll. Arts, 1972-77, mem. bd. govs., 1985; mem. bd. govs. Punjab Council Arts, 1984-87; advisor Lahore Environ. Com. Prin. works include Quaid-e-Azam Library, Free Mason Hall Bldg., Shakir Ali Mus., Alhamra Arts Ctr., Nat. Meml., Hotel Sheraton Lahore, Holiday Inn Lahore, Lahore Zoo, Performing Art Ctr., Peshawar, Oil and Gas Devel. Corp. Bldg., Islamabad. Recipient Environ. award for pub. bldgs. Environ. mag., 1981-82; Nat. Coll. Arts fellow, 1973. Mem. Pakistan Inst. Architects (mem. council), Pakistan Council Architects (vice chmn.), Lahore Conservation Soc. (founder, treas.). Club: Punjab. Home: 1 2 Habitat Housing Jail Rd, Shadman-II, Lahore Punjab, Pakistan Office: 8-F/3 New Muslim Town, Lahore Punjab, Pakistan

D'ADAMO, DOMINIC FRANK, financial services co. exec.; b. N.Y.C., Mar. 2, 1947; s. Michael and Anna D'Adamo; B.B.A. in Acctg., Baruch Coll., 1968, M.B.A. in Fin. & Investments, 1977; m. Susan Zozzaro, June 29, 1968; children—Michele, Dominic, John, Paul. Audit mgr. Arthur Andersen & Co., N.Y.C., 1968-69, 70-76; asst. controller Marsh & McLennan, Inc., N.Y.C., 1976-77, v.p., dep. controller, 1979-82, v.p., controller U.S. ops., 1982-83, mng. dir., controller-worldwide ops., 1983—; dir. acctg. Marsh & McLennan Cos., Inc., N.Y.C., 1977-79. Treas. Rockland County Scholarship Fund, 1979-83; bd. dirs. Rockland County Youth Football Program; mem. Clarkstown (N.Y.) PTA, 1977—. Served as 1st lt. U.S. Army, 1969-70. Beta Alpha Psi scholar, 1968; C.P.A., N.Y. Mem. Am. Inst. C.P.A.s (mem. ins. agts. and brokers task force 1980—), N.Y. State Soc. C.P.A.s (award of honor 1968), Fin. Execs. Inst., Assn. M.B.A. Execs.

DAENECKE, ERIC, lawyer, former UN advisor; b. Bklyn., Jan. 24, 1914; s. August and Ida (Brosowski) D.; B.S., Am. U., Washington, 1944, M.A., 1947, Ph.D., 1950; J.D., U. Balt., 1954; LL.M. cum laude, U. Manila, 1964; D.C.L., U. Santo Tomas, Manila, 1966; m. G. Alma Schwenn, Apr. 5, 1936 (dec.); children: William Eric, Maryellen Daenecke Lawlor; m. 2d, Teresa Oakley Jones, Apr. 17, 1981. Chief of finance GAO and Dept. Labor, Washington, 1935-56, public adminstrn. adviser Dept. State, 1957-70; interregional advisor UN, N.Y.C., 1970-77; tchr. Strayer Coll., Washington, 1951-56, U. Md. Far East Br., 1967-70, grad. law U. Santo Tomas, Manila, 1964-66; minister Christian Ch., Washington, 1953-56. Mem. Am. Inst. C.P.A.s, Fed. Bar Assn., Am. Acctg. Assn., Rosicrucian Order. Club: Lawyers. Author: Tales of Mullah Nasr-Ud-Din, 1960; More Tales, 1961. Home: 5640 Wood St Port Orange FL 32019

DAFGARD, LENNART, ambassador; b. Vanersborg, Sweden, Sept. 28, 1930; s. Otto and Doris (Mikaloff) D.; m. Agneta Anckarman, Jan. 28, 1959; children: Jan, Anna, Maria. Degree in Law, U. Stockholm, 1955. Joined Diplomatic Service of Sweden, 1955; assigned Diplomatic Service of Sweden, Geneva, Buenos Aires, Karachi (Pakistan), Mozambique and Bonn (Fed. Re, public Germany), 1956-77; Swedish del. to EC Diplomatic Service of Sweden, Brussels; asst. under-sec. Ministry Fgn. Affairs, Stockholm, 1980-85; ambassador to Turkey Ministry Fgn. Affairs, 1985—; asst. under-sec. Ministry for Fgn. Affairs, Stockholm, 1980-85. Home: Pl 8167, 611 90 Nykoping Sweden Office: Embassy of Sweden, BP3 Kavaklidere, 06692 Ankara Turkey

DAFNI, REUVEN, organization executive; b. Zagreb, Yugoslavia, Nov. 11, 1913; arrived in Israel, 1936; s. Max and Regina (Schwartz) Kandt; m. Rinna Grossman, 1948 (div. 1959); children: Tally, Yoram; m. Betty Ebling, 1960. Student, Vienna U., 1934-35, Columbia U., 1954, Hebrew U., 1980-82. Consul gen. State of Israel, Los Angeles, 1948-51; spokesman Ministry of Fgn. Affairs, Jerusalem, 1951-53; head Israel Info. Ctr., N.Y.C., 1954-57; dir. gen. Am.-Israel Cultural Found., Tel Aviv, 1958-60, Sports and Phys. Edn. Authority, Jerusalem, 1960-65; consul gen. State of Israel, Bombay, India, 1965-69; ambassador to Kenya State of Israel, 1969-73; head N.Am. div. Fgn. Ministry of Israel, Jerusalem, 1973-75; ambassador to Thailand State of Israel, 1975-79; vice chmn. Yad Vashem, The Holocaust Martyrs' and Heroes' Remembrance Authority, Jerusalem, 1980—. Bd. dirs. Jerusalem Theatre, 1980-84, Jerusalem Acad. of Music, 1980—, David Yellin Tchrs. Sem., 1981—; mem. exec. bd. Sovlanut, Movement for Tolerance, Jerusalem, 1982—. Served to lt. Brit. Army, 1940-45. Home: 56 Hapalmah, Jerusalem 92583, Israel Office: Yad Vashem, PO Box 3477, Jerusalem 91034, Israel

DA FONSECA, AUGUSTO JOSEPH, psychiatric social worker; b. Elizabeth, N.J., May 18, 1952; s. Abilio and Emilia (Rodrigues) da F.; B.A., U. Miami (Fla.), 1975; M.S.W., Barry U. Sch. Social Work, Miami Shores, Fla., 1977; m. Maryann Tokasz, Aug. 7, 1976; children—Amanda Marie, Andrea Augusta. Clin. social worker Mt. Carmel Guild Community Mental Health Center, Newark, 1977-78; psychiat. clinician dept. psychiatry Elizabeth Gen. Med. Ctr., 1978-81; psychiat. social worker U. Medicine and Dentistry of N.J.-N.J. Med. Sch., Newark, 1982-86; social service adminstr. Ironbound Ednl. and Cultural Ctr., Newark, 1986-87, nephrology social worker Alexian Bros. Hosp, Elizabeth, 1988—. Active council of nephrology social workers Nat. Kidney Found. N.J.; Democratic committeeman, Elizabeth, 1977-82. Mem. Nat. Assn. Social Workers, Am. Orthopsychiat. Assn., Nat. Bd. Examiners in Clin. Soc. Work (cert.), The Soc. for Clin. and Experimental Hypnosis (assoc.), The Internat. Soc. Hynosis. Clubs: KC, Elizabeth Portuguese Lions (sec. 1983-84, pres. 1984-85), Portuguese Instructive Social (Elizabeth), Portuguese Am. Congress of N.J. (Newark) (dir. 1986—), AM. Bd. Examiners Clin. Social Work (diplomate), Soc. Clin. and Exptl. Hypnosis, Internat. Soc. Hypnosis. Home: 973 Grove St Elizabeth NJ 07202

DAGGETT, ROBERT SHERMAN, lawyer; b. La Crosse, Wis., Sept. 16, 1930; s. Willard Manning and Vida Naomi (Sherman) D.; m. Lee Sullivan Burton, Sept. 16, 1960; children: Ann Sherman, John Sullivan; m. Helen Ackerman, July 20, 1976. A.B. with honors in Polit. Sci. and Journalism, U. Calif.-Berkeley, 1952, J.D., 1955. Bar: Calif. 1955, U.S. Supreme Ct. 1967. Assoc. firm Brobeck, Phleger & Harrison, San Francisco, 1958-66, ptnr., 1966—; counsel Calif. Senate Reapportionment Com., 1972-73; adj. prof. evidence and advocacy Hastings Coll. Law, 1982—; demonstrator-instr. Nat. Inst. for Trial Advocacy, 1981—, Hastings Ctr. for Trial and Appellate Advocacy, 1981-88, mem. adv. bd., 1983—, Am. Law Inst., 1988—; vol. pro tempsmall claims judge San Francisco Mcpl. Ct., 1981-88; arbitrator San Francisco Superior Ct., 1984—; Instr. No. Dist. Fed. Practice Origram, 1982—, mem. teaching com., 1983—. Bd. editors: Calif. Law Rev., 1953-55; contbr. articles to profl. jours. Rep. Pacific Assn. AAU, 1973; bd. dirs. San Francisco Legal Aid Soc.; bd. visitors Coll. V U. Calif.-Santa Cruz. Served to 1st lt. JAGC U.S. Army, 1958-62. Walter Perry Johnson scholar, 1953. Mem. ABA, State Bar Calif. (chmn. local adminstrv. com. 1964-65), San Francisco Bar Assn. (past dir.), Am. Judicature Soc., Am. Law Inst., Order of Golden Bear, Phi Delta Phi, Theta Xi. Republican. Club: Bohemian, Commonwealth, Commercial (San Francisco). Office: Brobeck Phleger & Harrison Spear St Tower 1 Market Plaza San Francisco CA 94105

D'AGNESE, HELEN JEAN, artist; b. N.Y.C.; d. Leonardo and Rose (Redavid) De Santis; m. John J. D'Agnese, Oct. 29, 1942; children—John, Linda, Diane, Michele, Helen, Gina, Paul. Student CUNY, 1940-42; student Atlanta Coll. Art, 1972-76. One-man shows: Maude Sullivan Gallery, El Paso, 1964, John Wanamaker Gallery, Phila., 1966, U. N.Mex., 1967, Karo Mancuci Gallery, San Francisco, 1968, Tuskegee Inst. Carver Mus., 1968, Lord & Taylor Gallery, N.Y.C., 1969, Harmon Gallery, Naples, Fla., 1970, Fountainbleau, Miami, 1970, Reflections Gallery, Atlanta, 1972, Williams Gallery, Atlanta, 1973, Atlanta Coll. of Art, 1976-80, Americana Gallery, Mineola, Tex., 1977, E. M. Howard Gallery, Amelia Island, Fla., 1978, Haitian Primitives Gallery, 1981, Highland Gallery, Atlanta, 1987, others; group shows: Musseo des Artes, Juárez, México, 1968, Benedictine Art Show, N.Y.C., 1967, Southeast Contemporary Art Show, Atlanta, 1968, Atlanta U., 1969, Red Piano Gallery, Hilton Head, S.C., Terrace Gallery, Atlanta, Ann. Bible Heritage Art Exhibit, Marietta, Ga., 1976, Nat. Judaic Theme Exhbn., Atlanta, 1976, Crystal Britton Gallery, Atlanta; represented in permanent collections: Pres. Jimmy Carter, Juarez (Mexico) Art Mus., Vatican Mus., Rome, Nassau (Fla.) County Pub. Library. Judge art show Mt. Loretto Acad., El Paso, 1967; commd. sculptor of Bob Marley in Limestone, 1985; art demonstration and lectr. Margaret Harris Sch., Atlanta, 1970; artist-in-residence Montessori Sch., Atlanta, 1978-79. Recipient Gold medal Accademia Italia delle Arti, Italy, 1979, Calvatone, 1982, Golden Flame award, 1986; 1st place sculpture award Tybee Island Art Festival, 1982, Golden Flame award Parliamento U.S.A., 1987, Golden Palette award Academia Europea, 1986, 87, Gold medal Internat. Parliament for the Arts, 1982. Mem. Nat. Mus. of Women in the Arts (chartered), Arts Alliance Amelia Island, Nat. Mus. Women in Arts (chartered). Address: 3240 S Fletcher Ave Fernandina Beach FL 32034 Office: Fine Art Gallery 14 1/2 N 4th St Fernandina Beach FL 32043

D'AGOSTINO, RALPH BENEDICT, mathematician, statistician, educator, consultant; b. Somerville, Mass., Aug. 16, 1940; s. Bennedetto and Carmela (Piemonte) D'A.; m. Lei Lanie Carta, Aug. 28, 1965; children: Ralph Benedict, Lei Lanie Maria. A.B., Boston U., 1962, M.A., 1964; Ph.D., Harvard U., 1968. Lectr. math. Boston U., 1964-68, asst. prof., 1968-71, assoc. prof., 1971-76, prof. math. and stats., 1976—, chmn. math. dept., dir. stats. cons. unit, 1986—, dir. stats. unit Framingham Heart Study, 1985—, dir. biostats program, 1988—, lectr. law, 1975—, prof. pub. health, 1982—, assoc. dean Grad. Sch., 1976-78; vis. lectr. Am. Statis. Assn., 1975-86, 1988—; spl. scientist Boston City Hosp., 1981—; cons. stats. United Brands, 1968-76, Diabetes and Arthritis Control Unit, Boston, 1971-75, City of Somerville, Mass., 1972, ednl. div. Bolt, Beranek & Newman, 1971, Harvard Dental Sch., 1969, Lahey Clinic Found., 1973—, Walden Research, 1974-79, FDA Biometrics Div. and Over-the-Counter Div., 1975—, Arnold & Porter, 1980, Bedford Research Assn., 1976-81, Corneal Scis., 1976, Biotek, 1979—, GCA, 1979—, Lever Bros., 1982—, Conrail, 1981, FBI, 1984, Ctr. Psychiat. Rehab., Boston U., 1985—, NIMH, 1985, Dade Clin. Assays, 1986—, Millipore, 1983—, VLI Corp., 1984—, New Eng. Coll. Optometry, 1985—, Dupont Corp., 1985, Bristol Myers, 1986, Tufts New Eng. Med. Ctr., Med. Decision Making Div. and Health Services Research Unit, 1986, Am. Inst. of Research in the Social Scis., 1983—, New England Research Insts., 1987—, Thompson Med., 1987—, Chesebrough-Pond's, Inc., 1988—, other research insts.; mem. fertility and maternal health drugs adv. com. FDA, 1978-81, life support subcom., 1979-81, drug abuse adv. com., 1987—, task force on design and analysis in dental and oral research, 1979—, health tech. com. Harvard U., 1986—, NIH Consensus Panel on Liver Transplantation, 1983, NIH Consensus Panel of Fresh Frozen Plasma, 1984, NIH Consensus Panel on Geriatric Assessment Methods for Clin. Decision Making, 1987, task force Office Tech. Assessment, 1980; prin., co-prin. investigator, or sr. statistician on grants Nat. Ctr. Health Services Research, 1976, USAF, 1980-85, Nat. Heart Lung Blood Inst., 1982—, Nat. Cancer Inst., 1985-87, Nat. Inst. Criminal Justice, 1982-85, Nat. Ctr. Child Abuse and Neglect, 1982-85, Robert Wood Johnson Found., 1981-85, Social Security Adminstrn., 1982-86, Motor Vechicle Mem. Assn., 1987, NIOSH, 1985, Nat. Insts. Aging, 1986—; grant/contract reviewer Nat. Acad. Sci., 1979—, Nat. Ctr. for Health Services Research, 1976, NIH, 1983, NSF, 1987. Author: (with E.E. Cureton) Factor Analysis, An Applied Approach, 1983 (with Shuman and Wolfe) Mathematical Modeling, Applications in Emergency Health Services, 1984, (with Stephens) Goodness of Fit Techniques, 1986; assoc. editor: Am. Statistician, 1972-76, Statistics in Medicine, 1981—; editor: Emergency Health Service Rev., 1981—, book reviewer, Houghton Mifflin, Holden-Day, Duxbury Press, Prentice Hall, 1969—; contbr. articles to profl. jours. Recipient Spl. Citation, FDA Commr., 1981, Metcalf award for excellence in teaching Boston U., 1985. Mem. Am. Statis. Assn. (pres. Boston chpt. 1972, v.p. 1971, mem. nat. council 1973-75, vis. lectr. 1976-78, 80—), Inst. Math. Stats., Am. Soc. Quality Control, Biometrics Soc., Am. Pub. Health Assn. (chmn. sect. emergency health services 1982-83, governing council 1983-85), Phi Beta Kappa, Sigma Xi. Home: 5 Everett Ave Winchester MA 01890 Office: Boston U Dept Math 111 Cummington St Boston MA 02215

DAGOUSSET, PIERRE EDMOND, business executive; b. Gentilly, France, Feb. 15, 1931; s. Edmond and Marie-Louise (Foucault) D.; m. Christiane Drouets, 1958; children: Jacques, Bernard, Georges. Degree in Engring., Ecole Nat. Superieure des Industries Agricoles et Alimentaires, Paris, 1952; Inst. D'Adminstrn. Des Enterprises De La Faculte De Droit Et Des Scis. Econs. de Paris, 1958, Centre De Perfectionnement Dans L'Adminstrn. Des Affaires De La Chambre De Commerce et D'Industrie De Paris, Paris, 1963. Chief GEO S.A., Paris, 1954-58; dir. Promodag, Nogent sur Marne, France, 1958-72; pres. Etrave S.A., Paris, 1960—. Contbr. articles to profl. jours., 1957-70. Served to capt. arty. French Army. Roman Catholic. Office: Etrave SA, 38 Av Daumesnil, 75012 Paris France

DAGUM, CAMILO, economist, educator; b. Argentina, Aug. 11, 1925; immigrated to Can., 1972, naturalized, 1978; s. Alexander and Nazira (Hakim) D.; Ph.D. (Gold medal summa cum laude), Nat. U. Cordoba, 1949, (hon.) U. Bologna, 1988, Nat. U. Cordova, 1988; m. Estela Bee, Dec. 22, 1958; children—Alexander, Paul, Leonardo. Mem. faculty Nat. U. Cordoba, 1950-66, prof. econs., 1956-66, dean Faculty Econ. Scis., 1962-66; sr. research economist Princeton U., 1966-68; prof. Nat. U. Mex., 1968-70; vis. prof. Inst. d'Etudes du Devel. Econ. and Social, U. Paris, 1967-69, U. Iowa, 1970-72; prof. econs. U. Ottawa (Ont., Can.), 1972—, chmn. dept., 1973-75, mem. acad. senate, 1981-84, bd. govs., 1983-84; pres. Cordoba Inst. Social Security, 1962-63; cons. to govt. and industry, 1956—; research prof. U. Rome, 1956-57, London Sch. Econs., 1960-62, Inst. Sci. Econmique Appliqué, Coll. France, 1965; vis. fellow Birkbeck Coll., U. London, 1960-61, Australian Nat. U., 1985; guest scholar Brookings Instn., 1978-79; vis. prof. U. Siena, Italy, 1987, 88. Mem. Acad. Council Research Ctr. on Income Distbn., U. Siena, 1986—. Served as res. officer Argentine Army, 1948. Decorated Pro-Patria Gold medal, 1948; hon. prof. Inst. Advanced Studies, Salta, Argentina, 1972; extraordinary prof. Cath. U. Salta, 1981—. Mem. Internat. Inst. Sociology, Internat. Statis. Inst., Statis. Soc., Econ. Soc., Econ. History Soc. Argentina, U.S. Eastern Econ. Assn., Econometric Soc., Am. Statis. Assn., Am. Econ. Assn., Can. Econ. Assn., Can. Statis. Soc., Assn. Social Econs. Roman Catholic. Author books on econ. theory; also editor econ. and statis. jours.; also articles. Home: 408 Buena Vista Rd, Rockcliffe Park, ON Canada K1M 0W3 Office: Dept Econs, Faculty Social Scis, U Ottawa, Ottawa, ON Canada K1N 6N5

DAHBANY, AVIVAH, psychologist; b. Bklyn., Jan. 3, 1951; d. Hyman and Esther (Levy) D.; BA, CCNY, 1974, MS, 1978. Fellow in Clin. Psychology Albert Einstein Coll. Medicine, 1976-77; psychologist Adams Sch., N.Y.C., 1977-78; dir. spl. edn., psychologist Dov Revel Yeshiva, Forest Hills, N.Y., 1978-79; psychologist Franklin Twp. Public Schs., Somerset, N.J., 1979—; adj. lectr. CCNY, 1977-78; adj. instr. Monmouth Coll., 1981, 88, Raritan Valley Community Coll., 1987—; psychol. cons. Robert Wood Johnson Meml. Hosp., Laurie Devel. Inst., Child Evaluation Ctr., 1985—. Mem. N.Y. Assn. Sch. Psychologists (chairperson student certification task force 1977-78), Am. Psychol. Assn., Nat. Assn. Sch. Psychologists, NEA. Office: Pupil Personnel Services 1755 Amwell Rd Somerset NJ 08873

DAHER, WASSEF YUSEF, airline executive; b. Jerusalem, Palestine, Jan. 27, 1940; s. Yusef Wassef and Ellen Matuk (Hajjar) D.; m. Nahia Shafiq Bahhous, Apr. 25, 1965; children—Yusef, Usama, Sani, Sana. Student Ibrahimiyeh Coll., Jerusalem, 1959. Office boy Swissair, Jerusalem, 1955-59, booking clk., 1959-63, sales promoter, 1963-64; sales rep. Scandinavian Airlines, Jerusalem, 1965-75, dist. sales mgr., 1976—. Editor daily sports column Elkuds newspaper, 1968-71, Alfajr newspaper, 1971-73. Vice pres. Jerusalem Players, 1961; pres. Legion of Mary, Jerusalem, 1963; sec. supreme bd. dirs. YMCA, Jerusalem, 1976; treas. Justice and Peace Commn., Jerusalem, 1978. Greek Catholic. Club: Skal (treas. 1981-82). Office: Scandinavian Airlines, Azzahra St, PO Box 19055, East Jerusalem Israel

DAHINDEN, JUSTUS, architect; b. Zurich, Switzerland, May. 18, 1925; s. Joseph and Eugenie (Kraus) D.; diploma architect Fed. High Sch. Tech., Zurich, 1949, Dr. sc. techn., 1956; m. Marta Arquint, Dec. 23, 1950; children—Zeno, Ivo, Delia. Pvt. practice architecture, Zurich, 1955—; prof. Vienna Tech. U., 1974; vis. prof. Faculty Architecture and Urbanism, Buenos Aires U. 1988—, prof. Internat. Acad. Architecture, 1988—. Recipient 12 1st prizes nat. and internat. competitions; award for excellence in design of Uganda Martyrs' Shrine, Mityana, Uganda, Heart of Jesus Cath. Ch., Buchs, Switzerland, Coronation of our Lady Cath. Ch., Zurich, from Guild for Religious Architecture at St. Louis Nat. Conf. on Religious Architecture, 1969; award for superlative achievement interior design for Hostellerie RigiKaltbad, Institutions mag., 1969; award for superlative achievement for interior design Tantris Restaurant, Institutions mag., 1959; Grand Prix Internat. d'Urbanisme et d'Architecture Paris/Cannes, 1979; Grand Prix d'Architecture, CEA, Paris, 1981; Spl. award, Bronze medal World Biennale of Architecture, Sofia, 1981, Silver medal, 1983; Spl. award Nat. Peace Com. Hon. fellow AIA; mem. Groupe International d'Architecture Prospective Paris/Zurich, Société Internationale des Artistes Chretiens (v.p., hon. pres.). Research on new urban structure, Akro-Polis, floating urban structures. Outstanding works include: National Shrines of Mityana and Namugongo, Uganda, 1969; numerous Cath. Chs. in Switzerland, Italy, Germany, Africa, China; Pyramidal Office Bldg., Zurich, 1970; Swiss vacation village Twannberg, 1970; Trigon village, Doldertal, Zurich, 1975; project for Floating Hotel Perle-du-Caire, Cairo, 1979; Leisure City at Munich, Germany, 1975; House of the Oriels, Zurich, 1983. Author: Standortbestimmung der Gegenwartsarchitektur, 1956; New Trends in Church Architecture, 1966; Urban Structures for the Future, 1971; Radio-City et Ville de Loisir, Centre d'Etudes Architecturale à Bruxelles, 1972; Thinking-Feeling-Acting, 1973, Justus Dahinden Architecture Monograph, 1987. Home: Kienastenwiesweg 41, 8053 Zurich Switzerland Office: Heuelstrasse 21, 8032 Zurich Switzerland

DAHL, ALV ANDREAS, psychiatry educator, psychoanalyst; b. Sarpsborg, Norway, Oct. 23, 1944; s. Nils Ludvig and Mari (Strengehagen) D.; m. Liv Inger Nerhagen, July 11, 1970 (div. 1981); children—Nils Ludvig, Sigrun; m. Margareta Falk, June 11, 1983 (separated 1987); 1 child, Christian Andreas. M.D., Oslo U., 1969. Resident in psychiatry Modum bads nervesanatorium, Vikersund, Norway, 1973-74; registrar in psychiatry Psychiat. Clinic, Oslo U., 1974-77, now chmn. com. psychiat. studies Faculty Medicine; sr. registrar psychiatry Gaustad Hosp., Oslo, 1977-79, research psychiatrist Inst. Psychiatry, 1979-86; assoc. prof. psychiatry U. Oslo; lectr. Inst. Psychotherapy, Oslo. Contbr. articles to profl. jours. Mem. Norwegian Doctors Assn., Norwegian Psychiat. Assn. (splty. bd. 1977-80, bd. psychotherapy 1981—), Norwegian Psychoanalytic Soc. Home: Olaf Bulls vei, 64 0765 Oslo 7 Norway Office: Dept Psychiatry, PO Box 85 Vindern, 0319 Oslo 3 Norway

DAHL, ANDREW WILBUR, health services executive; b. N.Y.C., Feb. 19, 1943; s. Wilbur A. and Margret L. Dahl; B.S., Clark U., 1968; M.P.A., Cornell U., 1970; Sc.D., Johns Hopkins U., 1974; m. Janice White, Sept. 4, 1965; children—Kristina, Jennifer, Meredith. Staff asst. Md. Comprehensive Health Planning Agy., Balt., 1970-72; dir. planning St. John Hosp., Detroit, 1972-79; exec. v.p., chief operating officer St. Clair Health Corp., Detroit, 1979—; pres., chief exec. officer United Health System, Detroit, 1983-88; v.p. devel. Hosp. Corp. Am. Mgmt. Co., 1988—; instr. U. Mich. Bur. Hosp. Adminstrn., 1981—. New Detroit Health Com., 1977—; bd. dirs. Detroit Sci. Ctr., 1984—; mem. Nat. Com. for Quality Health Care, Washington, 1984—; bd. dirs. Forum Health Care Planning. Served with USN, 1965-67. Recipient Disting. Service award Mich. Jaycees, 1977, Outstanding Contbns. to Profl. Mgmt. award, Cornell U., 1980. Mem. Am. Coll. Hosp. Adminstrs., Am. Hosp. Assn., Am. Public Health Assn., Internat. Health Econs. and Mgmt. Inst. Mich. Hosp. Assn. Methodist. Club: Grosse Pointe Hunt, Detroit Athletic. Office: One Park Plaza Nashville TN 37202

DAHL, ARLENE, actress, cosmetic executive; b. Mpls., Aug. 11, 1928; d. Rudolph and Idelle (Swan) D.; m. Marc A. Rosen; children: Lorenzo Lamas, Carole Christine Holmes, Rounseville Andreas Schaum. Student, U. Minn., Mpls. Inst. Art, Minn. Coll. Music, Minn. Bus. Coll. Pres. Arlene Dahl Enterprises, 1952-77; v.p. Kenyon & Eckhart, 1967-72, pres. Woman's World div., 1967-72; internat. dir. Sales and Mktg. Execs. Internat., 1972-75; fashion dir. O.M.A., 1975-78; pres. Dahlia Parfums, Inc., 1975—, Dahlia Productions, Inc., 1978-81, Dahlmark Prodns., 1981—, Lasting Beauty Ltd., 1986—; nat. beauty advisor Sears Roebuck Co., 1970-75. Author: Always Ask a Man, 1965, 12 Beautyscope books, 1968, rev. edit., 1978, Arlene Dahl's Secrets of Hair Care, 1970, Arlene Dahl's Secrets of Skin Care, 1972, Beyond Beauty, 1980, Arlene Dahl's Lovescopes, 1983; actress: (Broadway plays) including Mr. Strauss Goes to Boston, Questionable Ladies, Cyrano de Bergerac, (Broadway musical), Applause (Tony award), (films) including (debut) My Wild Irish Rose, The Bride Goes Wild, Reign of Terror, A Southern Yankee, Ambush, The Outriders, Three Little Words, Watch the Birdie, Scene of the Crime, Inside Straight, No Questions Asked, Desert Legion, Slightly Scarlet, Sangaree, Caribbean Gold, Jamaica Run, Diamond Queen, Here Come the Girls, Bengal Brigade, Kisses for My President, Woman's World, Journey to the Center of the Earth, Wicked as They Come, She Played with Fire, Les Poneyettes, Du Blé Enliases, The Land Raiders, The Way to Kathmandu, Fortune is a Woman, The Big Bank Role, Who Killed Maxwell Thorn?, (TV shows) Lux Video Theatre, 1952-53; guest starring appearances on The Love Boat, Fantasy Island, Love American Style, One Life to Live, 1981-84, Night of 100 Stars, 1983, Happy Birthday Hollywood, 1987; hostess (TV series): Pepsi-Cola Theatre, 1954, Opening Night, 1958, Arlene Dahl's Beauty Spot, 1966, Arlene Dahl's Starscope, 1979-80, Arlene Dahl's Lovescope, 1980-82; played throughout U.S. in One Touch of Venus, The Camel Bell, Blithe Spirit, Liliom, The King and I, Roman Candle, I Married an Angel, Bell, Book and Candle, Applause, Marriage Go Round, Pal Joey, A Little Night Music, Forty Carats, Life With Father, Murder Among Friends; (nightclub acts) Flamingo Hotel, Las Vegas, Latin Quarter, N.Y.C.; internat. syndicated beauty columnist, Chgo. Tribune/ N.Y. News Syndicate, 1950-70; designer sleepwear for A.N. Saab & Co., 1952-57, In Vogue with Arlene Dahl (Patterns), 1980-85. Hon. dir. Girl Scouts U.S., 1961—; mem. Father Flannagan's Boys Town; internat. chair Pearl Buck Found.; bd. dirs. Hollywood Mus. Recipient 8 Laurel awards Box Office Mag., Hollywood Walk of Fame star, Coup de Chapeau Deaville Film Festival award, 1982; named Best-Coiffed, 3 times, Woman of Yr., Advt. Club of N.Y.C., 1969, Mother of Yr., 1979. Mem. Author's Guild, Acad. Motion Picture Arts and Scis., Commanderie des Bontemps de Medoc, Nat. Acad. TV Arts and Scis., Internat. Platform Assn., Sierra Club, Nat. Trust Hist. Preservation, The Film Soc., Smithsonian Inst. Office: Dahlmark Prodns PO Box 116 Sparkill NY 10976

DAHL, GERALD LUVERN, psychotherapist, consultant, author; b. Osage, Iowa, Nov. 10, 1938; s. Lloyd F. and Leola J. (Painter) D.; B.A., Wheaton Coll., 1960; M.S.W., U. Nebr., 1962; PhD in psychotherapy (Hon.), Internat. U. Found., 1987; m. Judith Lee Brown, June 24, 1960; children—Peter, Stephen, Leah. Juvenile probation officer Hennepin County Ct. Services,

1962-65; cons. Citizens Council on Delinquency and Crime, Mpls., 1965-67; dir. patient services Mt. Sinai Hosp., Mpls., 1967-69; clin. social worker Mpls. Clinic of Psychiatry, 1969-82, G.L. Dahl & Assocs., Inc., Mpls., 1983—; asso. prof. social work Bethel Coll., St. Paul, 1964-83; spl. instr. sociology Golden Valley Luth. Coll., 1974-83; pres. Strategic Team-Makers, Inc., 1985—. Founder, Family Counseling Service, Minn. Baptist Conf.; bd. dirs. Edgewater Baptist Ch., 1972-75, chmn., 1974-75. Mem. AAUP, Am. Assn. Behavioral Therapists, Pi Gamma Mu. Author: Why Christian Marriages Are Breaking Up, 1979; Everybody Needs Somebody Sometime, 1980, How Can We Keep Christian Marriages from Falling Apart, 1988. Office: 4825 Hwy 55 Suite 140 Golden Valley MN 55422

DAHL, HARRY WALDEMAR, lawyer; b. Des Moines, Aug. 7, 1927; s. Harry Waldemar and Helen Gerda (Anderson) D.; m. Bonnie Sorensen, June 14, 1952; children: Harry Waldemar, Lisabeth (dec.), Christina. BA, U. Iowa, 1950; JD, Drake U., 1955. Bar: Iowa 1955, U.S. Dist. Ct. (no. and so. dists.) Iowa 1955, U.S. Supreme Ct 1965, Fla. 1970, Nebr. 1983, Minn. 1984. With Steward & Crouch, Des Moines, 1955-59; Iowa dep. indsl. commr. Des Moines, 1959-62; commr. 1962-71; of counsel Underwood, Gillis and Karcher, Miami, 1972-77; adj. prof. law Drake U., Des Moines, 1972—; exec. dir. Internat. Assn. Indsl. Accident Bds. and Commns., 1972-77; pres. Workers Compensation Studies, Inc., 1974—, Workers' Compensation Services, Inc., 1978—, Hewitt, Coleman & Assocs. Iowa, Inc., 1975-79; mem. adv. com. Second Injury Fund, Fla. Indsl. Relations Commn. Author: Iowa Law on Workmen's Compensation, 1975; editor: ABC Newsletter, 1964-77. Served with USNR, 1945-46. Recipient Adminstrs. award Internat. Assn. Indsl. Accident Bds. and Commns., 1967. Mem. Am. Trial Lawyers Assn., ABA, Iowa Bar Assn., Fla. Bar (bd. govs. 1988—), Nebr. Bar Assn., Minn. Bar Assn., Internat. Bar Assn., Am. Soc. Law and Medicine (council 1975-82), Iowa Assn. Workers' Compensation Lawyers (co-founder, past pres.), Def. Research Inst., Coll. of Workers Compensation Inc. (co-founder, regent), Swedish Pioneer Hist. Soc., Am. Swedish Inst., Des Moines Pioneer Club, East High Alumni Assn. (pres. 1975-76), Order of Coif. Lutheran. Lodges: Masons, Shriners, Sertoma (chmn. bd. dirs. 1974-75). Home: 3005 Sylvania Dr West Des Moines IA 50265 Office: 974 73 St #16 Des Moines IA 50312

DAHLBERG, JOYCE KAREN, communications company executive; b. Mpls., Sept. 30, 1943; d. Elon Clinton and Adelynne Elizabeth (Mitchell) Tuttle; m. Curtis Leroy Dahlberg, Dec. 23, 1967; children: Eric Curtis, Curtis Elon. BA cum laude, Hamline U., 1965; postgrad. U. Minn., community colls., 1965—. Tchr. English, Ind. Sch. Dist. 281, Robbinsdale, Minn., 1965-68; patient fin. rep. Univ. Hosps., U. Minn., Mpls., 1968-70; space analyst health scis. U. Minn., Mpls., 1970-71; freelance photographer, writer, editor for bus. communications, mags., newspapers, Mpls., 1975—; freelance franchise communications cons.; speaker various confs. and meetings; instr. continuing edn., 1988—. Editor: (newsletters) Friday Council for High Potential Children, 1981— (sec. 1981-82, pres. 1985-88), Minn. Park Suprs. Assn., 1980-86; writer ednl. videotapes Osseo TV/Media Prodns., 1978-81 (Upper Miss. Ednl. Videotape Competition award 1979), also pub. relations materials, software and tech. manuals, poetry, children's stories. Active numerous coms. United Methodist Ch., Fridley, Minn., 1978—, coordinator Year of Child, 1979; active YWCA Program Council, 1975-78, No. Suburban YWCA, Mpls.; vol. tchr. OMNIBUS, Fridley Schs., 1982, mem. community edn. tchr., 1985-86, mem. parent adv. com., 1985-87, others; citizen ambassador People to People Internat. to Republic of China, 1988. Mem. Women Entrepreneur People Network, Women in Communications (continuing edn. com., 1984-86), Minn. Council on Gifted and Talented (pres. Fridley chpt. 1985-88, newsletter edit. 1981—, sch. rep. 1982-84, advocate with State Ho. Reps. 1985-86), Fridley Council for High Potential Children, Freelance Communicators Network (charter, publicist), Am. Soc. Profl. and Exec. Women. Methodist. Address: 205 Rice Creek Blvd NE Minneapolis MN 55432

DAHLGREN, BO ARNE BERTIL, pension fund executive; b. Maltesholm, Scania, Sweden, Mar. 5, 1924; s. Åke and Lillie D.; m. Ingrid Wallner, June 20, 1949 (div. 1974); children: Elisabeth, Claes; m. Wanija de Jounge, May 9, 1977. Grad., U. Gothenburg, Sweden, 1948. Asst. v.p. AB Iföverken, Bromölla, Sweden, 1949; v.p. AB Iföverken, Malmö, Sweden, 1964-67; pres. AB Företagsfinans, Malmö and Stockholm, 1967-84; pres. pension fund Trefond Investments, Stockholm, 1984—. Author: Nycken till styrelserummet, 1983, Rösten på stämman, 1987. Lodge: Rotary. Home: Götavägen 10 A, S-18261 Djursholm Sweden Office: Trefond Investments, Hamngatan 6 5 tr, S-11147 Stockholm Sweden

DAHLGREN, JOHN ROBERT, military officer; b. Washington, Feb. 26, 1959; s. John Onsgard and Lois Faye (Reed) D.; m. Judy Neuman Prescott, Apr. 26, 1986. AA, N.Mex. Mil. Inst., 1980; BA, W.Va. U., 1983. Commd. 2d lt. U.S. Army, 1980, advanced through grades to capt., 1985; forward observer F.A., Fairmont, W.Va., 1981-82; with ordinance officer basic course Ordinance Corp., Aberdeen, Md., 1984; mgr. weapons systems matrix Ordinance Corp., Rock Island, Ill., 1984—. Mem. Nat. Hist. Preservation Trust, Ducks Unlimited, Pheasants Forever, Phi Theta Kappa (hon.). Republican. Lutheran. Clubs: Officer's, Arrowhead Hunt, BMW. Home: 3430 Winston Dr #4 Bettendorf IA 52722 Office: Hdqrs Armanent Munitions Chem Command Rock Island Arsenal 390 Rodman Ave Rock Island IL 61299

DAHLIN, ELIZABETH CARLSON, university administrator; b. Worcester, Mass., July 26, 1931; d. Alden Gustaf and Elizabeth Christine (Peterson) Carlson; m. Douglas Gordon Dahlin, June 27, 1953; children: Christine Elizabeth, Cynthia Jean, Constance May. BA, Wellesley Coll., 1953; postgrad. Harvard U., 1953, 64; MA, George Washington U., 1971. Substitute tchr. Fairfax County, Va., 1958-77; asst. folklife specialist, concessions mgr. Smithsonian Instn., Washington, 1976-77; asst. to exec. dir. Nat. Sch. Vol. Program, Alexandria, Va., 1978-80; asst. to v.p. devel. George Mason U., Fairfax, Va., 1980-83, dir. devel., 1983-87; exec. dir. George Mason U. Found., 1983—; v.p. for univ. devel., 1987—; bd. dirs. George Mason Bank Shares, Inc.; George Mason Bank. Treas., bd. dirs. Nation's Capital Council Girl Scouts U.S., 1972-78, award, 1978; chief election judge Fairfax County Electoral Bd., 1967-75; chmn. Belle Haven precinct Mount Vernon dist. Fairfax County Democratic Com.; bd. dirs. Alexandria Symphony, 1983-88; deacon United Ch. of Christ; mem. alumni council Wellesley Coll., 1970, 81. Brown U. grad. fellow, 1953. Mem. Va. Women's Polit. Caucus, Council Advancement and Support Edn., Profl. Women's Network, Textile Mus., Smithsonian Assocs., Nat. Aviation Club, AAUW, George Washington U. Alumni Council (edn. council), Arlington C. of C. (bd. dirs. 1984—), Phi Delta Kappa. Clubs: Wellesley (bd. dirs. 1969—, treas. 1978-80, pres. 1980-82), Harvard (Washington); Fort Myer Officer's. Home: 6041 Edgewood Terr Alexandria VA 22307 Office: George Mason U Devel House 4400 University Dr Fairfax VA 22030

DAHLIN, ROLF BRORSSON, mechanical engineer, researcher; b. Stockholm, Feb. 14, 1926; s. Bror and Sigrid (Hellström) D.; m. Hjördis Petersson, Sept. 25, 1958; children: Henrik, Eva, Ragnar. MS, Chalmers Tech. U., 1954. Researcher Ab Bofors, Karlskoga, Sweden, 1954-56, SAAB, Linköping, Sweden, 1956-58, Swedish Air Force, Stockholm, 1958-60; tech. mgr. Citograf Ab, Karlskrona, Sweden, 1960-68; researcher Ab UVA, Bromma, Sweden, 1968—. Contbr. articles to profl. jours; U.S. patentee in office machine, balancing apparatus, vibratory device. Mem. Am. Math. Soc., Svenska Matematiker Samfundet, Chalmerska Ingeniörsföreningen. Home: Kärrgränd 49, Vällingby 16246, Sweden

DAHLING, GERALD VERNON, lawyer; b. Red Wing, Minn., Jan. 11, 1947; s. Vernon and Lucille Alfrieda (Reuter) D.; m. Edell Marie Villella, July 26, 1969; children: David (dec.), Christopher, Elizabeth, Mary. BS, Winona (Minn.) State Coll., 1968; MS, U. Minn., 1970; PhD, Harvard U., 1974; JD, William Mitchell Coll. of Law, 1980. Bar: U.S. Patent Office 1979, Minn. 1980, Ind. 1980, U.S. Dist. Ct. (so. dist.) Ind. 1980. Patent atty. Eli Lilly and Co., Indpls., 1980-84, mgr. biotech. patents, 1984-86, asst. patent counsel biotech., 1986—. Mem. ABA, Ind. Bar Assn., Am. Intellectual Property Law Assn. (biotech. task force). Democrat. Roman Catholic. Home: 5362 Washington Blvd Indianapolis IN 46220 Office: Eli Lilly & Co Corporate Ctr Indianapolis IN 46285

DAHM, HELMUT JOHANNES, research institute administrator; b. Remagen, Germany, July 8, 1925; s. Hans and Helene (Schwamm) D.; m. Annemarie Hermann, Aug. 6, 1955; 1 son, Andreas. PhD, U. Mayence (W.Ger.), 1955; Habilitation, U. Munich (W.Ger.), 1974. Mem. editorial bd. Problems of the East, U.S. Embassy, Bonn., W.Ger., 1955-58; mem. editorial bd. Ost-Probleme, Fed. Office for Press and Info., Bonn., 1958-69, editor-in-chief, 1960-62; head first dept. Fed. Inst. for East European and Internat. Studies, Cologne, W.Ger., 1962—; prof. history of ideas and philosophy Fed. Inst. East European and Internat. Studies, Cologne, 1983—; head philosophy sect. 2d World Congress for Soviet and East European Studies, Garmisch-Partenkirchen, W.Ger., 1980. Author books, including: Dialectics in the Change of Soviet Philosophy, 1963, Deterrence or People's War (The Military Doctrines of the Soviet Union and The People's Republic of China), 1968, Mutiny on the Knees: The Crisis of the Marxist Conception of World and Man, 1969, Democratic Socialism: the Czechoslovakian Model, 1971, Vladimir Solovyev/Max Scheler, 1975; Main Features of Russian Thought, 1979; The Failed Escape, 1982; Ethics: Critique of the Communist 'Justification of the Good' , 1986, Socialist Theory of Crisis: The Soviet Turning-An Illusion, 1987; (with F. Kool) Technique of Power, 1974; (with Th. J. Blakeley and George L. Kline) Philosophical Sovietology: The Pursuit of a Science, 1988; contbr. numerous articles, chpts. to profl. publs., encys.; editorial bd. Studies in Soviet Thought, 1961—, Asian Thought and Soc., 1976—; editorial bd. series: Sovietica, 1961—. Decorated Fed. Cross of Merit. Mem. German Assn. Sci. and Presence (head philos. dep. 1979—), East Acad. Koenigstein (head scholarly council 1983—). Mem. Christian Democratic Party. Roman Catholic. Home: Im Tannenbusch 26, D-5300 Bonn 1 Federal Republic of Germany Office: Fed Inst for East European, & Internat Studies, Lindenbornstrasse 22, D-5000 Cologne 30 Federal Republic of Germany

DAHMEN, ERIK VERNER HARALD, economics educator; b. Halmstad, Sweden, Sept. 14, 1916; s. Elof and Selma Elvira (Manthe) D.; m. Margit Brandt, 1942; children: Jan, Harald, Elva. PhD, Lund U., Sweden, 1950; hon. doctorate, Swedish Bus. Sch. Finland, 1985. Dir. Inst. for Econ. Research, Stockholm, 1949-50; prof. econs. and social history Stockholm Sch. Econs., 1958-86; chmn. bd. Valand Ins. Corp., Stockholm, 1976-86, Inst. Econ. History Research, Stockholm, 1976—; mem. econs. facutly U. Lund, Sweden, 1988—; econ. advisor Stockholm Enskilda Banken, 1959-71, Skandinaviska Enskilda Banken, 1972—. Author: Entrepreneurial Acitivity in Swedish Industry, 1950, The Problem of Capital Formation, 1959, 1959, Pricing the Enviroment, 1968, Economies in Transformation, 1984, The Precondition for Economic Growth, 1988. Mem. Royal Acad. Engring. Scis., Royal Acad. Scis., Royal Acad. Letters, History, and Antiquities, Finnish Sci. Soc. Home: Rattarebacken 24, 13150 Nacka Sweden Office: Skandinaviska Enskilda Banken, 10640 Stockholm Sweden

DAHN, HANS, organic chemistry educator; b. Kassel, Ger., Jan. 2, 1919; s. Richard and Flora (Kaufmann) D.; m. Alice Winkler (div.); 1 son, Michael. Dr. phil., U. Basel (Switzerland), 1944. Privat-docent, U. Basel, 1950, chargé de cours, 1951, prof. extraordinaire, 1954-61, prof. ordinaire and dir. Inst. Organic Chemistry, U. Lausanne (Switzerland), 1961—. Contbr. articles to profl. jours. Bd. dirs. Swiss Nat. Sci. Found., 1970-81. Mem. Swiss Chem. Soc. (pres. 1968-69), Am. Chem. Soc. Office: Institut de Chimie Organique de, l'Universite rue de la Barre 2, 1005 Lausanne Switzerland

DAHN, INGE RUBEN, medical educator; b. Gothenburg, Sweden, Apr. 20, 1926; s. K. Ivan W. and Ester B. (Tillroth) D.; m. Jane A.M. Stranne, July 7, 1951; children—Mette, Martin, Torsten, Tove. Dr. Med., U. Lund, Sweden, 1965. Med. diplomate, Sweden. Asst. surgeon County Council, Kristianstad, Sweden, 1955-59, Lund, 1960-64; asst. prof. surgery U. Lund, 1965-74, asst. prof. adminstrv. medicine, 1975-81, asst. prof. social medicine, 1982—; cons. Nat. Bd. Health, Sweden, 1972-73; planning County Council, Malmö hus County, Sweden, 1973-77, cons. health sci., 1983—. Author: Surgery in Sweden, 1973; Lack-Surplus of Doctors, 1978. Contbr. articles to profl. jours. Fellow Swedish Med. Assn. Home: Svenska Vagen 63,, S-222 39 Lund, Sweden Office: Health Sci Centre, Vardcentralen S-250, 10 Dalby Sweden

DAHRENDORF, RALF GUSTAV, social scientist, educator; b. Hamburg, Germany, May 1, 1929; s. Gustav and Lina (Witt) D.; Dr.phil., U. Hamburg, 1952; Ph.D., London Sch. Econs., 1954; 14 hon. hon. degrees from European and Am. univs.; m. Ellen de Kadt. Privatdozent sociology U. Saar, W. Germany, 1957; fellow Center for Advanced Studies in Behavioral Scis., Palo Alto, Calif., 1957-58; prof. sociology U. Hamburg, W. Ger., 1958-60, U. Tubingen, 1960-66; prof. U. Constance, 1966-69, dean faculty social scis., 1966-67; vis. prof. various European, N. Am. univs.; mem. Fed. Parliament, Govt. of Fed. Republic Germany, 1969-70, parlimentary sec. of state in German Fgn. Office, 1969-70; mem. Commn. of the European Communities, 1970-74; dir. London Sch. Econs., 1974-84. Warden St. Anthony's Coll., Oxford, 1987—; trustee, Ford Found., 1976-87; mem. Council of British Acad., 1980-83; chmn. bd. Friedrich-Naumann Stiftung, 1982-87. mem. Hansard Soc. of Electoral Reform, 1975-76; mem. Royal Commn. on Legal Services, 1976-79; mem. Com. to Review the Functioning of Fin. Instns., 1977-80; mem. German PEN Centre, 1971—. Decorated hon. Knight Comdr. Order Brit. Empire, also by govts. of Senegal, Luxembourg, W. Ger., Austria, Belgium. Fellow Anglo German Soc. (presidium), British Acad., Royal Soc. Arts, Royal Coll. Surgeons (hon.); mem. Am. Acad. Arts and Scis. (hon.), Nat. Acad. Scis. (fgn. asso.), Am. Philos. Soc., Royal Irish Acad. (hon.), others. Mem. Free Dem. Party W. Ger. Author: Marx in Perspective, 1953; Industrie-und Betriebssoziologie, 1956; Class and Class Conflict, 1959; Die angewandte Aufklä rung, 1963; Gesellschaft unf Demokratie in Deutschland, 1965; Pfade aus Utopia, 1967; Essays in Theory of Society, 1968; Konflikt und Freiheit, 1972; Plä doyer fü r die Europä ische Union, 1973; The New Liberty, 1975; Life Chances, 1980; On Britain, 1982; Die Chancen der Krise, 1983 (all trans. into many langs.). Address: St Anthony's Coll, Oxford OX2 6JF, England Other: London Sch Econ & Polit Sci, Houghton St, London WC2A 2AE, England

DAI, AILIAN, dance company administrator; b. Trinidad, W.I., May 10, 1916; Arrived in People's Republic of China, 1940; d. Fredrick Yao Dai and Irene lau; m. Chien-yu Yeh, 1941 (div. 1952); stepdaughter, Ming Ming Yeh. Student, Trinity Coll. of Music, Trinidad, 1930; studied, Anton Dolin, Margaret Crashe and Marie Rambert, London, 1931-39; student, Joos-Leeder Sch. of Dance, Dartington Hall Devon, Eng., 1939-40. Head Nat. Opera Sch. Dance, Chung King, People's Republic of China, 1942-43, dance sect Nat. Inst. Social Edn., Chung King, 1943-44, Dance Group Yucai Sch., Chung King, 1944-47; dir. Dance Team of North China U., Beijing, 1949-53, Cen. Folk Song and Dance Ensemble, Beijing, 1953-56; prin. Beijing Dance Sch., 1954-64; artistic dir. Cen. Ballet of China, Beijing, 1964-66, artistic advisor, 1980—; v.p. Internat. Dance Council, Paris, 1982-86, UNESCO, 1986—. Choreographer Lotus Dance, 1953, Tibetan Spring Dance, 1953, Flying Apsaras Dance, 1955. Mem. standing com. China People's Polit. Consultative Conf., Beijing, 1983—, Internat. Juries of Dance and Ballet Bucharest, 1953, Moscow, 1955, Turino, 1983, Jackson, Miss., 1986, Tokyo, 1987, N.Y.C., 1987, Paris, 1988. Mem. China Dancers Assn. (pres. 1949, v.p. 1953—), Internat. Council of Kinetographie Laban/Labanotation, China Ballet Soc. (pres.). Office: Cen Ballet of China, 3 Tai Ping St, Beijing People's Republic of China

DAI, CHUANZENG, nuclear scientist; b. Ningpo, Chekiang, China, Dec. 26, 1921; m. An-ping Yu; 3 children. B.Sc., South-West Assn. U., Kunming, China, 1943; Ph.D., Liverpool U. (Eng.), 1951. Assoc. research fellow Inst. Atomic Energy, Beijing, China, 1951-56, research fellow, 1956-63, div. head, 1956-63, dep. dir., 1963-82, dir., 1982-85, hon. dir., 1986—. Vice chmn. Chinese nuclear power safety specialist com., 1986—. Mem. Academia Sinica (math. and physics div.), Nuclear Power Soc. (exec. v.p. 1984—). Office: Inst Atomic Energy, PO Box 275, Beijing People's Republic of China

DAI, SHU-HO, chemical machinery educator emeritus; b. Beijing, May 16, 1923; s. Ming-Zheng Dai and Wei-Xin Xu; m. Jia-Xhen Chu, Oct. 1947; children: Dai, Qi. BS, Nat. Central U., Chungking, People's Republic of China, 1946. Mem. faculty Nat. Central U., Nanjing, People's Republic of China, 1947-49, U. Nanjing, People's Republic of China, 1950-52; lectr. Nanjing Inst. Tech., People's Republic of China, 1953-58; sr. lectr. Nanjing Inst. Chem. Tech., People's Republic of China, 1959-77, prof. chem. machinery, 1978-85, vice chmn. dept. chem. machinery,, 1958-77, chmn. dept., 1978-86, chmn. dept. emeritus, 1986; cons. Xerox Co., Rochester, N.Y., 1981-82; vis. prof. U. Rochester, 1980-82. Author: (with others) Silicate Industrial Equipment, 1958, Cement Product Equipment, 1959, Process Equipment Design, 1961, 65, 80, Analysis in Process Equipment, 1987. Mem. Chinese Soc. Chem. Engring. (councilor 1978—), Chinese Soc. Chem. Machinery (councilor 1979-83, head of the councilors 1984—), Juangsu Province Br. Chinese Soc. Chem. Engring. (councilor 1978—), Am. Soc. Engring. Sci. Office: Nanjing Inst Chem Tech, No 5 New Model Rd, Nanjing Jiangsu 210009, People's Republic of China

DAICHES, DAVID, emeritus English literature educator, author; b. Sunderland, Eng., Sept. 2, 1912; s. Salis and Flora (Levin) Daiches; m. Isobel Mackay, July 27, 1937 (dec. Aug. 1977); children—Alan Harry, Jennifer Rachel, Elizabeth Mackay; m. 2d, Hazel Margaret Newman, Dec. 22, 1978 (dec. Sept. 1986). M.A., U. Edinburgh (Scotland), 1934, D.Litt. (hon.), 1976; D.Phil., U. Oxford (Eng.), 1937; L.H.D. (hon.), Brown U., 1964; Docteur de l'Université (hon.), Sorbonne, U. Paris, 1973; D.Litt. (hon.), U. Sussex, Brighton, Eng., 1978, U. Glasgow, 1987; D.Univ. (hon.), U. Stirling (Eng.), 1980. Bradley fellow Balliol Coll., Oxford U., 1936-37; asst. prof. English, U. Chgo., 1940-43; 2d sec. Brit. Embassy, Washington, 1944-46; prof. English, Cornell U., 1946-51; univ. lectr. English, Cambridge U. (Eng.), 1957-61, fellow Jesus Coll., 1957-62; dean Sch. English Studies, U. Sussex, 1961-67, prof. English, 1961-77, prof. emeritus, 1977—; LD Lit. (hon.), U. Glasgow, 1986. dir. Inst. for Advanced Study in Humanities, Edinburgh U. (Scotland), 1980-86, Gifford lectr., 1983. Author over 40 books, including: The Novel and the Modern World, 1939; A Study of Literature, 1948; Robert Burns, 1950; Two Worlds, 1956; Critical Approaches to Literature, 1956; Literary Essays, 1956; Milton, 1957; A Critical History of English Literature, 1960; More Literary Essays, 1968; Scotch Whisky, 1969; Sir Walter Scott and his World, 1971; (autobiography) A Third World, 1971; Robert Burns and his World, 1971; Prince Charles Edward Stuart, 1973; Robert Louis Stevenson and His World, 1973; Moses, 1975; James Boswell and His World, 1976; Scotland and the Union, 1977; Glasgow, 1977; Edinburgh, 1978; Literature and Gentility in Scotland, 1982; Robert Fergusson, 1983; God and the Poets, 1984. Editor: Fletcher of Saltoun: Selected Political Writings and Speeches, 1979; Edinburgh: A Traveller's Companion, 1986. Fellow Royal Soc. Lit., Royal Soc. Edinburgh; hon. mem. Assn. for Scottish Lit. Studies (pres. 1979-84), MLA; mem. Saltire Soc. (pres. 1980-87). Club: Scottish Arts (Edinburgh).

DAILEY, FRED WILLIAM, hotel exec.; b. Aurora, Ill., Feb. 3, 1908; s. Louis A. and Frances (McCoy) D.; m. Elizabeth Murphy, Apr. 22, 1946; children—Michael K., Pam Sue Hinman. Builder, operator tourist resorts, 1933-42; builder, So. Calif., 1946-52; pres. Mokuleia Assos., Mokuleia Polo Farms, Inc., Waikiki Corp., A.D. Corp. Adv. bd. Hawaii, Army; past mem. Honolulu Bd. Water Supply. Served as maj. AUS, World War II. Decorated Purple Heart. Mem. U.S. Air Force Assn., C. of C., Am. Hotel Assn. (past dir.), Hawaii Hotel Assn. (past pres.), Hawaii Horse Show Assn. (past pres.), Hawaii Polo and Racing Assn. (pres.), U.S. Polo Assn. (gov.). Clubs: Los Angeles Athletic; Hawaii Polo (Honolulu); Santa Barbara Polo; Big Bend Ranch (pres.) (Korbel). Author: Blood, Sweat and Jeers; One Man's Meat, Polo Is A Four Letter Word. Address: 2003 Kalia Rd Honolulu HI 96815 Address: Mokuleia Polo Farm Inc Gahu HI 96815

DAILY, FAY KENOYER, botany educator; b. Indpls., Feb. 17, 1911; d. Fredrick and Camellia Thea (Neal) Kenoyer; A.B., Butler U., 1935, M.S., 1952; m. William Allen Daily, June 24, 1937. Lab. technician Eli Lilly & Co., Indpls., 1935-37, Abbott Labs., North Chicago, Ill., 1939, William S. Merrell & Co., Ohio, 1940-41; lubrication chemist Indpls. Propellor div. Curtiss-Wright Corp., 1945; lectr. botany Butler U., Indpls., 1947-49, instr. immunology and microbiology, 1957-58, lectr. microbiology, 1962-63, mem. herbarium staff, 1949-87, curator cryptogamic herbarium, 1987—. Grantee Ind. Acad. Sci., 1961-62. Mem. Am. Inst. Biol. Sci., Bot. Soc. Am., Phycol. Soc. Am., Internat. Phycol. Soc., Ind. Acad. Sci., Torrey Bot. Club, Sigma Xi, Phi Kappa Phi, Sigma Delta Epsilon. Republican. Methodist. Co-author book on sci. history. Contbr. articles on fossil and extant charophytes (algae) to profl. jours. Home: 5884 Compton St Indianapolis IN 46220

DAILY, LOUIS, ophthalmologist; b. Houston, Apr. 23, 1919; s. Louis and Ray (Karchmer) D.; B.S., Harvard U., 1940; M.D., U. Tex. at Galveston, 1943; Ph.D., U. Minn., 1950; m. LaVerl Daily, Apr. 5, 1958; children—Evan Ray, Collin Derek. Intern, Jefferson Davis Hosp., Houston, 1943-44; resident in ophthalmology Jefferson Davis Hosp., 1944-45, Mayo Found., Rochester, Minn., 1947-50; individual practice medicine, specializing in ophthalmology, Houston, 1950—; asso. prof. clin. ophthalmology U. Tex-Houston, 1972-86 , Baylor Med. Sch., Houston, 1950—. Vice pres. bd. dirs. Mus. Med. Sci., 1973-85, pres., 1980-82. Served as lt. (j.g.) USNR, 1945-46. Diplomate Am. Bd. Ophthalmology. Fellow A.C.S., Internat. Coll. Surgeons; mem. Soc. Prevention of Blindness (med. chmn. Tex. 1968-70), Contact Lens Assn. Ophthalmologists (exec. bd. 1976-78), Tex. Ophthal. Assn. (pres. 1963-64), Houston Ophthal. Soc. (pres. 1970-71), numerous other med. socs., Sigma Xi, Alpha Omega Alpha. Jewish. Clubs: Doctors, Harvard (dir. 1965-66) (Houston). Editorial bd. Jour. Pediatric Ophthalmology, 1964-68; asso. editor Eye, Ear, Nose and Throat Monthly, 1962-65, Jour. Ophthalmic Surgery, 1970; contbr. numerous articles to profl. publs., also contbr. to books. Home: 2523 Maroneal St Houston TX 77030 Office: 1517 Med Towers Houston TX 77030

DAIN, STEPHEN JOHN, optometrist, educator, researcher; b. Wakefield, Yorkshire, Eng., Apr. 25, 1945; arrived in Australia, 1973; s. Sidney John and Margery (Impey) D.; m. Alison Theresa Wise, Aug. 9, 1969; children: Claire Elizabeth, Timothy Michael. BSc with honors, City U., London, 1968, PhD, 1972. Mng. optometrist G.C. Bateman Ltd., Guildford, Eng., 1972-73; research fellow dept. optometry U. Melbourne, Australian, 1973-75; lectr. Sch. Optometry, U. New S. Wales, Kensington, Kensington, Australia, 1976-82, sr. lectr., 1982—; cons. to govt. and industry; lectr. Australian and New Zealand Assn. for Advancement of Sci., 1983. Mem. Internat. Research Group on Color Vision Deficiencies, Color Soc. Australia (treas. 1985—), Econs. Soc. Australian and New Zealand. Mem. Uniting Church of Australia. Office: Univ New S Wales, PO Box 1, Kensington New South Wales 2033, Australia

DAJANI, MOHAMAD HUSSEIN, engineer; b. Irbia, Jordan, May 26, 1952; s. Hussein Taher and Abla Anis (Houry) D.; m. Carmen Luigi Sabatini, May 9, 1979; children: Dara, Diala, Dana. BArch, U. Studies of Faculty of Architecture, Florence, Italy, 1977. Architect Dib and Dib, Beirut, 1977-78; site engr. Nat. Indsl. Contracting Co., Doha, Qatar, 1978-82, project engr., 1982—. Mem. Jordan Syndicate of Architects and Engrs. Home: PO Box 3713, Doha Qatar Office: Nat Indsl Contracting Co, PO Box 3713, Doha Qatar

DAK, TEJ MAL, rural sociologist; b. Udaipur, India, Sept. 1, 1936; s. Bhura Lal and Mithoo Bai D.; m. Bhanwar Dak, Apr. 23, 1959; children: Pushpender, Vandana, Hem Lata. BA, Rajasthan U., 1957, MA in Sociology, 1959; PhD in Sociology, Punjab U., 1977. Sr. instr. Social Edn. Organizers Tng. Ctr., Udaipur, India, 1961-66; lectr. in sociology Extension Edn. Inst., Nelokheri, India, 1966-76; vice prin. Extension Edn. Inst., Nelokheri, 1976-81; assoc. prof. Haryana Agrl. U., Hisar, India, 1981—. Author: Social Research, 1959, Rural Sociology in India, 1963, Social Inequalities and Rural Devel., 1982; editor: Caste and Class in Agrarian Society, 1985, Aging in India: The Challenge for Society, 1987, Women and Work in Indian Society, 1988; contbr. over 75 papers to profl. publs. Mem. Indian Sociol. Soc. Office: Haryana Agrl U, Dept Sociology, Hisar Haryana 125 004, India

DAKIN, ARTHUR HAZARD, writer; b. Boston, Jan. 25, 1905; s. Arthur Hazard and Emma Frances (Sahler) D.; A.B., Princeton U., 1928, M.A., 1929, Ph.D., 1933; D. Phil., Oxford U., 1938. Author: Von Hügel and the Supernatural; Man the Measure; chpts. in Audiovisual Aids to Instruction (edited by W. Exton) and The Heritage of Kant (edited by G.T. Whitney and D.F. Bowers); A Paul Elmer More Miscellany; Paul Elmer More. Comdr., USNR ret.; exec. officer U.S. Naval Tng. Sch., Hampton, Va., and officer-in-charge Advance Base Reshipment Depot Battalion, Iroquois Point, Oahu, T.H., World War II. Mem. Am. Philos. Assn., Huguenot Soc., Soc. Colonial Wars, Saint Nicholas Soc. City N.Y., Metaphys. Soc. Am., Phi Beta Kappa.

Clubs: Algonquin (Boston); Century, Princeton, University (N.Y.C.). Home: 355 S Pleasant St Amherst MA 01002

DAL, GUNNAR, author; b. Iceland, June 4, 1923; s. Sigurd and Margret (Halldorsdottir) Davidsson; student U. Edinburg, 1950-51, Calcutta U., 1951-53, U. Wis., 1956-57; m. Elisabet, Oct. 22, 1975; children—Gunnar, Jonas, Gudvardur. Tchr., Keflavik Grammar Sch., 1968-76, Grammar Sch. of Breidholt, Reykjavik, 1976-78; editor Nutiminn and Kjordaemabladid, 1959-62; schoolmaster Party Sch. of Progressive Party, 1960-62. Recipient Lit. awards from State, 1950—. Authors Found. awards, 1976, 77, Radio and TV prize, 1976. Mem. PEN, Authors Soc., Union Icelandic Authors. Author: (poems) Being, 1949, The Sfnix, 1953; Forcast by the Stars, 1954; Oktoberpoems, 1959; The Six Darsanas, 1962; The Voices of Dawn, 1964; Plato, 1966; Aristotoles, 1966; (novels) Wealth and Fame, 1968, Youth at War, 1970, Kamala, 1976; Indian Philosophy, 1972; Greek Philosophy, 1975; Collection of Poems, 1977; The World in His Hand, 1978; Existentialism, 1978; Western Philosophy, 1979; (poems), The Age of the Fool (poems), 1979; Guru Govinda (novel), 1980; 100 Poems of Lackjartorg, 1982; The Modern World View, 1983; (poems) Between Friends, 1984, City Poems, 1986, Land of My Mothers, 1988. translator: The Prophet (Kahlil Gibran), 1958; The Crescent Moon (Tagore), 1964. Home: Hringbraut 43, Reykjavik Iceland

DALAI LAMA, (TENZIN GYATSO), supreme temporal and religious head Tibet; b. Taktser, Amdo province, Tibet, July 6, 1935; D. Buddhist Philosophy, Monasteries Sera, Drepung and Gaden, Lhasa, 1959. Enthroned Dalai Lama XIV, Lhasa, 1940; was requested to assume full polit. power, 1950; fled to Chumbi in South Tibet on Chinese invasion, 1950; negotiated with China, 1951; fled to India after abortive revolt of Tibetan people against Communist Chinese, 1959. Mem. nat. com. Chinese People's Polit. Consultative Conf., 1951-59; hon. chmn. China Buddhist Assn., 1953-59; del. Nat. Productivity Council, 1954-59, vice chmn. standing com.; chmn. preparatory com. Autonomous Region Tibet, 1955-59. Decorated Magsaysay award, Lincoln, Palketta and Alber Schweitzer Humanitarian awards. Author: My Land and My People, 1962; The Opening of the Wisdom Eye, 1963; An Introduction to Buddhism, 1965; Key to the Middle Way, 1971; Universal Responsibility and Good Heart, 1977; Four Essential Buddhist Commentaries, 1982; Kindness, Clarity and Insight, 1984; A Human Approach to World Peace, 1984 and others. Address: Thekchen Choeling, Dharmsala 176219, Himachal Pradesh India

DAL CANTO, MAURO CARLO, neuroscientist, educator; b. Soriano, Italy, Jan. 1, 1944; s. Alvaro and Eggi Dal C.; came to U.S., 1969, naturalized, 1976; M.D., U. Pisa (Italy), 1967; m. Mariafiora Neri, Jan. 4, 1968; children—Richard, Albert. Intern, L.I. Coll. Hosp., Bklyn., 1969-70; resident in pathology and neuropathology Albert Einstein Coll. Medicine, Bronx, N.Y., 1970-74; assoc. pathology Northwestern U. Med. Sch., Chgo., 1974-75, asst. prof. pathology and neurology, 1975-77, assoc. prof., 1977-81, prof. pathology and neurology, 1981—; dir. neuropathology Children's Meml. Hosp., Chgo., 1978-81, Northwestern U. Med. Sch., 1981—; cons. Evanston (Ill.) Hosp. Nat. Multiple Sclerosis Soc. grantee, 1976, 79, NIH grantee, 1976—. Mem. HIH Neurology C Study Section, 1984—; mem. editorial bd. Jour. Neuropathology and Exptl. Neurology, 1987—. Mem. Am. Assn. Neuropathologists, AAAS, Soc. for Neurosci. Roman Catholic. Contbr. articles to profl. jours. Home: 430B W Webster Ave Chicago IL 60614 Office: Northwestern U Med Sch Dept Pathology 303 Chicago Ave Chicago IL 60611

DALE, LEON ANDREW, educator, arbitrator; b. Paris, May 9, 1921; m. Arlene R. Dale; children: Glenn Roy, Melinda Jennifer. B.A., Tulane U., 1946; M.A., U. Wis., 1947, Ph.D., 1949. Grad. asst. in econs. U. Wis., 1946-48; Asst. prof. labor econs. U. Fla., 1949-50; internat. economist AFL, Paris, 1950-53; AFL rep. at nat. labor convs. Greece, 1951, Naples, Italy, 1951, Switzerland, Sweden, Norway, Belgium, Austria, Luxembourg, Gt. Britain, 1950-53; cons. U.S. Govt., 1954-56; internat. economist U.S. Dept. Labor, Washington, 1956-59; chief econ. sect. Embassy of Morocco, Washington, 1959-60; prof., chmn. dept. mgmt. and indsl. relations, dir. internat. ctr., coordinator courses for fgn. students U. Bridgeport, Conn., 1960-69; prof. mgmt. and human resources Calif. State Poly. U., Pomona, 1969—; acting chmn. bus. mgmt. dept. Calif. State Poly. U., summer 1973, coordinator internat. activities Sch. Bus. Adminstrn., 1969-77; lectr. Internat. Confedn. Tree Trade Unions Summer Sch., Wörgl, Austria, 1951; lectr. on Am. labor UN, Stockholm, 1952; lectr. U. Wis., Milw., 1960; vis. prof. Columbia U., 1966, 67, Bernard Baruch Sch. Bus. and Pub. Adminstrn., 1966-69; cons., arbitrator, fact-finder State of Conn., 1964-69; Am. del., speaker 3d Internat. Symposium on Small Bus., Washington, 1976, 4th Internat. Symposium on Small Bus., Seoul, Korea, 1977, 5th Internat. Symposium on Small Bus., Anaheim, Calif., 1978, 6th Internat. Symposium on Small Bus., Berlin, 1979; also mem. U.S. steering com. Internat. Symposium on Small Bus.; sr. cons. Am. Grad. U., Covina, Calif., 1981-82; adj. prof. econs. Nat. U., San Diego, 1981-86, Pepperdine U., 1986; discussion leader Calif. Inst. Tech. Internat. Conf. on Combining Best of Japanese and U.S. Mgmt., Anaheim, 1981; lectr. on indsl. relations to execs. Miller Brewing Co., Irwindale, Calif., 1983; cons. Agy. Internat. Devel., N'Djamena, Republic of Chad, 1987; cons. to Minister for Planning, Republic of Chad; cons., instr. behavior courses U. Chad.; instr. mgmt. internat. ctr. Calif. State Ploytech. U., Pomona, 1988. Author: Marxism and French Labor, 1956, A Bibliography of French Labor, 1969; video tape Industrial Relations and Human Resources, 1982, U.S. Industrial Relations of Today and Tomorrow, 1987; contbr. articles to profl. jours. Served with U.S. Army, 1942-45. Named Outstanding Educator of Am., 1972, 73; recipient U. Bridgeport Faculty Research and Experimental Fund grant, 1962, fellowship econs. U. Wis., 1949. Mem. Am. Arbitration Assn. (nat. panel arbitrators, nat. public employment disputes settlement panel), Indsl. Relations Research Assn., Am. Acad. Polit. and Social Sci., Soc. Profls. Dispute Resolution (charter). Club: Racing-Club de France. (Paris). Home: 30 S La Senda Laguna Beach CA 92677 Office: Calif State Poly U Pomona CA 91768

DALE, MARTIN ALBERT, investment banking consultant; b. Newark, Jan. 3, 1932; s. Philip D. and Lucie M. (Mintz) D.; B.A., Princeton, 1953; postgrad. (Fulbright fellow) U. Strasbourg (France), 1953-54; M.A. in Internat. Econs. with honors, Tufts U., 1955; m. Joan C. Dale, Apr. 3, 1954 (div. 1977); children—Charles, W. Gregory, Pamela, Eric; m. m. Berteline Baier, Nov. 21, 1980. Fgn. service officer U.S. Dept. State, 1955-60; pvt. counsellor, econ. adviser Prince Rainier III of Monaco, 1960-64; v.p., exec. asst. to pres. Grand Bahama Port Authority Ltd., Freeport, 1965-67; sr. v.p. fin., adminstrn. and ops. Revlon Internat. Corp., N.Y.C., 1967-72; corporate sr. v.p., dir. office strategic projects W.R. Grace & Co., N.Y.C., 1972-82; investment banking cons., 1983—; dir. Henkel of Am., Inc. Biotherapeutics, Inc; chmn. bd. of trustee Lycée Francais de N.Y. Republican. Clubs: Princeton (South Fla.). Home: 6061 Collins Ave Apt 16-F Miami Beach FL 33140

D'ALESSANDRO, EDWARD G., lawyer; b. Newark, Nov. 20, 1929; s. Orazio and Aida (Alexander) D'A.; m. Joan Elena D'Alessandro, June 29, 1957; children—Donna, Jan, Edward G., Jill. B.A., Rutgers U., 1951; LL.B, J.D., Boston U., 1954. Bar: N.J. 1954, N.Y. 1981, U.S. Dist. Ct. N.J. 1954, U.S. Ct. Appeals (3d cir.) 1956, U.S. Supreme Ct. 1959. Assoc., Anthony Calandra, Esq., 1955-57; asst. prosecutor Essex County, 1957-59; ptnr. Friedman & D'Alessandro, 1959-76; sr. ptnr. D'Alessandro, Sussman & Jacovino , Esqs. and predecessors, 1976—; adv. bd. Carteret Savs. & Loan Assn., 1st Nat. State Bank N.J.; gen. csl. Morristown Housing Authority; csl. Essex County Republican Com., 1968-69; former csl. Newark Housing Authority, Essex County Osteo. Soc.; spl. csl. N.J. Hwy. Dept., N.J. Turnpike Authority. Bd. trustees W. Essex Gen. Hosp.; bd. dirs. Newark Boys Club, Newark Police Athletic League; mem. Garden State Ballet Found., N.J. Symphony Found., Spl. Adv. Council Future of N.J., Colonial Symphony Soc.; former csl. Patrolmen's Benevolent Assn. Served with U.S. Army, 1954. Recipient Charles E. Rome award, 1952, 53; cert. civil and criminal trial atty. Mem. ABA, N.J. Bar Assn., Essex County Bar Assn., Am. Trial Lawyers Assn., Nat. Assn. Def. Lawyers in Criminal Cases, Am. Judicature Soc., Am. Arbitration Assn., Morris County Bar Assn. Clubs: Met., Met. Opera (N.Y.C.); Morris County (N.J.) Country; Confrerie de la Chaine des Rotisseurs, Tarrantine (Maine).

DALEY, KEITH IZETT, supermarket chain executive; b. Clarendon, Jamaica, Jan. 19, 1938; s. Charles and Amy Bell (Shaw) D.; student Coll. Arts and Scis. Tech., 1960-63, U. W.I., 1968-71; m. Leonie Patricia Hanson, June 10, 1967; children—Keith Michael, Karen Amy, Rodney Oliver. Storekeeper Ewan D. Macdougal Ltd., Kingston, 1958-63; fin. controller Nat. Packaging Corp., Kingston, Jamaica, 1965-73, v.p., 1973-76; exec. v.p. Masters Corp. Ltd., Kingston, 1977—; mng. dir. Allied Stores Ltd., 1978—; dir. Nat. Continental Corp., Nat. Agencies Ltd., Caldon Fin. Merchant Bank, Devel. Services Ltd., K.A.R. Ltd. Chmn. bd. govs. Lister Mair/Gilby Sch. for Deaf; mem. exec. bd. Jamaica Assn. for Deaf; mem. Jamaica Council for Handicapped; bd. dirs. Scouts Assn. Jamaica. Recipient Nat. Honour Officer of Order of Distinction Govt. of Jamaica, 1987. Mem. Adminstrv. Mgmt. Soc. (asst. sec.), Jamaica Rifle Assn. Methodist. Clubs: Kingston Cricket, Liguanea, Rotary of Kingston (past pres.). Home: 3 Pine View Red Hills, Saint Andrew Jamaica Office: Allied Stores Ltd, 1 Tobago Ave, Kingston 5 Jamaica

DALEY, TIMOTHY PATRICK, police officer, security consultant; b. Little Rock, Jan. 15, 1947; s. Robert Patrick and Eloise Francis (Sisco) D.; m. Bettye Lou Cox, Oct. 14, 1967; 1 dau., Robyn Renae. B.S., U. Ark.-Little Rock, 1974; cert. FBI Nat. Acad., Quantico, Va., 1977. Patrolman, Little Rock Police Dept., 1969-75, sgt., 1975-79, lt., 1979-81, capt., 1981—; cons. Pleasant Valley Country Club, Little Rock, 1976—; chmn. Ark. Bd. Pvt. Investigators and Security Guard Agencies; lobbyist Ark. Mcpl. Police Assn.; trustee Little Rock Police Pension Fund Bd., 1984—; appointed mem. Gov.'s Task Force on Crime, 1984-85, Ark. Law Enforcement Officers Meml. Com., treas., 1985—; dir. Fulfill a Dream, Inc. Pres. Pleasantree Property Owners Assn., 1981. Named Officer of the Month, Sertoma Club, 1971, 72, 75. Mem. Ark. Mcpl. Police Assn. (pres. 1983), Internat. Assn. Chiefs of Police, Nat. Assn. Crime Prevention, FBI Nat. Acad. Assocs. (sec.-treas. Ark. chpt. 1985, 2d v.p. 1986). Clubs: Black River Canoe (v.p. 1985-86), Big Lake (Little Rock). Lodge: Fraternal Order Police (recognition award 1983). Home: 15 Kings Ct Little Rock AR 72211 Office: Little Rock Police Dept 700 W Markham St Little Rock AR 72201

DALI, SALVADOR, artist; b. Figueras nr. Barcelona, Spain, May 11, 1904; s. Salvador and Felipa (Domeneck) D.; m. Gala Dali, Sept., 1935. Student pub. and pvt. schs., Bros. of Marist Order, Figueras; student, Sch. Fine Arts, Madrid, 1921-26. Influenced by Italian Futurists, 1923-25; became a Surrealist, Paris, 1929; designed jewelry, furniture and art nouveau decorations, 1929-31; designer films of Luis Bunuel; symbolic interpretations of legend of William Tell and Millet's The Angelus, 1934; series of beach scenes at Rosas, Spain, literal pictures of his dreams, 1934-46; decorated residence of Edward James, London, 1936; designed Dali's Dream House, N.Y. World's Fair, 1939; designed ballets including Bacchanale, Met. Opera, 1939; Labyrinth book, costumes, scenery; Cafe de Chiuita, Spanish Festival, Met. Opera, 1942; one-man shows include Julien Levy Gallery, N.Y.C., 1933, Arts Club, Chgo., 1941, Dalzell Hatfield Galleries, Los Angeles, Mus. Modern Art, N.Y.C., Knoedler Gallery, N.Y.C.; exhibited in numerous group shows, Paris, London, Barcelona, N.Y.C.; retrospective exhbn., Rotterdam, 1970-71; author: (autobiography) Secret Life of Salvador Dali, 1942, Diary of a Genius, 1965, The Unspeakable Confessions of Salvador Dali, 1976. Recipient $5000 Huntington Hartford Found. award, 1957. Address: care Carstairs Gallery 11 E 57th St New York NY 10022 *

DALIGAND, DANIEL, engineer, association executive, expert witness; b. Lyon, France, June 14, 1942; s. Maurice and Pierina Maria (Grandelli) D.; m. Christiane Elisabeth H. Agobian, Dec. 17, 1966. M. in Chem. Enging., ICPI, 1965. Cert. engr. Engr., SNIP, Paris, 1967-72, gen. sec., 1972—; adminstrv. sec. Eurogypsum, Paris, 1971—; sec. 13 mem. jury best craftsmanship in plaster work soc., Paris, 1982, 86; counsellor for technol. edn., 1986—. Author: (with J. Gibaru) Le Platre, 1981; (with others) Le Platre, Physico chimie, fabrication, 1982; Le Platre—Techniques de l'Ingenieur, 1986; editor: Platre Info. Jour. Office: Syndicat Nat des Inds, 3 rue Alfred Roll, 75849-Cedex, 17 Paris France

DALLA CHIARA, MARIA LUISA, philosopher, educator; b. Pola, Yugoslavia, Oct. 7, 1938; d. Pietro and Herta (Scopini) Dalla C.; m. Giuliano Scabia, July 11, 1960 (div. 1985); children: Marco, Scabia. Laurea, U. Padova, Italy, 1961. Prof. logic U. Florence, 1970—. Author books and articles. Mem. Italian Soc. for Logic and Philosophy Sci. (pres. 1987). Home: Via Panciatichi 38/5, Florence Italy Office: U Florence, Via Bolognese 52, Florence Italy

DALLA CHIESA, ROMEO, bank executive; b. Leghorn, Italy, Oct. 15, 1924; s. Romano and Maria Laura (Bergonzi) D.; m. Ebba Tamm (div.); children: Magnus, Umberto, Carlo, Marco, Riccardo. LLD, U. Rome; postgrad. bus. econs., Am. U. With head office Banca D'Italia, Rome, 1943-49, World Bank, Washington, 1949-58; loan officer Far East dept., gen. mgr. European Econ. Community loans European Investment Bank, Luxembourg, 1958-81; gen. fin. advisor Banca Nazionale del Lavoro, Rome, 1981-82; chmn. bd. dirs. Banco Di Roma, SPA, Rome, 1983—; economist, econ. advisor Govts. Panama and Thailand; vice chmn. Banco Di Roma, Paris, 1984; chmn. Rominvest, Rome, 1985, Finroma, Rome, 1986; hon. bd. dirs. European Investment Bank. Named Grande Ufficiale Della Repubblica Italiana, 1985. Mem. Assonime Assn. Fra Le Soc. Italiane Per Azioni (bd. dirs. 1983), Nomisma Soc. di Studi Economici SPA (bd. dirs. 1984), Inst. for Applied System Analysis (adv. bd. 1985), Camera De Commercio Italo-Sovietica (bd. dirs. 1987), Assn. Bancaria Italiana (bd. dirs. 1983), Internat. Council for New Initiatives in East-West Cooperation. Office: Banco di Roma, Viale Tupini, 00144 Rome Italy

DALLEAS, BRUNO RENE, physician; b. Bordeaux, France, Dec. 14, 1950; s. Rosny Rene and Monique Marie (Defontaines) D. MD, U. Bordeaux, 1978, D. Psychiatry, 1982, diploma in speech pathology, 1983, diploma in nutrition, 1987. Resident Vauclaire Hosp., Montpon, France, 1977-80, Garderose Hosp., Libourne, France, 1980-82, Charles Perrens Hosp., Bordeaux, 1982-84; med. cons. Pellegren Hosp., Bordeaux, 1984—. Author: Human Voice Characters, 1987. Mem. Internat. Assn. Phonetics, French Soc. Phonetics, Union French Phoneticists. Clubs: Facette, Passion des Arts. Home: Moulin de Peyfroment, 33750 Saint Quentin de Baron France

DALMIA, VISHNU HARI, cement company executive; b. India, May 1924; s. Shri Jaidayal Dalmia. With Tata Airlines, Indian Nat. Airways; chmn. Dalmia Dairy Industries Ltd., Golden Tobacco Co. Ltd., Sree Meenakshi Mills Ltd.; pres. Dalmia Cement (Bharat) Ltd., New Delhi; dir. Dalton Property Co. Ltd., Manchester, Eng., Export-Import Bank of India. Mem. India Tourism Adv. Bd.; bd. govs. Indian Inst. Tourism and Travel Mgmt.; mng. trustee Dalmia Charitable Trust; joint mng. trustee Shri Krishna Janmasthan Seva Sansthan; mem. 1st Wage Bd. for Cement Industry, 1958, Bonus Com. for Sugar Industry Uttar Pradesh, 1966. Vishnu H. Dalmia award for best book in Rajasthani lang. presented annually in his honor. Mem. Internat. Vegetarian Union (hon. v.p.), Indian Fedn. UN Assns. (v.p.), World Fedn. UN Assns. (internat. v.p. 1973-77), Internat. C. of C. (pres. Indian nat. com. 1976-77), Fedn. Indian Chambers Commerce and Industry (chmn. Indian sect. Indo-Netherlands econ. cooperation com., chmn. subcom. on tourism), Cement Mfrs. Assn. (pres. 1968-70), Indian Sugar Mills Assn. (pres. 1969-70), All Indian Distillers Assn. (pres. 1963-64). Office: Dalmia Cement (Bharat) Ltd, Hansalaya, 15 Barakhamba Rd, New Delhi 110001 India

DALRYMPLE, STEPHEN HARRIS, computer scientist, consultant; b. Austin, Tex., Dec. 2, 1932; s. Dewey Culberson and Marian Francis (Harris) D.; m. Sonia Beatrice Curd, Nov. 28, 1952; children—Sheri Lynn, Cindy Marie, Stephen Harris, Terrance Christopher. B.A., U. Tex., 1954, M.A., 1959. Staff mem. Los Alamos Sci. Lab., N.Mex., 1954-60; unit chief, sr. advisor Autonetics, Anaheim, Calif., 1960-65, 67-69; sr. specialist Planning Research Corp., Westwood, Calif., 1965-67; dir. ops. Central Computer Corp., Anaheim, Calif., 1969-70; br. chief McDonnell Douglas Astronautics, Huntington Beach, Calif., 1970-81; sr. computer scientist Sci. Applications Internat. Corp., La Jolla, Calif., 1981—. Pres. Tustin High PTO, Calif., 1974; scoutmaster Orange County council Boy Scouts Am., 1971. AEC grad. fellow, Los Alamos, N.Mex., 1958. Mem. Assn. Computing Machinery, IEEE, Math. Assn. Am., Acacia. Republican. Clubs: Soc. Am. Magicians, Internat. Brotherhood of Magicians. Home and Office: 1332 Arloura Way Tustin CA 92680

DALSKOV, TIM, energy technology executive, b. Copenhagen, May 13, 1945; M.A. in Econs., U. Copenhagen, 1973; B.Commerce, Copenhagen Sch. Bus. Adminstrn., 1975. With A.P. Moller (Maersk), 1972-84; exec. v.p. Semco Internat. and Dancare, Copenhagen, 1984-86; sr. cons. AIM Internat. Mktg. Cons., Copenhagen, 1986-87; sales dir. Kosan Teknova, Copenhagen, 1987-88; mng. dir. Volund Varmeteknik (Heat Technology Ltd., 1988—; external lectr. Copenhagen Sch. Bus. Adminstrn., 1976—. Served to 1st lt. Danish Army, 1964-66. Active UN, Cyprus, 1971. Club: Fgn. Trade (chmn. 1981-83). Home: Fredensvej 1, 2950 Vedbaek Denmark Office: Volund Varmeteknik A/S, 6920 Videback Denmark

DALTON, ROBERT I., JR., textile executive, broker, consultant, researcher; b. Charlotte, N.C., Apr. 2, 1921; s. Robert I. and Edith (Gossett) D.; m. Gwin Barnwell, Nov. 16, 1946; children—Millie, Edith. B.S. in Textile Engring., N.C. State U. Vice pres. sales Whitin Machine Works, Whitinsville, Mass., 1946-67; pres. Cocker Machine and Foundry, Gastonia, N.C., 1967-70, Tech-Tex Inc., Charlotte, 1970—, Gossett-Dalton Co., Charlotte, 1973—, dir., 1955—; bd. dir. Cadmus Communication Co., Richmond, Va., 1983—, Am.-Truetzschler, Charlotte, 1976—, N.C. Nat. Bank, Charlotte, 1962—; chmn. bd. trustees Brevard (N.C.) Coll., 1987—. Pres. Charlotte Symphony Orch., 1979-80; mem. bd. edn. Mecklenburg County, Charlotte, 1957-58; chmn. nat. bd. dirs. Handicapped Orgn. Women, Inc., 1986; chmn. bd. trustees Brevard Coll, 1987—. Served to maj. U.S. Army, 1943-46, ETO. Mem. Phi Psi. Methodist. Clubs: Charlotte City (pres. 1980-81), Charlotte Country. Avocations: tennis; photography. Home: 5900 Sardis Rd Charlotte NC 28226

DALVI, RAMESH R., toxicologist, educator, consultant; b. Bombay, India, Nov. 8, 1938; s. Rajaram S. and Sumitra R. (Sawant) D.; m. Rekha B. Jadhav, Jan. 22, 1969; children—Rajan, Samir. B.Sc. with honors, U. Bombay, 1962, B.Sc.Tech., 1964, M.Sc. Tech., 1967; Ph.D., Utah State U., Logan, 1972. Diplomate Am. Bd. Toxicology. Research fellow Univ. Grants Commn., New Delhi, 1964-67; biochemist Hindustan Lever, Ltd., Bombay, 1967; sci. research officer Bhabha Atomic Research Ctr., Bombay, 1967-69; grad-research fellow Utah State U., 1969-72; postdoctoral fellow Vanderbilt U., Nashville, 1972-74; asst. prof. to prof. toxicology Tuskegee (Ala.) U., 1974—; cons. Nat. Acad. Scis., Boston U. Editorial bd., internat. adv. bd.: Tropical Veterinarian, 1982—, mem. bd. reviewers Am. Jour. Vet. Research, 1987-89; contbr. articles to profl. jours., chpt. in book. Recipient award So. Regional Edn. Bd., 1975; Tuskegee U. Faculty Achievement award, 1985-86; numerous research grants, 1975—. Mem. Soc. Toxicology, Am. Coll. Vet. Toxicologist, Am. Chem. Soc., Am. Soc. Vet Physiol. Pharmacology, AAAS, Inst. Food Tech., Internat. Soc. Study of Xenobiotics, Am. Assn. Vet. Med. Colls., Pharm. Soc. Japan, Sigma Xi. Home: 1243 Ferndale Dr Auburn AL 36830 Office: School Vet Medicine Tuskegee U Tuskegee AL 36088

DALY, CHARLES, microbiologist; b. Cork, Ireland, Jan. 20, 1946; s. Eugene and Julia (O'Callaghan) D.; m. Michele C. Lachance, Sept. 23, 1974; children: Cathal, Andrew David. BSc in Dairying, U. Cork, 1967, MSc in Dairying, 1968; PhD, Oreg. State U., 1973. Lectr. Univ. Coll., Cork, 1973-82, assoc. prof. microbiology, 1982—, dean food sci. and tech. faculty, 1987—. Author: Cheese Starter Cultures, 1987; contbr. articles to profl. publs. Grantee, Commn. European Communities, 1986. Mem. Soc. Applied Bacteriology. Roman Catholic. Office: Univ Coll, Western Rd, Cork Ireland

DALY, JAMES JOSEPH, newspaper executive; b. Jersey City, June 11, 1916; s. Bernard B. and Anna (Leiner) D.; m. Catherine Mary Adams, June 26, 1937; children—Ann Daly Heller, Catherine Daly Kline. Student, St. Peters Coll. Classified advt. mgr. N.Y. Sun, 1946-49, World Telegram Sun, 1950-55; with Washington Post, 1955—, v.p., gen. mgr., 1965-72; exec. v.p. Washington Star, 1975-77, chmn. exec. com., dir., 1977-78; mem. exec. com. Newspaper I. Mem. exec. com. Washington Conv. and Visitors Bur., 1969-72; chmn. v.p. Tenafly (N.J.) Community Chest, 1955; budget com. Washington Health and Welfare Council, 1961-64; Bd. dirs. United Givers Fund, Washington Bd. Trade, Better Bus. Bur., ARC; trustee Am. Cancer Soc., Fed. City Council, 1977-78. Served with AUS, 1943-45. Mem. Washington Advt. Club, John Carroll Soc., Silurians. Clubs: Rotary. (Washington), Columbia Country (Washington), Pisces (Washington); Boca Raton (Fla.); Delray Beach Yacht (Fla.); Boca Raton Hotel and Club. Home: 700 S Ocean Blvd Boca Raton FL 33432

DÁM, LÁSZLÓ, ethnographer, museum director; b. Budapest, Hungary, Mar. 15, 1945; s. Lajos and Irma (Laboncz) D.; m. Gabriella Erdei, July 5, 1969 (div. 1981); children: László, Zsuzsanna; m. Magdolna Rácz, Sept. 10, 1981; 1 child, Edit. Univ Dr, L. Kossuth U., Debrecen, Hungary, 1968. Asst. prof. ethnography L. Kossuth U., 1968-84; dir. István Báthori Mus., Nyirbator, Hungary, 1984—. Author: A Nagy-Sárrét népi epiteszete, 1975, Építkezés, 1980, A Nyirseg népi építészete, 1982, Nepi építkezés... Gömörben, 1986. Mem. Hungarian Soc. Ethnography (Janko Janos award 1981), Internat. Hungarian Philol. Soc. Mem. Hungarian Socialist Workers Party. Roman Catholic. Home: Fay St 27, 4300 Nyirbator Hungary Office: Istvan Bathori Mus, Karolyi St 15, 4301 Nyirbator Hungary

DAMACHI, NICHOLAS AGIOBI, industrial engineer, educator; b. Obudu, Nigeria, Mar. 16, 1953; came to U.S., 1972; s. Justin Jabekong and Justina Lami (Ogar) D. B.S.I.E., Ohio State U., 1976, M.S., 1978; Ph.D., U. Cin., 1981. Tchr., Obudu, Nigeria, 1972; systems engr., Div. of Water, City of Columbus, Ohio, 1977-79; indsl. engring. cons. Dosimeter Corp., of Am., Cin., 1980; grad. research lectr. U. Cin., 1979-81, adj. asst. prof. 1981-82, asst. prof. indsl. engring., mng. dir., 1982—. Mem. bd. trustees, Cin. Freestore; Lamic (Nigeria) Ltd. Mem. Inst. of Indsl. Engrs., Am. Soc. for Quality Engrs., Am. Water Works Assn., Human Factors Soc. (chartered), Alpha Pi Mu. Roman Catholic. Contbr. articles to profl. jours. Office: U Cin Dep of Engring Cincinnati OH 45221

DAMAN, HARLAN RICHARD, allergist; b. N.Y.C., Nov. 1, 1941; s. D. Leon and Frances (Weissler) D.; AB cum laude, Harvard U., 1963; MD, Albert Einstein Coll. Medicine, 1967. Diplomate Am. Bd. Pediatrics, Am. Bd. Allergy and Immunology. Intern, then resident Yale-New Haven Hosp./Med. Ctr., 1967-69; fellow in allergy and clin. immunology Nat. Jewish Hosp. Research Ctr./U. Colo. Med. Ctr., Denver, 1971-73; clin. asst. prof. pediatrics Albert Einstein Coll. Medicine, N.Y.C., 1974—; chief pediatric outpatient allergy, dir. pediatric allergy clinic Bronx Mcpl. Hosp. Ctr., 1982—; mem. teaching staff dept. pediatrics Mt. Sinai Hosp. and Med. Ctr./Sch. Medicine, 1976—. Co-editor: Psychobiologic Aspects of Allergic Disorders, 1986; contbr. chpt. to Outpatient Medicine, 1980; contbr. articles on pulmonary function testing in asthmatic disorders. Served to maj. M.C., USAF, 1969-71. Fellow Am. Acad. Pediatrics, Am. Coll. Allergists, Am. Coll. Chest Physicians, Am. Acad. Allergy; mem. N.Y., Westchester (ednl. program dir. 1978—, treas. 1980-81, pres. 1982-83) allergy socs., Westchester Acad. Medicine. Office: 769 Kimball Ave Yonkers NY 10704

D'AMATO, ALFONSE M., senator; b. Bklyn., Aug. 1, 1937; m. Penelope Ann Collenburg, 1960; children: Lisa, Lorraine, Daniel, Christopher. B.S., Syracuse U., 1959, J.D., 1961. Bar: N.Y. 1962. Adminstr. Nassau County, 1965-68; receiver of taxes Town of Hempstead, 1971-77, presiding supr., vice chmn. County bd. suprs., 1977-80; senator 97th-100th Congresses, 1980—; mem. various subcoms. Appropriations Com., Banking, Housing and Urban Affairs Com., Small Bus. Com., Joint Econ. Com.; co-chmn. Senate Caucus on Internat. Narcotics Control, 1987—; chmn. Internat. Commn. on Security and Cooperation in Europe; mem. Helsinki Commn.; founder, co-chmn. Senate Anti-Terrorism Caucus. Mem. Island Park Vol. Fire Dept. Republican. Roman Catholic. Clubs: K.C, Lions, Sons of Italy. *

D'AMATO, ANTHONY ROGER, recording company executive; b. N.Y.C., Jan. 21, 1931; s. Agostino and Luisa (Galiani) D'A.; m. Gabrielle Hilton, June 26, 1958; children—Luisa, Jennie, Tania, Joanna, Antonia. B.A. in Music and English Lit. cum laude (Founders Day award 1956), N.Y. U., 1956; MI.A. (teaching fellow), Brandeis U., 1957. Artist and repertoire dir. stereophonic div. Decca Record Co., Ltd., Eng., 1958-78; pres. TDA Prodns. Ltd., N.Y.C., 1978—; exec. dir. Winnipeg (Man., Can.) Symphony Orch., 1979-80; v.p. artist and repertoire AudioFidelity Enterprises, N.Y.C., 1980-81; mng. dir. Mantovani Prodns., Mantovani Orch., N.Y.C., 1982—; mng. cons. Leopold Stokowski, 1964-72. Served with USMCR, 1951-53.

Recipient Grand Prix du Disque, Charles Cros award rec., 1969. Mem. Assn. Cultural Execs. Can., Winnipeg C. of C., Phi Beta Kappa.

DAMBERG, BO IVAR BERNDT, banker; b. Helsingborg, Sweden, Dec. 1, 1937; s. Ruben and Signe (Bremberg) D.; m. Margareta Ahlberg, June 20, 1966; children—Fredrik, Martin. LL.B., Lund U., 1961; M.B.A., Stockholm Sch. Econs., 1963. With Stockholm Sch. Econs., 1962-63, Gen. Export Assn. Sweden, Stockholm, 1963-64, Sundsvallsbanken, Stockholm, 1964-70, Platzer Bygg, Stockholm, 1970-71, Svenska Handelsbanken, Stockholm, 1971, exec. v.p., 1976—. Home: 40 Gronviksvagen, Bromma Stockholm Sweden Office: Svenska Handelsbanken, Stockholm Sweden

D'AMBROSIO, DANIELE ATTILIO, consumer products company; b. Milan, Oct. 5, 1957; s. Giordano Bruno and Maria (Garavaglia) D'A.; m. Marina Danna, June 29, 1987. B in Engring., U. Rome, 1981. Brand asst. Procter & Gamble, Rome, 1983-84, asst. brand mgr., 1984-85, brand mgr., 1985—; tchr. Communication Study Ctr., Rome, 1986-87, coordinator, 1987—; cons. in field. Served with Italian Navy, 1981-83. Office: Procter & Gamble, Via C Pavese 385, 00144 Rome Italy

D'AMICO, GIUSEPPE, nephrologist; b. Messina, Sicily, Italy, Sept. 6, 1929; s. Gaetano and Gaetana (Trifiletti) D'A.; m. Anna Maria Allegri, July 11, 1957; 1 son, Stefano. M.D., State U. Milan, 1952; L. Docenza in Internal Medicine, State U. Milan, 1964. Traineeship in endocrinology Chgo. Med. Sch., 1957-58; asst. prof. dept. internal medicine State U. Med. Sch., Milan, Italy, 1964-67, head div. nephrology San Carlo Hosp., Milan, 1967—. Contbr. articles to profl. jours. Recipient Ganassini Internat. award Ganassini Found., 1961; Fulbright travel grantee, 1957; NIH grantee, 1957. Mem. Italian Soc. Nephrology (pres. 1980-83), European Dialysis Transplant Assn. (exec. council), Internat. Soc. Nephrology (council), N.Y. Acad. Sci. Home: Viale Papiniano, 22/B, Milan Italy Office: San Carlo Hosp, Via Pio II 3, Milano Italy

DAMSBO, ANN MARIE, psychologist; b. Cortland, N.Y., July 7, 1931; d. Jorgen Einer and Agatha Irene (Schenck) D. B.S., San Diego State Coll., 1952; M.A., U.S. Internat. U., 1974, Ph.D., 1975. Commd. 2d lt. U.S. Army, 1952, advanced through grades to capt., 1957; staff therapist Letterman Army Hosp., San Francisco, 1953-54, 56-58, 61-62, Ft. Devers, Mass., 1955-56, Walter Reed Army Hosp., Washington, 1958-59, Tripler Army Hosp., Hawaii, 1959-61, Ft. Benning, Ga., 1962-64; chief therapist U.S. Army Hosp., Ft. McPherson, Ga., 1964-67; ret. U.S. Army, 1967; med. missionary So. Presbyterian Ch., Taiwan, 1968-70; psychology intern Naval Regional Med. Ctr., San Diego, 1975, pre-doctoral intern, 1975-76, postdoctoral intern, 1975-76, chief, founder pain clinic, 1977-86; adj. tchr. U. Calif. Med. Sch., San Diego; lectr., U.S., Can., Eng., France, Australia, cons. forensic hypnosis to law enforcement agys. Contbr. articles to profl. publs., chpt. to book. Tchr. Sunday sch. Methodist Ch., 1945—. Fellow Am. Soc. Clin. Hypnosis; mem. San Diego Soc. Clin. Hypnosis (pres. 1980), Am. Phys. Therapy Assn., Calif. Soc. Clin. and Hypnosis (bd. govs.), Internat. Soc. Clin. and Exptl. Hypnosis, Am. Assn. Univ. Women, Internat. Platform Assn., AAUW, Ret. Officers Am. Republican. Club: Toastmasters (local pres.). Lodges: Job's Daus., Zonta. Home and Office: 1062 W 5th Ave Escondido CA 92025

DAMUS, ROBERT GEORGE, lawyer, government official; b. San Bernardino, Calif., June 24, 1945; s. Shibli and Margaret (Saliba) D.; m. Pamela Claire Aldridge, Aug. 28, 1976; children—David Alexander, Elizabeth Anne. B.A. magna cum laude, Harvard U., 1967, J.D. cum laude, 1972; B.A., M.A. (1st class scholar), St. John's Coll., Cambridge U. (Eng.), 1969. Bar: Calif. 1972. Teaching fellow dept. econs. Harvard Coll., Cambridge, Mass., 1970-71; lectr. law U. Warwick, Coventry, Eng. 1972-73; assoc. McCutchen, Black, Verleger & Shea, Los Angeles, 1973-80; gen. trial atty. fed. programs br., civil div., U.S. Dept. Justice, Washington, 1980-82, asst. dir., 1982-85; asst. gen. counsel Office Mgmt. and Budget, Exec. Office of Pres. of U.S., 1985-87, acting gen. counsel, 1987-88, acting dep. gen. counsel, 1988—. Recipient Spl. Achievement awards Dept. Justice, 1981, 83; Wright prize in Econs., Cambridge U. (Eng.), 1972. Club: Harvard Varsity. Office: Exec Office Bldg 17th and Pennsylvania Aves NW Washington DC 20503

DANAHER, MALLORY MILLETT, actress, photographer; b. St. Paul; d. James Albert and Helen Rose (Feely) Millett; B.A., U. Minn.; m. Thomas C. Danaher, Mar. 1985; 1 child by previous marriage, Kristen Vigard. Active with N.Y. Theatre, 1971-84, mem. original cos. of Annie and The Best Little Whorehouse in Texas, 1977; appeared in stage roles in Dodsworth, Berkshire Theatre Festival, 1978, Hedda Gable, Kennedy's Children; also on Love of Life, CBS-TV, 1978-79, NBC Movie of the Week, Eischied: Only the Pretty Girls Die, 1979; Edward Albee's Everything in the Garden (dir. Shelley Winters), Actors' Studio, 1980—, also Another World, NBC, New Line Cinema: Alone in the Dark; appeared in House of Blue Leaves, Berkshire Theatre Festival, 1981, Tootsie, Columbia Pictures, Tornado, Lincoln Ctr. Library Theatre, Stella, N.Y.C., Rainbow Dancing; Cocteau's one-character play The Human Voice at Deutsches-Haes, NYU; Full Moon and High Tide, Actors Studio; off-Broadway prodn. Loose Connections, Judith Anderson Theatre; exhibitor of photography: Third Eye Gallery, N.Y.C., 1974-75, Modernage Discovery Gallery, N.Y.C., 1976-79, Gallery of St. Clement's, N.Y.C., 1979; author: Fatherless Child.

DANCEWICZ, JOHN EDWARD, investment banker; b. Boston, Mass., Feb. 12, 1949; s. John Felix and Teresa Sophia (Lewandowski) D.; m. Barbaragail Jarrett, Jan. 23, 1971; children: John Lawrence, Jill Elizabeth. BA in Econs., Yale U., 1971; MBA, Harvard U., 1973. Project adminstr., cons. Nat. Shawmut Bank Boston, 1972-73; v.p., mgr. U.S. investment banking Continental Ill. Nat. Bank Chgo., 1973-82; sr. mng. dir., mgr. corp. fin. Bear Stearns & Co. Inc., Chgo., 1982—; bd. dirs. Standard Havens, Inc., Kansas City, Mo. Contbr. articles to profl. jours. Active Yale U. Schs. Com., Spl. Gifts Com.; sec. Harvard Bus. Sch. sect. Mem. Mid. Am. Com., Assn. for Corp. Growth, Scholarship and Guidance Assn. (bd. dirs., treas. 1982—). Clubs: Economic, University, East Bank, Mid-America (Chgo.). Home: 969 E Spring Ln Lake Forest IL 60045 Office: Bear Stearns & Co Inc 3 First Nat Plaza Chicago IL 60602

DANCO, KATHARINE LECK, educator; b. Wilton, Conn., June 11, 1929; d. Walter Charles and Katharine (Elmendorf) Leck; m. Leon A. Danco, Aug. 25, 1951; children—Suzanne, Walter. R.N., Roosevelt Hosp. Sch. Nursing, 1950, R.N., N.Y., Ohio. Vice pres., treas. Univ. Services Inst., Cleve., 1968—, v.p., treas. Center for Family Bus., Cleve., 1973—, faculty, 1970—, seminar dir., 1971—; also dir. syndicated columnist numerous trade mags., 1978—, The Family in Bus., Cleve., 1978—. Author: From the Other Side of the Bed, 1980; contbr. articles to profl. jours. Bd. dirs. Julie Billiart Sch., Cleve., 1976—. Episcopalian. Home: 28230 Cedar Rd Pepper Pike OH 44122 Office: Ctr for Family Bus PO Box 24268 Cleveland OH 44124

DANCZ, ROGER LEE, musician; b. Ludington, Mich., May 25, 1930; s. Roy Stanley and Viola Lenore (Boston) D.; B.Mus. cum laude, Stetson U., 1952; Mus.M., Peabody Coll., 1958; m. Phyllis Ann Jones, June 2, 1952; 1 son, Steven. Dir. instrumental music Martin County Schs., Stuart, Fla., 1952-53; profl. trumpet player, 1951-65; dir. bands, U. Ga., Athens, 1955—, asso. prof., 1971—; guest condr., adjudicator South and Southwest. Served with U.S. Army, 1953-55. Recipient Music in Sports award Broadcast Music Inc., 1976; Sandy Beaver award Superior Teaching, 1981. Mem. Nat. Assn. Jazz Educators (past pres. Ga. chpt.), Ga. Music Educators Assn. (past pres.), Coll. Band Dirs. Nat. Assn. (past pres. So. div.), Music Educators Nat. Conf., Gridiron Soc., Phi Beta Mu (past pres. Ga. chpt.), Phi Mu Alpha Sinfonia, Pi Kappa Lambda, Ye Mystic Krewe, Kappa Kappa Psi. Columnist Athens Banner-Herald, 1970—; commentator radio program Invitation to Jazz.Sta. WUGA, Athens, 1987— . Home: 680 Pinecrest Dr Athens GA 30605 Office: U Ga Sch Music Athens GA 30602

DANDAPANI, S., management consultant; b. June 23, 1921; B.A. with honors; M.A. in Sociology; cert. in bus. mgmt., social welfare, indsl. relations Calcutta U.; diploma in social policy Inst. Social Studies, The Hague; Ph.D. in Sociology. With Indian Rys., 1946-65, divisional comml. supt., until 1965; dep. dir. Ministry of Rys., Govt. of India, New Delhi, 1965-75; cons., adv. Internat. Labor Orgn. UN, N.Y.C., 1973-76, cons. FAO, 1979; UN cons. dept. internat. econ. and social affairs, 1980-81; also cons. to Govt. Liberia; joint chief Internat. Coop. Alliance, London, 1976-80; FAO cons. to Sultanate of Oman, 1980, now mgmt. cons. Recipient State award, Govt. of Bahrain. Fellow Brit. Inst. Mgmt., Inst. Sales Mgmt., Inst. Adminstrv. Acctg.; mem. Inst. Rail Transport, Sociol. Assn. India, Anthrop. Assn. Bombay. Author: Sale A Profile: An Introduction to Sales Management in Retailing; Business Switch: An Introduction to Business Management in Retailing; Retionalization of Consumer Movement in Western Europe; Fundamentals of Social Survey and Research Methods; Facts From Figures; Research and Planning Methodology for Co-Op Enterprises; The Role of a Nominated Director in A Consumer Co-op Society; editor: (with K.P. Kornholz) Productivity in Retailing; Membership and Cooperative Effectiveness; (with G.V.J. Pratt) Statistics: A Management Tool. Home: 10 Holly Grove, Kingsbury, London NW9 8QU, England

DANDAVATE, MADHU, Indian political leader, physicist; b. Ahmed Nagar, Maharashtra, Jan. 21, 1924; ed. Royal Inst. Sci., Bombay. Active in Independence Movement, later in Quit India Movement, 1942; leader passive resistance Goa campaign, 1955; participant Samyukta Maharashtra Movement for formation Maharashtra State; mem. Praja Socialist Party, from 1948, chmn. Maharashtra unit, later joint sec. All-India Praja Socialist Party; active Land Liberation Movement, 1969; assoc. with Maharashtra Citizens' Def. Com. during conflicts with People's Republic China and Pakistan; mem. Maharashtra Legis. Council, 1970-71, Lok Sabha from Rajapur, 1971—; vice prin., head physics dept. Siddhartha Coll. Arts and Scis., Bombay, until 1971; mem., 1977, then leader Janata Party; minister of railways India, 1977-80. Author: Gandhiji's Impact on Socialist Thinking; Three Decades of Indian Communism; Evolution of Socialist Policies; Kashmir: a Test for Secularism; Myth and Mystery of Congress Socialism; Bharatiya Swarajwad (in Marathi). Address: care Janata Party, 7 Jantar Mantar Rd, New Delhi 110001, India *

DANDAVINO, RITA RACHELE, urban planner, architect; b. Montreal, Ont., Can., June 16, 1953; d. Francis and Matilde (Marchi) D. BArch, U. Montreal, 1976; M in Urban Planning, McGill U., 1979. Technician NRC, Ottawa, 1975; technician, planner City of Montreal, summers 1977-80; planner Laval Plan, Montreal, 1980; planner Daniel Arbour & Assocs., Lavalin and Montreal, Can., 1981-84, Montreal, 1986—, Merauke, Indonesia, 1984-86; research asst. Commn. Biens Culturels, Montreal, Que., 1981-82; bd. dirs. Societe Immobiliere Vieux Port Montreal subs. Can. Lands Co. Ltd., 1981-84. Que. Govt. scholar, 1977-79; grantee Can. Mortgage and Housing Corp. Study Bursary, 1977-79; McGill U. scholar, 1977-79; French Govt. scholar, 1981. Mem. Corp. Urbanistes Que., Can. Inst. Planners, Ordre Architectes Que., Assn. Vieux Port (exec. com. 1978-80), Icomos Can. (bd. dirs. 1987—). Home: 7331 Ave de Chateaubriand, Montreal, PQ Canada H2R 2L7 Office: Service de L'Habitation, Et du Devel Urbain, 275 rue Notre Dame Est, Montreal, PQ Canada H2Y 1C6

DANDRIDGE, WILLIAM SHELTON, orthopedic surgeon; b. Atoka, Okla., May 21, 1914; s. Theodore Oscar and Estelle (Shelton) D.; m. Pearl Sessions, Feb. 3, 1941; children:, Diana Dawn, James Rutledge. B.A., U. Okla., 1935; M.D., U. Ark., 1939; M.S., Baylor U., 1950. Intern, St. Paul's Hosp., Dallas, 1939-40; surg. residence Med. Arts Hosp., Dallas, 1940; commd. 1st lt. USAF, advanced through grades to lt. col., 1950; chief reconditioning service and reconstructive surgery Ashburn Gen. Hosp., McKinney, Tex., 1945-46; neurosurg. resident Brooke Army Med. Center, San Antonio, 1946-47; orthopedic surg. resident, 1947-50; chief orthopedic service and gen. surgery Francis E. Warren AFB, Cheyenne, Wyo., Travis AFB, Susan, Calif., 1950-51; chief orthopedic service and gen. surgery Shepherd AFB, 1951-52; comdg. officer, chief orthopedic service, chief gen. surgery Craig AFB Hosp., Selma, Ala., 1952-53; practice medicine specializing in orthopedic surgery, Muskogee, Okla., 1954-69, 72—; courtesy staff Muskegon Gen. Hosp.; orthopedic cons. McAlester (Okla.) Gen. Hosp., VA Hosp., Muskogee. Exec. mem. Eastern Okla. council Boy Scouts Am. Fellow ACS, Internat. Coll. Surgeons; mem. Am. Fracture Assn., Nat. Found. (adviser 1958-61), N.Y. Acad. Scis., Okla. State, Pan-Am., So., Aerospace med. assns., AMA, So. Orthopaedic Assn., Eastern Okla. Counties med. socs., S.W. Surg. Congress, Am. Rheumatology Soc., Air Force Assn. (life). Republican. Methodist. Mason (32 deg., K.T. Shriner, Jester), Lion. Club: Muskogee Country. Contbr. articles to profl. jours.; research and evaluation of various uses of refrigerated homogenous bone. Home: 3504 University Blvd Muskogee OK 74401 Office: 1601 W Okmulgee St Muskogee OK 74401

DANEELS, AXEL JEAN HERMAN ADRIEN EDWARD, computer scientist; b. Ghent, Belgium, Sept. 15, 1941; arrived in Switzerland, 1968; s. Alfred Adrien Camille and Francine (Duquesne) D.; m. Bernadette De Witte, Feb. 10, 1968; children: Eugenie, Jean-Francois. Grad. in Elec. and Mech. Engring., State U., Ghent, 1964, PhD, 1970; MSc, Cambridge U., 1967. Fellow Proton Synchrotr. div. European Orgn. for Nuclear Research, Geneva, 1968-70, sect. leader, 1970-77, dep. group leader, 1977-87, mem. tech. bd. for process controls, chmn. application software, 1987—; cons. Hahn Meitner Inst., Berlin, 1978, Los Alamos Nat. Lab., Upton, N.Y., 1984—; vis. scientist Acad. Sci and Tech. U., Prague, Czechoslovakia, 1987. Contbr. articles on high energy physics controls to profl. jours. Mem. Instn. Elec. Engrs., Soc. Royale Belge Ing. et Industrie, European Phys. Soc. (founder, chmn. exptl. physics control systems group), Cambridge Soc. (founder). Clubs: Royal Philotaxe (Antwerp, Belgium); Terrasse (Geneva); Country Bonmont (Cheserex, Switzerland). Home: Rive aux Foulques, Route Suisse 98, CH-1296 Coppet Switzerland Office: CERN, CH-1211 Geneva 23 Switzerland

DANEK, MARITA MCKENNA, counseling educator, educational administrator; b. Garden City, N.Y., June 7, 1942; d. James A. and Mary Rita (Noble) McKenna; m. Joseph Gerard Danek, June 18, 1966; children: Joseph, Jennifer, Geoffrey. BA, Catholic U., 1964; MEd, U. Md., 1970, PhD, 1979. Vocat. rehab. counselor State of Md., Bladensburg, 1966-70; counselor Model Secondary Sch. for Deaf, Washington, 1970-73; asst. prof. rehab. counseling Dept. Counseling, Gallaudet Coll., Washington, 1979-83, assoc. prof., 1983-87, prof., 1987—, dir. rehab. counseling (deafness) program, 1981—. Contbr. articles to profl. jours. Rehab. Services Adminstrn. fellow, 1976-78, D.C. Services for Independent Living grantee, 1982; Women's Ednl. Equity Act grantee, 1982; Nat. Inst. Handicapped Research grantee, 1984; Switzer scholar, 1985; recipient Rehabilitation Educator of Yr. award, 1986. Mem. Am. Assn. Counseling and Devel., Am. Deafness and Rehab. Assn., Am. Psychol. Assn., Nat. Rehab. Assn. Office: Gallaudet U 113 Fowler Hall Washington DC 20002

DANELIUS, HANS CARL YNGVE, ambassador; b. Stockholm, Apr. 2, 1934; s. Sven Carl and Inga Elisabet (Svensson) D., m. Hannah Helena Schadee, 1961; children: Fredrik, Margareta, Robert, Erik Johan. BL, Stockholm U., 1955, D honoris causa, 1988. Cert. lawyer. Lawyer Swedish Courts, 1957-64; mem. Secretariat European Commn. Human Rights, Strasbourg, France, 1964-67; asst. judge Swedish Court Appeal, Stockholm, 1967-68; legal advisor Swedish Ministry Justice, Stockholm, 1968-71, Swediah Ministry Foreign Affairs, Stockholm, 1971-74; under sec. Swedish Ministry Fgn. Affairs, Stockholm, 1974-84; ambassador to Netherlands Sweden, The Hague, 1984—. Author: Mänskliga Rättigheter, 1975, 3d edit., 1984. Mem. European Commn. Human Rights, Permanent court Arbitration. Home: Lange Voorhout 28, 2514 EE The Hague The Netherlands Office: Swedish Embassy, Neuhuyskade 40, 2596 XL The Hague The Netherlands

DANELSKI, DAVID JOSEPH, political scientist, lawyer, educator; b. Green Bay, Wis., Oct. 29, 1930; s. Peter Anthony and Magdalen Agnes (Piontek) D.; m. Jeanne C. Parmer, June 12, 1954; children—Christine, Catherine, David, Ann, Rebecca. Student, St. Norbert Coll., 1948-50; LL.B., DePaul U., 1953; B.A., Seattle U., 1955; M.A., U. Chgo., 1957, Ph.D. (Louis E. Asher fellow 1957-58, Univ. fellow 1958-59), 1961. Bar: Ill. 1953, Wash. 1955. Ptnr. Patrick & Danelski, Mt. Vernon, 1955-56; research atty. Am. Bar Found., Chgo., 1957-59; instr., asst. prof. polit. sci. U. Ill., Urbana, 1959-60; asst. prof. polit. sci. U. Wash., 1961-64; lectr., asso. prof. polit. sci. Yale U., 1964-70; prof. govt. Cornell U., Ithaca, N.Y., 1970-73, Goldwin Smith prof. govt., 1973-79, univ. ombudsman, 1973-75; ptnr. Schroeter, Goldmark & Bender, Seattle, 1978-79; prof. polit. sci. Stanford U., 1979-84; dean faculty, v.p. acad. affairs, Cecil and Louise Gamble prof. polit. sci. Occidental Coll., Los Angeles, 1984-87; Mary Lou and George Boone prof., dir. univ. program in Washington Stanford (Calif.) U., 1987—. Author: A Supreme Court Justice Is Appointed, 1964, Rights, Liberties and Ideals, 1983; author, editor: (with Glendon Schubert) Comparative Judicial Behavior, 1969; editor: (with Joseph Tulchin) The Autobiographical Notes of Charles Evans Hughes, 1973; Contbr. articles to profl. jours. Served to lt. (j.g.) USNR, 1953-55. Recipient Sr. Fulbright-Hays award to Japan, 1968-69, E. Harris Harbison prize for gifted teaching Danforth Found., 1970, Humanities and Scis. Dean's award for disting. teaching Stanford U., 1981; Walter E. Meyer research fellow, 1962-63; John Simon Guggenheim fellow, 1968-69; Center for Advanced Study in Behavioral Scis. fellow, 1970-71; Japan Found. fellow, 1975; Sr. specialist East-West Center, 1965, 67. Mem. Am. Polit. Sci. Assn., Law and Soc. Assn., Wash. Bar Assn. Office: Stanford in Washington 2661 Connecticut Ave NW Washington DC 20008

DANEY, WILLIAM CHESTER, physician; b. Pueblo, Colo., Nov. 18, 1934; s. William Lawrence and Isabel (Stevenson) D.; m. Barbara Julia Packan, July 27, 1956; children—Colette Marie, Tamra Kay, William C. Jr., Randall Todd. B.A. magna cum laude in Zoology, U. Colo.-Boulder, 1956; M.D., U. Colo.-Denver, 1960. Diplomate Am. Bd. Emergency Medicine Am. Bd. Family Practice. Intern St. Anthony Hosp., Denver, 1960-61; resident in internal medicine St. Mary-Corwin Hosp., Pueblo, 1961; pvt. practice, Pueblo, Colo., 1962-76; Staff St. Mary-Corwin Hosp., Pueblo, 1972-82, dir. emergency dept., 1976-82; chmn. dept. emergency medicine St. Mary's Hosp., Grand Rapids, Mich., 1982—, dir. Emergency Care Ctr., 1983—; project med. dir. Kent County Emergency Med. Services, 1985—; chmn. Kent County Med. Soc. Emergency Med. Services com.; pres. Grand River Emergency Med. Group, Grand Rapids, 1982—; del. to Colo. State Med. Soc., Pueblo, 1968; asst. prof. medicine Mich. State U., Lansing, 1983—; examiner Am. Bd. Emergency Medicine, Lansing, 1981—. Mem. Pueblo Arts Council, Colo., 1969-71; Pueblo Civic Symphony, Colo., 1968-72; patron Grand Rapids Opera, Mich., 1984—; mem. advanced cardiac life support com. Mich. Heart Assn. Recipient Physicians Recognition award AMA, 1984, 86; Spl. Recognition award Scenic Trails Council Boy Scouts Am., Mich., 1984. Fellow Am. Coll. Emergency Physicians (bd. dirs. Mich chpt., Spl. Service award Colo. chpt. 1981); mem. Kent County Med. Soc., Kent County Emergency Med. Services Council, Am. Acad. Med. Dirs., Nat. Assn. EMS Physicians (charter mem. 1985—), Soc. Tchrs. Emergency Medicine, Univ. Assn. Emergency Medicine. Club: Cascade Country (Grand Rapids). Avocations: Fly fishing, photography, astronomy, camping, travel. Home: 1631 Mont Rue SE Grand Rapids MI 49506 Office: Dir Emergency Care Ctr 200 Jefferson SE Grand Rapids MI 49503

DANFORTH, ARTHUR EDWARDS, finance executive; b. Cleve., Jan. 23, 1925; s. Arthur Edwards and Jane (Hillyard) D.; m. Elizabeth Wagley, Mar. 17, 1956; children: Hillyard Raible, Nicholas Edwards (dec.), Jonathan Ingersoll, Elizabeth Wagley, Michael Stowe. B.A., Yale, 1949. With Hayden Miller Co., Cleve., 1949-54, First Nat. City Bank (predecessor to Citibank N.A.), N.Y.C., 1954-63; asst. mgr. Buenos Aires office First Nat. City Bank (predecessor to Citibank N.A.), 1959-61; treas. Bunge Corp., N.Y.C., 1963-65; sr. v.p., treas. Colonial Bank & Trust Co., Waterbury, Conn., 1965-70; chmn., chief exec. officer Farmers Bank of Del., Wilmington, 1970-76; prin. Danforth Group, New Canaan, Conn. Former bd. dirs. United Way of Del., Boys Club of Wilmington, Grand Opera House Inc. of Del., NCCJ, Audubon Soc. Conn., Greater Wilmington Devel. Council. Served as ensign USNR, 1945-46. Clubs: Sankety Head Golf (Nantucket, Mass.), Nantucket Yacht; Yale (N.Y.C.). Home: 260 Whiting Pond Rd Fairfield CT 06430 Office: 21 Locust Ave New Canaan CT 06840

DANFORTH, JOHN CLAGGETT, U.S. senator, lawyer, clergyman; b. St. Louis, Sept. 5, 1936; s. Donald and Dorothy (Claggett) D.; m. Sally B. Dobson, Sept. 7, 1957; children: Eleanor, Mary, Dorothy, Johanna, Thomas. B.A. with honors, Princeton U., 1958; B.D., Yale U., 1963, LL.B., 1963, M.A. (hon.); M.A. hon. degrees: L.H.D., Lindenwood Coll., 1970; L.HD., Ind. Central U.; LL.D., Drury Coll., 1970, Maryville Coll., Rockhurst Coll., Westminster Coll., Culver-Stockton Coll., St. Louis U.; D.D., Lewis and Clark Coll.; H.H.D., William Jewell Coll.; S.T.D., Southwest Bapt. Coll. Bar: N.Y. 1964, Mo. 1966. With firm Davis Polk Wardwell Sunderland & Kiendl, N.Y.C., 1964-66, Bryan, Cave, McPheeters and McRoberts, St. Louis, 1966-68; atty. gen. State of Mo., 1969-76; U.S. senator from Mo. 1976—; ranking mem. Senate com. commerce, sci. and transp.; mem. Senate fin. com., Senate budget com; ordained deacon Episcopal Ch., 1963, priest, 1964; asst. rector N.Y.C., 1963-66; assoc. rector Clayton, Mo., 1966-68, Grace Ch., Jefferson City, 1969; hon. assoc. St. Albans Ch., Washington, 1977—; chmn. Mo. Law Enforcement Assistance Council, 1973-74. Republican nominee U.S. Senate, 1970. Recipient Distinguished Service award St. Louis Jr. C. of C., 1969, Disting. Missourian and Brotherhood awards NCCJ, Presdl. World Without Hunger award, 1985; Disting. Lectr. award Avila Coll.; named Outstanding Young Man Mo. Jr. C. of C., 1968; Alumni fellow Yale U., 1973-79. Mem. Mo. Acad. Squires, Alpha Sigma Nu (hon.). Republican. Office: 497 Russell Senate Bldg Washington DC 20510-2501 *

DANFORTH, WILLIAM HENRY, physician, university chancellor; b. St. Louis, Apr. 10, 1926; s. Donald and Dorothy (Claggett) D.; m. Elizabeth Anne Gray, Sept. 1, 1950; children—Cynthia Danforth Noto, David, Ann, Elizabeth. A.B., Princeton U., 1947; M.D., Harvard U., 1951. Intern Barnes Hosp., St. Louis, 1951-52; resident Barnes Hosp., 1954-57; now mem. staff; asst. prof. medicine Washington U., St. Louis, 1960-65; asso. prof. Washington U., 1965-67, prof., 1967—, vice chancellor for med. affairs, 1965-71, chancellor, 1971—; pres. Washington U. Med. Sch. and Asso. Hosps., 1965-71; program coordinator Bi-State Regional Med. Program, 1967-69; dir. Ralston Purina Co., McDonnell Douglas Corp.; mem. nat. adv. heart and lung council Nat. Heart and Lung Inst., 1970-74; chmn. Med. Ctr. Redevel. Corp., 1973-84, vice chmn. 1984—. Trustee, chmn. bd. Danforth Found.; trustee Am. Youth Found., 1963—, Princeton U., 1970-74; pres. St. Louis Christmas Carols Assn., 1958-74, chmn., 1975—. Served with USN, 1952-54. Named Man of Yr. St. Louis Globe-Democrat, 1978. Fellow AAAS, Am. Acad. Arts and Scis.; Mem. Nat. Acad. Scis. Inst. Medicine. Home: 10 Glenview Rd Saint Louis MO 63124 Office: Washington U Saint Louis MO 63130

DANG, MARVIN S. C., lawyer; b. Honolulu, Feb. 11, 1954; s. Brian K.T. and Flora (Yuen) D. BA with distinction, U. Hawaii, 1974; JD, George Washington U., 1978. Bar: Hawaii 1978, U.S. Dist. Ct. Hawaii 1978, U.S. Ct. Appeals (9th cir.) 1979. Atty. Gerson, Steiner & Anderson and predecessor firms, Honolulu, 1978-81; owner, atty. Law Offices of Marvin S.C. Dang, Honolulu, 1981—; bd. dirs. Foster Equipment Co. Ltd., Honolulu, 1986—; sr. v.p., bd. dirs. Rainbow Fin. Corp., Honolulu, 1984—. Chmn., vice chmn., mem. Manoa Neighborhood Bd. Honolulu, 1979-82, 84-87; pres., v.p., mem., Hawaii Council on Legal Edn. for Youth, Honolulu, 1979-86; state rep. and asst. minority floorleader Hawaii State Legislature, Honolulu, 1982-84; mem. Hawaii Bicentennial Commn., Honolulu, 1986—. Recipient Cert. of Appreciation Hawaii Speech-Language-Hearing Assn., Honolulu, 1984. Mem. ABA (standing com. on law and the electoral process 1985—, spl. com. on youth edn. for citizenship 1979-85, Hawaii state membership chmn. 1983—, exec. council young lawyers div. 1986—), Nat. Assn. Realtors, Hawaii State Bar Assn., Hawaii State Jaycees (one of ten Outstanding Young Persons of Hawaii 1983), Honolulu. Republican. Club: Plaza of Hawaii (Honolulu). Home: 108 Waokanaka Pl Honolulu HI 97817 Office: Suite 575 Cen Pacific Plaza 220 S King St Honolulu HI 96813

D'ANGELO, CHRISTOPHER SCOTT, lawyer; b. Phila., Aug. 30, 1953; s. George Anthony and Antonia Scott (Billett) D'A.; m. Betsy Hart Josephs, May 22, 1982; children: John Robert, Christopher Hart, Caroline Colt. Student, Episc. Acad., 1971; BA with honors, U. Va., 1975, JD, 1978. Bar: Pa. 1978, U.S. Dist. Ct. (ea. dist.) Pa. 1978, U.S. Ct. Appeals (3d cir.) 1978, U.S. Supreme Ct. 1981. From assoc. to sr. assoc. Montgomery, McCracken, Walker & Rhoads, Phila., 1978—; organizer, bd. dirs., counsel The Bank of Brandywine Valley, West chester, Pa., 1987—; mem. Products Liability adv. council., 1986—, case selection com., 1988—. Co-founder (U. Va. newsweekly) The Declaration, 1973-75. Mem. Internat. Vis. Ctr., Phila., 1982—, bd. dirs. 1987—, chmn. long range fin. com., 1987—, counsel for COMPASS (young profl. and spl. events div. of ctr. 1982—, exec. com.), 1982—; mem. selection com. Jefferson Scholar U. Va., Phila., 1980-84, chmn. 1981-82; fundraiser U.S. Ski Team, Phila., 1979—, chmn. 1982-83, 87; fundraiser Acad. Natural Scis., Phila., 1979-88; chmn. ann. giving fund Episc. Acad., 1983-88; bd. mgrs. Episc. Acad. Alumni Soc., Merion, Pa., 1983—, treas. 1984-85, v.p. 1985-88, pres. 1988—; treas., exec. com. Phila. Art Alliance, 1980-85, bd. dirs., 1980-86; bd. dirs. English Speaking Union U.S.' 1979-82, chmn. young mem. group, 1980-83; bd. dirs. English Speaking Union Phila., 1980-88, chmn. fin. com. 1985-88; counsel honor com. and judiciary com. U. Va., 1977-78; deanery del. Episc. Diocese of Pa., Merion Deanery, 1987—. Mem. ABA, Pa. Bar Assn. (exec. com. young lawyers div. 1982-88), Phila. Bar Assn., Acad. Natural Scis., Anthenaeum, Phila. Mus. Art, Phila. Zoo. Republican. Clubs: Merion Cricket (Haverford); Rittenhouse (Phila.) (treas. 1982-87, chmn. ho. com. 1980-83, bd. dirs. 1980-87, sec. admissions com. 1986—), Penn., IV Street, The Assemblies. Office: Montgomery McCracken Walker & Rhoads 3 Pkwy 20th Floor Philadelphia PA 19102

DANGERS, WILLIAM HENDRICKS, development economist; b. Ft. Smith, Ark., Apr. 11, 1948; s. Thomas Carter and Alice Patricia (Greer) D.; m. Xuyen Thi Bui Thi Xuyen, Feb. 1, 1975; 1 dau., Diem Thi Bui. B.S. in Banking and Fin., U. Ark.-Fayetteville, 1970; student Hendrix Coll., 1966-67. Economist Philippine Dept. Social Welfare, Davro City, 1971-72; comml. cons. Ch. World Services, Vietnam, 1974-75; fin. advisor Govt. of Papua New Guinea, 1975-77, economist, 1980-83; devel. cons. Ch. World Service, Thailand and Bangladesh, 1977-80, S. Asia Region, 1983-85, Indochina, 1985—.

DANGLER, LEROY STOUT, retired educational administrator, retail store owner; b. Wayside, N.J., July 13, 1916; s. Charles Edmund and Joan (Stout) D.; m. Julia Ziccardi, Apr. 17, 1943 (dec.). BA, Montclair State U., 1938; MA, Middlebury Coll., 1946; postgrad. U. Pa., U. Va., Rutgers U., NYU. Cert. secondary sch. tchr., N.J. Tchr. Burlington City High Sch., N.J., 1939-46; instr. U. Pa., Phila., 1946-47, Lafayette Coll., Easton, Pa., 1947-49; civil engr. John Meehan & Son, Phila., 1949-53; engr. RCA Govt. Services, Cherry Hill, N.J., 1953-61; owner, operator Pocoshock Custom Crafts (formerly Roy's Crafte Shoppe Ltd.), Chesterfield, Va., 1984—; bus. adminstr. St. Mary's Hall-Doane Acad., Burlington, 1973-84; bus. adminstr., elder Presbyn. Ch., Burlington, 1966—. Trustee Library Co. of Burlington, 1970-84, Snowden Naines Meml. Library, Burlington, 1975—; founder Julia Z. Dangler Meml. Scholarship, 1977—. Served with U.S. Army, 1942-45. Mem. AAAS, Nat. Wildlife Fedn. (life), Smithsonian Instn. (donor), Am. Mus. Natural History, Franklin Inst., N.Y. Acad. Scis., Am. Hort. Soc., Oceanic Soc., Cousteau Soc., Nat. Audubon Soc., Am. Forestry Assn., Nature Conservancy, Asia Soc. (assoc.), Va. Mus., Save the Bay Found., Woodworkers Assn. N.Am., Sierra Club, World Wildlife Fund, Wilderness Soc., Fraternal Order of Police, Am. Legion, Nat. Rifle Assn. Republican. Home and Office: 3202 Able Terr Chesterfield VA 23832

DANGOUR, ABRAHAM SION, manufacturing company executive; b. Marseilles, France, May 2, 1924; came to Eng., 1952; widowed; children: Anthony, Armand, Jonathan. Grad., Baghdad Law Coll. Dir. Iraq Advt. Agy., Baghdad, 1945-51, London, 1952-60; dir. The Metal Tray Mfg. Co., Ltd., London, 1961-82, Britannia Gateways, London, 1983—; market researcher Mid. East countries. Home: 20 Woodstock Rd, London W4, England Office: 66 Padenswick Rd, London W6 6UB, England

DANGREMOND, DAVID W., museum consultant, educator; b. Norristown, Pa., June 8, 1952; s. James L. and Joan O. (Kross) D.; m. Mary Plant Spivy, Oct. 18, 1980; 1 child, Samuel Plant Chapin. BA cum laude, Amherst Coll., 1974; MA, U. Del., 1976, Yale U., 1987. Dir. Webb-Deane-Stevens Mus., Wethersfield, Conn., 1976-80, Bennington Mus., Vt., 1980-86; adj. prof. art history U. Hartford, Conn., 1977-80; tutor Historic Deerfield, Mass., 1975; trustee Williamstown (Mass.) Regional Art Conservation Lab., 1981-86, Florence Griswold Mus., Old Lyme, Conn., 1987—; adv. bd. Gunston Hall Plantation, Lorton, Va., 1985—; dir. Attingham Summer Sch., Shropshire, England, 1980—; profl. adv. bd. Victoria Mus., Portland, Maine, 1985—; bd. overseers Strawberry Banke Mus., Portsmouth, N.H., 1987—; mem. mus. com. Conn. Hist. Soc., Hartford, 1987—; exec. com. Yale U. Art Gallery Assocs., 1987—. Foreword author: Heritage Houses: the American Tradition in Connecticut 1660-1900, 1979; contbr. articles to jours. Bd. dirs. Hartford Architecture Conservancy, Conn., 1978-80; adv. bd. Deacon John Grave Found.; mem. art and antiques council Conn. Pub. TV, Hartford, 1977-80; mem. concert com. Vermont Symphony Orch., Burlington, 1980-86; div. head United Way of Bennington County, 1982-84; del. Gov's Conf. on Future of Vt.'s Heritage, Montpelier, 1982; sr. warden St. Peter's Episcopal Ch., 1985—. Fellow Historic Deerfield, 1973; Winterthur fellow H.F. duPont Winterthur Mus., 1974-76; Sir George Trevelyan scholar Attingham summer sch., Shropshire, Eng., 1976. Mem. Am. Assn. for State and Local History (state awards chmn.), New Eng. Mus. Assn. (exec. com., 1985—), Am. Assn. Mus. (accreditation vis. com., mus. assessment program cons.), Vt. Mus. and Gallery Alliance (pres., 1983-86), Greater Hartford Assn. of Historic Houses (bd. dirs.), Am. Assn. Museums (accreditation vis. com), Decorative Arts Soc., Soc. Archtl. Historians, Antiquarian & Landmarks Soc. Conn. (hist. house com. 1987—), Coll. Art Assn. Episcopalian. Clubs: Univ. (Hartford); Soc. Colonial Wars (New Haven); Century (N.Y.C.). Home: Ferry Rd Old Lyme CT 06371 Office: Yale U Box 2009 New Haven CT 06520

DANIEL, ALEX VAN, electronics engineer; b. Marietta, Ga., Mar. 25, 1958; s. Thomas Jerrel and Ruby Wylene (Brown) D. B.E.E.T., So. Tech. Inst., Marietta, 1983. Quality control technician OECO Corp., Portland, Oreg., 1976; quality control insp. G.J. Aigner Co., Marietta, 1977-78; biomed. electronics technician Emory U. Hosp., Atlanta, 1981-82; field service engr. Life Services, Marietta, 1983-85; field service engr. CooperVision Inc., Irvine, Calif., 1985—. Mem. Engring. in Medicine and Biology Soc. of IEEE, Oceanic Engring. Soc. of IEEE, Lasers and Electro-Optics Soc. of IEEE. Office: Laser Div CooperVision Inc 17701 Cowan Ave PO Box 19587 Irvine CA 92713

DANIEL, ELEANOR SAUER, economist, real estate executive; b. N.Y.C., Feb. 8, 1917; d. Charles Peter and Elsie Edna (Dommer) Sauer; m. John Carl Daniel, Dec. 31, 1952; children: Victoria Ann, Charles Timothy. BA magna cum laude (Bardwell fellow), Mt. Holyoke Coll., 1936; MA (Perkins fellow), Columbia U., 1937. Economist, U.S. Steel Co., N.Y.C., 1938; lectr. econs. Bklyn. Coll., 1939-40; with Mut. Life Ins. Co. N.Y., N.Y.C., 1940-74, asst. v.p., 1972-74, sr. econ. adviser, 1972-74; economist Fed. Home Loan Bank, N.Y.C., 1974-75; v.p., dir. Daniel Realty Cos., N.Y.C., 1975—; pres. Midtown Daniel; dir., chmn. fin. com. Atlantic City Electric Co. and Atlantic Energy, Inc.; former mem. bd. mgrs. U.S. Savs. Bank Newark; mem. Pres.'s Task Force Fed. Credit Programs, 1968-69; mem. N.J. Gov.'s Econ. Recovery Com., 1975-76; mem. econ. adv. bd. U.S. Sec. Commerce, 1971-73; mem. bus. research adv. council U.S. Bur. Labor Statistics, 1966-86. Author: (with J.J. O'Leary and S.F. Foster) Our National Debt and Our Savings; contbr. articles to profl. jours. Former trustee Blue Shield of N.J., trustee fellow Mt. Holyoke Coll., also past vice chmn., mem. fin. com., trustee. Mem. Am. Econ. Assn., Am. Fin. Assn. (past dir.), Phi Beta Kappa. Home: 34 North Dr East Brunswick NJ 08816

DANIEL, GERARD LUCIAN, physician, drug company executive; b. Swanton, Vt., May 6, 1927; s. Edward and Exzilia (Perron) D.; AB, St. Michaels Coll., 1950; MD, U. Vt., 1954; m. Armande Renee Messier, Nov. 24, 1949; children: Suzanne Beatrice Foley. Practice medicine, Brattleboro, Vt., 1955-59; chief clin. medicine Dept. Army, Washington, 1959-63, chief life scis. div., 1963-70; med. dir. Pacific Region, Sterling/Winthrop Internat., Minami Azabu, Tokyo, 1970-73, internat. dir. clin. research Winthrop Products Inc., N.Y.C., 1973-75; corp. med. dir. Rhone-Poulenc, Inc., N.Y.C., 1975-78; exec. v.p. Lipha Chems. Inc., N.Y.C. subs. Air Liquid, France, 1978-81, pres., 1981—, dir., 1984—, DEY Labs., Inc., Napa, Calif., 1988—; pub. health officer State of Vt., 1958-59; mem. adv. com. Multiple Sclerosis, 1959-60; chmn. Pharm. Dels. Japan, Tokyo, 1972-73; mem. planning com. White House Conf. Aging, 1980-81. Recipient Achievement award NASA, 1963; Intelligence Merit medal, 1970. Mem. AMA, Am. Mgmt. Assn. (pres. assoc.), AAAS, Assn. Former Intelligence Officers, Med. Execs. Assn. N.Y.C., Washington Acad. Medicine, Fed. Execs. Alumni Assn. Contbr. sci. and technol. articles to profl. jours. Home: Carnegie House Suite 2Q 100 W 57th St New York NY 10019 Office: 660 Madison Ave New York NY 10021

DANIEL, KENNETH RULE, former iron and steel manufacturing company executive; b. Milford, Conn., Oct. 13, 1913; s. Cullen Coleman and Margaret Estelle (Elliott) D.; m. Virginia Moody Simpson, June 11, 1938; children: Kenneth Rule, Cullen Coleman, Robert Tennent Simpson, William Francis McKemie. B.S., U. Ala., 1936, Profl. Degree in Mech. Engring., 1957, D.Sc., 1980. Registered profl. engr. Ala. With Am. Cast Iron Pipe Co., Birmingham, Ala., 1936-78; chief engr. Am. Cast Iron Pipe Co., 1948-55, v.p. engring., 1955-59, v.p. engring. and purchases, 1959-61, exec. v.p., 1961-63, pres., 1963-78, also dir., dir. various subsidiaries, 1963-78; vice chmn. bd. 1st Ala. Bank of Birmingham, 1977-86; Sesquicentennial hon. prof. U. Ala., 1981. Mem. Ala. Bd. of Registration for Profl. Engrs. and Land Surveyors, 1967-87; mem. regional adv. council Conf. Bd., 1967-78, Ala. Export Council, 1966-69; bd. dirs. Community Chest, 1965-78, Jr. Achievement, 1964-78, Birmingham Centennial Corp., 1968-73, Warrior Tombigbee Devel. Assn., 1963-78; gen. co-chmn. United Appeal, 1964, chmn. indsl. div., 1958; chmn. Radio Free Europe, Birmingham, 1966; mem. Jefferson County Judicial Commn., 1967-72; chmn. adv. bd. Salvation Army, 1968-69, mem. adv. council home and hosp., mem. nat. adv. council, 1976—; trustee Foundry Ednl. Found. (pres. 1964-65); trustee, mem. exec. com. So. Research Inst.; chmn. bd. trustees Jefferson County Cooper Green Hosp.; bd. visitors Berry Coll., Mt. Berry, Ga., 1968-78. Served to lt. col. AUS, 1941-46, ETO. Decorated Bronze Star, Legion of Merit; Croix de Guerre France; recipient Gold Knight of Mgmt. award Nat. Mgmt. Assn., 1965, William Booth award Salvation Army, 1967, Henry Laurence Gantt medal Am. Mgmt. Assn. and ASME, 1977; Exec. of Yr. award Nat. Mgmt. Assn., 1978; named Engr. of Year Birmingham Engring. Council, 1967; Paladium medal Am. Assn. Engring. Socs. and Nat. Audubon Soc., 1986; elected to Ala. Acad. Honor, 1982, Nat. Mgmt. Assn. Hall of Fame, 1987. Fellow ASME (chmn. Birmingham sect. 1950-51, hon. mem. 1984); mem. NAM (dir. 1967-70), Asso. Industries Ala. (bd. dirs. 1963-78), Birmingham Area C. of C. (pres. 1969), Assn. Iron and Steel Engrs. (chmn. Birmingham Sect. 1954, nat. dir. 1955), Am. Ordnance Assn. (pres. Birmingham post 1964), Am. Foundrymen's Soc. (Thomas W. Pangborn Gold Medal award 1974), Am. Soc. for Engring. Edn., Engring. Soc. Birmingham, Newcomen Soc. N. Am., Sigma Alpha Epsilon, Theta Tau, Tau Beta Pi. Methodist (past chmn. bd. stewards). Clubs: Birmingham Country, The Club, Mountain Brook, Downtown (Birmingham); N.Y. Athletic (N.Y.C.). Lodges: Masons (knight comdr. Ct. of Honor), Kiwanis. Home: 3212 Brookwood Rd Birmingham AL 35223 Office: PO Box 2727 Birmingham AL 35202

DANIEL, MARTYN CHARLES, screenwriter, director; b. Manchester, Eng., Sept. 16, 1962; s. Brian and Jean Mary (Shaw) D. Diploma, Salford (Eng.) Coll., 1982. Comml. artist Garret Baulcombe Assocs., Manchester, 1982-83, Barnaby and Tarr Advt., Manchester, 1983; resident artist M.W.A. Advt., Manchester, 1983-84; prodn. artist Bowden, Dyble, Hayes and ptnrs., Manchester, 1984-86; freelance screenwriter, dir. Eng., 1986—; mng. dir. Ada Mary Shaw Film Co. Ltd. Author: (screenplays) Sonderkommando Ten, 1982, Saddened Water, 1987; (play) Venezia, 1984. Mem. Lit. Guild. Mem. Church of England. Home and Office: 69 Norfolk Ave, Near Thornley Park, Denton, Manchester M34 2WL, England

DANIEL, ROLF W., psychologist; b. Rochester, N.Y., July 18, 1953; s. Gunther F. and Dorothy (Green) D.; m. Aimee J. Robinson, Feb. 21, 1986; B.A., St. John Fisher Coll., 1975; M.S., St. Francis Coll., 1977; Ed.D., Ball State U., 1982. Behavioral clinician Ft. Wayne (Ind.) State Hosp., 1977-79, mental health adminstr., 1979; dir. psychology Northeast Ind. Spl. Edn. Coop., Corunna, 1982-86; hearing officer div. spl. edn., Ind. Dept. Edn., 1987—; instr. St. Joseph's Hosp. Sch. Nursing, Ft. Wayne, 1983—instr. St. Francis Coll., Ft. Wayne, 1981—; pvt. practice in psychology, Ft. Wayne, 1984—; cons. to Huntington Meml. Hosps. Addictions Unit, 1986—. Mem. learning disabilities task force Ind. Council Adminstrs. in Spl. Edn. Mem. Am. Psychol. Assn., Nat. Assn. Sch. Psychologists, Ind. Psychol. Assn. (pres.-elect div. I 1987). Democrat. Roman Catholic. Office: 6079 Stoney Creek Dr Fort Wayne IN 46825

DANIEL-DREYFUS, SUSAN B. RUSSE, civic worker; b. St. Louis, May 30, 1940; d. Frederick William and Suzanne (Mackay) Russe; m. Don B. Faerber, Nov. 27, 1962 (div. Nov. 1968); 1 child, Suzanne Mackay; m. Marc Andre Daniel-Dreyfus, Aug. 9, 1969; 1 child, Cable Dunster. Student, Smith Coll., 1958-60, Corcoran Sch. Fine Arts, 1960-61, Washington U., St. Louis, 1961-62. Mng. ptnr. Communications, Inc., 1980-82; asst. dir. Harvard Bus. Sch. Fund, Cambridge, 1982-86; pres. SCR Assocs. Corp., Cambridge, 1986—; mem. bd. advisors Odysseum, Inc.; bd. dirs. Future Mgmt. Systems. Mem. St. Louis-St. Louis County White House Conf. on Edn., 1966-68; mem. Mo. 1st Gov.'s Conf. on Edn., 1966, 2d Conf., 1968; bd. dirs. Tunbridge Sch., 1973-78, St. Louis Smith Coll.; hon. bd. dirs. New Music Circle; mem. woman's bd. dirs. Washington U., New Music Circle, 1963-67; mem. woman's bd. Mo. Hist. Soc.; bd. dirs. Non-Partisan Ct. Plan for Mo., Young Audiences Inc., 1967-69; bd. dirs. Childrens Art Bazaar, 1968-70; founder St. Louis Opera Theater; chmn. Art. Mus. Bond Issue election St. Louis, 1966; jr. bd. dirs. St. Louis Symphony, 1966-68, Opportunities Indsl. Center, Boston; legis. chmn. bd. dirs. Boston LWV, 1969-72; mem. council, bd. dirs. Jr. League Boston, 1970-72, 74-76, v.p. Bd. of Family Counseling Services-Region West, Boston, 1979—; pres. Family Counseling Bd., Brookline, Mass.; bd. govs. Tunbridge Sch.; trustee Chestnut Hill Sch., Boston, Brookline Friendly Soc.; mem. steering com. ann. fund Boston Children's Hosp. Med. Center, 1980-84; v.p. Nat. Friends Bd., Joslin Diabetes Found., 1980-83; mem. corp. bd. Joslin Diabetes Ctr.; v.p. bd. dirs. Boston Ctr. Internat. Visitors, 1979-82; Boston bd. dirs. Mass. Soc. Prevention of Cruelty to Children, 1980-84; exec. v.p. Ctr. for Middle East Bus., 1978-82; pres. bd. Brookline Community Fund, 1984—; overseer Old Sturbridge Village, 1987—. Mem. Colonial Dames, Soc. Art Historians. Clubs: Women's City (dir.) (Boston); Vincent (dir.). Home: 120 Middlesex Rd Chestnut Hill MA 02167

DANIELL, ROBERT F., diversified manufacturing company executive; b. Milton, Mass., 1933; married. Grad., Boston U. Coll. Indsl. Tech., 1954; DSc (hon.), U. Bridgeport; LLD (hon.), Trinity Coll., Boston U. With Sikorsky Aircraft, Stratford, Conn., 1956-82, design engr., from 1956, program mgr., 1968-71, comml. mktg. mgr., 1971-74, v.p. comml. mktg., 1974-76, sr. v.p. mktg., 1976-77, exec. v.p., 1977-80, chief exec. officer, 1980-82, pres., 1981-82; with United Technologies (parent co.), Hartford, Conn., 1982—, v.p., 1982-83, sr. v.p. def. systems, 1983-84, pres., chief operating officer, dir., 1984—, chief exec. officer, 1986—, chmn. bd. dirs., 1987—; bd. dirs. The Travelers Corp., Hartford, Conn., Shell Oil Co., Houston. Bd. trustees Boston U., Naval Aviation Mus. Found., Inc., Falcon Found.; corporator Inst. of Living. Served with U.S. Army, 1954-56. Fellow U. Bridgeport. Office: United Techs Corp United Techs Bldg Hartford CT 06101

DANIEL-LESUR, JEAN YVES, composer; b. Paris, Nov. 19, 1908; s. Robert and Alice (Thiboust) L.; student Paris Conservatoire, 1919-29; m. Simone Lauer, Mar. 30, 1943; children—Christian, Beatrice (Mrs. J. P. Brichant). Pianist, organist Basilica of Sainte-Clotilde, 1927-37, Benedictine Abbey, Paris, 1937-44; prof. counterpoint Schola Cantorum, 1935-57, prof. composition, 1957-64, dir., 1957-61, hon. dir., 1966—; composer music for films; mus. adviser Radiodiffusion-Television Franç aise, Paris, 1967—; prin. insp. music Ministry Cultural Affairs, 1969-71, insp. gen. Mem. French commn. UNESCO, 1958—. Decorated comdr. Legion of Honor, comdr. Nat. Order of Merit, comdr. Order Arts and Letters; recipient grand prize Gen. Council Seine, 1964, Ville de Paris, Conseil Municipale, 1969; prix Samuel-Rousseau, Acadé mie des Beaux-Arts. Mem. l'Academie Charles Cros (prés l'honneur), l'Institut de France, Royal Acad. Belgium. Club: Racing (France). Composer numerous works, including Chamber Concerto for piano and orchestra, 1953; Cantique des Colonnes for voice and orch., 1954; Le Bal du Destin (ballet), 1954; Elegie 2 guitars, 1956; Dance Symphony, 1956; Mass of Joy, 1960; Fantasy for 2 pianos, 1962; Three etudes for piano, 1962; Song of Songs, 1964; Andrea del Sarto (opera), 1968; Counter-Fugue for 2 pianos, 1970; Nocturne pour hautbois et orchestre, 1974; Symphonie, 1975; Intermezzo for violin and piano, 1977; Novelette for flute and piano, 1977; Ondine (opera) 1982, La Reine Morte, 1987. Contbr. articles to profl. jours. Office: Institut de France, 23 Quai de Conti, 75006 Paris France Address: 82 Blvd Flandrin, 75116 Paris France

DANIELS, LYDIA M., medical records administrator; b. Louisville, Dec. 21, 1932; d. Effort and Gladys T. (Turner) Williams; student Calif. State U., Hayward, 1967, 69, 70, 71, 72, Golden Gate U., 1979, 86, 87; cert. Samuel Merritt Hosp. Sch. Med. Record Adminstrs., 1959; student Central State Coll., Ohio, 1950-52; children by previous marriage—Danny Winston, Jeffrey Bruce, Anthony Wayne. Sec. chemistry dept. Central State Coll., Wilberforce, Ohio, 1950-52; co-dir. Indian Workcamp, Pala Indian Reservation, Pala, Calif., 1956-58; clk.-typist Camarillo (Calif.) State Hosp., 1956-58; student med. record adminstr. Samuel Merritt Hosp., Oakland, Calif., 1958-59, asst. med. record adminstr., 1962-63, asst. chief med. record adminstr., 1965, chief med. record adminstr., 1965-72; med. record adminstr. Albany (Calif.) Hosp., 1964-65; asst. med. record adminstr. Children's Hosp., San Francisco, 1960; co-dir. interns in community service Am. Friends Service Com., San Francisco, 1960-61; med. record adminstr. Pacific Hosp., Oakland, Calif., 1963-64; med. record cons. Tahoe Forest Hosp., Truckee, Calif., 1969-73; chief med. record adminstr. Highland Gen. Hosp., Oakland, 1972-74; dir. med. record services U. Calif. San Francisco Hosps. and Clinics, 1975-82; mgr. patient appointments, reception and registration Kaiser-Permanente Med. Ctr., 1982-88; dir. ambulatory services, 1988—; adj. prof. mgmt., office automation Golden Gate U., 1978—. Girl scout leader Oakland area council, 1960-62; Sunday sch. tchr. Soc. of Friends, Berkeley, Calif., 1961-63, mem. edn. com., 1965-68; mem. policy and adv. bd. Far West Lab. Demonstration Sch., Oakland, 1973—. Recipient Mgmt. Fellowship award U. Calif., San Francisco, 1979-80. Mem. Am. Med. Record Assn., Calif. Med. Record Assn. (editorial bd. 1976-77, pres. 1974-75), East Bay Med. Record Assn. (chmn. edn. com. 1971-72, pres. 1969-70), Assn. Systems Mgmt., Am. Mgmt. Assn., San Francisco Med. Records Assn. (pres.-elect 1982-83, pres. 1983-84). Author: Health Record Documentation: A Look at Cost, 1981; Inservice Training as a Tool in Managing the Changing Environment in the Medical Record Department, 1983; the Budget as a Management Tool, 1983. Issues editor Topics in Health Record Management, Parts I and II, 1983. Home: 545 Pierce St #1105 Albany CA 94706 Office: Kaiser-Permanente Med Ctr 280 W MacArthur Blvd Oakland CA 94611

DANIELS, MARCEL LUDOLPHE C.M., marketing communications specialist; b. St. Joris-Weert, Belgium, Feb. 14, 1952; s. Karel Lodewijk and Sylvia Johanna (Bollen) D.; m. Marie-Louise Vertongen, May 25, 1979; children: Thomas, Helene. MA in Interpreting cum laude, Leuven Cath. U., 1975. Freelance translator London, 1975-78; mgr. pub. relations Caterpillar Overseas, Brussels, 1978-80; mgr. mktg. communications Raychem Corp., Leuven, Belgium, 1980-86; dir. translations Crosby Assocs. Internat., Winter Park, Fla. and Brussels, 1986-87; mktg. communications mgr. Exxon Chem. Internat., Brussels, 1987—; founder, owner Lang. and Communication Systems, 1987—; owner, translator Lang. Cons., Brussels, 1986. Co-founder Boy Scouts Unit, St. Joris-Weert, 1966. Belgian Ministry Cultural Affairs scholar, Moscow, 1976-77. Mem. Internat. Assn. Bus. Communicators, Internat. TV Assn. Roman Catholic. Home: Stationsstraat 14, B-3060 Bertem Belgium Office: Exxon Chem Internat, Mechelsesteenweg 363, B 1950 Kraainem Belgium

DANIELS, MICHAEL ALAN, lawyer; b. Cape Girardeau, Mo., Mar. 6, 1946. B.S. in Speech, Northwestern U., 1968, M.A. in Polit. Sci., 1969; J.D., U. Mo., 1973. Bar: Fla. 1974, U. S. Supreme Ct. 1983. Spl. asst. for polit. sci. research Office Naval Research, Washington, 1969-71; legal aid Edwards, Seigfried, Runge and Hodge, Mexico, Mo., 1972-73; corp. atty. CACI, Inc., Washington, 1974-77; exec. v.p. gen. counsel Datex, Inc., Washington, 1977-78; chmn. bd., pres. Internat. Pub. Policy Research Corp., Falls Church, Va., 1978-87; v.p. Sci. Applications Internat. Corp., Washington, 1986—; pres. U.S. Global Strategy Council. Mem. Republican Nat. Com., Internat. Affairs Council, Nat. Security Adv. Council; mem. investment policy adv. com. Office U.S. Trade Rep., 1982—. Recipient Outstanding Fed. Securities Law Student award U. Mo., 1973. Mem. ABA (chmn. working group on law, nat. security and tech., standing com. law and nat. security 1984—), Fla. Bar Assn., Fed. Bar Assn. (chmn. internat. law com. 1979-86), Internat. Studies Assn. Office: SAIC 1710 Goodrich Dr McLean VA 22102

DANIELS, SAMUEL SOLOMON, management consultant; b. Lyallpur, Punjab, India, Feb. 9, 1936; s. Solomon Joshua and Ruth Solomon (Kusukar) D.; m. Dhun Mistry, Nov. 21, 1964; children: Ruth Dinaz. BE in Electro-Mech. Engring., Bombay U., 1957, diploma Bus. Mgmt. in Packaging Tech., 1969; diploma in Mktg. Mgmt., Indian Inst. Mgmt., 1972. Work study engr., head packaging devel., mgr. over-the-counter product mktg. Glaxo Internat., Bombay, 1960-69; divisional mgr. Larsen & Toubro Ltd., Bombay, 1969-79; gen. mgr. Suhail & Saud Bahwan Llc., Muscat, Oman, 1979-80; dir. Pt. Kalbe Farma Group, Jakarta, Indonesia, 1980-83; mktg. advisor Pt. Dafa/Ultra Jaya, Jakarta, 1983-85; tech. advisor Pt. Tempo Group, Jakarta, 1985-87; pvt. practice tech. cons. Jakarta, 1987—; sr. cons. Indonesian Packaging Fedn., Indonesian Packaging Inst.; mem. faculty Indian Inst., Bombay U., 1964-87. Contbr. articles to profl. jours.; inventor gravity liquid filler. Mem. packaging planning commn., New Dehli and Bombay, 1964-80. Served as squadron leader, pilot, Indian Air Force, 1962-64. Australian Govt. scholar, 1959. Fellow Inst. Indsl. Technicians; mem. World Packaging Orgn., Inst. Mktg. Mgmt., Inst. Engr., Inst. Mech. Engrs., Inst. Bus. Economy and Fin., Nat. Council for Sci. and Tech. (mem. expert com. on packaging), World Packaging Fedn. Clubs: Petroleum (Jakarta); United Servies (Bombay). Home: JL Cemput Tengah II/20 Pav, Jakarta 10510, Indonesia

DANIELS, VINCENT S., mining equipment company executive; b. Plainfield, N.J., Mar. 22, 1945; d. Vincent G. and Anna Carmela (Spisso) D.; m. Marianne K.M. Klee, Aug. 30, 1968; children—Jonathan Vincent Klee, Sebastian Nickolas Klee. B.S., U. Tampa, 1973; M. Internat. Mgmt., Am. Grad. Sch. Internat. Mgmt., Glendale, Ariz., 1974. Pres., Hassdan Internat., Glendale, 1974; dist. mgr. Bucyrus-Erie, South Milwaukee, Wis., 1975-76; pres. Disc, South Plainfield, N.J., 1976-79, Minequip Corp. Miami, 1980—; cons., pres. Daniels Internat. Sales & Cons., Miami, 1983—; cons. Paranapanema S.A., Sao Paulo, 1982—;bd. dirs. Minequip Ltda, La Paz, Bolivia, also Santiago, Chile, Lima, Peru and Rio de Janeiro, Brazil, Bogota, Colombia, 1983—. Contbr. articles to profl. jours. Mem. Republican Com. South Plainfield, 1976-79. Served to capt. U.S. Army, 1963-72; Vietnam, Greece, Ger. Decorated Air medal, Bronze Star, Purple Heart. Mem. Soc. Mining Engrs., Am. Mgmt. Assn., Mining Club, Inc., ARRL (life), Am. Legion. Club: World Trade. Home: 190 Los Pinos Ct Coral Gables FL 33143 Office: Minequip Corp 7777 NW 54th St Miami FL 33166

DANJCZEK, DAVID WILLIAM, manufacturing company executive; b. Phillipsburg, N.J., Sept. 29, 1951; s. William Emil and Erna (Lob) D. BSFS, Georgetown U., 1973; postgrad. Waseda U., 1973-74, Loyola U., Los Angeles, 1977-78. Contract adminstr. Aero Products, Woodland Hills, Calif., 1974-76, sr. contract adminstr., 1976-78; dir. internat. ops. Litton Industries, Washington, 1978—; adj. faculty Georgetown U. Trustee, treas. Athenaeum Mus., Alexandria, Va., 1983—. Mem. Nat. Security Indsl. Soc., Soc. Internat. Affairs, Electronic Industries Assn. (chmn. export-import com.), Washington Internat. Trade Assn., Machinery and Allied Products Inst. Republican. Roman Catholic. Clubs: University, Internat. Aviation. Avocations: squash, bridge. Home: 3800 N Fairfax Dr Arlington VA 22203 Office: Litton Industries 490 L'Enfant Plaza SW Washington DC 20024

DANJCZEK, WILLIAM EMIL, engring. supplies mfg. co. exec.; b. Prague, Czechoslovakia, June 4, 1913; s. Emil and Gabriele (Schich) D.; grad. St. Stevens Coll., Prague, 1931; Dr.Juris, Charles U., 1935; postgrad. Columbia, 1941, 50; m. Mary Anne Webb, Jan. 24, 1980; children by previous marriage—Helgi (Mrs. William Downes), Billie (Mrs. Mark Jorgensen), Thomas Arthur, Michael Harvey, David William. Mem. Legal and Gen. Assurance Soc., Ltd., London, 1933; market researcher Koh-inoor, Budweis, Czechoslovakia, 1935-37, Koh-inoor (Gt. Brit.), Ltd., Croydon, Eng., 1938-39; export mgr. Kohinoor, Inc., Bloomsbury, N.J., 1939-46, dir., v.p., 1947; pres. Koh-I-Noor Rapidograph, Inc. Koh-I-Noor (Can.) Ltd., 1947-75, hon. chmn. bd., 1975—; pres. Moser Jewel Co., Perth Amboy, N.J., 1970—, chmn., 1978. Bd. visitors Georgetown U. Sch. Fgn. Service, 1979—. Decorated knight St. Gregory; recipient Disting. Citizen Salesmanship award Sales and Mktg. Execs., 1966; Gold Americanism medal DAR, 1968. Mem. Pencil Makers Assn., Inc. (past pres.), Phillipsburg C. of C. (past pres., named Outstanding Citizen 1976). Club: Rotary (dir. Rancho Bernardo, Calif., past pres. Phillipsburg, N.J.). Home: 18233 Verano Dr San Diego CA 92128 Office: 100 North St Bloomsbury NJ 08804

DANK, LEONARD DEWEY, medical illustrator, audio-visual consultant; b. Birmingham, Ala., Dec. 21, 1929; s. George and Ellen (Balsam) D.; B.A. in Zoology, Cornell U., 1952; grad. Sch. Med. Illustration, Mass. Gen. Hosp., 1955; m. Beryl Eileen Jealous, Sept. 30, 1961; 1 dau., Amelia Theresa. Staff med. artist, plastic surgery clinic Manhattan Eye, Ear & Throat Hosp., 1955-57, Eye Bank for Sight Restoration, 1957-59; owner Leonard D. Dank Med. Illustration Studio, 1959-79; pres. Med. Illustrations Co., 1979—(all N.Y.C.); cons. med. illustrator St. Luke's Hosp., 1961-83, trans-vision div. Milprint, Inc., 1965—, Woman's Hosp., 1963-83, H.S. Struttman, Inc., 1964—, Home Library Press, 1960-70 (all N.Y.C.), Synapse Communications, Inc. (Conn.), 1973-75, Contemporary Orthopaedics and Contemporary Surgery, 1981-85, P.W. Communications, Inc., 1982—, Esquire Mags. Health and Fitness Clinic, 1985—. Recipient 1st prize certificate merit A.M.A., 1959, 1st prize citation of merit in motion picture program A.C.S., 1959, 62; Better Teller award Assn. Indsl. Advertisers, 1973, Outstanding Sci. Book award for Children Nat. Sci. Tchrs. Assn., 1982, Cert. of Merit Soc. of Illustrators, 1986. Mem. Assn. Med. Illustrators, Guild Natural Sci. Illustrators. Roman Catholic. Co-author: Gynecologic Operations, 1978; med. illustrator for numerous med. books, jours., elementary textbooks, juvenile books, encys. Home and Office: 800 Cox's Ln Cutchogue NY 11935

DANKO, WIKTOR LEON, mathematics educator, researcher; b. Karlino, Poland, July 3, 1948; s. Aleksander and Ryta Janina (Zakrzewska) D.; m. Zofia Kaszewska, Feb. 7, 1970; children: Aleksander Antoni, Anna Ryta. M of Math., U. Warsaw, 1971, D of Math., 1976, postgrad. degree, 1985. Tutor U. Warsaw, Bialystok, Poland, 1975-85; asst. prof. Bialystok div. U. Warsaw, 1986—; assoc. prof. U. Caen, France, 1985-86. Contbr. articles, revs. to profl. publs. Mem. Polskie Towarzystwo Matematyczne, Am. Math Soc. Home: Mieszka I 8 m35, 15-058 Bialystok Poland Office: U Warsaw Bialystok div, Akademicka 2, 15-267 Bialystok Poland

DANNEELS, GODFRIED CARDINAL, archbishop of Mechelen-Brussel; b. Kanegem, Belgium, Jun. 4, 1933. Ordained priest Roman Catholic Ch., 1957; prof. liturgy and sacramental theology Cath. U. Louvain (Belgium), 1969-77; consecrated bishop of Antwerp, 1977; apptd. archbishop of Mechelen-Brussel (Belgium), 1979; elected mem. gen. secretariat Synod of Bishops, 1981; elevated to Sacred Coll. of Cardinals, 1983. Mil. bishop, Belgium; pres. Belgian Episcopal Conf. Mem. Congregation of Cath. Edn., Congregation of Doctrine of Faith, Congregation of Bishops, Congregation of Evangelisation, Congregation of Divine Worship, Council for Pub. Affairs of the Ch., Secretariate. Address: Aartsbisdom, Wollemarkt 15, B-2800 Mechelen Belgium

DA NOBREGA, MAILSON FERREIRA, government official; b. Cruz do Espírito Santo, Brazil, May 14, 1942. Student, Colegio Lins de Vasconcelos, Joao Pessoa, Brazil, 1962, Faculdad de Ciencias Economica, 1974. With Banco do Brazil, 1964-77, Ministry of Industry and Commerce, Brazil, 1977-79, Ministry of Fin., Brazil, 1979—; now minister of fin. Brazil. Office: Ministry of Fin, Brasilia Brazil *

DANON, ABRAHAM, pharmacologist, educator; b. Sofia, Bulgaria, Mar. 2, 1939; arrived in Israel, 1940.; s. Gabriel and Zelma (Bejarano) D.; m. Batya Arzi, Nov. 7, 1963; children: Orna, Gabriel, Noam. MD, Hebrew U., Jerusalem, 1965, PhD, 1971. Intern Hadassah Hosp., Jerusalem, 1964; research assoc. Hebrew U., Jerusalem, 1967-70; fellow U. Pitts., 1970-71; research assoc. Vanderbilt U., 1971-74; sr. lectr., dir. clin. pharmacology Ben-Gurion U. and Soroka Med. Ctr., Beer-Sheva, Israel, 1974-79, assoc. prof., dir. clin. pharmacology, 1979—; cons. Ministry of Health, Jerusalem, 1975—. Contbr. articles to profl. jours. Served in Israeli Def. Army, 1965-67. Merck Internat. fellow, 1970-72. Mem. Israel Soc. Physiology and Pharmacology, Israel Soc. Endocrinology. Home: 14 Arava St, Omer 84965, Israel Office: Ben-Gurion U, PO Box 653, Beer-Sheva Israel

DANON, AMBRA, costume designer; b. Rome. Student, Acad. Costume Design, Rome, Acad. Dramatic Art, Rome. Costume designer for theatre, films, opera, and TV. Mem. Acad. Motion Picture Arts and Scis. (art dir. br., Acad. award nomination 1980). Home: 4 Piazza Priscilla, 00199 Rome Italy

DANON-BOILEAU, HENRI, retired psychiatrist, author; b. Buenos Aires, July 23, 1918; s. Danon and Wienberg B.; m. Martine Seligman; children: Laurent, Caroline. MD, U. Paris, 1953. Served with French Army, 1939-45; intern Hosp. Psychiat. de la Seine, Paris, 1948-52; head of clinic U. Paris, 1954-55, med. cons., 1956-60; mem. staff Found. Santé des Etudiants de France, Paris, 1956-81; cons. Hosp. Henri Rouselle, Paris, 1956-60; med. dir. Maison U. Medico-Psychologie, Paris, 1956-81. Contbr. more than 40 articles to profl. jours.; author: (scholarly) Les Etudes et L'Echec, 1984; (novels) Le Chemin de Tout le Monde, 1971, Vertiges, 1986, Une Rue à Traverser, 1987. Decorated Croix de Guerre (three), 1944, Medaille Militaire. Fellow Soc. Medico-Psychologuique; mem. Paris Psychoanalytical Soc., L'Evolution Psychiat., Soc. Med. Psycho-Somatique. Home and Office: 34 Quai de Bethune, 75004 Paris France

DANSER, MARY HELEN, pharmacist; b. Dawson Springs, Ky., Mar. 8, 1940; d. Maurice and Emma Louise (Thorn) Lisanby; m. Richard Allen Danser, June 8, 1963 (dec. Apr. 1976); 1 child, Richard Allen Jr. AA, Lindsey Wilson Jr. Coll., 1961; BS in Pharmacy, U. Ky., 1965. Intern U. Ky. Med. Ctr., 1965; intern, pharmacist Hubbard & Curry Druggists, Lexington, Ky., 1965-66; chief pharmacist Ky. Dept. Mental Health, Frankfort, 1966-73, Ky. Bur. Health Services, 1973-84; pharmacy services program mgr. Ky. Dept. Mental Health Cabinet for Human Resources, Frankfort, 1984—; cons. in field; instr. Coll. Law Enforcement Dept. Traffic Safety, Eastern Ky. U., 1968-84, vis. lectr.; instr. Jefferson County Police Dept., Louisville, Ky., 1985—. Recipient Scouters Training award, 1988. Mem. pastor/parish com. 1st Meth. Ch., Lexington, 1971-77, adminstrv. bd., 1972-74; chmn. com. Troop 276, Boy Scouts Am., Lexington, 1984—; youth counselor Antioch Christian Ch., 1984-86. Recipient Scouters Tng. award Boy Scouts Am., 1988; named to Hon. Order Ky. Cols., 1988. Mem. Bluegrass Pharm. Assn. (chair peer rev. com. 1986-87), Ky. Soc. Hosp. Pharmacists (sec. 1970), Am. Soc. Hosp. Pharmacists (panelist 1975-77). Democrat. Mem. Christian Ch. (Disciples of Christ). Avocations: gardening, sewing. Home: 3175 Paris Pike Lexington KY 40511 Office: Dept Mental Health 275 E Main St Frankfort KY 40621

DANSEREAU, FRED EDWARD, JR., behavioral scientist, educator; b. Yeadon, Pa., Sept. 20, 1946; s. Fred Edward and Catherine (Kennedy) D.; B.S., St. Josephs Coll., 1968; M.A., U. Ill., 1970, Ph.D., 1972. NSF fellow in behavioral sci. U. Ill., 1968-72; asst. prof. organizational behavior City U.N.Y., 1972-73; asso. prof. organizational behavior State U.N.Y., Buffalo, 1973—; cons. various orgns. Mem. Am. Psychol. Assn., Acad. Mgmt., AAAS, AAUP, Phi Kappa Phi. Author: Theory Testing in Organizational Behavior: The Varient Approach, 1984; contbr. articles and chpts. to profl. publs. Home: 60 Groton Dr Williamsville NY 14221 Office: SUNY 212 Crosby Hall Buffalo NY 14214

D'ANTONIO, GREGORY DOUGLAS, lawyer; b. Tucson, Oct. 6, 1951; s. Lawrence Patrick and Rosemary Catherine (Kane) D'A.; m. Judith Ann Furst, Sept. 8, 1979; 1 child, John Lawrence. B.A., U. Ariz., 1973, J.D., 1976. Bar: Ariz. 1976, U.S. Dist. Ct. Ariz. 1976, U.S. Ct. Mil. Appeals 1979. Sole practice, Tucson, 1979—. Served to capt. JAGC, U.S. Army, 1976-79. Mem. ABA, Assn. Trial Lawyers Am., Pima County Bar Assn., State Bar Ariz. Address: 70 W Cushing St Tucson AZ 85701

DANTZIG, RUDI VAN, choreographer, artistic director; b. Amsterdam, Netherlands, Aug. 4, 1933; s. Murk van and Berendina (Homburg) D.; H.B.S., Inst. voor Kunstnijverheid, 1950-52; studied ballet with Sonia Gaskell. With Sonia Gaskell's Co. Ballet-Recital, 1952-54; with Netherlands Ballet, 1954-59; with Netherlands Dance Theatre, 1959-60; with Netherlands Nat. Ballet, 1960—, artistic dir., 1968—; choreographer London Dance Theatre, Ballet Rambert, The Royal Ballet, Harkness Ballet, Houston Ballet, Ballet of Munich, Bat-Dor, Nat. Ballet Washington, Nat. Ballet Can., Asami Ballet Tokyo, Ballet Berlin, Am. Ballet Theatre, Royal Danish Ballet, Houston Ballet, Viennese Opera Ballet, Royal Winnipeg Ballet, Hungarian State Ballet, Finnish Nat. Ballet, Paris Opera Ballet, Hamburg Opera Ballet; works include: Night Island, 1955, Family Circle, 1958, Jungle, 1961, Monument for a Dead Boy, 1965, Romeo and Juliet, 1966, Moments, 1967, Epitaph, 1968, Astraal, 1969, On The Way, 1970; (for Rudolf Nureyev) The Ropes of Time, 1970, Painted Birds, 1971, Are Friends Delight or Pain'9 , 1972, The Unfinished, 1973, Ramifications, 1974, Orpheus, 1974, Couples, 1974, Movements in a Rocky Landscape, 1974, Collective Symphony, 1975, Blown in a Gentle Wind; (with Wade Waithall) for Rudolf Nureyev), 1975, Ginastera, 1976, Four Last Songs, 1977, Gesang de Jü nglinge, 1978, About a Dark House, 1978, Ullysses, 1978, (with Toer van Schayk) Life, 1979, Underneath My Feet, 1981, Room at the Top, 1982, No Man's Land, 1983, I Just Simply Keep My Breath, 1984, In Praise of Follie, 1984, For We Know Not What We Do, 1985. Decorated Ridder van Oranje Nassau; recipient prize City of Amsterdam, 1958, Prix de la Critique, 1955, 60. Author: Nureyev, a Biography, 1975; Ballet and Modern Dance, 1975; The Cry of the Firebird, 1977; Olga De Haas, A Memory, 1979; For a Lost Soldier, 1986 Follie, 1984; film of his life by Jan Vrijman: Rudi van Dantzig, portrait of a choreographer, 1972. Works also performed Europe, U.S.A., USSR, S.Am. Home: Emmastraat 27, Amsterdam The Netherlands Office: Het Nationale Ballet, Marnixstraat 427, 1071 HN Amsterdam The Netherlands *

DANUSUGONDHO, SUMARTO, public health physician, educator; b. Malang, Indonesia, Aug. 24, 1936; s. Soemargo Danusugondho and Asiani Nitiwidigdo; m. Siti Parwati Soeradibrata, Dec. 5, 1965; children: Radityo Tribawono Anindito, Sulistyanto Nirboyono. MD, U. Airlangga Surabaya, 1963; D of Pub. Health, U. N.C., 1982. Lectr. dept. pub. health U. Airlangga, Surabaya, Indonesia, 1963—; chmn. coordinating body community medicine U. Airlangga, Surabaya, 1976-79, asst. dean for research and community service, 1977-79, chmn. lab. dept. health adminstrn. and health edn., 1979—, dir. grad. program in pub. health, 1985—, prof. pub. health, 1987—; cons. WHO, Dacca, Bangladesh, 1978-79, AID, Jakarta, 1986, 87; vis. prof. U. Hawaii, 1987. Mem. editorial bd. Jour. Indonesian Pub. Health, 1983—. Mem. Indonesian Med. Assn., Indonesian Pub. Health Assn. Islam. Home: Dharmawangsa Dalam Selatan 14, Surabaya 60286, Indonesia Office: U Airlangga Faculty Medicine, Dharmahusada 47, Surabaya 60131, Indonesia

DANYLOW, PETER, historian, analyst; b. Hamburg, Fed. Republic Germany, Sept. 4, 1951; s. Hans and Gerda (Klingsporn) D.; m. Jutta Stephan, Apr. 14, 1975; children. PhD, U. Hamburg, 1980. Research fellow Deutsche Forschungsgemeinschaft U. Hamburg, 1980-83; research fellow German Soc. Fgn. Affairs, Bonn, Fed. Republic Germany, 1983—. Author: Foreign Relations Between Albania, Yugoslavia and the U.S.S.R. 1944-1967, 1982; co-author: Changes in the German Question?, 1985; contbr. articles to profl. jours. Mem. German Soc. Fgn. Affairs, German Soc. U.N. Home: Wittelsbacherstr 7, D-5300 Bonn Federal Republic of Germany

DANZIS, COLIN MICHAEL, lawyer; b. Newark, May 3, 1938; s. Sidney and Selma (Colin) D.; B.A., Wesleyan U., 1960; LL.B., N.Y. U., 1962, LL.M. in Taxation, 1963; m. Jo-Ann Fine, Nov. 16, 1963; children—Mitchell, Nicholas. Admitted to N.J bar, 1964; partner firm Lum, Hoens, Abeles, Conant & Danzis, Newark, 1971—; dir. Pottermeter Corp. Pres. bd. govs. Newark Acad., 1971-75, trustee, 1973—. Mem. Am., N.J., Essex County bar assns., Beta Theta Pi. Clubs: West Orange Tennis, Jockey. Office: 103 Eisenhower Pkwy Roseland NJ 07068

DAO, HUNG TRONG, architect, Canadian provincial government official; b. Hanoi, Vietnam, Mar. 27, 1936; came to Can., 1967; s. Cuong Trong Dao and Hoa Thi Nguyen; m. Thanh Hoa Hoang, Jan. 2, 1962; children: Tien, Linda, Mylene. Diploma in Earthquake Engring., Internat. Inst. Seismology and Earthquake Engring., Tokyo, 1966; BArch, Laval U., 1970, MArch, 1974; M of Pub. Adminstrn., U. Que., Can., 1985. Dir. archtl. dept. Indsl. Complex An Hoa, South Vietnam, 1963-65; architect St. Gelais and Tremblay, Ste. Foy, Que., 1970-75; dir. archtl. programming Que. Ministry Justice, Ste. Foy, 1975—. Fellow UNESCO, Paris, 1965, Housing Corp. Can., 1970-72; scholar Assn. Overseas Tech. Scholarships, Japan, 1966. Mem. Adminstrs. Assn. Que., Royal Inst. Architecture Can., Vietnamese Assn. (pres. Que. sect. 1976, pres. adminstrv. council 1985). Home: 3321 Quatre Saisons, Sainte Foy, PQ Canada G1X 2L5 Office: Ministry of Justice, 1200 Route de l'Eglise, Sainte Foy, PQ Canada G1V 4M1

DAOUD, GEORGE JAMIL, hotel and motel consultant; b. Beirut, Oct. 20, 1948; came to U.S., 1958, naturalized, 1970; s. Jamil G. and Shafika E. Daoud; B.S., N.Y.U., 1967; M.P.S., Cornell U., 1969; m. Barbara A. Fisco, Apr. 30, 1972: 5 children. Gen. mgr. Holiday Inn, New London and Groton, Conn., 1974-75, Gentle Winds Beach Resort, St. Croix, V.I., 1975-78; pres., cons. Motor Inn Mgmt., Inc., Dayton, Ohio, 1973—; pres. Central Services Group, Inc., First Group, Inc., Host Mgmt., Inc., The Inn Group, Inc., , 1981—, Metro Markets, Inc., Triad Ventures, Inc. (all Dayton), 1980-86; v.p. V.I. Hotel and Motel Assn., 1976. Mem. Am. Hotel and Motel Assn. (mem. Ednl. Inst., cert. hotel adminstr.), Ohio Hotel and Motel Assn., Nat. Assn. Rev. Appraisers, Cert. Real Estate Rev. Appraisers. Republican. Roman Catholic. Club: Masons. Office: Host Mgmt Inc 18 W 1st St Suite 100 Dayton OH 45402

DAOUD, MOHAMED, physicist; b. Tunis, Tunisia, Mar. 31, 1947; came to France, 1964; s. Hassen Daoud and Beya (Bahri) D. Maitrise, Ecole Normale Superieure, Saint Cloud, 1968-70, D.E.A., 1972, (hon.) Agregation, 1971; These, U. Paris VI, 1977. Research assoc. Commissariat a Energie Atomique, C.E.A. Saclay, 1974-78, physicist, 1980—; physicist Boston U., 1978-80. Recipient Grand Prix, Groupement Français de Polymers, 1978, prix C.E.A., 1986. Mem. Societe Française de Physique, Am. Phys. Soc. Office: CEN Saclay, Lab Leon Brillouin, 91191 Gif/Yvette France

DAPP, THOMAS EDWARD, construction company executive; b. Milw., Feb. 8, 1941; s. Jean Godfred and Verna Clara (Schumann) D.; BSCE, U. Wis., 1964, MBA, 1965; postgrad., Ind. U., 1971—; m. Susan Daine Ricker, June 24, 1967; children—Nicole Jeanine, Jason Thomas. Project engr. Ryan Inc. of Wis., Milw., 1965-66, systems and prodn. mgr., Janesville, 1966-67, eastern div. and structures mgr., Chgo. and Indpls., 1967-73; pres. Gradex, Inc., Indpls., 1973—; v.p. Midwest Racquetball, Inc., Indpls., 1978—; pres. Dapp, Inc., 1979—; partner Heatherlea Devel., 1979—; sec. Knollwood Valley Devel., Indpls., 1985—; pres. TriState Constrn. Co., Inc., Indpls., 1983—, Concrete Corp. Indpls., 1983—; sec.-treas. Excon, Inc., Indpls., 1985—. Bd. dirs. Ind. Hwys. for Survival; bd. dirs., sec. Build Ind. Council; nat. dir. AGC, Op. Engring Jr. Registered profl. engr., Ind. Mem. ASCE, Nat. Soc. Profl. Engrs., Ind. Constructors Assn. (past bd. dirs., pres.) Gen. Contractors. Am. Road Builders Assn., U. Wis. Alumni Assn., Ind. C. of C. (v.p.), Beta Gamma Sigma, Tau Epsilon. Clubs: Ind. Econ., Sierra, Woodland Country, Carmel Racquet, Brookshire Golf, Kokomo Racquetball, Racquetball Plus, Hoosier Roadrunners, U.S. Golf Assn. Home: 1315 Fairbanks Dr Carmel IN 46032 Office: 6810 N Shadeland Ave Indianapolis IN 46220

DAPPLES, EDWARD CHARLES, geologist, educator; b. Chgo., Dec. 13, 1906; s. Edward C. and Victoria (Gazzolo) D.; m. Marion Virginia Sprague, Sept. 2, 1931; children—Marianne Helena, Charles Christian. B.S., Northwestern U., 1928, M.S., 1934; M.A., Harvard, 1935; Ph.D., U. Wis., 1938. Geologist Ziegler Coal Co., 1928; geologist Truax-Traer Coal Co., 1928-32, mine supt., 1932; instr. Northwestern U., 1936-41, asst. prof., 1941, asso. prof., 1942-50, prof. geol. scis., 1950-75, prof. emeritus, 1975—; geologist Ill. Geol. Survey, 1939, Sinclair Oil Co., 1945-50, Pure Oil Co., 1950; dir. Evanston Exploration Corp; sr. vis. scientist U. Lausanne, Switzerland, 1960-61; vis. prof. U. Geneva, Switzerland, 1970. Author: Basic Geology for Science and Engineering, 1959, Atlas of Lithofacies Maps, 1960. Fellow Geol. Soc. Am., Soc. Econ. Geologist; mem. Am. Inst. Mining Engrs. (Legion of Honor), Assn. Petroleum Geologists, Internat. Assn. Sedimentologists, Soc. Econ. Paleontologists and Mineralogists (pres. 1970, hon. mem. 1974), Am. Inst. Profl. Geologists (pres. Ill.-Ind. sect. 1979, pres. Ariz. 1982, hon. mem. 1986), Geochem. Soc., Assn. Engring. Geologists. Home: 13035 98th Dr Sun City AZ 85351

DAPPRICH, JOHN WILLIAM, interior designer; b. Dearborn, Mich., Mar. 6, 1937; s. Elton and Ellen (Ketchum) D.; student Easter U., 1956-57; diploma Kendall Sch. Design, 1962. Interior designer Burdines Dept. Stores, Miami, Fla., 1963-64, restaurant at Ponce De Leon Lodge, St. Augustine, Fla., Jordan Marsh Dept. Store, Miami, 1964-66; interior designer Waldo Perez Interiors, Coconut Grove, Fla., 1967-68; owner Dapprich Interiors, Coconut Grove, 1968-70; dir. interior design Deltona Corp., Miami, 1970—. Served with AUS, 1957-59. Mem. AID. Interior designer penthouse Joe Garagiola, Marco Island, 1970, also interior designer for Jack Paar, Key Biscayne, 1972, Henry Kissinger, Key Biscayne, 1972, Gene Sarazen, Marco Island, 1972, Ken Venturi, Marco Island, Adm. Rickenbacker, Senator George Smathers, Ara Parseghian, Naples Beach Club Hotel, Airport Regency Hotel, Quail Creek Country Club, Kings Bay Yacht and Country Club and Hotel, Jupiter Hilton Hotel (Fla.); TV commls. for Bob Griese of Miami Dolphins; hotels include Marco Beach Hotel, Marco Island, Fla., Key Biscayne (Fla.) Hotel, Tierra Verde Hotel, St. Petersburg, Fla., The Palace Hotel, Phila., J.F.K. Internat. Hotel, N.Y.C., Belmont Hotel, Bermuda, LAX Hotel, Los Angeles, Miami Spring Villas, Miami. Home: 3927 Douglas Rd Coconut Grove FL 33133

DAPRON, ELMER JOSEPH, JR., advertising executive; b. Clayton, Mo., Jan. 14, 1925; s. Elmer Joseph and Susanna (Kruse) D.; m. Sharon Kay Neuling, Feb. 22, 1977 (dec. Apr. 1987). Employed in constrn. bus., Fairbanks, Alaska, 1947-48; tech. writer-editor McDonnell-Douglas Corp., St. Louis, 1948-57; free-lance writer, Paris, France, 1957; with Gardner Advt. Co., St. Louis, 1960-78, v.p. 1969-78; sr. v.p. Kenrick Advt. Inc., 1978—; pres. Cornucopia Communications, Inc., 1979—. Producer syndicated radio and TV show Elmer Dapron's Grocery List; advt. and mktg. cons. to govt. and industry; daily commentator The Grocery List Armed Forces Radio Network (world wide). Mem. Gov.'s Energy Commn., 1977—. Mem. Nat. Dem. Com. Served with USMCR, 1943-45; PTO; 50-51; Korea. Recipient advt. awards including New Filming Techniques award Internat.-Film Festival. Hon. fellow Harry Truman Library Inst. Mem. Nat. Agrl. Mktg. Assn. (v.p. 1970—, trustee Miss. Valley Farm Mktg. (Man of Yr. 1974), Assn. R.R. Advt. and Mktg. (nat. membership chmn.) , Marine Corps League (nat. vice comdt. 1967-69). Clubs: Media, Presidents, St. Louis Track. Democrat. Contbr. articles to publs. Home: 300 Mansion House Center St Louis MO 63102 Office: 319 N 4th St Saint Louis MO 63102

DARANY, TIBOR ENDRE, electronics company executive; b. Budapest, Hungary, Nov. 4, 1935; came to U.S., 1957; s. Henry and Olga (Fenakel) D.; m. Brita Maria Stadter; 1 child, Vanessa. BS in Engring., Columbia U., N.Y.C., 1960; MBA, CUNY, 1965. Asst. mgr., engr. Burndy Electra, Mechelen, Belgium, 1963-64; area mgr. Burndy Japan, Tokyo, 1965-68; engr. Burndy Corp., Norwalk, Conn., 1960-62, mgr. exports, 1969-78, dir. internat. div., 1979-84, v.p., 1985—. Home: 974 North St Greenwich CT 06831 Office: Burndy Corp Richards Ave Norwalk CT 06856

DARBO, BAKARY BUNJA, vice-president of Gambia; b. Dumbutte, Oct. 8, 1946; 3 children. Degree with honors in Modern Langs., U. Ibadan, 1967; cert. of proficiency in French Lang. and Civilization, U. Abidjan, 1966. Asst. divisional commr., divisional commr. Provincial Adminstrn., Basse and Kerewan, 1967-71; asst. sec. Prime Minister's Office Ministry External Affairs, 1968-70; dir. econ. and tech. affairs Senegambian Permanent Secretariat, 1971-74; mgr. coml. banking ops. G.C.&D. Bank, 1974-79; high commr. of Gambia to Republic of Senegal, 1979-81; minister of info. and tourism, 1981; v.p. of Gambia, 1982—. Address: Office of the President, State House, Banjul The Gambia

DARCY, GEORGE ROBERT, public relations company executive; b. Rochester, N.Y., Aug. 23, 1920; s. George N. and Agnes (Hogan) D.; m. Martha Louise Harbrecht, Apr. 5, 1950; children: George H., Patricia A., Kevin B., Michael J., Elizabeth A. A.B., U. Rochester, 1942. Coll. rep. McGraw-Hill Book Co., N.Y.C., 1947-48; editor indsl. and bus. books McGraw-Hill Book Co., 1949-52; mgr. book div. F.W. Dodge Corp., N.Y.C., 1952- 54; sr. v.p. adminstrn. Rumrill Co., Inc., Rochester, 1954-59; pres. Darcy Communications, Inc., Rochester, 1959-76; also dir.; chmn. bd., chief exec. officer Hutchins/Darcy Inc., 1971-76; pres. Darcy Internat. Counselors, Inc., Brooklandville, Md., 1976—; v.p. Internat. Pub. Relations Group Cos., Inc., 1977—; chmn., chief exec. officer Internat. Pub. Relations Co., Inc., Washington, 1986—; mem. Pub. Affairs Council, Washington, 1987—; bd. dirs. Darcy Communications, Inc., Denver, Marenco, Inc., Miami, Fla. Pub. information chmn. U.S. Golf Assn. Open Championship, 1968; mem. Monroe County Human Relations Commn., 1970-75, vice chmn., 1972-75; chmn. County Monroe Indsl. Devel. Agy., 1972-76, Independents for Rockefeller, Monroe County, 1970; mem. advisory bd. Am. Humane Assn., 1976-78; trustee Penfield (N.Y.) Bd. Edn., 1959-60, Meml. Art Gallery, U. Rochester, 1968-74; bd. dirs. Met. Rochester Devel. Council, 1972-77. Served to lt. (s.g.) USNR, 1942-46. Mem. Public Relations Soc. Am. (del. nat. assembly 1964-67), Rochester C. of C. (trustee), U. Rochester Assos. (chmn.). Home: 6 Old Boxwood Ln Lutherville MD 21093 Office: Darcy Internat Counselors PO Box 813 Brooklandville MD 21022

DARCY, JAMES J., steel company executive; b. Buffalo, July 24, 1947; s. Edward S. and Angeline H. (Szalkiewicz) D.; m. Afaf Atiyeh, May 23, 1976; 1 child, Joshua. A.D. in Info. Services, Bryant and Stratton Coll., 1967; B.S. in Acctg., Tri-State U., 1970; postgrad. cert. McGill U., 1983. Programmer/analyst Bethlehem Steel Corp., Pa., 1970-79, supr. keypunch, 1979, supr. data entry, 1979-80, network mgr., 1980-82, tech. support mgr., 1982-83, spl. asst. productivity, 1983-85, sr. systems cons., 1985-87, project mgr. human resources and info. systems dept., 1987—. Cons. Jr. League, Bethlehem, 1984. Recipient Cert. of Achievement U.S. Army, 1972. Mem. Data Processing Mgmt. Assn. (bd. dirs. 1985—), Human Resources Resources Profls., Internat. Assn. Quality Circles, Internat. Platform Assn., Alpha Kappa Psi (v.p., service award 1969). Republican. Roman Catholic. Lodges: Sertoma (sgt. at arms 1974-75), Knights (treas. 1975-76). Office: Bethlehem Steel Corp A208 Martin Tower Bethlehem PA 18016

DARDEN, MARY DUNLAP, management consultant; b. Richmond, Va., Aug. 10, 1952; d. Oscar Bruton and Ann Wingfield (Johnson) D.; BS in Math. and Edn., Va. Poly. Inst. and State U., 1974; MBA, U. Richmond, 1984. Mktg. rep. IBM, Richmond, 1974-78; territorial saleswoman Swan, Inc., Richmond, 1978, dir. ops., 1978-83; pres. Cygnet, Inc., mgmt. cons., 1980-83; v.p. Lee-Darden Assocs. Inc., Richmond, 1983—. Bd. dirs., sec.-treas. Va. Small Bus. Financing Authority, 1984-86; Va. del. White House Conf. on Small Bus., 1986. Named to 100 Percent Club, IBM, 1976, 77. Mem. St. Mary's Hosp. Aux., Richmond Assn. Women Bus. Owners (sec. 1983-84, pres. 1984-85). Presbyterian. Home: 4104 Park Ave Richmond VA 23221 Office: Lee-Darden Assocs Inc 1606 Santa Rosa Rd Suite 240 Richmond VA 23229

DARGHOUS, NABIL KAMEL, manufacturing executive; b. Beirut, Mar. 26, 1954; arrived in Saudi Arabia, 1982; s. Mohamed Kamel and Alensa Malaké (Halabi) D.; m. Linda Kathleen Caravan, 1978; children: Mazin, Soraya. M in Engring., Am. U. Beirut, 1975; postgrad., Alexander Hamilton Coll., 1987; MBA, Strayer Coll., Washington, 1988. Registered profl. engr. Project mgr. Westinghouse, Jeddah, Saudi Arabia, 1976-77; sales exec. Johnson Controls Internat., London, 1977-78; area mgr. Johnson Controls Internat., Riyadh, 1978-79; project dir. Johnson Controls Internat., London, Italy, 1979-82; gen. mgr. Johnson Controls Internat., Saudi Arabia, 1982-84, mng. dir., 1984—. Mem. Jeddah C. of C., Am. Businessmen Jeddah. Moslem. Office: Johnson Controls Systems, PO Box 79 Westlea Down, Swindon SN5 7DD, England

DARIOTIS, TERRENCE THEODORE, lawyer; b. Chgo., Feb. 28, 1946; s. Theodore S. and Dorothy Mizzen (Thompson) D.; m. Jeanne Elizabeth Gibbons, Oct. 24, 1970; children—Sara Mizzen, Kristin Elizabeth, Jennifer Ann. B.A. in Philosophy, St. Joseph's Coll., Rensselaer, Ind., 1969; J.D., Loyola U., 1973. Bar: Ill. 1973, Fla. 1975, U.S. Supreme Ct. 1978. Law clk. to presiding justice Appellate Ct. of Ill. (2d dist.), Waukegan, Ill., 1973-74; assoc. Keith Kinderman, Tallahassee, 1975-76; sole practice, Tallahassee, 1976-82; ptnr. Kahn & Dariotis, P.A., Tallahassee, 1982—; adj. prof. Fla. State U. Coll. Bus., 1987—. Mem. Ill. State Bar Assn. Roman Catholic. Office: Kahn and Dariotis PA 227 E Virginia St Tallahassee FL 32301

DARKES, ANNA SUE, religious organization administrator, writer; b. Lebanon, Pa., Feb. 5, 1927; d. John W. and Anna S. (Flinchbaugh) Darkes; diploma Lebanon Bus. Coll., 1945, Phila. Coll. Bible, 1949. Bookkeeper, E. H. Gerhart & Co., Jonestown, Pa., 1945-47; missionary Scripture Memory Mt. Mission, 1950-73; mem. Corp. Calvary Fellowship Homes, 1979—; co-founder, exec. dir. Faith Venture Visuals, Inc., Lititz, Pa., 1972—; co-founder

Mayking Bapt. Ch., 1958; overseas seminar lectr., Australia, Japan, New Zealand, Ireland, Ecuador, Brazil, Holland. Recipient Alumna of Yr. award Phila. Coll. Bible, 1977. Author: Sailing on Life's Sea, 1973; Pioneering of Life's Trail, How To Be Saved and Know It, 1974; Exploring God's Word, 1975; God of Space, 1976; Campsites of Victory, 1977; Christ Our Shepherd, 1978; How to Make and Use Overhead Transparencies, 1977; 80 Cool Ideas for Your Summer Outreach, 1984; author, filmer video tng. tapes 30 Whys and Ways of Overhead Use, The Basics for Making Transparencies, Teaching Your Overhead Good Manners and New Tricks, 1983, The Innovative Teaching Team: You and Your Overhead Projector, 1987; designer Faith Venture Visual's Instaframe. Office: 510 E Main St Lititz PA 17543

DARKO, DENIS FRANK, physician; b. Indpls., July 13, 1947; s. Charles O. and Agnes Mary (Lauck) D.; m. Ann Marie Barker, Oct. 15, 1983; 1 child, Emily Marie. BS in Physics, U. Notre Dame, 1969; MD, Ind. U., 1975. Diplomate Am. Bd. Psychiatry and Neurology. Research technician biols. div. Eli Lilly Co., Indpls., 1970, U. Colo. Sch. Medicine, 1971; resident physician family practice Scotsdale (Ariz.) Meml. Hosp., 1975-76; resident physician psychiatry Good Samaritan Med. Ctr., Phoenix, 1977-80, chief resident in psychiatry, 1979-80; pvt. practice psychiatry, Scottsdale, Ariz., 1980-83; cons. psychiatrist Phoenix Indian Med. Center, 1980-81; supr. psychiatry residency program Maricopa Med. Center, 1980-83; instr. pre-med. program Ariz. State U., 1980-83; instr. family practice residency program, 1980-83; fellow in consultantion/liaison psychiatry U. Calif.-San Diego Med. Ctr., 1983-84, fellow in psychopharmacology and psychobiology Clin. Research Center, 1984-85; asst. prof. psychiatry U. Calif., San Diego Sch. Medicine, 1985—, attending physician Univ. Hosp., 1985—; ward chief San Diego VA Med. Ctr., 1985-87, staff psychiatrist, 1985—, med. dir. mental health clinic, 1987-88, chief psychiatric emergency clinic, 1988—; dir. Mood Disorders Research Clinic U. Calif. San Diego Sch. Medicine and San Diego Vets. Administrn. Med. Ctr., 1987—, NIMH Mental Health Clin. Research Ctr., 1987-88. Editorial reviewer Am. Jour. Psychiatry, 1986—, Internat. Jour. of Psychiatry in Medicine, 1987—, Jour. of Neuropsychiatry and Clin. Neurosciences,1988—. Recipient review article award Am. Coll. Allergists, 1986; USPHS fellow, 1972, ACP fellow, 1988. Mem. Am. Phys. Soc., Am. Chem. Soc., ACP, Am. Psychiat. Assn., Central Neuropsychiat. Assn., Am. Psychosomatic Soc., Calif. Psychiat. Assn., San Diego Soc. Psychiat. Physicians. Office: U Calif San Diego Sch Medicine Dept Psychiatry M-003 La Jolla CA 92093

DARLING, ALBERTA STATKUS, art museum executive, marketing professional; b. Hammond, Ind., Apr. 28, 1944; d. Albert William and Helen Anne (Vaicunas) Statkus; m. William Anthony Darling, Aug. 12, 1967; children—Elizabeth Suzanne, William Anthony. B.S., U. Wis., 1967. English tchr. Nathan Hale High Sch., West Allis, Wis., 1967-69, Castle Rock High Sch., Colo., 1969-71; community vol. work, Milw., 1971—; cons. orgn. devel., Milw., 1982—; dir. mktg. and communications Milw. Art Mus., 1983—. A founder Goals for Greater Milw. 2000, 1980-84; co-chair Action 2000, 1984-86; bd. dirs., exec. com. United Way, Milw., 1982—, chair project 1985, 1984-85, chmn. policy com. 1988; founder Today's Girls/Tomorrow's Women, Milw., 1982—; pres. Jr. League Milw., 1980-82, Planned Parenthood Milw., 1982-84, Future Milw., 1983-85; vice chmn. State of Wis. Strategic Planning Council, 1988—, chmn. small bus./entrepreneur com.; mem. Greater Milw. Com.'s Mktg. Task Force, 1987-88; chmn. United Way Policy Com., 1987-88; participant Bus. Ptnrs. White House Conf., 1987. Recipient Vol. Action award Milw. Civic Alliance, 1984, Community Service award United Way, 1984, Leader of Future award Milw. Mag., 1985, Nat. Assn. Community Leadership Orgn. award, 1986, Today's Girls/Tomorrow's Women Leadership award, 1987, Future Milw. Community Leadership award, 1988. Mem. Greater Milw. Com., TEMPO Profl. Women, Am. Mktg. Assn. (Marketer of Yr. 1984), Pub. Relations Soc. Am., Internat. Assn. Bus. Communicators. Republican. Avocations: travel, art history, contemporary Am. lit., golf, tennis. Home: 1325 W Dean Rd Milwaukee WI 53217 Office: Beckley/Myers/Flad Inc 825 N Jefferson Milwaukee WI 53202

DARLING, JOHN ROTHBURN, JR., educator, university administrator; b. Holton, Kans., Mar. 30, 1937; s. John Rothburn and Beatrice Noel (Deaver) D.; m. Melva Jean Fears, Aug. 20, 1958; children: Stephen, Cynthia, Gregory. A.A., Graceland Coll., 1957; B.S., U. Ala., 1959, M.S., 1960; Ph.D., U. Ill., 1967. Divisional mgr. J.C. Penney Co., 1960-63; grad. teaching asst. U. Ill., Urbana, 1965-66; asst. prof. mktg. U. Ala., Tuscaloosa, 1966-68; assoc. prof. mktg. U. Mo., Columbia, 1968-71; prof. administrn., coordinator mktg. Wichita State U., 1971-76; dean, prof. mktg. Coll. Bus. and Adminstrn., So. Ill. U., Carbondale, 1976-81; v.p. acad. affairs, prof. bus. Tex. Tech U., Lubbock, 1981-86; provost, v.p. acad. affairs, prof. mktg. Miss. State U., Mississippi State, 1986—; mktg. research cons. Southwestern Bell, 1970; sr. v.p. Boothe Advt., Wichita, 1972; pres. Bus. Research Assos., 1972-76; cons. Bus. Research assocs., 1976-82; spl. cons. FTC, Washington, 1972-75, U.S. Dept. Justice, 1973-74, Atty. Gen., State of Kans., 1972-76, Dist. Atty., 18th Jud. Dist., Wichita, 1972-76. Author: (with Harry A. Lipson) Marketing Fundamentals, Text and Cases, 1974; contbr. articles to profl. jours. Bd. dirs. Outreach Found., 1973-79, v.p., 1975-77; bd. trustees Graceland Coll., Lamoni, Iowa, 1976-82; mem. mgmt. com. Park Coll., Kansas City, 1976-79. Mem. Am. Assn. Higher Edn., Internat. Council Small Bus., Am. Mktg. Assn., Acad. Internat. Bus., Am. Econs. Assn., So. Bus. Adminstrn. Assn., So. Mktg. Assn., So. Econs. Assn., Midwest Bus. Adminstrn. Assn., Sales and Mktg. Execs. Internat., Beta Gamma Sigma, Phi Kappa Phi, Omicron Delta Kappa, Phi Delta Kappa, Mu Kappa Tau, Pi Sigma Epsilon, Alpha Kappa Psi, Chi Alpha Phi, Alpha Phi Omega. Home: 622 Sherwood Rd Starkville MS 39759 Office: Miss State U Office of Provost Mississippi State MS 39762

DARLING, SCOTT EDWARD, lawyer; b. Los Angeles, Dec. 31, 1949; s. Dick R. and Marjorie Helen (Otto) D.; m. Cynthia Diane Harrah, June 1970 (div.); 1 child, Smokie; m. Deborah Lee Cochran, Aug. 22, 1981; children: Ryan, Jacob. BA, U. Redlands, 1972; JD, U.S.C., 1975. Bar: Calif. 1976, U.S. Dist. Ct. (cen. dist.) Calif. 1976. Assoc. atty. Elver, Falsetti, Boone & Crafts, Riverside, 1976-78; ptnr. Falsetti, Crafts, Pritchard & Darling, Riverside, 1978-84; sr. ptnr. Darling, Medof & Miller, Riverside, 1984—; grant reviewer HHS, Washington, 1982—; judge pro tem Riverside County Mcpl. Ct., 1980, Riverside County Supreme Ct., 1987; bd. dirs. Tel Law Nat. Legal Pub. Info. System, Riverside, 1978-80. Author, editor: Small Law Office Computer Legal System, 1984. Bd. dirs. Youth Adv. Com. to Selective Service, 1968-70, Am. Heart Assn. Riverside County, 1978-82, Survival Ministries, 1986—; atty. panel Calif. Assn. Realtors, Los Angeles, 1980—; pres. Calif. Young Reps., 1978-80; mem. Govt. Issue Forum, Riverside, 1970—; presdl. del. Nat. Rep. Party, 1980-84; asst. treas. Calif. Rep. Party, 1981-83; Rep. Congl. candidate, Riverside, 1982; treas. Riverside Sickle Cell Found., 1980-82, recipient Eddie D. Smith award; pres. Calif. Rep. Youth Caucus, 1980-82; v.p. Riverside County Red Cross, 1982-84; mem. Citizen's Univ. Com., Riverside, 1978-84, World Affairs Council, 1978-82, Urban League, Riverside, 1980-82. Calif. Scholarship Fedn. (life). Named one of Outstanding Young Men in Am., U.S. Jaycees, 1979—. Mem. ABA, Riverside County Bar Assn., Speaker's Bur. Riverside County Bar Assn., Riverside Jaycees, Riverside C. of C. Lodge: Native Sons of Golden West. Office: Darling Miller & King 7121 Magnolia Ave Riverside CA 92504

DARLINGTON, JARED LLOYD, computer scientist; b. Woodbury, N.J., Oct. 12, 1933; s. Charles Joseph and Eleanor (Collins) D.; m. Vehanoush Hemayag Ourfalian, June 12, 1960. B.A., Swarthmore Coll., 1954; M.A., Yale U., 1956, Ph.D., 1957. Instr., Conn. Coll., New London, 1957-59, Wellesley Coll., Mass., 1959-60; research asst. MIT, Cambridge, 1960-65; research assoc. Bonn U., Fed. Republic Germany, 1965-68, 75-77, Gesellschaft für Mathematik und Datenverarbeitung, St. Augustin, Fed. Republic Germany, 1968-74, 78—; vis. research prof. Rutgers U., New Brunswick, N.J., 1975; vis. researcher U. Edinburgh, Scotland, U. Waterloo, Ont., Can., U. Tex., RCA Sarnoff Lab., Princeton, N.J. Contbr. articles on computer sci. to profl. jours. Mem. Gesellschaft für Informatik. Club: Am. Embassy (Bonn). Home: Im Tannenbusch 3, D-5300 Bonn 1 Federal Republic of Germany Office: Gesellschaft für Mathematik und Datenverarbeitung mbH, Postfach 1240, D-5205 Saint Augustin 1 Federal Republic of Germany

DARMOJUWONO, JUSTIN CARDIN, retired archbishop; b. Godean, Yogyakarta, Indonesia, Nov. 2, 1914; s. Yoseph Surodikoro and Mary Ngatinah. Diploma, Tchr. Sch., Muntilan, Indonesia, 1935, Minor Sem., Yogyakarta, 1942, Major Sem., Yogyakarta, 1947, Gregorian U., Rome, 1955. Ordained Roman Cath. priest, 1947. Tchr. Minor Sem., 1947-48; priest local parish Yogyakarta, 1948-50, Klaten, Indonesia, 1950-54, Surakarta, Indonesia, 1956-62; priest, vicar gen. Semarang, Indonesia, 1962-63; archbishop Semarang, 1963-81; ret. 1981; bishop Indonesian Army, 1964-81; cardinal 1967—. Mem. S. Congregation Divine Cult. Home: Kamfer Raya 49, Semarang 50237, Indonesia

DARMSTANDLER, HARRY MAX, business executive, retired air force officer; b. Indpls., Aug. 9, 1922; s. Max M. and Nonna (Holden) D.; m. Donna L. Bender, Mar. 10, 1957; children: Paul William, Thomas Alan. B.S., U. Omaha, 1964; M.S., George Washington U., 1965; grad., Nat. War Coll., 1965. Commd. 2d lt. USAAF, 1943; advanced through grades to maj. gen. USAF, 1973; served with (15th Air Force), Europe, 1943, (5th Air Force), Korea, 1952; comdr.-in-chief Pacific 1960-63, served with joint chiefs of staff, 1965-68; supreme comdr. (Allied Powers Europe), 1969-71; comdr. 12th Air Div. SAC, 1972, dep. chief of staff for plans, 1973; spl. asst. to chief of staff USAF, 1974-75; chmn. bd. Rancho Bernardo Savs. Bank, San Diego; ptnr. Allied Assocs. and D&H Inc., Colorado Springs, Colo.; cons. Mid. East matters; trustee Palomar Pomerado Health Found, San Diego; bd. dirs. Clean Found, San Diego. Author numerous articles on nat. def. requirements. Decorated D.S.M. with oak leaf cluster, Legion of Merit with oak leaf cluster, D.F.C., Air medal with 3 oak leaf clusters; research fellow UCLA, 1969. Mem. AIAA, Order Daedalians, Eagle Scout Alumni Assn., Phi Tau Alpha. Club: Bernardo Heights Country (San Diego) (pres.). Home: 12284 Fairway Pointe Row San Diego CA 92128 Office: 16456 Bernardo Ctr Dr San Diego CA 92128

DARNALL, ROBERTA MORROW, university official; b. Kemmerer, Wyo., May 18, 1949; d. C. Dale and Eugenia Stayner (Christmas) Morrow; B.S., U. Wyo., Laramie, 1972; m. Leslie A. Darnall, Sept. 3, 1977; children: Kimberly Gene, Leslie Nicole. Tariff sec., ins. adminstr. Wyo. Trucking Assn., Casper, 1973-75; asst. clerical supr. Wyo. Legislature, Cheyenne, 1972-77; congl. campaign press aide, 1974; pub. relations dir. in Casper, Wyo. Republican Central Com., 1976-77; asst. dir. alumni relations U. Wyo., 1977-81, dir. of alumni, 1981—; exec. com. Higher Edn. Assn. Rockies. Mem. Council Advancement and Support Edn. (membership com.), Higher Edn. Assn. Rockies, Am. Soc. Assn. Execs., Laramie C. of C. (pizzazz and acad. instns. com.), PEO (courtesy com., officer), Sigma Delta Chi. Republican. Episcopalian. Lodge: Soroptimist (mem. pub. relations com.). Home: 1172 Frontera Dr Laramie WY 82070 Office: Box 3137 University Sta Laramie WY 82071

DAROFF, ROBERT BARRY, neurologist; b. N.Y.C., Aug. 3, 1936; s. Charles and May (Wolin) D.; m. Jane L. Abrahams, Dec. 4, 1959; children: Charles II, Robert Barry, Jr., William Clayton. B.A., U. Pa., 1957, M.D., 1961. Intern Phila. Gen. Hosp., 1961-62; resident in neurology Yale-New Haven Med. Center, 1962-65; fellow in neuro-ophthalmology U. Calif. Med. Center, San Francisco, 1967-68; prof. neurology, assoc. prof. ophthalmology U. Miami (Fla.) Med. Sch.; also dir. ocular motor neurophysiology lab. Miami VA Med. Center, 1968-80; Gilbert W. Humphrey prof., chmn. dept. neurology Case Western Res. U. Med. Sch.; also dir. dept. neurology Univ. Hosps., Cleve., 1980—; chief neurology clinic Cleve. VA Med. Ctr.; mem. med. adv. bd., chmn. sci. program com. Myasthenia Gravis Found.; mem. nat. adv. eye council sensory and motor disorders vision panel NIH., 1980-83; mem. steering com. neurological disorders in comml. dirvers U.S. Dept. Transportation, chmn. task force, 1987. Book rev. editor: Neuro-ophthalmology, 1981-86, mem. editorial bd., 1987—; assoc. editor: Jour. Biomed. Systems, 1970-72; mem. editorial bd. Annals of Neurology, 1977-86, Archives of Neurology, 1976, Neurology and Neurosurgery Update Series, 1978—, Headache, 1908-86; editor: Neurological Progress, Annals of Neurology, 1981-84; editor-in-chief Neurology, 1987—; contbr. numerous articles to profl. jours. Chmn. Young Tae Kwon Do Acad., N. Miami, 1977-80; bd. dirs. Benign Essential Blepharospasm Research Found., 1983—. Served as officer M.C. USAR, 1965-67. Mem. Am. Neurol. Assn. (program adv. com. 1977-78, chmn. 1978; membership adv. com. 1980-83, chmn. 1981-83; nominating com. 1984; chmn. Annals of Neurology oversight com. 1984-86; councillor, 1980-82; sec. 1985—), AMA, Am. Neurotology Soc., Am. Acad. Neurology (chmn. sci. program com. 1973-75, exec. bd. 1987—), Soc. Neurosci., Rocky Mountain Neuro-ophthalmology Soc. (bd. dirs. 1980-86), Assn. Research in Vision and Ophthalmology, N.Am. Neuro-ophthalmology Soc. (bd. dirs. 1986—), ACP (neurology subcom. med. knowledge self assessment program V 1977-80), Barany Soc., Am. Assn. Study Headache, Internat. Headache Soc., Internat. Soc. Neuro-ophthalmology, Clin. Eye Movement Soc., AAAS, Assn. Profs. Neurology, Am. Epilepsy Soc., World Fedn. Neurology (fin. com. 1985—, chmn. pubs. subcom. 1987—, exec. com. Research Group on Neuro-Opthalmology 1987—), Am. Soc. Clin. Pharmacology and Therapeutics, Council of Biology Educators, Neuro-Opthalmology Congress (orgn. com. 1983-88), Alpha Omega Alpha. Office: Dept Neurology Univ Hosps Cleveland OH 44106

DARROW, WILLIAM RICHARD, pharmaceutical company executive; b. Middletown, Ohio, Sept. 7, 1939; s. Richard William and Nelda Virginia (Darling) D.; B.A., Ohio Wesleyan U., 1960; M.D., Western Res. U., 1964; Ph.D., Case-Western Res. U., 1969; m. Janet Elizabeth Swan, June 20, 1964; children—James William, Susan Elizabeth, Margaret Ellen. Intern, Univ. Hosps., Cleve., 1964; sr. clin. research asso. CIBA Pharm. Co., 1969, asst. dir. clin. pharmacology, 1969-70; dir. clin. pharmacology CIBA-GEIGY Corp., 1970-75, exec. dir. clin. research, 1975-76; sr. v.p. research, med. dir. Wallace Labs. div. Carter Wallace, Inc., Cranbury, N.J., 1976-80; med. dir. Schering Labs. div. Schering-Plough Corp., Kenilworth, N.J., 1980, v.p. med. and regulatory affairs, 1981-82, sr. v.p. med. ops., 1982—. Chmn. research com. N.J. Health Scis. Group, 1973-76, mem. exec. com., 1973-74, 76-86, treas. 1977-80, v.p., 1980-86, Bernards Twp. Bd. Health; 1979—, v.p., 1980, pres., 1981-85, 86—. Roche award, 1962; USPHS postdoctoral fellow, 1965-69. Mem. AMA, Drug Info. Assn., N.J. Acad. Scis., Phi Gamma Delta, Phi Rho Sigma, Omicron Delta Kappa, Pi Delta Epsilon. Republican. Presbyterian. Home: 42 Palmerston Pl Basking Ridge NJ 07920 also: 521 E Lake Rd Penn Yan NY 14527 Office: Galloping Hill Rd Kenilworth NJ 07033

DARSONO, CHARLES LUKMAN, primate cons.; b. Belinyu, Bangka, Aug. 20, 1930; s. Tjin Lin and Moy Fa (Lo) D.; student public schs.; m. Shanti Setyo, Feb. 1, 1973; children—Anastasia, Richard. Sr. clk. producing dept. Standard Vacuum Petroleum, Sei-Gerong, Palembang, 1951-55; gen. contractor P.T. Stanvac, Indonesia, Sei-Gerong, 1955-57; civil engring. constrn. contractor West Irian Jaya, Sorong, 1968-70; mng. dir. C. V. Primex, Jakarta, 1971—. Mem. Indonesian Primatol. Soc., Primate Research Found., Indonesian Ornithol. Soc., Internat. Council Bird Preservation, Gt. Britain Primatol. Soc., Internat. Primatol. Soc., Internat. Primatol. Soc., Indonesian Zool. Parks Assn. Roman Catholic. Address: Cengkar Primelab, Jalan Jurumudi 51, Kebon Besar, Tangerang Indonesia Office: Globa Bldg, Lantai IV Blok D/5 JL, Hayam Wuruk, Jakarta Barat, Indonesia

DARTIGUENAVE, LAURENT, management consultant; b. Paris, June 17, 1952; s. Christian and Jacqueline (Dayras); m. Guyonne de Varax, Apr. 28, 1984; 1 child, Pauline. BBA, IAE, Paris, 1981; degree in engring., Ecole Centrale de Lyon, 1975. Project mgr. Renault, Paris, 1977-82; cons. Arthur Young, Paris, 1982-86, mgr., head of strategy, consultancy dept., 1987—. Home: 20 Rue Alphonse De Neuville, 75017 Paris France Office: Arthur Young Conseil, Tour Manhattan, 92095 Paris France

DARVIN, ROBERT W., furniture importing company executive; b. New Brunswick, N.J., Oct. 21, 1938; s. Julius and Goldie D.; m. Gretchen A. Gibbons, Oct. 28. Student, Rutgers U., 1956, 72, Columbia U., 1962-64. Midwest regional mgr. Walton Labs., Irvington, N.J., 1962-65; mgr. N.E. Fla. Jim Walter Corp., Tampa, 1963-66; founder, pres. Scandinavian Design Inc., Natick, Mass., 1965—; pres. Scandinavian Gallery Inc.; chmn. bd. Cambridge Dry Goods Co.; partner Am. Resource & Cons. Group; guest lectr. M.B.A. program Babson Coll. Editor, pub.: Darvin Theory econ. newsletter, 1977—. Mem. Mass. Fgn. Bus. Council. Served with USNAF, 1970-75. Recipient commendation Danish Minister Fgn. Affairs, 1978, Danish medal of honor and diploma Prince Henrik of Denmark; named One of Outstanding Retailers in Am. Home Furnishings Daily. Mem. Am. Mgmt. Assn., Nat. Home Furnishing Assn. (dir.), Furniture Assn. New Eng. (gov.), Young Presidents' Orgn., Am. Numismatic Assn., Nat. Speakers Assn. Office: 603 Worcester Rd Natick MA 01760

DARWICH, SAMIR A., management consultant; b. Damascus, Syria, Nov. 10, 1937; s. Amin and Samia D.; m. Ghada Liane, June 10, 1972; children: Nayla, Makram. Grad. in Law, Damascus U., 1960; student in polit. and econ. sci., U. St. Joseph, Beirut, 1962, student in bus. adminstrn., 1963-64. Columnist Al Ayam Daily, Damascus, 1955-56; asst. editor Bur. des Documentation Arabes, Damascus, 1957-62, dir., editor, 1962-64, pres., 1964—; pres., gen. mgr. OFA Holdings S.p.P., Damascus, 1975—; pres. OFA Bus. Cons. Ctr., Damascus, 1975—; dir. OFA Renseignements Commerciaux, 1964—; pres. OFA-Petroconsult, Ltd., Lebanon, 1988. Author surveys and essays on Middle Eastern politics and economy. Decorated Italian Medal of Merit. Mem. Anti-Cancer Soc., Syrian Equestrian Fedn. (pres.), Interarab Econ. Soc. Office: OFA-Holdings, SpP 67 Shahbandar Sq, Damascus Syria

DARWIN, FRED ARRANTS, business consultant; b. Chattanooga, May 28, 1913; s. Fred Perry and Alexandra Allen (Arrants) D.; m. Hope Genung Sparks, Sept. 30, 1939 (dec. 1987); children—Fred Arrants, Hope Darwin Beisinger. Student, U. Chattanooga, 1929-31; BS U.S. Naval Acad., 1935; MS, Harvard U., 1936. Registered profl. engr. Sr. supr. traffic dept. Western Union Telegraph Corp., Chgo., 1936-41; asst. dir. engring. Hazeltine Electronics Corp., N.Y.C., 1946-49; exec. dir. com. guided missiles research and devel. bd. Dept. Def., Washington, 1949-54; mgr. guided missiles Crosley div. Avco Mfg. Corp., Cin., 1954-56; mgr. missile electronics McDonnell Aircraft Corp., St. Louis, 1956-61, gen. mgr. electronic equipment div., 1961-63; asst. to pres. Librascope group Gen. Precision, Inc., 1963-65; bus. counselor, owner Gen. Bus. Services, Dallas, 1966—; mem. spl. com. radio tech. commn. for aeros. Dept. State, Dept. Navy, 1946; cons. del. UN Provisional Internat. Civil Aviation Orgn., 1946; mem. Stewart spl. com. Nat. Guided Missiles Program, 1950, Gardner spl. com., 1953. Contbr. articles to profl. jours.; originator word transponder; inventor multiple-coincidence mixer used in pulse-train coding. Served to comdr. USNR, 1941-46. Recipient citations Sec. Navy, USAAF. Mem. IEEE, Aero. Weights Engrs., Harvard Grad. Soc., E. Dallas C. of C., Naval Acad. Alumni Assn., Alpha Lambda Tau. Democrat. Presbyterian. Club: Harvard. Home: 11805 Neering Dr Dallas TX 75218

DAS, DILIP KUMAR, cytopathologist; b. Balia, Cuttack, India, May 14, 1951; s. Narasinha Charan and Snehalata (Dei) D.; m. Rashmibala Pattanayak, June 25, 1988. MBBS, MKCG Med. Coll., Berhampur, Orissa, 1973; MD in Pathology, PGIMER, Chandigarh, 1978, PhD in Cytology, 1984. Jr. resident pathology Postgrad. Inst. Med. Edn. and Research, Chandigarh, 1976-77; asst. dir. Cytology Research Ctr., New Delhi, India, 1982-86, dep. dir., 1986—; W.H.O. fellow Karolinska Hosp., Stockholm, 1985-86. Recipient Cert. of Merit, PGIMER, 1978; tutor cum research scholar, 1978-82. Mem. Indian Assn. Pathologists and Microbiologists (life), Indian Acad. Cytologists (exec. council 1985-87), Indian Soc. Oncology. Home: Vill, Rameswar, Puri Orissa, India Office: Maulana Azad Med Coll, Cytology Research Ctr ICMR, New Delhi India

DAS, SAJAL, polymer chemist, material scientist; b. Ranchi, India, Jan. 2, 1951; came to U.S., 1980, naturalized, 1983; s. Dhirendra Nath and Surama Das. B.S. with honors, Ranchi U., India, 1972, M.S., 1975; Ph.D., Indian Inst. Tech., Kharagpur, 1980. Vis. asst. prof. N.C. State U., Raleigh, 1980-82; research assoc. Wright State U., Dayton, 1982-83, U. Akron, Ohio, 1984; project mgr. Allied Signal Inc., Morristown, N.J., 1984—. Contbr. articles to profl. jours. and chpts. to books. Patentee in field. Fellow Allied Resins and Chemical Ltd., Calcutta, India, 1977. Mem. Am. Chem. Soc. (polymer chemistry and polymeric material divs.). Home: 3683-A Hill Rd Parsippany NJ 07054

DAS, SAMIR KUMAR, corporate personnel executive; b. Calcutta, Bengal, India, Jan. 20, 1939; s. Susil Chitta and Sarasi Bala (Mohapatra) D.; m. Zeenat Neemuchwala, Mar. 8, 1972 (div. 1986); children: Swagata, Saurav. BA with hons., U. Calcutta, 1959, DSW, 1962; MBA, U. Hawaii, 1968. Personnel officer Handustan Steel, Ltd., Durgapur, India, 1960-69, Air-India, Bombay, India, 1969-72; personnel mgr. The Metal Box Co. of India, Calcutta, 1972-74; gen. mgr. personnel and corp. planning Voltas, Ltd., Bombay, 1974-84; group v.p. personnel United Breweries Group, Bombay, 1984—; vis. prof. Jamnalal Bajaj Inst. Mgmt. Studies, Bombay, 1976—; cons. in field. Author: (presidential address) Personnel Profession in India, 1985. Fellow British Inst. Mgmt.; mem. Nat. Inst. Personnel Mgmt. (Profl. Excellence award 1986), Indian Soc. Tng. and Devel., Am. Soc. Tng. and Devel., Inst. Personnel Mgmt., Am. Alumni Assn. (pres. 1980). Baptist. Clubs: Bombay Gymkhana, Royal Presidency Golf. Home: Acropolis Near Colaba PO, 400005 Bombay India Office: United Breweries Group, 1 Grant Rd, 560001 Bangalore India

DASCALESCU, CONSTANTIN, prime minister of Romania; b. Breaza, Romania, 1923; ed. Bucharest Acad. Econ. Studies. Joined Romanian Communist Party, 1945; active in oilworkers trade union, 1947-49; held various offices in adminstrn. Central Com. of Romanian Communist Party before 1965; dep. to Grand Nat. Assembly, 1965—, mem. state council, 1973—; mem. central com. Romanian Communist Party, 1965—, sec., 1976-82; prime minister Govt. of Romania, 1982—. Decorated Hero of Socialist Labour; other nat. orders and medals. Office: care Cen Com, Romanian Communist Party, Bucharest Romania *

DASCHLE, THOMAS ANDREW, senator; b. Aberdeen, S.D., Dec. 9, 1947; m. Linda Hall Daschle; children: Kelley, Nathan, Lindsay. B.A., S.D. State U., 1969. Fin. investment rep.; chief legis. aide, field coordinator Sen. James Abourzek, 1973-77; mem. 96th-97th Congresses from 1st S.D. Dist., 98th-99th Congresses at large, 1983-87; U.S. senator from S.D. 1987—. Served to 1st lt. USAF, 1969-72. Democrat. Office: US Senate 317 Hart Senate Bldg Washington DC 20510-4103

DASH, JEAN MICHAEL, French educator; b. Port of Spain, Trinidad, July 20, 1948; s. Wallace and Elsie (Jarrette) d.; m. cheryl Marlene Brown, July 19, 1972; 1 child, Lauren Jeanine Claire. BA with spl. honors, U. W.I., 1969, PhD, 1973. Lectr. French U. W.I., Cave Hill, Barbados, 1972-74, U. Ahmadu Bello, Kano, Nigeria, 1974-76; sr. lectr., chmn. dept. French U. W.I., Mona, Jamaica, 1976—; cons. editor U. Va. Press, 1986—. Author: Literature and Ideology in Haiti, 1981, Haiti and the United States, 1988; translator: The Ripening, 1985. Decorated Chevalier des Palmes Academiques, Govt. of France, 1988; Sr. Fulbright fellow, Washington, 1983. Mem. Jamaica Assn. French Tchrs., Alliance Francaise (mem. exec. com. 1983-87). Office: U W I Dept French, Mona, Kingston 7, Jamaica

DASH, SITA KANTHA, nutritionist; b. Tunpur, Orissa, India, Nov. 15, 1942; came to U.S., 1969, naturalized, 1977; s. Nila K. and Duti (Sarangi) D.; m. Kalpana M. Mohapatra, June 18, 1967; children—Rajesh, Dave S. D.V.M., Orissa Vet. Coll., Bhubaneswar, India, 1964; M.S., S.D. State U., 1970, Ph.D., 1973. Cert. animal scientist. Vet. surgeon Kakatpur Vet. Clinic, India, 1964-68; asst. project officer Orissa Vet. Service, Bhubaneswar, India, 1968-69; research asst. S.D. State U., Brookings, 1969-73; dir. regulatory services S.D. Dept. Agr., Pierre, 1973-81; pres. UAS Labs. and United Agri-Services, Inc., Mpls., 1981—. Mem. AVMA, Am. Dairy Sci. Assn., Am. Soc. Animal Sci., Assn. Am. Feed Control Ofcls., S.D. Acad. Sci., Minn. Veterinary Med. Assn., S.D. Veterinary Med. Assn., Council Agrl. Sci. and Tech., North Central Assn. Dairy, Food, Feed and Drug Control Ofcls., Am. Feed Mfrs. Assn., Nat. Feed Ingredient Assn., N. Cen. Food Mfrs. Assn., Sigma Xi. Democrat. Hindu. Club: Lions. Contbr. articles to profl. jours. Developed DDS-acidophilus tablets and capsules for human use: Keto-Nutri-Aid, Calf Lacto Bolus, others. Home: 210 E 107th St Circle Bloomington MN 55420 Office: UAS Labs 9201 Penn Ave S Suite 10 Bloomington MN 55431

DASSIOS, GEORGE, mathematics educator; b. Patras, Greece, Jan. 22, 1946; s. Theodore and Helen (Kalliafas) D.; m. Helen Apostolatos, Sept. 6, 1970; children—Constantine, Theodore. Univ. diploma, U. Athens, 1970; M.S., U. Ill., 1972, Ph.D., 1975; Dozent, Nat. Tech. U. Athens, 1980. Lectr. U. Patras, Greece, 1975-77, prof. math., 1981—; lectr. Nat. Tech. U. Athens, 1977-80, asst. prof. math., 1980-81. Contbr. articles to profl. jours.; author textbooks. Regional pres. Greek Math. Soc., Patras, 1983; exec. mem. Balkan Union Mathematicians, 1983. Greek Ministry of Sci. Research and Tech. grantee, 1984; European Common Market grantee, 1985. Mem. Am. Math. Soc., Math. Assn. Am., Acoustical Soc. Am., Internat. Assn. Math. Physics, Greek Math. Soc., Greek Assn. Theoretical and Applied Mechanics. Club:

Movie. Avocations: open field sports; stamp collecting; photography. Home: 186 Korinthou St, 26221 Patras Greece Office: U Patras, Dept Math, 26110 Patras Greece

DASTON, LORRAINE JENIFER, historian, educator; b. East Lansing, Mich., June 9, 1951; d. Paul George and Marie Panoria (Arhondy) D.; m. Gerd Johann Gigerenzer, Oct. 25, 1985; 1 child, Thalia. AB, Harvard U., 1973, PhD, 1979; diploma, U. Cambridge, Eng., 1974. Asst. prof. Harvard U., Cambridge, Mass., 1980-83, Princeton (N.J.) U., 1983-86; assoc. prof. Brandeis U., Waltham, Mass., 1986—. Author: Classical Probability in the Enlightenment, 1988; co-editor: The Probabilistic Revolution, 1987; adv. editor ISIS, 1985—. Jr. fellow Columbia U., 1979; fellow Zentrum für interdisziplinäre Forschung, Bielefeld, Fed. Republic Germany, 1982-83, Wissenschaftskolleg, Berlin, 1987-88. Mem. Am. Hist. Assn., History Sci. Soc. (council 1986—), Phi Beta Kappa, Sigma Xi. Office: Brandeis U Dept History Waltham MA 02254

DASTON, MELISSA GAIL, educational consultant; b. Brockton, Mass., Sept. 8, 1954; d. Paul George and Marie Panoria (Arhondy) D.; BA, Duke U., 1976; MA, U. Md., 1978, MBA, 1980, MS., 1987. Dir. guidance Queen Anne Sch., Upper Marlboro, Md., 1977-79; instr. Coll. Bus. and Mgmt., U. Md., College Park, 1979-80; chmn. div. bus. Miss. Indsl. Coll., Holly Springs, 1980-81; research assoc. U. Md. Univ. Coll., 1981; ednl. specialist Dept. Def., Washington, 1982—; instr. U. Md., 1981—; chmn. bd. Birch Run HOA, Inc., 1983-86; bus. cons.; vis. fellow Howard U., 1981. Author: How to Run a Microteaching Workshop, 1979; How to Organize and Lead a Faculty Development Workshop or Seminar, 1981; How to Begin a Faculty Development Program, 1982. Woodrow Wilson fellow adminstrv. intern, 1980-81. Mem. Am. Mktg. Assn. Home: 15745 Haynes Rd Laurel MD 20707 Office: Def Intelligence Coll Washington DC 20340-5485

DATHE, JOHANNES MARTIN, manufacturing company executive; b. Habelschwerdt, Silesia, Germany, Aug. 10, 1930; s. Max Arno and Marie Helene (Lemmert) D.; m. Renate Viecenz. Degree, Tech. Sch., Stuttgart, Fed. Republic Germany, 1955, Tech. Sch., Karlsruhe, Fed. Republic Germany, 1962. Cert. engr. Scientist Dornier GmbH, Friedrichshafen, Fed. Republic Germany, 1958-65, Industrieanlagen Betriebs GmbH, Ottobrunn, Fed. Republic Germany, 1965—; group leader Betriebs Mfg., Ottobrunn, Fed. Republic Germany, 1968-70, dir., 1970-77, mging. dir., 1978—; lectr. Tech. U., Munich, 1969-85, prof., 1985—. Author: Modern Project Planning, 1971; contbr. numerous articles to profl. jours. Mem. German Soc. for Ops. Research. Office: Industrieanlagen Betriebs GmbH, Postfach, D 8012 Ottobrunn Bavaria, Federal Republic of Germany

DATTA, BISWA NATH, mathematics educator, computer scientist; b. Bighira, India, July 1, 1941; came to U.S., 1980; s. Nirmal Kumar and Sudha (Rani) D.; m. Karabi Sarkar, June 16, 1972; children—Rajarshi, Rakhi. B.Sc., U. Calcutta, 1960, M.Sc., 1962; M.Sc., McMaster U., Can., 1970; Ph.D., U. Ottawa, Can., 1972. Lectr. math. U. Ottawa, 1972-73, Ahmadu Bello U., Zaria, Nigeria, 1973-75; assoc. prof. U. Estadual De Campinas, Brazil, 1975-80; vis. assoc. prof. Pa. State U., University Park, 1980-81; prof. No. Ill. U., DeKalb, 1981—; vis. scientist Gas Turbine Research Establishment, Bangalore, India, 1973-74; vis. prof. U. Ill., Urbana, 1985, Israel Inst. Technology, Haifa, Israel, Indian Inst. Sci., Bangalore, India, U. Bielefeld, Fed. Republic Germany, U. Calif., San Diego, 1987-88; leader del., liaison from U.S. to Internat. Conf. on Math. Theory of Networks and Systems, Stockholm, 1985; organizer, chmn. sessions on interaction between linear algebra, numerical linear algebra and systems theory, U.S. coordinator internat. conf., Valencia, Spain, 1987—. Author: Advanced Numerical Linearal Algebra (in Portuguese), 1984. Editor: Contemporary Mathematics, 1985; mng. editor Linear Algebra in Signal Systems and Control, 1987; founding editor Siam Jour. on Matrix Analysis and Applications; contbr. articles, revs. to profl. jours. Rep.-at large Internat. Bd. Internat. Matrix Group lin. Algebra Community. Grantee, Air Force, 1983—, NSF, No. Ill. U., 1981. Mem. Am. Math. Soc. (chmn. summer research conf. 1984), Soc. Indsl. Applied Math. (chmn. linear algebra in signals, systems and control 1986), Calcutta Math. Soc. Hindu. Current work: Solving mathematical problems arising in electrical engineering (control and systems theory) using computers, developing algorithms for super computers. Subspecialties: Algorithms; Numerical analysis (mathematics). Home: 7 Cari Ct DeKalb IL 60115

DAUB, MERVYN AUSTIN, economics educator; b. Kitchener, Ont., Can., Sept. 11, 1943; s. Alvin H. and Lulu N. (Roeder) D.; m. Agnes S. Lefas, Oct. 28, 1972. B.Com., Queen's U., 1966; M.B.A., U. Chgo., 1968, Ph.D., 1971. Prof. econs. Queen's U. Kingston, Ont., 1971—; vis. scholar Cambridge U., Eng., 1973, Monash U., Australia, 1979; vis. prof. U. Paris-12, 1980, 81, U. Rennes, France, 1982. Author: Canadian Economic Forecasting, 1987; contbr. articles to profl. jours. Policy advisor Liberal Party Can., 1980—; commr. Ontario Energy Bd., 1986-88. Internat. Optimists scholar, 1962-66; U. Chgo. fellow, 1966-71; Foote, Cone, Belding scholar, 1967; Sears Roebuck Found. fellow, 1968; Am. Mktg. Assn. Consortium fellow, 1967; Nat. Bur. Econ. research grantee, 1967; Can. Council fellow, 1973-74, 79-80; SSHRC travel award, 1981-82; SSHRC grantee, 1982-84. Mem. Can. Econs. Assn., Am. Econs. Assn., Royal Econ. Soc., Econometric Soc., Can. Assn. Adminstrv. Scis. Avocations: skiing; photography; travel. Home: Rte 1, Upper Brewers, Seeleys Bay, ON Canada Office: Queens U, Sch Business, Kingston, ON Canada K7L 3N6

DAUGHTON, DONALD, lawyer; b. Grand River, Iowa, Mar. 11, 1932; s. F.J. and Ethel (Edwards) D.; children by previous marriage: Erin, Thomas, Andrew, J.P. B.S.C., U. Iowa, 1953, J.D., 1956. Bar: Iowa, 1956, Ariz., 1958. Assoc., Snell & Wilmer, Phoenix, 1959-64, Browder & Daughton, Phoenix, 1964-65, Browder, Gillenwater & Daughton, 1967-72; ptnr. Daughton Feinstein & Wilson, Phoenix, 1972-86, Daughton, Hawkins & Bacon P.C., 1986-87, Bryan, Cade, McPheeters and McRoberts, 1988—; judge Superior Ct. Ariz., 1956-67; asst. county atty. Polk County, 1958-59; chmn. Phoenix Employees Relations Bd., 1976; pres. Maricopa County Legal Aid Soc., 1971-73. Served to 1st lt. JAG, USAF, 1956-58. Fellow Am. Bar Found. (founder); mem. ABA (state bar del. ho. of dels., 1984-87, state del. 1987—), State Bar Ariz. (chmn. pub. relations com. 1980-84, chmn. jud. evaluation poll com. 1984—), Iowa State Bar, Maricopa County Bar Assn. (dir. 1962-64), 9th Cir. Jud. Conf. (lawyer rep. 1981-84), Ariz. Acad., Nat. Acad. Arbitrators. Club: Univs. Phoenix, Paradise Valley Country. Home: 7214 N 6th Way Phoenix AZ 85020 Office: Bryan Cave McPheeters & McRoberts 2800 Central Ave 21st Floor Phoenix AZ 85012

DAULT, RAYMOND ARTHUR, educator; b. Muskegon, Mich., June 30, 1923; s. Joseph F. and Eloise M. (Grosselin) D.; A.B., Mich. State U., 1950; M.B.A., Ind. U., 1969; m. Joyce J. Martin, Oct. 19, 1946; 1 dau., Suzanne Raye. Asst. reservation mgr. Bismarck Hotel, Chgo., 1950; asst. mgr. Ind. Meml. Union, Ind. U., Bloomington, 1950-53, mgr. Union Bldg. Med. Center, Indpls., 1953-70; assoc. prof. restaurant, hotel and instnl. mgmt. Ind.-Purdue U., Indpls., 1970-74, prof., 1974—, Frank E. Burley disting. prof. Sch. Engring. and Tech., 1986—; cons. Nat. Sanitation Found., Ann Arbor, Mich., 1970-72, Com. for a Quality Environ., 1970-73, Am. Hotel and Motel Assn., 1968—. Pres. Speedway (Ind.) Bd. Zoning Appeals, 1959-63. Served with AUS, 1943-46. Recipient Keys to N.Y.C., 1968, New Orleans, 1968, Elizabethtown, Ky., 1968, Oklahoma City, 1974, Indpls., 1974, Cleve., 1975, Cin., 1975, Louisville, 1975, South Bend, 1978; named Coll. and Univ. Food Operator of Yr., Internat. Foodservice Mfrs. Assn., 1970, Alumnus of Yr., Mich. State U. Sch. Hotel, Restaurant and Instnl. Mgmt., 1972; Hall of Fame civic category Civil Town of Speedway, 1978; recipient Outstanding Faculty Mem. award Purdue U. Sch. Engring. and Tech., Indpls., 1976, 81; Key to City of Indpls., 1984; cert. food exec. Mem. Nat. Restaurant Assn., Ind. Hotel and Motel Assn. (exec. v.p.), Indpls. Hotel and Motel Assn. (exec. v.p.), Assn. Coll. Unions Internat., Mich. State U. Motel and Restaurant Alumni Assn. (pres. 1970-73), Am. Legion, Hon. Order of Ky. Cols. Clubs: K.C., Lions. Contbr. over 460 articles on food service and lodging to profl. publs. in U.S., Can. and Australia. Home: 2312 N Fisher St Speedway IN 46224 Office: 799 Michigan St Indianapolis IN 46202

D'AURIA, MICHAEL MARTIN, college official; b. N.Y.C., Dec. 1, 1927; s. Al Joseph and Mary Ann (Lynch) D'A.; m. Joan Ann Lebkuecher, Oct. 1, 1955; 1 child, Denise Marie. B.A., Hillyer Coll., 1948; LL.B., J.D., St. John's U., 1951; LL.M., NYU, 1955. L.H.D. (hon.), Shaw U., 1979. County judge Nassau County, Mineola, N.Y., 1964-65; pvt. practice law, D'Auria, Bond, Corin and DeVito, Jericho, N.Y., 1966-68, 71-74; justice Supreme Ct. State of N.Y., Mineola, 1969-71; spl. asst. provost N.Y. Inst. Tech., Old Westbury, 1976-82, sr. v.p., 1983—, dir. Ctr. Labor and Indsl. Relations, 1977-83; dir. West Indian Holding Corp. Author: Legal Terms and Concepts in Criminal Justice, 1979; author plays: Youth and the Law, 1965; Narcotics and Youth, 1969. Served as col. U.S. Army, 1945-47, PTO. Mem. Criminal Justice Educators of N.Y. (chmn. 1978-82) (spl. award, 1980), Northeastern Assn. Criminal Justice Educators (pres. 1980-81) (spl. awards 1979-86). Republican. Roman Catholic. Clubs: Kiwanis Internat. (internat youth coordinator 1968-70) Brookville Taxpayers Assn. (v.p./sec. 1976-80). Lodges: Knights Columbus (chmn. 1968-70), Sons of Italy (exec. com. 1965-67). Home: 30 Rolling Dr Brookville NY 11545 Office: NY Inst Tech Old Westbury NY 11568

DAUS, DONALD GEORGE, lawyer, federal government official; b. Melrose Park, Ill., Nov. 17, 1931; s. George A. and Lillian M. (Culham) D.; m. Martha Joanne, Sept. 1, 1957; children—Robert Donald, Frederic George. B.S. in Chem. Engring. with honors, U. Ill., 1953; M.S., Mich. State U., 1954; J.D. with honors, George Washington U., 1966, LL.M. with highest honors, 1973. Bar: D.C. 1967, Va. 1969. Chem. engr. with industry, 1954-64; patent examiner U.S. Patent Office, Washington, 1964-73, supervisory patent examiner, 1973—. Served to capt. JAG Corps, USNR, 1970—. NIH fellow, 1953. Mem. ABA, Am. Intellectual Property Law Assn., Am. Chem. Soc., Judge Advs. Assn., Patent Office Soc. (chmn. 1981, bd. govs. Jour. 1977-80), Nat. Assn. of Securities Dealers (securities arbitrator), Am. Arbitrator Assn., Order of Coif, Phi Alpha Delta, Alpha Chi Sigma. Contbr. articles to profl. jours. Home: 2230 Primrose Dr Falls Church VA 22046 Office: US Patent and Trademark Office Washington DC 20231

DAUSSET, JEAN, immunologist; b. Toulouse, France, Oct. 19, 1916; s. Henri and Elizabeth D.; AB, Lycee Michelet, 1939; MD, U. Paris, 1945; m. Rose Mayoral, Mar. 17, 1962. Dir. lab. Nat. Transfusion Ctr., 1950-63; prof. immunohematology U. Paris VII, 1963-77; prof. exptl. medicine College de France, Paris, 1977-87; dir. research unit on immunogenetics Hopital Saint-Louis, Paris, 1969-84; dir. Human Polymorphism Study Ctr., Paris, 1986—. Served to capt., World War II. Recipient Nobel prize in physiology and medicine, 1980, Honda prize Honda Found. Japan, 1987. Mem. Academie des Sciences de l'Institut de France, Am. Acad. Arts and Sci., Nat. Acad. Scis. (Washington). Research in field of man's histocompatibility system, 1952—. Office: Hosp Saint-Louis, Place du Docteur Fournier, 75010 Paris France

DAUSSMAN, GROVER FREDERICK, consulting engineer; b. Newburgh, Ind., May 6, 1919; s. Grover Cleveland and Madeline (Springer) D.; student U. Cin., 1936-38, Carnegie Inst. Tech., 1944-45, George Washington U., 1948-56; B.S. in Elec. Engring., U. Ala., 1963, postgrad., 1963-64, 77; postgrad. Indsl. Coll. Armed Forces, 1955, 63; Ph.D. (hon.), Hamilton State U., 1973; m. Elli Margrite Kilian, Dec. 27, 1941; children—Cynthia Louise Daussman Quinn, Judith Ann, Margaret Elizabeth Daussman Davidson Cooper. Coop. engr. Sunbeam Elec. Mfg. Co., Evansville, Ind., 1936-38; engr., draftsman Phila. Navy Yard, 1941-42; resident engr., supr. shipbldg. USN, Neville Island, Pa., 1942-45; engr. Pearl Harbor Navy Yard, 1945-48; sect. head Bur. Ships, USN, Washington, 1948-56; head guidance and control tech. liaison Army Ballistic Missile Agy., Huntsville, Ala., 1956-58, chief program coordination Guidance and Control Lab., 1958-60; chief program coordination Astrionics Lab., Marshall Space Flight Center (Ala.), 1960-63, dir's staff asst. for advanced research and tech., 1963-70; engring. cons., 1970—; project dir. fallout shelter surveys Mil Dept. Tenn., 1971-73; head drafting dept. Alverson-Draughon Coll., Huntsville, 1974-77; instr. Ala. Christian Coll., 1977-79; engring. draftsman Reisz Engring., 1979; chief engr. Sheraton Motor Inn, 1979; sr. engr. Sperry Support Services, 1980; asso. Techni-Core Profls., Huntsville, 1980-81; elec. engr. Reisz Engring., Huntsville, 1981-86; tutor in mathematics, scis. and engring. Ednl. Opportunity Ctr., Huntsville, 1986. Chmn. community spl. gifts com. Madison County Heart Assn., 1965; mem. Population Action Council. Recipient cert. of recognition, 1945, cert. of service USN, 1946; performance award cert. U.S. Army, 1960; certs. of appreciation AIEE, 1960, 61, 62, Ala. Soc. Profl. Engrs., 1982; IEEE Centennial Medal, 1984, IEEE Honor Role of Outstanding Vols., 1986, IEEE Ednl. Activities Award, 1987, award for disting. services Huntsville sect. IEEE, 1964; award for contbn. to successful launch of 1st Saturn V, George C. Marshall Space Flight Center, 1967, also award of achievement for contbn. to 1st manned lunar landing, 1969; Apollo achievement award NASA, 1969; named Engr. of Yr., 1968, 69, 82. Registered profl. engr., Ala., Va., D.C.; cert. fallout shelter analyst, Dept. Def. Fellow Explorers Club, Redstone Arsenal Officers Club; mem. Planetary Soc. (charter), Hellenic Profl. Assn. Am. (hon.), U. Ala. Alumni Assn., Ala. (state dir. 1962-65, 68-71, 85—, chpt. pres. 1966-67), Nat. socs. profl. engrs., AARP, Am. Inst. Urban and Regional Affairs, The Cousteau Soc., IEEE (life mem., sect. chmn. N. Ala. sect. 1961-62; founder and chmn. engring. mgmt. chpt. 1964-65, mem. Region 3 exec. com. 1969-79, mem. inst. research com. 1965-67, mem. adminstv. com. of engring. mgmt. soc. 1966-86, sec. soc. 1968-85, regional del.-dir. S.E. region, mem. inst. bd. dirs. 1972-73), Am. Def. Preparedness Assn. (post dir. Tenn. Valley 1963-66), AAAS, Internat. Platform Assn., AIAA, Nat. Assn. Retarded Children, Huntsville Assn. Tech. Socs. (founder; sec. 1969-70; v.p. 1970-71), Am. Soc. Naval Engrs., U.S. Naval Inst., Assn. U.S. Army, Missile, Space and Range Pioneers (life), Nat. Assn. of Retired Fed. Employees, NASA Retirees Assn. (v.p. 1973-74, pres. 1974—). Democrat. Mem. United Ch. of Christ (treas. 1959-61, ch. council 1964-66; sec. ch. council, program com. chmn. ch. council 1965-66; vice moderator Ala.-Tenn. assn. 1965-68; bd. dirs. Southeast conf. 1965-66, mem. budget and finance com. 1965-66). Hon. mem. editorial adv. bd. Am. Biog. Inst., 1975-87. Home: 1910 Colice Rd SE Huntsville AL 35801 Office: 2205 University Dr Suite G Huntsville AL 35805

DAUTZENBERG, HERBERT CHRISTOPH, infosystems specialist; b. Aachen, Fed. Republic Germany, June 27, 1941; s. Paul Ferdinand and Antonia Maria (Gilles) D.; m. Ursula Jaeger, Nov. 21, 1969; children: Paul Benedikt, Johannes Gregor, Thomas Herbert. Diploma in engring., Tech. U. Aachen, 1967, PhD in Engring., 1976. Asst. programmer Computer Ctr., Tech. U. Aachen, 1967-70, dep. mgr. research Computer Sci. Dept., 1973-76, mgr. software engring. Computer Ctr.,, 1977-79, mgr. adminstr., 1980-86, mgr. Cen. Dept. Info. and Mgmt.,, 1984-86; mgr. info. systems Stawag, Aachen, 1986—; cons. Bergbaufor-schung, Essen, Fed. Republic Germany, 1969-80. Author: Fortran IV, 1980; co-author: Computer Science, 1977. Chmn. bd. parents Inda Gymnasium, Aachen, 1986-87. Mem. Cologne C. of C. (cons. 1966—). Home: Meischenfeld 60, D-5100 Federal Republic of Germany Office: Stawag, Lombardenstr 12-22, D-5100 Aachen Federal Republic of Germany

DAVACHI, FARZIN, pediatric cardiologist; b. Tehran, Iran, June 25, 1935; came to U.S., 1963, naturalized, 1972; s. Gholam Hussayn and Nosrat (Mohajer) D.; M.D., Mashad U., 1961; m. Nancy Ozias, May 27, 1969; children—Alexander, Todd, Christine. Intern, Ottawa Civic Hosp., 1962, resident, 1963; resident Duval Med. Center, 1964; fellow U. Miami, 1964, Ohio State U., 1965, U. Minn., 1966-68; asst. prof. pediatrics Meharry Med. Coll., 1968-70; dir. pediatrics, chief staff Port Harcourt (Nigeria) Gen. Hosp., 1970-72; asst. dir. dept. pediatrics St. Barnabas Med. Center, Livingston, N.J., 1972-75; lectr. N.J. Coll. Medicine, Rutgers Med. Sch., 1972-75; clin. prof. Meharry Med. Coll., 1975—, also dir. dept. med. edn.; chief of staff, dir. pediatrics, prof., chmn. dept. pediatrics Mama Yemo Hosp., Kinshasha, Zaire, 1975—. Pres. bd. dirs. Am. Sch. Kinshasa, 1984-86; cons. WHO, 1987—. Recipient Gold award Am. Acad. Pediatrics, 1973. Fellow Am. Acad. Pediatrics, Am. Coll. Cardiology, Am. Coll. Angiology; mem. Zairian Soc. Cardiology (co-founder), Zairian Soc. Pediatrics (founder, pres.), Essex County, N.J. med. socs., AMA. Editor-in-chief Jour. Medico Chirurgical, Kinshasa, 1976. Contbr. articles to profl. jours. Address: B P 4697, Kinshasa 2 Zaire

DAVANT, JAMES WARING, investment banker; b. McComb, Miss., Dec. 1, 1917; s. Guy Hamilton and Em Reid (Waring) D.; m. Mary Ellis Westlake, Apr. 4, 1942; children—Mary Diane, John Hamilton, Patricia Jean (Mrs. Coleman Dupont Donaldson). Student, U. Va., 1939. With Paine, Webber, Jackson & Curtis, 1945—, gen. partner, 1956—, mem. policy com., 1963—, mng. partner, 1964—, pres., chief exec. officer, 1970-71, chmn. bd., chief exec. officer, 1971-80; chmn. Paine Webber Inc., 1974-81, now dir., ret., 1981; chmn. Assn. Stock Exchange Firms, 1966-68; bd. dirs. N.Y. Stock Exchange, 1972-77, past chmn. cen. market com.; bd. dirs. Lanxide Corp., A.G.F. Reins. Chmn. nat. adv. council Nat. Cystic Fibrosis Research Found.; bd. dirs. Securities Industry Assn., 1973-78, Manhattan Eye, Ear and Throat Hosp.; chmn. central market com. Stock Exchange. Served to lt. comdr. USNR, 1940-45. Mem. Council Fgn. Relations. Episcopalian. Clubs: Links, River, Brook, Economic (chmn. 1976-77, trustee), Pilgrims of U.S., Bond (gov. 1965—, pres. 1972—) (N.Y.C.). also: 200 E 66th St New York NY 10021 also: Cherrywood Locust Valley NY 11560 also: 4600 Ocean Blvd Delray Beach FL 33435 Office: 1221 Ave of Americas 45th Floor New York NY 10020

DAVENPORT, DONALD AMES, electrical engineer; b. Boston, June 11, 1916; s. Frank Ames and Doris (McKechnie) D.; student Lowell Inst. of M.I.T., 1935-40; m. Alma Wilton, Feb. 21, 1941; children—Donna, Alma. Resident engr. Stone & Webster Engring. Corp., 1936-49; chief engr. Herlihy Midcontinent Co., 1949-53; chief engr. Asso. Research, Inc., 1953-55; pres., chief engr. Davenport Mfg. Co., Chgo., 1955-60, gen. mgr. Davenport Mfg. div. Duncan Electric Co., Inc., 1960-62; dir. research Sola Basic Research div. Basic Products Corp., 1962-66; pres., chmn. bd. Constant Voltage Co., Chgo., 1966-68, 70-73, Electron Mfg. Co., Chgo., 1968-69, Electro-Magnetic Corp., Chgo., 1969-70; pres., dir. Micron Industries Corp., Stone Park, Ill., 1973-83; cons. mgr. TFC Assocs., Inc., Augusta, Ga. 1983—. Profl. elec. engr., Ill. Mem. IEEE. Home: 607 Wellesley Dr Augusta GA 30909

DAVENPORT, FOUNTAIN ST. CLAIR, electronic engineer; b. Harmony, N.C., Jan. 16, 1914; s. Dennis F. and Margaret E. (Winfield) D.; BS, U. Miami, 1950; postgrad. U. Miami, U. Balt., Johns Hopkins, U. Fla., Rollins Coll., Brevard Engring. Coll., 1952-64; MS, Fla. Inst. Tech., 1970; m. Jane Helena Hermann, June 11, 1948 (dec. Sept. 1973); 1 dau., Sylvia Jane; m. Joyce Allen Huff, Mar. 16, 1974 (dec. 1983); m. Florence Cereceda Ryan, May 19, 1985. Engr., Bendix Aviation Corp., Towson, Md., 1951-53; project engr. Vitro Labs., Eglin AFB, Fla., 1953-55; engr. A, RCA Missile Test Project, Patrick AFB, Fla., 1955-60; supr. radar engring., guided missiles range div. Pan Am. World Airways, Inc., Patrick AFB, Fla., 1960-65, sr. systems engr. Aerospace Services Div., 1965-77; pvt. practice cons. engring., 1977-82; pres. Davenport Enterprises, Inc., 1982—. Cons. N.R.C., Churchill Research Range, Man., Can., 1966-67; faculty Fla. Inst. Tech., 1958-60, 62-63, mem. edn. com., 1964, adj. faculty physics and aerospace scis., 1979—. Mem. Friends Brevard Assn. for Advancement of Blind. Served with USN, 1934-37; with USNR, 1942-45. Life mem. Friends Melbourne Library. Mem. IEEE (life), Am. Defense Preparedness Assn.(life), Assn. Physics Tchr., (life), Missile and Space Pioneers (life), Assn. Physics Tchrs., Soc. Wireless Pioneers (life), Amnesty Internat. Lodge: Mason (32 deg.). Home: 371 Cocoanut Dr Indialantic FL 32903

DAVENPORT, GEORGE KEEFE, management executive; b. N.Y.C., Dec. 30, 1937; s. Fred Morris and Dorothy Frances (Keefe) D.; B.A., Lehigh U., 1959; B.S. in Indsl. Mgmt., C.W. Post Coll., 1962; cert. orgn. devel. W. Ga. Coll., 1978; m. Phyllis Joan Dallin, Oct. 12, 1963; children—Dierdre Kirsten, Christopher Prescott. Indsl. engr., Grumman Aircraft Co., Bethpage, N.Y., 1955-62; sales rep. IBM, Jacksonville, Fla., 1962-67; prin. engr. Reliability Engring. Bendix Co., Cape Kennedy, Fla., 1967-70; area mgr. Xerox Data Systems, Jacksonville, 1970-76; br. mktg. mgr. energy Sperry Univac Co., Bellaire, Tex., 1976-80; partner Norr Davenport-World Wide Fin. Services; dir. Advanced Communications Inc.; chmn. West Main Corp., Site Improvers, Inc., G.K. Davenport, Inc., Haglund Boat Works, Inc.; pres., chmn. Greenland Devel. Corp., 1984—; asso. prof. indsl mgmt. U. Fla., Brevard Coll., 1967-72; mem. quality control and reliability adv. com. Brevard Jr. Coll., Cape Kennedy, 1967-72; mem. fund raising com. 5th Congl. Dist. Fla., 1970. Recipient New Technology Utilization award NASA, 1969. Mem. Am. Mgmt. Assn., Instrument Soc. Am., Data Processing Mgmt. Assn., Am. Inst. Indsl. Engrs., Soc. Am. Mil. Engrs. Methodist. Clubs: Ponte Vedra (Jacksonville, Fla.); Univ. (Houston). Author: Statistical Calibration, 1967; Reliability Objectives, 1970; Introduction to Data Processing, 1971, others; contbr. articles to profl. jours. Home: 11415 Beacon Dr Jacksonville FL 32225 Office: 3156 Leon Rd Jacksonville FL 32216

DAVENPORT, WILLIAM WYATT, educator, writer; b. N.Y.C., Apr. 26, 1915; s. William Ashley and Pauline Jameson (Tilley) D.; m. Mary Roselle Riggin; children: Anthony Wyatt, Anne D. Arredondo. BA, Columbia U., 1937, MA, 1938. Asst. prof. English U. Hawaii, Honolulu, 1946-48, assoc. prof., 1948-54, prof. English and journalism, 1954-57; freelance writer Paris, 1957-68; dir. Reid Hall Columbia U., Paris, 1968-74, Northwood Inst. Europe, Paris, 1974—. Author: Belgium, 1955, Scandinavia, 1956, Austria, 1957, Fodor's Guide to the Hawaiian Islands, 1958, The Jet Age Guide to Europe, 1962, The Dolphin Guide to Paris, 1963, The Dolphin Guide to Rome, INDIA: A Personal Guide, 1964, the Monterey Peninsula, 1965, Art Treasures in the Far West, 1966, THE SEINE: From its Source to Paris to the Sea, 1968, GYRO! The Life and Times of Lawrence Sperry, 1978; author, dir. art films; contbr. articles to profl. jours. including National Geographic Mag. Democrat. Roman Catholic. Clubs: Univ. (v.p. 1960-68), Am. (v.p. 1964-68, Paris). Home: Domaine de St Martin, 83630 Moissac, 83630 Aups France Office: Northwood Inst Europe, Paris France

DAVENPORT-HINES, RICHARD PETER TREADWELL, historian; b. Hampstead, Eng., June 21, 1953; s. John Hines and June Patricia (Treadwell) Pearson; m. Frances Jane Davenport, May 20, 1978; children, Hugo Denzil Rufus, Cosmo Rory Hector Albertyn. B.A., Selwyn Coll., Cambridge, Eng., 1975, M.A., 1979; Ph.D., Cambridge U., Eng., 1979. Research officer Bus. History Unit, London Sch. Econ., 1983-86; historian Glaxo Pharm. Group, London, 1983—. Editor: Jour. Business History, 1984-88 Author: Dudley Docker, 1984, Speculators and Patriots, 1986; Markets and Bagmen, 1986, Business in the Age of Reason, 1987, Enterprise, Management and Innovation in British Business in Asia since 1860, 1988. Contbr. articles to profl. jours. Treas. Pembridge Sq. Garden Trust, Kensington, Eng., 1981-83. Fellow Royal Hist. Soc. Liberal; recipient Wolfson Literary prize, 1985, Wadsworth Lit. prize, 1986. Avocation: bunburing. Home: 51 Elsham Rd, Holland Pk, London W14 8HD, England

DAVER, BULENT, political science educator, lawyer; b. Istanbul, Turkey, Sept. 28, 1928; s. Abidin and Zeynep (Leman) D. B.A. in Polit. Sci., Ankara U. (Turkey), 1950, B.A. in Law, 1952, Ph.D., 1955. Lic. lawyer Turkey. Researcher, N.Y.U., N.Y.C., 1955-56; assoc. prof. Faculty of Polit. Sci., U. Ankara, 1960-68, prof., 1969—, chmn. dept. polit. sci., from 1967; mem. Commn. of Human Rights, Council of Europe, Strasbourg, France, 1965-81. Author: Separation of Religion and State in Turkey, 1955; Emergency Situations and Exceptional Powers, 1960; Modern Political Doctrines, 1969; Reference Guide in Political Science, 1973; Human Rights and Turkey: An Appraisal, 1975; Introduction to Political Sciences, 1975. Served to Lt., Turkish Army, 1957-58, Korea. Rockefeller Found. fellow, Columbia U., 1961-63. Mem. Internat. Polit. Sci. Assn. Club: Anadolu (Ankara). Home: Oran Sitesi 48/8, Ankara Turkey Office: Siyasal Bilgiler Fakultesi, U Ankara, Ankara Turkey *

DAVERAT, JEAN VINCENT, surgeon; b. Orthez, France, Feb. 2, 1927; s. André and Madeleine (Aran) D.; m. Nicole Bebear, Sept. 23, 1956; children: Pierre, Bernard, Vincent. MD, Faculty Medicine, U. Bordeaux. Resident med. surgeon U. Faculty Medicine, Bordeaux, 1950-54, anatomic asst., 1955, house surgeon, 1956-57; head surgical dept. Hosp., Dax, France, 1958—, chmn. med. cons. com. 1979—; mem. Council of Teaching Faculty Bordeaux, 1979—. Mem. Town Council, Dax, 1965—, dep. mayor, 1971-77. Served to lt. Med. Service, 1951-52. Recipient Silver medal French Sport and Cultural Fedn. 1974, Medal Youth and Sport 1978, Medal French Bridge Fedn. 1985. Mem. Surgery Soc. Bordeaux, French Surgery Assn. Clubs: Bridge (pres. 1963—), Local Sport Soc. (pres. 1978—) (Dax). Lodge: Rotary (pres. 1973-74). Avocations: bridge; tennis. Home: 36 Rue de la Republique, Dax, 40100 Landes France Office: Hosp Dax, Ave Yves du Manoir, 40100 Landes France

DAVEY, GRAHAM CHARLES LEONARD, psychology educator; b. Lutterworth, Eng., Oct. 10, 1949; s. Raymond Thomas and Olga Betty (Barrett) D. BA in Psychology with honors, Univ. Coll., Bangor, Wales, 1971, PhD in Psychology, 1974. Lectr. in psychology Sheffield (Eng.) U., 1974-76; lectr. in psychology City U., London, 1976-85, reader, 1985—. Author: Animal

Learning and Conditioning, 1981, Ecological Learning Theory, 1988; editor: Applications of Conditioning Theory, 1981, Animal Models of Human Behavior, 1983, Cognitive Processes and Pavlovian Conditioning in Humans, 1987; co-editor: Human Operant Conditioning and Behavior Modification, 1987. Sci. Research Council grantee, London, 1979-82, Wellcome Trust grantee, London, 1980-81, Nuffield Found. grantee, London, 1981; Sci. and Engring. Research Council grantee, London, 1983-86. Mem. British Psychol. Soc., Psychonomic Soc. Am., Exptl. Psychology Soc., Behavioral and Brain Scis., Animal Behaviour Soc. Office: The City Univ, Northampton Sq, London ECIV OHB, England

DAVEY, JEREMY ROBERT NICHOLAS, philosopher, educator; b. London, Aug. 8, 1950; s. Robert Trevor and Mary Covington (Damer) D.; m. Barbara Smith; children: Felix, Cecily. BA with honors, U. York, Eng., 1972; MA, U. Sussex, Eng., 1973; PhD, U. Sussex, 1981. Lectr. philosophy City U., London, 1976-79, Manchester (Eng.) U., 1979-80; sr. lectr. philosophy South Glamorgan Inst., Cardiff, Eng., 1980—; lectr. Cardiff Art Sch., 1981—, extra mural dept. U. Coll., Cardiff, 1982—, Goldsmiths Coll., London, 1985-86. Editor spl. edit. Brit. Jour. of Phenomenology, 1983; contbr. articles to profl. jours. Mem. Amnesty Internat., London, 1982—, Civil Liberties Council, London, 1983—. Research fellow Merchant Taylors Guild, London, 1977; travel grantee Brit. Council, London, 1983, 86; recipient research award Leathersellers Trust, London, 1974. Mem. Brit. Soc. Phenomenology (sec. 1985—). Home: 81 Plymouth Rd, Penarth, South Glamorgan CF6 2DE, England Office: South Glamorgan Inst, Cyncoed Rd, Cardiff, South Glamorgan CF2 2XE, England

DAVEY, LYCURGUS MICHAEL, neurosurgeon; b. N.Y.C., Feb. 20, 1918; s. Michael Marco and Elizabeth (Delaveris) D.; m. Artemis Diana Pappas, June 7, 1942; children: Michael Dean, Elaine Anne, Elizabeth. BA, Yale U., 1939, MD, 1943. Diplomate: Am. Bd. Neurol. Surgery. Surg. intern New Haven Hosp., 1943-44, asst. resident in surgery, 1946-50, William Harvey Cushing fellow, 1947-48, resident neurosurgeon, 1951-52; asst. resident in neurosurgery Hartford Hosp., 1950-51; clin. clk. Nat. Hosp., London, summer 1954; clin. instr. neurosurgery Yale U., 1952-60, asst. clin. prof., 1960-68, asso. clin. prof., 1968-77, clin. prof., 1977—; practice medicine, New Haven, 1952—; attending neurosurgeon Meriden-Wallingford Hosp., Hosp. St. Raphael, VA Hosp., West Haven; assoc. sect. chief emeritus Yale-New Haven Med. Center. Served to comdr. USNR, 1942-46, 52-54; capt. Res. ret. Fellow ACS, Internat. Coll. Surgeons; mem. AMA, Conn. Med. Soc. (pres. sect. on neurosurgery), Conn. Soc. Neurol. Surgeons, New Haven County Med. Soc. (pres. 1987), New Haven Med. Assn. (pres. 1972), Harvey Cushing Soc., New Eng. Neurosurg. Soc., Congress Neurol. Surgeons (disting. service award, 1966), Assn. Research in Nervous and Mental Diseases, Soc. Med. Cons. to Armed Forces. Home: 1010 Hartford Turnpike North Haven CT 06473 Office: 60 Temple St New Haven CT 06510 also: 2 Church St S New Haven CT 06519

DAVID, CLIVE, architect; b. Manchester, Eng., June 6, 1934; came to U.S., 1957, naturalized, 1962; s. Marcus Wiener and Claire Rose (Levy) Wiener Kattenburg. Student, Blackpool Tech. Coll., 1951-52, Royal Coll. Art, 1955-57. Designer Chippendale's, London, 1955-57; asst. to pres. pub. relations Maybruck Assocs., N.Y.C., 1959; Ea. regional dir. City of Hope, Phila., 1960-62; pres. Clive David Assocs., N.Y.C., Clive David Enterprises div. Party Enterprises Ltd., Beverly Hills, Calif., Party Enterprises, Ltd., Beverly Hills, 1962—; Lectr. Party Planning par excellence, 1966—. Arranger major parties including Miss Universe Coronation Ball, Miami Beach, 1965, State visit of Queen Elizabeth and Prince Philip, Duke of Edinburgh, Bahamas, 1966, An Evening at the Ritz-Carlton, Boston, 1967, 69, Un Ballo in Maschera, Venice, 1967, An Evening over Boston, 1968, M.G.M. Cavalcade of Style, Los Angeles, 1970, Symposium on Fund Raising through Parties, Los Angeles, 1970, Great Midwest Limestone Cave Party, Kansas City, 1972, Une Soiree de Gala, Phila., 1972, 11th Anniv. of the Mike Douglas Show, Phila., 1972, The Mayor's Salute to Volunteers, Los Angeles, 1972, Twenty Fifth Anniv. Salute to Israel, Jerusalem, 1973, The Bicentenary, 1976, The World Affairs Council Silver Ball, Boston, 1977, The Ohio Theatre Jubilee, Columbus, 1978, Mayor's Salute to Vols., 1978, Dedication and Gala Performance, Northwestern U. Performing Arts Ctr., 1980, Metromedia Gala, Los Angeles Bicentennial, 1981, The Albemarle Weekend, Charlottesville, 1985, The La Costa Weekend, Carlsbad, 1987, The Embassy Ball, N.Y.C., 1987, The Lagoon Cycle Premiere, Los Angeles, 1987; contbr. articles to profl. publs. Served with Royal Arty. Brit. Army, 1953-55. Recipient Freedom Found. award Valley Forge, Pa., 1961, City of Hope award Phila., 1962, Mayor's medal for vol. services Los Angeles, 1972, Shalom award State of Israel, 1974, Mayor's medal City of Columbus; named hon. citizen City of Columbus. Mem. AFTRA. Jewish. Home: Beekman Tower Mitchell Pl New York NY 10017 Office: 282 S Reeves Dr Beverly Hills CA 90212

DAVID, EDWARD EMIL, JR., electrical engineer, business executive; b. Wilmington, N.C., Jan. 25, 1925; s. Edward Emil and Beatrice (Liebman) D.; m. Ann Hirshberg, Dec. 23, 1950; 1 dau., Nancy. B.S., Ga. Inst. Tech., 1945; M.S., MIT, 1947, Sc.D., 1950; D.Engring. (hon.), Stevens Inst. Tech., 1971, Poly. Inst. Bklyn., 1971, U. Mich., 1971, Carnegie-Mellon, 1972, Lehigh U., 1973, U. Ill.-Chgo., 1973, Rose-Hulman Inst. Tech., 1978, U. Fla., 1982, Rensselaer Poly. Inst., 1982, Rutgers U., 1984, N.J. Inst. Tech., 1985, U. Pa., 1985. Exec. dir. research Bell Telephone Labs., Murray Hill, N.J., 1950-70; sci. adviser to Pres. Nixon; dir. Office Sci. and Tech., Washington, 1970-72; exec. v.p. Gould, Inc., 1973-77; ind. cons. 1977, 86—; v.p. Exxon Corp., N.Y.C., 1978-80; pres. Exxon Research and Engring. Co., Florham Park, N.J., 1977-86, EED, Inc., Bedminster, N.J., 1986—; dir. Materials Research Corp., Orangeburg, N.Y., Lord Corp., Erie, Pa., Gen. Sci. Corp., Landover, Md., Supercomuter Systems, Inc., Eau Claire, Wis., Intermagnetics Gen. Corp., Guilderland, N.Y.; cons. Nat. Security Council, 1974-77; mem. def. sci. bd. Dept. of Def., 1974-75; tech. adv. bd. Chrysler Corp.; chmn. Nat. Task Force on Tech. and Soc.; U.S. rep. to NATO Sci. Com.; mem. White House Sci. Council, N.J. Commn. on Sci. and Tech. Author: (with Dr. J.R. Pierce) Man's World of Sound, 1958, (with Dr. J.R. Pierce and W.A. van Bergeijk) Waves and the Ear, 1960, (with Dr. J.G. Truxal) The Man-Made World, 1969 (Lanchester prize Operations Research Soc. Am. 1971); contbr. articles to profl. jours. Mem. Bicentennial adv. com. Chgo. Mus. Sci. and Industry, 1974-75; mem. adv. bd. Office of Phys. Scis., NRC, 1976-81; mem. Pres.'s Commn. on Nat. Medal of Sci., 1975-78; mem. vis. com. to div. phys. scis. U. Chgo., 1976—; mem. adv. council Humanities Inst., 1976—; trustee Aerospace Corp., 1974-81, chmn. bd. trustees, 1975-81; life mem. corp. MIT, 1974—, also mem. exec. com., energy adv. bd.; bd. dirs. Summit (N.J.) Speech Sch., 1967-70; mem. Marshall Scholarships Adv. Council.; mem. adv. and resource council Princeton U.; mem. cons. sci. com. Chateaubriand Scholarships; trustee Carnegie Instn. of Washington, 20th Century Fund. Served with USNR, 1943-46. Recipient Outstanding Young Engr. award Eta Kappa Nu, 1954, George W. McCarty award Ga. Inst. Tech., 1958, award Summit Jr. C. of C., 1959, ASME award merit, 1971, Harold Pender award Moore Sch. U. Pa., 1972, N.C. award, 1972, award for disting. contbn. Soc. Research Adminstrs., 1980, N.J. Sci. and Tech. medal, 1982, Indsl. Research Inst. medal, 1983, Scientist of Yr. award R & D Mag., 1984, Fahrney medal Franklin Inst., 1985, Pub. Service award Conf. Bd. Math. Scis., 1985. Fellow IEEE, Acoustical Soc. Am., Am. Acad. Arts and Scis., AAAS (dir. 1974-75, 77-80, 80-82, pres. 1977-78, chmn. bd. dirs. 1979-80), Audio Engring. Soc.; mem. Am. Philos. Soc., Nat. Acad. Sci., Assn. Computing Machinery, Am. Soc. for Engring. Edn., Engring. Soc. Detroit, Nat. Acad. Engring. (Bueche award 1984), Nat. Acad. Pub. Adminstrn. Office: EED Inc Box 435 Bedminster NJ 07921

DAVID, LEON THOMAS, judge, educator, former army officer; b. San Francisco, Aug. 25, 1901; s. Leon Kline and Ella Nancy (Thomas) D.; A.B., Stanford, 1924, J.D., 1926; M.S. in Pub. Adminstrn., U. So. Calif., 1935, Dr. Pub. Adminstrn., 1957; m. Henrietta Louise Mellin, May 22, 1927; children—Carolyn L. Eskra, Leon Colby. City editor Vallejo (Calif.) Times, 1920-21; free-lance journalist, 1921-26; admitted to Calif. bar, 1926, U.S. Supreme Ct., 1932; pvt. practice law; mem. Malcolm & David, Palo Alto, Calif., 1926-31; dep. and acting city atty. Palo Alto, 1926-31; mem. faculty Sch. Law, U. So. Calif., 1931-34, Sch. Pub. Adminstrn., 1934-41, 1947-67; sr. asst. city atty. Los Angeles, 1934-41, 46-50; spl. counsel Los Angeles Harbor Commn., 1939-41; judge Municipal Ct., Los Angeles Jud. Dist., 1950-53; judge Superior Court, 1953-67, appellate dept., 1958-60, ret., 1967; asso. justice pro tem Calif. Ct. Appeal, 1969-73. Mem. Calif. Gov.'s Adv. Com. Law Enforcement, 1959-67. Chmn. legal aid com. State Bar Calif. intermittently to 1950, chmn. state bar com. history of law, 1975-78; bd. dirs., past pres. Los Angeles Legal Aid Found. Served from 2d lt. to maj. F.A.-O.R.C., 1924-42; from lt. col. to col., AUS, 1942-61; comdt. U.S. Army Sch. for Spl. Services, 1942-43, chief Spl. Services, N. Africa and Mediterranean theaters of operation, 1943-45; col. AUS (ret.), 1961. Decorated Legion of Merit (U.S.), Hon. Officer Order Brit. Empire, Medaille d'Honneur d'Or (France), Medalha do Guerra (Brazil), Comdr. Crown of Italy; recipient Reginald Heber Smith medal for distinguished legal aid service to indigent, 1962. Mem. Los Angeles Bar Assn., Contra Costa County Bar Assn., Am. Legion (past comdr.), Calif. Judges Assn. (life), Stanford, U. Calif., U. So. Calif. Alumni assns., Calif. Hist. Soc., Mt. Diablo Amateur Radio Club, Soc. Mayflower Descendants, Phi Alpha Delta, Phi Kappa Phi, Pi Sigma Alpha, Blue Key, Order of Coif. Mason (K.T., 32d degree, Shriner), DeMolay Legion of Honor (life). Presbyn. (elder, mem. laws and regulations com., social edn. and action com. Los Angeles Presbytery, 1965-69), World Affairs Council, San Francisco, 1987—. Clubs: Commonwealth, Kiwanis (pres. Palo Alto 1931, Los Angeles 1962, lt. gov. Div. 1 Calif.-Nev.-Hawaii dist. 1967). Author: Municipal Liability for Tortious Acts and Omissions, 1936; Administration of Public Tort Liability in Los Angeles, 1939; Tort Liability of Public Officers, 1940; Law and Lawyers, 1950; Role of the Lawyer in Public Administration, 1957; Law of Local Government, 1966; Old 89, My Horse, and Other Tales, Essays and Verse, 1974; History of State Bar of California, 1979; also articles in field of municipal law, ct. procedure and practice, legal history, legal aid, pub. adminstrn. Home: 240 Kuss Rd PO Box 656 Danville CA 94526

DAVID, ROBERT JEFFERSON, lawyer; b. New Roads, La., Aug. 10, 1943; s. Joseph Jefferson and Doris Marie (Olinde) D.; m. Stella Marie Scott, Jan. 21, 1967; children: Robert J. Jr., Richard M. BA, Southeastern La. U., 1966; JD, Loyola U., New Orleans, 1969. Bar: U.S. Dist. Ct. (ea. dist.) La. 1969, U.S. Dist. Ct. (mid. dist.) La. 1969, U.S. Dist. Ct. (we. dist.) La. 1975. Assoc. Kierr, Gainsburgh, Benjamin, Fallon & Lewis, New Orleans, 1969-74; ptnr. Kierr, Gainsburgh, Benjamin, Fallon, David & Ates, New Orleans, 1974—; adj. faculty Tulane U. Sch. Law, New Orleans, 1979-81. Staff mem. Loyola U. Law Review, 1967-69. Reader/recorder for La. Blind and Handicapped, 1986—; charter mem. Lawyers for Alliance for Nuclear Arms, New Orleans, 1986—; pres. Arden Cahill Acad. PTL, New Orleans, 1979-80. Mem. ABA, Fed. Bar Assn., La. State Bar Assn. (asst. examiner commn. on bar admissions 1974—, spl. ins. commn. 1974-82, mem. med.-legal interprofl. com. 1987—), La. Bar Found., Assn. Trial Lawyers Am., La. Trial Lawyers Assn. (bd. govs. 1981-83, contbg. editor Civil Trial Tactics manual 1981), Loyola U. Law Alumni Assn. (bd. dirs.), Kappa Sigma, Phi Alpha Delta. Home: 2559 Eton St New Orleans LA 70114 Office: Kierr Gainsburgh et al 1718 1st NBC Bldg New Orleans LA 70112

DAVIDS, ROBERT NORMAN, petroleum exploration geologist; b. Elizabeth, N.J., Apr. 27, 1938; s. William Scheible and Anna Elizabeth (Backhaus) D.; A.B. in Geology, U. Va., 1960; M.S., Rutgers U., 1963, Ph.D., 1966; m. Carol Ann Landauer, Apr. 20, 1957; 1 son, Robert Norman. With Exxon Co. USA, 1966—, micropaleontologist, New Orleans, 1965-71, uranium geologist, Denver, 1971-72, Albuquerque, 1972-78, supervisory geologist Tex. area exploration, Corpus Christi, 1978-80, N.W. area supr., 1981, dist. geologist so. dist., New Orleans, 1981-84, div. exploration tng. coordinator, spl. trades unit geologist, 1984-86; geol. trng. advisor, Houston, 1986—. Formerly active local Little League Baseball, Jr. Achievement. NSF grad. fellow, 1964-65. Mem. Geol. Soc. Am., AIME, Soc. Econ. Paleontologists and Mineralogists (treas. Gulf Coast sect. 1971), Am. Assn. Petroleum Geologists, Explorers Club, Krewe of Endymion, Sigma Xi, Beta Theta Pi. Author papers. Home: 173 Golden Shadow Circle The Woodlands TX 77381 Office: PO Box 2180 Houston TX 77252-2180

DAVIDSEN, ARTHUR FALNES, astrophysicist, educator; b. Freeport, N.Y., May 26, 1944; s. Andrew and Anna (Falnes) D.; m. Anita Clare Saltz, June 4, 1966; children: Andrew, Alexander (dec.), Austin. A.B., Princeton U., 1966; M.A., U. Calif.-Berkeley, 1972, Ph.D., 1975. Sci. liason officer Naval Research Lab., Washington, 1970-71; research asst. U. Calif., Berkeley, 1971-75; asst. prof. Johns Hopkins U., Balt., 1975-78, assoc. prof., 1978-80, prof. physics, 1980—, prof. physics and astronomy, 1984—, dir. Ctr. Astrophys. Scis., 1985-88; dir. Assn. Univs. for Research in Astronomy, Washington, 1979—; chmn. Johns Hopkins Space Telescope Inst. Com., 1979-81; mem. Space Telescope Inst. Council, 1982—; co-investigator Space Telescope Faint Object Spectrograph, 1978—; prin. investigator Hopkins Ultraviolet Telescope Project, 1979—; mem. space sci. working group Assn. Am. Univs., 1984—; eme. NASA Space and Earth Sci. Adv. Com., 1987-88. Contbr. articles to profl. jours. Served to lt. (j.g.) USNR, 1968-71. Recipient Helen B. Warner prize Am. Astron. Soc., 1979; Alfred P. Sloan fellow, 1976-80. Fellow AAAS (astronomy sect. chmn. 1989-90); mem. Am. Astron. Soc. (councilor 1981-84), Internat. Astron. Union (U.S. nat. com., co-chmn. 20th gen. assembly local organizing com. 1984-88), Royal Astron. Soc., Astron. Soc. Pacific, Explorers. Office: Johns Hopkins U Ctr for Astrophysical Sci Baltimore MD 21218

DAVIDSON, GEORGE A., JR., utility company executive; b. Pitts., July 28, 1938. BS, U. of Pitts., 1960. Chmn., chief exec. officer, dir. Consol. Natural Gas Co., Pitts. Office: Consol Natural Gas Co 4 Gateway Ctr CNG Tower Pittsburgh PA 15222 *

DAVIDSON, JOHN HUNTER, agriculturist; b. Wilmette, Ill., May 16, 1914; s. Joseph and Ruth Louise (Moody) D.; m. Elizabeth Marie Boynton, June 16, 1943; children—Joanne Davidson Hildebrand, Kathryn Davidson Bouwens, Patricia. B.S. in Horticulture, Mich. State U., 1937, M.S. in Plant Biochemistry, 1940. Field researcher agrl. chems. Dow Chem. Co., Midland, Mich., 1936-42, with research and devel. dept. agrl. products, 1946-72, tech. adviser research and devel. agrl. products, 1972-80, tech. adviser govt. relations, 1980-84, cons., 1984—. Served to lt. USNR, 1945. Mem. Am. Chem. Soc., Am. Soc. Hort. Sci., Weed Sci. Soc., Am. Pathol. Soc., N.Y. Acad. Sci., Phi Kappa Phi, Alpha Zeta. Republican. Presbyterian. Club: Exchange of Midland. Contbr. articles on plant pathology and weed control to profl. jours. Home: 4319 Andre Midland MI 48640 Office: Dow Chem Co PO Box 1706 Midland MI 48640

DAVIDSON, JOHN KEAY, III, diabetologist; b. Lithonia, Ga., Mar. 30, 1922; s. John Keay, Jr. and Laura Elizabeth (Lovingood) D.; m. Mary Evelyn Coney, May 30, 1952; children—John Keay, IV, Dorothy Elizabeth, Anne Ralston, Georgia Dial. B.S., Emory U., 1943, M.D., 1945; Ph.D. in Physiology (Am. Diabetes Assn. research fellow), U. Toronto, Ont., Can., 1965. Surg. intern Grady Meml. Hosp., Atlanta, 1945-46; resident in medicine Grady Meml. Hosp., 1948-49, Emory U. Hosp., Atlanta, 1949-50, New Eng. Center Hosp., Boston, 1950-51; assoc. prof. physiology and medicine U. Toronto Faculty Medicine, 1966-68; mem. faculty Emory U. Med. Sch., 1968—, prof. medicine, dir. diabetes unit, 1970—. Author: (diet sect.): Diabetes Guide Book, 3d edit, 1979; editor: Clinical Diabetes Mellitus, A Problem-Oriented Approach, 1986. Served with AUS, 1946-47. Fellow A.C.P.; mem. Am. Diabetes Assn. (dir. 1970-76, dir. postgrad. course 1980—, chmn. com. public affairs 1973-74, chmn. com. food and nutrition 1975-76, Outstanding Tchr. of Yr. award 1979, Charles H. Best medal, 1986), AMA, Am. Physiol. Soc., Endocrine Soc., Am. Soc. Internal Medicine, Can. Physiol. Soc. Methodist. Club: Druid Hills Golf. Home: 1075 Lullwater Rd NE Atlanta GA 30307 Office: 1365 Clifton Rd NE Atlanta GA 30322

DAVIDSON, JOHN KENNETH, SR., sociologist, educator; b. Augusta, Ga., Oct. 25, 1939; s. Larcie Charles and Betty (Corley) D.; m. Josephine Frazier, Apr. 11, 1964; children: John Kenneth, Stephen Wood. Student, Augusta Coll., 1956-58; B.S. in Edn, U. Ga., 1961, M.A., 1963; Ph.D., U. Fla., 1974. Asst. prof. dept. psychology and sociology Armstrong State Coll., Savannah, Ga., 1963-67; asst. prof. sociology Augusta Coll., 1967-74; acting chmn., asst. prof. dept. sociology Ind. U., South Bend, 1974-76; assoc. prof. sociology U. Wis., Eau Claire, 1976-78; prof. U. Wis., 1978—, asst. spl. projects to dean grad. studies and univ. research, 1987—, chmn. dept. sociology, 1976-80; cons. family life edn.; research cons. dept. ob-gyn Med. Coll. Ga., Augusta, 1969-74, pediatrics, 1972-73, also assoc. dir. health care project, 1971-73, research instr., summer 1971, research assoc., summer 1972-73, research cons. dept. community dentistry, 1974-79; program coordinator Community Devel. in Process Phase II and III, Title I Higher Edn. Act of, 1965, 1970; mem. sociology and anthropology com. Univ. System Ga., 1970-74, chmn. curriculum sub-com., 1970-72; dir. Sex Edn., The Public Schs. and You project Ind. Com. on Humanities, 1975. Assoc. editor: Jour. Marriage and the Family, 1975-85, Sociological Inquiry, 1986—; reviewer: Jour. Deviant Behavior, 1979—, Sociological Spectrum, 1985—; contbr. articles to profl. jours. Past state chmn. pub. affairs Ind. Assn. Planned Parenthood Affiliates, 1975-76; past mem. Eau Claire Coordinating Council; Former bd. dirs. Planned Parenthood North Cen. Ind., also past chmn. pub. affairs com., 1975-76; former bd. dirs., 1st v.p. and mem. resources allocation com. Wis. Family Planning Coordinating Council; former bd. dirs. and mem. exec., info., internat. and edn. coms., chmn. social sci. research com. Assn. for Vol. Sterilization; chmn. citizens adv. bd. Eau Claire and Chippewa Falls Planned Parenthood clinics; bd. dirs. Planned Parenthood of Wis., Inc.; former mem. Eau Claire County Adv. Health Forum, Eau Claire County Task Force on Family Planning. Mem. Am. Sociol. Assn., Am. Home Econs. Assn., Wis. Home Econs. Assn., Wis. Sociol. Assn., So. Sociol. Soc., Mid-South Sociol. Assn., Midwest Sociol. Soc., Nat. Council Family Relations (past chmn. com. standards and criteria for cert., former mem. devel. com. and cert. com.), Wis. Council Family Relations (bd. dirs., exec. com., past pres.), Soc. Sci. Study Sex, Soc. Study Social Problems, Augusta Coll. Alumni Soc., U. Fla. Alumni Soc., U. Ga. Alumni Soc., Groves Conf., Pres.'s Club U. Wis.-Eau Claire, Kappa Delta Pi, Phi Kappa Phi, Phi Theta Kappa, Alpha Kappa Delta (editor nat. newsletter 1979-83, past mem. exec. council). Episcopalian. Home: 1305 Nixon Ave Eau Claire WI 54701 Office: Dept Sociology U Wis Eau Claire WI 54702

DAVIDSON, PETER MACDONALD, sales executive; b. Saffron Walden, Essex, England, Nov. 1, 1946; s. Kenneth MacDonald and Rita (Crawte) D.; m. Elizabeth Mary Hawkes, July 24, 1972; children: Matthew MacDonald, Zöe. Cert. full tech., Cambridge Coll. of Arts and Tech., 1968. Engr. design British Gas Corp., Peterborough, Eng., 1968-71, British Steel Corp., Corby, Eng., 1971-75; sales engr. Acrow (Automation) Ltd., London, 1975-79; sales mgr. Electrolux Constructor, Luton, Eng., 1979—. Mem. Inst. of Engrs. Home: 106 Debden Rd, Saffron Walden CB11 4AL, England Office: Electrolux Constructor, Oakley Rd, Luton LU4 9QE, England

DAVIDSON, RALPH PARSONS, publishing company executive; b. Santa Fe, Aug. 17, 1927; s. William Clarence Davidson and Doris Parsons Stanton; m. Lou Hill; children: William A., R. Andrew, Ross H., Scott H., Sydney E., Mary Elizabeth. BA in Internat. Relations, Stanford U., 1950; postgrad., Alliance Française, Paris, 1951. With CIA, 1952-54; advt. salesman Life mag., 1954-56; European advt. dir. Time mag., London, 1956-62; mng. dir. Time-Life Internat., N.Y.C., 1967—; pub. Time mag., 1972-78; chmn. exec. com. Time Inc.; pres., chief exec. officer Kennedy Ctr. for the Performing Arts, Washington, 1988—; bd. dirs. Allied-Signal Co., First Interstate Bancorp; lectr. communications Stanford U. Trustee Nat. Urban League, Ocean Trust Found., Com. for Econ. Devel.; chmn. exec. com. Bus. Com. for Arts; mem. Pres.'s Commn. Exec. Exchange; bd. dirs. N.Y. City Ballet; mem. Statue of Liberty-Ellis Island Centennial Commn. Served with USNR, World War II. Mem. Stanford U. Alumni Assn. (pres. 1972-73), Explorers Club. Clubs: River (N.Y.C.); American (London). Office: Time Inc Rockefeller Ctr Time & Life Bldg New York NY 10020 *

DAVIDSON, VAN MICHAEL, JR., lawyer; b. Baton Rouge, Nov. 26 1945; s. Van Michael Sr. and Elizabeth Lamoine (Arnold) D.; m. Judith Ann Begue, Aug. 5, 1967; children: Van Michael III, Catherine Annette, Mary Elizabeth. BA in History, La. State U., 1968; JD, U. Miss., 1973. Bar: Miss. 1973, U.S. Dist. Ct. (no. dist.) Miss. 1973, U.S. Ct. Mil. Appeals 1974, U.S. Supreme Ct. 1978, U.S. Ct. Claims 1979, U.S. Tax Ct. 1980, U.S. Ct. Appeals (5th cir.) 1981, La. 1982, U.S. Dist. Ct. (we. and mid. dists.) La. 1982, U.S. Dist. Ct. (no. dist.) Tex. 1982, U.S. Ct. Appeals (Fed. cir.) 1982, U.S. Dist. Ct. (so. dist.) Miss. 1985, U.S. Dist. Ct. (ea. dist.) La. 1985, D.C., 1987. Commd. 2d lt. U.S. Army, 1968, advanced through grades to maj., 1980, resigned, 1981; forward observer U.S. Army, Ft. Bragg, N.C., 1968; battery battalion officer U.S. Army, Ft. Bliss, Tex., 1968-69, battery comdr., 1969-70; command spokesman IV U.S. Army, Vietnam, 1970-71; trial counsel U.S. Army, New Ulm, Fed. Republic Germany, 1974-77; trial atty. contact appeals div. U.S. Army, Washington, 1978-81; ptnr. Carmouche, Gray & Hoffman, Lake Charles, La., 1981-87; sole practice Lake Charles, 1987—; chmn. bd. dirs. Southwest Legl Services Agy., Lake Charles. Contbr. articles to profl. jours. Mem. meml. com. La. Vietnam Vets. Served to lt. col. USAR. Decorated Bronze Star, Vietnamese Gallantry Cross with Palm, Meritous Service medal with one oak leaf cluster. Mem. ABA, Fed. Bar Assn., Assn. Trial Lawyers Am., Indsl. Coll. Armed Forces, Armed Services Contract Trial Lawyers Assn., Am. Def. Preparedness Assn., Phi Delta Phi. Republican. Presbyterian. Home: 1525 N Greenfield Circle Lake Charles LA 70605 Office: 4820 Lake St Lake Charles LA 70602

DAVIDSON, WILLIAM G(EORGE), III, lawyer, accountant, fin. and mgmt. cons.; b. Ft. Benning, Ga., Oct. 28, 1938; s. William George and Dorothea Kathryn (Wright) D.; B.S., U.S. Naval Acad., 1960; M.B.A. in Fin., U. Pa., 1970; J.D., Suffolk U., 1974. Bar: Ohio 1975, Md. 1980, D.C. 1981, U.S. Tax Ct. 1980, U.S. Ct. Claims 1983, U.S. Ct. Appeals (D.C. cir.) 1983, U.S. Supreme Ct. 1980, Va. 1985; C.P.A., Md. Electronics engr., systems analyst Phila. Naval Shipyard, 1968; fin. analyst Allied Chem. Corp., N.Y.C., 1969; fin. analyst, staff acct. Dennison Mfg. Co., Framingham, Mass., 1969-74; corp. controller Premix, Inc., North Kingsville, Ohio, 1974-78; owner, mgr. W.G. Davidson and Assocs., Inc., mgmt. and fin. cons., Rockville, Md., 1978-87; mem. faculty Lake Erie-Garfield Coll., Painesville, Ohio, 1977-78, Washington, 1981-87, Benjamin Franklin U., 1981-87, Montgomery Coll., 1983—; head. dept. acctg. and taxation, Southeastern U, Washington, 1981—; del. White House Conf. on Small Bus., 1980. Active Vols. in Tech. Assistance, 1970-75; mem. fiscal affairs com. Montgomery County, Md., 1983-84. Served to lt. comdr., USN, 1960-67. Mem. ABA, Am. Inst. C.P.A.s, Md. Bar Assn., Bar Assn. Montgomery County; Fairfax Bar Assn., Va. State Bar Assn., Rockville C. of C., Fin. Execs. Inst., Nat. Assn. Accts., U.S. Naval Acad. Alumni Assn., Naval Res. Assn., Suffolk Law Sch. Assn. Washington. Roman Catholic. Lodges: Kiwanis (past dir. Ashtabula, Ohio); Civitan (Rockville).

DAVIE, EUGENE NEWTON, international language center executive; b. Oakland, Calif., Apr. 3, 1942; s. Eugene Newton and Marjorie Inez (Sifford) D.; m. Mary Jane Whitelam, May 19, 1967 (div. Feb. 1968). BA, San Francisco State U., 1965; postgrad. Syracuse U., 1968-69, U. Calif. and U. Hawaii, 1961-63. With Burman-Johnson & Assocs., 1965-66; tchr. spl. children San Raphael Mil. Acad., 1966-67; head English dept. St. Hilda's and Hughes Sch., 1969-69; with LanFranco Corp., San Francisco, 1972—, pres., 1976—, chmn. bd., 1979—; guest lectr. Soviet Consulate. Mem. San Francisco Tb and Lung Assn.; bd. dirs. San Francisco Spring Opera, also mem. exec. and planning coms.; mem. San Francisco Opera Fair., English Speaking Union of San Francisco. Tenn. squire, 1973. Mem. Theta Alpha Phi. Episcopalian. Office: Four Leaf Towers 5110 San Selite W-333 Houston TX 77056

DAVIES, DANIEL R., educator; b. Plymouth, Pa., Feb. 21, 1911; s. John R. and Minnie (Kocher) D.; m. Winifred Evans, June 14, 1941 (div. July 1975); children: Cathie, Wendy; m. Nancy Church Edwards, Sept. 9, 1975. A.B., Harvard U., 1933; A.M., Bucknell U., 1943; Ph.D., Columbia U., 1946. Tchr. Forty Fort (Pa.) High Sch., 1934-44, head dept. English, 1940-44; asst. supt. schs. Briarcliff Manor, N.Y., 1944-45; asst. dept. edn. adminstrn. Columbia, 1945-46, asst. prof. edn., exec. officer div. adminstrn. and guidance, 1946-49; assoc. prof., exec. officer Tchrs. Coll., 1949-50; prof. edn., dir. coop. program in edn1. adminstrn. Tchrs. Coll. (Middle Atlantic region), 1950-59; del. Coop. Center for Ednl. Adminstrn., 1955-59; assoc. dir. Indsl. Mgmt. Work Conf., Columbia U. Sch. Engring., and Indsl. Research Conf., 1955-60; exec. dir. U. Council for Edn. Adminstrn., 1958-59; editorial cons. A.C. Croft Publs., New London, Conn., 1958-60; dir. research and devel. Croft Ednl. Services, 1960-66; v.p. research, devel. and dir. Croft Cons. Services, Tucson, 1966-71; pres. Davies-Brickell Assocs., Ltd., 1972-88, Davies-Taylor Assocs., Inc., 1987—; chmn. bd. Doris Lemke Realty, Inc., Bisbee, Ariz., 1981-83; lectr. U. Ariz., 1962-64; vis. prof. San Diego State, summer 1957, U. N.Mex., summer 1960, Okla. A. and M., summer 1963, Tex. A. and M., U. Scranton, summer 1964, U. Nebr., summer 1971; mem. Nat. Com. Advancement Ednl. Adminstrn., 1955-57; cons. Lilly Endowment, Inc., 1976-77; head policy cons. Calif. Sch. Bds. Assn., 1976-81; dir. policy services Conn. Assn. Bds. Edn., 1978-88; head policy cons. N.J. Sch. Bds. Assn., 1977-82; spl. cons. on installing Davies-Brickell System in schs.,

U.S.A., Can., also Am. Schs., France, Holland, Greece, Italy.; organizing dir. First Nat. Bank Bisbee. Author: numerous books including Dynamics of Group Action, 8 vols, 1954; (with V. Anderson) Patterns of Educational Leadership, 1956, (with H.M. Brickell) Davies-Brickell System for School Board Policy Making, 1957, 17th edit., 1988, Calif. edits., 1977-80, Conn. edit., 1978-86, Nebr. edit., 1983-84, Board Policy Letter, 1958-71, (with R.T. Livingston) You and Management, 1958, (translated into Japanese, 1968), (with Margaret Handlong) Teaching of Art, 1962, The Administrative Internship, 1962, (with D.E. Griffiths) Executive Action, 1962-68, (with W.S. Elsbree, Louise H. Nelson) Educational Sec., 1962-67, Catholic Schools Adaptation of the Davies-Brickell System, 1968, (with Father James R. Dineen) New Patterns for Catholic Education, 1968, (with Catherine Davies Armistead) In-Service Education, 1975. Pres. bd. dirs. Ariz. Theatre Co., 1976-79; v.p. bd. dirs. Copper Queen Community Hosp., Bisbee, 1985—; pres., founder The Bisbee Found., Inc., 1986—. Named Citizen of Yr. Bisbee C. of C., 1983; Ford Found. grantee Europe, 1961. Fellow AAAS; mem. NEA, AAUP, Nat. Soc. Study Edn. (contbr. Yearbook 1954), Am. Assn. Sch. Adminstrs., Nat. Conf. Profs. Ednl. Adminstrn. (exec. com., sec.-treas. 1948-58), Phi Delta Kappa. Club: Bisbee Country. Lodge: Bisbee Rotary (pres. 1984-85). Home: Casa del Jubilado PO Box 757 Naco AZ 85620 Office: San Jose Sq #11 Bisbee AZ 85603

DAVIES, DAVID KEITH, geologist; b. Barry, Eng., Oct. 10, 1940; came to U.S., 1966, naturalized, 1973; s. Buller T. and Muriel G. (Champ) D.; m. Ruth Margaret Mary Gilbertson, Dec. 12, 1964; children: Mark James, John Phillip. B.S., U. Wales, 1962, Ph.D., 1966; M.S., La. State U., 1964. Asst. prof. Tex. A. and M. College Station, 1966-68, assoc. prof., 1968-70, asst. dean, 1968-70; prof. U. Mo., Columbia, 1970-77; chmn. dept. geoscis., dir. Reservoir Studies Inst., Tex. Technol. U., Lubbock, 1977-80; dir. Tex. Commerce Bank, Kingwood, 1984—; pres. David K. Davies & Assos., Inc., Houston, 1980—. Contbr. articles to profl. jours. Mem. Planning and Zoning Commn. Columbia, Mo., 1979-80. Recipient A. I. Levorsen Meml. award Am. Assn. Petroleum Geologists, 1978. Fellow Geol. Soc. Am.; mem. Am. Assn. Petroleum Geologists, Soc. Econ. Paleontologists and Mineralogists, Soc. Petroleum Engrs. of AIME (disting. lectr. 1984-85), Phi Kappa Phi. Home: 2210 Long Valley Kingwood TX 77345 Office: 1410 Stonehollow Dr Kingwood TX 77339

DAVIES, DONALD THOMAS, hospital administrator, Air Force officer; b. Chgo., June 12, 1948; s. Brettland Lloyd and Catherine (Dobesh) D.; m. Inta Eva Delmage, Apr. 20, 1968; children—Donald Thomas, Alicia, Melissa, Sebastian. B.B.A., Chaminade U., 1974; M.B.A., Philips U., 1984. Commd. 2d lt. U.S. Air Force, 1975, advanced through grades to maj., 1985; asst. adminstr. U.S. Air Force Hosp., Rantoul, Ill., 1975-78; chief med. placement U.S. Air Force, Chgo., 1978-81; adminstr. U.S. Air Force Clinic, Enid, Okla., 1981-83, U.S. Air Force Hosp., Lubbock, Tex., 1983-85, US Air Force Hosp., Misawa, Japan, 1985-88; staff officer Hdqrs. Pacific Air Forces Office Command Surgeon, Hickam AFB, Hawaii, 1988—. Mem. West Tex. Hosp. Assn., Am. Coll. Hosp. Adminstrs. (presiding officer 1985—, cert.), Tex. Hosp. Assn., Am. Hosp. Assn., Delta Mu Delta. Republican. Roman Catholic. Avocations: camping; golf; bowling.

DAVIES, EDWARD WILLIAM, oil company executive; b. Neath, Glamorgan, S. Wales, Apr. 28, 1937; s. David Emlyn and Ruby Maud (Durose) D.; m. Lynne Maureen Hadley, Sept. 30, 1965; children: Denise Elisabeth Claire, Geraldine Louise Jane. HNC and Endorsements in Chem. Engring., Neath Tech. Coll., 1958; postgrad. Instn. Chem. Engrs., 1961. Chartered engr. Process engr. Conoco Ltd., Immingham, Eng., 1965-72; supt. process engring. Gulf Oil Raffinaderij B.V., Europoort, Holland, 1972-79; coordinator mfg. Gulf Oil Co., Internat., London, 1979-82; refiner mgr. Kuwait Petroleum Refining (Danmark) A/S, Skaelskoer, 1982-86, mng. dir., 1982-86; mng. dir. Kuwait Petroleum Europoort B.V., 1986—. Mem. The Engring. Council, Instn. Chem. Engrs., Instn. Gas Engrs., Inst. Petroleum. Christian. Office: Kuwait Petroleum Europoort BV, PO Box 7180, 300HD Rotterdam The Netherlands

DAVIES, GLADSTONE, mineralogist; b. Pretoria, Transvaal, Republic of South Africa, Oct. 10, 1952; s. Gladstone and Getroulina (Botha) D.; m. Gwenda Hilda Greer, Oct. 5, 1977; children: Michelle Susan, Gwenda Claire. BSc, U. of the Wiwatersrand, Johannesburg, Republic of South Africa, 1973, BSc with honors, 1974, PhD, 1983. Geologist Geol. Survey, Pretoria, 1975-76; researcher Chamber of Mines, Johannesburg, 1978; microprobe operator U. of the Witswatersrand, Johannesburg, 1979-81, postdoctoral researcher, 1982-83; chief researcher Council for Sci. and Indsl. Research, Pretoria, 1984—. Mem. Geol. Soc. South Africa, Mineral. Soc. South Africa. Home: 504 Mirage St, Pretoria 0181, Republic of South Africa Office: NBRI-Council for Sci and Indsl, Research PO Box 395, Pretoria 0001, Republic of South Africa

DAVIES, JOHN PICTON, investment adviser, counselor; b. Ton Pentre, Glamorgan, Wales, Jan. 19, 1920, came to Can., 1947; s. Sydney William and Sarah (Jones) D.; m. Iris Eleanor Bentley, May 28, 1958, (dec. 1969); children—Tudor Craddock, Morgan Clayton, Trevor Roderick; m. Beverley Ann Lewis, Dec. 20, 1969. B.A., Cambridge U., 1941, M.A., 1946. Chartered fin. analyst. Engr. Sir Alexander Gibb & Ptnrs., London, 1946-47, Bell Can., Toronto, Ont., 1947-48; staff cons. Woods Gordon, Toronto, 1948-52; research dir. Leethan Simpson, Montreal, Que., Can., 1952-55; stockbroker Burns Bros., Montreal, 1955-57; mgr. Edper Investments Ltd., Montreal, 1957-62; asst. v.p. UNAS Investments, Ltd., Toronto, 1962-70; pvt. practice as investment counsellor and adv. Polymetric Cons.s Ltd., Don Mills, Ont., 1970—. Author and editor Polymetric Report. Served to lt. Third Brit. Infantry Div., 1943-46. Scholar Brit. Govt., 1938, Corpus Christi Coll., 1939. Mem. Inst. Chartered Fin. Analysts, Assn. Profl. Engrs. Ont. (cert.), Fin. Analysts Fedn. Mem. United Ch. Can. Avocations: violin; sailing; skiing; reading; walking; classical music. Home: 84 Valentine Dr, Don Mills, ON Canada M3A 3J8

DAVIES, MICHAEL KEVIN, cardiologist; b. Birmingham, West Midlands, Eng., May 9, 1951; s. Gordon William John and June Moreen (Murphy) D. BA, Cambridge (Eng.) U., 1972, MB, BChir., 1975, MA, 1976, MD, 1983. Sr. house officer Nat. Health Service, Leicester, Eng., 1976-78; Birmingham, Eng., 1978; Sheldon research fellow, hon. registrar West Midlands Regional Health Authority, 1978-80, hon. cons. cardiologist, 1984—, instr. ambulance service, 1985; lectr. cardiovascular medicine U. Birmingham, 1980-84, sr. lectr., 1984—; hon. sr. registrar in cardiovascular medicine Cen. and East Birmingham Health Dists., 1980-84; com. mem. Brit. Heart Found., Solihill, Birmingham, 1986—. Contbr. articles to med. jours. Mem. Royal Coll. Physicians, Med. Research Soc., Brit. Cardiac Soc. Mem. Ch. of Eng. Home: 12 Mellish Rd, Walsall, West Midlands W54 2ED, England Office: U Birmingham East Hosp Dept, Cardiovascular Medicine, Birmingham B9 5ST, England

DAVIES, PAUL THOMAS GRANT, neuroscientist; b. Wrexham, Wales, May 12, 1955; s. David Frank and Doreen May (Davidson) D. MB, BChir, Cambridge (Eng.) U., 1979, MA, 1980. Research fellow Acad. Unit Neurosci., Charing Cross Hosp., London, 1985—; hon. registrar The Princess Margaret Migraine Clinic, London, 1985—. Author: Answers to Migraine, 1987; contbr. numerous articles to med. jours. Migraine Trust research fellow, 1985—. Mem. Royal Soc. Medicine, Royal Coll. Physicians. Mem. Ch. of Eng. Office: Charing Cross Hosp Neurosci Unit, Fulham Palace Rd, London W6 8RF, England

DAVIES, PETER MAXWELL, composer, conductor; b. Manchester, Sept. 8, 1934; s. Thomas and Hilda Davies; student Manchester U.; Mus.B. with honors, Royal Manchester Coll. Music, 1956; Mus.D. (hon.), Edinburgh U., 1979, Manchester U., 1983, Bristol U., 1984, Open U., 1986; LL.D. (hon.), Aberdeen U., 1981; LittD (hon.), U. Warwick, 1986; student of Goffredo Petrassi, Rome, 1957; Harkness fellow Grad. Music Sch., Princeton U., 1962-64. Dir. music Cirencester Grammar Sch., 1959-62; vis. composer Adelaide (Australia) U., 1966; co-dir. Pierrot Players, 1967-70; artistic dir. The Fires of London, 1971-87; prof. composition Royal No. Coll. Music, Manchester, Eng., 1978-80; founder, dir. St. Magnus Festival, Orkney Islands, 1977-86, pres., 1986—; artistic dir. Dartington Summer Sch. Music, 1979-84; participant UNESCO Conf. Music Edn., Sydney, Australia, 1965; lectr. tours, Europe, Australia, N.Z., U.S., Can., Brazil; vis. prof. composition Harvard U., spring 1985; series sch. broadcasts BBC-TV; assoc. condr./composer Scottish Chamber Orch., 1985—. Composer works for piano, orch., and solo instruments, also theatre works including: Quartet Movement for string quartet, 1952, Sonata for trumpet and piano, 1955, Five Klee Pictures, 1959, rev., 1979, William Byrd: Three Dances, 1959, Five Voluntaries, 1960, The Shepherd's Calendar, 1965, Notre Dame des Fleurs, 1966, Eight Songs for a Mad King for male voice and instrumental ensemble, 1969, Missa Super l'Homme Arme, 1968, Vesalii Icones, 1969, Blind Man's Buff (masque), 1972, Miss Donnithorne's Maggot for mezzo-soprano and instrumental ensemble, 1974, Stevie's Ferry to Hoy, 1975, The Martyrdom of St. Magnus, 1976, The Two Fiddlers (opera for children), 1978, Le Jongleur de Notre Dame (masque), 1979, sacred and secular choral and instrumental works including: O Magnum Mysterium, 1960, Veni Sancte Spiritus, 1963, Westerlings, 1977, Taverner (opera), 1970, Symphony, 1976, Salome (ballet), 1978, Kirkwall Shopping Songs (for children), 1979, Solstice of Light, 1979, Black Pentecost, 1979, The Lighthouse (chamber opera), 1979, Cinderella (children's opera), 1980, The Yellow Cake Review (cabaret), 1980, Symphony No. 2, 1980, The Rainbow (sing-spiel), 1981, The Medium, 1981, Little Quartet No. 2 (string quartet), 1981, Hill Runes, solo guitar, 1981, The Bairns of Brugh, instrumental ensemble, 1981, Three Tenor Arias from The Martyrdom of St. Magnus, 1981, Lullabye for Lucy, 1981, Salome, 1981, Brass Quintet, 1981, Songs of Hoy, 1981, Seven Songs Home, 1981, Sea Eagle, 1982, Image, Reflection, Shadow, 1982, Sinfonia Concertante, 1983, Into the Labyrinth, 1983, The Number 11 Bus, 1984, Cello Concerto, 1987, various others. Fellow Royal No. Coll. Music, 1978; Hon. mem. Royal Acad. Music; decorated comdr. Order Brit. Empire, 1981. Mem. Accademia Filarmonica Romana, Royal Philharm. Soc. (hon.), Schs. Music Assn. (pres. 1983—), Composer's Guild Gt. Britain (pres. 1986—). Address: care Mrs Judy Arnold, 50 Hogarth Rd Flat 3, London SW5 England also: Hoy, Orkney Islands Scotland

DAVIES, RAY GEORGE ANDREW, horticulturist, water gardening company executive; b. Crewe, Chesire, Eng., Oct. 15, 1939; s. Sidney Thomas and Marguerete (Martin) D.; m. Pauline Margaret Coffin, Sept. 14, 1965; 1 child, Sarah Lisa. NCH, Celyn Coll., 1963. Trainee horticulturalist Crewe Parks, Cheshire, 1955-62; asst. head gardener Reaseheath Coll., Nantwich, 1963-65; prin. Davies Enterprises, Shavington, Crewe, 1965-70, Stapeley Water Gardens Ltd., 1970—; mng. dir., chmn. Stapeley Water Gardens Ltd., Stapeley Nantwich, Cheshire; mng. dir. Perrys Hardy Plant Farm Ltd., Enfield, 1976—, Proops Manufacturing Ltd., Burton-on-Trent, 1980—. Author: (with others) The Stapeley Book of Water Gardens, 1985. Chmn. Hop Trust Charity Multiple Sclerosis, Crewe, 1985. Mem. Internat. Water Lily Soc. (founder, life), Water Lily Soc. Md. U.S.A., (dir. 1986—). Anglican. Avocations: shooting, swimming. Office: Stapeley Water Gardens Ltd, London Rd, Stapeley Nantwich, Cheshire CW5 7LH, England

DAVIES, TREVOR, religious organization administrator; b. Liverpool, Merseyside, Eng., Jan. 10, 1940; s. Arthur Stanley and Alice (Hughes) D.; m. Dorothy Irene Blair, July 31, 1965; children: Rosalind Jane, Alistair James. BS with honors, U. Birmingham, 1962; Diploma in Social Work, Home Office, London, 1963. Probation officer Manchester (Eng.) City Cts., 1963-65; lectr. social adminstrn. Lancaster Poly., Coventry, Eng., 1965-68, sr. lectr. social policy, 1968-72; dep. head social affairs sect. personnel div. European Orgn. Nuclear Research, Geneva, 1972-78; dir. personnel office World Council Chs., Geneva, 1978—; cons. Joint Inspection Unit UN, Geneva, 1977-78, World Intellectual Property Orgn., Geneva, 1977, Joint Working Group on Social Security U. Geneva, 1986—; pres. social commn., mem. exec. com. Fedn. Internat. Non-Govtl. Orgns. in Geneva, 1978—. Mem. vestry com. Holy Trinity Ch., Geneva, 1973-80; Ferney Voltaire elder Crossroads Community Ch., 1981—. Mem. Soc. Suisse Gestion Personnel. Anglican. Office: World Council Chs, 150 Rte de Ferncy, 1211 Geneva Switzerland

DAVILA, ENRIQUE, medical educator, physician; b. Bogota, Colombia, Dec. 28, 1948; came to U.S., 1974; s. Enrique Patricio Davila and Elvira (Davila) D.; m. Luz Elena; children: Luz Elena, Michelle, Laura, Alejandra. Bachiller, Gimnasio Campestre, Bogota, 1965; M.D., Nat. U. Colombia, Bogota, 1973. Diplomate Am. Bd. Internal Medicine, Am. Bd. Hematology and Oncology. Intern Nassau Hosp., Mineola, N.Y., 1974-75; resident in medicine U. Miami, Fla., 1975-78, chief med. resident, 1980-81, asst. prof. medicine, 1981-86, asst. prof. oncology, 1982-86; chief oncology sect. Miami VA Med. Ctr., 1984-86; practice medicine specializing in oncology, Miami Beach, 1986—; fellow in hematology/oncology U. Pa., Phila., 1978-80; cons. Pan Am. Health Orgn., 1982-86. Fellow ACP; mem. Dade County Med. Assn., Fla. Med. Assn., Nat. Surgical Adj. Breast Cancer Study Group, Mt. Sinai Community Clin. Oncology Program, Sociedad Colombiana de Hematologia, Am. Soc. Clin Oncology, Am. Soc. Hematology. Home: 2300 S Miami Ave Miami FL 33129 Office: 1688 Meridian Ave Suite 702 Miami Beach FL 33139

DAVIN, JAMES MANSON, investment banker; b. Allentown, Pa., Dec. 24, 1945; s. James Thomas and Louise (Manson) D.; m. Christine Sims, Feb. 27, 1971; children: James Christian, Alexander Manson, Nicholas. BS in Bus. Adminstrn., Georgetown U., 1967; grad. Bondurant Sch. of High Performance Driving, Sonoma, Calif., 1978. Succesively asst. to treas., asst. mgr., mgr., asst. v.p., v.p. corp. fixed income trading, mng. dir. underwriting, syndicate nat. mktg. mgr. First Boston Corp., N.Y.C., 1969-87, mng. dir. internat. equity dept., 1987-88; sr. v.p., 1988. Davin Motorsports; bd. dirs. Internat. Convertible Growth Fund Mgmt. Co. Served with U.S. Army, 1967-69. Counselor, Georgetown U. Mem. N.Y. Investment Assn., Securities Industry Assn. (mem. N.Y. dist. com., dist. bus. conduct com., fin. com., adv. bd., bd. dirs., chmn. bd. govs.), Bond Club of N.Y., Nat. Assn. Securities Dealers (bd. dirs., dist. bus. conduct com.), Pa. Soc. Roman Catholic. Club: Saucon Valley Country (Bethlehem, Pa.). Home: 1120 Park Ave New York NY 10021

DAVINSON, DONALD EDWARD, college administrator; b. Middlesbrough, Yorkshire, Eng., July 20, 1932; s. Henry and Mary Isabel (Johnson) D.; m. Ann Kennedy, July 6, 1957; children: Roger, Joanna, Deborah. D in Pub. Adminstrn., U. London, 1964, BSc, 1969. Asst. Pub. Library, Middlebrough, 1949-56; chief asst. Pub. Library, Warrington, Eng., 1956-58; chief librarian Pub. Library, Dukinfield, Eng., 1958-59; bus. librarian Pub. Library, Belfast, Northern Ireland, 1959-62; head sch. Leeds (Eng.) Poly., 1962-85, asst. dir., 1985—; mem. Council for Nat. Acad. Awards, Eng., 1976-82, Library Adv. Council, Eng., 1979-82; cons. Brit. Library, 1985; vis. lectr. Brit. Council, 1977. Author: Bibliographic Control, 1960, Periodical Collection, 1960, Reference Service, 1961, Theses and Dissertations, 1977. Served as cpl. Brit. Army, 1950. Mem. Library Assn., Inst. Info. Scientists. Mem. Conservative Party. Lodge: Masons, St. Germain (sec. 1982—), Salebeia (sec. 1983—). Home: Meadowfields, Main St, South Duffield, Selby YO8 7ST, England Office: Leeds Poly, Calverley St, Leeds LS1 3HE, England

DAVIS, A. DANO, grocery store chain executive. Student, Stetson U. With Winn-Dixie Stores Inc., Jacksonville, Fla., 1968—, corp. v.p., mgr. Jacksonville div., 1978-80, sr. v.p. and regional dir. Jacksonville and Orlando (Fla.) and Atlanta divs., 1980-82, pres., 1982-88, chief exec. officer, 1982—, chmn., 1988—, also bd. dirs. Office: Winn Dixie Stores Inc 5050 Edgewood Ct Jacksonville FL 32203 *

DAVIS, ALEXANDER SCHENCK, architect; b. San Francisco, Jan. 3, 1930; s. William Schenck and Amelia (Francisco) D.; B.A. with honors in Architecture, U. Calif.-Berkeley, 1953, M.A. in Architecture (D. Zelinsky & Sons Found. Grad. scholar), 1957; m. Nancy Leah Barry, Oct. 21, 1953; children—Arthur Barry, Laurel Davis Bowden, Pamela Davis Bennett. With Hammarberg & Herman, Architects, El Cerrito, Calif., 1956-62; project architect Bonelli, Young & Wong, Architects and Engrs., San Francisco, 1962-67; chief architect Earl & Wright, Cons. Engrs., San Francisco, 1967-73; constrn. mgr. Fisher Devel., Inc., San Francisco, 1973-74; project architect Keller & Gannon, Cons. Engrs., San Francisco, 1974-77; individual practice architecture, Albany, Calif., 1977-81, El Cerrito, Calif., 1986—. Served with USCGR, 1951-56, active duty 1953-55. Registered architect, Calif., Alaska, U.K.; cert. Nat. Council Archtl. Registration Bds. Fellow Soc. Am. Registered Architects, mem. AIA, Royal Inst. Brit. Architects, Soc. Am. Mil. Engrs., Constrn. Specifications Inst. Home and Office: 928 Contra Costa Dr El Cerrito CA 94530

DAVIS, ALICE J., municipal employee; b. Galveston, Tex., Aug. 4, 1929; d. Joseph Edward Reagan and Gertrude Bertha Reagan Zeller; m. Bob J. Davis, Oct. 22, 1948; 1 child, Paula Lynn Davis Baughman. A.A., San Jacinto Coll., 1966; B.S., Western Ill. U., 1976. With office staff various automobile dealerships, Houston, 1951-68, Yeast Printing Co., Macomb, Ill., 1974-77; clk. Office of City Clk., City of Macomb, 1977-86. Youth program leader 1st Meth. Ch., Pasadena, Tex., 1960-63; mem. choir Wesley United Meth. Ch., Macomb, 1968—, worship com., 1987-88, chmn. Alter Guild, 1987-88; area chmn. Macomb United Way, 1970-71, program chmn., 1984-85. Mem. Univ. Faculty Women, Macomb Home Econs. Assn. (pres. 1981-82, treas. 1987-88), Kappa Omicron Phi, Phi Kappa Phi, Beta Sigma Phi (treas. 1987-88), Xi Epsilon Rho (pres. 1981-82, 86-87). Lodges: Eastern Star, White Shrine, Deer. Office: Office of City Clerk Macomb IL 61455

DAVIS, ALVIN GEORGE, international trade consultant; b. Chgo., May 10, 1918; s. Isadore and Mary (Wasserman) D.; m. Rose Lorber, Dec. 14, 1940 (dec. 1980); children—Fred Barry, Glenn Martin; m. June Elizabeth Davis, May 24, 1982. With Sears Roebuck & Co., 1936-40; gen. partner, sales mgr. Ritz Mfg. Co., 1940-41; buyer hobby dept. The Fair, 1941-43; mgr. hobby div. Central Camera Co., wholesalers, 1944; pres., gen. mgr. Nat. Model Distbrs., Inc., 1945-63; pres. Hobbycraft Exports, 1946-62; pub., editor Cyclopedia Pub., Inc., 1949-62; dir. internat. operations Aurora Plastics Corp., 1951-62, v.p. internat. div., 1962-70; v.p. Aurora Plastics Can., Ltd., 1963-70; mng. dir. Aurora Plastics Nederland N.V., 1964-70, Aurora Plastics Co. U.K. Ltd., Croydon, Eng.; expert cons. U.S. and Fgn. Comml. Service, Hong Kong; EDP internat. trade and distbn. cons.; internat. trade cons. until 1984; sr. internat. trade specialist U.S. Comml. Service, U.S. Dept. Commerce, 1971-84; lectr. Stuart Sch. of Bus. Adminstrn., Ill. Inst. Tech., Midwest Credit Assn.; dir. Rowe Industries (HK) Ltd., Rowe Industries (Taiwan) (Singapore), Rowe Industries Ltd. Mem., chmn. People to People Com.; meet mgr. USN/Plymouth Corp. Cadet Procurement Program Internat. Model Plane Qualification Championships, 1948-52; scoutmaster, past mem. fin. com. Chgo. council Boy Scouts Am.; info. officer, dep. comdr. CAP. Recipient Berkeley award, 1957, Hobbies award of merit Hobby Industry Assn., 1960, Meritorious award of honor, 1975. Fellow Inst. Dirs. (London), Hobby Industry Am. (hon. life); mem. Nat. Rifle Assn. (life), Soaring Soc. Am., Airplane Owners and Pilots Assn., Acad. Model Aeros. (contest dir. 1936-70), Nat. Model R.R. Assn. (life), Model Industry Assn. (dir. 1952-60, sec. 1954-57, pres. 1957-59), Hobby Industry Assn. (hon. life), Chgo. Aeronuts (hon.). Lodges: Masons (32 deg.), Shriners. Contbr. articles on internat. merchandising to trade mags. Pub., Cyclopedia of Hobbies, 1946-62; editor Dartnell-Internat. Trade Handbook; contbg. editor Brittanica Jr., 1949. Office: 9-A Dragon Terr, Suite #3, Causeway Bay Hong Kong

DAVIS, ANDREW HAMBLEY, JR., lawyer; b. Fall River, Mass., Feb. 10, 1937; s. Fall River, Mass., Feb. 10, 1937; s. Andrew Hambley and Doris (Baker) D.; m. Gail D. Perry, July 21, 1962; children: Andrew W., Katherine B., Joshua P. AB, Brown U., 1960; LLB, U. Va., 1962. Bar: R.I. 1963, Mass. 1962. Ptnr., Swan, Jenckes, Asquith & Davis, Providence, 1962-79; ptnr. Davis, Jenckes, Kilmarx & Swan, Providence, 1979—; sec., dir. Union Wadding Co., Uncas Mfg. Co., Potter Hazelhurst Advt. Co. Pres., Bethany Home of R.I., 1966; bd. dirs., exec. com. Bradley Hosp.; bd. dirs. Moses Brown Sch., R.I. Philharmonic Orch., 1967—. Mem. ABA, R.I. Bar Assn., Boston Bar Assn., Estate Planning Council, Am. Coll. Probate Council. Clubs: University, Acoaxet Golf, Agawam Hunt, Elephant Rock Beach, Art, Hope. Lodge: Masons. Home: 9 Harbour Rd Barrington RI 02806 Office: 1420 Hospital Trust Tower 1 Hospital Trust Plaza Providence RI 02903

DAVIS, ANTHONY, data processing executive; b. London, Jan. 14, 1938; s. Simon and Celia (De Grasse) D.; m. Rosa Karp, June 4, 1961; children: Richard John, Andrew James, Ruth Helen. BSc, U. London, 1959; BS (hon.), Pacific Western U. With IBM U.K., London, 1960-1976, sales rep., 1964-69, mktg. mgr., 1969-72, branch mgr., 1972-76; mgr. profl. sales devel. IBM Europe, Paris, 1976-77; mng. dir. Strategic Sales Tng. Internat. Ltd., Harrow, 1977—; bd. dirs. First Nat. Sales Devel., London, Strategic Sales Tng., Harrow. Author: Selling Professional Services, 1984; scriptwriter: (videos) Importance of Qualification, 1982, Presenting Change, 1985. Mem. Brit. Computer Soc. (cert.), Brit. Inst. Mgmt., Inst. Mktg. Conservative. Jewish. Club: Dyrham Park (London).

DAVIS, ARTHUR HORACE, diplomat; b. Brockton, Mass., Oct. 6, 1917; s. Arthur Horace and Hazel E. (Cubbage) D.; m. Marian Esther James, Sept. 29, 1945 (dec.); children: Cynthia, Karen, Susan, Arthur Horace. Student, U. Colo., 1956-62. Lic. real estate broker, Colo. Meteorologist Pan Am. Grace, Santiago, Chile, 1945-56, United Air Lines, Denver, 1956-62; v.p. Van Frellick Assocs., Denver, 1962-64; pres. New Englewood Colo., Denver, 1964-68, Villa Enterprises Inc., Denver, 1968-77, Arthur Davis Assocs., Denver, 1976-82; U.S. Ambassador to Paraguay Asuncion, 1982-85; U.S. Ambassador to Panama Washington, 1985—. Author Martin T. McMahon-Diplomatico en el Estridor de las Armas, 1985. Chmn. Jefferson County Republican Central Com., Denver, 1963-67. Served with USAAF, 1942-45. Mem. Am. Meteorol. Soc., Bd. Realtors, Inst. Real Estate Mgmt., Internat. Council Shopping Ctrs., Am. Fgn. Service Assn. Methodist. Club: International. Office: care US Dept of State Embassy of Panama Washington DC 20520

DAVIS, BOB J., transportation educator; b. Grand Saline, Tex., June 27, 1927; s. Frank H. and Minnie Kathryn (Crocker) D.; B.B.A., U. Houston, 1957, M.B.A., 1961, J.D., 1966; m. Alice Joyce Reagan, Oct. 22, 1948; 1 dau., Paula Lynn. Admitted to Tex. bar, 1966; traffic rep. Texaco, Inc., Houston, 1951-61; traffic mgr. Republic Steel Corp., Cleve., 1961-67; mem. faculty Western Ill. U., Macomb, 1967—, prof. transp., 1970-83, dir. exec. devel., 1970-83; mem. Macomb Planning Commn., 1971-75; mem. Macomb Mcpl. Airport Authority, 1980-84, chmn., 1988—. Served with USNR, 1944-47. Recipient Sam Harper award Purchasing Agts. Assn. Houston, 1957; named Traffic Man of Yr., Transp. Club Houston, 1966; Regional Educator of Yr., Delta Nu Alpha, 1980, 81, Regional Man of Yr., 1982, Mayleben award, 1982; Coll. Bus. Tchr. of Yr., Western Ill. U., 1981. Mem. Assn. Transp. Practitioners (Clyde B. Aitchison award 1966), Am. Soc. Transp. and Logistics, Internat. Material Mgmt. Soc., Ill. Pub. Airports Assn. (bd. dirs. 1982-84, 88—), Phi Kappa Phi (disting. mem. 1982). Methodist. Lodge: Masons. Author books, bibliographies, reports, articles in field. Home: 1111 E Grant St Macomb IL 61455 Office: Western Ill U 900 W Adams St Macomb IL 61455

DAVIS, BRUCE GORDON, educational administrator; b. Fulton, Tex., Sept. 2, 1922; s. Arthur Lee and Clara Katherine (Rouquette) D.; B.A., U. Tex., 1950; M.Ed., U. Houston, 1965; m. Mary Virginia Jackson, Aug. 31, 1946; children—Ford Rouquette, Barton Bolling, Katherine Norvell Davis McLendon. Tchr., Edison Jr. High Sch., Houston, 1951; tchr. Sidney Lanier Jr. High Sch., Houston, 1957-60, asst. prin., 1966-74, prin., 1974—; tchr. Johnston Jr. High Sch., Houston, 1960-66; prin. Sidney Lanier Vanguard Sch., Houston, 1974-82. Served with USMC, 1942-45; with U.S. Army, 1951-57. Mem. Nat. Assn. Secondary Sch. Prins., Tex. Assn. Secondary Sch. Prins., Houston Profl. Adminstrs., U.S. Army Officers Res. Assn., Houston Congress Tchrs., Am. Legion. Republican. Presbyterian. Club: Masons. Home: 6614 Sharpview St Houston TX 77074 Office: 2600 Woodhead St Houston TX 77098

DAVIS, CALVIN DE ARMOND, historian, educator; b. Westport, Ind., Dec. 3, 1927; s. Harry Russell and Abbie Jane (Moncrief) D. A.B., Franklin Coll., Ind., 1949; M.A., Ind. U., 1956, Ph.D., 1961. Tchr. Wilson Sch., Columbus, Ind., 1949-51, 53-54; asst. prof. history Ind. Central Coll., Indpls., 1956-57; teaching assoc. Ind. U., 1958-59; asst. prof. history U. Denver, 1959-62; asst. prof. history Duke U., Durham, N.C., 1962-64, assoc. prof., 1964-76, prof., 1976—; cons. NEH, 1974. Author: The United States and the First Hague Peace Conference, 1962 (Albert J. Beveridge award 1961), The United States and the Second Hague Peace Conference, 1976. Served to cpl. U.S. Army, 1951-53. Mem. Am. Hist. Assn., Orgn. Am. Historians, Soc. Historians Am. Fgn. Relations, Conf. Peace Research in History (council 1979-81). Mem. Christian Ch. Home: 907 Monmouth Ave Durham NC 27701 Office: Dept History Duke U Durham NC 27706

DAVIS, CHERYL MARIE, computer company executive; b. Winona, Minn., Dec. 30, 1945; d. George W. and Beverly F. (Cieminski) Wos; A.B. in English with honors in humanities, Stanford U., 1968; postgrad. Ga. State

U., 1974-75, U. Tex., Austin, 1975-81; m. John Nicholas Davis, Aug. 24, 1985; child, Patrick Robert Davis; children by previous marriage—David Austin Russell, Timothy Francis George Russell, Cristi Lynn Traver, Pamela Cindy Traver. Programmer Fairchild Semiconductor, Mountain View, Calif., 1966-67; programming mgr. adminstrn. computing Stanford (Calif.) U., 1969-74; mgmt. info. systems dir. Ga. State U., Atlanta, 1974-75; software engring. mgr. INTEL, Austin, Tex., 1976-81, product mktg. mgr., 1982-84; dir. Wollongong Group, Palo Alto, Calif., 1985—; bd. dirs. Coll. and Univ. Systems Exchange, 1974-76, Info. Success Systems, 1972. Tchr. religious edn. St. Theresa Sch., 1976-78, St. Thomas More Sch., 1978-79, mem. fin. com. St. Thomas More, 1978-79. Recipient Bausch & Lomb award, 1964, Nat. Sci. Fair award, 1964. Mem. Phi Kappa Phi. Republican. Roman Catholic. Club: Stanford Alumni. Contbr. papers to profl. publs. and confs. Home: 985 Eastwood Place Los Altos CA 94022 Office: Wollongong Group 1129 San Antonio Rd Palo Alto CA 94303

DAVIS, CHESTER R., JR., lawyer; b. Chgo., Aug. 30, 1930; s. Chester R. and Mead (Scoville) D.; m. Anne Meserve, Mar. 3, 1962; children: John Chester, Julia Snow, Elizabeth Meserve. Grad., Phillips Exeter Acad., 1947; A.B., Princeton, 1951; LL.B., Harvard, 1958. Bar: Ill. 1958, U.S. Dist. Ct. (no. dist.) Ill. 1958. Ptnr. Bell, Boyd & Lloyd and predecessor firms, 1968—. Assoc. Rush-Presbyn.-St. Luke's Med. Center, Chgo., 1964—, Adlai Stevenson Inst. Internat. Affairs, 1968—, Newberry Library, Chgo., 1974—; mem. Winnetka (Ill.) Zoning Commn. and Bd. Appeals, 1974-79; mem. Winnetka Plan Commn., 1976-82, 84-88; chmn. Spl. Joint. Com. of Winnetka Zoning Bd. and Plan Commn. to Revise Land Use Ordinances, 1978-83; village trustee Village of Winnetka, 1984-88; sec., bd. dirs. Vascular Disease Research Found.; mem. alumni council Phillips Exeter Acad.; chmn. Winnetka Interchurch Council, 1981-84. Served to lt. (j.g.) USNR, 1952-56, now capt. Decorated Navy Commendation Medal, 1984; recipient New Trier Dist. Award of Merit Boy Scouts Am., 1982. Mem. ABA, Ill. Bar Assn., Chgo. Bar Assn. (chmn. com. civil practice 1969-70, chmn. land use and zoning com. 1980-82, chmn. real property law com. 1983-84), Am. Soc. Internat. Law, Am. Judicature Soc., Am. Arbitration Assn. (nat. panel arbitrators), U.S. Naval Inst., Naval Res. Assn., Am. Planning Assn., Urban Land Inst., Chgo. Mortgage Attys. Assn., Harvard Law Soc. Ill. (past pres.), Harvard Law Sch. Assn. (nat. v.p. 1970-71). Episcopalian. Clubs: University (Chgo.), Economic (Chgo.), Law (Chgo.), Legal (Chgo.); Princeton (N.Y.C.), Nassau (Princeton, N.J.). Home: 670 Blackthorn Rd Winnetka IL 60093 Office: 3 First Nat Plaza Chicago IL 60602

DAVIS, COLIN REX, conductor; b. Weybridge, Eng., Sept. 25, 1927; s. Reginald George and Lilian (Colbran) D.; student Royal Coll. Music, London, 1944-49; m. April Cantelo, 1949 (div. 1964); children—Suzanne, Christopher; m. Ashraf Naini, 1964; 3 children. Household Cav. for Nat. Service, 1946-48; asst. condr. BBC, Scottish Orch., 1957-59; mus. dir. Sadler's Wells Opera Co., London, 1961-65; chief condr. BBC Symphony Orch., 1967-71; music dir. Royal Opera House, Covent Garden, London, 1971-84; prin. guest condr. London Symphony Orch., Boston Symphony Orch., 1974-84; chief condr. Bavarian Radio Symphony Orch., 1983—; condr. Bayreuth Festival, 1977. Decorated comdr. Order Brit. Empire. Office: care 7A Fitzray Park, London N6 6HS, England *

DAVIS, CRAIG CARLTON, aerospace co. exec.; b. Gulfport, Miss., Dec. 14, 1919; s. Craig Carlton and Helen Lizette (Houppert) D.; B.S., Ga. Inst. Tech., 1941; J.D., Harvard U., 1949; children—Kimberly Patricia, Craig Carlton. Instr. aeros. Escola Tecnica de Aviacao, Sao Paulo, Brazil, 1946; contract adminstr. Convair, Fort Worth, 1949-51; mgr. contracts and pricing, atomics internat. and autonetics divs. N.Am. Aviation, Anaheim, Calif., 1954-62, asst. corp. dir. contracts and proposals, El Segundo, Calif., 1963-70; dir. contracts Aerojet Electro Systems Co., Azusa, Calif., 1971-81, v.p., 1982—. Served with AUS, 1941-45; USAF, 1951-53, to col. res., 1953-66. Mem. ABA, Fed. Bar Assn., D.C. Bar Assn., Res. Officers Assn., Harvard U. Alumni Assn., Ga. Tech. Alumni Assn. Republican. Episcopalian. Club: Harvard. Home: 10501 Wilshire Blvd Apt 1208 Los Angeles CA 90024 Office: Aerojet Electro Systems Co 1100 W Hollyvale St Azusa CA 91702

DAVIS, DAISY SIDNEY, educator; b. Bay City, Tex., Nov. 7, 1944; d. Alex. C. and Alice M. (Edison) Sidney; m. John Dee Davis, Apr. 17, 1968; children—Anaca Michelle, Lowell Kent. BS, Bishop Coll., 1966; MS, East Tex. State U., 1971; MEd, Prairie View A&M and Mech., 1980. Cert. lifetime elem. tchr., Tex.; mid-mgmt. administrator. Tchr., Dallas pub. schs., 1966— Coordinator, Get Out the Vote campaign, Dallas, 1972, 80, 84, 88. Recipient Outstanding Tchr. award Dallas pub. schs., 1980, Jack Lowe award for ednl. excellence, 1982; Free Enterprise scholar So. Meth. U., 1987; Constitutionalism fellow U. Dallas, 1988; named to Hall of Fame, Holmes Acad., 1979. Mem. NEA, Tex. State Tchrs. Assn., Classroom Tchrs. Dallas (faculty rep. 1971-77), Dallas County History Tchrs., Afro-Am. Daus. Republic of Tex. (founder), Zeta Phi Beta. Democrat. Baptist. Club: Jack & Jill, (Dallas) (rec. sec., v.p.). Home: 1302 Mill Stream Dr Dallas TX 75232 Office: 9339 S Polk St Dallas TX 75232

DAVIS, DAVID, psychiatrist, educator; b. Liverpool, Eng., Oct. 5, 1927; came to U.S., naturalized, 1966; s. Solomon A. and Bertha (Finkelstein) D.; m. Phyllis Burman, 1952; children: Jonathan Paul, Jeremy Mark, Timothy Spenser. M.B., Ch.B., Glasgow (Scotland) U., 1949, M.D., 1974; Diploma in Psychol. Medicine, Conjoint Bd. of Royal Colls. Physicians and Surgeons, Eng., 1954. House officer Stobhill Gen. Hosp., Glasgow, 1949-50; locum gen. practice London, 1952; registrar in psychiatry St. Crispin Hosp., Northampton and South Ockendon Hosp., Essex, Eng., 1952-55; Fulbright traveling scholar, research fellow in psychiatry Washington U., St. Louis; vis. physician in psychiatry Washington U., 1955-57; registrar in psychiatry Bethlem Royal and Maudsley Hosps., U. London Postgrad. Inst. Psychiatry, 1957-59; sr. hosp. med. officer in psychiatry Borocourt Hosp., Henley, Eng.; with service at other hosps. 1959-60; asst. prof. psychiatry U. Mo., Columbia, 1960-61, assoc. prof., 1961-68, prof., 1968-86, prof. emeritus, 1986—, dir. inpatient psychiatry service, 1960-68, chief sect. gen. psychiatry, dir. edn. and tng., 1964-68, dir. community cons. program, 1966-72, chmn. dept. psychiatry, 1968-69, asso. chmn. dept. psychiatry, 1971-75, 77-86; disting. prof. U. Tex. Med. Br., Galveston, 1986-87, acting chmn. dept. psychiatry and behavioral scis., 1986—, vice chmn., 1987—; clin. dir. univ. service Mid-Mo. Mental Health Ctr., 1967-74, acad. head, 1968-69, assoc. acad. head, dir. research and tng., chief sect. gen. psychiatry, 1970-75, chmn. dept. psychiatry, acad. head, 1975-76, chief psychiatry, 1977-83, chmn. dept. psychiatry, acad. head, 1983-84; vis. scientist NIMH, 1969-70; vis. prof. U. Edinburgh, Scotland, 1976-77; vis. faculty fellow in community psychiatry Lab. Community Psychiatry, Harvard U. Med. Sch., 1965-67; disting. vis. prof. dept. psychology Bowling Green State U. (Ohio), Apr. 1983; examiner N.Y. State Dept. Mental Hygiene, 1970—; cons. in field. Contbr. articles to med. publs.; cons. editor Jour. Operational Psychiatry. Pres. Congregation Beth Shalom of Mid-Mo., 1981-83; bd. trustees Congregation B'nai Israel, Galveston, Tex., 1988—. Served as flight lt. RAF, 1950-52. Recipient award for teaching excellence U. Mo. Residents, 1975, 85; Guhlman award for clin. excellence, 1985; Royal Soc. Medicine Wellcome fellow, 1957-59; Am. Fund for Psychiatry teaching fellow, 1961-62; NIMH grantee, 1965-67. Fellow Am. Psychiat. Assn. (rep. and liaison Royal Coll. Psychiatrists 1979-86), AAAS, Royal Soc. Health, Royal Coll. Psychiatrists, Am. Coll. Psychiatrists, Mo. Acad. Psychiatry (pres. 1970); mem. Can. Psychiat. Assn., Mid-Continent Psychiat. Assn., Assn. Mental Health (chmn. adv. com. 1968-74), AAUP, Internat. Assn. Social Psychiatry, Am. Assn. for Social Psychiatry (program com. 1985-87, awards com. 1987—), N.Y. Acad. Scis., Central Mo. Psychiat. Soc. (pres. 1974, chmn. ethics com. 1977-86), Mo. Psychiat. Assn. (pres. 1975), AMA, Galveston County Med. Soc., Tex. Med. Assn., Tex. Soc. Psychiatric Physicians, Brit. Med. Dir., Brit. Med. Register, Mo. Acad. Psychiatry (counselor 1975), N.Am. Soc., Royal Coll. Psychiatrists (founding chmn. 1978-85), World Psychiat. Assn. (expert com. on clin. psychopathology), Fulbright Alumni Assn., Poetry Roundtable of Galveston Artists Guild, Sigma Xi, Phi Beta Pi (mem. adv. bd. Profls. Inst., 1987). Clubs: University, Pelican. Lodge: B'nai B'rith (pres. 1965-66). Office: Dept Psychiatry and Behavioral Scis U Tex Med Br 1200 Graves Bldg Galveston TX 77550

DAVIS, DAVID MACFARLAND, film and television executive; b. St. Charles, Ill., Mar. 23, 1926; s. Harrold Henry Davis and Bernice (MacFarland) Goodstein; m. Sylvia Asin, Apr. 26, 1948 (div. 1970); children—Lynn (dec.), Scott Burr, Matthew Todd; m. Marcia DeSilva, Sept. 27, 1970; 1 child, Adam Owen. B of Music Edn., Northwestern U., 1947; MS, U. Pa., 1951. Producer, dir. Sta. WFIL-AM-FM-TV, Phila., 1947-51; instr. Temple U., Phila., 1947-51; TV prodn. coordinator Mich. State U., East Lansing, 1951-52; prodn. mgr. Sta. WMAL-TV, ABC News, Washington, 1952-53; dir. programs Sta. WUNC-TV, Greensboro, N.C., 1953-56; sta. mgr. Sta. WGBH-TV, Boston, 1956-67; dir. programming Instruction TV Trust, Tel Aviv, 1967-68; program officer-in-charge Ford Found., N.Y.C., 1968-79; pres., chief exec. officer Pub. TV Playhouse Inc., American Playhouse, N.Y.C., 1980—; cons. German Marshall Fund, Washington, 1979-81. Exec. producer documentary film Robert Frost: A Lover's Quarrel with the World, 1962 (Oscar award 1963); producer, dir.: (TV series) Aaron Copland: Music of the 20's, 1966, Lotte Lenya: World of Kurt Weill, 1967. Mem. Nat. Acad. TV Arts and Scis., Brit. Acad. Film and TV Arts, Media Com. of the Indo-US Sub-com. on Edn. and Culture. Club: Ischoda Yacht (Norwalk, Conn.). Avocations: sailing, playing trumpet, conducting. Office: Am Playhouse 1776 Broadway New York NY 10019

DAVIS, DON R(AY), insurance consultant, executive recruiter; b. Washingtonville, Ohio, Jan. 27, 1924; s. Ivan Wilbur and Sarah (Barton) D.; m. Louise Endress Hall, Nov. 15, 1952; children: Don Scott, Timothy John, Wendy Louise. B.A., Ohio Wesleyan U., 1948. Home office group rep. Aetna Life Ins. Co., Detroit, 1948-51; dist. group supr. N.Y. Life Ins. Co., Cleve., 1951-58; regional group mgr. Paul Revere Life Ins. Co., Detroit, 1958-60; ins. agt. Dore Agy., Detroit, 1960-61; asst. v.p. sales Safeco Life Ins. Co., Seattle, 1961-68; pres. Am. Life Ins. Co. subs. Am. Internat. Group, Wilmington, Del., 1968-76; sr. v.p. Continental Corp., N.Y.C., 1976-82; cons. ins. 1983-85, cons. ins. exec. recruiting, 1985—; mem.exec. com., mem. program com. Pacific Ins. Conf., 1981—. Former dir. Diners Club Internat., Nat. Life Ins. Can. (chmn.), Loyalty Life Ins. Co. (chmn.), Nat. Ben Franklin Life (chmn.), Continental Life-U.K. (chmn.), Underwriters Adjusting Co., Am. Life Ins. Co., Del., Continental Hellas Ins., Greece. Served to sgt. USMC, 1943-46, PTO, China. Mem. Nat. Assn. Life Underwriters. Republican. Club: Wilmington Country. Home: 66 Elvira Ln Fairfield CT 06430 Office: Danforth Group 21 Locust Ave New Canaan CT 06840

DAVIS, DONALD IRVIN, psychiatrist, family therapist; b. Portland, Oreg., Oct. 18, 1942; s. Aubrey Milton and Clara Ethel (Dickson) D.; B.A. magna cum laude (NSF grantee), Harvard Coll., 1964; M.D., U. Pa., 1968; m. Susan Lynn Rabinowitz, Aug. 16, 1964; children—Kenneth Bernard, Joshua Ian. Intern, Case-Western Res. U. Hosps. Cleve., 1968-69; resident in psychiatry U. Chgo.-Billings Hosp., 1969-72; clin. asso. Alcoholism Clin. Research Lab., Nat. Inst. on Alcohol Abuse and Alcoholism, NIMH, Washington, 1972-74; clinic instr. Georgetown U., 1973-74; asst. prof. psychiatry and behavioral scis. George Washington U., 1974-79, attending psychiatrist, dir. family therapy program, psychiat. inpatient unit, 1977-79, clin. asso. prof. psychiatry, 1979-87, clin. prof. psychiatry, 1987—; trainee in family therapy Family Therapy Inst. D.C., 1975-76, med. cons., 1976-77; co-founder, dir. Family Therapy Inst. Alexandria (Va.), 1978—; condr. profl. workshops, panels, U.S. and abroad. Served to lt. comdr. USPHS, 1972-74. Nat. Inst. Drug Abuse grantee, 1974-77; Nat. Inst. Alcohol Abuse and Alcoholism grantee, 1974-77, Diplomate Am. Bd. Psychiatry and Neurology; cert. master practitioner neuro-linguistic programming. Fellow Am. Psychiat. Assn., Am. Orthopsychiat. Assn., Am. Assn. Marriage and Family Therapy (approved supr.); mem. Nat. Assn. Neuro-Linguistic Programming (charter), Physicians for Social Responsibility, Am. Family Therapy Assn. (charter), Washington Psychiat. Soc., No. Va. Psychiat. Soc. (exec. com. 1981-82), Alexandria Med. Soc., Va. Med. Soc., Am. Med. Soc. on Alcoholism and other Drug Dependencies, Phi Rho Sigma. Democrat. Jewish. Author: Alcoholism Treatment: An Integrative Family and Individual Approach, 1986. Research, publs. on alcoholism, the family, family therapy, neuro-linguistic programming. Office: 220 S Washington St Alexandria VA 22314

DAVIS, ELIZABETH STOUT, retired educator, writer; b. Salem, Ind., Mar. 12, 1907; d. Arthur Lindley and Bettye Collier (Wilson) Stout; m. James Brown Davis, Nov. 14, 1931 (dec. 1977); 1 child, Elizabeth Jane. Student Ogontz Jr. Coll., 1922-26. Mem. staff, reporter Fortune mag., N.Y.C., 1929-32; pres. Mary & Alexander Laughlin Children's Ctr., Sewickley, Pa., 1955-58. Author: (poems) Excuse for Singing, 1951. Pres. Allegheny County Garden Club, Pitts., 1962-64, regent Kenmore Nat. Shrine, Fredericksburg, Va., 1972—; past bd. dirs. N.Y. Kingergarten Assn., Judson Health Ctr., mem. Murray Hill com. of the visiting nurse. Recipient citation ARC, 1943-46. Mem. Nat. Soc. Colonial Dames (chmn. Pitts. com.). Republican. Episcopalian. Club: Naples Yacht. Home: 1900 Gulf Shore Blvd N Apt 506 Naples FL 33940

DAVIS, EVELYN MARGUERITE B., artist, organist, pianist; b. Springfield, Mo.; d. Philip Edward and Della Jane (Morris) Bailey; student pub. schs., Springfield; student art Drury Coll.; piano , organ student of Charles Cordeal; m. James Harvey Davis, Sept. 22, 1946. Sec., Shea and Morris Monument Co., before 1946; past mem. sextet, soloist Sta. KGBX; past pianist, Sunday sch. tchr., mem. choir East Avenue Bapt. Ch.; tchr. Bible, organist, pianist, vocal soloist and dir. youth choir Bible Bapt. Ch., Maplewood, Mo., 1956-69, also executed 12 by 6 foot mural of Jordan River; pvt. instr. piano and organ, voice, Croma Harp, Affton, Mo., 1960-71, St. Charles, Mo., 1971-83; Bible instr. 3d Bapt. Ch., St. Louis, 1948-54; pianist, soloist, tchr. Bible, Temple Bapt. Ch., Kirkwood, Mo., 1969-71; asst. organist-pianist, vocal soloist, tchr. Bible, Bible Ch., Arnold, Mo., 1969; faculty St. Charles Bible Bapt. Christian Sch., 1976-77; ch. organist, pianist, soloist, Bible tchr., dir. youth orch., music, floral arranger Bible Bapt. Ch., St. Charles, 1971-78; organist, vocal soloist, floral arranger, Bible tchr. Faith Missionary Bapt. Ch., St. Charles, 1978-82; organist, floral arranger Bellview Bapt. Ch., Springfield, Mo., 1984—; tchr. piano, organ, voice, organist, Springfield, Mo., 1983-84; interior decorator and floral arranger. Fellow Internat. Biog. Assn. (life), Am. Biog. Inst. Research Assn. (life); mem. Nat. Guild Organists, Nat. Guild Piano Tchr. Auditions, Internat. Platform Assn. Composer: I Will Sing Hallelujah, (cantata) I Am Alpha and Omega, Prelude to Prayer, My Shepherd, O Sing unto The Lord A New Song, O Come Let Us Sing unto The Lord, The King of Glory; The Lord Is My Light and My Salvation; O Worship the Lord in the Beauty of Holiness; The Greatest of These is Love; also numerous hymn arrangements for organ and piano. Home: RFD 2 Box 405 Rogersville MO 65742

DAVIS, EVELYN Y., editor, writer, publisher; b. The Netherlands, Aug. 16, 1929; d. Herman H. and Marian (Witteboom) DeJong; m. William Henry Davis, 1957 (div. 1958); m. Marvin Knudsen, 1969 (div. 1970). Student, Western Md. Coll., George Washington U., N.Y. Inst. Fin. Editor, pub., Highlights and Lowlights, 1964—. Mem. Luther Rice Soc. (life). Republican. Episcopalian. Home: Watergate East 2510 Virginia Ave NW Washington DC 20037 Office: Highlights and Lowlights Watergate Office Bldg 2600 Virginia Ave NW Suite 215 Washington DC 20037

DAVIS, FERD LEARY, JR., legal educator, lawyer, consultant; b. Zebulon, N.C., Dec. 4, 1941; s. Ferd L. and Selma Ann (Harris) D.; m. Joy Baker Davis, Jan. 25, 1963; children: Ferd Leary III, James Benjamin, Elizabeth Joy. BA, Wake Forest U., 1964, JD, 1967; LLM, Columbia U., 1984. Bar: N.C. 1967. Editor Zebulon (N.C.) Record, 1958; tchr. Davidson County Schs., Wallburg, N.C., 1966; ptnr. Davis & Davis and related law firms, Zebulon and Raleigh, N.C., 1967-76; asst. prosecutor Wake County Dist. Ct., Raleigh, 1968-69; town atty., Town of Zebulon, 1969-76; dean Campbell U. Sch. Law, Buies Creek, N.C., 1975-86, prof. law, 1975—; dir. Inst. for Study Practice of Law and Socioecon. Devel., 1985—; pres. The Davis Cons. Group, Inc., Buies Creek, 1987—; cons. U. Charleston, W.Va., 1979. Assoc. editor Wake Forest U. Law Review. Trustee Wake County Pub. Libraries, 1971-75, Olivia Raney Trust, 1969-71; mem. N.C. State Dem. Exec. Com., 1970-72; mem. N.C. Gen. Statutes Commn., 1977-79. Served with USAR, 1959-66. Babcock scholar Wake Forest U., 1963-67; Dayton Hudson fellow Columbia U., 1982-83. Mem. ABA, N.C. Bar Assn., N.C. State Bar, Phi Delta Phi, Delta Theta Phi. Democrat. Baptist. Office: Campbell U Sch of Law Box 158 Buies Creek NC 27506 also: The Davis Cons Group Inc Box 279 Buies Creek NC 27506

DAVIS, F(RANCIS) GORDON, public relations executive; b. Bloomfield, Ind., May 21, 1908; s. Francis Gordon and Grace (Bryan) D.; m. Margaret Aletha Smith, July 13, 1931; children: Margaret Jayne Davis Johnson, Marilyn Grace Davis Johnson. Student Wayne State U., 1925-27, postgrad., 1929-30; BA, U. Mich., 1929, postgrad., 1930, 42; postgrad. Cleve. Inst. Art, 1936-37, Western Res. U., 1938-39. Reporter, aviation editor, editorial writer Buffalo Times, 1930-33; feature, editorial, sci. writer Cleve. Press, 1934-42; pub. relations dir. Mich. Blue Cross-Blue Shield, Detroit, 1942-46; exec. dir. Mich. Health Council, Detroit, 1943-46; owner F. Gordon Davis & Assocs., Roscommon, Mich., 1946—. Mem. Pub. Relations Soc. Am., Am. Hosp. Assn. (life; chmn. pub. relations adv. com. 1965, mem. 1968-71, chmn. Conf. Affiliated Soc. Pres. 1969), Ohio Hosp. Assn. (hon.), Am. Soc. Hosp. Pub. Relations (pres. 1968-69), Mich. (pres. 1975-76), Southeastern Mich. (pres. 1973-74) hosp. pub. relations assns. Club: Higgins Lake Boat (dir. 1962-65). Contbr. articles to profl. jours. Died Nov. 6, 1987. Home and Office: 127 Forest Trail Roscommon MI 48653

DAVIS, FRANCIS KAYE, university administrator; b. Scranton, Pa., May 4, 1918; s. Francis Kaye and Anna Jane (Wooten) D.; m. Ida Mae Lamplugh, Sept. 25, 1941 (div. 1977); children—Richard Kaye, Frances Kay; m. Gloria Mae Griffith, Aug. 18, 1978. B.S., West Chester U., Pa., 1939; M.S., MIT, 1944; Ph.D., NYU, 1957. Mem. faculty Drexel U., Phila., 1946—, head dept. physics, 1963-70, dean Coll. Sci., 1970—; staff meteorologist WFIL-TV, Phila., 1947-71; cons. in field. Contbr. articles to tech. and popular publs. Served to capt. USAAF, 1942-45. Recipient Disting. Service award Chapel of Four Chaplains, Phila., 1967, Disting. Alumnus award Westchester U., 1968, Sci. and Tech. award City of Phila., 1974, Robert Morris award Welsh Soc., 1975. Fellow Am. Meteorol. Soc.; mem. Am. Inst. Med. Climatology (charter, bd. dirs. 1960—), Am. Acad. Forensic Sci., Am. Phys. Soc., Sigma Xi, Sigma Pi Sigma, Phi Kappa Phi. Republican. Methodist. Clubs: Cosmos (Washington); Spring Haven (Wallingford, Pa.); Port Royal (Hilton Head Island, S.C.). Home: 639 Niblick Ln Wallingford PA 19086 Office: Coll Sci Drexel U Philadelphia PA 19104

DAVIS, FRANCIS RAYMOND, priest; b. Washington, Feb. 10, 1920; s. Frank Raymond and Ruth Madeline (Donovan) D.; B.A., St. Bernard's Sem., Rochester, N.Y., 1941; M.L.S., Cath. U. Am., 1953. Ordained priest Roman Cath. Ch., 1945; asst. pastor St. Ambrose Ch., Rochester, 1945-50; prof. lit. St. Bernard's Sem., 1950-51, librarian, 1950-69, prof. speech., 1958-67; pastor Our Lady Lourdes Ch., Elmira, N.Y., 1969-78; pastor St. Mary's Ch., Dansville, N.Y., 1978-80, St. Patrick's Ch., Corning, N.Y., 1980—. Mem. Chemung county gen. edn. bd. Diocese of Rochester, 1971-78; mem. exec. com. Chemung County (N.Y.) Council Aging, 1972-76; mem. adv. com. Chemung County Office for Aging, 1973-78; mem. exec. com. Ecumenical Preaching Mission, 1977-78; bd. dirs. All Saints' Acad., Corning, 1986—, founder. Fellow Internat. Biog. Assn.; mem. ALA, Cath. Library Assn. (officer sem. sect. 1958-61), Ch. and Synagogue Library Assn. (nominating com. 1979), Elmira Vicinity Ministerial Assn. (officer 1972-73). Author articles and book revs. Home and Office: 274 Denison Pkwy E Corning NY 14830

DAVIS, FRANK TRADEWELL, JR., lawyer; b. Atlanta, Feb. 2, 1938; s. Frank T. and Sue (Burnett) D.; m. Winifred Storey, June 23, 1961; children: Frank, Frederick, Gordon. A.B., Princeton U., 1960; J.D., George Washington U., 1963; LL.M., Harvard U., 1964. Bar: Ga. 1963, U.S. Ct. Appeals (5th cir.) 1963, D.C. 1966, U.S. Supreme Ct. 1968, U.S. Ct. Appeals (11th cir.) 1982. Assoc. Hansell, Post Brandon & Dorsey, Atlanta, 1964-67; ptnr. Hansell & Post, Atlanta, 1968-77, 79-86, Long, Aldridge & Norman, 1986—; mng. ptnr., gen. counsel Pres.'s Reorgn. Project office of Pres., 1977-79; vis. instr. U. Ga. Law Sch., 1964-66, Ga. State U. Law Sch., 1988—. Author: Business Acquisitions, 1977, (2d edit.), 1982; contbr. articles to legal jours. Bd. dirs. Nat. Inst. Justice, 1980-81; bd. dirs. Westminster Schs., 1969—, chmn. bd. dirs., 1984—; sr. warden All Saints' Episcopal Ch., 1982; bd. dirs. Va. Sem., 1980—, exec. com., 1985—; mem. Atlanta Charter Commn.; chmn. Atlanta Crime Commn., 1979; mem. bd. councilors Carter Presdl. Ctr., 1988—. Served to lt. USNR, 1960-62. Mem. Am. Law Inst., Atlanta C. of C. (bd. dirs. 1975-77). Democrat. Clubs: Piedmont Driving (Atlanta); Chevy Chase (Md.). Lodge: Rotary (bd. dirs., sec. Atlanta chpt. 1988—). Home: 9 Nacoochee Pl NW Atlanta GA 30305 Office: 134 Peachtree St Atlanta GA 30303

DAVIS, HELEN NANCY MATSON (MRS. CHAUNCEY D. DAVIS), real estate broker, civic worker; b. Zanesville, Ohio, Nov. 18, 1905; d. Austin F. and Georgianna (Hale) Matson; grad. high sch.; m. Chauncey D. Davis, May 1, 1924; children—James Harvey, Robert Lee. Real estate broker, South Bend, Wash., 1964—. Chmn. Park Bd., South Bend, 1955—; ofcl. Pacific County Bicentennial Pageant, Dedication Ft. Columbia, 1959; trustee Pacific County Hist. Soc. Named Woman of Yr. Pacific County C. of C., 1949, 61. Mem. Nat. League Am. Pen Women, Dramatists Guild Inc., Propaelaeum Study Club, Chinook Indian Tribe (hon.), The Dramatist Guild N.Y., Nat. League Am. Pen Women, Delta Kappa Gamma (hon.). Republican. Methodist. Rebekah. Club: Garden (South Bend). Composer: Washington, My Home (ofcl. state song Wash.), 1959; Eliza and the Lumberjack (mus. play) (ofcl. territorial centennial play Wash.), 1954. Home: 606 W 2d St South Bend WA 98586 Office: 705 Robert Bush Dr South Bend WA 98586

DAVIS, HELENA LANG, human relations consultant, writer, psychotherapist; b. Richmond, Va., Sept. 21, 1942; d. Harold and Regina (Lang) Pfeffer; m. Richard Earl Davis, Dec. 18, 1966(div. 1988); 1 dau., Rebekah Caroline Beatty Davis. B.A., U. Md., 1965; secondary teaching credential San Francisco State U., 1972, postgrad. in Am. Indian edn., 1973-75; postgrad. in curriculum design, U. San Francisco, 1978-80; MA in Counseling U. San Francisco, 19887; cert. Psychosynthesis Tng. Program, 1986, advanced Psychosynthesis Tng. Program, 1987. Instr. Native Am. studies U. San Francisco, 1971-72; Emergency Sch. Aid Act reading coordinator San Francisco Unified Sch. Dist., 1973-75, chmn. native Am. sub-com., 1974; tchr. English and lang. arts Ramah Navajo High Sch., N.Mex., 1976; coordinator acad. support services U. San Francisco, 1979-80; fgn. expert East China Normal U., Shanghai, People's Republic China, 1980-81; dir. School Initiatives program Community Bd. Ctr. for Policy and Tng., San Francisco, 1982-85, assoc. dir., 1985-86; founder, exec. dir. Connections, 1986—; intern Cath. Schs. Family Counseling Program, U. San Francisco, 1987-88; cons. Human Rights Commn., San Francisco, 1973-74, Filipino Edn. Ctr., San Francisco, 1974-75, Title IV Am. Indian Edn. Project, San Francisco, 1974-75, J. Gary Mitchell Film Productions, 1984—, Paul Rupert Assocs., 1986—, Camp Thoreau-In-Vermont, 1985-86, British Columbia Justice Inst., 1985-86; curriculum cons. Chinese-Am. People's Friendship Assn., San Francisco, 1975-76; program cons. UN U. for Peace, Costa Rica, 1984; mem. Consortium on Peace Research, Edn. and Devel., 1984; adv. bd. Meadowlark Camp for Peace; dir. Alice B. Northrop Meml. Camp, 1987; program organizer Third Nat. Conf. on Peacemaking and Conflict Resolution, Denver, 1986; co-founder World Mediation Congress, 1985; mem. steering com. San Francisco Sch. Arts, 1986-87. Author: Conflict Resolution for Youth: An Experiential Approach, 1982; China Year, 1981; Indians in America's Past, 1971; author, editor: Conflict Manager Program Implementation and Training Manual, 1983; The Teacher as Trainer in Conflict Management Programs, 1984, (with Judith Bach) Birthing and Rebirthing Peace- Building Communities: Experiments in Social Psychosynthesis, 1988; producer, dir. video film: Mission: Possible, 1988. Contbr. articles to Profl. jours. Mem. Parents Coalition, 1984, M.H. deYoung Mus., 1978-84. Mem. Calif. Acad. Sci., Am. Soc. for Tng. and Devel., Nat. Assn. Mediators in Edn. (co-founder, steering com. 1984), Am. Assn. Psychosynthesis Practitioners (co-founder 1987), Calif. Assn. for Marriabe and Family Therapists, Mass. Assn. of Mental Health Practitioners, Am. Assn. for Counseling and Devel., Pi Lambda Theta (rec. sec. 1973-74, nat. conf. del. 1975), Phi Delta Kappa. Office: Connections PO Box Housatonic CA 01236

DAVIS, HENRY BARNARD, JR., lawyer; b. East Grand Rapids, Mich., June 3, 1923; s. Henry Barnard and Ethel Margaret (Turnbull) D.; m. Margaret Lees Wilson, Aug. 27, 1947; children—Caroline Dellenbusch, Laura Davis Jackson, George B. B.A., Yale U., 1945; J.D., U. Mich., 1950; LL.D., Olivet Coll., 1983. Bar: Mich. 1951; U.S. Dist. Ct. (we. dist.) Mich. 1956, U.S. Ct. Apls. (6th cir.) 1971, U.S. Supreme Ct. 1978. Assoc. Allaben, Wiarda, Hayes & Hewitt, 1951-52; ptnr. Hayes, Davis & Dellenbusch, Grand Rapids, 1952—. Mem. Kent County Bd. Commrs., 1968-72, Community Mental Health Bd., 1970—, past chmn.; trustee, sec. bd. Olivet Coll., 1965—; chair Grand Rapids Historic Preservation Com., 1977-79. Republican. Trustee, East Congregational Ch., 1979-81. Served with USAAF, 1943-

46; Philippines. ABA, Mich. Assn. Professions, Mich. Bar Assn., Grand Rapids Round Table (pres. 1969). Lodge: Masons. Home: 30 Mayfair Dr NE Grand Rapids MI 49503 Office: 535 Fountain St NE Grand Rapids MI 49503

DAVIS, HENRY RICHARD, commercial real estate company executive; b. Pahokee, Fla., Oct. 3, 1948; s. Henry Albert and Greta (Blechschmidt) D.; A.A., Palm Beach Jr. Coll., 1968; B.A., Fla. Atlantic U., 1969; m. Gail Ann Hayford, Oct. 28, 1972; children—Kyle Taylor, Brad Geoffrey. Merchandiser Walden Book Co. div. Carter Hawley Hale Stores, Inc., Stamford, Conn., asst. buyer, 1969-70, buyer, 1970-72, regional mgr., 1972-73, asst. dir. store ops., 1973-74, asst. dir. real estate, 1975-76, dir. real estate, 1976-79; v.p. leasing Pembrook Mgmt., N.Y.C., 1978-84; v.p., dir. leasing Corp. Property Investors, 1985—. Mem. exec. bd. Ridgefield Jaycees, 1976-77; mem. Ridgefield Republican Town Com., 1975-77, chmn. orgn. com., treas., 1976-77; justice of peace State of Conn., 1977-81; mem. bd. Norwalk Jr. Soccer ssn; mem. Fla. Atlantic U. Found. Mem. Internat. Council Shopping Centers, Am. Mgmt. Assn., Urban Land Inst., Order Ky. Cols., Phi Alpha Theta. Baptist. Club: Silvermine Golf. Home: 6 Cricklewood Ln Norwalk CT 06851 Office: 3 Dag Hammarskjold Plaza New York NY 10017

DAVIS, HERBERT HAYWOOD, JR., investment banker; b. Omaha, Mar. 23, 1924; s. Herbert H. and Olga (Metz) D.; m. Nell Evans, Feb. 17, 1945; children—Herbert H., Deborah Davis. B.C.E., Cornell U., 1948. chmn. bd. Weigh Tronix, Inc., Fairmont, Minn.; owner Miracle Hill Golf and Tennis Ctr.; dir. Chief Automotive System, Inc., Grand Island, Nebr., Arts Way Mfg., Armstrong, Iowa. Clubs: Omaha Country, Omaha Press; La Quinta Hotel Golf (Calif.), Thunderbird Country (Rancho Mirage, Calif.), Firethorn Golf (Lincoln, Nebr.). Home: 939 S 106th Pl Omaha NE 68114

DAVIS, JACQUELINE MARIE VINCENT (MRS. LOUIS REID DAVIS), child development educator, academic administrator; b. Birmingham, Ala.; d. Jud Fred and Marie (Yates) Vincent; m. Louis Reid Davis, July 17, 1943. A.B. cum laude, Birmingham So. Coll., 1943; M.A., Columbia, U., 1950; M.S., U. Ala., 1958, Ed.D., 1961; postgrad., U. Va., George Washington U. Tchr. Fork Union (Va.) Mil. Acad., 1943-46; tchr. Fork Union (Va.) Mil. Acad., Ft. Belvoir, Va., 1946-48; tchr., adminstrv. asst., supr. Quantica (Va.) Post schs., 1950-52; instr., prof. dept. child devel. and family life U. Ala. Sch. Home Econs., 1952-57, assoc. prof., 1957-67; prof. child devel., dir. U. Ala. Sch. Home Econs. (Child Devel. Ctr.), 1967—; mem. grad. council, adminstr. head start tng. program, dir. U. Ala. Sch. Home Econs. (Ala. Presch. Inst.), 1964—; mem. NASA scholarship selection bd. U. Ala., 1966; mem. Gov.'s Advisory Com. on Day Care, 1963-66, State Adv. Com. on Children and Youth, 1960—; coordinator Head Start supplementary tng. programs State of Ala. Contbr. articles to profl. jours. Adviser, mem. selection com. Tombigbee council Girl Scouts U.S.A., 1961-66; cons. Tuscaloosa Community Action Program, 1965-66; chmn. Ala. Advisory Com. Children and Youth, 1978—. Mem. Nat. Assn. for Edn. of Young Children (mem. planning bd. 1963-64), U.S. Nat. Com. for Early Childhood Edn., World Orgn. for Early Childhood Edn., Southeastern Council Family Relations, So. Assn. Children Under Six (pres. 1961, mem. exec. bd. 1961—, chmn. 19th ann. conf.), Ala. Assn. Children Under Six (pres. 1963-64), Ala. Home Econs. Assn. (chmn. profl. sect. family life and child devel. 1963—, v.p. mem. governing bd. 1969-70), Comparative Edn. Soc., NEA, Am. Home Econs. Assn., Phi Beta Kappa, Kappa Delta Pi, Kappa Delta Epsilon. Methodist. Home: 47 Guilds Wood Tuscaloosa AL 35401 Office: PO Box 1211 University AL 35486

DAVIS, JERROLD CALVIN, artist; b. Chico, Calif., Nov. 2, 1926; s. Charles R. and Moira E. (Ryan) D.; M.A., student of John Haley and Felix Ruvolo, U. Calif., Berkeley, 1953. One-man shows of paintings include: Instituto Brazil Estados Unidos, Rio de Janeiro, 1950, Calif. Palace of Legion of Honor, San Francisco, 1958, Carmen Waugh Gallery, Santiago de Chile, 1962, Newport Harbor (Calif.) Art Mus., 1973, Richmond (Calif.) Art Center, 1980; group shows include: Nat. Salon of Brazil, 1950, Sao Paulo (Brazil) Bienale, 1951, Pitts. Internat., 1958, U. Ill., Urbana, 1959, 61, 63, Calif. Palace of Legion of Honor, 1960, 61, 63, Amon Carter Mus., Ft. Worth, 1962, UCLA Art Gallery, 1964, Los Angeles County Mus., 1965, U. Ariz., Tucson, 1967, Newport Harbor Art Mus., 1981; represented in permanent collections: Carnegie Inst., Pitts., Santa Barbara (Calif.) Mus., Flint (Mich.) Inst. Art, San Francisco Mus. Modern Art. Recipient Bronze medal award Nat. Salon of Brazil, 1951, Calif. Palace of Legion of Honor award, 1960, 62; Sigmund Martin Heller fellow, 1953, Guggenheim fellow, 1959. Address: 66 Twain Ave Berkeley CA 94708

DAVIS, JESSE EDWIN, JR., wood products executive; b. Atlanta, Feb. 4, 1910; s. Jesse Edwin and Eufa (Swilling) D.; B.S., Ga. Sch. Tech., 1933; LL.B., Woodrow Wilson Coll., 1937; m. Sarah Etta Fitzpatrick, Apr. 7, 1938; children—Carolyn W. (Mrs. Edward W. Riser), Sarah K. (Mrs. M. Rick Taylor), Jesse Edwin III, Marion H. Admitted to Ga. bar, 1937; sales rep. Atlantic Steel Co., 1937-43, Tidewater Supply Co., 1943-49; v.p., treas. Thackston-Davis Supply, 1949-59; with Marwin Co., Columbia, S.C., 1959—, chmn. bd., treas., 1959—; chmn. bd. Apollo Estates, Columbia. Mem. Columbia Com. of 100. Chmn. religious work com. Columbia YMCA, 1956—, bd. dirs.; trustee United Community Services. Mem. Sigma Chi, Alpha Kappa Psi, Pi Delta Epsilon. Baptist (deacon). Mason (Shriner), Lion. Home: 4829 Carter Hill Rd Columbia SC 29206 Office: PO Box 9126 Atlas Rd Columbia SC 29290

DAVIS, JOANNE HERRING, foreign service officer, consultant; b. San Antonio; d. W. Dunlap and Maelan McGill (Johnson); m. Robert R. Herring (dec.); children—Beau S. King, Robin D. King; m. Lloyd K. Davis. Ed., U. Tex. TV talk show hostess, editor Sta. KHOU TV, Houston, 1963-72, Sta. KPRC-TV, Houston, 1973-75; hon. consul gen. Pakistan and Morocco, Houston, 1973—; cons. LTV, WEDTECH, CONTRAVES; bd. dirs. First Bank Houston, Coronado Oil Co., Kittinger Furniture, Internat. Films Prodns. Inc.; hostess numerous fgn. ministers, princes, ambassadors including Kings of Sweden, Jordan, Morocco, Pres. of Egypt, Pres. of Pakistan, Shah of Iran, Prime Minister of Belgium, Houston. Knighted, King of Belgium; Decorated, Pres. Pakistan. Bd. dirs. Lindbergh Fund, Moroccan Am. Found., Houston Ballet, Houston Youth Symphony. Republican. Presbyterian. Clubs: Lyford Cay; Met. (N.Y.C.); Rivers Oaks Country, Ramada, Houston.

DAVIS, JOHN TERRANCE, surgeon; b. Phila., Apr. 11, 1941; s. John Warren and Jean (MacClelland) D.; B.A., Williams Coll., 1963; M.D., U. Pa., 1967; m. Barbara Brewer, July 10, 1965; children—James Melvin, John Gregory. Intern, Hosp. of U. Pa., Phila., 1968, resident in surgery Grad. Hosp., 1968-73, resident in cardiothoracic surgery, 1975; mem. faculty Med. Coll. Ohio, Toledo, 1975—, assoc. prof. surgery, chief div. thoracic and cardiovascular surgery, 1979-88, prof. surgery, 1988; also assoc. prof. pediatrics; chief of staff Med. Coll. Hosps., 1986-88. Fellow A.C.S.; mem. Toledo Surg. Soc. (pres. 1985-86), Soc. Thoracic Surgery, Am. Assn. Thoracic Surgery. Sigma Xi. Author papers in field. Office: CS 10008 Toledo OH 43699

DAVIS, L(LOYD) WAYNE, research company executive; b. Medicine Lodge, Kans., July 16, 1929; s. Lloyd and Edith Elda (Furnas) D.; B.S. in Engring. Physics (Summerfield scholar), U. Kans., 1952; M.S. in Elec. Engring. (fellow), U. N.Mex., 1959; m. Betty Louise Pyke, Sept. 7, 1963; 1 son, William W.; children by previous marriage—Robert L., Cheryl S. Staff mem. systems analysis dept. Sandia Corp., Albuquerque, 1952-56, cons., 1956-57; research physicist Dikewood Corp., Albuquerque, 1957-60, sr. research physicist, 1960-64, head weapons effects div., 1964-67, dep. tech. dir., 1967-69, asst. v.p., 1969-72, sec., 1970-80, dir., 1971-82, v.p., 1972-77, sr. v.p., 1977-80, pres., chmn. bd., 1980-82; v.p. Kaman Scis. Corp., gen. mgr. Dikewood Div., Albuquerque, 1982-83; sci. cons., 1983—. Mem. IEEE (sr.), Am. Phys. Soc. (S.E. sect.), Sigma Xi, Phi Kappa Phi, Tau Beta Pi, Sigma Tau, Sigma Pi Sigma, Kappa Mu Epsilon, Beta Gamma Sigma, Delta Sigma Pi, Sigma Chi. Republican. Mem. Christian Ch. Research on nuclear weapons effects and phenomenology effects on personnel and complex mil. systems; developed urban nuclear-casualty prediction model for high-yield nuclear bursts from Japanese data base over many years; presented paper in Eng. on Japanese Blast Casualty Experience at Brit. Home Office (Govt.) request, 1984. Home: 4411 Altura Ave NE Albuquerque NM 87110

DAVIS, MARK HEZEKIAH, JR., electrical engineer; b. Knoxville, Tenn., Oct. 5, 1948; s. Mark Hezekiah and Grace Carson (Owens) D.; m. Susan Nakamura, July 14, 1977; 1 dau.: Michelle Grace. B.S. in E.E, U. Tenn., 1972, M.S., 1973. Devel. engr. Westinghouse Electric Corp.-U.S. AEC, Pitts. and Oakridge, 1969-76; sr. research engr. N.L. Petroleum Service, Houston, 1977-79; mgr. research and devel. Advanced Ocean Systems div. Hydril Corp., Houston, 1980-81; engring. mgr. Schlumberger Corp., Sugarland, Tex., 1981-82; dir. electronics devel. Tech. for Energy Corp., Knoxville, Tenn., 1982-84; mgr. digital signal processing N.E.C. Electronics, Mountain View, Calif., 1984—. Pres. N.W. Houston United Civic Assn., 1980-81. Robert Miller scholar, 1971; U. Tenn. Nat. Alumni scholar, 1972; U.S. AEC grantee, 1973. Mem. IEEE (sr.), Am. Soc. Engring. Edn., Optical Soc. Am., Electro-Chem. Soc., Marine Tech. Soc., Soc. Photo-Optical Instrumentation Engrs. Current Work: Fiber optic sensors and communications systems and high temperature electronics in geosci. Subspecialties: Ocean engineering; Fiber optics. Home: PO Box 118 Knoxville TN 37901 Office: NEC Electronics Mountain View CA 94035

DAVIS, MARTIN S., diversified company executive; b. N.Y.C. With Samuel Goldwyn Prodns., N.Y.C., 1947-55, Allied Artists Pictures Corp. N.Y.C., 1955-58; with Paramount Pictures Corp., N.Y.C., 1958-69, v.p., 1962-66, exec. v.p., chief operating officer, mem. exec. com., dir., 1966-69; sr. v.p. Gulf & Western, Inc., 1969-74, exec. v.p., mem. exec. com., from 1974, chmn. and chief exec. officer, 1983—, also dir.; bd. dirs. Primeriera Corp., N.Y.C. Ptnrship. Bd. dirs. Primerica Corp., Nat. Multiple Sclerosis Soc., John Jay Coll. Criminal Justice; bd. trustees Carnegie Hall, Com. for Econ. Devel., Fordham U. Served with AUS, 1943-46. Club: Economic (N.Y.) (bd. trustees). Office: Gulf and Western Inc 1 Gulf and Western Plaza New York NY 10023

DAVIS, MARVIN ARNOLD, manufacturing company executive; b. St. Louis, Nov. 16, 1937; s. Sam and Pauline (Neuman) D.; m. Trudy Brenda Rein, Aug. 11, 1968; children: Julie, Jeffrey. BS in Chem. Engring., WashingtonU., St. Louis, 1959; MBA in Fin.and Mktg., WashingtonU., 1966. Lead engr. Standard Oil Calif., San Francisco, 1962-64; product mgr. Shell Chem. Co., N.Y.C., 1966-69; group controller Pfizer, Inc., N.Y.C., 1969-75; exec. v.p. Good Hope Industries, New Orleans, 1975-77; pres., chief exec. officer Reed Industries, Inc., Stone Mountain, Ga., 1978—; pres. Sentrex Ltd., Atlanta, 1977-82; v.p. Sentry Ins., 1982-84; cons. Grisanti Galef Goldress, 1984—; instr. Fairleigh Dickinson U., 1968-71; lectr. Washington U., 1966, 77; also cons. Author: The Profit Prescription, 1985, Turnaround, 1987. Active Seville Recreation Assn. Served to lt. USNR, 1959-62. Recipient scholarship Washington U., 1959, fellow, 1968. Mem. DeKalb C. of C., Beta Gamma Sigma, Alpha Chi Sigma. Jewish. Club: Horseshoe Bend Country. Office: 19701 Hamilton Ave Torrance CA 90502-1335

DAVIS, MILTON WICKERS, JR., chemical engineer, educator; b. Frederick, Md., Apr. 5, 1923; s. Milton Wickers and Elizabeth Howard Griffith (Wood) D.; m. Roberta B. McIntyre, Dec. 18, 1948; 1 child, Gaither Griffith; m. Jane Crayton, May 21, 1955; 1 son, Richard Render; m. Harriett P. Ackerman, Dec. 24, 1977. B.E., Johns Hopkins U., 1943; M.S., U. Calif.-Berkeley, 1949, Ph.D., 1951. Research asst. U. Calif. Radiation Lab., 1947-50; research engr. atomic energy div. duPont Co., Wilmington, Del., 1950-54; research supr. duPont Co. (Savannah River plant), Aiken, S.C., 1954-62; Weisiger prof. chem. engring. U. S.C., Columbia, 1962—. Contbr.: Chemical Processing of Nuclear Fuels, 1970; patentee catalyzed hydrogenation and dehydrogenation processes, 1985, extraction Cesium and Strontium from nuclear waste, 1985, catalysts for synthesis of ammonia, 1986. Served to lt. USNR, 1943-46, PTO. Fellow Am. Inst. Chem. Engrs.; mem. Am. Chem. Soc., Md. Soc. War of 1812, Delta Phi. Episcopalian. Clubs: Sea Pines, Island (Hilton Head Island, S.C.). Address: PO Box 242 Columbia SC 29202

DAVIS, MINNIE DELORES, consultant; b. Laurens, S.C., Oct. 27, 1945; d. John Ed and Minnie Florie (Watts) D. BA, No. Ill. U., 1967; MBA, U. Chgo., 1973. Tchr. pub. schs., Chgo., 1967-72; internal auditor Container Corp. Am., Chgo., 1973-74; sr. corp. auditor NCR Corp., Dayton, Ohio, 1974-76; project specialist J.I. Case Co., Racine, Wis., 1976-79, sr. fin. analyst, 1979-81; dir. strategic planning Peoples Gas Co., Council Bluffs, Iowa, 1981-84; sr. cons. Arthur D. Little Inc., Washington, 1984-88; owner Watts Jendy Cons., 1988—; vis. prof. Black Exec. Exchange Program. Chmn. family services com. United Way, Omaha, 1984, steering com. 1983-84; bd. dirs. Racine area United Way, 1979-81; mem. Foster Care Rev. Bd., Racine County, 1978-80, Ft. Valley Coll. Bus. Adv. Bd., Ga., 1979-81. Awarded key to city Office of the Mayor, Daytona Beach, Fla., 1979. Mem. Nat. Council Negro Women, The Planning Forum (bd. dirs. capital chpt. 1987—), Soc. Exec. and Profl. Women, Nat. Assn. Female Execs., Strategic Mgmt. Soc., Black MBA Assn., Eta Phi Beta Gamma. Baptist. Club: SouthEast Service. Home: 2701 Park Ctr Dr B1009 Alexandria VA 22302

DAVIS, MULLER, lawyer; b. Chgo., Apr. 23, 1935; s. Benjamin B. and Janice (Muller) D.; m. Jane Lynn Strauss, Dec. 28, 1963; children: Melissa Jane, Muller, Joseph Jeffrey. Grad. with honors, Phillips Exeter (N.H.) Acad., 1953; B.A. magna cum laude, Yale U., 1957; J.D., Harvard U., 1960. Bar: Ill. 1960, U.S. Dist. Ct. (no. dist.) Ill. 1961. Practice law Chgo., 1960—; assoc. Jenner & Block, 1960-67; ptnr. Davis, Friedman, Zavett, Kane & MacRae, 1967—; lectr. continuing legal edn., matrimonial law and litigation Legal adviser Michael Reese Med. Research Inst. Council, 1967-82. Contbr. articles to law jours.; author (with Sherman C. Feinstein) The Parental Couple in a Successful Divorce; mem. editorial bd. Equitable Distbn. Jour., 1984—. Bd. dirs. Infant Welfare Soc., 1975—, pres., 1978-82. Served to capt. U.S. Army, Ill. N.G., 1960-67. Fellow Am. Acad. Matrimonial Lawyers, Am. Bar Found.; mem. Fed. Bar Assn., ABA, Ill. Bar Assn., Chgo. Bar Assn. (matrimonial com., sec. civil practice com. 1979-80, vice chmn. 1980-81, chmn. 1981-82), Chgo. Estate Planning Council, Law Club Chgo. Republican. Jewish. Clubs: Tavern, Lake Shore Country. Home: 1020 E Westleigh Rd Lake Forest IL 60045 Office: 140 S Dearborn St Chicago IL 60603

DAVIS, PAMELA CRALLE, financial executive; b. Norfolk, Va., June 4, 1945; d. Ryland Paul and Kathleen (Cralle) Davis; BA, Fla. State U., 1966; MBA, NYU, 1975; student Mary Baldwin Coll., 1963-64. Stewardess, Delta Air Lines, Inc., Atlanta, Houston, Miami, 1967-70, sales, N.Y.C., 1970-72, mgr., 1972-74; fin. analyst Student Loan Mktg. Assn., Washington, 1975-77, mgr. corp. planning, 1977-79, dir. corp. planning, 1979-80; v.p. mktg. Inter-science Group, Inc., 1980-81; pres. Valkyrie Fin. Group, Ltd., 1981—. Advisor, McLean Community Center, Fairfax County Council of Arts; bd. dirs. Cybron Corp., Entrepreneurship Inst. Marcus Nadler fellow, 1974; NYU Univ. Tuition scholar, 1974. Mem. N. Am. Soc. Corp. Planning (v.p. Washington chpt. 1979-80), Kappa Kappa Gamma, Beta Gamma Sigma. Club: NYU. Home: 2004 Freedom Ln Falls Church VA 22043

DAVIS, RALPH, research chemist; b. Huntington, Ind., Aug. 14, 1917; s. Floyd Anderson and Rozella (Burton) D.; m. Muriel Evelyn Wait, Aug. 11, 1940 (dec. 1975); children—Robert S., Norman W. B.A., Huntington Coll., 1939; M.A., Ind. U., 1942. Tchr. Leo High Sch., Ind., 1939-41; research asst. in chemistry Ind. U., Bloomington, 1941-42; analytical chemist Dow Chem. Co., Midland, Mich., 1942-49, chem. researcher, 1949-82, ret. 1982. Patentee in field of fluorine and halogen chemistry. Contbr. articles to sci. jours. Active Boy Scouts Am., 1950-63. Mem. Am. Chem. Soc., AAAS, Sigma Xi. Republican. Methodist. Avocations: gardening; photography. Address: 1160 Poseyville Rd R7 Midland MI 48640

DAVIS, REBECCA WING, accountant; b. Provo, Utah, Apr. 23, 1953; d. Sherman William and Martha Elayne (Hinckley) W.; m. Michael Whitaker Davis, Aug. 11, 1983; children: Margaret Jeanne, Joseph Michael, Jessica Ann. Student Brigham Young U., 1971-72; B.S., U. Utah, 1976, M.B.A., 1982. Typist, pool supr. Haskins & Sells, Salt Lake City, 1977-78; real estate salesperson Ken Mayne Inc., Salt Lake City, 1978-79; exec. sec. Eimco PMD, Salt Lake City, 1979-80; legal sec. Richard G. Cook, P.C., Salt Lake City, 1980; fin. analyst E-Systems, Inc., Salt Lake City, 1982-83; acct. U. Utah, Salt Lake City, 1983—. Campaign worker Frances Farley for Congress, Salt Lake City, 1982. Mem. Women in Communications. Democrat.

DAVIS, ROBERT ALDINE, college president; b. Broxton, Ga., June 15, 1928; s. Robert Aldine and Leda Estelle (Palmer) D.; m. Phyllis Clough, Aug. 5, 1955; children: Robert Aldine III, Phyllis Blaine, Palmer Clough. B.B.A., U. Ga., 1949; M.Div., Emory U., 1952; S.T.M., Yale U., 1959; D.D., Pfeiffer Coll., N.C., 1970; L.H.D., Westmar Coll., 1977. Ordained to ministry United Methodist Ch., 1952; dir. Wesley Found., Va. Poly. Inst., Blacksburg, 1952-59, Ga. Inst. Tech., Atlanta, 1959-62; assoc. dir. bd. higher edn. United Meth. Ch., Nashville, 1962-69; pres. Brevard (N.C.) Coll., 1969-76, Fla. So. Coll., Lakeland, 1976—; mem. univ. senate United Meth. Ch.; pres. Fla. Ind. Colls. Fund., 1978-80; mem. adv. com. bd. govs. U. N.C., 1972-76; sec. N.C. Assn. Ind. Coll., 1970-74; mem. 2d Dist. Ct. Appeal Jud. Nominating Com., 1982-86. Pres. Brevard United Way, 1970, Brevard C. of C., 1975; bd. dirs. Lakeland YMCA, 1976-79; mem. Fla. Research and Devel. Com.; trustee Polk Mus. Art, 1986—. Danforth scholar, 1958-59; named Young Man of Yr. Blacksburg C. of C., 1957, mem. Fla. Council of 100, 1979—; recipient Outstanding Service award Brevard C. of C., 1975. Mem. Nat. Assn. Ind. Colls. and Univs., Ind. Colls. and Univs. Fla. (pres. 1980-82, 87—); Fla. Assn. Colls. and Univs. (pres. 1985-87); Mem. Internat. Assn. Univ. Pres. (dir. N.Am. council), Lakeland C. of C. (dir. 1977—), Omicron Delta Kappa, Phi Kappa Phi, Beta Gamma Sigma. Club: Rotary (past pres. Brevard). Office: Fla Southern Coll Lakeland FL 33801

DAVIS, ROBERT D., grocery store chain executive; b. 1931; married. Grad., U. Fla., 1953. With Winn-Dixie Stores, Inc., Jacksonville, Fla., 1955—, asst. treas. and sec., 1961-65, v.p. fin., from 1965, vice-chmn., 1982-83, chmn., chief fin. officer, 1983—, also bd. dirs. Served with U.S. Army, 1953-55. Office: Winn-Dixie Stores Inc 5050 Edgewood Ct Jacksonville FL 32203 *

DAVIS, ROBERT H., financial executive; b. Phila., Mar. 26, 1943; student Los Angeles Valley Coll., 1965-67, Alexander Hamilton Inst., 1965-68, Grad. Sch. of Credit and Fin. Mgmt., Stanford U., 1977-80, Pepperdine U., 1981; 1 dau., Michelle R. Fin. cons., Montepelier, Idaho, 1976-78; asst. controller, credit mgr. Wyo. Machinery Co., Casper, 1978-79; controller/sec.-treas., dir. John E. Burns Drilling Co., Casper, 1979—; comptroller, v.p. Philip Crosby Assocs., Inc., Winter Park, Fla., 1984—; v.p., treas. Crosby Assocs. Internat., Inc., Winter Park, Fla.; mgmt/ cons. and legal investigator, Langley, Wash., fin. cons. Western Energy Co., Huey's Smoked Meats, Nashville, Trans-Equip., Casper, Three Percent, Inc., Riverton, Wyo., 1979-80. Adv. bd. dirs. Highland Park Community Ch., 1980—. Served with USNR, 1961-63. Mem. Nat. Assn. Credit Mgmt. (state rep. 1979, 80, founder, chmn. Casper Credit Group), Credit Mgrs. Assn. So. Calif. (dir. bus. re-orgn. and bankruptcy 1973-74), Credit Research Found., Am. Mgmt. Assn., Practicing Law Inst. (assoc.), Stanford U. Alumni Assn., Internat. Platform Assn. Club: Order of Demolay (sr. award 1960). Author: Leasing as a Secondary Source of Financing in the Heavy Equipment Industry.

DAVIS, RONALD FRANKLIN, mechanical engineer, real estate broker; b. Asheville, N.C., June 17, 1943; s. Edgar Franklin and Geneva Snow (Kuykendall) D.; m. Karen Starleaf, Aug. 2, 1980. BS in Aerospace Engring., N.C. State U., 1968; postgrad. in aerospace engring. U. Tenn. Space Inst., Tullahoma, 1968-70; MBA, U. So. Calif., 1985. Engring. scientist/specialist McDonnell Douglas Astronautics Co., Huntington Beach, Calif., 1970-80; sr. engr. Interstate Electronics Corp., Anaheim, Calif., 1980-81; engring. specialist Ford Aerospace & Communications Co., Newport Beach, Calif., 1981-85; dep. program mgr. JWP Communication Mfg. Co., Long Beach, Calif., 1985-87; mgr., systems engr. BDM Corp., Tacoma, Wash., 1987-88; sr. program mgr. ELDEC Corp., Lynnwood, Wash., 1988—. Author: (with K. Starleaf) Microkey, 1982. Served with USAF, 1961-65. Mem. AIAA, Am. Mgmt. Assn. Office: ELDEC Corp PO Box 100 Lynnwood WA 98046-0100

DAVIS, RUTH MARGARET (MRS. BENJAMIN FRANKLIN LOHR), former government official, business executive; b. Sharpsville, Pa., Oct. 19, 1928; d. W. George and Mary Anna (Ackermann) D.; m. Benjamin F. Lohr, Apr. 29, 1961. B.A., Am. U., 1950; M.A., U. Md., 1952, Ph.D., 1955. Statistician FAO, UN, Washington, 1946-49; mathematician Nat. Bur. Standards, 1950-51; head operations research div. David Taylor Model Basin, 1955-61; staff asst. Office Dir. Def. Research and Engring., Dept. Def., 1961-67; asso. dir. research and devel. Nat. Library Medicine, 1967-68; dir. Lister Hill Nat. Center for Biomed. Communications, 1968-70; dir. Inst. for Computer Scis. and Tech., Nat. Bur. Standards, 1970-77; dep. undersec. def. for research and engring. 1977-79; asst. sec. resource applications U.S. Dept. Energy, 1979-81; pres. Pymatuning Group Inc., 1981—; bd. dirs. Control Data Corp., United Telecommunications Inc., Air Products and Chems., Varian Assocs., BTG, Inc., Premark Internat., Inc., Prin. Fin. Group, Ins.; trustee Consol. Edison Co. of N.Y., Aerospace Corp.; lectr. U. Md., 1955-57, Am. U., 1957-58; vis. prof. computer sci. U. Pa., 1969-72; adj. prof. U. Pitts.; cons. Office Naval Research, Washington, 1957-58; mem. Md. Gov.'s Sci. Adv. Council, 1971-77; chmn. nat. adv. council Electric Power Research Inst., 1975-76. Contbr. articles to profl. jours. Trustee Inst. Def. Analysis; bd. visitors Cath. U. Am.; adv. bd. U. Calif.-Berkeley Sch. Engring. Recipient Rockefeller Tech. Mgmt. award, 1973; Fed. Woman of Yr. award, 1973; Systems Profl. of Yr. award, 1973; Computer Sci. Man of Yr. award, 1979; Disting. Service medal Dept. Def., 1979; Disting. Service medal Dept. Energy, 1981; gold medal Dept. Energy, 1981; Ada A. Lovelace award, 1984. Fellow AIAA, Soc. for Info. Display; mem. AAAS, Am. Math Soc., Math Assn. Am., Nat. Acad. Engring., Nat. Acad. Pub. Adminstrn., Washington Philos. Soc., Phi Kappa Phi, Sigma Pi Sigma. Office: Pymatuning Group Inc 2000 N 15th St Suite 707 Arlington VA 22201

DAVIS, SHIRLEY CAROL SPENCE, nurse; b. Drexel Hill, Pa., Sept. 8, 1938; d. William Lloyd and Hilda Irene (Marshall) Spence; m. Davis Louis Davis, Feb. 6, 1960 (dec. May 1979); 1 son, David Louis. Diploma in nursing Orange Meml. Hosp., 1959; student in nursing Lake Superior State Coll., 1977-78; BS in Nursing, U. South Fla., 1981, MS in Nursing, 1985. Cert. critical care RN. Operating room nurse Eastern Maine Gen. Hosp., Bangor, 1960-62, S. Community Hosp., Oklahoma City, 1972-75; staff nurse recovery room float team Doctors Hosp., Shreveport, La., 1969-70; infectious care unit nurse Bayfront Med. Ctr., St. Petersburg, Fla., 1970-71, staff nurse float team to med./surg./neurol. units, 1978-85, James A. Haley VA Hosp., Tampa, Fla., 1985—, Fla. Surg. Intensive Care, 1985. Vol., Family Services, Scott AFB, Ill., 1975-77, ARC, Scott AFB, Ill., 1975-77. Mem. Am. Nurses Assn., Fla. Nurses Assn., Am. Heart Assn., Sigma Theta Tau. Republican. Methodist. Clubs: Squadron Wives (Barksdale AFB) (treas. 1965-66), Officers' Wives. Home: 30 Sycamore Ct Palm Harbor FL 33563 Office: James A Haley VA Hosp 13000 Bruce B Downs Blvd Tampa FL 33612

DAVIS, STANLEY CLINTON, government association commissioner; b. London, Dec. 6, 1928; s. Sidney and Lily (Levine) D.; m. Frances Jane Lucas, 1954; four children. LLB, London U., 1950. Mem. Hackney Borough Council, London, 1959-71, mayor, 1968-69; mem. parliament Hackney Cen., London, 1970-83; parliamentary undersec. of state Dept. Trade, London, 1974-79; opposition spokesman for trade Brit. House Commons, London, 1979-81, opposition spokesman for fgn. affairs, 1981-83; mem. Commn. of the European Communities, Brussels, Belgium, 1985-88. Pres. Hackney br. Multiple Sclerosis Soc., London, 1968—; mem. bd. deps. Brit. Jews, London, 1972-74, 79-84; chmn. adv. com. Pollution of the Sea, London, 1984-85. Mem. Assn. Profl. Exec. Clerical and Computer Staff, Nat. Union of Marine, Aviation and Shipping Transport Officers (hon.), Council of Justice (Brit. sect. Internat. Commn. Jurists, hon.), Law Soc. (mem. parliamentary relations sub-com. 1979-83). Jewish. Clubs: Rotary, Reform (London). Office: Care Commn of the European Communities, 200 rue de la Loi, 1049 Brussels Belgium

DAVIS, STANLEY NELSON, hydrologist, educator; b. Rio de Janeiro, Brazil, Aug. 6, 1924; s. Nelson Caryl and Mary Faye (Caulkins) D.; m. Barbara Jean Wickham, Apr. 14, 1949 (div.); children: Gerald Nelson, Ruth Ann, Darlene Grace, Randall Wayne, Betty Jean, Nancy Faye.; m. Augusta G. Felty, Feb. 12, 1982; children—Tara Devi, Locana Kamala. B.S. in Geology, U. Nev., 1949; M.S., U. Kans., 1951; Ph.D., Yale, 1955. Geologist U.S. Bur. Reclamation, 1949, Mo. Geol. Survey, 1952, 53, 55; instr. U. Rochester, 1953-54; mem. faculty Stanford, 1954-67, prof. geology, 1965-67; prof. geology U. Mo., 1967-73, chmn. dept., 1969-72; asso. dean Coll. Arts and Scis., 1972-73; prof. geology Ind. U., Bloomington, 1973-75; prof. hydrology U. Ariz., Tucson, 1975—; head dept. hydrology and water resources U. Ariz., 1975-79; Vis. prof. U. Chile, Santiago, 1960-61; tchr.

Bowling Green U., summer 1963, Princeton, summer 1965, U. Hawaii, fall 1966; instr. U. Oriente in Venezuela, summer 1967-68, 72; lectr. Am. Geol. Inst.; mem. East Greenland Expdn., Arctic Inst. N. Am., summer 1959; cons. to govt. and industry, 1955—. Author: Hidrogeologia, 1961, (with R.M. DeWiest) Hydrogeology, 1966, (with P. Reitan and R. Pestrong) Geology, Our Physical Environment, 1976; also articles. Served with AUS, 1943-46, PTO. Fellow Geol. Soc. Am., AAAS; mem. Assn. Ground Water Scientists and Engrs., Am. Geophys. Union, Assn. Engring. Geologists, Soc. Econ. Paleontologists and Mineralogists, Nat. Water Resources Assn., Sigma Xi. Home: 6540 W Box Canyon Dr Tucson AZ 85745 Office: Dept Hydrology and Water Resources U Ariz Tucson AZ 85721

DAVIS, SUSAN LYNN RABINOWITZ, psychiat. social worker, family therapist, trainer; b. Bklyn., Feb. 27, 1944; d. Murray and Jeanette (Baumgarten) Rabinowitz; B.A., Conn. Coll. for Women, 1964; M.S.S. (NIMH grantee), Bryn Mawr Coll., 1968; m. Donald Irvin Davis, Aug. 16, 1964; children—Kenneth Bernard, Joshua Ian. Caseworker, Phila. State Reception Center, Phila. Gen. Hosp., 1965-66; field work Eastern Pa. Psychiat. Inst., Phila., 1966-67, Child Devel. Center, Bryn Mawr Coll., 1967-68; social worker Mental Devel. Center, Case Western Res. U., 1968-69; clin. instr. Northwestern U. Med. Sch., 1969-70; co-leader parent-student group U. Chgo. Lab. Schs., 1972; trainee in family therapy Family Therapy Inst. Washington, 1975-76; pvt. practice family therapy, Alexandria, Va., 1972-78; co-founder, asso. dir. Family Therapy Inst. Alexandria 1978—; developer, co-dir. Habit Mgmt. Workshops, Alexandria, 1981—; cons. local schs.; workshop presenter and panelist, local, nat., internat. mental health meetings; trainer Neurolinguistic Programming; faculty Vir. Poly. Inst. Co-chmn. Com. To Assess Future of Burgundy Farm Sch., Alexandria, 1977-78; active in campaigning for polit. candidates. Lic. social worker, Md., Va.; cert. neurolinguistic programming. Fellow Am. Orthopsychiat. Assn.; mem. Internat. Physicians for Prevention of Nuclear War, Nat. Assn. Social Workers, Acad. Cert. Social Workers, Am. Family Therapy Assn., LWV, NOW, Center for Study Democratic Instns., Common Cause. Contbr. articles to profl. jours. Home: 7805 Elba Rd Alexandria VA 22306 Office: 220 S Washington St Alexandria VA 22314

DAVIS, VIRGINIA MARIE, financial analyst, consultant; b. Chgo., Mar. 17, 1947; d. Robert Frank and Verne J. (Van Cata) Davis; divorced; children: Jack R. R. Barnette, Christopher D. M. Barnette, David T. J. Neuburger. Student Moorpark Coll., Calif., 1984-86. Ins. lic., Calif.; ordained to ministry Temple of Light, 1977. Sales mgr. Grand Plaza Hotel, Rosemont, Ill., 1975-77; pastor, founder God's House, Evanston, Ill., 1977-80; athletics bus. mgr. Pepperdine U., Malibu, Calif., 1980-82, budget and planning analyst, 1984-87; mktg. rep. GNA, Long Beach, Calif., 1987—; field underwriter N.Y. Life Ins. and Annuity Corp. Cons., Calif., 1984-87; founder budget control assistance co. My Manager, 1986; mgmt. cons. Checkbook, Thousand Oaks, Calif., 1984—; dir., founder Ins.. Seminars, Ventury County, Calif., 1984-85; cons. Farmers Ins., Simi Valley, Calif., 1985-86; dir., lectr. Alternative Med. Treatment, 1977-78. Author: Herbology, 1976. Com. chairperson Ventura council Boy Scouts Am., 1982-84; pres., founder Pepperdine Hiker's Club, 1985-86; affirmative action adv. com. Pepperdine U., 1985-87, sec., 1987, officer, 1986-87. Recipient Vol. of Yr. award Boy Scouts Am. Troop 799, 1982-84; State of Ill. scholar, 1965; Swedish Covenant Hosp., 1965. Mem. Nat. Assn. Life Underwriters. Republican. Club: Toastmasters (Malibu, Calif.)(adminstv. v.p. 1987). Lodge: Zonta (asst. treas. and budget chairperson local club 1984). Avocations: cross country hiking; herbology; geology.

DAVIS, WANDA ROSE, lawyer; b. Lampasas, Tex., Oct. 4, 1937; d. Ellis DeWitt and Julia Doris (Rose) Cockrell; m. Richard Andrew Fulcher, May 9, 1959 (div. 1969); 1 child, Greg Ellis; m. Edwin Leon Davis, Jan. 14, 1973 (div. 1985). BBA, U. Tex., 1959, JD, 1971. Bar: Tex. 1971, Colo. 1981, U.S. Dist. Ct. (no. dist.) Tex. 1972, U.S. Dist. Ct. Colo. 1981, U.S. Ct. Appeals (10th cir. 1981, U.S. Supreme Ct. 1976. Atty. Atlantic Richfield Co., Dallas, 1971; assoc. firm Crocker & Murphy, Dallas, 1971-72; prin. Wanda Davis, Atty. at Law, Dallas, 1972-73; ptnr. firm Davis & Davis Inc., Dallas, 1973-75; atty. adviser HUD, Dallas, 1974-75, Air Force Acctg. and Fin. Ctr., Denver, 1976—; co-chmn. regional Profl. Devel. Inst., Am. Soc. Mil. Comptrollers, Colorado Springs, Colo., 1982; chmn. Lowry AFB Noontime Edn. Program, Exercise Program, Denver, 1977-83; mem. speakers bur. Colo. Women's Bar, 1982-83, Lowry AFB, 1981-83; mem. fed. ct. liaison com. U.S. Dist. Ct. Colo., 1983; mem. Leaders of the Fed. Bar Assn. People to People Del. to China, USSR and Finland, 1986. Contbr. numerous articles to profl. jours. Bd. dirs. Pres.'s Council Met. Denver, 1981-83; mem. Lowry AFB Alcohol Abuse Exec. Com., 1981-84. Recipient Spl. Achievement award USAF, 1978; Upward Mobility award Fed. Profl. and Adminstrv. Women, Denver, 1979. Mem. Fed. Bar Assn. (pres. Colo. 1982-83, mem. nat. council 1984—, Earl W. Kintner Disting. Service award 1983, 1st v.p. 10th cir. 1986—), Colo. Trial Lawyers Assn., Bus. and Profl. Women's Club (dist. IV East dir. 1983-84, Colo. pres. 1988—), Am. Soc. Mil. Comptrollers (pres. 1984-85), Denver South Met. Bus. and Profl. Women's Club (pres. 1982-83), Denver Silver Spruce Am. Bus. Women's Assn. (pres. 1981-82; Woman of Yr. award 1982), Colo. Jud. Inst., Colo. Concerned Lawyers, Profl. Mgrs. Assn., Fed. Women's Program (v.p. Denver 1980), Colo. Woman News Community adv. bd., 1988—, Dallas Bar Assn., Tex. Bar Assn., Denver Bar Assn., Altrusa, Zonta, Denver Nancy Langhorn Federally Employed Women. (pres. 1979-80). Christian. Office: Air Force Acctg and Fin Ctr AFAFC/JAL Denver CO 80279

DAVIS, WARREN EARL, trade association executive; b. Seattle, Apr. 13, 1926; s. Earl A. and Madelyn L. Davis; B.A. in Polit. Sci., U. So. Calif., 1947; M.S. in Bus. Adminstrn., Calif. State U., Sacramento, 1968; m. Kathleen Dale Neely, Oct. 4, 1952; children—Stephen, Pamela, Julie, Jennifer. Ins. underwriter Pacific Indemnity Co., Los Angeles, 1947-51; mgr. prodn. control Aerojet-Gen. Corp., Sacramento, 1959-69; corp. planner Fairchild Camera & Instrument Corp., Mountain View, Calif., 1969-78; dir. govt. affairs Semicondr. Industry Assn., San Jose, Calif., 1978-84, v.p. pub. affairs, 1984-86, v.p., 1986—; instr. internat. bus. San Jose (Calif.) State U. Sch. Bus., 1977-82. Served to lt. comdr. USNR, 1944-46, 51-53, 55-59. Mem. World Affairs Council No. Calif., Army and Navy Club, Phi Delta Theta. Republican. Contbr. articles to profl. jours. Home: 13682 Manteca Way Saratoga CA 95070

DAVIS, WARREN FREDERICK, physicist; b. Norwood, Mass., Sept. 4, 1941; s. Leon Bigelow and Lydia Virginia (Lenhart) D.; S.B., M.I.T., 1970, Ph.D., 1979; m. Sharon Joy Tramer, Oct. 4, 1963 (div. Feb. 1981); children—Naomi Susan, Bjoren Kurt; m. Georgia Christou Papaefthymiou, Sept. 10, 1983; 1 child, Hrysoula Leona. Mathematician, Sylvania Electronic Systems, Needham, Mass., 1963-64; mathematician, programmer Info. Processing Service, Newton, Mass., 1964-65; scientist, programmer Arcon Corp., Wakefield, Mass., 1965-69; cons. Max Planck Institut für Radioastronomie, Bonn, W.Ger., 1970, 71-73; sr. scientist Arcon Corp., Wakefield, 1973-76; mgr. applications devel. Computer Design and Applications, Newton, Mass., 1980-81; physicist Smithsonian Astrophys. Obs., Cambridge, Mass., 1981-82; cons. dept. psychology M.I.T., Cambridge, 1976—, pres. Davis Assocs., Inc., 1987—; participated in Symposium on Econ. Conversion, USSR Acad. Scis., 1984. Contbg. author: The Militarization of High Technology, 1984. Co-founder, pres. emeritus High Tech. Profls. for Peace, Cambridge, Mass.; N.E. regional v.p. Peacework Alternatives, Louisville, 1985. Recipient Bausch & Lomb Hon. Sci. award, 1959; M.I.T. Apollo 11 commendation, 1969; U.S. Sr. Scientist award Alexander von Humboldt Stiftung, 1972. Mem. Am. Phys. Soc., Fed. Am. Scientists, AAAS, N.Y. Acad. Scis., Math. Assn. Am., Sigma Xi. Home: 43 Holden Rd West Newton MA 02165

DAVIS, WILLIAM COLUMBUS, educator, writer, lecturer; b. Birmingham, Ala., Aug. 28, 1910; s. William Columbus and Maude (Gray) D.; m. Mildred J. Dorman, July 24, 1948 (dec.); m. Dorothy A. Fleetwood, Feb. 14, 1987. A.B., U. Ala., 1931, M.A., 1932; M.A., Harvard U., 1943, Ph.D., 1948. Adminstrv. positions U.S. Senate, 1933-46; asst. prof. history U. Ga., 1948-51; faculty George Washington U., 1951-66, prof. Latin Am. history and govt., 1960-66, dir. Latin Am. studies, 1952-66; prof. internat. affairs, dir. Latin Am. studies, dir. lecture program, only permanent mem. faculty Nat. War Coll., Washington, 1963-74;; dir., participant numerous radio, TV programs in field; lectr. various colls., univs.; vis. prof. Samford U., 1983—. Author: The Last Conquistadores: The Spanish Intervention in Peru and Chile, 1863-1866, 1950, The Columns of Athens, 1951; co-author: Soviet Bloc Latin American Activities and Their Implications for United States Foreign Policy, 1960; editor: Index to the Writings on American History, 1902-1940, 1956, Am. Hist. Assn's Guide to Historical Literature, 1960; contbr. numerous articles on recent Latin Am. devels. to various publs. Mem. Phi Beta Kappa, Pi Kappa Phi. Baptist. Home: 1323 Darnall Dr McLean VA 22101

DAVIS-HARRIS, JEANNETTE GARDRINE, educator, historian; b. Glastonbury, Conn.; d. James Robert and Jeannette Gardrine (Nelson) Davis; B.S. (Easthampton Lions Club scholar, DAR award, Lotta Crabtree scholar, Commonwealth of Mass. scholar), U. Mass., Amherst, 1953, M.Ed., 1972, Ed.D., 1974; spl. studies Boston U., 1961-62, Westfield State Coll., 1971; children—Paul Anthony, Catherine Gardrine. Med. missionary, bacteriologist Order of Holy Cross, Bolahun, Liberia, 1953-55; research instr., chemist Mass. Dept. Agr., Amherst, 1955-56; virologist Mass. Dept. Pub. Health, Boston, 1956-58; bacteriologist-in-charge Lahey Clinic, Boston, 1958-65; grad. research asst. in microbiology U. Mass., Amherst, 1965-66, teaching asst. anthropology, 1967-68; community organizer, cultural and ednl. programmer No. Ednl. Services, Inc., Springfield, Mass., 1967-69; chmn. social studies dept., tchr. Classical High Sch., Springfield Pub. Schs., 1969-78; ednl. specialist Mass. Dept. Edn., West Springfield, 1978-87, Chicopee, 1987—; adj. instr. Springfield Tech. Community Coll., 1977, Holyoke Community Coll., 1973, 75; adj. assoc. prof. Springfield Coll., 1976; vis. lectr. Am. Internat. Coll., 1971-73, 81, Elms Coll., Chicopee, Mass., 1984; adj. lectr. Afro-Am. studies U. Mass., Amherst, 1982-84; vis. lectr. African history Our Lady of Elms Coll., Chicopee, Mass., 1984; ednl. adminstr., photographer in Africa, Am. Forum for Internat. Study, Cleve., summer 1972, 73; instr. Elder Hostel, Western New Eng. Coll., Springfield, summer 1985; cons. African and Afro-Am. studies; corporator Easthampton Savs. Bank, 1980—; mem. nat. bd. cons. Parting Ways Mus. Afro-Am. Ethnohistory, Inc., Plymouth, Mass., 1980—. Trustee Springfield Library and Mus. Assn., 1979-83; corporator Easthampton Pub. Library 1985-86; bd. tribunes Sta. WGBY-TV, 1979-83, exec. com., 1980-83; Mass. State Senate intern, 1976; bd. dirs. World Affairs Council of Conn. Valley, 1983-84; mem. Mayor's Com. for 350th Celebration, Springfield, Mass., 1983-86; mem. Mass. Gov.'s Spl. Commn. for Commemoration 350th Anniversary Arrival of Africans to Mass., 1984—; mem. Easthampton Town Charter Commn., chmn., 1985-86. Mass. Found. Humanities and Public Policy grantee, 1982; recipient Brethren Community Service award, 1985; cert. tchr., Mass.; cert. Mus. Research in Archaeology. Mem. Nat. Assn. Supervision and Curriculum Devel., Mass. Assn. Supervision and Curriculum Devel. (exec. bd. 1981-85), Assn. Study of Afro-Am. Life and History (pres. Western Mass. br. 1980-81); mem. Bd. Contributers Holyoke Transcript Telegram, 1986-87; elected Easthampton Bd. Selectmen, 1987—, vice-chair 1988, town meeting mem. 1987—. Author: Springfield's Ethnic Heritage: The Black Community, 1976, 2d edit., 1982; co-author Africa units in textbook Unfinished Journey, 1980, A History of the World, 1985; photographer-author documentary exhibit The African-Afro-American Connection, 1982; contbr. articles to publs.; co-author curriculum guides; cons., advisor, textbook Freedom's Trail, 1976. Home: 15 Reservation Rd Easthampton MA 01027 Office: Macek Dr Chicopee MA 01013

DAVISON, BETSY JANE, training consultant; b. Cleve., Dec. 22, 1921; d. Alexander Stuart and Helen Eva (Chapman) D.; student Albion (Mich.) Coll., 1941-43; B.A., U. Chgo., 1943; M.A., Tchrs. Coll., Columbia U., 1952. Civilian recreation dir. U.S. Army and Air Force Overseas, 1945-55; command recreation dir. Hdqrs. U.S. Air Forces in Europe, Ger., 1956-58; coordinator student activities Kean (N.J.) Coll., 1959-66; cons. edn. and tng. Assn. Jr. Leagues, N.Y.C., 1966-70; dir. tng. Mental Health Materials Center, N.Y.C., 1971-76; tng. cons. APC Skills Co., N.Y.C., 1977-78; dir. tng. and confs. Child Welfare League Am., N.Y.C., 1979-83; tng. cons., 1983—. Mem. Am. Soc. Tng. and Devel., Am. Adult Edn. Assn., Kappa Delta Pi, Pi Lambda Theta, Delta Sigma Rho, Alpha Lambda Delta. Author tng. manuals. Home and Office: 333 E 43d St New York NY 10017

DAVISON, MICHAEL CHARLES, psychologist; b. London, May 17, 1943; arrived in New Zealand, 1966; s. Kenneth Charles and Marjorie Emily (Thompson) D.; children: Eleanor Kate, Joseph Michael. BS with honors, Bristol (Eng.) U., 1966; PhD, Otago (New Zealand) U., 1969; DSc, Auckland (New Zealand) U., 1982. Lectr. U. Otago, 1968, Univ. Coll. London, 1968-69; lectr. psychology U. Auckland, 1969-72, sr. lectr., 1972-79, assoc. prof. 1979-87, personal chair, 1987—. Author: The Matching Law, 1987; contbr. articles to profl. jours. Commonwealth scholar, 1966-69. Fellow Royal Soc. New Zealand, New Zealand Psychol. Soc. (Hunter prize 1978). Mem. Labour Party. Office: U Auckland Dept Psychology, Auckland New Zealand

DAVY, PHILIP SHERIDAN, civil engineer; b. Madison, Wis., July 12, 1915; s. Francis Joseph and Mathilda Sarah (Femrite) D.; B.S. in Civil Engring., U. Wis., 1937, M.S. in Civil Engring. with high honors, 1938; m. Caecilia Magdalen Thiemann, Feb. 8, 1939; children—Katherine Agnes (Mrs. William Bathurst), Patricia Mary (Mrs. Steven Sciborski), Michael Francis, Barbara Jean (Mrs. John Salassa), Thomas Henry, Margaret Theresa (Mrs. Douglas Claeys). Engr., Frank J. Davy & Son, cons. engrs., La Crosse, Wis., 1938-41, Permutit Co., N.Y.C., 1946; v.p. Davy Engring. Co., cons. engrs., La Crosse, 1947-56, pres., 1956—; lectr. seminars U. Wis., 1950-75, Wis. Dept. Natural Resources, 1970-82; mem. Gov.'s Com. on Wis. Water Resources, 1965-66; mem. region 1 adv. bd. to Wis. Dept. Resource Devel., 1966-68; chmn., 1968. Campaign chmn. United Fund, La Crosse, 1961, 72, bd. dirs., pres., 1962-65; com. chmn. Gateway Area council Boy Scouts Am., 1948-52, bd. mem., 1953-66, v.p., 1967-70, pres., 1971-73, v.p. area 1 central region, 1978-81, bd. dirs. East central region, 1983—; bd. dirs., mem. fin. and adminstrn. com. Diocese of La Crosse, 1970-86, chmn., 1974-77; campaign chmn. La Crosse joint hosp. fund drive-St. Francis and Luth. hosps., 1977; bd. dirs. River Center U.S.A., 1980, pres., 1981-82. Served to lt. col. C.E., AUS, 1937-46; mem. Res., 1946-75. Decorated Army Commendation medal with oakleaf cluster; knight comdr. Holy Sepulchre (Vatican), knight comdr. with star Diocese of LaCrosse; recipient Silver Beaver, St. George, Silver Antelope, Disting. Eagle Scout awards Boy Scouts Am.; diplomate Am. Acad. Environ. Engrs.; registered profl. engr., Wis., Minn., Iowa, Mich., Ill., Ind. Fellow ASCE (Disting. Service award Wis. sect. 1979); mem. Am. Water Works Assn. (trustee, chmn. Wis. sect. 1957, 60, George Warren Fuller award 1985), AAAS, Water Pollution Control Assn., La Crosse County Hist. Soc. (dir. 1978-82, pres. 1982-83), Nat. Soc. Profl. Engrs. (dir. 1967-70), Wis. Soc. Profl. Engrs. (v.p. 1965-67, pres. 1974-75, Engr. of Yr. in Pvt. Practice award 1967, named Engr. of Yr. 1970) Am. Pub. Works Assn., Greater La Crosse C. of C. (dir. 1959-62, exec. bd. 1964-67, pres. 1968 named Man of Yr. 1973), Scabbard and Blade, Tau Beta Pi, Chi Epsilon, Phi Kappa Phi. Clubs: La Crosse, La Crosse Country. Lodges: La Crosse Elks, K.C. (3 deg., 4th deg.), Serra, Downtown La Crosse Rotary (bd. dirs. 1984-85, pres. 1986-87). Home: 3482 Woodbridge Ct La Crosse WI 54601 Office: 115 S 6th St La Crosse WI 54601

DAWE, DONALD BRUCE, literature educator; b. Geelong, Victoria, Australia, Feb. 15, 1930; s. Alfred James and Mary Ann (Hamilton) D.; m. Gloria Desley; children: Brian, Jamie, Katrina, Melissa. BA, U. Queensland, Australia, 1969, MA, 1975, PhD, 1980; LittB, U. New Eng., New South Wales, Australia, 1973. Secondary tchr. Downlands Sacred Heart Coll., Toowoomba, Australia, 1969-71; lectr. lit. Darling Downs Inst. Advanced Edn., Toowoomba, 1971-80, sr. lectr., 1980-83, 85—, sr. teaching fellow, 1983-84; writer-in-residence, U. Queensland, 1984. Author: Condolences of the Season, 1971, Sometimes Gladness, 1978, Towards Sunrise, 1986, Speaking in Parables: A Reader, 1987. Mem. Assn. for Study Australian Lit., South Pacific and Commonwealth Lang. and Lit. Soc., Australian Assn. Tchrs. English. Roman Catholic. Office: Darling Downs Inst Advanced Edn, Sch Arts, Darling Heights, 4350 Toowoomba Australia

DAWE, GERALD CHARTRES, eductor, poet; b. Belfast, Antrim, Ireland, Apr. 22, 1952; s. Gordon Aubrey Dawe and Norma Fitzgerald (Bradshaw) Richardson; m. Dorothea Melvin, Sept. 28, 1979; children: Iarla, Olwen Chartres. BA with honors, U. Ulster, Ireland, 1974; MA, U. Coll. Galway, Ireland, 1978. Library asst. fine arts Belfast City Library, 1974-78; tutor, asst. lectr. in English U. Coll. Galway, 1978—; asst. lectr. Trinity Coll., Dublin, 1988—; editor writing in the West, Galway, 1979, 84, Krino Literary Mag., Galway, 1986—. Author: (poems) Sheltering Places, 1978, The Lundys Letter, 1985; editor: (anthology) The Younger Irish Poets, 1982; co-editor: (with Edna Longley) (essays) Across a Roaring Hill, 1985; contbr. poems, numerous essays and critical articles to newspapers and jours. Macaulay fellow Arts Council of Ireland, 1984, fellow Hawthorden Internat., 1987. Mem. Internat. Assn. Study of Anglo-Irish Lit. and Lang. Office: U Coll Galway, Dept English, Galway Ireland

DAWES, CHARLES EDWARD, retired manufacturing company executive; b. Peoria, Okla., Feb. 7, 1923; s. Charles Gates and Lottie (Nonkesis) D.; A.A., Joplin (Mo.) Jr. Coll., 1950; B.S., U. Ark., 1953; m. Lorraine Mercer, Apr. 16, 1948; children—Charla Rene, Kevin Lawrence. Mgr. mfg. Vickers, Inc., Joplin, 1953-57; sales engr. Sebastian Diesel Co., Joplin, 1957-59; gen. mgr. Duplex Mfg. Co., Ft. Smith, Ark., 1959-77; v.p. Flanders Industries, Inc., from 1977, now ret. Chief, Ottawa Indians of Okla.; sr. counselor Inter-tribal Songchiefs Okla. Bd. dirs. Ark.-Okla. Regional Edn. and Promotion Assn., Old Fort Militia; trustee St. Edward Mercy Med. Center; bd. dirs., pres. Abilities Unlimited, Inc.; bd. dirs., mem. exec. com. Ft. Smith United Fund; mem. adv. bd. Seneca Indian Sch. Served with USAAF, 1943-46. Mem. Am. Soc. Tool and Mech. Engrs., Ft. Smith C. of C. (dir.), Personnel Assn. N.W. Ark., Western Ark. Purchasing Assn., Mfg. Execs. Assn. (pres. Ft. Smith), Nat. Congress Am. Indians, Okla. Inter-Tribal Council. Republican. Presbyterian. Mason. Home: PO Box 32 Quapaw OK 74363 Office: 318 Kentucky St Quapaw OK 74363

DAWES, DAVID FORD, real estate developer; b. Muskogee, Okla., July 29, 1909; s. Maurice and Ethel (Ford) D.; student Okla. U., 1928; m. Dorothy Louise Snyder, Jan. 5, 1933; children—David Alan, Stuart Edward, Mary Louise (dec.). With Bellante Dawes Realty Co., Inglewood, Calif., 1946-48; owner David Realty, Inglewood and Torrance, Calif., 1948-69; pres. Western Land & Devel. Corp., Carlsbad, Calif., 1969—. Sec., Boys Club Carlsbad, 1973, 74, 76-77, v.p., 1975. Mem. San. and Flood Control Commn. Dist. 1 San Diego County, 1974—. Mem. Calif. Assn. Realtors (state dir. 1959, 60, 74, 75), Carlsbad Bd. Realtors (pres. 1974), Carlsbad C. of C., Gardena Bd. Realtors (past pres.). Clubs: Elks, Rotary, Masons (32 deg.; worshipful master 1984), KT, Shriners. Home: 3428 Don Juan Dr Carlsbad CA 92008 Office: 5200 El Camino Real Carlsbad CA 92008

DAWES, PETER, international holding company executive; b. Horsham, Eng., Sept. 19, 1952; s. John and Elizabeth May (Walker) D.; m. Sharon Ann Johnson, June 22, 1974; children: William, Katherine, Luke. Asst. sec. Fisons PLC, Cambridge, Eng., 1977-83; co. sec. Huntingdon (Eng.) Internat. Holdings PLC, 1983—. Fellow Inst. Chartered Secs. and Adminstrs. Office: Huntingdon Internat Holdings, Huntingdon PE18 6ES, England

DAWKINS, JOHN SYDNEY, minister of employment, education and training for Australia; b. Perth, Australia, Mar. 2, 1947; s. Al Dawkins; m. Kate Lowese George, Dec. 15, 1973; children: Kezia, Finnian. Student, Scotch Coll.; Diploma in Agr., Roseworthy Agrl. Coll., Australia; B in Econs., U. Western Australia. Mgr. family farm, nr. Perth; former staff Bur. Agrl. Econs. Australia; staff Australian Dept. Trade and Industry, 1971-72; mem. Australian Ho. of Reps., Canberra, 1974-75, 77—, opposition spokesman for edn., 1980-83, opposition spokesman for industry and commerce, 1983, minister for fin., 1983, minister assisting prime minister for pub. service matters, from 1983, minister of trade, 1984-87, minister assisting prime minister for youth affairs, from 1984, minister of employment, edn., tng., 1987—; press officer Western Australia Trades and Labor Council, 1976-77. Mem. nat. exec. Australian Labor Party, v.p., from 1982. Office: Parliament House, Canberra 2600, Australia *

DAWLEY, DONALD LEE, business educator, information systems specialist; b. Amanda, Ohio, Feb. 21, 1936; s. Stanley Bernel and Alice Opel (Santee) D.; m. T. Jane Bokay, Nov. 24, 1957; children: Donald Wayne, Douglas Lee, Denise Jane. BS in Edn., Kent State U., 1959; AA in Bus., U. Calif., Victor Valley, 1966; MBA in Bus., U. Hawaii, Far East div., 1968; MS in Logistics Engring., Air Force Inst. Tech., Dayton, Ohio, 1970; D in Bus. Adminstrn., George Washington U., 1980-81. Cert. systems profl., data processor. Enlisted USAF, 1959, advanced through grades to lt. col.; with data processing and logistics inspection Hdqrs. USAF, Washington, 1973-75; with data processing plans Def. Logistics Agy., Washington, 1973-75, Air Force Logistics, Dayton, 1978; resigned USAF, 1979; from instr. to assoc. prof. decision scis. Miami U., Oxford, Ohio, 1979—, asst. chair Mgmt. Info. Systems, 1985—; cons. J.M. Smucker Co., Orrville, Ohio, 1982, McCullough-Hyde Hosp., Oxford, 1986—; speaker in field. Author: Auditor Data Processing Knowledge Requirements, 1984; also articles. Decorated Medal of Honor (foreign), Bronze Star. Mem. Data Processing Mgmt. Assn. (internat. com., sec./treas. 1987, bd. dirs. 1988—), Assn. for Systems Mgmt., Assn. for Ednl. Data Systems, Soc. Data Educators, Assn. Computing Machinery, Ohio Mgmt. Info. Systems Dirs. Assn. (founder, past pres.), Beta Gamma Sigma, Omnicron Delta Kappa. Baptist. Home: 323 Sandra Dr Oxford OH 45056 Office: Miami Univ Decision Scis Dept 221 Culler Oxford OH 45056

DAWLEY, ROBERT MICHAEL, music educator; b. Buffalo, June 3, 1948; s. Morris D. and Grace (Carrow) D.; Mus.B., Eastman Sch. Music, 1970; M.A., N.E. Mo. State U., 1972; D.Ed., U. Ill., 1979; postgrad. U. Ariz., Haverford Coll., Temple U., U. Ind., U. Ill., U. Tenn. at Knoxville; m. Ofelia Vasquez, June 2, 1973; children—Robert Albert, Edward Michael. Dir. Youth Symphony, Corpus Christi, Tex., 1972-74; violinist Corpus Christi Symphony, 1972-74; 1st violinist Tucson Symphony, 1975-76; dir. orch., jazz ensemble (founder) Hillsdale Coll. (Mich.), 1978-80; asst. prof. music Purdue U., West Lafayette, Ind., 1980-85, Pembroke State U. of U. N.C., 1986—; 1st viola Lafayette Symphony and Quartet, 1980-81; charter mem. Music Edn. for Handicapped, Inc., presenter papers at regional, nat. and internat. meetings. U. Mich. fellow, 1978; NEH fellow, summer 1980, Purdue Research Found. grantee, 1981-83. Mem. Coll. Music Soc., Music Educators Nat. Conf., Music Educators Book Soc., Am. String Tchrs. Assn., Nat. Sch. Orch. Assn., N.C. Music Educators Assn., Internat. Soc. for Music Edn., Nat. Assn. Jazz Edn., Phi Delta Kappa, Pi Kappa Lambda. Democrat. Composer: Six Bagatelles for String Quartet Demonstration, 1980; contbr. articles to profl. jours. Home: 2601 Riverwood Ave Lumberton NC 28358 Office: Music Dept Pembroke State U Pembroke NC 28372

DAWSON, EARL BLISS, obstetrics-gynecology educator; b. Perry, Fla., Feb. 1, 1930; s. Bliss and Linnie (Callaham) D.; B.A., U. Kans., 1955; student Bowman Gray Sch. Medicine, 1955-57; M.A., U. Mo., 1960; Ph.D., Tex. A. & M. U., 1964; m. Winnie Ruth Isbell, Apr. 10, 1951; children—Barbara Gail, Patricia Ann, Robert Earl, Diana Lynn. Research instr. dept. obstetrics and gynecology U. Tex. Med. br., Galveston, 1963-67, research asst. prof., 1967-70, research asso. prof., 1970-86, assoc. prof. obgyn., 1986—; cons. Interdeptl. Com. on Nutrition for Nat. Defense, 1965-68; cons. Nat. Nutrition Survey, 1968-69. Served with USNR, 1951-52. Nutrition Research fellow, 1960-61; NSF scholar, 1961-62; NIH Research fellow, 1962-63. Mem. Am. Chem. Soc., Tex., N.Y. acads. scis., AAAS, Am. Inst. Physicists, Am. Inst. Nutrition, Am. Soc. Clin. Nutrition, Soc. Environ. Geochemistry and Health, Sigma Xi, Phi Rho Sigma. Baptist. Mason. Club: Mic-O-Say (Kansas City, Mo.). Contbr. numerous articles to profl. jours. Home: 15 Chimney Corners LaMarque TX 77568 Office: U Tex Med Br Dept Ob-Gyn Galveston TX 77550

DAWSON, JUDITH M. SHEEHAN, educational administrator; b. Honolulu, Nov. 3, 1939; d. Wade Edmund and Barbara Montague (Guard) Sheehan; m. Donald D. Dawson, Apr. 4, 1964 (div. Aug. 1979); children—Mark Lynn, Starr Montague. Student Wellesley Coll., 1957-59; B.A., U. Calif.-Berkeley, 1962; M.A., U. Hawaii, 1977. Exec. sec. Halekulani Hotel, Honolulu, 1962-64; reservations mgr. Waikiki Grand Hotel, Honolulu, 1964-65; community relations officer East-West Ctr., Honolulu, 1965-66; dir. devel. Punahou Sch., Honolulu, 1978—. Bd. dirs. Boys Club Am., Honolulu, 1982—; trustee, v.p. Atherton Family Found., Honolulu, 1980—; trustee Hawaiian Mission Childrens Soc., 1982—, pres., 1986—. Mem. Hawaii Soc. Fund-Raising Execs. (trustee, bd. dirs. 1983—), Oriental Art Soc. (bd. dirs. 1979—). Republican. Episcopalian. Club: Oahu Country (Honolulu). Home: 3155 Kaohinani Dr Honolulu HI 96817 Office: Punahou Sch 1601 Punahou St Honolulu HI 96822

DAWSON, ROBERT EDWARD, ophthalmologist; b. Rocky Mount, N.C., Feb. 23, 1918; s. William and Daisy (Wright) D.; B.S., Clark Coll., 1939;

M.D., Meharry Med. Coll., 1943; m. Julia Belle Davis, Mar. 10, 1950; children—Dianne Elizabeth, Janice Elaine, Robert Edward, Melanie Lorraine. Diplomate Am. Bd. Ophthalmology (examiner 1979-82). Intern, Homer G. Phillips Hosp., St. Louis, 1943-44, resident, 1944-46; preceptor Duke Hosp., 1946-50, clin. instr. ophthalmology, 1968-70; practice ophthalmology, Durham, N.C., 1946-55, 57-88; mem. attending staff ophthalmology Lincoln Hosp., Durham, 1946-55; cons. ophthalmology N.C. Central U. Health Service, Durham, 1950-64; chief ophthalmology and otolaryngology Lincoln Hosp., Durham, 1959-76; mem. attending staff ophthalmology Watts Hosp., Durham, 1966-76; mem. attending staff ophthalmology Durham County Gen. Hosp., v.p. med. staff, 1976-88; med. dir. Lincoln Hosp., Durham, 1968-70; lectr. ophthalmology Lincoln Hosp. Sch. Nursing, 1948-56; clin. asso. Duke U., 1969-75, clin. asst. prof. ophthalmology, 1975-87; cons. in ophthalmology Eye Ctr., Duke U., 1986—; mem. N.C. Adv. Com. on Med. Assistance, 1972-85; mem. adv. bd. N.C. State Commn. for Blind, 1965-75; mem. Gov.'s Adv. Com. Med. Assistance; regional surg. dir. Eye Bank Assn. Am., Inc., 1968-79. Mem. Durham Council Human Relations, 1967-69; mem. Pres. Com. on Employment of Handicapped, 1971-79. Bd. dirs. Durham County Tb Assn., 1950-54, Better Health Found., 1960-66, Durham Community House, 1966-68, Lincoln Community Health Center, Am. Cancer Soc., Durham United Fund, Durham County Mental Health Center, 1976-79, Found. for Better Health of Durham County Gen. Hosp., 1975-79; bd. dirs., v.p. Nat. Soc. Prevention of Blindness; trustee Durham Acad., 1969-72; life trustee Meharry Med. Coll.; trustee emeritus N.C. Central U.; mem. bd. mgmt. Meharry Med. Coll. Alumni Assn.; bd. assocs. Greensboro Coll., N.C.; chmn. bd. dirs. Lincoln Pvt. Diagnostic Clinic; bd. visitors Clark Coll., Atlanta. Served as maj., M.C., USAF, 1955-57. Recipient Disting. Service award Clark Coll., 1984, Nat. Assn. Equal Opportunity in Higher Edn., 1985. Fellow A.C.S., Acad. Ophthalmology; mem. Nat. Soc. to Prevent Blindness (v.p.), Am. Assn. Ophthalmology, Soc. Eye Surgeons, AMA, Nat. Med. Assn. (trustee 1971-80, pres. 1979-80, Disting. Service award 1983), Pan Am. Med. Assn. (diplomate), Old North State Med. Soc. (pres. 1966-67), Durham Acad. Medicine (pres. 1967-68), NAACP (life), Durham Bus. and Profl. Chain, C. of C., Meharry Nat. Alumni Assn. (past pres.), Alpha Omega Alpha, Alpha Phi Alpha (past pres.), Sigma Pi Phi (pres.), Chi Delta Mu. Democrat. Mem. A.M.E. Ch. (stewards bd. 1968—). Mason (32 deg., Shriner). Club: Toastmasters (pres. 1969-70). Home: 817 Lawson St Durham NC 27701 Office: 512 Simmons St Durham NC 27701

DAWSON, WILLIAM LEVI, composer, conductor; b. Anniston, Ala., Sept. 26, 1899; s. George W. and Eliza M. (Starkey) D.; m. Cornella D. Lampton, May 25, 1927 (dec. Aug. 1928); m. Cecile D. Nicholson, Sept. 21, 1935. Student composition, orchestration, Washburn Coll.; Mus. B., Horner Inst. Fine Arts, Kansas City, Mo., 1925; M. Composition, Am. Conservatory Music, Chgo., 1927; Mus. D., Tuskegee Inst., 1955, Ithaca Coll., 1982; postgrad., Eastman Sch. Music; LL.D., Lincoln U., 1978. Dir. music, Topeka, Kansas City, 1921-25, then 1st trombonist, Chgo. Civic Symphony Orch., dir., Tuskegee Inst. Sch. Music, Tuskegee Choir; led: opening Tuskegee Choir at, Radio City Music Hall, 1932-33, on many tours, in concert series, NBC, CBS, ABC; guest condr. numerous state choral festivals, choral groups in, Spain, under auspices, Dept. State, 1956, Kansas City Philharmonic Orch., 1966, Nashville Symphony Orch., 1966, Talladega Choir and Mobile Symphony Orch., 1968, Wayne State U. Glee Club, 1970, 74, Balt. Symphony Orch., 1975; condr. symposium choral music, Huntingdon Coll., Montgomery, Ala., 1976 (Winner Rodman Wanamaker contest for composition 1930, 31, Chgo. Daily News contest for band condrs. 1929); Composer: numerous arrangements Negro folk songs for voices Break, Break; with orch. Trio in A; violin, cello, piano Sonata in A; violin and piano Negro Folk Symphony. Recipient award and citation U. Pa. Glee Club, 1967; recipient Alumni Achievement award U. Mo. at Kansas City, 1963, award and citation Am. Choral Dirs. Assn., 1975; named to Ala. Arts Hall of Fame, 1975; recipient Paul Heinecke citation of merit, 1983, Alumni Merit award Tuskegee Inst., 1983. Mem. Phi Mu Alpha Sinfonia (hon.). Address: PO Box 1052 Tuskegee Institute AL 36088

DAXNER, MICHAEL FRITZ ROBERT, university administrator; b. Vienna, Austria, Oct. 27, 1947; arrived Fed. Republic Germany, 1974; PhD, U. Vienna, 1972. Adminstr., sec. of Sci. and Research Vienna, 1970-73; prof. U. Osnabrueck, Fed. Republic Germany, 1974-86, pres., 1986—. Author, editor 5 books; contbr. numerous articles to profl. jours. Del. OECD-IMTEC, Paris, 1972-74, Council of Europe, Strasbourg, 1972-74. Mem. Arbeitsgembinschaft f r Hochschuldidaktik, Bund Demokr. Wissenschaftler, Gewerkschaft Erziehung und Wissenschaft (exec. bd. Lower Saxony 1977-86). Office: U Oldenburg, PO Box 2503, D 2900 Oldenburg Federal Republic of Germany

DAY, DANIEL EDGAR, government information officer; b. Montgomery, Ala., Dec. 10, 1913; s. Thomas and Gertrude (Ford) D.; m. Sanone Nickerson, Jan. 18, 1942; children: Sandra Ann (Mrs. James Johnson), Gregory Alan. Student, Crane Jr. Coll., Chgo., 1932-33, Am. U., 1946, 62, 64, U. Chgo., 1958. With Robert S. Abbott Pub. Co., Chgo., 1929-40; asst. city editor Robert S. Abbott Pub. Co., 1936-40; enlisted USNG, 1938; enlisted as sgt. U.S. Army, 1941, advanced through ranks to lt. col., 1952; asst. chief, then chief Negro interest sect. Bur. Pub. Relations, War Dept., Washington, 1943-46; stationed (Hdqrs. 8th Army), Japan, 1946-49, (82d Airborne Div.), Ft. Bragg, NC, 1950-51, (maj. port), Korea, 1952-53, (Japan Procurement Agy.), Yokohama, 1953-55; prof. mil. sci. Fla. A & M U., Tallahassee, 1955-61; ret. 1961; Washington corr. Nat. Newspaper Pubs. Assn., 1961-66; adminstrv. officer USDA, Washington, 1966; info. specialist HUD, Washington, 1966-68; dep. dir. pub. information div. HUD, 1968-70, pub. information officer, 1970-73, dep. dir. news services div., 1973-74, info. officer, 1975-84. Mem. Nat. Assn. Govt. Communicators (dir. 1974). Clubs: Nat. Press (chmn. membership com. 1983), Pigskin, Capital Press (Washington). Home: 8212 Eastern Ave NW Washington DC 20012

DAY, EDWARD FRANCIS, JR., lawyer; b. Portland, Maine, Nov. 4, 1946; s. Edward Francis and Anne (Rague) D.; m. Claire Ann Nicholson, June 27, 1970; children: Kelley Ann, John Edward. BA, St. Anselm Coll., 1968; JD cum laude, U. Maine, 1973; LLM in Taxation, NYU, 1976. Bar: N.J. 1973, U.S. Dist. Ct. N.J. 1973, U.S. Tax Ct. 1974, N.Y. 1981. Assoc. Hannoch, Weisman, Stern & Besser, Newark, 1973-74; assoc. Carpenter, Bennett & Morrissey, Newark, 1975-78, ptnr., 1979—; inst. employee benefits and taxation The Am. Coll., Valley Forge, Pa., 1981-82; bd. dirs. Weiss-Aug. Co., Inc., East Hanover, N.J., 1986—. Editor Maine Law Rev., 1972-73. Mem. Allenhurst (N.J.) Planning Bd., 1985-87, vice chmn.; scoutmaster Council Boy Scouts Am., Ocean Twp., 1987—; mem. Nat. Ski Patrol, Denver, 1985—. Served as sgt. U.S. Army, 1968-70. Named One of Outstanding Young Men of Am., 1979. Mem. ABA, N.J. Bar Assn., Essex County Bar Assn., Estate Planning Council of No. N.J. Roman Catholic. Clubs: Deal (N.J.) Golf and Country (bd. dirs. 1985—); Jersey Coast (Red Bank, N.J.) (v.p. 1976-77). Lodge: KC. Home: 225 Spier Ave Allenhurst NJ 07711 Office: Carpenter Bennett & Morrissey 3 Gateway Ctr Newark NJ 07102

DAY, EMERSON, physician; b. Hanover, N.H., May 2, 1913; s. Edmund Ezra and Emily Sophia (Emerson) D.; m. Ruth Fairfield, Aug. 7, 1937; children: Edmund Perry, Robert Fairfield, Nancy, Bonnie, Sheryl. B.A., Dartmouth Coll., 1934; M.D., Harvard U., 1938. Intern Presbyn. Hosp., N.Y.C., 1938- 40; fellow in cardiology Johns Hopkins U., 1940-42; asst. resident medicine N.Y. Hosp., 1942; med. dir. internat. div. Trans World Airline, N.Y.C., 1945-47; asst. prof. preventive medicine and pub. health Cornell U. Med. Coll., 1947-50, assoc. prof. clin. preventive medicine and pub. health, 1950-54, prof. preventive medicine Sloan Kettering div., 1954-64; chmn. dept. preventive medicine Meml. Hosp., N.Y.C., 1954-63; dir. Strang Cancer Prevention Clinic, 1950-63; mem., chief div. preventive medicine Sloan-Kettering Inst., N.Y.C., 1954-64; cons. in geriatrics Cold Spring Inst., Cold Spring-on-Hudson, N.Y., 1952-57; dir. N.Y.C. Dept. Health Cancer Detection Center, 1947-50, Strang Clinic, Inc., 1963-66, PMI-Strang Clinic, 1966-69; pres. Preventive Medicine Inst., 1963-69, hon. pres., 1969—; v.p., med. dir. Medequip Corp., 1969-76, sr. med. cons., 1976-82; med. v.p. Health Mgmt. Internat., Inc., 1982-84; med. dir. Physicians for Med. Cost Containment, Inc., 1984—; prof. medicine Northwestern U. Med. Sch., 1976-81, prof. emeritus, 1981—; assoc. dir. Northwestern U. Cancer Center, 1976-81; med. dir. Portes Cancer Prevention Center, 1978-79; attending physician Northwestern Meml. Hosp., 1976-81, vis. physician, 1981—; lectr. Cook County Grad. Sch. Med., 1977—; mem. Northwestern U. Med. Assocs., 1980-81; med. dir., chmn. dept. internal medicine Chgo. Splty. Hosp. and Med. Center, 1981-84; affiliate staff physician Evanston, Glenbrook hosps., 1976—; attending physician, mem. med. bd. James Ewing Hosp., Meml. Hosp., N.Y.C., 1950-64; sr. mem. PMX Med. Group, N.Y.C., 1956—70; adj. prof. biology N.Y. U., 1965-70; mem. cancer detection com. Internat. Union Against Cancer, 1954-70; pres. N.Y.C. div. Am. Cancer Soc., 1963-64; med. cons. Medidata Health Services, Inc., 1985—. Contbr. numerous articles to profl. jours. Served as flight surgeon ATC USAAF, 1942-45. Recipient Bronze medal Am. Cancer Soc., 1956, professorship in early detection Ill. div., 1976-79. Fellow ACP, N.Y. Acad. Medicine, N.Y. Acad. Scis. (pres. 1965), Am. Pub. Health Assn., Am. Occupational Med. Assn., Am. Geriatrics Soc., Internat. Acad. Cytology (hon.); mem. Am. Soc. Cytology (founding mem., pres. 1958, now hon. mem., Papanicolaou award 1978), Am. Soc. Preventive Oncology, Internat. Health Evaluation Assn., Soc. for Advanced Med. Systems (founding dir. 1969-81), Am. Assn. Med. Systems and Informatics (founding dir. 1981-84), Harvey Soc., Ill., Chgo. med. socs., AMA, Phi Beta Kappa, Alpha Omega Alpha, Zeta Psi. Club: Century Assn. (N.Y.C.). Home and Office: 320 Pebblebrook Dr Northbrook IL 60062

DAY, JAMES MICHAEL, hospital administrator, game designer; b. Toledo, Jan. 26, 1951; s. Cecil W. and Edith (Gaspari) D.; m. Merry Livingston, May 24, 1980; 1 child, Andrea. BBA, U. Toledo, 1973; MHA, Cen. Mich. U., 1986. Inventory analyst, cost acct. Questor Co., Toledo, 1971-75; asst. purchasing agt. Riverside Hosp., Toledo, 1975-76, purchasing agt., 1976-78, dir. purchasing, 1978-81, dir. materiel mgmt., 1981-84, dir. materiel and info. services, 1984-87; v.p. support services Balt. County Gen. Hosp., 1987—; designer computer software materiel mgmt. system. Mem. Northwest Ohio Hosp. Council, Am. Hosp. Assn., Ohio Hosp. Assn., Am. Soc. Hosp. Purchasing and Material Mgmt. (sr.), Md. Hosp. Assn., Md. Assn. Healthcare Execs. Republican. Roman Catholic. Clubs: Chgo. Wargamers Assn., Metro Detroit Gamers. Home: 49 Six Notches Ct Catonsville MD 21228 Office: Balt County Gen Hosp 5401 Old Court Rd Randallstown MD 21133

DAY, JOHN DENTON, wholesale industrial sales compsny executive, cattle and horse rancher, trainer; b. Salt Lake City, Jan. 20, 1942; s. George W. and Grace (Denton) Jenkins; student U. Utah, 1964-65; BA in Econs. and Bus. Adminstrn. with high honors, Westminster Coll., 1971; m. Susan Hansen, June 20, 1971; children—Tammy Denton, Jeanett. Riding instr., rangler vinta wilderness area, U-Ranch, Neola, Utah, 1955-58; with Mil. Data Cons., Inc., Los Angeles, 1961-62, Carlseon Credit Corp., Salt Lake City, 1962-65; sales mgr. sporting goods Western Enterprises, Salt Lake City, 1965-69, Western rep. PBR Co., Cleve., 1969-71; dist. sales rep. Crown Zellerbach Corp., Seattle and Los Angeles, 1971-73; pres. Dapco paper, chem., instl. food and janitorial supplies, Salt Lake City, 1973-79; owner, pres. John D. Day, mfrs. reps., 1972—; dist. sales mgr. Surfonics Engrs., Inc., Woods Cross, Utah, 1976-78, Garland Co., Cleve., 1978-81; rancher, Heber, Utah, 1976—, Temecula, Calif., 1984—; sec. bd. Acquadyne. Group chmn. Tele-Dex fund raising project Westminster Coll. Served with AUS, 1963-64. Recipient grand nat. award for engring. design and craftmanship Internat. Custom Car Show, San Diego, 1962; Key to City, Louisville, 1964; Dally team roping heading and heeling champion, 1982. Mem. Internat. Show Car Assn. (co-chmn. 1978-79), Am. Quarter Horse Assn. (high point reining champion 1981, sr. reining champion 1982, working cowhorse champion), Utah Quarter Horse Assn. (champion AMAT reining 1979, 80, AMAT barrel racing 1980), Profl. Cowhorseman's Assn. (world champion team roping, heeling 1986, high point rider 1985, world champion stock horse rider 1985-86, world champion working cowhorse 1985, PCA finals open cutting champion, 1985, 86, 87, PCA finals 1500 novice champion 1987, PCA finals all-around champion 1985, 86, 87, first on record registered Tex. longhorn cutting contest, open champion, founder, editor newsletter 1985—), Intermountain Quarter Horse Assn. (champion AMAT reining 1979, 80, 81). Contbr. articles to jours. Home and Office: 76 Dgts # 2 PO Box 1297 Temecula CA 92390 also: Rockin D Ranch #2 Box 1297 Temecula CA 92390 also: Ranch #2 John D Day Tng Ctr 39935 East Benton Rd Temecula CA 92390 also: Rockin D Ranch #1 Box 4 Heber City UT 84032

DAY, MELVIN SHERMAN, information company executive; b. Lewiston, Maine, Jan. 22, 1923; s. Israel and Frances (Goldberg) D.; m. Louisa Walker; children: Cynthia Day Solganick, Wendy Day Levin, Robert Marshall. BS, Bates Col., 1943; postgrad. U. Tenn., 1953-54. Chemist, Metal Hydrides Inc., Beverly, Mass., 1943-44, Tenn. Eastman Corp., Oak Ridge, 1944-46; sci. analyst AEC, Oak Ridge, 1946-48, asst. chief tech. info. service extension, 1950-56, chief, 1956-58, dir. tech. info. div., Washington, 1958-60; dep. dir. Tech. Info. and Ednl. Programs Office, NASA, Washington, 1960-61, dir. Sci. and Tech. Info. div., 1961-67, dep. asst. adminstr. tech. utilization, 1967-70; head Office Sci. Info., NSF, Washington, 1970-72; dep. dir. Nat. Library Medicine, HEW, Bethesda, Md., 1972-78; dir. Nat. Tech. Info. Service Dept. Commerce, 1978-82; v.p. Info. Tech. Group, 1982-84; v.p. Research Publs., Arlington, Va., 1984-86; sr. v.p. Herner & Co., 1986-88; pres. M.Day Cons. Internat., Inc., Arlington, Va., 1988—; cons. Internat. Atomic Energy Agy., 1960; adviser OECD, 1970, 75; U.S. mem. info. policy group; U.S. mem. NATO Tech. Info. Panel, 1960-70, 79-82, chmn., 1970; chmn. com. on sci. and tech. info. Fed. Council, 1970-72, chmn. com. on intergovtl. sci. relations, 1969-70; chmn. Sci. Info. Exchange Adv. Bd., 1963-69, mem. Chem. Abstracts Adv. Bd., 1964-68; mem. Fed. Library Com., 1968-78, chmn. exec. bd., 1973-75; U.S. mem. adv. com. on libraries, documentation and archives UNESCO; pres. abstracting bd. Internat. Council Sci. Unions, 1977-83; bd. dirs. Internat. Council for Sci. and Tech. Info., 1983—, Inst. for Internat. Info. Programs, 1985—, del. numerous panels, also cons., adviser, lectr. in field. Mem. editorial bd. Health Communications and Informatics. Bd. visitors U. Pitts. Grad. Sch. Info. Sci., 1977-83; trustee Found. Ctr., 1974-78, trustee Engring. Info. Inc., 1981-84. Served with U.S. Army, 1944-46. Recipient Sustained Superior Performance award AEC, 1960, Exceptional Service medal NASA, 1971, Superior Service award USPHS, 1976. Fellow Am. Soc. Advancement Sci.; mem. Am. Soc. Info. Sci. (chmn. internat. relations com. 1972-75, pres. 1975-76, council 1975-77, editorial bd. bull.), Am. Chem. Soc., N.Y. Acad. Sci., Spl. Libraries Assn., Am. Soc. Cybernetics (bd. dirs. 1975-79), Am. Library Assn., Venezuelan Acad. Scis. (hon. corr.), Internat. Council Sci. and Tech. Info. (hon.) Home: 4309 Chesapeake St NW Washington DC 20016

DAY, RICHARD EARL, lawyer, educator; b. St. Joseph, Mo., Nov. 2, 1929; s. William E. and Geneva C. (Miller) D.; m. Melissa W. Blair, Feb. 2, 1951; children: William E., Thomas E. BS, U. Pa., 1951; JD with distinction, U. Mich., 1957. Bar: Ill. 1957, D.C. 1959, S.C. 1980. Assoc. Kirkland & Ellis, Chgo., 1957-58, Howrey Simon Baker & Murchison, Washington, 1958-61; asst. prof. law U. N.C., Chapel Hill, 1961-64; assoc. prof. Ohio State U., Columbus, 1964-66, prof. 1966-75; prof. U. S.C., Columbia, 1975-76, 80-86, dean, 1977-80, John William Thurmond chair prof. of law, 1986—; cons. U.S. Office Edn., 1964-66; course dir. Ohio Legal Ctr. Inst., Columbus, 1970-75; vis. prof. law U. Southampton (Eng.), fall 1988. Author: The Intensified Course in Antitrust Law, 1972, rev. edit., 1974; book rev. editor Antitrust Bull., 1968-71, adv. bd., 1971—; adv. bd. Antitrust and Trade Regulation Report, 1973-76, Jour. Reprints for Antitrust Law and Econs., 1974—. Ohio commr. Nat. Conf. on Uniform State Laws, 1967-75, S.C. commr., 1977-80; mem. Ohio Gov.'s Adv. Council Internat. Trade, 1972-74, S.C. Jud. Council, 1977-80; chmn. S.C. Appellate Def. Council, 1977-80, S.C. Com. Intellectual Property and Unfair Trade Practices Law, 1981—. Named John William Thurmond Disting. Prof. Law. Served to lt. USNR, 1952-55. Mem. ABA, S.C. Bar Assn. (bd. govs. 1977-80), Am. Law Inst., Am. Intellectual Property Law Assn. Methodist. Home: 204 Barnwell St Columbia SC 29205 Office: Law Center U SC Main and Green Sts Columbia SC 29208

DAY, RONALD ELWIN, banker; b. Randolph, Vt., Dec. 15, 1933; s. John Ellis and Esther Murle (Tabor) D.; A.A., Pasadena City Coll., 1958, student, 1958-59; B.A., U. Calif., Santa Barbara, 1961; M.B.A., UCLA, 1962; m. Elizabeth Jean McKeage, June 26, 1955; children—Gary Alan, Kathi Ellen, Judy Anne, Jeffrey Evan. Internal auditor North Am. Aviation, Downey, Calif., 1962-64; systems and procedures mgr. Proto Tool Co., Los Angeles, 1964-65; computer programmer First Nat. Bank, Boston, 1966-67; project mgr., 1967-73, systems analyst 1974-77, system planning com. chmn., trust div., 1977—, trust info. mgmt. system adminstr., 1977—. Served with USAF, 1952-56. Mem. Soc. Advancement of Mgmt., Inst. Internal Auditors, Nat. Geog. Soc., Indsl. Mgmt. Club, Boston Computer Soc., Assn. Systems Mgmt., Alpha Gamma Sigma. Republican. Clubs: U.S. Ski Assn., Indian Guides. Home: 2 Bigham Rd North Reading MA 01864 Office: 1st Nat Bank Boston 100 Federal St Boston MA 02105

DAY, STACEY BISWAS, physician, educator, health science administrator, author; b. London, Dec. 31, 1927; s. Satis B. and Emma L. (Camp) D.; m. Noor Kassam Kanji, May 6, 1952 (div. 1969); children: Kahlil A., Selim M.; m. Nasreen Y. Fazelbhoy, June 7, 1970 (div. 1973); m. Ivana Podvalova, Oct. 18, 1973. M.D., Royal Coll. Surgeons, Dublin, Ireland, 1955; Ph.D., McGill U., 1964; D.Sc., Cin. U., 1971. Intern King's County Hosp., SUNY Downstate Ctr., 1955-56; resident fellow in surgery U. Minn. Hosp., 1956-60; hon. registrar St. George's Hosp., London, Eng., 1960-61; lectr. exptl. surgery McGill U., Montreal, Que., Can., 1964; asst. prof. exptl. surgery U. Cin. Med. Sch., 1968-70; assoc. dir. basic med. research Shriner's Burn Inst., Cin., 1969-71; from asst. to assoc. prof. pathology, head Bell Mus. Pathobiology U. Minn., Mpls., 1970-74; dir. biomed. communications and med. edn. Sloan-Kettering Inst., N.Y.C., 1974-80; mem. Sloan-Kettering Inst. for Cancer Research, 1974-80; mem. adminstrv. council, field coordinator 1974-75; prof. biology Sloan Kettering div. Grad. Sch. Med. Sci. Cornell U., ret., 1980; clin. prof. medicine div. behavioral medicine N.Y. Med. Coll., 1980—; prof. biopsychosocial medicine, chmn. dept. community health U. Calabar (Nigeria) Sch. Medicine, 1982-85; prof. internat. health, dir. Internat. Ctr. for Health Scis. Meharry Med. Coll., Nashville, 1985—, dir. WHO Collaborating Ctr. ICHS, 1987—; founding dir. WHO Collaborating Ctr., Nashville, 1987; adj. prof. family and community medicine U. Ariz. Coll. Med. Scis., Tucson, 1985—; Arris and Gale lectr. Royal Coll. Surgeons, Eng., 1972, vis. lectr., Ireland, 1972; vis. prof. U. Bologna, 1977; vis. prof. health communications U. Santiago, Chile, 1979-80; vis. prof. Oncologic Research Inst., Tallinn, Estonia, 1976, All India Insts. Health, 1976, Univ. Maiduguri, 1982; moderator med. cartography and computer health Harvard U., 1978, Acad. Scis., Czechoslovakia, 1987; cons. Pan Am. Health Assn., 1974—, U.S.-USSR Agreement for Health Cooperation, 1976, WHO Collaborating Centre Meharry Med. Coll., Nashville, 1985, liaison officer NAFEO/AID, 1986—; mem. expert com. for health, manpower devel., WHO, 1986—, cons. div. strengthening health care resources WHO, Geneva, 1987—; pres., chmn., pub. Cultural and Ednl. Prodns., Montreal, U.S.A., 1966-85; advisor to dean Med. Coll., Faculty Medicine and Health Scis., ABHA, Province of Asir, Saudi Arabia, 1981; cons. advisor to rector Universidad Autonoma Agraria Antonio Narro, Saltillo, Mexico, 1987—; cons. U.S. Dept. Edn. Office Spl. Edn. Region X, San Francisco, 1986—, bd. dirs. Internat. Health, African Health Consultancy Service, Nigeria; bd. dirs., v.p. Am. sci. activities Mario Negri Research Found., 1975-80; hon. founding chmn., bd. dirs. Lambo Found. U.S.; pres., exec. dir. Internat. Found. for Biosocial Devel. and Human Health, 1978-86; cons. Inst. Health, Lyfford Cay, Bahamas, 1981, Govt. Cross River State, Nigeria, Itreto State and H.H. Obong of Calabar, Nat. Bd. Advs., Am. Biog. Inst., 1982—; cons. community health and health communications Navaho Nation, Sage Meml. Hosp., Ganado, Ariz., 1984; founder, cons. Primary Self-Health Clinics, Oban, Ikot Oku Okono, and Ikot Imo, Nigeria, 1982-84; appointed ambassador Gov. State of Tenn., 1986—; adj. clin. prof. medicine N.Y. Med. Coll. Writer, 1965—; Author: verse Collected Lines, 1966; play By the Waters of Babylon, 1966; verse American Lines, 1967; play The Music Box, 1967; Three Folk Songs Set to Music, 1967, Poems and Etudes, 1968; novel Rosalita, 1968; The Idle Thoughts of a Surgical Fellow, 1968, Edward Stevens-Gastric Physiologist, Physician and American Statesman, 1969; novella Bellechasse, 1970; A Leaf of the Chaatim, 1970, Ten Poems and a Letter from America for Mr. Sinha, 1971, Curling's Ulcer: An Experiment of Nature, 1972, Tuluak and Amaulik: Dialogues on Death and Mourning with the Innuit Eskimo of Point Barrow and Wainwright, Alaska, 1974, East of the Navel and Afterbirth: Reflections from Rapa Nui, 1976, Health Communications, 1979, The Biopsychosocial Imperative, 1981, What Is Survival: The Physician's Way and the Biologos, 1981; editor: Death and Attitudes Toward Death, 1972, Membranes, Viruses and Immune Mechanisms in Experimental and Clinical Disease, 1972, Ethics in Medicine in a Changing Society, 1973, Communication of Scientific Information, 1975, Trauma: Clinical and Biological Aspects, 1975, Molecular Pathology, 1975; (with Robert A. Good) series Comprehensive Immunology, 9 vols., 1976-80; Cancer Invasion and Metastasis-Biologic Mechanisms and Therapy, 1977, Some Systems of Biological Communication, 1977, Image of Science and Society, 1977, What Is a Scientist, 1978, Sloan Kettering Inst. Cancer Series, 1974-80; editor-in-chief, mem. editorial bd.: Health Communications and Informatics, 1974-80; editor-in-chief: The American Biomedical Network: Health Care System in America Present and Past, 1978, A Companion to the Life Sciences, Vol. 1, 1979, A Companion to the Life Sciences, Vol. 2: Integrated Medicine, 1980, A Companion to the Life Sciences, Vol. 3: Life Stress, 1981, Advance to Biopsychosocial Health, 1984; editor-in-chief, mem. editorial bd.: Health Communications and Biopsycho. Social Health; editor: (with others) Cancer, Stress and Death, 1979, 2d edit., 1986, Computers for Medical Office and Patient Management, 1981, Readings in Oncology, 1980, Biopsychosocial Health, 1981; editor: Primary Health Care Guidelines: A Training Manual for Community Health, 2d edit., 1986; mem. editorial bd.: Psyche et Cancer, Switzerland, Psychoonocologia (Eupsycha); also co-editor various publs.; contbr. articles to profl. lit.; producer TV and radio health edn. programs, Nigeria. Served with Brit. Army, 1946-49. Recipient Moynihan medal Assn. Surgeons Gt. Britain and Ireland, 1960, Reuben Harvey triennial prize Royal Coll. Physicians, Ireland, 1957, Disting. scholar award Internat. Communication Assn., 1980, Sama Found. medal, 1982; named to Hon. Order Ky. Cols.; named Chieftan Ntufam Ajan of Oban Ejagham People, Cross River State, Nigeria, 1983; recipient Chieftan Obong Nsong Idem Ibibio Nigeria, 1983, Mgbe (Ekpe) honor Nigeria, commendation WHO address Fed. Govt. Nigeria, Calabar, 1983, Leadership in Internat. Med. Health citation Pres. U.S., 1987, WHO medal, 1987, Agromedicine citation Commr. of Agr., State of Tenn., 1987, Assembly citation State of N.Y., 1987, Citation Congl. Record., 1987; Maestro Honorifo, U. Autonoma Agraria, Coahuila, Mex., 1987; presented Key to the City of Nashville, 1987; addresses presented by people of Ikot Imo, Nsit Anyang, Oban, 1982-84, Commendation from King of Calabar, 1984; Ciba fellow Can., 1965; Stacey Day award named in his honor by Fed. Minister and Gov. of Cross River State, Calabar Med. Ctr., Nigeria, 1986. Fellow Zool. Soc. London, Royal Micros. Soc., Royal Soc. Health, World Acad. Arts and Scis., Japanese Found. for Biopsychosocial Health (internat. hon. fellow and most disting. mem.), African Acad. Sci., African Acad. Med. Scis. (founding); mem. Am. Burn Assn., Internat. Burn Assn., Can. Authors Assn., N.Y. Acad. Scis., AAAS, AMA, Am. Assn. History Medicine, Am. Inst. Stress (dir.), Am. Anthrop. Assn., Am. Rural Health Assn. (v.p. internat. sci. affairs, dir.), Am. Cybernetics Assn., Soc. Med. Anthropology, Arctic Soc. N.Am., Harvey Soc., Soc. Medical Geographers U.S.S.R. (hon.), Council Biology Editors, Musk Ox Circle, Sigma Xi, numerous others. Club: U. Minn. Alumni (charter). Home: 6 Lomond Ave Spring Valley NY 10977

DAYAN, RODNEY S., lawyer; b. Seattle, May 3, 1933; s. Jesse Charles Dayan and Thelma (Spencer) Dorsey; m. Barbara Heustis, Aug. 27, 1958; children: Christopher, Amanda. AB, Princeton U., 1955; LLB, Columbia U., 1961; LLM, NYU, 1967. Bar: N.Y. 1962. Assoc. Cadwalader, Wickersham & Taft, N.Y.C., 1961-69, ptnr., 1969—; Frequent chmn., panelist on legal or investment banking. Chmn. Bd. Examiners Montclair Dept. Pub. Safety, N.J., 1976-80; mem. Montclair Bd. Edn., 1971-75, Montclair Bd. Sch. Estimate, 1972-75. Keasby fellow New Coll. Oxford U., 1955-56. Mem. ABA (fed. regulation securities com. 1972-78), N.Y. State Bar Assn., Assn. of Bar of City of N.Y. (securities regulations com. 1973-76, commodities regulation com. 1976-77). Clubs: Down Town (N.Y.C.); Montclair Golf; Pennask Lake Fishing and Game (British Columbia, Can.). Office: Cadwalader Wickersham & Taft 100 Maiden Ln New York NY 10038

DAYEZ, NOEL ETIENNE, printing executive; b. Uccle, Belgium, Dec. 23, 1932; s. Paul and Jeanne (Gobbe) D.; m. Micheline Gillon, May 4, 1957; children—Sophie, Donatienne, Nicolas, Charlotte. Doctor Laws, U. Louvain, 1956. Br. mgr. Bank Credit du Nord Belge, Antwerp, 1956-64; v.p. sales Scaldia, Antwerp, 1965-71; sales and mktg. v.p. Intermills SA, Wemmel, Belgium, 1972-79, chief exec. officer, 1980-83; chief exec. officer Internat. Label Co., Cy-Clarksville (T.N.E.) USA, 1984-87, mng. dir., 1988—; dir. Illochroma Group Belgium Office. Roman Catholic. Home: 65 Av Van Gysel, B1810 Wemmel Belgium Office: Illochroma Group, 13 Rue du Chateau D'Or, 1180 Brussels Belgium

DAYRIT, MARIA LOURDES (LOUDETTE) LIMJUCO, small business owner, gourmet cooking instructor; b. Manila, Nov. 18, 1950; d. Francisco

Sr. and Pat (Limjuco) D. BBA, St. Theresa's Coll., Quezon City, 1972. Owner Le Cordon Bleu Food Products, Quezon City, Philippines, 1972-80; dir., owner Le Cordon Bleu Ecole de Cuisine Manille, Manila, 1975—, owner, 1975—; owner Loudette L. Dayrit Culinary Art Prodns., Manila, 1984—, Le Cordon Bleu Foods Enterprises, Manila, 1988—. Hostess TV shows Spicy Fry Day, 1976, and She, 1983-84. Recipient Cert. Appreciation Nutritionist-Dietitians Assn. of Philippines, 1978, Plaque of Appreciation Jaycees Philippines, 1979. Mem. Hotel and Restaurant Assn. of Philippines, Internat. Assn. Cooking Profls. Roman Catholic. Mailing Address: PO Box 423, 1502 Greenhills, Metro Manila Philippines

DE, BIBHAS RANJAN, physicist, researcher; b. Silchar, India, Jan. 22, 1946; came to U.S., 1968; s. Binod Bihari and Lila (Rakshit) D.; m. Gopa Sarkar, Jan. 16, 1971. BS with honors, U. Calcutta, 1967; M.S., U. Mich., 1970; Ph.D., U. Calif.-La Jolla, 1973. Research asst. U. Mich., Ann Arbor, 1969-71; asst. research physicist U. Calif.-La Jolla, 1974-75; guest researcher Royal Inst. Tech., Stockholm, 1974; vis. scientist Lunar and Planetary Inst., Houston, 1976-79; sr. physicist Sci.-Atlanta Inc., Atlanta, 1979-80; sr. research physicist Exxon, Houston, 1980-81, Chevron, La Habra, Calif., 1981-85, sr. research assoc., 1985—. Contbr. chpts. to The Sea, 1974, Planetary Satellites, 1977. Guest editor Astrophysics and Space Sci., 1979, 88. Author: (poetry) On Grunion Shore, 1987; contbr. articles to profl. jours., poetry to nat. and internat. lit. mags. Patentee in field. Nat. scholar Govt. of India, 1967; UNESCO fellow, 1968. Mem. Am. Phys. Soc., IEEE, N.Y. Acad. Scis., Acad. Am. Poets, World Poetry Soc., Phi Kappa Phi. Hindu. Office: Chevron Oil Field Research Co PO Box 446 La Habra CA 90631

DEACON, MARGARET BRENDA, historian; b. West Kilbride, Ayrshire, Scotland, Jan. 30, 1942; d. Sir George Edward Raven and Margaret Elsa (Jeffries) D.; m. David Quentin Seward, Sept. 18, 1982. BA, Oxford U., Eng., 1963, MA, 1967. Research fellow Inst. Oceanographic Scis., Surrey, Eng., 1963-68; research asst. sci. studies unit Edinburgh (Scotland) U., 1969-72; research asst. Nat. Maritime Mus., London, 1973-78; research fellow Inst. for Advanced Studies, 1979; Hartley research fellow Dept. Oceanography Southampton (Eng.) U., 1980-82, hon. research fellow, 1982—. Author: Scientists and the Sea, 1650-1900, 1971, Oceanography: Concepts and History, 1978; contbr. articles to profl. jours. Fellow Soc. Nautical Research, Challenger Soc., Royal Geograph. Soc., Royal Meteorol. Soc. (mem. specialist group on history of meteorology and oceanography 1982—); mem. Commn. Oceanography of the Internat. Union for History and Philosophy of Sci. (hon. v.p. 1987—), Hakluyt Soc. Mem. Ch. of Eng. Home: Montefiore House, Wessex Ln Southampton, Hampshire SO9 3TD, England Office: University Southampton, Dept Oceanography, Southampton SO9 5NH, England

DEAKIN, JAMES, writer, former newspaperman; b. St. Louis, Dec. 3, 1929; s. Rogers and Dorothy (Jeffrey) D.; m. Doris Marie Kanter, Apr. 14, 1956; 1 son, David Andrew. A.B., Washington U., St. Louis, 1951. Mem. staff St. Louis Post-Dispatch, 1951-81, Washington corr., 1953-80, White House corr., 1955-80; adj. assoc. prof. journalism George Washington U., 1981-87; fellow Woodrow Wilson Internat. Center for Scholars, 1980-81. Author: the Lobbyists, 1966, Lyndon Johnson's Credibility Gap, 1968, Straight Stuff, 1984; co-author: Smiling Through The Apocalypse, 1971, The Presidency and The Press, 1976, The American Presidency, Principles and Problems, Vol. II, 1983, The White House Press on the Presidency, 1983; also numerous articles. Recipient Distinguished Alumnus citation Washington U., 1973, Merriman Smith award for White House reporting, 1977; Markle Found. grantee, 1981. Mem. White House Corrs. Assn. (pres. 1974-75). Home: 402 W West St Southport NC 28461

DEAL, ERNEST LINWOOD, JR., banker; b. Florence, Ala., Jan. 5, 1929; s. Ernest Linwood and Nell W. (Willingham) D.; m. Mary Cooper, Dec. 27, 1952; children: Theresa Lynn, Sarah Street, Matthew Cooper, Jennifer Willingham. Student, Florence State Coll., 1947-49; B.S., U. Ala., 1952; postgrad., Southwestern Grad. Sch. Banking, So. Meth. U., 1961. V.p. Tex. Commerce Bank, Houston, 1956-65; sr. v.p. Capital Nat. Bank, Houston, 1965-71; pres., chief exec. officer Fannin Bank, Houston, 1971-82, chmn., chief exec. officer, 1982; chmn., chief exec. officer InterFirst Bank, Houston, 1983, First City Nat. Bank, Houston, 1984—; bd. dirs. Cherokee Resources Corp., N.Y. Mem. bd. visitors M.D. Anderson Hosp., Houston, 1971—; past chmn. Houston Parks Bd.; chmn. Local Organizing Com. U.S. Olympic Festival, 1986; chmn. bd. trustees Kinkaid Sch.; trustee Southwestern Grad. Sch. Banking. Served to lt. (j.g.) USNR, 1952-55. Mem. U. Ala. Alumni Assn., Houston C. of C. (dir., exec. com.), Am. Bankers Assn. (governing council, state v.p., govt. relations council 1977-82, v.p. 1978-79), Tex. Bankers Assn. (dir.), Phi Gamma Delta, Delta Sigma Pi, Omicron Delta Kappa. Republican. Presbyterian. Clubs: Houston Country, Ramada (treas.), Petroleum. Office: First City Nat Bank Houston 1001 Main St PO Box 2557 Houston TX 77252

DEAL, GEORGE EDGAR, corporate executive, management consultant; b. Marion, Ind., July 31, 1920; s. Harold Everett and Esther Victoria (Kendall) D.; m. Ruth Florence McFarland, Nov. 4, 1945; children: Joan Deal Eklund, Georgia Deal Ashcraft, Sharon Deal Ferdyiwek, Frank Kendall, Susan Melanie, Marylise Tobin. Student, Ind. Wesleyan U., 1937-39; B.S. with high distinction, Ind. U., 1941, M.S., 1942; postgrad., Am. U., 1942, Harvard U., 1943, Columbia U., 1948; D.B.A., George Washington U., 1970. Indsl. specialist WPB, 1942; dept. mgr. Macy's, N.Y.C., 1947-49; supt. Bloomingdale's, N.Y.C., 1949-53; v.p. The Kroger Co., Washington, 1953-63; asst. to pres. Bionetics Research Labs., Falls Church, Va., 1964-67; dir. Grad. Mgmt. Sch., Am. Mgmt. Assn., Saranac Lake, N.Y., 1967-69; sr. research assoc. Logistics Mgmt. Inst., Washington, 1969-70; pres. Mgmt. Factors Orgn., McLean, Va., 1970—; pres. San Luis Aurum Inc., 1976—; v.p. Cañonex de Oro, 1978—; faculty study dir. Nat. Grad. U., bd. advisors Coll. Democracy; chmn. sec. navy's adv. bd. edn. and tng., 1972-75; spl. asst. to dir. LIFE Internat.; cons. to pres. Coalinga Resources Inc. Author; contbr. articles to profl. jours. Mem. Greater Washington Health and Welfare Council, 1966-67; mem.-at-large Nat. council Boy Scouts Am. Served to capt. USNR, 1942-47, 50-52. Fellow Washington Acad. Scis.; mem. Nat. Council Assns. in Policy Scis. (steering com.), Councils Retail Mchts. (dir. Tenn. and Ala. councils 1954-60), Inst. of Mgmt., AAAS, Ops. Research Soc. Am. (assoc. editor 1969-73), Acad. Mgmt., Strategic Mgmt. Soc., Am. Mktg. Assn., World Future Soc., Soc. for Internat. Devel., Am. Inst. Mgmt., Internat. Inst. Strategic Studies, Navy League U.S., Cath. Acad. Scis. (v.p.), Beta Gamma Sigma. Republican. Roman Catholic. Lodges: Masons (Scottish Rite), Equestian Order Knights of the Holy Sepulchre in Jerusalem. Home and Office: 6245 Park Rd McLean VA 22101

DEAL, TIMOTHY, foreign service officer; b. St. Louis, Sept. 17, 1940; s. Edward F. and Loretta (Fuemuller) D.; m. Jill Brady, Sept. 5, 1964; children—Christopher, Bart. B.A., U. Calif.-Berkeley, 1962; postgrad., San Francisco State Coll., 1964-65, Am. U., 1972-73. With U.S. Embassy, Tegucigalpa, Honduras, 1966-68, Warsaw, Poland, 1969-72, econ. counselor, London, 1981-85; various fgn. service assignments Dept. State, Washington, 1972-76; sr. staff mem. Nat. Security Council, The White House, Washington, 1976-81; dep. U.S. Rep. U.S. Mission To OECD, Paris, 1985-88; dir. office Eastern European/Yugoslav affairs Dept. State, 1988—. Served to capt. U.S. Army, 1963-65. Recipient Performance Pay Award U.S. Dept. State 1984, 85, 86; Outstanding Service Cash award Nat. Security Council 1980. Avocations: theater; cinema; horse racing; sports. Home: 5721 Mac Arthur Blvd Washington DC 20016 Office: US Dept State Dir EUR/EEY 2201 C St NW Washington DC 20520

DEAL, WILLIAM BROWN, physician, university dean; b. Durham, N.C., Oct. 4, 1936; s. Harold Albert and Louise Brown D.; m. Elizabeth French Grayson, Aug. 30, 1958; children: Kimberly Cawthorne, Kathleen Louise. A.A., Mars Hill Coll., 1956; A.B., U. N.C., 1958, M.D., 1963. Intern Shands Hosp., Gainesville, Fla., 1963-64; chief resident, instr. dept. medicine U. Fla., Gainesville, 1969-70; mem. faculty U. Fla., 1970—, prof., 1975—, assoc. dean Coll. Medicine, 1973-77, v.p. health affairs, dean Coll. Medicine, 1978-80, dean, assoc. v.p. clin. affairs Coll. Medicine, 1980—; dir. Univ. Med. Ctr., Jacksonville, Fla., mem. liaison com. on med. edn., 1982—, vice chmn. bd. dirs., 1987—; dir. First Union Bank, Gainesville; dir., sec.-treas. Shands Teaching Hosp., Inc. Contbr. articles to med. jours. Served with USNR, 1964-66. Recipient Disting. Service award U. N.C., 1979. Fellow ACP, mem. AMA (chmn. med. schs. sect.), Assn. Am. Med. Colls. (adminstrv. bd. council of deans 1981—, exec. council 1986—), So. Council Med. Deans (chmn. 1982-83), Alpha Omega Alpha (bd. dirs.), Beta Theta Pi. Republican. Presbyterian. Club: Cosmos (Washington). Office: Box J-215 J Hillis Miller Health Center Gainesville FL 32610

DEALESSANDRO, JOSEPH PAUL, insurance company executive; b. Bklyn., Apr. 9, 1930; s. Peter Charles and Lucy Rose (Doganiero) DeA.; m. Dorothy Joan Sivillo, Nov. 7, 1962 (dec. 1966). Student, Bklyn. Coll., 1947-51, N.Y. U. Coll. Ins., 1958. Mgr. Am. Ins. Co., N.Y.C., 1952-60, Century Ins. Co., N.Y.C., 1960-62, St. Paul Ins. Co., N.Y.C., 1962-67; pres. Nat. Union Ins. Co., N.Y.C., 1967-87, also dir.; sr. v.p., dir. Am. Internat. Underwriters, 1970-87; exec. v.p., dir. Am. Home Assurance Co., 1973-87; chief exec. officer Comml. Credit Ins. Services Inc., 1987—, also chmn. bd. dirs.; sr. v.p. Comml. Credit Co., 1987—, Am. Credit Indemnity Ins. Co., 1987—, The Select Ins. Co., 1987—; also chmn., pres., chief exec. officer, dir. Atlantic Ins. Co., Dallas; pres., dir. Am. Internat. Global Assistance Corp.; chmn. bd. Am. Internat. Group Polit. Risk Inc.; tchr., condr. seminars Coll. of Ins.; dir. Commerce & Industry Ins. Co., United Guarantee Corp., Greensboro, N.C. Contbg. author: The Insurance Business Handbook; Contbr. articles to ins. jours. Bd. dirs. St. Vincent's Home; trustee Statue of Liberty Anniversary Com. Named Ky. Col.; recipient Man of Yr. award N.Y.C. United Jewish Appeal and Fedn. Jewish Philanthropies, 1985, 87, Humanitarian award Brandeis U., 1988. Mem. Am. Mgmt. Assn., Am. Risk Mgrs. Assn. Roman Catholic. Clubs: Grand Centurians. Lodges: K.C., Knights of Malta, Knight Comdrs. of Grand Cross. Office: Atlantic Ins Co PO Box 1771 Dallas TX 75221

DE ALWIS, SUSANTA, diplomat; b. Colombo, Sri Lanka, Aug. 17, 1932; s. Leslie and Emily De Alwis; m. Achala Pandita Gunawardene; children: Chamini, Darshini, Ruvan. LLB, U. Ceylon, 1954; LLM (Oxon) (Internat. Law), Oxford U., 1961. Barrister of the Gray's Inn, Eng.; atty.-at-law Sri Lankan Law Coll. Asst. news editor Daily News-Lake House, Colombo, 1953-57; asst. high commr. Sri Lanka Madras, India, 1962-66; charge d'affaires Embassy Sri Lanka, Indonesia, 1966-68; AMB/permanent rep. UN & Specialized Agys Geneva, Unido- Vienna, 1974-78; pres. U.N. Trade and Devel. Bd., Geneva, 1977-78; Sri Lankan ambassador to Japan and Republic of Korea 1980-84; Sri Lankan ambassador to U.S. and Mex. Washington, 1986—; chmn. Bur. of Non-Aligned Countries, Colombo, 1976; pres. Intelsat Assembly, 1987—; cons. UN, N.Y.C., 1978—. Author: Non-Alignment--A Critical Evaluation of the New Society, 1979. Exec. dir. Washington Vihara, 1970-74. Buddhist. Home: 2503 30th St NW Washington DC 20008 Office: Embassy of Sri Lanka 2148 Wyoming Ave NW Washington DC 20008

DEAN, DENIS ALLEN, lawyer; b. Detroit, Jan. 29, 1942; s. Allen and Mildred Ella (Stevens) D.; m. Sherrilynn J. Huerkamp, Mar. 16, 1973; children: Denis Allen, Daron Andrew. B.A., U. Miami (Fla.), 1963, J.D., 1966. Bar: Fla. 1966, U.S. Supreme Ct. 1971. Research asst. State Atty.'s Office, Dade County, Fla., 1964-66; asst. state atty. 11th Jud. Cir. of Fla., 1966-70; assoc. Eugene P. Spellman, Miami, 1970-79; ptnr. Dean & Hartman, P.A., Miami, 1979—; instr. criminal law and procedure Dade Jr. Coll., 1969-71; mem. N.Y.S.E. Bd. Arbitration, 1973—. Mem. ABA, Dade County Bar Assn., Assn. Trial Lawyers Am. Democrat. Presbyterian. Club: Dade County Police Benevolent Assn. (hon. mem.). Home: 12680 Hickory Rd North Miami FL 33181 Office: PBA Bldg 10680 NW 25st Ste 200 Miami FL 33172

DEAN, EDWIN BECTON, federal agency cost estimator; b. Danville, Va., Feb. 7, 1940; s. Edwin Becton and Lois (Campbell) D.; m. Deirdre Anne Jacovides, Aug. 16, 1964; children: Jennifer E., Kristin R., Brian N. BS in Physics, Va. Poly. Inst. and State U., 1963, MS in Math., 1965; postgrad., George Washington U., 1974-77. Technician, assoc. engr. Johns Hopkins U. Applied Physics Lab., Laurel, Md., 1959-64; physicist, mathematician, electronic engr., and ops. research analyst Naval Surface Weapons Ctr., Silver Spring, Md., 1964-79; owner Gen. Bus. Services and Beta Systems Virginia Beach, 1979-84; treas. Communique Inc., Virginia Beach, Va., 1980-81; registered rep. First Investors Corp., Arlington, Va., 1971-85; dir. Tips Club of Va. Beach, Inc., 1980-82; computer specialist Naval Supply Systems Command, Norfolk, Va., 1982-83; head cost estimating office NASA-Langley Research Ctr., Hampton, Va., 1983—. NASA fellow, 1963-65. Mem. IEEE, Internat. Soc. Parametric Analysts (bd. dirs.), Inst. for Cost Analysis, Assn. for Computing Machinery, Inst. for Mgmt. Sci., AIAA, N.Y. Acad. Sci., Ops. Research Soc. Am., Area Council Econ. Edn., Internat. Nuclear News Service, Sigma Pi Sigma, Pi Mu Epsilon, Phi Kappa Phi. Office: MS 444 NASA-Langley Research Ctr Hampton VA 23665

DEAN, JOHN AURIE, chemist, author, emeritus educator; b. Sault St. Marie, Mich., May 9, 1921; s. Aurie Jerome and Gertrude (Saw) D.; m. Elizabeth Louise Cousins, June 20, 1943 (div. 1981); children: Nancy Elizabeth, Thomas Alfred, John Randolph, Laurie Alice, Clarissa Elaine; m. Peggy DeHart Beeler, Oct. 23, 1981; stepchildren: Diane Barbara, Lisa Lynn, James Edward, Jonathan Curtis. B.S. in Chemistry, U. Mich., 1942, M.S. in Chemistry, 1944, Ph.D., 1949. Teaching fellow in chemistry U. Mich., Ann Arbor, 1942-44, 45-46; lectr. in chemistry U. Mich., 1946-48; chemist X-100 Phase Manhattan Project Chrysler Corp., Detroit, 1944-45; assoc. prof. chemistry U. Ala., Tuscaloosa, 1948-50; asst. prof. chemistry U. Tenn., Knoxville, 1950-53; assoc. prof. U. Tenn., 1953-58, prof. chemistry, 1958-81, prof. emeritus, 1981—; cons. Union Car Nuclear Div., Oak Ridge, 1953-74, Stewart Labs., Knoxville, 1968-81; vis. lectr. Peoples Republic of China, 1985. Author: Instrumental Methods of Analysis, 7 edits., 1948, 51, 58, 65, 74, 81, 88; Flame Photometry, 1960, Chemical Separation Methods, 1969, Flame Emission and Atomic Absorption Spectrometry, vol. 1, 1969, vol. 2, 1971, vol. 3, 1975, Lange's Handbook of Chemistry, 11th edit. 1973, 12th edit. 1979, 13th edit. 1985, Handbook of Organic Chemistry, 1986, Solutions Manual for Instrumental Methods of Analysis, 7th edit., 1988; contbr. articles to profl. jours. and chpts. to books. lectr. Peoples Republic of China, 1985. Mem. Am. Chem. Soc. (Charles H. Stone award Carolina-Piedmont sect. 1974), Soc. Applied Spectroscopy (chmn. SE sect. 1971-73, editor newsletter 1984—), Archaeol. Inst. Am., E. Tenn. Soc. (pres. 1980-81), U.S. Naval Inst. (life), Oriental Inst., U. Mus. Pa., Sigma Xi, Phi Kappa Phi. Presbyterian. Address: 201 Mayflower Dr Knoxville TN 37920-5871

DEAN, JOHN GUNTHER, ambassador; b. Germany, Feb. 24, 1926; came to U.S., 1939, naturalized, 1944; s. Joseph and Lucy (Askenaczy) D.; m. Martine Duphenieux, Dec. 26, 1952; children: Catherine Dean Curtis, Paul, Joseph. B.S. magna cum laude, Harvard U., 1947, M.A., 1950; Doctorate, U. Paris, 1949. With ECA, Am. embassy, Paris, 1950-51, Am. embassy, Brussels, 1951-53; asst. econ. commr. Am. embassy, Saigon, 1953-56; polit. officer Am. embassy, Laos, 1956-58; consul Am. consulate, Togo, 1959-60; chargé d'affaires Am. embassy, Mali, 1960-61; with Dept. State, Washington, 1961-65; polit. officer Am. embassy, Paris, 1965-69; regional dir. CORDS in Central Vietnam, 1970-72; dep. chief mission Am. embassy, Laos, 1972-74; ambassador to Cambodia, 1974-75, to Denmark, 1975-78, to Lebanon, 1978-81, to Thailand, 1981-85, to India, 1985—; adv. U.S. delegation to UN, 1963. Served to 2d lt. AUS, 1944-46. Fellow Center for Internat. Affairs Harvard, 1969-70. Clubs: Harvard (N.Y.C.); Kenwood Golf and Country (Washington). Office: US Ambassador to India Dept of State Washington DC 20520

DEAN, LYDIA MARGARET CARTER (MRS. HALSEY ALBERT DEAN), author, food and nutrition consultant; b. Bedford, Va., July 11, 1919; d. Christopher C. and Hettie (Gross) Carter; m. Halsey Albert Dean, Dec. 24, 1941; children: Halsey Albert Jr., John Carter, Lydia Margarae. Grad., Averett Coll.; B.S., Madison Coll., 1941; M.S., Va. Poly. Inst. and State U., 1951; postgrad., U. Va., Mich. State U.; D.Sc., Ph.D., UCLA Med. Sch., 1985. Dietetic intern, therapeutic dietitian St. Vincent de Paul Hosp., Norfolk, Va., 1942; physicist U.S. Naval Operating Base, Norfolk, 1943-45; clin. dietitian Roanoke Meml. Hosps., 1946-51; asso. prof. Va. Poly. Inst. and State U., 1946-53; community nutritionist Roanoke, Va., 1953-60; dir. dept. nutritions and dietetics Southwestern Va. Med. Center, Roanoke, 1960-67; food and nutrition cons. Nat. Hdqrs. A.R.C., Washington, 1967—; staff and vol. Nat. Hdqrs. A.R.C., 1973—; nutrition scientist, cons. Dept. Army, Washington, 1973—, Dept. Agr., 1973—; pres. Dean Assoc.; cons., assoc. dir. Am. Dietetic Assn., 1975—; coordinator new degree program U. Hawaii, 1974-75; dir., nutrition coordinator programs HHS, Washington, 1975—; mem. task force White House Conf. Food and Nutrition, 1969—; chmn. fed. com. Interagy. Com. on Nutrition Edn., 1970-71; tech. rep. to AID and State Dept.; chmn. Crusade for Nutrition Edn., Washington, 1970—; participant, cons. Nat. Nutrition Policy Conf., 1974. Author: (with Virginia McMasters) Community Emergency Feeding, 1972, Help My Child How To Eat Right, 1973, rev., 1978, The Complete Gourmet Nutrition Cookbook: The Joy of Eating Well and Right, 1978, The Stress Foodbook, 1980, rev. edit., 1982; contbr. articles to profl. jours. Trustee World U. Fellow Am. Pub. Health Assn., Internat. Inst. Community Service; mem. Am. Dietetic Assn., Bus. and Profl. Women's Clubs (cons. 1970—, pres. 1981-82), Am. Home Econs. Assn. (rep. and treas. joint congl. com.), AAUW, Inst. Food Technologists. Home: 7816 Birnam Wood Dr McLean VA 22102

DEAN, MICHAEL MENAHEM, lawyer; b. Phila., Jan. 7, 1933; s. David Justin and Lena (Gassel) D.; children from previous marriage: Benjamin, Gillian, Jessica; m. Sandra, June 25, 1978. B.A., Antioch Coll., 1954; J.D. cum laude, U. Pa., 1957. Bar: Pa. 1957. Assoc. Wolf & Block, Phila., 1957-62, 63-66; ptnr. Wolf, Block, Schorr & Solis-Cohen, Phila., 1966—; Fulbright fellow recorder tribal law Sch. Oriental and African Studies U. London, London, Nairobi, Kenya, 1962-63; counsel, dir., exec. com. Council Labor and Industry, Phila., 1970—; dir., exec. com., Univ. City Sci. Ctr., Phila., 1974-86, counsel, 1974—; counsel Food Distbn. Ctr., Phila., 1974—, Rouse & Assocs., Malvern, Pa., 1972—, Posel Enterprises, Phila., 1975—, Klein Realty Co., Phila., 1980—; exec. com. Wolf, Block, Phila., 1981-83. Bd. dirs., exec. com. Cen. Phila. Devel. Corp., 1974—, pres., 1987—; counsel, bd. dirs., exec. com., chmn. endowment trust Diagnostic and Rehab. Ctr., Phila., 1980—; mem. Phila. Mayor's Econ. Roundtable, 1985—; bd. dirs. Greater Phila. Econ. Devel. Coalition, 1987—. Mem. ABA, Pa. Bar Assn., Phila. Bar Assn., Order of Coif, Downtown Council Greater Phila. C. of C. Club: Locust. Office: Wolf Block Schorr & Solis-Cohen 12th floor Packard Bldg Philadelphia PA 19102

DEAN, STANLEY ROCHELLE, psychiatrist; b. Stamford, Conn., Feb. 13, 1908; s. Jacob and Gerta (Rochelle) D.; m. Marion Jamieson, Nov. 8, 1967; children: Lori Dean Schonfeld, Michael Louis. B.S., U. Mich., 1930, M.D. cum laude, 1934. Diplomate: Am. Bd. Psychiatry and Neurology. Intern Hurley (Mich.) Hosp., 1934-35; resident in psychiatry Taunton (Mass.) State Hosp., Boston Psychopathic Hosp., 1935-37; sr. physician Fairfield State Hosp., Newtown, Conn., 1937-40; practice medicine specializing in psychiatry Stamford, 1940-64; specializing in schizophrenia family and marriage counseling Miami, Fla., 1964—; emeritus staff Stamford Hosp., St. Joseph's Hosp., Stamford; clin. prof. psychiatry U. Fla., U. Miami, Fla.; founder Research in Schizophrenia Endowment, 1958-62. Author-editor: Schizophrenia: the First Ten Dean Award Lectures, 1973, Psychiatry and Mysticism, 1975; (with Robert Cancro) Research in the Schizophrenic Disorders: The Stanley R. Dean Award Lectures, 2 vols., 1984. Contbr. articles to profl. jours. Recipient prize for research New Eng. Psychiat. Assn., 1942, Silvano Arieti award Am. Acad. Psychoanalysis, 1987, Pioneer in Research award Nat. Alliance for Mentally Ill, 1987; Stanley R. Dean award named in honor Fund Behavioral Scis. and Am. Coll. Psychiatrists. Fellow Am. Psychiat. Assn. (joint commn. pub. affairs), Am. Coll. Psychiatrists, Royal Coll. Psychiatrists (Gt. Brit.); mem. Am. Assn. Social Psychiatry (pres. 1980-82), Alpha Omega Alpha, Phi Kappa Phi. Address: 1800 NE 1145h St Miami FL 33181

DE ANDRADE, CARLOS ALBERTO FILIPE, city manager, consultant; b. V F Campo, Azores, Portugal, July 24, 1941; s. Jacinto and Luisa (Filipe) de A.; m. Nelly Franco, Oct. 15, 1966; children: Filipe, Miguel. M in Econs., Inst. Superior de Ciências Económicas e Financeiras, 1975. Dir. Matrena-Sociedade Industrial de Papeis, SA, Lisbon, Portugal, 1965-79, Gremetal-Montages Industriais, LDA, Bucelas, Portugal, 1979-81, Edifer, SA, Amadora, Portugal, 1981-88; construcões Técnicas, SA., Lisbon, Portugal, 1988—. Author monographs in field. Served to lt. Portuguese Military Police, 1962-65. Mem. Associação Fiscal Portuguesa, Associação Portuguesa Economistas. Democrat. Roman Catholic. Home: Rua de Ceuta Lote 158-11th D, 1495 Linda-a-Velha Portugal Office: Edifer SA, Rua das Fontainhas, 2700 Amadora Portugal

DEANE, JAMES GARNER, editor, conservationist; b. Hartford, Conn., Apr. 5, 1923; s. Julian Lowrie and Miriam (Grover) D. B.A., Swarthmore Coll., 1943. Mem. editorial staff Washington Star, 1944-60; edn. editor Washington Star, 1952-57, classical recs. critic, 1952-60; ind. researcher, vol. in conservation activity 1961-68; asso. editor Nat. Parks Mag., 1968-69, editor, 1969; asst. editor The Living Wilderness, Washington, 1969-71; exec. editor The Living Wilderness, 1971-75, editor, 1975-81; now editor Defenders mag., Washington, 1981—; Washington corr. Mus. Courier, 1945-55; contbg. editor High Fidelity mag., 1953-55; mem. com. transp. environ. rev. process Transp. Research Bd. NRC, 1974-77; Am. co-chmn. Can. U.S. Environ. Council, 1975—. Bd. dirs. Arctic Internat. Wildlife Range Soc., 1979—; trustee Com. of 100 on Federal City, 1967—, 1st vice chmn., 1967-69; chmn. Potomac Valley Conservation and Recreation Council, 1967. Served with AUS, 1946-47. Recipient award Edn. Writers Assn., 1956, Public Service award Washington Newspaper Guild, 1956, Charles Carroll Glover award Nat. Park Service, 1967. Club: City Tavern. Home: 4200 Cathedral Ave NW Washington DC 20016 Office: 1244 19th St NW Washington DC 20036

DEANS, GRAEME KETCHESON, management consultant; b. Montreal, Que., Can., Aug. 2, 1961; s. Sidney Alfred Vindin and Barbara (Ketcheson) D.; m. Julia Lyndon Wilson, July 4, 1987. BSChemE, Queen's U., 1983; MBA, Dartmouth Coll., 1987. Asst. chem. engr. Hulett Sugar, Tongaat, South Africa, 1982; jr. field engr. Schlumberger Internat., Pau, France, 1983-85; field engr. Sfax, Tunisia, 1984-85; sr. field engr. Madrid, 1985; market devel. specialist Corning (N.Y.) Glass Works, 1986; assoc. cons. Booz, Allen & Hamilton Inc., N.Y.C., 1987—. Office: Booz Allen & Hamilton Inc 101 Park Ave New York NY 10178

DE ARAUJO SALES, EUGENIO CARDINAL, archbishop of Rio de Janeiro; b. Acari, Brazil, Nov. 8, 1920; d. Celso Dantas and Josefa de A.S.; student Seminary Fortaleza City. Ordained priest Roman Catholic Ch., 1943, consecrated bishop, 1954, elevated to cardinal, 1969; Sede Plena apostolic adminstr., Natal, 1962, Salvador, 1964; archbishop, Salvador, 1968-71, Rio de Janeiro, 1971—; mem. Council Pub. Affairs, Sacred Congregation Bishops, Evangelization, Oriental Chs., Cath. Edn., Commns. for Social Communication and Culture, Cardinal Council Organic and Econ. Problems. Editor: The Pastors Voice. Address: Gloria 446, 20241 Rio de Janeiro Brazil

DEARING, JOHN WILLIAM, metals company executive; b. Sydney, N.S., Can., Aug. 22, 1956; s. Harry and Rita Marie (LeBlanc) D.; m. Shirley Margaret Weren, July 17, 1982; 1 child, Kyle John. BBA, Carleton U., Ottawa, Ont., Can., 1984, cert. mng. for quality, 1986. Sheet metal apprentice Western Plumbing and Heating Ltd., Sydney, 1977-78; metal technician Viking Helicopter Ltd., Carleton Place, Ont., 1979-80; lead hand Ea. Aircraft Structural Repair, Arnprior, Ont., 1980-81; lead hand Pryor Metals Ltd., Ottawa, 1981-82, supr. shipping and receiving, 1981-82, material mgr., 1982-86, quality assurance mgr., 1986—, safety dir., 1981—, cons. customer design, 1983—. Troop leader Boy Scouts of Can., Chesterville, Ont., 1986—. Served with Can. Armed Forces, 1976-79. Named Hon. Citizen, City of Waterbury, Conn., 1987. Roman Catholic. Home: 6 Riverside Dr PO Box 708, Chesterville, ON Canada K0C 1H0 Office: Pryor Metals Ltd, 2623 Fenton Rd, Ottawa, ON Canada K1G 3N3

DEARMON, THOMAS ALFRED, automotive industry financial executive, life insurance executive; b. Montgomery, Ala., Dec. 28, 1937; s. Thomas A. and Rose (Giardina) D.; m. Leigh Caroline Smith, Dec. 28, 1963; children—Jacob Thomas, Joshua Carter. B.B.A., U. Okla, 1961; J.D., Oklahoma City U., 1968. Bar: Okla. 1968. C.P.A., Okla. Audit mgr. Arthur Andersen & Co., Oklahoma City, 1961-68; account exec. F.I. DuPont, Oklahoma City, 1968-73; v.p., sec. Fred Jones, Inc. and Fred Jones Mfg. Co., 1973—; pres., bd. dirs. Century Mgmt. Co., Century Life Assurance, Oklahoma City, 1983—, Century Property and Casualty Ins. 1987—, Century Producers Life Ins., 1988—; mem. investment com. Fred Jones Industries, a Ltd. Ptnrship, Oklahoma City, 1985—; sec., bd. dirs. Hist. Preservation Inc., Oklahoma City, 1984—. Served with U.S. Army, 1963. Mem. Oklahoma Bar Assn., Oklahoma Soc. CPA's, Fin. Execs. Inst. Democrat. Methodist. Lodge: Downtown Lions (pres. 1985-86). Office: 123 S Hudson St Oklahoma City OK 73102

DEAVER, PETE EUGENE, civil engineer; b. Ft. Worth, Mar. 8, 1936; s. Elmer Jack and Mattie Alline (Kelley) Deaver; student Cramwell Inst., 1957; B.S., U. Tex., Arlington, 1968; m. Birdie Jo Foster, Apr. 30, 1954; children—Pete Eugene, Stephen Lewis, Mickey Jo, Robert. Aircraft engr. Gen. Dynamics Corp., Ft. Worth, 1957-61; project engr. ejection seat studies Kirk Engring. Co., Bethpage, N.Y., 1961-64; sr. engr. Ling Tempco Vought Aeros., Dallas, 1964-65; stress engr. Boeing Aircraft Co., Seattle, 1965-66; sr. aero. engr. Gen. Dynamics Corp., Albuquerque, 1966-74; owner, operator Deaver Engring. Co., cons. constrn. and petroleum industry, Midland, Tex., 1974-84. Served with USNR, 1952-54. Registered profl. engr., N.Mex., Tex. Mem. Tex. Water Pollution Control Assn., NW Tex. Water Utilities Assn., Am. Helicopter Soc., Soc. Exploration Geophysicists, Tex., Nat. socs. profl. engrs. Baptist. Club: Masons (32 deg.). Author: Basic Stress Analysis for Engineers and Draftsmen, 1967; Drilling Manual for Rotary Drilling, 1981. Home: 2200 Sharpshire Ln Arlington TX 76014

DEAVER, PHILLIP LESTER, lawyer; b. Long Beach, Calif., July 21, 1952; s. Albert Lester and Eva Lucille (Welton) D. Student, USCG Acad., 1970-72; BA, UCLA, 1974; JD, U. So. Calif., 1977. Bar: Hawaii 1977, U.S. Dist. Ct. Hawaii 1977, U.S. Ct. Appeals (9th cir.) 1978, U.S. Supreme Ct. 1981. Assoc. Carlsmith, Wichman, Case, Mukai & Ichiki, Honolulu, 1977-83, ptnr., 1983-86; mng. ptnr. Bays, Deaver, Hiatt, Kawachika & Lezak, Honolulu, 1986. Mem. ABA (forum com. on the Constrn. Industry), AIA (affiliate Hawaii chpt.). Home: 2471 Pacific Heights Honolulu HI 96813 Office: Bays Deaver Hiatt Kawachika & Lezak PO Box 1760 Honolulu HI 96806

DEBAENE, CHRISTIAN FRANQOIS DEBAENE, hotel executive; b. Paris, Dec. 19, 1953; s. Jacques and Nicole (Vaissier) D.; m. Faugeras Penelope, Oct. 4, 1986. BS in Engring., Inst. Indsl. du Nord, Lille, France, 1976; MS in Engring., U. Calif., Berkeley, 1977; MBA, INSEAD, Fontainebleau, France, 1986. Asst. to pres. Thomson Consumer Goods, Paris, 1981-83, mktg. mgr. Europe, 1983-85; devel. mgr. IBIS Hotel Chain-Accor Group, Paris, 1987—; guest speaker H.E.C. and ISG, Paris, 1983-86. Contbr. articles to profl. jours. French Govt. scholar, 1976-77. Home: 58 Rue Victor Hugo, 92400 Courbevoie France Office: Sphere IBIS Group Accor, 6-8 Rue du Bois Briard, 91021 Cedex Evry France

DEBAKEY, GEORGE TOUFEE, trade association executive; b. Ft. Dodge, Iowa, Oct. 2, 1949; s. George Joseph and Marge (Armstrong) DeB.; m. Jimmie Lou Crook; children: John, Robert. BS, Drake U., 1972; M in Internat. Mgmt., Am. Grad. Sch. Internat. Mgmt., Phoenix, 1973; MBA, So. Meth. U., 1974. Internat. mktg. analyst Rockwell Internat., Dallas, 1974-76; asst. to mng. dir. Rockwell Internat., London, Eng., 1976-77; mgr. internat. relations Rockwell Internat., Washington, 1977-78; dir. Middle East div. Rockwell Internat., Cairo, 1978-82; dir. internat. mktg. Rockwell Internat., Washington, 1982-83; v.p. Fleet Fin. Group, Providence, 1983-85; dep. asst. sec. Dept. Commerce, Washington, 1985-87; exec. dir. ADAPSO, Washington, 1987—; bd. dirs. Informant newsletter Dallas High Tech. Trade Ctr., MIT Enterprise Forum, Washington. Republican. Presbyterian. Home: 5303 Marlyn Dr Bethesda MD 20816 Office: ADAPSO 1300 N 17th St Arlington VA 22209

DEBAKEY, LOIS, writer, lecturer, editor, scholar; b. Lake Charles, La.; d. S.M. and Raheeja (Zorba) DeBakey. B.A. in Math., Tulane U., 1949, M.A. in Lit. and Linguistics, 1959, Ph.D. in Lit. and Linguistics, 1963. Asst. prof. English Tulane U.; asst. prof. sci. communication Tulane Med. Sch., 1963-65; assoc. prof. sci. communication Tulane U. Med. Sch., 1965-67; prof. Tulane Med. Sch., 1967-68, lectr., 1968—, adj. prof., 1981—; prof. sci. communication Baylor Coll. Medicine, Houston, 1968—; mem. biomed. library rev. com. Nat. Library Medicine, Bethesda, Md., 1973-77, bd. regents, 1981-86, cons., 1986—; lit. selection tech. rev. com., 1988—; Permanent Paper Task Force, 1986—; dir. courses in med. communication ACS and other orgns.; mem. nat. adv. council U. So. Calif. Ctr. for Continuing Med. Edn., 1981—; mem. adv. com. Soc. for Preservation of Eng. Lang. and Lit. (SPELL), 1986—; steering com. Plain English Forum, 1984—; founding bd. Friends Nat. Library Medicine, 1985—; cons. legal writing com. ABA, 1983—; former cons. Nat. Assn. Standard Med. Vocabulary. Sr. author: The Scientific Journal: Editorial Policies and Practices, 1976; co-author: Medicine: Preserving the Passion, 1987; mem editorial bd.: Tulane Studies in English, 1966-68, Cardiovascular Research Center Bull., 1971-83, Health Communications and Informatics, 1975-80, Forum on Medicine, 1977-80, Grants Mag, 1978-81, Internat. Jour. Cardiology, 1981-86, Excerpta Medica's Core Jours. in Cardiology, 1981—, Health Communications and Biopsychosocial Health, 1981-82, Internat. Angiology, 1985—; mem. usage panel: Am. Heritage Dictionary, 1980—; cons. Webster's Medical Desk Dictionary, 1986; contbr. articles on biomed. communication and sci. writing, literacy, also other subjects to profl. jours., books, encys., and pub. press. Recipient Disting. Service award Am. Med. Writers Assn., 1970, Bausch & Lomb sci. award., John P. McGovern award Med. Library Assn., 1983. Mem. Internat. Soc. Gen. Semantics, Inst. Soc., Ethics and Life Scis., Council Biology Editors (dir. 1973-77, chmn. com. on editorial policy 1971-75), Council Basic Edn. (spl. commn. writing 1977-79), Soc. Tech. Communication, So. Assn. Colls. and Schs. (exec. council Commn. on Colls. 1975-80), AAAS, NIH Alumni Assn., Nat. Council Tchrs. English (com. on tech. sci. writing, conf. on coll. composition and communication), Assn. Tchrs. Tech. Writing, Dictionary Soc. N.Am., Nat. Assn. Sci. Writers, Soc. for Health and Human Values, Com. of Thousand for Better Health Regulations, Golden Key Nat. Honor Soc. (hon.), Phi Beta Kappa. Office: Baylor Coll Medicine One Baylor Plaza Houston TX 77030

DEBAKEY, MICHAEL ELLIS, cardiovascular surgeon; b. Lake Charles, La., Sept. 7, 1908; s. Shaker Morris and Raheeja (Zorba) DeB.; m. Diana Cooper, Oct. 15, 1936; children: Michael Maurice, Ernest Ochsner, Barry Edward, Denis Alton, Olga Katerina; m. Katrin Fehlhaber, July 1975. B.S., Tulane U., 1930, M.D., 1932, M.S., 1935, LL.D., 1965; Docteur Honoris Causa, U. Lyon, France, 1961, U. Brussels, 1962, U. Ghent, Belgium, 1964, U. Athens, 1964; D.H.C., U. Turin, Italy, 1965, U. Belgrade, Yugoslavia, 1967; LL.D., Lafayette Coll., 1965; M.D. (hon.), Aristotelean U. of Thessaloniki, Greece, 1972; D.Sc., Hahnemann Med. Coll., 1973, numerous others. Diplomate Nat. Bd. Med. Examiners, Am. Bd. Surgery, Am. Bd. Thoracic Surgery. Intern Charity Hosp., New Orleans, 1932-33, asst. surgery, 1933-35; asst. surgery U. Strasbourg, France, 1935-36, U. Heidelberg, Fed. Republic of Germany, 1936; instr. surgery Tulane U., New Orleans, 1937-40, asst. prof., 1940-46, assoc. prof., 1946-48; prof., chmn. dept. surgery Baylor (Tex.) Coll. Medicine, 1948—, v.p. med. affairs, 1968-69, chief exec. officer, 1968-69, pres., 1969-79, chancellor, 1979—, dir. Nat. Heart and Blood Vessel Research and Demonstration Ctr., 1975-85, dir. DeBakey Heart Ctr., 1985—; surgeon-in-chief Ben Taub Gen. Hosp., 1963—; sr. attending surgeon Meth. Hosp.; clin. prof. surgery U. Tex. Dental Br., Houston; cons. surgery VA Hosp., St. Elizabeth's Hosp., M.D. Anderson Hosp., St. Luke's Hosp., Tex. Children's Hosp., Tex. Inst. Rehab. and Research Brooke Gen. Hosp., Brooke Army Med. Ctr., Ft. Sam Houston, Tex., Walter Reed Army Hosp., Washington.; mem. med. adv. com. Office Sec. Def., 1948-50, Ams. for Substance Abuse Prevention, 1984; Med. Adv. Bd., Internat. Brotherhood Teamsters, 1985—; chmn. com. surgery NRC, 1953, mem. exec. com., 1953; mem. com. med. services Hoover Commn.; Friends of Nat. Library of Medicine (founding bd. dirs.), 1985—; chmn. bd. regents Nat. Library Medicine, 1959; past mem. nat. adv. heart council NIH; mem. Nat. Adv. Health Council, 1961-65, Nat. Adv. Council Regional Med. Programs, 1965—, Nat. Adv. Gen. Med. Scis. Council, 1965, Program Planning Com., Com. Tng., Nat. Heart Inst., 1961—; mem. civilian health and med. adv. council Office Asst. Sec. Def.; chmn. Pres.'s Commn. Heart Disease, Cancer and Stroke, 1964; mem. adv. council Nat. Heart Lung and Blood Inst., 1982-87; mem. Tex. Sci. and Tech. Council, 1984-86. Author: (with Robert A. Kilduffe) Blood Transfusion, 1942, (with Gilbert W. Beebe) Battle Casualties, 1952, (with Alton Ochsner) Textbook of Minor Surgery, 1955, (with T. Whayne) Cold Injury, Ground Type, 1958, A Surgeon's Visit to China, 1974, The Living Heart, 1977, The Living Heart Diet, 1985; editor: Yearbook of Surgery, 1958-70; chmn. adv. editorial bd.: Medical History of World War II; editor Jour. Vascular Surgery, 1984—; contbr. over 1150 articles to med. jours. Mem. Tex. Constl. Revision Commn., 1973. Served as col. Office Surgeon Gen. AUS, 1942-46; now Col. Res.; cons. to Surgeon Gen. 1946—. Decorated Legion of Merit, 1946, Independence of Jordan medal 1st class, Merit Order of Republic 1st Class Egypt, , comdr. Cross of Merit Pro Utiliate Hominum Sovereign Order Knights of Hosp. of St. John of Jerusalem in Denmark; recipient Rudolph Matas award, 1954, Internat. Soc. Surgery Disting. Service award, 1957, Modern Medicine award, 1957, Roswell Park medal, 1959, Leriche award Internat. Soc. Surgery, 1959, Great medallion U. Ghent, 1961, Grand Cross, Order Leopold Belgium, 1962, Albert Lasker award for clin. research, 1963, Order of Merit Chile, 1964, St. Vincent prize med. scis. U. Turin, 1965, Orden del Libertador Gen. San Martin Argentina, 1965, Centennial medal Albert Einstein Med. Ctr., 1966, Gold Scalpel award Internat. Cardiology Found., 1966, Disting. Faculty award, 197,; Eleanor Roosevelt Humanities award, 1969; Civilian Service medal Office Sec. Def., 1970, USSR Acad. Sci. 50th Anniversary Jubilee medal, 1973, Phi Delta Epsilon Disting. Servic, 1974, La Madonnina award, 1974, 30 Yr. Service award Harris County Hosp. Dist., 1978, Knights Humanity award honoris causa Internat. Register Chivalry, Milan, 1978, diploma de Merito Caja Costarricense de Seguro Social, San Jose, Costa Rica, 1979, Disting. Service plaque Tex. Bd. Edn., 1979, Britannica Achievement in Life award, 1979, Medal of Freedom with Distinction Presdl. award, 1969, Disting. Service award Internat. Soc. Atherosclerosis, 1979, Centennial award ASME, 1980, Marian Health Care award St. Mary's U., 1981, Clemson U. award, 1983, Humana Heart Inst. award, 1985, Theodore E. Cummings award, 1987, Nat. Med. of Sci. award 1987, others; named Dr. of Yr., Med. World News, 1965, Med. Man of Yr., 1966, Disting. Service Prof., Baylor U., 1968, Humanitarian Father of Yr., 1974, Tulane U. Alumnus of Yr., 1974, Tex. Scientist of Yr., Tex. Acad. Sci., 1979. Fellow ACS (Ann. award Southwestern Pa. chpt. 1973), Inst. of Medicine Chgo. (hon.); mem. Am. Coll. Cardiology (hon. fellow), Royal Soc. Medicine, Halsted Soc., Am. Heart Assn., So. Soc. Clin. Research, AAAS, Southwestern Surg. Congress (pres. 1952), Soc. Vascular Surgery (pres. 1953), Soc. Vascular Surg. Edn. & Research Found. (pres. 1988), AMA (Disting. Service award 1959, Hektoen Gold medal), Am. Surg. Assn. (Disting. Service award 1981), So. Surg. Assn., Western Surg. Assn., Am. Assn. Thoracic Surgery (pres. 1959), Internat. Cardiovascular Soc. (pres. 1958, pres. N.Am chpt. 1964), Assn. Internat. Vascular Surgeons (pres. 1983), Mex. Acad. Surgery (hon.), Soc. Clin. Surg., Nat. Acads. Practice Medicine, Soc. Univ. Surgeons, Internat. Soc. Surgery, Soc. Exptl. Biology and Medicine, Hellenic Surg. Soc. (hon.), Bio-med. Engring. Soc. (bd. dirs. 1968), Houston Heart Assn. (mem. adv. council 1968-69), Soc. Nacional de Cirugia (Cuba), C. of C., Sigma Xi, Alpha Omega Alpha. Democrat. Episcopalian. Club: University (Washington). Office: Baylor Coll Medicine One Baylor Plaza Houston TX 77030

DEBAKEY, MICHAEL MAURICE, investment company executive; b. New Orleans, July 20, 1939; s. Michael E. and Diana (Cooper) DeB.; m. Delia Revoredo, Dec. 29, 1962; children—Delia, Michael, Denise. B.A., U. south, 1963; B. Fgn. Trade, Am. Inst. Fgn. Trade, 1964. Gen. mgr. Texaco, Inc., Lima, Peru, 1962-68; pres. Interam. Devel. Reps., Lima, 1968-70; mng. gen. ptnr. Paso Grande Investments, Houston, 1980-86; chmn., chief exec. officer Challenge Air Transport, Miami, 1981-87; pres. Paso Grande Holdings, Inc., Houston, 1986—, Tex. Med. Capital Corp., Houston, 1985—, MSupply Corp., 1987—; dir., Houston Biomed., Inc., Socorro Investment Corp.; advisor to minister tourism, Peru. Mem. Houston C. of C. Club: Nacional, Lima Golf and Tennis. Home: Á lvarez Calderó n 760, San Isidro, Lima Peru Office: 1900 Yorktown Suite 450 Houston TX 77056

DEBAKEY, SELMA, science communication educator, writer, editor, lecturer; b. Lake Charles, La.. B.A., Newcomb Coll., Tulane U., New Orleans, postgrad. Dir. dept. med. communication Alton Ochsner Med. Found., New Orleans, 1942-68; prof. sci. communication Baylor Coll. Medicine, Houston, 1968—; editor Cardiovascular Research Ctr. Bull., 1970-84. Author: (with A. Segaloff and K. Meyer) Current Concepts in Breast Cancer, 1967; former editor: Ochsner Clinic Reports, Selected Writings from the Ochsner Clinic; mem. editorial bd. Internat. Angiology, 1985—; contbr. articles in field. Mem. Soc. Tech. Communication, Assn. Tchrs. Tech. Writing, Am. Med. Writers Assn. (past bd. dirs.; publ., nominating, fellowship, constn., bylaws, awards, and edn. coms.), Council Biol. Editors (past mem. trn. in sci. writing com.), Soc. Health and Human Values, Modern Med. Monograph Awards Com., AAAS, Nat. Assn. Standard Med. Vocabulary (former cons.). Office: Baylor Coll Medicine One Baylor Pl Houston TX 77030

DEBEAR, RICHARD STEPHEN, library planning consultant; b. N.Y.C., Jan. 18, 1933; s. Arthur A. and Sarah (Morrison) deB.; m. Estelle Carmel Grandon, Apr. 27, 1951; children—Richard, Jr., Diana deBear Fortson, Patricia deBear Talkington, Robert, Christopher, Nancy. B.S., Queens Coll. CUNY, 1953. Sales rep. Sperry Rand Corp., Blue Bell, Pa., 1954-76; pres. Library Design Assocs., Plymouth, Mich., 1976—, Am. Library Ctr., Plymouth, 1981—; bldg. cons. to numerous libraries, 1965—. Mem. ALA, Mich. Library Assn. Office: Library Design Assocs Inc 859 S Main St Plymouth MI 48170

DEBEER, WILLIAM ALLAN, engineer; b. Somerset West, Cape, Republic S. Africa, Jan. 7, 1938; s. Allan John and Florence Winifred (Wallis) DeB.; m. Deirdre Roisin, Nov. 4, 1977; children: Patrick Cormac, Conor William. BSc in Engring., U. Cape Town, Republic S. Africa, 1959; BA with honors, U. Stellenbosch, Republic S. Africa, 1969. Registered profl. engr. Trainee Assoc. Electrical Industries, Manchester, England, 1960-62; applications engr. Assoc. Electrical Industries, Rugby, England, 1962-65, Johannesburg, 1965-68; adminstr. mgr. Searle Bush Africa, Ltd., Johannesburg, 1970-73; mng. dir. Winder Controls, Ltd., Germisson, Republic S. Africa, 1974—. Mem. London IEEE (assoc.), S. African IEEE. Mem. Progressive Fed. party. Anglican. Clubs: S. African Country, Old Edwardians. Home: PO Box 75076, 2047 Garden View Republic of South Africa Office: Winder Controls Ltd, 56 Stanley St, 1401 Germisson Transvaal, Republic of South Africa

DE BELINKO, GEORGE, retired mining engineer; b. Kharkow, Russia, Nov. 22, 1910; came to France, 1920, naturalized, 1932; s. Leo and Mary (Groubbe) DeB.; grad. Nat. High Mining Sch., 1931; D.Sc., U. Louvain (Belgium), 1934; m. Jane Matras le Billoy De La Dyardiere, July 11, 1952. Engr., Germany, 1931-34; free-lance prospector, Africa, 1935-40; engr. Penarroya Cy., Morocco, 1946-56, dir., 1951-58; engr. Cerphos, Aubervilliers, France, 1958-76, chief engr., 1967-76; pvt. cons., Paris, 1975-84, ret., 1984. Served as vol. with Free French Army, 1940-46. Decorated Legion d'Honneur. Mem. AIME, AAAS, N.Y. Acad. Scis., Soc. Geology Applied to Mineral Deposits, IAGOD, Soc. Mineral Industry (France, award medal 1977), French Sedimentologists' Assn. Contr. articles to French Acad. Scis. and tech. jours. Home: Les Strelitzias, Rue Pauline, 06160 Juan-Les-Pins France

DEBELJAK, ALES, writer, editor; b. Ljubljana, Yugoslavia, Dec. 25, 1961; s. Pavel and Maria (Mohar) D. BA in Philosophy, Comparative Lit., U. Ljubljana, 1985; postgrad., U. Iowa, Syracuse U. Chief editor Tribune, Ljubljana, 1982-83, Problems, Ljubljana, 1986—; cons. Glej, Ljubljana, 1985-87; advisor for lit. Nat. Endowment for Arts and Culture, Ljubljana, 1986-87. Author: Exchanges, Exchanges, 1982, Names of the Death, 1985 (Golden Bird award 1985), Dictionary of Silence, 1987, Figures of Melancholy, 1988; translator: The Social Construction of Reality (Peter L. Berger and Thomas Luckmann) 1966; editor: American Metafiction, 1988. Recipient Seven Leaders award Yugoslav Youth Assn., 1985. Fellow Nat. Endowment for Arts and Culture; mem. Comparative Lit. Soc. Slovenia (exec. bd. 1986—), Slovene Writer's Soc. (exec. bd. 1986—), Poets, Essayists, Novelists. Home: 14 Gotska, 61000 Ljubljana Slovenia, Yugoslavia Office: Research Inst FSPN, Kardeljeva Pl 5, Ljubljana Slovenia, Yugoslavia

DEBENEDETTI, CARLO, entrepreneur; b. Turin, Italy, Nov. 14, 1934. Student, Polytech. U., Turin, Italy; PhD (hon.), Wesleyan U., 1986. Chmn., chief exec. officer Gilardini, Turin, Italy, 1972-76; chief exec. officer Fiat, Turin, 1976; vice chmn., chief exec. officer Ing. C. Olivetti and Co., Ivrea, Italy, 1978-83; chmn., chief exec. officer Ing. C. Olivetti and Co., Ivrea, 1983—; vice chmn., chief exec. officer CIR, Cofide; founder, vice chmn. Euromobiliare; chmn. Cerus, S.F.G.; dir. Ctr. Strategic Internat. Studies, Washington; mem. Internat. ady. bd. Morgan Guaranty Trust, N.Y., European Ady. Com., N.Y. Stock Exchange; bd. dirs. Shearson Lehman Bros. Holdings, N.Y. Named Cavaliere del Lavoro Republic of Italy, 1983, Officier, Légion d'Honneur Republic of France, 1987. Mem. Royal Swedish Acad. Engring. Scis., Confindustria (v.p. 1983). Office: Ing C Olivetti and C SpA, via Jervis 77, 10015 Ivrea To Italy

DEBERNARDI, ENZO ENRICO CESARE, utility company executive; b. Asuncion, Paraguay, Nov. 18, 1925; s. Antonio and Maria (Orillier); m. Maria del Rosario Cano, Oct. 8, 1928; children: Antonio, Roberto. D in Engring., Politecnico di Torino, Italy, 1950. Adminstr. gen. Ande, Asuncion, 1959-64, pres., 1964—; prof. emeritus U. Asuncion, 1987—; dir. gen. adj. Itaipu Binacional, Asuncion, 1974-76, dir. gen. Paraguayo, 1986—. Elected senator, Asuncion, 1983. Mem. Cen. Paraguayo de Engring. (pres. 1973-75). Mem. Colorado Party. Clubs: Centenario, Yacht and Golf (Asuncion). Office: Administracion Nacional De Elec, Tricidad Ande P Cardozo 560, Asuncion Paraguay

DEBEUCKELAERE, STEF, telecommunications executive; b. Antwerp, Belgium, Nov. 29, 1957; s. Jan and Mia (Greeve) D. Commerce A2, St. Eligius, Antwerp, 1978. Product mgr. Interpieaces (spare parts), Brussels, 1985-86; program dir. Radio Annick, Antwerp, 1982-85, Radio Contact, Antwerp, 1986—. Mem. Contact Radio Franchising (bd. dirs. 1986—). Home: Vlotstraat 30, B-2231 Ranst, Antwerp Belgium Office: Radio Contact, Hof Ter Lo 7/47, B-2200 Antwerp Belgium

DE BIE, ALEXIS IRÉNÉE DU PONT, educational psychologist; b. Bryn Mawr, Pa., Dec. 3, 1943; s. Johannes Cornelis and Marie Alexia du Pont (Ortiz) de Bie; m. Joan Farley, Mar. 7, 1980; children: Natacha Alexia, Denis Eglimez, Alexis Irénée, Jr. BA, U. Paris, 1966; diploma psychiat. nursing, psychol. counseling Charenton Psychiat. Hosp., Paris, 1966-68; BA, Columbia Pacific U., 1985, PhD, 1987. Lectr. tchr. edn. Ontario Inst. Studies in Edn., 1971-72; psychol. counsellor Ky. East/West Bluegrass Mental Health Comprehensive Care Ctr., Lexington, 1972-74; cons., tchr. Nat. Assn. for Gifted Children, Washington, 1964-76. Chmn., Psychosynthesis Found. Fla., Inc., Palm Beach, 1978—. Disting. fellow Am. Bd. Master Educators, 1986. Mem. AAAS, Am. Assn. Adult and Continuing Edn., Am. Guild Hypnotherapists, Am. Assn. Profl. Hypnotherapists, Am. Assn. Gifted Children, Nat. Assn. Creative Children and Adults, Assn. Transpersonal Psychology, Devel. Council of Ctr. for Creativity, Innovation and Leadership, Am. Geriatric Soc., Soc. Accelerated Learning, Fla. Assn. for Gifted, Nat. Psychiat. Assn., Assn. Humanistic Psychology, Internat. Freedom Found, N.Y. Acad. Scis., Am. Assn. Profl. Hypnotherapists, Am. Assn. Adult & Continuing Edn., AAAS, Teh Renaissance Project Internat. (dir. gen.). Lodges: Masons, Rotary. Avocation: Sailing.

DE BLAUWE, JOZEF LEO, hospital administrator; b. Antwerp, Belgium, July 5, 1940; s. Camillus Leo and Magdalena (Versavel); m. Gilberte Marie Dobbelaere, Dec. 24, 1964; children: Didier, Tanguy. Degree in Acctg., St. Eligius Coll., Antwerp, 1963. Chief acct. SOBEMI, Canmanuf, Brussels, 1967-69; fin. analyst Continental Grain, Antwerp, 1969-70; chief acct., asst. fin. mgr. Sidal N.V. Aluminum semis producer, Duffel, Belgium, 1970-87; fin. adminstr. dir. St. Vincentius Hosp., Antwerp, 1987—; lectr. Tech. High Sch., Mechelen, Belgium, 1969-83; cons. in field. Mem. Christian Employers and Mgrs. Assn. (adminstr./treas. Antwerp chpt. 1983), Nat. Coll. Accts. of Belgium-Brussels (auditor 1987), Inst. Accts. Belgium. Roman Catholic. Club: Fifty-One Internat. (Antwerp). Home: De Goudvink 22, 2232 Schilde Belgium Office: Saint Vincentius Hosp, Saint Vincentius St 20, 2018 Antwerp Belgium

DEBOCK, FLORENT ALPHONSE, corporation controller; b. LaLouviere, Belgium, Feb. 3, 1924; came to U.S., 1954, naturalized, 1959; s. Benoit and Elvire (Verbeke) DeB.; m. Mary C. Murray, July 2, 1960; 1 child, Mark Steven. Tchr. diploma, Inst. Ste. Marie, Arlon, Belgium, 1944; Accountant diploma, Inst. Professionel Superieur de Belgigue, 1953; postgrad., La Salle Extension U., Chgo., 1956. CPA, D.C. Govt. auditor U.S. Army Audit Agy., Engr. Procurement Center, Europe, 1946-54; auditor Touche, Ross, Bailey & Smart, N.Y.C., 1954-61; controller Armor Elevator Co. (and affiliates), Queens, N.Y., 1962-64; controller subsidiary of Eaton, Yale & Towne, Dusseldorf, Germany, 1964-67; group controller bus. furnishings group Litton Industries, N.Y.C., 1967-68; controller Levitt & Sons, homebldg. div. ITT, Lake Success, N.Y., 1969-71, Intermodulex NDH Corp., White Plains, N.Y., 1971-74, Watch Case Corp. div. Zale Corp., Long Island City, N.Y., 1974-82; corp. controller Am. Gemsmiths, Inc., N.Y.C., N.Y., 1982-86; controller Loren Rings, Inc., N.Y.C., 1986—, Budoff Inc., Secaucus, N.J., 1986—. Served with inf. Belgian Army, 1945-46. Decorated War of 1940-45 Commemorative medal, 1940-45 Vol. medal. Mem. Am. Inst. CPA's, N.Y. State Soc. CPA's, Nat. Assn. Accountants. Home: 123 99th St Brooklyn NY 11209 Office: Budoff Inc 1375 Paterson Plank Rd Secaucus NJ 07094

DE BOER, MARTINUS STEPHANUS JOHANNES, transport company executive; b. Nieuwveen, The Netherlands, Oct. 11, 1930; s. Leonardus and Alida Geertruida (Meijer) De B.; m. Wilhelmina Agatha Petronella Dijsselbloem, June 26, 1957; children: Marie-Jose, Leon. With Airfreight div. William H. Muller & Co., Amsterdam, The Netherlands, 1948-51; mgr. shipbroker div. N.V. Kon. Holl. Lloyd, Amsterdam, 1951-60; sales mgr. Airfreight R.S.K., Schiphol, 1960-62; dir. inland freight N.V. van Gend & Loos, Utrecht, The Netherlands, 1962—; pres. European Express Consortium, 1983—, LTV Lockhorst, Leusden, 1979—. Bd. dirs. Eemland Coll., Amersfoort, 1977, Stichting Landdag Spierdistrofie, Baarn, 1979—. Served with Dutch Army, 1951-52. Roman Catholic. Lodge: Rotary. Home: Landweg 323, 3833 VK Leusden The Netherlands Office: N V van Gend & Loos BV, Randhoeve 225, PO Box 199, 3990 DD Houten The Netherlands

DE BOISDEFFRE, PIERRE NERAUD LE, diplomat; b. Paris, Nov. 7, 1926; m. Beatrice Wiedemann Goiran, Nov. 6, 1957; children: Christian, Lionel, Olivier. Bachelor's, Stanislas Coll., Paris, 1943; Licencié, Faculté de Droit, Paris, 1946; diploma, Ecole Libre des Scis. Polits., Paris, 1946; postgrad., Ecole Nat. Adminstrn., Paris, 1947-49. Gen. mgr. Nat. French Broadcast, 1963-68; cultural counsellor French Embassy, London, 1968-71, Brussels, Belgium, 1971-77; ambassador Govt. of France, Montevideo, Uruguay, 1981-84, Bogota, Colombia, 1984—. Decorated Legion of Honor Govt. France, 1981, Nat. Order of Merit, 1988. Roman Catholic. Clubs: Traveller's, London, Royal Gaulois, Brussels. Office: Embassy of France, Avenida 39, No 7-84, Bogota Colombia

DEBON, KURT GUENTHER, Sinologist; b. Munich, Germany, May 13, 1921; s. Kurt Martin and Isa Luise (Bestehorn) D.; Ph.D., U. Munich, 1953; m. Gertraude Therese Eisemann, Mar. 11, 1960; children—Bettina Luise, Reinhard Guenther. Lectr., prof. Sinology, U. Cologne, 1953-68; dir. Sinol. Inst., U. Heidelberg, 1968-86. Mem. Deutsche Morgenländische Gesellschaft, European Assn. Chinese Studies. Author: Ts'ang-lang's Gesprächeü ber die Dichtung, 1962; Lob der Naturtreue, 1969; Grundbegriffe der chinesischen Schrifttheorie, 1978; Schiller und der chinesische Geist, 1983; Oscar Wilde and Taoism, 1986. Editor: Ostasiatische Literaturen (—Neues Handbuch der Literaturwissenschaft, Band 23), 1984. Home: 6 Im Rosengarten, 6903 Neckargemuend Federal Republic of Germany

DE BOUCHARD D'AUBETERRE, HUBERT GUY (COMTE DE), former company executive, sculpteur; b. Mercoeur, France, Nov. 10, 1912; s. Raoul Gaspard Savary and Vera Helene Marie (de Caprara de Montecucoli) B. d'A.; m. Alba Maria de Filkiewitch Beck, Nov. 28, 1944; children—Guy, Vera, Anne, Amaury, Yvan. Student schs., France, Monte Carlo. Chief of staff Apport-Rural Normandy, 1935-39; Officer French Army, 1939-40, WWII; Sec. Secours Nat. Nice, 1942; French Red Cross, 1943-44, Served in French resistance, WWII, Served in U.S. Army, 1944; mgr. Societe Transp. Industry, Nice, 1946-51; travel export mgr. Ste Camuscognac, Paris and Cognac, 1952-68; country mgr. Ste. Grand Marnier, Paris, 1967-74. Mem. Hunt Assn. Mercoeur (chmn. 1966-72), Football Assn. Mercoeur (chmn. 1969-85), War Vets. Assn. Mercoeur (chmn. 1969-85), Am. Legion. Roman Catholic. Clubs: Recherches Celtiques (Vichy); Saint Odilon (Mercoeur); Association entraide Noblesse Francaise (Paris). Home: Chateau de Fontaride, 43100 Mercoeur France

DEBRECZENI, JÚLIA, language professional, literary translator, educator; b. Pécs, Baranya, Hungary, July 3, 1960; d. László and Mária (Pál) D.; m. Miklós Törkenczy, June 30, 1984. MA in Hungarian Lit., Eötvös Loránd U., Budapest, Hungary, 1983, MA in English, 1983. Cert. internat. tchr. English as fgn. lang. Freelance translator Budapest, 1982-85; lectr. József Attila U., Szeged, Hungary, 1985-86; project cons. Has-Soros Found., Budapest, 1986—.

DEBREU, GERARD, educator, economist; b. Calais, France, July 4, 1921; came to U.S., 1950, naturalized, 1975; s. Camille and Fernande (Decharne) D.; m. Françoise Bled, June 14, 1945; children: Chantal, Florence. Student, Ecole Normale Supérieure, Paris, 1941-44, Agrégé de l'Université, 1946; DSc, U. Paris, 1956; Dr. Rerum Politicarum honoris causa, U. Bonn, 1977; D. Scis. Economiques (hon.), U. Lausanne, 1980; DSc (hon.), Northwestern U., 1981; Dr. honoris causa, U. des Scis. Sociales de Toulouse, 1983, Yale U., 1987. Research assoc. Centre Nat. De La Recherche Sci., Paris, 1946-48; Rockefeller fellow U.S., Sweden and Norway, 1948-50; research assoc. Cowles Commn., U. Chgo., 1950-55; assoc. prof. econs. Cowles Found., Yale, 1955-61; fellow Center Advanced Study Behavioral Scis., 1960-61; vis. prof. econs. Yale U., fall 1961; prof. econs. U. Calif. at Berkeley, 1962—, prof. math., 1975—, Univ. prof., 1985—; Guggenheim fellow, vis. prof. Center Ops. Research and Econometrics, U. Louvain, 1968-69, vis. prof., fall 1971, winter, 1972; Erskine fellow U. Canterbury, Christchurch, New Zealand, 1969, 87, vis. prof., 1973; Overseas fellow Churchill Coll., Cambridge, Eng., spring 1972; vis. prof. Cowles Found. for Research in Econs., Yale U., fall 1976; vis. prof. U. Bonn, 1977; research assoc. CEPREMAP, Paris, fall 1980; faculty research lectr. U. Calif. Berkeley, 1984-85, univ. prof., 1985—; vis. prof. U. Sydney, Australia, June-July, 1987. Author: Theory of Value, 1959, Mathematical Economics: Twenty Papers of Gerard Debreu, 1983; Asso. editor: Internat. Econ. Rev, 1959-69; mem. editorial bd.: Jour. Econ. theory, 1972—; mem. adv. bd.: Jour. Math. Econs, 1974—. Served with French Army, 1944-45. Decorated chevalier Légion d'Honneur; recipient Nobel Prize in Econ. Scis., 1983, Commandeur de l'Ordre du Merite, 1984; sr. U.S. Scientist awardee Alexander von Humboldt Found. Fellow Am. Acad. Arts and Scis., AAAS, Econometric Soc. (pres. 1971); Disting. fellow Am. Econ. Assn.; mem. Am. Philos. Soc., Nat. Acad. Scis., French Acad. Scis. (fgn. assoc.). Office: U Calif Dept of Econs Berkeley CA 94720

DE BRUYNE, PATRICK, electrical company executive, engineer; b. Tournai, Belgium, Dec. 28, 1948; arrived in Switzerland, 1971; s. Gabriel and Lucienne (Cornu) De B.; m. Viviane Riviere, Aug. 28, 1971; children: Yves, Vinciane. Grad. elect. engring., Faculte Poly. Mons, Belgium, 1971. Registered profl. engr., Switzerland. Research ctr. scientist BBC Brown Boveri Ltd., Switzerland, 1973-75; group leader testing BBC Semiconductor Div., Switzerland, 1976-77, quality control mgr., 1978-80, devel. mg r., 1978-81; mktg. mgr. BBC Semiconductor Div., Lenzburg, Switzerland, 1982-83; gen. mgr. BBC High Power Semiconductors Div., Lenzburg, Switzerland, 1984-87, v.p., gen. mgr., 1987—. Contbr. articles to profl. jours.; 8 patents light triggering, protection explosion integral, HF device. Mem. IEEE, Assn. des ingenieurs de la Faculte Polytechnique de Mons., Soc. Royale Belge des Electriciens. Roman Catholic. Office: Asea Brown Boveri Ltd, Subdivision EKS, 5401 Baden Switzerland

DE BRUYNE, PAUL, diversified companies executive; b. Dendermonde, Belgium, June 11, 1953; s. Georges and Marie-Louise (Saelemans) DeB.; m. Nicole Heuvinck, Aug. 25, 1978; children: Wim, Pieter. Degree in Civil Engring., Free Univ., Brussels, 1978. Cert. engr. Researcher Bell Telephone, Antwerp, Belgium, 1978-83; mgmt. dir. Micro Systems Group (8 cos.), Belgium, 1983—; also bd. dirs. Micro Systems, Dendermonde/Gent; bd. dirs. numerous cos. Mem. Koninklijke Vlaamse Ingenieurs Vereniging, Jaycees (pres. Demdermonde chpt. 1987, judge in Ct. of Commerce). Home: Sint Christiana St 21, 9330 Dendermonde Belgium Office: Micro Systems Group, Desguinlei 92 (7), 2018 Antwerp Belgium

DEBS, BARBARA KNOWLES, academic administrator; b. Eastham, Mass., Dec. 24, 1931; d. Stanley F. and Arline (Eugley) Knowles; m. Richard A. Debs, July 19, 1958; children: Elizabeth, Nicholas. BA, Vassar Coll., 1953; postgrad., Radcliffe Coll., 1956-58; PhD, Harvard U., 1967; LLD, N.Y. Law Sch., 1979; LHD, Manhattanville Coll., 1985. Instr. art Vassar Coll., 1955-56; freelance translation editor Ency. of World Art div. McGaw-Hill Pub., N.Y.C., 1959-62; asst. prof. art history Manhattanville Coll., Purchase, N.Y., 1968-73, assoc. prof., 1973-77, prof., 1977-86, pres., 1975-85; bd. dirs. AMF Inc., 1978-85. Contbr. articles on Renaissance and contemporary art to profl. publs. Mem. N.Y. Council Humanities, 1978-85; mem. Westchester Med. Ctr. Hosp. Implementation Bd., 1978-84; mem. Westchester County Bd. Ethics, 1979-84; trustee N.Y. Law Sch., 1979—; trustee Geraldine R. Dodge Found., 1985—; trustee N.Y. Hist. Soc., 1985-87, chmn. collections com., 1985-87; bd. dirs. Internat. Found. for Art Research, 1985—, trustee Com. Econ. Devel., 1985—, mem. council on fgn. relations, 1983—; mem. Commn. Ind. Colls. and Univs. of N.Y., 1977-79; mem. com. on higher edn., adv. council to Dems. N.Y. State Senate, 1979-85. AAUW Nat. fellow and Ann Radcliffe fellow, 1958-59; Am. Council Learned Socs. grantee, 1973; Fulbright fellow Scuola Normale, Pisa, Italy, 1953, U. Rome, 1954. Mem. Am. Council on Edn. (chmn. commn. acad. affairs 1977-79), Young Audiences (nat. dir. 1977-80), Hundred Club of Westchester (bd. dirs.), Renaissance Soc. of Am., Coll. Art Assn., Phi Beta Kappa. Club: Cosmopolitan.

DEBUS, ELEANOR VIOLA, business management company executive; b. Buffalo, May 19, 1920; d. Arthur Adam and Viola Charlotte (Pohl) D.; student Chown Bus. Sch., 1939. Sec., Buffalo Wire Works, 1939-45; home talent producer Empire Producing Co., Kansas City, Mo., sec. Owens Corning Fiberglass, Buffalo; public relations and publicity Niagara Falls Theatre, Ont., Can.; pub. relations dir. Woman's Internat. Bowling Congress, Columbus, Ohio, 1957-59; publicist, sec. Ice Capades, Hollywood, Calif., 1961-63; sec. to controller Rexall Drug Co., Los Angeles, 1963-67; bus. mgmt. acct. Samuel Berke & Co., Beverly Hills, Calif., 1967-75; Gadbois Mgmt. Co., Beverly Hills, 1975-76; sec., treas. Sasha Corp., Los Angeles, 1976—; bus. mgr. Dean Martin, Shirley MacLaine, Debbie Reynolds; pres. Tempo Co., Los Angeles, 1976—. Mem. Nat. Assn. Female Execs., Nat. Notary Assn., Nat. Film Soc., Am. Film Inst. Republican. Lodge: Order Eastern Star. Contbr. articles to various mags. Office: Tempo Co 1900 Avenue of Stars #1230 Los Angeles CA 90067

DEBUSK, EDITH M., lawyer; b. Waco, Tex., Apr. 12, 1912; d. Otto Clifton and Margaret (Hatcher) Mann; m. Manuel C. DeBusk, June 13, 1941. LL.B., Dallas Sch. Law, 1941; Cert., So. Meth. U. Sch. Law, 1941. Atty. Regional Atty.'s Office (O.P.A.), Dallas, 1942; assoc. atty. Office of Karl F. Steinmann, Balt., 1943-46; mem. firm DeBusk & DeBusk, 1946—; bd. dirs. DeBusk Corp.; officer Met. Hosp. Corp. Former mem. Gov.'s Com. on Aging; dir. Dallas Citizens Commn. on Action for Aging, Inc.; del. to White House Conf. Children and Youth, 1960, Conf. on Aging, 1961; mem. Dallas Bd. Adjustment, 1963-65; former bd. dirs. Dallas United Cerebral Palsy Assn., Tex. Soc. Aging, Dallas County Community Action Com., Inc.; trustee Found. for Cranio-Facial Deformities, Nina Fay Calhoun Scholarship Fund Trust; former mem. adv. council Sr. Citizens Found., Inc.; former mem. div. aging Council of Social Agys., Citizens Traffic Commn.; former sec., legal adviser Tex. Fedn. Bus. and Profl. Women's Clubs; bd. visitors Freedoms Found. at Valley Forge. Named Woman of the Month Dallas Mag., 1948; Woman of Week Balt., 1945; recipient George Washington honor medal Freedoms Found. Fellow Tex. Bar Found. (life); mem. State Bar Tex., ABA (chmn. com. state and local taxation 1979-81), Dallas Bar Assn. (numerous coms.), Women's Council of Dallas County (legis. com.), Bus. and Profl. Women's Club Dallas (past pres.), Nat. Assn. Women in Constrn. (hon.), Delta Kappa Gamma (hon.), Kappa Beta Pi (past dean province IV). Presbyn. Club: Altrusa (Dallas) (pres. internat. 1963-65). Home: 7365 Elmridge Dr Dallas TX 75240 Office: DeBusk & DeBusk 13117 Meandering Way Dallas TX 75240

DECALO, SAMUEL, political science educator; b. Sofia, Bulgaria, Nov. 19, 1937; came to U.S., 1961; s. Eliezer and Joy (Nachmias) D.; m. Roma Lewandowska, Feb. 24, 1974; children: Ruth, Niv. BS, U. Ottawa, Ont., Can., 1961; MA, U. Pa., 1962, PhD, 1970. Instr. PMC Colls., Chester, Pa., 1964-65; asst. prof. U. R.I., Kingston, 1965-70; assoc. prof. grad. faculty New Sch. Social Research, N.Y.C., 1970-76; prof., chmn. U. Botswana, Gaborone, 1977-81; sr. lectr. U. W.I., St. Augustine, Trinidad and Tobago, 1982-84; prof., head dept. comparative African govt. U. Natal, Durban, South Africa, 1984—. Author: Coups and Army Rule in Africa, 1976, Historical Dictionary of Benin, 1977, 2d edit. 1987, Historical Dictionary of Tojo, 1978, 2d edit., 1987, Historical Dictionary of Chad, 1979, 2d edit. 1987, others; mem. editorial bd. Jour. Contemporary African Studies, Documents in Communist Affairs jour. Human Scis. Research Council Ad-Hoc grantee, 1987-88. Fellow Am. Polit. Sci. Assn., African Studies Assn., Royal African Soc.

DE CAMP, WILLIAM SCHUYLER, retired army officer; b. Ft. Monroe, Va., Sept. 24, 1934; s. John Taylor and Barbara Virginia (Meister) deC.; m. Anne Lindsey Draper, July 25, 1959; children: William Schuyler, Jr., Philip Draper, Timothy Laurent. A.A., U. Calif.-Berkeley, 1954, A.B., 1956; M.A., Tulane U., 1965, Ph.D., 1970; student, Army War Coll., 1972-73, Armed Forces Staff Coll., 1969-70. Commd. 2d lt. U.S. Army, 1956, advanced through grades to maj. gen., 1980; bn. comdr., brigade exec. officer U.S. Army, Vietnam, 1968-69; spl. asst. to Army Chief of Staff, Washington, 1970-72; army assoc. Sch. Advanced Internat. Studies Johns Hopkins, 1972-73; dep. to asst. dep. chief staff for ops. and planning U.S. Army, Washington, 1973-75; brigade comdr. W. Ger., 1975-76; spl. asst. to chief staff SHAPE, Belgium, 1976-77; asst. comdr. 3d Div. W. Ger., 1977-79; joint chiefs rep. NATO-Warsaw Pact MBFR Negotiations, Vienna, 1979-80; dir. Interam. Region Office Sec. Def., 1981-84. Pres. Mantua PTA, Fairfax, Va., 1973-74; instl. rep. Boy Scouts Am. Recipient awards Boy Scouts Am.; awards PTA; awards Landkreis Kitzingen, W. Ger.; decorated Silver Star, Legion of Merit with oak leaf cluster, Meritorious Service medal with cluster, D.F.C., Bronze Star, Def. Disting. Service medal, Army Disting. Service medal, Air medals with V, numerous others. Mem. Assn. U.S. Army, U.S. Armor Assn., Pi Sigma Alpha. Episcopalian. Home: 8912 Lynnhurst Dr Fairfax VA 22031-3226 Office: DAI PO Box 2224 Merrifield VA 22116

DECARAVA, ROY R., photographer, educator; b. N.Y.C., Dec. 9, 1919; s. Andrew DeCarava and Alfreda Anglero; m. Sherry Forsythe, June 16, 1947; children—Susan, Wendy, Laura. Student Cooper Union Art Sch., N.Y.C., 1938-40; Ph.D. (hon.), R.I. Sch. Design, 1985. Worked in N.Y. as sign painter and display artist, 1936-37, tech. draftsman, 1939-42, comml. artist and illustrator, 1944-58; freelance photographer for various advt. agys., rec. and TV cos., mags. including Scientific American, Fortune, McCall's, Look, Newsweek, Time, Life, 1959-68, 75—; contract photographer Sports Illustrated mag., N.Y.C., 1968-75; founder, dir. A Photographers Gallery, N.Y.C., 1954-56, Kamolinge Workshop for Black Photographers, N.Y.C., 1963-66; adj. prof. photography Cooper Union Inst., 1969-72, assoc. prof., 1975-78; prof. art Hunter Coll., from 1978; one-man shows: 44th Street Gallery, N.Y.C., 1950; Countee Cullen Br. N.Y. Pub. Library, 1951; Little Gallery N.Y. Pub. Library, 1954; A Photographers Gallery, N.Y.C., 1955; Studio Mus., Harlem, N.Y., 1969; Sheldon Meml. Art Ctr. U. Nebr., Lincoln, 1970; U. Mass., Amherst, 1974; Mus. Fine Arts, Houston, 1975; Corcoran Gallery, Washington, 1976; Benin Gallery, N.Y.C., 1976; Witkin Gallery, N.Y.C., 1977; Light Work Gallery, Syracuse, N.Y., 1977; Port Washington Pub. Library, N.Y.C., 1978; Friends of Photography, Carmel, Calif., 1980; Akron Art Inst. (Ohio), 1980; group exhbns. include: Mus. Modern Art, N.Y.C., 1953, 55, 78, Met. Mus. Art, N.Y.C., 1964, Nat. Gallery of Can., Ottowa (toured Can. and U.S.), 1967, Ctr. Creative Photography, U. Ariz., Tucson, 1980, Tampa (Fla.) Mus., 1983, Barbican Art Gallery, London (toured Eng.), 1985, Fotografiska Museet, Stockholm, 1986; represented in permanent collections: Mus. Modern Art, N.Y.C., Met. Mus. Art, N.Y.C., Harlem Art Collections, N.Y. State Office Bldg., N.Y.C., Andover Art Gallery Phillips Acad. (Mass.), Corcoran Gallery; Atlanta U., Sheldon Meml. Art Gallery U. Nebr., Mus. Fine Arts, Houston, Ctr. for Creative Photography U. Ariz., Tucson; mem. curatorial council Studio Mus., Harlem, N.Y., 1976. Books: The Sweet Flypaper of Life (text by Langston Hughes), 1955, 2d edit., 1984; Photographs/DeCarava, 1981; The Sound I Saw, 1983 (exhibited throughout Japan and Near East 1986). Recipient Art Service award Mt. Morris United Presbyn. Ch., N.Y.C., 1969; Benin Creative Photography award, 1972; Artistic and Cultural Achievement award Community Mus. of Bklyn., 1979; named hon. citizen of Houston, 1975; Guggenheim fellow, 1952. Served with U.S. Army, 1943. Mem. Am. Soc. Mag. Photographers. Office: care Witkin Gallery 41 E 57th St New York NY 10022 *

DE CARBONNEL, FRANÇOIS ERIC, management consultant; b. Paris, Dec. 7, 1946; came to U.S., 1979; s. Charles Eric and Elizabeth (Chevreux) De C.; diploma Ecole Centrale, Lyon, France, 1970; M.S. in Indsl. Administrn. (Smith award), Carnegie-Mellon U., 1972; m. L. Vercambre, Feb. 16, 1968; children—Geoffroy, Antoine, Thomas, Matthieu. With Boston Cons. Group, 1972-81, v.p., dir., Chgo., 1979-81; exec. v.p., chief operating officer Strategic Planning Assos., Inc., Washington, 1981-83, pres., 1983—. Mellon fellow 1971. Author: Les Mecanismes Fondamentaux de la Competitivite, 1980, La Victoire de Reagan, 1984. Office: 2300 N St NW Washington DC 20037

DE CARO, MARC CLEMENT, designer, artist; b. Paris, May 28, 1920, came to U.S. 1926; s. George Louis and Fernande Marie (Ressie) Vallee DeC.; m. Cleo Williams, Aug. 30, 1943; children—Marc Frederic, George Claude. Student, Cleve. Art Inst., 1947-50, Art Students League of N.Y., 1950-51. Freelance designer and artist, Bronx, N.Y. Executed murals Stewart Air Force Base; Passenger Terminal, N.Y.; Philip Morris Inc. Hdqrs. Richmond, Va. Served as 2nd lt. USAAF, 1941-45, ETO.

DE CARVAJAL PÉREZ, JOSÉ FEDERICO, Spanish government official; b. Málaga, Spain, Mar. 14, 1930; s. Federico and Magdalena De C.; m. Matilde González Barandilla, May 25, 1958; children: Jose Federico, Gador, Pablo. Student, Colegio Calasancis, Colegio El Pilar, El Colegio Torres; grad. law sch., Madrid. Senator Auila, Spain, 1977; mem. Parlimentary Assembly, Council Europe, 1977; v.p. Socialist Group, 1978-79; 1st v.p. Spanish Group Interparlimentary Union, 1978; senator Madrid, 1982, 86; pres. High Council 2d legislature, Madrid, 1982, High Council 3d legislature, Madrid, 1986; now pres. Spanish Senate, Madrid. Mem. Coll. Lawyers. Office: Senate, Plaza de la Mariva Espanola 8, 28013 Madrid Spain *

DE CASTRO, JOSÉ MANUEL BORGES, trading company executive; b. Lisbon, Portugal, Aug. 9, 1939; s. Jose Borges and Maria Helena (Carvalho) De C.; m. Maria de Rosario Ramalho de Castro, Feb. 8, 1964; children: Frederico, Gonzalo, Diogo, Tomás. Degree in langs., Institut Rosseau, Neuchatel, Switzerland, 1956; degree in auto engring., Chelsea Coll. of Engring., London, 1962. Engring. mgr. Ford Motor Co., Azambuja, Portugal, 1963-66; mgr. Metalurgica Duarte Ferreira, Tramagal, Portugal, 1969-70, dir., exec. v.p., 1971-75; dir. Engesa, S.A., São Paulo, Brazil, 1975-79; pres., gen. mgr. Emco Wheaton subs. Masco Group, Rio de Janeiro, 1979-81; v.p. ea. hemisphere Emco Wheaton subs. Masco Group, London, Ont., Can., 1981-86; exec. v.p., gen. mgr. Planco Pão de Açucar Group, Lisbon, 1986—. Served with Portuguese Army, 1966-69. Christian Democrat. Roman Catholic. Office: Planco SA, Rua Castilho 75-8 Esq, 1200 Lisbon Portugal

DECAUDAVEINE, ALAIN ALBERT, physician; b. Crulai, Orne, France, June 10, 1925; s. Louis and Cecile (Hadengue) D.; m. Micheline Charpentier; children: Beatrice, Isabelle, MarieJoëlle, MarieAgnes, Benedicte. MD, U. Paris, 1951. Intern Hosp. of Perpetual Help of Paris Pvt. Hosps., 1948-52; practice medicine Paris Med. U., 1948-52; gen. practice medicine Le Portel, France. Mem. Med. Doctor's Order (vice chmn. 1986). Home and Office: 10 Rue Victor Hugo, 62480 Le Portel France

DE CHAMPLAIN, VERA CHOPAK, artist, painter; b. Kulmbach, Germany, Jan. 26, 1928; Am. citizen; d. Nathaniel and Selma (Stiefel) Florsheim; m. Albert Chopak de Champlain, 1948. Student, Art Students League, N.Y.C., 1950-60; spl. studies with Edwin Dickinson, 1962-64. Art dir., tchr. Emanuel Ctr., N.Y.C., 1967—. One person show Consulate Fed. Republic of Germany, N.Y.C., 1986, Fusco Gallery, N.Y.C., 1969-70, B. Altman Gallery, N.Y.C., 1982; exhibited group shows including Munich, W. Ger., 1966, Rudolph Gallery, Woodstock, N.Y., 1967, Artists Equity Gallery, N.Y.C., 1970-77, Lever House, N.Y.C., 1974, 80, 85; Avery Fisher Hall-Cork Gallery, N.Y.C., 1970, 82, 83, 84, 87, Fontainebleau Gallery, N.Y.C., 1972, 73, 74, NYU, 1978, Met. Mus., 1979, Muriel Karasik Gallery, Westhampton Beach, N.Y., 1980; represented in permanent collections Butler Inst. Am. Art, Youngstown, Ohio, Ga. Mus. Art, Athens, Slater Mus., Norwich, Conn., Webster Coll., St. Louis, Evansville Mus. Arts and Sci. (Ind.), Smithsonian Instn., Archives Am. Art, Washington; traveling exhibition in U.S. 1988—. Recipient award in portrait painting, Hainesfalls, N.Y., 1965, First Prize-World award, Acad. Italia, Parma, 1985, 87; subject of TV interview, 1984. Fellow Royal Soc. Arts (London); mem. Artists Equity Assn. N.Y., Arts Students League (life), Nat. Soc. Arts and Letters (art chmn. 1969—), Kappa Pi (life). Clubs: Woman Pays, Liederkranz City of N.Y. (trustee 1979—). Home: 230 Riverside Dr New York NY 10025

DECHAMPS, BRUNO JOSEF GERHARD, newspaper editor; b. Aachen, Fed. Republic Germany, Apr. 4, 1925; s. Paul and Kitty (Herman) D.; m. Annemarie Rueben, Aug. 7, 1952; children: Claudius, Nicola, Daniel, Madeleine. MA, Fordham U., 1949; PhD, Heidelberg (Fed. Republic Germany) U., 1952. Copy editor Deutsche Zeitung-Wirtschafts Zeitung, Stuttgart, Fed. Republic Germany, 1952-56; copy editor Frankfurter Allgemeine Zeitung, 1956-66, editor, 1966—. Author: Macht und Arbeit der Ausschuesse, 1954, Ueber Pferde, 1957. Recipient German Fed. Order of Merit, 1985, Order of St. Gregorius Pope John Paul II, 1985. Roman Catholic. Office: Frankfurther Allgemeine Zeitung, Hellerhofstr 2-4, Postfach 100808, 6000 Frankfurt 1 Federal Republic of Germany

DECHERNEY, DEANNA SAVER, interior designer; b. Phila., Mar. 5, 1943; d. Martin and Bessie (Pitkoff) Saver; m. Alan Hersh DeCherney, June 26, 1965; children—Peter, Alexander, Nicholas. B.F.A., U. of Arts, 1966. Designer, Paul Planert Design Assocs., Pitts., 1967-68; assoc. designer Temple U., 1969-72; dir. interiors P.A.E., Tokyo, Japan, 1972-74; pres. The Nat. Design Service, Woodbridge, Conn., 1981—; instr. Paier Coll. Art, 1975—, instr., Post Coll., 1987—. Bd. dirs. Chamber Orch. of New Eng. 1975—; bd. dirs. The Neighborhood Music Sch., 1979-85. Mem. Am. Soc. Interior Designers (pres. Conn. 1983, 84, 87 88), Interior Design Educator Council (assoc.). Address: 83 Maplevale Dr Woodbridge CT 06525

DE CIUTIIS, VINCENT LOUIS, hospital administrator, anesthesiology educator; b. N.Y.C., Oct. 11, 1924; s. Alfredo Vincent and Chiara Mary (Giannone) de C.; m. Claire Adele Ostuni, June 28, 1947 (div. 1976); children: Vilia, Nadine, Vincent, Mario, Elena, Michael, Elisa, Carl; m. Patricia Therese Paulson, June 3, 1976; children: James, Marianna, Michelle, Donald. BA, Columbia U., 1945; MD, N.Y. Med. Coll., 1948; grad. Med. Sch. Walter Reed Army Med. Ctr., 1954; MBA, Pepperdine U., 1976; grad. U.S. Army Command and Gen. Staff Coll., 1986. Diplomate Am. Bd. Anesthesia. Intern Met. Hosp., N.Y.C., 1948-49, resident in anesthesia, 1949-51; resident Fitzsimons Army Hosp., Denver, 1952-53; chief anesthesiology U.S. Army Hosp., Ft. Dix, N.J., 1951-52, Misericordia Hosp., Bronx, 1958-62, Torrance Meml. Hosp., Calif., 1971-79; chief anesthesiology, assoc. prof. Met. Hosp. N.Y. Med. Coll., N.Y.C., 1956-58; asst. prof. UCLA Med. Sch., Los Angeles, 1958-86, assoc. prof., 1986—; prof. surgery, anesthesiology Coll. Osteo. Medicine U. of the Pacific, Stockton, Calif., 1985; adminstr. Riviera Community Hosp., Torrance, 1963-64; adminstr., med. dir. Surg. Ctr. S. Bay, Torrance, 1979—; cons. U.S. Army Hosp., Ft. MacArthur, Calif., 1965-71; dir. med. edn. Torrance Meml. Hosp., 1972-76. Producer/dir. med. documentary with KNBC, 1972; inventor intravenous catheter laryngoscope, 1973; contbr. articles to profl. jours. Served to lt. col. U.S. Army, col. Res. Decorated World War II Victory medal, Korean Service medal, Commendation ribbon. Fellow Am. Coll. Anesthesiologists; mem. AMA, Los Angeles County Med. Assn., Calif. Med. Assn., Disabled Am. Vets., Assn. Mil. Surgeons U.S. Republican. Roman Catholic. Home: 254 Via Linda Vista Redondo Beach CA 90277 Office: Alternacare Corp Surg Ctr of S Bay 23500 Madison St Torrance CA 90505

DECKELBAUM, NELSON, lawyer; b. Washington, Apr. 1, 1928; s. Fred and Rose (Egber) D.; m. Louann Jacobs, Oct. 19, 1952; children: David Alan, Todd Stuart. B.S., Georgetown U., 1950, J.D., 1952. Bar: D.C. 1952, Md. 1957, U.S. Supreme Ct. 1966. Practice law Washington, 1952—; sr. partner Deckelbaum & Ogens, Chartered, 1974—; Staff mem. Commn. on Govt. Security, 1956. Chmn. Democratic precinct, Montgomery County, Md., 1958. Served with USAF, 1952-54. Named in Best Lawyers in Am. Mem. Am., Md., D.C. bar assns., Am. Judicature Soc., Georgetown University Alumni Assn. Democrat. Jewish. Clubs: Woodmont Country, Amity, Univ. Home: 4201 Cathedral Ave NW Washington DC 20016 Office: Deckelbaum & Ogens 1140 Connecticut Ave NW Washington DC 20036 also: 10240 River Rd Potomac MD 20814

DECKER, ALFRED MARIE, research institute administrator; b. La Calamine, Belgium, Oct. 22, 1925; s. Nicolas and Erna (Bailly) D.; m. Françoise L. Hinnisdaels. Degree in Chem. Civil Engring., U. Liege, Belgium, 1949, DSc in Appliqués, 1956. Research engr. Ctr. Recherches Metallurgiques Asbl, Liege, 1951—, also mng. dir., bd. dirs.; lectr. phys. chemistry steel making U. Liege, 1962-73. Patentee in field. Recipient Lauréat de la Fondation A. Galopin, 1957, Prix L. Melsens Royal Acad. Scis., 1964, Medaille Reaumur Soc. Française Metallurgie, 1974, Sr. R. Hadfield medal Metals Soc., 1980. Mem. European Com. Steel Research, Belgian Welding Inst., Internat. Iron and Steel Inst. (steel tech. com.). Lodge: Rotary. Office: Ctr de Recherches Metallurgies, 11 Rue Ernest Solvay, 4000 Liege Belgium

DECKER, BRIAN CECIL, medical publisher; b. St. Catharines, Ont., Can., Feb. 1, 1949; s. Cecil Hubert and Dorothy Lillian (Lloyd) D.; m. Sandra Hamill, Nov. 8, 1986; children: R. Adam, Ashley E., Ryan Thomas, Jeffrey Brian. BS, McMaster U., Hamilton, Ont., 1971. Salesman W.B. Saunders, Toronto, Can., 1970-71; med. editor W.B. Saunders, Phila., 1972-78; v.p., pub. Stratton Intercontinental, N.Y.C., 1978-81; chief exec. officer, chmn., pub. B.C. Decker Inc., Toronto, 1981-85, Decker Electronic Pub. Inc., Burlington, Ont., 1985—. Bd. dirs. Opera Hamilton. Mem. Am. Med. Pub. Assn. Office: Decker Electronic Pub Inc, 3228 S Service Rd, Burlington, ON Canada L7N 3H8

DECKER, JAMES THOMAS, psychotherapist; b. Dayton, Ky., Jan. 16, 1944; s. Frank and Edith (Mountain) D.; m. Jane Campbell Fisher, May 6, 1972; children: Peter Campbell, James Mountain, Christina Campbell. AA, Los Angeles Pierce Coll., 1970; BA, Calif. State U., Northridge, 1972; MSW, SUNY, Stony Brook, 1974; PhD, U. Minn., 1976. Research asst. U. Minn., Mpls., 1974-76; asst. prof. San Diego State U., 1976-78; dir., assoc. prof. U. Tex., El Paso, 1978-80; dir. cons. Kern View Hosp., Bakersfield, Calif., 1980-82; exec. dir. J.T. Decker Profl. Group, Bakersfield, Calif., 1982—; adj. prof. Calif. State Coll., Bakersfield, 1981—; sch. psychotherapist Friends Sch., Bakersfield, 1983—; nursing mgmt. cons. Meml. Hosp., Bakersfield, 1983—; out placement cons. Tosco Inc., Bakersfield, 1983—; employee asst. coordinator various orgns., Bakersfield, 1982—. Contbr. articles to profl. jours. Bd. dirs. Consumer Credit Counselors, Bakersfield, 1982—; chmn. Human Resources Com., Bakersfield, 1980-85; bd. dirs. Health Care Mgmt. Adv. Council, Bakersfield, 1982—; bd. dirs. United Way., San Diego and El Paso, Tex., 1977-80. Served with U.S. Army, 1960-64. Recipient Outstanding Alumni award Sch. Social Work, SUNY. Mem. Assn. Labor Mgmt. Adminstrs. and Cons. on Alcoholism, Nat. Assn. Social Workers (cert.). Home: 231 Oleander St Bakersfield CA 93304 Office: JT Decker Profl Group 2428 West St Bakersfield CA 93301

DECKER, KURT HANS, lawyer, lecturer, researcher; b. Phila., Sept. 23, 1946; s. Hans Emil and Gertrude Elsa (Nestler) D.; m. Hilary McAllister, Aug. 13, 1973; children—Kurt Christian, Allison McAllister. B.A. in History, Thiel Coll., 1968; M.P.A., Pa. State U., 1973; J.D., Vanderbilt U., 1976; LL.M. in Labor, Temple U., 1980. Bar: Pa. 1976, U.S. Tax Ct. 1977, U.S. Ct. Internat. Trade 1977, U.S. Ct. Claims 1979, U.S. Dist. Ct. (mid. dist.) Pa. 1976, U.S. Dist. Ct. (ea. dist.) Pa. 1980, U.S. Ct. Appeals (3d cir.) 1980, U.S. Supreme Ct. 1980. Asst. atty. gen. Gov.'s Office, Pa. Bur. Labor Relations, Harrisburg, 1976-79; counsel Stevens & Lee, Reading, Pa., 1979—; adj. asst. prof. Indsl. Relations St. Francis Coll., Pa., 1985—; seminar speaker Reading/Berks Area C. of C., 1980, Dickinson Sch. Law, 1983, Reading Area Community Coll., 1985—; researcher in field. Author: Employee Privacy: Law and Practice, 1987, Employee Privacy Forms and Procedures, 1988; adminstrv. editor Vanderbilt Jour. Transnat. Law; bd. editors Jour. Collective Negotiations in Pub. Sector, 1982—; contbr. chpts. to books, articles to profl. jours. Served with U.S. Army, 1968-72. Decorated Army Commendation medal. Mem. ABA (sect. labor and employment law), Pa. Bar Assn. (sect. labor and employment law, News Media award 1985), Phila. Bar Assn., Berks County Bar Assn., Am. Soc. Personnel Adminstrn., Am. Soc. Pub. Adminstrn., Internat. Personnel Mgmt. Assn., Sigma Phi Epsilon, Phi Alph Delta. Lutheran. Office: Stevens & Lee 607 Washington St Reading PA 19601

DECKER, PETER W., Bible college official, former chemical company executive; b. Grand Rapids, Mich., Mar. 20, 1919; s. Charles B. and Ruth E. (Thorndill) D.; B.S., Wheaton Coll., 1941; postgrad. Northwestern U., 1942-43, U. Mich., 1958-60; D.Sc. (hon.), London Inst. Applied Research, 1973, LL.D., 1975; m. Margaret I. Stainthorpe, June 10, 1944; children—Peter,

Marilyn, Christine, Charles. Advt. dept. Hotels Windermere, Chgo., 1942, Princess Pat Cosmetics, Chgo., 1943; market research investigator A.C. Nielson Co., Chgo., 1944-48; pres. Peter Decker Constrn. Co., Detroit, 1948-60; sales mgr. Century Chem. Products Co., Detroit, 1961-62, v.p., 1962-63, pres., 1963-75; sr. partner G & D Advt. Assos., 1967-78; v.p., treas., exec. dir. Christian Edn. Advancement, Inc., 1975-77, exec. dir., 1978—; registrar, instr. N.T. Greek and Theology Birmingham (Mich.) Bible Inst., 1973—; prof. Midwestern Baptist Coll., 1984—, dir. student fin. aid, 1984—, trustee, 1985—; mem. exec. com., 1986—. Neighborhood commr. Boy Scouts Am., 1961-66, merit badge counselor; emeritus, 1979—; mem. Bd. Rev., Beverly Hills, Mich., 1957-63; chmn. bd. review Southfield Twp., Mich., 1964-67; bd. dirs., past pres. Beverly Hills Civic Assn.; bd. dirs. Mich. Epilepsy Center and Assn., 1957-71, exec. com., 1962-67. Mem. Detroit Soc. Model Engrs. (pres. 1958, 62, dir. 1955-71), Chem. Splty. Mfg. Assn., AAAS, Nat. Geog. Soc., Internat. Platform Assn., ASTM, Smithsonian Instn. Assos., Archaeol. Inst. Am., Bibl. Archaeol. Soc., Bible-Sci. Assn., Creation Research Soc., Mich. Student Fin. Aid Assn., Midwest Assn. Student Fin. Aid Adminstrs. Republican (sustaining mem. Oakland County, Mich.). Baptist (trustee, instr. Bible Inst.). Author: Getting To Know New Testament Greek. Home: 32210 Rosevear Dr Beverly Hills Birmingham MI 48009 Office: 280 E Lincoln Birmingham MI 48009

DECKER, ROBERT OWEN, history educator; b. Lafayette, Ind., Nov. 6, 1927; s. Samuel Owen and Helen Dale (Noble) D.; A.B., Butler U., 1953; A.M., Ind. U., 1958; Ph.D., U. Conn., 1970; m. Margaret Ann Harris, May 30, 1948; 1 dau., Terry Lynn Decker DeIulis. Instr., Sch. City of LaPorte (Ind.), 1956-59; instr. Cen. Conn. State U., New Britain, 1959-63, asst. prof., 1963-73, assoc. prof., 1973-77, prof. history, 1977—; evaluator manuscripts Wesleyan U. Press, 1977—; advisor Nat. Endowment for Humanities, 1977—, Connecticut River Found. Mem. Christian Activities Council, Hartford, 1965—, pres., 1972-74, 76-78; dir. Hartford (Conn.) InnerCity Exchange, 1971-81, chmn. bd., 1977-80; chmn. state legis. adv. com. Conn. Developmental Disabilities Council, 1973-75; evaluator programs Conn. Humanities Council; Historian Christian Activities Council, 1983—, Rocky Hill (Conn.) Congl. Ch., 1985—, Conn. 350th Com., 1985—; justice of peace, 1985—, constable Rocky Hill, 1986—; apptd. town historian. Served with U.S. Army, 1946-48, 50-51. Asian Studies grantee, 1959; Am. Studies grantee, 1959; Danforth grantee, 1962; Munson Maritime grantee, 1961; Smithsonian Inst. grantee, 1963. Mem. Orgn. Am. Historians, Am., New Eng., Conn. hist. assns., Assn. for Study of Conn. History, AAUP, New London County Hist. Soc., Am. Waldensian Aid Soc. (pres. Hartford chpt. 1986—), Phi Alpha Theta. Republican. Congregationalist (life deacon). Club: Masons. Author: Whaling Industry of New London, 1973; The Whaling City: A History of New London, 1976; A Student Guidebook to American History, 1983; Hartford and Immigrants, 1986; The New London Merchants, 1986; contbr. articles and book revs. to profl. jours. Home: 2623 Main St Rocky Hill CT 06067 Office: Cen Conn State U Dept History New Britain CT 06050

DECKINGER, ELLIOTT LAWRENCE, advertising agency executive, marketing educator; b. N.Y.C., Apr. 17, 1917; s. Isaac and Mollie (Rose) D.; m. Adele Victoria Kay, June 7, 1941; children: Matthew, Nancy. B.S., N.Y. U., 1936, M.S., 1939, Ph.D., 1947. With Biow Co., N.Y.C., 1937-56; research and media dir. Biow Co., 1941-56; with Grey Advt., Inc., N.Y.C., 1956—; sr. v.p., gen. mgr. Internat. Grey Advt., Inc., 1965-82; cons. Grey Advt., Inc., 1982—; assoc. prof. mktg. St. John's U., 1982-87, disting. prof., 1987—. Author: Careers in Advertising, 1984; contbr. articles to profl. publs. Active Boy Scouts Am., 1955—, mem. nat. public relations com., 1972—, mem. nat. com. internat. scouting, 1973. Named Scouter of Year for communication arts in N.Y.C., 1976; named to Market Research Hall of Fame, 1984; recipient Pres.'s medal St. John's U., 1987. Mem. Copy Research Council (past pres.), Market Research Council (past pres.), Radio and TV Research Council (past pres.), Advt. Research Found. (past chmn.), Internat. Advt. Assn., Am. Mktg. Assn. Home: Box 960 Jamaica NY 11431 Office: St John's U Utopia and Grand Central Pkwys Jamaica NY 11439

DE CLERCK, HERVÉ, food products executive; b. Pau, France, Feb. 5, 1945; s. Jean de Clerck and Colette (de Courson) de la Villeneuve; m. Christine Zafiropulo, Mar. 6, 1968; children: Sophie, Isabel. Diploma, Inst. Supérieur du Commerce Paris, 1968; internat. sr. mgmt. program, Harvard U., 1985. Brand mgr. Colgate Palmolive, France, 1970-72; devel. mgr. Colgate Food Div., France, 1972-74; gen. mgr. Synapse Consumer Research, France, 1974-77; owner/founder Self Mktg., France, 1974—; pres., chief exec. officer Benton & Bowles, Inc., France, 1977-85; also v.p. Benton & Bowles, N.Y.C.; chief operating officer Lesieur Cotelle, France, 1985-87; gen. mgr. Lesieur Alimentaire, France, 1987—; bd. dirs. Imprimerie Adminstrv. Cen., Ordinalpha, Secodip. Author: Relations Agences-Annonceur, 1976; founder, Marketing Mix mag., 1986. Served to lt. French armed forces, 1968-69. Mem. Colgate Bus. Club (co-founder, 1983). Roman Catholic. Home: 33 Blvd d'Angleterre, 78110 le Vesinet France Office: Lesieur, 122 Avenue du Gen Leclerc, 92103 Boulogne Billancourt France

DE CLERCQ, ANDRE GUSTAVE, gynecologist; b. Ghent, Belgium, Dec. 10, 1941. BSc, U. Ghent, 1963, MD, 1967. Resident Faculty Med. Dept. OB Gyn, Ghent, 1967-71; lectr. Faculty Med. Rwanda, Butare, 1971-74; gynecologist Centre Hospitalier, Kigali, 1974—; head of gynecology dept. Centre Hospitalier, 1974—. Contbr. articles to profl. jours. Program dir. Pathfinder Fund, Rwanda, 1972-74; cons. UNDP, Rwanda, 1987. Mem. Flerish Soc. Obstetrics & Gynecology, Royal Belgium Soc. Gynecology & Obstetrics. Home: BP 934, Kigali Rwanda Office: CHK, BP 650, Kigali Rwanda

DECLERCQ, GUIDO VICTOR ALFONS, investment company executive; b. Ardooie, Belgium, Apr. 21, 1928; s. Gerard V. Declecq and Gabrielle Deboutte; m. Josine Ghekiere, Apr. 26, 1957; children: Dominik, Magda, Beatrijs, Philip, Pieter, Marijke. Student econs., U. Leuven, Belgium, 1945-50, student philosophy, 1950-53; student econs., Columbia U., 1951-52. Mng. dir. West-Flanders Devel. Council, Bruges, Belgium, 1954-57, Bank van Roeselare, Belgium, 1957-62; advisor Banque Lambert, Brussels, 1963-70; gen. adminstr. Katholieke U. Leuven, 1967-82; chmn., chief exec. officer Investco N.V., Brussels, 1982—; chmn. Fidisco N.V., Brussels, 1982—; pres. Orda-B N.V., Leuven, 1971—; bd. dirs. HSA-Spaarbank N.V., Antwerp, Belgium, GEVAERT N.V., Antwerp, Transurb Consult, Brussels, VTW-Prado N.V., Kortrijk, Belgium, BeneVent, Brussels, MezzaFinance, Luxembourg; chmn. Gresford, Dublin, Amaten Holdings, Dublin , vice chmn. KB LuxLease, Luxembourg. Author: Structurele Werkloosheid, 1954; Kust en Hinterland, 1956, Ieper, Economische Situatie, 1957. Pres. Internat. Assn. Cons. in Higher Edn. Instns., London, 1981; mem. editorial bd. Industry and Higher Edn., Guilford, Surrey, U.K., 1987. Recipient John Fraser Meml. award Australian Teriary Inst. Cons. Cos. Assn., 1987. Office: Investco NV, Regentlaan 54 (box 2), 1000 Brussels Belgium

DE CLERCQ, WILLY, common market commissioner, barrister; b. Ghent, Belgium, July 8, 1927; s. Frans and Yvonne (Catry) de C.; LL.D.; m. Fernande Fazzi, 1953; 3 children. Barrister, Ct. of Appeal, Ghent; with Gen. Secretariat UN, N.Y.C., 1952; mem. Chamber of Reps. Belgium for Ghent-Ekloo, Brussels, 1958—, dep. prime minister in charge budget, 1966-68, dep. prime minister, 1973-74, minister fin., 1974-77, minister fin., 1981—, vice prime minister, minister fin. and fgn. trade, 1981-85; acting pres., mem. European Parliament, 1979-81; mem. Fedn. European Liberal and Democratic Parties, 1980-85; mem. Commn. European Communities, 1985—; pres. interim com. IMF, 1971-77, 83-85; prof. U. Ghent, U. Brussels. Pres. Partij voor Vrijheid en Vooruitgang, Belgium, 1971-73, 77-81. Office: Commn of European Communities, 200 rue de la Loi 200, 1049 Brussels Belgium

DE CONCINI, DENNIS, U.S. senator, lawyer; b. Tucson, May 8, 1937; s. Evo and Ora (Webster) DeC.; m. Susan Margaret Hurley, June 6, 1959; children: Denise, Christina, Patrick Evo. B.A., U. Ariz., 1959, LL.B., 1963. Bar: Ariz. 1963. Mem. firm Evo DeConcini, Tucson; ptnr. DeConcini & McDonald, Tucson, 1968-73; dep. Pima County atty. Sch. Dist. 1, 1971-72, county atty., 1972-76; U.S. Senator from Ariz. 1977—; mem. Senate Appropriations com., Judiciary com., subcom. on Treasury, Postal Service, and gen. govt., subcom. on def., subcom. energy and water devel., subcom. on fgn. ops., subcom. on interior and related agys., subcom. on State, Justice, Commerce and Judiciary, subcom. on Constitution, subcom. on immigration, select com. on Indian Affairs, select com. on Vet.'s Affairs; formerly pres., now dir. Shopping Centers, Inc.; chmn. Judiciary subcom. on Patents, Copyrights, Trademarks, Antitrust, Cts., Tech. and the Law;. Chmn. legis. com. Tucson Community Council, 1966-67; mem. major gifts com., devel. fund drive St. Joseph's Hosp., 1970, mem. devel. council, 1971-73; mem. major gifts com. Tucson Mus. and Art Center Bldg. Fund, 1971; adminstr. Ariz. Drug Control Dist., 1975-76; precinct committeeman Ariz. Democratic Party, 1958—; mem. Pima County Dem. Central Com., 1958-67, Dem. State Exec. Com., 1958-68; state vice chmn. Ariz. Dem. Com., 1964-66, 70-72; vice chmn. Pima County Dem. Com., 1970-73. Served to 2d lt. JAG U.S. Army, 1959-60. Named Outstanding Ariz. County Atty., 1975. Mem. Am., Ariz., Pima County bar assns., Nat. Dist. Attys. Assn., Ariz. Sheriffs and County Attys. Assn., Am. Judicature Soc., Ariz. Pioneer Hist. Soc., NAACP, U. Ariz. Alumni Assn., Tucson Fraternal Order Police, Phi Delta Theta, Delta Sigma Rho, Phi Alpha Delta. Roman Catholic. Clubs: Nucleus (Tucson), Old Pueblo (Tucson), Pres.'s U. Ariz. (Tucson), Latin Am. (Tucson), Latin Am. Social (Tucson). Office: 328 Hart Senate Bldg Washington DC 20510 *

DE CONINGH, EDWARD HURLBUT, electric company executive; b. Chgo., July 2, 1902; s. Frederic Benjamin Edward and Lucy (Peck) de C.; m. Virginia Scott Mueller, Nov. 7, 1927 (dec. 1964); children—Mary (Mrs. Oliver F. Emerson), Edward Hurlbut, Virginia (Mrs. Harold C. Fleming); m. Martha Hooker Washburn, 1965. A.B., Princeton, 1922; student, U. Grenoble (France), 1922; B.S., Mass. Inst. Tech., 1925. Apprentice Am. Steel Foundries, 1925; sec. Laudryette Mfg. Co., Cleve., 1926-27; tech. editor Dust Recovering and Conveying Co., Cleve., 1928-33; ptnr., chief engr. Mueller Electric Co. (now Mueller Electric Co., Inc.), Cleve., 1933-66, chmn. bd., 1966-; dir. Emerson Press, Inc., Midwest Screw Products, Inc. Pres. Cleve. Welfare Fedn., 1956-59; campaign chmn. Cleve. United Appeal, 1961, 62; pres. Cleve. Community Chest, 1964-65; Vice chmn. trustees Smith Coll., 1962-72; trustee Greater Cleve. Asso. Found., 1967-70, Cleve. Inst. Music; vice chmn. bd. trustees Case Western Res. Univ., 1973-75; trustee Laurel Sch., 1970-76. Recipient Outstanding Service award Cleve. Welfare Fedn., 1959, Distinguished Service award Cleve. United Appeal, 1963; 1967 Cleve. medal for pub. service. Mem. Phi Beta Kappa, Tau Beta Pi, Chi Phi. Clubs: Cleveland Skating, Union, University (Cleve.). Home: 23799 Stanford Rd Shaker Heights OH 44122 Office: Mueller Electric Co Inc 1583 E 31st St Cleveland OH 44114

DECORNEZ, DANIEL, ophthalmologist; b. Reims, Marne, France, Sept. 19, 1938; s. Maurice and Yvonne (Leclerc) DeC.; m. Roseline Bouton; children: Christophe, Stephane, Arnaud, Helene. Degree in Opthalmology, Med. Faculty Reims, France, 1968; MD, Med. Faulty Paris, 1969. Internship U. Hosp. Ctr., Reims, 1964-69, ophthalmologist, 1968-69; dept. head ophthalmologist Hosp. Ctr., Briancon, France, 1969—; cons. ophthalmology Health Resort Founds., Briancon, 1969—; ophthalmology instr. Nurses Coll., ophthalmology examiner Ministry of Health, Marseille, France. Mem. Med. Trade Assn., Hosp. Doctoral Trade Assn., Med. Dept. Council. Roman Catholic. Avocations: skiing, water skiing, fishing, travel. Home: Rt De Puy Saint Pierre 122, 05100 Briancon France Office: Hosp Ctr, Consulting Room, Place De L'Europe, 05100 Briancon France

DECOURCELLE, GUY ADRIEN, clothing company executive; b. Amiens, France, May 10, 1932; s. Raymond and Simone (Persyn) D.; m. Claudine Paule Lemay, Dec. 28, 1959; children: Thierry, Philippe, Francois, Florence. Engr. Diploma, Ecole Centrale, Paris, 1959. Mine engr. H.B.N.P.C., Douai, France, 1959-70; devel. mgr. Martel Catala, Selestat, France, 1970-72; gen. mgr. PIM subs. Martel Catala, Marokolsheim, France, 1972-78; mktg. mgr. Martel Catala, Selestat, 1982-83, ops. dir., 1983—. Served to lt. French Air Force, 1960-62. Office: Martel Catala, 3 Rte De Strasbourg, F-67600 Selestat France

DE CRAENE, JACQUES MARIA, plastics company executive, retired judge, arbitrator; b. Gent, Belgium, May 16, 1929; s. Robert and Marthe (Rosez) de C.; m. Marie-Thérèse Claes, Feb. 24, 1954; children: Guido, Erik, Kristin. Cert. Latin-Greek, Sint-Lievenscollege, Antwerp, Belgium, 1948. Commr. Vlaams Verbond der Katholieke Scouts, Belgium, 1956; founder, owner de Craene Plastics Engring., Monaco, 1983—; RIGI Ltd., Antwerp, 1948—, RIGI-OMNIA Ltd., Antwerp, 1986—, RIGI-MEDIA, Inc., Antwerp, 1975—, Profl. Info. Media Ltd., St. Hellier, C.I., 1985—; judge Social Ct., Antwerp, 1974-82. Pub. Plastics Bull., 1972—; contbr. articles to profl. jours.; speaker in field. Mem. Soc. Plastics Engrs. (founder Benelux Sect. 1972, pres. 1978-80, exec. com. and v.p. internat. affairs 1982-88, award for meritorious services 1979), Pres.'s Cup, Plastics Engrs Arbitration Council Internat. (pres. 1982—). Roman Catholic. Home: Leopoldslei 56, B2130 Brasschaat Belgium Office: RIGI Ltd, Noorderlaan 33, B2030 Antwerp Belgium

DECRANE, ALFRED CHARLES, JR., petroleum company executive; b. Cleve., June 11, 1931; s. Alfred Charles and Verona (Marquard) DeC.; m. Joan Elizabeth Hoffman, July 3, 1954; children: David, Lisa, Stacie, Stephanie, Sarah, Jennifer. B.A., U. Notre Dame, 1953; J.D., Georgetown U., 1959. Bar: Va. bar 1959, D.C. bar 1959, Tex. bar 1961, N.Y. bar 1966. Legal dept. Texaco, Inc., Houston, 1959-64, N.Y.C., 1964-66; asst. to vice chmn. bd. Texaco, Inc., 1965-67, asst. to chmn. bd., 1967-68, gen. mgr. producing dept. Eastern hemisphere, 1968-70, v.p., 1970-76, sr. v.p., gen. counsel, 1976-77, sr. v.p., dir., 1977-78, exec. v.p., 1978-83, pres., 1983-86, chmn. bd. dirs., 1987—; dir. CIGNA Corp. Trustee Council for Econ. Devel. Served to lt. USMCR, 1954-55. Mem. ABA (sect. sec. 1964-67, co-founder Natural Resources Law Jour. mineral law sect., council mem. minerals sect.). Home: 55 Valley Rd Bronxville NY 10708 Office: Texaco Inc 2000 Westchester Ave White Plains NY 10650

DE CROO, HERMAN FRANCIS, member of Belgian House of Representatives; b. Brakel, Belgium, Aug. 12, 1937; s. Alfons and Germaine (Wauters) De C.; Doctorate in law, Université Libre de Bruxelles, 1961; m. Françoise Desguin, Sept. 16, 1961; children—Alexander, Ariane. Barrister at law, 1961—; mayor of Michelbeke (Belgium), 1964-71; rep. Belgian Parliament, 1968—; minister of Nat. Edn., 1974-77; minister of P.T.T. and pensions, 1980; minister of communications and P.T.T., 1981-85; pres. liberal faction Cultural Council, 1972-74; leader liberal faction Ho. of Reps., 1977-80; minister of communications and fgn. trade, 1985—; prof. Faculty of Law, U. Brussels, 1973—; chmn. European Council of Ministers of Transport, 1982, 86, Liberal Study Centre Paul Hymans, Brussels. Chmn. Princess Liliane Found., Mediatheek voor Vlaamse Gemeenschap musical found. Chmn. Autoworld (vet. cars) Collection, 1986—. Decorated comdr. Order of King Leopold; comdr. Nordstjarneorder (Sweden). Mem. Belgian Liberal Study Center (pres.), Found. for Pediatry (pres.), Liberal Internat. Assn. (internat. v.p., vice-chmn.). Club: Rotary Internat. Author: numerous books; contbr. articles to profl. jours. Home: 57 Lepelstraat, Michelbeke-Brakel 9660, Belgium Office: Liberal Study Centre, 37-39 rue de Naples, Brussels Belgium

DE CUENCA, LUIS ALBERTO, poet, Greek and Latin philology researcher; b. Madrid, Spain, Dec. 29, 1950; s. Juan Antonio De Cuenca and Mercedes Prado; m. Julia Barella; 1 child, Álvaro. Degree, U. Autónoma, Spain, 1973, PhD, 1976. Full researcher Consejo Superior Investigaciones Cientificas, Madrid. Author: (poetry) Elsinore, 1972, Scholia, 1978, La Caja de Plata (Critica award 1985), 1985, El Otro Sueño, 1987. Home: Don Ramon De la Cruz 28, Madrid 28001, Spain Office: CSIC, Duque de Medinaceli 6, Madrid 28014, Spain

DE CUEVAS, ELIZABETH, sculptor; b. St. Germain en Laye, France, Jan. 22, 1929 (Am. citizen); d. George and Margaret (Strong) de C.; 1 child, Deborah Carmichael. Student, Vassar Coll., 1946-48; AB, Sarah Lawrence Coll., 1952; student, Art Students League, N.Y.C., 1963-68. One-woman shows include Lee Ault Gallery, N.Y.C., 1977-78, Tower Gallery, Southampton, N.Y., 1980, Iolas-Jackson Gallery, N.Y.C., 1983-85, Guild Hall Mus., East Hampton, N.Y., 1985, Kerr Gallery, N.Y.C., 1988—; exhibited in group shows at Guild Hall, East Hampton, 1980, Art Students League of N.Y., 1982, Bruce Mus., Greenwich, Conn., 1984, 85, Tower Gallery, N.Y.C., 1984, Andre Zarre Gallery, N.Y.C., 1985, Kouros Gallery, N.Y.C. and Ridgefield, Conn., 1985, Susan Blanchard Gallery, N.Y.C., 1985-86, Ruth Vered Gallery, East Hampton, 1986-87, Benton Gallery, Southampton, 1987—, Kerr Gallery, 1988—; represented in pvt. collections. Club: Vassar of N.Y.

DEDEURWAERDER, JOSE JOSEPH, automotive executive; b. Brussels, Dec. 31, 1932; s. Louis and Philippine (Pater Not) D.; m. Nelly Antoinette Clemens, May 15, 1954; 1 child, Joelle Cabassol. Grad. in tech. engring, Ecole Technique Moyenne Superieure, Belgium, 1953. Mfg. dir. Renault, Belgium, 1958-67; indsl. dir. Renault, Argentina, 1967-73; chief exec. officer Renault Mexicana, Mexico, 1973-76; plant dir. Renault, Douai, France, 1976-81; exec. v.p. Am. Motors Corp., Detroit, 1981-82, pres., chief operating officer, 1982-84; pres., chief exec. officer Am. Motors Corp., Southfield, Mich., 1984-86, vice chmn., chmn. exec. com., 1986—. Served as officer Belgium Navy, 1952-53. Mem. Automotive Hall of Fame (bd dirs.). Office: American Motors Corp 27777 Franklin Rd Southfield MI 48034 *

DEDIJER, VLADIMIR, author; b. Belgrade, Feb. 4, 1914; m. Olga Popovic, 1943 (dec.); m. Vera Krizman, 1944; 4 children. Ph.D., Belgrad U. Lt. col. Army of Yugoslavia, World War II; Yugoslav del. UN Gen. Assemblies, 1945, 46, 48, 49, 51, 52; mem. Yugoslav del. to Peace Conf., Paris, 1946; mem. central com. League of Communists Yugoslavia, 1952-54; prof. modern history Belgrade U., 1954-55; defender right of M. Djilas to free speech, 1954, 56, 81, 85; expelled from Central Com., League of Communists, 1954; sentenced to 6 months on probation, 1955; Simon Sr. fellow Manchester U., 1960-62, hon. fellow; fellow St. Antony's Coll., Oxford, 1962-63; research assoc. Harvard Univ., 1963-64; vis. prof. Cornell Univ., 1964-65, MIT, 1969, Brandeis U., 1970-71, U. Mich., 1971, 74, 81, 83; pres. Bertrand Russell's Internat. War Crimes Tribunal, 1964—; mem. Serbian Acad. Scis., 1968, pres. genocide com.; mem. Order of Liberation of Yugoslavia; mem. Nuremberg Council for Publ. of Documents on Post-Nuremberg Trials, 1987, Russell Hist. Com. on Waldhem, 1987. Publs. include: Partisan Diary, 1945; Notes from the United States, 1945; Paris Peace Conf. 1948; Yugoslav-Albanian Relations, 1949; Tito, 1952; The Beloved Land, 1962; Sarajevo, 1963; The Battle Stalin Lost, 1969; History of Yugoslavia, 1973; New Documents for Tito's Biography, 1984, Vatikan and Jasenovack, 1987. Address: Gorkiceva 16/V, 2-4 Ljubljana Yugoslavia

DEDIU, MICHAEL MIHAI, mathematician, computer scientist, researcher, consultant; b. Iasi, Romania, Nov. 6, 1943; s. Virgil V. and Ana M. (Condurache) D.; m. Sofia D. Scarlat, July 22, 1964; children—Ovidiu, Horatiu. M.S., U. Bucharest (Romania), 1966; Ph.D., Inst. Math., Bucharest, 1972. Cert. tchr., Ohio. Researcher, Inst. Math., Bucharest, 1967-75; asst. prof. U. Bucharest, 1972-73; researcher Inst. Physics, Bucharest, 1975-76, U. Turin (Italy), 1977-78; vis. research assoc. Case Western Res. U., Cleve., 1978-83; computer scientist, mathematician Cleve. Bd. Edn., 1979-84; prin. software engr. Applicon-Schlumberger, Burlington, Mass., 1984-85, Encode Tech. Inc., Nashua, N.H., 1985-86, Adcole Corp., Marlborough, Mass., 1986—; cons., pres. Dr. Dediu Inst. Mem. Presdl. Task Force, 1982—. Recipient Consiglio Nazionale delle Richerche, Italy, 1977, Mathematischesinstitut, Oberwolfach, W.Ger., 1977. Mem. Am. Math. Soc., Math. Assn. Am., Soc. Indsl. and Applied Math., Computer Soc. of IEEE. Republican. Club: Library of Computer Scis. Author: Lens Spaces, 1972; Immersions of Projective Spaces in Euclidean Spaces, 1973; Vector Fields on Three Dimensional Lens Spaces, 1974; The General Theory of Life. Home: 230 North St Tewksbury MA 01876 Office: 669 Forest St Marlborough MA 01752

DE DONNEA, FRANCOIS-XAVIER, government official; b. Edegem, Belgium, Apr. 29, 1941; s. Xavier de Donnea de Hamoir and Beeckmans de West-Meerbeeck; m. Comtesse de Villegas de Saint Pierre Jette, Apr. 29, 1967. B. in Applied Econs., Cath. U. Louvain, Belgium, 1963, B. in Economical Scis., 1968; MBA, U. Calif., Berkeley, 1965; D. in Economical Scis., Erasmus U., Rotterdam, The Netherlands, 1971. Asst. and prof. Cath. U. of Louvain, 1967; chief of staff State Sec. to Economical Affairs, 1974-76; dep. chief of staff Minister of Fgn. Trade, 1976-77; adminstr. Belgian Office of Fgn. Trade, 1977-79; adminstr., mem. Study Ctr.'s Office of Nuclear Energy, Md., 1975-81; co-opt senator, senator 1981-85; gen. polit. sec. Liberal Reforming Party, 1982-83; mem. common council City of Brussels, 1983; pres. Senatorial Commn. for Fins., 1983; state sec. Cooperation for Devel., 1983-85; minister of nat. def. and minister of Brussels region 1985—. Mem. Liberal Reforming Party. Served with Belgian Army. Office: Ministry of Nat Def, Rue Lambermont 8, 1000 Brussels Belgium also: Ministry of Brussels Region, Boulevard du Regent 21-23, 1000 Brussels Belgium

DE DUVE, CHRISTIAN RENÉ, chemist, educator; b. Thames-Ditton, Eng., Oct. 2, 1917; s. Alphonse and Madeleine (Pungs) de D.; M.D., U. Louvain (Belgium), 1941, Ph.D., 1945, M.Sc., 1946; Dr. honoris causa, univs. Turin, Leiden, Sherbrooke, Lille, Cath. U. Santiago (Chile), U. René Descartes, Paris, State U. Ghent, State U. Liege, Gustavus Adolphus Coll., St. Peter, Minn., U. Rosario (Argentina), U. Aix-Marseille II, U. Keele, Katholieke Universitet Leuven, Karolinska Inst., Stockholm; m. Janine Herman, Sept. 30, 1943; children: Thierry, Anne, Françoise, Alain. Lectr. physiol. chemistry faculty medicine Cath. U. Louvain, 1947-51, prof., head dept. physiol. chemistry, 1951-85, emeritus prof., 1985—; prof. biochem. cytology Rockefeller U., N.Y.C., 1962-74, Andrew W. Mellon prof., 1974-88, prf. emeritus, 1988—; vis. prof. Albert Einstein Coll. Medicine, Bronx, N.Y., 1961-62, Chaire Francqui State U. Ghent, 1962-63, Free U. Brussels, 1963-64, State U. Liège, 1972-73; Mayne guest prof. U. Queensland, Brisbane, Australia, 1972. Pres. Internat. Inst. Cellular and Molecular Pathology, Brussels, 1974—. Mem. Conseil d'Adminstrn. du Fonds Nat. de la Recherche Scientifique, 1958-61; mem. Conseil de Gestion du Fonds de la Recherche Scientifique Medicale, 1959, 61; mem. Commn. Scientifique du Fonds de la Recherche Scientifique Medicale, 1958, 61; mem. Comite des Experts du Conseil Nat. de la Politique Scientifique, 1958-61; mem. adv. bd. Ciba Found.; mem. adult devel. and aging research and tng. rev. com. Nat. Inst. Child Health and Devel., NIH, 1970-72; mem. adv. com. for med. research WHO, 1974-79; mem. sci. adv. com. Max Planck-Inst. für Immunbiologie, 1975-78, Ludwig Inst. Cancer Research, 1985—, Mary Imogene Bassett Research Inst., 1986—, Clin. Research Inst. Montreal, 1986—; mem. biology adv. com. N.Y. Hall of Sci., 1986—. Recipient Prix des Alumni, 1949, Prix Pfizer, 1957, Prix Francqui, 1960, Prix Quinquennal Belge des Sciences Médicales, 1967 (Belgium); Gairdner Found. Internat. award merit (Can.), 1967; Dr. H.P. Heineken prize (Netherlands), 1973; Nobel prize for physiology or medicine, 1974; Harden award Biochem. Soc. (Gt. Britain), 1978; Theobald Smith award Albany Med. Coll., 1981; Jimenez Diaz award, 1985. Fellow AAAS; mem. Royal Acad. Medicine, Royal Acad. Belgium, Am. Chem. Soc., Biochem. Soc., Am. Soc. Biol. Chemists, Pontifical Acad. Sci., Am. Soc. Cell Biology (council 1966-69), Soc. Chimie Biologique, Soc. Belge Biochim. (pres. 1962-64), Deutsche Akademie der Naturforscher Leopoldina, Koninklyke Akademie voor Geneeskunde (Belgium), European Assn. Study Diabetes, European Molecular Biology Orgn., European Cell Biology Orgn., Internat. Soc. Cell Biology, N.Y. Acad. Scis., Soc. Belge de Physiologie, Sigma Xi; fgn. asso. Am. Acad. Arts and Scis., Nat. Acad. Scis. (U.S.), Royal Soc. London (fgn. mem.), Académie des Sciences de Paris, Académie des Sciences d'Athen, Royal Soc. of London; numerous hon. memberships. Mem. editorial bd. Subcellular Biochemistry, 1971-87, Preparative Biochemistry, 1971-80, Molecular and Cellular Biochemistry, 1973-80. Office: Rockefeller U 1230 York Ave New York NY 10021 also: ICP, 75 Avenue Hippocrate, B-1200 Brussels Belgium

DEE, HELEN YUCHENGCO, insurance company executive; b. Manila, Philippines, May 18, 1944; d. Alfonso Tiaoqui and Paz Bau (Sycip) Yuchengco; m. Peter Sycip Dee, July 18, 1964; children—Michael Patrick Y., Michele Marie Y., Johanna Y. B.S. in Commerce, Assumption Convent, Manila, 1963, MBA De La Salle U., Manila, 1987. Asst. to pres. Malayan Ins. Co., Inc., Manila, 1963-70, v.p., 1970-72, sr. v.p., 1972-74, exec. v.p., 1974-82, pres., 1982—; chmn. bd. Z Fishing Corp., Manila, First Nationwide Assurance Corp., Manila; chmn. Manila Meml. Park Cemetery, Makati, 1983—; pres., bd. dirs. Malayan Ins. Co., Inc.; pres. Hydee Mgmt. & Resource Corp., Manila, 1977—, Y Realty Corp., Manila, 1976—, Enrique T. Yuchengco, Inc., Manila, 1963—; exec. v.p., bd. dirs. House of Investments, Inc., Makati, Malayan-Zurich Ins. Co. Inc., Manila, 1974—; bd. dirs. Pan Malayan Ins. Corp., Zamboanga Wood Products, Inc., Nat. Reinsurance Corp., Seafront Resources Corp., First Malayan Leasing and Fin. Corp., HI Eisai Pharms., Inc.; chmn. bd. dirs. Am. Bristol Ins. Co., Malayan Zurich Ins. (Guam); vice chmn. Malayan Overseas Ins. Corp., Taipei, 1986—; bd. dirs. Mico Equities, Inc.13; dir. Pacific Data Corp., Philippine Global Communications, Inc., Philippine Rock Products, Inc., Eastern Gen. Reins. Corp., Philmark, Inc., Philippine Fuji Xerox Corp.; mem. adv. bd. Rizal Comml. Banking Corp.; vice chmn. Asean Ins. Coll. working com., 1985—; trustee Ins. Inst. for Asia and the Pacific, Manila, 1985-88. Chmn., 10th Nat. Fire Safety Conv., Safety Orgn. Philippines, Inc., 1983; mem. Community

Chests and Councils of Philippines, 1975—, Goodwill Industries Philippines, 1983—; trustee Philippine Philharm. Soc., Manila, 1985—; mem. Young Pres. Orgn., 1987—. Mem. Philippine Insurers Club (pres. 1975-76), Ins. and Surety Assn. Philippines (pres., chmn. 1982-84), Asean Ins. Council (chmn. 1982-84, adv. bd. 1985—), Internat. Ins. Soc., Inc. (charter 1987—). Office: Malayan Ins Co Inc, 500 Q Paredes St, Manila Philippines 2805

DEE, PETER SYCIP, banker; b. Pasay, Metro Manila, Nov. 18, 1941; s. George Dee and Mary (Mary SyCip) D.; m. Helen Yuchengco; children: Michael Patrick, Michele Marie, Johanna Marie. B.S. Commerce, De La Salle U., Manila, 1965; spl. banking curse Am. Inst. Banking, 1966. Asst. v.p. Rizal Commercial Banking Corp., Manila, 1963-71; pres., chief operating officer China Banking Corp., Manila, 1972—, dir., 1977—; pres. CBC Venture Capital; dir. Trans-Pacific Ins. Co. (Australia) Ltd., 1970—, First CBC Capital (Asia) Ltd., Hong Kong, 1980—, CBC Fin., Manila, 1980—; alt. dir. Asean Fin. Corp., Singapore, 1981-86. Bd. dirs. Cityland Devel. Corp., Jr. Achievement of Philippines, 1986-87; dir. Oriental Holdings Corp., Phillipine Pacific Captial Corp., Sinclair Inc., HI-Mktg. Corp.; treas, dir. D.D.D., Inc.; asst. treas., dir. Dee C. Chaun Investment Corp.; mgr., ptnr. Silver Flacon Ins. Agy., Ltd.; pres., dir. GDSK Devel. Corp. Mem. Fin. Exec. Inst. Philippines, Jaycee Internat. (senator). Clubs: Baguio Country (Baguio City); Wack Wack Golf and Country (Manila). Home: 1150 Tamarind Rd, Dasmarinas Village, Makati, Mento Manila Philippines Office: China Banking Corp, Dasmarinas St, Metro Manila Philippines

DEE, ROBERT FORREST, retired pharmaceutical company executive; b. Cin., July 8, 1924; s. Raymond H. and Mary (Owen) D.; m. Virginia Winston Verner, Sept. 10, 1948 (div. 1979); children: Jacqueline, Robert R., John, Catherine, Thomas; m. 2d Jean T. Tanney, Jan. 2, 1980; 1 child, Patrick. A.B., Harvard U., 1946; LL.D. (hon.), Phila. Coll. Pharmacy and Sci., 1978; L.H.D. (hon.), Med. Coll. Pa., 1979. With SmithKline Corp., Phila., 1948-87; successively market research analyst, asst. to adminstrv. v.p., dir. Animal Health div., dir. consumer, animal and instrument products, v.p., dir. consumer, animal and instrument products, exec. v.p., pres., chief exec. officer, chmn.; bd. dirs. United Techs. Corp., Air Products and Chems. Inc.; mem. adv. bd. Volvo Internat. Bd. dirs. U.S. Council for Internat. Bus., Com. Econ. Devel.; trustee Heritage Found. Served with AUS. Mem. Nat. Assn. Mfrs. (chmn. exec. com.), Bus. Council, Conf. Bd., Council Fgn. Relations, Mgmt. Execs. Soc. Episcopalian. Office: Smith Kline Beckman Corp 1 Franklin Plaza Philadelphia PA 19101

DEEG, EMIL WOLFGANG, manufacturing company executive; b. Selb, Germany, Sept. 20, 1926; s. Fritz and Trina (Poehlmann) D.; came to U.S., 1967, naturalized, 1975; Dipl. Physiker, U. Wuerzburg, 1954, Dr. rer. nat., 1956; m. Hedwig M.S. Kempf, Aug. 25, 1953; children—Wolfgang, Martin, Bernhard, Renate. Research asst. Max Planck Inst., Wuerzburg, 1954-59; mem. tech. staff Bell Telephone Labs., Allentown, Pa., 1959-60; research asso. Jenaer Glaswerk Schott U. Gen., Mainz, Germany, 1960, dir. research, 1960-65; asso. prof. physics and solid state sci. Am. U., Cairo, 1965-67; mgr. ceramic research Am. Optical Corp., Southbridge, Mass., 1967-71, mgr. materials research, 1971-73, dir. process and materials research, 1973-75, dir. inorganic materials research and devel., 1975-77, tech. adviser, 1977-78; sr. scientist Anchor Hocking Corp., Lancaster, Ohio, 1978-79, mgr. materials research and devel., 1979-80; mgr. glass tech. Bausch & Lomb, Rochester, N.Y., 1980-82; mgr. glass and fiber devel. Mead Office Systems, Richardson, Tex., 1982-84; project mgr. AMP, Inc., Harrisburg, Pa., 1984—; mem. Internat. Commn. on Glass, 1963-81. Pres., PTA, Woodstock, Conn., 1970-71; committeeman Mohegan council Boy Scouts Am., 1967-73; trustee Woodstock Acad., 1971-78; overseer Old Sturbridge Village, Inc.; chmn. Optical Info. Center, Southbridge, 1976-77. Served with German Army, 1944-45. Fellow Am. Ceramic Soc.; mem. Optical Soc. Am., Nat. Inst. Ceramic Engrs., Brit. Soc. Glass Tech., Soc. Advancement Materials and Process Engring. Club: Lions (pres. Woodstock chpt. 1975; zone chmn. dist. 23 C, Lions Internat. 1976-78), Contbr. chpts. to books, articles to profl. jours. Author: (with H. Richter) Glas im Laboratorium, 1966. Patentee in field. Home: 501 Ohio Ave Lemoyne PA 17043 Office: 2901 Fulling Mill Rd Middletown PA 17057

DEEGAN, JOHN ANTHONY, scientific instrument company executive; b. Slough, Buckingham, Eng., Apr. 1, 1933; arrived in Fed. Republic Germany, 1977; s. John Newman and Joy Marjorie (Gray) D.; m. Michaela Maria Weingärtner; children: Nigel, Sacha, Natalie. Degree in chemistry, Acton Tech. Coll., 1955. Mgr. research & devel. Elga Ltd., High Wycombe, Eng., 1960-67; mng. dir. Bruker Spectrospin Ltd., Coventry, Eng., 1967-77, Bruker Japan Co. Ltd., Tokyo, 1975-77; geschäftsführer Oxford Instruments GmbH, Heidelberg, Fed. Republic of Germany, 1977-83; dir. nuclear magnetic resonance Europe Diasonics Sonotron GmbH, Heidelberg, Fed. Republic of Germany, 1983—. Mem. Gesellschaft Deutscher Chemiker. Home: Mönchbergweg 79, 6900 Heidelberg Federal Republic of Germany

DEEIK, KHALIL GEORGE, economist, financing company executive; b. Bethlehem, Jordan, Nov. 12, 1937; s. George Said Diek and Wadiea (Jalil) Lama; m. Jalileh Mary Marzouka, Aug. 22, 1965; children—George, Ramzi, Nader. B.A., Sacramento State U., 1961, M.A., 1964; Ph.D., U. So. Calif., 1972. Prin., adminstr. Manzinata Sch., Hyanpom, Calif., 1964-65; mgr. Gen. Trading Co., Alkhobar, Saudi Arabia, 1966-69; program dir., instr. Krebs Coll., North Hollywood, Calif., 1969-72; mng. dir., v.p. Olayan Saudi Investment Co., Olayan Financing Co., Jeddah, Saudi Arabia, 1973—; bd. dirs. Saudi Polyester Products Co., Jeddah, 1984—; exec. com. mem. Saudi Arabian Constrn. and Repair Services Co., Jeddah, 1984—; hon. lectr. King Abdulaziz U., Saudi Arabia, 1979; faculty mem., program coordinator Century U., Calif., 1978—. Mem. Internat. Educators Assn. (v.p. 1970-72), Phi Delta Kappa, Phi Delta Epsilon. Club. Marquis (U.S.A.). Office: Olayan Financing Co, PO Box 8772, Riyadh 11492, Saudi Arabia

DEER, JAMES WILLIS, lawyer; b. Reading, Pa., Mar. 14, 1917; s. Irvin E. and Rosemary (French) D.; m. Marion M. Hawkinson, July 31, 1943 (dec. 1987); 1 child, Ann Marie. AB, Oberlin Coll, 1938; JD, U. Mich., 1941. Bar: Ohio 1941, N.Y. 1948. Legal staff SEC, 1942-45; practice in N.Y.C., 1945—; mem. firm Holtzmann, Wise & Shepard, 1954—; bd. dirs. Arts Way Mfg. Co., Inc., Selvac Corp., Am. Diversified Enterprises, Inc., Techsci. Industries, Applied DNA Sytems, Inc., Allegheny & Western Energy Corp. Mem. Am., N.Y. State bar assns., Phi Beta Kappa, Phi Alpha Delta. Home: 611 Shore Acres Dr Mamaroneck NY 10543 also: Barr Terr 50 East Dr Delray Beach FL 33444 Office: 745 Fifth Ave New York NY 10151

DEERING, ALLAN BROOKS, soft drink company executive; b. Chappaqua, N.Y., Apr. 1, 1934; s. Clarence and Muriel (Lee) D.; B.A., Columbia U., 1956; m. Carol Ann Werle, Apr. 14, 1957; children—Peter Brooks, Andrew Werle. Systems analyst IBM Corp., White Plains, N.Y., 1956-58; EDP mgr. R. H. Donnelly Corp. N.Y.C., 1958-68; dir. systems and data processing W. R. Grace & Co., N.Y.C., 1968-76, asst. v.p., 1975, dir. info. systems SCM Corp., N.Y.C., 1976-81; dir. mgmt. info. services Pepsi Co., 1981-86, v.p. mgmt. info. services, 1986—. Mem. Mayor's Industry Adv. Bd. for Data Processing, N.Y.C., 1978, adv. bd. Pace U. Sch. Computer Sci., Omicron. Mem. Data Processing Mgmt. Assn., Soc. Mgmt. Info. Systems, N.Y. Computer Execs. Roundtable. Clubs; Rocky Point, Old Greenwich Yacht, Milbrook. Home: 3 Perkley Ln Riverside CT 06878 Office: Anderson Hill Rd Purchase NY 10577

DE ESCONDRILLAS DAMBORENEA, JOSE MARIO, corporate executive; b. Mar. 27, 1934. Dr. Indsl. Engring., Escuela Técnica Superior de Ingenieros Industriales, Bilbao. Head engr. for heat treatment and quality control Olarra S.A., 1960-67, tech. and prodn. v.p., 1963-67; chief engr. for heat treatment and quality control Aceros de Llodio S.A., 1962-63; tech. and prodn. v.p. Made S.A., 1963-64; head prodn. dept. S.E. De Construccion Naval, Reinosa works, 1967-69, tech. and prodn. v.p., 1969-70, pres., 1970-75; pres. for Vizcaya area Gen. Electrica Española S.A., 1975-76; tech. and indsl. v.p. Empresa Nat. Siderurgica S.A., 1976; chmn., chief exec. officer Unión de Explosivos Rio Tinto S.A., 1983—; chmn. Check S.A.; mem. European adv. council AT&T. Mem. Atlantic Inst. for Internat. Affairs; chmn. Consejo Social de la U. Nat. de Edn. a Distancia. Office: Union Explosivos Rio Tinto SA, Paseo Castellana 20, Madrid Spain

DE FACQ, EUGENE AUGUSTA, government consultant; b. Dendermonde, Flanders, Belgium, May 13, 1931; s. Julien J. and Angela (Verleyen) DeF.; m. Gertrude G. De Rycker, Oct. 20, 1954; children: Hans, Kris, Wim, Paul, Katia, Nik, Ben, Keysha. Laureate, Royal Conservatory Sch. Drama, Ghent, Belgium, 1952; MA in Applied Psychology, U. Ghent, 1954. Faculty assoc. U. Pa., Phila., 1956-57; sr. asst. U Ghent, 1954-64; prof. Univ. Faculties Antwerp, Belgium, 1961-71; dir. Berenschot Mgmt. Cons., Brussels, 1964-69; senator Belgian Parliament, Brussels, 1968-79; co-dir. UN Indsl. Devel. Orgn., Brussels, 1980-84; joint chief staff Minister Fgn. Trade, Brussels, 1979; project cons. Belgian Govt. and EEC, Brussels, 1979—; bd. dirs. Interface, U Ghent., 1988—; cons. govt. cos. and internat. orgns., Europe, Asia, Africa, Middle East, 1968—. Contbr. articles on indsl. psychol., sociol., polit. and internat. affairs to profl. jours. Del. UN Gen. Assembly 5th Com., N.Y.C., 1968-80, UN Conf. on Trade and Devel., Nairobi, 1976. Decorated Leopold Order, Kingdom of Belgium, 1977; named to Council Fgn. Trade, Belgian Govt., 1979, Hon. Consul, Liberia, 1977-79. Mem. Internat. Circle Flanders (pres. 1985—), UN Assn. (v.p. 1984—) Auvex Audio Visuals for Export (v.p. 1986—), Rugos Internat. Coop. (sec. bd. 1986—). Roman Catholic. Home: James-Ensorlaan 11, 9820 Ghent Belgium Office: St Pieters Niewstraat 25, U of Ghent Rectorate, B-9000 Ghent Belgium

DEFAZIO, LYNETTE STEVENS, dancer, choreographer, educator, chiropractor; b. Berkeley, Calif., Sept. 29; d. Honore and Mabel J. (Estavan) Stevens; student U. Calif., Berkeley, 1950-55, San Francisco State Coll., 1950-51; D. Chiropractic, Life-West Chiropractic Coll., San Lorenzo, Calif., 1983, BA in Humanities, New Coll. Calif., 1986; children—Joey H. Panganiban, Joanna Pang. Diplomate Nat. Sci. Bd.; eminence in dance edn., Calif. Community Colls. dance specialist, standard services, childrens ctrs. credentials Calif. Dept. Edn. Contract child dancer Monogram Movie Studio, Hollywood, Calif., 1938-40; dance instr. San Francisco Ballet, 1953-64; performer San Francisco Opera Ring, 1960-67; performer, choreographer Oakland (Calif.) Civic Light Opera, 1963-70; fgn. exchange dance dir. Academie de Danses-Salle Pleyel, Paris, France, 1966; dir. Ballet Arts Studio, Oakland, 1960—; teaching specialist Oakland Unified Sch. Dist.-Childrens Ctrs., 1968-80; instr. Peralta Community Coll. Dist., Oakland, 1971—, chmn. dance dept., 1985—; cons., instr. extension courses UCLA, Dirs. and Suprs. Assn., Pittsburg Unified Sch. Dist., Tulare (Calif.) Sch. Dist., 1971-73; researcher Ednl. Testing Services, HEW, Berkeley, 1974; resident choreographer San Francisco Childrens Opera, 1970—, Oakland Civic Theater; ballet mistress Dimensions Dance Theater, Oakland, 1977-80; cons. Gianchetta Sch. Dance, San Francisco, Robicheau Boston Ballet, TV series Patchwork Family, CBS, N.Y.C.; choreographer Ravel's Valses Nobles et Sentimentales, 1976. Author: The Opera Ballets; A Choreographic Manual, Vols. I-V, 1986. Recipient Foremost Women of 20th Century, 1985, Merit award San Francisco Children's Opera, 1985. Mem. Profl. Dance Tchrs. Assn. Am. Author: Basic Music Outlines for Dance Classes, 1960, rev., 1968; Teaching Techniques and Choreography for Advanced Dancers, 1965; Basic Music Outlines for Dance Classes, 1965; Goals and Objectives in Improving Physical Capabilities, 1970; A Teacher's Guide for Ballet Techniques, 1970; Principle Procedures in Basic Curriculum, 1974; Objectives and Standards of Performance for Physical Development, 1975. Asso. music arranger Le Ballet du Cirque, 1964, Techniques of a Ballet School, 1970, rev., 1974; asso. composer, lyricist The Ballet of Mother Goose, 1968; choreographer: Walses Nobles Et Sentimentales (Ravel); Cannon in D for Strings and Continuo (Pachelbel), 1979. Home and Office: 4923 Harbord Dr Oakland CA 94618

DEFELICE, EUGENE VINCENT, lawyer; b. Miami, Fla., Sept. 2, 1958; s. Eugene Anthony DeFelice and Charlene Cecilia Petsch. BA, Rutgers Coll., 1980; JD, Seton Hall U., 1983. Bar: N.J. 1983. Assoc. Lynch, Mannion, Martin, Benitz, & Lynch, P.A., New Brunswick, N.J., 1983-86; atty. Hoffmann-LaRoche Inc., Nutley, N.J., 1986—. Vol. Spl. Olympics, Bergen County area, 1988. Named Eagle Scout, Boy Scouts Am. Mem. ABA (labor and employment law sect.), N.J. Bar Assn., Assn. Trial Lawyers Am. Avocation: flying. Office: care Hoffmann-LaRoche Inc 340 Kingsland St Nutley NJ 07110

DEFOOR, JAMES ALLISON, II, lawyer; b. Coral Gables, Fla., Dec. 6, 1953; s. James Allison Sr. and Marjorie (Keen) DeF.; m. Terry Ann White, June 24, 1977; children: Melissa Anne, Mary Katherine. BA, U. So. Fla., 1976; JD, Stetson U., 1979; MA, U. So. Fla., 1979. Bar: Fla. 1979, U.S. Dist. Ct. (so. dist.) Fla. 1980, U.S. Ct. Appeals (5th cir.) 1981, U.S. Ct. Appeals (11th cir.) 1982. Asst. state's atty. 16th Cir., Key West, Fla., 1980-83, dir. narcotics task force, 1981-83; judge Monroe County, Plantation Key, Fla., 1983-87; assoc. Cunningham, Albritton, Lenz, Warner, Bragg & Miller, Plantation Key, 1987—; pres. Keen Fruit Corp., Key West, 1979-83, 85—; adj. faculty St. Leo Coll., Key West, 1980-81, U. So. Fla., Ft. Myers, Fla., 1981-82, Fla. Internat. U., Miami, 1985, U. Miami Law Sch., 1985—; bd. of trustees U. of South, Sewanee, Tenn., 1983—; faculty Nat. Jud. Coll., Reno, Nev., 1985-86. Chmn. Monroe County Rep. Exec. Com., 1987-88. Named one of Five Outstanding Young Men in Fla., Jaycees, 1984, Ten Outstanding Young Men in Am., Jaycees, 1985; Merit award Fla. Crime Prevention Commn., 1982. Mem. ABA, Fla. Bar Assn., Monroe County Bar Assn., Lawyers in Mensa, Fla. Keys Bar Assn. Republican. Episcopalian. Clubs: St. Petersburg (Fla.) Yacht, Ocean Reef (Key Largo, Fla.); Islamorada (Fla.) Fishing.

DEFRAIN, DENNIS ALLEN, education director, retired army officer; b. Fairbury, Nebr., Mar. 3, 1943; s. Howard Willis and Anna Pauline (Eisenhauer) De F.; m. Carol Jean Daugherty, Nov. 21, 1964; 1 child, Darren Craig. BSc, U. Nebr., 1965; MSc, U. So. Calif., 1972; EdD, Cath. U. Am., 1983. Commd. 2d lt. U.S. Army, 1965, advanced through grades to lt. col., 1982; adminstrv. officer 2d Bn., 15th Arty., Ft. Wainwright, Alaska, 1965-66, unit comdr., 1966-67; adminstrv. officer Adv. Team 55, Rach Gia, Vietnam, 1968-69; unit comdr. 2d Bn., 59th Arty., El Paso, Tex., and Schwabach, W.Ger., 1970-71, personnel mgr., Schwabach, 1971-73; asst. prof. U. Wis.-Oshkosh, 1973-76; personnel mgr. U.S. Army Personnel Ctr., Alexandria, Va., 1976-78; faculty devel. adminstr., instructional technologist Command and Gen. Staff Coll., Ft. Leavenworth, Kans., 1979-82; prof. mil. sci. Weber State Coll., Ogden, Utah, 1982-85 , dir. distance edn., 1985—. Dir. youth bowling Ft. Leavenworth Youth Activities, 1979-80, dir. rifle marksmanship, 1981-82; mem. adv. bd. Layton High Sch. Decorated Bronze Star medal, Army Commendation medal, Meritorious Service medal with two oak leaf clusters. Mem. Mil. Testing Assn., Nat. Univ. Continuing Edn. Assn., Am. Assn. for Adult and Continuing Edn., Layton C. of C. (bd. dirs., pres.), Alliance for Distance Learning, Alpha Gamma Rho. Home: 2762 E Brinton Way Layton UT 84041 Office: Weber State Coll Ogden UT 84408

DEFRASNE, HERVE, human resources management company official; b. St. Mande, France, May 27, 1957; s. Jean-Claude and Michele (Verquin) D.; m. Sylvie Pineau, Sept. 10, 1983; 1 child, Hugo. MBA, Jacksonville U., 1983. Salesman Control Data Co., Paris, 1983-86; cons. Mercuri Urval, Paris, 1986—. Served to lt. French Army, 1978-79. Home: Rue de Charenton 261-263, 75012 Paris France Office: Mercuri Urval, 14 Bis Rue Daru, 75008 Paris France

DE FURSTENBERG, MAXIMILIEN CARDINAL, ecclesiastic; b. Heerlen, Netherlands, Oct. 23, 1904. Ordained priest Roman Catholic Ch., 1931; titular archbishop of Palto and apostolic del. to Japan, 1949; internuncio, 1952, when Japan established diplomatic relations with Vatican; apostolic del. to Australia, N.Z. and Oceania, 1960; nuncio to Portugal, 1962-67; elevated to Sacred Coll. Cardinals, 1967; prefect of Congregation for Oriental Chs., 1969-74; chamberlain Sacred Coll. Cardinals, 1983—; mem. Council for Public Affairs of Ch. Grand master Equestrian Order Holy Sepulchre of Jerusalem. Address: Piazza del S Uffizio 11, 00193 Rome Italy also: Via della Conciliazione 34, Rome Italy *

DEGBOR, ANKU FRANCIS, civil service executive, educator; b. Kpando, Akpini, Ghana, Feb. 8, 1940; arrived in Republic South Africa, 1978; s. Cletus Kodjo and Magdalena (Odonkor) D.; m. Bernada-Celestine Mabre; children: William Ankutse, Joycelyn Abra, Ebenezer Yao, David Kwame, Frances Yaosi. Cert. in advanced craft, Accra (Ghana) Poly., 1966, full tech. cert. in bldg., 1971; diploma in advanced tech. teaching, Kumasi (Ghana) Advanced Tech. Tchrs. Coll., 1969. Tech. tchr. Ghana Edn. Service, Koforidua, 1969-74; head dept. craft/civil engring. Lesotho Edn. Service, Maseru, Lesotho, 1974-78; dep. prin. Lusikisiki Br. Ngqungqushe Tech. Inst. Transkei Edn. Service, Umtata, Republic South Africa, 1978-86; chief dir. tng. Transkei Civil Service, Umtata, 1986—; Cert. tech. tchr. Licentiate Inst. Bldg. (chartered technician), City Guilds London Inst. (advanced grade); fellow Profl. Bus. Tech. Mgmt. Roman Catholic. Lodge: Rotary (head vocat. service Umtata chpt. 1983—). Home: 3 Jasmine St, Umtata Transkei 5100, Republic of South Africa

DEGENNARO, VINCENT ANTHONY, surgeon; b. Hoboken, N.J., Apr. 30, 1946; s. Robert G. and Grace (Impreveduto) DeG.; A.B. cum laude, Lafayette Coll., 1968; M.D., SUNY, Downstate Med. Coll., 1972; m. Geraldine Gifford, Dec. 26, 1970; children—Robert, Steven, Vincent, Kristen. Intern, St. Vincents Hosp. and Med. Center, N.Y.C., 1972-73; resident in surgery, 1973-77; fellow in surgery Lahey Clinic, Boston, 1977-78; chief surg. edn. St. Vincent's Hosp., N.Y.C., 1978—; practice medicine specializing in surgery, N.Y.C., 1978-80; mem. staff St. Joseph's Hosp. and Med. Center, Paterson, N.J.; asst. prof. surgery N.Y. Med. Coll., Valhalla, N.Y. Am. Cancer Soc. fellow, 1976-77; diplomate Am. Bd. Surgery, Am. Bd. Colon and Rectal Surgery. Fellow Am. Soc. Colon Rectal Surgeons, ACS; mem. N.Y. Acad. Medicine, N.Y. Soc. Colon Rectal Surgeons, N.Y. Surg. Soc., N.J. Soc. Colon Rectal Surgeons, N.Y. Cancer Soc., Phi Beta Kappa. Club: Unico Nat. Office: 1960 NE 47th St Fort Lauderdale FL 33308

DEGENSZEJN, RICARDO EMANUEL, industrial company executive, engineer; b. Warsaw, Poland, May 4, 1934; arrived in Brazil, 1941; s. Jerzy and Helena D.; m. Rachel "Lola" Yallouz, Aug. 16, 1958; children: Debora, Vivian E. Elizabeth. BS in Engring., MIT, 1955; grad. in higher polit. and strategic studies, Brazilian War Coll. Cert. engr. Tech. dir. CIA. Quimica Indsl. de Laminados, Rio De Janeiro, 1955-65, gen. dir., 1965-70; alternately v.p. and pres. Cia. Quimica Indsl. de Laminados (Formiplac Group), Satipel Indsl. S/A. (Formiplac Group), Minasplac S/A. Ind. Reflorestamento (Formiplac Group), Formiplac Nordeste S/A. (Formiplac Group), Rio De Janeiro, Taquari, Uberaba and Recife, Brazil, 1970-87; pres. Formiplac Group, Rio De Janeiro, Taquari, Uberaba and Recife, 1988—; v.p. Indsl. Ctr. Rio de Janeiro, 1983-87. Contbr. articles to periodicals. Recipient Estado Da Guanabara medal, Cruzeiro Do Sul medal. Mem. Indsl. Fdn. Rio de Janeiro (counselor, v.p., merit medal 1985), Young Pres.'s Org. (pres. Brazil chpt. 1977-78). Jewish. Clubs: Iate, Itanhangá Golf. Home: AV Vieira Souto, 86/302 Rio de Janeiro 22420, Brazil Office: Quimica Indsl de Laminados, AV Automóvel Clube, 10976 Rio de Janeiro 21530, Brazil

DEGHETTO, KENNETH ANSELM, engineering and construction company executive; b. Clifton, N.J., Apr. 1, 1924; s. Anselm and Linda (Zanetti) DeG.; m. Helen Zschack, Nov. 5, 1944; children: Donna, Glenn. B.S., U.S. Mcht. Marine Acad., 1943; B.Mech. Engring., Rensselaer Poly. Inst., Troy, N.Y., 1950. Registered profl. engr., N.Y., N.J., Wash., Fla., Alaska. With Foster Wheeler Corp., Livingston, N.J., 1951—, dir., 1973—, v.p., 1973-76, exec. v.p., 1976-85, chmn. bd., 1983-87; chmn. bd. Foster Wheeler Internat. Corp., Livingston, N.J., 1975-85, also bd. dirs. Mem. bd. overseers N.J. Inst. Tech.; mem. Rensselaer Council; nat. chmn. U.S. Mcht. Marine Acad. Kings Point Challenge. Served to lt. USNR, 1943-46. Fellow ASME, Brit. Inst. Mech. Engrs.; mem. Nat. Assn. Corrosion Engrs., Sigma Xi, Tau Beta Pi, Tau Pi Sigma. Lutheran. Clubs: Royal and Ancient Golf (St. Andrews, Scotland); Montclair (N.J.) Country. Home: 42 Cornell Dr Livingston NJ 07039 Office: Foster Wheeler Corp Perryville Corp Pk Clinton NJ 08809-4000

DE GIVENCHY, HUBERT JAMES MARCEL TAFFIN (GIVENCHY), fashion designer; b. Beauvais, France, Feb. 20, 1927; s. Lucien and Béatrice (Badin) Taffin de G. Ed., Ecole nationale supérieure des beaux-arts. Faculty of Law U. Paris; Apprenticeship fashion houses of Lelong, 1945-46, Piquet, 1946-48, Fath, 1948-49, Schiaparelli, 1949-51; opened his own fashion house, Paris, 1952-56; pres., dir. gen. Givenchy-Couture, 1954—. Designer costumes for films Breakfast at Tiffany's, 1961, Charade, 1963, Paris When It Sizzles, 1964, How To Steal a Million, 1966. Decorated chevalier Legion of Honor. Address: 3 Ave George V, F-75008 Paris France *

DEGOS, CLAUDE-FRANCOIS, neurology professor; b. Villers sur Mer, Calvados, France, Oct. 12, 1939; s. Robert and Monique (Lortat-Jacob) D.; m. Catherine Anzani, Jan. 18, 1968; children: Louis, Thomas, Marie. MD, U. Paris, 1970; degree in med. edn., U. Paris VI, 1976. Cert. neurologist Nat. Med Council, 1974. Intern various hosps., Paris, 1965-70; sr. resident Faculty of Medicine, Paris, 1970-76; neurologist various hosps., Paris, 1976—; prof., chmn. neurology dept. U. Paris, St. Joseph Hosp., 1976 ; V.p. U. Paris; mem. med. bd. St. Joseph Hosp. (pres. 1986-87); chief neurologic dept. contbr. numerous articles to profl. jours.,; mem editorial bd. La Revue du Practicien, 1972—. Mem. Intersyndicat. of Physicians, Surgeons, Biologists, and Specialists of Paris Hosps. (pres. 1985—), French Nat. Soc. of Neurology (bd. mem., treas.), European Union of Med. Specialists (bd. mem., treas.), Nat. Assn. of French Physician Specialists of Nervous System Diseases (gen. sec.), French Soc. Neuropsychology. Roman Catholic. Home: 66 Blvd Auguste Blanqui 66, 75013 Paris France Office: Hosp St Joseph, 7 Rue Pierre Larousse, 75014 Paris France

DE GRANDPRÉ, ALBERT JEAN, telecommunications company executive; b. Montreal, Que., Can., Sept. 14, 1921; s. Rol and Aline (Magnan) de G.; m. Hélène Choquet, Sept. 27, 1947; children: François, Liliane, Suzanne, Louise. BA, Coll. Jean de Brébeuf, 1940; B.C.L. (Gold medalist), McGill U., 1943. Bar: Montreal 1943. Partner firm Tansey, de Grandpré, Bergeron & Monet, Montreal, 1949-65; gen. counsel Bell Can., Montreal, 1966; v.p. law Bell Can., 1966-68, exec. v.p. adminstrn., 1968-70, exec. v.p. Eastern region, 1970-73, pres., 1973-76, dir., mem. exec. com., 1972—, chmn., chief exec. officer, 1976-83; chmn., chief exec. officer parent co. Bell Can. Enterprises, Inc. (now BCE Inc.), 1983—; mem. internat. adv. bd. Goldman, Sachs & Co., N.Y.C., Chem. Bank, N.Y.C.; dir. E.I. du Pont de Nemours & Co., Wilmington, Del., Toronto-Dominion Bank, TransCan. PipeLines, No. Telecom. Ltd., Seagram Co. Ltd., Stelco Inc., Sun Life Assurance Co. of Can., Chrysler Can. Ltd., Chrysler Corp.; bd. dirs. B.C.E., Inc., Bell Can. Chancellor McGill U., 1984—. Named companion Order of Can., Q.C. Mem. Canadian Bar Assn. (life), Assn. Canadian Gen. Counsel (emeritus), Bar Province of Que., Conf. Bd. N.Y. (trustee). Roman Catholic. Clubs: St. James (Montreal), St. Denis (Montreal), Mt. Royal (Montreal), Forest and Stream (Montreal); Toronto, York (Toronto); Mt. Bruno Country; University. Office: BCE Inc, 2000 McGill Coll Ave, Montreal, PQ Canada H3A 3H7

DEGRASSI, LEONARD RENE, art historian, educator; b. East Orange, N.J., Mar. 2, 1928; s. Romulus-William and Anna Sophia (Sannicolo) DeG.; m. Dolores Marie Welgoss, June 24, 1961; children: Maria Christina, Paul. BA, U. So. Calif., 1950, BFA, 1951, MA, 1956; postgrad., Harvard U., 1953, U. Rome, 1959-60, UCLA, 1970-73. Tchr. art Redlands (Calif.) Jr. High Sch., 1951-53, Toll Jr. High Sch., Glendale, Calif., 1953-61, Wilson Jr. High Sch., Glendale, 1961; mem. faculty Glendale Coll., 1962—, prof. art history, 1974—, chmn. dept., 1972. Prin. works include: (paintings) high altar at Ch. St. Mary, Cook, Minn., altar screen at Ch. St. Andrew, El Segundo, Calif., 1965-71, altar screen at Ch. of the Descent of the Holy Spirit, Glendale, 14 Stas. of the Cross at Ch. of St. Benedict, Duluth, Minn; also research, artwork and dramatic work for Spaceship Earth exhbn. at Disney World, Orlando, Fla., 1980. Decorated knight Order of Merit of Republic of Italy, 1972; knight Grand Cross Holy Sepulchre (Papal); knight St. John of Jerusalem, 1974; Cross of Merit, 1984. Mem. Art Educators Assn., Glendale Art Assn., Egypt Exploration Soc. London, Am. Research Ctr. Egypt, Tau Kappa Alpha, Kappa Pi, Delta Sigma Rho. Office: 1500 N Verdugo Rd Glendale CA 91206

DE GROOT, ADRIAAN DINGEMAN, educator; b. Santpoort, Netherlands, Oct. 26, 1914; s. Adrianus and Dingena Albertina (Schotman) DeG.; Ph.D., U. Amsterdam, 1946; D.Psychol. and Pedagogical Scis. (hon.), State U. Ghent, 1972; m. Elsa V.C. Van Embden, Apr. 11, 1963; children by previous marriage—Elsa, Pauline, Frans, Koen, Martyn. Secondary sch. tchr. math., Arnheim, The Hague, 1941-43; staff psychologist, co-dir. Psychologisch Instituut, The Hague, 1942-46; psychol. advisor Philips Elec. Ltd., Eindhoven, 1946-49; lectr. U. Amsterdam, 1948-50, prof. applied psychol. and methodology, 1950-61, prof. methodology, behavioral scis., 1961-79; extraordinary prof. State U. Groningen, 1980-85. Mem. Royal Netherlands Acad. Arts and Scis., Netherlands Inst. Psychologists, Am. Psychol. Assn. (affiliate mem.). Author: Thought and Choice in Chess, 1966; Saint Nicholas, A Psychoanalytic Study of His History and Myth, 1966; Methodology,

Foundations of Inference and Research in the Behavioral Sciences, 1969; editor: (with Nico H. Frijda) Otto Selz. His Contribution to Psychology, 1981; contbr. articles to profl. jours. Founder Nat. Inst. Ednl. Testing, Arnheim, Netherlands, 1968. Research on intuitive processes, unification of behavioral sci. methodology, methods of concept analysis. Home: 7 Middenstreek, 9166LL Schiermonnikoog The Netherlands Office: State University of Groningen, 31-32 Grote Markt, 9712HV Groningen The Netherlands

DE GROOT, ROLAND RALPH, art director; b. Batavia, Indonesia, Dec. 5, 1939; arrived in The Netherlands, 1947; s. Willem Frederick and Sophie (Saueressig) De G.; m. Maryke Van Der Elst, Dec. 21, 1963; children: Ralph, Niels, Mita. Student, Sch. Fine Arts, Haarlem, Netherlands and Amsterdam. With Toonder Studios, Amsterdam, Netherlands, 1960-62, Bellvision Studios, Brussels, 1962-63; designer Dutch Broadcasting Co., Hilversum, Netherlands, 1963-68; art dir. Dutch Broadcasting Co., Hilversum, 1968-86; mem. publicity dept. Cong. Ctr., The Hague, 1968-69. Set designer for plays Vrijdag, Blauw, Blauw, others; for films Kort Amerikaans, 1970, Turkish Delight, 1970, Soldier of Orange, 1972, Keetje Tippel, 1973, Doctor Vlimmen, 1977, Boezem Vriend, 1982, De Zwarte Ruiter, 1982, Lucky Star, 1982, The Fourth Man, 1984; for opera Satyricon. Recipient Nipkov award, 1973, Arts award City of Bussum, 1985, Eurovision Song Contest award 1970, 76, 80, 84. Home: 9 Koedyklaan, 1046 KW Bussum The Netherlands Office: NOB Room 407 Hoofdgebouw, Box 10 Dutch TV, Hilversum The Netherlands

DEGRUCHY, ALAN B., consulting engineer; b. Bklyn., Oct. 4, 1932; s. William C. and Ethne L. deGruchy; IE, Indsl. Mgmt. Inst., 1956; degree in Bus. Adminstrn., Temple U., 1958. Apprentice, E.G. Budd Co., 1954-58; quality control mgr. Cutler Metal Products Co., 1958-62; plant mgr. Falco Products Co., 1962-63; chief engr. Met-Pro, Inc., 1963-66; project engr. Day & Zimmerman, Inc., 1966-72; corp. cons. engr. C.S.I., Bridgewater, N.J., 1972—; mng. dir. Thermalite, Inc., Rocky Mount, N.C., 1987—. Mem. Am. Inst. Indsl. Engrs., Am. Soc. Quality Control. Club: Masons. Inventor automatic process and assembly machines. Office: Thermalite Inc 500 S Church St Rocky Mount NC

DE GRYSE, BOB FRANÇOIS, archeologist, federal official; b. Ostend, Belgium, May 12, 1925; s. Oscar and Jeanne (Reilzen) DeG.; m. Simonne Legaey, May 6, 1952. M Archeology and Art History, U. Ghent, Belgium, 1958; M European Cultural History, Coll. Europe, Bruges, Belgium, 1960. Reporter Volksgazet, Antwerp, Belgium, 1948-69; desk chief Belga News Agy., Brussels, 1970-79; dir. in chief Ministry of Fin., Brussels, 1980—; archeologist Loterie Nat., Brussels, 1959—. Author: The Games of Zeus, 1982, Karnak, Egypt's Glory, 1984, Re, Suncult in Egypt, 1986 (Legion d'Honneur 1987). Recipient Gold medal of Paris, 1971, Gold medal Order of the Crown, 1986, Chevallier de la Legion d'Honneur, 1987.

DEGUILLAUME, JEAN-CHARLES, biophysicist; b. Paris, July 23, 1949; s. Jean-Jules Deguillaume and Georgette-Emilienne Plana; m. Marie-Claude Lavedrine, May 12, 1979; children: Thibaut, Laure. MD, U. Paris, 1977. cons. in fields of phlebology, hemodynamics. Served as maj. French health forces. Mem. French. Soc. Phlebology, French Soc. Angeiology. Office: 12 Av des Sapins, 95290 L'Isle Adam France

DE GUNZBURG, JEAN-LOUIS, bank executive; b. Paris, Dec. 4, 1935; m. Dagmar Haumersen. BA, Middlebury Coll., 1958. Mgr. Bank of Am., San Francisco and Paris, 1958-65; exec. Samuel Montagu, London, 1965-69; chmn. Banque Franck, S.A., Geneva, 1969—. Mem. Swiss Pvt. Bankers Assn. Office: Banque Franck SA, 1 Rue Toepffer, 1206 Geneva Switzerland

DEHAAN, NORMAN RICHARD, architect; b. Chgo., July 8, 1927; s. Peter Arend and Clara Anna (Nordstrom) DeH.; m. Christopher Welles, Dec. 1957 (div. Jan. 1963). Student, Ill. Inst. Tech., 1944-45. project dir. AID, Dept. State, Korea, 1958-61; est. Norman DeHaan Asso., Chgo., 1964—; pres. Norman DeHaan Asso., Inc., 1967—; regional rep. Nat. Accessions Com., Dept. of State's Art in Embassies Program, 1965-75; v.p. The Bright New City Inc.; mem. Sculpture Chgo. Steering Com., 1985—; v.p. Chgo. Wildflower Works; U.S. del., exec. com. Internat. Fed. Interior Designers and Architects, 1987—. Art dir., Country Life Ins. Co., Chgo., 1947-48, archtl. and interior designer, Sidney Morris & Assos., Chgo., 1948-53, designer, architect, UN Korean Reconstrn. Agy., 1953-54, archtl. adviser, Office of Pres. Korea, 1953-55, asst. dir. design, Container Corp. of Am., Chgo., 1955-57. Dir. Lake Michigan Regional Planning Council, 1963-76; trustee Columbia Coll., Chgo., 1976-84, Chgo. Sch. Architecture Found., 1966-71. Served with USNR, 1945-46; with C.E. U.S. Army, 1950-52. Fellow Am. Soc. Interior Designers (nat. pres. 1974-75, chmn. Ednl. Found.); mem. AIA (nat. chmn. com. interior architecture 1976-78, bd. dirs. Chgo. chpt. 1981-87, pres. Chgo. chpt. 1985-86, pres. Chgo. chpt. found. 1986-87), Internat. Fedn. Interior Architects and Designers (del. 1973-87, exec. bd. 1988—). Clubs: Cliff Dwellers, Arts Club, Casino (Chgo.). Home: 237 Menomonee St Chicago IL 60614 Office: Norman DeHaan Assoc Inc 355 N Canal St Chicago IL 60606

DE HARTOG, JAN, writer; b. Haarlem, Holland, Apr. 22, 1914; s. Arnold Hendrik and Lucretia (Meyjes) de H.; m. Marjorie E. Mein, Sept. 1961; children—Sylvia, Arnold, Nicholas, Catherine, Eva, Julia. Student, Amsterdam Naval Coll., 1930. Author: plays Skipper Next to God, 1946, This Time Tomorrow, 1947, The Fourposter, 1951, William and Mary, 1964; novels The Lost Sea, 1951, The Distant Shore, 1952, The Little Ark, 1954, A Sailor's Life, 1956, The Spiral Road, 1957, The Inspector, 1960, Waters of the New World, 1961, The Artist, 1963, The Hospital, 1964, The Call of the Sea, 1966, The Captain, 1966, The Children, 1968, The Peaceable Kingdom, 1971, The Lamb's War, 1979, The Trail of the Serpent, 1983, Star of Peace, 1984, The Commodore, 1986; musical I Do, I Do, 1966. Mem. Soc. of Friends. *

DEHAVEN, ERNEST THOMAS, association executive; b. Hiram Twp., Ohio, Aug. 7, 1928; s. Ernest Roy and Bertha Catherine (Thomas) DeH.; m. Barbara Ann Hoskin, Aug. 21, 1955; children—Matthew, Stephen, Catherine. A.B., Hiram Coll., 1949; M.H.A., Va. Commonwealth U., 1957. Lic. nursing home adminstr., Iowa. Adminstr. Albert Schweitzer Meml. Hosp., St. Mark, Haiti, 1958-59, Jackman Meml. Hosp., Bilaspur, India, 1959-64; asst. adminstr. Lake County Meml. Hosp., Painesville, Ohio, 1965-67; adminstr. Carroll County Meml. Hosp., Carrollton, Ky., 1967-77; exec. dir. Wesley Manor, Frankfort, Ind., 1977-82; adminstr. Ramsey Meml. Home, Des Moines, 1982—; regional ops. dir. Nat. Benevolent Assn., 1985—. Served with AUS, 1953-54. Mem. Am. Coll. Health Care Adminstrs., Am. Coll. Hosp. Adminstrs. (cert.), Am. Mgmt. Assn., Des Moines Choral Soc. Mem. Christian Ch. (Disciples of Christ). Avocation: Choral singing. Home: 7008 Townsend St Des Moines IA 50322 Office: Ramsey Home 1611 27th St Des Moines IA 50310

DEHAVEN, KENNETH LE MOYNE, retired physician; b. The Dalles, Oreg., Mar. 28, 1913; s. Luther John and Dora (Beeks) DeH.; m. Ledith Mary Ewing, Jan. 11, 1937; children: Marya LeMoyne DeHaven Keeth, Lisa Marguerite DeHaven Jordan, Camille Suzanne DeHaven. BS, North Pacific Coll. Oreg., 1935; MD, U. Mich., 1946. Intern USPHS Hosp., St. Louis, 1947; intern Franklin Hosp., San Francisco, 1947-48, resident, 1949; clinician Dept. Pub. Health, City San Francisco, Dept. V.D., 1949-51; practice gen. medicine, Sunnyvale, Calif., 1955-87; mem. staff El Camino Hosp., Mt. View, Calif., San Jose (Calif.) Hosp. Pres. Los Altos Hills Assn. Served to capt., USAF, 1952-55. Fellow Am. Acad. Family Practice; mem. Calif. Med. Assn., Santa Clara Couty Med. Soc., Royal Astron. Soc. Can., Brit. Astron. Assn., Astron. Soc. Pacific, Sunnyvale C. of C. (bd. dirs. 1955-56), Alpha Kappa Kappa. Republican. Club: Book (San Francisco). Lodge: Masons. Home: 9348 E Casitas Del Rio Dr Scottsdale AZ 85255

DEHECQ, JEAN-FRANÇOIS, mathematician; b. Jan. 1, 1940. Prof. math. 1962-64; with Soc. Nat. des Petroles d'Aquitaines, Paris, 1965-73, adminstr., 1969-70, ops. engr., 1970-71, dir. devel., 1971-73; v.p. Sonofi, Paris, 1973-82, exec. v.p., 1982-88, chmn., chief exec. officer, 1988—; bd. dirs. Diagnostics Pasteur, Chory S.Am., Sanofi Inc. U.S.A. Served with French army, 1964-65. Mem. Sovereign Order of Malta (officer of merit), Nat. Order Merit (knight). Office: Sanofi, 40 Ave George V, 75008 Paris France

DEHEUVELS, RENÉ, mathematics professor; b. Roubaix, France, Mar. 22, 1923; s. Jules and Suzanne (Galens) Deheuvels; m. France Lagarde, July 16, 1947; 1 child, Paul. Agrégé in math., Ecole Normale Supérieure, Paris, 1945; DSc, U. Paris, 1953. Prof. Istanbul (Turkey) Tech. U., 1947-51; researcher Nat. Ctr. Sci. Research, Paris, 1951-53; with The Inst. for Adv. Study Princeton (N.J.) U., 1953-55; prof. U. Lille, France, 1955-59, Ecole Poly., Paris, 1957-80, Yale U., New Haven, Conn., 1959-60, U. Paris, 1960—; pres. Ecole Pratique des Hautes Etudes, Paris, 1975-78. Editor: Formes Quadratiques, 1981; contbr. articles to profl. jours. Mem. Jury Elie Faure. Mem. Calvinist Ch. Home: 14 Ave du Chateau, 92340 Bourg-la-Reine France Office: Inst Henri Poincare, 11 Rue Pierre-et-Marie Curie, Paris France

DE HODGINS, OFELIA CANALES, materials scientist; b. Mexico City, Oct. 25, 1943; d. Fernando Canales Rocha and Leana Del Olmo de Canales; B.S., U. Mex., 1972, M.S. in Physics; M.S. in Materials Sci., U. Va., 1977, M.S. in Engring. Physics, 1983; m. Garry Hodgins, Aug. 24, 1974; 1 son, Alfonso Sidarta. Prof. math. Instituto Freinet de Mex., Mexico City, 1971-72; asst. prof. thermodynamics U. Mex., 1972-73; asst. prof. math. Instituto Politecnico Nacional, Mexico City, 1973-74; sr. researcher Lab. of Ultracentrifuges, Nuclear Inst. Mex., 1973-76; staff engr. data systems div. dept. components and application assurance IBM Corp., Poughkeepsie, N.Y., 1981—. Recipient Lit. prize U. Mex., 1970; Nat. Applied Research Instrumentation prize, 1973-74; Dorothea Buck fellow, 1975-76. Mem. Mexican Soc. Physics, Am. Soc. Metals, Electron Microscopy Soc. Am., Am. Nuclear Soc., Soc. for Exptl. Stress Analysis, Sigma Xi. Contbr. articles to profl. jours. Dorothea Buck fellow, 1975-76; recipient Nat. Prize of Sci., Mexico, 1974. Mem. Mexican Soc. Physics, Am. Soc. Metals, Am. Nuclear Soc., Electron Microscopy Soc., Am. Phys. Soc. Address: 612 Granite Springs Rd Yorktown Heights NY 10598 Office: IBM Corp Advanced Substrate Tech D/33Q B-300/40-E Poughkeepsie NY 12601

DEHOUVE, DANIELE, social anthropologist; b. Avallon, Yonne, France, Oct. 10, 1945; d. André and Paulette (Balthazard) D.; m. Flatischler Franz, Mar. 23, 1974; children: David, Nadia, Nelly. PhD, U. Paris, 1970; doctorat ès Lettres et Scis. Humaines, Ecole des Hautes Etudes en Scis. Sociales, Paris, 1985. Lectr. U. Paris X, 1969-76; asst. prof. U. Nantes (France), 1970-72; researcher Centre Nat. de la Recherche Scientifique, Paris, 1972—. Author: Corvée des saints et Luttes de marchands, 1974, El tequio de los santos y la competencia entre los mercaderes, 1976; reviewer L'Homme, 1970—. Fellow Société des Americanistes; mem. Am. Anthrop. Assn. Home: 24 Bd Raspail, 75007 Paris France Office: Laboratoire d'Ethnologie, U Paris X 2 rue de Rouen, 92001 Nanterre France

DEIBLER, BARBARA ELLEN, librarian; b. Pottsville, Pa., Aug. 11, 1943; d. Samuel Elwood and Miriam Elizabeth (Houser) D. BA, Pa. State U., 1965; MS, Drexel U., 1966. Cataloger State Library Pa., Harrisburg, 1966-82, head cataloger, 1972-82, rare book librarian, 1980—, asst. coordinator collection mgmt., 1982—. Librarian Hist. Soc. Schuylkill County, 1971-77. Mem. Am. Acad. Polit. and Social Scis., Acad. Polit. Sci., Soc. Polit. Enquiries (sec. 1987—), Schuylkill County Allied Artists (dir. 1976-77), Pa. Library Assn., Hist. Soc. Pa. Baptist. Clubs: Pilot of Pottsville (rec. sec. 1974-75, dir. 1975-77), Pilot of Harrisburg (pres. 1979-81, 87-88, treas. 1978-79, dir. 1981-83, 88—, sec. 1983-85, v.p. 1985-87). Author: Pennsylvania German Barn Signs: For Protection or Just for Nice, 1978, Simplified Cataloging for Libraries, 1978, The State Library of Pennsylvania: The Philadelphia Years, 1982, Books of State: A Peripatetic Collection, 1983, A Treasure Trove of Books, 1986, How Libraries Stack Up With Authors, 1987, Anne Royall's Visit to Carlisle in 1828, 1987. Home: 2285 W Norwegian St Pottsville PA 17901 Office: State Library Pa Box 1601 Harrisburg PA 17105

DEICHES, ISADORE WILLIAM, author, researcher; b. London, Sept. 9, 1933; s. David and Doris (Wilcocks) D.; m. Jennifer Margaret Humphrey, Apr. 30, 1981. Dir., Amalgamated Bus. Machines Ltd., 1952-64; free-lance aircraft accident researcher, 1965; dir. Amalgamated Bus. Machines Ltd., 1966-82; free-lance author, researcher, broadcaster on subject of B.C. aeronautics, 1983—; cons. Egyptology, time energy. Active Hosp. Radio, 1981-82, Moorfield's Eye Hosp., London. Served with RAF, 1950-52, U.S. Army, 1966. Mem. Soc. Psychical Research (London). Author: Pyramids, 1983; Aeronautics, C. 3225 B.C. - 1783 A.D., 1983; discoverer method employed by the ancient Egyptians and the true purpose of the need for pyramid constrn.; discoverer world's first aircraft and gliders; recorded in glider and balloon sections of Guiness Book of Records. Home and Office: 14 Railway Square, Brentwood Essex, England

DEIGHTON, LEN, author; b. London, Feb. 18, 1929; m. Shirley Thompson. Author: The Ipcress File (also motion picture), 1963; Horse under Water, 1963; Funeral in Berlin, 1964; An Expensive Place to Die, 1967; Action Cook Book Guide to Eating, 1965; Ou est le Garlic, or Len Deighton's French Cook Book, 1966; Billion Dollar Brain, 1966; Only When I Larf, 1968; Bomber, 1970; Declarations of War (short stories), 1971; Close-Up, 1972; Spy Story, 1974; Yesterday's Spy, 1975; Twinkle Twinkle Little Spy, 1976; Catch a Falling Spy, 1976; Fighter, 1977; SS-GB, 1979; Blitzkrieg, 1979; XPD, 1981; Goodbye Mickey Mouse, 1982; Berlin Game, 1984; Mexico Set, 1985; London Match, 1986; Winter: A Novel of a Berlin Family, 1988. Office: care Jonathan Cape Ltd, 30 Bedford Sq, London England also: 25 Newman St, London W1 England *

DEIHL, RICHARD HARRY, savings and loan association executive; b. Whittier, Calif., Sept. 8, 1928; s. Victor Francis and Wilma Aileen (Thomas) D.; m. Billie Dantz Beane, Mar. 24, 1952; children: Catherine Kent, Michael, Victoria, Christine. A.B., Whittier Coll., 1949; postgrad., UCLA, 1949, U. Calif.-Berkeley, 1949-50. With Nat. Cash Register Co., Pomona, Calif., 1955-59; trainee Rio Hondo Savs. & Loan, Calif., 1959-60; loan cons. Home Savs. & Loan Assn. (now Home Savs. Am., A Fed. Savs. & Loan Assn.), Los Angeles, 1960-63; loan agt., supr., v.p. Home Savs. & Loan Assn. (now Home Savs. Am., A Fed. Savs. & Loan Assn.), 1964, loan service supr., 1964, v.p. ops., v.p. loans, 1965, exec. v.p., 1966, pres., 1967-84, chief exec. officer, 1967-84, chmn., 1984—, also dir.; chief exec. officer, dir. H.F. Ahmanson Co., 1984—; bd. dirs. Fed. Home Loan Bank, Atlantic Richfield Good Samaritan Hosp. Contbr. articles to profl. jours. Served to 1st lt. USAF, 1951-55. Decorated D.F.C., Air medal with three clusters. Republican. Club: Fairbanks Ranch Country (Rancho Santa Fe). Office: H F Ahmanson & Co 3731 Wilshire Blvd Los Angeles CA 90010 also: Home Savs of America 1001 Commerce Dr Irwindale CA 91706

DEINES, HARRY J., agricultural and livestock company executive; b. Loveland, Colo., Nov. 5, 1909; s. John and Mary (Maseka) D.; B.M.E., U. Colo.; grad. Advanced Mgmt. Program, Harvard; m. Eleanor Vrooman, 1932; children: Gretchen Deines Langston, Mark, Katrina, Stephen. Advt. mgr. Gen. Electric Co., 1930-45; v.p. Fuller & Smith & Ross, 1945-49; gen. advt. mgr. Westinghouse Electric Corp., 1949-53; v.p. J. Walter Thompson, N.Y.C., 1953-56, Fuller & Smith & Ross, N.Y.C., 1956-59; exec. v.p., dir. Campbell, Mithun, Inc., Mpls., 1959-71; mng. partner Deines Agr. & Livestock Co., Ft. Collins, Colo., 1971—; pres. Collectors' Books Ltd. Home and Office: 1707 Country Club Rd Fort Collins CO 80524

DEINZER, GEORGE WILLIAM, public welfare organization administrator; b. Tiffin, Ohio, Nov. 1, 1934; s. Harvey Charles and Edna Louise (Harpley) D.; A.B., Heidelberg Coll., 1956; postgrad. Washington U., 1956-57. Asst. to dir. phys. plant Heidelberg Coll., 1957-58, admissions counselor, 1958-60, dir. admissions, 1960-71, dir. fin. aids, asso. dir. admissions, 1971-80; exec. dir. Tiffin-Seneca United Way, 1980-85; adminstr. Seneca County (Ohio) Dept. Human Services and Children's Services, 1985—. Voting rep. Coll. Entrance Examination Bd., 1963-80; fin. aid cons. Nat. Collegiate Athletic Assn.; cons. Ohio Scholarship Funds, 1960-61. Pres., chmn. allocations com., bd. dirs. United Way; pres. lay bd. Mercy Hosp.; treas., bd. dirs. N.W. Ohio Health Planning Assn., co-chmn. steering com., 1984; mem. legis. com. Ohio Citizens Council, 1981—, human services task force, 1984—; pres. Seneca County Mus.; treas. Tiffin Theatre, Inc.; mem. Seneca Indsl. and Econ. Devel. Corp. Bd., 1983—; chmn. Tiffin Area Devel. and Pub. Relations Dirs., 1984—. Mem. Organ Hist. Soc. Mem. Nat., Ohio (regional coordinator, treas., state trainer, chmn. needs analysis com.) assns. student fin. aid adminstrs., Ohio Athletic Conf. Fin. Dirs. (past chmn.), Internat. Platform Assn., Am. Personnel and Guidance Assn., Am. Coll. Personnel Assn., Council Ohio United Way Execs., Farm Bur., Ohio Hist. Soc., U.S. Naval Inst., Buckeye Sheriffs Assn., N.W. Ohio and Ohio Human Service Dirs., Beta Beta Beta. Republican. Lodges: Rotary (dir., pres. 1982-83), Elks. Contbr. articles to profl. jours. Home: 197 Jefferson St PO Box 904 Tiffin OH 44883

DEISSLER, ROBERT GEORGE, fluid dynamicist; b. Greenville, Pa., Aug. 1, 1921; s. Victor Girard and Helen Stella (Fisher) D.; m. June Marie Gallagher, Oct. 7, 1950; children—Robert Joseph, Mary Beth, Ellen Ann, Ann Marie. B.S., Carnegie Inst. Tech., 1943; M.S., Case Inst. Tech., 1948. Researcher Goodyear Aircraft Corp., Akron, OH, 1943-44; aero. research scientist NASA Lewis Research Ctr., Cleve., 1947-52; chief fundamental heat transfer br. NASA Lewis Research Ctr., 1952-70, staff scientist, sci. cons. fluid physics, 1970—. Contbr. articles to profl. jours. Served as lt. (j.g.) USNR, 1944-46. Recipient Max Jacob Meml. award ASME/Am. Inst. Chem. Engrs., 1975; NACA/NASA Exceptional Service award, 1957, Outstanding Publ. award, 1978. Fellow AIAA (Best Paper award 1975, Tech. Achievement award 1981), ASME (Heat Transfer Meml. award 1964); mem. Am. Phys. Soc., Soc. Natural Philosophy, Sigma Xi. Roman Catholic. Home: 4540 W 213 St Fairview Park OH 44126 Office: NASA Lewis Research Ctr 21000 Brookpark Rd Cleveland OH 44135

DEITZ, ROBERT DAVID, manufacturing company executive; b. Cleve., Dec. 26, 1926; s. Joseph H. and Irene (Mates) D.; m. Sallie Eisen, Jan. 26, 1950; children—Jo-Anne Deitz Daniels, Diana Deitz Russel. B.B.A., Case Western Res. U., 1948. Export mgr. Consol. Paint and Varnish Corp., Cleve., 1948-57; v.p. Consol. Protective Coatings Corp. and subs. Consol. Inter-Continental Corp., Consol. Protective Coatings Ltd., Cleve., Montreal, Que., Can., 1957, pres., 1958—; dir. Hastings Pavement corp., L.I., N.Y. Chmn. budget com. United Way Services, Cleve., 1972-75; trustee Mt. Sinai Med. Ctr., Cleve., 1971-78; pres. Jewish Vocat. Service, 1970-73; vice chmn. Dist. Export Council, Dept. Commerce, 1975-83; pres. Menorah Park Jewish Home for Aged, Beachwood, Ohio, 1976-78. Served with USMC, 1945-46. Recipient Kane award Jewish Community Fedn., 1965; Man of Yr. award Orgn. Rehab. Tng., 1981. Office: Consol Protective Coatings Corp 202 Ohio Savs Plaza Cleveland OH 44114

DE JAGER, CORNELIS, astronomer; b. Texel, Netherlands, Apr. 29, 1921; s. Jan and Cornelia (Kuyper) de J.; Ph.D. cum laude, U. Utrecht, 1952; Dr. (hon.), U. Wroclaw (Poland), 1975, U. Paris, 1976; m. Duotsje Rienks, Apr. 10, 1947; children—Els, Jan, Sieds, Corrie. Asst. theoretical physics and astronomy univs. Utrecht and Leiden, 1945-46; mem. faculty U. Utrecht, 1947-86, prof. space physics, 1960-86, mng. dir., then chmn. council Astron. Inst., 1963-83. Mem. Internat. Astron. Union (asst. gen. sec. 1967-70, gen. sec. 1970-73), Internat., Council Sci. Unions (pres. com. space research, 1972-78, 82-86, world pres. 1978-80). Recipient Karl Schwarzschild medal, Astron. Gesellschaft, 1974, Hale medal Am. Atron. Soc., 1988, Cospar medal Internat. Cooperation in Space Sci., 1988. Mem. Royal Netherlands Arts and Scis. (fgn. sec. 1985—); asso. Royal Astron. Soc. London (Gold medal 1988); fgn. mem. Internat. Acad. Astronautics (chmn. sect. basic scis. 1984—), Royal Belgium Acad., Royal Acad. Liege, Deutsche Akademie Leopoldina, Indian Nat. Scis. Acad., Acad. Européene. Author: The Hydrogen Spectrum of the Sun, 1952; Structure and Dynamics of the Solar Atmosphere, 1959; The Solar Spectrum, 1963; Highlights of Astronomy, 1974; Image Processing Techniques in Astronomy, 1975; The Brightest Stars, 1980; also articles.

DE JARNETTE, JAMES EDWARD, psychoanalyst, psychotherapist; b. Atlanta, Mar. 22, 1948; s. Charles Nathan and Sarah Holmes (Phillips) deJ. B.A., Shorter Coll., 1970; M.A., W. Ga. Coll., 1971; Ph.D., Sussex Coll., 1973. Exec. dir. Middle Ga. Counseling Center, Macon, 1972-80; exec. dir. Power Ferry Psychotherapy Clinic, 1976-80, deJarnette and Assocs., Beverly Hills, Calif., 1979—; chmn. bd. Leonidas Ltd., Inc.; dir. Alpha-Omega Enterprises, Inc.; chmn. bd. trustees Center for Meditative Living, Inc. Bd. dirs. Ga. Mental Health Assn., 1975, Macon/Bibb County Mental Health Assn., 1975. Fellow Am. Orthopsychiat. Assn., Am. Acad. Behavioral Sci.; mem. Am. Mental Health Couselors Assn., Nat. Psychiat. Assn., Internat. Soc. Adlerian Psychology, Mensa, Tripple Nine Soc. Pi Gamma Mu. Republican. Episcopalian. Contbr. articles to profl. jours. Home: 8535 W Knoll Dr Apt 215 Los Angeles CA 90069

DE JESUS, ANTONIO COSTALES, rural development and reconstruction and primary health care specialist; b. Manila, June 11, 1940; s. Roman Banting and Alberta (Costales) de J.; m. Mary Ellen Garfes, Dec. 27, 1972; children: Roman Miguel, Maria Katrina, Antonio Carlo, Erick Daniel. MD, U. Philippines, 1964; MPH, Johns Hopkins U., 1977. From intern to med. resident Mercy Hosp., Pitts., 1964-66; resident Mt. Sinai-Elmhurst Hosp., N.Y.C., 1966-68; fellow in community medicine Albert Einstein-Montfiore Martin Luther King Health Ctr., N.Y.C., 1968-69; internist NE Neighborhood Health Ctr., N.Y.C., 1969-70; asst. prof. community helath U. Philippines, Laguna Bay, 1971-72; health specialist Internat. Inst. Rural Reconstrn., Silang, Cavite, Philippines, 1972-79, v.p., 1979—; cons., tech. dir. Philippine Council on Health Research and Devel., Nat. Sci. and Tech., Manila, 1982-87; cons. health care World Bank Mission, Nairobi, Kenya, 1986. Contbr. articles on rural devel. and primary health care to jours. Office: Internat Inst Rural Reconstrn, IIRR Silang, Cavite Philippines 2720

DE JESÚS, NYDIA ROSA, physician, anesthesiologist; b. Humacao, P.R., Sept. 8, 1930; d. Manuel Aurelio De Jesus and Luz María González. BS, U. P.R., 1949, MD, 1955; cert. med. tech., Sch. Tropical Medicine, San Juan, P.R., 1950; cert. anesthesiology, Columbia Presbyn. Med. Ctr., 1958. Diplomate Am. Bd. Anesthesiology. Dir. dept. anesthesiology U. Hosp. & Sch. Medicine, San Juan, 1960-65; dir. div. anesthesiology P.R. Med. Ctr., San Juan, 1965-76; vis. prof. anesthesiology Harvard Med. Sch., Boston, Mass., 1973-74; dean acad. affairs Med. Scis. Campus, U. P.R., San Juan, 1976-78; dir. cardiovascular surg. ctr. P.R. Med. Ctr., San Juan, 1980-85; prof. anesthesiology U. P.R. Sch. Medicine, San Juan, 1965—, dean, 1986—; dir. intensive care unit Univ. Hosp., San Juan, 1974-75; chief sect. anesthesiology VA Hosp., San Juan, 1963-76; mem. cardiovascular commn. Sec. of Health, Commonwealth of P.R., 1985; cons. div. medicine, health resources adminstrn. Bur Health Manpower, USPHS, 1977-79; pres. cons. bd. Pediatric U. Hosp., San Juan, mem. bd. dirs., 1986. Fellow Am. Coll. Anesthesiology; mem. ACP, N.Y. Acad. Scis., AAAS, Am. Soc. Anesthesiology. Home: No 8 Jardines De Vedruna Rio Piedras PR 00927 Office: Univ of P R Sch of Medicine GPO Box 5067 San Juan PR 00936

DEJMEK, KAZIMIERZ KAZIMIERZ, theatre director, actor; b. Kowel, Poland, May 17, 1924; s. Henryk and Wlodzimiera D.; m. Irena, 1945; m. Danuta, 1954; 2 children. Student, State Theatrical Acad., Lódz. Actor, Rzeszów, Jelenia Góra Companies, 1945, Teatr Wojska Polskiego Lódz, 1946-49; founder, gen. dir. Teatr Nowy, Lódz, 1949-61; head State Theatrical Acad., Lódz, 1952-55; gen. mgr., artistic dir. Teatr Nowy, Lódz, 1975-81, Teatr Polski, Warsaw, 1981—. Productions include opera Franc-tireur (Carl Maria von Weber), 1978, Revange (Fedro), 1978, Vatzlav (Mrozek), 1978, Krakowiacy i Górale (Boguslawski), 1978. Decorated comdr. Cross of Order Polonia Restituta; Order of Banner of Labour (2d class); recipient state prizes (2d & 3d class), prize of Minister of Culture and Art (1st class), Alfred Jurzykowski Found. award, 1975; Gottfried von Herder Prize, 1979. Address: Ul Rajcow 8, 00-220 Warsaw Poland *

DE JONG, DAVID SAMUEL, lawyer, educator; b. Washington, Jan. 8, 1951; s. Samuel and Dorothy (Thomas) De J.; m. Alisa Green, Jan. 5, 1980. BA, U. Md., 1972; JD, Washington and Lee U., 1975; LLM in Taxation, Georgetown U., 1979. Bar: Md. 1975, U.S. Dist. Ct. Md. 1977, U.S. Tax Ct. 1977, U.S. Ct. Appeals (4th cir.) 1978, U.S. Supreme Ct. 1979, D.C. 1980, U.S. Dist. Ct. D.C. 1983, U.S. Ct. Claims, U.S. Ct. Appeals (fed. cir.) 1983; CPA, Md. Atty. Gen. Bus. Services Inc., Rockville, Md., 1975-80; ptnr. Stein, Sperling, Bennett, De Jong, Driscoll, Greenfeig & Metro P.A., Rockville, 1980—; adj. prof. Southeastern U., Washington, 1979-85, Am. U., Washington, 1983—; instr. U. Md., College Park, 1986—, Montgomery Coll., Rockville, 1983. Co-author: J.K. Lasser's Personal Tax Strategies for 1989; Notes and comments editor Washington and Lee U. Law Rev., 1974-75. V.p. Seneca Whetstone Homeowners Assn., Gaithersburg, Md., 1981-82, pres. 1982-83. Mem. ABA, Md. Bar Assn., Montgomery County Bar Assn., D.C. Bar Assn., Am. Inst. CPA's, Md. Assn. CPA's, D.C. Inst. CPA's, Am. Assn. Atty.-CPA's, Phi Alpha Delta. Office: Stein

Sperling Bennett De Jong Driscoll Greenfeig & Metro 25 W Middle Ln Rockville MD 20850

DE JONG, GERRIT, engineer, consultant; b. Rotterdam, The Netherlands, Mar. 13, 1927; s. Teije and Saapke (Hoekstra) de J.; m. Johanna Alberta Bosman, Oct. 6, 1956; children: Gerritje Ch. G., Saapke, Teije, Marike, Engelina J.H. Cert., Tech. Coll., Leeuwarden, The Netherlands, 1950, Advanced Tech. Coll., 's-Hertogenbosch, The Netherlands, 1954. Lic. mech. and control engr. Asst. research lab. Kon. Ned. Hoogovens en Staalfarieken, Ijmuiden, The Netherlands, 1951-66; successively asst. project engr., project engr., sr. project engr., project mgr. Hoogovens Groep B.V., Ijmuiden, 1966-81; cons. maintenance dept. Hoogovens Group B.V., Ijmuiden, 1984-87; cons. ESTS, Ijmuiden, 1981-84, Ingenieursbureau de Jong, Obdam, The Netherlands, 1986—. Contbr. articles to profl. jours.; patentee in field. Mem. Koninklijk Insttituut van Ingenieurs, Nat. Geog. Soc. Home and Office: Kelderswerf 81, 1713 WH Obdam The Netherlands

DE JONG, STEF J. M. CHR., executive search consultant, business educator; b. The Hague, Netherlands, Aug. 10, 1955; s. Peter L.F. and Janie H.A. (van Wieringen) de J.; m. Carole M. Schouwey, Oct. 27, 1984. Lic., Grad. Inst. Internat. Studies, Geneva, 1978; diploma, Grad. Inst. European Studies, Geneva, 1983. Market research methodologist Philips, Netherlands, 1976-79; asst. prof. internat. bus. adminstrn. Am. Coll. of Switzerland, Leysin, 1980-84; bus. devel. strategist, exec. search cons. mergers and aquisitions Boyden Assocs., Geneva, 1984—; logistics officer CASIN, Geneva, 1979-83; assoc. prof. European U., Antwerp and Montreux, 1985—, Colgate U., 1982, Hertog Jan Coll., Netherlands, 1977. Co-author: Marketing Research, 1985-86; also translator and editor; contbr. articles to profl. jours. Mem. World Services Forum. Dutch/Swiss C. of C., Ctr. Europeén de la Culture. Roman Catholic. Home: 31 route de Moulin-Roget, 1237 Avully Geneva Switzerland Office: Boyden Assocs, 4 rue de la Scie, 1207 Geneva Switzerland

DEJONG, WILLEM ALEXANDER, health science association administrator; b. Steenwijkerwold, Overijssel, The Netherlands, Oct. 5, 1925; m. Elizabeth A.A. van der Ploeg, Sept. 19, 1953; children: Anne E., Idske E., Lieke G. MS in Chem. Engring., Tech. U., Delft, The Netherlands, 1952. Research engr. Royal/Dutch Shell Labs., Amsterdam, The Netherlands, 1952-64; vis. scientist Houston Research Lab. Shell Oil Co., Deer Park, Tex., 1964-65; dept. head Shell Internat. Research, Amsterdam, 1965-66; prof. Chem. Tech. Tech. U., 1966-80, dean dept. chem. tech., 1976-78; pres. Netherlands Orgn. Applied Sci. Research, The Hague, The Netherlands, 1980—. Mem. Royal Netherlands Chem. Soc., Royal Netherlands Inst. Engrs. Home: Gevers Deynootweg 129, 2586 HL The Hague The Netherlands Office: Netherlands Orgn Applied Sci, Research, PO Box 297, 2501 BD The Hague The Netherlands

DE JONGE, GERRIT, communications company executive; b. Schiedam, The Netherlands, Aug. 22, 1947; s. Roelof and Jacoba Adriana (Pellicaan) de J.; m. Christiana Pietronella van Ry, Nov. 22, 1967; 1 child, G. Arthur. Research technician Magneto Chemie NV, Schiedam, 1965-67; lab. mgr. Schiecarton NV, Schiedam, 1967-69; product sales mgr. Tamson NV, Zoetermeer, The Netherlands, 1969-72; sales and service mgr. United-Techs. Packard-Becker BV, Delft, The Netherlands, 1972-82; mng. dir. Autophon Telekommunikatie BV, Woerden, The Netherlands, 1982-88; dir. sales and mktg. PTT-CWP, The Hague, 1988—. Contbr. articles to chemistry jours. Mem. Nederlands Centrum Directeuren. Home: Rietkraag 51, 3121 TC Schiedam The Netherlands Office: Autophon Telekommunitatie BV, Polanerbaan 13N, 3447 GN Woerden The Netherlands

DEJONGE, KRIN, industrial and consumer products company executive; b. Terneuzen, The Netherlands, Feb. 16, 1941; arrived in Belgium, 1968; s. Pieter and Jacomina (De Kraker) De J.; m. Elizabeth Lillian Mance, June 8, 1968; children: Krin Alexandre, Erik Mance. BA, U. Oreg., 1966, MBA, 1967. Brand mgr. Procter & Gamble Co., Brussels, 1968-70, Brooke Bond Liebig, Antwerp, Belgium, 1971-72; group product mgr. Colgate-Palmolive Co., Amsterdam, 1972-79; subs. mgr. Hellesens A.G., Brussels, 1979-80; mktg. dir. Internat. Playtex Co., Brussels, 1981-85; internat. bus. mgr. Avery Fasson, Turnhout, Belgium, 1986—. Served with Dutch Army, 1961-62. Fulbright scholar U. Oreg., 1965. Home: 2 Huizenweg 73-33, 1200 Brussels Belgium Office: Avery Fasson, Tieblokkenlaan 1, 2300 Turnhout Belgium

DE JONGE, MARINUS, religious literature educator; b. Vlissingen, The Netherlands, Dec. 9, 1925; s. Jacobus and P. Dorothea (Kloosterman) de J.; m. Vera Abrahams, Feb. 10, 1951; children: Christiaan, Henriëtte, Anne D. Student, U. Leiden, The Netherlands, 1945-50, U. Manchester, Eng., 1951-52; ThD, U. Leiden, The Netherlands, 1953. Ordained to ministry Netherlands Reformed Ch., 1952. Minister Netherlands Reformed Ch., Wedde, The Netherlands, 1952-56, Blija, The Netherlands, 1956-61, Barchem, The Netherlands, 1961-62; lectr. of New Testament Faculty of Theology U. Groningen, The Netherlands, 1962-65, reader Early Christian and Intertestamentary Lit., 1965-66; prof. of New Testament and Early Christian Lit. U. Leiden, 1966—; Manson Meml. lectr. U. Manchester, 1970; vis. prof. New Testament Yale U., New Haven, Conn., 1981. Author: The Testaments of the Twelve Patriarchs: A Study of their Text, Composition and Origin, 1953, The Letters of John, 1968, Jezus: Inspirator en Spelbreker, 1971, Jesus: Inspiring and Disturbing Presence, 1974, Jesus: Stranger from Heaven and Son of God, 1977, Cristology in Context: The Earliest Christian Response to Jesus, 1988, (with C. Haas and J.L. Swellengrebel) A Translator's Handbook on the Letters of John, 1972, (with H.M.J. van Duyne) Words and Signs: Encounters with Jesus in the Gospel of John, 1978, (with H.W. Hollander, H.J. de Jonge and Th. Korteweg) The Testaments of the Twelve Patriarchs: A Critical Edition of the Greek Text, 1978, (with H.M.J. van Duyne) From Text to Interpretation: Exercises in Listening to the New Testament, 1982, (with H.W. Hollander) The Testaments of the Twelve Patriarchs: A Commentary, 1985; editor, co-author (book) Studies on the Testaments of the Twelve Patriarchs Text and Interpretation, 1975; editor Outside the Old Testament, 1985; contbr. articles to profl. jours. Mem. Soc. Biblical Lit., Studiorum Novi Testament Soc. (pres. 1985-86), Colloquium Biblicum Lovaniense (pres. 1975). Home: Libellenveld 1g, 2318 VE Leiden The Netherlands Office: Theologisch Inst, Post Box 9515, 2300 RA Leiden The Netherlands

DEKKER, DIRK JAN, business executive; b. Amsterdam, Oct. 31, 1930; s. Arie Dekker and Louise Wilhelmina Koetsier; m. Cathelijne Adriaanse, Feb. 27, 1928; children: Elise, Caroline. Doctorate, U. Amsterdam, 1955. Dir. High Authority European Coan and Steel Community, Luxembourg, 1958-65; sr. advisor DAS Harvard U., Monrovia-Liberia, 1965-67; dir. Commn. of European Communities, Brussels, 1967-86; sec. gen. European Bus. and Innovation Ctr. Network assn. sans but lucratif, Brussels, 1986—. Served to 1st lt. Royal Dutch Airforce, 1956-58. Mem. various econ. assns. Home: Schaveistraat 23, 1900 Overijse Belgium Office: EBN assn sans but lucratif, rue Belliard 205, 1040 Brussels Belgium

DEKKER, WISSE, electrical products manufacturing executive. Chmn. supervisory bd. N.V. Philips Gloeilampenfabrieken, Eindhoven, The Netherlands, now pres. Office: NV Philips, Gloeilampenfabrieken, Groenewoudseweg 1, Eindhoven The Netherlands also: Philips Industries NV, 5621 BA Eindhoven The Netherlands *

DEKKERS, GER(RIT) (HENDRIK), photographer; b. Borne, Aug. 21, 1929; m. Hilda Hartsuiker, 1954; children—Henriette, Jose. Studied graphics Acad. Art, Enschede, 1950-54. Free-lance artist, photographer, Enschede, 1954-76, Giethoorn, The Netherlands, 1975—; mem. photo sect. Gebonden Kunstenfederatie, 1969—. One-man shows: Rijksmuseum Kröller-Müller, Otterlo, The Netherlands, 1972, Museum Bochum-Kunstammlung (W.Ger.), 1973, Neue Galerie-Kunstammlung Ludwig, Aachen, W.Ger., 1973, Stedelijk Mus., Amsterdam, The Netherlands, 1974, Haagse Germeentemuseum, The Hague, The Netherlands, 1974, Palais des Beaux-Arts, Brussels, 1975, Galleria del Cavallino, Venice, Italy, 1975, Kunstmuseum, Aarhus, Denmark, 1976, Print Gallery Pieter Brattinga, Amsterdam, 1976, 79, Galerie M, Bochum, 1976, Rijksmuseum Kröller-Müller, Otterlo, 1977, Museum Boymans-van Beuningen, Rotterdam, The Netherlands, 1977, Gemeentemuseum, Arnhem, Netherlands, 1978, De Vishal, Haarlem, The Netherlands, 1978, Hayden Gallery, MIT, Cambridge, 1979, Provincaal Begijnhof, Hasselt, Belgium, 1979, Kunstcentrum Markt 17, Enschede, The Netherlands, 1980, Rijksplanologische Dienst, The Hague, The Netherlands, 1980, Studium Generale, Wageningen, The Netherlands, 1981, Städtische Galerie, Nordhorn, W.Ger., 1981; represented in permanent collections: Rijksmuseum Kröller-Müller, Otterlo, Stedelijk Mus., Amsterdam, Mus. Boymans-van Beuningen, Haagse Gemeentemuseum, The Hague, Gemeentemuseum, Ministry of Culture, The Hague, Posts-Telegraph-Telephone, The Hague, Mus. Ludwig, Cologne, W.Ger., Kunsthalle, Hamburg, W.Ger., Mus. Bochum-Kunstammlung; photographer: (with introduction by R.W.D. Oxenaar) Planned Landscape: 25 Horizons, 1977; co-editor Graven en Begrave in Overijssel, 1980. Served with Dutch Army, 1948-50; Indonesia. Recipient stipendium City of Amsterdam, 1976; Dutch Ministry Culture grantee, 1970, 71, 75, 76. Address: Dwarsgracht 31, 8355 CV Giethoorn The Netherlands *

DE KLERK RUBIN, VICKI B., theater executive; b. N.Y.C., Oct. 3, 1956; d. Warren J. Rubin and Naomi (Weil) Feil; m. Pieter de Klerk, June 24, 1987; 1 child, Helena Adriana. BFA, Boston U., 1978; MBA, Fordham U., 1983. Asst. mng. dir. Circle in the Square Theater, N.Y.C., 1978-79; mng. dir. Chelsea Theater Ctr., N.Y.C., 1980-81; free-lance theatrical producer N.Y.C., 1982-85, free-lance fin. cons. to arts orgns., 1982-85; bus. mgr. Circle Repertory Co., N.Y.C., 1985-86, Mickery Theater, Amsterdam, The Netherlands, 1986-87; rep. Fedn. Am. Women's Clubs Overseas, Vienna, 1988—.

DEKMEJIAN, RICHARD HRAIR, political science educator; b. Aleppo, Syria, Aug. 3, 1933; came to U.S., 1950, naturalized, 1955; s. Hrant H. and Vahede V. (Matossian) D.; m. Anoush Hagopian, Sept. 19, 1954; children: Gregory, Armen, Haig. B.A., U. Conn., 1959; M.A., Boston U., 1960; Middle East Inst. cert., Columbia U., 1964, Ph.D., 1966. Mem. faculty SUNY, Binghamton, 1964-86; prof., chmn. dept. polit. sci. U. So. Calif., Los Angeles, 1986—; also master Hinman Coll., 1971-72; lectr. Fgn. Service Inst., Dep. State, 1976—; vis. prof. Columbia U., U. Pa., 1977-78; dir. Ctr. for Research and Devel. Inc.; cons. Dept. State, AID, USIA, UN. Author: Egypt Under Nasir, 1971, Patterns of Political Leadership: Israel, Lebanon, and Egypt, 1975; Islam in Revolution, 1985. Contbr. articles to profl. jours. Pres. So. Tier Civic Ballet Co., 1973-76. Served with AUS, 1955-57. Mem. Am. Polit. Sci. Assn., Middle East Inst., Middle East Studies Assn., Internat. Inst. Strategic Studies, Internat. Polit. Sci. Assn., Pi Sigma Alpha, Phi Alpha Theta. Home: 331 W Wilson Ave Glendale CA 91203 Office: U So Calif Dept Polit Sci Los Angeles CA 90007

DE KORTE, RUDOLF WILLEM, government official; b. The Hague, The Netherlands, July 8, 1936; married; 2 children. Ph.D. in Math. and Natural Scis., Leiden U., 1964; postgrad., Harvard U. Bus. Sch., 1964. With various cos., Hong Kong, 1964-66, Ethipia, 1967-68; gen. sales mgr. Unilever-Emery NV, 1969-71, dir., 1972-77; mem. Lower House of Parliament, The Netherlands, 1977-86; minister home affairs 1st Lubbers govt., The Netherlands, 1986; deputy prime minister, minister econ. affairs 2d Lubbers govt., The Netherlands, 1986—. Sec. People's Party for Freedom and Democracy, 1971-78; mem. Wassenaar municipal council, 1978-82. Office: M of Econ Affairs, Com Nuclear, Energy, Bezuidednhoutseweg 30, POB 20101, 2500 EC The Hague The Netherlands *

DE KOSTER, GUUS, pulp and paper industry executive; b. Medan, Indonesia, Dec. 16, 1931; came to N.Z., 1952; s. Jacobus Barend and Josepha Adolphina Eugenia (Moormann) deK.; m. Mary Agnes May Gaelic, Mar. 4, 1953; children—Mark, Maria, Clive, Lisa, Kurt. Diplomate Mcpl. U., Amsterdam, 1951. Liaison officer N.Z. Forest Products, Kinleith, 1955-67, asst. gen. sales mgr., Penrose, Auckland, N.Z., 1967-69, sales mgr., 1969-79, regional mktg. mgr., Christchurch, South Island, N.Z., 1979-82, spl. duties officer, Penrose, 1982-84; mgmt. cons., facilitator, Auckland, 1985—; gen. mgr. Downstage Theatre, Wellington, N.Z., 1984; mgr. Sails Sci., 1986-87. Mem. found., edn. com. Export Inst. Auckland, 1971-73; exec. Export Inst., Christchurch, 1980-82; Liaison Civil Def., Tokoroa, N.Z., 1959-60; sec. Auckland Ethnic Council, 1987—. Mem. N.Z. Inst. Printing (assoc. 1982), Australian and N.Z. Pulp and Paper Industry Appita (sec.-treas. Auckland 1969-72), Rate Payers Assn. (exec. 1984), N.Z. Futures Trust Inc. (regional convenor 1985—, trust bd. mem. 1985—), Canterbury C. of C. (councillor). Roman Catholic. Clubs: Canterbury (Christchurch); Comml. Travellers (Auckland). Avocations: acting; directing; singing; piano playing; tutoring drama and stagecraft.

DE KOSTER, HENRI JOHAN, industrialist, Netherlands politician; b. Leiden, Netherlands, Nov. 5, 1914; C.Econ., Amsterdam U., 1936. Asst. commr. gen. Netherlands Govt. Food Purchasing Bur., N.Y.C., 1945-46; mng. dir. Desleutels Flour Mill, Leiden, 1947-67; pres. Netherlands Flour Milling Assn., 1954-67, Netherlands Fedn. Industries, 1961-67, Union Indsl. Fedns. of EEC, 1962-67; mem. Dutch Parliament, 1967-77; sec. state for fgn. affairs, 1967-71; minister of def., 1971-73; v.p. Fedn. Liberal and Democratic Parties in EEC, 1975-79; mem. Senate of States Gen. of Netherlands, 1977-80; state councillor, 1980-85; pres. Europa Nostra, 1984—; pres. Parliamentary Assembly of Council of Europe, 1978-81. Served with Resistance, World War II. Decorated Mil. Bronze Lion, grand officer Order Orange Nassau, knight Netherlands Lion; grand cordon Order Merit (Luxembourg); comdr. Order Couronne (Belgium); gt. cross 1st class Fed. Republic Ger.; comdr. 1st class Order Austria. Office: 35 Lange Voorhout, The Hague 2514-EC, The Netherlands

DEKSTER, BORIS VENIAMIN, mathematician, educator; b. Leningrad, USSR, Oct. 8, 1938; arrived in Can., 1974; s. Veniamin Moisey Zeigerman and Faina Aron Dekster; m. Nadezhda Sergey Prokopets, Feb. 7, 1969 (div. May 1985); 1 child, Sonya. Master's degree Leningrad U., 1962; Ph.D., Steklov Inst., Leningrad, 1971. Research assoc. U. Toronto, Ont., Can., 1974-78, asst. prof., 1981-86, assoc. prof. Mt. Allison U., New Brinswick, Can., 1986— ; asst. prof. U. Notre Dame, Ind., 1979-81. Contbr. articles on differential geometry and convexity to profl. jours. NSF grantee, 1980-81; Can. Natural Scis. Research Council grantee, 1981—. Mem. Am. Math. Soc. Home: 9 Raworth Heights, Sackville, NB Canada E0A 3C0 Office: Erindale Campus of U Toronto, Mississauga, ON Canada L5L 1C6 also: Mount Allison Univ, Sackville, NB Canada E0A 3C0

DELACATO, JANICE ELAINE, learning consultant; b. Bklyn., June 6, 1926; d. Frode Siegfried and Vilma (Riis) Fernstrom; m. Carl Henry Delacato, June 20, 1951; children—Elizabeth Delacato Putnam, Carl Henry, David Fernstrom. A.B., Bryn Mawr Coll., 1948. Tchr., Rydal Hall, Ogontz Sch., Pa., 1948-49, The Spence Sch., N.Y.C., 1949-50, Chestnut Hill Acad., Phila., 1950-52; co-dir. The Chestnut Hill Reading Clinic, Phila., 1951-65, Delacato & Delacato, Cons. in Learning, Phila., 1972—; mgr. Morton (Pa.) Book Store, 1972—; co-dir. The Delacato & Delacato Conf. on Autism and Learning Disabilities, 1979-82. Chmn. fund-raising com. Springside Sch., 1969-71; treas. Main St. Fair Antiques Booth, Chestnut Hill Hosp., 1965-77. Recipient Main St. Fair award Chestnut Hill Hosp., 1972. Mem. AAUW. Republican. Unitarian. Club: Phila. Cricket. Editor newsletter Temple U. Med. Center Women's Aux., Phila., 1953-65; class editor Bryn Mawr Coll. Alumnae Bull., 1966-79. Home: The Glen 700 Thomas Rd Philadelphia PA 19118 Office: Delacato and Delacato Plymouth Plaza Suite 107 Meeting PA 19462

DELACOUR, YVES JEAN CLAUDE MARIE, technology information executive; b. Pamiers, Ariege, France, June 24, 1943; s. Jacques and Marie-Louise (Rambaud) D.; m. Elisabeth Peu-Duvallon; children—Thibault, Gauthier. Engr. French Naval Acad., 1965; B.S. in Econs., Fin., Institut d'Etudes Politiques, 1972; M.B.A., Stanford U., 1975. Commd. ensign, 1965, advanced through grades to lt. de Vaisseau, 1971; naval officer Helicopter Carrier Jeanne d'Arc, French Navy, 1965-69; in charge of communications dept. Destroyer, Toulon, 1966-69; staff mem. Navy Dept., Paris, 1969-73; credit officer Banque de l'Indochine et de Suez, Paris, 1975-77; pres. Transasia Corp., Paris, 1978—, pres. Internat. Data Group, France, 1980-86, v.p., 1986—. Home: 22 rue de la Federation, 75015 Paris France Office: IDG France, 12 Ave George V, 75008 Paris France

DE LA CRUZ, ELIAS ALEJANDRO, computer company executive; b. Santiago, Chile, Dec. 23, 1950; s. Miguel Angel and Ilma Paz (Cross) D.; m. Isabel Margarita Weinstein; children: Beatriz, Elias, Vicente, Isabel, Juan Pablo. Mktg. Mgmt. degree, I.P.E.V.E., Santiago, 1971; Mktg. degree, New So. Wales Inst. Tech., Sydney, Australia, 1973. Sales mgr. Nylex Corp., Sydney, 1972-73, Olivetti of Australia, Sydney, 1973-75; sales mgr. Burroughs de Chile SA, Santiago, 1975-78, div. mgr., 1981-83; br. mgr. Burroughs de Chile SA (became Unisys Corp.), Santiago, 1983-84; exec. dir. Unisys Chile, Santiago, 1985—; gen. mgr. Santiago Trading Ltd., 1978-80. Club: Prince of Wales Country. Office: Unisys Chile Corp, 325 Avenida Los Leones, Santiago Chile

DE LA CRUZ-CROSS, JOSE MIGUEL, diplomat; b. Santiago de Chile, Chile, Mar. 21, 1952; s. Miguel De La Cruz and Ilma (Cross) De Aguirre; m. Maria Ines Castro, Dec. 12, 1984; 1 child, Jose Miguel, Maria Jose, Alejandra Francisca. Student, U. Chile Law Sch., Santiago, 1970-74; grad. in Diplomatic Studies, Acad. Diplomática Chile, Santiago, 1975; diploma in French, Alliance Franciase Paris, 1976. 3d sec. Chilean Embassy, Tokyo, 1977-78; 1st sec. Lima, Peru, 1978-81, Caracas, Venezuela, 1981-85; 1st sec., consul Managua, Nicaragua, 1985, Guatemala, 1985-87; 1st sec. fgn. service Ministerio de Relaciones Exteriores, Santiago de Chile, 1987—; del. Chile Sistema Economico Latinoamericano meetings, 1981-85, Guatemalan meetings, 1985, OAS meetings, 1976, 86. Contbr. articles to profl. jours.; photographic exhibit Sala Siriaco Guatemala, 1987. Decorated Orden del Sol del Peru, Peruvian Govt., 1986. Mem. Diplomatic Assn. Lima (bd. dirs. 1981), Diplomatic Assn. Guatemala (bd. dirs. 1986). Roman Catholic. Club: Santiago Wanderers (Valparaiso, Chile); Club de la Union (Santiago). Office: Ministerio de Ralaciones Exteriores, Palacio de La Moneda, Santiago Chile

DE LA FUENTE, GONZALO, marketing professional; b. Madrid, Oct. 10, 1935; s. Jesús and María (de la Revilla) de la F.; m. María Eugenia Rodríguez de Liévana; children: María Eugenia, Inés María. Grad. in Econ. and Comml. Scis., U. Madrid. Statistician Nat. Office Stats., Madrid, 1957-65; stat. research dept. mgr. A.C. Nielsen Co., Madrid, 1965-70, mktg. services sr. exec., 1970-75, mktg. services mgr., 1975—, new products mgr., 1978—; lectr. in field. Co-author: Manual for Market Research, 1979. Mem. Spanish Assn. for Market and Opinion Researchers, Royal Automobile Club. Home: Paseo de San Francisco, de Sales 23, 28003 Madrid Spain Office: AC Nielsen Co SA, Luchana 23, 28010 Madrid Spain

DELAGE, GILLES PASCAL, international company sales executive; b. Paris, Apr. 23, 1953; s. Joseph and Raymonde (Lavie) D.; m. Dominique Jeanine M. Berna, Mar. 19, 1976; children—Thibault, Matthieu, Guillaume. M.B.A./Descaf, Ecole Supé rieure de Commerce, Amiens, France, 1976; DEUG, Bus. Rights U., Paris, 1977. Fin. exec. Creusot Loire Entreprises, Paris, 1977-79; export and fin. dep. mgr. Trindel, Paris, 1979-82; fin. mgr. Spie Batignolles, Velizy, France, 1983-86; internat. sales mgr. FECHOZ, Paris, 1986-87; Asia v.p. Spie Batignolles, Cergy Pontoise, France, 1987— . Served with French Air Force, 1976-77. Mem. Association des Diplomes de L'ESCAE-Amiens (pres. 1976-87). Roman Catholic. Avocations: golf; skiing; tennis. Home: 7 rue Marco Polo, 78180 Montigny le Bretonneux France Office: Spie Batignolles, 202 Quai de Clichy, 92111 Clichy France

DELAHOUSSE, PIERRE JEAN, physician; b. Roubaix, France, Jan. 28, 1936; s. Jean-Stanislas and Eveline (Mullier) D.; m. Michele Pressat, July 11, 1964; children: Anne-Michele, Marie-Agnes, Pierre-Denis. MD, External Univ. Hosp Lille, 1961; Laureate Medicine, Paris Acad. Medicine, 1962; grad., Internat. Sch., Sophrologia, Barcelona, 1979. Practice medicine Roubaix, France, 1963—. Contbr. author Cancer: Dynamique et Eradication, 1971. Served to capt. of medicine, French Armed Forces, 1961-63. Mem. Mcpl. Fedn. Sophrologian Medicine, Sci. Acad. Rome. Roman Catholic. Lodge: Lions. Home: Rue de Barbieux 50, 59100 Roubaix France Office: Rue de College 96, 59100 Roubaix France

DE LA MADRID HURTADO, MIGUEL, former president of Mexico; b. Colima, Mexico, Dec. 12, 1934; s. Miguel de la M. and Castro (Alicia) Hurtado; m. Paloma Cordero, June 27, 1959; children: Margarita, Miguel, Enrique, Federico, Gerardo. Licenciatura, Faculty Law Nat. AUtonomous U. Mexico, Mexico City, 1957; M.P.A., Harvard U., 1965. Prof. constl. law Nat. Autonomous U. Mexico, Mexico City, 1958-68, prof. comparative law Inst. Juridical Research, 1958-68; dept. dir. pub. credit Mexican Ministry Fin. and Pub. Credit, Mexico City, 1965-70, gen. dir. pub. credit, 1972-75, undersec. fin. and pub. credit, 1975-79; dep. dir. fin. Petroleos Mexicanos, Mexico City, 1970-72; sec. planning and budget Mexican Ministry Planning and Budget, Mexico City, 1979-81; pres. Mexico, 1982-88; adv. Mexican Soc. Indsl. Credit, Mexican Ins. Co. Aeromexico, Nat. Bank Fgn. Commerce, Nat. Savs. Bank, Nat. Cinematographic Bank, Nat. Sugar Financing Commn., Nat. Pub. Works Bank; has represented Govt. Mexico at various internat. confs. on econ. issues, including those of Internat. Monetary Fund, World Bank, Interam. Devel. Bank and Interam. Econ. and Social Council. Author: Studies on Constitutional Law, 1977. Researcher Inst. Polit. Econ. and Social Studies Instl. Revolutionary Party. Recipient scholar Banco de Mexico, 1964. Mem. Barra Mexicana de Abogados (Mexican Bar Law), Instituto Iberoamericano de Derecho Constitucional (Iberoam. Inst. Constl. Law), Sociedad Mexicana de Planificacion (Mexican Planning Soc.), Instituto de Administraction Publica (Inst. Pub. Adminstrn.). Mem. Instl. Revolutionary Party. Office: Pres de la Republica, Palacio Nacional, Mexico City Mexico 06220

DELANEY, ANDREW, retired insurance company executive, consultant; b. Vienna, Ohio, Aug. 2, 1920; s. John David and Elizabeth L. (Wurstner) D.; m. Wynelle Shellhouse, Apr. 5, 1947; 1 dau., Janet Lynn; m. Pauline Mills, July 31, 1982. B.A., Oberlin Coll., 1942; B.S., NYU, 1942. Actuarial trainee Equitable Life Assurance Co., N.Y.C., 1946-49; asst. actuary Union Central Life Ins. Co., Cin., 1949-54; v.p. actuary Am. Gen. Life Ins. Co., Houston, 1954-68, sr. v.p., 1968-76, sr. v.p., chief investment officer, 1976-82, vice chmn. bd., chief investment officer, 1982-85; ret. Am. Gen. Life Ins. Co., 1985; fin. cons. Fireman's Fund Corp., 1985—; bd. dirs. Cullen Ctr. Bank & Trust, Houston, Fireman's Fund. Corp., Novato, Calif., AOA Corp., Dallas. Life bd. dirs. Big Bros., Houston, 1969—; trustee Found. for Retarded, 1982—, Oberlin Coll., 1981—; past chmn. bd. trustees Emerson Unitarian Ch., Houston. Served to capt. USAF, 1942-46. Fellow Soc. Actuaries (bd. govs.). Republican. Clubs: Houston Racquet, Forest, Ramada (Houston); Braeburn. Home: 2831 Sackett Houston TX 77098 Office: Suite 830 2727 Allen Pkwy Houston TX 77019

DELANEY, EDWARD NORMAN, lawyer; b. Chgo., Sept. 16, 1927; s. Frederick E. and Wynifred (Ward) D.; m. Carole P. Walter, May 31, 1950; children: Deborah Delaney Rogers, Kathleen Delaney Langan, Edward Norman II, Dorian A. LLB, Loyola U., Chgo., 1951; LLM, NYU, 1959. Bar: Ill. 1952, Minn. 1961, U.S. Supreme Ct. 1963, Mo. 1974, D.C. 1975. Staff Office Chief Counsel, IRS, N.Y.C., 1955-60; atty. Investors Diversified Services Inc., Mpls., 1960-73; v.p., gen. counsel investment adv. group Investors Diversified Services Inc., 1968-73; sr. v.p., gen. counsel Waddell & Reed and United Investors Life Ins. Co., Kansas City, Mo., 1974; ptnr. firm Bogan & Freeland, Washington, 1975-81; prin. Delaney, Bitonti & Wilhelm, Chartered, Washington, 1981—; chmn. tax com. Investment Co. Inst., 1963-74; bus. adv. com. SEC Inter-Agy. Task Force Offshore Funds, 1970-71. Active fundraiser Ctr. for Performing Arts, Kansas City, Mo., 1974; bd. dirs. Civic Orch., Mpls., 1963-68, pres., 1966-68; mem. lawyers com. Washington Performing Arts Soc. Served with USMCR, 1945-46. Fellow Am. Bar Found.; mem. ABA (council tax sect. 1974-77, vice chmn. tax sect. 1978-81, chmn. tax sect. 1983-84), Fed., Minn., Hennepin County, Mo., D.C. bar assns., Am. Law Inst., Am. Coll. Tax Counsel. Clubs: Congl. Country, Univ., Georgetown, Capitol Hill (Washington). Home: 9405 Tobin Circle Potomac MD 20854 Office: Delaney Bitonti & Wilhelm 1629 K St NW Washington DC 20006

DELANEY, ELEANOR CECILIA COUGHLIN, educator; b. Elizabeth, N.J.; d. John C. and Eleanor C. (Fadde) Coughlin; B.S., Sch. Edn. Rutgers U., 1930, M.A., 1939; Ph.D., Columbia U., 1954; 1 son, John. Tchr. public schs., Elizabeth, N.J., 1927; prin. Woodrow Wilson Sch., Elizabeth, 1941-55; prof. Grad. Sch. Edn., Rutgers U., New Brunswick, N.J., 1955-87, prof. emeritus, 1987—, chmn. dept. ednl. adminstrn. and supervision, 1974—; vis. prof. William and Mary Coll., U. Mex., Columbia U.; ednl. cons. sch. systems, N.J., N.Y., Va., 1950—; con. U.S. Dept. State, Health and Edn., coordinator Intern-Am. Affairs. Mem. Elizabeth Charter Commn., 1960-61; chmn. Mayor's Adv. Commn. on Urban Devel., 1962-64, Elizabeth Human Relations Commn., 1968-75; mem. Elizabeth Bd. Edn., 1972-79, pres., 1973-76; mem. exec. bd. Union County chpt. ARC; mem. exec. bd. Vis. Nurse and Health Assn., 1977—; pres., 1981-85. Mem. AAUW, Nat., N.J. edn. assns., Dept. Elem. Sch. Prins., AAUP, AAAS, Am. Ednl. Research Assn., Kappa Delta Pi (counelor 1970-87, Nat. Honor Key), Pi Lambda Theta, Phi Delta Kappa. Author: Spanish Gold, Lands of Middle America, Our Friends in South America, Science-Life Series, Book 4; Persistent Problems in Education. Contbr. articles to profl. mags. Home: 220 W Jersey St Elizabeth NJ 07202

DELANEY, HERBERT WADE, JR., lawyer; b. Leadville, Colo., Mar. 30, 1925; s. Herbert Wade and Marie Ann (Garbarino) DeL.; m. Ramona Rae Ortiz, Aug. 6, 1953; children—Herbert Wade III, Paula Rae, Bonnie Marie Manshel. B.S., U. Denver, 1949, LL.B., 1951. Bar: Colo. 1951, U.S. Supreme Ct. 1959. Sole practice, Denver, 1953-61; faculty U. Denver, Colo., 1960-61;

ptnr. Salazar & DeLaney, Denver, 1961-64, DeLaney & West, Denver, 1964-65; sole practice, Denver, 1965—. Served as capt. JAG's Dept., USAF, 1951-53. Mem. Colo. Trial Lawyers Assn., Assn. Trial Lawyers Am., Colo. Bar Assn., Denver Bar Assn., Am. Legion, Phi Alpha Delta. Club: Footprinters (Denver). Lodges: Masons, Elks. Office: Empire Park Suite 606 1355 S Colo Blvd Denver CO 80222

DELANEY, PHILIP ALFRED, banker; b. Chgo., Nov. 18, 1928; s. Walter J. and Kathryn M. (McWilliams) D.; m. Patricia O'Brien, June 21, 1952; children—Sharon Ann, Philip A., Nancy, Mary Beth. B.S. magna cum laude, U. Notre Dame, 1950; M.B.A., U. Chgo., 1956; postgrad., U. Wis. Grad. Sch. Banking, 1960. Trainee A.G. Becker & Co., Chgo., 1950; broker/dealer A.G. Becker & Co., 1951-52; with Harris Trust & Savs. Bank, Chgo., 1952—; exec. v.p., chief credit officer Harris Trust & Savs. Bank, 1980-84, pres., 1984—; pres. holding co. Harris Bankcorp, Inc., Chgo., 1984—, also bd. dirs.; prin. Chgo. United; bd. dirs. DeSoto, Inc., Des Plaines, Ill., Bankmont Fin. Corp., Harris Brokerage Services, Inc., Evanston Hosp., Chgo. Bd. dirs. Catholic Charities Chgo., Chgo. Conv. and Visitors Bur., Evanston Hosp.; mem. Chgo. Com., Chgo. Council Fgn. Relations; assoc. Northwestern U.; Chief Crusader United Way/Crusade of Mercy; mem. adv. council Chgo. Urban League; mem. citizens bd. Loyola U., Chgo. Served to 2d lt. USMC, 1951. Mem. Am. Bankers Assn., Am. Inst. Banking, Am. Mgmt. Assn., Assn. Res. City Bankers, Bankers Club Chgo., Chgo. Assn. Commerce and Industry, Robert Morris Assocs., U. Chgo. Alumni Assn., Mid Am. Com., Econ. Club of Chgo. Roman Catholic. Clubs: Commercial, Commonwealth, Economic, Notre Dame (Chgo.), North Shore Country, Chgo. Office: Harris Bankcorp Inc 111 W Monroe St PO Box 755 Chicago IL 60690

DELAP, J. Q., JR., gas company executive; b. Liberal, Kans., May 29, 1948; s. J.Q. and Estella Fern (Cook) D.; m. Ellen Rubin, Oct. 22, 1983; children: J.Q. (Jake), Tiffani Jaye. BSME, Rose-Hulman Inst., 1970; MBA, Pepperdine U., 1978. Engr. Panhandle Eastern Pipeline Co., Kansas City, Mo., 1970-74; mgr. hydrocarbon sales Anadarko Prodn. Co., Houston, 1974-76; mgr. gas liquids acquisition No. Gas Products Co., Houston, 1976-77; mgr. gas supply Gulf Coast region, Farmland Industries, Inc., crude oil rep. Gulf Coast region CRA, Inc., Houston, 1977-79; pres. La. Energy and Devel. Corp., New Orleans, 1979—; pres. Loutex Energy Inc., Delta Gas Inc., 1980—, La. State Gas Corp., 1981—, Gas Systems Network, Inc., 1981—, NorthCan Energy, Inc., 1988—. Bd. advisors Rose-Hulman Inst., 1980. Mem. ASME, Am. Gas Assn., La. Gas Assn. (bd. dirs.), Natural Gas Men of Houston, Natural Gas Men of New Orleans. Presbyterinian. Club: Petroleum (Houston). Home: 2115 Forest Falls Dr Kingwood TX 77345 Office: 334 Carondelet St Suite 400 New Orleans LA 70130

DE LARROCHA, ALICIA, concert pianist; b. Barcelona, Spain, May 23, 1923; d. Eduardo and Teresa (De La Calle) de L.; m. Juan Torra, June 21, 1950; children: Juan, Alicia. Grad. (prize extraordinary, Gold medal), Acad. Marshall, Barcelona. Debut, Barcelona, 1929, solo recitalist, concert pianist maj. orchs. in, Europe, U.S., Can., Central and S. Am., S. Africa, N.Z., Australia, Japan; dir. Acad. Marshall, 1959—; rec. artist: Hispavox, CBS, Decca-London; records.: (Grammy award 1974, 75, 1st Gold medal Merito a la Vocacion 1972). Recipient Harriet Cohen Internat. Music award, 1968; Paderewski Meml. medal, 1961; Grand prix du Disque Acad. Charles Cros, 1960, 74; Edison award, 1968; decorated Order Civil Merit Order Isabel la Catolica, Spain). Mem. Musica en Compostela (dir.), Hispanic Soc. Am. (corr.), Internat. Piano Archives (hon. pres.). Address: care Columbia Artists Mgmt 165 W 57th St New York NY 10019 *

DELASHMET, GORDON BARTLETT, newsprint executive; b. Moss Point, Miss., Dec. 19, 1928; s. Thomas Lewis and Ione (Broome) DeL.; m. Barbara Harris, Sept. 11, 1971; 1 child, Katherine Casey. BA, U. Miss., 1950. Salesman Internat. Paper, Montreal, 1955-63, regional mgr., Atlanta, 1963-68; exec. v.p. Clarendon Paper Sales, Atlanta, 1968-73; v.p. sales Abitibi Newsprint Corp., Atlanta, 1973-77; sr. v.p. Abitibi-Price Sales Corp., N.Y.C., 1977-80, exec. v.p., 1980—. Patron South Africa Air Force Mus. Served to capt. U.S. Army, 1950-54, prisoner of war, Korea. Recipient Fred Hoyt award, Atlanta Rotary, 1976; Award of Excellence, Sigma Chi Frat., 1983, Significant Sig, 1987. Mem. Can. Pulp and Paper Assn., Am. Paper Inst., Sigma Chi. Republican. Clubs: Commerce, Union League, Wee Burn Country, Capital City, Tournament Players. Lodge: Masons (Knight Comdr. Ct. of Honor, 1987). Avocations: golfing, goose and duck hunting, salmon fishing. Home: 10 Granaston Ln Darien CT 06820

DE LASZLO, DAMON PATRICK, electronics company executive, economist; b. London, Oct. 8, 1942; s. Patrick David and Deborah Hamar (Greenwood) de L.; m. Sandra Daphne Hacking, July 18, 1972; children: Lucy Deborah, Robert Damon, William Patrick. Student, Gordonstoun Sch., Scotland, Rosenberg Coll., Switzerland. Commd. 2d lt. Army of U.K., 1962, advanced through grades to capt., ret., 1970; exec. Harwin Engrs.; bd. dirs. Trust Co. of West, Calif., 1980—. chmn. Econ. Research Council, London, 1981—. Fellow Royal Soc. of Arts. Home: A2 Albany, London W1V 9RD, England Office: Harwin Engrs SA, Fitzherbert Rd, Portsmouth PO6 1RT, England

DE LAURENTIIS, DINO, motion picture producer; b. Torre Annunziata, Italy, Aug. 8, 1919; s. Rosario Aurelio and Giuseppina (Salvatore) De L.; m. Silvana Magnano, July 17, 1949; children: Veronica, Rafaella, Francesca. Ed. high sch. and comml. sch., Centro Sperimentale di Cinematografia, Rome. Prin. De Laurentiis Entertainment Group Studios, Wilmington, 1984—; prin. De Laurentiis Entertainment Group, Inc., 1986—, now chmn. bd.; with Embassy Pictures, 1985; prin. De Laurentiis Entertainment Ltd., Australia, 1986—; purchased Embassy Pictures, 1985; formed De Laurentiis Entertainment Ltd. (Australia), 1986. Mem. actor's sch., Expt. Film Center, Rome, 1937-39, organized first film prodn. co., 1941; productions include Bitter Rice, 1952, Ulysses, 1955, War and Peace, 1956, La Strada, 1956 (Acad. award), Nights of Cabiria, 1957 (Acad. award), This Angry Age, 1958, The Tempest, 1959, Under Ten Flags, 1960, The Best of Enemies, 1962, Barabbas, 1962, Three Faces of a Woman (Soraya), 1964, The Bible, 1966, Barbarella, 1967, Anzio, 1967, Waterloo, 1970, Valachi Papers, 1972, The Stone Killer, 1973, (moved to N.Y. 1973), Serpico, 1974, Death Wish, 1974, Mandingo, 1975, Three Days of the Condor, 1975, (moved to Los Angeles 1975), Lipstick, 1976, Face to Face, 1976, Buffalo Bill and the Indians, 1976, The Shootist, 1976, King Kong, 1976, Orca, 1977, The Serpent's Egg, 1977, King of the Gypsies, 1978, The Great Train Robbery, 1978, The Brink's Job, 1979, Hurricane, 1979, Flash Gordon, 1980, Ragtime, 1981, Striking Back, 1982, Conan The Barbarian, 1982, The Dead Zone, 1983, Firestarter, 1984, The Bounty, 1984, Conan The Destroyer, 1984, Dune, 1984, Cat's Eye, 1985, Red Sonja, 1985, Year of the Dragon, 1985, Marie, 1985, Silver Bullet, 1985, Raw Deal, 1986, Maximum Overdrive, 1986, Tai-Pan, 1986, Blue Velvet, 1986, 1986, King Kong Lives, 1986, Manhunter, 1986, Trick or Treat, 1986, Crimes of the Heart, 1986, Date With an Angel, 1987, The Bedroom Window, 1987, From the Hip, 1987, Million Dollar Mystery, 1987, Traxx, 1987, Weeds, 1987, Rampage, 1987, Collision Course, 1987, Dracula's Widow, 1987, Pumpkinhead, 1987, Adult Education, 1987. Office: De Laurentiis Entertainment Group 8670 Wilshire Blvd Beverly Hills CA 90211 *

DE LA VEGA DOMINGUEZ, JORGE, government official; b. Comitán, Chiapas, Mexico, 1931. Degree in Econ., Nat. Autonomous U. Mexico. With Ministry of Economy, Mexico, 1949-55; prof. economy theory, pub. financing, and economy problems of Mexico Nat. Poly. Inst., Mexico, 1957-65, dir. economy faculty, 1963-65; former chmn. Bank for Retail Trade, Tampico, Mexico; former dep. dir. Bank for Retail Trade, Mexico City, Mexico, Diesel Nat., S.Am., Mexico; former chief dept. pub. spending Ministry of the Presidency, Mexico; former dep. XLV Legis., Mexico; sales mgr. Nat. Co. Popular Foodstuffs, Mexico; gen. dir. Inst. Polit., Econ., and Social Studies, Instl. Revolutionary Party, Mexico; former gen. dir. Nat. Co. Popular Foodstuffs, Mexico; former gov. State of Chiapas, Mexico; former sec. commerce Mexico; former gen. coordinator Nat. Commn. Nourishing and Foodstuffs, Mexico; former gen. coordinator regional programs Ministry Agriculture and Hydraulic Resources, Mexico; now pres. nat. exec. com. Instl. Revolutionary Party, Mexico. Mem. Mexico's Coll. Economists (former pres.). Address: Instl Revolutionary Party, Insurgentes Norte 61, 06350 Mexico, DF Mexico *

DEL CAMPO, MARTIN BERNARDELLI, architect; b. Guadalajara, Mexico, Nov. 27, 1922; s. Salvador and Margarita (Bernardelli) Del C.; B.A., Colegio Frances Morelos, Mexico City, 1941; Archtl. degree Escuela Nacional de Arquitectura, Mexico City, 1948; m. Laura Zaikowska, May 25, 1945; children—Felicia, Margarita, Mario. Came to U.S., 1949. Partner, Del Campo & Fruiht, architects, Santa Rosa, Cal., 1955-56, Del Campo & Clark, San Francisco, 1957-63; mgr. Hotel Victoria, Oaxaca, Mexico, 1964-67; pres. Gulli-Del Campo, architects, San Francisco, 1968-70; partner Del Campo Assos., San Francisco, 1977-81; pres. Del Campo-Giffels, Architects-Engrs., 1981—; pres., dir. City Fed. Savs., Oakland, Calif., 1974—. Lectr. archtl. design Coll. Environmental Design, U. Calif., Berkeley, 1973-74. Mem. AIA (sec. exec. com. 1970—). Archtl. works include: Calif. Med. Facility South, Vacaville, Phillip Burton Fed. Bldg. remodeling, San Francisco. Address: 1601 Shrader San Francisco CA 94117

DELECOUR, MICHEL ROGER, physician, educator; b. Lille, France, May 29, 1925; s. Georges and Estelle (Frey) D.; 1 child, Suzanne. MD. Resident Lille (France) U., 1947, physician, 1952, fellow, 1953, assoc. prof., 1963, chmn., 1971—; dir. residency tng. program in ob-gyn., Lille, France, 1971—, midwives tng. program, Lille, 1971—; mem. African and Malgache Conseil of Superior U., editorial bd. Revue de Gynecology-Obstetrics et Biology de la Reproduction. Author: Abrege de Gynecology, 1975; co-author: (encylopedie) Medical and Chirurgical. Recipient Palmes Académiques, 1968, Légion d'Honneur, 1987. Mem. French Coll of Obstetricians and Gynecologists, Perinatal French Soc. (founding), Med. Ethics Com., Bd. French Speaking Fedn. Obstetricians and Gynecologists. Roman Catholic. Club: Tastvin (Clos Vougeot) (comdr.). Office: Clinique Gynécologique, et Obstétricale, 12 rue Malpart, 59000 Lille France

DELEDICQUE, ALAIN-GEORGES, rehabilitation physician; b. Roubaix, Nord, France, Jan. 17, 1944; s. Georges-Paul and Yvonne (Destailleur) D.; m. Brigitte Poillion (div. 1980); 1 child, Robin; m. Danielle Gedon, Sept. 29, 1981; children: Roland, Carole. Grad. in medecine, U. Lille, France, 1969; grad. in rehab. phys. medecine, U. Paris, 1971. Medecin dir. Thalassotherapy, Oleron, France, 1973-77; medecin chief Thalassotherapy, Carnac, France, 1978-83, Quiberon, France, 1983—; sr. spine cons.; expert Cour d'Appel, Poitiers, France, 1974-78. Author: The Thalassoth, 1978, The Fitness, 1986. Mcpl. conseiller, St. Trojan, France, 1976. Mem. Societe Francaise de Thalassotherapie (treas.). Republican. Roman Catholic. Lodge: Rotary. Office: Thalassotherapy, F56170 Quiberon Brittany, France

DELEMARRE, BEN JOHANNES, cardiologist; b. Roermond, Limburg, Netherlands, Mar. 24, 1950; s. Ben Martinus and Mieke (Lampe) D.; m. Henriette Aleida van de Waal, Mar. 30, 1977; children: Eveline, Steven. MD, Ryks U., Leiden, Netherlands, 1976. Fellow in internal medicine Elisabeth's Gasthuis, Haarlem, Netherlands, 1976-80; fellow in cardiology Wilhelmina Gasthuis, Amsterdam, 1980-83; cardiologist Academical Med. Ctr., Amsterdam, 1983—. Contbr. articles to profl. jours. Home: Burg Dedelstraat 22, 1391 GD Abcoude Utrecht, The Netherlands Office: Academical Med Ctr, Meibergdreef 9, Amsterdam The Netherlands

DELEURAN, AAGE, journalist; b. Korsor, Denmark, Oct. 11, 1925; s. Holger Johannes and Agnete (Lorentsen) D.; m. Birthe Braae, 1955. Staff reporter Korsor Avis, 1942, Berlingske Aftenavis, 1945; corr. Berlingske Tidende, Paris, 1952-56, asst. editor-in-chief, 1961, exec. editor, 1967, editor-in-chief, 1970—; dir. Berlingske House, 1975—; chmn. Soc. Danish Press History, 1966—, Ritzau's News Agy., 1971-76, 1980-85. Author: April 40, 1965. Decorated comdr. Order of Dannebrog; officier Legion d'honneur. Mem. Assn. Danish Newspapers (vice chmn. 1979-85, chmn. 1985). Office: 34 Pilestraede, 1147 Copenhagen K Denmark

DELFONT, BERNARD, Lord Delfont of Stepney, business executive, impresario, film executive; b. Tokmak, Russia, Sept. 5, 1909; s. Isaac and Olga (Winogradsky) D.; m. Carole Lynne, 1946; children—Susan, Jennifer, David. Entered theatrical mgmt. in Britain, 1941; 1st London prodn., 1942; since presented numerous shows in London; re-introduced variety to West End at London Casino, 1947-48, presenting Laurel and Hardy, Sophie Tucker, Lena Horne, Olsen and Johnson, Mistinguett; presented London Experience, Piccadilly, summer shows in seaside resorts; presenter ann. Royal Variety Performance, 1958-78; converted London Hippodrome into Talk of the Town theatre restaurant, 1958, also presented entertainment; exec. chmn. First Leisure Corp. Plc.; dir. Bernard Delfont Orgn., Blackpool Tower Co.; chmn., chief exec. officer Trust House Forte Leisure Ltd., 1981-82 others; v.p. Asso. Film Distbn. Corp., Inc., 1978; recent prodns. include: (with David Merrick) The Roar of the Greasepaint-The Smell of the Crowd, 1965, Pickwick, 1965; (with Arthur Lewis) Barefoot in the Park, 1965, Funny Girl, 1966; (with Michael Codron) The Killing of Sister George, 1965; (with Geoffrey Russel) The Matchgirls, 1966; (with others) The Odd Couple, 1966, Martha Graham Dance Co., 1967, Sweet Charity, 1967, The Four Musketeers, 1967, Golden Boy, 1968, Hotel in Amsterdam, 1968, Time Present, 1968, Mame, 1969, Your Own Thing, 1969, What the Butler Saw, 1969, Cat Among the Pigeons, 1969, Carol Channing with Her 10 Stout-Hearted Men, 1970, The Great Waltz, 1970, Danny La Rue at the Palace, 1970, Kean, 1971, Rabelais, 1971, Children of the World, 1971, Lulu, 1971, Applause, 1972, Threepenny Opera, 1972, The Good Old Bad Old Days, 1972, The Unknown Soldier and his Wife, 1973, The Danny La Rue Show, 1973, The Wolf, 1973, Brief Lives, 1974, The Good Companions, 1974, Sammy Cahn's Songbook, 1974, Cinderella (Twiggy), 1974, Harvey, 1975, 1975, Dad's Army, 1975; The Plumber's Progress, Queen Danniella, 1975; Mardi Gras, 1976; LeGrande Eugene, 1976; Tommy Steele Anniversary Show nat. tour, 1976; Val Doonican tour, 1977; Danny LaRue Show tour, 1977; An Evening with Tommy Steele, 1979; It's All Right If I Do It, 1977; Beyond the Rainbow, 1978; Charley's Aunt, 1979; Tommy Steele, 1980; It's Magic, Best Little Whorehouse in Texas, 1981; Underneath the Arches, 1982; Little Me, 1984. Pres., Entertainment Artistes Benevolent Fund. Named companion Grand Order Water Rats; knighted, 1974; created life peer, 1976. Mem. Saints and Sinners. Club: Variety of Gt. Britain (past pres.). Office: First Leisure Corp Plc, 7 Soho St, Soho Square, London W1V 5FA, England also: EMI Ltd, 20 Manchester Sq, London W1, England

DELFS, ROBERT A., JR., journalist; b. Long Beach, Calif., June 18, 1948. BA, Stanford U., 1970, MA, 1972; MA, Princeton U., 1976. Corr. China economy Far Eastern Econ. Rev., Hong Kong, 1981-86, bureau chief, Beijing correspondent, 1986—. Author: The Good Food of Sichuan, 1974; co-author: China, 1986. Fgn. Corr. (Hong Kong) (bd. govs. 1984-85), Royal Hong Kong Yacht. Office: Diplomatic Service Housing, Jianguomenwai 7-1-93, Beijing Peoples Republic of China

DELGADO, JOSÉ MANUEL RODRIGUEZ, neurobiologist; b. Ronda, Malaga, Spain, Aug. 8, 1915; s. Rafael R. Amérigo and Amada Delgado; m. Carolina Stoddard; children: Jose Carlos, Linda. MD, Madrid U., D Sci; MA, Yale U., 1967. Prof. physiology Yale U., New Haven, 1953-74, Autonomous U., Madrid, 1971-78; dir. research Ramon y Cajal Ctr, Madrid, 1974-85, LBE Pharma, Madrid, 1985—; head Est. Neurobiologicos, Madrid, 1985—. Contbr. numerous articles to profl. jours. Recipient Gold medal Am. Psychiatric Soc., 1971, Internat. Soc. Biol. Psychiatry. Fellow N.Y. Acad. Scis.; mem. numerous sci. orgns. Office: LBE Pharma, Velazquez 31, 28001 Madrid Spain

DELGADO, JOSEPH RAMON, business executive; b. Chgo., Mar. 4, 1932; s. Joseph Ramon and Florence (Nelson) D. BA in English, U. Ill., 1958. With Campbell-Mithun Advt., Chgo., 1960-68, purchasing agt., dir. office services, 1964-68; purchasing agt., asst. to pres., asst. to treas. Maxant Button & Supply Co., Chgo., 1968-70; asst. purchasing agt., administrv. asst. Soiltest, Inc., Evanston, Ill., 1970-82; v.p., asst. to pres. S.W. Chgo. Corp., 1982—, also bd. dirs. Mem. Lyric Opera Subscription Com., 1957; observer Joint Civic Com. on Elections, 1965; election judge primary and gen. elections, 1968, 70. Served with AUS, 1952-54. Mem. Purchasing Agts. Assn. Chgo. (co-chmn. publicity and pub. relations com. 1963-64), U. Ill. Alumni, Illiniweks, Chgo. Symphony Soc. (charter). Lutheran. Republican. Clubs: Whitehall, Barclay, International (Chgo.). Dance choreographer for various groups and individuals. Office: 3605 NE 32d Ave Fort Lauderdale FL 33308

DE LIMA, CLARA ROSA, theatre administrator, writer; b. Port of Spain, Trinidad and Tobago, July 27, 1922; d. Yldefonso and Rosario (Hernandez) De L.; student Notre Dame Coll., Md., 1935-38, L.I. U., 1945-48. Dir., shareholder Y. De Lima & Co., Port of Spain, 1943—; exec. sec. bank, 1954-68; v.p. City Playhouse of Trinidad, 1975—; publicity mgr. Music Festival, 1976; chmn. Trinidad and Tobago Opera Co., 1977; dir. Art Creators; free-lance journalist; writer Thoughts for Radio Trinidad, weekly travel programme, 1979; pub. relations adminstr. Friends of the Mus., 1985; mem. Found. for Orch. for Trinidad and Tobago, 1986; social worker, 1970-80; commentator on arts on radio. Author: (verse) Thoughts and Dreams, 1973; Dreams Non-Stop, 1974; Reminiscing, 1975; (novels) Tomorrow Will Always Come, 1965; Not Bad Just a Little Mad, 1975; Currents of the Yuna, 1978; Countdown to Carnival, 1980; Kilometre Nineteen, 1980. Mem. Nat. Status of Women, 1982-83, Com. Nat. Days and Festivals. Recipient Palme d 'Oro Accademiche, Centro Studi e Scambio Internazionale, Acad. Leonardo Da Vinci, and Oscar Modiale of Citti de Boretto, 1980; diploma of merit Academia Internazionale de Iblea, Ragusa, Italy; Rotary Found. Paul Harris fellow, 1983. Mem. Authors Guild Am., Met. Opera Guild, Music Found. Trinidad & tobago (chmn. working com. 1986—). Home and Office: Aldegonda Park, 7 Saint Anns Rd, Port of Spain Trinidad and Tobago

DELISI, CHARLES, biophysicist; b. N.Y.C., Dec. 9, 1941; s. Jack and Phyllis DeL.; Ph.D. in Physics, N.Y. U., 1969; m. Lynn Moskowitz, Aug. 11, 1968; children—Jacqueline, Daniel. Postdoctoral fellow chemistry and biophysics Yale U., 1969-72; sr. lectr. engring. and applied sci., 1971-72; engr. Sperry Rand Corp., N.Y.C., 1963-65; staff scientist theoretical div. Los Alamos Nat. Lab., 1972-75; chief theoretical immunology NIH, Bethesda, Md., 1975-85, spl. asst. Office of the Dir., NIH, 1978-79, chief math. biology, 1982-84; dir. Office Health and Environment Research, U.S. Dept. Energy, 1985-87; prof., chmn. dept. biomath sci. Mt. Sinai Sch. Medicine, 1987—; bd. spl. examiners U.S. civil Service commn., 1982-84; theory adv. com. Los Alamos Nat. Lab.; bd. sci. adv. molecular vaccines Protein Database Inc., co-devel. of aids vaccines; mem. numerous editorial bds. profl. jours. Author: Antigen-Antibody Interactions, 1976; Physical Chemistry Surface Events and Biological Regulation, 1978; Regulatory Implications of Immune Response Dynamics, 2 vols., 1982; Cell Surface Dynamics, 1984; contbr. numerous articles to profl. jours. Home: 270 Chestnut Dr Roslyn NY 11576 Office: Mt Sinai Sch Medicine 1 Gustave Levy Pl New York NY 10029

DELIVANIS, DIMITRIOS JOHN, economics educator; b. Vienna, Austria, Apr. 3, 1909; arrived in Greece, 1913; s. John D. and Helen J. (Triantafyllidis) D.; m. Maria Amvrosios Negreponti, May 7, 1959; 1 child, Helen. Degree in econs., U. Athens, Greece, 1930, degree in law, 1931; PhD in Econs., U. Paris, 1934. Counselor Prometheus Econ. and Tech. Corp., Athens, 1935-38; asst. prof. econ. Athens U., 1938-44; prof. Pantics Sch. Polit. Scis., Athens, 1939-45; prof. U. Thessaloniki, Greece, 1944-74, prof. emeritus, 1974—; econ. counselor Internat. Com. for Foodstuffs, 1943-45; rep. of Greece Gen. Assembly UN; com. mem. Econs. and Fin. Problems, 1973-77; corr. mem. Acad. Barcelona, Spain, 1967—, Acad. Athens, 1984—, Inst. Acad. Moral and Polit. Scis., Paris, 1987—. Author books; contbr. numerous articles to jours. Undersec. of State Ministry of Welfare, Athens, 1939-41. Decorated various decorations Govts. of Greece, France. Mem. Greek Econ. Assn. (pres. 1971-74), French Econ. Assn., Brit. Royal Econ. Soc., German Verein for Socialpolitik. Clubs: Athens, Athens Tennis. Home: Voukourestiou 50, 106-73 Athens Greece Office: U Thessaloniki, Thessaloniki Greece

DELL, ERNEST ROBERT, lawyer; b. Vandergrift, Pa., Feb. 6, 1928; m. Karen D. Reed, May 8, 1965; children: Robert W., John D., Jane C. B.S., U. Pitts., 1949, M.Litt., 1953; J.D., Harvard U., 1956. Bar: Pa. 1957, U.S. Supreme Ct. 1961; C.P.A., Pa. Ptnr. firm Reed Smith Shaw & McClay, Pitts., 1956—; adj. prof. law Duquesne U. Law Sch., Pitts., 1960-86; bd. dirs. Atty's. Liability Assurance Soc. Inc., Chgo., Atty's. Liability Assurance Soc. (Bermuda) Ltd. Mem. ABA, Pa. Bar Assn., Allegheny County Bar Assn., Pa. Inst. C.P.A.'s. Home: 119 Riding Trail Lane Pittsburgh PA 15215 Office: Reed Smith Shaw & McClay Mellon Sq 435 6th Ave Pittsburgh PA 15219

DELLA CLARA, FRANCO ABIS, physician; b. Sorengo, Switzerland, May 23, 1940; s. Hermes Lorenzo and Elisa Catharina (Flisch) D.; Maturité Classique, U. Geneva, 1962, Fed. Med. diploma, 1969; M.D., U. Zurich, 1974. Intern, Geneva Univ. Hosp. and Zurich Univ. Hosp., 1969-75; specialist in internal medicine Foederatio Medicorum Helveticorum, Zurich, 1975; supervising physician, head intensive care unit Ospedale Civico Lugano (Switzerland), 1975-87; pvt. practice specializing in intensive care medicine, Lugano, 1987—. Mem. N.Y. Acad. Scis., Swiss, German, European Soc. Intensive Care Medicine, Swiss Geneal. Soc. Roman Catholic. Contbr. articles to med. and hist. jours., geneol. publs. Home: 12 D'Alberti, 6900 Lugano Switzerland

DELLA SANTA, RAFFAELLO, banker; b. Rome, Sept. 26, 1938; s. Giulio and Anna (La Penna) Della S.; married, Oct. 7, 1963; children: Alba, Stefano. Laurea Economia Commercio, U. Sapienza, Rome, 1966. Br. mgr. Cassa Risparmio Roma, 1976-79, deputy mgr. fgn. dept., 1980-81, area br. mgr., 1982-86, internat. cen. mgr., 1987—. Contbr. articles to profl. jours. Roman Catholic. Club: Le Magno Lie. Office: Cassa di Risparmio Roma, Via del Corso 320, 00100 Rome Italy

DELL'ERGO, ROBERT JAMES, lawyer; b. Berkeley, Calif., Mar. 2, 1918; s. Cosmo A. and Lilian James (Rennie) Dell'E.; divorced; children: Robert, Marilee, Richard. BA with honors, U. Calif., Berkeley, 1939, JD, 1942. Assoc. Brobeck, Phleger & Harrison, San Francisco, 1946; ptnr. Millington & Dell'Ergo, Redwood City, Calif., 1947-57, Dell'Ergo & Tinsley, Redwood City, 1971—; sole practice Redwood City, 1957-71; bd. dirs. Whitevale Inc., Menlo Park, Calif. Chmn. Com. for Ct. Reorganization, San Mateo County, Calif., 1954, Com. to Elect John F. Kennedy, San Mateo County; mem. Redwood City 6 Yr. Plan com.; past chmn. bd. trustees Sequoia Union High Sch. Dist., San Mateo County, trustee, 1951-57. Served to lt. USNR, 1942-46, PTO. Mem. ABA, Calif. Bar Assn., San Mateo County Bar Assn. (pres. 1954, chmn. various coms.), Internat. Platform Assn., Sequoia Club, Redwood City C. of C. (pres. 1958), Am. Legion. Democrat. Club: Redwood City Antlers. Lodges: Elks, Sons of Italy, Redwood City (pres., chmn. grand lodge law commn.), Native Sons. Office: Dell'Ergo & Tinsley 1900 Broadway Suite 200 Redwood City CA 94063

DELLIMORE, JEFFREY WEBSTER, development banker; b. St. Vincent, W.I., Jan. 28, 1943; s. John and Nellie (Gumbs) D.; B.Sc., U. W.I., 1966; Ph.D., U. London, 1971; m. Jeanette Regina Rudder, Jan. 1, 1969; children—Imari John Albert, Chike Akil Jeffrey, Kiran Hamilton Jeffrey. Lectr., U. W.I., Cave Hill Campus, Barbados, 1970-79, sr. lectr., 1979-81; asst. dir., head tech. and energy unit Caribbean Devel. Bank, Barbados, 1980-84, chief project officer for tech. cooperation, 1984—. Mem. mgmt. com. Caribbean Appropriate Tech. Centre, 1981—; chmn. Caribbean Appropriate Tech. Com., 1977-80. Recipient U. W.I. Overseas award, 1966; Commonwealth scholar, 1969; Can. Heart Found. vis. scientist award, 1979; Overseas Devel. Adminstrn. (U.K.) fellow, 1973. Mem. Biophys. Soc., Internat. Soc. Biorheology. Anglican. Contbr. articles to profl. jours. Home: 7 The Mount, Saint George, Barbados West Indies Office: PO Box 408, Wildey, Saint Michael, Barbados West Indies

DELLORA, RALPH STEPHEN, accountant; b. Melbourne, Victoria, Australia, Oct. 9, 1940; s. Alexander John and Ida Gwendolyne (Anderson) D.; m. Maria Gloria Bathan, Dec. 4, 1976. B of Bus. in Acctg., Curtin U. Tech., Perth, Australia, 1981. Assessor State Taxation Office, Melbourne, 1957-62, Office Commonwealth Taxation, Melbourne, 1964-71; registrar of accts. Papua New Guinea, Port Moresby, 1972-84; sr. corp. examiner Office Corp. Affairs Victoria, Melbourne, 1985—. Fellow Inst. Chartered Secs. and Adminstrs., Australian Soc. Accts., Nat. Inst. Accts. (Victorian Div. Councillor, Chmn. Nat. Acctg. Standards Com.), Papua New Guinea Assn. Accts. Inc.; mem. Nat. Assn. Accts., N.Y. Acad. Sci., The Planetary Soc., Alumni Assn. Advanced Internat. Program in Oil and Gas Fin. Mgmt., Curtin U. Tech. Alumni Assn., Baseball Umpires Assn. Victoria, Australian Cricket Soc. (life), Inst. Arbitrators Australia (assoc.), Securities Inst. Australia, Inst. of Internal Auditors of Australia, Econ. Soc. of Australia, Victorian Cricket Umpires Assn. Inc., Council of Petroleum Accts. Socs. Roman Catholic. Clubs: Queensland Cricketers (Wollongabba, Australia); Dandenong Cricket (Victoria). Home: 75 James St, 3060 Fawkner Victoria, Australia Office:

Office Corp Affairs Victoria, 471 Lt Bourke St, Melbourne Victoria, Australia

DELMEZ, JACQUES EDMOND EMILE JULES, telecommunications marketing executive; b. Deux-Acren, Hainaut, Belgium, July 27, 1933; s. Albert and Julienne (Detry) D.; m. Jacqueline Arnould, Aug. 17, 1959; children: Bernard, Veronique. Grad., St. Augustus Coll., Enghiem, Belgium, 1953, Ecole Technique Superieure de l'Etat Anderlecht, Brussels, 1962. With staff MBLE, Brussels, 1955-59, head mobile radio dept., 1959-74, head mktg. comml. telecom, 1979, head mktg. def. telecom, 1979—; bd. dirs. Air Command and Control System Co. S.A., Brussels, Eurair S.A., Brussels. Mem. Armed Forces Communications and Electronics Assn. (pres. Benelux chpt. 1985-86), Old Crows. Roman Catholic. Home: CH de Tervueren 84, 1410 Waterloo Belgium Office: MBLE, 82 Rue des 2 Gares, 1070 Brussels Belgium

DEL MUNDO, AMELITA GLORIANI, plastic and reconstructive surgeon, burn specialist; b. Manila, Dec. 30, 1949; d. Rufo Agrimano del Mundo and Geronima Panganiban (Gloriani) D. BS cum laude, U. Philippines, 1970, MD (outstanding grad. in academics), 1974. Diplomate Philippine Bd. Plastic Surgery. Resident in plastic surgery and burn treatment Philippine Gen. Hosp., Manila, 1976-79; fellow in plastic and reconstructive surgery Showa Med. Sch., Tokyo, 1979-80; fellow in acute burn care U. Tex. Health Sci. Ctr., Dallas, 1980-81; fellow in reconstructive burn surgery U. Tex. Med. Sch., Houston, 1981-82; cons. physician Philippine Med. Children's Hosp., Quezon City, 1983—; staff surgeon San Juan de Dios Hosp., Pasay City, Philippines, 1984—, De Los Santos Med. Ctr., Quezon City, 1983—, Emmanuel Community Hosp., Manila, 1983—; asst. prof. surgery Dr. Nicanor Reyes Found. Far Eastern U., Manila, 1984—; frequent speaker on surgery. Contbr. articles, research reports to profl. jours. Recipient many awards and honors for med. achievement. Fellow Philippine Assn. Plastic Surgeons (pub. relations officer 1984-85), Philippine Coll. Surgeons; mem. Philippine Med. Assn., Am. Burn Assn., Internat. Soc. for Burn Injuries, Internat. Confedn. Plastic Surgeons, Philippine Soc. for Burn Injuries (founder, 1st sec. 1983-86), Philippine Soc. Aesthetic Plastic Surgeons (charter mem. and 1st pub. relations officer 1985-86). Roman Catholic. Home: 1751 Almeda, Santa Cruz, Manila 2805, Philippines Office: Far Eastern U Hosps, Dr Nicanor Reyes St, Sampaloc, Manila 2806, Philippines also: JAERRELANT del Mundo's Service Ventures, 1759 Almeda, Santa Cruz, Manila 2805, Philippines

DELOACH, CARTHA DEKLE, business executive; b. Claxton, Ga., July 20, 1920; s. Cartha Calhoun and Eula Mary (Dekle) DeL.; m. Barbara Owens, Apr. 22, 1945; children: Barbara Elaine, Cartha Dekle, Thomas O., Theresa M., Gregory D., Sharon Marie, Mark Christopher. B.A., Stetson U., 1942; student, Law Sch., 1941-42, J.D. (hon.), 1966; J.D. (hon.), Lincoln Coll., 1968. With FBI, 1942-70, asst. dir., 1959-65, asst. to dir., 1965-70; v.p. corporate affairs Pepsico, Inc., Purchase, N.Y., 1970-85; chmn. bd. Atlantic Savs. Bank, 1985—. Chmn. Cultural Council Hilton Head, S.C., Rep. Pary of Beaufort County, S.C.; chmn., pres. bd. dirs. J. Edgar Hoover Found., 1964—; bd. dirs. Banking Instns. Served with USN, 1944-46. Recipient Dist. Alumni award Stetson U., 1958; Pres.' Medal St. John's Coll., 1967; George Washington Honor medal Freedoms Found., 1967, 68, 69, 72; named Man of Year Nat. Assn. State Dirs. Vets. Affairs, 1964. Mem. Am. Legion (dept. comdr. 1958, nat. vice comdr. 1959, chmn. nat. pub. relations commn. 1959-78, Man of year award 1963), Stetson U. Alumni Assn. (dist. Alumnus award 1966), Knights of Malta, Pi Kappa Phi, Phi Alpha Delta. Home: 50 Gull Point Rd Hilton Head Island SC 29928

DEL OLMO LETE, GREGORIO, philologist, educator; b. Aranda de Duero, Spain, Apr. 17, 1935; s. Manuel Del Olmo and Celedonia Lete; m. Isabel Roura Romagosa, June 15, 1979. Lic., Pontifical Bibl. U., Rome, 1963; ThD, Pontifical U., Salamanca, Spain, 1969; D in Semitic Philology, Complutense U., Madrid, 1972. Asst. prof. Pontifical U., Salamanca, 1965-70; agregate prof. Cen. U., Barcelona, Spain, 1975-84, prof. Hebrew lang. and lit., 1984—. Author: La vocación del lider enant Israel, 1973, Mitos y Leyendas de Canaan, 1981, Interpretacion de la Mitologia Canaán, 1984; co-author El diwán de Yosef sbn Saddig, 1987; co-editor Los Fenicios en la Peninsula Ibérica, 1986, Semitistas Catalanes del siglo XVIII, 1988; jour. editor Aula Orientalis, 1983—. Recipient medal Coll. France, Paris, 1985; grantee Spanish Council Investigation, Barcelona, 1984-87. Mem. Assn. Biblica Española, Assn. Española de Orientalistas, World Union Jewish Studies, European Assn. Jewish Studies. Home: Valencia 3A 40 la, 08015 Barcelona Spain Office: Facultad Filologia Universidad, Gran Via 585, 08007 Barcelona Spain

DELON, ALAIN, actor; b. Sceaux, France, Nov. 8, 1935; s. Fabien and Edith (Arnold) D.; m. Francine-Nathalie Canovas, Aug. 13, 1964; 1 child, Anthony. Student, Cath. Boarding Sch., Bagneux, France. Motion picture appearances include Quand la Femme S'en Mele, 1957, Sois Belle et Tais-Toi, 1957, Faibles Femmes, 1958, Le Chemin des Ecoliers, 1959, Plein Soleil, 1959, Rocco et Ses Freres, 1960, Quelle Joie de Vivre, 1961, Les Amours Celebres, 1961, L'Eclisse, 1961, Le Diable et Les Dix Commandements, 1962, Le Guepard, 1962, Melodie en Sous Sol, 1962, La Tulipe Noire, 1963, Les Felins, 1963, L'Insoumis, 1964, La Rolls Royce Jaune, 1964, Once a Thief, 1964, Les Centurions, 1965, Paris Brule-T-Il?, 1965, Texas Across the River, 1966, Les Aventuriers, 1966, Le Samourai, 1967, Histoires Extraordinaires, 1967, Diaboliquement Votre 1967, Adieu l'ami, 1968, Girl on a Motorcycle, 1968, La Piscine, 1968, Jeff, 1968, Die Boss, Die Quietly, 1970, Borsaling, 1970, Le Cercle Rouge, 1971, Madly, 1971, Doucement Les Basses, 1971, Red Sun, 1971, La Veuve Coudac, 1971, Assassination of Trotsky, 1971, Le Professuer, 1972, Scorpio, 1972, Traitement de Choc, 1972, Les Granges Brulées, 1973, Big Guns, 1973, Deux Hommes dans La Ville, 1973, La Race des Seigneurs, 1973, Les Seins de Glace, 1974, Borsalino and C deg., 1974, Zorro, 1974, Flic Story, 1975, Le Gitan, 1975, Mr. Klein, 1975, Comme un Boomerang, 1976, Le Gang, 1976, Armaguedon, 1976, L'Homme Pressé, 1977, Mort d'un Pourri, 1977, Attention Les Enfants Regardent, 1977, Airport 80, 1979, Trois Hommes a Abattre, 1980, Pour La Peau d'un Flic, 1981, Le Choc, 1982, Le Battant, 1982, Un Amour de Swann, 1983, Notre Histoire, 1984, Parole de Flic, 1985, Le Passage, 1986; stage appearances include Tis Pity She's a Whore, 1961, 62, Les Yeux Creves, 1967. Served with French Marine Corps, 1953-55, Indo-China. Recipient Prix David de Donatello, Taormina Festival, 1972. Club: Monte Carlo Yachting. Address: 4 rue Chambiges, 75008 Paris France

DELORENZO, SUSAN SMITH, insurance company executive, transportation executive; b. Boston, June 8, 1945; d. W. Arthur and Jane (Cowan) Smith; m. Arthur E. DeLorenzo, June 26, 1965 (div. June 1973); children—Arthur E., Jr., Dana Leigh. A.A.S., Green Mountain Coll., 1965; student Onondaga Community Coll., 1968, 76, Syracuse U., 1976-78, Rochester Inst. Tech., 1978-80; profl. courses Solomon S. Hoebner Sch., Am. Coll., 1982—, Ryan Fin and Ins. Tng. Seminar, 1987. Lic. ins. rep. Paralegal, legal sec. Frank E. Visco, Cortland, N.Y., 1971-76; exec. sec. trust and investment Lincoln 1st Bank N.A., Syracuse, N.Y., 1976-78; personnel asst. Brewer-Titchener Corp., Cortland, 1978-80; regional life adminstr. U.S. Life Ins. Co., Syracuse, 1980-81; regional sales adminstr. Nat. Benefit Life Ins. Co., White Plains, N.Y., 1981-82, nat. dir. regional sales adminstrn., N.Y.C., 1982-84, asst. v.p., nat. dir. sales adminstrn., 1984-85; v.p. ops. Nat. Fin. Corp., Stamford, Conn., 1985-87, bus. mgr. Traynor Ford, Traynor Volkswagen-Pugeot & Trainer Motors, Inc., Brigeport, Fairfield, Conn., 1987—. Mem. Nat. Assn. Female Execs., Nat. Assn. Life Underwriters, Life Suprs. Assn., Nat. Orgn. for Women, Women Life Underwriters Conf. of NALU, Fairfield Network Exec. Women, Women in Mgmt. Home: 1001 Village Dr Brewster NY 10509 Office: Traynor Motors Inc 2269 Post Rd Fairfield CT 06430 also: 355 E Kings Hwy Fairfield CT 06430

DELORME, JACQUES, pediatrician; b. Antibes, France, Aug. 6, 1950; s. Georges and Odette (Bachelard) D.; m. Annie Merme, July 21, 1973; children: Arnaud, Xavier. MD, U. Marseille, 1973. Intern Martiques Hosp., France, 1975-78, attache de consultation en premier, 1979; practice medicine specializing in pediatrics Martiques, 1979—; charge d'enseignement clin. à la faculte Marseille, 1986—. V.p. Assn. des Parents d'eleve, Ecole de St. Pierre, Martiques, 1983-85, CES Pablo Picasso, Martiques, 1985—. Mem. Pediatrician Union. Roman Catholic. Home: Lavigne de la Gravade, 13500 Martiques Saint Pierre France Office: 10 rue Jean Roque, 13500 Martiques France

DE LOS REYES, JR. TELESFORO JAVELLANA, physician; b. Iloilo City, Philippines, May 7, 1932; s. Telesforo Eligio and Elena Matti (Javellana) de los R.; m. Erlinda Encanto Gelvezon, Jan. 27, 1963; children: Maria Elena, Telesforo III, Isabelo, Antonia Erlinda. MD, U. Santo Tomas, Manila, 1959. Resident Dr. Jose Locsin Meml. Hosp., Silay City, Philippines, 1961-63, Montelibano Meml. Regional Hosp., Bacolod City, Philippines, 1963-66; gen. practice medicine Bacolod City, 1966—; clinic physician Ma-ao Planters Assn., Bago City, 1966-85; retainer physician Social Security System Regional Office, Bacolod City, 1967—; co. physician 1st Farmers Milling Co., 1st Farmers Assn., Talisay, Philippines, 1968-82, Bormaheco, Inc., Bacolod City, 1970—, Negros Bottlers Inc., Bacolod City, 1970—; cons. dept. medicine Riverside Med. Ctr., Bacolod City, 1976—; head med. dept. Azucar Mgmt. and Devel. Corp., Bacolod City, 1987—. Recipient recognition award U. Santo Tomas Alumni Assn., 1980; named Outstanding Thomasian, 1986. Fellow Phillipine Acad. Family Physicians (bd. dirs. 1972-82), Philippine Occupational and Indsl. Med. Assn. (diplomate, pres. 1976-82, Most Outstanding Pres. award 1982); life mem. Philippine Med. Assn. (dist. councilor Western Visayas 1975-76, community service award 1974, plaque of honor 1976), Negros Occidental Med. Soc. (pres. 1974, Most Outstanding Physician award 1974); mem. Philippine Assn. Mil. Surgeons. Roman Catholic. Lodge: Lions (pres. Bacolod City 1971-72, zone chmn. 1972-73, dep. dist. gov. 1973-74, cabinet treas. 1976-77, dist. gov. 1984-85, dist. gov.'s leadership award 1985). Home: Henrietta Village, Bacolod City 6001, Philippines Office: Philamlife Bldg, Suite 2, Galo St, Bacolod City 6001, Philippines

DELOST, FRANK PETER, medical electronics company executive; b. Toronto, Ont., Can., Sept. 8, 1946; s. Frank and Donna Marie (Ropac) D.; m. Margaret Jane Godsoe, Dec. 27, 1973 (div. 1988); 1 child, Derek; m. Candace Lorraine Graham, Aug. 1988; children: Margie, jeff, Peter. Student, Kent State U., 1966-68, Ryerson Poly. Inst., Toronto, 1968-70, City U., Vancouver, B.C., Can., 1981-83. Pres. Delwood Electronics Ltd., Vancouver, 1975—, also bd. dirs.; sales mgr. Bard Can. Inc., Mississauga, Ont., 1976-86; v.p. Techlem Med. Systems Inc., Mississauga, 1986—, also bd. dirs.; bd. dirs. A.T.G. Healthcare Products, Mississauga; cons. Wasteco Sanitation, Willowdale, Ont., 1983—. Mem. Can. Med. Mfrs. Assn., Can. Mfrs. Assn., Mississauga C. of C. Roman Catholic. Clubs: Hollyburn Country (West Vancouver); Balmy Beach (Toronto), Meadowvale Racquet.

DELPHIN, JACQUES MERCIER, psychiatrist; b. Cap Haitien, Haiti, Apr. 26, 1929; s. Alexander and Sonia (Bernadin) D.; came to U.S., 1959, naturalized, 1972; B.S., Lycee Nat. Phillipe Guerrier, 1950; M.D., Faculty Medicine Port-au-Prince, Haiti, 1957; m. Marlene Lavitola Mastroti, Aug. 26, 1967; children—Patrick, Barthold, Beverly, Miriam, Matthew, Janice. Intern, St. Luke's Hosp., Newburgh, N.Y., 1960; resident in psychiatry Hudson River Psychiat. Center, Poughkeepsie, N.Y., 1961-64; dir. psychiat. day hosp. Hudson River State Hosp., Poughkeepsie, N.Y., 1966-69; dir. psychiat. day hosp. Community Mental Health Center, Poughkeepsie, 1969-74, now supervising psychiatrist; attending physician St. Francis Hosp., Poughkeepsie, 1968—; med. dir. Mother Cabrini Home, West Park, N.Y., 1974—; practice medicine specializing in psychiatry, Poughkeepsie, 1968—. Commr., Dutchess County Dept. Mental Hygiene, Poughkeepsie, 1973-74. Fellow Am. Psychiat. Assn. (pres. Mid-Hudson br. 1974-76). Republican. Roman Catholic. Kiwanian (dir. Poughkeepsie 1968). Author: Chants du Passe, poems, 1951; Rythmes et Fleurs, poems, 1953; Une Robe au Destin Librarie Garneau, 1972. Home: Schutzvill Rd Clinton Corners NY 12541 Office: Community Mental Health Ctr 230 North Rd Poughkeepsie NY 12601 also: 84 Haight Ave Poughkeepsie NY 12603

DELPORTE, ANTOON GUSTAAF, architect; b. Harelbeke, West Vlaanderen, Belgium, Sept. 2, 1923; arrived in India, 1946; s. George Gaston and Marguerite Alice (Kimpe) D. MPhil, S.H. Coll., Shembaganur, India, 1949; M of Theology, S.M. Coll., Kurseong, India, 1956; diploma in architecture, AA Sch. Architecture, London, 1973. Prin. St. Joseph High Sch., Torpa, India, 1958-59, St. Xavier High Sch., Doranda, India, 1960-62; social worker Cath. Ch., Lohardaga, India, 1962-70; architect Ranchi (India) Jesuit Soc. and Cath. Archdiocese, 1974—. Works include numerous health and community ctrs., homes and schs. Mem. Architectes Sans Frontieres. Roman Catholic. Home and Studio: Manresa House, Purulia Rd, Ranchi Bihar, India 834001

DEL POZO VEINTIMILLA, LUIS GUILLERMO, hospital administrator; b. Quito, Ecuador, Feb. 23, 1954; s. Guillermo Del Pozo Sierra and Julia Veintimilla Palacios; m. Maria Meza, Apr. 12, 1986; 1 child, Guillermo Andres. MD, Central U., 1978; cert. in cardiology, Japan Cardiovascular Ctr., 1983. Assoc. prof. Nat. U., Loja, Ecuador, 1979-82; dir. Hosp.-Health Ctr. Vilcabamba, Loja, 1980—; cardiovascular researcher WHO, 1983—. Pres. Vilcabamba Com. Pro. Library and Kindergarten, 1979, Vilcabamba Community Devel. Com., 1980, Nat. Reconstrn. Front, Vilcabamba, 1984, Vilcabamba Pro Aging Def. Assn., 1986. Roman Catholic. Lodge: Rotary. Home and Office: Vilcabamba, PO Box 801, Loja Ecuador

DELPUECH, JEAN-JACQUES, chemistry educator; b. Sumene, Gard, France, Sept. 6, 1934; s. Raymond Roger and Jeanne Antonie (Vivens) D.; m. Annie Coubris, Sept. 15, 1954; children—Alain, Sylvie. Student, Ecole Nat. Superieure des Industries Chimiques, Nancy, 1954-57; M.Sc., U. Nancy, 1956; Professorship, Ecole Normale Superieure, Paris, 1958, Thesis, 1965. Research worker Centre National de la Recherche Scientifique, France, 1960-62; asst. Ecole Normale Superieure, Paris, 1962-66; asst. prof. U. Grenoble, France, 1966-68; prof. chemistry U. Nancy, France, 1968—; dir. Laboratoire de Chimie Physique Organique, U. Nancy and Centre National de la Recherche Scientifique, France, 1970. Author: Practical NMR Spectroscopy, 1980; (with M.L. and G.J. Martin): NMR of Newly Accessible Nuclei, 1984. Contbr. articles on chemistry and spectroscopy to profl. jours. Patentee in field. Mem. nat. com. Centre National de la Recherche Scientifique, Paris, 1975-80, 80-83, 87—, Conseil Nat. des Universités, 1987—. Served with French Air Force, 1958-60. Recipient Chevalier Palmes Academiques, French Ministry of Edn.; officer Palmes Academiques; recipient Bronze medal Centre National de la Recherche, 1966, Silver medal, 1975. Mem. Am. Chem. Soc., Societe Chimique de France, Chem. Soc. Gt. Britain, Societe de Chimie Physique. Home: 16 Rue du Plateau, F-54520 Laxou France Office: Laboratoire de Chimie Physique, Organique, U de Nancy 1, 54506 Vandoeuvre-les-Nancy Cedex BP 239, France

DEL RENZIO, TONI ROMANOV, art critic; b. Tsarskoe, Selo, Russia, Apr. 15, 1915; s. Antonio Carlo and Nina Mariia (Romanova) Del R.; m. Doris Lilian Miller, Dec. 13, 1971; children: (quadruplets) Lydia Maria Eugenia, Tamara Xenia Antonina, Ivan Carlo Agostino, PlerLuigi Alessandro. Illustrator various places, 1937-40; art editor Nat. Trade Press, 1948-51; prin. lectr. art Canterbury Coll. Art, Eng., 1975—. Contbr. articles to profl. jours.

DEL RIEGO DE DEL CASTILLO, LILIA, mathematician; b. Mexico City, June 11, 1948; d. Antonio and Lilia (Senior) Del Riego; m. Luis del Castillo, Sept. 26, 1969; children: Guillermo, Cecilia, Alejandro. MS in Math., U. Nat. Autónoma de México, 1969; PhD, U. Med. et Scientifique de Grenoble, France, 1973. Prof. math., sci. faculty U. Nat. Autónoma de México, Mexico City, 1973-75; researcher Inst. de Math. U. Nat. Autónoma de México, 1974-75; prof. math. U. Autónoma Metropolitana, Mexico City, 1975-86; vis. prof. U. de Yucatán, Mérida, 1982-83; vis. researcher Inst. Fourier, Grenoble, 1983. Contbr. articles to profl. jours. Mem. Soc. Matemática Mexicana, Am. Math. Soc., Assn. Women in Math., Capitulo Mérida Soc. Mexicana de Computación en la Educación (pres.). Office: Centro de Inv Cientifica, de Yucatan Apartado, Postal 87, 97310 Cordemex Mexico

DEL SANTO, LAWRENCE A., retail merchandising company executive; b. 1934; married. B.S., U. San Francisco, 1955. With Household Merchandising Inc., Des Plaines, Ill., from 1957, with advt. dept. subs. Vons Grocery Co., 1957-58, asst. advt. mgr., 1958-61, advt. mgr., 1961-68, mgr. sales and mdse., 1968-71, sr. v.p., 1971-73, pres., chief exec. officer, 1973-75, corp. sr. v.p., 1975-79, exec. v.p., from 1979, also bd. dirs.; exec. v.p. Lucky Stores Inc., Dublin, Calif., to 1986, pres., 1986—, also bd. dirs. Served with U.S. Army, 1955-57. Office: Lucky Stores Inc 6300 Clark Ave Dublin CA 94568 *

DELTOMBES, PHILIPPE GEORGES, engineering company executive, educator; b. Paris, Oct. 31, 1947; s. Jacques Arthur and Marie Antoinette (Delasalle) D.; m. Aline Helene Lespes, Aug. 17, 1977; 1 child, Valerie Francoise. Diploma ESME Engring., Paris, 1972. Registered profl. engr., France. Engr. Tex. Instrument Co., Paris, 1973-77, sales controller, 1977-80; strategic planning mgr. Thomson CSF Telecom, Paris, 1980-84; mktg. dir. Thomson SemiCondrs., 1984—; prof. indsl. engring. Paris Dauphine U., 1983—. Home: 3 Blvd des Jeux Olympiques, 78000 Versailles Yvelines, France Office: SGS Thomson, 7 Ave Galieni, 94253 Gentilly France

DEL TORO, ILIA, retired teacher, educator; b. Ponce, P.R., July 17, 1918; d. Gerardo Gabriel and Angela (Robledo) del T. B.A., U. P.R., Rio Piedras, 1940; M.A. in Edn., N.Y. U., 1958. Elem. tchr. State Dept. Instruction, 1941-44; tchr. high sch. social studies, 1944-57; instr. high sch. social studies, Coll. Edn., U. P.R., 1957-59; officer external resources, 1975-76, assoc. prof., 1979-86, coordinator student teaching, 1979-86, supr. student teaching, methods in high sch. social studies, edn. sociology, elem. edn. in social studies, curriculum and teaching dept., 1959-81, coordinator Inst. Family Fin., 1962-69, coordinator EPDA/U.S. Project, 1970-75. Puerto Rican del. to Edith Macy Girl Scout Camp, 1947; v.p. Liceo Ponceñ o North Zone Ex Alumnae Chpt. Mem. Assn. Supervision and Curriculum Devel. (nat. bd.), Assn. Tchr. Educators., Nat. Council Social Studies, NEA, P.R. Tchr. Assn., Assn. Tchr. Educators (pres. Puerto Rican chpt.), Future World Soc., Smithsonian Instn., Phi Delta Kappa (pres. of ceremonials, 1978, 84-85, outstanding educator, San Juan chpt. Diamond Jubilee, 1981), Delta Kappa Gamma (state founder, 1976, chpt. pres., 1978-80, state pres. 1983-85, Golden Gift Fund scholar Leadership/Mgmt. seminar Exec. Devel. Ctr. U. Ill. 1983-85, mem. internat. exec. com., mem. state bd. 1987—). Roman Catholic. Contbr. papers in field. Home: 506 Parque de Las Fuentes Hato Rey PR 00918

DE LUBAC, HENRI SONIER CARDINAL, theologian, writer; b. Cambrai Nord, France, Feb. 20, 1896; s. Maurice Sonier de Lubac and Gabrielle de Beaurepaire. Hon. degree, U. Notre Dame, South Bend, Ind., Cath. U. Chile, Univ. Innsbruck, Austria. Prof. Cath. theology U. Lyon, France, 1929-61; created Cardinal 1983; Deacon St. Maria in Dominica, 1984—. Author: Catholicisme, 1938, Corpus Mysticum, 1944, Proudhon et le Christianisme, 1945, Le Fondement Theologique des Missions, 1946, Surnaturel, 1946, Histoire et Esprit, 1950, Aspect du Bouddhisme, 2 vols., 1951, 55, Rencontre du Bouddhisme et de l'Occident, 1952, Meditation sur l'Eglise, 1953, Nouveau Paradoxes, 1955, Sur les Chemins de Dieu, 1956, Exégèse Médiévale, 4 vols., 1959-64, La Pensee Religieuse du Père Teilhard de Chardin, 1962, La Prière du Père Teilhard de Chardin, 1964, L'Eglise dans La Crise Actuelle, 1969, La Structure du Symbole des Apôtres, 1971, Teilhard et Notre Temps, 1971, Les Eglises Particulieres dans L'Eglise Universelle, 1972, Dieu Se Dit Dans L'Histoire, 1974, Pic de la Mirandole, 1975, Teilhard Posthume--Reflexions et Souvenirs, 1977, La Postérité Spirituelle de Joachim de Flore, 1979, La Revélation Divine, 1983, Théologie D'Occasion, 1984, Correspondance Commentee entre G. Marcel et G. Fessard, 1985, Entretien autour de Vatican II, 1985, Lettres de M. Etienne Gilson au P. de Lubac, 1986. Served with French Armed Forces, 1914-18. Decorated Légion d'Honneur, Croix d'Guerre. Mem. Acad. Moral Sci. and Politics. Home: 42 rue de Grenelle, 75007 Paris France *

DE LUCA, ANTHONY JAMES, psychoanalyst, theologian; b. N.Y.C.; s. James Carl and Antoinette (Scarano) DeL.; B.A., St. John's U., 1957; S.T.B., Catholic U. Am., 1961; B.S., Queens Coll., 1963; M.A., Fordham U., 1965; Ph.D., 1971; M.A., St. John's U., 1973; cert. in psychoanalysis and psychotherapy Postgrad. Center Mental Health, 1975. Asst. prof. philosophy and psychology Notre Dame Coll., N.Y.C., 1967-71, Fordham U., N.Y.C., 1972-73; exec. dir Am. Inst. for Creative Living Inc., Bklyn., S.I., N.Y., Morrisville, Pa., and East Brunswick, N.J., 1972—; assoc. pastor Bklyn Diocese, Roman Catholic Ch., 1961-67, cons. Marriage Tribunal, 1967—; chaplain to students Fedn. Christian Ministries; dean Internat. Sch. for Mental Health Practitioners, S.I. and Pa.; cons. N.Y.C. Police Dept., 1980—; dean Internat. Sch. Mental Health Practitioners, Morrisville, Pa. Mem. S.I. Mental Health Council, 1975—. Lic. psychologist, Pa., marriage counselor, N.J., sch. psychologist, N.Y., N.J. Fellow Am. Orthopsychiat. Assn.; mem. Am. Psychol. Assn., Am. Philos. Assn., Am. Sociol Assn., Am. Group Psychotherapy Assn., Am. Assn. Marriage and Family Therapists (supr.), Am. Found Religion and Psychiatry, N.Y. Soc. Clin. Psychologists, Am. Assn Psychoednl Therapists (adv. bd.), Council Register Health Providers in Psychology. Author: Freud and Future Religious Experience, 1976. Home: 2295 Victory Blvd Staten Island NY 10314 also: 78 N Pennsylvania Ave Morrisville PA 19067

DELUCCHI, GEORGE PAUL, accountant; b. Richmond, Calif., Apr. 20, 1938; s. George Carl and Rose Caroline (Golino) D. BA, San Jose State U., 1959. Ptnr. Delucchi, Swanson & Co., Santa Clara, Calif., 1968-74, Delucchi, Swanson & Sandival, Santa Clara, 1974-76, Delucchi, Sandoval & Co., Santa Clara, 1976-77, Wolf & Co., San Jose, Calif., 1977-78; v.p. Lautze & Lautze, San Jose, 1978-82, also bd. dirs.; sr. ptnr. G.P. Delucchi & Assocs. (name changed to Delucchi, Robinson, Streit & Co., Santa Clara, 1982—. Treas. Crippled Children Soc., San Jose, 1967-71, San Jose Catholic Social Service, 1986—, F. Schmidt Found. for Youth; bd. dirs. Serra Med. Found., Mission City Community Fund; pres. Santa Clara Police Activity League, 1977-78; bd. fellows Santa Clara U., 1975—. Served to lt. U.S. Army, 1959-62. Mem. Am. Inst. CPA's, Calif. Soc. CPA's. Republican. Roman Catholic. Club: Sainte Claire (San Jose), Civic. Lodges: Elks (Santa Clara exalted ruler 1969-70). Rotary (bd. dirs. Santa Clara chpt. 1986—). Home: 774 Circle Dr Santa Clara CA 95050 Office: 2075 De La Cruz Blvd #200 Santa Clara CA 95050

DELUCCIA, EMIL ROBERT, civil engineer; b. Brighton, Mass., Sept. 20, 1904; s. Emil James and Edna Laura (Hewes) de L.; m. Margaret McCutcheon, Jan. 16, 1932; children: Margaret Crichton, Jane Hewes. BS in Civil Engring, Mass. Inst. Tech., 1927. Registered profl. engr., D.C., Oreg. Surveyman and transitman Met. Water Supply Commn., Enfield, Mass., 1927-29; engr. designer Stone and Webster Engring. Corp., 1929-31; engr. insp. and designer U.S. Engr. Office, Charleston, W.Va., 1931-33; asso. engr. and chief of design sect. U.S. Engr. Office, Huntington, W.Va., 1933-38, FPC, 1938-51; gen. engring. cons. and mgr. Yale hydroelectric project and others Pacific Power & Light Co., 1951, v.p., chief engr., 1952-66, sr. v.p., 1966-69; pres. Oreg. Grad. Center, 1969-72; cons. engr. 1969—; v.p. Overseas Adv. Assos., Inc., 1973—; sr. engr. cons. on dams and hydroelectric projects 1938-40; chief, power supply br. Nat. Def. Power staff, 1940-41; asst. dir. Nat. Def. Power staff and asst. chief Bur. of Elec. Engring. (also cons. on power to OPM and WPB), chief Bur. of Power, 1944—; head group econ. and energy studies South Vietnam, 1971-72, 74-75; U.S. del. Internat. Conf. on High Dams, Stockholm, 1948, Internat. Conf. on High Tension Elec. Systems, Paris, 1948; chief U.S. delegation Internat. Conf. High Tension Lines, Paris, 1950; U.S. del. World Power Conf., London, Eng., 1950; U.S. ofcl. Negotiation Treaty with Canada for division of water at Niagara Falls; cons. to UN, Japan, 1961, AEC, Nat. Security Resources Bd.; chmn. Internat. Passamaquoddy Bd. Engrs., U.S. Com. on Large Dams; mem. Tech. Indsl. Disarmament Com. for German and Japan Elec. Power Industry; vice-chmn. bd. dirs. Oreg. AAA. Contbr. to Ency. Brit., Ency. Americana. Served with ROTC, Mass. Inst. Tech.; 2d lt. ORC, 1927; commd. capt. and advanced through grades to lt. col. AUS, 1942-45; with SHEAF, 1944, ETO; ret. as lt. col. ORC, 1956. Decorated medal of merit Legion of Merit; medal of Merit 1st class South Vietnam; named Oreg. Engr. of Year, 1962; recipient Aubrey R. Watzek award Lewis and Clark Coll., 1986. Fellow IEEE, ASCE; mem. Soc. Am. Mil. Engrs. (dir., recipient Goethals medal award 1963), AIM, VFW, Am. Geophys. Union, Am. Legion, Internat. Assn. High Tension Lines, Internat. Assn. Hydraulic Research, Internat. Assn. Large Dams, Am. Automobile Assn. Clubs: Army-Navy Country (Arlington, Va.); Cosmos (Washington); Arlington, University, Waverly Country (Portland). Lodges: Masons (Ware, Mass.); Shriners. Home: 1275 S Skyland Dr Lake Oswego OR 97034

DE LUCE, VIRGINIA, entertainer; b. San Francisco, Mar. 25, 1921. Attended Bishop-Lee Sch. of Theatre, Beacon Hill, Boston, Mass. Model John Roberts Powers, Harry Conover; dir. New Wrinkle Theatre; actress 20th Century Fox Film Corp., Columbia Pictures, Paramount Pictures, also commercials; pres. Soc. Prodns., Cosmic Sci. Inst., Earth Jazz, Texloid Products. Actress: (musicals and plays) including Kiss Me Kate, Brigadoon,

Can Can, Pal Joey, Will Success Spoil Rock Hunter, Twelfth Night, Emperor Jones, Pygmalion and Galatea, White Iris, Leave It To Psmith, The Sacrifice, Bonanza, The Beggars' Opera, (Broadway play) Who Was That Lady, (musical revues) Vaudeville at Palace Theatre, New Faces at Royale Theatre, Chic at Orpheum Theatre, Billy Barnes' Rev. at Carnegie Hall, Have A Heart at Madison Sq. Garden; producer: (concert) Blue Dove's Many Feathers; appeared in hotel shows and cabarets including Ritz Carlton Hotel, Montreal, Can., Le Cabaret, Toronto, Can., Copacobana Palace, Rio De Janeiro, Brazil, Copacobana, N.Y.C., Comedy Club, N.Y.C., Twelfth Night Club, N.Y.C., Waldorf Astoria, N.Y.C., Biltmore Bowl, Los Angeles, Golden Horseshoe, Disneyland, Calif., Hotel Roosevelt, New Orleans, Scotch and Sirloin, Los Angeles, #1 Fifth Avenue, N.Y.C., Di Maggio's Yacht Club, San Francisco, Leon & Eddie's, N.Y.C., The Ballroom, N.Y.C., Mayfair, Boston, Pirates' Den, Hollywood, Calif., Trocadero, Hollywood, House of Vienna, N.Y.C., Blue Angel, N.Y.C., Lambs' Club, N.Y.C.; advance "man" for Spike Jones Orch., Coast to Coast Tour; appearances in TV shows including Play of the Week (NTA), Repetoire Workshop, Tonight Show, Sgt. Bilko series, others, also radio shows, local and network telethons; appeared in rodeos Leo Carillo, Roy Rogers Rodeos, Coliseum, Los Angeles; author, composer: The Boston Nod, (scripts, songs and poetry) Dallas Sal, Spider, Give All His Love to Her, Great Sun, Victory, Making Up-Silent Song, Pow Wow Smile, Saga of Jini, When Love is Near, The Thorns of Summer; author: Your Own Voice, My Learning Path, Crystal Gazing Lessons, Your Heart's Desire, Lucky Break; creator astrological paintings, datascope, delineations, Dog-O-Scope, Cat-O-Scope; also painter, fashion designer and songwriter. Mem. Rep. Town Com., Weston, Mass.; alt. Senator Silver Haired Legis., Mass.; asst. to mgr. Eisenhower-Nixon Bandwagon Hdqtrs., N.Y.C.; creator theme, chmn. entertainment Inaugural Ball Pres. Nixon; asst. coordinator, dir. pub. relations Mass. Satellite Inaugural Ball for Pres. Reagan, 1980; precinct dir. Re-elect Pres. Reagan, 1984; coordinator Dr. Richard A. Jones for Senator campaign, Weston; speaker, writer LWV Candidate Night; apptd. election officer Town of Weston, also apptd. fence viewer; author Mass. Legis. House bills; bd. dirs. Arts and Crafts Assn.; mem. Environment Task Force, Mass.; past mem. numerous other civic orgns., bds.; vol. worker, performer for charities. Named to Times Square Hall of Fame; recipient Theatre World award, Yale U. Drama Salute. Mem. Am. Guild Variety Artists, Screen Actors' Guild, Actor's Equity Assn., AFTVRA, Franklin County C. of C., Am. Legion, Mass. Fedn. Rep. Women (bd. dirs.), Nat. Rifle Assn., Gun Owners' League, Am. Fedn. Astrologers, Gun Owners' Action League (past treas. Los Angeles chpt.), Am. Indian Movement (former treas. Los Angeles chpt.), U.S Coast Guard Womens' Aux.

DELUCIA, GENE ANTHONY, government administrator, computer company executive; b. Methuen, Mass., Feb. 20, 1952; s. Antonio Gitano and Carmen Theresa (Carpenito) DeL. B.S., Boston Coll., 1973; M.B.A., Northeastern U., 1980. Project mgr. Delphi div. Arthur D. Little Inc., Lowell, Mass., 1975-78, gen. mgr., eastern region, 1978-80; systems devel. mgr. Wang Labs. Inc., Lowell, 1980-82, computer technician mgr., 1982-83; asst. to commr. Dept. Pub. Welfare, Boston, 1983-86; pres., chief exec. officer Computer Innovations Inc., Lowell, 1983-86; pres., Corp. Investment Bus. Brokers, North Andover, Mass., 1986-88; v.p. Maximus Inc., Falls Church, Va., 1988—. Treas., St. Lucy's Catholic Youth Orgn., Methuen, 1968, pres., 1969; mem. St. John's Men's Guild, Lowell, 1980—. Mem. Data Processing Mgmt. Assn. Democrat. Avocations: skiing; running; racquetball; electronics. Home: 24 Winsor Park Rd Lowell MA 01852 Office: Maximus Inc 125 Technology Dr 4th Floor Wortham MA 02154

DELUMEAU, JEAN, religion educator; b. Nantes, France, June 18, 1923; s. Leon and Claire (Seguinaud) D.; m. Jeanny Le Goff, Sept. 2, 1947; children: Jean-Pierre, Marie-Christine, Jean-Christophe. Student, Agrege d'Histoire, 1947, Ecole Francaise, Rome, 1948-50; DLitt, U. Paris, 1955. Prof. faculty of letters U. Rennes, France, 1955-70; prof. U. Pantheon-Sorbonne, Paris, 1970-74, Coll. de France, Paris, 1974—. Author: Le Christianisme va-t-il Mourir?, 1977, La Peur en Occident, 1978, La Peche et la Peur, 1983, La Cas Luther, 1983, Ce Que Je Crois, 1985. Home: 29 Rue des Lauriers, 35510 Cesson-Sevigne France Office: Coll de France, 11 Place Marcelin Berthlot, Cedex5, 75231 Paris France

DE LUQUE, ORLANDO RAFAEL, biochemistry educator, researcher; b. Riohacha, Colombia, Mar. 18, 1933; came to U.S., 1961; s. Alfredo De Luque and Maria Francisca Rosado; m. Edith Andrade, Dec. 16, 1958; children—Mabel, Orlando, Ivette, Sandra. B.S., Nat. U., 1959; M.A., So. Ill. U., 1964; Ph.D., U. R.I., 1969. Research asst. So. Ill. U., Carbondale, 1961-62; postdoctoral fellow U. Conn., Farmington, 1969-71; vis. prof. CIEA Poly. Inst., Mexico City, 1973-74; prof. Zulia U., Maraciabo, Venezuela, 1978-84; prof. biochemistry Inter Am. U., Arecibo, P.R., 1984-86, cons., 1983—; prof. biochemistry Ponce (P.R.) Sch. Medicine, 1986—. Contbr. articles to profl. jours. Fellow Rockefeller Found., 1962-64, Conn. Heart Assn., 1969; Nat. U. scholar, 1955, U. R.I. scholar, 1967. Mem. Am. Chem. Soc., AAAS, Phi Sigma. Roman Catholic. Office: Inter Am U of PR PO Box UI Arecibo PR 00613

DELVALLE HENRIQUEZ, ERIC ARTURO, former president of Panama; b. Panama, Republic of Panama, Feb. 2, 1933; m. Mariela Diaz; children: Mariela, Eric Antonio, Lourdes del Carmen. Student, Collegio Javier, 1948-53, La. State U., 1953-56. Past pres. several bus., Panama; 1st v.p. Panama, to 1985, pres., 1985—. Mem. Industrialist Syndicate of Panama, Panamanian Assn. Bus. Execs. *

DEL VECCHIO, MARY ANN, language professional, educator; b. Cortland, N.Y., Aug. 8, 1956; d. Ardin Mario and Frances (Romano) Del V.; m. George Nocolas El-Hage, Aug. 18, 1979. BA, State U. Coll., Cortland, 1977; MA, Cornell U., 1982, postgrad., 1978—. Cert. tchr. N.Y. Bilingual tester State U. Coll., 1975-76, translator, 1974-76; italian teaching asst. Cornell U., Ithaca, N.Y., 1979-81; English instr. Lebanese U., Fanar, Lebanon, 1981-83, Am. U. of Beirut, Lebanon, 1983; systems engr. IBM, Monterey, Calif., 1984—; lectr. Cornell U., 1980, Columbia U., 1979, Middlebury (Vt.) Coll., 1978; bibliographer Panorama de l'actualite, Beirut, 1981. Vol. Am. Cancer Assn., Cortland, 1970, Cystic Fibrosis Assn., Cortland, 1969; tchr. St. Anthony's Cath. Ch., Cortland, 1974-77. Nat. French Honor Soc. scholar, State U. Coll., 1977, Presdl. scholar, 1977; research grantee Cornell U., 1978. Mem. Modern Lang. Assn., Nat. Assn. Tchrs. of Italian. Club: Italian (Ithaca).

DELWART, JEAN-MARIE, chemical company executive; b. LaTeste de, France, Apr. 30, 1940; s. Jean and Marie (Taymans) D.; m. Janine DeGryse, July 2, 1967; children—Nathalie, Olivia, Charles-Emmanuel. M. Chemistry, U. Louvain (Belgium), 1963, B. Philosophy, 1959. Product mgr. Owens-Corning Fiberglas Europe, Brussels, Belgium, 1966-69; mng. dir. Floridienne S.A., Brussels, 1970-80, chmn., 1980—; chmn. Biotec S.A., Brussels, 1975—. Avocation: tennis. Home: ave Louise 479, 1050 Brussels Belgium Office: Floridienne SA, Ave Louise 479 Box 45, 1050 Brussels Belgium

DELYANNIS, LEONIDAS THEODORE, engineer; b. Athens, Greece, Nov. 8, 1926; came to U.S., 1957, naturalized, 1963; s. Theodore L. and Xanthi (Mamouri-Goura) D.; B.S., Greek Mil. Acad., 1947; B.S., Greek Tech. Mil. Coll., 1954; M.S., U. Ill., 1958; m. Georgia H. Alexander, Feb. 21, 1957; children—Theodore, Harry-Michael. Chief structural engr. Ben. Dyer & Assos., Hyattsville, Md., 1958-60; chief bridge engr. David Volkert & Assocs., Washington, 1960-70; pres. L.T. Delyannis & Assocs., Arlington, Va., 1970—; program chmn. Internat. Symposium on Concrete Bridge Design, Toronto, Ont., Can., 1967, Chgo., 1969; chmn. dist. adv. council SBA, 1980-82; mem. Va. Bd. Geology, 1981-82. Mem. Arlington County Planning Commn., 1976-80; mem. inaugural com. for Nixon-Agnew Inauguration, 1968, 72; alt. del. Republican Nat. Conv., 1972, 76; chmn. Va. Rep. Nationalities Council, 1970-76; bd. dirs. Arlington Dance Theater, 1973-77. Registered profl. engr., Ala., Md., Va. D.C. Mem. ASCE, Nat. Soc. Profl. Engrs., Am. Concrete Inst. (com. on concrete bridge design), Am. Hellenic Inst. (sec.-treas.), Soc. Am. Mil. Engrs., Am. Concrete Inst., Internat. Assn. for Bridge and Structural Engring, AHEPA. Mem. Greek Orthodox Ch. Clubs: Republican Capitol Hill (life); Washington Golf and Country. Contbr. papers to tech. lit. Home: 2769 N Randolph St Arlington VA 22207 Office: 3030 Clarendon Blvd Arlington VA 22201

DE MAEYER, EDWARD, virologist; b. Mechelen, Belgium, June 4, 1932; s. Pieter Jan. and Maria Louisa (Van Aken) De M.; M.D., U. Louvain, 1957; Agrege de l'Enseignement Superieur, 1964; m. Jaqueline Guignard, June 3, 1961. Research fellow Children's Hosp., Boston and Harvard U., 1958-60; research asso. Rockefeller Inst., 1960-61; lectr. virology U. Louvain (Belgium), 1961-65; maitre de recherche CNRS, France, 1966-74, dir., 1975—; chef Laboratoire Institut Curie; tchr. microbiology Pasteur Inst. Fulbright fellow, 1958-61; Prix Antoine Lacassagne de la Ligue Nationale Francaise Contre le Cancer, 1988. Lederle Internat. fellow, 1959-60; recipient Jean-Louis Camus prize, Paris, 1971, Prix Gaston Rousseau de l'Academie des Sciences, Paris, 1976, Soc. de Microbiologie Francaise. Mem. Socié té de Microbiologie Franç aise, Am. Soc. Microbiology, Am. Assn. Immunologists, AAAS, Internat. Soc. for Interferon Research (pres. 1984, 85), Sigma Xi. Contbr. numerous articles to sci. jours. Home: 34 Ave Saint Laurent, 91400 Orsay France Office: Inst Curie Bât, 110 Centre Universitaire, 91405 Orsay France

DEMANET, JEAN-CLAUDE, medical educator, internist; b. Waterloo, Brabant, Belgium, Feb. 26, 1930; s. Leon and Simone (Paret) D.; m. Anne Bastenie; children—Marie, Helene. M.D., Free U. Brussels, 1954, Ph.D. in Medicine (hon.), 1967. Asst. physician Univ. Hosp., Leiden, Netherlands, 1955, Hopital Cantonal, Geneva, 1957-58; asst. physician St. Pierre Hosp., Brussels, 1958-62, staff physician, 1962-70, chief internal medicine and hypertension, 1971—; prof. medicine Free U. Brussels, 1971—, researcher exptl. lab. medicine, 1952-55, 58-67; cons. physician in cardiology and medicine Civil Hosp., Vilvoorde, Belgium, 1962-70; chmn. postgrad. teaching in internal medicine U. Brussels, 1978—. Contbr. numerous articles on hypertension, nephrology, water and electrolytes metabolism and clin. medicine to med. publs. Expert mem. Belgian and Benelux Drug Adminstrn., Brussels, 1970—. Served to comdr M.C., Belgian Army, 1955-56. Decorated officer Ordre de Leopold II (Belgium). Mem. Academie Royale de Medecine de Belgique (corr.), Belgian Hypertension Com. (founder-mem.; pres. 1976-80), Internat. Soc. Hypertension, Internat. Soc. Nephrology, Belgian Soc. Internal Medicine, Collège des Médecins de l'Agglomé ration Bruxelloise (pres. 1984-88). Club: Fondation Universitaire (Brussels). Home: 51 rue d'Alconval, 1420 Braine l'Alleud, Brabant Belgium Office: Clinique Medicale, Hosp St Pierre, 322 rue Haute, 1000 Brussels Belgium

DEMANGINUWE, ROY DEGOROGORE, federal official; b. Feb. 6, 1922; s. Demanginuwe Areri Deminginuwe and Eibarere (Magdalena) Aurob. Student, Nauru Tech. Sch. Mgr. The Royal Store, Nauru, 1936—; mem. parlaiment Republic Nauru, 1968-80, 83—. Councillor Nauru Local Govt., 1951—. Democrat. Roman Catholic. Home: Akwida Valley, House #7, Anetan Nauru Office: Royal Store, PO Box 308, Anetan South Pacific, Nauru

DE MARCO, GUIDO, government official; b. Valletta, Malta, July 22, 1931; s. Emmanuel and Giovanna (Raniolo) De M.; m. Violet Saliba, 1956; children: Mario, Giannella, Fiorella. BA in Econs., Philosophy, and Italian, St. Aloysius Coll., 1952; LLD, Royal U. of Malta, 1955. Apptd. Crown Counsel Republic of Malta, 1964-66, elected parliament mem., 1971, 76, 81, 87; parliamentary spokesman for Nationalist Party, Justice and Parliamentary Affairs Com., 1973—; elected sec. gen. Nationalist Party, Malta, 1973-77; elected dep. leader Nationalist Party, 1977, 82; dep. prime minister Republic of Malta, 1987—, minister interior and justice, 1987—; rep. Maltese Parliament in Council of Europe Parliamentary Assembly, 1967—, v.p. rules and procedures com. Pres. Students Rep. Council, 1953, editor Encounter and Leader orgns. Nationalist Youth Movement during student years; organizer Nat. Congress Maltese Students, 1953; advocate for gen. elections Nationalist Party; founder numerous Nationalist Party dels.; active mem. Legal Com. of Council of Europe; v.p. Europe Parliamentary Assembly Christian Dem. Group. Mem. Commonwealth Parliamentary Assn. (exec. com.). Home: L'Orangerie, Mile End, Hamrun Malta Office: The Palace, Valletta Malta *

DEMARCO, ROLAND R., foundation executive; b. Mt. Morris, N.Y., July 21, 1910; s. Marion and Mary (Scalzette) DeM.; m. Lydia Hees, June 23, 1934; children—Richard, Ronald, Lynn. Diploma, Geneseo State Tchrs. Coll., 1930; B.S., N.Y. State Coll. Tchrs., 1934; A.M., Columbia U., 1937, Ph.D., 1942; student, U. Munich, Germany, 1937, Shrivenham Am. U., Eng., 1945, Officers Candidate Sch., 1944, Air Intelligence Sch., 1944; LL.D., Chungang U., Seoul, Korea, 1959; D.Litt., Sung Kyun Kwan U., Seoul, 1969, Hanyang U., Seoul, 1974. Instr. Gowanda Pub. Schs., 1930-34; dir. social studies East Islip High Sch., N.Y., 1934-38; instr. social scis. Coll. Charleston, 1939; instr. social scis. Columbia U., 1939-40, vis. prof., 1946-47; prof. history, head dept. social scis. Ala. State Tchrs. Coll., 1940-46, pres. dept., dean, 1949, adminstrv. head, 1949-50, pres., 1950-52; pres. Finch Coll., 1952-70, pres. emeritus, cons., 1970-75; chmn., chief exec. officer Internat. Human Assistance Programs, Inc., N.Y.C., 1973-82, hon. chmn., 1982-84, 85—, pres., chief exec. officer, 1984-85; head history dept. Finch Jr. Coll., 1947-49; curriculum cons. Jackson County Schs., Ala., 1940-43; mem. Nat. Adv. Council Edn. Disadvantaged Children, 1971-73; exec. vice chmn., chmn. ednl. adv. com. Am.-Korea Found., 1953-64, pres., 1964-68, 71-73, hon. chmn., 1968-71, chmn., chief exec. officer, 1973-75. Author: The Italianization of African Natives, 1943, The Comeback Country, Vol. I: Light of the East, an Insight into Korea, 1972. Contbr. articles to profl. jours. Trustee Allen Stevenson Sch. Boys, pres., 1956-58; bd. dirs., treas. Council Higher Ednl. Instns., N.Y.C.; pres. All Am. Open Karate Championships, 1965-80, Karate Championships North Am., 1967-80; v.p. World Taekwan Do Fedn., 1973-82; trustee Universidad Politecnica de P.R., San Juan, 1974-85; bd. dirs. Am. Behavioral Scis., 1967-80. Served to 1st lt. USAAF, 1943-46. Decorated Order Cultural Merit Nat. medal (Korea); named hon. citizen of Seoul, 1964; knight officer Order of Merit (Italy); recipient Disting. Alumni award SUNY, 1969, Disting. Alumni award Coll. Arts and Sci. at Geneseo, 1971. Mem. Am. Hist. Assn., Am. Acad. Polit. and Social Sci., NEA, Nat. Council Social Studies, N.Y. Assn. Deans and Guidance, Soc. Advancement Edn., Acad. Polit. Sci., Academia Tiberna, Internat. Sports Fedn., Phi Delta Kappa, Kappa Delta Pi (scholar 1939-40). Club: University. Home: 1400 East Ave Rochester NY 14610 also: Avoca NY 14809 Office: Internat Human Asst Programs Inc 360 Park Ave S New York NY 10010

DE MARGITAY, GEDEON, acquisitions and management consultant; b. Budapest, Hungary, Mar. 6, 1924; s. Joseph and Anne (de Bessenyei) de M.; came to U.S., 1953, naturalized, 1958; student U. Budapest Grad. Sch. Econs., 1941-44, Ecole des Scis. Politiques, Paris, 1946-48; m. Virginia Varet Martin, Dec. 30, 1963. With N.Y. Times, 1947-50, European info. div. Mut. Security Agy., 1950-53; with N.Y. Times, 1954-61; chief exec. Magnum Photos, Inc., N.Y.C., 1961-63; with Time Inc., 1964-75, dir. mktg. services Time/Life TV, 1975; dir. broadcast and corp. planning NBC, 1975-78; acquisitions and mgmt. cons., N.Y.C., 1978—. Mem. The Planning Forum, Assn. for Systems Mgmt., Internat. Radio-TV Soc., World Future Soc., Am. Acad. Polit. and Social Sci. Republican. Presbyterian. Co-author: Broadcasting: The Next Ten Years, 1977. Address: 65 E 96th St New York NY 10128

DEMARTINO, ANTHONY GABRIEL, cardiologist, internist; b. Bronx, Oct. 7, 1931; s. Agostino and Vincenzina (Clarizia) DeM.; B.S. cum laude, Iona Coll., 1953; M.D., SUNY, 1957; m. Marlene Mignone, Aug. 8, 1964; children—Anthony Augustin, Laura Jean. Intern, Univ. div. Kings County Med. Center, Bklyn., 1957-58, med. resident, 1960-62; fellow cardiopulmonary Cornell U., N.Y. Hosp., 1962-64; acting chief medicine Fordham div. Misericordia Fordham Affiliation, Bronx, 1964-65; physician in charge cardiac lab. Misericordia-Fordham Affiliation, 1965-69; attending physician dept. medicine and cardiology Our Lady of Mercy Med. Ctr., Bronx, 1967—; assoc. attending physician Lawrence Hosp., Bronxville, N.Y., 1977—; practice medicine, specializing in cardiology and internal medicine, Bronx, 1964—; v.p. med. bd. Misericordia Hosp. Med. Center, Bronx, 1973-75, pres., 1975-77; clin. asst. prof. medicine N.Y. Med. Coll., 1971—; hon. police surgeon N.Y.C. Trustee, Misericordia Hosp., 1977-83. Served to capt., M.C., U.S. Army, 1958-60. Nat. Heart Inst. fellow, 1962-64. Diplomate Nat. Bd. Med. Examiners, Am. Bd. Internal Medicine (cardiovascular disease). Fellow ACP, Am. Coll. Cardiology, Council Clin. Cardiology of Am. Heart Assn., Am. Coll. Chest Physicians, Am., Internat. colls. angiology, N.Y. Cardiol. Assn.; mem. Am. Soc. Internal Medicine, AMA, Westchester County, N.Y. County med. socs. Roman Catholic. Club: N.Y. Athletic. Contbr. articles to profl. jours; editorial bd. N.Y. Med. Quar., 1980-84. Office: 4350 Van Cortlandt Park E Bronx NY 10470 also: 77 Pondfield Rd Bronxville NY 10708

DEMAS, WILLIAM GILBERT, banker, economist; b. Port-of Spain, Trinidad, Nov. 14, 1929; s. Herman and Audrey (Walters) D.; m. Norma Taylor, 1958; 1 dau. Student Queen's Royal Coll., Trinidad, Emmanuel Coll., Cambridge. Head econ. planning div. Govt. Trinidad and Tobago, 1959-66, permanent sec. Ministry Planning and Devel., 1966-68, econ. adviser to Prime Minister, 1968-69; sec. Gen. Commonwealth Caribbean Regional Secretariate, 1970-74; pres. Caribbean Devel. Bank, St. Michael, Barbados, 1974—; dir. Central Bank. Author: Economics of Development in Small Countries, 1965; Planning and the Price Mechanism in the Context of Caribbean Economic Integration, 1966. Recipient Humming Bird Gold medal (for public service). Office: Caribbean Devel Bank, PO Box 408, Wildey, Saint Michael Barbados *

DE MASSA, JESSIE G., media specialist. BJ, Temple U.; MLS, San Jose State U., 1967; postgrad., U. Okla., U. So. Calif. Tchr. Palo Alto (Calif.) Unified Sch. Dist., 1966; librarian Antelope Valley Joint Union High Sch. Dist., Lancaster, Calif., 1966-68, ABC Unified Sch. Dist., Artesia, Calif., 1968-72; dist. librarian Tehachapi (Calif.) Unified Sch. Dist., 1972-81; also media specialist, free lance writer, 1981—. Contbr. articles to profl. jours. Mem. Statue of Liberty Ellis Island Found., Inc. Fellow Internat. Biog. Assn.; mem. Calif. Media and Library Educators Assn., Calif. Assn. Sch. Librarians (exec. council), AAUW (bull. editor, assoc. editor state bull., chmn. publicity 1955-68), Nat. Mus. Women in Arts (charter), Hon. Fellows John F. Kennedy Library (founding mem.). Home: 9951 Garrett Circle Huntington Beach CA 92646

DEMATTEO, GENE JOSEPH, investment executive; b. Jan. 30, 1933; m. Katherine Preyer; children—Gene Joseph, Kevin, Elizabeth, Cynthia, Robin, Randall, Kendall. Ed. JMCA Jr. Coll., 1952. Chmn. bd. Nat. Capital Corp., Hamden, Conn.; pres., dir. cos. including Nat. Investment Trust, Wichita, Kans., Country Club Apts., Inc., Greensboro, N.C., others. Bd. dirs. Ocean Learning Inst., 1978—. Clubs: Hartford (Conn.); Fairfield County Hunt (Fairfield, Conn.), Ocean Reef (Key Largo, Fla.); Beach (Palm Beach, Fla.), Sankaty Head Golf (Siasconset, Mass.), Beach & Tennis (Pebble Beach, Calif.), Figure Eight Island (N.C.), Surf (Surfside, Fla.). Home: Stonehenge 785 Smith Ridge New Canaan CT 06840 also: 830 S Ocean Blvd Palm Beach FL 33480 also: 17 Mile Dr Pebble Beach CA 93953 also: 700 Country Club Dr Greensboro NC 27408 Office: DeMatteo Bldg 2911 Dixwell Ave Hamden CT 06518

DEMAY, JOHN ANDREW, lawyer; b. Phila., Sept. 5, 1925; s. John Andrew and Anne Elizabeth (Mamaux) DeM.; m. Helen Louise Duffy, Sept. 2, 1950; children—John, Patrick, Ann, Mary, Theresa, Michael, Elizabeth, Stephen, Paul, David, Maureen. B.A. in Econs., U. Pitts., 1949, J.D., 1952. Bar: Pa. 1953, U.S. Dist. Ct. (we. dist.) Pa. 1953, U.S. Ct. Appeals (3d cir.) 1960, U.S. Ct. Appeals (2d cir.) 1965, U.S. Supreme Ct. 1965, U.S. Dist. Ct. (we. dist.) N.Y. 1968, U.S. Dist. Ct. (no. dist.) Ohio 1981. Law clk., Ct. Common Pleas, Pitts., 1952-53; asst. U.S. atty. We. Dist. Pa., 1953-57; ptnr. McArdle, Harrington & McLaughlin, Pitts., 1957-67; sole practice, Pitts., 1967-80; ptnr. DeMay, DeMay & Donnelly, P.C., Bethel Park, Pa., 1980—. Served to maj. CE USAR, 1950-70. Mem. ABA, Pa. Bar Assn., Allegheny County Bar Assn., Assn. Trial Lawyers Am., Acad. Trial Lawyers Allegheny County, Order Coif. Republican. Roman Catholic. Author: The Plaintiff's Personal Injury Case: It's Preparation, Trial and Settlement, 1977, Discovery-How To Win Your Case Without Trial, 1982. Home: 7166 Keith Rd Bethel Park PA 15102 Office: 4800 Library Rd Bethel Park PA 15102

DEMBELE, MAMADOU, government official. Prime minister Mali, 1986-88, minister of pub. health and social affairs, 1988—. Office: Ministry of Pub Health, Bamako Mali *

DE MELO, EURICO, Portugese government official; b. Santo Tirso, Portugal, Sept. 2, 1925. Grad. in engring., U. Porto, 1950. With Social Dem. Party, Portugal, 1974—, v.p. Nat. Polit. Commn.; minister internal affairs VI Constitutional Govt., 1980-81; mem. nat. council VIII Congress; mem. Portugal Parliament; minister internal affairs X Constitutional Govt.; chmn. dist. polit. com. Braga, Portugal; civil gov. Braga, 1975-76; now dep. prime minister, minister nat. def. Portugal, Lisbon. Address: Office Dep Prime Minister, Lisbon Portugal *

DE MENT, IRA, lawyer; b. Birmingham, Ala., Dec. 21, 1931; s. Ira Jr. and Helen (Sparks) DeM.; m. Ruth Lester Posey; 1 child, Charles Posey. AS, Marion Mil. Inst., 1951; AB, U. Ala., 1953, LLB, 1958, JD, 1969. Bar: Ala. 1958, U.S. Dist. Ct. (mid. dist.) Ala. 1958, U.S. Ct. Appeals (5th cir.) 1958, U.S. Supreme Ct. 1966, U.S. Dist. Ct. (so. dist.) Ala. 1967, U.S. Dist. Ct. D.C. 1972, U.S. Ct. Appeals (D.C.) 1972, U.S. Tax Ct. 1972, U.S. Customs and Patents Appeals 1976, U.S. Dist. Ct. (no. dist.) Ala. 1977. U.S. Ct. Appeals (11th cir.), 1981, U.S. Ct. Mil. Appeal 1972. Law clk. Sup. Ct. Ala., 1958-59; asst. atty. gen. State of Ala., 1959, spl. asst. atty. gen., 1966-69, 81—; asst. U.S. atty., Montgomery, Ala., 1959-61; sole practice Montgomery, 1961-69, 77—; acting U.S. atty. Mid. Dist. Ala. 1969, U.S. atty., 1969-77; asst. atty., legal advisor to police and fire depts. City of Montgomery, 1965-69; instr. Jones Law Sch., 1962-64; instr. Montgomery Police Acad. 1964-77; lectr. constl. law Ala. Police Acad., 1971-75; instr. law enforcement U. Ala., 1967, mem. adj. faculty New Coll., 1974-75, adj. prof. psychology, 1975—; spl. counsel to Gov. State Ala., 1980-88, gen. counsel Commn. on Aging, 1980-82. Served to lt. col. USAR, 1953-74; now maj. gen. USAFR. Recipient Disting. Service award Internat. Assn. Firefighters, 1975; Rockefeller Pub. Service award, Woodrow Wilson Sch. Pub. and Internat. Affairs Princeton U., 1976; named Alumnus of Yr. Marion Mil. Inst., 1988. Mem. Am. Arbitration Assn. (mem. nat. panel arbitrators), Nat. Dist. Attys. Assn., ABA, Fed. Bar Assn., D.C. Bar Assn., Ala. Bar Assn. (mem. editorial adv. bd. The Alabama Lawyer 1966-72), Assn. Trial Lawyers Am., Ala. Trial Lawyers Assn., Montgomery County Trial Lawyers Assn., Am. Judicature Soc., Fraternal Order Police, Ala. Peace Officers Assn., Res. Officers Assn. U.S., Air Force Assn., Nat. Assn. Former U.S. Attys., Phi Alpha Delta. Republican. United Methodist. Clubs: Montgomery Country and Beauvoir, Masons, Shriners. Address: PO Box 4163 Montgomery AL 36103

DE MERE-DWYER, LEONA, medical artist; b. Memphis, May 1, 1928; d. Clifton and Leona (McCarthy) De Mere; BA, Rhodes Coll., Memphis, 1949; M.Sc., Memphis State U., 1984; m. John Thomas Dwyer, May 10, 1952; children—John, DeMere, Patrice, Brian, Anne-Clifton DeMere Dwyer, McCarthy-DeMere Dwyer. Med. artist for McCarthy DeMere, Memphis, 1950-80; pres. Aesthetic Med. & Forensic Art, 1984—; speech therapist, Memphis, 1950-82; lic. embalmer, funeral dir., 1981; lectr. on med. art univs., conf., assns.; cons. in prostheses Vocat. Rehab. Services; bereavement counselor. Organizer Ladies of St. Jude, Memphis, 1960; active Brooks Art Gallery League of Memphis; leader Confraternity of Christian Doctrine, St. Louis Cath. Ch., 1966-67; vice dir. Tellico Hist. Found., 1980-80; mem. exec. bd. Chickasaw council Boy Scouts Am.; active Republican campaign coms. Lic. Fedn. Internationale de'Automobile, (internat. car racing), 1972; recipient Disting. Service award Gupton-Jones Coll. Mortuary Sci., 1981; Silver Sons of the Am. Revolution medal, 1985. Mem. Assn. Med. Illustrators, Am. Assn. Med. Assts., Emergency Dept. Nurses Assn., Am. Physicians Nurses Assn., Am. Soc. Plastic and Reconstructive Surgeons Found. (guest mem., cons.), Women in Law (chmn. assos.), FORUM, Nat. Death Edn. Soc., Exec. Women Am., Brandeis U. Women, DAR (1st v.p. regent 1980), UDC (pres. Nathan Bedford Forrest chpt.), Cotton Carnival Assn. (chairperson children's ct. 1968-70), Pi Sigma Eta, Kappa Delta (adv.), Kappa Delta Pi. Clubs: Tennessee, Royal Matron Amaranth (Faith Ct.), Sertoma (1st female mem. Memphis, 1st female life mem. Sertoma Internat.) (Memphis). Contbr. articles to profl. jours. Home: 660 W Suggs Dr Memphis TN 38119

DEMETRESCU, MIHAI CONSTANTIN, computer company executive, scientist; b. Bucharest, Romania, May 23, 1929; s. Dan and Alina (Dragosescu) D.; M.E.E., Poly. Inst. of U. Bucharest, 1954; Ph.D., Romanian Acad. Sci., 1957; m. Agnes Halas, May 25, 1969; 1 child, Stefan. Came to U.S., 1966. Prin. investigator Research Inst. Endocrinology Romanian Acad. Sci., Bucharest, 1958-66; research fellow dept. anatomy UCLA, 1966-67; faculty U. Calif.-Irvine, 1967—, asst. prof. dept. physiology, 1971-78, assoc. researcher, 1978-79, assoc. clin. prof., 1979-83; v.p. Resonance Motors, Inc., Monrovia, Calif., 1972—; pres. Neurometrics, Inc., Irvine, Calif., 1978-82; pres. Lasergraphics Inc., Irvine, 1982-84, chmn., chief exec. officer, 1984—. Mem. com. on hon. degrees U. Calif.-Irvine, 1970-72. Postdoctoral fellow UCLA, 1966. Mem. Internat. Platform Assn., Am. Physiol. Soc., IEEE (sr.). Republican. Contbr. articles to profl. jours. Patentee in field. Home: 20 Palmento Way Irvine CA 92715 Office: 17671 Cowan Ave Irvine CA 92714

DEMETRIOU, ANDREAS PANTELI, psychology educator; b. Strongylo, Cyprus, Aug. 15, 1950; arrived in Greece, 1970; s. Pantelis and Lysimachi (Konstantinou) Panteli D.; m. Julia Tsakalea; children: Pantelis, Demetris. BA in Psychology and Edn. with honors, Aristotelian U., Thessaloniki, Greece, 1975, PhD in Psychology, 1983. Asst. psychology lab Aristotelian U., 1975-83, lectr. psychology, 1983-86, assoc. prof., 1986—; prof. Psychology In Service Tchrs. Tng. Sch., Thessaloniki, 1983—; vis. research fellow dept. psychology U. Melbourne, Australia, 1988. Author, editor: The Neo-Piagetian Theories of Cognitive Development: Toward an Integration Amsterdam: North-Holland, 1988; contbr. articles to profl. jours. Recipient Australian Govt. Grad. Studies award, 1978, U.S. Dept. Navy cons. visitors award, 1985. Mem. European Assn. for Resefarch on Learning and Instrn. (nat. rep. 1985—, mem. editorial bd. newletter 1987—). Home: Ethnikis Aminis 40, 54621 Thessaloniki Greece Office: Aristotelian U, Psychol Lab, 54006 Thessaloniki Greece

DEMETRIUS, JAMES KLEON, classicist, educator; b. Chicopee Falls, Mass., Aug. 23, 1924; s. James Demetrius and Bess Stephens. Student, NYU, 1945, U. N.D., 1946-47; B.A., U. Iowa and Bklyn. Coll., 1948; M.A., Columbia U., 1949, postgrad., 1950-58; Ph.D. (hon.), WU, 1982; hon. degree, Madras, India. Instr. Greek, Spanish, Italian Iona Coll., 1953-59; asst. prof. Spanish, ancient history Widener Coll., 1959-62; asst. prof. Spanish Wash. Coll., 1962-63; asso. prof. Greek and Spanish Bloomfield Coll., 1963-68; vis. prof. fgn. langs. St. Francis Coll., 1971-72; prof. ancient and modern langs. Touro Coll., 1972; research in Spain and Latin Am., 1973—; chmn. English and fgn. lang. dept. Interboro Jr. Coll., N.Y.C.; speaker U. Ky., 1958; honored speaker, Barry Chase Meml. lectr. The Grecian Concept of Education and Its Meaning to Us Today Bloomfield Coll., 1968, The Originality of the Greek Genius Harvard U., 1986—; hon. speaker Unification Theol. Sem., 1985, New Platz, 1985, Princeton U., 1987, Dumbarton Oakes, Washington, 1987. Author: Greek Scholarship in Spain and Latin America, 1966; monographs An Essay on Greek Influences on Spanish Literature, 1961, Los Griegos en Espana, 1962, A Bibliography of Greek Studies in Spain, 1962, Nikos Kazantzakis in Spain, 1968, (with Dr. Luis Leon) Spanish Grammar Explained, 1972, Modern Greek Poetry, 1974, Homer: Europe's First Humanist, 1974, S. They Thought Theocritus Was Dead, 1985; The Greek Genius, 1986, Romanticism and the Greeks, 1986; columnist: Grecian World, 1961—; numerous articles and studies and notes contbd. to Folia Humanistica, Spain, St. Francis Bull., Greek Gazette London, Boletin de estudios helenicos, Spain, Greek Star, Slavic Rev, Filosofia Oggi, Balkan Studies; book rev. editor, mem. editorial bd.: Numerous articles and studies and notes contbd. to Hellenic Times, 1974—. Recipient awards for excellence in teaching, student bodies in Bloomfield Coll., 1968, awards for excellence in teaching, student bodies in St. Francis Coll., 1972; Fellow Athens, Greece, 1977. Mem. Classical Assn. Spain, Hellenic Soc. London, Royal Inst. Philosophy (Eng.), Classical Assn. Spain, Internat. Hispanist Assn., Am. Assn. Teachers of Spanish and Portuguese, AAUP, Medieval Soc. Am., Am. Classical League, Soc. Ancient Greek Philosophy, Alpha Sigma Phi.

DE MEY, HUBERT ROLAND, psychology educator; b. Antwerp, Belgium, Mar. 25, 1946; Arrived in The Netherlands, 1971; s. Roger and Rosa (Arnou) DeM. M, State U. Gent, Belgium, 1970; PhD, Cath. U. Nijmegen, The Netherlands, 1981. Staff mem. Inst. for the Mentally Retarded, Rolde, The Netherlands, 1971-74; jr. asst. Dept. Clin. Psychol., Nijmegen, 1974-81; sr. asst. Dept. Clin. and Personality Scis., Nijmegen, 1981—. Editor: Gedrag & Gezondheid. Mem. Am. Assn. for Behavioral Analysis, Dutch Assn. for Behavior Therapy. Office: Cath U Nijmegen, PO Box 9104, 6500HE Nymegen The Netherlands

DE MEYER, JOSEPH ALEXANDRE AUGUST, clinical psychologist; b. Amsterdam, Netherlands, June 13, 1950; came to U.S., 1977; s. Joseph François and Constance Maria (van Delft) de M.; m. Elizabeth Maria Meijers, Feb. 17, 1978; children—Robert Joseph, Melanie Constance. Doctoral degree State U. Leyden (Netherlands), 1977. Clin. psychologist Retreat Hosp., Decatur, Ala., 1977-80; clin. dir. North Central Ala. Mental Health Center, Decatur, 1980-83; dir adult outpatient psychiatry, 1985-86; dir. child and adolescent psychiatry Jersey City Med. Ctr. (N.J.), 1984-88; pvt. practice, 1984—; attending psychologist Chilton Meml. Hosp., adj. prof. Am. Inst. Psychotherapy, Huntsville, Ala., 1981-83; candidate William Alanson White Inst., N.Y.C., 1983-87. Cert. psychoanalyst; Lic. psychologist, Ala., N.J. Mem. Am. Psychol. Assn., N.J. Psychol. Assn., William Alanson White Psychoanalytic Soc., Netherlands Inst. Psychologists, N.J. Psychologists in Pvt. Practice. Home: 23 Pitman Pl Wayne NJ 07470 Office: 20 W 74th St New York NY 10023

DE MICOLI, SALVATORE, non-ferrous metals commodity executive; b. Pieta, Malta, May 21, 1939; came to U.S., 1954; s. Anthony and Jane (Camilleri) De M.; m. Irma L. Gil, Sept. 25, 1966; children: Mark, Marisa, Martin. Asst. sec. AMAX/Ametalco Inc., N.Y.C., 1956-72; v.p. N.C. Trading Co. Inc., N.Y.C., 1972-73; exec. v.p. Cerro Sales Corp., N.Y.C., 1973—; bd. govs. Commodity Exchange Inc., N.Y.C., 1982—. Clubs: Copper (N.Y.C.). Home: 286 Bayview Ave S Massapequa NY 11758 Office: Cerro Sales Corp 540 Madison Ave New York NY 10022

DE MIGUEL, JESUS MANUEL, sociologist, educator; b. San Sebastian, Spain, Dec. 28, 1947; s. Diego de Miguel and M. Angeles Rodriguez; m. Melissa G. Moyer, Mar. 21, 1979; children: Carolina G., Robert W. D in Polit. Sci., U. Complutense, Madrid, 1971; PhD in Sociology, Yale U., 1976. Chmn. dept. sociology U. de Oviedo, Asturias, Spain, 1983-87, chmn. dept. econs., 1987—; vis. prof. U. Calif., Berkeley, 1985-86; advisor WHO, Copenhagen, 1981-87, Minister of Health, Spain, 1983-86. Author: Sociology in Spain, 1979, Control de Natalidad, 1981, La Amorosa Dictadura, 1984, La Salud Publica del Futuro, 1985. Mem. Socialist Trade Union, 1980. Grantee Fulbright Commn., Social Sci. Research Council, Rockefeller Found., Am. Council Learned Socs. Mem. Am. Sociol. Assn., Internat. Sociol. Assn., European Soc. Med. Sociologists. Mem. Partido Socialista. Home: Osio 45 (1-13), 08034 Barcelona Spain Office: Universidad de Barcelona, Facultad de Sociologia, Avenida Diagonal 690, 08034 Barcelona Spain

DE MIGUEL MORNET, MANUEL LORENZO, racing car accessories company executive; b. Lerida, Spain, Apr. 17, 1945; s. Manuel Jacinto and Suzanne Marie (Mornet) deMF; m. Mable Serena Gutierrez, Mar. 22, 1973; children—Bernard, Eric. Cert. math., physics, chemistry Faculté des Sciences, Bordeaux, France, 1966; Mech. Engr., Instituto Universitaire de Technologie, Talence, France, 1970. Gen. mgr., founder IRESA, S.A., Lerida, Spain, 1971—; dir. Alimentos Rapidos S.A. Burger King franchise, Zaragoza. Contbr. articles on Ferrari cars to profl. jours. Served with French Army, 1969-70. Mem. Am. C. of C. in Spain. Roman Catholic. Club: Ferrari Owners (founder). Home: Campode Marte 37, Lerida Spain Office: IRESA, Pol Indust El Segre, Lerida Spain

DEMILLIERE, BERNARD HENRI JOSEPH, ophthalmologist; b. Maligny, Côte-D'Or, France, Jan. 24, 1931; s. René and Joséphine (Gagliardi) D.; divorced; children: Etienne, Lucie. Intern St.-Luc Hosp., Lyon, France, 1956-60; asst. St.-Luc Hosp., Lyon's Hosps., 1960-64; mem. faculty medicine and pharmacy Lyon U., 1964; chief cons. ophthalmology service Mutualiste Clinic, Lyon, 1965; chief ophthalmologist Jeanne d'Arc Clinic, Lyon, 1979—; dir. clinic edn. U. Lyon; researcher ocular immunology Soc. Ophthaomology, Lyon, French Ophthalmology Soc., Paris. Served to lt. French mil. health services, 1958-60. Lodge: Lions. Home: 241 Montee des Roches, 69760 Limonest Rhone, France Office: 322 Ave Berthelot, 69008 Lyon Rhone, France

DEMING, W(ILLIAM) EDWARDS, statistics educator, consultant. BS, U. Wyo., 1921, LLD (hon.), 1958; MS, U. Colo., 1924, LLD (hon.), 1987; PhD, Yale U., 1928; ScD (hon.), Rivier Coll., 1981, Ohio State U., 1982, Md. U., 1983, Clarkson Inst. Tech., 1983; D in Engring. (hon.), U. Miami, 1985; LLD (hon.), George Washington U., 1986, D in Engring. (hon.), 1987; DSc (hon), U. Colo., 1987. Instr. engring. U. Wyo., 1921-22; asst. prof. physics Colo. Sch. Mines, 1922-24, U. Colo., 1924-25; instr. physics Yale U., 1925-27; math. physicist USDA, 1927-39; adviser in sampling Bur. of Census, 1939-45; prof. stats. NYU Grad. Sch. Bus. Adminstrn., N.Y.C., from 1946; cons. research, industry, 1946—; statistician Allied Mission to Observe Greek Elections, 1946; cons. sampling Govt. India, 1947, 51, 71; adviser in sampling techniques Supreme Command Allied Powers, Tokyo, 1947-50, High Commn. for Germany, 1952, 53; mem. UN Sub-Commn. on Statis. Sampling, 1947-52; lectr. various univs., Germany, Austria, 1953, London Sch. Econs., 1964, Institut de Statistique de U. Paris, 1964; cons. Census Mex., Bank of Mex., Ministry Economy Mex., 1954, 55; cons. Statistisches Bundesamt, Wiesbaden, Fed. Republic Germany, 1953, Central Statis. Office Turkey, 1959—, China Productivity Ctr., Taiwan, 1970, 71; Inter Am. Statis. Inst. lectr., Brazil, Argentina. Author: Quality, Productivity, and Competitive Position, 1982, Out of the Crisis, 1986; contbr. numerous articles to profl. publs. Decorated 2d Order medal of the Sacred Treasure (Japan); elected Most Disting. Grad., U. Wyo., 1972; recipient Taylor Key award Am. Mgmt. Assn., 1983; enshrinedin the Engring. and Sci. Hall of Fame, 1986. Fellow Am. Statis. Assn., Royal Statis. Soc. (hon.), Inst. Math. Stats.; mem. Am. Soc. Quality Control (hon. life, Shewhart medal 1955), Internat. Statis. Inst., Philos. Soc. Washington, World Assn. Pub. Opinion Research, Market Research Council, Biometric Soc. (hon. life), ASTM (hon.), Union Japanese Scientists and Engrs. (hon. life) (tchr. and cons to Japanese industry 1950-52, 55, 60, 65—, honored in establishment of Deming prizes), Japanese Statis. Assn. (hon. life), Deutsche Statistische Gesellschaft (hon. life), Ops. Research Soc. Am., Nat. Acad. Engring., Dayton Hall of Fame. Home and Office: 4924 Butterworth Pl Washington DC 20016

DE MITA, LUIGI CIRIACO, prime minister Italy; b. Fusco, Avellino, Italy, Feb. 2, 1928. Mem. Chamber Deps., Benevento-Avellino-Salerno, Italy, 1963, 72—; nat. counsellor Christian Dem. Party, 1964, later vice sec.; under-sec. for the interior Italy, Rome, minister industry and commerce, 1973-74, minister fgn. trade, 1974-76, minister without portfolio with responsibility for the Mezzogiorno, 1976-79; sec. gen. Christian Dem. Party, 1982—; prime minister Italy, Rome, 1988—. Address: Christian Dem Party, Piazza del Gesu 46, 00186 Rome Italy *

DEMOEN, BALDWIN MICHEL, finance executive; b. Esen, Flanders, Belgium, Jan. 10, 1947; s. Gabriel Demoen and Marie-Louise Vereecke; married, Dec. 20, 1974; children: Ruth, Niels. Grad., Hoger Inst. Bestuurs en Handelswetenschappen, Gent, Belgium, 1969. Various acctg. positions Belgium, 1969-71; cash mgr. Europe and Africa divs. Del Monte, Belgium, 1971-75; credit mgr. div. Dow Chem., Belgium, 1975-80, treas., 1980-83; treas. France div. France, 1983-86; treas. Mid-East and Africa divs. Geneva, 1986-87; treas. Mid-East, Africa and Ea. Europe divs. Geneva and Vienna, 1988—. Home: 20 D Av Vercheres, 1226 Geneva Switzerland Office: Dow Chem Mid-East Africa, 17 B Ancienne Rt, 1218 Geneva Switzerland

DEMONSABERT, WINSTON RUSSEL, chemist, consultant; b. New Orleans, June 12, 1915; s. Joseph Francis and Davida Elizabeth (Gullett) deM.; B.S. in Chemistry, Loyola U., New Orleans, 1937; M.A. in Edn., Tulane U., 1945, Ph.D. in Chemistry, 1952; m. Eleanor Ray Ranson, Aug. 8, 1955; children—Winston Russel. Asst. prof. Loyola U., New Orleans, 1948-49, assoc. prof., 1949-55, prof., 1955-66; chief chemist Nat. Center for Disease Control, Dept. Health and Human Services, Atlanta, 1966-69, chief contract liaison br. Nat. Center for Health Services Research, 1969-73, chief extramural programs Bur. Drugs, FDA, Rockville, Md., 1973-79, scientist adminstr. office of interagy sci. coordination, office of commr. FDA, after 1979; now cons., govt. liaison environ. chemistry and toxicology; assoc. prof. Tulane U., 1957-58; research chemist Am. Cyanamid Co., 1957-58; v.p. Interagy. Testing Com. Committeeman Boy Scouts Am., New Orleans and Atlanta; mem. curriculum coms. New Orleans Pub. Sch. Bd., 1965. Fellow Am. Inst. Chemists (chmn. La. chpt. 1958-60, chmn. Ga. chpt. 1968-69, pres. D.C. chpt. 1982-83), AAAS; mem. Am. Chem. Soc. (chmn. La. sect. 1954, alt. councilor 1957-66). Roman Catholic. Contbr. to encys. and profl. jours. Home: 4317 Lake Trail Dr Kenner LA 70065 Office: 869 Taft Pl New Orleans LA 70119

DE MONTEBELLO, PHILIPPE LANNES, museum administrator; b. Paris, May 16, 1936; came to U.S., 1951, naturalized, 1955; s. Roger L. and Germaine (de Croisset) de M.; m. Edith Bradford Myles, June 24, 1961; children: Marc, Laure, Charles. B.A. magna cum laude, Harvard U., 1961; M.A., NYU Inst. Fine Arts, 1963; LL.D. (hon.), Lafayette Coll., 1979; D.H.L. (hon.), Bard Coll., 1981; D.F.A. (hon.), Iona Coll., 1982. Asso. curator European paintings Met. Mus. Art, N.Y.C., 1963-69; vice dir. for curatorial and ednl. affairs Met. Mus. Art, 1974-77, acting dir., 1977-78, dir., 1978—; dir. Mus. Fine Arts, Houston, 1969-74; mem. adv. bd. Skowhegan Sch. Painting and Sculpture, N.Y.C.; mem. Council Museums and Edn. in the Visual Arts, Columbia Adv. Council Depts. Art History and Archeology. Author: Peter Paul Rubens, 1969; contbr. to mus. bulls., various exhbn. catalogs. Trustee, mem. exec. com. NYU Inst. Fine Arts. Served to 2d lt. AUS, 1956-58. Recipient NYU Grad. Sch. Alumni Achievement award, 1978; Woodrow Wilson fellow, 1961-62; Gallatin fellow, 1981. Mem. Assn. Art Mus. Dirs. (future directions com.), Am. Fedn. Arts (trustee, exec. com.), Coll. Art Assn., Am. Assn. Mus. Home: 1150 Fifth Ave New York NY 10028 Office: Met Mus of Art 82d St at Fifth Ave New York NY 10028

DE MONTLIBERT, CHRISTIAN ANNE PAUL, sociology educator; b. Orleans, France, July 28, 1937; m. Nadia Warlamow, Dec. 19, 1959; children: Catherine, Renaud, Ariane. BA in Psychology, U. Paris, 1959, PhD in Sociology, 1974; postgrad., Sorbonne U., Paris, 1965. Asst. research Lab. Social Psychology, Sorbonne U., 1959-61; researcher Inst. for Adult Tng., Nancy, France, 1963-73; prof. sociology U. Strasbourg, France, 1973—, prof. Archtl. and Urbanism Sch., 1975—; researcher Sch. Social Arts U. Strasborg, France, 1975—, mem. sci. and adminstrv. coms., 1978-83; dir. research Cress U., Strasborg, 1977—; cons. Council of Europe, Strasbourg, 1978-80; mem. sci. com. Regional Council Alsace, Strasbourg, 1984—. Author: The Architects, 1970, Sociology of Work, 1972, The Youngs and the Work, 1980, The Social Worker, 1987; contbr. articles to profl. jours. Mem. French Sociol. Soc., Assn. Qualite de la Sci. Francaise. Office: U Strasbourg II, Rue Descartes, 67000 Strasbourg France

DE MORAIS MIGUENS, ÁLVARO JOSÉ, plastic company executive; b. Porto, Douro, Portugal, Feb. 3, 1941; s. Mario G. Gonçalves and Maria Alberta (Pereira De Morais) Miguens; m. Maria Manuela G. Silveira Assis, Aug. 26, 1967; children: Sofia Gabriela, Cristina Isabel, Diana Patricia. B in Chem. Engring., U. Oporto, Porto, 1963; cert in mgmt. (hon.), Conservatoire Nat. des Arts et Metiers, Paris, 1963-64. Asst. engr. Fabr. Port Borracha Lda, Porto, 1968-70; chief engr. Vila Conde, Portugal, 1970-76; product dir. 1976-80, tech. and product dir., 1980—; owner, founder Policel, Maia, Portugal, 1978—. Served to lt. Engring. Corps Portugese mil., 1966-68. Mem. Social-Democratic Party. Roman Catholic. Home: Rua S Miguel 323, 4470 Maia Portugal

DE MOUCHY, DUCHESSE, corporate executive; b. N.Y.C., Jan. 31, 1935; arrived in Luxembourg, 1967; d. Clarence Douglas and Phyllis Chess (Ellsworth) Dillon; m. James Brady Mosely (annuled 1963); 1 child, Her Royal Higness Joan Dillon Moseley Bryan; m. His Royal Higness, His Royal Highness Prince Charles of Luxembourg (dec. 1977); children: Princess Cahrlotte, Prince Robert; m. Philippe de Noailles Duc de Mouchy. Asst. editor The Paris Rev., 1958-65; pres. Domaine Clarence Dillon S.Am., Paris, 1975—, Infirmes des Moteurs Cerebraux-Kräzbierg, Dudelange, Luxembourg, 1977—; pres. Union Banques Suisses, Luxembourg, 1977-82. Mem. Am.-Luxembourg Soc. (pres. 1967-78). Club: Inner-Wheel (Luxembourg) (pres. 1968-78). Office: Domaine Clarence Dillon SA, Chateau Haut Brion, 26 Rue de la Pepiniere, 75008 Paris France

DE MOUSSET, LAURA DIAZ-LABROUSSE, painter and sculptor; b. Lima, Peru, Feb. 13, 1952; d. Carlos Wendorff Diaz and Luisa (Labrousse) Cambana; m. Cedric Melchior de Mousset, Apr. 8, 1976; children: Yann Erik, Christelle Alexia. Student, Jarque Painting, Lima, Peru, 1976-81; studies with C. Galvez, Lima, Peru, 1978-80; student of Velarde, 1979; studies with Michel, Brussels, 1981-86. Art tchr. Ecole Française De Seoul, Republic of Korea, 1987—; specialist teaching art to the handicapped. Editor: Designs in Creativity, 1968; numerous solo and group exhibitions in Peru, Belgium, Republic of Korea; sculptures, paintings permanently displayed in various homes and offices throughout Belgium, France, Peru, Canada, U.S.A., Netherlands, Eng., Luxembourg. Mem. Union Feminine Artistique Culturelle Salons Internationaux. Club: Sadan-Seoul (Republic of Korea). Home: 330-288 Sungbuk Dong, Sungbuk-ku Seoul Republic of Korea

DEMUTH, NINA LEWIS, chemical company executive; b. Benton, Ill., July 14, 1921; d. William Henry and Agnes Clara (Landreth) Lewis; m. Herbert Willard Demuth, Feb. 16, 1947; 1 child, Nina Dale (dec.). Student Nassau Coll., 1976—. With Barbour Co., Inc., St. Louis, 1939-47, v.p., 1943-47; pres. Demuth Co., Garden City, N.Y., 1948—, Demuth Service Corp., Garden City, 1955—, Demuth Devel. Corp., Garden City, 1958. Contbr. articles to profl. publs. Mem. Parenteral Drug Assn. (bd. dirs. 1977-79), Parenteral Drug Assn. Found. for Pharm. Scis. (incorporator 1979, pres. 1979-83, bd. dirs. 1979—, treas. 1984—), Huguenot Soc. Methodist. Office: PO Box 242 Garden City NY 11530

DENAMUR, THOMAS JOSEPH, dentist; b. Green Bay, Wis., Aug. 20, 1950; s. Lloyd Francis and Muriel Janet (Delfosse) DeN.; m. Lynn Marie Vetter, Aug. 26, 1972; children: Christopher Thomas, Nicole Lynn. BS in Chemistry, St. Norbet Coll., 1972; DDS, Marquette U., 1976. Lic. dentist, Wis. Gen. practice dentistry Algoma, Wis., 1976—; cons. dentist Algoma Meml. Hosp., 1985-86. Contbr. articles to profl. jours. Mem. Concerned Citizens Com. St. Mary's Ch., 1982, Algoma Citizens Together, 1984. Fellow Acad. Gen. Dentistry; mem. Am. Equilibration Soc., Soc. Occlusal Studies, Wis. Dental Assn. (alternate del. 1986), Bay Lakes Dental Soc., Chgo., Brown Door Kewanee Dental Soc. (bd. dirs. 1983-86, peer rev. com. 1984-86), Chgo Dental Soc. (assoc.), Am. Assn. Functional Orthodontists (Hon. Mention Case Solvers 1986), Omicron Kappa Soc. Lodges: Algoma Optimists (v.p. 1979-80, pres. 1980-81, Honor Club mem. 1981). Home: 520 Ohio St Algoma WI 54201 Office: 800 Jefferson St Algoma WI 54201

DENBOW, NICHOLAS JOHN, marketing executive; b. Leeds, Eng., June 1, 1946; s. Ernest John and Freda Margaret (Dockray) D.; children: Tamasine A., Nicholas C. MA in Elec. Scis. with honors, Cambridge (Eng.) U., 1967. Mgmt. trainee, devel. engr. Plessey Electronics, London, 1970-75; bus. planner Brit. Oxygen Welding Products Div., London, 1970-75; new product mgr. controls and instrumentation div. Bestobell Mobrey, Slough, Eng., 1975-80, product mgr., 1980-81, mktg. mgr. in electronics, 1983—; with product mktg. Sarasota Automation, Winchester, Eng., 1981-83. Patentee in field. Mem. Inst. Measurement and Control. Home: 7 Carisbrooke Close, Alresford Winchester, Hants SO24 9PQ, England Office: Bestobell Mobrey, 190 Bath Rd, Slough SL1 4DN, England

DEN BUTTER, FRANK ARTHUR GIJSBERT, economist; b. Schiedam, The Netherlands, Mar. 29, 1948; s. Gijsbert and Guurtje (Schild) Den B.; m. Jeanette W.A. van den Eelaart, May 22, 1987. D in Econs., U. Amsterdam, 1973; PhD in Econs., Eramus U., Rotterdam, The Netherlands, 1986. Research assoc. Econ. Inst. Bldg. Industry, Amsterdam; research mem. De Nederlandsche Bank NV, Amsterdam, 1973-78, asst. chief, 1979-88; prof. Econ. Free U., Amsterdam, 1988—; cons. OECD, Paris, 1983; lectr. Tech. U., 1981, Hilversum (The Netherlands) C. of C., 1987—. Author: Model and Theory in Macroeconomics, 1987, Seasonal Adjustment and Policy Diagnosis, 1988; contbr. articles to profl. jours. Mem. Vereniging voor de Staathuishoudkunde, European Econ. Assn. Home: Dorpsstraat 24, 1191 BJ Ouderkerk The Netherlands Office: Free Univ, PO Box 7161, 1007 MC Amsterdam The Netherlands

DENCH, JUDITH OLIVIA, actress; b. York, Eng., Dec. 9, 1934; d. Reginald Arthur and Eleanora Olave (Joses) D.; student Central Sch. Speech Tng. and Dramatic Art (Gold medal, Elsie Fogarty prize, William Poel Meml. prize); Litt.D. (hon.), Warwick U., 1978, York U., 1983; m. Michael Williams, Feb. 5, 1971; 1 child, Tara Cressida Frances. Theatrical appearances include: (Old Vic) Hamlet, Midsummer Night's Dream, Twelfth Night, 1957-58, The Importance of Being Earnest, As You Like It, Romeo and Juliet, 1959-61; (Venice Festival) Romeo and Juliet (Paladino d'Argentino), 1961; (Royal Shakespeare Co., Stratford) The Cherry Orchard, Measure for Measure, Midsummer Night's Dream, A Penny for a Song, 1961-62; (Oxford Playhouse) The Alchemist, The Three Sisters, Romeo and Jeanette, 1964; (Oxford and London) The Promise, 1966-67; (London) Sally Bowles in Cabaret, 1968; (Royal Shakespeare Co., London) Twelfth Night, A Winter's Tale, London Assurance, 1970; (Royal Shakespeare Co., Stratford) The Merchant of Venice, The Duchess of Malfi, 1971; tour of Japan with Twelfth Night, 1972; (London) London Assurance, 1973; (Oxford and London) The Wolf, 1974; (London) The Good Companions, 1974-75, The Gay Lord Quex, 1975; (Royal Shakespeare Co., Stratford) Much Ado About Nothing, The Comedy of Errors, Macbeth (SWET Best Actress award for Lady Macbeth), King Lear, 1976-77; Cymbeline, 1979; (Royal Shakespeare Co., London) Pillars of the Community, The Way of the World, 1977-78, (Aldwych) Juno and the Paycock (SWET Best Actress award, Evening Standard Drama award for Best Actress, Plays and Players award for Best Actress, Variety Club award Actress of Yr.), 1981, A Kind of Alaska, The Importance of Being Earnest (Standard Best Actress award, Plays and Players award for best actress), Pack of Lies (Plays and Players award SWET Best Actress award); films: He Who Rides a Tiger, A Study in Terror, Four in the Morning (Brit. Film Acad. Most Promising Newcomer award 1965), A Midsummer Night's Dream, The Third Secret, Dead Cert, Wetherby, 1985, A Room with a Room, 84 Charing Cross Road; TV appearances include: Major Barbara, Talking to a Stranger (Best TV Actress of Yr. award 1967), Jackanory, Luther, Neighbours, Marching Song, Days to Come, The Comedy of Errors, Macbeth, Village Wooing, Love in a Cold Climate, A Fine Romance, The Cherry Orchard, Going Gently; Saigon, (film) Wetherby, 1985. Decorated Order Brit. Empire. Mem. Religious Soc. of Friends. *

DENEUVE, CATHERINE (CATHERINE DORLEAC), actress; b. Paris, Oct. 22, 1943; d. Maurice Dorleac and Renee Deneuve; m. David Bailey, 1965 (div. 1970); children: Christian Vadim, Chiara Mastroianni. Ed., Lycée La Fontaine, Paris. Motion picture appearances include Les Petits Chats, 1956, Les Collegiennes, 1956, Les portes claquent, 1960, Les Parisiennes, 1961, Et Satan conduit le bal, 1962, Vacances portugaises, 1963, Le Vice et la Vertu, 1963, Les Parapluies de Cherbourg, 1964 (Golden Palm of Cannes Festival), La Chasse à l'homme, 1964, Les Plus belles escroqueries du monde, 1964, Un Monsieur de compagnie, 1964, Repulsion, 1965, Coeur à la gorge, 1965, Le Chant de Ronde, 1965, La Vie de Chateau, 1965, Les créatures, 1966, Les Demoiselles de Rochefort, 1966, Benjamin, 1967, Manon 70, 1967, Belle de Jour, 1967 (Golden Lion of Venice Festival), Meyerling, 1967, La Chamade, 1968, The April Fools, 1968, La Sirène du Mississippi, 1968, Tristana, 1969, It Only Happens to Others, 1971, Dirty Money, Hustle, 1975, Lovers Like Us, 1975, Act of Aggression, 1976, March or Die, 1977, La Grande Bourgeoise, 1977, The Last Metro, 1980, A Second Chance, 1981, Reporters, 1982, The Hunger, 1983, Fort Saganne, Scene of the Crime. Home: 36 Ave Georges-Mandel, 75116 Paris France *

DE NEVERS, ROY OLAF, retired aerospace company executive; b. Strasburg, Sask., Can., Dec. 30, 1922; s. Edouard Albrecht V.V. and Christy Helen (Hunt) de N.; divorced; children Gregory Frank (dec.), Sara Dianne. BS in Econs., U. London, 1963; BA in Econ. History, U. Winnipeg (Can.), 1971. Served to lt. comdr. Royal Can. Navy, 1946-67; chief contract adminstr., aircraft repair and overhaul Bristol Aerospace Ltd., Winnipeg, MB, Can., 1968-83; originator co. operating procedure Bristol Aerospace Ltd., Winnipeg, Man., Can., 1983-86. Editor aero. mag., 1956-60. Served to flight lt. Royal Can. Air Force, 1941-45. Decorated DFC, 1945, Aircrew Europe Star, 1945, France and Germany Clasp, 1945, Def. medal, 1945. Mem. Can. Aeoros. and Space Inst. (assoc. fellow). Mem. Adventist Ch. Clubs: Royal Air Force (London), Fleet Air Arm Officers (London). Address: Group 2 Box 9 Route 1, Anola, MB Canada R0E 0A0

DENG XIAOPING, government official People's Republic of China; b. Guang'an, Sichuan, China, Aug. 24, 1904. Attended French Sch., Chungking, Far Eastern U., Moscow; m. Cho Lin; children: Deng Pufang, Deng Chifang, Deng Rong, Deng Maomao. Joined Chinese Comminist

Party, 1926; dean edn. Chungshan Mil. Acad., Shensi, 1926; polit. commissar 7th Red Army, 1929; chief staff 3d Corps, Red Army, 1930; dir. propaganda dept. 1st Front Army on Long March, 1934-36; polit. commissar Sino-Japanese War; mem. 7th Cen. Com., Chinese Communist Party, 1945; polit. commissar 2d Field Army, People's Liberation Army, 1948-54; vice premier, 1952; mem. State Planning Commn., 1952-54; vice chmn. Chinese People's Polit. Consultative Conf., 1953, mem. Standing Com., 1954-59; minister of fin. 1953-54; vice chmn. Nat. Def. Council, 1954-67; 1st sec. East China Bur., Chinese Communist Party, 1949, sec.-gen. Cen. Com., 1953-56, mem. Politburo, 7th Cen. Com., 1955-67, mem. Politburo and Standing Com., sec.-gen. 8th Cen. Com., 1956, mem. 10th Cen. Com., 1973, mem. Politburo, 1974-76, vice chmn. Cen. Com., 1975-82, mem. Standing Com., 1975, vice chmn. mil. affairs com., 1975-76; chief gen. staff People's Liberation Army, 1977-80; mem. Politburo, 11th Cen. Com., 1977, mem. 12th Cen. Com., 1982-87, vice chmn. party, 1977, chmn. Nat. Com., from 1978; vice chmn. Nat. Def. Council, 1954-67; removed from office during Cultural Revolution, 1967, removed from office, 1976; chmn. Cen. Mil. Com., Chinese Communist Party, 1981—, chmn. Cen. Adv. Com., 1982-88. Avocation: swimming. Address: Office of Chmn, Cen Mil Commn, Beijing People's Republic of China

DENHAM, WILLIAM ERNEST, JR., clergyman, counselor; b. Louisville, Oct. 8, 1911; s. William E. and Myrtle (Lane) D.; m. Priscilla Kelley, June 27, 1941 (dec.); children: William Ernest III, James Kelley, Priscilla, Elizabeth Denham Thompson; m. 2d, Louise D. Yelvington, Nov. 23, 1974. A.B., Washington U., 1933; Th.M., So. Bapt. Theol. Sem., 1940, Ph.D., 1944; postgrad. U. Tex., Austin, 1971-73. Cert. counselor, Tex. Sec. Bapt. Student Union, Mo. Baptist Conv., 1933-35, Atlanta, 1935-37; pastor 1st Bapt. Ch., Newport, Tenn., 1944-47, Macon, Ga., 1947-52, River Oaks Bapt. Ch., Houston, 1952-64, 1st. Bapt. Ch., Austin, 1964-75; dir. Counseling and Pastoral Care Ctr., Austin, 1975-87, dir. spiritual growth, 1987—; mem. bd. Bapt. Radio Commn., So. Bapt. Conv.; exec. com. mem. Bapt. Gen. Conv., Tex.; first bd. chmn. Houston Bapt. U. Mem. Family Meditation Assn. (cert.), Am. Assn. Marriage and Family Therapists, Am. Assn. Sex Educators, Counselors and Therapists, Am. Assn. Pastoral Counselors (diplomate), Omicron Delta Kappa. Democrat. Lodges: Rotary, Kiwanis. Contbr. articles to profl. jours. Office: Counseling and Pastoral Care Ctr 3701 N Lamar Ave Austin TX 78705

DE NICOLA, PETER FRANCIS, holding company executive; b. N.Y.C., Oct. 28, 1954; s. Louis Joseph and Nancy Eleanor (Maddi) DeN.; B.S., NYU, 1976, M.B.A., 1978. Pres., founder P.F. DeNicola, Inc., N.Y.C., now Stamford, Conn., 1976-84; acct. Main Hurdman, N.Y.C., 1978-81; tax mgr. Gen. Signal Corp., Stamford, 1981-83; tax mgr. Emery Air Freight Corp., Wilton, Conn., 1983-85; dir. taxes A.I. Internat. Corp., N.Y.C., 1985—. Recipient Ferdinand W. Lafrentz acctg. award, 1977 C.P.A., Conn., N.Y. Mem. Tax Soc. NYU, Assn. M.B.A. Execs., Am. Mgmt. Assn., Stamford Tax Assn. (sec.-treas. 1988—), Nat. Assn. Accts., NYU Commerce Alumni Assn. (dir. 1978—, corr. sec. 1978-79, rec. sec. 1979-81, chmn. budget com. 1987—, chmn. Annual Bus. Conf. 1988), Am. Inst. C.P.A.s (fed. tax and tax acctg. coms. 1984—), N.Y. Soc. C.P.A.s (fed. and state tax com. 1983-85, depreciation and investment tax credit com. 1986-87), Conn. Soc. C.P.A.s, Tax Execs. Inst., Round Table Assn. of U.S. (co-founder 1986, nat. treas. 1987-88, pres. 1988—, del. to internat. convention, 1987), Estate Planning Council Westchester County, Round Table 3 of Greenwich (Conn.) (dir. 1984—, v.p. 1985-86, pres. 1986-88), Internat. Platform Assn. Republican. Roman Catholic. Clubs: NYU, Rockefeller Ctr. (N.Y.C.), Landmark, Long Ridge (Stamford); Saw Mill River Racquet (Mt. Kisco, N.Y.); Lakeover Country (Bedford Hills, N.Y.); St. James's (Antigua). Author: Legal Liability of Tax Return Preparers, 1978. Contbr. articles to tax and investment periodicals. Home: PO Box 4637 Stamford CT 06907 Office: A I Internat Corp 650 Fifth Ave New York NY 10019

DE NICOLAI, LINDA JANE, librarian; b. St. Annes, Lancashire, Eng., Mar. 7, 1962; arrived in Australia, 1968; d. Knud and Sheila Margaret (Burn) Hasberg; m. Oliver David de Nicolai, Aug. 19, 1983. B of Applied Sci., Western Australian Inst. Tech., Perth, 1981. Librarian Dwyer Durack, Perth, 1981-85, Hungerfords K.M.G., Perth, 1982-84, Ilbery Barblett & O'Dea, Perth, 1982-85, Fed. Ct. Australia, Perth, 1984-85, Atty.-Gen.'s Dept., Perth, 1985—. Editor: Union List of Law Reports in Western Australian Libraries, 1986; author: Index to Legislation Reproduced in Looseleaf Services, 1987. Recipient Queen's Guide award Girl Guides Assn., 1977, Wendy Rogers Meml. award Western Australian Inst. Tech., 1981. Mem. Library Assn. Australia (assoc.), Australian Law Librarians Group (sec. Western Australia chpt. 1984-87, treas. 1987—). Anglican. Office: Atty-Gen's Dept, 251 Adelaide Terr, Perth 6000, Australia

DENIS, ROBERT, video company executive; b. Buenos Aires, May 30, 1938; s. Julio Roberto and Dolores (Pereiras) D.; m. Kouka Denis, Oct. 20, 1967; children: Lisa Berenice, Alexandra, Jessica. BA, Buenos Aires U., 1963. TV dir. Channel 13, Buenos Aires, 1962-77, producer, 1965-77; cons. Buenos Aires, 1977-79; TV producer, dir. Channel 9, Buenos Aires, 1979-82; dir. films Videofilms S.A., Buenos Aires, 1983-84, pres., cons., 1988—; producer, dir. Crustel TV, Buenos Aires, 1985-87, cons., 1985—; cons. Capitalvision Inc., Miami, Fla., 1985—. Named Best TV Dir. Martin Fierro, 1973, 75, Best TV Producer Martin Fierro, 1976, Best TV Producer-Dir. Cruz de Plata, 1976. Mem. Union Civica Radical Party. Roman Catholic. Home: Parana 1331-F2, 01018 Buenos Aires Argentina

DENIUS, FRANKLIN WOFFORD, lawyer; b. Athens, Tex., Jan. 4, 1925; s. S.F. and Frances (Cain) D.; m. Charmaine Hooper, Nov. 19, 1949; children: Frank Wofford, Charmaine. B.B.A., LL.B., U. Tex. Bar: Tex. 1949. Practiced in Austin 1949—; past sec.-treas., dir. Telcom Corp.; pres., chief exec. officer, chmn. bd. So. Union Co.; dir. Tex. Commerce Bank-Austin; past legal counsel Austin Better Bus. Bur. Chmn. spl. schs. div. United Fund, 1960, Pacesetters div., 1961, Schs. div., 1964; 1st v.p. United Fund; chmn. steering com. sch. bond campaign, past trustee Austin Ind. Sch. Dist., 1964; past pres. Young Men's Bus. League Austin; past pres., exec. council Austin Ex-Students Assn. U. Tex.; co-chmn. LBJ U. Tex. Library Found.; mem. chancellor's council, pres.'s assos. U. Tex.; bd. dirs. Tex. Research League; advisory trustee Schreiner Coll. Decorated Silver Star medal with four oak leaf clusters, Purple Heart; recipient Outstanding Young Man of Austin award Jr. C. of C., 1959. Mem. ABA, Tex., Travis County bar assns., Tex. Philos. Soc. Presbyterian (deacon, elder). Clubs: Longhorn (past pres.), West Austin Optimists (past dir.), Headliners (pres., sec. bd. trustees, mem. exec. com.). Lodge: Masons. Home: 3703 Meadowbank Dr Austin TX 78703 Office: Tex Commerce Bank Bldg Suite #700 700 Lavaca Austin TX 78701-3102

DENIUS, HOMER RAINEY, electronics company executive; b. Appomattox, Va., Jan. 31, 1914; s. Frank E. and Margaret (Watters) D.; m. Grace Evelyn Pence, June 26, 1936; children—Chris F., Sandra Jeanne (Mrs. Robert Keeley), Homer R. Student U. Cin.; D.Sc. (hon.), Fla. Inst. Tech., 1964. Mgmt. exec., 1943—; chmn. bd. Electro-Sci. Mgmt. Corp., Melbourne, Fla., 1968—. Mason (32 deg.). Methodist. Office: 1600 Sarno Rd Suite 214 Melbourne FL 32935

DENJOY, JEAN FABRICE, physician; b. Paris, Jan. 1, 1925; s. Arnaud and Therese (Chevresson) D.; m. Caroline Adams Byrd, Apr. 27, 1957; children: Isabelle, Hughes-Arnaud, William Fabrice. MD, U. Paris, 1950; Diplome, Dommage Corporel, 1963. Intern Inst. Cancer, Villejuif, France, 1947-49; attache Hosp. St. Louis, Paris, 1971-76; practice medicine specializing in gen. medicine Paris, 1955—. Served with French Army, 1945. Mem. Ste. France Cancerologie Privee (archivist 1982—), Assn. Medicine Victimes d'Accidents. Club: Amis du Musee de Blerancourt. Home: 16 Ave Parmentier, 75011 Paris France Office: 104 Ave Parmentier, 75011 Paris France

DENKER, HENRY, playwright, author, director; b. N.Y.C., Nov. 25, 1912; s. Max and Jennie (Geller) D.; m. Edith Rose Heckman, Dec. 5, 1942. LL.B., N.Y. Law Sch., 1934. Bar: N.Y. 1935. Practiced law N.Y.C., 1935-38; exec. Research Inst. Am., N.Y.C., 1936-37; tax cons. Standard Stats. subs. Standard and Poor, N.Y.C., 1937-39; lectr. dramatic writing Am. Theatre Wing, 1961-63, Coll. of the Desert. Writer, dir., producer: (radio series) The Greatest Story Ever Told, N.Y.C., 1947-57; author: (Broadway plays) Time Limit, 1956, A Far Country, 1961, Venus at Large, 1962, A Case of Libel, 1964, What Did We Do Wrong, 1968, Something Old, Something New, 1976, Horowitz and Mrs. Washington, 1979; (off-Broadway) The Name of The Game, 1967; A Sound of Distant Thunder, 1969, The Headhunters, 1974; (screenplays) The Heartfarm, 1970; The Hook, Twilight of Honor, Time Limit, A Time for Miracles, 1980, Outrage, 1984; writer, dir., producer numerous TV dramas, 1950-66; TV spls. include Give us Barrabas, 1964; Neither are we Enemies, 1971, The Choice, The Court Martial of Lieutenant Calley, Mother Seton, 1980, Love Leads The Way, 1985, Outrage, 1986, Case of Libel, 1986; author: I'll Be Right Home, Ma, 1949, My Son, the Lawyer, 1950, Salome, Princess of Galilee, 1954, That First Easter, 1956, The Director, 1970, The Kingmaker, 1972, A Place for the Mighty, 1973, The Physicians, 1975, The Experiment, 1976, The Starmaker, 1977, The Scofield Diagnosis, 1977, The Actress, 1978, The Error of Judgement, 1979, Horowitz and Mrs. Washington, 1979, The Warfield Syndrome, 1981, Outrage!, 1982, The Healers, 1983, Kincaid, 1984, Love Leads the Way, 1985, A Case of Libel, 1985, Robert, My Son, 1985, Judge Spencer Dissents, 1986, The Choice, 1987, The Retreat, 1988. Mem. council Dramatists Guild, N.Y.C., 1967-69. Recipient Peabody award, 1949; Christopher award, 1953; Emmy award, 1948. Mem. Acad. TV Arts and Scis. (council), Authors League Council. Jewish. Address: 241 Central Park W New York NY 10024

DENKEWALTER, KIM RICHARD, lawyer; b. Chgo., May 7, 1948; s. Walter J. and Doris A. (Gast) D.; m. Laura Kim Thompson, May 28, 1988. B.A., Loyola U., Chgo., 1971; J.D., Chgo.-Kent Coll. Law, 1974. Bar: Ill. 1974, U.S. Dist. Ct. (no. dist.) Ill. 1974, U.S. Ct. Appeals (7th cir.) 1977, U.S. Supreme Ct. 1979. Ptnr., Abramovic, Denkewalter & Ryan, Northfield, Ill., 1974-79; pres. Denkewalter & Assocs., Northfield, 1979—; real estate broker, Chgo., 1978—; guest lectr. Am. Coll. Emergency Physicians, Rosemont, Ill., 1979-84. Pres. 539 Stratford Condo Assn., Chgo., 1985-86, sec. 1985-86, bd. dirs. 1985-86, treas. 1985-86; mem. Hoopis Fin. Group, Northfield, Ill. Served to staff sgt. USAR, 1970-76. Named EMT-A (hon.) Ill. Dept. Pub. Health, 1983. Mem. Ill. State Bar Assn., Chgo. Bar Assn., Assn. Trial Lawyers Am., ABA. Club: Brookwood Country. Home: 215 Ashbury Circle Park Ridge IL 60068 Office: Denkewalter & Angelo 790 Frontage Rd Northfield IL 60093

DENKOWSKA, ZOFIA BOGUMILA, mathematician, educator; b. Rzeszow, Poland; d. Piotr and Marcjanna (Kruszyna) Kazienko; m. Zdzislaw Denkowski, June 2, 1968; children: Bartlomiej, Maciej. MS, Jagellonian U., Krakow, Poland, 1971, PhD in Math., 1975. Asst. Jagellonian U., 1971-76, asst. prof. math., 1976—, cons. lang.; vis. prof. U. Rennes, Poitieres, France, 1986, U. Orsay, Paris, 1988. Contbr. articles to profl. jours. Mem. Polish Math. Soc., Am. Math. Assn., Polish Assn. Translators. Office: U Jagellonian Inst Math, Reymonta 4, 30059 Krakow Poland

DENKTAS, RAUF RAIF, Cypriot politician; b. Ktima, Paphos, Cyprus, Jan. 27, 1924; s. M. Raif bey; m. Aydin Munir, 1949; 4 children. Ed., English Sch., Nicosia, Cyprus, Lincoln's Inn, London. Practice law, Nicosia, 1947-49; Jr. Crown Counsel, 1949-52, Crown Counsel, 1952-56, acting Solicitor-Gen., 1956-58; pres. Fed. Turkish Cypriot Assns., 1958-60; pres. Turkish Communal Chamber, 1960; in exile for political reasons, 1963-68; v.p. Cyprus, 1973—; pres. Turkish Federated State of Cyprus, 1975-83; pres. Turkish Republic of Northern Cyprus, 1983—. Author: Secrets of Happiness, 1943; Hell Without Fire, 1944; A Handbook of Criminal Cases, 1955; Five Minutes to Twelve, 1966; The AKRITAS Plan, 1972; A Short Discourse on Cyprus, 1982; The Cyprus Problem, 1973; A Discourse with Youth, 1981; The Cyprus Triangle, 1982. Address: Office of President, Turkish Republic of Northern Cyprus, Lefkosa via Mersin 10 Turkey

DENMAN, ROY, British diplomat; b. June 12, 1924; s. Albert Edward and Gertrude Ann D.; attended St. John's Coll., Cambridge (Eng.) U.; m. Moya Lade, 1966; 2 children. War service, 1943-46; maj. Royal Signals, Joined BoT, 1948; asst. pvt. sec. to successive pres., 1950-52; 1st sec. Brit. embassy, Bonn, W. Ger., 1957-60; mem. U.K. del., Geneva, 1960-61; counsellor, Geneva, 1965-67; under-sec., 1967-70, BoT; dep. sec. DTI, 1970-74, Dept. Trade, 1974-75; 2d permanent sec. Cabinet Office, 1975-77; dir.-gen. for external affairs Commn. of European Communities, Brussels, 1977-82; mem. negotiating del. Commn. European Communities, 1970-72, head del., Washington, 1982—; mem. Brit. Overseas Trade Bd., 1972-75. Decorated CB, Order of St. Michael and St. George. Club: United Oxford and Cambridge Univ. Office: Suite 707 2100M St NW Washington DC 20037

DENMARK, JOHN CLIFFORD, psychiatrist; b. Liverpool, Eng., Feb. 15, 1924; s. Frank Lindley and Florence (Webster) D.; m. Frances Murray, Mar. 1, 1945; children: John Alexander, Kathleen Frances Bulmer. MB ChB, Liverpool U., 1952, MRCS LRCP, 1952; DPM, 1958; M of Psychological Medicine, Liverpool U., 1975. Licentiate Royal Coll. Physicians. Practice medicine specializing in psychiatry Preston, Eng.; hon. cons. Nat. Nose, Throat and Ear Hosp., London; hon. psychiatrist Royal Nat. Inst. for Deaf, London; hon. prof. U. Alta., Can., 1985. Contbr. articles to profl. jours. Served with Royal Navy, 1942-46. Recipient La Decoration au Merite Social Internat. World Fedn. Deaf, 1975, Bronze award BMA Annual Film Competition, Tribune award, 1985. Fellow Royal Coll. Psychiatrists; mem. Royal Coll. Surgeons. Mem. Church of England. Office: Dept Psychiatry for Deaf, Whittingham Hosp, Preston Lancashire England

DENMARK, LAWRENCE JAY, concrete products company executive; b. Miami Beach, Fla., Apr. 8, 1953; Irving J. and Evelyn (Kohn) D. B.S., Antioch Coll., Yellow Springs, Ohio, 1975; M.S., Univ. Coll. North Wales, 1975; Ph.D., Univ. Without Walls, Yellow Springs, 1980. Notary pub., Fla.; cert. tchr., Fla. Tchr., Dade County Pub. Sch. System, Miami, 1970, 75; research staff U. Miami, 1971, U. Calif.-San Diego, 1972, W. Indies Lab., St. Croix, 1973; v.p. Denmark Art Stone Co., Miami, 1975—, pres., 1986—, chief exec. officer, 1984—; dir. Denmark Cast Stone Co., Reil Advt., Denmark Synergisms, Oceana Lab., Tectona Industries; cons. in field.; bd. dirs. Alfred P. Sloan Found., Yellow Springs, Ohio, 1974-75. Mem. Am. Mgmt. Assn., S. Fla. Builders Assn., Nat. Precast Concrete Assn., AAAS, Fla. Nurseryman's Assn., Internat. Oceanographic Found. Lodge: Rotary. Office: Denmark Art Stone Co 12351 NW 7th Ave Miami FL 33168

DENNELL, ROBIN WILLIAM, prehistory educator; b. Plymouth, Devon, Eng., Apr. 1, 1947; s. Ernest and Suzanne (Furneaux) D. BA with hons., Pembroke Coll., 1969, MA, 1973, PhD, 1977. Lectr. archeology and prehistory dept. U. Sheffield, Eng., 1973-83, sr. lectr., 1983—; reviewer research grants U.S., Can. and Australia, 1979—. Author: Early Farming in South Bulgaria, 1978, European Economic Prehistory, 1983; contbr. numerous articles to profl. jours. Office: U Sheffield, Dept Archeology and Prehistory, Sheffield S10 2TN, England

DENNEY, AL B., JR., motion picture producer; b. Waco, Tex., Mar. 15, 1935; s. Albert B. and Mary E. (Fason) D.; m. Christine Denney; 1 son, Rick L. Student San Antonio Jr. Coll., 1953, 57-58, Tex. Chiropractic Coll., 1953, 57-58. Owner, screen writer, newsreel cameraman, location mgr., lighting dir., stunt driver Ind. Artists Prodns., Winnetka, Calif., 1965—; owner/broker DenReal Co., 1961—; owner/designer The Dennehy Touch, 1972—. Served with USMC, 1953-56. Recipient awards Brit. Broadcasting Co., Cannes Film Festival, Underwater Film Festival. Mem. Dirs. Guild Am., Internat. Photography Guild, I.A., Underwater Photographer Soc., Am. Soc. Lighting Dirs., Acad. TV Arts and Scis., Am. Film Inst., Internat. Platform Assn., VFW, Am. Legion. Republican. Lodge: Elks. Office: 20360 Haynes St Winnetka CA 91306

DENNEY, TALBERT L., real estate investment broker, antique and classic automobile dealer; b. Leedey, Okla., Apr. 23, 1928; s. James Harden and Myrtle Mae (Eaton) D.; student pub. schs., Stockton, Calif.; m. Barbara Pilcher, Feb. 17, 1951; children: Melanie Ann, Monica Susan. Owner cleaning co., Portland, Oreg. and Santa Barbara, Calif., 1959-67; co-founder, pres. Servpro Industries, Inc., Rancho Cordova, Calif., 1967-78, chmn. bd. 1978-84; condr. seminars on principles of success. Served with U.S. Army, 1950-52. Mem. Am. Mgmt. Assn., Internat. Franchise Assn, Airplane Owners and Pilots Assn., Am. Bonanza Soc. Office: PO Box 1648 Gardnerville NV 89410

DENNING, MICHAEL MARION, computer company executive; b. Durant, Okla., Dec. 22, 1943; s. Samuel M. and Lula Mae (Waitman) D.; m. Suzette Karin Wallance, Aug. 10, 1968 (div. 1979); children—Lila Monique, Tanya Kerstin, Charlton Derek; m. Donna Jean Hamel, Sept. 28, 1985; 1 child, Caitlin Shannon. Student USAF Acad., 1963; B.S., U. Tex., 1966; B.S., Fairleigh Dickinson U., 1971; M.S., Columbia U., 1973. Mgr. systems IBM, White Plains, N.Y., 1978-79, mgr. service and mktg., San Jose, Calif., 1979-81; nat. market support mgr. Memorex Corp., Santa Clara, Calif., 1981, v.p. mktg., 1981-82; v.p. mktg. and sales Icot Corp., Mountain View, Calif., 1982-83; exec. v.p. Phase Info. Machines Corp., Scottsdale, Ariz., 1983-84; exec. v.p. Tricom Automotive Dealer Systems Inc., Hayward, Calif., 1985-87; pres. ADS Computer Services, Inc., Toronto, Ont., Can., 1985-87; pres. Denning Investments, Inc., Palo Alto, Calif., 1987—. Served with USAF, 1962-66; Vietnam. Mem. Phi Beta Kappa, Lambda Chi Alpha (pres. 1965-66). Republican. Methodist. Home: H-1030 Parkwood Way Redwood City CA 94061 Office: Denning Investments Inc O-525 Univ Ave Suite 203 Palo Alto CA 94301

DENNIS, DONALD PHILIPS, association executive; b. Kenton, Ohio, Nov. 3, 1916; s. Ray H. and Ella Maude (Snodgrass) D.; B.A., Wittenberg Coll., 1939; M.A., U. Minn., 1942; m. Helen Frances Hogue, Dec. 25, 1939; children—Donna Frances, Nancy Petiya, Katherine E. Page, M. Anne Toccafondi. Mgr., Kans. Assn. Municipal Utilities, 1941-42; exec. dir. Fed. Union, Inc., 1946-49; asso. exec. dir. Atlantic Union Com., 1949-52, dir., 1953; bus. mgr., asst. sec.-treas. Fgn. Policy Assn., 1953-79, v.p., 1980-86. Sec., dir. Fed. Union, Inc., 1961-84; sec., dir.Assn. to Unite the Democracies (U.S.); chmn. commn. for Internat. Assn. to Unite the Democracies; pres. Rye Forum; mem. U.S. del. to Atlantic Congress, London, 1959, to Chinese Peoples Inst. Fgn. Affairs, 1979; bd. govs., exec. com. Atlantic Union Com., 1953-61. Served as lt. (j.g.), staff comdr. 7th Fleet, USNR, 1943-45. Mem. Assn. Internat. Relations Clubs (nat. exec. com. 1958-65), Nat. Council Christian Social Action (internat. relations com. 1953-63). Sigma Delta Chi, Phi Mu Delta. Presbyterian (elder). Home and Office: 9 Charlotte St Rye NY 10580

DENNIS, DOROTHY (MRS. LESTER JOHN DENNIS), insurance broker; b. Esther, Mo., Oct. 18; d. William Arthur and Rosalie (Jinkerson) Bates; student Washington U. Coll., 1937-40; m. Lester John Dennis, June 8, 1940 (dec. Dec. 1947); children: Bytell, June D. Bytell. Property mgr. Ralph D'Oench Co., realtors, 1944-46; fleet sales mgr. Rauscher Chevrolet Co., 1948-50; pres. Automotive Cons., Inc., 1950-60; propr. Dorothy Dennis Ins. Co., 1951—; pres. Fgn. Cars, Ltd., Inc., 1956-60; founder, pres. Hosp. Television, Inc., 1959—, Birthday Photographs, Inc., 1959-82, Media Projects Co., 1986-87; founder, pres. Dennis Enterprises, Kirkwood, Mo., 1987—; pioneer woman in automobile sales cons. field, 1951-60; founder, pres. Ambassador Services Co., 1968-72. Bd. dirs. women's div. Better Bus. Bur. Greater St. Louis, 1956-62, Grand Jurors Assn. St. Louis County, 1971-76; mem. adv. bd. St. Mary on the Mount Hosp. and Rehab. Center, 1982—; mem. St. Louis County Bd. Election Commrs., 1957-61; adv. bd. SSM Rehab. Inst., 1982—. Named Woman of Distinction, City of Kirkwood, Mo., 1986. Hist. research and compilation data on founder of order of nuns devoted to adminstrn. hosps. and edn. hosp. personnel, 1960—. Home: 522 Dougherty Ferry Rd Bedford Oaks Kirkwood MO 63122

DENNIS, SAMUEL SIBLEY, III, lawyer; b. Boston, June 23, 1910; s. Samuel Sibley and Helen M. (Ferguson) D.; m. Lillian Elena Williamson, Aug. 19, 1938; children: Nancy Anne (dec.), Ellen Ferguson. AB, Harvard U., 1932, MBA, 1934, LLB, 1938. Bar: Mass. 1938. Sr. ptnr. Hale & Door, 1951—; v.p. Standex Internat. Corp., Andover, Mass., 1955—, also bd. dirs., mem. exec. com. and gen. counsel; bd. dirs. Vaponics, Inc., Knott Tool & Mfg. Co., Augat, Inc., A.T. Cross Co., Dresher Inc., French River Industries; former mem. vis. com. of bd. overseers Law Sch., former co-chmn. bequest Com. Bus. Sch., Harvard U., past mem. com. stockholder responsibility. Pres. Roxbury Latin Sch., 1972-84, life trustee, vice chmn., 1984—; mem. corp. Jordan Hosp., Plymouth; past trustee Leslie Coll.; bd. dirs. Joint Ctr. for Econ. Edn., Montgomery Found., Fairchild Fellows. Served to col. C.E., AUS, 1941-45, now col. Res. Decorated Legion of Merit. Mem. ABA, Mass. Bar Assn., Boston Bar Assn., Mil. Order World Wars, Harvard Bus. Sch. Assn., Harvard Law Sch. Assn. (former bd. govs.), World Affairs Council. Clubs: Harvard U. (Boston and Miami, Fla.); Duxbury Yacht; Country (Brookline, Mass.); Key Largo, Anglers, Coral Reef, Ocean Reef; Masons. Home: 52 Essex Rd Chestnut Hill MA 02167 also: 175 Washington St Duxbury MA 02332 Office: Hale and Dorr 60 State St Boston MA 02109

DENNIS, SHIRLEY MAE, federal agency administrator; b. Omaha, Feb. 26, 1938; d. Millard and Iantha (Hall) Haynes; m. William D.C. Dennis, Dec. 28, 1968; children: Pamela Peoples, Robin, Sherrie. Student Cheyney State Coll., 1955-56; A.S. in Bus. Adminstrn., Temple U., 1985; J.D. (hon.), Lincoln U., 1986. Sales and office mgr. Tucker and Tucker, Phila., 1961-67; equal opportunity specialist Redevel. Authority Phila., 1967-68; housing dir. Urban League of Phila., 1969-71; pub., founder Infill mag., Phila., 1972-79; mng. dir. Housing Assn. Delaware Valley, Phila., 1971-79; sec. Pa. Dept. Community Affairs, Harrisburg, 1979-86; dir. Women's Bur., U.S. Dept. of Labor, Washington, 1986—; chairperson Pa. Housing Fin. Agy., 1979-86, Pa. Martin Luther King, Jr. Holiday Commn., Local Govt. Records Com.; mem. Pa. Gov.'s Econ. Cabinet; sec. Pa. Indsl. Devel. Authority. Mem. sustaining adv. bd. Abington Meml. Hosp., 1981-82; bd. dirs. Abington Meml. Health Care Corp., 1983—; mem. Crestmont Bapt. Fed. Credit Union, 1970—; pres. Willow Grove br. NAACP, 1972-80, mem. exec. bd. Pa. State Conf. br., 1976-86; mem. Coalition of 100 Black Women, Phila. Tribune Charities. Recipient Assn. Black Journalists award, 1978, Nat. Freedom award, 1980, Pub. Service award Pa. Fedn. Bus. and Profl. Women's Clubs, 1980, Woman of Yr. award Black Women's Collective, 1981, Community Service award Nat. Assn. Negro Bus. and Profl. Women, 1981, Leadership award Pa. Tribune Charities. Mem. Community Info. Exchange, Nat. Conf. Women Execs in State Govt. (bd. dirs. 1985), Nat. Conf. State Housing Fin. Chairpersons (exec. com. 1983-85), Council of State Community Affairs Agys. (exec. bd. 1980-85). Republican. Baptist. Columnist Phila. Tribune, Phila. Daily News, 1974-75; author HADV housing series, Phila. Daily News, 1974; producer film Floodplain: The Path of Nature's Power, 1984 (award). Home: 1656 Easton Rd Willow Grove PA 19090 Office: Dept Labor Women's Bur 200 Constitution Ave NW Washington DC 20210

DENNISH, GEORGE WILLIAM, III, cardiologist; b. Trenton, N.J., Feb. 14, 1945; s. George William and Mary Ann (Bodnar) D.; A.B. magna cum laude, Seton Hall U., 1967; M.D., Jefferson Med. Coll., 1971; m. Kathleen Macchi, June 28, 1969; children—Andrew Stuart, Brian George, Michael John. Intern, Naval Hosp., Phila., 1971-72, jr. asst. resident, 1972-73, sr. asst. resident, 1973-74; fellow cardiovascular diseases Naval Regional Med. Center, San Diego, 1974-76, dir. coronary care unit, 1977-78; practice medicine specializing in cardiology, San Diego, 1974—, pvt. practice, 1978—; v.p. Splty. Med. Clinic, La Jolla and San Diego, 1982—; staff cardiologist Naval Regional Med. Center, Faculty Medicine, San Diego, 1976—; dir. spl. care units Scripps Meml. Hosp., La Jolla, 1981—, chmn. cardiology div., 1987—; chief medicine Scripps-Encinitas Hosp., 1983—; asst. clin. prof. medicine U. Calif., San Diego, 1976—. Bd. dirs. San Diego County Heart Assn.; founder, pres., Cardiovascular Inst., La Jolla. Served to lt. comdr. USNR, 1971—. Decorated Knight of Holy Sepulchre; recipient Physician's Recognition award AMA, 1974-77; diplomate Am. Bd. Internal Medicine (sub-splty. cert. in cardiovascular diseases), Nat. Bd. Med. Examiners. Fellow ACP, Am. Coll. Cardiology, Am. Heart Assn. (clin. council), Am. Coll. Chest Physicians, Am. Coll. Angrology mem. Am. Soc. Internal Medicine, AAAS, Am. Coll. Clin. Pharmacology, N.Y. Acad. Scis., Am. Fedn. Clin. Research, N.Am. Soc. Pacing and Electrophysiology. Roman Catholic. Club: Old Mission Players, K.C. Contbr. articles to med. jours. Home: 15696 El Camino Real PO Box 2302 Rancho Santa Fe CA 92067 Office: 351 Santa Fe Dr Suite 200 Encinitas CA 92024 Other: 9844 Genesee Ave Suite 400 La Jolla CA 92037

DENNISON, RONALD WALTON, engineer; b. San Francisco, Oct. 23, 1944; s. S. Mason and Elizabeth Louise (Hatcher) D.; m. Sandra Lee Johnson; children—Ronald, Frederick. B.S. in Physics and Math., San Jose State U., 1970, M.S. in Physics, 1972. Physicist, Memorex, Santa Clara, Calif., 1970-71; sr. engr. AVCO, San Jose, Calif., 1972-73; advanced devel. engr. Perkin Elmer, Palo Alto, Calif., 1973-75; staff engr. Hewlett-Packard, Santa Rosa, Calif., 1975-79; program gen. mgr. Burroughs, Westlake Village, Calif., 1979-82; dir. engring., founder EIKON, Simi Valley, Calif., 1982-85; sr. staff technologist Maxtor Corp., San Jose, 1987—; materials. Author tech. publs. Served to sgt. USAF, 1963-67. Mem. IEEE, Am. Vacuum Soc., Internat. Soc. Hybrid Microelectronics, Am. Nat. Standards Inst. (com. rigid disks), Disk Equipment and Materials Assn. Republican. Methodist. Mem. Aircraft Owners and Pilots Assn., Internat. Comanche Soc., Ventura County Aviators Assn. Home: 2764 Granvia Place Thousand Oaks CA 91360

DENNY, WILLIAM MURDOCH, JR., investment management executive; b. Schenectady, N.Y., June 10, 1934; s. William Murdock and Ione Elizabeth (Lundy) D.; ScB in Chemistry, Brown U., 1958; MBA in Fin., Drexel U., 1974; m. Delores Gay Shillady, June 11, 1966; children: Ellen Gay, Nancy Beth, Linda Ann. Mem. mgmt. staff chem. specialities div. Pennwalt Corp., Phila., 1961-73; pres. Denny Fin. Enterprises, Paoli, Pa., 1974—; chmn. mgmt. com. Houston-County Coal Co. Interests, Crockett, Tex., 1987—. Bd. dirs. United Way of North Central Chester County, 1980-83. Served to lt. comdr. USN, 1959-61. Mem. Fin. Analysts Fedn., Fin. Analysts Phila., Navy League U.S., Phi Kappa Psi. Episcopalian. Clubs: Brown U. (pres. 1979-81) (Phila.); Aronimink Golf (Newtown Square, Pa.); Yacht of Hilton Head Island (S.C.); Sea Pines. Home: 6 Anthony Dr Malvern PA 19355

DE NOBLET D'ANGLURE, COUNT FRANÇOIS, physician; b. Berlin, Fed. Republic Germany, May 7, 1947; s. Count Jean and Nicole (De Sevin) De N. BA, U. Paris, 1967, postdoctoral in homeopathy and acupuncture, 1977-80; Dr. in Medicine, U. Besançon, France, 1977. Practice medicine specializing in acupuncture and honeopathy Paris, 1980—. Named Honour's and Devotion's Knight, Sovereign Order St. John of Jerusalem and Malta, 1986. Mem. French Soc. Phyto-Aromatherapy. Roman Catholic. Club: French Nobility Assn. (Paris). Home and Office: 21 Ave Jean Moulin, 75014 Paris France

DENOEUX, JEAN-PAUL, dermatologist; b. Amiens, Somme, France, Apr. 26, 1942; s. Pierre and Therese-Marie (Debouverie) D.; m. Michele Plouchart, Mar. 26, 1966; children: Olivier, François. MD, U. Picardy, Amiens, 1969. Interne U. Regional Hosp., Amiens, 1967-72; chef de clinique Faculty Medicine, Amiens, 1972-78; asst. U. Regional Hosp., Amiens, 1972-78; prof. dermatology and venereology Faculty Medicine, Amiens, 1978—; head dermatology and venereology dept. U. Regional Hosp., Amiens, 1981—; founder, chmn. Picardy study group on AIDS, H.I.V. infection; pub. service physician anti-venereal diseases, Amiens, 1974—. Contbr. numerous articles to profl. jours. Mem. Assn. French-Speaking Dermatologists and Syphiligraphists, French Soc. Dermatology and Syphiligraphy, European Soc. Pediatric Dermatology, Dermatol. Research Soc. Roman Catholic. Lodge: Lions. Office: Univ Regional Hosp, Dept Dermatology and Venereology, South Hosp, 80030 Amiens Cedex France

DENOIX, GILLES HUBERT, reconstructive surgeon; b. Paris, Apr. 22, 1924; s. Leon Auguste and Christine Marie (Rigolot) D.; m. Therese Albertine Foucart, July, 9, 1955; children: Monique (Mrs. T.M. Gaudard), Antoine, Jean-Luc. MD, U. Paris, 1953. Cert. specialist in stomatology 1964, Maxillo-facial surgery 1979. Practice medicine specializing in reconstructive surgery Paris; chargé de cours la Faculté de Medecine de Paris VII, 1981—; attaché Des Hospitaux de Paris, 1973; asst. Hosp. St. Joseph de Paris, 1973, Hosp. de la Région Parisienne, 1979; chef de service Centre Hospitalier, Creil, France, 1979—; expert Cour d' Appel, Paris, 1972. Editor: Cahiers de Stomatologie et de Chirurgie Maxillo-Faciale, 1977—. Fellow Internat. Assn. Oral Surgery. Home and Office: 71 Rue de Monceau, 75008 Paris France

DENOOYER, LAMBERT DAVID, banker; b. Lawton, Okla., Mar. 27, 1946; s. Lambert and Margaret Josephine (Van Houten) DeN.; student Bucknell U., 1964-66; B.S. in Mech. Engring., Newark Coll., Engring., 1969; M.B.A., Fairleigh Dickinson U., 1980; m. Karen Ann Hartford, June 27, 1970; children—Lambert David, Kelly Ann. Asso. engr. Gen. Dynamics Co., San Diego, 1969-71, sr. mech. engr., Avenel, N.J., 1971-73; asso. Mortgage Brokerage Services, East Orange, N.J., 1973-74; v.p. United Mortgage and Real Estate Corp., East Orange, N.J., 1974-76, Heathecote Equities, Ft. Lee, N.J., 1976-78; analyst Midlantic Mortgage Corp., Newark, 1978-82, asst. v.p., 1982-84; asst. v.p. First Fidelity Bank N.A., North Jersey, 1984-85, v.p., 1985-88; v.p. and mgr. comml. real estate lending, Ensign bank, FSB, Fort Lee, N.J., 1988—; cons. Recipient profl. devel. award Newark Coll. Engring., 1967. Mem. Mortgage Bankers Assn. (young mortgage bankers com., income property investment com.), N.J. Mortgage Bankers Assn., Delta Mu Delta. Roman Catholic. Club: KC. Home: 21 Crescent Dr Convent NJ 07961 Office: Ensign Bank FSB 2011 Lemone Ave Fort Lee NJ 07024

DENOVIO, SUSAN WILLIAMS, advertising agency executive; b. Phila., Feb. 9, 1948; d. William Clinton and Catherine Irene (Currie) Williams; m. Carl James DeNovio, Aug. 9, 1969 (div. 1982); 1 child, Nicole Marie. BA Journalism, Rider Coll., 1969. Coordinator publications Ocean County Coll., Toms River, N.J., 1969-72; pub. info. officer Burlington County Coll., Pemberton, N.J., 1972-73, asst. to pres. for pub. info., 1973-75; freelance copywriter, Yardley, Pa., 1978-80; mng. editor Ad World, Inc., Levittown, Pa., 1980-83; founder, pres. Catalyst Communications, Inc., Newtown, Pa., 1983-88, Vista Communications Inc., Newtown, 1988—; mktg. cons. Mercer County Small Bus. Devel. Ctr., Trenton, N.J., 1983-84; instr. continuing edn. Bucks County Community Coll., Newtown, 1985-87. Editor, contbg. author: Bucks' Fortune, 1983. Bd. dirs. YWCA of Bucks County, Langhorne, Pa., 1984—, recording sec., 1984-86. Recipient Outstanding Service award Bd. Trustees Burlington County Coll., 1975; cert. of Recognition Bucks County Community Coll., 1985; Addy award Phila. Club Advt. Women, 1985, Neographics Silver award Greater Del. Valley Graphic Arts Assn., 1986. Mem. Lower Bucks County C. of C., Greater Phila. C. of C., Pi Delta Epsilon. Republican. Roman Catholic. Office: Vista Communications Inc Newtown Indsl Commons 111 Pheasant Run Newtown PA 18940

DENSCHLAG, JOHANNES OTTO, chemistry educator; b. Worms, Germany, July 1, 1937; s. Johannes and Hiltrud (Schildhauer) D.; m. Ilse Schlüter, Dec. 28, 1965; children: Marie Karoline, Johannes Peter, Gabriele Gisela. Diploma in chemistry, Mainz U., Fed. Republic of Germany, 1961, doctorate degree, 1965, habilitation, 1971. Research assoc. U. Mich., Ann Arbor, 1965-66; instr. U. Calif., Irvine, 1966-67; privatdozent U. Mainz, 1972, auBerplanmäBiger prof., 1972-73, prof., 1973—; vis. prof. Univ. Kyoto, Kumatori, Japan, 1974. Contbr. articles to profl. jours. Mem. Gesellschaft Deutscher Chemiker, Hochschulverband. Roman Catholic. Office: Inst für Kernchemie, Saarstr 20, D-6500 Mainz Federal Republic of Germany

DENSMORE, DANA, educator, publisher, computer technologist; b. Washington, Mar. 27, 1945; d. Russell Wykoff and Donna Claire Allen; B.A., St. John's Coll., 1965. Founder, Ja Shin Do Acad., Washington, 1974-82; founder, dir. Artemis Inst. Boston, Washington, Los Angeles, Santa Fe, 1978—; systems programmer Apollo Project, MIT, 1966-72, Space Shuttle, 1972-77; sr. product planner Nixdorf Computer Corp., 1980-82, faculty mem. St. Johns Coll., Santa Fe, 1987—; founder A Woman of Power, self-empowerment tng. for women, 1980—, Awareness Energetics, tng. for mind-body integration, 1982—; founder Creative Ptnrng Relationship Empowerment Tng., 1987—, co-convenor Feminist Computer Tech. Project, 1979; cons. Women's Satellite Project, 1978; bd. dirs., cons., editor Women's Inst. for Freedom of Press, 1972—. Editor, pub. No More Fun and Games, 1968-72; editor, pub. Black Belt Woman, mag., 1975-76; pub. The Artemis Path, 1983—. Home: PO Box 4787 Santa Fe NM 87502

DENT, ERNEST DUBOSE, JR., physician; b. Columbia, S.C., May 3, 1927; s. E. Dubose and Grace (Lee) D.; student Presbyn. Coll., 1944-45; M.D., Med. Coll. S.C., 1949; m. Dorothy McCalman, June 16, 1949; children—Christopher, Pamela; m. 2d, Karin Frehse, Sept. 6, 1970. Intern U.S. Naval Hosp., Phila., 1949-50; resident pathology USPHS Hosp., Balt., 1950-54; chief pathology USPHS Hosp., Norfolk, Va., 1954-56; asso. pathology Columbia (S.C.) Hosp., 1956-59; pathologist Columbia Hosp., S.C. Baptist Hosp., also dir. labs., 1958-69; with Straus Clin. Labs., Los Angeles, 1969-72; staff pathologist St. Joseph Hosp., Burbank, Calif., Hollywood (Calif.) Community Hosp., 1969-72; dir. labs. Meml. Hosp. of Glendale, 1972—. Diplomate clin. pathology and pathology anatomy Am. Bd. Pathology. Mem. Am. Cancer Soc., AMA, Los Angeles County Med. Assn. (pres. Glendale dist. 1980-81), Calif. Med. Assn. (councillor 1984—), Am. Soc. Clin. Pathology, Coll. Am. Pathologists (assemblyman S.C. 1965-67; mem. publs. com. bull. 1968-70), Los Angeles Soc. Pathologists (trustee 1984-87), Los Angeles Acad. Medicine, S.C. Soc. Pathologists (pres. 1967-69). Lutheran. Author papers nat. med. jours. Home: 1526 Blue Jay Way Los Angeles CA 90069 Office: 1420 S Central Ave Glendale CA 91204

DENTINGER, RONALD LEE, comedian, speaker; b. Milw., Feb. 14, 1941; s. William Cassel and Kathryn Faye (Ritzman) D.; m. Kaylee Ann Kasten, Aug. 28, 1965; children: Ronald Lee Jr., Joann Jean. Officer Milw. Police Dept., 1962-67; dist. mgr. Am. Automobile Assn., Madison, Wis., 1967-71; gen. mgr. Don Q Inn, Dodgeville, Wis., 1971-85; comedian, speaker, Dodgeville, 1976—; humorist quoted in comedy mags., books; jokes sold to Rodney Dangerfield, 1980—, Joan Rivers, The Tonight Show, Saturday Night Live, 20/20 Show, Time Mag. Pres. Hidden Valley Tourism Region, Wis., 1984. Named Funniest Person in Wis., Showtime-TV Network, 1985. Mem. Nat. Speakers Assn., Wis. Profl. Speakers Assn., Dodgeville C. of C. (pres. 1984). Home and Office: PO Box 151 Dodgeville WI 53533

DENTON, RAY DOUGLAS, insurance company executive; b. Lake City, Ark., May 16, 1937; s. Ray Dudney and Edna Lorraine (Roe) D.; B.A., U. Mich., 1964, postgrad., 1969-70; J.D., Wayne State U., 1969, postgrad., 1964-65; m. Cheryl Emma Borchardt, Mar. 9, 1964; children—Ray D., Derek St. Clair, Carter Lee. Claims rep. Hartford Ins. Co., Crum & Forster, Detroit, and Am. Claims, Chgo., 1962-73; partner Chgo. Metro Claims, Oak Park, Ill., 1974-75; founder, pres. Ray D. Denton & Assocs., Inc., Hinsdale, Ill., 1975—. Mem. Pi Kappa Alpha, Phi Alpha Delta. Home: 4532 Howard Western Springs IL 60558 Office: 930 N York Suite 1 Hinsdale IL 60521

DENTON, ROGER MARIUS, lawyer; b. Galveston, Tex., Feb. 23, 1946; s. Dan N. and Frances Elizabeth (Hotopp) D; m. Beverly Joyce Bauer; 1 child, Michael. B.A., Loyola U., New Orleans, 1968, J.D., 1971. Bar: La. 1971, U.S. Dist. Ct. (ea. dist.) La. 1971, U.S. Ct. Appeals (5th cir.) 1971, U.S. Supreme Ct. 1976. Pres. Roger M. Denton, P.C., Metairie, La., 1971—. Vice-chmn. Jefferson Parish Charter Adv. Bd., 1980; chmn. East Jefferson chpt. ARC, 1980-81; pres. Civic Council East Jefferson, 1975-76; pres. Willowdale Civic Assn., 1973-74; bd. dirs. Lafreniere Park Found., 1982-87, sec., 1986-87; pres. Friends of Lafreniere Park, 1983-84; trustee United Way of Greater New Orleans, 1983—, vice chmn. bd. of trustees, 1986—; bd. dirs., mem. exec. com. S.E. La. chpt. ARC, 1983-85, bd. dirs., 1983-88. Served to capt. USAR. Recipient award of merit ARC, 1969; Silver Beaver award Boy Scouts Am., 1976 . Mem. ABA, La. Bar Assn. (ho. of dels. 1987—), Fed. Bar Assn., Jefferson Bar Assn., Assn. Trial Lawyers Am., La. Trial Lawyers Assn., New Orleans Acad. Trial Lawyers, New Orleans and River Region C. of C. (bd. dirs. 1981-83, chmn. East Jefferson Council 1982), Veterans Blvd. Bus. Assn. (pres. 1982), Internat. Platform Assn. Republican. Roman Catholic. Club: Rotary (pres. 1978-79, dist. chmn. Internat. Service, 1985-87, mem. dist. coordinating com. 1985-87, Paul Harris Fellowship 1987). Author La. Civil Practice Forms, 1985. Assoc. editor Loyola Law Rev., 1970-71; editor Jefferson Bar Assn. Record, 1979-80. Home: 2401 Elise Ave PO Box 73789 Metairie LA 70033 Office: 1900 Veterans Blvd Suite 104 Metairie LA 70005

D'ENTREMONT, EDWARD JOSEPH, infosystems engineer, educator; b. Lynn Mass., June 25, 1954; s. Joseph Albenie and Gertrude Grace (Flattery) D'E. B.A. in Math., Salem State Coll., 1972-76; M.S. in Applied Math., Northeastern U., 1982. Floor supr. Jordan Marsh Co., Peabody, Mass., 1972-76; sci. programmer Electronics Corp. Am., Cambridge, Mass., 1977, Sulivan and Cogliano, Waltham, Mass., 1977; software engr. Raytheon Service Co., Burlington, Mass., 1977-86, Raytheon Missile Systems div., Bedford, Mass., 1986—. Editor-in-chief Salem State Coll. Yearbook, 1975, 76. Campaign worker presdl. campaigns, 1968-72, City Council and State Rep., Lynn, 1976, Dukakis for Gov., Lynn, 1982. Mem. Am. Math. Soc., Math. Assn. Am., Soc. Indsl. and Applied Math., IEEE, IEEE Computer Soc., N.Y. Acad. Scis., Assn. Computing Machinery, St. Mary's High Alumni Assn., Salem State Alumni Assn., Northeastern Alumni Assn. Democrat. Roman Catholic. Club: Lexington Racquet and Swim. Home: 50 York Rd Lynn MA 01904

DENVER, DANIEL JOSEPH, utilities executive, nuclear engineer; b. N.Y.C., Dec. 21, 1944; s. Daniel Joseph and Katherine Ann (Boland) D.; m. Maureen Diane Conroy, June 11, 1966; children: Daniel Thomas, Molly Kathryn, Tammy Maureen, Katherine Eileen. Registered profl. engr., Va. Scientist Westinghouse Bettis Atomic Power Lab., West Mifflin, Pa., 1967-71; assoc. engr. Pub. Service Electric and Gas Co., Newark, 1971-73; sr. reactor physicist Yankee Atomic Electric Co., Westboro, Mass., 1973-77; v.p. ops. Energy, Inc., Idaho Falls, 1977-88; mgr. nuclear engring. Houston Light and Power Co., 1988—. Mem. fin. com. Town of Holliston, Mass., 1975-76. Fellow Atomic Energy Commn. MIT, 1966-67. Mem. Am. Nuclear Soc., ASME. Roman Catholic. Home: 125 Arrowwood Rd Lake Jackson TX 77566 Office: Houston Light and Power Co PO Box 1700 Houston TX 77011

DENYS, R. B., diplomat; b. Rio de Janeiro, Oct. 12, 1927; s. Odylio and Maria Heiza (Bayma) D.; m. Suzanne S. Denys, Dec. 16, 1957; children: Renata, Jean Francois. Degree in Law, U. Rio de Janeiro, 1951. Consulate gen. Brazil Barcelona, Spain, 1970-74; Brazilian ambassador to El Salvador San Salvador, 1974-79; Brazilian Ambassador to Senegal Dakar, 1979-85; Brazilian ambassador to Costa Rica San Jose, 1985-88; Brazilian ambassador to Tunisia Tunis, 1988—. Office: Brazilian Embassy, Edificio Plaza Artilleria 7, Calle 4, San Jose Costa Rica

DENYSYK, BOHDAN, business executive; b. Kornberg, Germany, Feb. 13, 1947; came to U.S., 1949; s. John and Maria (Zelenewich) D.; m. Halina Bubela, June 28, 1969; children: Maria H., Danya L., Adrienne Y., Alexis M. B.S., Manhattan Coll., 1968; M.S., Cath. U. Am., 1971; Ph.D., Union Exptl. Colls. and Univs., 1981. Project mgr. Naval Weapons Lab., Dahlgren, Va., 1968-72; scientist Naval Med. Research Inst., Bethesda, Md., 1972-75; program mgr. Naval Surface Weapons Ctr., Dahlgren, 1975-78; dept. head E.G. & G. Inc., Rockville, Md., 1978-81; dep. asst. sec. U.S. Dept. Commerce, Washington, 1981-83; dir. civil programs IBM Corp., 1983-86; pres. DLR Assocs., Arlington, Va., 1972-80, 83—; sr. v.p. Global U.S.A., 1986—; mem. Congl. Adv. Panel on China, 1985—. Contbr. articles to profl. jours. Mem. Presdl. Transition Team, Washington, 1981; regional dir. Rep. Nat. Com., 1980; dir. pub. relations Ukranian Nat. Info. Service, 1976-80; mem. Pres.'s Export Council, 1981—, Presdl. Awards Commn., 1986-87; exec. dir. Md. Reagan-Bush Campaign, 1984; pres. Phi Mu Alpha Sinfonia, 1967-68; nat. dir. for coalitions Dole for U.S Pres. campaign. Navy fellow, 1969-72; Regents scholar, 1964-68. Mem. AIAA, Am. Def. Preparedness Assn., Am. Phys. Soc. Republican. Roman Catholic. Home: 1301 19th Rd S Arlington VA 22202

DEOUL, NEAL, electronics company executive; b. N.Y.C., Feb. 27, 1931; s. George and Pearl (Hirschfeld) D.; B.S. in Physics, Coll. City N.Y., 1952; postgrad. Rutgers U., 1954-55; LL.B., Bklyn. Law Sch., 1959; m. Bernice Kradel, Dec. 25, 1955 (div.); children: Cara Jan, Stefani Neva, Evan Craig; m., Kathleen B. Davis, June 20, 1982; 1 child, Shannon Rae. Engr., Signal Corps, U.S. Army, Evans Signal Lab., Belmar, N.J., 1952-55; engr. Airborne Instruments Lab., Deer Park, N.Y., 1955-56; sales mgr. FXR, Inc., Woodside, L.I., 1956-60; admitted to N.Y. State bar, 1960; pres. Microwave Dynamics Corp., Plainview, L.I., 1960-61, Paradynamics, Inc., Huntington Station, N.Y., 1961-64; mgr. Servo Corp. Am., Hicksville, N.Y., 1964-66; v.p. Trio Labs., Inc., Plainview, N.Y., 1966-69; exec. v.p. Microlab/FXR, Livingston, N.J., 1969-74; pres. Neal Deoul Assocs., Owings Mills, Md., 1974—. Mem. IEEE (sr.), N.Y. State Bar Assn., Md. Bar Assn., Young Pres.'s Orgn., Profl. Group Engring. Mgmt., Am. Arbitration Assn. Home and Office: 3104 Caves Rd Owings Mills MD 21117

DEPAOLIS, POTITO UMBERTO, food co. exec.; b. Mignano, Italy, Aug. 28, 1925; s. Giuseppe A. and Filomena (Macchiaverna) deP.; Vet. Dr., U. Naples, 1948; Libera Docenza, Ministero Pubblica Istruzione (Rome, Italy), 1955; m. Marie A. Caronna, Apr. 10, 1965. Came to U.S., 1966, naturalized, 1970. Prof. food service Vet. Sch., U. Naples, Italy, 1948-66; retired, 1966; asst. prof. A titre Benevole Ecole Veterinaire Alfort, Paris, France, 1956; vet. inspector U.S. Dept. Agr., Omaha, 1966-67; sr. research chemist Grain Processing Corp., Muscatine, Iowa, 1967-68; v.p., dir. product devel. Reddi Wip, Inc., Los Angeles, 1968-72; with Kubro Foods, Los Angeles, 1972-73, Shade Foods, Inc., 1975—; pres. Vegetable Protein Co., Riverside, Calif., 1973—, Tima Brand Food Co., 1975—, Dr. Tima Natural Foods, 1977—. Fulbright scholar Cornell U., Ithaca, N.Y., 1954; British Council scholar, U. Reading, Eng., 1959-60; postdoctoral research fellow NIH, Cornell U., 1963-64. Mem. Inst. Food Technologists, Italian Assn. Advancement Sci., AAAS, Vet. Med. Assn., Biol. Sci. Assn. Italy, Italian Press Assn., Greater Los Angeles Press Club. Contbr. articles in field to prol. jours. Patentee in field. Home: 131 Groverton Pl Bel Air Los Angeles CA 90077 Office: 8570 Wilshire Blvd Beverly Hills CA 90211 also: 6878 Beck Ave North Hollywood CA 91605

DEPARDIEU, GERARD, actor; b. Chateauroux, France, Dec. 27, 1948; s. René and Alice (Marillier) D.; ed. Ecole Communale, Cours d'art Dramatique de Charles Dullin, Ecole d'art Dramatique de Jean Laurent Cochet; m. Elisabeth Guignot, 1970; children: Guillaume, Julie. Actor in short films Le Beatnick et le Minet, 1966, Nathalie Granger, 1971; feature films include: les Gaspards, 1974, les Valseuses, 1974, 1900, 1975, la Dernière femme, 1975, Pas si mé chant que ça, 1975, Sept morts sur ordonnance, 1975, Maitresse, Barocco, 1976, René la Canne, 1976, Baxter verra Baxter, 1976, Dites-lui que je l'aime, 1977, le Camion, 1977, Preparez vos mouchoirs, Rêve de singe, 1978, Le sucre, 1978, Loulou, 1980, le Dernier Metro (Cesar award for best actor, France), 1980, Tartuffe, 1984, numerous others, latest being Le Grand Frere, Danton, La Lune Dans le Caniveau, 1983; stage appearances include: Boudu sauvé des eaux, 1968, les Garçons Galapagos, 1971, Home, 1972, la Chevauchée sur le lac de Constance, 1974, Les Insensés sont en Voie D'extinction, 1978, also TV series.

DEPASS, ERNEST T., mechanical engineer, consultant; b. Memphis, Apr. 26, 1926; s. Ernest T. and Lillian (Klenke) DeP.; B.S. in Elec. Engring., U. Tenn., 1948, B.S. in Mech. Engring., 1949; postgrad. U. Ariz., 1950, Columbia, 1950-51; m. Henrietta Marie Green, May 1, 1949; 1 son, Paul Jeffrey. Asst. plant engr. Am. Finishing Co., Memphis, 1943-47; asst. to chief engr. Standard Brands, Inc., N.Y.C., 1951-53; mgr. process engring. Johnson & Johnson, New Brunswick, N.J., 1953-63; mgr. packaging machinery design and devel. Union Camp Corp., Princeton, N.J., 1963-69; v.p. mfg. and engring. Whitman's Chocolates div. Pet Inc., Phila., 1969-79; engring. cons., 1979—. Served to lt. (j.g.), USNR, 1949-51. Mem. Soc. Plastics Engrs., Soc. Mfg. Engrs. (cert.), Am. Mgmt. Assn. Research in field. Home: RD 1 Woodland Terr Bound Brook NJ 08805 Office: 9701 Roosevelt Blvd Philadelphia PA 19114

DE PATOUL, DOMINIQUE, airline executive; b. Overpelt, Limburg, Belgium, Oct. 26, 1938; s. Jack Chevalier and Veronica (Fallon) De P.; m. Claire De Bethune, Sept. 5, 1964 (div. May 1980); m. Genevieve Lechien, Sept. 14, 1985; children—Christopher, Manuela, Alexander, Olivia. D. in Law, U. Louvain, 1963; M.Econs., City of London Coll., 1964. With Sabena Airlines, Ankara, Turkey, 1968-70, Warsaw, Poland and Beirut, 1970-75, Kinshasa, Zaire, 1975-80, regional mgr., Nairobi, Kenya, 1980-86, gen. mgr. Cen. and South Africa, Kinshasa, Zaire, 1986—. Author: Impertinent Guide to Lebanon, 1973. Served as res. officer Belgium Air Force, 1964. Avocations: golf; tennis; skiing. Home: Sabena 35 Rue, Cardinal Mercier, 1000 Brussels Belgium Office: Sabena Airlines, Kinshasa Zaire

DEPAUW, GOMMAR ALBERT, priest, former educator; b. Stekene, Belgium, Oct. 11, 1918; came to U.S., 1949, naturalized, 1955; s. Desiré and Anna (Van Overloop) De P. Diplomate Classical Humanities, Coll. St. Nicholas, Belgium, 1936; JCB, U. Louvain, 1943, JCL, 1945; Juris Canonici Dr., Catholic U. Am., 1953. Ordained priest Roman Cath. Ch., 1942. Parish priest, chaplain Cath. Social Action, Ghent, Belgium, 1945-49, N.Y.C., 1949-52; successively prof. moral and fundamental dogmatic theology and canon law sem. div., assoc. prof. philosophy coll. div. Mt. St. Mary's Coll., Emmitsburg, Md., 1952-65, dean studies maj. sem. div., 1954-64, mem. council adminstrn., 1957-65; Theol. adviser II Vatican Ecumenical Council, 1962-65; founder-pres. Cath. Traditionalist Movement, Inc., 1964—. Author: The Educational Rights of the Church, 1953, The Rebel Priest, 1965, The Traditional Roman Catholic Mass, 1977; co-author: New Catholic Ency; contbr. to: Homiletic and Pastoral Rev.; editor: Sounds of Truth and Tradition, Quote ... Unquote; producer Latin radio mass, various religious phonograph records, audio and video cassettes. Served with Inf. M.C. Belgian Army, 1939-45. Decorated Honor cross Free Polish Forces. Mem. Internat. Platform Assn., Cath. Theol. Soc. Am. Canon Law Soc. Am., Am. Cath. Philos. Assn., Nat. Cath. Ednl. Assn., AAUP, Univ. Prof. for Acad. Order. Home: 210 Maple Ave Westbury NY 10166 Office: Pan Am Bldg Suite 303E New York NY 10166

DE PAUW KNOWLAND, DECIA, real estate and financial company executive; b. Hove, Belgium, Mar. 12, 1942; d. John Charles Knowland and Daphne J. (Lyons) Reavey; m. Charles De Pauw, 1971 (dec. 1984); children: Dorothee, Olivia, Caroline. Dir. World Trade Ctr., Brussels, Belgium, 1970-72, Compagnie de Promotion and World Trade Ctr., Brussels, 1985—; dir. Cell Industries, Can., 1987—. Home: Chemin de Vieusart 16, 1300 Wavre Belgium Office: WTC & CDP, 162 Bd Emile Jacquemain, 1000 Brussels Belgium

DE PELSMAKER, PAUL PIETER, photographic company executive; b. Aalst, Belgium, Mar. 17, 1929; s. Maurice and Rachel (Sevens) De P.; m. Lutgarde Boon, Apr. 25, 1955; children: Lieve, Helena, Marc, Peter. BCE, U. Louvain (Belgium), 1953. Asst. mgr. Div. Graphic & Reprographic AGFA-GEVAERT N.V., Mortsel, Belgium, 1954-62, mgr., 1962-69, gen. mgr., 1969-74, asst. dir., 1974-82; co. dir. of Graphic Communication Systems Div. AGFA-GEVAERT N.V., Mortsel, Belgium, 1982—; bd. dirs. Compugraphic Corp., Wilmington, Mass. Contbr. articles to profl. jours. Recipient Golden medal The Photographic Soc., Vienna, 1977. Office: AGFA-GEVAERT NV, Graphic Communication Systems Div, Septestraat 27, B-2510 Mortsel Belgium

DE PETRIS, CARLA NICOLE CAPIRONE, fine arts consultant; b. Torino, Italy; came to U.S., 1956, naturalized, 1961; d. Giovanni Giuseppe and Albina Luigia (Ferraris) Capirone di Montanaro; ed. Italian and Calif. schs.; cert. in arts mgmt. U. Calif.; m. Wilmer Anthony DePetris, Dec. 4, 19S5; 1 son, Walther Gian Carlo. Internat. cons. fine arts, interior design and hist. preservation, Sonoma, Calif., 1969—; co-owner Fine Arts Research Assos.; tchr. art and art appreciation Sonoma Cath. Elem. Sch.; Arabian horse breeder, Am. Saddlebred breeder. Bd. dirs. Cath. Social Service, 1967-69, treas., 1968, Sensura Sister's Cities Assn., World Affairs Council; active Pacific Mus. Soc., San Francisco 1968-69, Internat. Visitor Ctr. , San Francisco; pres. Sonoma League Hist. Preservation, 1979; sec.-treas. Sonoma Land Trust, 1977-78; founder St. Francis the Ch. Mouse; diocese interior decorator and appraiser; archtl. rev. commr. City of Sonoma; adv. com. Sonoma Parks and Recreation; bd. dirs. Sonoma County Art Council; chmn. spl. events Pres.'s Assos., Sonoma State U. Recipient award Sonoma Parks and Recreation, 1975; Calif. State Office Preservation grantee, 1978. Mem. Associated Photographers Internat. Republican. Research on archtl. style and social devel. from 1840-1940 in So. Sonoma County.

DEPEW, THOMAS ANDREW, mission adminstrator; b. Pittsfield, Mass., Nov. 30, 1927; s. George Edward and Rose Delma (Major) D. BA, U. N.Y., 1950; M in Religious Edn., Maryknoll, N.Y., 1955. Ordained priest Roman Cath. Ch., 1955. Pastor, educator Maryknoll Mission, Huehuetenango, Guatemala, 1955-60; diocesan consultor Prelature Huehuetenango, Guatemala, 1960-65, dir. edn., 1958-65; asst. superior Maryknoll Mission, Cen. Am., 1960-65; new missionary Maryknoll Mission, Caracas, Venezuela, 1965-66, asst. superior, 1966-74, superior, 1974-77, coordinator, adminstr., 1977-85, adminstr. formation ctr., 1985—; pres. Ecumenical Assn., Caracas, 1970-72. Home: Apartado Postal 30319, Correos de Pro-Patria, 1030-A Caracas Venezuela Office: Catia Formation Ctr, Casa #4 Vereda #2 Urdaneta, 1030 Caracas Venezuela

DEPEYRE, NICOLE MELINA, perfume company executive; b. Yokohama, Japan, Nov. 16, 1926; d. Pierre Marcel and Anne Yvonne (Serre-Genestoux) D.; 1 child, Fabienne Melchior de Montarnal. Baccalaureat, Lycee, Paris, 1946; diploma Ecole des Langues Orientales, 1949. Press attachee Japan Trade Recovery Orgn., Brussels, 1958-59; profl. buyer Christian Dior Couture, Paris, 1959-68; pub. relations and promotion dir. for Asia and Pacific, Parfums Christian Dior, Tokyo, 1968—; cons. Comité National des Conseillers du Commerce Exterieur de La France, Paris, Japan chpt., 1984—. Author: Work in Harmony (in Japanese), 1981. Mem. Amnesty Internat., Tokyo, 1975. Decorated Chevalier de l'Ordre National du Merite, 1985. Mem. Tokyo Fgn. Corrs. Club. Roman Catholic.

DEPEYROT, MICHEL YVES-LOUIS, engineering company executive; b. Montauban, Tarn & Garonne, France, Aug. 19, 1940; s. Olivier Louis and Marthe (Favant) D.; m. Laura Chapman, June 22, 1967; children: Gilles,

Thierry, Alexa, Joelle, Valerie. Degree in engring., Ecole Sup. D'Electricite, Paris, 1963; PhD, Stanford U., 1968; doctorate, U. Grenoble, France, 1976. Dir. research Centre Automatique Ensmp, Fontainebleau, France, 1968-70; product mgr. CII, Louveciennes, France, 1971-74; mgr. engring. DEC, Maynard, Mass., 1975-80; v.p. engring. Thomson-EFCIS, Grenoble, France, 1981-85; chmn., pres. Dolphin Integration S.A., Meylan, France, 1985—; research dir. INRIA, Rocouencourt, France, 1971-76. Author: Automata and Control Science, 1974. Served as capt. with French Navy, 1963-65. Roman Catholic. Clubs: Horseback Riding, CHA (Grenoble). Home: Fontclaire, 22 Rte de Chartreuse, 38700 Corenc-le-Haut La Tronche, France Office: Dolphin Integration SA, Zirst/8 Chemin Des Clos, Meylan France 38240

DE PFYFFER, ANDRE, lawyer; b. Lucerne, Switzerland, Nov. 3, 1928; s. Leodegar and Anna (Carvalho) de P.; Baccalaureat, U. Berne, 1947; postgrad. U. Geneva, 1947-50, 54; married; children—Corinne, Francois. Admitted to Geneva Lawyers Assn., 1952, since practiced in Geneva; ptnr. firm Mes. de Pfyffer, Argand, Troller & Assocs.; dir. IC Industries (Internat.) S.A., Volvo Suisse S.A., Cederroth Internat. S.A., Banque Paribas (Suisse) S.A., Groupe Bruxelles Lambert, (chmn.) Banque Scandinave en Suisse S.A.; v.p. Pargesa Holding, S.A. Mem. Internat. Law Assn., Circle de la Terrasse. Home: 41 Quai Wilson, Geneva Switzerland Office: 6 Rue Bellot, Geneva Switzerland

DE PINGRE, MAJOR, office supply co. exec.; b. Leesville, La., May 31, 1928; s. Adrien Edward and Madeline Ethel (Kirby) deP.; B.A., La. State U., 1952; m. Patricia Lee Catron, Mar. 27, 1953; children—Benny Louis, Margaret Ann. Pres., Meadow Park Nursing Center, Shreveport, La., 1959—; pres. Major Office Supply; sec. Tremade, Inc., 1963-72. Pres. Webster Parish Tb Assn., 1958-59; treas. New March of Dimes, 1959-60, publicity chmn., 1956-60; pres. Am. Field Service, Webster Parish chpt., 1960-61; publicity chmn. Charlie Hennigan Day, 1964; pres. Minden Little Theatre, 1964-66; chmn. comml. div. Webster United Fund, 1964; chmn. camping and activities com. Yatasi council Boy Scouts Am., 1960-61, dist. commr., 1960-61, 66; pres. chpt. A.R.C., 1965-66; publicity chmn. Webster's Centennial, 1971; v.p. Com. to Get Mus., 1974; mem. Cultural Affairs Com., 1973; co-chmn. United Way, South Webster, 1985, sect. leader, 1987. Mem. Webster Parish Democratic Exec. Com., 1960-74. Bd. dirs. Webster Parish Cancer Bd., Easter Seal Soc. Served with USN, 1946-48. Recipient Outstanding Jaycee Local Pres. State La., Jr. C. of C., 1959-60, Distinguished Service award Jr. C. of C., 1969. Mem. Am. Legion (publicity chmn. 1958-59), Minden C. of C. (dir. 1961-62), Minden Jr. C. of C. (pres. 1959-60), Jr. C. of C. (life mem., senator 1986), Webster Parish La. State U. Alumni Assn. (pres. 1962-63). Baptist (deacon). Club: Tennis and Aquatic (Minden). Author: History of the First Baptist Church, 1844-1969, 1969. Office: 116 Pearl St Minden LA 71055

DE POKOMANDY, GABRIEL, lawyer; b. Oroshaza, Hungary, July 7, 1944; s. Alexander and Irene (Csizmadia) De P.; B.A., Coll. de Levis (Que., Can.), 1965; license in Law, Laval U., 1968; s. Louise Sirois, Dec. 11, 1971; children—Erik, Alexandra. Atty. firm Rouleau, Carrier & Assos., Baie Comeau, Que., 1968-72; crown prosecutor, Sept Iles, Que., 1973; sr. partner firm De Pokomandy, Besnier & Assocs., Sept-Iles, 1974—; tchr. bus. law Regional Coll., 1972-79; legal adviser Fedn. des Jeunes Chambres du Can. Francais, 1978-83. Vice-pres., Jeune Chambre de Baie-Comeau, 1971-72; pres. Jeune Chambre de Sept-Iles, 1973-74, Mcpl. Environ. Com., Sept-Iles, 1976-78; pres. Conseil de Gestion Scout-Guide, Sept-iles Inc., 1983-84; pres. local com. P.Q. Hearth Found., Sept-Iles, 1979-80; v.p. Sept-Iles Mus., 1976-79, pres. 1985-88. Mem. Barreau Du Que., Canadian Bar Assn., Quebec Bar Assn. (pres. north shore sect. 1984-86). Roman Catholic. Club: Richelieu. Home: 11 Pampalon, Sept Iles, PQ Canada G4R 1T9 Office: 865 Laure, Sept Iles, PQ Canada G4R 1Y6

DEPPE, HENRY A., insurance company executive; b. S.I., N.Y., July 1, 1920; s. Herman and Marie Deppe; student Cornell Sch. Hotel Adminstrn., 1943; m. Florence Chieffo, Aug. 8, 1943; children—Katherine, Marlaina, Lynda. Agt. Travelers Life Ins. Co., White Plains, N.Y., 1946-49; dist. mgr. Mass. Life Ins. Co., White Plains, 1949-57; gen. agt. Guardian Life Ins. Co., White Plains, 1956-87 ; pres. Nat. Pension Service, Inc., White Plains, 1957-85, chmn. bd., chief exec. officer, 1985—; chmn. bd. Nat. Pension Service Inc.; bd. dirs. YOREC Corp.; mem. faculty C.L.U. Inst.; guest lectr. N.Y. State Trial Lawyers Assn., Fairleigh Dickinson Pension Inst., IRS, C.W. Post Tax Inst., various other profl. assns. and ednl. instns.; bd. dirs. Nat. Bank Stamford. Pres., Young Republicans Club of Westchester County (N.Y.), 1954-55, Ossining (N.Y.) PTA, 1963-64, Multiple Sclerosis Soc. Westchester, 1964, 65; pres. Estate Planning Council of Westchester; founder Tax Inst., Iona Coll., co-chmn. inst., 1976-78; bd. dirs. ARC, Westchester County, N.Y.; pres., bd. dirs. N.Y. Fertility Research Found. Served to lt., inf., U.S. Army, 1942-46. Recipient Nat. Sales Achievement award, 1966; Fred E. Hamilton award, 1975; David Ben Gurion Friendship award, 1975; Guest of Honor award United Jewish Appeal Fedn., 1978; Leadership award State of Israel, 1979; Disting. Citizen award, Westchester-Putnam Council Boy Scouts Am., 1986. Mem. Assn. Advanced Life Underwriters, Internat. Assn. Fin. Planners, Am. Pension Conf., Am. Soc. Pension Actuaries, Am. Soc. C.L.U.s, Life Underwriters Assn. Westchester (pres. 1949-50), Nat. Assn. Pension Cons. and Adminstrs. (treas.), Fertility Research Assn. (pres. bd. dirs. 1982-83), Nat. Assn. Health and Welfare Plans, Million Dollar Round Table (life and qualifying), Golden Key Soc. (founder), Top of Table, Ten Million Dollar Forum, Research Agys. Group, White Plains C. of C. Club: Sleepy Hollow Country. Home: 1500 S Ocean Blvd Boca Raton FL 33432 Office: Nat Pension Service 1025 Westchester Ave White Plains NY 10601

DEPPELER, JAMES GREGORY, mgmt. cons. agency exec.; b. N.Y.C., Feb. 10, 1946; s. John Howard, Jr. and Muriel Dolores (Hecker) D.; B.Engring., Stevens Inst. Tech., 1968, M.Mgmt. Sci., 1971, postgrad., 1971—; m. Wende Cyrille Somers, June 9, 1979; children—James Gregory Jr., Hillary Somers. Engr., Jersey Central Power and Light Co., Asbury Park, N.J., 1968-71; internal cons. Gen. Pub. Utilities Corp., Morristown, N.J., 1971-73; sr. cons. Fantus Co., South Orange, N.J., 1973-77; v.p. Bus. Mktg. Corp., N.Y.C., 1977-80; chmn. Deppeler Assos., Manasquan, N.J., 1980—; dir. Econ. Geography Assos., Marlton, N.J., World Trade Services, Portland, Maine. Environ. commr. Borough of Brielle (N.J.), 1973-81, mem. bd. adjustment, 1979—, chmn. 1985—. Mem. Am. Soc. Metals, AIME, Am. Soc. Profl. Cons., Am. Assn. Econ. Developers (dir. 1979—), Barnegat Bay Yacht Racing Assn. (del. 1981—), Squan Tri Sail Offshore Racing Assn. (pres. 1984—, bd. dirs. 1980—). Club: Manasquan River Yacht (Brielle) (trustee 1974—, sec. 1980-81, rear commodore 1982-83, vice commodore 1984, commodore 1985—). Researcher urban devel. problems of major cities, geographically variable costs for corp. facilities. Home: 519 Harris Ave Brielle NJ 08730

DE PREE, WILLARD AMES, ambassador to Bangladesh; b. Zeeland, Mich., Nov. 1, 1928; s. Adrian and Edith (Kroeze) De P.; m. Elisabeth Pierrou, Aug. 1956; children: Carin, Thomas, Peter, Birgitta, Susan, Anita. BA with honors, Harvard U., 1950; MA, U. Mich., 1952; LLD (hon.), Hope Coll., 1978. Dep. chief of mission Am. Embassy, Freetown, Sierra Leone, 1968-70; mem. policy planning staff U.S. Dept. State, Washington, 1972-76; U.S. ambassador to Mozambique 1976-80, sr. insp., 1980-81, exec. asst. to under sec. for mgmt., 1982-83; dir. mgmt. ops. U.S. Dept. State, Washington, 1983-87; U.S. ambassador to Bangladesh 1987—; teaching asst. U. Mich., Ann Arbor, 1952-53. Served with U.S. Army, 1954-56. Rotary Found. fellow, 1950-51. Mem. Am. Fgn. Service Assn. Office: Am Embassy Dhaka Bangladesh care Dept State Washington DC 20520 *

DEPUKAT, THADDEUS STANLEY, optometrist; b. Chgo., Feb. 3, 1936; s. Stanley Frank and Genevieve Josephine (Skorupinski) D.; m. Melanie Ann Gadomski, Sept. 7, 1963 (dec. Jan. 1987); children—Brian Ted, Todd Steven. Student Loyola U., 1954-56; B.S., Ill. Coll. Optometry, 1960, O.D., 1960. Clin. instr. Ill. Coll. Optometry, Chgo., 1960-61, assoc. prof., 1961-66; optometrist, Downers Grove, Ill., 1966—; trustee Ill. Coll. Optometry, 1982—. Contbr. articles to profl. jours. Active mem. United Fund Bd., Downers Grove, 1966-69, Suburban Cook County-Dupage County Health Systems Agy., 1976-77; del. White House Conf. on Children, Washington, 1970. Recipient Tribute of Appreciation Ill. Coll. Optometry Alumni Assn., 1982. Fellow Am. Acad. Optometry, AAAS, Coll. Optometrists in Vision Devel.; mem. Ill. Optometric Assn. (Disting. Service award, 1982; pre. 1978-80, v.p. pub. health 1974-76), Ill. Coll. Optometry Alumni Assn., Am. Optometric Assn., West Suburban Optometric Assn. (pres. 1974), Optometric Extension Program. Lodge: Lions (v.p. 1982-85, pres. 1985-86, named Lion of Yr. 1986, award of appreciation 1986). Avocations: camping; computers; reading. Office: 1043 Curtiss Downers Grove IL 60515

DERAMUS, WILLIAM NEAL, III, railroad executive; b. Pittsburg, Kans., Dec. 10, 1915; s. William Neal and Lucile Ione (Nicholas) D.; m. Patricia Howell Watson, Jan. 22, 1943; children: William Neal IV, Patricia Nicholas Fogel, Jean Deramus Wagner, Jill Watson Dean. A.A., Kansas City Jr. Coll., 1934; A.B., U. Mich., 1936; LL.B., Harvard U., 1939. Transp. apprentice Wabash R.R. Co., St. Louis, 1939-41; asst. trainmaster Wabash R.R. Co., 1941-43; asst. to gen. mgr. K.C.S. Ry. Co., Kansas City, Mo., 1946-48; asst. to pres. C.G.W. Ry. Co., Chgo., 1948; pres., dir. C.G.W. Ry. Co., 1949-57, chmn. exec. com., 1954-57; pres., dir. M.-K.-T. R.R., 1957-61; chmn. bd. MAPCO, Inc., Tulsa, 1960-73, chmn. exec. com., 1973-81, now dir.; pres., dir. Kansas City So. Lines, Mo., 1961-73; chmn. bd. Kansas City So. Lines, 1966-80; pres. Kansas City So. Industries, Inc., Mo., 1962-71, chmn. bd., 1966—; dir. Bus. Men's Assurance Co., Kansas City, Kansas City Royals. Served from capt. to maj. Transp. Corps, Mil. Ry. Service AUS, 1943-46, overseas, India. Mem. Beta Theta Pi. Clubs: Chgo.; Kansas City (Kansas), River (Kansas City), Mission Hills Country (Kansas City), Mercury (Kansas City); Lodge: Rotary (Kansas City). Home: 37 LeMans Ct Prairie Village KS 66208 Office: Kansas City So Industries Inc 114 W 11th St Kansas City MO 64105

DERANI, MARCOS ZARZUR, paper company executive; b. São Paulo, Brazil, Nov. 20, 1957; s. Oswaldo Benchara and Ivette (Zarzur) D.; m. Tania Maria Salem; 1 child, Eduarda. Degree in law, U. Mackenzie, São Paulo, 1981. Dir. Ripasa S/A Celulose e Papel, São Paulo, 1977—. Clubs: Jockey, Monte Libano. Home: Largo Sao Bento 64, 50 Andar Brazil Office: Ripasa S/A Celulose e Papel, Largo São Bento 64-40 andar, 01029 Sao Paulo Brazil

DERDENGER, PATRICK, lawyer; b. Los Angeles, June 29, 1946; s. Charles Patrick and Drucilla Marguerite (Lange) D.; m. Jo Lynn Dickins, Aug. 24, 1968; children—Kristin Lynn, Bryan Patrick, Timothy Patrick. B.A., Loyola U., Los Angeles, 1968; M.B.A., U. So. Calif., 1971, J.D., 1974; LL.M. in Taxation, George Washington U., 1977. Bar: Calif. 1974, U.S. Ct. Claims 1975, Ariz. 1979, U.S. Ct. Appeals (9th cir.) 1979, U.S. Dist. Ct. Ariz. 1979, U.S. Tax Ct. 1979, U.S. Supreme Ct. 1979. Trial atty. honors program Dept. Justice, Washington, 1974-78; ptnr. Lewis and Roca, Phoenix, 1978—; adj. prof. taxation Golden Gate U., Phoenix, 1983—; mem. Ariz. State Tax Ct. Legis. Study Commn. Author: Arizona State and Local Taxation, Cases and Materials, 1983, Arizona Sales and Use Tax Handbook, 1988, Advanced Arizona Sales and Use Tax, 1987; author (with others) State and Local Taxation. Bd. dirs. North Scottsdale Little League. Served to capt. USAF, 1968-71. Recipient U.S. Law Week award Bur. Nat. Affairs, 1974. Mem. ABA (taxation sect., various coms.), Ariz. Bar Assn. (taxation sect., various coms., chmn. state and local tax com., chmn. continuing legal edn. com.), Maricopa County Bar AsBar Assn., Nat. Assn. Bond Lawyers, Inst. Property Taxation, Inst. Sales Taxation, Inst. Sales Taxation, Phoenix Met. C. of C., Ariz. C. of C. (tax com.), Phi Delta Phi. Clubs: Sereno Soccer (bd. dirs.), U. So. Calif. Alumni (bd. dirs., pres.-elect) Home: 9501 N 49th Pl Paradise Valley AZ 85253 Office: Lewis and Roca 2200 First Interstate Bank Plaza 100 W Washington St Phoenix AZ 85003

DEREGOWSKI, JAN BRONISLAW, psychology educator; b. Pinsk, Poland, Mar. 1, 1933; s. Jan and Szczeslawa Helena (Enskajt) D.; m. Eva Loft Nielsen, 1958; children: Sven Marek, Niels Tadeusz, Anna Halina. BSc, U. London, 1960, BA, 1965, PhD, 1968; DSc, U. Aberdeen, Scotland, 1988. Various engring. and ops. research positions Ministry of Overseas Dept., London, 1956-64; research fellow U. Zambia, 1965-69; lectr. U. Aberdeen, 1969-77, sr. lectr., 1977-81, reader, 1981-86, prof., 1986—. Fellow Brit. Psychol. Soc., Netherlands Inst. Advanced Studies; mem. Nat. Acad. Psychology (del.). Office: U Aberdeen, Dept Psychology, Aberdeen AB1 7XS, Scotland

DEREGT, JOHN STEWART, real estate development executive; b. San Francisco; s. Christian Anthony and Mary Margaret (Stewart) deR.; B.C.E., U. Santa Clara, 1950; m. Mal Padgett, Mar. 21, 1981; children—Kenneth, Thomas, James, Lauren, Mary, Jordan, Keith, Stewart. Pres. Carl Holvick Co., Palo Alto, Calif., 1957-75; v.p. Holvick deRegt Koering, Sunnyvale, Calif., 1960-75, pres., owner 1975-86; indsl. and office park counsel Urban Land Inst., 1978—; pres., owner Golden Eagle Devel. Co., Inc., 1987—. Contbr. feature articles to Corporate Times, Santa Clara, Calif. Mem. bd. regents Bellarmine High Sch., San Jose, 1977—; bd. dirs. Food Bank, San Jose, Calif., 1980—, San Mateo County Devel. Assn., San Mateo, Calif., 1975—; YMCA, 1984—; adv. bd. Santa Clara U. Sch. Bus., 1984— ; mem. Exec. Com., 1980—. Served with U.S. Army, 1951-53. Mem. Nat. Assn. Indsl. Office Parks. Club: Sharon Heights Country (Menlo Park, Calif.). Home: 1700 Sand Hill Rd #408 Palo Alto CA 94304 Office: 1230 Oakmead Pkwy 212 Sunnyvale CA 94088

DERENDINGER, PIERRE FRITZ, aerospace components manufacturing company executive; b. Nyon, Vaud, Switzerland, Oct. 29, 1943; s. Fritz and Hedwige (Stalder) D.; m. Genevieve DeMaeyer; children: Alizée, Maeva. M.E., Fed. Inst. Tech., Zurich, 1970. Mgr. prodn. Derendinger & Cie S.A., Geneva, Switzerland, 1970-75, pres., gen. mgr., 1975—; Office of Promotion of Geneva Industry, 1975-87, Union of Small Businesses, Geneva, 1974—. Served with Swiss Army, 1963-64. Roman Catholic. Club: Société Nautique. Home: 73 Rue des Eaux-Vives, 1207 Geneva Switzerland Office: Derendinger & Cie SA, 7 Ch du Champ des Filles Geneva, Plan-les-Ouates, 1228 Geneva Switzerland

DERGALIS, GEORGE, artist, educator; b. Athens, Greece, Aug. 31, 1928; s. Demetrios and Zina (Alehina) D.; MFA, Accademia Belle Arti, Rome, 1951; diploma Boston Museum Sch., 1956-59; m. Margaret Murphey; 1 child by previous marriage, Alexis. One-man shows Woodstock Gallery, London, 1974, Cámara de Comercio de Medellín, Colombia, 1980, Galesburg Civic Art Ctr., Ill., 1985, Hotel Meridien, Boston, 1987; exhibited in group shows New Eng. Drawing, 1979, Ariz. Nat., 1980, Tampa Mus., 1983-84, others; represented in permanent collection De Cordova Mus., Worcester Acad., Museo de Zea, Colombia, also pvt. collections; instr. Boston Mus. Sch., 1961-69, De Cordova Mus., Lincoln, Mass., 1961—; pvt. instrn. Wayland, Mass., 1969—; chmn., curator Festival Bostonians for Art and Humanity, 1976; chmn. curator prison art Inst. Contemporary Art Boston, 1975-76; artist-in-residence Partners of Ams., Colombia, 1979; lectr. Helicon, Harvard U., 1981. Trustee, Graham Jr. Coll., 1971; hon. dir. Boston Ballet, 1971. Served with USAF, 1951-54. Recipient Prix de Rome, 1951; William Paige scholar, 1959; Civilian merit award U.S. Army Hist. Soc., 1969; Gold medal Accademia Italia delle Arte, 1980. Mem. Internat. Sculpture Assn., Alumni Assn. Boston Mus. Sch. (pres., 1966, 67), Copley Soc. Boston (v.p. and art chmn. 1978, Excellence in Technique award 1978), Lit. and Arts, DeCordova Mus. Home: 72 Oxbow Rd Wayland MA 01778

DER HAROOTIAN, KHOREN, sculptor; b. Ashodvan, Armenia, Apr. 2, 1909; came to U.S., 1921, naturalized, 1954; s. Haroutun and Nevart (Mouradian) Der Haroutunian; m. Hermine Ohanesyan, May 13, 1939 (dec. 1977); m. Yolanda Pirulis, 1979. Student, Worcester Art Mus. Sch. Sculptor, painter one-man shows, Caz-Delbos Galleries, N.Y.C., 1929, Jamaica (B.W.I.) Museum, Kingston, 1931, 38, 43, Worcester (Mass.) Art Museum, 1932, Kraushaar Galleries, N.Y.C., 1945, outdoor exhbn., N.Y.C., 1948, Art Alliance, Phila., 1950, Zwemmer Gallery, London, 1964, Armenian Gen. Benevolent Union Gallery, N.Y.C., 1965, Rockland Community Coll., Suffern, N.Y., 1967, Contemporaries Gallery, N.Y.C., 1967, Galerie Bernheim-Jeune, Paris, 1971, Artists' House and Gallery, Erevan, Armenia, USSR, 1971, Sculpture Ctr., N.Y.C., 1975; Mother of Ararat, Armenian Govt., 1977; exhbn., AGBU Gallery, N.Y.C., 1980, outdoor exhbn., Armenian Ch., N.Y.C., 1981, Worcester, Mass., 1981; commd. 15 foot sculpture from native volcanic stone, Armenian Govt., 1982-84; sculptor, painter retrospective exhbn., Mus. of Etchmiazin, Holy City of Armenia, 1983, two-man show, Gallery Ten, Inc., Mt. Vernon, N.Y., 1975, Mass., 1981, annual and group shows, Whitney Mus. Am. Art, Pa. Acad. Fine Arts, Chgo. Art Inst., U. Nebr., Worcester, Cranbrook, Springfield, Toledo, Cin. museums, Des Moines Art Ctr., Ohio U., Phila. Mus. Art, Audubon Artists exhbns., Sculptors Guild exhbns., John Herron Art Inst., Indpls., various London galleries, Royal Acad., London, 1964, 65, Royal Glasgow (Scotland) Inst., 1964; represented in permanent collections Met. Mus. Art, N.Y.C., Worcester Art Mus., Jamaica (B.W.I.) Mus., Pa. Acad. Fine Arts, Whitney Mus. Am. Art, N.Y.C., Ariz. State Coll., Newark Art Mus., Bezelel Nat. Mus., Israel, Jerusalem Mus. Art, Our Lady Queen of Angels Sem., Albany, N.Y., Armenian State Art Mus., Erevan, Pushkin Mus. Art, Moscow, pvt. collections in U.S., Eng., Venezuela, Holland, France, Germany, Italy, W. Indies; exhibited work in marble, U.S. Pavilion, Brussels World's Fair, 1958, USIS, Florence, Italy, 1963; commd. to carve figure Christ and 4 Martyrs for Diocese bldg. Armenian Ch. and Cultural Ctr., N.Y.C., 1959, Beaver for Bernard Baruch City Coll., 1962, 2 8-foot bronze sculptures for facade, SS. Mesrob and Sahag Armenian Apostolic Ch., Wynnewood, Pa., 1973, 24-foot bronze monument Meher with 4 high relief panels by, Phila. Armenian Bicentennial Commemoration Com. for Fairmount Park, 1974, 30-foot bronze monument World Peace Dedicated to All Mankind, Moscow, 1985. Recipient 1st prize Springfield Art Assn., 1944; Gold medal Audubon Artists 7th Ann. Exhbn., 1949; 1st prize sculpture 8th Ann. Exhbn., 1950; commn. Phila. Internat. Sculpture Exhbn., 1949; commn. for 9-foot granite Inventor Fairmount Park Art Assn., 1950; George D. Widener Meml. Gold Medal Pa. Acad. Fine Arts, 1954; exhbns. and monetary award with citation Nat. Inst. Arts and Letters, 1954; Medal of Honor Gruppo Donatello, Florence, 1962; Citation of Honor Gov. of Mass., 1981; Key to City Worcester, Mass, 1981. Mem. Fedn. Modern Painters and Sculptors. Home: RFD 9 West Castle Rd Orangeburg NY 10962

DERMODY, JOHN, oceanographer; b. Needham, Mass., Mar. 28, 1924; s. Frank J. and Frances (Frawley) D.; m. Tommy Anne Black, Mar. 5, 1950; children—Grant M., Robin Anne, Todd F. B.S., Holy Cross Coll., 1945; postgrad. U. Wash., 1957-58; MIT, 1959. With U.S. Coast and Geodetic Survey, 1948-56; oceanographer U. Wash., Seattle, 1957-75; mgr. programs U. Alaska, Fairbanks, 1976-79; lab. dir. Ocean Inst. of Wash., Seattle, 1979-81; tech. mgr. Raven Systems & Research, Seattle, 1981—. Contbr. articles to profl. jours. Served with USN, 1942-46. Adult leader Boy Scouts Am., Seattle, 1968-74; exec. sec. Pres.'s Commn. on Marine Sci., Engring. and Resources, 1967-68; mem. Gov.'s Tech. Com., Alaska, 1976-79. Recipient award of yr. U.S. Dept. Commerce, 1956. Mem. Soc. Naval Architects and Marine Engrs., Inst. of Navigation, The Hydrographic Soc., Marine Tech. Soc. Republican. Roman Catholic.

DE ROBURT, HAMMER, president of Nauru; b. Nauru, Sept. 25, 1923; ed. Geelong Tech. Coll., Victoria, Australia. Tchr., 1940-42, 51-57; deported by Japanese, 1942-46; ednl. liaison officer Dept. Nauruan Affairs, 1947-51; mem. Nauru Local Govt. Council, 1955-68; pres. Republic of Nauru, 1968-76, 78—, also minister comml. aviation, minister internat. affairs, minister island devel. and industry, minister external affairs, pub. service, leader of opposition, 1976-78. Address: Office of Pres, Yaren Nauru *

DE ROOIJ, NICOLAAS FRANS, microelectronics educator, consultant; b. Bergen op Zoom, North-Brabant, Netherlands, Jan. 3, 1951; s. Nico and Johanna (van Willegen) de R.; m. Alie Wildvank, May 26, 1979; children—Nicolien, Marjolein. MSc., State Univ., Utrecht, Netherlands, 1975; Ph.D., Twente Univ. of Tech., Enschede, Netherlands, 1978. Jr. scientist Twente Univ. of Tech., 1975-78; research scientist Cordis Europa N.V., Roden, Netherlands, 1979-82; full prof. microelectronics Univ. Neuchâ tel, Switzerland, 1982—; lectr. Fed. Inst. Tech., Lausanne, Switzerland, 1983—, Zurich, 1987; chmn. internat. steering com. Transducers, 1987—. also cons. Contbr. articles and tech. papers to profl. jours.; mem. editorial bd. Sensors and Actuators, Sensors and Materials. Mem. IEEE, Electrochem. Soc., Royal Netherlands Chem. Soc. Office: Inst of Microtech, U Neuchâtel, Rue Breguet, 2000 Neuchâtel Switzerland

DEROOST, FRED EDWARD, industrial company executive; b. St. Joost-ten-Node, Belgium, Feb. 21, 1930. Lic. Handels- en Fin. Wetenschappen, U. Faculteit St. Aloysius, Ehsal, Brussels, 1953. Acct. Cotonco, Zaïre, 1954-59; head buyer Vandemoortele Izegem, Belgium, 1959-74; gen. mgr. Vamo Mills Izegem, Belgium, 1974-87. Mem. Soya Working Group Fediol (pres.). Office: NV Vamo Mills, Prins Albertlaan 12, 8700 Izegem Belgium

DE ROOVER, MARTIN C(ORNELIUS) M(ARIA), international transport executive; b. Hoogstraten, Antwerp, Belgium, June 25, 1938; s. Louis and Maria (Siemons) DeR.; m. Andrée B.T.C. Dely, Feb. 19, 1966; children: Ruben, Ilja. Degree in Comml. and Consular Scis., St. Ignatius, Antwerp, 1961. Accts. exec. Ned. Lloyd Ins., Antwerp, 1963-66; pub. relations FINANCIA, Antwerp, 1966-67; mgr. Claver Import & Distbrn., Merksem, Belgium, 1968-72; mgr. and gen. mgr. Group NAVEX, Antwerp, 1972—; advisor to Ministry of Trade, Brussels, 1976—; comml. ct. judge maritime chamber Ministry of Justice, Antwerp, 1983—. Named Knight Order Leopold II Ministry of Econ. Affairs, 1980. Mem. World Trade Ctr. Assn., Assn. Antwerp Port Interests, Internat. Freight Forwarders Assn., Baltic & Maritime Council. Roman Catholic. Home: Esmoreitlaan 1/b 2, B-2050 Antwerp Belgium Office: NAVEX, Brouwersvliet 15, B-2000 Antwerp Belgium

DE ROSA, ALFONSO MICHAEL, investment banker; b. Neptune, N.J., Mar. 31, 1943; s. Salvator Paul and Julia Mary (Vaccaro) DeR.; B.S. in B.A., Georgetown U., 1964; M.B.A., Am. U., 1966; m. Susan Lowe, Sept. 12, 1965 (div.); children—Christina Beth, Lisa Anne, Michael, Matthew. Account exec. Reynolds & Co., Washington, 1966-69, nat. sales devel., N.Y.C., 1969-70, mgr. regional instl. dept., Washington; v.p., resident mgr. Hayden Stone, Washington, 1971-73; v.p., resident mgr. Hornblower, Weeks, Hemphill, Noyes (merged with Shearson Loeb Rhoades), Washington, 1973—; v.p. Shearson Lehman Bros., 984—; co-chmn. Georgetown U. Alumni cons. Mem. lay adv. council Center for Applied Research in the Apostolate. Mem. Washington Soc. Investment Analysts, John Carroll Soc. Republican. Roman Catholic. Clubs: Kenwood Golf and Country, Bond of Washington (past pres., bd. govs.). Home: 3964 Georgetown Ct NW Washington DC 20007 Office: Shearson Lehman Bros Inc 1700 Pennsylvania Ave 10th Floor Washington DC 20006

DE ROSNAY, GERARD, textile company executive; b. Orleans, Loiret, France, Mar. 5, 1940; came to Can., 1966; s. Gaston de Rosnay and Genevieve du Boisberranger; separated; children: Gilles, Nathalie, Marc, Caroline. Directeur regional Armstrong World Industries Ltd., Montreal, 1970—. Home: 832 Dollard, Outremont, PQ Canada H2V 3G7 Office: Armstrong World Industries Ltd, 6911 Decarie Blvd, Montreal, PQ Canada H3W 3E5

DEROUANE, ERIC GERARD, chemist, educator; b. Peruwelz, Belgium, July 4, 1944; s. Gerard Joseph and Marcelle (Gjsens) D.; B.A., U. Liege, 1965, D.Sc., 1968; M.A., Princeton U., 1968; m. Claudine Grizeau, May 27, 1967; 1 dau., Daphne. Research scientist Belgian Nat. Sci. Found., 1967-73; mem. faculty U. Namur, 1973—, prof. chemistry, 1976—; research scientist Mobil R & D, 1982-84; cons. to industry; sec. research group catalysis Council of Europe. Recipient Stas-Spring prize, 1968, Wetrems award Belgica Acad. Scis., 1975. Mem. Belgian Chem. Soc. (award 19—), Belgian Phys. Soc., Am. Chem. Soc., Chem. Soc. Lodon, Sigma Xi. Author over 200 papers in field; editor: Electronic Structure and Reactivity of Metal Surfaces, 1976; editor-in-chief Jour. Molecular Catalysis. Home: 56 rue de Champs Verts, 5020 Namur Belgium Office: 61 rue des Bruxelles, 5000 Namur Belgium

DE ROY, STEPHANE, physician, surgeon, researcher; b. Brussels, Brabant, Belgium, Dec. 12, 1924; s. Herman and Caroline (Struelens) deR.; m. Monique Lecocq, Aug. 1, 1952 (div. 1962); 1 child, Francoise; m. Anne-Marie Dunesme, Aug. 29, 1981; 1 child, Axel. M.D., U. Brussels, 1951. Asst. surgeon Brugmann Hosp., Brussels, 1951-53, U.L.B. Section Geriatric surgery, Brussels, 1955-61, adj. surgeon, 1961-62, chief dept. surgery, 1962-75; asst. in anatomic pathology ULB St. Pieters Hosp., Brussels, 1951-53; researcher in physiology ULB, Brussels, 1945-48; med. dir. Warner Lambert Co., Glaxo, Brussels, 1953-78. Contbr. articles to profl. jours. Recipient Chevalier Ordre Leopold King and Govt. Belgium, 1975. Fellow. Internat. Coll. Angiology. Roman Catholic. Clubs: Cercle Royal Gaulois, Assn. Atlantique Belge. Avocations: music; piano; swimming. Office: 3 ave des Violettes, 1640 Rhode St, Genese Belgium

DERR, KENNETH T., oil company executive. m. Donna Mettler, Sept. 12, 1959; 3 children. B.M.E., Cornell U. With Chevron Corp. (formerly Standard Oil Co. of Calif.), 1960—, v.p., 1972-85; pres. Chevron U.S.A., Inc. subs. Chevron Corp., 1978-84; head merger program Chevron Corp. and Gulf Oil Corp., 1984-85; vice-chmn. Chevron Corp., 1985—; bd. dirs. Citicorp. Trustee Cornell U.; bd. dirs. Citicorp. Mem. Am. Petroleum Inst. (dir.). Clubs: Orinda Country (Calif.); Pacific Union. Office: Chevron Corp 225 Bush St San Francisco CA 94104

DERR, THOMAS SIEGER, religion educator; b. Boston, June 18, 1931; s. Thomas Sieger and Mary Ferguson (Sebring) D.; m. Virginia Anne Bush, June 9, 1956, (div. 1977); children—Peter Bulkeley, Laura Seely, Mary Williams; m. Janet Hackman, Apr. 12, 1980 (div. 1985); 1 child, Philip Henry; m. Linda Vincent, Feb. 14, 1986. A.B., Harvard U., 1953; M.Div., Union Theol. Sem., 1956; Ph.D., Columbia U., 1972. Ordained to ministry, United Ch. of Christ, 1956. Researcher World Council Chs., Geneva, 1961-62; asst. chaplain Stanford U., Calif., 1956-59; asst. chaplain Smith Coll., Northampton, Mass., 1963-65, asst. prof. religion, 1965-71, assoc. prof., 1972-77, prof., 1977—; cons. World Council Chs., 1965—; dir. Ctr. on Religion and Soc., N.Y.C.; mem. complemental faculty Rush Med. Coll., Chgo., 1979-84. Author: The Political Thought of the Ecumenical Movement, 1972; Ecology and Human Need, 1975; Church State, and Politics, 1981; Barriers to Ecumenism: The Holy See and the World Council of Churches on Social Questions, 1983; Believable Futures of American Protesantism, 1988. Contbr. articles to profl. jours. Danforth Found. grantee, 1959-60, 65-66; Inst. for Advanced Study of Religion, U. Chgo. fellow, 1981. Mem. Soc. for Christian Ethics. Avocations: sailing; skiing; travel. Home: 60 Harrison Ave Northampton MA 01060 Office: Smith Coll Northampton MA 01063

DERRICKSON, WILLIAM BORDEN, business executive; b. Milford, Del., May 30, 1940; m. Patricia Jean Hayes, Feb. 1, 1964; children—Stephen Russel, Michael Scot. B.S.E.E., U. Del., 1964; diploma, Harvard Bus. Sch., 1979. Registered profl. engr. Supr. elec. maintenance Delmarva Power, Salisbury, Md., 1964-68; instrumentation engr. Hercules, Inc., Wilmington, Del., 1968-69, Sun Shipbldg., Chester, Pa., 1969-70; dir. project Fla. Power & Light Co., Juno Beach, Fla., 1970-84; sr. v.p. Pub. Service Co. N.H., Manchester, 1984-85; pres. New Hampshire Yankee Electric Co., Seabrook, 1985-87, WPD Assocs., Inc., 1986—; Nuclear advisor Tenn. Valley Authority Bd. Dirs., 1987; pres., chief operating officer Quadrex Corp., Campbell, Calif., 1988—. Contbr. articles to profl. publs. Named Constrn. Man of Yr. ENR/McGraw-Hill Publs., 1984. Mem. Am. Nuclear Soc., Atomic Indsl. Forum, Project Mgmt. Inst., Nat. Soc. Profl. Engrs., N.H. Soc. Profl. Engrs. Republican. Home: PO Box 1017 North Hampton NH 03862 Office: Quadrex Corp 1700 Dell Ave Campbell CA 95008

DERRY, JAMES LEWIS, air transport executive, business educator; b. Chgo., May 11, 1952; s. Freeman Wayne and Lorraine (Youpel) D.; m. Patricia Joy Bylsma, Oct. 2, 1952; children: Juliane, Sarah Lynn. BA, Concordia Coll., 1973; postgrad., Internat. Peoples Coll., Elsinsor, Denmark, 1974-75, U. Bergen, Norway, 1975; MBA, Maharishi Internat. U., 1986. English tchr. AIS Sproglaboratorium, Oslo, Norway and Odense, Denmark, 1975-80; sheep farmer, Aal, Norway, 1980-84; vis. instr. Maharishi Internat. U., Fairfield, Iowa, 1986—; mktg. dir. Derry Air, Aal, 1986—; bd. dirs. Geiteryggen Flysenter Inc., Skien, Norway; mem. faculty Maharishi Internat. U., Oslo; cons. in field. Mem. Aircraft Owners and Pilots Assn., Orgn. of Bus. Profls. Practicing the TM Technique. Mem. Venstre Party. Lutheran. Clubs: Klanten Flyklubb (Gol, Norway); Dagali Flyklubb (Norway). Home: Tveitemovegen 3, N-3570 Aal Norway Office: Derry Air, N-3570 Aal Norway

DERSH, RHODA E., management consultant, business executive; b. Phila., Sept. 10, 1934; d. Maurice S. and Kay (Wiener) Eisman; m. Jerome Dersh, Dec. 23, 1956; children: Debra Lori, Jeffrey Jonathan. BA, U. Pa., 1955; MA, Tufts U., 1956; MBA, Manhattan Coll. Sch. Bus., 1980. Interpreter, Consul of Chile, 1954-57; various teaching and staff positions Albright Coll., Mt. Holyoke Coll., Amherst Coll., Marple Newtown Sch., 1957-64; systems designer Systems Inc., Reading, Pa., 1964-67; pres., chief exec. officer Profl. Practice Mgmt. Assocs., Reading, 1976—; pres., chief exec. officer Pace Inst.; chief exec. officer Pace Inst., Reading, 1981—; pres., chief exec. officer Pace Mgmt., Inc., 1983—; pres. Wordserv, 1984—, State Bd. Pvt. Lic. Schs., 1987—; cons. dir. pub. sch. budget study project City of Reading, 1967-78, chmn. comprehensive community plan task force, 1973-75, chmn. pub. service cons. project, 1980—; panel chmn. budget allocations United Way, 1974-76; del. White House Conf. on Children Youth, 1970; co-founder World Affairs Council, Reading and Berks County, 1963-65; chmn. Berks County Com. for Children Youth, 1968-72; commr. Trial Ct. Nominating Commn. of Berks County (Pa.), 1982-84; bd. dirs. United Way of Berks County, 1984-87; chmn. programs Leadership Berks, mem. Bd. of Pvt. Lic. Schs., Pa., 1987—. Recipient grant AAUW Ednl. Found.; Outstanding Womens award Jr. League Reading; Trendsetter award YWCA, 1985; accredited ind. cons. Mem. Inst. Community Affairs (exec. com. 1975-79), Pa. Assn. Pvt. Sch. Bus. Adminstrs. (bd. dirs. 1985—), LWV, Berks County C. of C. (bd. dirs. 1983-86, chmn. edn. com. 1983-85), AAUW, Am. Mgmt. Assn., Am. Acad. Ind. Cons. (pres. 1978-80), Nat. Com. Citizens in Edn., Am. Acad. Polit. Social Sci., Nat. Assn. Female Execs., Reading and Berks C. of C (bd. dirs., chmn. edn. com., Entrepreneur of Yr. 1985). Lodge: Rotary (mem. Club of Reading 1987—). Author: The School Budget is Your Business, 1976, Business Management for Professional Offices, 1977, The School Budget: It's Your Money, It's Your Business, 1979, Improving Public School Management Practices, 1979, Part-Time Professional and Managerial Personnel: The Employers View, 1979; contbr. articles to profl. jours. Office: 606 Court St Reading PA 19601

DE RU, HENDRIK JAN, law educator; b. Leiden, The Netherlands, Sept. 9, 1948; s. Cornelis and Nelia Everharda (van der Burgh) de R.; m. Maaike Anneke van Oord, Sept. 1, 1971; children: Cornelis, Govert Nanne, Barbara, Nelia. LLM, Free U. of Amsterdam, 1972; LLD, U. Ultrecht, 1981. Researcher U. Strasbourg, France, 1972-73; lectr. law Cath. U., Nijmegan, The Netherlands, 1973-78; lectr. Free U. of Amsterdam, 1978-87, prof. constl., adminstrv. law, 1987—; cons. various govtl. depts., pub. enterprises, The Netherlands; mem. Adminstrv. Ct., The Netherlands, 1982—; vis. prof. U. Calif., Berkeley, 1984-85. Author: Staatsbedrijven en staatsdeelnemingen, 1981, Deregulering, 1984, Staat, markt en recht, 1987, Privatisering in de praktijk, 1987, Pryst de wet zich uit de markt, 1988; editor-in-chief Ars Aequi, 1973-78. Mem. Com. Socio-Econ. Council, The Hague, 1986—. Research grantee The Netherlands Orgn. for Sci. Research, 1984-85. Mem. Internat. Inst. Adminstrv. Scis. (pub. enterprise com. 1982—). Lodge: Rotary. Home: Bredestraat 39, 6674 AX Herveld The Netherlands Office: Free U Sch of Law, PO Box 7161, 1007 MC Amsterdam The Netherlands

DERUCHER, KENNETH NOEL, civil engineering educator; b. Messina, N.Y., Jan. 24, 1949; s. Kenneth John and Vienna May (MacDougall) D.; m. Barbara Eileen Frick, Apr. 15, 1978; 1 son, Kenneth James. AA, Erie County Tech. Coll., Buffalo, 1969; BCE, Tri-State U., Angola, Ind., 1971; MS, U. N.D., 1973; PhD, Va. Poly. Inst., 1977. Asst. prof. civil engring. U. Md., Coll. Park, 1976-79; research cons. Civil Design Corp., Laurel, Md., 1979-80; assoc. prof., Stevens Inst. Tech., Hoboken, N.J., 1980-82, head dept. civil engring., 1982—, prof., 1985—; research cons. various govt. orgns.; cons. engr. 1983. Author: Structural Analysis and Design, 1980, Materials for Civil and Highway Engineering, 1981, others; contbr. numerous articles to profl. jours. Pres. Marcel Lake Property Owners Assn., 1986-88. Mem. ASCE (dir. N.J. sect. 1981-82, awards chmn. N.J. br. 1980-83, v.p. 1981-82, pres. 1983-84, Educator of Yr. local student chpt. 1981), Sigma Xi (sec. Stevens Inst. Tech. chpt. 1977-79). Office: Dept Civil & Ocean Engring Stevens Inst Tech Castle Point Station NJ 07030

DERUNGS, ADOLF, management company executive; b. Uors, Grison, Switzerland, Aug. 20, 1935; s. Gion Giusep Derungs and Emerita Collenberg; m. Savoldelli Milli, Oct. 10, 1964; children: Patrizia, Mirella. Internal auditor Nestle Co., Vevey, Switzerland, 1961-65; controller Franke Norm, Aarburg, Switzerland, 1965-67; credit mgr. Polysar Internat., Fribourg, Switzerland, 1967-68; cash mgr. Ciba-Geigy, Basle, Switzerland, 1968-74; fin. exec. Swisspharmia, Cairo, 1974-78; treas. Soc. Internat. Pirelli, Basle, 1978-82; corp. fin. officer Pirelli Soc. Gen., Basle, 1982-85, chief auditor, 1985—. Home: Allmendgasse 20, CH-4148 Pfeffingen Switzerland Office: Pirelli Soc Gen, St Jakobstrasse 54, CH-4052 Basle Switzerland

DERWIN, JORDAN, lawyer, consultant, actor; b. N.Y.C., Sept. 15, 1931; s. Harry and Sadie (Baruch) D.; m. Barbara Joan Concool, July 4, 1956 (div. 1970); children—Susan Lee, Moira Ellen; m. Joan Linda Wolfberg, May 6, 1973. B.S., NYU, 1953, J.D., 1959. Bar: N.Y. 1959, U.S. Dist. Ct. (so. and ea. dists. N.Y.) 1960, U.S. Ct. Appeals (2d. cir.) 1960, U.S. Supreme Ct. 1962. Arthur Garfield Hays research fellow NYU, 1958-59, research assoc. Duke U. Sch. of Law, Durham, N.C., 1959-60; assoc. Brennan, London, Buttenwieser, N.Y.C., 1960-64; sole practice Jordan Derwin, N.Y.C., 1964-70; gen. counsel N.Y.C. Off Track Betting Corp., 1970-74; assoc. gen. counsel Gen. Instrument Corp., N.Y.C., 1974-79; cons., 1980—. Author (with F. Hodge O'Neal), Expulsion or Oppression of Business Associates: Squeeze Outs in Small Business, 1960; actor in various films, TV programs, commls. 1980—; contbr. articles to prof. jours. Served to lt. j.g., USNR, 1953-56, Korea, Vietnam. Mem. Am. Soc. of Mag. Photographers, Screen Actors Guild (dir. nat. bd. 1982—, sec. N.Y. br. 1983-87, 12th nat. v.p. 1984-87, 4th nat. v.p. 1987—, 1st v.p. N.Y. br. 1987—), AFTRA (dir. N.Y. local 1980-83, 87—, dir. nat. bd. 1981—), Motion Picture Players Welfare Fund (trustee 1987—), Actors Equity Assn., Phi Delta Phi. Home and Office: 305 E 86 St New York NY 10028

DERZAI, MATTHEW, telecommunications company executive; b. Heerlerheide, Limburg, The Netherlands, Sept. 2, 1928; s. Matt Derzai and Angela Ocepek; m. Karen Adele Stokes, June 14, 1958; children: Melinda Anne, Cynthia Kim, Wendy Cheryl. B of Applied Sci., U. Toronto, Can., 1955. Registered profl. engr. Engr. Bell Can., Montreal, 1954-64, staff engr., 1967-75; engr. AT&T, N.Y.C., 1964-67; head dept. tech. services Internat. Telecommunications Union, Geneva, 1975-79; computer services engr. Canadian Telecommunications Carriers Assn., Ottawa, Ont., Can., 1979-83; gen. mgr., sec.-treas. Frequency Coordination System Assn., Ottawa, 1983—. Contbr. articles to profl. jours. Mem. IEEE, Assn. Profl. Engrs. Ontario. Office: Frequency Coordination, System Assn, 1 Nicholas St, Suite 700, Ottawa, ON Canada K1N 7B7

DERZAW, RICHARD LAWRENCE, lawyer; b. N.Y.C., Mar. 6, 1954; s. Ronald Murray and Diana (Diamond) D. B.A. magna cum laude, Fairleigh Dickinson U., 1976; J.D., Ohio No. U., 1979. Bar: Fla. 1979, U.S. Dist. Ct. (so. dist.) Fla. 1981, U.S. Ct. Appeals (5th cir.) 1981, U.S. Ct. Appeals (11th cir.) 1981, (2d cir.), 1988, N.Y. 1982, U.S. Dist. Ct. (ea. dist.) N.Y. 1986, U.S. Tax Ct. 1986, U.S. Supreme Ct., 1988. Sole practice, Boca Raton, Fla., 1979-82, N.Y.C., 1982—. Mem. ABA, N.Y. State Bar Assn., Fla. Bar Assn., Am. Arbitration Assn., Assn. of Bar of City of N.Y., Fed. Bar Council, Phi Alpha Delta, Phi Zeta Kappa, Phi Omega Epsilon. Lodge: Lions of Boca Raton (treas. 1981-82). Home: 32 Pecan Valley Dr New City NY 10956

DESAI, KIRIT NAVNITRAI, polymer chemist; b. Bilimora, Gujarat, India, Feb. 9, 1949; came to U.S., 1971; s. Navnitrai R. and Vinaben (Vina) D.; m. Kailash Ratilal Desai, Mar. 21, 1975; children: Nirav K., Shivani. B.Sc. in Chemistry, Gujarat U., India, 1968; M.Sc., 1970; M.S. in Chemistry, St. Joseph's U., 1974, M.B.A., 1984. Research specialist U. Pa., Phila., 1974—. Contbr. articles to profl. jours. M.G. Sci. Inst.-India merit scholar, 1964-68; Indian Rys. fellow, 1968-70. Mem. Am. Chem. Soc. (polymer div.), Am. Chem. Inst., Internat. Confedn. Thermal Analysis, N.Am. Thermal Analysis Soc., Am. Mgmt. Assn., Delaware Valley Thermal Analysis Forum. Home: 740 Providence Rd Aldan PA 19018

DESAI, RASHMI C., physics educator; b. Amod, India, Nov. 21, 1938; came to U.S., 1962; s. Chimanlal P. and Savita (Vakil) D.; m. Kalpakam Shanker, May 2, 1963; children—Anuj, Aparna. BS with honors, Bombay U., India, 1957; PhD, Cornell U., 1966. Sci. officer Bhabha Atomic Research Ctr., Bombay, 1957-62; research assoc. MIT, Cambridge, 1966-68; asst. prof. U. Toronto, Ont., Can., 1968-71, assoc. prof., 1971-78, prof., 1978—, prof. physics and coordinator grad. studies, 1983-87; vis. assoc. Calif. Inst. Tech., 1975; vis. scientist IBM, San Jose, Calif., 1981-82; vis. prof. U. Mainz, Fed. Republic of Germany, 1987, Inst. for Nonlinear Sci., U. Calif.-San Diego, La Jolla, 1988. Author: (with others) Advances in Chemical Physics, Vol. 46, 1981, Interfacial Dynamics, 1986; contbr. articles to profl. jours. Chmn., trustee Nirvan Bhavan, Toronto, 1979-81; trustee Indo-Can. Cultural Ctr., Toronto, 1981—, Nat. Sci. and Engring. Research Council Can. grantee, 1968—. Mem. Can. Assn. Physicists (sec. 1970-71), Am. Phys. Soc., Am. Assn. Physics Tchrs., Sun Workstations Users Group Toronto.

DESAI, SURESH VITHOBA, trading company executive; b. Margao, India, Mar. 13, 1950; s. Vithoba Ganesh and Rukminibai Vithoba (Rukminibai) D.; m. Maya Suresh, Feb. 17, 1984; 1 child, Dipti. BSc, Bombay U., 1973. Ptnr. Goa Trade Link Service, Margao, 1975—; ptnr. M/S Success Enterprises, Cuncolim, Philippines, 1979—, M/S Shobsan Mktg. Agys., 1987—; bd. dirs. Desai Trade Well Mktg. Agys. Adv. com. Cuncolim Ednl. Soc., 1988—. Mem. Mahatma Gandhi Market Shop Owners Assn. (pres. 1981-86), Navelim Villagers Union (life). Club: Alem de Margao (sec. 1985-86). Lodge: Lions (pres. Margao club 1988—). Office: Goa Trade Link Service, Martires Dias Rd Opp New Era High Sch, Margao 403 601, India

DE SAINT-JORRE, GEOFFROY BERNARD MICHEL, surgeon; b. Saint-Lo, Manche, France, May 7, 1943; s. Jean and Edith (d'Annoville) de S.-J.; m. Elizabeth Prevost, Dec. 8, 1967; children—Nicholas, Gregoire, Victoire. Bacalaureat philosophie, Lycee Lakanal, Sceaux, France, 1961; M.D., Paris U., 1968. Intern, Hopitalx de Paris; chef de clinique Asst. des Hopitaux de Paris, 1976; surgeon, maxillofacial surgery Foch Hosp., Suresnes, France, 1977—. Author: Medical Dictionary Flamnarion, 1971. Mem. French Plastic and Reconstructive and Aesthetic Soc., French Maxillofacial Soc., European Cranio Facial Soc. Home: 10 Rue Kleber, 92130 Issy Les Moulineaux France Office: 59 rue Geoffroy Saint Hilaire, 75005 Paris France

DE SAINT PHALLE, THERESE, author; b. N.Y.C., Mar. 7, 1930; d. Alexandre and Helen Georgia (Harper) de St. Phalle; grad. high sch.; m. Baron Jehan de Drouas, Dec. 30, 1950; 1 son, Henri. Works include: (novels) La Mendigote, 1966, La Chandelle, 1967, Le Tournesol, 1968, Le Souverain, 1970, La Clairiere, 1974 (pub. as The Clearing in U.S. 1978), Le Metronome, 1980, Le Programme, 1985, L'Odeur de la Poudre, 1988; also TV films, motion picture scripts, short stories, articles; editor Flammarion, 1971-84. Vice pres., gen. mgr. Stock Pubs.; mem. French com. United World Colls. Mem. PEN, Cavalier King Charles Spaniel Club, Les Amis de Colette, Les Amis des Roses, Les Amis d'Alexandre Dumas, Les Gens du Livre (pres.), Islam et Occident, S.O.S. Paris, Nat. Women's Forum, Club L. , Cercle de l'Union Interallie'e. Roman Catholic. Home: 46 Blvd, Emile Augier, 75116 Paris France Office: 103 blvd Saint Michel, 75005 Paris France

DE SALVA, SALVATORE JOSEPH, pharmacologist, toxicologist; b. N.Y.C., Jan. 14, 1924; s. Nicola Carlo and Frances Agnes (Caldarella) De S.; m. Elaine Mae Radloff, June 14, 1948; children: Salaine Claire De Salva Bonanne, Christopher Joseph, Stephanie De Salva Farrelly, Steven William, Gregory Vincent, Peter Nicholas, Philip Anthony, Diedre De Salva Berry. BS, Marquette U., 1947, MS, 1949; postgrad., U. Ill., Chgo., 1951-53; PhD, Stritch Sch. Medicine, Loyola U., Chgo., 1958. Research and teaching asst. Marquette U., Milw., 1947-49; research biochemist Milw. County Gen. Hosp., 1954; instr. U. Ill., Chgo., 1951-52; asst. prof. Chgo. Coll. Optometry, 1951-53; pharmacologist Armour Pharm. Lab., Chgo, 1953-59; sect. head Colgate Palmolive Co., Piscataway, N.J., 1959-66, sr. research assoc., 1966-72, mgr., 1972-76, assoc. dir. research for pharmacology and toxicology, 1976-83, dir. research pharmacology and toxicology, 1983-88, worldwide ops. dir., 1988—; lectr. Loyola U., 1957-59; mem. technician tng. N.J. Council for Research and Devel., Rutgers U., 1969-72. Editor: Symposium for Biomedical Electronic Instrumentation, 1965; contbr. articles to profl. jours.; patentee in field. Mem. Park Forest (Ill.) Mosquito Abatement Program, 1952-55, Franklin Twp. (N.J.) Sch. Bd., 1969-70, Somerset (N.J.) Bd. Health, 1965-67, Cath. Youth Orgn., Somerset; v.p. Cedar Hill Swim Club, Somerset; active Boy Scouts Am., Somerset, 1965-67; trustee Franklin Twp. Day Care Ctr., 1969. Served with USN, 1942-46. Mem. AAAS, Soc. Exptl. Biology and Medicine, Am. Soc. Pharmacology and Exptl. Therapeutics, Soc. Toxicology, Internat. Union Pharmacology (toxicology sect.), N.Y. Acad. Scis., Sigma Xi. Roman Catholic. Office: Colgate Palmolive Co 909 River Rd Piscataway NJ 08854

DE SANTO, DONALD JAMES, psychologist, educational administrator; b. Bklyn., July 5, 1942; s. Vincent James and Rose Ann (Dowd) DeS.; B.A. cum laude, St. Francis Coll., N.Y., 1964; M.A. in Clin./Child Psychology, St. John's U., 1966, profl. diploma, 1976; m. Loretta DePippo, Aug. 25, 1962; children—Dolores, Jennifer, Marisa. Asst. law librarian Dewey, Ballantine, Bushby, Palmer & Wood, N.Y.C., 1960-64; research asst. St. John's U., N.Y., 1964-65, teaching fellow, 1965-66, project dir. 2 federally funded grants, 1975-76; dir. The Rugby Sch., Freehold, N.J., 1977—. Mem. Youth Guidance Com., Freehold, 1983—, chmn. econ. devel. com., 1984—; mem. Econ. Devel. Com., Freehold, 1983—; mem. Zoning Bd. Adjustment, Freehold. Contbg. editor Channels jour. special educators, 1986—. Recipient Fire Prevention medal, N.Y.C., 1954; citation for outstanding contbn. to arts in edn. N.J. Commr. Edn., 1981; Title VIb Fed. grantee, 1972-78. Mem. Am. Psychol. Assn. (pub. relations com. div. 16), Nat. Assn. for Retarded Citizens, Council for Exceptional Children, N.J. Assn. Schs. and Agys. for Handicapped (sec., conf. chmn. 1983-84, pub. relations chmn. 1984-86), Assn. for Help Retarded Children, Monmouth County Hist. Assn., Psi Chi, Phi Delta Kappa. Roman Catholic. Home: 222 Park Ave Freehold NJ 07728 Office: PO Box 1403 Glendola NJ 07719

DESCHAMPS, JEAN PIERRE, physician; b. Paris, Mar. 20, 1941; s. Roger and Marcelle (Vanhamme) D.; m. Genevieve Blangille, Jan. 11, 1964; children: Emmanuelle, Marie, Pierre, Anne. MD, Faculte Medecine, Nancy, France, 1969. Intern Centre Hosp. Regional, Nancy, 1964-69; chef de clinique Faculte de Medecine, 1969-75, prof., 1978; prof. Centre Internat. de l'Enfance, Paris, 1975-77; dir. gen. Centre de Medecine Preventive, Nancy, 1987—; Author: Mother and Child Health, 1984, Pregnancy in Adolescence, 1976, Public Health, Community Health, 1980; editor Rev. Francaise de Sante Publique, other books and articles. Conseiller mcpl., Villers les Nancy, 1970-75. Named Medecin sous lt. Internat. Coop., 1964-65. Mem. Soc. Francaise de Sante Publique (sec. gen. 1983), Club Internat. Pediatrie Sociale (pres. 1983). Office: Centre de Medecine Preventive, 2 Ave du Doyen J, 54500 Parisot Vandoeuvre France

DESCHE, PIERRE MAURICE, orthopedic surgeon; b. Paris, May 31, 1936; s. Pierre Hardy and Madeleine (Desche) Zizine; m. Micheyle Marie-Alice-Chaillou;children: Eric, Marion, Elsa. MD, U. Paris, 1968. Resident in surgery Assistance Publique, Paris, 1964-68; sr. resident asst. Assistance Publique Paris U. Med. Sch., 1968-71; asst. prof. Tour's U. Med. Sch., 1971-76; orthopaedic surgeon Ctr. Orthopedique, Dracy Le Fort, France, 1976-86, Clinque Aumont, Versailles, France, 1986—; cons. Clinosa SA, Lyon, 1976-84, De Puy SNC, Paris, 1984. Contbr. articles to profl. jours.; inventor in field. Bd. dirs. College National des Chirurgiens Francaise, Paris, 1979. Mem. Soc. Internat. Surgery Orthopaedics, French Soc. Surgery Orthopaedics. Rasseblenent Pour La Republique. Roman Catholic. Clubs: France-Amerique, La Bidoche. Home: 7 Residence la Rose Raie, 78000 Versailles France Office: Clinique Aumont, 52 Ave de Saint Cloud, 78000 Versailles France

D'ESCOTO, MIGUEL, Nicaraguan minister foreign affairs, priest; b. Hollywood, Calif., Feb. 5, 1933 (parents Nicaraguan citizens). BA, Maryknoll Coll., 1956; MA in Religious Edn., Maryknoll Sem., N.Y., 1961; MS in Comparative Journalism, Columbia U., 1962. Ordained priest Roman Catholic Ch., 1961. Founder Inst. for Neighborhood Action and Research, Santiago, Chile, 1963-69; dir. social communications Maryknoll Sem., N.Y.C., 1969-79, pub. Orbis Books; editor, pub. Maryknoll Mag.; founder Nicaraguan Fund for Integral Community Devel.; active Sandinista Front for Nat. Liberation, 1975—, founder Group of 12; fgn. minister of Nicaragua, Managua, 1979—.79—. *

DESERTI, LUIGI, food distribution executive; b. Argenta, Italy, June 21, 1915; m. Dora Veronesi, May 21, 1941; 1 child, Marina. Degree in Economy and Commerce, Bologna U., 1940. Chmn., D&C Compagnia, Bologna, 1950—, Oltremare Industria, Bologna, 1960-85; v.p. Credito Romagnolo, Bologna. Mem. Town Council Bologna, 1964-70; dir. Associazione Italiana Perl'arbitrato, 1979—, Confcommercio, Roma, 1983—. Decorated comdr. Order of Jerusalem Holy Sepulchre; officer Order du Merite Agricole (France); cavaliere del Lavoro, cavaliere di Gran Croce (Italy); officer Brit. Empire, 1986. Mem. Am. C. of C. (chmn. Bologna br. 1956-66), Industry Coop. Programme (chmn. Rome br. 1974-76), Unione Italiana Vini (chmn. Milan br. 1977-83), Italian Inst. Foreign Trade (chmn. Rome chpt. 1978-82). Club: Rotary (pres. 1968-69) (Bologna). Office: Via Nannetti 1, 40069 Zola Predosa Bologna, Italy

DESGRANGES, JEAN-PIERRE, physician; b. Angouleme, Charente, France, Apr. 29, 1941; s. Pierre and Suzanne (Fraisse) D.; m. Janyvonne LeGoff, April 14, 1970; children: Sebastienne, Jean-Malo. Grad., Coll. St. Paul, Angouleme, 1958; MD, Faculteé Medecine, Bordeaux, France, 1970. Gen. practice med. Lanvallay, France, 1971—. Roman Catholic. Home and Office: 21 Rue de la Prevalaye, 22100 Lanvallay, Dinan France

DE SILVA, COLIN, business executive, author, actor; b. Ceylon, Feb. 11, 1920; came to U.S., 1962, naturalized, 1972; s. John William and Rose Mary (Weerasinghe) de S.; children: Devayani, Cherine-Parakrama Chandrasoma. With Ceylon Civil Service, 1945-56, asst. sec. def., 1949-53, commr. nat. housing, 1953-56; diplomatic service 1953; mng. dir. Colombo Agencies, Ltd., also Colombo Indsl. Agencies, Ltd., 1957-62; exec. dir. Ceylon Mineral Waters, Ltd., 1957-62; dir. Vavasseur Trading Co., Ltd., 1957-62; pres., dir., owner Bus. Investment, Ltd., Honolulu, 1964—, West Coast Bus. Investment, Ltd., Portland, Oreg., 1970—, Econ. Devel. and Engring. Cons., Inc., Honolulu, 1965—; chmn. Gen. Mgmt. Corp., Honolulu, 1973—; pioneer in condominium devel., 1963—; chmn., dir. Condominium Mgmt., Inc.; lectr., cons. Peace Corps, 1962-66; econ. and fin. cons. nat. tourism studies. Del. Commonwealth Prime Ministers Conf., 1949, UN Housing Conf., 1955; chief liaison officer Commonwealth Fgn. Ministers Conf., 1949; pres. Ceylon Assn. Iron and Steel Mchts., 1956-62. Past chmn. bd. Opera Players of Hawaii; exec. com. Internat. C. of C., Ceylon, 1958-62; chmn. gen. importers com., mem. gen. council Ceylon Nat. C. of C., 1958-62; dir., past pres. McCully Bus. and Profl. Assn.; past dir. Waikiki Improvement Assn.; Trustee Kandyan Art Assn., 1946-49, Hawaii Pacific Coll., 1968-70. Mem. Screen Actors Guild, Honolulu, Portland chambers commerce, Smithsonian Instn. Home: 1040 Kealaolu Ave Honolulu HI 96816 Office: Pacific Tower Suite 2700 Honolulu HI 96813

DE SILVA, SEMBUKUTTIGE HENRY CORNELIUS, government irrigation official; b. Galle, Sri Lanka, Nov. 29, 1928; s. Sembukuttige Cornelius and Margret (Ediriweera) de. S.; m. Chandra Weeraratne Jayasuriya, July 4, 1960 (div. 1969); children—Nilanth, Rukmanthi; m. 2d Illekuttige Trixie Hema Fernando, July 27, 1970. B.Sc.Eng., Battersea Polytech., London, 1956; D.H.E., Technol. U. Delft (Netherlands), 1965. Asst. irrigation engr. Irrigation Dept., Sri Lanka, 1957-60, engr., 1960-67, div. engr., 1968-72, chief engr., 1973-77, dep. dir., 1978-79, sr. dep. dir., 1980-85, dir. irrigation, 1985—; f sec. Sri Lanka Nat. Com. on Large Dams, 1984—. Author articles and papers. Fellow Inst. Engrs. Sri Lanka; mem. Inst. Civil Engrs. (London), Franco Ceylon Technologists (pres. 1981-83, 84-85, 85-86), Netherlands Alumni Sri Lanka (sec. 1970-83, 85-88). Buddhist. Home: 21/28 Polhengoda Rd, Colombo 5 Sri Lanka Office: Irrigation Dept, Colombo 7 Sri Lanka

DESIND, PHILIP, art dealer, mathematical statistician; b. N.Y.C., Feb. 28, 1910; s. Max and Bertha (Gleichenhaus) D.; m. Anne Feuer (dec.); children—Barbara Harriet, Herbert Stephen. B.S., CCNY, 1934, M.S., 1938; postgrad. Columbia U., 1938-42. Works project supt. in charge of remedial reading program, Works Project Adminstrn., N.Y.C., 1936-42; statistician, ships program War Prodn. Bd., Washington, 1942-45; math. statistician U.S. Navy dept., Washington, 1945-61, U.S. Postal Service, 1962-71; dir. Capricorn Galleries, Bethesda, Md., 1964—; adj. prof. Am. U., 1956-71, Cath. U., 1961-64, Howard U., 1960-62, U. Md., 1961; statis. cons., 1971-81. Contbg. author: Teaching Children to Read, 1938; author: Reading Tastes of High School Students, 1939; contbr. articles to profl. jours. Designer system for counting mail for U.S. Postal Service. Recipient Meritorious award U.S. Postal Service, 1965. Mem. Am. Statis. Assn. Office: Capricorn Galleries 4849 Rugby Ave Bethesda MD 20814

DESNICK, ROBERT JOHN, human geneticist; b. Mpls., July 12, 1943; s. Theodore David and Celia Janice (Marcus) D. B.A., U. Minn., 1965, Ph.D., 1970, M.D., 1971. Diplomate: Nat. Bd. Med. Examiners. Research assoc. U. Minn., Mpls., 1970-72; intern and resident dept. pediatrics U. Minn., 1971-73, asst. prof. pediatrics, 1973-75, asst. prof. lab. medicine and pathology, 1973-75; asst. prof. U. Minn. (Dight Inst. Human Genetics), 1973-75, assoc. prof. pediatrics, 1975-77; asso. prof. genetics and cell biology U. Minn. (Coll. Biologic Sci.), 1975-77; assoc. prof. U. Minn. (Dight Inst.), 1975-77, prof. pediatrics, 1977; Arthur J. and Nellie Z. Cohen prof. pediatrics and genetics and chief div. med. genetics Mt. Sinai Sch. Medicine, N.Y.C., 1977—; dir. Mt. Sinai Ctr. Jewish Genetic Diseases, 1981—; attending physician pediatrics Mt. Sinai Hosp.; cons. physician pediatrics Beth Israel Med. Ctr., N.Y.C., City Ctr. Hosp. Elmhurst, N.Y.; med. adv. bd. Nat. Tay-Sachs and Allied Diseases Assn., 1975—, Nat. Neurofibromatosis Found., 1978-81; Med. adv. bd. Nat. Found. Jewish Genetic Diseases, 1981—, Am. Porphyria Assn., 1984—, Nat. MPS Soc., 1987—; bd. dirs. Soc. Inherited Metabolic Diseases, 1983—; mem. N.Y. Gov.'s Adv. Com. on Genetics, 1982—; mem. med. adv. bd. Mucolipidosis IV Found. Editor: Enzyme Therapy in Genetic Diseases, 1972, 79, Molecular Genetic Modification of Eucaryotes, 1978, Gaucher Disease: A Century of Delineation and Research, 1982, Animal Models of Inherited Metabolic Diseases, 1982, Recent Advances in Inborn Errors of Metabolism, 1987; mem. editorial bd.: Enzyme, 1979—, Am. Jour. Human Genetics, 1980-84, Clinica Chemica Acta, 1984—; contbr. articles to sci. jours. USPHS fellow, 1968-70; recipient Ross award Soc. Pediatric Research, 1972; C.J. Watson award U. Minn. Med. Sch., 1973; NIH Research Career Devel. award, 1975-80; E. Mead Johnson award Am. Acad. Pediatrics, 1981. Mem. Am. Soc. Human Genetics, Genetics Soc. Am., Minn. Human Genetics League (dir. 1970-77), Soc. Complex Carbohydrates, Behavior Genetics Assn., Am. Fedn. Clin. Research, Am. Soc. Biochemistry and Molecular Biology, AAAS, Midwest Soc. Pediatric Research, Soc. Pediatric Research, Soc. Exptl. Biology and Medicine, Am. Soc. Exptl. Pathology, Central Soc. Clin. Research, Soc. Study Social Biology, Soc. Study Inborn Errors of Metabolism, N.Y. Acad. Sci., European Soc. Human Genetics, Harvey Soc. (sec. 1984—), Soc. Inherited Metabolic Diseases, Am. Pediatric Soc., Am. Soc. Microbiology, Am. Assn. Physicians, Am. Soc. Clin. Investigation, Japanese Soc. Inherited Diseases (hon.), Nat. Mucopolysaccharidosis Soc. (med. adv. bd.), 1987—, Sigma Xi. Office: CUNY Mt Sinai Sch Medicine Fifth Ave and 100th St New York NY 10029

DE SOFI, OLIVER JULIUS, data processing executive; b. Havana, Cuba, Dec. 26, 1929; s. Julius A. and Edith H. (Zsuffa) DeS.; B.S. in Math. and Physics, Ernst Lehman Coll., 1950; postgrad. in agronomy U. Havana, 1952, B.S. in Aero. Engring., 1956; came to U.S., 1956, naturalized, 1961; m. Phyllis H. Dumich, Feb. 14, 1971; children—Richard D., Stephen R., Kerri L. Dir. EDP tech. services and planning Am. Airlines, N.Y.C., 1968-70; dir. Sabre II, Tulsa, 1970-72; v.p. data processing and communications Nat. Bank of N. Am., Huntington Station, N.Y., 1972-76, sr. v.p. data processing and communications, 1976-78, sr. v.p. systems and ops., 1978-79, sr. v.p. adminstrn., N.Y.C., 1979-80, exec. v.p. adminstrn. group, 1980-83; exec. v.p. data processing methodologies and architecture Anacomp, Inc., Ft. Lee, N.J. and Sarasota, Fla., 1983-84; v.p. corp. devel. Computer Horizons Corp., N.Y.C., 1984-86; pres., chief exec. officer Coast to Coast Computers Inc., Sarasota, 1986—; lectr. program for women Adelphi Coll. Mem. Data Processing Mgmt. Assn., Computer Exec. Round Table, Am. Mgmt. Assn., Sales Execs. Club, Bank Adminstrn. Inst., AAAS, Internat. Platform Assn., Nat. Rifle Assn. Republican. Club: Masons (Havana).

DESOMOGYI, AILEEN ADA, retired librarian; b. London, Nov. 26, 1911; d. Harry Alfred and Ada Amelia (Ponten) Taylor; immigrated to Can., 1966; B.A., Royal Holloway Coll., U. London, 1936, M.A., 1939; M.L.S., U. Western Ont., 1971; m. Leslie Kuti, Nov. 22, 1958; m. 2d, Joseph DeSomogyi, July 8, 1966. Librarian in spl. and public libraries, Eng., 1943-66; sr. instr. Nat. Coal Bd., 1957; charge regional collection S.W. Ont., Lawson Library, U. Western Ont., 1967-71; cataloger Coop. Book Centre Can., 1971; mem. staff E. York (Ont.) Public Library, 1971-74; librarian Ont. Ministry Govt. Services Mgmt. and Info. Services Library, 1975-78, Sperry-Univac Computer Systems, Toronto (Ont.) Central Library, 1980-81. Fellow Internat. Biographical Assn.; Mem. Internat. Platform Assn., English Speaking Union, Can. Orgn. for Devel. Through Edn., Royal Can. Geog. Soc., Consumers Assn. Can., Can. Wildlife Fedn., Ont. Humane Soc., Internat. Fund Animal Welfare, Endangered Animal Sanctuary, U. Western Ont. Alumni Assn., Royal Holloway and Bedford New Coll. Assn., Am. Biog. Inst. Research Assn. (dep. gov., nat. bd. advisors), Can. Mental Health Assn., John Howard Soc., Met. Toronto Zool. Soc., Toronto Humane Soc. Roman Catholic. Contbr. articles to profl. jours. Home: 9 Bonnie Brae Blvd, Toronto, ON Canada M4J 4N3

DESPOTOPOULOS, CONSTANTINE, philosopher; b. Smyrna, Greece, Feb. 8, 1913; s. John Despotopoulos and Stella Samouchou; m. Olga Tsakatika, Apr. 13, 1979. Lic., U. Athens, Greece, 1933, PhD, 1939, Agregation, 1943. Lectr. philosophy Free Sch. Athenaion, Athens, 1955-56; prof. philosophy of law U. Nancy, France, 1969-75; prof. philosophy Panteios Sch. Polit. Sci., Athens, 1975-80; dir. ctr. research Greek Philosophy Acad., Athens, 1984—. Author: Philosophy of Law, 1954, Political Philosophy, 1975, 83, Philosophy I, II, II, 1978, 80, 82, Political Philosophy of Plato, 1980, also 15 other books. Served as lt. Greek Army, 1941. Mem. Greek Philos. Soc. (pres. 1979-81, hn. pres. 1985), Hestia Nea Snyrna (hon.), League Lawyers (hon.), European Soc. Culture (exec. bd. 1982). Greek Orthodox. Home: Pratinou St 99, 11634 Athens Greece Office: Acad Athens, Panepistimiou 28, 10679 Athens Greece

DESROCHERS, GERARD CAMILLE, surgeon; b. Marlboro, Mass., June 8, 1922; s. Emery Hector and Eliane (Lemire) DesR.; A.B., Coll. of Holy Cross, 1944; M.D., Tufts Coll., 1947; m. Ellen Franklin, Sept. 27, 1959; children—Gerard, Emery, Lewis, Anthony. Gen. rotating intern St. Mary's Hosp., Waterbury, Conn., 1947-48; straight surg. intern Boston City Hosp., 1949-50, asst. resident surgeon, 1950-51; resident in surgery New Eng. Med. Center, Boston, 1955-57; practice medicine specializing in surgery, Manchester, N.H.; gen. surgeon staff Cath. Med. Center, Manchester; med. dir. Sea Supply Corp., Bangkok, Thailand, 1953-54. Incorporator, Cath. Med. Center; incorporator Thomas More Found., Merrimack, N.H.; adv. bd. Lincoln Inst.; mem. N.H. Right to Life Com.; mem. bd. of policy Liberty Lobby; mem. New Eng. Med. Ethics Forum. Served as 1st lt. M.C., U.S. Army, 1970. Mem. Manchester Med. Soc., Hillsboro County Med. Soc., Internat. Coll. Physicians and Surgeons. Home: 402 Sagamore St Manchester NH 03104 Office: 648 Belmont St Manchester NH 03104

DESSALET, SAMUEL ROBERT, treasurer; b. York, Pa., Apr. 14, 1932; s. Jack Rose and Ethel (Werner) D.; B.S. in Commerce, Rider Coll., 1957; m. Nancy Lee Ashmore, Jan. 29, 1953; children—Deborah Lee, Sharon Lynne, Theresa Louise, Samuel Robert. Staff acct. Price Waterhouse & Co., Newark, 1957-61; mem. controller's staff Remington Rand Systems Div., N.Y.C., 1961; sr. bus. analyst, asst. sect. head Bayonne and Bayway Refineries, Humble Oil & Refining Co., Bayonne and Linden, N.J., 1961-65; chief acct., tax mgr. Bro Dart Industries, Newark, 1965-67; dir. corp. acctg. No. Natural Gas Co., Omaha, 1967-68; controller Nat. Poly Products div. No. Petrochem. Co., Mankato, Minn., 1968-83; treas.-sec. Nat. Poly Products, Inc., Mankato, Minn., 1983-86, chief fin. officer, 1986—, bd. dirs. Winland Electronics, Inc., Playtronics Inc. Loaned exec. Mankato Area United Way, 1978; trustee Centenary United Methodist Ch., Mankato, 1972-81, treas., 1977-81; bd. dirs. Multi-Ch. Found., Inc., 1974-81, chmn. bd., 1978-81. Served with AUS, 1952-54. C.P.A., Minn., N.J., Nebr. Mem. Am. Inst. C.P.A.s, N.J. Soc. C.P.A.s, Nebr. Soc. C.P.A.s, Minn. Soc. C.P.A.s, Nat. Assn. Accts. (pres. South Central Minn. chpt. 1976-77, nat. dir. 1978-80, del. Minn. Council). Republican. Club: Mankato Exchange (1st v.p. 1973). Home: 10 N Hill Ct Rt 5 Mankato MN 56001 Office: 2111 3d Ave PO Box 1180 Mankato MN 56001

DE STRATCLUT, ALECSANDR CUIL (ALASTAIR BOYD KYLE), merchant banker; b. London, Mar. 12, 1931; s. Allan Granger and Dora Jessie Ellen (Taylor) Kyle; m. Corinne Lois Silverman, Aug. 28, 1959; children: Joshua Reis, Peredur Thomas, Julia Dora; m. 2d, Mary Carmela Giarrizzo, Mar. 3, 1969; children: Allan Salvatore, Kentigern Sigvard. Student, St. John's Coll., 1947-49; AB, U. Michoacán, 1951; postgrad., U. Havana, 1951-52, U. Chgo., 1959. Child actor radio, stage and TV 1940-44; radio dir. Clyde de Mex. S.A., Acapulco, 1950; salesman Radiovision Internacional, Mexico City, 1951; with Atlantic Union Com., N.Y.C., 1953-54; with investment dept. Grace Internat. Devel. Co., N.Y.C., 1955-56; v.p., bd. dirs. Index & Retrieval Systems, Inc., N.Y.C. and Woodstock, Vt., 1957-62; prin. Alec Kyle & Co., N.Y.C., 1962-66; pres. Inst. Computer Assisted Instrn., Inc., Doylestown, Pa., 1967-70; mng. ptnr. Corp. Fin. Cons., Phila. and Princeton, N.J., 1971-82; prin. Cromwell & Kyle, Fountainville, Pa. and Fairfield, Conn., 1982-85, Kyle & Hayes-Morrison, Frazer, Pa. and Jamestown, R.I., 1986—; trustee Ymddiriedolaeth Llinach Brenhiniaeth y Cwmbriaid, 1963—; chmn. Strathclyde Corp., Phila.; seminar leader and lectr. in field. Co-founder, bd. dirs. Am. Council on NATO, 1954-57; sec. dir. No. New England passenger R.R. Conf., 1960-62; co-founder, sec. Fountainville Hist. Farm Assn., Bucks County, Pa., 1972—; cons. preservation agrl. land Buckingham (Pa.) Twp., 1978-79; pres. New Britain (Pa.) Twp. Democratic Orgn., 1974-78; mem. exec. bd. Bucks County Dem. Com., 1974-78; chmn. Nat. Task Force on Religion and Animal Rights, 1981-85; bd. dirs. Pa. Soc. Prevention of Cruelty to Animals, 1987—; chmn. Internat. Network for Religion and Animals, 1985-88, treas. 1988—; lay reader, dep. convs., mem. coms. Episcopal Diocese Pa.; vestryman St. Paul's Ch., Doylestown, Pa., vestryman Anglican Ch. of the Incarnation, Telford, Pa. Recipient Suprs. commendation Buckingham Twp., 1979. Mem. Newcomen Soc., Inst. Effective Mgmt. (v.p. 1978—), Assn. Corp. Growth, Am. Mgmt. Assn. (cons.), Family Assn. Cumbrian Dynasty (convenor), Welsh Soc. Phila. (steward 1982-84, 2d v.p. 1984-86, v.p. 1986—), Royal Stuart Soc., Cymdeithas Madog, Celtic League Am., Internat. Com. for the Def. of the Breton Lang. (bd. dirs. Am. br., 1984—), Mensa, Phila. Vegetarian Soc. Clubs: St. Andrew's, Atheneum (Phila.), St. Andrew's (Mexico City), Cercle des Princes (Paris), Sloane (London). Home: Garden End Belvoir, Grantham Lincs England Office: 7 Frame Ave PO Box 925 Frazer PA 19355

DE SWAAN, ABRAM, sociology educator; b. Amsterdam, The Netherlands, Jan. 8, 1942; s. Meier and Hennie (Roos) De S.; m. Ellen Louise Ombre, Dec. 27, 1973; 1 child, Meik. MA in Polit. Sci. with honors, U. Amsterdam, 1966, PhD in Social Scis. with honors, 1973. Assoc. prof. sociology U. Amsterdam, 1973-77, prof., 1977—, dean grad. sch. sociology, 1987—. Author: numerous books, including In Care of the State, 1988; contbr. articles to profl. jours. Office: Sociologisch Inst, Oude Hoogstraat 24, 1012 CE Amsterdam The Netherlands

DESWARTE, SYLVIE MARIE, art historian; b. Lyon, France, Sept. 25, 1945; d. Francis Gabriel and Monique (Garnier) D.; m. Alberto Machado Rosa, Mar. 17, 1976; 1 child, Maya. BA, U. Paris Sorbonne, 1969, MA, 1970, PhD, 1974. Pub. asst., exhbn. asst. Ctr. Beaubourg, Paris, 1974-78; Prix de Rome, French Acad., Rome, 1978-80; researcher art history Nat. Ctr. Sci. Research, Paris, 1981—. Author: Les Enluminures de la Leitura Nova, 1977, L'Architecture et les Ingenieurs, 1979, As Imagens das Idades do Mundo, 1987. Mem. Portuguese Nat. Acad. Fine Arts Lisbon. Home and Office: 1 Pl Bellecour, 69002 Lyon France

DE TARLE, ANTOINE, media executive; b. Lyon, Rhone, France, Sept. 23, 1939; s. Antoine and Marie (de Sambucy) de T.; m. Florence Bernard; children: Antoine, Virginie. Diploma, Hautes Etudes Comml., Paris, 1963. Mem. staff Nat. Assembly, Paris, 1965-69, chief counsel on broadcasting, 1969-81; gen. sec. Nat. Inst. Audiovisual, Paris, 1981-82; gen. mgr. TV Francaise, Paris, 1982-85, SEDECO-Quest France, Paris, 1985—; bd. dirs. Phricommunication, Paris. Author: Television and Political Life, 1979, Newspapers and Democracy, 1980; contbr. articles to profl. jours. Mem. Internat. Inst. Communication. Roman Catholic. Clubs: Cincinnati (Washington); Travellers (Paris). Home: 26 rue Singer, 75016 Paris France Office: SEDECO, 114 Champs Elysées, 75008 Paris France

DETREVILLE, ROBERT TREAT PAINE, physician, retired air force officer; b. Beaufort, S.C., Feb. 19, 1925; s. Benjamin Ellis and Ruth Claghorn (Saffold) DeT.; m. Janice Suzanne Mundy, Nov. 26, 1953; children: Suzanne, Anne Hamilton, Janice Mundy, Nancy Beaumont, George Mundy. B.S., The Citadel, 1948; M.D., Med. Coll. S.C., 1948; Sc.D. in Indsl. Medicine, U. Cin., 1956; grad., Sch. Aviation Medicine. Diplomate: occupational medicine Am. Bd. Preventive Medicine. Rotating intern St. Francis X. Infirmary, Charleston, S.C., 1947-48, Roper Hosp., Charleston, 1948-49; practice gen. medicine Charleston County, 1949-51; commd. 1st lt. USAF, 1951; advanced through grades to col. M.C.; chief phys. standards USAF (Surgeon Gen.'s Office, hdqrs. Air Material Command), Wright-Patterson AFB, Ohio, 1952-53; dep. chief profl. services div. USAF, 1956-59; chief Aerospace Med. Br., Norton AFB, Calif., 1959-60; chief health and safety, ballistic systems div. Air Force Systems Command, Inglewood, Calif., 1960-61; comdr. Tactical Airlift Clinic (AFRES) Greater Pitts. Internat. Airport, 1974-75; maj. command asst. occupational med. services Air Force Logistics Center, Wright-Patterson AFB, 1975-77; dir. aerospace medicine USAF Med. Center, Wright-Patterson AFB, 1977-79; spl. asst. to comdr. for occupational and hyperbaric medicine, dir. base med. services USAF Med. Center, 1979-80; cons. occupational medicine to comdr. USAF Occupational Environ. Health Lab., Brooks AFB, Tex., 1980-85; ret. 1985; asst. clin. prof. indsl. health U. Cin., 1958-59; asst. prof. indsl. health, dept. preventive medicine and indsl. health Coll. Medicine, 1961-63; vis. lectr. occupational medicine U. Calif. Med. Center, Los Angeles, 1960-61, USAF Sch. Aerospace Medicine, 1965—, U. Tex. Grad. Sch. Pub. Health, San Antonio, 1981—; co. physician Ethyl Corp., 1961-62, asst. med. dir., 1962-63; mng. dir. Indsl. Hygiene Found. Am., Mellon Inst., Pitts., 1963-68; adv. fellow Mellon Inst. of Carnegie-Mellon U., 1968-72; pres. Indsl. Health Found. Am., Inc., 1968-72; cons. Triangle Health Ctr., 1972-75, Southwest Research Inst., 1985—; adj. prof. occupational medicine U. Pitts. Grad. Sch. Pub. Health, 1963-75; assoc. clin. prof. community medicine dept. Wright State U., 1977-80; cons. staff div. medicine dept. occupational health West Pa. Hosp., 1963-75; sr. research cons. Inst. for Devel. Human Resources, Am. Insts. for Research, 1972-73; mil. cons. USAF surgeon gen., 1977-85; USAF liaison mem. NRC Com. on Toxicology, 1956-60, occupational health med. surveillance com., Dept. Def., 1982-85; cons. staff San Antonio State Chest Hosp., 1985—. Editorial bd.: Jour. Occupational Medicine, 1961-67. Mem. bd. Oakmont Carnegie Library, 1966-75. Fellow Am. Acad. Occupational Medicine (chmn. publs. com. 1962-65, now emeritus), ACP; mem. emeritus Am. Conf. Govtl. Indsl. Hygienists, AMA, Tex. Med. Assn., Bexar County Med. Soc. Episcopalian. Home: 6310 Mallard Point San Antonio TX 78239

DETTMER, ROBERT GERHART, soft drink company executive; b. Parsons, Kans., Sept. 11, 1931; s. Ira Gerhart and Dema (Hinze) D.; m. Patricia Isabel York, Aug. 20, 1955; children: Stephanie, Constance, Robert Brantley. Student, U.S. Naval Acad., 1949-52; B in Bus. and Engring. Adminstrn., MIT, 1955; MBA, Harvard U., 1957. Engr. Lincoln Electric Co., Cleve., 1957-60; assoc. Booz, Allen & Hamilton, Cleve., 1960-64; propr. Robert G. Dettmer, Investment Mgmt., Cleve., 1964-66; v.p. ops. Tasa Corp., Pitts., 1966-68; pres. Scott Aviation div. A-T-O, Lancaster, N.Y., 1968-70, George J. Meyer Mfg. div., Milw., N.Y., 1970-72, N.Am. Van Lines subs. PepsiCo, Inc., Fort Wayne, Ind., 1973-76; v.p. fin. mgmt. and planning parent co. N.Am. Van Lines subs. PepsiCo, Inc., Purchase, N.Y., 1976-79; pres. Pepsi Cola Bottling Group subs., Purchase, N.Y., 1979-86; exec. v.p., chief fin. officer PepsiCo., Purchase, N.Y., 1986—; bd. dirs. Pantesote, Inc., 1978. Chmn. bd. Am. Movers Conf., 1974-76; trustee Miss Porter's Sch., 1978-84, Manhattanville Coll., 1986—. Served with USN, 1949-52. Mem. MIT Alumni Assn., Harvard Bus. Sch. Alumni Assn., U.S. Naval Acad. Alumni Assn., Delta Tau Delta, Tau Beta Pi. Clubs: Harvard Bus. Sch. of Westchester-Fairfield County (chmn. bd. 1977-80), Harvard Bus. Sch. of Greater N.Y. (chmn. bd. 1982-83). Lodge: Masons. Home: 80 Round Hill Rd Greenwich CT 06831 Office: Pepsico Inc Purchase NY 10577

DETWILER, PETER MEAD, investment banker; b. Detroit, June 7, 1928; m. Linda Forte, 1986; children: Mary, Elizabeth, Susan. B.A., Trinity Coll., 1950; M.B.A., Harvard, 1953. With Holly Carburetor Co., Detroit, 1953; research analyst, asst. to dir. Schroder Wagg & Co. Ltd., London, Eng., 1954-55; exec. asst. to mng. dir. and chmn. Ever-Ready Razor Products, London, 1955-57; asst. to pres. A.S.R. Products Co., N.Y.C., 1957-61; with Philip Morris, Inc., N.Y.C., 1961; v.p. E.F. Hutton & Co., Inc., N.Y.C., 1961-64; v.p., voting stockholder E.F. Hutton & Co., Inc., 1964-70, dir., 1968—, sr. v.p., 1970-72; vice chmn. bd. E.F. Hutton & Co., Inc. and E.F. Hutton Group, Inc., 1972—; chmn. bd. E.F. Hutton Group, Inc., 1974—; bd. dirs. Learning Techs. Inc., Jacksonville, Fla., Tesoro Petroleum Corp., San Antonio; pres., dir. Fifth 78th St Corp., N.Y. Trustee Upper Raritan Watershed Assn., Far Hills, N.J., Purnell Sch., Pottersville, N.J.; bd. dirs. Am.-Swiss Assn.; bd. govs., mem. exec. com. , sr. vice chmn. Flight Safety Found., from 1981. Mem. N.Y. Soc. Security Analysts, Fin. Analysts Fedn., Delta Psi. Clubs: Somerset Lake and Game (Far Hills, N.J.); Knickerbocker, Wings (N.Y.C.); Turf (London); Essex Hunt, Essex Foxhounds, Larger Cross Rd. Gun (Peapeack, N.J.); Hyannis Port Yacht (Mass.). Home: High Stoy Farm Box 360 Larger Cross Rd Gladstone NJ 07934 Office: 2440 Larger Cross Rd Gladstone NJ 07934

DEUKMEJIAN, GEORGE, governor of California; b. Albany, N.Y., June 6, 1928; s. C. George and Alice (Gairdan) D.; m. Gloria M. Saatjian, 1957; children: Leslie Ann, George Krikor, Andrea Diane. BA, Siena Coll., 1949; JD, St. John's U., 1952. Bar: N.Y. 1952, Calif. 1956, U.S. Supreme Ct. 1970. Partner firm Riedman, Dalessi, Deukmejian & Woods, Long Beach, Calif., to 1979; mem. Calif. Assembly, 1963-67; mem. Calif. Senate, 1967-79, minority leader; atty. gen. State of Calif., 1979-82, gov., 1983—; former dep. county counsel Los Angeles County. Mem. exec. bd. Long Beach council Boy Scouts Am. Served with U.S. Army, 1953-55. Mem. Long Beach Bar Assn., Am. Bar Assn., State Bar Calif., Long Beach C. of C. (past dir.), Navy League, YMCA. Republican. Episcopalian. Clubs: Lions, Elks. Office: Office of Gov State Capitol Sacramento CA 95814

DEUPREE, MARVIN MATTOX, business consultant, accountant; b. Woodbine, Iowa, Oct. 8, 1917; s. Archie Orin and Pearl (Mattox) D.; m. Katherine Anita Beard, Aug. 18, 1951; children: Marvin Mattox, Meredith Ann. B.A. with high distinction, State U. Iowa, 1941; M.B.A. with distinction, U. Pa., 1948. C.P.A., N.Y., Ill., Mich., La., Iowa, Va., N.C. Instr. acctg. U. Pa., 1947-48; with Arthur Andersen & Co. (C.P.A.s), 1948-75, partner, 1960-75, mem. policy com. on acctg. and auditing, 1962-72; bus. cons. 1975—; pres. Emporium Specialties Co., Inc., 1977—; adj. asso. prof. NYU Grad. Sch. Bus. Adminstrn., 1973-76. Contbr. articles to profl. jours. Served as officer USNR, 1943-46. Mem. Am. Inst. C.P.A.s, N.Y. State, Ill. socs. C.P.A.s, Nat. Assn. Accts., Am. Acctg. Assn., Phi Beta Kappa. Episcopalian. Clubs: Wall Street (N.Y.C.); Executives (Chgo.), Wharton Graduate Business School (Chgo.), University (Chgo.). Home: 5 Academy Rd Ho Ho Kus NJ 07423 Office: 1345 Ave of Americas New York NY 10019

DEUPREE, ROBERT MARSHALL, physician, retired government official; b. Elizabeth, Colo., Dec. 26, 1912; s. Elmer Burton and Mary Ayer (Griffin) DeuP.; student Santa Ana Coll., 1930-33, Los Angeles City Coll., 1937-38; D.O., Coll. Osteo. Physicians and Surgeons, 1942; M.D., Met. U., 1948; postgrad. UCLA, 1952-53; A.B., Calif. State U., Fullerton, 1962; M.A., Calif. State U., Long Beach, 1963; PhD (Nat. Inst. Dental Health fellow) Purdue U., 1963-64; m. Harriett Ann Janetos, Oct. 11, 1963; children—Carol J., R. Scott. Intern, Wilshire Hosp., Los Angeles, 1942-43, resident in neurology, 1943-44; practice medicine, Los Angeles, 1944-57, El Monte, Calif., 1957-58, Newport Beach, Calif., 1958-59; dir. Rush-Merced Clinic, 1957-58; asso. med. dir. Aerojet Gen. Corp., Azusa, Calif., 1967-69, Am. Airlines, Los Angeles, 1969; ships surgeon U. Calif. Scripps Inst. Oceanography, 1969; area med. officer Div. Fed. Employee Health, USPHS, Los Angeles, 1970-85; head dept. internal medicine and radiology Hiss Orthopedic Clinic, Los Angeles, 1953-57; instr. differential diagnosis Coll. Osteo. Physicians and Surgeons, Los Angeles, 1945-49; instr. med. terminology N. Orange Community Coll. Dist., 1966-78; pres., Deustar Internat. Corp.; research fellow VA Hosp., Long Beach State Coll., UCLA Inst. Laryngol. Research, 1962-63. Diplomate in aerospace medicine and occupational medicine. Fellow Royal Soc. Health, N.Y. Acad. Scis., Am. Occupational Med. Assn., Am. Aerospace Med. Assn. (assoc.); mem. Royal Soc. Medicine, Aviation Hall of Fame (charter), Asclepiad. Author, editor: DeuPree International Emergency Medical Translations, 1972; co-author: Travis' Handbook of Speech Pathology and Audiology, 1972; editor Jour. Pro-Re-Nata, 1947-50; author, producer med. motion pictures, U.S. Navy, 1950-51; cons. med. TV, Films, 1952—. Home: 2625 W Huckleberry Rd Santa Ana CA 92706

DE URRUTIA Y LOPEZ, LUCILO ROBERTO, civil engineer; b. Havana, Oct. 31, 1927; came to P.R., 1967, naturalized, 1973; s. Julian Jose and Maria Brigida (Lopez) de U.; B.Sc. in Civil Engring., Havana U., 1952; m. Lucille Craib Espinosa, Dec. 30, 1971. Engr., M.A. Glez. del Valle Orgn., Cuba, 1952-59; prin. Constructora Diana, Cuba, 1959-60; engr. Havana Municipality, 1960; investing engr. Dept. Industries, Cuba, 1960-66; project mgr. Promotora Tecnica, Spain, 1966-67; chief engr. Highland Realty, P.R., 1967-76; prin. Lucilo R. de Urrutia & Assos., Santurce, P.R., 1976—; cons. E.R. Enterprises, Developers, 1980-82. Registered profl. engr., P.R., N.Y., N.J., Tenn., Fla. Fellow ASCE; mem. Nat. Soc. Profl. Engrs., Am. Water Works Assn., P.R. Inst. Civil Engrs., P.R. Instn. Engrs. and Land Surveyors, Cuban Inst. Civil Engrs. (sec. 1961), Am. Arbitration Assn., Nat. Geog. Roman Catholic. Home: 11E Laguna Gardens III Isla Verde PR 00913-6409

DEUTSCH, BARRY JOSEPH, management development company executive; b. Gary, Ind., Aug. 10, 1941; s. Jack Elias and Helen Louise (La Rue) D.; B.S., U. So. Calif., 1969, M.B.A. magna cum laude, 1970; m. Gina Krispinsky, Feb. 20, 1972. Lectr. mgmt. U. So. Calif., Los Angeles, 1967-70; pres., founder The Deutsch Group, Inc., mgmt. cons. co. tng. upper and middle mgmt., Los Angeles, 1970—, chmn. bd., 1975—; founder, chief exec. officer, chmn. bd. Investment Planning Network, Inc., 1988—; dir. Red Carpet Corp. Am., 1975-77, United Fin. Planners, 1984-86. Chmn. bd. govs. Am. Hist. Center, 1980—. Served with M.I., U.S. Army, 1964-66. Mem. Am. Mgmt. Assn., Am. Soc. Bus. and Mgmt. Cons.'s, Am. Soc. Tng. and Devel., Internat. Mgmt. by Objectives Inst. Author: Leadership Techniques, 1969; Recruiting Techniques, 1970; The Art of Selling, 1973; Professional Real Estate Management, 1975; Strategic Planning, 1976; Employer/Employee: Making the Transition, 1978; Managing by Objectives, 1980; Conducting Effective Performance Appraisal, 1982; Advanced Supervisory Development, 1984. Home: 4509 Candleberry Ave Seal Beach CA 90740

DEUTSCH, MARTIN BERNARD JOSEPH, editor, publisher; b. Karlsruhe, Fed. Republic of Germany, Apr. 7, 1931; came to U.S., 1939, naturalized, 1948; s. Benedikt and Margarethe (Zivi) D.; m. son, Kenneth. Student in history and journalism, CCNY, 1953; student in Eng. lit., Columbia U., summer 1955. CCNY coll. corr. N.Y. Times, 1953-55; mng. editor The Beachcomber, Long Beach I., N.J., summers 1952, 53; reporter Southwest American, Ft. Smith, Ark., 1954-55; mng. editor Travel Courier and Travel Weekly, 1955-67; sr. v.p., editor, pub. OAG Travel Mags. div. Ofcl. Airline Guides, Inc., Dun & Bradstreet Co., N.Y.C., 1967—; guest instr. U. Mass., 1975; speaker travel and transp. industry. Monthly columnist, Up Front, Frequent Flyer mag., 1980—. Mem. Upper Manhattan Community Planning Bd., 1965; mem. travel adv. bd. U.S. Dept. Commerce, U.S. Travel Service, 1977-81. Served with U.S. Army, 1953-55. Recipient various awards for travel journalism. Mem. Travel Industry Assn. Am. Club: Sky (N.Y.). Home: 106 Pinehurst Ave New York NY 10033 Office: 888 Seventh Ave New York NY 10106

DEUTSCH, MICHEL, radiologist; b. Strasbourg, France, Feb. 5, 1928; s. Abraham and Marguerite (Levy) D.; m. Elise Elmaleh, Sept. 21, 1959; children: Jean Philippe, Bruno. MD, U. Strasbourg, 1954, diploma in medicine of work, 1955, diploma in gastroenterology, 1959; diploma in radiology, U. Paris, 1963. Practice medicine specializing in radiology Paris. Served as med. comdr. officer French Armed Forces. Recipient Chevalier du Merite, 1984. Fellow French Soc. Radiology. Home: Ave des Voir Paupliers 13c, 75015 Paris France Office: Rue Beranger 21, 75003 Paris France

DEUTSCH, NINA, concert pianist, actress; b. San Antonio, Mar. 15; d. Irvin and Freda Deutsch; B.S., Juilliard Sch. Music; M.M.A., Yale U., 1973. Concert pianist, 1958—; recording artist Vox Prodns.; only woman to record complete solo piano music of Charles Ives, 1976; recs. include: piano arrangement of Variations on Am. (Ives); freelance writer on music for N.Y. Times, UPI and mags., 1974—; music cons. Joe Franklin Show, WOR-TV, 1975—; entertainer Home Lines Cruises, N.Y.C., 1987—; exec. v.p. Internat. Symphony. Author: (play) Portrait of Clara Wieck Schumann. Bd. dirs. Metzner Found. for Overseas Relief; Ft. Lee coordinator Channel 13, 1974. Grantee Nat. Endowment for Arts, 1975, Phillips Petroleum Found., 1982; Tanglewood fellow, 1966; recipient award for Am. music Nat. Fedn. Music Clubs, 1975; Oberlin Coll. scholar. Mem. Music Critics Assn., Publicity Club

N.Y., Dramatist Guild, Music Critics Assn. Avocations: swimming, baking. Home: 410 Hazlitt Ave Leonia NJ 07605

DEVADASON, FRANCIS JAWAHAR, librarian; b. Tirunelvely, Tamil Nadu, India, Nov. 5, 1947; s. Y. Gnanathangam and Ruthmoni Devadason; m. Irene Renuka, Dec. 27, 1978; children: Frederick Ajit, Catherine Anisha, Caroline Anitha. BS in Physics, U. Madras, India, 1966; B of Library Sci., U. Madras, 1968; AD, DRTC, ISI, Bangalore, India, 1969-70; PhD, Karnatak U., Dwarwad, India, 1984. Cert. librarian info. scientist. Librarian Aditanar Coll., Tiruchendur, India, 1968-69, 70-74, IIT Computer Ctr., Madras, 1974-76; asst. librarian Indian Inst. Mgmt., Bangalore, 1976-77; faculty lectr. Documentation Research and Tng. Ctr., Bangalore, 1977-87; asst. dir. Cen. Leather Research Inst., Madras, 1987—. Mem. edit. rev. bd. Pergamon Press, N.Y.C., 1981—; edit. asst. IFCA Directory, 1986; contbr. articles to profl. jours. Mem. Indo-U.S. sub-commn. Sci. and Tech. Mem. Inst. Info. Tech. (v.p. 1987), Madras Library Assn., Working Group on Info. Sics., Soc. Conceptual and Content Analysis by Computer, Dept. German, Russian and East Asian Langs. Bowling Green State U. Home: Hoggville 11 Agaram Rd, Tanbaram East 600059, India

DEVAPRIAM, EMMA, curator; b. Kodaikanal, India, Aug. 5, 1933; d. Gideon and Mary (Zachariah) D.; came to Australia, 1975. B.A., Stella Maris Coll., Madras, India, 1955, M.A., 1964; Ph.D., Case-Western Res. U., 1972. Tutor in fine arts Stella Maris Coll., 1955-62, lectr., 1962-67; asst. curator Cleve. Mus. Art, 1972; student adv. U.S. Ednl. Found. in India, Madras, 1974-75; asst. curator Nat. Gallery of Victoria, Melbourne, Australia, 1975-76, sr. curator European painting, 1976—; mem. Syllabus Com. High Schs., Madras, 1957-59; chmn. Syllabus Com. Art History in Madras U., 1963-67. Fulbright scholar, 1967-68. Mem. Art History Assn. U.S.A., 1967-72, Australian Art Galleries Assn. Office: National Gallery of Victoria, 180 S Kilda Rd, Melbourne Victoria 3004, Australia

DE VARIS, PANAYOTIS ERIC, architect; b. Lefkas Island, Greece, Dec. 29, 1932; came to U.S., 1960; s. Christos and Angelika (Contorrigopoulo) De V.; m. Eleonore Guthmann, Dec. 29, 1962 (div. July 1964); 1 child, Suzanne; m. June Julia Johnson, Aug. 19, 1968 (div. Apr. 1973); children—Angelika, Christos. M.Arch., Ecole des Beaux Arts, Paris, 1960; grad. cert. in bus. adminstrn., L.I. U., 1981. Registered architect; cert. Nat. Council Archtl. Registration Bds. Architect, Caleb Hornbostel, Architect, N.Y.C., 1960-62, Brown, Lawford & Forbes, Architects, N.Y.C., 1962-64, Tams Engrs. and Architects, N.Y.C., 1964-65; sr. designer Emery Roth & Sons, Architects, N.Y.C., 1965-72; sr. architect AT&T, N.Y.C., 1972—; prin., architect, planner, designer P. Eric De Varis, Architect, N.Y.C., 1960-84; author, lectr. in field of cybernetics; juror furniture design competition Corp. Design mag., 1984, 85, 86, 87, Annual Design Awards N.Y. State Assn. Architects. Contbr. articles to trade mags. Mem. exec. com. Architects for Social Responsibility, 1982-86. Recipient tech. excellence award Western Electric Co., Inc., 1983. Mem. AIA (chmn. corp. architects, mem. steering com. 1963—), Nat. Inst. for Archtl. Edn. Club: Hellenic U. (N.Y.C.). Office: AT&T 222 Mt Airy Rd Basking Ridge NJ 07920

DE VERDIER, CARL-HENRIC ANDERS OLOF, physician, educator; b. Stockholm, Sweden, June 30, 1924; s. Anders and Hedvig (Steuch) de V.; Med. kand., U. Uppsala, 1946, Med. lic., 1957, Med. Dr., 1957; m. Karin Margareta Ruback, Sept. 6, 1952; children—Kerstin, Britt-Marie, Ulla, Katarina. USPHS research fellow McArdle Lab. for Cancer Research, Madison, Wis., 1958-59; asst. prof. clin. chemistry Med. Faculty Uppsala, 1961; research fellow Swedish Med. Research Council, 1961-64; asst. head physician, dept. clin. chemistry Univ. Hosp., Uppsala, 1965-68, head physician, 1968—, prof., dir. dept., 1976—. Mem. bd. Nordic Clin. Chemistry project Nordic Council, 1977, European Com. Clin. Lab. Standard. Hon. mem. Swedish Soc. Clin. Chemistry, Finnish Soc. Clin. Chemistry. Contbr. articles to profl. jours; research in biochemistry, clin. chemistry and hematology. Home: Talgoxvagen 6 A, S-752 52 Uppsala Sweden Office: University Hospital, Uppsala S-751 85, Sweden

DEVESI, BADDELEY, governor-general Solomon Islands; b. Oct. 16, 1941; s. Mostyn Tagabasoe Norua and Laisa Oru; attended St. Stephen's Sch., Auckland, N.Z., Ardmore Tchrs. Coll., Auckland; m. June Marie Barley; 7 children. MLC and mem. Exec. Council, 1967-69; head master St. Nicholas Sch., Honiara, Solomon Islands, 1968; edn. officer and lectr., 1970-72; dist. officer, 1973; dist. commr. and clk. to Malaita Council, 1974, permanent sec., 1976; sec. ministry of work and pub. utilities, ministry of transport and communication, 1977; dep. chmn. Solomon Islands Broadcasting Corp., 1976; gov.-gen. Solomon Islands, Honiara, 1978—; chancellor U. of South Pacific, from 1980. Commr., Boy Scouts Assn., 1968; capt. Solomon Islands team, 2d South Pacific Games, 1969. Office: Govt House, Honiara Solomon Islands *

DEVI, D. RADHA, demographic-economics researcher; b. Trivandrum, Kerala, India, July 27, 1940; s. Sankara Kunjukrishna and Dakshayani Amma Pillai; m. Mundayat Ravindran. MA in Econs., U. Kerala, India, 1961, MSc in Demography, 1966; MA in Sociology, U. N.C., 1973; PhD in Econs., U. Mysore, India, 1980. Sr. research asst. U. Kerala, 1967-70; sr. social scientist Gandhigram Inst. Rural Health and Family Welfare Trust, Madurai, Tamil Nadu, India, 1977-80; reader Internat. Inst. for Population Scis., Bombay, 1980—. Contbr. articles to profl. jours. Mem. Indian Assn. for Study of Population (life). Hindu. Office: Internat Inst for Population Scis, Govandi Station Rd, Deonar, Bombay 400088, India

DE VICQ DE CUMPTICH, BARON EMMANUEL, professional association director; b. Soignies, Hainaut, Belgium, Dec. 27, 1933; s. Baron Charles and Marie-José (van Cutsem) de Vicq de C.; m. Chantal de Limon Triest, Sept. 2, 1961; children: Arnaud, Caroline. Student, U. Va., 1951-52; LLM, Cath. U. de Louvain, Belgium, 1957, Lic. in Polit. and Social Sci., 1960; MBA, Insead, Fontainebleau, France, 1963. Program dir. Mgmt. Ctr./Europe, Brussels, 1961-62; brand mgr. Procter & Gamble Benelux S.A., Brussels, 1963-68, Procter & Gamble GmbH, Frankfurt, Fed. Republic Germany, 1969-70; mng. dir. Ted Bates S.A., Brussels, 1970-82; gen. mgr. Ets. Debaise-Hannecart, Binche, Belgium, 1983-84; cons. Maes & Lunau (Ward Howell subs.), Brussels, 1984-85; mng. dir. Union Belge Des Annonceurs (U.B.A.), Brussels, 1986—; bd. dirs. Com. Belge for Distbn., Brussels. Mem. Insead Alumni Assn. Belgium (v.p. 1984—). Club: Cercle Gaulois (Brussels). Home: Diepestraat 205, 1980 Tervuren Belgium Office: Union Belge Des Annonceurs, 54 rue des Colonies, 1000 Brussels Belgium

DE VILLEMEJANE, BERNARD, mining and metallurgy executive; b. Marseilles, France, Mar. 10, 1930; s. Pierre and Marie-Therese (Getten) de V.; m. Françoise Boucheronde, Oct. 1, 1965; children—Pierre, Francois-David. Grad. Ecole Poly., 1949, Ecole des Mines, Paris, 1952. With dept. mining and geology French W. Africa, 1955-60; with Ministry of Industry, Paris, 1960-61; engring. cons. Banque Rothschild, Paris, 1961-62; with Penarroya, 1963, chmn. and chief exec. officer Penarroya, 1971-86, bd. dirs. 1986; pres. Eramet-SLN, 1971-73, chmn. bd., chief exec. officer, 1974-83, bd. dirs. 1983; pres. Imetal, 1974—, bd. chmn., chief exec. officer, 1979—; bd. dirs. Copperweld Corp. (US), Minemet SA (Switzerland), Penarroya Espana (Spanish). Decorated knight Legion of Honor, officer Order of Merit, Grand Cross Order del Merito Civil (Spain), Comdr. Order of L'etoile Equatoriale (Gabon). Home: 102 rue d'Assas, 75006 Paris France Office: IMETAL Tour Maine Montparnasse, 33 Ave du Maine Cedex 15, 75755 Paris France

DEVINE, C. ROBERT, publishing company executive; b. Clarksburg, W.Va., June 13, 1917; s. James J. and Frances M. (Ryan) D.; m. Louise C. Williams, Mar. 27, 1943 (div.); children: Mallory C., Rodney W., Ian C.; m. Gisele Edenbourgh Lichine, Dec. 23, 1966. Grad., Princeton U., 1938; L.H.D., Fairleigh Dickinson U., 1976. Promotion, research dir. U.S. News Pub. Co., 1946-48, asst. advt. dir., 1948-55; exec. bus. dept. Reader's Digest, N.Y.C., 1955-58; advt. dir. internat. edits. Reader's Digest, 1958-60, pres. Latin Am. div., 1960, asst. gen. mgr., 1960-66, dep. gen. mgr. internat. edits., 1966; v.p. dir. corp. and public affairs Reader's Digest Assn., Inc., 1970-82. Bd. dirs. Met. Opera Assn., 1973-83; bd. dirs. Am. Hosp. Istanbul; trustee Am. U. Cairo; bd. dirs. Gen. Douglas MacArthur Found., Vail-Deane Sch. Served from pvt. to maj. AUS, World War II. Decorated Bronze Star medal. Mem. Council on Fgn. Relations, Internat. Advt. Assn. (chmn., chief exec. officer 1976-80, pres. 1962-64), Assn. Ex-Mems. Squadron A, XIIIth Corps Assn., Mil. Order Fgn. Wars, Assn. U.S. Army (v.p. N.Y. chpt.), Fgn. Policy Assn., Internat. Fedn. Periodical Press (v.p. 1978-79, pres. 1979-81, chmn. 1981-83), English-Speaking Union, World Press Inst. (chmn. 1982-84), Nat. Inst. Social Scis., Nat. Found. for Facial Reconstruction (bd. dirs.), Pub. Relations Soc. Am. Clubs: Union (N.Y.C.), Squadron A (N.Y.C.), Dutch Treat (N.Y.C.), River (N.Y.C.); Pilgrims U.S; Travellers (Paris). Home: 101 E 69th St New York NY 10021

DEVINE, CHARLES JOSEPH, JR., urologist, educator; b. Norfolk, Va., Feb. 23, 1923; s. Charles Joseph and Julia Vera (Campbell) D.; m. Rae Lou Ellis, Sept. 30, 1950; children—Charles Joseph III, Paul E., Jane C., David C., Rachel A. B.A., Washington and Lee U., 1943; M.D., George Washington U., 1947. Diplomate: Am. Bd. Urology, Nat. Bd. Med. Examiners. Intern Brady Inst., Johns Hopkins Hosp., 1947-48; fellow in urology Cleve. Clinic, 1948-50; resident in urology U.S. Naval Hosp., Phila., 1951; with Devine Fiveash Urology, Ltd., Norfolk, Va., 1952—; pres. Devine Fiveash Urology, Ltd., 1975-84; chief urology Med. Center Hosps., 1979-80; pres. med. staff Norfolk Gen. Hosp., 1970; chmn. dept. surgery DePaul Hosp., 1965-66; chief of urology Children's Hosp. of King's Daus., 1977-85; cons. staff Gen. Hosp. of Virginia Beach, Va.; cons. in urology Lake Taylor City, U.S. Naval hosps., VA Center, Hampton, Va.; clin. coordinator for urology Eastern Va. Med. Sch., 1973-75, prof., chmn. dept. urology, 1975—; clin. dir. pediatric urology program Bur. Crippled Children of Va., Norfolk; mem. Project Hope, Alexandria, Egypt, 1977; Royal Australasian Coll. Surgeons Found. lectr., 1982, condr. symposia; producer med. motion pictures, TV surg. presentations; vis. prof. univs.; presenter profl. meetings. Author: Urology in Practice, 1978; mem. editorial bd.: Jour. Urology, 1978—, Weekly Updates in Urology, 1978—; contbr. numerous articles to profl. jours., chpts. in books. Served to lt. M.C. USNR, 1950-52. Fellow A.C.S. (pres. Va. chpt. 1967), Am. Acad. Pediatrics, Am. Soc. Plastic and Reconstructive Surgeons (asso.); mem. AMA, Med. Soc. Va., Norfolk Acad. Medicine, Am. Urol. Assn. (awards), Va. Urol. Soc. (pres. 1968), Tidewater Urol. Assn., Societe Internationale d'Urologie, Am. Assn. Genitourinary Surgeons, Soc. Pediatric Urology, Soc. Univ. Urologists, Genitourinary Reconstructive Surgeons (founding pres. 1987-88), So. Med. Assn., Seaboard Med. Soc., AAAS, N.Y. Acad. Scis., Alpha Tau Omega, Nu Sigma Nu. Roman Catholic. Clubs: Norfolk Yacht and Country (Norfolk), Harbor (Norfolk); U.S. Yacht Racing Union, Cruising of Va. Home: 2034 Hunters Trail Norfolk VA 23518 Office: 400 W Brambleton Ave Suite 100 Norfolk VA 23510

DEVINE, MICHAEL BUXTON, lawyer; b. Des Moines, Oct. 25, 1953; s. Cleatie Hiram, Jr., and Katherine Ann (Buxton) D. Student St. Peter's Coll., Oxford U., Eng., 1975; B.A. cum laude, St. Olaf Coll., 1976; M.P.A., Drake U., 1980, J.D., 1980; diploma in Advanced Internat. Legal Studies, U. Pacific extension Salzburg, Austria, 1986; LLM in Internat. Bus. Legal Studies, U. Exeter, Eng., 1988. Bar: Iowa 1980, U.S. Dist. Ct. (no. and so. dists.) Iowa 1980, U.S. Ct. Appeals (8th cir.) 1980, Nebr. 1985, Supreme Ct. 1985, Minn. 1986, D.C. 1986., N.Y. 1987, Wis. 1987, Colo. 1988; Assoc. Bump & Haesemeyer, P.C., Des Moines, 1980-85; sole practice, Des Moines, 1985—; legal intern Herbert Oppenheimer, Nathan & Vandyk, London, England, 1986. Scholar St. Olaf Coll., 1972-76; nat. alt. U.S. Presdl. Mgmt. Intern Program, 1980. Mem. ABA, Fed. Bar Assn. (chmn. state of Iowa SBA export assistance program 1983-85, treas. Iowa chpt. 1984-85, exec. com. 1985—), Iowa Bar Assn., Nebr. Bar Assn., Minn. Bar Assn., D.C. Bar Assn., Internat. Bar Assn., Polk County Bar Assn., Phi Alpha Theta, Pi Alpha Alpha, Phi Alpha Delta. Presbyterian. Home and Office: 2611 40th St Des Moines IA 50310

DEVINE, RICHARD ARTHUR, architect, construction company executive; b. Green Bay, Wis., Sept. 7, 1937; s. Arthur Joseph and Florence Irene (Olson) D.; divorced; children—Craig Richard, Charlotte Adrienne, Derek Joseph. B.A., Lawrence Coll., 1959; B.Arch., U. Ill., 1963, M.S., 1964. Registered architect, Ill., Calif.; registered profl. engr., Calif. Structural engr. A. C. Martin & Assocs., Los Angeles, 1964-67, constrn. adminstr., 1968-76; project mgr. Conrad Engrs., Van Nuys, Calif., 1967-68; gen. mgr. Contempo Vans, Warren, Ohio, 1976-79; constrn. mgr. L. L. Farber, Inc., Pompano Beach, Fla., 1979-80; owner Devine Constrn. Co., Geneva, Ill., 1980-85; architect, constrn. mgr. Perman Constrn./Goodman Realty Group, Chgo., 1985-88; project mgr., Capitol Constrn. Group Inc., Wheeling, Ill., 1988—. Dist. chmn. Boy Scouts Am., St. Charles, Ill., 1984-86, vice chmn., 1983, dist. commr., 1982, dist. tng. chmn., 1986-88; various dist. and unit positions, St. Charles, Canfield, Ohio and Los Angeles, 1960-82, v.p. Geneva Music Boosters, 1984-85, pres., 1985-86. Inland Steel-Ryerson Found. fellow, 1963-64; recipient award of Merit, Ruberoid Matico Urban Design Competition, 1963; Fidelity award for Outstanding Community Service, Fidelity Fed. Savs. and Loan Assn., 1973; Dist. Award of Merit, Mid-Valley Dist., Gt. Western council Boy Scouts Am., 1974, Wood badge, 1974, Order of Arrow-Ordeal, 1970, Order of Arrow-Brotherhood, 1972, Order of the Arrow-Vigil, 1987, Scouters Tng. award, 1971, Scouters Key, 1976, Silver Beaver award, Two Rivers council, 1986; Top Ten award, Albert C. Martin and Assocs., 1974, 75. Mem. Structural Engrs. Assn. Soc. Calif., Gargoyle (nat. scholastic hon. soc.), Scarab (rat. archtl. profl. hon. soc.), Phi Kappa Tau. Republican. Lutheran. Home: 13/D Horne St Saint Charles IL 60174 Office: 123 N Wacker Dr Chicago IL 60606

DEVINE, STANLEY BEVAN, oil company executive, geologist; b. Warwick, Australia, Aug. 23, 1938; s. Stanley Arthur and Isabel (Avery) D.; m. Margaret Elizabeth Bushell, June 11, 1966; children—Josephine, Brendan, Matthew, Timothy. Cert. in teaching Queensland Tchrs. Coll. (Australia), 1957; B.Sc., U. Queensland, 1963; Ph.D., La. State Univ., 1971. Gen. mgr., chief exec. Sagasco Resources Ltd., Adelaide, 1978—; councillor, mem. exec. com. Australian Mineral Found., Adelaide, 1981—. mem. industry adv. bd. Nat. Ctr. for Petroleum Geology and Geophysics, 1985—;mng. editor Petroleum Exploration Soc. Australia Jour., 1982—; editorial advisor Oil and Gas Australia, 1982—; contbr. articles to profl. jours. Fellow Australian Inst. Dirs.; mem. Petroleum Exploration Soc. Australia (coordinator disting. lectures 1978-84, pres. 1981-83), Am. Assn. Petroleum Geologists (cert. petroleum geologist). Home: 4A Borthwick Ct, Beaumont South Australia 5066, Australia Office: Sagasco Resources Ltd, 60 Hindmarsh Sq, GPO Box 2576, Adelaide SA 5000, Australia

DEVINEY, MARVIN LEE, JR., chemical company research scientist, administrator; b. Kingsville, Tex., Dec. 5, 1929; s. Marvin Lee and Esther Lee (Gambrell) D.; B.S. in Chemistry and Math., S.W. Tex. State U., San Marcos, 1949; M.A. in Phys. Chemistry, U. Tex. at Austin, 1952, Ph.D. in Phys. Chemistry, 1956; cert. profl. chemist; m. Marie Carole Massey, June 7, 1975; children—Marvin Lee III, John H., Ann-Marie K. Devel. chemist Celanese Chem. Co., Bishop, Tex., 1956-58; research chemist Shell Chem. Co., Deer Park, Tex., 1958-66; sr. scientist, head group phys. and radiochemistry Ashland Chem. Co., Houston, 1966-68, mgr. sect. phys. and analytical chemistry, 1968-71, mgr. sect. phys. chemistry div. research and devel., Columbus, Ohio, 1971-78, research assoc., supr. applied surface chemistry, Ashland Ventures Research and Devel., 1978-84, supr. electron microscopy, advanced aerospace composites, govt. contracts, 1984—; adj. prof. U. Tex., San Antonio, 1973-75. Mem. sci. adv. bd. Am. Petroleum Inst. Research Project 60, 1968-74. Mem. ednl. adv. com. Columbus Tech. Inst., 1974-84, Central Ohio Tech. Coll., 1975-82. Served to lt. col., USAR. Humble Oil Research fellow, 1954. Fellow Am. Inst. Chemists (pres. Ohio Inst. 1978-82, nat. com. mem. 1985—); mem. Ohio, Tex. acads. scis., Am. Def. Preparedness Assn., Electron Microscopy Soc. Am., Materials Research Soc., SAMPE Composite Soc., N.Am. Catalysis Soc., Am. Soc. Composites, Am. Chem. Soc. (chmn. chpt. exec. bd. 1969, bus. mgr. nat. div. Petroleum Chemistry, 1986—, Best Paper award rubber div. 1967, 70, Hon. Mention awards 1968, 69, 73; symposia co-chmn., co-editor books on catalysis-surface chemistry 1985, carbon-graphite chemistry 1975), Engr.'s Council Houston (sr. councilor 1970-71), Sigma Xi, Phi Lambda Upsilon, Alpha Chi, Sigma Pi Sigma. Co-author govt. research contract reports; contbr. numerous articles to profl. jours.; patentee in field. Home: 6810 Hayhurst Worthington OH 43085 Office: Box 2219 Columbus OH 43216

DEVISÉ, PIERRE ROMAIN, city planner, educator; b. Brussels, Belgium, July 27, 1924; came to U.S., 1935, naturalized, 1958; s. Victor Pierre and Madeleine (Cupers) DeV.; m. Margaret Ahern, Nov. 17, 1978; children: Peter Charles, Daniel Romain. B.A., U. Chgo., 1945, M.A., 1958; Ph.D., U. Ill., 1985. Chancellor Belgian Consul, Chgo., 1945-47; comml. attache Belgian Consul, 1947-56, Belgian Consulate Gen., Chgo.; planning dir. Hyde Park-Kenwood Conf., 1956-57; research planner Northeastern Ill. Planning Commn., 1958-60; sr. planner Chgo. City Planning Dept., 1961-63; asst. dir. Hosp. Planning Council for Met. Chgo., 1964-70, Ill. Regional Med. Program, 1971-73; prof. urban scis. U. Ill., 1973-81; prof. pub. adminstrn. Roosevelt U., Chgo., 1982—; Lectr. De Paul U., 1962—; vis. lectr. U. Mich., 1966, U. Hawaii, 1968, U. Ill., 1969, 70, U. Iowa, 1971, U. Chgo., 1972; prin. investigator Chgo. Regional Hosp. Study, 1966—; exec. dir. Chgo. Commn. to Study Conv. Week Disorders, 1968-70; cons. Chgo. Commn. on Human Relations, 1966—, Chgo. Model Cities Program, 1968—, Cook County Council Govts., 1968—, Comprehensive Health Planning, Inc., 1971—; Census Bur., 1973—, U.S. Senate Health Subcom., 1974, HEW, 1975—, Ho. Ways and Means Com., 1975—, Senate Banking Com., 1976—. Author: monographs including Suburban Factbook, 1960, Social Geography of Metropolitan Chicago, 1960, Chicago's People, Jobs and Homes, 1963, Chicago's Widening Color Gap, 1967, Chicago's Apartheid Hospital System, 1968, Chicago, 1971, Ready for Another Fire, 1971, Misused and Misplaced Hospitals and Doctors, 1973, Chicago's Future, 1976, Chicago: Transformations of an Urban System, 1976, Chicago in the Year 2000, 1978; Descent From the Summit, 1985. Mem. Am. Statist. Assn., Chgo. Assn. Commerce and Industry, Am. Soc. Pub. Adminstrn., Am. Pub. Health Assn., Assn. Am. Geographers, Nat. Council Geog. Edn., Planned Parenthood Assn. Chgo., Old Town Boys Club. Club: City (Chgo.). Home: 1712 W Henderson Chicago IL 60657 Office: Roosevelt U 430 S Michigan Ave Chicago IL 60605

DE VIVO, GIANCARLO, economics educator; b. Naples, Italy, Oct. 18, 1946; s. Filippo and Sara (Albi-Marini) De V.; m. Roberta Barbati, Oct. 18, 1980; children: Giulia Sara, Guido Piero. Degree in Law, U. Naples, 1968, postgrad., 1970. Lectr. econs. U. Florence, Italy, 1973-74; lectr. econs. U. Modena, Italy, 1974-82, assoc. prof., 1982-86; assoc. prof. U. Naples, 1986—; acad. vis. U. Cambridge, Eng., 1979-80, affiliated lectr., 1987-88. Author: Ricardo and His Critics, 1984; joint editor Contbns. to Polit. Economy, U.K., 1981—; contbr. articles to profl. jours. Research fellow U. Florence, 1971-73. Fellow Soc. Italiana Degli Economisti. Home: Via Egiziaca A Pizzofalcone, 43, Naples 80132, Italy Office: U Naples Dept Econs Social Scis, Via Santa Lucia 20, Naples 80132, Italy

DEVLIN, ROBERT MANNING, insurance company executive; b. Bklyn., Feb. 28, 1941; s. John Manning and Norma (Hall) D.; m. KatharineBareis, Sept. 13, 1961; children: Michael Hall, Matthew Bareis. BA in Econs., Tulane U., 1964. C.L.U. Various positions Mut. Life Ins. Co. N.Y., 1964-77; v.p., asst. to pres. Calif. Western States Life Ins. Co., Sacramento, 1977-80, sr. v.p., 1980; exec. v.p., dir. Life and Casualty Ins. Co. Tenn., Nashville, 1980-83; exec. v.p. Am. Gen. Life & Accident Ins. Co., 1983-84, exec. v.p. mktg., 1984-86; exec. v.p. Am. Gen. Corp., Houston, 1986; pres., chief exec. officer, dir. Am. Gen. Life Ins. Co. Tex., Am. Gen. Life Ins. Co. Del., Houston and Del., 1986—; Chmn bd. Am. Gen. Securities; bd. dirs. Calif.-Western State Life Ins. Co., Nat. Life and Accident Ins. Co. Mem. Am. Soc. C.L.U.s, Nat. Assn. Life Underwriters. Roman Catholic. Clubs: Belle Meade Country (Nashville); Univ.; Heritage. Home: 2129 Brentwood Dr Houston TX 77019 Office: Am Gen Life Ins Co 2727 Allen Pkwy Houston TX 77019

DEVOL, GEORGE CHARLES, JR., manufacturing executive; b. Louisville, Feb. 20, 1912; s. George C. and Elsa (Vance) D.; m. Evelyn R. Jahelka, Dec. 31, 1938; children—Christine, George C. III, Robert Vance, Suzanne. Pres., United Cinephone Corp., N.Y., 1933-39; project engr. Sperry Gyroscope Co., Garden City, N.Y., 1939-41; gen. mgr. Gen. Electronic Industries, Greenwich, Conn., 1941-45; pres. Devol Research Co., Ft. Lauderdale, Fla., 1947—, Automatic Mfg. Systems, Inc., Ft. Lauderdale, 1984—. Clubs: Ocean Reef, Key Largo (Fla.); Lago Mar (Ft. Lauderdale, Fla.). Patentee 40 electronic, mech. devices including 1st comml. robot called Unimation. Address: 990 Ridgefield Rd Wilton CT 06897 also: 1543 SE 13th St Fort Lauderdale FL 33316

DE VOOGD, FRANK, sales and marketing executive; b. Heemstede, The Netherlands, Apr. 16, 1944; s. Johannes Marie Jacoba Wilhemina (Rothengatter) de V.; m. Philippine van de Linde, Apr. 25, 1967; children: Saskia, Charlotte, Sebastiaan. Grad., Christelijk Lyceum, Haarlem, Holland. Student trainee Bloksma N.V., Diemen, The Netherlands, 1967-68, United Lubricants Ltd., London, 1967, Eximport SPRL, Brussels, 1968-69; comml. dir. Somla SRPL, Brussels, 1969-74, sales mgr. Benelux Don Internat. S.A., Manage, Belgium, 1974-80, mktg. and distbn. sales dir., 1981-85, mktg. and sales dir., 1985—; bd. dirs. Don France S.A., Argenteuil, France, Don Deutschalnd GmbH, Wiesbaden, Fed. Republic Germany, Don Italia S.R.L., Torino, Italy, Don Internat. S.A. Manage Belgium, 1985. Mem. Autotechnica (organizing com. internat. trade shows 1987—), Fedn. Materiel Automation (v.p. mfrs. com. 1986—). Clubs: Brabantse Golf (Melsbroek); Schepdaal Tennis. Office: Don Internat SA, Chaussee de Nivelles 95/97, 6538 Manage Belgium

DEVORE, KIMBERLY K., sales executive; b. Louisville., June 19, 1947; d. Wendell O. and Shirley F. DeV.; student, Xavier U., 1972-76; AA, Coll. Mt. St. Joseph, 1979. Patient registration supr. St. Francis Hosp., Cin., 1974-76; cons., bus. mgr. Family Health Care Found., Cin., 1976-77; exec. dir. Hospice of Cin., Inc., 1977-80; pres. Micro Med, 1979-86; v.p. Sycamore Profl. Assn., 1979-86; ptnr. Enchanted House, 1979-86, sec., 1979-80, treas. 1980-83; dist. sales rep. Control-O-Fax, 1986, dist. sales mgr., br. sales mgr., 1987, nat. dealer devel. rep., 1987—; bd. dirs. Nat. Hospice Orgn., 1979-82, chmn. long-term planning com., fin. com., ann. meeting com., 1979-82, sec., 1980-81. treas., 1981-82; bd. dirs. Hospice of Miami Valley, Inc., 1982-86, also chmn. personnel com., by-laws com. Mem. Greater Cin. Soc. Fund Raisers, Better Housing League; Mem. service and rehab. com. Hamilton County Unit, Am. Cancer Soc., 1977-78. Mem. Ohio Hospice Assn. (co-founder, state chmn., pres., 1978-83), Nat. League for Nursing, Ohio Hosp. Assn., Nat.Fedn. Bus. and Profl. Women's, Ohio Fedn. Bus. and Profl. Women's, Cin. Bus. and Profl. Women's (pres. 1973-75).

DE VOS, JOHNNIE, palaeontologist; b. Hilversum, The Netherlands, Dec. 15, 1947; s. Franciscus Bernardus and Gerarda (De Heus) D.; m. Maria Sebilla van der Schans, July 9, 1971; children: Debby, Sebilla. BS, Utrecht U., 1969, MA, 1973, PhD, 1983. Biology tchr. secondary Goois Modern High Sch., Bussum, 1976-79; curator Dubois Collection Rijksmuseum van Natural History, Leiden, 1979—; part-time curator Pal.-Min. Cabinet of Tylers Mus., Haarlem, 1981—; curator of large fossil mammals Rijksmuseum van Geol. and Min., Leiden, 1984—; sci. assoc. Inst. Human Origins, Berkeley, Calif., 1987—. Home: Zeverijnstraat 420, 1216 HA Hilversum The Netherlands Office: Rijksmuseum Natural History, Raamsteeg 2, 2311 PL Leiden The Netherlands

DE VRIES, ERNST BART, software development company executive; b. Bussum, Noord-Holland, The Netherlands, May 16, 1939; s. Henry Louis Jan and Adriana Cornelia (De Leeuw) de V.; m. Louise Delfgaauw, Apr. 8, 1963; children: Wouter, Inger. Student, Technische Hoge Sch., Delft, Netherlands, 1956-58. Developer software, firmware Philips Computer Industry, Apeldoorn, The Netherlands, 1965-72; mgr. spl. projects Philips Data Systems, Apeldoorn, The Netherlands, 1972-79, mgr. software support, 1979-86; mgr. system software devel. Philips Telecom and Data Systems, Apeldoorn, The Netherlands, 1986—; state del. Exin, Utrecht, The Netherlands, 1985—. Sec. Netherlands Red Cross, Apeldoorn, 1972-78, mem. hon. com., 1978—; chmn. com. Nature Edn., Apeldoorn, 1980-86. Served to 1st lt. The Netherlands army, 1959-65. Mem. Netherland Genootschap Voor Informatica. Liberal. Club: Algemene Nederlandse Wielryders Bond (The Hague, Netherlands). Home: Hoornbloem 129, 7322 AR Apeldoorn The Netherlands Office: Philips Telecom and Data Systems, PO Box 245, 7300 AE Apeldoorn The Netherlands

DEVRIES, MARTEN WILLIAM, psychiatrist educator; b. Amsterdam, Limburg, the Netherlands, Feb. 14, 1948; came to U.S., 1956, returned to The Netherlands, 1983; s. Hendrik and Teuny Antonia (van de Klashorst) deV.; m. M. Rachel Rappise, Dec. 27, 1969 (div. June 1978); m. Nancy A. Nicolson, Apr. 2, 1982; children: Willem A. and Christopher H.J. BA, Harvard U., 1970, MD, U. Rochester, N.Y., 1975, postgrad. in psychiatry, 1979. Research assoc., child devel. research unit U. Nairobi (Kenya), 1974-75; intern, then resident Strong Meml. Hosp., Rochester, N.Y., 1975-79; asst. prof. anthropology U. Rochester, 1976-78; vis. scientist Z.I.F. Center for

Interdisciplinary Studies, Bielefeld, Fed. Republic of Germany, 1977-78; psychiatry instr. Harvard Med. Sch., Boston, 1979-82; assoc. in edn. human devel. lab. Harvard Grad. Sch. Edn., Cambridge, Mass., 1979-81; lectr. Harvard Med. Sch., Boston, 1982-87; prof. social psychiatry U. Limburg, Maastricht, The Netherlands, 1983—; chmn. Internat. Inst. for Psycho-Social and Ecological Research, Maastricht, 1985—; cons. WHO World Bank Project Hope, Kenya, Swaziland, 1981—; Dutch rep. European Med. Council, Brussels, 1985—; expert cons. NIMH, Washington, 1987—. Author, editor: The Use & Abuse of Medicine, 1982; guest editor: Special Issue, Jour. of Investigating Mental Disorders, Nerves, and Mental Disease, 1987; contbr. articles to profl. jours. Recipient Harvard scholarship, 1966-70, Benjamin Rush Psychiatry prize U. Rochester, 1975; Mac Arthur Found., NIMH, ZWO research grantee, 1981—. Mem. Am. Psychiat. Assn., Soc. for Study of Psychology-Culture, Assn. Med. Anthropology, World Psychiat. Assn. (mem. Epid. and transcultural sects.), Dutch Psychiat. Assn., Workgroup in Social Psychiatry (sec. 1987—). Home: St Lambertuslaan 4, 6211 KB Maastricht The Netherlands Office: U Limburg Dept Social, Psychiatry, PO Box 616, 6200 MD Maastricht The Netherlands

DEW, JESS EDWARD, chemical engineer; b. Okemah, Okla., July 18, 1920; s. Jess Edward and Colleen Avara (Norman) D.; m. Mary Ann Burns, Jan. 3, 1944; children: Anne, Stephen Dodson, David Burns; m. 2d, Sarah Shimoon Kelley, Feb. 4, 1984. Student, Okla. Mil. Acad., 1939-41; BS in Chem. Engring., U. Okla., 1943; MS in Chem. Engring., MIT, 1948. Registered profl. engr., Okla. Asst. chem. engr. Exxon Corp., Baytown, Tex., 1943-47; chem. engr. Amoco Oil Co., Tulsa, 1948-52; v.p. engring. John Deere Chem. Co., Pryor, Okla., 1952-63; gen. supt. John Deere Planter Works, Moline, Ill., 1963-65; v.p. mfg. Arkia Chem. Corp., Helena, Ark., 1965-69; project mgr. Chem. Constrn. Co., N.Y.C. hdqrs., 1969-74, posts included Gt. Britain, 1969-71, Argentina, 1971, Saudi Arabia, 1971-72, Algeria, 1972-74; ind. cons. engr., 1974-78; constrn. mgr. W.R. Holway & Assocs., Tulsa, 1978-82; v.p., gen. mgr. R.L. Frailey, Inc., Tulsa, 1982-86, ret., 1986; pres., bd. dirs. Pryor Indsl. Conservation Co., 1961-63. Contbr. articles to profl. jours. and chpts. to books; patentee in field. Mem. Pryor Mcpl. Utility Bd., 1955-60, Pryor City Council, 1962-63, Rivers and Harbor Commn., Helena, 1966-70; adv. bd. Sacred Heart Acad., 1967-69; bd. dirs. Helena United Fund, 1969. Mem. Am. Inst. Chem. Engrs., ASME, Am. Chem. Soc., Nat. Eagle Scout Assn., Am. Philatelic Soc., Sigma Xi, Beta Theta Pi, Alpha Chi Sigma, Tau Beta Pi. Republican. Roman Catholic. Clubs: Tulsa, Muskogee Country. Lodge: Elks, Rotary. Home: 600 N 45th St Muskogee OK 74401

DE WAARD, JOHANNES, government agency administrator; b. Velzen, Netherlands, June 4, 1936; s. Johannes and Dieuwertje Frederika (Brands) de W.; Engr., Coll. Engring., Haarlem, Netherlands, 1957; 1st lt., Sch. Res. Officieren Verbinding, Ede, Netherlands, 1958; m. Margarete Halfar, 1982; children by previous marriage: Ronald, Marcel, Richard. Research and devel. engr. Brown Boveri Cie, Baden, Switzerland, 1959-63, CONTRAVES, Zuerich, Switzerland, 1963-64; with European Space Sci. and Tech.Ctr, Delft/Noordwijk, Netherlands, 1964-72, test dir., launch ops. mgr., 1968-72; study mgr. space lab. phase A, European Space Agy., Paris, 1972-73, mission mgr. ASSESS 1 and 2, 1973-76; head ops. and crew activities ESA-SPICE, Porz-Wahn, W.Ger., 1976-79; cons. on German spacelab utilization program DFVLR, Porz-Wahn, 1979-81; cons. on peaceful uses of outer space to UN, N.Y.C., 1981-82; with European Space Agy., Office of Dir. Gen., Overath, W.Ger., 1982, project mgr. Meteosat Exploitation Project, 1983—. Mem. AIAA, Planetary Soc., Dutch Aerospace Soc. Contbr. numerous articles on manned space activities and exploitation meteorol. satellites to profl. publs. Office: European Space Agency/European, Space Ops Ctr, D-6100 Darmstadt Federal Republic of Germany

DE WAARD, JOHANNES MARTINUS, management consultant; b. Delft, The Netherlands, Jan. 20, 1930; s. Jan Adriaan and Catharina Jacomina (Vader) De W.; m. Alida Aletta Bekkers, June 27, 1958; children: Gert-Jan, Henk. MA, Tech. U. Delft, 1958; postgrad. in mgmt., Inst. Social Scis., 1963. Cert. elec. engr. Engr. Vanandel BV, Rotterdam, The Netherlands, 1958-60; mgr. ITT Holland, The Hague, The Netherlands, 1960-64; mgmt. cons. Ydo, Amsterdam, The Netherlands, 1964-70, Bilthoven, The Netherlands, 1970—. Mem. Royal Inst. Engrs., Order Mgmt. Cons. Home and Office: Kruislaan 1, 3721 AL Bilthoven The Netherlands

DE WAART, EDO, conductor; b. Amsterdam, Netherlands, June 1, 1941. Grad. with honors for oboe, Amsterdam Conservatoire, 1962. Oboist, Concertgebouw Orch., Amsterdam, 1963-64, asst. condr., 1966-67; asst. to Leonard Bernstein, N.Y. Philharm., 1965-66; condr. Rotterdam (Netherlands) Philharm., 1967-79, also prin. condr., music dir.; founding condr. Netherlands Wind Ensemble, 1967-71; condr., music dir., San Francisco Symphony Orch., 1977-85; music dir. Minn. Orch., 1986—; guest condr., Amsterdam Concertgebouw, Berlin Philharm., Boston Symphony, Chgo. Symphony, London Symphony, Cleve. Orch., N.Y. Philharm., Phila. Orch.; condr.: new prodn. Lohengrin, Beyreuth Festival, summer 1979; new prodn. Wagner's Ring, San Francisco Opera, 1985; rec. artist, Philips Records, rec. with major European orchs. including, New Philharmonia, English Chamber Orch., Royal Philharmonic Orch., Dresden State Orch. Recipient 1st prize Metropoulos Competition, N.Y.C., 1964. Office: Minn Orch 1111 Nicollet Mall Minneapolis MN 55403

DEWAR, MICHAEL JAMES STEUART, chemistry educator; b. Ahmednagar, India, Sept. 24, 1918; came to U.S., 1959, naturalized, 1980; s. Francis and Nan (Keith) D.; m. Mary Williamson, June 3, 1944; children: Robert Berriedale Keith, Charles Edward Steuart. B.A., Oxford (Eng.) U., 1940, D.Phil., 1942, M.A., 1943. Imperial Chem. Industries fellow Oxford U., 1945; phys. chemist Courtaulds Ltd., 1945-51; prof. chemistry, head dept. Queen Mary Coll., U. London, Eng., 1951-59; prof. chemistry U. Chgo., 1959-63; Robert A. Welch prof. chemistry U. Tex., 1963—; Reilly lectr. U. Notre Dame, 1951; Tilden lectr. Chem. Soc. London, 1954; vis. prof. Yale U., 1957; Falk-Plaut lectr. Columbia U., 1963; Daines Meml. lectr. U. Kans., 1963; Glidden C. lectr. U. Kans., 1964; William Pyle Phillips visitor Haverford Coll., 1964, 70; Arthur D. Little vis. prof. MIT, 1966; Marchon vis. lectr. U. Newcastle (Eng.), 1966; Glidden Co. lectr. Kent State U., 1967; Gnehm lectr. Eldg. Technische Hochschule, Zurich, Switzerland, 1968; Barton lectr. U. Okla., 1969; Disting. vis. lectr. Yeshiva U., 1970; Kahlbaum lectr. U. Basel, Switzerland, 1970; Benjamin Rush lectr. U. Pa., 1971; Kharasch vis. prof. U. Chgo., 1971; Venable lectr. U. N.C., 1971; Phi Lambda Upsilon lectr. Johns Hopkins U., 1972; Firth vis. prof. U. Sheffield, 1972; Foster lectr. SUNY-Buffalo, 1973; Five Colls. lectr., Mass., 1973; Sprague lectr. U. Wis., 1974; spl. lectr. U. London, 1974; lectr. chem. edn. Fla. State U., 1975; disting. Bicentennial prof. U. Utah, 1976; Bircher lectr. Vanderbilt U., 1976; Pahlavi lectr., Iran, 1977; Michael Faraday lectr. U. No. Ill., 1977; Priestley lectr. Pa. State U., 1980; research scholar lectr. Drew U., 1984; J. Clarence Karcher lectr. U. Okla., 1984; cons. to industry. Author: Electronic Theory of Organic Chemistry, 1949, Hyperconjugation, 1962, Introduction to Modern Organic Chemistry, 1965, Computer Compilation of Molecular Weights and Percentage Compositions of Organic Compounds, 1969, The Molecular Orbital Theory of Organic Chemistry, 1969, The PMO Theory of Organic Chemistry, 1975; also articles. Recipient Harrison Howe award Am. Chem. Soc., 1961, S.W. regional award, 1978, Robert Robinson Lecture, Chem. Soc., 1974, G.W. Wheland Meml. medal U. Chgo., 1976, Evans award Ohio State U., 1977, James Flack Norris award, 1984, Nichols medal, 1986, Auburn-G.M. Kosolapoff award Am. Chem. Soc., 1988; hon. fellow Balliol Coll., 1974. Fellow Royal Soc. (Davy medal 1982), Am. Acad. Arts and Scis., Chem. Soc. London; mem. Am. Chem. Soc., Nat. Acad. Sci., Sigma Xi. Home: 6808 Mesa Dr Austin TX 78731

DE WARDT, JOHN PELHAM, oil company executive; b. Tadworth, Surrey, Eng., July 22, 1955; s. Robert Hugh and Mary Pelham (Hankins) de W.; m. Susan Lee Holder, Feb. 19, 1983; children: Winston Pelham, Rebecca Anne. BSME, U. of Newcastle-Upon-Tyne, Eng., 1976. Ops. engr. Nederlandse Aardoilie Maatschappij, Assen, Holland, 1976-80; staff drilling engr. Scallop Corp., Houston, 1980-83; head drilling engring. Thai Shell Exploration and Prodn. Co., Bangkok, 1983-85; head ops. contracts Sarawak Shell Berhad, Miri, Malaysia, 1985—. Mem. Instn. Mech. Engrs. (grad.), Soc. Petroleum Engrs. Club: Hash House Harriers (Miri) (treas. 1987—). Office: Sarawak Shell Berhad, Lutong, Miri Sarawak Malaysia

DE WARREN, ROBERT, dancer, choreographer, ballet director. Dancer Royal Ballet, London; prin. dancer Stuttgart Ballet, Fed. Republic of Germany, Frankfurt Ballet, German Dem. Republic, Nat. Ballet of Uruguay; ballet master, choreographer Nat. Ballet of Iran, 1965-71; artistic dir. Northern Ballet Theatre, Manchester, Eng., 1976-87, La Scala Opera Ballet, Milan, 1987—. Recipient Theatre award Manchester Evening News, 1984. Office: La Scala Opera Ballet, Teatro alla Scala, 20121 Milan Italy other: care Mark Kappel 252 W 76th St Suite 6E New York NY 10023 *

DEWART, DOROTHY BOARDMAN, clinical psychologist, consultant, researcher; b. Boston, Aug. 19, 1948; d. Thomas Dennie and Dorothy (Potter) Boardman. B.A. in Psychology and Sociology, Salem Coll., 1972; M.A. in Clin. Psychology, Xavier U., 1976; postgrad., U. Cin., 1975-77; Ph.D. in Clin. Psychology, Temple U., 1981. Research asst. Cin. Ctr. Devel. Disorders, 1974-75, psychology trainee, 1975, U. Cin., 1975-76, Rollman' Psychiat. Inst., Cin., 1975-76; psychologist Cen. Psychiat. Clinic, Cin., 1976-77; asst. dir. Pyschol. Services, Clermont Gen. and Tech. Coll., U. Cin., 1976-77; supr. Psychol. Services Ctr., Temple U., 1978, clin. asst., 1980, psychology intern, 1980-81, staff psychologist, dept. psychiat. and chronic pain clinic, 1981-82; cons. maxillo-facial pain clinic, 1981—, clin. instr. dept. psychiatry, 1981—. Profl. com. Wissahickon Hospice, Chestnut Hill, Pa. Research Incentive Fund grantee Temple U. Hosp., 1981—; Pew Meml Trust grantee, 1981—; recipient NIMH assistantship, 1977-78. Mem. Am. Psychol. Assn., Phila. Soc. Clin. Psychologists, Am. Pain Soc. Research in psychotherapy with patients who present significant physical illness; research in effects of tryptophan on chronic pain; clin. assoc. Am. Bd. Med. Psychotherapists, 1987; clin. instr. dept. psychiatry Temple U. Hosp., Phila. Home and Office: 748 St George's Rd Philadelphia PA 19119

DEWEY, DONALD WILLIAM, magazine editor and publisher, writer; b. Honolulu, Sept. 30, 1933; s. Donald William and Theckla Jean (Engeborg) D.; m. Sally Rae Ryan, Aug. 7, 1961; children: Michael Kevin, Wendy Ann. Student, Pomona Coll., 1953-55. With Pascoe Steel Corp., Pomona, Calif., 1955-56, div. Reynolds Aluminum Co., Los Angeles, 1956-58, Switzer Panel Corp., Pasadena, Calif., 1958-60; sales and gen. mgr. Western Pre-Cast Concrete Corp., Ontario, Calif., 1960-62; editor, pub. R/C Modeler Mag., Sierra Madre, Calif., 1963—, Freshwater and Marine Aquarium Mag., Sierra Madre, 1978—; pres., chmn. bd. R/C Modeler Corp., Sierra Madre, 1963—. Author: Radio Control From the Ground Up, 1970, Flight Training Course, 1973, For What It's Worth, Vol. 1, 1973, Vol. 2, 1975; contbr. articles to profl. jours. Sustaining mem. Rep. Nat. Com., 1981—; charter mem. Nat. Congl. Club, 1981—; mem. Rep. Presdl. Task Force, 1981—, U.S. Senatorial Club, 1983—, 1984 Presdl. Trust, Conservative Caucus, Nat. Tax Limitation Com., Nat. Conservative Polit. Action Com.; assoc. Meth. Hosp. of Southern Calif. Served with Hosp. Corps, USN, 1951-53. Mem. Oceanic Soc., Internat. Oceanograpnic Found., Internat. Assn. Aquatic Animal Medicine, Fedn. Am. Aquarium Socs., Am. Philatelic Soc., Am. Topical Assn., Marine Aquarium Soc., APS Writers Unit 30, Nat. Trust for Historic Preservation, Am. First Day Cover Soc., United Postal Stationery Soc., Confederate Stamp Alliance, Am. Air Mail Soc., Bur. Issues Assn., Am. Revenue Assn., C.Z. Study Group, Pitcairn Islands Study Group, Pet Industry Joint Adv. Council, Sierra Madre Hist. Soc., Friends of Sierra Madre Library, Internat. Betta Congress, Nat. Fisheries Assn., Am. Killifish Assn., Am. Catfish and Loach Assn., Am. Wildlife Fedn., Greater Los Angeles Zoo Assn., Am. Indian Heritage Found., Los Angeles County Arboretum Assn., Calif. Hist. Soc., Internat. Platform Assn. Republican. Episcopalian. Home: 410 W Montecito Ave Sierra Madre CA 91024 Office: 144 W Sierra Madre Blvd Sierra Madre CA 91024

DEWHURST, WILLIAM GEORGE, psychiatrist, educator, administrator, researcher; b. Frosterley, Durham, Eng., Nov. 21, 1926; came to Can., 1969; s. William and Elspeth Leslie (Begg) D.; m. Margaret Dransfield, Sept. 17, 1960; children—Timothy Andrew, Susan Jane. B.A., Oxford U., Eng., 1947, B.M., B.Ch., 1950; MA, Oxford U., 1961; D.P.M. with distinction, London U., 1961. House physician, surgeon London Hosp., 1950-52, jr. registrar, registrar, 1954-58; registrar, sr. registrar Maudsley Hosp., London, 1958-62, cons. physician, 1965-69; lectr. Inst. Psychiatry, London, 1962-64, sr. lectr., 1965-69; assoc. prof. psychiatry U. Alta., Edmonton, Can., 1969-72, prof., 1972—, chmn. dept. psychiatry, 1975—, co-dir. Neurochem. Research Unit, 1979—, hon. prof. pharmacy and pharm. scis., 1979—, hon. prof. oncology, 1983—; cons. psychiatrist Royal Alexandra Hosp., Edmonton, Edmonton Gen. Hosp.; chmn. med. council Can. Test Com., 1977-79, Royal Coll. Test Com. in Psychiatry, 1971-80, examiner, 1975—. Co-editor: Neurobiology of Trace Amines, 1984, Pharmacotherapy of Affective Disorders, 1985; also conf. procs. Referee Nature, Can. Psychiat. Assn. Jour., Brit. Jour. Psychiatry; mem. editorial bd. Neuropsychobiology, Psychiat. Jour. U. Ottawa. Contbr. articles to profl. jours. Mem., chmn. Edmonton Psychiat. Services Steering Com., 1977-80; chmn. Edmonton Psychiat. Services Planning Com., 1985—; mem. Provincial Mental Health Adv. Council, 1973-79, Mental Health Research Com., 1973—, Edmonton Bd. Health, 1974-76, Can. Psychiat. Research Found., 1985—; bd. dirs. Friends of Schizophrenics, Ctr. Gerontology, Alta., Can. Psychiat. Research Found.; grant referee Health & Welfare Can., Med. Research Council Can., Ont. Mental Health Found., Man. Health Research Council, B.C. Health Research Found. Served to capt. Royal Army M.C., 1952-54, Hong Kong. Fellow Can. Coll. Neuropsychopharmacology (pres. 1982-84), Am. Psychopathol. Assn., Am. Coll. Psychiatrists, Am. Psychiat. Assn., Royal Coll. Psychiatrists, Royal Coll. Physicians and Surgeons Can. (nucleus speciality com. 1987—); mem. Alta. Psychiat. Assn. (pres. 1973-74), Can. Psychiat. Assn. (pres. 1983-84), Royal Coll. Physicians, Alta. Coll. Physicians and Surgeons, Alta. Med. Assn., AAAS, Am. Assn. Chmn. Depts. Psychiatry, Assn. for Acad. Psychiatry, Brit. Med. Assn., Can. Assn. Anglican. Club: Faculty (Alta.). Office: U Alberta, Dept Psychiatry, 1E7 44 Mackenzie Centre, 8440-112 St, Edmonton, AB Canada T6G 2B7

DEWILT, HENK G.J., business executive; b. Hulst, Zeeland, The Netherlands, Sept. 17, 1940; m. Josephine van Oosterbosch; 4 children. Degree in Engring., H.T.S. Breda, 1960; MS, U. Tech., 1966; D, U. Eindhoven, 1969. Scientist U. Tech., Eindhoven, The Netherlands, 1962-69; adminstr. U. Tech., Eindhoven, 1971-72; scientist State Lab. Chem. Engring., Tokyo, 1970; lectr. Univ. Groningen, The Netherlands, 1972-75; research and devel. mgr. Douwe Egberts, Utrecht, The Netherlands, 1975-80, mgr. corp. strategy, 1980-81, gen. mgr. tech., 1981-86, mem. bd. mgmt., 1986—; prof. State U. Bus. Adminstrn., Groningen, 1981-86; cons., 1966-75. Patentee in field; contbr. numerous articles to profl. jours. Office: Douwe Egberts NV, Keulsekade 143, 3532 AA Utrecht The Netherlands

DE WOUTERS, BARON GUY, investment company executive; b. Paris, Oct. 1, 1930; s. Charles and Elisabeth (duLuart) de W.; m. Elisabeth Roche de la Rigodiere, Nov. 19, 1962; children—Camille, Guillaume, Juliette, Charlotte. LL.B., U. Louvain, 1950, econs. degree, 1951. Chmn., chief exec. officer Belgian Shell Co., Brussels, 1974-80; head strategic planning Shell Internat., London, 1980-83; mng. dir. Société Generale de Belgique, Brussels, 1985—; chmn. Oranje Nassau Group, The Hague, 1984-87; pres. Tractebel, Brussels, 1987—; dir. Tanks Holdings, London, Petrofino, Brussels, Dillo Read Ltd., London, Havas, Paris. D ecorated Order Leopold, Ordre de la Couronne. Clubs: Automobile (Paris, London); Queens (London). Avocations: tennis; skiing; collecting books and modern paintings.

DE WREE, EUGENE ERNEST, manufacturing company executive; b. Fairbanks, Alaska, June 26, 1930; s. Henry Joseph and Bertha Agnes DeWree; m. Shirley May Russo, Apr. 16, 1955; children: Angela Kathryn, Mary Rebecca, Thomas Albert Babette Gabrielle, Jane Elizabeth. BSME Cogswell Engring. Coll., 1955; MBA Stanford U., 1959. Project engr. Heat & Control Co., San Francisco, 1955-59; chief applications engr., then market mgr. Wesix Electric Heater Co., San Francisco, 1959-65; account mgr. Fisher Controls, San Francisco, 1965-76; market and sales mgr. TRW Mission, Houston, 1976-80; v.p. mktg.-sales Houston Heat Exchange, 1980-82; mktg. mgr. Anderson, Greenwood & Co., 1982—; sr. partner Affiliated Products Inc.; pres. DeWree Enterprises, DeWree Rental Properties; ptnr., dir. Constrn. Info. Services, Cismap, TVMP; dir. Creative Capers, San Francisco and Houston. Mem. Belmont (Calif.) Personnel Bd., 1965; com. chmn. Boy Scouts Am., 1970; bd. dirs. Cypress Forest Pub. Utility Dist. of Harris County, Tex., 1981, 83, 85, 86—, Harris County Regional Water Supply; pres. Water Bd. Served to capt., arty. U.S. Army, 1951-53; Korea. Named Outstanding Jaycee of Yr., 1966. Mem. Am. Mgmt. Assn., Am. Nuclear Soc., Valve Mfg. Assn., Instrument Soc. Am. (sr.), Assn. Water Bd. Dirs., Water Pollution Control Fedn., Sales and Mktg. Execs. Republican. Roman Catholic. Clubs: Pine Forest Country, Plaza; Engrs. (San Francisco). Home: 16203 Champions Dr Spring TX 77373 Office: 13231 Champion Forest Dr Suite 110 Houston TX 77069

DEXHEIMER, HENRY PHILLIP, II, insurance agency executive; b. Dayton, Ohio, Sept. 16, 1925; s. Henry Phillip and Helene Francis (Veach) D.; B.S. in Commerce, U. So. Calif., 1952; children—James Phillip, Jana Helene. Sales account exec. with various cos. and newspapers, 1946-51; broadcasting sales exec. Sta. KBIG, KTLA-TV, Los Angeles, 1952-58; broadcasting sales exec. Sta. KFXM, San Bernardino, Calif., 1956-57, pres., 1956-57; founder, owner, pres. Dexheimer Co., Los Angeles, 1958—. Served with inf. and adj. gen.'s dept. U.S. Army, 1943-46; PTO. Recipient Sammy award Los Angeles Sales Execs. Club, 1955; Silver Sales trophy Radio Advt. Bur. N.Y., 1955; named Agt. of Year, Los Angeles office Travelers Ins. Cos., 1978, 83, 84, 85; Hal Parsons award, 1978, 83, 84, 85. C.L.U. Mem. Am. Soc. C.L.U.s (nat. dir. Travelers chpt. 1972-73, 80-81), Am. Coll. Life Underwriters, Advt. Assn. West, Radio and TV Soc. Hollywood, Life Ins. and Trust Council Los Angeles, Los Angeles Life Underwriters Assn. (dir. 1963-65, v.p. 1967-69), Million Dollar Round Table (life, honor roll), World Affairs Council Los Angeles, Internat. Assn. Fin. Planners, Am. Art Council, Decorative Art Council of Los Angeles County Art Mus., Alpha Delta Sigma, Phi Kappa Tau. Republican. Presbyterian. Clubs: Town Hall (Los Angeles); Beverly Hills Men's (Calif.); Masons (32 degree), Shriners, Legion of Honor. Office: Dexheimer Co Marina Bus Ctr 13160 Mindanao Way Suite 222 Marina del Rey CA 90292

DEXTER, DALLAS-LEE, insurance executive, consultant; b. Rockville Center, N.Y., Nov. 30, 1950; d. David D. and Jane (Nesbitt) D.; m. Leonard Eugene Carter, Nov. 6, 1975 (div. 1982). Student numerous dance courses; B.S., Mills Coll., 1972; M.A., Tchrs. Coll. Columbia U., 1974; postgrad. Nat. U. Mex., 1974, Lesley Coll., 1974, Fgn. Service Inst., 1977, Johns Hopkins Sch. Advanced Internat. Studies, 1982, Middle East Inst., 1982-83, U. N.C., 1982-86. Cert. ins., securities, teaching. Tchr. Am. Sch., Hawalli, Kuwait, 1975-76, Copenhagen Internat. Sch., 1977-79, Rygaards Internat. Sch., Hellerup, Denmark, 1980-81; mktg. contractor Nat. Right to Work Com., 1986—, 21st Century Telemedial Mktg. Services, Inc., 1986, sales mgr. Best Programs, Inc., Arlington, Va., 1987—; cons. Mark V Assocs., Inc., N.Y.C., 1982-86, Success, Inc., Palm Beach, Fla., 1985-86, Resources Planning Systems, 1983-86, Mgmt. Engring. Affiliates, Calabasa, Calif., 1984, Aerojet Gen., Washington, 1983; ednl. cons. Mayors Program on Summer Youth Employment, Washington, 1986, Islamic Saudi Acad. of Kingdom of Saudi Arabia, Dunn Loring, Va., 1986-87; mktg. cons. Nat. Right to Work Com., Springfield, Va., 1986—; cons., adminstr. Kingdom Of Saudi Arabia: Islamic Saudi Acad., 1986-87; sales rep. First Investors Corp., Arlington, Va., 1985-86; assoc. Potomac Ins. and Fin. Planning Group, Rockville, Md., 1985—; mgr. telesales div. Best Programs, Inc., Arlington, Va., 1987—; dancer Twyla Tharp Dance Co., 1969-70, James Cunningham Co., 1970, others; . Campaign worker Reagan-Bush, Washington, 1983-84; active Rock Creek Women's Republican Club, Chevy Chase Women's Rep. Club, Montgomery County Rep. Club, Nat. Fedn. Rep. Women; mem. women's com. Nat. Symphony Orch.; charter mem., sponsor Assn. of Friends of Mus. Modern Art of Latin Am. Mem. Nat. Assn. Life Underwriters, U.S. C. of C., D.C. Life Underwriters Assn., Nat. Assn. Female Execs. (network dir. 1985—), Internat. Educators Inst., World Affairs Council, Soc. for Internat. Devel., Middle East Inst., Middle East Studies Assn., Nat. Acad. TV Arts and Scis., Am. Def. Preparedness Assn., Air Force Assn., AAUW, Phi Delta Kappa. Unitarian. Clubs: Renaissance Women, Columbia Univ., University. Avocations: Travel; theatre; music; dance; painting. Home: 1280 21st St NW Washington DC 20036 Office: Best Programs Inc 2700 S Quincy St Suite 200 Arlington VA 22206

DEXTER, HELEN LOUISE, dermatologist, consultant; b. Cin., July 28, 1908; d. William Jordan and Katherine (Weston) Taylor; A.B., Bryn Mawr Coll., 1930; M.D., Columbia U., 1937; postgrad. U. Cin. Coll. Medicine, 1948-50; m. Morrie W. Dexter, Jan. 27, 1937; children—Katharine, Helen Dexter Dalzell, Elizabeth Taylor Dexter Potsubay, William Taylor. Intern, Jersey City Med. Center, 1938-39; internist Cin. Babies Milk Fund, Maternal Health Clinic, 1938-45; clinician U. Cin. Med. Sch., 1938-48, lectr. dept. dermatology, 1948-53; practice medicine specializing in dermatology, Clearwater, Fla., 1954-—; dermatology cons. VA, 1955-—; investigation of carcinogenic effects of shale oil U.S. Bur. Mines, Rifle, Colo., 1950. Mem. Clearwater Power Squadron Aux.; bd. dirs. Girls Clubs Pinellas County; commr. Town of Belleair, 1980. Recipient Ina Clay trophy Intercollegiate Ski Champion, 1928-30. Mem. AMA, Soc. Investigation Dermatology, Am. Acad. Dermatology, S.E. Dermatol. Assn. (v.p. 1963-64), Fla. Dermatol. Soc. (pres. 1959), Fla. Soc. Dermatology (pres.), Noah Worcester Dermatol. Soc., Am. Archaeol. Soc., Pan-Am. Dermatol. Soc., Soc. Tropical Dermatology. Presbyterian. Club: Clearwater Yacht Carlovel Yacht. Contbr. articles to profl. jours. Address: 409 Bayview Dr Belleair FL 34616

DEXTER, IAN PHILLIP, automotive executive; b. Strathfield, Australia, Sept. 22, 1935; s. Leslie Horton and Eleanor Mary Greig (Anderson) D.; m. Vivienne Elizabeth Cope, Dec. 20, 1967 (div.); 1 son, Guy Phillip. M.B.A., Harvard U., 1967. Mem. profl. motor racing team, Europe, U.S.A., 1959-63; used car mgr. Renault Australia, Sydney, 1965-68; leasing mgr. Hastings Deering P.L., Lidcombe, New South Wales, Australia, 1968-70, sales and mktg. mgr., 1970-73; chmn., mng. dir. Ian Dexter Racing Pty Ltd., New South Wales, 1974—; cons. to auto industry, 1974—. Mem. Historic Sports and Racing Car Assn. Mem. Ch. of Eng. Clubs: Royal Automobile, Mercedes-Benz. Contbg. editor nat. and internat. automotive publs.; contbr. articles in automotive history to mags.

DEXTER, JOHN, opera, stage and film director; b. Derby, Eng., Aug. 2, 1925; s. Harry James and Rose D. Dir. English Stage Co.; dir. plays Yes - and After, 1957, Each in His Wilderness, 1958, Chicken Soup with Barley, 1958, Roots, 1959, The Kitchen, 1959, This Year, Next Year, 1960, I'm Talking About Jerusalem, 1960, South, 1961, The Keep, 1961, England, Our England, 1962, The Blood of the Bambergs, 1962, Jackie the Jumper, 1963, Saint Joan, 1963, Hobson's Choice, Othello, Royal Hunt of the Sun, 1964, Armstrong's Last Goodnight, 1965, Black Comedy, 1965, The Storm, 1966, A Woman Killed with Kindness, 1971, Tyger, 1971, The Misanthrope, 1973, Equus, N.Y.C., 1973, 74, The Party, 1973, Phaedra Britannica, 1975, Do I hear a Waltz?, N.Y.C., 1965, Benevenuto Cellini, 1966, Black Comedy and White Lies, N.Y.C., 1967, Wise Child, 1967, The Old Ones, 1972, In Praise of Love, 1973, Equus, N.Y.C., 1974, Pygmalion, 1974, M. Butterfly, N.Y.C., 1988; dir. prodns. of Un Ballo in Maschera, I Vespri Sicliani, From the House of the Dead, Hamburg State Opera, Boris Godurov, Billy Budd, all at Hamburg State Opera; dir. Sadler's Wells Opera prodn. The Devils of Loudon, Nat. Theatre prodn. Gallileo, 1980, Shoemaker's Holiday, 1981, Paris Opera prodn. I Vespri Siciliani; dir. prodns. Met. Opera, N.Y.C., 1974-81, advisor, 1981-84, including Le Prophete, Dialogues of the Carmelites, Lulu, 1976-77, Rigoletto, 1977-78, Billy Budd, The Bartered Bride, Don Pasquale, Don Carlo, 1978-79, Die Entfuhrung aus dem Serail, 1979, The Rise and Fall of the City of Mahagonny, Don Carlo, 1979, Parade, 1981, Stravinsky, 1981, The Portage to San Cristobal, 1982, Gigi , The Cocktail Party, in London, from 1985; films The Virgin Soldiers, 1969, The Sidelong Glances of a Pigeon Kicker, 1970, I Want What I Want, 1972; assoc. dir. plays Nat Theatre, 1963-66, 71-75. Recipient Tony award for Best Dir. of a Drama, 1975, 1988. Office: 142A Portland Rd, Holland Park, London W11, England *

DEYSHER, PAUL EVANS, training consultant; b. Reading, Pa., Oct. 16, 1923; s. Paul Stauffer and Ida Estelle (Evans) D.; m. Myrtle Constance Stover, June 17, 1950; children—David Paul, Mark Edward. B.S., Albright Coll., 1945; M.Ednl. Adminstrn., Temple U., 1949. Math. and sci. teacher Lebanon City (Pa.) Sch. Dist., 1950-56; asst. high sch. prin. Ocean City Sch. (N.J.) Dist., 1956-57; high sch. prin. Yeadon Sch. (Pa.), Dist., 1957-60; mgr. personnel adminstrn. Philco Corp., Phila., 1960-66; tng. specialist AMP Inc., Harrisburg, Pa., 1966-80, supr. mgmt. tng., 1980-85, mgr. mgmt. tng. and devel., 1986; cons. and lectr. in field. Co-author: Transistor Fundamentals, 1962; contbr. chpts. to books and articles to profl. jours. Treas. Friends of Spang Crest Retirement Home, Lebanon, Pa.; pres., Albright Coll.-Lebanon County Alumni chpt., 1979—; trustee Albright Coll., Reading, Pa., 1985—. Mem. NEA (life), Am. Soc. Personnel Adminstrn. (cert., sr. profl. in human resources), Am. Soc. Training & Devel. (past pres.), Phi Delta Kappa. Republican. Lutheran. Club: Lebanon Coin. Lodge: Kiwanis. Home: 39 S Mill St Cleona PA 17042

DE YTURRIAGA, JOSE ANTONIO, Spanish diplomat, international law educator; b. Granada, Spain, Oct. 12, 1936; s. Enrique and Maria (Barberan) de Y.; m. Mavis Anne Saldanha, June 24, 1964; children—Enrique, Ana Lilian, Maria Victoria. Degree in Law, U. Sevilla, 1958; LL.D., U. Madrid, 1965; Sec. Spanish Embassy, Monrovia, Liberia, 1965-67; consul, Spanish Consulate, Dusseldorf, Germany, 1967-70; legal advisor Minister of Fgn. Affairs, Madrid, 1970-75; cultural counsellor Spanish Embassy, Lisbon, Portugal, 1975-76; dep. dir. gen. air maritime coop. Minister Fgn. Affairs, Madrid, 1976-81, head legal dept., 1981-82, sec. gen., 1982-83; ambassador Spanish Embassy, Baghdad, Iraq, 1983-87, Dublin, Ireland, 1987—. Served to lt. Spanish Marines, 1958. Decorated caballero y comendador Orden de Isabel la Católica; comendador Orden Mérito Civil; cruz de primera Orden Mérito Naval; chevalier Ordre Merit Maritime; caballero y comendador Orden Carlos III. Mem. Inst. Hispano-Luso-Americano de Derecho Internat., Assn. Argentina de Derecho Internat., Internat. Law Assn., Jurisconsulte de Intelsat, Internat. Inst. of Space Law. Home: Spanish Embassy, Ailesbury House, Ailesbury Rd, Dublin-4 Ireland

DEZON COSTA HASSLOCHER, MARCEL, diplomat. Former ambassador from Brazil to Maputo, Mozambique; now ambassador to Rabat, Morocco, 1986—. Office: Ambassade du Bresil, 1-Charia Marrakech, Rabat Morocco

DE ZULUETA, PHILIP FRANCIS, banker; b. Oxford, Eng., Jan. 2, 1925; s. Francis and Marie Louise (Lyne-Stephens) De Z.; m. Marie Louise Hennessy, Sept. 14, 1955; children—Louise, Francis. M.A. (scholar), New Coll., Oxford U. With Fgn. Service, 1949-53, pvt. sect. to Prime Minister, 1955-63, asst. sec. treasury, 1962; with Hill Samuel & Co., Ltd., 1964-72, dir., 1965-72; spl. adviser to bd. Hong Kong and Shanghai Banking Corp., 1981-85; chmn. Antony Gibbs Holdings Ltd., 1975-81, chief exec., 1973-75; chmn. Tanks Consolidated Investments p.l.c., 1983—; bd. dirs. Union Miniere, Belgium, Abbotts Lab., others. Served to capt. Welsh Guards, 1943-47. Decorated knight bachelor U.K.; knight Sovereign Mil. Order of Malta; officer Legion d'Honneur. Conservative. Roman Catholic. Clubs: Beefsteak, Pratt's, Whites (London); Jockey (Paris). Home: 3 Westminster Gardens, Marsham St, London SW1 P4JA, England Office: 6 John St, London WC1 N2ES, England

D'HAEN, ELSA JOSEPHINA MARIE, artist; b. St. Amandsberg, Belgium, Jan. 31, 1926; d. Firmin and Beorgette (Wallaert) d.; m. Alexander Clemens Wauters, July 15, 1947 (dec. 1965). Degree in Teaching, Normal Sch., Gent, Belgium, 1944; student, Gent Conservatoire, 1945-50; pvt. studies with Alexander Wauters, 1946. Author: Catalogues van het oeuvre Alexander Wauters, 1976; painter of drawings and water colors; exhbns. include Gent, 1948, 50, 75, Antwerpen, 1954, Brugge 1966, Oostende 1971. Address: Wintertuinstraat 6, Ghent 9000, Belgium

DHAINAUT CRÉMER, MICHEL EUGÈNE PIERRE, international agricultural trader; b. Bueno Aires, Argentina, Sept. 10, 1927; arrived in Spain, 1963.; s. Donatien and Thérése (Crémer) D.; m. Marie-France Audit; children: Caroline, Florence, Jean-Michel. Degree in Econs., U. Argentina, 1949. Trader Am. Sohr, Buenos Aires, 1945-48; purchasing mgr. Inteco-Etam, Buenos Aires, 1984-54; owner Garchel Soc. Responsabilidad Ltd., Buenos Aires, 1954-57; trader La Plata Cereal Co. SA, Buenos Aires, 1957-61, André & Co. SA, Lausanne, Switzerland, 1961-63; mgr. Silor SA, Madrid, 1963—; councillor Transcatalana S.A., Barcelona, Spain. Served with the Argentinian Army, 1946-48. Mem. French C. of C. Club: Real, Puerta de Hierro (Madrid). Home: Ave Miraflores 46 Bis, 28035 Madrid Spain Office: Silor SA, Gen Pardiñas 114, 7B, 28006 Madrid Spain

DHANABALAN, SUPPIAH, minister of foreign affairs for Singapore; b. Singapore, Aug. 8, 1937; m. Tan Khoon Hiap, 1963; 2 children. BA with honors in Econs., U. Malaya, Singapore, 1960. Asst. sec. Ministry of Fin., Singapore, 1960-61; sr. indsl. economist Econ. Devel. Bd., Singapore, 1961-68; v.p., exec. v.p. Devel. Bank Singapore, Singapore, 1968-78; sr. minister of state Ministry of Nat. Devel., Singapore, 1978-79; sr. minister of state Ministry of Fgn. Affairs, Singapore, 1979-80, minister, 1980—; minister Ministry of Culture, Singapore, 1981-84, Ministry of Community Devel., Singapore, 1984-86, Ministry of Nat. Devel., Singapore, 1987—; mem. of parliament People's Action Party, Kallang Constituency, 1976—. Office: Ministry of Fgn Affairs, St Andrew's Rd, Singapore 0617, Singapore

DHESI, AUTAR SINGH, economics educator; b. Jalandhar, India, July 9, 1936; s. Milkha Singh and Bakhshish Kaur (Rakhi) D.; m. Harbhahan Kaur, Dec. 12, 1976 (div. Mar. 1984). BS, Panjab U., 1957; postgrad diploma in Devel. Adminstrn., Leeds U., 1966; MS in Econs, U. Surrey, 1968; M. in Sociology, U. Birmingham, 1971, PhD, 1974. Freelance journalist London, 1960-74; lectr. Lanchester Poly., Coventry, Eng., 1971-72; assoc. prof. econs. Guru Nanak Dev U., Amritsar, India, 1975-83, prof., 1983—; chmn. Punjab Sch. Econs., 1984-87, dean, 1986-87; cons. World Bank Washington, 1982, Ministry Indsl. Devel., New Delhi, 1986—; mem. panel indsl. economists Indian Planning commn., New Delhi, 1986—; mem. Punjab Planning Bd., Chandigarh, India, 1987—. Author: Human Capital Formation and Its Utilization, 1979; founder, editor Indian Jour. Quantitative Econs., 1985—; contbr. articles to profl. jours. Indian Council Social Sci. research grantee, 1982, Cen. Water Commn. research grantee, 1987. Mem. Indian Econmetric Soc. (council 1986—), Indian Econ. Assn. (life). Home: House B-1, Guru Nanak U Campus, Amritsar 143005, India Office: Guru Nanak Dev U, Punjab Sch Econs, Amritsar 143005, India

DHIR, KRISHNA SWAROOP, management professional, educator; b. Calcutta, India, Mar. 21, 1944; s. Hari Das and Sushila Devi (Kochhar) D.; m. Shailaja Nair, July 3, 1983; children: Devika, Radhika. BS in Tech., Indian Inst. Tech., Bombay, 1966; MS in Chem. Engring., Mich. State U., 1967; MBA (Rama Watumull scholar), U. Hawaii, 1968; DBA, U. Colo., 1975. Process control engr., mgr. pilot plant Borg-Warner Chems. Co., Washington, W.Va., 1969-72; head dept. bus. W.Va. U., Parkersburg Ctr., 1971-72; vis. prof. quantitative methods U. Hawaii, Honolulu, 1974; asst. prof. mgmt. Clarkson Coll. Tech., 1975-76; mgmt. adv. Pharm. div. CIBA-Geigy Ltd., Basle, Switzerland, 1976-82; assoc. prof. mgmt. sci. U. Colo., Boulder, 1979-82; assoc. prof. mgmt. U. Denver, 1982-87; dir. M.I.M. degree program, 1986-87; prof., head dept. bus. adminstrn. The Citadel, Charleston, S.C., 1987—; vis. prof. mgmt. and stats. U. Bombay, G.S. Med. Coll. and King Edward VII Meml. Hosp., India, 1985. Lt. col. S.C. Militia, 1987—; mem. adv. bd. Info. Res. Mgmt. Assn., 1988—. Recipient gold medal St. John's Ambulance Assn. India, 1956; U.P. Bd. Edn. merit scholar, India, 1959. Mem. Am. Soc. for Quality Control (edn. chmn. Mid-Ohio Valley 1971-72), Instn. Indsl. Engring. of India, Indian Inst. Ind. Engrs., Decision Scis. Inst., Acad. Internat. Bus., Acad. Mgmt., Beta Gamma Sigma, Sigma Iota Epsilon. Contbr. numerous articles to profl. jours. and chpts. in books; made policy formulation studies for conservation Gir Forest ecosystem, Western India, 1975-79. Avocations: photography, camping, travel. Office: The Citadel Dept Bus Adminstrn Charleston SC 29409-0215

DIACONU, ADRIAN, robotics company official; b. Posesti, Roum, France, Mar. 29, 1959; s. Stephan and Florica D. Student, Hautes Etudes Industrielles, France, 1982; grad., Conservatoire National des Arts et Metiers, France, 1983. Cert. engr., France. Project engr. Moismont SA, France, 1983-85; project engr. Setradis-Bertelsmann France, Noyelles/Lens, 1985-87, mgr. indsl. research and devel., 1987—; cons. Roboplast Robotics, France, 1983. Inventor in field. Home: 27 Rt de la Neuville,, 59710 Attiches-Pont A Marcq France Office: Setradis Bertelsmann France, Rue du Docteur Schaffner, 62221 Noyelles/Lens France

DIALLO, ABDOUL AZIZ, library director; b. Nioro, Mali, Malienne, Mar. 23, 1953; parents Mamoudou Alfa and Rella Sow Diallo; m. Adam Fanta Diakite, Apr. 20, 1980; children: Fatimata, Mamoudou, Madani. Grad., ecole normale supérieure, Bamako, Mali, 1977. Historian Ministry Arts, Culture, Bamako, Mali, 1978-80; dir. gen. National Library, Bamako, 1980-82; chief of div. Patrimoine Culturel, Bamako, 1982—. Author: Orgines et Fractionnement des Peul du Haut-Senegal, 1987. Mem. Publications Enfartines Fayida, Assn. Sauvegarde Patr Culture Comité National ICOMOS, (pres.). Musulmane. Home: Daoudabougou comite 3, Bamako Mali 159 Office: Inst of Sci Humaines, Ave Kassé, Bamako Mali 159

DIALLO, FALILOU, research association administrator; b. Dakar, Senegal, June 16, 1955; s. Seydou and Aminata (Ly) D. B of History, U. Dakar, 1979; M of History, diploma in polit. sci., U. Paris Sorbonne, 1981, D of History, 1983. Prof. human scis. and arts Coll. Jean-Jaures ville pinte, France, 1981-82; prof. Coll. Marie Curie Les Lilas, France, 1981-82, Coll. Evariste Gallois Epinay, Seine, France, 1982-83, Coll. Joliot Curie Stains, France, 1983-85; coordinator regional research and documentation Ctr. for Cultural Devel., African Cultural Inst., Dakar, 1985—; chmn. African Research Assn. Cauri, Paris, 1983-84; cons. UNESCO-Breda, Senegal, 1986. Editor: ICA Info. Mag., 1986, Mag. African Coutural Inst., 1987. Mem. Assn. Senegalaise Professeur d'histoire et géographie, Revue Panafricaine Recherches Scientifiques et d'Etudes Politiques, Maison de l'Europe Paris, Assn. Francaise Droit et Culture. Home: PO Box 5263 Dakar Fan N, Dakar Senegal Office: African Cultural Inst, 13 Ave Pdt Bourguiba PO Box 1, Dakar Senegal

DIAMANDOPOULOS, PETER, philosopher, educator; b. Irakleion, Crete, Greece, Sept. 1, 1928; came to U.S., 1948, naturalized, 1964; s. Theodore George and Rita (Mouzenides) D.; m. Maria Blackstock, 1980; children: Theodore, Cybele, Ariadne, Patricia. Diploma with honors, Athens Coll., 1947; A.B. cum laude, Harvard U., 1951; M.A., Harvard, 1956, Ph.D., 1957. Instr. philosophy Bates Coll., 1958; instr., then asst. prof. philosophy U. Md., 1958-62; mem. faculty Brandeis U., 1962-77, prof. philosophy, 1964-77, dean faculty, 1965-71, chmn. dept. philosophy and history of ideas, 1972-76, faculty mem. bd. trustees, 1974-77; pres. Calif. State U.-Sonoma, Rohnert Park, Calif., 1977-83; pres. emeritus Calif. State U.-Sonoma, 1983—; Univ. Trustees' prof. Calif. State U., San Francisco, 1983-85; pres., trustee Adelphi U., Garden City, N.Y., 1985—; dir. internat. studies Adlai Stevenson Inst., Chgo., 1969-74; cons. history of sci. Smithsonian Instn., 1959-62; bd. trusteesAdelphi Acad., Athens Coll., 1987—. Chmn., bd. advisers U.S. Command and Gen. Staff Coll., 1987; mem. U.S. Congl. Adv. Bd. Mem. Am. Philol. Assn., Am. Philos. Assn., Mind Assn., Aristotelian Soc., Hellenic Soc., AAAS, Assn. Am. Colls., Council for Greek Am. Affairs (dir. 1986—), Assn. Governing Bds. Univs. and Colls., N.Y. Acad. Scis., Newcomem Soc. N.Am. Clubs: Harvard (Boston); Commonwealth (San Francisco); University, The Links, The Union League (N.Y.C.). Home: 55 Brompton Rd Garden City NY 11530 Office: Adelphi U Presdl Suite Levermore 100 Garden City NY 11530

DIAMOND, DAVID LEO, composer; b. Rochester, N.Y., July 9, 1915; s. Osias and Anna (Schildhaus) D. Student, Cleve. Inst. Music, 1927-29, Eastman Sch. Music, U. Rochester, 1930-34, Am. Conservatory, Fontainebleau, France, summers 1937, 38, New Music and Dalcroze Inst., N.Y. C., 1934-36; pvt. studies with Roger Sessions, N.Y.C.; pvt. studies with Nadia Boulanger, Paris. Tchr. composition Met. Music Sch., N.Y.C., 1950; lectr. on Am. music Seminar in Am. Studies Schloss Leopoldskron, Salzburg, Austria, 1949; Fulbright prof. U. Rome, 1951-52; Slee prof. music U. Buffalo, 1961, 63; prof., chmn. dept. composition Manhattan Sch. Music, N.Y.C., 1965-67; composer-in-residence Am. Acad. in Rome, 1971-72, Juilliard Sch. Music, 1973—; vis. prof., U. Colo., Boulder, 1970, U. Denver, 1983, other univs. Contbr. to Jour. Modern Music, Music Quar., N.Y. Herald Tribune; compositions include 9 symphonies, concertos for violin, cello, piano and flute, 11 string quartets, chamber music, 52 preludes and fugues for the piano, sonatas, choral music and songs, solo symphony for organ, scores for motion pictures, and other forms of instrumental music; composer music for Columbia albums Fourth String Quartet, Romeo and Juliet, 4th Symphony (performed by Bernstein, N.Y. Philharm. Orch.); composer, condr.: original score for Margaret Webster prodn. of The Tempest, 1944-45, incidental music for Cheryl Crawford prodn. of Tennessee Williams' The Rose Tattoo, 1951, music for This Sacred Ground (setting of Lincoln's Gettysburg Address), 1962; composer (ballets) Tom (e.e. cummings), 1936, The Dream of Audubon (Glenway Wescott), 1941; commd. works include: (opera) The Noblest Game, Nat. Opera Inst., 1975, Secular Cantata (James Agee poems), N.Y. State Arts Council, A Song for Hope (Elie Wiesel), Second Sonata for Violin and Piano, Library of Congress McKim Fund, Second Sonata for Cello and Piano, Concerto for Flute and Orch., Sonata for Flute and Piano (for Jean-Pierre Rampal); works performed by major orchs. and other well known music orgns., throughout U.S. and abroad. Recipient numerous major awards and prizes, 1935—, including: Prix de Rome; Paderewski award, Juilliard Pub. award, Stravinsky award ASCAP, Naumberg Rec. award for Nonet and String Quartet No. 9, William Schuman Lifetime Achievement award 1986; NEA grantee, Rockefeller Found. grantee, 1983; Guggenheim fellow, 1938, 42, 58; Elfrida Whiteman scholarship, 1935. Mem. Am. Acad., Nat. Inst. Arts and Letters. Address: 249 Edgerton St Rochester NY 14607

DIAMOND, HARVEY JEROME, machinery manufacturing company executive; b. Charlotte, N.C., Dec. 7, 1928; s. Harry B. and Jeanette (Davis) D.; m. Betty L. Ball, May 22, 1953; children: Michael, Beth, David, Abby. BS, U. N.C., 1952. Sales mgr. Dixie Neon Supply House, Charlotte, 1950-61; pres., gen. mgr. Plasti-Vac, Inc., Charlotte, 1961—; pres., gen. mgr. Diamond Supply, Inc., 1971-84, chmn. bd. dirs., 1984—; pres. Plastic Prodn., Inc., 1973—, PVI Internat. Corp., 1980—; mem. dist. export council Dept. Commerce, 1979—; del. White House Conf. on Small Bus., 1980; bd. dirs. U.S. Free Trade Zone No. 57, 1983. Author: (manual) Introduction to Vacuum Forming, 1976; patentee inverted clamping frame system for vacuum forming machines, process of vacuum forming plastics with vertical oven. Chmn. Mecklenburg Dem. Party, 1974-75, treas., 1972-74; del. Dem. Nat. Conv., 1972; bd. advisors Pfeiffer Coll., Misenheimer, N.C., 1977—; participant White House Conf. on Small Bus., 1978, White House Conf. on anti-inflation initiatives, 1978. Served with U.S. Army, 1952-54. Recipient award for Activity in U.S. Trade Mission to S.Am., Dept. Commerce, 1967, March of Dimes award, 1966, Excellence in Exporting award N.C. Trade Club, 1981. Mem. Soc. Plastic Engrs., Soc. Plastics Industry, So. States Sign Assn. (bd. dirs. 1983—), Nat. Electric Sign Assn. Metrolina World Trade Assn. (v.p. 1982-83), Metrolina World Trade Club (pres. 1983-84), N.C. World Trade Assn. (bd. dirs. 1983-86, gen. chmn. ann. conv. 1984). Jewish. Lodge: Masons. Home: 9400 White Hemlock Ln Matthews NC 28105 Office: PO Box 5543 Charlotte NC 28205

DIAMOND, PHILIP ERNEST, lawyer; b. Los Angeles, Feb. 11, 1925; s. William and Elizabeth (Weizenhaus) D.; m. Dorae Seymour (dec.); children—William, Wendy, Nancy; m. 2d, Jenny White Carson. B.A., UCLA, 1949, M.A., 1950; J.D., U. Calif.-Berkeley, 1953. Bar: Calif. 1953, U.S. Dist. Ct. (no., ea. and cen. dists.) Calif. 1953, U.S. Ct. Appeals (9th cir.) 1953. Law clk. to presiding justice Calif. Dist. Ct. Appeals, 1953-54; assoc. Landels & Weigel, San Francisco, 1954-60; ptnr. Landels Weigel & Ripley, San Francisco, 1960-62; sr. ptnr. Landels, Ripley & Diamond, San Francisco, 1962—; bd. dirs. Pierre Deux West, Berkley Ballet Theatre. Pres. Contra Costa Sch. Bd. Assn., 1966-68. Served with USN, 1943-46. Mem. ABA, Calif. State Bar Assn., San Francisco Bar Assn., Phi Beta Kappa. Democrat. Clubs: Commonwealth, Merchants and Exchange. Office: 450 Pacific Ave San Francisco CA 94133

DIAMONDSTONE, LAWRENCE, paper company executive; b. N.Y.C., Mar. 27, 1928; s. Harry A. and Sally (Margulies) D.; B.S., U. Ill., 1950; m. Helen O'Connor, Dec. 8, 1984; 1 child, Cynthia Ann. Founder, pres., chief exec., chmn. bd., officer Newbrook Paper Div., N.Y.C., 1958—, Cottonwood Converting Div., Memphis, 1971—, Garden State Converters Div., Bayonne, N.J., 1973—, Triangle Mktg. Corp., N.Y.C., 1975—. Home: 2 Beekman Pl New York NY 10022 Office: 32 Bleecker St New York NY 10012

DIANA, PRINCESS, Her Royal Highness the Princess of Wales; b. July 1, 1961; d. Earl of Spencer and the hon. Mrs. Shand-Kydd (formerly Lord and Lady Althorp); student Riddlesworth Hall, Norfolk, Eng., W. Heath Sch., nr. Sevenoaks, Kent, Eng., Chateau D'Oex, Switzerland; m. Charles, Prince of Wales, July 29, 1981; children: William Arthur Philip Louis (Prince William of Wales), Henry Charles Albert David. Formerly tchr. kindergarten, London. Office: Buckingham Palace, London SW1 England *

DIANA, JOHN NICHOLAS, physiologist; b. Lake Placid, N.Y., Dec. 19, 1930; s. Alphonse Walton and Dolores (Mirto) D.; m. Anita Louise Harris, May 8, 1966; children: Gina Sue, Lisa Ann, John Nicholas. B.A., Norwich U., 1952; Ph.D., U. Louisville, 1965. Asst. prof. physiology Mich. State U. Med. Sch., 1966-68; asso. prof., then prof. U. Iowa Med. Sch., 1969-78; prof. physiology, chmn. dept. La. State U. Med. Center, Shreveport, 1978-85; dir. cardiovascular research ctr. U. Ky., 1985-87, assoc. dean research and basic sci., 1987-88; dir. T&H Research Inst., 1988—; cons. Nat. Inst. Neurol. Diseases and Stroke, 1973-75, Nat. Heart, Lung and Blood Inst., 1974—, mem. cardiovascular and renal study sect., 1980-85; research com. Iowa Heart Assn., 1974-77, bd. dirs., 1977-79; mem. cardiovascular study sect. Am. Heart Assn., 1981-84. Author papers, abstracts in field. Served with AUS, 1952-54; Served with USAR, 1961-62. NIH postdoctoral fellow, 1965-67. Mem. Am. Fedn. Clin. Research, Am. Physiol. Soc. (editorial bd. jour. 1974-78), Microcirculation Soc. (pres. 1977-78, editorial bd. jour. 1979-85), Am. Heart Assn. (fellow council circulation), N.Y. Acad. Scis., La. Heart Assn. (dir. 1979-81, research com. 1978-82), Sigma Xi. Democrat. Home: 3656 Eleuthera Ct Lexington KY 40509 Office: U Ky Dean's Office Coll Medicine 900 Rose St Room MN140D Lexington KY 40546

DIANZANI, MARIO UMBERTO, pathology educator; b. Grosseto, Italy, June 13, 1925; s. Edgardo and Irma (Bocelli) D.; m. Maria Assunta Mor, Aug. 18, 1956; children: Irma, Chiara, Umberto, Paola. Degree in medicine, U. Siena, Italy, 1948, degree in pharmacy, 1950; doctor hon., Brunel U., London, 1978. Asst. in gen. pathology U. Siena, 1948-50, prof. gen. pathology, 1964-65; asst. in gen. pathology U. Genoa, Italy, 1950-58; prof. gen. pathology U. Cagliari, Italy, 1958-64, U. Turin, Italy, 1965—; rector magnificus U. Turin, 1984. Author textbook of gen. pathology, 1970. Recipient Premio Feltrinelli, Accademia del Lincei, Rome, 1979. Roman Catholic. Home: Corso D'azeglio 118, 10126 Torino Italy Office: U Torino, Via PO 17, 10100 Torino Italy

DIAZ, A. MICHEL, administrator and researcher in computer and control science; b. Carcassonne, France, July 27, 1945; s. Melchor and Pilar (Villa) D.; Licences Physique I and II, Toulouse U., 1966; Dr.Sci., U. Paul Sabatier, 1974; m. Monique Philipot, Apr. 10, 1969; children—Nicolas, Sandrine. Mem. LAAS du CNRS, 1968—; asst. prof. Inst. Tech., Toulouse U., 1969-70; researcher at CNRS, French Nat. Center for Sci. Research, Toulouse, France, 1970—, head team computer sci., 1975—; head European Esprit-Software Engring. Distributed Systems project, 1984-88; lectr. in field; mem. internat. sci. coms. Mem. IEEE, Assn. Francaise pour la Cybernetique Economique et Technique, Internat. Fedn. Info. Processing, Internat. Standardization Orgn., Assn. Francaise pour la Normalisation. Author: Introd al Diseno Assistido por Ordenador de Circuitos Electronicos, 1977; editor: Protocol Specification, Testing and Verification V, North Holland, 1986; contbr. articles to profl. jours. and congresses. Office: LAAS du CNRS, 7 Av Cl Roche, Toulouse France

DIAZ, JOSE IGNACIO, economist; b. San Fernando, Apure, Venezuela, Feb. 17, 1953; s. Jose Ignacio and Temilda (Retali) D.; m. Dionne Malpica; 1 child, Jose Ignacio. BS, Liceo M.J. Sanabria, Valencia, Carabobo, 1969; postgrad., U. De Carabobo, 1976, MBA, 1984; PhD, Columbia Pacific U., San Rafael, Calif., 1985. Comptroller C.A. Facegra, Valencia, Carabobo, Venezuela, 1976-77, Disnaca, Valencia, Carabobo, Venezuela, 1976—; pres. Siproinca, Valencia, Carabobo, Venezuela, 1978-80, Polyconomics C.A., Valencia, Carabobo, Venezuela, 1986—, Grupo Consultor Gerencial, Valencia, Carabobo, Venezuela, 1979—; gen. mgr. Venetank, Valencia, Carabobo, Venezuela, 1979-80, Inlobla, Valencia, Carabobo, Venezuela, 1980—; assoc. prof. sch. econs. U. De Carabobo, Valencia, Carabobo, Venezuela, 1979—, prof. grad. sch. bus., 1985—; bd. dirs. Lobsa; cons. in field. Author: Sistemag De Informacion, 1980, Estudios De Mercado, 1985, Pronosticos Y Proyecciones, 1986. Mem. Registro Ministerio De Fomento, Assn. Profs., Assn. Coll. Economists, Assn. Execs., Am. Mgmt. Assn. Roman Catholic. Club: Hacienda Country. Home: PO Box 382, Valencia Carabobo Venezuela Office: Grupo Consultor Gerencial, Avenida Bolivar E/ S El Vinedo, Valencia Carabobo Venezuela

DIAZ, RHODORA DAMASO, pediatrician, educator; b. Iloilo City, Iloilo, Philippines, Sept. 23, 1947; d. Benjamin Maderazo and Pacita (Menol) Damaso; m. Crispin Ylanan Diaz; children: Crispin Emmanuel, Larisa Julia, Daniel Benjamin. BS, U. Philippines, Iloilo City, 1966; MD, U. Philippines, Manila, 1971. Resident in pediatrics Newark Beth Israel Med. Ctr., 1972-74, chief resident in pediatrics, fellow in neonatology, 1974-75, fellow in infectious diseases, 1975-76; instr. pediatrics Cebu Inst. Medicine, Cebu City, Philippines, 1976-79, assoc. prof., 1980-87; asst. prof. pediatrics Cebu Dr.'s Coll. of Medicine, Cebu City, 1979—; cons. Cebu Velez Gen. Hosp., 1976-80, Cebu Dr.'s Hosp., Cebu City, 1976—, Chong Hua Hosp., 1976—, Perpetual Secour Hosp., 1976—. Contbr. articles to profl. jours. Mem. Philippine Pediatric Soc. (diplomate, pres. Cebu chpt. 1985-87). Office: M Diaz Bldg, Don Jose Avila St Room 202, Cebu City Cebu, Philippines

DIAZ DE LA VEGA, VICTOR MANUEL, cardiologist; b. Guamuchil, Sinaloa, Mex., Mar. 22, 1951; s. Alfredo Diaz Angulo and Josefina (De La Vega Cota) De Angulo; m. Ruth Gurria Treviño, Dec. 6, 1986; 1 child, Victor. MD, Univ. Nacional Autonoma De Mexico, 1974. Resident internal medicine San Barnabas Med. Ctr., Livingston, N.J., 1975-76, Hosp. L. Cardenas Issste, Chihuahua, Mex., 1976-77; resident cardiology Inst. Nat. De Cardiologia, Mex. City, 1977-81; chief resident cardiology Inst. Nat. De Cardiologia, 1981-82; fellow research Hammersmith Hosp. Royal Post Grad. Sch. London, 1982-83; med. dir. Gabinete De Cardiologia De Sinaloa (Mex.), 1983—; pres. Sociedad De Cardiologia Del Noroeste, Culiacan, Sinaloa, 1986-88. Mem. Sociedad Mex. De Cardiologia, Sibic Internat., Soc. Española De Cardiologia, Soc. De Cardiologia Del Noroeste De Mexico (pres. 1986-88). Clubs: Raquet (Culiacan, Sinaloa), Orleans (Guamuchil, Sinaloa) (sec. 1983—). Home: Blvd Universitarios #2517, Culiacan Mexico Office: Gabinete En Cardiologia De Sin, Edif La Lonja #80, Culiacan Mexico

DIAZ-ORELLANA, HECTOR, entrepreneur, accountant, tax consultant; b. San Pedro Sula, Honduras, May 30, 1936; s. Adan Diaz and Ricarda Orellana; m. Alba Engracia Ramirez, May 14, 1964 (div. July 1982); children: Hector Gustavo, Luis Fernando, Wendy Denisse, Sandy Cecelia, Eduardo Rafael; m. Nora Edith Lopez, Feb. 15, 1986; children: David Antonio, Adán Alejandro. BSBA, Cen. Mo. State U., Warrensburg, 1960. CPA, Honduras, Guatemala, Eng. Acct. Price Waterhouse, Los Angeles, 1960-61; 1st asst. Price Waterhouse, Mex. City, 1962; sr. acct. Price Waterhouse, Guatemala City, 1962-65; mgr., ptnr. Price Waterhouse, San Pedro Sula, 1965—; pres., chief exec. officer Parches y Accesorios, S.A.; Agencia de Viajes Brenda, S.A.; Honduras Magic Tours, S.A.; Cen. Impresora, S.A., Nippon HD, S.A., San Pedro Sula, 1980—. Author: High Dynamic Planning, 1984. Mem. No. Honduran-Am. C. of C. (dir. 1987-88), Cómoro de Commercio Industria de Cortes (dir., econ. advisor 1980-88). Club: Lima Golf (La Lima, Honduras). Lodge: Rotary (treas. San Pedro Sula chpt. 1974-77). Office: Parches y Accesorios SA, 3a Ave SO #93, San Pedro Sula Honduras

DÍAZ SEIJAS, PEDRO VICENTE, language professional, educator; b. Valle de la Guárico, Llanos, Venezuela, Dec. 24, 1921; s. Guillermo Diaz Sanes and Juana Seijas de Diaz; m. Gladys Campos de Diaz, July 16, 1958; children: Euridice, Pedro, Manuel, Aimara. Student, Pedagógico Caracas, Venezuela, U Cent., Caracas. Titular prof. Inst. Santos Michelina, Caracas, 1946-58; dir. Inst. Univ. Pedagógico, Barquisimeto, Venezuela, 1959; nat. supr. Ministry of Edn., Caracas, 1960-63; v.p. Inst. Nat. Culture, Caracas, 1964-66; ministro consejero Embajada de Venezuela en Mex., 1967; titular prof. Inst. Pedagógico de Caracas, 1968-77; cultural dir. U. Simón Rodriguez, Caracas, 1978-83; pres. Venezuelan Acad. Lang., Caracas, 1984—. Author: Historia y Antologia de la Literatura Venezolana, La Novela y el Cuento Venezuela. Council mem. Ministry Culture, Caracas, 1983; assessor Nat. Council Edn., Caracas, 1986; pres. cultural commn. Dem. Action, 1983; senator Nat. Congress, 1983. Decorated 27 de Junio medal, Ministry Edn.; Andres Bello 1st, 2d and 3d class, Gov. Venezuela. Mem. Real Acad. Española, Acad. Lengua de Honduras, PEN Club Internat., Acad. Arts Puerto Rico. Democrat. Roman Catholic. Office: Acad Venezolana De La Lengua, Bolsa a San Francisco, Caracas 1010, Venezuela Home: Av del Centro Quinta "Gladys", Urb Miranda, Caracas 1010, Venezuela

DIBELA, SIR KINGSFORD, governor general of Papua New Guinea; b. Mar. 16, 1932; s. Norman Dibela and Edna Dalauna; m. Winifred Tomolarina, 1952; 6 children. Student St. Paul's Primary Sch., Dogura. Primary sch. tchr. and tchr., 1949-63; pres. Weraura Local Govt. Council, 1963-77; mem. Parliament, Papua New Guinea, 1975-82; speaker of Nat. Parliament, 1977-80; gov. gen. of Papua New Guinea, 1983—. Avocations: golf; cricket.

DI BERNARDO, GIULIANO, sociologist, philosopher; b. Penne, Abruzzo, Italy, Mar. 1, 1939; s. Vincenzo and Angela (Leopardi) Di B.; m. Anna Maria Manci, Dec. 7, 1968; children: Jacopo, Silvia Maria. Diploma in Sociology, U. Trento, Italy, 1967. Lectr. philosophy U. Trento, Italy, 1966-70, assoc. prof. philosophy sci., 1971-78, chair dept., 1979—, head dept., 1980-84. Mem. Acad. Internat. de Philosophie des Scis., Italian Soc. Logic and Philosophy of Scis., Italian Soc. of Philosophy. Lodges: Zamboni De Rolandis; Masons (33 degree). Home: Localita Mesiano di Povo, 38050 Trento Italy Office: Univ of Trento, Via Verdi 26, 38100 Trento Italy

DIBIAGGIO, JOHN A., university administrator; b. San Antonio, Sept. 11, 1932; s. Ciro and Acidalia DiBiaggio; m. Carolyn Mary Enright, June 29, 1957; children: David John, Dana Elizabeth, Deirdre Joan. AB, Eastern Mich. U., 1954, D of Edn. (hon.), 1985; DDS, U. Detroit, 1958, LHD (hon.), 1985; MA, U. Mich., 1967; DSci. (hon.), Fairleigh Dickinson U., 1981; LLD (hon.), Sacred Heart U., Bridgeport, Conn., 1984, U. Md., 1985; DHL (hon.), U. New Eng., 1987. Gen. practice dentistry New Baltimore, Mich., 1958-65; asst. prof., asst. to dean, dept. chmn. sch. dentistry U. Detroit, 1965-67; asst. dean student affairs U. Ky., Lexington, 1967-70; prof., dean sch. dentistry Va. Commonwealth U., Richmond, 1970-76; v.p. for health affairs, exec. dir. health ctr. U. Conn., Farmington, 1976-79; pres. U. Conn., Storrs, 1979-85, Mich. State U., East Lansing, 1985—; mem. Gov.'s Comn. on Jobs and Econ. Devel., 1985—, Mich. Council of State Coll. Pres., 1985—; mem. project for pub. and community services Edn. Commn. of States, 1985—; mem. Nat. Bd. Examiners, 1987; bd. dirs. Mich. Biotech. Inst., 1985—, Mich. High Tech. Task Force, 1985—, Mich. Materials and Processing Inst., 1985—, Am. Council on Edn., 1987—; mem. Mich. China Council, 1985—; mem. MUCIA Council of Pres., 1987-88. Author: (with others) Applied Practice Management: A Strategy for Stress Control, 1979; edit. bd. Michigan Woman, 1987—; contbr. articles to profl. jours. Chmn. adv. com. dental scholars R.W. Johnson Found; mem. Pres. Com. for Argonne Nat. Lab. 6, 1986—; trustee U. Detroit, 1979-86; bd. overseers Sch. Dentistry, U. Pa., 1979-86. Decorated Order of Merit, Italy; recipient Leadership award Sacred Heart U., Disting. Profl. of Yr. award Mich. Assn. Profls., 1985, Disting. Alumni award Eastern Mich. U., 1986, Pierre Fauchard Dental award, 1987; named Man of Yr., City of Detroit, 1985. Fellow Am. Coll. Dentists, Internat. Coll. Dentists; mem. ADA (cons. jour.), Mich. Dental Assn., Am. Assn. Dental Schs., Internat. Assn. Dental Research, Am. Pub. Health Assn., Am. Assn. Higher Edn., Assn. Acad. Health Ctrs., Nat. Assn. State Univs. and Land Grant Colls. (chmn. 1986-87), Phi Kappa Phi, Omicron Kappa Upsilon, Beta Gamma Sigma, Alpha Omega, Alpha Sigma Chi, Alpha Lambda Delta. Home: 1 Abbott Rd East Lansing MI 48824 Office: Mich State U 450 Administration Bldg East Lansing MI 48824

DICARLO, LOUIS MICHAEL, educator; b. N.Y.C., Jan. 17, 1903; s. Amedeo and Theresa (Glacomo) DiC.; m. Marian E. Warcup, Sept. 17, 1947. B.A., Union Coll., 1932; certificate of proficiency, Clarke Sch. for Deaf, 1936; M.S., Mass. State U., 1937; Ed.D., Columbia, 1948. With N.Y. State Police, 1923-26; social worker 1932-35; tchr. pub. schs. New Rochelle, N.Y., 1938-47; faculty Ind. U., 1942; faculty dept. audiology and speech pathology Syracuse U., 1947-62, prof., 1952-68, chmn. dept., 1952-62; clin. prof. otolaryngology Upstate Med. Sch., Syracuse, 1959-86; vis. prof. audio and speech pathology U. Hawaii, 1964-65; vis. prof. Ithaca Coll., 1968-69, acting dean, 1971-73; vis. prof. U. Alaska, 1963, U. Calif.-Long Beach, 1964; chief audiology and speech pathology VA Hosp. Syracuse, 1966-84, N.Y. State Crippled Children's Assn., Sunnyview Orthopaedic and Rehab. Hosp., Schenectady; with Gordon D. Hoople Hearing and Speech Center; dir. speech pathology Syracuse Rehab. Center; cons. Pineland Hosp. and Tng. Center, Pownal, Maine. Author: Speech after Laryngectomy, 1958, Our Educational Dilemma: The Deaf, 1964; contbr. articles profl. jours., fiction to mags. Bd. dirs. United Cerebral Palsy Assn. of Syracuse; aux. bd. Graham Alexander Assn. Served with U.S. Army, 1919-23; with AUS, 1942-45. Recipient Archibold high scholarship prize, Warner prize, meritorious award VA, 1981; named spl. edn. tchr. of year N.Y. State Dept. Spl. Edn., 1973. Fellow Am. Speech, Lang. Hearing Assn. (honors 1981); mem. Am., N.Y. State, Syracuse psychol. assns., Alexander Graham Bell Assn. for Deaf, Speech Assn. Eastern States, Acoustical Soc. Am., Nat. Council Psychol. Aspects of Disability, Am. Assn. Mental Deficiency, Council Exceptional Children (Hammond prof. 1960), N.Y. State Speech and Hearing Assn. (pres. 1962-63, honors 1971, Silver Anniversary award 1984), Acad. Rehab. Audiology (life). Home: 9413 Rt 46 Western NY 13486

DICELLO, JOHN FRANCIS, JR., physicist, educator; b. Bradford, Pa., Dec. 18, 1938; s. John Francis and Nicolina Camille (Costello) D.; m. Shirley Ann Rodgers, Aug. 25, 1962; children—John Francis III, Paul T. B.S., St. Bonaventure U., 1960; M.S., U. Pitts., 1962; Ph.D., Tex. A&M U., 1968. Instr. St. Bonaventure U., 1962-63; Univ. grad. fellow Tex. A&M U., College Station, 1963-65; AEC-Assoc. Western Univs. grad. fellow Los Alamos Nat. Lab., 1965-67, staff scientist, 1973-84; research assoc., research scientist Columbia U., N.Y.C., 1967-73; faculty U. N.Mex., Los Alamos, 1980-82; prof. physics Clarkson U., Potsdam, N.Y., 1982—. Contbr. articles to profl. jours. Bd. dirs. N.Mex. div. Am. Cancer Soc., 1978-82. Recipient Young Scientist travel award Am. Assn. Physicists in Medicine, 1972. Mem. Am. Assn. Physicists in Medicine, IEEE (div. electromagnetics and radiation), Radiation Research Soc., Am. Phys. Soc. (div. biology and accelerator physics), Am. Assn. Univ. Profs., Sigma Xi, Sigma Pi Sigma. Roman Catholic. Research in field of physics, dosimetry, microdosimetry, radiation biology, hyperthermia, cancer research, integrated circuits, accelerator and nuclear physics; cons. with Fermilab and Loma Linda U. on first clinically dedicated proton accelerator designed for cancer therapy. Office: Clarkson Univ Dept Physics Potsdam NY 13676

DICK, ALBERT BLAKE, III, former manufacturing company executive, corporate director; b. Chgo., Mar. 10, 1918; s. Albert Blake and Helen (Aldrich) D.; m. Elisabeth York, Sept. 14, 1940; children: Albert Blake IV, John Howard, Frederick Aldrich; m. Susan Drake Bent, Aug. 20, 1960. Student, Yale U., 1938-39. With A.B. Dick Co., 1939-82, holding various positions in purchasing, mfg., sales, and controllers divs., dir., 1946-82, treas., 1947-60, pres., 1947-61, chmn., 1961-82; dir. Northern Trust Bank-Lake Forest (Ill.). Life trustee Ill. Inst. Tech.; trustee mem. exec. bd. Rush-Presbyn.-St. Luke's Med. Center; dir. Lake Forest Hosp. Served with USN, 1942-45. Clubs: Economic, Chicago, Attic, Commercial, Metropolitan (Chgo.); Onwentsia (Lake Forest); Cotton Bay (Eleuthera, Bahamas); Old Elm (Ft. Sheridan, Ill.); Birnam Wood Golf, The Valley (Santa Barbara, Calif.), The Valley Montecito. Home: 1550 N Green Bay Rd Lake Forest IL 60045 Office: AB Dick Co Box 312 249 Market Sq Lake Forest IL 60045

DICK, NEIL ALAN, architectural engineer; b. Cleve., June 15, 1941; s. Harvey L. and Rose (Flom) D.; B.Arch., Ohio State U., 1965; M.B., Cleve. State U., 1966; m. Bonnie M. Natarus, Sept. 3, 1967; 1 dau., Rory D. Exec. v.p. J.R. Hyde & Assos., Pitts., 1967-70; dir. tech. and market devel. Stirling Homex Corp., Avon, N.Y., 1970-72; sr. housing coordinator Nat. Housing Corp., Cleve., 1972-74; fin. and estate analyst Conn. Gen. Corp., Cleve., 1974-76; sr. v.p., dir. mktg. Cannon Design Inc., Grand Island, N.Y., 1976-82, also dir.; exec. v.p. Greiner, Inc. (formerly Daverman, Inc.), subs. Greiner Engring. Inc., Grand Rapids, Mich., 1983-88, Foty & Van Dyke, div. G.M., Green Bay, Wis., 1988—; bd. dirs. West Mich. Telecommunications Found., AIDS Found. Kent County; mem. bd. trustees Kendall Coll. Art & Design, Grand Rapids Art Mus., Grand Rapids C. of C. Found. (bd. dirs.), treas., Amherst (N.Y.) Democratic Com.; zone chmn., county fin. chmn., mem. exec. com. Erie County Dem. Com.; mem. Mich. Dem. State Com.; treas. Mich. 5th Congl. Dist. Dem. Com. Recipient Service award Erie County Dem. Com., 1979, Mem. Soc. Mktg. Profl. Services (regional coordinator), Buffalo Area C. of C., Am. Hosp. Assn., Nat. Trust Hist. Preservation, Ohio State U. Alumni Assn., Mich. C. of C., Buffalo Mus. Sci., Albright Knox Art Gallery, Alpha Rho Chi. Jewish. Clubs: Economic, Peninsular, Cascade Hills. Lodge: Rotary (Grand Rapids). Home: c/o Foty & Van Dyke 2737 S Ridge Rd Green Bay WI 54307-9012 Office: 82 Iona Ave NW Grand Rapids MI 49503

DICKENS, DORIS LEE, psychiatrist; b. Roxboro, N.C., Oct. 12; d. Lee Edward and Delma Ernestine (Hester) Dickens; B.S. magna cum laude, Va. Union U., 1960; M.D., Howard U., 1966; m. Austin LeCount Fickling, Oct. 15, 1975. Intern, St. Elizabeth's Hosp., Washington, 1966-67, resident, 1967-70; staff psychiatrist, dir. Mental Health Program for Deaf, St. Elizabeth's Hosp., Washington, 1970-87. Bd. dirs. Nat. Health Care Found. for Deaf; med. officer Region 4 Community Mental Health Ctr., Washington, Commn. on Mental Health, 1987—. Recipient Dorothea Lynde Dix award, 1980; diplomate Nat. Bd. Med. Examiners. Mem. Am. Psychiat. Assn. (achievement awards bd. 1988—), Washington Psychiat. Soc., Alpha Kappa Mu, Beta Kappa Chi. Author: How and When Psychiatry Can Help You, 1972; You and Your Doctor; contbg. author: Hearing and Hearing Impairment, 1979; contbg. author Counseling Deaf People, Research and Practice. Home: 12308 Surrey Circle Tantallon MD 20022

DICKENS, MICHAEL HUGH, physicist, consulting company executive; b. Clevedon, Somerset, Eng., July 11, 1943; s. Reginald William and Marjorie Eileen (Williams) D.; m. Jill Randall, Aug. 5, 1967; children: Charlotte Elise, Julius Christian. BSc, London U., 1965; MS, Northeastern U., 1970; PhD in Physics, MIT, 1974; diploma, Inst. Mktg., Cookham, Eng., 1986. Mem. research and devices staff Elec. Research Assocs., Leatherhead, Eng., 1965-67, Microwave Assocs. Inc., Burlington, Mass., 1967-70; research fellow MIT, Cambridge, 1970-74; postdoctoral fellow Clarendon Labs, Oxford (Eng.) U., 1974-79; applications engr., exec. Cryogenic Cons. Ltd., London, 1979-83, exec. dir., 1983—. Contbr. articles to profl. jours. Mem. Inst. Physics, Inst. Mktg. Home: 3 Toonagh, Maidens Green, Winkfield, Windsor England Office: Cryogenic Cons Ltd, Metrostore Bldg, 231 The Vale, London W37Q5, England

DICKERMAN, ALLEN BRIGGS, business executive; b. Mt. Dora, Fla., Oct. 22, 1914; s. M. Marcellus and Emma (Dickerman) Javens; A.B., Hamilton Coll., 1936; M.B.A., Harvard U., 1941; Ph.D., Syracuse U., 1956; m. Stella M. Brower, May 15, 1943; children—Elizabeth (Mrs. Peter L. Thompson), Joanna (Mrs. Owen Parsons), Laura; m. Luise E. Peake, July 23, 1985. Instr., Harvard Bus. Sch., 1941-42; instr. U. Rochester, 1946-49; asso. prof. bus. adminstrn. Syracuse U., 1949-74, Internat. Bus. Research fellow, 1971, dir. internat. mgmt. devel. dept., 1960-74; prof. internat. bus., dir. Internat. Devel., Coll. Bus. Adminstrn., U. S.C., Columbia, 1974-85; pres. Carolina Internat. Devel. Assocs., Inc., Columbia, 1985—; advisor to univs., Colombia, Brazil, Philippines, Costa Rica, Venezuela, Indonesia. Mem. S.C. Dist. Export Council, 1976-81. Served with USNR, 1942-46. Mem. Acad. Internat. Bus., Delta Upsilon, Greater Columbia C. of C. Republican. Episcopalian. Author: Training Japanese Managers, 1974. Home: 4828 Citadel Ave Columbia SC 29206 Office: PO Box 11486 Columbia SC 29211

DICKERSON, E(ARL) TUCKER, finance company executive, lawyer; b. Selmer, Tenn., May 2, 1929; s. Andrew Leroy and Grace Dexter (Chumbler) D.; m. Joyce Collins, July 10, 1954 (div. 1975); children—Jennifer D. Cook, Earl T., Gregory A.; m. Suzanne Frensdorf Sondheim, Oct. 3, 1976. B.A., Lambuth Coll., Jackson, Tenn., 1950; grad. sch. credit and fin. mgmt. Stanford U., 1986; J.D., Vanderbilt U., 1956. Bar: Tenn., 1956. Sole practice, Manchester, Tenn., 1956-61, Memphis, 1962-65; judge gen. sessions Coffee County ct., Manchester, 1961-62; atty. Gen. Innkeeping Acceptance Corp. subs. Holiday Inns, Inc., Memphis, 1965-69, mgr. 1969-77, pres., 1977—; dir. Nat. Comml. Fin. Assn., N.Y.C., 1980-85; dir. gen. innkeeping Acceptance Corp.; dir. GIAC Leasing Corp., Holiday Corp. Credit Union. Alderman City of Manchester, 1960-62. Served to sgt. U.S. Army, 1950-52; Korea. Mem. Memphis and Shelby County Bar Assn., Tenn. Bar Assn. Unitarian. Home: 461 N Mendenhall Memphis TN 38117 Office: 3779 Lamar Ave Memphis TN 38117

DICKERSON, FREDERICK REED, lawyer, educator; b. Chgo., Nov. 11, 1909; s. Fred George and Rena (Reed) D.; m. Jane Morrison, June 14, 1939; children: Elizabeth Ann (Mrs. David D. Brown), John Scott, Martha Reed. Grad., Lake Forest Acad., 1927; AB, Williams Coll., 1931; LLB, Harvard U., 1934; LLM (Univ. fellow 1938-39), Columbia U., 1939, JSD, 1950; LLD (hon.), Ind. U., 1986. Bar: Mass. 1934, Ill. 1936, U.S. Supreme Ct. 1943. Assoc. Goodwin, Procter & Hoar, Boston, 1934-35, McNab, Holmes & Long, Chgo., 1936-38; asst. prof. law Washington U., St. Louis, 1939-40, U. Pitts., 1940-42; atty. OPA, 1942-47; asst. legis. counsel U.S. Ho. of Reps., 1947-49, Joint Army-Air Force Statutory Revision Group; chmn. com. on codification, dep. asst. gen. counsel U.S. Dept. Def., 1949-58; prof. law Ind. U., 1958-83, prof. emeritus, 1983—, assoc. dean, 1971-75; disting. vis. prof. law So. Ill. U., 1976, 80; pres. F.G. Dickerson Co., Chgo., 1948-82; chmn. commn. on uniform laws State of Ind., 1969-81; mem. Ind. Statute Revision Commn., 1969-70, adv. bd. Ctr. Semiotic Research: Law, Govt., Econs.; cons. Dept. Def., 1958-59, 66, FAA, 1960-65, Dept. Transp., 1967-69, Pres.'s Com. on Consumer Interests, 1967-68, Commn. on Govt. Procurement, 1971-72, Gen. Acctg. Office, 1973-76; lectr. Northwestern U., 1938, Am. U., 1956, 58, Practising Law Inst., 1961, 79, U.K. Govt. Legal Officers' Course, 1972, U.S. CSC, 1971-76, lectr. Center for Adminstrv. Justice, 1975-79. Author: Products Liability and the Food Consumer, 1951, Legislative Drafting, 1954, 2d edit., 1986, Fundamentals of Legal Drafting, 1965, 2d edit., 1986, Interpretation and Application of Statutes, 1975; editor: Legal Problems Affecting Private Swimming Pools, 1961, Product Safety in Household Goods, 1968, Professionalizing Legislative Drafting—The Federal Experience, 1973, Proc. International Seminar and Workshop on the Teaching of Legal Drafting, 1977, Cases and Materials on Legislation, 1978, Materials on Legal Drafting, 1981; mem. editorial bd.: Jurimetrics Jour., 1962-85; bd. advisors: Jour. of Legislation, 1977-85; contbr.: articles to Harper's mag., Esquire, Ency. Americana. Mem. Arlington Civic Symphony, 1950-53; pres. Chevy Chase Citizens Assn., 1955-56, Friends of Music, Ind. U., 1972-73. Recipient Disting. Civilian Service award Dept. Def., 1957, award Assn. Am. Law Schs., 1983; Ford Found. law faculty fellow Harvard U., 1961-62; Am. Assembly fellow, 1968. Mem. Am. Law Inst., Nat. Conf. Commrs. on Uniform State Laws, ABA (chmn. standing com. law and tech. 1968-69, chmn. standing com. legis. drafting 1969-73, chmn. com. on lang. sci. and formal systems 1982-87), Ind. Bar Assn., Monroe County Bar Assn., Pierian Sodality of 1808, Order of Coif, Phi Alpha Delta, Phi Gamma Delta. Methodist. Home: 870 Woodscrest Dr Bloomington IN 47401

DICKERSON, WILLIAM ROY, lawyer; b. Uniontown, Ky., Feb. 15, 1928; s. Benjamin Franklin and Honor Mae (Staples) D. B.A. in Acctg., Calif. State U.; J.D., UCLA, 1948. Bar: Calif. 1959. Dep. atty., ex-officio city prosecutor City of Glendale, Calif., 1959-62; assoc. James Brewer, Los Angeles, 1962-68, LaFollette, Johnson, Schroeter & DeHaas, Los Angeles, 1968-73; sole practice, Los Angeles, 1973—; arbitrator Los Angeles Superior Ct; judge pro tem Los Angeles Mcpl. Ct., Small Claims Ct., Traffic Ct.; lectr. and speaker in field. Bd. dirs. LosFeliz Improvement Assn., Zoning Commn.; co-chmn. Streets and Hwys. Commn. Mem. ABA, Calif. Bar Assn., Los Angeles County Bar Assn., Soc. Calif. Accts., Assn. Trial Lawyers Am., Century City Bar Assn., Fed. Bar Assn., Nat. Soc. Pub. Accts., Assn. So. Calif. Def. Counsel, Am. Film Inst., Internat. Platform Assn. Home and Office: 813 N Doheny Dr Beverly Hills CA 90210

DICKEY, JAMES, poet, novelist, filmmaker, critic; b. Atlanta, Feb. 2, 1923; s. Eugene and Maibelle (Swift) D.; m. Maxine Syerson, Nov. 4, 1948 (dec. 1976); children—Christopher Swift, Kevin Webster; m. Deborah Dodson, Dec. 30, 1976; 1 dau., Bronwen Elaine. Student, Clemson Coll., 1942; B.A., Vanderbilt U., 1949, M.A., 1950. Poet in residence Reed Coll., Portland, Oreg., 1963-64, San Fernando (Calif.) Valley State Coll., 1964, U. Wis., 1966; cons. in poetry Library of Congress, 1966-68; now poet in residence, prof. English U. S.C., Columbia. Author: poems Into The Stone, 1960, Drowning with Others, 1962, Helmets, 1964, Two Poems of the Air, 1964, Buckdancer's Choice, 1965, reissued 1982 (Nat. Book Award of poetry 1966); criticism The Suspect in Poetry, 1964; Poems, 1957-67; poems The Eye-Beaters, 1970; criticism Babel to Byzantium, 1968, reissued 1981; novel Deliverance, 1970, Alnilam, 1987; belles-lettres Self-Interviews, 1970; criticism Sorties, 1971; prose poem Jericho, 1974; poems The Zodiac, 1976; prose poem God's Images, 1977; children's poem Tucky the Hunter, 1978, Bronwen, The Traw and the Shape-Shifter, 1986; poems The Strength of Fields, 1979, Scion, 1980; Deliverance: A Screenplay, 1981; poems Puella, 1982, Falling, May Day Sermon and Other Poems, 1982; author: poems The Early Motion, 1981, False Youth: Four Seasons, 1983; belles-lettres Night Hurdling, 1983; poems The Central Motion, 1983. Served with USAAF and USAF, World War II, Korea. Decorated Air medal.; recipient Union League prize, 1958, Vachel Lindsay award, 1959, Longview award, 1959; Melville Cane award, 1965-66; Prix Medicis (France), 1971, Levinson prize, 1981; Sewanee Rev. fellow, 1954-55; Guggenheim fellow, 1962-63; Nat. Inst. grantee, 1966. Mem. Nat. Inst. Arts and Letters, Am. Acad. Arts and Letters. Address: 4620 Lelias Ct Lake Katherine Columbia SC 29206 Office: Dept of English Univ of SC Columbia SC 29208 *

DICKIE, JAMES ARNOLD, banker; b. Morden, Man., Can., Mar. 15, 1931; s. James Arnold and Jamesina Henderson (Burnett) D.; m. Marie Adeleen Matthews, July 10, 1954; children: Barbara Maureen, Cathleen Lynn, Patrick Glen. Diploma, Harvard U., 1969. Asst. gen. mgr. Toronto Dominion Bank, Ont., 1975-77; v.p., gen. mgr. Toronto Dominion Bank, Ont., Man., 1978-79; sr. v.p. Toronto Dominion Bank, Ont., 1979—; bd. dirs. Ont. Safety League, Toronto, 1981—. Club: Blvd. (Toronto). Office: Toronto-Dominion Bank, King & Bay Sts PO Box 1, TD Ctr, Toronto, ON Canada M5K 1A2

DICKINSON, CHARLES CAMERON, III, theologian, educator; b. Charleston, W.Va., May 13, 1936; s. Charles Cameron and Frances Ann (Saunders) D., Jr.; m. JoAnne Walton. BA cum laude, Dartmouth Coll., 1958; BD, Pitts. Theol. Sem., 1965; PhD, U. Pitts., 1973. Prof. English, Greek and N.T. Ecole de Theologie Kimbanguiste, Zaire, 1972; asst. prof. systematic theology and philosophy Union Theol. Sem., Richmond, Va., 1974-75; asst. prof. religion and philosophy Morris Harvey Coll., Charleston, 1975-79; prof. Am. Coll. of Rome, 1979; research prof. U. Charleston, 1980-81; curatorial assoc. manuscript collections Andover-Harvard Theol. Library, 1981-86; vis. scholar Christ Ch., Oxford (Eng.) U., 1979, Harvard U. Div. Sch., 1980; prof. linguistics and lit. Hebei Tchrs U., Shijiazhuang, Hebei Province, China, 1983-84; dir. Univ. Press Edits./Mountain State Press, Charleston, 1980-83; lectr. Harvard Med. Sch., 1985—. Author articles, revs. in field. Bd. dirs., mem. ednl. council River Sch., Charleston, 1978-81; bd. dirs. Charleston Chamber Music Soc., Kanawha Valley Youth Orch., Charleston Ballet, W.Va. Opera Theater, Kanawha Pastoral Counseling Center. Served with USMC, 1958-61. Entrance fellow Chgo. Theol. Sem., 1962; Chgo. U. Div. Sch. scholar, 1962. Fellow Royal Soc. Arts; mem. Karl Barth Soc. N.Am. (dir.), Am. Acad. Religion, Soc. Bibl. Lit., Am. Theol. Soc., Am. Philos. Assn., Am. Assn. Advancement Humanities, AAAS, W.Va. Philos. Soc., W.Va. Assn. Humanities, Internat. Bonhoeffer Soc., English Speaking Union (U.S., France chpts.), Cercle de l'Union Interalliée, Am. Club Paris. Democrat. Clubs: Edgewood Country (Charleston); Wichita, University (Wichita Falls, Tex.); University (Pitts.); Harvard (Boston, Dallas, France). Lodge: Rotary (chmn. Charleston club student exchange com. 1978-79). Home: 2100 Santa Fe #903 Wichita Falls TX 76309 Office: 1111 City National Bldg Wichita Falls TX 76301

DICKINSON, DAVID WALTER, engineer, educator; b. Troy, N.Y., Mar. 29, 1946; s. Edward Irwin and Charlotte Crescentia (Raschke) D.; m. Christine Ann Donnelly, Nov. 18, 1972; children—Kara Ann, Rebecca Jane, Johanna Lee. B.S. in Materials Engring., Rensselaer Poly. Inst., 1967, Ph.D., 1972. Engring. specialist Olin Corp. Research, New Haven, 1972-74; sr. welding research engr. Republic Steel Research, Independence, Ohio, 1974, group leader welding, 1974-79, supr. cold rolled, 1979-83, sect. chief flat rolled, 1983—; prof. Ohio State U., Columbus, 1984—; dir. research Edison Welding Inst., 1985-87; chmn. dept. welding engring. Ohio State U., 1987—. Author: Welding in the Automotive Industry, 1981. Patentee in field. Mem. adv. bd. Lakeland Community Coll., Mentor, Ohio, 1979-82, Cuyahoga Vocat. Sch., Brecksville, Ohio, 1975-83; mem. acad. bd. Highland Sch. Dist., Hinckley, 1983-84; swim team coach YMCA, Wallingford, Conn., 1972-74; youth advisor Lutheran Ch., Hinckley, 1978-83; synod del. Lutheran Ch. Am., Ohio, 1983; del. Ch. council Lutheran Ch., Hinckley, 1979-84. Recipient Excellence in Oral Presentation award Soc. Automotive Engrs., 1981, Lasting Significance award, 1982; Painter Meml. fellow ASTM, 1970. Mem. Am. Welding Soc. (v.p. 1989—, chmn. Cleve. sect. 1979-80, dir. 1982—; Dist. Meritorious award 1981, McKay-Helm award, 1982), Welding Research Council, Internat. Inst. Welding, Am. Soc. for Metals, Welding Acad. Am. Welding Soc. (chmn. 1980—), Joining Div. Council Am. Soc. Metals, Alpha Sigma Mu (pres. 1970-71). Home: 195 Stonefence Ln Dublin OH 43017 Office: Edison Welding Inst 1100 Kinnear Rd Columbus OH 43212

DICKINSON, FAIRLEIGH STANTON, JR., former manufacturing company executive; b. Rutherford, N.J., Dec. 9, 1919; s. Fairleigh Stanton and Grace Bancroft (Smith) D.; m. Mary Elizabeth Harrington, June 25, 1946; children: Ann Bancroft, Tracy Harrington. BA cum laude, Williams Coll., 1941, LLD, 1973; LHD, Bard Coll., St. Peter's Coll. With Becton, Dickinson & Co., Rutherford, 1941-77; pres. Becton, Dickinson & Co., 1948-73, chmn. bd., 1973-77, chief exec. officer, 1973-74, also dir.; chmn. bd. dirs. Nat. Community Bank, Rutherford. Mem. N.J. Senate, 1968-71; hon. bd. govs. Hackensack (N.J.) Hosp.; bd. dirs. Coast Guard Acad. Found.; trustee Vineyard Open Land Found., Bennington Coll., Edward Williams Coll., Fairleigh Dickinson U. Served to lt. comdr. USCGR, 1941-46. Decorated Order Vasco Nunez de Balboa Panama; recipient Distinguished Pub. Service award USCG; Pres.'s medal Hunter Coll. of CUNY; Hon. fellow Wolfson Coll. Cambridge, Eng.). Fellow Royal Soc. Arts; mem. N.Y. Acad. Scis., N.J. Hist. Soc. (trustee), Phi Beta Kappa, Delta Upsilon. Clubs: University (N.Y.C.), N.Y. Yacht (N.Y.C.), Williams (N.Y.C.); Edgartown (Mass.) Yacht, St. Croix (V.I.) Yacht. Home: 160 Fairmount Rd Ridgewood NJ 07450 Office: Rutherford NJ

DICKINSON, JANE W., club woman; b. Kalamazoo, Sept. 27, 1919; d. Charles Herman and Rachel (Whaler) Wagner; student Hollins Coll., 1938-39; B.A., Duke U., 1941; M.Ed., Goucher Coll., 1965; m. E.F. Sherwood Dickinson, Oct. 23, 1943; children—Diane Jane Gray Clem, Carolyn Dickinson Vane. Exec. sec. Petroleum Industry Com., Balt., 1941-43; exec. sec. Sherwood Feed Mills Inc., Balt., 1943-79. Mem. exec. com. Children's Aid Md., 1960-61; mem. bd. women's aux. Balt. Symphony Orch., 1958-60; dist. chmn. Balt. Cancer Drive, 1958; dist. chmn. Balt. Mental Health Drive, 1957; co-chmn. Balt. United Appeal, 1968; bd. mgrs. Pickersgill Retirement Home. Mem. Alpha Delta Phi. Republican. Episcopalian. Clubs: Three Arts (sec. 1958-60, bd. govs. 1960-64, 67—, pres. 1970-72) (Balt.); Women's (bd. govs. 1960-64, 86-88) (Roland Park); Cliff Dwellers Garden. Home: 1708 Killington Rd Baltimore MD 21204

DICKINSON, JOANNE WALTON, lawyer, writer; b. Windsor, N.C., Nov. 17, 1936; d. John Odell and Lois (King) Walton; m. Charles Cameron Dickinson III; children: Richard E.P. Eaton, John W.T. Eaton, Edward V.H. Eaton. Student Wake Forest Coll., 1961-62; BA, W.Va., U., 1975, JD, 1978. Bar: W.Va. 1978. Actress, W.Va., 1968-78; contbg. editor Victorian Poetry W.Va. U., Morgantown, 1970-75; assoc. Love, Wise, Robinson & Woodroe, Charleston, W.Va., 1978-82; adj. prof. U. Charleston, 1982—; prof. Hebei Tchrs. U., Shijiazhuang, Hebei Province, People's Republic China, 1983-84; lectr. Erikson Ctr./Harvard Med. Sch., 1985-88; lead articles editor W.Va. Law Rev., Morgantown, 1977-78; asst. editor Mountain State Press, Charleston, 1980-83. Contbr. articles to profl. jours. Bd. dirs. Women's Health Ctr., Charleston, 1980-81; bd. dirs. Legal Aid Soc., Charleston, 1980-81. Recipient 1st prize Nathan Burke Competition ASCAP, W.Va., 1977. Fellow Royal Soc. Arts; mem. W.Va. State Bar Assn., ABA, Phi Beta Kappa. Clubs: University (Wichita Falls, Tex.); Harvard (Boston), Athenaeum (Boston). Home: 2100 Santa Fe #903 Wichita Falls TX 76309 Office: 1111 City National Bldg Wichita Falls TX 76301-3309

DICKINSON, PETER, composer; b. Lytham St. Annes, Lancashire, England, Nov. 15, 1934; s. Frank and Muriel (Porter) D.; m. Bridget Jane Tomkinson, July 29, 1964; children: Jasper Edward Peck, Francis Charles Porter. Student, Leys Sch., Cambridge, Eng., 1948-53; MA, Queens' Coll., Cambridge, Eng., 1957; fellow Rotary Found., Juilliard Sch. Music, 1958-59; FRSA (hon.), Royal Soc. Arts, London, 1981. Tchr. free lance, N.Y.C., 1958-61; lectr. Coll. St. Mark and St. John, London, 1962-66, Birmingham U., Eng., 1966-70; tchr. free lance, London, 1970-74; prof. music Keele U., Staffordshire, Eng., 1974-84; composer free lance, London, 1984—; pres. London Concert Choir, 1987—; bd dirs. Trinity Coll. Music, London, 1984—. Composer orchestral, chamber, choral, vocal music; recorder as pianist; contbr. articles to profl. jours. Mem. Assn. Profl. Composers (founder), Royal Soc. Musicians. Office: care Novello and Co, 9 Lower James St, London NW5 1TX, England

DICKINSON, RICHARD HENRY, accountant; b. Long Beach, Calif., June 16, 1944; s. Everett I. and Gertrude T. (Frear) D.; B.S., U. Wis.; B.B.A., Siena Coll., 1973; m. Georgette M. Turner, Jan. 27, 1968; children—Eric, Christine, Brent. Asso. accountant Alexander Varga, C.P.A., Catskill, N.Y., 1973; controller Hocker Power Brake Co., Inc., Evansville, Ind., 1974; dep. controller Watervliet (N.Y.) Arsenal, Dept. Def., 1975-76; auditor Melvin I. Weiskopf, C.P.A., Saratoga Springs, N.Y., 1977; owner, prin. Richard H. Dickinson, C.P.A., Ballston Spa, N.Y. and Saratoga Springs, N.Y., 1978-83; owner Dickinson & Co., C.P.A.s, Saratoga Springs, 1984—; lectr. Siena Coll., Loudonville, N.Y., 1983—. Served with U.S. Army, 1967-70. Decorated Silver Star, Bronze Star; C.P.A. Mem. Am. Inst. C.P.A.s, Nat. Assn. Accts., Am. Inst. Corporate Controllers, Delta Epsilon Sigma, Alpha Kappa Alpha. Republican. Lutheran. Clubs: Masons, Rotary (pres. Ballston Spa chpt. 1979). Home: 4 Ritchie Place Saratoga Springs NY 12866 Office: 439 Maple Ave Saratoga Springs NY 12866

DICKINSON, TERENCE, science author, science journalist, lecturer; b. Toronto, Ont., Can., Nov. 10, 1943; s. Reginald Chapman and Anna Teresa (Duz) D.; m. Susan Harriett Beard, June 24, 1967. Technician, Communications Dept. Ont. Govt., 1964-67; sci. asst. McLaughlin Planetarium, Toronto, 1967-70; asst. dir. Strasenburgh Planetarium, Rochester, N.Y., 1970-73; editor Astronomy mag., Milw., 1973-75, Ont. Sci. Centre, Toronto, 1975-76; free lance sci. journalist, 1976—; weekly newspaper columnist Toronto Star, 1981—; commentator, cons. CBC, Toronto, 1978—; part time teaching master St. Lawrence Coll., Kingston, Ont., 1977—; contbg. editor Maclean's mag., Toronto, 1976-84, Equinox mag., Camden, East Ont., 1984—. Author: Sky Guide, 1977, Nightwatch, 1983, Halley's Comet Returns, 1984, The Universe and Beyond, 1986, Exploring The Night Sky, 1987, Skywatch, 1988; contbr. over 800 articles to newspapers and mags. Columnist Kingston Whig-Standard, 1977-82. Recipient Author's award, Found. for Advancement Can. Letters, 1982, 84, 86, award Can. Sci. Writers Assn., 1985, Hughes Aerospace Writing award, 1985. Mem. Royal Astron. Soc. Can. (life), AIAA, AAAS, Astron. Soc. of Pacific, Am. Inst. Physics, Can. Sci. Writers Assn. Home and Office: Box 10, Yarker, ON Canada K0K 3N0

DICKSON, BRIAN, chief justice of Canada; b. Yorkton, Sask., Can., May 25, 1916; s. Thomas and Sarah Elizabeth (Gibson) D.; m. Barbara Melville Sellers, June 18, 1943; children: Brian H., Deborah I. Dickson Shields, Peter G., Barry R. LL.B., U. Man., 1938, LL.D., 1973; D.Cn.L., St. John's Coll., 1965; LL.D., U. Man., 1973, U. Sask., 1978, U. Ottawa, 1979, Queen's U., 1980, Dalhousie U., 1983, York U., 1985; LL.D. U. B.C., 1986, U. Toronto, 1986, Laurentian U., 1986, Yeshiva U., 1987, McGill U., 1987; D.C.L., U. Windsor, 1988. Bar: Man. 1940, created Queen's counsel 1953; privy counselor. Mem. firm Aikins, MacAulay & Co., Winnipeg, Man., 1945-63; judge Ct. of Queen's Bench of Man, 1963-67, Ct. of Appeal for Man., 1967-73; justice Supreme Ct. of Can., Ottawa, Ont., 1973-84, chief justice, 1984—; Dep. Gov. Gen.; chmn. Adv. Council Order of Can.; chmn. Can. Judicial Council. Chancellor Diocese of Rupert's Land, Ch. of Eng., 1960-71; chmn. bd. govs. U. Man., 1971-73. Served with Royal Canadian Arty., 1940-45; hon. col. 30th Field Rgt. Royal Can. Arty. Decorated Knight Order St. John; named hon. prof. U. Man., 1985. Hon. fellow Am. Coll. Trial Lawyers; mem. Law Soc. Man. (life bencher), Heraldry Soc. Can. (vice patron), Order of the Buffalo Hunt. Mem. Anglican Ch. Can. Club: Rideau. Office: Supreme Ct of Can, Ottawa, ON Canada K1A 0J1

DICKSON, PAUL, clergyman; b. Lakeland, Fla., Sept. 9, 1905; s. David B. and Coral (Patrick) D.; m. Anna Elizabeth Clarke, May 24, 1930; 1 son, David Franklin. Student, Stetson U., 1922-26; Ph.D. cum laude, Ludwigs-Maxmillians U., Munich, Germany, 1951; M.A., Columbia, 1954, Ed.D., 1960. Commd. 1st lt. U.S. Army, 1934-38; exec. asst. mgr. Southwest Hotels Co., Memphis and Kansas City, Mo., 1938-39; gen. mgr. Commonwealth Hotel, Kansas City, Mo., 1939-40; returned to active duty as capt. U.S. Army, 1940, advanced through grades to col., 1953; various assignments U.S. mil. schs. and inf. divs. 1940-45; prof. mil. sci. and tactics Denver pub. schs., 1945-47; assigned U.S. Army Europe, 1947-49; mem. faculty (U.S. Mil. Acad.), 1949-55; ret. 1956; dean Munich Campus U. Md., 1957-61; asso. prof. fgn. lang. edn. Fla. State U., 1961-63, prof., 1963-69; dir. staff devel. Pinellas County schs., Fla, 1969-72; ordained to ministry Episcopal Ch., 1970; asst. rector Ch. of Ascension, Clearwater, Fla., 1972-77; asso. rector Ch. of Ascension, 1978—; lang. cons. south Fla. Edn. Center, 1962-64; adv. council N.E. Conf. Teaching Fgn. Langs, 1963-67. Author: Das Amerikabild in der deutschen Emigrantenliteratur seit 1933, 1951, Visible Vocabulary to Accompany German Military Readings, 1954, Foreign Language Instruction, 1960, Ins Deutsche Hinein, 1963, Articulated Language Learning, 1964, Foreign Language Education, 1966; Editor: Deutsche Sprachlehre, 1954, German Military Readings, 1954. Pres., chmn. bd. Fla. Gulf Coast Art Center, 1974-77. Decorated Bronze Star medal; Medaille de Reconnaissance France; named officer d'Academie Francaise. Mem. Modern Lang. Assn. Am. (regional fgn. lang. cons. 1963—), Am. Assn. Tchrs. French, German, Spanish and Portuguese, NEA, Fla. Edn. Assn. (pres. modern lang. sect. 1965-68), Assn. Higher Edn., South Atlantic Modern Lang. Assn., Assn. Supervision and Curriculum Devel., So. Humanities Conf., Pi Kappa Phi. Episcopalian (lay reader, vestryman, clk. deacon, priest). Home: 1100 Ponce de Leon Blvd Apt 304 South Clearwater FL 34616

DICKSON, PAUL WESLEY, JR., physicist; b. Sharon, Pa., Sept. 14, 1931; s. Paul Wesley and Elizabeth Ella (Trevethan) D.; m. Eleanor Ann Dunning, Nov. 17, 1952; children—Gretchen Ann, Heather Elizabeth, Paul Wesley. B.S. in Metall. Engring., U. Ariz., 1954, M.S., 1954; Ph.D. in Physics, N.C. State U., 1962. With Westinghouse Electric Corp., Large, Pa., 1963-84, mgr. weapon systems, 1965-68, mgr. advanced projects, 1969-72, mgr. reactor analysis and core design, Madison, Pa., 1972-79, tech. dir., Oak Ridge, 1979-84; with EG & G Idaho, Idaho Falls, 1984—, mgr. new tech. devel., 1984-87, reactor projects and programs, 1987—; mem. adv. com. on advanced propulsion systems NASA, Washington, 1970-72; mem. adv. com. reactor physics AEC/Dept. Energy, 1974-79; mem. rev. com. applied physics Argonne (Ill.) Nat. Lab., 1978-83, chmn., 1980; mem. rev. com. engring. physics Oak Ridge Nat. Lab., 1982-86, chmn. 1986; mem. sci. and tech. adv. com. Argonne Nat. Lab., 1985—. Contbr. numerous sci. articles to profl. publs. Served to capt. USAF, 1955-63. Fellow Am. Nuclear Soc.; mem. Am. Phys. Soc., N.Y. Acad. Scis., AIME, AAAS, Scabbord and Blade, Sigma Xi, Phi Kappa Phi, Tau Beta Pi, Phi Lambda Upsilon, Sigma Pi Sigma. Republican. Methodist. Subspecialties: Nuclear fission; Nuclear engineering. Current work: Nuclear reactor development. Home: 4850 Loma Circle Idaho Falls ID 83401

DICKSON-PORTER, CLAUDIA BLAIR, librarian; b. Memphis, Oct. 22, 1925; d. Walton Avery and Annie Laurie (Tate) Tucker; B.S., U. Nebr., Omaha, 1964; M.L.S., N. Tex. State U., Denton, 1971, Ph.D., 1979; m. Benjamin A. Dickson, June 5, 1945 (div.); children—Susan Dickson Morrison, Andrea Dickson Darby, Donna Dickson Stephens, Reid W., Bryan A.; m. 2d, William G. Porter, Feb. 8, 1978. Tchrs. schs. in Nebr. and Hawaii, 1964-71; librarian Nat. Assn. Retarded Citizens, Arlington, Tex., from 1971; dir. Regional Office TAS VI, Research and Tng Center in Mental Retardation Tex. Tech. U.; dir. planning Tex. Planning Council for Devel. Disabilities, Tex. Dept. Mental Health/Mental Retardation, 1979-80; program specialist Office of Devel. Disabilities, Office of Human Devel., Fed. Region VI, Dallas, 1980-82, grants mgmt. specialist Office of Fiscal Ops., 1982-83; Head Start Community rep. Adminstrn. for Children, Youth and Families, 1983-84; program specialist So. Region Adminstrn. on Developmental Disabilities, Fed. Region VI, 1984—; tchr. community services courses El Centro Jr. Coll., Dallas Recipient Disting. Alumnus award North Tex. State U., 1984. Mem. Spl. Libraries Assn., Southwestern, Tex. library assns., Am. Assn. Mental Deficiency, Council Exceptional Children, Soc. S.W. Archivists, Local History Soc., Phi Delta Kappa. Author, compiler in field. Home: 2413 Lakeside Dr Arlington TX 76013 Office: 1200 Main Tower Dallas TX 75202

DI DIEGO, DOMENICO, marketing executive; b. Atessa, Chieti, Italy, Jan. 8, 1944; s. Camillo and Paolina (Sabatini) Di D.; m. Carla Scandroglio, May 10, 1974; 1 child, Paolo. Dr., U. Studi, Padova, Italy, 1968. Jr. scientist Montedison Research Ctr., Mantova, Italy, 1970-72, Castellanza, Italy, 1973-75; sr. scientist Monte Polimeri Research Ctr., Rho, Italy, 1976-80; mgr. tech. service Monte Polimeri Research Ctr., Rho, 1980-85; mgr. mktg. Vedril SPA, Rho and Milan, 1985—; lectr. Poly. Design Sch., Milan, 1981-84, U. Milan, 1984-86. Contbr. articles to profl. jours. Patentee in field. Served to lt. arty. Italian Army, 1970-72. Mem. Soc. Plastics Engrs. (affiliated), Enteunificazione Italiana, Comite Europeen Normalization. Republican. Roman Catholic. Club: G.M. Football (Gorla Maggiore, Italy). Home: Via Giotto 2, 21050 Gorla Maggiore Varese Italy Office: Vedril SPA, Via Pregnana 63, 20017 Rho Milan Italy

DI DRUSCO, GIOVANNI, materials company executive; b. Muggia/Trieste, Italy, July 13, 1930; s. Giuseppe and Margherita (Zaccaria) Di D.; m. Laura Landi; children: Fabia, Isotta. D in Chem. Engring., U. Bologna, Italy. Mgr. dept. process devel. research Research Centre Montedison Group, Ferrara, Italy, 1956-60; dir. process devel. dept. Montedison Group, Ferrara, Italy, 1960-69; coordinator process devel., tech. Montedison Group, Milan, Italy, 1970-74; dir. factory ops. Montedison Group, Ferrara, 1975-77; dep. gen. mgr. Plastic Material div. Montedison Group, Milan, 1978-82; v.p. Himont Inc., Wilmington, Del., 1983-84; chief exec. officer, pres. Ausimont Spa, Milan, 1985-86; pres. Dutral Spa, Milan, 1985—; chief exec. officer Adv. Comp. Materials Group, 1987—; bd. dirs., adviser numerous corporations. Home: Via Palestro 47, 44100 Ferrara Italy Office: Montedison Spa, Via Principe, Eugenio, 1/5-20155 Milano Italy

DIEBOLD, PAUL HORST, civil engineer; b. Singen, Baden, Germany, May 21, 1944; s. Albert Paul and Berta (Brunner) D.; m. Mechthild Luise Lange, Oct. 24, 1967; children—Jens Oliver, Silja Chantal, Nicolas Fabian. B.S. in Civil Engring., Tech. Coll., Wiesbaden, Fed. Republic Germany, 1971; B.A., U. South Africa, Pretoria, 1981; M.B.A., Century U., Beverly Hills, Calif., 1984. Sr. engr. Wolhuter Cons., Windhoek, Namibia, 1972-74; br. mgr. BSB Cons., Tripoli, Libya, 1975-76; supt. Escom, Kriel, South Africa, 1977-81; project leader Motor Columbus Inc., Baden, Switzerland, 1981-85; prin., exec. dir. Paul Diebold Co., Baden, 1985—; owner Paul Diebold, Engring. Mgmt.; tchr. applied economy E. Schmidheiny Found., Holderbank, Switzerland, 1983. Served with C.E., Swiss Army, 1964—. Mem. Soc. Profl. Engrs. Germany, Alumni Assn. U. South Africa, Alumni Assn. Century U., C. of C. Aargau. Mem. Evangelical-Reformed Ch. Lodge: Rotary (local officer 1979-82). Avocations: skiing; tennis; music. Home: im Chrumbacher 28, 5406 Baden Switzerland Office: Meinrad Lienert-Strasse 1, 8003 Zürich Switzerland

DIEDERICHS, JOHN KUENSTING, investment company executive; b. Chgo., July 16, 1921; m. Janet Barbara Wood, Sept. 16, 1953. AB, U. Chgo.; postgrad., MIT, Northwestern U. Sales and market planning adminstr. Pan Am. World Airways, N.Y.C. and Chgo., 1946-49; regional sales mgr. Pan Am.-Grace Airways, N.Y.C. and Chgo., 1949-52; mem. profl. mgmt. cons. staff Booz Allen and Hamilton, Chgo., 1952-55; chmn. techno-econs. dept. Ill. Inst. Tech. Research Inst., Chgo.; v.p. Johnson and Assocs., Mgmt. Cons., 1962-63; v.p. research and corp. devel. Chgo. Mill and Lumber Co., 1962-65; v.p. corp. planning and devel. Sunbeam Corp., Chgo., 1965-82; owner, investment counselor Diederichs & Assocs., 1982—; associated with John C. Stanley, London, 1982—, Eric von Stolzenberg, Zurich, Pacific Corporate Fin., Inc., La Jolla, Calif.; chmn., chief exec. officer WFMT, Inc., Chgo. Mag., 1985-86, bd. dirs. WFMT, Inc., 1976-86; bd. dirs. Mich. Bldg. Corp., 1978-82; trustee WTTW-TV, Chgo. Mem. Investment Co. Inst., Tech. Assn. of the Graphic Arts, Photographic Scientists and Engrs., Internat. Soc. Econometricians. Clubs: Chicago, Tavern, International. Office: Diederichs & Assocs 333 N Michigan Av Suite 1214 Chicago IL 60601-4002

DIEDRICH, RICHARD JOHN, insurance company executive; b. St. Paul, June 5, 1936; s. Carl Anthony and Alice V. (May) D.; student Macalester Coll., 1953-54; B.S., U. Minn., 1959; m. Judith Parish, Aug. 12, 1961; children—Pamela H., Stuart B., John C. With St. Paul Fire and Marine Ins. Co., 1959—, gen. mgr., Cleve., 1973-77, v.p. fidelity and surety bond dept., St. Paul, 1977-80, divisional v.p. property underwriting, 1980-82, v.p. underwriting ops., 1983-85, v.p. planning and corp. devel., 1985-86, v.p. and gen. mgr. New Eng. region, Holyoke, Mass., 1986—. Trustee, Salem Found., 1979—; mem. exec. bd., exploring chmn. Hiawatha council Boy Scouts Am., Syracuse, N.Y., 1967-72, vice chmn. exploring, mem. exec. bd. Greater Cleve. council, 1973-77, v.p., mem. exec. bd. Indianhead council, St. Paul, 1977-86, mem. internat. com., 1981—; mem. U.S. Found. for Internat. Scouting, 1982—; mem. exec. bd. St. Paul Chamber Orch., 1982-83; mem. exec. bd. Sci. Mus. Minn., 1980-86; mem. exec. bd. Big Bros. Greater Cleve., 1975-76, Minn. Opera Co., 1978-80; trustee Oakland Cemetery Assn., 1979-86, Bay State Med. Ctr., Springfield, Mass., 1987—; exec. bd., v.p. Exploring, Pioneer Valley council Boy Scouts Am.; exec. v.p. Compas, 1984-86. Served with USAF, 1954-58. Recipient William E. Spurgeon award Greater Cleve. council Boy Scouts Am., Silver Beaver award; Baden-Powell fellow World Scout Found. Mem. Mass. Med. Joint Underwriting Assn. (bd. dirs. 1986—), N.H. Med. Joint Underwriting Assn. (bd. dirs. 1986—), R.I. Med. Malpractice Joint Underwriting Assn. (bd. dirs. 1986). Republican. Roman Catholic. Clubs: Colony (Springfield); Pool and Yacht; Longmeadow Country. Office: St Paul Fire and Marine Ins Co 489 Whitney Ave Holyoke MA 01040

DIEHL, SAYLOR FLORY, statistician; b. Nokesville, Va., Nov. 8, 1919; s. Daniel Saylor and Vernie (Flory) D.; A.B., Bridgewater Coll., 1943; student George Washington U., 1943-45, Am. U., 1945-50; m. Nettie Ruth Mathison, Aug. 31, 1946; children—Linda Jean, Wayne Bruce. Specialist Air Intelligence, USAF, Washington, D.C. 1949-51; analyst commodity industry Nat. Prodn. Authority, Washington, 1951-53; analytical statistician Bur. Personnel, U.S. Navy, Washington, 1953-54; head work measurement br. Office Indsl. Relations, exec. office Sec. of Navy, Washington, 1954-57; supervisory survey statistician Census Bur. Washington, 1957-62; ednl. research specialist U.S. Office Edn., Washington, 1962-80. Mason (32 deg., Shriner, K.T., grand master grand council Royal and Select Masters of Md., grand gov. Md. York Rite Sovereign Coll., great chief of grand council of knight masons 1976), Knights of Templar (grand commander of grand commandery 1983), R.A.M. (grand high priest of grand chot. 1975). Author: The Presiding Officer. Home: 11505 Carroll Ct Upper Marlboro MD 20772

DIEMER, FERDINAND PETER, govt. ofcl.; b. N.Y.C., Oct. 16, 1920; s. Ferdinand Francis and Cunigunda Marie (Kolm) D.; B.S.E.E., Cooper Union U., 1948; M.S.E.E., N.Y.U., 1950; m. Maureen Margaret Davoren, May 8, 1952; children—Margretta, Jeanne Marie, Ferdinand, Dolores, Peter, Mary, Maribeth, Paul, Leon. Dir. spl. projects, asst. dir. engring. Martin Marietta Corp., Balt., 1961-66; mgr. command, control, communications systems TRW, Inc., McLean, Va., 1966-71; phys. sci. adminstr. Navy Oceanographic Sci., Office Naval Research, Arlington, Va., 1971-80; energy info. adminstr., dir. systems engring. U.S. Dept. Energy, Washington, 1980—; cons. dept. indsl. engring. Columbia U., Nat. Oceans Com., U. Miami, 1965-71; grad. lectr. applied sci. and engring. U. So. Calif., Am. U., 1959-71; dep. dir. Agard Internat. Tech. Conf., 1978; dir. Primars Sci. Internat. Conf., U. Manchester (Eng.), 1979. Active various community drives. Served with Signal Corps, U.S. Army, 1944-46; ETO, PTO. Recipient Outstanding Performance award USN, 1978. Mem. IEEE (life, chmn. computer soc.), AAAS, Assn. Computing Machinery, Instrument Soc. Am., Soc. Indsl. and Applied Math., Engring. Soc. Balt., N.Y. Acad. Scis., Armed Forces Electronic Communication Assn. Author: Advanced Concepts in Ocean Measurements, 1978; Processes in Marine Remote Sensing, 1982. Home: 5307 Springlake Way Baltimore MD 21212-3413 Office: Dept Energy 1000 Independence Ave Washington DC 20585

DIEMERT, JOHN PETER, business educator; b. Crooked Creek, Alta., Can., Jan. 18, 1932; s. Frank J. and Martha Matilda (Hoffard) D.; m. Helen Krall, July 4, 1953; children: Brian, Allan. Justice of peace, notary pub. Province of Alta., 1970-75; coordinator entrepreneurship No. Lights Coll., Dawson Creek, B.C., Can., 1975—. Author: (with others) Entrepreneurship Manufacturing Course, 1986. Chmn. Spirit River (Alta.) Sch. Div., 1968-75, Dawson Creek Econ. Devel. Commn., 1977-80; 2d v.p. Alta. Sch. Trustees Assn., 1973-75; mem. task force Hosp. Labour Relations Bd., Vancouver, B.C., 1986-87, exec. com. Dawson Creek and Dist. Hosp., 1984-87; bd. dirs. Dawson Creek Recreation Commn., 1972-75, No. Inst. Resources, 1987—. Mem. Conservative Party. Roman Catholic. Lodges: Rotary (pres. Dawson Creek club 1977-78), KC, Elks (ruler 1968-69). Home: 10701 Pinecrest Ln, Dawson Creek, BC Canada V1G 4M6 Office: No Lights Coll, 11401 8th St, Dawson Creek, BC Canada V1G 4M6

DIENER, ROYCE, health care services company executive; b. Balt., Mar. 27, 1918; s. Louis and Lillian (Goodman) D.; m. Jennifer S. Flinton; children: Robert, Joan, Michael. BA, Harvard U.; LLD, Pepperdine U. Comml. lending officer, investment banker various locations to 1972; pres. Am. Med. Internat., Inc., Beverly Hills, Calif., 1972-75, pres., chief exec. officer, 1975-78, chmn., chief exec. officer, 1978-85, chmn. bd., 1986-88, chmn. exec. com., 1986—; bd. dirs. Calif. Econ. Devel. Corp., Advanced Tech. Venture Funds, Am. Health Properties, AMI Healthcare Group, plc. Author: Financing a Growing Business, 1966, 3d edit., 1978. Bd. visitors Grad. Sch. Mgmt., UCLA; mem. vis. com. Med. Sch. and Sch. Dental Medicine, Harvard U.; trustee Andrus Gerontol. Inst., U. So. Calif.; bd. dirs. Los Angeles Philharm. Assn., Los Angeles chpt. ARC, Heritage Sq. Mus., Santa Monica. Served to capt. USAF, 1942-46, PTO. Decorated D.F.C. with oak leaf cluster. Mem. Los Angeles C. of C. (bd. dirs.), Calif. C. of C. (bd. dirs.), Calif. Bus. Round Table (bd. dirs.). Clubs: Harvard, Regency, California Yacht, Riviera Country (Los Angeles); Marks (London). Office: Am Med Internat Inc 414 N Camden Dr Beverly Hills CA 90210

DIENER, THEODOR OTTO, plant pathologist; b. Zurich, Switzerland, Feb. 28, 1921; came to U.S., 1949, naturalized, 1955; s. Theodor Emanuel and Hedwig Rosa (Baumann) D.; m. Sybil Mary Fox, May 11, 1968; children by previous marriage: Theodor W., Robert A., Michael S. Diploma, Swiss Fed. Inst. Tech., 1946; DSc, Nat. Swiss Fed. Inst. Tech., 1948. Asst. Swiss Fed. Inst. Tech., Zurich, 1946-48; plant pathologist Swiss Fed. Exptl. Sta., Waedenswil, 1949-50; asst. prof. plant pathology R.I. State U., Kingston, 1950; asst. plant pathologist Wash. State U., Prosser, 1950-55; asso. plant pathologist Wash. State U., 1955-59; research plant pathologist Agrl. Research Service, USDA, Beltsville, Md., 1959-88; prof. botany, sr. staff sci. Agr. Biotechnology Ctr., U. Md., College Park, 1988—; lectr. univs. and research insts.; Regents' lectr. U. Calif., Riverside, 1970; A.W. Dimock lectr. Cornell U., 1975; Andrew D. White prof.-at-large Cornell U., 1979-81; James Law Disting. lectr. N.Y. State Coll. Vet. Medicine, Cornell U., 1981; Disting. lectr. Boyce Thompson Inst. for Plant Research, Cornell U., 1987. Author: Viroids and Viroid Diseases, 1979; editor: The Viroids, 1987; assoc. editor jour. Virology, 1964-66, 74-76, editor jour., 1967-71; mem. editorial com. jour. Ann. Rev. Phytopathology, 1970-74, Annales de Virologie, 1980—; contbr. articles to sci. publs. Recipient Campbell award Am. Inst. Biol. Scis., 1968, Gov.'s Citation Atate of Md., 1988, E.C. Stakman award U. Minn., 1988, Alexander von Humboldt award, 1975, Superior Service award USDA, 1969, Disting. Service award, 1977, Wolf Prize in Agr., 1987, U.S. Nat. Medal of Sci., 1987, E.C. Stakman award U. Minn., 1988. Fellow Am. Phytopath. Soc. (Ruth Allen award 1976, Disting. Service award, 1988), N.Y. Acad. Scis., Am. Acad. Arts and Scis.; mem. AAAS, Nat. Acad. Scis., Leopoldina, German Acad. Natural Scientists. Home: 4530 Powder Mill Rd PO Box 272 Beltsville MD 20705 Office: Plant Virology Lab Agrl Research Center USDA Beltsville MD 20705

DIEPGEN, EBERHARD, mayor of West Berlin; b. Berlin, Nov. 13, 1941; s. Erik and Erika (Kruger) D.; m. Monika Adler; children—Anne-Katrin, Frederick-Paul. Student in jurisprudence, Free U. Berlin. Parliamentary leader Christian Democratic Union Ho. of Reps., Berlin, vice parliamentary chmn., mgr. exec. com. of land, 1975, chmn. central com., 1979—, chmn. central com. Ho. of Reps. 1981-84; mayor of West Berlin, 1984—. Address: Regierender Burgermeister, West Berlin Federal Republic of Germany

DIERCKS, CHESTER WILLIAM, JR., capital goods manufacturing company executive; b. Urbana, Ill., Oct. 15, 1926; s. Chester William and Anna (Gude) D.; m. Marie Johnson, Aug. 5, 1950; children: Chester William, III, Lisa Beth. B.S. in Gen. Engring., Iowa State U., Ames, 1950; M.S. in Indsl. Mgmt. (Sloan fellow), MIT, 1962. Gen. mgr. med. services, x-ray and splty. transformer div. Westinghouse Electric Co., Pitts., 1950-71; with Allis-Chalmers Corp. (and subs.), 1971-77, dir. Mgmt. Services, v.p., staff exec. Mgmt. Services, group exec., v.p. Indsl. Elec. Group, group exec., v.p. Elec. Products Group, sr. exec. v.p., chief fin. officer, 1976-77; pres., chief exec. officer Siemens-Allis, Inc., 1978-85, Utility Power Corp., Atlanta, 1978—; bd. dirs. 1st Atlanta Corp., 1st Nat. Bank Atlanta; bd. dirs. Equipment Innovators Inc.; past dir. Fiat-Allis Inc., Marine Corp., Clow Corp., Siemens-Allis, Siemens Elec. Ltd.; mem. Industry Sector Adv. Com. to 1974 Trade Reform Act, 1976-77; mem. mgmt. adv. council Coll. Mgmt., Ga. Inst. Tech. Bd. dirs. Japan Am. Soc.; bd. visitors Emory U., Berry Coll., Mt. Berry, Ga.; past bd. govs. Soc. Alfred P. Sloan Fellows, MIT; elder Peachtree Presbyn. Ch., Atlanta. Served to 1st lt. U.S. Army, 1945-47. Mem. Nat. Elec. Mfrs. Assn. (past bd. govs. mem. long range planning com., chmn. govt. & internat. policy com.), Machinery and Allied Products Inc., Atlanta C. of C. (past exec. com. mem., 1st v.p. bd. dirs.), Fla. Council of 100, Fin. Execs. Inst. Clubs: Capital City (Atlanta); Ashford, Stadium, Elec. Mfrs. Home: 4545 Powers Rd Marietta GA 30067 Office: Utility Power Corp 1020 Cambridge Sq Suite A Alpharetta GA 30201

DIERCKS, FREDERICK OTTO, government official; b. Rainy River, Ont., Can., Sept. 8, 1912; s. Otto Herman and Lucy (Plunkett) D.; m. Kathryn Frances Transue, Sept. 1, 1937; children: Frederick William, Lucy Helena. B.S., U.S. Mil. Acad., 1937; M.S. in Civil Engring., MIT, 1939; M.S. in Photogrammetry, Syracuse U., 1950. Registered profl. engr., D.C. Commd. 2d lt. U.S. Army, 1937, advanced through grades to col., 1952; comdg. officer U.S. Army Map Service, Washington, 1957-61, Def. Intelligence Agy., 1961-63; dep. engr. 8th U.S. Army, Korea, 1963-64; dir. U.S. Army Coastal Engring. Research Ctr., 1964-67; ret. 1967; assoc. dir. U.S. Coast and Geodetic Survey (now Nat. Ocean Survey), Rockville, Md., 1967-74; U.S. mem. commn. cartography Pan Am. Inst. Geography and History, OAS, 1961-67, alt. U.S. mem. directing council, 1970-74, exec. sec. U.S. sect., 1975-87. Decorated Legion of Merit, Grand Cross Order of King George II (Greece); Comdr. Most Exalted Order of White Elephant (Thailand). Fellow ASCE, Soc. Am. Mil. Engrs. (Colbert medal); mem. Am. Soc. Photogrammetry (hon., pres. 1970-71, Luis Struck award), Am. Congress on Surveying and Mapping, Sigma Xi. Republican. Presbyterian. Clubs: Army-Navy, Cosmos (Washington). Lodge: Masons (Fort Leavenworth, Kans.). Home: 9313 Christopher St Fairfax VA 22031

DIERSEN, INGE EMMA, German literature educator; b. Hamburg, Germany, Dec. 7, 1927; d. Karl and Elsbeth (Lewecke) D. Grad., Oberschule, Berlin, 1947; diploma in German, Humboldt U., Berlin, German Democratic Republic, 1952, PhD, 1954, Dr. in Habilitation, 1963. Prof. German lit. Humboldt U., Berlin, 1959-88, prof. emeritus, 1988—. Author: Thomas Mann, 1959, 75, 85, Anna Seghers, 1965, Georg Büchner, 1988. Mem. Internat. Vereinigung für Germanische Sprach- und Literaturwissenschaft. Home: Friedrich-Engels-Strasse 44, 1110 Berlin German Democratic Republic

DIESEL, JOHN PHILLIP, multinational corporation executive; b. St. Louis, June 10, 1926; s. John Henry and Elsa A. (Poetting) D.; m. Rita Jan Meyer, June 12, 1949; children: Holly, Gretchen, John, Dana. B.S., Washington U., St. Louis, 1951. Exec. asst. div. mgr. McQuay-Norris Mfg. Co., St. Louis, 1951-57; ptnr. Booz, Allen & Hamilton, Inc., Chgo., 1957-61; v.p. ops. Ops. Research, Inc., Santa Monica, Calif., 1961-62; v.p., treas., dir. Mgmt. Tech., Inc., Los Angeles, 1962-63; dir. mktg. and planning A.O. Smith Corp., Milw., 1963-65, dir. mfg. and engring., 1965-67, v.p. mfg. and planning, 1967-70, group v.p., 1970-72; chmn. bd. Armor Elevator Can., Ltd., 1970-72; chmn. bd., pres. Armor Elevator Co., Inc., 1970-72; pres., chief exec. officer Newport News (Va.) Shipbldg. & Dry Dock Co., 1972-78, chmn. bd., 1976-78; exec. v.p. Tenneco Inc., Houston, 1976-79, pres., 1979—, also dir.; dir. Cooper Industries, Inc., Aluminum Co. of Am. Served with USNR, 1944-47. Methodist. Clubs: Pine Valley Golf, Seminole Golf, Metropolitan. Office: Tenneco Inc PO Box 2511 Houston TX 77002 *

DIETL, CHARLES ALBERT, surgeon; b. Eng., July 27, 1948; came to Argentina, 1948; s. Carlos Enrique and Martha J. (Marfort) D.; m. Maria Marta Marenco, Dec 21 1972; children: Mariana, Johnny, Deborah. MD with honors, U. Buenos Aires, 1971. Intern St. Vincent Hosp., Portland, Oreg., 1973-74; resident in surgery St. Vincent Hosp. and U. Oreg., Portland, 1974-78; resident in cardiopulmonary surg. U. Oreg., Portland, 1978-80; cardiovascular and chief pediatric heart surgeon Inst. de Cardiologia y Cirugia Toracica y Cardiovascular Hosp. Guemes and Fundacion Favaloro, Buenos Aires, 1980. Recipient physician's recognition AMA, 1981. Fellow Am. Coll. Cardiology; mem. Am. Bd. Surgery, Am. Bd. Thoracic Surgery, Am. Coll. Cardiology, Soc. Argentina de Cardiologia y Cirugia Cardiovascular Infantil (founding mem. 1985), Soc. Argentina de Cardiologia (hon.), Soc. Arrgentina de Pediatria. Home: Lafinur 3163 #2, Buenos Aires 1425, Argentina

DIETRICH, BRUCE LEINBACH, planetarium and museum administrator, astronomer, educator; b. Reading, Pa., Oct. 10, 1937; s. Harold Richard and Emily Jeanette (Leinbach) D.; m. Renee Carol Long, Nov. 25, 1959; children—Dodson Bruce, Katie Ellen. B.S., Kutztown U., 1960; M.S., SUNY-Oswego, 1969. Tchr. Reading Pub. Schs., 1960-67; curator space sci. Reading Mus., 1967-69, dir. planetarium, 1969—, dir., 1976—; prof. astronomy Reading Area Community Coll., 1972—. Contbr. articles to profl. jours. V.p. Reading Musical Found., 1980—, trustee, 1987—. Named Kellogg Mus. Profl., 1987; NSF grantee, 1965-67. Fellow Internat. Planetarium Soc. (chmn. awards com.); mem. Can. Assn. of Planetariums Mid-Atlantic Planetarium Soc., AAAS, AAM. Club: Torch (Reading) (pres. 1987). Lodge: Kiwanis (pres. 1969). Home: 1546 Dauphin Ave Wyomissing PA 19610 Office: Reading Pub Mus and Art Gallery 500 Museum Rd Reading PA 19611

DIETRICH, GEORGE CHARLES, chemical company executive; b. Detroit, Feb. 5, 1927; s. George Sylvester and Catherine Elizabeth (Cable) D.; B.S., U. Detroit; m. Dorothy Ann Flanigan, Aug. 21, 1954; children—Linda Marie, Elizabeth Ann, George Charles. Field sales mgr. Allied Chem. Co., Chgo., 1960-64; dir. sales Aerosol Research Co., North Riverside, Ill., 1964—; pres. Aeropres Corp., Chgo., 1964-65, Diversified Chems. & Propellants Co., Westmont, Ill., 1965—, also dir.; chmn. bd. ChemSpec Ins. Ltd.; dir. Am. Nat. Bank, De Kalb, Ill., Diversified CPC Internat., Anaheim, Calif., Klockner CPC Internat.; bd. dirs., chmn. Consumers Specialties Ins. Co., Wilmington, Del., Expert Mgmt. Systems, Phoenix; pres., chief exec. officer Gen. Energy Internat. Served with USNR, 1945-46. Mem. Chem. Splty. Mfrs. Assn. (gov., chmn. bd.), Chgo. Drug and Chem. Assn., Chgo. Perfumery Soap and Extract Assn., Nat. Paint and Coatings Assn., World Univ. Roundtable, Internat. Platform Assn., Econs. Club Chgo., Execs. Club Chgo. Roman Catholic. Clubs: Butler Nat. Golf; Boca Raton (Fla.) Hotel and Club; Butterfield Country. Home: 1 Charleston Rd Hinsdale IL 60521 Office: Diversified CPC Internat Durkee Rd PO Box 490 Channahon IL 60410-0490

DIETRICH, MARLENE (MARIA MAGDALENA VON LOSCH), actress; b. Berlin, Germany; d. Edward and Josephine (Felsing) von Losch; ed. Augusta Victoria Sch., Berlin; m. Rudolf Siebet, May 13, 1924; 1 dau., Maria. Began as violinist; debut as actress in Broadway, Berlin; 4 years with Max Reinhardt; later in film The Blue Angel (German); came to U.S., 1930, and since starred in motion pictures, including: Martin Roumagnec (French), 1946, Golden Earrings, 1947, Foreign Affair, 1948, Stage Fright, 1950, No Highway in the Sky, 1951, Rancho Notorious, 1952, numerous others the latest including The Monte Carlo Story, 1957, Around the World in 80 Days, 1956, Witness for the Prosecution, 1958. Judgment at Nuremberg, 1961; Just a Gigolo, 1978; also appears in night clubs and theatres. Recipient Spl. Tony award, 1967-68. Author: Marlene Dietrich's ABC, 1962; My Life Story, 1979. Toured Army Service Camps, Europe, 1945; concert tour U.S., 1973. Address: care Regency Artists Ltd 9200 Sunset Blvd Suite 823 Los Angeles CA 90069 *

DIETRICH, SUZANNE CLAIRE, instructional designer; b. Granite City, Ill., Apr. 9, 1937; d. Charles Daniel and Evelyn Blanche (Waters) D.; B.S. in Speech, Northwestern U., 1958; M.S. in Pub. Communication, Boston U., 1967; postgrad. So. Ill. U., 1973—. Intern, prodn. staff Sta. WGBH-TV, Boston, 1958-59, asst. dir., 1962-64, asst. dir. program Invitation to Art, 1958; cons. producer dir. dept. instructional TV radio Ill. Office Supt. Pub. Instruction, Springfield, 1969-70; dir. program prodn. and distbn., 1970-72; instr. faculty call staff, speech dept. Sch. Fine Arts So. Ill. U., Edwardsville, 1972—, grad. asst. for doctoral program office of dean Sch. Edn., 1975-78; research asst. Ill. public telecommunications study for Ill. Public Broadcasting Council, 1979-80; cons. and research in communications, 1980—; exec. producer, dir. TV programs Con-Con Countdown, 1970, The Flag Speaks, 1971. Roman Catholic. Home: 1011 Minnesota Ave Edwardsville IL 62025

DIETZ, KARSTEN, data processing executive; b. Hamburg, Fed. Republic Germany, Oct. 3, 1947; s. Gottlieb and Gertrud (Heyden) D.; m. Christa H. Grell, Aug. 2, 1978; children: Julia, Lena. M of Computer Sci., U. Hamburg, 1978. Sr. systems engr. M&S Computing, Hamburg, 1978-80, mgr., 1980-82; products mgr. European hdqrs. Intergraph, Hoofddorp, The Netherlands, 1982-84; tech. dir. Intergraph Germany, Munich, 1984-86, Hamburg, 1986—. Home: Am Ehrenmal 2, D2000 Hamburg 71, Federal Republic Germany Office: Intergraph Abt Pgh, Uberseering 9, D2000 Hamburg 60, Federal Republic Germany

DIETZ, WILLIAM RONALD, banker, consultant; b. Seattle, Nov. 25, 1942; s. William Phillip and Helen Mae (Wilson) D.; m. Elizabeth R. Daoust; 1 child, David Phillip. BA, U. Wash., 1964; MBA, Stanford U., 1968. Fin. cons. 1st Nat. City Bank, N.Y.C., 1968-70; v.p., mgr. Citicorp Subs. Mgmt. Office, Citicorp, N.Y.C., 1971-74; chmn. Citicorp Factors, Inc., N.Y.C., 1974-75; v.p., mgr. N.Y., N.J. and Conn. comml. banking Citibank N.A., N.Y.C., 1976-78; sr. v.p., gen. mgr. Eastern region corp. banking Citibank N.A., 1978-81, sr. v.p., head Caribbean Basin div., 1982-84; pres. Charter Assocs. Ltd., 1984—; bd. dirs. Chase Packaging Corp. Contbg. author: Marketing Financial Services. Mem. policy com. Bank Mgmt. Inst., SUNY-Buffalo. Served to lt. USNR, 1964-66. Mem. Delta Tau Delta. Club: University (N.Y.C.). Home and Office: 2204 Decatur Pl NW Washington DC 20008 also: 2003 N Ocean Blvd Boca Raton FL 33431

DIETZ, WOLFGANG, parliamentary librarian; b. Leipzig, Ger., Aug. 30, 1921; s. Rudolf and Martha (Reichelt) D.; m. Gisela Selige, Oct. 31, 1963; children—Hartmut, Helgard, Silke. Diploma, U. Leipzig, 1954; postgrad. Deutsche Staatsbibliothek, Berlin, 1954-56. Librarian, Univ. Library, Leipzig, 1956, Deutsche Bü cherei, Leipzig, 1957-58; parliamentary librarian Deutscher Bundestag, Bonn, 1958-86; cons. various instns., 1987—; mem. various profl. adv. coms.; chair steering com. for network between Parliamentary Library and state libraries, 1977-86; chair gen. steering com. Eurodocdel Project, European Com., 1984-86. Author profl. articles. Served with German Army, 1940-47; NATOUSA; POW, U.S.A., 1943-46. Decorated Cross of Merit 1st class (W. Ger.); recipient Silver medal of the German Diet, 1986. Mem. Assn. Parliamentary and Adminstrv. Libraries W. Ger. (chair 1975-85), Internat. Fedn. Library Assns. (chair sect. parliamentary libraries 1979-83, chair div. of gen. research libraries 1979-83, mem. profl. bd.).

DIETZSCH, STEFFEN MICHAEL, philosopher; b. Chemnitz, German Dem. Republic, Aug. 21, 1943; s. Ruth Dietzsch; m. Birgit Scherf, Dec. 30, 1966; children: Caroline, Benjamin. D of Philosophy, U. Leipzig, Dem. Republic of Germany, 1973; DSc in Philosophy, Acad. of Sci., Berlin, 1986. Researcher Cen. Inst. of Philosophy, Acad. of Sci., Berlin, 1973-83, head of dept., 1983—. Author: (biography) F.W.J. Schelling, 1978; editor Nachtwachen von Bonaventura, 1980, J.W. Ritter, Fragmente, 1984, A. Panormite, Hermaphroditus, 1986, I. Kant, Von den Träumen der Vernunft, 1979; mem. editorial bd. German Jour. of Philosophy, 1985—. Office: Cen Inst of Philosphy, Otto Nuschke Strasse 10/11, 1080 Berlin German Democratic Republic

DIETZ Y RUIZ, CONRADO RODOLFO, mechanical engineering consultant; b. Mexico City, Feb. 23, 1939; s. Gustavo Dietz and Guillermina Ruiz; m. Argelia Diaz Flores, July 19, 1969; 1 child, Argelia. Mech. Engr., Escuela Superior de Ingenieria Mecanica y Electrica IPN, 1961. Projects dir. Altos Hornos de Mexico SA, Monclova, 1962-70; supt. Simpson SA de CV, Toluca, 1971-74; plant mgr. Metacarb SA de CV, Lerma, 1975-77; supt. Durit SA de CV, Toluca, 1978-80; plant mgr. Talleres de Hornos SA de CV, Lerma, 1981—. Mem. Asociacion Mexicana de Ingenieros Mecanicos y Electricistas AC. Roman Catholic. Avocations: Motorcycles; computers; swimming; sailing. Office: Apartado Postal 659, 50000 Toluca Mexico

DIEUZAIDE, JEAN (YAN), photographer; b. Grenade-sur-Garonne, France, June 20, 1921; m. Jacqueline Manuquet, 1950; children—Michel, Marie-Francoise. Ed. at secondary sch., Nice, France, 1938-40; prep. yr. for St.-Cyr Mil. Sch. Free-lance photographer, Toulouse, France, 1944—; founder, art dir. Galerie du Château d'Eau, Toulouse, 1974—; established Jean Dieuzaide Gallery, Toulouse, 1976; instr. in photography workshops Rencontres Internationales de Photographie, Arles, France, from 1969; instr. Ecole Audio-visuelle de Saint-Cloud, Paris, 1978; chmn. artistic com. Fédération Internationale d'Art Photographique, from 1970. One-man shows: Publicity Club, Paris, 1948, Inter-Club, Toulouse, 1952, Galerie d'Orsay, Paris, 1955, Knights of St. Joan, Toulouse, 1955, Augustin Mus., Toulouse, 1960, Mcpl. Mus., Sete, France, 1961, Galeria Imagen y Sonido, Barcelona, Pavillon de Marsan, Paris, 1962, Mcpl. Mus., Tel Aviv, 1963, Cloister Gallery, Moissac, France, 1964, Cultural Ctr., Toulouse, 1965, 71, Tangueil U., Toulouse, 1966, Assn. Culture and Photog. Art, Avignon, France, 1967, Maison des Quatres Vents, Paris, 1968, Fiat Cultural Ctr., Turin, 1969, Musée Réattu, Arles, France, 1970, Toussaint Gallery, Angers, France, 1970, Galerie de l'Oeuvre, Toulouse, 1971, Ecole des Beaux-Arts, Tourcoing, France, 1976, Musée Nicéphore Niepce, Chalon-sur-Sâone, France, 1977, Galerij Paule Pia, Antwerp, Belgium, 1978, Credit Commercial de France, Toulouse, 1979, Galerie Le Trepied, Geneva, 1981, Fondation NAtionale de la Photographie, Lyon, France, 1983, Musée de Colmar, France, 1984, Réfectoire des Jacobins, Toulouse, 1986; recent group shows include: Le Trepied Galerie Photo, Geneva, 1981, Photographer's Gallery, London, 1981, Centre Culturel, Boulogne-Billancourt, France, 1981, Photokina 82, Cologne, 1982, Pavillon des Arts, Paris, 1984, Mus. Ludwig, Cologne, 1984, Palacio del Infantado, Guadalajara, Spain, 1985; represented in permanent collections: Bibliothè que Nationale, Paris, Musé e Ré attu, Musé e Nicephore Niepce, Musé e Cantini, Marseilles, France, Het Sterckshof Mus., Antwerp, Met. Mus. Art, N.Y.C., Va. Mus., Norfolk; books: (with text by Jean Sermet) The South of Spain, 1953; (with text by Jean Peyrade) St. Sernin de Toulouse, 1955; (with text by Yves Bottineau) Spain, 1955, Portugal, 1956, The Ways to Santiago, 1961; (with text by Victor Beyer) Pictures of Alsace, 1956; (with text by Antonio Borio) Sardinia, 1957; (with text by Ml de St-Pierre) Treasures of Turkey, 1957; (with text by Marcel Durliat) Roussillon Roman, 1958, Roman en Espagne, 1962; (with text by Rd Ritter) Basque Country, 1958, Bé arn-Bigorre, 1958; (with text by P. Wolff) History of Toulouse, 1958, Voix et Images de Toulouse, 1962; (with text by P. de Gorsse) Blue Guide of the Pyrenees, 1959; (with text by M. Vidal) Romanesque Quercy, 1959; (with text by Edouardo Junyent) Catalogne Romane, 1960; (with text by Robert Mesuret) Toulouse and Haut-Languedoc, 1961, Dialogues Avec la Lumière, 1979, Voyages en Ibérie, 1983, Toulouse d'Hier et d'Aujourdhi, 1984, others. Decorated chevalier Order of Merit, officier Ordre des Arts et Lettres; recipient French Cup for portraits Fédération Internationale de d'Art Photographique, 1951, French Cup for indsl. research and Edouard Belin medal, 1957, French Cup for landscape photography, 1967; Niepce prize, 1955, Internat. prize Colour Tourist Poster Competition, New Delhi, 1956, French Nat. prize for posters, 1959, Nadar Book prize, 1961, Lucien Lorell Cup, Bordeaux, France, 1969, Clemence Isaure prize Languedoc Acad., 1979, Grand Prix de la Ville de Paris, 1985. Hon. mem. French Com. of Photog. Art. Address: 7 rue Erasme, 31400 Toulouse France *

DIEZ BORQUE, JOSÉ-MARIA, Spanish literature educator; b. Gómara, Soria, Spain, Aug. 15, 1947; s. Sotero Diez and Evelia Borque; m. Angela Ena Bordonada, July 28, 1972; children: Javier, Jaime, Laura. Grad. in Philology, U. Zaragoza, Spain, 1970; D in Philology, U. Complutense, Madrid, 1975. Prof. U. Zaragoza, 1970-71; prof. U. Complutense, 1971-77, titular prof., 1978—; researcher in field; mem. confs. worldwide. Author 30 books on Spanish lit., 100 articles and monographs. Mem. CIS del CSIC, Assn. J. Hispanistas. Home: Isla de Oza 26, Villa Flor, 28035 Madrid Spain Office: U Complutense, Faculty Filologia, Madrid Spain

DIFFEY, TERENCE J., philosopher, educator; b. Poole, Eng., July 1, 1938; s. Perc Charles and Elsie Florence May (Gale) D.; m. Carole Theresa O'Driscoll, Sept. 8, 1962; children: William, Elizabeth, Catherine. BA in Philosophy and English Lit., Bristol U., 1960, PhD, 1966. Tutorial fellow U. Sussex, Brighton, Eng., 1962-63, asst. lectr., 1963-65, reader in philosophy, 1978—; tutor in philosophy U. Coll., Cardiff, Wales, 1961-62. Editor Brit. Jour. Aesthetics, 1977—; author: Tolstoy's What is Art?, 1985; contbr. articles to profl. jours. Mem. Brit. Soc. Aesthetics, Aristotelian Soc. Buddhist. Office: U Sussex, Arts Bldg, Falmer BN1 9QN, England

DI FRANCO, FIORENZA, university administrator; b. Budapest, Hungary, June 19, 1932; (parents Italian citizens); d. Oscarre and Olga (Czako) DiF.; 1 child, Olga. Doctorate, U. Rome, 1965; MA, Case-Western Res. U., 1965, PhD, 1969; MLS, Vatican Sch. Library Sci., Vatican City, 1974. Asst. prof. Notre Dame Coll., Cleve., 1965-66, Kent (Ohio) State U., 1966-67; prof. Case-Western Res. U., Cleve., 1968-72, U. Mo., St. Louis, 1972-74; prof., exec. directress J. Cabot Internat. Coll., Rome, 1976—. Author: Le Théâtre de Salacrou, 1970, Il Teatro di Eduardo, 1975, Eduardo, 1978, Eduardo da Scugnizzo a Senatore, 1983, Le Commedie di Eduardo, 1984. Grantee Wright-Plaisance Found., 1967-68, Ministry Fgn. Affairs, Rome, 1974-77. Home: Via Porta Fabbrica 9, 00165 Rome Italy Office: J Cabot Internat Coll, Via Massaua 7, 00162 Rome Italy

DI FURIA, GIULIO, psychiatrist; b. Ariano, Irpino, Italy, Oct. 24, 1925; came to U.S., 1953, naturalized, 1959; s. Oto Maria and Vincenza (Scauzillo) di F.; m. Marion Ann Ramputi, Mar. 27, 1955; children: Renzo, Diane, Robert, Richard, Julieann, Paul. M.D., Bologna (Italy) U., 1951. Chief hosp. services Medfield State Hosp., Harding, Mass., 1957-58; mem. staff Western State Hosp., Fort Stellacoom, Wash., 1958—; supt. Western State Hosp., 1963-80; asst. clin. prof. psychiatry and pharmacology U. Wash. Sch. Medicine, 1965—. Contbr. profl. jours. Recipient citation for outstanding service to Wash. in mental health, 1964. Fellow Am. Psychiat. Assn., Am. Geriatric Soc., N. Pacific Soc. Neurology and Psychiatry; mem. Am. Assn. Med. Supts. Mental Hosps. (mem. council 1971—). Address: 2125 1st Ave Seattle WA 98121

DIGGES, EDWARD S(IMMS), JR., lawyer; b. Pitts., June 30, 1946; s. Edward S. and Maria Jane (McHugh) D.; m. Wendy L. Knowk May 31, 1969; children: Courtney, Edward III, Ashley, John, Brittany. AB, Princeton U., 1968; JD, U. Md., 1971. Bar: Md. 1972, D.C. 1981, U.S. Supreme Ct. 1975. With staff of gov. State of Md., Annapolis, 1973; ptnr. Piper & Marbury, Washington and Balt., 1977-84; founding, mng. ptnr. Digges, Wharton & Levin, Annapolis, 1984—; instr. Advanced Bus. Law, Johns Hopkins U., 1975-78; lectr. Civil Procedure, U. Balt. Law Sch., 1976-78; mem. govs. commn. to revise Md. code, 1978—. Contbr. articles to profl. jours. Mem. Alumni Council Mercersburg Acad., 1982-88, pres. 1987-88; bd. advisors Indian Creek Sch., 1982-88, chmn. 1986-88; pres. Beacon Hill Community Assn., 1978-86. Served U.S. Army R.O.T.C. 1970-71. Fellow Am. Bar Found., Md. Bar Found.; mem. ABA, Md. State Bar Assn. (bd. govs. 1981-82), D.C. Bar Assn., Bar Assn. Balt. City (treas. 1982-83), Anne Arundel County Bar Assn., Am. Law Inst., Am. Bd. Trial Adv. (pres. Md. chpt. 1984—), Inn XIII, Am. Inns of Ct. (Master of the Bench 1986—), Internat. Assn. Def. Counsel, Fedn. Ins. and Corp. Counsel, Am. Judicature Soc., Md. Assn. Def. Trial Counsel (pres. 1978), Def. Research and Trial Lawyers Assn., Scribes. Democrat. Roman Catholic. Clubs: Ctr., Mcht.'s (Balt.); Annapolis Yacht, So. Md. Soc. (bd. govs., pres. 1988); Mid Ocean (Bermuda); Chester Golf and Country (Chestertown). Home: Hinchingham Chestertown MD 21620-0209 Office: 225 Duke of Gloucester St Annapolis MD 21401-6610

DIGIOVANNI, LEONARD JEROME, educational administrator; b. Bklyn., July 8, 1928; s. Robert and Katherine DiG.; B.S., Fordham U., 1950; B.S. in Edn., CCNY, 1951; M.S. in Edn., Rutgers State U., 1957; Ed.D., N.Y.U., 1970; m. Erika Busch, June 22, 1952; children—Angela, Leonard, Robert, Nina, William. Prin., Plainedge (N.Y.) Public Schs., 1957-72; prin. dist. curriculum coordinator South Plainfield, N.J., 1972-75; coordinator elem. edn., West Orange, N.J., 1975-76; supt. schs., Fairfield, N.J., 1976-78; cons., program coordinator N.J. State Edn. Dept., 1978-80; sec. bd. bus. adminstrn. Springfield (N.J.) Bd. Edn., 1980-85, interim supt. of schools, 1986-87; sec. bd. bus. adminstrn. Belleville (N.J.) Bd. Edn., 1987—; lectr. Rutgers State U.; adj. prof. edn.; instr. St. John's U., Keane Coll.; instr. Command and Gen. Staff Coll., 1972-74. Bd. dirs. Pooled Ins. Programs N.J., 1984-87. Served with U.S. Army, 1951-53, served to maj. USAR. NSF grantee, 1959; recipient Founders Day award NYU, 1970. Mem. NEA, Nat. Elem. Prins. Assn., N.Y.U. Roundtable, Watchung Arts Council (cofounder), Wildwood Crest Townhouse Condo Assn. N.J. (v.p. 1983, treas. 1987, bd. dirs. 1984-87), Assn. Sch. Bus. Officials Internat., Internat. Platform Assn. Clubs: Optimists Internat., Masons. Home: 27 Upper Mountain Ave Montclair NJ 07043 Office: Belleville Bd Edn Belleville NJ 07109

DIGMAN, LESTER ALOYSIUS, management educator; b. Kieler, Wis., Nov. 22, 1938; s. Arthur Louis and Hilda Dorothy (Jansen) D.; m. Ellen Rhomberg Pfohl, Jan. 15, 1966; children: Stephanie, Sarah, Mark. BSME, U. Iowa, 1961, MSIE, 1962, PhD, 1970. Registered profl. engr., Mass. Mgt. cons. U.S. Ameta, Rock Island, Ill., 1962-67; mgmt. instr. U. Iowa, Iowa City, 1967-69; head applied math. dept. U.S. Ameta, Rock Island, Ill., 1969-74, head managerial tng. dept., 1974-77; assoc. prof. mgt. U. Neb., Lincoln, 1977-84; dir. grad. studies in mgmt. U. Neb., 1982—; prof. mgt. U. Neb., Lincoln, 1984-87; Leonard E Whittaker Am. Charter disting. prof. mgmt. U. Nebr., Lincoln, 1987—; cons. various orgns., 1963-72; sec. treas. Mgmt. Services Associates Ltd., Davenport, Iowa, 1972-77; owner L.A. Digman and Assocs., Lincoln, 1977—; gen. ptnr. Letna Properties, Madison, Wis., 1978—. Author: Strategic Management, 1986; Network Analysis for Management Decisions, 1982; also articles. Recipient Dist. award SBA, 1980, certs. of appreciation Dept. of Def., 1972. Mem. Decision Scis. Inst. (charter) (assoc. program chmn. 1985-86, program chmn. 1986, pres. 1987-88), Strategic Mgmt. Soc. (founding), Acad. of Mgmt. The Planning Forum, Pan Pacific Bus. Assn., Inst. Mgmt. Scis., Ops. Research Soc. Am. Roman Catholic. Clubs: Hillcrest Country (Lincoln). Home: 7520 Lincolnshire Rd Lincoln NE 68506 Office: U Nebr 219 CBA Lincoln NE 68588

DIGNAN, THOMAS GREGORY, JR., lawyer; b. Worcester, Mass., May 23, 1940; s. Thomas Gregory and Hester Clare (Sharkey) D.; m. Mary Anne Connor, Sept. 16, 1978; children—Kellyanne E., Maryclare E. B.A., Yale U., 1961; J.D., U. Mich., 1964. Bar: Mass. 1964, U.S. Supreme Ct. 1968. Assoc. firm Ropes & Gray, Boston, 1964-74; ptnr. firm Ropes & Gray, 1974—; spl. asst. atty. gen. State of Mass., 1974-76; dir. Boston Edison Co. Asst. editor: Mich. Law Review, 1963-64; contbr. articles to profl. jours. Bd. dirs. Family Counseling and Guidance Ctrs., Inc., 1967-76, 78—, v.p., 1983-87, pres. 1987—; bd. dirs. Gov.'s Mgmt. Task Force, 1979-81; mem. fin. com. Town of Sudbury, 1982-85; moderator Town of Sudbury, 1985—; bd. advisers Environ. Law Ctr., Vt. Law Sch., 1981—; mem. vis. com. U. Mich. Law Sch. Mem. Am. Bar Assn., Mass. Bar Assn., Boston Bar Assn., Assn. Internationale du Droit Nucleaire, Am. Nuclear Soc., Am. Law Inst., Order of the Coif.; mem. Phi Delta Phi. Republican. Roman Catholic. Clubs: Downtown, Union. Home: 8 Saddle Ridge Rd Sudbury MA 01776 Office: Ropes and Gray One International Pl Boston MA 02110

DI GREGORIO, MARIO AURELIO UMBERTO, historian, educator; b. Milan, Italy, May 23, 1950; s. Giorgio Rosario and Annamaria (Fontana-Rossi) Di G. Degree in philosophy, Milan U., 1973; MA in History, Cambridge U., 1978; PhD in Anatomy, U. Coll., London, 1980. Research fellow Darwin Coll., Cambridge, Eng., 1978-81; research assoc. Darwin Correspondence, Cambridge, 1985-87; affiliated lectr. faculty of history Cambridge U., 1987—; vis. prof. biology, history, Hiram Coll., Ohio. Author: T.H. Huxley's Place in Natural Science, 1984, Darwin's Library, 1988. British Council Royal Soc. grantee, 1976-79, 78-81. Fellow Linnean Soc. London, Cambridge Philos. Soc.; mem. Brit. Soc. History Sci., Soc. History Natural History, Wagner Soc. Clubs: Univ. Pitts., United Oxford and Cambridge Univ. Home: 42 York St, Cambridge England Office: Darwin Coll, Silver St, Cambridge England CBE 9EU

DI JOSEPH, STEVEN, lawyer; b. N.Y.C., June 5, 1948; s. Arnold Edward and Christine (Mariano) Di J.; m. Jill Di Joseph, Aug. 2, 1976; children: Robin Brett, Justin Steven. B.A., N.Y.U., 1970; J.D., Bklyn. Law Sch., 1973. Bar: N.Y. 1974, U.S. Dist. (so. and ea. dists.) N.Y. 1974, U.S. Ct. Appeals (2d and 5th cirs.) 1974, U.S. Supreme Ct. 1977. Asst. dist. atty. Kings County, N.Y., 1973-75; assoc. Siff & Newman, P.C., N.Y.C., 1975-81, ptnr., 1982-83; mng. atty., Morris J. Eisen, P.C., N.Y.C., 1983-84, Peter E. DeBlasio P.C., N.Y.C., 1984-86; sr. ptnr., DiJoseph & Gluck, N.Y.C., 1986—; lectr. on appellate practice; cons. in field. Mem. ABA, (com. rules criminal procedure and evidence 1977-79, vice chmn. com. appellate practice 1983—). N.Y. Bar Assn. (award 1981), N.Y. County Lawyers Assn., Nat. Dist. Attys. Assn., Lawyer to Lawyer Consultation Panel. Author: The Liberalization of Discovery Rules with Respect to Relevant Medical Records and Related Materials, 1981. Contbr. articles on law to profl. jours. Office: 233 Broadway New York NY 10279

DIKE, AZUKA ANTHONY, educator; b. Awka, Nigeria; s. Johnson Chukwuemeka and Nwakelundu (Mottoh) D.; m. Virginia Weisell, July 19, 1970; children: Ejimaria, Ijeoma, Nkem, Chinelo, Chinweze. BA, Brandeis U., 1960-64; MA, Columbia U., 1966, PhD, 1974. Tchr. Ch. Missionary Schs., eastern provinces, Nigeria, 1953-59; instr. Montclair State Coll., Upper Montclair, N.J., 1967-68, Keuka Coll., Keuka Park, N.Y., 1968-69, Marymount Coll., Tarry Town, N.Y., 1969-72; asst. prof. Ramapo State Coll., Maywah, N.J., 1972-75; sr. lectr. U. Nigeria, Nsukka, Nigeria, 1975—; dept. head U. Nigeria, 1982-85; coordinator social services, 1979-82. Fellow Am. Anthrop. Assn.; mem. Internat. Union Anthrop. and Ethnol. Scis., Commn. on Urban Anthropology and Documentation. Home: 8 Mbonu Ojike St, Nsukka Nigeria Office: U Nigeria, Dept Sociology & Anthropology, Nsukka Nigeria

DIKSHIT, GANESH DATTA, mathematician, educator; b. Varanasi, Uttar Pradesh, India, July 10, 1935; arrived in New Zealand, 1968; s. Baldev and Roopkali (Chaube) D.; m. Malti Ojha, July 1, 1957; children: Ritu, Anshu, Shikha, Rashmi, Devesh. BA, B.R. Coll., Agra, 1954; MA, U. Allahabad, 1956, DPhil., 1960. Lectr. U. Allahabad, India, 1960-66, 67-68, U. Nigeria, Nsukka, 1966-67; sr. lectr. U. Auckland, New Zealand, 1968—. Assoc. editor Math. Chronicle, 1976-79; contbr. articles to profl. jours. Served as 2d lt. Nat. Cadet Corps (India), 1963-66. Life mem. Indian Math. Soc., Allahabad Math. Soc. (asst. editor Indian Jour. Maths. 1962-69, assoc. editor 1977—), Indian Sci. Congress; mem. Am. Math. Soc., New Zealand Math. Soc. Home: 79 Empire Rd, Epsom, Auckland 1003, New Zealand Office: Dept Maths, U Auckland, Pvt Bag, Auckland 1001, New Zealand

DIKTAS, CHRISTOS JAMES, lawyer; b. Hackensack, N.J., June 17, 1955; s. Christos James and Elpiniki (Angelou) D. Student U. Salonika (Greece), 1976, U. Copenhagen (Denmark), 1976. BA, Montclair State Coll., 1977; JD, Calif. Western Sch. Law, 1981. Bar: N.J. 1982, U.S. Dist. Ct. N.J. 1982. Law sec. Honorable James F. Madden, Superior Ct. Judge, Hackensack, N.J., 1981-82; sr. assoc. Klinger, Nicolette, Mavroudis & Honig, Hackensack, 1982-85; ptnr. Montecallo & Diktas, Hackensack, 1985-86, Biagiotti, Marino, Montecallo & Diktas, Hackensack, 1986—; asst. counsel Bergen County, 1986-87; atty. zoning bd. adjustment Borough Cliffside Park, N.J., 1986; atty. planning bd. Borough Ridgefield, N.J., 1987—; adj. prof. law Montclair (N.J.) State Coll., 1988—. Editor lead articles Calif. Western Internat. Law Jour., 1980-81. Campaign dir. Kingman for Senate Com., Bergen County, N.J., 1983; mcpl. coordinator Kean for Gov. campaign, 1985; asst. treas. Arthur F. Jones for Congress, 9th Congl. Dist., 1986—. Mem. ABA, N.J. Bar Assn., Bergen County Bar Assn., Order of Am. Hellenic Edn. Progressive Assn., Phi Alpa Delta (parliamentarian Campbell E. Beaumont chpt. 1978-81). Republican. Greek Orthodox. Lodge: Sons of Pericles (5th dist. gov. 1976-77, supreme gov. 1977-78). Home: 243 Columbia Ave Cliffside Park NJ 07010 Office: Biagiotti Marino Montecallo & Diktas 294 Union St Hackensack NJ 07601

DILÃO, RUI MANUEL AGOSTINHO, physicist; b. Lisbon, Portugal, July 13, 1955; s. Artur Eduardo Ramalho and Maria Manuela da Piedade Agostinho D.; m. Ana Maria Oliveira Noronha e Menezes da Costa; children: Joana Ramos. Licenciatura in Physics, Faculty Scis. Lisbon, 1980; PhD in Physics, Tech. U. Lisbon, 1986. Asst. New U. Lisbon, 1980-81; asst. Tech. U. Lisbon, 1981-85, asst. prof., 1985-86, aux. prof., 1986; sr. fellow European Orgn. Nuclear Research, Geneva, 1986—. Contbr. articles to profl. jours. Mem. Am. Math. Soc. (reviewer 1984), Soc. Indsl. Applied Math., N.Y. Acad. Scis., Portuguese Physics Soc., Associacao de Ciência E Tecnologia Para Desenvolvimento. Home: care R Carlos Calisto, 3 3 Esq, 1400 Lisbon Portugal Office: Cern SPS div, CH 1211, Geneva Switzerland

DILKS, ELIZABETH THOMAS S., poet, clubwoman; b. North Merion, Bryn Mawr, Pa., July 21, 1917; d. Benjamin and Elizabeth Jones (Thomas) Shank; m. John Henry Dilks, June 17, 1945; student Louis Shenk Voice

Studios, Phila., 1939-42, Pison Acad. of Appreciation of Arts, Phila., 1941-43, Taylor Coll., Phila., 1943-45. Author, illustrator poetry: His and Hers, 1976, A Drop in the Bucket; contbr. poetry to mags. and various anthologies in American Poetry, Contemporary Poets of America. Recipient Soc. Disting. Am. award, 1976; poem hung at Christian C. Sanderson Mus. Fellow Internat. Acad. Poets, The World Literary Acad. Eng. (hon.); mem. Acad. Am. Poets and Writers, Pa. Acad. Fine Arts, Poets and Writers N.Y., Nat. League Am. Pen Women (Phila. chpt.), Internat. Platform Assn., Acad. Am. Poets, Christian C. Sanderson Mus. (life), DAR (Downtown chpt.), Chester County Library, G. Wilson Peale House, Phila. Clubs: Whitford Country (Exton, Pa.), Mercedes-Benz of Am. Home: 394 Carlton Pl Exton PA 19341

DILL, KENNETH AUSTIN, pharmaceutical chemistry educator; b. Oklahoma City, Dec. 11, 1947; s. Austin Glenn and Margaret (Blocker) D. S.B., Mass. Inst. Tech., 1971, S.M., 1971; Ph.D., U. Calif.-San Diego, 1978. Damon Runyon-Walter Winchell fellow Stanford (Calif.) U., 1978-81; asst. prof. chemistry U. Fla., Gainesville, 1981-82; asst. prof. pharm. chemistry and pharmacy U. Calif., San Francisco, 1982-85, assoc. prof., 1985—. PEW Found. scholar. Contbr. numerous sci. articles to profl. publs. Patentee in field. Mem. Am. Chem. Soc., Am. Phys. Soc., Biophys. Soc., AAAS. Office: Univ Calif Pharm Chemistry Dept San Francisco CA 94143

DILLABER, PHILIP ARTHUR, infosystems specialist, consultant; b. Springfield, Mass., Aug. 24, 1922; s. Ralph E. and Grace (Holman) D.; m. Jacqueline M. Bertin, July 16, 1946; children: Anne Erline (Mrs. Donald Youngblood), Katherine Marie, John Philip, Patricia Elizabeth. BA, Am. Internat. Coll., 1949; MBA, Ind. U., 1950; postgrad. U. Mich., Ind. U., 1950-54; PhD, Pacific Western U., 1985. Clk. research and devel. div. Springfield Armory, 1946-47; research asst. dept. econs. Ind. U., 1951, lectr. econs., 1955-57; orgn. and methods examiner U.S. Air Force, Gulfport, Miss., 1952-53; mgmt. analyst 5th U.S. Army, Chgo., 1954-61; program progress and resources mgmt. analyst Continental Army Command, Ft. Monroe, Va., 1962-66; adminstrv. officer U.S. Army NIKE-X System Office, Alexandria, Va., 1967; program analyst Office Asst. Chief Staff Force Devel., Dept. Army, Washington, 1967-71; budget analyst Office Dep. Chief Staff Logistics, Dept. Army, Washington, 1971-74, Office Dep. Chief Staff Research, Devel. and Acquisition, 1974-80; analyst Info. Spectrum, Inc., Arlington, Va., 1980-87, Nat. Def. Exec. Reserve, 1985—; guest lectr. econs. Purdue U., 1959-61. Served with AUS, 1943-46. Mem. Am. Econ. Assn., Am. Soc. Pub. Adminstrn., Beta Gamma Sigma.

DILLARD, DUDLEY, economist, educator; b. Ontario, Oreg., Oct. 18, 1913; s. John James and Frances (Cunning) D.; m. Louisa Gardner, August 22, 1939; children: Lorraine Gardner (Mrs. William C. Gray), Amber Frances (Mrs. Douglas G. Kelly). B.S., U. Calif., 1935, Ph.D., 1940; vis. scholar, Harvard, 1939, Columbia, 1940. Teaching asst. U. Calif., 1935-36, Flood fellow in econs., 1936-37, research asst., 1937-38, teaching asst., 1938-39; Newton Booth Travelling fellow 1939-40; instr. econs. U. Colo., 1940-41, U. Del., 1941-42; faculty U. Md., 1942—, chmn. dept. econs., 1951-75, acting provost div. behavioral and social scis., 1976-77; vis. asso. prof. econs. Columbia, 1948-50, vis. prof., summer, 1951, 55, 58; cons. U.S. Army, 1945-46. Author: The Economics of John Maynard Keynes, 1948; (with others) Post-Keynesian Economics, 1954; Economic Development of North Atlantic Community, 1967; (with others) The Policy Consequences of John Maynard Keynes, 1985, The Foundations of Keynesian Analysis, 1988; Editorial bd.: Jour. Econ. History, 1948-54; Contbr. profl. jours. Chmn. Gov.'s Com. on Employment in Md., 1962-64; mem. Gov.'s Adv. Com. on Manpower Devel. and Tng., 1962-67; Mem. U.S. exec. bd. Am. Coll. in Paris, 1966-86, chmn., 1979-81. Recipient Veblen-Commons award, 1986. Mem. Am. Econ. Assn., So. Econ. Assn. (pres. 1976-77), Eastern Econ. Assn. (exec. bd. 1982-85, pres. 1987-88), Assn. Evolutionary Econs. (pres. 1979), History Econs. Soc. (v.p. 1982-83), Econ. History Soc., AAUP, Phi Beta Kappa, Pi Gamma Mu, Beta Gamma Sigma, Beta Alpha Psi. Club: Cosmos (Washington, District of Columbia). Home: 7007 Forest Hill Dr University Park Hyattsville MD 20782 Office: Dept Econs U Md College Park MD 20742

DILLARD, EARLE STERLING, insurance company executive; b. Man, W.Va., Apr. 24, 1925; s. Andrew Sterling and Margaret Grace (Keiffer) D.; m. Naomi Ruth Ferrell, Aug. 31, 1947; children: Dan Earle, Cherilyn Ruth, David Ferrell, Kevin Andrew, Kerry Paul, Julie Beth. Student, Marshall U., 1953-54. Supr. agts. Security Ins. Co., Huntington, W.Va., 1948-54; pres. Dollar Stores Corp., Huntington, 1971-79, Harlo Corp., Huntington, 1971-82; pres., treas. Bloss & Dillard, Inc., Huntington, 1954—; pres. Ins. Mgrs., Inc., Columbus, Ohio, 1977-84, Agts. Ins. Markets, Inc., Richmond, Va., 1979-86; bd. dirs. Huntington Fed. Savs. Loan Assn.; chmn. bd. Rubberlite, Inc., Accufacts Investigations Inc., 1986—, Wee IV Inc., 1986—, I.P.F. Corp., 1987—. Chmn. Huntington Mayor's Adv. Com., 1967-69, 86—; pres. Huntington YMCA, 1969-71, Marshall U. Big Green Scholarship Found., 1981-83. Served with USCG, 1943-46, ETO. Named W.Va. Ins. Agts. Co. Man of Yr., 1977, YMCA Layman of the Yr., 1964. Mem. W.Va. Ins. Assn. (pres. 1969), Am. Assn. Mng. Gen. Agts. (pres. 1974-75), W.Va. Surplus Lines Assn. (pres. 1979-80), U.S.A. Alliance (pres. 1985-87), Am. Legion, VFW, C. of C. Baptist. Clubs: Guyan Country, Wild Dunes Country. Lodges: Masons, Lions (pres. 1964-65). Home: 1934 S Englewood Rd Huntington WV 25701 Office: 1925 Adams Ave Huntington WV 25704

DILLARD, JOHN MILTON, counselor, educator, author; b. Prenter, W.Va., July 25, 1936; s. John Milton and Lucy (Martin) D.; divorced; children: Scott Maurice, Brian Milton. Student, W.Va. State Coll., 1957-58; BS in Elem. Edn., Wilberforce U., 1964; EdM in Sch. Counseling, SUNY, Buffalo, 1971, PhD in Counselor Edn., 1975; postgrad. in higher edn. adminstrn., Okla. State U., Buffalo, 1981-82. Tchr. elem. sch. Buffalo, 1964-72, tchr. basic adult edn., 1966-69, elem. sch. guidance counselor, 1972-76; clin. teaching asst. dept. counseling and ednl. psychology SUNY, Buffalo, 1974-75, adj. asst. prof., 1975-76; vis. asst. prof. U. Carabobo (Venezuela), Buffalo, summer 1978; assoc. prof. counseling and student personnel, dept. applied behavioral studies in edn. Okla. State U., Stillwater, 1976-84, also coordinator higher student personnel adminstrn. programs; prof. ednl. psychology and ednl. adminstrn. Tex. A&M. U., College Station, 1985—, also coordinator of coll. student personnel program, coordinator univ. lecture series, 1985-86; chmn. 1986 Conf. on Career Devel. of Women; cons. devel. workshop presentation; co-chmn. Inquiry Group on Career Devel.; speaker in field; mem. Nat. Council Accreditation Tchr.'s Edn. Bd. Examiners, 1988-91. Author: Multicultural Counseling: Toward Ethnic and Cultural Relevance in Human Encounters; Lifelong Career Planning; Systematic Interviewing: Communication Skills for Professional Effectiveness; also numerous articles; cons. editor Jour. Cross Cultural Psychology; assoc. editor Coll. Student Affairs Jour.; adv. editor Jour. Ednl. Psychology; cons. editor, bd. dirs. Jour. Ednl. Internat. Student Personnel, 1979-80; mem. editorial bd. Jour. Voc. Behavior, Coll. Student Affairs Jour., Jour. of Coll. Student Devel. Mem. Internat. Assn. Cross-Cultural Psychology, Am. Psychol. Assn., Am. Assn. Counseling and Devel., Am. Ednl. Research Assn. (chmn. career counseling and vocat. devel. panel), Am. Psychol. Assn., So. Assn. for Coll. Student Affairs, Am. Sch. Counselor Assn., Okla. Sch. Counselor Assn. (past v.p.), Phi Delta Kappa, Kappa Alpha Psi. Office: Tex A&M U Dept Ednl Psychology 704 Harrington Edn Ctr College Station TX 77843

DILLE, JOHN FLINT, JR., broadcasting executive, editor, publisher; b. Chgo., Nov. 14, 1913; s. John Flint and Phoebe Minerva (Crabtree) D.; m. Jayne Paulman, Apr. 9, 1938; children—John Flint III, Joanne Paulman Barrett. A.B., U. Chgo., 1935, A.M., 1956; Litt.D. (hon.), Tri-State Coll., Ind., 1965. Producer newspaper features Nat. Newspaper Syndicate, Chgo., 1935-52; chmn. Federated Media; pub. Elkhart (Ind.) Truth, Greencastle (Ind.) Banner-Graphic; operator WTRC-AM-WYEZ-FM, Elkhart and South Bend, Ind., WQHK-AM, WMEE-FM, Ft. Wayne, Ind., WCUZ, WCUZ-FM, Grand Rapids, Mich., WCKY, WWEZ-FM, Cin., KSKS, KVLT-FM, Tulsa; dir. emeritus First Nat. Bank Elkhart;. vice chmn. Ind. Toll Rd Commn., 1961-66; chmn. Minority Broadcaster Investment Fund. Served to lt. comdr. USNR, World War II. Recipient Disting. Journalism award U. Minn., 1977. Mem. Am. Soc. Newspaper Editors, U. Chgo. Alumni Assn. (past pres.), Nat. Assn. Broadcasters (chmn. joint bd. dirs. 1965-67), Broadcast Pioneers, Chief Execs. Orgn. (past pres.), Elkhart C. of C. (past pres., dir.), Alpha Delta Phi, Sigma Delta Chi. Episcopalian (past vestry). Clubs: National Press, International (Washington); Elcona Country (Elkhart) (dir., incorporator); University (Chgo.); Lost Tree, Old Port Yacht (North Palm Beach, Fla.); Everglades. Home: 1 Holly Ln Elkhart IN 46514 also: 11450 Turtle Beach Rd North Palm Beach FL 33408 Office: PO Box 487 Elkhart IN 46515

DILLEHAY, DAVID ROGERS, pyrotechnist; b. Shreveport, Sept. 21, 1936; s. Thomas Jefferson, Jr. and Rachel (Todd) D.; B.A. in Chemistry, Rice U., Houston, 1958; Ph.D. in Chemistry, Clayton U.-St. Louis, 1983; m. Marilyn Heath, Nov. 23, 1957; children—David, Janet. With Morton Thiokol Corp., Marshall, Tex., 1958—, process engrng. supr., 1979-81, spl. projects supr., 1981-84, research and devel. projects supr., 1984—. Recipient award U.S. Army Material Command, 1969; named Image Maker for Marshall of 1983, Marshall C. of C. Mem. Am. Mgmt. Assn., Am. Def. Preparedness Ass-. (1st v.p. La. chpt. 1981, pres. Ark.-La.-Tex. chpt. 1982, nat. council rep. 1983), Internat. Pyrotechnics Soc. (sec. 1980-83, v.p. 1984-86, pres., 1986—), R Assn., Thiokol-Longhorn Mgmt. Club, Ark.-La.-Tex. Wireless Assn. Roman Catholic. Author, patentee in field. Home: 107 Ashwood Terr Marshall TX 75670 Office: PO Box 1149 Marshall TX 75670

DILLING, KIRKPATRICK WALLWICK, lawyer; b. Evanston, Ill., Apr. 11, 1920; s. Albert W. and Elizabeth (Kirkpatrick) D.; m. Betty Ellen Bronson, June 18, 1942 (div. July 1944); m. Elizabeth Ely Tilden, Dec. 11, 1948; children—Diana Jean, Eloise Tilden, Victoria Walgreen, Albert Kirkpatrick. Student, Cornell U., 1939-40; B.S. in Law, Northwestern U., 1942; postgrad., DePaul U., 1946-47, L'Ecole Vaubier, Montreux, Switzerland; Degre Normal, Sorbonne U., Paris. Bar: Ill. 1947, Wis., Ind., Mich., Md., La., Tex., Okla., U.S. Dist. Ct. (ea. dist.) Wis., U.S. Ct. Appeals (2d, 3d, 5th, 7th, 8th, 9th, 10th, 11th, D.C. cirs.), U.S. Supreme Ct. Ptnr. Dilling & Dilling and predecessors, Chgo., 1948—; gen. counsel Nat. Health Fedn., Cancer Control Soc.; dir. Dillman Labs.; v.p. Midwest Medic-Aide, Inc.; spl. counsel Herbalife (U.K.) Ltd., Herbalife Australasia Pty., Ltd.; lectr. on pub. health law. Contbr. articles to profl. publs. Bd. dirs. Nat. Health Fedn., Adele Davis Found. Served to 1st lt. AUS, 1943-46. Mem. ABA, Ill. Bar Assn., Chgo. Bar Assn., Assn. Trial Lawyers Am., Cornell Soc. Engrs., Am. Legion, Air Force Assn., Pharm. Advt. Club, Delta Upsilon. Republican. Episcopalian. Clubs: Rolls Royce Owners', Tower, Cornell U., Chicago. Home: 1120 Lee Rd Northbrook IL 60062 also: Casa Dorado Indian Wells CA 92260 Office: 150 N Wacker Dr Chicago IL 60601

DILLINGHAM, MARJORIE CARTER, foreign language educator; b. Bicknell, Ind., Aug. 20, 1915; m. William Pyrle Dillingham, (dec. 1981); children: William Pyrle (dec.), Robert Carter, Sharon Dillingham Martin. PhD in Spanish (Delta Kappa Gamma scholar and fellow), Fla. State U., 1970. High sch. tchr., Fla.; former instr. St. George's Sch., Havana; former mem. faculty Panama Canal Zone Coll., Fla. State U., U. Ga., Duke U.; dir. traveling Spanish conversation classes abroad. U.S. rep. (with husband) Hemispheric Conf. on Taxation, Rosario, Argentina. Named to Putnam County Hall of Fame, 1986. Mem. Am. Assn. Tchrs. Spanish and Portuguese (past pres. Fla. chpt.), Fla. Edn. Assn. (past pres. fgn. lang. div.), La Sociedad Honoraria Hispanica (past nat. pres.), Fgn. Lang. Tchrs. Leon County, Fla. (pres.), Delta Kappa Gamma (pres.), Phi Kappa Phi, Sigma Delta Pi, Beta Pi Theta, Kappa Delta Pi, Alpha Omicron Pi, Delta Kappa Gamma. Home: 2109 Trescott Dr Tallahassee FL 32312

DILLON, FRANCIS PATRICK, human resources executive, management consultant; b. Long Beach, Calif., Mar. 15, 1937; s. Wallace Myron and Mary Elizabeth (Land) D.; B.A., U. Va., 1959; M.S., Def. Fgn. Affairs Sch., 1962; M.B.A., Pepperdine U., 1975; m. Vicki Lee Dillon, Oct. 1980; children—Cary Randolph, Francis Patrick Jr., Randee, Rick. Traffic mgr., mgr. personnel services Pacific Telephone Co., Sacramento and Lakeport, Calif., 1966-69; asst. mgr. manpower planning and devel. Pan-Am. World Airways, N.Y.C., 1969-71; mgr. personnel and orgn. devel. Continental Airlines, Los Angeles, 1971-74; dir. personnel Farwest Services, Inc., Irvine, Calif., 1974; dir. human resources Bourns, Inc., Riverside, Calif., 1974-80; dir. employee and community relations MSI Data Corp., 1980-83; pres. Pavi Enterprises, 1983—; mgmt. cons., 1983—; pres., chief exec. officer Personnel Products & Services Inc., 1984—; pres. Meditrans Inc. Bd. dirs. Health Services Maintenance Orgn., Inc., Youth Services Center, Inc.; vol. precinct worker. Served to lt. comdr. USN, 1959-66; asst. naval attaché, Brazil, 1963-65. Recipient Disting. Service award Jaycees, 1969; Jack Cates Meml. Vol. of Year award Youth Service Center, 1977. Mem. Assn. Internal Mgmt. Cons.'s, Am. Soc. Personnel Adminstrn., Personnel Indsl. Relations Assn., Am. Soc. Tng. and Devel. Republican. Episcopalian. Clubs: Mission Viejo Sailing, YMCA Bike, Mission Viejo Ski, Caving, Toastmasters (pres. 1966-67), Have Dirt Will Travel. Office: Personnel Products & Services Inc 3700 S Susan Suite 100 Santa Ana CA 92704

DILLON, HOWARD BURTON, civil engineer; b. Hardyville, Ky., Aug. 12, 1935; s. Charlie Edison and Mary Opal (Bell) D.; m. Bonny Jean Garard, May 19, 1962; 1 child, Robert Edward. BCE, U. Louisville, 1958, MCE, 1960; postgrad., Okla. State U., 1962, Mich. State U., 1962-65. Registered profl. engr., Ind. Instr. U. Louisville, Ky., 1958-60; from assoc. prof. to prof. Ind. Inst. Tech., Ft. Wayne, 1960-62; NSF fellow Okla. State U., Stillwater, 1962; NSF grantee, instr. Mich. State U., East Lansing, 1962-67; head civil engring. dept. MW Inc. Cons. Engrs., Indpls., 1967-83; project mgr. civil div. SEG Engrs. & Cons., Indpls., 1983—; asst. dir. to local pub. road needs study for Ind., 1970; mem. design com. for dams in Ind., 1974—; spl. cons. to Ind. Dept. Nat. Resources on dams, 1980—; mem. infrastructure com. for State of Ind., 1984—. Contbr. articles to profl. jours. Committeeman Wayne 52 precinct, Indpls., 1972-86; vice-ward chmn. Wayne South Twp., Indpls., 1986-87. Hazelett and Erdal scholar, 1957-58, W.B. Wendt scholar U. Louisville. Mem. ASCE (Outstanding Civil Engring. Grad. award 1958), NSPE, Am. Soc. Engring. Edn., Am. Soc. for Testing and Materials, Internat. Soc. Found. Engrs., Internat. Acad. Sci., Constrn. Specifications Inst., Chi Epsilon. Democrat. Baptist. Lodge: Optimists (pres. Suburban West chpt. 1972-74, bd. dirs. Suburban West 1974-78, lt. gov. Ind. dist. 1973-74). Home: 6548 Westdrum Rd Indianapolis IN 46241 Office: SEG Engrs and Cons Inc Century Bldg 36 S Pennsylvania St Suite 360 Indianapolis IN 46204

DILLON, J. PAT, telecommunications engineer; b. Long Beach, Calif., Sept. 10, 1945; s. Joseph C. and Mary (Friend) D.; m. Kathleen Doffing, Sept. 14, 1974; children—Shondra L., Jeffrey J. Student U. Colo., 1963-67. Chemist, Longmont Foundry (Colo.), 1965-67; metallurgist Dow Chem. Co., Rocky Flats, Colo., 1967-68; chemist Great Western Sugar Co., Longmont, Colo., 1968-70; engr. Mountain Bell Co., Boulder, Colo., 1970-72; cons. engr. Henkels & McCoy, Blue Bell, Pa., 1972-80; staff engr. Northwestern Bell Co., Mpls., 1980-85; sr. communications specialist Burnup and Sims, Camarillo, Calif., 1985—; owner, mgr. Papillon Enterprises, Apple Valley, Minn., 1982-85, Camarillo, 1985—; co-owner Butterfly Boutique, Apple Valley, 1981-85; owner Country Craftworks, Camarillo, 1986—, TelCom Tech, Port Hueneme, Calif., 1987, Camarillo, 1987—. Author: (pamphlet) How to Save Money Building Your Own House. Mem. Minn. Ind. Businessmen, Innovators Council (award 1982). Roman Catholic. Home: 6267 Calle Bodega Camarillo CA 93010 Office: Burnup & Sims 751 Daily Dr Suite 300 Camarillo CA 93010

DILLON, MICHAEL ROY, transportation executive; b. London, Nov. 23, 1938; s. John Roger and Sarah Elizabeth Jessie (Wilmott) D.; m. Phyllis Elizabeth Grace Draeger, Mar. 2, 1963; children: Susan Elizabeth, Patricia Ann. Cert. of Edn., Thomas Calton Sch., London, 1955. Shipping clk. P&O Group Cos., London, 1953-57; sr. forwarding clk. Shipping and Coal Co. Ltd., Rochester, Eng., 1959-63; clk. Sommerfeld and Thomas Ltd., Kent, Eng., 1963-71; supr., asst. mgr. then mgr. Powell Duffryn Shipping Services Ltd., Tilbury Essex, Eng., 1972-84; mgr. Decotrans Ltd., Tilbury Essex, Eng., 1985-86; rep. U.K. Leipzig Fair Agy., London, 1986—. Hon. treas. London-Berlin Com., 1986—. Served with Brit. Army, 1957-59. Fellow Inst. Freight Forwarders; mem. Inst. Chartered Shipbrokers, Brit. Inst. Mgmt. Home: 34 Ash Crescent, Higham Village, Kent ME3 7BA, England Office: Leipzig Fair Agy in Gt Britain, Queensgate Ctr, Orsett Rd, Grays, Essex RM17 5DJ, England

DILLON, PHILLIP MICHAEL, construction company executive; b. Ypsilanti, Mich., July 15, 1944; s. Robert Timothy and Maxine Helen (Elliott) D.; student Mich. State U., 1962-66; m. Phyllis Louise Brooks, Jan. 21, 1978; children: Richard, Debora, Michael, Robert, Karen. Store mgr. Morse Shoe, Inc., Detroit, 1964-68, asst. dir. store planning and constrn., Canton, Mass., 1968-72; dir. store planning and constrn. Stride Rite Corp., Boston, 1972-74; sr. v.p. Capitol Cos., Inc., Arlington Heights, Ill., 1974-81; chmn. bd., chief exec. officer Standard Cos., Inc., Palatine, Ill., 1982-83; co-owner, sr. v.p. Eagle Constrn. Corp., 1983-88; chief exec. officer Dillon Enterprises Ltd., Lemont, Ill., 1988—. Mem. Inst. Store Planners, Urban Land Inst. Roman Catholic. Club: Green Acres Sportsman. Office: 50 E New Ave Lemont IL 60439

DILLON, ROBERT MORTON, association executive; b. Seattle, Oct. 27, 1923; s. James Richard and Lucille (Morton) D.; m. Mary Charlotte Beeson, Jan. 6, 1943; children: Robert Thomas, Colleen Marie Dillon Brown, Patrick Morton. Student, U. Ill., 1946-47; B. Arch., U. Wash., 1949; M.A. in Architecture, U. Fla., 1954. Registered architect, Fla. Designer-draftsman Williams and Longstreet (Architects), Greenville, S.C., 1949-50, William G. Lyles, Bissett, Carlisle & Wolff (Architects), Columbia, S.C., 1949-50, Robert M. Dillon and Wm. B. Eaton (Architects), Gainesville, Fla., 1952-55; staff architect Bldg. Research Adv. Bd., Nat. Acad. Scis.-NRC, Washington, 1955-56; project dir. Bldg. Research Adv. Bd., Nat. Acad. Scis.-NRC, 1956-58, exec. dir., 1958-77; exec. sec. U.S. nat. com. for Conseil Internat. du Batiment, 1962-74; Sec. U.S. Planning Com. 2d Internat. Conf. on Permafrost, Yakutsk, USSR, 1972-74; exec. asst. to pres. Nat. Inst. Bldg. Scis., Washington, 1978-81, v.p., 1982-84, acting controller, 1983-84; exec. v.p. Am. Council Constrn. Edn., Washington, 1984—; Asst. prof. architecture Clemson Coll., 1949-50; instr., asst. prof. architecture U. Fla., 1950-55; lectr. structural theory and design Catholic U. Am., 1956-62; guest lectr. Air Force Inst. Tech., Wright-Patterson AFB, 1964-65; distinguished faculty Acad. Code Adminstrn. and Enforcement, U. Ill., 1972; Professorial lectr. engrng. George Washington U., 1973-77, 81-82; vis. prof. architecture U. Utah, 1978; vis. prof. Coll. Environ. Design, U. Okla., 1984, adj. assoc. prof. bldg. sci., 1985-87. Author: (with S.W. Crawley) Steel Buildings: Analysis and Design, 1970, 3d edit., 1983; contbg. author: Funk and Wagnall's New Ency, 1972; editor-in-chief Guide to the Use of NEHRP Provisions in Earthquake Resistant Design of Bldgs., 1987. Cons. Ednl. Facilities Labs., N.Y.C., 1958-71; Mem. adv. com., low-income housing demonstration program HUD, Washington, 1964-67; mem. working groups U.S.-USSR Agreement on Housing and Other Construction, 1975—; mem. sub-panel on housing White House Panel on Civilian Tech., Washington, 1961-62; mem. advs. to the F. Stuart Fitzpatrick Meml. Award Trustee, 1969-84, chmn., 1974-78; mem. adv. panel Basic Homes Program OEO and HUD, 1972-77; mem. Nat. Adv. Council on Research in Energy Conservation, 1975-78; mem. adv. com. Council Am. Bldg. Ofcls., 1976-87; mem. tech. council on bldg. codes and standards Nat. Conf. of States, 1977-78. Served with USNR, 1942-45. Mem. AIA (mem. com. on research for architecture 1962-67, chmn. 1969, chmn. com. archtl. barriers 1967-68, mem. nat. housing com. 1970-72, 84-85), Nat. Acad. Code Adminstrn. (trustee 1976-80, mem. exec. com. 1978-82, mem. new bd. dirs. 1980-82, 83-84, sec.-treas. 1981-82), Md. Soc. Architects, ASCE (task com. on cold regions 1977-79, tech. council on codes and standards, exec. com. 1976-81, sec, tech. council on codes and standards, exec. com. 1977-78, mem. tech. council on cold regions engring., exec. com. 1976-84, vice chmn. 1980-81, chmn. 1981), Am. Inst. Steel Constrn. (profl.), Sigma Lambda Chi. Home: 811 Arrington Dr Silver Spring MD 20901 Office: 1015 15th St NW Suite 700 Washington DC 20005

DIMANT, JACOB, internist; b. Rehovot, Israel, Apr. 27, 1947; s. Simcha and Ita D.; came to U.S., 1972, naturalized, 1977; M.D., Hadassah Med. Sch., Hebrew U., Jerusalem, 1972; m. Rose Bea Jearolmen, Sept. 11, 1974. Intern, Maimonides Med. Center, Bklyn., 1972-73, resident in medicine, 1973-75, chief resident in medicine, 1975-76; fellow in rheumatology Downstate Med. Center, Bklyn., 1976-78; practice medicine specializing in internal medicine and rheumatology, Bklyn., 1975—; dir. rheumatology Maimonides Med. Center, Bklyn., 1978—, assoc. dir. med. edn., 1978-80; med. dir. Prospect Park Nursing Home, Bklyn., 1977-87, Crown Nursing Home, Bklyn., 1983—, Clove Lakes Nursing Home and health related facility, Staten Island, N.Y., 1985—; asst. prof. medicine SUNY, Bklyn., 1978—. Arthritis Found. of N.Y. fellow, 1977-78. Diplomate Am. Bd. Internal Medicine and Rheumatology, Am. Bd. Quality Assurance and Utilization Rev. Physicians. Named hon. police surgeon N.Y.C. Police Dept., 1982—. Fellow ACP, Am. Rheumatism Assn. (co-founder), Am. Fedn. Clin. Research; mem. Am. Geriatric Soc., N.Y. Rheumatism Assn., Am. Fedn. Clin. Research, Am. Geriatric Soc., Am. Med. Dirs. Assn., N.Y. Med. Dirs. Assn. Contbr. articles to med. jours. Office: Kingsboro Med Group 3457 Nostrand Ave Brooklyn NY 11229

DIMBATH, MERLE F., economic consultant, business educator; b. Dayton, Ohio, Mar. 21, 1939; s. Merle S. and Zella (Shadowens) D.; children—Merle, Richard, Sesilie, Eric. B.S. in Commerce, U. Va., 1961; M.A. in Mktg., U. Fla., 1962, Ph.D. in Econs. and Bus. Adminstrn., 1964. Qualified econ. expert witness state and fed. cts., Fla. Chmn. dept. econs. and bus. Fla. So. Coll., Lakeland, 1967-77; supt. pub. instrn. Polk County, Fla., 1968-69; exec. dir. Fla. Pub. Sch. Bd., Tallahassee, 1969; land developer, real estate and mortgage broker, investments, Lakeland, Fla., 1971-80; pres. Dimbath Devel. Co., Lakeland, 1971—; econ. research and cons. Dimbath & Assocs., Stuart, Fla., 1980—; assoc. prof. Coll. Bus. and Pub. Adminstrn., Fla. Atlantic U., Boca Raton, 1981—; money reporter sta. WPEC-TV, West Palm Beach, Fla., 1982-87. DuPont scholar, 1957-61; Ford Found. fellow, 1963-64. Mem. Am. Econ. Assn., Nat. Assn. Bus. Economists, So. Econ. Assn. Home: 1240 SW Dyer Point Rd Palm City FL 34990 Office: River One 309 E Osceola St Suite 105 Stuart FL 34994 also: 3601 E Ocean Blvd Suite 202 Stuart FL 33494

DIMBLEBY, DAVID, broadcast journalist, newspaper company executive; b. London, Oct. 28, 1938; s. Richard Dimbleby and Dilys Thomas; m. Josceline Gaskell, 1967; 1 son, 2 daus. Student Charterhouse, Christ Ch., Oxford, U. Paris, U. Perugia. News reporter BBC, Bristol, 1960-61; presenter and interviewer various sci., religious, and polit. programs, BBC-TV, 1961-63, fgn. affairs film reporter and dir., 1964-65, spl. corr. CBS News, 1966; reporter Panorama, BBC-TV, 1967-69, presenter, 1974-77, 1980-81, presenter 24 Hours BBC-TV, 1969-72, Dimbleby Talk-In, 1972-74, Nationwide, BBC-TV, 1982; People and Power, 1982-83, This Week Next Week, 1984—; mng. dir. Dimbleby Newspaper Group, 1966-86, chmn., 1986—; chmn. Wadsworth Borough News Ltd., 1986—; reporter The White Tribe of Africa BBC-TV, 1979 (Royal TV Soc. Supreme Documentary award). Address: 14 King St, Richmond, Surrey TW9 1NF, England *

DIMCA, ALEXANDRU, mathematics educator, researcher; b. Constantza, Romania, July 21, 1953; s. Gheorghe and Silvia D.; m. Gabriela Sladescu, June 1, 1981; children: Alexandru Ioan, Gheorghe Constantin. Grad., Bucharest U., Romania, 1977; PhD in Math., U. Bucharest, 1981. Math. diplomate. Sr. reseacher dept. math. Nat. Inst. Scientific and Tech. Creation, Bucharest, 1980—. Author: Real and Complex Singularities, 1987; contbr. articles to profl. jours. Recipient Prize Romanian Acad. Geometry, 1985. Mem. Am. Math. Soc. Office: Inst Math, Str Academiei 14, Bucharest 70109, Romania

DI MEANA, CARLO RIPA, journalist, political leader; b. Marina di Pietrasanta, Lucca, Italy, Aug. 15, 1929; m. Marina Punturieri. Editor Il Lavoro, Unitá, 1950-53; Italian rep. to Internat. Student Union Prague, Czechoslovakia, 1953-56; founder weekly publ. Nuova Generazione, Italy, 1956; founder, chief editor mag. Passato e Presente, 1957—; editor pub. house Feltrinelli and Rizzoli, 1957-66; sec.-gen. Club Turati, Milan, 1967-76; councilor for Lombardy 1970; chmn. Venice Biennale, 1974-79, mem. council, 1979-82; dir. internat. relations (PSI) Italian Socialist Party, 1979-80; mem. Nat. Assembly of the PSI; PSI rep. Leadership of Union of European Socialist Parties; mem. European Parliament 1979-84; pres. Inst. Internat. Econ. Cooperation and Devel. Problems, 1983—; mem. Commn. of European Communities, 1985—. Author: Un viaggio in Vietnam, 1956, Dedicato a Raymond Roussel e alle sue impressioni d'Africa, 1965, Il governo audiovisivo, 1973. Pres. Fernando Santi Inst.; vice chmn. Internat. Com. for Solidarity with the Afghan People; bd. dirs. La Scala Theatre. Mem. Federazione Unitaria della Stampa Italiana all'Estero (pres.). Club: Crocodile (founder). Home: Rue de la Loi 200, 1049 Brussels Belgium

DI MENZA, SALVATORE, psychologist; b. Chgo., May 2, 1938; s. Salvatore and Bartalomea (Gallina) diM. A.B., DePaul U., 1960, M.A., 1964; postgrad. Loyola U., 1961-64, Ill. Inst. Tech., 1964, 72. Dir. research Ill. Drug Abuse Program, Chgo., 1972-73; dir. mgmt. systems Ill. Drug Abuse Program, 1973; dir. drug abuse div. Joint Commn. Accreditation of Hosps.,

Chgo., 1973-76, assoc. program dir. for planning and devel., 1976-78; mng. partner Health Resources Mgmt. Systems, Chgo., 1978-80; pres. AGI, Rolling Meadows, Ill., 1981-84; v.p. J.W. Crawford Assos., Inc., Chgo., 1979-85; research and eval. cons. Cook County Research and Eval. Project, Inc., Chgo., 1985-86; spl. asst. to dir., Nat. Inst. on Drug Abuse, Rockville, Md., 1986—; cons. bus. formation and mgmt.; developer nat. standards for providing mental health treatment services, also large scale employee assistance programs and mental health services for industry. Recipient Superior Achievement award State of Ill., 1972. Fellow Royal Soc. Health; mem. Am. (asso.), Ill. psychol. assns., Am. Pub. Health Assn., Alcohol and Drug Problems Assn., Am. Health Planning Assn., Assn. Mental Health Adminstrs. Contbr. articles to profl. jours. Home: 10101 Grosvenor Pl Rockville MD 20852 Office: Nat Inst Drug Abuse 5600 Fishers Ln Rockville MD 20857

DI MICELI, CAROLINE REGINA, English educator; b. London, May 27, 1959; arrived in France, 1981; d. Charles Victor and Maria Regina (Mackay) Mann. m. Philippe Francios Bernard De Miceli, July 16, 1983; 1 child, Mathieu Charles Vincent. Degree with first class honors in English Lit., U. London, 1980; diploma in French Lit. and Civilization, U. Sorbonne, 1981; Maitrise, U. Montpellier, 1983, Agregation in English, 1984, DEA in English Lit., 1984. English tchr. Lycee Louis Feuillade, Lunel, France, 1984-85, Ces Le Chailloux, Imphy, France, 1985-87, Lycee Clemenceau, Montpellier, France, 1987—. Recipient Francis Ralph Allen prize Westfield Coll., 1980. Home: Villa 4 Plan Des Pastourelles, 34430 Saint Jean de Vedas France

DIMINO, FRANKLIN JOSEPH, lawyer; b. Bklyn., Feb. 4, 1933; s. Joseph Frank and Anna Elizabeth (Laserinko) D.; m. Joan E. Maceli, Dec. 26, 1955; children—Lynn, Mark, Glen, Robyn. B.A., Queens Coll.; J.D., NYU, 1961. Bar: Calif. 1962. Asso., Parker, Stanburg, McGee, Peckham & Garrett, 1962-69; ptnr. Garrett & Dimino Inc., 1969-80; ptnr. Dimino & Card, Santa Ana, Calif., 1980—; chmn. bd. Bank San Clemente. Served with USAF as capt. Mem. Calif. Bar Assn., Fed. Bar Assn., ABA, Am. Judicature Soc., Assn. Trial Lawyers Am., Lawyer Pilots Bar Assn., Am. Trial Lawyers Assn., Assn. So. Calif. Def. Counsel, Orange County Bar Assn. Roman Catholic. Office: 1633 E 4th St Suite 120 Santa Ana CA 92701 also: 300 El Camino Real San Clemente CA 92672

DIMITRACOPOULOS, GEORGE ULYSSES, physician, microbiologist, educator; b. Athens, Greece, Dec. 9, 1940; s. Ulysses George and Maria (Moditou) D.; M.D., Faculty of Medicine, U. Athens, 1965, cert. in lab. medicine, 1970; m. Despina Saroglou, July 8, 1972; children—Maria, Ulysses. Asst., dept. microbiology Faculty of Medicine, U. Athens, 1968-72, lectr., 1974-77, docent, 1977-79; postdoctoral teaching/research fellow dept. microbiology Coll. Medicine and Dentistry N.J., Newark, 1972-74; prof., chmn. dept. microbiology Sch. Medicine, U. Patras (Greece), 1979—, mem. intern subcom. for phage typing of staphylococci. Served with Health Service, Greek Army, 1966-68. Council of Europe fellow, London, 1976. Mem. Am. Soc. Microbiology, N.Y. Acad. Sci., AAAS, Am. Public Health Assn., Sigma Xi. Author numerous books. Contbr. articles to profl. jours. Office: Dept Microbiology, Sch of Medicine Univ Patras, Patras Greece

DIMITRIOU, GEORGIOS CONSTANTIN, data processing executive and consultant; b. Volos, Greece, July 5, 1947; s. Constantin and Soi (Panetsou) D. Dipl. Math., T.H. Darmstadt, Fed. Republic Germany, 1973, La. State U., 1972. Systems analyst European Space Ops. Ctr., Darmstadt, 1972-76; mgr. Michanologistiki, Salonica, Greece, 1977-78; EDP cons. Software Devel. & Cons., Salonica, 1978-83; mgr. Datapac, Salonica, 1983-84; info. systems cons., Salonica and Munich, Fed. Republic Germany, 1984—; lectr. on computing Greek Productivity Ctr., Aristotelian U. Contbr. articles on computers to profl. jours. Mem. Assn. Computing Machinery, IEEE, Gesellschaft fur Informatik, Deutsche Gesellschaft fur Operations Research, Am. Math. Soc., Greek Math. Soc., Am. Assn. for Artificial Intelligence. Office: Nikis 77, Salonica 54621 Greece

DIMITROV, BOYAN GRIGOROV, historian, scientist; b. Pernik, Bulgaria, July 29, 1922; s. Grigor Dimitrov and Raina Grigorova (Hadjieva) Popov; m. Roza Crumova Trendafilova, Aug. 16, 1953; children: Svetlana, Rositsa. Grad., U. Sofia, Bulgaria, 1949; MA, Acad. Social Scis., 1959; PhD in History, U. Sofia, 1979. Sr. asst. Higher Party Sch., Sofia, 1950-52, asst. prof., 1953-55; postgrad. student Acad. Social Scis., Moscow, 1955-59; assoc. prof., sr. research assoc. Higher Party Sch., Inst. History, Sofia, 1964-72; prof. Inst. History, Cen. Com. Bulgarian Communist Party, Sofia, 1972—; sub-mgr. Inst. History, Sofia, 1975. Author: 18 sci. books and brochures, more than 130 publs.; compiler and editor of 34 sci. collections. Sec. Cen. Com. Bulgarian Hist. Soc., Sofia, 1970-76; mem. bd. mgrs. Model Community Centre Svetlina, Sofia, 1940. Named Honoured Scientist, Bulgarian Council of State, 1981; recipient several awards Dimitrov Joung Communist League, other insignia of honour from govt. and Sofia. Mem. Sci. Councils Modern History, Sci. Com. History (chmn. 1975), Higher Certifying Commn. (mem. presidium 1980-83), World Congresses of Historians (participant 1970, 80, 85). Bulgarian Communist.

DIMITROV, ILCHO IVANOV, historian; b. Sofia, Bulgaria, June 3, 1931; s. Ivan and Yordanka Dimitrov; m. Bella Mois Dimitrova; children: Ivan Ilchev, Ralitza Ilcheva. PhD in History, Sofia U., 1963, Dr. History, 1976. Asst. prof. Sofia U., 1959-71, assoc. prof., 1971-74, prof. history, 1974—; head Bulgarian history dept., assoc. mem. Bulgarian Acad. Scis., 1981—, coordinating sec., 1977-78, dep. pres., 1984-86. Author: Bourgeois Opposition in Bulgaria (1939-1944), 1969, The Prince, the Consitution and the People, 1972, Bulgarian-Italian Political Relations, 1923-1943, 1976, The Bulgarian Democratic Public Against Fascism and War (1934-44), 1976, Bulgaria in the Balkans and in Europe, 1980, 2d edit., 1983, Bulgaria and Britain on the Eve and the Outbreak of the War (1938-41), 1983, One Hundred Years Ago-Bulgaria's Reunion with Eastern Romelia in 1885, 1986, 2d. edit., 1988. Rector Sofia U., 1979-81; dir. Bulgarian Studies Cen., 1984-86, Minister of Edn., 1986; mem. Cen. Com. Bulgarian Communist party, 1981. Decorated People's Republic of Bulgaria Order, 1981, The Cyril and Methodius Order, 1985. Mem. Bulgarian History Research Soc. Bulgarian Communist party. Office: Sofia U, 15 Russky Blvd, 1504 Sofia Bulgaria

DIMITROVA, GHENA, opera singer; b. Beglej, Bulgaria, May 6, 1941. Début Sofia (Bulgaria) Opera; singer laureate Internat. Competition, Treviso, Italy, 1972; appearances in France, Italy, Spain, S. America and Moscow; appears in opera houses of Vienna, Austria, Munich, Paris, Hamburg, Federal Republic of Germany, Berlin, Madrid, Barcelona, Spain, Rome, Naples, Italy, Zürich, Switzerland; recordings include Nabucco and Oberto, Conte di San Bonafacio. Recipient Gold medal and First prize Fourth Internat. Competition for Young Singers, Sofia, 1970, Golden Archer and Giovanni Zenatello prizes, 1981. Address: care SA Gorlinsky Ltd, 33 Dover St, London W1X 4NJ, England *

DIMMA, WILLIAM ANDREW, real estate executive; b. Montreal, Que., Can., Aug. 13, 1928; s. William Roy and Lillian Noreen (Miller) D.; m. Katherine Louise Vacy Ash, May 13, 1961; children: Suzanne Elizabeth Irene, Katherine Lillian Louise. BA in Sci., U. Toronto, Can., 1948; MMP, Harvard U., 1956, DBA, 1973; MBA, York U., Toronto, 1969. Registered profl. engr., Ont. With Union Carbide Can Ltd., 1948-69, exec. v.p., dir., 1967-69; dean Faculty Adminstrv. Studies York U., 1973-75; pres., dir. Torstar Corp., Toronto, 1976-78, Toronto Star Newspapers Ltd., 1976-78, A.E. LePage Ltd., Toronto, 1979-85; pres., chief exec. officer Royal LePage Ltd., Toronto, 1985-86, dep. chmn., 1986—; bd. dirs. Continental Bank, Canron Inc., Interprovincial Pipelines Ltd., London Life Ins. Co., Trizec Corp., Can. Reassurance Co., Can. Reinsurance Co., Polysar Energy and Chems. Corp., Silcorp Ltd., Sears Can. Ltd., Trilon Fin. Corp., C.D. Howe Inst. Bd. govs. York U.; trustee Toronto Hosp. for Sick Children, Jr. Achievement Can., Ont. Press Council; bd. dirs. Trillium Found, York U. Devel. Corp. Sir Bertram Whindle scholar; Elmslie Meml. scholar, 1944; Can. Council fellow, 1970-73. Clubs: Toronto, Toronto Golf, York (Toronto), Mark's (London). Home: 17 Dunloe Rd, Toronto, ON Canada M4V 2W4 Office: 33 Yonge St, Suite 1000, Toronto, ON Canada M5E 1S9

DIMSON, ELROY, business educator; b. London, Jan. 17, 1947; m. Helen Sonn, July 1, 1969; children: Jonathan, Susanna, Benjamin, Daniel. BA, Newcastle upon Tyne, Eng., 1968; M in Commerce, Birmingham U., 1970; PhD, U. London, 1979. Diplomate London Inst. Mktg. Planning officer Tube Investments, Birmingham, Eng., 1968-69; ops. research mgr. Unilever Ltd., London, 1970-72; mng. dir. Elroy Dimson Assocs., London, 1987—; bd. dirs. pension fund London U., 1982—; non-exec. dir. Mobil Trustee Co., 1984—; sr. lectr. fin. London Bus. Sch. 1974—, dir. MBA program 1986—; vis. prof. U. Calif., Berkeley, U. Chgo., U. Hawaii, U. Brussels, European Inst. for Advanced Studies in Mgmt. Author: Stock Market Anomalies, 1988, Cases in Corporate Finance, 1988; co-editor Risk Measurement Service, 1979—, articles to profl. jours. Adviser London Securities and Investment Bd., 1986—. Recipient research award Dean Witter Found., 1981, Ea. Fin. Assn., 1984. Mem. European Fin. Assn., Am. Fin. Assn. Office: London Bus Sch, Sussex Pl, Regents Park, London NW1 4SA, England

DINET, RENÉ GEORGES, physician; b. St. Cirgues, France, Apr. 27, 1923; s. Philippe Joseph and Auastasie (Gay) D.; m. Nicole Boetsch (dec.); m. Piereette Marguerite Laulanie (div. 1966); children: Jean-Philippe, Anne, Nicole, René. MD, Med. Facility Paris, 1951; Cert. Cancerology, Med. Faculty Paris, 1952, Cert. in Indsl. Medicine, 1953. Pvt. practice medicine Paris, 1951—; physician Bus and Subway Paris, 1952-63, Lizabelh Ardeu, Paris, 1965-72; physician French Ry. Service, 1972—, mem. disability commn., 1975—. Served with French Army. Home and Office: 82 Blvd Haussmann, 75008 Paris France

DING, SHISUN, university administrator; b. Shanghai, People's Republic of China, Sept. 5, 1927; s. Ruonong Ding and Huixian Liu; m. Linlin Gui, Mar. 10, 1956; children: Songqing, Gan Ding. Grad., Tsinghua U., Beijing, 1950; Doctorate (hon.), Soka U., Tokyo, 1950. Lectr. math. Peking U., Beijing, 1954-79, prof., 1979—, chmn. dept. math., 1981-82, pres., 1984—. Author numerous books and papers in field of math. Mem. Math. Soc. Beijing (pres. 1986-89). Home and Office: Peking Univ, Hai Dian, Beijing Peoples Republic of China

DINGES, RICHARD ALLEN, entrepreneur; b. Englewood, N.J., June 17, 1945; m. Kathie A. Headley; children: Kelly, Courtney. Grad., Jersey City State Coll., 1967; MEd, U. Hawaii, 1972; postgrad., William Peterson Coll., 1974-79. Cert. sch. adminstr.; cert. sch. spl. services dir., N.J., Ariz., Hawaii. Pres. Def. Industry Assocs., Sierra Vista, Ariz., 1979—, Fed. Career Cons., Sierra Vista, Ariz., 1985; dir. Nat. Scholarship Locators, Sierra Vista, 1985—. Editor: Guide to U.S. Defense Contractors, 1985, 87, 10 Step Guide to College Selection, Salary Negotiations for Military, How to Survive the Job Interview. Mem. Cochise County Merit Commn. (vice-chmn.). Home: 2713 Pawnee Dr Sierra Vista AZ 85635 Office: 2160 E Fry Blvd Suite 400 Sierra Vista AZ 85635

DINGMAN, MICHAEL DAVID, industrial company executive; b. New Haven, Sept. 29, 1931; s. James Everett and Amelia (Williamson) D.; m. Jean Hazlewood, May 16, 1953 (div.); children: Michael David, Linda Channing (Mrs. Michael S. Cady), James Clifford; m. Elizabeth G. Tharp, Apr. 13, 1984; children: James Tharp, David Ross. Student, U. Md. Various mgmt. positions Sigma Instruments, Inc., Braintree, Mass., 1954-64; gen. and ltd. ptnr. Drexel Burnham Lambert, Inc. (formerly Burnham & Co.), N.Y.C., 1964-70; pres., chief exec. officer, bd. dirs. Wheelabrator-Frye, Inc., Hampton, N.H., 1970-83; chmn. bd. Wheelabrator-Frye Inc., Hampton, N.H., 1977-83; pres., bd. dirs. The Signal Cos., Inc., La Jolla, Calif., 1983-85, Allied-Signal Inc., Morristown, N.J., 1985-86; chmn. bd., chief exec. officer The Henley Group, Inc., La Jolla, 1986—; bd. dirs. Ford Motor Co., Time Inc. Trustee John A. Hartford Found. Mem. IEEE (mem. adv. bd.). Clubs: Links, Bd. Room, N.Y. Yacht (N.Y.C.); Union (Boston); Cruising of Am. (Conn.); Bohemian (San Francisco), Fairbanks Ranch Country; Lyford Cay (Nassau); La Jolla Country, San Diego Yacht. Office: The Henley Group Inc Liberty Lane Hampton NH 03842

DING MOU-SHIH, former federal agency administrator; b. Yunnan, Taiwan, Republic of China, Oct. 10, 1925; m. Shih mei-Chang; 2 children. Student, U. Paris. Reporter Cen. News Agy., Republic of China, 1956-58; cons. Ministry Fgn. Affairs, Republic of China, 1958-60, sect. chief West Asian Affairs Dept., 1960-62; first sec. Chinese Mission to European Office of UN, Republic of China, 1962; chargé d'affaires Chinese Embassy, Republic of Rwanda, Republic of China, 1962-65; ambassador to Rwanda Chinese Embassy, Republic of China, 1965-67, ambassador to Zaire, 1967-72; dir. African Affairs Dept. Ministry Fgn. Affairs, Republic of China, 1973-75; dir. Dept. Cultural Affairs Kuomintang, Republic of China, 1976-78; dir. gen. Govt. Info. Office, Republic of China, 1975-78; adminstrv. vice minister of fgn. affairs Republic of China, 1978-79; ambassador to Korea Chinese embassy, Republic of China, 1979-82. Office: Ministry of Fgn Affairs, Taipei Republic of China *

DINKELSPIEL, PAUL GAINES, investment banking and public financial consultant; b. San Francisco, Feb. 12, 1935; s. Edward Gaines and Pauline (Watson) D.; A.B., U. Calif.-Berkeley, 1959. Gen. ptnr. Stone & Youngberg, San Francisco, 1961-71; 1st v.p. Shearson/Lehman and predecessor firms, San Francisco, 1971-79; pres., chmn. bd. dirs. Dinkelspiel, Belmont & Co., Inc., investment banking and pub. fin. cons., San Francisco, 1979—. Served with AUS, 1959-60. Mem. Mcpl. Fin. Officers Assn., Am. Water Works Assn., San Francisco Mcpl. Forum, Pub. Securities Assn. (public fin. com.), Sigma Chi. Clubs: San Francisco Comml., Commonwealth of Calif., Mcpl. Bond, N.Y. World Trade. Home: PO Box 727 Stinson Beach CA 94970 Office: One California St San Francisco CA 94111

DINKINS, GENE LYNN, civil engineer; b. El Paso, Tex., Apr. 6, 1951; s. Holly Walker and Lucille (Huggins) D.; B.S. in Chem. Engring. (R.F. Poole scholar), Clemson (S.C.) U., 1973; m. Nancy Ruth Cox, Dec. 30, 1972; children—Gene Lyn, Sanford Benjamin, Mary Lucille. BS in Civil Engring. U. S.C., 1975, M. Engring., 1985. Chem. engr. Dow-Badische Co., Anderson, S.C., 1973; surveyor and engr.-in-tng., then v.p. Isaac B. Cox & Son, Inc., Columbia, S.C., 1973-79; pres. Cox and Dinkins, Inc., engrs. and surveyors, Columbia, 1979—; mem. adv. com. indsl. drafting Midlands Tech. Coll., Columbia, 1980—. Mem. Richland County Planning Commn., 1980—, vice chmn., 1983-87, chmn., 1987—. Registered profl. engr., S.C.; registered profl. land surveyor, S.C. Mem. Nat. Soc. Profl. Engrs., Nat. Assn. Homebuilders, S.C. Soc. Profl. Engrs., S.C. Soc. Registered Land Surveyors, Am. Congress Surveying and Mapping, Chi Psi, Phi Kappa Phi, Tau Beta Pi. Episcopalian. Home: 3409 Monroe St Columbia SC 29205 Office: 614 Holly St Columbia SC 29205

DINKINS, JANE POLING, management consultant, EDP specialist; b. Van Wert, Ohio, Oct. 11, 1928; d. Doyt Carl and Kathryn (Sawyer) Poling; BBA, So. Meth. U., 1974. Stewardess, instr. stewardesses, chief stewardess Am. Airlines, 1946-50; exec. sec., adminstrv. asst. Southland Royalty Co., Ft. Worth, 1956-63; exec. sec. Charles E. Seay, Inc. and C.W. Goyer, Jr., Dallas, 1963-68; systems analyst, programmer Southland Life Ins. Co., Dallas, 1968-69, 1st. Nat. Bank, Dallas, 1969-72, Occidental Life Ins. Co., Los Angeles, 1972-73; systems analyst, programmer Pacific Mut. Life Ins. Co., Newport Beach, Calif., 1973-74, mgr. mut. fund subs., 1975; systems analyst, programmer Info. Services Div. TRW, Orange, Calif., 1975-79; EDP auditor Union Bank, Los Angeles, 1979; sr. EDP auditor Security Pacific Nat. Bank, Glendale, Calif., 1979-80, asst. v.p., Los Angeles, 1981; mgmt. cons. Automation Program Office, Fed. Res. Bank, Dallas, 1982-85; pres. Poling & Assocs., Inc., 1985—. Mem. Am. Mgmt. Assn., EDP Auditors Assn., Quality Assurance Inst. (cert. quality analyst), Data Processing Mgmt. Assn., Sigma Kappa. Republican. Methodist. Club: University (Dallas). Home and Office: 5990 Arapaho Rd Apt 3D Dallas TX 75248-3712

DINKOV, VASILIY ALEXANDROVICH, Soviet government official; b. 1924. Student Azerbaijan Azizbekov Indsl. Inst. Engring. tech. work in gas industry; mem. CPSU, 1946; head main dept. for gas prodn. USSR Ministry of Gas Industry, 1966-70, dep. minister, 1970-79, 1st dep. minister gas industry, 1979-81, minister, 1981-85; minister of oil industry, 1985—; mem. USSR Supreme Soviet (10th convocation). Recipient State Prize, Order of Lenin, Hero of Socialist Labour, 1984. *

DINNIMAN, ANDREW ERIC, educator; b. New Haven, Oct. 10, 1944; s. Harold and Edith (Stephson) D.; B.A., U. Conn., 1966; M.A., U. Md., 1969; Ed.D., Pa. State U., 1978; m. Margo Portnoy, June 8, 1969; 1 dau., Alexis. Student personnel worker U. Md., 1969-71, U. Denver, 1971-72; mem. faculty West Chester (Pa.) State U., 1972—, asso. prof. history, 1972—; dir. Ctr. for Internat. Programs, 1986—. Chmn. Chester County Dem. Com., 1979-85; mem. Pa. Dem. State Com., 1982—, mem. exec. com., 1984—; chmn. Eastern Pa. Dem. County Chmn. Assn., 1982-85; mem. Dem. Nat. Com., 1984—; v.p. Downington Area (Pa.) Sch. Bd., 1975-79; mem. Central Chester County Vocat.-Tech. Sch. Bd., 1978-79. Recipient Bicentennial award Pa. Sch. Bds. Assn., 1976, Outstanding Acad. Service award Commonwealth Pa., 1977, Human Rights award W. Chester State U. chpt. NAACP, 1980. Mem. Orgn. Am. Historians, Chester County Hist. Soc., Pa. Soc. Jewish. Author: Book of Human Relations Readings, 1980; also articles. Home: 467 Spruce Dr Exton PA 19341 Office: West Chester State U Dept History West Chester PA 19383

DION, PIERRE, physician; b. Quebec City, Que., Can., Aug. 23, 1947; s. Roland and Mary (Koolery) D.; m. Diane Martel, Oct. 2, 1971; children—Alexandre, Nicolas, Louis-Etienne, Francois-Xavier, Genevieve. B.A., U. Laval, 1968, B.Sc., 1972, M.D., 1973. Intern, Chicoutimi Gen. Hosp., Que., 1973-74; resident Enfant Jé sus Hosp., Que., 1977-78; gen. practice, Alma, Que., 1978-85; mem. staff Centre Hospitalier Chaveau, Que., 1985—. Scout master Boy Scouts Can., Alma, 1982-85. Served to capt. Air Force, 1971-77. Mem. Coll. Physicians and Surgeons Ont. Roman Catholic. Avocations: winter skiing; mountain hiking; painting; sailing; flying; ornithology. Home: 28 Myrtilles, Loretteville, PQ Canada G2A 3J7 Office: 2350 Bastien Neufchatel, Quebec City, PQ Canada G2B 1B5

DION, PIERRE, sales executive; b. Montreal, Que., Can., Nov. 16, 1948; s. Floribert and Marguerite (Moran) D.; m. Sharon Lynn Gibbs, Oct. 2, 1971; children: Pierre-Justin, Pierre-Martin. Diploma in bus. adminstrn., Montreal U., 1968; diploma in mktg., St. Foy Coll., 1971; MBA, Southland U., 1986. Sales rep. Bell Can., Montreal, 1968-71; mktg. rep. Xerox of Can. Ltd., Montreal, 1971-73; sr. mktg. rep. IBM of Can. Ltd., Montreal, 1973-75; dist. mgr. Investors Syndicate Ltd., Montreal, 1975-77; wholesaler Loto-Que., Montreal, 1977-80; sales and mktg. cons. Montreal, 1981-86; regional mgr. sales and customer service Automatic Data Processing Co., Montreal, 1986—. Author: Professional Selling Skills, 1980. Mem. Par Club, Xerox of Can. Ltd., Montreal, 1971-72, Pres. Club, IBM of Can. Ltd., Montreal, 1974. Mem. Montreal Bd. Trade, MBA Assn. Can. Roman Catholic. Home: 321 Lanthier #114, Pointe-Claire, PQ Canada H9S 5K6

DIONNE, GERALD FRANCIS, research physicist; b. Montreal, Que., Can., Feb. 5, 1935; came to U.S., 1964, naturalized, 1980; s. Louis Philip and Clare Isabel (Flood) D.; m. Claudette Leblanc, June 29, 1963; 1 child, Stephen. BS summa cum laude, Concordia (Can.) U., 1956; B of Engring. magna cum laude, McGill U., 1958, PhD in Physics, 1964; MS, Carnegie-Mellon U., 1959. Jr. engr. IBM Corp., Poughkeepsie, N.Y., 1959-60; sr. engr. Sylvania Electric Products, Woburn, Mass., 1960-61; research asst., lectr. McGill U., Montreal, Que., Can., 1964; sr. research assoc. Pratt & Whitney Aircraft, North Haven, Conn., 1964-66; research staff mem. Lincoln Lab., MIT, Lexington, 1966—; guest lectr., grad. student research adv. NRC of Can. fellow, 1961-63. Contbr. articles to sci.jours. Mem. Am. Phys. Soc., IEEE (sr.), Corp. Profl. Engrs. Que., Sigma Xi. Researcher in magnetism, magnetoelastic and magneto-optic phenomena, oxide superconductivity, microwave, submillimeter-wave and surface physics. Home: 182 High St Winchester MA 01890 Office: 244 Wood St Lexington MA 02173

DIONYSIOU, DEMETRIOS, mathematics educator and researcher; b. Athens, Sept. 11, 1939; s. Dionysius Demetrios and Demeter Dion (Kateva) D.; children: Dennis, Demeter, Evita. BSc in Math., U. Athens, 1963; BSc Spl. in Math., U. London, 1969, PhD in Math., 1973. Math. tchr. secondary schs. Greece, 1965-70; lectr. math. U. Athens, 1970-80; prof. Hellenic Air Force Acad., Attica, Greece, 1980—; head math. dept. Hellenic Air Force Acad., Attica, 1980—. Author numerous researches math., physics and books; referee, editorial bd. dirs. jour. Astrophysics and Space Science. Served to 2d lt. Greek army, 1963-65. Mem. Math. Assn. Am., Math. Assn. Greece, Internat. Astron. Union, Royal Astron. Soc., Joint Assn. for Geophysics, N.Y. Acad. Scis., Convocation of the U. London. Home: 18 Amassias, 11634 Athens Greece Office: Hellenic Air Force Acad, Dekelia, Attica Greece

DIOSO, DANIEL VICENTE, retired physician, science administrator; b. Pandan, Antique, Phillipines, July 21, 1919; s. Mariano Dioso Sardañas and Bonifacia (Amante) D. MD in Surgery, U. Santo Tomas, Manila, 1947; cert. pub. health, U. The Philippines, Manila, 1970. Tchr. high sch. Pandan, 1947-49; rural health physician Phillipine Dept. Health, Pandan, 1949-79; ret. Pandan, 1979; acting chief (p.t.) emergency hosp. Dept. Health Philippines, 1975-77. Author: (poems) Verismilitude, 1954, Trajectory, 1959. Mem. Philippine Med. Assn. Mem. Nacionalista Party. Roman Catholic. Lodge: KC. Address: Candari St, Pandan 5617, Philippines

DIOUF, ABDOU, president Republic of Sénégal; b. Louga, Sénégal, Sept. 7, 1935; ed. Lycée St. Louis, Sénégal, Dakar Faculty of Law, 1955-58; Lic. in Public Law and Polit. Sci., Faculty of Law, U. Paris, 1959. Dir. tech. coop., also minister planning Senegal, 1962; dir. cabinet of pres. of republic, 1963-64; asst. sec.-gen., later sec.-gen. govt., 1964-68; minister planning and industry, 1968-70, prime minister, 1970-80, pres. Republic of Sénégal, 1981—. Former chmn. Council of Ministers Orgn. Sénégal River Basin States, Orgn. Africa Unity; sec.-gen. Socialist Party; pres. Confederation de la Senégambie. Co-recipient Africa Prize for Leadership, 1987. Address: Office of Pres, Dakar Senegal *

DI PILLO, GIANNI, applied mathematics educator; b. Rome, Feb. 1, 1942. Laurea, U. Rome, 1966. Researcher U. Rome, 1968-72, assoc. prof., 1975-80; assoc. prof. U. Calabria, Cosenza, Italy, 1972-75; prof. U. Salerno, Italy, 1981, U. Rome La Sapienza, 1982—. Editor: Metodi e Algoritmi per l'Ottimirazione, 1984, Stochastic Programming, 1986, Control Applications of Nonlinear Programming, 1986. Office: U Roma La Sapienza, Via Eudossiana 18, 00184 Rome Italy

DI PONIO, CONCETTA CELIA, automobile manufacturing company systems security coordinator; b. Detroit, June 2, 19; d. Antonio and Mary (Franciosi) Di P.; B.B.A. magna cum laude, U. Detroit, 1973, M.A., 1974, M.B.A., 1975; A.C. cum laude, Henry Ford Community Coll., 1969. Various clerical positions F.W. Woolworth Co., Detroit, 1940-41; office mgr., instr. Design and Engring. Inst., Detroit, 1947-52; propr., mgr. TRI-D Constrn. Co., Detroit, 1955-68; instr. bus. Detroit Coll. Bus., Dearborn, Mich., 1975—; mgmt. tchr. Henry Ford Community Coll., Dearborn, 1979—; with Ford Motor Co., Dearborn, 1942—, div. prodn. surplus liaison, 1952-55, statis. analytical coordinator, 1955-66, parts program coordinator, 1966-74, mgmt. info. system programmer analyst, 1974-81, systems security coordinator, parts and service div., 1981—, Italian translator of letters, corr. and blue prints, 1960—; chmn. M.B.A. confs., 1973-76. Founder 9 collegiate councils U. Detroit, 1977—, pres. univ. bd. dirs., 1978—; chmn. Juvenile Diabetes Found. Trial hon, 1982—; pres. council, rep. St. Eugene Parish Council, 1983—, mem. Grand River vicariate, 1983—, also eucharistic minister, lector. Recipient Lawrence Canjar Woman of Yr. award U. Detroit, 1974-75; Divisional Community Services award Ford Motor Co., 1973, Nat. Citizen of Yr. award, 1973, Nat. Town Crier award, 1973; Top Ten Working Woman award Detroit C. of C., 1969; M.B.A. award, 1974-76; Centennial Alumni award, 1976; Dowling award U. Detroit, 1980; Down Jones Wall St. award. Mem. Am. Mgmt. Assn., Am. Bus. Women's Assn., Nat. Assn. for Female Execs., Nat. Bus. Edn. Assn., Women's Econ. Club: Ford Motor Employee Recreation Assn., U. Detroit Nat. Alumni Assn. (pres. 1978—), Sparks Wheelchair Basketball Assn., Alpha Sigma Nu (pres. 1973—), Beta Gamma Sigma, Phi Gamma Nu (pres. 1971-72), Phi Gamma Nu Alumnae (pres. 1973-77), Alpha Sigma Lambda, Alpha Kappa Psi. Clubs: Old Timers, Quarter Century, Ford Motor Girls (pres. 1965-69). Home: 3086 Devon Brook Dr Bloomfield Hills MI 48013 Office: Ford Motor Co Parts and Service Div 4 Parklane Blvd Rm #233 Dearborn MI 48126

DIPPOLDSMANN, PETER, lawyer, researcher; b. Hessen, Fed. Republic Germany, 1944. Grad., Philipps-Universität Marburg/L, Fed. Republic Germany, 1975. Cert. assessor. Lektor Verlag, Fed. Republic Germany, 1977-80; researcher Gesellschaft für Mathematik und Datenverarbeitung, Fed. Republic Germany, 1980—; Mitglied des Vorstands der Deutschen Verienigung für Daten schutz, Fed. Republic Germany, 1981—; lektor articles, 1971—. Served to lt. German Air Force, 1965-67. Office: Gesellschaft für Mathematik, und Datenverarbeitung, Postfach 1250, D-5205 Saint Augustin 1 Federal Republic of Germany

DIPRETE, EDWARD D., governor of Rhode Island; b. Cranston, R.I., July 8, 1934; s. Frank A. and Maria (Grossi) DiP.; m. Patricia Hines, Aug. 18, 1956; children: Edward D., Dennis, Nancy, Patricia, Mary Ellen, Kathleen, Thomas. Student, Coll. of Holy Cross, Worcester, Mass. Councilman City of Cranston, 1975-79, mayor, 1979-85; gov. State of R.I., 1985—; dir. Ind. Ins. Agts. Bd. dirs. R.I. Lung Assn. Served to lt. comdr. USN. Recipient Man of Yr. award Italian-Am. War Vets., 1983, Outstanding Contbns. award Boy Scouts Am., 1984. Mem. Cranston C. of C. (bd. dirs. 1983), Order of Sons of Italy. Republican. Roman Catholic. Office: 222 State House Providence RI 02903 *

DI PRIMA, STEPHANIE MARIE, educational administrator; b. Chgo., Aug. 29, 1952; d. Joseph and Ann Marie (Albate) DiP. BA in English, Rosary Coll., 1974; MEd in Adminstrn. and Supervision, Loyola U., Chgo., 1979. Tchr. St. Vincent Ferrer Sch., River Forest, Ill., 1974-78, Our Lady of Hope Sch., Rosemont, Ill., 1978-81, Sacred Heart Sch., Winnetka, Ill., 1981-84; prin. St. Monica Sch., Chgo., 1984—. Mem. Nat. Cath. Ednl. Assn., Nat. Assn. Elem. Sch. Prins., Ill. Prins.' Assn., Assn. Supervision and Curriculum Devel., Ill. Assn. Supervision and Curriculum Devel., Women in Mgmt., Archdiocesan Prins.' Assn., Urban Gateways Prins. Coalition for Arts. Avocations: piano, reading, theatre and fine arts, needlecrafts, travel. Office: 5115 N Montclare Ave Chicago IL 60656

DIRENZO, GORDON JAMES, sociologist, psychologist, educator; b. North Attleboro, Mass., July 19, 1934; s. Santo and Giulia (Petti) DiR.; m. Mary Kathleen Ryan, July 6, 1968; children: Maria Giulia, Chiara Veronica, Marco Santo. B.A., U. Notre Dame, 1956, M.A., 1957, Ph.D., 1963; postgrad., Harvard U., 1959, Columbia U., 1963-65, U. Colo., 1964. Diplomate: cert. social psychologist, sociologist; lic. psychologist, Del. Instr. Coll. of St. Rose, Albany, N.Y., 1957-59; Instr. U. Portland, Oreg., 1961-62; asst. prof. Fairfield (Conn.) U., 1962-66; asso. prof. Ind. U., South Bend, 1966-70; prof. sociology U. Del., Newark, 1970—; mem. faculty Siena Coll., Albany (N.Y.) Med. Center, 1958-59, U. Notre Dame, 1960-61, Coll. White Plains, 1963-65, Bklyn. Coll., 1965, Western Conn. State Coll., 1964; mem. faculty SUNY, Stony Brook, 1980, Cortland, 1966; affiliate mem. med. and dental staff Med. Center Del., Wilmington, 1976—, St. Francis Hosp., Wilmington, 1980—, Northeastern Hosp., Phila., 1982-85; pres. Behavioral Cons., Newark, 1975—; dir. Sociol. Cons. Group, North Attleboro, Mass., 1963-75; Fulbright-Hays prof. U. Rome, 1968-69, U. Bologna, Italy, 1980-81. Contbr. articles to profl. jours.; author: Personality, Power and Politics, 1967, Concepts, Theory and Explanation in the Behavioral Sciences, 1966, Personality and Politics, 1974, We, the People: American Character and Social Change, 1977, Sociological Perspectives, 1987, Personality and Society, 1985. U. Notre Dame fellow, 1959-60; Ford Found. grantee, 1960; Italian Ministry of Edn. fellow, 1960; NSF fellow, 1964; Nat. Endowment for Humanities grantee, 1975; Del. Inst. Med. Edn. and Research grantee, 1975; recipient Disting. Service award Am. Assn. Family Practice, 1980, 82, 84. Fellow Am. Sociol. Assn.; mem. Am. Psychol. Assn., AAUP, AAAS, Assn. Behavioral Scis. in Med. Edn., Soc. Personality and Social Psychology, Am.-Italian Hist. Assn. (nat. exec. council 1977-80), Fulbright Alumni Assn., Internat. Sociol. Assn., Clin. Sociology Assn., Internat. Soc. Polit. Psychology (charter), Soc. Psychologists in Medicine, Internat. Polit. Sci. Assn., Soc. for Study Social Problems, Soc. Psychol. Study Social Issues, Eastern Sociol. Soc., Alpha Kappa Delta. Home: 28 Deer Run Little Baltimore Farms Newark DE 19711 Office: Dept Sociology U Del Newark DE 19716

DIRKS, KENNETH RAY, pathologist, medical educator, army officer; b. Newton, Kans., Feb. 11, 1925; s. Jacob Kenneth and Ruth Viola (Penner) D.; m. Betty Jean Worsham, June 9, 1946; children: Susan Jan, Jeffrey Mark, Deborah Anne, Timothy David, Melissa Jane. M.D., Washington U., St. Louis, 1947. Diplomate: Am. Bd. Pathology. Rotating intern St. Louis City Hosp., 1948, asst. resident in gen. surgery, 1948-49; resident in pathology VA Hosp., Jefferson Barracks, Mo., 1951-53; resident in pathology, asst. chief lab. service VA Hosp., Indpls., 1953-54; resident in pathology Letterman Army Hosp., San Francisco, 1956-57; fellow in tropical medicine and parasitology La. State U., Central Am., 1958; asst. in pathology Washington U. Sch. Medicine, 1952-53; asst. chief lab. service VA Hosp., Jefferson Barracks, 1953; instr. pathology U. Ind. Med. Center, Indpls., 1953-54; commd. capt. M.C. U.S. Army, 1954, advanced through grades to maj. gen., 1976; dir. research Med. Research and Devel. Command, Washington, 1968-69; dep. comdr. Med. Research and Devel. Command, 1969-71, comdr., 1973-76; asst. surgeon gen., research and devel. U.S. Army, 1973-76; dep. comdr., comdr. Med. Research Inst. Infectious Diseases, Ft. Detrick, Frederick, Md., 1972-73, comdr. Fitzsimons Army Med. Center, Denver, 1976-77; supt. Acad. Health Scis., Ft. Sam Houston, Tex., 1977-80; assoc. prof. to prof. pathology and lab. medicine Coll. Medicine, Tex. A&M U., College Station, 1980—; asst. dean Coll. Medicine, Tex. A&M U., College Station, 1985—. Contbr. articles to med. jours. Decorated D.S.M., Legion of Merit with oak leaf cluster, Meritorious Service medal, Army Commendation medal with oak leaf cluster. Fellow Coll. Am. Pathologists, Internat. Acad. Pathology. Address: 2513 Oak Circle Bryan TX 77802

DIRKS, LEE EDWARD, newspaper executive; b. Indpls., Aug. 4, 1935; s. Raymond Louis and Virginia Belle (Wagner) D.; m. Barbara Dee Nutt, June 16, 1956 (div. Jan. 1985); children: Stephen Merle, Deborah Virginia, David Louis; m. Mary Catherine Israel Dietz, June 27, 1987; stepchildren: Brian Michael Dietz, Holly Laureen Dietz. B.A., DePauw U., 1956; M.A., Fletcher Sch. Law and Diplomacy, 1957. Reporter Boston Globe, 1957, Nat. Observer, Washington, 1962-65; news editor Nat. Observer, 1966-68; securities analyst specializing in newspaper stocks Dirks Bros., Ltd., Washington, 1969-71, Delafield, Childs, Inc., Washington, 1971-75, C.S. McKee & Co., Washington, 1975-76; asst. to pres. Detroit Free Press, 1976-77, v.p., gen. mgr., 1977-80; pres. Lee Dirks & Assoc., Detroit, 1980—; lectr. Am. Press Inst., 1971—. Author: Religion in Action, 1965; pub.: Newspaper Newsletter, 1970-76. Bd. dirs. Nat. Ghost Ranch Found., Santa Fe, 1973—. Served to capt. USAF, 1957-61. Named Religion Writer of Yr. Religious Newswriters Assn., 1964. Fellow Religious Pub. Relations Council; mem. Phi Beta Kappa, Lambda Chi Alpha. Unitarian. Clubs: Nat. Press (Washington); Oakland Hills (Detroit). Home: 3150 Kernway Dr Bloomfield Hills MI 48013 Office: 255 E Brown St Suite 210 Birmingham MI 48011-1526

DIRSCHERL, KLAUS, literature educator; b. Weiden, Fed. Republic Germany, Dec. 13, 1940. PhD, U. Munich, 1972, Dr.Phil. Habil., 1979. Prof. U. Fed. Republic Germany, 1980-82; prof. U. Passau, Fed. Republic Germany, 1982—, dean faculty philosophy. Author: Zur Typologie Baudelaires, 1975, Der Roman der Philosophen, 1985. Office: U Passau, Innstrasse 25, D-8390 Passau Federal Republic of Germany

DI SANTO, GRACE JOHANNE DEMARCO, poet; b. Derby, Conn., July 12, 1924; d. Richard and Fannie De Marco; m. Frank Michael Di Santo, Aug. 30, 1946; children: Frank Richard, Bernadette Mary, Roxanne Judith. Student in journalism, NYU, 1941-43; AB in English, Belmont Abbey Coll., 1974. Newswriter Australian Assn. Press, N.Y.C., 1942-43; staff reporter Ansonia Sentinel, Derby, 1943-45; feature writer, drama critic Bridgeport Herald, New Haven, 1945-46; editor monthly bull. Pa. State Coll. Optometry, Phila., 1947-48; free-lance writer, 1949-54; founder, pres. bd. dirs. Investors Ltd., Morganton, N.C., 1966-67; freelance writer. Author: (poetry) The Eye is Single, Portrait of the Poet as Teacher: James Dickey; contbr. The Dream Book: An Anthology of Writings by Italian-American Women. Pres., Burke County chpt. N.C. Symphony Soc., 1968-70; mem. exec. bd. Community Concerts Assn., 1962-71; trustee N.C. Symphony Soc., 1965-68, 69-70, North State Acad., Hickory, N.C., 1974—; bd. advisors Belmont Abbey Coll., 1986—. Recipient Oscar Arnold Young Meml. award, 1982. Republican. Roman Catholic. Clubs: Grandfather Golf and Country (Linville, N.C.); Mimosa Hills Golf. Address: 218 Riverside Dr Morganton NC 28655 also: Grandfather Golf and Country Club Linville NC 28646

DISBROW, RICHARD EDWIN, utility executive; b. Newark, Sept. 20, 1930; s. Milton A. and Madeline Catherine (Segal) D.; m. Patricia Fair Warner, June 27, 1953 (div. Sept. 1972); children: John Scott, Lisa Karen; m. Teresa Marie Moser, May 12, 1973. B.S., Lehigh U., 1952; M.S. in Elec. Engring., Newark Coll. Engring., 1959; M.S. in indsl. mgmt., MIT, 1965. With Am. Electric Power Service Corp., N.Y.C., 1954-80; with Am. Electric Power Service Corp., Columbus, Ohio, 1980—, transmission and distbn. mgr., 1967-70, controller, 1970-71, v.p., controller, 1971-74, exec. v.p., 1974-75, vice chmn. bd., 1975-79, pres., chief adminstrv. officer, 1979-84, pres., chief operating officer, 1985—, dir.; pres., dir. Am. Electric Power Co.; dir. Banc Ohio Nat. Bank, 1986; instr. Newark Coll. Engring., 1959-64; mem. N.J. Engrs. Com. For Student Guidance, 1960-64; indsl. commr., Piscataway, N.J., 1960-64; mem. vis. com. dept. mech. engring. and mechanics Lehigh U., 1960-64; trustee Franklin U.; bd. visitors N.J. Inst. Tech; v.p., bd. dirs. Columbus So. Power Co., Ind. Mich. Power Co., Wheeling Electric Co., Windsor Coal Co. Served to 1st lt. USAF, 1952-54. Sloan fellow MIT. Mem. Edison Electric Inst. (dir.), Psi Upsilon, Eta Kappa Nu. Clubs: Columbus Athletic, Worthington Hills Country. Office: Am Electric Power Co Inc 1 Riverside Plaza Columbus OH 43215

DISHEROON, FRED RUSSELL, lawyer; b. Hot Springs, Ark., Nov. 21, 1931; s. Andrew Russell and Ruth Fayrene (Bearden) D.; m. Laurel Joan Picou, Apr. 1, 1961 (div. Dec. 1977); children—Terri Suzanne, John Frederick. A.B., Hendrix Coll., 1953; J.D., So. Meth. U., 1956; LL.M. in Environ. Law, George Washington U., 1976. Bar: Tex. 1956, U.S. Ct. Appeals (1st, 5th, 6th, 8th, 9th, 10th, and 11th cirs.), U.S. Supreme Ct. 1964, Va. 1974. Atty. Superior Ins. Co., Dallas, 1960-64; claims atty. Sentry Ins. Co., Dallas, 1964-67; litigation counsel Stigall, Maxfield & Collier, Dallas, 1967-69; sole practice, Dallas, 1969-70; asst. gen. counsel for litigation C.E., U.S. Army, Washington, 1970-75; spl. litigation counsel Dept. Justice, Washington, 1975—; instr. environ. law U. Ala.-Huntsville, 1979-82; lectr. law George Washington U., 1981-86. Editor Southwestern Law Jour., 1955-56. Served to col. JAGC, USAR. Recipient numerous outstanding performance awards U.S. Army, Dept. Justice, Sr. Exec. Service Meritorious award Dept. Justice, 1984. Mem. Sr. Execs. Assn., Res. Officers Assn. Home: PO Box 6464 Arlington VA 22206 Office: Dept Justice Land and Natural Resources Div 1000 Pennsylvania Ave NW Room 7332 Washington DC 20530

DISHOP, RICHARD THOMAS, automotive dealer; b. Wauseon, Ohio, Aug. 24, 1942; s. Albert Henry and Amelia A. D.; m. Janice Elain Longstreet, July 5, 1973; children: Teresa, Anthony, Jodi. Student U. Automotive Mgmt., New Orleans, 1980. Barber, 1961-64; gen. mgr. Turnpike Travelers, Bowling Green, Ohio, 1967-71; owner, operator Dishop Ford Yugo Nissan, Bowling Green, 1972—; owner, operator RTD & Assos., collection agy., 1972-75; mem. Mid Am. Bank Adv. Bd., 1971-80, pres., 1972. Mem. Rep. Nat. Task Force. Named to Outstanding Young Men Am., U.S. Jaycees, 1973; recipient Quality Dealer award Datsun, 1975, 80, 82-83, 86, 87, Quality Dealer award Ford Motor Co., 1985, Disting. Dealer award Ford Motor Co., 1985. Mem. Am. Imported Automobile Dealers Assn., Nat. Auto Dealers Assn., Bowling Green Auto Dealers (sec.-treas. 1978-88), Ohio Auto Dealers Assn. Lutheran. Clubs: Falcon, Bowling Green State U. Pres.'s. Lodge: Elks. Home: 14251 Gorrill Rd Bowling Green OH 43402 Office: Dishop Ford-Yugo-Nissan Rt 25 Bowling Green OH 43402

DISLE, MICHEL, graphic designer; b. Neuilly-sur-Seine, France, Oct. 26, 1934; s. André and Lucie (Davesne) D.; divorced; children: Caroline, Olivier. Grad., Ecole Nat. Supérieure des Arts Appliqués, Paris, 1956, Cours Supérieur d'Esthétique Indsl., Paris, 1957. Asst. art dir. Publicis, Paris, 1960-65; jr. art dir. McCann-Erickson, Paris, 1965-69; art dir. Ted Bates, Paris, 1969-72; co-founder, creative dir. Carré Noir, Paris, 1973—. Creator personal emblem for French pres. Francois Mitterrand, 1982. Roman Catholic. Home: 109 Blvd Bineau, 92200 Neuilly-sur-Seine France Office: Carre Noir, 82 Blvd des Batignolles, 75017 Paris France

DI SPIGNO, GUY JOSEPH, psychologist, consultant; b. Bklyn., Mar. 6, 1948; s. Joseph Vincent and Jeanne Nina (Renna) DiS.; BS, Carroll Coll., 1969; MA (fellow), No. Ill. U., 1972; MEd, Loyola U., 1974; PhD, Northwestern U., 1977; m. Gisela Riba, May 23, 1979; children: Michael Paul, Abie Francis. Instr., No. Ill. U., DeKalb, 1969-70; chmn. humanities dept. Quincy (Ill.) Boys' High Sch., 1970-71; dir. religious edn. St. Mary's Ch., DeKalb, 1971-72; dir. edn. Immaculate Conception Parish, Higland Park, Ill., 1972-77; dir. human resources Am. Valuation Cons., Des Plaines, Ill., 1977-79; psychologist Hay Assocs., Chgo., 1979-80; v.p. psychol. services Exec. Assets Corp., Chgo., 1980-82; dir. mgmt. devel. and personnel services Borg-Warner Corp., Chgo., 1982-84; ptnr., cons. psychologist Medina & Thompson, Chgo., 1984—. Mem. Highland Park Human Relations Commn., 1975-77, Home Owners and Businessmen's Assn., Highland Park, 1976-77; mem. legis. com. Vernon Hills (Ill.) Sch. Bd.; soccer coach, Am. Youth Soccer Orgn., Glenview, Ill. Clifford B. Scott scholar, 1967. Mem. Community Religious Edn. Dirs. (nat. vice chmn. 1971-73), Am. Psychol. Assn., Ill. Psychol. Assn., Nat. Registry Health Service Providers in Psychology, Am. Personnel and Guidance Assn., Carroll Coll. Alumni Counsel, Phi Alpha Theta, Sigma Phi Epsilon. Contbr. articles to profl. jours. Home: 3710 Maple Leaf Dr Glenview IL 60025 Office: 100 S Wacker Dr Suite 1710 Chicago IL 60606

DISSTON, HARRY, author, business executive, horseman; b. Red Bank, N.J., Nov. 23, 1899; s. Eugene John Kauffmann and Frances Matilda Disston; A.B., Amherst Coll., 1921; m. Valerie Ivy Duval, Mar. 26, 1930 (dec. 1951); children—Robin John Duval, Geoffrey Whitmore (dec.); m. Catherine Sitler John, Aug. 26, 1960. With N.Y. Telephone Co., 1921-32, with AT&T, N.Y.C., 1932-60, exec. tng. student, dist. traffic supt., sales engr., dist. mgr., adv. staff engr., adv. staff exec. ind. co. relations, 1951-60; coordinator devel. activities, placement dir. Grad. Sch. Bus. Adminstrn., U. Va.; v.p. Equine Motion Analysis, Ltd., 1979-82; sr. v.p., dir. leasing Equivest Fin. Services Corp., Charlottesville, Va., 1986-88; pres. Harwood Corp., Ltd.; dir. AMVEST Horse Leasing Co., Charlottesville, Aide-de-camp to gov. Va.; chmn. Louisa County Electoral Bd.; mem. Va. Bd. Mil. Affairs; chmn. fin. com. Republican party Va.; chmn. Louisa County Rep. Com.; v.p. pres., dir. Park Ave. Assn.; mem. exec. com. Episcopal Diocese of Va., also pres. council, region 15; trustee Grant Monument Assn., Va. Outdoors Found.; bd. dirs. Atlantic Rural Expn.; bd. dirs., treas. Lee-Jackson Found.; chmn., bd. dirs. Charlottesville-Albemarle Clean Community Commn., 1978-84. Served from maj. to col., cav. and gen. staff corps, 1941-46; PTO; comdg. officer 107th Regtl. Combat Team, N.Y.N.G., 1947-57; brig. gen. ret. Awarded Legion of Merit, Bronze Star with oak leaf cluster; comdr. Order of Boliver; Philippine Liberation Medal; Medal of Merit with Swords, Free Poland. Mem. Am. Horse Shows Assn. (judge, steward, tech. del.), Vets. 7th Regt., N.Y. Soc. Mil. and Naval Officers World Wars (past pres.), Vet. Corps Arty., Mil. Order Fgn. Wars, Mil. Order World Wars, Am. Legion, Res. Officers Assn. (chpt. pres.), St. Georges Soc., St. Andrews Soc., Va. Thoroughbred Assn., U.S. Pony Clubs (gov.), Phi Beta Kappa, Phi Kappa Psi. Clubs: Torch (past pres. Charlottesville-Albermarle); Union; Amherst; Church of New York; Farmington Country, Greencroft, Jack Jouett Bridle Trails (pres.) (Charlottesville, Va.); Pilgrims of U.S.; Keswick Hunt, Keswick of Va. Author: Equestionnaire, 1947; Riding Rhymes, 1951; Know About Horses, 1961; Young Horseman's Handbooks, 1962; Elementary Dressage, 1971; Beginning Polo, 1973; Beginning the Rest of Your Life, 1980; columnist Daily Progress, Cen. Virginian; several mag. articles on mil., equine and bus. subjects; contbr. to Ency. Brit. Home: Hidden Hill Farm Keswick VA 22947 Office: 2955 Ivy Rd Suite 302 Charlottesville VA 22901

DISTEFANO, PETER ANDREW, insurance executive; b. N.Y.C., Nov. 26, 1939; s. Peter Julian and Marie Antoinette (Onorato) D.; student City Coll. San Francisco, 1965, Costa Mesa (Calif.)-Orange Coast Coll., 1975; cert. enrolled employee benefits, Wharton Sch., U. Pa., 1980; cert. profl. ins. agt., 1987; children: Diane, Daniel, Donald. Agt., Mut. N.Y., San Francisco, 1971-73; regional mgr. Hartford Ins. Group, Santa Ana, Calif., 1972-77; v.p. Lachman & Assos., Inc., ins., Lafayette, Calif., 1977-80; pres., owner Distefano Ins. Services, Benicia, Calif., 1980—; lectr., cons. risk mgmt., employee benefits. Pres. Contra Costa/Solano County Easter Seal Soc. Served with USNR, 1957-62. Recipient various ins. sales awards; registered profl. disability and health ins. underwriter. Fellow Acad. Producer Ins. Studies; mem. Nat. Assn. Health Underwriters, Nat. Assn. Life Underwriters, Soc. Registered Profl. Health Underwriters, Nat. Assn. Security Dealers, Internat. Found. Employee Benefit Plans, Profl. Ins. Agts. Calif./Nev. Soc. (cert.), Oakland/East Bay Assn. Life Underwriters. Greek Orthodox. Office: Distefano Ins Services Inc 845 First St PO Box 696 Benicia CA 94510

DISTELHORST, CRAIG TIPTON, savings and loan executive; b. Pitts., Nov. 3, 1941; s. Carl Frederick and Josephine Harris (Smith) D.; m. Judith Ann Harrill, Oct. 6, 1979. BS, Washington and Lee U., 1963; JD, George Washington U., 1966. Bar: N.Y. 1969, D.C., 1967. Sr. v.p., sec. Home Fed. Savs., Greesboro, N.C., 1976-79; v.p. Mortgage Guaranty Ins. Corp., Milw., 1979-82; exec. v.p., chief operating officer Benjamin Franklin Savs. and Loan, Houston, 1982-84, pres., 1984-85, chmn. exec. com., 1985-86; pres., chief exec. officer, Village Savs. and Loan, Houston, 1986—, chmn. bd., 1988; bd. dirs. Security Capital Credit Corp. Hartford, Conn., Foster Ins. Mgrs., Inc., Houston, Lloyds Mgmt. Corp., Houston, Security Capital Lloyds, Houston. Mem. corp. bd. dirs. Milw. Sch. Engring., 1980—; vol. steering com. United Craftsman, Bedford-Stuyvesant, N.Y., 1968-69; chmn. support program, George Washington U. Law Sch., 1969; mem. Mo. Rep. State Com., 1972-74; adv. Ret. Sr. Citizens Vol. Program, Nevada, Mo., 1975-76; vol. Juvenile Probation Officer, Nevada, 1974-76; bd. dirs. Mo.-Kans. Regional council Boy Scouts Am., 1975-76; bd. dirs. Greater Greensboro Housing Found., N.C., 1978-79; state fin. chmn. for election Gov. Kit Bond of Mo., 1972; chmn. Vernon County United Fund, Nevada, 1975, Nevada City Planning Commn., 1973-75, Mo. Mcpl. Bond Com., 1978-79; vice chmn., bd. dirs. United Arts Council Greensboro, 1979; mem. Nevada City Council, 1975-76; mem. 25th anniversary class reunion com. Washington and Lee U., 1987-88. Mem. Phi Delta Phi. Presbyterian. Club: Kingwood Country. Lodges: Elks, Rotary (bd. dirs. 1975-76, chmn. program 1974-76). Avocations: jogging, swimming, sailing, snow skiing. Home: 4615 Breezy Point Dr Kingwood TX 77345 Office: Village Savs Assn 11 Greenway Plaza Houston TX 77025-1102

DI TADA, DANIELA LYDIA, interior decorator; b. Buenos Aires, July 29, 1965; d. Esteban Guarino and Lydia Maria Carmen (Bruhn) diT. Bachiller, Instituto Martin y Omar, Buenos Aires, 1983. Interior decorator Consejo de Mujeres, Buenos Aires, 1983-87. Roman Catholic. Club: Centro Naval. Home: Rawson 2580 38A, Olivos, 1636 Buenos Aires Argentina Office: Av Maipú 3366, Olivos, 1636 Buenos Aires Argentina

DITHRIDGE, BETTY, civic worker; b. Los Angeles, Sept. 11, 1920; d. Thomas Edward and Louise (Miles) Mitchell; m. Andrew Morrison Dithridge, May 11, 1940; 1 child, Andrew Morrison Jr. Student, UCLA, 1937-39. Boy scout and cub scout leader Los Angeles Orphan's Home Soc., 1952-69, sec. extension com., 1959-61, chmn., 1966-68; vol. worker USO; mem. Los Angeles Jr. Philharmonic Com., 1949—; active Symphonies for Youth Concerts, 1958-59; founder, chmn. San Marino Protection Com., 1971-72; sec. Los Angeles County Grand Jury, 1974-75; bd. dirs. Pasadena chpt. ARC, 1961-62, Vol. Service Bur. Pasadena; bd. dirs., treas. Wilshire Community Police Council, 1979-81; mem. citizens adv. com. Los Angeles Olympics Organizing Com., 1982-84; dir. Capistrano Bay Community Services Dist., 1987—. Recipient awards for work with local youth groups. Mem. Wilshire C. of C. (chmn. women's bur. 1957-59), Los Angeles C. of C. Assocs. Los Angeles City Coll., Orange County Marine Inst., Friends of Huntington Library, D.A.R., Friends of San Juan Capistrano Library, San Juan Capistrano Hist. Soc., Los Angeles Grand Jurors Assn., Alpha Phi, Sigma Alpha Iota. Home: 35411 Beach Rd Capistrano Beach CA 92624

DITKOWSKY, KENNETH K., lawyer; b. Chgo., July 12, 1936; s. Samuel J. and Lillian (Plavnik) D.; m. Judith Goodman, Aug. 9, 1959; children—Naomi, Deborah, R. Benjamin. B.S., U. Chgo.; J.D., Loyola U., Chgo. Bar: Ill. 1961, U.S. Dist. Ct. (no. dist.) Ill. 1962, U.S. Ct. Apls. (7th cir.) 1973, U.S. Tax Ct. 1973, U.S. Sup. Ct. 1975. Ptnr., Ditkowsky & Contorer, Chgo., 1961—. Mem. Ill. Bar Assn., Chgo. Bar Assn. Club: Kiwanis. Address: 6150 Forest Glen Chicago IL 60646

DITTENHAFER, BRIAN DOUGLAS, banker, economist; b. York, Pa., Aug. 15, 1942; s. Nathaniel Webster and Evelyn Romaine (Myers) D.; m. Miriam Marcy, Aug. 22, 1964; 1 child. B.A., Ursinus Coll., 1964; M.A., Temple U., 1966, postgrad. (Univ. fellow) (G.E. Found fellow), 1967-71. Personnel asst. Philco Corp., Phila., 1965-66; teaching asst. Temple U., Phila., 1966-67; research asso. Temple U., 1968-69; bus. economist Fed. Res. Bank of Atlanta, 1971-76; v.p., chief economist Fed. Home Loan Bank of N.Y., N.Y.C., 1976-79, sr. v.p., chief fin. officer, 1979-80, exec. v.p., 1980-85, pres., 1985—. Deacon Central Presbyn. Ch., 1981-84; bd. dirs. N.Y. Council Econ. Edn., 1983—; trustee Fin. Instns. Retirement Fund., 1985—. Mem. Nat. Assn. Bus. Economists, Am. Econ. Assn., Am. Fin. Assn., Am. Real Estate and Urban Econ. Assn., N.Y. Assn. Bus. Econs., Omicron Delta Epsilon. Club: Forecaster's of N.Y. (sec.-treas. 1982-84). Office: Fed Home Loan Bank of NY One World Trade Ctr 103rd Floor New York NY 10048

DITTERICH, ERIC KEITH VON, clergyman; b. East Melbourne, Victoria, Australia, Feb. 8, 1913; s. Richard and Christiana (Shand) D.; B.A., B.D., Dip.Ed., Queen's Coll., Melbourne U.; m. Nancy Moyle Russell, Aug. 6, 1940; children—Anne (Mrs. Roger T. McLeod), Helen (Mrs. Kenneth I. Williams), Elizabeth (Mrs. Ross S. Fraser), Robert J.R., Julianne B. Pardee. Ordained to ministry Methodist Ch., 1940; minister in East Malvern, 1946-50, Benalla, 1950-55, Horsham, 1955-58; chmn. Wimmera Dist., 1955-58; mng. treas. Meth. Gen. Conf. Supernumerary Fund, 1958-77; mng. treas. Uniting Ch. in Australia Beneficiary Fund, 1977-80, chmn., 1980; dir. Meth. Publishing House, Melbourne, 1945-77; convener Uniting Ch. Pub. Agy., 1977-79. Pres., Victoria and Tasmania Conf., Meth. Ch., 1969-70; mem. Joint Commn. for Uniting Ch. in Australia, 1966-72; chmn. Meth. World Council Com. Pub. Interests 1971-76. Pres. council Queen's Coll., U. Melbourne, 1965-68; pres. council Wesley Coll., Melbourne, 1966-81, hon. fellow, 1983; trustee F.J. Cato Charitable Fund, 1977—, chmn., 1982. Served as chaplain Royal Australian Air Force, 1940-46; chaplain Citizen Air Force, 1948-70, Nepean Presbytery, 1981-84. Decorated mem. Order Brit. Empire. Mem. Royal Philatelic Soc., Royal Automobile Club. Lodge: Rotary (past pres.). Club: Port Philip Probus. Author: Food Available to Air Crew shot down in Tropical Areas, 1942, The Church on Active Service, 1945, Some Distortions of the Christian Faith, 1953, A Methodist Member's Manual, 1956, Three Curious Creeds, 1961, Our Faith and Its Fruits, 1965, Inflation, The Church and The Ministry, 1973, others. Home: 1574 High St, Glen Iris Victoria 3146, Australia Office: 94 Queen St, Melbourne Victoria, Australia

DIVINSKY, DANIEL JORGE, publisher; b. Buenos Aires, Apr. 1, 1942; s. José and Renée Ana (Wexselblatt) D.; m. Ana Mari a Teresa Miler, July 25, 1970; 1 child: Emilio. JD, U. Buenos Aires, 1962. Bar: Buenos Aires, 1963, La Plata. Sole practice Buenos Aires, 1963-73; ptnr. Divinsky and Finkelberg, Buenos Aires, 1963-73; gen. dir. Ediciones de la Flor, Buenos Aires, 1967-76, 83—; dir. Biblioteca Ayacucho, Caracas, Venezuela, 1978-83; editorial counselor El Diario de Caracas, 1979-83; gen. dir. Radio Belgrano, Buenos Aires, 1984-85; editor Revista Plural, Buenos Aires, 1984—; mem. administrn. council Plural Found., Buenos Aires, 1984—. Home: Rep de la India 2789, 10 B, 1425 Buenos Aires Argentina Office: Ediciones de la Flor, Anchoris 27, 1280 Buenos Aires Argentina

DIVONE, LOUIS VINCENT, aerospace engineer, educator; b. N.Y.C., July 24, 1934; s. Dominic and Christina Agnes (Cassa) D.; B.Aero. Engring., Poly. Inst. Bklyn., 1955; M.S., M.I.T., 1956; m. Judene Frances Smith, Aug. 10, 1968. Mem. tech. staff Jet Propulsion Lab., Calif. Inst. Tech., 1956-67, 69-72; program mgr. NASA, 1962-63; cons. Dept. Transp., 1968-69; dir. wind energy systems NSF, 1973-74; dir. wind energy systems ERDA, 1975-76; dir. Wind Energy Tech. div. Dept. Energy, Washington, 1977-83, dir. Office Solar Electric Techs., 1982-84, 86—; spl. asst. to dir. market planning and research Grumman Aerospace Corp., 1984-85; professorial lectr. George Washington U., 1976-84; cons. Wind Energy Working Group, UN, 1979-81; chmn. wind energy exec. com. Internat. Energy Agy., 1978-82. Recipient Apollo Achievement award NASA, 1970, Spl. Achievement award ERDA, 1976; Spl. Cash award, 1979, Sr. Exec. Service award, 1980 (both Dept. Energy), Pres.'s. Exec. Exchange Program appointment, 1984-86. Mem. AAAS, AIAA, Sr. Exec. Assn., Smithsonian Assos., Antique Airplane Assn., Nat. Trust for Hist. Preservation, Nat. Aviation Club, Cessna 180 Owners Club, Sigma Xi, Tau Beta Pi. Contbr. papers to profl. symposia. Patentee variable area rocket nozzle, self-attaching fluid coupling. Home: 2530 Leeds Rd Oakton VA 22124 Office: 1000 Independence Ave Washington DC 20585

DIWOKY, ROY JOHN, petroleum executive; b. Council Bluffs, Iowa, Dec. 4, 1910; s. Adolph and Ann (Koncal (Diwoky); m. Doris M. Hendricks, Apr. 17, 1933; children—Roy James (dec.), Linda. B.S., State U. Iowa, 1933, M.S., 1934; student, Harvard Bus. Sch., 1948. With Standard Oil Co., Ind.), Whiting (Ind.) Refinery, 1935-49; asst. gen. supt. Standard Oil Co., 1948-49; exec. asst. to pres., dir., v.p. Pan-Am. So. Corp., New Orleans, 1949; exec. v.p. and dir. Pan-Am. So. Corp., 1950-56; gen. mgr. mfg., dir.

Am. Oil Co., 1956-57; pres., chief exec. officer, dir. Commonwealth Oil Refining Co., Inc., 1957-61; pres., chief exec. officer, dir. Crown Central Petroleum Corp., 1961-67, cons. and dir.; treas., sec., dir. Liquilux Gas Service, Inc., also Bottle Service, Inc., 1968-74; cons., dir. Liquilux Gas Service, Ponce, P.R., 1974—. Mem. Am. Petroleum Inst. (mem. gen. refining com.), Am. Chem. Soc., Am. Inst. Chem. Engrs., New Orleans C. of C., Nat. Petroleum Refiners Assn. (dir.), 25 Yr. Club Petroleum Industry, Phi Gamma Delta. Clubs: Internat. House (New Orleans), Petroleum (New Orleans); Chicago (Ill.); Dorado Beach (San Juan, P.R.); Deportivo (Ponce, P.R.), Yacht (Ponce, P.R.); Maryland, Baltimore Country; Ridglea Country (Ft. Worth). Home: 4005 Winding Way Fort Worth TX 76126

DIX, GERALD BENNETT, educator; b. Salford, Eng., Jan. 12, 1926; s. Cyril and Mabel Winifred (Bennett) D.; m. Lois Nichols, July 23, 1963; 3 children. BA with honors in Architecture, U. Manchester, 1950, Diploma in Town and County Planning with distinction, 1951; MLA, Harvard U., 1954. Chartered architect, chartered town planner. Asst. lectr. U. Manchester, Eng., 1951-53; chief architect-planner Municipality of Addis Ababa, Ethiopia, 1954-56; planning officer Singapore Improvement Trust, 1957-59; sr. research fellow U. Sci. & Tech., Kumasi, 1959-63; sr. planner ODA U.K. Govt., 1963-65; lectr./sr. lectr. U. Nottingham, Eng., 1965-70, prof. planning, 1970-75; prof. civic design U. Liverpool, Eng., 1975-88, prof. emeritus, 1988, provice chancellor, 1984—; planner UN, Ghana, 1962; mem. Historic Areas Advt. Com., U.K., London, 1986-88; dir. plan project Govt. Cyprus, 1967-73, Govt. Alexandria, Egypt, 1980—. Editor: Third World Planning Rev., 1978—; assoc. editor: Town Planning Rev., 1976—; editorial bd. Ekistics, 1974—. Fellow Royal Town Planning Inst.; mem. World Soc. Ekistics (pres. 1987—). Mem. Ch. of Eng. Club: Athenaeum. Home: 13 Friars Quay, Norwich NR3 1ES, England Office: Dept Civic Design, Univ Liverpool, PO Box 147, Liverpool L69 3BX, England

DIX, RALPH EUGENE, office supply company executive; b. Leavenworth, Kans., July 16, 1926; s. Grover Webster and Mary Alice Dix; student public schs., Leavenworth; m. Mary Margaret DeCoursey, Dec. 2, 1944; children—Ralph Eugene, Carey Ann. Grocery store clk., 1947-48; owner Ralph's Grocery, 1948-60; in material control Gen. Motors Corp., 1949-59; salesman Sears Roebuck & Co., Leavenworth, 1959-68; owner Dix & Son Office Supply, Leavenworth, 1968—; sr. partner Platte Office Supply, Parkville, Mo., 1978—; partner Discount Carpet Warehouse, Leavenworth, 1978—; consul for Guatemala, 1981—. Mem. Leavenworth Urban Renewal Bd., 1969—; bd. dirs. Leavenworth Downtown Assn., 1974-75; Guatemalan consul Midwest region. Served with U.S. Army, 1944-46. Mem. Leavenworth C. of C. (dir. 1970-72), V.F.W., Am. Legion. Republican. Lodge: Eagles. Home: 2608 S 14th St Leavenworth KS 66048 Office: 413-415 Delaware St Leavenworth KS 66048

DIX, WILLIAM LESLIE, manufacturing executive. married; 3 children. Grad., Geelong Coll., Australia, 1941. Chartered sec., Australia. Various positions Ford Motor Co., Australia and Canada; dir. fin. Ford Motor Co. of Australia Ltd., 1965-72, pres., chief exec. officer, 1981—; staff dir. fin. Ford Asia-Pacific Inc., 1972-73, regional dir., 1973-77; v.p. export ops. Ford of Europe, 1977-79; pres. Ford Japan, 1979-81. Commr., dep. chmn. Australian Telecommunications Commn.; mem. Nat. Tennis Centre Trust, Geelong Coll. Council. Decorated officer Order of Australia, 1987. Fellow Australian Soc. Accts., Australian Inst. Mgmt.; mem. Fed. Chamber Automotive Industries (past pres.), Automotive Industry Council (chmn.), Australian Mfg. Council, Bus. Council Australia. Office: Ford Motor Co of Australia Ltd, 1735 Sydney Rd, Campbellfield Victoria 3061, Australia

DIXON, ALAN JOHN, U.S. senator; b. Belleville, Ill., July 7, 1927; s. William G. and Elsa (Tebbenhoff) D.; m. Joan Louise Fox, Jan. 17, 1954; children: Stephanie Jo, Jeffrey Alan, Elizabeth Jane. B.S., U. Ill., 1949; LL.B., Washington U., St. Louis, 1949. Bar: Ill. 1950. Practiced in Belleville, 1950-76; police magistrate City of Belleville, 1949; asst. atty. St. Clair County, Ill., 1950; mem. Ill. Ho. of Reps., 1951-63, Ill. Senate, 1963-71; minority whip; treas. State of Ill., 1971-77, sec. of state, 1977-81; U.S. Senator from Ill., 1981—. Mem. Am. Legion, Belleville C. of C. Democrat. Office: US Senate 331 Hart Senate Bldg Washington DC 20510-1301 *

DIXON, CARL FRANKLIN, lawyer; b. Mansfield, Ohio, Feb. 17, 1948; s. Carl Hughes and Elizabeth (Kauffman) D.; m. Barbara Wagner, Dec. 27, 1969; children—Clare Elizabeth, Jane Allison. B.A., Ill. Wesleyan U., 1970, B.S., 1970; M.A. Fletcher Sch. Law and Diplomacy div. Tufts U., 1974; JD, U. Chgo., 1974. Bar: Ill. 1975, U.S. Dist. Ct. (no. dist.) Ill. 1975, Ohio 1983. Assoc., Keck, Mahin & Cate, Chgo., 1974-78; ptnr. Dixon & Kois, Chgo., 1978-82; assoc. Porter, Wright, Morris & Arthur, Cleve., 1982-85, ptnr., 1986-87; v.p., sec., gen. counsel Weston, Inc., Cleve., 1987—. Recipient Adlai E. Stevenson award UN Assn., 1970; Edward R. Murrow fellow, 1971. Mem. ABA, Greater Cleve. Bar Assn., Phi Kappa Phi. Republican. Episcopalian. Clubs: Union League (Chgo.), Clifton (Lakewood, Ohio), Cleve. Athletic. Home: 31011 Manchester Ln Bay Village OH 44140 Office: Weston Inc 3615 Superior Ave Cleveland OH 44114

DIXON, EVA CRAWFORD JOHNSON, librarian; b. Evinston, Fla., Aug. 28, 1909; d. William Alpheus and Willie (Crawford) Johnson; AB with honors in Edn., U. Fla., 1937, MA, 1948; postgrad. Fla. State U., 1950, Appalachian State Tchrs. Coll., 1955; m. Thomas Gordon Dixon, Dec. 14, 1935 (div. 1944). Tchr. English, librarian Jefferson High Sch., Monticello, Fla., 1945-47; audio-visual dir. Jefferson County Schs., 1948-50; tchr. English, librarian Meigs (Ga.) High Sch., 1954-55; librarian Chipola Jr. Coll., Marianna, Fla., 1955-57, dir. library services, 1958-80, emeritus, 1980—, chmn. student aid and scholarship com., 1961-65; parliamentarian Fla. Gov.'s on Library on Info. Services, 1977-78; parliamentary workshop Tchr., Crystal River, Gainsville and Inverness, Fla., 1984-86. Elder, 1st Presbyterian Ch. Marianna, 1976—, chmn. witness/evangelism com., 1978-80, parliamentarian Fla. Presbytery, 1979-82. Recipient DAR Honor medal, 1984; prof. registered parliamentarian, 1985. Mem. Jefferson County Edn. Assn. (pres. 1948-50), Fla. Edn. Assn. Honor Socs. (chmn. 1950-51), Bus. and Profl. Women's Club (pres. 1958-59, 62-63), Fla. Fedn. Bus. Profl. and Women's Clubs (dist. dir. 1962-63), Women of 1st Presbyn. Ch. (pres. 1962-65), Nat. Assn. Parliamentarians (tchr., 1983—, v.p., program chmn. Jacksonville Mace unit 1983-84, edn. com. 1985-87, workshop coordinator at conv., 1987), Am. Inst. Parliamentarians (sec. Jacksonville area 1984), Fla. State Assn. Parliamentarians (edn. chmn. 1985-87, scholarship com. 1987—, contbr. articles The Fla. Parliamentarian jour. 1985-88), Kappa Delta Pi. Contbr. articles to profl. jours. Home: 6621 Shindler Dr Jacksonville FL 32222

DIXON, JOBIE, marketing executive; b. Sumter, S.C.; m. Celeste Bahadosingh; children—Chris, Watts, Jean Louise. pub. schs., Sumter, S.C. Promotion supr. Procter & Gamble, Cin. Ohio, 1966-69; Account exec. Doyle Dane Bernbach, N.Y.C., 1969-72; sr. account supr. Kincaid Agy., Charlotte, N.C., 1972, Cargill, Wilson & Acree, Atlanta, 1973; exec. v.p., dir. client services Pringle Dixon Pringle, Atlanta, 1974—; mem. White House Conf. on Small Bus., Ga. Bus. Council, Ga. Small Bus. Council, Econ. Devel. Council. Advt. strategist 3 presdl. campaigns; bd. dirs. AMA. Mem. Assn. Travel Mktg. Execs., Atlanta C. of C., Atlanta Coll. Arts, S.E. Tourism Soc., Fin. Instns. Mktg. Assn. Clubs: Cherokee Town and Country, Ainsley Golf. Home: 120 River Ridge Ln Roswell GA 30075 Other: 6 Spring Park Dr, Kingston Jamaica West Indies Office: 3340 Peachtree Rd Atlanta GA 30026

DIXON, JOHN EDWARD, food company executive; b. Halifax, N.S., Can., Apr. 21, 1933; came to U.S., 1974, naturalized, 1983; s. Edward Sterling and Flora Elizabeth (McDonald) D.; m. Marion Doris Jaqueline, June 16, 1956; children—Steven, Lynn, Glenn, Heather, Jeffrey. B.Sc. with honors, Queens U., 1955. Assoc. mgr. product devel. for Asia Procter & Gamble, Cin., 1974-75; dir. internat. research and devel. Pillsbury Co., Mpls., 1975-77, dir. corp. research and devel., 1977-79, v.p. new product devel., 1979-81, v.p. research and devel., 1981-86; v.p. tech. Pillsbury Co., 1986-88, v.p. ops., 1988—. Mem. Chem. Inst. Can., Indsl. Research Inst., Inst. Food Technologists. Presbyterian. Office: Pillsbury Pillsbury Ctr Minneapolis MN 55402

DIXON, LAWRENCE PAUL, insurance company executive; b. N.Y.C., Oct. 23, 1938; s. Clinton DeForge and Frances Margaret (Van Deusen) D.; BS, Fordham, U., 1960; m. Barbara Carell, June 18, 1960; children—Laurie Jean, Gregory, Linda, Kenneth; m. Zelen Wilde, July 3, 1981. Sr. underwriting officer Chubb & Son, Inc., Short Hills, N.J., 1960-73; sr. v.p. Contractors Coverage Corp., Great Neck, N.Y., 1973-76; v.p., ptnr. Global Planning Corp., Great Neck, 1976-78; pres. Dixon Brokerage, Inc., Melville, N.Y., 1978—, Ledd Co. Inc., Melville, 1975—; bd. dirs. Ebony Internat.; pres. Tiburn Services Ltd., Melville. Mem. U.S. Congl. Adv. bd., mem. The Pres.'s Com., Rep. Presdl. Task Force, Rep. Nat. State Elections Com., Am. Security Council Found.; pres. Fathers Club LaSalle Mil. Acad., chmn. Beef-o-Rama, 1982. Mem. Profl. Ins. Agts., Ind. Ins. Agts., Am. Subcontractors Assn., Subcontractors Trade Assn., Assn. Gen. Contractors, Advancement Commerce and Industry, Old Chester Hills Civic Assn., Gen. Contractors Assn. Republican. Clubs: Northport Yacht, Drug and Chem., Huntington Yacht, Green Turtle Yacht, North Palm Beach Yacht, Familiares (bd. dirs.), Ducks Unltd. (sponsor). Home: 35 Bunkerhill Dr Huntington NY 11743 Office: 150 Broadhollow Rd Melville NY 11747

DIXON, MICHAEL FREDERICK, pathologist; b. London, Mar. 7, 1941; s. Frederick and Doris (Langley) D.; m. Judith Loughton Bilsby, Aug. 28, 1965; children: Mark, Jane, Anna. M in Surgery, U. Edinburgh, Scotland, 1965, MD, 1980; M in Pathology, London U., 1972. Lectr. pathology U. Edinburgh, 1968-70; lectr. U. Leeds, Eng., 1970-80, sr. lectr., 1980—. Author: Aids to Pathology. Sr. steward Christchurch, Ilkley, Eng., 1985; chmn. Ilkley Council Chs., 1987. Fellow Royal Coll. Pathologists; mem. Internat. Acad. Pathology (council mem. British div. 1985-87), Path. Soc. Great Britain and No. Ireland (mem. com. 1988—), Assn. Clin. Pathologists, British Soc. Gastroenterology. Methodist. Clubs: Ilkley 41 (chmn. 1984), Ilkley Round Table (chmn. 1978). Home: 2 Tarn Villas, Ilkley LS29 8RH, England Office: Leeds Univ, Leeds LS2 9JT, England

DIXON, NORMAN FRANK, psychology educator; b. London, May 19, 1922; s. Henri Jacques and Edith Mary (O'Connor) D. BA in psychology with honors, U. Reading, Berkshire, Eng., 1953, PhD in Psychology, 1956; DSc, U. London, 1978; PhD (hon.), U. Lund, Sweden, 1983. Served with Bomb Disposal Units, Royal Engrs. 21st Army Group, Brit. Army (World War II), 1940-50; lectr. Univ. Coll. U. London, 1954-71, reader, 1971, prof. emeritus psychology, 1987—. Author: Subliminal Perception: the Nature of a Controversy, 1971, On the Psychology of Military Incompetence, 1976, Preconscious Processing, 1981, Our Own Worst Enemy, 1987. Named mem. Order of the Brit. Empire, 1944; recipient Carpenter medal for disting. research U. London, 1975. Fellow Brit. Psychol. Soc. Office: Dept Psychology Univ Coll, U London, London England

DIXON, PETER BISHOP, economist,; b. Melbourne, Australia, July 23, 1946; s. Herbert Bishop and Margaret Vera (Langbourne-Smith) D.; m. Orani Limpaamara, July 20, 1968; children: Janine Margaret, Barbara Bishop. B in Econs., Monash U., Melbourne, 1968; AM, Harvard U., 1970, PhD, 1972. Economist IMF, Washington, 1972-74, Res. Bank Australia, Sydney, 1974-75; sr. lectr. Monash U., 1975-78; assoc. dir. Impact Econ. Research, Melbourne, 1975-78; prof. econs. Latrobe U., Melbourne, 1978-83; vis. prof. Harvard U., Cambridge, Mass., 1983; prof., dir. U. Melbourne Inst. Applied Econs. and Research, 1984—; chmn. editorial bd. Australian Econ. Rev., Melbourne, 1984—. Author: ORANI: A Multisectoral Model of the Australian Economy, 1982; contbr. 70 articles to profl. jours., 1972—. Co-recipient Research medal Royal Soc. Victoria, Melbourne, 1983. Fellow Australian Acad. Soc. Scis.; mem. Econ. Soc. Australia. Office: U Melbourne Inst Applied, Econs and Soc Research, 3052 Parkville Australia

DIXON, RICHARD DEAN, lawyer, educator; b. Columbus, Ohio, Nov. 6, 1944; s. Dean A. and Katherine L. (Currier) D.; m. Kathleen A. Manfrass, June 17, 1967; children—Jennifer, Lindsay. B.S. in Elec. Engring., Ohio State U., 1967, M.S. in Elec. Engring., 1968; M.B.A., Fla. State U., 1972, J.D., 1974. Bar: Fla. 1975, U.S. Dist. Ct. (mid. dist.) Fla. 1975, U.S. Patent and Trademark Office, 1975, Colo. 1985, U.S. Dist. Ct. Colo. 1985. Telemetry systems engr. Pan Am. World Airways, Patrick AFB, Fla., 1968-72; sole practice, Melbourne and Orlando, Fla., 1975-80; sr. counsel Harris Corp., Melbourne, 1980-85; corp. counsel Ford Microelectronics, Inc., Colorado Springs, Colo., 1985—; adj. prof. bus. law U. Central Fla., Cocoa, 1977, Fla. Inst. Tech., Melbourne, 1980-84. Cooper Industries Engring. scholar Ohio State U., 1964-67. Mem. Licensing Execs. Soc., Am. Intellectual Property Law Assn., Am. Corp. Counsel Assn., ABA, Sigma Iota Epsilon, Eta Kappa Nu, Phi Eta Sigma. Home: 225 Woodmoor Dr Monument CO 80132 Office: Ford Microelectronics Inc 10340 State Hwy 83 Colorado Springs CO 80908

DIXON, ROBERT CLYDE, communication systems engineer, consultant; b. Greensboro, N.C., Jan. 8, 1932; s. Earnest Patrick and Alma Leona (Moore) D.; m. Nancy Tom Zurborg, July 9, 1955; children—David Thomas, Theresa Anne, Robert Weldon. B.S. in Elec. Engring., Pacific States U., 1961; M.S. in Systems Engring., West Coast U., 1968; cert. bus. for tech. personnel, UCLA, 1971, profl. designation in bus., 1972. Registered profl. engr., Calif. Sr. engr. Magnavox Research Labs., Torrance, Calif., 1959-68; staff engr. TRW, Redondo Beach, Calif., 1968-71; sr. research engr. Northrop Corp., Palos Verdes, Calif., 1971-74; sr. tech. staff asst. Hughes Aircraft Co., Fullerton, Calif., 1974-75; chief scientist, Irvine, Calif., 1982-84; pres. Spectrack Systems Inc., Cypress, Calif., 1975-82; cons. R.C. Dixon & Assocs., Cypress, 1975—; chief scientist Spread Spectrum Scis., Palmer Lake, Colo., 1981—; lectr. UCLA, Westwood, 1975—, George Washington U., 1976—. Author: Spread Spectrum Systems, 1976, 84; editor: Spread Spectrum Techniques, 1976; contbr. articles to tech. jours. Elder's pres. Ch. of Jesus Christ of Latter Day Saints, Cypress, 1975, mem. High Council, 1977-83. Served with USN, 1951-55. Mem. IEEE (sr. mem., co-editor spl. issue communications transactions 1978, mem. prceedings editorial bd.), Armed Forces Communications and Electronic Assn. Mormon. Home: 14717 Perry Park Rd Palmer Lake CO 80133 Office: Spread Spectrum Scis PO Box 100 Palmer Lake CO 80133

DIXON, ROBERT MORTON, soil scientist; b. Leon, Kans., May 30, 1929; s. William Gill and Vivian (Marshall)D.; B.S., Kans. State U., 1959, M.S., 1960; Ph.D., U. Wis., 1966; children—James, Curtis, Donna, Gregory. Instr., Kans. State U., Manhattan, 1959-60; irrigation specialist Ford Found., Cairo, 1967; research soil scientist U.S. Dept. Agr., 1960-85, Tucson, 1973-85; water infiltration control specialist AID, Port-au-Prince, Haiti, 1977; agrl. cons. U.S. Agy. Internat. Devel., Haiti, 1978; People-to-People Irrigation del. People's Republic of China, 1982. Served with U.S. Army, 1954-56. Mem. Internat. Soc. Soil Sci., Am. Soc. Agronomy, Am. Geophys. Union, Am. Soc. Agrl. Engrs., Soil Sci. Soc. Am., Soil Conservation Soc. Am., Internat. Platform Assn., Soc. Range Mgmt., Ariz.-Nev. Acad. Sci., Land Imprinting Found. (organizer 1986, chmn. 1986—). Democrat. Unitarian. Contbr. articles to profl. jours. Patentee land imprinter. Home and Office: 1231 E Big Rock Rd Tucson AZ 85718

DIXON, SHIRLEY JUANITA, restaurant owner; b. Canton, N.C., June 29, 1935; d. Willard Luther and Bessie Eugenia (Scroggs) Clark; m. Clinton Matthew Dixon, Jan. 3, 1953; children: Elizabeth Swanger, Hugh Monroe III, Cynthia Owen, Sharon Fouts. BS, Wayne State U., 1956; postgrad. Mary Baldwin Coll., 1958, U. N.C., 1977. Acct., Standard Oil Co., Detroit, 1955-57; asst. dining room mgr. Statler Hilton, Detroit, 1958-60; bookkeeper Osborne Lumber Co., Canton, N.C., 1960-61; bus. owner, pres. Dixon's Restaurant, Canton, 1961—; judge N.C. Assn. Distributive Edn. Assn., state and dist., 1982—; owner Halbert's Family Heritage Ctr., Canton. V.p. Haywood County Assn. Retarded Citizens Bd., 1985—; bd. commrs. Haywood Vocationals Opportunities, 1985—; dist. dir. 11th Congl. Dist. Democratic Women, 1982—; state Teen-Dem. advisor State Dem. party, 1985—; del. 1988 Dem. Nat. Conv., Atlanta; alderwoman Town of Canton, N.C.; vice-chair Gov.'s Adv. Council on Aging, State N.C., 1982—; 1st v.p. crime prevention Community Watch Bd., State N.C., 1985, 86; mem. Criminal Justice Bd., N.C. Assembly on Women and the Economy; chair. Western N.C. Epilipsey Assn., Haywood County N.C. Mus. Historu, 1987—; co-chair Haywood County Commn. on the Bi-Centennial of Constn., 1987—; bd. dirs. Canton Recreation Dept., Western N.C. Alzheimers and Related Disorders Assn., 1987—, N.C. Conf. for Social Services, 1987—. Recipient Outstanding Service award Crime Prevention from Gov., 1982, Gov.'s Spl. Vol. award, 1983, Outstanding Service award N.C. Community Watch Assn., 1984, Community Service award to Handicapped, 1983-84, Outstanding Service award ARC, 1988; named Employer of Yr. for Hiring Handicapped N.C. Assn. for Retarded Citizens, 1985. Mem. NOW, Women's Polit. Caucus, Nat. Assn. Female Execs., Internat. Platform Assn., Women's Forum N.C., Canton Bus. and Profl. Women's Club (pres. 1974-79; Woman of Yr. 1984). Democrat. Episcopalian. Club: Altrusa. Avocation: softball club. Home: 104 Skyland Terrace Canton NC 28716 Office: Dixon's Restaurant 30 N Main St Canton NC 28716

DIXON, WILLIAM CORNELIUS, lawyer; b. Dexter, N.Y., July 1, 1904; s. Frank and Celia (Potter) D.; m. Arvilla Pratt, Nov. 20, 1934; children—Anne Arvilla, Nancy Cornelia. A.B., U. Mich., 1926, J.D., 1928. Bar: Ohio 1928, Calif. 1948, Supreme Ct. U.S 1948. Asso. Holliday-Grossman-McAfee, Cleve., 1928-32; asst. dir. law Cleve., 1932-33, practiced law, 1933-38; justice Supreme Ct. Ohio, 1938; spl. asst. in anti-trust div. to atty. gen. U.S. Dept. Justice, 1944-54, chief asst. trial sect. anti-trust div., 1945, apptd. chief West Coast offices Anti-trust div., 1946, chief trial counsel for Govt. U.S. versus Standard Oil Co. Calif. et al, 1948, chief Los Angeles Office, 1948-54; pvt. law practice Los Angeles, 1954-59; asst. atty. gen. in charge state anti-trust enforcement Calif., 1959-63; legal adviser and mem. Joint War and State Depts., Zaibatsu Mission to Japan, 1946. Dir. relief for Ohio under Emergency Relief Act, 1938-39; moderator Los Angeles Assn. Congl. Chs., 1957; moderator Congl. Conf. So. Calif. and S.W., 1960; mem. constn. commn. United Ch. of Christ; mem. United Ch. Bd. for Homeland Ministries, 1962-65. Papers included in Truman Library, Library of Contemporary History, U. Wyo., Ohio State U. and UCLA libraries. Mem. Calif., Los Angeles bar assns., Delta Sigma Rho, Pi Kappa Alpha. Democrat. Home: 1188 Romney Dr Pasadena CA 91105 Office: Subway Terminal Bldg 417 S Hill St Los Angeles CA 90013

DIZ, ADOLFO CESAR, economist; b. Buenos Aires, May 12, 1931; s. Agustín Diz and Elisa Aristizabal; m. Martha Solari, 1959; five sons. Student Univ. de Buenos Aires, Univ. Chicago. Instr. stats. Univ. de Buenos Aires, 1951-55, 1958-59; prof. stats. Univ. Nacional de Tucumán, 1959-60, dir. Inst. Econ. Research, 1959-65, prof. stats. and econometrics, 1960-61, 1964, prof. monetary theory, 1962, 1965-66; exec. dir. Internat. Monetary Fund (IMF), 1966-68; envoy extraordinary and minister plenipotentiary, Argentine Fin. Rep. Europe, 1969-73; dir. Ctr. for Latin America Monetary Studies, 1973-76, Per Jacobsson Found., 1976—; pres. Banco Central de la República Argentina, 1976-81; mem. Argentine socs., Am. Econ. Assn., Econometric Soc. Author: Money and Prices in Argentina, 1935-62 in varieties of Monetary Experience, Money Supply Models (in Spanish); contbr. articles on econs. to publs. Address: Callao Ave 2049-P6 (1024), Buenos Aires Argentina *

DIZDAREVIC, RAIF, Yugoslavian president; b. Fojnica, Bosnia and Herzegovina, Yugoslavia, 1926. With Nat. Liberation struggle, 1943; mem. League of Communists, 1945—, mem. Presidency Central Com. of Bosnia and Herzegovina, 1974—; in pub. offices of Bosnia and Herzegovina, 1945-51; with Ministry Fgn. Affairs, Yugoslavia, 1951-54; sec. and charge d'affairs Yugoslav embassy, Bulgaria, 1951-54; 1st sec. Yugoslav embassy, Moscow, 1956-59; counsellor Yugoslav embassy, Prague, Czechoslovakia, 1963-67; sec. Council of Confederacy of Trade Unions of Yugoslavia, 1967-72; asst. fed. sec. for fgn. affairs, 1972-74; council pres., mem. council presidency Confederacy of Trade Unions of Bosnia and Herzegovina, 1974-78; mem. presidency Republican Conf. of Socialist and Workers Party of Bosnia and Herzegovina, 1975-78; mem. presidency of Cen. Com. of League of Communists of Bosnia, Herzegovina, 1974-84, 84—; mem. Cen. Com. League of Communists of Yugoslavia; pres. presidency Socialist Republic of Bosnia and Herzegovina and pres. Council for Overall Nat. Def., 1978-82; mem. Council for Nat. Def. Yugoslavia, 1978-83; fed. sec. fgn. affairs SFR of Yugoslavia, 1984; del. Fed. Chamber of Assembly Yugoslavia, 1982—, pres. assembly, 1982-83; fed. sec. fgn. affairs, 1984-87; minister of fgn. affairs Yugoslavia, Novi Beograd, until 1988, v.p., 1987-88, pres., 1988—. Various Yugoslav and fgn. decorations. Office: care Fed Exec Council, Bul Lenjina 2, 11075 Novi Beograd Yugoslavia

DJAHANBAKHCH, OVRANG, obstetrician, gynecologist, lecturer, consultant; b. Babol, Iran, Oct. 21, 1944; came to Great Britain 1967; s. Ibrahim and Foroughiyeh (Bassari) D.; 1 child, Mathew Charles. MD, Med. Sch., Istanbul, Turkey, 1967, MPhil, London U., 1983, MD, 1984. Clin. research fellow Med. Research Council, Edinburgh, Scotland, 1979-81; lectr., sr. registrar Royal Free Hosp. Med. Sch., London, 1981-85. Contbr. articles to profl. med. jours. Contbr. many chpts. to med. books; lectr. various med. group. Mem. Royal Coll. Obstetricians and Gynecologists, William Blair Bell Research Soc., Endocrine Soc. Home: 23 Cannon Pl, London NW3, England Office: London Hosp Med Coll, Dept Ob-Gyn, London E1, England

DJAKABABA, CORNELIUS MALO, international trading and construction company executive; b. Rara, Sumba, Indonesia, Dec. 8, 1935; s. Yosef B. Malo and Maria D. Horo; m. Eden Y. Dalisay, June 4, 1966; children—Marian, Nelden, Yosef. B.S.C., U. San Carlos, 1962; M.S.C., U. Santo Tomas, 1965. Tchr., high sch., Sumba, Indonesia, 1957-58; Philippine Women's U., Manila, 1963-64; asst. v.p. Aguinaldo Devel. Corp., Manila, 1963-70; gen. mgr. Kayan River Timber Co., Jakarta, 1970-78; pres., dir. Pt. Atlantica Wisesa, Jakarta, 1978—. pres., dir. Pt. Adikara Agung, Jakarta, 1976—, Pt. Sekawan Agung Mulia, Jakarta, 1976-82. Vice chmn. Nusenggara Timur Cultural Assn., Jakarta, 1976—, Inna Ama Social Found., 1980—; adviser, sponsor Civic Assn. Sumba, Jakarta, 1976—; chmn. Catholic Civic Group, Jakarta, 1979—. Mem. Bus. and Fin. Club (pres. 1960-62), Photographic Club (pres. 1960-62). Lodge: Rotary (hon. sec. 1983-84). Address: Kav A 36, Permata Hijau, Jakarta 12210, Indonesia

DJELANTIK, ANAK AGUNG MADE, physician; b. Karangasem, Bali, Indonesia, July 21, 1919; s. Anak Agung Bagus and Djero Selaga D.; m. Astri Henriette Zwart; children: Bulantrisna, Suryawati, Madelief, Widura, Merti. MD, U. Amsterdam, The Netherlands, 1946. Pub. health officer Govt. of Indonesia, outer islands: Buru, Sumbawa, North Sulawesi, 1948-54, Buleleng, North Bali, 1954-58; chief of health services Govt. of Indonesia, Bali, 1958-68; dir. main hosp. Govt. of Indonesia, Denpasar, Bali, 1960-68; dean med. sch. Udayana U., Denpasar, 1962-64, lectr. pub. health, 1962—; malariologist WHO, Manila, Iraq, Somalia, Afghanistan, 1969-79, Pakistan, India, Nepal, 1980-83; cons. UNICEF, 1983. Author: Balinese Paintings, 1986. Dir. Red Cross, Sulawesi and Bali, 1954-68; co-founder Council for the Arts and Culture, Bali, 1960, Dance Acad., Denpasar, 1966; treas. Sch. Found. Cipta Dharma, Denpasar, 1982—; chmn. Walter Spies Found., Denpasar, 1983—, Rudolf Bonnet Found., Denpasar, 1983—; bd. dirs. Udayana U., 1980—. Mem. Indonesian Med. Assn. (bd. med. ethics 1987—). Home and Office: Janan Sanur, 101 Bunderan Renon, Denpasar Bali, Indonesia

DJOJOKUSUMO, DJAROT, safety engineer, company executive; b. Yogyakarta, Indonesia, Feb. 3, 1936; s. B.P.H. and B.R.A.Y. D.; m. Ida Hamid King, May 18, 1943; children: Ira Murhajati, Sari Damayanti, Tomi Kurniawan. Insinyur degree, Gajah Mada U., 1961. Supt. tech. installation PT Pupuk Sriwidjaja, Jakarta, Indonesia, 1962; supt. process engring. PT Pupuk Sriwidjaja, Palembang, 1964; safety/inspection mgr. PT Petrokimia Gresik, Indonesia, 1971, tech., ops. mgr., 1972, plant mgr., 1977, tech. and prodn. dir., 1978-82, tech. dir., 1982; pres. PT Pupuk Isakander Muda, Lhok Seumawe, Indonesia, 1982—, also bd. dirs. Recipient award of appreciation, Pres. Upakarti, Satya Lencana Pembangunan. Home: Jl Niaga Hijau Raya #26, Pondok Indah, Jakarta Sela tan Indonesia Office: Jl Medan Banda Aceh, PO Box 21, Lhok Seumawe Indonesia

DJORDJEVIC, MIODRAG (BORISLAV), photographer; b. Valijevo, Yugoslavia, Dec. 12, 1919; m. Branka Petrovic, 1956 (div. 1968); m. Dusanka Miljkovic, 1978; 1 son, Nenad. Student in medicine U. Belgrade (Yugoslavia), 1939-49, M.D., 1968; self-taught in photography. Free-lance artist, photographer, Belgrade, 1947—; prof. photography Sch. Design, Belgrade, 1968-78; head dept. photography and film Med. Ctr., U. Belgrade, 1978—. One-man shows: Dom zljeznicara, Belgrade, 1951, Stanko Vraz, Belgrade, 1952, Graficki kolektiv, Belgrade, 1957, 66, Cultural House, Nova Huta, Poland, 1961, Mus. Applied Arts, Belgrade, 1963, City Mus., Subotica, Yugoslavia, 1963 (travelled to City Mus., Rovinj, Yugoslavia 1964), Nadezda Petrovic (retrospective), Cacak, Yugoslavia, 1966, City Mus., Rovinj, Yugoslavia, 1966, Dum Panuz Kunstatu, Brno, Czechoslovakia, 1967, Kamen mali, Cavtat, Yugoslavia, 1968, Applied Arts Gallery, Belgrade, 1970, GUF Gallery, Zagreb, 1970, Mus. Applied Arts, Belgrade, 1971 (travelled to Cultural House, Cacak, 1972), Stadtmuseum, Erlangen, W.Ger.,

1972, Students' Centre, Novi Sad, Yugoslavia, 1972, Avenida das Nacoes Gallery, Brasilia, Brazil, 1976 (travelled to Tower Gallery, Nis, Yugoslavia 1977), Museu de Arte Moderna, Sao Paulo, Brazil, 1977, Mus. Modern Arts, Belgrade, 1978 (travelled to Mus. Modern Arts, Skopje, Yugoslavia, 1979, and Gallery Modern Arts, Zagreb, 1980), Gallery of Arts, Shanghai, China, 1979; represented in permanent collections: Mus. Applied Arts, Belgrade, Mus. Modern Arts, Belgrade, Serbian Acad. Sci. and Arts, Belgrade, Begrade Galery Cveta Zuzoric, 1985, Sarajevo, A. Galery Skenderius, 1985, Rovinj Muzeum, 1986; Mus. Modern Arts, Skopje, Gallery Contemporary Arts, Zagreb, Monastery Chilander, Athos, Greece, Museu de Arte Contemporante, Sao Paulo, Museu de Arte Moderna, Sao Paulo; books: (with introduction by Mandic Sveta) Studenica, 1963; (with introduction by Anton Paulentic) Rovinj, 1963; (with others) Art on the Soil of Yugoslavia: From Prehistoric Times to the Present, 1971; Istorija Beograda, 3 vols., 1974; Icones Byzantines, 1977; (with an introduction by Pavle Savic) Hilander, 1978; (with an introduction by Nebojsa Tomasevic) Tisnikar, 1979; (with others, with an introduction by No Myth) China, 1980; (introduction by Paul Miller) Famous Fresks Bizantines. Served with Yugoslav Nat. Liberation Army, 1941-45. Recipient Janez Puhar award Yugoslav Photography Exhbn., 1953; First prize Internat. Exhbn. Photography, Federation Internationale Public de l'Art Photographique, Cologne, 1956, First prize Exposicion Internacional Universitaria de Fotografia de Montant, Madrid, 1957, Golden Plate award Yugoslav Photography Exhbn., Osjek, 1958; Artist of Photography award Federation Internationale de l'Art Photographique, 1961, award of Excellence, 1972; ULUPUS award, Belgrade, 1963, Master of Photography award Assn. Photographers Yugoslavia, 1969, October Salon award, Belgrade, 1975. Office: Stanka Vraza 6, 11000 Belgrade Yugoslavia

DJURANOVIC, VESELIN, Yugoslavian government official; b. Martinici, Yugoslavia, May 17, 1925; s. Vjera D.; m., 3 children. Joined partisan movement, 1941, League of Yugoslav Communist Youth, 1941, League of Communists of Yugoslavia, 1944; various party posts after war; pres. central com. Youth Orgn. Montenegro; dir. Radio Titograd, 1953-54; editor-in-chief Pobjeda newspaper, 1954-58; chmn. central bd. Montenegro Socialist Alliance of Working People, 1962-63; mem. ideological com. of central com. Montenegro League Communists, then mem. central com. Yugoslav League Communists, 1964—; pres. exec. council (state premier) Socialist Republic of Montenegro, 1963-66; sec. exec. com. of central com. Montenegro League Communists, 1967-68, pres., 1968-77; pres. (prime minister) Fed. Exec. Council Yugoslavia, from 1977, mem. Presidency of Central Com., 1978-82; pres. Socialist Republic of Montenegro, 1982—. Address: Fed Exec Council, Bul Lenjina 2, 11075 Novi Beograd Yugoslavia

DJUROVIC, MIRČETA, educator; b. Danilovgrad, Montenegro, Yugoslavia, Aug. 5, 1924; s. Marko Djurovic and Rumica Raspopovic; m. Jana Kažic, Aug. 7, 1960; children: Goran, Natalija, Marina. B in Econs., U. Belgrade, Yugoslavia, 1949; postgrad., Inst. Social Studies, Belgrade, 1951; PhD in Econs., U. Belgrade, Belgrade, 1956. Asst. Sci. Soc., Titograd, Yugoslavia, 1951-60; asst. prof. Faculty of Economy, Titograd, 1960-71, dean, 1960-64, prof., 1971—; pres. Montenegrin Acad. Scis. and Arts, Titograd, 1985—; rector Titograd U., 1974-78, prof. Author: Commercial Capital of Montenegro in the Second Half of the XIX Century and at the Beginning of the XX Century, 1958, Monetary Offices in Montenegro, 1959, Stock Companies in Montenegro, 1959, Montenegrin Finances: 1860-1915, 1960, Changes in Montenegrin Social-Economic Structure, 1964, Functional Capability of Means in Montenegrin Enterprises, 1967, Political Economy I, II, III-1970, 1976. Rep. Parliament of Montenegro, Titograd, 1967-71; mem. cen. com. Communist League of Montenegro, 1974, 85—, Yugoslav Communist League, 1979-82. Recipient July 13 prize Parliament of Montenegro, Titograd, 1961, Ochtoich prize, 1978. Mem. Fed. Econ. Council. Mem. Christian Orthodox Ch. Home: Beogradska 6, 81000 Titograd Yugoslavia Office: Montenegrin Acad of Scis & Arts, 81000 Titograd, Rista Stijovica 5 Yugoslavia

DLAB, VLASTIMIL, mathematics educator, researcher; b. Bzi, Czechoslovakia, Aug. 5, 1932; came to Can., 1968; s. Vlastimil Dlab and Anna (Stuchlikova) Dlabova; m. Zdenka Dvorakova, Apr. 27, 1959 (div.); children—Dagmar, Daniel Jan; m. Helena Briestenska, Dec. 18, 1985; children: Philip Adam, David Michael. R.N.Dr., Charles U., Prague, Czechoslovakia, 1956, C.Sc., 1959, Habilitation, 1962, D.Sc., 1966; Ph.D., U. Khartoum, Sudan, 1962. Research fellow Czechoslovak Acad. Scis., Prague, 1956-57; lectr., sr. lectr. Charles U., Prague, 1957-59, reader, 1964-65; lectr., sr. lectr. U. Khartoum, Sudan, 1959-64; research fellow, sr. research fellow Inst. Advanced Studies, Australian Nat. U., Canberra, 1965-68; prof. math. Carleton U., Ottawa, Ont., Can., 1968—, chmn. dept., 1971-74; vis. prof. U. Paris VI, Brandeis U., U. Bonn, U. Tsukuba, U. Sao Paulo, U. Stuttgart, U. Poitiers, Nat. U. Mex., U. Essen, U. Bielefeld, Hungarian Acad. Scis., Budapest, U. Warsaw, U. Normal Beijing, U. Vienna, Czechoslovakian Acad. Scis. Author: Representations of Valued Graphs, 1980, An Introduction to Diagrammatical Methods, 1981; editor proc. internat. confs., 1974, 79, 84, 87; contbr. numerous articles to profl. jours. Recipient Diploma of Honour Union Czechoslovak Mathematicians, 1962; Can. Council fellow, 1974; Japan Soc. Promotion of Sci. sr. research fellow, 1981; sci. exchange grantee Nat. Scis. and Engring. Research Council Can., 1978, 81, 83, 85, 88. Fellow Royal Soc. Can. (convenor 1977-78, 80-81, council mem. 1980-81); mem. Can. Math. Soc. (council, chmn. research com. 1973-77, editor Can. Jour. Math.), London Math. Soc., Am. Math. Soc., Math. Assn. Am. Roman Catholic. Home: 277 Sherwood Dr, Ottawa, ON Canada K1Y 3W3 Office: Carleton Univ, Ottawa, ON Canada K1S 5B6

DLAMINI, SOTSHA ERNEST, prime minister of Swaziland; b. Mankayane, Swaziland, May 27, 1940; married; 5 daughters, 4 sons. Cert., Inst. Personnel Mgmt., Mgmt. Services Ltd. Clk. for timber logging firm Republic South Africa, 1959-60; from constable to asst. commr. in charge of criminal investigations dept. Swaziland Police Force, 1961-84; chief indsl. relations officer Ubombo Ranches Ltd., 1984-86, asst. personnel mgr., 1986; prime minister Kingdom Swaziland, Mbabane, 1986—. Address: Office Prime Minister, Mbabane Swaziland *

D'LAURO, FRANK ANDREW, JR., real estate development executive; b. Phila., Nov. 11, 1940; s. Frank Andrew and Dorothy (Adams) D'L.; grad. Hill Sch., 1958; B.A., Washington and Lee U., 1962; M.Arch., U. Pa., 1965. Architect, FKWP, Phila., 1967-68; project mgr., exec. v.p., pres. Frank A. D'Lauro Co., Phila., 1968—; pres. D'Lauro Devel. Corp., 1974—, D'Lauro Corp., 1979—; mem. regional exec. bd. Continental Bank, Phila. Chmn., Montgomery County Young Republican Fedn., 1970-72; mem. Montgomery County Rep. Finance Com., 1972—; bd. dirs. Young Republicans of Pa., 1972-74; chmn. Montgomery County Housing Authority, 1976—. Bd. dirs., v.p. Big Bros. Assn. Phila., pres. 1985—; bd. dirs. Sacred Heart Hosp., 1980—; pres. Youth Recreation Assn. Montgomery County, 1979—. Served to capt. U.S. Army, 1965-67; Vietnam. Decorated Bronze Star with oak leaf cluster, Soldiers medal; recipient award of merit Big Bros. Phila., 1972. Mem. Carpenters Co. Phila., Pa. Soc. S.R., Sigma Nu. Clubs: Union League, Racquet Philadelphia Cricket (Phila.). Office: 218 E Willow Grove Ave Philadelphia PA 19118

D'LOWER, DEL, importing company executive; b. Warsaw, Poland, Sept. 21, 1912; came to U.S., 1919; s. Max and Estere (Gerlatky) D.; m. Helen Fuchs, June 5, 1937 (dec. Mar. 1980); 1 child, Esther Ann. Student, CCNY, 1931-32, U. Tulsa, 1942-44, New Sch., N.Y.C., 1960-63, 81-82. Cosmetologist, Seligman & Latz, N.Y.C., 1936-41, Del's, Tulsa, 1941-46; beauty salon owner Delby, N.Y.C., 1946-75; greeting card mfr., 1972; pres. Delby System Importers, N.Y.C., 1975—. Author: Ginny the Pretty White Doe, 1973; composer: High Cheek Bones, 1960; patentee in field. Fellow ASCAP. Jewish. Avocations: creative writing, composing, poems, plays. Office: Delby System Importers 450 7th Ave New York NY 10123

DLUBAK, ZBIGNIEW, photographer; b. Radonsko, Poland, Apr. 26, 1921. Self-taught in photography, painter, 1946—; free-lance photographer, 1948—; founder mem. Grupa 55 artists group, 1955-56; co-founder Galeria Permafo, Wroclaw, Poland, 1970-74. One-man shows: Club of Young Artists and Scientists, Warsaw, Poland, 1948, Contemporary Gallery, Warsaw, 1967, Internat. Press and Book Club Ruch, Warsaw, 1970, Galeria Od Nowa, Poznan, Poland, 1970, (3-person) Galeria Bod Mona Liza, Wroclaw (travelled to Contemporary Gallery, Warsaw), 1971, Galeria Permafo, Wroclaw, 1971 (2), Gallery of Actual Art (Znak), Bialystock, Poland, 1974, Galeria Labirynt, Lublin, Poland, 1975, Galeria Remont, Warsaw, 1975, Salon of Contemporary Art, Lodz, Poland, 1976, Mus. Fine Arts, Lodz, 1978, Inst. Polonais, Paris, 1981; retrospective exhbn. Nat. Mus., Warsaw, 1981; group shows include: Club of Young Artists and Scientists, Warsaw, 1948, Zacheta Galeria, Warsaw, 1957, 66, 84, Galeria Remont, 1973, Galerie Paramedia, W. Berlin, 1974, Jose Clement Orosco Gallery, Mexico City, 1975, Albright-Knox Art Gallery, Buffalo, 1976, Rencontres Internationales de la Photographie, Arles, France, 1978, Internat. Ctr. Photography, N.Y.C., 1979 (travelled to Mus. Contemporary Art, Chgo., Zacheta Galeria, Warsaw, Mus. Fine Arts, Lodz, and Whitechapel Art Gallery, London, 1979-80), Centre Georges Pompidou, Paris, 1981; represented in permanent collections: Nat. Mus. Art, Warsaw, Nat. Mus. Art, Poznan, Nat. Mus. Art, Wroclaw, Mus. Contemporary Art, Lodz, Kunsthalle, Bochum, W.Ger., Mus. Modern Art, N.Y.C.; author: Wybrane Teksty o Sztuce, 1977; contbr. articles to profl. publs.; chief editor Fotografia mag., 1953-72; editorial com. Polish Art Rev., 1971-72. Kosciuszkowsko Found. scholar, 1972. Mem. Union of Polish Art Photographers (pres. 1979—). Address: Pulawska 24a M 26, 02-512 Warsaw Poland *

D'LUHY, JOHN JAMES, investment banker; b. Passaic, N.J., Sept. 18, 1933; s. John George and Leonora (Fila) D'L.; m. Gale Rainsford, Dec. 7, 1968; children: Amanda, Pamela. AB, Trinity Coll., 1955; MBA, U. Pa., 1959. Lic. amateur radio operator KZEXI, pvt. pilot. Jr. exec. trainee Merrill Lynch, N.Y.C., 1956-58, with over-the-counter research dept., 1959-60; assoc. syndicate dept., investment mgmt., investment banking Lazard Freres & Co., N.Y.C., 1960-68; sr. v.p., ptnr., dir. money mgmt. and venture capital divs. R.W. Pressprich & Co., N.Y.C., 1968-72; dir. money mgmt. and pvt. placements Wood Walker & Co., N.Y.C., 1972-73; pres. U.S. Oil Co., 1973-83, chmn., 1983-84; investment advisor Dominick & Dominick, Inc., 1986—, investment broker, 1988—; adviser Hampshire Coll., Mass; trustee Collier Services Found., Marlboro, N.J., 1986—; pvt. investor, 1983-86. Founding mem. U.S. Naval War Coll. Found., Newport, R.I. Served with USNR, 1955. Fellow Frick Mus.; mem. Investment Assn. N.Y. (bd. dirs. 1967, chmn. capital and money markets com.), Bond Club of N.Y., N.Y. Soc. Security Analysts (sr. analyst), Am. Radio Relay League. Roman Catholic. Clubs: University (council exec. com., treas. 1979-83), Thursday Evening (N.Y.C.); Spring Lake (N.J.) Bath & Tennis, Bond. Home: 115 Ludlow Ave Spring Lake NJ 07762 Office: Dominick & Dominick Inc Valley Park 2517 Rt 35 Bldg D-101 Manasquan NJ 08736

DMITRIEV, ALEKSANDER, conductor; b. Leningrad, USSR; ed. Leningrad Conservatory under Kudriavtseva, Tiulin and Rabinovich. Condr., Karelian Radio and TV Symphony Orch., 1961, prin. condr., from 1962; prin. condr. Maly Opera and Ballet Theatre, Leningrad, 1973-77, Symphony Orch. of Leningrad Philharm., 1977—. Recipient prize 2d USSR Competition for Condrs., 1966. Recs. include: Miaskovsky's Violin Concerto; Balakirev's Piano Concerto; Medtner's Piano Concerto No. 1. Address: care Symphony Orch of, Leningrad Philharmoniya, U1 Brokskogo 2, Leningrad USSR *

DOAMARAL, DIOGO FREITAS, Portuguese politician, educator; b. Povoa de Varzim, Portugal, July 21, 1941; s. Duarte P.C. and Maria Filomena (Campos) Trocado; m. Maria Jose Salgado Sarmento de Matos, 1965; 4 children. Ed., Lisbon U. Prof. administrv. law Lisbon U., 1968—, Portuguese Catholic U., 1978—; mem. Council of State, Portugal, 1974-75, mem. Parliament, 1975, 1976—, dep. Prime Minister and Minister Fgn. Affairs, 1980-81, dep. Prime Minister and Minister of Def., 1981-83; pres. Centre Democrat Party, 1974-82; pres. European Union of Christian Democrats, 1981-82. Author: A Utilizacao do Dominio Publico Pelos Particulares, 1965, A Execucao das Sentencas dos Tribuanais Administrativos, 1967, Conceito e natureza do recurso hierarquico, 1981. Office: care Partido do Centro, Democratico Social, Largo do Caldas 5, Lisbon Portugal Address: Casa 50, Quinta da Marinha, 2750 Cascais Portugal *

DOAN, XUYEN VAN, lawyer; b. Hadong, Vietnam, Apr. 1, 1949; came to U.S., 1975; s. Quyet V. Doan and Binh T. Kieu; m. Binh Thanh Tran, 1980; children: Quy-Bao, Ky-Nam. Licence en droit, U. Saigon Law Sch., Vietnam, 1971; MBA, U. Ark., 1977; JD, U. Calif., Hastings, 1982. Bar: Saigon 1972, Calif. 1982. Sole practice Costa Mesa and San Jose, Calif., 1982-84; ptnr. Doan & Vu, San Jose, 1984—. Author: Of the Seas and Men, 1985. Named Ark. Traveler Ambassador of Good Will, State of Ark., 1975. Office: Doan & Vu Law Firm Doan & Vu Bldg 556 N First St Suite 100 San Jose CA 95112

DOANE, HAROLD EVERETT, record company executive; b. N.Y.C., Oct. 17, 1904; s. Thomas J. and Mary S. (Blaisdell) D.; student Edison Sch. Arts, 1919-23, Columbia, 1924; m. Mary G. Gardner, Dec. 20, 1936 (div. 1941); m. Faith S. Tracy, Oct. 17, 1943 (div. 1966); children—Priscilla Clare (Mrs. Ramiro Tello-Saldano), Richard Henry Tracy; m. 3d Vivian Dillon Dunn, May 3, 1966. Asst. cameraman D.W. Griffith Orienta Point Studios, Mamaroneck, N.Y., 1921-22; radio announcer sta. WGBU, Fulford, Fla., 1925-26, WBNY, N.Y.C., 1926-27, WMCA, 1927 WKBQ, 1927-28; owner radio sta. WCOH, Mt. Vernon, N.Y., 1928-29; research engr., N.Y.C., 1929-35; dir. Gramercy Pictures Corp., N.Y.C., 1935-37; producer Spotlight Prodns., Inc., 1940-41; tech. operations dir. War Finance Com., N.Y. State div. U.S. Treasury Dept., N.Y.C., 1941-44; gen. mgr. Art Records, Miami, Fla., 1945-59, pres., 1959—. Mem. nat. adv. bd. Am. Security Council. Mem. Nat. Acad. Rec. Arts and Scis., N.Y. Advt. Club. Republican. Home: 5800 SW 17th Ct Plantation Isles FL 33317 Office: Art Records Mfg Co PO Box 15032 Fort Lauderdale FL 33318

DOAT, LOUIS PIERRE MARIE, psychiatrist; b. Toulouse, Haute Garonne, France, June 2, 1937; s. Marie Charles and Madeleine (Hom) D.; m. Valerie Joan Mason; 1 child, Jacqueline. MD, Toulouse U., 1969, cert. specialist in psychiatry, 1970. Intern in psychiatry Hosp. Psychiatrique, Montauban, France, 1966-70; child psychiatrist Clinique de Chateau, Sollies-Pont, Var, France, 1970—, I.M.P. La Bergerie, Pegomas, France, 1977—; psychoanalyst, discussion group leader Freudian Sch. Paris, Toulon, 1982—. Roman Catholic. Lodge: Lions. Office: Clinique du Chateau, Rue de la Republique, 83210 Sollies Pont Var 8, France

DOBBINS, JAMES JOSEPH, artist; b. Woburn, Mass., Aug. 12, 1924; s. William John and Delia (Feeney) D.; m. Dorothy Esther Fitzpatrick, Jan. 20, 1951; children: Patricia Dobbins Osborn, William, Mary Dobbins Hintlian, James Joseph, Rita Dobbins McGoldrick, Mark, Dorothy Dobbins Claflin, Christopher, John, Maura. Student, Cornell Coll., Mt. Vernon, Iowa, 1945; B.S., Mass. Coll. Art, 1951; student, Boston U. Grad. Sch. Edn., 1951-52. Tchr. Boston pub. schs., 1952; editorial cartoonist Woburn (Mass.) Times, 1947-51, Lowell (Mass.) Sun, 1952-53, N.Y. Daily News, 1953, Boston Post, 1953-56, Boston Herald Traveler, 1956-72, Boston Herald Am., 1972-76, Manchester Union Leader, N.H. Sunday News, 1977—. Author: Dobbins Diary of the New Frontier, 1964; Original drawings donated to, Syracuse U. Library. Mem. Diocese of Boston Ecumenical Commn., 1975-77; trustee Cath. Charities for Diocese of Boston.; bd. dirs. Marr Boys and Girls Club, Dorchester, Mass. Served with USNR, 1943-45. Decorated D.F.C., Air medal; recipient two Freedoms Found. 1st prizes, 14 honors medals; Christopher Lit. award, 1958; grand prize Internat. Competition Wayne State U., 1960; certificate of merit Syracuse U., 1969; named Outstanding Young Man Boston Jaycees, 1957. Mem. Nat. Cartoonist Soc., Assn. Am. Editorial Cartoonists. Democrat. Catholic. Clubs: Boston Press (pres. 1967-68), Winchester Country. Home: 1 Swan Rd Winchester MA 01890 Office: 35 Amherst St Manchester NH 03105

DOBBS, DONALD EDWIN ALBERT, public relations executive; b. Ft. Wayne, Ind., Oct. 8, 1931; s. Edmund F. and Agnes (Stempnick) D.; B.S., Marquette U., 1953; m. Beatrice A. Spieker, July 27, 1957; children: Margaret L. Howard, Christopher E.J., Laura C. Pribe. Reporter, Cath. Chronicle, Toledo, 1953; with pub. relations dept. Nat. Supply Co., Toledo 1955-59; employee communications exec. Prestolite Co., an Eltra Co., Toledo, 1959-61, public relations dir., 1961-80, dir. communications, 1980-83; mgr. external affairs Allied Electronic Components Co., an Allied Corp. Co.; pres. Dobbs & Assocs. Pub. Realtions and Advt., 1984—. Past chmn. Maumee Valley Hosp. Sch. Nursing Com.; pres. Internat. Inst., Toledo, 1970-73; past chmn. Child Nutrition Center, Toledo; past mem. Ohio Adv. Council Vocat. Edn.; vice chmn. Mayor's Citizen Devel. Forum; chmn., past pres. Mercy Hosp. adv. bd.; past pres. bd. dirs. Crosby Gardens; past pres. Ohio Friends of Library; past chmn. Salvation Army; past pres. Toledo Council of World Affairs, Toledo Hearing and Speech Center, Friends of Toledo/Lucas County Library; past pres. bd. dirs. Internat. Park; v.p. Toledo Opera Assn.; bd. dirs. Ohio Library Found. Served with AUS, 1953-55. Mem. Marquette U. Alumni Assn. N.W. Ohio (past pres., area dir.), Soc. Profl. Journalists, Public Relations Soc. Am. (past pres. N.W. Ohio), Automotive Public Relations Council (past pres.), Cath. Interracial Council (past pres.). Democrat (past nat. com. Wis. Young Dems.). Roman Catholic. Lodge: Kiwanis (past pres. Toledo, Mid-City Athletic League, Youth Found.; lt. gov. 1974-75). Home: 2433 Meadowwood Dr Toledo OH 43606 Office: PO Box 2964 Toledo OH 43606

DOBBS, GEORGE ALBERT, retail corp. exec.; b. Nashville, Oct. 16, 1943; s. Albert F. and Ruby Lee (Haynes) D.; B.A., Cornell U., 1966, M.B.A., 1972; Retail store mgr. Alterman Foods, Atlanta, 1960-72; ind. mng. cons. George A. Dobbs & Assos., Decatur, Ga., 1972-78; retail mgr. K-Mart Corp., Decatur, 1978—; notary public, 1976—. Named Small Bus. Mgr. of Year, Dekalb Businessman's Assn., 1974. Mem. Ga. Small Bus. Mgrs. Assn. (Recognition cert. for contbns. 1976), Dekalb Businessmen's Assn., Dekalb Sheriff's Posse, Ga. Sheriff's Assn. Republican. Baptist. Clubs: Capital City, Masons, Shriners. Address: 108 Thistle Ln Hermitage TN 37076 Office: K-Mart Corp 2901 Clairmont Rd NE Atlanta GA 30033

DOBERKAT, ERNST ERNST, computer science professor; b. Breckerfeld, North Rhine Westphalia, Fed. Republic Germany, Aug. 17, 1948; s. Erich P. and Johanna (Plaschke) D.; m. Gudrun W. Röll, May 9, 1975; children: Julia Kathrin. MS in Math., U. Bochum, Fed. Republic Germany, 1973; PhD in Math., U. Paderborn, Fed. Republic Germany, 1976; Habilitation, U. Hagen, Fed. Republic Germany, 1980. Mathematician FEoLL GmbH, Paderborn, 1973-76; adj. faculty U. Bonn, Fed. Republic Germany, 1976-78, U. Hagen, 1978-81; assoc. prof. Clarkson U., Potsdam, N.Y., 1981-85; full prof. computer sci. U. Hildesheim, Fed. Republic Germany, 1985—. Author: Automata Theory, 1981, Pascal Programming, 1981, 2d edit. 1985, 3d edit., 1987; contbr. sci. papers in field. Mem. IEEE, Assn. Computing Machinery, Gesellschaft für Informatick, Deutsche Mathematikerverein. Home: Schulstrasse 14B, D-3201 Algermissen Federal Republic of Germany Office: U Hildesheim, Samelsonplatz 1, D-3200 Hildesheim Federal Republic of Germany

DOBES, WILLIAM LAMAR, JR., dermatologist; b. Atlanta, Apr. 16, 1943; s. William Lamar and Sara (Wilson) D.; B.A., Emory U., 1965, M.D., 1969; m. Martha Husmann, June 16, 1966; children—Margaret Alison, William Shane. Intern Grady Meml. Hosp., Atlanta, 1969-70; fellow dermatology Mayo Clinic, 1970-71; fellow U. Miami, 1971-73; clin. instr. Emory U. Sch. Medicine, Atlanta, 1973-77, asst. prof. dermatology, 1977-83, assoc. prof., 1983—, dir. immunofluorescense lab.; mem. staff Crawford Long, West Paces Ferry, Grady Meml., Ga. Bapt., Piedmont hosps. (all Atlanta); dir. Skin Cancer Project, Emory Univ., 1981—; chmn. profl. edn. unit Atlanta unit Am. Cancer Soc., also bd. dirs., pres., 1986-87, chmn. bd. 1987—. Grantee Dermatology Found. Research award, 1979; mem. Ga. med. bd. Lupus Found. Diplomate Am. Bd. Dermatology. Mem. Soc. Investigative Dermatology, Am. Acad. Dermatology (chmn. com. quality assurance 1982-84; adv. council 1985—, task force on standards of care 1987—); So. Med. Assn. (vice chmn. 1983), Ga., Pan Am. med. assns., AMA, A.C.P., Am. Soc. Dermatologic Surgery, Ga. Dermatol. Assn. (pres. 1986-87), Atlanta Dermatol. Assn. (pres. 1979), N.Am. Clin. Dermatologic Soc., Soc. Tropical Dermatology, Med. Assn. of Atlanta (bd. dirs. 1985—, chmn. communications com. 1985—), Med. Assn. of Ga. (Interspeciality Council 1984), Atlanta Clin. Soc., Emory U. Med. Alumni Assn. (pres. 1980), Phi Delta Theta (past pres.), Phi Chi (past pres.). Club: Cherokee Town & Country (Atlanta). Contbr. articles to profl. jours. and texts. Home: 2898 Rivermead Dr Atlanta GA 30327 Office: 478 Peachtree St Atlanta GA 30308 also: Emory U Sch Medicine Dept Dermatology Atlanta GA 30308

DOBKIN, DONALD IRWIN, metal treating company executive; b. N.Y.C., July 9, 1922; s. Isidor and Rebecca (Silverman) D.; m. Rosalyn Goldberg, June 15, 1956; children: Robert, Lisa. BS, CCNY, 1942; postgrad., Lehigh U., 1942, Columbia U., 1946-47. Copywriter, accounts exec. Wiley, Frazee, Davenport Advt., N.Y.C., 1946-48; copy chief, accounts exec. Lancaster Advt., N.Y.C., 1948-50; gen. mgr. Ace Metal Treating Corp., Elizabeth, N.J., 1950-59; sales mgr., dir., sec. L-R Metal Treating Corp., Newark, 1959-68; v.p. sales, sec., dir. Thermo Nat Industries, Inc., Newark, 1968—. Served with U.S. Army, 1942-46, ETO. Decorated Combat Inf. Badge. Mem. Am. Soc. for Metals, Soc. Mfg. Engrs., N.J. Tool and Die Mfrs. Assn., Sigma Alpha Mu. Home: 4 Tilden Ct Livingston NJ 07039 Office: Thermo Nat Industries Inc 108-34 Johnson St Newark NJ 07105

DOBKIN, IRVING BERN, entomologist, sculptor; b. Chgo., Aug. 9, 1918; m. Frances Berlin, July 1, 1941; children: Jane, Joan, David, Jill. B.S. cum laude, U. Ill., 1940; postgrad., Ill. Inst. Tech., 1941-42. With War Dept., 1942; chmn., pres. Dobkin Pest Control Co., Chgo., 1946-79; Pres., dir. Sculptors Guild Ill., 1964-86; lectr. schs. and assn.; life mem. Art Inst. Chgo., Chgo. Natural History Museum (life mem.), N. Shore Art League, Evanston Art Center, Mus. Contemporary Art, Chgo. Exhibits include, Art Inst. Chgo., McCormick Pl., Chgo., Old Orchard. Assoc. mem. Smithsonian Instn.; asso. mem. Peabody Mus. Natural History, Yale U.; pres. Suburban Fine Art Ctr., 1983-84; asso. mem. Adler Planetarium Assn. Served to lt. USN, 1943-46, PTO. Mem. Entomol. Soc. Am., Am Registry Profl. Entomologists, Fedn. Am. Scientists, AAAS, Am. Inst. Biol. Scis., UN Assn., Oceanographic Soc., Malacology Soc. Am.; asso. mem. Sierra Club, Chgo. Acad. Sci., Archeol. Inst. Am., Calif. Acad. Sci., AIA, Am. Schs. Oriental Research, Geog. Soc. Am., Nat. Audubon Soc., Ill. Audubon Soc., Am. Indian Affairs Fedn., S.W. Indian Fedn., Nat. Wildlife Soc., Save the Redwoods Soc., Wilderness Soc., Nat. Parks and Conservation Assn., Am. Harp Soc., Chgo. Harp Soc., Am. Forestry Assn., Am. Fedn. Mineral Socs., Explorers Club, Primitive Arts Soc. Chgo., Chgo. Horticulture Soc., UN Assn. U.S., Chgo. Zool. Soc., Midwest Paleontol. Soc., Stratford Theatre Found., Renaissance Soc., Internat. Flamenco Soc., Ensemble Espanol (bd. dirs.), Council on Fgn. Relations. Home: 306 Maple Ave Highland Park IL 60035

DOBRACZYNSKI, JAN, author; b. Warsaw, Poland, 1910; s. Anthony and Valerie (Markiewicz) D.; ed. High Sch. Commerce, 1932; m. Danuta Kotowicz, June 2, 1935; children—Jan (Mrs. Kus), Aleksandra (Mrs. Kadzinska). Served with Armed Forces, World War II; now comdr. Res. Decorated comdr., officer cross Order Polonia Restituta, Virtuti Militari Cross; Golden Cross of Merit; Silver Cross of Merit with Swords. Mem. Polish PEN, Polish Writers Assn. (mem. directorate 1964—). Author numerous novels including: Firing Lava, 1937; Invaders, 1946; Sacred Sword, 1949; The Key of Wisdom, 1951; Letters of Nicodemus, 1952; The Church of Chocholow, 1954; The Invincible Armada, 1960; Hands of the Wall, 1960; To Drain the Sea, 1961; Blue Helmets on the Dam, 1964; Voices of the Time, 1966; Overtaken, 1967; The Burnt Bridges Left Behind, 1969; Poisoners, 1974; The Gates of Leipzig, 1976; The Shade of the Father, 1977; Samson and Delilah, 1979; Ann's Marriage, 1981; Earth of the Gospel, 1982; Ann's Children, 1983; Anyone Who Puts You To Death, 1985, The World of the Ashes, 1985, The Birds Sing, The Fishes Hear, 1987. Address: 42 Hetmanska St, 04305 Warsaw Poland

DOBRIANSKY, LEV EUGENE, educator, economist, diplomat; b. N.Y.C., Nov. 9, 1918; s. John and Eugenia (Greshchuk) D.; m. Julia Kusy, June 29, 1946; children: Larisa Eugenia, Paula Jon. B.S. (Charles Hayden Meml. scholar), NYU, 1941, M.A., 1943, Hirshland polit. sci. fellow, 1943-44, Ph.D., 1951; LL.D., Free Ukrainian U. at U. Munich, Germany, 1952. Faculty NYU, 1942-48; asst. prof. econs. Georgetown U., 1948-52, assoc. prof., 1952-60, prof., 1960—, chmn. dept., 1953-54; exec. mem. Inst. Ethnic Studies, 1957—; dir. Inst. Comparative Econ. and Polit. Systems, 1970—; faculty Nat. War Coll., 1957-58; U.S. ambassador to Bahamas 1982-86; pres. Global Economic Action Inst., 1987—; cons. Dept. State, 1971—, USIA, 1971—; lectr. on Soviet Union, Communism, U.S. fgn. policy; chmn. Nat. Captive Nations Com., Inc., 1959—; pres. Ukrainian Congress Com. Am., 1949-82, Am. Council for World Freedom, 1976-79; mem. Economists Nat. Com. on Monetary Policy; strategy staff mem. Am. Security Council, 1962—; econs. editor Washington Report; mem. Pres.'s Commn. on Population, 1974-75; cons. Corpus Instrumentorum, Kreber Found.; mem. Am. Com. to Aid Katanga Freedom Fighters, Emergency Com. Chinese

Refugees. Author: A Philosophico-Economic Critique of Thorstein Veblen, 1943, The Social Philosophical System of Thorstein Veblen, 1950, Free Trade Ideal, 1954, Communist Takeover of Non-Russian Nations in USSR, 1954; co-author: The Great Pretense, 1956, Veblenism: A New Critique, 1957, Captive Nations Week Resolution, 1959, The Crimes of Khrushchev, 1959, Shevchenko Statue Resolution, 1960, Decisions for a Better America, 1960, Vulnerabilities of USSR, 1963, Nations, Peoples, and Countries in the USSR, 1964, The Vulnerable Russians, 1967, U.S.A. and the Soviet Myth, 1971; pub.: Revista Americana, 1977; editor: Europe's Freedom Fighter: Taras Shevchenko, 1960, Tenth Anniversary of the Captive Nations Week Resolution, 1969, The Bicentennial Salute to the Captive Nations, 1977, Twentieth Observance and Anniversary of Captive Nations Week, 1980; asso. editor: (1946-62) Ukrainian Quar., chmn. editorial bd.,, 1962; contbr.: Peace and Freedom Through Cold War Victory, 1964, Nationalism in the USSR and Eastern Europe, 1977, Ukraine in a Changing World, 1978; articles to profl. jours. Planning mem. Freedom Studies Center, Boston; asst. sec. Republican Nat. Conv., 1952; adviser Rep. Nat. Com., 1956; mem. Com. on Program and Progress of Rep. Party, 1959; asst. to chmn. Rep. Nat. Conv., 1964; vice chmn. nationalities div. Rep. Nat. Com., 1964; sr. adviser United Citizens for Nixon-Agnew, 1968; exec. mem. ethnic div. Com. to Reelect the Pres., 1972; advisor to Gov. Reagan, 1980; issues dir. Republican Nat. Com., 1980; chmn. Ukrainian Catholic Studies Found., 1970-73; bd. govs. Charles Edison Youth Fund, 1976—; mem. expert adv. bd. NBC, Washington, 1977—. Lt. col. (res.) 352d Mil. Govt. Civil Affairs 1958; col. U.S. Army Res., 1966. Recipient Freedoms Found. award, 1961, 73; Shevchenko Freedom award Shevchenko Meml. Com., 1964; Shevchenko Sci. Soc. medal, 1965; Hungarian Freedom Fighters' Freedom award, 1965; Latvian Pro Merito medal, 1968; Freedom Acad. award Korea, 1969; Wisdom award of honor Calif., 1970; named Outstanding Am. Educator, 1973; decorated D.S.M., 1973; Georgetown U. Centennial medal of honor, 1982; Ellis Island medal of honor, 1986; Thomas C. Corcoran award, 1987. Mem. Free World Forum (exec. com.), Acad. Polit. Sci., Nat. Acad. Econs. and Polit. Sci., AAUP, Am. Acad. Polit. and Social Sci., Am., Cath. econ. assns., Am. Finance Assn., Nat. Soc. Study Edn., Shevchenko Sci. Soc., U.S. Global Strategy Council, Social Inst. of Washington, Global Econ. Action Inst., Council Am. Ambassadors, NYU Alumni Assn., Internat. Cultural Soc. Korea (hon.), Gold Key Soc., Beta Gamma Sigma, Delta Sigma Pi. Clubs: Capitol Hill (Washington), International (Washington), University (Washington).

DOBRIANSKY, PAULA JON, government official; b. Alexandria, Va., Sept. 14, 1955; d. Lev Eugene and Julia Kusy D. BS summa cum laude, Sch. Fgn. Service, Georgetown U., 1977; MA, Harvard U., 1980, postgrad., 1980—. Adminstrv. aide Dept. Army, Washington, 1973-76; staff asst. Am. embassy, Rome, 1976; research asst. joint econ. com. U.S. Congress, Washington, 1977-78; NATO analyst Bur. Intelligence and Research, Dept. State, Washington, 1979; staff mem. NSC, White House, Washington, 1980-83, dep. dir. European and Soviet affairs, 1983-84, dir. European and Soviet affairs, 1984-87; dep. asst. sec. of state for Human Rights and Humanitarian Affairs, 1987—; assoc. Ctr. for Internat. Affairs, Harvard U., Cambridge, Mass. Fulbright-Hays scholar, 1978: Rotary Found. fellow, 1979; Ford Found. fellow, 1980. Mem. Internat. Inst. Strategic Studies, Am. Polit. Sci. Assn., Council on Fgn. Relations, Phi Beta Kappa, Phi Alpha Theta, Pi Sigma Alpha. Club: Harvard (bd. dirs. 1982-85) (Washington). Office: Dept State Human Rights & Humanitarian Affairs 2201 C St NW Washington DC 20520

DOBRINSKY, HERBERT COLMAN, university administrator; b. Montreal, Quebec, Can., Apr. 6, 1933; came to U.S., 1962; s. Victor and Lillian D.; m. Dina Loebenberg, Dec., 1954; children—Deborah Kramer, Tova Cohen, Aaron David. B.A., Yeshiva U., 1954, M.S. in Edn., 1959, D. in Edn., 1980; Semikha (rabbinic ordination), Rabbi Isaac Elchanan Theological Sem., Yeshiva U., 1957. Rabbi, Beth Israel Synagogue, Halifax, N.S., Can., 1958-62; assoc dir. div. communal services Yeshiva U., N.Y.C., 1962-73, dir. rabbinic placement, 1964-73, dir. Sephardic community activities program div. of communal service, 1964-80, exec. asst. to pres., 1973-80, v.p. univ. affairs, 1980—. Author: A Treasury of Sephardic Laws and Customs, 1986. Office: VP Univ Affairs Yeshiva U 500 W 185th St New York NY 10033

DOBRITT, DENNIS WILLIAM, physician, researcher, pain management specialist; b. Detroit, July 13, 1953; s. Walter Peter and Catherine Janet (Auito) D.; m. Kitty Louise Burros, June 21, 1980; children: Carol Ann, Julie Marie. BS magna cum laude, Western Mich. U., 1975; DO, Phila. Coll. Osteopathic Medicine, 1981. Diplomate Nat. Bd. Osteopathic Examiners, Am. Bd. Anesthesiology. Intern Garden City (Mich.) Hosp., 1981-82, emergency physician, 1982-83; emergency physician McPherson Hosp., Howell, Mich., 1983-84; resident physician Providence Hosp., Southfield, Mich., 1983-85, fellow, 1985-86, attending physician, 1986-88, attending anesthesiologist, 1986—; attending physician Botsford Hosp., Farmington Hills, Mich., 1986-87; asst. clin. prof. coll. osteopathic medicine Mich. State U., Ann Arbor, 1987—; dir. Ctr. for Pain Control, Farmington Hills, 1986-87, Farmbrook Pain Control Ctr., Southfield, 1987—; pres. Pain Control Cons., Farmington Hills, 1987—. Editor newsletter Osteo. Pain Mgmt. News, 1987-88; guest editor Mich. Osteo. Jour., 1987-88; contbr. articles to profl. jours. Active Mich. Osteopathic Polit. Action Com., 1987-88. Mem. AMA, Am. Osteo. Assn., Am. Soc. Anesthesiology, Internat. Anesthesiology Research Soc., Am. Pain Soc., Internat. Assn. for Study of Pain. Democrat. Roman Catholic. Club: One on One (West Bloomfield, Mich.), Mich. Apple Users Group. Office: 29877 Telegraph Rd Suite 200 Southfield MI 48034

DOBRYNIN, ANATOLY F., Soviet ambassador to U.S.; b. Krasnaya Gorka, Nov. 16, 1919; m. Irina Nikolaevna; 1 child, Yelena. Grad., tech. coll.; M.S. in History. Mem. Soviet Diplomatic Service, 1944—; asst. to dep. minister fgn. affairs 1949-52; counselor Ministry Fgn. Affairs, 1955, 60-61, head Am. dept., 1960-62; counselor Soviet embassy, Washington, 1952-54; minister-counselor Soviet embassy, 1954-55; adviser Soviet del. 11th session UN Gen. Assembly, 1956; mem. Soviet del. London Conf. on Suez Canal, 1956; mem. secretariat UN, 1957, undersec. without portfolio, 1957, undersec. charge dept. polit. and security council affairs secretariat, 1957-60; ambassador to U.S. 1962-86; mem. secretariat Cen. Com. Communist Party, Moscow; mem. Communist Party of Soviet Union, 1945—, candidate mem. cen. com., 1966-71, mem. cen. com., 1971—, head internat. dept., 1986—; lectr. course on Soviet-Am. relations State Inst. Internat. Relations, Moscow. Office: care Cen Com Communist Party, Moscow USSR *

DOBSON, ALASTAIR GRAHAM, bank and trust company executive; b. Hanover, West Germany, Oct. 5, 1948; came to Switzerland, 1980; s. James Richard Easton and Dorothy Margaret (Ritchie) D.; m. Annie Magdelaine Bissoo, May 12, 1977; children—Alexandra, Andrew. LL.B., St. Andrews U., St. Andrews, Scotland, 1969; postgrad. U. Coll. London, 1969-70. With Bank of Scotland, Edinburgh, 1970-74; trust officer Royal Bank Trust Co., Cayman Islands, 1974-75, 77-79, Georgetown, Guyana, 1975-77; dir., mgr. Kleinwort Benson Trustee S.A., Geneva, 1979-84; dir. Kleinwort Benson Internat. Trust Corp., New Brunswick, Can., 1981-84; mng. dir. Hoogewerf Trust Co. S.A., 1984-86; chief exec. officer Gibraltar and Iberian Bank Ltd., 1987-88; bd. dirs., gen. mgr. Citco (Suisse) S.A., Anglo-Saxon Trust Co. Ltd. (B.V.I.), Anglo-Saxon Trust Co. (Guernsey) Ltd., Anglo-Saxon Trust Co. (Cyprus) Ltd. Fellow Inst. Can. Bankers; mem. Inst. Bankers Scotland (assoc.), Inst. Bankers. Mem. Ch. of Scotland. Office: Citco (Suisse) S A, 1 Ave, Ruchonnet, CH-1001 Lausanne Switzerland

DOBSON, CLIFFORD BRIGGS, psychology educator, researcher, consultant; b. Bradford, Yorkshire, Eng., Feb. 5, 1931; s. William Briggs and May (Bartle) D. Cert. edn. St. John's Coll., York, Eng., 1953; diploma edn. U. Leeds, 1957; licentiate diploma Coll. Preceptors, London, 1960; M.S., U. Bradford, 1973, Ph.D., 1977. Tchr., Yorkshire, Eng., 1953-70; head psychology St. Michael's Coll., Leeds, Eng., 1970-85; tchr. fellow Langwith Coll., U. York, 1977; hon. vis. research fellow Sch. Studies in Psychology, U. Bradford (Eng.), 1979-85, dir. psychosocial oncology research, clin. oncology unit, 1985-87; dir. Cancer Support Ctr., Bradford, West Yorkshire, Engl., 1987—; cons. psychologist, West Yorkshire Police Authority, 1986—; research psychologist Yorkshire Regional Cancer Orgn., 1983—. Author: (with others) Understanding Psychology, 1980; (with R.B. Burns) Experimental Psychology, 1981; Approaching Psychology, 1982; Stress: the Hidden Adversary, 1983; (with R.B. Burns) Introductory Psychology, 1983; contbr. articles to profl. jours. Served with Brit. Army, 1949-51. Fellow Royal Soc. Health, Royal Soc. Medicine; mem. Brit. Psychol. Soc. (assoc.), Assn. Study Med. Edn., Brit. Psychosocial Oncology Group. Mem. Ch. of Eng. Office: Cancer Support Ctr, 72 Vicar Ln, Bradford West Yorkshire BD7 1DP, England

DOBZYNSKI, JOSEPH MARTIN, corporate operational specialist; b. Chgo., Jan. 30, 1954; s. Walter and Alice (Brace) D.; m. Debra Ruth Crawford, Apr. 16, 1977; children: Joseph Jr., Mindy. AA in hotel-motel mgmt., Career Acad., 1973; AA in Polit. Economics, Henry George Inst.; wine diploma, Italian Trade Commn., French Trade Commn., Calif. Wine Inst. Cert. stress mgmt. specialist; cert. in parapsychology. Sous chef Playboy Club Internat., Chgo., 1973-75; exec. chef The Bradly House, Palm Beach, Fla., 1975-77; chef dir. East Indian Co., Winter Park, Fla., 1977-80, Ellwood Greens Club, Genoa, Ill., 1980-84; food dir. Bally Corp., Chgo., 1984-85; corp. food and beverage cir. Riverwalk Corp., Geneva, Ill., 1985—; instr. Kishwaukee Jr. Coll., Malta, Ill., 1981-82; vocat. food judge Ill. Dept. Edn., Springfield, 1983; speaker Bremen (Ill.) High Sch. Career Day, 1982. Contbr. articles to profl. jours.; inventor hibernate freezing. vice chmn. Genoa-Kingston Vocat. Council, 1981; wine chmn. Festival of the Vine, Geneva C. of C., 1986. Recipient Silver medal Am. Culinary Fedn., 1982, Medals (4), Chgo. Culinary Arts Salon, 1981-83, Second place Crab Cooking Olympics, San Francisco, 1982, Entree award Boyle's Co., 1986. Mem. Les Amis du Vin (chpt. dir. 1981—, Cavalier award 1982), The Am. Inst. Food (assoc.) Chgo. Chef Apprentice Program (chmn. 1981-82, Plaque, 1982), Soc. Wine Educators, Am. Wine Soc. Home: 306 S Genoa St Genoa IL 60135

DOCKHORN, ROBERT JOHN, physician; b. Goodland, Kans., Oct. 9, 1934; s. Charles George and Dorotha Mae (Horton) D.; m. Beverly Ann Wilke, June 15, 1957; children: David, Douglas, Deborah. A.B., U. Kans., 1956, M.D., 1960. Diplomate: Am. Bd. Pediatrics. Intern Naval Hosp., San Diego, 1960-61; resident in pediatrics Naval Hosp., Oakland, Calif., 1963-65; resident in pediatric allergy and immunology U. Kans. Med. Center, 1967-69, asst. adj. prof. pediatrics, 1969—; resident in pediatric allergy and immunology Children's Mercy Hosp., Kansas City, Mo., 1967-69; chief div. Children's Mercy Hosp., 1969—; practice medicine specializing in allergy and immunology Prairie, Kans., 1969—; clin. prof. pediatrics and medicine U. Mo. Med. Sch., Kansas City, 1972—; founder, chief exec. officer Internat. Med. Tech. Cons., Inc., Prairie Village, Kans. Contbr. articles to med. jours.; co-editor: Allergy and Immunology in Children, 1973. Fellow Am. Acad. Pediatrics, Am. Coll. Allergists (bd. regents 1976—, v.p. 1978-79, pres.-elect 1980-81, pres. 1981-82), Am. Acad. Allergy; mem. AMA, Kans. Med. Soc., Johnson County Med. Soc., Kans. Allergy Soc. (pres. 1976-77), Mo. Allergy Soc. (sec. 1975-76), Joint Council Socio-Econs. of Allergy (dir. 1976—, pres. 1978-79). Home: 8510 Delmar Ln Prairie Village KS 66208 Office: 5300 W 94th Terr Prairie Village KS 66207

DOCKSON, ROBERT RAY, savings and loan executive; b. Quincy, Ill., Oct. 6, 1917; s. Marshall Ray and Letah (Edmondson) D.; m. Katheryn Virginia Allison, Mar. 4, 1944; 1 child, Kathy Kimberlee. A.B., Springfield Jr. Coll., 1937; B.S., U. Ill., 1939; M.S. in Fgn. Service, U. So. Calif., 1940, Ph.D., 1946. Lectr. U. So. Calif., 1940-41, 45-46, prof., head dept. mktg., 1953-59; dean U. So. Calif. (Sch. Bus. Adminstrn.); and prof. bus. econs. 1959-69; vice chmn. bd. Calif. Fed. Savs. & Loan Assn., Los Angeles, 1969-70; pres. Calif. Fed. Savs. & Loan Assn., 1970-77, chmn., 1977—, chief exec. officer, 1973-83; chmn. CalFed Inc., 1984—, chief exec. officer, 1984-85, also dir.; instr. Rutgers U., 1946-47, asst. prof., 1947-48; dir. Bur. Bus. and Econ. Research, 1947-48; economist Western home office Prudential Ins. Co., 1948-52, Bank of Am., San Francisco, 1952-53; econ. cons., 1953-57; dir. McKesson Corp., IT Corp., Pacific Lighting Corp., Transam. Capital Fund, Inc., Transam. Income Shares, Inc., Internat. Lease Fin. Corp., Computer Scis. Corp. Am. specialist for U.S. Dept. State; mem. Town Hall, 1954—, bd. govs., 1963-65, hon. bd. govs., 1965—, pres., 1961-62; Trustee John Randolph Haynes and Dora Haynes Found., Rose Hills Meml. Park Assn., Com. for Econ. Devel., Calif. Council for Econ. Edn.; trustee, pres. Orthopedic Hosp.; bd. councilors Grad. Sch. Bus. Adminstrn., U. So. Calif.; bd. regents, chmn. univ. bd. Pepperdine U.; chmn. housing task force Calif. Roundtable. Served from ensign to lt. USNR, 1942-44. Decorated Star of Solidarity Govt. of Italy.; Recipient Asa V. Call Achievement award; Disting. Community Service award Brandeis U.; Whitney M. Young Jr. award Urban League, 1981, Albert Schweitzer Leadership award; Man of Yr. award Nat. Housing Conf., 1981; Industrialist of Yr. award Calif. Mus. Sci. and Industry, 1984. Mem. Calif. C. of C. (pres. 1980, dir. 1981—), Los Angeles C. of C. (dir.), Am. Arbitration Assn., Newcomen Soc. North Am., Hugh O'Brian Youth Found., Phi Kappa Phi (Diploma of Honor award 1984), Beta Gamma Sigma. Clubs: Bohemian, California, Los Angeles Country, One Hundred, Silver Dollar, Birnam Wood Golf, Thunderbird Country. Office: CalFed Inc 5670 Wilshire Blvd Los Angeles CA 90036

DOCKSTADER, EMMETT STANLEY, construction company executive; b. Elmira, N.Y., Nov. 7, 1923; s. Roy S. and Gertrude (Everts) D.; B.C.E. cum laude, Syracuse U., 1947; m. Ruth Norma Emery, May 11, 1946; children—Deborah Ruth, David Stanley. Engr., Am. Bridge Co., Elmira, 1948-50; field engr. Sessinghaus & Ostergaard, Inc., Erie, Pa., 1950-53, project mgr., 1953-58, v.p., 1958-69; gen. mgr. constrn. div. H.H. Robertson Co., Ambridge, Pa., 1969-71; sr. v.p., sec. Sessinghaus & Ostergaard, Inc., Erie, 1972-79; constrn. exec. Gilbane Bldg. Co., Providence, R.I., 1979-84; pres., dir. Sessinghavs & Ostergaard Inc., Erie, 1984-86; cons. constrn. mgmt., 1986—; dir. Promac Corp., Research Triangle, N.C. Mem. Erie Port Commn., 1967-69. Bd. govs. Pastoral Counseling Center of Greater Providence, corporator Boston Seaman's Friend Soc., Inc. Served with USNR, 1944-46. Registered profl. engr., R.I., Pa., W.Va., Ga., N.C. Mem. Nat. Soc. Profl. Engrs., Erie Mannerchor, SAR. Mem. Ch. of the Covenant (trustee). Mason (32 deg.), Rotarian. Clubs: Erie Yacht, Y Mens (past pres.). Home: 125 Lincoln Ave Erie PA 16505 Office: 2221 Peninsula Dr Erie PA 16505

DOCKSTADER, JACK LEE, electronics executive; b. Los Angeles, Dec. 14, 1936; s. George Earl and Grace Orine (Travers) D.;m. Kerry Jo King, Oct. 24, 1987; children: Travis Adam Mayer, Bridget Olivia Mayer. student UCLA, 1960-70. Rate analyst Rate Bur., So. Pacific Co., Los Angeles, 1954-57; traffic analyst traffic dept. Hughes Aircraft Co., Fullerton, Calif., 1957-58, Culver City, Calif., 1958-59, traffic mgr. Hughes Research Labs., Malibu, Calif., 1959-70, materiel mgr., 1970-75; materiel mgr. Hughes Aircraft Co., Culver City, 1975-80, prodn. materiel mgr. Electro-Optical and Data Systems Group, El Segundo, Calif., 1980-84, mgr. materiel total quality 1984-85, mgr. cen. materiel ops. and property mgmt. 1987—. Mem. adv. council transp. mgmt. profl. designation program UCLA, 1966-80, mem. Design for Sharing Com., 1977-82; adv. com. transp. program Los Angeles Trade Tech. Coll., 1970-80. Served with USNR, 1954-76. Mem. UCLA Alumni Assn., Nat. Contracts Mgmt. Assn., Naval Enlisted Res. Assn., Hughes Aircraft Co. Mgmt. Club, Delta Nu Alpha (pres. San Fernando Valley chpt. 1965-66, v.p. Pacific S.W. region 1969-71, region man of year 1971). Republican. Presbyn. Home: PO Box 3156 Redondo Beach CA 90277 Office: PO Box 902 El Segundo CA 90245

DODD, CHARLES GARDNER, physical chemist; b. St. Louis, Jan. 26, 1915; s. Harry Gardner and Ruth Esther (Hauskins) D.; m. Edel Marie Bovbjerg, June 10, 1943; children—Sally Little, Karen Elise, Mary Bartlett, Frederick Porter. B.S., Rice U., 1940; M.S., U. Mich., 1945, Ph.D., 1948. In academic wor; and with Fed. Bur. Mines; with Continental Oil Co., Owens-Ill. Tech. Ctr., Philip Morris Research Center, Warner Lambert Co.; pres. Conn. Tech. Cons., Inc., Stratford, 1980—; cons. surface modification techniques, surface chemistry and physics, materials sci.; importer, distbr. sci. instruments, chmn. Gordon Research Conf. on Chemistry at Interfaces, 1957. Contbr. articles to sci. and tech. publs. Fellow AAAS, Am. Inst. Chemists; mem. AIME Metall. Soc., Am. Vacuum Soc., Am. Chem. Soc., Am. Soc. Metals. Club: Chemists. Home: 581-B North Trail Stratford CT 06497 Office: Conn Tech Cons Inc PO Box 524 Stratford CT 06497

DODD, CHRISTOPHER J., senator; b. Willimantic, Conn., May 27, 1944; s. Thomas J. and Grace (Murphy) D. B.A. in English Lit., Providence Coll., 1966; J.D., U. Louisville, 1972. Bar: Conn. 1973. Vol. Peace Corps, Dominican Republic, 1966-68; mem. 94th-96th Congresses from 2d Conn. Dist.; U.S. Senator from Conn. 1980—. Served with AUS, 1969-75. Democrat. Office: US Senate Washington DC 20510

DODD, DARLENE MAE, nurse, air force officer; b. Dowagiac, Mich., Oct. 11, 1935; d. Charles B. and Lila H. Dodd; diploma in nursing Borgess Hosp. Sch. Nursing, Kalamazoo, 1957; grad. U.S. Air Force Flight Nurse Course, 1959, U.S. Air Force Squadron Officers Sch., 1963, Air Command and Staff Coll., 1973; BS in Psychology and Gen. Studies, So. Oreg. State Coll., 1987, postgrad., 1987; Commd. 2d lt. U.S. Air Force, 1959, advanced through grades to lt. col., 1975; staff nurse, Randolph AFB, Tex., 1959-60, Ladd AFB, Alaska, 1960-62, Selfridge AFB, Mich., 1962-63; Cam Rahn Bay Air Base, Vietnam, 1966-67, Seymour Johnson AFB, N.C., 1967-69, Air Force Acad., 1971-72; flight nurse 22d Aeromed. Evacuation, Tex., 1963-66; chief nurse Danang AFB, Vietnam, 1967; flight nurse Yokotu AFB, Japan, 1969-71; clin. coordinator ob/gyn and flight nurse, Elmendorf AFB, Alaska, 1973-76; clin. nurse coordinator obstetrics-gynecology and pediatric services USAF Med. Center, Keesler AFB, Miss., 1976-79, ret., 1979. Decorated Bronze Star, Meritorious Service medal, Air Force Commendation medal (3). Mem. So. Oreg. Hist. Soc., DAV, Ret. Officers Assn., Vietnam Vets. Am., VFW, Uniformed Services Disabled Retirees, Psy Chi, Phi Kappa Phi. Clubs: Psychology, Women of Moose. Home: 712 W 1st St Phoenix OR 97535

DODD, JOE DAVID, safety engineer, consultant, administrator; b. Walnut Grove, Mo., Jan. 22, 1920; s. Marshall Hill and Pearl (Combs) D.; m. Nona Bell Junkins, Sept. 17, 1939; 1 dau. Linda Kay Dodd Helmick. Student SW Mo. State U., 1937-39, Wash. U., 1947-55. Cert. profl. safety engr. Calif. Office asst. retail credit co., Kansas City, Mo., 1939-42; bus driver City of Springfield (Mo.), 1945-47; ops., engring., and personnel positions Shell Oil Co., Wood River (Ill.) Refinery, 1947-66; health and safety dept. mgr. Martinez Mfg. Complex, Calif., 1966-83, retired 1983; exec. dir. Fire Protection Tng. Acad., U. Nev.-Reno; rep. Shell Oil Co., Western Oil and Gas Assn., 1970-81. Mem. Republican Presdl. Task Force. Served with USMC, 1942-45. Decorated Presdl. Citation. Mem. Western Oil and Gas Assn. (Hose Handler award 1972-81, Outstanding mem. award), Am. Soc. Safety Engrs., Veterans Safety, State and County Fire Chiefs Assn., Peace Officers Assn., Nat. Fire Protection Assn. Presbyterian (elder). Established Fire Protection Tng. Acad., U. Nev.-Reno, Stead Campus.

DODD, ROGER JAMES, lawyer; b. Sewickley, Pa., Sept. 15, 1951; s. Carl Roger and Dorothy Maude (Barley) D.; m. Emily Elizabeth Lilly, June 9, 1974; children—Matthew A., Andrew J. BA in Econs., Bucknell U., 1973; JD, U. Pitts., 1976. Ga. 1976, Fla. 1977, U.S. Ct. Appeals (5th cir.) 1976, U.S. Ct. Appeals (11th cir.) 1981, U.S. Dist. Ct. (mid. dist.) Ga. 1976, U.S. Dist. Ct. (no. dist.) Ga. 1983, U.S. Dist. Ct. Fla. 1983, U.S. Supreme Ct. 1987, USAF Ct. of Mil. Review, 1987, U.S. Ct. of Mil. Appeals, 1987. Ptnr., Blackburn, Bright, Edwards, Dodd & Joseph, Valdosta, Ga., 1976-87; prin. Roger J. Dodd, P.C., Valdosta, 1987—; spl. asst. atty. gen. State of Ga., 1979-85; mem. faculty Nat. Coll. Criminal Def., 1986—, Ga. Inst. Trial Advocacy, 1986—; bd. dirs. Ga. Inst. Trial Advocacy, 1986—; guest lectr. Mercer U. Sch. Law., Ga. State U. Sch. Law. Contbr. articles to profl. jours., newspapers. Bd. dirs. Lowndes Country Assn. Retarded Citizens, Valdosta, 1977, Valwood Sch., Valdosta, 1984-86. Named Outstanding Law Day Chmn., State Bar Ga., 1977. Mem. Ga. Assn. Criminal Def. Lawyers (v.p. 1982-83, bd. dirs. 1982—, Pres.'s award 1982, exec. v.p. 1984, pres. 1986), State Bar Ga. (mem. exec. com. family law sect., 1986, sec. criminal law section, 1987—), Ga. Trial Lawyers Assn. (contbr. articles), Assn. Trial Lawyers Am., Nat. Assn. Criminal Def. Lawyers, Valdosta Bar Assn. (sec.-treas. 1977-78), Ga. Assn. Sch. Bd. Attys., MENSA, Nat. Inst. Trial Advocacy (Advance Trial Advocacy Skills 1985), Internat. Platform Assn.; fellow Am. Acad. Matrimonial Lawyers Assn., Ga. Bar Found. Libertarian. Presbyterian. Clubs: William Pitt (Pitts.), William Bucknell Assn. Lodge: Elks. Home: 1415 Williams St Valdosta GA 31601 Office: PO Box 1066 613 N Patterson St Valdosta GA 31603

DODD, TED BYRON, environmental scientist; b. Tyler, Tex., Oct. 1, 1952; s. James Byron and Roxie Fayne (Mitchum) D.; B.S., Sam Houston State U., 1979; m. Cynthia Ann Duren, June 12, 1971; children—Justin Tyler Jackson, Kristin Nicole Jane. Chemist, City of Huntsville (Tex.), 1977-79, City of Conroe (Tex.), 1979; plant chemist Pilot Industries Tex., Houston, 1979-80; ops. mgr. People's Nat. Utilities, Houston, 1980-85; environ. scientist Coe Utilities Inc., Pinehurst, Tex.; systems adminstr. H&J Water Co., 1985-86; pres. Am. Utilities Co., 1985-88; owner Republic Water Systems Tex., Houston, 1977-88; dir. pub. works City of Perryton, Tex., 1988—; cons. Demar Engring., Champ's Utilities, West Montgomery Utilities Corp. Served with USAF, 1971-75. Mem. Am. Chem. Soc., Am. Water Works Assn., Sam Houston Water Utilities Assn. (2d v.p.), Green Forest Water Utilities Assn. Republican. Baptist. Home: 3313 S Ash Perryton TX 79070 Office: 110 S Ash Perryton TX 79070

DODGE, THEODORE AYRAULT, geological mining consultant, drilling company executive; b. Chgo., Jan. 17, 1911; s. Robert Elkin Neil and Katherine Eleanor (Staley) D.; m. Isabelle Stebbins, June 15, 1935; children—Eleanor Dodge Gray, Janet, Richard Neil, Thomas Marshall. A.B. in Geology, Harvard Coll., 1932; A.M. in Geology, Harvard U., 1935, Ph.D. in Geology, 1936; M.A. in Geology, U. Wis., 1933. Registered geologist, Ariz. Geologist, sr. geologist Cerro de Pasco Copper Corp., Morococha, Peru, 1935-38; geologist, petroleum engr. various cos., 1939-41; geologist Anaconda Copper Mining Co., Las Cruces, N.Mex., 1941-42; geologist, acting chief geologist Cananea Consol. Copper Co., Cananea, Mexico, 1942-45; cons. geologist various companies, Ariz. and Mex. 1946-70; mgr. Christmas div. Inspiration Consol. Copper Co., Christmas, Ariz., 1971-75; pres. Hoagland & Dodge Drilling Co., Inc., Tucson, 1976—; instr. geology U. So. Calif., Los Angeles, 1940. Contbr. articles to profl. jours. Fellow Geol. Soc. Am., Mineral. Soc. Am.; mem. Ariz. Geol. Soc. (pres. 1955), Soc. Econ. Geologists, Am. Inst. Mining Engrs., Phi Beta Kappa, Sigma Xi. Baha'i. Club: Mining of the Southwest (Tucson). Home and Office: 1770 N Potter Pl Tucson AZ 85719

DODSON, OSCAR HENRY, numismatist, museum consultant; b. Houston, Jan. 3, 1905; s. Dennis S. and Maggie (Sisk) D.; m. Pauline Wellbrock, Dec. 17, 1932; 1 child, John Dennis. BS, U.S. Naval Acad., 1927; grad., U.S. Naval Postgrad. Sch., 1936; MA in History, U. Ill., 1953. Commd. ensign USN, 1927, advanced through grades to rear adm., 1957; moblzn. planning officer Bur. Naval Personnel, 1945-48; comdg. officer U.S.S. Thomas Jefferson, 1949-50; prof. naval sci. U. Ill., 1950-53; comdr. Landing Ship Flotilla, Atlantic Fleet, 1954-55; chief staff U.S. Naval mission to Greece, 1955-56, 1st Naval Dist., Boston, 1956-57; ret. 1957; asst. prof. history U. Ill., 1957-59; dir. Money Mus., Nat. Bank Detroit, 1959-65; dir. World Heritage Mus., U. Ill., Urbana, 1966-73, now dir. emeritus; acting dir. Champaign County Hist. Mus., 1980-81; mem. numis. adv. com. Smithsonian Instn., 1946; mem. Ann. Assay Commn., 1948, U. Ill. Found. Pres.'s Council, U.S. Naval Acad. Found.; visited numis. socs. under auspices State Dept., USSR, Finland, Poland, Austria, Denmark, 1959. Author: Money Tells the Story, 1962; contbg. editor Coinage Mag., 1973—; contbr. articles to profl. and numis. jours. Decorated Silver Star. Fellow Am. Numis. Soc., Royal (London) Numis. Soc., Explorers Club; mem. Am. Numis. Assn. (life, Farran Zerbe award 1968, bd. govs. 1950-55, pres. 1957-61), Am. Mil. Inst., Archeaeol. Inst. Am., U. Ill. Alumni Assn. (Loyalty award 1966), U.S. Naval Acad. Alumni Assn., SAR. Clubs: Rotary (pres. Champaign 1972-73), Yacht (N.Y.C.); Army-Navy (Washington); Champaign Country, Circumnavigators, Torch. Office: 486 Lincoln Hall U Ill 702 S Wright St Urbana IL 61801

DODSON, TIMOTHY DANIEL, disaster management specialist, financial consultant, realtor, investor; b. Washington, Apr. 17, 1951; s. Tom and Elizabeth (Pera) D.; m. Elizabeth Murrie Orman, Apr. 8, 1978 (div. July 1983). Student UCLA, 1969; B.A. in Philosophy, George Mason U., 1975; postgrad in hydrology, Dartmouth Coll., 1982; postgrad. in water resources MIT, 1982. Lic. real estate agt. Acctg. technician U.S. Naval Ordnance Sta., Indian Head, Md., 1976-77; loan collection agt. office of edn. HEW, Washington, 1977-78; program policy specialist Fed. Ins. Adminstrn., Fed. Emergency Mgmt. Agy., Washington, 1978-83, sr. exec. asst., 1983-85; program analyst, 1985-87; realtor, 1985—; owner, founder "Toad Hall", 1978—. Patron, Middleburg Wine Festival, Va., 1982, sponsor, 1983; donor Friends of U.S. Congressman Frank Wolf Republican-Va., Washington, 1982-83, Friends of U.S. Senator John Warner Rep.-Va., Washington, 1982-83. Recipient Letter of Commendation U.S. Congress, 1979, 83, White House, 1980, State of Nev., 1983. Mem. Millenia Soc., Mensa, Tropical Plants Unlimited (pres. 1972-75), D and D Investments (pres. 1980—), Nat.

Trust Historic Preservation, Internat. Platform Assn., People to People Sports Com., Capitol Hill Equestrian Soc. Clubs: Desiree, Middleburg Tennis Assn., Mile High. Club: Washington Ski, Myo-Sym Karate, Potomac Polo, Wash. Internat. Horse Show. Avocations: polit. and charity fundraising, entertaining, travel, mixologist, ecdysiast auditioner, oenophile, numismatist, weight lifting, karate, piano, guitar. Home: Route 1 Box 199A Aldie VA 22001

DOE, SAMUEL K., head of state of Liberia; b. Tuzon, Liberia, May 6, 1952; ed. Marcus Garvey Meml. High Sch.; m. Nancy Doe; 2 children. With Liberian Army, from 1973, acting 1st sgt., Monrovia, 1973-75, adj. 3d Bn., 1975-79; overthrew Pres. William Tobert in coup d'etat, 1980; head of state, chmn. People's Redemption Council, 1980—. Address: People's Redemption Council, Monrovia Liberia also: Executive Mansion, Capitol Hill, Sinkor, PO Box 9001, Monrovia Liberia *

DOEK, JAKOB EGBERT, law educator, deputy judge; b. Nieuw-Amsterdam, Drente, The Netherlands, May 1, 1942; s. Toni Jantinus Wilhelminus and Femmigje (de Leeuw) D.; m. Maarje de Best, Sept. 16, 1966 (div. Oct. 1981); children: Afelonne J.M., Cherieke S., Mirthe S., Amanja F.; m. Marretje Petronella E Van der Valk, Aug. 30, 1984. Mem. faculty Free U., Amsterdam, The Netherlands, 1967; legal advisor dept. for child protection, dept. for legis. Ministry Justice, The Hague, The Netherlands, 1969-74; assoc. prof. law Free U., Amsterdam, 1974-78; judge juvenile Alkmar Dist. Ct., 1978-82, Dist. Ct., The Hague, 1982-84; prof. law Free U., Amsterdam, 1985-87, dean, 1988—; Mem. adv. bd. Found. for Figth against anti-Semitism, Rotterdam, The Netherlands, 1983—, Parents and Tchrs. against Violence in Edn., Los Angeles, 1985—, Nat. Council on Family Violence, Washington, 1985—; organizer Internat. Congress, Third Internat. Congress on Child Abuse and Neglect, Amsterdam, 1981, Internat. Congress Juvenile and Family Ct. Magistrates, Amsterdam, 1982. Contbd. numerous articles to profl. jours. Mem. Internat. Assn. Juvenile and Family Ct. Magistrates (bd. dirs. 1982-86), Internat. Soc. for Prevention Child Abuse and Neglect (v.p. 1981-82, pres. 1982-84, coordinating v.p. for developing countries 1984—), Def. for Children Internat. (founding mem., bd. dirs. 1979-86), Dutch Soc. for the Prevention Child Abuse and Neglect (pres. 1977—), Dutch Soc. for Family and Juvenile Law (founding mem. 1978, bd. dirs. 1978-82, pres. 1987—). Home: Verdistraat 26, 2162 A V Lisse The Netherlands Office: Vrije U Free U, Postbus 7161, 1007 MC Amsterdam The Netherlands

DOELLE, LESLIE LASZLO, acoustical engineering educator, consultant; b. Budapest, Hungary, Oct. 28, 1913; emigrated to Can., 1957; s. Julius and Hermina (Wohl) D.; m. Eva Marer, Apr. 17, 1940; children—Robert, Judy. Educated Tech. U., Budapest, 1936; M.Arch., McGill U., Montreal, 1964. Cert. acoustical engr., Can. Acoustical cons., Montreal and Toronto, 1958—; aux. prof. McGill U., Montreal, 1964-86; vis. prof. U. Toronto, 1981-86. Author: Acoustics in Architectural Design, 1964; Environmental Acoustics, 1972 (translated to Japanese, Chinese, Indonesian). Contbr. articles on acoustics to profl. jours. Vice pres. York Condominium Corp. 96, Toronto, 1983. Mem. Assn. Profl. Engrs. Ont., Order Engrs. Que., Can. Acoustical Assn. Lodge: Royal Victoria. Home: 5 Kenneth Ave, North York, ON Canada M2N 4V7

DOERFER, GERHARD, language educator; b. Königsberg, Fed. Republic Germany, Mar. 8, 1920; s. Franz and Adina (Bruchmann) D.; m. Ingeborg Blüthner, Apr. 6, 1957. Grad. high sch., Berlin, 1948. Doctor philosophy Freie U., Berlin, 1954-60; asst. prof. U. Göttingen, Fed. Republic Germany, 1960-66, assoc. prof., 1966-70, prof., 1970—; bd. dirs. Seminar für Turkologie und Zentralasienkunde, Göttingen, 1970—. Author: Türkische u. Mongolische Elemente im Neupersischen, 4 vols., 1975, Mongolo-Tungusica, 1985; contbr. numerous articles to profl. jours. Recipient Atatürk medal Republic Turkey, 1981. Mem. Societas Uralo-Altaica, Mongolia Soc., Société Finno Ougrienne, Türk Dil Kurumu (hon.), Türkisch-deutscher Freundeskreis (hon.), Körösi Csoma Soc. (hon.). Lutheran. Office: Seminar Turkologie, Zentralasienkunde, Papendiek 16, 3400 Göttingen Federal Republic of Germany

DOERFLING, HANK, aerospace engineer; b. San Pedro, Calif., Nov. 3, 1936; s. Laurence Howard and Julia Margret (Rusbarsky) D.; B.S. in Physics, Oreg. State U., 1958, M.S., 1963; M.Pub. Adminstrn., Pepperdine U., 1975; m. Elaine Carole; children—Howard, Carrie, Cassie, Tony, Evon. Analyst, No. Am. Aviation Co., Downey, Calif., 1963-64; mem. tech. staff TRW Systems Redondo Beach, Calif., 1964-66, adminstrv. and project mgr. Logicon, San Pedro, Calif., 1966-77; mgr. data processing mgmt. info. div., space and communications group Hughes Aircraft Co., El Segundo, Calif., 1977—. Mem. Hermosa Beach Improvement Commn., 1970-72, chmn., 1971-72; mem. City of Hermosa Beach City Council, 1972-80, mayor, 1973-74, 79-80; pres. South Bay Cities Assn., 1975-76; commr. South Coast (Calif.) Regional Coastal Commn., 1977-80, Calif. Coastal Commn., 1978-80. Served with USN, 1958-61. Mem. Hermosa Beach C. of C. (bd. dirs. 1970-71), League Calif. Cities, Sigma Pi Sigma. Home: 1011 2d St Hermosa Beach CA 90254 Office: Hughes Aircraft Co 650 N Sepulveda Blvd El Segundo CA 90245

DOERMANN, PAUL EDMUND, surgeon; b. Kodaikanal, India, Aug. 3, 1926; s. Carl M. and Cora (Knupke) D.; m. W. Ernestine McPherson, May 3, 1953; children—William McPherson, Marcia, Paula Michelle, Diana, Charles. Student, Ohio State U., 1944; B.S., Capital U., 1947; M.D., U. Mich., 1951. Diplomate Am. Bd. Surgery. Intern Louisville Gen. Hosp., 1951-52, resident in surgery, 1952-53; resident in surgery Milw. County Hosp., 1955-58; med. missionary Lutheran Mission Hosp., Madang, New Guinea, 1958-69; surgeon Linvill Clinic, Columbia City, Ind., 1960-61; practice medicine specializing in surgery Huntington, Ind.; pres. med. staff, chief surg. service Huntington Meml. Hosp.; pres. Huntington Surg. Corp. Served from 1st lt. to capt., AUS, 1953-55. Luth. Acad. scholar; Paul Harris fellow. Fellow ACS; mem. Huntington County Med. Soc., Christian Med. Soc., Am. Assn. Physicians and Surgeons, Pvt. Doctors Am., Huntington C. of C. Lutheran. Lodge: Rotary (Paul Harris fellow). Home: 5503 West 500 North Huntington IN 46750 Office: 1751 N Jefferson Huntington IN 46750

DOESCHER, WILLIAM FREDERICK, public relations executive, publisher; b. Utica, N.Y., Dec. 9, 1937; s. Frederick William and Katherine Ann (Kipp) D.; B.A. in Econs., Colgate U., 1959; M.A. in Journalism, Syracuse (N.Y.) U., 1961; postgrad. in advanced mgmt. Columbia U., 1973; m. Linda Blair, Nov. 25, 1977; children: Michelle Blair, Douglas C. Doescher, Marc H. Blair, Cinda L. Doescher. Pub. relations assoc., editor Chase Manhattan News, Chase Manhattan Bank, N.Y.C., 1961-65; mgr. press relations Inmont Corp., 1965-66; asst. corp. relations mgr. U.S. Plywood Corp., 1966-67; pub. affairs mgr. Eastern region Champion Internat. Corp., 1967-69, mgr. advt. services, then dir. corp. advt., 1969- 71; v.p. advt. and pub. relations Drexel Heritage Furnishings, Inc., 1971-78; v.p. communications Dun & Bradstreet, Inc., 1978-83, v.p. pub. relations and advt., 1983—, also pub. D&B Reports mag., N.Y.C., 1978—. Bd. dirs., Nat. Easter Seal Soc. ; past pres. Nat. Combined Health Appeal; past pres. Scarsdale, N.Y. Civic Club. Served with USAR, 1959-65. Mem. Public Relations Soc. Am. Author numerous articles in mags., periodicals. Office: 299 Park Ave New York NY 10171

DOGHUDJE, CHRISTOPHER AWUSA, advertising company executive; b. Usiefrun, Nigeria; s. Michael Ovien and Cecilia Yabreghagha (Oghenekaro) D.; m. Anne Mararosue Aziza, Apr. 23, 1973; children: Ejiro, Nosodere, Bevughe. BA in Mass Communications, Lagos (Nigeria) U., 1967; postgrad., Columbia U., 1975. Client service and tng. dir. Ogilvy, Benson & Mather, Ltd., Lagos, 1972-78; client service cir. Lintas, Ltd., Lagos, 1975-85, mng. dir., 1986—. Editor: How To Get the Best Results from an Advertising Agency, 1982; author: Advertising in Nigerian Perspective, 1985; contbr. articles to profl. jours. Mem. Assn. Advt. Practitioners in Nigeria (sec. edn. com. 1978-82), Nigerian Inst. Mgmt. (guest speaker advt. courses 1976—), Am. Mgmt. Assn., Metaphysics Research Group Nigeria. Roman Catholic. Home: 7 Bola Shadipe St, Lagos Nigeria Office: Lintas Ltd, PO Box 551, Lagos Nigeria

DOHENY, DONALD ALOYSIUS, lawyer, business exec.; b. Milw., Apr. 20, 1924; s. John Anthony and Adelaide (Koller) D.; m. Catherine Elizabeth Lee, Oct. 25, 1952; children: Donald Aloysius, Celeste Hazel Doheny Kennedy, John Vincent, Ellen Adelaide, Edward Lawrence II, William Francis, Madonna Lee. Student U. Notre Dame, 1942-43; BME, Marquette U., 1947; JD, Harvard, 1949; M in Indsl. Engring. Washington U., St. Louis, 1956. Bar: Wis. 1949, Mo. 1949, U.S. Supreme Ct. 1970; registered prof. engr., Mo. Asst. to civil engr. Shipbuilding div. Froemming Bros., Inc., Milw., 1942-43; draftsman, designer The Heil Co., Milw., 1944-46; assoc. Igoe, Carroll & Keefe, St. Louis, 1949-51; asst. to v.p. and gen. mgr., chief prodn. engr., gen. adminstr., dir. adminstrn. Granco Steel Products subsidiary Granite City Steel, Granite City, Ill., 1951-57; asst. to pres. Vestal Labs., Inc., St. Louis, 1957-63; exec. v.p., dir. Moehlenpah Engring., Inc., Hydro-Air Engring., Inc., 1963-67; pres. dir. Foamtex Industries, Inc., St. Louis, 1967-75; exec. v.p., dir. Seasonal Industries, Inc., N.Y.C., 1973-75; sole practice, St. Louis, 1967-81; ptnr., Doheny & Doheny, Attys., St. Louis, 1981—, Doheny & Assocs. Mgmt. Counsel, St. Louis, 1967—; pres., dir. Mktg. & Sales Counsel, Inc., St. Louis, 1975—; pres., dir. Mid-USA Sales Co., St. Louis, 1976—; pres., bd. dirs. Profl. Bus. Exchange, Inc., St Louis, 1986, Prestige Offices and Properties, Inc., St. Louis, 1987; lectr. bus. orgn. and adminstrn. Washington U., 1950-74; lectr. Grad. Sch. Bus., St. Louis U., 1980—. Served with AUS, 1943-44; 1st lt. Res., 1948-52. Mem. ABA, Am. Judicature Soc., Am. Marketing Assn. (nat. membership chmn. 1959), Mo. Bar Assn., Wis. Bar Assn., Fed. Bar Assn., Bar Assn. St. Louis (gen. chmn. pub. relations 1955-56, vice chmn., sec.-treas. jr. sect. 1950, 51), Marquette Engring. Assn. (pres. 1946-47), Engring. Knights, Am. Legion, Tau Beta Pi, Pi Tau Sigma. Clubs: Notre Dame (pres. 1955, 56), Marquette (pres. 1961), Harvard (St. Louis); Stadium, Engineers, Mo. Athletic. Office: 12000 Bldg 11960 Westline Industrial Dr Suite 330 Saint Louis MO 63146 also: Mchts Laclede Bldg 408 Olive St Suite 400 Saint Louis MO 63102

DOHERTY, GEORGE WILLIAM, research psychologist, counselor; b. N.Y.C., Oct. 18, 1941; s. William George and Catherine Marguerite (Nierenhausen) D.; B.S., Pa. State U., 1964; M.S., Miss. State U., 1977; postgrad. Baylor U., 1972, North Texas State U., 1979. Cert. Nat. Acad. Cert. Clin. Mental Health Counselors. Program coordinator, dir. youth devel. program Econ. Opportunities Advancement Corp., Waco, Texas, 1968-71; psychol. counselor, parent tng. Counseling or Referral Assistance Services, Phila., 1973-75; psychologist III, Rural Clinics Community Counseling Ctr., Ely, Nev., 1980-85; counselor, researcher, Ely, 1985-86; evaluator San Luis Valley Comprehensive Community Mental Health Ctr., 1987—; mem. faculty No. Nev. Community Coll., Ely, 1980-85; co-chmn. human rights com. Blue Peaks Devel. Ctr., Alamosa, Colo., 1988—. Served to capt. U.S. Air Force, 1964-68. Fellow Am. Biog. Inst. (life, commemorative medal of honor); mem. Am. Psychol. Assn. (assoc.), Western Psychol. Assn., Tex. Psychol. Assn., Nev. Psychol. Assn., Inter-Am. Soc. Psychology, Internat. Assn. Applied Psychology, Assn. Behavior Analysis, Am. Assn. Counseling and Devel., Biofeedback Soc. Am., Assn. Counselor Edn. and Supervision (chmn. task force and interest group community counseling 1984-85), Western Assn. Counselor Edn. and Supervision, Assn. Measurement Edn. and Guidance, Am. Mental Health Counselors Assn., Air Force Assn., World Future Soc., AAAS, Pa. State U. Alumni Assn., Smithsonian Assoc., Irish-Am. Cultural Inst., O'Dochartaigh Family Research Assn., Am. Legion, Wilderness Soc., Nat. Audubon Soc. Democrat. Home: PO Box 567 Alamosa CO 81101 Office: San Luis Valley CCMHC Alamosa CO 81101 also: Monte Vista CO 81144

DOHERTY, THOMAS JOSEPH, financial services company executive; b. Cambridge, Mass., Oct. 20, 1933; s. Thomas Joseph and Margaret Cecelia (O'Connell) D.; m. Carol Anne Conroy, Jan. 5, 1957; children: William, John, Robert, Susan. AB cum laude, Suffolk U., Boston, 1961. With Merrill Lynch, Pierce, Fenner & Smith Inc., N.Y.C., 1958—; v.p. Merrill Lynch, Pierce, Fenner & Smith Inc., 1978—; mng. dir. Merrill Lynch White Weld Capital Markets Group, 1979-83; pres., chief exec. officer Merrill Lynch Specialists, Inc., 1985—; trustee Cin. Stock Exchange, 1979-83; mem. Am. Stock Exchange, N.Y. Stock Exchange; bd. govs. Pacific Stock Exchange, 1984—. Served with AUS, 1953-55. Mem. Security Traders Assn. N.Y., Nat. Security Traders Assn. (chmn. exchange liaison com. 1986-87), Gen. Alumni Assn. Suffolk U. (bd. dirs. 1976-77). Republican. Roman Catholic.

DOHMEN, FREDERICK HOEGER, retired wholesale drug company executive; b. Milw., May 12, 1917; s. Fred William and Viola (Gutsch) D.; B.A. in Commerce, U. Wis., 1939; m. Gladys Elizabeth Dite, Dec. 23, 1939 (dec. 1963); children—William Francis, Robert Charles; m. 2d, Mary Alexander Holgate, June 27, 1964. With F. Dohmen Co., Milw., 1939-82, successively warehouse employee, sec., v.p., 1944-52, pres., 1952-82, dir., 1947—, chmn. bd., 1952-82. Bd. dirs. St. Luke's Hosp. Ednl. Found., Milw., 1965-83, pres., 1969-72, chmn. bd., 1972-73; bd. dirs. U. Wis.-Milw. Found., 1976-79, bd. visitors, 1978-88, emeritus mem. 1988—; assoc. chmn. Nat. Bible Week, Laymen's Nat. Bible Com., N.Y.C., 1968-82, council of adv., 1983—. Mem. Nat. Wholesale Druggists Assn. (chmn. mfr. relations com. 1962, resolutions com. 1963, mem. of bd. control 1963-66), Nat. Assn. Wholesalers (trustee 1966-75), Druggists Service Council (dir. 1967-71), Wis. Pharm. Assn., Miss. Valley Drug Club, Beta Gamma Sigma, Phi Eta Sigma, Delta Kappa Epsilon. Presbyn. Clubs: University, Town (Milw.). Home: 3903 W Mequon Rd 112 N Mequon WI 53092

DOI, MASAYUKI, credit card company executive; b. Amagasaki, Japan, Aug. 1, 1933; s. Masaharu and Tae (Shimizu) D.; m. Kazuko Yamamoto, Dec. 7, 1962; children: Masataka, Yasuhiro. BA in Econs., Kwansei Gakuin U., Nishinomiya, Hyogo, 1957. Various positions The Sumitomo Bank Co., Ltd., Osaka, Japan, 1957-73, br. mgr., 1973-83; mng. dir. The Sumitomo Credit Service Co., Ltd., Osaka, 1983—; adv. internat. risk Visa Internat. Service Assn., San Francisco, 1987. Office: The Sumitomo Credit, Service Co Ltd, 5-2-10 Shinbash, Minato-ku, Tokyo 105, Japan

DOI, TAKAKO, congresswoman; b. Kobe, Hyogo, Japan, Nov. 30, 1928; parents: Niroichi and Kiyo Doi. BA, Doshisha U., Kyoto, Japan, 1951, M of Laws, 1956. Lectr. Doshisha U., 1958-63, Kanseigakuin U., Nishinomiyo, Japan, 1963-68, Seiwa Women's U., Nishinomiyo, 1968-69; mem. Japanese Ho. of Reps., 1969—. Socialist vice chair, Tokyo, 1983-86, chair, 1986—. Home: Nishinomiya, Hyogo Japan Office: Shugiin Daini Giinkaikan, 2-1-2 Nagata-cho, Chiyoda-ku Tokyo 100, Japan

DOISNEAU, ROBERT SYLVAIN, photographer; b. Gentilly, France, Apr. 14, 1912; s. Gaston and Sylvie (Duval) D.; m. Pierrette Reine Chaumaison, 1932; children—Annette, Francine. Ed. Ecole Estienne, Paris, 1925-29. Freelance photographer Agence Rapho, Paris, 1946—. Exhibited one-man shows including: La Fontaine des Quatre Saisons, Paris, 1951, Limelight Gallery, N.Y., 1959, Art Inst. Chgo., 1960, Bibliothè que Nationale, Paris, 1968, Internat. Mus. Photography, Rochester, N.Y., 1972, Witkin Gallery, N.Y., 1974, 78, La Galerie et Fils, Brussels, 1975, Photo Art, Basle, 1976, Galerie Agathe Gaillard, Paris, 1978, Musee d'Art Moderne, Paris, 1979, Gallery for Fine Photography, New Orleans, 1981, Datar, 1985, Un Ceraui R.D., Rome, 1986, 88; represented in permanent collections Musé e d'Art Moderne, Paris, Bibliothè que Nationale, Paris, Musé e Nicé phore Niepce, Chalon-Sur-Saô ne, France, Victoria and Albert Mus., London, Mus. Modern Art, N.Y.C., Internat. Mus. Photography, Rochester, N.Y., New Orleans Mus. Art, Center for Creative Photography, U. Ariz., Tucson. Author 12 books, including 3 Seconds from Eternity, 1981, Doisuar, 1983. Decorated chevalier Lé gion d'Honneur. Home: 46 Pl Jules Ferry, 92000 Montrouge France Office: Agence Rapho, 8 rue d'Alger, 75001 Paris France

DOJKA, EDWIN SIGMUND, civil engineer; b. Niagara Falls N.Y., Dec. 20, 1924; s. Zygmunt Joseph and Felixa (Pasek) D.; BCE, Rensselaer Poly. Inst., 1951; m. Jean L. Keller, July 9, 1949; children—Paul, Gail Dojka Rutkowski, Jay. Structures engr. Bell Aircraft Corp., Wheatfield, N.Y., 1951-52; design engr. Hooker Electro Chem. Corp., Niagara Falls, N.Y., 1952-55; civil engr. City of Niagara Falls (N.Y.), 1955-58, asst. city engr., 1958-60, dep. city engr., 1960-63, city engr., 1963-79; city engr. City of North Tonawanda, 1979-85; mem. sewer commn., plumbing bd., 1963-85, mem. planning bd., 1963-66, bd. equalization rev., 1963-71; mem. Niagara County Planning Bd., 1978—, Traffic Safety Commn., 1979-85. Mem. United Fund Community Budget Com., 1962-68; mem. Community Ambassador Gen. Com., 1958, 59; Fleet Safety adv. commr., Niagara Falls, 1960-68; bd. assos. Mt. St. Mary's Hosp., 1969-70. Served with inf. AUS, World War II; ETO. Decorated Bronze Star, Purple Heart, Combat Infantryman's badge. Registered profl. engr., land surveyor, N.Y. Fellow ASCE; mem. Soc. Am. Mil. Engrs., Am. Pub. Works Assn., Am. Water Works Assn., Nat. Soc. Profl. Engrs., Water Pollution Control Fedn., Am. Planning Control Fedn., Am. Planning Assn., Inst. for Engring., Am. Arbitration Assn. (comml. panelist 1978—), DAV, Am. Legion, 102d Inf. Div. Assn., AMVETS Meml. Day Assn., Boys Club Alumni Assn., VFW, Pulaski Civic League, Polish Legion Am. Vets., Mil. Order Purple Heart 40 and 8, 2d Armored Div. Assn., Hon. Order Ky. Cols., Sigma Xi, Chi Epsilon, Tau Beta Pi. Roman Catholic. Clubs: Echo, Sertoma, Elks, First Friday, K.C., Dom Polski. Home and Office: 509 80th St Niagara Falls NY 14304

DOKIC, PETAR, chemist, educator; b. Novi Sad, Yugoslavia, Oct. 18, 1941; s. Pavle and Milica (Bijuklic) D.; m. Kler Miroslava, Oct. 2, 1965; children: Ljubica, Milica. Diploma in Engring., Faculty Tech., Novi Sad, 1964, MSc, 1971, PhD, 1974. Asst. Faculty Tech., Novi Sad, 1965-75, asst. prof., 1980-85, assoc. prof. colloid chemistry, 1985, vice dean, 1975-77, pres. council Inst. Applied Chemistry, 1980-84, pro rector univ., 1983-87; postdoctoral research Queen Elizabeth Coll., London, 1977-78; pres. Commn. for Sci. and Edn. Union Univs. Yugoslavia, 1985-87. Contbr. over 80 articles in colloid chemistry to profl. jours. Pres. assembly for high and secondary edn. Province of Vojvodina, 1977-83; mem. exec. council, pres. com. for scis. and informatics Assembly Socialistic Autonomous Province of Vojvodina, 1987—. Fellow Eisenhower Exchange, Phila., 1987. Mem. Serbian Chem. Soc., Chem. Soc. Province Vojvodina, Fed. Com. for Sci. and Tech., Council Cen. for Comparative Studies on Technol. and Social Progress. Home: Sonje Marinkovic 21, 21000 Novi Sad Yugoslavia Office: 2 V Vlahovica, 21000 Novi Sad Yugoslavia

DOKURNO, ANTHONY DAVID, lawyer; b. Gardner, Mass., Mar. 14, 1957; s. Anthony Chester and Damey Anteena (Aleson) D.; m. Andee J. Rappazzo. BA, Holy Cross Coll., 1979; JD, Vt. Law Sch., 1982. Bar: Mass. 1982, U.S. Ct. Mil. Appeals 1986, U.S. Supreme Ct. 1987. Sole practice Fitchburg, Mass., 1982—. Served to lt. USNR, 1986—. Mem. ABA (internat. law and practice sect., sci. and tech. sect.), Mass. Bar Assn., Fed. Bar Assn., Am. Trial Lawyers Assn., Phi Beta Kappa. Home: 1600 S Eads St #826N Arlington VA 22202

DOLAN, BEVERLY FRANKLIN, diversified company executive; b. Augusta, Ga., 1927; married. Grad., U. Ga., 1952; grad. Advanced Mgmt. Program, Harvard U., 1969. Pres., co-founder E-Z Go Car Corp., 1954-60; with Textron Inc., Providence, 1960—, pres. Homelite div., 1976-79, corp. exec. v.p. ops., 1979-80, pres., 1980—, chief operating officer, 1980-85, chief exec. officer, 1985—, chmn., 1986—, also dir.; dir. First Union Corp., Allendale Mut. Ins. Co. Served with AUS, 1952-54. Office: Textron Inc 40 Westminster St Providence RI 02903 *

DOLAN, JAMES VINCENT, lawyer; b. Washington, Nov. 11, 1938; s. John Vincent and Philomena Theresa (Vance) D.; m. Anne McSherry Reilly, June 18, 1960; children: Caroline McSherry, James Reilly. A.B., Georgetown U., 1960, LL.B., 1963. Bar: U.S. Dist. Ct. 1963, U.S. Ct. Appeals (D.C.) cir. 1964, U.S. Ct. Appeals (4th cir.) 1976. Law clk. U.S. Ct. Appeals D.C., 1963-64; assoc. Steptoe & Johnson, Washington, 1964-71, ptnr., 1971-82; mem. Steptoe & Johnson Chartered, Washington, 1982-83; v.p. law Union Pacific R.R., Omaha, 1983—. Co-author: Construction Contract Law, 1981; contbr. articles to legal jours.; editor-in-chief: Georgetown Law Jour., 1962-63. Mem. ABA, D.C. Bar Assn., Barristers. Republican. Roman Catholic. Clubs: Congressional Country (v.p. 1982, pres. 1983), Metropolitan; Omaha Country. Home: 9789 Frederick St Omaha NE 68124 Office: Union Pacific RR 1416 Dodge St Omaha NE 68179

DOLAN, MARYANNE MCLORN, writer, educator, lecturer; b. N.Y.C., July 14, 1924; d. Frederick Joseph and Kathryn Cecilia (Carroll) McLorn; m. John Francis Dolan, Oct. 6, 1951; children—John Carroll, James Francis McLorn, William Brennan. B.A., San Francisco State U., 1978, M.A., 1981. Tchr. classes and seminars in antiques and collectibles U. Calif.-Berkeley, U. Calif.-Davis, U. Calif.-Santa Cruz, Coll. of Marin, Kentfield, Calif., Mills Coll., Oakland, Calif., St. Mary's Coll., Moraga, Calif., 1969—; tchr. writing Dolan Sch., 1978—; owner antique shop, Benicia, Calif., 1970—. Author: Vintage Clothing, 1880-1960, 1983; Collecting Rhinestone Jewelry, 1984; weekly columnist The Collector, 1979—; contbr. articles to profl. jours. Mem. AAUW, Internat. Soc. Appraisers, Calif. Writers Club, Internat. Platform Assn. Republican. Roman Catholic. Home: 138 Belle Ave Pleasant Hill CA 94523 Office: 191 West J St Benicia CA 94510

DOLAN, VINCENT GERARD, international administration and finance executive; b. N.Y.C., Oct. 12, 1927; s. Vincent Lawrence and Elizabeth Mable (Cummings) D.; B.A., St. Lawrence U., Canton, N.Y., 1955; s. Carrie Marie Knopf, Apr. 14, 1959. Trainee, Chase Manhattan bank, N.Y.C., 1956-57, asst. accounts mgr. Columbian Carbon Internat., Inc., N.Y.C., 1957-59; export credit mgr. Dorr-Oliver, Inc., Stamford, Conn., 1959-65; supr. credit/collection documentation control IGE Export div. Gen. Electric Co., N.Y.C., 1965-66; mgr. Western hemisphere credit accts. RCA Corp., N.Y.C., 1966-71; cons., analyst S.J. Rundt Assos., Inc., N.Y.C., 1971-72; credit supr. export div. Ford Motor Co., Newark, 1972-79; mgr. credit/collections Harris Corp. Info. Systems Internat. Div., Melbourne, Fla., 1979-83, mgr., distbr. adminstrn., 1983-86, mgr. internat. adminstrv. support, 1986— . Served with USMC, 1945-49, 50-51. Mem. Am. Soc. Internat. Execs., Alpha Tau Omega. Roman Catholic. Died Apr. 10, 1988. Home: 1301 Wisteria Way Richardson TX 75080 Office: 16001 Dallas Pkwy Dallas TX 75380-9022

DOLANC, STANE, Yugoslavian government official; b. Hrastnik, Slovenia, Nov. 16, 1925; grad. Ljubljana U. Law Sch. Mem. Communist Party of Yugoslavia, 1944—; commd. officer Yugoslav People's Army, advanced through grades to col.; ret., 1960; former dep. to Republican Assembly of Slovenia; dir. Ljubljana Sch. Polit. Sci., 1963-67; mem. central com. League of Communists of Slovenia, 1964—; mem. central com. League of Communists of Yugoslavia, 1969—, sec. exec. bur., 1972-78, mem. central com. presidency, sec., 1979; fed. sec. of Interior, 1982-83; v.p., 1988—, also mem. Presidency; mem. Fed. Exec. Council, from 1984; mem. Yugoslav del. 3d Nonaligned Summit Conf., Lusaka, 5th Conf., Colombo. Office: SavezKomunista Jugoslavije, Bulevar Lenjina 6, Novi Beograd Yugoslavia *

DOLE, ELIZABETH HANFORD, Republican campaigner, former secretary of transportation; b. Salisbury, N.C., July 29, 1936; d. John Van and Mary Ella (Cathey) Hanford; m. Robert Joseph Dole (U.S. Senator from Kans.), Dec. 6, 1975. B.A. with honors in Polit. Sci., Duke, 1958; postgrad., Oxford (Eng.) U., summer 1959; M.A. in Edn., Harvard U., 1960, J.D., 1965. Bar: D.C. 1966. Staff asst. to asst. sec. for edn. HEW, Washington, 1966-67; practiced law Washington, 1967-68; assoc. dir. legis. affairs, then exec. dir. Pres.'s Com. for Consumer Interests, Washington, 1968-71; dep. dir. Office Consumer Affairs, The White House, Washington, 1971-73; commr. FTC, Washington, 1973-79; chmn. Voters for Reagan-Bush, 1980; dir. Human Services Group, Office of Exec. Br. Mgmt., Office of Pres.-Elect, 1980; asst. to Pres. for pub. liaison 1981-83; sec. U.S. Dept. Transp., 1983-87; with Robert Dole for Presdl. Campaign, 1987-88; participant 1988 Presdl. and Congl. campaigns; mem. nominating com. Am. Stock Exchange, 1972, N.C. Consumer Council, 1972. Trustee Duke U., 1974-88; mem. council Harvard Law Sch. Assocs.; hon. chmn. bd. overseers Duke U. Comprehensive Cancer Ctr., 1988—; mem. vis. com. John F. Kennedy Sch. Govt. Harvard U., 1988—. Recipient Arthur S. Flemming award U.S. Govt., 1972, Humanitarian award Nat. Commn. Against Drunk Driving, 1988, Disting. Alumni award Duke U., 1988; named one of Am.'s 200 Young Leaders, Time mag., 1974, one of World's 10 Most Admired Women, Gallup Poll, 1988. Mem. Phi Beta Kappa, Pi Lambda Theta, Pi Sigma Alpha.

DOLE, ROBERT J., U.S. senator; b. Russell, Kans., July 22, 1923; s. Doran R. and Bina D.; m. Elizabeth Hanford, Dec. 1975. Student, U. Kans., U. Ariz.; A.B., Washburn Mcpl. U., Topeka, 1952, LL.B., 1952; LL.D. (hon.), Washburn U., Topeka, 1969. Bar: Kans. Mem. Kans. Ho. of Reps., 1951-53; sole practice Russell, Kans., 1953-61; Russell County atty. 1953-61; mem. 87th Congress from 6th Dist., Kans., 88th-90th congresses from 1st Dist., Kans.; mem. U.S. Senate from Kans., 1968—, Senate majority leader, 1984—, Senate Rep. leader, 1987—; chmn. Republican Nat. Com., 1971-73; Rep. vice-presdl. candidate, 1976. Chmn. Dole Found. Served with AUS, World War II. Decorated Purple Heart (2), Bronze Star with cluster. Recipient Horatio Alger award Horatio Alger Assn. Disting. Ams., 1988. Mem. Am. Legion, VFW, DAV, 4-H Fair Assn., Kappa Sigma.

Methodist. Clubs: Masons, Shriners, Elk, Kiwanis. Home: Russell KS 67665 Office: 141 Hart Senate Bldg Washington DC 20510-3401

DOLEAC, CHARLES BARTHOLOMEW, lawyer; b. New Orleans, Sept. 20, 1947; s. Cyril Bartholomew and Emma Elizabeth (St. Clair) D.; m. Denise Kilfoyle, Feb. 2, 1972; children: Keith Gabriel, Jessa Lee. BS cum laude, U. N.H., 1968; JD, NYU, 1971. Bar: Mass. 1972, N.H. 1972, Maine 1973. Law clk. to Justice Grimes N.H. Supreme Ct., Concord, 1972-73; assoc. Boynton, Waldron, Dill & Aeschliman, Portsmouth, N.H., 1973-76; ptnr. Boynton, Waldron, Doleac, Woodman & Scott, Portsmouth, 1977—; delegation mem. on tour of Chinese legal system Chinese Ministry of Justice, 1982; del. to Peoples Republic of China/U.S. joint session on trade investments and econ. law Chinese Ministry of Justice/U.S. Dept. Justice, Beijing, 1987; pres. bd. of trustees Strawbery Banke, Inc.; prop. Portsmouth Athenaeum. Mem. citizens adv. council Portsmouth Community Devel. Program, 1976-77; pres. bd. dirs. Seacoast United Way, 1976; chmn. Portsmouth Bd. of Bldg. Appeals, 1976-77; chmn. stewardship com. Soc. Preservation New Eng. Antiquities, 1980-84, trustee. Fellow NEH, Aspen Inst. Fellow N.H. Bar Found.; mem. Mass. Bar Assn., Maine Bar Assn., N.H. Bar Assn. , Assn. Trial Lawyers Am., N.H. Trial Lawyers Assn., Maine Trial Lawyers Assn., Japan Soc. of N.H. (pres.). Home: Little Harbor Rd Portsmouth NH 03801 Office: Boynton Waldron Doleac et al 82 Court St Portsmouth NH 03801

DOLGIN, STEPHEN MARK, teacher, social worker; b. San Francisco, Dec. 22, 1949; s. David Aubrey and Ruth (Ogurak) D.; B.A., U. Minn., 1972, M.S.W., 1976; M.B.A. in Health Services Mgmt., Golden Gate U., 1982; postgrad., San Francisco State U., 1987—. Social caseworker Contra Costa County Social Services Dept., Richmond, Calif., 1979-81; social ins. claims examiner Social Security Adminstrn., Richmond, Calif., 1982-84; exercise project officer tour Army Res., 1984-85; vets. service officer Dakota County, Minn., 1987; secondary tchr. South San Francisco Sch. Dist., 1987—. Served with U.S. Army, 1976-79; maj. USAR. Mem. CAP (cadet program officer, Sr. Mem. of Yr. award 1980), Assn. U.S. Army (former chpt. exec. bd.), Am. Philatelic Soc., Res. Officers Assn., (v.p. med. service dept. Calif. 1983-84), Toastmasters Internat. (club pres., sec. 1984, Competent Toastmaster award), Air Force Assn., Mil. Order World Wars (chpt. sr. v.p.), Am. Legion. Home: 3815 Susan Dr J-8 San Bruno CA 94066

D'OLIER, H(ENRY) MITCHELL, lawyer; b. Chgo., June 10, 1946; s. Henry and Helen Elizabeth (Mitchell) D'O.; m. Barbara Ann Miller, June 12, 1971; children: Jason Mitchell, Justin Frank, Jordan Henry. BA in English and Gen. Sci., U. Iowa, 1968, JD with distinction, 1972. Bar: Iowa 1972, Hawaii 1972. Assoc. tax Goodsil, Anderson, Quinn & Stifel, Honolulu, 1972-77; ptnr. tax, health, mgmt. coms. Goodsill, Anderson, Quinn & Stifel, Honolulu, 1977—; bd. dirs. Reyn's Men's Wear Inc., Kamuela, Hawaii. Note and comment editor Iowa Law Rev., 1971. Chmn., co-chmn. Friends Of Fred Hemmings, Honolulu, 1984, 86, 88; chmn., vice-chmn. profl. div. campaign Aloha United Way, 1982-84; clk., deacon Cen. Union Ch., 1983-85; bd. dirs. Hawaii Theatre Ctr., 1988—, Boys' and Girls' Club Honolulu, 1977—, v.p., pres.-elect 1987, pres., 1988—. Mem. ABA (tax and health law sects.), Nat. Health Lawyers Assn., Am. Coll. Hosp. Attys., Hawaii State Bar Assn. (tax sect.), Order of Coif, Omicron Delta Kappa. Republican. Club: Plaza (Honolulu). Lodge: Rotary (bd. dirs. Honolulu club 1988—). Home: 1704 Kumakani Loop Honolulu HI 96821 Office: Goodsil Anderson Quinn & Stifel 130 Merchant St Suite 1600 Honolulu HI 96813

DOLIN, LONNY H., lawyer; b. Youngstown, Ohio, Jan. 24, 1954; d. Lawrence Joseph and Sonya (Sacks) Heselov ; m. Raphael Dolin, June 19, 1976; children: Nathaniel, Brooke. AB, Georgetown U., 1976; JD, Cath. U., 1979. Bar: Vt. 1980, N.Y. State Ba, 1984, U.S. Dist. Ct. (we. dist.) N.Y. 1984. Assoc. Downs, Rachlin & Martin, Burlington, Vt., 1979-81; sole practice Burlington, 1981-84; assoc. Harris, Beach, Wilcox, Rubin & Levey, Rochester, N.Y., 1984—; of counsel to U.S. Congressman Fred J. Eckert, N.Y., 1985—; bd. dirs. Monroe County Legal Services Corp. Mem. Pittsford Town and County Com., N.Y., 1983—, Town of Pittsford Bd. of Zoning Appeals, N.Y., 1984—; chmn. Monroe County Comparable Worth Task Force, Rochester, 1985—, Fred J. Eckert Women's Adv. Council, Rochester, 1985—; del. The Jud. Dist. N.Y., Rochester, 1985; bd. dirs. Nat. Council Jewish Women. Recipient Corpus Juris Secundum award West Pub. co., 1979. Mem. ABA, Vt. Bar Assn., N.Y. Bar Assn., Monroe County Bar Assn., Greater Rochester Women's Bar Assn. (treas. 1986), Assn. Trial Lawyers Am., N.Y. State Trial Lawyers Assn. Republican. Home: 22 Fletcher Rd Pittsford NY 14534 Office: Harris Beach et al 130 E Main St Rochester NY 14604

DOLINER, NATHANIEL LEE, lawyer; b. Daytona Beach, Fla., June 28, 1949; s. Joseph and Asia (Shaffer) D.; m. Debra Lynn Simon, June 5, 1983. B.A., George Washington U., 1970; J.D., Vanderbilt U., 1973; LL.M. in Taxation, U. Fla., 1977. Bar: Fla. 1973, U.S. Tax Ct. 1973, U.S. Dist. Ct. (mid. dist.) Fla. 1974. Assoc. Smalbein, Eubank, Johnson, Rosier & Bussey, P.A., Daytona Beach, Fla., 1973-76; vis. asst. prof. law U. Fla., Gainesville, 1977-78; assoc. Carlton, Fields, Ward, Emmanuel, Smith & Cutler, P.A., Tampa, Fla., 1978-82, ptnr., 1982—, chmn. tax, corp. and securities dept., 1984—, treas. 1985-86, bd. dirs., 1983-87, 88-89. Bd. dirs. Big Bros./Big Sisters of Greater Tampa, Inc., 1980-82., dist. commnr. Gulf Ridge council Boy Scouts Am., 1983; bd. dirs. Child Abuse Council, Inc. 1986—, Am. Heart Assn. (bd. dirs. Hillsborough County chpt. 1987—), Mem. ABA (vice chmn. continuing legal education com. tax sect. 1986-88, chmn. 1988—, chmn. subcom. on sales and exchanges, partnership com. ABA Tax Sect. 1986-88; com. on negotiated acquisitions bus. law sect.), Fla. Bar Assn. (mem. exec. com. tax sect. 1980-83, tax cert. com. 1987-88, vice chair 1988—); Greater Tampa C. of C. (chmn. Ambassadors Target Task Force of Com. of 100, 1984-85), Anti-Defamation League (regional bd. mem. 1986—, exec. com. 1987—), Tampa Jewish Fedn. (chmn. community relations com. 1986-87, bd. dirs. 1986-88). Clubs: Tampa Rotary (bd. dirs. 1986—), The Tampa Club (bd. dirs., sec. 1987—). Home: 3207 Tarabrook Dr Tampa FL 33618 Office: Carlton Fields Ward et al 777 S Harbour Island Blvd 5th Floor Tampa FL 33602

DOLING, JOHN FRANCIS, urban policy educator; b. Bristol, Eng., Apr. 7, 1946; s. Henry James and Eileen Rosina (Harris) D.; m. Ann Brown, July 3, 1976; children: Sophie, Thomas, Samuel. BA, U. London, 1967; MSc, U. Birmingham, 1970, PhD, 1973. Town planner Town Planning dept. City of Exeter, Devon, Eng., 1967-69; lectr., then sr. lectr. social and urban policy U. Birmingham, Eng., 1972—; prof. U. Tampere, Finland, 1988; expert group mem. Swedish Council Bldg. Research, Stockholm, 1984-85; chmn. adv. group Joseph Rowntree Meml. Trust, York, Eng., 1985—; external examiner U. Salford, Eng., 1987—, Inst. Housing, London, 1987—. Author: Planning for Engineers and Surveyors, 1981, Public Control of Private Rented Housing, 1984, The Property Owning Democracy, 1988. Grantee, J. Rowntree Meml. Trust, 1982-86, Social Sci. Research Council, 1980. Mem. Ch. of England. Home: 6 Park Hill Rd, Harborne Birmingham B17 9SL, England Office: U Birmingham, PO Box 363, Birmingham B15 2TT, England

DOLJACK, BARBARA LYNN, publishing company executive; b. Cleve., Mar. 14, 1942; d. Rudolph Frank and Mary Jean Doljack; student Ohio Dominican Coll., 1960-62, Tobe-Coburn Sch. Fashion Careers, N.Y.C., 1963. With Bloomingdale's, N.Y.C., 1963-66, asst. fashion dir., 1964-66; sr. merchandising coordinator Seventeen Mag., N.Y.C., 1966-69, merchandising editor, 1969-71, merchandising dir., 1971-76; dir. promotion services Seventeen mag., 1976-82, mktg. dir. direct merchandising, pub. relations, promotion, composing and buy-by-mail depts., 1982—; dir. promotion services Panorama mag., 1979-81. Mem. exec. alumnae com. The Tobe-Coburn Sch., 1976-79, also mem. industry adv. com.; mem. various coms. The Floating Hosp., 1978—; pres. exec. com. Friends of Henry St. Settlement, 1976-78, adv. com., 1979—. Recipient Mehitabel award, 1979; The T award Tobe-Coburn Sch., 1968. Mem. N.Y. Jr. League, Mktg. Communications Execs. Internat. (chpt. bd. dirs. 1977-79), Advt. Women of N.Y., Nat. Home Fashions League, Women in Communications, The Fashion Group (v.p. bd. govs. 1981-83). Club: Gardiner's Bay Country. Home: 310 E 70 St New York NY 10021 Office: 850 Third Ave New York NY 10022

DOLL, PADDY ANN, psychologist, educator; b. Shreveport, La., July 31, 1928; d. Charles and Helen (D'Artois) D. B.A., Centenary Coll., 1948; M.A., La. State U., 1952; Ph.D., U. Houston, 1969. Lic. psychologist, La. Personnel dir. Doll Bros., Shreveport, 1948-54, v.p., Doll Investments, 1954-78, pres., 1978—; asst. prof. McNeese State U., Lake Charles, La., 1956-61; teaching fellow U. Houston, 1961-64; asst. prof. dept. psychology Loyola U., New Orleans, 1964-71, assoc. prof., 1971-87, prof., 1987—, chmn. dept., 1966-69, 76-78, 81-85; psychol. dir. St. Mary's Residential Sch. for Mentally Retarded, Clarks, La., 1953-56; prof. Notre Dame Sem., New Orleans, 1968-71; cons. in field; mem. La. State Bd. Examiners Psychology, 1978-82, sec.-treas., 1978-79, vice-chmn., 1979-82. Author: Toplevel Executives, 1965. Contbr. articles to profl. jours. Bd. dirs. La. Assn. Retarded Children, 1952-56; bd. dirs. Magnolia Sch., New Orleans, 1966-69. Mem. Am. Psychol. Assn., Southwestern Psychol. Assn., La. Psychol. Assn., Southeastern Psychol. Assn., AAAS, Phi Sigma Iota, Sigma Pi Sigma, Psi Chi, Delta Omicron, Delta Phi Alpha. Republican. Roman Catholic. Office: Loyola U Psychology Dept 6363 Saint Charles Ave New Orleans LA 70118

DOLL, WILLIAM ELDER, JR., educator; b. Detroit, Jan. 29, 1931; s. William Elder and Anne (Moran) D.; B.A. in Philosophy, Cornell U., 1953; M.A., Boston U., 1960; Ph.D. in Edn., Johns Hopkins U., 1972; m. Mary Elizabeth Aswell, June 25, 1966; 1 son, William Campbell. Tchr., Mass., Colo. and N.Y. State, 1954-64; headmaster Valley Sch., Owings Mills, Md., 1964-67; mem. faculty SUNY Coll.-Oswego, 1971-85. Assoc. prof. edn., 1975-85, chmn. dept. elem. edn., 1980-82, coordinator, 1983-85; dir. tchr. preparation programs U. Redlands, Calif., 1985-87; assoc. prof. curriculum La. State U., Baton Rouge, 1988—. Mem. Fulton Bd. Edn., 1983-85. Grantee SUNY, 1979, 80. Mem. Am. Ednl. Research Assn., Am. Ednl. Studies Assn., Assn. Supervision and Curriculum Devel., John Dewey Soc., Philosophy of Edn. Soc., Soc. Profs. Curriculum, Soc. Profs. Edn. Democrat. Roman Catholic. Author papers in field. Home: 69 Belle Grove Destrehan LA 70047 Office: Peabody Hall Louisiana State Univ Baton Rouge LA 70803

DOLLERUP, ERIK CAY KREBS, philologist; b. Buenos Aires, Argentina, Nov. 12, 1939; arrived Denmark, 1946; s. Jens Peter and Margot Marie (Krebs) D.; m. Aase Poulsen, June 9, 1972 (div. 1976); 1 son, Carsten; m. Susanne Jorgensen, June 20, 1981; children: Karen Marie, Niels Peter. Cand. mag., U. Copenhagen, 1970. Jr. research asst. Dept. English, U. Copenhagen, 1970-73, sr. research asst., 1973-76, sr. lectr., 1976—, founder research unit exptl. studies in reader response, 1984; cons. linguistic services EEC, Brussels, 1974, 75. Author: Denmark, Hamlet and Shakespeare, 1975; Omkring Sproglig Transmission, 1978; contbr. numerous articles to profl. jours.; editor: Volve: Scandinavian Views on Science Fiction, 1978. Chmn. adv. com. on univ. affairs Dansk Magisterforening, Copenhagen, 1977-80. Served with Danish Army, 1958-59. Mem. Internat. Reading Assn., MLA, World Assn. Applied Linguistics, Assn. Univ. Tchrs. (exec. bd. 1986-87), Det Filologisk Historiske Samfund. Home: Engtoftevej 4 iitv, DK-1816 Fredensborg Denmark Office: Dept English, Njalsgade 80, DK-2300 Copenhagen V Denmark

DOLMANS, SERVÉ MARIE JOSEPH EDMOND, surgeon; b. Maastricht, S. Limburg, Netherlands, Mar. 6, 1946; came to Belgium, 1958, naturalized, 1985; s. Pierre Hubert Marie and Hubertha Anna Maria (Niesten) D.; m. Christine Marie Marthe Julienne Brasseur, May 5, 1973; children—Marie-Madeleine, Pierre, Guillaume, Serve Jr., Bieuc, Michel. Degree with highest distinction, St. Joseph Coll., St. Pieters-Wol, Brussels, 1964; degree with highest distinction in medicine U. Louvain, Leuven, 1968, M.D. with distinction, 1972. Diplomate in gen. surgery. Attache etranger Acad. Hosp., Bordeaux, France, 1977-78; sci. resident, Acad. Hosp., Leuven, Belgium, 1978-79; chief resident Acad. Hosp., Antwerp, Belgium, 1979-80; surgeon in chief Elisabeth Hosp., Antwerp, 1980—; cons. microsurgeon Acad. Hosp., Antwerp, 1980—. Contbr. articles to sci. jours. Grantee Nat. Fund for Med. Research, 1978-79. Fellow Internat. Microsurg. Soc.; mem. Royal Belgian Soc. for Surgery, Belgian Soc. Med. Specialists, AO Internat. (Belgian sect.). Avocation: painting. Home: 66 Avenue de la Chapelle, 1200 Brussels Belgium

DOLTO-TOLITCH, CATHERINE, family practitioner; b. Le Croisic, France, Aug. 8, 1946; d. Boris Ivanovitch and Fransoise Marette Dolto; m. Ranko Tolitch, Nov. 12, 1984. B, Ecole De Theatre, 1966; D of Sociology, Sorbonne, 1970. Contbr. articles to profl. jours. Office: Cabinet Medical, 21 Rue Cujas, 75005 Paris France

DOMACHOWSKI, WALDEMAR STANISLAW, psychologist, educator; b. Poznan, Poland, Jan. 3, 1948; s. Tadeusz Domachowski and Irena (Maciejeszczak) Domachowska; m. Lidia Siatka, Jan. 28, 1984; 1 child, Irena. MA in Psychology, U. Poznan, 1973, PhD in Psychology, 1982. Lic. psychologist Commn. Ministry of Health, 1985, Commn. of Inst. of Psychology of Adam Mickiewicz U., 1973. Psychologist Mental Hosp., Koscian, Poland, 1973-75; asst. lectr. Adam Mickiewicz U. Inst. Psychology, Poznan, 1975-81; mem. sci. bd. Adam Mickiewicz U. Inst. Psychology, 1978-84, U. Poznan, 1979-83; asst. prof. Adam Mickiewicz U. Inst. Psychology, 1982—; cons. Mental Hosp. 1975-83, Ct. of Province, Poznan, 1973-83. Contbr. articles in field. Mem. adv. bd. Ctr. Intercultural Communication Marquette U., 1982. Recipient Rector's award Rector U., Poznan, 1979, 84. Mem. Polish Psychol. Soc. (bd. award 1982), European Assn. Exptl. Social Psychology. Club: Wagabunda. Home: Leczycka 11, 61-044 Poznan Szamarzewskiego 89, Poland Office: Adam Mickiewicz U, Inst Psychology, Stalingradka 89, 66-987 Poznan Poland

DOMANSKI, RYSZARD, economics educator; b. Wzdol, Kielce, Poland, Jan. 17, 1928; s. Pawel and Bronislawa (Szabla) D.; m. Irena Dunowska, July 26, 1952; children—Anna, Barbara. M.A. in Econs., Central Sch. Stats. and Planning, Poland, 1952; Ph.D. in Econs., Sch. Econs. Krakow, Poland, 1958; Dr.Sc. Geography, Poznan U., Poland, 1963. Lectr. Sch. Econs., Poznan, 1956-63, assoc. prof., 1963-69, pres., 1969-79, prof., 1969—; vis. lectr. U. Pa., Phila., 1966-67; vis. scholar U. Wash., Seattle, 1971; research scholar Internat. Inst. for Applied Systems Analysis, Luxenburg, Austria, 1980. Author: Complexes of Transport Networks, 1963; Economic Geography, 1979; Theoretical Foundations of Economic Geography, 1982. Contbr. articles to profl. jours. Vice pres. Poznan Assn. of Friends of Scis., 1978—. Recipient research award Polish Acad. Sci., 1978, Porvince of Poznan, 1984. Mem. Com. for Space Economy of Polish Acad. Sci., World Acad. Arts and Scis. (exec. com.), Regional Sci. Assn. (pres. 1981-82). Roman Catholic. Avocation: classical music. Home: Szafirowa 8, Szafirowa 8, 60-592 Poznan Poland Office: Akademia Ekonomiczna, Marchlewskiego 146/150, 60-967 Poznan Poland

DOMBEY, NORMAN DAVID, theoretical physicist; b. London, Aug. 4, 1938; s. Harry and Hetty (Morovitch) D.; m. Henrietta Mary Roberts, July 14, 1967; children—Daniel Michael, Natasha Abigail Leah. B.A., Magdalen Coll., Oxford, 1959; Ph.D., Calif. Inst. Tech., 1961. Lectr. U. Sussex, Brighton, East Sussex, U.K., 1964-69, reader theoretical physics, 1969—, assoc. fellow sci. policy research unit, 1974—; lectr. Royal Soc., Poland, 1987; vis. physicist Harvard U., 1967-68; collaborator Los Alamos Nat. Sci. Lab., N.Mex., 1978-79, 85—; specialist advisor House of Commons Select Com. on Energy, 1979-81. Contbr. articles to profl. jours., chpts. to books. Mem. Royal Inst. Internat. Affairs, London, 1984—, British Pugwash Group, London, 1975—. British Council fellow, Moscow, 1962; Leverhulme grantee, 1983. Office: U Sussex Physics Bldg, Brighton East Sussex United Kingdom BN1 9QM

DOMBROWSKI, FRANK PAUL, JR., pharmacist; b. Nashua, N.H., May 10, 1943; s. Frank Paul and Yvonne Joan (Paris) D.; B.S., Mass. Coll. Pharmacy, 1965, M.S., 1967; m. Eleanor Cassady, June 15, 1968; children—Michael, Peter, Laura, Cheryl, Douglas. Pharmacist, Androscoggin Valley Hosp., Berlin, N.H., 1974-75, Eastern Maine Med. Center, 1975-77; dir. pharm. services and central supply Concord Hosp., N.H., 1977-82; founder, pres. Hosp. Home Health Care of NH, 1982—, Hosp. Home Health Care of Maine, 1986; commr. N.H. Bd. of Registration of Pharmacy; cons. nurse anesthetist sch. Concord Hosp. Served with U.S. Army, 1968-74. Decorated Combat Inf. badge, Bronze Star medal, Army Commendation medal. Fellow Am. Acad. Med. Adminstrs.; mem. Am. Pharm. Assn., Am. Soc. Hosp. Pharmacists, N.H. Pharm. Assn., N.H. Soc. Hosp. Pharmacists, Nat. Assoc. Retail Druggists. Club: Lions (chpt. pres.). Home: RFD 1 Broadcove Dr Contoocook NH 03229 Office: 835 Hanover St Suite 104 Manchester NH 03104

DOMENICI, PETE (VICHI DOMENICI), U.S. senator; b. Albuquerque, May 7, 1932; s. Cherubino and Alda (Vichi) D.; m. Nancy Burk, Jan. 15, 1958; children: Lisa, Peter, Nella, Clare, David, Nanette, Helen, Paula. Student, U. Albuquerque, 1950-52; BS, U. N.Mex., 1954, LLD (hon.); LLB, Denver U., 1958; LLD (hon.), Georgetown U. Sch. Medicine; HHD (hon.), N.Mex. State U. Bar: N.Mex. 1958. Tchr. math. pub. schs. Albuquerque, 1954-55; ptnr. firm Domenici & Bonham, Albuquerque, 1958-72; mem. U.S. Senate from N.Mex. 1972—; mem. energy and natural resources com., chmn. subcom. on energy research and devel.; mem. com. on environ. and public works; chmn. budget com.; mem. spl. com. on aging; mem. Presdl. Adv. Com. on Federalism. Mem. Gov.'s Policy Bd. for Law Enforcement, 1967-68; chmn. Model Cities Joint Adv. Com., 1967-68; mem. Albuquerque City Commn., 1966-68, chmn. and ex-offico mayor, 1967. Mem. Nat. League Cities, Middle Rio Grande Council Govts. Home: 120 3rd St NE Washington DC 20002 Office: 434 Dirksen Senate Office Bldg Washington DC 20510 Other: 135 E 50th St #5L New York NY 10022-7515 *

DOMES, JURGEN OTTO, political scientist, educator; b. Lubeck, Germany, Apr. 2, 1932; s. Alfred and Freia (Johannsen) D.; m. Marie-Luise Nath, Apr. 29, 1977. Ph.D., Heidelberg U., 1960. Asst. polit. sci. Heidelberg U., 1960-62; vis. assoc. prof. Nat. Chengchi U., Taipei, 1963-64; jr. asso. prof. polit. sci. Free U., Berlin, 1964-69, sr. assoc. prof., 1969-75; prof. polit. sci., dir. research unit on Chinese and Asian politics The Saar U., Saarbrucken, W. Ger., 1975—, v.p., 1982-84. Recipient Sophie-Charlotte Mé daille fü r Kunst und Wissenschaft, 1975. Mem. Council on Am. Affairs, Saarland br. German Polit. Sci. Assn., German Assn. Acad. Freedom, German Assn. East Asian Studies, German Assn. Univ. Profs., Internat. Council Future of Univ. Christian Democratic Union. Author numerous books latest including Die Aussenpolitik der VR China, 1972; Internal Politics of China, 1973; China nach der Kulturrevolution, 1975; China After the Cultural Revolution, 1977; Sozialismus in China Dö rfern, 1977; Politische Soziologie der VR China, 1980; Taiwan im Wandel, 1981; Government and Politics in People's Republic of China, Time of Transition, 1985, P'eng Te-Huai, The Man and the Image, 1985. Home: Kleewag 2a, Sulzbach-Huhnerfeld Federal Republic of Germany Office: Inst fur Politikwissenschaft, U des Saarlandes, D-6600 Saarbrucken Federal Republic of Germany

D'OMÉZON, YVES PAUL CHRISTIAN, physician; b. Marseille, France, Nov. 20, 1939; s. Guy Pierre and Madeleine Nicole (Martel) d'O.; m. Carole M.L. Lombardo, Aug. 22, 1968; children: Eric, Benoit. Student, Faculté de Medecine, 1955-66, MD, 1971. Externe des hopitaux Concours de 1960, Marseille, 1960-65, interne des hopitaux, 1965; médecin asst. des hopitaux Chef de Clinique Rhumatologique a la Faculté, Marseille, 1971-77; médecin chef Centre de Rééducation ORSAC, Marseille, 1981—. Editor various books, 1973-78. Mem. Société Francaise de Rhumatologiqie, Assn. Francaise de Lutte Antirumatismale, Soc. Francaise de Nutrition, Soc. Pour le Devel. de Recherches sur le Magnesium. Lodge: Lions. Home: 429 Rue Paradis, 13008 Marseille France Office: 39 Rue Brandis, 13005 Marseille France

DOMINGO, PLACIDO, tenor; b. Madrid, Spain, Jan. 21, 1941; s. Placido and Pepita (Embil) D.; m. Marta Domingo; children: Jose, Placido, Alvaro Maurizio. Student, Conservatory in Mexico City. Made operatic debut, 1961; debut, Met. Opera, 1968; star tenor with opera cos. including, La Scala, Covent Garden, Hamburg State Opera, Vienna State Opera, N.Y.C. Opera, San Francisco Opera, Nat. Hebrew Opera in Tel-Aviv; leading roles: 50 operas including Don Rodrigo, Tosca, Andrea Chenier, Don Carlo, Carmen, La Boheme, Ernani; appeared in film: La Traviata, 1983, Carmen, 1984, Othello, 1986; recs. for RCA including Save Your Nights For Me, 1985. Recipient Grammy award Best Latin Pop Performance, 1984. Office: care Eric Semon Assocs Inc 111 W 57th St New York NY 10019 also: care Stafford Law Assocs, 26 Mayfield Rd, Weybridge Surrey KT13 8XB, England *

DOMINGUE, GERALD JAMES, microbiology, immunology and urology educator, researcher; b. Lafayette, La., Mar. 2, 1937; s. Edgar Paul and Sarah Ann (Prejean) D.; m. Marie H. Dugas, Aug. 30, 1958 (div. 1980); children: Andrea, Yvonne, Michelle, Gerald Jr., Marcel; m. Kathryn H. Colbert, June 20, 1981 (div. 1985). BA in Bacteriology, U. Southwestern La., 1958; PhD in Med. Microbiol. and Immunology, Tulane U., 1964. Postdoctoral research fellow Children's Hosp., asst. research instr. pediatrics SUNY, Buffalo, 1965-66; dir. microbiol. Snodgras Lab. of Pathology and Bacteriology, St. Louis, 1966-67; instr. microbiology St. Louis U., 1966-67; asst. prof. microbiology, immunology and urology Tulane U., New Orleans, 1967-70, assoc. prof. microbiology, immunology and urology, 1970-74, prof. microbiology, immunology and urology, 1974—; lectr. microbiology sch. dentistry Washington U., St. Louis, 1966-67; vis. prof., lectr. Peruvian Urol. Assn., Lima, 1973, First Internat. Congress Bacteriology, Jerusalem, 1973, Internat. Convocation Immunology, Buffalo, 1974, World Health Orgn. Conf. on Sperm Immunology, Aarhus, Denmark, 1974, European Soc. Exptl. Urol. Research, Wurzburg, Fed. Republic Germany, 1976, Internat. Seminar L-Forms, Montpellier, France, 1976, U. Melbourne, Royal Melbourne Hosp., Australia, 1978, XII Internat. Congress Microbiology, Munich, 1978, Internat. Symposium Vaccines and Vaccinations, Institut Pasteur, Paris, 1985; speaker U. Montpellier Sch. Medicine, 1985, 4th Internat. Congress on Pyelonephritis, Gotebor, Sweden, 1986, Orion Diagnostica, Helsinki, Finland, 1986, Nat. Inst. Hygiene, Warsaw, Poland, 1986, Symposium on Molecular Biology and Infectious Diseases, Institut Pasteur, 1987; mem. com. for infection control So. Bapt. Hosp., 1971-75, Charity Hosp. La., 1977—, Tulane U. Hosp., 1977—; mem. infectious disease com. St. Louis City Hosp., 1966-67; mem., reviewer, visitor project sites NIH Grant Review Study Sects., 1967—; cons. bacteriology So. Bapt. Hosp., New Orleans, 1968-84, Tulane U. Hosp., 1978-83, Med. Tech. Corp., Somerset, N.J., 1983—; research cons. VA Hosp., New Orleans, 1970-78; cons., mem. tech. adv. bd. Analytab Products, Inc., N.Y.C., 1972-77. Author, editor: Cell Wall-Deficient Bacteria, 1962; editorial bd. cons. numerous jours.; contbr. over 100 articles to profl. jours. and chpts. to books. Pres. France-Louisiane de la Nouvelle Orleans, 1985—; apptd. mem. Council for Devel. of French Lang. in La.; mem. Met. Area Com., New Orleans, 1987, Bur. Govtl. Research, New Orleans, 1987; mem. Mayor's Com. New Orleans-Paris Cultural Exchange, 1988. Served with La. N.G., USAR, 1955-63. Guaranty scholar U. Southwestern La., 1958; grantee NIH, 1970—, NSF, Kaiser Research Found., Schlieder Found., Armour Pharm. House, VA, Cadwallader Family Donation, Med. Tech. Corp., Orion Diagnostica. Fellow Am. Acad. Microbiology, Infectious Disease Soc. Am.; mem. Am. Soc. Microbiology (divisional lectr. 1978, found. lectr. 1979-80), Soc. for Exptl. Biology and Medicine, AAAS, Am. Assn. Univ. Profs., Fedn. Am. Scientists, Southwestern Assn. Clin. Microbiology (editor newsletter 1983-85, pres. 1985-86), Sigma Xi. Republican. Roman Catholic. Home: 3540 rue Michelle New Orleans LA 70114 Office: Tulane U Sch Medicine 1430 Tulane Ave New Orleans LA 70112

DOMINIONI, ANGELO MARIA FRANCESCO, import-export co. exec.; b. Naples, Italy, Jan. 31, 1932; came to U.S., 1968; s. Giacinto Enrico and Jole (Vuturo) D.; student U. Messina (Italy), 1950-56; m. Valerie Ann Morrone, Aug. 25, 1971; 1 dau., Silvana Laura. With Securities Dept., Banco Di Sicilia, Milan, 1958-62; with SFI S.p.A., Milan, Italy, 1962-66; with Galbani S.p.A., Milan, Italy, 1966—, pres. Bel Paesesales Co. Inc. div., Galbani Inc., Brick, N.J., 1981—, also dir.; mktg. cons. Mem. Am. Mgmt. Assn., Nat. Cheese Inst., Nat. Assn. Specialty Trade. Republican. Club: Metedeconk River Yacht. Home: 47 Mizzen Rd Brick NJ 08723 Office: 445 Brick Blvd Suite 203 Brick NJ 08723

DOMJAN, LASZLO KAROLY, newspaper executive; b. Kormend, Hungary, Apr. 19, 1947; came to U.S., 1956; s. Frank and Violet (Pinter) D.; m. Louise Replogle, June 6, 1969; children: Andrew P., Eric S. BJ, U. Mo., 1969. Copy editor St. Louis Globe-Democrat, 1969; reporter, bureau chief UPI, St. Louis, 1969-81; reporter, night city editor St. Louis Post-Dispatch, 1981—, exec. city editor, 1987—. Journalistic writings include: author, editor Dioxin: Quandary for the 80's, 1983 (numerous awards), author, reporter series Hungary: Thirty Years After, 1986. Active Leadership St.

Louis, 1987—. Recipient Herb Trask award Sigma Delta Chi, St. Louis, 1968. Roman Catholic. Office: St Louis Post-Dispatch 900 N Tucker Blvd Saint Louis MO 63101

DOMM, ALICE, lawyer; b. Phila., May 22, 1954; d. William Donald and Alice Frances (Day) D.; m. Richard Coles Grubb, Sept. 26, 1987. B.A., Gettysburg Coll. (Pa.), 1976; J.D., Rutgers U., 1981. Bar: N.J. 1981, Pa. 1981. Atty., juvenile sect. chief Office of the Pub. Defender, New Brunswick, N.J., 1982—; assoc. prof. Glassboro Coll. (N.J.), 1980-81. Bd. dirs. Police Athletic League, New Brunswick, 1982-85; mem. Middlesex County Youth Services Commn., New Brunswick; steering treas. Middlesex County Women Lawyers Com.; mem. Gov.'s Council on Child Abuse and Neglect, Middlesex County, Gov.'s com. childrens Services Planning Juvenile Justice Subcom.; mem. Middlesex County Commn. Child Abuse and Missing Children, Criminal Justice Planning Com. Middlesex County. Mem. ABA, N.J. Bar Assn., Middlesex County Bar Assn. (trustee), Middlesex County Women's Bar Assn. (steering com., treas.), Assn. Criminal Def. Lawyers N.J. Office: Office Pub Defender 172 New St New Brunswick NJ 08903

DOMMERMUTH, WILLIAM PETER, marketing consultant, educator; b. Chgo.; s. Peter R. and Gertrude (Schnell) D.; m. H. Joan Hasty, June 6, 1959; children: Karin, Margaret, Jean. B.A., U. Iowa; Ph.D., Northwestern U., 1964. Advt. copywriter Sears, Roebuck & Co., Chgo.; sales promotion mgr. Sears, Roebuck & Co.; asst., then asso. prof. mktg. U. Tex., Austin, 1961-67; asso. prof. U. Iowa, Iowa City, 1967-68; prof. So. Ill. U., Carbondale, 1968-86, U. Mo., St. Louis, 1986—; Cons. bus. firms. Author: (with Kernan and Sommers) Promotion: An Introductory Analysis, 1970, (with Andersen) Distribution Systems, 1972, (with Marcus and others) Modern Marketing, 1975, Modern Marketing Management, 1980, Promotion: Analysis, Creativity and Strategy, 1984; contbr. articles to profl. jours. Mem. Am. Mktg. Assn. (v.p. St Louis chpt.), Am. Psychol. Assn., So. Mktg. Assn., Midwest Mktg. Assn., Phi Beta Kappa, Beta Gamma Sigma, Theta Xi, Delta Sigma Pi. Club: Frontenac Racquet. Home: 7242 S Roland Blvd Pasadena Hills MO 63121 Office: U Mo 1304 SSB Tower 8001 Natural Bridge Rd Saint Louis MO 63121

DOMONDON, OSCAR, dentist; b. Cebu City, Philippines, July 4, 1924; s. Antero B. and Ursula (Maglasang) D.; D.M.D., Philippine Dental Coll., 1951; D.D.S., Loma Linda U., 1964; m. Vicky Domondon. children—Reinelda, Carolyn, Catherine, Oscar. Came to U.S., 1954, naturalized, 1956. Dentist, Manila. (Philippines) Sanitarium and Hosp., 1952, U.S. embassy, Manila, 1952-54; pvt. practice dentistry, Long Beach, Calif., 1964—. Dentist, Children's Dental Health Center, Long Beach, part-time, 1964-68; past mem. Calif. State Bd. Dental Examiners. Past pres., Filipino Community Action Services, Inc. Served with AUS, 1946-49, 54-60. Fellow Acad. Dentistry International, Acad. Gen. Dentistry, Internat. Inst. Community Service, Acad. Internat. Dental Studies, Internat. Coll. Dentists, Am. Coll. Dentists; mem. Am. Soc. Dentistry Children, ADA, Am. Acad. Oral Radiology (award 1964), Internat. Acad. Orthodontists, Am. Soc. Clin. Hypnosis, Am. Endodontic Soc., Western Conf. Dental Examiners and Dental Sch. Deans, Fedn. of Assns. of Health Regulatory Bds., Calif. Assn. Fgn. Dental Grads. (past pres.), Filipino Dental Soc. (past pres.), Philippine Tech. and Profl. Soc. (v.p.), Am. Acad. Dentistry for Handicapped, Am. Assn. Dental Examiners, Nat. Assn. Filipino Practicing Dentists in Am. (pres.), Pierre Fauchard Acad., Acad. Continuing Edn. Republican. Lodges: Lions (past pres.), Elks (past chmn. rangers), Masons. Home: 3570 Aster St Seal Beach CA 90740 Office: 3714 Atlantic Ave Long Beach CA 90807

DÖMÖSI, PÁL BÉLA, mathematician, scientific advisor; b. Munkács, Hungary, Oct. 29, 1943; s. Pál Dömösi and Erzsébet Balázs; m. Éva Rápolti, Mar. 12, 1977; children: Enikö, Réka, Boglárka. Diploma in teaching, U. A. József, Szeged, Hungary, 1966, diploma in math., 1969; candidate of scis., Hungarian Acad. Sci., Budapest, 1983; Doctor of Univ., U. L. Kossuth, Debrecen, Hungary, 1983. Asst. mathematician Hungarian Cable Work, Szeged, 1966-67; computer operator U. A. József, Szeged, 1967-68; mathematician Bldg. Co. So. Hungary, Szeged, 1968-79; aspirant Hungarian Acad. Sci., Budapest, 1979-82; sci. advisor U. L. Kossuth, Debrecen, Hungary, 1982—; lectr. Karl Marx U. Econs., Budapest, 1982—. Contbr. articles to profl. jours.; mem. reviewer Math. Revs., R.I., 1976—. Mem. Janos Bolyai Math. Soc., J. Neumann Computer Sci. Soc., Am. Math. Soc. Home: Thuri András u 10/B, H-4034 Debrecen Hungary Office: Univ L Kossuth, Egyetem ter 1, H 4032 Debrecen Hungary

DOMPKE, NORBERT FRANK, photography studio executive; b. Chgo., Oct. 16, 1920; s. Frank and Mary (Manley) D.; m. Marjorie Gies, Dec. 12, 1964; children: Scott, Pamela. Grad. Wright Jr. Coll., 1939-40; student Northwestern U., 1946-49. Cost comptroller, budget dir. Scott Radio Corp., 1947; pres. TV Forecast, Inc., 1948-52, editor Chgo. edit. TV Guide, 1953, mgr. Wis. edit., 1954; pres. Root Photographers, Inc., Chgo., 1955—. Adv. com. photography & audiovisual tech., So. Ill. U., 1980-81; adv. bd. Gordon Tech. High Sch., 1979-86. Served with USAAC, 1943-47. CPA, Ill. Mem. United Photographers Orgn. (pres. 1970-71), Profl. Photographers Am., Profl. Sch. Photographers Am. (v.p. 1966-67, 87—, sec.-treas. 1967-69, pres. 1969-70, dir. 1971-78, treas. 1985-86, sec. 1986-87, pres. 1988—), Ill. Small Bus. Men's Assn. (dir. 1970-73), Chgo. Assn. Commerce and Industry (edn. com. 1966—), NEA, Nat. Sch. Press Assn., Ill. High Sch. Press Assn., Nat. Collegiate Sch. Press Assn., North Cen. Assn. (visitation com. 1986), Chgo. Bible Soc. (bd. advisors), Ill. C. of C. Co-founder T.V. Guide, 1947. Clubs: Barclay, Whitehall, International; Tonquish Creek Yacht, Plaza. Home: 990 N Lake Shore Dr Chicago IL 60611 Office: 1131 W Sheridan Rd Chicago IL 60660

DON, NORMAN STANLEY, research psychologist; b. Port Chester, N.Y., Oct. 2, 1934; s. William and Betty (Berson) D.; m. Ruth Stevens Tolman, June 28, 1958; children—Bronson Whitmarsh, Brent Tolman. M.S., U. Chgo., 1960; Ph.D., Union Grad. Sch., 1974. Researcher U. Chgo., 1961-65; cons. in field industry, fed., state govt., 1965-74; research assoc. Dept. Psychiatry, U. Chgo., 1974-75; investigator Am. Dental Assn., Chgo., 1976-80; pvt. practice psychology, cons., Chgo., 1975-81; dir., pres. Kairos Found., Chgo., 1981—; research assoc. U. Ill., Chgo., 1982—; lectr. in field; cons. in field. Author: The Transpersonal Crisis, 1983; contbr. articles to profl. jours.; discoverer/prin. investigator: The Canonical Effect, 1974. Epilepsy Found. Am. fellow, 1975. Mem. Biofeedback Soc. Ill. (dir. 1976-79), Am. Psychol. Assn., Biofeedback Soc. Am., AAAS. Address: Kairos Found 405 N Wabash Ave Chicago IL 60611

DONAHOO, STANLEY ELLSWORTH, orthopaedic surgeon; b. St. Joseph, Mo., Dec. 3, 1933; s. Charles Ellsworth and Opal (Cole) D.; m. Cheryl R. Donahoo; children—Shan Maureen, Brian Patrick, Mary Kathleen, Jane Eileen; stepchildren: Trina Person, Kevin Person. MD, U. Wash., 1963. Resident, Duke U., Durham, N.C., 1967-68, U.S. Naval Hosp., Oakland, Calif., 1963-67; commd. lt., U.S. Navy, 1963 advanced through grades to lt. comdr. (orthopaedic surgeon), 1971, ret. 1971; practice medicine, specializing in orthopaedic surgery, Roseburg, Oreg., 1971—; chief surgery Mercy Hosp., Roseburg, 1973-74; chief surgery Douglas Community Hosp., Roseburg, 1973, chief of staff, 1974—; cons. Guam Meml. Hosp., codir. rehab. unit, 1970-71; cons. orthopaedic surgery VA Hosp., Roseburg, 1971—; chmn. Douglas County (Oreg.) Emergency Med. Services Com., 1973-74. Trustee Douglas Community Hosp., 1975. Served with AUS, 1952-55. Diplomate Am. Bd. Orthopaedic Surgery. Fellow Am. Acad. Orthopaedic Surgeons (admissions com. region 14), North Pacific Orthopaedic Assn. (v.p. 1984-85); mem. Piedmont Orthopaedic Soc., AMA, Oreg. Med. Assn. (mem. sports medicine com., ins. and fee rev. com. 1981), Guam Med. Soc. (pres. 1970), Am. Trauma Soc. (founding mem.), Roseburg C. of C. (bd. govs. 1978—). Home: 205 Wildfern Dr Winchester OR 97495 Office: 1813 W Harvard St Suite 201 Roseburg OR 97470

DONAHUE, CHARLES BERTRAND, II, lawyer; b. Hampton, Iowa, Apr. 17, 1937; s. Charles Bertrand and Alta Margaret (Sykes) D.; m. Brenda K. Kumpf, July 18, 1961 (div. 1980); children—Kaylie Elizabeth, Megan Elizabeth; m. Kathleen L. Komnenovich, June 27, 1987. AB, Harvard Coll., 1959; JD cum laude, Cleve.-Marshall Coll. Cleve. State U., 1967. Bar: Ohio 1967, Fla. 1973. Subcontract mgr. Westinghouse Corp., Pitts., 1962-63; contract mgr. TRW, Inc., Cleve., 1963-67; ptnr. Calfee, Halter & Griswold, 1967-79; mng. ptnr. Donahue & Scanlon, Cleve., 1979—; adj. faculty Cleve.-Marshall Coll., 1973-79; dir. AExcel Corp., Life Systems, Inc., Lortec Power Systems, Inc., Vitec, Inc. Served to capt. USAF, 1959-62. Delta Theta Phi scholar, 1967; recipient Spl. Merit award, Cleve. State U., 1973, Spl. Merit award, Ohio Legal Ctr. Ins., 1972, 74. Mem. Ohio State Bar Assn., Fla. State Bar Assn., Greater Cleve. Bar Assn., Estate Planning Council, Cleve.-Marshall Law Alumni (pres., trustee 1972). Republican. Episcopalian. Clubs: Harvard (Kingswood, Ohio and Cleve.). Avocations: traveling, cooking, reading. Home: 827 Brick Mill Run Rd Westlake OH 44145 Office: Donahue & Scanlon 3300 Terminal Tower Cleveland OH 44113-2294

DONAHUE, HAYDEN HACKNEY, mental health institute administrator, medical educator, psychiatric consultant; b. El Reno, Okla., Dec. 4, 1912; s. Henry Hilton and Mame (Hackney) D.; m. Patricia Toothaker; children—Erin Kathleen, Kerry Shannon, Patricia Marie. B.S., U. Kans., 1939, M.D., 1941. Cert. mental hosp. adminstr.; cert. mental health adminstr. Draftsman, topographer Wilson Constrn. Co., Salina, Kans., 1934; constrn. engr. Pub. Works Adminstrn., State of Kans., 1935-37, efficiency engr. Dept. Inspections and registration, 1937; intern U. Ga. Sch. Medicine Hosp., 1941-42, resident in psychiatry, 1942; resident in aviation medicine Army Air Force Sch. Aviation Medicine, 1943; resident in psychiatry Ark. State Hosp., Little Rock, 1959-61; asst. chief hosp. ops. VA, Washington, 1946; exec. officer, acting mgr. VA Hosp., North Little Rock, Ark., 1946-49; dir. edn. and research Ark. State Hosp., Little Rock, 1949-51; asst. med. dir. Tex. Bd. for Hosps. and Spl. Schs., 1951-52; dir. mental health State of Okla., 1952-59; dir. projects Ark. State Hosp., 1959-61; supt. Central State Hosp., Norman, Okla., 1961-79; asst. dir. dept. mental health State of Okla., 1966-70, dir. dept. mental health, 1970-78; dir. Okla. Inst. for Mental Health Edn. and Tng., Norman, 1979—; cons. in psychiatry Ark. Health Dept., 1949-51, Okla. Crime Bur., 1964—, Base Hosp., Tinker Field, 1964-70; chief cons. Okla. State Penitentiary, 1963-79; cons. to NIMH, 1969-70, USMC, Viet Nam, 1970; instr. medicine and psychiatry U. Ga. Sch. Medicine, 1942; lectr. in psychiatry AAF Redistbn. Ctr., Atlantic City, 1944; lectr. lect. legal medicine U. Tex. Sch. Law, 1952; lectr. Homicide Inst., U. Okla, U. Tex., 1953-67; lectr. scholarly lecture series U. Okla. 1965-70, mem. faculty and adv. com. U. Okla. Health Sci. Ctr., 1975-78; clin. prof. psychiatry U. Okla. Sch. Medicine, 1967-87, emeritus clin. prof. psychiatry and behavioral scis., 1988—; assoc. prof. pysychiatry U. Ark. Sch. Medicine, 1949-51, 1960-61, U. Okla. Sch. Medicine, 1958-67, also numerous others; bd. dirs., treas. Pan Am. Tng. Exchange in Psychiatry, 1961-63; mem. ABA Commn. on Mentally Disabled, 1973-80; pres. L.F. Am. Coll. Psychiatrists, 1975-76. Contbr. numerous articles to profl. jours. Advisor Okla. com. President's Com. on Employment of Handicapped, 1957-59, 61—; mem. Okla. Health Planning Commn. Served with M.C., USAAF, 1942-46. Recipient Health Planning award Okla. Health Planning Council, 1978, Bowis award, 1978; Outstanding Service award Okla. Health Welfare Assn., 1967; Donahue Appreciation Day declared State of Okla., 1959; elected to Okla. Hall of Fame, 1968, numerous other awards. Fellow AAAS, Am. Assn. for Mental Deficiency, ACP, Am. Psychiat. Assn. (life, pres. Okla. dist. br. 1963, del. Okla. 1957-95, 66-81, chmn. budget com., treas. 1966-80, treas., dir., exec. com. 1969-73, vice chmn. counsil internal affairs 1981—, Disting. Service award 1984), Am. Geriatrics Soc., Am. Assn. Psychiat. Adminstrs. (pres. 1974-75, dir. 1967-75, com. on continuing edn. 1979—); mem. AMA, Nat. Assn. for Mental Health (program dir., profl. adv. com. 1970-78), Okla. Med. Assn. (chmn. council pub. and mental health 1962-70, ho. of dels. 1964—, A.H. Robins Community Service award 1979), Cleveland-McClain County Med. Soc., Oklahoma County Med. Soc., Okla. Health Planning Commn., Mid-Continent Psychiat. Assn. (pres. 1962-66), Am. Med. Correctional Assn. Nat. Acad. Religion and Mental Health, Nat. Rehab. Assn., Am. Rehab. Assn., Okla. Rehab. Assn. (pres. 1969), ABA (commn. mentally disabled 1973-80, mem. exec. com. 1973-80), Norman C. of C. Methodist. Lodge: Rotary. Home: 1109 Westbrooke Terr Norman OK 73072 Office: Okla Inst for Mental Health Edn Tng PO Box 151 Norman OK 73030

DONAHUGH, ROBERT HAYDEN, library administrator; b. St. Paul, May 20, 1930; s. Robert Emmett and Elmyra Elanore (Hayden) D. B.A., Coll. St. Thomas, 1952; M.A., U. Minn., 1953. Instr. English and speech Robert Coll., Istanbul, Turkey, 1956-57; head tech. services Canton (Ohio) Public Library, 1957-62; asst. dir. Public Library of Youngstown and Mahoning County, Ohio, 1962-79; dir. Public Library of Youngstown and Mahoning County, 1979—. Author: Evaluation of Reference Resources in 8 Public Libraries in 4 Ohio Counties, 1970; contbr. book revs. to Library Jour., 1958—; contbr. radio program WYSU-FM, 1976—. Served with M.P. U.S. Army, 1954-56. Mem. ALA, Ohio Library Assn. (pres. 1975, Ohio Librarian of Yr. 1983-84), Midwest Fedn. Library Assns. (pres. 1979-83). Lodges: Elks, Rotary. Home: 509 Ferndale Ave Youngstown OH 44511 Office: 305 Wick Ave Youngstown OH 44503

DONALD, ALEXANDER GRANT, psychiatrist; b. Darlington, S.C., Jan. 24, 1928; s. Raymond George and Chesnut Evans (McIntosh) D.; m. Emma Louise Coggeshall, Oct. 25, 1958; children: Sandy, Mary Chesnut, Marion Lide. B.S., Davidson Coll., 1948; M.D., Med. U. S.C., 1952. Diplomate: Am. Bd. Psychiatry and Neurology. Intern Jefferson Med. Coll., 1952-53; resident in psychiatry Walter Reed Hosp., 1956-59; dir. Mental Health Clinic, Florence, S.C., 1962-66; dept. commr. S.C. Dept. Mental Health, 1966-67; dir. William S Hall Psychiat. Inst., Columbia, 1967—; prof., chmn. dept. neuropsychiatry and behavioral scis. Sch. Medicine, U. S.C., Columbia, 1975—, assoc. dean student affairs, 1982—. Served to maj. U.S. Army, 1953-62. Fellow Am. Coll. Psychiatrists, So. Psychiat. Assn., Am. Psychiat. Assn. (pres. S.C. dist. br. 1967), Am. Coll. Mental Health Adminstrn.; mem. AMA, Columbia Med. Soc. (v.p. 1981, del. 1981). Presbyterian. Office: U SC Sch Med Dept Neurology PO Box 202 Columbia SC 29202

DONALDSON, GEORGE BURNEY, chemical company executive; b. Oakland, Calif., Mar. 16, 1945; s. George T. and L.M. (Burney) D.; m. Jennifer L. Bishop, Feb. 16, 1974; children: Dawn Marie, Paul Matthew. AS in Criminology, Porterville Coll., 1972. Police officer City of Lindsay (Calif.), 1966-67; distbn. mgr. Ortho div. Chevron Chem. Co., Lindsay, 1967-73; safety specialist Wilbur-Ellis Co. Fresno, Calif., 1973-77, safety dir., 1977-79, dir. regulatory affairs, 1979—; industry rep. to White House Inter-Govtl. Sci. Engring., and Tech. Adv. Panel, Task Force on Transp. of Non-Nuclear Hazardous Materials, 1980; industry rep. Transp. Research Bd.'s Nat. Strategies Conf. on Transp. of Hazardous Materials and Wastes in the 1980's, Nat. Acad. Scis., 1981, Hazardous Materials Transp. Conf., Nat. Conf. of State Legislatures, 1982; chair industry/govt. task force for unique on-site hazardous waste recycling, devel. task force for computerized regulatory software and data base system, devel. task force modifying high expansion foam tech. for fire suppression; hazardous materials adviser, motor carrier rating com. Calif. Hwy. Patrol, 1978-79. Served with U.S. Army, 1962-65. Mem. Western Agrl. Chems. Assn. (chmn. transp., distbn. and safety com., outstanding mem. of year 1981, govtl. affairs com.), Nat. Agrl. Chems. Assn. (past chmn. transp. and distbn. com., occupational safety and health com., environ. mgmt. com., state affairs com.), Am. Soc. Safety Engrs., Calif. Fertilizer Assn. (transp. and distbn. com., environ. com.), Fresno City and County C. of C. (agrl. steering com., govt. affairs com.), Calif. C. of C. (environ. policy com.), Am. Legion. Republican. Lodge: Elks. Office: 191 W Shaw Ave Suite 107 Fresno CA 93704

DONALDSON, JOHN CECIL, JR., consumer products company executive; b. Bklyn., Dec. 8, 1933; s. John Cecil and Josephine (Greason) D.; m. Marilyn J. Smith, Aug. 29, 1959; children: Susan, John III. AB, Brown U., 1956; MBA, U. Pa., 1959; student, Bentley Sch. of Acctg., Boston, 1957, LaSalle Law Sch., Chgo., 1959. Various positions Gen. Motors Corp., Flint, Mich., 1960-71; zone mgr. Gen. Motors Corp., Buffalo, 1971-76; zone mgr. Gen. Motors Corp., Newark, 1976-77, mgr. forward product planning, 1977-78; from dir. sales and mktg. to v.p. Corbin Ltd., 1979-85; exec. v.p. and gen. mgr. TMG Corp., N.Y.C., 1986—; pres. Gen. Motors Exec. Club, Newark, N.J., 1977-78. Mem. Am. Mktg. Assn. Republican. Home: 36 Nottingham Way Millington NJ 07946

DONALDSON, LESLIE WELLINGTON (LES), JR., research institute executive; b. Washington, Dec. 29, 1953; s. Leslie W. and Conchita (Newman) D.; m. Karen E. Mitchell, June 19, 1976; children: Adrienne S. Donaldson, Brittany L. BS in Chem. Engring., Newark Coll. Engring., 1974; postgrad., Loyola U. Chgo., 1988—. Process engr. Airco, Inc., Murray Hill, N.J., 1974-77; project engr. Celanese Corp., Louisville, 1977-83; project mgr. indsl. research and devel. Gas Research Inst., Chgo., 1983-86, mgr., 1986—. Mem. Am. Inst. Chem. Engrs., Am. Ceramic Soc. Republican. Avocations: racquetball, golf. Office: Gas Research Inst 8600 W Bryn Mawr Ave Chicago IL 60631

DONALDSON, TAMSIN JANE, linguist, educator; b. London, July 31, 1939; came to Australia, 1969; d. Willmot Ayton and Phoebe Mary (Nance) Procter; m. Charles Ian Donaldson, Mar. 6, 1962; children: Benjamin, Sadie. BA, Oxon (Somerville Coll.), Oxford, 1962; diploma in pub. and social adminstrn., Oxon, 1964; MA, Oxon (Somerville Coll.), Oxford, 1967; PhD in linguistics, Australian Nat. U., Canberra, 1977. Tchr. English Brit. Council, 1961-62, Oxford City Edn. Authority, 1965-69; lectr. Sch. Australian Linguistics, Darwin Community Coll., 1979, 81; audiographer Australian Inst. Aboriginal Studies, Canberra, 1979-86; lectr. Sydney U., Dept. Anthropology, Australia, 1982, 83; research affiliate Australian Inst. Aboriginal Studies, 1984; postdoctoral fellow Soc. for Humanities, Cornell U., Ithaca, N.Y., 1987-88; cons. in linguistics Anutech, Canberra, 1984. Author: Ngiyambaa, the Language of the Wangaaybuwan, 1980; co-editor Seeing the First Australians, 1985, Songs of Aboriginal Australia, 1987; contbr. articles to jours. Abortion counselor Women's Liberation Orgn., Canberra, 1972-74. RecipientEthel Mary Grant Read research grant Royal Zool. Soc., New South Wales, 1986, numerous other scholarship and project grants, 1972-88. Office: Soc for Humanities Cornell U Ithaca NY 14853-1110

DO NASCIMENTO, ALEXANDER CARDINAL, archbishop; b. Malanje, Angola, Mar. 1, 1925. Ordained priest Roman Catholic Ch., 1952; prof. dogmatic theology in maj. sem. of Luanda (Angola); editor Cath. newspaper O Apostolada; in exile, Lisbon, Portugal, 1961-71, returned to Angola, 1971; then prof. Pius XII Inst. Social Scis.; consecrated bishop of Malanje, 1975; consecrated archbishop of Lubango and apostolic adminstr. of Onjiva, 1977; held hostage by Angolan guerrillas in 1982; elevated to Sacred Coll. of Cardinals, 1983; titular see, St. Mark in Agro Laurentino. Mem. Congregation for Evangelization of Peoples. Address: Arcebispado CP 231, Lubango Angola *

DONATI, GIAN CARLO, trading company executive; b. Parma, Italy, Sept. 3, 1929; s. Severino and Gabbi Anita Gian Carlo; m. Milena Cocconi, July 6, 1952; 1 child, Patrizia. Grad. in mktg., U. Parma, Italy, 1956. With Banca Comml. Italy, Milan, 1947-52; mgr. Ente Fiere, Parma, 1952-74; internat. dir. Salvarani SpA, Parma, 1974-78; chmn. bd. dirs. Intermktg. Corp., Parma. Contbr. articles to profl. jours. Decorated Commendatore Republic of Italy, 1977. Mem. Confedn. Italiana Dirigenti D'Azienda. Roman Catholic. Home: Via Corsica 139, Brescia Italy Office: Viale Tanara 43, 43100 Parma Italy

DONATI, ROBERT MARIO, physician, educational administrator; b. Richmond Heights, Mo., Feb. 28, 1934; s. Leo S. and Rose Marie (Gualdoni) D. B.S. in Biology, St. Louis U., 1955, M.D., 1959. Diplomate: Am. Bd. Nuclear Medicine, bd. dirs., 1980-86, vice chmn. 1984-85, chmn. 1985-86. Intern St. Louis City Hosp., 1959-60; asst. resident John Cochran Hosp., St. Louis, 1960-62; fellow in nuclear medicine St. Louis U., 1962-63; practice medicine specializing in nuclear medicine St. Louis, 1963—; mem. staff John Cochran Hosp., 1963-83, St. Louis U. Hosp., 1963—; mem. faculty St. Louis U. Sch. Medicine, 1963—, asst. prof. internal medicine, 1965-68, assoc. prof., 1968-74, prof., 1974—, prof. radiology, 1979—, dir. div. nuclear medicine, 1968-87, sr. assoc. dean, 1983—; exec. assoc. v.p. Med. Ctr., 1985—; acting v.p. Med. Ctr., 1986; chief nuclear medicine services St. Louis VA Med. Center, 1968-79, chief of staff, 1979-83; adj. prof. medicine Washington U. Sch. Medicine, 1979-83; Del. Am. Bd. Med. Spltys., 1982—, fin. com., 1984-87; councilor Federated Council Member Medicine Orgns., 1981-85. Editor: (with W. T. Newton) Radioassay in Clinical Medicine, 1974; Contbr. articles to profl. jours. Mem. Presdl. Adv. Commn. on VA, 1972; Bd. dirs. Inst. for Health Mgmt., Inc., 1976-78, Alliance for Community Health Inc., 1986—, Ind. Colls. and Univs. of Mo., 1985, Affiliated Med. Transport, Inc., 1985—, Healthline Mgmt. Services, Inc., 1986—; mem. HEW Task Force on Health Effects of Ionizing Radiation, 1978-79; mem. desegregation monitoring and adv. com. U.S. Dist. Ct., 1980-82; mem. Multi-Hosp. Systems Nat. Adv. Com., 1982-84. Served to capt. AUS, 1966-68. Decorated Army Commendation medal; recipient VA Disting. Service award, 1983. Mem. AMA (residency rev. com. for nuclear medicine 1978-80), St. Louis Med. Soc., Am. Fedn. for Clin. Research (councilor 1967-70), Central Soc. Clin. Research, AAUP, N.Y. Acad. Scis., Soc. Exptl. Biology and Medicine, Soc. Nuclear Medicine (acad. council 1970 , bd. trustee 1977-81, assoc. chmn. sci. program 1978, mem. publs. com. 1979—, chmn. 1982-83), Am. Coll. Nuclear Physicians, Am., Internat. socs. hematology, Soc. Med. Consultants to Armed Forces, Sigma Xi, Alpha Omega Alpha, Phi Beta Kappa. Roman Catholic. Clubs: Cosmos (Washington); Racquet (St. Louis). Home: 5335 Botanical Ave Saint Louis MO 63110 Office: St Louis U Sch Medicine 1325 S Grand Blvd Saint Louis MO 63104

DONATO, ALFRED VIRGIL, electrical engineer, consultant; b. N.Y.C., Feb. 8, 1917; s. Philip and Mary (Tafuri) D.; m. Josephine Louise Marsiglia, Sept. 7, 1947; 1 child, Beverly. BS Elect. Engring. NYU, 1940; MS in Electric Ship Propulsion, Poly., Inst., 1943. Cert. profl. engr., Md. Elec. engr. marine Gibbs & Cox, N.Y.C., 1940-45, Gen. Elec., Schenectady, N.Y., 1945-47, Bethleham Steel Ship Building, Balt., 1947-50, Gen. Services Adminstrn., Washington, 1950-53; interdisciplinary supervisory elec. engr. Dept. of Army Corps of Engrs. New Dist., N.Y.C., 1953—; cons. elec., Bklyn., 1980—; cons. estimator, Bklyn., 1968—. Author: Load Shedding brochure (Significant Achievement award Corps of Engrs., 1983), 1982. Mem. legis. adv. com. N.Y. State Senator, 21st Dist., Albany, 1979; mem. Republican Nat. Com., Washington; supporter St. Anselmi Catholic Ch., Bklyn. Recipient Superior Performance award Corps of Engrs., 1967, 76, Significant Achievement award Corps of Engrs., 1984, 85, Outstanding Leadership award Corps of Engrs., 1987. Mem. Soc. Naval Architects and Marine Engrs., Am. Mil. Engrs., AIEE, N.Y. Acad. Scis. Clubs: Crescent Hill, Athletic. Avocations: ship and airplane models. Office: Dept Army Corps Engrs NY Dist 26 Federal Plaza New York NY 10278

DONATONI, FRANCO, composer, educator; b. Verona, Italy, June 9, 1927; s. Silvio and Dolores (Stefanucci) D.; student conservatory Bologna and Rome; m. Susan Park, Sept. 20, 1958; children—Roberto, Renato. Prof. composition U. Bologna, 1953-55, U. Milan, 1955-67, 69—, Turin, 1967-69; docent composizione conservatorio Verdi, Milan, 1969-78; tchr. course Accademia di Santa Cecilia, Rome, 1978; docente course advanced composition Acad. Chigiana, Siena, 1970; composer: Puppenspiel, 1961; Sezioni, 1960; Per Orchestra, 1962; Quartetto IV, 1963; Asar, 1964; Puppenspiel (2), 1965; Souvenir, 1967; Etwas ruhiger im Ausdruck, 1967; Doubles II, 1969-70; Questo, 1970; To Earle Two, 1971-72; Lied, 1972; Voci, 1973; Espressivo, 1974; Duo pour Bruno, 1975; Lumen, 1975; Ash, 1976; Portrait, 1976-77; Diario 76, 1977; Toy, 1977; Spiri, 1977; Arie, 1978; Nidi, 1979, The Heart's Eye, 1979-80, L'ultima Sera, 1980, Tè ma, 1981, Fili, 1981. Recipient Marzotto prize, 1966; Koussevitzky prize, 1968; others. Address: 39 via Bassini, 20133 Milan Italy *

DONCKERWOLCKE, EDMOND CESAR, textile executive, consultant; b. Brussels, Belgium, July 10, 1924; s. Leonce and Bertha (Demyttenaere) D.; Atheneum Bachelor, 1942; m. Elsa Billen, Oct. 10, 1944; children—Susan, Solange, Eddy, Hedwige, Jaques, Rose, David, Frank, Serge. Mgr., Cotolana, Brussels, 1944-52; free-lance rep. Belgian textile industries, 1952-57; pres. SACOTIL, Geneva, Switzerland, 1957-77; counselor, adv. Belgian textile firms, 1977-81; cons., 1981—. Adv., Chinese art studies, 1970—; adminstr. Ars Asiatica, Flanders/Belgium, 1980—. Served with Belgian Resistance, 1942-44. Decorated Medal of Resistance, Medal of War. Research in Chinese art, Wei and Tang period, 1980—. Address: 66 Dr Van Bockstaelestraat, 9218 Ledeberg Belgium

DONDELINGER, ALBERT, banker; b. Redange/Attert, Luxembourg, Mar. 22, 1934; s. Jean and Simone (Lamborelle) D.; 1 child, Sandrine. Bachelor, Coll. St. Michel, Brussels, 1952; LL.D., Belgium Cath. U. Louvain, 1958. Trainee State Savs. Bank Luxembourg, 1959; spl. trainee World Bank and IMF, 1961; attache Banking Control Commn., Luxembourg, 1959-64, prin. insp., 1964, joint mgr., 1965, vice commr., 1966-67, commr., 1968-76; pres., mng. dir. Banque Internationale à Luxembourg, 1977—; alt. gov. for Luxembourg at IBRD - World Bank, 1967-76; mem. European Monetary Com., 1971-76; mem. bd. Institut Belgo-Luxembourgeois du Change, 1972-76; advisor to group of twenty in charge internat. monetary system reform, later assoc. mem. IMF interim com., 1972-76; mem. bd. European Monetary Cooperation Fund, also mem. govs.' com. EEC Central Banks, 1973-76; co-chmn. commn. for fin. affairs Conf. for Internat. Econ. Cooperation, Paris, 1975-76; pres. Luxembourg nat. com. European League for Econ. Cooperation; chmn. bd. BIL (Asia) Ltd., Singapore, Société Électrique de l'Our; dir. Luxair S.A., Société de la Bourse de Luxembourg S.A., Philips Internat. Fin. S.A., La Compagnie Luxembourgeoisede Télédiffusion, other companies; mem. monetary commn. Internat. C. of C. Pres. Cercle Artistique de Luxembourg; bd. dirs. Found. Prince Henri-Princesse Maria Teresa for integration of disabled persons. Decorated comdr. Ordre de la Couronne (Belgium); comdr. Ordre Nat. (Ivory Coast); officier Ordre Nat. du Mé rite (France); officier Ordre de la Couronne de Chêne, officier Ordre Nat. du Mérite (Luxembourg). Fellow Internat. Bankers Assn.; mem. Luxembourg Bankers Assn. (chmn. 1977-78), Institut Internat. d'Etudes Bancaires. Clubs: Rotary Internat. (Luxembourg-Kiem); Overseas Bankers (London). Avocations: photography, golf, skiing, tennis. Home: rue de Cents, L-1319 Luxembourg Luxembourg

DONE, DEREK EDWIN, economist; b. London, Nov. 11, 1932; s. Harold William and Ivy Mabel Marion (Last) D.; m. Margaret Rogers, Oct. 25, 1967; 1 child, Stephen. BSc, U. Coll., London, 1954; MSc in Econs., Birkbeck Coll., London, 1977. Long-range planner Brit. European Airways, London, 1959-62; mkt. research officer Brit. Overseas Airways Corp., London, 1962-63; asst. economist Transport Holding Co., London, 1963-69; economist Nat. Bus Co., London, 1969-70; asst. corp. planning mgr. Brit. Airways, London, 1974-77, econ. research mgr., 1977—; vis. lectr. econs. City U., London, 1984-87; mem. exec. com. Brit. Airways Trade Union Council. Contbr. articles to profl. jours. Mem. Assn. Supr., Tech. and Managerial Staffs (treas. 1984-87), IATA (chmn. traffic forecasting group 1978); fellow Chartered Inst. Transport, Inst. Travel and Tourism, Royal Statistical Soc. Social and Liberal Democrat. Methodist. Home: 13 Harwood Rd, Marlow SL7 2AR, England Office: British Airways, PO Box 10 Heathrow Airport, Hounslow TW6 2JA, England

DONEGAN, CHARLES EDWARD, lawyer, educator; b. Chgo., Apr. 10, 1933; s. Arthur C. and Odessa (Arnold) D.; m. Patty Lou Harris, June 15, 1963; 1 son, Carter Edward. B.S.C., Roosevelt U., 1954; M.S., Loyola U., 1959; J.D., Howard U., 1967; LL.M., Columbia, 1970. Bar: N.Y. 1968, D.C. 1968, Ill. 1979. Pub. sch. tchr. Chgo., 1956-59; with Office Internal Revenue, Chgo., 1959-62; labor economist U.S. Dept. Labor, Washington, 1962-65; legal intern U.S. Commn. Civil Rights, Washington, summer 1966; asst. counsel NAACP Legal Def. Fund, N.Y.C., 1967-69; lectr. law Baruch Coll., N.Y.C., 1969-70; asst. prof. law State U. N.Y. at Buffalo, 1970-73; assoc. prof. law Howard U., 1973-77; vis. assoc. prof. Ohio State U., Columbus, 1977-78; asst. regional counsel U.S. EPA, 1978-80; prof. law So. U., Baton Rouge, 1980—; sole practice law Chgo. and Washington, 1984—; arbitrator steel industry, 1972—, U.S. Postal Service, New Orleans, D.C. Superior Ct., 1987—, Fed. Mediation and Conciliation Service, 1985—; vis. prof. law La. State U., summer 1981; real estate broker; mem. bd. consumer claims Dist. D.C., 1988—. Author: Discrimination in Public Employment, 1975; Contbr. articles to profl. jours., to Dictionary Am. Negro Biography. Active Americans for Democratic Action. Named Most Outstanding Prof. So. U. Law Sch., 1982; Ford Found. scholar, 1965-67; Ford Found. fellow Columbia U., 1972-73; Nat. Endowment for Humanities postdoctoral fellow in Afro-Am. studies Yale, 1972-73. Mem. ABA (vice chmn. com. edn. and curriculum local govt. law sect. 1972—, mem. pub. edn. com. sect. local govt. 1974—, chmn. liaison com. AALS), Nat. Bar Assn., D.C. Bar Assn., Chgo. Bar Assn., Fed. Bar Assn., Cook County Bar Assn., Am. Arbitration Assn. (arbitrator), Nat. Conf. Black Lawyers (bd. organizers), Assn. Henri Capitant, Roosevelt, Loyola, Howard and Columbia alumni assns., Alpha Phi Alpha, Phi Alpha Kappa, Phi Alpha Delta. Home: 4315 Argyle Terrace NW Washington DC 20011 Office: 601 Indiana Ave NW Suite 900 Washington DC 20004 also: 30 W Washington Suite 1300 Chicago IL 60602

DONEHUE, JOHN DOUGLAS, newspaper executive; b. Cramerton, N.C., July 5, 1928; s. John Sidney and Annie (Shepherd) D.; m. Mary Phelps, Jan. 9, 1952 (dec. 1964); children: Teresa Jean, Marilyn Phelps; m. Sylvia Louise McKenzie, Feb. 11, 1966 (dec. Nov. 1971); children: Hayden Shepherd, John Douglas; m. Virginia Kirkland, June 28, 1975; children: Anne Mikell, Robertson Carr. Student Am. Press Inst., Columbia U., 1965, 71-73; D. of Humane Letters (hon.), Bapt. Coll., 1985. Sports writer Charleston, S.C. News and Courier, 1947, copy editor, 1956, state editor, 1959-62, city editor, 1962-68, mng. editor, 1968-71, promotion dir., 1971—, v.p. for corp. pub. relations, 1975—, compiler News and Courier Style Book, 1969; sports editor Orangeburg (S.C.) Times and Dem., 1948-50; polit. reporter Montgomery (Ala.) Advertiser, 1954-55; faculty advisor Bapt. Coll. at Charleston Student Newspaper; spl. adviser comdt. 7th USCG dist. for establishment dist.-wide pub. info. program, 1960-61; journalism lectr. Bapt. Coll., Charleston Coll.; sec. 1st bd. founders, 1969. Guest commentator Nat. Pub. Radio. Chmn. adv. bd. Salvation Army; chmn. regional adv. council S.C. Dept. Youth Services; chmn. United Way Planning Bd.; bd. dirs. S.C. Tricentennial Parade Com., 1972; pres. Palmetto Safety Council; Lay reader, vestryman, sr. warden Episc. Ch. Served with S.C. N.G., 1948-50, USAF, 1950-54, USMCR, 1955-56, USAR, 1956-59, USCGR, 1959-66, USNR, 1966-75. Recipient Freedoms Found. award, 1969, S.C. Family of Yr. award, Am. Advt. Fedn. Silver Medal award, 1987. Vets. Adminstrn. citation for Meritorious Service, 1971. Mem. John Ancrum Soc. of Soc. Prevention Cruelty to Animals, Carolina Art Assn., YMCA, Internat. Newspaper Promotion Assn., S.C. Press Assn. (pres. 1985), Air Force Assn. (dir. Charleston council), Navy League (v.p. Charleston council), Charleston Trident C. of C. (pres. 1983), Toastmasters Internat. (charter mem. Okinawa club), Okinawa Soc. Clubs: Downtown Athletic, Toastmasters Internat. (charter mem. Okinawa club). Lodge: Rotary (Charleston) (pres. 1974-75). Home: 66 Bull St Charleston SC 29401 Office: The News & Courier 134 Columbus St PO Box 758 Charleston SC 29401

DONELSON, ANGIE FIELDS CANTRELL MERRITT, real estate executive; b. Hermitage, Tenn., Dec. 2, 1914; d. Dempsey Weaver and Nora (Johnson) Cantrell; student public and pvt. schs., Hermitage, Nashville; m. Gilbert Stroud Merritt, Dec. 15, 1934 (dec.); 1 son, Gilbert Stroud; m. 2d, John Donelson, Jr., VII, Apr. 23, 1966 (dec.); step-children—John, Agnes Donelson Williams (dec.), William Stockley. Pres., So. Woodenware Co., Nashville, 1955-61, So. Properties, Co., Inc., Hermitage, 1961—. Chmn. comml. flower exhibits Tenn. State Fair, 1951; committeewoman and v.p. Davidson County Agrl. Soil and Conservation Community Com., 1959-60; bd. mem. Nashville Symphony Assn., 1961-64, regional council mem., 1977-79; chmn. bd. Nashville Presbyn. Neighborhood Settlement House; founding bd. mem. Davidson County Cancer Soc.; bd. mem. Nashville Vis. Nurse Service; dist. chmn., speakers bur. Am. Red Cross. Proclaimed First Lady Donelson-Hermitage Community, 1986. Mem. Vanderbilt U. Aid, Peabody Coll. Aid, Tenn. Hist. Soc., Descs. of Ft. Nashboro Pioneers (bd. dirs. 1984-87), English Speaking Union. Presbyterian. Clubs: Ladies Hermitage Assn. (dir. 1949—), DAR, (chpt. regent 1941), Lebanon Rd. Garden Club (pres. 1947), Horticulture Soc. Davidson County (v.p. 1949). Clubs: Ravenwood Country, Centennial, Belle Meade. Contbr. to books and mags. on history of Tenn. Home: Stone Hall Stones River Rd Hermitage TN 37076 Office: Lebanon Rd Hermitage TN 37076

DONG, XIJIU, dance historian, educator; b. Jinan, Peoples Republic of China, Feb. 10, 1927; d. Lianreng and Xiaochi (Xue) D.; m. Chao Tong, May 2, 1952; children: Jin Zhu, Panpan Zhu, Honghong Zhu, Ying Zhu. BA, Beijing U., 1949. Sec. Chinese Ctr. Drama Acad., Beijing, 1952-73; dep. dir. Dance Inst. Acad. Arts China, Beijing, 1973—, chmn. dept. dance Grad. Sch., 1981—. Author: Ancient Chinese Dance History, 1983; (with others) Ancient Chinese Dancers Story, 1983. Mem. Chinese Nat. Dancers Assn. (mem. presidium), Dunhuang and Turpan Learned Soc. (bd. dirs. 1983—, chairwoman dance assn. 1985), Gen. History of Chinese Dance (chief editor 1987—). Office: Acad Arts China, 17 Qian Hai W St, Beijing Peoples Republic of China

DONG FU-RENG, economist, educational administrator, educator; b. Ningbo, People's Republic of China, July 26, 1927; s. Dong Jun-min and Zhao Jue-ying; m. Liu Ai-nian, Aug. 1, 1957; children—Dong, Xin-nian, Dong, Xin-zhong. Student Wuhan U., China, 1946-50; postgrad. Moscow Nat. Econ. Inst., 1957. Asst. Wuhan U., 1950-52, lectr., 1957-58; co-head research group Econs. Inst. CASS Beijing, People's Republic of China, 1959-76, co-dir. inst., 1979-85, dir., 1985—, sr. research fellow, 1979—, v.p. Grad. Sch., 1982-85, dir. Econ. Inst., 1985—; prof. econs. Beijing U., 1979-86, prof. econs., Wuhan Univ. and China's Peoples Univ., 1986—; vis. fellow St. Anthony's Coll. and Wolfson Coll., Oxford (Eng.) U., 1985; dep. Nat. People's Congress, 1988—, mem. standing com., 1988—, v.p. econ. and fin. standing com., 1988—. Author: Dynamic Analysis of USSR National Income, 1959, Socialist Reproduction and National Income, 1980, Theoretical Problems of the Chineese Economy in the Great Transformation, 1981, On Sun Ye-fang's Socialist Economic Theory, 1983, Dong Fureng's Selected Works, 1985, On Economic Development Strategies, 1988; editor-in-chief Jour. Econ. Research, 1985—. Mem. Union of Chinese Socs. for Econ. Research (sec.-gen. 1981-87), Chinese Acad. Social Scis. (council 1982-85). Office: Econ Inst CASS, 2 Yuetan Beixiaojie, Beijing People's Republic of China

DONIS, PETER P., agricultural machinery manufacturing company executive; b. Madison, Wis., May 30, 1924; s. Peter A. and Katherine A. (Gray) D.; m. Mildred Eva Niesen, June 23, 1948; children: David Lee, Diana Louise, Paul Andrew. B.B.A., U. Wis., 1948. With Caterpillar Tractor Co., Joliet, Ill., 1956—, plant mgr., 1963-74; v.p. Caterpillar Tractor Co., Peoria, Ill., 1975-77, exec. v.p., 1977-85, pres., chief operating officer, 1985—, also bd. dirs.; dir. Home Fed. Savs. and Loan Assn., Peoria. Trustee Joint Council on Econ. Edn.; trustee Western U. Regional Adv. Council, Adv. Council of Ill. 2000 Found. Mem. Ill. State C. of C. (bd. dirs.). Club: Country (Peoria). Office: Caterpillar Inc 100 NE Adams St Peoria IL 61629 *

DONIZETTI, MARIO, painter; b. Bergamo, Italy, Jan. 23, 1932; s. Giuseppe and Luigie (Animelli) D.; m. Costanza Andreucci, Jan. 16, 1958. Founder, Center for Research and Divulgation of the Techniques of the Arts; exhibited in one-man shows Ranzini Gallery, Milan, 1955, LaBussola Gallery, Turin, 1959, Rotta Gallery, Genova, 1961, Leitheimer-Schloss Gallery, Donauworth, 1972, Bauer Gallery, Hannover, 1974; group shows Cohen Gallery, London, 1961, Nat. Gallery, London, Quadriennale di'Roma-Premio Suzzara, Museo d'Arte Moderne, Ambrosiana Pinacotea, Pinseotee, Milan, 1983, others; represented in permanent pvt., public collections Italy, Germany, France, Switzerland, USSR, U.S., U.K.; commd. portraits include Edwige Feuillè re, Jean-Louis Barrault, Marcel Marceau, Vittorio Gassman, Valentina Cortese, Carla Fracci, Lady Diana Spencer (Time mag. cover Apr. 20, 1981), Indira Gandi (Time mag. cover, Nov. 1984), Pope John Paul II (Time mag. Feb. 1985); frescoes hist. Basilica Pontida, 1958. Contbr. articles and philos. essays on art to jours. and revs. Discoverer the glazed and varnished egg-yolk tempera. Home: 13 via Rocca, Bergamo Italy Office: 11 Colleoni, Bergamo Italy

DONKERS, JAN MATTHEUS, journalist, literary editor; b. Amsterdam, The Netherlands, June 15, 1943; s. Jan M. and Johanna Dorothea (Reekers) D.; m. Tineke Funhoff, Mar. 1967 (div. 1983); 1 child, Sander. M of Sociology, U. Amsterdam, 1966. Editor De Revisor mag., Amsterdam, 1974-75; feature writer Haagse Post mag., Amsterdam, 1970—; literary editor Avenue mag., Amsterdam, 1975—; staff editor Vpro Radio, Amsterdam, 1976—; writer-in-residence U. Tex., Austin, 1986-87. Author: Opgeruimde Verhalen, 1973, Ouders Van Nu, 1975, Gevoel Voor Verhoudingen, 1978, Amerika, Amerika, 1982, (drama) Een Maand Later, 1985. Mem. PEN, Vereniging Van Letter-zundigen. Home: 5 R Vinheleskade, Amsterdam 1071 SN, The Netherlands Office: Vpro Radio, F Gravelandseweq 65, Hilversum The Netherlands

DONKIN, ROBERT GORDON, management consultant, automatic control engineer; b. Cleve., Apr. 16, 1923; s. Robert Forster and Louise (Hess) D.; B.S.M.E., Case Inst. Tech., 1944; postgrad. U.S. Naval Acad., 1944; m. Marilyn Ann Mitzel, Dec. 23, 1944; children—Marilyn Ann Donkin Walters, Elizabeth Louise Donkin Ayers, Diana Jeanne Donkin Grigg. Design engr. Townmotor Corp., 1946-47; chief engr. Webster Products Corp., 1947-48; chief mech. designer Swartwout Co., 1949-50, asst. gen. supt., 1951-54, mgr. steam specialties mfg., 1955-56; gen. supt. Rockwell Mfg. Co., Chgo., 1957-58, works mgr., 1959-62, gen. mgr., Tulsa, 1962-63; mng. asso., gen. mgmt. cons. div. mgmt. services Arthur Young & Co., Tulsa, 1964-66, prin., 1967-68, dir., partner, 1969-73; pres. Indsl. Relations Services, Inc., Tulsa, 1973-83; exec. v.p. Selindex, Inc., 1976-84; pres. ABC Systems, Tulsa, 1983—; designer, author ABCSYS Software. Served to ensign USNR, 1942-46. Mem. Am. Prodn. and Inventory Control Soc. (pres. Tulsa chpt. 1975-76), Phi Delta Theta. Republican. Methodist. Club: Mason. Patentee centrifuge. Home and Office: 5408 E 38th St Tulsa OK 74135

DONKO, ALFONS FRANZ, electrical engineer; b. Vienna, Austria, May 31, 1924; s. Franz Josef and Olga Elisabeth (Spacil) D.; M.A. in Elec. Engring., U. Tech. Vienna, 1953; m. Gabriele Ute Spensberger, Jan. 13, 1962. Tech. officer industry dept. AEG-Union, Vienna, 1953-57, export dept. AEG-Allgemeine Elektricitäsges., Frankfurt/Main, W. Ger., 1957-61; safety engr., asst. to tech. mgmt. Danubia Petrochemie, Vienna-Schwechat, 1961-63; mng. dir. petroleum industry equipment Kutscha Ltd., Vienna, 1963-68; dep. mng. dir. Austrian Standards Inst., Vienna, 1968—; cons. in field of tech. equipment; mem., chmn. various nat. and internat. standards coms. and working groups. Served with German Army, 1942-45. Recipient Silver sign of honor Republic of Austria. Mem. Austrian Assn. Elec. Engrs., Austrian Fund Promotion Research Devel., Permanent Internat. Assn. Navigation Congresses, Mensa. Conservative. Roman Catholic. Contbr. articles profl. jours. Home: Münichreiterstrasse 30, A-1130 Vienna Austria Office: Österr Normungsinst, Postfach 130, A-1021 Vienna Austria

DONLON, WILLIAM JAMES, lawyer; b. Colorado Springs, Colo., Apr. 22, 1924; s. John Andrew and Kathleen M. Donlon; m. Josephine A. Janssen, July 19, 1946; children—William James, Gregory A., Michele, Dru Ann Lees. Student Colo. Coll., 1941-43; B.S., U. Denver, 1949, J.D., 1950. Bar: Colo. 1950, Ohio 1964, Ill. 1969, U.S. Dist. Ct. Colo. 1956 (no. dist.) Ill. 1974, U.S. Ct. Apls. (10th cir.) 1957, U.S. Ct. Apls. (5th cir.) 1970, U.S. Ct. Apls. (7th cir.) 1974, U.S. Ct. Apls. D.C. 1979, U.S. Supreme Ct. 1965. Dep. clk. U.S. Dist. Ct. Denver, 1949-50; solo practice, Denver, 1953-63; gen. counsel Brotherhood Ry., Airline and S.S. Clks., Freight Handlers, Express and Sta. Employees, Rosemont, Ill., 1963-78, Rockville, Md., 1963-86; instr. labor U. Ill., 1972-78. Served with USAAF, 1942-45. Decorated Air medal with 2 oak leaf clusters. Mem. ABA (council sect. labor and employment law 1977-86), Ill. Bar Assn., D.C. Bar Assn., Am. Legion, Phi Alpha Delta, Phi Delta Theta. Democrat. Roman Catholic.

DONNALLY, PATRICIA BRODERICK, fashion editor; b. Cheverly, Md., Mar. 11, 1955; d. James Duane and Olga Frances (Duenas) Broderick; m. Robert Andrew Donnally, Dec. 30, 1977. B.S., U. Md., 1977. Fashion editor The Washington Times (D.C.), 1983-85, The San Francisco Chronicle, 1985—. Recipient Atrium award, 1984, 87, Lulu award, 1985, 87. Mem. San Francisco Fashion Group, Inc. Avocation: travel. Home: 1 Lansdale San Francisco CA 94127-1608 Office: The San Francisco Chronicle 901 Mission St San Francisco CA 94103

DONNAY, JEAN-MICHEL, industrial company executive; b. Toulouse, France, Sept. 16, 1948; s. Jean and Odette (Reyynaud) D.; m. Helene Goldenberg; children: Romain, Laurene. Maitrise en Droit Prive, Faculte de Droit, Toulouse, 1972. With Airlec Industries, Aubervilliers, France. Office: Airelec Industries, 32 Rue du Landy, 93308 Aubervilliers France

DONNE, DAVID LUCAS, business executive; b. Aug. 17, 1925; s. Cecil Lucas and Marjorie Nicholls Donne; m. Jennifer Margaret Duncan, 1957 (dec. 1975); 3 children; m. Clare Yates, 1978. MA, U. Oxford, Eng.; MBA, Syracuse (N.Y.) U., 1953. Bar: Middle Temple, 1949. With Charterhouse Group, 1963-64, William Baird, 1964-67; dep. chmn. Dalgety, 1975-77, chmn., 1977-86; bd. dirs. ASDA-MFI Group plc, 1984—, chmn., 1986—; bd. dirs. Royal Trust Bank, British Coal. Bd. dirs. Royal Opera House Devel. Land Trust, 1985—. Club: Royal Thames Yacht. Office: 21 Hertford St, London W1Y 7DA, England *

DONNELL, BRUCE BOLTON, stage director; b. San Francisco, Feb. 7, 1946; s. Otto Dewey Jr. and Jean (Bolton) D. AB, Columbia Coll., 1967; MA, Columbia U., 1970. Mem. staging staff opera cos. San Francisco, Toronto, Memphis, N.Y.C., Newark, Geneva, Paris, Palermo, Tehran, Netherlands, San Diego, Buenos Aires, and Santa Fe, 1972-75; stage dir. Met. Opera, N.Y.C., 1975—; trustee nat. adv. bd. Santa Fe Opera, 1983—; judge Internat. Competition for Verdian Voices, Busseto, Italy, 1981—. Bd. dirs. Sullivan Found. Recipient Emmy for Outstanding Program Achievement in Performing Arts, 1983-84. Mem. Nat. Inst. Music Theater (trustee), Am. Guild Mus. Artists (bd. govs. N.Y.C. 1983—). Office: Met Opera Lincoln Center New York NY 10023

DONNELL, JOHN RANDOLPH, petroleum executive; b. Findlay, Ohio, June 22, 1912; s. Otto Dewey and Glenn (McClelland) D.; m. Margaret Louise Watt, Feb. 1, 1939 (dec.); children: John Randolph, Ann (Mrs. R. Kennedy Davis), William Watt, Thomas Blakeman, Richard Holmes; m. Maureen Nahas, July 31, 1981. B.S., Case Inst. Tech., 1934. Spl. rep. Marathon Oil Co., Findlay, 1938; asst. to mgr. prodn. Marathon Oil Co., 1944-50, treas., 1950-54, v.p. supply and transp., 1954-61, dir., 1954-73, v.p. charge internat. activities, 1961-65, sr. v.p. internat., 1965-67, sr. v.p. corporate planning, 1967-69, sr. v.p. finance and planning, 1969-73; pres. Marathon Internat. Oil Co., 1961-67; dir. First Nat. Bank Findlay, 1939-83, chmn. bd., 1947-83; dir. Toledo Trust Co., 1958-80, Toledo Trustcorp., Inc., 1970-80. Pres. Bd. Edn. Findlay, 1944-54; Trustee Case Western Res. U., Cleve.; Regional chmn. Boy Scouts Am., 1953-56, mem. nat. exec. bd., 1953-83; bd. dirs. World Scout Found. Mem. Sigma Xi, Tau Beta Pi. Presbyn. Clubs: Country (Findlay); Toledo, Belmont Country (Toledo); The Country, Chagrin Valley Hunt, Union (Cleve.); Rolling Rock (Ligonier, Pa.); Sky (N.Y.C.); Beach, Everglades (Palm Beach, Fla.). Home: 77 Locust St Perrysburg OH 43551 also: 300 Parc Monceau Palm Beach FL 33480

DONNELLY, GERARD KEVIN, retail executive; b. N.Y.C., July 2, 1933; s. Joseph R. and Margaret M. (Siefert) D.; B.B.A. in Acctg., Pace U., 1957; cert. in indsl. relations Colgate U., 1966; m. Maria McAllister, Aug. 29, 1964; children—Gerard K., Peter F., Deirdre A., Patrick J., James V. Asst. controller Allied Stores Corp., N.Y.C., 1957-65; gen. auditor Lone Star Industries, N.Y.C., 1965-67; controller, asst. sec. Computer Applications, Inc., N.Y.C., 1967-70; pres. Rhodes S.W., Phoenix, 1970-75; sr. v.p. Hart Schaffner & Marx, Chgo., 1975-81; chmn. bd., chief exec. officer Hughes & Hatcher, Inc., Phila., 1981-83; sr. v.p., dir. Macys-N.E. Inc., N.Y.C., 1983—. Mem. County Com., Queens County, N.Y., 1955-64; commr. parks and recreation, Manalapan Twp., N.J., 1967-68; bd. dirs. Central Bus. Dist. Assn., Detroit, 1981-83. Served with USN, 1951-53. Mem. Nat. Retail Mchts. Assn., Am. Mgmt. Assn., Internat. Council Shopping Centers, Menswear Retailers Am. Roman Catholic. Clubs: Birmingham (Mich.) Country, N.Y. Athletic, Celtic Soccer Football (referee), KC (4 deg.). Home: 15 Autumn Hill Princeton NJ 08540 Office: 151 W 34th St New York NY 10001

DONNELLY, JAMES, atomic energy company executive; b. Wishaw, Lanarkshire, Scotland, Mar. 22, 1931; came to Can., 1974, naturalized; s. Peter and Mary (Morris) D.; m. Brenda Marks, Mar. 29, 1956; 4 children. Degree in Electrical Engring., Royal Tech. Coll., Glasgow, 1953. Dir. Gen. Electric Co., Rugby, U.K., 1954-74; v.p. forestry products Internat. Systems and Controls Corp., Inc., Montreal, Que., Can., 1974-78; pres., chief exec. officer Atomic Energy of Can., Ottawa, Ont., 1978—; dir. Can. Nuclear Assn., Toronto, Can. Major Projects Assn., Can. Nat. Com.-World Energy Conf., Ottawa, Nuclear Project Mgrs., Inc.; chmn. adv. bd. Ctr. Nuclear Engring. U. Toronto. Mem. U.K. Inst. Elect. Engrs. Clubs: Cercle Universitaire, Ottawa Athletic, Royal Ottawa Golf. Home: TH3 111 Echo Dr, Ottawa, ON Canada K1S 5K8 Office: Atomic Energy of Can Ltd, 275 Slater St, Ottawa, ON Canada K1A 0S4

DONNELLY, THOMAS EDWARD, JR, pharmacology educator; b. Chelsea, Mass., Sept. 16, 1943; s. Thomas Edward and Catherine Sutherland (Ross) D.; m. Thorkatla Thorkelsdottir, Jan. 31, 1975; children: Karina, Erling. BS, Mass. Coll. Pharmacy, 1966; MA, Harvard U., 1968; PhD, Yale U., 1972. Registered pharmacist. Post-doctoral fellow U. Copenhagen, 1972-73; biochemist Leo Pharm. Products Co., Ballerup, Denmark, 1973-74; research assoc. Emory U., Atlanta, 1974; asst. prof. U. Nebr. Med. Ctr., Omaha, 1974-78, assoc. prof. pharmacology, 1978—. Contbr. articles to profl. jours. Coach soccer YMCA, Omaha, 1984-88. Grantee NIH, 1966-72, 76-81, 84—, Am. Heart Assn., Dept. Health Nebr., 1983-85, 87—. Mem. AAAS, N.Y. Acad. Scis., Am. Soc. Pharmacology and Exptl. Therapeutics. Democrat. Home: 10713 Valley St Omaha NE 68124 Office: U Nebr Med Ctr 42d St and Dewey Ave Omaha NE 68105

DONNEM, ROLAND WILLIAM, lawyer; b. Seattle, Nov. 8, 1929; s. William Roland and Mary Louise (Hughes) D.; m. Sarah Brandon Lund, Feb. 18, 1961; children: Elizabeth Prince, Sarah Madison. B.A., Yale U., 1952; J.D. magna cum laude, Harvard U., 1957. Bar: N.Y. 1958, U.S. Dist. Ct. (ea. and so. dists.) N.Y. 1959, U.S. Ct. Appeals (2d cir.) 1959, U.S. Ct. Claims 1960, U.S. Tax Ct. 1960, U.S. Supreme Ct. 1963, U.S. Ct. Appeals (3d cir.) 1969, D.C. 1970, U.S. Ct. Appeals (D.C. cir.) 1970, Ohio 1976, U.S. Dist. Ct. (no. dist.) Ohio 1980, U.S. Ct. Appeals (7th cir.) 1980, U.S. Ct. Appeals (6th cir.) 1984. With Davis Polk & Wardwell, N.Y.C., 1957-63, 64-69; law sec. appellate div. N.Y. Supreme Ct., N.Y.C., 1963-64; dir. policy planning antitrust div. Justice Dept., Washington, 1969-71; v.p., sec., gen. counsel Standard Brands Inc., N.Y.C., 1971-76; v.p. law Chessie System, Cleve., 1976-78, sr. v.p. law, 1978-86; ptnr. Meta Ptnrs., real estate devel., 1984—; dir., v.p. registered security rep. Cidco Investment Services, Inc., Cleve., 1985—; dir., v.p. Cidco Mgmt. Co., Inc., Cleve., 1986—; chmn., chief exec. officer Med. Facilities Devel. & Mgmt., Inc. and Retirement Developers, Inc., Cleve., 1985—; dir., sec., v.p. Meta Mgmt. INc., Cleve., 1987—. Mem. editorial bd. Harvard Law Rev., 1955-57. Bd. dirs., fin. v.p. Presbyn. Home for Aged Women, N.Y.C., 1972-76; bd. dirs., treas. James Lenox House, Inc., 1972-76; trustee Food and Drug Law Inst., 1974-76; trustee, sec. Brick Presbyterian Ch., 1974-76. Served from ensign to lt. (j.g.) USNR, 1952-54. Mem. ABA, N.Y.C. Bar Assn., D.C. Bar Assn., Ohio Bar Assn., Greater Cleve. Bar Assn., Am. Law Inst., Nat. Panel Arbitrators, Am. Arbitration Assn., Def. Orientation Conf. Assn., Yale U. Alumni Assn. Cleve. (treas. 1982-84, del. 1984-87, trustee), Assn. Yale Alumni (bd. govs. 1987—, fellow), Phi Beta Kappa. Republican. Presbyterian. Clubs: Tuxedo (N.Y.); Union (N.Y.C.); Capitol Hill, University, Metropolitan, Chevy Chase (Washington); Union, Racquet, Kirtland, Cleve. Wine and Food, Mid Day (Cleve.). Home: 2945 Fontenay Rd Shaker Heights OH 44120 Office: Med Facilities Devel & Mgmt Inc 1250 Superior Ave The Park Mall Cleveland OH 44114

DONNER, JÖRN JOHAN, film director, writer; b. Helsinki, Finland, Feb. 5, 1933; s. Kai Reinhold and Greta (von Bonsdorff) D.; B.A. in Polit. Sci. and Lit., Helsinki U., 1958; m. Inga-Britt W.; 1954 (div. 1962); children—Johan, Jakob; m. Jeanette Bonnier, 1974. Film critic various jours., 1951-62, including Dagens Nyheter, Stockholm; lit. critic various jours. in Sweden and Finland, 1951—; founder Finnish Film Archive, 1957; dir. Swedish Film Prodn. Cos., including Europa Film and Sandrews, 1963-66; founder, dir. Jö rn Donner Prodns., 1966-74; mem. bd. Marimekko Textile Co., several hotel cos.; dir. Swedish Film Inst., 1972-75. Mem. Helsinki City Council, 1968-72. Recipient Finnish State prizes Premio Opera Prima. Venice Film Festival, 1963; Vittorio Sica prize, Sorrento, 1978. Author: Report from Berlin, 1958; The Personal Vision of Ingmar Bergman, 1962; writer, pub. 21 books; writer, dir. 12 films including The World of Ingmar Bergman, 1975, Men Can't Be Raped, 1978. Address: 12 Pohjoisranta, Helsinki SF 00170 Finland *

DONNET, JEAN BAPTISTE, physical chemist, educator, scientific consultant; b. Pontgibaud, France, Sept. 28, 1923; s. Antoine and Marie (Berouhard) D.; Ph.D. in Chem. Engring., U. Strasbourg (France), 1953; m. Suzanne Rittiman, Dec. 21, 1968; children by previous marriage—Anne-Michele, Pierre-Antoine, Marie-Christine. With Centre National de Recherche Scientifique, 1946-53, successively stagiaire, attaché, chargé de recherche; prof. dep. dir. U. Haute-Alsace, Mulhouse, France, 1958-73, dir., 1973-77, prof., pres. U. Haute-Alsace, 1977—, fundator, head Research Center of Physico-Chemistry of Solid Surfaces, 1967-86. Served to maj. French Air Force, 1977. Decorated officer de la Legion d'Honneur et de l'Ordre du Mérite, commdr. Acad. Palmes; recipient Gold medal Société pour l'Encouragement de l'Industrie Nationale, 1976; Silver medal French Assn. Advancement of Sci., 1979; George Skakel Meml. award Am. Carbon Soc., 1981, Karl Harris medal Deutsche Kautschuk. Gessels, 1985 George Colwin medal Plastic award Rubber Inst., Eng., 1988. Fellow Plastic and

Rubber Inst. (London indsl. bd.), mem. AAAS, Am. Chem. Soc. (Rubber div.), Société Française de Chimie Physique, Societe Chimique de France, Soc. Plastic Engrs., French Assn. Rubber and Plastic Engrs. Club: Rotary. Author: Elastomers, 1958; Les Noirs de Carbone, 1965; Carbon Black 1976; Carbon Fiber, 1984, Active Carbon, 1988. Contbr. 250 articles in field to profl. jours. Office: 24 ave President Kennedy, Mulhouse France

DONOHOO, DONOVAN L., accountant; b. Buford, Ohio, Dec. 23, 1936; s. Lawrence Earl and Mary Elizabeth (Remley) D.; m. Beverly Ann Thatcher, Mar. 8, 1958; children: Douglas, Donovan Jr., Dennison, Duane, Daren. BBA in Acctg., Cin. U., 1960. CPA, Ohio, Fla. Asst. treas., controller Am. Fin. Corp., Cin., 1962-66; treas. Thriftway Supermarkets, Cin., 1962-66; ptnr. Storch, Donohoo & Storch, Cin., 1966-73; pres. D.L. Donohoo & Co., Batavia, Ohio, 1973—; v.p. Donohoo Computer Services, Batavia, 1984—. Elder Ch. of Christ, Owensville, Ohio; pres. Clermont Christian Assembly, Amelia, Ohio, 1973; bd. dirs. YMCA, Batavia, 1985. Fellow Ohio Soc. CPA's (v.p. Cin. 1982, sec. Cin. 1983, bd. dirs. 1985-88); mem. Am. Inst CPA's., Fla. Inst. C.P.A.'s. Republican. Lodges: Rotary, Masons (32 Degree), Shriners (mem. clown unit 1961—, dir. 1980-84). Home: 4691 S Rt 132 Batavia OH 45103 Office: D L Donohoo & Co 247 Main St Batavia OH 45103-2978

DONOHUE, CARROLL JOHN, lawyer; b. St. Louis, June 24, 1917; s. Thomas M. and Florence (Klefisch) D.; m. Juanita Maire, Jan. 4, 1943 (div. July 1973); children: Patricia Carol Donohue Stevens, Christine Ann Donohue Smith, Deborah Lee Donohue Wilucki; m. Barbara Lounsbury, Dec. 1978. A.B., Washington U., 1939, LL.B. magna cum laude, 1939. Bar: Mo. 1939. Assoc. Hay & Flanagan, St. Louis, 1939-42; asso. Salkey & Jones, 1946-49; partner Husch, Eppenberger, Donohue, Cornfeld & Jenkins, St. Louis, 1949—. Author articles in field. Campaign chmn. ARC, St. Louis County, 1950; mem. adv. com. Child Welfare, St. Louis, 1952-55; exec. com. Slum Clearance, 1949, bond issue com., 1955; bond issue com. St. Louis County Bond Issue, screening and supervisory coms., 1955-61, county citizen's com. for better law enforcement, 1953-56, chmn. com. on immigration policy, 1954-56, Mayor, Olivette, Mo., 1953-56; chmn. Bd. Election Commrs., St. Louis County, 1960-65; chmn. com. Non-Partisan Ct. Plan; vice-chmn. bd. Regional Commerce and Growth Assn.; bd. dirs. Downtown St. Louis, Inc., Civic Entrepreneurs Orgn.; bd. dirs. Gateway Mayors Emeritus. Served to lt. USNR, 1942-45. Decorated Bronze Star medal, Navy and M.C. medal. Mem. Mo. Bar Assn. (past mem. bd. govs., chmn. annual meeting, editor jour. 1940-41), ABA, St. Louis Bar Assn. (past pres., v.p., treas.), Order of Coif, Omicron Delta Kappa, Sigma Phi Epsilon, Delta Theta Phi. Club: Mo. Athletic. Address: 100 N Broadway Saint Louis MO 63102

DONOSO, JOSÉ, author; b. Oct. 5, 1924; s. Jose and Alicia D.; m. Maria P. Serrano, 1961; 1 child; ed. Instituto Pedagogico, U. Chile; A.B., Princeton U. English conversation Catholic U. Chile, 1952; tchr. techiques of expression Sch. Journalism, U. Chile; journalist Revista Ercilla, Santiago, 1959-64; vis. lectr. Writers' Workshop, English dept. U. Iowa, 1966-67. Recipient Premio Municipal de Santiago, 1955; Chile-Italia prize for journalism, 1960; prize William Faulkner Found., 1962. Author: (short stories) Veraneo y otras Cuentos, 1955, Charleston, 1960; (novels) Coronacion, 1962, Este Domingo, 1960, El Lugar sin Limites, 1966, Casa de Campo (Critics award for best novel in Spanish), 1979, La Misteriosa Desaparición de la Marquesita de Loria, 1980, El Jardin de la Lado, 1981; Tri-Quarterly Anthology of Contemporary Latin American Literature, 1969; El Obsceno Pájaro de la Noche, 1971; (anthology) Cuentos, 1971; (novellas) Tres novelitas burguesas, 1973. Office: Castellon de la Plana 17, Madrid 6, Spain *

DONOVAN, JOHN JOSEPH, JR., real estate broker and developer; b. Oakland, Calif., Mar. 10, 1916; s. John Joseph and May Ella (Coogan) D.; Ph.B., Santa Clara U., 1938; postgrad. Stanford U., 1938-40, Harvard U., 1942; m. Margaret Mary Abel, June 7, 1941; children—John Joseph III, Mary Margaret Donovan Szarnicki, Patricia Anne Donovan Jelley, Eileen Marie, Marian Gertrude Corrigan, George Edwin, Michael Sean. Sales mgr. Universal Window Co., Berkeley, Calif., 1940-41, v.p., 1946-49, pres., chmn. bd., 1949-66; real estate broker and developer, 1966—. Mem. aluminum window mfrs. adv. com. NPA, 1951-52; chmn. pace setters com., commerce and industry div. Alameda County United Crusade, 1961. Mem. Republican small businessmen's com., Alameda County, Calif., 1946. Bd. dirs. Providence Hosp., 1970-80, also Found., 1980-82; bd. dirs. Apostleship of the Sea Center, 1968-85, Hanna Boy's Center, Sonoma County, 1976-79; mem. Oakland Mayor's Internat. Welcoming Center, 1972-77; trustee, treas. Serra Internat. Found., 1980-87, pres., 1981-82; mem. Sierra Bicentennial Commn., 1983-86; mem. membership enrollment maj. div. San Francisco Bay Area council Boy Scouts Am., 1984—; mem. bd. Jesuit Sch. Theology, Berkeley, 1982-85, Grad. Theol. Union, Berkeley, 1982-85. Served from ensign to lt. Supply Corps, USNR, 1940-46; in U.S.S. General Ballou; capt. Res. Named knight St. Gregory the Gt., Pope John XXIII, 1962 (pres. Oakland diocese 1970—); decorated Cross of Comdr. Merit, 1978, Cross of Comdr. of Merit with swords Order of Malta, Rome, 1981; named grand officer of merit, Order of Malta with swords, 1983, Knight Grace and Devotion, Order of Malta, 1987, Knight of Obedience, Order of Malta, 1988; invested and decorated Knight of Grace, Sacred Mil. Constantinian Order of St. George, 1988. Mem. Western Archtl. Metal Mfrs. Assn. San Francisco (dir. 1956-65, exec. com. 1958-65, pres. 1959-60), Aluminum Window Mfrs. Assn. N.Y.C. (dir. 1950-58, 1st v.p. 1955-56), Newcomen Soc. N.Am., Naval Order U.S., Navy Supply Corps Assn. San Francisco Bay Area (2d v.p. 1970—), Father Junipero Serra 250th Anniversary Assn. (v.p., sec.), Internat. Council Shopping Centers, AIM (pres.'s council), Naval Res. Assn., Western Assn. Knights of Malta (chmn. admissions com. 1975-81 dir. 1976—, chancellor 1981-84), VFW. Roman Catholic. Clubs: Berkeley Serra (charter mem.); Comml., Commonwealth, Pacific-Union (San Francisco); Monterey Peninsula Country (Pebble Beach, Calif.); Claremont Country (Oakland, Calif.), Army-Navy (Washington). Home: 2 Lincolnshire Dr Oakland CA 94618 Office: PO Box 11100 Oakland CA 94611

DONSIMONI, MARIE-PAULE JOSEPH, economics educator, consulting company executive; b. Paris, Jan. 2, 1950; d. Francois and Jacqueline (Heste) D. DES in Econs., U. Paris, 1972, DEA in Math., 1972; MA in Econs., Harvard U., 1976, PhD in Econs., 1978. Asst. prof. Columbia U., N.Y.C., 1978-81; assoc. prof. U. Catholique de Louvain, Belgium, 1981—; dir. European service Data Resources Inc., Brussels, 1986—. Home: 30 Rue du Gen Patton, 1050 Brussels Belgium Office: UCL, 3 Place Montesquieu, 1348 Louvain-la-Neuve Belgium

DOODOH, ALFONS FRANCIS, electronics company executive; b. Menado Celebes, Indonesia, July 13, 1939; s. Frits Hendrik and Judith Imelda (Wantania) D.; grad. Econ. Faculty, Mahadjaja U., 1968, Nasional U., 1978; M, Kennedy Western U., 1986; PhD in Economics (hon.), 1987; m. Esther Magdalena Ontoh, Feb. 25, 1967; children—Mila, Remy, Gisella, Reza, Fifi. With Vet. Shipping Corp., 1960-65, gen. mgr., Jakarta, 1962-65; mng. dir. Pt. Neptune Electronic Services Corp., Jakarta, 1965—; pres., dir. Underwater Services Co., P.T. Teratai Utara. Mem. Indonesia Ship Officers Assn., Indonesia Shipbldg. Industry Assn. (dir.), AMA, Indonesian Profl. Divers Assn., Underwater Constrn. and Engring. Assn., Indonesian Distbrs. Assn., Indonesian C. of C. and Industry. Roman Catholic. Home: Jalan M No 1502-3 Blok F IV, Kavpolri Jelambar, Jakarta Indonesia Office: 12 Jalan Cilincing Tg, Jakarta Utara, Indonesia

DOODY, BARBARA PETTETT, computer specialist; b. Cin., Sept. 18, 1938; d. Philip Wayne and Virginia Bird (Handley) P.; student Sinclair Coll., Tulane U.; 1 son, Daniel Frederick Reasor, Jr. Owner, mgr. Honeysuckle Pet Shop, Tipp City, Ohio, 1970-76; office mgr. Doody & Doody, C.P.A.s, New Orleans, 1976-77, computer ops. mgr., 1979—; office mgr. San Diego Yacht Club, 1977-79. Mem. DAR, UDC, Jamestown Soc., Magna Charta, So. Dames, Colonial Dames of 17th Century, Nat. Soc. Daughters of 1812, Daus. Am. Colonists, Dames Ct. Honor. Republican. Lutheran. Home: 16 Cypress Covington LA 70433 Office: 1160 Commerce Bldg New Orleans LA 70112

DOOGE, JAMES CLEMENT IGNATIUS, engineer, former Irish diplomat; b. Birkenhead, Eng., July 30, 1922; s. Denis Patrick and Veronica Catherine (Carroll) D.; C.B.S., Dun Langhaire; B.E., B.Sc., Univ. Coll., Dublin, 1942, M.E., 1952; M.S., U. Iowa, 1956; Dr.Agr.Sci. (hon.), U. Wageningen, 1978, Dr. Tech. (hon.), 1980; m. Veronica O'Doherty, Nov. 25, 1946; children—Colm, Diarmuid, Cliona, Dara, Meliosa. Jr. civil engr. Irish Office Public Works, 1943-46; design engr. E.S.B., 1946-58; prof. civil engring. Univ. Coll., Cork, 1958-70, Univ. Coll., Dublin, 1970-81, 82-84; minister for fgn. affairs, Ireland, 1981-82; leader Irish Senate from 1983; mem. Council of State, 1973-77. Recipient Horton award Am. Geophys. Union, 1959. Mem. Instn. Civil Engrs. Ireland (pres. 1968-69, Kettle Premium and Plaque, 1948, Mullins Medal, 1951, 62), Royal Irish Acad. (sec.), Internat. Assn. Hydrological Scis. (pres. 1975-79). Mem. Fine Gael Parliamentary Party. Roman Catholic. Office: University Coll, Earlsford Terr, Dublin 2 Ireland *

DOOLEY, ARCH RICHARD, business administration educator; b. Oklahoma City, Feb. 1, 1925; s. Archibald E. and Grace (Moore) D.; m. Patricia Folts, Sept. 5, 1953; children—Arch Richard, Christopher Folts. A.B., Yale, 1944; M.B.A., Harvard, 1950, D.C.S., 1960. Asst. prof. Oklahoma City U., 1946-47; asst. prof., asst. dean bus. U. N.C., 1950-54; mem. faculty Harvard Grad. Sch. Bus. Adminstrn., 1954—, prof., 1965—, Jesse Philips prof. mfg., 1969—; mem. vis. faculty Keio (Japan) U., U. Western Ont., Inst. Panamericano de Alta Dirección de Empresa, Mexico, Exec. Tng. Inst. Philippines, Singapore Mgmt. Inst., Instituto Centroamericano de Administración de Empresas, Nicaragua, U. de Carabobo, Venezuela; mem. adv. bd. Instituto Estudios Superiores Empresas, Spain, Instituto Internacional de San Telmo, Spain; cons. to govt. and industry, 1952—. Author: Business Management Credit Bureaus, 1953, (with others) Casebooks in Production Management-Basic Problems, Concepts and Techniques, rev. edit, 1968, Production Operating Decisions in the Total Business Strategy, 1964, Operations Planning and Control, 1964, Wage Administration and Worker Productivity, 1964. Served as officer USNR, World War II. Mem. Acad. Mgmt., Beta Theta Pi. Home: 21 Summit Rd Lexington MA 02173 Office: Harvard Business Sch Soldiers Field Boston MA 02163

DOOLEY, J. GORDON, food scientist; b. Nevada, Mo., Nov. 15, 1935; s. Howard Eugene and Wilma June (Vanderford) D.; B.S. with honors in Biology, Drury Coll., Springfield, Mo., 1958; postgrad. (NSF grantee) U. Mo., Rolla, 1961, (NSF grantee) Kirksville (Mo.) State Coll., 1959; M.S. in Biology (NSF grantee), Brown U., 1966; postgrad. bus. mgmt. Alexander Hamilton Inst., 1973-75, No. Ill. U., 1964. Tchr. sci. Morton West High Sch., Berwyn, Ill., 1963-64; dairy technologist Borden Co., Elgin, Ill., 1964-65; project leader Cheese Products Lab., Kraft Corp., Glenview, Ill., 1965-73; sr. food scientist Wallerstein Co. div. Travenol Labs., Inc., Morton Grove, Ill., 1973-77; mgr. food sci. GB Fermentation Industries, Inc., Des Plaines, Ill., 1977-79, mgr. product devel., 1979-82; group leader Food Ingredients div. Stauffer Chem. Co., Clawson, Mich., 1982-84; sr. research scientist Schreiber Foods, Inc., Green Bay, Wis., 1984-87, Ridgeview, LaCrosse, Wis., 1987—; sci. lectr. seminars, Mexico, 1975; assoc. mem. Ad Hoc Enzyme Tech. Com., 1978—; dairy research adv. bd. Utah State U. Recipient Spoke award Nevada (Mo.) Jr. C. of C., 1960. Mem. Am. Dairy Sci. Assn., Inst. Food Technologists, Am. Chem. Soc., Cousteau Soc., Am. Inst. Biol. Scis., Nat. Sci. Tchrs. Assn., Whey Products Inst., Beta Beta Beta, Phi Eta Sigma. Republican. Presbyterian. Clubs: Toastmasters Internat. (pres. Baxter Labs. club 1976-77); Brown U. (Chgo.). Patentee in food and enzyme tech. field; contbr. sci. articles to profl. jours. Home: 723 Pleasant Ct Onalaska WI 54602 Office: Ridgeview 2340 Enterprise Ave La Crosse WI 54602

DOOLEY, JO ANN CATHERINE, publishing company executive; b. Cin., Nov. 24, 1930; d. Joseph Frank and Margaret Mary (Flynn) Dooley; ed. U. Cin., 1966. Clk., Castellini Co., Cin., 1949-52; IBM operator Kroger Co., Cin., 1952; asst. acct. Gardner Publs., Inc., Cin., 1953-67, treas., sec., 1967—, dir., 1983—, v.p. fin., 1986—, also trustee employees profit sharing trust, trustee retirement trust. Mem. Am. Soc. Women Accts. (advt. mgr. Woman CPA 1979-81, nat. pres. 1982-83, treas. 1984—, trustee Ednl. Found., achievement award), Cin. Women's Forum, Nat. Assn. Female Execs. Roman Catholic. Office: 6600 Clough Pike Cincinnati OH 45244

DOORNBOS, JOHANNES FOKKO, trading company executive; b. Rotterdam, Netherlands, Jan. 8, 1923; s. Johannes Fokko and Ludwina (Koot) D.; ed. Bus. Sch., Oudenbosch, 1940; C.E. Engring. Sch. M.T.S., Rotterdam, 1943; m. Margaretha Maria Hyna, Jan. 8, 1950; children—Robert Fokko, Johannes Fokko, Founder, pres. Doornbos Tech Bedr BV, Rotterdam, Netherlands, 1941—, also internat. subsidiaries; mem. adv. bd. Nederlandsche Middenstandsbank, Switzerland; mem. adv. bd. Security Pacific Bank; exec. com. Internat. Lausanne; cons. internat. investments. Mem. Am. C. of C. Netherlands, Associated Equipment Distbrs. Assn. U.S., Vereniging van FabriKanten van en Handelaren in Bouwmachines, Mijn en Wegenbouw machines en Transportmiddelen. Internat. Pipeline Contractors Assn. Roman Catholic. Clubs: Minnesota, Pool and Yacht (St. Paul); Vennemeer; Yacht Club de Monaco. Home: 1 Ave de Grande Bretagne, Les Floralies, Apt 8A, Monte Carlo Monaco Office: 12 Brecvaartstraat, 3044 AH Rotterdam The Netherlands

DORAN, DORIS JEANNE, librarian; b. Chambersburg, Pa., July 19, 1932; d. John Franklin and Kathleen Elmira (Cooke) Fraker; m. Francis Joseph Doran, Feb. 5, 1955; children: Brenda Lou, Polly Ann. BS, Wilson Coll., 1954; MLS, U. Md., 1970, postgrad., 1976-77. Asst. buyer Joseph Horne Co., Pitts., 1955-56; dir. research library Sears Roebuck & Co., Chgo., 1956-58; project officer contracts John I. Thompson Co., Washington, 1967-69, staff asst. to v.p. info. sci. div., 1969-70; program officer grants div. Nat. Library of Medicine, Bethesda, Md., 1970-79, program analyst Office of Dir., 1980-82; project dir. Nat. Med. Audiovisual Center, 1979; asst. for network devel. VA, Washington, 1982-84; co-owner, treas., gen. mgr. Gilran Lighting Products, Springfield, Va., 1970—; project mgr. Preservation Microfilm Project, REMAC Info. Corp., 1987-88, Nat. Library Medicine; acquisitions specialist Nat. Tech. Info. Service, 1988—. Mem. Am. Library Assn., Med. Library Assn., Nat. Assn. Female Execs. Home: 4816 Cloister Dr Bethesda MD 20852

DORATI, ANTAL, composer, conductor; b. Budapest, Hungary, Apr. 9, 1906; came to U.S., 1941, naturalized, 1947; s. Alexander and Margit (Kunwald) D.; m. Klara Korody, 1929 (div.); 1 dau., Antonia; m. Ilse von Alpenheim, 1971. Student composition and piano, Acad. of Music, Budapest, diploma, 1924; student, U. Vienna, Austria, 1923-25; D.Mus., Macalester Coll., 1957; hon. doctorates, George Washington U., 1975, U. Md., 1976. Condr., Budapest Royal Opera House, 1924-28, Dresden State Opera, 1928-29, Munster State Opera, 1929-32, Ballet Russe de Monte Carlo, 1933-37, mus. dir. original, Ballet Russe, 1938-40, Ballet Theatre, 1940-44, mus. dir., Dallas Symphony Orch., 1945-49, Mpls. Symphony Orch., 1949-60, chief condr., BBC Symphony Orch., London, 1962-66, Stockholm Philharmonic, 1966-74, music dir., Washington Nat. Symphony, 1969-77, sr. condr., Royal Philharmonic Orch., London, 1974-78, condr. laureate, Royal Philharmonic Orch., 1978-81, music dir., Detroit Symphony Orch., 1977-81, condr. laureate, 1981—, condr. laureate, Stockholm Symphony, 1981—; guest condr. all maj. orchestras, U.S., Europe, Latin Am., Australia; compositions include string quartet, quintet for oboe and strings, divertimento for small orchestra, Am. serenades for string orchestra, cello concerto The Way; cantata The Two Enchantments of Li Tai Pe; lyric scene for baritone and small orchestra Symphony; for large orch. Missa brevis; for mixed choir and percussion instruments Magdalena; ballet Madrigal Suite; chorus and orch. Chamber Music for Soprano and String Orchestra; night music for flute and small orch. Bartok Variations; piano solo The Voices; song cycle; ballet arrangements include Harvest Time; recs. for, Mercury Record Co., EMI, Philips, RCA-Victor, London-Decca. Decorated Royal Order of Vasa (Sweden); chevalier Ordre des Arts et Lettres (France); Order Arts and Letters (Austria). Mem. Royal Acad. Music London (hon.). Office: care Columbia Artists Mgmt 165 W 57th St New York NY 10019 also: Royal Philharm Orch, 56 Kingsway, London WC2B 6DX, England *

DORE, BONNY ELLEN, film and television production company executive; b. Cleve., Aug. 16, 1947; d. Reber Hutson and Ellen Elizabeth (McNamara) Barnes; m. James Llewellyn Metz, Feb. 20, 1977 (div. Aug. 1986); m. Sanford Astor, May 22, 1987. BA, U. Mich., 1969, MA, 1975. Cert. tchr., Mich. Dir., tchr. Plymouth (Mich.) Community Schs., 1969-72; gen. mgr. Sta. WSDP-FM, Plymouth, 1970-72; prodn. supr. pub. TV N.Y. State Dept. Edn., 1972-74; producer TV series Hot Fudge Sta. WXYZ-TV, Detroit, 1974-75; mgr. children's programs ABC TV Network, Los Angeles, 1975, dir. children's programs, 1975-76, dir. prime time variety programs, 1976-77; dir. devel. Hanna-Barbera, Los Angeles, 1977; v.p. devel. and prodn. Krofft Entertainment, Los Angeles, 1977-81, Centerpoint Prodn., Los Angeles, 1981-82; pres., owner in assn. with Orion TV The Greif-Dore Co., Los Angeles, 1983-87, Bonny Dore Prodns. Inc., Los Angeles, 1988—. Producer (TV series) The Krofft Superstar Hour, 1978 (2 Emmy awards 1979), (mini-series) Sins, 1986, (comedy series CBS) First Impressions, 1987-88, (mini-series HBO) Sister Ruth, 1988, numerous others; exec. producer (mini-series) Sister Ruth, 1988-89). Named Outstanding Young Tchr. of Yr., Cen. States Speech Assn., 1973; Cert. of Appreciation, Gov. of Mich., 1985, City of Beverly Hills, Calif., 1985. Mem. Women in Film (v.p. 1978-81, pres. 1980-81), Women in Film Found. (trustee 1981—), Acad. TV Arts and Scis., Beverly Hills C. of C. (cons. 1985), Exec. Roundtable Los Angeles (trustee 1987—). Home: 15150 Dickens Condo 307 Sherman Oaks CA 91403 Office: Orion TV Studios 1888 Century Park E 6th Floor Los Angeles CA 90067

DORET, MICHEL R., architect, engineer; b. Haiti, Jan. 5, 1938; came to U.S., 1962; s. Raymond Doret and Marie Rigaud; m. Liselotte Ruth Bencze, Nov. 10, 1970. B in Letters and Philosophy, Coll. St. Martial, Port-au-Prince, 1958; BA, Pace U., 1970; MA, NYU, 1972; Degree in Engring./Architecture, U. d'Etat d'Haiti, Port-au-Prince, 1981; PhD, George Washington U., 1982. Cert. math., French, Spanish tchr., N.Y., architect/engr., Haiti. Ind. architect/engr., researcher, writer Pétion-Ville, Haiti. Author: Glossary of Basic Technical Terminology for Architects, 1982, Situation Poésie 83, 1984, The Gingerbread Style, 1985, Poetesses genevoises francophones, 1986, Abrégé de II Histoire de l'architecture d'Haiti and the Gingerbread Style, 1987, Volutes, 1988, Destinée Tragique, 1988; editor Compte Rendus de la Societé Haitienne d'Histoire et de Geographie d'Haiti; contbr. articles to profl. jours.; patentee in field. Served with U.S. Army, 1963-65, Vietnam. Recipient Martin Luther King Jr. award NYU, 1970-71, several N.Y. State Scholar Incentive awards, 1971-73, prix France-Suisse de la Fondation Michel-Ange-Monaco, 1987; teaching fellow George Washington U., 1977-78. Mem. Acad. Réunion, N.Y. Acad. Scis., Modern Lang. Assn., ASCE, Soc. Profl. Engrs., Coll. de L'Ordre Nat. des Ingenieurs et Architectes Haitiens, Soc. des gens de Lettres de France, Assn. des Ecrivains de Langue Française, Pi Delta Phi, Phi Sigma Iota. Roman Catholic. Home: Le Verger, 01210 Ornex Maconnex France Office: CP 15 558, Pétion-Ville Haiti

DORFMAN, ALLEN BERNARD, international management consultant; b. N.Y.C., Mar. 30, 1930; s. Harry and Jean (Schreiber) D.; m. Elaine Turbé, Jan. 9, 1955; children: Nancy Ann, Jeffrey David. BBA summa cum laude, 1952; postgrad. mgmt. studies, Harvard Bus. Sch. From mem. exec. tng. squad to sr. mgmt. R.H. Macy's, N.Y.C., 1954-67; asst. gen. mdse. mgr., v.p., mem. mgmt. com. N.Y. div. Allied Stores Corp., N.Y.C., 1967-69; v.p., gen. mdse. mgr. hard and soft goods, mem. exec. com. Town & Country Full Line Discount Stores div. Lane Bryant Corp., N.Y.C., 1969-71; pres., dir. Nat. Bellas Hess Inc., Kansas City, Mo., 1971-73; corp. sr. v.p. and pres., chief exec. officer retail div. Jewelcor, Inc., N.Y.C., 1973-77; corp. v.p., dir. corp. ops., mem. exec. com. Vornado, Inc., Garfield, N.J., 1977-78; chmn. bd., chief exec. officer Allen B. Dorfman Assocs., 1978—; prof. Grad. Sch., L.I. U., evenings. Bd. dirs., exec. v.p. Am. Cancer Soc.; bd. dirs. Kings Point Civic Assn. Served with AUS, 1952-54. Recipient award Advt. Club N.Y., Torch of Liberty award Nat. Anti-Defamation League. Mem. Mass Retailing Inst., Nat. Retail Mchts. Assn., Nat. Assn. Catalog Showroom Merchandisers Inc., Adelphi Coll. Found., Boy Scouts Am., Boys Club, Philharmonic Assn., Police Athletic League, Beta Gamma Sigma, Eta Mu Pi, Sigma Alpha. Club: Wildwood Country (Kings Point, N.Y.) (pres., dir.). Office: Allen B Dorfman Chmn Allen B Dorfman Assos The Polo Club-Penthouse Villa 17588-C. Ashbourne Ln Boca Raton FL 33496

DORGAN, ROBERT THOMAS, construction equipment manufacturing executive; b. Chgo., Apr. 22, 1925; s. Walter H. and Juanita M. (Corbett) D.; m. Shirley M. Schomer, May 10, 1947; children: Robert Thomas, Linda Lee. Student in mgmt., U. Chgo., 1958-60; BA, Roosevelt U., Chgo., 1976. With Internat. Harvester Co., 1946-81, machine operator, 1946-48, mgmt. trainee, 1948-49, mgr. various positions, Chgo. and Louisville, 1949-73, mgr. mfg. ops. Farmall Plant, Rock Island, Ill., 1973-81; plant mgr. Twin Disc, Inc., Rockford, Ill., 1981-82; exec. v.p. Trojan Industries, Inc., Batavia, N.Y., 1982-83, pres., chief operating officer, 1983-87, also bd. dirs. Advisor Jr. Achievement, Chgo., 1953-55; active Big Bros. program, Chgo., 1958-59; bd. dirs. YMCA, Rock Island, Ill., 1979-81, C. of C. Genesee County, N.Y., 1984-87; mem. adv. com. State Univs. of N.Y., 1985-87; mem. adv. bd. Salvation Army, Rock Island, 1976-81; mem. State of N.Y. Finger Lakes Regional Econ. Devel. Council, 1984-86; chmn. bus. adv. com. Devel. Ctr., Genesee Coll., 1984-86; chmn. Genesee County chpt. Am. Heart Assn., 1984-86; pres., chief exec. officer Genesee Community Coll. Found., Batavia, 1987-88; treas. Catastrophic Illness Assistance Found., Elmhurst, Ill., 1987—; bd. dirs. Jr. Holy Name Soc., Chgo., 1959-63, Upper Rock Island YMCA, 1979-81, Franciscan Hosp., Rock Island, 1980-81. Served with U.S. Army, 1943-46. Named Man of Yr. for youth work, St. Turibius Cath. Ch., Chgo., 1961, Father of Yr., Chgo. Tribune, 1962. Mem. Am. Soc. Quality Control (sr.), Soc. Automotive Engrs. (sr.), Soc. Mfg. Engrs. (cert. mfg. engr.), Am. Def. Prepardness Assn. (bd. dirs. Iowa-Ill. chpt. 1977-82). Roman Catholic. Lodge: Rotary (bd. dirs. 1983-87). Home and Office: 7102 S Summit Rd Darien IL 60559

DORIA, ANTHONY NOTARNICOLA, college dean; b. Savona, Italy, June 2, 1927; s. Vito Sante and Jolanda (Giampaolo) Notarnicola. M.B.A., Wharton Sch., U. Pa., 1953; LL.M. (equivalent), U. Paris, 1960; D.Jr., U. Rome, 1962. Prof. history, bus. and internat. law Community Coll. at Suffolk County, Selden, N.Y., 1960-65, L.I. U., Southampton, N.Y., 1964-65; founder, pres. Royalton Coll. Sch. Internat. Affairs, S. Royalton, Vt., 1965-72; dean Royalton Coll. Sch. Internat. Affairs (Royalton Coll. Law Study Center), 1974—; founder, dean Vt. Law Sch., 1972-74; cons. internat. law and orgns.; panelist Am. Arbitration Assn.; mem. Vt. Gov.'s Commn. on Student Affairs, 1972-75. Author: Italy and the Free World, 1945, The Conquest of the Congo, 1947, Influences in the Making of Foreign Policy in the United States of America, Great Britain, and France, 1953, Introduction to International Law, 1976. Candidate for U.S. Senate, 1986. Served with underground resistance movement World War II. Recipient Merit cert. UN; citation Boy Scouts Am., 1965. Mem. Am. Judicature Soc., Internat. Bar Assn., Internat. Law Assn., Am. Soc. Internat. Law, AAUP, Acad. Polit. Sci., Noble Assn. Chevaliers Pontificaux (life). Clubs: Elysee (Paris); Pen and Pencil. Home: The Royalton Inn South Royalton VT 05068 Office: Royalton Coll Law Study Ctr South Royalton VT 05068

DORIA, MARIO A., ceramics company executive; b. Mexico City, May 27, 1952; s. Mario and Carmen (Serrano) D.; m. Rosa Elena Dicostanzo, July 1, 1978; children: Mario A., Jorge A. BS, Inst. Tech. de Monterrey, Mex., 1978. Cert. mech. and elec. engr. Maintenance chief Ladrilleras A. La Huerta S.A., Toluca, Mex., 1978-80; plant mgr. Ladrilleras A. La Huerta S.A., Toluca, 1980-82, chief exec. officer, 1981—; cons. Ladrillera Jalisciense S.A. Home: Ferando Quiroz 239, 50120 Toluca MEXICO Office: Ladrilleras Asociadas La Huerta SA, Avila Camacho 40-301, 53390 Naucalpan MEXICO

DORIEL, JOSEPH D., government administrator; b. Stolin, Poland, May 15, 1929; arrived in Israel, 1947; s. Itzhak and Judith (Seldin) D.; m. Shulamith Henich, Dec. 27, 1951; children: Tamar, Amnon, Dalia. BSME, Technion U., Haifa, Israel, 1952, diploma in engring., 1953. Prodn. engr. Israel Mil. Industries, Tel Aviv, 1952-53, head prodn. planning and control, 1953-55; mgr., ptnr. The Functional Planning Co., Tel Aviv, 1956-79; adviser to minister Ministry of Transport, Jerulalem, 1979-80; chmn. Pub. Mgmt. Efficiency Bd., Jerulalem, 1981-84; dir. gen. Israel Inst. Productivity, Tel Aviv, 1985—; bd. dirs. Crystal Co. Ltd., Ramat Gan, Israel. Author: A New Approach to National Security, 1974, Systems Madness, 1981; inventor parking card system, 1971. Served with Israeli Air Force, 1948-49. Mem. Assn. Mgmt. Cons. (chmn. 1981-85). Mem. Heruth Party. Office: Israel Inst Productivity, Henrietta Szold 4 Box 33010, Tel Aviv 61330, Israel

DORIN, ANDRICA, mathematician; b. Hunedoara, Romania, Mar. 12, 1956; s. Andrica Manole and Maria (Nelega) A.; m. Bandea Zamfria, Mar. 7, 1981; children: Andrica Tudor, Andrica Teodora. DSc in Math., Faculty of Math, Cluj-Napoca, Romania, 1981. Tchr. A. Muresanu Sec. Sch., Dej,

Cluj, Romania, 1981-85; prof. math. U. Cluj-Napoca, 1985—. Contbr. articles to profl. jours.; author numerous books in math.; reviewer Zentralblatt für Mathematik, Math. Rev. Mem. Math. Assn. Am., Math. Soc. Romania. Mem. Romanian Communist Party. Club: Univ. Lodge: Cluj-Napoca. Home: Str Pepinierei Nr 38, BL I ScA Ap 11, 4650 Dej, Cluj Romania Office: Cluj-Napoca Faculty Math, & Physics Kogalniceanu, 1, 3400 Cluj-Napoca Romania

DORIN, BERNARD J., ambassador; b. Beauvais, Picardie, France, Aug. 25, 1929; s. Robert G. and Jacqueline (Goumard) D.; m. Christine M.L du Bois de Meyrignac, Apr. 30, 1943; children: Hélène, Sophie, Alban, Philippe. Diploma, Sch. Polit. Sci., Paris, 1950, Ecole Nat. Adminstrn., France, 1956; Student, Harvard U., 1970. Ambassador French Govt., Haiti, 1972-75; dir. Francophonie French Govt., Paris, 1975-78; ambassador French Govt., South Africa, 1978-81; Under sec. State for Am. Affairs French Govt., Paris, 1981-84; ambassador French Govt., Brazil, 1984-87, Japan, 1987—. Named officier de la Legion d'Honneur, officier de L'Ordre Nat. du Merite, commdr. des Palmes Academiques. Lodge: Order of Malta. Office and Home: Embassy of France, 4-11-44 Minami-Azabu, Minato-ku, Tokyo Japan

DORLAND, BYRL BROWN, civic worker; b. Greenwich, Utah, Apr. 25, 1915; d. David Alma and Ethel Myrle (Peterson) Brown; teaching cert. Brigham Young U., 1937; B.S., Utah State Coll., Logan, 1940; grad. John Robert Powers Sch. Profl. Women, N.Y.C., 1980; m. Jack Albert Dorland, June 11, 1944; children—Lynn Elise Dorland Trost, Lee Allison. Sch. tchr., Utah, 1937-39, 40-42; restored Washington Irving's graveplot in Sleepy Hollow Cemetery, North Tarrytown, N.Y. (named Nat. Hist. Landmark 1972); nat. dir. Washington Irving Graveplot Restoration Program, 1968—, designer landmark plaque for grave; mem. Nat. Council State Garden Clubs, 1959—; pres. Potpourri Garden Club, Westchester, N.Y., 1966—; nat. chmn. for graveplot programs Washington Irving Bicentennial, 1983-84; dir. Dorland Family Graveyard Restoration, N.J. Hist. Landmark, 1983—. Recipient May Duff Walters trophy Nat. Council State Garden Clubs, 1974; nat. trophy Nat. Historic Landmark Com., 1974; citation Keep Am. Beautiful, 1974. Mem. Nat. Trust for Historic Preservation (Pres.'s award 1977), Nat. Historic Soc. Am., Gen. Soc. Mayflower Desc., Internat. Washington Irving Soc. (founder, pres. 1981—), Nat. Assn. for Gravestone Studies (hon.), Herb Soc. Am., DAR. Home and Office: 10 Castle Heights Ave Tarrytown NY 10591

DORLAND, DODGE OATWELL, investment banker; b. N.Y.C., Feb. 27, 1948; s. Joseph Warner and Marion (Dodge) D.; m. Bonita Gillette Zeese, Jan. 9, 1971. Diploma, Choate Sch., 1966; BA, Colgate U., 1970; MBA, NYU, 1975. With Mfrs. Hanover Trust Co., N.Y.C., 1970-77, asst. sec., 1974-77; with Bank of Montreal Trust Co., N.Y.C., 1977-86, v.p., 1979-86, v.p. communications unit, 1982-86, U.S. industry coordinator for communications, 1983-86; v.p. Shearson Lehman Bros., Inc., N.Y.C., 1986-87; v.p. media and communications fin. Gen. Electric Corp., 1987—; bd. dirs. So. Telecom, Inc., West Ga. Cable, Inc. Author: The Communications Industry: An Informational Overview, 1983; contbr. papers in field to profl. jours. Treas. Learning for Living Inst., N.Y.C., 1977-81; chmn. bd. dirs. 325 E. 72d St. Apts., N.Y.C., 1978-81; participant NYU Grad. Sch. Bus. Mgmt. Decision Lab., 1977-79, now bd. dirs.; mem. investment com. Assn. for Relief of Elderly Inc., 1984—. Mem. Nat. Cable TV Assn., Nat Assn. Broadcasters, Cellular Telecommunications Industry Assn., The Elfun Soc. N.Y., Drama League N.Y., Broadcast Fin. Mgmt. Assn., Telocator Network of Am., Cellular Telecommunications Industry Assn., Media and Entertainment Analysts Assn. N.Y., Am. Film Inst., Smithsonian Inst., Vets. Corp. Arty., SAR, Soc. Colonial Wars, Mil. Order Loyal Legion of U.S., Holland Soc. Republican. Episcopalian. Clubs: Yale (N.Y.C.); Meadow, Bathing Corp. (Southampton, N.Y.)., Toastmasters (v.p. Mfrs. Hanover chpt. 1975-78). Home: 103 E 75th St New York NY 10021 Office: Gen Electric Capital Corp 535 Madison Ave Suite 2700 New York NY 10022

DORMANN, JUERGEN, chemical company executive; b. 1940. Student, U. Heidelberg, Fed. Republic Germany. Chmn., chief exec. officer, dir. Hoechst Celanese Corp., N.Y.C. Office: Hoechst Celanese Corp Rt 202-206 N Somerville NJ 08876 also: Hoechst Celanese Corp 1211 Ave of the Americas New York NY 10036 *

D'ORMESSON, JEAN See ORMESSON, JEAN D'

DORMINEY, HENRY CLAYTON, JR., allergist; b. Tifton, Ga., May 15, 1949; s. Henry Clayton and Virginia (Petty) D.; m. Diane Louise Thiel, Sept. 29, 1978. BS, Davidson Coll., 1971; MD, U. Iowa, 1975. Diplomate Am. Bd. Internal Medicine, Am. Bd. Allergy and Immunology; lic. physician, Ky., Iowa, Ga. Med. intern, U. Iowa Hosps. and Clinics, Iowa City, 1975-76, med. resident, 1976-78, allergy and immunology fellow, 1978-80; practice medicine specializing in allergy and clin. immunology Allergy and Dermatology Assos. Tifton, P.C. (Ga.), 1981—; mem. staff Tifton Gen. Hosp., chmn. peer rev./credentials com., 1986-87. Assoc. editor, contbng. author Vital Signs, 1969-71. Recipient Physician's Recognition award AMA, 1979, 85, Lee Willingham III trophy Davidson Coll., 1987; VA grantee, 1978-80, Am. Coll. Allergy grantee, 1980. Mem. ACP, Am. Acad. Allergy (travel grantee 1980), Tift County Med. Soc. (sec., treas. 1983-84, v.p. 1984-85, pres. 1985-86), Med. Assn. Ga., N.Y. Acad. Sci. Democrat. Lodge: Rotary (Spl. Merit award, founder Tifton Directory). Home: 1001 N Ridge Ave Tifton GA 31794 Office: 1409 B Tift Ave Tifton GA 31794

DORNBERG, JOHN ROBERT, journalist; b. Erfurt, Germany, Aug. 22, 1931; came to U.S., 1939; s. Robert Egon and Lily (Weisner) D.; m. Ursula Stalph, July 3, 1956 (div. 1976); 1 child, Stephan; m. Jane Haynes Green, Mar. 4, 1977. Student, U. Denver, 1953. Account executive Harry Shubart Pub. Relations, Denver, 1952-54; news editor The Overseas Weekly, Frankfurt, Fed. Republic Germany, 1956-63; corr. Newsweek Mag., Bonn, Fed. Republic Germany, 1963-67; bur. chief Newsweek Mag., Vienna, Moscow and Munich, 1967-73; free lance fgn. corr., writer Munich, 1973—. Author: The Other Germany, 1968, The New Tsars, 1972, Brezhnev, 1974, Munich 1923, 1982. Served as pfc. U.S. Army, 1954-56. Mem. Fgn. Press Assn. Fed. Republic Germany. Club: Overseas Press of Am. (N.Y.C.). Home and Office: Kafka Strasse 8, 8000 Munich Federal Republic of Germany

DORNER-ANDELORA, SHARON AGNES HADDON, educator; b. Morristown, N.J., Nov. 3, 1943; d. William P. and Eleanor (Dygert) Haddon; BA in Bus. Edn., Montclair State Coll., 1965, MA in Bus. Edn., 1970, MA in Guidance and Counseling, 1978; EdD in Vocat.-Tech. Edn., Adminstrn. and Supervision, Rutgers U., 1982; m. Robert Andelora, Feb. 17, 1985; children—Wendy, Meridith. Tchr., Morris Knolls High Sch., 1965-70; tchr. Katherine Gibbs Sec. Sch., Montclair, N.J., 1973-74; tchr. Leonia (N.J.) High Sch., 1974-75; tchr. bus. Woodcliff Sch., Woodcliff Lake, N.J., 1976—, adminstrv. intern to supt., 1980—; tchr. adult sch. Sussex Vocat. Sch., County Coll. Morris, Randolph, N.J. Judge, Election Bd., Montclair, 1972-82. Mem. Assn. Supervision and Curriculum Devel., Am. Vocat. Assn., Am. Vocat. Research Assn., N.J. Vocat. Assn., NEA, N.J. Edn. Assn., Bergen County Edn. Assn., Woodcliff Lake Edn. Assn. (sec. 1976-84), N.J. Bus. Edn. Assn. (co-editor Observer), Nat. Bus. Edn. Assn., Eastern Bus. Edn. Assn., Consumers League (dir. 1979—), N.J. Coll. Ednl. Leaders (v.p. 1985—, treas. 1983-84, Northeastern regional rep. 1982-83), Northeast Coalition Ednl. Leaders, Delta Pi Epsilon (pres. Beta Phi chpt. 1979-80, v.p. 1978-79, sec. 1976-78, newsletter editor 1974-76, nat. com. 1980-84, nat. council rep. 1981-88, nat. historian 1987—, chmn. nat. com. 1982-84), Sigma Kappa (nat. alumnae province officer 1977-81, nat. alumnae dist. dir. 1981-87), Phi Delta Kappa (pres. 1980-82 treas. 1975-79, 82-84, council del. 1977-80, 84-86, research rep. 1986-88, found. rep. 1988—), Omicron Tau Theta (pres. Delta chpt. 1987-88, v.p. 1986-87, nat. parliamentarian 1986-88). Lodges: Daus. of Nile, N.J. Eastern Star. Mem. adv. bd. Today's Sec., 1981-82. Home: 28 College Ave Upper Montclair NJ 07043 Office: 134 Woodcliff Ave Woodcliff Lake NJ 07675

DORNSIFE, SAMUEL JONATHAN, interior designer; b. Williamsport, Pa., Feb. 4, 1916; s. Henry Albert and Lizzie Lottie (Spatz) D.; D.F.A. (hon.). Lycoming Coll., 1976. Pvt. practice interior design, 1934—, designer in charge restorations including Gallier House, New Orleans, 1971—, San Francisco Plantation, Garyville, La., 1973-77, Hermann-Grima House, New Orleans, 1976—, White House of Confederacy, Richmond, Va., 1983; cons. on restoration Hermitage, Nashville, Biltmore, Asheville, N.C., Gov.'s Mansion, Jefferson City, Mo., Devereaux, Salt Lake City, Genesse Village, Mumford, N.Y., Gov.'s Mansion, Columbia, S.C., Edmondston-Alston House, Charleston, S.C., Maxwell Mansion, Phila., Iolani Palace, Honolulu, 1982—; lectr. Columbia U., Cornell U., Lycoming Coll; participant symposia Sotheby's, N.Y.C., Victorian Soc. in Am., Natchez Antiques Forum, Decorative Arts Soc. Mem. bd. Lycoming County Hist. Soc., 1950-82, Greater Williamsport Community Arts Council, 1970—; advisor to Hist. Architecture Rev. Bd., Williamsport; mem. archtl. tech. adv. com. Williamsport Area Community Coll., 1983—. Served with U.S. Army, 1942-46. Recipient commendation for carpet design for Iolani Palace, Resources Council, 1983. Fellow Royal Soc. Arts (London); mem. Am. Soc. Interior Designers (preservation award 1980), Soc. Archtl. Historians, Assn. for Preservation Tech., Decorative Arts Soc., Victorian Soc. Am. (dir. 1970-77), Victorian Soc. U.K., Furniture History Soc., Nat. Trust for Historic Preservation. Episcopalian. Author intro. and bibliogrpahy: Exterior Decoration, 1975, Some Sources for 19th Century Drapery Designs, 1975; sects. on wallpaper Ency. Victoriana, 1975, 19th Century Carpet Technology, 1981. Home and Office: 974 Hollywood Circle Williamsport PA 17701

DORO, MARION ELIZABETH, political scientist, educator; b. Miami, Fla., Oct. 9, 1928; d. George and Alma (Carram) D. B.A., Fla. State U., 1951, M.A., 1952; Ph.D. (Bennett fellow), U. Pa., 1959. Instr. polit. sci. Wheaton Coll., Norton, Mass., 1958-60; Ford Found. Area Studies fellow U. London, Kenya, Africa, 1960-62; asst. prof. Conn. Coll., New London, 1962-65; assoc. prof. Conn. Coll., 1965-70, prof., 1970—, Lucy Marsh Haskell prof. govt., 1983—, dir. grad. studies, 1975-79, chmn. dept. govt., 1981-84, 87—; assoc. So. Africa research program Yale U., 1988—. Editor: (with N. Stultz) Governing in Black Africa, 1970, 2d edit., 1986, Africa Contemporary Record; editor: African Contemporary Record, 1988—; mem. editorial bd.: African Studies Rev.; contbr. articles and book revs. to profl. jours. Fulbright fellow Makerere U., Kampala, Uganda, 1963-64; sr. research fellow Radcliffe Inst., Cambridge, Mass., 1968-69; vis. research fellow, Am. Philos. Soc. grantee East Africa Inst. Social Sci. Research, 1971-72; AAUW Am. fellow, sr. assoc. St. Anthony's Coll., Oxford U., 1977-78; vis. faculty fellow Yale U., 1984-85. Mem. Am. Polit. Sci. Assn. (publ. com. 1987—), N.Eng. Polit. Sci. Assn. (chmn. status women com. 1972-75, exec. council 1973-75), Northeast Polit. Sci. Assn. (exec. council 1974-76, 82-84), African Studies Assn. (dir. program nat. meetings 1976), AAUP, AAUW, Soc. Fellows Radcliffe Inst. (exec. council 1979-84), Phi Beta Kappa, Phi Kappa Phi, Pi Sigma Alpha. Office: Conn Coll PO Box 1457 New London CT 06320

DORON, CHAIM RAPHAEL, insurance company executive; b. Buenos Aires, Mar. 26, 1928; arrived in Israel, 1953; s. Moises and Ana (orlean) Derechinski; m. Noemi Gutman; children: Yshaihau, Amos, Hana. MD, U. London, 1952, Degree in Pub. Health, 1961. Regional med. officer K. Holim, Negev, Israel, 1961-68, head med. div., 1968-72, dep. chmn., 1972-76, chmn., bd. dirs., Tel Aviv—1976—. Office: Kupat H Health Ins, Gen Fed Labour, 101 Arlozorov St, Tel Aviv 62098, Israel

DORONINA, TATYANA VASILIYEVNA, actress; b. Sept. 12, 1933; grad. Studio Sch. Moscow Art Theatre, 1956. Appeared at Leningrad Lenin Komsomol State Theatre, 1956-59, Leningrad Maxim Gordy State Bolshoi Drama Theatre, 1959-66; Moscow Arts Theatre, 1966-71, Majakovski Theatre, Moscow, 1971-83, Moscow Arts Theatre, 1983—; leading roles include: (theatre) Zhenka Shulzhenko in Factory Girl, Lenochka in In Search of Happiness, Sophia in Wit Works Woe, Nadya Rozoyeve in My Elder Sister, Nadezhda Polikarpovna in The Barbarians, Lushka in Virgin Soil upturned, Nastasya Filippovna in the Idiot, Valka in Irkutsk Story, Oxana in Loss of the Squadron; (films) Nadya in Elder Sister, Natasha in Again about Love, Nivra in Three Poplars on Plushchikha Street. Mem. RSFSR. Office: care Moscow Theatre, 22 Tverskoi Blvd, Moscow USSR *

DOROSCHAK, JOHN Z., dentist; b. Solochiw, Ukraine, Feb. 11, 1928; s. William and Anna (Stroczan) D.; came to U.S., 1950, naturalized, 1954; student U. Minn., 1955-57, B.S., 1959, D.D.S., 1961; m. Nadia Zahorodny, June 30, 1962; children—Andrew, Michael, Natalie, Maria. Pvt. practice dentistry, Mpls., 1961—. Cons., St. Joseph's Home for Aged, Mpls., 1974-77, Holy Family Residence, St. Paul, 1977-84. Mem. steering com. St. Anthony West Neighborhood, Mpls., 1971-72; chmn. Mpls. dentists com. Little Sisters of the Poor Devel. Program, 1975; Webelos leader troop 50, Boy Scouts Am., 1975-76; pres. N.E. Regional Sch. Assn. Parents and Tchrs., 1978-79; bd. dirs. East Side Neighborhood Service, 1972; treas. Plast Inc., Ukrainian youth orgn., Mpls., 1979-83; mem. Sr. Citizen Centers Health Adv. Com., Mpls., 1979-83. Served with AUS, 1953-55. Mem. Am. Dental Assn., Minn. Dental Assn. (com. on dental care access 1980-83), Minn. Soc. Preventive Dentistry (dir. 1977-83, treas. 1979-83), Am. Soc. Dentistry for Children, Mpls. Dist. Dental Soc. (nursing home com. 1974—, chmn. 1979-82, 84—, emergency care com. 1983-84), Ukrainian Med. Assn. (sec.-treas. Minn. chpt. 1971-75), Ukrainian Profl. Club, Psi Omega. Mem. Ukrainian Catholic Ch. (campaign chmn. 1966-80, mem. ch. com. 1965—). Club: University Minnesota Alumni (charter mem.). Home: 919 Main St NE Minneapolis MN 55413 Office: Broadway and University Profl Bldg 230 NE Broadway Minneapolis MN 55413

DORR, ROBERT CHARLES, patent lawyer; b. Denver, Jan. 7, 1946; s. Owen and Rose Esther (Tudek) D.; m. Sandra Leah Gehlsen, Feb. 25, 1971; children—Bryan, Aric. B.S.E.E., Milw. Sch. Engring., 1968; M.S.E.E., Northwestern U., 1970; J.D., U. Denver, 1975. Bar: Colo. 1975, U.S. Dist. Ct. Colo. 1975, U.S. Patent Office 1975. Mem. tech. staff Bell Labs., Naperville, Ill., 1968-72, patent staff, Denver, 1975-76; ptnr. Dorr, Carson, Sloan & Peterson, Denver, 1976-86, sr. ptnr., 1986—; ptnr. Internat. Practicum Inst., Denver, 1979—; owner The Lawyers Edge, Inc., 1985—; seminar speaker various profl. orgns. Contbr. articles to profl. jours. Active Citizens Com. for Retention of Judges, Denver, 1984. Milw. Sch. Engring. scholar, 1964-68; named Outstanding Young Man Am., 1976. Mem. Douglas-Elbert County Bar Assn. (pres. 1983—), IEEE, AAAS, ABA, Colo. Trial Lawyers Assn., Sigma XI. Republican. Roman Catholic. Home: 519 Willowlake Dr PO Box 116 Franktown CO 80116 Office: Dorr Carson Sloan & Peterson 3010 E 6th Ave Denver CO 80222

DORR, ROBERT SIBLEY, publisher; b. Norwalk, Conn., Sept. 21, 1932; s. Sanders M. and Emma Millicent (Barron) D.; student public schs. Norwalk; With Acorn Press, Ridgefield, Conn., 1951-64; with Data Publs., Inc., Danbury, Conn., 1964—, pres., 1969—. Mem. Nat. Rifle Assn., Aircraft Owners and Pilots Assn., Internat. Platform Assn., Nat. Pilots Assn., Exptl. Aircraft Assn. Republican. Methodist. Club: Nat. Press. Office: Danbury Airport Wibling Rd Danbury CT 06810

DÖRRBECKER, DETLEF W., art historian; b. Frankfurt, Fed. Republic of Germany, Jan. 4, 1951; s. Klaus and Ruth (Pennrich) D. MA, Johann Wolfgang Goethe U., Frankfurt, 1979; PhD, U. Trier, Fed. Republic of Germany, 1986. Lectr. art history U. Trier, Fed. Republic of Germany, 1979-86, asst. prof., 1986—. Co-compiler ann. bibliography, Blake/An Illustrated Quar. U. N.Mex., Albuquerque, 1977-84, bibliographer, U. Rochester, N.Y., 1984—; contbr. articles to profl. jours. Research grantee Studienstiftung des Deutschen Volkes, 1978-79. Mem. Swiss Inst. for Art Research. Office: Fach Kunstgeschichte im FB III, PO Box 3825, D-5000 Trier Federal Republic of Germany

DORRIE, CHARLES THEODORE, manufacturing company executive; b. N.Y.C., June 25, 1925; s. Charles Frederick and Agnes Christine (Andersen) D.; student public schs., N.Y.C.; div.; children: Richard Stephen, Suzanne Christine Dorrie Metz. Chief tool designer and supr. Hilton Tool & Machine Co., Bronx, N.Y., 1947-52; chief design engr. tools and machinery Edwards Engring. Corp., Pompton Plains, N.J., 1952-70; pres., dir. Karlo Mfg. Co., Inc., Ringwood, N.J., 1970—; bd. govs. Tool Makers Inst. Pres., Pets Poison Protection Assn., Inc. Served with USMC, 1942-45; PTO. Recipient Soc. Mfg. Engrs. award. Mem. Soc. Mfg. Engrs. (cert. mfg. technologist, past chmn. chpt. 102, editor SME Bull.), N.J. Tooling and Mfg. Assn. (pres., dir.). Home: 112 Cedar Ave Pompton Lakes NJ 07442 Office: 236 Margaret King Ave Ringwood NJ 07456

DORRITIE, JOHN FRANCIS, pharmaceutical advertising agency executive; b. N.Y.C., Feb. 26, 1934; s. George D. and Mary C. (Pollock) D.; m. Carol Kelley, July 23, 1960; children: George, Teresa, John, Carol Jean. B.S., Iona Coll., 1955. Product mgr., asst. advt. mgr. Sandoz Pharms., 1957-65; v.p. account services Sudler & Hennessey, Inc., 1965-68; founder, pres. Stat-Kit, Inc., 1968-69; exec. dir. Council for Interdisciplinary Communications in Medicine, N.Y.C., 1970; sr. v.p. Sudler & Hennessey, N.Y.C., 1970-77; exec. v.p. Sudler & Hennessey, 1977-79; pres. Dorritie & Lyons Inc., 1979—. Served with U.S. Army, 1955-57. Mem. Am. Mktg. Assn., Pharm. Advt. Club, Midwest Pharm. Advt. Club, Soc. Advanced Med. Systems., AAAS, N.Y. Acad. Scis. Roman Catholic. Home: 8 Gable Rd New City NY 10956 Office: 655 Third Ave New York NY 10017

DORSETT, CHARLES IRVIN, mathematics educator; b. Lufkin, Tex., Sept. 25, 1945; s. C.B. and Dorothy Alice (Smith) D. B.S., Stephen F. Austin State U., Nacogdoches, Tex., 1967, M.S., 1968; Ph.D., N. Tex. State U., 1976. Cert. secondary sch. tchr., Tex. Instr. Stephen F. Austin State U., 1968-71; lectr. N. Tex. State U., Denton, 1976-77, 78-79; asst. prof. La. Tech U., Ruston, 1977-78, assoc. prof., 1982—; lectr. Tex. A&M U., College Station, 1979-82; reviewer Zentralblatt Für Mathematik und Ihre Grenzgebrite, 1983—; referee Indian Jour. Pure and Applied Math., 1986—, INdian Jour. Math., 1986—, Bulletin of the Faculty of Sci., Assiut Univ.; Physics and Math., 1986—. Contbr. articles to profl. publs. Recipient Cert. for Excellence in Research, La. Tech U., 1984-85, La. Tech. Sigma Xi Research award, 1987. Mem. Am. Math. Soc., Sigma Xi. Baptist. Avocations: mathematical research, farming. Home: Route 9 Box 4290 Lufkin TX 75901 Office: La Tech U Dept Math and Stats Ruston LA 71272

DORSEY, JEREMIAH EDMUND, pharmaceutical company executive; b. Worcester, Mass., Oct. 15, 1944; s. Jeremiah Edmund and Mary Theresa Dorsey; A.B., Assumption Coll., Worcester, 1966; M.B.A., Fairleigh Dickinson U., 1978; m. Nadia S. Vidach, Dec. 6, 1970; children—Todd Edmund, Jaime Erin, Megan Elizabeth, Kelly Ann. With Johnson & Johnson, New Brunswick, N.J., 1970-88, nat. indsl. engring. mgr., 1975-76, supt. ops. and maintenance, from 1976, now dir. ops. and mem. mgmt. bd.; v.p. ops. and sales Johnson & Johnson Dental Products Co.; pres. ops. The Karlin Group, Bridgeton, N.J.,1988—; pres. J.E. Dorsey Co. Active N.J. Commn. for Discharge Up-grade, Appalachian Trail Conf.; mem. alumni bd. dirs. Assumption Coll.; mem. adv. com. U. P.R. Sch. of Pharmacy; mem. mil. acad. selection com. U.S. Senate; vice chmn. N.J. Vietnam Vets. Leadership Program; mem. Mercer County Pvt. Industry Council (N.J.), N.J. SR-92 Coalition. Served with U.S. Army, 1966-69; Vietnam. Decorated Bronze Star with 2 oak leaf clusters, Purple Heart with 4 oak leaf clusters, Army Commendation medal, Air medal with oak leaf cluster; Medal of Honor, Gallantry Cross (Vietnam); recipient Corp. Affirmative Action award, 1981. named Mgr. of Yr., Johnson & Johnson, 1974-75. Mem. Sierra Club, Spl. Forces Assn., Smithsonian Assocs., DAV, Soc. First Div., Tiger Karate Soc. (Black Belt), Delta Epsilon Sigma. Roman Catholic. Clubs: K.C.; Johnson & Johnson Mgmt. Editor: Spl. Forces Assn. News. Home: 10 Eastern Dr Kendall Park NJ 08824 Office: The Karlin Group Dutch Neck Rd PO Box 160 Windsor NJ 08520

DOS, SERGE JACQUES, surgeon, physiology researcher; b. Paris, Jan. 24, 1934; came to U.S., 1957; s. Octave Pierre Marie and Fernande Lucienne (Daire) D.; m. Rasma Kupers, Aug. 19, 1966; children: Soshana, Yasmin, Maiya. M.D., U. Paris, 1964; Ph.D. in Physiology, U. Minn., 1965. Diplomate Am. Bd. Surgery. Lab. instr. physiology U. Minn., Mpls., 1962-65; instr. in surgery Cornell U., N.Y.C., 1971-73; asst. prof. surgery SUNY-Stony Brook, 1973, asst. prof. clin. physiology, 1973-76; surgeon St. John's Episcopal Hosp., Smithtown, N.Y., 1978—; research com. VA Hosp., Northport, N.Y., 1974-76. Contbr. chpt. to book. USPHS trainee., 1962-65; various research grants NIH; various research grants Am. Heart Assn.; various research grants pvt. labs.; Laureate (Silver Medal) Faculty of Medicine U. Paris, 1966. Fellow N.Y. Acad. Scis.; mem. Am. Fedn. Clin. Research, AAAS, Am. Physiol. Soc., Assn. Acad. Surgery. Current Work: Physiology, history. Subspecialties: Surgery; Cardiac surgery.

DOSANJH, DARSHAN S(INGH), aeronautical engineer, educator; b. Sultanwind, Punjab, India, Feb. 21, 1921; came to U.S., 1946, naturalized, 1965; s. S. Arur and Inder (Hundal) D.; B.Sc. (honours) Physics, Punjab U., India, 1944, M.S., 1945; M.S. in Aero. Engring., U. Mich., 1948; Ph.D. in Aeros., Johns Hopkins U., 1953; m. Harwant K. Gill, Mar. 18, 1957; children—Amrita K., Kiren K., Rajit S. Research assoc. U. Md. Inst. Fluid Dynamics and Applied Math., 1955-56; assoc. prof. mech. and aerospace engring. Syracuse (N.Y.) U., 1956-62, prof., 1962—; vis. prof. Coll. Aeros., Cranfield, Eng., 1961-62; Fulbright-Hayes sr. faculty research fellow and vis. prof. Southampton (Eng.) U., 1971-72. NATO fellow, 1967. Mem. AIAA (aeroacoustics tech. com.; assoc. fellow); mem. Acoustical Soc. Am., Am. Phys. Soc., ASME, Am. Soc. Engring. Edn., AAUP. Editor: Modern Optical Methods in Gas Dynamics Research, 1971; Effects of Noise on Hearing, 1976; contbr. numerous articles to sci. jours. Home: 5176 Brockway Ln Fayetteville NY 13066

DOSEN, KOSTA, logician; b. Belgrade, Serbia, Yugoslavia, June 5, 1954; s. Milenko and Hristina (Milosevic) D.; m. Tatjana Ostrogorski, June 24, 1984. BA in Philosophy, U. Belgrade, 1977; PhD in Math. Logic, Oxford (Eng.) U., 1981. Asst. prof. Math. Inst., Belgrade, 1982—; asst. prof. faculty of sci. U. Belgrade, 1985—; vis. asst. prof. dept. philosophy U. Notre Dame, South Bend, Ind., 1986-87. Author: Hilbert's Problems and Logic, 1986; contbr. articles to profl. jours. Mem. Assn. Symbolic Logic, Serbian Philosophical Soc. Orthodox Christian. Home: General Zdanova 19, 11000 Belgrade Yugoslavia Office: Math Inst, Knez Mihailova 35, 11000 Belgrade Yugoslavia

DOSKACH, ANNA GRIGORYEVNA, geographer; b. Leningrad, USSR, Feb. 26, 1911; d. Grigori Lazarevich and Sophia (Evgenyevna) D.; m. Anatoli Illarionovich Dvoryadkin, Sept. 27, 1940; 1 child: Yurii Anatolyevich. Dip., Leningrad State U., 1933; PhD in Geography, Acad. Sci., USSR, 1940. Researcher 1st grade Inst. Geography Acad. Sci., USSR, 1933-36, sr. researcher, 1937—; cons. in field. Author books; contbr. articles to profl. jours. Recipient Badge of Honor Presidium of Supreme Soviet of USSR, 1946. Mem. Geog. Soc. Acad. Sci. USSR, Knowledge Soc. Home: Apt 264 Bldg 5, 6 Obruchev St, Moscow USSR Office: Inst Geog Acad Sci USSR, 29 Staromonetny per, Moscow USSR

DOS SANTOS, JOSE EDUARDO, president of Angola; b. Aug. 28, 1942; s. Edwardo Avelino and Jacinta Paulino. Grad. Patrice Lumumba U., Moscow, 1969; various mil. course in telecommunications. Joined Movimiento Popular de Libertação de Angola (MPLA), 1961; went into exile, 1961; founder, v.p. MPLA Youth, Leopoldville, Congo (now Kinshasa, Zaire); returned to Angola and participated in war against Portuguese, 1970-73; mem. MPLA Central Com. 2nd Polit. Bur., 1974—, then chmn.; coordinator MPLA Fgn. Relations Dept., 1975-79; sec. Central Com. for Edn., Culture and Sport; then sec. Nat. Reconstruction; sec. Econ. Devel. and Planning, 1977-79; minister of planning, pres. Nat. Planning Commn., 1978-80; dep. prime minister, then pres. of Angola, 1980—, now also minister of state for social and econ. affairs; mem. polit. bur. Popular Movement for the Liberation of Angola. Office: Oficio de Presidente, Luanda Angola *

DOTO, PAUL JEROME, accountant; b. Newark, July 22, 1917; s. Anthony and Edith Margaret (Mascellaro) D. BS, NYU, 1947. Registered mcpl. acct., N.J.; registered pub. sch. acct., N.J. Acct. John Hewitt Foundry Co., East Newark, N.J., 1941-43; acct. S.D. Leidesdorf & Co., N.Y.C., 1947-56; CPA Peat Marwick Mitchell & Co., N.Y.C., 1956-64; asst. controller Lincoln Ctr. for the Performing Arts Inc., N.Y.C. 1964-69; controller Seton Hall U., South Orange, N.J., 1969-74, Belart Products, Applied Coatings, Maddock, Inc., N.J., 1974-80, Internat. Trading Sales, Inc., Pan Atlantic Paper Co., N.Y.C., 1980; cons. Controller's Office, City N.Y., 1966. Bd. dirs. Parkway, Ltd., 1973-78. Served with AUS, 1943-46. Mem. Nat. Police Hall of Fame. Mem. N.Y. State Soc. CPA's (chmn. govtl. accounting com. 1963-64, chmn. internal control quest on aid of municipalities N.Y. State), Am. Inst. CPA's, Cath. Accts. Guild (bd. govs. 1961-64), N.J. Soc. CPA's, N.Y. State Soc. CPA's, Am. Accounting Assn., Fin. Execs. Inst., N.Y. Assn. Profs., Smithsonian Assocs. (charter), Am. Legion, Am. Mus. Natural Hist. N.Y.C. (assoc.) Address: PO Box 2508 Bloomfield NJ 07003

DOUB, WILLIAM OFFUTT, lawyer; b. Cumberland, Md., Sept. 3, 1931; s. Albert A. and Fannabelle (Offutt) D.; m. Mary Graham Boggs, Sept. 12,

1959; children: Joseph Peyton, Albert A., II. A.B., Washington and Jefferson Coll., 1953; LL.B., U. Md., 1956. Bar: Md. 1956, D.C. 1974. With law dept. B. & O. R.R., 1955-57; assoc. Bartlett Poe & Claggett, Balt., 1957-61; ptnr. Niles Barton & Wilmer, Balt., 1961-71; commr. AEC, 1971-74; ptnr. LeBoeuf, Lamb, Leiby & MacRae, Washington, 1974-77, Doub & Muntzing, Washington, 1977—; chmn. Minimum Wage Commn., Balt., 1964-66; peoples' counsel Md. Pub. Service Commn., 1967-68, chmn., 1968-71; vice chmn. Washington Met. Area Transit Commn., 1968-71; mem. President's Air Quality Adv. Bd., 1970-71; mem. exec. adv. com. FPC, 1969-71, Nat. Gas Survey, 1975-78; pres. Great Lakes Conf. Pub. Utility Commrs., 1971; mem. nat. adv. bd. Am. Nat. Standards Inst., 1975-80; mem. Md. Adv. Com. Retardation, 1969-71. Mem. Adminstrv. Conf. U.S., 1973-75; chmn. U.S. Energy Assn. Inc. World Energy Conf., 1978-80, U.S. del., 1974, 77, 80, 83, 86; vice chmn. World Energy Conf., 1986—; mem. adv. groups Nat. Acad. Public Adminstrn., NSF; presdl. appointee as rep. to So. States Energy Bd., 1983—; trustee Thomas Alva Edison Found., mem. exec. com., 1983—, v.p., 1985—; bd. govs. Middle East Inst., exec. com., 1985—. Clubs: Met., City Tavern (Washington); East India (London). Home: 6 Warde Ct Potomac MD 20854

DOUCE, CLAUDE-LOUIS, advertising executive; b. St. Maurice, France, Oct. 10, 1937; s. Louis-Léandre and Odette (Louis-Jean) D.; m. Evelyne Baglin, June 4, 1962; children: Valérie, Frédéric, Chantal, Emilie. BEPC, Brevet Comml.; postgrad., Harvard U., 1969. Account executive Havas Conseil, Paris, 1957-72, account supr., 1968-69, bus. mgr., 1970-72; founder Belier Conseil, Neuilly-Sur-Seine, France, 1972, chmn., chief exec. officer, 1976; chmn., chief exec. officer Group Belier, Neuilly-Sur-Seine, 1980—, Groupe BELIER/WCRS, 1987; vice chmn., chief exec. officer Eurocom, 1986. Named chevalier Order Nat.du Mérite, chevalier Order de la Légion d'Honneur. Named Chevalier Order Nat. du Mérite. Office: Groupe BELIER/WCRS, 27-29 reu des Poissonniers, 92200 Neuilly Sur Seine France

DOUCET, JEAN, parasitologist, educator; b. Paris, Mar. 4, 1919; s. Leon and Louise (Renaud) D.; m. Martine Geismar, Mar. 3, 1948 (div. June 1957); 1 child, Catherine Doucet Simonelli; m. Andree Labuzan, Sept. 20, 1958 (div. June 1973); 1 child, Beatrice Doucet Vacher. Baccalaureat Philo., Lycee Voltaire, Paris, 1937; M.D., U. Paris, 1947, Dr.Sci., 1965, Agreg.Fac.Medici, 1965. With Office de la Recherche Scientifique et Technique d'Outre-mer, 1948—, dir. research, 1962-66; maitre de conference agrege des Facultes de Medecine, Abidjan, 1966, prof. lectr., 1966-74; titulaire prof. U. Abidjan, 1974-82; U. Nice, 1982—; chief lab. med. entomology Inst. Recherche Sci., Madagascar, 1948-51; chief lab. med. parasitology Inst. d'Enseign Recherche Tropicale Abidjan, 1951-65; chief lab. Centre Hospitalier Abidjan, 1966-82, Nice, 1982—; dir. lab. Analyses Med. Inst. U. Tech. Abidjan, 1969-77. Author: Les Anopheles de Madagascar, 1950, Les Serpents de Cote d'Ivoire, 1964, Contribution a l'etude des Pentastomes, 1965. Conbr. articles to profl. jours. Decorated Chevalier Legion d'Honneur, officier Palmes Academiques, Croix de Guerre. Mem. Assn. French Experts Coop. Tech. Internat., Soc. French Parasitologie, Soc. French Mycol. Med., Internat. Soc. Human Animal Mycology, Royal Soc. Tropical Med. Hygiene, AAAS, Soc. French Microbiology; hon. mem. Soc. Belge Med. Tropical, Mensa, Planetary Soc., Nat. Geog. Soc. Clubs: NR Explorer's (N.Y.C.) (fellow). Lodge: Lions. Home: 3 Boulevard du Parc Imperial, 0600 Nice France Office: Faculte de Medecine, av de Vallombrose, Nice France

DOUCETTE, DAVID ROBERT, computer systems company executive; b. Pitts., Feb. 2, 1946; s. Mary Alyce (Newland) D. B.S.E.E., Poly. Inst. Bklyn., 1968, M.S.E.E., 1970, Ph.D., 1974. Asst. prof. elec. engring. Poly. Inst. N.Y., 1973-74; assoc. prof. computer sci., 1975-82, prof., 1982—; sr. staff specialist advanced planning Grumman Data Systems Corp., Bethpage, N.Y., 1979-80, program mgr., 1979-80, mgr. graphics systems, 1980-84, from asst. dir. to dir. interactive systems support, 1984-86, dir. interactive systems, 1986—. Active Friends of Long Island Heritage, Nassau County Hist. Soc., Garden City Hist. Soc. Mem. IEEE (past sect. chmn.), Assn. Computing Machinery (past chpt. chmn.), L.I. Forum for Tech. (dir.), AIAA (sect. dir.), Planetary Soc., Am. Space Found., Sigma Xi, Tau Beta Pi, Eta Kappa Nu. Club: University of L.I. (dir.), Long Island Early Fliers. Home: 146 Washington Ave Garden City NY 11530 Office: Grumman Data Systems Corp Bethpage NY 11714

DOUGAL, ARWIN ADELBERT, educator, electrical engineer; b. Dunlap, Iowa, Nov. 22, 1926; s. Adelbert Isaac and Goldya (White) D.; m. Margaret Jane McLennan, Sept. 3, 1951; children: Catherine Anne, Roger Adelbert, Leonard Harley, Laura Beth. B.S., Iowa State U., 1952; M.S., U. Ill., 1955, Ph.D., 1957. Registered profl. engr., Tex. Radio engr. Collins Radio Co., Cedar Rapids, Iowa, 1952; research asst., research asso., asst. prof., asso. prof. U. Ill., Urbana, 1952-61; prof., mem. grad. faculty, dir. labs. for electronics and related sci. research U. Tex., Austin, 1961-67; prof. U. Tex., 1969—; dir. Electronics Research Center, 1971-77, sec. grad. assembly, 1972-74; dir. Austron, Inc., 1977 82; asst. dir. def. research and engring. for research Office Sec. Def., Washington, 1967-69; cons. Tex. Instruments, Inc., Dallas, Gen. Dynamics Corp., Ft. Worth, U. Calif. Los Alamos Sci. Lab. Contbr. articles to profl. jours. Faculty sponsor U. Tex. Conservative Democrats Club, 1966-67; sr. mem. CAP, 1984—. Served with USAF, 1946-49. Recipient Teaching Excellence awards U. Tex. Students Assn., 1962, 63, Spl. award for outstanding service as program chmn. S.W. IEEE Conf. and Exhbn., 1967; Outstanding Grad. Adviser award Grad. Engring. Council, U. Tex., 1971; Disting. Advisor award Grad. Engring. Council, U. Tex., 1977, 84; Teaching Achievement award Grad. Engring. Council, U. Tex., 1977; Profl. Achievement citation in engring. Iowa State U. Alumni Assn., 1975. Fellow Am. Phys. Soc., IEEE (dir. 1980-81, Centennial medal 1984, Student Br. Citation 1988); mem. Am. Soc. Engring. Edn., Optical Soc. Am., Sigma Xi, Phi Kappa Phi, Tau Beta Pi, Eta Kappa Nu, Pi Mu Epsilon, Phi Eta Sigma. Presbyn. (elder). Club: Lakeway Yacht and Country. Home: 6115 Rickey Dr Austin TX 78731

DOUGHERTY, JAMES, orthopaedic surgeon; b. Lawrence, Mass., July 31, 1926; s. James A. and Maude D. (Dillard) D.; m. Rita Buchman; children—James (dec.), Charles, Janice, Jonathan, Christopher. B.S., Trinity Coll., Hartford, Conn., 1950; M.D., Albany Med. Coll., N.Y., 1951. Diplomate Am. Bd. Orthopaedic Surgery. Intern, U. Chgo. Clinics, 1951-52, resident, 1951-56; instr., 1955-56; chmn. div. orthopaedic surgery SUNY, Syracuse, 1958-59; prof. clin. surgery Albany Med. Coll., 1960—; chmn. med. staff Albany Med. Ctr., 1987—. Contbr. articles to profl. jours. Mem. Bd. Edn. Ravena-Coeymans-Selkirk Central Schs., Ravena, N.Y., 1960-75. Served with U.S. Army, 1944-46. Fellow Am. Acad. Othopaedic Surgeons; mem. Crawford Campbell Soc. (pres. 1978-84), Northeastern Regional Assn. Sports Medicine (chmn. 1984—), Alpha Omega Alpha, Sigma Psi. Baptist. Home: Onesquethaw Creek Rd Feura Bush NY 12067 Office: 1 Executive Park Dr Albany NY 12203

DOUGHERTY, JOHN CHRYSOSTOM, III, lawyer; b. Beeville, Tex., May 3, 1915; s. John Chrysostom and Mary V. (Henderson) D.; m. Mary Ireland Graves, Apr. 18, 1942 (dec. July 1977); children: Mary Ireland, John Chrysostom IV; m. Bea Ann Smith, June 1978 (div. 1981); m. Sarah B. Randle, 1981. BA, U. Tex., 1937; LLB, Harvard, 1940; diploma, Inter-Am. Acad. Internat. and Comparative Law, Havana, Cuba, 1948. Bar: Tex. 1940. Atty. Hewit & Dougherty, Beeville, 1940-41; ptnr. Graves & Dougherty, Austin, Tex., 1946-50, Graves, Dougherty & Greenhill, Austin, 1950-57, Graves, Dougherty & Gee, Austin, 1957-60, Graves, Dougherty, Gee & Hearon, Austin, 1961-66, Graves, Dougherty, Gee, Hearon, Moody & Garwood, Austin, 1966-73, Graves, Dougherty, Hearon, Moody & Garwood, Austin, 1973-79, Graves, Dougherty, Hearon & Moody, Austin, 1979—; spl. asst. atty. gen., 1949-50; Hon. French Consul, Austin, 1971-86; lectr. on tax, estate planning, probate code, community property problems; mem. Tex. Submerged Lands Adv. Com., 1963-72, Tex. Bus. and Commerce Code Adv. Com., 1964-66, Gov.'s Com. on Marine Resources, 1970-71, Gov.'s Planning Com. on Colorado River Basin Water Quality Mgmt. Study, 1972-73, Tex. Legis. Property Tax Com., 1973-75. Co-editor: Texas Appellate Practice, 1964, 2d edit., 1977; contbr. Bowe, Estate Planning and Taxation; Texas Lawyers Practice Guide, 1967, 71, How to Live and Die with Texas Probate, 1968, 5th edit., 1988, Texas Estate Administration, 1975, 78; mem. bd. editors: Appellate Procedure in Tex., 1964, 2d edit., 1982; contbr. articles to legal jours. Bd. dirs. Grenville Clark Fund at Dartmouth Coll., 1976—; past bd. dirs. Advanced Religious Study Found., Holy Cross Hosp., Sea Arama, Inc., Nat. Pollution Control Found., Austin Nat. Bank; trustee St. Stephen's Episcopal Sch., Austin, 1969-83, U. Tex. Law Sch. Found., 1974—. Served as capt. C.I.C. AUS, 1941-44, JAGC, 1944-46, now maj. Res. Decorated Medaille Française France, Medaille d'honneur en Argent des Affairs Etrangeres France, Chevalier, L'Ordre Nat. du Merite. Fellow Am. Bar Found., Tex. Bar Found., Am. Coll. Probate Counsel, Am. Coll. Tax Counsel, Tex. State Bar Coll.; mem. Am. Arbitration Assn. (mem. nat. panel arbitrators 1958—), Inter-Am. Bar Assn., ABA (mem. ho. dels. 1982—), Travis County Bar Assn. (pres.-elect 1978, pres. 1979-80), State Bar Tex. (chmn. sect. taxation 1965-66, pres.-elect 1978, pres. 1979-80, chmn. State Bar Coll. Bd. 1983-84), Am. Judicature Soc. (bd. dirs. 1986—), Internat. Law Assn., Am. Fgn. Law Assn., Am. Law Inst., Am. Soc. Internat. Law (exec. council 1959-62), World Assn. Lawyers, Internat. Acad. Estate and Trust Law (exec. com. 1986—), Am. Assn. Internat. Council Jurists, Cum Laude Soc., Phi Beta Kappa, Phi Eta Sigma, Beta Theta Pi (bd. dirs. Tex. Beta Students Aid Fund 1947-85). Presbyterian. Lodge: Rotary. Home: 6 Green Lanes Austin TX 78703 Office: 2300 First Republic Bank Tower Austin TX 78701 also: PO Box 98 Austin TX 78767

DOUGHERTY, RUSSELL ELLIOTT, lawyer, retired air force officer, association executive; b. Glasgow, Ky., Nov. 15, 1920; s. Ewell Walter and Bess (House) D.; m. m Geralee Shaaber, Apr. 26, 1943 (dec. Jan. 1978); children: Diane Ellen, Mark Elliott, William Bryant; m. Barbara Brooks Lake, Sept. 1978. A.B., Western Ky. U., 1941; J.D., U. Louisville, 1948; grad., Nat. War Coll., 1960; LL.D., U. Akron, 1975, U. Nebr., 1976, U. Louisville, 1977; D.Sc., Westminster Coll., 1976, Embry-Riddle Aeronautical U., 1986. Bar: Ky. bar 1948. Also U.S. Supreme Ct.; commd. 2d. lt. USAAF, 1943; advanced through grades to gen. USAF, 1972; various staff and command assignments in Far East Air Forces, SAC, U.S. European Command, World War II; dir. European region Office of Sec. of Def., 1965-67; dep. chief of staff for plans and operations Hdqrs. USAF, 1970; comdr. 2d Air Force (Strategic Air Command), 1971; chief of staff Supreme Hdqrs. Allied Powers Europe, 1972-74; comdr.-in-chief Strategic Air Command and dir. U.S. Strategic Target Planning, 1974-77, ret., 1977; exec. dir. Air Force Assn., 1980-86; corp. atty. McGuire, Woods, Battle and Boothe, 1986—; bd. dirs. Enron Corp.; vice chmn. bd. trustees Aerospace Corp.; mem. Def. Sci. Bd.; planned Operation Powerflight Mission, 1957; U.S. planner Stanleyville (Republic Congo) Rescue Operation, 1964; trustee Inst. Def. Analysis. Bd. visitors Nat. Def. U.; bd. dirs. Atlantic Council of U.S., Falcon Found., Air Force Assn. Decorated D.S.M. USAF; (3), D.S.M. Dept. Def.; (2), Legion of Merit; (3), Bronze Star.; recipient Outstanding Alumnus award Western Ky. U., 1976, David Sannoff award Armed Forces Communications and Electronics Assn., 1980, Gen. Thomas D. White Nat. Def. award U.S. Air Force Acad., 1983; named Man of Yr. Nat. Jewish Hosp., 1976, Man of Yr. Los Angeles Philanthropic Soc.d, 1976, Disting. Grad., Louisville Law Sch., 1984, Outstanding Alumnus Ky., Gov. and Ky. Advocates, 1987. Mem. Ky. Bar Assn., Omicron Delta Kappa, Phi Alpha Delta, Lambda Chi Alpha. Home: Forest Hills 2359 S Queen St Arlington VA 22202 Office: 8280 Greensboro Dr Suite 900 McLean VA 22102 Other: The Aerospace Corp 2350 E El Segundo Blvd El Segundo CA 90245

DOUGLAS, DWIGHT OLIVER, university administrator; b. Mt. Carmel, Ill., May 7, 1941; s. Dwight Oliver and Jeannette Elizabeth (Moyer) D.; m. Carol Jane Brunson, June 2, 1963; children: Terri, Staci, Dana. B.S., Eastern Ill. U., 1962, M.S., 1966; D.Ed., U. Tenn., 1972. Asst. dir. residence halls U. Tenn., Knoxville, 1969-71, dir. residence halls, 1971-72; dir. housing U. Ga., Athens, 1972-74, dean student affairs, 1975-78, assoc. v.p. acad. affairs, 1978-80, v.p. student affairs, 1980—. Contbr. articles to profl. jours. Pres. PTA Council Clarke County, 1978; pres. Gaines Sch. PTA, 1977-78. Mem. Nat. Assn. Student Personnel Adminstrs. (state dir. Ga. 1982-84), So. Assn. Coll. Student Affairs, Ga. Personnel Assn., Phi Delta Kappa, Kappa Delta Pi, Omicron Delta Kappa. Methodist. Club: Gridiron. Office: U Ga 201 Academic Bldg Athens GA 30602

DOUGLAS, EDWARD FRANKLIN, artist, photographer; b. San Rafael, Calif., May 6, 1943; arrived in Australia, 1973; s. Glen Franklin and Thelma Viola (Rais) D.; m. Nancy Wehrheim, Aug. 8, 1965 (div. 1970). A.A., Coll. of Marin, Kentfield, Calif., 1963; student San Francisco Art Inst., 1964-65; B.F.A., San Francisco State U., 1967, M.F.A., 1969. Founding mem. Visual Dialogue Found., San Francisco, 1969; tchr. photography Coll. Marin, Kentfield, Calif., 1969-73; farmer, studio owner, Nimbin, N.S.W., Australia, 1974-75; tchr. Sydney Coll. of the Arts, 1976-77; head photo studies South Australian Sch. Art, 1977—. One-man shows include Australian Centre Photography, Sydney, 1975, 82, Sydney Coll. Arts, 1976, Contemporary Art Soc., Parkside, S. Australia, 1978, Developed Image Gallery, Adelaide, 1982, Christine Abrahams Gallery, Melbourne, 1983; group exhbns. include Australian Centre Photography, 1980-84, Tasmanian Sch. Art, Hobart, 1985; represented in permanent collections Australian Centre Photography, Sydney, Gallery South Australia, Adelaide, Mus. Modern Art, N.Y.C., Bibliotheque Nat., Paris, Internat. Mus. Photography, Rochester, N.Y., Australian Nat. Gallery, Canberra, San Francisco Mus. Modern Art; contbr. articles and photographs to profl. jours. Recipient Grand Prix, Le Provençal du Festival d'Avignon, France, 1971; Visual Arts Bd. equipment grantee, 1976, spl. projects grantee, 1981; CSR Project grantee, 1982-83; Commn., Parliament House Constrn. Authority, 1984. Home: 26 Charles Sturt Ave, Grange South Australia 50221, Australia Office: South Australian Sch Art, Holbrooks Rd, Underdale South Australia, Australia *

DOUGLAS, HERBERT PAUL, JR., beverage company executive; b. Pitts., Mar. 9, 1922; s. Herbert Paul and Ilessa May (France) D.; m. Rozell Reid, Jan. 3, 1950; children—Barbara Joy, Herbert Paul III. B.S., U. Pitts., 1948, M.S., 1950. Sales rep. Pabst Brewing Co., So. Eastern states, 1950-58; dist. mgr. Pabst Brewing Co., 1958-63; control states rep. Schieffelin & Co., N.Y.C., 1963-65; nat. spl. markets mgr. Schieffelin & Co., 1965-68, v.p. nat. spl. markets, 1968-83, v.p. urban market devel., 1983—; lectr. West Chester Coll., Chester, Pa., 1972. Com. mem. Phila. chpt. Fight for Sight, 1974-75; chmn. Black Athletes Hall of Fame, 1974; mem. 1976 U.S. Olympic Com. Recipient Olympic medal for track and field, 1948; Beverage Industry award Urban League Guild, 1974; Black Book award as outstanding businessman, 1986; Dr. Martin Luther King Jr. award N.Y. Bottle and Cork, 1986, Athlete of Yr. Pitts., 1948, Bicentennial medallion U. Pitts, 1987; inducted into Varsity Lettermen Club of Distinction U. Pitts., 1980; Hon. Pittsburgher medallion, 1986. Mem. Sales Execs. Club of New York (exec. bd.). Baptist. Club: Elk. Home: 407 Rices Mill Rd Wyncote PA 19095 Office: 30 Cooper Sq New York NY 10003

DOUGLAS, LLOYD EVANS, supervisory computer systems programmer; b. N.Y.C., Oct. 5, 1951; s. Calvin and Lurline (Brown) D.; m. Janet Aline St. Laurent, Jan. 20, 1979 (div. 1984). B.S., CCNY, 1972; M.S., Miami U., Oxford, Ohio, 1974; postgrad. Boston U., 1974-76. Teaching fellow Boston U., 1975-76; sr. teaching fellow Boston U., 1976-76; mathematician U.S. Dept. Navy, Newport, R.I., 1976-78, computer specialist, 1978-80; ops. research analyst U.S. Dept. Army, Ft. Monmouth, N.J., 1980-83; computer specialist GSA, Washington, 1983-84; head central systems mgmt. NSF, Washington, 1984—. N.Y. State Regents scholar, 1968-72. Mem. Math. Assn. Am., Am. Math. Soc., Fed. Automatic Data Processing Users Group. Democrat. Lutheran. Home: 5544 Karen Elaine Dr #1521 New Carrollton MD 20784 Office: NSF Office Info Systems 1800 G St NW Washington DC 20550

DOUGLAS, MARION JOAN, labor negotiator; b. Jersey City, May 29, 1940; d. Walter Stanley and Sophie Frances (Zysk) Binaski; children: Jane Dee, Alex Jay. BA, Mich. State U., 1962; MSW, Sacramento State Coll., 1971; MPA, Calif. State U.-Sacramento, 1981. Owner, mgr. Linkletter-Totten Dance Studios, Sacramento, 1962-68, Young World of Discovery, Sacramento, 1965-68; welfare worker Sacramento County, 1964-67, welfare supr., 1968-72, child welfare supr., 1972-75, sr. personnel analyst, 1976-78, personnel program mgr., 1978-81, labor relations rep., 1981—; cons. State Dept. Health, Sacramento, 1975-76; cons. in field. Author/editor: (newsletter) Thursday's Child, 1972-74. Presiding officer Community Resource Orgn., Fair Oaks, Calif., 1970-72; exec. bd. Foster Parent's Assn., Sacramento, 1972-75; organizer Foster Care Sch. Dist. liaison programs, 1973-75; active Am. Lung Assn., 1983-87; rep. Calif. Welfare Dirs. Assn., 1975-76; county staff advisor Joint Powers Authority, Sacramento, 1978-81; mem. Mgmt. Devel. Com., Sacramento, 1979-80; vol., auctioneer sta. KVIE Pub. TV, Sacramento, 1970-84, 88—; adv. bd. Job and Info. Resource Ctr., 1976-77; spl. adv. task force coordinator Sacramento Employment and Tng. Adv. Council, 1980-81; vol. leader Am. Lung Assn., Sacramento, 1983-86 Calif. Dept. Social Welfare ednl. stipend, 1967-68, County of Sacramento ednl. stipend, 1969-70. Recipient Achievement award Nat. Assn. Counties, 1981. Mem. Mgmt. Women's Forum, Indsl. Relations Assn. No. Calif., Indsl. Relations Research Assn., Nat. Assn. Female Execs., Mensa. Republican. Avocations: real estate, nutrition. Home: 7812 Palmyra Dr Fair Oaks CA 95628 Office: County of Sacramento Dept Personnel Mgmt 700 H St Sacramento CA 95814

DOUGLAS, SIR WILLIAM (RANDOLPH), judge; b. Barbados, W.I., Sept. 24, 1921; m. Thelma Ruth Gilkes, Apr. 4, 1951; 2 children. BA with honors, McGill U., 1942; LLB, U. London, 1948. Bar: 1947. Sole practice Barbados, 1948-50; dep. registrar Supreme Ct., Barbados, 1950-55; resident magistrate Jamaica, 1955-59, asst. atty. gen., 1959-62, solicitor gen., 1962, Puisne judge, 1962-65; chief justice Barbados, 1965-86; ambassador to U.S. and permanent rep. to OAS 1986-87; acted as Gov.-Gen. Barbados, 1965-86; mem. exec. council World Assn. Judges, 1967-75; mem. jud. com. of several appeals Her Majesty's Privy Council, London, 1979—; mem. com. experts on application of convs. and recommendations Internat. Labour Orgn., Geneva, 1975—, dep. judge ILO Adminstrv. Tribunal, 1982; mem. Adminstrv. Tribunal Inter-Am. Devel. Bank, Washington, 1982-86; mem. Inter-Am. Juridicial Com., Rio de Janeiro, 1977-81, chmn., 1981; chmn. Council on Legal Edn. for Commonwealth Caribbean, 1971-77; participant various confs., seminars, and workshops, 1970-87. Pres. Barbados Civil Service Assn., 1954-55, Barbados Assn. for Blind and Deaf, 1966-87, Barbados Arts Council, 1967-74, Caribbean Council for Blind, 1968-75, Barbados Boy Scouts Assn., 1971-87, UN Assn. Barbados, 1974-87, Barbados Council for Handicapped, 1979-84; mem. council Bellairs Inst. McGill U., 1966-87, Royal Commonwealth Soc. for Blind, 1975—; chmn. Barbados chpt. Duke of Edinburgh's Award Scheme, 1957-61; patron Barbados Amateur Athletic Assn., 1976-88. Named Knight Bachelor, 1969, Privy Councillor, 1977, Knight Comdr. Most Disting. Order St. Michael and St. George, 1983. Office: Embassy of Barbados 2144 Wyoming Ave NW Washington DC 20008

DOUGLASS, HARRY ROBERT, hospital and health care consultant, architect, educator; b. McCook, Nebr., Mar. 27, 1937; s. Harry William and Irma Ruth Douglass; divorced; 1 son, William Robert. B.Arch., U. Nebr., 1963; M.Arch. in Hosp. Planning, U. Minn., 1965; grad. owner, pres. mgmt. program Harvard U. Bus. Sch., 1983. Chmn., chief exec. officer Robert Douglass Assocs. Inc., Hosp. Cons., Houston, 1973-88, merged with Deloitte, Haskins & Sells, 1988, ptnr., 1988—, also bd. dirs.; assoc. prof. Rice U., U. Tex. Sch. Pub. Health, 1973-75; adj. prof. health care planning Rice U., 1975—. AIA-Am. Hosp. Assn. Joint fellow, 1964-66. Fellow Am. Assn. Hosp. Cons., Am. Inst. Architects; mem. Soc. Hosp. Planners, AIA (nat. com. on architecture for health), Am. Assn. Hosp. Planning (dir. 1975-80), Am. Mgmt. Assn., Houston C. of C. (health com.). Episcopalian. Contbr. articles to profl. jours.; rep. exec. bd. WHO, Managua, 1972; organizer, dir. internat. seminar in hosp. and health care Panamerican Health Orgn., U. San Martin, Buenos Aires, 1971; designer, planned of numerous archtl. projects; recipient numerous design awards, including Presdl. Silver medal for Charles River Project, Boston, 1984. Clubs: Houston, City. Home: 1905 Wroxton Houston TX 77005 Office: Douglass Group Deloitte Haskins & Sells 1200 Travis Houston TX 77002

DOUILLARD, NATHALIE PIERRE OUVAROFF, social worker; b. Kiev, USSR, Sept. 9, 1911; arrived in France, 1912; d. Serge and Nathalie (Tereschenko) Ouvaroff; m. Pierre Douillard, June 19, 1939. Ed. pvt. schs., Paris. V.p. social work 5 Brittany hosps., 1945—. Decorated Legion of Honor, Croix de Guerre a etoile. Home: Moulin de Pontours, 29262 Ploudalmezeau, Plouguin France Office: Centre Hygiene Alementaire, 232 Rue Jean Jaures, F-29200 Brest France

DOUMA, HARRY HEIN, social service agency administrator; b. Richmond, N.Y., Mar. 12, 1933; s. Hein and Ida D. (Van Der Veer) D.; m. Carole Marie Piening; June 21, 1958; children:Daniel H., Deborah Joy, Crystal A. BA in Philosophy, Shelton Coll., 1960; MDiv, Faith Theol. Sem., 1965. Ordained to ministry, 1965. Pastor Port Monmouth (N.J.) Ch., 1955-60; chaplain Edward R. Johnstone Tng. and Research Ctr., Bordentown, N.J., 1960-65; pastor Times Beach (Mo.) Bible Ch., 1965-67, 1st Bapt. Ch., Pilot Knob, Mo., 1967-76; founder, pres., pastor Penuel, Inc., Ironton, Mo., 1973—. Author The Book of Revelation for the Layman, 1971. Mem. Rep. Presdl. Task Force. Served with USN, 1953-55. Mem. Full Gospel Bus. Men's Fellowship Internat. Home: 326 Michael Ln Rt 1 Box 593 Ironton MO 63650 Office: Penuel Inc Box 367 Lake Killarney-Ironton MO 63650

DOURNOVO, PIERRE ALEXANDRE, physician; b. Paris, Nov. 10, 1945; s. Alexandre Jean and Tatiana (Savitsky) D.; m. Marianne Faye Thibaut; children: Nathalie, Julien. MD, U. Paris, 1974; grad., Inst. Polit. Scis., Paris, 1986. House physician various hosps., Paris, 1970 74; head of clinic Bichat Hosp., Paris, 1974-81; head dept. pneumology Eaubonne Hosp., France, 1983—; cons. physician Am. Hosp., Paris, 1981—. Contbr. articles to profl. jours. Mem. French Soc. Pneumolgy, French Soc. Internal Med. Home: 16 rue Edouard Vaillant, Saint Ouen 93400, France Office: Eaubonne Hosp, rue du Docteur Roux, Eaubonne 95600, France

DOUTT, GERALDINE MOFFATT, educational administrator; b. Warren, Mich., Apr. 16, 1927; d. Stanford and Wilhelmine (Ewaldt) Moffatt; married, 2 children. B.S. in Occupational Therapy, Eastern Mich. U., Ypsilanti, 1952, M.A. in Edn., 1959; E.D.S. in Spl. Edn., Wayne State U., Detroit, 1968; m. Robert G. Doutt; children—Eric Robert, Gerald George. Tchr., Van Dyke Pub. Schs., Warren, 1963-65, tchr. educable mentally impaired, 1965-67, tchr. cons. for emotionally impaired, 1967-69, dir. spl. edn., 1969—. Chmn. Macomb County Interagy. Council, 1968-69. Mem. Mich. Assn. Dirs. Spl. Edn., Nat. Council Exceptional Children, Delta Kappa Gamma. Home: 22919 Playview St Saint Clair Shores MI 48082 also: Treasure Island Higgins Lake PO Box 412 Higgins Lake MI 48627 Office: 22100 Federal St Warren MI 48089

DOVALE, ANTONIO JOSEPH, JR., chemical engineer; b. Newark, Feb. 25, 1954; s. Antonio Joseph and Rose (Bevacqua) DoV. BS in Chem. Engring., N.J. Inst. Tech., 1975; m. Fern Louise Crandall, Oct. 17, 1981. Sr. process engr. M.W. Kellogg Co., Hackensack, N.J., 1975-84; mgr. FGD systems Wheelabrator Air Pollution Control, Pitts., 1984—. Registered profl. engr., N.J., Mass. Mem., Conn., Fla. Mem. Am. Inst. Chem. Engrs., Sigma Xi, Omega Chi Epsilon, Tau Beta Pi. Roman Catholic.

DOVE, DONALD AUGUSTINE, city planner, educator; b. Waco, Tex., Aug. 7, 1930; s. Sebert Constantine and Amy Delmena (Stern) D.; m. Cecelia Mae White, Feb. 9, 1957; children—Angela Dove Gaddy, Donald, Monica, Celine, Austin, Cathlyn, Dianna, Jennifer. B.A., Calif. State U.-Los Angeles, 1951; M.A. in Pub. Adminstrn., U. So. Calif., 1966. Planning and devel. cons. D. Dove Assocs., Los Angeles, 1959-60; supr. demographic research Calif. Dept. Pub. Works, Los Angeles, 1960-66, environ. coordinator, Sacramento, 1971-75; dir. transp. employment project State of Calif., Los Angeles, 1966-71, chief Los Angeles Region transp. study, 1975-84; chief environ. planning Calif. Dept. Transp., Los Angeles, 1972-75; dir. U. So. Calif. Praetors, Los Angeles, 1984-87; panelist, advisor Pres. Conf. on Aging, Washington, 1970—, Internat. Conf. on Energy Use Mgmt., 1981; guest lectr. univs. western U.S., 1969—. Author: Preserving Urban Environment, 1976; Small Area Population Forecasts, 1966. Chmn. Lynwood City Planning Commn., Calif., 1982—; pres. Area Pastoral Council, Los Angeles, 1982-83; mem., del. Archdiocesan Pastoral Council, Los Angeles, 1979-86, Compton Community Devel. Bd., Calif., 1967-71. Served to cpl. U.S. Army, 1952-54. Mem. Am. Planning Assn., Am. Inst. Planners (transp. chmn. 1972-73), Calif. Assn. of Mgmt. (pres. 1987-88), Am. Inst. Cert. Planners, Assn. Environ. Profls. (co-founder 1973). Democrat. Roman Catholic. Lodges: Optimists (sec. 1978-79), K.C., Knights of Peter Claver. Home: 11356 Ernestine Ave Lynwood CA 90262 Office: Calif Dept Transp 120 S Spring St Los Angeles CA 90012

DOVER, KENNETH JAMES, educator, Greek scholar; b. Croydon, Eng., Mar. 11, 1920; s. Percy Henry and Dorothy Valerie (Healey) D.; student Balliol Coll., Oxford (Eng.) U., 1938-40, 45-47, M.A., 1946, D.Litt., 1974, student Merton Coll., 1948; LL.D., Birmingham U., St. Andrews U.; D.Litt., U. Bristol, U. Liverpool, U. London, St. Andrews U., U. Liverpool, U.

Durham; m. Audrey Ruth Latimer, Mar. 17, 1947; children—Alan Hugh, Catherine Ruth. Fellow, tutor Balliol Coll., Oxford (Eng.) U., 1948-55, pres. Corpus Christi Coll., 1976-86, hon. fellow; prof. of Greek, St. Andrews U., 1955-76; chancellor St. Andrews U., 1981—; prof.-at-large Cornell U., 1983—; vis. lectr. Harvard U., 1960; Sather vis. prof. U. Calif., 1967. Served with artillery Brit. Army, 1940-45; mentioned in dispatches. Created Knight, 1977. Fellow Brit. Acad. (pres., 1978-81); mem. Hellenic Soc. (pres., 1971-74), Classical Assn. (pres., 1975), Am. Acad. Arts and Scis., Netherlands Acad. Arts and Scis. Club: Athenaeum. Author: Greek Word Order, 1960; Lysias and the Corpus Lysiacum, 1968; Aristophanic Comedy, 1972; Greek Popular Morality in the Time of Plato and Aristotle, 1974; Greek Homosexuality, 1978; The Greeks, 1980; contbr. to other books and articles; editor: Aristophanes' Clouds, 1968; Theocritus, 1971; Plato, Symposium, 1980. Home: 49 Hepburn Gardens, Saint Andrews KY16 9LS Scotland Office: British Acad, 20-21 Cornwall Terrace, London NW1 4QP England *

DOVLETOGLOU, PAUL CHRISTOS, pharmacist; b. Thessaloniki, Greece, May 4, 1939; s. Christos and Catherine (Pasmatzoglou) D.; m. Smaragda Paul Nomikou, Dec. 20, 1970; 1 son, Christos. Pharm. Degree, Thessaloniki U., 1964. With pharm. div. Bristol Hellas Ltd., Thessaloniki, 1967-68, sales supr. pharm. div., 1969-70; sales mgr. pharm. div. Bristol Hellas AEBE, Athens, Greece, 1971-72, mgr., 1973-78, dir., 1978—, v.p. bd. dirs., 1978-83; owner Comml. House of Pharm. Products, Athens, 1984—; pres. Panhellenic Union of Pharmacists, Athens, 1982—. Served as officer-pharmacist Greek Army, 1965-67. Mem. Greek Mgmt. Assn., Greek Mktg. Inst. Clubs: Lions Possidon (v.p.), Vouliagmeni Nautical (Athens). Office: Menandrou 68, 104 32 Athens Greece

DOVRING, KARIN ELSA INGEBORG, author, playwright; b. Stenstorp, Sweden, Dec. 5, 1919; came to U.S., 1953, naturalized, 1968; grad. Coll. Commerce, Gothenburg, Sweden, 1936; M.A., Lund (Sweden) U., 1943, Ph.D., 1951; Phil. Licentiate, Gothenburg U., 1947; m. Folke Dovring, May 30, 1943. Journalist several Swedish daily newspapers and weekly mags., 1940-60; tchr. Swedish colls.; research assoc. of Harold Lasswell Yale U., New Haven, 1953-78; fgn. corr. Swedish newspapers, Italy, Switzerland, France and Germany, 1956-60; vis. prof. Internat. U., Rome, 1958-60, Gottingen (W.Ger.) U., 1962; lectr. numerous univs. including Yale U., U. Wis., McGill U., U. Iowa; research assoc. U. Ill., Urbana, 1968-69; invited contbr. Spl. Sci. Research Council, 1988; free-lance writer, journalist, 1960—; radio and TV interviews; books include Songs of Zion, 1951, Land Reform as a Propaganda Theme, 3d edit. 1965, Road of Propaganda, 1959, Optional Society, 1972; Frontiers of Communication, 1975, (short stories) No Parking This Side of Heaven, 1982; Harold D. Lasswell: His Communication with a Future, 1987; Forked Tongue? Body-Snatched English in Political Communications, 1988, contbr. numerous articles to mags.; writer Ill. Alliance to Prevent Nuclear War, radio theater. Recipient Swedish Nat. award for short stories Bonniers Pub. House Stockholm, 1951; lit. awards Internat. Acad. Leonardo da Vinci, Rome, 1982-83. Mem. NOW, Société Jean Jacques Rousseau (hon. life), Inst. Freedom of Press (life asso.). Democrat. Address: 613 W Vermont Ave Urbana IL 61801

DOW, JEAN LOUISE, school system business manager; b. Mattoon, Ill., Dec. 20, 1955; d. Paul Leroy and Maria (Brandlhofer) Smith; m. Chris Alan Pfeiffer, June 1, 1974 (div. Nov. 1979); 1 child, Lisa Marie; m. Bradley Ray Elder, Sept. 4, 1982 (div. Mar. 1985); m. John W. Dow, Aug. 1, 1986. B.S. in Bus., Eastern Ill. U., 1977, M.B.A., 1980. Office mgr. ED Buxton & Assocs., Charleston, Ill., 1974-77; personnel mgr. Unibuilt Structures, Charleston, 1977-80; bus. mgr. Eastern Ill Area Spl. Edn., Mattoon, 1980—. Ill. Assn. Sch. Bus. Ofcls. (scholarship 1984, com. mem. 1984—), Assn. Sch. Bus. Ofcls., Ill. Adminstrs. Spl. Edn. Republican. Kappa Delta Pi. Baptist. Avocations: sewing; jogging; swimming; racquetball; tennis.

DOW, THOMAS WENDELL, psychiatrist; b. Boston, Oct. 7, 1939; s. Wendell Adams and Elise Rose (Mullaney) D.; B.S., Boston Coll., 1961; M.D., U. Vt., 1965; postgrad. McGill U., 1968-71; m. Anne Campbell Shea, June 11, 1960; children—David Wendell, Abra Elise. Intern, Lakeland (Fla.) Gen. and Polk County (Fla.) hosps., 1965-66; resident psychiatry Douglas Hosp., Verdun, Que., 1968-69, Jewish Gen. Hosp., Montreal, 1969-71; practice medicine specializing in psychiatry Orlando, Fla., 1971—; mem. staffs Orlando Regional Med. Center, chmn. dept. psychiatry, 1983-85; clin. dir. West Lake Hosp., 1984—; mem. staff Fla. Hosp., Lucerne Gen. Hosp.; psychiat. cons. Orlando Regional Med. Center Community Mental Health Center, 1972-84, Cath. Social Services, 1973-77, Hillcrest Halfway House, 1971-73, Orange County Sch. System, 1977—; v.p. med. staff West Lake Hosp., Longwood, Fla., 1984-86, pres. 1986-88; clin. asst. prof. U. S. Fla. Coll. Medicine, 1978—. Mem. citizens advocacy com. Emotionally Disturbed Children of Central Fla., Orlando. Trustee, chmn. planning and evaluation com. Mental Health Bd. Central Fla., 1974-80; bd. dirs., chmn. profl. adv. com. Thee Door of Orange County Drug Abuse Program, 1971-74; bd. dirs. Orange County Mental Health Assn. Served to capt. M.C., USAF, 1966-68. Recipient Sir William Osler medal, 1965; diplomate Am. Bd. Psychiatry and Neurology. Fellow Am. Psychiat. Assn.; mem. Can. Psychiat. Assn., Am. Group Psychotherapy Assn., Am., So., Fla. med. assns., Orange County Med. Soc., Fla. Psychiat. Soc. (br. pres. 1975—), Am. Soc. Adolescent Psychiatry, Fla. Psychiat. Cons. (v.p.), Am. Acad. Child Psychiatry. Democrat. Unitarian. Club: Bay Hill Country. Home: 6083 Tarawood Dr Orlando FL 32819 Office: 201 S Orange Ave Suite 620 Orlando FL 32801

DOW, WILLIAM GOULD, electrical engineer, educator; b. Faribault, Minn., Sept. 30, 1895; s. James Jabez and Myra Amelia (Brown) D.; m. Edna Lois Sontag., Oct. 24, 1924 (dec. Feb. 1963); children—Daniel Gould, David Sontag; m. Katherine Bird Keene, Apr. 2, 1968; stepchildren—John S. Keene, Margaret Keene Hannan, Karen Keene Day. B.S., U. Minn., 1916, E.E., 1917; M.S.E., U. Mich., 1929; D.Sc. (hon.), U. Colo., 1980. Registered profl. engr., Mich. Diversified engring. and bus. experience 1917-26; faculty, dept. elec. engring. U. Mich., Ann Arbor, 1926-65; prof. elec. engring. U. Mich., 1945-65, chmn. dept. elec. engring., 1958-64, prof. emeritus, 1966—; sr. research geophysicist Space Physics Research Lab., 1966-71; electronics cons. Nat. Bur. Standards, 1945-55; research staff Radio Research Lab., Harvard, 1943-45, assignment, U.K., winter 1944-45; sci. adv. com. Harry Diamond Labs., 1953-64; bus. mgr. Lang. Studies Abroad, Spain, summers, 1965-74; Mem. vacuum tube devel. com. NDRC, World War II; (European vacuum tube research survey), 1953; mem. rocket and satellite research panel, 1946-60; U.S. tech. panel on rocketry IGY, 1956-59; made world tour for space research and engring. edn. survey, 1969-70; Charter mem. bd. trustees Environmental Research Inst. Mich., 1972—. Author: Fundamentals of Engineering Electronics, 1937, rev. 1952, Very High Frequency Techniques (co-author), 2 vols, 1947; Contbr. tech. articles in field. Served as lt. C.E. U.S. Army, World War I. Recipient medal, award in elec. engring. edn. IEEE, 1963. Fellow IEEE (bd. editors 1941-54), Engring. Soc. Detroit, AAAS; mem. AAUP, Am. Phys. Soc., Am. Inst. Aeros. and Astronautics, Am. Geophys. Union, Nat., Mich. socs. profl. engrs., Am. Astronautical Soc., N.Y. Acad. Scis., Am. Soc. Engring. Edn., Am. Welding Soc., Nat. Electronics Conf. (dir. 1949-52, chmn. bd. 1951), Sigma Xi, Tau Beta Pi, Eta Kappa Nu. Episcopalian. Clubs: Mason. (Minn.), Cosmos (Washington). Home: 915 Heatherway Ann Arbor MI 48104

DOWBEN, CARLA LURIE, lawyer, educator; b. Chgo., Jan. 22, 1932; d. Harold H. and Gertrude (Geitner) Lurie; m. Robert Dowben, June 20, 1950; children: Peter Arnold, Jonathan Stuart, Susan Laurie. AB, U. Chgo., 1950; JD, Temple U., 1955; cert., Brandeis U., 1968. Bar: Ill. 1957, Mass. 1963, Tex. 1974, U.S. Supreme Ct., 1974. Assoc. Conrad and Verges, Chgo., 1957-62; exec. officer MIT, Cambridge, Mass., 1963-64; legal planner, Mass. Health Planning Project, Boston, 1964-69; assoc. prof. Life Scis. Inst., Brown U., Providence, 1970-72; asst. prof. health law U. Tex. Health Sci. Ctr., Dallas, 1973-78, assoc. prof., 1978—; ptnr. Brice and Mankoff, Dallas; cons. to bd. dirs. Mental Health Assn., 1958-86, Ft. Worth Assn. Retarded Citizens, 1980—, Advocacy, Inc., 1981-85. Contbr. articles to profl. jours.; active in drafting health and mental health legis., agy. regulations in several states and locat govts. Mem. ABA, Tex. Bar Assn., Dallas Bar Assn., Nat. Health Lawyers Assn., Hastings Inst. Ethics, Tex. Family Planning Assn. Quaker. Home: 7150 Eudora Dr Dallas TX 75230 Office: Brice and Mankoff 300 Crescent Ct Dallas TX 75201-1841

DOWD, JAMES PATRICK, bookseller; b. Chgo., Apr. 26, 1937; s. James Patrick and Mary Margaret (Healy) D.; m. Frances Marie Allevato, Aug. 4, 1962; children—Mary Frances, Daniel James, Matthew Joseph. Student Wright Jr. Coll., 1956-58, Harper Coll., 1984, Elgin Community Coll., 1986, AS, 1988. With Spraying Systems Co., Wheaton, Ill., 1958-78, owner operator Dowd's Book Shoppe, St. Charles, Ill., 1978-80. tech. specialist Fermi Nat. Accelerator Lab., Batavia, Ill., 1980—, task order adminstr., 1986-88, fabrication specialist, 1986-88; mem. SSC task force, 1984-88, Elgin (Ill.) Community Coll., 1986-88; hist. cons. Potawatomi Indian Statue Com., St. Charles. Editor: Life of Black Hawk, 1974. Author: Built Like A Bear, 1979; Custer Lives, 1983, The Potawatomi-A Native American Legacy, 1988. Contbr.: Images of the Mystic Truth, 1981. Served with U.S. Army, 1961-63. Mem. Midwest Bookhunters. Roman Catholic. Chgo. Corral of Westerners (hon.). Avocations: collector of scarce and rare western Americana. Home: 38 W 281 Toms Trail Dr Saint Charles IL 60175 Office: Fermi Nat Accelerator Lab PO Box 500 MS 314 Batavia IL 60510

DOWD, MICHAEL BURKE, architect; b. Alexandria, Va., Dec. 1, 1958; s. Thomas John and Catherine Jean (Burke) D.; m. Hilary Mackenzie, Aug. 16, 1986. BA, U. Wash., 1980, MArch, 1983. Registered architect, Wash., Oreg. Designer Charles Bergmann, Architect, Seattle, 1983, Ibsen Nelsen & Assocs., Seattle, 1983-84, GBD Architects, Portland, Oreg., 1984—. Contbr. and Portland correspondent to ARCADE Jour., 1983—; archtl. drawings and projects of projects published in various mags. and jours. Recipient Blue Ribbon ARCADE Jour., 1985, 1st prize Arts N.W., 1982, Portland Landmarks Commn. award, 1986, Design award City of Beaverton, 1987. Mem. AIA (exhbn. Portland Oreg. chpt. 1988). Home: 2722 SW Rutland Terr Portland OR 97201 Office: GBD Architects 920 SW 3d Ave Suite 4000 Portland OR 97204

DOWD, PETER JEROME, public relations executive; b. Bklyn., Oct. 5, 1942; s. Jerome Ambrose and Mary Agnes (Young) D.; m. Brenda Badura, Nov. 25, 1972; 1 child, Kelly Ann. A.B., Fordham U., 1964. Reporter UPI, N.Y.C., 1964-66; account exec. Hill and Knowlton, N.Y.C., 1966-71; v.p. Hill and Knowlton, 1971-74; sr. v.p., mgr. Hill and Knowlton (Los Angeles office), 1974-78, mng. dir. Western region, 1978-80, exec. v.p., 1980; ptnr. Haley, Kiss & Dowd, Inc., Los Angeles, 1980-83; group v.p. Am. Med. Internat., 1983—; instr. U. So. Calif., Calif. State U., Fullerton; gen. mgr., pub. relations Tecaco, Inc., 1988—. Bd. dirs. Cath. Big Bros.; trustee Center for Non-profit Mgmt. Mem. Public Relations Soc. Am. (dir. Los Angeles chpt.), Town Hall West (v.p., dir.). Republican. Roman Catholic. Club: Jonathan (Los Angeles). Office: 414 N Camden Dr Beverly Hills CA 90210

DOWDY, JOHN WESLEY, JR., minister; b. Muskogee, Okla., Nov. 15, 1935; s. John Wesley and Floy Weaver (Thurston) D.; m. Joycelyn Adele Pinnell, June 9, 1956; children: Barbara Annette, Gina Marie (dec.). AA, Southwest Baptist Coll., 1954; BA, Southwest Mo. State U., 1956; M in Div., Midwestern Baptsit Theol. Sem., 1962, D in Ministries, 1974. Pastor Cedar City (Mo.) Baptist Ch., 1956-59, First Baptist Ch., Maysville, Mo., 1959-64, Tabernacle Baptist Ch., Kansas City, Mo., 1964-75; dir. Christian social ministries Metro Mission Bd., Kansas City, 1975-78; dir. Christian social ministries Mo. Baptist Convention, Jefferson City, Mo., 1978-80, dir. missions dept., 1980-88, dir. missions evangelism div., 1988—; field supr., adj. prof. D of Ministries program Midwestern Baptist Theol Sem., Kansas City, Mo., 1976—; cons. SBC Home Mission Bd., Atlanta, 1976—. Pres. Inter Faith Chaplian's Commn. of Mo., Jefferson City, 1983—; bd. dirs. Am. Field Service, Jefferson City, 1985-88. Mem. So. Baptist Convention Research Soc., So. Baptist Social Service Soc., Futurist Soc. Am. Home: 1004 Winston Dr Jefferson City MO 65101 Office: Mo Baptist Convention 400 E High Jefferson City MO 65101

DOWELL, ANTHONY JAMES, ballet dancer; b. London, Feb. 16, 1943; s. Arthur Henry and Catherine Ethel D. Studied with, June Hampshire; student, Royal Ballet Sch. Dancer Covent Garden Opera Ballet, 1960; dancer Royal Ballet, 1961-78, prin. dancer, 1966—, asst. to dir., 1984-85, assoc. dir., 1985-86, artistic dir., 1986—; guest artist Am. Ballet Threatre, N.Y.C., 1977-79. Created: dance roles in ballets The Dream, 1964, Monotones, 1965, Jazz Calendar, 1968, Shadowplay, 1967, Enigma Variations, 1968, Meditation, 1971, Anastasia, 1971, Triad, 1972, Pavane, 1973, Manon, 1974, Four Schumann Pieces, 1975, A Month in the Country, 1976, Contre Dances, 1979; appeared in: film Valentino; guest artist: Nat. Ballet Can., 1979, 81. Comdr. Order Brit. Empire.; Recipient award Dance mag., 1972. Office: care Peter S Diggins Assocs 133 W 71st St New York NY 10023 Address: Royal Ballet, Royal Opera House, Covent Garden, London WC2E 9DD England *

DOWELL, RICHARD PATRICK, professional services executive, consultant; b. Washington, Apr. 21, 1934; s. Cassius McClellan and Mary Barbara (McHenry) D.; m. Eleanor Craddock Halley, Dec. 23, 1957 (div. Sept. 1973); children: Richard Patrick Jr., Robert Paul, Christopher Lee; m. Sandra Susan Humm, June 16, 1974; children: Ethan Leslie Smith, Allison Courtney Smith. BS, U.S. Mil. Acad., 1956; MA, Stanford U., 1961, post-grad., 1962; postgrad., The Am. U., 1971-80; grad., The Nat. War Coll., 1975. Commd. 2d lt. USAF, 1956, advanced through grades to lt. col., 1974, ret., 1976; mgr. The BDM Corp., Fairfax, Va., 1977-79; sr. analyst Analytic Services, Inc., Arlington, Va., 1979-81, div. mgr., 1981-84, v.p., 1984—. Contr. articles to profl. jours. Pres. Alexandria (Va.) Taxpayer's Alliance, 1983. Decorated Bronze star, Air medal with 13 oak leaf clusters, D.F.C. with one oak leaf cluster. Mem. Mil. Ops. Research Soc., Air Force Assn. Republican. Roman Catholic. Home: 414 Franklin St Alexandria VA 22314 Office: Analytic Services Inc 1215 Jefferson Davis Hwy Suite 800 Arlington VA 22202

DOWLING, EMILIA MARIA, psychologist; b. Bogota, Colombia, Nov. 5, 1941; arrived in Eng., 1972.; d. Ernesto Calvo and Maria Mercado de Calvo; m. John Richard Dowling, June 6, 1974; children: Robert, Paul. Degree in Profl. Psychology, Javeriana U., Bogota, 1967; postgrad., Tavistock Clinic, 1972-73; MSc, U. Wales, 1977; postgrad., Inst. Sci. Tech., Cardiff, Wales, 1977. Lic. clin. psychologist. Lectr., tutor clin. psychology Javeriana U., 1968-71; head child psychology dept. Hosp. Infantil, Bogota, 1968-71; child psychotherapist Wandsworth Child Guidance Clinic, London, 1972-73; sr. clin. psychologist The Family Inst., Cardiff, 1973-77, acting prin. family therapist, 1977-79, research psychologist, 1973-77; prin. clin. psychologist child, family dept. Tavistock Clinic, London, 1982—; cons. London schs., 1982—; tutor clin. tng. Inst. Family Therapy, London, 1980—; organzing tutor advanced course on working with systems Tavistock Clinc, London, 1982—; hon. tchr. Brunel U., London, 1987—. Author/editor: The Family and the School, A Joint Systems Approach to Problems with Children, 1985; contbr. articles to profl. jours.; mem. editorial bd. Jour. Family Therapy, London, 1982-86, assessor, 1981—. Mem. Brit. Psychol. Soc. (grad., div. clin. psychology), Assn. Family Therapy, Assn. Child Psychology and Psychiatry. Roman Catholic. Home: 29 Lynmouth Rd, London N2 9LR, England Office: Tavistock Clinic, Dept Child and Family, 120 Belsize Ln, London NW3, England

DOWLING, JACQUES MACCUISTON, sculptor, painter, writer; b. Texarkana, Tex., Oct. 19, 1906; d. Charles Edward and Viola John (Estes) MacCuiston; Tchrs. Certificate, Coll. Marshall, 1923; studied art Loyola U., Frolich's Sch. Fine Art, Los Angeles, NAD, Art Students League, N.Y.C.; Ph.D., Colo. State Christian Coll. One woman shows include Fedn. Dallas Artists, 1950, 52, Rush Gallery, 1958, Sartor's Gallery, 1958, Sheraton-Dallas Hotel, 1960, Dallas Meml. Auditorium, 1960; exhibited in group shows at Dallas Mus. Fine Arts, Mus. of N.Mex., Fedn. Dallas Artists, Sartor's Galleries, Ney Art Mus., Oak Cliff Soc. of Fine Arts, Sartor's Gallery, Shuttles Gallery, Sheraton-Park Internat. Platform Assn., 1966-68, Phillips Mills Art Assn., 1967-74, Yardley Ann. Exhbn., 1968-73, Tinicum Art Festival, 1968, Woodmere Art Gallery (life mem.), 1972-74, others; selected sculpture 1st S.W. ann. show Mus. N.Mex., 1958; represented in permanent collections several corps., many pvt. homes. Recipient 1st Sculpture Fedn. Dallas Artists, 1950-54, pinned (all awards jewels), 1961; Recipient Sweepstakes award SW Ann. Art Show, 1953, Hon. Cert. award Dallas Fed. Bus. Assn., 1964; two 1st awards N.J. Fedn. Womens Clubs, 1972, two 1st award, 1974, 1st and 2d award 1975, Gold medal Accademia Italia, 1979, Golden Centaur award Accademia Italia, 1982, Gold medal Internat. Parliament (U.S.A.) of Safety and Peace, 1983, Centro Studi e Ricerche delle Nazioni, Parma, Italy, 1986, statue of victory, 1983; Oscar d' Italia, Accademia Italia, 1985; named Cavalier of Arts, Accademia Bedriacense, 1985, many others, including 3 awards for journalism, 1962-63; 2 Golden Flame awards World Parliament (U.S.A.), 1986. Fellow Internat. Inst. Arts and Letters (life); mem. Cousteau Soc. (founding), U.S. Chess Fedn., Am. Contract Bridge League, Internat. Acad. Lit., Arts and Sci. (hon. life mem., Tommaso Campanello with gold medal award 1972), C. of C. South Hunterdon (charter). Republican. Episcopalian. Mem. Order Eastern Star (past grand officer; past matron). Address: 2005 Halmrock Pl Sun City Center FL 33570

DOWLING, JOHN MALCOLM, economist; b. Pitts., July 4, 1939; s. John Malcolm and Mary Muriel (Snyder) D.; m. Nancy Hehn, June 18, 1966 (div., 1987); children: Kelly Pierce, Gregory Scott. BA, U. Pitts., 1961, MA, 1963, PhD, 1968. Asst. prof. U. Colo., Boulder, 1965-71, assoc. prof., 1971-75, prof. econs., 1975-83; sr. economist Asian Devel. Bank, Manila, 1981-85, asst. chief economist, 1985—; vis. lectr. U. Reading, Eng., 1967-68, Fulbright lectr. Tehran (Iran) U., 1971-72, Thamassat U., Bangkok, 1976-78; cons. various law firms, 1968-80. Author, editor: Readings in Econometric Theory, 1970, Development Strategy for Pakistan, 1985, Development Strategy for Indonesia, 1987; contbr. articles to profl. pubis. Fulbright fellow, 1971-72, 76-78, Rockefeller Found. fellow, 1979. Mem. Econometric Soc., Am. Econ. Assn. Democrat. Roman Catholic. Office: Asian Devel Bank, PO Box 789, Manila 2800, Philippines

DOWLING, MICHAEL LESLIE, mathematician; b. Apia, Western Samoa, July 27, 1957; s. Leslie Robert and Gweneth Ashworth (Taylor) D. BSc, U. Auckland, New Zealand, 1973; MSc with honors, U. Auckland, 1974; Dr. rer. nat., Carolo Wilhelmina U., Braunschweig, Fed. Republic Germany, 1987. Jr. lectr. dept. math. U. Auckland, New Zealand, 1975-76; lectr. part-time Poly. Cen. London, 1977-78; mathematician Gesamthoschschule Essen, Fed. Republic Germany, 1979-80, Deutsche Forschungs-und Versuchsanstalt fur Luft and Ramfahrt, Gottingen, Fed. Republic Germany, 1981-84, Carolo-Wilhelmina U., Braunschweig, Fed. Republic Germany, 1985—. Contbr. articles to profl. jours. Grantee U. Grants Com. New Zealand, 1974. Mem. Am. Math. Soc., Deutsche Mathematiber Vereinigung, Gesellschaft fur Angewandte Mathematick Mechanik. Office: Carolo Wilhelmina U Braunschweig, Pockelsstr 14, Braunschweig Federal Republic of Germany

DOWNEY, PATRICK JAMES, barrister; b. Timaru, New Zealand, May 1, 1927; s. Patrick and Mary Elizabeth (Quested) D.; m. Krystyna Kolodynska, July 26, 1968. Student, Sacred Heart Coll., Auckland, New Zealand, 1945; MA, Auckland U., 1950; LLB, Victoria U., Wellington, New Zealand, 1958. Bar: Supreme Ct., New Zealand, 1959. Ptnr. Marshall, Page, Gibson & Sheat, Wellington, New Zealand, 1962-66, Phillips, Shayle, George & Co., Wellington, 1966-78; chief Human Rights Commn., Wellington, 1978-83; chmn. Corp. Radio New Zealand, 1973-75; bd. dirs. New Zealand Broadcasting Corp., 1973-77; legal pub. dir. Butterworths Pub. Co., 1984—; chmn. Union Membership Exemption Tribunal, 1986—. Founder, editor Comment quar., 1960-70; editor New Zealand Law Jour., 1983—. Bd. dirs. Royal New Zealand Ballet; dep. chmn. New Zealand Sch. Dance; past pres. Wellington Film Soc. Decorated Queen's Jubilee medal. Mem. New Zealand Law Soc. (chmn. standing com. Lawasia, 1986—), Lawasia (alternate councillor 1987—), Internat. Commn. Jurists (council mem. New Zealand sect.). Roman Catholic. Club: Wellington. Home: 48 Nicholson Rd, Wellington New Zealand Office: 205-207 Victoria St, Box 5096, Wellington New Zealand

DOWNEY, RICHARD RALPH, lawyer, accountant, management consultant; b. Boston, Apr. 22, 1934; s. Paul Joseph and Evelyn Mae (Butler) D.; B.S., Northeastern U., 1958; M.B.A., Harvard U., 1962; J.D., Suffolk U., 1979; LL.M., Boston U., 1981; children—Richard Ralph, Janice M., Erin C., Timothy M. Mem. audit staff Price Waterhouse & Co., Boston, 1962-64, asso. Assos. for Internat. Research, Inc., Cambridge, Mass., 1964-68, v.p., 1968—, also dir.; admitted to Mass. bar, 1979, Fed. bar, 1980. Treas., 1580 House Condominium Trust, 1979-80. C.P.A., Mass., Mem. Am. Inst. C.P.A.'s, Mass. Soc. C.P.A.'s, Am. Bar Assn., Mass. Bar Assn., Boston Bar Assn. Clubs: Algonquin; Harvard (Boston, N.Y.C.). Home: 25 Washington Ave Cambridge MA 02140 Office: 1100 Massachusetts Ave Cambridge MA 02138

DOWNEY, WILLIAM GERALD, JR., lawyer; b. Bklyn., June 20, 1914; s. William Gerald and Mary Veronica (Ryder) D.; m. Ellen Wagle, Apr. 22, 1942 (dec. Nov. 1944); 1 child, William Gerald III (dec.); m. Laufey Arnadottir, June 5, 1947; children—Robert, Richard, Elizabeth, Mary, Catherine, William Gerald IV, Karen. B.S.S., CCNY, 1937; M.A., Cath. U. Am., 1938; J.D., Georgetown U., 1951; diploma Trinity Coll., Dublin, Ireland, 1976. Bar: D.C. 1951, Va. 1955, U.S. Ct. Mil. Appeals 1952, U.S. Supreme Ct. 1963. Fellow in internat. law Cath. U. Am., 1936-37, Georgetown U., 1937-40; commd. 2d lt. Inf., U.S. Army, 1936, advanced through grades to col. JAGC; served in various locations in U.S., Iceland, Eng., France, Germany, Formosa; ret., 1955; sr. ptnr. Downey & Lennhoff, Springfield, Va., 1955-85, of counsel Duvall, Blackburn, Hale & Downey, Fairfax, Va., 1986—; founder, v.p., past chmn. No. Va. Bank, Springfield; prof. law Soochow U., Taipei, Formosa, 1952-53. Decorated Army Commendation medal. Mem. D.C. Bar Assn., Va. Bar Assn., Fairfax County Bar Assn., Phi Alpha Delta. Roman Catholic. Clubs: Army-Navy (Washington); Army-Navy Country (Arlington, Va.). Contbr. articles to jours. Office: Duvall Blackburn Hale & Downey 4031 University Dr Suite 202 Fairfax VA 22030

DOWNING, JAMES CHRISTIE, lawyer; b. Los Angeles, Dec. 17, 1924; s. Dorman Perkins and Merle Grace (Christie) D.; m. Betty Griggs, Dec. 23, 1949; children—Colleen, James, Kimberly, Kelly, Kathleen. B.S., U. Calif., 1949; LL.B., U. Calif.-San Francisco, 1952. Bar: Calif. 1953, U.S. Dist. Ct. (no. dist.) Calif. 1953, U.S. Dist. Ct. (ea. dist.) Calif. 1975, U.S. Ct. Appeals (9th dir.) 1953. Assoc. Walkup, Downing, Shelby, Bastian, Melodia, Kelly & O'Reilly, and predecessors, San Francisco, 1954-59, ptnr., 1959-70, exec. v.p., 1970-84; ptnr. Downing & Downing, 1985—; lectr. Calif. Continuing Edn. of Bar Program. Served in AC, U.S. Army, 1943-45. Decorated Air medal with 5 oak leaf clusters. Fellow Am. Coll. Trial Lawyers; mem. ABA, State Bar Calif., Bar Assn. San Francisco (vice chmn. trial practice com. 1970), Calif. Trial Lawyers Assn., San Francisco Trial Lawyers Assn. (pres. 1972), Am. Bd. Trial Advs. (nat. exec. com. 1970-73, nat. sec. 1971, nat. chmn. membership 1972-73, 76-77, nat. pres. 1974, pres. San Francisco chpt. 1974, Calif. Trial Lawyer of Yr. 1978), Internat. Soc. Barristers, Internat. Acad. Trial Lawyers. Republican. Club: Bankers of San Francisco. litigation. Office: Downing & Downing 2121 N California Blvd Suite 1010 Walnut Creek CA 94596

DOWNS, HARTLEY H., III, chemist; b. Ridgewood, N.J., Oct. 21, 1949; s. Hartley Harrison and Jennie Mae (Smith) D.; B.S., Grove City Coll., 1971; M.S., Indiana U. of Pa., 1973; Ph.D., W. Va. U., 1978; student U. Colo., 1976-78; m. Cindy Marie Millen, June 19, 1976; children—Kathryn Marie, Jennifer Anne, Susanna Jayne. Postdoctoral research asso. chemistry dept. U. So. Calif., Los Angeles, 1977-78; staff chemist corp. research labs. Exxon Research and Engring. Co., Linden, N.J., 1978-81, Houston, 1981-83, Annandale, N.J., 1983-86; research scientist, surface chemistry group supr., Baker Performance Chemicals, Houston, 1986—. Recipient Stan Gillman award U. Colo., 1977, Union Carbide award W. Va. U., 1975, Sigma Xi award Indiana U. of Pa., 1973. Mem. Am. Chem. Soc., Soc. Petroleum Engrs., Sigma Xi, Phi Lambda Upsilon. Presbyterian. Contbr. articles to profl. jours.; patentee in field.

DOWNS, JON FRANKLIN, educator, director; b. Bartow, Fla., Sept. 15, 1938; s. Clarence Curtis and Frankie (Morgan) D.; student Ga. State Coll., 1956-58; BFA, U. Ga., 1960, MFA, 1969. Dir. The Beastly Purple Forest (marionettes) U. Ga., 1968, Dracula: A Horrible Musical, DeKalb Coll., 1971, Streetcar Named Desire, DeKalb, 1974, Brigadoon, DeKalb, 1981, West Side Story, 1983, Amadeus, 1984, Noises Off, 1986, The Three Musketeers, 1988, numerous others; actor Wedding in Japan, N.Y.C., 1960, Dark at the Top of the Stairs, N.Y.C. and tour, 1961, A Life in the Theatre, DeKalb Coll., 1981, numerous others; designer Sweeney Todd, DeKalb Coll., 1970, Romulus, 1971, Grass Harp, 1972, others: drama dir. DeKalb Coll., Clarkston, Ga., 1969—. Writer, dir. plays Tokalitta, Gold!, The Vigil: on tour of Ga., summers 1973, 74, 75, 76. Ga. Dept. Planning and Budget arts sect. grantee, 1973, 74. State and Nat. Bicentennial Commn. grantee,

1975. Mem. Southeastern Theatre Conf. (state rep. 1971-73), Ga. Theatre Conf. (exec. bd. 1970-73 79-82). Author: The Illusionist, 1979. Home: 1124 Forrest Blvd Decatur GA 30030 Office: DeKalb Coll Dept Theatre Clarkston GA 30021

DOYEN, GEROLD KAI MENNO, theoretical physical chemist; b. Bremerhaven, Germany, Aug. 21, 1946; s. Karl Gerold and Renate (von Heiden) D.; m. Vera Jeannette Mesen Araya, July 20, 1977. Diploma in Physics, Tech. U., Hannover, West Germany, 1972; Dr. rer. nat., Ludwig-Maximilians U., Munich, West Germany, 1975, Dr. rer. nat. (Habilitation), 1981; venia legendi, 1984. Fellow, U. Liverpool (Eng.), 1975-76; sci. asst. U. Munich, 1976-82, Akademischer Oberrat, 1982-84. Contbr. articles in field to profl. jours. Heisenberg fellow Deutsche Forschungsgemeinschaft, 1984. Mem. Deutsche Physikalische Gesellschaft, Deutsche Bunsen Gesellschaft. Office: Inst fur Physikalische Chemie, Theresienstrasse 37, D-8000 Munchen 2 Federal Republic of Germany

DOYLE, ANTHONY IAN, librarian; b. Liverpool, Eng., Oct. 24, 1925; s. Edward and Norah (Keating) D. BA, Cambridge (Eng.) U., 1945, MA, 1949, PhD, 1953. Asst. librarian Durham (Eng.) U. Library, 1950—, keeper of rare books, 1958-82, reader in bibliography, 1972-85; Lyell reader in bibliography Oxford (Eng.) U., 1967. Contbr. articles to profl. jours. Hon. sec. Bow Trust, Durham, 1975—; trustee City of Durham Trust. Fellow Leverhulme Trust Fund, 1979-80, Henry E. Huntington Library, 1980; recipient Israel Gollancz prize Brit. Acad., 1983. Mem. Surtees Soc. (v.p.), Bibliog. Soc. London (v.p.), Early English Text Soc. (mem. council), Com. Internat. Paleographie Latine. Roman Catholic. Office: Durham U Library, Palace Green, Durham DH1 3RN, England

DOYLE, CONSTANCE TALCOTT JOHNSTON, physician; b. Mansfield, Ohio, July 8, 1945; d. Frederick Lyman IV and Nancy Jean Bushnell (Johnston) Talcott; m. Alan Jerome Demsky, June 13, 1976; children—Ian Frederick Demsky, Zachary Adam Demsky. B.S., Ohio U., 1967; M.D., Ohio State U., 1971. Diplomate Am. Bd. Emergency Medicine. Intern, Riverside Hosp., Columbus, Ohio, 1971-72; resident in internal medicine Hurley Hosp. and U. Mich., Flint, 1972-74, emergency physician Oakwood Hosp., Dearborn, Mich., 1974-76, Jackson County (Mich.) Emergency Services, 1975—; survival flight physician U. Mich. helicopter rescue service, 1983—; disaster cons., co-chmn. emergency med. services disaster com. Region II EMS, 1978-79; course dir. advanced cardiac life support and chmn. advanced life support com. W.A. Foote Meml. Hosp., Jackson, 1979—, others; clin. instr. emergency services, dept. surgery U. Mich., 1981—; instr. Jackson County Emergency Med. Technician refresher courses, Jackson Community Coll. Bd. dirs. Jackson County Heart Assn., 1979-83. Fellow Am. Coll. Emergency Physicians (Mich. disaster com., dir. Mich. 1979—, chmn. Mich. disaster com. 1979-85, mem. nat. disaster med. services com. 1983-85, chmn., 1987-88; cons. disaster mgmt. course Fed. Emergency Mgmt. Agy., 1982—, treas. 1984-85, emergency med. services com. 1985, pres. 1986-87, councillor 1986—); mem. ACP, Am. Med. Women's Assn., Mich. Assn. Emergency Med. Technicians (bd. dirs. 1979-80), Mich., Jackson County med. socs., Sierra Club. Jewish. Contbg. author: Clinical Approach to Poisoning and Toxicology, 1983; contbr. articles to profl. publs. Home: 1665 Lansdowne Rd Ann Arbor MI 48105 Office: WA Foote Hospital East Emergency Dept Jackson MI 49201

DOYLE, FRANK LAWRENCE, hydrogeologist, executive; b. San Antonio, Oct. 16, 1926; s. William Michael and Elizabeth Lillian (Black) D.; m. Giovanna Maria Scorza, June 9, 1962; 1 son, Michael Joseph. BS in Geology, U. Tex.-Austin, 1950; MS, La. State U., 1955; PhD, U. Ill., 1958. Registered geologist, Calif.; cert. profl. geol. scientist. Instr., St. Mary's U., San Antonio, 1950-53, asst. prof. geology, 1958-60, assoc. prof., 1960-62, chmn. dept. geology, 1961-62; prof. geology Seeligson Engring. Com., San Antonio, 1952-53; asst. geologist Ill. Geol. Survey, Urbana, 1956-58, assoc. geologist/research affiliate, 1959-61; geologist U.S. Geol. Survey, Mont., 1955, Colo., Ariz., 1962-63; assoc. prof. U. Conn., 1963-65; con. hydrogeologist, Panama, Nicaragua, Algeria, 1965-71; regional geologist N.Ala., Geol. Survey Ala., 1971-77; cons. Kenneth E. Johnson Environ. and Energy Ctr., U. Ala., Huntsville, 1971-77, adj. prof. hydrology, chmn. environ. sci. program Sch. Sci. and Engring., 1971-77; cons. hydrogeologist Fla., 1977-78; chief hydrogeologist Metcalf and Eddy, Inc., Boston, 1978-79; sr. hydrogeologist/program mgr. for waste mgmt. research U.S. Nuclear Regulatory Commn., Washington, 1979-84; environ. rev. officer, geologist, hydrologist Office of Sec., U.S. Dept. of Interior, Washington, 1984-87; systems scientist, geologist, hydrologist The MITRE Corp., McLean, Va., 1987—; mem. U.S. Nat. com. on Geology, Nat. Research Council; alt. U.S. delegation to 27th Internat. Geol. Congress, Moscow, 1984. Sr. author: Environmental Geology and Hydrology, Huntsville and Madison County, Alabama, 1975; co-editor: Karst Hydrogeology, 1977. Active Huntsville/Madison County Local Govt. Study Com., Huntsville Solid Waste Mgmt. Com., 1972-75. Served with U.S. Army, 1945-46. U. Ill. fellow, 1954-55. Fellow Geol. Soc. Am.; mem. Am.Assn. Petroleum Geologists (del. 1975-76), Internat. Assn. Hydrogeologists (gen. chmn. 12th Internat. Congress 1975, adv. council 1977-80, sec.-treas. U.S. com. 1980-84, chmn. U.S. com. 1984—), Am. Geophys. Union, Am. Inst. Profl. Geologists, Assn. Ground Water Scientists and Engrs., Sigma Xi, USPHS (reserve scientist dir.).

DOYLE, IRENE ELIZABETH, electronic sales executive, nurse; b. West Point, Iowa, Oct. 5, 1920; d. Joseph Deidrich and Mary Adelaide (Groene) Schulte; m. William Joseph Doyle, Feb. 3, 1956. R.N., Mercy Hosp., 1941. Courier nurse Santa Fe R.R., Chgo., 1947-50; indsl. nurse Montgomery Ward, Chgo., 1950-54; rep. Hornblower & Weeks, Chgo., 1954-56; v.p. William J. Doyle Co., Chgo., 1956-80, Ormond Beach, Fla., 1980-88. Served with M.C., U.S. Army, 1942-46. Mem. Electronic Reps. Assn. Republican. Roman Catholic. Club: Oceanside Country (Ormond Beach).

DOYLE, JOHN ROBERT, JR., writer; b. Dinwiddie County, Va., Jan. 22, 1910; s. John Robert and Marian Stickley (Binford) D.; m. Clarice Alise Slate, June 13, 1942; 1 child, Gwendolen Binford Doyle Hurst. B.A., Randolph-Macon Coll., 1932; M.A., U. Va., 1937, Bread Loaf Sch. English, 1941; postgrad., U. N.C., 1944-45. Head dept. English Dinwiddie High Sch., Va., 1932-40; instr. English Clemson U., 1940-41; asst. prof. English The Citadel, 1941-44, asst., 1946-57, assoc. prof., 1957-63, prof., 1963-75, prof. emeritus, 1975—, dir. Fine Art Series, 1965-75; lectr. in physics U. N.C., 1944-45; lectr. lit. Stephens Coll., 1945-46; vis. prof. Am. lit. Univs. Cape Town and the Witwatersrand, 1958. Author books including: The Poetry of Robert Frost, 1962; William Plomer, 1969; Francis Carey Slater, 1971; Thomas Pringle, 1972; Arthur Shearly Cripps, 1975; William Charles Scully, 1978. Founding editor The Citadel Monograph Series. Contbr. articles and essays to periodicals. Pres., Charleston Civic Ballet, 1963-65; chmn. fine arts events S.C. Tri-Centennial, 1970. Recipient Smith-Mundt grant to S. Africa, 1958, Daniel Disting. Teaching award, 1968, Algernon Sidney Sullivan award, The Citadel, 1971. Mem. Poetry Soc. S.C. (past pres., dir. writing group 1947-75, award of merit 1971), MLA (chmn. conf. So. lit. 1965, world lit. written in English 1967), Am. Studies Assn. (past dir.), Coll. English Assn., Va. Writers Club, Phi Beta Kappa. Home and Office: Rives Ave McKenney VA 23872

DOYLE, MATTHEW WALLACE, data processing, telecommunications executive; b. N.Y.C., Dec. 11, 1958; s. Bertram Wilbur and Flora Elaine (Wallace) D. BSEE, U. Md., 1980; MBA, Howard U., 1985. Mgr. Vitro Corp., Silver Spring, Md., 1981—. Author: Finance 1 Users Guide, 1981. Mem. D-Com Computer Assocs. (pres. 1984—), Assn. MBA Execs., Black Engrs. Soc. Democrat. Home: 811 Kersey Rd Silver Spring MD 20902 Office: Vitro Corp 14000 Georgia Ave Silver Spring MD 20910

DOYLE, RICHARD HENRY, IV, lawyer; b. Elgin, Ill., Aug. 8, 1949; s. Richard Henry and Shirley Marian (Ohms) D.; m. Debbie Kay Cahalan, Aug. 2, 1975; children—John Richard, Kerry Jane. B.A., Drake U., 1971, J.D., 1976. Bar: Iowa 1976, U.S. Dist. Ct. (no. and so. dists.) Iowa 1977, U.S. Ct. Appeals (8th cir.) 1977, U.S. Supreme Ct. 1986. Asst. atty. gen. Iowa Dept. Justice, Des Moines, 1976-77; assoc. Lawyer, Lawyer & Jackson, Des Moines, 1977-79; assoc. Law Offices of Verne Lawyer & Assocs., Des Moines, 1979—. Contbr. articles to profl. jours. Served with U.S. Army, 1971-73. Fellow Iowa Acad. Trial Lawyers; mem. Assn. Trial Lawyers Am., Assn. Trial Lawyers Iowa, ABA (jud. adminstrn. and tort and ins. practice sects.), Am. Judicature Soc., Iowa Bar Assn., Polk County Bar Assn. (law library trustee 1986—), SAR (registrar Iowa 1983—), Phi Alpha Delta (chpt. pres. 1975), Republican. Presbyterian. Home: 532 Waterbury Circle Des Moines IA 50312 Office: Law Offices Verne Lawyer & Assocs 427 Fleming Bldg Des Moines IA 50309

DOYLE, WALTER ARNETT, pedodontist, orthodontist, educator; b. Los Angeles, Aug. 9, 1933; s. Walter and Ruth D.; m. Betty Ann Parrot, Dec. 27, 1957 (div. June 1975); children—Shannon, Elizabeth, Sarah, Walter; m. Elizabeth Lewis, July 17, 1977. D.D.S., Emory U., 1959; M.S.D., Ind. U.-Indpls., 1961; postgrad., Boston U., 1974-76. Diplomate Am. Bd. Pedodontics, Am. Bd. Orthodontics. Pvt. practice pedodontics, Lexington, Ky., 1962—, pvt. practice orthodontics, Lexington, 1976—; instr. pedodontics Ind. U., 1961-62; instr. pedodontics U. Ky., 1964-65, guest lectr. dept. community dentistry, 1972-74, asst. field prof., 1972-74; vis. assoc. prof. pedodontics Northwestern U., 1972-74; vis. clin. prof. pedodontics Boston U. Sch. Grad. Dentistry, 1975—; mem. staff Good Samaratin, St. Joseph, Central Baptist, Humana hosps.; cons., contbr. Health Info. Systems, Inc.; dental cons. Medcom, Inc.; bd. dirs. Ky. Dental Service Corp., 1964-69; S.S. White Centennial teaching fellow; pres. Doyle Seminars and Internat. Symposia. Contbr. articles to profl. jours. Trustee Hunter Found., 1972-74; mem. Bluegrass Trust for Historic Preservation, 1968—, Lexington Council for Arts, 1976—; alumni area rep. Boston U. Recipient award for leadership in dental progress Thomas Hinman, 1972, 76; Lexington Council Arts fellow; fellow, U. Ky., 1984—. Fellow Am. Acad. Pedodontics, Internat. Coll. Dentists, Am. Coll. Dentists. Mem. Am. Soc. Preventive Dentistry (pres. Ky. unit 1972), Am. Soc. Dentistry for Children (mem. exec. council 1972—, pres. 1976-77), Internat. Assn. Dental Research, Am. Dental Assn., Assn. Pedodontic Diplomates (pres.-elect. 1968), Southeastern Soc. Pedodontics (pres. 1968), Ky. Soc. Dentistry for Children (pres. 1963), Psi Omega, Lexington C. of C. Clubs: Lexington Polo, Keeneland, Sierra, Ind. U. Century. Home: 3284 Paris Pike Lexington KY 40511 Office: 1628 Nicholasville Rd Lexington KY 40503

DOYLE, WILLIAM JAY, II, business consultant; b. Cin., Nov. 7, 1928; s. William Jay and Blanche (Gross) D.; B.S., Miami U., Oxford, Ohio, 1949; postgrad. U. Cin., 1950-51, Xavier U., 1953-54, Case Western Res. U., 1959-60; m. Joan Lucas, July 23, 1949; children—David L., William Jay, III, Daniel L. Sales rep. Diebold, Inc., Cin., 1949-52, asst. br. mgr., 1953-57, asst. regional mgr., Cin., 1957-62, regional mgr., Cin., 1962-74; founder, chief exec. officer Central Bus. Group div. Central Bus. Equipment Co., Cin., 1974—, dir. parent co. and divs.; mem. area contractor's council Spacesaver Corp., 1985-87; speaker on bus systems, security concepts. Mem. Armstrong Chapel, Methodist ch., Indian Hill, Ohio, adminstrv. bd. 1987-88. Mem. Bus. Systems and Security Mktg. Assn. (nat. dir. 1977-79, 81-83, nat. pres. 1981-83, 84-85), Nat. Assn. Accts. Republican. Clubs: Kenwood Country, Masons, Shriners. Contbr. articles to co. and trade publs.; developer new concepts in tng., cash and securities handling, mobile and mechanized storage and filing, and other areas of bus. systems. Home: 6250 S Clippinger Dr Cincinnati OH 45243 Office: 10839 Indeco Dr Cincinnati OH 45241

DOYRAN, TURHAN, author; b. Ankara, Turkey, June 20, 1926; s. Ahmet and Sabriye Doyran; student U. Ankara, U. Genoble, Sorbonne, Inst. Internat. Studies Paris, Ansaldi Acad. Photography, Nat. Conservatory Arts and Trades; m. Madeleine, Aug. 17, 1953; 1 dau., Selma. Exhibited photographs in Paris, Istanbul, Ankara, Rotterdam, The Hague, Milan, Bologna, Stuttgart, Mü nchen. Author: (poetry) Siirler, 1955, Sehir, 1959, Partir, 1962, Gecilmez, 1962; Le Jour, 1962; Il Faut bien, 1962; Comme Autre-fois, 1964; Jene suis pas de Bologne, 1967; The Tree, 1967; The Way, 1975; The Mirror, 1975; Photo-Graphies, 1980; Les Rois Demeurent, 1984; The Rain, 1986; others; (plays) La Promesse, 1946, L'Offense, 1947, La Préméditation, 1961, Marée Haute, 1965, Le Mobile, 1967. Recipient award Cannes Cinema Festival; award Leonardo da Vinci Acad. Poetry, 1964; Prix Comité Européen Arts et Culture, 1985; named Artist of Yr. Plastic Arts, Turkey, 1987. Home: 8 rue de Cambodge, 75020 Paris France

DOZIER, WELDON GRADY, real estate development marketing company executive; b. Gainesville, Tex., Oct. 21, 1938; s. Weldon G. and Dorothy M. (Woods) D.; B.A., Union U., 1962; postgrad. North Tex. State U.; m. Pamela Kay Kerns, Dec. 15, 1978. Mgr., Hybrid Computer Center sponsored by NASA, Denton, Tex., 1962-69; EDP mgr. Continental Ins. Cos., Atlanta, 1970-72; dist. systems mgr. 14 states for TRW Data Systems, Inc., 1973-75; pres. Property Mktg., Inc., Denison, Tex., 1976—; cons. in field. Mem. Nat. Speakers Assn., Internat. Platform Assn., Am. Land Developers Assn., Lake Texoma Assn., Denison C. of C. Republican. Baptist. Clubs: Woodlawn Country (Sherman, Tex.); Rod and Gun Country (Denison); Toastmaster (sec., treas., v.p., pres.). Author: The Bell, 1982; False Echoes, 1983. Home: P O Box 165179 Irving TX 75016 Office: 330 W Chesnut St Denison TX 75020

DRABBLE, MARGARET (MRS. CLIVE SWIFT), writer; b. June 5, 1939; d. John Frederick and Kathleen Marie (Bloor) D.; m. Clive Swift, May 27, 1960 (dec. dissolved 1975); children—Adam, Rebecca, Joseph; m. Michael Holroyd, 1982. B.A. with honors, Newnham Coll. Cambridge U., 1960. Author: novels A Summer Bird-Cage, 1963, The Garrick Year, 1964, The Millstone, 1965, Jerusalem the Golden, 1967, The Waterfall, 1969, The Needle's Eye, 1972, The Realms of Gold, 1975, The Ice Age, 1977, The Middle Ground, 1980; short stories Hassan's Tower, 1966, The Reunion, 1968, The Gifts of War, 1970; play Birds of Paradise, 1969, The Radiant Way, 1987; screenplay A Touch of Love, 1969; also: screenplay Wordsworth, 1966, Arnold Bennett, A Biography, 1974, For Queen and Country: Britain in the Victorian Age, 1978, A Writer's Britain, 1979; editor: Oxford Companion to English Literature, 5th edit., 1985. Recipient Rhys Meml. prize, 1966, Black Meml. prize, 1968, E.M. Forster award, 1973. Office: care AD Peters & Co, 10 Buckingham St, London WC2, England

DRAKE, DAVID C. M., banker; b. 1941. Joined Lloyds Bank Plc, Eng., 1958; asst. mgr. Sevenoaks, 1971-75; personal asst. to gen. mgrs., head office 1975-77; br. mgr. From, 1977-79; asst. to gen. mgr., head office 1979, asst. treas., head office, 1980-81; dep. regional gen. mgr. Birmingham, 1981-84, regional dir., gen. mgr., 1984-87; pres., chief exec. officer, dir. Lloyds Bank Can., Toronto, 1987—. Mem. Can. Bankers Assn. (dep. chmn. schedule B fgn. banks' exec. com.). Office: Lloyds Bank Can, 130 Adelaide St W, Toronto, ON Canada M5H 3R2

DRAKE, ERVIN MAURICE, composer, author; b. N.Y.C., Apr. 3, 1919; B of Social Sci., CCNY, 1940; studies with Tibor Serly, Jacob Druckman; s. Max and Pearl Edith (Cohen) D.; m. Ada Sax, May 28, 1947 (dec. Mar. 1975); children: Linda Shifra, Betsy Jennifer; m. Edith Bein Berman, Nov. 19, 1982. Composer popular songs including I Believe, It Was a Very Good Year, Tico Tico, Perdido, Al Di La, A Room Without Windows, Good Morning Heartache, Come to the Mardi Gras, The Rickety Rickshaw Man, Across the Wide Missouri, My Friend, Father of Girls, Quando Quando Quando, Sonata, Made for Each Other, One God; composer, lyricist: What Makes Sammy Run?, 1965; composer music, lyrics and libretto for Her First Roman, 1968; lyricist, co-librettist, composer music Florence of Arabia, 1985; composer music, lyrics, and co-librettist Oils of Araby, 1986, Songs in Sophisticated Ladies 1983-84, Shades of Harlem, 1985 and Lady Day, 1987; writer, composer and/or producer TV programs including: To Our First Lady With Music, 1956, Yves Montand on Broadway, 1961, Timex Comedy Hour, 1962, Accent on Love, 1959, The Jane Froman Show, 1952-55, Sing It Again, 1948-50; scored TV series Sherlock Holmes and Dr. Watson, 1981; scored films: Lady Sings the Blues, 1972, Heartbeat, 1943, Across the Wide Missouri, 1951, Arch of Triumph, 1948, Holiday in Mexico, 1944, Bathing Beauty, 1944, Foreign Intrigue, 1956, Rome Adventure, 1961, Affair at the Villa Florita, 1961, Two for the Guillotine, 1962. Recipient Christopher award, 1953, Sylvania award, 1956, Aggie award, 1976, ASCAP award, 1973; nominee Nat. Acad. Rec. Arts and Scis. award for What Makes Sammy Run?; award of honor entertainment lawyers div. United Jewish Appeal/Fedn. Jewish Philanthropies, 1982; named to Songwriters Hall of Fame, Nat. Acad. Popular Music, 1982. Mem. Songwriters Guild Am. (pres. 1973-82, sec. 1982—, Aggie award 1976), The Songwriter's Guild Am. (pres. 1973-82), ASCAP, Authors League, Dramatists Guild, Writers Guild Am. East., Townsend Harris High Alumni Assn. (composed music and lyrics of offl. fight song and Alma Mater 1986), CCNY Alumni Assn. (Townsend Harris medal 1986). Democrat. Clubs: Lake Success Golf, Spaulding Hole-in-One.

DRAKE, FRANK ROBERT, mathematics educator; b. Sheffield, Eng., June 23, 1936; s. Arnold and Winifred Helen (Bennett) D.; m. Verna Carol M. Chapman, June 14, 1958; children: Robert, Ann. BA, U. (Eng.) Cambridge, 1959, PhD, 1963. Lectr. in pure math. U. (Eng.) Leeds, 1962-72, sr. lectr., 1973—; vis. lectr. U. Wash., Seattle, 1972-73; head dept. pure math. U. Leeds, 1978-82. Author: Set Theory: An Introduction To Large Cardinals, 1974; contbr. articles math. logic to acad. jours. Served to lance cpl. Royal Corps Signals, Brit. Army, 1954-56. Mem. Brit. Logic Colloquium (sec. 1971—), London Math. Soc., Am. Math. Soc., Assn. for Symbolic Logic (chmn. European com. 1986—). Christian Scientist. Office: U Leeds, Dept Pure Math, Leeds LS2 9JT, England

DRAKE, LYNN ANNETTE, physician; b. Albuquerque, Aug. 4, 1945; d. Olen Lester and Lucille Susan (Henry) Drake; BA, Adams State Coll., 1966, MA, 1967; MD, U. Tenn., 1971. Instr. math. Adams State Coll., Alamosa, Colo., 1966-67; intern City of Memphis Hosp., 1971-72, resident in dermatology, 1972-75, chief resident, 1974-75; mem. faculty dept. medicine, div. dermatology U. Tenn. Center Health Scis., also Med. Practice Group, Inc.; asst. prof. dermatology Emory U., Atlanta; chief dermatology VA Med. Center, Atlanta; dir. devel., policy and planning Mass. Gen. Hosp.; with dept. dermatology Harvard Med. Sch.; chmn. chemosurgery tag group VA; instr. advanced cardiac life support Am. Heart Assn.; mem. emergency room com. St. Joseph Hosp. Vol., Am. Cancer Soc., 1973-75; dir. policy and planning dept. dermatology and Wellman Labs Photomedicine Harvard, Mass. Gen. Hosp., Boston, 1988—. Diplomate Am. Bd. Dermatology (chmn. com. health care quality assurance 1984—). Robert Wood Johnson Health Policy fellow, 1986-87. Fellow Am. Acad. Dermatology (bd. dirs. 1987—); mem. Soc. for Investigative Dermatology, Am. Acad. Dermatology (com. on health planning), Women's Med. Assn., ACP, Ga. Dermatology Soc., Atlanta Dermatology Soc. (program chmn.), Am. Assn. Med. Colls., Council Acad. Scis., Women's Dermatology Soc. (housestaff liaison com., nominating com., pres. 1984-86). Dermatology Found. Home: One Longfellow Pl #2418 Boston MA 02114

DRAKE, MALCOLM ERNEST, architect; b. Erode, S. India, Mar. 27, 1933; s. Sidney Malcolm and Coral Mary (Fisher) D.; B.Arch., Sir J.J. Sch. Art, Bombay, 1958; postgrad. Hammersmith Sch. Architecture, London, 1968-70, Univ. Coll., London, 1972, 76; m. Gillian Dudley Ward, Nov. 20, 1971. Job architect firms in Bombay, 1957-62; partner S.R. Fernando, architects, Madras, 1962-67; prin. exec. architect London Transp. Exec., 1976-83; cons. architect Property Devel. div. Ministry of Transport, 1983-85, mgr. property planning and office accommodation, State Transport Authority, 1985—. Recipient Best Student prize, Bombay, 1954, Prof. Robert W. Cable prize architecture, 1954; Indian Govt. scholar, 1954. Registered architect, Victoria, U.K. Asso. Royal Inst. Brit. Architects. Royal Australian Inst. Architects, Incorporated Assn. Architects London, Inst. Arbitrators, Brit. Inst. Mgmt.; mem. Royal Soc. Health. Roman Catholic. Author papers in field. Home: 149 Manningham Rd, Lower Templestow, 3107 Victoria Australia

DRANE, JOHN WILLIAM, clergyman, religious educator; b. Hartlepool, Eng., Oct. 17, 1946; s. John Wallace and Marjorie (Ireland) D.; m. Olive Mary Fleming, Sept. 16, 1967; children: Andrew James Jonathan, Mark Samuel Paul, Alethea Joy Frances. MA with 1st class honors, U. Aberdeen, Scotland, 1969; PhD, U. Manchester, Eng., 1972. Ordained to ministry Bapt. Ch. Minister Bapt. Ch., Eng., 1971-73; prof. religious studies U. Stirling, Scotland, 1973—; mission convener Scottish Chs. Council, 1984—; mem. joint ministerial bd. Bapt. Union Scotland, 1985—; mem. evangelism com. Brit. Council of Chs., 1985—. Author: Introducing the New Testament, 1986, Introducing the Old Testament, 1987; contbr. articles to profl. and religious jours. Mem. Studiorium Novi Testamenti Societas, Writers Guild, Soc. Authors. Home: 39 Fountain Rd, Bridge of Allan FK9 4AU, Scotland Office: U Stirling, Dept Religious Studies, Stirling FK9 4LA, Scotland

DRAPER, WILLIAM W., corporation executive; b. Edmonton, Alta., Oct. 1, 1933; s. Walter Jay and Martha Ann (Richards) D.; m. Maxine Gladys Slocum, May 31, 1952; children: Linda Coleen, Bonetta Gay, James William. CLU. Life underwriter Standard Life Assurance Co., 1955-65; asst. Ont. mgr. Can. C. of C., 1965-67; gen. mgr. Sault St. Marie C. of C., 1967-72, Winnipeg C. of C., 1972—; corp. sec. Winnipeg Bus. Devel. Corp., 1979—; bd. dirs. Chamber Ins. Corp. Can., Winnipeg. Pres. Kirkfield Westwood Community Club, 1977-78; Winnipeg Symphony Orch., 1981-82; v.p. Manitoba Theater Centre, 1979-80. Mem. C. of C. Execs. (pres. 1976-77), Can. Soc. Assn. Execs. (chmn. bd. 1987—), Jr. Chamber Internat. (life senator 1963—), Jr. Chamber (v.p. 1959-61). Club: Carleton (Winnipeg), Canadian. Office: Winnipeg Chamber of Commerce, 500-167 Lombard Ave, Winnipeg, MB Canada R3B 3E5

DRAZEN, ALLAN, economics educator; b. St. Louis, Aug. 30, 1950; arrived in Israel, 1982; s. Michael and Helen (Sichel) D. SB, MIT, 1972, PhD, 1976. Asst. prof. econs. U. Chgo., 1976-82; vis. fellow Inst. Internat. Econ. Studies, Stockholm, 1986-87; vis. assoc. prof. U. Pa., 1987-88; sr. lectr. Tel-Aviv U., 1982—. Contbr. articles to profl. jours. Grantee NSF, Washington, 1979, 1987. Mem. Am. Econ. Assn., European Econ. Assn., Phi Beta Kappa. Jewish. Home: 801 Swarthmore Saint Louis MO 63130

DRAZEN, LEONARD, securities company executive; b. Balt., Dec. 27, 1913; s. Jacob and Fannie (Kriegel) D.; B.S., U. Md., 1954; m. Sylvia Michelsohn, Apr. 27, 1941; 1 child, George Hilary. Enlisted as pvt. Signal Corps, U.S. Army, 1936, commd. 1st lt., 1941, advanced through grades to col., 1962; served PTO, World War II; ret., 1966; mgr. field services SE Asia, Page Communications Engrs. Inc., Honolulu, 1966-67; mgr. plans and programs Control Data Corp., Honolulu, 1969-70; pres. First Hawaiian Investment Corp. (formerly Drazen Assos., Inc.), Honolulu, 1970-73; Hawaii rep. ITT Fed. Electric Corp., Honolulu, 1970-73; pres., chmn. bd. Olympia Corp., Honolulu, 1974—; dir. Real Estate Services, Inc. Decorated Army Commendation ribbon with 2 oak leaf clusters. Mem. Armed Forces Communications Electronics Assn. (pres. Hawaii chpt. 1964, Man of Month, Mar. 1978), Ret. Officers Assn., Mil. Order World Wars, Sojourners. Clubs: Masons, Shriners. Home: 917 Koloa St Honolulu HI 96816 Office: 680 Ala Moana Honolulu HI 96813

DREBUS, RICHARD WILLIAM, pharmaceutical company executive; b. Oshkosh, Wis., Mar. 30, 1924; s. William and Frieda (Schmidt) D.; m. Hazel Redford, June 7, 1947; children—William R., John R., Kathryn L. BS, U. Wis., 1947, MS, 1949, PhD, 1952. Bus. trainee Marathon Paper Corp., Menasha, Wis., 1951-52; tng. mgr. Ansul Corp., Marinette, Wis., 1952-55; asst. to v.p. Ansul Corp., 1955-58, marketing mgr., 1958-60; dir. personnel devel. Mead Johnson & Co., Evansville, Ind., 1960-65; v.p. corporate planning Mead Johnson & Co., 1965-66, internat. pres., 1966-68; v.p. internat. div. Bristol-Myers Co. (merger Mead Johnson Internat. div. with Bristol-Myers Co. Internat. div.), N.Y.C., 1968-77, sr. v.p., 1977-78, v.p. parent co., 1978-85, sr. v.p. pharm. research and devel. div., 1985—; Trustee Quinnipal Coll. Bd. dirs. Wallingford Symphony, Wallingford-Meriden United Way, chmn. 1988—, Jr. Achievement S.E. Conn., Meriden-Wallingford Mfrs. Assn., Meriden Silver Mus. Served with inf. AUS, 1943-45. Decorated Combat Inf. Badge, Purple Heart, Bronze Star. Mem. Am. Psychol. Assn., N.Y. Acad. Scis., Wallingford C. of C. (bd. dirs.), Meriden C. of C. (bd. dirs.), U. Wis. Bascom Hill Soc., Phi Delta Kappa. Clubs: Oshkosh Country; Oshkosh Power Boat. Home: PO Box 867 Wallingford CT 06492 Office: PO Box 5100 5 Research Pkwy Wallingford CT 06492-7660

DRECHSEL, EDWARD RUSSELL, JR., utility company executive; b. Webster, Mass., Dec. 29, 1927; s. Edward R. and Eva A. (Kullas) D.; m. Marcella Marie Japko, Dec. 26, 1950; children: E. Russell, Carl M. BSEE, Worcester Poly. Inst., 1949; MSEE, N.J. Inst. Tech., 1956; grad. pub. utilities exec. program, U. Mich.; intermittent coursework, Rutgers U. Registered profl. engr., N.J. Sales mgr. Jersey Cen. Power and Light Co., Lakewood, N.J., 1959-60, div. engr., 1960-64, dist. supt., 1969-84; supt. div. ops. Jersey Cen. Power and Light Co., Old Bridge, N.J., 1984-87, Lakewood, N.J., 1987—; ptnr. Cornucopia Enterprises, Wrightstown. Mem. Friends of the Gardens, Monmouth County, Bklyn. Botanic Gardens; bd. dirs. Tom's River (N.J.) C. of C., 1978-84; bd. dirs. N.J. Shade Tree Fedn., New Brunswick, 1982-86; v.p. No. Hanover Twp. Bd. Edn., 1982-83, pres. 1985-86; chmn. No. Hanover Shade Tree Commn., 1985-86, Zoning Bd. of Adjustment, No. Hanover, 1985-86; mem. Sayreville Indsl. Commn.; past chmn. Ocean County Traffic Safety Commn., Raritan Valley C. of C. Served to staff sgt. Signal Corps., U.S. Army, 1950-53. Mem. IEEE (sr.), Nat. Soc. Profl. Engrs., N.J. Soc. Profl. Engrs., Internat. Soc. Arborists, Internat. Soc. Arbiculture, Am. Forestry Assn., N.J. Fedn. Shade Tree Commns., Air Force Assn. (life), Nat. Rifle Assn. (life), Am. Legion, Pa. Horticulture Soc., N.J. Pesticide Assn., Raritan Valley Regional C. of C., Ocean County Employees Legis. Com., Burlington County Employees Legis. Com., Monmouth County Employees Legis. Com. Republican. Roman Catholic. Home: Box 67-2 RD 2 Larrison Rd Wrightstown NJ 08750 Office: Jersey Cen Power & Light Co 55 River Ave Lakewood NJ 08701

DREESMANN, ANTON CASPAR RUDOLPHUS, retailing and services company executive; b. Amsterdam, Netherlands, May 2, 1923; s. Willem Jozef R. and Anna Maria (Peek) D.; grad. student in Law, U. Amsterdam, 1947, Econs., 1949, Ph.D. in Econs. cum laude, 1963; m. Marianne Leonie VanderSpek, Jan. 22, 1955; children—Anton, Pieter, Quinten, Marc, Barbara. Mng. dir. Vroom & Dreesmann Den Haag N.V., The Hague, 1954-73, Vedemij Den Haag N.V., The Hague, 1971-73; chmn. bd., chief exec. officer Vendex Internat. N.V. c.a., retailing and services group, Amsterdam, 1973-88, v.p. adv. bd., 1988—; prof. faculty econ. scis. U. Amsterdam, 1973—; dir. Algemene Bank Nederland N.V., Dillard's, Little Rock, Minit Internat. S.A., N.V. Koninklyke Byenkorf, Beheer KBB, De Vleeschmeesters BV, Esdex V.O.F., Barnes & Noble Book Stores Inc. Mem. exec. bd. Catholic Nat. Party, 1950-55, Cath. Peoples Party, 1955-66; bd. dirs. Mater Amabilis Schs., 1953-56, Found. Soc. and Industry, 1971-76, Found. Econ. Research, U. Amsterdam, 1968-75, Assn. Trust fund for Social Scis. and Univ. Fund Found., Rotterdam, 1974—; mem. council Rockefeller U., 1981—; mem. Adv. Com. Indsl. Affairs, 1981. Decorated knight Order of Nederlandse Leeuw, 1981; Comdr. in Order of Orange-Nassau. Fellow Internat. Acad. Mgmt.; mem. Nat. Retail Mchts. Assn. (internat. com. 1976—; Retailer of Yr. 1981), Internat. Mgmt. and Devel. Inst., Orgn. Large Scale Retailers (dir. 1965—), Orgn. Large Scale Splty. Retailers, (chmn. 1972—), C. of C., Netherlands-Brit. C. of C. (gen. council 1971—), Dutch Soc. for Sci. (dir. 1979—), Dutch Inst. Mktg. (gen. council 1966-76), Dutch Inst. Mgmt. (gen. council 1968-80), Assn. Distbn. Econs. (trustee 1964—). Author: Evolutie en Expansie, 2 parts, 1963; Familie-problemen in het Bedrijf, 1966; (with A. W. Luyckx) Moderne Winkelcentra, 1966, Steden in Steigers, 1968; Konkurrenz, Konzentration und Kooperation im Textileinzelhandel, 1967; Vernieuwing en Vooruitgang, Prae-advies Vereniging voor Distributie-Economie, 1969; Dynamiek in de Distributie, 2 parts, 1974; contbg. author: Fortschrift im Betrieb, 1970; Neuerungsorientierte Unternehmungsfü hrung, 1971; Spiegel van Onroerend Goed, 1977; Amsterdam Hoofdstad'9 , 1977; Dynamik im Handel, 1978; Reflecties op Limperg, 1979; others. Contbg. numerous articles to profl. jours. Chmn. editorial bd. Inkoop monthly, 1986-75, Modern Markt, bi-weekly, 1970-72. Christian Democrat. Roman Catholic. Home: 16 Rijksweg W, 1251 CK Laren The Netherlands Office: 6 De Klencke, 1083 HH Amsterdam The Netherlands

DREI, CLAUDIO CAFIERO GUIDI, composer, conductor; b. Buenos Aires, Aug. 17, 1927; m. Bella Haydee Ambrosioni. Profesorado il Musica, Conservatorio Nacional, Buenos Aires; student in composicion, Conservatorio J. Rossini, Pesaro, Italy. Prof. il soffeo y teoria superior y armonia, maestro en composicion musical. Dir. de estudio Teatro Lirico Argentino, La Plata, 1960-82, dir. artistico, 1972-73, 1980-82; dir. de estudios Teatro Lirico Colon, Buenos Aires, 1973-76, 1983-86, dir. artistico, 1976; rector Inst. Musical, Avellaneda, Argentina, 1979-81; jurados de composicion Sec. Cultura Mpl., Buenos Aires, 1972-75, 1984-86; jurados internat. S.O.D.R.E., Montevideo, Uraguay, 1980; jurado Orch. Sinfonica, Bahia Blanca, Argentina, 1979-80. Compositor: (ballet) Lupapag, 1969, El Trappa, 1987; (opera) Medea (Mpl. de Buenos Aires award 1971); (cantata) Calvario (Sec. de Cultura Nacional award 1982); various musica vocal de camara (Fondo Nacional de las Artes awards 1975, 77). Mem. Assn. Argentina de Compositores. Home: Chacabuco 337, Banfield Buenos Aires, Argentina 1828 Office: Teatro Colon, Cerrito 618, Buenos Aires Argentina 1010

DREISBACH, JOHN GUSTAVE, investment banker; b. Paterson, N.J., Apr. 24, 1939; s. Gustave John and Rose Catherine (Koehler) D.; BA, NYU, 1963; m. Janice Lynn Petitjean; 1 child, John Gustave Jr. With Shields & Co., Inc., 1965-68, Model, Roland & Co., Inc., N.Y.C., 1968-72, F. Eberstadt & Co., Inc., N.Y.C., 1972-74; v.p. Bessemer Trust Co., 1974-78; pres. Community Housing Capital, Inc., 1978-80; chmn., pres. John G. Dreisbach, Inc., Santa Fe, N.Mex., 1980—; JGD Housing Corp., 1982—; bd. dirs., pres. The Santa Fe Investment Conf., 1986— Served with USAFR, 1964. Mem. Mensa, Santa Fe C. of C. Republican. Episcopalian. Clubs: St. Bartholomew's Community, Essex, Hartford, Amigos del Alcalde. Office: 1 Sunflower Circle Santa Fe NM 87501-8503

DRENNAN, JOSEPH PETER, lawyer; b. Albany, N.Y., Apr. 15, 1956; s. Richard Peter and Ann Marie (Conlon) D.; m. Adriana Sonia Miramontes, Sept. 26, 1987. BA in Polit. Sci., U. Richmond, 1978; JD, Cath. U. of Am., Washington, 1981. Bar: D.C. 1981, U.S. Dist. Ct. D.C. 1983, U.S. Ct. Appeals (fed. cir.) 1983, Va. 1984, U.S. Ct. Appeals (D.C. cir.) 1984, U.S. Dist. Ct. (no. dist.) Va. 1987, U.S. Ct. Appeals (4th cir.) 1987, U.S. Dist. Ct. (no. dist.) Miss. 1988. Sole practice Washington, 1981—. Mem. ABA, Assn. Trial Lawyers Am., Bar Assn. D.C. Republican. Roman Catholic. Club: Univ. Washington. Home: 1425 S Eads St #1305 Arlington VA 22202-2847 Office: 1420 16th St NW Washington DC 20036-2218

DRESCHHOFF, GISELA AUGUSTE MARIE, physicist, educator; b. Moenchengladbach, Germany, Sept. 13, 1938; came to U.S., 1967, naturalized, 1976; d. Gustav Julius and Hildegard Friederike (Krug) D. Ph.D., Tech. U. Braunschweig (Ger.), 1972. Staff scientist Fed. Inst. Physics and Tech. Ger., 1965-67; research assoc. Kans. Geol. Survey, Lawrence, 1971-72; vis. asst. prof. physics U. Kans., 1972-74; dep. dir. radiation physics lab. Space Tech. Ctr., 1972-78, assoc. dir., 1979-83, co-dir., 1984—, adj. asst. prof. physics, 1974; assoc. program mgr. NSF, Washington, 1978-79. Patentee identification markings for gemstones. Named to Women's Hall of Fame, U. Kans., 1978; recipient Antarctic Service medal U.S.A., 1979; recipient NASA Group Achievement award, 1983. Mem. Am. Phys. Soc., Am. Geophys. Union, AAAS, Am. Polar Soc., Antarctican Soc., U.S. Naval Inst., Sigma Xi. Club: Explorers. Home: 2908 W 19th Lawrence KS 66044 Office: Space Tech Ctr 2291 Irving Hill Dr Lawrence KS 66045

DRESKIN, ERVING ARTHUR, pathologist; b. Newark, Jan. 9, 1919; s. Harry and Sarah Molly (Krulvetsky) D.; B.S., Tulane U., 1940, M.D., 1943; m. Jeanet Irma Steckler, May 9, 1943; children—Richard Burgas, Stephen Charles, Jeanet Elizabeth, Rena Lynn. Intern, Newark Beth Israel Hosp., 1943-44; resident in pathology, instr. pathology U. Ill. Coll. Medicine, Chgo., 1946-49, Am. Cancer Soc. fellow, 1949-50; asso. pathologist Grant Hosp., Chgo., 1949-50; chief pathologist, dir. labs. and Blood Bank, Greenville (S.C.) Hosp. System, 1950-85; med. dir. Carolina Blood Center, 1980—; cons. pathologist to hosps.; professorial lectr. Clemson U.; clin. prof. pathology Med. U. S.C.; past pres., chmn., exec. com. Pathology Assn. Greenville, Pa.; bd. dirs. United Way Greenville County, 1973-76; treas. Greater Greenville Community Found., 1980-81, bd. dirs., 1980-83; pres. Temple of Israel, Greenville, 1966-68. Served to lt. (s.g.) M.C., USNR, 1944-46. Diplomate Am. Bd. Pathology. Fellow Am. Soc. Clin. Pathologists, Coll. Am. Pathologists (S.C. regional commr. for lab. accreditation); mem. Am. Assn. Blood Banks (v.p. 1962, sec. 1963-65, pres. 1965-66), S.C. Soc. Pathologists (pres. 1957-59), AMA, S.C. Med. Assn., Alpha Omega Alpha. Clubs: Rotary, Poinsett. Home: 60 Lake Forest Dr Greenville SC 29609 Office: Greenville Hosp System 701 Grove Rd Greenville SC 29605

DRESSEL, HENRY FRANCIS, lawyer; b. Bklyn., Apr. 11, 1914; s. Henry Philip and Ernestine (Delmar) D.; A.B., Washington Sq. Coll., N.Y. U., 1943, J.D., 1949; m. Rose Marie Valentine, Nov. 24, 1937; 1 dau., Diana (Mrs. Anthony P. Fradella). Admitted to N.Y. bar, 1949; asso. corp. law firm Chadbourne, Stanchfield & Levy (and its successors), N.Y.C., 1933-43; pvt. practice law, N.Y.C., 1950-86; ptnr. Dressel & Altman, P.C.; of counsel Berger & Steingut 1986—. Served from ensign to lt. USNR, 1943-46. Named hon. col. Okla., 1958, Okie, 1969. Mem. ABA, N.Y. State Bar Assn., Assn. Bar City of N.Y., N.Y. County Lawyers, Am. Judicature Soc., Justinian Soc., Internat. Footprint Assn., Phi Delta Phi. Democrat. Episcopalian. Clubs: Danish Athletic, N.Y. University. Home: 8365 Shore Rd Brooklyn NY 11209 Office: 600 Madison Ave New York NY 10022

DREW, JANE BEVERLY, architect; b. Thornton Heath, Surrey, Eng., Mar. 24, 1911; d. Harry Guy Radcliffe and Emma Spering (Jones) D.; m. Edwin Maxwell Fry, Apr. 24, 1942; children—Jennifer, Georgina Alliston. LL.D. (hon.), U. Ibadan (Nigeria), 1960; hon. doctorate Open U., Milton Keynee, Eng., 1973; LittD, Newcastle U., 1987. Ptnr., Alliston E. Drew, Eng., 1934-39; prin. Jane B. Drew, Eng., 1939-45; ptnr. Fry Drew & Ptnrs., Seven Oaks, Eng., 1945—; asst. town planning advisor to resident minister W. African colonies, 1944-45; sr. architect Indian Capitol Project, Chandigari, 1951-54; Beamis prof. MIT, Boston, 1961; vis. prof. Harvard U., Boston, 1970. Editor: Architect's Year Book, 1984; author: (with E. Maxwell Fry) Architecture for Children, 1944; Architecture in the Humid Tropics, 1956. Hon. fellow AIA, Nigerian Inst. Architects; hon. assoc. Inst. Contemporary Arts.; mem. Archtl. Assn. (past pres.), Royal Inst. Am. Architects (hon.), Indian Inst. Architects. Mem. Labour Party. Home: West Lodge, Cotherstone, Castle Barnard, County Durham England Office: Fry Drew Knight & Creamer, Seven Oaks Kent, England also: 63 Gloucester Pl, London W1H 4DJ, England

DREW, PAUL, entrepreneur; b. Detroit, Mar. 10, 1935; s. Harry and Elizabeth (Schneider) Schlachman; m. Dove Ann Austin, Sept. 9, 1961. B.A., Wayne State U., Detroit, 1957. Disc jockey stas. in Port Huron, Mich. and Atlanta, 1955-67; program dir. Sta. WQXI, Atlanta, 1966-67, Sta. CKLW, Detroit, 1967-68; program cons. Storer Broadcasting Co., Phila., 1968-69; program dir. RKO Radio stas. in, Detroit, San Francisco, Washington and Los Angeles, 1970-73; v.p. programming RKO Radio stas. in, 1973-77; pres. Paul Drew Enterprises, Los Angeles, 1977—, Red Carpet Mktg., U.S.A. and Japan, 1978—, PAD Entertainment, Hollywood, Calif., 1980—; personal mgr. Pink Lady, outside Japan, 1978; partner Teacup/Teaspoon Music Pub. Co., 1978; chmn. Billboard Internat. Programming Conf., 1976; commr. Calif. Motion Picture Council. Del. Democratic Nat. Conv., 1976; mem. Dem. Nat. Com., Calif. Dem. Com., Dem. Nat. Fin. Council. Named DeeJay of Year Sixteen Mag., 1965; Program Dir. of Year Bill Gavin Report, 1967; recipient Superior Achievement award RKO Radio, 1973; also numerous gold records for contbs. toward million selling records. Mem. Nat. Acad. Rec. Arts. and Scis., Am. Advt. Fedn., Am. Film Inst., Hollywood Radio and TV Soc., Los Angeles World Affairs Council, Town Hall Calif., Japanese-Am. Citizens League., Japan Am. Soc. Clubs: Variety, Friars, Frat. of Friends, Music Center. Home: 2151 N Hobart Blvd Los Angeles CA 90027 Office: Sunset-Gower Studios 1438 N Gower Hollywood CA 90028

DREWRY, GUY CARLETON, author; b. Stevensburg, Va., May 21, 1901; s. Rev. Samuel Richard and Julia Harriett (Pinckard) D.; student public schs. Va.; m. Margaret Elizabeth McDonald, Apr. 2, 1942; children—Barbara Louise, Guy Carleton. Asso. editor The Lyric, 1929-49; vis. lectr. English, Am. poetry Hollins Coll., 1952-53; instr. creative writing U. Va. Extension Div. Named Poet Laureate of Commonwealth of Va., 1970. Contbr. poetry to The Dial, later The Nation, The New Republic, Poetry; A Magazine of Verse also Voices. Work appears in N.Y. Times, N.Y. Herald Tribune, The Georgia Rev., Prairie Schooner, Sat. Rev., Queen's Quar., Va. Quar. Rev., Yale Rev.; included in following anthologies: American Writing, Lyric Virginia Today, Moult's Best Poems, Virginia Reader, Poetry Awards (1949, 51), Lyric Virginia Today, No. 2, The Best Poems of 1956. Author: (poetry) Proud Horns, 1933, The Sounding Summer, 1948; A Time of Turning, 1951, The Writhen Wood, 1953, Cloud Above Clocktime, 1957. Winner The Voices award, 1940; Poetry awards prize for best book of poetry pub. in 1951; Poet Laureate Va., 1970—. Mem. Poetry Soc. Va. (pres. 1952-55), Poetry Soc. of Am. (regional v.p.) Author: (lyrics) To Love that Well, 1975. Editor: Southern Issue of Voices. Home: 2305 Maiden Ln SW 2 Roanoke VA 24015

DREYER, RONALD FRED, political scientist; b. Zurich, Switzerland, Aug. 3, 1950; s. Heinz and Irene (May) D.; m. Marilyn Jean Pigott, June 1, 1983. Degree in polit. sci., Grad. Inst. Internat. Studies, Geneva, 1974; diploma in devel. studies, Inst. Devel. Studies, Geneva, 1974; PhD in Polit. Sci., U. Geneva, 1984. Research fellow Grad. Inst. Internat. Studies, 1985—; research assoc. Univ. Zimbabwe, Harare, 1986-88; vis. fellow Ctr. Fgn. Relations, Dar-es Salaam, Tanzania, 1988; vis. lectr. diplomacy tng. program Univ. Nairobi, Kenya, 1985, 88; cons. UN Inst. Tng. and Research, Conakry, Guinea, 1987. Author: The Official Mind of Imperialism, 1987; contbr. articles to profl. jours. Mem. Royal African Soc., Soc. suisse d'études africaines. Home: 2 rue Nicole, 1260 Nyon Switzerland Office: Grad Inst Internat Studies, PO Box 36, 1211 Geneva 21 Switzerland

DREYER, THOMAS PRINS, mathematics educator; b. Joubertina, Republic South Africa, May 31, 1937; s. Nicolaas Bernard and Albertina (Prins) D.; m. Catharina Maria Stals, July 30, 1960; children: Johanna Jacomina, Anita Maria, Nicolaas Bernard. BSc, Stellenbosch U., Republic South Africa, 1956, BSc (hon.), 1957, MSC, 1959, PhD, 1972; AM, Harvard U., 1960. Lectr. U. Stellenbosch, 1957-59, 62-68, sr. lectr., 1959-75, assoc. prof., 1976-79, prof. math., 1980—. Contbr. articles to profl. jours. Chmn. sch. com. Stellenbosch, 1979-85; mem. sch. bd. Stellenbosch Area County, 1983—; mem. exec. bd. Voortrekker Youth Orgn., Pretoria, Republic South Africa, 1985—. Frank Knox Meml. fellow Harvard U., 1959; decorated Orde van die Wawiel, 1984, Orde van die Fakkel, 1988, Voortrekker Youth Orgn.; recipient Cornwall and York prize, 1959. Mem. Am. Math. Soc., S. African Akademie Vir Wetenskap en Kuns, S. African Math. Soc., Math. Assn. S. Africa. Mem. National Party. Mem. Dutch Reformed Ch. Office: U Stellenbosch, Dept Applied Math, Stellenbosch Republic of South Africa

DREZDZON, WILLIAM LAWRENCE, mathematics educator; b. Milw., Feb. 19, 1934; s. Edward Kenneth and Mildred Mary (Schneider) D.; B.S. in Math., St. Mary's U., 1957; M.S. in Math. (Esso Oil Co. fellow), Ill. Inst. Tech., 1964; m. Frances Anita Sikes; children—Gregory Francis, Andrea Louise. Tchr. math., chemistry St. Michael's High Sch., Chgo., 1957-59, Lane Tech. High Sch., Chgo., 1959-66; software design engr. A.C. Electronics div. Gen. Motors, Oak Creek, Wis., 1966-67; prof. math., chmn. dept. Kennedy-King Coll., Chgo., 1967-71; prof. math. and learning lab. coordinator Oakton Community Coll., Des Plaines, Ill., 1971—; vis. prof. U. New Orleans, 1982-84; cons. nat. calculus survey, 1975. NSF grantee, 1961-65; Chgo. Bd. Edn. grantee, summer 1964; NSF coop. program, 1971, 72; Chautauqua Course grantee, 1975-80. Mem. Math. Assn. Am. (chmn. jr. coll. com. Ill. sect., 1971-74), No. Ill. Math. Assn. Community Colls. (founding pres., 1971, 72), Am. Math. Assn. Two-Yr. Colls. (chmn., 1975, pres. 1979), Nat. Math. Assn., Ill. councils tchrs. math., Ill. Assn. Community Colls. (pres. 1979), Met. Mathematics Club of Gtr. Chgo., Adler Planetarium Soc., Ill. Assn. Personalized Learning Programs, Analytic Psychology Club of Chgo., Delta Epsilon Sigma. Regional editor Math. Assns. of Two-Year Colleges Jour., 1970-82; author: Curriculum Guide of Transfer Courses for the Ill. Community College Board, 1974; Math. Research and Teaching Techniques, 1973, 76; contbr. articles to jours. Home: 1600 Ashland Ave Des Plaines IL 60016 Office: Oakton Community College 1600 E Golf Rd Des Plaines IL 60016

DRIES, LOUIS JOSEPH, transportation executive; b. St Vith, Liège, Belgium, Nov. 30, 1948; arrived in Canada, 1967; s. Paul and Helena (Eicher) D.; m. Joan L. Macleod, Apr. 24, 1971; children: John-Paul, Stephen, Andrew, Eric. Grad., Canadian Inst. Traffic and Transp., Toronto, 1974. Dist. mgr. Daymond, Mississauga, Ont., Can., 1977-84; plant mgr. Daymond, Chatham, Ont., 1984-85; logistics mgr. Alchem Inc., Burlington, Ont., 1985—. Mem. Can. Inst. Traffic and Transp. (chmn. 1978, internal auditor 1982-84, pres. 1984-85; recipient J.T. MacKenzie Gold Medal, 1974), Can. Assn. Physical Dist. Mgmt. Roman Catholic. Home: 24 Carl Dr RR#1, Waterdown, ON Canada L0R 2H0 Office: Alchem Inc, 1055 Truman Str, Burlington, ON Canada L7R 3Y9

DRIGGS, MARGARET, educator; b. Kansas City, Kans., June 30, 1909; d. William Foster and Lillian Edith (Landers) Brazier; m. J.W. Quarrier, Nov. 26, 1933 (div. July 1945); children: John Chilton, Philip Harrington, Camille Elizabeth; m. Howard R. Driggs, Sept. 26, 1933 (dec.). AB, U. Kans., 1930; postgrad. Hofstra Coll., 1960, Grad. Sch. Library Sci., Pratt Inst., 1964-65. Contbr. Kansas City Star and Johnson County (Kans.) Herald, 1930-33; editor Am. Trails Series, filmstrips; nat. dir. pub. relations Am. Pioneer Trails Assn., 1948; chmn. pub. relations NYU Faculty Women's Club, 1950-54; nat. 1st v.p. Assn. Parents and Friends Kings Point, 1957-58; mem. Nat. Council Coll. Publs. Advisers, 1958; staff adviser Nexus (yearbook), Hofstra Coll., 1961; mem. faculty Westover Sch., Middlebury, Conn., 1964-65; dir. devel. pub. relations, asst. to dean Cathedral Sch. of St. Mary, Garden City, N.Y., 1965, also yearbook adviser; chmn. guides N.J. Gov.'s Mansion, 1975-82; chmn. docents N.J. Hist. Soc., 1982-86; curator Driggs Collection of Americana. Mem. women's council Hofstra Coll., 1959-60; mem. U.S. Com. for UN Children's Fund, 1957; mem. Friends of Princeton Univ. Library, 1975; mem. Princeton Med. Ctr.Aux.; chair civilian hostesses 15th Ann. U.S. Army Mus. Conf., Princeton, 1986. Recipient Disting. Service citation Am. Pioneer Trails Assn., 1943, medals Am. Yearbook, Columbia Scholastic Press Assn., 1970, pin for vol. work in Princeton, 1976, French-Am. Alliance medal, cert. and hist. house tile award N.J. Hist. Soc., 1984; Margaret Brazier Driggs Collection of Americana established at U. Kans., 1953, at Hofstra Coll., 1961. Mem. ALA, Internat. Platform Assn., Assn. Coll. and Research Libraries, Princeton Hist. Soc., Nat. Trust Hist. Preservation, Smithsonian Assocs., Women's Bd. of N.J. Hist. Soc., Met. Mus. Art, Women's Coll. Club Princeton, Amiga of Orgn. of Am. States, Pi Delta Epsilon (grand councilman 1960-61). Clubs: NYU; Faculty (hon. life), Present Day (Princeton), Gold Medal (pin and citation for achievement 1930-1980, Kans.). Editor: New Light on Old Glory, 1950, Pitch Pine Tales, 1951, Nick Wilson, 1951, George, The Handcart Boy, 1952, The Old West Speaks, 1956, When Grandfather Was a Boy and Western Cowkid, 1957 (all by Howard R. Driggs); contbg. editor Nat. Assn. Ind. Schs. Archives, Harvard, 1965; editor and photographer Vive Rochambeau, Vive Washington. Home: 135 Princeton Arms S Cranbury NJ 08512

DRILL, LOIS H., retail jeweler; b. Cin., Oct. 10, 1934; d. Harry H. and Idah (Gelshof) Herrman; m. Edwin L. Drill, June 3, 1956; children—Ann Drill Bernstein; Robert Mark. Student U. Cin. Co-owner, mgr. The Two of Us Fine Jewelry Boutique, Cin. Mem. Alpha Zeta Omega Ladies Aux., Dental Aid Fund for Handicapped Children, Jewish Hosp. Ladies Aux., Adath Israel Sisterhood, Hadassah, Am. Women's Orgn., Ruth Lodge. Mem. Retail Jewelers Am. Republican.

DRISCOLL, CONSTANCE FITZGERALD, educator, author; b. Lawrence, Mass., Mar. 29, 1926; d. John James and Mary Anne (Leecock) Fitzgerald; A.B., Radcliffe Coll., 1946; postgrad. Harvard U., U. Hartford (Conn.), U. Bridgeport (Conn.), Worcester (Mass.) State Coll.; m. Francis George Driscoll, Aug. 21, 1948; children—Frances Mary, Martha Anne, Sara Helene, Maribeth Lee. Secondary sch. tchr., North Andover, Mass., 1946-48; book reviewer N.Y.C. and Boston pubs., 1955-64; asst. conf. edn. dir. U. Hartford, 1964-68; lectr. Pace U., N.Y.C., 1973-74; edn. commentary Radio WVOX, New Rochelle, N.Y., 1974-75; asst. ednl. adv. Nat. Girl Scouts, 1972-74; pres., owner, dir. Open Corridor Schs. Cons., Inc., Bronxville, N.Y., 1972—, pres., dir. Open Corridor Schs., Inc., Oxford, Mass., 1984—; creator in-service edn. programs pub. schs., Norwalk, Conn., 1983—; assoc. Worcester State Coll. (Mass.) 1984—, Fitchburg State Coll., 1986-87; cons. in-service tchr. edn. programs, Norwalk, Yonkers, N.Y., 1987—; tutor, cons. Wincester County sch. dist., 1989—. Author curriculum materials. Recipient Educator award Nat. Council ARC, Washington, 1985, Edn. award Nipmuc Am. Indian Council, Webster, Mass, 1985. Home: 338 Main St Oxford MA 01540 Office: Box 564 Oxford MA 01540

DRISCOLL, JAMES PATRICK, economic policy advisor, consultant; b. Cardiff, Wales, Apr. 24, 1925; s. Henry James and Honorah (Flynn) D.; m. Jeanne Lawrence Williams, Apr. 16, 1955; children—Fiona E.L., Jonathan J.L. B.A. with 1st class honors, Univ. Coll., Cardiff, 1950. Asst. lectr. econs., indsl. relations Univ. Coll., 1950-53; research fellow Council of Europe, Luxembourg, 1953; Advisor, then econ. dir. and dep. dir. gen. Brit. Iron and Steel Fedn., London, 1953-67; mng. dir. corp. strategy, advisor Brit. Steel Corp., London, 1967-80; dir. Nationalized Industries Chmns. Group, London, 1975—; observer Nat. Econ. Devel. Council, London, 1977—; chmn., mng. dir. Woodcote Cons. Ltd., London, 1980—. Contbr. articles in field to profl. jours. Dep. chmn. Univ. Conservative Fedn., 1949-50; dep. chmn. U.K. Young Conservatives, 1950; dep. chmn. Brit. Nat. Union Students, 1951-53; mem. ct. govs. Univ. Coll., Cardiff 1970—. Served to lt. Royal Marines, 1944-45. Fellow Univ. Coll., Cardiff, 1986—, Royal Soc. Arts, Royal Econ. Soc., Internat. Iron and Steel Inst. (chmn. econ. com. 1975-78), Confedn. Brit. Industry (mem. council 1981—). Conservative. Anglican. Home: Foxley Hatch, Birch Ln, Purley Surrey, England Office: Nationalised Industries Chmns Group, Hobart House, Grosvenor Pl, London SW1, England

DRISKO, ELLIOT HILLMAN, social service executive, therapist; b. Columbia Falls, Maine, Aug. 19, 1917; s. Eri Haskell and Susie Farnsworth (Allen) D.; B.A. cum laude, Colby Coll., 1939; M.S., Boston U., 1941; Ed.D., Columbia U., 1960; m. Elizabeth Winship, Oct. 17, 1942; children—Elliot Hillman, James Winship. Family counselor Children's Aid Soc., Niagara Falls, N.Y., 1941-42; supr. psychiat. social work Mason Gen. Hosp., Brentwood, N.Y., 1944-46; intake supr. Family Service Soc., Yonkers, N.Y., 1946-49, exec. dir., 1950-87; pvt. practice marriage and family therapy, Yonkers, 1965—; founder Yonkers Homemaker Service, 1953, Big-Brother-Big Sister program, 1963, Senior Service Center, 1971; chmn. N.Y. State Council of Family Service Agys. 1959-61, exec. bd., 1974; N.Y. State del. White House Conf. Children and Youth, 1960; mem. adv. council Westchester County (N.Y.) Dept. Social Services, 1975-85; Yonkers Youth Bd., Mayor's Com. on Aging; cons. public relations Family Service Assn. Am., 1960-71. Treas., Yonkers Community Planning Council, 1970-81; chmn. Yonkers unit Internat. Year of Child, UN Assn./U.S., 1977; bd. dirs. Yonkers council Boy Scouts Am.; mem. home care com. Yonkers Office for the Aging; mem. Police Athletic League. Served in U.S. Army 1942-46. Recipient Yonkers Community Service award Family Service Soc., 1964; Jenkins Meml. Community Service award Yonkers PTA Council, 1967; Service Above Self award Rotary, 1980. Fellow Am. Assn. Marriage and Family Therapists; mem. Acad. Cert. Social Workers (pres. Westchester County chpt. 1971-72), Nat. Assn. Social Workers (chmn. com. third-party payment N.Y. State chpt. 1974-79), Westchester Assn. Psychiat. Social Workers, Am. Assn. Sex Educators and Therapists, Soc. for Sci. Study of Sex, NCCJ. Author: Parent-Teen Age Codes in the United States, 1960; contbr. articles to popular magazines. Home: 10 Mitchell Ave Yonkers NY 10701 Office: Family Service Soc 219 Palisade Ave Yonkers NY 10703

DRIZUL, ALEKSANDR ARVIDOVICH, science academy administrator, historian; b. Pskov, Latvia, USSR, June 29, 1920; s. Arvid Y. and Milda I. (Trauberg) D.; m. Irina A. Maslennikova, Sept. 29, 1943; 1 child, Viktoria A. Grad. history, Archival Inst., Moscow, 1942; postgrad., State Pedagogical Inst., Moscow, 1943-44, Inst. History, Moscow, 1944-46. Learned sec. Inst. History, Riga, USSR, 1946-70; dep. dir. then dir. Latvian Soviet Socialist Republic Acad. Scis., Riga, from 1963, academician, sec. Dept. Social Scis., 1963-70, v.p., from 1975; mem. Nat. Com. Historians, Moscow, 1975—; leader Latvian sect. Acad. Council of History of Great Oct. Revolution, from 1960. Author: Lenin and the Revolutionary Movement in Latvia, 1980, History of the Great October Revolution in Latvia, 1987; author, editor: History of Latvian Soviet Socialist Republic, 1986 (State prize 1987). Dep. Supreme Soviet of Latvian Soviet Socialist Republic, from 1967, dep. chmn. of presidium, 1967-84, chmn., from 1985; sec. cen. com. Latvian Communist Party, 1970-75. Decorated Order of Lenin Presidium Supreme Soviet, Moscow, 3 Orders of Red Banner Presidium Supreme Soviet; recipient medal USSR Peace Com., 1973. Mem. Latvian Soviet Socialist Soc. of Knowledge. Office: Latvian SSR Acad Scis, #19 Turgenev St, Riga USSR

DROMS, WILLIAM GEORGE, college dean, finance educator; b. Schenectady, Aug. 20, 1944; s. George William and Frances (Maguire) D.; m. JoAnn Gilberti, June 17, 1967; children: Courtney, Justin. AB, Brown U., 1966; MBA, George Washington U., 1971, DBA, 1975. Prof. Georgetown U., Washington, 1973—, assoc. dean Sch. Bus. Adminstrn., 1978-81, 87—; cons. Dennis M. Gurtz and Assoc., Inc., D.C., 1983-87 , Minn. Mut. Life, 1986—. Author: (with others) The Dow Jones Irwin Guide to Personal Financial Planning, 1986; (with others) Personal Financial Management, 1986, (with others) Dow Jones-Irwin No-Load Mutual Funds, 1986, (with others) The Life Insurance Investment Advisor, 1988, Finance and Accounting for Nonfinancial Managers, 1983, The Dow Jones Irwin Mutual Fund Yearbook, 1984, 85. Contbr. numerous articles to profl. jours. Served to lt. USN, 1966-70. Fellow Inst. Chartered Fin. Analysts; mem. Am. Fin. Assn., Eastern Fin. Assn., Fin. Analysts Fedn., Fin. Mgmt. Assn. D.C. Soc. Investment Analysts, AAUP. Republican. Roman Catholic. Avocations: tennis, fishing, golf. Office: Georgetown U Sch Bus Adminstrn Washington DC 20057

DROTNING, PHILLIP THOMAS, retired oil company official, business and government consultant; b. Deerfield, Wis., July 4, 1920; s. Edward Clarence and Martha (Skaar) D.; student U. Wis., 1937-41; m. Loretta Jayne Taylor, Nov. 3, 1964; children—Meredith Anne, Maria Kristina, Misya Kerri. Reporter, Wis. State Jour., Madison, 1943-44; editorial page writer Milw. Jour., 1944-45; freelance author, 1945-47; exec. sec. to gov. Wis., 1948-55; v.p. Northwest Airlines, Inc., 1956-61; spl. asst. to adminstr. NASA, Washington, 1961-65; exec. communications cons. Standard Oil Co. (Ind.), 1965-66; mgr. communications Am. Oil Co., Chgo., 1967-68; dir. urban affairs Amoco Corp., Chgo., 1968-72, dir. pub. affairs ops., 1973, dir. corp. social policy, 1973-85; ret., 1985; vis. fellow Am. Enterprise Inst. for Pub. Policy Research, Washington, 1985—; cons. to bus. and govt., 1985—. Bd. dirs., first v.p. Child Care Assn. Ill., 1973-76, pres., 1976-78; bd. dirs. T.R.U.S.T., Inc., 1976—, pres., 1979-81. Served with USMCR, 1941-43. Mem. Pub. Relations Soc. Am., Nat. Assn. Mfrs. (chmn. urban affairs com. 1969-71), Nat. Minority Purchasing Council (dir. 1972-84, pres. 1972-77). Club: Plaza (Phoenix). Author: A Guide to Negro History in America, 1968; Black Heroes in our Nation's History, 1969; A Job with a Future in the Petroleum Industry, 1969; Up from the Ghetto, 1970; New Hope for Problem Drinkers, 1977; Taking Stock: A Woman's Guide to Corporate Success, 1977; Putting the Fun in Fundraising, 1979; How To Get Your Creditors off Your Back without Losing Your Shirt, 1979; You Can Buy a Home Now, 1982; editorial advisory bd. The Chicago Reporter, 1971-85. Contbr. numerous articles to pubs.

DROUGHT, ROSE ALICE, gerontology consultant; b. Milw., Aug. 4, 1903; student U. Ill., 1924-25, Layton Sch. Art, 1931; BA, U. Wis., 1924, MA, 1926, PhD (Carnegie fellow), 1931; postgrad. U. Ariz., No. Ariz. U., Ariz. State U., U. Sydney, Australia, 1970, U. London, 1972. Exec. camp dir. Girl Scouts U.S.A., 1934-48; free-lance writer, 1948-54; tchr. spl. edn. Phoenix Elem. Schs., 1954-69; dir. Community Council Project on Aging, 1969-74; dir. Area Agy. on Aging, Region I, Ariz., 1974-78, exec. dir., 1977-82, dir. emeritus, 1982—; cons. Internat. Ctr. Social Gerontology, 1978; del. White House Conf. on Aging, 1971-81; mem. adv. com. curriculum and internships No. Ariz. U., 1978; mem. multidisciplinary com. on gerontology Ariz. State U., 1978-81; adj. prof. Sch. Social Work, 1981-82; cons. in gerontology; mem. sr. adult faculty Scottsdale Community Coll., 1983—; camp planning cons. YMCA, YWCA, ch. camps, pvt. camps, 1935—; dir. internat. encampment Girl Guides and Girl Scouts, Adelboden, Switzerland, 1939-1940; dir. Outdoor Edn. Inst., Marquette, U., Milw., summer 1963; guest lectr. Ariz. State U., 1966-81, Glendale Community Coll., Mem. adv. bd. Salvation Army; mem. Phoenix Housing Commn., Phoenix Nutrition Council; chmn. Phoenix Pub. Housing Adv. Bd., 1973-78; cons. Phoenix Chinese Sr. Citizens Assn., 1980—. Mem. exec. bd. Sr. Citizens Council Maricopa County, 1983—. Recipient Ann. awards Ariz. State Fair, 1953—; Disting. Service award United Cerebral Palsy Ariz., 1962-63, citation, 1965, cert. appreciation ARC, 1965; Floyd Adams award, 1972; citation Nat. Ret. Tchrs. Assn., 1973; citation of merit Gov. Ariz., 1974, 76, Gov.'s citation as Sr. Citizen of Yr., 1985; disting. service award Scottsdale Community Coll. Sr. Adult Program, 1982; recognition award for contbn. to nutrition Ariz. Dietetic Assn., 1984. Mem. Ariz. Acad. Pub. Affairs, Am. Camping Assn. (dir. 1945-48, pres. Wis. sect. 1946-48, pres. Coronado sect. 1960-62, v.p. region VIII, 1961-62, lifetime campcraft instr.), NEA (del. to World Assemblies of Teaching Profession, Vancouver, B.C., Can. 1967, Dublin 1968, Sydney 1970, Kingston, Jamaica 1971, London 1972, Nairobi, Kenya 1973, Singapore 1974, Washington 1976), Ariz. Edn. Asn. (editorial bd. 1968-74), Assn. Outdoor Edn., Council Exceptional Children, Assn. Educators Homebound and Hospitalized Children, Nat. Assn. Area Agys. on Aging (dir. 1974-80, v.p. 1979-80), Ariz. Assn. Area Agys. on Aging (pres. 1974-77), Nat. Wildlife Fedn., Nat. Sch. Pub. Relations Assn. (pres. Ariz. chpt. 1968-69), Gerontol. Soc., Western Gerontol. Soc., Nat. Council on Aging, Internat. Platform Assn., Delta Kappa Gamma. Democrat. Author: A Camping Manual, 1943; Services and Facilities for Meeting the Needs of Older Americans, 1973; The Community College-A Resource for Older Americans-Older Americans-A Resource for the Community, 1974; What the Older Person Will be like—A Look to the Future, 1976; Ministries for Senior Adults—Let's Go Beyond the Horizon, 1983; editor: Conservation in Camping, 1952; Phoenix Elementary Classroom Tchrs. Assn. Press, 1965-68; The Elderly Arizonan, 1976, updated 1978; editor The Sr. Observer (Gov.'s Adv. Council on Aging, 1985-87; acting editor Camping Mag., 1945-46. Home: PO Box 353 Chandler AZ 85224

DROULLARD, STEVEN MAURICE, jewelry company executive; b. Pampa, Tex., June 28, 1951; s. Maurice Erskin and Betty (Bonnett) D.; m. Alessia Passalacqua, Dec. 31, 1978. Grad. gemology, Gemological Inst Am., Santa Monica, Calif., 1985. Lic. broadcaster, 1972. Asst. to pres. Standard Coal Co., San Francisco, 1976-78; pres. Adamas Gem Services, Kailua-kona, Hawaii, 1978-82; v.p. Intergem, Inc., Denver, 1982-85, pres., 1985-87, also bd. dirs.; pres., chmn. bd. GMA Inc., 1988—; cons. Wells Communications, Boulder, Colo., 1984—; mem. bd. advisors Colo. Computing Mag., Boulder, 1985—; bd. dirs. Computer Sci. Tech., Inc. Contbr. articles to mags.; also cons. The Great American Sapphire, 1985. Named Bus. Assoc. of Yr. Am. Bus. Women Assoc., 1981. Mem. Gemological Inst. Am. Alumni Assn. (charter, pres. Colo. chpt. 1987—), Accredited Gemologists Assn., Am. Gem Trade Assn., Gem Mcht. Assocs. (pres. 1986), Kailua-Kona C. of C. (v.p. 1981). Office: GMA Inc 451 E 58th Ave #2220 Denver CO 80216

DROZDZIEL, MARION JOHN, aeronautical engineer; b. Dunkirk, N.Y., Dec. 21, 1924; s. Steven and Veronica (Wilk) D.; B.S. in Aero. Engring., Tri State U., 1947, B.S. in Mech. Engring., 1948; postgrad. Ohio State U., 1948, Nigara U., 1949-51, U. Buffalo, 1951-52; m. Rita L. Korwek, Aug. 30, 1952; 1 son, Eric A. Stress analyst Curtiss Wright Corp., Columbus, Ohio, 1948; project engr. weight analysis Bell Aerospace Textron, Buffalo, 1949-52, stress analyst, 1952-60, asst. supr. stress analysis, 1960-64, chief stress analysis propulsion, 1964-79, chief engr. stress and weights, 1979-84, staff scientist, 1984-85, cons. structures and fractures, 1985—. Served with AUS, 1944-47; PTO. Recipient cert. of achievement NASA-Apollo, 1972; cert. commendation U.K. NATO program, 1982. Mem. AIAA (Membership Chairman's award, 1988), Soc. Reliability Engrs., U.S. Naval Inst., Am. Space Found., Nat. Conservancy, Nat. Audubon Soc., Am. Acad. Polit. and Social Sci., Acad. Polit. Sci., AAAS, Union of Concerned Scientists, Air Force Assn., Nat. Space Soc., Soc. Allied Weight Engrs., Planetary Soc., Am. Mgmt. Assns., Bibl. Archeology Soc., Archeol. Inst. Am., Cousteau Soc., Smithsonian Assocs., Buffalo Audubon Soc., Bell Mgmt. Club. Republican. Roman Catholic. Club: Quarter Century. Home: 152 Linwood Ave Tonawanda NY 14150 Office: 152 Linwood Ave Tonawanda NY 14150

DRUCKER, PETER FERDINAND, writer, consultant, educator; b. Vienna, Austria, Nov. 19, 1909; came to U.S., 1937, naturalized, 1943; s. Adolph Bertram and Caroline D.; m. Doris Schmitz, Jan. 16, 1937; children: Kathleen Romola, J. Vincent, Cecily Anne, Joan Agatha. Grad., Gymnasium, Vienna, 1927; LL.D., U. Frankfurt, 1931; 16 hon. doctorates, U.S. and fgn. univs. Economist London Banking House, 1933-37; Am. adviser for Brit. banks, Am. corr. Brit. newspapers 1937-42; cons. maj. bus. corps. U.S., 1940—; prof. philosophy, politics Bennington Coll., 1942-49; prof. mgmt. NYU, 1950-72, chmn. mgmt. area, 1957-62, disting. univ. lectr., 1972—; Clarke prof. social sci. Claremont Grad. Sch. (Calif.), 1971—; prof. dept art Pomona Coll., Calif., 1979-85. Author: The End of Economic Man, 1939, The Future of Industrial Man, 1941, Concept of the Corporation, 1946, The New Society, 1950, Practice of Management, 1954, America's Next Twenty Years, 1957, The Landmarks of Tomorrow, 1959, Managing for Results, 1964, The Effective Executive, 1966, The Age of Discontinuity, 1969, Technology; Management and Society, 1970, Men, Ideas and Politics, 1971, Management: Tasks, Responsibilities, Practices, 1974, The Unseen Revolution: How Pension Fund Socialism Came to America, 1976, People and Performance, 1977, Management, An Overview, 1978, Adventures of a Bystander, 1979, Managing in Turbulent Times, 1980, Toward the Next Economics and Other Essays, 1981, The Changing World of the Executive, 1982, Innovation and Entrepreneurship, 1985; The Frontiers of Management, 1986; (fiction) The Last of All Possible Worlds, 1982, The Temptation to Do Good, 1984; producer: movie series The Effective Executive, 1969, Managing Discontinuity, 1971, The Manager and the Organization, 1977, Managing for Tomorrow, 1981; producer 25 audiocassette series on leadership in the non-profit inst., 1988. Recipient gold medal Internat. U. Social Studies, Rome, 1957; Wallace Clark Internat. Mgmt. medal, 1963; Taylor Key Soc. for Advancement Mgmt., 1967; Presdl. citation NYU, 1969; CIOS Internat. Mgmt. gold medal, 1972; Chancellor's medal Internat. Acad. Mgmt., 1987. Fellow AAAS (council), Internat., Am., Irish Acads. Mgmt., Brit. Inst. Mgmt. (hon.), Am. Acad. Arts and Scis.; mem. Soc. for History Tech. (pres. 1965-66), Nat. Acad. Pub. Adminstrn. (hon.).

DRUCKER, ROLF, audio-video engineering company exec.; b. Nuremberg, Ger., Sept. 15, 1926; came to U.S., 1941, naturalized, 1945; s. Benno and Erna (Engel) D.; student CCNY, 1950; m. Olga M. Lenk, Oct. 22, 1950; children—Jane L., Robert S., Alice S. Engr., Sta. WNYC, 1946-48; tech. dirs. Sta. ABC-TV, N.Y.C., 1948-77, v.p. ops. and engring. Sta. WNET-TV, N.Y.C., 1977-83; dir. electronic graphics ABC-TV, 1983—; owner Audio-video Engring. Co., Merrick, N.Y., 1969—. Designed video effects keyer, 1951, automatic video delay line, 1967, video hum-stop coil, 1969. Served with U.S. Army, 1944-46. Recipient Emmy award Nat. Acad. TV Arts and Scis., Innsbruck, Austria, 1976. Mem. Soc. Motion Picture and TV Engrs., Royal TV Soc., PBS Engring. Com., World Ship Soc. Home: 65 Nancy Blvd Merrick NY 11566 Office: 356 W 58th St New York NY 10019

DRUMHELLER, GEORGE JESSE, motel and hotel chain owner; b. Walla Walla, Wash., Jan. 30, 1933; s. Allen and Ila Margaret (Croxdale) D.; student Wash. State U., 1951-52, Whittier Coll., 1955-58; m. Carla Rene Cunha, May 4, 1965 (div. 1985). Asst. mgr. Olympic Hotel, Seattle, 1959; jr. exec. Westin Hotels, Seattle, 1959-63; founder, pres. George Drumheller Properties, Inc., motel holding co., Pendleton, Oreg., 1963—; founder, chmn. bd. Dalles Tapadera, Inc., motel and hotel holding co., The Dalles, Oreg., 1964-77; founder, pres. Lewiston Tapadera, Inc. (Idaho), motel holding co., 1970-77; founder, pres. Yakima Tapadera, Inc. (Wash.), 1971-77; founding partner Drumheller & Titcomb (Tapadera Motor Inn), Ontario, Oreg., 1972-84; merger with Tapadera motel holding cos. and George Drumheller Properties, Inc., 1978—, founder Tapadera Budget Inns, Kennewick and Walla Walla, Wash., 1981-85, also merged with George Drumheller Properties, Inc., 1986; engaged in farming, eastern Wash., 1958-80. Served with USCG, 1952-55. Mem. Am. Hotel and Motel Assn. (nat. dir. 1980-84, pres.'s exec. com. 1983-84), Oreg. Hotel Motel Assn. (dir. 1974-78), Wash. State Lodging Assn. (dir., v.p. 1976-84). Clubs: Spokane, Walla Walla Country, Washington Athletic, J.D. Shea, LaJolla Beach and Tennis, Kona Kai, San Diego. Home: 3132 Morning Way La Jolla CA 92037 Office: George Drumheller Properties Inc PO Box 1234 Walla Walla WA 99362

DRUMMOND, MALCOLM MCALLISTER, electronics engineer; b. London, Eng., Sept. 22, 1937; came to U.S., 1966, naturalized, 1977; s. George James and Winifred Ethel (Jaye) D.; BS in Elec. Engring. with honors, City U., London, 1961; Registered profl. elec. engr. m. Linda Jerome Banning, May 25, 1968; 1 dau., Heather Lynn. Engr., Brit. Fgn. Office, Cheltenham, Eng., 1964-66; sr. engr. Gen. Dynamics Corp., Rochester, N.Y., 1966-70; tech. rep. Tymshare Inc., Rochester, 1970-72; project engr. Sybron Corp., Taylor Instrument Co., Rochester, 1972-85, Hampshire Instruments Corp. 1985—; dir. Care & Service Inc., 1982—, pres. 1986—. Christian Sci. minister for VA Hosp., 1974-80. Mem. IEEE (sr., chmn. Rochester sect. 1979—, past chmn. pension task force 1983-84, Region I PAC coordinator 1980-82, Area D chmn. 1982-85, ASIC seminar chmn. 1987—), Engrs. and Scientists Joint Com. on Pensions (vice chmn. 1983-84, IEEE rep. 1982-85), Mgmt. Soc. (past chmn.), Computer Soc. (past pres.), Instrument Soc. Am., Rochester Engring. Soc. (dir. 1979-83), Am. Mgmt. Assns., Inst. Elec. Engrs. (Gt. Brit.). Home: 60 Marberth Dr Henrietta NY 14467 Office: Hampshire Instruments Corp 10 Carlson Rd Rochester NY 14610

DRUMMOND, OLIVER LEE, city official; b. Van Nuys, Calif., Oct. 7, 1947; s. Joseph Lester and Ollie Lee (Rodabaugh) D.; m. Deborah Louise Clark, Oct. 14, 1970; 1 dau., Deborah Lee. B.S. in Criminology, Calif. State U.-Long Beach, 1974; advanced grad. cert. in exec. mgmt. Pacific Christian Coll., 1979; postgrad. in human behavior Newport U., 1979—; L.H.D. (hon.) Newport Internat. U., 1979; LL.D. (hon.) Van Norman U., 1980. Community coll. lifetime tchr. credential, Calif.; basic, intermediate, advanced and mgmt. certs., exec. cert. Calif. Dept. Justice. Police officer Santa Ana (Calif.) Police Dept., 1970-75, sgt., 1975-78, lt., 1978-82; chief of police Hanford (Calif.) Police Dept., 1982—; instr. Advanced Investigators Acad., Saddleback Coll., 1981-83. Mem. sch. site council Kings River-Hardwick Sch., 1982—, mem. sch. attendance rev. bd., 1982—; bd. dirs. Kings County Vol. Bur., 1982—, chmn., 1985. Served with Army N.G., 1969-75; served to lt., Mil. Police Corps, USAR, 1972-76. Recipient Profl. Service award Santa Ana Police Dept., 1982; Meritorious Service/Valor award Santa Ana Police Benevolent Assn., 1973; named Chief of Yr., Calif. Law Enforcement Mgmt. Ctr., 1982. Mem. Internat. Assn. Chiefs of Police, Internat. Police Assn., ABA (criminal justice sect.), Calif. Peace Officers Assn. (law and legis. com.), Calif. Chiefs Assn., Calif. Police Chiefs Assn. (standards and ethics com., tng. com.), Calif. Assn. Police Tng. Officers, Calif. Assn. Adminstrn. of Justice Educators, Calif. Robbery Investigators Assn., Kings County Peace Officers Assn., League of Calif. Cities (1st v.p. police chiefs sect.), Hanford C. of C. (dir. 1983, pres. 1985, mem. ambassador corps, City Employee of Yr. award 1982, President's award 1984), SAR (Law Enforcement Commendation medal), Lodge: Rotary (sgt.-at-arms 1983-84). Office: 425 N Irwin St Hanford CA 93230

DRURY, ALLEN STUART, writer; b. Houston, Sept. 2, 1918; s. Alden Monteith and Flora (Allen) D. B.A., Stanford U., 1939; Litt.D. (hon.), Rollins Coll., 1961. Editor Tulare (Calif.) Bee, 1940-41; county editor Bakersfield Californian, 1941-42; mem. Senate staff U.P.I., Washington, 1943-45; free lance corr. 1946; nation editor Pathfinder mag., 1947-53; nat. staff Washington Evening Star, 1953-54; mem. Senate staff N.Y. Times, 1954-59; polit. contbr. Reader's Digest, 1959-62. Author: Advise and Consent, 1959, A Shade of Difference, 1962, A Senate Journal, 1963, That Summer, 1965, Three Kids in A Cart, 1965, Capable of Honor, 1966, "A Very Strange Society,", 1967, Preserve and Protect, 1968, The Throne of Saturn, 1971, Courage and Hesitation, 1971, Come Nineveh, Come Tyre, 1973, The Promise of Joy, 1975, A God Against the Gods, 1976, Return to Thebes, 1976, Anna Hastings, 1977, Mark Coffin, U.S.S, 1979, Egypt: The Eternal Smile, 1980, The Hill of Summer, 1981, Decision, 1983, The Roads of Earth, 1984, Pentagon, 1986. Served with AUS, 1942-43. Recipient Pulitzer prize for fiction Advise and Consent, 1960. Mem. Sigma Delta Chi (nat. award for editorial writing 1941), Alpha Kappa Lambda. Clubs: Nat. Press (Washington), Cosmos (Washington), University (Washington); Bohemian (San Francisco). Address: care The Lantz Office 888 Seventh Ave New York NY 10106

DRYDEN, ROBERT EUGENE, lawyer; b. Chanute, Kans., Aug. 20, 1927; s. Calvin William and Mary Alfreda (Foley) D.; m. Jetta Rae Burger, Dec. 19, 1953; children: Lynn Marie, Thomas Calvin. A.A., City Coll., San Francisco, 1947; B.S., U. San Francisco, 1951, J.D., 1954. Bar: Calif. 1955; diplomate: Am. Bd. Trial Advs. Assoc. Barfield, Dryden & Ruane (and predecessor firm), San Francisco, 1954-60, jr. ptnr., 1960-65, gen. ptnr., 1965—; lectr. continuing edn. of the bar, 1971-77. Served with USMCR, 1945-46. Fellow Am. Coll. Trial Lawyers, Am. Bar Found; mem. ABA, San Francisco Bar Assn., State Bar Calif., Am. Judicature Soc., Assn. Def. Counsel (dir. 1968-71), Def. Research Inst., Internat. Assn. Ins. Counsel, Fedn. Ins. Counsel, Am. Arbitration Assn., U. San Francisco Law Soc. (mem. exec. com. 1970-72). U. San Francisco Alumni Assn. (bd. govs. 1977), Phi Alpha Delta. Home: 1320 Lasuen Dr Millbrae CA 94030 Office: Barfield Dryden & Ruane Suite 3125 1 California St San Francisco CA 94111

DRYER, DOROTHEA MERRILL (MRS. EDWIN JASON DRYER), lawyer; b. Salt Lake City; d. George Edmund and Lillian (Chapman) Merrill; A.B., Stanford, 1936; LL.B., Yale, 1940; m. Edwin Jason Dryer, Feb. 28, 1942; children—Diana Claire Dryer Wright, Faith Ellen. Admitted to Utah bar, 1941, U.S. Supreme Ct. bar, U.S. Ct. Mil. Appeals; clk. to Chief Justice Wolfe, Utah Supreme Ct., 1941; atty. Bur. Immigration, Dept. Justice, Washington, 1941-42; practiced in Salt Lake City, 1943-47, Washington, 1948—; dep. county atty., Salt Lake City, 1947-48. Fellow Am. Assn. Criminology; mem. Am., Fed., Utah bar assns., Nat. Assn. Women Lawyers, Am. Judicature Soc., Nat. Assn. for Gifted Children, Assn. for Gifted, Oral History Assn., Kappa Kappa Gamma. Unitarian. Clubs: Jr. League Washington; Potomac Bus. and Profl. Women's; Nat. Lawyers. Home: 5126 Palisade Ln NW Washington DC 20016

DRYFOOS, NANCY, sculptor; b. New Rochelle, N.Y., Mar. 28; d. Richman and Edith (Harris) Proskauer; m. Donald Dryfoos. Cert. Sarah Lawrence Coll., 1939; postgrad. Columbia U. Extension Sch., 1945-46. One-person shows include: Contemporary Arts Gallery, N.Y.C., 1952, Silvermine Guild Gallery, 1954, Wellons Gallery, 1956, Bodley Gallery, 1958, Collectors Gallery, 1960, Dime Savs. Bank, Bklyn., 1969, Lincoln Savs. Bank, N.Y.C., 1975-76, Donnell Library, N.Y.C., 1987 (pen and pen and brush show winner 1988); group shows include: Pa. Acad. Fine Arts, 1947, Syracuse Mus., 1948, Bklyn. Mus., 1952, Corcoran Gallery, 1954, Nat. Acad. Fine Arts, N.Y.C., 1952-76, Lincoln Savs. Bank, 1987, Donnell Library Ctr., 1987, others; v.p. Fine Arts Fedn. of N.Y. Contbr. articles to profl. publs. Named Winner of the Solo Exhbn. Sculpture Pen and Brush, 1988. Fellow Nat. Sculpture Soc. (recording sec. 1973, bd. dirs. 1988—); mem. Allied Artists America (Medal of Honor 1978), Audubon Artists (exhbn. dir. 1983-84, asst. treas. 1987-88, prize), Am. Soc. Contemporary Artists (dir., exhbn. dir., prize), Contemporary Artists Guild (dir.), N.Y. Soc. Women Artists (dir.), Fine Arts Fedn. N.Y. (v.p.), Pen and Brush Club, Nat. Trust for Hist. Preservation, Network Visual Arts Ctr. (dir.), Brandeis Creative Arts Commn. (dir.), Artists Equity Assn. (bd. dirs. 1978-80). Avocations: printmaking, enameling. Home: 45 E 89th St New York NY 10128

DRZEWIECKI, KRZYSZTOF TADEUSZ, plastic surgeon; b. Warsaw, Poland, Feb. 23, 1944; came to Denmark, 1971, naturalized, 1977; s. Tadeusz and Jadwiga (Kubiak) D.; m. Joanna Kotowska, Mar. 22, 1971. M.D., Med. Acad., Warszawa, Poland, 1967, U. Copenhagen, 1973; D.Sc.(Med.), U. Odense, Denmark, 1981. Jr. doctor Med. Acad., Warsaw, 1967-71; jr. doctor U. Hosp., Odense, 1971-74, surg. resident, 1974-76, sr. registrar plastic surgery, 1976-79; sr. registrar plastic surgery U. Hosp., Arhus, Denmark, 1979-80; head dept. plastic surgery Finseninst. Copenhagen, 1981-86; head dept. plastic surgery Rigshospitalet, Copenhagen, 1987—; mem. exec. com. bd. doctors, 1985; chmn. Danish Melanoma Group, Copenhagen, 1983—; bd. doctors Rigs Hosp., Copenhagen, 1985. Co-author: Cutaneous Melanoma, 1985, Kirurgisk Kompendium, 1987; contbr. articles to profl. publs. Recipient award Haandvaerkersparekassens Fond, 1977. Mem. Danish Soc. Surgery, Danish Soc. for Plastic and Reconstructive Surgery (sec.), Scandinavian Soc. for Plastic and Reconstructive Surgery (exec. com. 1985), Danish Cancer Soc., Danish Soc. for Head and Neck Oncology. Roman Catholic. Clubs: Skovshoved Sejlklub, Copenhagen Amateur Sail. Avocations: alpine skiing; cross country skiing; sailing. Office: Rigshospitalet, Dept Plastic Surgery, Blegdamsvej 9, 2100 Copenhagen Denmark

DU, ROMEO REGNER, orthopedic surgeon, educator; b. Cebu, Philippines, Jan. 20, 1939; s. Guillermo Velasquez and Rafaela Bascon (Regner) D.; m. Elvira Fuentes, Sept. 8, 1986; children: Julie Anne, John Arnold, Anthony Romeo. MD, U. Santo Tomas, 1965. Diplomate Philippine Bd. Orthopedic Surgery. Resident in surgery UP-PGH Med. Ctr., Manila, 1967-68, Nat. Orthopedic Hosp., Quezon City, Philippines, 1969-74; orthopedic surgeon Mt. Apo Gen. Hosp., Davao Med. Ctr., Brokenshire Meml. Hosp., Davao City, Philippines, 1974-76; fellow Dutches of Kent Children's Orthopedic Hosp., Hong Kong, 1976-77, Nat. Health Service Hosps., Eng., Scotland, 1978-83; chief orthopedic surgeon City Hosp., Cebu City, 1984—; lectr. Queen Mary Hosp., Hong Kong, 1976-77, Hong Kong U., 1977-78; cons. Cebu Doctors Hosp., 1984—; mem. faculty SWU-MHAM, Cebu City, 1984—, CDH and Cullas Med. Coll., Cebu City, 1984—. Co-author manual on spinal surgery; contbr. articles to profl. publs. Fellow Philippine Orthopedic Assn.; mem. Philippine Coll. Surgeons, Philippine Med. Assn., Brit. Med. Assn., Ateneo Alumni Assn. Roman Catholic. Lodge: Rotary. Office: 101 M Diaz Bldg, Osmena Blvd, Cebu Philippines

DUARTE, CRISTOBAL G., physician, educator, researcher, scientist; b. Concepión, Paraguay, July 17, 1929; s. Cristobal Duarte and Emilia Miltos. B.S., Colegio de San José Asuncion, 1947; M.D., Nat. U. Asunción, 1953. Intern De Goesbriand Meml. Hosp., Burlington, Vt., 1956; resident in medicine Carney Hosp. and St. Elizabeth's Hosp., Boston, 1956-58; fellow in medicine Lahey Clinc, Boston, 1959; fellow hypertension and renal medicine Hahnemann Hosp., Phila., 1960; assoc. in medicine U. Vt. Coll. Medicine, 1962-65; clin. investigator VA, 1966-68, staff physician, 1968-73; dir. Renal Function Lab., Mayo Clinic and Found., Rochester, Minn., 1973-77; asst. prof. lab. medicine Mayo Med. Sch., 1973-77; commd. lt. col. U.S. Army, 1977; assoc. prof. medicine and physiology Uniformed Services U. Health Scis., Bethesda, Md., 1977-84, attending in medicine Walter Reed Army Med. Ctr., Washington, 1977-84; chief nephrology service Bay Pines VA Med. Ctr., 1984—; assoc. prof. medicine U. South Fla., Tampa, 1984-87; med. officer cardio-renal drug products FDA, Rockville, Md., 1987—. Editor: Renal Function Tests, 1980; contbr. articles to profl. jours., chpts. to books. Recipient cert. of accomplishment VA, 1969; physician's recognition award AMA, 1981, 86; Cordell Hull Found. fellow, 1958-59. Fellow Am. Coll. Nutrition; mem. Nat. Kidney Found., Latin Am. Soc. Nephrology, Am. Fedn. Clin. Research, Am. Physiol. Soc., Am. Soc. Pharmacology and Exptl. Therapeutics, Midwest Salt and Water Club, Am. Soc. for Clin. Research, Central Soc. for Clin. Research, Am. Soc. Nephrology, Sigma Xi. Roman Catholic. Current Work: Radio-contrast-induced renal failure. Subspecialty: Nephrology.

DUARTE, RAMON GONZALEZ, nurse; b. San Fernando, Calif., Jan. 5, 1948; s. Salvador Revelez and Juanita (Gonzalez) D.; m. Sophia Constant Garabedian, Apr. 17, 1983; children: David Ramon, John Robert. AA in Nursing, Los Angeles Valley Coll., 1972; student, Calif. State U., Los Angeles, 1972-76. RN; Cert. Bd. Nephrology Examiners. Staff nurse hemodialysis unit U. So. Calif. Med. Ctr., Los Angeles, 1971-75; charge nurse self care hemodialysis unit Kaiser Found. Hosp., Los Angeles, 1976, Culver City (Calif.) Dialysis Services, Inc., 1981-82; adminstrv. head nurse hemodialysis unit Valley Prebyn. Hosp., Van Nuys, Calif., 1976-78; adminstrv. head nurse Kidney Dialysis Care Units, Lynwood, Calif., 1980-81; ind. nursing contractor Nursing Services in Nephrology, Van Nuys, 1982—, clin. instr., researcher, 1980—, dir. research, 1988—; coordinator clin. research Valley Dialysis Assocs., Inc., Van Nuys, 1978-80; mem. research com. Valley Presbyn. Hosp. Research; founder, pres. Dialysis Mus. Council, chmn. So. Calif. Dialysis Earthquake Preparedness Commn.; mem. council nephrology nurses and technicians, mem. allied profl. adv. com., chmn. allied health profl research grant com. Nat. Kidney Found. Inc.; mem. sci. adv. council Nat. Kidney Found. So. Calif. Mem. editorial bd. Dialysis and Transplantation mag.; contbr. articles to med. publs. Founder Mus. Hope, Van Nuys. Recipient Dedicated Service award Hemodialysis Found., 1976; named Allied Health Profl. of Yr. Nat. Kidney Found. So. Calif., 1986; scholar Am. G.I. Forum, 1966, Am. Legion Forty and Eight Coll., Los Angeles Valley Coll. Associated Students. Mem. Am. Assn. Artificial Internal Organs, Am. Assn. Nephrology Nurses and Technicians, Kidney Found. So. Calif., Am. Assn. Critical Care Nurses, Ind. Nurses' Assn., Nat. Assn. Patients on Hemodialysis and Transplantation Inc., Am. Soc. Nephrology, N.Y. Acad. Scis. Democrat. Roman Catholic. Home and Office: 6849 Oak Park Ave Van Nuys CA 91406

DUARTE FUENTES, JOSÉ NAPOLEÓN, president of El Salvador; b. Nov. 23, 1925; m. Inés Durán; children: Inés Guadalupe, José Napoleón, José Alejandro, Maria Eugenia, Maria Elena, Ana Lorena. M in Engring., U. Notre Dame. Founder Christian Dem. Party, 1960, sec.-gen., 1960-64, 68-70, pres., 1972—; practicing civil engr. before 1964; mayor San Salvador, 1964-70; elected pres. Republic of El Salvador, 1972; imprisoned, then exiled to Venezuela 1972-79, returned to El Salvador, 1979, after mil. coup served as mem. Ruling Junta, 1980-82; pres. Republic of El Salvador, 1984—. Office: Office of President, Govt House, San Salvador El Salvador

DUBAY, GWEN ANN, sales and marketing professional; b. Lewiston, Maine, Mar. 25, 1951; d. Ronald N. and Alice M. (Fellows) Johnson; widowed Feb. 1985; children: Ty Brandon, Tara Lee. BA in Sociology, U. Maine, Orono, 1972. Social worker State of Maine, Bangor, 1972; office mgr. S.C. Clayton Co., Marlboro, Mass., 1972-74; sec., treas. Dubay Sales & Mktg., Zionsville, Ind., 1983-85, pres., 1985—; sales adminstr. Woods Wire Products, Inc., Carmel, Ind., 1985—; vis. artist intern Ind. Arts Commn., Indpls., 1983-84. treas. PTO, Zionsville, 1982-83; vol. tchr. for gifted Eagle

Elem. Sch., Zionsville, 1983-85. Republican. Methodist. Home: 200 Governors Ln Zionsville IN 46077 Office: Woods Wire Products Inc 510 Third Ave SW Carmel IN 46032

DUBE, JOHN, lawyer; b. Montreal, Que., Can., July 14, 1899; came to U.S., 1926, naturalized, 1945; s. Joseph Edmond and Marie Louise (Quintal) D.; m. Liliane Hibbert, 1981; 1 son by previous marriage, John Edmund. B.L., B.S., Montreal U., 1920, B.C.L., 1923; licentiate in Civil Law, Paris U., 1924; postgrad., U. Oxford, 1925. Bar: Montreal 1925, N.Y. 1945, apptd. king's counsel 1941, now Queen's counsel 1941, U.S. Supreme Ct. 1941, U.S. Treasury Dept 1941. Assoc. Coudert Bros., N.Y.C. and Paris office, 1926-32, Nice, France, 1933-40; practice N.Y.C., 1945—; Past pres. Le Moulin Legumes Corp., Wilmington, Del.; past v.p. Bengue, Inc., Union City, N.J.; consul of Monaco, N.Y.C., 1949—; now consul gen.; dep. permanent observer for Monaco at UN, 1956-71, permanent observer, 1971—. Past trustee Soc. Rehab. Facially Disfigured; co-founder and co-comdr. Anglo-Am. Ambulance Corps., Cannes, France, 1939-40. Decorated Comdr. Order of Grimaldi (Monaco). Mem. Union Interallié e (Paris), Assn. Bar City of N.Y., ABA, Internat. Bar Assn., Am. Fgn. Law Assn., Am. Soc. Internat. Law, Soc. Fgn. Consuls, Société de Legislation Comparee. Clubs: Rockefeller Ctr. Luncheon, Sky (assoc.). Home: 18 Royal Palm Way Apt 309 Boca Raton FL 33432

DUBEN, ALAN ROBERT, anthropologist; b. N.Y.C., Feb. 26, 1943; s. Frederick N. and Edith Dubetsky; m. Ipek Aksugur, Aug. 12, 1967. BA, SUNY, Binghamton, 1964; MA in Social Anthropology, U. Chgo., 1968, PhD in Social Anthropology, 1973. Asst. prof. anthropology, dir. program in anthropology and edn. NYU, N.Y.C., 1972-76; lectr. European div. U. Md., Turkey, 1977; lectr. dept. social scis. Bogazici U., Istanbul, Turkey, 1977-78, lectr. social anthopology, 1980-84, coordinator undergrad. and grad. programs in sociology, 1980-82; research assoc. dept. anthropology Hunter Coll., CUNY, 1984-85, 86—; cons. Orgn. Econ. Cooperation and Devel., Paris, 1979-80, AID, Washington, 1985, Dar Al-Handasah Cons., 1985-86; sr. advisorEa. Mediterranean and Mid. East Region Internat. Union of Local Authorities, Istanbul, Turkey, 1988—; cons. in field. Editor: A Reader in Social Anthropology, 1979; mem. editorial bd. Toplum ve Bilim, 1988; contbr. articles to profl. jours. Active Dostlar Chamber Musicians. Ford Found. fellow in internat. devel., 1966-67, NIMH fellow, 1967-72; research grantee NIMH, 1969-71, NSF, 1986-87, Wenner-Gren Found. for Anthrop. Research, 1986-87, Rockefeller Found., 1987, Mid. East research grantee Ford Found./Population Council/Internat. Devel. Research Centre, 1982-84, 85-86. Mem. Am. Anthrop. Assn., Internat. Union Anthrop. and Ethnol. Scis. Home: #6 Sircaci Sokak, Rumelihisari Istanbul, Turkey

DUBERG, JOHN EDWARD, aeronautical engineer, educator; b. N.Y.C., Nov. 30, 1917; s. Charles Augustus and Mary (Blake) D.; m. Mary Louise Andrews, June 11, 1943; children—Mary Jane, John Andrews. B.S. in Engring, Manhattan Coll., 1938; M.S., Va. Poly. Inst., 1940; Ph.D., U. Ill., 1948; grad., Fed. Exec. Inst., 1971. Engr. Cauldwell-Wingate Builders, N.Y.C., 1938-39; research asst. U. Ill., 1940-43; research engr. NASA, 1943-46; chief structures Langley Labs., NASA, Hampton, Va., 1948-56; research engr. Standard Oil Co. Ind., 1946-48; with Ford Aeros., Glendale, Calif., 1956-57; mem. faculty U. Ill., 1957-59; mem. staff Langley Research Center, NASA, 1959-79, assoc. dir., 1968-79; research prof. aeros. George Washington U., 1979—; dir. Joint Inst. Advanced Flight Scis., 1971-79; mem. materials adv. bd. Nat. Acad. Sci., 1950; mem. subcom. profl. and sci. manpower Dept. Labor, 1971; mem. indsl. adv. com. U. Va., 1978-80; president's adv. council Christopher Newport Coll., 1973-76, vice chmn., 1976; dir. Newport News Savs. Bank. Contbr. articles to profl. jours., chpts. to books. Trustee United Way Va. Peninsula, 1963—; chmn. Hampton Roads chpt. ARC, 1984-86. Recipient Outstanding Leadership award NASA, 1977. Fellow AIAA (DeFlorez award 1977), AAAS; mem. Va. Acad. Scis., N.Y. Acad. Scis., Am. Soc. Engring. Edn. (dir.), Engrs. Club Peninsula (pres. 1955), Soc. Engring. Scis. (dir.). Episcopalian. Clubs: James River Country, Rotary (pres. Newport News 1967-68). Home: 4 Museum Dr Newport News VA 23601 Office: GWU/JIAFS NASA Langley Research Ctr M/S 269 Hampton VA 23665

DUBES, GEORGE RICHARD, geneticist; b. Sioux City, Iowa, Oct. 12, 1926; s. George Wesley and Regina Eleanor (Kelleher) D.; m. Margaret Joanne Tumberger, July 25, 1964; children: George Richard, David Frank, Deanna Marie, Kenneth Wesley, Deborah Joanne, Keith Timothy. B.S., Iowa State U., 1949; Ph.D., Calif. Inst. Tech., 1953. Research assoc. McCollum-Pratt Inst. for Research in Micronutrient Elements, Johns Hopkins U., 1953-54; research assoc. sect. virus research dept. pediatrics U. Kans. Sch. Medicine, Kansas City, 1954-56, asst. prof., 1956-60, assoc. prof., 1960-64; head viral genetics Eppley Cancer Inst.-U. Nebr. Med. Ctr., Omaha, 1964-68, assoc. prof. dept. med. microbiology (now dept. pathology and microbiology), 1964-81, prof., 1981—; vis. lectr. U. Baghdad, (Iraq), 1977, U. Mosul, (Iraq), 1977. Author: Methods for Transfecting Cells with Nucleic Acids of Animal Viruses; A Review, 1971; contbr. articles to sci. jours. Co-pres. Adams Sch. PTA, Omaha, 1976-77; mem. citizens adv. com. Omaha Pub. Schs., 1977-80. Served with AUS, 1945-46. Fellow AEC, 1951-52; fellow Caltech McCallum, 1951-52; grantee Nat. Inst. Allergy and Infectious Diseases, 1966-69, NIH Gen. Research Support, 1964-72. Mem. Am. Assn. Cancer Research, AAAS, Am. Genetic Assn., Am. Inst. Biol. Scis., Am. Soc. Microbiology (pres. Missouri Valley br. 1983-84), Biometric Soc., Genetics Soc. Am., Nebr. Acad. Scis. (co-chmn. biol. and med. scis. sect. 1983-85), Internat. Soc. Oncodevelopmental Biology and Medicine, N.Y. Acad. Scis., Sigma Xi. Home: 7061 Starlite Dr Omaha NE 68152 Office: U Nebr Coll Medicine Dept Pathology and Microbiology 42d and Dewey Ave Omaha NE 68105

DUBIEF, JEAN, climatologist; b. Rennes, France, Oct. 28, 1903; s. Henry Georges Adolphe and Berthe (Biver) D.; Ingenieur, Ecole Nat. Superieure Agronomique, Algeria, 1920; Sc.D., U. Alger, 1953; m. Marguerite Tenthorey, Feb. 19, 1954; 1 son, Yves. Mem. staff Inst. Meteorology and Earth Physics Algeria, 1924-62 also Faculty Scis.; chief Obs. Phys. de Globe, Tamanrasset, Algeria, 1931-42; adj. physician Inst. Earth Physics, Paris, 1962-68. Served with French Army, 1939-40, 42-45. Decorated chevalier Legion of Honor, du Merite Saharien, du Merite Agricole; officer Palmes Academiques. Mem. Union Geodesique et Geophysique Internat., Geographie Soc. Paris, Assn. French Geographers. Roman Catholic. Clubs: La Rahia; Explorers (N.Y.C.). Author: Essai sur L'Hydrologie Superficielle du Sahara, 1953; Le Climat du Sahara, Vol. 1, 1959, Vol. 2, 1963; also articles. Address: 150 Rue de l'Universite, 75007 Paris France

DUBIN, E. BEVERLY, photographer, graphic artist, designer; b. Los Angeles, Dec. 11, 1945; d. Beatrice Winograd. Student, U. Miami, Fla., 1963-64, Emerson Coll., 1964-66, New Sch. for Social Research, 1966-67; BFA, San Francisco Art Acad., 1971; MA in Art, Lone Mountain Coll., 1973; postgrad., U. Calif., 1971-73, Screen Printing Acad., 1973. Lectr. in field. One woman shows Circle Gallery, San Francisco, 1972, Old Ways Gallery, Oakland, Calif., 1973; group shows including Renaissance Pleasure Faire, 1970-80, Wonder Fair, Oakland, 1970, Gt. Himalaya Cookie Co., San Francisco, 1974, Squaw Valley (Calif.) Art Ctr., 1984; author: Roll Your Own, 1973, Water Squatters, 1975, (poems and photographs) Show and Tell, 1985; designer: (album cover) Firebyrd, 1985; painted mural Beth Israel Synagogue, Greeley, Colo., 1988; photographs appeared in Clear Creek mag., 1972, San Francisco Examiner/Chronicle, 1973, Oakland Telegraph, 1973, Bookpaper, 1975. Office: PO Box 189 San Anselmo CA 94960

DUBIN, JAMES MICHAEL, lawyer; b. N.Y.C., Aug. 20, 1946; s. Benjamin and Irene (Wasserman) D.; m. Susan Hope Schraub, Mar. 15, 1981; children—Alexander Philip, Elizabeth Joy. B.A., U. Pa., 1968; J.D., Columbia U., 1974. Bar: N.Y. 1975, D.C. 1984, U.S. Dist. Ct. (so. and ea. dist.) N.Y. 1975, U.S. Ct. Appeals (2d cir.) 1975. Assoc. Paul, Weiss, Rifkind, Wharton & Garrison, N.Y.C., 1974-82, ptnr. 1982—. Bd. editors Columbia Law Rev., 1973-74. Bd. dirs. FOJP Service Corp., 1988—; bd. dirs. YM-YWHA of Mid-Westchester, Scarsdale, N.Y., 1983-86, chmn. budget and fin. com., 1984-85; chmn. Cable Oversight Com., Harrison, N.Y., 1983-85; dir. Reiss Media Enterprises, Inc., 1985-86. Served with U.S. Army, 1969-71. Mem. ABA, Assn. Bar City N.Y., Phi Delta Phi. Club: Sunningdale Country (Scarsdale); Hemisphere (N.Y.C.). Office: Paul Weiss Rifkind Wharton & Garrison 1285 Ave of Americas New York NY 10019

DUBININ, NIKOLAI PETROVICH, biologist; b. Jan. 4, 1907; grad. Moscow State U., 1928. With Moscow Zootech. Inst., 1928-32; with Inst. Exptl. Biology, USSR Acad. Sci., 1932-48, Inst. Forestry, 1949-55, Inst. Biophysics, 1955-56, dir. Inst. Cytology and Genetics, Sibirian br. USSR Acad. Scis., 1957-60, dir. Inst. Gen. Genetics, Moscow, 1966—, prof., 1935—. Recipient Darwin medal, 1962, Mendel medal, 1965, medal for cosmic research, 1965, Purkyniana Universitatis Brunensis medal, 1966, Lenin prize, 1966, Stribrnou plaketu za zasluhi o vedu a lidstvo, 1967; named to Lenin Order, 1967, 1980, Order of Oct. Revolution, 1975; numerous others. Mem. USSR Acad. Sci., Soc. Geneticists Gt. Britain (hon.), Brno U. (hon.); fgn. mem. Nat. Acad. Scis., Am. Acad. Arts and Scis., German Acad. Leopoldina, Yugoslavian Acad. Scis. and Arts, Polish Acad. Scis. Author: Birds of the Lower Ural Valley Forests, 1953; Problems of the Physical and Chemical Bases of Heredity, 1956; Problems of Radiation Genetics, 1961; Population Evolution and Radiation, 1966; Population Genetics and Selection, 1967; Horizons of Genetics, 1970; Genetics and the Future of Mankind, 1971; General Genetics, 1970, 76, 86; Perpetual Motion, 1973, 75; Potential DNA Changes and Mutations, 1978; Mutagenesis and Environment, 1978; Who is Man, 1983; New at Modern Genetics, 1986; others. Mem. Communist Party. Address: Inst Gen Genetics Acad USSR, Gubkin Str 3 B-333 GSP-1, 117809 Moscow USSR

DUBININ, YURIY VLADIMIROVICH, ambassador; b. Nalchik, USSR, Oct. 7, 1930; m. Liana Dubinin; children: Natalia, Irina Tatyana. Grad., Moscow State Inst. Internat. Relations, 1954, PhD in History, 1978. Mem. Diplomatc Service, 1955—, USSR Ministry of Fgn. Affairs, 1959-63, 68-78; 1st sec., embassy councellor USSR Embassy in France, 1963-68; USSR ambassador to Spain 1978-87, permanent rep. to UN, 1987—; ambassador to USA USSR, Washington, N.Y.C, 1986—. Author: USSR-France: Experience of Cooperation, 1978; contbr., translator articles in field. Recipient several govt. awards. Office: Embassy of the Union of the Soviet Socialist Republics 1125 16th St NW Washington DC 20036

DUBOIS, GAZELL MACY, architect, consultant; b. Balt., Dec. 20, 1929; came to Can., 1958; s. Benjamin Victor and Lilly (Sneidman) DuB.; m. Sarah Buchanan, Jan. 26, 1957; children—Mark Benjamin, Lindsay; m. 2d, Helga Plumb, Oct. 20, 1975; children—Colin, Marc. B.S., Tufts U., 1951; M.Arch., Harvard U., 1958. Registered profl. engr., Ont. Designer, The Architects Collaborative, Cambridge, Mass., 1957-58; architect designer John B. Parkin, Toronto, Ont., 1958-59; architect Robert Fairfield Architects, Toronto, 1959-61; architect-ptnr. Fairfield & DuBois, Architects, Toronto, 1961-75, DuBois Plumb & Assocs., Toronto, 1975—. Prin. archtl. works Art Centre Central Tech. Sch., 1964, ECE Office Bldg., 1968, The Oaklands Apts., 1983. Mem. Yonge-St. Clair Task Force, Toronto, 1966-75. Served to lt. (j.g.) USN, 1951-54. Recipient Massey medals, 1964, 68; Gov. Gen. medal, 1983. Fellow AIA (hon.), Royal Archtl. Inst. Can. (pres. 1982-83); mem. OAA (chmn. 1970-71), Royal Acad. Arts (academician 1971). Home: 43 Farnham Ave, Toronto, ON Canada M4V 1H6 Office: DuBois Plumb & Assocs, 76 Richmond St E, Toronto, ON Canada M5C 1P1 also: Royal Arch Inst of Can, 328 Somerset W, Ottawa, ON Canada K2P 0J9 *

DUBOIS, GERARD CLAUDE EUGENE ALBERT, anesthesiologist; b. St. Hilaire le Vouhie, France, Apr. 20, 1936; s. Eugene Marcelin Jean Aime and Edith Marie Elizabeth (Foucher) D.; m. Michelle Marie Fernande Chataigner, Mar. 19, 1966; children: Jocelyn, Geraldine; 1 child by previous marriage, Caroline. B of Math., Poitiers Lycee, France, 1955; B of Biology, Poitiers U., France, 1955; MD, FAulte de Medicine, Paris, 1964. Gen. practice medicine Vigneulle-Pont A Mousson, France, 1964-68; resident Faculte de Medicine U. Nancy, France, 1969-71; asst. physician anesthesiology Gen. Hosp. Nancy, 1970-72; anesthetist physician Gen. Hosp. C.H.U., Caen, France, 1972-76, C.H.U. Univ., 1976—. Contbr. articles to profl. jours. Mem. Men's Rights League, paris, 1982—; pub. friend Nat. Police Children's Home, Paris, 1985—. Served to capt. French Army, 1963-64. Mem. Pediatric Anesthetist Reanimator Assn., Analgesia Reanimation French Soc. Roman Catholic. Home: 3 clos du perthuis lebisey, Herouville Saint Clair France F14200 Office: CHU Gen Hosp, Cote de Nacre, Caen France F14000

DUBOIS, MARK BENJAMIN, utility official; b. Peoria, Ill., Sept. 27, 1955; s. Benjamin John and Marjorie Abigail (Black) DuB.; m. Jeri Rene Simmons, May 24, 1975; 1 son, Benjamin Robert. B.S. with high distinction, U. Ariz., 1977; M.A., U. Kans., 1981. Research asst. State Biol. Survey Kans., Lawrence, 1978-81; systems programmer Central Ill. Light Co., Peoria, 1982-84, operating software supr., 1984-85, gen. supr. data processing ops. sect., 1985—; part-time instr. nat. sci. and computer literacy Midstate Coll., 1987—. Bd. dirs. Spl. People Encounter Christ, Peoria, 1982-83; treas. Religious Edn. Activities for Community Handicapped, Peoria, 1978-81; cons. Jr. Achievement, 1987—. Mem. AAAS, Data Processing Mgmt. Assn., Internat. Union for Study Social Insects, Entomol. Soc. Am., Cen. States Entomol. Soc., Kans. Acad. Sci., Soc. Systematic Zoology, Sigma Xi. Contbr. articles on entomology and personal computer software to profl. jours. Home: 208 Oakwood Circle Washington IL 61571 Office: Central Illinois Light Co 300 Liberty St Peoria IL 61602

DUBOW, ARTHUR MYRON, private investor, lawyer; b. Chgo., Sept. 18, 1933; s. David and Matilda (Polster) D.; m. Isabella Goodrich Breckinridge, Mar. 2, 1962 (div. Dec. 1983); children: Charles Stewart, Alexandra Breckinridge; m. Barbara J. Shattuck, Dec. 27, 1986. A.B., Harvard U., 1954, LL.B., 1957. Bar: N.Y. 1962. Assoc. firm Webster Sheffield Fleischmann Hitchcock & Chrystie, N.Y.C., 1960-64; v.p., dir. Back Bay-Orient Enterprises, Inc., Boston, 1965-68; pres. Back Bay-Orient Enterprises, Inc., 1968-76; pres., dir. Bayorient Holding Corp., Boston, 1969-76; pres. Korea Capital Corp., N.Y.C., 1968-76, Fortune Capital Ltd., Boston, 1979-84; pres., dir. Boston Co. Energy Advisers, 1981-85; dir. Sulpetro Can. Ltd., Calgary, Alta., 1966-76, chmn. exec. com., 1974-76; dir. Sulpetro Internat. Ltd., Dallas, 1973-76, chmn. exec. com., 1974-76; dir. Castle Convertible Fund, Inc., Spectra Fund, Inc., Alger Funds, Coolidge Investment Corp., Herald Prodns., Inc., Internat. Basic Economy Corp., 1977-80, Allegheny & Western Energy Corp., 1978-81, Calif. Energy Co., 1980-86, Devel. & Resources, Inc., 1977-80; fellow Center for Internat. Affairs, Harvard U., 1976-77. Mem. mgmt. com. Parenting mag., 1986—. Mem. vis. com. dept. visual and environ. studies, dept. East Asian langs. and civilizations Harvard U.; bd. dirs. Inst. Ednl. Leadership, Sabre Found., Thomas Jefferson Forum; chmn. bd. dirs. Potomac Assocs., Inc., Washington; mem. nat. adv. com. on accreditation and instl. eligibility U.S. Dept. Edn., 1982-86; co-chmn. New Am. Filmmakers' Series, Whitney Mus. Am. Art, N.Y.C., 1970-76; mem. adv. bd. Sch. Advanced Internat. Studies, Johns Hopkins U., 1980-86; trustee Augustus St. Gaudens Meml., 1980-86, Arthur Dubow Found., 1986—; mem. nat. fin. com. George Bush for Pres., 1980; mem. Council on Fgn. Relations. Served with U.S. Army, 1957-59. Clubs: Harvard of N.Y. and Somerset; Tavern (Boston).

DUBOWSKI, JANEK KAZIMIERZ, art therapy educator, consultant, researcher; b. Mansfield, Nottinghamshire, Eng., Mar. 24, 1953; d. Joseph and Angela (Burak) D. BA with honors, Leeds Poly., Yorkshire, 1975; PhD, Hertfordshire Coll. Art & Design, St. Albans, 1983. Sr. art therapist Cell Barnes Hosp., St. Albans, 1977-83; lectr. Hertfordshire Coll. Art & Design, St. Albans, 1983—. Editor: Art Therapy as Psychotherapy in Relation to the Mentally Handicapped, 1985, Image and Enactment in Childhood, 1987. Research scholar Rank Xerox, Eng., 1979. Roman Catholic. Office: Hertfordshire Coll Art, & Design, 7 Hatfield Rd, Saint Albans Hertfordshire England

DUBROVSKI, DAVID ISRAELIEVICH, philosopher; b. Orehov, USSR, Mar. 3, 1929; s. Israel Solomonovich and Yuta Israelievna (Frimer) D.; m. Kovaleva Evgenja, Aug., 1958 (div. Sept. 1968); 1 child, Irina. Magister philosophy, State Univ. Kiev, USSR, 1952, candidate philosophy, 1962; PhD, State Univ. Rostov, USSR, 1969. Sch. tchr. Donetsk, USSR, 1952-57; prof. Med. Inst., Donetsk, 1957-70, State Univ., Moscow, 1971-87; leading scientist Inst. Philosophy, Acad. of Sci. USSR, Moscow, 1987—. Author: Psychic Phenomena and Brain, 1971, Information, Consicenceness, Brain, 1980, Problem of Ideal, 1983; staff editor Philos. Scis. mag., 1971—; contbr. articles to profl. jours. Served with Russian inf., 1943-45. Decorated Order of the Gt. Patriotic War. Mem. Philos. Soc. USSR (dep. chmn. Moscow sect., 1983—, bd. dirs. 1987), Philos. Psychoregulation and Self-improvement Soc. USSR (head sect. 1987—), Union of Journalists USSR. Office: Inst Philosophy, Volkhonka st 14, Moscow 119842, USSR

DUBRULE, PAUL JEAN-MARIE, hotel and restaurant company executive; b. Tourcoing, France, July 6, 1934; s. Paul and Suzanne (Mamet) D.; 3 children. Diploma Institut Hautes Etudes Commerciales, Geneva, 1958. Asst. to Bernardo Trujillo, Dayton, Ohio, 1962-63; co-chmn., chief exec. officer ACCOR, France, 1967—. Decorated Chevalier de l'Ordre National du Merite et Legion d'Honneur (France). Home: 121 rue Saint Merry, 77300 Fontainebleau France Office: ACCOR, 2 rue de la Mare Neuve, 91021 Evry Cedex France

DUBUC, CARROLL EDWARD, lawyer; b. Burlington, Vt., May 6, 1933; s. Jerome Joachim and Rose (Bessette) D.; m. Mary Jane Lowe, Aug. 31, 1963; children: Andrew, Steven, Matthew. BS in Acctg., Cornell U., 1955; LLB, Boston Coll., 1962; postgrad. NYU, 1966-67. Bar: N.Y. 1963, D.C. 1972, U.S. Supreme Ct. 1970, U.S. Ct. Claims 1975, U.S. Ct. Appeals (2d cir.) 1965, U.S. Ct. Appeals (4th cir.) 1977, U.S. Ct. Appeals (7th cir.) 1984, U.S. Ct. Appeals (5th and 9th cirs.) 1985, U.S. Ct. Appeals (fed. cir.) 1988, U.S. Ct. Internat. Trade 1988. Assoc. Haight Gardner Poor & Havens, N.Y.C., 1962-70, ptnr., 1970-83, resident ptnr. D.C. office, 1975-83; sr. ptnr. Finley, Kumble, Wagner, Heine, Underberg, Manley, Myerson & Casey, Washington, 1983-87, Laxalt, Washington, Perito & Dubuc, 1988—. Served as capt. AC, USN, 1955-59. Mem. ABA (past chmn. com. aviation law 1985-86, chmn. subcom. aviation ins.), N.Y. State Bar Assn. (past chmn. aviation law com.), D.C. Bar Assn., Fed. Bar Assn., Assn. Bar City N.Y. (aeros. com.), Maritime Law Assn. U.S., Nav. Aviation Commandery (vice comdr.), Internat. Assn. Ins. Counsel (aviation law com.), Fedn. Ins. Counsel (aviation law com.), Sigma Chi. Clubs: World Trade Ctr., Wings (N.Y.C.); Univ., Capitol Hill (Washington); Congrl. Country (Potomac, Md.). Home: 2430 Inglewood Ct Falls Church VA 22043 Office: Laxalt Washington Perito & Dubuc & Dubuc 1120 Connecticut Ave Nw Washington DC 20036 also: Laxalt, Washington, Perito & Dubuc 780 Third Ave New York NY 10017

DUCANN, SIR EDWARD (DILLON LOTT), financial executive; b. May 28, 1924; s. C.G.L. and Janet (Murchie) deC.; m. Sallie Innes Murchie, 1962; 3 children. MA in Law, U. Oxford, Eng. V.p. Somerset and Wilts Trustee Savs. Bank, 1956-75; founder Unicorp Group of Unit Trusts, 1957; bd. dirs. Lonrho plc, 1972, joint dep. chmn., 1983-84, chmn., 1984—; M.P. Tauton div. of Somerset 1956-87, econ. sec. to the treasury, 1962-63; minister of trade Bd. of Trade, 1963-64; chmn. Barcleys Unicorn Ltd. and assoc. cos., 1957-72, Keyser Ullman Holdings Ltd., 1970-75, Cannon Assurance Ltd., 1972-80; past bd. dirs. James Beattie Ltd.; vis. fellow U. Lancaster Bus. Sch., 1970-82. Author: Investing Simplified, 1959; contbr. articles to profl. jours. Mem. Lord Chancellor's adv. com. on pub. records, 1960-62, Conservative Parliamentary Fin. Group, 1961-62, select com. on House of Lords Reform, 1962, select com. on Privilege, 1972-87, Pub. Accounts Commn., 1984-87, Conservative Parliamentary European Community Group, 1985-87, All-Party Maritime Affairs Parliamentary Group, 1984-87, Conservative Party Orgn., 1965-67; joint hon. sec. U.N. Parliamentary Group, 1961-62; chmn. select com. on pub. accounts, 1974-79; liaison Com. of Select Com. Chairmen, 1974-83; founder select com. on treasury and civil service affairs, 1979-83; vice-chmn. Brit. Am. Parliamentary Group, 1978-81; joint leader Brit.-Am. Parliamentary Group dels. to U.S., 1978, 80; leader Joint Brit. Parliamentary Group del. to China, 1982; mem. panel of judges Templeton Found., 1984—; mgmt. council GB-Sasa Kawa Found., 1984—. Served with Royal Navy Vol. Res., 1943-46. Mem. Assn. Unit Trust Mgrs. (chmn. 1961), Brit. Ins. Brokers Assn. (v.p. 1978—), Assoc. Ins. Brokers (patron). Clubs: Carlton, Pratt's, Royal Thames Yacht, House of Commons Yacht. Office: 9 Tufton Ct, Tufton St, London SW1, England also: Bothay Barton, Greenham, Wellington, Somerset England *

DUCCI, RAUL VALENZUELA, engineering consultant firm executive; b. Santiago, Chile, June 19, 1947; s. Raul Ducci Claro and Adriana Valenzuela; m. Loreto Cornu Pizarro, Dec. 12, 1970; children—Raul, Pedro Jose, Juan Cristobal, Martin, Pablo, Gonzalo, Francisco . C.E., U. de Chile, 1969. Site engr. Cometro Ltda, Santiago, 1970-75, plant mgr., 1976-77; mng. dir. Raul Ducci Y Cia, Santiago, 1971—, Figueiredo Ferraz Chile, Santiago, 1978—. Vice pres. Juventud Nacional, Santiago, 1969-70. Roman Catholic. Club: Los Leones Golf (Santiago). Home: El Rodeo 13008, Santiago Chile Office: Figueiredo Ferraz Chile, P O Box 10098, Callao 3181, Santiago Chile

DUCK, ROBERT WILLIAM, geologist, educator; b. York, Yorkshire, Eng., Mar. 30, 1955; s. William and Joyce Amelia (Curry) D.; m. Elizabeth Ann Doctor, July 29, 1978; children: Jennifer, Colin. BS with honors, U. Dundee, Scotland, 1977, PhD, 1982. Research fellow U. Dundee, 1980-83; Research fellow Royal Soc. Edinburgh, 1983-85, lectr., 1985-88; lectr. U. St. Andrews, Scotland, 1988—; course tutor Open U., Dundee and Stirling, Scotland, 1982-84. Contbr. articles on sedimentology and geophysics to profl. jours. Mem. Fellow Geol. Soc. London; mem. Instn. Geologists (assoc.), Brit. Assn. Advancement Sci. (com. mem. Tayside and Fife br. 1983—). Home: 29 Ogilvy St, Tayport, DD6 9NF Fife Scotland Office: U St Andrews, Dept Geography & Geology, Purdie Bldg, St Andrews, Fife KY16 9ST, Scotland

DUCKHAM, BARON FREDERICK, historian, educator; b. Leeds, Yorkshire, Eng., May 20, 1933; s. Kenneth Luzon and Edith Faith (Baron) D.; m. Helen Gertrud Ebbe Wegener; Mar. 30, 1959; children: Christopher Michael John, Katrin Sarah, Jonathan Stephen Andrew. BA, Manchesterr U., Eng., 1954, MA, 1956; Cert. in Edn., Leeds (Eng.) U., 1955. Lectr. Further Edn. Colls., Redcar, Reading, Eng., 1958-62, Doncaster Coll. Edn., Yorkshire, Eng., 1962-64; sr. lectr. Doncaster Coll. Edn., Vorkshire, Eng., 1964-66; from lectr. to sr. lectr. Strathclyde U., Glasgow, Scotland, 1966-78; prof. history U. Wales St. David's Coll., Lampeter, Wales, 1978—; lectr. Sheffield U., Yorkshire, 1964-66. Author several books; editor Transport History; contbr. numerous articles to profl. jours. Churchwarden The Ch. in Wales, Betws Bledrws, 1979-86. Fellow Royal Hist. Soc. (Fellowship award 1969); mem. Hist. Assn., Econ. Hist. Soc. Anglican. Home: Bronllan near Lampeter, Dyfed SA48 8NY, Wales Office: St Davids U Coll, College St, Lampeter Dyfed SA48 ED, Wales

DUCOFFE, KEITH RICH, advertising executive; b. Atlanta, June 13, 1950; s. Arnold Lionel and Emily (Rich) D.; m. JoAnn Cardon, May 6, 1984; children—Lauren S., Caroline P., Aaron R. B.F.A., U. Ga., 1973; M.Product Design, N.C. State U.-Raleigh, 1978. Designer, Schuss Design, Columbus, Ohio, 1975-76; instr. Sch. of Design, N.C. State U., Raleigh, 1976-78; free lance designer, 1977-78; account exec. Alpha Bet Group, Atlanta, 1978-80; v.p. account services Creative Services, Inc., Atlanta, 1981-85; exec. v.p. Gitel Ducorp, 1985-86; pres. Group One Advt., Atlanta, 1986—; mem. faculty N.C. State U., Art Inst. of Atlanta, 1978-80; dir. Southeast Wholesale Furniture Co. Bd. dirs., v.p. Forrest Place Condominium Assn., Atlanta, 1980-82. Mem. Soc. for Photog. Edn., Friends of Photography, Orchid Soc. Am. Jewish. Clubs: Porsche of Am., Mercedes Benz. Contbr. articles to profl. jours. Home: 5455 Errol Pl Atlanta GA 30327 Office: 8 Piedmont Ctr Suite 500 Atlanta GA 30305

DUCROT, JÉRÔME JEAN, film director; b. Oran, Algeria, June 10, 1935; came to France, 1972; s. Ducrot Jean and Abadie Helen D.; children from previous marriage: Cecile, Natasha; m. Rocher de Gerigné Aurelie; 1 child, Amandine. Prin. Jerome Ducrot Studio, Questembert, France. Served to lt. paratroopers, French Army, 1954-58. Mem. Dir's. Guild Am. Roman Catholic. Home and Office: Bespérué, 56230 Questembert France

DUDA, RICHARD MICHAEL, osteopathic physician; b. Toledo, Aug. 6, 1942; s. Michael Eugene and Margaret Julia (Veselka) D.; m. Deborah Ann Kosakowski, Jan. 14, 1972; children—Richard Michael, Bridget Ann. Student U. Toledo, 1960-63; D.O., Chgo. Coll. Osteo. Medicine, 1967. Intern Doctors Hosp., Columbus, Ohio, 1967-68, Mercy Hosp., Toledo, 1970-71; resident Med. Coll. Ohio, 1971-74; practice specializing in emergency medicine, Toledo, 1974—; dir. emergency services Mercy Hosp., Toledo, 1981—; pres. Mercy Emergency Services, Inc., Toledo, 1981—, Phillips Med. Ctr., Inc., 1984-86, Demms Co., 1984—; mem. Monroe Med. Control Bd., Emergency/Med. Service Council, 1985—; asst. prof. clin. emergency medicine Ohio Univ. Coll. Osteopathic Medicine, 1986—. Mem. Lucus County (Ohio) Drug Abuse Adv. Bd.; bd. dirs. Med. Direction Lucus County, 1984—; mem. U.S. Senatorial Bus. Adv. Bd.; co-founder, mem.

Republican Presdl. Task Force. Served as capt. M.C., U.S. Army, 1967-70. Mem. Am. Trauma Soc. (founding mem.), Am. Coll. Sports Medicine, Am. Coll. Emergency Physicians, AMA, Toledo Acad. Medicine, Soc. Law and Medicine, Ohio State Med. Assn. Roman Catholic. Club: Exchange. Office: 2200 Jefferson Ave Toledo OH 43624

DUDLEY, HORACE CHESTER, scientist; b. St. Louis, June 28, 1909; s. Horace Chester and Rhoda Olivette (Mc Adoo) D.; A.B., SW Mo. State Coll., 1931; Ph.D. in Chemistry, Georgetown U., 1941; postgrad. U. Calif., 1948, N.Y. U., 1957; m. Thelma Avis Scott, June 13, 1935 (dec.); children—Jeanette, David; m. 2d, Joan Marie Kallenback, Nov. 6, 1954; children—Robert, Susan. Lab. asst. U.S. Bur. Standards, Washington, 1931-32; jr. chemist Bur. Chemistry, U.S. Dept. Agr., Washington, 1933-34; asst. chemist div. med. research Chem. Warfare Service, Edgewood Arsenal, Md., 1934-36; biochemist USPHS, Bethesda, Md., 1936-42; commd. lt., U.S. Navy, 1942, advanced through grades to capt., 1955; explosives specialist, comdg. officer units PTO, 1942-47; head div. biochemistry Naval Med. Research Inst., Bethesda, 1947-52; head sect. allied sci. Med. Service Corps, Washington, 1949-52; head radioisotope lab., dept. radiology Naval Hosp., St. Albans, N.Y., 1952-62; ret., 1962; prof. physics, chmn. dept. physics, U. So. Miss., Hattiesburg, 1962-69; prof. radiation physics, chief physicist U. Ill. Med. Center, Chgo., 1969-77, ret., 1977; with Rad. Safety Assocs., 1976-85; mem. com. coop. clin. studies, mem. med. library staff VA Med. Center, Hines, Ill., 1980-85. cons. in field. Decorated Bronze Star, Sec. Navy Medal; recipient Nat. prize Am. Chem. Soc., 1929; Outstanding Alumnus award Southwest Mo. State U., 1982; grantee AEC, 1963-64, NSF, 1963, 65, U. Ill., 1970, 72, U. So. Miss., 1965, 66, 67. Fellow AAAS; mem. Am. Phys. Soc., Health Physics Soc., Am. Assn. Physics Tchrs., Am. Assn. Physicists in Medicine, Am. Bd. Health Physics (cert.), Sigma Xi. Club: Masons. Author: New Principles in Quantum Mechanics, 1959; Morality of Nuclear Planning, 1976; Theory of Neutrino Sea as Generalized, Energy-Rich Medium, 1977. Contbr. articles to profl. publs. Patentee in field. Home: 405 W 8th Pl Hinsdale IL 60521

DUDLEY, MERLE BLAND, clergyman; b. Norfolk, Va., Feb. 19, 1929; s. Harry Roy and Merle (Garrett) D.; B.A., Lynchburg Coll., 1950; M.Div., Union Theol. Sem., 1954; M.A., Presbyn. Sch. Christian Edn., 1969; Ph.D., Glasgow (Scotland) U., 1973; m. Lillie M. Pennington, Oct. 12, 1950; children—Carter Bland, Jane Merle. Ordained to ministry Presbyterian Ch., 1954; pastor McQuay Meml. Presbyn. Ch., Charlotte, N.C., 1954-56, Holmes Presbyn. Ch., Cheriton, Va., 1956-59; asst. pastor First Presbyn. Ch., Roanoke, Va., 1959-60; pastor Christ Presbyn. Ch., Virginia Beach, Va., 1960-67; asso. pastor First Presbyn. Ch., Winston-Salem, N.C., 1967-70; pastor Westminster Presbyn. Ch., Waynesboro, Va., 1971—; mem. adj. faculty dept. philosophy and religion Blue Ridge Community Coll., Weyers Cave, Va., 1977—. Mem. Am. Acad. Religion, Soc. Bibl. Lit., Ch. Service Soc., Am. Schs. Oriental Research, Waynesboro Ministers' Assn. (pres. 1978-79), Va. Hist. Soc., Va. Soc. Sons of Am. Revolution, Jamestowne Soc. Republican. Presbyterian. Club: Rotary (pres. 1974-75) (Waynesboro, Va.). Author: New Testament Preaching and Twentieth Century Communication, 1973. Home: 1900 Mount Vernon St Waynesboro VA 22980 Office: 1904 Mount Vernon St Waynesboro VA 22980

DUDRICK, STANLEY JOHN, surgeon, educator; b. Nanticoke, Pa., Apr. 9, 1935; s. Stanley Francis and Stephania Mary (Jachimczak) D.; m. Theresa M. Keen, June 14, 1958; children: Susan Marie, Paul Stanley, Carolyn Mary, Stanley Jonathan, Holly Anne, Anne Theresa. B.S. cum laude, Franklin and Marshall Coll., 1957; M.D., U. Pa., 1961. Intern Hosp. of U. Pa., Phila., 1961-62, resident, 1962-67; practice medicine specializing in surgery Phila., 1967-72, Houston, 1972—; chief surg. services Hermann Hosp., 1972-80; prof. surgery U. Tex. Med. Sch., Houston, 1972-82, clin. prof. surgery, 1982—, chmn. dept. surgery, 1972-80; cons. in surgery M.D. Anderson Hosp. and Tumor Inst., 1973—, clin. prof. surgery, cons. to pres., 1982—; sr. cons. surgery and medicine Tex. Inst. for Rehab. and Research, 1974—; mem. Anatomical Bd., State of Tex., 1973-78; examiner Am. Bd. Surgery, 1974-78, bd. dirs., 1978-84, sr. mem., 1984—, also mem. and chmn. various coms.; chmn. sci. adv. com. Tex. Med. Ctr. Library, 1974; mem. food and nutrition bd. NRC-Nat. Acad. Scis., 1973-75; mem. sci. adv. com. Nat. Found. for Ileitis and Colitis; mem. anesthesia and trauma study sect. NIH, 1982-86. Editor: Manual of Surgical Nutrition, 1975, Manual of Preoperative and Postoperative Care, 1983; assoc. editor: Nutrition in Medicine, 1975—; editorial cons.: Jour. of Trauma, 1972-76; editorial bd.: Annals of Surgery, 1975—, Infusion, 1978—, Nutrition and Cancer, 1980—, Nutrition Support Services, 1980-86, Jour. Clin. Surgery, 1980-83, Nutrition Research, 1981—, Intermed. Communications Nursing Services, 1981—; others.; Contbr. chpts. to books, articles to profl. jours. Bd. dirs. Found. for Children, Houston, Harris County unit Am. Cancer Soc.; trustee Franklin and Marshall Coll., 1985—, overseers bd., 1986—. Decorated knight Order St. John of Jerusalem Knights Hopitaller; recipient VA citation for significant contbn. to med. care, 1970; Mead Johnson award for research in hosp. pharmacy, 1972; Seale Harris medal So. Med. Assn., 1973; AMA-Brookdale award in medicine, 1975; Great Texan award Nat. Found. Iletis and Colitis, 1975; Modern Medicine award, 1977; Disting. Alumnus citation Franklin and Marshall Coll., 1980; WHO, Houston, 1980; Stinchfield award Am. Acad. Orthopedic Surgery, 1981; Bernstein award Med. Soc. of State of N.Y., 1986 numerous others. Fellow ACS (vice chmn. pre and post operative com. 1975, gov. 1979-85, com. on med. motion pictures 1981—), Philippine Coll. Surgeons (hon.), Am. Coll. Nutrition (Grace A. Goldsmith award 1982); mem. AMA (council on food and nutrition 1971-76, exec. com. 1975-76, council on sci. affairs 1976-81, Goldberger award in clin. nutrition 1970), Am. Surg. Assn., Am. Pediatric Surg. Assn. (hon.), Am. Soc. Nutritional Support Services (bd. dirs. 1982-87, pres. 1984, Outstanding Humanitarian award 1984) Soc. Univ. Surgeons (exec. council 1974-78), Assn. for Acad. Surgery (founders group), Internat. Soc. Parenteral Nutrition (exec. council 1975—, pres. 1978-81), So. Med. Assn. (chmn. surgery sect. 1984-85), Houston Gastroent. Soc., Tex. Surg. Soc., Tex. Med. Assn. (com. nutrition and food resources), Harris County Med. Soc., Am. Radium Soc., Am. Soc. Parenteral and Enteral Nutrition (pres. 1977, bd. advs. 1978—, chmn. bd. advisers 1978, Vars award 1982, Rhoads lectr. 1985, Dudrick award named in his honor), Am. Gastroent. Assn., Soc. Surg. Oncology, James Ewing Soc., Ravdin-Rhoads Surg. Assn., Excelsior Surg. Soc. (Edward D. Churchill lectr. 1981), Soc. Surg. Chairmen, So. Surg. Assn., Southwestern Surg. Congress, Southeastern Surg. Congress, Surg. Biology Club II, Surg. Infection Soc. (chmn. membership com 1987—), Western Surg. Soc., Halsted Soc., Allen O. Whipple Surg. Soc., Am. Inst. Nutrition, Soc. Clin. Surgery, Am. Soc. Clin. Investigation, Soc. for Surgery of Alimentary Tract, Am. Trauma Soc. (founders group), Am. Assn. for Surgery of Trauma, Soc. Clin. Surgery, Am. Soc. Clin. Nutrition, Am. Burn Assn., AAAS, AAUP, Phi Beta Kappa, Sigma Xi, Alpha Omega Alpha. (sec.-treas. Houston chpt. 1982-83). Club: Houston Doctors (gov. 1973-76). Home: 527 Saddlewood Ln Houston TX 77024 Office: Pa Hosp Dept of Surgery Surgeon in Chief Eighth & Spruce St Philadelphia PA 19107

DUER, ELLEN ANN DAGON, physician; b. Balt., Feb. 3, 1936; d. Emmett Paul and Annie (Sollers) Dagon; A.B., George Washington U., 1959; M.D., U. Md., 1964; postgrad. Johns Hopkins U., 1965-68; m. Lyle Jordan Millan IV, Dec. 21, 1963; children—Lyle Jordan V, Elizabeth Lyle, Ann Sheridan Worthington.; m. T. Marshall Duer, Jr., Aug. 23, 1985. Intern, Union Meml. Hosp., Balt., 1964-65; resident anesthesiology Johns Hopkins Hosp., Balt., 1965-68, fellow in surgery, 1965-68; practice medicine specializing in anesthesiology, Balt., 1968—; attending staff Union Meml. Hosp., Church Home and Hosp., Franklin Sq. Hosp., Children's Hosp., James Lawrence Kernan Hosp., Balt., 1982—; co-chief anesthesiology James Kernan Hosp., 1983—, med. dir. out-patient surgery dept., 1987—; faculty Church Home and Hosp., Balt., 1969—, affiliate cons. emergency room, 1969—, mem. med. audit and utilizations com., 1970-72, mem. emergency and ambulatory care com., 1973-74, chief emergency dept., 1973-74; cons. anesthesiologist Md. State Penitentiary, 1971; fellow in critical care medicine Md. Inst. Emergency Medicine, 1975-76; mem. infection control com. U. Md. Hosp., 1975—; instr. anesthesiology U. Md. Sch. Medicine, 1975—; staff anesthesiologist Mercy Hosp., 1978—, audit com., 1979-80, 82; med. dir. outpatient surgery Kernan Hosp., 1987—. Mem. AMA, Am. Coll. Emergency Physicians, Met. Emergency Dept. Heads, Am., Md. socs. anaesthesiologists, Balt. City Med. and Chiurgical Soc., Internat. Congress Anaesthesiologists, Internat. Anaesthesia Research Soc., Am., Md. horse shows assns. Clubs: L'Hirondelle; Annapolis Yacht; Chesapeake Bay Yacht Racing Assn. Episcopalian. Address: 1011 Wagner Rd Ruxton MD 21204

DUESENBERG, RICHARD WILLIAM, lawyer; b. St. Louis, Dec. 10, 1930; s. (John August) Hugo and Edna Marie (Warmann) D.; m. Phyllis Evelyn Buehner, Aug. 7, 1955; children: Karen, Daryl, Mark, David. B.A., Valparaiso U., 1951, J.D., 1953; LL.M., Yale U., 1956. Bar: Mo. 1953. Prof. law N.Y. U. Sch. Law, N.Y.C., 1956-62; dir. Law Ctr. Publs. N.Y. U. Sch. Law, 1960-62; sr. atty. Monsanto Co., St. Louis, 1963-70; asst. gen. counsel, asst. sec. Monsanto Co., 1975-77, sr. v.p., sec., gen. counsel, 1977—; dir. law Monsanto Textiles Co., St. Louis, 1971-75; corp. sec. Fisher Controls Co., Marshalltown, Iowa, 1969-71, Olympia Industries Inc., Spartanburg, S.C., 1974-75; vis. prof. law U. Mo., 1970-71; faculty Banking Sch. South, La. State U., 1967-83; mem. legal adv. com. Chem. Mfrs. Assn., Washington, 1980—. Author: (with Lawrence P. King) Sales and Bulk Transfers Under the Uniform Commercial Code, 2 vols, 1966, rev., 1984, New York Law of Contracts, 3 vols, 1964, Missouri Forms and Practice Under the Uniform Commercial Code, 2 vols, 1966; editor: Ann. Survey of Am. Law, N.Y. U., 1961-62; mem. bd. contbg. editors and advisors: Corp. Law Rev, 1977-86; contbr. articles to law revs., jours. Mem. adv. council Southwestern Legal Found., Dallas, 1977—, lawyers adv. council NAM, Washington, 1980, Adminstrv. Conf. of U.S., 1980-86, legal adv. com. N.Y. Stock Exchange, 1983-87, corp. law dept. adv. council Practising Law Inst., 1982; bd. dirs. Bach Soc. St. Louis, 1965-86, pres. 1973-77; bd. dirs. Valparaiso U., 1977—, chmn. bd. visitors Law Sch. 1966—, Luth. Charities Assn., 1984-87, vice chmn. 1986-87; bd. dirs. Luth Med. Ctr., St. Louis, 1973-82, vice chmn., 1975-80; bd. dirs. The Nat. Jud. Coll., 1984—. Served with U.S. Army, 1953-55. Named Disting. Alumnus Valparaiso U., 1976. Fellow ABA (chmn. com. uniform comml. code 1976-79, council sect. corp., banking and bus. law 1979-83, sec. 1983-84, chmn. 1986-87); mem. Am. Law Inst., Luth. Acad. Scholarship, Am. Arbitration Assn. (nat. panel arbitrators 1960, bd. dirs. 1987—), Mo. Bar Assn., St. Louis Bar Assn., Internat. Bar Assn., Assn. Gen. Counsel, Am. Soc. Corp. Secs. (securities com., bd. dirs. 1983—, chmn. 1987-88), Am. Judicature Soc., Mont Pelerin Soc., Order of Coif. Home: One Indian Creek Lane Saint Louis MO 63131 Office: Monsanto Co 800 N Lindbergh Blvd Saint Louis MO 63167

DUESENBERG, ROBERT H., corporate lawyer; b. St. Louis, Dec. 10, 1930; s. Hugo John August and Edna Marie (Warmann) D.; m. Lorraine Freda Hall, July 23, 1938; children: Lynda Renee, Kirsten Lynn, John Robert. BA, Valparaiso (Ind.) U., 1951, LLB, 1953; LLM, Harvard U., 1956. Bar: 1953, U.S. Supreme Ct. 1981. Sole practice St. Louis, 1956-58; atty. Wabash R.R. Co., St. Louis, 1958-65, Norfolk & Western Ry. Co., St. Louis, 1962-65; atty., assoc. gen. counsel Pet Inc., St. Louis, 1965-77, v.p., assoc. gen. counsel, 1977-80, v.p., gen. counsel, 1980-83; v.p., gen. counsel Gen. Dynamics Corp., St. Louis, 1984—; bd. dirs. Pipe Systems Inc., St. Louis, Gerber-Barthel Truck and Tractor Inc., Belleville, Ill. Contbr. numerous articles to profl. jours. Sec., treas., legal advisor Am. Kantorei, St. Louis, 1970-75; mem. Council on World Affairs, St. Louis, 1975—; mem. Mo. Coordinating Bd. for Higher Edn., Jefferson City, 1976-83, chmn. 1978-81; mem. pres. council Valparaiso U., Ind., 1979—, Mo. Higher Edn. Loan Authority, 1982-84. Served as corp. U.S. Army, 1953-55. Recipient Disting. Alumnus award Valparaiso U., 1982. Mem. ABA, Mo. Bar Assn., St. Louis Bar Assn. (chmn. antitrust com. 1971-73, v.p. bus. law sect. 1972-73, chmn. 1973-74), Machine and Allied Products Inst. (legal counsel 1986—), Am. Corp. Counsel Assn., S.W. Legal Found. (adv. bd.), Aerospace Industry Assn. (legal com. 1986—), Nat. C. of C. (antitrust policy com. 1981-88), Northwestern U. Corp. Counsel Ctr. adv. bd., 1988—. Republican. Lutheran. Club: Harvard (St. Louis). Home: 9026 Whitehaven Dr Saint Louis MO 63123 Office: Gen Dynamics Corp Pierre Laclede Ctr Saint Louis MO 63105

DUESING, KLAUS GERHARD, philosopher, educator; b. Cologne, Rhineland, Fed. Republic of Germany, Sept. 3, 1940; s. Walter and Hildegard (Schulze) D.; m. Edith Kallert, Aug. 23, 1977. MD, U. Cologne, 1967. Collaborator Hegel Archives, Bonn, Fed. Republic of Germany, 1967-68, Bochum, Fed. Republic of Germany, 1969-76; prof. Inst. for Philosophy, U. Bochum, 1977-80, Inst. for Philosophy, U. Siegen, Fed. Republic of Germany, 1980-83; prof., co-dir. Inst. for Philosophy and Husserl Archives, U. Cologne, 1983—; expert Deutsche Forschungsgemeinschaft, Bonn, 1984—. Author 4 books; editor 1 book. Mem. Internat. Hegel Vereinigung. Office: U Cologne Inst for Philosophy, Albertus Magnus Platz, D 5000 Cologne Rhineland, Federal Republic of Germany

DUFAU, DANIEL GEORGES, dermatologist; b. Paris, Mar. 15, 1952; s. Jacques and Yvette (Ringoot) D.; married, Sept. 5, 1987. MD, U. Paris, 1980, cert. in dermatology, 1982. Diplomate French Bd. Dermatology. Dermatologist St. Louis Hosp., Paris, 1982—; practice medicine specializing in dermatology Paris, 1983—. Office: 129 Rue Caulaincourt, 75018 Paris France

DUFF, WILLIAM GRIERSON, electrical engineer; b. Alexandria, Va., Dec. 16, 1936; s. Johnnie Douglas and Annetta Osceola (Rind) D.; B.E.E., George Washington U., 1959, postgrad., 1959-72; M.S., Syracuse U., 1969; D.Sc. in Elec. Engring., Clayton U., 1977; m. Sandra K. Via, June 25, 1983; children—Warren David, Valerie Lynn, Dawn Elizabeth, Deborah Arleen, Kelly Juanita. Mgr. advanced systems tech. dept. Atlantic Research Corp., Alexandria, 1959—; asst. prof. Capitol Inst. Tech., Greenbelt, Md., 1972—; instr. Interference Control Technologies, Don White Cons., Inc., Gainesville, Va. Counselor, Meth. Sr. High Youth Group, 1965-73. Recipient Good Citizenship award DAR, 1955; Math. award George Washington High Sch., Alexandria, 1955. Fellow IEEE (pres. EMC Soc., assoc. editor group newsletter 1970—); mem. AIEE (Best Paper award 1961), George Washington U. Engring. Alumni Assn. (pres. 1963-64, Engring. Alumni Service award 1980), Sigma Tau, Theta Tau. Clubs: Springfield Golf and Country; Occoquan (Va.) Water Ski (pres. 1976). Author: EMI Handbook, vol. 5, EMI Prediction and Analysis Techniques, 1972; Mobile Communications, 1976; contbr. articles to profl. jours. Home: 7601 South Valley Dr Fairfax Station VA 22039 Office: 5390 Cherokee Ave Alexandria VA 22312

DUFFEY, JOSEPH DANIEL, university chancellor; b. Huntington, W.Va., July 1, 1932; s. Joseph I. and Ruth (Wilson) D.; m. Anne Wexler, 1974; children: Michael, David. A.B., Marshall U., Huntington, 1954; S.T.M., Yale U., 1964; B.D., Andover Newton Theol. Sch., 1957; Ph.D., Hartford Sem. Found., 1969; L.H.D., CUNY, 1978, U. Cin., 1978; Litt.D., Dickinson Coll., Pa., 1978, Centre Coll., Ky., 1977, Gonzaga U., Wash., 1980; LL.D., Monmouth Coll., 1980, CCNY, Amherst Coll., Bethany Coll., Austin Coll., Alderson-Broadus Coll., Adelphi U., Central Fla. Asst. prof. Hartford (Conn.) Sem., 1960-63; assoc. prof. and dir. Center for Urban Studies, 1965-70; fellow Harvard U. Kennedy Sch. Govt., 1971; adj. prof. and fellow Calhoun Coll., Yale U., 1971-73; exec. officer AAUP, 1974-76; asst. sec. for edn. and cultural affairs Dept. State, 1977; chmn. NEH, 1977-81; chancellor U. Mass., Amherst, 1982—; mem. U.S. del. 20th and 21st Gen Confs., UNESCO, 1978, 80; mem. exec. com. Nat. Council on Competitiveness Govt. and Industry Univ. Panel, Nat. Acad. Scis.; bd. dirs. Bay Bank of Springfield (Mass.). Contbr. numerous articles to profl. jours. Bd. dirs. Woodrow Wilson Internat. Ctr. for Scholars, East-West Ctr., Western Mass. Area Devel. Corp., Jewish Theol. Sem. Library, Springfield Symphony; del. Dem. Nat. Conv., 1968, 72; Dem. candidate for U.S. Senate, State of Conn., 1970. Decorated Order of Leopold IV (Belgium); recipient Tree of Life award Nat. Jewish Fund, 1987; Rockefeller fellow, 1966-68. Mem. Council on Fgn. Relations, Century Assn. Clubs: Cosmos, Fed. City (Washington); Century (N.Y.); Colony. Office: U Mass Office Chancellor Amherst MA 01003

DUFFIELD, GERVASE ELWES, publisher, editor; b. Oxford, Eng., June 1, 1935. MA, U. Oxford, Eng.; postgrad., U. Cambridge, Eng. Editor The Churchman, News Extra, News Today, Courtenay Publications Series; pub. Elizabeth Collie Assocs., Abingdon, Eng.; editorial dir. Appleford Pub. Group. Editor: The Churchman, News Extra, News Today; contbr. chpts. to books and articles to profl. jours. Mem. standing com. Ch. Eng. Gen. Synod, Archbishop's Intercommunion Commn.; elected mem. British Council Churches. Mem. Ch. of Eng. Home: Appleford House, Appleford, Abingdon Oxford OX14 4PB, England Office: Elizabeth Collie Assocs, Appleford, Abingdon, Oxford OX14 4PB, England

DUFFUS, ALLAN FERGUSON, architect, consultant in restoration and conservations; b. Halifax, N.S., Can., June 16, 1915; s. Allan Walker and Edith Gwendolyn (MacKinlay) D.; m. Caroline Elizabeth Hendry, Aug. 3, 1945; children—Sylvia Jean, Graeme Ferguson, Roslyn Elizabeth, Heather Anne. Pre-engring. cert. Dalhousie U., 1933; B.Arch., McGill U., 1938; D. Engring. (hon.), Tech. U. N.S., 1978. Registered architect, N.S. Prin., founding mem. Duffus Romans Architects, Halifax, 1946-56, Duffus Romans & Single, Halifax, 1956-64, Duffus Roman Kundzing & Rounsefell, Halifax, 1964-72, Duffus Romans Kundzins Roussefell Ltd., Halifax, 1972-80; pres. Archtl. Resource Cons. Ltd., Halifax, 1980—; pres. Heritage Trust of N.S., Halifax, 1969-72; gov. Heritage Can., Heritage Found. Can., Ottawa, Ont., 1974-79. Co-author: Thy Dwellings Fair, 1982; More Stately Churches, 1983. Vice chmn. Landmarks Commn., Halifax. Served to lt. comdr. Can. Navy, 1942-45. Fellow Royal Archtl. Inst. Can. (dean Coll. Fellows 1969-72, pres. 1973-74), AIA (hon.); mem. N.S. Assn. Architects (pres. 1955, 65), Halifax Found. Mem. United Ch. of Canada. Clubs: Halifax, Royal N.S. Yacht Squadron, Liberal Party of N.S. Century (Halifax). Office: Archtl Resource Cons, 1359 Barrington St, Halifax, NS Canada B3J 1Y0 *

DUFFY, FRANCIS CUTHBERT, architect; b. Berwick Upon Tweed, Eng., Sept. 3, 1940; s. John Austin and Annie (Reed) D.; m. Jessica Mary Bear, Sept. 4, 1965; children—Sibylla, Eleanor, Katya. diploma with honors, Archtl. Assn., London, 1964; M.Arch., U. Calif.-Berkeley, 1971; Ph.D., Princeton U., 1974. Archtl. asst. NBA, London, 1964-67; architect JFN Assocs., N.Y.C., London and Brussels, 1971-74; ptnr. DEGW Architects, London, 1974—; chmn. Bldg. Use Studies, London, 1980—. Author: Planning Office Space, 1976; co-author: Original ORBIT Studies, 1983, N. Am. edit., 1985, The Changing City, 1988; editor: The Office Book, 1982; Facilities, 1983—; contbr. articles to profl. jours. Harkness fellow Commonwealth Fund of N.Y., 1967-69; Charles Grosvenor Osgood fellow, 1970; Leverhulme Trust fellow, 1975. Mem. Royal Inst. Brit. Architects (assoc., council mem. 1988—), Archtl. Assn. (hon. sec. 1976), Environ. Design Research Assn., Internat. Assn. Applied Psychology. Mem. Labour Party. Roman Catholic. Club: Princeton (N.Y.C.). Home: 195 Liverpool Rd, London N1 ORF, England Office: DEGW Architects & Space Planners, 8-9 Bulstrode Pl, Marylebone Ln, London W1M 5FW W1M 5FW, England

DUFFY, JOHN CHARLES, statistician, teacher; b. Glasgow, Scotland, Mar. 6, 1949; s. Thomas Anthony and Catherine (Croft) D.; m. Rosemary Clare Arthur, Sept. 14, 1970; children: Catherine, John, Stephen. BS, U. Edinburgh, Scotland, 1969; MS, U. Reading, Eng., 1970. Statistician Brit. Steel Corp., Motherwell, Scotland, 1970; lectr. stats. U. Edinburgh, 1971—; statistician MRC Unit for Epidemiol. Studies in Psychiatry, Edinburgh, 1971—. Editor stats. entries in Chambers Dictionary Sci. and Tech., 1987; contbr. papers to jours. Recipient Best Paper 1984 award Study Group for Use Computers in Survey Analysis, 1985; grantee Scotch Whisky Assn., London, 1981, Sci. and Engring. Research Council, London, 1986. Fellow Royal Stats. Soc. (mem. social stats. sect. 1984—); mem. Scotland Assn. Univ. Tchrs. (pres. 1988—), Edinburgh Assn. Univ. Tchrs. (pres. 1982-85). Roman Catholic. Home: 11 Davidson Park, Edinburgh EH4 2PF, Scotland Office: U Edinburgh Dept Stats, Kings Bldgs, Edinburgh EH9 3JZ, Scotland

DUFFY, JOHN LESTER, pathologist; b. Huntington, N.Y., Jan. 26, 1927; s. Lester Maurice and Mildred (Aitken) D.; m. Katherine Dann Smyth, June 21, 1952; children: Mary, Sarah, John. A.B., Columbia U., 1948; M.D., N.Y. Med. Coll., 1952. Diplomate Am Bd. Pathology, Nat. Bd. Med. Examiners. Intern Nassau County Med. Center (formerly Meadowbrook Hosp.), East Meadow, N.Y., 1952-53; resident Nassau County Med. Center (formerly Meadowbrook Hosp.), 1953-58; assoc. dir. med. tech. program, assoc. chmn. dept. pathology and labs., 1959-84, cons. in pathology; practice medicine specializing in pathology Nassau County Med. Center (formerly Meadowbrook Hosp.), East Meadow, 1984—; asst. clin. prof. pathology N.Y. Med. Coll., 1966-70, clin. assoc. prof. pathology, 1970-71; asso. prof. pathology SUNY-Stony Brook, 1971-79, prof. pathology, 1979-84, clin. prof. pathology, 1984—. Served to capt. M.C. AUS, 1955-57. Fellow Coll. Am. Pathologists; Fellow Am. Soc. Clin. Pathologists, Nassau Acad. Medicine; mem. AMA, N.Y. State, Nassau County med. socs., N.Y. State Assn. Public Health Labs., Internat. Acad. Pathology, N.Y. Acad. Scis., Internat. Soc. Nephrologists. Office: Nassau County Med Ctr East Meadow NY 11554

DUFFY, LAWRENCE KEVIN, biochemist, educator; b. Bklyn., Feb. 1, 1948; s. Michael and Anne (Browne) D.; m. Geraldine Antoinette Sheridan, Nov. 10, 1972; children—Anne Marie, Kevin Michael. B.S., Fordham U., 1969; M.S., U. Alaska, 1972, Ph.D., 1977. Teaching asst. dept. chemistry U. Alaska, 1969-71, research asst. inst. arctic biology, 1974-77; postdoctoral fellow Boston U., 1977-78, Roche Inst. Molecular Biology, 1978-80; research asst. prof. U. Tex. Med. Br., 1980-82; asst. prof. neurology (biol. chemistry) Harvard Med. Sch., Boston, Mass., 1982-87, adv. biochemistry instr., 1983-87 ; instr. gen. and organic chemistry Roxbury Community Coll., Boston, 1984-87; assoc. prof. Biochem., U. Alaska, Fairbanks, 1987—. Contbr. articles to profl. jours. Disaster control coordinator Warren County CD, N.J., 1979; treas. youth Commn., Acton, Mass., 1984. Served as lt. USNR, 1971-73. NSF trainee, 1971; J.W. McLaughlin fellow, 1981; W.F. Milton scholar, 1983. Recipient Alzheimers Disease and Related Disorders Assoc. Faculty Scholar award, 1987. Mem. Am. Soc. Neurochemists, Am. Soc. Biol. Chemists, N.Y. Acad. Sci., Am. Soc. Zoologists, Am. Chem. Soc. (chem. edn. com. 1984; Analytical Chemistry award 1969), Intern Soc. Toxinologists, Sigma Xi. Phi Lambda Upsilon. Roman Catholic. Office: Inst Arctic Biology U Alaska Fairbanks AK 99775

DUFFY, MICHAEL FRANCIS, marketing educator; b. Bklyn., July 21, 1950; s. Lambert Francis and Cecelia Teresa (Bruscinski) D.; m. Patricia Marie Dunn, Sept. 1, 1973; 1 child, Elizabeth Camille. AS, Fla. Inst. Tech., 1970; BA, U. South Fla., 1974; MBA, Calif. State U., Carson, 1982; PhD, U. So. Calif., 1985. Environ. analyst Hillsborough/Pasco County govts., Tampa, Port Richey, Fla., 1975-77; pvt. practice field geologist San Antonio, 1977-80; sr. lectr. mktg. U. Otago, Dunedin, New Zealand, 1986—; cons. Ministry Agr. and Fisheries, Invermay, New Zealand, 1986-87; instr. Mktg. Inst. New Zealand, Auckland, 1987. Mem. editorial rev. bd. Jour. Global Mktg., Harrisburg, Pa., 1987—; contbr. chpts. to textbooks. Served to Capt. USAF, 1980-86. Otago Research grantee, 1987, New Zealand Univ. grantee, U.S., Can., 1987. Fellow New Zealand Inst. Mgmt.; mem. Am. Mktg. Assn. Republican. Presbyterian. Office: U Otago, PO Box 56, Dunedin New Zealand

DUGAN, KIMIKO HATTA (MRS. WAYNE ALEXANDER DUGAN), anatomist, educator; b. Kyoto City, Japan, Oct. 21, 1924; came to U.S., 1948, naturalized, 1956; d. Shinzo and Sano (Hatta) Hatta; student U. Md., 1957-58; B.A., Okla. Coll. Women, 1961; M.S., U. Okla., 1965, Ph.D., 1970; m. Wayne Alexander Dugan, Aug. 18, 1947 (dec. Aug. 1971). Grad. fellow dept. anatomy Sch. Medicine, U. Okla., Oklahoma City, 1964-69, instr. dept. anat. sci. Coll. Medicine, 1969-71, asst. prof., 1971-78, asso. prof., 1978—. Recipient Undergrad. Chemistry Achievement award Okla. Coll. Women, 1960; elected to U. Sci. and Arts Okla. (formerly Okla. Coll. Women) Alumni Hall of Fame, 1977. Mem. Am. Assn. Anatomists, AAAS, AAUW, Okla. Acad. Sci., Am. Chem. Soc., Am. Soc. Zoologists, Electron Microscopy Soc. Am., N.Y. Acad. Sci., Internat. Soc. Developmental Comparatvie Immunology, Sigma Xi. Episcopalian. Home: 1139 NW 63d St Oklahoma City OK 73116 Office: U Okla Health Scis Ctr Coll Medicine Dept Anat Scis PO Box 26901 Oklahoma City OK 73190

DUGAN, MAUREEN BLACK, realty company executive; b. Manchester, Eng., Feb. 4, 1937; came to U.S., 1957, naturalized, 1962; d. William Henry and Kathleen Mary (Cleaver) Jackson; grad. Felt and Tarrant Comptometer Sch., Eng., 1953; student Alamogordo br. N.Mex. State U., 1959-60, 62-63; m. Charles J. Dugan, Nov. 1979; 1 dau., Karen Elizabeth Black. Office mgr., personnel dir. J.C. Penney Co., Alamogordo, 1958-66; exec. sec. to project mgr. Re-entry System div. Gen. Electric Co., Holloman AFB, 1967-68; soc. editor, columnist Alamogordo Daily News, 1968-73; regional corr. El Paso (Tex.) Times, 1968-75; free lance writer and photographer; script writer Film Unit 505, Alamogordo, 1971; realtor asso. Shyne Realty, Alamogordo, 1975-77, West Source Realtors, 1977-80; owner, broker Hyde Park West Realty Co., 1980—. Pres., Alamogordo Music Theatre, 1971-72, Zia Endowment Inc., 1984-85. Mem. planning com. tourism, recreation, convs. Gov. of N.Mex., 1965; mem. N.Mex. State Film Commn., 1973-74; life mem. Aux. of Zia Sch. for Handicapped Children, pres. Aux., 1975-76, 80-82, mem. sch. bd., 1982-83. Recipient service award Nat. Found., March of Dimes, 1971; Americanism medal DAR, 1972; named Career Woman of Yr., Alamogordo chpt. Am. Bus. Women's Assn., 1971. Mem. Alamogordo C. of C. (chmn.

convs. and motion picture com. 1965—), Nat. Assn. Realtors, Internat. Real Estate Fedn., Realtors Assn. N.Mex., Alamogordo Bd. Realtors (chmn. public relations com., v.p. 1981-82, pres.-elect 1982-83, pres. 1983-84), N.Mex. Opera Guild. Home: 1206 Desert Eve Dr Alamogordo NM 88310 Office: PO Box 2021 Alamogordo NM 88310

DUGAN, MICHAEL THOMAS, II, judge; b. Indpls., May 26, 1944; s. Michael Thomas and Ella Joyce (Cox) D.; m. Kathleen W. Dugan, May 14, 1983; 1 son, James P. B.S., Murray State U., 1965; J.D., Ind. U., 1969, MBA, Ind. U., 1987. Bar: Ind. 1969, U.S. Dist. Ct. (so. dist.) Ind. 1969, U.S. Dist. Ct. (no. dist.) Ind. 1970, U.S. Ct. Apls. (7th cir.) 1970, U.S. Tax Ct. 1971. Broadcaster Sta. WNBS, Murray, Ky., 1964-65; bailiff Marion County (Ind.) Probate Ct., 1966-66; housing insp. Marion County Health and Hosp. Corp., 1967; tchr. Indpls. Pub. Schs., 1967-68; instr. English Ind. U.-Purdue U., Indpls., 1970-71; ptnr. Poore, Popcheff, Wurster & Dugan, Indpls., 1969-74; judge Marion County Superior Ct., 1975-86; presiding judge civil div., 1980, 84. Mem. nat. adv. council Eureka (Ill.) Coll.; bd. dirs. Julian Ctr.; v.p. Nat. Sports Festival, Indpls., 1982; bd. dirs. Circle Theater Assocs., Indpls. Humane Soc., Met. YMCA, Crossroads of Am. council Boy Scouts Am.; Democratic nominee Ind. Ho. of Reps., 1972; press sec. Ind. State Young Democrats, 1970; mem. Mayor's Task Force on Recreation, 1969-70. Mem. ABA (sect. corp., banking and bus. law, sect. internat. law), Indpls. Bar Assn., Bar Assn. 7th Fed. Cir., Indpls. Lawyers Assn. (Trial Judge of Yr.), Ind. Judges Assn., Am. Arbitration Assn., Am. Assn. Conciliation Cts., Am. Mgmt. Assn., Indpls. C. of C., Indpls. Legal Aid Soc., Ind. U. Sch. Law Alumni Assn. (pres. bd. dirs.), NAACP (life), Common Cause, So. Poverty Law Ctr., Sigma Chi. Methodist. Club: Indpls. Athletic. Home: 3144 Sandpiper Dr S Indianapolis IN 46268 Office: Marion Superior Ct 507 City County Bd W Indianapolis IN 46204

DUGERSUREN, MANGALYN, former Mongolian minister foreign affairs; b. Galuut Bomon, Mongolia, Feb. 15, 1922; student Inst. Internat. Relations, Moscow. Schoolmaster, 1941-44; dep. head, later head dept. Ministry Fgn. Affairs Mongolia, 1951-53; sec. central com. Mongolian Revolutionary Youth League, 1953-54; dep. minister of justice, 1954-56, dep. minister of fgn. affairs, 1956-58; ambassador to India, 1958-62; 1st dep. minister fgn. affairs, 1962-63; minister fgn. affairs, 1963-68, 76-88; permanent rep. to UN, 1968-72, to UN Office at Geneva and other internat. orgns., 1972-76. Mem. central com. Mongolian People's Revolutionary Party; dep. to Peoples Ct. Hural (parliament), 1963-69, from 1977. Office: Ministry of Foreign Affairs, Ulan Bator Mongolia *

DUGGAN, CAROL COOK, researcher; b. Conway, S.C., May 25, 1946; d. Pierce Embree and Lillian Watkins (Eller) Cook; m. Kevin Duggan, Dec. 29, 1973. B.A., Columbia Coll., 1968; M.S., U. Ky., 1970. Reference asst. Richland County Pub. Library, Columbia, S.C., 1968-69, asst. to dir., 1970, chief adult services, 1971-82; dir. Maris Research, Columbia, 1982—; lectr. mem. Friends of Richland County Pub. Library, 1977—, Greater Columbia (S.C.) Literacy Council, 1973—; mem. worship com. Washington St. United Meth. Ch., Columbia, 1985-86, mem. staff-parish relations com., 1986—, mem. history and archives com., 1988—. Recipient Sternheimer award, 1968. Mem. ALA (councilor 1980-82, chmn. state membership com. 1979-83), S.C. Library Assn. (sec. 1976, exec. bd. 1976, 78-82), S.C. Pub. Library Assn. (pres. 1980-81), Beta Phi Mu. Methodist (exec. bd. United Methodist Women 1983—). Club: PEO (pres. 1983-85 , chmn. amendments and recommendations com. 1983-85, historian 1986-87, treas. State conv., 1987-88), Columbia Coll. Afternoon of S.C. Home: 2101 Woodmere Dr Columbia SC 29204

DUGGAN, KEVIN, data processor; b. St. Louis, Feb. 29, 1944; s. Leo Patrick and Jean Claire (McHenry) D.; BA, U. S.C., 1977, MA, Webster U., 1988; m. Lillian Carol Cook, Dec. 29, 1973. With S.C. Nat. Bank, Columbia, 1970-79, mgr. tech. support, 1978-79; dir. info. sci. tech., Midlands Tech. Coll., Columbia, 1979—; cons. electronic data processing. Mem. Richland County Friends of Library, Literacy Council S.C., chmn. fin. com., 1987—; chmn. stewardship com., 1982-86; mem. evangelism and membership coms., 1982-86; mem. council on ministries, 1982—; mem. exec. com., 1987—; mem. adminstrv. bd. Washington St. United Meth. Ch. Served with USMC, 1963-67. Decorated Bronze Star (3). Mem. Assn. Systems Mgr., IBM Users Group, Data Processing Mgmt. Assn., Palmetto Fencing Soc., Amateur Fencing League Am. Methodist. Lodge: Rotary. Office: PO Box 2408 Columbia SC 29202

DUGGAN, T(HOMAS) PATRICK, management consultant; b. Hartford, Conn., Mar. 17, 1946; s. Edward O. and Mildred B. (Balf) D.; A.B., Providence Coll., 1968; postgrad. in mgmt. Western New Eng. Coll., 1969-71; m. Marcia McCormack, Aug. 31, 1968 (div. 1978); children—Mary-Christina, T. Patrick; m. Ann Hailey, Sept. 21, 1985. Mgr., Travelers Mgmt. Services, Hartford, 1968-75; mgr. mgmt. cons. services Coopers & Lybrand, N.Y.C., 1975-79; prin., dir. ins. mgmt. cons. services Hay Assocs., N.Y.C., 1979-84; exec. v.p., nat. dir. bus. Strategy cons. group Alexander & Alexander Mgmt. Cons. Services, N.Y.C., 1984; pres. Duggan Cons. Assocs., Greenwich, Conn., 1984—. Served to 1st lt., inf. USAR, 1968-75. Mem. Human Resource Planning Soc., Am. Mgmt. Assn., Ins. Accounting and Statis. Assn. (session chmn. 1975-79). Clubs: Golf of Avon, Hartford (Conn.). Home: 5 September Ln Weston CT 06883

DUGGER, JOHN SAMUEL, architect, educator; b. Rochester, N.Y., May 24, 1952; s. John Samuel and Mary Lucile (Celentano) D.; m. Katherine Rose Koob, June 12, 1976. B.F.A., R.I. Sch. Design, 1974, B.Arch., 1975. Registered architect, Mass., N.H., cert. Nat. Council of Archtl. Registration Bds., 1983. Chief designer Interface Architects, Newton, Mass., 1977-78; designer Aldrich div. Carlson Group, Cochituate, Mass., 1979-80; archtl. cons., 1981; chief architect, v.p. Channel Bldg. Co., Andover, Mass., 1982-84; pres., chief exec. officer Arch-Works Inc., Lawrence, Mass., 1984-86; design instr. Boston Archtl. Ctr., 1982—; cons. Sanborn Regional High Sch. Bldg. Com., Kingston, N.H., 1978-79. Photographer, etymologist: Architectural Illustration (P.S. Oles), 1979; illustrator books, pamphlets, reports for New Eng. historians. Bd. dirs. Andover Com. for a Better Chance, 1987—. Mem. Andover Conservation Commn., 1985—. Mem. AIA, Constrn. Specifications Inst., Soc. for Comml. Archeology (co-founder, dir. 1977-81). Republican. Club: Lions Office: 15 Railroad St Andover MA 01810

DUGGIN, MICHAEL JOHN, physics educator; b. Dorking, Surrey, Eng., July 30, 1937; came to U.S., 1979; s. Walter J. and Winnifred L. (Button) D.; m. Maggie Amelia Beveridge, July 16, 1978; children—John Bruce, Blake Michael. B.Sc., Melbourne (Austrlia) U., 1959; Ph.D., Monash U., Melbourne, 1965. Teaching fellow Monash U., Melbourne, Australia, 1962-64; postdoctoral fellow U. Pitts., 1965, asst. prof., 1966; research scientist CSIRO, Sydney, Australia, 1967-71, sr. research scientist, 1971-79; prof. physics, dept. forest engring. Coll. Environ. Sci. and Forestry SUNY-Syracuse, 1979—; cons. in field. Contbr. numerous articles to profl. jours. Fellow Inst. of Physics, Royal Astron. Soc., Optical Soc. Am., AIAA (assoc.); mem. IEEE (sr.), Am. Inst. Physics, Am. Soc. Photogrammetry, Internat. Remote Sensing Assn., Soc. of Photo-Optical Instrumentation Engrs. Research in physics of remote sensing processes; fundamental remote sensing research; spectral reflectance factor measurement; remote sensing data acquisition and analysis optimization, image analysis and infrared study. Home: 212 Robinhood Ln Camillus NY 13031 Office: SUNY 308 Bray Hall Syracuse NY 13210

DUHME, CAROL MCCARTHY, civic worker; b. St. Louis, Apr. 13, 1917; d. Eugene Ross and Louise (Roblee) McCarthy; A.B., Vassar Coll., 1939; m. Sheldon Ware, June 12, 1941 (dec. 1944); 1 son, David; m. 2d, H. Richard Duhme, Jr., Apr. 9, 1947; children—Benton (dec.), Ann, Warren. Tchr. elem. sch., 1939-41, 42-44; moderator St. Louis Assn. Congregational Chs., 1952; dir. Christian edn. First Congregational Ch., St. Louis, 1987—, trustee, 1964-66, mem. ch. council, 1974-75, 88—, bd. deaconesses, 1978-81, bd. deacons, 1982-85, chmn. bd. Christian Edn., 1988—; former bd. dirs. Community Music Schs., St. Louis, Community Sch., Ch. Women United, John Burroughs Sch., St. Louis Bicentennial Women's Com., St. Louis Jr. League; pres. St. Louis Vassar Club; pres. bd. dirs. YWCA, St. Louis, 1973-76; bd. dirs. North Side Team Ministry, 1968-84, Chautauqua (N.Y.) Instn., 1971-79, mem. adv. council to bd., 1987—; Mo. Bapt. Hosp., 1973—; exec. com. bd. dirs. Eden Theol. Sem., 1981—, presdl. search com. 1986—; sec. bd. dirs. UN Assn., St. Louis, 1976-84; pres. bd. dirs. Family and Children's Service Greater St. Louis, 1977-79; mem. chancellor's long-range planning com. Washington U., 1980-81, mem. Nat. Council, Sch. Social Work, 1987—; chmn. Benton Roblee Duhme Scholarship Fund; pres., trustee Joseph H. and Florence A. Roblee Found., St. Louis, pres. 1984—; chmn. Chautaugua Bell Tower Scholarship Fund. Mem. corp. assembly Blue Cross Hosp. Service of Mo., 1978-86. Recipient Mary Alice Messerley award for volunteerism Health and Welfare Council St. Louis, 1971; Vol. of Yr. award, YWCA, 1976; Woman of Achievement award St. Louis Globe Democrat, 1980. Home: 8 Edgewood Rd Saint Louis MO 63124

DUKAKIS, MICHAEL STANLEY, governor of Massachusetts; b. Brookline, Mass., Nov. 3, 1933; s. Panos and Euterpe (Boukis) D.; m. Katharine (Kitty) Dukakis, 1963; children: John, Andrea, Kara. BA, Swarthmore Coll., 1955; LLB, Harvard U., 1960. Bar: Mass. 1960. Mem. firm. Hill and Barlow, Boston, 1960-74; gov. State of Mass., Boston, 1975-79, 83—; Mem. Mass. Ho. of Reps., 1962-70; lectr., dir. Intergovtl. Studies, John F. Kennedy Sch. Govt., Harvard U., 1979-82; chmn. Indsl. and Entrepreneurial Economy Com., Policy Commn. Dem. Nat. Com.; chmn. New Eng. Gov.'s Conf.; chmn. Econ. Devel. Com. for Coalition of NE Govs.; moderator Pub. TV program The Advocates, 1970-73; Democratic nominee for Pres. U.S., 1988. Served with U.S. Army, 1955-75, Korea. Mem. Nat. Gov.'s Assn. (vice chmn. com. on econ. devel. and tech. innovation 1984, chmn. com. on econ. devel. and tech. innovative 1985-87, exec. com. 1987). Office: Office of Governor State House Room 360 Boston MA 02133

DUKALY, ALI MOHAMMED, librarian, researcher; b. Tamzawa, Fezzan, Libya, Jan. 5, 1952; s. Mohammed Dukaly Hisnawi and Masooda (Mohammed) El-Hadi; m. Khadija Ali Ibrahim, June 9, 1977; children: Najah, Malek, Nadya, Nasreen. BA in History, Garyounis U., Benghazi, Libya, 1976; MLS, Atlanta U., 1982. Chief librarian Faculty of Edn., Sebha Libya, 1976-78; chief librarian Sebha U., 1982-85, univ. staff mem., researcher, 1982—. Contbr. articles to profl. jours. Mem. ALA, Arab Assn. for Librarians and Inf. Specialists, Tunis, IFLA, Indian Library Assn., Libyan Assn. for Profl. Librarians. Home: Sebha U, PO Box 18758, Sebha Libya Office: Sebha U, PO Box 18758, Sebha Libya

DUKE, ANGIER BIDDLE, academic administrator, retired diplomat; b. N.Y.C., Nov. 30, 1915; s. Angier Buchanan and Cordelia (Biddle) D.; m. Robin Chandler Lynn, May 12, 1962; 1 son, Angier Biddle; children by previous marriage: A. St. George B., Maria-Luisa B. Duke, Dario B. Student, Yale U., 1934-37; LL.D., Iona Coll., 1957, Duke U., 1969; L.H.D., L.I. U., 1967. Pres. Duke Internat. Corp., N.Y.C., 1945-48; apptd. 2d sec. U.S. Fgn. Service, 1949; with Am. embassy, Buenos Aires, Argentina, 1949; spl. asst. to ambassador Am. embassy, Madrid, 1951; U.S. ambassador to El Salvador, 1952-53; v.p. CARE, 1958-60; pres. Am. Immigration and Citizenship Com., 1960-64; chief of protocol White House and Dept. State, 1961-65; ambassador to Spain, 1965-68; chief of protocol Dept. State, 1968; ambassador to Denmark, 1968-69; commr. civic affairs and pub. events N.Y.C., 1973-76; chmn. N.Y.C. Dem. Com., 1976-77; pres. The Spanish Inst., N.Y.C., 1977-79, chmn., 1983-87; chmn. N.Y. State Council on Ethnic Affairs, 1978-79; pres. Nat. Com. on Am. Fgn. Policy, Inc., N.Y.C., 1978-79; ambassador to Morocco, 1979-81; chmn. U.S.-Japan Found., N.Y.C., 1981-86; spl. adv. The Aspen Inst., Colo., 1981—; pres. Internat. Rescue Com., 1954-60; chmn. Dem. State Com. Nationalities and Intergroup Relations, 1960, Appeal of Conscience Found., 1974—. Commr. L.I. State Park, 1955-61; trustee L.I. U., 1981—, chancellor Southampton campus; chmn. World Affairs Council L.I., 1981—; bd. dirs. Ctr. for Jewish Life, Duke U., 1987, FDR Four Freedoms Found. Served from pvt. to maj. AUS, 1940-45; officer in charge Paris sect. Air Transport Command, 1945. Decorated by govts. Gt. Britain, France, Spain, Haiti, Morocco, Sweden, Greece and Denmark. Mem. Council Fgn. Relations, Fgn. Policy Assn. (bd. dirs.), Fgn. Service Assn., Council Am. Ambassadors (vice chmn.), The Pilgrims, SAR, Soc. Colonial Wars. Clubs: Brook (N.Y.C.), River (N.Y.C.), Racquet and Tennis (N.Y.C.); Travellers (Paris); Buck's (London). Address: Long Island U Chancellor's Office Southampton Campus Southampton NY 11968

DUKE, LAWRENCE KENNETH, banker; b. Lexington Park, Md., Mar. 7, 1956; s. Marvin Leonard and Judith Anne (Jackoway) D. BSMechE, MIT, 1978; BS in Polit. Sci., SUNY, 1982; MBA, Harvard Bus. Sch., 1984. Registered engr. in tng., Minn. Asst. mgr., treasury div. Citibank NA, Dubai, United Arab Emirates, 1984-86; chief dealer, treasury div. Midland Bank, London, 1986; dep. gen. mgr., treasury div. Nomura Bank Internat., London, 1986—. Recipient Cert. of Recognition, Gov. of Guam, 1970, Navy Achievement medal, Sec. of the Navy, 1982. Mem. Forex Assn. (internat. mgr. 1984—). Home: 30 Prospect Pl, Wapping Wall, London E1 9SP, England Office: Nomura Bank Internat, 24 Monument St, London EC3R 8AJ, England

DUKES, PHILIP DUSKIN, plant pathologist, educator; b. Reevesville, S.C., Jan. 16, 1931; s. Henry L. and Roberta E. (Reeves) D.; m. Marlene Hart, July 28, 1956; children—MarLa Hart, Philip Duskin Jr. B.S., Clemson U., 1953; M.S., N.C. State U., 1960, Ph.D., 1963; student Colo. State U., 1957. Plant chief clk. Davison Chem. Corp., Savannah, Ga., 1953-54; asst. county agt. S.C. Extension Service, Saluda, 1956-58; research asst. N.C. State U., Raleigh, 1958-62; asst. prof. U. Ga., Tifton, 1962-67, asso. prof. plant pathology, 1967-70, research plant pathologist U.S. Vegetable Lab., U.S. Dept. Agr., Charleston, S.C., 1970—; mem. Tobacco Variety Adv. Com., 1967-70; chmn. Tobacco Disease Evaluation Com., 1969-70; mem. Sweet-potato Disease Com., 1970—, chmn., 1970-80. Mem. local bd. SSS. Served with Signal Corps, U.S. Army, 1954-56. Recipient Ware research award for excellence in horticultural research, 1979. Mem. Internat. Soc. Plant Pathology, Am. Phytopath. Soc., Internat. Soc. Tropical Root Crops, So. Assn. Agrl. Scientists, Nat. Sweetpotato Collaborator Group (vice-chmn. 1984-85, chmn. 1986-87), Sigma Xi, Phi Kappa Phi, Alpha Zeta. Methodist (lay speaker). Research on physiology of phytopathogenic fungi, physiology of parasitism of root and stem pathogens, breeding disease resistant vegetables. Address: US Vegetable Lab 2875 Savannah Hwy Charleston SC 29414

DULBECCO, PATRICK, physiologist; b. Tours, France, Apr. 11, 1947; s. Serge and Renee (Ledoux) D.; m. Patricia Mathis, Aug. 21, 1971; children: Laurent, Fanny. MD, U. Tours, Cert. in Sports Medicine. Cert. medicine, France. Tchr. French Red Cross, Tours, 1972-74; tchr. physiology French Edn., Nice, 1982, Tours, 1987—, Le Cannet, 1988—; head med. dept. Reg. Ctr. Physical and Sports Edn., Antibes, 1980. Mem. French Swimming Fedn. (nat. med. com.), French Nat. Soc. Sport Medicine. Club: Ambassador (Antibes). Home: Villa Estournel Chemin Orangerie, 06600 Antibes France Office: 13 Boulevard Foch, 06600 Antibes France

DULBECCO, RENATO, biologist, educator; b. Catanzaro, Italy, Feb. 22, 1914; came to U.S., 1947, naturalized, 1953; s. Leonardo and Maria (Virdia) D.; m. Gulseppina Salvo, June 1, 1940 (div. 1963); children: Peter Leonard (dec.), Maria Vittoria; m. Maureen Muir; 1 dau., Fiona Linsey. M.D., U. Torino, Italy, 1936; D.Sc. (hon.), Yale U., 1968, Vrije Universiteit, Brussels, 1978; LL.D., U. Glasgow, Scotland, 1970. Asst. U. Torino, 1940-47; research asso. Ind. U., 1947-49; sr. research fellow Calif. Inst. Tech., 1949-52, asso. prof., then prof. biology, 1952-63; sr. fellow Salk Inst. Biol. Studies, San Diego, 1963-71; asst. dir. research Imperial Cancer Research Fund, London, 1971-74; dep. dir. research Imperial Cancer Research Fund, 1974-77; disting. research prof. Salk Inst., La Jolla, Calif., 1977—; prof. pathology and medicine U. Calif. at San Diego Med. Sch., La Jolla, 1977-81, mem. Cancer Ctr.,; vis. prof. Royal Soc. Great Britain, 1963-64, Leeuwenhoek lectr., 1974; Clowes Meml. lectr., Atlantic City, 1961; Harvey lectr. Harvey Soc., 1967; Dunham lectr. Harvard U., 1972; 11th Marjory Stephenson Meml. lectr., London, 1973, Harden lectr., Wye, Eng., 1973, Am. Soc. for Microbiology lectr., Los Angeles, 1979; Mem. Calif. Cancer Adv. Council, 1963-67; adv. bd. Roche Inst., N.J., 1968-71, Inst. Immunology, Basel, Switzerland, 1969-84; chmn. sr. council Internat. Assn. Breast Cancer Research, 1980-84; pres., trustee Am.-Italian Found. for Cancer Research. Trustee LaJolla Country Day Sch. Recipient John Scott award City Phila., 1958; Kimball award Conf. Pub. Health Lab. Dirs., 1959; Albert and Mary Lasker Basic Med. Research award, 1964; Howard Taylor Ricketts award, 1965; Paul Ehrlich-Ludwig Darmstaedter prize, 1967; Horwitz prize Columbia U., 1973; (with David Baltimore and Howard Martin Temin) Nobel prize in medicine, 1975; Targa d'oro Villa San Giovanni, 1978; Mandel Gold medal Czechoslovak Acad. Scis., 1982; named Man of Yr. London, 1975; Italian Am. of Yr. San Diego County, Calif., 1978; hon. citizen City of Imperia (Italy), 1983; Guggenheim and Fulbright fellow, 1957-58; decorated grand ufficiale Italian Republic, 1981; hon. founder Hebrew U., 1981. Mem. Nat. Acad. Scis. (Selman A. Waksman award 1974), Am. Acad. Arts and Scis., Am. Assn. Cancer Research, Internat. Physicians for Prevention Nuclear War, Accademia Nazionale dei Lincei (fgn.), Accademia Ligure di Scienze e Lettre (hon.), Royal Soc. (fgn. mem.). Club: Athenaeum. (London). Home: 7525 Hillside Dr La Jolla CA 92037

DULCHINOS, PETER, infosystems specialist; b. Chicopee Falls, Mass., Feb. 2, 1935; s. George and Angeline D.; B.S.E.E., Mass. Inst. Tech., 1956, M.S.E.E., 1957; M.S. Engring. Mgmt., Northeastern U., 1965; J.D., Suffolk Law Sch., 1984; m. Thalia Verros, Aug. 28, 1960; children—Matthew George, Paul Constantine, Gregory Peter. Bar: Mass. 1984, U.S. Dist. Ct. (Mass.) 1984, U.S. Ct. Appeals (1st cir.) 1985, U.S. Supreme Ct. 1988. With Sylvania Co., Waltham, Mass., 1957-61, Needham, Mass., 1963-66, Tech Ops, Burlington, Mass., 1961, RCA, Burlington, 1962-63; with Raytheon Co., Bedford, Mass., 1966—, computer ops. mgr. tactical software devel. facility Patriot Ground Computer System, 1977-86, proprietary data mgr., 1986—; lectr. Fitchburg State Coll., 1985—; corporator Central Savs. Bank, Lowell, Mass., 1980—; sec.-treas. U. Lowell Bldg. Authority, 1974-85. Mem. human studies subcom. Bedford VA Hosp., 1987—; pres., Chelmsford Republican Club, 1964-70; chmn. Chelmsford Rep. Town Com., 1972-76; assoc. Town Counsel for Tyngsborough (Mass.), 1985-87; chmn. Chelmsford Bd. Health, 1972-87; mem. Nashoba Tech. High Sch. Com., 1970-71. Served to 2d lt., Signal Corps, U.S. Army, 1957-58. Registered profl. engr., Mass., N.H. Mem. IEEE, Mass. Bar Assn., Boston Patent Law Assn. Republican. Greek Orthodox. Home: 211 Wellman Ave North Chelmsford MA 01863 Office: Raytheon Co Hartwell Rd Bedford MA 01730

DÜLFFER, JOST, historian, educator; b. Siegen, Westfalen, Fed. Republic of Germany, Feb. 24, 1943. PhD, U. Freiburg, Fed. Republic of Germany, 1972; habilitation, U. Cologne, Fed. Republic of Germany, 1979. Asst. prof. history U. Cologne, 1972-82, privatdocent, 1979-82, prof. modern history, 1982—. Author: Weimar, Hitler and the Marine, 1973, Hitler's Städte, 1978, Regeln gegen den Krieg? Die Haager Friedenskonferenzen 1899-1907 in der Internationalen Politik, 1981, National Sozialismus und traditionelle Machteliten, 1985, (with others) Inseln als Brennpunkte Internationaler Politik, 1986, (with others) Bereit zum Krieg. Kriegsmentalität im Wilhelminischen Deutschland, 1986, Deutschland als Kaiserreich 1871-1918, 1987. Home: Lochnerstrasse 20, D 5000 Cologne Federal Republic of Germany Office: U Cologne Dept Modern History, Albertus Magnus Platz, D 5000 Cologne Federal Republic of Germany

DULLES, FREDERICK HENDRIK, lawyer; b. N.Y.C., Mar. 12, 1942; s. William Winslow and Joanna (deLeu) D.; m. Martine Pred'homme, Aug. 26, 1977; 1 dau., Emilie Pred'homme. A.B. cum laude, Harvard U., 1964; J.D., Columbia U., 1968, M.B.A., 1968. Admitted to D.C. bar, 1971, N.Y. bar, 1972; asso. firm Shearman & Sterling, N.Y.C. and Paris, 1971-80; counsel Philip Morris Inc., N.Y.C., 1980, asst. gen. counsel, 1981-83, dir. counsel EFTA-Eastern Europe-Middle East-Africa region, Lausanne, Switzerland, 1983—; internat. exec. Assn. Internationale des Etudiants en Sciences Economiques et Commerciales, 1961-66, U.S. gen. counsel, 1977-80. Served to lt. Security Group Command, USNR, 1968-71. Decorated Navy Achievement medal. Mem. Am. Bar Assn., Assn. Bar City N.Y., Am. Mgmt. Assn., Internat. Bar Assn. Republican. Club: Harvard (N.Y.C.). Home: 7 Chemin des Colombaires, 1096 Cully Switzerland Office: Philip Morris Europe SA, Ave de Cour 107, Case Postale, 1001 Lausanne Switzerland

DULUDE, RICHARD, glass manufacturing company executive; b. Dunbarton, N.H., Apr. 20, 1933; s. Joseph Phillip and Anna (Lenz) D.; m. Jean Anne MacDonald, Sept. 11, 1954; children: Jeffrey, Jonathan, Joel. BME, Syracuse (N.Y.) U., 1954; postgrad., MIT, 1969. With Allis Chalmers Mfg. Co., Milw., 1954-55; with Corning (N.Y.) Glass Works, 1957—, v.p., gen. mgr. tech. products div., 1972-75, v.p., gen. mgr. European ops., 1975-78, pres. European div., 1978-80, dir. mktg. and bus. devel., 1980-83, pres. Telecommmunications and Elect. group, 1983-85, group pres., 1985—, chmn., chief exec. officer Corning Europe, 1987—, also bd. dirs.; bd. dirs. N.H. Land Mgmt., Inc., Optical Fibers Ltd., U.K., Fibre Optique, France, Corning Internat. Corp., Siecor Corp., Siemens Communications Systems, Inc., Siecor GmbH, Fed. Republic of Germany; mem. adv. council Sch. Engring. Clarkson U.; mem. engring. adv. bd. Syracuse U. Patentee combination space lighting, heating and ventilation fixture. Bd. dirs. Corning YMCA.; Past bd. dirs. Better Vision Inst., N.Y.C., Am. Sch., Paris, Am. Hosp., Am. C. of C., Paris; trustee Syracuse U., Clarkson U. Served to 1st lt. AUS, 1955-57. Mem. Optical Soc. Am., Illuminating Engring. Soc., Nat. Ski Patrol System (past bd. dirs.). Club: Travellers (Paris). Home: RD 2 Spencer Hill Corning NY 14830 Office: Corning Glass Works Houghton Park Corning NY 14831

DUMAS, ELNORA JEANETTE, psychotherapist; b. Elmira, N.Y., Oct. 24, 1938; d. Henry and Ira Mae (Lewis) D.; B.S., Howard U., 1960, M.S.W., 1962; postgrad. New Sch. for Social Research, 1979-80; doctoral candidate Fordham U., 1980. Supr., Bronx (N.Y.) State Hosp., 1968-71; asst. dir., then dir. Project Teen Aid, Bklyn., 1967-68; supr. N.Y.C. Soc. Meth. Ch., Headstart Program/Foster Home Care Div., Bur. Child Welfare, 1964-67; cons. Pre-Kindergarten Headstart, N.Y.C., 1969-71, Maternal and Infant Care Family Planning Project, N.Y.C., 1963-64; caseworker Community Service Soc./Warwick State Tng. Sch., 1962-63; pvt. practice psychotherapy, Bklyn., 1971—; supr. prison health services N.Y.C. Dept. Health; cons. Reed & DiSalvo Assos., N.Y.C., 1971; sec. Psychiat. Outpatient Clinics Am., 1971; asst. sec. Bklyn. Psychiat. Centers, 1974—; pres. Bushwick Mental Health Clinic, 1974—. Den mother Boy Scouts Am., Bklyn., 1975; vol. Internat. Center Fgn. Students and Businessmen, Bklyn., 1977, Vol. Literacy Program, 1980—; transp. hostess Nat. Dem. Conv., 1976. Cert. social worker, N.Y. State. Mem. Nat. Assn. Social Workers, Acad. Cert. Social Workers, Nat. Assn. Black Social Workers, Coalition of 100 Black Women, NAACP, Lambda Kappa Mu (Gamma chpt.). Democrat. Roman Catholic. League K.C. Aux. Home: 361 Clinton Ave Brooklyn NY 11238 Office: 35 W 9th St Suite 1B New York NY 10011

DUMAS, LAWRENCE, lawyer; b. Talladega, Ala., Oct. 12, 1908; s. William Lawrence and Mary (Hicks) D.; A.B. summa cum laude, Davidson Coll., 1929; J.D., Harvard U., 1932; LL.M., George Washington U., 1933; J.D., Georgetown U., 1935; m. Donald Berry, Dec. 4, 1940; children—Mary Aleta Dumas Schanbacher, Lawrence, William Berry, John Hicks. Admitted to Ala. bar, 1932, D.C. bar, 1933; atty. Fed. Farm Bd. and PWA, 1932-36; practice in Birmingham, Ala., 1936-43, 44—; atty. OPA, asst. U.S. atty., 1943-44; mem. firm Cabaniss, Johnston, Gardner, Dumas & O'Neal; mem. Ala. Constn. Commn., 1970-77; mem. Indsl. Securities Adv. Council, 1975-78; mem. Ala. Ho. of Reps., 1947-55, Ala. Senate, 1959-66; chmn. Ala. Legis. Council, 1955, 63. Chmn. adv. bd. local Salvation Army; trustee Carraway Meth. Med. Center. Mem. Am. Judicature Soc., Ala. Bar Found., Am. (Ala. chmn. jr. bar conf. 1947), Ala., Birmingham bar assns. Methodist (ofcl. bd.). Clubs: Masons, Shriners (potentate Zamora temple 1967), Birmingham Exchange (pres. 1958-59). Contbr. articles to legal jours. Home: 3251 Dell Rd Birmingham AL 35223 Office: First Nat Southern Natural Bldg Birmingham AL 35203

DUMAS, RÉMI FRANCOIS, accountant, consultant; b. Rivieres, Gard, France, Jan. 12, 1945; s. Gustave Leon and Rosilla (Rouquette) D.; m. Claudie Dupuis, May 8, 1970 (div. May 1987); children: Francois, Olivier. MBA, Montpellier (France) Bus. Sch., 1964-67; PhD, Inst. D'Adminstrn. Enterprises, Paris, 1968-72. CPA, France. Acctg. trainee IFEC Pub. Accts., Paris, 1967-68, Peat Marwick Mitchell, Paris, 1968-69, Ernst & Whinney, Paris, 1969-70; acct. Coop., Brazzaville, Peoples Republic of Congo, 1969-71, Credit Lyomais, Paris, 1971-72; controller Leasco France, Neuilly, 1972-76, Am. Express France, Rueil Malmaison, 1976-78; pres., chief exec. officer Etudes Comptables Fins Cons. Group, St. Leu La Forêt, France, 1979—; bd. dirs. Soc. Anonyme D'Entreprise Comptabilite, St. Leu La Forêt. Bd. dirs. Caisse D'Assurance Vieillesse Experts Comptables Commissaires Aux Comptes Pension Fund, Paris, 1987—. Mem. Inst. Pub. Accts., Nat. Inst. Statutory Auditors (dep. dir. 1985—), Regional Inst. Statutory Auditors (treas. Versailles chpt. 1985—0, St. Leu La Forêt C. of C. (bd. dirs. 1987—). Roman Catholic. Office: Etudes Comptables Fins Cons Group, Les Diablots BP53, 95320 Saint Leu La Foret France

DUMAS, ROLAND, French government official, lawyer, journalist; b. Limoges, France, Aug. 23, 1922; s. Georges and Elisabeth (Lecanuet) D.; m. Anne-Marie Lillet, 1964; 2 sons, 1 daughter. Ed., U. Paris, U. London. Bar: Paris 1950. Sole practice law Paris, from 1950; journalist Socialiste Limousin, Paris, 1967—; mem. French Nat. Assembly, Paris, 1956-58, 67-68, 81-83, 86—; minister European affairs France, Paris, 1983-84, minister fgn. affairs, 1984-86, 88—. Decorated Legion of Honor. Address: Nat Assembly, 75355 Paris France *

DUMITRESCU, TUDOR, mathematics researcher; b. Sinaia, Prahova, Romania, July 31, 1955; s. Ion and Georgeta (Munteanu) D. Diploma in Math., U. Bucharest, 1979. Analyst Ctr. Cybernetics for Indsl. Bldgs., Bucharest, 1979-80; researcher dept. cybernetics Acad. Econ. Studies, Bucharest, 1980—. Contbr. articles to profl. jours. Mem. Romanian Math. Soc., Am. Math. Soc. Mem. Romanian Communist Party. Home: C A Rosetti, Bucharest 70209, Romania Office: Acad Econ Studies, Calea Dorobantilor 15-17, Bucharest 71131, Romania

DUMITRIU, PETRU, writer; b. Bazias, Romania, May 8, 1924; s. Petre and Theresia (von Debretzy) D.; student Ludwig-Maximilians U., Munich; m. Irene Medrea, 1955; 2 daus. Chief editor Viata Romaneasco, Bucharest, 1953-55; mgr. State Pub. House for Lit. and Art, Bucharest, 1955-58; editor S. Fischer Verlag, Frankfurt am Main, Ger., 1963-67; books: The Boyars, 1956, Meeting at the Last Judgement, 1961, Incognito, 1962, The Extreme Occident, 1964, Die Transmoderne, 1965, Les inities, 1965, The Sardinian Smily, 1967, L'homme aux yeux gris, 1968, Retour a Milo, 1969, Le beau voyage, 1969, To the Unknown God, 1982; chmn. Council of Pub. Houses Ministry of Culture, Bucharest, 1958-60. Recipient Romanian State prize for lit., 1949, 52, 56, Star of the Republic. Address: Seilerstrasse 12, D-6000 Frankfurt am Main Federal Republic of Germany *

DUMMETT, MICHAEL ANTHONY EARDLEY, philosopher, educator; b. June 27, 1925; s. George Herbert and Iris (Eardley-Wilmot) D.; ed. Christ Ch., Oxford; Ph.D. (hon.), U. Nijmegen, 1983;m. Ann Chesney, 1951; 5 children (2 dec.). Asst. lectr. philosophy Birmingham U., 1950-51; Commonwealth Fund fellow U. Calif., Berkeley, 1955-56; reader in philosophy of math. U. Oxford, 1962-74; fellow All Souls Coll., Oxford, 1950-79, sr. research fellow, 1974-79, sub-warden, 1974-76, emeritus fellow, 1980; Wykeham prof. logic, U. Oxford and fellow New Coll., Oxford, 1979—; vis. lectr. U. Ghana, 1958; vis. prof. Stanford U., 1964, 66, U. Minn., 1968, Princeton U., 1970, Rockefeller U., 1973; William James lectr. in philosophy Harvard U., 1976; founder mem. Oxford Com. for Racial Integration, 1965, chmn., 1966; mem. exec. com. Campaign Against Racial Discrimination, 1966-67; mem. legal and civil affairs panel Nat. Com. for Commonwealth Immigrants, 1966-68; chmn. Council for Welfare of Immigrants, 1970-71. Author: Frege: Philosophy of Language, 1973, 2d edit., 1981; The Justification of Deduction, 1973; Elements of Intuitionism, 1977; Truth and Other Enigmas, 1978; Immigration: where the debate goes wrong, 1978; Catholicism and the World Order, 1979; The Game of Tarot, 1980; Twelve Tarot Games, 1980; The Interpretation of Frege's Philosophy, 1981; Approaches to Language, 1983; Frege: Traditional Influence, 1984; Voting Procedures, 1984; The Visconti-Sforza Tarot Cards, 1986; contbr. articles to profl. jours. Served in Brit. Army, 1943-47. Mem. Am. Acad. Arts and Scis. (hon. fgn.). Address: 54 Park Town, Oxford OX2 6SJ England *

DUMONT, SERGE, educational administrator; b. Douai, France, Feb. 6, 1934; s. Edmond Arthur and Maria Conchita (Mazure del Rio Navarro) D.; m. Christiane Leonide Nizart, July 18, 1956; 1 son, Philippe Christian. B. Lang. Arts, U. Lille, France, 1958, M.A. in English, 1959, diploma of edn., 1961. Tchr. modern langs., France, 1961-71; vice prin. Lycee Paul Duez, Cambrai, France, 1971-75; dir., prin. Lycee Polyvalent Classique Moderne Technique, Fourmies, France, 1975-80; dir., prin. Lycee Marcel Gimond, Aubenas, France, 1980—; dir. student's folk music and dances Lille U., 1953-56; dir. courses in French for immigrants, Cambrai, 1963-69; dir. lang. lab. Cambrai C. of C., 1966-75; bd. dirs. Credit Mut. Bank Cambrai, 1971-75, Crédit Mut. Bank Aubenas, 1987—; concert violinist, pianist, composer. Contbr. articles to profl. publs. Dir. Thierache Ctr. Profl. Tng. and Futher Edn. for Adults, Fourmies, 1975-80. Officer Order of the Palmes Academiques (pres. Ardè che sect. 1985—). Lodge: Rotary (Aubenas). Address: Lycee Marcel Gimond Bd de l'Europe,, Aubenas 07200 France

DU MUOI, government official; b. N.Vietnam, 1911. Vice chair and minister of Building Dem. Republic of Vietnam, 1974-76; vice chair Socialist Republic of Vietnam, 1976-88, chmn., 1988—, also minister of constrn., 1976-77, minister of capital constrn., industry, communications, transport and postal services, 1977, chair Econ. Affairs Bd. in Office of the Chair, 1976—; alt. mem. Politbureau of Communist Party of Vietnam, 1976—, now full mem. Decorated Order of the October Revolution, 1987. Office: Council of Ministers, Hanoi Socialist Republic of Vietnam *

DUNAIEF, LEAH S., newspaper editor, publisher, writer; b. N.Y.C., Aug. 21, 1940; d. Rudolph and Mollie (Rosenthal) Salmansohn; m. Ivan F. Dunaief, Feb. 24, 1963; children: Joshua, Daniel, David. BA, Barnard Coll., 1962; MBA, Columbia U., 1982. Writer, researcher Time, Inc., N.Y.C., 1963-67; founder editor, pub. The Village Times, Setauket, N.Y., 1976—, now pres., chmn. bd.; founder, editor, pub. The Village Beacon, Rocky Point, N.Y., 1986—, The St. James Times, 1988—, The Port Jefferson Times, 1988—; pub. Suffolk Lawyer, Suffolk County Bar Assn. Contbr. The New York Times; contbr., researcher Time Life Sci. Library. Mem. Speaker Stanley Fink's Small Bus. Commn. for L.I., Congessman Mrazek's Women's Issues Com.; assoc. trustee Dowling Coll., Oakdale, N.Y.; mem. edn. com. Mus. at Stony Brook; bd. dirs. Stony Brook Found. Realty, SUNY; mem adv. bd. W. Averill Harriman Coll. Policy Analysis and Pub. Mgmt. SUNY at Stony Brook; chmn. adv. com. Barnard Mag. Barnard Coll. Columbia U.. Recipient numerous media awards from state and nat. press assns; named Woman of Yr. in Communications, Town of Brookhaven, 1987. Mem. N.Y. Press Assn. (pres. 1984-85, 3d place best column), Nat. Newspaper Assn. (state chmn. 1982—, 1st Place award for investigative reporting 1985), L.I. Press Club (1st Place award for best weekly column 1987). Office: Village Times 185 Route 25A Box VT Setauket NY 11733

DUNANT, JEAN HENRI FREDERIC, surgeon, medical educator; b. Geneva, Nov. 12, 1934; s. Robert Plantamour and Gertrude Alice D.; m. Yvonne Barlatey, July 19, 1967; 1 child, Nicolas. M.D., U. Basel, 1961. Mem. dept. surgery Univ. Hosp., Basel, Switzerland, 1961—, dep. chief dept. vascular surgery, 1969-77, assoc. prof. surgery, 1975—; practice medicine specializing in vascular surgery, Basel, 1977—. Contbr. numerous med. articles to profl. jours. Serving as col. M.C., Swiss Army. Fellow ACS; mem. Swiss Soc. Surgery, Swiss Soc. Angiology, Internat. Coll. Surgeons, Internat. Soc. Cardiovascular Surgery, Internat. Coll. Surgery, Internat. Union Angiology. Home: Luftmattstrasse 12, Basel CH-4052 Switzerland

DUNBAR, CHARLES EDWARD, III, lawyer; b. New Orleans, Apr. 19, 1926; s. Charles Edward and Ethelyn (Legendre) D.; m. Marguerite Stephanie Dinkins, July 23, 1959; children: Ladd Dinkins, Charles Edward IV, Ethelyn Legendre, George Bauer II. B.A., Tulane U., 1949, LL.B., 1951. Bar: La. 1951. Since practiced New Orleans; of counsel firm Phelps, Dunbar, Marks, Claverie & Sims. Mem. citizens adv. com. Bur. Child Welfare, New Orleans, 1955-62, chmn., 1961; citizens adv. com. Juvenile Ct. New Orleans, 1960-65, chmn., 1964; charter mem. Information Council Americas, bd. dirs., 1964-68; Del. Republican Nat. Conv., 1968, 72, 76, 88; Presdl. elector, 1980; mem. La. Rep. state central com.; former mem. Orleans Parish Rep. exec. com.; finance chmn. New Orleans Rep. party, 1969; Bd. dirs. La. Civil Service League, 1960—, vice chmn., 1964-69, pres., 1970; bd. govs. Tulane U. Med. Center.; former bd. dirs. Internat. House, New Orleans; mem. host com. Rep. Nat. Com., 1988. Served with USNR, 1944-46. Mem. Fed., Am., La., New Orleans bar assns., Maritime Law Assn. U.S., Assn. Average Adjustors, Am. Legion, Phi Beta Kappa, Delta Kappa Epsilon, Phi Delta Phi. Roman Catholic. Clubs: Boston (New Orleans), La. (New Orleans), Stratford (New Orleans), Round Table (New Orleans), International House (New Orleans). Home: 411 Fairway Dr New Orleans LA 70124 Office: Phelps Dunbar Marks et al 400 Poydres St 13th Floor Texaco Center New Orleans LA 70130

DUNCAN, ANSLEY MC KINLEY, aerospace co. mgr.; b. Homer City, Pa., Jan. 25, 1932; s. William McKinley and Marion Melissa (Davis) D.; student U. Denver, 1955-57, Pa. State U., 1957-59. Engring. adminstr. RCA, Van Nuys, Calif., 1959-61; program evaluation coordinator N.Am. Aviation, Anaheim, Calif., 1961-66; mfg. supr., Rockwell Internat., Anaheim Calif., 1966-70, program adminstr., 1970-76, program controls mgr., 1976-81, plans/schedule advisor, 1981—. Served with USN, 1951-55. Home: 12600 Willowood Ave Garden Grove CA 92640 Office: 3370 Miraloma Ave Anaheim CA 92803

DUNCAN, DAVID FRANK, community health specialist, educator; b. Kansas City, Mo., June 26, 1947; s. Chester Frank and Maxine (Irwin) D.; B.A., U. Mo., Kansas City, 1970; postgrad. Sam Houston State U., 1971; Dr.P.H., U. Tex., 1976; 1 foster son, Kevin Rheinboldt. Research asst. U. Kans. Bur. Child Research, 1967-68; supr. Johnson County Juvenile Hall, Olathe, Kans., 1968-70; asst. to warden Draper Correctional Center, Elmore, Ala., summer 1970; supr. Harris County Juvenile Hall, Houston, 1970-71; project dir. Who Cares, Inc. Drug Abuse Treatment Center, Houston, 1971-73; exec. dir. Reality Island Halfway House, Houston, 1974-75; research asso. Tex. Gov.'s Office, Austin, summer 1975; research asso. Inst. Clin. Toxicology, clin. toxicologist Ben Taub Gen. Hosp., Houston, 1975-76; asst. prof. health sci. SUNY, Brockport, 1976-78, asso. prof., 1978, acting chmn. dept. health sci., summer 1978; vis. prof. health environ. research U. Cologne, Fed. Republic Germany, 1986; prof. health edn., coordinator community health program So. Ill. U., Carbondale, 1978—; chmn. So. Ill. Health Edn. Task Force, 1979—; bd. dirs. Ill. Pub. Health Continuing Edn. Council; cons. to numerous health, edn. instns. Mem. Am. Public Health Assn. (past chmn. sect. mental health), Ill. Public Health Assn. (exec. council), Am. Coll. Epidemiology, Soc. Epidemiologic Research, AAAS, Ill. Acad. Sci., N.Y. Acad. Sci. Democrat. Methodist. Author: Drugs and the Whole Person, 1982, Health Education: A Transatlantic Perspective, 1987, Epidemiology-Basis for Disease Prevention and Health Promotion, 1988; contbr. articles to profl. jours.; editorial bd. Health Values, 1980—, also assoc. editor ; Jour. Drug Edn., 1981—, Internat. Jour. Mental Health, 1982-83. Home: 306A S Oakland Carbondale IL 62901 Office: So Ill U Health Edn Dept Carbondale IL 62901-6618

DUNCAN, DORIS GOTTSCHALK, information systems educator; b. Seattle, Nov. 19, 1944; d. Raymond Robert and Marian (Onstad) D.; m. Robert George Gottschalk, Sept. 12, 1971 (div. Dec. 1983). B.A., U. Wash., Seattle, 1967, M.B.A., 1968; Ph.D., Golden Gate U., 1978. Cert. data processor, systems profl., data educator. Communications cons. Pacific NW Bell Telephone Co., Seattle, 1968-71; mktg. supr. AT&T, San Francisco, 1971-73; sr. cons., project leader Quantum Sci. Corp., Palo Alto, Calif., 1973-75; dir. analysis program Input Inc., Palo Alto, 1975-76; dir. info. sci. dept. Golden Gate U., San Francisco, 1982-83, mem. info. systems adv. bd., 1983—; lectr. acctg. and info. systems Calif. State U., Hayward, 1976-78, assoc. prof., 1978-85, prof., 1985—; cons. pvt. cos., 1975—; speaker profl. groups and confs. Author: Computers and Remote Computing Services, 1983; contbr. articles to profl. jours. Loaned exec. United Good Neighbors, Seattle, 1969; nat. committeewoman, bd. dirs. Young Republicans, Wash., 1970-71; adv. Jr. Achievement, San Francisco, 1971-72. Mem. Data Processing Mgmt. Assn. (1982, Meritorious Service award, Bronze award 1984, Silver award 1986, dir., edn. chmn. San Francisco chpt. 1984-85, sec. and v.p. 1985, pres. 1986, nat. grantee 1984, assoc. dir., by-laws chmn. 1987; nat. bd. dirs. spl. interest group in edn. 1985—), Am. Inst. Decision Scis., Western Assn. Schs. and Colls. (accreditation evaluation team), Assn. Computing Machinery. Club: Junior (Seattle). Subspecialties: Information systems (information science); Database systems. Current work: curriculum development, professionalism in data processing field, professional certification, industry standards, computer literacy and user education, design of data bases and data banks. Office: Sch of Bus and Econs Calif State U-Hayward Hayward CA 94542

DUNCAN, JOHN C., minerals company executive; b. N.Y.C., Sept. 29, 1920; s. John C. and Doris (Bullard) D.; m. Barbara Doyle, Dec. 12, 1942; children: Lynn Duncan Tarbox, Wendy, Craig, Gale Duncan Simmons. BA, Yale U., 1942. With W.R. Grace & Co., 1946-70, exec. v.p. charge Latin Am. ops., 1960-64, exec. v.p., dir. corp., 1964-70; sr. v.p. St. Joe Minerals Corp., 1971, pres., 1971-82, then chmn. bd., chief exec. officer; chmn. bd. dirs. Cyprus Minerals Co., 1985—, also bd. dirs.; bd. dirs. BF Goodrich Co., Westvaco Corp., Irving Bank Corp., Irving Trust Co., The France Fund Inc.; chmn., bd. dirs. Acción Internat.; bd. dirs., Ams. Soc. Council for Ams. Served to capt., F.A., AUS, 1942-46, CBI. Presbyterian. Clubs: Links, Yale (N.Y.C.); Round Hill (Greenwich).

DUNCAN, PAUL, printmaker, communications consultant; educator; b. Columbia, S.C., July 10, 1909; s. William Whiteford and Myrtle Frances (Gibson) D.; B.A., U. Ala., 1934; postgrad. Corcoran Sch. Art, 1967-75, Georgetown U., 1973-74; m. Gwendolyn Margaret Drolet, Feb. 6, 1937; children—Paula Duncan Hereford, Denis Duncan Hasty, Jean Laurens Duncan Lott. With Montgomery (Ala.) Advertiser, 1926-30, Anniston (Ala.) Star, 1934, Knoxville News-Sentinel, 1935-36, AP, Montgomery and Birmingham, Ala., 1937-42; with Office of Govt. Reports, Nat. War Labor Bd., Office Economic Stabilization of Exec. Office Pres., Washington, 1942-46; adminstrv. asst. U.S. Senator Lister Hill, Washington, 1946-51; dir. info. and reports Tech. Coop. Adminstrn. Dept. State, Washington, 1951-53; information cons. Pres.'s Com. on Scientists and Engrs., Washington, 1956-58; owner, cons. on mass communications and pub. affairs co., Washington, 1953-77. Prints exhibited in Corcoran Gallery Art, 1969-71. Decorated Comdr. Most Noble Order Crown, King of Thailand, 1960. Recipient First prize printmaking, Corcoran Sch. Art, 1971. Mem. Phi Gamma Delta. Democrat. Presbyterian. Author: Motivate, Teach, Train, 1952 (handbook). Editor: The Scientific Revolution: Challenge and Promise, 1959; contbr. articles to various publs. Home and Studio: Magnolia Springs AL 36555

DUNCAN, RICHARD LEE, JR., educational psychologist; b. Lincoln, Nebr., June 1, 1940; s. Richard L. Duncan; m. Charlotte Fish; children: Dana, Dwight, Derick, Denise, Darlene. BA in Edn., Ariz. State U., 1963, MA in Counseling and Ednl. Psychology, 1965; EdD in Psychology, Western Colo. U., 1975. Cert. elem. and secondary tchr., counselor, psychologist, adminstr. Psychologist Mesa (Ariz.) Pub. Schs., 1969-71, guidance cons., 1971-74, dir. Title III, 1973-74, head psychologist, 1974-76, dir. psychol. services, 1976-87, pres. clin. communications systems, 1978—, regional dir., 1987—; cons. nat. tng. on Stanford Binet Intelligence Test, edit. IV, 1986—; adj. prof. Ariz. State U., 1982—; vis. faculty Mesa Community Coll., 1969—. Editor: Creative Action Counseling Techniques and Useful Strategies, 1976. Bd. dirs. Maricopa County Youth Services Bur., Tri-City Community Behavioral Health Ctr., 1983—, pres., 1986-87; active Boy Scouts Am., YMCA (mem. LYFE found. bd. dirs.), Right to Life Assn. Recipient Merit award Boy Scouts Am., 1986. Mem. Nat. Assn. Sch. Psychologists, Ariz. Assn. Sch. Psychologists (pres. 1970-71), Am. Personnel and Guidance Assn., Ariz. Personnel and Guidance Assn. (pres. 1975-76), Am. Sch. Counselors Assn., Ariz. Sch. Counselors Assn., Kappa Delta Pi, Phi Delta Kappa. Mormon. Home: 651 S Alba Circle Mesa AZ 85204 Office: 549 N Stapley Dr Mesa AZ 85203

DUNCAN, ROBERT MICHAEL, banker, lawyer; b. Oneida, Tenn., Apr. 14, 1951; s. Robert C. and Barbara (Taylor) D.; m. Joanne Kirk, June 3, 1972; children—Robert Michael. B.A., Cumberland Coll., 1971; J.D., U. Ky., 1974; postgrad. U. Wis., 1977-80, Harvard Bus. Sch., 1983. Vice pres. Inez Deposit Bank, Ky., 1974-77, exec. v.p., 1977-81, pres., chief exec. officer, 1981—; pres., chief exec. officer Community Holding Co., Inez, 1983—, First Nat. Bank, Louisa, Ky., 1984—; ptnr. Kirk Ins. Agy., 1978—; dir. First Nat. Bank, Louisa, Cin. Br. of the Cleve. Fed. Reserve Bank, 1987-90; chmn. Morehead State U., 1985-86; trustee, sec. Alice Lloyd Coll., Pippa Passes, Ky., 1978—; del. Republican. Nat. Conv., 1972-76; trustee Highlands Regional Med. Ctr., 1977. Named Cumberland Coll. Outstanding Alumnus, 1976; Outstanding Young Man, Ky. Jaycees, 1982; U. Ky. fellow, 1978. Mem. Am. Bankers Assn., Edn. Devel. and Policy Council, Ky. Bankers Assn. (pres. 1985-86, dir.), ABA, Ky. Bar Assn., Ky. C. of C. (dir.). Baptist. Club: Kiwanis (lt. gov. 1983-84). Home: PO Box 331 Inez KY 41224 Office: PO Box 365 Main St Inez KY 41224

DUNCAN, VIRGINIA IRWIN, lawyer; b. Parker Dam, Calif., May 7, 1949; d. George Gothic and Virginia E. (Dick) Irwin; m. Richard Vaughn Duncan, Jan. 25, 1971; 1 dau., Jessica Von. B.S. in Spl. Edn., No. Ariz. U., 1972, B.S. in Elem. Edn., 1972, M.A. in Spl. Edn., 1978; J.D., U. Ariz., 1983. Cert. tchr. elem. edn., spl. edn., learning disabled, gifted, mentally retarded, blind, Ariz.; bar: Ariz. 1983. Dir., instr. spl. edn. program Beaver Creek Sch. Dist., Rimrock, Ariz., 1975-78; instr. Yavapai Community Coll., Verde Campus, Ariz., 1977-78; tchr. Verde Valley Sch., Sedona, Ariz., 1978, Beaver Creek Sch., Rimrock, 1972-79; assoc. Joyce & Frankel, P.A., Sedona, 1983-87; ptnr. Joyce, Levin & Duncan, P.A., 1988—; bd. dirs. Verde Valley Guidance Clinic. Recipient Am. Jurisprudence award Lawyers Coop. Pub. Co. and Bancroft-Whitney Co., 1982, Samuel M. Fegtly award U. Ariz., 1982; Am. Field Service fgn. exchange student, 1966. Mem. ABA, Ariz. Bar Assn., Phi Kappa Phi, Phi Delta Phi. Democrat. Home: PO Box 3275 Sedona AZ 86340 Office: Joyce Levin & Duncan PA PO Box 3984 Sedona AZ 86340

DUNCOMBE, RAYNOR LOCKWOOD, astronomer; b. Bronxville, N.Y., Mar. 3, 1917; s. Frederic Howe and Mabel Louise (Taylor) D.; m. Julena Theodora Steinheider, Jan. 29, 1948; 1 son, Raynor B. B.A., Wesleyan U., Middletown, Conn., 1940; M.A., State U. Iowa, 1941; Ph.D., Yale U., 1956. Astronomer U.S. Naval Obs., Washington, 1942-62; dir. Nautical Almanac Office, 1963-75; prof. aerospace sci. U. Tex., Austin, 1976—; research asso. Yale U. Obs., 1948-49; lectr. dynamical astronomy U. Md., 1963, Yale Summer Inst., 1959-70, Office Naval Research Summer Inst. in Orbital Mechanics, 1971, NATO Advanced Study Inst., 1972; cons. orbital mechanics Projects Vanguard, Mercury, Gemini, Apollo, USN Space Surveillance System; mem. NASA space scis. steering com., NASA research adv. panel in applied math., 1967; adviser Internat. Com. on Weights and Measures, Internat. Radio Consultative Com., Internat. Telecommunications Union; mem. Nat. Acad.-NRC astronomy survey com., 1970-72. Author: Motion of Venus, 1958, Coordinates of Ceres, Pallas, Juno and Vesta, 1969; editor: (with V.G. Szebehely) Methods in Celestial Mechanics, 1966, Dynamics of the Solar System, 1979; (with D. Dvorak and P.J. Message) The Stability of Planetary Systems, 1984; assoc. editor: Fundamentals of Cosmic Physics, 1971; exec. editor: Celestial Mechanics, 1977-85; contbr. articles to profl. jours. Recipient Superior Achievement award Inst. Navigation, 1967. Fellow Royal Astron. Soc., AAAS (sect. chmn.); assoc. fellow AIAA; mem. Internat. Astron. Union (pres. com. on ephemerides), Am. Astron. Soc. (chmn. div. dynamical astronomy 1970), Inst. Navigation (councillor 1960-64, v.p. 1964-66, pres. 1966-67, Hays award 1975), ASME (sponsor applied mechanics div. 1968-70), Internat. Assn. Insts. Nav. (v.p.), Assn. Computing Machinery, Sigma Xi. Club: Nat. Aviation (Washington). Home: 1804 Vance Circle Austin TX 78701 Office: Dept Aerospace Engring U Tex Austin TX 78712

DUNDON, MARGO ELAINE, museum director; b. Cleve., July 3, 1950; d. Elmer Edward and Ruth Ann (Dreger) Buckeye. BS in Communications cum laude honors coll., Ohio U., 1972; postgrad. in Mus. Studies, U. Okla, 1987—. Mem. gen. staff Grout Mus. History and Sci., Waterloo, Iowa, 1974-75; coordinator edn. Grout Mus. History and Sci., Waterloo, 1976-78, co-dir., 1979-87, dir., 1988—. Chairperson Waterloo Hist. Preservation Commn., 1987—, cultural com. Visitors and Conv. Bur., Waterloo, 1988—, My Waterloo Days, 1982, 83, leadership award, 1982; mem. Jr. League; bd. dirs. Resources Plus, Waterloo-Cedar Falls, Iowa, 1986—. Am. Law Inst.-ABA scholar, 1979, 86; recipient Mayor's Vol. Performance award, Waterloo, 1983. Mem. Am. Assn Mus. (site surveyor nat. assessment program 1982—, site examiner nat. accreditation commn. 1987—, regional councilor 1988—), Midwest Mus. Conf. (pres. 1988—), Iowa Mus. Assn. (pres. 1984-86). Club: Quota (Waterloo) (pres. 1982). Office: Grout Mus History & Sci 503 South St Waterloo IA 50701

DUNGAN, WILLIAM JOSEPH, JR., insurance broker, economics educator; b. New London, Conn., Mar. 19, 1956; s. William Joseph and Alpha (Combs) D.; m. Janet Dudek, May 28, 1983. BS in Biology, Old Dominion U., 1978, postgrad. in Econs., 1978-80; postgrad., Wharton Sch., U. Pa., 1984-85, Coll. for Fin. Planners, 1983-84. CLU; Chartered fin. cons. Rep. Prudential Ins. Co., Norfolk, VA., 1979-80; assoc. Russ Gills and Assocs., Va. Beach, Va., 1980—; instr. Tidewater Community Coll., Va. Beach, Va., 1979—. Mem. Internat. Assoc. Fin. Planning, Nat. Assoc. Life Underwriters, Inst. Cert. Fin. Planners, Inst. Cert. Employee Benefits Specialists, Am. Soc. CLU's, Million Dollar Round Table. Republican. Club: Norfolk Va. Beach Exec. Home: 4201 Mercedes Ct Virginia Beach VA 23455 Office: Russ Gills and Assocs 144 Business Park Dr #201 Virginia Beach VA 23462

DUNHAM, DONALD HARRISON, insurance consultant; b. Davies County, Mo., Sept. 15, 1913; s. Emory H. and Zula (Crain) D.; A.A., Pomona Coll., 1935; LL.B., Nat. U., Washington, 1941, LL.M., 1942; J.D., George Washington U., 1968; m. Lillian Mae Ingram, Aug. 21, 1941; 1 dau., Carol-Lynn Shirley. Instr. ins., office mgmt. Nat. Inst. Tech., Washington, 1946-47, dist. mgr. group dept. Mass. Mut. Life Ins. Co., 1947-48; regional mgr. group dept. U.S. Life, N.Y.C., 1948-50; region and group dir. Eastern Seaboard, Minn. Mut. Life Ins. Co., 1950-51; dir. retirement, safety and ins. dept., also contbg. editor Rural Electrification mag. Nat. Rural Electric Coop. Assn., 1951-58; asst. v.p. Church Life Ins. Corp., 1958-59, adminstrv. v.p., 1959-64, v.p., mgr., 1964-72, dir., 1962-72, mem. exec. com., 1964-72; sec. Ch. Agy. Corp., Ch. Finance Corp., 1966-72; asst. v.p. govt. relations Ch. Pension Fund P.E. Ch., 1959-72; dep. asst. adminstr. Tex. State Bd. Ins., 1972-74; dep. asst. adminstr., ins. contract specialist Tex. Dept. Human Services, 1974-77, adminstr. contractual devel., compliance rev., purchased health services, 1977-84 , HMO specialist, 1975-84 ; ins. cons., Dunham Assocs., 1950—; ins. cons. Nat. Telephone Coop. Assn.; mem. Gov.'s Com. on Nat. Health Ins. and Com. on Aging, 1977-78. Chmn. adv. com. problems aging to Borough Council, 1959-72; vice chmn. planning bd. Borough of New Providence, 1966-72; chmn. New Providence Indsl. Devel. Com., 1970-72; mem. Md. Gov.'s Citizens Com. Traffic Safety, 1951-72, Pres.'s Conf. Traffic Safety, Indsl. Safety; nat. safety counsel Ins. Conf. of Coop. League U.S. Served with USNR, 1944-46. Mem. A.I.M. (fellow pres.'s council), Am. Legion (post comdr.), Minn. State Soc. (past pres.), V.F.W., D.A.V., Nat. Assn. Ins. Commrs. (Episcopal Ch. rep. 1958-72), Group Health Fedn. Am., Nat. Health Lawyers Assn., Group Health Assn. Am., Nat. Assn. HMO Regulators, U.S. Power Squadron (No. N.J. safety com.), Kappa Sigma Kappa, Sigma Delta Kappa, Delta Psi Omega (mem. bishop's com. 1959-72). Mason (32 deg.). Clubs: Kenwood Golf and Country (Chevy Chase, Md.); Lucaya Golf and Country (Freeport, Grand Bahamas); Craftsman. Home and office: 409 Cherokee Dr Temple TX 76504

DUNHAM, WOLCOTT BALESTIER, oncologist, researcher; b. Boston, June 15, 1900; s. Theodore and Josephine (Balestier) D.; m. Isabel Bosworth, Oct. 7, 1940; children—Wolcott Balestier, Anne Huntington Dunham Ewart. Student, Harvard Coll., 1920-22; A.B., Columbia U., 1924, M.D., 1928. Diplomate Am. Bd. Med. Microbiology. Asst. bacteriologist N.Y. Postgrad. Med. Sch. and Hosp., 1936-46; research biologist VA Hosp., Memphis, 1946-61, Asst. dir. profl. services for research, 1956-61, assoc. chief staff, 1961-68; vis. investigator Jackson Lab., Bar Harbor, Maine, 1968-76; assoc. research prof. Linus Pauling Inst., Palo Alto, Calif., 1978-83, sr. scientist, 1983—. Author articles. Non-govtl. orgn. observer Parliamentarians Global Action at UN Third Spl. Session on Disarmament, 1988. Recipient Civic award VA, 1967. Fellow ACP, N.Y. Acad. Medicine, N.Y. Acad. Scis.; mem. Am. Assn. Immunologists, Am. Soc. for Microbiology, Am. Tissue Culture Assn., Physicians for Social Responsibility. Democrat. Episcopalian. Club: Harvard (N.Y.C.). Home: 270 W Floresta Way Menlo Park CA 94025 Office: 440 Page Mill Rd Palo Alto CA 94306

DUNLAP, ESTELLE CECILIA DIGGS (MRS. LEE A. DUNLAP), educator; b. Washington, Sept 26, 1912; d. John F. and Mary F. (Chasley) Diggs; B.S., D.C. Tchrs. Coll., 1937; M.S., Howard U., 1940, doctoral degree World U., Internat. Univ. Found. (hon.); m. Lee A. Dunlap, May 16, 1941; children—Gladys Dunlap Carpenti, Dolly Dunlap Sparkman. Tchr. math. Garnet-Patterson Jr. High Sch., Washington, 1941-56, head dept. math., 1950-56; tchr. math., sci. MacFarland Jr. High Sch., Washington, 1956-72. Vis. instr. math. D.C. Tchrs. Coll., 1963—. Mem. N.W. Boundary Civic Assn., Washington, 1954—, rec. sec., 1964-66. Recipient Bronze medal for peace Albert Einstein Internat. Acad., 1986; NSF fellow, 1959. Fellow Intercontintental Biog. Assn.; mem. AAAS, Nat. Edn. Council, Nat. Council Tchrs. Math. Nat. Aviation Edn. Council, Internat. Platform Assn., Washington Performing Arts Soc., Soc. Indsl. and Applied Math., Am. Ordnance Assn., Am. Math. Soc., Math. Assn. Am., Washington Urban League. Washington Opera Soc., UN Assn., Met. Opera Guild, Smithsonian Assos.,

Fgn. Policy Research Inst., Assos. Nat. Archives, Nat. Ret. Tchrs. Assn., Nat. Trust for Historic Preservation, Nat. Symphony Orch. Assn., Arena Stage Assn., U.S. Olympic Soc., AAUW, Internat. Inst. Community Service. Republican. Clubs: U.S. Senatorial (founding); Stardusters' V.I.P. (Waldorf, Md.) Home: 719 Shepherd St NW Washington DC 20011

DUNLOP, FRANK, theatre director; b. Leeds, Eng., Feb. 15, 1927; s. Charles Norman and Mary (Aarons) D.; B.A. with honors in English, University Coll., London, hon. fellow, 1978; postgrad. Shakespeare Inst., Old Vic Sch., London. Dir. of Piccolo Theatre, Manchester, Eng., 1954, Arts Council Midland Theatre Co., 1955; asst. dir. Bristol Old Vic, 1956; dir. Nottingham Playhouse, 1961-63; author and dir. of Les Freres Jacques at Adelphi Theatre, London; asso. dir. Nat. Theatre, London, prodns. include: Edward II, The White Devil, Macrune's Guevara, Home and Beauty, The Captain of Kopenick, also adminstrv. dir.; founder Young Vic Theatre, London, 1969, dir., 1969—, plays include: The Taming of the Shrew, The Comedy of Errors, The Maids and Deathwatch, The Alchemist, Bible One, French Without Tears, Much Ado About Nothing, Macbeth, Antony and Cleopatra, King Lear; dir. plays Belgian Nat. Theatre, including: Pantagleise, 1970, Antony and Cleopatra, 1971, Pericles, 1973; dir. Midsummer Night's Dream at Edinburgh (Scotland) Festival and Saville Theatre, London, 1967; dir. Joseph and the Amazing Technicolor Dreamcoat at Bklyn. Acad. Music, N.Y.C., dir. BAM Theatre Co., plays include: The Three Sisters, The New York Idea, The Devil's Disciple, The Play's the Thing, Julius Caesar; Broadway prodns.: Sherlock Holmes, Scapino, Habeas Corpus, Camelot. Bd. dirs. Edinburgh Internat. Festival, 1984—. Decorated comdr. Brit. Empire. Office: Edinburgh Internat Festival, 21 Market St, Edinburgh EH1 1BW Scotland Other: care Ernest Nives 200 W 57th St New York NY 10019

DUNN, DEAN ALAN, oceanographer, geologist, educator; b. Groton, Conn., Nov. 11, 1954; s. Edward Daniel Jr. and Margaret Elizabeth (Smillie) D.; m. Jana Marie Adams, May 24, 1986. B.S. in Biology cum laude, U. So. Calif., 1976, B.S. in Geology, 1977; Ph.D. in Oceanography, U. R.I., 1982. Lab. technician geology dept. U. So. Calif., Los Angeles, 1975-77; geophys. asst. Union Oil Co., Santa Fe Springs, Calif., summer 1976; grad. teaching asst. geology dept. Fla. State U., Tallahassee, 1977-78; grad. research asst. oceanography U. R.I., Kingston, 1978-82; staff scientist deep sea drilling project U. Calif., San Diego, 1983-86; asst. prof. geology U. So. Miss., Hattiesburg, 1983-86, assoc. prof., 1986—, vis. assoc. prof. Ctr. Marine Sci., 1987; summer faculty fellow U.S. Naval Oceanographic Office, Bay St. Louis, Miss., 1988; cruise scientist oceanography cruises U. So. Calif., 1976-77; shipboard scientist oceanography cruises U. R.I., 1979; shipboard sedimentologist deep sea drilling project, 1982; shipboard sci. rep., sedimentologist, 1983; lead scientist Oceanography Cruises, Naval Oceanographic office, 1988. Author: (with others) Initial Reports of the Deep Sea Drilling Project, vol. 85, 1985; co-editor, author vol. 93, 1987; contbg. author: Physical Geology, 1989; contbr. articles to profl. jours. Named Nat. Merit scholar, 1972-77, Trustee scholar U. So. Calif, 1972-77, Dolphin scholar U.S. Navy, 1973-77. Mem. Am. Assn. Petroleum Geologists, Geol. Soc. Am., Am. Geophys. Union, Soc. Econ. Paleontologists and Mineralogists, Mensa, Sigma Xi, Sigma Gamma Epsilon. Presbyterian. Avocations: photography, bicycling, racquetball, reading, music. Home: PO Box 8506 Hattiesburg MS 39406 Office: U So Miss Dept Geology S Sta Box 5044 Hattiesburg MS 39406

DUNN, FLOYD EMRYL, neurologist, psychiatrist, consultant; b. Wilkes-Barre, Pa., Apr. 25, 1910; s. Adrian Anson and Frances Amanda (Culver) D.; m. Wilda Kathryn Lauer, Aug. 14, 1943; children—Kathryn Alice (dec.), Deborah Lee. Student, Temple U., 1929-32; D.O., Phila. Coll. Osteo. Medicine, 1936. Diplomate Am. Osteo. Bd. Neurology and Psychiatry. Resident in neurology, psychiatry Still-Hildreth Hosp., 1941-45, staff psychiatrist, 1945-49; chmn. div. neurology, psychiatry Kirksville Coll. Osteo. Medicine, 1945-48, Kansas City Coll. Osteo. Medicine, U. Health Scis., Mo., 1949-68; mem. staff VA Hosp., Knoxville, Iowa, 1968-76, chief psychiatry service, 1970-76; clin. prof. neurology, psychiatry Coll. Osteo. Medicine, Des Moines, 1970-74; mem. Nat. Bd. Examiners for Osteo. Physicans and Surgeons, 1965-74, Excellence award, 1974, cons. neurology, psychiatry, Chgo., 1974—; cons., examiner sect. of disability determinations Mo. Dept. Elem. and Secondary Edn., Jefferson City, 1985—. Author: (monograph) History of the American College of Neuropsychiatrists, 1984. Contbr. articles to profl. jours. Mem. Iowa Adv. Council on Mental Health Ctrs., Des Moines, 1972-78, Central Regional Adv. Council for Comprehensive Psychiat. Services, Columbia, Mo., 1978-86. Fellow Am. Coll. Neuropsychiatrists (life, sec.-treas. 1948-52, pres. 1954-55, 63-64, Disting. Service award 1967, Disting. Fellow award 1984), Am. Assn. on Mental Deficiency; mem. Am. Osteo. Assn. (life, editorial cons. publs. 1958—, del. 1960-69, pres.'s adv. council 1973), Mo. Assn. Osteo. Physicians and Surgeons (hon. life, del. 1958-69, v.p. 1969-70), Phi Sigma Gamma (pres. grand council 1952-53, council sec.-treas. 1953-59, editor Speculum 1959-65, Meritorious Service award 1965, exec. sec.-treas. grand council 1980—), Alpha Phi Omega. Republican. Methodist. Lodges: Lions (pres. Gravois Mills, Mo. chpt. 1984-85, sec. 1985—, del. to internat. conv. 1985, 86, 87), Masons, Elks. Avocations: photography; travel; journalism. Home: Route 3 Box 504-A Gravois Mills MO 65037

DUNN, JESSIE JOYCE, psychotherapist, consultant; b. Pineville, Mo., July 16, 1930; d. Silas and Lucretia (Packwood) Clark; m. Robert E. Dunn, Dec. 13, 1958 (div. 1970); 1 child, Jonathan. BA in Soc. and Justice magna cum laude, U. Wash., 1974, MSW, 1977. Counselor Salvation Army, Seattle, 1977-78; therapist Divorce Lifeline, Seattle, 1977-84; pvt. practice specializing in psychotherapy Seattle, 1980—; practicum instr. U. Wash. Sch. Social Work, 1980-81. Screen clients Mcpl. Probations and Parole, Seattle, 1974; bd. dirs. Seattle Counseling, 1973-74, v.p.; coordinator of adult single programs Univ. Unitarian Ch., Seattle, 1979-83. Mem. Nat. Assn. Social Workers, Phi Beta Kappa. Democrat.

DUNN, JOHANNA ALEXANDRA READ, investment banker; b. N.Y.C., Mar. 7, 1946. B.A. summa cum laude, Barnard Coll., 1965; M.A. cum laude, Columbia U., 1967, Ph.D. magna cum laude, 1970; postgrad. The Sorbonne, U. Paris, 1969-70. With McKinsey & Co., Inc., N.Y.C., 1967; mng. editor European Bus., Paris, 1969-70; co-founder, chief bus. editor Tempo Economico, Lisbon, Portugal, 1970-74; chief fin. writer for Expresso Lisbon, 1970-74; fgn. correspondent Manchester Guardian, Portugal, 1973-74; communications cons. Citicorp, 1975-76, Norton Simon Inc., 1975-76, Council of Americas, 1975-76; communications specialist N.Y. Stock Exchange, Inc., 1976-78; exec. asst. to office of chmn. N.Y. Stock Exchange, 1978-79, asst. v.p. corp. planning, 1979-80; v.p. mktg. planning and support N.Y. Futures Exchange, 1980-81; asst. v.p. market ops. N.Y. Stock Exchange, 1981-83, asst. v.p. mktg. group, 1984-85; asst. v.p. communications dept., 1985-87; pres., chief exec. officer Stephen R. Petschek Investment Bankers, Greenwich, Ct., 1988—; cons. State Edn. Dept., State U. N.Y., 1975-81. Mem. Pres.'s Council Marymount Manhattan Coll., 1981—; mem. Cardinal's Com. of Laity for the 1980's, Archdiocese of N.Y. Woodrow Wilson vis. fellow, 1979-81; bd. dirs. Spl. Citizens Unltd. Inc., 1980—. Mem. Fin. Women's Assn., Investment Assn. N.Y., Bond Club, Wall St. Planning Group (v.p.), Phi Beta Kappa. Democrat. Presbyterian. Author: Counterpoint: A Book of Modern Poetry, Depois de 25 de Abril, Photo Exposé of 1974 Portugese Revolution; contbg. author Business: Its Nature and Environment; contbr. numerous poems to lit. publs. Avocations: hunting, horseback riding, photography, swimming, music. Home: 750 Park Ave New York NY 10021 Office: Stephen R Petschek Investment Bankers 34 Simmons Ln Greenwich CT 06830

DUNN, JOHN MICHAEL, association executive; b. Los Angeles, July 22, 1927; s. John Michael and Mary Janet (Murphy) D.; m. Mary Frances Hobbs, Nov. 17, 1950; children: Alan Michael, Neal Patrick. A.B., Harvard U., 1948; M. Pub. Adminstrn., Princeton U., 1959, M.A., 1960, Ph.D., 1961; grad., Nat. War Coll., 1967. Commd. 2d lt. U.S. Army, 1949, advanced through grades to maj. gen., 1971; personal asst. ambassador to Vietnam, 1963-64; asst. to v.p. of U.S. 1969-74; exec. dir. Council Internat. Econ. Policy, Office of Pres., 1974-76; pres. Can Mfrs. Inst., Washington, 1976—. Contbr. articles, reviews to profl. and popular jours. Decorated D.S.M., Legion of Merit, Silver Star, Bronze Star, Purple Heart; named Knight Comdr., Royal Order of Phoenix, Greece; recipient numerous fgn. decorations including Knights of Malta, Knights of Saint Denis. Mem. Pi Eta. Clubs: Pisces, City, Capitol Hill, 1925 F Street. Home: 2707 N Nelson St Arlington VA 22207 Office: Can Mfrs Inst 1625 Massachusetts Ave NW Washington DC 20036

DUNN, JOHN RAYMOND, JR., stockbroker; b. Pittsfield, Mass., Aug. 24, 1937; s. John Raymond and Margaret Mary (Coyne) D.; m. Rosemary Caine 1973; 1 son, John Raymond III, A.B., Boston Coll., 1960. Ins. agt. John Hancock Ins. Co., Boston, 1964-67; dist. mgr. Nat. Life Ins. Co., Montpelier, Vt., 1967-74; gen. agt. United Life & Accident Ins. Co., Concord, N.H., 1974—; stockbroker, regional mgr. Cornerstone Fin. Services, Inc., Boston, 1974-80; stockbroker, br. mgr. Weinrich, Zitzman, Whitehead Fin. Services, Inc., St. Louis, 1980—; pres. Dunn Assocs., Amherst, Mass., 1965—; field adv. mem. Pres. Adv. Council CFS-Div. Weinrich, Zitzman, Whitehead, Inc., 1982—; dir. Parents and Tchrs. for Social Responsibility, Moretown, Vt., 1982-85 ; lectr. in field; free-lance writer Investment Dealer Digest, 1980. Coordinator Wheels for Life Bike-a-Thon, Amherst St. Jude's Children's Hosp., 1988. Mem. Republican Town Com., Amherst, Mass., 1980—; dist. mgr. Chubb Securities Leaders' Club. Recipient Outstanding Agts. award, Nat. Life Ins. Co., 1971; Golden Circle award, Cornerstone Fin. Services, Inc., 1979; Outstanding Underwriter award, United Life & Accident Ins. Co., 1976; Equity Prodn. award Chubb Securities Corp., 1985, 86; named to White Mountain Club, 1974—(Club award 1984, 85, 86, 87), Leaders Club, 1985; recipient Spl. Achievement Broker award, Cornerstone Fin. Services, 1980; Outstanding Broker award, Weinrich, Zitzman Whitehead Fin Services, Inc. 1983, Spl. Products award, Weinrich, Zitzman, Whiteman Fin. Services, Inc., 1983, Total Revenues award, Weinrich, Zitzman, Whitehead Fin. Services, Inc., 1983, Equities award, Weinrich, Zitzman, Whiteman Fin. Services, Inc., 1983. Roman Catholic. Club: White Mountain.

DUNN, LYDIA, trading company executive; b. Hong Kong, Feb. 29, 1940; d. Yin Chuen Yeh and Yin-chu Bessie (Chen) D. BS, U. Calif., Berkeley, 1963; LLD (hon.), Chinese U. Hong Kong, 1984. Dir. John Swire & Sons (HK) Ltd., Republic of China, 1969—, Hong Kong and Shanghai Banking Corp., Hong Kong, 1981—; exec. dir. Swire Pacific, Ltd., Hong Kong, 1982—; dir. Cathay Pacific Airways, Ltd., Hong Kong, 1985—; chmn. Swire & Maclaine Ltd., Swire Loxley Ltd., Camberley Enterprises Ltd., Swire Mktg. Ltd., Internat. Adv. Bd. Volvo AB. Author: In the Kingdom of the Blind, 1983. Mem. Hong Kong Legis. Council, 1976-88, exec. council, 1982, sr. mem., 1985-88; chmn. Hong Kong Trade Devel. Council, 1983—; bd. dirs. Mass Transit Ry. Corp., 1979-85; active World Wildlife Fund, Hong Kong, 1982-85. Decorated officer Order of Brit. Empire , comdr. Order of Brit. Empire (England); named Justice of Peace Hong Kong Govt., 1976; recipient Trade award Prime Minister of Japan, 1987. Mem. Trade Policy Research Centre (council mem. London chpt.), Internat. Council of Asia Soc., Hong Kong Mgmt., Fedn. Hong Kong Industries (gen. com. 1978-83), Hong Kong Gen. C. of C. Office: John Swire & Sons (HK) Ltd, 5/F Swire House 9 Connaught Rd, Hong Kong Hong Kong

DUNN, M(ORRIS) DOUGLAS, lawyer; b. Ionia, Mich., Nov. 1, 1944; s. Morris Frederick and Lola Adella (Gee) D.; m. Jill Lynn Fasbender, July 22, 1967; children—Brooks, Gillian, Joshua. B.S. in Mech. Engring., U. Mich., 1967; J.D., Vanderbilt U., 1970. Assoc. Winthrop Stimson, Putnam & Roberts, N.Y.C., 1970-78, ptnr. 1978-84; sr. v.p., mng. dir. Shearson Lehman Bros. Inc., N.Y.C., 1984-85; ptnr. Milbank, Tweed, Hadley & McCloy, N.Y.C., 1985—. Contbr. articles to profl. jours. Mem. ABA (corp. fin. com. in Pub. Utility law sect., vice chmn. 1980-86, chmn. 1986—, council mem. 1987—, fed. regulation of securities com. bus. and law sect. mem. 1981—), N.Y.C. Bar Assn. (chmn. nuclear tech. and law com. bus. and banking law sect. 1976-77), Internat. Bar Assn. (vice chmn. com. K 1986—), alumni bd. Vanderbilt U. Law Sch., 1987—. Chatham Fish and Game. Club: Down Town (N.Y.C.), Canoe Brook Country (Summit, N.J.). Home: 72 Chandler Rd Chatham NJ 07928 Office: Milbank Tweed Hadley & McCloy 1 Chase Manhattan Plaza New York NY 10005

DUNN, NOEL LEE, insurance company executive; b. Cleve., Jan. 18, 1942; s. Leon John and Ruth (Slyh) D.; B.A., U. N.C., 1964. Mktg. supr. Aetna Casualty and Surety, Charlotte, N.C., 1964-69; partner Pilot Ins. Agy., Winston Salem, N.C., 1969-86; pres., chief exec. officer Rollins Burdick Hunter of N.C., Inc., 1987— bd. dirs. First Union Nat. Bank; v.p. Mgmt. Oecisions. Trustee Nat. Nature Conservancy, 1978-80, 81—, also vice chmn., N.Am. Wildlife Found. ; dir. Nat. Audubon Soc., 1978—, vice chmn., 1985—; trustee Ducks Unltd., 1974-82, sr. v.p., 1976-81, trustee imeritus, 1981—; hon. pres. Izaak Walton League Am., 1978; trustee N.C. Sch. Arts Found., 1976-80; chmn. steering com. N.C. Sch. of Arts, 1980—; bd. dirs. Southeastern Center for Contemporary Art, Winston-Salem, 1976—, chmn. bd. trustees, 1977-79; chmn. steering com. Awards in Visual Arts, 1980-82; trustee Forsyth County Nature Sci. Center, 1978-82. Mem. Devel. Council U. N.C. C.P.C.U. Republican. Episcopalian. Clubs: Rotary; Old Town (Winston-Salem); Union League (N.Y.C.); University (Houston); Long Hope, Athletic (Charlotte). Office: Box 203 Winston-Salem NC 27102

DUNN, RICHARD JOSEPH, investment counselor; b. Chgo., Apr. 5, 1924; s. Richard Joseph and Margaret Mary (Jennett) D.; A.B., Yale U., 1948; LL.B., Harvard U., 1951; M.B.A., Stanford U., 1956; m. Marygrace Calhoun, Oct. 13, 1951; children—Richard, Marianne, Anthony, Gregory, Noelle. Admitted to Tex. bar, 1952; mem. firm Carrington, Gowen, Johnson & Walker, Dallas, 1951-54; investment counselor Scudder, Stevens & Clark, San Francisco, 1956-84, v.p., 1965-77, sr. v.p., 1977-84, gen. partner, 1974-84; ret., 1984. Mem. Democratic State Central Com., Calif., 1962; mem. San Francsico Dem. County Central Com., 1963-66; bd. dirs. Mercy High Sch., 1978-81. Served with AUS, 1943-46. Decorated Purple Heart. Mem. Knight of the Sovereign Mil. Hospitaller Order of St. John of Jerusalem of Rhodes and of Malta 1978— (Officer Cross of Merit, 1986, Chancellor 1987, bd. of dirs. 1987—), Knight of the Sacred Mil. Constantinian Order of St. George 1988—. Roman Catholic. Home: 530 Junipero Serra Blvd San Francisco CA 94127

DUNN, ROBIN, television executive; b. Mount Gambier, Australia, Mar. 11, 1935; s. Percy Henry and Elsie Clair (Bradford) D.; m. Marie Woolfitt Stott, Jan. 16, 1965; children: Stephen Donald, Nigel Robin, Tina Louise. A, South Australia Inst. Tech., 1963. Printing clk. 20th Century Fox Film Corp., Adelaide, South Australia, 1954-61; sales rep. Lever and Kitchen, Adelaide, 1961-65; sales rep. South Australian Telecasters Ltd., Adelaide, 1965-71, sales mgr., 1971-85, mktg. mgr., 1985-88, Christmas appeal mgr., 1988—. Mem. Advt. Inst. Australia (assoc.). Liberal. Mem. Ch. Australia. Club: Marcom (Adelaide). Office: South Australian Telecasters, 45-49 Park Terrace, 5081 Gilberton Australia

DUNN, RONALD HOLLAND, engineer; b. Balt., Sept. 15, 1937; s. Delmas Joseph and Edna Grace (Holland) D.; m. Verona Lucille Lambert, Aug. 17, 1958; children: Ronald H., Jr. (dec.), David R., Brian W. Student U. S.C., 1956-58; BS in Engring., Johns Hopkins U., 1969. Field engr. Balt. & Ohio R.R., Balt., 1958-66; chief engr. yards, shops, trackwork DeLeuw, Cather & Co., Washington, 1966-73; mgr. engring. support Parsons-Brinckerhoff-Tudor-Bechtel, Atlanta, 1973-76; dir. railroad engring. Morrison-Knudsen Co., Inc., Boise, Idaho, 1976-78; v.p. Parsons Brinckerhoff-Centec, Inc., McLean, Va., 1978-83; v.p., area mgr., tech. dir. ry. engring., profl. assoc. Parsons Brinckerhoff Quade & Douglas, Inc., McLean and Pitts., 1983-84; dir. transp. engring. R.L. Banks & Assocs., Inc., Washington, 1984; pres. R.H. Dunn & Assocs., Inc., Fairfax, Va., 1984—; insp. ry. and rail transit facilities, Europe, 1980, 82, 84, China and Hong Kong, 1985; involved in engring. of 15 railroads and 16 rail transit systems throughout N. Am.; guest Japan Railway Civil Engring. Assn., 1972, French Nat. Railroads and Paris Transport Authority, 1988; mem. adv. com. track engrs. U.S. Dept. Transp., 1968-71. Chmn. Cub Scout Pack, Boy Scouts Am., 1972-73, committeeman, 1973-75, troop committeeman, 1979-85, chmn. transp. com. Mem. Am. Mgmt. Assn., Am. Ry. Engring. Assn., ASCE, Am. Public Transit Assn., Soc. Am. Mil. Engrs., Roadmasters and Maintenance of Way Assn. of Am., Am. Ry. Bridge and Bldg. Assn., Constrn. Specifications Inst., Nat. Soc. Profl. Engrs., Transp. Research Bd., Soc. Profl. Mgmt. Cons., Can. Soc. Civil Engring., Can. Urban Transit Assn., Inst. Transp. Engrs., Ry. Tie Assn., Inst. of Rapid Transit, Phi Kappa Sigma. Methodist. Office: 10608 Orchard St Fairfax VA 22030

DUNN, WENDELL EARL, III, management consultant, business educator; b. Boca Raton, Fla., Aug. 20, 1945; s. Wendell Earl Jr. and Lillian (Daniels) D.; m. Kathleen Ann Riley, Mar. 29, 1981. B.A., Johns Hopkins U., 1966; M.B.A., U. So. Calif., 1973; Ph.D., U. Mich., 1981. Asst. to dir. personnel Johns Hopkins U., Balt., 1967-68; pilot project mgr. Chlorine Tech. Ltd., Sydney, Australia, 1968-71; energy analyst Alex Brown & Sons, Balt., 1973-74; lectr. bus. adminstrn. U. Mich., Ann Arbor, 1977-80; asst. prof. bus. adminstrn. Coll. of William and Mary, Williamsburg, Va., 1980-81; prin. W.E. Dunn & Assocs., Phila., 1981—; lectr. mgmt. Wharton Sch. U. Pa., Phila., 1981-82, 84—, course head Entrepreneurship & New Ventures (grad.), 1986—, mem. faculty MBA Program, 1988; adj. assoc. prof. Columbia U., 1983-84; mem. planning com. N.J. workshops U.S. Dept. Commerce Nat. Innovation, 1986, leader N.Y.C. workshops, 1987. Contbr. articles to profl. jours.; mem. editorial bd. Jour. of Bus. Venturing, 1987—. Active Luth. Student Found., Ann Arbor, 1978-80; cons. Bus. Vols. for Arts, Phila., 1982-83; active Luth. Retirement Homes, Phila., 1983-84. Robert Rodkey Found. fellow, 1974-75. Mem. Acad. Mgmt., Strategic Mgmt. Soc., Am. Soc. Inventors (bd. dirs. 1984-87, nat. pres. 1985-86), Beta Gamma Sigma, Phi Kappa Phi. Republican. Clubs: Down Town (bd. govs. 1986—), Faculty of U. Pa. Avocations: sailing, gardening. Home: 443 Gladstone Ave Haddonfield NJ 08033 Office: W E Dunn & Assocs PO Box 2036 Haddonfield NJ 08033

DUNN, WILLIAM DAVID, lawyer, writer; b. Tampa, Fla., July 2, 1933; s. Thomas Henry and Eleanor (Stephens) D. B.S. in Journalism, Fla. State U., 1953; J.D., U. Fla., 1958; postgrad. in French studies U. Paris, 1965-66, in art history Ecole du Louvre, Paris, 1966-67. Bar: N.Y. 1972, U.S. Dist. Ct. (so. and ea. dists.) N.Y. 1974. Night news editor Nippon Times, Tokyo, 1954-55; arts editor St. Petersburg Times, Fla., 1958-65; bur. chief MacNens News Agy., Paris, 1965-66; account exec. Foote, Cone & Belding, Paris, 1967-68; editorial dir. Advt. Trade Publs., N.Y.C., 1968-70; def. atty. Legal Aid Soc., N.Y.C., 1972—. Editor monthly mag. Art Direction, 1968-70, FotoTimes, 1970-71. Area coordinator Gt. Books Found., discussion groups, Fla., 1959-63; mem. coordinating council Great Decisions, fgn. policy discussion groups, St. Petersburg, Fla., 1961-64; bd. dirs. Fla. Arts Council, 1963-65, Performing Arts Alumni Theatre, N.Y.C., 1983—; mem. adv. bd. New Mus., N.Y.C., 1975—. Served with U.S. Army, 1953-55. Recipient Key to City, Mayor of St. Petersburg, 1965. Mem. N.Y. State Bar Assn., New York County Bar Assn., N.Y. State Defenders (bd. dirs. 1976—, amicus curiae com. 1983—, treas. 1985—), Gold Key, Alpha Tau Omega, Delta Sigma Pi. Democrat. Clubs: Union (Tokyo); American (Paris). Home: 77 W 85th St Apt 2-C New York NY 10024 also: 2118 Marjory Ave Tampa FL 33606 Office: Legal Aid Soc 80 Lafayette St New York NY 10013

DUNNE, DIANE C., advertising executive; b. Milw.; d. Francis and Ruth Carolyn (Borman) Cantine; 1 child, Dana Philip. B.S., Marquette U., 1970; Exec. M.B.A., NYU, 1985. Mgr. advt. NBC, N.Y.C., 1975-77; dir. advt. CBS, N.Y.C., 1977-80; dir. advt. Bloomingdale's, N.Y.C., 1980—; dir. 750 Park Ave. Corp., N.Y.C., 1985—. Author: Guidelines to Advertising All News Radio, 1976. Author: Guidlines for Catalogue Copywriters, 1987; asst. editor Am. Cancer Soc., Gourmet Guide for Busy People by Famous People, 1985, The Internat. Directory of Disting. Leadership; contbr. articles to profl. jours. Chmn. Am. Cancer Soc., N.Y.C., 1980—; chair St. James Ch. Feed the Homeless com., N.Y.C., 1984—; mem. pastoral and worship com. St. James Altar Guild. Mem. Fashion Group (co-chair regional com.), Women's Econ. Roundtable (mem. program and membership coms.), N.Y.U. Exec. MBA Assn. Episcopalian. Avocations: opera; jogging; skiing; squash. Home: 750 Park Ave New York NY 10021 Office: Bloomingdales 155 E 60th St New York NY 10022

DUNNINGTON, WALTER GREY, JR., lawyer, food and tobacco company executive; b. N.Y.C., Feb. 5, 1927; s. Walter Grey and Allen (Gray) D.; m. Jacqueline Cochran, Apr. 26, 1958; m. Patricia MacPhee, Sept. 21, 1972; children: Walter Grey III, India M. BA, U. Va., 1948, LLB, 1950. Bar: N.Y. 1952. Assoc. Rathbone, Perry, Kelley & Drye, N.Y.C., 1950-54; ptnr. Dunnington, Bartholow & Miller, N.Y.C., 1954-75, sr. ptnr., 1976-81; sr. v.p., gen. counsel Standard Brands Inc., N.Y.C., 1981; exec. v.p., gen. counsel Nabisco Brands, Inc., East Hanover, N.J., 1981-87; sr. v.p., dep. gen. counsel RJR Nabisco, Inc., N.Y.C., 1987-88, counsel to pres., chief exec. officer, 1988—; mem. legal steering com. Grocery Mfrs. Am., Inc., Washington; bd. dirs. Brittania Industries, Ltd., Bombay, Nabisco Brands, Toronto, Ont., Canada. Bd. govs. N.Y. Hosp., N.Y.C.; trustee Algernon Sydney Sullivan Found., Morristown, N.J., Boys' Club N.Y., N.Y.C., Sprague Found., N.Y.C., Food and Drug Law Inst., Washington; trustee emeritus Woodberry Forest Sch., Va. Served with USNR, 1945. Mem. ABA, Assn. Bar City N.Y., N.Y. State Bar Assn. Episcopalian. Clubs: Brook (N.Y.C.) (v.p., sec., gov.); Racquet and Tennis (N.Y.C.); Nat. Golf Links Am. (Southampton, N.Y.) (v.p., dir.); Deepdale (L.I., N.Y.); Somerset Hills Country (Bernardsville, N.J.). Home: Roxiticus Rd PO Box 479 Gladstone NJ 07934 Office: RJR Nabisco Inc 100 DeForest Ave East Hanover NJ 07936

DUNROSSIL, JOHN WILLIAM MORRISON (2D VISCOUNT), governor of Bermuda; b. May 22, 1926; s. William Shepherd Morrison D.; m. 1951 (div.), 3 sons, 1 dau.; m. Diana Mary Cunliffe, 1969; 2 daus. Ed. Oriel Coll., Oxford U. Joined Commonwealth Relations Office, 1951; pvt. sec. to Sec. of State, 1952-54; 2d sec., Canberra, Australia, 1954-56; assigned Commonwealth Relations Office, 1956-58; 1st sec., acting dep. high commr., Dacca, E. Pakistan, 1958-60; 1st sec., Pretoria/Capetown, S.Africa, 1961-64; assigned Fgn. Office, 1964-68, Diplomatic Service Adminstrv. Office, 1965; on loan to Intergovtl. Maritime Consultative Orgn., 1968-70; counsellor, head of chancery, Ottawa, 1970-75; counsellor, Brussels, 1975-78; high commr. of Fiji, Republic Nauru and Tavalu, 1978-82; high commr. Barbados, Antigua and Barbuda, St. Vincent and Grenadines, St. Lucia, Commonwealth of Dominica, and Grenada, also Brit. Govt. rep. to West Indies Assoc. States, 1982-83; gov. and comdr.-in-chief Bermuda, 1983—. Served as flight lt. RAF, 1945-48. Decorated knight Order Hosp. St. John Jerusalem, companion Order St. Michael and St. George. Clubs: Royal Air Force, Royal Commonwealth Soc.; Cercle Royal Gaulois (Brussels). Address: care Fgn and Commonwealth Office, Downing St, London SW 1 England also: Govt House, Hamilton Bermuda *

DUNST, KLAUS HERMANN, strategic planning executive; b. Bad Schwartau, Fed. Republic of Germany, Aug. 22, 1946; s. Hermann Gustav and Ingeborg Alice (Maass) D.; m. Inez Carolinn Rupprecht, Aug. 4, 1968; children: Kirsten Caroline, Christian Edward. BA summa cum laude, U. Minn., 1968; MS in Indsl. Adminstrn., Carnegie Mellon U., 1970; Dr. Rer. Pol. (PhD), Technische Hochschule, Darmstadt, Fed. Republic Germany, 1978. Mgmt. cons. The Boston Cons. Group, 1970-72; project mgr. Kearney Mgmt. Cons., Dusseldorf, Fed. Republic Germany, 1972-79; dep. dir. strategic planning Siemens AG, Munich, Fed. Republic Germany, 1979-81; dir. corp. planning Siemens Corp., Iselin, N.J., 1981-82; v.p. bus. analysis and strategic planning Siemens Corp. Research & Support, Inc., Iselin, 1982—. Author: Portfolio Management, 1979. Resident mem. Deutsche Verein, N.Y.C., 1984. Mem. Phi Beta Kappa. Lutheran. Home: 3 Jaywood Manor Dr Bricktown NJ 08723 Office: Siemens Corp 186 Wood Ave S Iselin NJ 08830

DUNTON, JAMES GERALD, association executive; b. Circleville, Ohio, Nov. 10, 1899; s. Oscar Howard and Florence (Nightengale) D.; A.B., Harvard U., 1923, M.Ed., 1928; m. Dorothy Winfough, Oct. 10, 1944. Freelance author, 1925-34; Fed. Projects dir., Ohio, 1935-37; spl. rep. Fed. N.W. Ter. Sesquicentennial Commn., 1938; editor Ohio Democracy, 1939-40; Ohio field rep. Office Govt. Reports, Exec. Office of Pres., 1940-41; dir. spl. activities Office Sec. Def., 1950-61; exec. dir. Va. Health Care Assn., 1965-75, spl. rep., 1975—; Washington rep. Am. Chess Found., 1962-81; adv. council Oliver Wendell Holmes Assn., 1966—. Mem. vets. com. Presdl. Inaugurations, 1965, 69, 77; pres. Nat. Capital USO, Washington, 1966-67, mem. nat. council, 1966—; mem. Va. State Adv. Com. Adult Services, 1972; disting. sponsor 100th Anniversary 1st Battle of Bull Run, 1961. Served with Ambulance Corps, A.E.F., U.S. Army, 1918-19, to maj. AUS, World War II, Korea. Recipient cert. of appreciation Nat. Press Club, 1955, Commendation award Pres.'s Com. on Employment of Handicapped, 1963; decorated Army Commendation medal; hon. fellow Truman Library Inst. Mem. Nat. Assn. Execs., U.S. Army Hon. Ret. Res., SAR, Am. Legion (Nat. Comdr.'s award 1975), Vets. World War I, DAV, VFW, U.S. Army Ambulance Service Assn., Mil. Order World Wars, Ohio Soc. Washington, Soc. of Va. (pres. 1984—). Presbyterian (elder). Club: Harvard (Washington). Author: Wild

Asses, 1925; Murders in Lovers Lane, 1927; Maid and a Million Men, 1928; Counterfeit Wife, 1930; Honey's Money, 1933; Queen's Harem, 1933; (anthology) C'est La Guerre, 1927. Contbr. articles to mags., newspapers. Address: 2820 Bisvey Dr Falls Church VA 22042

DUPÉRÉ, JEAN, mining company executive; b. Montreal, Que., Can., Nov. 19, 1942; m. Michèle Thibert Dupéré, Dec. 18, 1975; children: Mathieu, Simon, Catherine. BA, Jean-De-Brébeouf, Montreal, 1966; B in Civil Law, McGill U., Montreal, 1969. Bar: Que., Can. Assoc. Byers, Casgrain, Montreal, 1969-78; exec. v.p. Lake Asbestos of Que., Black Lake, 1978-81; pres., chief exec. officer Lake Asbestos of Que., 1981—, Lab Chrysotile Inc., Thetford Mines, Que., 1986—; bd. dirs. Francomet, France, Capco Pipe, Ala., Ark. and Ind. Mem. Can. Inst. Mining, Que. Asbestos Mining Assn., Asbestos Inst. Can. (chmn. bd. 1984), Asbestos Internat. Assn., Asbestos Internat. Assn. N.Am. Home: 632 Laflamme St, Thetford Mines, PQ Canada G6G 3G7 Office: Lab Chrysotile Inc, 835 Mooney PO Box 459, Thetford Mines, PQ Canada G6G 5T5

DU PLESSIS, BAREND JACOBUS, minister of finance Republic of South Africa; b. Johannesburg, Republic of South Africa, Jan. 19, 1940; s. Jan Hendrik and Martha Johanna Wilhelmina (Botha) Du P.; m. Antoinette Van Den Berg, Jan. 6, 1962; children: Jean Henri, Vanessa, Charl Guillaume, Berno Jacques. BS, Potchefstroom U. Christian Higher Edn.; grad., Tchrs. Tng. Coll., Potchefstroom. Tchr., Hoëer Seunskool Helpmekaar, Johannesburg, 1962; adminstrv. sec. SABC, Johannesburg, 1962-68; systems engr., mktg. rep. IBM (SA), Johannesburg, 1968-74; M.P., 1974—, minister edn. and tng., 1983, minister of fin., 1984—. Mem. National Party. Office: Ministry of Fin, 240 Vermeulen St, Pretoria 0002, Republic of South Africa *

DU PLOOY, ROBERT ABRAHAM, former South African ambassador to France; b. Bloemfontein, South Africa, July 5, 1921; s. Jacob Bester and Eileen Beryl (Wicks) du P.; m. Giulia Vera Bonino, Oct. 10, 1945; 1 son, Robert Etienne. B. Econs., U. South Africa, 1949, LL.B., 1952; J.D., U. Cologne (W. Ger.), 1958. Bar: South Africa 1953. Home: 90 Murray St, Brooklyn, 0001 Pretoria Republic of South Africa

DUPOND, PATRICK, ballet dancer; b. Paris. Studied with Max Bozzoni and at Paris Opera Sch. Mem. Paris Opera Ballet, 1974—, promoted through corps, prin. dancer (étoile), 1980—; appeared in Giselle, The Sleeping Beauty, Romeo and Juliet, Don Quixote, La Bayadere, Le Corsaire pas de deux, Etudes, Balanchine's Rubies, Petit's The Phantom of the Opera and Queen of Spades, Song of the Earth, Daphnis and Chloe, A Midsummer Night's Dream, Bolero, Firebird, Schema, La Sonatine Beaurocratic, Vaslav (created for him by John Neumeier), Alvin Ailey's Precipice; appeared as guest artist with numerous internat. dance cos.; appeared at Met. Opera's Centennial Celebration, 1984. Recipient Gold medal, spl. citation for tech. excellence Varna competition, 1976. Office: care Paris Opera Ballet, 8 rue Scribe, F-75009 Paris France also: care Paul Szilard Prodns 161 W 73rd St New York NY 10023 *

DUPONG, WILLIAM GREGG, physician; b. Bklyn., Aug. 31, 1911; s. David William and Bertha (Ferris) D.; B.S., Columbia U., 1935; M.D., L.I. Coll., 1939; m. Jessie MacLeman, Feb. 7, 1942. Intern, Norwegian Hosp., Bklyn., 1939-40; resident Swedish Hosp., Bklyn., 1940-41; practice medicine, specializing in occupational medicine and surgery, Bklyn., 1942—; mem. staff Lutheran Med. Center; exam. physician N.Y. Telephone Co., 1943-53, med. dir., L.I., 1953-66, L.I., Upstate N.Y. Telephone, 1966-69, Manhattan, Bklyn., Queens, 1969-75, med. dir. clin. tech., 1975-76; dir. clin. lab. N.Y.C. Dept. Health, 1965-77; cons. Workers' compensation N.Y.C. Law Dept., 1976—; lectr. dept. environ. medicine Coll. Medicine Down-State Med. Center; chmn. indsl. medicine com. Luth. Med. Center, mem. tissue rev. com., legal def. com., 1982—; mem. impartial specialist adv. com., mem. rehab. adv. com. N.Y. State Workers' Compensation Bd.; chmn. Council Tb and Health Assns. N.Y. Mem. Park Slope Civic Council, 1958—. Diplomate in occupational medicine Am. Bd. Preventive Medicine; diplomate Am. Bd. Family Practice (recert. 1976, 82); certified instr. cardiopulmonary resuscitation N.Y. Heart Assn. Fellow Am. Coll. Preventive Medicine, Am. Acad. Family Practice, Am. Acad. Compensation Medicine, Indsl. Med. Assn., N.Y. Indsl. Med. Assn., N.Y. Acad. Medicine, Am. Acad. Occupational Medicine, Am. Pub. Health Assn.; mem. N.Y. Pub. Health Assn., Royal Soc. Health, AMA, N.Y. State (sec. sect. occupational medicine 1975, sec. 1976, vice chmn. sect. legal medicine and workers' compensation 1977-78, chmn. 1978—), Kings County (chmn. adv. com. on indsl. medicine, chmn. indsl. health com., pub. health com. 1968—, mem. workers' compensation com. 1968—, chmn. 1976-80, peer rev. com. 1971—) med. socs., Am., N.Y. heart assns., Bklyn. Tb and Respiratory Disease Assn. (dir., exec. com., med. adv. com., v.p. 1965-68, pres. 1968-70), Am. Lung Assn. (rep. dir. bd. dirs. 1965-80), Assn. Tchrs. Preventive Medicine, N.Y. State Acad. Gen. Practice (indsl. med. adv. com. 1969—), Nat. Council on Alcholism, Am. Acad. Compensation Medicine (gov. 1971—). Methodist. Club: Masons. Contbr. articles to profl. jours. Home: 555 1st St Brooklyn NY 11215

DUPONT, DANIEL, ambassador; b. Paris, June 7, 1931; s. Louis Jacques and Jeanne Louise (Mathias) D.; m. Athena Alonzo; children: Sylvie, Isabelle, Charles, Etienne. BA in Law, U. Paris, 1954; diploma, Ecole Nationale France d'Outre-Mer, Paris, 1955. Adminstr. overseas service Govt. Mauritania, 1958-61; sec. Laos embassy French Ministry of Fgn. Affairs, Vientiane, 1962-65; 1st sec. Seoul, Korea, 1965-69; 2d counsellor Bonn, Fed. Republic of Germany, 1972-77; 1st councillor Antananapivo, Madagascar, 1980-84; French ambassador to Fiji, 1984—; lectr. in field. Contbr. articles to profl. jours. Served as lt. French Army, 1956-58. Decorated Knight of Nat. Order of Merit, Legion of Honor, Officer Gen. Merit, Officer of Order Mil. Cols., Veteran's Cross. Roman Catholic. Home: 36 Rue des Fontaines, 92310 Sevres France Office: French Embassy, Pvt Mail Bag, Suva 1 Fiji

DUPONT, JOHN, television producer, director, writer; b. Troy, N.Y., June 5, 1948; s. William and Marian Theresa (Northrup) D. A.A.S. in Media Tech., Pima Community Coll., Tucson, 1982. Organist, 1959-71; Organ sales mgr. Muller Music Ctr., Tucson, 1973-74; printed circuit bd. digitizer Compuroute, Inc. Dallas, 1974-77; computer operator for various firms, Tucson, 1977-79; TV producer/dir. Tucson Med. Ctr., 1979—; music instr. Baldwin Music Ctr., Tucson, 1982-85. Composer numerous songs. Served with U.S. Army, 1971-73. Republican. Roman Catholic. Office: Tucson Med Ctr 5301 E Grant Rd Tucson AZ 85733

DU PONT, ROBERT LOUIS, JR., physician; b. Toledo, Mar. 25, 1936; s. Robert Louis and Martha Ireton (Lancashire) DuP.; m. Helen Gayden Spink, July 14, 1962; children: Elizabeth, Caroline. BA, Emory U., 1958; MD, Harvard U., 1963. Diplomate Am. Bd. Psychiatry and Neurology. Intern Western Res. U., 1963-64; resident in psychiatry Harvard Med. Sch., 1964-66; clin. assoc. NIH, 1966-68; research psychiatrist, acting assoc. dir. for community services D.C. Dept. Corrections, Washington, 1968-70; practice medicine specializing in psychiatry 1968—; adminstr. Narcotics Treatment Adminstrn., D.C. Dept. Human Resources, 1970-73; acting adminstr. Alcohol, Drug Abuse and Mental Health Adminstrn., HEW, Rockville, Md., 1974; dir. Nat. Inst. on Drug Abuse, HEW, Rockville, 1973-78, Spl. Action Office for Drug Abuse Prevention, Exec. Office Pres., Washington, 1973-75; pres. Inst. for Behavior and Health Inc., 1978—, Am. Council for Drug Edn., 1980-85; U.S. del. UN Commn. on Narcotic Drugs, 1973-78; mem. Coordinating Council on Juvenile Justice and Delinquency Prevention, Dept. Justice, 1974-78; assoc. clin. prof. psychiatry and behavioral scis. George Washington Med. Sch., 1972-80; clin. prof. psychiatry Georgetown U. Med. Sch., 1980—; vis. assoc. clin. prof. psychiatry Harvard U. Med. Sch., 1978-84; chmn. Ctr. Behavioral Medicine, 1978—; v.p. Bensinger, DuPont Assocs., Inc, 1982—. Contbr. articles in fields of drug abuse, criminology and mental health to profl. jours.; appeared on Good Morning America, ABC-TV, 1978-80. Bd. dirs. Washington Soc. for Performing Arts, 1972-76; mem. adv. com. Washington Jr. League, 1972-76. Served to surgeon (maj.) USPHS, 1966-68. Fellow Am. Psychiat. Assn.; mem. Washington Psychiat. Soc., World Psychiat. Assn., Pan Am. Med. Assn., Phobia Soc. Am. (pres. 1982-85). Home: 8708 Susanna Ln Chevy Chase MD 20815 Office: 6191 Executive Blvd Rockville MD 20852

DUPORTAIL-HEUSSAFF, HELÉNE MARIE, gynecologist; b. Brittany, France, Nov. 7, 1949; divorced; children: Christelle, Matthieu. MD, U. France, Nantes, 1974; specialist in gynecology, U. France, Angers, 1977. Practice medicine specializing in gynecology Nantes, 1979—. Roman Catholic. Home: Bel-Air, La Chapelle sur Erdre, 44240 Nantes France Office: 3 bis Blvd des Belges, 44000 Nantes France

DUPREE, SAMUEL HARDY, JR., senior software analyst; b. Phila., Feb. 25, 1953; s. Samuel H. and Louise D. B.S., Pa. State U., 1974, M.S., 1978. Programming cons. Computation Ctr., Pa. State U., 1975-78; instr. physics and computer sci. Rose-Hulman Inst. Tech., 1978-81; programmer/analyst Gen. Electric Fed. and Electronic Systems Div., Phila., 1981-86, sr. software analyst, 1986—. Mem. Am. Astron. Soc., Soc. Indsl. and Applied Math., Astron. Soc. Pacific, IEEE Computer Soc., Assn. Computing Machinery. Baptist. Office: Gen Electric Fed & Electronic Div PO Box 8555 Philadelphia PA 19101

DUPREY, JEAN, pediatrician; b. Rouen, France, June 27, 1947; s. Maurice and Française (Isaac) D.; m. Marie-Claude Fievet, 1977; children: Marie, Amelie. MD, U. Rouen, 1976. Intern, then resident Internat. Cen. Hospitaulier Lier Univesitaire de Lille, France, 1973-78; practice medicine specializing in pediatrics and allergies Temps Partiel Cen. Hospitaulier Maubeuge (France) Depuis, France, 1979—. Contbr. articles to profl jours. Mem. French Pediatric Soc., French Allergy Soc. Roman Catholic. Home: Le Prieure, 1 Rue Vauban, 59600 Maubeuge France

DUPUIS, MICHELE, library director; b. Montreal, Que., Can., July 22, 1944; d. Gabriel and Yolande (Dubois) D. BA in Art History, U. Montreal, 1978, MLS, 1980. Asst. librarian Bibliothèque Municipale de repentigny, Que., 1964-76; dir. Bibliothèque Monicipale des Deux-Montagnes, Que., 1980-83; art and architecture slide curator Nat. Gallery of Can., Ottawa, Ont., Can., 1984-85; dir. Bibliothèque Pierrefonds Dollard-des-Ormeaux, Que., 1985—. Mem. Assn. des Directeurs des Bibliothèques Publique du Que., Corp. Bibliothèques Profl. du Que., Conférence des Directeurs des Bibliothèques Publique. Office: Bibliothèque Pierrefonds, Dollard-des-Ormeaux, 13555 Blvd, Pierrefonds, PQ Canada H9A 1A6

DUPUIS, RUSSELL DEAN, electrical engineer, research scientist; b. Kankakee, Ill., July 9, 1947; s. Rudolph William and Evelyn Marie (Hoevet) D.; m. Dana Elizabeth Gammage, Nov. 19, 1973; 1 child, Elizabeth Anne. BEE, U. Ill., 1970, MEE, 1971, PhD in Elec. Engring., 1973. Mem. tech. staff Tex. Instruments Corp., Dallas, 1973-74, Rockwell Internat. Corp., Anaheim, Calif., 1975-79; mem. tech. staff AT&T Bell Labs., Murray Hill, N.J., 1979-85, disting. tech. staff mem., 1985—. Contbr. articles to profl. jours. Recipient Disting. MTS award AT&T-Bell Labs., 1985, Young Scientist award GaAs Symposium, 1986, Disting. Alumnus award U. Ill., 1987. Fellow IEEE (Morris Liebmann award 1985); mem. Am. Phys. Soc., Electrochem. Soc., Electronics Materials Com. Office: AT&T Bell Labs 600 Mountain Ave Murray Hill NJ 07974-2070

DUPUY, ELBERT NEWTON, obstetrician, gynecologist, educator; b. Parral, W.Va., Oct. 19, 1904; s. Elbert Stephenson and Lillian (Dixon) DuP.; m. Ruth Christine Griffenhagen, May 7, 1938; children: James Newton, Karl Frederick Griffenhagen, William Edwin Stuart. BS, U. W.Va., 1930, Duke U., 1932. Diplomate Am. Bd. Ob/gyn. Intern Ch. Home and Infirmary, Balt., 1933; resident in obstetrics U. Hosp., Balt., 1934-36; fellow Rotunda Hosp., Dublin, Ireland, 1931; practice medicine specializing in Ob/gyn Beckley, W.Va., 1936-42, Quincy, Ill., 1946-84; mem. staff Blessing Hosp., 1946-84, chief ob/gyn, 1975-77; assoc. clin. prof. ob/gyn So. Ill. U., Springfield. Mem. Nat. Council Boy Scouts Am., 1968—; trustee Robert Morris Coll., Carthage, Ill., 1964-69, Spastic Paralysis Research Found., 1956—. Served with M.C., U.S. Army, 1942-46. Decorated Silver Star, Bronze Star; recipient Silver Beaver award Boy Scouts Am., 1972. Fellow Am. Coll. Ob/gyn. (founder), ACS, Royal Soc. Medicine (Eng.), Am. Acad. Geriatrics, Am. Acad. Psychosomatic Medicine, Royal Soc. Health (Eng.), Edn. and Sci. Found. if Ill. Med. Sco. (founder); mem. AMA (Physician's Recognition award), World Soc. Med. Assns., Cen. Assn. Obstetricians and Gynecologists, Assn. Mil. Surgeons, Ill. State Med. Soc. (past pres., past chmn. bd. trustees), Adams County Med. Soc. (past pres.). Clubs: University (Chgo.); Quincy Country. Lodges: Masons, Shriners, Jesters, Kiwanis Internat. Home: 18 Country Club Dr Quincy IL 62301

DUPUY, HOWARD MOORE, JR., lawyer; b. Portland, Oreg., Mar. 15, 1929; s. Howard Moore and Lola (Dunham) D.; m. Anne Irene Hanna, Aug. 26, 1950; children—Loanne Kay, Brent Moore. B.A., U. Portland, 1951; postgrad., Willamette U., Salem, Oreg., 1951; LL.B., Lewis and Clark Coll., 1956. Bar: Oreg. bar 1956. Since practiced in Portland; assoc. Green, Richardson, Green & Griswold, 1956; ptnr. Morton & Dupuy, 1957-67, Black & Dupuy (and predecessor firm), 1968—. Mem. fin. com. Oreg. Rep. Cen. Com., 1962. Served with AUS, 1946-47. Mem. Am., Oreg., Multnomah County Bar Assns., Am. Arbitration Assn. (nat. panel arbitrators), World Trade Club, Oregon Trial Lawyers Assn., Am. Judicature Soc. Club: World Trade (Portland). Home: 16116 NE Stanton St Portland OR 97230 Office: Black and Dupuy 400 SW 6th Ave Suite 800 First Farwest Bldg Portland OR 97204

DUPUY, TREVOR NEVITT, historian, research executive; b. S.I., N.Y., May 3, 1916; s. Richard Ernest and Laura (Nevitt) D.; m. Jonna Sløk Bjerggaard, Oct. 16, 1968 (dec. Apr. 1982); 1 child, Signe Sløk; children (by previous marriage): Trevor Nevitt, Richard Ernest II, George McVicar, Laura Nevitt, Charles Geissbuhler, Mirande Elisabeth, Arnold Christian, Fielding Davis. Student, St. Peter's Coll., 1933-34; B.S., U.S. Mil. Acad., 1938; grad., Joint Services Staff Coll., Latimer, Eng., 1948-49; student, Harvard Grad. Sch. Pub. Adminstrn., 1953-54. Commd. 2d lt. U.S. Army, 1938, advanced through grades to col., 1953; prof. mil. sci. and tactics Harvard, 1952-56, mem. original faculty Def. Studies program, 1954-56; dir. mil. history program Ohio State U., 1956, 57; ret. 1958; vis. prof. internat. relations program Rangoon (Burma) U., 1959-60; mem. internat. studies div. Inst. Def. Analyses, 1960-62; pres., exec. dir., bd. dirs. Hist. Evaluation and Research Orgn., 1962—; pres. bd. dirs. T.N. Dupuy Assos., Inc., 1971-83, Data Memory Systems, Inc., 1983—. Author: (with R.E. Dupuy) To The Colors, 1942, Faithful and True, 1949, (with R.E. Dupuy) Military Heritage of America, 2d edit., 1984, Campaigns of the French Revolution and of Napoleon, 1956, (with R.E. Dupuy) Brave Men and Great Captains, 1960, 84, Compact History of the Civil War, 1960 (Fletcher Pratt award), Civil War Land Battles, 1960, Civil War Naval Actions, 1961, Military History of World War II, 19 vols, 1962-65, (with R.E. Dupuy) Compact History of the Revolutionary War, 1963, Military History of World War I, 12 vols, 1967, The Battle of Austerlitz, 1968, Modern Libraries for Modern Colleges: Research Strategies for Design and Development, 1968, Ferment in College Libraries: The Impact of Information Technology, 1968, Military History of the Chinese Civil War, 1969, (with R.E. Dupuy) Encyclopedia of Military History, 4th edit, 1986, Military Lives, 12 vols, 1969, (with Grace P. Hayes) Revolutionary War Naval Battles, 1970, (with Gay M. Hammerman) Revolutionary War Land Battles, 1970; editor, contbr. to Holidays, 1965, (with John A. Andrews and Grace P. Hayes) Almanac of World Military Power, 1970, 72, 74, 80, (with Gay M. Hammerman) Documentary History of Arms Control and Disarmament, 1973, (with Gay M. Hammerman) People and Events of the American Revolution, 1974, (with R.E. Dupuy) An Outline History of the American Revolution, 1975, A Genius for War: The German Army and General Staff, 1807-1945, 1977, 84, Numbers, Prediction and War, 1978, 85, Elusive Victory: The Arab-Israeli Wars, 1947-1974, 1978, 84, The Evolution of Weapons and Warfare, 1980, 84, (with Paul Martell) Great Battles of the Eastern Front, 1982, Options of Command, 1984, (with Paul Martell) Flawed Victory: The Arab-Israeli Conflict and the 1982 War in Lebanon, 1986, Understanding War: Military History and a Theory of Conflict, 1986, (with Curt Johnson, Grace P. Hayes) Dictionary of Military Terms, 1986/87. Trustee Coll. Potomac. Decorated Legion of Merit, Bronze Star with combat V, Air medal; Brit. Distinguished Service Order; Chinese Nat. Govt. Cloud and Banner (2 grades). Mem. Am. Hist. Assn., Am. Mil. Inst. (pres. 1958-59), Assn. U.S. Army, Internat. Inst. Strategic Studies, U.S. Naval Inst. Home: 1324 Kurtz Rd McLean VA 22101 Office: 10392 Democracy Ln Fairfax VA 22030

DUPUY-BOURY, MARIE-CATHERINE, advertising executive; b. Neuilly, France, May 12, 1950; d. Jean-Pierre Dupuy and Maria Poidatz; children: Pierre-Marie Dru, Francois Marie Dru; m. Boury Paul, Sept. 12, 1987. Copy writer Dupuy-Compton, Neuilly, 1970-81, creative dir., 1981-83; creative dir., co-founder Boulet Dru Dupuy Petit, Boulogne, 1984—. Office: B D D P 162, 164 Rue de Billancourt, 92100 Boulogne France

DURAN, JOSE EMILIO, mining engineer; b. Turon, Asturias, Spain, May 27, 1927; s. Emilio and Maria (Zalona) D.; m. Maria Isabel Leguina, Oct. 12, 1959; children—Isabel/Jose Emilio. DEng, Sch. Mines, Madrid, 1955; postgrad. Gen. Electric Co., Phoenix, 1969, Escuela M.S. Trabajo, Oviedo, 1974, Organizacion Indsl. Sch., Madrid, 1980. Mine supt. Solvay & Co., Lieres, Asturias, 1955-56; enging. mgr. Minersa, Ribadesella, Asturias, 1956-62; chief engr. quarry quality control/ops. research Ensidesa, Aviles, Asturias, 1962-73; inspector Direccion Ministerio de Industria, Oviedo, Asturias, 1973-85; mining law advisor; prof. Sch. Mines, Oviedo, 1969-80; mine evaluator local govt., Oviedo, 1975-83; Spain's rep. Safety and Health Commn. for Mining and Extractive Industries. Mem. Colegio Ingenieros de Minas. Roman Catholic. Clubs: Tennis, Centro Asturia (Oviedo). Home: Gonzalez Besada n deg 4, Oviedo, Asturias Spain Office: Direccion Regional de Mineria, Plaza de Espana, Oviedo Spain

DURAN, PEDRO VICTOR MANUEL, cardiologist; b. Tampico, Mex., June 29, 1936; s. Francisco and Amparo (Rodriguez) D.; m. Bertha Lilia Fernandez, May 26, 1973; children: Monica, Lilian, Julieta. MD, Faculty medicine, Tampico, 1961. Cert. cardiologist, Consejo Mexicano de Cardiologia. Resident in internal medcine Inst. Nat. Cardiologist, Mexico City, 1964-67; fellow internal med. cardiology Wayne State U., Detroit, 1967-68; prof. cardiology Faculty Med., Tampico, 1968—, asst. dean, 1970-74; asst. dir. Hosp. Gen. de Tampico, 1983—. Mem. Mex. Soc. Cardiology, Mex. Assn. Internal Med., Am. Coll. Cardiology, Consejo Mexicano de Cardiology. Roman Catholic. Lodge: Rotary. Office: Altamira 110 PTE, 89000 Tampico Mexico

DURAND, GUY, surgeon, gynecologist; b. Aurillac, Cantal, France, Nov. 3, 1932; s. Alfred and Anna (Pons) D.; m. Claudine Pizon, Dec. 21, 1954; children: Thierry, Geraud. MD, Faculte Medecine, Clermont Ferrand, France, 1962. Intern des Hopitaux-Clermont Ferrand, 1955-59; chief surg. clinic Faculte de Clermont Ferrand, 1962-64; surgeon clinique St. Jacques, 1963-79; chief surgeon Centre Hosp., Saint Flour, Cantal, France, 1968-71, 1971—; Chief clinic Faculte Medecine, 1962-64. Decorated Croix Valeur Militaire, 1961. Mem. Coll. Gynecologues et Obstetriciens Françcis. Roman Catholic. Lodge: Rotary. Office: Centre Hosp, 2 Ave Mallet, Saint-Flour, 15100 Cantal France

DURAND, PAOLO VINCENZO, science facility administrator; b. Celle Ligure, Italy, Apr. 30, 1922; s. Giovanni and Beatrice (Delfino) D.; m. Gabriella Pozzi, Apr. 16, 1956; children: Andrea, Paola, Stefano, Chiara. MD, U. Genova, Italy, 1947, degree in Pediatrics, 1949. Asst. physician pediatric clinic Inst. Giannina Gaslini, Genova, 1951-56, vice-head physician pediatric clinic, 1956-59, head physician infectious diseases dept., 1959-62, head physician III pediatric div., 1962—, sci. dir., 1983—. Author: Disorders Due To Intestinal Defective Carbohydrate Digestion and Absorption, 1964; co-author: Genetic Errors of Glycoprotein Metabolism, 1982. Pres. Santa Chiara Acad., Genova, 1979-81. Recipient Fieschi, Com. of Genoa, 1984, L'Uomo e la Scienza per un domani migliore, Com. of Genoa, 1985. Mem. Italian Soc. Paediatrics (councillor 1979-82), European Soc. Pediatric Research, European Study Group of Lysosomal Storage Disease (councillor 1979-82), Commn. European Communities (project leader of concerted action on inborn metabolic diseases Med. and Pub. Health Research Programme). Roman Catholic. Lodge: Rotary. Home: Viale Causa 7/4, 16145 Genoa Italy Office: Giannina Gaslini Inst, Via V Maggio 39, 16148 Quarto-Genoa Italy

DURAND-REVILLE, LUC, business executive; b. Cairo, Apr. 12, 1904 (parents French citizens); s. Maurice and Jeanne (Reville) Durand; m. Françoise Warnod, Mar. 28, 1926; children: Eveline Durand-Reville Lobry, Eric, Blaise. Lic. en Droit diplôme H.E.C. Pres. various colonial cos. in Africa, 1934—; mem. French Senate, 1945-58; mem. Econ. and Social Council France, 1958-74; v.p. Cie Optorg, Puteaux, 1970—; hon. chmn. Acad. Comml. Scis., Acad. Overseas Scis., Soc. Polit. Econs.; corr. Inst. of France; hon. v.p. Internat. C. of C.; bd. dirs. European League Econ. Community. Served to capt. French Army, 1939-45. Decorated officer Legion of Honor, comdr. Nat. Order Merit; knight comdr. Order Brit. Empire; comdr. Palmes Acadé miques. Mem. Mt. Pelerin Soc. Mem. Radical Party. Mem. Evangelical Ch. Club: Cercle Republicain. Author numerous books and articles on developing countries. Home: 16 rue Leconte de Lisle, 75016 Paris France Office: 5 rue Bellini, Puteaux 92806 France

DURANT, FREDERICK CLARK, III, consultant aerospace history and space art; b. Ardmore, Pa., Dec. 31, 1916; s. Frederick Clark, Jr. and Cornelia Allen (Howel) D.; m. Carolyn Griscom Jones, Oct. 4, 1947; children: Derek C. (dec.), Carolyn M., William C., Stephen H. B.S. in Chem. Engring, Lehigh U., 1939; postgrad., Phila. Mus. Sch. Indsl. Arts, 1946-47. Registered profl. engr., D.C., Mass. Engr. E.I. duPont de Nemours & Co., Inc., 1939-41; rocket engr. Bell Aircraft Corp., 1947-48; dir. engring. Naval Air Rocket Test Sta., 1948-51; cons. Washington, 1952-53; mem. sr. staff Arthur D. Little, Inc., 1954-57; dir. Maynard Ordnance Test Sta., 1954-55; exec. asst. to dir. Avco-Everett Research Lab., 1957-59; dir. pub. and govt. relations, research and advanced devel. div. Avco Corp., Wilmington, Mass., 1959-61; sr. rep. Bell Aerosystems Co., Washington, 1961-64; asst. dir. and head astronautics dept. Nat. Air and Space Mus., Smithsonian Instn., Washington, 1964-80; cons. 1980—; dir. Nat. Space Soc., Washington, 1982—; conservator Bonestell Space Art and Space Art Internat.; dir. Arthur C. Clarke Found. U.S. Inc.; participant ann. congresses Internat. Astronautical Fedn., 1951—, pres., 1953-56; mem. organizing com. Project Orbiter, 1954. Author: First Steps toward Space, 1975, Worlds Beyond: The Art of Chesley Bonestell, 1983; Contbg. editor: Missiles and Rockets, 1956-58; contbr. to: Funk & Wagnalls Year Book; contbr.: space terms Am. Heritage Dictionary; Ency. Brit. Served to comdr. as naval aviator USNR, 1941-46,48-52. Recipient spl. medal L'Assn. Pour l'Encouragement de l'Aeronautique et de l'Astronautique, 1963, Charles A. Lindbergh award Smithsonian Instn., 1976, hon. 6 Dan Karate-Do, Japan, 1978. Fellow Am. Astronautical Soc., AIAA, Am. Rocket Soc. (pres. 1953); mem. Internat. Acad. Astronautics (co-chmn. history com. 1981—), Nat. Space Club (gov. 1961), Nat. Space Club (Disting. Service award 1982); hon. fellow or mem. numerous fgn. rocket and space flight socs. Club: Cosmos. Home: 109 Grafton St Chevy Chase Village MD 20815

DURAS, MARGUERITE, writer; b. Giadinh, Indochina, Apr. 4, 1914; d. Henri and Marie (Legrand) Donnadieu; ed. in Saigon and Paris. Sec. to minister for the colonies, 1935-41; writer, 1943—; works include: Les Impudents, 1943, La Vie Tranquille, 1944, Marin de Gibraltar, 1952, Les Petits Chevaux da Tarquinia, 1953, Des Journeés Entieres Dans las Arbres, 1954, Le Square, 1955, Les Viaduc de la Seine et Oise, Hiroshima Mon Amour (film), Dix heures et Demie du Soir en Ete, 1960, L'Apres-Midi de Monsieur Andesmas, 1962, Le Ravissement de Lol V. Stein, 1964, Theatre I, Le Vice-Consul, 1965, Amante Anglaise, 1967, Theatre II (5 pieces), 1958, Detruire, Dit-Elle, 1969, Suzanna Ardier (piece), 1969, L'Amour, 1972, Nathalie Granger, 1973, India Song (scenario), 1973, Les Parleuses (with Xaviere Gauthier), 1974, Une Aussi Longue Absence (with Jariot Gerard), 1961, Les Lieux de Marguerite Dumas (with Michelle Porte), 1977, L'Eden Cinema, 1977, The Lover (Ritz Paris Hemingway prize), 1985, Destroy, She Said, 1986, Little Horses of Tarquinia, 1986; has also written for theater and film. Recipient Prix Jean Cocteau, Grand Prix Academie du Cinema. Address: 5 rue Saint-Benoit, 75006 Paris France *

DURBEN, MARIA-MAGDALENA, writer, editor; b. Berlin, July 8, 1935; d. Bernhard and Eva (Klein) Block; grad. Paedagogische Hochschule Erfurt and Berlin, 1958; Dr. h.c., U. Danzig, 1977; Litt.D., Free U. Karachi (Pakistan), 1978, World Acad. Lang. and Lit., Sao Paulo, 1978; H.H.D., Bodkin Bible Inst., U.S., 1979; Litt.D., World Acad. Arts and Culture, Taipei, 1981; m. Wolfgang Durben, Dec. 22, 1967; children—Roman, Claudia, Friederike. Governess, Berlin, 1958-61; tchr. German lang., Berlin, 1961-65; mentor for tchrs. of German, Berlin, 1965-68; writer, editor, Beckingen-Saar, Ger., 1968—; editor: Essays aus juengster Zeit, Franzi Ascher-Nash, 1976; editor anthology Diagonalen, 1976; Mauern (Lyrik), 1978; Mauern (Prose), 1978; (with F. Durben) Drei Tropfen Mondlicht-Lebenszeichen aus fünf Jahrzehnten, 1983; co-editor UNIO Mag., 1968-78; editor Bunte Blä tter, 1974-78; mem. central com. Lit. Union, 1968-82; mem. Internat. Cultural

Council, 1983—; chmn. 2d World Congress Poets, Taipei, Taiwan, 1973; founder Literarische Teestunden in der Durbenburg, 1974-82, Literarischer Turmtee, 1983—; organizer poetry festivals and lit. competitions, 1974-82. Recipient Prosa-Preis ECON-Jubilaeumswettbewerb, Dü sseldorf, 1974; Internat. Man and Woman Laureate award UPLI, Academia Asiatica, 1975; Lyrik-Preis Wettbewerb Zwei Menschen, 1976; Poet of Mankind award Academia Antero de Quental, Sao Paulo, 1978; Prosapreis Atrioc-Jubiläums-Wettbewerb Bad Mergentheim, 1984; named Internat. Woman 1975 with Laureate Honors; Ordem do Mérito, Dame Grand Cross (Brazil), 1978; Excellence in Lit., Internat. Soc. Lit., Yorkshire, Eng., 1979. Mem. Melbourne Shakespeare Soc., Der Turmbund, Gesellschaft für Literatur und Kunst (Austria), Regensburger Schriftstellergruppe, United Poets Laureate Internat. (hon.), Cosmosynthesis League (hon.), Internationaler Autorenkreis Plesse. Author: (short stories) Wenn der Schnee fällt, 1974, 78; (poetry) Gruss an Taiwan, 1974; (dialogue) (with Claudia Durben) Ein Stückchen von Gott, 1974; (Kalender) (with Wendolin) Ein Berliner schnuppert Saarluft, 1977; (poems) Unterm Glasnadelzelt, 1976; (love poems) Roter Rausch und weisse Haut, 1976; (short stories) Wenn das Feuer fällt, 1976, Wenn die Asche fällt, 1976; (poems of fools) Wenn die Maske fällt, 1977; (travel book) Zwischen Knoblauch und Chrysanthemen, 1979; Haiku mit Stäbchen, 1980; (short stories, cassette) Liebe oder so, 1981; (fairy-tale) Da schrie der Schatten fürchterlich, 1975; (poems) Schaukle am blauen Stern, 1975; (poems) Lichtrunen, 1977; (poems) Fernweh, 1983; Atemnester, 1983; Lieb' ein Loch in die Welt, 1983; Und das Licht war Liebe, 1983; (short stories and poems) Die Lesung, 1985; (poems) Zehn Liebeslieder für Tobias, 1985. Address: 8 Schulstrasse, D6645 Beckingen Federal Republic of Germany

DURBNEY, CLYDROW JOHN, clergyman; b. St. Louis, Sept. 27, 1916; s. Earl Elmer and Conetta Mae D.; A.B., Gordon Coll. Theology and Missions, 1950; B.D., Eden Theol. Sem., 1953; S.T.M., Concordia Theol. Sem., 1954, postgrad. 1954-59; postgrad Eden Sem., 1973-75; D.D., Am. Bible Inst., 1980; Cultural doctorate in Sacred Philosophy, World U., 1982; m. Mattie Lee Neal, Oct. 27, 1968. Ordained to ministry Nat. Bapt. Ch., 1952. Clk., U.S. Post Office, St. Louis, 1941-54; instr. Western Bapt. Bible Coll., St. Louis, 1954-67; asst. pastor Central Bapt. Ch., St. Louis, 1954, pastor, 1983; ghetto evangelist Ch. on Wheels, 1952-84; pastor, founder Saints Fellowship Ch., 1984—. Served with AUS, 1942-46; ETO. Decorated Bronze Star. Recipient Disting. World Service award Central Bapt. Ch. Prayer Aux., 1974. Mem. Internat. Platform Assn., Inst. Research Assn., Gordon Alumni Assn., Anglo Am. Acad., Nat. Geog. Soc., Smithsonian Instn. Republican. Author: With Him in Glory, 1955; Adventures in Soul Winning, 1966; contbr. to New Voices in Am. Poetry, 1972—. Home: 8244 Addington Dr Berkeley MO 63134

DURDY, JAMES DIRK, marketing professional; b. Denver, Nov. 24, 1957; s. James G. and Elizabeth (Collins) D. BA in Biol., Colo. State U., 1980. Cert. emergency med. technician, in CPR, and as a CPR instr. Founder, mgr. firewood service 1974-75; owner/operator DD and Y Springling System, 1978-81, summers; pres., dir., chief ops. officer Mt. Experience Inc., Littleton, Colo., 1982—; cons. Roo Mark, Victoria, Australia, 1986—. Tchr. CPR and emergency first aid Red Cross throughout Colo., mem. Idaho Mt. Search and Rescue Team. Named Outstanding Young Man in Am., 1985. Republican. Roman Catholic. Home: 6010 S Detroit St Littleton CO 80121 Office: Roo Mark, 16 Wooten Cres, Longwarrin Victoria Australia 3910

DURENBERGER, DAVID FERDINAND, U.S. senator; b. St. Cloud, Minn., Aug. 19, 1934; s. George G. and Isabelle M. (Cebulla) D.; m. Gilda Beth (Penny) Baran, Sept. 4, 1971; children by previous marriage: Charles, David, Michael, Daniel. B.A. cum laude in Polit. Sci, St. Johns U., 1955; J.D., U. Minn., 1959. Bar: Minn. bar 1959. Mem. firm LeVander, Gillen, Miller & Durenberger, South St. Paul, 1959-66; exec. sec. to Gov. Harold LeVander, 1967-71; counsel for legal and community affairs, corporate sec. H.B. Fuller Co., St. Paul, 1971-78; mem. U.S. Senate from Minn., 1978—. Co-chmn. NAIA Football Bowl Playoff, 1963; div. chmn. United Fund of South St. Paul, 1965; chmn. citizens sect. Minn. Recreation and Park Assn., 1971-72; mem. South St. Paul Parks and Recreation Commn., 1971-72; chmn. Metro Council Open Space Adv. Bd., 1972-74; commr. Murphy-Hanrehan Park Bd., 1973-75; chmn. Save Open Space Now, 1974, Close-Up Found. Minn., 1975-76, Social Investment Task Force, Project Responsibility, 1974-76, Spl. Service div. St. Paul Area United Way, 1973-76; chmn. bd. commrs. Hennepin County Park Res. Dist.; vice chmn. Met. Parks and Open Space Bd.; exec. vice chmn. Gov.'s Commn. on Arts; exec. dir. Minn. Constl. Study Commn., Supreme Ct. Adv. Com. on Jud. Responsibility; pres. Burroughs Sch. PTA, Mpls.; chmn. Dakota County Young Republican League, 1963-64; dir., legal counsel Minn. Young Rep. League, 1964-65; co-chmn. State Young Rep. League, 1965; del. State Rep. Conv., 1966, 68, 70, 72; first vice chmn. 1st Dist. Rep. Party, 1970-72; vice chmn. 13th ward Rep. Party Mpls., 1973-74; bd. dirs. Met. Parks Found., Pub. Service Options, Inc., St. Louis Park AAU Swim Club, Minn. Landmarks, 1971-73, Pub. Affairs Leadership and Mgmt. Tng., Inc., 1973-75, U. Minn. YMCA, 1973-75, Community Planning Orgn., Inc., St. Paul, 1973-76, Project Environment Found., 1974-75, Urban Lab., Inc., 1975, Nat. Recreation and Park Assn., Within the System, Inc., 1976-77; trustee Children's Health Center and Hosp., Inc., Mpls.; mem. exec. com. Nat. Center for Vol. Action, Minn. Charities Rev. Council. Served as 2d lt. U.S. Army, 1955-56; as capt. Res., 1957-63. Named Outstanding Young Man in South St. Paul, 1964, One of Ten Outstanding Young Men in Minn., 1965. Mem. Am., Minn., 1st Dist. bar assns., Corp. Counsel Assn., St. Johns U. Alumni Assn. (pres. Twin Cities chpt. 1963-65, nat. pres. 1971-73), Mpls., St. Paul Area chambers commerce, Gamma Eta Gamma (chancellor 1958-59, v.p. Alumni Assn. 1965-75). Roman Catholic. Club: K.C. Office: US Senate 154 Russell Senate Bldg Washington DC 20510-2301 *

DURIEU, BERNARD HENRI, food products executive, controller; b. Lille, France, Jan. 28, 1944; s. Henri Emile and Thérèse (Dupont) D., m. Geneviève Michoux, June 11, 1973; children: Cyril, Murielle, Christophe. Diploma, Hautes Etudes Commerciales, 1967; MBA, U. Pa., 1970. Sales inspector B.S.N., France, 1968-69; sr. cons. Arthur Andersen Co., Paris, 1971-73; controller Martini & Rossi, Paris, 1974-80; group controller Gen. Beverage Corp., Brussells, 1980-84; gen. mgr., chmn. Cie Francaise Grands Vins, Paris, 1985—; interim cons. ISSEC, Paris, 1980-86. Mem. Assn. Dirs. Financiers and Contrôleurs Gestion, Assn. Française Auditers Internes. Roman Catholic. Home: 11 rue de la Chine, 75020 Paris France Office: Compagnie Francaise Grands, Vins, Rue Eiffel, 77220 Tournan-en-Brie France

DU RIVAULT, CLAUDE, corporate financial executive; b. Poitiers, France, Aug. 26, 1928; s. René and Odette (Pillard) du R.; m. Purificacion Gonzalez y Gonzalez; children: Thècle, Pétronille, Apollin, Florent. Licencié en droit, U. Paris; degree in Econs., Yale U. Gen. mgr. Chemetron Corp., Huntington, W.Va., 1963-77; pvt. practice fin. enterprises cons. Puteaux, France, 1980—. Club: Cercle de l'opinion (Paris). Lodge: Xavier de la Fourneire. Home and Office: du Rivault Cons, 14 Rue Anatole France, 92802 Puteaux France

DURKEE, JEAN KELLNER, home economist; b. Chgo., Feb. 7, 1932; d. Herbert Ernest and Lucy (Stevens) Kellner; m. Robert Rosswell Durkee Jr., Oct. 3, 1953; children: Robert Rosswell III, Mark, Todd. BS in Home Econs., U. Tex., 1953. Dir. 1st Presbyn. Nursery Sch. and Kindergarten, Lafayette, La., 1954-56; dir. Grace Presbyn. Nursery Sch. and Kindergarten, Lafayette, 1965-67; pres. Tout de Suite, Inc., Lafayette, 1978—; tchr. microwave cooking. Author, pub.: Tout de Suite la Microwave, I, 1977, II, 1980; author: Voilà! Lafayette Centennial Cookbook, 1884-1984, 1983, (with others) (column) Blades and Waves, 1978-83; producer: (video) Microwave Cooking-Tout de Suite, 1985. Pres. Lafayette Natural History Mus.; Lafayette Jr. League, 1959-60; bd. dirs. Vol. Ctr. Lafayette, 1988—. Mem. Am. Home Econs. Assn., Home Economists in Bus., La. Home Econs. Assn. Internat. Microwave Power Inst., Internat. Assn. Cooking Profls. (cert.), P.E.O. (pres. chpt. 1961-62), Lafayette C. of C. (bd. dirs. 1987—). Republican. Methodist. Club: Chez Amis Women's (pres. 1957-58). Office: PO Box 30121 Lafayette LA 70503

DURKIN, HENRY PAUL, marketing executive; b. Staab, Czechoslovakia, June 24, 1940; s. Edward James and Barbara (Wachter) D.; BA, Fordham U., 1962; m. Jane Elizabeth Lewis, Apr. 27, 1968; children—Jennifer Marie, Peter Christopher, Elizabeth Amy. Dir. publicity Arlington House Publishers, New Rochelle, N.Y., 1967-69; dir. advt., publicity, promotion Walker & Co., N.Y.C., 1969-72; dir. subsidiary rights World Publ. Co., N.Y.C., 1972-73; dir. subs. rights, asso. editor Hawthorn Books, N.Y.C., 1973-76; publ. cons., Westfield, N.J., 1976-77; v.p. Publishers Mktg. Enterprises, Inc., N.Y.C., 1977-81; v.p. direct response mktg. Book World Promotions Inc., Vineland, N.J., 1981—; pres. Durkin Media Publ. Cons., Plainfield, N.J., 1976-88, Success Books, Plainfield, 1984-88, Gourmet House, Plainfield, 1984-87. German Acad. Exchange Service scholar, Rheinische Friedrich Wilhelms U., Bonn., 1962-63; N.Y. State Regents scholar, 1958-62. Author: 44 Hours to Change Your Life, 1974; contbr. articles to profl. jours. Home: 1159 Gresham Rd Plainfield NJ 07062 Office: 3669 N Mill Rd Vineland NJ 08360

DURLACH, MARCUS RUSSELL, mechanical engineering consultant, artist; b. Bklyn., Jan. 27, 1911; s. Marcus Russell and Nellie Kinard (Schureman) D.; M.E., Stevens Inst. Tech., 1933; M.Sc., Cornell U., 1946; m. Jeannette Vivian Lorber, June 29, 1941; children—Marcus Russell, Richard Stevens. Tchr. Bklyn. Tech. High Sch., 1934-41; test engr., supr. U.S. Navy, Charleston, S.C., 1941-45; asso. prof. engring. U. S.C., Columbia, 1945-52; cons. engr., sr. partner Durlach, O'Neal & Jenkins, Columbia, 1946—. Mem. S.C. Bd. Engring. Examiners. Exhibited in one-man shows at Columbia Coll., Ft. Jackson Gallery, Columbia Mus. Art; exhibited in group shows at Columbia Gallery, Columbia Mus. Art; represented in permanent collections. Chmn. curriculum com. Midlands Tech. Inst., Columbia, 1969-78. Recipient various art awards. Registered profl. engr., N.C., S.C., Ga., Nev., Wis. Fellow Am. Soc. M.E. (profl. practice com. 1972—), Am. Soc. Heating Ventilation Air Conditioning Engrs.; mem. Artists Guild Columbia (pres. 1973-74), S.C. Guild of Artists, Nat. (dir. 1966-69), S.C. (pres. 1964), Columbia (pres. 1957) socs. profl. engrs., S.C. Watercolor Soc. (pres.), So. Watercolor Soc. (pres. 1979—), SAR. Lodge: Rotary (pres. club 1963-64). Home: 6025 Lakeshore Dr Columbia SC 29206 Office: 2119 Santee Ave Columbia SC 29205

DU ROCHER, JAMES HOWARD, lawyer; b. Racine, Wis., Aug. 4, 1945; s. Howard James and Frances Ann (Rasmussen) DuR.; m. Rosalyn Ann, Sept. 2, 1972; children—Jessica Lynn, James Howard, Emily Rosalyn. Student U.S. Mil. Acad., 1963-65, Ripon Coll., 1965-66; J.D., U. Wis., 1969. Bar: Wis. Assoc. Stewart, Peyton, Crawford & Josten, Racine, 1969-78; ptnr. Josten, DuRocher, Murphy & Pierce, S.C., Racine, 1978—. Bd. dirs. Racine Area United Way, 1973-79, v.p., 1977-79; chmn. Park Trails Dist. Boy Scouts Am., 1979-82; bd. dirs. Careers for Retarded Adults, Inc., 1982, pres., 1983; bd. dirs. A-Center of Racine, Inc., 1978-82, pres., 1985; deacon Atonement Lutheran Ch., Racine, 1978-81; mem. adv. bd. Children's Service Soc. Wis. Served as capt. JAGC, U.S. Army, 1969-73. Decorated Bronze Star. Mem. State Bar Wis., ABA, Fed. Bar Assn. Club: Mason, Rotary. Home: 5531 Whirlaway Ln Racine WI 53402 Office: 927 Main St PO Box 1815 Racine WI 53401

DUROSELLE, JEAN-BAPTISTE, university professor, writer, author of historical books; b. Paris, Nov. 17, 1917; s. Albert and Jeanne (Peronne) D.; m. Christiane Viant, Oct. 1, 1940; children: Henri, Genevieve, Dominique, Michel. BS, Ecole Normale Superieure, Paris, 1938; PhD, Ecole Normale, Paris, 1949; PhD (hon.), U. Notre Dame, 1977, U. Liege, Belgium, 1982. Tchr. Lycées, various locations, 1943-45; asst. prof. U. Sorbonne, Paris, 1945-49; prof. various univs., Saarland and France, 1950-58, Found. Nationale des Sciences Politiques, Paris, 1958-64; prof. U. Paris, 1966-84, emeritus prof., 1983—; pres. Inst. History Internat. Contemporary Relations, Paris, 1968—, Publs. de la Sorbonne, 1967—. Author 20 books and over 300 articles to profl. jours. Served to lt. artillery French Army, 1939-40. Mem. Am. Hist. Assn., Am. Philos. Soc., Royal Acad. of Belgium, Academie des Sciences Morales et Politique (hon. pres.). Roman. Catholic. Home: 5 rue de Naples, 78150 Roquencourt le Chesnay France Office: Institut De France, 23 quai de Conti, 75006 Paris France

DUROVIC, LUBOMIR JAN, Slavonic languages educator; b. Vazec, Czechoslovakia, Feb. 9, 1925; arrived in Sweden, 1966; s. Jan and Olga Maria Anna (Palicova) D.; m. Ludmila Ruzekova, June 30, 1951; children—Vladimir, Natasa. PhDr., Comenius U., Bratislava, 1951; DSc, Czechoslovak Acad. Scis., Prague, 1966. Asst. Comenius U., Bratislava, Czechoslovakia, 1951-56, assoc. prof., 1956-66, prof., 1967-70, head dept. Russian, 1955-57; lectr. State U., Uppsala, Sweden, 1966-69, assoc. prof., 1969-72; prof. Royal U., Lund, Sweden, 1972—, head dept. Slavic Langs., 1972—. Author: Modalnost, 1956, Paradigmatics of Russian, 1964, 70; editor: Slavica Lundensia 1-2, 1973—, Russian Linguistics Jour. 4-12, 1978—. Mem. Czechoslovak Soc. Scis. & Arts, Royal Soc. Humanities, Scandinavian Assn. Slavicists (pres. 1987—). New Soc. Letters at Lund. Lutheran. Home: Spexarevagen 5B, S-223-71 Lund Sweden Office: Dept Slavonic Langs, Finngatan 12, S-223 62 Lund Sweden

DÜRR, HEINZ, communication equipment manufacturing executive; b. Stuttgart, Fed. Republic Germany, July 16, 1933; m. Heide Dürr; 3 children. Student, Tech. U., Stuttgart, 1957-80. Mgr., mng. dir. Dürr GmbH (formerly Otto Dürr GmbH), Stuttgart, 1957-80; chmn. mng. bd. AEG Aktiengesellschaft, Berlin, since 1980, Daimler-Benz AG, Berlin, since 1986; chmn. bd. Olympia Aktiengesellschaft, Wilhelmshaven, since 1980; bd. dirs. Thyssen Industrie AG, Essen, Frankfurter Allianz-Aktiengesellschaft; mem. adv. council Dresdner Bank AG, Franfurt, 1980—. Mem. Cen. Assn. Elect. and Electronics Industry of Germany (presidency mem. 1984—), Metal Industry Assn. Germany (pres. 1975-80). Office: AEG Aktiengesellschaft, Theodor-Stern-Kai 1, D-6000 Frankfurt 70 Federal Republic of Germany

DURRELL, GERALD MALCOLM, zoologist, author; b. Jamshedpur, India, Jan. 7, 1925; s. Lawrence Samuel and Louisa Florence (Dixie) D.; m. Jacqueline Sonia Rasen, 1951 (div.); m. 2d, Lee Wilson McGeorge, 1979. Ed. pvt. tutors; L.H.D. (hon.), Yale U., 1972. Student keeper Whipsnade Park, 1945-46; mem. zool. collecting expdn., Brit. Cameroons, 1947, 48, Brit. Guiana, 1949, Argentina, Paraguay, 1953, Brit. Cameroons, 1956, Trans-Argentine, 1958, N.Z., Australia, Malaysia, 1961, Sierra Leone, 1964, Mexico, 1968, Mauritius, 1976, 77, India/Assam, 1978, Madagascar, 1981; established own zoo, Jersey, Channel Islands, 1959; founder Jersey Wildlife Preservation Trust, 1964, dir., 1964—; lectr. in field; Appeared on broadcasts, BBC; 4 maj. TV series on animals; author: The Overloaded Ark, 1952; Three Singles to Adventure, 1953; The Bafut Beagles, 1953; The Drunken Forest, 1955; My Family and Other Animals, 1956; Encounters with Animals, 1959; A Zoo in My Luggage, 1960; The Whispering Land, 1962; Menagerie Manor, 1964; Two in the Bush, 1966; Rosy is my Relative (novel), 1968; Birds, Beasts and Relatives, 1969; Fillets of Plaice, 1971; Catch Me a Colobus, 1972; Beasts in my Belfrey, 1973; The Stationary Ark, 1976; Golden Batrs and Pink Pigeons, 1977; The Garden of the Gods, 1978; the Picnic and Suchlike Pandemonium, 1979; The Mockery Bird, 1981; The Ark on the Move, 1981; Amateur Naturalist, 1982; How to Shoot an Amateur Naturalist, 1984, Durrell in Russia, 1986; children's books: The New Noah, 1956; Island Zoo, 1961; Look at Zoos, 1961; My Favourite Animal Stories, 1963; The Donkey Rustler, 1968; The Talking Parcel, 1974, The Fantastic Flying Journey, 1987. Decorated Order Brit. Empire. Fellow Internat. Inst. Arts and Letters, Inst. Biology, Zool. Soc.; mem. Brit. Ornithologists Union. Office: Jersey Wildlife Preservat Trust, Les Augres Manor, Trinity, Jersey Channel Islands

DURRELL, LAWRENCE GEORGE, author; b. Julundur, India, Feb. 27, 1912; s. Lawrence Samuel and Louise Florence (Dixie) D.; ed. Coll. of St. Joseph, Darjiling, India, also St. Edmund's Coll., Canterbury, Eng.; 2 daus. Formerly with Brit. fgn. service; press attache, Belgrade, Yugoslavia; dir. Brit. Inst., Cordoba, Argentina; dir. pub. relations, Dodecanese Islands; press attache, Alexandria, Egypt; sr. press officer Brit. embassy, Cairo; dir. Brit. Inst., Kalamata, Greece; sr. press officer, Athens, Greece; dir. pub. relations Govt. of Cyprus, 1954-56; spl. corr. for Economist in Cyprus, 1953; lectr. lit. for Brit. Council in Greece and Argentina. Fellow Royal Soc. Lit. Author: (novels) Panic Spring, 1937, The Black Book, 1938, Prospero's Cell, 1945, Cefalu, 1947, Reflections on a Marine Venus, 1953, Justine, 1956. Bitter Lemons, 1956, Balthazar, 1958, Mountolive, 1958, Clea, 1960, Tunc, 1968; Nunquam, 1970; (humor) Stiff Upper Lip, 1958, Esprit de Corps, 1957; (verse) Private Country, 1943, Cities, Plains and Peoples, 1946, On Seeming to Presume, 1948, Tree of Idleness, 1955, Selected Poems, 1956, Sappho (play), 1950, Acte (play), 1962, An Irish Faustus (play), 1964; Collected Poems, 1960; Selected Poems, 1953-1963, 1964; The Ikons and Other Poems, 1967; Sauve Qui Peut, 1967; (criticism) A Key to Modern Poetry, 1952; (translation) Pope Joan, 1948; A Private Correspondence, 1963; Spirit of Place, quintet The Quinx, 1984; letters and essays on travel, 1969; also articles mags., newspapers; editor: The Henry Miller Reader, 1959. Address: care Nat and Grindlay's Bank, 13 St James Sq, London SW1 England *

DURRENMATT, FRIEDRICH, writer; b. Konolfingen, Switzerland, Jan. 5, 1921; s. Reinhold and Hulda (Zimmermann) D.; m. Lotti Geissler, 1946 (dec.); 3 children; m. Charlotte Kerr, 1984. Ed., U. Berne, 1941-42, U. Zurich, 1941. Author plays: Es steht geschrieben, Der Blinde, Romulus der Grosse, Die Ehe des Herrn Mississippi, Ein Engel kommt nach Babylon, Der Besuch der alten Dame, Frank V, Die Physiker, Herkules und der Stall des Augias, Der Meteor, Die Wiedertaufer, König Johann (after Shakespeare), Play Strindberg, Titus Andronicus (after Shakespeare), Porträt eines Planeten, Der Mitmacher, Die Frist, Die Panne, Achterloo, Rollenspie; plays for radio: Der Doppelganger, Der Prozess um des Esels Schatten, Nächtliches Gespräch mit einem verachteten Menschen, Stranitzky und der Nationalheld, Herkules und de Stall des Augias, Das Unternehmen der Wega, Abendstunde im Spätherbst; fiction: Der Richter und sein Henker, Der Verdacht, Das Versprechen; prose: Pilatus, Der Nihilist, Der Hund, Der Theater-direktor, Der Tunnel, Grieche sucht Griedhin, Im Coiffeurladen, Das Bild des Sisyphos, Dir Sturz, Dramaturgisches und Kritisches, Stoffe I-III, Minotauras, Der Auftrag, Theaterschriften und Reden, Gerechtigkeit und Recht, Zusammenhänge, Friedrich Schiller, Sätze aus Amerika, Gespräch mit Heinz Ludwig Arnold, Frankfurter Rede, Lesebuch, Einstein-Vortrag.

DURRETT, DEWEY BERT, real estate, ranching; b. Belington, W.Va., May 16, 1929; s. Dewey Lee and Bernice Cinthy (Simon) D.; m. Pauline Ann Stefanik, May 3, 1958; children: Bryan Price, Keith Simon, Craig Steven. BS, W.Va. U., 1951; MS, U. Mass., 1957; student, Air U., Maxwell AFB, Ala., 1964, 67; cert. nat. security mgmt., Indsl. Coll. Armed Services, 1968. Capt. Delta Airlines, Boston, 1957-85; owner, chief exec. officer Durrett Enterprises, Salem, N.H., 1967—. Mem. Credit Bur. of Greater Lawrence, Mass., 1978—. Served to lt. col. USAFR, 1951-79. Durrett Hall named after him Erickson Alumni Ctr. W.Va. U., 1986; recipient Am. Farmer Degree award Future Farmers Am., 1949. Mem. Air Force Assn., Res. Officers Assn., Airline Pilots Assn., Aircraft Owners and Pilots Assn., Salem Contractors Assn., Greater Lawrence Rental Assn., Found. N.Am. Wild Sheep, Nat. Rifle Assn., Exptl. Aircraft Assn., Am. Legion, Nat. Cattlemen's Assn., W.Va. Cattlemen's Assn., N.H. Aviation Assn., Alpha Gamma Rho (Outstanding Alumnus 1977), Sphinx, Alpha Zeta. Clubs: Internat. C-180-185 (Phoenix) (bd. dirs. 1985—); Cub (Mt. Pleasant, N.Y.); Marmon (Willoughby, Ohio). Home: 377 Main St Salem NH 03079 Office: Durrett Enterprises 373 Main St Salem NH 03079

DURSIN, HENRY LOUIS, opinion survey company executive; b. Woonsocket, R.I., May 3, 1921; s. Henry and Mary Regina (Butler) D.; m. Margaret Alice Smith, Apr. 20, 1943 (dec.); children: Henry Peter, Philomene Louise, Margaret Elizabeth, Stefanie Marie; m. Marie Ann Novosedlik, May 22, 1982. AB with honors, Brown U., 1942; MBA, Harvard U., 1948. Supr. corp. research Gen. Electric Co., N.Y.C., 1948-63; supr. corp. research Harper-Atlantic Sales Co., N.Y.C., also dir. research and promotion, 1963-67; dir. research ORC Caravan Surveys Co., Princeton, N.J., 1968-70, pres., 1970—; v.p. Opinion Research Corp., Princeton, 1970-74, sr. v.p., 1974—. Chmn. agy. com. United Fund No. Westchester, 1960-68, pres. 1967-68; v.p. Westchester County United Fund, co-chmn. agy. com. 1966-67. Served with USAAF, 1942-46. Mem. Am. Assn. Pub. Opinion Research. Roman Catholic. Club: Harvard (N.Y.C). Home: 42 Bear Brook Rd Princeton NJ 08540 Office: Opinion Research Corp Box 183 Princeton NJ 08540

DURVASULA, SRIRAMA SASTRI, lawyer; b. Vizag, India, Mar. 1, 1938; came to U.S., 1970; s. Reddi Pantulu and Varahalamma D.; m. Nagasundari, May 21, 1967; children—Padmaja, Suryaprakash. I.Sc., A.V.N. Coll., Vizag, 1954; B.L., Andhra U., Vizag, 1957; LL.M., George Washington U., 1971. Bar: D.C. 1974, Md. 1977, U.S. Supreme Ct. 1977. Advocate, High Ct., Andhra Pradesh, India, 1958—; sole practice, Silver Spring, Md., 1974—; mem. faculty Law Sch., George Washington U., Washington, 1972-75; assoc. gen. counsel Md. Nat. Capital Park and Planning Commn., Silver Spring, 1973—; legal counsel Embassy of India, Washington, 1975—, Permanent Mission of India to UN, N.Y.C., 1980—. Contbr. articles to profl. publs. Pres. India Cultural Coordination Com., Washington, 1974-79. Mem. ABA, D.C. Bar Assn., Md. State Bar Assn. Democrat. Hindu. Lodge: Masons (worshipful master 1965-66). Home: 2707 Silverdale Dr Silver Spring MD 20906 Office: Md Nat Capital Park and Planning Commn 8787 Georgia Ave Silver Spring MD 20907

DURYEA, LOVEJOY REEVES, interior designer; b. Bronxville, N.Y., May 7, 1944; d. Rosser and Elizabeth Lovejoy (Street) Reeves; B.A., St. John's Coll., 1967; m. William M. Duryea, Jr., Aug. 7, 1976; children—Robert Atwell, David Rosser McShane. Sr. copywriter Compton Advt. Co., N.Y.C., 1967-70; copywriter Avon Products Inc., N.Y.C., 1970-71, copychief, 1971-73, group-coordinator, 1973-74, mgr., 1974, creative mgr., 1975, project mgr., 1975-76, mgr. nat. rep. recruiting, 1976-80, cons., 1980-86; pres. Dorset Design, 1980-82; bd. dirs. Alderney Design Ltd., Boothroy Stuart Ltd.; faculty Sch. Visual Arts, 1987—; bd. dirs. St. John's Coll., 1983, bd. visitors, bd. govs., sec. and mem. exec. com.; dir. Boothsroy Stuart Ltd. founder N.Y. chpt. Achievement Rewards Scientists Found. Inc., 1972, dir. at large, 1974-76, dir., 1975-76, membership chmn., 1976-77, 1st v.p., 1978-79, chmn. exec. com., 1979-80; active Jr. League N.Y., 1968-76. Recipient cert. of achievement Avon Products Inc., 1978. Clubs: Leash, Cold Spring Harbor Beach; Nat. Arts, Doubles.

DUSINBERRE, JULIET ANNE STAINER, educator and writer; b. Great Everdon, Northamptonshire, Eng., Oct. 21, 1941; d. John Ranald and Theophania (Cecil) Stainer; m. William Warner Dusinberre, July 9, 1966; children: Edward John, Martin William. BA, Oxford U., 1963; PhD, U. Warwick, 1969; MA, Oxford U., 1973, Cambridge U., 1982. Extramural lectr. English U. Birmingham (Eng.), 1967-79; vis. research scholar Radcliffe Inst., Harvard U., Cambridge, Mass., 1971-72; research fellow Clare Hall, Cambridge, Eng., 1979-80; fellow, lectr. Girton Coll., Cambridge, Eng., 1980—. Author: Shakespeare and the Nature of Women, 1975, Alice to the Lighthouse, 1987. Address: Girton Coll, Cambridge CB3 OJG, England

DUSOLD, LAURENCE RICHARD, chemist, computer specialist; b. Chgo., Nov. 15, 1944; s. Henry E. and Colette M. D.; B.S. in Chemistry, Purdue U., 1966; M.S., U. N.C., 1969; postgrad. Wayne State U., 1969-71; m. Karen A. Marsh, Aug. 29, 1970; children—Amy, Lauren, Patricia, Amanda. Research chemist, residue analysis and methods investigation br. Bur. Foods, FDA, Washington, 1971-75, chemist, computer specialist, div. chemistry and physics, 1975-81; sr. chemist, computer specialist, div. of chemistry and physics, 1981-86, chief telecommunications and scientific computer support, 1986—; mem. faculty, evening div. U. Md., 1973—. Recipient Commendable Service award FDA, Commnr.'s Spl. Citation award. Mem. Am. Chem. Soc., N.Y. Acad. Scis., Assn. Computing Machinery (chmn. SIGAPL, D.C. chpt. 1978-86), Greater Washington Fed. Agy. APL Users Group (co-chmn.), AAUP, Alpha Chi Sigma, Phi Lambda Upsilon. Republican. Roman Catholic. Contbr. articles to profl. jours. Office: FDA 200 C St SW Washington DC 20204

DUSSAIX, FRÉDÉRIC-FRANCOIS, dermatologist; b. Paris, Aug. 2, 1952; s. Olivier-Paul and Hélène (Chavatte) D. MD, Paris Hosp. Bichat, 1981, D in Dermatology, 1983. Diplomate in dermatology. Intern then resident Clinique Tarnier, 1980-83; medecin office de vulgarisation pharmaceutique Formation des Déléques Médicaux, Paris, 1978-79; dermatologist Clinique Tarnier, Paris, 1980-83; gen. practice dermatology Paris, 1981—. Vol. physician Amnesty Internat., Paris, 1984—. Mem. Paris Medecin Soc. (medecin du travail office de recherche scientifique des. territoires d'outre mer 1980-86). Roman Catholic. Home: 9 Rue du Centre, Neuilly, 92200 Seine France Office: 50 Rue de Bourogue, 75007 Paris France

DUTILLEUX, HENRI PAUL JULIEN, composer; b. Angers, France, Jan. 22, 1916; s. Paul and Therese (Koszul) D.; m. Joy Genevieve, Sept. 17, 1946. Ed., Conservatoire Nat. de Paris. Head musical illustrations French Radio, 1944-63; lectr. Ecole Normale de Musique de Paris, 1944-71, prof. composition, 1961-70; guest lectr. Conservatoire National Supérieur de Paris, 1970-71; composer: Sonata for Piano, 1947; First Symphony, 1951; Le Loup (ballet), 1953; 3 Sonnets de Jean Cassou, 1954; Second Symphony Le Double, 1959; Metaboles, 1965; Tout un monde lointain, 1970; Ainsi la nuit, 1976; Timbres espace mouvement ou La nuit Etoilée, 1978; 3 Strophes sur le nom de Sacher, 1982, L'arbre des songes; Concerto for Violin and Orchestra, 1985; Mystere de l'Instant, 1987. Recipient Prix de Rome, Villa Medici, 1938, Grand Prix National de Musique, France, 1967, Prix Mondial du Disque, 1976, 83; prix Internat. Maurice Ravel, 1987, Prix Internat. Music Council UNESCO, 1987. Mem. Academie Royale de Belgique (assoc.), Am. Acad. Arts and Letters (hon.). Address: 12 rue St-Louis-en-l'Ile, 75004 Paris France

DUTOIT, ALEXIS, clothing company executive; b. De Aar, Cape Province, South Africa, Mar. 9, 1938; d. David Fredrick and Pauline (Naude) D. Diploma sheep and wool expert, Grootfontein Coll. Agriculture, Middleburg, Cape Province, 1958. Woolseller, Farmers Co-co Union, Durban, Natal, South Africa, 1959-63; with Jeromes Exclusive Men's Clothing Co., Durban, 1964-72; owner, mgr. Snowgoose Clothing Pty Ltd., Amanzimtoti, Natal, 1973—, mng. dir., 1973—; dir. Conlor Flats Pty Ltd., Durban, Port Natal Housing and Investment Co., Durban, Pick and Shovel Restaurants, Durban, Switzerland Restaurant, Durban. Home: 9 Conlor Holden Ave, Durban, Natal 4001 Republic of South Africa Office: Snowgoose Clothing Pty Ltd, PO Box 296, Amanzimtoti, Natal 4125, Republic of South Africa

DUTOIT, CHARLES, conductor; b. Lausanne, Switzerland, Oct. 7, 1936. Studied at, Conservatory of Lausanne, Acad. Music, Geneva, Academia Musicale Chigiana, Siena, Conservatory Benedetto Marcello, Venice, Italy; attended session in conducting, Berkshire Music Center, Tanglewood, Mass. Formerly violinist with Lausanne Chamber Orch.; debut as condr. with Bern Symphony Orch., Switzerland, 1963; condr. and asst. music dir., Bern Symphony Orch., 1964, later music dir.; condr. and artistic dir., Radio-Zurich Orch., Switzerland, 1967; also guest condr. Vienna Opera; mus. dir. Nat. Symphony Orch. of Mex.; appointed regular condr. Goteborg Orch., Sweden, 1975; music dir., condr., Montreal Symphony Orch., 1977—; prin. guest condr. Minn. Orch., 1982-85; guest condr. all major orchs., S.Am., Europe, Japan, Australia, U.S., Can. and Israel., rec., Deutsche Gramophon, Erato, CBS, Decca/London. Recipient Canadian Music Council medal, 1988. Office: care Orch Symphonique Montreal, 85 St Catherine W Suite 900, Montreal, PQ Canada H2X 3P4

DUTTA BARUAH, BHABENDRA NARAYAN, business executive, journalist; b. Nalbari, India, Dec. 1, 1939; s. Harinarayan and Parbati Dutta Baruah; B.A., Bombay U., 1962; married; 1 dau. Dir. Dutta Baruah & Co., Sreeguru Press, Uma Press, Saptahik Nilachal; editor Assamese daily, Monikut, quar. mag., Saptahik Nilachal; vis. lectr., Boston and Moscow. Active Youth Welfare and Red Cross; pres. Sreemanta Shankar Mission, Guwahati; past v.p. Indian Red Cross Soc.; chmn. Nalbari Municipality. Recipient best service award Indian Red Cross. Mem. All India Small and Medium Newspapers Fedn. (gen. sec.), All Assam Newspaper and Periodicals Assn. (gen. sec.). Clubs: Gauhati Town. Lodge: Rotary (Gauhati West). Author: Banjara; Moscowarpara Preyasilai, Krishnajeena; Preethibir Nanadesh; Sasitra Sishu Path; Juijhala Daorat. Office: Editor Saptahik Nilachal, College Hostel Rd PO Box 135, Gauhati 781001, India

DUTTON, BRIAN GORDON, information consultant; b. Liverpool, Lancashire, Eng., May 2, 1930; widowed; children: David Brian, Andrew. BSc. with honors, U. Liverpool, 1952, PhD, 1955. Sr. research chemist I.C.I. Plc., Cheshire, Eng., 1956-65; librarian I.C.I. Plc., Cheshire, 1965-74, mgr. info. services, 1974-86; pvt. practice info. cons. Devon, 1987—. Author: Chemical Industry-Economic and Social Aspects, 1972; contbr. articles to profl. jours.; patentee in field. Mem. ct. U. Liverpool, 1953—; gov. Sir Thomas Boteler Sch., Warrington, Edn., 1958-62. Fellow Royal Soc. Chemistry, Inst. Info. Scientists; mem. Soc. Chem. Industry, Assn. Info. Mgmt. (chmn. 1988—).

DUTTON, DAVID JOHN, historian, educator; b. Birmingham, Eng., Mar. 25, 1950; s. Frank and Gladys Annie (Massey) D. BA, London U., 1971, PhD, 1975. Lectr. Liverpool (Eng.) U., 1974-85, sr. lectr., 1985—. Author: Austen Chamberlain, 1985; contbr. articles to hist. jours., 1978—. Grantee Brit. Acad., 1984. Fellow Royal Hist. Soc.; mem. Hist. Assn. Mem. Conservative Party. Anglican. Home: Dale Hall, Elmswood Rd, Liverpool 18 England Office: U Liverpool, 8 Abercromby Sq, Liverpool L69 3BX, England

DUTTON, DENIS LAURENCE, philosopher, educator; b. Los Angeles, Feb. 9, 1944; came to New Zeland, 1984; s. William and Thelma (Hansen) D.; m. Margit Stoll, Apr. 7, 1969; children: Sonia, Benjamin. AB in Philosophy, U. Calif., Santa Barbara, 1966, PhD in Philsophy, 1973. Prof. philosphy U. Mich., Dearborn, 1973-84; sr. lectr. philosphy of art U. Canterbury, Christchurch, New Zealand, 1984—; vis. prof. philosphy Claremont (Calif.) Grad. Sch., 1979-80; chmn. New Zealand Com. Sci. Investigation of Claims of Paranormal, 1985—. Editor: The Concept of Creativity in Science and Art, 1982, THe Forger's Art, 1983; editor Philosophy and Lit. Jour., 1976—; contbr. articles to scholarly publs. Devel. worker Peace Corps, India, 1966-68. Mem. Am. Soc. Aesthetics (trustee 1982-850, Brit. Soc. Aesthetics, Royal Soc. New Zealand Philosophy Assn., Canterbury Astronomical Soc. Mem. New Zealand Labor Party. Home: 30 Tyndale Pl, Christchurch New Zealand Office: U Canterbury, Sch Fine Arts, Christchurch New Zealand

DUTTON, ROBERT EDWARD, JR., medical educator; b. Milford, N.H., Aug. 11, 1924; s. Robert Edward and Mildred Beatrice (Prior) D.; m. Cynthia Baldwin, June 15, 1958; children: Elizabeth Helen, Leila Baldwin. Student, Gettysburg Coll., 1942-43, The Citadel, 1943-44, Johns Hopkins U., 1944-45; M.D., Med. Coll. Va., 1949. Intern Boston City Hosp., 1950-51, resident, 1953-54; resident SUNY, Syracuse, 1954-56; instr. medicine SUNY, 1956-59; asst. prof. environ. medicine and medicine Johns Hopkins U., 1964-68; asso. prof. physiology Albany Med. Coll., Union U., 1968-74, asso. prof. medicine, 1970-77, prof. physiology, 1974-86, prof. medicine, 1977-86; prof. biomed. engring. Rensselaer Poly. Inst., 1972—; cons. pulmonary div. VA hosps., 1968-69. Contbr. articles to profl. jours. Served with AUS, 1943-46; Served with USAF, 1951-53. Nat. Heart Inst. postdoctoral fellow, 1959-61. Mem. Am. Physiol. Soc., Am. Thoracic Soc. (pres. Eastern sect.), Internat. Union Physiol. Scis., Biomed. Engring. Soc., Am. Fedn. Clin. Research, Johns Hopkins Med. and Surg. Assn., Sigma Xi (pres. SUNY-Albany chpt. 1983-84), Sigma Zeta. Office: Rensselaer Poly Inst Troy NY 12180-3590

DUTY, TONY EDGAR, lawyer, judge, historian; b. Golinda, Tex., May 14, 1928; s. Tony and Glennie Mae (Butler) D.; m. Kathleen Lou Lear; children—Valerie Ann, Barbara Diane, Dan Richard. Student, U. Colo., 1947-49; B.B.A., Baylor U., 1952, J.D., 1953. Bar: Tex. 1954, U.S. Dist. CT. (we. dist.) Tex. 1970, U.S. Ct. Appeals (5th cir.) 1978, U.S. Ct. Appeals (11th cir.) 1981, U.S. Supreme Ct. 1982, U.S. Dist. Ct. (no. dist.) Tex. 1983. Sole practice Waco, Tex., 1954-56, 64—; 1st asst. atty City of Waco, 1957-63; mcpl. judge City Woodway, Tex., 1963-80, City of Lacy-Lakeview, Tex., 1976-78, City of Beverly Hills, Tex., 1976-78, City of Waco, 1957-87, City of Bellmead, Tex., 1964-86; prof. bus. law, corps. and real estate Baylor U., 1976-78; ptnr. Indian Creek Estates; dir. Shannon Devel. Co., Telco Systems Inc., Sun Valley Water and Devel. Co., Inc., Hewitt Devel. Co., Woodway Seed and Garden Co., Inc. Author: The Coronado Expedition, 1540-1542, 1970, James Wilkinson: 1757-1825, 1971, Champ D'Asile, 1972, The Home Front: McLennan County in the Civil War, 1974; contbr. articles to hist. jours. Mem. Waco Plan Commn., 1966-69, Waco-McLennan County Library Commn., 1968-72, chmn., 1971-72; mem. Waco Fire and Police Civil Service Commn., 1975-81, chmn., 1980-81; mem. Waco Am. Revolution Bicentennial Commn., 1974-76; chmn. Waco Heritage '76, 1974-76; mem. McLennan County Hist. Survey Commn., 1970—; chmn. Ft. House Mus., Waco, 1968-72; bd. dirs. Waco Heritage Soc., 1960—. Served with USAF, 1946-49. Mem. State Bar Tex., Waco-McLennan County Bar Assn., Waco-McLennan County Def. Lawyers Assn. (v.p.), 5th Cir. Bar Assn., Delta Theta Phi. Democrat. Baptist. Lodges: Masons, K.P. Home: 613 Camp Dr Waco TX 76710 Office: 2317 Austin Ave Waco TX 76701

D'UVA, ROBERT CARMEN, insurance and real estate broker; b. Castelpetroso, Italy, Aug. 25, 1920; s. Gabriele and Bettina D'Uva; m. Josephine C. Del Riccio, Sept. 5, 1948; children: Robert Gary, Gary James, James Joseph. Student, Rutgers U., 1946-47, postgrad., 1950-51; BA in Acctg., Seton Hall U., 1949. Spl. rep. Manhattan Life Ins. Co. of N.Y., 1949—; real estate sales rep. David Cornheim Agy., Newark, 1950-51; pvt. practice ins. and real estate broker Newark, 1951—; ptnr. Romaine Realty Co., Newark, 1962-83; gen. agt. Md. Am. Gen. Ins. Cos.; pres. Diversified Variable Annuities, Inc., Newark, 1968—, Del-Gior Corp., Bloomfield, N.J., 1971—, Diversified Ins. Agy., Inc., Caldwell, N.J., 1973—. Bd. dirs. Newark Boys Club, pres. Broadway unit, 1967; pres. real estate bd. of Newark, Irvington and Hillside, N.J. Served as cpl. Q.M.C. AUS, 1942-46, PTO. Mem. Nat. Real Estate Brokers Assn., Nat. Security Dealers Assn., N.J. Real Estate Assn., Nat. Assn. Real Estate Bd., Life Underwriters Assn., Ind. Ins. Agts. Assn. Roman Catholic. Lodge: Lions (North Newark) (pres., dep. dist. gov. 1964). Home: 27 Howland Circle W Caldwell NJ 07006 Office: Diversified Variable Annuities Inc 316 Mount Prospect Ave Newark NJ 07104 also: Del-Gior Corp 115 Bloomfield Ave Caldwell NJ 07006 also: Diversified Ins Agy Inc 41 Bloomfield Ave Caldwell NJ 07006

DUVAL, (CHARLES) GAETAN, deputy prime minister and minister of justice of Mauritius, lawyer; b. Rose Hill, Mauritius, Oct. 9, 1930; s. Charles R. and Rosina M. Duval; divorced; 1 child. Ed., Royal Coll., Curepipe, Mauritius, Lincoln's Inn, London, and Faculty of Law, U. Paris. Mem. Town Council, chmn. Curepipe, from 1960; mem. Legis. Council, Curepipe, from 1960; mem. Mcpl. Council, Port Louis, Mauritius, 1969—; Minister of Housing, Lands and Town and Country Planning, 1964-65; mem. London Constl. Conf., 1965; leader Parti Mauritien Social Democrate, 1966—; mem. Legis. Assembly for Grand River North-west and Port Louis West, 1967; leader of opposition, 1967-69; minister External Affairs, Tourism and Emigration, 1969-73; mayor City of Port Louis, 1969-71, lord mayor, 1981-84, 81—; mayor Town of Curepipe, 1976-79; pres. Assn. Touristique de l'Ocean Indien, 1973; chmn. S. African Regional Tourism Council, 1973; dep. prime Minister, Mauritius, 1983—; atty. gen., minister of justice, 1983-86, minister tourism and labor, 1986— . Decorated grand officier de l'Ordre de Lion, grand officier de l'Ordre Nat. du Tchad; commandeur de la Legion d'Honneur (France); queen's counsel, knight bachelor. Avocations: horse riding, bee keeping. Office: Parti Mauricien Social Democrate, Place Foch, Port Louis Mauritius *

DUVAL, LEON-ETIENNE CARDINAL, archbishop of Algiers; b. Chenex, France, Nov. 9, 1903. Ordained priest Roman Catholic Ch., 1926, bishop of Constantine, Algeria, 1947; archbishop of Algiers, Algeria, 1954—; elevated to Sacred Coll. Cardinals, 1965; titular ch. St. Balbina. Office: Archeveche, 13 rue Khelifa-Boukhalfa, Algiers Algeria also: Vatican City Vatican *

DUVIER, FRITS ALGOT, financial consultant; b. Frederiksberg, Denmark, Aug. 27, 1932; arrived in Isle of Man, 1980; s. Borge Fritz Phillip and Karen Marie (Madsen) D.; m. Annie Margit Jensen, Feb. 3, 1960 (dec.); children—Jeanette, Pernille. Student Copenhagen Comml. Coll., 1949-50, Danish Coll. Commerce, 1953-54. Sales promotion mgr. fiber div. Dupont de Nemours & Co., Denmark, 1956-58; export sales mgr. Zeuthen & Aagaard, C Copenhagen, 1959-60; sales mgr. Minnesota Mining & Mfg., Copenhagen, 1960-65; v.p. sales and mktg. No. Feather Co. Ltd., Copenhagen, 1965-74; comml. and fin. cons., Denmark, Eng., Ireland, Isle of Man, 1974—; bd. dirs. Statorpacks Ltd., Tromode Ind. Est., FDC Ltd., Isle of Man, Margrethe Thormar's Found., Denmark, Robust Mouldings Ltd., Wrexham, Wales, U.K. Manx Project Devel. Services Ltd., Douglas, Isle of Man, Manx Design Research and Devel. Ltd., Douglas. Home and Office: Woodbourne House, 3 Woodbourne Sq, Douglas Isle of Man

D'VER, ABBOTT SIMON, veterinarian, toxicologist; b. Teaneck, N.J., Mar. 24, 1939; s. Morris D'Ver and Lillian D'Ver Sirkin; m. Judith Z. Stern, Sept. 4, 1977; children: Marc, Ilana. Student Cornell U., 1957-59; V.M.D., U. Pa., 1963. Accredited veterinarian U.S. Dept. Agr. Assoc. Am. Soc. Prevention Cruelty to Animals, N.Y.C., 1965-66; dir. lab. animal services Hoffmann-La Roche, Nutley, N.J., 1966-72; pres. White Eagle Lab., Doylestown, Pa., 1972—; chmn. Biodyne Corp., 1985—; adj. prof. Union Grad. Sch., Yellow Springs, Ohio, 1970-74; cons. SUNY-Delhi, 1979—, Harcum Jr. Coll., 1981—; dir. BioDyne Corp., Doylestown. Author: Assistant Animal Technician Manual, 1972. Assoc. editor Lab. Animal Bull., 1965-66. Pres. Bd. Health, Dumont, N.J., 1971-72. Served to capt. U.S. Army, 1963-65. Mem. AVMA, Am. Assn. for Lab. Animal Sci., Am. Assn. Indsl. Veterinarians, N.J. Soc. for Med. Edn. (trustee 1968-72), Am. Assn. for Lab. Animal Practioners, Mid Atlantic Soc. Toxicology, Middle Atlantic Reproduction and Teratology Assn. Home: 1142 N Glenwood St Allentown PA 18104

DWEK, CYRIL S., banker; b. Kobe, Japan, Nov. 9, 1936; s. Nessim S. and Alice (Stambouli) D.; children: Nevil, Alicia. B.S., Wharton Sch., U. Pa., 1958. With Trade Devel. Bank, Geneva, Switzerland, 1962-65; with Republic Nat. Bank of N.Y., 1966—, dir., 1967—, exec. v.p., 1973—, vice chmn., 1983—; dir. Republic N.Y. Corp., 1974—, vice chmn., 1983—; Bd. advisers Brazilian Inst. Bus. Programs, Pace U. Mem. Brazilian Am. C. of C. (dir.). Club: Racing Club de France (Paris). Office: Republic NY Corp 452 Fifth Ave New York NY 10018

DWIGGINS, CLAUDIUS WILLIAM, JR., chemist; b. Amity, Ark., May 11, 1933; s. Claudius William and Lillian (Scott) D.; B.S., U. Ark., 1954, M.S., 1956, Ph.D. (Am. Oil Co. fellow, Coulter-Jones scholar), 1958. With U.S. Dept. of Energy, Bartlesville (Okla.) Tech. Center, 1958-83, chemist, 1958-60, project leader surface physics project, 1960-65, project leader petroleum composition research project, 1965-80, supervisory research chemist, thermodynamics div., 1980-83; sr. chemist Nat. Inst. Petroleum and Energy Research, 1983-84; cons., 1984—. Mem. Am. Chem. Soc., N.Y. Acad. Scis., AAAS, Am. Crystallographic Assn., Am. Inst. Physics, Sigma Xi (sec. 1966-67), Alpha Chi Sigma, Delta Sigma Phi (treas. 1952). Contbr. articles to profl. jours. Home: 1211 S Keeler St Bartlesville OK 74003

DWORKIN, MICHAEL LEONARD, lawyer; b. Bridgeport Ct., Oct. 10, 1947; s. Samuel and Frances (Stein) Dworkin; m. Christina Lyn Hildreth, Sept. 25, 1977; children: Jennifer Hildreth, Amanda Hildreth. BA in Gov. with honors, Clark U., 1969; JD with honors, George Washington U., 1973. Bar: D.C. 1973, Calif. 1975, U.S. Ct. Appeals (9th cir.) 1982, U.S. Supreme Ct. 1978, U.S. Claims Ct. 1983. Atty. FAA, Washington, Los Angeles, 1973-77, United Airlines, San Francisco, 1977-81; sole practice, San Francisco, 1981—; instr. Embry Riddle Aeronautical U., San Francisco, 1980-81; dir. Poplar Ctr., San Mateo, Calif. Jonas Clark scholar Clark U., 1966-69. Mem. ABA, Lawyer Pilot's Bar Assn., Nat. Transp. Safety Bd. Bar Assn. (regional v.p. 1986-87, chmn. rules com. 1985-88), Aircraft Owners and Pilots Assn., Soaring Soc. Am., Internat. Soc. Air Safety Investigators (bd. dirs. San Francisco regional chpt.), State Bar Calif., D.C. Bar Assn. Jewish. Office: 1 Embarcadero Ctr Suite 370 San Francisco CA 94111

DWORZAN, HELENE LIBERMAN, novelist, poet, playwright; b. Paris, France, Mar. 13, 1925; d. Ansjel and Rebecca (Weiripp) Liberman; came to U.S., 1950, naturalized, 1952; student Lycee Victor Hugo, Paris, 1937-43, New Sch. for Social Research, 1952-53; B.A., Richmond Coll., 1974; m. George R. Dworzan; 1 son, Patrice Olivier; m. 2d. Donald H. Reiman, 1975. Translator, Robin Internat./Cinerama, N.Y.C., 1954-59; freelance translator NBC, 1962-72; asso. editor Chelsea, lit. rev., 1970-81; tchr. French, Lang. Inst., N.Y.C., 1970-73, Riverdale Country Sch., N.Y.C., 1973-86; founder, dir. Continuum, poetry and fiction readings, 1970-76. Recipient novel grant Material Jewish Claims against Germany, 1961, Short Story award Dial Press, 1953; Prairie Schooner prize for fiction, 1978. Mem. Authors League Am., Dramatists Guild. Author: (novel) Le Temps de la Chrysalide, 1957; also short stories and poems in various publs. Address: 6495 Broadway Riverdale NY 10471

DWYER, DENNIS D., information systems manager; b. Oak Park, Ill., July 19, 1943; s. John J. and Jessie M. Dwyer; m. Carolyn R. Schultz, Apr. 29, 1967; children: David, Julianne. Various positions Harris Bank, Chgo., 1967-85, mgr. info. systems equipment planning, 1983-86, v.p. info-systems equipment planning and acquisition, 1986—; resolutions chmn. Cooperating Users of Burroughs Equipment, Detroit, 1978-82; cons. Burroughs mainframe computers. Pres. Hunting Ridge Homeowners Assn., 1983-85, Palatine Plan Commn., 1984—. Home: 1032 Raven Ln Palatine IL 60067-6649 Office: Harris Bank PO Box 755 Chicago IL 60690-0755

DWYER, TERRENCE EDWARD, health association executive; b. Ft. Wayne, Ind., June 6, 1945; s. Michael Kenneth and Maxine Marie (Berkhimer) D.; A.B., Harvard U., 1967; M.P.A., U. Mich., 1968. Teaching fellow in polit. sci. U. Mich., 1968-72, research asso. Sch. Public Health, 1973-74; research asso. Pres.'s Adv. Council. on Exec. Orgn., White House, 1969-70; lectr. in polit. sci. Eastern Mich. U., 1972-73; asso. dir. Mich. Profl. Standards Rev. Orgn. Support Center, East Lansing, Mich., 1974-76; exec. dir. Empire State Peer Rev. Orgn., Inc. (formerly Profl. Standards Rev. Orgn. Central N.Y.), Syracuse, 1976-87 ; exec. dir. Med. Soc. Va. Rev. Orgn., Richmond, 1987—; dir. Am. Med. Rev. Research Ctr., 1985—, sec., mem. exec. com., 1985—. Mem. Am. Med. Peer Rev. Orgn. (dir., chmn. chief exec. officers sect. 1982-85), Am. Public Health Assn., Am. Soc. Public Adminstrn., Am. Polit. Sci. Assn., Am. Acad. Polit. and Social Scis., Acad. Polit. Sci. Republican. Clubs: Harvard-Radcliffe of Central N.Y., Univ. of Syracuse, Harvard of Va., Downtown of Richmond.

DY, CYNTHIA HERNANDEZ, pharmacologist educator; b. Manilla, June 27, 1953; d. Marcelo Yap and Zenaida Baron (Galgo) Hernandez; m. Frankie Chua Dy, Nov. 7, 1977; children: Kristine Cheryll, Franciene Dianne, Michelle Bianca. BS in Chemistry, Far Eastern U., Manilla, 1973, MD, 1977. Asst. prof. pharmacology Far Eastern U., Manilla, 1979—; asst. prof. Fatima Med. Coll., Manilla, 1980—. A.H. Robbins Scholar, 1977. Fellow Phillipine Soc. Clin. Experimental Pharmacology. Roman Catholic. Home: 193 Apo Sta, Quezon City Metro Manila, Philippines Office: Beauty Clinic, 56 Spinach St, Valle Verde Metro Manila, Philippines

DYCK, GEORGE, medical educator; b. Hague, Sask., Can., July 25, 1937; came to U.S., 1965; s. John and Mary (Janzen) D.; m. Edna Margaret Krueger, June 27, 1959; children: Brian Edward, Janine Louise, Stanley George, Jonathan Jay. Student, U. Sask., 1955-56; B. Christian Edn., Can. Mennonite Bible Coll., 1959; M.D., U. Man., 1964; postgrad., Menninger Sch. Psychiatry, 1965-68. Diplomate Am. Bd. Psychiatry and Neurology, Royal Coll. Physicians and Surgeons (Can.) in Psychiatry. Fellow community psychiatry Prairie View Mental Health Center, Newton, Kans., 1968-70; clin. dir. tri-county services Prairie View Mental Health Center, 1970-73; prof. U. Kans., Wichita, 1973—; chmn. dept. psychiatry U. Kans., 1973-80; med. dir. Prairie View, Inc., 1980—. Bd. dirs. Mennonite Mut. Aid, Goshen, Ind., 1973-85, Chmn., 1982-85; bd. dirs. Mid-Kans. Community Action Program, 1970-73, Wichita Council Drug Abuse, 1974-76. Fellow Am. Psychiat. Assn. (pres. Kans. dist. br. 1982-84, dep. rep. 1984-86, rep. 1986—, cert. in adminstrv. psychiatry 1984); mem. AMA, Kans. Med. Soc., Kans.-Paraguay Ptnrs. (treas. 1986). Mennonite. Home: 1505 Hillcrest Rd Newton KS 67114 Office: Prairie View Inc 1901 E 1st St Newton KS 67114

DYCK, RANDALL JOHN, data processing manager, marketing support; b. Boissevain, Man., Can., Aug. 19, 1958; s. George Abraham and Ruth Edna (Drader) D.; m. Ee Pai Chew, Dec. 29, 1980. B.Sc. in Math. and Computer Sci., Brandon Univ., 1978; postgrad. Univ. Man., 1978-79; cert. in Bus. Adminstrn., Red River Community Coll., 1982. Certified systems prof. Sci. programmer Burroughs Bus. Machines, Winnipeg, Man., Can., 1978-79; bus. programmer Northern Sales Ltd., Winnipeg, 1979-80; programmer analyst Group West Mgmt. Support, Winnipeg, 1980-81; systems analyst Spectra Computer Services, Winnipeg, 1981-84; systems cons. J.D.A. Software, Calgary, Alta., Can., 1984-86; systems cons., Spectrum Info. Systems, Calgary, Alb., Can., 1986-87; data processing mgr., Can. Tire Corp., Calgary, 1987—. Recipient award for excellence Univ. Man. Alumni, 1976; Univ. scholarship Brandon U., 1977; IBM grantee, 1977. Mem. Assn. Computing Machinery, Data Processing Mgmt. Assn., Can. Inst. Mgmt., Soc. Mgmt. Accts.; Inst. Data Processing Mgmt. Avocations: European fencing; judo. Home: 128 Woodvalley Rise SW, Calgary, AB Canada T2W 5L7 Office: Can Tire, 3516-8 Ave NE, Calgary, AB Canada T2A 6K5

DYER, ANDREW ROY, manufacturing executive; b. Nashville, Apr. 30, 1951; s. Andrew Johnson and Gladys Marie (Kelly) D. B.S., U. Tenn., 1973; B.E., Vanderbilt U., 1974; M.B.A., U. Tenn., 1975. Prin. systems analyst Teledyne Brown Engring., Huntsville, Ala., 1976-78; ops. auditor Data Design Labs., Cucamonga, Calif., 1978-80; sr. acctg. systems analyst Calif. Federal, Los Angeles, 1980-81; sr. mem. tech. staff Teledyne Systems Co., Northridge, Calif., 1981—. Sustaining mem. Mount Wilson Obs. Assn., Pasadena, 1983—. Named Best Econ. Forecaster of the Year, So. Calif. Corp. Planning Assn., 1980; Sturges Meml. scholar, U. Tenn., 1976. Fellow Brit. Interplanetary Soc.; mem. AIAA, IEEE, Planning Forum, World Future Soc. Los Angeles (pres. 1979-80), Orgn. for Advancement of Space Industrialization and Settlement, Los Angeles Astron. Soc., Orange County Astronomers. Home: 22446 Burbank Blvd Woodland Hills CA 91367 Office: Teledyne Systems Co 19601 Nordhoff St Northridge CA 91324

DYER, CROMWELL ADAIR, JR., lawyer, international organization official; b. St. Louis, Sept. 9, 1932; came to Netherlands, 1973; s. Adair and Tompie Leora (Giles) D.; m. Margaret Copeland Peickert, June 12, 1958 (div. Aug. 1976); children—Gretchen, Jack, Julie, Stephen; m. Susan Aynesworth, Aug. 20, 1977; stepchildren—Carol, Amanda, Donne Brown. B.A., U. Tex.-Austin, 1954, J.D., 1961; LL.M., Harvard U., 1971. Bar: Tex. 1961, U.S. Dist. Ct. (no. dist.) Tex. 1965, U.S. Ct. Apls. (5th cir.) 1965, U.S. Dist. Ct. (ea. dist.) Tex. 1966, U.S. Ct. Apls. (11th cir.), 1982. Law clk. FTC, Washington, 1960; staff atty. So. Union Gas Co., Dallas, 1962-64; assoc. Dedman & May, Dallas, 1964-65, White, McElroy & White, Dallas, 1965-67; sole practice, Dallas, 1967-73; 1st sec. Hague Conf. on Pvt. Internat. Law, 1973—; observer or cons. to intergovernmental orgns.; conductor seminars. Author articles in field. Served to lt. (j.g.) U.S. Navy, 1954-57. Mem. jury for award of Diploma in Internat. Law, Hague Acad., 1980, 84, 85, 86, 87, dir. studies, 1985; course on Unfair Competition in Private International Law, 1988. Mem. Internat. Bar Assn., ABA, Am. Soc. Internat. Law, Inter-Am. Bar Assn., Am. Fgn. Law Assn., Dallas Bar Assn. Club: Club du jeudi (pres. 1983-85) (The Hague). Home: Jozef Israelslaan 18, The Hague 2596 AP, The Netherlands Office: Hague Conference on Pvt. International Law, Javastraat 2c, The Hague 2585 AM, The Netherlands

DYER, FREDERICK CHARLES, writer, consultant; b. St. Louis, Feb. 17, 1918; s. George Leo and Katherine Mary (Dobson) D.; m. Lucrecia E. Herrera-Ibarguen, 1946; children: John R., Michael G., Lisa M. Dyer Fitzpatrick. B.A., Holy Cross Coll., 1938; M.B.A., Dartmouth Coll., 1948. Edni. writer, editor tng. publs. Bur. Naval Personnel, 1948-58, asst. for spl. projects, leadership staff, 1958-64; spl. asst. to Undersec. Navy U.S. Navy, 1964-66; asst. for spl. projects Office Civilian Manpower Mgmt., Dept. Navy, 1966-68; dir. program analysis div. Navy Publs. and Printing Service, Washington, 1968-74; profl. lectr. George Washington U., 1956-60; adj. prof. Drexel Inst. Tech., 1962-67; profl. lectr. Am. U., 1967-73; adv. Ctr. for Applied Research in Apostolate, 1979-85. Author, co-author: Putting Yourself Over in Business, 1957, Executive's Guide to Handling People, 1958, Executive's Guide to Effective Speaking and Writing, 1962, Blueprint for Executive Success, 1964, Bureaucracy vs. Creativity, 1965, rev. edit., 1969, How to Make Decisions About People, 1966, The Petty Officer's Guide, 6 edits., 1952-66, The Enjoyment of Management, 1971, 82; contbr. more than 70 articles to profl. jours.; contbg. editor The Pope Speaks mag., 1954-64, Wall St. Rev. of Books, 1977-82. Mem. Town Council Somerset, Md., 1962-64; chmn. U.S. Civil Service Task Force on Mgmt. Edn. for Computers, 1965-66. Served with USNR, 1943-46; PTO; Navy Dept., 1948-52; ret. comdr., 1961. Mem. Authors Guild, Authors League Am., Washington Ind. Writers. Clubs: Columbia Country (Chevy Chase, Md.); Cosmos (fin. and hist. coms.), Nat. Press (library com.), Army and Navy (Washington). Home and Office: 4509 Cumberland Ave Somerset MD 20815-5459

DYER, ROBERT FRANCIS, JR., internist; b. Washington, Nov. 18, 1926; s. Robert Francis and Sallie Antoinette (Worley) D.; A.B., U. Mich., 1951; M.D., George Washington U., 1955; cert. Postgrad. Med. Sch. Harvard U., 1958; m. Doris Anne Swain, June 27, 1970; children—Robert Francis, William Edward, Anne-Marie Helen Sallie, Scott Robertson McGavin. Intern, George Washington U. Hosp., 1955-56; resident in medicine D.C. Gen. Hosp., 1956-57, VA Hosp., Washington, 1957-58; chief resident physician George Washington U. Hosp., 1958-59; chief of staff Herndon (Va.) Med. Center, 1960-61, U.S. Army Hosp., Ft. Lewes, Del., 1963-65; chief of medicine U.S. Army Hosp., Ft. Indiantown Gap, Pa., 1962-63, dep. comdr., 1964-65; practice medicine specializing in internal medicine, Washington and Chevy Chase, Md., 1965—; chmn. dept. medicine Sibley Hosp., 1986—, vice-chmn. continuing edn. com., 1987-88; mem. staffs George Washington

U. Hosp., Washington Hosp. Center, Drs. Hosp. (all Washington); dir. Research Lab. on Eosinophil Effect of Heparin, Washington, 1959-71; asst. clin. prof. medicine George Washington U., 1963—; dir. clin. research Police and Fire Clinic, Washington, 1964—, acting chief of medicine, 1970, clinic adminstr., 1973-75, clinic dir., 1973—; dep. med. dir. Washington Nat. Airport, 1961; nat. med. dir. Emphysema Control Com., 1967-70; med. cons. bd. ARC, 1985—; sr. internist med. review bd., D.C. Dept. Labor, 1983—; mem. D.C. Mayor's Adv. Bd. on Emergency Med. Service, 1974-75; chmn. bd. Protective Service Physicians, Washington, 1973-80; lectr. U.S. Park Police Acad., Alexandria, Va., 1964-76, D.C. Fire Tng. Acad., 1964—; chief med. flight surgeon Met. Police, Washington, 1968—, U.S. Park Police Helicopter Corps, 1970—; cons. in medicine D.C. Gen. Hosp., Walter Reed Army Hosp., VA, George Washington U. Hosp. Cardiology Clinic. Bd. dirs. Bd. Police and Fire Surgeons, Washington, 1963—, sec., 1964-71, chmn., 1973—; founder, dir. Police and Fire Surgeons Library, 1976—; chmn. bd. dirs. D.C. Bd. Police and Fire Surgeons, 1973—. Served with M.C., U.S. Army, 1945-47, to col., 1956-65; Korea. Decorated Knight Order of St. Lazarus; recipient E. H. Hill award U. Mich., 1950, Citizenship award Am. Legion, 1954, Osler award George Washington U., 1954; diplomate Nat. Bd. Med. Examiners. Fellow Internat. Coll. Angiology, Am. Coll. Angiology, Am. Geriatrics Soc., Royal Soc. Health, InterAm. Coll. Physicians, Am. Occupational Med. Assn., Am. Acad. Med. Dirs.; mem. Am. Soc. Clin. Research, George Washington U. Med. Soc., D.C. Med. Soc. (pres. sect. occupational medicine 1979-80, inter-splty. bd. 1975, chmn. state com. on environ. and occupational health 1980—, pres.-elect, med. editor Metro-Intercom 1977-80), Nat., Nat. Capital (dir., exec. sec. 1979-80, v.p. 1980—, occupational med. assns.1981-83), AMA, Am. Soc. Internal Medicine, U.S. Assn. Mil. Surgeons, So. Med. Assn., Pan Am. Med. Soc. (pres. 1981-83), Internat. Assn. Fire Chiefs (sec. med. sect. 1973-76), SAR (v.p. chpt. 1974-76, pres. 1976-77, state pres. 1976-78, surgeon gen. 1979-80), Descs. Colonial Physicians (gov. gen. 1974—), Sons of Union Vets. (state comdr. 1980-81), Washington Assembly, Am. Assn. Police Physicians and Surgeons (founder 1976), Washington Med. and Surg. Soc. (exec. sec. 1977-78, pres. 1978-79), Hippocrates-Galen Med. Soc. (chmn. bd. 1976-77), George Washington U. Faculty Club, Soc. Colonial Wars (gov. chpt. 1969-72, mem. resolutions com. 1972—, dep. gov. gen. 1978-81), D.C. Med. Soc. (ho. of dels. 1985—), Sovereign Mil. Order of Temple U.S.A. (nat. pres. 1984—), Delta Deuteron (pres. 1950), Phi Sigma Kappa (scholarship award 1950), Phi Chi (v.p. 1965, pres. 1977—). Clubs: Army and Navy (pres. Augustur Gardner Post Soc. 1983-84), Univ., Kenwood Golf and Country, George Washington U.; Annapolis Yacht; Royal Health (London). Med. editor Met. Intercom Jour., 1973-80; contbr. articles to profl. jours. Home: 5608 Albia Rd Westwood Bethesda MD 20816 Office: 5530 Wisconsin Ave NW Washington DC 20815

DYKSTRA, DAVID ALLEN, business executive; b. Kalamazoo, Feb. 5, 1938; s. Alle and Elizabeth (VanderHorst) D. m. Kathryn Ann DeNio, Aug. 4, 1962 (div. Nov. 1985); children: Brian Thayer, Kristen Lee, Holly Beth. BBA, Western Mich. U., 1966. Pres. Allied Waste Inc., Portage, Mich., 1970-80, Dykert Enterprises, Portage, 1981—; cons. Waste Industry, Mich., 1976-82; owner Dairy World Yogurt Shops. Bd. dirs. Portage C. of C., 1980-83, mem. econ. devel. com.; alt. del. Rep. Conv., Mich., 1984. Mem. Safari Club Internat., Lakes Area Conservation Club. Republican. Methodist. Club: Beacon, 300 of Western Mich. U. Lodge: Sertoma (pres. Kalamazoo club 1978). Home: 7221 W VW Ave Schoolcraft MI 49087 Office: The Windjammer 275 Romence Ave Portage MI 49081

DYKSTRA, WILLIAM DWIGHT, business executive, consultant; b. Grand Rapids, Mich., June 15, 1927; s. John Albert and Irene (Stablekamp) D.; m. Ann McGuiness, Nov. 5, 1957; children: William Hugh, Mary Irene. AB, Hope Coll., 1949; MBA, Ind. U., 1950. Asst. mgr. Ply-Curves, Inc., 1950, originator magnesium metal furniture 1951; pres. mfg. co. Dwight Corp., 1952-56; pres. W.D. Dykstra Group, 1956—; ptnr. Dykstra Assos.; bd. dirs. Sheldon Co., Graphic Murals, Inc. Author: Management and the 4th Estate; New Profits for Management. George F. Baker Scholar selector; elder Dutch Reformed Ch. Recipient Outstanding Furniture Merit award, 1955, Vehicle Color Design award, 1967, P.I.A. Graphic award, 1971, Am. Advt. Fedn. award, 1971, 73, 76, Disting. Entrepreneur Alumnus award Ind. U., 1983. Mem. Am. Econs. Assn., Am. Inst. Graphic Arts (Packaging award 1965, 67), Acad. Polit. Sci., Am. Mktg. Assn. (Mktg. Man of Yr. 1981), Soc. Packaging and Handling Engrs., Phi Kappa Psi, Pi Kappa Delta. Republican. Clubs: Charlevoix Yacht (Mich.). Home: 1145 Edison St NW Grand Rapids MI 49505 Office: Old Tallmadge Grange Hall 0-1845 W Leonard Rd Grand Rapids MI 49504

DYMOND, LEWIS WANDELL, lawyer; b. Lansing, Mich., June 28, 1920; s. Lewis Wandell and Irene (Parker) D.; m. Betty Louise Blood, Sept. 6, 1942; children: Lewis W., Jean Ann; m. Joann Surrey, Sept. 3, 1966; 1 son, Steven Henry. J.D. cum laude, U. Miami, 1956. Bar: Fla. 1957. With Nat. Airlines, Inc., Miami, Fla., 1938-62; mechanic, agt., sta. mgr., flight dispatcher, ops. mgr., pilot, v.p. ops., maintenance and engring. Nat. Airlines, Inc., 1955-62; pres., chief exec. officer, dir. Frontier Airlines, 1962-69. Mem. Com. of 100, Miami. Mem. U. Miami Alumni Club, Phi Kappa Phi, Phi Alpha Delta. Clubs: Mason (32, Shriner), Union League (N.Y.C.), Cherry Hills Country, Denver, Petroleum of Denver, Garden of the Gods (Colorado Springs, Colo.), Palm Bay, Surf (Miami, Fla.), Miami, La Gorce Country (bd. dirs.) (Miami Beach, Fla.). Office: Taylor Brion Buker and Greene 1111 S Bayshore Dr Miami FL 33131

DYOTT, RICHARD BURNABY, electrical engineer, researcher; b. Tientsin, China, June 19, 1924; came to Eng., 1936; came to U.S., 1979; s. Hugh Felton and Winifred Okell (Weaver) D.; m. Jean Margaret Butler, Oct. 18, 1952; children—Rosemary Jane, Penelope Anne, Caroline Mary. B.Sc. in Engring., U. London, 1949, D. Sc., 1985. Research engr. Gen. Electric Co., London, 1949-67; sect. leader Brit. Telecom Research, London, 1967-75; research fellow Imperial Coll., London U., 1975-79; dir. optical fiber research and devel. Andrew Corp., Chgo., 1979—. Contbr. numerous papers to profl. publs. Patentee in field. Fellow Instn. Elec. Engrs. (Electronics award 1979); mem. IEEE, Optical Soc. Am. Office: Andrew Corp 10500 W 153d St Orland Park IL 60462

DYSLI, MICHEL, data processing executive; b. Chaux-De-Fonds, Switzerland, May 20, 1954; m. Sept. 5, 1984; 1 child, Nicolas. Diploma Informatique de Gestion, U. Neuchatel, 1986. Analyst Teled, Neuchatel, Switzerland, 1980-84, Assut, Lausanne, Switzerland, 1985; cons. and dir. Deltec-System, Neuchatel, 1980—; prof. CPLN, Neuchatel, 1985—. Home: Acacias 12, Neuchatel 2000, Switzerland Office: Deltec-System Gare 53, Box 1652, Neuchatel 2002, Switzerland

DYTZ, EDISON, electronics engineer, consultant; b. Santo Angelo, Rio Grande do Sul, Brazil, Feb. 25, 1935; s. Wenceslau and Irena (Ludtke) D.; m. Nilda Bastos, Dec. 15, 1956 (div. 1975); children—Susana, Edison, Cristina, Sergio, Monica, Ana Claudia; m. Jane Lynn Garrison, June 9, 1980; children—Marcos, Marcio. Grad. in Mil. Engring., Academia Militar de Agulhas Negros, 1956; grad. in elec. engring. Instituto Militar de Engenharia, 1960; M.S. in Bioengring., Universidade Federal do Rio de Janeiro, 1979. Cert. elec. engr. Commd. lt. Brazilian Army, 1951, advanced through grades to lt. col., 1977, ret. 1979; prof. Univ. de Brasilia, 1967—; head communications service to Presidency, Brazilia, 1972-75; sec. informatics SEI, Brasilia, 1980-85; cons. Dytz Informatica e Automacao Ltda., Brasilia, 1985, UN-Sistema Economico Latino-Americano, N.Y.C., 1985. Author: A Informatica no Brasil, 1987. Collaborator: A Questao da Informatica, 1985, Ciencia & Tecnologia, 1984. Head delegations: UNESCO Informatics Third World, 1984, confs. Brazil-W.Ger., 1983, Brazil Brazil-China and Argentina, 1984; coordinator bill info. Brazilian Congress, 1984. Decorated medals Portuguese govt., 1973, Paraguay govt., 1972, Venezuelan govt., 1972; recipient Rio Branco/Pacificador medal, Brazil, 1974. Methodist. Avocations: Gardening; tennis. Home: Shin QL 14, Conj 5 Casa 10, DF 71 500 Brasilia Brazil

EADS, LYLE WILLIS, retired government inspector; b. Ida Grove, Iowa, June 29, 1916; s. David J. and Bertha E. (McGonigle) E.; m. Betty Boles, Dec. 22, 1946; children—Diane, Mary Ellen. Enlisted U.S. Navy, 1934, advanced through grades to comdr., ret., 1964; asst. inspector gen. Naval Sea Systems Command, Washington, 1966-84, ret. 1984—. Author: Survival Amidst the Ashes, 1978. Decorated Merito Naval Degree of Knight, Republic of Brazil, Rio de Janeiro. Mem. DAV, Am. Legion, Mil. Order of Purple Heart, Am. Ex-Prisoners of War, Inc., Ret. Officers Assn., Nat. Adv. Bd., Am. Security Council, Internat. Platform Assn. Methodist. Lodge: Masons. Avocation: writing. Home: 401 S Carlyn Spring Rd Arlington VA 22204

EAGLES, JOHN MORTIMER, psychiatrist; b. Newport-on-Tay, Fife, Scotland, Oct. 21, 1952; s. Philip Mortimer and Robina Mary (Renn) E.; m. Janette Isobel Rorke, Jan. 17, 1978; children: Katherine Mary, Jane Lesley. MB, ChB, Aberdeen (Scotland) U., 1977; MPhil, Edinburgh (Scotland) U., 1984. Med. house officer Grampian Health Bd., Aberdeen, 1977-78; cons. psychiatrist Grampian Health Bd., 1985—; sr. house officer Lothian Health Bd., Edinburgh, 1978-79, registrar in psychiatry, 1979-82; lectr. in mental health U. Aberdeen, 1982-85, hon. sr. lectr., 1985—; psychiat. tutor Aberdeen Postgrad. Tng. Scheme in Psychiatry, 1987—, sr. registrar tutor, 1986-87. Author (with D. A. Alexander): Multiple Choice Questionnaire Examinations in Psychiatry, 1986. Mem. Royal Coll. Psychiatrists. Mem. Brit. Labour Party. Home: 41 Binghill Park, Milltimber, Aberdeen Grampian AB1 0EE, Scotland Office: Royal Cornhill Hosp Ross Clinic, 26 Cornhill Rd, Aberdeen Grampian AB9 2ZF, Scotland

EAGLETON, WILLIAM LESTER, JR., foreign service officer; b. Peoria, Ill., Aug. 17, 1926; s. William Lester and Mary Louise (Chandler) E.; m. Francoise Bosworth, Oct. 12, 1948 (div. 1966); children—Diane, Marc, Richard, Robert, Philip; m. Kathleen Flannigan, Mar. 18, 1967; children—Anthony Brian, John Patrick, Mary Louise. BA, Yale U., 1948; postgrad., Inst. D'Etudes Politiques, Paris, 1948-49. Joined U.S. Fgn. Service, 1949; 3d sec. embassy U.S. Fgn. Service, Madrid, 1950-51, Damascus, Syria, 1951-53, Beirut, 1953-54; pub. affairs officer U.S. Fgn. Service, Kirkuk, Iraq, 1954-55; assigned Dept. State, 1956-59; consul Tabriz, Iran, 1959-61; charge d'affaires embassy U.S. Fgn. Service, Nouakchott, Mauritania, 1962-64; 1st sec. embassy U.S. Fgn. Service, London, 1964-66; with Woodrow Wilson Sch. Pub. and Internat. Affairs, 1966-67; consul gen. U.S. Fgn. Service, Democratic Yemen, 1967, charge d'affaires, 1967-69; chief U.S. interests sect. Swiss embassy, Algiers, Algeria, 1969-74; assigned Dept. State, 1974-76; diplomat-in-residence Colo. State U., 1976-77; posted to Am. embassy, Tunis, Tunisia, 1977-78; charge d'affaires Am. embassy, Tripoli, Libya, 1978-80; chief U.S. interests sect. Baghdad, Iraq, 1980-84; ambassador Am. embassy, Syria, Damascus, 1984-88; dep. commr. gen. UNRWA, Vienna, 1988—. Author: The Kurdish Republic of 1946, 1963, Introduction to Kurdish Rugs and Other Weavings, 1988. Office: US Ambassador to Syria Dept of State Washington DC 20520

EAGLSTEIN, ABRAHAM SOLOMON, government official; b. Munich, Germany, June 27, 1946; came to U.S., 1949; arrived in Israel, 1971; s. Howard and Rose (Richman) E.; m. Celia Jeanette Hanfling, June 18, 1973; children: Shammai Meir, Yael Sarah, Rafael Moshe. BS in Psychology, Purdue U., 1967; MS in Edn. Research, Ind. U., 1969, PhD in Edn. Research, 1970. Social caseworker Jackson County, Mo., 1965; dir. U.S. Office Edn. Research Grant, 1968-69; research assoc. Columbia U. Tchrs. Coll. Dept. Spl. Edn., 1970-71; evaluation researcher Moadon Shalom, Israel Inst. Applied Social Research, 1972-74; dir. research dept. Ministry Labor and Social Affairs, 1975—; lectr. dept. spl. edn. Hebrew U., 1972-78, Bar Ilan U., 1974-75, Jerusalem Girls Coll., 1975-80; research dir. project for tng. minimally brain damaged children, 1975; sabbatical Brookdale Inst. Gerontology and Human Devel., 1983-84; Israel rep. info. exchange system Ctr. for Social Devel. and Humanitarian Offices UN; mem. adv. panel Minister Labor and Social Affairs on Mental Retardation, 1977-80; mem. Jerusalem Working Group for Blind, 1978-80; nat. corr. UN European Social Devel. Program. Mem. editorial bd. Soc. and Welfare; contbr. articles to profl. jours. Trustee Beersheba Ctr. for Rehab. Blind, 1975-78; bd. dirs. Jerusalem Inst. for Research in Contemporary Jewish Issues. Fellow Ind. U. Research Tng. program, 1967-68. Jewish. Office: Ministry Labor and Social Affairs, 10 Yad Haruzim St, Jerusalem Israel

EAKIN, THOMAS CAPPER, sports promotion executive; b. New Castle, Pa., Dec. 16, 1933; s. Frederick William and Beatrice (Capper) E.; m. Brenda Lee Andrews, Oct. 21, 1961; children: Thomas Andrews, Scott Frederick. B.A. in History, Denison U., 1956. Life ins. cons. Northwestern Mut. Life Ins. Co., Cleve., 1959-67; dist. mgr. Putman Pub. Co., Cleve., 1968-69; regional bus. mgr. Chilton Pub. Co., Cleve., 1969-70; dist. mgr. Hitchcock Pub. Co., Cleve., 1970-72; founder, pres. Golf Internat. 100 Club, Shaker Heights, Ohio, 1970—; founder, pres., dir. Cy Young Mus., 1975-80; pres. TCE Enterprises, Shaker Heights, Ohio, 1973—; founder, pres. Ohio Baseball Hall of Fame, 1976—, Ohio Baseball Hall of Fame Celebration, 1977-79, Ohio Baseball Hall of Fame and Mus., 1980—, Ohio Sports Hall of Fame, 1985—, Ohio Assn. of Sports Hall of Fames, 1985—, Ohio Sports Council, 1985—; founder, chmn. Ohio Baseball Hall of Fame Golf Invitational, 1980—, Ohio Baseball Hall of Fame media award, 1981; bd. dirs. New Hope Records, Greater Toledo Sports Hall of Fame; trustee Newcomerstown Sports Corp., 1975-80; founder, nat. chmn. Cy Young Centennial, 1967; founder, nat. chmn. Cy Young Golf Invitational, 1967-79, (champion 1967, 1969-72, 1979); mem. adv. bd. Cleve. Indian Old Timers Com., 1966-67, Portage County Sports Hall of Fame (Ohio), 1983—, Sportsbeat, 1985—, Cleve. Sports Legends Found., 1988—, Sch. Calendar Co. Inc., 1984, Madison (Ohio) Hist. Soc., 1988—; hon. dir. Tuscarawas County (Ohio) Old Timers Baseball Assn., 1972—, commendation, 1970; Ohio exec. sponsor chmn. World Golf Hall of Fame, Pinehurst, N.C., 1979—; founder, pres. Toledo Baseball Bluecoats, 1984—, Tuscarawas County Sports Hall of Fame, 1980—; mem. adv. bd. Damascus Steel Casting Co., 1987—; founder, chmn. Ohio Baseball Hall of Fame Lifetime Achievement award, 1987—; mem. disting. citizens adv. bd. Am. Police Hall of Fame & Mus., 1987—. Feature story in Amateur Athletics World, 1982; mem. adv. bd. M&M Publs., 1987—. Fund drive rep. Boy Scouts Am., Cleve., 1959-60, United Appeal, 1959-63, Heart Fund, 1963-64; mem. Cleve. Council Corrections, 1971-73; mem. adv. bd. Cuyahoga Hills Boys Sch., Warrensville Heights, Ohio, 1971—, Camp Hope, Warrrensville Twp., 1973—, Fitness Evaluation Services, Inc., 1977-79, Interact Club of Twinsburg (Ohio), 1981—, The Old Time Ball Players Assn. of Wis., Greater Youngstown Old Timers Baseball Assn.; mem. research bd. advisors Am. Biog. Inst., 1986—; founder, bd. dirs. TRY (Target/Reach Youth), 1971—, Interact Club Shaker Heights, 1971—; mem. exec. com. Tuscarawas County Am. Revolution Bicentennial Commn., 1974-76; trustee Tuscarawas County Hist. Soc., 1978-81; bd. dirs. Shaker Hts. Youth Center, 1975, Tuscarawas Valley Tourist Assn., 1979-81, Buckeye Tourist Assn., 1979-80; mem. adv. bd. Ohio Racquetball Assn., 1981-82; bd. trustees Nat. Jr. Tennis League, 1985-87; mem. adv. bd. Middlefield Hist. Soc., 1986—; hon. trustee Clinton (Ohio) Hist. Soc., 1987—; mem. adv. bd. Windsor (Ohio) Hist. Soc., 1987—. Served with AUS, 1956-58. Recipient commendation award Cy Young Centennial Com., 1967, commendation award Tuscarawas County C. of C., 1967, commendation award Sporting News, 1968, commendation awards Gov. James A. Rhodes, Ohio, 1968, 75, 78, commendation award Gov. John J. Gilligan, Ohio, 1972, commendation award Newcomerstown (Ohio) C. of C., 1967, commendation award N.C. Senate, 1984, commendation award State of Pa. Senate, 1984, Disting. Service award, Hubbard, Ohio, 1986; Outstanding Contbn. to Baseball award baseball commr. William Eckert, 1967; Sport Service award Sport mag., 1969, Feature Cover Story Personality award Amateur Athlete's World mag., 1982; Civic Service award Cuyahoga Hills Boys Sch., 1970; citation of merit La. Stadium and Expn. Dist., 1972; Presdl. commendations Nixon, Ford, Reagan; Disting. Service award Camp Hope, 1974; Founder's award Interact Club Shaker Heights, 1974; Gov.'s Award for community action State of Ohio,d of achievement Ohio Assn. Hist. Socs., 1975; named to Order of Long Leaf Pine, State of N.C., 1984; Chief Newawatowes award Newcomerstown C. of C., 1975; Proclamation award, Thomas C. Eakin Day City of Cleve., 1974, and in numerous Ohio cities 1984-86, Ohio First Record (only person to ever have a day in his honor proclaimed by one city or village in every county in Ohio): Thomas C. Eakin day, State of N.Mex., 1987; Outstanding Alumnus award Phi Delta Theta Alumni Club, Cleve., 1975; commendation states of La., N.C., Ohio Senate, House of Rep.; certificate of merit Tuscarawas County Am. Revolution Bicentennial Commn., 1976; Appreciation award Am. Revolution Bicentennial Adminstrn., 1977; Cert. of Merit State of La., 1978; Gov.'s Award State of Ohio, 1978; named Hon. Citizen City of New Orleans, 1978, City of Memphis, 1986, City of Little Rock, 1986, numerous Ohio cities; Founder's award TRY, Target/Reach Youth 1979; inducted into Chautauqua Sports Hall of Fame (N.Y.), 1983, hon. bd. dirs., 1982—; Sch. Calendar Co. Inc. Hall of Fame, 1987; Commissioners' award Trumbull County Ohio, 1985; honor resolution New Orleans City Council, 1984; Commendation, N.C. Senate, 1984, Pa. Senate, 1984; Gov.'s citation State of Md., 1987, Hon. West Virginian award Gov. W.Va., 1987; recipient various honors resolutions, tributes and commendations; named to hon. order Ky. Cols., 1986, Can. Internat. Friendship award Premier of Ont., Can., 1985, Significant Achievement award Rotary Internat. 1970-71. Fellow Intercontinental Biog. Assn.; fellow Am. Biog. Inst.; mem. Tuscarawas County Hist. Soc. (trustee 1978-81), Shaker Hist. Soc. (trustee 1980-82), Internat. Platform Assn., English Speaking Union, Denison U. Cleve. Men's Club (v.p. 1964-65), Merrick Art Gallery (assoc. 1980—), Soc. for Am. Baseball Research, Phi Delta Theta (pres. Cleve. alumni club 1970, Appreciation award 1971, dir. 1971-75, exec. com. nat. Lou Gehrig award com. 1975—, trustee Ohio Iota chpt. 1979-82). Baptist (mem. bd. 1966-69). Clubs: Executive (Woodmere, Ohio); PGA Nat. Golf (Palm Beach Gardens, Fla.) (internat. mem.); Legend Lake Golf (Chardon, Ohio); Univ. Sch. Tennis (Shaker Heights), Beachwood Athletic. Lodge: Rotary (pres. Shaker Heights 1970-71, founder and chmn. club's internat. student exchange program U.S. and Can. 1965-70, Outstanding Young Rotarian award 1962, founder, chmn. Henry G. Duchscherer Meml. award com., 1971, trustee V. Blakeman Qua Scholarship Fund 1972-73, Wahoo (dir. 1975-77). Address: 2729 Shelley Rd Shaker Heights OH 44122

EALY, LAWRENCE ORR, writer, educator; b. Ocean City, N.J., Sept. 17, 1915; s. Vance Lawrie Orr and Nelle Gray (Rohm) E.; m. Margaret A. Scott, Aug. 10, 1942 (dec. 1945); 1 son, Grant Haertter. A.B., Temple U., 1934; LL.B., U. Pa., 1937, M.A., 1947, Ph.D., 1951; Litt.D., Rider Coll., 1982; student, Navy Supply Corps Sch., Grad. Sch. Bus. Adminstrn., Harvard, 1941. Bar: Ohio bar 1938, Pa. bar 1941. Pvt. practive law Steubenville, Ohio and Phila., 1938-41; instr. history Temple U., 1947-51, asst. prof., 1951-54, asso. prof., 1954-58; lectr. Naval Res. Officers Sch., 1956-57, Rutgers U., 1954-55; Ernest J. King prof. history Naval War Coll., Newport, R.I., 1958-59; provost, dean of faculties, prof. history Hobart Coll., William Smith Coll., 1959-62; dean, prof. history and govt. Rider Coll., Trenton, N.J., 1962-66; v.p. coll. Rider Coll., 1966-70. Author: Under the Puppet's Crown, 1939, Tacony Farm, 1942, Republic of Panama in World Affairs, 1951, reprinted, 1971, Yanqui Politics and the Isthmian Canal, 1971, I Joined the Navy and Saw World War II, 1988; Mem. bd.: Am. Jour. Legal History, 1957-80. Mem. Pa. Citizens Com. for Eisenhower, 1952; Trustee Temple U. Alumni Fund Council, 1947-51, Ednl. Found. of Alpha Chi Rho, 1956-57. Served from ensign to comdr. USNR, 1941-46. Recipient Christian R. and Mary F. Lindbach award, 1973. Mem. Pa., Phila. bar assns., Ret. Officers Assn., Pa. Soc. N.Y., Am. Legion, Phi Beta Kappa, Phi Alpha Theta, Pi Gamma Mu, Delta Sigma Pi, Alpha Chi Rho, Pi Delta Epsilon. Episcopalian. Clubs: Torch (Trenton, N.J.) (pres. 1966-67); Pa. Soc. N.Y. Lodge: Elks. Home: Society Hill Towers Apt 20-A 200 Locust St Philadelphia PA 19106

EAPEN, ELDHO, accountant, management consultant; b. Kothamangalum, Kerala, India, May 14, 1949; s. Nainen and Sosamma (Pothen) E.; m. Suzy Alexander, July 16, 1978; children: Smita Susan, Viniet Eapen, Revathi Anna. B in Commerce, U. Kerala, India, 1969. Chartered acct., auditor D. Rangaswany & Co., Chartered Accts., Madras, India, 1969-75; working ptnr. Cherian & Cherian, Chartered Accts., Kerala, 1975-76; audit supr. Arthur Young, Bader al Bazie & Co., Kuwait, 1976-82; sr. auditor Burgan Bank, S.A.K., Kuwait, 1982—; cons. Philrae Cons. (P) Ltd., Bangalore, Karnataka, 1986—. Fellow Inst. Chartered Accts. of India; mem. Brit. Inst. Mgmt., Inst. Internal Auditors. Mem. Christian Ch. Office: Burgan Bank SAK, PO Box 5389, Ahmed Al Jaber St 13054, Kuwait

EARLE, VICTOR MONTAGNE, III, lawyer; b. N.Y.C., June 13, 1933; s. Victor Montagne and Marian Jeanette (Litonius) E.; m. Lois MacKennan, Dec. 28, 1955 (div. Jan. 1980); children: Jane Stewart, Susan Elizabeth, Anne McCallum; m. Karen Peterson Howard, Aug. 24, 1985. A.B., Williams Coll., 1954; LL.B., Columbia U., 1959. Bar: N.Y. 1960, U.S. Supreme Ct. 1963. Law clk. to Hon. Leonard P. Moore U.S. Ct. Appeals 2d Circuit, 1959-60; assoc. firm Cravath, Swaine & Moore, N.Y.C., 1960-68; gen. counsel Peat, Marwick, Mitchell & Co., N.Y.C., 1968-86, Peat, Marwick Internat., 1978-86; ptnr. Cahill, Gordon & Reindel, N.Y.C., 1986—; lectr. constl. and corp. law issues, U.S. and abroad. Contbr. articles to profl. jours. and popular mags. Served with U.S. Army, 1954-56. Mem. Am. Bar Assn., N.Y. State Bar Assn., Internat. Bar Assn., Assn. Bar City N.Y. (judiciary com. 1983-86), Am. Law Inst., Lawyers Com. Civil Rights under Law (trustee), Legal Aid Soc. (dir. 1980-86), Fund for Modern Cts. (dir.), Columbia Law Sch. Alumni Assn. (dir.). Office: Cahill Gordon & Reindel 80 Pine St New York NY 10005

EARLE, WILLIAM GEORGE, lawyer; b. Monroe, Mich., July 10, 1940; s. George Nelson and Ruth Elizabeth (Davies) E.; m. Cassandra Jane Mayer, Mar. 12, 1966; children—Dana, William, George. Student Yale U., 1958-59; A.B., U. Mich., 1963, LL.B., 1966. Bar: Fla. 1967, U.S. Ct. Appeals (2d cir.), U.S. Ct. Appeals (5th cir.) 1967, U.S. Dist. Ct. (so. dist.) Fla. 1967, U.S. Supreme Ct. 1972, U.S. Ct. Appeals (11th cir.) 1981; cert. civil trial lawyer, advocate. Law clk. to judge U.S. Ct. Appeals (5th cir.), 1966-67; trial atty. organized crime and racketeering sect. Dept. of Justice, 1967-69; ptnr. Kelly, Black, Black, Earle & Patchen, Miami, Fla., 1969-84; ptnr. Earle & Patchen, 1984—; bd. dirs. Fla. Bar Found., 1984—. Mem. emeritus nat. com. law sch. fund U. Mich., also mem. Pres.'s Club; chmn. eminent domain com. Fla. Bar, 1975-77. Mem. ABA (vice chmn. com. on condemnation 1987-88), Fla. Bar Assn. (civil trial adv. nat. bd. trial advocacy 1984—, bd. dirs.), Dade County Bar Assn., Fed. Bar Assn. Episcopalian. Contbr. articles to profl. jours. Club: U. Mich. (Miami). Office: 1000 Brickell Ave Suite 660 Miami FL 33131

EARLOUGHER, ROBERT CHARLES, SR., petroleum engineer; b. Kans., May 6, 1914; s. Harry Walter and Annetta (Partridge) E.; m. Jeanne D. Storer, Oct. 6, 1937; children: Robert Charles, Jr., Janet Earlougher Craven, Anne Earlougher O'Connell. Grad., Colo. Sch. Mines, 1936. Registered profl. engr., Calif., Okla., Tex., Kans. Supr. core lab. The Sloan and Zook Co., Bradford, Pa., 1936-38; co-owner, cons. Geologic Standards Co., Tulsa, 1938-45; owner, cons. Earlougher Engring., Tulsa, 1945-73, pres., 1988—; chmn., cons. Godsey-Earlougher, Inc., Tulsa, 1973-76, Petroleum Cons. div. Williams Bros. Engring. Co., Tulsa, 1976-88. Patentee in field. Recipient Disting. Achievement award Colo. Sch. Mines, 1960;. Mem. AIME (Anthony F. Lucas Gold medal 1980, hon. mem. 1985—), Am. Petroleum Inst. (chmn. mid-continent dist. 1961-62, citation for service 1964), Ind. Petroleum Assn. Am. (bd. dirs. 9 yrs.), Interstate Oil Compact Commn. (oil recovery com. 1947—), Soc. Petroleum Engrs. (hon.; Disting. Service award 1973), Tau Beta Pi. Republican. Episcopalian. Clubs: Tulsa, Southern Hills Country (Tulsa). Lodge: Masons. Home: 2135 E 48th Pl Tulsa OK 74105 Office: 3316 E 21st St Tulsa OK 74114

EARLY, BERT HYLTON, lawyer, legal search consultant; b. Kimball, W.Va., July 17, 1922; s. Robert Terry and Sue Keister (Hylton) E.; m. Elizabeth Henry, June 24, 1950; children—Bert Hylton, Robert Christian, Mark Randolph, Philip Henry, Peter St. Clair. Student, Marshall U., 1940-42; A.B., Duke U., 1946; J.D., Harvard U., 1949. Bar: W.Va. 1949, Ill. 1963, Fla. 1981. Assoc. Fitzpatrick, Marshall, Huddleston & Bolen, Huntington, W.Va., 1949-57; asst. counsel Island Creek Coal Co., Huntington, W.Va., 1957-60, assoc. gen. counsel, 1960-62; dep. exec. dir. ABA, Chgo., 1962-64, exec. dir., 1964-81; sr. v.p. Wells Internat., Chgo., 1981-83, pres., 1983-85; pres. Bert H. Early Assocs. Inc., Chgo., 1985—; instr., Marshall U., 1950-53; cons. and lectr. in field. Bd. dirs. Morris Meml. Hosp. Crippled Children, 1954-60, Huntington Pub. Library, 1951-60, W.Va. Tax Inst., 1961-62, Huntington Galleries, 1961-62; mem. W.Va. Jud. Council, 1960-62, Huntington City Council, 1961-62; bd. dirs. Community Renewal Soc., Chgo., 1965-76, United Charities Chgo., 1972-80, Am. Bar Endowment, 1983—, sec. 1987—, Hinsdale Hosp. Found., 1987—, Internat. Bar Assn. Found., 1987—; mem. vis. com. U. Chgo. Law Sch., 1975-78; trustee David and Elkins Coll., 1960-63. mem., Hinsdale Plan Commn., Ill., 1982-85. Served to 1st lt. AC, U.S. Army, 1943-45. Life Fellow Am. Bar Found., Ill. State Bar Found. (charter); mem. Am. Law Inst. (life), Internat. Bar Assn. (asst. sec. gen. 1967-82), ABA (Ho. of Dels. 1958-59, 84—, chmn. Young Lawyers div. 1957-58, Disting. Service award Young Lawyers div. 1983), Nat. Legal Aid and Defender Assn., Am. Jud. Soc. (bd. dirs. 1981-84), Fla. Bar, W.Va. State Bar, Chgo. Bar Assn. Presbyterian. Clubs: Harvard (N.Y.C.); Metropolitan (Washington); University, Economic (Chgo.); Hinsdale Golf (Ill.). Office: Bert Early Assocs 111 W Washington St Suite 1421 Chicago IL 60602-2708

EARLY, GERALD LEE, cardiovascular and thoracic surgeon, educator; b. St. Joseph, Mo., June 10, 1947; s. Abram Lee and Arline Joyce (Stein) E.; m. Shauna R. Roberts, 1 dau., Jennifer Lynn. B.A., Central Methodist Coll., Fayette, Mo., 1969; M.D., U. Mo.-Kansas City, 1973; M.A., U. Mo.-Columbia, 1975. Diplomate Nat. Bd. Med. Examiners, 1974, Am. Bd. Surgery, 1980, Am. Bd. Thoracic Surgery, 1983. Intern, Kansas City Gen. Hosp. and Med. Ctr., 1973-74; resident in internal medicine Pensacola Ednl. Program, 1974-75; resident in surgery U. Mo.-Kansas City, 1976-79, in thoracic surgery Ohio State U., 1979-81; dir. dept. emergency medicine Pensacola (Fla.) Ednl. Program, 1975-76; dir. cardiovascular and thoracic surgery Truman Med. Ctr., Kansas City, Mo., 1982-83; clin. asst. prof. surgery U. Mo.-Kansas City, 1982—. Recipient Meritorious Service award West Fla. Heart Assn., 1976; named Surgery Resident of Yr., Truman Med. Ctr., 1978, 79; USPHS Reproductive Biology Tng. grantee, 1970-71. Fellow Am. Coll. Surgeons, Am. Coll. Chest Physicians; mem. Jackson County Med. Soc., Mo. Med. Assn., AMA, Assn. Acad. Surgery, Soc. of Thoracic Surgeons, Kans. City Surg. Soc., Kans. City Cardiology Roundtable, Kansas City Pulmonary Round Table. Methodist. Contbr. articles sci. jours. Office: 6700 Troost St 348 Rockhill Med Bldg Kansas City MO 64131

EARLY, JACK JONES, foundation executive; b. Corbin, Ky., Apr. 12, 1925; s. Joseph M. and Lela (Jones) E.; m. Nancye Bruce Whaley, June 1, 1952; children: Lela Katherine, Judith Ann, Laura Hattie. A.B., Union Coll., Barbourville, Ky., 1948; M.A., U. Ky., 1953, Ed.D. (So. scholar 1955-56), 1956; B.D., Coll. of Bible, Lexington, Ky., 1956; D.D., Wesley Coll., Grand Forks, N.D., 1961; LL.D., Parsons Coll., 1962, Iowa Wesleyan Coll., 1972; Litt.D., Dakota Wesleyan U., 1969; L.H.D., Union Coll., Barbourville, Ky., 1979; D.Adminstrn., Cumberland Coll., 1981. Ordained to ministry Methodist Ch., 1954; pastor Rockhold Circuit, Ky., 1943-44, Craig's Chapel and Laurel Circuit, London, Ky., 1944-47, Trinity Ch., Oak Ridge, summer 1945, Hindman Ch., Ky., 1947-52; dean of men Hindman Settlement Sch., 1948-51; assoc. pastor Park Ch., Lexington, Ky., 1952-54; asst. to pres., dean Athens Coll., Ala., 1954- 55; v.p., dean of coll. Iowa Wesleyan Coll., Mount Pleasant, 1956-58; pres. Dakota Wesleyan U., 1958-69, Pfeiffer Coll., Misenheimer, N.C., 1969-71; exec. dir. Am. Bankers Assn., Washington, 1971-73; pres. Limestone Coll., Gaffney, S.C., 1973-79; exec. dir. edn. Combined Ins. Co. Am., Chgo., 1979-82, v.p., exec. dir. edn. and communications, 1982-84; pres. Ky. Ind. Coll. Fund, Louisville, 1984—. Active Boy Scouts Am.; mem. pres.' adv. council North Park Coll.; mem. Felician adv. bd. Felician Coll.; mem. Ky. Ho. of Reps., 1952-54; bd. dirs. S.D. Found. Pvt. Colls., S.D. Meth. Found., Nat. Council on Youth Leadership, Ctr. for Citizenship Edn., YMCA, Motivational Inst., Mid-Am. chpt. ARC, 1980—, W. Clement and Jessie V. Stone Found., Northbrook Symphony Orch.; v.p. Religious Heritage Am. Recipient Spoke award Mitchell Jr. C. of C., 1959, Disting. Service award, 1960; Disting. Service award S.D. Jr. C. of C., 1960, Gaffney Jaycees, 1979; named Outstanding Former Kentuckian, 1963; hon. fellow Wroxton Coll., Oxfordshire, Eng. Mem. Ky. Chpt. Assn. Execs., Jr. C. of C. (dir. 1959), C. of C., Blue Key, Kappa Delta Pi, Phi Delta Kappa (dir. Northwestern U. 1980—), Kappa Phi Kappa, Alpha Psi Omega, Theta Phi, Pi Tau Chi. Republican. Club: Rotary. Home: 9002 Hurstwood Ct Louisville KY 40222 Office: Ky Ind Coll Fund 201 Breckinridge Ln Louisville KY 40207

EARLY, JOHN COLLINS, lawyer; b. N.Y.C., Jan. 24, 1919; s. Ernest Rhea and Elizabeth Jane (Collins) E.; m. Eleanor Livingston, Dec. 21, 1941; children—Elizabeth, Alison, Nancy. B.A. cum laude, Princeton U., 1940; J.D., Harvard U., 1947. Bar: N.Y. 1947, U.S. Tax Ct. 1948, U.S. Supreme Ct. 1951, U.S. Ct. Claims 1954, U.S. Ct. Mil. Appeals, 1956. Assoc. McCanliss & Early, N.Y.C., 1947-48, ptnr., 1950—; assoc. Conboy, Hewitt, O'Brien & Boardman, 1948-50. Past pres. United Campaign of Madison and Florham Park, N.J.; past v.p., trustee Kent Place Sch., Summit, N.J. Served to maj. U.S. Army, 1941-46; ETO. Decorated Bronze Star. Mem. Assn. Bar City N.Y., ABA, N.Y. State Bar Assn. Republican. Episcopalian. Clubs: Down Town Assn., Princeton, Church (N.Y.C.); Nassau, Charter (Princeton, N.J.). Home: Dellwood Park S Madison NJ 07940 Office: 90 Broad St New York NY 10004

EARMAN, VELMA PORTER, lighting fixture designer, consultant; b. New Orleans, July 31, 1910; d. Albert Arthur and Mabel (Long) Porter; m. John William Hulsey, Feb. 18, 1933 (dec. 1957); children: Carroll Joan, Gloria Faye; m. Clarence G. Earman, Jr., Sept. 25, 1963. Student So. Meth. U., 1928-30, Dallas Art Inst., 1930-31. Free-lance fashion designer, Dallas, 1930-33; tchr. art and Spanish lang., Dallas Pub. Schs., 1933-36; owner, contractor Hulsey Constrn. Co., Dallas, 1936-57; owner, designer A.A. Porter Lighting Co., Inc., Dallas, 1958-85, ret., 1985; pvt. practice dress, archtl., and horticultural design, Dallas, 1988—; cons. in field. Campaign worker Dallas Republican party. Christian Scientist. Avocation: gardening.

EARNEST, JACK EDWARD, lawyer; b. Dallas, June 18, 1928; s. William Hubert and Uma Mae (Jolly) E.; m. Billie Jo Young, Aug. 1, 1953; children: Laura Ellen, Jack Edward. Student (Founders scholar), Vanderbilt U., 1944-46; B.B.A., So. Methodist U., 1948, LL.B., 1952; postgrad., Stanford U., summer 1967. Bar: N.Y. 1962, Tex. 1952, U.S. Supreme Ct. 1957. With Mobil Oil Corp., 1946-79; v.p. natural gas N. Am. Mobil Oil Corp., Houston, 1970-76; v.p. natural gas (worldwide) Mobil Oil Corp., N.Y.C., 1976-79; pres., chief operating officer Transcontinental Gas Pipe Line Corp., Houston, 1979-80; sr. v.p., gen. counsel Tex. Eastern Corp., Houston, 1981-83. Mem. Southeastern Gas Assn., So. Gas Assn. (dir.), Interstate Natural Gas Assn. Am. (dir.), Am. Bar Assn., Natural Gas Supply Assn. (chmn. 1979). Methodist. Clubs: Jesters, Wee Burn Country, Univ. of Houston, Ramada. Office: 4600 Post Oak Pl Houston TX 77027

EASBEY, MARION MORIARTY, writer, retired telephone company official; b. New Bedford, Mass., Apr. 8, 1930; d. Walter Vincent and Marion Elizabeth (Rigby) Moriarty; B.S., U. R.I., 1947-51; student Bell System Center for Tech. Edn., 1973-86. Service rep. N.E. Telephone & Northwestern Bell, Providence and St. Paul, 1952-58; office supr. Northwestern Bell, St. Paul, 1958-63, engring. staff asst., 1963-64; engring. technician, asso. engr. and engr. Northwestern Bell, St. Paul and N.E. Telephone, Providence, 1967-79, project mgr. N.E. Telephone, Framingham, Mass., 1979-86; engr. chief clk. Northwestern Bell, 1964-67. Practical politics instr. St. Paul C. of C., 1970; Lake Elmo Precinct chmn. and county conv. del., 1973; bd. dirs., co-chmn. privacy com. ACLU. Recipient cert. of Accomplishment, CAP, 1968, cert. of Merit, 1968. Mem. Common Cause (state network chmn. 1976-79), Assn. Mgmt. Women, Nat. Assn. Female Execs., Am. Mgmt. Assn., AAUW, ACLU, NOW. Democrat Unitarian. Club: Appalachian Mountain. Home: PO Box 9556 Warwick RI 02889

EASLEY, GEORGE WASHINGTON, construction executive; b. Williamson, W.Va., Mar. 14, 1933; s. George Washington and Isabel Ritchie (Saville) E.; student U. Richmond, 1952-56; children—Bridget Bland, Kathy Clark, Saville Woodson, Marie Alexis, Isabell Roxanne, George Washington, Laura Dean. Hwy. engr. Va. Dept. Hwys., Richmond, 1956-62; dep. city mgr. City of Anchorage, 1962-68; prin. assoc. Wilbur Smith & Assos., Los Angeles, 1969-70; commr. pub. works State of Alaska, Juneau, 1971-74; exec. v.p. Burgess Internat. Constrn. Co., Anchorage, 1974, pres., 1975; pres., chmn. bd. George W. Easley Co., Anchorage, 1976-86 ; pres. Alaska Aggregate Corp., Fairbanks Sand & Gravel Co., 1986—; chmn. bd. Central Services, Inc. DBA Yellow Cab of Anchorage, 1982—; bd. dirs. Totem Ocean Trailer Express, Inc., Life Ins. Co. Alaska. Mem. New Capital Site Planning Commn. State of Alaska, 1981—; bd. dirs. Anchorage YMCA. Recipient commendations City of Anchorage, 1966, Greater Anchorage, Inc., 1969, Ketchikan C. of C., 1973, Alaska State Legis., 1974, Gov. of Alaska, 1974; named one of Outstanding Young Men, Anchorage Jaycees, 1964. Registered profl. engr., Calif. Mem. U.S. C. of C. (nat. com. on small bus.), Alaska C. of C. (dir. 1978—, chmn. 1982-83), Anchorage C. of C. (sec.-treas. 1976, v.p. 1977, pres.-elect 1978, pres. 1979-80, dir. 1982-88, Gold Pan award 1969, 77), Hwy. Users Fedn. Alaska (dir. 1972—, treas. 1974—), Orgn. Mgmt. of Alaska's Resources (past dir.), Am. Pub. Works Assn., Anchorage Transp. Commn. (past chmn.), Associated Gen. Contractors (dir. Alaska chpt. 1978—, chpt. treas. 1980-81, sec. 1981, pres. 1984, nat. com. labor relations, Hard Hat award, 1985), Am. Mil. Engrs. (v.p. Alaska chpt. 1978), Ak. Trucking Assn. (bd. dirs. 1986—), Inst. Mcpl. Engrs., Inst. Traffic Engrs., Internat. Orgn. Masters, Mates and Pilots (hon.), Common Sense for Alaska (past pres.), Commonwealth North (charter). Democrat. Presbyterian. Club: San Francisco Tennis. Lodge: Rotary. Home: 333 M St #210 Anchorage AK 99501 Office: 7800 Lake Otis Blvd Anchorage AK 99507

EASTAUGH, FREDERICK ORLEBAR, lawyer; b. Nome, Alaska, June 12, 1913; s. Edward Orlebar and Lucy Evelyn (Ladd) E.; m. Carol Benning Robertson, Aug. 8, 1942; children: Robert Ladd, Alison Benning Eastaugh Farnan. BA, U. Wash., 1937; D Humanities (hon.), U. Alaska, 1982. Bar: Alaska 1948, U.S. Ct. Appeals (9th cir.) 1956, U.S. Supreme Ct. 1958. With Alaska Steamship Co., Seattle, 1934-39; acct. Pan Am. Airways, Juneau, Fairbanks, Seattle and San Francisco, 1940-46; clk. Robertson, Monagle & Eastaugh , Juneau, 1946-48, ptnr., 1948-88; Royal Norwegian Consul for Alaska, 1951-87; commr. Nat. Conf. Uniform State Laws, 1962-69; mem. Alaska Land Use Adv. Com., 1984-86. Founder, bd. dirs. Develop Juneau, Inc.; pres. U. Alaska Found., Fairbanks, 1981-82; bd. dirs. Alaska Resource Devel. Council; trustee Pacific Legal Found., 1983-86. Named Citizen of Yr., Juneau C. of C., 1977. Fellow ABA Found.; mem. ABA, Alaska Bar Assn., Rocky Mt. Mineral Law Found., Alaska C. of C. (pres. 1955-56, named Outstanding Alaskan 1978). Republican. Episcopalian. Home: PO Box 210609 12555 Auke Nu Dr Auke Bay AK 99821 Office: Robertson Monagle & Eastaugh 240 Main St Suite 800 Court Plaza Bldg Juneau AK 99801

EASTHOPE, ANTONY KELYNGE, English educator; b. Portsmouth, Eng., Apr. 14, 1939; s. Kelynge Bryan Easthope and Mary Lilian Revington; m. Carol-Ann Hudak, June 20, 1964 (div. 1968); m. Diane Garside, Feb. 1, 1971; children: Annabeth, Catherine, Kelynge. BA, Cambridge U., 1961, MA, 1965, MLitt, 1967. Vis. instr. Brown U., Providence, 1964-65; lectr. Warwick (Eng.) U., 1967-68; sr. lectr. English and cultural studies Manchester (Eng.) Poly., 1969—; charter fellow Wolfson Coll., Oxford U., 1984-85; disting. vis. scholar U. Adelaide, Australia, 1986. Author: Poetry as Discourse, 1983, What a Man's Gotta Do, 1986, British Post-Structuralism, 1988. Mem. Labour Party. Home: 27 Victoria Ave, Didsbury, Manchester M20 8QX, England Office: Manchester Polytechnic, Dept English, Manchester M15 6BX, England

EASTON, GLENN HANSON, JR., management and insurance consultant, federal official; b. N.Y.C., Mar. 11; s. Glenn Herman and Cornelia Blanchard (Hanson) E.; m. Jeanne Milhall, June 15, 1944; children: Jeanne, Glenn Hanson III, Michelle, Carol. Assoc. in Bus. Adminstrn., U. Pa., 1949, B.A. in Econs., 1950; M.B.A., NYU, 1959. CLU, Am. Coll. Life Underwriters. Various positions to asst. traffic mgr. Keystone Shipping Co., Phila., 1940-54; various positions to mgr. transp. econs. div. Standard-Vacuum Oil Co., White Plains, N.Y., 1954-59; various positions to cons. to pres. S.R. Guggenheim Found., N.Y.C., 1959-84; pres. Glenn Easton & Assocs. (mgmt. and ins. cons.), Port Chester, N.Y., 1970—; polit. appointee U.S. Dept. Labor, Washington, 1982—; assoc. prof. mgmt. L.I. U., Brookville, N.Y., 1971-72. Rep. candidate for congressman, N.Y., 1972, 74, 80; pres. local Rep. Club, 1973-74; mem. Westchester County Rep. Com., 1972-83; Rep., Conservative and Ind. candidate for supr. Town of Rye, N.Y., 1973, 75, 79, 81, Rep. candidate for councilman, 1977; vice-chmn. Ind. Conservative Caucus, Westchester, 1977-83; exec. v.p. bd. trustees New York-Phoenix Schs. Design, 1968-74. Served to comdr. USNR, 1943-46, 50-54, 70, PTO. Mem. Soc. Naval Architects and Marine Engrs. (life), Pa. Jr. C. of C. (1948-57), C. of C., Naval Res. Assn. (life mem.; v.p. Westchester chpt.), Militia Assn. N.Y. (life), Westchester Organ Soc. (v.p.), Met. Organ Soc. of Va., No. Va. Ragtime Soc., U.S. Capitol Hist. Soc., Pi Gamma Mu, Sigma Kappa Phi, Phi Delta Theta. Clubs: Masons, Shriners, Kiwanis, Elks.

EASTWOOD, DANA ALAN, banker; b. Poughkeepsie, N.Y., June 1, 1947; s. Donald Edward and Edith Margaret (Davis) E.; m. Cynthia Carol Allen, Jan. 1, 1984; children: Athena Yvonne, Ashlee Lyn, Alysa Bryhn. Diploma, Am. Inst. Banking, Washington, 1980; Diploma with highest honors, Paralegal Inst., Phoenix, 1983. Proprietor Eastwood Studio, Hyde Park, N.Y., 1965-70; credit rep. Bankers Trust of Hudson Valley, Poughkeepsie, 1970-73; installment loan supr. Poughkeepsie Savs. Bank, 1973-75, installment loan mgr., 1975-78, consumer loan officer, 1978-79, compliance officer, 1979-87, compliance officer, data security adminstr., 1987—; pres., chmn. bd. Consumer Credit Assn. of Mid-Hudson Valley, Poughkeepsie, 1973-75; 1st v.p. Consumer Credit Group of N.Y. State, N.Y.C., 1978-79; 1st v.p. Internat. Consumer Credit Assn., Dist. 2, N.Y. and N.J., 1978-79; mem. consumer credit com. Savs. Banks Assn. of N.Y. State, N.Y.C., 1982-85. Author: Gravity Park, 1978; editor The Right Banker, 1979-82; also numerous modern acrylic paintings. Mem. legis. adv. com. State Assemblyman Emeel S. Betros, Albany, N.Y., 1970-76; mem. consumer edn. adv. com. Dutchess County Cooperative Extension Assn., Millbrook, N.Y., 1975-77. Recipient Award for Outstanding Leadership Consumer Credit Assn. Mid-Hudson Valley, Poughkeepsie, 1974, John C. Corliss Meml. award, 1977, Dedicated Service award Consumer Credit Group N.Y. State, N.Y.C., 1979. Fellow Soc. Cert. Consumer Credit Execs.; mem. Mid-Hudson Compliance Assn. (founding), Internat. Platform Assn. Home: 7 Carriage House Ct Hyde Park NY 12538 Office: Poughkeepsie Savs Bank FSB 21 Market St PO Box 31 Poughkeepsie NY 12602-0031

EASTWOOD, MYLES ERIC, lawyer; b. Springfield, Mass., Mar. 9, 1945; s. Eric and Allison Fairlee (Judd) E.; m. Linda Lee Revai, Dec. 29, 1975; 2 children. AB (Lovett Sch. scholar), U. N.C., 1967; JD (law scholar), Emory U., 1970; MBA, Ga. State U., 1982. Bar: Ga. 1970. Assoc. Lanier, Freeman, Elliott & Price, Atlanta, 1975-76; acting chief Edn. and Adminstrv. Law div. Office of Gen. Counsel Region IV, HEW, Atlanta, 1977-80; asst. U.S. atty. No. Dist. of Ga., Atlanta, 1980-87; assoc. Jones, Brown and Brennan, Atlanta, 1988—; treas., bd. mem., Campus Internat., Inc., 1987—. Contbr. articles to profl. jours. Served to lt. USN, 1971-75; to capt. USNR, 1968-71, 75—. Recipient Outstanding Merit award Ga. State U., 1979. Mem. Ga. Internat. Trade Assn. (scholar 1979), ABA (standing com. on legal assistance to mil. personnel), Fed. Bar Assn. (pres. Atlanta chpt. 1984-85), Atlanta Bar Assn., Internat. Legal Soc. Tokyo, Plaintiff Employment Lawyers Assn., U.S. Naval Inst. (life), Naval Reserve Assn. (life), Retired Officers Assn. (life). Democrat. Episcopalian. Club: Lawyers. Lodge: Kiwanis (Northside Atlanta chpt., chmn. com. 1977-78, 80-81, dir. 1982-84, treas. 1985-86, pres.-elect 1986-87, pres. 1987-88, co-chmn. Internat. Students Reception 1979-81). Office: 1900 One Gregory Ctr 500 W Peachtree St NW Atlanta GA 30308

EATON, ALVIN RALPH, research and development administrator; b. Toledo, Ohio, Mar. 13, 1920; s. Alvin Ralph and Katherine (Hasel) E.; A.B. (Miller scholar), Oberlin Coll., 1941; M.S., Calif. Inst. Tech., 1943; m. Kathleen Steiner, Aug. 15, 1942 (div.); children—Eric Lloyd, Alan Ralph; m. 2d Ellen Griffiths Phillips, Oct. 3, 1970. Engr. So. Calif. Co-op. Wind Tunnel, Pasadena, 1944-45; with The Johns Hopkins U. Applied Physics Lab., Silver Spring, Md., 1945-75, Laurel, Md., 1975—, mem. prin. profl. staff, 1950—, supr. aerodynamics, dynamics and guidance analysis groups, 1949-54, program supr. supersonic missile and weapon system programs, 1954-64, supr. missile systems div., 1964-73, faculty evening coll. grad. sch. 1973-75, supr. fleet systems dept. 1973-83, asst. dir. for tactical systems Applied Physics Lab. 1973-79, asst. dir., 1979-86, assoc. dir., 1986—, also mem. Johns Hopkins U. adv. bd. for Applied Physics Lab. Chmn. Def. Sci. Bd. Task Force, 1977-78, mem. task forces 1979-83; cons. to under sec. def. for research and engring., 1977-83, chmn. and mem. special NATO and U.S. task forces 1977—, mem. under sec. def. high energy laser rev. group, 1981-83, mem. under sec. def. durability of electronic countermeasures rev. group, 1983-86; mem. Navy Planning and Steering adv. Group for Surface Ship Security, 1979-82, chmn. and mem. subgroups 1979-82; cons. to Asst. Sec. of Army for research, devel. and acquisition, 1969-74, 80-86, chmn., Asst. Sec. of Army ind. rev. panel for major Army air def. system, 1980-86; mem. Army Sci. Bd., 1980-86; chmn. panel on adv. syst. test, 1980-81; dep. chmn. summer studies on sci. and engring. personnel and future dev. goals, 1982-83, mem. several subgroups 1982-83, mem. subgroup on ballistic missile def., 1984-86; chmn. atmospheric scis. lab. effectiveness rev., 1985; chmn., asst. sec. army research, devel. and acquisition ind. rev. panel for anti-tactical missile program, 1986—; dep. chmn., exec. bd. Air Armaments Systems Div. of the Am. Def. Preparedness Assn., 1984—. Trustee Howard County (Md.) Gen. Hosp., 1977-85, chmn. fin. com., treas. 1979-81, vice-chmn., 1981-83, chmn., 1983-85, chmn. Community Relations Council, 1988—; mem. editorial bd. Journal of Defense Research, 1988—. Recipient Meritorious Pub. Service award USN, 1957, Distinguished Pub. Service award USN, 1975. Mem. Balt. Council on Fgn. Affairs, Phi Beta Kappa, Sigma Xi, The Hudson Inst. (fellow), The Explorers Club (fellow). Methodist. Clubs: Cosmos (Washington); Rolling Road Golf (Balt.); Oyster Reef Golf (Hilton Head, S.C.). Lodge: Rotary. Inventor in field; contbr. articles to profl. jours. Home: 6701 Surrey Ln Clarksville MD 21029 Office: Johns Hopkins Rd Laurel MD 20707

EATON, BERRIEN CLARK, lawyer, author; b. Chgo., Feb. 12, 1919; s. Berrien Clark and Gladys (Hambleton) E.; m. Donna K. Prestwood; children: Theodore Hambleton, Ann Berrien. Student, Williams Coll., 1936-38; B.S., U. Va., 1940, LL.B., 1948, J.D., 1970. Bar: Mich. 1948, Ariz. 1969, Ga. 1971. Practiced in Detroit, 1948-69, Phoenix, 1969—; assoc. Miller, Canfield, Paddock & Stone, 1948-58, partner, 1958-69; mem. Leibsohn, Eaton, Gooding & Romley, P.C., 1971-79; partner Gray, Plant, Mooty, Mooty & Bennett, Phoenix, 1979-80; mem. firm Eaton, Lazarus, & Dodge Ltd., 1981—; instr. Wayne State U. Law Sch., 1954-69; prof. U. Ga. Law Sch., 1970-71; lectr. at law Ariz. State U. Coll. Law, 1970-71. Author: Professional Corporations and Associations, 6 vols., updated twice annually; co-author: tax newsletter employee benefits VEBA report, 1984-87; editor, co-author: Working with Employee Benefits and VEBA's, 4th vol.; editorial bd. jour. Estate Planning; Notes editor Va. Law Rev.; contbr. articles to profl. jours. Served to capt. F.A., AUS, 1941-46. Decorated Bronze Star. Fellow Am. Coll. Probate Counsel, Am. Coll. Tax Counsel (regent 1980-86); mem. ABA, (past com. chmn. tax sect.), Mich. Bar Assn. (past chmn. tax sect.), Detroit Bar Assn. (past chmn. tax sect.), Ariz. Bar Assn. (past chmn. tax sect.), Ga. Bar Assn., AAUP, Valley Estate Planning Council, Am. Law Inst. (program chmn.), Nat. Coll. Tax Practice (bd. trustees), Newcomen Soc. N.Am., Order of Coif, Raven Soc., Kappa Alpha. Episcopalian. Clubs: Paradise Valley Country, Waweatonong. Home: 7239 N Mockingbird Ln Paradise Valley AZ 85253 Office: Eaton Lazarus & Dodge 3636 N Central 12th Floor Phoenix AZ 85012

EATON, CURTIS HOWARTH, banker, lawyer; b. Twin Falls, Idaho, Sept. 3, 1945; s. Curtis Turner and Wilma (Howarth) E.; m. Mardo Ohlsson, Aug. 2, 1969; 1 child, Dylan Alexander. B.A., Stanford U., 1969; M.P.A., Johns Hopkins U., 1971; J.D., U. Idaho, 1974. Bar: Idaho 1974. Atty., Idaho Atty. Gen.'s Office, Boise, 1974-76, Stephan, Slavin, Eaton, Twin Falls, 1976-82; exec. v.p. Twin Falls Bank & Trust, 1982-84, pres., 198—, also bd. dirs.; bd. dirs. San Francisco Fed. Res., Salt Lake City. Bd. dirs. United Way of Magic Valley, 1978—, Sr. Citizens, 1978-82, Twin Falls C. of C., 1983—; trustee YFCA, 1981—; pres. Coll. So. Idaho Found., 1986-88. Mem. Idaho Bar Assn., Assn. Trial Lawyers Am.

EATON, EDGAR PHILIP, JR., manufacturing executive; b. Milw., Jan. 17, 1923; s. Edgar P. and Dorothy (Morgenthau) E.; B.S. in Mech. Engring., Mass. Inst. Tech., 1944; M.S. in Bus. Adminstrn., Boston U., 1948; m. Rita Beverly Shachat, June 7, 1945 (div.); children—Richard Michael, Randall Charles; m. Helen Yansura. Asst. plant engr. Gen. Dynamics Corp., Groton, Conn., 1944-45; sales engr., supr. Allis Chalmers Mfg. Co., Boston, 1945-49, sales mgr., asst. to pres., 1949-51; exec. v.p. Carbone Corp., Boonton, N.J., 1951-56, pres., 1957—, also dir.; pres. Carbone-Lorraine Industries Corp., 1974—; chmn. bd. Advance Carbon Products, Inc., San Gabriel, Helecoflex Corp., Carbone Lorraine Corp., Montreal, Que., Can., Carbone-Ferraz, Rockaway, N.J., Xetron Corp., Cedar Knolls, N.J., Carbone U.S.A. Corp.; dir. N.J. Blue Shield and Blue Cross; cons. to mgmt. personnel. Active Urban League; chmn. United Fund, 1959-60, 60-61; chmn. Morris County Community Chest, 1959-60, 60-61, pres., 1963-64; chmn. Morris-Sussex Regional Health Facilities Planning Council, 1960-79; chmn. hosp. governing bds. Am. Hosp. Assn., 1968-69; bd. dirs. Morristown Mem. Hosp., Morris Mus., 1985—, Ctr. for Addictive Illness Corp.; pres. Winston Sch., 1979—. Served with AUS, 1942-43. Mem. Young Pres.'s Orgn. (chmn. 1963-64), ASME, IEEE, Am. R.R. Assn., Nat. Elec. Mfrs. Assn. (treas., dir.), Assn. Iron and Steel Engrs. Club: Rockaway River Golf. Author: The Marketing of Heavy Power Equipment, 1948. Home: 30 Colonial Dr Convent Station NJ 07961 Office: Carbone Lorraine Industries Corp 400 Myrtle Ave Boonton NJ 07005

EATON, GEORGE BENJAMIN, army officer; b. Portland, Oreg., Sept. 12, 1958; s. Donald Barnett and Joan Carolyn (Turner) E.; m. Annette Louise Zemek, June 7, 1981. BA cum laude, Knox Coll., 1980; MA in Internat. Relations U. So. Calif., 1987, postgrad. U. Minn. Commd. 2d lt. U.S. Army, 1980, advanced through grades to capt., 1984; material readiness officer 7th Div. Support Command, Ft. Ord, Calif., 1983-84; logistics plans officer Hdqrs. VII Corps, Apo, N.Y., 1984-86; commdr. supply and transport troop, 2d Armoured Cavalry Regiment, 1986-88. Tech. dir. 4th St. Playhouse/Cabaret Theater, Ft. Ord, 1980-83. Decorated Civic Service award, 1982; Meritorious Service medal, 1986; recipient Herbert W. Alden award, 1984. Mem. Assn. U.S. Army, Phi Delta Theta. Republican. Episcopalian. Avocations: running; scale modeling; collecting books. Home: 6704 Sheridan Ave S Richfield MN 55423

EATON, JOEL DOUGLAS, lawyer; b. Miami, Fla., Oct. 31, 1943; s. Joe Oscar and Patricia (MacVicar) E.; m. Mary Benson, June 24, 1967; children: Douglas, Darryl, David. BA, Yale U., 1965; JD, Harvard U., 1975. Bar: Fla. 1975, U.S. Dist. Ct. (so. dist.) Fla. 1976, U.S. Ct. Appeals (5th cir.) 1976, U.S. Supreme Ct. 1978, U.S. Ct. Appeals (11th cir.) 1981. Ptnr. Podhurst, Orseck, Parks, Josefsberg, Eaton, Meadow & Olin, P.A., Miami, 1975—. Served with USN, 1965-71. Decorated Air medal with Bronze Star and numeral 14, Navy Commendation medal with 2 gold stars, Cross of Gallantry (Vietnam). Mem. Acad. Fla. Trial Lawyers, ABA, Am. Law Inst., Assn. Trial Lawyers Am., Dade County Bar Assn., Fla. Bar Assn. (appellate rules com. 1981—). Democrat. Office: Podhurst Orseck Parks et al City Nat Bank Bldg Suite 800 25 W Flagler St Miami FL 33130

EATON, RICHARD GILLETTE, surgeon; b. Forty Fort, Pa., Dec. 3, 1929; s. Walter L. and Ruth (Shaw) E.; B.A., Franklin and Marshall Coll., 1951; M.D., U. Pa., 1955; m. Du Ree Hunter, June 13, 1954; children— Holly, Hillary. Intern, U. Pa. Grad. Hosp., 1956; gen. surg. resident Peter Bent Brigham Hosp., Boston, 1957; orthopedic resident Children's Hosp. Med. Center, Mass. Gen. Hosp. and Peter Bent Brigham Hosp., Boston, 1959-62; hand surgery fellow J.W. Littler, Roosevelt Hosp., N.Y.C., 1962, now attending orthopedic surgery and reconstrn., chief hand surgery service; prof. clin. surgery Columbia Coll. Physicians and Surgeons, N.Y.C. Ruling elder Huguenot Presbyn. Ch., Pelham, N.Y. Served to capt., M.C., U.S. Army, 1957-59. NIH fellow, 1963-64. Diplomate Am. Bd. Orthopedic Surgeons. Mem. Am. Acad. Orthopedic Surgery, Am. Orthopaedic Assn., Am. Soc. Surgery of Hand, A.C.S., Interurban Orthopedic Club, N.Y. Acad. Medicine, J.W. Littler Soc., N.Y. Soc. Surgery of Hand. Author: Joint Injuries of the Hand, 1971; also articles. Home: 640 Ely Ave Pelham Manor NY 10803 Office: Roosevelt Hosp 428 W 59 St New York NY 10019

EATON, ROBERT EDWARD LEE, retired air force officer, public relations and management executive; b. Hattiesburg, Miss., Dec. 22, 1909; s. Malcolm Jasper and Sallie Lucinda (Huff) E.; student U. Miss., 1926-27, Mass. Inst. Tech., 1936-37, Command and Gen. Staff Sch., 1942; B.S., U.S. Mil. Acad., 1931; m. Jo Kathryn Rhein, Jan. 1, 1939; children—Robert Edward Lee, Sallie, Charles. Commd. 2d lt., inf. U.S. Army, 1931; trans. to Air Corps, 1933; promoted through grades to maj. gen., 1947; operations officer 5th Bomb Squadron, 1935; weather officer, 1937; comdg. officer 7th Air Base Group, 1941; regional control officer 2d Weather Region, 1941; chief weather central div. A.A.F. hdqrs., 1942; comdg. officer 451st Bomb Group, Zone of Interior and Italy, 1943-44; dep. dir. operations U.S. Strategic Air Forces, Europe, 1944-45; office asst. chief air staff personnel A.A.F. hdqrs., 1945; Office of Dir. Information, 1946; dep. dir. Office of Legislative Liaison, Office of Sec. Def., 1949; dir. Legislation and Liaison Office of Sec. Air Force, 1951-53; comdr. Sixth Allied Tactical Air Force, Izmir, Turkey, 1953-55; comdr. 10th Air Force, Selfridge AFB, Mich., 1955-59; asst. chief staff res. forces, hdqrs., 1959-62, ret.; pres. Eaton Assos., Inc., pub. relations and mgmt. consultants, Washington, 1962—. Decorated Silver Star with oak leaf cluster, Legion of Merit, D.F.C. with oak leaf cluster, Bronze Star medal, Air medal with four oak leaf clusters, D.S.M., Croix de Guerre (France). Mem. Miss. State Soc. of Washington, Am. Legion (nat. comdr. 1973-74), 40 and 8. Episcopalian. Mason. Clubs: Columbia Country, Army-Navy, Metropolitan, Burning Tree (Washington); Pine Valley Golf (Clementon, N.J.). Home: 4921 Essex Ave Chevy Chase MD 20815 Office: 1725 K St NW Suite 1111 Washington DC 20006

EBAN, ABBA, former foreign minister of Israel; b. Cape Town, South Africa, Feb. 2, 1915; s. Abram and Alida (Solomon) E.; ed. U. Cambridge (Eng.); Hon. Dr., NYU, Boston U., U. Md., U. Cin., Temple U., others; m. Susan Ambache, 1947; 1 son, 1 dau. Liaison Officer Allied Hdqrs with Jewish Population in Jerusalem, 1940; chief instr. Middle East Arab Centre in Jerusalem; joined service of Jewish Agy., 1946; liaison officer with UN Spl. Com. on Palestine, 1947, rep. provisional Govt. of Israel to UN, 1948, permanent rep., 1949-59; ambassador to U.S., 1950-59; minister without portfolio, 1959-60; minister of edn., 1960-63; dep. prime minister, 1963-66; minister of fgn. affairs, 1966-74; mem. Knesset, 1959—; chmn. com. security and fgn. affairs, 1984—; vis. prof. Columbia U., 1974; mem. Inst. Advanced Study, Princeton U., 1978; pres. Weizmann Inst. Sch., 1958-66. Fellow World Acad. Arts and Scis., Am. Acad. Arts and Scis., Am. Acad. Polit. Sci. Author: The Modern Literary Movement in Egypt, 1944; Maze of Justice, 1946; Voice of Israel, 1957; Tide of Nationalism, 1959; My People, 1968; My Country, 1972; Abba Eban: An Autobiography, 1977; The New Diplomacy, 1983, Heritage: Civilization and the Jews, 1984. Office: The Knesset, Jerusalem Israel

EBAUGH, DAVID PAUL, clergyman, engr.; b. Indpls., June 22, 1930; s. Paul Edward and Gladys Rachael (Ruddick) E.; m. Betty LeTourneau, Apr. 9, 1950; children—Michael, Marcellene, Diane, Rosalie. Tool and test equipment engr. IBM, Lexington, Ky., 1956-62; sr. indsl. engr. Goodyear Aerospace Corp., Akron, 1962-64; methods engr. AMP, Inc., Harrisburg, Pa., 1965-67; ordained to ministry Ind. Assembly of God Ch., 1968; founder, pres. David Ebaugh Bible Sch., Harrisburg, 1968—; pastor Ch. of Revelation, 1982—. Served with USN, 1947-52. Mem. IEEE (profl. diploma 1959), Soc. Am. Value Engrs., Am. Inst. Indsl. Engrs., Am. Soc. Tool and Mfg. Engrs. Clubs: Christian Businessmen's Com. (pres. Lexington chpt. 1960), Full Gospel Businessmen's Com. (pres. Harrisburg chpt. 1967). Author numerous publs. on religious topics. Home and Office: 102 Park Terr Harrisburg PA 17111

EBAUGH, FRANK WRIGHT, consulting industrial engineer, investments executive; b. New Orleans, July 31, 1901; s. John Lynn and Mary (Wright) E.; m. Elizabeth Brown, Feb. 22, 1930; 1 dau., Betty Jane (Mrs. Gordon B. McFarland, Jr.). B in Chem Engring., Tulane U., 1923. Engr., asso. mgmt. Tex. Co., 1923-34; partner retail firm, Jacksonville, Tex., 1934-54; mgr., partner Ebaugh & Brown Investments, Jacksonville, 1955-61; prin. Frank W. Ebaugh, Profl. Engr., Cons.; dir., mem. fin. com. Palestine Savs. & Loan Assn. (Tex.); dir. Superior Savs. Assn. Pres. Upper Neches River Mcpl. Water Authority; bd. dirs. Neches River Conservation Dist., 1966-71, Tex. Indsl. Devel. Council; vice chmn. Tex. Mapping Adv. Com.; sec. Texas Coordinating Water Com.; pres. Neches River Devel. Assn., 1966-69; panel chmn. Cherokee County (Tex.) War Price and Ration Bd., 3 years; mem. Library Bd., 1976-79. Mem. regional com. Girl Scouts Am. Named Man of Month East Tex. C. of C., 1953, Man of Yr., Lions Club, 1953; honored by resolution Tex. Senate, 1967, Appreciation plaque Jacksonville Library, 1969. Registered profl. engr., Tex. Mem. NSPE (life), Tex. Soc. Profl. Engrs. (life, chmn. water com.), East Tex. Soc. Profl. Engrs., E. Tex. C. of C., Am. Chem. Soc. (life), AAAS, Tex. Acad. Sci., Nat. Trust for Historic Preservation. Presbyn. (elder, trustee). Rotarian. Clubs: Headliners (Austin); Country of Jacksonville (past pres.). Patentee Ebaugh Mixer. Home: 428 S Patton St Jacksonville TX 75766 Office: Box 1031 Jacksonville TX 75766

EBB, NINA ZDENKA, author; b. Pilsen, Czechoslovakia, May 21, 1923; came to U.S., 1946 (Holocaust survivor, 4 yrs. Terezin), naturalized 1951; d. Alfred and Emma (Wolfner) Goldscheider; m. Stanley J. Ebb; children—Alaine Ebb Hoornbeck, John Stuart. B.S. in Edn., U. Bridgeport, 1976; M.A. in Art and Humanities, U. New Haven, 1983. Supr. Lang. Lab., Newton High Sch., Mass., 1958-73. Translator: What Does to Enlighten Mean? (Moses Maimonides), 1980. Author: Terezin, 1985. Mem. nat. women's com. Brandeis U., 1975-88. Avocations: travel; swimming; skiing; hiking; reading. Address: 157A South Trail Stratford CT 06497

EBERHARD, FRANZ VALENTIN, association executive; b. St. Johann, Carinthia, Austria, Feb. 1, 1947; s. Johann and Theresia (Krušic) E.; m. Irmgard Kothmaier, Aug. 4, 1968; children: Christoph, Stephan. LLD, U. Vienna, Austria, 1970; D Polit. Sci., U. Paris, 1973. Lectr. U. Vienna, 1970-82, U. Paris II, 1972-73; sec. Constl. Ct., Vienna, 1974-78; sec. gen. Austrian Rectors' Conf., 1978-82; dir. European Centre Higher Edn., UNESCO, Bucharest, Romania, 1982-86; sec. gen. Internat. Assn. Univs., Paris, 1987—; dir. Internat. Univs. Bur., Paris, 1987—. Editor in chief Higher Edn. in Europe, 1982-86; co-editor Adminstrv. Law and Adminstrv. Sci., 1976-82; pub. dir. Higher Edn. Policy, 1988—; contbr. articles on pub. law, polit. sci. and higher edn. to profl. jours. Office: Internat Assn Univs, 1 Rue Miollis, 75015 Paris France

EBERHART, STEVEN W., psychologist; b. St. Louis, Oct. 12, 1952; s. Carl A. and Cora H. (Kruckeberg) E. BA in Psychology, So. Ill. U., 1974; MS in Psychology, Western Ill. U., 1980; EdS in Sch. Psychology, U. Iowa, 1984, PhD in Sch. Psychology, 1986. Lic. psychologist, Minn.; cert. sch. psychologist, Minn., Iowa; cert. clin. psychologist, Ky. Mental health technician Anna (Ill.) State Hosp., 1974-78; clin. psychologist Barren River Comprehensive Care, Bowling Green, Ky., 1980-82; sch. psychologist Meeker and Wright Spl. Edn. Co-op, Cokato, Minn., 1985—. Contbr. article to profl. jours. Ill. State scholar. Mem. Nat. Assn. Sch. Psychologists, Minn. Sch. Psychologist Assn., Minn. Soc. Clin. Hypnosis, Mensa. Home: 10453 295th St Saint Joseph MN 56374

EBERLY, WILLIAM ROBERT, biology educator; b. North Manchester, Ind., Oct. 4, 1926; s. John H. and Ollie M. (Heaston) E.; m. Eloise L. Whitehead, June 30, 1946; children—Diana Sue, Brenda Kay, Sandra Jo. B.A., Manchester Coll., 1948; M.S., Ind. U., 1955, Ph.D., 1958. Tchr. music and sci. Laketon and Somerset pub. schs., Wabash County, Ind., 1947-52; teaching asst. dept. zoology Ind. U., Bloomington, 1952-55; asst. prof. Manchester Coll., North Manchester, 1955-60, assoc. prof., 1960-67, prof. biology, 1967—, dir. Environ. Studies, 1971—, chmn. biology dept., 1986—, chmn. natural sci. div., 1986—; cons. Ind. Dept. Natural Resources, Indpls., 1968, 76-82; vis. scientist U. Uppsala Inst. Limnology, Sweden, 1963-64; mem. biology educators del. People to People Citizen Ambassador Program to China, 1988. Author: History of Church of the Brethren in Northwestern Ohio, 1982. Contbr. articles to profl. jours. Mem. Ind. Pesticide Rev. Com., Indpls., 1971-83. Named Sagamore of Wabash, Ind. Gov., 1983; Ind. scholar Indpls. Star newspaper, 1984; recipient Best Educator award Gage Inst., Indpls., 1988. Fellow Ind. Acad. Sci. (founder/editor spl. monograph series of publs. 1968—, chmn. publs. com. 1977-80, pres. 1982, chmn. constn. rev. com. 1983—); mem. Am. Soc. Limnology and Oceanography, Am. Inst. Biol. Scis., Internat. Assn. Theoretical and Applied Limnology, Nat. Assn. Biology Tchrs., Beta Beta Beta. Republican. Mem. Ch. of Brethren. Avocations: fishing; historical and genealogical research. Home: 304 Sunset Ct North Manchester IN 46962 Office: Dept Biology Manchester College North Manchester IN 46962

EBERSOLE, J. GLENN, JR., public relations and marketing executive; b. Lancaster, Pa., Feb. 8, 1947; s. J. Glenn and Marie Christine (Stoner) E.; student Ohio No. U., 1965-67; BSCE, Pa. State U., 1970, M in Engring. Sci., 1973; m. Helen Walton, July 11, 1970. Research technician Pa. State U., University Park, 1968-70; civil engring. intern Pa. Dept. Transp., Harrisburg, 1970-71, asst. dist. design liaison engr., 1971, head research and spl. studies Bur. Traffic Engring., 1971-76; asst. chief engr.-traffic Pa. Turnpike Commn., Harrisburg, 1976-78; chief transp. engr. Huth Engrs., Inc., Lancaster, 1978-81; exec. engr. GSGSB, Clarks Summit, Pa., 1981-82; founder and chief exec. J.G. Ebersole Assocs., Lancaster, Pa., 1982—; founder, chief exec. The Renaissance Group TM, Lancaster, Pa., 1983—; part-time lectr. Pa. State U.; mem. pub. relations com. Assoc. Bldgs. and Contractors. Contbr. articles to profl. jours. Ch. sch. tchr., lector Ch. of the Apostles, mem. ch. council, ch. steering com. for long range planning, chmn. ch. brochure com., chmn. cable TV com., communications com.; past chmn. Rapho Twp. Planning Commn.; mem. regional devel. council Pa. State U.; bd. dirs., mem. devel. com. Actors Co. of Pa. Registered profl. engr., Pa., Vt., Md., Del., N.J. Bd. dirs. Actors Co. of Pa. Mem. Am. Mktg. Assn. (dir., past Cen. Pa. chpt. pres.), ASCE, Inst. Transp. Engrs., NSPE, Associated Builders and Contractors, Inc. (pub. relations com.), Internat. Platform Assn., Am. Road and Transp. Builders Assn. (transp. safety adv. council), Lancaster C. of C. (govt. affairs com., chmn. golf com. 1985-87, long range transp. task force), Pa. Soc. Profl. Engrs., Am. Mgmt. Assn., Pa. Soc., Pa. Hwy. Info. Assn., Pa. State Alumni Assn. (regional devel. council), Phi Eta Sigma, Alpha Sigma Phi. Clubs: Penn State of Lancaster County (past pres., dir.), Hershey Country. Lodges: Shriners, Masons (past master Mount Joy, Pa. club). Home and Office: 1305 Wheatland Ave Lancaster PA 17603

EBERT, GLADYS EILEEN MEYER, home economist, adult education specialist, counselor; b. Wellsburg, Iowa, Jan. 16, 1921; d. Eilert J. and Juliet O'Ressa (Thompson) Meyer; B.A., U. No. Iowa, 1942; M.S., Iowa State U., 1967, M.S., 1968, Ph.D., 1978; m. George Henry Ebert, Sept. 16, 1950; children—George Meyer, Ann Louise, Barbara Eileen. Tchr., McGregor (Iowa) High Sch., 1942-43, Sigourney (Iowa) High Sch., 1943-44, Wellsburg (Iowa) High Sch., 1944-46, Nevada (Iowa) High Sch., 1946-52, Freeborn (Minn.) High Sch., 1952-53, Westmarshall Community Sch., State Center, Iowa, 1962-65; research asst. home econs. Iowa State U., Ames, 1965-67, instr. home econs., 1967-78, asst. prof., 1979—, acting coordinator Office of Distance Learning Programs, summer 1980; vis. prof. S.D. State U., summer 1977; mem. Iowa Task Force on Needs of Incarcerated Mothers, 1981-82; dir. Vocat. Edn. Fundes. Project to Assist Mesquakie Am. Indians Single Parents Gain Edn. for meaningful employment, 1986—; participant profl. confs. Mem. Am. Home Econs. Assn., Iowa Home Econs. Assn., Am. Vocat. Edn. Research Assn., Am. Ednl. Research Assn., Adult Edn. Research Assn., Assn. Tchr. Edn., Nat. Assn. Tchr. Educators for Home Econs., AAUW, Phi Delta Kappa, Omicron Nu, Theta Theta Epsilon, Phi Delta Gamma, Alpha Chi Omega. Presbyterian (deacon, elder). Contbr. articles to profl. jours. Home: 2114 Greenbriar Circle Ames IA 50010 Office: Iowa State U Coll Family Consumer Scis Ames IA 50010

EBERT, JAMES DAVID, research biologist; b. Bentleyville, Pa., Dec. 11, 1921; s. Alva Charles and Anna Frances (Brundege) E.; m. Alma Christine Goodwin, Apr. 19, 1946; children—Frances Diane, David Brian, Rebecca Susan. A.B., Washington and Jefferson Coll., 1942, Sc.D., 1969; Ph.D., Johns Hopkins, 1950; Sc.D., Yale, 1973, Ind. U., 1975; LL.D., Moravian Coll., 1979. Jr. instr. biology Johns Hopkins, 1946-49, Adam T. Bruce fellow biology, 1949-50, hon. prof. biology, 1956-86; hon. prof. embryology Johns Hopkins (Sch. Medicine), 1956-86; instr. biology Mass. Inst. Tech., 1950-51; asst. prof. zoology Ind. U., 1951-54, asso. prof., 1954-56, Patten vis. prof., 1963; dir. dept. embryology Carnegie Instn. of Washington, 1956-76, pres., 1978-87, trustee, 1987; dir. Chesapake Bay Inst. Johns Hopkins U., 1987—; vis. scientist med. dept. Brookhaven Nat. Lab., 1953-54; Philips vis. prof. Haverford Coll., 1961; instr. in charge embryology tng. program Marine Biol. Lab., summers 1962-66, trustee, 1964—, pres., 1970-78, dir., 1970-75, 77-78; mem. Commn. on Undergrad. Edn. in Biol. Scis., 1963-66; mem. vis. com. for biol. and phys. scis. Western Res. U., 1964-68; Mem. panels on morphogenesis and biology of neoplasia of com. on growth NRC, 1954-56; mem. adv. panel on genetic and developmental biology NSF, 1955-56, mem. divisional com. for biology and medicine, 1962-66, mem. univ. sci. devel. panel, 1965-70, adv. com. for instl. devel., 1970-72; mem. panel basic biol. research in aging Am. Inst. Biol. Sci., 1957-60; mem. panel on cell biology NIH, USPHS, 1958-62, mem. child health and human devel. tng. com., 1963-66; mem. bd. sci. counselors Nat. Cancer Inst., 1967-71, Nat. Inst. Child Health, 1973-77; mem. Com. on Scholarly Communication with People's Republic of China, 1978-81; mem. vis. com. to dept. biology Mass. Inst. Tech., 1959-68; mem. vis. com. biology Harvard, 1969-75, Princeton, 1970-76; chmn. bd. sci. overseers Jackson Lab., 1976-80; mem. Inst. Medicine. Author: (with others) The Chick Embryo in Biological Research, 1952, Molecular Events in Differentiation Related to Specificity of Cell Type, 1955, Aspects of Synthesis and Order in Growth, 1955, Interacting Systems in Development, 2d edit, 1970, Biology, 1973, Mechanisms of Cell Change, 1979; Mem. editorial bd.: (with others) Abstracts of Human Developmental Biology; editor: (with others) Oceanus; Contbr. (with others) articles to profl. jours. Trustee Jackson Lab., Worcester Found., Associated Univs. Served as lt. USNR, 1942-46. Decorated Purple Heart. Fellow AAAS (v.p. med. scis. 1964), Am. Acad. Arts and Scis., Internat. Soc. Developmental Biology; mem. Nat. Acad. Scis. (chmn. assembly life scis. 1973-77, v.p. 1981—, chmn. Govt., Univ., INdustry Research Roundtable, 1987—), Am. Philos. Soc., Am. Inst. Biol. Scis. (pres. 1963, Pres.'s medal 1972), Am. Soc. Naturalists, Am. Soc. Zoologists (pres. 1970), Soc. Study Growth and Devel. (pres. 1957-58), Phi Beta Kappa, Sigma Xi, Phi Sigma. Home: 4100 N Charles St Baltimore MD 21218 Office: Johns Hopkins U Chesapeake Bay Inst Suite 340 The Rotunda 711 W 40th St Baltimore MD 21211

EBIGBO, PETER ONYEKWERE, psychology educator; b. Orlu, Imo, Nigeria, Aug. 1, 1947; s. George Akamobi and Sussanna Ehidiozo (Uzoaru) E.; m. Hildegard Maria Raab, Mar. 25, 1975; children: Njikoha, Alanna, Anozie, Esther. Lic. in Philosophy, Bigard Cath. Sr. Srm., Enugu, Nigeria, 1968; haupt diplom in psychologie, Julius Maximilian Bavarian U., Wuerzburg, Fed. Republic Germany, 1974, PhD in Psychology, 1977. Clin. psychologist U. Nigeria Teaching Hosp., Enugu, 1977-78; cons., lectr. U. Nigeria Coll. Medicine, Enugu, 1978-82, cons., sr. lectr., 1982—; cons. Enugu State Psychiat. Hosp., 1985—. Co-editor: Textbook of Clinical Psychology, 1987; editor: Child Labur in Africa, 1987; co-editor Jour. African Psychology; contbr. articles to profl. jours. Founding chmn. Afamefuna Charitable Orgn. for Early Furtherance of Handicapped Children, Enugu, 1982—; co-founder, cons. Therapeutic Daycare Ctr. and Boarding Sch. for Mentally Retarded Children, Enugu, 1978—. Mem. Nigerian Assn. Clin. Psychologists (exec.), Internat. Council Psychologists, European Working Group for Psychosomatic Cancer Research (research council 1984—), African Network for Prevention and Protection Against Child Abuse and Neglect (exec., asst. sec. 1984—), Inst. Advancement of Health. Roman Catholic. Clubs: Peoples of Nigeria, Enugu Sports. Office: Therapeutic Daycare Ctr &, Boarding Sch Complex, Enugu, Anambra Nigeria also: U Nigeria Coll Medicine, Enugu, Anambra Nigeria

EBINER, ROBERT MAURICE, lawyer; b. Los Angeles, Sept. 2, 1927; s. Maurice and Virginia (Grand) E.; m. Paula H. Van Sluyters, June 16, 1951; children—John, Lawrence, Marie, Michael, Christopher, Joseph, Francis, Matthew, Therese, Kathleen, Eileen, Brian, Patricia, Elizabeth, Ann. J.D., Loyola U., Los Angeles, 1953. Bar: Calif. 1954, U.S. dist. ct. (cen. dist.) Calif. 1954. Solo practice, West Covina, Calif., 1954—; judge pro tem Los Angeles Superior Ct., 1964-66, arbitrator, 1979—; judge pro tem Citrus Mcpl. Ct., 1966-70; instr. law Alhambra Evening High Sch., 1955-58; mem. disciplinary hearing panel Calif. State Bar, 1968-75. Bd. dirs. West Covina United Fund, 1958-61, chmn. budget com. 1960-61; organizer Joint United Funds East San Gabriel Valley, 1961, bd. dirs. 1961-68; bd. dirs. San Gabriel Valley Cath. Social Services, 1969—, pres., 1969-72; bd. dirs. Region II Cath. Social Service, 1970—, pres. 1970-74; trustee Los Angeles Cath. Welfare Bur. (now Cath. Charities), 1978—; charter bd. dirs. East San Gabriel Valley Hot Line, 1969-74, sec., 1969-72; charter bd. dirs. N.E. Los Angeles County unit Am. Cancer Soc., 1973-78, chmn. by-laws com. 1973-78; bd. dirs. Queen of the Valley Hosp. Found., 1983—, sec., 1988—; organizer West Covina Hist. Soc., 1982—; active Calif. State Democratic Central Com., 1963-68. Served with AUS, 1945-47. Recipient Los Angeles County Human Relations Commn. Disting. Service award, 1978; named West Covina Citizen of Yr., 1986. Mem. ABA, Calif. Bar Assn., Los Angeles County Bar Assn., Fed. Ct. So. Dist. Calif. Assn., Los Angeles Trial Lawyers Assn., Eastern Bar Assn. Los Angeles County (pres. Pomona Valley 1965-66), West Covina C. of C. (pres. 1960), Am. Arbitration Assn. Clubs: K.C., Bishop Amat High Sch. Booster (bd. dirs. 1973—, pres. 1978-80), Kiwanis (charter West Covina, pres. 1976-77, lt. gov. div. 35 1980-81, Kiwanian of Yr. 1978, 82, Disting. Lt. Gov. 1980-81, bd.dirs. Cal-Nev-Ha Found. 1986—). Office: 1502 W Covina Pkwy West Covina CA 91790

EBITZ, ELIZABETH KELLY, lawyer; b. LaPorte, Ind., June 9, 1950; d. Joseph Monahan and Ann Mary (Barrett) Kelly; m. David MacKinnon Ebitz, Jan. 23, 1971 (div. 1981). A.B. with honors, Smith Coll., 1972; J.D. cum laude, Boston U., 1975. Bar: Maine, Mass, U.S. Supreme Ct. Law clk. Boston Legal Assistance Project, 1973-75; law clk., assoc. Law Offices of John J. Thornton, Boston, 1974-76; ptnr. Ebitz & Zurn, Northampton, Mass., 1976-79; assoc. Gross, Minsky, Mogul & Singal, Bangor, Maine, 1979-80; sole practice, pres. Elizabeth Kelly Ebitz, P.A., Bangor, 1980—. Pres. Greater Bangor Rape Crisis Bd., 1983-85; bd. dirs. Greater Bangor Area Shelter, 1985—, Maine Women's Lobby, 1986—, No. Maine Bread for the World, 1987—; mem. various peace, feminist and hunger orgns., Bangor, 1982—. Named Young Career Woman of Hampshire County, Nat. Bus. and Profl. Women, Northampton, 1979. Mem. ABA, Assn. Trial Lawyers Am., Sigma Xi. Democrat. Roman Catholic. Home: 111 Maple St Bangor ME 04401 Office: 15 Columbia St PO Box 641 Bangor ME 04401

EBY, LAWRENCE THORNTON, chemist; b. South Bend, Ind., May 3, 1916; s. Ralph C. and Edna May (Thornton) E.; B.S. cum laude in Chem. Engring., U. Notre Dame, 1938, M.S. magna cum laude, 1939, Ph.D. magna cum laude, 1941; m. Claudine Isabelle Hart, June 8, 1941; children—Jane Sue, Claudia Ann. Research chemist Esso Research & Engring. Co., Linden, N.J., 1941-57; asst. mgr. market devel. Enjay Chem. Co., Elizabeth, N.J., 1957-64; pres. Protective Treatments, Aeroplast Corp. and Dellrose Industries, Dayton, Ohio, 1964-65; dir. devel. Chrysler Corp., Trenton, Mich., 1965-67; mgr. polymer div. USG Corp., Des Plaines, Ill., 1967-73, assoc. dir. research, 1973-82, prin. assoc., Libertyville, Ill., 1982-85, dir. research, 1985-86; cons., lectr. in field. Chmn., Mental Health Found., Linden, N.J., 1954-55. Recipient Honor award U. Notre Dame, 1965. Mem. Am. Chem. Soc. (dir. 1963-65), Am. Inst. Chemists, AAAS, Comml. Devel. Assn., Chem. Mktg. Research Assn., Soc. Plastics Engrs., Assn. Iron and Steel Engrs., Am. Indsl. Hygiene Assn., TAPPI, Am. Assn. Textile Chemists and Colorists, Soc. Automotive Engrs., Internat. Union Testing and Research Labs. for Materials and Structures, Soc. Research Adminstrs., Research Dirs.' Assn. Chgo., Midwest Chem. Mktg. Assn., Akron Rubber Group, Alpha Chi Sigma. Presbyterian. Patentee in field; contbr. articles to profl. jours. Home and Office: 102 S Kennicott Ave Arlington Heights IL 60005

ECCARD, WALTER THOMAS, lawyer; b. Bklyn., May 19, 1946; s. Walter Stanley and Alice Lorenza (Thomas) E.; m. Joan Elizabeth Dufel, July 31, 1983; 1 child, David Thomas; 1 stepchild, Anne Linder. B.A., Capital U., 1968; M.A., U. Okla., 1973; J.D., Vanderbilt U., 1977. Bar: D.C. 1978, U.S. Dist. Ct. D.C. 1978. Assoc. LeBoeuf, Lamb, Leiby & MacRae, Washington, 1977-80; atty. adv. U.S. Dept. Treasury, Washington, 1980-85, asst. gen. counsel banking and finance, 1985-86, ptnr. Brown & Wood, Washington, 1986—. Author: (textbook chpt.) Nurses, Nurse Practitioners, 1985. Served to capt. USAF, 1968-72. Recipient Performance award U.S. Dept. Energy, 1982, U.S. Dept. Treasury, 1984, 85, Meritorius Service award, 1986, Spl. Appreciation Adminstrn. award U.S. HHS, Washington, 1983. Mem. ABA, Order of Coif. Lutheran. Home: 9836 Dellcastle Rd Gaithersburg MD 20879 Office: Brown & Wood One Farragut Sq Washington DC 20006

ECCLES, SIR JOHN CAREW, physiologist; b. Melbourne, Australia, Jan. 27, 1903; s. William James and Mary (Carew) E.; M.B., B.S., Melbourne U., 1925; M.A., Oxford U., 1929, D.Phil., 1929; LL.D., Melbourne U., 1965; D.Sc. (hon.), U. B.C., 1966, Cambridge U., 1960, U. Tasmania, 1964, Gustavus Adolphus, 1967, Marquette U., 1967, Loyola U., 1969, Yeshiva U., 1969, Charles U., Prague, 1969, Oxford U., 1974, U. Fribourg, 1981, U. Torino, 1983, Georgetown U., 1984, U. Tsukuba, Japan, 1986; m. Irene Miller, 1928; 9 children; m. 2d, Helena Táboriková, 1968. Research fellow Exeter Coll., Oxford U., 1927-34, tutorial fellow Magdalen Coll., 1934-37; dir. Kanematsu Meml. Inst. Pathology, Sydney (Australia) Hosp., 1937-43; prof. physiology Otago U., Dunedin, N.Z., 1944-51; prof. physiology Australian Nat. U., Canberra, 1951-66; mem. AMA/E.R.F. Inst. Biomed. Research, Chgo., 1966-68; disting. prof. SUNY, Buffalo, 1968-75. Decorated knight bachelor, 1958; Royal medal Royal Soc., 1962; Order of the Rising Sun; Gold and Silver Stars, 1986; Cothenius medal Deutche Akademie der Naturforscher Leopoldina; Nobel prize in physiology and medicine (with A. L. Hodgkin and A. F. Huxley), 1963. Fellow Royal Soc., 1941, Australia Acad. Sci. (pres. 1957-61); mem. Pontifical Acad. Scis., Am. Philos. Soc. (hon.), Accademia Nazionale del Lincei (fgn. hon.), Nat. Acad. Sci. (fgn. asso.), Am. Physiol. Soc. (fgn. hon.), ACP (hon.), Am. Acad. Arts and Scis. (fgn. hon.), Max Planck Soc. (hon.). Author: (with others) Reflex Activity of the Spinal Cord, 1932; The Neurophysiological Basis of Mind: The Principles of Neurophysiology, 1953; The Physiology of Nerve Cells, 1957; The Physiology of Synapses, 1964; (with Ito, Szentagothai) The Cerebellum as a Neuronal Machine, 1967; The Inhibitory Pathways of the Central Nervous System, 1968; Facing Reality, 1970; The Understanding of the Brain, 1973; (with Karl Popper) The Self and Its Brain, 1977; (with others) Molecular Neurobiology of the Mammalian Brain, 1978, 2d edit., 1987; (with W. Gibson) Sherrington, His Life and Thought, 1979; The Human Mystery, 1979; The Human Psyche, 1980; (with D.N. Robinson) The Wonder of Being Human: Our Brain, Our Mind, 1984. Research, numerous publs. on the physiology of synapses of the nervous system and chem. transmitters. Home: Cáa la Grá, CH-6611 Contra Ticino, Switzerland

ECEVIT, BULENT, former prime minister Turkey, journalist, politician; b. Istanbul, Turkey, May 28, 1925; s. Fahri and Nazli E.; BA, Robert Coll., 1944; Faculty Linguistics, Ankara, 1944-46, Sch. Oriental and African Studies, London U., 1946-48; m. Rahsan Aral, Aug. 22, 1946. Mem. press and publicity dept. Turkish Govt., 1944-46; ofcl. Turkish Press Attache's Office, London, 1946-50; news editor Ulus, Ankara, 1950-53, polit. columnist, 1956-60; polit. columnist Halkci and Ulus, Ankara, 1954-56; M.P., 1957-60, 61-80; prime minister, 1974, 78-79 (resigned); mem. Constituent Assembly, 1960; minister labor, 1961-65; polit. columnist Milliyet, 1965; sec.-gen. Republican People's Party, 1965-71, chmn., 1972-80; detained after coup, Sept. 1980, released Oct. 1980; jailed 3 times for expressing polit. views, 1981-82; guest writer Winston-Salem (N.C.) Jour., 1954-55. Served to lt. Turkish Army, 1951-52. Rockefeller Found. fellow Harvard U., 1958. Moslem. Author: Poems, 1976; poems pub. in W.Ger., USSR, Romania, Yugoslavia, and Denmark; (polit. works) Left of Center, 1966, The System Must Change, 1968, Ataturk and the Revolution, 1970, Conversations, 1974, Democratic Left, 1974, Foreign Policy, 1975, Workers and Peasants Together, 1976, Poems, 1976, New Developments in the Exploitative System; also translations. Address: Or-an Sitesi 69/5, Ankara Turkey *

ECHAVE RASINES, CARLOS, security company executive; b. Madrid, Spain, Feb. 11, 1950; s. Ceferino Echave and Emilia Rasines; m. Mercedes Espot Pinol, Mar. 20, 1976; children: Isabel, Ignacio, Javier, Amaya, Maria, Carlos, Begoña. Electronics Engr., Escuela Tecnica Superior Ingenieros de Telecommunicacion, 1967-73; M.B.A., Instituto de Estudios Superiores de la Empresa, Barcelona, Spain, 1973-75. Exec., Zardoya Otis, Madrid, 1974; chief industry and markets Renfe, Madrid, 1975-77; internat. mgr. Magisterio Espanol, Madrid, 1977-80; gen. mgr. group Sistemas de Control y Seguridad S.A., 1980—. Home: Conjunto Balsain N1, Las Rozas, Madrid Spain Office: SCS SA, Marques de Urqui 34, 28008 Madrid Spain

ECHENIQUE-ELIZONDO, MIGUEL, surgeon, educator; b. Zarauz, Basque Country, Spain, Dec. 4, 1948; s. Miguel Echnique and Lucia Elizondo; M.D., U. Zaragoza (Spain), 1972, Ph.D., 1977; m. Patro Chueca, Oct. 26, 1976; 1 son, Alejo. Trainee in surgery U. Zaragoza, 1969-75, asst. prof. surgery, 1972-77, gen. surgeon Univ. Hosp., 1975-77; chief of surgery Aranzazu Hosp., San Sebastian, Spain, 1978—; prof. surgery U. Pais Vasco, 1978—. Recipient Zaragoza award Royal Acad. Medicine, 1976, Sociedad de Endrocinologia (Madrid) award, 1976; Fundacion Murua-Balzola grantee, 1968-77, Comisaria Proteccion Escolar grantee, 1969-72. Mem. Sociedad Espanola de Angiologia, Sociedad Espanola de Patologia Digestiva, Internat. Acad. Proctology, Internat. Coll. Surgeons, Sociedad de Estudios Vascos-Euzko Ikazkuntza, Academia de Ciencias Medicas de Bilbao. Basque Nationalist. Roman Catholic. Clubs: Zarauz Golf, Jaizkibel Golf (San Sebastian). Contbr. articles to sci. jours. Home: 3 Nuevo Igueldo, San Sebastian Spain Office: Clinica Martin Santos, Parque Alcolea, San Sebastian Spain

ECHOLS, IVOR TATUM, educator, assistant dean; b. Oklahoma City, Dec. 28, 1919; d. Israel E. and Katie (Bingley) Tatum; A.B., U. Kans., 1942; postgrad. (A.R.C. scholar) U. Nebr., 1945-46; M.S. in Social Work (Nat. Urban League fellow, Porter R. Lee fellow), Columbia, 1952, postgrad. (NIMH fellow), U. So. Calif., 1961-62, D.S.W., 1968; m. Kenneth Johnston, Dec. 28, 1948 (div. June 1951); 1 dau., Kalu Helene; m. 2d, Sylvester J. Echols, June 13, 1954 (div. 1976); 1 son, Kim Arnett. Tchr. social studies high sch., Holdenville, Okla., 1942-43, Geary, Okla., 1943-45; caseworker A.R.C., Chgo., 1946-47; resident group worker, Dosoris House for Teen-Age Girls, Community Services Soc., N.Y.C., 1950-51; supr. group work Walnut Grove Center Neighborhood Clubs, Oklahoma City, 1948-51; program dir. Camp Lookout YWCA, Denver, 1951; dir. program services Presbyn. Neighborhood Services, Detroit, summer 1960, supr. group work Merrill-Palmer Inst., Detroit, 1951-70; asst. dir. Merrill-Palmer Camp, Dryden, Mich., 1951-59; prof. Sch. Social Work, U. Conn., West Hartford, 1970—, now also asst. dean; del. Inter-Univ. Consortium of Social Devel., Hong Kong, 1980; mem. Conn. adv. com. U.S. Commn. Civil Rights. Mem. Ad

Hoc Com. Citizens Concerned with Equal Ednl. Opportunity, Detroit, 1964—; cons. to N.E.A. Conf. Family Camping Washington, 1959, ednl. film Scott Paper Co., Phila., 1963, 64; summer study skills project Presbyn. Ch. Bd. Nat. Missions, Knoxville, Tenn., 1965—; sec. United Neighborhood Centers Am.; pres. Protestant Community Services, Detroit, 1969-70. Recipient Educator Human Rights award UN Assn. , 1987, Sojourner Truth award Detroit chpt. Nat. Assn. Negro Bus. and Profl. Women, 1969, UN Assn. award for Edn. and Women's Rights, 1987; named Conn. Social Worker of Year, 1979. Mem. Nat. Assn. Colored Women's Clubs (participant White House Conf. on Children and Youth 1960), A.M.E. Ministers Wives, Acad. Certified Social Workers, Delta Sigma Theta. Mem. A.M.E. Ch. Home: 51 Chestnut Dr Windsor CT 06095 Office: U Conn 1800 Asylum Ave W Hartford CT 06007

ECKBO, BJORN ESPEN, economics educator; b. Oslo, Norway, June 2, 1952; came to Can., 1981; s. Per Leo Eckbo and Ranveig (Hoffgaard) Borsum; m. Sigrid Alsaker, June 20, 1975; children—Sigrid Camilla, Claus Espen, Hannah Cathrine. B.Commerce, Norwegian Sch. Econs., Bergen, 1975, M.B.A., 1977; M.S., U. Rochester, 1980, Ph.D., 1981. Prof. econs. U. B.C., Vancouver, Can., 1981—; vis. prof. UCLA, 1985-86; cons. U.S. FTC, Washington, 1984, Consumer and Corp. Affairs Can., Ottawa, 1985. Contbr. articles to sci. jours. Fellow Norwegian Sch. Econs., 1979-81, U. Rochester, 1981, Batterymarch fellow, 1987-88; recipient Harry G. Johnson award Can. Econs. Assn., 1987. Mem. Am. Econ. Assn., Am. Fin. Assn., Can. Econ. Assn., European Fin. Assn. Avocations: music; literature; outdoors. Home: 4633 W 8 Ave, Vancouver, BC Canada Office: U BC Faculty Commerce, Vancouver, BC Canada V6T 1Y8

ECKDAHL, DONALD EDWARD, manufacturing company executive; b. Los Angeles, Apr. 29, 1924; s. Edward Bernhard and Esther Amelia (Nystrom) E.; m. Barbara D. Crease, May 1, 1981; children by previous marriage: Karin, Robert. B.S.E.E., U. So. Calif., 1944, M.S.E.E., 1949. Project engr. Northrop Aircraft Corp., Hawthorne, Calif., 1946-50; founder, v.p. ops. Computer Research Corp., Hawthorne, 1950-53; v.p., gen. mgr. data processing div. NCR Corp., Hawthorne, 1953-70; sr. v.p. engring. and mfg. group NCR Corp., Dayton, Ohio, 1970-81, ret., 1981; sr. v.p. McCray, Shriver, Eckdahl and Assocs., Inc., Los Angeles, 1982-84; pres., chief exec. officer, chmn. bd. Multiflow Computer Inc., Branford, Conn., 1984—. Served with USNR, 1943-46. Mem. IEEE, Assn. Computing Machinery. Republican. Lutheran. Address: 10 Cambridge Dr Madison CT 06443

ECKERBERG, C. LENNART, diplomat; b. Malmö, Sweden, July 2, 1928; s. Enar L. and Dagmar (Liljedahl) E.; m. Willia Foster Fales, May 29, 1965; children: John Fales, Alice R. D., Christopher Fales. Degree in law, U. Stockholm, 1953. With Swedish Fgn. Ministry, London, Warsaw (Poland), Stockholm, Washington, 1955-71; disarmament ambassador Geneva, 1971-75; minister Washington, 1975-77; undersec. for polit. affairs Stockholm, 1979-83; ambassador to Tanzania, Dar es Salaam, 1977-79, Fed. Republic of Germany, Bonn, 1983—. Home: Alter Fronhof, D-5047 Wesseling-Urfeld Bundesrepublik, Federal Republic of Germany Office: Swedish Embassy, Allianzplatz, 5300 Bonn 1 Federal Republic of Germany

ECKERED, THOMAS HARALD, nuclear safety organization executive; b. Stockholm, Sweden, July 20, 1941; s. Harald R. and Sally M. (Lindgren) E.; m. Mikaela Bjurner, July 15, 1967 (div. 1979); children—Sara, Karin; m. 2d, Mona Sundberg, Apr. 21, 1981; children—David, Emma. M. Aero. Engring., Royal Inst. Tech., Stockholm, 1965. Research and devel. engr., project mgr. Swedish Aero. and Mech. Industry, Stockholm, 1965-71; sci. adviser Swedish Delegation to OECD, Paris, 1972-75; dep. dir. Swedish Nuclear Power Inspectorate, Stockholm, 1975-80; pres. RKS (Nuclear Safety Bd. of the Swedish Utilities), Stockholm, 1980-86; spl. asst. internat. and supplier div., Inst. of Nuclear Power Ops., Atlanta, 1987—; co-chmn. Internat. Nuclear Fuel Cycle Eval. Working Group 7, Vienna, 1978-80; bd. dirs. Swedish Nat. Radiation Protections Inst., Stockholm, 1976-80, mem. emergency planning bd., 1981-86. Mem. Swedish Nuclear Soc. (chmn. 1983-84), Swedish Soc. Mech. Engrs. (treas. 1982-83), European Nuclear Soc. (v.p.). Home: 52 Woodsford Sq, London W14 8DS, England Office: Inst Nuclear Power Ops, 262A Fulham Rd, London SW10 9EL, England

ECKERMANN, ANNE-KATRIN, anthropologist; b. Luneburg, Germany, Sept. 1, 1946; came to Australia, 1958. BA with honors, U. Queensland, Brisbane, Australia, 1968, MA, 1973, PhD, 1977. Tutor U. Queensland, Brisbane, 1969, 73; research fellow Australian Inst. Aboriginal Studies, Canberra, Australia, 1970-72, 1974-76; lectr. Armidale Coll. Advanced Edn., New South Wales, Australia, 1977-83, sr. lectr., 1984-86; prin. lectr. anthropology Armidale Coll. Advanced Edn., New South Wales, 1987—; cons. in field. Contbr. articles to profl. jours. Mem. Reg. Council of Tech. and Further Edn., New Eng. Region, 1985—, mem. state council, Sydney, 1986—, mem. bd. studies, 1987. Commonwealth scholar, 1966; Australian Inst. Aboriginal Studies research fellow, 1970-72, 74-76. Mem. Australian Anthropology Soc., Australian Inst. Aboriginal Studies, Med. Anthropology Soc. Australia, Australian Assn. Research in Edn. Home: 196 Markham St, Armidale, New South Wales 2350, Australia Office: Armidale Coll Advanced Edn, Mossman St, Armidale Australia

ECKERT, MICHAEL, physicist; b. Munich, May 17, 1949; s. Josef and Hildegard (Schwankl) E. Diploma in Physics, Tech. U., Munich, 1976; D Nat. Scis., U. Bayreuth, Fed. Republic Germany, 1979. Research in radiation risk analysis Gesellschaft fur Strahlenund Umweltforschung, Munich, 1980-81; research in history of physics Deutches Mus., Munich, 1981-84, research in history of nuclear energy, 1985—. Author: Geheimrat Sommerfeld, 1984, Kristalle, Elektronen, Transistoren, 1986.

ECKHARDT, WILLIAM BOYDEN, credit union executive; b. Bellefonte, Pa., Aug. 31, 1949; s. Boyden and Maxine Alice (Young) E.; BBA, Oreg. State U., 1971. Adminstrv. officer Alaska U.S.A. Fed. Credit Union, Anchorage, 1971-72, ops. mgr., 1972-74, asst. gen. mgr., 1974-79, pres., 1979—; chmn. bd. Alaska USA Ins., Inc., 1986—; chmn. Alaska Option Services Corp.; dir. Alaska League Services Corp. Mem. Credit Union Execs. Soc. (pres. Alaska council 1975-88), Alaska Credit Union League (pres. Anchorage chpt. 1979-81), Credit Union Nat. Assn. (dir.). Club: Elks, Commonwealth North. Home: 12850 Ben Ct Anchorage AK 99515 Office: Mail Pouch 6613 4000 Credit Union Dr Anchorage AK 99502

ECKL, WILLIAM WRAY, lawyer; b. Florence, Ala., Dec. 2, 1936; s. Louis Arnold and Patricia Barclift (Dowd) E.; m. Mary Lynn McGough, June 29, 1963; children—Eric Dowd, Lynn Lacey. B.A., U. Notre Dame, 1959, LL.B., U. Va., 1962. Bar: Va. 1962, Ala. 1962, Ga. 1964. Law clk. Supreme Ct. of Ala., 1962; ptnr. Gambrell, Harlan, Russell & Moye, Atlanta, 1965-68, Swift, Currie, McGhee & Hiers, Atlanta, 1968-82, Drew, Eckl & Farnham, Atlanta, 1983—. Served to capt. JAGC, USAR, 1962-65. Mem. Def. Research Inst., State Bar of Ga. Roman Catholic. Clubs: Lawyers of Atlanta, Brookwood Hills. Home: 348 Camden Rd Atlanta GA 30309 Office: 880 W Peachtree St PO Box 7600 Atlanta GA 30357

ECKLUND, JOHN EDWIN, lawyer, researcher; b. Jamestown, N.Y., Apr. 3, 1916; s. J. Edwin and Sagrid M. (Johnson) E.; m. Mary Theodora Sizer, Oct. 29, 1942 (dec. Dec. 1973); children—Hilda Ecklund Ollmann, Peter J., Elizabeth Ecklund Berger, John Edwin; m. Constance L. Cryer, Mar. 22, 1975. B.A., Yale U., 1938, LL.B., 1941, M.A. (hon.), 1966. Bar: Conn. 1941, U.S. Dist. Ct. Conn. 1946, U.S. Ct. Appeals (2d cir.) 1950. Assoc. Wiggin & Dana, New Haven, Conn., 1941, 46-51, ptnr., 1951-66; of counsel Yale U., New Haven, 1957-66, treas., 1966-78, researcher legal history, 1978—; bd. govs. Yale U. Press, 1966-78. Case editor Yale Law Jour., 1940-41. Contbr. articles to profl. jours. Bd. dirs. New Haven Symphony Orch., 1948-58, Yale New Haven Hosp., 1966-78; chmn. Woodridge Town Plan and Zoning Commn., 1954-64. Served to lt. (s.g.) USNR, 1941-46. Recipient Alpheus Henry Snow prize, Yale U., 1938. Mem. ABA, New Haven County Bar Assn., Order of Coif. Republican. Episcopalian. Clubs: Yale (N.Y.C.); Mory's Graduate (New Haven) (gov. 1970-76). Home: 27 Cedar Rd Woodbridge CT 06525

ECKSTEIN, MARLENE R., vascular radiologist; b. Poughkeepsie, N.Y., Sept. 6, 1948; d. Marc and Lola (Charm) E.; A.B., Vassar Coll., 1970; M.D., Albert Einstein Coll. Medicine, 1973. Diplomate Nat. Bd. Med. Examiners; cert. Am. Bd. Radiology. Intern in medicine Yale-New Haven Med. Center, 1973-74, resident in diagnostic radiology, 1974-77; asst. radiologist, chief vascular radiology sect. South Nassau Communities Hosp., Oceanside, N.Y., 1977-78, asso. radiologist, chief vascular radiology sect., 1978-81, asst. dir. dept. radiology, chief vascular radiology sect., 1981-83; asst. prof. clin. radiology SUNY-Stony Brook Med. Sch., 1980-83; instr. radiology, Harvard Med. Sch., 1983-84, asst. prof., 1984—; asst. radiologist Mass. Gen. Hosp., 1983-87, assoc. radiologist, 1987—. Mem. exec. com. and hosp. chmn. United Jewish Appeal of Physicians and Dentists of Nassau County (N.Y.), 1981-83. Fellow Am. Coll. Angiology, Soc. Cardiovascular and Interventional Radiology; mem. Internat. Platform Assn., Am. Coll. Radiology, Am. Inst. Ultrasound in Medicine, Mass. Radiol. Soc., Am. Assn. Women Radiologists, Am. Med. Women's Assn., AMA, Mass. Med. Soc., New Eng. Soc. Cardiovascular and Interventional Radiology (pres. 1985-86), Radiol. Soc. N.Am., Designer and developer line of vascular catheters. Home: 4 Longfellow Pl Apt 2708 Boston MA 02114 Office: Vascular Radiology Sect Mass Gen Hosp Boston MA 02114

ECO, UMBERTO, educator, author; b. Jan. 5, 1932; s. Giulio Eco and Giovanna Bisio; m. Renate Ramge, Sept. 24, 1962; children—Stefano, Carlotta. Student Univ. degli Studi, Turin. With Italian TV, 1954-59; asst. lectr. aesthetics Univ. Turin, 1956-63, lectr., 1963-64; lectr. Faculty Arch. U. Milan, 1964-65; prof. visual communications U. Florence, 1966-69; prof. semiotics Milan Poly., 1970-71, U. Bologna, 1971—; vis. prof. NYU, 1969-70, 1976, Northwestern U., 1972, Yale U., 1977, 80, 81, Columbia U., 1978. Columnist, L'Espresso, 1965; editor VS, 1971—. Author: Il Problema Estetico in San Tommaso, 1956, Sviluppo dell'Estetica Medioevale, 1959, Opera Aperta, 1962, Diario Minimo, 1963, Apocalittici e Integrati, 1964, L'Oeuvre Ouverte, 1965, La Struttura Assente, 1968, Il Costume di Casa, 1973, Trattato di Semiotica Generale, 1975, A Theory of Semiotics, 1976, The Role of the Reader, 1979, Il Nome della Rosa, 1981, Semiotics and the Philosophy of Language, 1984, Sette anni de desiderio, 1977-83, 1984, Travels in the Hyperreality, 1986 (Italian Lit. award), Art and Beauty in the Middle Ages, 1986 (Italian Lit. award). Recipient Prix Medici, 1982, McLuhan Teleglobe prize, 1985. Address: Via Melzi d'Eril 23, Milan Italy

ECOLE, JEAN JOSEPH, philosophy and metaphysics researcher; b. Craon, France, Mar. 2, 1920; s. Ernest and Marie (Goupil) E. License, U. Rennes, France, 1947, Doctorat, 1956. Prof. philosophy Coll. Mayenne, France, 1945-55; prof. metaphysics U. Angers, France, 1955-70; researcher Centre Nat. de la Recherche Scientifique, Paris, 1970-85. Author: La Métaphysique de l'être dans la Philosophie de Lavelle, 1957; La Metaphysique de l'être dans la Philosophie de Blondel, 1959, Introduction à l'Opus Metaphysicum de Wolff; Index Auctorum ad Quos Wolffius Remittit, 1985. Editor: Ontologia-Cosmologia-Psychologia Empirica-Psychologia Rationalis-Theologia Naturalis-Logica of Christian Wolff, 1962-83. Decorated officier Légion d'Honneur. Roman Catholic. Home: 58 Route Stratégique, Col des Quatre Chemins, 06300 Nice France

ECONOMIDES, PHAEDROS, trading company executive; b. Nicosia, Cyprus, Apr. 16, 1945; s. Christofis and Maria (Vassiliadou) E.; m. Anastasia Loizidou, Nov. 9, 1969; children—Alina, Mania. B.Sc. in Engring., U. London, 1968. Dept. mgr. Cyprus Import Corp., Ltd., Cyprus, 1969-73, mng. dir., 1973—; mng. dir. Economides Drilling Co., Cyprus, 1982—; tech. dir. Saudi Cypriot Drilling Co., Saudi Arabia, 1983-87 ; v.p. Vehicle Importers Assn., Cyprus, 1982-85, pres., 1985-87; dir. Employers and Industralists Fedn., Cyprus, 1983—, v.p., 1986-88, pres. 1988— . Mem. Fedn. Internat. Automobile (Cyprus rep., Paris, 1978—), Fedn. Internat. du Sport Automobile (Cyprus rep., Paris, 1978—), Cyprus Profl. Engrs. Assn., Cyprus Automobile Assn. (pres. 1985—), OFA Auto Club (chmn. 1978-80). Office: Cyprus Import Corp Ltd, PO Box 1632, Nicosia Cyprus

EDAGAWA, MASARU, architect; b. Tsuchiura, Ibaraki, Japan, Feb. 8, 1950; s. Isamu and Rin (Takagi) E.; m. Yumiko Fukushima, Oct. 10, 1976; children: Kei, Ayumu. B in Engring., U. Kanagawa, Yokohama, Kanagawa, 1975. Registered architect. Pres. Edagawa Archtl. Planning, Ltd., Tsuchiura, 1969—. Mem. Tsuchiura Architects Assn. Home and Office: 4-1-36 Namiki, 300 Tsuchiura Japan

EDDLEMAN, WILLIAM ROSEMAN, lawyer; b. Shelby, N.C., May 21, 1913; s. William Peter and Nellie Holland (Roseman) E.; student U. N.C., 1930-34, Pace Inst., 1934-35, Washington Coll. Law, 1935-37; LLB, Gonzaga U., 1939; Licenciado en Derecho, Nat. U. Mex., 1968, m. Ruth Carolyn Phelps, Aug. 31, 1952 (dec. Aug. 1966); 1 son, William Lammers; m. 2d, Elizabeth Dorothy Carp, Nov. 1, 1966 (dec. June 1985); M. 3d, Sarah J. Seawell, Sept. 21, 1985. Admitted to Wash. bar, 1939, U.S. Supreme Ct. bar, 1945, Mexican bar, 1968, Tex. bar, 1972; mem. firm Eddleman & Wheeler, Seattle, 1946-64, Perez, Verdia, Eddleman, 1963-64; with Parker Sch. Internat. Law, Columbia, 1964, Facultad de Derecho, Nat. U. Mex., 1964-67; mem. firm Carp & Eddleman, Dallas, 1972—, Bufete-Eddleman, Mex., 1968—; del. Internat. Bar Assn. meeting, Mexico, 1964; del. Inter-Am. Bar Assn. meeting, Mexico, 1944; ABA del. to Inter-Am. Bar Assn., 1984. Exec. bd. Chief Seattle council Boy Scouts Am., 1959-61. Republican dist. leader, 1949-52, mem. exec. com., 1950-52. Mem. Inter-Am. (chmn. com. legal aspects devel. and integration 1978—, council 1981—), Internat. (charter patron), Am. (nat. chmn. younger lawyers 1948-49, ho. dels. 1949-50), Wash. (chmn. war readjustment and traffic court coms. 1944-46), Dallas (internat. com. 1974-81), Tex. (internat. sec. 1980—, lawyer referral and immigration law 1987—), Whitman County (pres. 1943-44) bar assns., Fedn. Ins. Counsel (v.p. 1960-61), Am. Soc. Internat. Law, Am. Fgn. Law Assn., Dallas Internat. Lawyers, Comml. Law League Am. (pres. 1961-62), Nat. Geneal. Soc., Selden Soc., SAR (chpt. pres. 1981, chancellor 1983, pres. Tex. 1985-86, v.p. gen. 1987—), La Acad. Mexicana de Derecho Internat. Episcopalian (vestryman). Odd Fellow (sovereign grand rep. 1954), Lion (dir. 1963-64). Author: Legal Aspects of LAFTA, 1967; Full Faith and Credit in Federal Systems, 1968; Conflicts-Private International Law, 1969; Legal Aspects Current Latin American Integration and Development, 1979, Latin American Regional Devel. and Debt, 1985. Home: 7149 Northaven Dallas TX 75230 Office: 3232 Republic Tower Dallas TX 75201

EDE, STUART JOHN, librarian, information consultant; b. London, May 7, 1948; s. Melville William and Doris Lilian (Towner) E.; m. Maureen Brittan, July 17, 1969; children: Beth, Kate, Gareth. BSc with honors, U. Manchester, Eng., 1969. Research asst. U. Manchester Inst. Sci. and Tech., 1969-72, Nat. Cen. Library, London, 1973; head records planning Brit. Library Lending Div., Boston Spa, Eng., 1974-79, dep. head computing, 1979-80, head lending (records), 1980-84; head service devel. Brit. Library Document Supply Ctr., Boston Spa, 1984-86; dir. consultancy services Brit. Library, Boston Spa, 1986—. Contbr. articles to profl. jours. Mem. Instn. Profl. Civil Servants (founding sec. Brit. library br. 1973-74). Office: The Brit Library, Boston Spa, Wetherby, West York LS23 7BQ, England

EDELL, DENNIS NELSON, advertising executive; b. Newark, Dec. 4, 1946; s. Morton and Joan E. (Gutterson) E.; m. Leslie Ann Howatt; children: Laura, Esther, Anna. BA, U. Pa., 1968; student in mgmt. tng., U. Western Ont., London, Can., 1983. V.p. mktg. Hampton Techs., Inc., Charlottetown, P.E.I., Can., 1979-81; ptnr. Island Energy Assocs. Cons. Group, Ottawa, Ont., 1980-83; pres. Mediaplus Advt., Ottawa, 1983—. Served with USN, 1968-70. Mem. Am. Mktg. Assn., Can. Direct Mktg. Assn. (bd. dirs., v.p. Ottawa chpt.), Ottawa-Carleton Econ. Devel. Corp., Ottawa Advt. and Sales Assn. (1st pl. awards 1987). Office: Mediaplus Advt, 205-149 Second Ave, Ottawa, ON Canada K1S 4N6

EDELMAN, ALVIN, lawyer; b. Chgo., Dec. 12, 1916; s. Leon and Sally (Kramer) E.; m. Rose Marie Slossy, Sept. 22, 1940; children: Marilyn Frances Edelman Snyder, Stephen D., Leon F. B.S. in Law, Northwestern U., 1938, J.D., 1940. Bar: Ill. 1940. Practiced in Chgo., 1940—; pres. Edelman & Edelman, Chartered, and predecessors, 1973—; gen. counsel Internat. Coll. Surgeons; lectr. Internat. Mus. Surg. Sci. and Hall of Fame; chmn. wills and gifts com. Medinah Temple of Masonic Shrine, Chgo., 1975-79; pres. Lawyers Shrine Club of Medinah Temple, 1971-73. Contbr. articles to profl. jours. Fellow Am. Coll. Probate Counsel; mem. ABA, Ill., Chgo. (chmn. grievance com. 1971-72) Bar Assns., Phi Beta Kappa (pres. Chgo. area assn. 1975-85), Phi Beta Kappa Assocs. (bd. dirs. 1985—, nat. v.p. 1986—). Lodges: Monroe, Elks (past exalted ruler) (Chgo.).). Home: 1100 Oak Ridge Dr Glencoe IL 60022 Office: 1 N LaSalle St Chicago IL 60602

EDELMAN, GERALD MAURICE, biochemist, educator; b. N.Y.C., July 1, 1929; s. Edward and Anna (Freedman) E.; m. Maxine Morrison, June 11, 1950; children: Eric, David, Judith. B.S., Ursinus Coll., 1950, Sc.D., 1974; M.D., U. Pa., 1954, D.Sc., 1973; Ph.D., Rockefeller U., 1960; M.D. (hon.), U. Siena, Italy, 1974; D.Sc., Gustavus Adolphus Coll., 1975; Sc.D., Williams Coll., 1976. Med. house officer Mass. Gen. Hosp., 1954-55; asst. physician hosp. of Rockefeller U., 1957-60, mem. faculty, 1960—, assoc. dean grad. studies, 1963-66, prof., 1966-74, Vincent Astor disting. prof., 1974—; mem. biophysics and biophys. chemistry study sect. NIH, 1964-67; mem. Sci. Council, Ctr. for Theoretical Studies, 1970-72; assoc., sci. chmn. Neurosciences Research Program, 1980—, dir. Neuroscis. Inst., 1981—; mem. adv. bd. Basel Inst. Immunology, 1970-77, chmn., 1975-77; non-resident fellow, trustee Salk Inst., 1973-85; bd. overseers Faculty Arts and Scis., U. Pa., 1976-83; trustee, mem. adv. com. Carnegie Inst., Washington, 1980-87; bd. govs. Weizman Inst. Sci., 1971-87, mem. emeritus. Trustee Rockefeller Bros. Fund., 1972-82. Served to capt. M.C. AUS, 1955-57. Recipient Spencer Morris award U. Pa., 1954; Ann. Alumni award Ursinus Coll., 1969; Nobel prize for physiology or medicine, 1972; Albert Einstein Commemorative award Yeshiva U., 1974; Buchman Meml. award Calif. Inst. Tech., 1975; Rabbi Shai Shacknai meml. prize Hebrew U.-Hadassah Med. Sch., Jerusalem, 1977; Regents medal Excellence, N.Y. State, 1984; Hans Neurath Prize, U. Washington, 1986; Sesquicentennial Commemorative award Nat. Library Medicine, 1986. Fellow AAAS, N.Y. Acad. Scis., N.Y. Acad. Medicine; mem. Am. Philos. Soc., Am. Soc. Biol. Chemists, Am. Assn. Immunologists, Genetics Soc. Am., Harvey Soc. (pres. 1975-76, Am. Chem. Soc., Eli Lilly award biol. chemistry 1965), Am. Acad. Arts and Scis., Nat. Acad. Sci., Am. Soc. Cell Biology, Acad. Scis. of Inst. France (fgn.), Japanese Biochem. Soc. (hon.), Pharm. Soc. Japan (hon.), Soc. Developmental Biology, Council Fgn. Relations, Sigma Xi, Alpha Omega Alpha. Office: Rockefeller Univ 1230 York Ave New York NY 10021

EDELMAN, MARK LESLIE, ambassador; b. St. Louis, June 27, 1943; s. Marvin and Ruth Faye (Goldstein) E.; m. Nancy M. Wasell, May 12, 1973. A.B., Oberlin Coll., Ohio, 1965; portgrad., George Washington U., 1965-66. Budget analyst USIA, Washington, 1965-67; researcher Planning Research Corp., Washington, 1968; budget examiner Office Mgmt. and Budget, Washington, 1968-72; budget dir. State of Mo., Jefferson City, 1973-76; legis. asst. U.S. Senate, Washington, 1977-81; dep. asst. sec. Bur. Internat. Orgn. Affairs U.S. Dept. State, Washington, 1981-83; exec. sec. Agy. for Internat. Devel., Washington, 1983-84, asst. adminstr. Bur. for Africa, from 1984; ambassador U.S. Embassy, Cameroon, 1987—. Mem. exec. bd. Washington Oberlin Alumni Assn., 1966-72; class v.p. Oberlin Coll., 1982-84. Republican. Office: US Embassy, Rue Nachitigal BP 817, Yaounde Cameroon

EDELMAN, PAUL STERLING, lawyer; b. Bklyn., Jan. 2, 1926; s. Joseph S. and Rose (Kaminsky) E.; m. Rosemary Jacobs, June 15, 1951; children: Peter, Jeffrey. AB, Harvard U., 1946, JD, 1950. Bar: N.Y. 1951, U.S. Dist. Ct. (so. and ea. dists.) N.Y. 1954, U.S. Ct. Appeals (2d cir.) 1965, U.S. Supreme Ct. 1967. Ptnr. Kreindler & Kreindler, N.Y.C., 1953—; legal advisor Andre Doria TV show, 1984. Author: Maritime Injury and Death, 1960; editor: Maritime Law Reporter, 1987—; columnist N.Y. Law Jour. Served with U.S. Army, 1944-46. Mem. ABA (past chmn. admiralty com., toxic and hazardous substances litigation com., mem. long range planning com. 1982-84, mem. TIPS council 1984, Soviet-Am lawyers conf. Moscow 1987), N.Y. State Bar Assn. (INCL award 1980, chmn. INCL sect. 1982-83, editor Ins. Jour. 1973—), Assn. Trial Lawyers Am. (past chmn. admiralty coms.), Maritime Law Assn., World Peace Through Law Ctr. Democrat. Jewish. Clubs: Hudson Valley Tennis; Hastings on Hudson (past chmn., planning bd.). Home: 57 Buena Vista Dr Hastings-on-Hudson NY 10706 Office: 100 Park Ave New York NY 10017

EDELMAN, ROBERT JOEL, clinical psychologist; b. Basingstoke, Hampshire, Eng., July 21, 1951; s. Joel and Rita (Finkelbloch) E. BS in Geography and Geology, U. London, 1972, BS in Psychology, 1977, PhD in Psychology, 1981, MPhil in Clin. Psychology, 1984. Lectr. Bulmershe Coll. Edn., Reading, Berkshire, Eng., 1981-82, U. Sheffield, Eng., 1984-86, U. Surrey, Guildford, Eng., 1986—; tutor Open U., London, 1980—; vis. lectr. City U., London, 1987—; clin. psychologist SW Surrey Dist. Health Authority, 1987—. Author: The Psychology of Embarassment, 1987; contbr. numerous articles to profl. jours. Fellow Brit. Psychol. Soc. (assoc.); mem. Brit. Assn. Behavioral Psychotherapy, Internat. Soc. for Study Individual Differences, Brit. Soc. Exptl. and Clin. Hypnosis, Soc. Reproductive and Infant Psychology. Office: U Surrey Dept Psychology, Guildford GU2 5XH, England

EDELMANN, OTTO KARL, music educator; b. Vienna, Austria, Feb. 5, 1917; s. Wenzel and Maria (Krystufek) E.; widowed; m. Ilse-Maria Straub, Apr. 13, 1960; children: Elisabeth, Peter-Alexander, Paul-Armin. Diploma, Univ. Music, Vienna, 1938. Mem. States-Theater, Gera, Germany, 1938, Nuremburg, Germany, 1939, Staatsoper Vienna, 1948-78. Author: Ein Meistersinger aus Wien, 1987; appeared in opera houses throughout world, including Met. Opera, N.Y.C., Opera House, Rio de Janeiro; appeared on numerous opera records. Served with German mil., 1940-47, prisoner of war, USSR. Recipient Order of Daneborg (Denmark) 1962; Cross of Honor Republic of Austria, Cross of Sci. and Arts Republic of Austria, Medal of Gold City of Vienna, 1987. Address: Breitenfurterstrasse 547, Vienna-Kalksburg 1237, Austria

EDELSTEIN, WOLFGANG, academic institute administrator; b. Freiburg, Germany, June 15, 1929; s. Heinz and Charlotte (Schottländer) E.; m. Ilse Rosenkranz, May 10, 1967 (div. 1975); m. Monika Keller, Aug. 23, 1980; children: Anna Lilja, Benjamin Tomas. Licence ès-lettres, U. Paris Sorbonne, 1953; PhD, U. Heidelberg, 1962. Staff mem. Odenwaldschule, Ober Hambach, Fed. Republic Germany, 1954-63, dir. studies, 1961-63; sr. researcher Max Planck Inst. Human Devel. and Edn., Berlin, 1963-81, co-dir., 1981—; chief sci. advisor Ministry Edn., Reykjavik, Iceland, 1966-84; cons. Orgn. Econ. Cooperation and Devel., Paris, 1968-70. Author: Eruditio und Sapientia, 1965, School, Learning, Society (in Icelandic), 1988; contbr. articles to sci. jours. Mem. German Psychol. Assn., German Sociol. Assn., Internat. Soc. for the Study of Behavioral Development, German Educational Research Assn., Soc. for Research in Child Development. Office: Max Planck Inst for Human Devel, Lentzealle 94, D-1000 Berlin 33 Federal Republic of Germany

EDEN, JOHN DERRICK, mining engineering consultant; b. Didsbury, Eng., Oct. 22, 1933; s. John William and Edith (Smith) E.; m. Norma Lee, Sept. 28, 1958. A.C.S.M., Camborne Sch. Mines, 1958; M.S., U. Tenn., 1969; M.Phil., Oxford U., 1972, D.Phil., 1975. Chartered engr., U.K. Mine capt., mine supt. N.W.D. Mining Co. div. Union Carbide, N.W. Dist., Guyana, 1958-60; mining engr. Pahang Consol. Co., Malaysia, 1960-64; mining engr. Tenn. ops. Am. Zinc Co., Mascot, Tenn., 1964-70; sr. cons. mining engr. Brit. Mining Cons. Ltd., London, 1975-82; sr. cons. mining engr. Seltrust Cons., Seltrust Engring., London, 1982-86; mining engring. cons. Goldfields Group, London, 1986-88; free-lance cons. mining engr., Hertfordshire, 1988—; cons. mining engr. Overseas Devel. Adminstrn., London, 1976—. Contbr. numerous reports to profl. publs. Social Sci. Research Council research fellow Oxford U., 1970-75. Fellow Instn. Mining and Metallurgy (mem. editorial bd.); mem. AIME, Mining Assn. UK (mem. council). Mem. Ch. of Eng. Clubs: Mining (London); Hertford. Home and Office: West Bush House, Hailey Ln, Hertford Heath, Hertfordshire England

EDGAR, JAMES MACMILLAN, JR., management consultant; b. N.Y.C., Nov. 7, 1936; s. James Macmillan Edgar and Lilyan (McCann) E.; B. Chem. Engring., Cornell U., 1959, M.B.A. with distinction, 1960; m. Judith Frances Storey, June 28, 1958; children—Suzanne Lynn, James Macmillan, Gordon Stuart. New product rep. E.I. duPont Nemours, Wilmington, Del., 1960-63, mktg. services rep., 1963-64; with Touche Ross & Co., 1964-78, mgr., Detroit, 1966-68, partner, 1968-71, partner in charge, mgmt. services ops. for No. Calif. and Hawaii, San Francisco, 1971-78, partner Western regional mgmt. services, 1978; prin. Edgar, Dunn & Conover, Inc., San Francisco, 1978—; mem. San Francisco Mayor's Fin. Adv. Com., 1976—, mem. exec. com., 1978—, Blue Ribbon com. for Bus., 1987—; mem. Alumnae Resources adv. bd., 1986—, mem. San Francisco Planning and Urban Research Bd., 1986—; mem. alumni exec. council Johnson Grad. Sch. Mgmt. Cornell U., 1985—, Cornell Council, 1970-73. Recipient Award of Merit for outstanding pub. service City and County of San Francisco, 1978; Honor award for outstanding contbns. to profl. mgmt. Johnson Grad. Sch. Mgmt., Cornell U., 1978. CPA, cert. mgmt. cons. Mem. Assn. Corp. Growth (v.p. membership San Francisco chpt. 1979-81, v.p. programs 1981-82, pres. 1982-83, nat. bd. dirs. 1983-86), Am. Inst. C.P.A.s, Calif. Soc. C.P.A.s, Am. Mktg. Assn., Inst. Mgmt. Cons. (regional v.p. 1973-80, dir. 1975-77, bd. v.p. 1977-80), San Francisco C. of C. (bd. dirs. 1987—, v.p. econ. affairs 1988—, mem. exec. com. 1988—), New Main Library Found. Bd., Tau Beta Pi. Clubs: Univ., Commonwealth of San Francisco, Marin Rod and Gun. Patentee nonwoven fabrics. Home: 10 Buckeye Way Kentfield CA 94904 Office: Edgar Dunn & Conover Inc 847 Sansome St San Francisco CA 94111

EDGE, DAVID OWEN, science educator; b. High Wycombe, Eng., Sept. 4, 1932; s. Stephen Rathbone Holden and Kathleen Edith (Haines) E.; m. Barbara Corsie, Feb. 21, 1959; children: Aran Kathleen, Alastair Clouston, Gordon. BA in Physics, Cambridge U., 1955, MA, 1959, PhD in Radio Astronomy, 1959. Producer Sci. Talks BBC, London, 1959-66; dir. Sci. Studies Unit Edinburgh (Scotland) U., 1966—, Reader Sci. Studies, 1979—, mem. Univ. Ct., 1983-86. Co-author: Astronomy Transformed, 1976; co-editor: Science in Context, 1982; joint editor Social Studies Sci. 1971-82, editor, 1982—. Hdqrs. adviser Scout Assn., Scotland, 1967-85; cir. steward Meth. Ch., Edinburgh and Forth Cir., 1984-86. Soc. for Humanities fellow Cornell U., 1973. Fellow Royal Astron. Soc., Royal Soc. Arts; mem. Soc. for Social Studies Sci. (council 1980-81, pres. 1985-87), N.Y. Acad. Scis., Internat. Soc. for Optical Engring., Sci. Tech. Soc. Assn., Oral History Soc., Soc. for Study Theology, Brit. Soc. for Social Responsibility in Sci., History of Sci. Soc., Brit; Soc. for History of Sci., Brit. Assn. for Advancement Sci., AAAS, Philosophy of Sci. Assn., Union Concerned Scientists, Scout and Guide Grad. Assn. (pres., former chmn.), Australasian Assn. for History, Philosophy and Social Studies of Sci., European Assn. for Study of Sci. and Tech. Mem. Social and Liberal Democrats. Home: 25 Gilmour Rd, Edinburgh EH16 5NS, Scotland Office: Edinburgh U Sci Studies Unit, 34 Buccleuch Pl, Edinburgh EH8 9JT, Scotland

EDGELL, GEORGE PAUL, lawyer; b. Dallas, Mar. 9, 1937; s. George Paul and Sarah Elizabeth (McDonald) E.; B.S. in Aero. Engring., U. Ill., 1960; J.D., Georgetown U., 1967; M.B.A., Roosevelt U., 1983, B.G.S. in Computer Sci., 1986; m. Karin Jane Williams; 1 son, Scott Rickard. Admitted to Va. bar, 1967, D.C. bar, 1968, Ill. bar, 1980; patent examiner U.S. Patent Office, Washington, 1963-65; ptnr. firm Schuyler, Birch, McKie & Beckett, Washington, 1969-80, assoc., 1965-69; group patent counsel Gould Inc., Rolling Meadows, Ill., 1980-86, asst. chief patent counsel, 1986—. Vol. tutor Hopkins Ho., 1968-69; officer St. Stephen's Dads' Club, 1975-77. Served with USMC, 1960-63. Mem. ABA, D.C., Ill., Va. Bar Assns., Am. Intellectual Property Law Assn., Licensing Execs. Soc. Republican. Presbyterian. Clubs: Army Navy Country, Meadow. Home: 5403 Chateau Dr Rolling Meadows IL 60008 Office: Gould Inc Intellectual Property Law Dept 10 Gould Ctr Rolling Meadows IL 60008

EDGERTON, RICHARD, restaurant/hotel owner; b. Haverford, Pa., May 2, 1911; s. Charles and Ida (Bonner) E.; LL.D. (hon.), Berry Coll., Mt. Berry, Ga.; m. Marie Lytle Page, Oct. 24, 1936; children—Leila, Margaret, Carol. Pres./owner Lakeside Inn Properties, Inc., Mt. Dora, Fla., 1935—; co-owner 28 Burger King restaurants, Pa., 1967—; gen. mgr., pres. Buck Hill Falls (Pa.) Co., 1961-65 ; pres., chief exec. officer Eustis Sand Co., Mt. Dora, Fla., 1961—founding dir. Fla. Service Corp., Tampa; v.p., dir. 1st Nat. Bank, Mt. Dora. Mem. Gov.'s Little Cabinet, 1955-61. Trustee emeritus Berry Coll.; bd. dirs. Mt. Dora Community Trust Fund; trustee emeritus Lake Sumter Community Coll. Served to lt. USNR, 1944-46; ETO. Mem. Am. (dir.), Fla. (hon., past pres.) hotel and motel assns., N.H. Hotel Assn. (past pres.), Newcomen Soc., Welcome Soc., Pa. Soc. Clubs: Miami; Mt. Dora Yacht, Mt. Dora Golf. Home: 3d and McDonald Sts Mount Dora FL 32757 Office: 234 W 3d Ave Mount Dora FL 32757

EDGERTON, WILLIAM B(ENBOW), foreign language educator; b. Winston-Salem, N.C., Mar. 11, 1914; s. Paul Clifton and Annie Maude (Benbow) E.; m. Jewell Mock Conrad, June 6, 1935; children: Susan, David. B.A., Guilford Coll., 1934; M.A., Haverford Coll., 1935; Ph.D., Columbia U., 1954. Tchr. French. German, Spanish, English in secondary schs. U.S. and France, 1935-39; faculty French and Spanish Guilford Coll., 1939-47; faculty Russian lit. Pa. State U., University Park, 1950-56, U. Mich., Ann Arbor, 1954-55, Columbia U., N.Y.C., 1956-58; prof. Slavic langs. and lits. Ind. U., Bloomington, 1958-83, prof. emeritus, 1983—, chmn. Slavic dept., 1958-65, 69-73, acting dir. Russian and East European Inst., 1981-82; cons. Ford Found., 1952-61; mem. joint com. on Slavic studies Am. Council Learned Socs., 1951-62; chmn. 1958-61. Gen. editor: Columbia Dictionary of Modern European Literature, 1980; translator, editor: Satirical Stories of Nikolai Leskov, 1969; editor: Ind. Slavic Studies, III, 1963, Ind. Slavic Studies, IV, 1967, Am. Contributions to the Fifth Internat. Congress of Slavists, 1963; contbr. articles to profl. internat. jours. Bd. dirs. Am. Friends Service Com., 1956-59; trustee Guilford Coll., 1969—; mem. vis. com. for Slavic Studies Harvard U., 1967-77; mem. adv. com. Nat. Humanities Ctr., 1978—. Recipient Josef Dobrovsky medal Czechoslovak Acad. Sci., 1968; Am. Council Learned Socs. fellow, 1948-50; Guggenheim fellow, 1963-64. Mem. MLA (exec. council 1962-65), Am. Assn. Advancement Slavic Studies (pres. 1961), Internat. Comparative Lit. Assn., Am. Com. Slavists (chmn. 1958-78), Internat. Com. Slavists (Am. rep., 1958-78; hon. 1978—). Democrat. Quaker. Home: 1801 E Maxwell Ln Bloomington IN 47401 Office: Ballantine 502 Ind U Bloomington IN 47405

EDGREN, GUSTAF ADOLF, labor employment administrator; b. Stockholm, Nov. 9, 1935; s. Anders Fredrik and Irma Eleonora (Magnusson) E.; m. Margareta Karin Thelne, Aug. 28, 1940; children: Anders, Johan. BA in Econs. and Stats., Stockholm U., 1961. Dir. research The Cen. Orgn. of Salaried Employees, Sweden, 1965-69, Devel. Authority, Sweden, 1969-71; asst. dir. gen. Swedish Internat. Devel. Authority, Sweden, 1971-73, 79-82; chiefemployment promotion div. Ministry of Labour, Nairobi, Kenya, 1973-76; br. chief Internat. Labour Office, Geneva, 1976-79; asst. dir. gen. Swedish Internat. Devel. Authority, 1979-82; state sec. devel. cooperation Ministry of Fgn. Affairs, 1982-85; chief Asian Employment Program Internat. Labour Office, New Delhi, 1986—; dir. research Internat. Confedn. of Free Trade Unions African Research Office, Kampala, Uganda, 1962-65. Mem. Social Dem. Party. Office: Internat Labour Office-ARTEP, Box 643, New Delhi 110001, India

EDMUNDSON, IAN GRAHAM, electrical engineer, technical marketing engineer; b. Rugby, Warwickshire, Eng., July 28, 1947; s. John and Julia (Zeital) E.; m. Vivien Mary Eccles, July 25, 1970; children: Jamie, Benjamin, Imogen. Electrical and electronic engr. grad., Hatfield Poly., Eng., 1975. Devel. engr. Tex. Instruments Ltd., Bedford, Eng., 1969-77, mktg. engr., 1978-83; devel. engr. Hunting Engring. Ltd., Ampthill, Eng., 1977-78; customer support SGS Semicondr. Ltd., Aylesbury, Eng., 1983-88; sales exec. SGS Thomson Microelectronics, Marlow, Eng., 1988—. Office: SGS Thomson Microelectronics, Planar House, Parkway, Globe Park, Marlow, Bucks SL7 IYL, England

EDSALL, HOWARD LINN, consulting executive; b. N.Y.C., Nov. 17, 1904; s. John Linn and Alise (Stoughton) E.; student pub. schs., pvt. tutoring; m. Florence S. Small, July 5, 1930 (dec. 1986); children: Florence Linn (Mrs. Robert James Whitehouse). Sea-going radio operator, marine div. RCA, 1920-25, advt. and sales promotion mgr. electron tube div., 1944-47; with Curtis-Martin Newspapers, Inc., 1926; mktg., sales promotion exec., plans writer R.E. Lovekin Corp., 1928-34, Bridge & King, 1934-35. E.F. Houghton Co., 1935-37; co-founder, dir. G.S. Rogers & Co., Chgo., 1937-40, Ajax Metal Co. & Affiliates, 1940-44; exec. cons. Rockport Press, The Reporter, Household Fin. Corp., 1948; v.p., dir. Craven & Hedrick, AM TV's The Big Story, 1949-53; exec. v.p. Fred Wittner Advt., N.Y.C., 1953-57; sec., dir. Plastomics Products Co., Inc., 1946; pres., founder AIMS, Inc. (counselors to profl. mgrs.), 1959; ptnr. Bonniview Lodge. Lake Penage, Whitfish, Ont., Can. Mem. Re-Employment Planning Assocs., 1966; dir. spl. events UN Council, 1944-45. Mem. Am. Soc. Metals (bd. editors 1944-47), Jewelry Industry Council (advt. dir. 1951), Soc. Profl. Mgmt. Cons. (charter 1960, v.p., dir. 1967-69), Inst. Mgmt. Cons. (founder-mem.), Poets and Writers Am. Fiction Writers (dir.), SAR. Clubs: Pen and Pencil (Phila.); Morse Telegraph; Listentome (N.J.). Author: An Unexplored Musical Resource, 1944; Borrow & Prosper, 1946; Management Consultant and Reporter, 1968; The How You Can Borrow and Prosper Kit, 1972; co-author One To Ten Thousand Copies, 1963; cons. editorial bd. Jour. Mgmt. and Bus. Consulting, 1976; author: Song of Free Men, 1985 (awarded Presdl. commn. 1986), Society of Wireless Pioneers, 1986; contbr. fiction and articles to nat. U.S. and fgn. mags. Inventor Violute, 1939. Home: 39A North Mountain Ave Montclair NJ 07042

EDSON, HERBERT ROBBINS, hospital executive; b. Upper Darby, Pa., Dec. 26, 1931; s. Merritt Austin and Ethel Winifred (Robbins) E.; m. Rose Anne McGowan, July 25, 1970; children: Patricia Anne, David William, Merritt Austin III, Herbert Robbins, Jr. BA, Tufts U., 1955; MBA, U. Pa., 1972. Commd. 2d lt. USMC, 1955, advanced through grades to major, 1967, adminstr., mgr., supr. various orgns., 1955-72; controller III Marine Amphibious Force and 3d Marine Div. USMC, Camp Butler, Japan, 1972-73; dir. acctg. Marine Corps Supply Activity USMC, Phila., 1973-75; ret. USMC, 1975; cons. acctg. Ardmore, Pa., 1975-77; chief fin. officer Mercy Meml. Hosp. Corp., Monroe, Mich., 1977—. Co-pres. Custer Elem. Sch. Parent Tchr. Orgn., Monroe, 1985-87; v.p., trustee Christ Evang. Luth. Ch., Monroe, 1981-86; treas., chmn. Taylor Endowment Fund com. St. Paul's Evang. Luth. Ch., Ardmore, Pa., 1974-76, trustee, chmn. property com., 1976. Decorated Purple Heart, Navy Commendation medal, Combat Action ribbon. Mem. Nat. Assn. Accts., Am. Hosp. Assn., Healthcare Fin. Mgmt. Assn., U.S. Naval Inst. (life), Marine Corps Inst., First Marine Div. Assn. (life), Edson's Raiders Assn. (1st Marine Raider Bn., hon. life), The Ret. Officers Assn. (life), Nat. Rifle Assn. (life), Monroe County C. of C. (dir. 1982-84). Republican. Lutheran. Club: Marine's Meml. (San Francisco); Monroe Rod and Gun, Army and Navy (Washington). Home: 526 Scott St Monroe MI 48161 Office: Mercy Meml Hosp Corp 740 N Macomb St Monroe MI 48161

EDSTROM, JOHN OLOF, educator, industrialist; b. Stockholm, May 11, 1926; s. Johan and Martha Torborg (Andersson) E.; dipl.ing., Royal Inst. Tech., 1950, tech.lic., 1953, dr.sci., 1958; m. Gunnel Kling, Nov. 24, 1950; 1 child, Ingeborg. Research asst. Royal Inst. Tech., Stockholm, 1950-53, prof. ferrous metallurgy, 1960—, prof. prodn. tech., 1977—; research asso. U. Minn., Mpls., 1954; research metallurgist Jernkontoret, Stockholm, 1955-57; head metall. research dept. Sandvik Co., Sandviken, Sweden, 1958-60, v.p. research and devel., 1960-65, exec. v.p., 1965-70; pres. Norrbotten Steelworks, Luleå , Sweden, 1970-76; chmn. Swedish Welding Commn., 1986—; chmn. U. Luleå , 1970-77; hon. prof. E. China Inst. Metallurgy, 1987—. Decorated comdr. Order of Vasa; recipient Bergs medal Royal Inst. Tech., 1973. Mem. Royal Swedish Acad. Engring. (dir. 1979-82), Inst. Metal Research (dir. 1970—), MEFOS (dir. 1970—), Swedish Inst. Prodn. Engring. Research (dir. 1977-80), AIME, Metal Soc., Iron and Steel Inst. Japan (hon.), Svenska Metallografforbundet, Verein Deutsche Eisenhuttenleute. Clubs: Rotary, Svenska Bergsmannaforeningen, Sankt Orjans Gille. Contbr. articles to profl. jours.; patentee in field; inventor. Home: 2E Orrspelsvagen, 18275 Stocksund Sweden Office: Royal Inst Tech, Dept Prodn Tech, 25 Drottning Kristinas vag, 10044 Stockholm Sweden

EDVINSSON, JOHAN HENRIK LEIF, export company executive; b. Upsala, Sweden, Mar. 8, 1946; s. Johan Edvin and Siri Ingrid Adèle (Ludwigsson) J.; m. Gunilla Elisabeth Hedlund, July, 7, 1973; children: Marie, Sophie. Degree in civil econs., U. Lund, Sweden, 1970; MBA, U. Calif., Berkeley, 1974. Cons. Saljkonsult AB, Malmo, Sweden, 1970-73; sr. cons. Saljkonsult AB, Stockholm, 1974-76; sr. cons., bus. developer PA Internat., Stockholm, 1976-80; sr. ptnr Consultus AB, Stockholm, 1980-82; pres. Consultus Internat. AB, Stockholm, 1982—; CTC chmn. bd. PA Internat., London, 1978-80; spl. adv. Ministry Fgn. Trade and Affairs Swedish Govt., Stockholm, 1983-84; researcher Ctr. Service Research, Karlstad, Sweden, 1986; mem. adv. bd. Promethee, Paris and N.Y.C., 1987, Swedish Coalition of Services Industries, 1985—; bd. dirs. several export oriented cos. Contbr. to profl. jours. Served with Swedish Army, 1970-71. Sweden-Am. Found. scholar, 1973, research scholar Mktg. Tech. Ctr., 1981. Mem. Am. Mktg. Assn., Swedish Coalition Service Industries. Lutheran. Club: U.S.A. Office: Consultus Internat AB, Dobelnsgatan 64, S-11352 Stockholm Sweden

EDWARDES, MICHAEL OWEN, business executive; b. Port Elizabeth, South Africa, Oct. 11, 1930; s. Denys Owen and Audrey Noel (Copeland) E.; ed. St. Andrew's Coll., Grahamstown, South Africa; law degree Rhodes U., Grahamstown; m. Mary Margaret Finlay, Dec. 27, 1958; children: Susan, Judy, Penelope. Mgmt. trainee Chloride Group, London, from 1951, mem. main bd., 1969—, chief exec. officer, from 1972, exec. chmn., from 1974, non-exec. dep. chmn., 1977-82, non-exec. chmn., 1982—; chmn. ICL Pub. Ltd. Co., 1984—; chmn. Brit. Leyland (now BL Ltd.), 1977-82; chmn. Mercury Communications Ltd., 1982-83; non-exec. chmn. Hill Samuel S. Africa, 1982—; non-exec. dir. Hill Samuel, mcht. bankers; mem. Nat. Enterprise Bd., 1975-77; mem. council Confedn. Brit. Industry, 1974-81, mem. pres.'s com., 1981—; mem. Queen's Award for Industry Rev. Com., 1975; pres. Comite des Constructeurs d'Automobile du Marche Commun, 1979. Author: Back From The Brink, 1983. Bd. dirs. Internat. Mgmt. and Devel. Inst., Washington, 1972—. Decorated knight Order Brit. Empire, 1979; named Young Businessman of Yr., Guardian newspaper, 1975. Fellow Brit. Inst. Mgmt. (vice chmn. from 1977), Instn. Mech. Engrs. (hon.). Clubs: RAC (London); Rand (Johannesburg, South Africa); Jesters. Office: Chloride Group PLC, 52 Grosvenor Gardens, London SW1A 0AU, England *

EDWARDS, BERT TVEDT, accountant; b. Washington, Aug. 23, 1937; s. Archie Campbell and Geniana (Rasmussen) E.; m. Susan Elizabeth Dye, July 18, 1964; children: Christopher Andrew, Stacey Elizabeth. BA, Wesleyan U., 1959; MBA, Stanford U., 1961. CPA, D.C., Va., N.C., La. With Arthur Andersen & Co., Washington, 1961-69, 70—, mgr., 1965-69, 70-71, ptnr., 1971—; fin. v.p. Leisure Time Industries, Inc., 1969-70. Trustee Barker Found., 1968-78, treas., 1968-71, 1st v.p., 1971-72, pres., 1972-75; trustee, treas. Population Reference Bur., Inc., 1975—; bd. dirs. Jr. Achievement Met. Washington, Inc., 1973-87, treas., 1973-74, 2d v.p., 1974-75, 1st v.p., 1975-77, pres., 1977-78, chmn., 1978-80; dir., treas. Heritage Walk Homes Corp., 1975-80; mem. spl. adv. commn. for indsl. and comml. devel. D.C. City Council, 1972-74; chmn. Nat. Bus. Leadership Conf., 1978; co-chmn. annual conf., 1987; class agt. Wesleyan U. Ann. Fund, 1970-85; Wesleyan U. Alumni Council, 1985—. Served with AUS, 1962-63. Recipient Outstanding Achievement award Stanford U., 1982, Outstanding Publ. award Soc. Mil. Comptrollers, 1983, Bronze Leadership award Jr. Achievement, 1979, Silver Leadership award, 1981; Victor Royall fellow Stanford U., 1960-61. Mem. Am. Inst. CPAs (state and local govt. acctg. com. 1984-85, 85—, subcom. fed. govt. acctg. and auditing 1981-84, mem. ad hoc task force univ. audit 1985-87, mem. task force quality of govt. audit 1986-87, author, editor single audit course 1985, 86, 87, 88), D.C. Inst. CPAs (chmn. membership com. 1973-74, SEC com. 1974-75, govt. acctg. com. 1979-81), Va. Soc. CPAs, Nat. Assn. Accts., Am. Acctg. Assn., Md. Mcpl. League, Healthcare Fin. Mgmt. Assn., Assn. Sch. Bus. Ofcls., Govt. Fin. Officers Assn., Md. Pub. Fin. Officers Assn., Assn. Govt. Accts., Govt. Fin. Officers Assn. Met. Washington, Met. Washington Bd. Trade, Wesleyan U. Alumni Club Washington (treas. 1968-70, pres. 1970-73), Univ. Club (mem. bd. admissions 1976-82, chmn. 1980-82, bd. govs. 1982-85). Methodist. Home: 10712 Stapleford Hall Dr Potomac MD 20854-4449 Office: 1666 K St NW Washington DC 20006

EDWARDS, CARL NORMAND, management consultant; b. Norwood, Mass., Jan. 22, 1943; s. Wilfred Carl and Cecile Marie-Anne (Pepin) E.; m. Mary Louise Buyse, Jan. 22, 1982. Student Brdigewater State Coll.; MEd, Suffolk U., 1969; postgrad. Harvard U. Cons. dept. social relations Harvard, 1966-69, research fellow, 1969-71, lectr. social relations, 1971-72; cons. research psychologist Cambridge Computer Assocs., Mass., 1966—; assoc. clin. prof. psychiatry Tufts U. Sch. Medicine, 1971—, research social psychologist Tufts-New Eng. Med. Center, 1969—; dir. Four Oaks Research Inst., Norfolk, Mass., 1974—; sr. assoc. for policy planning and research Justice Resource Inst., 1971—; field faculty grad. program Goddard Coll., Plainfield, Vt., 1972-82; chmn. bd. dirs. MEDx Systems, Ltd., Dover, Mass., 1985—; chmn. bd. trustees Ctr. for Birth Defects Info. Services, Inc., Dover, 1984—; tchr. seminars; cons. to major corps., govt. agys. and pub. instns. in human dynamics and pub. policy; lectr., thesis adviser, program devel. cons. schs., colls., insts. Contbr. articles to profl. jours., monographs, revs. Mem. USNG, 1963-64. Mem. Am., Mass. psychol. Assns., Soc. for Psychol. Study Social Issues, Peace Research Soc., Nat. Pilots Assn., Nat. Trust for Hist. Preservation. Clubs: Harvard (Boston); Appalachian Mountain, Norfolk Hunt, Blue Ridge Hunt. Author: Drug Dependence: Social Regulation and Treatment Alternatives. Contbr. articles to profl. jours., monographs, revs. Home: Four Oaks Off Springdale PO Box 279 Dover MA 02030

EDWARDS, CHARLES HENRY, JR., surgeon; b. Goldsboro, N.C., Dec. 22, 1920; s. Charles Henry and Lillie Estelle (Thornton) E.; B.A., U. N.C., 1940, postgrad. in medicine, 1940-42; M.D., Thomas Jefferson U., 1944; m. Betty Shea, Mar. 11, 1950; children—Charles Henry, Christopher G. Intern, Pa. Hosp., Phila., 1944; resident in gen. surgery Halloran VA Hosp., S.I., 1947-51; surg. resident Martland Hosp., Newark, 1951-52; practice gen. and vascular surgery, Newark, 1951-55, Glen Ridge, N.J., 1955-71, Montclair, N.J., 1971—; mem. surg. staff St. Vincent's, St. James, United Hosp. of Newark, St. Barnabas, Riverside hosps.; med. dir. Riverside Hospice, Boonton, N.J., 1976-78; clin. asst. prof. surgery N.J. Coll. Medicine and Dentistry, Newark, 1966—; med. dir. Individual Freedom Found. Ednl. Trust, 1976—. Bd. dirs. Citizens Freedom Found. N.Y./N.J., 1980—. Served to capt., M.C., U.S. Army, 1944-47. Diplomate Am. Bd. Surgery. Fellow ACS; mem. AMA, N.J. State, Essex County med. socs. Lodges: Masons (32 deg.), Shriners. Home: 19 Club Rd Upper Montclair NJ 07043 Office: 5 Roosevelt Pl Montclair NJ 07042

EDWARDS, DEL M(OUNT), business executive; b. Tyler, Tex., Apr. 12, 1953; s. Welby Clell and Davida (Mount) E.; m. Susan Alicia Pappas, 1984 (div. 1986). AA cum laude, Tyler Jr. Coll., 1974; BBA, Baylor U., 1976. Corp. coordinator Dillard Dept. Stores, Inc., Ft. Worth, 1976-77; v.p. W.C. Supply, Inc., Tyler, 1977—; pres., owner Walker Auto Spring, Inc., Shreveport, La., 1978-88, Edwards & Assocs., Inc., 1984—; v.p. W.C. Square, Inc., 1976—. Mem. planning com. Tyler Heritage Tour, 1982-83; Originator Designer Show-Case, Tyler, 1983; founder, chmn. Rose Garden Trust Fund, 1981-87; bd. dirs. Carnegie History Ctr., 1984-85 ; pres. Smith County Youth Found., 1986-87, bd. dirs., 1984—; East Tex. Baylor Club, 1986-87; chmn. Sr. Citizens Day ann. program, East Tex. Fair, 1979—, bd. dirs. 1984—; mem. Bd. Assocs. East Tex. Bapt. U., Marshall, 1987—; trustee Timberline Bapt. Camp and Conf. Ctr., 1987—. Mem. Council Fleet Specialists, Tyler Area C. of C., Smith County Hist. Soc. (chmn. bd. govs. 1984-85, 87-88, pres. 1984-85), mem. Smith County Hist. Commn., 1984-85, Hist. Tyler, Inc., Tyler Jaycees (v.p. 1982-83, dir. 1981-85), Nat. Trust for Hist. Preservation, , SCV (treas. camp 124, 1979-83). Baptist. Clubs: Tyler Petroleum, Willow Brook Country (Tyler). Home: 3415 S Keaton Ave Tyler TX 75701 also: Mountwood Ranch Rt 2 Box 305 Tyler TX 75704 Office: WC Square Front at Bonner Tyler TX 75710

EDWARDS, DILAWAR MUMBY, educator; b. Sagar, Madhya Pradesh, India, Feb. 26, 1943; came to U.S., 1967; s. Seth Jason and Doris Mary (Bernard) E.; m. Esther Orine Thomas, Jan. 19, 1974; children: Karuna Ruth, Dilawar Mark, Anugraha Hannah, Dileshu Matthew. I.Sc., St. Aloysius' Coll., Jabalpur, India, 1961; BE with 1st class honors, Govt. Engring. Coll., Jabalpur, India, 1966; ME (I.), Indian Inst. Sci., Bangalore, 1967; M.Sc. in Edn., Ind. U. Bloomington, 1969, PhD, 1970. Assoc. prof., dir. CCTV, N.C. Cen. U., Durham, 1970-72; prof. California U. of Pa., 1972-80, prof. dept. ednl. studies, chmn. dept., 1981-84, chmn. secondary edn. adv. council, 1981-84, prof. dept. ednl. studies, prof. comparative religions East and West, Sch. Grad. Studies and Continuing Edn., Nat. Elderhostel Program, 1984—; cons. research design and instrnl. message design N.C. Central U., Durham, 1970-72; hon. sec. Dr. Edwards Inst. for Homoeopathy and Evangelism, Inc., California, Pa., 1977—; mgr. DIL Records, California, Pa., 1979—; council mem. Am. Council Ramabai Mukti Mission, Clinton, N.J., 1985—; mem. Internat. Edn. Council California U. of Pa., 1986—. Artist, record albums: Jesus is Lord and Saviour, 1980, Faith of Our Fathers Living Faith, 1980; speaker, soloist numerous chs., Bible confs., convs., concerts, recitals, retreats, radio and TV broadcasts, 1958—; soloist Asian Christian Youth Congress, Hyderabad, India, 1965, Far East Broadcasting Co., Manila, Philipines, Bangalore, India, 1966-67, Ind. U. Opera Theatre, Bloomington, 1969. Recipient India State Bd. Tech. Edn. Merit Scholarship award, 1961-65; All India Council for Tech. Edn. Ministry of Sci. Research and Cultural Affairs Scholarship awardee, 1966-67; Ind. U. Alumni Assn. Alumni awardee, 1967-69. Mem. Assn. for Ednl. Communications and Tech. (mem. evaluation team nat. conv. 1978), Am. Ednl. Research Assn., The Gideons Internat. (life; pres. Washington County East Camp 1986-87, meml. Bible chmn. 1987—, soloist state conv., Pitts., 1986 , Winston-Salem, 1987, internat. conv., Columbus, Ohio 1988), Phi Delta Kappa. Independent Bible Baptist. Office: U Pa Dept Ednl Studies California PA 15419

EDWARDS, GLORIA BANKS, human relations facilitator, management consultant, educator; b. Yonkers, N.Y., Sept. 18, 1932; d. Richard Henry and Pinkie (Moore) Banks; m. Esmond Herbert Edwards, Aug. 7, 1954 (div. May 1961). B.S., Tchrs. Coll. Columbia U., 1961, M.A., M.Ed., 1977, Ed.D., 1985. Nat. cert. counselor. Research assoc. Met. Applied Research Ctr., N.Y.C., 1969-70; spl. projects coordinator N.Y. Urban Coalition, N.Y.C., 1970-77; field faculty advisor Vt. Coll., 1983—; adj. asst. prof. Herbert H. Lehman Coll., Bronx, N.Y., 1981-84; sr. assoc. Arawak Consulting Corp., N.Y.C., 1984-86; human relations facilitator Yonkers (N.Y.) Bd. Edn., 1986—. Contbr. articles to profl. jours. Mem. Lincoln Nurses Assn. Democrat. Baptist. Club: L'54 (N.Y.C.). Avocations: sculptoring; sketching. Office: Yonkers Bd of Edn Ednl and Cultural Arts Ctr 1109 N Broadway Yonkers NY 10701

EDWARDS, HARRY LAFOY, lawyer; b. Greenville, S.C., July 29, 1936; s. George Belton and Mary Olive (Jones) E.; m. Suzanne Copeland, June 16, 1956; 1 dau., Margaret Peden. LLB, U. S.C., 1963, JD, 1970. Bar: S.C. 1963, U.S. dist. ct. S.C. 1975, U.S. Ct. Apls. (4th cir.) 1974. Assoc. Edwards and Edmunds, Greenville, 1963; v.p., sec., dir. Edwards Co., Inc., Greenville, 1963-65; atty. investment legal dept. Liberty Life Ins. Co., Greenville, 1965-67, asst. sec., asst. v.p., head investment legal dept., 1967-70; asst. sec. Liberty Corp., 1970-75; asst. v.p. Liberty Life Ins. Co., 1970-75; sec. Bent Tree Corp., CEL, Inc., 1970-75; sec., dir. Westchester Mall, Inc., 1970-75; asst. sect. Libco, Inc., Liberty Properties, Inc., 1970-75; sole practice, Greenville, 1975—. Com. mem. Hipp Fund Spl. Edn., Greenville County Sch. System; mem. Boyd C. Hipp II Scholarship Com. Wofford Coll., Spartanburg, S.C.; scholarship com. mem. Liberty Scholars, U. So. Calif., 1984, 86-88; editor U.S.C. law rev., 1963 . Served with USAFR, 1957-63. Mem. ABA, S.C. Bar Assn., Greenville County Bar Assn., Phi Delta Phi. Baptist. Clubs: Greenville Lawyers, Poinsett (Greenville). Home: 106 Ridgeland Dr Greenville SC 29601 Office: PO Box 10350 Federal Station Greenville SC 29603

EDWARDS, HENRY PERCIVAL, psychology educator, dean; b. Bogota, Colombia, Sept. 5, 1939; arrived in Can., 1953; s. Henry Percival and Rosalbina (Contreras) E.; m. Frances M. Lamontagne, Aug. 31, 1963; children: Jane, Henry, Rosann, Robert. BA in Pre-Med., Loyola U., Montreal, Can., 1961; MA in Psychology, U. Ottawa, Can., 1965, PhD in Psychology, 1967. Lectr. in psychology U. Loyola, Montreal, 1965-66; prof. psychology U. Ottawa, 1967—; dean faculty Social Scis. U. Loyola, 1985—; program evaluation cons. Ottawa Separate Sch. Bd., 1970-78, Carleton Bd. Edn ., Nepean, Can., 1981-87. Contbr. articles to profl. jours. Recipient Paul Pimsleur award for research in fgn. lang. evaluation Am. Council on Teaching of Fgn. Langs., 1986. Fellow Can. Psychol. Assn.; mem. Ont. Psychol. Assn., Am. Assn. State Psychology Bds. (exec. com. 1985-88). Roman Catholic. Office: Univ of Ottawa, Social Scis, 550 Cumberland, Ottawa, ON Canada K1N 6N5

EDWARDS, IAN KEITH, obstetrician, gynecologist; b. Spartanburg, S.C., Mar. 2, 1926; s. James Smiley and Georgina (Waters) E.; m. Glenda Melissa Joselyn, Dec. 27, 1968; children—Darien, Jennifer, Carol, Terry. A.B., Duke U., 1949, M.D., 1953. Diplomate Am. Bd. Ob-Gyn. Spl. study pediatrics St. Bartholomew's Hosp., London, 1952; resident in ob-gyn Grady Meml. Hosp., Atlanta, 1955-58; chief ob-gyn Valley Forge Army Hosp., Pa., 1958-61; practice medicine specializing in ob-gyn Olney, Ill., 1969—; ptnr. Trover Clinic, Madisonville, Ky., 1961-68, Weber Med. Clinic, Olney, 1969—; dir. dept. ob-gyn Weber Med. Clinic, 1970-74, 78-83, chmn. bd. dirs., 1983-87, med. dir., 1987—; chief of staff Hopkins County Hosp., Ky., 1967-68, Richland Meml. Hosp., Olney, 1974-76; clin. instr. ob-gyn U. Ky. Med. Ctr., Lexington, 1965-68; cons. Childbirth Edn. League; del. Ill. Sec. Dist. VI. Contbr. articles to med. jours. Mem. Found. com. Olney Central Coll. Served to capt. M.C., U.S. Army, 1954-55; Korea. Fellow Am. Coll. Obstetricians and Gynecologists (exec. com. Ill. sect.); mem. AMA, Phila. Obstet. Soc., S.E. Ill. Consortium Maternal and Fetal Welfare, Ill. Assn. Maternal and Child Health, N.Y. Acad. Scis., Am. Acad. Med. Dirs., Am. Group Practice Assn. (nat. mktg. com., clin. editorial cons.), Ill. Med. Soc., Hopkins County Med. Soc. (pres. 1968), Richland Med. Soc. (pres. 1974-76), Ill. Soc. Ob-Gyn., Am. Soc. Colposcopists and Cervical Pathology, Am. Assn. Gynecologic Laparoscopists, Am. Legion, VFW. Democrat. Methodist. Office: Weber Med Clinic 1200 N East St Olney IL 62450

EDWARDS, JAMES EDWIN, lawyer; b. Clarkesville, Ga., July 29, 1914; s. Gus Calloway and Mary Clara (McKinney) E.; m. Frances Lillian Stanley, Nov. 22, 1948; children—Robin Anne Edwards Ralston, James Christopher, Clare Wilkson. Student U. Tex. 1931-33; B.A., George Washington U., 1935, J.D. cum laude, 1946. Bar: Fla. 1938, D.C. 1981, Va 1987. Practice law, Cocoa, Fla., 1938-42; hearing and exam. officer USCG, 1943-45; div. asst. State Dept., Washington, 1945-50; practice law Ft. Lauderdale, Fla., 1951-55, 59-77; mem. firm Bell, Edwards, Coker, Carlon & Amsden, Ft. Lauderdale, 1956-59; sole practice, Coral Springs, Fla., 1977-81, 84-85; asst. city atty. Fort Lauderdale, 1961, 63-65; mem. firm. Edwards & Leary, Coral Springs, 1981-84; mem. panel Am. Arbitration Assn., 1984—. Commr., Coral Springs, 1970-76, mayor, 1972-74; mem. bd. suprs. Sunshine Water Mgmt. Dist., 1976-80; chmn. Ft. Lauderdale for Eisenhower, 1952; pres. Fla. Conservative Union, Broward County, 1976. Served to lt. USCGR, 1943-45, to lt. col. JAG, USAFR, 1950-68. Mem. SAR. Presbyterian. Club: English Speaking Union (Charlottesville, Va.). Lodge: Rotary. Author: Myths About Guns, 1978. Home and Office: PO Box 88 Keswick VA 22947-0088

EDWARDS, JOHN WILLIAM, business executive; b. Fitchburg, Mass., Feb. 1, 1930; s. Junius Griffith and Sylvia Emma (Mallioux) E.; A.B., Columbia Coll., 1952; postgrad. study in law Georgetown U., 1958; m. Lillian Elizabeth O'Dowd, July 5, 1952; children—Christopher, John, Steven. Gen. mgr. info. systems div. Polaroid Corp., Cambridge, Mass., 1966-71; asst. to commr. U.S. Customs Service, Washington, 1971-73; v.p. systems No. Telecom Ltd., Montreal, Que., Can., 1974-76; v.p. info. systems GATX Corp., Chgo., 1976-85; sr. v.p. Household Fin. Services, Chgo., 1986—. Chmn. Sudbury (Mass.) Sch. Bd., 1962-69; co-chmn. membership Decordova Mus., Lincoln, Mass., 1968-69; community chmn. United Fund, Sudbury, 1965-66; adv. bd. Nat. Orgn. on Disability, 1985—. Served to lt. USNR, 1953-57. Mem. Soc. Info. Mgmt., Ret. Officers Assn. Clubs: Met. (Chgo.); Edgartown Yacht. Contbr. numerous articles on info. systems to profl. jours. Home: 154 Quicksand Pond Rd Little Compton RI 02837 Office: 2700 Sanders Rd Prospect Heights IL 60070

EDWARDS, MARIE BABARE, psychologist; b. Tacoma; d. Nick and Mary (Mardesich) Babare; B.A., Stanford, 1948, M.A., 1949; m. Tilden Hampton Edwards (div.); 1 son, Tilden Hampton Edwards III. Counselor guidance center U. So. Calif., Los Angeles, 1950-52; project coordinator So. Calif. Soc. Mental Hygiene, 1952-54; pub. speaker Welfare Fedn. Los Angeles, 1953-57; field rep. Los Angeles County Assn. Mental Health, 1957-58; intern psychologist UCLA, 1958-60; pvt. practice, human relations tng., counselor tng. Mem. Calif., Am., Western, Los Angeles psychol. assns., AAAS, So. Calif. Soc. Clin. Hypnosis, Internat. Platform Assn. Author: (with Eleanor Hoover) The Challenge of Being Single, 1974, paperback edit., 1975. Office: 6100 Buckingham Pkwy Culver City CA 90230

EDWARDS, MICHAEL PAUL, electrical engineer; b. Lemay, Mo., Apr. 13, 1950; s. William Riley and Mary Lena (Curry) E.; m. Joyce Jeanette Reich, Apr. 14, 1973. BEE, U. Mo., Rolla, 1973; MBA, Wash. U., St. Louis, 1986. Elect. engr. McDonnell-Douglas, St. Louis, 1973-75, 1977-79; mgr. engring. Autocontrol, Inc., St. Louis, 1974-77; mgr. computer services Anheuser-Busch Cos., St. Louis, 1979—. Vol. ARC. Mem. IEEE (sr.), Engrs. Club (membership com.), Soc. Mfgr. Engrs. (sr.), Eta Kappa Nu, Beta Gamma Sigma. Republican. Congregationalist. Club: Engineers (St. Louis). Home: 7002 Stony Ridge Rd Saint Louis MO 63129 Office: Anheuser Busch Cos One Busch Pl 202-3 Saint Louis MO 63118

EDWARDS, PETER GEOFFREY, historian; b. Watford, Eng., Aug. 29, 1945; came to Australia, 1950; s. Geoffrey and Joan M. (Nunn) E.; m. Jean B. Tait, Oct. 1, 1971; children: Kirsten Joanna, Nicola Louise. BA with honors, U. Western Australia, 1967; PhD, Oxford (Eng.) U., 1971. Research historian Australian Dept. Fgn. Affairs, Canberra, 1972-75; research fellow Australian Nat. U., Canberra, 1975-78; master St. Mark's Coll., U. Adelaide, Australia, 1978-83; ofcl. historian Malaya, Vietnam Australian War Meml., Canberra, 1983—; mem. bur. Commn. for the History of Internat. Relations, 1985—. Author: Prime Ministers and Diplomats, 1983; editor: Australia Through American Eyes, 1979, documents on Australian fgn. policy, 1975-79. Fellow Duke U., 1976, Harkness fellow, 1975; Rhodes scholar Oxford U., 1967. Mem. Assn. for History of Australian Def. and Fgn. Policy (pres. 1985—), Australian Inst. Internat. Affairs (research com. 1984—). Office: Australian War Meml, GPO Box 345, Canberra 2601, Australia

EDWARDS, PETER STUART ALLENBY, solicitor; b. Beckenham, Kent, England, May 28, 1948; s. Randall and Eileen Muriel (Allenby) E.; m. Helene Alice Marguerite Anne Chantal de Cabrol de Moute, Oct. 10, 1981. MA, Magdalen Coll., Oxford, 1969. Cert. solicitor, Eng., Wales, 1972, Hong Kong, 1976; notary public, Hong Kong, 1986. Articled clk. Richards, Butler & Co., London, 1970-72; asst. solicitor Richards, Butler & Co., 1972-75; asst. solicitor Johnson, Stokes & Master, Hong Kong, 1975-78, ptnr., 1979—. Mem. Law Soc. of Eng. and Wales, Law Soc. of Hong Kong, Hong Kong Soc. of Notaries, Internat. Fiscal Assn. (deputy chmn. Hong Kong br. 1979-87. chmn. 1987—). Anglican. Clubs: Royal Soc. St. George (com. mem 1984—, v.p. 1987-88), Hong Kong Backgammon (pres. 1980-82), Hong Kong, Royal Hong Kong Jockey, United Oxford and Cambridge. Home: 34B Mount Kellett Rd, The Peak, Hong Kong Hong Kong Office: Johnson Stokes & Master, Princes Bldg 18th Fl, Hong Kong Hong Kong

EDWARDS, RAY CONWAY, engineering corporation executive; b. Belleville, Ont., Can., Sept. 1, 1913; s. Ernest Alfred and Augusta (Fee) E.; B.A., UCLA, 1935; m. Marjorie Baisch; children—David, Douglas, Ruth, Diane, Robert (dec.), Helen. Engr., Carrier Corp., Syracuse, N.Y., 1935-42; physicist Gen. Lab., U.S. Rubber Co., Passaic, N.J., 1942-46; acoustical cons., founder, chmn. bd., pres. Edwards Engring. Corp., Pompton Plains, N.J., 1947—; founder, chmn. bd. Spi-Rol-Fin Corp., 1954-58; mfr. air conditioning and refrigeration equipment, gas treatment and pollution control equipment for petroleum industry; patentee in field. Registered profl. engr. N.Y., N.J., Va., Pa. Mem. ASHRAE (life), Theta Delta Chi. Home: 396 Ski Trail Smoke Rise Butler NJ 07405 Office: 101 Alexander Ave Pompton Plains NJ 07444

EDWARDS, RICHARD AMBROSE, lawyer, business educator; b. Roachdale, Ind., May 10, 1922; s. Ralph A. and Bess May (McCampbell) E.; children—Craig Richard, Barbara F. A.B., Ind. U., 1947; LL.B. Harvard U, 1949; Ph.D. (Curtis fellow), Columbia U., 1952. Bar: Ind., U.S. Supreme Ct. 1954. Instr. Rutgers U., 1949-51; assoc. prof. pub. law and govt. Lafayette Coll., 1952-56; dir. research U.S. Commn. on Govt. Security, Washington, 1956-57; assoc. dir. legislative research Columbia Law Sch., N.Y.C., 1957-58; assoc. gen. counsel Health Ins. Assn. Am., N.Y.C., 1958-66; v.p. head public relations dept. Assos. Investment Co., South Bend, Ind., 1966-68; sr. v.p., head govt. and industry relations dept. Met. Life Inst. Co., N.Y.C., 1968-85; Frederick R. Kappel prof. bus.-govt. relations U. Minn. Sch. Mgmt., 1985. Author: (with N.T. Dowling) American Constitutional Law, 1954; editor: Index Digest of State Constitutions, 1958. Trustee Nat. Mcpl. League. Served to capt. U.S. Army, World War II, Korea. Decorated Bronze Star. Mem. Am. Bar Assn., Am. Acad. Mgmt., Assn. Life Ins. Counsel, Phi Beta Kappa. Republican. Presbyterian. Home: 111 Marguette Ave S Apt 2401 Minneapolis MN 55401 Office: 271 19th Ave S Minneapolis MN 55455

EDWARDS, RYAN HAYES, baritone; b. Columbia, S.C., Aug. 5, 1941; s. William Munroe and Dorothy LeGrande (Sawyer) Faucett; m. Leila Scelonge; children: Geoffrey C., Trevor B. Mus.B., U. Tex., 1964; Mus.M., Tex. Christian U., 1971. Scholar, Juilliard Am. Opera Center, N.Y.C., 1968-71, debut, N.Y.C. Opera, 1971, Hollywood Bowl, 1973, New York Philharmonic, 1971, Los Angeles Philharmonic, 1971, San Francisco Opera Co., 1975, Miami Opera Co., 1976, Boston Opera, 1976, Teatro del Liceo, Barcelona, 1973, Royal Festival Hall, London, 1974, 75, Met. Opera Co., 1976, radio debut, O.R.T.F., Paris, 1973-74, assoc. prof. voice-opera, Northwestern U., Evanston, Ill., 1982. Rockefeller grantee, 1968-69; Nat. Opera Inst. grantee, 1970-72; Edwin H. Mosler Found. grantee, 1970-74; William Mathews Sullivan Mus. Found. grantee, 1971-72. Mem. Am. Guild Musical Artists, Actors Equity, Phi Mu Alpha, Lambda Chi Alpha. Office: care Robert Lombardo Assocs 61 W 62d St New York NY 10023

EDWARDS, SAMUEL FREDERICK, physicist, educator; b. Swansea, U.K., Feb. 1, 1928; ed. Cambridge U., Harvard U.; D.Sc. (hon.), univs. Bath, Edinburgh, Loughborough, Salford, Birmingham, Strasbourg; m. E.M. Merriell, 1953; 1 son, 3 daus. Mem. Inst. Advanced Study, Princeton, N.J.; research fellow U. Birmingham; prof. U. Manchester; now Cavendish prof. physics Cavendish Lab., Cambridge U.; dir. Lucas Industries, Steetley Industries; chmn. Sci. Research Council U.K., 1973-77, Def. Sci. Adv. Council, 1977-80; chief sci. advisor U.K. Dept. Energy, 1983-88. Fellow Royal Soc. (Davy medal 1985), Inst. Physics (Maxwell medal, Guthrie medal), Royal Soc. Chemistry, Inst. Math. (Gold medallist 1986); mem. Am. Phys. Soc. (High Polymer Physics prize), Brit. Assn. Advancement of Sci. (chmn. 1977-82, pres. 1988—). Club: Athenaeum. Contbr. articles to sci. jours. Home: 7 Penarth Pl, Cambridge CB3 9LU, England Office: Cavendish Lab, Cambridge CB3 OHE, England also: care Royal Soc, 6 Carlton House Tce, London SW1Y 5AG, England

EECKHOUDT, LOUIS RAYMOND, economics educator; b. Horrues, Hainaut, Belgium, Jan. 17, 1944; s. Robert R. and Marie-Louise (Decorte) E.; m. Genviève Gilmant, Feb. 9, 1968 (div. Apr. 1976); children: Veronique, Stéphanie (dec.), Luc; m. Béatrice Plisnier, Sept. 10, 1980. Lic. in Comml., Cath. Faculties Mons, Belgium, 1965; Lic. in Econs., Cath. U. Louvain, Belgium, 1967; PhD in Econs., Mich. State U., 1970. Asst. prof. econs. Cath. Faculties Mons, 1970-73, assoc. prof., 1973-76, prof., 1976—; Prof. (part time) Cath. U. Lille, 1970—. Author: L'Équilibre Macro-Economique, 1976; contbr. articles to profl. jours. Served as sgt. Belgian Army, 1972-73. Hoover Inst. fellow, 1967. Mem. Am. Risk and Ins. Assn., European Soc. for Med. Decision Making (bd. dirs.), European Fin. Assn. (bd. dirs.). Roman Catholic. Home: Rue Vilaine 10, B-7000 Mons Belgium Office: Cath Faculties Mons, 151 Chausseé Binche, Mons Belgium

EELLS, RICHARD, emeritus business educator; b. Cashmere, Wash., Aug. 5, 1917; s. Fred K. and Sophia (Fox) E. A.B., Whitman Coll., 1940, LL.D., 1982; M.A., Princeton, 1942. Fellow Library of Congress, 1945-46, chief div. aeros., 1946-50, Guggenheim chair aeros., 1949-50; field dir. Near East Coll. Assos., 1950-52; ednl. cons. Gen. Electric Co., N.Y.C., 1952-53; mgr. pub. relations research Gen. Electric Co., 1953-56, mgr. pub. policy research, 1956-60; founder, pres. Richard Eells and Assocs. Inc., 1961—; sr. researcher Grad. Sch. Bus., Columbia U., N.Y.C., 1959-60; adj. prof. Grad. Sch. Bus., Columbia U., 1960-85, adj. prof. bus. emeritus, 1985—; dir., editor Studies of the Modern Corp., 1964-85, mem. nat. devel. bd., 1974—, counselor to dean, 1975—, spl. adviser to pres., 1977—, chmn. bd., 1985—; ct.-apptd. observer U.S. Ct., Berlin, 1979; John M. Olin Disting. Lectr. Berry Coll., 1980; cons., adviser IBM; cons., adviser Gen. Electric Co., Kaiser Cos., Rockefeller Bros. Fund, Com. for Econ. Devel., Continental Group, Ashland Oil Co.; Mem. adv. research bd. Nat. Merit Scholarship Corp., 1957-59; pres. Found. Study Human Orgn.; trustee Arkville Erpf Fund, 1962-82, also sec. and treas.; dir. Midgard Found., 1958-87. Author: Corporation Giving in a Free Society, 1956, The Meaning of Modern Business: An Introduction to the Philosophy of Large Corporate Enterprise, 1960, (with Clarence Walton) Conceptual Foundations of Business, 1961, 3d edit., 1974 (McKinsey Found. Acad. Mgmt. award), The Business System: Readings in Ideas and Concepts, 1967, Man in the City of the Future, 1968, The Government of Corporations, 1962, The Corporation and the Arts, 1967, (with Kenneth G. Patrick) Education and the Business Dollar, 1969, Global Corporations: The Emerging System of World Economic Power, 2d edit, 1976, (with Neil H. Jacoby and Peter Nehemkis) Bribery and Extortion in World Business, 1977, International Business Philanthropy, 1979, The Political Crisis of the Enterprise System, 1980; author: (with Peter Nehemkis) Corporate Intelligence and Espionage, 1984. Trustee New Eng. Conservatory Music, 1974-78, Next Century Found., 1970—, Southeastern Coll., Athens, Greece, 1987—, Biopolitics Internat. Orgn., Athens, 1987—; trustee, v.p., treas. Weatherhead Found., 1958-87; bd. overseers Whitman Coll.; bd. founders Acad. Gerontol. Edn. and Devel.; spl. advisor The New York Botanical Garden, 1987-88; bd. dirs. Aging-in-Am. Served with USAAF, 1943-45. Alfred P. Sloan Found., grantee, 1956; Rockefeller Found. grantee, 1963. Mem. Nat. Inst. Social Scis., The Pilgrims, Phi Beta Kappa. Episcopalian. Clubs: Metropolitan (N.Y.C.); Church; Cosmos (Washington). Home: 251 E 51st St New York NY 10022

EFCAVITCH, J. WILLIAM, biochemist; b. Phila., Dec. 8, 1952; s. William and Beatrice (Donnelly) E.; m. Patricia Ann Books, June 6, 1981; children: John Adam, Sasha Nicole, Ryan Patrick. B.A., LaSalle Coll., 1974; Ph.D., Ohio U., 1978. Research assoc. U. Colo., 1978-81; project dir. DNA synthesizer Applied Biosystems, Foster City, Calif., 1981-87; project dir. HPEC Applied Biosystems, 1987—. Contbr. articles to profl. jours. Current work: Automation of synthetic chemistry, biochemistry, molecular biology processes. Subspecialties: Molecular biology; Organic chemistry. Home: 857 South Rd Belmont CA 94002

EFFREN, JOHN KENNETH, research and consulting firm executive, educator, researcher, consultant; b. Hackensack, N.J., Apr. 21, 1949; s. Mack and Evelyn (Taylor) E.; m. Alyce Brie Stein, Jan. 17, 1976 (div. Nov. 1981). B.S., Hobart and William Smith Colls., 1971; M.S., New Sch. for Social and Polit. Research, 1974; Ph.D., Hofstra U., Am. West U., 1982. Cons., researcher Manhattan Psychiat. Ctr., N.Y.C., 1974-75; staff psychologist Bergen Pines Hosp., Paramus, N.J., 1976-78; research psychologist Cornell-Northshore Univ. Hosp, Manhasset, N.Y., 1977-78; exec. dir. Biofeedback Inst. Fla., Ft. Lauderdale, 1979-80, Biofeedback Ctr. N.J., Middletown, 1980-81; pres., chmn. bd. Patient Referral Systems, N.Y.C., 1980—; pres. Profl. Practice Developers, N.Y.C., 1972—; adj. prof. Adelphi U., Garden City, N.Y., 1980—; spl. cons. AMA, ADA, APA, Washington, 1980—; nat. adviser weekly radio broadcasts Nat. Physicians Radio Network, Stamford, Conn., 1985—; lectr. in field. Author: A Psychobehavioral Approach to Marketing, 1985; author papers in practice mktg.; inventor computer-assisted neuropsychodiagnostic test device. Foster parent Internat. Foster Parents Plan, 1982—; active Students Against Drunk Driving, 1984—. Recipient various honors and citations, 1974—. Mem. Assn. Media Psychology (charter), Am. Psychol. Assn., Eastern Psychol. Assn., Pub. Relations Soc. of Am. (accreditation 1987), Physicians for Social Responsibility. Office: Profl Practice Developers 1 Pennsylvania Plaza Suite 100 New York NY 10119

EFRON, SAMUEL, lawyer; b. Lansford, Pa., May 6, 1915; s. Abraham and Rose (Kaduchin) E.; m. Hope Bachrach Newman, Apr. 5, 1941; children: Marc Fred, Eric Michael. B.A., Lehigh U., 1935; LL.B., Harvard U., 1938. Bar: Pa. 1938, D.C. 1949, N.Y. 1967. Atty. forms and regulations div., also registration div. SEC, 1939-40; Office Solicitor Dept. Labor, 1940-42; asst. chief real and personal property sect. Office Alien Property Custodian, 1942-43; chief debt claims sect., also asst. chief claims br. Office Alien Property, Dept. Justice, 1946-51; asst. gen. counsel internat. affairs Dept. Def., 1951-53, cons., 1953-54; partner firm Surrey, Karasik, Gould & Efron, Washington, 1954-61; exec. v.p. Parsons & Whittemore, Inc., N.Y.C., 1961-68; now partner Arent, Fox, Kintner, Plotkin & Kahn, Washington.; Mem. internat. relations vis. com. Lehigh U. Author: Creditors Claims Under the Trading with the Enemy Act, 1948, Foreign Taxes on United States Expenditures, 1954, Offshore Procurement and Industrial Mobilization, 1955, The Operation of Investment Incentive Laws with Emphasis on the U.S.A. and Mexico, 1977. Served to lt. USNR, 1943-46. Decorated Order of the Lion of Finland 1st class. Mem. Am., Fed., Inter-Am. bar assns., Am. Soc. Internat. Law, Assn. Bar City N.Y., Bar Assn. D.C., Phi Beta Kappa. Clubs: Army-Navy (Washington), Cosmos (Washington), Harvard, Internat. (Washington), Nat. Press (Washington), University (Washington), Fed. Bar (Washington); Harvard (N.Y.C.), Lehigh (N.Y.C.), Lotos (N.Y.C.). Home: 3537 Ordway St NW Washington DC 20016 Office: 1050 Connecticut Ave NW Washington DC 20036

EGAN, JOHN FREDERICK, electronics executive; b. Council Bluffs, Iowa, Feb. 25, 1935; s. Frederick Emerson and Ruth Pauline (Russell) E.; m. Anne B. Patterson, June 14, 1958; children: John Jr., James Michael. AB in Physics with honors, Grinnell Coll., 1957; MEE, Northwestern U., 1958, PhD in Elec. Engring., 1961. Tech. dir. computer systems, Electronics Systems div. USAF, Bedford, Mass., 1964-67; sr. staff specialist intelligence Office Dir. Def., Research and Engring., Washington, 1967-71; chief scientist command support Office Chief Naval Ops., Washington, 1971-73; group dir. fed. systems Sanders Assocs., Inc., Nashua, N.H., 1973-77; v.p. Sanders Assoc., Inc., Nashua, N.H., 1977-87; group v.p. Lockheed Corp., 1987—; mem. exec. panel Chief Naval Ops., Washington, 1971—. Chmn. alumni fund Grinnell Coll., 1972—; trustee Nashua Symphony Orch., 1976—. Served with USAF, 1961-64. Baker scholar, 1953-57; Transp. Ctr. fellow, 1957-61. Mem. IEEE, Inst. Aeros. and Astronautics, Nat. Security Indsl. Assn. (mem. exec. com. communications, command and control 1970—), Assn. for Computing Machinery. Office: Lockheed Electronic Systems Group C S 2050 NHQ 1-719 Nashua NH 03061-2050

EGAN, SIR JOHN (LEOPOLD), automobile executive; b. Nov. 7, 1939; m. Julia Emily Treble, 1963; 2 daughters. BSc (hons.), London U., 1961, MSc in Econs., 1968. Petroleum engr. Shell Internat., 1962-66; gen. mgr. Al-Delco Replacements Parts Op. Gen. Motors Ltd., 1968-71; mng. dir. Leyland Cars Parts div. Leyland Cars BLMC, 1971-76, also parts and service dir., 1971-76; corp. parts dir. Massey Ferguson, 1976-80; chmn., chief exec. Jaguar Cars Ltd., 1980-85, Jaguar plc, 1985—. Decorated Knight, 1986. Club: Warwick Boat. Office: Jaguar plc, Brown's Lane, Coventry CV5 9DR, England *

EGAN, SHIRLEY ANNE, retired nursing educator; b. Haverill, Mass.; d. Rush B. and Beatrice (Bengle) Willard. Diploma, St. Joseph's Hosp. Sch. Nursing, Nashua, N.H., 1945; B.S. in Nursing Edn., Boston U., 1949, M.S., 1954. Instr. sci. Sturdy Meml. Hosp. Sch. Nursing, Attleboro, Mass., 1949-51; instr. sci. Peter Bent Brigham Hosp. Sch. Nursing, Boston, 1951-53, ednl. dir., 1953-55, assoc. dir. Sch. Nursing, 1955-59, med. surg. coordinator, 1971-73, assoc. dir. Sch. Nursing, 1973-79, dir., 1979-85; cons. North Country Hosp., 1985-86; infection control practitioner 1986-87; nurse edn. adviser AID (formerly ICA), Karachi, Pakistan, 1959-67; prin. Coll. Nursing, Karachi, 1959-67; dir. Vis. Nurse Service, Nashua, N.H., 1967-70; cons. nursing edn. Pakistan Ministry of Health, Labour and Social Welfare, 1959-67; adviser to editor Pakistan Nursing and Health Rev., 1959-67; exec. bd. Nat. Health Edn. Com., Pakistan; WHO short-term cons. U. W.I., Jamaica, 1970-71; mem. Greater Nashua Health Planning Council. Contbr. articles to profl. publs. Bd. dirs. Matthew Thornton health Ctr., Nashua, Nashua Child Care Ctr.; vol. ombudsman N.H. Council on Aging; mem. Nashua Service League. Served as 1st lt., Army Nurse Corps., 1945-47. Mem. Trained Nurses Assn. Pakistan, Nat. League for Nursing, St. Joseph's Sch. Nursing Alumnae Assn., Boston U. Alumnae Assn., Brit. Soc. Health Edn., Cath. Daus. Am. (vice regent ct. Bishop Malloy), Statis. Study Grads. Karachi Coll. Nursing, Sigma Theta Tau. Home: Rte 1 Box 1268A Natchitoches LA 71457

EGAWA, SHIRO, banker; b. Nagasaki-shi, Japan, Oct. 30, 1922; s. Tadaharu and Muh E.; m. Akiko Egawa, Dec. 5, 1950; children—Midori, Mayumi. B.A. in Econs., U. Tokyo, 1947. Mgr. Hiroshima br. I.B.J., Japan, 1962-70; dir. Nippon Credit Bank, Ltd., Tokyo, 1970-72, mng. dir., 1972-75, dep. pres., 1975-82, pres., 1982—. Office: Nippon Credit Bank Ltd, 1-13-10 Kudan-kita, Chiyoda-ku, Tokyo 102 Japan *

EGERVARI, TIBOR JANOS, artistic director, theatre arts educator; b. Budapest, Hungary, May 21, 1938; arrived in Can., 1965; s. Laszlo and Klara (Petö) E. Diploma, École Supérieure d'Art Dramatique, Strasbourg, France, 1960. Stage dir., prof. Centre Dramatique de l'Est, Strasbourg, France, 1960-65; asst. artistic dir. Nat. Theatre Sch., Montreal, Que., Can., 1965-71; prof. theatre U. Ottawa (Ont.), 1971—, chmn. dept. theatre 1974-77, 79-84, 87—, mem. univ. senate, 1980—, univ. bd. govs., 1986-87; artistic dir. Théâtre du Peuple, Bussang, France, 1972-85. Contbr. articles to publs. in field. Mem. exec. com. of Bd. Nat. Theatre Sch., Montreal, 1979—; mem. jury for various grant agys., 1975—. Free Europe scholar, 1957-60. Jewish.

EGGERS, PAUL WALTER, lawyer; b. Seymour, Ind., Apr. 20, 1919; s. Ernest H. and Ottelia W. (Carre) E.; m. Frances Kramer, Dec. 29, 1946; 1 son, Steven Paul; m. Virginia McMillin, Feb. 23, 1974. B.A., Valparaiso U., 1941; J.D., U. Tex.-Austin, 1948. Bar: Tex. 1948. Sole practice, Wichita Falls, Tex., 1948-52; ptnr. Eggers, Sherrill & Pace, Wichita Falls, 1952-69; gen. counsel U.S. Treasury Dept., Washington, 1969-70; sole practice, Dallas, 1971-75; pres. Eggers & Wylie, P.C., Dallas, 1977-79, Eggers & Greene, P.C., Dallas, 1979—, Tower, Eggers and Greene, Inc., 1987—. Chmn. Wichita County Republican Club; mem. Pres.'s Task Force Narcotics and Dangerous Drugs, chmn. Tex. Gov.'s Task Force on Drug Abuse, 1987—; Republican candidate for gov. of Tex., 1968, 70; Treasury Dept. liaison with White House on Minority Affairs; trustee Episc. Ch. Bldg. Fund, 1972-84; sr. warden vestry St. Michael and All Angels Episc. Ch. of Dallas, 1983-85; dir. St. Michael and All Angels Found.; chancellor Episc. Diocese of Dallas, 1978—, pres. Corporation, 1983—; chmn. Gov.'s Task Force on Drug Abuse, 1987—; pres. Texans' War on Drugs Found., 1987—. Served to maj. USAAF, World War II. Recipient Silver Anniversary All-Am. award Sports Illustrated, 1966, Layman of Yr. award Episc. Diocese of Dallas, 1968; Disting. Alumnus award Valparaiso U., 1978. Mem. ABA, Fed. Bar Assn., Am. Judicature Soc., Dallas Estate Planning Council, Tex. Bar Assn., Vis. Nurse Assn. (bd. dirs. 1982—), Vis. Nurse Assn. Found. (bd. dirs. 1984—), Vis. Nurses Assn. Tex. (hon. life mem.), Dallas Bar Assn. Republican. Clubs: Brook Hollow Golf (Dallas); Met., Capitol Hill (Washington). Office: Suite 3220 1999 Bryan St Dallas TX 75201

EGI, YASUSHI, pharmaceutical executive; b. Osaka, Japan, Oct. 20, 1929; s. Kohso and Tamiko (Kaneko) E.; m. Chieko Uchiyama, Apr. 21, 1957; children: Anna Egi Kino, Takeshi. BA in mktg., Kobe City U. Fgn. Studies, 1952. Pres., chief exec. officer PMP Fermentation Products, Inc., Milw., 1985-87; dir. overseas ops. Fujisawa Pharm. Co., Ltd., Osaka, 1980—, gen. mgr. new product, 1987—; pres., chief exec. officer Rainbow Tourist, Inc., Osaka, 1984—. Mem. Japan Pharm., Med., and Dental Supply Exporters Assn. (chmn. gen. adminstrn. com. 1980-84). Mem. Liberal Dem. Party. Home: 1-19-1 Higashi Kori, 573 Hirakata Japan Office: Fujisawa Pharm Co Ltd, #3 Doshomachi 4-chome, Higashi-ku, Osaka Japan

EGLOFF, JULIUS, III, geologist; b. Washington, Sept. 19, 1946; s. Julius and Cassandra Mary Sue (Adreon) E.; m. Cassie LeAnn Tumlin, Feb. 17, 1980; children—Cassandra Desiree, Julius Tristan, Heidi Sara Louise. B.S. in Geology, U. Miami, 1969, postgrad. Oreg. State U., 1972, La. State U., 1979-80, U. R.I., 1986-87. With Nautical Chart div. Cartographic Br., U.S. Naval Hydrographic Office, Suitland, Md., 1965; with Deep Ocean Surveys div. Geology and Geophysics Br., U.S. Naval Oceanographic Office, Washington, 1966, with Deep Ocean Vehicle Br., 1967, oceanographer Global Ocean Floor Analysis Research Project Code 038, 1968-76; geologist, oceanographer Seafloor Geoscis. div. Code 361, U.S. Naval Ocean Research and Devel. Activity, Bay St. Louis, Miss., 1976—; chief exec. officer Re-Evaluations Co., Pass Christian, Miss., 1980—; chief geologist, pres. Deep Ventures, Ltd. Oil and Gas and Minerals Exploration Co., Inc., 1983-86 . Contbg. author: The Bermuda Triangle, 1974, Atlantis: The Eighth Continent, 1984. Contbr. articles to profl. publs. Fellow Explorers Club; mem. Am. Assn. Petroleum Geologists, Baton Rouge Geol. Soc., New Orleans Geol. Soc., Am. Geophysical Union. Republican. Avocations: research of historical and undiscovered shipwrecks and archaeological subjects. Home: PO Box C Pass Christian MS 39571 Office: US Naval Ocean Research and Devel Activity Seafloor Geoscis Div Code 361 Nat Space Tech Labs Bay Saint Louis MS 39529 Other: 229 Panorama Dr Washington DC 20743

EGNER, BERTHOLD KARL, business executive; b. Karlsruhe, Ger., July 23, 1939; came to France, 1976; s. Karl Friedrich and Elisabeth Paula (Dörflinger) E.; m. Nicole Elisabeth Duprey, Sept. 3, 1965; children: Cyril, Christian, Benjamin. MA in Econs., U. Mainz, Fed. Republic of Germany, 1965; MBA, INSEAD, Fontainbleau, France, 1970. Fin. controller Villeroy and Boch, Fed. Republic of Germany, 1965-69; mgr. mktg. Ideal Standard Europe, Brussels, 1970-76; dir. mktg. Kleber-Colombes, Paris, 1976-81; dir. sales and mktg. Lafarge-Coppee, Paris, 1981-83; mng. dir. Gail Internat., Paris, 1983-84; dir. mktg. and sales Paulstra Hutchinson, Paris, 1984-85; mng. dir. VDO Instruments, Paris, 1986—; lectr. Protestant Edn. Ctr., Lubeck, Ger., 1965-67. Mem. Belgian Mgmt. Assn. Roman Catholic. Avocations: literature, painting, tennis, golf. Home: 7 Ave Victor Hugo,

95160 Montmorency Val D'oise, France Office: VDO Instruments, 6-8 Ave S Allende, 93805 Erinay Seine, France

EGSTRAND, BJARNE FRIDLEF, managing director; b. Fredericia, Denmark, Oct. 28, 1939; s. Arvid Emil and Henny Helena (Christensen) Andersen; m. Yvet Poulsen; children—Claus, Henrik, Susanne. M.S., Danish Tech. High Sch., Copenhagen, 1963. Product mgr. Dansk Shell, Denmark, 1964-71; mgr. mktg. devel. Svenska Shell, Sweden, 1972-74; project exec. Shell Internat., London, 1974-76; pub. relations mgr., personnel mgr., retail mgr. Dansk Shell, Copenhagen, Denmark, 1976-80; mng. dir. Domi A/S, Glostrup, Denmark, 1980-85, Saab Biler A/S, Kvistgaard, Denmark, 1985—. Mem. Danish Automobil Importers Assn. (chmn. 1983—). Home: Laagegude 134, 2980 Kokkedal Denmark Office: Saab Biler A/S Port Husvej 4, PO Box 34, DK-3490 Kvistgaard Denmark

EHIAMETALOR, EGBE THOMAS, educator; b. Enugu, Nigeria, Sept. 28, 1948; married; children. BS, Murray State U., 1974, MS, 1976; EdD in Ednl. Adminstrn., Tex. So. U., 1979. Grad. asst. Murray (Ky.) State U., 1975-76; instr. Tex. So. U., Houston, 1977-79; lectr. ednl. adminstrn. and founds. U. Benin, Benin City, 1979-83; sr. lectr. U. Benin, 1983—, head dept. adult edn. and extramural studies, 1986—; cons. Gallow Indsl. Supply Inc., Houston, 1979, Internat. Trade Venture Ltd., Nigeria, 1979-80, Evans Bros. Ltd., Nigeria, 1988—; participant numerous seminars and confs., 1980—. Author: Classroom Management: Evaluation and Methods, 1985, Business and Economics Education: Principles and Methods, 1987; co-author: Introduction to Administration of Schools in Nigeria, 1985, Business Studies for Junior Secondary Schools, 3 vols., 1986; mem. editorial bd. Benin Jour. Ednl. Studies, 1981-82; contbr. articles to profl. jours. Nigerian Fed. Govt. scholar, 1977-79. Mem. Nigerian Ednl. Research Assn. (editor-in-chief jour., conf. coordinator 1982, 83, 86, pres. 1987—). Home: 47 Akhionbare St, Govt Reservation Area, Benin City Nigeria Office: U Benin, Dept Ednl Adminstrn and Founds, Benin City Nigeria

EHLE, JOHN MARSDEN, JR., writer; b. Asheville, N.C., Dec. 13, 1925; s. John M. and Gladys (Starnes) E.; m. Gail Oliver, Aug. 30, 1952 (div. Apr. 1967); m. Rosemary Harris, Oct. 22, 1967; 1 dau., Jennifer Anne. BA, U. N.C., 1949; DFA (hon.), N.C. Sch. Arts, 1981; DHL (hon.), Berea Coll., 1986, U. N.C., Asheville, 1987. Faculty U. N.C., Chapel Hill, 1951-63; spl. asst. to Gov. Terry Sanford, Raleigh, N.C., 1963-64; program officer Ford Found., N.Y.C., 1964-65; spl. cons. Duke U., 1976-80. Author: novels Move Over, Mountain, 1957, Kingstree Island, 1959, Lion on the Hearth, 1961, The Land Breakers, 1964, The Road, 1967, Time of Drums, 1970, The Journey of August King, 1971, The Changing of the Guard, 1975, The Winter People, 1981, Last One Home, 1983; biographies The Free Men, 1965 (Mayflower Soc. cup), The Survivor, 1968, Shepherd of the Streets, 1960; non-fiction The Cheeses and Wines of England and France, with Notes on Irish Whisky, 1972, Trail of Tears: The Rise and Fall of the Cherokee Nation, 1988; pub. also, in several fgn. countries. Mem. White House Group for Domestic Affairs, 1964-66, Nat. Council Humanities, 1966-70; exec. com. Nat. Book Com., N.Y.C., 1972-75, N.C. Sch. of Arts Found., Winston-Salem, 1970-75; mem. awards commn. Mary Reynolds Babcock Found., Winston-Salem, N.C., 1985—. Served with inf. AUS, 1944-46. Recipient Walter Raleigh prize for fiction, 1964, 67, 70, 75, 84, State of N.C. award for Lit., 1972; Gov.'s award for disting. meritorious service, 1978; Lillian Smith prize, 1982; Disting. Alumnus award U. N.C.-Chapel Hill, 1984; Thomas Wolfe prize, 1984; W.D. Weatherford award, 1985. Mem. Authors League, P.E.N. Democrat. Methodist. Club: Century (N.Y.C.). Home: 125 Westview Dr NW Winston-Salem NC 27104 Office: care Candida Donadio 231 W 22d St New York NY 10011

EHLEN, PETER, philosopher; b. Berlin, May 16, 1934. Lic. philosophy, Berchmanskolleg, Pullach, Fed. Republic of Germany, 1958; Lic. theology, St. Georgen, Frankfurt, Fed. Republic of Germany, 1964; PhD, Freie U., Berlin, 1977. Prof. Hochschule für Philosophie, Munich, 1975—; bd. dirs. Ostakademie Königstein, Fed. Republic of Germany, 1979-86; cons. editor Studies of Soviet Thought, Boston. Author: Soviet Ethics, 1972, Marxist Philosophy, 1982. Mem. Soc. of Jesus. Home: Kaulbach St 31, 8000 Munich 22 Federal Republic of Germany

EHLERS, ELEANOR MAY COLLIER (MRS. FREDERICK BURTON EHLERS), civic worker; b. Klamath Falls, Oreg., Apr. 23, 1920; d. Alfred Douglas and Ethel (Foster) Collier; B.A., U. Oreg., 1941; secondary tchrs. credentials Stanford, 1942; m. Frederick Burton Ehlers, June 26, 1943; children—Frederick Douglas, Charles Collier. Tchr., Salinas Union High Sch., 1942-43; piano tchr. pvt. lessons, Klamath Falls, 1958—. Mem. Child Guidance Adv. Council, 1956-60; mem. adv. com. Boys and Girls Aid Soc., 1965-70 ; mem. Gov.'s Adv. Com. Arts and Humanities, 1966-67; bd. mem. PBS TV Sta. KSYS, 1988, Friends of Mus. U. Oreg., 1966-69, Arts in Oreg., 1966-68, Klamath County Colls. for Oreg.'s Future, 1968-70 ; co-chmn. Friends of Collier Park, Collier Park Logging Mus., 1986-87, sec. 1987—; chpt. pres. Am. Field Service, 1962-63; mem. Gov.'s Com. Governance of Community Colls., 1967; bd. dirs. Favell Mus. Western Art and Artifacts, 1971—, Community Concert Assn., 1950-80 , pres., 1966-74; established Women's Guild at Merle West Med. Ctr., 1965, trustee hosp. sec. bd. trustees, 1962-65, 76—, mem. bldg. com. 1962-67, mem. planning com., chmn. edn. and research com. hosp. bd., 1967—. Named Woman of Month, Klamath Herald News, 1965; named grant to Oreg. Endowed Fellowship Fund, AAUW, 1971; recipient greatest Service award Oreg. Tech. Inst., 1970-71, Internat. Woman of Achievement award Quota Club, 1981, U. Oreg. Pioneer award, 1981. Mem. AAUW (local pres. 1955-56), Oreg. Music Tchrs. Assn. (pres. Klamath Basin dist. 1979-81), P.E.O. (Oreg. dir. 1968-75, state pres. 1974-75, trustee internat. Continuing Edn. Fund 1977-83, chmn. 1981-83), Pi Beta Phi, Mu Phi Epsilon, Pi Lambda Theta. Presbyterian. Address: 1338 Pacific Terr Klamath Falls OR 97601

EHLERS, JÜRGEN, geologist, lecturer; b. Hamburg, Fed. Republic of Germany, May 2, 1948; s. Friedrich Christoph and Emilie (Schröder) E.; m. Uta Schmidt, Dec. 9, 1983; 1 child, Ann-Kathrin. Diploma in geography, U. Hamburg, 1974, DSc, 1978. Researcher Geog. Inst., U. Hamburg, 1977; geologist Geol. Survey, Hamburg, 1978-85, head mapping dept., 1986—; researcher U. Cambridge, Eng., 1986; examiner Quaternary geology U. Bergen, Norway, 1982; lectr. U. Lund, Sweden, 1985; life mem. Clare Hall, U. Cambridge, 1986—. Author: The Morphodynamics of the Wadden Sea, 1988; editor: Glacial Deposits in Northwest Europe, 1983; mem. editorial bd.: Palaeogeography, Palaeoclimatology, Palaeoecology Jour., Amsterdam, 1986—. Mem. Internat. Glaciological Soc., Internat. Assn. Sedimentologists, Quaternary Research Assn. Home: Hellberg 2 A, D 2059 Witzeeze Federal Republic of Germany Office: Geol Survey, Oberstrasse 88, D 2000 Hamburg 13 Federal Republic of Germany

EHLERS, KENNETH WARREN, physicist; b. Dix, Nebr., Aug. 3, 1922; s. Walter Richard and Clara (Sievers) E.; B.S., U. Colo., 1943; postgrad. Okla. A&M Coll., 1943-44, MIT, 1945; PhD in Physics, U. Calif., Berkeley, 1969; m. Marion Catherine Ward, Mar. 4, 1947; 1 son, Gary Walter. Head electronic aids dept. Landing Aids Exptl. Sta., Arcata, Calif., 1946-50; sr. physicist Lawrence Berkeley Lab., U. Calif., Berkeley, 1950—; cons. Brobeck Industries, Berkeley, 1961—, Avco Corp., Tulsa, 1962-65, Applied Radiation Corp., 1962-65, Cyclotron Corp., Berkeley, 1965—, New Eng. Nuclear, Phys. Dynamics, Sci. Applications Internat. Corp., 1984—. Served with USNR, 1942-46. Named Emeritus U. Calif. Berkeley Bd. Regents, 1986; Ford Found. scholar, Santiago, Chile, 1970-72. Fellow IEEE, Am. Phys. Soc.; mem. Am. Vacuum Soc., AAAS. Methodist. Contbr. numerous articles to profl. jours.; editorial bd. Rev. Sci. Instruments, 1966—; inventor in field. Home: 3129 Via Larga Alamo CA 94507 Office: U Calif Lawrence Berkeley Lab Bldg 4 Berkeley CA 94720

EHLERS, LARRY LEE, engineering executive; b. Kansas City, Mo., Mar. 10, 1953; s. Rufus Arndt and Wanda Marie (Pickett) E.; m. Teresa Ann Gunter, Jan. 24, 1981; children: Megan Ann, Austin Lee. MS, Purdue U., 1976; BME, Gen. Motors Inst., 1977. Lic. profl. engr., Kans. Environ. engr. Gen. Motors Corp., Kansas City, Kans., 1976-79; corp. plant engr. Bendix/King div. Allied-Signal, Inc., Olathe, Kans., 1979—. Mem. Internat. Communications Assn. (voting), DBX Users Assn. (bd. dirs. 1985—, pres. 1987-88), Assn. Energy Engrs., Am. Inst. Plant Engrs., MidAm. Telecommunications Assn., Midwestern Soc. Telephone Engrs., Internat. Teleconferencing Assn. Libertarian. Lutheran. Home: 11512 W 108th St Overland Park KS 66210 Office: Allied Signal Inc Bendix/King Div 400 N Rogers Rd Olathe KS 66062

EHLERS, THOMAS MARTIN, investments and retail consultant; b. Worthington, Minn., Feb. 6, 1937; s. Martin Andrew and Genevieve Ellen (Rust) E.; m. Sandra Joan McCartney, Apr. 12, 1964; children—Joseph, Genevieve, T. Michael. B.A., Hamline U., 1959; M.S.R., NYU, 1960. Exec. trainee Daytons, Mpls., 1960; v.p. Ehlers of Redwood Falls (Minn.), 1961-70, pres., 1971—, also bd. dirs.; bd. dirs. Ehlers Apparel, Inc., 1987—; pres. Boxrud Bldg. Corp., 1985—; v.p. MGT Investment Corp. Home: 595 N Lake Spicer MN 56288 Office: 219 S Washington St Redwood Falls MN 56283

EHLERS ZURITA, FREDERICO ARTURO, television executive; b. Quito, Ecuador, Nov. 30, 1945; s. Frederick Arthur and Dolores (Zurita) Ehlers; m.Sylvia Moncayo, Aug. 17, 1968 (div. Nov. 1974); 1 child, Raul Ernesto; m. Maria de Lourdes Morelli, Dec. 18, 1974; children: Carolina, Fernando. Student, Davidson Coll., Charlotte, N.C., 1964-65, Universidad Cen., Quito, 1965-69, Radio Nederland Tng. Ctr., Hilversun, Holland, 1972. Prodn. dir. Nat. TV Channel 8, Quito, 1970-74; pub. relations dir. Latin Am. Energy Assn., Quito, 1975; audiovisual dept. dir. Cath. U., Quito, 1976-78; ind. TV dir. Quito, Cartagena (Andean Pact), Quito, 1980—; cons., Lima, Peru, 1982-83; dir. TV series Nuestra Am., 1980-83 (nominated for UNESCO Simon Bolivar award); dir. Chimborazo documentary, 1980, TV series Hablenos de Nosotros, 1978-79, Nuestra Primera Historia documentary, 1977. Spl. del. World Population Congress, UN, Geneva, Bucharest, 1973. Fulbright scholar, 1965; scholar Nederland Tng. Ctr., 1972. Mem. Ecuadorean Film Assn., Casa de Nuestra Am. Izquierda Democratica. Office: PO Box 6097, Quito Ecuador

EHMANN, ANTHONY VALENTINE, lawyer; b. Chgo., Sept. 5, 1935; s. Anthony E. and Frances (Verweil) E.; m. Alice A. Avina, Nov. 27, 1959; children—Ann, Thomas, Jerome, Gregory, Rose, Robert. B.S., Ariz. State U., 1957; J.D., U. Ariz., 1960. Bar: Ariz. 1960, U.S. Tax Ct. 1960, U.S. Sup. Ct. 1968. Spl. asst. atty. gen., 1961-68; mem. Ehmann and Hiller, P.C., Phoenix, 1969—. Republican dist. chmn. Ariz., 1964; pres., mem. exec. com. Theodore Roosevelt council Boy Scouts Am., Recipient Silver Beaver award Boy Scouts Am., 1982, Bronze Pelican award Cath. Com. on Scouting, 1981. C.P.A., Ariz. Mem. State Bar Ariz. (chmn. tax sect. 1968, 69), Central Ariz. Estate Planning Council (pres. 1968, 69). Republican. Roman Catholic. Clubs: Rotary (Phoenix); KC (grand knight 1964, 65) (Glendale, Ariz.). Office: 4722 N 24th St Suite 350 Phoenix AZ 85016

EHN, ERIK JOHAN, banker; b. Uppsala, Sweden, Dec. 7, 1927; s. Oskar and Inez (Lidforss) E.; m. Gun Ljungstrom, June 13, 1964; 1 child, Anna. B.A., U. Uppsala, 1954; postgrad. U. Wis., U.S.A., 1955-56, 59, U. Uppsala, 1956-57. Mktg. cons. Ekonomisk Foretagsledning AB, Stockholm, 1960-61; mgr. Sparframjandet, Stockholm, 1961-63; mgr. Sundsvallsbanken, Umea, Sweden, 1963-70, asst. gen. mgr., Stockholm, 1970-76, gen. mgr. and chief exec. officer, 1976-86; gen. mgr., chief exec. officer, Nordbanken, 1986—, dir., 1987—; chmn. Graningeverkens AB, Stockholm, Atrium AB Industri-Renting AB; dir. Swedish Wine & Spirit Corp., Stockholm. Mem. Swedish Touring Club (dep. chmn.). Office: Nordbanken, PO Box 7133, S-103 87 Stockholm Sweden

EHNERT, ROLF, educator, researcher; b. Chemnitz, East Germany, Nov. 9, 1939; came to West Germany, 1950;; s. Werner and Else (Seifert) E.; m. Helga Zwikirsch, Sept. 1, 1966 (dec. June 1978); m. Franoise Aubret, 1987. Staatsexamen Deutsch, Französisch, U. Tübingen, 1966, PhD, 1976. Lectr. German lang, lit. U. Oulu, Finland, 1966-74; akademischer oberrat Deutsch als Fremdsprache Deutsch älterer Sprachstufen U. Bielefeld, West Germany, 1974—; lectr. German and French U. Poitiets Inst. langue française La Rochelle, 1966-68; dir. Arbeitskreis Deutsche als Fremdsprache, Deutscher Acad. Austauschdienst, Bonn, 1976—. Author and editor numerous books; contbr. artilces to profl. jours. Chmn. bd. examiners Tongji U., People's Republic China, Shanghai, 1983, 85. Mem. oswald-von-Wolknstein Gesellschaft, Gesellschafür Jnterkulturelle Germanistik. Office: U Bielefeld, Nordrhein Westfalen Federal Republic of Germany

EHRENPREIS, SEYMOUR, pharmacology educator; b. N.Y.C., June 20, 1927; s. William and Ethel (Balk) E.; m. Bella R. Goodman, June 30, 1953; children: Mark, Eli, Ira. B.S., CCNY, 1949; Ph.D., NYU, 1954. Mem. faculty dept. pharmacology Chgo. Med. Sch., prof., 1976—, chmn. pharmacology, 1976-85; grants reviewer NSF, 1977-83, March of Dimes, 1983; vis. prof. Showa Med. Sch., Tokyo, 1985. Editor: Neurosciences Research, vols. 1-5, 1967-75, Revs. of Neurosci., vols. 1-3, 1974-77, Methods in Narcotics Research, 1974, Degradation of Endogenous Opoids, 1983; mem. editorial bd.: Jour. Medicinal Chemistry, 1969-72. Served with USN, 1945-46. Recipient Meritorious Service award Coll. Pharm. Sci., Columbia U., 1976; recipient Parker award Chgo. Med. Sch., 1981, Vis. Prof. award Japan Soc. Promotion Sci., 1974, cert. of merit for research Showa Med. Sch., 1985. Fellow N.Y. Acad. Sci. (chmn. cholinergic mechanisms conf. 1966), Am. Inst. Chemists, AAAS; mem. Am. Soc. Pharmacology and Exptl. Therapeutics, Sigma Xi. Office: Univ Health Sci Chgo Med Sch 3333 Green Bay Rd North Chicago IL 60064

EHRENTHAL, FRANK FREDERIC, architect, educator; b. Budapest, Hungary, Jan. 22, 1910; s. Alexander S. and Eugenie (Deutch) E.; came to U.S., 1939, naturalized, 1944; student U. Padua, Italy, 1928-29, Brunn Inst. Tech., Czechoslovakia, 1929-32; D.Arch., U. Firenze, Italy, 1935; L.H.D. (hon.), Starr King Sch. for Ministry, Berkeley, 1966; m. Julie Ann Deutch, 1941; children—Robert, Ann, Sylvia. Asso. various archtl. firms, Czechoslovakia, Italy, U.S., 1931—; pvt. practice architecture, San Francisco, 1946-63; vis. lectr. various colls., 1948-63; prof. architecture and urban design Pa. State U., 1963-66, Okla. State U., 1966-68; prof., chmn. grad. urban design program Center for Urban and Regional Studies, Coll. Architecture, Va. Poly. Inst. and State U., Blacksburg, 1968-69, prof., chmn. grad. urban and regional planning and urban design programs Environ. and Urban Systems div. Coll. Architecture and Urban Studies, 1969-70, prof. urban and regional studies, chmn. grad. urban design program, 1970-80, prof. emeritus, 1980—. Recipient 1st and Grand prize Archtl. Forum, NAMP Internat. Competition, 1952, honorable mention Franklin Delano Roosevelt Meml. Competition, Washington, 1960, Spl. honorable mention Centro Direzionale Fontivegge Bellocchio Internat. Competition, Perugia, Italy, 1971, hon. mention Rainbow Center Plaza Competition, Niagara Falls, 1972. Past chmn. com. on extension San Francisco Council Chs.; past mem. com. on extension Calif.-Nev. Council Chs.; past mem. Mayor's San Francisco Forward Com. Task Force, Fedn. Am. Scientists; founder Centre Citizens Planning Assn. (Pa.). Mem. AIA, Am. Planning Assn., Va. Citizens Planning Assn. (past dir.), Environ. Designers and Planners for Social Responsibility (founder), Architects/Designers/Plannersfor Social Responsibility (founding dir. nat. bd.). Contbr. articles to profl. jours.; work featured in various profl. publs. Home: 140 Agnes Ct Vallejo CA 94589

EHRENZWEIG, JOEL, veterinarian; b. Bklyn., Mar. 14, 1943; s. William B. and Malvina (Heisler) E.; B.S., CCNY, 1965; D.V.M., Ont. Vet. Coll., 1970; m. Ellen Beth Rodburg, Oct. 21, 1973; children—Regina, Rachel, Jesse, Julie, Jill, Elizabeth. Assoc. veterinarian Davis Animal Hosp., Stamford, Conn., 1970-72; dir. Animal Hosp. Bklyn., 1972-86, Riverside Animal Hosp., 1982-85, The Country Vet., Needham, Mass., 1987—; coordinator ABC-TV Heartworm Disease Testing Clinic, 1978-83; mem. com. on vocat. tng. N.Y.C. Dept. Edn.; mktg. and mgmt. cons.; phys. fitness cons. Cycle Dog Food Div., 1981-82. Mem. AVMA, Can., N.Y. State vet. med. assns., Ont., N.Y.C. vet. assns., Am. Animal Hosp. Assn., Royal Coll. Vet. Surgeons (London), Vet. Radiology Soc., Am. Assn. Feline Practitioners, Am. Assn. Animal Welfare Veterinarians, Vet. Orthopedic Soc., Am. Vet. Runners Assn. (founder, pres. 1979-84). Contbg. editor Pet News mag., 1975-78. Contbr. articles to veterinary jours.

EHRHARDT, MANFRED GUENTHER, chemist; b. Hamburg, Fed. Republic of Germany, Aug. 28, 1933; s. Ernst Guenther and Margarete C.E. (Foelsche) E.; m. Antje Marie Louise Geib, Mar. 7, 1968; children: Katja Susan, Miriam Elisabeth. BS, Kiel (Fed. Republic of Germany), 1962, MS in Chemistry, 1964, DSc, 1966. Research fellow Inst. for Marine Research, Kiel, 1967-69, assoc. scientist, 1972-81, acting dir. dept. marine chemistry, 1981-83, sr. scientist, 1983—; research fellow Woods Hole (Mass.) Oceanographic Instn., 1969-71; mem. group experts for methods, standards and intercalibration Intergovtl. Oceanographic Commn., UNESCO, also cons., Alexandria, Egypt, 1980, 86, Kuwait, 1982, Bangkok, 1986, Rio de Janeiro, Brazil, 1987; mem. Internat. Council for Exploration of Sea, Fed. Republic of Germany, 1985—. Co-editor: Methods of Seawater Analysis, 1983, Marine Chemistry jour., 1977; contbr. articles to profl. jours. Grantee Ministry for Research and Tech., Fed. Republic of Germany, 1980-85, Deutsche Forschungsgemeinschaft, 1970-80, 85-87, Exxon Corp., 1986. Mem. Gesellschaft Deutscher Chemiker, Bermuda Biol. Sta. for Research, Inc. Office: Inst for Marine Research, Duesternbrooker Weg 20, D-2300 Kiel Federal Republic of Germany

EHRHORN, RICHARD WILLIAM, electronics company executive; b. Marshalltown, Iowa, Jan. 21, 1934; s. Theodore Raymond and Zelda Elizabeth (Axtell) E.; B.S.E.E., U. Minn., 1955; M.S.E.E., Calif. Inst. Tech., 1958; m. Marilyn Patrick, Aug. 1, 1959; children: Scott Patrick, Kimberlee Dawn. Sr. engr. Gen. Dynamics Corp., Pomona, Calif., 1956-60; sr. research engr. Calif. Inst. Tech. Jet Propulsion Lab., Pasadena, 1960-63; mgr. advanced devel. lab. Electronic Communications Inc., St. Petersburg, Fla., 1963-68; gen. mgr. Signal/One div., 1968-70; pres. Ehrhorn Tech. Ops., Inc., Canon Cityand Colorado Springs (Colo.), 1970—. Bd. dirs. Fremont County (Colo.) Econ. Devel. Council, 1978-84; trustee, bd. dirs. St. Thomas More Hosp., Canon City, 1981-88; trustee First United Meth. Ch., Canon City, 1980-85; mem. Fremont Re-1 Dist. Bd. Edn., 1983-88, pres., 1985-88. Mem. IEEE (sr.; chmn. sect. 1967-68), Mfrs. Roundtable, Armed Forces Communications and Electronics Assn., Am. Radio Relay League, Radio Club Am., Quar. Century Wireless Assn. Author: (with others) Principles of Electronic Warfare, 1959; patentee in field. Office: PO Box 888 Canon City CO 81212

EHRLE, WILLIAM LAWRENCE, lawyer, association executive; b. Colorado City, Tex., Dec. 11, 1932; s. Frank Lawrence and Mary Elma (Hinds) E.; m. Sandra Faye Luckey, Aug. 3, 1963; children—Sharon Elaine, William Lawrence, Rhonda Kay. B.A., McMurry Coll., 1953; J.D., U. Tex., 1961. Bar: Tex. 1961. Asst. gen. counsel Lone Star Gas Co., Dallas, 1961-67; pres. Coaches Life Ins. Co., El Paso, Tex., 1967-70; sole practice, Austin, Tex., 1970-78; pres., gen. counsel Tex. Manufactured Housing Assn., Austin, 1978—; dir. Nat. Manufactured Housing Fedn., Washington, 1978—; mem. adv. council Fed. Nat. Mortgage Assn., Dallas, 1983-84. Mem. Tex. Ho. of Reps., 1957-63. Served as 1st lt. USMC, 1953-56. Office: Tex Manufactured Housing Assn PO Box 14428 Austin TX 78761

EHRLICH, CLARENCE EUGENE, physician, educator; b. Rosenberg, Tex., Oct. 19, 1938; s. Oscar Lee and Gertrude Gene (Walzel) E.; children—Tracey Janet, Bradley Scott, Suzanne Margaret. BA, U. Tex., 1961; MD, Baylor Coll. Medicine, 1965. Diplomate Am. Bd. Ob-Gyn (mem. div. gynec. oncology 1982—, dir. 1985—). Intern Phila. Gen. Hosp., 1965-66; resident Charity Hosp.-Tulane U., New Orleans, 1966-69; asst. prof. Ind. U., Indpls., 1973-77, assoc. prof., 1977-81, prof., chmn. ob/gyn dept., 1981—. Contbr. articles to profl. publs., chpts. in books. Served to major USAF, 1969-71. Grantee USPHS, 1975-78, Upjohn Co., 1976-81, Gynecol. Group, 1978-80, 80-84, Eli Lilly & Co., 1982-85. Mem. AAAS, Am. Assn. Cancer Research, Am. Coll. Obstetricians and Gynecologists, ACS, AMA, Am. Radium Soc., Am. Soc. Clin. Pharmacology and Therapeutics, Am. Soc. Parental and Enteral Nutrition, Am. Soc. Clin. Oncology, Am. Soc. Colposcopists and Colpomicroscopists, Assn. Profs. Gynecology and Obstetrics, Sigma Xi, others. Office: Ind U Med Ctr 926 W Michigan St Indianapolis IN 46223

EHRLICH, CLIFFORD JOHN, hotel executive; b. N.Y.C., Nov. 17, 1938; s. Joseph George and Eugenia Marie (Rybacky) E.; m. Patricia Marie Stankunas, June 20, 1964; children: Susan, Brian, Scott. B.A. in Econs., Brown U., 1960; J.D., Boston Coll., 1965; H.H.D. (hon.), Bethany Coll., 1986. With Monsanto Co., 1960-73; personnel supt. Monsanto Co., Miamisburg, Ohio, 1969-73; dir. labor relations, then v.p. employee relations Marriott Corp., Washington, 1973-78; sr. v.p. human resources Marriott Corp., 1978—; instr. Georgetown U., 1986. Served with USAFR, 1962. Mem. MacIntyre Group, Personnel Roundtable, Employee Relations Com. of Bus. Roundtable. Club: Congl. Country. Home: 9128 Vendome Dr Bethesda MD 20817 Office: Marriott Corp 1 Marriott Dr Washington DC 20058

EHRLICH, CYRIL, historian, educator; b. London, Sept. 13, 1925; s. Henry and Diana (Jacobs) E.; m. Felicity Bell-Bonnett; children: Ruth, Paul, Robert. BS in Econs., London Sch. Econs., 1950, PhD, 1958. Lectr. Makerer Coll., Uganda, 1952-61; lectr., reader Queen's U., Belfast, No. Ireland, 1961-74, prof. history, 1974-86, prof. emeritus social and econ. history, 1986—. Author: The Piano: A History, 1976, The Music Profession in England, 1986; contbr. articles to profl. jours. Mem. Royal Musical Assn., Econ. History Soc. Home and Office: 8 Chilswell Rd, Oxford OX1 4PJ, England

EHRLICH, FREDERICK, surgery consultant, geriatrician, rehabilitation specialist; b. Czernowitz, Bukowina, USSR, Mar. 23, 1932; came to Australia, 1947; s. Alexander and Klara (Schneider) E.; m. Shirley Rose Eastbourne, Sept. 26, 1959; children—Paul, Rachel, Simon, Adam, Miriam, Mark. M.B., B.S. (hons.), Med. Faculty, U. Sydney, 1955; B.A., Macquarie U., Sydney, 1970, Ph.D., 1979; Dip.Phys. and Rehab. Medicine, Australian Postgrad. Fedn. in Medicine, Canberra, 1974. Intern, Royal Newcastle Hosp., N.S.W., 1955, rotating resident, 1955-57; resident surg. officer Charing Cross and Fulham Hosp., London, 1958-59; surg. registrar Royal Newcastle Hosp., 1959-63; dir. surg. service State Psychiat. Service, Sydney, 1962-75; prin. advisor State Geriatric and Rehab. Service, N.S.W., 1975-77; pvt. practice cons. surgeon, Sydney, Australia, 1979—; hon. cons. Sydney Hosp., 1977—; cons. geriatrics and rehab. Hornsby Hosp., Sydney, 1977—, orthopaedic surgery Spastic Ctr. New South Wales; vis. gen. and orthaepdic surgeon Marrickville Dist. Hosp., Sydney, 1977—, also chmn. med. bd., Chatswood Community Hosp., Sydney, 1978—, Concord Hosp, 1987—. Cons. Subnormal Children's Welfare Assn., Multiple Sclerosis Soc., 1968-75. Author: Chronic Illness in New South Wales, 1977 and more than 40 monographs; editor: The Demography of Disability, 1969; New Thinking on Housing for the Aging, 1973; Aging in a Metropolis, 1974; Rehabilitation and Geriatric Services; Report of a Task Force, 1978. Fellow Royal Coll. Surgeons Eng., Royal Coll. Surgeons Edinburgh; mem. Australian Coll. Rehab. Medicine (found. mem.), Royal Coll. Psychiatrists, Total Care Found. (hon. life), Adv. Council on Visually Handicapped (hon. life), Australia Assn. Gerentology (pres. New South Wales div.), New South Wales Council on Aging (chmn.). Jewish. Home: Box E11, St James, Sydney 2000, New South Wales Australia

EHRLICH, GEORGE EDWARD, physician, pharmaceutical executive; b. Vienna, Austria, July 18, 1928; came to U.S., 1938, naturalized, 1944; s. Edward and Irene (Elling) E.; m. Gail S. Abrams, Mar. 30, 1968; children: Charles Edward, Steven L. Abrams, Rebecca Ann Abrams. A.B. cum laude, Harvard U., 1948; M.B., M.D., Chgo. Med. Sch., 1952. Intern Michael Reese Hosp., Chgo., 1952; resident Francis Delafield Hosp., N.Y.C., 1955, Beth Israel Hosp., Boston, 1956, New Eng. Center Hosp., Boston, 1957; fellow rheumatology NIH, Bethesda, Md., 1958, Hosp. for Spl. Surgery, N.Y.C., 1959-61; asst. attending physician Hosp. for Spl. Surgery, 1960-64; spl. fellow Sloan Kettering Inst., 1960-61; instr. medicine Cornell U., 1960-64; dir. Arthritis Center, chief rheumatology Albert Einstein Med. Center and Moss Rehab. Hosp., Phila., 1964-80; asst. prof. medicine Temple U., 1964-67, asso. prof. medicine, 1967-72, prof. medicine, 1972-80, asso. prof. rehab. medicine, 1964-74, prof., 1974-80; vis. lectr. U. Pa., 1964-80; prof. medicine, dir. div. rheumatology Hahnemann U., Phila., 1980-83; v.p. Anti-Inflammatory/Endocrine CIBA-Geigy Pharmaceuticals, Summit, N.J., 1983-86; head cen. med. affairs CIBA-Geigy Ltd., Switzerland, 1987-88; cons. in field; adj. prof. clin. medicine NYU Med. Ctr., 1984—. Author: Differential Diagnosis of Rheumatoid Arthritis, 1972, Oculocutaneous Manifestations of Rheumatic Diseases, 1973, Total Management of the Arthritic Patient, 1973, Rehabilitation Management of Rheumatic Conditions, 1980, 2d edit., 1986, (with J. Fries) Prognosis, 1981, (with H.E. Paulus) Controversies in the Clinical Evaluation of Analgesic-Anti-Inflammatory-Antirheumatic Drugs, 1981; (with P. Utsinger, N. Zvaifler) Rheumatoid Arthritis, 1985; editor: Jour. Albert Einstein Med. Center, 1966-71, Arthritis and Rheumatic Diseases Abstracts, 1968-71; editorial bd.: Inflammation, 1974-88, Psychosomatics, 1977-83, Sexual Medicine Today, 1977-84, Jour. Rheumatology, 1982—, Immunopharmacology, 1985—, Med. Problems Performing Artists, 1985—; contbr. articles to profl. jours. Pres. Eastern Pa. chpt. Arthritis Found., 1970-72; mem. Phila. Mayor's Sci. and Tech. Adv. Council, 1972-81; chmn. ad hoc adv. com. Bur. Drugs, FDA, 1971. Served to comdr. M.C. USNR, 1953-55; Res. to 1975. Recipient citations City Phila., 1969, 74, Distinguished Alumnus award Chgo. Med. Sch., 1969; decorated Cavaliere Order of Star of Italian Solidarity. Fellow A.C.P., Am. Geriatric Soc., Phila. Coll. Physicians, Am. Coll. Clin. Pharmacology, Am. Rheumatism Assn. (com. for publ. Arthritis and Rheumatism 1977-79, mem. editorial bd. 1980-83); mem. Am. Soc. Clin. Therapeutics, Am. Coll. Rehab., AMA (editorial bd. Jour. 1972-82), Am. Fedn. Clin. Research, Assn. Mil. Surgeons (Philip Hench award 1971), Am. Med. Writers Assn., Brit. Assn. Rheumatology and Rehab. (overseas mem., editorial bd. 1979-82), Alpha Omega Alpha. Club: Harvard (Boston, N.Y.C.). Home: One Independence Pl Apt 1101 6th St and Locust Walk Philadelphia PA 19106

EHRLICH, GERALDINE ELIZABETH, food service management consultant; b. Phila., Nov. 28, 1939; d. Joseph Vincent and Agnes Barbara (Campbell) McKenna; m. S. Paul Ehrlich, Jr., June 20, 1959; children: Susan Patricia, Paula Jeanne, Jill Marie. BS, Drexel Inst. Tech., 1957—. Supervisory dietitian ARA Service Co., Phila. and San Francisco, 1959-65; dietary mgmt. cons. HEW, Washington, 1967-68; nutrition cons., hypertension research team U. Calif. Micronesia, 1970; regional sales dir. Marriott Corp., Bethesda, Md., 1976-78; dir. sales and profl. services Coll. and Health Care div. Macke Co., Cheverly, Md., 1978, gen. mgr., 1978-79; v.p. ops., div., 1979-80, pres. Health Care div., 1980-81; regional v.p. Custom Mgmt. Corp., Alexandria, Va., 1981-83, v.p. mktg., 1983-87; v.p. mktg. and health-care sales Morrison's Custom Mgmt., Mobile, Ala., 1987-88; internat. v.p. sales, ARA Services, Phila., 1988—; cons. mktg. The Green House, Tokyo, 1987—; chmn. bd. Mktg. Matrix, Falls Church, Va., 1984—. Mem. Health Systems Agy. No. Va., 1976-77; chmn. Health Care Adv. Bd. Fairfax County Va., 1973-77; vice chmn. Fairfax County Community Action Com., 1973-77; treas. Fairfax County Dem. Com., 1969-73; trustee Fairfax Hosp., 1973-77; bd. dirs. Tennis Patrons, Washington, 1984—. Mem. Internat. Women's Assn., Am. Mgmt. Assn., Nat. Assn. Female Execs., Roundtable for Women in Food Service, Soc. Mktg. Profls. Club: Internat. (Washington). Avocation: reading. Home: 6512 Lakeview Dr Falls Church VA 22041 Office: Morrison's Custom Mgmt 209 Madison St Alexandria VA 22314

EHRLICH, LESLIE SHARON, communications executive; b. Bklyn., July 30, 1952; d. Abraham and Evelyn (Kuznetz) E.; m. Lee Marc Kaswiner, Aug. 11, 1979; children: Adam Jason, Jessica Sara. BA, Hofstra U., 1973; paralegal cert., Adelphi U., 1974; MA, Montclair State U., 1977; JD, Pace U., 1981. Owner Paralegal Corp., Newark, 1975-77; supr. paralegal AT&T, N.Y.C., 1977-79, law clk. with sales dept., 1979-81; mgr. state regulatory N.Y. Telephone Co., N.Y.C., 1981-82; atty. Bell Communications Research, N.Y.C., 1983-84; mgr. contracts AT&T-IS, Morristown, N.J., 1984-86; mgr. contracts, adminstrn. and policies Timeplex, Woodcliff Lakes, N.J., 1986-87; v.p., gen. counsel M&SD, Lyndhurst, N.J., 1987-88; ptnr. Avarini and Avarini, Jersey City, 1988—; prin. Guarini & Guarini, Lyndhurst, 1988—; adj. prof. Am. Paralegal Inst., South Orange, N.J., 1982-83, Seton Hall, Newark, 1983-84. Chairperson Nat. Council Jewish Women, N.J., 1981-82, Edn./Programming, Suburban Jewish Ctr., Florham Park, N.J., 1984—; attendee Brookings Inst., Washington, 1986. Mem. ABA (vice chairperson young lawyers corp. council sect. 1984-88, pub. utility com. 1986—, student liaison antitrust com. 1979-80, Silver Key award 1979, Gold Key award 1980), N.Y. Bar Assn., N.J. Bar Assn., Exec. Women of N.J. Democrat. Jewish. Home: 8 Pheasant Way Florham Park NJ 07932 Office: M&SD Lyndhurst NJ 07071

EICH, PETER HEINRICH, publishing executive; b. Turckheim, France, Apr. 9, 1944; s. Heinrich and Frieda (Model) E.; m. Ilona Monika Buchleither, Sept. 29, 1972; children: Elisabeth, Johannes. Educated pub. schs., Karlsruhe, Fed. Republic Germany. Bookseller Braunsche Buchhandlung, Karlsruhe, 1965-66, 68; mktg. asst. Arena-Verlag, Wurzburg, Fed. Republic Germany, 1969-74; head div. Deutsche Verlagsanstalt, Stuttgart, Fed. Republic Germany, 1969-74; mktg. mgr. Ernst Klett Verlag, Stuttgart, 1975-77; pub. asst. Hippokrates Verlag, Stuttgart, 1977-80; mktg. and devel. mgr. Georg Thieme Verlag, Stuttgart, 1981—; copy editor Optimales Lesen, 1972. Bd. dirs. Social Dem. Party, Stuttgart-Birkach, 1978-83. Mem. Absatzkommission Arbeits Gemeinschaft Zeitschriften-Verlage Börsenvereins (chmn. 1985—), Zentralausschuss Werbewirtschaft (presdl. bd. 1985—). Home: Heidestrasse 48 B, D-7000 Stuttgart Federal Republic of Germany Office: Georg Thieme Verlag, Rudigerstrasse 14, D-7000 Stuttgart 30, Federal Republic of Germany

EICHER, WOLF, gynecologist/obstetrician, educator, physician; b. Stuttgart, Germany, Apr. 11, 1940; Student Med. Sch., U. Munich, Fed. Republic Germany, 1959-61; student Med. Sch., U. Lausanne, Switzerland, 1962, Med. Sch., U. Strasbourg, France, 1962-63; M.D., Med. Sch., U. Heidelberg, Fed. Republic Germany, 1965. Practice medicine specializing in ob-gyn, Worms, Fed. Republic of Germany, 1967-70; gynecologist-obstetrician U. Heidelberg, 1970-75; gynecologist-obstetrician, prof. ob-gyn U. Munich, Fed. Republic Germany, 1975-83, U. Mannheim/Heidelberg, 1983—. Author: Transsexualismus, 1984. Editor: Sexualmedizin in der Praxis, 1980, Sexology, 1988, Plastic Surgery in the Sexually Handicapped, 1988. Pres. 8th World Congress for Sexology, 1987. Mem. Soc. for Sci. Study Sex, Gesellschaft zur Forderung Sexualmedizinischer Fortbildung (pres.), Gesellschaft fur Praktische Sexualmedizin (v.p.). Office: Diakonissenkrankenhaus, Speyerer Strasse 91-93, 6800 Mannheim Federal Republic of Germany

EICHHORN, GUNTHER LOUIS, chemist; b. Frankfurt am Main, Fed. Republic of Germany, Feb. 8, 1927; s. Fritz David and Else Regina (Weiss) E.; m. Lotti Neuhaus, June 25, 1964; children: David Mark, Sharon Julie. A.B. in Chemistry, U. Louisville, 1947; M.S., U. Ill., 1948, Ph.D., 1950. Asst. prof., then asso. prof. chemi.try La. State U., 1950-57; commd. officer USPHS, 1954-57; asso. prof. chemistry Georgetown U., 1957-58; guest scientist Naval Med. Research Inst., 1957-58; chief sect. molecular biology Gerontology Research Center, Nat. Inst. Health, NIH, Balt., 1958-78; chief lab. cellular and molecular biology and head sect. inorganic biochemistry Gerontology Research Center, Nat. Inst. Aging, NIH, 1978—; pres. Nat. Inst. Child Health and Human Devel. Assembly Scientists, 1972-73; mem. panel nickel NRC, 1974; distinguished lectr. Mich. State U., 1972; Watkins vis. prof. Wichita State U., 1983; organizer symposium Internat. Conf. Bioinorganic Chemistry, Netherlands, 1987; lectr. Internat. Conf. Molecular Mechanisms of Metal Toxicity and Carcinogenicity, Urbino, Italy, 1988; Henry Lardy lectr. S.D. U.; condr. seminars, lectr. in field. Editor: Inorganic Biochemistry, 1973; co-editor: Advances in Inorganic Biochemistry, 1978—; mem. editorial bds. profl. jours.; author papers in field. Gen. Aniline and Film Co. grantee, 1949; postdoctoral fellow Ohio State U., summers 1951, 52; recipient Woodcock medal U. Louisville, 1947; Md. Chemist award, 1978; NIH Dir.'s award, 1979; Sr. Exec. Service bonus award, 1982. Fellow AAAS, Am. Inst. Chemists, Gerontol. Soc. (fin. com. 1980-82, research and edn. com. 1982-83); mem. Am. Chem. Soc., N.Y. Acad. Scis., Am. Inst. Biol. Chemists, Biophys. Soc. Home: 6703 97th Ave Seabrook MD 20706 Office: Gerontology Research Ctr NIH Nat Inst on Aging Baltimore MD 21224

EICHHORN, WOLFGANG FRIEDRICH, economics educator; b. Ansbach, Ger., Aug. 18, 1933; s. Max Franz and Charlotte (Geldner) E.; M.A. in Math., U. Würzburg, 1959, M.A. in Econs., 1964, Ph.D., 1962, Habilitation in Math., 1966; m. Heidrun Dagmar Tiedmann, Mar. 7, 1964; children—Christian, Saskia. Sci. asst. U. Würzburg, 1959-66, asst. prof. math., 1966-69; prof. econs. U. Karlsruhe, 1969—; vis. prof. U. Waterloo, Ont., Can., 1967, 72, 87, U. Bonn, 1973, U. So. Calif., 1973, U. Calif., Berkeley, 1978, Tech. U. Lisbon, 1982, U. B.C., Vancouver, 1983, Fed. U., Rio de Janeiro, 1986; research counsel Munich Reins. Co. Mem. German Math. Soc., Soc. Applied Math. and Mechanics, Econometric Soc., Soc. Math., Econ. and Ops. Research, others. Evang. Lutheran. Author books including Functional Equations in Economics, 1978; editor several books including Measurement in Economics; co-editor sci. jours. and monograph series; contbr. numerous articles to profl. jours. Office: 12 Kaiserstrasse, Universität, D-7500 Karlsruhe 1 Federal Republic of Germany

EICHNER, CLAUS-RAINER, naval architect; b. Duisburg, Fed. Republic Germany, Apr. 22, 1949; s. Heinz and Christamaria (Bade) E.; m. Laura Helina Puukari-Eichner, June 12, 1980; 1 child, Meri Johanna. MSc in Engring. Naval Architecture, RWTH, Aachen, Fed. Republic Germany, 1976, MBA in Wirtschaft Engring., 1979. Asst. inst. fuer Prouktionssystematik am WZL, Aachen, 1975-78; project engr./mgr. Blohm and Voss AG Shipyard, Hamburg, Fed. Republic Germany, 1979-81; head engring. adminstrn., project mgr. Deminex GmbH, Essen, Fed. Republic Germany, 1982—; cons. KSRC, Kuwait, 1981. Contbr. articles to profl. jours.; author presentations for internat. offshore confs. Mem. Schiffbautechnische Gesellschaft, Gesellschaft fuer Projektmanagement. Lutheran. Home: Hoelterhoffstr 17, D-5620 Velbert Federal Republic of Germany Office: Deminex GmbH, Dorotheenstr 1, D-4300 Essen Federal Republic of Germany

EICHNER, EDUARD, gynecologist; b. Cleve., Nov. 11, 1905; s. Nathan Jacob and Dora (Guren) E.; A.B., Case Western Res. U., 1925, M.D., 1929; m. Helen Augusta Short, Sept. 11, 1931; children—William Eduard, Judith Eichner Henderson. Intern, St. Alexis Hosp., Cleve., 1929-30; resident obstetrics St. Ann Hosp., Cleve., 1930-31; proctor-tng., intervals obstetrics and gynecology Mt. Sinai Hosp., Cleve., 1932-36; gen. practice medicine, Cleve., 1931-37; practice medicine specializing in obstetrics and gynecology, Cleve., 1938-86; obstetrician, gynecologist, dir. family planning clinic Mt. Sinai Hosp., Cleve., 1954-72, assoc. vis. physician, dir. family planning, 1972-78, cons., 1978—; assoc. clin. prof. obstetrics and gynecology Case Western Res. U. Sch. Medicine, Cleve., 1973-81, clin. emeritus dept. reproductive biology, 1981—; med. dir. preterm, 1974-77, cons., 1977-86; mem. med. adv. bd. Met. Health Planning Com., Cleve. Dist., 1974-80; clin. adv. bd. Cuyahoga County Bd. Mental Retardation, Cleve., 1969-76. mem. Am. Com. on Maternal Welfare, Chgo., 1947-60. Trustee Circle Workshop, Cleve., Parents Vol. Assn., Cleve., 1972-82. Served with USNR, 1942-46. Recipient Disting. Achievement and Service award Mt. Sinai Hosp., 1979; awards for original investigation Am. Coll. Obstetricians and Gynecologists, 1954, 63, Ohio Med. Assn., 1955, 63, A.C.S., 1955, Modern Medicine, 1956; diplomate Am. Bd. Ob-Gyn. Fellow A.C.S., Am. Coll. Obstetrics and Gynecology, Internat. Coll. Surgeons (chmn. 1966, v.p. internat. sect. obstetrics-gynecology 1979); mem. AMA, Central Assn. Obstetricians and Gynecologists, Endocrine Soc., Soc. for Exptl. Biology and Medicine, Am. Fertility Soc., Am. Inst. Biologic Sci., Internat. Soc. for Research in Reproduction, Pan-Pacific Surg. Assn., Pan-Am. Med. Soc., N.Y. Acad. Sci., Med. Alumni Assn. Case Western Res. U. (pres. 1967), Cleve. Soc. Obstetricians and Gynecologists (pres. 1960), N.E. Ohio Gynecologic Cancer Group (chmn. edn. 1978-81), Cleve. City Club, Sigma Xi, Kappa Nu, Phi Lambda Kappa. Contbr. numerous articles to profl. jours. Home: 3333 Daleford Rd Shaker Heights OH 44120

EICHSTÄDT, HERMANN WERNER, cardiology educator; b. Alten-Buseck/Giessen, W. Ger., Feb. 15, 1948; s. Karl Heinz and Elisabeth Magdalena (Froese) E.; med. student U. Mainz, 1968; cand. med. U. Düsseldorf, 1971, M.D., 1974; m. Regina Altmann, Nov. 20, 1949; children—Björn, Kerstin, Bastienne. Intern, Univ. Hosp., Düsseldorf, 1974, Augusta Hosp., Düsseldorf, 1974-75; researcher, Düsseldorf, 1972-74; resident cardiol. clinic, Bad Krozingen, W. Ger., 1975-77; resident U. Tübingen (W. Ger.), 1977-79; lectr. dept. cardiology, cons. internal medicine Free U. Berlin, 1979—; mem. directory radiology and internal medicine Universitätsklinikum Charlottenburg, Berlin, 1981—, prof. cardiology, 1985—. Fellow Am. Coll. Chest Physicians, Internat. Coll. Angiology; mem. N.Y. Acad. Scis., German Soc. Internal Medicine, Profl. Assn. Internists, German Soc. Cardiology, European Soc. Cardiology (working group on isotopes), German Soc. Cardiovascular Surgery, German Heart Found. Roman Catholic. Contbr. numerous articles to English, French and German jours. Editor books and monographs. Home: 61 Konstanzerstrasse, 1000 Berlin 15, Federal Republic of Germany Office: 130 Spandauer Damm, 1000 Berlin 19 Federal Republic of Germany

EIDLIN, FRED HOWARD, political science educator; b. Rochester, N.Y., Nov. 16, 1942; citizen of U.S. and Can.; s. Ephraim Mark and Eva (Szmulewicz) E.; m. Anne Chambers Boehringer, Dec. 9, 1972; children—Carl, Eric, Alena. B.A. Dartmouth Coll., 1964; M.A., Ind. U., 1968; Ph.D., U. Toronto, 1980; Cert. d'Etudes Polit., Inst. d'Etudes Polit., Paris, 1963. Policy asst. Radio Free Europe, Munich, Fed. Republic Germany, 1968-69; lectr. U. Guelph, Ont., 1973-79, asst. prof., 1979-83, assoc. prof. polit. sci., 1983—; dir. Founds. Polit. Theory Group U.S., 1981, 82; organizer Colloquium for Critical Approach to Sci. and Philosophy, Guelph, 1982. Bd. editors Philosophy Social Scis., Toronto, 1982. Author: Logic of Normalization, Soviet Intervention in Czechoslovakia, 1980. Editor: Constitutional Democracy, 1983. Editor Popper Newsletter, 1981—. Co-translator: For a Humane Economic Society, 1985; translator: Communist Party in Power, 1987. Grantee Soc. Sci. and Human Research Council Can., 1984, 85. Exchange sr. scholars and specialists Nat. Research Council Can.-USSR, Strasbourg, France, 1987, IREX (U.S.) Exchanges with German Dem. Republic. Mem. Am. Polit. Sci. Assn., Can. Polit. Sci. Assn., Internat. Polit. Sci. Assn., Société Québécoise de Science Politique, Am. Assn. Advancement Slavic Studies, Internat. Sociol. Assn. Liberal. Anglican. Home: 123-295 Water St, Guelph, ON Canada N1G 2X5 Office: U Guelph, Dept Polit Studies, Guelph, ON Canada N1G 2W1

EIFLER, CARL FREDERICK, retired psychologist; b. Los Angeles, June 27, 1906; s. Carl Frederick and Pauline (Engelbert) E.; Ph.D., Ill. Inst. Tech., 1962; B.D., Jackson Coll.; m. Margaret Christine Aaberg, June 30, 1963; 1 son, Carl Henry; 1 adopted son, Byron Hisey. Insp., U.S. Bur. Customs, 1928-35, chief insp., 1936-37, dep. collector, 1937-56; bus. mgr. Jackson Coll., Honolulu, 1954-56, instr., 1955-56; grad. asst. instr., research asst. Ill. Inst. Tech., Chgo., 1959-62; psychologist Monterey County Mental Health Services, Salinas, Calif., 1964-73; ret., 1973. Served with U.S. Army, 1922-23, 40-47; col. ret. Decorated Combat Infantryman's Badge, Legion of Merit with 2 oak leaf clusters, Bronze Star medal, Air medal, Purple Heart. Mem. Am., Western States, Calif., Monterey County psychol. assns., AAUP, Res. Officers Assn. (Hawaii pres. 1947), Assn. Former Intelligence Officers (bd. govs., Western coordinator), Pearl Harbor Survivors, 101 Assn., Assn. U.S. Army, Vets. of OSS (western v.p.), Am. Law Enforcement Officers Assn., Nat. Intelligence Study Center, Security and Intelligence Fund, Ret. Officers Assn., Psi Chi. Clubs: Masons, KT, Shriners, Elks, Nat. Sojourners. Contbg. author Psychon. Sci., vol. 20, 1970; co-author: The Deadliest Colonel; author, pub.: Jesus Said. Home: 22700 Picador Dr Salinas CA 93908

EIG, NORMAN, investment company executive; b. Passaic, N.J., Mar. 9, 1941; s. Edward H. and Mary (Friedman) E.; m. Barbara Minkin, Feb. 1, 1964; children: Andrew, Alissa, Karin. BS, Ohio State U., 1963; MBA, Columbia U., 1965. Asst. controller Silver Burdett Co., Morristown, N.J., 1965; controller Juliet Footwear, East Paterson, N.J., 1965-68; security analyst Brimberg and Co., N.Y.C., 1968; portfolio mgr. EFC Mgmt., N.Y.C., 1968-69, Scherl, Egener and Co., N.Y.C., 1970-71; exec. v.p. Internat. Research and Devel., Princeton, N.J., 1971-72; pres. Rotunda Advisors, Princeton, 1972-73; ptnr. Oppenheimer and Co., N.Y.C., 1973-82, Lazard Freres and Co., N.Y.C., 1982—; bd. dirs. Lazard Freres Spl. Equity Fund, N.Y.C., Quest for Value Fund, N.Y.C. Mem. corp. adv. bd. Sch. Social Work Columbia U., N.Y.C., 1986—; trustee Jewish Community Found., East Orange, N.J., 1985-86, Newark Acad., Livingston, N.J., 1986—. Mem. Internat. Found. Employee Benefit Plans. Jewish. Clubs: City Athletic (N.Y.C.); Greenbrook Country (North Caldwell, N.J.). Office: Lazard Freres & Co 1 Rockefeller Plaza New York NY 10020

EIGEN, MANFRED, physicist; b. Bochum, Germany, May 9, 1927; s. Ernst E. and Hedwig (Feld) E.; ed. physics and chemistry U. Gottingen (Germany); hon. degrees Harvard U., U. Chgo., Washington U., St. Louis, Nottingham U.; m. Elfriede Muller; 2 children. Sci. asst. Inst. Phys. Chemistry, U. Gottingen, 1951-53; mem. staff Max Planck Inst. Phys. Chemistry, Gottingen, 1953—, now chmn.; vis. lectr. Cornell U. Co-recipient Nobel prize in chemistry, 1967. Mem. Bunsen Soc. Phys. Chemistry (Bodenstein Preis), Faraday Soc., Nat. Acad. Scis. Author tech. papers. Studies on evolution of biol. macromolecules; research on control of enzymes. Address: Max Planck Inst, 3400 Gottingen-Nikolausberg Federal Republic of Germany *

EIKREM, LYNWOOD OLAF, business executive; b. Lansing, Mich., June 11, 1919; s. Arthur Rudolph and Gatha (Zupp) E.; m. Margaret Rosemarie McDonough, July 13, 1946; children: Margaret, John, Marie, Jeanne. BS, Mich. State U., 1941; MS, MIT, 1948. Assoc. prof. chemistry La. Poly. Inst., 1946; tech. dir. Jarrell-Ash Co., Newtonville, Mass., 1949-53; project engr. Baird-Atomic, Cambridge, Mass., 1953-59; staff engr. Geophysics Corp. Am., Bedford, Mass., 1959-60; mgr. product devel. dept. David W. Mann Co. div. Geophysics Corp. Am., Lincoln, Mass., 1960-63, dir. mktg., Burlington, Mass., 1963-65; v.p. mktg. Applied Research Labs. subs. Bausch & Lomb Inc., Sunland, Calif., 1965-72; dir. mktg. Darling & Alsobrook, Los Angeles, 1972-75; prin. Darling, Paterson & Salzer, 1975-79; pres. Paterson & Co., 1979-81; chmn. Strategic Directions Internat., 1981—. Fellow Am. Inst. Chemists; mem. Optical Soc. Am., ASTM, N.Y. Acad. Scis., Sales and Mktg. Execs. Assn., VFW. Lodge: K.C. Home: 605 N Louise St #201 Glendale CA 91206 Office: Strategic Directions Internat 6242 Westchester Pkwy Suite 100 Los Angeles CA 90045

EIN, MELVIN BENNETT, government official; b. Hammond, Ind., Apr. 2, 1932; s. David and Rose (Chayken) E.; A.B., Ind. U., 1955; B.S., State U. N.Y., 1976; M.B.A., Am. U., 1976; m. Connie Chong, Dec. 9, 1957; children—Esther, Deborah, Michael P., Ruth, Nathan S., Sarah. Chief repair parts br. Engr. Sect. 8th. U.S. Army, Seoul, S. Korea, 1958-63; mgr. regional adminstrv. services Fed. Hwy. Adminstrn., Homewood, Ill., 1963-67; supply mgmt. officer U.S. Fgn. Service, U.S. Dept. State, AID, Am. Embassy, Vientiane, Laos, 1967-75; head material br. Naval Research Lab., Washington, 1975-76; chief material br. FAA, Nat. Aviation Facilities Exptl. Center, Atlantic City, 1976-78, emergency preparedness officer, 1978-79, chief material mgmt. br. Dept. Transp., Washington, 1979-83; supply mgr. Comptroller of the Currencysury, Adminstr. Nat. Banks, Washington, 1983—; lectr. in field. Served to 1st lt. U.S. Army, 1955-58. Recipient Sustained Superior Performance award Fed. Hwy. Adminstrn., 1965, HUG award FAA, 1978. Mem. Internat. Material Mgmt. Soc. (profl. certified in material mgmt.), Nat. Property Mgmt. Assn. (cert. profl. property mgr.), Adminstrv. Mgmt. Soc. (certified adminstr. mgr.), Sigma Alpha Mu. Democrat. Jewish. Clubs: Toastmasters (Able award 1976). Home: 1509 Beech Ln Mays Landing NJ 08330 Office: Comptroller of Currency Adminstr Nat Banks 490 L'Enfant Plaza SW Washington DC 20219

EINAV, BEN-AMI, public relations professional, orchestra administrator; b. Bucarest, Romania, May 6, 1947; arrived in Israel, 1960; s. Heinrich and Miriam (Kusman) Weiner; m. Hedva Avnon, Oct. 29, 1970; children: Dalit, Orly. BA, Hebrew U., Jerusalem, 1971, MA in Communication cum laude, 1974. Research dir. Israel Inst. Applied Social Research, Jerusalem, 1971-74; spokesman Technion-Israel Inst. Tech., Haifa, 1974-85; dir. gen. Haifa Symphony Orch., 1985—; lectr. Haifa U., 1976-82; pub. relations cons., No. Israel, 1980-85. Fellow Israel Painters and Sculptors Assn.; mem. Internat. Pub. Relations Assn., Israel Pub. Relations Assn., Israel Assn. Editors of Periodicals. Home: 21A Sea Rd, Haifa 34741, Israel Office: Haifa Symphony Orch, PO Box 5210, 50 Pevsner St, Haifa 31052, Israel

EINODER, CAMILLE ELIZABETH, educator; b. Chgo., June 15, 1937; d. Isadore and Elizabeth T. (Czerwinski) Popowski; student Fox Bus. Coll., 1954; B.Ed. in Biology, Chgo. Tchrs. Coll., 1964; M.A. in Analytical Chemistry, Gov.'s State U., 1977; MA in Adminstrn. and Supervision, Roosevelt U., 1986; postgrad. m. Joseph X. Einoder, Aug. 5, 1978; children—Carl Frank, Mark Frank, Vivian Einoder, Joe Einoder, Tim Einoder, Sheila Einoder, Jude Einoder. Secretarial positions, Chgo., 1955-64; tchr. biology Chgo. Bd. Edn., 1964—, tchr. biology and agr., 1975-81, tchr. biology, agr. and chemistry, 1981—; human relations coordinator Morgan Park High Sch., Chgo., 1980—, tchr. biology Internat. Studies Sch., 1983—; career devel. cons. for agr. related curriculum. Bds. dirs., founding mem., author constn. Community Council, 1970—; bd. dirs., edn. cons. Neighborhood Council, 1974; rep. Chgo. Tchrs. Union, 1969. Mem. Phi Delta Kappa. Home: 10637 S Claremont St Chicago IL 60643 Office: 1744 W Pryor St Chicago IL 60643

EINSELE, CARL, retired publisher; b. Zurich, Switzerland, July 3, 1919; s. Karl Friedrich and Marie-Louise (Ott) E.; m. Nelly Birkhauser, Apr. 17, 1947; children—Sylvia, Peter. Lic. phil., U. Zurich, 1945. Recipient Julius Adams Stratton prize for cultural achievement Friends of Switzerland Inc. of Boston, 1982. Mem. Swiss Pubs. Assn. Lodge: Lions (Basel). Home: Hafenrainstrasse 18, CH-4104 Oberwil BL Switzerland

EINSTEIN, STANLEY, psychologist; b. N.Y.C., July 5, 1934; s. Abraham and Rebecca (Siskind) E.; m. Sarah Wenger, Aug. 31, 1958; children: Tamar Reva, Joshua Gregory. BA in Psychology cum laude, CCNY, 1957, MA in Social Psychology, 1958; MA in Clin. Psychology, U. Pa., 1960; PhD in Psychology, Yeshiva U., 1964. Staff psychologist Riverside Hosp., N.Y.C., 1960-63; psychologist, researcher dept. psychiatry, asst. prof. psychiatry N.Y. Med. Coll., N.Y.C., 1963-67; dir. N.Y. Council Alcoholism, N.Y.C., 1967-69; asst. dir. div. drug abuse, assoc. prof. Dept. Pub. Health N.J. Coll. Medicine, Newark, 1969-73; assoc. prof. dept. criminology Bar Ilan U., Ramat Gan, Israel, 1974-85; assoc. prof. dept. criminology, dept. psychology Hebrew U., Jerusalem, 1977-81; founder, dir. Jerusalem Ctr. Drug Misuse Intervention, 1976-84; pvt. practice psychology N.Y.C., 1964-73, Jerusalem, 1984—; presenter numerous lectures, workshops, seminars. Founder, editor-in-chief Internat. Jour. of the Addictions, Altered States of Consciousness, Drug Forum, Social Pharmacology, Violence, Aggression and Terrorism, Decisions, Issues and Alternatives; weekly columnist Star Ledger, Newark, 1972, Newark News, 1973. Recipient Pace Setter award Nat. Inst. Drug Abuse, 1979. Mem. Am. Psychol. Assn., Israel Psychol. Assn. Home: care Wenger 864 Sumerest Dr NW Atlanta GA 30327 Office: Mesidu, 113/41 E Talpiot, Jerusalem Israel

EIRICH, FREDERICK ROLAND, educator, chemist; b. Vienna, Austria, May 23, 1905; came to U.S., 1947, naturalized, 1953; s. Otto George and Hermine (Perlhefter) E.; m. Maria Dorothea Dehne, Feb. 1, 1936; children-Ursula D., Richard S. Moeller, Susan H. Ph.D., U. Vienna, 1929, Dr. Phil. habil., 1938; M.A., U. Cambridge, Eng., 1939. Research asso., lectr. U. Vienna, 1934- 38, U. Cambridge, 1939-47; mem. faculty Poly. Inst., Bklyn., 1948—; prof. Poly. Inst., 1952—; distinguished prof. 1969—, dean research, 1967-70; vis. prof. U. Uppsala, 1950; Unilever prof. U. Bristol, 1965; vis. scientist Lab. Chem. Evolution, U. Md., 1985—; cons. Govt. Com. Chems., Plastics and Rubber Industry. Author, editor numerous books and research papers. Recipient A. Humboldt Found. award, 1980; Bingham Medal, 1983, M. Huggins award, 1985. Fellow N.Y. Acad. Sci. (chmn. chem. sect. 1952-53), Faraday Soc., Internat. Inst. Fracture Mechanics (hon.); mem. Am. Chem. Soc. (chmn. colloid div. 1960, Distinguished Service award 1975, Merit award Rubber Div. 1978), AAAS (chmn., councillor Gordon Confs. 1959-65), Soc. Rheology (pres. 1972-73), Am. Phys. Soc. (gov. bd. 1970-74), Sigma Xi (research award 1970). Home: 22 Deerfield Ave Tuckahoe NY 10707 Office: 333 Jay St Brooklyn NY 11201

EISDORFER, CARL, psychiatrist, health care executive; b. Bronx, N.Y., June 20, 1930. B.A., NYU, 1951, M.A., 1953, Ph.D., 1959; M.D., Duke U., 1964; postgrad. in health systems mgmt., Harvard U., 1981. Lectr. in psychology Duke U. Med. Ctr., Durham, N.C., 1959-72, intern in medicine, 1964-65, psychiat. trainee, 1964-67, dir. tng., research coordinator Ctr. for Study Aging and Human Devel., 1965-70, prof. psychiatry and med. psychology, 1968-72, dir. med. studies behavioral scis. program, 1970-72, head div. med. psychology dept. psychiatry, 1970-72, dir. Ctr. for Study Aging and Human Devel., 1970-72; founding dir. Inst. on Aging, U. Wash., Seattle, 1977-79, prof., chmn. dept. psychiatry and behavioral scis. Sch. of Medicine, adj. prof. psychology, 1972-81; sr. scholar in residence Inst. Medicine, Nat. Acad. Scis., Washington, 1979-80; prof. psychiatry and neurosci. Albert Einstein Coll. Medicine, N.Y.C., 1981-85; chief exec. officer Montefiore Med. Ctr., N.Y.C., 1981-85; prof., chmn. dept. psychiatry U. Miami, Fla., 1986—; also dir. Ctr. on Adult Devel. and Aging U. Miami; chief div. mental health Jackson Meml. Med. Ctr., 1986—; coordinator Community Mental Health Services, Halifax County N.C., 1969-70; vis. prof. U. Calif., 1969-70, U. Calif.-Berkeley, 1969-70; H.T. Dozer vis. prof. geriatrics and psychiatry Ben Gurion U., Negev, Israel, 1980; cons. NIH, Bethesda, Md., Robert Wood Johnson Found., numerous others. Editor-in-chief Ann. Rev. Gerontology and Geriatrics, 1978—; cons. editor Ency. of Aging, 1984—; mem. editorial bd. Alzheimers Disease and Related Disorders-Internat. Jour., Aging and Human Devel., Western Jour. Medicine, Neurobiology of Aging: Exptl. and Clin. Research; contbr. numerous articles to profl. jours.; also books. Served with U.S. Army, 1954-56. Recipient Kesten award Ethel Percy Andrus Gerontology Ctr., U. So. Calif., 1976, Potamkin prize, 1982, Disting. Alumnus award Duke U. Sch. of Medicine,

1985. Fellow Soc. Behavioral Medicine, N.Y. Acad. Medicine, Am. Psychol. Assn. (chmn. div. adult devel. and aging 1970-71, task force on aging 1971-73, award for disting. contbns. 1981, award for contbns. on aging research 1985), Gerontol. Soc. Am. (pres. 1971-72, Robert W. Kleemeier award 1969, Joseph Freeman award div. clin. medicine 1979), Am. Geriatrics Soc. (Edward B. Allen award 1974), Am. Psychiat. Assn. (Jack Weinberg Meml. award 1984), Am. Coll. Psychiatrists, AAAS; mem. Am. Soc. Aging (pres. 1980-82), Am. Fed. Aging Res. (pres. 1986-88), Sigma Xi, Alpha Omega Alpha. Office: U Miami Sch Medicine Dept Psychiatry D-29 PO Box 016960 Miami FL 33101

EISELE, JOHN ALLAN, physicist, astronomer, theologian; b. Chgo., Oct. 25, 1929; s. Anton Joseph and Anne Josephine (Bodeck) E.; m. Nancy Crisman, Aug. 3, 1957; children: Jeffery Allan, Jane Katherin. Student U. Chgo., 1947-53, U. Pitts., 1953-57; Ph.D., Ohio State U., 1959. Theoretical physicist, Research Lab., Westinghouse Co., Pitts., 1955-56, atomic power dept., 1956-57; asst. prof. physics So. Ill. U., 1959-62; assoc. prof. physics Tex. A&M U., 1962-65; research physicist Naval Research Lab., Washington, 1965—; vis. research scientist U. Calif., Berkeley, 1964; assoc. prof. physics U. Md., 1965—; astronomy instr. Smithsonian Instn., 1973; pres. Nat. Book Co. Am., Washington, 1965-71; lectr. sci. and the Bible, also radio and TV appearances. NSF grantee, 1961-62. Fellow Washington Acad. Scis. (bd. dirs.), Am. Phys. Soc., Nat. Capitol Astronomers (pres. 1972-74), Astron. Soc. Pacific, Research Engring. Soc. Am., Sigma Xi. Author: Advanced Quantum Mechanics and Particle Physics, 1964, Astrodynamics, Rockets, Satellites, and Space Travel, 1967, Modern Quantum Mechanics with Applications to Elementary Particle Physics, 1969, (with R.M. Mason) Applied Matrix and Tensor Analysis, 1970; Scientific Highlights from the Book of Job, 1982, Our Animal Friends Now and Hereafter on the Renewed Earth, 1985, Biblical Chronology and the Dating of the Crucifixion, 1987, Three Important Steps to Salvation, 1987, The Star of Bethlehem, 1987, Heaven and the Renewed Earth, 1988, The Marvels and the Mysteries of Orion, 1988; contbr. articles to profl. jours. Home: 3310 Curtis Dr Apt 202 Suitland MD 20746 Office: Space Systems and Tech Div US Naval Research Lab Code 7701 Washington DC 20032

EISELE, WILLIAM DAVID, insurance agency executive; b. Iron Mountain, Mich., July 31, 1927; s. David Christian and Muriel Elizabeth (Ockstadt) E.; B.S., U. Mich., 1950; m. Helen Jeanne Holmberg, Dec. 27, 1953; children—David, Meg. Ins. agt. Employers Mut. of Wausau, Milw., 1951, West Bend, Wis., 1952-53, Watertown, Wis., 1953-56, Orlando, Fla., 1957, Tampa, Fla., 1958; pres. William D. Eisele & Co., Clearwater, Fla., 1959—. Charter pres. Heritage Presbyn. Housing Project, 1971-72; town commr., Belleair Shore, Fla.; elder Presbyn. Ch. Recipient disting. alumni service award U. Mich., 1975. Mem. Fla. Assn. Ins. Agts., Clearwater-Largo-Dunedin Insurors (past pres.), U. Mich. Alumni Assn. (dir., v.p.). Clubs: Clearwater Rotary; U. Mich. (organizer, past pres. Pinellas County, Fla.). Office: 1012 E Druid Rd Clearwater FL 34616

EISEMANN, MARTIN RAIMUND, psychology educator and researcher; b. Marktheidenfel, Bavaria, Fed. Republic Germany, Dec. 30, 1950; arrived in Sweden, 1975; s. Hans and Anna (Dümig) E.; m. Carina Ringmor Nyström; children: Linnéa, Eric. BA, U. Würzburg, Fed. Republic Germany, 1975; MSc, U. Umeå, Sweden, 1978; PhD, U. UmeÅ, Sweden, 1985. Research assoc. dept. Psychiatry U. UmeÅ, 1978-85, assoc. prof. med. psychology, 1987—; research coordinator WHO-Collaborating Ctr., Umeå, 1985—. Contbr. articles to profl. jours. Mem. Swedish Assn. Behavioral Medicine, Internat. Assn. Scientists Against Nuclear Arms. Home: Akterstigen 1, S-91024 Obbola Sweden Office: U Umea, Dept Psychiatry, S-901 85 Umea Sweden

EISEN, ALAN G., public relations executive; b. N.Y.C., Feb. 11, 1929; s. Nathan and Edna Eisen; B.A., Temple U., 1952; m. Joanne Fink. Dir. radio and TV, City of Phila., 1951-52; dir. pub. relations Greater N.Y. councils Boy Scouts Am., 1952-54; asst. dir. press relations Music Corp. Am., 1954-56; v.p. Ruder & Finn, N.Y.C., 1956-63; pres. Alan G. Eisen Co., Inc., Old Bethpage, N.Y., 1963—. Chmn. pub. relations Glen Cove Bicentennial Commn. Mem. Pub. Relations Soc. Am. (accredited), Nat. Rifle Assn. (life). Club: Matinecock Rod and Gun. Author: Foodbook, 1973. Home: Frog Pond Farm Route 2 Box 310 Narrowsburg NY 12764 Office: 1188 Round Swamp Rd Old Bethpage NY 11804

EISEN, LEONARD, food and retail company executive; b. Toronto, Ont., Can., Oct. 14, 1934; s. Harry Mendle and Anne Miriam (Grossman) E.; m. Merle Faye Dover, June 18, 1958; children: Rhonda Lynn Eisen Shore, Beth Francis. Chartered Acct., Inst. Chartered Accts. (Toronto) Ont., 1957; BA in Econs., York U., Toronto, 1977. Chartered acct. Mgr. corp. fin. Vise, Rumack, Seigel, Kurtz & Co., Toronto, 1960-63; ptnr. Bernard C. Kurtz & Co., Toronto, 1963-64; v.p. fin. and adminstrn. WIMCO Steel Sales Ltd., Toronto, 1964-68; v.p. fin., dir. adminstrn. Toronto Iron Works Ltd., 1965-68; dir. corp. acctg. The Oshawa Group Ltd., Toronto, 1968-70, asst. treas., 1970-74, treas., 1974—. Bd. govs., vice chmn., chmn. budget and fin. com. Beth Tzedec Synagogue, Toronto, 1983—. Fellow of Inst. Chartered Accts. Ont.; mem. Can. Tax Found. (bd. govs. and chmn. audit and fin. com. 1984-87, chmn. investment com. 1984—), Retail Council of Can. (mem. tax com.). Office: The Oshawa Group Ltd, 302 East Mall, Etobicoke, Toronto, ON Canada M9B 6B8

EISENBEISS, RICHARD FELIX, chemical manufacturing company executive; b. Heidelberg, Germany, Dec. 18, 1927; m. Annabelle Fischer, Sept. 25, 1958; children—R. David, Philip William. Student, U. Basel (Switzerland), 1950, U. Heidelberg, 1952. Vice pres. Cervessa Corp., N.Y.C., 1954-58; pres. Kissel & Wolf Gmbh, Wiesloch, W.Ger., 1958—; pres. Albert Rose Chems. SA, Bern, Switzerland, 1973—; dir. Albert Rose Chems. Ltd., Wilmington, Del., 1963—; dir. Albert Rose Chems. (India) Pty Ltd., Bombay, Suntrak Ltd., London. Mem. C. of C. Deutschland-Schweiz, List Soc. Dusseldorf, Acad. Screen Printing Tech. Contbr. articles to profl. jours. Office: 10 Thunstrasse, 3005 Bern Switzerland

EISENBERG, HOWARD EDWARD, psychologist, educator, consultant; b. Montreal, Que., Can., Aug. 5, 1946; s. Harold and Elsie (Goldbloom) E.; m. Nancy Roberta Jeffries, Jan. 10, 1976; children—Taryn Noelle, Jory Michael, Meredith Kate. B.Sc. with honors in Psychology, McGill U., 1967, M.Sc., 1971, M.D.C.M., 1972. Intern Sunnybrook Med. Ctr., U. Toronto, 1973; research asst. psychology dept. McGill U., 1966-69, research asst. gerontology unit Alan Meml. Inst. Psychiatry, McGill U., 1968, clin. fellow Clarke Inst. Psychiatry, U. Toronto, 1973; lectr. Centre for Continuing Edn., York U., 1973-78, Sheridan Coll., Oakville, 1974-76; supr. individual directed study Faculty Environ. Studies, York U., 1975; lectr. dept. interdisciplinary studies U. Toronto, 1975; instr. ind. studies program, Innis Coll., U. Toronto, 1975-78, lectr. 1976-81, spl. conf. coordinator, 1977-79, lectr. Sch. Continuing Studies, 1977—; assoc. dir. edn. and growth opportunities program York U., 1975-76, dir. E.G.O. program, 1976-78; lectr. Sch. Adult Edn., McMaster U., 1980—; instr. profl. and mgmt. devel. Humber Coll., 1982-85; pvt. practice psychotherapy, Toronto, Ont., 1973—; pres. Synectia Cons., Inc., Toronto, 1980-84, Synectia Prodns., Inc., 1974—. Author: Inner Spaces, 1977, The Tranquility Experience, 1987; contbr. articles to profl. jours. McGill scholar, 1966-67; Quebec scholar, 1967-68; Earle C. Anthony fellow, 1967-68; Ont. Arts Council grantee, 1977. Mem. Can. Med. Assn., Ont. Med. Assn. (past chmn. sect. ind. physicians), Can. Psychiat. Assn., Can. Council on Working Life, Orgnl. Devel. Can., Assn. for Humanistic Psychology. Address: 219 St Clair Ave W, Suite 102, Toronto, ON Canada M4V 1R3

EISENBERG, JOSEPH MARTIN, psychologist; b. Bklyn., June 19, 1944; s. David and Dora (Levine) E.; B.A. in Psychology magna cum laude, C. W. Post Coll., 1966; M.A. in Psychology, U. Alta., 1969, Ph.D. in Psychology, 1971; m. Susan Joan Kahn, Aug. 16, 1980; children—Ian, Lara, Jason, Davida. Psychol. diagnostician, counselor dept. psychology U. Alta. (Can.), 1969-70; field researcher Dept. youth Alta., 1967-69; assoc. dir. Toronto (Ont.) YMCA Centre for Counseling and Human Relations, 1970-71; counselor, cons. York Regional Sch. Nursing, Toronto, 1970-71; chief psychologist Salvation Army House of Concord, Toronto, 1971-72; dir. outpatient service St. Vincent Hosp. Community Mental Health Center, Erie, Pa., 1972-73; dir. Erie County Center for Learning Disabilities, 1973-74; pvt. practice psychology, Erie and Balt., 1972—; v.p. in charge personnel and communications Bridge Energy Corp., Balt., 1981—; pres. Reason House, Balt., 1981—; spl. cons. Md. Children and Family Services, Inc.; mem. profl. adv. bds. Balt. Assn. Children with Learning Disabilities, Feingold Assn.; cons. Mormac Ltd., 1979—; forensic cons. Howard County/Balt. County/Carroll County, Office of Public Defenders and Balt. City Solicitor's Office, 1977—. Chmn., Carroll County Child Abuse Consultation Com., 1978-80; dir. Psychol. Services for the Metabolic Nutrition Program, 1986—; mem. profl. adv. bd. Catonsville Group Home, 1980-81. Recipient Richard P. Runyon award, 1966; cert., lic., Md. and Tex.; cert. clin. hypnotherapist, Negotiation Inst. Mem. Am. Psychol. Assn., Md. Psychol. Assn., Assn. Advancement of Psychology, Balt. Assn. Cons. Psychologists, Balt. County C. of C. (exec. dialogue program), Psi Chi, Phi Theta. Co-author computer software; contbr. articles to profl. jours. Office: 204 E Joppa Rd Penthouse Suite 10 Towson MD 21204

EISENMANN, OLIVIER DAPHNIS, concert organist; b. Zürich, Switzerland, June 7, 1940; s. Will E. and Eva (Westphal) E. Doctor, U. Zü rich, 1972; student Will E. Eisenmann, Conservatory Lucerne, 1945-59, Eduard Kaufmann, Stiftsorganist, 1962-72. First performed as pianist, 1948; pianist, accompanist, 1957—; organist, 1972—; artistic dir. several internat. concert series. Performed in concerts and tours in Europe, U.S., Australia, Mexico City, Washington Cathedral, Riverside Ch., N.Y., Seattle, Boston, Notre Dame de Paris, Bonn Münsterbasilika, St. Paul's Cathedral, London, cathedrals in Worcester, Dublin, Haarlem, Amsterdam, Oslo, Stockholm, Berlin, Madrid, Budapest, Helsinki; festivals in Bonn, Trier Cathedral, Rostock, Naples, Czechoslovakia, Verona and Internat. Hong Kong Arts Festival; radio and TV programs, a dozen records, including CD's. Editor LNN Lucerne, 1971-76. Author: Friedrich der Grosse im Urteil seiner schweizerischen Mitwelt, 1972. Contbr. articles to booklets and newspapers. Mem. Internat. Soc. for New Music (Swiss sect.). Address: Chalet Brisenblick, 6353 Weggis, Lucerne Switzerland

EISENSCHITZ, TAMARA SYBIL, information science educator; b. London, July 19, 1950; d. Robert Karl and Eva (Laufer) E. BSc, Queen Mary Coll., 1971; PhD, U. Edinburgh, 1974; MSc, City U. London, 1978. Research fellow Deutsches Elektronen Synchrotron-Hamburg, Fed. Republic Germany, 1975-76, Carlton U., Ottawa, Can., 1976-77; patent searcher New Product Mgmt., London, 1978-79; lectr. Victoria U., Wellington, New Zealand, 1979-80, City U. London, 1981—. Author: Inventors' Information Guide, 1985, Patents, Trademarks and Designs, 1987; contbr. articles to profl. publs. Mem. Inst. Info. Scientists, Inst. Patentees and Inventors. Office: City U Northampton Sq, London EC1V OHB, England

EISENSTADT, SHMUEL NOAH, sociologist, educator; b. Warsaw, Poland, Sept. 10, 1923; s. Michael and Rosa (Baruchin) E.; came to Israel, 1935; m. Shulamith Yaroshevsky, Sept. 6, 1948; children—Michael, Irit Meir, Alexander. M.A., Hebrew U. of Jerusalem, 1944, Ph.D. in Sociology, 1947; postdoctoral studies London Sch. Econs., 1947-48; D Polit. Sci. (hon.) U. Helsinki, 1986. With Hebrew U. of Jerusalem, 1946—, chmn. dept. sociology, 1951-69, Rose Isaacs prof. sociology, 1959—, dean Faculty of Social Scis., The Eliezer Kaplan Sch. Econs., 1966-68; fellow Ctr. for Advanced Studies in Behavioral Scis., Stanford, Calif., 1955-56; vis. mem. London Sch. Econs., 1958; vis. prof. U. Oslo, 1958, U. Chgo., 1960, 71, MIT, 1962-63, Harvard U., 1968-69, 75-81, U. Mich., 1970, U. Zurich, 1975, Stanford U., 1984, 86, 87, 88,U. Wash., 1986; others; fellow Netherlands Inst. for Advanced Study, Wassenaar, 1973; Simon vis. prof. U. Manchester, 1978; vis. fellow Australian Nat. U., 1978; research fellow Hoover Inst., 1986. Author: The Absorption of Immigrants, 1955, 2d edit., 1978; From Generation to Generation, 1956, 2d edit., 1970; Essays on Sociological Aspects of Political and Economic Development, 1961; The Political Systems of Empires, 1963, 1969; Modernization, Protest and Change, 1966; Israeli Society, 1968; Political Sociology of Modernization (Japanese), 1968; Tradition, Change and Modernity, 1975; The Form of Sociology (with M. Curelaru), 1976; Revolution and the Tranformation of Societies, 1973; (with L. Roniger) Patrons, Clients and Friends, 1984; (with A. Shachar) Culture, Society and Urbanization, 1986, Transformation of Israeli Society, 1985. Editor: Comparative Social Problems, 1964; The Decline of Empires, 1967; Comparative Perspectives on Social Change, Post-Traditional Socieites, 1973, other books in field. Contbr. numerous articles to profl. jours. Mem. editorial bd. Comparative Studies in Society and History, Econ. Devel. and Cultural Change, Comparative Politics, Am. Behavioral Scientist, Comparative Polit. Studies, Youth and Soc., Jour. Polit. and Mil. Sociology, Civilizations, other profl. jours. Recipient Kaplun prize in Social Scis., 1969; Rothschild prize in Social Scis., 1970; Israel prize in Social Scis., 1973; Balzan prize, 1988. Fellow London Sch. of Econs. and Polit. Sci.; mem. Am. Sociol. Assn. (McIver award 1964), Internat. Sociol. Assn. (coms. on polit. sociology, social stratification), Am. Acad. Arts and Scis., Am. Philos. Soc., Inst. Comparative Civilizations (Brussels), Soc. for the Study of Internat. Problems (trustee Switzerland), Nat. Acad. Scis. (assoc.), Israel Acad. Scis. and Humanities, Israel Council of Community Relations (chmn. 1960-64), Israeli Sociol. Assn. (pres. 1969-71). Office: The Hebrew U, Mount Scopus, Jerusalem Israel

EISENSTEIN, THEODORE DONALD, pediatrician; b. N.Y.C., July 4, 1930; s. Harry and Myra (Drexler) E.; student N.Y. U., 1948-49; A.B., Johns Hopkins U., 1952; M.D., Albany Med. Coll., 1956; m. Ellen Roob, Dec. 9, 1956; children—Janet, Stephen. Pediatric intern Kings County Med. Center, Bklyn., 1956-57; resident in pediatrics N.Y. Hosp., N.Y.C., 1957-59; NIH vis. fellow in pediatric endocrinology Columbia-Presbyn. Med. Center, N.Y.C., 1961-62; practice medicine specializing in pediatrics, West Caldwell, N.J., 1962—; full attending staff St. Barnabas Med. Center, clin. chmn. dept. pediatrics; v.p. Pediatric Assos. West Essex, P.A.; asst. clin. prof. pediatrics Columbia U. Coll. Phys. and Surg., 1970—; clin. asst. prof. pediatrics N.J. Coll. Medicine and Dentistry, Rutgers U., 1970—; Mem. alumni council N.Y. Hosp.-Cornell Med. Center. Served with M.C., USAF, 1959-61. Diplomate Am. Bd. Pediatrics. Fellow Am. Acad. Pediatrics; mem. AMA, Acad. Medicine N.J., Am. Diabetes Assn., AAAS, Soc. Practitioners Columbia-Presbyn. Med. Center, Albany Med. Coll. Alumni Assn., Am. Physicians Fellowship, N.J. Med. Sch. Faculty Orgn. Jewish. Research on pediatric endocrinology, human growth hormone. Home: 7 Byron Rd North Caldwell NJ 07006 Office: 700 Passaic Ave W Caldwell NJ 07006

EISENZIMMER, BETTY WENNER, insurance agency executive; b. Twisp, Wash., July 25, 1939; d. Bren William and Julia Emogene (Salmon) Wenner; m. Erwin LeRoy Cook, June 19, 1955 (div. 1960); 1 child, Richard Jeffrey; m. Jerome Anthony Eisenzimmer, Feb. 18, 1966. Cert. in gen. ins. Ins. Inst. Am., 1981; cert. profl. ins. woman. Clk. typist MR Ins., Seattle, 1957-59; records clk. Assigned Risk Plan, Seattle, 1959-61; acct. asst. Robinson Jenner, Inc., Seattle, 1961-66; sec., acct. asst. Falkenberg & Co., Seattle, 1966-75, adminstrv. asst., 1975-77; ins. agt., corp. officer Service Ins. Inc., Seattle, 1975—; mem. adv. bd. Sch. Ins., Wash. State U. Coll. Bus., 1981—. Asst. editor Today's Ins. Woman, 1980-81. Exec. bd. Wash. chpt. Cystic Fibrosis Found., 1978-86, pres., 1983-85; mem. Wash. State Centennial Speakers' Bur., 1987—; mem. long range planning com. Cedar Cross United Meth. Ch., 1986-87, mem. worship com., 1988—. Recipient Disting. Service award Cystic Fibrosis Found., 1984; named Vol. of Yr., Wash. chpt. Cystic Fibrosis Found., 1980. Mem. Seattle C. of C., Ins. Women Puget Sound (pres. 1970-72, Ins. Woman of Yr. 1978, 81, Industry award 1984), Ins. Women's Assn. Seattle (chmn. 1992 conf., Ins. Woman of Yr. 1981), Nat. Assn. Ins. Women (nat. sec. 1976-77, regional dir. 1981-82, mem. exec. bd. 1976-77, 81-82, You Make the Difference award 1977, Regional IX Lace Speakoff winner 1983), Ind. Ins. Agts. and Brokers Wash. (edn. com. 1982-83), Ind. Ins. Agts. and Brokers King County (chmn. bylaws 1984-85), Profl. Ins. Agts. Wash. (edn. com. 1982-86, chmn. 1983-86), Wash. Ins. Council (mem. speakers bur. 1980—), Women's Bus. Exchange, Women's Profl. and Managerial Women's Network, Nat. Assn. Life Underwriters, Women Life Underwriters Conf. (nat. bd. dirs., region I dir. 1987-88), Acad. Producer Ins. Studies (fellow of acad.), Network of Exec. Women, Seattle Assn. Life Underwriters, Nat. Assn. Female Execs. Club: Toastmasters (pres. Wallingford chpt. 1986-87, ednl. v.p. 1987-88, dist. 2 area 5 gov. 1987-88, Gov.'s Honor Roll dist. 2 1987, designated able toastmaster 1987 and other awards and positions). Home: 8932 240th St SW Edmonds WA 98020 Office: Service Ins Inc 332 Securities Bldg Seattle WA 98101

EISERER, LEONARD ALBERT CARL, publishing executive; b. Polar, Wis., June 3, 1916; s. Herman Frederick and Anna Elizabeth (Schnieder) E.; m. Lorraine Elizabeth Hickey, June 28, 1941; children—Carol Jean, Elaine Roberta, Leonard Arnold, Beverly Arlene. B.A., Roosevelt U., Chgo., 1937; M.S. in Journalism, Northwestern U., 1939. Editor, Am. Aviation Publs., Inc., Washington, 1939-51, v.p., gen. mgr., 1952-57, exec. v.p., sec., 1958-62; pres., pub. Sports Age, Inc., Washington, 1962-63, chmn., pres., pub. Bus. Pubs., Inc., Silver Spring, Md., 1963—. Served to lt. USN, 1942-46. Mem. Air Pollution Control Assn., Water Pollution Control Fedn., Soc. Profl. Journalists, Newsletter Assn. Club: Nat. Press, University. Home: 9101 Sligo Creek Pkwy Silver Spring MD 20901 Office: Bus Pubs Inc 951 Pershing Dr Silver Spring MD 20910

EISMA, JOSE ALBARRACIN, physician; b. Jolo, Sulu, Philippines, Oct. 18, 1939; came to U.S., 1964, naturalized, 1973; s. Marcelo L. and Rosa A. (Albarracin) E.; A.A., Silliman U., Philippines, 1958; M.D., U. Santo Tomas (Manila), 1963; m. Lenora Womack, Sept. 14, 1977; children: Joseph Alan, John Mitchell, Gregory Mitchell, Teresa Lyn, Lorell Elizabeth, Julia Dawn. Rotating intern Wilson Meml. Hosp., Johnson City, N.Y., 1964-65, med. resident, 1965-67; med. resident Kingsbrook Jewish Med. Center, Bklyn., 1967-68; gen. internist Reynolds Army Hosp., Ft. Sill, Okla., 1971-73; resident in pulmonary disease Brooke Army Med. Center, Ft. Sam Houston, Tex., 1973-74; chief of medicine, med. dir. respiratory therapy dept. West (Tex.) Community Hosp., 1976—, bd. dirs., 1986. Served to col., M.C., Army N.G., 1975-80. Diplomate Am. Bd. Family Practice. Fellow Am. Acad. Family Physicians; mem. A.C.P., Am. Soc. Internal Medicine, Am. Thoracic Soc. Clubs: Res. Officers Assn., Tex. N.G. Assn., Assn. U.S. Army, Assn. Mil. Surgeons of U.S. Contbr. article to profl. publ. in field. Home: 1406 N Reagan St West TX 76691 Office: 300 N Reagan St West TX 76691

EISNER, LAWRENCE BRAND, lawyer, real estate developer; b. New Haven, Sept. 27, 1951; s. Robert Raphael and Anita Stanton (Brand) E.; m. Karen Marie Menne, Nov. 11, 1979; children: Benjamin, Anna, Julia. B.A., Union Coll., 1973; J.D., Georgetown U., 1976. Bar: Conn. 1976, D.C. 1978, Mass. 1982. Atty., adviser Commodity Futures Trading Commn., Washington, 1977-79; treas. Continental Lumber Co., West Haven, Conn., 1979-85; pres. Eisner Devel. Group, Hamden, Conn., 1985—. Mem. Conn. Bar Assn., D.C. Bar Assn., Phi Beta Kappa. Democrat. Jewish. Home: 88 Churchill Rd Hamden CT 06517 Office: Eisner Devel Group 2911 Dixwell Ave Hamden CT 06518

EISSMANN, WALTER JAMES, weight loss franchise owner; b. Newark, N.J., Apr. 20, 1939; s. Walter Curt Eissmann and Alice Delice (Irving) Clark; m. Dorothea Ann Donaldson, June 1, 1963; children—Patricia Helene, Walter William. B.S. in Indsl. Engring., Rutgers U., 1962. Account mgr. Gen. Electric, Engelwood Cliffs, N.J., 1962-67; regional sales mgr. Tymshare, Engelwood Cliffs, 1968-71, Buffalo, N.Y., 1971-73, Washington, 1973-74, v.p. mktg. service div., Cupertino, Calif., 1974-79, div. v.p., Cupertino, 1980-84; sr. v.p. McDonnell Douglas Corp., Cupertino, 1984-86; gen. ptnr. Archer Assocs., 1985—; bd. dirs. Softyme, Inc., 1984, NSF Corp., 1987—. Bd. dirs. Saratoga Little League, Calif., 1976-81, Saratoga Boosters, 1981-84; active Vienna Theatre Players, Va., 1973, mem. Church Men's Choir, Saratoga, 1980-82. Named to President's Club Tymshare, Golden Circle. Mem. Pi Tau Sigma. Republican. Club: Johnson Ranch Racquet (bd. dirs. 1988—). Office: Archer Assocs 1510 Arden Way Suite 300 Sacramento CA 95815

EITENBICHLER, ULRICH H., textiles executive; b. Kaufbeuren, Fed. Republic Germany, Sept. 1, 1934; s. Heinrich and Rosa (Hutner) E.; m. Maria Roth, Aug. 29, 1961; children: Patrick, Ulrike, Lucia. From apprentice to sales mgr. Spinnerei und Weberei Momm AG, Kaufbeuren, Federal Republic of Germany, 1951—. Home: AM Sonneneck 27B, D8950 Kaufbeuren Federal Republic of Germany Office: MOMM AG, D8950 Kaufbeuren Federal Republic of Germany

EITJE, MICHAEL, pension fund administrator; b. Amsterdam, The Netherlands, July 17, 1940. D in Econs., U. Amsterdam, 1967. Asst. acct. Klynfeld Kraayenhof, 1967-69; mgr. portfolio Brenca BV, 1969-85, sr. v.p., 1985-87, mng. dir., 1987—. Bd. dirs. Nederlands Israelietische Hoofdsynagoge of Amsterdam, 1965—, daily bd., 1971-73, 77-83, 87— ; mem. council NIK, 1966—; sec. treas. Pekidim & Amarcalim, S.A. Raufe Stichting, F. Friedmann's Stichting, 1984—; chmn. NIHS Pension Fund, 1973—. Mem. Fedn. Dutch Fin. Analysts. Jewish. Home: Soetendaal 58, 1081 BP Amsterdam The Netherlands

EJAZ, TAHSEEN EJAZ, physician; b. Chilas, Gilgit, Pakistan, Jan. 5, 1934; s. Alam and Jano Khan; m. Nelufar Khan, Jan. 14, 1948; children: Farrukh, Ambreen, Arsalan, Zeshan. FSC, Islamia Coll., Peshawar, Pakistan, 1958; MBBS, Khybar Med. Coll., Peshawar, 1967. Intern Leady Reading Hosp., Peshawar, 1967; asst. dir. Gilgit (Pakistan) Rural Health System, 1973-74, dir., 1974-81; coordinator drug abuse program Gilgit, 1979-84, convenor family planning program, 1986—; temp. advisor Internat. Workshop on Narcotics, Chianmai, Thailand, 1979; primary health care specialist, trained community health workers, Pakistan, 1973-81. Sec. gen. Pakistan People's Party, Gilgit, 1986. Mem. Pakistan Med. Assn. Home and Office: Ejaz Clinic, Airport Rd, Gilgit Pakistan

EJIRI, KOICHIRO, manufacturing executive; b. Yokohama, Japan, Sept. 1, 1920; m. Mitsuko Ejiri, Nov. 13, 1948; children: Yoichiro, Kensuke. BA in Laws, Tokyo Imperial U., 1943. With Mitsui and Co., Tokyo, 1943—; pres. Australia div. Mitsui and Co., Melbourne and Sydney, 1971-73; dir. Mitsui and Co., Tokyo, 1975-76, exec. mng. dir., 1977-81; pres. U.S.A. div. Mitsui and Co., N.Y.C., 1980-81; sr. exec. mng. dir. Mitsui and Co., Tokyo, 1982—, exec. v.p., 1983-84, pres., 1985—; chmn. European Community com. Keidanren, Tokyo, 1988—. Recipient Gov. award, State of N.Y., 1982, Blue Ribbon medal Japanese Govt., 1986. Office: Mitsui and Co, 2-1 Ohte-machi 1-chome, Chiyoda-ku, Tokyo 100, Japan

EJIRI, MASAKAZU, research robotics scientist; b. Takefu, Japan, Mar. 9, 1937; s. Tadashi and Sueo E.; m. Keiko Manda, Mar. 28, 1962; children—Manami, Yumika, Koki. B. Engring., Osaka U., 1959, D.Engring., 1967. Research scientist Hitachi Central Research Lab., Tokyo, 1959-67, sr. research scientist, 1968-77, chief research scientist, 1981-87; sr. chief research scientist, 1987—; asst. prof. U. Ill.-Chgo., 1967-68; v.p. HISL, Inc., Mountain View, Calif., 1977-81; lectr. U. Tokyo, 1982—, Waseda U., 1984—; Tokyo Inst. Tech., 1987—. Author: Robotics and its Applications, 1984, Industrial Image Processing, 1988, Artificial Intelligence, 1988; editor: Visual Pattern Recognition Technology, 1983; contbr. articles to profl. jours. Mem. Am. Assn. for Artificial Intelligence, Internat. Assn. Pattern Recognition, Soc. Instrument and Control Engrs. of Japan, Pattern Recognition Soc., IEEE. Avocations: tennis; skiing. Home: 4-18-17 Nakaarai, Tokorozawa, Saitama 359, Japan Office: Hitachi Central Research Lab, 1-280 Higashi-koigakubo, Kokubunji, Tokyo 185, Japan

EKANDEM, DOMINIC IGNATIUS CARDINAL, priest; b. Obio Ibiono, Nigeria, 1917; s. Paul Ino Ekandem Ubo and Nwa Ibong Umana; D.D., St. Paul's Major Sem., Enugu, 1941, Okpala, 1947. Ordained priest Roman Catholic Ch., 1947; priest in Nigeria, 1947-54; consecrated bishop, 1954; bishop of Ikot Ekpene, Akwa Ibom State, 1963—; chmn. Dept. Social Welfare, Cath. Secretariat of Nigeria, 1970; apostolic adminstr. of Port Harcourt, 1970-73; pres. Episcopal Conf. Nigeria, 1973-79; elevated to Sacred Coll. Cardinals, 1976; cardinal of St. Marcellus, 1976—. Decorated Order Brit. Empire; comdr. Order Niger, Order Fed. Republic of Nigeria; named Mission Superior of Abuja, 1981—; recipient 5 chieftancy titles in Nigeria. Mem. Assn. Episcopal Confs. of Anglophone West Africa (pres. 1977), Congregation for the Evang. of Peoples, Pioneer Total Abstinance Assn. Author: Shepherd Among Shepherds, 1979; also articles. Address: Bishop's Residence, PO Box 870, Ikot Ekpene, Akwa Ibom State Nigeria

EKBOM, TORSTEN GUNNAR, writer; b. Stockholm, Feb. 6, 1938; s. Karl-Axel Ekbom and Hedvig Charlotta Stålhane; m. Maud Arvidson, July 19, 1962; children Torun, Karin. Fil Kand, Stockholm U., 1962. Critic Dagens Nyheter, Stockholm, 1962. Co-editor: Rondo, 1961-65, Gorilla, 1966-67; author: Negationer, 1963, Spelöppning, 1964; Signalspelet, 1965, Spelmatriser for Operation Albatross, 1967, En galakväll på Operan, 1969, Europeiska Konserten, 1975, Molnbyggen, 1980, Tatlins torn, 1986. Mem. Acad. of Arts (hon.). Home: Döbelnsgatan 32D, S-75237 Uppsala Sweden

EKELUND, ULF RAGNAR, sport executive, editor; b. Stockholm, Dec. 16, 1943; s. Axel Gunnar and Ingrid (Bergh) E.; m. Genevieve Ann Elisabeth Weber, Mar. 18, 1967 (div. 1970). MA in Polit. Sci. and French, U. Stockholm, 1966; student Sorbonne, Paris, 1964. Clk., Swedish Consulate, Paris, 1965; prin. clk. Nat. Bd. Immigration, Stockholm, 1966-70, prin. asst. sec., 1970-75; chief editor Rev. Friidrott, Stockholm, 1978—; gen. sec. Swedish Amateur Athletic Assn., Stockholm, 1975-84, exec. dir., 1984—; mktg. cons. Internat. amateur Athletic Fedn., London, 1983—. Contbr. articles to profl. jours. Recipient Medal of Merit in Gold, Finnish Amateur Athletic Assn., 1978, Medal of Merit in Gold, Icelandic Amateur Athletic Assn. Mem. Children's Internat. Summer Villages (pres. 1978-82, hon. pres. 1982—), Swedish Assn. Children's Internat. Summer Villages. Office: Svenska-Fri-Idrotsforbundet, Sofiatornet Stadion, S-11433 Stockholm Sweden

EKENBERG, BERTIL LENNART EDWARD, computer scientist, educator; b. Vaxjo, Sweden, Apr. 23, 1947; s. Bengt A.E. and Ella V. (Ny) E. PhD in Computer Scis., Lund U., Sweden, 1978. Asst., Lund U., 1968-71, asst. master, 1971-82, sr. univ. lectr., 1982-86, sr. cons., 1986—; research worker, 1970-78, demonstrator, 1977-78, 81-82, bd. mem. dept. computer scis., 1982-86; cons. Alfa Laval, Lund, 1979, Enpece, Lund, 1985. Contbr. articles to profl. lit. Lutheran. Avocation: photography. Home: Dag Hammarskjolds vag 3 D, S-22364 Lund Sweden Office: Lund Computing Ctr, Box 783, S-22007 Lund Sweden

EKENSTIERNA, HARVEY SCOTT, public relations and advertising executive; b. Bayonne, N.J., Sept. 22, 1935; s. Harvey Conrad and Anne Janice (Scott) E.; m. Diana Stuart Johnson, Dec. 7, 1963; children: Scott Mercer, Susan Lynn, Karen Anne. BA, Marietta (Ohio) Coll., 1958. Reporter, photographer, sports editor Wildwood (N.J.) Leader, 1959-65; reporter, bur. chief, acting state editor Newark Evening News, 1965-70; asst. dir. pub. relations Kidde, Inc., Saddle Brook, N.J., 1970-74, dir. pub. relations, 1974-79, v.p. corp. communications, 1979-88; dir. pub. affairs and pub. relations Goody Products, Inc., Kearny, N.J., 1988—. Mem. West Milford Bd. Edn., Mem. North Jersey Press Assn., Meeting Planners Internat. Episcopalian. Home: 28 Frederick Dr West Milford NJ 07480 Office: Goody Products Inc 969 Newark Turnpike Kearny NJ 07032

EKMAN, MARIA, translator; b. Stockholm County, Sweden, Feb. 6, 1944; d. Eyvind and Cilla (Frankenhaeuser) J.; m. 1964 (div. 1976); 1 child. Freelance lit. translator Sweden, 1968—. Translator numerous lit. works including: Africa in Social Change (Peter C. Lloyd) 1969, Can Africa Survive? (Basil Davidson) 1976, The Dragon's Village (Yuan-tsung Chen) 1981, The Comfort of Strangers (Ian McEwan) 1981, Easy Travel to Other Planets (Ted Mooney) 1983, The Handmaid's Tale (Margaret Atwood) 1986, The Child in Time (Ian McEwan) 1988. Recipient Guaranteed Author's coin The Swedish Author's Fund, 1983—; Swedish Author's Fund grantee, 1976-82. Mem. Swedish Writers' Union (com. mem. translators' sect., 1976—), Swedish PEN Centre (com. mem. 1986—). Home: Borgargatan 2, S-11734 Stockholm Sweden

EKMAN, MATTS P., finance executive; b. Goteborg, Sweden, Dec. 3, 1946; s. Matts G. and Gudrun (Falkheden) E.; m. Christina Wiking-Johnsson; children: Caroline, Susanne, Charlotte, Sophie. Diploma in civil econs., U. Lund, Sweden, 1969; MBA, U. Calif., Berkeley, 1971. Asst. treas. Gränges AB, Stockholm, 1973-75, v.p. fin., 1976-79, exec. v.p. fin., 1980-81; v.p. fin., group treas. AB Electrolux, Stockholm, 1981—, also bd. dirs.; bd. dirs. Lamco, Liberia, Telefinans, Stockholm, Cominvest, Stockholm. Co-author: Corporate Finance in Multinational Companies, 1986; contbr. articles on corp. fin. to profl. jours. Mem. Swedisn Fedn. of Fin. Analysts, Soc. of Internat. Treas. Clubs: Stockholms, Köpmansklubb. Office: AB Electrolux, Luxbacken 1, S 10545 Stockholm Sweden

EKSTROM, ROBERT CARL, musician, music educator, choral director; b. Duluth, Minn., Mar. 26, 1917; s. Hans Birger and Hilda Sophia (Nelson) E.; m. Charlotte Virginia Tuttle, Dec. 28, 1940; children: Robert, Virginia, Carol, Richard, Lorrie, Cheryl. Diploma, Duluth Jr. Coll., 1937; BS in Music Edn., U. Minn., 1940, MEd in Music Edn., 1946; EdD in Music Edn., U. So. Calif., 1959. Cert. tchr., Minn., Calif., Ill. Head vocal dept. Sherburn (Minn.) Bd. Edn., 1940-41; instr. music Duluth Pub. Schs., 1941-52, 54-64; prof. music Pasadena (Calif.) City Coll., 1952-54; head music dept. Lindblom Tech. High Sch., chgo., 1964—; dir. and soloist Chgo. Choral Soc., 1970—; mem., oratorio dir. Chgo. Swedish Choral and Symphony Orch., 1964-74; mem., dir. Am. Union Swedish Singers, 1958—; choir dir. and soloist various chs. Minn., Calif., Ill., 1941—; music dir. Calif. Bur. Music, Los Angeles, 1951-59, Mayor's Cultural Com., Chgo., 1972-79, State St. Council, Chgo., 1975-79, various musical groups, 1949—; tenor soloist and singer radio, television, stage, others; recorded with Capitol Records; sang at coronation festivities Coronation of Queen Elizabeth II, London, 1953, Luth. World Fedn. Conv., Helsinki, 1963; gave command performance for King of Sweden, Stockholm, 1976; performed in six concert tours of Europe in many countries including Eng., Scotland, France, Germany, Holland, Sweden, Norway, Denmark, Finland, Austria, Italy, Switzerland, Greece, Spain, 1953, 63, 68, 73, 76, 80; sang with choir in more than sixty engagements, Europe, 1963; performed in musicals, on radio, on TV, in motion pictures and in numerous personal appearances worldwide. Author: The Male Voice, 1945, Correlation of Music Talent With Intelligence, 1946, Development of the Madrigal, 1947, Comparison of the Male Voice, 1959, Boys Life in Minnesota, 1986. Recipient Singers medal of Merit, Am. Union Swedish Singers, 1974. Mem. Am. Choral Dirs. Assn., Music Educators Nat. Conf., Associated Male Choruses Am. (dir. upper midwest dist., pres. 1949-52). Club: Ill. Athletic (Chgo.). Lodge: Masons (music dir. 1969—, Meritorious Service award 1980). Home: 2321 W 110th Pl Chicago IL 60643 Office: Chgo Choral Soc 12 S Michigan Ave Chicago IL 60603

EKSTRUM, PATRICIA SHELDON STRAUSS, business executive; b. Greenville, Miss., Feb. 7, 1941; d. Anson Hoisington and Beatrice Everett Sheldon; student Miss. State Coll. for Women, 1958-59; B.A., U. Miss., 1962; m. Willard Louis Ekstrum, Jr., Dec. 17, 1983; 1 dau., Anne Michelle. With U. Miss. Med. Center, Jackson, 1965-75, grant coordinator, workshop coordinator, in-house instr., 1975; legal sec., office mgr. Parks & Moss, Houston, 1975-77; adminstrv. asst. 3D/ Internat., Houston, 1977-79, spl. facilities coordinator, 1979-81, assoc. 1980-85, sr. assoc., 1985—; exec. asst., 1981—. Pres., bd. trustees Jackson Ballet Guild; co-founder, trustee Jackson Ballet Guild Sch., 1973-75; mem. Jackson Civic Arts Council, 1971-73; auction co-chmn. Jackson Symphony League, 1967-75; bd. dirs. Internat. Inst. of Edn., 1987—. Mem. Exec. Women Internat. Republican. Episcopalian. Club: Univ. (Houston).

EKVALL, BERNT, dentist; b. Nora, Sweden, June 25, 1915; s. Johan Alexis and Elin Karolina (Persson) E.; L.D.S., U. Stockholm, 1944; D.D.S., U. Mich., 1951; m. Margit Andersson, June 23, 1940 (div. 1982); 1 dau., Lucie Margita. Came to U.S., 1949, naturalized, 1954. With Swedish Govt. Dental Services, 1943-45; pvt. practice dentistry Sweden, 1945-49, Clinton, Mich., 1951-52, Dearborn, 1952-55, 57-58, Detroit, 1958-81, 87—, St. Clair, Mich., 1981-87; v.p. Scandinavian Am. Republican Club, 1960-68, pres., 1968-72; treas. Rep. State Nationalities Council, 1971-73; Bd. dirs. Scandinavian Symphony Soc., 1961-72; bd. mgrs. Hannan br. YMCA, 1962—, chmn. Eastside br., 1976. Served to capt. AUS, 1955-57. Fellow Royal Soc. Health, Acad. Dentistry Internat., Acad. Gen. Dentistry, Internat. Coll. Dentists, Am. Coll. Dentists; mem. Am., Mich. Dental Assns., Detroit Dist. Dental Soc., Detroit Dental Clinic Club (membership sec. 1972-73, sec. 1973-74, pres. 1975-76), Bunting Periodontal Study Club, Mich. Acad. Gen. Dentistry (sec. 1975-76, v.p. 1976-78, pres. 1978-80). Clubs: Prismatic Renaissance (Detroit); Grosse Pointe Hunt. Home: 1063 Woodbridge E Saint Clair Shores MI 48080 Office: 11110 Morang Detroit MI 48224

ELAMIN, ABDELATIF, ambassador; b. Khartoum, Sudan, May 30, 1951; s. Abdelatif Elamin Elamin and Fatima Medani; children: Housam, Sami. BC in Agriculture, Cairo U., 1957; student, London Sch. of Econs., 1963-64. Various govt. positions Sudan Govt., 1960-76; ambassador to Nigeria Sudan Govt., Ghana, Camaroon, 1977-78; ambassador to Sweden, Denmark, Norway, Finland Sudan Govt., 1978-83; mem. Council of Ministers in Charte of Manpower Devel., 1984; dir. gen. for polit. affairs Ministry of Fgn. Affairs; ambassador to Egypt Cairo, 1985—. Pres. Sudanese Diplomatic Assn., Khartoum, Sudan, 1975-77. Office: Embassy Dem Republic of Sudan, 4 Sharia El Ibrahim, Cairo Egypt

ELBAZ, JEAN SAUVEUR, plastic and aesthetic surgeon; b. Constantine, Algeria, July 28, 1933; s. Jonathan and Suzanne (Kalifa) E.; m. Beatrice Silvestre de Sacy, June 15, 1970; 1 child, Sophie. M.D., Med. Sch. Paris, 1963. Intern, Hosp. of Paris, 1956-60, resident, 1962-65; practice medicine, specializing in plastic and aesthetic surgery, Paris, 1963—; staff various hosps., Paris, 1963-78; asst. anatomy U. Paris, 1960-62; expert for Ct. of Paris, 1975—; prof. plastic and aesthetic surgery U. Paris, 1970. Author: Plastic Surgery of the Abdomen, 1979; Chirurgie Plastique de l'Abdomen, 1977; Mammary Prosthesis, 1982; Face Lifting, 1983. Served to maj. French Army, 1960-62. Recipient Internat. Prize award Plastic and Aesthetic Surgery Soc. Mexico, 1977. Mem. French Soc. Plastic and Aesthetic Surgery (dir.), French Coll. Plastic and Aesthetic Surgery (gen. sec.), Internat. Confedn. Plastic and Reconstructive Surgery, Internat. Soc. Aesthetic Plastic Surgery. Jewish. Club: Club 33 av Foch. Home and Office: 144 rue de Courcelles, 75017 Paris France

ELBERSON, ROBERT EVANS, food industry executive; b. Winston-Salem, N.C., Nov. 9, 1928; children: Nancy Ann, Charles Evans II. Grad., Choate Sch., 1946; B.S. in Engring, Princeton U., 1950; M.B.A., Harvard U., 1952. Mgmt. trainee Hanes Hosiery Mills Co., Winston-Salem, 1954-56; office mgr. Hanes Hosiery Mills Co., 1956-62, sec., 1959-62, v.p. mfg., 1962-65, mem. exec. com., dir., 1963-65; v.p. planning Hanes Corp. Hanes Hosiery Mills Co. (merger Hanes Hosiery Mills Co. and P.H. Hanes Knitting Co.), 1965-68, pres. hosiery div., v.p. corp., 1968-72, pres., chief exec. officer, 1972-79, dir., 1972-79; dir. Sara Lee Corp. (formerly Consol. Foods Corp.), 1979—, exec. v.p., 1979-82, vice chmn., 1982-83, pres., chief operating officer, 1983-86, vice chmn., 1986—; dir. W.W. Grainger Co., Skokie, Ill., Chgo., Sonoco Products Co., Hartsville, S.C. Bd. visitors Babcock Grad. Sch. Mgmt., Wake Forest U., 1977-83; trustee Salem Acad. and Coll., Winston-Salem, 1980—, Mus. Sci. and Industry, Chgo., 1984—. Served as lt. USAF, 1952-54. Office: Sara Lee Corp 3 First National Plaza Chicago IL 60602

ELBING, ALVAR OLIVER, educator, administrator, management consultant; b. Mpls., Sept. 24, 1928; s. Alvar O. and Martha A. (Malmquist) E.; m. Carol R. Jeppson, Aug. 3, 1950; children—Kristofer Erik, John Rolf. B.A., U. Minn., 1950; B.S., U. Calif.-Berkeley, 1956, M.S., Calif. State U.-Sacramento, 1959; Ph.D., U. Wash., 1962. Instr. human relations U. Wash., Seattle, 1959-62; prof. mgmt. Dartmouth Coll., Hanover, N.H., 1962-67; prof. mgmt. SUNY-Albany, 1967-72; prof. IMEDE, Lausanne, Switzerland, 1970-77; dir. Exec. and Environ. Ctr., Lousanne, Switzerland, 1977—; prof., dir. Inst. for Exec. Edn., Wake Forest U., Winston-Salem, N.C., 1983-85; vis. prof. U. Lausanne, 1972-78; cons. world-wide. Author: (with Carol Elbing) The Value Issue of Business, 1967; Behavioral Decisions in Organizations, 1970, 78; contbr. articles to profl. publs. Served to 1st lt. USAF, 1951-53; Fellow Ford Found., 1961-62; faculty research grantee Ford Found., Sloan Found., 1962-66. Mem. Am. Psychol. Assn., Am. Econ. Assn., European Found. for Mgmt. Devel.; Soc. for Psychol. Study Social Issues, Swiss-Am. C. of C., Beta Gamma Sigma. Home: rue de la Madeleine 16, 1003 Lausanne Switzerland Address: Granada Del Mar Christiansted Saint Croix VI 00820

ELBING, CAROL JEPPSON, business educator, administrator; b. West Ellis, Wis., Mar. 15, 1930; d. Ralph and Claire (Fredell) Jeppson.; m. Alvar O. Elbing, Aug. 3, 1950; children—Kristofer Erik, John Rolf. B.A., U. Minn., 1951; M.A., Calif. State U.-Sacramento, 1958; Ph.D., U. Wash., 1970. Instr. communication Am. River Coll., Sacramento, 1958-59, U. Wash., Seattle, 1959-62; lectr. Dartmouth Coll., Hanover, N.Y., 1962-66; research fellow, cons. IMEDE, Lausanne, Switzerland, 1970-77; co-dir. Exec. and Environ. Ctr., Lausanne, Switzerland, 1977—; assoc. prof. Sch. Bus. and Accountancy, Wake Forest U., Winston-Salem, N.C., 1982-85. Co-author: The Value Issue of Business, 1967. Mem. Phi Beta Kappa. Home and Office: rue de la Madeleine 16, 1003 Lausanne Switzerland also: Granada Del Mar Christiansted Saint Croix VI 00820

EL-CASSABGUI, MOURAD (GEORGE) MOURAD, business executive; b. Cairo, Nov. 1, 1928; s. Mourad Salib and Alexandra Rafoul (Khouri) El-C.; m. Amal Nessib Wehaiba, July 3, 1954 (div. Oct. 1958); children—Patricia, Mourad; m. Andree Meguid Wehaiba, Dec. 6, 1958; 1 child, Ashraf. Degree in Econs. and Bus., Am. U. in Cairo, 1970. Exec. asst. Mobil Oil Co., Cairo, 1949-55; area mgr. Kadry Mahmoud & Co., Suez, Egypt, 1955-59; mgr. logistics Gen. Desert Devel. Authority, Cairo, 1959-62; dir. personnel Am. U., Cairo, 1962-66, dir. housing and travel, 1966-68; pres., mng. dir. Mina Supplies Co., Cairo, 1968—; pres. Flame Enterprises, Athens, Tex., 1981—; pres. Cassabgui Oil Co., Seguin, Tex., 1982—; pres., mng. dir. Mina Oilfield Services Co., Cairo, 1983—. Mem. Egyptian Democratic Party. Roman Catholic. Avocations: philately, travel, yachting,Egyptian Arabian horse breeding. Home: 39 Ahmed Heshmat St, Zamalek, Cairo Egypt Office: Mina Oilfield Supplies & Services 18B, 26 July St, Cairo Egypt

ELCHARDUS, MARK, sociologist; b. Sint-Truiden, Belgium, Nov. 28, 1946; s. Gaston Elchardus and Maria Mathijs; children: David, Thomas. Licence, Vrije U., Brussels, 1971; PhD, Brown U., 1978. Research asst. Brown U., Providence, 1971-76; researcher Ministry Health and Family, Belgium, 1976-80; lectr. Vrije U., Brussels, 1978-82, prof. sociology, 1982—. Author various books on ednl. achievement and occupational ranking, 1979-82; contbr. articles to profl. jours. Mem. Vlaamse Vereniging Voor Sociologie, Am. Sociol. Assn., Internat. Sociol. Assn. Office: Vrije Univ, Pleinlaan 2, 1050 Brussels Belgium

EL DIB, MOUFID KAMAL, lawyer; b. Cairo, Nov. 15, 1929; s. Mohamed Kamal and Zinat (El Sayed) El D.; m. Hoda Abdel Hadi, Sept. 8, 1957; children: Hisham Moufid, Amr Moufid. BL, U. Cairo, 1952. Bar: high supreme court, court of cassation. Sr. ptnr. Yansouni, El Dib and Ptnrs., Alexandria, Cairo, Suez, Port Said, Egypt, 1952—; advisor various banks and oil cos. Hon. consul Chilean and Belgian Consulates, Alexandria. Mem. Egyptian Bar Assn., Internat. Bar Assn., Internat. Law Assn., Assn. Internat. Pour la Protection de Propriete Indsl., US Trademark Assn., Stanford Research Inst., Asia-Pacific Lawyers Assn., Egyptian Maritime Soc., Soc. Egyptianne d'Economie Politique de Statistique et de Legislation, Law of Sea Inst., Egyptian Am. Friendship Assn., Egyptian-Japanese Friendship Assn. Club: Les Ambassador, Alexandria Sporting, Shooting, Heliopolis, El Shams, Automobile, Sakara Country, Egyptian Maritime, El Gezierah. Home: 32 Lumumba St, Alexandria Egypt Office: Yansouni, El Dib & Bartners, 32 Blvd Saad Zaghloul, Alexandria Egypt

ELDRED, KENNETH MCKECHNIE, acoustical consultant; b. Springfield, Mass., Nov. 25, 1929; s. Robert Moseley and Jean McKechnie (Ashton) E.; m. Helene Barbara Koerting Fischer, May 31, 1957; 1 dau., Heidi Jean. B.S., MIT, 1950, postgrad., 1951-53; postgrad., UCLA, 1960-63. Engr. in charge vibration and sound lab. Boston Naval Shipyard, 1951-54; supervisory physicist, chief phys. acoustics sect. U.S. Air Force, Wright Field, Ohio, 1956-57; v.p., cons. acoustics Western Electro-Acoustics Labs., Los Angeles, 1957-63; v.p., tech. dir. sci. services and systems group Wyle Labs., El Segundo, Calif., 1963-73; v.p., dir. div. environ. and noise control tech. Bolt Beranek and Newman Inc., Cambridge, Mass., 1973-77; prin. cons. Bolt Beranek and Newman Am. Inc., 1977-81; dir. Ken Eldred Engring.; mem. exec. standards council Am. Nat. Standards Inst., 1979—, vice-chmn., 1981-83, chmn., 1985-87, bd. dirs., 1983-87; mem., past chmn. Acoustical Standards Bd.; mem. com. hearing, bioacoustics and biomechanics NRC, 1963—. Served with USAF, 1954-56. Fellow Acoustical Soc. Am. (standards dir. 1987—, past chmn. coordinating com. environ. acoustics); mem. Nat. Acad. Engring., Inst. Noise Control Engring. (pres. 1976, bd. dirs. 1987—), Soc. Automotive Engrs., Soc. Naval Architects and Marine Engrs., U.S. Yacht Racing Union. Club: Down East Yacht. Home: 722 Annursnac Hill Rd Concord MA 01742 Office: PO Box 1037 Concord MA 01742

ELDREDGE, WILLIAM AUGUSTUS, JR., lawyer; b. Memphis, July 21, 1925; s. William Augustus and Lucile (Crews) E.; m. Lee Campbell, Aug. 4, 1951; children: Michael Charles, Elizabeth Lee, William Augustus III. LL.B., U. Ark., 1949, J.D., 1969. Bar: Ark. 1949. Practiced in Little Rock, 1949—; ptnr. and counsel Friday, Eldredge & Clark (and predecessor firm), 1953—; vol. instr. legal medicine U. Ark. Sch. Medicine, 1954—; clin. prof. med. jurisprudence U. Ark., 1976—; asst. gen. atty. Union Pacific R.R. for state of Ark. Chmn. city and county campaign March of Dimes, 1959-61; chmn. Pulaski County chpt. Nat. Found., 1961-62. Served with USNR, 1944-46; 1st lt. JAG Corps U.S. Army, 1951-53. Recipient Little Rock Kappa Sigma Disting. Alumni award, 1965; U. Ark. Coll. Medicine Disting. Service award, 1978. Fellow Ark. Bar Found. (patron); mem. Am. Coll. Trial Lawyers, ABA, Ark. Bar Assn., Pulaski County Bar Assn. (past pres.), Fedn. Ins. Counsel, Def. Research Inst., Blue Key, Kappa Sigma, Delta Theta Phi. Methodist. Home: 6608 Granada St Little Rock AR 72205 Office: Friday Eldredge & Clark 2000 First Commercial Bldg Little Rock AR 72201

ELEN, BERNARD LOUIS JEAN, pharmaceutical company executive; b. Montegnee, Liege, Belgium, Nov. 6, 1935; s. Jean-Pierre and Marie Elisabeth (Vaes) E.; m. Simone Marie Smeets, July 9, 1960; 1 son, Alain Bernard. Student humanities, St-Barthelemy Coll., 1948-54, Catholic U. of Louvain, Belgium, 1954-58; grad. advt. and mktg. Comml. Sch. Liege, 1971; grad. bus. and fin. adminstrn. Comml. Chamber of Brussels, 1976; postgrad. in mgmt. Catholic U. of Louvain, 1978; M in Mgmt., Solvay Inst., Brussels U., 1987. Pharmaceutical detailman Parke, Davis and Cy., Belgium, 1960-64; pharm. detailman Pfizer, Belgium, 1964-66; hosp. detailman Bristol-Myers, Belgium, 1966-71; field sales mgr. Schering-Plough, Belgium, 1971-72; mktg. and sales mgr. Mead Johnson, Belgium, 1972-85; mktg. research mgr., Bristol-Myers, Belgium, 1986—; adminstr. Fichier Medical-AGIM, Brussels, 1976—; pres. security com. Mead Johnson, Brussels, 1979—. Creator advt. campaigns; Union des Professionnels de la Publicite, 1970 (Price award); Association des Chefs de Publicite de Belgique, 1971 (Price award). Served to 1st sgt. Royal Belgium Health Service, 1959-60, Ghent. Decorated Militaire 2eme class, 1968. Mem. N.Y. Acad. Scis. Home: Chaussee de Louvain 143, 1410 Waterloo Belgium Office: Bristol Benelux SA and, Mead Johnson Benelux SA, Chaussee del la Hulpe 185, 1170 Brussels Belgium

ELEQUIN, CLETO, JR., physician; b. Antique, Philippines, Oct. 18, 1933; s. Cleto and Enriqueta (Tengonciang) E.; M.D., Far Eastern U. (Philippines), 1957; m. Nancy Johnson, May 14, 1958; children—Tracy, Thomas Kyle, Stuart Scott. Rotating intern Good Samaritan Hosp., Lexington, Ky., 1957-58; gen. practice resident Central Bapt. Hosp., Lexington, 1958-59; psychiat. resident State Hosp., Danville, Pa., 1959-60, 61-62; psychiat. resident with child psychiatry State Hosp., New Castle, Del., 1962-63; staff physician Eastern State Hosp., Lexington, 1960-61, dir. Fayette County Project, dir. intensive treatment service, 1964-67, supt., 1969-71; dep. commr. Dept. Mental Health, State Ky., 1967-69; practice medicine, specializing in family practice, Pecos, Tex., 1971-72, Austin, Tex., 1974—; asst. dep. commr. Tex. Dept. Mental Health and Mental Retardation, Austin, 1973-74, dep. commr. mental health, 1974; attending psychiatrist U. Ky. Med. Center, 1964-71, Good Samaritan Hosp., 1969-71, Central Bapt. Hosp., 1966-71; cons. psychiatrist U. Ky. Student Health Service, 1965-71, Peace Corps, 1966-68, Bur. Rehab., State Ky., 1965-71, Blue Grass Community Care Center, 1967-71, Covington (Ky.) Community Care Center, 1969-71, Hazard Community Care Center, 1969-71, Danville (Ky.) Community Care Center, 1969-71, Maysville (Ky.) Community Care Center, 1969-71; clin. instr., asst. clin. prof. dept. psychiatry U. Ky. Med. Center, 1964-69, asso. clin. prof., 1969-71. Mem. Profl. Adv. Council Community Mental Health-Retardation Center, Lexington, 1967-71; mem. Lexington Hosp. Council, 1969-71. Mem. AMA, Am. Psychiat. Assn., Tex. Med. Assn., Travis County Med. Soc., Austin Psychiat. Soc., Assn. Med. Supts. Mental Hosps., Am. Acad. Family Physicians. Home: PO Box 1198 Buda TX 78610 Office: 942 Peyton Gin Rd Austin TX 78758

ELETA, GRACIELA QUELQUEJEU DE, civic worker; b. Panama, Republic of Panama, Oct. 8, 1939; d. Camilo and Isabel Constancia (Muller) Quelquejeu; m. Fernando Eleta A., Jan. 31, 1960; children—Graciela Del Carmen, Yolanda, Ximena Isabel, Diego. B.A., Rosemont Coll., 1969; diploma for teaching French in fgn. countries Inst. Francais Moderne, U. Fribourg, Switzerland, 1958. Sec. Nat. Assn. Concerts, Panama City, 1973—; pres., founder fin. com. Bolivar Home for Elders, Panama City, 1975, 76; pres. Panamanian Art Inst., Panama City, 1976, 77; fund raiser, v.p. Mus. Contemporary Art, Panama City, 1984, 85; mem. adv. bd. Panama Internat. Sch., Panama City, 1982—. Decorated Vasco Nunez de Balboa, Ministry Fgn. Affairs, Republic of Panama, 1983. Roman Catholic. Club: Panama Garden (pres. 1972), Hacia La Luz. Union (Panama City). Avocations: art collecting, tennis, race-horse breeding, horse-back riding, skiing. Home: PO Box 1795, Panama 1, Republic of Panama

EL-FAYOUMY, SAAD G. A., economist, banker, accountant, consultant; b. Cairo, Egypt, June 10, 1926; came to U.S., 1962, naturalized, 1973; s. Guirguis Awad El-Fayoumy and Labiba Youssef Boustarous (El-Sissi) El-F.; m. Joanne Patricia (Quinn), Sept. 8, 1963. B.A., Cairo U., 1949, M.A., 1960; Ph.D., NYU, 1972. Cert. acct., Egypt; C.P.A., Va. Chief insp., mgr., chief auditor, chief acct. Banque Misr, Egypt, 1949-61; under sec. econ. planning President's Council for Econ. Planning, Cairo, 1962; economist Egyptian interest section UN, N.Y.C., 1962-67; cons. to World Bank, Agrl. Bank of Sudan, Khartoum, Sudan, 1982-84; cons. U.S. AID; cons., vis. prof. Faculty Econs. Adminstrv. Scis. U. Jordan; prof. Norfolk State U., Va., 1967—; dir. Banking Edn. Ctr., Norfolk State U., 1974—; dir., vice-chmn. Hirschfeld Bank of Commerce, Virginia Beach, Va., 1976-78. Author: New Accounting Systems, 1984; New Budgeting Systems, 1984; Agriculture and Commercial Banking Techniques, 1984; contbr. articles to nat. and internat. jours. Founder-pres. Arab-Am. Assn. Va., Hampton Roads, Va., 1970; bd. dirs. World Affairs Council, Norfolk, 1970—; chmn. Faculty Benefits Commn., Faculty Senate of Va., 1969-81. Recipient Founders Day award, NYU, 1973. Fellow Va. Soc. C.P.A.s, mem. Am. Econ. Assn., Atlantic Econ. Soc., Am. Fin. Assn. Mem. Coptic Orthodox of Alexandria. Republican. Home: 652 Greentree Dr Virginia Beach VA 23452 Office: 650 Greentree Dr Virginia Beach VA 23452

EL GABALY, SHERIF-MOSTAFA, chemical company executive; b. Alexandria, Egypt, Feb. 15, 1949; s. Mostafa El Gabaly and Nabila (Hassan) Bassouny; m. Nevine Abdel Moneim Seif, Sept. 1977; children: Mostafa, Naela. BS in Chem. Engring., Cairo U., 1970; PhD in Chem. Engring., Higher Inst. of Chemical Tech., Sofia, Bulgaria, 1976. Research engr. Indsl. Orgn. of Arab League States, Cairo, 1976-77; petrochem. engr. Qatar Gen. Petroleum Corp., Doha, Qatar, 1977-80; gen. mgr. NE Africa dist. The Dow Chem. Co., Cairo, 1980—; bd. dirs. Internat. Fertilizer and Chem. Co., Egypt; chmn. Agrl. Com. of Am. Egyptian C. of C., 1985-87; mem. Industry and Energy Com., Egypt, 1986—. Mem. Am. C. of C. (bd. dirs. 1987). Home: 33 Mohamed Mazhar St, Zamalek, Cairo Egypt Office: Dow Chem Europe SA, 3 Abul Feda St Zamalek, PO Box 189, Cairo Egypt

EL-GARAWANI, IBRAHIM SAYED, cement manufacturing company executive; b. Tanta, Egypt, Nov. 22, 1950; s. El-Sayed El-Garawani and Zeinab Abu Chawarb; m. Hayat Ali Sultan, Mar. 2, 1980; children: Shaymā a, Karim, Maryam, Yahiya. B of commerce, Ain Shams U., 1975. Br. mgr. Hassan Sons & Co., Suez, Egypt, 1975-76; fin. controller Ministry Fin., Cairo, 1976-78; mgmt. acct. Sante Fe Internat. Services Inc. div. Aramco, Abqaiq, Saudi Arabia, 1978-83; fin. mgr. Saudi Kuwaiti Cement Mfg. Co., Dammam, Saudi Arabia, 1983; freelance mgmt. cons. Mem. Egyptian Syndicate Comml. Professions. Islam. Home: 33 Azab St, Kolali, Cairo Egypt Office: Saudi Kuwaiti Cement Mfg Co, P O Box 4536, Dammam 31412, Saudi Arabia

ELGER, WILLIAM ROBERT, JR., accountant; b. Chgo., Mar. 20, 1950; s. William Robert and Grace G. (LaVaque) E.; m. Kathryn Michele Johnson, July 10, 1971; children: Kimberly, William, Kristin, Joseph. AS in Applied Sci., Coll. of DuPage, Glen Ellyn, Ill., 1970; BS magna cum laude, U. Ill.-Chgo., 1972. CPA, Ill. Staff acct. Ernst & Whinney, Chgo., 1973, in-charge acct., 1973-74, sr. acct., 1974-78, mgr., 1978-82, sr. mgr., 1982-88; chief fin. officer U. Ill. Eye and Ear Infirmary, 1988—; presenter various confs. in field Ernst & Whinney, Chgo., 1980-88. Author, developer: (tng. course) Auditing Third Party Reimbursement, 1986, 87. Mem. Union League Civic and Arts Found., Chgo., 1982—, Union League Found. for Boy's and Girl's Clubs, Chgo., 1982—; treas. Newport Assn., Carol Stream, Ill., 1982-83; coach Tri-City Soccer Assn., St. Charles, Ill., 1984, 87. Mem. Healthcare Fin. Mgmt. Assn. (acctg. and reimbursement com. 1982-87, chpt. task force com. 1986, 87, auditing com. 1986, 87, Spl. Recognition award 1986), Ill. Soc. CPA's (mem. long-term healthcare com. 1983, hosps. com. 1988—),

Am. Inst. CPA's, Chgo. Health Execs. Forum. Methodist. Club: Union League (Chgo.). Home: 1505 Madison Ave Saint Charles IL 60174 Office: U Ill Eye & Ear Infirmary 1855 W Taylor Chicago IL 60612

ELGIZ, TURGUT CAN, construction company executive; b. Genova, Italy, Apr. 18, 1950; s. Bahattin and Muzdan (Kulaksizoglu) E.; m. Sevda Coklar, Aug. 26, 1977. Diploma in Engring. and Architecture, Tech. U. Istanbul, Turkey, 1973, PhD, 1978. Architect H. Bremi, Winterthur, Switzerland, 1969-70; assoc. prof. Tech. U. Istanbul, 1973—; architect, exec. dir. Elgiz Cons. Co., Istanbul, 1973-80, Giz Project and Constrn., Inc., Istanbul, 1980—. Author: Industrialization in School Buildings in Turkey, 1977. Mem. Turkey Chamber of Architects. Moslem. Lodge: Rotary. Home: Kalipci Sok Haznedar, Apt #156-10, Tesvikiye, Istanbul Turkey Office: Giz Project and Constrn Inc, Fur-Giz Bldg 80260, Kocamansur 115-21 Sisli, Istanbul Turkey

EL-HAGE, NABIL NAZIH, venture capitalist; b. Zhgarta, Lebanon, Sept. 2, 1958; came to U.S., 1975; s. Nazih Khalil and Odette Toufic (Melhem) El-H. BEE, Yale U., 1980; MBA with high distinction, Harvard U., 1984. Registered profl. engr. Mgmt. cons. McKinsey & Co., N.Y. and Brussels, 1980-82; fin. instr. Harvard U., Boston, 1984-85; venture investor TA Assocs., Boston, 1985—; bd. dirs. Intellicall, Inc., Dallas. Baker scholar Harvard U., 1984. Fellow Yale Sci. and Engring., Tau Beta Pi (treas. 1979-80). Mem. Maronite Christian Ch. Club: Yale of N.Y.C. Home: 153 North Ave Weston MA 02193 Office: Westwood Group Inc 855 Boylston St Boston MA 02116

EL HUSSEINI, AKRAM FEISSAL, corporate executive; b. Jerusalem, Sept. 29, 1947; arrived in Saudi Arabia, 1983; s. Feissal Hashim and Obeida El Husseini; m. Rola Saiham, Dec. 28, 1979; children: Fawaz, Adi. B in Commerce, Al Azhar U., Cairo, 1970. Auditor Saba and Co., Kuwait, 1970-72; sr. auditor Talal Abu-Ghazalem and Co., Kuwait, 1972-74; mgr. Manama, Bahrain, 1974-78; ptnr. Tunis, 1978-79; exec. ptnr. Manama, 1980-83, Jeddah, Saudi Arabia, 1983—. Mem. Arab Soc. Cert. Accts. Office: Talal Abu-Ghazaleh and Co, PO Box 2415, Jeddah 21451, Saudi Arabia

ELIA, MICHELE, mathematics educator; b. Berzano, Asti-Piemonte, Italy, Jan. 2, 1945; s. Luigi and Cristina (Fogliatti) E. Dr. engr., Politecnico di Torino, 1970. Researcher FIAT, Torino, Italy, 1970-71, Politecnico di Torino, 1971-77, assoc. prof. math., 1977—. Author: (with others) The Information Theory Approach to Communications, 1977. Contbr. articles to profl. jours. Mem. Unione Matematica Italiana, Am. Math. Soc., Math. Assn. Am., Soc. Indsl. and Applied Math., IEEE (sr.). Roman Catholic. Home: Via G Marconi 3, Castiglione Torinese, 10090 Torino Italy Office: Dipartimento di Elettronica-Politecnico, di Torino Corso Duca degli, Abruzzi 24, 10129 Torino Italy

ELIAHU, MORDECHAI, rabbi; b. Jerusalem, Israel, 1928; s. Ha Rau Salman Shlama E.; m. Shlita Azrani; 4 children. Ordained rabbi, 1951. Former judge, religious ct. of Beersheba, Israel; then Jerusalem regional judge, 1971-83; now judge Rabbinical High Sch., Jerusalem; also Sephardi Chief Rabbi of Israel, 1983—. Served with Israeli army. Office: Chief Rabbinate, Sephardic Community, Jerusalem Israel *

ELIAS, TASLIM OLAWALE, judge International Court of Justice; b. Nov. 11, 1914; ed. Igbobi Coll., Lagos, Nigeria; B.A., U. London; LL.B., LL.M., Univ. Coll., London; Ph.D.; postgrad. Inst. Advanced Legal Studies, London; LL.D., U. London, Dakar; Yarborough Anderson scholar Inner Temple, London, 1946-49; D.Litt., U. Ibadan, U. Lagos, U. Nsukka; LL.D., U. Ahmadu Bello U., Ile-Ife, Howard U., univs. Jodhpur, 1976, Hull, 1980, Dalhousie, 1983, Nairobi, 1983, Manchester, 1984, Buckingham, 1986; D.Sc. (Econ.), London, Lagos State U., Nigeria, 1987, U. Jos., Nigeria, 1987. Called to bar, 1947; created Queen's counsel, 1961; UNESCO fellow, Africa, 1951; Simon research fellow U. Manchester (Eng.), 1951-53; Oppenheim research fellow Inst. Commonwealth Studies, Nuffield Coll. and Queen Elizabeth House, Oxford, Eng., 1954-60; vis. prof. polit. sci. Delhi (India) U., 1956; mem. del. Nigerian Constl. Conf., London, 1958; fed. atty.-gen., also minister justice Nigeria, 1960-66, atty.-gen., 1966-72, commr. for justice, 1967-72; prof. law, dean faculty law U. Lagos, 1966-72; chief justice of Nigeria, 1972-75; judge, v.p. Internat. Ct. Justice, The Hague, Netherlands, pres., 1981-85. Mem. Internat. Law Commn., UN, 1961-75, chmn. com. constl. experts to draft Congo Const. 1961-62; mem. governing council U. Nigeria, 1959-66; gov. Sch. Oriental and African Studies, London U., 1957-60; mem. Council Legal Edn., 1962-72, chmn., 1973; chmn. Adv. Jud. Com., 1972-75, Internat. Law Commn. UN, 1970, Drafting Com. Protocol, Mediation, Conciliation and Arbitration, 1964, UN Conf. Law of Treaties, 1968-69, 13th Session Asian-African Legal Consultative Com., 1972; exec. Council Internat. Commn. Jurists, 1975—. Decorated comdr. Fed. Republic of Nigeria, 1963; recipient Nat. Merit award Fed. Republic of Nigeria, 1979. Fellow Delian Inst. Internat. Relations; mem. Nigerian Inst. Internat. Affairs (chmn.), Am. Soc. Internat. Law (hon.), Inst. Internat. Law (titular), Hague Acad. Internat. Law, Nigerian Soc. Internat. Law (pres. 1968—), Soc. Inner Temple (bencher), Curatorium Hague Acad. Internat. Law., World Assn. Internat. Relations., African Soc. Internat. and Comparative Law., African Assn. Internat. Law, Permanent Ct. Arbitration, Am. Acad. Arts and Scis., Internat. Acad. Comparative (assoc.), Soc Pub. Tchrs. Law, Am. Soc. Interan. Law. Author: Nigerian Land Law and Custom, 1951; Nigerian Legal System, 1954; Ghana and Sierra Leone: Development of their Laws and Constitutions, 1962; British Colonial Law: A Comparative Study, 1962; Government and Politics in Africa, 2d edit., 1963; Nature of African Customary Law, 2d edit., 1962; Nigeria: Development of its Laws and Constitution, 1965; Africa and Development of International Law, 1972; Modern Law of Treaties, 1974; New Horizons in International Law, 1979; The International Court of Justice and Some Contemporary Problems, 1983. Co-author: British Legal Papers, 1958; International Law in a Changing World, 1963; Sovereignty Within the Law, 1965; African Law: Adaptation and Development, 1965; Law, Justice and Equity, 1967; Nigerian Prison System, 1968; Nigerian Press Law, 1969; editor Nigerian Law Jour., 1968-73. Address: 20 Ozumba Mbadiwe St, Victoria Island, Lagos Nigeria also: Internat Ct of Justice, Peace Palace, 2517 KJ Hague The Netherlands

ELIASSON, JAN K., ambassador; b. Goteberg, Sweden, Sept. 17, 1940; s. John H. and Karin (Nilsson) E.; m. Kerstin E. Englesson; children: Anna, Emilie, Johan. Grad., Swedish Naval Acad., Stockholm, 1962; MA, Sch. of Econs., Goteborg, 1965. Attaché Ministry of Fgn. Affairs, Stockholm, 1965-67, head of section, 1974-77, dir., 1977-80, dep. undersec., 1980-82, undersec. for polit. affairs, 1983-87; 2d sec. Embassy of Sweden, Bonn, Fed. Republic of Germany, 1967-70; 1st sec. Embassy of Sweden, Washington, 1970-74; advisor Prime Minister's office, Stockholm, 1982-83; ambassador, permanent rep. to UN, N.Y.C., 1988—. Served to comdr. Swedish Mil. Reserves. Lutheran. Home: 117 E 64th St New York NY 10021 Office: Swedish Mission to UN 825 Third Ave New York NY 10022

ELIASSON, LEIF STURE RUDOLF, construction and building material company executive; b. Malmo, Sweden, May 29, 1939; s. Rudolf and Sonja (Nilsson) E.; m. Eva C. Kullgren, July 25, 1964; children—Johan L., Eva Stina S.B. M.C.E., Chalmers U., Gothenburg, 1963; M.B.A., Gothenburg Bus. U., 1964. Vice-pres. SV. Leca, Sweden, 1965-70; chief exec. officer Bird Cos. Internat., Denmark, Germany, Sweden and U.S.A., 1970—; pres. ECK Granit KB, Italy, Portugal, Saudi Arabia, Sweden, U.S.A., 1976—; chmn. Ljungmans Vaerksteder, Denmark, 1988—. Contbr. articles to profl. jours.; patentee in field. Rotary scholar, 1967. Mem. Swedish Civil Engring. Orgn. (del. 1964—, bd. dirs. 1967-70, chmn. 1971-72), Swedish Assn. Grad. Engrs. (del. 1963—); bd. mem. bus. orgns. and athletic clubs. Office: Bird Sweden AB, 52A Regementsgatan, 21748 Malmo Sweden

ELINDER, ULF CHRISTIAN, civil engineer; b. Karlstad, Varmland, Sweden, Aug. 21, 1940; s. Frans Elof and Ragnhild (Jonsson) E. Civil Engring. degree, KTH, Stockholm, 1968. Tchr. Gymnasium, Karlstad, Sweden, 1970-71; civil engr. Varml. Mus., Karlstad, 1975-78; researcher, Karlstad, 1977—. Club: Mensa. Author: The Dimensions of the Universe, 1980.

ELION, HERBERT A., optoelectronics company executive, physicist; b. N.Y.C., Oct. 16, 1923; s. Robert and Bertha (Kahn) E.; B.S. in Mech. Engring., CCNY, 1945; M.S., Bklyn. Poly. Inst., 1949, grad. in physics, 1954; PhD (hon) Hamilton State U., 1973. Registered profl. engr., Mass.; Pa., N.Y. Group leader RCA, Camden, N.J., 1957-59; pres. Elion Instruments, Inc., Burlington, N.J., 1959-64; assoc. dir. space sci. GCA Corp., Bedford, Mass., 1965-67; mng. dir. electro-optics Arthur D. Little Inc., Cambridge, Mass., 1967-79; pres., chief exec. officer Internat. Communications and Energy, Inc., Framingham, Mass., 1979—; pres. Aetna Telecommunications Cons., Centerville, Mass., 1981-85, also ptnr., Hartford, Conn.; pres., chief exec. officer Internat. Optical Telecommunications, Larkspur, Calif., 1981—; co-founder Kristallchemie M & Elion GmbH, Meudt, Fed. Republic Germany, 1961-64; cons. on data communications Exec. Office of Pres., Washington, 1978-79; cons. Ministry Internat. Trade and Industry, Tokyo, 1975-84; chmn. internat. conf. European Electro-optics Conf., Heeze, The Netherlands, 1972-78; internat. lectr. in field. Author, editor 27 books, including 11 on lightwave info. networks. Several Japanese and internat. world records in geothermal energy devel. Contbr. articles to profl. jours. Patentee in field. Pres. Elion Found., Princeton, N.J., 1960-67; founder Rainbow's End Camp, Ashby, Mass., 1960; elder Unitarian Ch., Princeton, 1963-64. Served with USN, 1944-46. Decorated Chevalier du Tastevin (France); recipient Presdl. awards Arthur D. Little Inc. Fellow Am. Phys. Soc.; mem. IEEE (sr.), Am. Phys. Soc., Optical Soc. Am., Soc. Photo Instrumentation Engrs., Sigma Xi, Epsilon Nu Gamma. Office: 900 Larkspur Landing Suite 230 Larkspur CA 94939 also: 900 Larkspur Landing Circle Suite 230 Larkspur CA 94934

ELIOT, LUCY CARTER, artist; b. N.Y.C., May 8, 1913; d. Ellsworth and Lucy Carter (Byrd) E. B.A., Vassar Coll., 1935; postgrad., Art Students League, 1935-40. tchr. painting and drawing Red Cross Bronx Vets. Hosp., N.Y.C., 1950, 51. Exhibited one-woman shows, Rochester Meml. Art Gallery, 1946, Cazenovia Coll., 1942, 47, 62, Syracuse Mus. Fine Arts, 1947, Wells Coll., 1953, Ft. Schuyler Club, Utica, N.Y., 1971, nat. shows, Pa. Acad. Fine Arts, Phila., 1946, 48, 49, 50, 52, 54, Corcoran Biennial, Washington, 1947, 51, Va. Biennial, Richmond, 1948, NAD, N.Y.C., 1971, 78, Butler Inst. Am. Art, 1965, 67, 69, 70, 72, 74, 81; represented in permanent collections: Rochester Meml. Art Gallery, Munson-Williams-Proctor Inst., also pvt. collections. Bd. dirs. Artists Tech. Research Inst., 1975-79. Recipient First prize Rochester Meml. Art Gallery, 1946; recipient Purchase prize Munson-Williams-Proctor Inst., 1949, Painting of Industry award Silvermine Guild, 1957, 1st prize in oils Cooperstown Art Assn., 1978. Mem. N.Y. Artists Equity, N.Y. Soc. Women Artists (pres. 1973-75), Audubon Artists (dir. oil 1983-85, chmn. awards 1986-88), Am. Soc. Contemporary Artists. Episcopalian. Clubs: Cazenovia (N.Y.); Cosmopolitan (N.Y.C.). Home: 131 E 66th St New York NY 10021

ELIZABETH, HER MAJESTY II (ELIZABETH ALEXANDRA MARY), Queen of U.K. of Gt. Britain and No. Ireland, and her other realms and Tys., head of the Commonwealth, defender of the faith; b. Apr. 21, 1926; d. King George VI (formerly Duke of York) and Queen Elizabeth (formerly Duchess of York); m. Prince Philip, Duke of Edinburgh, Nov. 20, 1947; children: Charles Philip Arthur George, Anne Elizabeth Alice Louise, Andrew Albert Christian Edward, Edward Antony Richard Louis. Succeeded to throne following death of father Feb. 6, 1952, crowned Queen, June 2, 1953. Address: Buckingham Palace, London England SW1 *

ELIZABETH (ANGELA MARGUERITE), HER MAJESTY, Queen Elizabeth The Queen Mother; b. Aug. 4, 1900; d. 14th Earl Strathmore; m. Duke of York (later His Majesty King George VI), 1923 (dec. 1952); children: Princess Elizabeth (later Her Majesty Queen Elizabeth), Princess Margaret Rose; reigned as Queen Consort, 1936-52. Lady Order of Garter, Lady Order of Thistle. Decorated Imperial Order Crown India, dame grand cross Royal Victorian Order. Address: Clarence House, St James's, London SW1 England also: Castle of, Mey Caithness-shire Scotland also: Royal Lodge, Windsor, Gt Park, Berkshire England *

EL-JISR, BASSEM, lawyer, educator; b. Beirut, Lebanon, Mar. 21, 1930; s. Cheick Mohammad and Montaha (Zein) El-J.; m. Aurora Araos. Lic. en Droit, U. Beirut, 1953; postgrad., Sorbonne, 1977. Sole practice law Beirut, 1956-59; editor, columnist various Lebanese and Arabic newspapers, 1959-62; dir. info. Ministry of Info., Lebanon, 1962; prof. law U. Lebanon, 1972-74; del. of Lebanon UNESCO, Paris, 1960-82; consellar Arab States League, Tunis, 1979-81; dir. gen. Inst. du Monde Arabie, Paris, 1984—. Co-founder, sec. gen. Lebanese Dem. party, 1969-74. Home: 8 Rue de Commandant Schloesing, 75116 Paris France Office: Inst du Monde Arabe, 23 Quai Saint Bernard, 75005 Paris France

ELKAMEL, FARAG MOHAMED, social scientist, educator, mass media expert; b. Aga, Egypt, Jan. 5, 1952; came to U.S., 1976, naturalized, 1983; s. M. Hafez and Hekmat E. (Metwali) E.; m. Martha Ann Solt, Mar. 22, 1981 (div. 1984). BA, U. Cairo, 1974; MA, U. Chgo., 1978, PhD, 1981. Prof. communication U. Cairo, 1981—; media adviser UNICEF, Amman, Jordan, 1984—, John Snow, Inc., Boston, 1983—; founder Ctr. Devel. Communication Cairo/Washington, 1985—, also dir.; adviser Ford Found., N.Y.C. and Cairo, 1984; cons. Johns Hopkins U., Balt., 1985. Author: Influence of Media, 1985; (UNICEF manual) Devel. Communication Strategies and Porgrams, 1985. Inventor in field. Ford Found. fellow, 1976, 85; U. Chgo. fellow, 1980. Mem. Nat. Council Internat. Health, Internat. Inst. Communication, U. Chgo. Alumni Assn. Club: Faculty (Cairo). Home: 1466 N Quinn Arlington VA 22209 Office: John Snow Inc 210 Lincoln St Boston MA 02111

EL-KHATIB, YOUSEF MOHAMMAD, maintenance, trade and contracting company executive; b. Dear Ghassanah, Jordan, Mar. 20, 1950; arrived in Saudi Arabia, 1972; s. Mohammad Yousef and Olyan Ismail (Eizyah) El-K.; married; 1 child, Mohammad. Cert. in mgmt., Alexander Hamilton Inst., N.Y.C., 1981. Receptionist Inter-Continental Hotels, Amman, Jordan, 1972; mgr. personnel adminstrn. Safami div. Williams Bros., Al-Khobar, Saudi Arabia, 1972-79; asst. gen. mgr., co. adminstr. Gen. Contracting Co., Amman, 1979; mgr. personnel and office orgn. Grand Met. Hotels, Amman, 1980-81; project mgr. Samama Co. Ltd., Medina, Saudi Arabia, 1981-85; br. mgr. Makkah, Saudi Arabia, 1985-87; adminstrn. mgr. Taif, Saudi Arabia, 1987—. Recipient Infection Control award King Fahd Hosp., Medina, 1983. Mem. Am. Mgmt. Assn. Home: PO Box 20350, Amman Jordon Office: Samama Co Ltd, PO Box 1497, Taif Saudi Arabia

EL-KHOURY, SHAWKI KHALIL, transportation executive; b. Mharbieh, Lebanon, Aug. 24, 1936; s. Khalil Antoine and Laurice Shukri (Zahar) K..; m. Raymonde Antoine Massoud, July 5, 1969; children: Khalil, Antoine. BBA, Am. U., Beirut, 1956, MBA, 1958. Sr. supr. accounts Trans Mediterranean Airways, Lebanon, 1958-59, acting chief acct., 1959-62, chief acct., 1962-69, dir. fin., 1965-69, dir. purchasing and stores, 1969-73, asst. v.p., 1974-76, v.p. adminstrn., 1977-86, exec. v.p., 1986—; bd. dirs. Lebanese Helicopter Co., Beirut, 1987. Mem. Lebanese Mgmt. Assn., Am. U. Alumni Assn.

EL-KHOURY, YOUSSEF SAAVOLLAH, judge, educator; b. Ain-Ikrine, Koura, Lebanon, Sept. 11, 1933; s. Saadallah and Maria El-K.; m. Diana Aurore-Zablith, Apr. 13, 1969; children: Charles, Christian, Claude. B in French Law, U. St. Joseph, Beirut, 1958, B in Lebanese Law, 1959; D in Pub. Law, U. René Descartes, Paris, 1980. Aux. justice Ministry of Justice, Beirut, 1957-59; probationary auditor Exchequer and Audit Office, Beirut, 1959-65, judge, 1965-83; gen. dir. Republic Presidency of Lebanon, Beirut, 1983; pres. Council of State, Beirut, 1983—. Author: The Relations Between Schools and Universities and the Public Administrative Attitudes, 1972, The Administrative Attributions of the Audit Office of Lebanon, 1980, The General Administrative Law, 1984, The Review of the Administrative Jurisdiction, 1986; contbr. articles on law. Maronite. Office: Court of the Council of State, Palais du Justice, Beirut Lebanon

ELKINS, JAMES ANDERSON, JR., banker; b. Galveston, Tex., Mar. 24, 1919; s. James Anderson and Isabel (Mitchell) E.; m. Margaret Wiess, Nov. 24, 1945; children—Elise, James Anderson III, Leslie K. B.A., Princeton U., 1941. With First City Nat. Bank, Houston, 1941—, v.p., 1946-50, pres., 1950; then chmn. bd., now sr. chmn. bd. First City Bancorp., Houston, 1982—; bd. dirs. Freeport-McMoran Inc., New Orleans, 1970—, Am. Gen. Cos., Houston, 1973—. Bd. dirs. Houston Grand Opera; trustee Tex. Children's Hosp., Baylor U. Coll. Medicine, 1970—. Episcopalian. Home: 101 Farish Circle Houston TX 77024 Office: 1st City Bancorp Tex Inc 1001 Fannin St Houston TX 77253 also: PO Box 2387 Houston TX 77001

ELKINS, JAMES PAUL, physician; b. Lincoln, Nebr., Mar. 20, 1924; s. James Hill and Antonia (Wohler) E.; M.D., U. Va., 1947; m. May Hollingsworth Reynolds, June 15, 1946; children—Patricia May Elkins Riggs, Paulette Frances Elkins Phillips, James Barrington. Cert. Emergency Med. Services Commn. Intern, DePaul Hosp., Norfolk, Va., 1947-48; resident in ob-gyn Alexandria (Va.) Hosp., 1948-49, Franklin Sq. Hosp., Balt., 1949-50, St. Rita's Hosp., Lima, Ohio, 1950, Tripler Army Hosp., Honolulu, 1953-54; practice medicine specializing in ob-gyn, Indpls., 1954-73; chief ob-gyn St. Francis Hosp., Beech Grove, Ind., 1965-66; mem. teaching staff Gen. Hosp., Indpls., 1954-73; dep. coroner Marion County, 1965-74; med. cons. disability determination div. Ind. Rehab. Services; examining physician Plasma Alliance Ctr. Served with AUS, 1949-54. Recipient Fred Deborde Award Ind. Golden Gloves, 1985. Mem. Am. Coll. Ob-Gyn, AMA, Ind. State Med. Assn., Marion County Med. Soc., Indpls. Press Club (hon. life), Police League Ind., Fraternal Order Police, Nat. Sojourners, 500 Festival Assos., Police League Ind., Ind. Sports Corp. (charter gold mem.), U.S. Auto Club (life), Phi Chi. Clubs: Ind. Pacers Booster (charter), Thundering Herd Booster Indpls. Colts (charter mem.). Lodges: Masons, Shriners (life). Home: 2045 Lick Creek Dr Indianapolis IN 46203 Office: 225 N New Jersey St Indianapolis IN 46204

ELKINS, STEVEN PAUL, architect; b. Ephrata, Wash., Feb. 18, 1949; s. Hugh Kyle Elkins and Fern Irene (Vining) Johnson; m. Linda Louise Harris, Aug. 6, 1977; children: Andrea Rouleau, Michael Rouleau, Jennifer. BArch, Wash. State U., 1972. Registered architect, Wash., Oreg. Designer, draftsman Eng & Wright Architects, Vancouver, B.C., Can., 1972-73, Harthorne-Hagen-Gross, Inc., Seattle, 1973-75, Leo A. Daly Co., Seattle, 1975-77; architect Lawrence Campbell & Assocs., Kent, Wash., 1977-81; prin. Steven P. Elkins Architects, Inc., Seattle, 1981—. Mem. community adv. com. Auburn (Wash.) Gen. Hosp., 1985—, mem. planning and bldg. com. Campus Way Covenant Ch., Federal Way, Wash., 1985—. Recipient Award of Excellence Wash. Precast Concrete Industry Assn., 1985, 86, Appreciation award Vocat. Indsl. Clubs Am., Wash., 1985, 86., Superintendant of Pub. Instrn., Auburn Sch. Dist., 1987. Mem. AIA (corp.), Nat. Trust for Hist. Preservation. Democrat. Protestant. Club: Washington Athletic. Home: 1326 183d Ave NE Bellevue WA 98008 Office: 610 Market St #201 Kirkland WA 98033

ELKLIT, JÖRGEN, political science educator; b. Frederiksverk, Denmark, Oct. 12, 1942; s. Hans F. and Sigrun (Johnsen) E.; m. Tove Henningsen, Mar. 12, 1966; children: Annedorte, Charlotte. Candidate degree in History, U. Aarhus, Denmark, 1970; PhD in Polit. Sci., U. Aarhus, 1988. Research fellow Inst. Polit. Sci., Aarhus, Denmark, 1970-72; asst. prof. U. Aarhus, Denmark, 1972-74; assoc. prof. Inst. Polit. Sci. U. Aarhus, Denmark, 1974—; head polit. sci. dept. U. Aarhus, Denmark, 1975-76, 80-81; mng. dir. publishing house Politica, Aarhus, 1980—; bd. dirs. Danish Nat. Bus. Archives; cons. various Danish polit. parties, 1980—. Author: The Census of 1845, 1970; author: (with others) National Identification in North Schleswig, 1978; editor: (with others) Electors and Electoral Behavior, 1984, 2d edition, 1986, From Open to Secret Voting, 1988; contbr. articles to profl. jours. Recipient Gold Medal U. Aarhus, 1969; research grantee Hist. Commn. West Berlin, 1982. Mem. Social Sci. History Assn., Danish Polit. Sci., The Jutland Soc. History. Home: Fredensvang Runddel 3, DK-8260 Viby Denmark

ELKOMOSS, SABRY GOBRAN, physicist; b. Elkoussia, Egypt, Apr. 2, 1925; immigrated to France, 1957, naturalized, 1959; s. Gobran Bishay and Rifka Morcos Elkomoss; B.Sc. in Math. with distinction, Alexandria U., 1949; M.Sc. in Physics, 1953; D.Scis. Physiques (French Govt. scholar 1951-52), U. Strasbourg (France), 1955; m. Arlette Meyer, Dec. 11, 1957; children—Anita, Alexander. Asst., Alexandria U., 1949-56; mem. staff Nat. Center Sci. Research, 1952-62; sr. research scientist, exec. adv. space and missile div. Douglas Corp., Santa Monica, Calif., 1963-64; sr. staff mem. space and missile div. Litton Industries, Beverly Hills, Calif., 1964-66; research scientist plasma div. McDonnell Corp., St. Louis, 1966-67; maitre recherches Nat. Center Sci. Research, Strasbourg, 1967—; lectr. U. Ein Shams, Cairo, also prof. physics Lycee Francais, Alexandria, 1956-57. Fulbright advanced scholar, 1959-61; postdoctoral asso. research U. Notre Dame, 1959-63. Mem. Am. Phys. Soc., New York Acad. of Sci. (sec. European study group solid state spectroscopy), Sigma Xi. Mem. Coptic Orthodox. Ch. Contbr. articles to profl. jours. Home: 21 Rue D'Oslo, Strasbourg 67000 France Office: 23 Rue du Loess, Strassburg 670 37, France

ELKUS, RICHARD J., JR., electronics company executive; b. San Francisco, Feb. 25, 1935; s. Richard J. and Ruth (Kahn) E.; m. Helen Morrison, Aug. 17, 1956; children—Miriam Lyster, Richard M., Kevin J. B.A., Stanford U., 1957; M.B.A., Dartmouth Coll., 1959. Product control mgr. Ampex Corp., Redwood City, Calif., 1959-64, asst. to pres., 1968-71, mem. ops. bd., 1969-71, gen. mgr. edn. and indsl. products div., 1969-71; pres., chief exec. officer, dir. Eyrle Co., Santa Clara, Calif., 1964-67; gen. mgr. Gould Med. Systems, Santa Clara, 1973-74; exec. v.p., gen. mgr. Geometrics, Inc., including fgn. subsidiaries, Sunnyvale, Calif., 1974-80; dir. Acacia Sales Corp., 1973-83; dir. Pacific Measurements, Inc., Sunnyvale, 1974-83, chmn., 1980-83; chmn., chief exec. officer, dir. Prometrix Corp., Santa Clara, 1983—; dir., vice chmn. bd. Integrated Systems, Inc., 1985—; bd. dirs. Tomex Corp., 1982-87. Mem. ex-officio N.H. Gov.'s Fee Schedule Com., 1958-59. Served to capt. USAF, 1957-65. Mem. Am. Mgmt. Assn. (pres.'s council), Am. Electronics Assn., Electronics Assn. Calif., Semicondr. Equipment and Materials Internat., Assn. for Corp. Growth, Assn. for Calif. Tort Reform. Republican. Clubs: Foothills Tennis and Swim (Palo Alto, Calif.); Menlo Circus (Atherton, Calif.); Sequoia (Redwood City); Commonwealth. Office: Prometrix Corp 3255 Scott Blvd Bldg 6 Santa Clara CA 95054

ELLAGA, ELIZABETH DELA VEGA, physician; b. Antique, Philippines, Mar. 20, 1955; d. Gil Samulde and Fidela (Dela Vega) E. BS in Biol. Scis., U. Philippines, Manila, 1976; MD, West Visayas State Coll., Iloilo, Philippines, 1981. Resident physician Gov. Mamerto Portillo Meml. Dist. Hosp., Antique, 1986, officer in charge, 1986-87, sr. resident physician, 1986—. Served to capt., Philippine Army, 1982, Res., 1985—. Mem. Philippines Med. Assn. Roman Catholic. Home: Poblacion 2, Hamtic, Antique 5607, Philippines

ELLEMANN-JENSEN, UFFE, Danish government official; b. Haarby, Denmark, Nov. 1, 1941; s. Jens Peter and Edith (Ellemann) J.; m. Alice Vestergaard, June 19, 1971; children: Claus, Helene, Karen, Jakob. M.A. in Econs., Copenhagen U., 1969. Editor, Berlingske Aften, Copenhagen, 1967-69; commentator TV-News Dept., Copenhagen, 1969-75; editor-in-chief Boersen, Copenhagen, 1975-77; mem. Danish Parliament, 1977—, minister fgn. affairs, 1982—, speaker Liberal Party, 1978-82, chmn. Com. on European Market Affairs, 1978-79; chmn. Liberal Party, 1984—. Author 5 books on econ. and polit. issues, 1970-76. Served to 1st lt. Danish Armed Forces, 1960-64. Recipient Robert Shumann prize, 1987 Office: Ministry Fgn Affairs, Asiatisk Plads 2, Copenhagen Denmark 1448

ELLENBERGER, DIANE MARIE, nurse, educator; b. St. Louis, Oct. 5, 1946; d. Charles Ernst and Celeste Loraine (Neudecker) E.; R.N., Barnes Hosp., St. Louis, 1970; B.S. in Nursing St. Louis U., 1976; M.S., U. Colo., 1977. Staff nurse hosps., clin. nurse, St. Louis, 1973-76; nurse clinician, Sedalia, Mo., 1977-78; nurse clinician, educator Bothwell Hosp., Sedalia, 1977-78; clin. nurse specialist, coordinator perinatal outreach edn. Cardinal Glennon Meml. Hosp. Children, St. Louis, 1978-80; instr. McKendree Coll., Lebanon, Ill., 1980; asst. prof. Maryville Coll., St. Louis, 1982-85; nurse cons. Carr, Korein, Schlichter, Kunin and Montroy Attys. at Law, 1986—;asst. prof. nursing, Webster U., St. Louis, 1988—; owner, operator

Diane Designs Needlepoint, St. Louis, 1981—. Served with Nurse Corps, USAF, 1970-72. Mem. Am. Nurses Assn., Nurses Assn. Am. Coll. Ob-Gyn, Nat. Perinatal Assn., Mo. Nurses Assn., Mo. Perinatal Assn. (v.p. 1980), Sigma Theta Tau. Mem. Divine Sci. Ch. Contbr. articles profl. jours. Office: 412 Missouri Ave East Saint Louis IL 62201

ELLER, DAVID GALLAWAY, oil and gas exploration and development company executive; b. Mexia, Tex., Mar. 13, 1938; s. James Marion and Myrtis (Gallaway) E.; m. Margaretha Sallen, Mar. 5, 1966 (dec. Nov. 1973); children: David Erik, Dirk Gustaf; m. 2d, Linda Schmuck, June 28, 1980. B.S., B.A., Tex. A&M U., 1959; postgrad. Stanford U., 1977. Mgr. Western Europe Warren & Co., Frankfurt, W.Ger., 1962-65; pres. Becco, Inc., N.Y.C., 1965-72; chmn., chief exec. officer Alcorn Internat., N.Y.C., London, 1967-72, Am. Nat. Petroleum Co., Houston, 1979-87, Granada Corp., Houston, 1972—; dir. Allied Bank of Tex., Houston. Bd. dirs. Houston Area Research Ctr., Houston Econ. Devel. Council, Houston Livestock Show and Rodeo, 1982-83; trustee Baylor U. Coll. Medicine; chmn. bd. regents Tex. A&M U. System, College Station, 1983—. Served as capt. U.S. Army, 1960-62. Mem. ASME, Houston C. of C. (bd. dirs.). Clubs: Houston Racquet, The Houstonian, The Plaza, Univ., Lakeside Country (Houston). Lodge: Tejas Vaqueros (dir. 1983—).

ELLERY, JOHN BLAISE, military training consultant, former educational administrator; b. N.Y.C., Feb. 3, 1920; s. William Hoyt and Thea (Kavanagh) E.; m. Ellen Jane Savacool, Sept. 21, 1946; children: Thea Jane, Martha Ann, Sarah Savacool, John Blaise, Jessica Joyce. A.B., Hamilton Coll., 1948; M.A., U. Colo., 1950; Ph.D., U. Wis., 1954. Instr. U. Colo., 1948-50; asst. prof. U. Iowa, 1952-56; assoc. prof. Wayne State U., 1957-61; prof., chmn. dept. English East Tenn. State U., Johnson City, 1961-66; sr. lectr. Njala U. Coll., West Africa, 1966-68; asst. to chancellor U. Wis., Stevens Point, 1968-74; vice chancellor U. Wis., 1974-80, acting chancellor, 1978-79, dean Coll. Natural Resources, 1970-72, dir. Ednl. Media Center, 1980-82; sec. of state Wis. Dept. Vet. Affairs, 1982-85; Omar N. Bradley lectr. U.S. Army Command and Gen. Staff Coll., 1985; Mem. Wis. Gov.'s Commn. on Edn., 1969; v.p. Wis.-Nicaragua Partners of Ams., 1979-80, pres., 1980-81, bd. dirs., exec. com., 1978—. Works include John Stuart Mill, 1964, Linguistic Impedance and Dialect Interference Among Certain African Tribes, 1970; also short stories, articles; contbg. author: Essays on Language and Literature, 1969. Served to ensign USNR, 1938-41; with inf. AUS, 1941-45; col. Army N.G. Decorated Silver Star, Bronze Star with oak leaf cluster, Purple Heart with oak leaf cluster, Conspicuous Service Cross; Croix de Guerre; Medaille Militaire Fourragere; recipient U.S. Army patriotic civilian service award. Mem. Ret. Officers Assn., Res. Officers Assn., Assn. of U.S. Army, Sigma Phi Epsilon, Sigma Tau Delta, Eta Sigma Phi. Office: 400 S Madison St Stoughton WI 53589

ELLETSON, ROGER CHANDOS, investment executive; b. Preesall, Lancashire, Eng., June 4, 1911; s. Harry Chandos and Katherine Helen (PhilipsP E.; m. Simone Therese Boudard, Nov. 20, 1938 (div. Dec. 1950); children: Lorraine Joan, Philip Roger; m. Pamela Mary Brown, Oct. 20, 1958; children: Anthony Leslie, Anne, Hope. Mng. dir. Smith and Philips, Witney, Oxford, Eng., 1937-39; chmn., mng. dir. R.C. Elletson and Co. and subs. cos., Lancashire, 1947—; fin. dir. Humphrey Lloyd, Manchester, 1967-80; oooo; chmn. Parry Sons and Hanson, Manchester, 1966-67; chmn. Crosses and Heaton, Bolton, Eng., 1970-78; underwriting mem. Lloyds of London, 1960—. Contbr. articles on recreation to local newspapers. Served to lt. British Army, 1939-45. Mem. Inst. Journalists. Clubs: Brooks' (London); Royal Lytham Golf. (Stannes). Home: Grey House, Forton, Preston PR3 0AN, England

ELLIE, YVONNE KISSINGER, principal; b. Wisconsin Rapids, Wis., Mar. 21, 1936; d. Alfred J. and Louise J. (Brockman) Kissinger; B.S., Coll. St. Teresa, 1958; M.S., U. Wis.-Stevens Point, 1978; postgrad. U. Wis.-Madison, 1979—; m. Gene C. Ellie, June 28, 1958; children—Gregory, Jean Marie, Katherine, Daniel, David, Brian. Tchr., Mpls. Pub. Schs., 1958, Lowell Sch., Moses Lake, Wash., 1958-59, Vesper Elem. Sch., Wisconsin Rapids, 1967-78, Mead, Howe, Woodside Schs., Wisconsin Rapids, 1978-79; adminstrv. intern Grove and Pitsch Elem. Sch., Wisconsin Rapids, 1979-80, prin., dir. community services, 1980-85, dir. human resources, 1985-87; prin. Howe Elem. Sch., Wisconsin Rapids, 1987—; mem. Wood County Environ. Edn. Com. Chmn. unified bargaining com. Central Wis. Uniserve Council, 1976-79. Mem. Wisconsin Rapids Tchrs. Assn. (pres. 1978-79), LWV, NEA, Wis. Edn. Assn. (council), Wisconsin Rapids Edn. Assn., Internat. Reading Assn., Wis. Reading Assn., Central Wis. Reading Assn., Wis. Community Edn. Assn., Nat. Assn. Elementary Prins., Assn. Wis. Sch. Adminstrs., Assn. Supervision and Curriculum Devel., Network Outcome Based Schs., Nat. Council Tchrs. of English, Wis. Math. Council, Phi Delta Kappa. Home: 990 1st Ave S Wisconsin Rapids WI 54494 Office: Howe Sch 2750 Wisconsin St Wisconsin Rapids WI 54494

ELLIG, BRUCE ROBERT, personnel executive; b. Manitowoc, Wis., Oct. 15, 1936; s. Robert Louis and Lucille Marie (Westphal) E.; B.B.A., U. Wis., 1959, M.B.A., 1960; 1 son, Brett Robert. With Pfizer Inc., N.Y.C., 1960—, mgr. compensation and personnel research, 1968-70, corp. dir. compensation and benefits, 1970-78, v.p. compensation and benefits, 1978-83, v.p. employee relations, 1983-85, v.p. personnel, 1985—; speaker at workshops, seminars and confs.; assoc. adv. council Commerce Clearing House. Mem. Mayor's Adv. Pay Commn., N.Y.C., 1977-78, chmn., 1980; mem. bus. sector staff Council on Wage and Price Stability, 1979-80; mem. Ctr. for Advanced Human Resource Studies Cornell U., Human Resource Roundtable, Presdl. Quadrennial Pay Commn., 1976, U.S. Civil Service Commn. Merit Pay Task Force, 1979; mem. adv. bd. Ky. Ednl. TV, 1987—. Mem. Am. Compensation Assn. (charter pres. Ea. region; publ. award 1980), Am. Soc. Personnel Adminstrs. (accredited sr. profl. human rsources, mem. human resources strategies and issues council), N.Y. Assn. Compensation Adminstrs. (charter pres.), NAM (employee benefits and compensation com.), Am. Mgmt. Assn. (human resource council; Wall of Fame 1983), N.Y. Personnel Mgmt. Assn. (past pres.; anniversary award of merit 1980), Bus. Roundtable (employee relations com.), Conf. Bd. Council Human Resources Research, N.Y. Indsl. Relations Assn., Pharm. Mfrs. Assn. (personnel sect.), Sr. Execs. Forum, U. So. Calif. Ctr. for Effective Orgs. (corp. adv. bd.), U. Wis. Bus. Sch. Alumni Assn. (bd. dirs.), Phi Beta Kappa, Phi Eta Sigma, Phi Kappa Phi, Delta Epsilon, Beta Gamma Sigma, Alpha Kappa Psi. Republican. Roman Catholic. Author: Compensation and Benefits: Analytical Strategies, 1978; Executive Compensation: A Total Pay Perspective, 1982; Compensation and Benefits: Design and Analysis, 1985; contbg. author: Encyclopedia of Professional Management, 1978; Handbook of Business Administration, 1984; cons. editor Compensation & Benefits Rev.; editorial bd., personnel adv. bd. Jour. Compensation & Benefits; contbr. articles to profl. jours. Office: Pfizer Inc 235 E 42d St New York NY 10017

ELLIN, MARVIN, lawyer; b. Balt., Mar. 6, 1923; s. Morris and Goldie (Rosen) E.; m. Stella J. Granto, Aug. 2, 1948; children: Morris, Raymond, Elisa. LL.B., U. Balt., 1953. Bar: Md. 1953, U.S. Supreme Ct. 1978. Practice law Balt., 1953—; mem. firm Ellin & Baker, 1957—; specialist in med. malpractice law; cons. med./legal trial matters lectr. ACS, U. Md. Law Sch., U. Balt. Law Sch., Md. Bar Assn., Bar Assn. Balt. City. Writer; producer ct. dramatizations featured on various TV and radio stas., Balt. Fellow Internat. Acad. Trial Lawyers. Home: 13414 Longnecker Rd Glyndon MD 21071 Office: 1101 Saint Paul St Baltimore MD 21202

ELLINGSEN, OLAV, mechanical equipment company executive; b. Byrne, Norway, Mar. 22, 1941; s. Brynjulf and Jenny (ness) E.; m. Liv Sorebo, July 19, 1969; 1 child, Bjarte Sorebo. Degree in Mech. Engring., Stavanger Tech. High Sch., 1966. Jr. engr. Norsk Hydro A/S, Oslo, 1966-67; mgr. Per Hetland Maskinfabrikk A/S, Bryne, 1967-70, Hatten & Jota A/S, Trysil, Norway, 1970-73, Industrikontakt, O. Ellingsen & Co., Floro, Norway, 1973—; chmn. bd. dirs. Kirkenes Engring. A/S, Kirkenes, Ellingsen and Assocs. A/S, Floro.; bd. dirs. Noride A/S, Floro, Consensus A/S, Bergen, Norway, Lifecare A/S, Oslo, Norway, Pertoleum Reservoi Cons. A/S, Oslo, Forest A/S, Oslo, NOrpigg Als, Höyanger. Inventor thermodynamic cuttings cleaning, thermodynamic enhanced oil recovery, artificial pancreas; patentee in field. Recipient diplomas Klerk, Bergen, 1986, Norwegian Inventors Assn., 1980. Mem. Norwegian Indsl. Fedn., Norwegian Inventors Assn., Norwegian Petroleum Soc. Conservative. Lutheran. Club: Flor Yacht (Floro) (chmn. 1986). Lodge: Odd Fellow. Home: Kleiva 20, 6900 Floro Norway Office: Ellingsen & Assocs A/S, Boks 133, 6901 Floro Norway

ELLIOT, JEFFREY M., political science educator, author; b. Los Angeles, June 14, 1947; s. Gene and Harriet (Sobsey) E. BA, U. So. Calif., 1969, MA, 1970; ArtsD in History, Carnegie-Mellon U., 1976; EdD, Laurence U., 1976; ArtsD in Govt., Claremont Grad. Sch., 1978; LittD (hon.), Shaw U., 1985; LLD (hon.), City U. of Los Angeles, 1986. Research asst. U. So. Calif., 1969-70; instr. polit. sci. Glendale Coll., 1970-72, Cerritos Coll., 1970-72; asst. prof. history and polit. sci. U. Alaska-Anchorage Community Coll., 1973-74; asst. prof. history and polit. sci., dean curriculum Miami-Dade Community Coll., 1974-76; asst. prof. polit. sci. Va. Wesleyan Coll., Norfolk, 1978-79; sr. curriculum specialist Edn. Devel. Center, Newton, Mass., 1979-81; prof. polit. sci. N.C. Central U., 1981—; disting. advisor on internat. relations, Congressman Mervyn M. Dymally (Dem. Calif.), 1985—. Author: 59 books, including Keys to Economic Understanding, 1976, Science Fiction Voices, 1979, Literary Voices, 1980, Analytical Congressional Directory, 1981, Deathman Pass Me By: Two Years on Death Row, 1982, Tempest in a Teapot: The Falkland Islands War, 1983, Kindred Spirits, 1984, Black Voices in American Politics, 1985, Urban Society, 1985, The Presidential-Congressional Political Dictionary, 1985, Nothing Can Stop the Course of History, 1986, The State and Local Government Political Dictionary, 1986, The Third World, 1987, Dictionary of Arms Control, Disarmament, and Military Security, 1988, Dictionary of American Government, 1988, Fidel, 1988, Conversations with Maya Angelou, 1988; contbr. 500 articles and revs. to profl. and popular jours.; contbg. editor Negro History Bull., 1976-80, West Coast Writers' Conspiracy, 1978-80. Mem. community services adv. council Miami (Fla.) Community Services, 1974-76; mem. Los Angeles Mayor's Adv. Com., 1971-72; speechwriter, research asst., campaign strategist U.S. Sen. Howard W. Cannon of Nev., 1969—; cons. Calif. Clean Environment Act, 1970-72. Recipient 50 literary and scholarly awards including Fair Enterprise Medallion award, 1965, Outstanding Polit. Sci. Scholar citation, 1970, Outstanding Tchr. award, 1971, Outstanding Am. Educator citation, 1975, Distinguished Service Through Community Effort award, 1976, Outstanding Research Prize, 1987, Disting. Scholarship award, 1987. Mem. Community Coll. Social Sci. Assn. (dir. 1970-77, pres. 1975-77), So. Assn. Colls. and Schs. (accreditation team 1974-76), AAUP, Am. Polit. Sci. Assn., Assn. Supervision and Curriculum Devel., Nat. Council for Social Studies, Rocky Mountain Social Sci. Assn., Am. Hist. Assn., Pi Sigma Alpha, Phi Delta Kappa. Home: 1419 Barliff Pl Durham NC 27712 Office: Dept Polit Sci NC Central U Durham NC 27707

ELLIOTT, DAVID ANTHONY, design educator; b. Cambridge, Eng., Oct. 31, 1943; s. Donald Reginald and Olga (Norcott) E.; m. Ruth Helen Small, Feb. 19, 1972 (div. Oct. 1987); m. Tam Dougan, Mar. 1988. BSc with honours, Southbank Poly., London, 1967; PhD, U. London, 1971. Asst. Harwell Atomic Energy Authority, Didcot, Eng., 1962-67; research officer Cen. Electricity Generating Bd., Portishead, Bristol, Eng., 1967-68; research asst. Chelsea Coll. U. London, 1968-70, research fellow Westfield Coll., 1970-71; lectr. design Open U., Milton Keynes, Eng., 1971082, sr. lectr., 1982—; cons. Greater London Enterprise Bd., 1982-83. Author: (with others) The Control of Technology, 1976, The Politics of Nuclear Power, 1978, The Lucas Plan, 1982, Enterprising Innovation, 1987; editor: Man Made, Futures, Politics of Technology. Grantee Sci. and Engring. Research Council, Social Sci. Research Council. Mem. Socialist Environ. and Resources (convenor energy group 1978—), Network for Alternative Tech. and Tech. Assessment (editor jour. 1978—). Mem. Labour Party. Home: 39 Holland Park, London W11 4UB, England Office: Open U Faculty TechWalton, Milton Keynes MK7 6AA, England

ELLIOTT, EDWARD, investment executive, financial planner; b. Madison, Wis., Jan. 11, 1915; s. Edward C. and Elizabeth (Nowland) E.; m. Letitia Ord, Feb. 20, 1943 (div. Aug. 1955); children: Emily, Ord; m. Melita Uihlein, Jan. 1, 1958; 1 dau., Deborah. B.S. in Mech. Engring, Purdue U., 1936. Engr. Gen. Electric Co., Schenectady, 1936-37; engr. Pressed Steel Tank Co., Milw., 1937-38, N.Y.C., 1939-41; dist. sales mgr. Pressed Steel Tank Co., Cleve., 1946-48, N.Y.C., 1949-54; sales mgr. Pressed Steel Tank Co., Milw., 1954-58; v.p. sales Cambridge Co. div. Carrier Corp., Lowell, Mass., 1958-59; mgr. indsl. and med. sales Liquid Carbonic div. Gen. Dynamics Corp., Chgo., 1959-61; v.p. Haywood Pub. Co., Chgo., 1961-63; pres. Omnibus, Inc., Chgo., 1963-67; gen. sales mgr. Resistoflex Corp., Roseland, N.J., 1967-68; investment exec. Shearson, Hammill & Co., Inc., Chgo., 1968-74; v.p. McCormick & Co., Inc., 1974-75, now v.p. Paine Webber, Inc., Naples, Fla., 1975—. Served with USAAF, 1941-46. Decorated officer Order Brit. Empire; inducted Indiana Basketball Hall of Fame. Mem. ASME, Air Force Assn., Inst. Cert. Fin. Planners, Internat. Assn. Fin. Planning, Phi Delta Theta. Republican. Episcopalian. Clubs: Shore Acres Golf (Lake Bluff, Ill.); Onwentsia (Lake Forest, Ill.); Milwaukee Country , University (Milw.); Chenequa Country (Hartland, Wis.); Lake (Oconomowoc, Wis.); Army-Navy Country (Arlington, Va.); Lafayette (Ind.) Country; Coral Beach (Paget Bermuda); Royal Poinciana Golf, Hole-in-Wall Golf, Naples Yacht, Naples Athletic (Naples). Lodge: Rotary. Home: 1285 Gulf Shore Blvd N Naples FL 33940 Office: Paine Webber Inc 1400 Gulf Shore Blvd N Naples FL 33940

ELLIOTT, FRANK WALLACE, lawyer; b. Cotulla, Tex., June 25, 1930; s. Frank Wallace and Eunice Marie (Akin) E.; m. Winona Trent, July 3, 1954 (dec. 1981); 1 dau., Harriet Lindsey; m. Kay Elkins, Aug. 15, 1983. Student, N.Mex. Mil. Inst., 1947-49; B.A., U. Tex., 1951, LL.B., 1957. Bar: Tex. 1957. Asst. atty. gen. State of Tex., 1957; briefing atty. Supreme Ct. Tex., 1957-58; prof. U. Tex. Law Sch., 1958-77; dean, prof. law Tex. Tech U. Sch. Law, 1977-80; pres. Southwestern Legal Found., 1980-86; ptnr. Baker, Mills & Glast, Dallas, 1987-88; of counsel Ramirez & Assocs., 1988—; parliamentarian Tex. Senate, 1969-73; dir. research Tex. Constl. Revision Commn., 1973. Author: Texas Judicial Process, 2d edit, 1977, Texas Trial and Appellate Practice, 2d edit, 1974, Cases on Evidence, 1980, West's Texas Forms, 20 vols, 1977—. Served with U.S. Army, 1951-53, 73-74. Decorated Purple Heart, Meritorious Service medal, Army Commendation medal. Mem. Am. Bar Assn., Judge Advs. Assn., Am. Judicature Soc., Am. Bar Found., Tex. Bar Found., Am. Law Inst., Southwestern Legal Found. (trustee), Internat. and Comparative Law Ctr. (adv. bd.). Home: 7710 Scotia Dr Dallas TX 75248 Office: 500 LTV Center 2001 Ross Ave Dallas TX 75201

ELLIOTT, GEOFFREY CHARLES, newspaper editor; b. Coventry, Eng., May 10, 1945; s. Alfred Stanley and Elsie (Wilday) E.; m. Lynda Barbara Williams; children: Joanne Marie, Nicholas John. Reporter Coventry Evening Telegraph, 1962-67, chief feature writer, 1969-72, dep. editor, 1973-79, editor, 1981—; editor Kent Messenger, Maidstone, 1979-81. Mem. Guild Brit. Newspaper Editors (chmn. W. Midlands guild 1987-88, chmn. parliamentary and legal com. 1983-86), Press Council. Anglican. Clubs: Round Table, Rugby, Maidstone, Coventry. Office: Coventry Evening Telegraph, Corporation St, Coventry CV1 1FP, England

ELLIOTT, INGER MCCABE, designer, textile company executive; b. Oslo, Feb. 23, 1933; d. David and Lova (Katz) Abrahamsen; came to U.S., 1941; naturalized, 1946; A.B. in History with honors, Cornell U., 1954; postgrad. Harvard U., 1955; A.M. (Jean Birdsall fellow), Radcliffe Coll., 1957; m. Osborn Elliott, Oct. 20, 1973; children by previous marriage—Kari McCabe, Alexander McCabe, Molly McCabe. Editor, East European Student and Youth Service, N.Y.C., 1957-60; photographer Rapho-Guillumette, U.S. and fgn. countries, 1960-73; pres. China Seas, Inc., N.Y.C., 1972—; tchr. Newton (Mass.) Pub. Schs., 1955-56. Mem. East Asia vis. com. Harvard U. Recipient Roscoe awards, 1978, 79, 80, 82-86. Mem. Am. Soc. Mag. Photographers, Am. Women's Econ. Devel. Corp., Com. of 200, Nat. Home Fashions League, Phi Beta Kappa. Author: Batik: Fabled Cloth of Java. Women Photographers, 1970; A Week in Amy's World, 1970; A Week in Henry's World, 1971; portfolio appeared in Infinity mag., 1969. Club: Cosmopolitan. Avocations: skiing, tennis. Home: 36 E 72nd St New York NY 10021 Office: 21 E 4th St New York NY 10003

ELLIOTT, IVAN A., lawyer; b. White County, Ill., Nov. 18, 1889; s. Benjamin Franklin and Nellie B. (Stroup) E.; m. Malen Stinson, Oct. 12, 1922; children—Ivan A., Norman J. Student, Ill. Wesleyan Acad., 1909-11, U. Ill., 1913; LL.B., Ill. Wesleyan U., 1916. Bar: Ill. 1917, U.S. Dist. Ct. (so. dist.) Ill. 1922, U.S. Ct. Appeals (7th cir.) 1930, U.S. Supreme Ct. 1953. Ptnr. Conger & Elliott, Carmi, Ill., 1919-49, 53-78, 78-86; dir. White County Abstract Co., White County Democratic Tribune; asst. atty. gen. State of Ill., 1932-40, atty. gen., 1949-53; city atty. City of Carmi, 1933-43; states atty. White County, Carmi, 1936-42; Home service sec. White County ARC, 1923-43; pres. grade sch. bd. Carmi Twp. 1933-43; Dem. state cen. committeeman 24th Congl. Dist., Ill., 1932-40. Served to lt. col., U.S. Army, 1917-1918, 1942-44, ETO. Mem. Ill. Bar Assn., ABA, White County Bar Assn., Chgo. Bar Assn., Carmi C. of C., White County Hist. Soc., Am. Legion (comdr. 1920-21, post service officer 1920-42), VFW, Sigma Phi Epsilon, Phi Alpha Delta. Presbyterian. Lodges: Kiwanis (pres. 1933), Elks. Home: 206 S 3d St Carmi IL 62821 Office: Farm Bur Bldg Carmi IL 62821

ELLIOTT, JOHN DORMAN, business executive; b. Oct. 3, 1941; s. Frank Faithful and Anita Caroline Elliott; m. Lorraine Clare Golder, 1965; 3 children. BCom (hons.), U. Melbourne, Australia, 1962, MBA, 1965. With BHP, Melbourne, 1963-65, McKinsey and Co., Melbourne, 1966-72; mng. dir. Henry Jones (IXL), 1972; mng. dir. Elders IXL (Henry Jones IXL merged with Elder Smith Goldsbrough Mort), 1981, acquired Carlton and United Breweries, 1983; chmn., chief exec. Elders IXL Ltd., 1985—. Federal treas. Liberal Party Australia, 1985—. Clubs: Melbourne, Australian, Savage, Royal Melbourne Tennis. Office: 546 Toorak Rd, Toorak, Victoria 3142, Australia *

ELLIOTT, JOHN FRANKLIN, clergyman; b. Neosho, Mo., June 11, 1915; s. William Marion and Charlotte Jeanette (Crump) E.; student Maryville Coll., 1933-35; A.B., Austin Coll., 1937; postgrad. Louisville Presbyn. Sem., 1937-38, U. Tenn., 1938, Dallas Theol. Sem., 1939-40; B.D., Columbia Theol. Sem., 1942, M.Div., 1971; D.Litt. (hon.), Internat. Acad., 1954; m. Winifred Margaret Key, July 6, 1939; children—Paul Timothy, Stephen Marion, Andrew Daniel. Ordained to ministry Presbyn. Ch., 1942; founder Emory Presbyn. Ch., Atlanta, 1941, Wildwood Presbyn. Ch., Salem, Va., 1950; pastor Wylam Presbyn. Ch., Birmingham, Ala., 1942-47, Salem Presbyn. Ch., 1947-51, Calvary Presbyn. Ch. Ind., Fort Worth, 1952-86 ; founder, pastor Grace Presbyn. Ch. Ind., Roanoke, Va., 1951-52; founder, headmaster Colony Christian Sch., Ft. Worth, 1968-86; founder dir. Grace Ministries, Ft. Worth, 1986— . Bd. dirs., pres. Salem (Va.) Nursing Assn., 1949; charter mem. Fellowship Independent Evang. Chs., 1950—, pres., 1967, nat. sec., 1971; founder, dir. Ft. Worth Home Bible Classes, 1954—; dir. Spanish Publs., Inc., 1969—; bd. dirs. Ind. Bd. for Presbyn. Home Missions, 1956-74; dist. committeeman Longhorn council Boy Scouts Am., Ft. Worth, 1960-66; bd. dirs. Union Gospel Mission, Ft. Worth, 1965-70, pres., 1968; mem. U.S. Coast Guard Aux., Ft. Worth, 1967—; pilot, chaplain, col. CAP, Ft. Worth, 1970-80 , chmn. nat. chaplain com., 1979-80, chief of chaplains, 1980-82 ; ministerial adviser bd. dirs. Reformed Theol. Sem., Jackson, Miss., 1973-83; chaplain Tex. Constl. Conv., 1974; bd. dirs. Scripture Memory Fellowship Internat., 1979-84, Graham Bible Coll., 1966-74; part-time chaplain Dallas Cowboys, Tex. Rangers, Kansas City Royals. Fellow Philos. Soc. Gt. Britain (Victoria Inst.), Royal Geog. Soc., Huguenot Soc. of London. Clubs: Ft. Worth, Ridglea Country, Ft. Worth Boat, Rotary. Home: 3980 Edgehill Rd Fort Worth TX 76116 Office: Ridglea Bank Bldg 6300 Ridglea Pl Suite 420 Fort Worth TX 76116

ELLIOTT, LEE ANN, psychologist; b. Tulsa, Jan. 22, 1923; d. John Lewis and Evelyn (Peters) Moore; m. Craig Judson Elliott (dec. Feb. 1971). B.S., Okla. State U., 1945; postgrad. UCLA, 1947-50. Part owner, Profl. Guidance Assocs., Sherman Oaks, Calif., 1961-66; mgr., dir., spokesperson Alpha Oxi Omega, North Hollywood, Calif., 1967—; vis. nurse Vis. Nurses Assn., Hollywood, Calif., 1977-78, 1978—. Mem. Republican Presdl. Task Force, U.S. Senatorial Club, 1984—. Fellow Nat. Assn. Female Execs., Smithsonian Inst.; mem. Internat. Platform Assn., Heritage Found. Avocations: dress design, writing. Home: 5251 Strohm St North Hollywood CA 91601 Office: Alpha Oxi Omega 5149 Bakman St North Hollywood CA 91601

ELLIOTT, ROBERT BETZEL, physician; b. Ada, Ohio, Dec. 8, 1926; s. Floyd Milton and Rose Marguerite (Betzel) E.; m. Margaret Mary Robichaux, Aug. 26, 1954; children: Howard A., Michael D., Robert Bruce, Douglas J., John C., Joan O. BA, Ohio No. U., 1949; MD, U. Cin., 1953. Diplomate Am. Bd. Family Pracitice. Intern Charity Hosp., New Orleans, 1953-54; resident in pathology Bapt. Meml. Hosp., Memphis, 1958-59; practice medicine specializing in family practice Ada, 1959—; mem. staff Ohio No. U. Health Service, Ada, 1960-70; Coroner Hardin County, 1973—. Served with U.S. Army, 1945-46, PTO. Mem. Ada Exempted Village Sch. Bd., 1960—, pres., 1966-69, 72—, v.p. 1971—. Named Ohio Family Physician of Yr., 1985. Mem. AMA, Ohio State Med. Assn., Hardin County Med. Soc. (pres. 1964), Am. Acad. Family Physicians, Ohio Acad. Family Physicians, Lima Acad. Family Physicians, Am. Coll. Health Assn. Democrat. Presbyterian. Lodges: Masons, Elks. Home: 4429 State Rt 235 Ada OH 45810 Office: 302 N Main St Ada OH 45810

ELLIOTT, SHIRLEY RAE, medical technologist; b. Binghamton, N.Y., Oct. 21, 1922; d. John Rook and Carrie Marie (Keeney) Reynolds; m. Floyd Strother Elliott, Nov. 13, 1943; children: Linda Rae, Teresa Marie, Rita Kay, Susan Irene, John Roger, Katherine Claire, Floyd Strother. Student, Duke U., 1940-42; student, U. Tex., 1942-43, Sch. Med. Tech. VA Med. Ctr., 1955-56. Research technologist VA Med. Ctr., Nashville, 1956, med. technologist microbiology, chemistry, 1956-59, med. technologist, supr., 1959-66, coagulation/parasitology, technologist, 1966-72, supr. med. technology, 1972-88. Named Mother of the Yr., Gallatin Jaycettes, 1976, others. Mem. Nat. Geographic Soc., Cousteau Soc., Duke Alumni Assn., Met. Opera Guild, Am. Soc. Med. Technologists (life), Internat. Soc. Med. Technologists, Tenn. Soc. Microbiology, Am. Soc. Clin. Pathologists., Cousteau Soc., DAR. Methodist. Clubs: Nat. Commodore, Iron Dukes. Home: 1007 Bentley Cir Gallatin TN 37066 Office: 1310 24th Ave S Nashville TN 37212

ELLIS, ALAN JOHN, educator; b. Walsall, Staffordshire, Eng., July 7, 1940; s. Charles Henry and Elsie Madeline (Price) E.; m. Jennifer Helen Mary Evans, Aug. 14, 1976; 1 child, David Stephen John. B.Sc. with 1st class honors, U. Birmingham, 1961; D.Phil., U. Oxford, 1965, D.Sc., 1979. Lectr. math. Univ. Coll. Swansea, Wales, 1964-72, sr. lectr., 1972-73, reader in math., 1973-81; prof., head dept. math. U. Hong Kong, 1981—vis asst. prof. Calif. Inst. Tech., Pasadena, 1968-69. Author: Banach Spaces of Continuous Functions, 1978; Basic Algebra and Geometry, 1982; joint author: Convexity Theory and its Applications, 1980. Contbr. articles to profl. jours. Fellow Inst. Math and Its Applications; mem. London Math. Soc., Am. Math. Soc., Hong Kong Math. Soc. (pres.). Office: Math Dept Univ Hong Kong, Pokfulam Rd, Hong Kong Hong Kong

ELLIS, DAVID DALE, lawyer; b. Columbus, Ga., Dec. 22, 1952; s. Audie Stammattee and Eva Grace (Thomas) E. B.A. cum laude Mercer U., Macon, Ga., 1974; J.D., Drake U., 1976, M.P.A., 1977. Bar: Iowa 1977, Ga. 1978, U.S. Dist. Ct. (no. dist.) Ga. 1979, U.S. Ct. Appeals (11th cir.) 1979, U.S. Supreme Ct. 1983, Tex. 1986. Instr. Grad. Sch., Drake U., Des Moines, 1977; claims adjuster Farm Bur. Ins. Co., Des Moines, 1977; assoc. firm Cotton, White & Palmer, Atlanta, 1978-82; mng. atty. Hyatt Legal Services, Marietta and Smyrna, Ga., 1982-84, regional ptnr., Houston, 1984-86; sr. assoc. Hughes & Hilbert P.C., 1986-87; sr. ptnr. Jeffers & Ellis, P.C., Houston, 1987—. Career awareness chmn. Houston council Boy Scouts Am., 1984-85; instr. project bus., legal advisor Jr. Achievement, Houston, 1984-85. Mem. Iowa Bar Assn., Ga. Bar Assn., State Bar Tex., Am. Soc. Tng. and Devel., Atlanta Jaycees (chmn. Empty Stockings Fund 1982, v.p. individual devel. 1983-84; Officer of Yr. 1984), U.S. Jaycees (life, ambassador award 1985, named JCI senator), Houston Jaycees (exec. v.p. 1986—, chmn. govt. affairs 1984-85, pres. 1987—), Tex. Jaycees (legal counsel 1985-87), ABA (chmn. bankruptcy com. 1985-87, co-chmn. 1987, chmn. 1987—), Atlanta Bar Assn., Houston Bar Assn., Houston Young Lawyers Assn., Tex. Young Lawyers Assn., Assn. Trial Lawyers of Am., Ga. Trial Lawyers Assn.Lodge: Masons. Office: Jeffers & Ellis PC 3013 Fountainview #275 Houston TX 77057

ELLIS, EDWARD PRIOLEAU, lawyer; b. Atlanta, May 31, 1929; s. Frampton E. and Eloise (Oliver) E.; m. Harriet L. Witham, Sept. 5, 1954; children: Harriet, Edward, Andrew. AB cum laude, U. Ga., 1951; LLB, Harvard U., 1956. Bar: Ga. 1956. Ptnr. Ellis, Moore & Simons, Atlanta, 1976—; pres. First Security and Exchange Co., Atlanta, 1965—. Pres. Peachtree Heights Civic Assn., Atlanta, 1985. Served to 1st lt. U.S. Army, 1952-54. Fellow Am. Coll. Probate Counsel; mem. Ga. Bar Assn. (chmn.

taxation sect.), Phi Beta Kappa. Home: 2804 Habersham Rd NW Atlanta GA 30305 Office: Ellis Moore & Simons 3015-B Piedmont Rd NE Atlanta GA 30305

ELLIS, ELDON EUGENE, physician; b. Washington, Ind., July 2, 1922; s. Osman Polson and Ina Lucretia (Cochran) E.; B.A., U. Rochester, 1946, M.D., 1949; m. Irene Clay, June 26, 1948 (dec. 1968); m. 2d, Priscilla Dean Strong, Sept. 20, 1969; children—Paul Addison, Kathe Lynn, Jonathan Clay, Sharon Anne, Eldon Eugene, Rebecca Deborah. Intern in surgery Stanford U. Hosp., San Francisco, 1949-50, resident and fellow in surgery, 1950-52, 55; Schilling fellow in pathology San Francisco Gen. Hosp., 1955; partner Redwood Med. Clinic, Redwood City, Calif., 1955—, med. dir., 1984-87; dir. Sequoia Hosp., Redwood City, 1974-82; asst. clin. prof. surgery Stanford U., 1970-80. Pres. Sequoia Hosp. Found., 1983—; pres., chmn. bd. dirs. Bay Chamber Symphony Orchestra, 1988—; mem. Nat. Bd. of Benevolence Evang. Covenent Ch., Chgo., 1988—. Served with USNR, 1942-46, 50-52. Named Outstanding Citizen of Yr., Redwood City, 1987. Mem. San Mateo County (pres. 1961-63), Calif. (pres. 1965-66), Am. (v.p. 1974-75) heart assns., San Mateo Med. Soc. (pres. 1969-70), San Mateo County Comprehensive Health Planning Council (v.p. 1969-70), Calif., Am. med. assns., San Mateo, Stanford surg. socs., Am. Coll. Chest Physicians, Calif. Thoracic Soc., Cardiovascular Council. Republican. Mem. Peninsula Covenant Ch. Club: Commonwealth. Home: 3621 Farm Hill Blvd Redwood City CA 94061 Office: Redwood Med Clinic 2900 Whipple Ave Redwood City CA 94062

ELLIS, FRED WILSON, pharmacology educator; b. Heath Springs, S.C., Apr. 24, 1914; s. George Dixon and Mary Jane (Hammond) E.; m. Elizabeth Ervin Landrum, Aug. 6, 1940; children: Barbara (Mrs. Glenn E. Minah), Marybeth, Frances (Mrs. Alan Segar), Frieda (Mrs. Lawrence G. Norris). B.S., U. S.C., 1936; postgrad., Yale U., 1936-37; M.S., U. Fla., 1938; Ph.D., U. Md., 1941; cert. in medicine, U. N.C., 1948; M.D., Duke, 1952. Asso. pharmacology Jefferson Med. Coll., 1942-44; faculty pharmacology U. N.C. Sch. Medicine, Chapel Hill, 1944—; prof. U. N.C. Sch. Medicine, 1964-80, prof. emeritus, 1980—; Vis. prof. pharmacology U. Ky. Med. Center; cons. Research Triangle Inst., N.C.; Mem. sci. adv. council Distilled Spirits Council U.S., Washington, 1973—; mem. peer rev. bd. Nat. Council on Alcoholism, N.Y.C., 1973-79; mem. N.C. Alcoholism Research Authority, 1974-84, vice-chmn., 1978-82; mem. psychopharmacology study sect. NIH; cons. N.C. Breath and Blood Analyser Tng. and Teaching Program;. Contbr. articles to sci. jours. Vice-chmn. Chapel Hill Bd. Edn., 1961-63, mem., 1963-67. Recipient Disting. Teaching award U. N.C., 1972, Vol. Service awards Nat. Council on Alcoholism, 1977, 78, Cert. of Appreciation as Outstanding North Carolinian, State of N.C., 1984, Disting. Service award U. N.C. Sch. Med., Chapel Hill, 1986. Postdoctoral fellow U. Md. Sch. Medicine, 1941-42; research grantee Nat. Inst. Alcohol Abuse and Alcoholism, 1977-83; research grantee Nat. Found. March of Dimes, 1977-79. Mem. AMA (cons. council pharmacy, chemistry, drugs), AAAS, Soc. Exptl. Biology and Medicine (sec. Southeastern sect. 1958-62), Am. Soc. Pharmacology and Exptl. Therapeutics, Research Soc. on Alcoholism (constn. com. 1979, membership com. 1978-85, chmn. 1980-85, chmn. fetal alcohol study group 1983, 84), Blue Key Soc. (hon.), Sigma Xi. Home: 805 Old Mill Rd Chapel Hill NC 27514

ELLIS, GEORGE EDWIN, JR., chemical engineer; b. Beaumont, Tex., Apr. 14, 1921; s. George Edwin and Julia (Ryan) E.; B.S. in Chem. Engring., U. Tex., 1948; M.S., U. So. Calif., 1958, M.B.A., 1965, M.S. in Mech. Engring., 1968, M.S. in Mgmt. Sci., 1971, Engr. in Indsl. and Systems Engring., 1979. Research chem. engr. Tex. Co., Port Arthur, Tex., 1948-51, Long Beach, Calif., Houston, 1952-53, Space and Information div. N.Am. Aviation Co., Downey, Calif., 1959-61, Magna Corp., Anaheim, Calif., 1961-62; chem. process engr. AiResearch Mfg. Co., Los Angeles, 1953-57, 57-59; chem. engr. Petroleum Combustion & Engring. Co., Santa Monica, Calif., 1957, Jacobs Engring. Co., Pasadena, Calif., 1957, Sesler & Assos., Los Angeles, 1959; research specialist Marquardt Corp., Van Nuys, Calif., 1962-67; sr. project engr. Conductron Corp., Northridge, 1967-68; information systems asst. Los Angeles Dept. Water and Power, 1969—. Instr. thermodynamics U. So. Calif., Los Angeles, 1957. Served with USAAF, 1943-45. Mem. Am. Chem. Soc., Am. Soc. for Metals, Am. Inst. Chem. Engrs., ASME, Am. Electroplaters Soc., Am. Inst. Indsl. Engrs., Am. Mktg. Assn., Ops. Research Soc. Am., Am. Prodn. and Inventory Control Soc., Am. Assn. Cost Engrs., Nat. Assn. Accts., Soc. Mfg. Engrs., Pi Tau Sigma, Phi Lambda Upsilon, Alpha Pi Mu. Home: 1344 W 20th St San Pedro CA 90731 Office: Dept Water and Power Los Angeles CA 90012

ELLIS, JAMES REED, lawyer; b. Oakland, Calif., Aug. 5, 1921; s. Floyd E. and Hazel (Reed) E.; m. Mary Lou Earling, Nov. 18, 1944 (dec.); children: Robert Lee, Judith Ann (dec.), Lynn Earling, Steven Reed. B.S., Yale, 1942; J.D., U. Wash., 1948; LL.D., Lewis and Clark U., 1968, Seattle U., 1981. Bar: Wash. 1949, D.C. 1971. Partner firm Preston, Thorgrimson, Horowitz, Starin & Ellis, 1952-69; Preston, Thorgrimson, Starin, Ellis & Holman, Seattle, 1969-72, Preston, Thorgrimson, Ellis, Holman & Fletcher, 1972-79; sr. partner firm Preston, Thorgrimson, Ellis & Holman, 1979—; dep. pros. atty., King County, 1952; gen. counsel Municipality of Met. Seattle, 1958-79. Mem. Nat. Water Commn., 1970-73; mem. urban transp. adv. council U.S. Dept. Transp., 1970-71; mem. Wash. Planning Adv. Council, 1965-72; pres. Forward Thrust Inc., 1966-73; chmn. Mayors Com. on Rapid Transit, 1964-65; Trustee Ford Found., 1970-82, mem. exec. com., 1978-82; bd. regents U. Wash., 1965-77, pres., 1972-73; trustee Resources for the Future, 1983—; mem. council Nat. Mcpl. League, 1968-76, v.p., 1972-76; chmn. Save our Local Farmlands Com., 1978-79, King County Farmlands Adv. Com., 1980-82; pres. Friends of Freeway Park, 1976—; bd. dirs. Nat. Park and Recreation Assn., 1979-82; bd. dirs. Wash. State Conv. and Trade Ctr., 1982—, vice chmn., 1982-86, chmn., 1986—. Served to 1st lt. USAAF, 1943-46. Recipient Bellevue First Citizen award, 1968, Seattle First Citizen award, 1968, Nat. Conservation award Am. Motors, 1968, Distinguished Service award Wash. State Dept. Parks and Recreation, 1968, Distinguished Citizen award Nat. Municipal League, 1969, King County Distinguished Citizen award, 1970, La Guardia award Center N.Y.C. Affairs, 1975, Environ. Quality award EPA, 1977, Am. Inst. for Public Service award, 1974, U. Wash. Recognition award, 1981. Fellow Am. Bar Found.; Mem. ABA (ho. dels. 1978-82, past chmn. urban, state and local govt. law sect.), Wash. Bar Assn., Seattle Bar Assn., D.C. Bar Assn., Am. Judicature Soc., Acad. Public Adminstrn., Council on Fgn. Relations, Mcpl. League Seattle and King County (past pres.), Order of Hosp. of St. John of Jerusalem, AIA (hon.), Order of Coif (hon.), Phi Delta Phi, Phi Gamma Delta. Club: Rainier (Seattle). Home: 903 SE Shoreland Dr Bellevue WA 98004 Office: 5400 Columbia Ctr Seattle WA 98104

ELLIS, LAWRENCE DOBSON, internist; b. Pitts., Oct. 11, 1932; s. Robert S. and Elizabeth (Dobson) E.; m. Jacqueline Coogan, June 8, 1954; children: Christine, Thomas, Holly Anne, Jerome. B.S., U. Notre Dame, 1954; M.D., U. Pitts., 1958. Diplomate: Am. Bd. Internal Medicine. Intern in internal medicine U. Pitts. Health Center Hosps., 1958-59; resident in internal medicine Presbyn.-Univ. Hosp., Pitts., 1959-60, 62-63, fellow in hematology, 1963-64; practice medicine specializing in internal medicine, hematology and oncology Pitts., 1964—; clin. asst. prof. medicine U. Pitts., 1966-71; clin. assoc. prof. U. Pitts, 1971-81; clin. prof. U. Pitts., 1981—; mem. active staff Presbyn.-Univ. Hosp., sec., treas. med. staff, 1972-76, v.p. med. staff, 1976-78, pres., 1978—; mem. cons. staff Shadyside Hosp., Pitts., 1964—, Allegheny County Bd. Health, 1976—; bd. commrs. Health Edn. Ctr., Pitts., 1976—; mem. Pa. State Bd. Medicine, 1986—, vice chmn. 1987—; mem. active staff Montefiore Hosp. Contbr. articles to profl. jours., chpts. to med. books. Trustee Leukemia Soc. Am., 1972—, chmn. profl. edn., 1973—, nat. pres., 1985-87; trustee Presbyn.-Univ. Hosp., 1981—, U. Pitts., 1986—. Served to lt. M.C. USN, 1960-62. Recipient Bicentennial medallion of distinction U. Pitts., 1987. Fellow ACP; mem. Pa. Med. Soc. (del. 1974—), Allegheny County Med. Soc. (pres. 1976, chmn. bd. 1977, bd. dirs. 1970—, Frederick M. Jacob Physician of Merit award 1981), Pitts. Acad. Medicine (pres. 1984), Royal Soc. Medicine, N.Y. Acad. Scis., AMA, Am. Soc. Hematology, Leukemia Soc. Am. (exec. com. 1978—, John J. Kenny award 1981), Med. Alumni Assn. U. Pitts. (pres. 1979-80), Alpha Omega Alpha. Republican. Roman Catholic. Clubs: Pitts. Field, Univ., Pitts. Athletic Assn. Office: 3471 Fifth Ave Suite 1111 Pittsburgh PA 15213

ELLIS, LESTER NEAL, JR., lawyer; b. Washington, Aug. 1, 1948; s. Lester Neal and Marie (Brooks) E.; m. Rhoda Goheen, June 14, 1970; children—Patrick Neal, Bret Hamilton, Ryan Renyer. B.S. U.S. Mil. Acad., 1970; J.D., U. Va., 1975. Bar: Va. 1975, U.S. Ct. Appeals (5th cir.) 1977, D.C. 1978, U.S. Ct. Appeals (4th and D.C. cirs.) 1979, U.S. Ct. Appeals (11th cir.) 1982. trial atty. litigation div. office JAG, Dept. Army, Washington, 1975-78; assoc. Hunton & Williams, Richmond, Va., 1978-84, ptnr., Raleigh, N.C., 1984—. Contbr. articles to profl. jours. Mem. Wake County Bd. Elections, 1986—, chmn., 1987—. Served to maj. U.S. Army, 1970-78. Recipient Judge Paul W. Brosman award U.S. Ct. Mil. Appeals, 1975. Mem. ABA, Va. Bar Assn. (spl. issues com. 1982—), D.C. Bar Assn. (ct. rules com. 1981—, Wake County bd. elections 1986—, chmn. 1987—), Phi Kappa Phi. Republican. Episcopalian. Home: 7204 Willmark Ct Raleigh NC 27612 Office: Hunton & Williams One Hanover Sq Raleigh NC 27602

ELLIS, MICHAEL MARTIN, sales executive; b. Pompton Plains, N.J., Aug. 19, 1959; s. Philip Richard and Irene (Preblo) E.; m. Vivian Jade Liu, Mar. 11, 1985. BA in Psychology, Mercer U., 1982, MBA, 1988. Br. sales mgr. GA Industries, Ltd. subs. Lee Guan Enterprises, Ltd., Taipei, Rep. of China, 1982-85; v.p. mktg. V.M.T. Industries, Ltd., Taipei, 1985—; bus. cons. Mizuki Tensei Indsl. Co., Ltd., Chia I Hsien, Rep. of China, 1986—, Top Standard Mfg. Co., Ltd., Taipei, 1986—, Chung Tai Iron Works Co., Ltd., Nei-hu, Rep. of China, 1986—, Yu Chuan Metal Co., Ltd., Shu-lin Taipei, 1986—. Democrat. Presbyterian. Lodge: Order of DeMolay (precept 1976-77). Home: Grant Island PO Box 285 Grant FL 32949-0285 Office: VMT Industries Ltd, 64 Hsin Sheng N 2d Floor, Rd Sect One, Taipei Republic of China

ELLIS, PATRICIA JASMINE, banker; b. Trinidad, Apr. 28, 1954; d. Rudolph Mark Allan and Alma (Joseph) Chambers; m. Garnett Leroy Ellis, Oct. 1, 1983; children: Gennyne, Phiona. BA, Hartwick Coll., 1977; MA, Fordham U., 1980. Tchr. music Bahamas Ministry Edn., Nassau, Bahamas, 1977-79; mgmt. trainee 1st Savs. and Loan, Nassau, Bahamas, 1980-81, human resources devel. officer, 1982-84; asst. v.p. human resources devel. 1st Home Banking Ctr., Nassau, Bahamas, 1984—. Mem. Am. Soc. Tng. and Devel., Am. Soc. Personnel Adminstrs., Am. Mgmt. Assn. Anglican. Office: 1st Home Banking Centre, P O Box N-3744, Nassau The Bahamas

ELLIS, ROBERT GRISWOLD, engineer; b. Kokomo, Ind., Dec. 28, 1908; s. Ernest Eli and Ethel (Griswold) E.; A.B., Ind. U., 1934; m. Rachel O. Burckey, Oct. 27, 1984. Mem. staff Ind. U., Bloomington, 1930-34; researcher Blackett-Sample-Hummert Inc., Chgo., 1934, asst. mgr. merchandising, 1935-36; prodn. mgr. Harvey & Howe, Inc., Chgo., 1936-37; Chgo./Midwest dist. mgr. L.F. Grammes & Sons, Inc., Allentown, Pa., 1937-45; with Ellis & Co., Chgo. and Park Ridge, Ill., 1945—, pres., chief engr., 1948—, mng. dir., chief engr. Ellis Internat. Co., Chgo. and Park Ridge, Ill., 1965—, chief engr. Ellis Engring. Co., Park Ridge, 1969—. Chmn. Citizens Com. for Cleaner and More Beautiful Park Ridge, 1957-60; trustee, treas. bd. dirs. 1st United Methodist Ch., Park Ridge, 1974-77. Recipient Civic Achievement award City of Park Ridge, 1959. Mem. Soc. Automotive Engrs., Armed Forces Communications and Electronics Assn. (life), Ind. U. Alumni Assn. (life), Quartermaster Assn. (pres. Chgo. chpt. 1957-58), Ind. Acad. Sci., Am. Powder Metallurgy Inst., Ill. Acad. Sci., Mfrs. Agts. Assn. Gt. Britain and Ireland,Internat. Union Comml. Agts. and Brokers, Am. Logistics Assn., Am. Soc. Metals, Indiana Soc. of Chgo. Republican. Clubs: Union League, Varsity (pres. Chgo. 1957), Ind. U. Alumni (pres. Chgo. 1956-57), Emeritus of Ind. U., Internat. Trade. Home: 643 Parkwood St Park Ridge IL 60068 Office: Box 344 306 Busse Hwy Park Ridge IL 60068-0344

ELLIS, WILLIAM GRENVILLE, educational administrator, management consultant; b. Teaneck, N.J., Nov. 29, 1940; s. Grenville Brigham and Vivian Lilian (Breeze) E.; m. Nancy Elizabeth Kempton, 1963; children—William Grenville, Bradford Graham. B.S. in Bus. Adminstrn., Babson Coll., 1962; M.B.A., Suffolk U., 1963; Ed.M., Westfield State Coll., 1965; Ed.D., Pa. State U., 1968; MLE (Sears Roebuck Found. scholar), Harvard U., 1980; IAL, MIT, 1984. Asst. prof. bus. Rider Coll., 1968-69; div. dir., assoc. prof. Castleton State Coll., 1969-72; exec. v.p., prof. Coll. of St. Joseph the Provider, Rutland, Vt., 1972-73; acad. v.p., dean grad. sch. Thomas Coll., Waterville, Maine, 1973-82; pres. Wayland Acad., Beaver Dam, Wis., 1982—; corporator 1st Consumers Savs., 1974-81, Maine Savs., 1981-83; bd. dirs. Marine Bank, 1983—. Trustee Marian Coll., 1988—, Wayland Acad., 1982—; auditor, Town of Castleton (Vt.), 1969-71; pres. Kennebee Valley Youth Hockey, Augusta, Maine, 1975-77; sec., bd. dirs. Beaver Dam Community Hosp. Named Cons. of Yr., SBA, 1975, 77; recipient Community Service award Rutland C. of C., 1973. Mem. Am. Psychol. Assn., Nat. Assn. Ind. Schs., Nat. Assn. Intercollegiate Athletics (cert. of merit 1979), North Central Assn. Colls. and Secondary Schs., Wis. Assn. Ind. Schs. (pres. 1984-86), Ind. Schs. Assn. Central States, Beaver Dam C. of C. (pres. 1985, 86), Cum Laude Soc., Alpha Chi, Pi Omega Pi, Alpha Delta Sigma, Delta Pi Epsilon, Phi Delta Kappa Clubs: Madison, Natanis, Old Hickory. Lodge: Rotary. Author: The Analysis and Attainment of Economic Stability, 1963; The Relationship of Related Work Experience to the Teaching Success of Beginning Teachers, 1968; contbr. numerous articles, abstracts to profl. publs. Home: 101 N University Ave Beaver Dam WI 53916 Office: Wayland Acad PO Box 398 Beaver Dam WI 53916

ELLIS, WILLIAM HARTSHORNE, actor, director, social psychologist; b. Cin., Dec. 5, 1929; s. William Hartshorne and Mary Morris (La Boiteaux) E.; m. Miriam Hubbard Roelofs, Dec. 22, 1950; children: Miriam, Howard, David, Jonathan. Student St. Pauls Sch., 1943-47, Kenyon, 1947-48; BFA, Art. Inst. of Chgo., 1953; MA, Columbia U., 1961; PhD, NYU, 1975. Cert. in psychoanalysis and psychotherapy Tng. Inst. for Mental Health Practitioners, 1977. Actor, dir., 1953-55; programmer trainee IBM, 1955; IBM systems and procedures adminstr. Singer Mfg. Co., 1956-59; pvt. practice individual and group psychotherapy, N.Y.C., 1961—; workshop and encounter group leader; applications of principles of sport psychology in the performing arts since 1985—; panel mem. Artist-Therapists for Artists, N.Y.C.; dir. Hartshorne Prodns., 1981—; actor, dir., producer, 1981—; staff mem. Ctr. for Holistic Health Care, S.I., N.Y., 1987—. Patentee drainboard, 1982. Founder, pres. Henderson Manor Revival Assn. New Brighton, N.Y., 1983—. Served with USN, 1948-49. Mem. Am. Psychol. Assn., Can. Psychol. Assn., Am. Acad. Psychotherapists, N.Y. Soc. Clin. Psychologists, Internat. Soc. Sport Psychology, Actors' Equity Assn., Screen Actors Guild, Soc. Stage Dirs. and Choreographers, AFTRA, Dramatists Guild, Am. Dirs. Inst. Clubs: Princeton, Players. Avocations: boardsailing, bicycling, flying, writing. Office: Hartshorne Prodns 88 Henderson Ave Staten Island NY 10301

ELLIS, WILLIAM HERBERT BAXTER, medical consultant, underwriter; b. Newcastle on Tyne, Northumberland, Eng., July 2, 1921; s. William Baxter and Georgina Isabella (Waller) E.; m. Margaret Mary Limb, July 22, 1948 (div. 1977); children—Penelope Ann Baxter Ellis Deakin, Christopher John Baxter. M.B., B.S., Durham U., Newcastle on Tyne, 1944, M.D., 1952. Commd. Surgeon lt. Royal Navy, 1945, advanced through grades to surgeon comdr., 1953; stationed in Malta, Farnborough and U.S.; with Inst. Aviation Medicine, Farnborough, Eng., 1950-56, Navy, Naval Navy Aviation Medicine Acceleration Lab., Johnsville, Pa., 1956-58; mem. main bd. BEWAC (U.K. and Nigerian Coy), 1964-70; med. cons. Plessey Coy, Phillips, Eng., 1972—, Sundstrand Ltd.; underwriter Lloyd's; dir. gen. Dr. Barnardos, London, 1970-72; county surgeon St. John Ambulance, Gloucestershire, Eng., 1979-86, comdr., 1987—; researcher in aviation field. Inventor audio airspeed for decklanding, 1952 (Gilbert Blane medal 1952); Author: Human Factors in Industry, Rehabilitation into Industry, 1983; Hippocrates, R.N., 1984. Vice-chmn. St. John Council, Gloucestershire, 1987—. Decorated Air Force Cross, Air Ministry, 1952.; named comdr. St. John. Mem. Royal Coll. Gen. Practitioners (research found. bd. 1962-78). Mem. Ch. of Eng. Clubs: Army and Navy, Naval and Mil. (London). Home: The Manor House, Compton Abdale, Cheltenham, Gloucestershire England GL54 4DR Office: care Midland Bank, 5 Threadneedle St, London EC2R 8BD, England

ELLIS, WILLIAM RUFUS, physicist, government official; b. Greenville, S.C., Jan. 22, 1940; s. William Rufus and Mary Louise (Rogers) E.; m. Gail Maxcine Gladden, Aug. 13, 1966; children—Benjamin Brian, Jaman Nathaniel. B.S., Clemson U., 1962; M.A., Princeton U., 1965, Ph.D., 1967. Vis. scientist A.E.R.E. Culham Lab., Abingdon, Eng., 1967-69; mem. staff Los Alamos Nat. Lab., 1970-73, assoc. group leader, 1974-75; chief open systems br. Office of Fusion Energy, ERDA, Washington, 1976-78; dir. mirror systems div. Dept. Energy, 1979-83; assoc. dir. research for gen. sci. and tech. U.S. Naval Research Lab., 1983—. Contbr. articles to profl. jours. Patentee in field. Vice chmn. Los Alamos County Council, 1975-76. NSF fellow, 1961; NASA grantee, 1962-66. Mem. Am. Phys. Soc. (div. plasma physics, exec. com. 1980), AAAS, Am. Geophys. Union, Am. Nuclear Soc. Home: 1613 Auburn Ave Rockville MD 20850 Office: US Naval Research Lab Code 4000 4555 Overlook Ave SW Washington DC 20375

ELLIS-MOSS, NESTA WYN, writer; b. Llanwrst, Wales, Nov. 25, 1940; came to U.S., 1979; d. Arthur Wyn and Ada Dorothy (Jones) Ellis; m. Edward Kiper Moss, Jan. 6, 1979. BSc, U. Liverpool, Eng., 1963. Pub. relations exec. Link Info. Services, London, 1966-68; editor Carpet World, London, 1968-70; pub. relations exec. Rawes and Ptnrs., London, 1970-71, Rank, Hovis and McDougal, London, 1971-73; free-lance writer, journalist, broadcaster Africa, Washington, Can., Eng., 1979—; dir., European v.p. Moss Internat., Inc., Washington and London. Author: Dear Elector, The Truth about MP's, 1974. Parliamentary candidate Liberal Party, Eng., 1966, 69, 74, European cand., Wales, 1979. Mem. Royal Instn. London, Nat. Union of Journalists, Ind. Programme Producers Assn. Office: Moss Internat Inc, 34 Montagu Sq, London W1H 1TL, England

ELLISON, LUTHER FREDERICK, oil executive; b. Monroe, La., Jan. 2, 1925; s. Luther and Gertrude (Hudson) E.; student Emory U., 1943-44; B.S. in Petroleum Engring., Tex. A&M U., 1949, B.S. in Geol. Engring., 1950; m. Frances Z. Williams, July 17, 1948; children—Constance Elizabeth, Carolyn Williams. Jr. petroleum engr. Sun Prodn. Co., Kilgore and McAllen, Tex., 1950-52, area petroleum engr., Garcia Field, Tex., 1952-54, Delhi (La.) unit engr., 1954-60, asst. region supt., Dallas, 1960-62, dist. drilling engr., Corpus Christi, 1962-63, dist. engr., McAllen, 1963-65, supr. engring., Dallas, 1965-66, div. chief petroleum engr., 1966-70, regional mgr. engring., 1970-75, region mgr., 1975-78, dir. devel., 1978-80, v.p. devel., 1980-84; div. v.p., dir. Sun Exploration and Prodn. Co., 1984-86, pres., bd. dirs., 1986—; pres., chief exec. officer Oil & Gas Exports, Inc., Dallas, 1986—, Am. Energy Enterprises Inc., Dallas, 1988—; pres., dir., mem. exec. com. Nabors-Sun Drilling Co.; dir., mem. exec. com. East Tex. Salt & Water Disposal Co.; pres. Oil & Gas Experts Inc., 1986; speaker in field. Vice pres. Northwood Jr. High Sch. PTA, Dallas, 1967-68, pres., 1968-69. Served with USNR, 1943-46. Registered profl. engr., Tex., La. Mem. Tex.-Mid-Continent Oil and Gas Assn. (Outstanding Achievement award 1964, chmn. area 1964-65, mgr. north region, operating com., Outstanding Performance award 1985—), Am. Petroleum Inst., Soc. Petroleum Engrs., Dallas Engrs. Club, Petroleum Engrs. Club, Dallas Petroleum Club, Dallas Energy Club, Parents League, Sigma Alpha Epsilon (pres. 1944-45). Presbyterian (elder). Clubs: Northwood (Dallas), Lions, Premier (Dallas). Home: 3 Castle Creek Ct Dallas TX 75240 Office: 6440 N Central Expressway Suite 613 Dallas TX 75206

ELLISON, ROBERT ALEXANDER, JR., investors association executive; b. New Rochelle, N.Y., Nov. 29, 1942; s. Robert Alexander and Eve (Poletynski) E.; m. Sona Araxe Sandalian, May 30, 1965. B.A., Ohio U., 1968. Tchr., U.S. AID, Rabat, Morocco, 1963-64, Am. Coll., Cairo Egypt, 1964-65; stockbroker for various cos., Canada, 1968-78; pres. Gold Bondholders Protective Council, Inc., Seattle, Wash., 1978—. Mem. Am. Econ. Assn., ABA (assoc.), Internat. Assn. Club: Economist (Seattle). Registered Fin. Planners. Author: Guidelines for Investment Management: Stocks, Bonds, Commodities and Gold, 1979; contbr. articles to profl. jours. Home: 2500 Canterbury Ln Suite 413 Seattle WA 98112 Office: Gold Bondholders Protective Council Inc PO Box 2283 Seattle WA 98111

ELLISON, RUSSELL HENRY, pharmaceutical executive; b. Vancouver, B.C., Can., Sept. 6, 1947; arrived in Switzerland, 1984; s. Earl Joseph and Lucille Georgina (Sheps) E.; m. Eloise Frances Graham, Mar. 29, 1977; children: Jonathan, Sammantha, Kirsten. MD, U. B.C., Can., 1972; MS in Community Health, London Sch. Tropical Medicine & Hygiene, 1979. Family physician Health & Human Resources, Queen Charlotte Islands, B.C., Can., 1974-77; regional med. dir. Africa Ciba Geigy, Pharm. Internat., Nairobi, Kenya, 1979-84; head disease control programs Basel, Switzerland, 1984-87, head med. ops., 1987—. Editor: III Africa Regional Conference on STD, 1983; contbr. articles to profl. jours.

ELLMANN, SHEILA FRENKEL, investment company executive; b. Detroit, June 8, 1931; d. Joseph and Rose (Neback) Frenkel; BA in English, U. Mich., 1953; m. William M. Ellmann, Nov. 1, 1953; children: Douglas Stanley, Carol Elizabeth, Robert Lawrence. Dir. Advance Glove Mfg. Co., Detroit, 1954-78; v.p. Frome Investment Co., Detroit, 1980—. Mem. U. Mich. Alumni Assn., Nat. Trust Hist. Preservation. Home: 28000 Weymouth St Farmington Hills MI 48018

ELLMANN, WILLIAM MARSHALL, lawyer, arbitrator; b. Highland Park, Mich., Mar. 23, 1921; s. James I. and Jeannette (Barsook) E.; m. Sheila Estelle Frenkel, Nov. 1, 1953; children: Douglas S., Carol E., Robert L. Student, Occidental Coll., 1939-40; AB, U. Mich., 1946; LLB, Wayne State U., 1951. Bar: Mich. 1951. Sole practice Detroit, 1951—; ptnr. Ellmann & Ellmann, 1970—; Spl. com. atty. gen. Mich. to study use state troops in emergencies, 1964-65; mem. exec. com. Inst. Continuing Legal Edn., 1964-68; mem. Mich. Employment Relations Commn., 1973—, chmn., 1983-86; commr. Mackinac Island State Park Commn., 1979-85, chmn., 1983-85. Author: A Reply to the Ambassador, 1988, (with Douglas S. Ellmann) How to Win at Arbitration, 1987. Served with USAAF, 1942-46. Fellow Am. Bar Found.; mem. Am. Arbitration Assn. (mem. adv. council), Nat. Acad. Arbitrators, ABA (ho. of dels. 1969-72), Detroit Bar Assn. (vice chmn. pub. relations com. 1959), State Bar Mich. (commr. 1959-69, pres. 1966-67, co-chmn. com. on qualification jud. candidates 1970-78, mem. Detroit News secret witness panel 1983—), Practicing Law Inst. (adv. council 1969-70, spl. asst. atty. gen. 1970-78), Sigma Nu Phi. Home: 28000 Weymouth Farmington Hills MI 48018 Office: 1575 Penobsot Bldg Detroit MI 48226

ELLRODT, ROBERT JEAN LOUIS, English linguist, humanist; b. Luchon, France, July 10, 1922; s. Ernest Bernard and Albane Jeanne (Maleplate) E.; m. Suzanne Jahier, Nov. 12, 1952; children—Axel, Isabelle, Genevieve. B.A., U. Aix, 1940, M.A., 1942; D. Lettres, U. Sorbonne, 1959. Lectr. English, U. Poitiers (France), 1949-50, U. Algiers (Algeria), 1950-57, U. Toulouse (France), 1957-61; prof. English, U. Sorbonne, Paris, 1961-66; prof. English, U. Nice (France), 1966-75, dean Faculty of Letters, 1967-71; prof. Sorbonne Nouvelle, 1975-86, pres. 1986—; chmn. dept. English, 1976-79. Author: Les Poè tes Métaphysiques Anglais, 1960, 73; Neoplatonism in the Poetry of Spenser, 1960. Editor: Genèse de la Conscience Moderne, 1982. Contbr. essays, articles to profl. publs. Decorated comdr. Palmes Academiques, officier de la Lé gion d'honneur; comdr. Order Brit. Empire. Corr. fellow Brit. Acad.; mem. Assn. Universitaire pour l'Entente et la Liberté (pres. 1977—), Société des Anglicistes de l'Enselgnement Superieur (pres. 1968-78, hon. pres. 1978—), Société d'Etudes Anglaises et Américaines des 17e et 18e Siècles (hon. pres. 1976—). Home: 15 Rue Olivier Noyer, Paris 75014 France Office: 5 Rue Ecole de Medecine, Paris 75006 France

ELLSTROM-CALDER, ANNETTE, clinical social worker; b. Duluth, Minn., Dec. 19, 1952; d. Raymond Charles Ellstrom and Ruth Elaine (Bloomquist) Larson; m. Jeffrey Ellstrom Calder, July 30, 1982. BA in Social Work, Psychology, Sociology, Concordia Coll., 1974; MSW, U. Wis., 1978. Group therapist N.D. State Indsl. Sch., 1973; social worker Fergus Falls (Minn.) State Hosp., 1974, Jackson County Dept. Social Services, Black River Falls, Wis., 1975-77; clin. social worker U. Wis. Hosp., Madison, 1979—; cons. Waupun (Wis.) Meml. Hosp., 1979-84; lectr. grad. sch. social work U. Wis., Madison, 1979—, lectr. U. Wis. med. sch., Madison, 1979-82, prin. investigator in research U. Wis. Hosp., Madison, 1985—. Editor: A Guide to Patients and Families, 1984; contbr. articles to profl. jours. Del. trustee, bd. dirs. Nat. Kidney Found., N.Y.C., 1983—, chmn. bd. dirs. Wis. chpt., Milw., 1985-87, vice chmn. 1983-85, sec. 1982-83, chmn. patient services com. 1981-82, bd. dirs. 1981—, chmn. nat. tng. and edn. com., N.Y., 1987—, mem. nat. patient services com. N.Y., 1987—; bd. dirs. Madison chpt., 1979—; mem. nat. research com. Am. Assn. Spinal Cord Injury Psychologists and Social Workers, N.Y.C., 1988. Recipient Health Advancement award Nat. Kidney Found. Wis., 1985, Vol. Yr. award Nat. Kidney Found. Wis., 1984, Vol. Service award Nat. Kidney Found. Wis., 1983, Nat. Nephrology Social Worker of Yr. Merit award Nat. Kidney Found. and Council of Nephrology Social Workers, 1987; hon. adoptee Winnebago Indian Tribe, 1978; named Outstanding Young Wisconsinite Wisc. Jaycees, 1988. Mem. Council Nephrology Social Workers (nat. v.p. 1984-86, nat. exec. com. 1984-86, Nat. Nephrology Social Worker Yr. award 1987), Nat. Assn. Social Workers, Pi Gamma Mu. Democrat. Home: 3538 Topping Rd Madison WI 53705 Office: U Wis Hosp 600 Highland Ave E5/ 620 Madison WI 53792

ELLSWEIG, PHYLLIS LEAH, psychotherapist, retired; b. Irvington, N.J., Apr. 19, 1927; d. Sumar and Jeanette (Geffner) Schwartz; m. Martin Richard Ellsweig, Dec. 25, 1947; children: Bruce, Steven. BS, East Stroudsburg U. (Pa.), 1947; EdM, Lehigh U., 1966, EdD, 1972. Tchr. Stroud Union High Sch., 1963-66; guidance counselor East Stroudsburg Schs., 1966-68; asst. prof. edn. East Stroudsburg U., 1968; staff psychologist, outpatient supr. Mental Health Center Carbon, Monroe and Pike Counties, Stroudsburg, 1968-80; pvt. practice in psychotherapy and clin. hypnosis Stroudsburg, 1969-87; mem. staff Pocono Hosp.; pub. speaker in field; cons. to schs., orgns. Mem. Am. Psychol. Assn., Pa. Psychol. Assn., Am. Soc. Clin. Hypnosis, Internat. Soc. Hypnosis, NOW (profl. cons. 1973—).

ELLSWORTH, CYNTHIA ANN, educator, financial consultant; b. Springfield, Ohio, Jan. 19, 1950; d. Donald Harry and Jeanne Marie (Glover) E. BE, Western Conn. State U., 1972; M in Spl. Edn., Ohio U., 1976; Postgrad., Ohio State U., 1985-86; MS in Counseling, U. Dayton, 1988. Tchr. LBD Fed. Hocking Schs., Stewart, Ohio, 1972-76, Southwestern City Schs., Grove City, Ohio, 1977—; supr. elmr. LBD Vinton County Schs., McArthur, Ohio, 1976-77; registered rep. Chubb Securities, W.L. Walker & Assocs., Columbus, Ohio, 1981—. Named one of Outstanding Young Women Am., 1980. Mem. Council Exceptional Children, Phi Delta Kappa. Home: 421 E Whittier St Columbus OH 43206 Office: W L Walker & Assocs 3677 Karl Rd Columbus OH 43224

EL MAGHOUR, KAMIL HASSAN, government official. Student, Cairo U. Legal advisor to oil industry Govt. of Libya, 1970, ambassador to UN, 1972-76, ambassador to France, 1976-78, ambassador to People's Republic of China, 1978-81, head petroleum secretariat, 1982-84, now sec. of fgn. liasion bur.; Libyan rep. Internat. Ct. of Justice, The Hague. Office: Fgn Liasion Bur, Tripoli Libya *

EL-MAHGOUB, RIFAAT, federal government official; b. Damietta, Egypt, Apr. 23, 1926; s. Sayed Ibrahim El-M; children: Omneya, Eiman, Aiman, Amira. Licenciate in law, Cairo U., 1948, diploma in pvt. law, 1949; diploma in pub. law, Paris U., 1950, diploma in econs., 1951, PhD in Econs. and Pub. Fin., 1953. Lectr. in law Cairo U., 1949, 1953, prof. econs. and polit. sci., 1964, dean Faculty Econs. and Polit. Sci., 1971, 72, 81; minister polit. affairs at the Presidency Govt. Egypt, 1972; atty. Ct. Cassation, State Council and Supreme Constl. Ct; dep. prime minister polit. affairs Govt. Egypt, 1975, 1st sec. gen. cen. com., 1975; speaker People's Assembly 1984, speaker Nile Valley Parliament; sec. gen. econ. com. for Egypt and Syria, 1958; counsellor to Pub. Banking Authority, 1963; mem. Nat. Council for Prodn., since 1972; mem., reporter Higher Council of Culture, since 1972; head permananet sci. com. for nominating prof. econs., pub. fin. and planning Egyptian univs. Author: Political Economy, 3 Vols., Effective Demand with Special Study for the Developing Countries, Public Finance, Redistribution of National Income Through Fiscal Policy. Recipient Decorations of Republic, 4th degree, 1959, 3d degree, 1964, 1st degree, 1975, Golden Medal of State, 1980, award Grand Cordon of Nile, 1980, Grand-Croix de l'ordre Royal de Danebrog-Danemark, 1986, Decoration Friendship 1st degree Dem. Republic Korea, 1986; Cairo U. scholar, 1949. Office: Peoples Assembly, Maglis El Shaab St, Cairo Egypt

ELMALEH, JOSEPH, investment banker; b. Beirut, Aug. 28, 1938; s. Elie Rene and Suzanne (Farhi) E.; B.Sc. in Chem. Engring., Israel Inst. Tech., Haifa, 1962; Ph.D., Imperial Coll., London U., 1968. Rep., Israeli Ministry Indsl. Devel. in Europe, 1962-68; lectr. ops. research Grad. Sch. Mgmt. Sci., Imperial Coll., 1968-73; mgmt. cons. Finind S.A., 1971-74; chmn. bd. Elmco Holdings Ltd., London, 1974-86; chmn. bd., chief exec. officer Isramco, Inc., 1983—; chmn. bd. J.O.E.L. (Jerusalem Oil Exploration Ltd.), 1982—. Served with Israeli Army, 1956 59. Leo Baeck research fellow, 1962 65. Clubs: Harmonie (N.Y.C.). Office: 1 Balfour Pl, London W1, England

ELMAN, GERRY JAY, lawyer; b. Chgo., Oct. 7, 1942; s. Earl Samuel and Lucille Paulyne (Greenberger) E.; children—Jason Farrel, Floren Haley. B.S., U. Chgo., 1963; M.S. in Chemistry, Stanford U., 1964; J.D., Columbia U., 1967. Bar: N.Y. 1967, U.S. Patent Office 1967, Pa. 1969, U.S. Supreme Ct. 1973, U.S. Dist. Ct. (so. and ea. dists.) N.Y., 1971, U.S. Dist. Ct. (ea. dist.) Pa. 1973, U.S. Dist. Ct. (mid. dist.) Pa. 1974, U.S. Ct. Appeals (fed. cir.), 1985. Assoc. Hubbell, Cohen and Stiefel, N.Y.C., 1967-68; patent atty., enzymes and health products Rohm and Haas Co., Phila., 1968-72; dep. atty. gen. Pa. Dept. Justice, Harrisburg, Pa., 1972-76; trial atty. middle Atlantic office antitrust div. U.S. Justice Dept., Phila., 1976-82; sole practice, Phila., 1982-83; ptnr. Elman Assocs., Phila., 1984-88, Lipton, Famiglio & Elman, Media, Pa., 1988—; instr. short course in computer law Temple U., Phila., 1984. Contbg. author: Lawyers' Microcomputer Users Group Jour., 1985—; editor: Columbia Jour. Transnat. Law, 1966-67; mem. adv. bd. Jour. Computer Law Reporter, 1983—; mem. editorial bd. Jour. Trademark Reporter, 1968; founder, editor-in-chief legal newsletter Biotechnology Law Report, 1982—. Chmn. Three Steps Nursery Sch., Phila., 1977; arbitrator Phila. Ct. Common Pleas, 1971-72, 1983—; arbitrator U.S. Dist. Ct. (ea. dist.) Pa., 1983—; arbitrator Am. Arbitration Assn. for computer disputes, 1987— . Mem. Am. Chem. Soc., Licensing Execs. Soc., Assn. Biotech. Cos., AAAS, ABA, Am. Intellectual Property Law Assn., Phila. Bar Assn. (chmn. jurimetrics com. 1975-77), Phila. Patent Law Assn. (chmn. biotech. subcom. 1982-86), Computer Law Assn., Phila. Area Computer Soc. Lodge: B'nai B'rith (v.p. Society Hill 1977). Home: 416 N Chester Rd Swarthmore PA 19081 Office: Lipton Famiglio & Elman 201 N Jackson St Media PA 19063

EL'MOHAMMED, ALI MALIK BELL, psychotherapist; b. Monroe, La., Mar. 12, 1944; s. Ali Malik and Lucille (Culpepper) eL-M.; m. Musette Bell, Mar. 23, 1974; children: Angela, Chris, Aliah, Ali IV. AAS in Social Work, NYU, 1971, BS in Secondary Edn., 1972, MS in Black Studies, 1973, MSW, 1975; PhD, Columbia Pacific U., 1982. Diplomate clin. social work; cert. permanent tchr., N.Y.; cert. social worker, N.Y., Mich. Project dir. Congress Racial Equality, N.Y.C., 1964-65; mental health worker Albert Einstein Coll. Medicine-Lincoln Community Mental Health Services, Bronx, N.Y., 1966-68, supr. community orgn., 1968-69, dir. community orgn., 1969-71, assoc. dir. dept. cons. and edn., 1971-75, clin. supr., 1975-77; clin. supr. Misericordia Hosp. Med. Ctr., Bronx, 1977-79; clin. social worker Mich. Inst. Mental Health, Diamondale, 1979-80; program supr. Riverwood Community Mental Health Services, St. Joseph, Mich., 1983-84; psychotherapist Genesee Psychiat. Ctr., Kalamazoo, Mich., 1980—, Kalamazoo Community Counselling, 1981—; mgr. assertive community treatment program Douglass Community Assn., Kalamazoo, 1985—; Adminstr. Cannan Counseling Service, Harlem, N.Y., 1978-79; mem. Council Against Domestic Assault, East Lansing, 1979-80; mem. steering com. Community Support Systems, Mich., 1984; mem. numerous community programs, N.Y.C., 1966-79. Trustee Kalamazoo Acad. Bd., 1985-86; chmn. Kalamazoo Civic Black Theatre, 1984-85; mem. Northside Task Force on Housing, Kalamazoo, 1986, Mich. Steering Com. on Community Support Systems, 1984, St. Martin's Episcopal Adv. Bd., 1984-85; mem. admission com. Mich. State U. Med. Sch., 1980-82. Recipient Outstanding Contribution award Island of Curacag, 1978, S. Bronx Action award, 1968. Fellow Am. Orthopsychiat. Assn.; mem. Nat. Assn. Black Social Workers, Nat. Assn. Social Workers, Am. Group Psychotherapy Assn. Muslim. Home: 1167 Mount Royal Dr Kalamazoo MI 49009 Office: Afram Cons Service G3300 Miller Rd #125 Flint MI 48507

ELMS, JAMES CORNELIUS, IV, aerospace and energy consultant; b. East Orange, N.J., May 16, 1916; s. James Cornelius and Iva Marguerite (Corwin) E.; m. Patricia Marguerite Pafford, Jan. 4, 1942; children: Christopher Michael, Suzanne, Francesca, Deborah. B.S. in Physics, Calif. Inst. Tech., 1948; M.A. in Physics, UCLA, 1950. Registered profl. engr., Calif. Stress analyst Consol. Aircraft Corp., San Diego, 1940-42; chief devel. engr. G.M. Giannini & Co., Pasadena, Calif., 1948-49; research assoc. in geophysics UCLA, 1949-50; mgr. dept. armament systems, div. autonetics N.Am. Aviation Co., Downey, Calif., 1950-57; mgr. dept. avionics Martin Co., Denver, 1957-59; exec. v.p. Crosley div. AVCO Corp., Cin., 1959-60; gen. ops. mgr. aeronutronic div. Ford Motor Co., Newport Beach, Calif., 1960-63; dep. dir. Manned Spacecraft Center NASA, Houston, 1963-64; dep. assoc. adminstr. for manned space flight Manned Spacecraft Hdqrs. NASA, Washington, 1965-66; dir. Electronics Research Ctr. NASA, Cambridge, Mass., 1966-70; cons. to adminstr. NASA as dep. dir. Space Shuttle Assessment Team NASA, Washington, 1975; corp. v.p., gen. mgr. div. space and info. systems Raytheon, Sudbury, Mass., 1964-65; dir. Trans. Systems Center, Dept. Transp., Cambridge, 1970-74; cons. to adminstr. ERDA, 1975-77; cons. to mgmt. of aerospace and energy cos. Newport Beach, 1975-81; cons. to adminstr. NASA, 1981-85; mem. space systems com. space adv. council NASA, 1970-77; cons. to dir., mem. adv. com. Strategic Def. Initiative Orgn., 1984—. Served to capt. USAAF, 1942-46. Recipient Spl. award NASA, 1964, Exceptional Service medal, 1969, Outstanding Leadership medal, 1970; Sec.'s award for meritorious service Dept. Transp., 1974. Fellow IEEE, AIAA (assoc.); mem. Nat. Acad. Engring., Am. Phys. Soc., Air Force Assn., Assocs. of Calif. Inst. Tech., Res. Officers Assn., Soaring Soc. Am., Aircraft Owners and Pilot's Assn., Explorers Club, Am. Legion. Episcopalian. Clubs: Balboa Yacht; Army and Navy; U.S. Air Force Open Mess. Home and Office: 112 Kings Pl Newport Beach CA 92663

EL-NOZAHI, AHMED MOHAMED, engineer, consultant; b. Samalut, Egypt, Aug. 26, 1940; s. Mohamed and Farida (Osman) El-N.; m. Soheir Ashor Helal, July 29, 1976; children—Mohamed, Mostafa, Farida. B.Sc. in Mining Engring., Assiut U. (Egypt), 1962; Diploma in Metall. Engring., Tech. U. Clausthal (West Germany), 1967, Dr. Engring., 1971. Sci. asst. Assiut U., 1962-64; sci. researcher Tech. Clausthal, 1965-71; head projects dept. Egyptian Metall. Orgn., Cairo, 1972-77; mgr. studies and cons. services Egyptian-Italian Engring. and Constrn. Co., Cairo, 1978-84; gen. mgr. Egyptian Italian Engring. and Constrn. Co., 1985—; lectr. Azhar U., Cairo, 1974-75, Mansoura U., 1987-88; cons. Arab Iron and Steel Union, Cairo, 1976-77; mem. Nat. Acad. Sci.-Industry Council, Cairo, 1983—. Bd. dirs., gen. sec. Assn. Egyptians Graduated in West Germany, 1973—. Mem. Egyptian Engring. Syndicate, Egyptian Businessmen Assn., Egyptian Engring. Assn. Club: Business (Cairo). Avocation: oil painting. Home: 30 Mahmoud Abu Eloyoon St, Heliopolis, Cairo Egypt Office: Egyptian-Italian Engring Constrn, 143 Omar Ibn El Khattab St, Al Maza 11341, Egypt

ELORANTA, JORMA OLAVI, investment company executive; b. Helsinki, Finland, Feb. 1, 1951; s. Voitto Olavi and Laina Esteri (Suontakanen) E.; m. Virpi-Liisa Pieninkeroinen, June 13, 1973; children: Pauliina, Tuomo. DI, U. Tech., Helsinki, 1975. Sec. gen. Nat. Union Finnish Students, Helsinki, 1976-78; cons., mgr. Oy Mec-Rastor AB, Espoo, Finland, 1979-84; pres. Finvest Inc., Helsinki, 1985—; chmn. bd. Travela, 1978-87; pres. Painokytkentä, 1981; exec. v.p. Hanke-Palsbo, 1982; bd. dirs. Dipoli. Recipient medal of merit Nat. Union Finnish Students, 1986. Office: Finvest Inc, Kumpulantie 15, 00520 Helsinki Finland

ELROD, EUGENE RICHARD, lawyer; b. Roanoke, Ala., May 14, 1949; s. James Woodrow and Selma Fromer (Steinbach) E. AB, Dartmouth Coll., 1971; JD, Emory U., 1974. Bar: Ga. 1974, D.C. 1976, U.S. Ct. Appeals (D.C. cir.) 1985, U.S. Ct. Appeals (5th cir.) 1987, U.S. Dist. Ct. D.C. 1987, U.S. Supreme Ct. 1987. Trial atty. Fed. Power Com., Washington, 1974-76; atty.-advisor Fed. Energy Adminstrn., Washington, 1977; assoc. Sidley & Austin, Washington, 1977-80, ptnr., 1981—; mem. adv. bd. The Keplinger Cos., Houston. Mem. selection com. for Woodruff scholars Emory U. Law Sch. Mem. ABA, D.C. Bar Assn., Ga. Bar Assn., Fed. Energy Bar Assn. (chmn. oil pipelne com. 1982-83, tax com. 1980-81, liaison with adminstrv. law judges 1986-87). Clubs: Dartmouth, Mt. Vernon Swimming and Tennis (Washington). Home: 4300 Hawthorne St NW Washington DC 20016 Office: Sidley & Austin 1722 Eye St NW Washington DC 20006

ELSANUSI, AHMED ELNOMAN ABDELLA, reinsurance executive; b. Omdurman, Sudan, May 6, 1935; s. Abdella and Fatima (Elsheikh Ahmed) E.; m. Ihsan Mohammed Ali Bakheit, June 15, 1966; children: Hassabelrasoul, Amina. BS in Social Studies, U. Khartoum, Sudan, 1960; MBA, U. Pa., 1969. Controller ins. Ministry Fin. and Econs., Khartoum, 1964-67, head econ. research unit, 1969-70, asst. undersec. govt. corps., 1969-79; mng. dir. Sudanese/Kuwaiti Bldg. and Constrn. Co., Khartoum, 1974-76; gen. mgr. Khartoum Motor Ins. Co. Sudan Ltd., 1976-77, The African Ins. Co., 1978-84; dep. gen. mgr. The African Reins. Corp., Lagos, Nigeria, 1984—; alternate bd. dirs. Shelter Afrique, Nairobi, Kenya, 1984—; adj. lectr. of ins. law U. Khartoum. Contbr. articles to profl. jours., papers to confs. Former chmn. Agrl. Reform Schemes Settlement and Payment Com. Mem. Sudanese Economist Assn., Grads. Club. Office: African Reins Corp, 46 Marina, Lagos Nigeria

ELSEN, SHELDON HOWARD, lawyer; b. Pitts., May 12, 1928; m. Gerri Sharfman, 1952; children: Susan Rachel, Jonathan Charles. A.B., Princeton U., 1950; A.M., Harvard U., 1952, J.D., 1958. Bar: N.Y. 1959, U.S. Supreme Ct. 1971. Mem. firm Orans, Elsen & Lupert, N.Y.C., 1965—; adj. prof. law Columbia Law Sch., 1969—; chief counsel N.Y. Moreland Act Commn., 1975-76; asst. U.S. atty. So. Dist. N.Y., 1960-64; cons. Pres's. Commn. Law Enforcement Adminstrn. Justice, 1967; mem. faculty Nat. Inst. Trial Advocacy, 1973. Contbr. articles to legal jours. Fellow Am. Coll. Trial Lawyers, Am. Bar Found.; mem. Am. Law Inst., Assn. Bar City N.Y. (v.p. 1988—, chmn. com. on fed. legislation 1969-72, mem. com. on judiciary 1972-75, chmn. com. on fed. courts 1983-86, chmn. nominating com. 1986-87, v.p. 1988—, chmn. com. on fed. legis.), Phi Beta Kappa. Home: 50 Fenimore Rd Scarsdale NY 10583 Office: 1 Rockefeller Plaza New York NY 10020

EL SHAZLY, EL SHAZLY MOHAMMED, national scientific committee executive; b. Dakahlia, Egypt, Nov. 18, 1923; s. Mohamed El Shazly and Amna Ahmed (Ghoneim) El S.; B.Sc., U. Cairo, 1943; Ph.D., U. London, 1951; diploma Imperial Coll. Sci. and Tech., 1951; m. Khayria Osman El Degwi, Mar. 3, 1983; 1 son. Hassan. Supt., Upper Egypt Mining Co., 1943-45; geologist dir. Geol. Survey/Mineral Research Labs., 1945-62; head geology and raw materials dep./undersec. state Atomic Energy Establishment, 1962-77; pres., chmn. Nuclear Materials Corp., Cairo, 1977-83; mem. com. remote sensing devel. Nat. Acad. Scis., Washington; v.p. Internat. Geol. Correlation Program Precambrian Mobile Zones. Decorated 1st Order Scis. and Arts, 1st Order Industry and Commerce, State Prize Geol. Scis.; 1st Order of Merit, Gold Medal of Mining and Quarrying. Mem. Arab Sci. Assn. (sec.-gen.), Geol. Soc. Egypt (sec. gen.), Egyptian Acad. Scis. Clubs: Nat. Sporting, Cairo Yacht, Co-author: The Mediterranean Sea; Sedimentation in Submarine Canyons, Fans and Trenches; The Indian Ocean; editor Egyptian Jour. Geology, 1957—; author papers, abstracts. Home: Street 14, Mokattam City, Cairo Egypt Office: 101 Kasr El Aini St, Cairo Egypt

ELSON, EDWARD ELLIOTT, distribution and retail executive; b. N.Y.C., Mar. 8, 1934; s. Harry and Esther (Cohn) E.; m. Suzanne Wolf Goodman, Aug. 24, 1957; children: Charles Myer, Louis Goodman, Harry Elson II. Grad., Phillips Acad., 1952; BA in Polit. Sci. with honors, U. Va., 1956; JD, Emory U., 1959. With Atlanta News Agy., Inc., 1959-86, pres., 1967-82, chmn. bd. dirs., pres., 1982-85, chmn. bd. dirs., 1985-86; pres. Airport News Corp., Atlanta, 1961-82, chmn. bd. dirs., 1982-85; pres. Elson's, Atlanta, 1963-82, chmn. bd. dirs., 1982-86; chmn. Gordon County Bank, 1979-83; chmn. bd. dirs. W.H. Smith & Son Holdings, PLC, 1985-88; bd. dirs. Citizens and So. Ga. Corp., Atlantic Am. Corp., Citizens and So. Trust. Co., Inc., Genesco, Inc., The Majestic Wine Corp., W.H. Smith Group plc. Mem. publs. com. Commentary Mag., 1967—, chmn., 1975-80. Bd. dirs. So. Regional Council, 1966—; bd. govs. Am. Jewish Com., 1966—, trustee, 1977—, chmn. bd. trustees, 1986—, v.p., 1982-84, treas., 1984-86; mem. Presdl. Commn. on Obscenity and Pornography, 1967-71, Nat. Adv. Commn. Pub. Edn. and Desegregation, 1976-77; mem. funds appeals rev. bd. City of Atlanta, 1971-73; mem. Atlanta-Fulton County Recreation Authority, 1973-80, vice chmn., 1975-80; mem. adv. com. to U.S. Commn. on Civil Rights, State of Ga., 1974—, chmn., 1974-82; chmn. bd. dirs. Nat. Pub. Radio, 1977-80; chmn. So. regional adv. com. to U.S. Commn. on Civil Rights, 1978; mem. pres.'s council Brandeis U., 1967—, dir. Reading is Fundamental program, 1975-86, fellow, 1979; bd. visitors U. Va., 1984—, trustee Med. Ctr., mem. exec. com., 1987—; trustee U. Va. Med. Ctr., 1987—, exec. com., 1987—; trustee Brown U., 1988—; bd. visitors Clark Coll., 1973—, chmn. bd. visitors, 1982; mem. alumni council Phillips Acad., Andover, Mass., 1973-76; mem. pres.'s council Agnes Scott Coll., 1973-82, chmn., 1975-82; trustee Talladega Coll., 1973—, U. Mid-Am., 1979-82, Am. Fedn. Arts, 1985—, Brenau Coll., 1986—, Hampton Inst., 1986—; chmn. adv. bd., bd. dirs. Southeastern Ctr. for Contemporary Art, 1976—; chmn. bd. vis. Emory U. Mus. Art and Archaeology, 1985—; chmn. U. Va. Bayley Mus., 1986—; chmn. resource planning com. Nat. Gallery, Washington, 1986—; Presdl. del. returning Crown of Stephen to Hungary, 1978. Recipient Robert B. Downs award Grad. Sch. Library Sci., U. Ill., 1971, Human Relations award Am. Jewish Com., 1975, Disting. Service award Nat. Pub. Radio, 1979, Inst. Human Relations award, 1982. Mem. Ga. Bar Assn., Atlantic Coast Ind. Distbrs. Assn. (bd. dirs. 1963-76), L.Q.C. Lamar Soc. (v.p. 1973-74, chmn. bd. dirs. 1974-80), Jewish Publ. Soc. (trustee 1974-82, 85—, v.p. 1986-87, pres. 1987—), Am. Jewish Hist. Soc. (exec. com. 1980—, v.p. 1982-85), Muscular Dystrophy Assn. Am. (v.p. 1972-73, mem. corp. 1973-74), U. Va. Alumni Assn. (bd. mgrs. 1982-84). Clubs: Commerce, Georgian (Atlanta); Farmington Country (Charlottesville, Va.); Univ. (N.Y.C.). Home: 65 Valley Rd NW Atlanta GA 30305

ELSTER, TOBY, petroleum geologist, oil company executive, planning and financial consultant; b. Calipatria, Calif., Feb. 15, 1923; s. Jack and Pauline (Gelles) E.; m. Mary M. Benest, 1949 (div. 1975); children: Marc, Louis, Paulette; m. T. Alayne Corbell, Jan. 28, 1979. BS in Bus. Adminstrn., Wichita State U., 1948, BA in Geology, 1950. Staff geologist, Nat. Coop. Refining Assn., Wichita, 1953-55, Petroleum, Inc., Wichita, 1955-56; cons., Wichita, 1956-68, 70—; sr. v.p. exploration Acme Oil Corp., Wichita, 1968-70; bd. dirs. Am. Consolidated Holding Corp. Author articles. Wing comdr CAP, Wichita, 1968-70, mem. CAP, 1965—, alumni counsel Wichita State U. Served to capt. USAFR, 1942-83. Mem. Soc. Ind. Profl. Earth Scientists (service award 1970, 72, chmn. Wichita chpt. 1970, nat. dir. 1971-72), Am. Assn. Petroleum Geologists, Kans. Geol. Soc., Soc. Exploration Geophysicists, Soc. Econ. Paleontologists & Mineralogists, Rocky Mountain Geol. Soc., Am. Arbitration Assn., VFW (life). Clubs: Petroleum, Cosmopolitan (Wichita). Lodges: Moose, Elks. Office: Pan-Western Petroleum Inc Board of Trade Ctr Suite 501 Wichita KS 67202

ELSTRODT, JUERGEN HEINRICH, mathematician, educator; b. Osnabrueck, Fed. Republic of Germany, Apr. 8, 1940; s. August Hermann and Luise (Petertoenjes) E.; m. Baerbel Anna Croeplin, July 30, 1965; children: Monika, Marion. Degree in Math., U. Muenster, Fed. Republic of Germany, 1965; DSc, U. Munich, 1970, Habilitation, 1974. Research asst. U. Munich, 1970-71, acad. advisor, 1971-74, prof., sci. advisor, 1974-76, prof., 1976—. Contbr. over 15 articles to math. jours. Mem. German Math. Soc., Am. Math. Soc. Home: Buenkamp 98, Muenster Federal Republic of Germany 4400 Office: Math Inst, U Muenster, Einsteinstrasse 62, Muenster Federal Republic of Germany

EL-TAHAN, MONA, civil engineer; b. Alexandria, Egypt, Aug. 27, 1950; came to Can., 1975; d. Salah and Nawall (Ameen) Shahwan; m. Hussein Wahba El-Tahan, Oct. 30, 1947; children: Tahmir, Yassir. BSc in Civil Engring., Cairo U., Egypt, 1975; M in Engring., Meml. U., St. John's, Nfld., Can., 1980, postgrad., 1981-83. Research/teaching asst. Meml. U., St. John's, Nfld., Can., 1976-80; ocean engr. Feng Nfld. Ltd.-Lavalin, St. John's, 1980-82; project engr. Feng Nfld. Ltd.-Lavalin, 1982-85, sr. research engr., 1985—. Contbr. articles to profl. jours. Merit fellow, Cairo U., 1970; grad. fellow, Meml. U., 1977-79; NRC Can. grantee, 1977-80. Mem. Assn. of Profl. Engrs., Women in Sci. and Engring., Marine Tech. Soc. (sec. 1983-84), Can. Council of Moslem Women (pres.), Can Meteorol. and Oceanographic Soc. Home: 5 Hampshire Pl, Saint John's, NF Canada A1A L4H5 Office: Feng NFLD Ltd, 189 Water St PO Box 268, Sta C, Saint John's, NF Canada A1C 5J2

ELTGROTH, MARLENE ANNE BUMGARNER, author, editor, educator; b. Yorkshire, Eng., Nov. 6, 1947; came to U.S., 1949, naturalized, 1965; d. Rowland and May (Whittaker) Skirrow; m. John Owen Bumgarner, June 17, 1967 (div. 1982); children: Doña Ana, John Rowland; m. Robert J. Eltgroth, Feb. 19, 1983; 1 child, Deborah Ruth. AA, Coll. San Mateo, 1967; BA, San Diego State Coll., 1970; MA, San Jose (Calif.) State U., 1982. Tech. editor electronics firms, 1967-70; coordinator Peer Counseling Center, Las Cruces, N.Mex., 1970-72; tchr. elem. sch., 1974-76, 82-84; owner, mgr. Morgan Hill Trading Post, natural food store, Morgan Hill, Calif., 1976-78; editor Natural Living Newsline, Morgan Hill, 1979-81; mgr. Natural Living Assocs., 1979—; dir. Morgan Hill Country Day Sch., 1980-82; instr. early childhood edn. Gavilan Coll., 1979—, coordinator child devel. programs, 1985—; new products editor Classroom Computer Learning mag., 1980-82. Leader, founder La Leche League of Morgan Hill, 1977-85; supt. Sunday Sch., St. John's Episc. Ch., 1982-85; coordinator Morgan Hill Community Garden, 1982-84; participant Leaders for the 80s, 1987. Named Woman of Achievement Santa Clara County, 1987. Mem. AAUW, Soc. Children's Book Writers, Nat. Newspaper Food Writers and Editors Assn., Calif. Press Women, Nat. Assoc. for Edn. of Young Children. Author: Book of Whole Grains, 1976, (contbr.) The People's Cookbook, 1977, Organic Cooking for (not-so-organic) Mothers, 1980, (contbr.) Real Food Places to Eat, 1981; food columnist San Jose Mercury, 1977-80, Gilroy Dispatch, 1984-86; sr. tech. writer Boole and Babbage, Inc., 1983-85; contbg. editor Mothering mag., 1981-87; contbr. articles to Mother's Manual, Baby Talk, Am. Baby, McCalls, Family Computing and others. Office: PO Box 1326 Morgan Hill CA 95037

ELTON, SIR ARNOLD, surgeon, consultant; b. London, Feb. 14, 1920; s. Max and Ada (Levy) E.; m. Billie Pamela Briggs, Nov. 9, 1953; 1 child, Michael Jonathan. L.R.C.P., Univ. Coll. London, 1943, M.B., B.S., 1943, F.R.C.S., 1946, M.S., 1950. House physician and surgeon, casualty officer Univ. Coll. Hosp., London, 1946; sr. surg. registrar Charing Cross Hosp., London, 1946-50; cons. surgeon Mt. Vernon and Harrow Hosps., London, 1950-70, Northwick Park Hosp., London, 1970—; surg. tutor Royal Coll. Surgeons, London, 1970-83; mem. govt. working group on breast screening. Contbr. articles to profl. jours. Chmn. Conservative Med. Soc., 1975—. Recipient Queen's Jubilee medal for community services, 1982; C.B.E., 1982, K.B., 1987. Fellow Hunterian Soc., Royal Soc. Medicine, Apothecaries Livery; mem. Thyroid Club. Clubs: Carlton, RAC, MCC. Avocations: tennis; music. Office: Wellington Hosp, The Consulting Rooms, Wellington Pl, London NW8, England

ELTON, GEOFFREY RUDOLPH, historian, educator; b. Tübingen, W. Ger., Aug. 17, 1921; s. Victor Leopold and Eva (Sommer) Ehrenberg; B.A., U. London, 1943, Ph.D., 1949; M.A., U. Cambridge, 1949, Litt.D., 1960; D.Lit. (hon.), U. Glasgow, 1980, U. Newcastle, 1981, U. Bristol, 1981, U. London, 1985, U. Göttingen, 1987; m. Sheila Lambert, Aug. 30, 1952. Asst. in history U. Glasgow, 1948-49; asst. lectr., U. Cambridge, 1949-54, lectr., 1954-63, reader Tudor studies, 1963-67, prof. English constl. history, 1967-84, Regius prof. modern history, 1983-88 . Served with Inf. and Intelligence Corps, 1944-46. Created knight, 1986. Fellow Brit. Acad. (publs. sec. 1981—), Royal Hist. Soc. (pres. 1973-77); mem. Selden Soc. (pres. 1984-86), Eccles. Hist. Soc. (pres. 1984-85), Am. Acad. Arts and Scis. (fgn. mem.). Author: Tudor Revolution in Government, 1953, and numerous other books. Avocations: joinery, gardening. Home: 30 Millington Rd, Cambridge CB3 9HP, England Office: Clare Coll, Cambridge CB2 1TL, England Other: British Acad, 20-21 Cornwall Terrace, London NW1 4QP England

ELWIN, JAMES WILLIAM, JR., university dean, lawyer; b. Everett, Wash., June 28, 1950; s. James William Elwin and Jeannette Georgette (Zichy-Litscheff) Sherman; m. Regina K. McCabe, Oct. 25, 1986. B.A., U. Denver, 1971, M.A., 1972; J.D., Northwestern U., 1975. Bar: Ill. 1975, U.S. Dist. Ct. (no. dist.) Ill. 1975, U.S. Ct. Appeals (7th cir.) 1977, U.S. Supreme Ct. 1980. Trial atty. antitrust div. U.S. Dept. Justice, Chgo., 1975-77; asst. dean Northwestern U. Sch. Law, Chgo., 1977-82, assoc. dean, 1982—, exec. dir. Corp. Counsel Ctr. Northwestern U., 1984—; planning dir. Corp. Counsel Inst., Chgo., 1983—; dir. Short Course for Pros. Attys., Chgo., 1981—, Short Course for Def. Lawyers in Criminal Cases, Chgo., 1979—. Bd. dirs. Legal Assistance Found. of Chgo., 1985—; vice chmn. Gov.'s Adv. Council on Criminal Justice Legislation, 1986—. Fellow German Academic Exchange Service, 1986. Mem. Chgo. Bar Assn. (bd. mgrs. 1983-85, bd. dirs.), Chgo. Bar Found. (v.p. 1988—), Ill. Inst. Continuing Legal Edn. (chmn. 1987-88), Am. Law Inst., Phi Beta Kappa, Pi Gamma Mu. Clubs:

Legal (sec.-treas. 1988—), Univ. (Chgo.). Office: Northwestern Univ Sch Law 357 E Chicago Ave Chicago IL 60611

ELY, DONALD JEAN, clergyman, educator; b. Frederick, Md., July 15, 1935; s. George Kline and Jennie Mabel (Boyer) E.; AB, Gettysburg Coll., 1955; BD, Lancaster Sem., 1958; MEd, Bloomsburg State U., 1972; m. Lois Jean Kirkpatrick, Aug. 27, 1967; children—Kathleen Rose, Stephen David, Yvonne Elaine. Ordained to ministry Evang. and Reformed Ch., 1958; pastor St. John Evang. and Reformed Ch., Riegelsville, Pa., 1958-61, Zion's Reformed Ch., Ashland, Pa., 1961-64, Augusta Reformed Parish, Sunbury, Pa., 1964-74, Salem United Meth. Ch., Middleburg, Pa., 1974-79, Salem Independent Brethren Ch., Middleburg, Pa., 1979-83; tchr. social studies Shikellamy High Sch., Sunbury, Pa., 1966—. Bd. dirs. Sunbury Area YMCA, 1966—, sec., 1973-80, 1988—; bd. dirs. Northumberland County unit Am. Cancer Soc., 1971-74, Snyder County unit, 1974-84; Rep. candidate state legis., 1982. Mem. Sunbury Area Ministerial Assn. (past pres.), Pa. Council Social Studies, Snyder County Hist. Soc. (pres. 1980-83, life mem.), Northumberland County Hist. Soc. (trustee 1972-82, life mem.), Union County Hist. Soc., Hist. Soc. Evang. and Reformed Ch., Hereditary Register of U.S., SAR (chaplain 1971—, chpt. pres. 1981-86), Ams. for Constl. Action, Am. Conservative Union. Lodges: Masons, Moose. Home: PO Box 765 Sunbury PA 17801 Office: 1149 Market St Sunbury PA 17801

ELY, MARICA MCCANN, interior designer; b. Pachuca, Mex., May 2, 1907 (parents Am. citizens); d. Warner and Mary Evans (Cook) McCann; m. Northcutt Ely, Dec. 2, 1931; children—Michael and Craig (twins), Parry Haines. B.A., U. Calif.-Berkeley, 1929; diploma Pratt Inst. of Art, N.Y.C., 1931. Free-lance interior designer, Washington and Redlands, Calif., 1931—; lectr. on flower arranging and fgn. travel, 1931—; prof. Sogetsu Ikebana Sch., Tokyo, 1972. Art editor (calendar) Nat. Capital Garden Club League, 1957-58. Pres. Kenwood Garden Club, Md.; bd. dirs. Nat. Library Blind, Washington; v.p. bd. dirs. Washington Hearing and Speech Soc., 1969; co-founder Delta Gamma Found. Pre-Sch. Blind Children, Washington. Finalist Nat. Silver Bowl Competition, Jackson-Perkins Co., 1966; garden shown on nat. tour Am. Hort. Soc., 1985. Mem. Calif. Arboretum Found., Redlands Hort. and Improvement Soc. (bd. dirs. 1982—), Yucaipa Valley Garden Club, Town and Country African Violet Soc., Hemerocallis Soc., Delta Gamma. Clubs: Redlands Country (Calif.); Washington, Chevy Chase (Washington); Berkeley Tennis (Calif.).

ELY, NORTHCUTT, lawyer; b. Phoenix, Sept. 14, 1903; s. Sims and Elizabeth (Northcutt) E.; m. Marica McCann, Dec. 2, 1931; children—Michael and Craig (twins), Parry Haines. A.B., Stanford U., 1924, J.D., 1926. Bar: Calif. 1926, N.Y. 1928, D.C. 1932, U.S. Sup. Ct. 1932. Practice law N.Y., 1926-29, D.C. and Calif., 1933—; exec. asst. to Sec. Interior, Washington, 1929-33; chmn. tech. adv. com. Fed. Oil Cons. Bd., Washington, 1931-33; represented Sec. Interior in negotiation of Hoover Dam power and water contracts 1930-33; counsel to Gov. of Okla. in negotiating Interstate Oil Compact, 1934-35; co-executor of estate of ex-Pres. Herbert Hoover, 1964-68; spl. counsel Colo. River Bd. of Calif., 1946-76 and various Calif. water and power agys.; spl. Asst. Atty. Gen. State of Calif., 1953-64 in Ariz. v. Calif.; mem. nat. Petroleum Council, 1968-76; counsel in 7 U.S. Supreme Ct cases involving rights in Colo., Columbia, Cowlitz, Niagara Rivers and fed. natural resource statutes; legal advisor to Ruler of Sharjah in boundary disputes with Iran, Umm al Qawain, and internat. arbitration of boundary with Dubai; counsel to Swaziland in internat. river dispute with Republic of South Africa and to Mekong Commn. (U.N.) in settling principles for devel. of Mekong Basin; counsel to govts. and cos. in determination of seabed boundaries in Gulf of Thailand, Mediterranean, East China, South China, Caribbean seas, Persian Gulf; represented U.S. Mining cos. in enactment of Deepsea Hard Minerals Act, & subsequent reciprocal internat. recognition of mining leases; gen. counsel Am. Pub. Power Assn., 1941-81; counsel Los Angeles, So. Calif. Edison Co. in renewal of Hoover Power contracts, 1980—; counsel to Govts. of Saudi Arabia, Turkey, People's Republic China, Algeria, Malagasy Republic, Ethiopia, Grenada, Thailand on mining and petroleum legis.; mem. U.S. del. to UN Conf. on application of Sci. and Tech. for Benefit Less Developed Areas, 1963, UN Conf. on mineral legislation, Manila, 1969, Bangkok, 1973; mem. bd. overseers Hoover Instn.; trustee Herbert Hoover Found., Hoover Birthplace Found. Author: Summary of Mining & Petroleum Laws of the World, Oil Conservation Through Interstate Agreement, The Hoover Dam Documents; co-author Law of International Drainage Basins, Economics of the Mineral Industries. Adv. bd. Ctr. Oceans Law Policy, U. Va. Fellow Am. Bar Found. (life); mem. ABA (chmn. natural resource sect. 1973-74, ho. dels. 1974-80, regulatory reform com.), Calif. State Bar Assn., D.C. Bar Assn., Am. Law Inst. (life), Internat. Law Assn. (chmn. Am. br. com. on deep sea mineral resources 1970-79), Internat. Bar Assn., Sigma Nu, Phi Delta Phi, Sigma Delta Chi. Republican. Clubs: Bohemian (San Francisco); California (Los Angeles); Metropolitan, Chevy Chase, University (Washington); Fortnightly (Redlands); Redlands Country, Berkeley Tennis (Calif.). Home: 222 Escondido Dr Redlands CA 92373 Office: Law Offices Northcutt Ely 300 E State St Redlands CA 92373

ELY, PARRY HAINES, dermatologist; b. Washington, Sept. 19, 1945; s. Northcutt and Marica (McCann) E.; B.A., Stanford U., 1967; M.D., U. So. Calif., 1971; m. Elizabeth Magee, June 20, 1969; children—Sims, Rebecca Jennings, Merideth Magee. Intern, U. So. Calif./Los Angeles County Hosp., 1971-72, resident in dermatology, 1972-75, chief resident, 1975; clin. instr. dermatology U. Calif., Davis, 1975-79, asso. clin. prof. dermatology, 1979—; practice medicine, specializing in dermatology, Roseville, Calif., 1975—; mem. staff Roseville Community Hosp. Bd. dirs. Am. Cancer Soc., Placer County, 1977-78. Served to lt. comdr. USNR, 1968-81. Winner, Nelson Paul Anderson Essay Contest, Pacific Dermatologic Assn., 1979. Fellow Am. Acad. Dermatology; mem. AMA, Calif. Med. Assn., Soc. Investigative Dermatology, Am. Soc. Dermatologic Surgery, Internat. Soc. Dermatoennui Research (pres. 1980-81), Soc. Internat. Tropical Dermatology, Sacramento Valley Dermatologic Soc., Phlebology Soc. Am., Royal Soc. Medicine (assoc.), Am. Soc. Dermatopathology, Wodehouse Soc., N. Am. Clin. Dermatology Soc., Noah Webster Dermatological Soc., Alpha Delta Phi. Quaker. Contbr. articles to profl. jours. Address: 10565 Brunswick #7 Grass Valley CA 95945

ELY, RICHARD GEORGE, historian, educator; b. Sydney, New South Wales, Australia, Nov. 29, 1934; s. Robert George Barkley and Nita Elizabeth (Hepworth) E.; m. Margaret Jean Miller, Feb. 22, 1962; children: Robert, Linda, Andrew. BA, U. Sydney, 1961; MA, U. Queensland, Australia, 1967; PhD, U. Tasmania, Hobart, Australia, 1976. Sr. lectr. history U. Tasmania, Hobart, 1970—. Author: Unto God and Caesar, 1976, In Search of the Central Society of Education, 1982; editor (with Jean Ely): Lionel Murphy: The Rule of Law, 1986. Chmn. council Elizabeth Coll., Hobart, 1986-87. Research Sch. of Social Scis. fellow Australian Nat. U., 1986. Mem. Australian and New Zealand History of Edn. Soc. (pres. 1981-82), Australian Studies Assn. Office: U Tasmania, Dept History, 7005 Hobart Australia

ELYTIS, ODYSSEUS, poet, essayist; b. Hercaleon, Crete, Greece, Nov. 2, 1911; ed. U. Athens, U. Paris; Dr. h.c. phil., U. Thessaloniki, 1975; Dr. h.c., U. Paris, 1980; D.Litt. (hon.), U. London, 1981. Contbr. to rev. Nea Grammata, 1935; art critic for newspaper Kathimerini, 1946-48; broadcasting and program dir. Hellenic Nat. Broadcasting Inst., 1945-46, 53-54; author: Clepsydras of the Unknown, 1937; Sporades, 1938, Orientations, 1940, Sun the First, 1943, An Heroic and Funeral Chant for the Lieutenant Los in Albania, 1946, To Axion Esti - It Is Worthy, 1959, Six Plus One Remorses for the Sky, 1960, The Light Tree and the Fourteenth Beauty, 1972, The Sovereign Sun, 1972, The Trills of Love, 1973, The Monogram, 1973, The Painter Theophilos, 1973, Steppoems, 1974, Offering My Cards to Sight, 1974, Second Writing, 1976, The Magic of Papadiamantis, 1976, Signalbook, 1977, Maria Nefeli, 1978. Rep. for Greece at Recontres Internat. de Geneve, 1948, Congrès de l'Association des Critiques d'Art, 1949, Incontro Romano della Cultura, 1960; mem. Nat. Theatre Adminstrv. Council, Consultative Com. of Greek Nat. Tourist Orgn. on Athens Festival. Served to 2d lt. Greek Army, World War II. Recipient First State Poetry prize, 1960; Nobel prize for lit., 1979; hon. citizen of Mytilene. Mem. Internat. Assn. Art Critics, Société Europeénne de Culture. Address: 23 Skoufa St, G-136 Athens Greece *

EL ZAYAT, ELHAMY MOSTAFA, travel company executive; b. Cairo, Dec. 26, 1942; s. Mostafa Fahmy and Fatma Mostafa Khalil (El-Khalifa) El Z.; m. Samira Mounir Farid; children: Shahira Elhamy, Noha Elhamy. BA in Mgmt., Cairo U., 1965; MA in Mgmt., Am. U. Cairo, 1972; PhD (hon.), Marquis Guiseppa Scicluna U., Del., 1987. Math. tchr. Lycee El Horreya, Cairo, 1960-66; sales rep. Pan Am., Cairo, 1967-70; mgr. Pan Am. World Airways, Tripoli, Libya, 1970-72; mgr. Egypt, Libya and Sudan Pan Am. World Airways, Cairo, 1972-77; owner, pres. Emeco Travel, Cairo, 1977—; chmn. Transworld Cons. and Trading Co., Cairo, 1977—, Oasis Travel, Cairo, 1980—. Recipient Golden Helm award Internat. Award Tourism, 1982. Mem. Am. C. of C. in Egypt (v.p.), Am. U. Cairo Internat. Alumni Com. (chmn.), European Meeting Incentive Conv. (pres.), Egyptian C. of C. (bd. dirs.). Office: Emeco Travel, 2 Talaat Harb St, 1294 Cairo Egypt

EMAMIRAD, HASSAN ALI, mathematics educator; b. Tehran, Iran, Nov. 28, 1943; came to France, 1964; s. Abdolhossein Emamirad and Mahin Banou (Mortazavi) Movahed; m. Fariba Mortazavi; 1 child, Kevin. M. of Applied Math., U. Strasbourg, France, 1969; Dr. 3d Cycle, U. Dijon, France, 1973; Dr. Etat in Math., U. Paris-Nord, 1983; habilitation in Mechanics, U. Pierre and Marie Curie, Paris, 1985. Asst. prof. math U. Dijon, 1971-73; jr. lectr. U. Tehran, 1973-76; head sect. applied math. Nuclear Research Ctr. Atomic Energy Orgn. of Iran, Tehran, 1976-80; asst. prof. mechanics U. Pierre and Marie Curie, 1981-85, U. Rouen, France, 1985-87; prof. math. U. Poitiers, France, 1987—. Contbr. articles to profl. math. jours. Mem. Société Mathematique France, Am. Math. Soc. Office: U Poitiers Math Dept, 40 ave du Recteur Pineau, 86022 Poitiers France

EMAN, HENNY, prime minister of Aruba, lawyer. Leader Arubaanse Volksparty; mem. Council of Ministers, 1986—; prime minister 1986—. Office: Office of Prime Minister, Oranjestad Aruba *

EMANUEL, BRIAN JOHN, management consultant; b. Brisbane, Queensland, Australia, Oct. 30, 1938; s. Henry John and Gertrude Elizabeth (McMahon) E.; m. Desley Joan Campbell, May 20, 1961; children: David John, Gillian Christine, Stephen Campbell. Assoc. in Accountancy, U. Queensland, 1960, Assoc. Australian Soc. Accts., 1962, B in Commerce, 1967. CPA, New South Wales. With Charles Elliott & Son, Queensland, 1956-68; mktg. rep. I.B.M. Australia Ltd., Queensland, 1968-72, mktg. mgr., 1972-73, br. mgr., 1973-77; nat. edn. mgr. I.B.M. Australia Ltd., New South Wales, 1977-81, mktg. mgr., 1981-82; mng. dir. Esprit Mgmt. Services Proprietary. Ltd., Sydney, New South Wales, Australia, 1982—; also bd. dirs. Esprit Ltd., Buckinghamshire, Eng., 1984—. Mem. Australian Soc. Accts. Mem. Liberal Party. Mem. Uniting Ch. Office: Esprit Mgmt Services Proprietary Ltd, 275 Alfred St, Suite 502, North Sydney, 2060 New South Wales Australia

EMBODY, DANIEL ROBERT, biometrician; b. Ithaca, N.Y., July 10, 1914; s. George Charles and Mary Madeline (Riceman) E.; BS, Cornell U., 1938, M.S., 1939, postgrad., 1939-42; postgrad. N.C. State Coll., summer 1940; m. Margaret Constance Gran, Mar. 21, 1946 (dec. Mar. 1961); children: James Michael, Daniel Robert, David Richard. Instr. limnology Cornell U., Ithaca, N.Y., 1940-42; sr. math. analyst Arnold Bernard & Co., N.Y.C., 1947-48; statistician Wash. Water Power Co., Spokane, 1949-53; head statistics sect. E.R. Squibb & Sons-Olin, New Brunswick, N.J., 1953-57, mgr. electronic data processing service center, 1958-63, coordinator sci. computations, 1964-65; math. statistician Bur. Ships, Navy Dept., Washington, 1965-67; biometrician Dept. Agr., Beltsville, Md., 1967-72, staff biometrician animal and plant health inspection service, Hyattsville, Md., 1972—; sr. ptnr. EIC Assocs., College Park, Md., 1981—; cons., Idaho Fish and Game Dept., 1950-60, U.S. Geol. Survey, 1953-58, N.J. Dept. Fish and Game, 1953-60. Served to lt. comdr. USNR, 1942-46, ETO. Mem. Am. Statis. Assn., Biometric Soc., Entomol. Soc. Am. (cert.), AAAS, N.Y. Acad. Scis., Am. Legion, Nat. Rifle Assn., Naval Res. Assn., Am. Fisheries Soc., Sigma Xi, Gamma Alpha. Contbr. articles to profl. jours. Home: 5025 Edgewood Rd College Park MD 20740 Office: USDA Fed Bldg Room 602 Hyattsville MD 20782

EMBRY, MICHAEL HEARD, mining company executive; b. Shreveport, La., Jan. 28, 1951; s. Woodrow Wilson and Annie Dell (Heard) E.; m. Kathy Ann Hill, July 28, 1984. BS in Bldg. Constrn., NE La. U., 1976. Cost analyst, scheduler Ford Bacon and Davis, Inc., Monroe, La., 1976-77; mgr. cost control, scheduling Ford Bacon and Davis, Inc., Salt Lake City, 1978-87, Newmont Mining Corp., Tucson, 1988—. Mem. Am. Assn. Cost Engrs. Democrat. Baptist. Home: 640 Parkview Dr Park City UT 84060 Office: Newmont Mining Corp 200 W Desert Sky Rd Tucson AZ 85737

EMERK, KAYA, biochemist; b. Ankara, Turkey, Nov. 10, 1945; s. Ali and Turkan (Hisim) E.; m. Oya Dizdaroglu, Oct. 12, 1970; children: Funda, Defne. BS magna cum laude, Ankara U., 1963, MS with honors, 1967; PhD with high honors, Hacettepe U., Ankara, 1970. Lectr. Hacettepe U. Sch. Medicine, Ankara, 1969-70; postdoctoral fellow Washington U., St. Louis, 1970-74; assoc. prof. Hacettepe U., St. Louis, 1975-82; prof. Marmara U., Istanbul, Turkey, 1983—; asst. dean Marmara U., 1985—; founding mem. Med. Sch. Found., Marmara U., 1986—, head, coordinator med. edn., 1986—, mem. univ. senate, 1985-87. head dept. biochemistry, 1983—. Author: Introduction to Human Chemistry, 1981; editor Biochemistry Jour., 1982-84; contbr. articles to profl. jours. Rep. Internat. Union Biochemistry, 1980-84, Fedn. European Biochem. Socs., 1979-83. Served to lt. Turkish Army, 1974-75. Scholar Agy. for Internat. Devel., 1971; NIH grantee Washington U., 1972-74. Mem. Turkish Assn. Chem. Engrs., Turkish Biochem. Soc. (founding mem.). Office: Marmara U Sch Medicine, Tabiye Cad, Istanbul Turkey 81326

EMERSON, ALTON CALVIN, physical therapist; b. Webster, N.Y., Sept. 29, 1934; s. Homer Douglas and Pluma (Babcock) E.; m. Nancy Ann Poarch, Dec. 20, 1955 (div. 1972); children: Marcia Ann, Mark Alton; m. Barbara Irene Stewart, Oct. 6, 1972. BS in Vertibrate Zoology, U. Utah, 1957; cert. phys. therapy, U. So. Calif., 1959. Staff phys. therapist Los Angeles County Crippled Children's Services, 1958-65; pvt. practice phys. therapy Los Angeles, 1966—; cons. City of Hope, Duarte, Calif., 1962-72; trustee Wolcott Found. Inc., St. Louis, 1972-86, chmn. bd. trustees, 1980-85. Recipient Cert. of Achievement, George Washington U., Washington, 1986. Mem. Temple City High Twelve Club (pres. 1971), Calif. Assn. High Twelve Clubs (pres. 1986), Aston Martin Owners Club. Lodges: Masons (master Camellia 1973, v.p. High Twelve Internat. Pasadena Scottish Rite Bodies), Royal Order Scotland. Home and Office: 287 W Ave de Las Flores Thousand Oaks CA 91360

EMERSON, ANDI (MRS. ANDI EMERSON WEEKS), sales and advertising executive; b. N.Y.C.; d. Willard Ingham and Ethel (Mole) E.; student Barnard Coll.; m. George G. Fawcett, Jr. (div.); children—Ann Emerson II, George Gifford III, Christopher Babcock; m. Kenneth E. Weeks (div.); 1 dau., Electra Ingham. Successively v.p. Eugene Stevens, Inc., N.Y.C.; pres., dir. Emerson Mktg. Agy., Inc., N.Y.C., 1960—; pres., dir. Mail Order Operating Co. Ltd., N.Y.C. and London, 1976—; pres., dir. Ingham Hall, Ltd., 1977-83; chmn. bd. Sonal World Mktg. Ltd., N.Y.C., and Delhi, India, 1983—; elected N.Y. State Del. to White House Conf. on Small Bus., 1986; instr. NYU, 1960-65, 87—. Block chmn. fund raising ARC, Multiple Sclerosis, Nat. Found., Crippled Children, Found. for Blind, 1954-63; vol. worker Children's Ward, Meml. Hosp., 1964-66, Hosp. for Spl. Surgery, 1967; mem. adv. com. African Students League, 1965-67; bd. dirs. Violet Oakley Meml. Found., Phila., 1964-81. Inducted into Silver Apple Hall of Fame, 1985. Mem. Nat. Assn. Women Business Owners, Direct Mktg. Assn., Sales Promotion Execs., Advt. Club, Mktg. Execs. Club, Direct Mktg. Club of N.Y. (treas. 1960-61), Mail Order Profls. Group, Soc. Profl. Writers, Direct Mktg. Creative Guild (pres. 1975—). Founder, chmn. The John Caples Awards, 1977—. Clubs: Ex-Mems. Squadron A, N.Y. Jr. League, Barnard. Home: 16 E 96th St New York NY 10128 Office: Emerson Mktg Agy Inc 44 E 29th St New York NY 10016

EMERSON, DONALD HOWARD GEORGE, computer educator, consultant; b. Simcoe, Ont., Can., Feb. 5, 1939; s. Maurice Howard and Marjorie Cleone (Ford) E.; m. Gwen E. Mingle, Aug. 18, 1962; children: Cheri Lea, Howard John. Student, Wilfred Laurier U., Kitchner, Can., 1983—. Ins. adjuster Norwich Union Fire Ins., Toronto, Ont., Can., 1958; self-employed Emerson China and Ladies Wear, Simcoe, Ont., Can., 1958-82; instr. computers Fanshawe Coll., Simcoe, 1982—. Named No. Telecom Nat. Inst. fellow, 1987. Club: Mensa Can. (Ont.). Home: 21 Warren Rd, Simcoe, ON Canada N3Y 2J7 Office: Fanshawe Coll, Box 10, Simcoe, ON Canada N3Y 4K8

EMERSON, K(ARY) C(ADMUS), scientific consultant; b. Sasakwa, Okla., Mar. 13, 1918; s. Earle Evans and Diva Elizabeth (Wilkins) E.; B.S., Okla. State U., 1939, M.S., 1940, Ph.D., 1949; m. Mary Rebecca Williams, Aug. 13, 1939; children—William K., James B., Robert E. Commd. officer U.S. Army, 1940, advanced through grades to col.; ret. from active duty, 1966; asst. prof. Okla. State U., 1946-49, adj. prof., 1971—; staff Armistice Commn., Korea, 1958-59; tech. liaison Office Chief Research and Devel., Army Dept., Washington, 1959-60; asst. for research Office Sec. Army, Washington, 1961-75, acting dep. asst. sec. Army, 1973-75, acting asst. sec. Army, 1975-76, dep. for sci. and tech., 1974-78; mem. Army Sci. Bd., 1978-84. Research assoc. Smithsonian Instn., 1960—, Fla. Dept. Agr. and Consumer Service, 1981—, Seminole Nation Museum, 1975—, Bishop Mus., 1983—; collaborator U.S. Dept. Agr., 1959—; instr. Far East br. U. Md., 1959; mem. Def. Com. on Research, 1967-78; U.S. Panel Systematics and Taxonomy, 1968—, NATO Panel I Long-term Studies, 1970-78, pres. Care and Rehab. of Wildlife, 1984-86; sec. Sanibel-Captiva Conservation Found., 1982-85; bd. dirs. Internat. Osprey Found. Decorated Legion of Merit, Bronze Star, Purple Heart; recipient 2 Exceptional Civilian Service awards Army; Outstanding Civilian Service award Dept. Def. Fellow Entomol. Soc. Am., Washington Acad. Sci., Explorers Club; mem. Biol. Soc. Washington (exec. bd. 1969-70), Soc. Tropical Medicine and Hygiene, Soc. Systematic Zoology, Wildlife Disease Assn., Entomol. Soc. Washington, AAAS, Sigma Xi, Alpha Zeta, Phi Sigma. Club: Cosmos (Washington). Author or co-author numerous books; mem. editorial bd. 2 sci. jours.; contbr. articles to profl. jours. Home: 560 Boulder Dr Sanibel FL 33957

EMERSON, THOMAS OLIVER, savings and loan executive; b. Albert Lea, Minn., July 15, 1920; s. Ralph Waldo and Letha F. (Johnson) E.; m. Alma Irene Schuetz, Sept. 2, 1942; children—James Alexander, Jack Thomas, Thomas Hall. Student U. Wash., 1939-41; grad. diploma Inst. Fin. Edn., Chgo., 1965. Real estate broker, Idaho. Messenger-teller, Coffman-Dobson Bank, Chehalis, Wash., 1936-39; bookkeeper-teller Peoples Nat. Bank, Seattle, 1939-42; flying instr. U.S. Army AC, 1943-45; owner/mgr. Emerson Flying Service, Coeur d'Alene, Idaho, 1946-49; chief exec. officer First Fed. Savs. & Loan, Coeur d'Alene, 1949-82, chmn. bd., 1983—. Author: Seaplanes from Coeur d'Alene, 1973; Hangar Flying, 1984. Mem. Coeur d'Alene City Council, 1956-60; trustee N. Idaho Coll., 1978-81. Served to capt. AC, U.S. Army, 1943-46. Named Outstanding Citizen of Coeur d'Alene, 1980. Mem. U.S. League Savs. Assns. (dir. 1971-72, nat. legis. com. 1976-81), Idaho League Ins. Savs. and Loans (past pres.), Am. Inst. Real Estate Appraisers, M.A.I. (retired), Coeur d'Alene C. of C. (dir. 1964-65). Republican. Clubs: Viking Booster (pres. 1966-67), Hayden Lake Country. Lodges: Rotary (pres. 1976-77), Elks, Eagles (Coeur d'Alene). Home: 1111 Mountain Ave Coeur d'Alene ID 83814 Office: First Fed Savs & Loan PO Box 400 Coeur d'Alene ID 83814

EMERSON, WILLIAM STEVENSON, retired chemist, consultant, writer; b. Boston, Mar. 25, 1913; s. Natt Waldo and Marion (Stevenson) E.; m. Flora Millicent Carter, Dec. 12, 1958. A.B., Dartmouth Coll., 1934; Ph.D., MIT, 1937. DuPont fellow U. Ill., Urbana, 1937-38, instr. chemistry, 1938-41; research chemist Monsanto Co., Dayton, Ohio, 1941-44, research group leader, 1944-51, asst. dir. cen. research dept., 1951-54, asst. dir. gen. devel. dept. St. Louis, 1954-56; mgr. cen. research dept. Am. Potash & Chem. Corp., Whittier, Calif., 1956-60; sr. staff assoc. Arthur D. Little, Inc., Cambridge, Mass., 1960-72, ret., 1972. Author: Guide to the Chemical Industry, 1983. Contbr. numerous articles to profl. jours. Patentee in field. Mem. Am. Chem. Soc. (chmn. Dayton sect. 1952), Am. Ornithologists Union, Am. Birding Assn., Phi Beta Kappa, Sigma Xi, Phi Lambda Upsilon. Republican. Club: Chemists (N.Y.C.). Avocations: fly fishing; birding; golf; squash; reading; philately. Home: Box 030 Bristol Rd Damariscotta ME 04543

EMERY, HENRY ALFRED, engineer; b. Northfield, N.H., Feb. 9, 1926; s. Henry A. and Ruth (Trask) E.; B.A., U. Maine, 1950; M.B.A., U. Denver, 1966; Petroleum Engr., Colo. Sch. Mines, 1956; m. Barbara Sadwith, June 10, 1971; children—Trask, Timothy, Ptarmigan. With Mobil Pipeline Co., 1950-53, Portland Montreal Pipeline Co., 1956-59; maintenance design engr., planning supr., engring. supt., project mgr. Pub. Service Co. Colo., 1959-72; pres. Computer Graphics Co., Denver, 1972-78; div. mgr. Kellogg Corp., Littleton, Colo., 1978-82; chmn., chief exec. officer Emery DataGraphic Inc., 1982-86; chmn., chief exec. officer Emery DataGraphic II Inc., Englewod, 1986-87; pres. Emery DataGraphic div. Harris-McBurney Co., 1987—. Registered profl. engr., Colo. Mem. Assn. Systems Mgmt., Rocky Mountain Ski Instrs. Assn., Profl. Ski Instrs. Am., Tau Beta Pi. Democrat. Home: 5680 S Big Canyon Dr Englewood CO 80111 Office: 6767 S Spruce Suite #140 Englewood CO 80112

EMERY, MARCIA ROSE, parapsychologist; b. Phila., Mar. 19, 1937; d. David Joshua and Naomi (Carner) Rose; B.A. in Psychology, Adelphi U., Garden City, N.Y., 1958; M.S. in Clin. Psychology, CCNY, 1960; M.A. in Social Psychology, New Sch. Social Research, 1964, Ph.D., 1968; m. Gordon M. Becker, 1970 (div.); m. 2d, James D. Emery, 1982; stepchildren—Stephen, Alicia, Jamie. Research asst. Office Instl. Research, Hunter Coll., N.Y.C., 1959-62, Community Service Soc., N.Y.C., 1962-65; lectr. psychology Hunter Coll., 1965-67; assoc. prof. psychology, chmn. M.A. program in community psychology Fed. City Coll., Washington, 1968-74; ind. practice psychology and astrological counseling, Hollywood, Fla., 1981—; pres. Intuitive Mgmt. Cons. Corp.; adj. faculty Aquinas Coll., Grand Rapids; psychologist Renaissance Revitalization Center, Nassau, Bahamas, 1975; lectr., coordinator counseling Coll. Bahamas, 1976-80; condr. workshops in parapsychology throughout U.S. Author: Developing Your Intuition: A Beginner's Guide; Manage Intuitively to Improve Decision Making and Problem Solving. Grantee NIMH, 1972. Mem. Am. Psychol. Assn., Assn. Humanistic Psychology, Parapsychol. Assn., Spiritual Frontiers Fellowship, Am. Soc. Psychical Research, Am. Fedn. Astrology, Assn. Past Life Research and Therapy. Mem. Unity Ch. Address: 3512 McCoy SE Grand Rapids MI 49506

EMHARDT, CHARLES DAVID, lawyer; b. Indpls., Feb. 13, 1931; s. John William and Martha Jack (Macdougall) E.; m. Ann Devaney, Nov. 12, 1954; children—John D., Carol A., Frederick D., Martha A., Lucy E. B.S. in Engring. Mechanics, Purdue U., 1952, A.S. in Elec. Engring. Tech., 1966; LL.B., Harvard U., 1955. Bar: D.C. 1955, Ind. 1958, U.S. Patent Office 1955. Patent atty. Western Electric Co., Washington, Balt., 1955-57; assoc. Harold B. Hood, Indpls., 1957-59, Lockwood, Woodard, Smith & Weikart, Indpls., 1959-64; ptnr. Woodard, Emhardt, Naughton, Moriarty & McNett and previous firm Woodard, Weikart, Emhardt & Naughton, Indpls., 1964—. Republican precinct committeeman, 1965-70. Served with Army NG, 1955-66. Mem. ABA, Ind. State Bar Assn. (chmn. pat. sect. 1967-68), Indpls. Bar Assn. (bd. 1979-81, ethics com. 1982-83). Presbyterian. Clubs: Woodstock, Indpls. Athletic, Masons, Shriners. Home: 4801 Fauna Ln Indianapolis IN 46234 Office: Woodard Emhardt Naughton et al 2000 1 Indiana Sq Indianapolis IN 46204

EMMANUEL, ANASTASE STEPHANOS, architect; b. Athens, Greece, May 13, 1943; arrived in United Arab Emirates, 1977; s. Stephanos Anastase and Heleni (Karamalis) E.; m. Ann Travers Hamilton, Oct. 4, 1972; 1 child, Stephan Ashley. Diploma in Architecture and Engring., Nat. Technol. U., Athens, 1966; MArch in Planning, Edinburgh (Scotland) U., 1968. Planner Planning Research Unit, Edinburgh, 1967-68; prin. A.S. Emmanuel & Assocs., Athens, 1968-77; sr. archtl. planner Doxiades Assocs., Athens, 1968-72; sr. planner Environ. Design Co., Athens, 1973-75; ptnr. Empetus Consultancy, Athens, 1974-77; architect, planner Pitria Co. Ltd. Cosn., Athens, 1975-77; chief town planner Dubai Municipality, United Arab Emirates, 1977-80; ptnr., regional dir. Candilis-Gredeso Cons., Dubai, 1980-83; prin. A.S. Emmanual & Assocs., Dubai, 1983—; cons. Tech. Assistance Recruitment Service, UN, N.Y.C., 1981—, Ctr. Human Settlements, UN, Nairobi, Kenya, 1981—. Designer domestic appliances; contbr. articles to profl. jours. Winner design competition U. Salonica, Greece, 1966, Dubai Municipality, 1982. Mem. Tech. Chamber Greec, Archtl. Assn. Greece, Internat. Union Architects, Soc. Engrs. United Arab Emirates, Internat. Soc.

City and Regional Planners. Greek Orthodox. Club: Six Continents Passport. Home and Office: PO Box 3807 Deira, Dubai United Arab Emirates

EMMANUEL, ARTEMIS, sociologist; b. Egypt, 1923; d. Stratis and Maria Dimitriadis; B.A., Am. U., Cairo; M.A., Columbia U.; Ph.D. in Sociology, Am. U., Washington, 1969; m. Philippe D. Emmanuel, 1955. Mem. faculty Webster Jr. Coll., Washington, 1963-65; professorial lectr. sociology George Washington U., also U. Md., Howard U., Washington, 1965-70; asst. prof. Am. U., 1970-71; lectr. Washington Internat. Center, 1964-71; research asso., seminar dir. Athens Center Ekistics, 1971-73; research fellow, sci. adviser Nat. Center Social Research, Athens, 1972-74, bd. dirs., 1973-74; prof. sociology Grad. Sch. Indsl. Studies, Piraeus, 1973—, vice rector Grad. Sch. Indsl. Studies, 1984—; lectr. Sch. Nat. Def., Athens; vis. prof. sociology Grad. Sch. Econs. and Comml. Studies, 1983—; adj. pres. bd. dirs. Center Planning and Econ. Research Greece; bd. dirs. Nat. Ctr. Pub. Adminstrn., 1985—. Mem. Internat. Sociol. Assn. (research council 1974-82, exec. com. of research com. on history sociology 1974-77), Am. Sociol. Assn., World Soc. Ekistics (mem. exec. council), AAAS, Greek Econs. Soc., Greek Polit. Sci. Assn., Hellenic Soc. Gerontology (a founder), Greek Eugenics Soc. Author: G. Tarde and the Sociology of Public Opinion, 1969; Public Opinion: A Sociological Review and Analysis, 1975; Scientific and Historical Foundations of Sociology, 1978, rev. edit., 1979; Sociology-Basic Problems, 1979; also articles. Home: 34 Solomou P Psychico, Athens Greece Office: 40 Caraoli and Demetriou, Piraeus Greece

EMMANUEL, MICHEL GEORGE, lawyer; b. Clearwater, Fla., May 16, 1918; s. George M. and Alexandra (Damianakes) E.; m. Betty Boring, Dec. 19, 1942; children: George Michel II, Martha Alexandra. B.S., U. Fla., 1940, LL.B., 1948; LL.M., NYU, 1949. Bar: Fla. 1948. Research fellow NYU, N.Y.C., 1948-49; ptnr. Mabry, Reaves, Carlton, Fields & Ward, Tampa, 1951-63; mem. firm Carlton, Fields, Ward, Emmanuel, Smith & Cutler, 1963—; mem. adv. com., lectr. NYU Tax Inst.; lectr. Estate Planning Inst. U. Miami. Contbr. articles to profl. jours. and yachting mags. Bd. dirs., past pres. Hillsborough County Crime Commn.; chmn. Mayor's Com. on Juvenile Delinquency; bd. dirs. Anclote Found., U. of South Fla. Found., Univ. Community Found., U. Tampa, Saunders Found., Fla. Hist. Soc., Univ. Community Hosp., Fla. Yacht Club Council, United Fund, Tampa Improvement Found., Fales Com., U.S. Naval Acad. Served to comdr. USNR, World War II. Decorated D.F.C., Air medal with 2 stars, Purple Heart; recipient Gov.'s award for distinguished service to State of Fla. Fellow Am. Coll. Probate Counsel, Am. Coll. Tax Counsel; mem. Am., Hillsborough County, Tampa bar assns., D.C. Bar, Fla. Bar (past chmn. tax sect.), Am. Judicature Soc., Tampa C. of C. (past pres.), U.S. C. of C. (taxation com.), Ancient and Secret Order of Quiet Birdmen, Sigma Chi, Phi Delta Phi. Episcopalian. Clubs: Ye Mystic Krewe of Gasparilla (past king), University (past pres.), Tampa Executives , Tampa, Tampa Yacht and Country, Tower (all Tampa); Gainesville (Fla.) Golf and Country; Cruising Club of Am. Lodge: Rotary (Tampa past pres.). Home: 2806 Terrace Dr Tampa FL 33609 also: Kritonos 9, Aegina Greece Office: One Harbour Pl Tampa FL 33602

EMMERICH, JOHN PATRICK, micro-computer co. exec.; b. N.Y.C., Feb. 15, 1940; s. Clifford L. and Anna V. E.; B.S., Fla. State U., 1970; M.B.A., Syracuse U., 1974. Vice pres., treas. Applied Devices Corp., Hauppage, N.Y., 1960-75; exec. v.p. Ontel Corp., Woodbury, N.Y., 1976-82; sr. v.p. Visual Tech. Inc., 1983—; bd. dirs. Ontel Corp., Lowell, Mass. Visual Tech. Internat. Inc., Lowell. V.p. N. Creek Property Owners Assn. (N.Y.), 1976. Recipient commendation U.S. Army, 1962, 64. Mem. U.S. Naval Inst., Am. Mgmt. Assn., Nat. Microfilm Assn., Am. Def. Preparedness Assn., Pres. Club, L.I. Assn. Bus. Commerce. Roman Catholic. Contbr. articles to profl. jours. Home: 34 Walden Pond Dr Nashua NH 03060

EMMERIJ, LOUIS JOHAN, corporate professional; b. Rotterdam, Netherlands, Dec. 25, 1934; s. Louis Johan Hendrik and Elisabeth (DeLege) E.; m. Gisela Schade, Nov. 13, 1964 (div. Nov. 16, 1977); 1 child, Karina; m. Vera Marinova, Dec. 10, 1977. Diploma in Econs., U. Paris, 1959; MA in Internat. Econs., Columbia U., N.Y.C., 1961; PhD, U. Paris, 1971; D. in Econs. (hons.), State U. of Ghent, Belgium, 1985. Research asst. Inst. d'Etudes Econs. et Sociales U. Paris, 1961-62; economist Directorate of Scientific Affairs, Orgn. Econ. Co-operation and Devel., Paris, 1962-70; dir. Internat. Labour Office World Employment Programme, Geneva, 1971-76; rector Inst. Social Studies, The Hague, Netherlands, 1976-85; pres. Orgn. Econ. Co-operation and Devel. Ctr., Paris, 1986—. Mem. Soc. Internat. Devel. (chmn. program com., mem. governing council). Club: North-South Roundtable, Rome. Office: OECD Devel Ctr, 94 rue Chardon Lagache, 75016 Paris France

EMMET, THOMAS ADDIS, JR., college administrator, consultant; b. Detroit, July 26, 1930; s. Thomas Addis and Leona Margaret (Schneider) E.; m. Anne Marie Baker, Mar. 3, 1972; children—Lynn, Anthony, William Novitsky. Ph.B., U. Detroit, 1952, M.Ed., 1954; Ed.S., Ed.D., U. Mich., 1963. Asst. dean U. Detroit, 1953-57, dean men, 1957-64, dean evening coll. arts and scis., 1964-66, asst. prof. higher edn., 1964-67; asst. exec. v.p. Marquette U., 1966-67, adj. prof. higher edn. Wayne State U., Detroit, 1968-70; spl. asst. to pres., prof. edn. Regis Coll., Denver, 1972—; pres. higher edn. exec. assocs., 1967-72, 84-86; chmn. bd. Higher Edn. Group, 1986—; pres. Thomas A. Emmet & Assos., 1972-84. Cons. collective negotiations in higher edn. Edn. Commn. of States, 1971—; cons. higher edn. Opinion Research Corp.; dir. leadership seminars, sr. adviser Am. Council on Edn., 1979-85. Staff dir. Mich. State Senate Student Unrest Com., 1968-69; exec. sec. Conf. Jesuit Student Personnel Adminstrs., 1956-64; sec. Council Student Personnel Assns. in Higher Edn., 1966-69. Recipient Bernard Webster Reed award, 1963, John P. McNichols award U. Detroit, 1986. Mem. Adult Student Personnel Assn. (v.p. 1961-64), Nat. Assn. Student Personnel Adminstrs. (editor Jour. 1962-63), Phi Kappa Phi, Alpha Sigma Nu, Alpha Sigma Lambda, Phi Delta Kappa, Phi Eta Sigma. Editor: The Academic Department and Division Chairman, 1972; Collective Bargaining in Postsecondary Institutions: The Impact on the Campus and the State, 1974; asso. editor Coll. and Univ. Bus., 1969-71; pub. The Department Advisor, 1985—. Home: 3941 E Orchard Rd Littleton CO 80121 Office: Regis Coll Dept Edn 50th St and Lowell Blvd Denver CO 80221

EMMETT, WALTER CHARLES, broker; b. Lawrence, Mass., July 6, 1925; s. Walter Thornton and Agnes Owens Emmett; student Dartmouth Coll., 1942-43, 46-47; m. Laurel Stinnett, Nov. 21, 1975; children—Jeffrey, Nancy, Scott; stepchildren—Wayne S. Dammier, Victoria Haile. Owner, pres. Emmett Bus. Brokers, Inc., Amarillo, Tex., 1978-85, 87—; dealer, operator, pres. Emmett-Simm's Motor Co., Inc., Panhandle, Tex., 1985-86; bus. broker Boston and Chamblin Realtors, Inc. 1986-87; owner Your Graphics Are Showing, Amarillo, 1977-79; salesman Ada Realtors, Amarillo, 1976-78; salesman Stevenson Motor, 1969-74, Russell Buick, 1974-76; lectr. Amarillo Jr. Coll.; ptnr. S.W.O.R.D., small bus. seminar prodns.; pres. Bus. Appraisal Services div. Emmet Bus. Brokers, cons. sales tng. and mgmt. Past bd. dirs. Maverick Boys Club; past mem. adv. com. on comml. art, fine arts adv. council Amarillo Coll., comml. arts adv. com. Amarillo Coll.; lay reader St. Andrew's Episcopal Ch., Amarillo. Served with A.C., USN, 1943-46. Lic. real estate broker, Tex. Mem. Inst. Cert. Bus. Counselors, Internat. Bus. Brokers Assn., Career Exchange Network, Am. Mktg. Assn. (Amarillo chpt.), Carl Himl Assocs., Tex. Assn. Bus. Brokers, Franchise Brokers' Network, Amarillo C. of C. (chmn. small bus. council). Episcopalian. Clubs: Amarillo, Downtown Kiwanis (bd. dirs. 1979-80, 1st v.p., pres.-elect 1988—), Masons, Shriners. Home: 2611 Henning St Amarillo TX 79106-4923 Office: Tex Commerce Bank Bldg Suite 303 2201 Civic Circle Amarillo TX 79109

EMOND, LIONEL JOSEPH, management consulting firm executive; b. Winnipeg, Man., Can., May 31, 1932; s. Henri R. and Anastasia E.; m. Elizabeth Boelen, Sept. 9, 1957; children: Catherine, Pierre, Marise, Robert. B in Commerce, McGill U., 1953, MBA, 1957. Chartered acct., Can. Pvt. practice auditing, 1953-55; with Shell Oil Co. of Can., Montreal, 1955-58; mgr. fiscal dept. Can. Chem. & Cellulose Co., 1958-60; asst. corp. controller Kruger Pulp & Paper Co., 1960-62, controller, 1962-65; mgr. fin. Dominion Bridge Co., Montreal, 1965-68; asst. gen. mgr. Churchill Falls Project, 1968-70; sr. fin. cons. Acres Internat., 1970-71; v.p. fin. Can. Gen. Ins. Co., 1971-75; v.p., treas. United Coops. of Ont., Toronto, 1976-80; v.p. fin. services The S.N.C. Group, Montreal, 1980-83; ptnr. Guerra Emond Internat. Mgmt. Cons., 1983-86; pres., Emondial, Inc., 1986—; lectr. fin. Concordia U. Mem. editorial bd. Cost and Mgmt., 1965—; contbr. articles to profl. jours. Pres. Etobicoke Rate Payers Assn., 1978-80; mem. bd. mgmt. Etobicoke Olympium, 1977-80; mem. exec. com. Canadian Coop. Credit Soc., 1977-80. Recipient citation Canadian Coop. Credit Soc., 1980. Mem. Fin. Exec. Inst. (pres. 1986-87), Inst. Chartered Accts., Soc. Mgmt. Accts., Am. Assn. Cost Engrs., Montreal Amateur Athletic Assn., Les Artisanats Centre-Ville Montreal (pres. 1984—). Roman Catholic. Home and Office: 203 Outremont Ave, Outremont, PQ Canada H2V 3L9

EMPLIT, RAYMOND HENRY, electrical engineer; b. Darby, Pa., May 2, 1948; s. Henry Raymond and Caroline Winifred (Parker) E.; m. Patricia Jean Jezl, Aug. 7, 1976; children—Eric, Susan. BS summa cum laude in Engring., U. Pa., 1978, MS in Engring., 1979. Engr., Custom Controls Co., Broomall, Pa., 1972-75, tech. dir., 1975-78, v.p., 1979-82; chief engr. Robertshaw Controls, Havertown, Pa., 1982-87; pres. Electronic Devel. Corp., Edgemont, Pa., 1987—. Patentee indsl. level instrumentation in U.S. and Can. Served with U.S. Army, 1968-71. Recipient Hugo Otto Wolf Meml. prize U. Pa., 1978. Mem. IEEE, U.S. Power Squadron, Eta Kappa Nu, Tau Beta Pi. Republican. Avocations: reading, wine, investing, real estate, boating. Home: 71 Sweetwater Rd Glen Mills PA 19342 Office: Electronic Devel Corp 5 Miller Rd Edgemont PA 19028

EMRICK, DONALD DAY, chemist, consultant; b. Waynesfield, Ohio, Apr. 3, 1929; s. Ernest Harold and Nellie (Day) E.; B.S. cum laude, Miami U., Oxford, Ohio, 1951; M.S., Purdue U., 1954, Ph.D., 1956 Grad. teaching asst. Purdue U., Lafayette, Ind., 1951-55; with chem. and phys. research div. Standard Oil Co. Ohio, 1955-64, research asso., 1961-64; cons., sr. research chemist research dept. Nat. Cash Register Co., Dayton, Ohio, 1965-72, chem. cons., 1972—. Mem. AAAS, Am. Chem. Soc., Phi Beta Kappa, Sigma Xi. Patentee in Field. Contbr. articles to profl. jours. Home: 4240 Lesher Dr Kettering OH 45429

ENBERG, HENRY WINFIELD, legal editor; b. Bethlehem, Pa., Oct. 4, 1940; s. Henry Winfield and Mildred Elizabeth (Jordan) E. B.S., U. Denver, 1962; LL.B., NYU, 1965. Bar: N.Y. 1967. Digester, Winthrop, Stimson, Putnam & Roberts, N.Y.C., 1965-69; sr. legal editor Practising Law Inst., N.Y.C., 1969—; bd. dirs. ZPPR Prodns., Inc. Contbr. articles. Republican. Episcopalian. Clubs: Wolfe Pack, Priory Scholars (N.Y.C.). Home: 250 W 27th St New York NY 10001 Office: Practising Law Inst 810 7th Ave New York NY 10019

ENCARNACIÓN, JOSÉ, JR., economist, educator; b. Manila, Philippines, Nov. 17, 1928; s. José and Teófila (Concepción) E.; m. Patricia Kearney, June 27, 1959; children—Paul, John, Mark, Riza. Ph.B., U. Philippines, Quezon City, 1950, M.A., 1954; Ph.D., Princeton U., 1960. Instr. philosophy U. Philippines, 1950-56, asst. prof. econs., 1960-62, assoc. prof., 1962-66, prof., 1966—; dean Sch. Econs., 1974—; instr. econs. Princeton U., N.J., 1959-60; vis. prof. U. Wis.-Madison, 1969-70; exec. dir. Philippine Ctr. for Econ. Devel., Quezon City, 1975—; mem. com. for devel. planning UN, N.Y.C., 1978-83; mem. sci. and tech. adv. com. WHO, Geneva, 1979-81. Contbr. articles to profl. pubs. Named to Ten Outstanding Young Men, Philippine Jaycees, 1963; Rockefeller Found. grantee, 1965; recipient Disting. Scholar award U. Philippines, 1968; elected academician Nat. Acad. Sci., 1979; citation as Nat. Scientist, Republic of Philippines, 1987. Mem. Philippine Econ. Soc. (pres. 1966-67), Econometric Soc., Philippine Statis. Assn., East Asian Econ. Assn. (exec. com. 1984—). Home: 59 Salvador St, Loyola Heights, Quezon City 1108, Philippines Office: U Philippines, Sch Econs, Quezon City 1101, Philippines

ENCEL, SOLOMON, education educator, consultant; b. Warsaw, Poland, Mar. 3, 1925; arrived in Australia, 1929; s. Gustav and Ethel (Kutner) E.; m. Diana Helen, Sept. 20, 1928; children: Vivien, Deborah, Daniel, Sarah. BA, U. Melbourne, 1949, MA, 1952, PhD, 1960. Lectr. U. Melbourne, Victoria, Australia, 1952-55; reader Australian Nat. U., Canberra, 1956-66; prof. U. New South Wales, Sydney, Australia, 1966—; commr. Edn. Commn. New South Wales, 1980-83; mem. Higher Edn. Bd. New South Wales, 1981-83; mem. Australian Sci. and Tech. Council, 1975. Author: Equality and Authority, 1970, Women and Society, 1974, Cabinet Government in Australia, 1974. Served with Australian Air Force, 1944-45. Fellow Australian Acad. Social Scis., Sociol. Assn. Australia (pres. 1969-71). Mem. Australian Labor party. Jewish. Club: U. New South Wales. Office: U New South Wales, PO Box 1, Kensington New South Wales 2033, Australia

END, HENRY, interior and industrial designer; b. Salford, Eng., Nov. 3, 1915; came to U.S. 1946; s. Maximillian and Adela (Blain) E.; m. Jessica Marion Claas, July 5, 1947; 1 child, Lindsay. Student architecture and art, St. Martin's Sch. Art, London, 1930; A.R.C.A., Royal Coll. Art, London, 1934. Founder, pres. Henry End Assoc, Miami, Fla., 1950—; founder Internat. Design Ctr. Los Angeles and Miami, 1960; designer sets 20th Century Fox, Warner Bros., Universal, Selznick. Interior designer hotels and restaurants, condominiums, office bldgs., including Cocoanut Grove, Los Angeles, Carlton Tower and Heathrow Hotel, London, Mayflower, Washington, Hotel Quito, Ecuador, El Conquistador, P.R., Carlton Beach, Bermuda, Lucayan Beach Hotel, Grand Bahama Island, Nassau Beach Hotel, Penta Hotels, London and Munich, Fed. Republic Germany, Ritz Carlton, Montreal, Que., Can., Seacoast Towers West, Seacoast Towers V, 733 Park Ave. Bldg., N.Y.C., The Whitehall, Chgo., Marriott chain motor hotels, tourist hotels for Govt. Tunisia, Hilton, Sheraton Brussels, Sheraton Buenos Aires, Argentina, Sonesta Internat., Hyatt Internat., Brussels, Montreal, Iran, Panama and Jamaica, Esso Hotel, Antwerp, Belgium, UN Hotel N.Y.C., S.S. Norway, Pavillion Hotel, Miami, Ledra Marriott, Athens, Lakeside Regent, Palm Beach, Fla.; designer feature exhibits Room of Tomorrow, Designs for Dining, Internat. Hotel Expn., N.Y.C., Chgo., Los Angeles, Internat. Restaurant Expn., Chgo., U.S. Rubber Pavilion, Coliseum, N.Y.C.; author: Interiors Book of Hotels and Motor Hotels, 1963, Interiors 2nd Book of Hotels, 1976, Hyatt Regency, Miami, Plaza Hotel, N.Y.C. Served with RAF, 1940-46. Recipient spl. citation AIA, awards Art Dirs. Club, Design Derby citation Société Culinaire Philanthropique, 13 design awards Instns. Mag.; named to Hall of Fame, Interior Design Mag., 1985. Fellow Royal Soc. Arts; mem. Am. Soc. Interior Designers (citation of merit, 2 design awards).

ENDERUD, WILBUR DONALD, JR., data processing cons.; b. Pueblo, Colo., Nov. 4, 1945; s. Wilbur Donald and Loretta Faye (Jackson) E.; B.A. in Math., San Diego State U., 1967; M.B.A., Calif. State U., Long Beach, 1972; children—Cynthia. From programmer to project leader Mattel, Inc., Hawthorne, Calif., 1967-72; dir. mgmt. info. systems Audio-Magnetics Corp., Gardena, Calif., 1972-75; founder, 1975, since owner, prin. cons. Don Enderud & Assocs. (now Mgmt. Info. Solutions, Inc.), Diamond Bar, Calif.; founding ptnr. New Century Leasing, Diamond Bar, 1978—. Served with USAR, 1968-69; Vietnam. Decorated Army Commendation medal. Mem. Assn. Computing Machinery, Aircraft Owners and Pilots Assn. Republican. Lutheran. Office: PO Box 4237 Diamond Bar CA 91765

ENDICOTT, ALAN GRATTAN, executive search company executive; b. Coventry, Eng., Oct. 23, 1934; s. Grattan John Endicott; m. Pauleen Ann Johnson, July 11, 1986; children: Richard, David. BS in Biochemistry, U. Birmingham, Eng., 1955. Chemist J. Sainsbury, 1959-61; mgr. prodn. Mars Ltd., 1961-64; works mgr. Cavenham Foods, 1964-66; resident cons. PA Cons., 1966-69; mng. dir. index printers Internat. Pub. Corp., 1969-70, mng. dir. Soutwark offset, 1970-71; dir. GKR, 1971-73; exec. search cons. Plumbley/Endicott & Assocs., Ltd., London, 1973—. Served to flight lt. RAF, 1956-59.

ENDIEVERI, ANTHONY FRANK, lawyer; b. Syracuse, N.Y., May 21, 1939; s. Santo and Anne Rose (Zeolla) E.; m. Arlene Rita McDonald, May 20, 1967; children: Anne C., Steven A. BA, Syracuse U., 1961, JD, 1965. Bar: N.Y. 1967, U.S. Dist. Ct. (no. dist.) N.Y. 1967, U.S. Ct. Appeals (2d cir.) 1969, U.S. Supreme Ct. 1970. Assoc. Ronald Crowley, Atty., North Syracuse, N.Y., 1965-67, Love, Balducci & Scaccia, Syracuse, 1967; sole practice, Camillus, N.Y., 1968—; appellate counsel Hiscock Legal Aid, Syracuse, 1968-70; asst. corp. counsel, prosecutor City of Syracuse, 1970-74; participant Nat. Coll. Advocacy, 1981-83, 86; speaker seminar, 1987. Mem. ministry program Syracuse Diocese Pre-Deacon Study, 1980-82. Served to maj. USMCR, 1972-88. Mem. N.Y. Bar Assn., ABA, Onondaga County Bar Assn., N.Y. Trial Lawyers Assn., Assn. Trial Lawyers Am. Democrat. Roman Catholic. Home: 205 Emann Dr Camillus NY 13031

ENDO, SHUSAKO, author; b. Tokyo, Mar. 27, 1923; s. Tsunehisa E. and Iku (Takei) E.; m. Junko Okada, Sept. 3, 1955; 1 son, Ryunosuke. B.A., Keio U., 1949; student French lit., Lyon U. (France), 1950-53. Author novels and plays including: Umi to Dokuyaku, 1958; Kuchibue wo Fuku Toki, Bara no Yakata (play), 1969, The Samurai, 1984; chief editor Japan Cath. Digest, 1954. Recipient Akutagana prize, for Shirophito, 1955; Tanizaki prize, 1967, Gru de Oficial de Ordem do Infante dom Henrique, Portugal, 1968 for Chinmoku; Sancti Silvestri, Pope Paul VI, 1970. Address: 3-35 Tamagawa-gakiren, 2 Chome Machida, Tokyo 194, Japan *

ENEBAKK, MAGNAR HENRY, newspaper executive; b. Trondheim, Norway, Apr. 28, 1929; s. Melker Andreas and Hanna (Pedersen) E.; m. Bjorg Ranvig, Apr. 28, 1956 (div. 1967); children: Harald, Hanne, Tor, Geir; m. Rigmor R.S. Enebakk, May 6, 1972; 1 child, Tim. Student, U. Oslo, 1959-61, Norwegian Sch. Econs. and Bus. Adminstrn., 1962-63. Personnel mgr. Afterposten, Oslo, 1963-68, circulation mgr., 1968-71, asst. circulation dir., 1976-73, circulation dir., 1973-85, v.p. circulation, 1985—. Author: Marketing of Newspapers, 1985. Served to maj. Norwegian Infantry, 1947-62, Norway, Fed. Republic of Germany, Korea, Middle East. Mem. Norwegian Publishers Assn. (chmn. several coms.), Internat. Circulation Mgmt. Assn. (bd. dirs. 1980-83), Direct Mktg. Assn., Norwegian Mktg. Assn., Norwegian Telemarketing Assn. (bd. dirs. 1987—); mem. numerous govt. newspaper coms. Lodge: Rotary (pres. 1987-88). Office: Aftenposten, Akersgt 51, N 0107, Oslo 1 Norway

ENFIELD, KURT FERDINAND, retired business machine retail company executive; b. Frankfurt, Germany, July 23, 1921; s. Henry and Alice (Bluethental) E.; came to U.S., 1939, naturalized, 1944; children: Gwen, Jill, Richard. Grad. Buxton Coll., Eng., 1937; Partner, Enfield's Camera Shop, Miami Beach, Fla., 1939-63; pres. Enfield's Bus. Products Co., Miami, 1955-85. Served with AUS, 1944-46. Decorated Bronze Star. Mem. Miami Beach C. of C., Bus. Products Council Assn. (pres. 1972-73), Nat. Microfilm Assn., Internat. Word Processing Assn. Democrat. Jewish. Clubs: Bayshore Service (pres. 1980-81), Tiger Bay Polit., Standard, Jockey, B'nai B'rith, U. Miami Founders; Club du Chateau (France). Office: 3141 NW 40th St Miami FL 33142

ENG, LAWRENCE (LARRY) PHILLIP, electrical engineer; b. Tulsa, Okla., June 7, 1957; s. Lawrence Eng and Daisy (Gee) Geere. B. in Chemistry, So. Meth. U., 1979, postgrad. in elec. engring., 1982-84. Lab. technician Children's Med. Ctr., Dallas, 1975-79; engr. Mostek, Carrollton, Tex., 1979-82, sr. engr. research and devel., 1982-84, head sect. research and devel., 1984-85; staff engr. Thomson Components Mostek Corp., Carrollton, 1985-87; engring. sect. mgr. SGS-Thomson Microelectronics, 1987—. Mem. IEEE, Am. Chem. Soc., Soc. Photo-Instrumentation Engrs. Patentee in field. Republican. Episcopalian. Home: 1909 Baxley Circle Carrollton TX 75006

ENG, NORMAN, civil engineer; b. Chgo., Dec. 21, 1952; s. Shang Hon (Eugene) and Hop Yee (Wong) E.; m. Candice (Wei June) Chiang, June 26, 1982; children: Timothy Eugene, Thomas Edison. BS in Civil Engring. (scholar), U. Calif., Berkeley, 1974. Prin. engr. EDS Nuclear Inc., San Francisco, 1975-78; advanced engr. Westinghouse Hanford, Richland, Wash., 1978-79; lead engr. Duke Power Co., Charlotte, N.C., 1979-80; project engr. URS/John A. Blume & Assocs., Engrs., San Francisco, 1980-81; project mgr. NUTECH Engrs., Inc., San Jose, Calif., 1981—. Bd. dirs. East Bay Asians Community Action, Oakland, Calif., 1973-74; tchr. Chinese Community Adult Sch., Oakland, 1975-77; sec. U.S. Jaycees, Berkeley, 1979-82. Recipient Ann. award San Francisco Bay Area Engring. Council, 1970. Mem. Am. Nuclear Soc., Am. Welding Soc., ASME, AAAS, Am. Concrete Inst., Am. Soc. Engring. Edn., N.Y. Acad. Sci., Nat. Soc. Profl. Engrs., Am. Soc. Civil Engrs., Am. Soc. Quality Control. Home: 3285 Padilla Way San Jose CA 95148 Office: NUTECH Engrs 145 Martinvale Ln San Jose CA 95119

ENG, WILLIAM, health educator; b. N.Y.C., July 30, 1950; s. George and Sarah E.; m. Emily Chan, Aug. 11, 1973; children—Jason, Jordan, Jared, Jesse. B.S. in Edn., CCNY, 1972, M.S. in Edn., 1973; Ed.D., NYU, 1978. Adminstrv. asst. CCNY, 1970-72; tchr. Stuyvesant High Sch., N.Y.C., 1971-72; adj. lectr., men's soccer coach York Coll., N.Y.C., 1972-73; asst. prof. health, dep. chairperson edn. dept. Baruch Coll., CUNY, N.Y.C., 1973—, athletic dir., 1978—, women's tennis coach, 1984—, men's soccer coach, 1980-82. Mem. legis. adv. com. State Senator Frank Padavan, Queens, N.Y. Mem. Met. Coll. Athletic Dirs. Assn. (v.p. 1984-86, treas. 1982-84, pres. 1986—), CUNY Athletic Conf. (v.p. 1985-86, treas., 1981-85, 87—), N.Y. Met. Intercollegiate Soccer Ofcls. Assn. Avocations: tennis; karate. Office: Baruch Coll CUNY 17 Lexington Ave New York NY 10010

ENGBERG, OLE HIERONYMUS, engineering educator; b. Odense, Denmark, Feb. 19, 1922; s. Jens F. and Julie (Zeuthen) E.; m. Ellen Andersen, Dec. 29, 1949; children—Lars, Henrik, Jens. M.Sc. Mech. Engring., Royal Tech. Highsch., 1941-47; Indsl. Cons., Danish Productivity Council, 1953-55. Design/field engr. Koppers Co./Rust Engring., Pitts., 1947-49; prodn. mgr. A/S Atlas, Copenhagen, 1949-53, 55-63; gen. mgr. service sector A/S Regnecentralen, Copenhagen, 1963-72, OE Consult, Holte, 1972—; asoc. prof. Danmarks Ingenior Akademi/DTH, Copenhagen, 1980—. Co-author ednl. film. Industry at Work, 1955; co-editor, author: White Paper on EDP, 1974; editor-in-chief: Report of EDP Education, 1983; co-editor, author Politikens Bog om EDB, 1985; contbr. articles to profl. jours. Chmn. Elers Kollegium, Copenhagen, 1979—, others. Mem. Dansk Databehandlingsforening (vice chmn. 1972-86), Dansk Standardiseringsrad (chmn. 1984—, TC184/DK), Danish State Ch. Home: Arnevangen 33, Holte DK 2840 Denmark

ENGDAHL, HORACE, critic; b. Karlskrona, Sweden, Dec. 30, 1948; s. Roland and Ann-Marie (Jonsson) E. Candidate in philosophy, U. Stockholm, 1970, PhD, 1987. Amanuensis dept. lit. history U. Stockholm, 1970-74, asst. prof. Inst. for English-Speaking Students, 1975-80; lit. critic Expressen (daily newspaper), Stockholm, 1980-82; lit. critic, dance critic Dagens Nyheter (daily newspaper), Stockholm, 1982—. Author: Den romantiska texten, 1986 (Tegner prize 1987); co-author: Hermeneutik, 1977; translator: Två dramer av H. von Kleist, 1982; editor Kris mag., 1977-87; contbr. articles to profl. jours. Served to lt. Swedish Army, 1967-68. Recipient Lundblad prize Swedish Acad., 1984. Home: Trädgårdsgatan 5, 111 31 Stockholm Sweden Office: Dagens Nyheter, 105 15 Stockholm Sweden

ENGEL, CHARLES ROBERT, educator, chemist; b. Vienna, Austria, Jan. 28, 1922; s. Jean and Lucie (Fuchs) E.; m. Edith H. Braillard, Aug. 6, 1951; children: Lucie Tatiana Engel Berthoud, Christiane Simonne Engel Vaillancourt, Francis Pierre, Marc Robert. BA, U. Grenoble, 1941; MSc, Swiss Fed. Inst. Tech., Zurich, 1947, DSc, 1951; State-DSc, U. Paris, 1970. Research fellow, asst. Swiss Fed. Inst. Tech., Zurich, 1948-51; asst. prof. med. research Collip Med. Research Lab. U. Western Ont., London, 1951-55; asso. prof. med. research U. Western Ont., 1955-58, hon. spl. lectr. chemistry, dept. chemistry, 1951-58; prof. chemistry Laval U., Quebec, Que., 1958—; vis. prof. Inst. de Chimie des Substances Naturelles CNRS, Gif-sur-Yvette, France, 1966-67. Editorial bd.: Steroids, 1964—; hon. editorial bd.: Current Abstracts of Chemistry, 1971-72, Index Chemicus, 1971-72; mem. editorial adv. bd.: Can. Jour. Chemistry, 1974; editor: Can. Jour. Chemistry, 1986—. Lt. for Can.-Que., Equestrian Order of Holy Sepulchre of Jerusalem, 1970—; bd. dirs. Cath. Culture Center, London, Ont. Decorated comdr. Equestrian Order of Holy Sepulchre of Jerusalem, 1964, comdr. with star, 1970, knight grand cross, 1973; knight Legion of Honor, France, 1985; medal Austrian Ministry of Edn. Fellow Chem. Inst. Can. (chmn. organic div. 1965-66, exec. med. div. 1966-78), Royal Chem. Soc. (London), Royal Soc. Chemistry; mem. Am., Swiss, French chem. socs., Canadian Biochem. Soc., N.Y. Acad. Scis., Order Chemists Que, Sigma Xi. Office: Dept Chemistry, Laval U, Quebec, PQ Canada G1K 7P4

ENGEL, VICTOR BOYNTON, construction industry company executive; b. Keokuk, Iowa, Jan. 29, 1914; s. Martin T. and Gertrude (Boynton) E.; AA Calif. Concordia Coll., 1935; various bus. and mil. schs.; BA, U. Calif. at

Berkeley, 1949; cert. Acad. Internat. Law, Hague, Netherlands, 1951; MA, Grad. Inst. Internat. Studies and U. Geneva, Switzerland, 1952; m. Dorothea Ann Messner, Mar. 18, 1944. Prof. constl. law, U.S. history U. Geneva, 1950-52; exec. mgr. Assn. Plumbing and Heating Contractors of Contra Costa County, Richmond, Calif., 1952-54; exec. dir. Contra Costa Builders Exchange, Concord, Calif., 1954—; pres. Constrn. Mgmt. Services, Inc., Metro-Mgmt. Services, Inc. Pres., Internat. Builders Exchange Execs., U.S., Can., 1962-63; chmn. Builders Exchange Council, 1971-72; pres. Builders Exchanges Constrn. Industry Conf., 1969-70. Mem. Contra Costa County Devel. Assn., Contra Costa Taxpayers Assn., Bay Area Coalition for Transp. Served with AUS, 1941-46. Recipient Dan Patrick award of merit Internat. Builders Exchange Execs., 1983. Mem. World Affairs Council No. Calif., Calif. Alumni Assn., Am. Soc. Assn. Execs., No. Calif. Soc. Assn. Execs., Assn. des Anciens l'Inst. Geneva. Clubs: Commonwealth (San Francisco); Concord Century, Toastmasters (Concord). Lodge: Rotary. Author: Significant Developments in American Society, 1952. Editor: Constrn. Weekly, 1954—. Home: 10 Gran Via Alamo CA 94507 Office: 115 Aspen Dr Pacheco CA 94553

ENGEL, WALBURGA VON RAFFLER, linguist, kinesicist; b. Munich, Ger., Sept. 25, 1920; d. Friedrich J. and Gertrud E. (Kiefer) von Raffler; D.Litt., U. Turin (Italy), 1947; M.S., Columbia U., 1951; Ph.D., Ind. U., 1953; came to U.S., 1949; naturalized, 1955; m. A. Ferdinand Engel, June 2, 1957; children—Lea Maxine, Eric Robert von Raffler. Faculty, Bennett Coll., Greensboro, N.C., 1953-55, Morris Harvey Coll. (now U. Charleston), W.Va., 1955-57, City Coll. of City U. N.Y., Adelphi U., 1957-58, NYU, 1957-59, U. Florence (Italy), 1959-60, Istituto Post Universitario Organizzazione Aziendale, Italy, 1960-61, Bologna Center of Johns Hopkins U., 1964; faculty Vanderbilt U., Nashville, 1965—, assoc. prof. linguistics, 1966-77, prof., 1977-86, prof. emeritus, 1986—, sr. research assoc. Inst. Pub. Policy Studies, 1986—; chmn. com. on linguistics Nashville Univ. Center, 1974-79; vis. prof. U. Ottawa, 1971-72, Inst. for Lang. Scis., Tokyo, 1976, Faculty Devel. course, Shanxi U., China, 1985; Nat. Sci. Found. prof., U. Florence, Italy, 1986-87; evaluator NSF, Nat. Endowment for Humanities and Can. Council; free lance journalist, 1949-58. Mem. AAUP, Internat. Linguists Assn. (chmn. nominating com. 1972), Kinesics Internat. (pres. 1988—), Linguistic Soc. Am. (emeritus 1986, chmn. anniversary film com. 1974), Internat. Assn. Applied Linguistics (research com. on discourse analysis), Internat. Sociol. Assn. (research com. on sociolinguistics), Societas Linguistica Europea, Inst. Nonverbal Communication Research, Internat. Assn. Study of Child Lang. (v.p. 1975-78), Lang. Origins Soc. (chmn. 23d internat. meeting 1987), Southeastern Conf. on Linguistics (hon.). Author: Il Prelinquaggio Infantile, 1964; Language Intervention Programs, 1975; (color film) Children's Acquisition of Kinesis; The Perception of Nonverbal Behavior, 1983, 85; editor: Child Language, 1975; co-editor: Baby Talk and Infant Speech, 1976, Views of Language, 1975, Aspects of Non-verbal Communication, 1977, 80 (transl. into Japanese); Language and Cognitive Styles, 1982; Language Acquisition and Developmental Kinesis, 1978; guest editor Word, Internat. Jour. Sociology of Lang.; adv. bd. Jour. Child Lang. (founder); contbr. 300 articles to profl. publs. Home: 372 Elmington Ave Nashville TN 37205

ENGEL, WILLIAM KING, neurologist, educator; b. St. Louis, Nov. 19, 1930; s. William Ernst and Opal (King) E.; m. Valerie Askanas; children: W. Keith, Peter J., Bradford C., Eve M. B.A., Johns Hopkins U., 1951; M.D., C.M., McGill U., 1955; M.D. (hon.), L'univ. d'Aix Marseille II, 1987. Diplomate: Am. Bd. Neurology and Psychiatry, Pan. Am. Med. Assn. (hon. life mem.). Intern U. Mich. Hosp., 1955-56; clin. assoc. Nat. Inst. Neurol. Diseases and Blindness, 1956-59; clin. clk. Nat. Hosp., London, 1959-60; with Nat. Inst. Neurol. Diseases and Stroke, 1960-81, chief med. neurology, 1963-78, chief neuromuscular diseases, 1978-81; clin. prof. neurology George Washington U., 1969-81; prof. neurology and pathology, chief div. neuromuscular diseases, dept. neurology U. So. Calif. Sch. Medicine, Los Angeles, 1981—; mem. med. bd. NIH, 1968-69;; founding dir. U. So. Calif. Neuromuscular Center, Hosp. of Good Samaritan, 1981—; Mem. med. adv. bd. St. Jude's Children's Research Hosp., Memphis, 1970-76, Myasthenia Gravis Found., 1970—, Amyotrophic Lateral Sclerosis Nat. Found., 1971-85, Los Angeles chpt. Muscular Dystrophy Assn., 1981—, Amyotrophic Lateral Sclerosis Soc. Am., 1980-85, (sci. adv. bd. 1982—); vis. prof., invited lectr., advisor internat. congresses in, Europe, S.Am., Can., Far East; cons. Nat. Naval Med. Center. Former Mem. editorial bd.: Archives of Neurology; contbr. numerous papers to profl. lit., poems to mags. Past pres. Citizens Assn., Bethesda, Md., Longhouse chief YMCA Indian Guides, 1965-66; past chmn. troop com. Boy Scouts Am.; mem. edn. adv. bd. Phronesis, Spain; nat. corp. mem. Muscular Dystrophy Assn., 1985-88, nat. v.p. 1988— , med. adv. bd. Los Angeles chpt., 1981—, bd. dirs. 1985—. Recipient Meritorious Service medal USPHS, 1971, various awards from Italian med. socs. Fellow Am. Acad. Neurology (S. Weir Mitchell award 1962; pres. VI Internat. Congress Neuromuscular Diseases, 1986); mem. AMA, Histochem Soc., Am. Soc. Cell Biology, Am. Assn. Neuropathologists, World Commn. Neuromuscular Disease (exec. com.), Am. Neurol. Assn., Los Angeles County Med. Assn., Société Belge d'Electromyographie (assoc.), Asociación de Distrofía Muscular de la República Argentina (hon. pres.), Soc. for Neurosci., Société Francaise de Neurologie (hon.). Office: U So Calif Neuromuscular Ctr Hosp Good Samaritan 637 S Lucas Ave Los Angeles CA 90017

ENGEL-ARIELI, SUSAN LEE, physician; b. Chgo., Oct. 7, 1954; d. Thaddeus S. Dziengiel and Marian L. (Carpenter) Kasper; m. Udi Arieli. BA, Northwestern U., 1975; MD, Chgo. Med. Sch., 1982. Med. technician G.D. Searle, Skokie, Ill., 1972, 73, assoc. dir., 1983-84, dir., 1984-86; research editorial asst. U. Chgo., 1974; research assoc. Loyola U., Maywood, Ill., 1977-78; intern Rush Pres St. Lukes Hosp., 1982-83; resident U. Chgo., 1983; mgr. Hosp. Products div. Abbott Labs, Abbott Park, Ill., 1986—; Vis. prof. Rush Presbyn.-St. Luke's Hosp., Chgo., 1985, faculty assoc., 1985; assoc. investigator, asst. prof. medicine King Drew Med. Ctr., UCLA, 1985—. Contbr. articles to profl. and scholarly jours. Bd. govs. Art Inst. of Chgo., 1985—, aux. bd., 1988—, mem. multiple benefit coms., 1984—, vice chmn. Capital Campaign, 1984-85; mem. pres. com. Landmark Preservation Council, Chgo., 1984—, chmn. multiple coms. polit. candidates, 1986; bd. dirs. Marshall unit Chgo. Boys Clubs, 1984—; mem. benefit com. Hubbard St. Dance Co. 10th Gala, 1988, Victory Garden's Theatre Annual Benefit, 1988. Internat. Coll. Surgeons fellow, 1982. Mem. AMA, Am. Coll. Physicians, Am. Fedn. for Clin. Research, So. Med. Assn., Ill. State Med. Soc., Chgo. Med. Soc., Am. Acad. Med. Dirs., Nat. Acad. Arts & Scis.

ENGELHARDT, HUGO TRISTRAM, JR., physician, educator; b. New Orleans, Apr. 27, 1941; s. Hugo Tristram and Beulah (Karbach) E.; m. Susan Gay Malloy, Nov. 25, 1965; children: Susan Elisabeth, Christina Tristram, Dorothea. B.A., U. Tex., Austin, 1963, Ph.D., 1969; M.D. with honors, Tulane U., 1972. Asst. prof. U. Tex. Med. Br., 1972-75, asso. prof., 1975-77; mem. Inst. Med. Humanities, 1973-77; Rosemary Kennedy prof. philosophy of medicine Georgetown U., 1977-82; sr. research scholar Kennedy Inst. Center for Bioethics, Washington, 1977-82; prof. depts. internal medicine and community medicine Baylor Coll. Medicine, Houston, 1983—, mem. Ctr. for Ethics, Medicine and Pub. Issues, 1983—; prof. Rice U., Houston, 1983—; chmn. adv. panel on infertility prevention and treatment for office of tech. assessment of the U.S. Congress, 1986-87. Author: Mind Body: A Categorial Relation, 1973, The Foundations of Bioethics, 1986; co-author: Bioethics: Readings and Cases, 1987; assoc. editor Ency. of Bioethics, 1973-78, Jour. Medicine and Philosophy, 1974-84 ; mem. editorial adv. bd.: Social Sci. and Medicine, 1976—, Theoretical Medicine, 1981—, Second Opinion, 1985—, Bioethics, 1987—, Jour. Medicine Ethics Law, 1987—; editor Jour. Medicine and Philosophy, 1984—; co-editor Philosophy and Medicine series, 1974—; editor (with others): Evaluation and Explanation in the Biomedical Sciences, 1975, Philosophical Dimensions of the Neuro-Medical Sciences, 1976, Philosophical Medical Ethics, 1977, Mental Health, 1978, Clinical Judgment, 1979, Mental Illness: Law and Public Policy, 1980, Concepts of Health and Disease, 1981, The Roots of Ethics: Science, Religion, and Values, 1981, New Knowledge in the Biomedical Sciences, 1982, Abortion and the Status of the Fetus, 1983, Scientific Controversies, 1987, The Use of Human Beings in Research, 1988. Mem. bioethics com. Nat. Found. March of Dimes, 1975—; mem. Masters and Johnson Dirs. Adv. Council. Fulbright fellow, 1969-70. Fellow Inst. Soc., Ethics and the Life Scis.; mem. Am. Philos. Assn. Home: 2802 Lafayette Houston TX 77005 also: HC 3 Box 1 New Braunfels TX 78132 Office: Baylor Coll Medicine Center for Ethics Medicine and Pub Issue Houston TX 77030

ENGELHARDT, JOHN HUGO, lawyer; b. Houston, Feb. 3, 1946; s. Hugo Tristram and Beulah Lillie (Karbach) E.; m. Jasmin Inge Nestler, Nov. 12, 1976; children: Angelique D, Sabrina N. BA, U. Tex., 1968; JD, St. Mary's U., San Antonio, 1973. Bar: Tex. 1973. Tchr. history Pearsall High Sch., Tex., 1968-69; examining atty. Comml. Title Co., San Antonio, 1975-78, San Antonio Title Co., 1978-82; sole practice, New Braunfels, Tex., 1973-75, 1982—; adv. dir. M Bank Brenham, Tex., 1983—. Mem. ABA, Coll. State Bar Tex., Pi Gamma Mu. Republican. Roman Catholic. Office: HC 3 Box 1 New Braunfels TX 78132

ENGELKING, ELLEN MELINDA, foundry pattern company executive, real estate broker; b. Columbus, Ind., May 12, 1942; d. Lowell Eugene and Marcella (Brane) E.; children: Melissa Claire Fairbanks John David Prohaska, Ellen Margaret Prohaska. Student Sullins Coll., 1961, Franklin Coll., 1961-62, Ind. U., 1963. Vice chmn., pres., chief exec. officer Engelking Patterns, Inc., Columbus, Ind., 1980—, dir., treas., chief exec. officer Engelking Properties, Inc., Columbus, 1980—; guest speaker Bus. Sch., Ind. U., Bloomington, 1985-86, Ball State U., Muncie, Ind., 1986. Campaign chmn. Am. Heart Assn., Bartholomew County, 1980-81; chmn. Mothers March of Dimes, Bartholomew County, 1967; sec. Bartholomew County Republican Party, 1976-80; bd. dirs. Found. for Youth, 1975-78, Quinco Found., 1978-79; protocol hostess Pan Am. Games X, Indpls., 1987. Mem. U.S. C. of C., Ind. C. of C., Ind. Mfg. Assn., Am. Foundrymens Soc., Internat. Platform Assn., Acad. of Model Aeronautics, Alumni Council of Franklin Coll., Delta Delta Delta. Roman Catholic. Avocations: study and present adaptation of Shaker work ethic, remote-controlled aircrafts, literature, oil painting. Office: Engelking Patterns Inc PO Box 607 Columbus IN 47202

ENGELL, HANS, Danish government official; b. Copenhagen, Oct. 8, 1948; s. Knud Engell Andersen. Journalist newspapers of Berlingske consortium, Copenhagen; head of press service Conservative People's Party, Copenhagen, 1978—; M.P., former minister of def. from 1982. Address: Conservative People's Party, Tordenskjoldsgade, 1055 Copenhagen K Denmark *

ENGELMANN, FOLKER, plasma physicist, educator; b. Lübeck, Germany, July 9, 1931; s. Helmut and Johanna (Rüdel) E.; Diploma in Physics, Technische Hochschule Munich, 1953, Ph.D., 1956; m. Christa Kursawe, July 28, 1951; children—Gunter, Roger, Rainer, Edda Desiree, Tiziana. Sci. asst. Technische Hochschule, Munich, 1953-60; physicist Euratom-Cea, Fontenay-aux Roses, 1960-88; physicist Euratom-Cnen, Frascati, Italy, 1963-75, head theory div., 1967-75; head theory div. Euratom-Fom, Fom-Instituut voor Plasmayfysica, Jutphaas, Netherlands, 1975-88 ; prof. theoretical physics U. Utrecht Netherlands, 1976-88 ; dep. head NET Team, GARCHING (Germany); lectr. U. Rome, 1965-75. Mem. European Phys. Soc. (bd. plasma physics div.), Dutch Phys. Soc., German Phys. Soc., Commn. Plasma Physics (chmn. IUPAP). Office: Boltzuannstr 2, D-8046 Garching Federal Republic of Germany

ENGERRAND, DORIS DIESKOW, educator; b. Chgo., Aug. 7, 1925; d. William Jacob and Alma Willhelmina (Cords) Dieskow; B.S. in Bus. Adminstrn., N. Ga. Coll., 1958, B.S. in Elementary Edn., 1959; M. Bus. Edn., Ga. State U., 1966, Ph.D., 1970; m. Gabriel H. Engerrand, Oct. 26, 1946 (dec. June 1987); children—Steven, Kenneth, Jeannine. Tchr., dept. chmn. Lumpkin County High Sch., Dahlonega, Ga., 1960-63, 65-68; tchr., Gainesville, Ga., 1965; asst. prof. Troy (Ala.) State U., 1969-71; asst. prof. bus. Ga. Coll., Milledgeville, 1971-74, asso. prof., 1974-78, prof., 1978—, chmn. dept. bus. info. systems and communications, 1978—; cons. Named Outstanding Tchr. Lumpkin County Pub. Schs., 1963, 66; Outstanding Educator bus. faculty Ga. Coll., 1975, Exec. of Yr. award, 1983. Fellow Am. Bus. Communication Assn. (v.p. S.E. 1978-80, 81-84), So. Mgmt. Assn., Nat., Ga. (Postsecondary Tchr. of Yr. award 10th dist. 1983, Postsecondary Tchr. of Yr. award 1984) bus. edn. assns., Am., Ga. (Educator of Yr. award 1984) vocat. assns., Profl. Secs. Internat., Office Systems Research Assn., Ninety-nines Internat. (chmn. N. Ga. chpt. 1975-76, named Pilot of Year N. Ga. chpt. 1973). Methodist. Contbr. articles on bus. edn. to profl. publs. Home: 1674 Pine Valley Rd Milledgeville GA 31061 Office: Ga Coll Milledgeville GA 31061

ENGERRAND, KENNETH GABRIEL, lawyer, law educator; b. Atlanta, June 30, 1952; s. Gabriel H. and Doris A. (Dieskow) E.; m. Anne Walts, Mar. 16, 1985; 1 child, Caroline Elizabeth Turner. B.A., Fla. State U., 1973; J.D., U. Tex., 1976. Bar: Tex. 1976, U.S. Dist. Ct. (so. dist.) Tex. 1977. U.S. Ct. Appeals (5th cir.) 1978, U.S. Supreme Ct. 1980, U.S. Ct. Appeals (11th cir.) 1981, U.S. Dist. Ct. (ea. dist.) Tex. 1987. Assoc. Royston, Rayzor, Vickery & Williams, Houston, 1976-80, Brown, Sims & Ayre, Houston, 1980; v.p., gen. counsel Huthnance Offshore Corp., Houston, 1980-86; assoc. Brown, Sims, Wise & White, Houston, 1986— ; adj. prof. law S. Tex. Coll. Law, Houston, 1979—. Columnist The Reporter, 1984-87; contbr. articles to profl. jours. Faculty advisor to spl. maritime edits. S. Tex. Law Jour., 1981—. Fund drive vol. Houston Grand Opera, 1985—, trustee, 1986—. Named Best Prof., S. Tex. Coll. Law, Houston, 1981-82, 83-84; recipient Outstanding Contrbn. to Community award, Houston Jaycees, 1983; Mem. ABA (vice chmn. admiralty and maritime law com., tort and ins. practice sect. 1986—), Maritime Law Assn., Order of Coif, Phi Beta Kappa, Phi Delta Phi. Republican. Methodist. Avocation: legal writing, cultivating roses. Home: 773 W Creekside Dr Houston TX 77024 Office: Brown Sims Wise & White 2000 Post Oak Blvd Suite 2300 Post Oak Central Houston TX 77056

ENGGAARD, KNUD, government official; b. Odder, Denmark, June 4, 1929; s. Jens Nielsen and Anna Skousgaard E.; m. Elsebeth Andersen, Jan. 12, 1962; children: Thomas, Jacob, Christian. MS in Engring. Sci., Royal Tech. U., Copenhagen, Denmark, 1954. With Swedish Engring. Co., 1956-58; chmn. Liberal Youth of Denmark, Denmark, 1959-62, Danish Youth Council, Denmark, 1962-64; M.P. Liberal Party, Denmark, 1964-77, 79-81, 84—, chmn. liberal group, 1970-71, 73-77, vice chmn., 1978; minister of interior Denmark, 1978-79, 86-87, minister of energy, 1982-86, minister of econ. affairs, 1987-88, minister of def., 1988—; chmn. Copenhagen Telefon Co., 1974-78; pres. Nordic Counsel, 1976-77; mem. Folketing, 1964-77, 79-81, 84—. Served as lt. Army Tech. Corps (Res.) 1955. Office: Ministry of Def, Slotsholmsgade 10, 1216 Copenhagen 12, Denmark *

ENGGASS, ROBERT, art historian; b. Detroit, Dec. 20, 1921; s. Clarence H. and Helen (Strasburger) E.; m. Catherine Ann Cavanaugh, June 27, 1949. B.A., Harvard U., 1946; M.A., U. Mich., 1950, Ph.D. (Rackham fellow), 1955. Instr. Bryn Mawr Coll., Haverford Coll., 1955-56; asst. prof. Williams Coll., 1956-57, U. Buffalo, 1957-58; assoc. prof. Pa. State U., 1958-65, acting head art history dept., 1963, chmn. grad. program, 1960-65; prof. art history, chmn. art dept. La. State U., 1965-66; prof. art history Pa. State U., 1966-71, U. Kans., Lawrence, 1971-78; grad. adv. U. Kans., 1973-76; Callaway prof. art U. Ga., Athens, 1979-88; disting. vis. prof. art history Va. Commonwealth U., Richmond, 1988—. Author: Baciccio, 1966, (with J. Brown) Italy and Spain 1600-1750 - Sources and Documents in Art History, 1970, Early 18th Century Sculpture in Rome, 1976 (Borghese prize 1977), (with Catherine Enggass) Vatican Library edit. Pio's Vite di Pittori, 1977, Malvasia's Reni, 1980, Ridolfi's Tintoretto, 1984; contbr. numerous articles to profl. jours. Served with USAAF, 1942. Am. Council Learned Socs. grantee-in-aid, 1958, 70, 76; Fulbright research scholar U. Rome, 1963-64; Kress Found. grantee, 1966, 67, 69, 70; U. Kans. grantee, 1971-77. Mem. Coll. Art Assn., AAUP, Inst. di Studi Romani, Royal Soc. Arts, Am. Soc. Eighteenth Century Studies (editorial bd. quar. jour. 1979-84), Southeastern Soc. 18th Century Studies (dir. 1984-87). Democrat. Club: Accademia degli Ippopotami. Home: 212 Stony Run Ln Baltimore MD 21210 Office: Bishop House U Ga Athens GA 30602

ENGL, RICHARD LUDWIG, tax consultant; b. Burghausen, W. Ger., June 28, 1950; s. Otto and Käthe (Fö rg) E.; m. Pascale Müller, July 14, 1975; children—Patrick R., Caroline A. Diplom-Kaufmann (M.B.A.), U. Regensburg (W. Ger.), 1975. Tax cons. (steuerberater). Tax dept. mgr. Procter & Gamble GmbH, Schwalbach, Taunus, W. Ger., 1976-77; assoc. Rädler, Raupach & Ptnrs., Munich, W. Ger., 1977-81, ptnr., 1982—; mem. supervisory bd. Heinr. Hill GmbH, Hattingen, W. Ger., 1983—, Deutscher Supermarkt GmbH, Düsseldorf, W. Ger., 1986—. Contbr. articles on taxes to profl. jours.; co-author German Income Tax Act. Mem. Tax Cons. Bar Assn. Home: Bertha Suttnerweg 7-A, 8033 Martinsried Federal Republic of Germany Office: Rädler Raupach & Ptnrs, Prinzregentenplatz 10, 8000 Munich Federal Republic of Germany

ENGLAND, LYNNE LIPTON, lawyer, speech pathologist, audiologist; b. Youngstown, Ohio, Apr. 11, 1949; d. Sanford Y. and Sally (Kentor) Lipton; m. Richard E. England, Mar. 5, 1977. B.A., U. Mich., 1970; M.A., Temple U., 1972; J.D., Tulane U., 1981. Bar: Fla. 1981. Cert. clin. competence in speech pathology and audiology. Speech pathologist Rockland Children's Hosp. (N.Y.), 1972-74, Jefferson Parish Sch., Gretna, La., 1977-81; audiologist Rehab. Inst. Chgo., 1974-76; assoc. Trenam, Simmons, Kemker, Scharf, Barkin, Frye & O'Neill, Tampa, Fla., 1981-84; asst. U.S. atty. for Middle Dist. Fla., Tampa, 1984-87, asst. U.S. trustee, 1987—. Editor Fla. Bankruptcy Casenotes, 1983. Recipient clin. assistantship Temple U., 1972-74. Mem. Am. Speech and Hearing Assn., Fla. Bar Assn., ABA, Hillsborough County Bar Assn., Assn. Trial Lawyers Am., ALTA, Am. Bankruptcy Inst., Fed. Bar Assn., Order of Coif. Jewish. Home: 3054 Wister Circle Valrico FL 33594 Office: US Trustees Office 4921 Memorial Hwy Suite 340 Tampa FL 33634

ENGLANDER, ALOIS GODFREY, publisher; b. Prague, Czechoslovakia, May 13, 1907; came to U.S., 1940, naturalized, 1947; s. Adolf and Luise (Hofmann) E.; student Law and Medicine, German U., Prague, 1931-34; m. Lida Matouskova, Sept. 15, 1948; children—Juno S., Lucky V.; children by previous marriage—Juliet S. Seaver, Lola M. Shumlin. Mem. mgmt. office Bohemian Discount Bank and Soc. of Credit, Prague, 1933; pub., Vienna, Austria, 1936-38, Sweden, 1939-40, N.Y.C., 1941-47, Vienna, 1947—; cons. Isovolta Inc., Vienna, 1959—; dep. chief, assimilated rank brig. gen., Displaced Persons Camps, UNRRA, 1946; founder, sec. gen. World Congress Alternatives and Environ., Vienna; co-founder, bd. mem. Austrian Fgn. Policy Assn., Vienna; founder, vice chmn. No to Zwentendorf (anti-atom); permanent rep., chief of mission (envoy) to IAEA, Vienna, now ret.; hon. consul of Honduras in Austria, now ret.; founder United Green Party of Austria, The Green Democrats. Served with Calif. State Guard, 1943-46. Decorated comdr. Lateran Cross. Mem. European C. of C. Vienna (founder, v.p.), Mexican C. of C. Vienna (pres.). Club: Lions (vice gov. 1955-58). Publisher non-fiction, former editor-in-chief UN World; author: Who Is Johnson, 1964, editor: First World Congress, 1980. Home and Office: 27/28 Graben, A-1010 Vienna Austria

ENGLER, GIDEON, physicist, researcher; b. Kosow, Poland, Mar. 16, 1936; arrived in Palestine, 1946; s. Baruch and Bluma (Hefter) E.; m. Maya Bitan, Oct. 23, 1966 (div. 1978); 1 child, Nogah. MSc, Hebrew U., Jerusalem, 1964, PhD, 1969. Research fellow U. Pitts., 1968-70; mem. research dept. Weitzmann Inst. Sci., Rehovot, Israel, 1970-73; sr. researcher Soreq Nuclear Research Ctr., Yavne, Israel, 1973—, Brookhaven Nat. Lab., Upton, N.Y., 1978-79, Nuclear Lab., Oxford, Eng., 1984-85. Editor: Nuclear Instruments and Methods, Volume 139, 1976; contbr. articles on nuclear physics to profl. jours.; non-fiction lit. critic Maariv Newspaper. Served as sgt. Israeli Air Force, 1954-57. Royal Soc. Research grantee, 1984. Mem. Am. Physical Soc., N.Y. Acad. Sci., British Soc. Aesthetics, Am. Soc. Aesthetics. Home: PO Box 2139, 76 121 Rehovot Israel Office: Soreq Nuclear Research Ctr, 70 600 Yavne Israel

ENGLISH, FRANCIS PETER, ophthalmologist; b. Cairns, Australia, May 31, 1932; s. Peter Bede and Mona (Elliott) E.; m. Leonie Therese Jones, May 31, 1975; children—Lawrence, James. M.B., B.S., U. Queensland, Australia, 1957. Glaucoma fellow Howe Lab., Harvard U., Cambridge, Mass., 1962-63; clin. asst. Moorfields Hosp., London, 1963-66; vis. prof. ophthalmology U. Okla., 1969; fellow retina service U. Tex., Houston, 1967-68; fellow in oculoplastic surgery Manhattan Eye and Ear Hosp., N.Y.C., 1969-70; fellow cornea service Retina Found., Boston, 1970-71; ophthalmic surgeon Repatriation Dept., Brisbane, Australia, 1972—; instr. ophthalmology U. Queensland, 1972—; cons. Australian Govt., 1979—. Author: Reconstructive and Plastic Surgery of the Eyelids, 1975; contbr. to Current Ocular Therapy (Fraunfelder), 1985, Techniques in Ophthalmic Plastic Surgery (Wesley), 1986. Contbr. articles to profl. jours. Recipient ophthalmic study tour award Grenfell Found., Can., 1968. Fellow Internat. Coll. Surgeons, Royal Coll. Surgeons, Royal Australian Coll. Ophthalmologists; mem. Australian Med. Assn., Internat. Oculoplastic Soc. (bd. dirs. 1982—). Clubs: Johnsonian (Brisbane); Tattersalls, United Services. Home: 41 Charlton St Ascot, Brisbane 4007, Australia Office: 113 Wickham Terr, Brisbane 4000, Australia

ENGLISH, RUTH HILL, artist, consultant, educator; b. Andover, Mass., Feb. 7, 1904; d. Herbert Hudson and Ada Jane (Wells) Hill; grad. Abbot Acad., Andover; received pvt. instrn.; m. A. Evans Rephart, June 28, 1929; children—Susan K. (Mrs. Howard K. Simpson), Katharine K. (Mrs. Christopher R. Barnes); m. 2d, E. Schuyler English, July 4, 1959. Faculty Hampton Inst., 1924-25, Bryn Mawr Art Center (later Main Line Center of Arts), 1945-65, Wayne Art Center, 1947-49; dir. Hedgeabout Studio, Gladwyne, Pa., 1965—; lectr., art cons. throughout East, 1960-70. Past mem. womens bd. Pa. Hosp.; mem. womens bd. Babies Hosp., 1934-39. Mem. Hist. Soc. Early Am. Decoration (pres. William Penn chpt. 1950-51), Pa. Craftsmans Guild (dir. 1952-54). Republican. Episcopalian. Clubs: Acorn, Skytop (Pa.), Athenaeum. Home: 47 E Wynnewood Rd Merion PA 19066 also: Skytop PA 18357 Studio: 1124 Rose Glen Rd Gladwyne PA 19035

ENGLISH, TERENCE ALEXANDER, cardiac surgeon; b. Pietermaritzburg, Natal, South Africa, Oct. 3, 1932; came to Eng., 1955; s. Arthur Alexander and Mavis Eleanor (Lund) E.; m. Ann Margaret Dicey, Nov. 23, 1963; children—Katharine, Arthur, Mary, William. B.Sc. in Engring., U. Witwatersrand, South Africa, 1954; M.B.B.S., Guy's Hosp. Med. Sch., London, 1962; M.A., Cambridge U., Eng., 1977. Med. diplomate. Intern Guy's Hosp., 1962-63, resident, 1964-65; surg. registrar Brompton Hosp., London, 1967; research fellow dept. surgery U. Ala., Birmingham, 1969; sr. registrar Nat. Heart and Chest Hosps., London, 1969-72; cons. surgeon Papworth and Addenbrooke's Hosps., Cambridge, 1973—; dir. Heart Transplant Research Unit, Cambridge, 1980—; cons. adviser Humana Hosp. Wellington, London, 1983—. Mem. editorial bd. Jour. for Heart Transplantation, 1981, Cardiology in Practice, 1983, Perfusion, 1985. Mem. Brit. Heart Found. (council 1983—), Gen. Med. Council (council 1983—), Soc. Thoracic and Cardiovascular Surgeons (council 1975-77), Brit. Thoracic Soc. (council 1976-78), Internat. Soc. for Heart Transplantation (pres. 1984-85); fellow Royal Coll. Surgeons of Eng. (council 1981—), Soc. Perfusionists of Great Britain and Ireland (pres. 1986-87). Travelling scholar Soc. Thoracic and Cardiovascular Surgeons, 1979; recipient Man of Yr. award Royal Assn. for Disability and Rehab., 1980; Price-Thomas award for disting. service to surgery, 1986. Conservative. Mem. Ch. of England. Avocations: reading; music; walking; tennis. Home: 19 Adams Rd, Cambridge CB3 9AD, England Office: Papworth Hosp, Papworth CB3 8RE, England

ENGMAN, LEWIS AUGUST, lawyer, former government official, former trade association executive; b. Grand Rapids, Mich., Jan. 6, 1936; s. H. Sigurd and Florence C. (Lewis) E.; m. Patricia Lynne Hanahan, Dec. 2, 1978; children: Geoffrey Ponton, Jonathan Lewis, Richard Ransford. A.B., U. Mich., 1957; postgrad., Univ. Coll. and London Sch. Econs., 1957-58; LL.B., Harvard U., 1961. Assoc., then partner law firm Warner Norcross & Judd, Grand Rapids, 1961-70, Washington, 1976-79; pres. Pharm. Mfrs. Assn., Washington, 1979-84; ptnr. Winston & Strawn, Washington, 1985—; mem. council Internat. Fedn. Pharm. Mfrs. Assns., 1979-84; pres. Nat. Drug Trade Conf., 1980; dir. legis. affairs Pres.'s Com. Consumer Interests, Washington, 1970; gen. counsel White House Office Consumer Affairs, Washington, 1970-71; asst. dir. Domestic Council, The White House, Washington, 1971-73; chmn. FTC, Washington, 1973-75; Mem. Council Adminstrv. Conf. of U.S., 1974-75, pub. mem., 1986—; life mem. 6th Cir. Jud. Conf. U.S.; Bd. advisors Columbia U. Ctr. for Law and Econ. Studies, 1975-79, Mich. Franchise Adv. Com., 1977-79; mem. Western Mich. Areawide Comprehensive Health Planning Unit, 1969-70; chmn. Kent County (Mich.) Health Planning unit, 1969-70. Mem. Friends of Art adv. bd. Grand Valley State Coll., 1969-70; mem. Kent County Republican Finance Com., 1965-70; bd. dirs. Opera Assn. Western Mich., 1967-69; bd. dirs. Grand Rapids Symphony Soc., 1964-70, pres., 1968-70; trustee Blodgett Meml. Hosp., 1968-70, sec., 1969-70; bd. dirs. Dyer-Ives Found., 1964—, sec., 1961-70. Mem. ABA (mem. council sect. anti-trust law 1973-75), Fed. Bar Assn., D.C. Bar Assn., State Bar Mich., Am. Soc. Internat. Law, Phi Beta Kappa, Delta Sigma Rho, Phi Kappa Phi, Phi Eta Sigma. Presbyterian. Clubs: Kent Country (Grand Rapids), University (Grand Rapids); George Town (Washington), Metropolitan (Washington). Office: Winston & Strawn 2550 M St NW Suite 500 Washington DC 20037

ENGSTEDT, LARS MAGNUS, physician, educator; b. Enkoping, Sweden, Sept. 23, 1920; s. B. Magnus and Karin (Eriksson) E.; m. Anne-Marie Ohlson, Dec. 30, 1948; children—Malin, Lotta, Magnus, Karolina. M.D., Karolinska Inst., 1946. Physician dept. internal medicine Karolinska Hosp., Stockholm, 1948-60, assoc. prof., 1960-66, prof., head dept. internal medicine Sodersjukhuset/Karolinska Inst., South Hosp., 1966-86; head clin. dept. Lab. Drug Control, Nat. Health Services, Stockholm, 1960-64. Contbr. articles to profl. jours. Mem. Swedish Soc. Hematology (pres. 1982-84), Swedish Physicians Against Nuclear Weapons (pres. 1981), Internat. Physicians for Prevention of Nuclear War (councillor 1983, v.p. 1985), Swedish Nat. Inst. for Radioactive Protection (bd. dirs. 1960-66). Address: Stromkarlsvagen 59, S-16138 Bromma Sweden

ENGSTROM, ARNE VILHELM, biophysicist; b. Stockholm, May 15, 1920; s. Axel Vilhelm and Margareta E.; M.D., U. Stockholm, 1946; m. Anna Lisa Orrdal, 1948; children—Vilhelm, Alexander. Prof. med. biophysics Karolinska Institutet, Stockholm, 1952—; chief sci. adv. Swedish Govt., 1966-75; dir. gen., head Nat. Swedish Food Adminstrn., Uppsala, 1975-87; vis. prof. Stanford U., U. Calif., 1951, 62; head Swedish sci. orgn. for UN Conf. on Environment; chmn. bd. Swedish Com. for Def. Research, Com. for Med. Orgn., Com. for Social Sci. Research; vice chmn. sci. com. OECD, Paris; pres. council European Molecular Biol. Lab., 1974-76. Decorated comdr. Polar Star; comdr. Order Brit. Empire; King's medal; Rockefeller fellow, 1951. Mem. Internat. Union Pure and Applied Biophysics (pres. 1962-70), Swedish Soc. Med. Scis. (pres. 1974), Royal Swedish Acad. Sci., Royal Swedish Acad. Engring. Scis., Royal Soc. Sci. Uppsala, Indian Acad. Sci., other internat. orgns. Author: X-ray Microanalysis in Biology and Medicine, 1962; co-author: Bone and Radiostrontium, 1957; Biological Ultrastructure, 1958; editor Quar. Revs. Biophysics; contbr. numerous articles to sci. jours. Home: Skeppargatan 48, 11458 Stockholm Sweden Office: Karolinska Institute, Dept Medical Physics, Stockholm Sweden

ENHORNING, CONSTANCE ELISABET, broadcasting executive; b. Kristianstad, Sweden, Oct. 22, 1945; came to The Gambia, 1969; d. Tage Enhorning and Britt Wadner. Studentkompetens in English and Swedish, Latinskolan, Malmo, Sweden, 1966. Producer Radio Syd, Malmo, 1964-66, gen. mgr., Banjul, The Gambia, 1972—; kanslisekreterare Skanes Turisttrafikforbund, Malmo, 1966-69; owner, operator restaurant/disco, shop on board M/S Cheeta, Banjul, The Gambia, 1969-71. Avocation: tennis. Home and Office: PO Box 279-280, Banjul The Gambia

ENJOJI, JIRO, newspaper company executive; b. Chiba Prefecture, Japan, Apr. 3, 1907; s. Teigo and Kei (Asano) E.; grad. Waseda U., Tokyo, 1933; m. Nobu Takeda, Nov. 23, 1938; children—Mrs. Taoko Yozo Miyamoto, Hajime. With Chugai Shogyo Shimpo, 1933-46; editor-in-chief Nihon Keizai Shimbun, 1946-47, dir., 1947-68, pres., 1968-76, chmn., 1976-80, adviser, 1980—. Dir. Tokyo Stock Exchange; dir. Investment Trusts Assn.; adv. Japan Devel. Bank; vice chmn. Japan Atomic Indsl. Forum, Inc. Chmn., Petroleum Council, Central Social Ins. Med. Council; committeeman Indsl. Structure Council, Coal Mining Council; mem. Adv. Com. on Energy; counsellor Econ. Planning Agy. Recipient Art award Edn. Ministry, 1963. Home: 5-2-7 Yoyogi, Shibuya-ku, Tokyo Japan Office: 5-9-1 Otemachi, Chiyoda-ku, Tokyo Japan

ENKVIST, NILS ERIK AUGUST, linguist, educator; b. Helsinki, Finland, Sept. 27, 1925; s. Ole Johannes and Ester (Makkonen) E.; m. Tua-Lill Ingegärd Elise Söderholm, Dec. 26, 1956; children: Kjell, Kristian, Elisabeth. MA, U. Mich., 1948, U. Helsinki, 1949; PhD, U. Helsinki, 1952; PhD (hon.), U. Stockholm, 1980; LittD (hon.), Purdue U., 1982, Adam Mickiewicz U., Poznań, Poland, 1984. Speech clinic asst. U. Mich., Ann Arbor, 1947-48; asst. in phonetics U. Helsinki, 1949-50, lectr. English, 1950-51; docent of English Åbo Akademi, Finland, 1952-57, Donner prof. English, 1957-84; dir. Research Inst. Åbo Akademi Found., Finland, 1978—; research prof. Acad. Finland, 1974-77; dist. prof. stylistics and text linguistics Åbo Akademi, 1984—; Vis. fellow Folger Library, Washington, 1964; vis. prof. English UCLA, 1965; vis. lectr. U. Cambridge, vis. fellow, Clare Hall, Cambridge U., Eng., 1972; dist. scholar in residence, Purdue U., West Lafayette, Ind., 1977, 85. Author: American Humour in England, 1953, The Seasons of the Year, 1957, Geoffrey Chaucer, 1964, Linguistic Stylistics, 1974, Stilforskning och Stilteori, 1974, Tekstilingvistiikan Peruskasitteita, 1975, (with others) Linguistics and Style, 1962; editor Approaches to Word Order, 1976, Impromptu Speech, 1982, Coherence and Composition, 1985. Pres. Soc. Linguistica Europaea, 1977-78; v.p. Fillm Fédération Internat. des Langues et Littératures Modernes, 1981-87, pres., 1988—. Served to 1st lt. Finnish Army, 1943-45. Recipient Hugo Suolahti prize Helsinki U., 1949, Elfving award Åbo Akademi, 1965, 74, Nyström prize Societas Scientiarum Fennica, Helsinki, 1986, Nordic prize Swedish Acad., 1988; named Knight Commander, Order of Lion Finland, 1967. Fellow Soc. Scientiarum Fennica (recipient medal 1988), Finnish Acad. Scis., Lund Soc. Letters, Royal Swedish Acad. of Letters, History and Antiquities; mem. MLA Am. (hon.), Academia Europea, Finnish Soc. Applied Linguistics (hon.), Philol. Soc., Modern Humanities Research Assn., Soc. Linguistica Europea, Linguistica Soc. Am., Internat. Assn. U. Profs. English, Finnish Assn. Applied Linguistics, Henry Sweet Soc. Home: Liljasaarentie 2F, 00340 Helsinki Finland Office: Åbo Akademi, 20500 Åbo Finland

ENLOE, CORTEZ FERDINAND, JR., magazine publisher, physician; b. Jefferson City, Mo., June 1, 1910; m. Mary Josephine Greenlee, May 4, 1963; children: Margaret Mary Greenlee, David Goodridge, Cynthia Holden. B.A., U. Mo., Columbia, 1932; postgrad., Ruperto Carola U. Heidelberg, Ger., Ludwig Maximillians U. Munich, Ger.; M.D. cum laude, U. Berlin, 1937; grad., Sch. Aviation Medicine, 1942, Command and Gen. Staff Coll., 1943. Diplomate: Am. Bd. Preventive Medicine. Research intern Charity Clinic, Berlin, 1936-37; intern St. Anthony Hosp., St. Louis, 1937-38; practice medicine, specializing in internal medicine; asst. med. dir. Winthrop Chem. Co., N.Y.C.; exec. v.p., gen. mgr. G.F. Harvey Co., Saratoga Springs, N.Y.; dir. profl. services and clin. research William R. Warner, Inc., N.Y.C.; v.p. Murray Breese Assos., N.Y.C.; chmn. bd., pres. Cortez F. Enloe, Inc., N.Y.C.; pres. Mediphone, Inc., Washington; sr. partner Enloe, Stalvey & Assocs., Washington; chmn. bd., pres. Nutrition Today, Inc., Annapolis, Md., 1964—; editor, pub. Nutrition Today mag., 1964—; mem. med. adv. bd. Nat. Assn. Human Devel., Washington, 1980—; hon. Militare Samfunn lectr. Oslo, 1980; v.p. Chindits Old Comrades Assn., Wolverhampton, U.K.; dir. Antarctic Nutrition Survey, 1968—; chmn. sci. adv. com. Am./Norwegian Trans Polar Expdn., 1968-69; ofcl. observer NATO High Arctic Exercises, 1980; Central European corr. Kansas City Star, 1933-37; cons. fed. adminstr. CD and dir. Office of Emergency Planning; adminstr. N.Y. State CD; cons. mem. Council Nat. Def., AMA; cons. Surgeon Gen. USAF; mem. N.Y. Gov's Adv. Com. Emergency Health Resources. Editor: The Flight Surgeon's Manual, 1954; contbr. articles to sci. jours. and yachting mags. Trustee Geriatrics Research Found. Served to maj. USAAF, 1946, CBI, PTO, ETO; med. advisor to Admiral Lord Louis Mountbatten, comdr. CBI. Decorated Legion of Merit, Air medal, Bronze Star, Antarctic medal, numerous others; recipient Faculty-Alumni Gold medal U. Mo., 1973, citation Jefferson City Public Schs., Nat. Air Power award Air Force Assn., 1955, Nat. Leica Photographers medal, 1939; Churchill scholar Westminster Coll., 1988; Churchill fellow Westminster Coll., Fulton, Mo. (life), fellow Churchill Meml. and Library, 1988. Fellow N.Y. Acad. Medicine, Royal Soc. Medicine (London), Royal Geog. Soc. (London), Aerospace Med. Assn., Am. Coll. Angiology, Am. Geriatrics Soc., Explorers Club; mem. AMA, N.Y. State Med. Soc. (chmn. space medicine sect.), County N.Y. Med. Soc., Am. Coll. Preventive Medicine, Am. Chem. Soc., AAAS, Endocrine Soc. (emeritus), Space Med. Soc., World Med. Assn., Hollywood (Calif.) Acad. Medicine (hon. life), Hakluyt Soc. (London), Air Force Assn. (life, past dir.), Soc. Med. Friends of Wine (hon. life). Clubs: N.Y. Yacht (Atalantis trophy 1964, D.S.M. 1967), Explorers of N.Y.

ENNERFELT, PER GORAN, conglomerate company executive; b. Norrkoping, Sweden, Mar. 6, 1940; s. Pewe and Dagmar (Tallroth) E.; m. Antonia Axson Johnson, 1984. Student Williams Coll., 1960; MBA, Stockholm Sch. Econs., 1963; MA, U. Stockholm, 1963. With Swedish Ironmasters Assn., Stockholm, 1963-66; personal asst. to head Axel Johnson Group, 1966-71; internat. banker Wells Fargo Bank, San Francisco, 1971-72; v.p. Axel Johnson AB, Stockholm, 1972-77, exec. v.p., chief operating officer, 1977-79, pres., chief exec. officer, 1979—; chmn. bd. Axel Johnson Petroleum AB, Stockholm, Axel Johnson Ore & Metals AB, Stockholm, Axel Johnson Internat. AB and other Johnson Cos. bd. dirs. Avesta AB, Avesta, Sweden, Svenska Handelsbanken, Hexagon AB. Contbr. articles to profl. jours. Vice chmn., dir. Com. Promotion of Trade Between the Soviet Union and Sweden, 1983—, Sweden-China Trade Council, 1980—; bd. dirs. Sweden Am. Found., 1982—, Inst. Eastern Econ. Affairs, 1973—, Wells Fargo Internat. Adv. Council, San Francisco, 1976—, SRI internat. adv. council, Menlo Park, Calif.. Mem. Gen. Export Assn. Sweden (vice chmn.), Internat. C. of C., Stockholm C. of C. Home: Lovsta, 19442 Upplands-Vasby Sweden Office: Axel Johnson AB, Jakobsbergsgatan 7, 10375 Stockholm Sweden

ENNIS, RUTH M., realtor; b. Toledo, Feb. 27, 1913; d. Charles Newton and Ethel J. (Wagoner) Detwiler; student pub. schs., Toledo; m. Arthur Waldo Holly, Jan. 19, 1935 (div.); 1 dau., Barbara Ann (Mrs. Lawrence J. Novak); m. 2d, Harry E. Beddoe, Sept. 29, 1948 (div. 1967); 1 son, Thomas Weston; m. 3d, Wilbur John Ennis, Feb. 14, 1974. Real estate broker Chas. N. Detwiler, realtor, Huntington Park, Calif., 1942-48, Harry E. Beddoe, realtor, Huntington Park and Downey, Calif., 1948-67; escrow officer Universal Escrow Co., Huntington Park, 1944, Advance Escrow Co., 1945-47; v.p. Beddoe Investments, 1957-68, Golden State Hawaiian Corp., 1964, now pres.; exec. v.p. Hawaiian Home Developers, to 1973. Precinct capt. Rep. Party, Buena Park, Calif., 1960, area chmn., 1962-72. Mem. Calif. Real Estate Assn., Ainaloa (Hawaii) Community Assn. (dir. 1966-78). Home: 39-860 Desert Greens Dr E Palm Desert CA 92260 also: 699 LaHou Hilo HI 96720 Office: 120 Pauahi St Suite 308 Hilo HI 96720

ENNIS, THOMAS MICHAEL, health foundation executive; b. Morgantown, W.Va., Mar. 7, 1931; s. Thomas Edson and Violet Ruth (Nugent) E.; m. Julia Marie Dorety, June 30, 1956; children—Thomas John, Robert Griswold (dec.). Student, W.Va. U., 1949-52; A.B., George Washington U., 1954; J.D., Georgetown U, 1960. Subrogation-arbitration examiner Govt. Employees Ins. Co., Washington, 1956-59; asst., legis. analyst to v.p. pub. affairs Air Transport Assn. Am., Washington, 1959-60; dir. ann. support program George Washington U., 1960-63; nat. dir. devel. Project HOPE, People to People Health Found., Inc., Washington, 1963-66; nat. exec. dir. Epilepsy Found. Am., Washington, 1966-74; exec. dir. Clinton, Eaton, Ingham Community Mental Health Bd., 1974-83; nat. exec. dir. Alzheimer's Disease and Related Disorders Assn., Inc., Chgo., 1983-86; exec. dir. John Douglas French Found., Los Angeles, 1986—; clin. inst. dept. community medicine and internat. health Georgetown U., 1967-74; adj. assoc. prof. dept. psychiatry Mich. State U., 1975-84; lectr. Univ. Ctr. for Internat. Rehab., 1977; cons. health and med. founds., related orgns.; cons. Am. Health Found., 1967-69, Reston, Va.-Georgetown U. Health Planning Project, 1967-70;. Contbr. articles on devel. disabilities, mental health and health care to profl. jours. Mem. adv. bd. Nat. Center for Law and Handicapped, 1971-74; advisor Nat. Reye's Syndrome Found.; mem. Internat. Bur. Epilepsy, Nat. Com. for Research in Neurol. Disorders, 1967-72; mem. nat. adv. bd. Developmental Disabilities/Tech. Assistance System, U. N.C., 1971-78, Handicapped Organized Women, Charlotte, N.C., 1984—; Nat. del. trustee, v.p. Nat. Capitol Area chpt., bd. dirs., exec. com. Nat. Kidney Found., 1969-74, Nat. trustee, 1970-74, pres., 1972—; bd. dirs. Nat. Assn. Pvt. Residential Facilities for Mentally Retarded, 1970-74; bd. dirs., mem. exec. com. Epilepsy Found. Am., 1977-84, Epilepsy Center Mich., 1974-83; nat. bd. dirs. Western Inst. on Epilepsy, 1969-72; bd. dirs., pres. Mich. Mid-South Health Systems Agy., 1975-78; sec. gen. Internat. Fedn. Alzheimer's Disease and Related Disorders, 1984-86. World Rehab. Fund fellow Norway, 1980. Mem. Nat. Rehab. Assn., Am. Pub. Health Assn., Nat. Epilepsy League (bd. dirs. 1977-78), Mich. Assn. Community Mental Health Bd. Dirs. (pres. 1977-79), AAAS, Phi Alpha Theta, Phi Kappa Psi. Office: John Douglas French Found 11620 Wilshire Blvd Suite 260 Los Angeles CA 90025

ENRIQUE Y TARANCON, VICENTE CARDINAL, Spanish ecclesiastic; b. Burriana, Castellon, June 14, 1907; s. Manuel E. Urios and Vicenta T. Fandos. Ed. Seminario Conciliar Rortosa, Tarragona and Universidad Pontificia Valencia. Adminstrv. asst. Vinaroz, 1930-33, Archpriest, 1938-43; Archipriest, Villarreal, 1943-46; Bishop of Solsona, 1946-64; gen. sec. Spanish Bishopric, 1956-64; Archbishop of Ovopie, 1964-69; Archibishop of Toledo, Primate of Spain, 1969-71; Archbishop of Madrid, 1971-83; elevated to Sacred Coll. Cardinals, 1969; mem. Sacred Congregations for Bishops, Divine Worship and Reform of Canon Law; mem. Spanish Acad., 1969. Author: La Renovació n Total de la Vida Cristiana, 1954, Los Seglares en la Iglesia, 1958, Sucesores de los Apostoles, 1960, La Parroquia, Hoy, 1961, El Misterio de la Iglesia, 1963, Ecumenismo y Pastoral 1964, La Iglesia en el Mundo de Hoy, 1965, El Sacerdocio a la Luz del Concilio Vaticano II, 1966, La Iglesia del Posconcilio, 1967, La Crisis de Fe en el Mundo Actual, 1968, Unidad y pluralismo en la Iglesia, 1969, Liturgia y lengua del pueblo, 1970, El magisterio de Santa Teresa, 1970. Avocations: musical composition; classical music. Address: care Palacio Arzobispal, Toledo Spain *

ENSENAT, LOUIS ALBERT, surgeon; b. Merida, Mexico, Oct. 24, 1916; s. Frank and Guadalupe F. (Ensenat) E.; B.S., Tulane U., 1938, M.D., 1941; M.Sc. in Medicine, U. Pa., 1953; m. Ruth Ogden, July 9, 1943; children—Gloria Louise, Tinita Ruth, Louis Albert, Rita Joan, Barbara Jean, Michael Monroe. Intern, Charity Hosp., New Orleans, 1941-42; resident surgery Charity Hosp., Monroe, La., 1942, Lakeshore Hosp., New Orleans, VA hosp., New Orleans, Batavia, N.Y.; fellow in surg. pathology Tulane U. Sch. Med.; preceptorship in surgery Biloxi (Miss.) VA Hosp.; staff surg. VA Hosp., Montgomery, 1946-52; pvt. practice surgery, Pasadena, Tex., 1952-63, New Orleans, 1963—; adminstr. Mercy Hosp. Pasadena, 1954-63, chief surgery, 1954-63; founder, dir. Gulf Coast Home Builders, Inc.; trustee Angiology Research Found., 1986—. Trustee, Big State Factors Corp. Served from lt. (j.g.) to lt. comdr. USN, 1942-46. Decorated Purple Heart, Bronze Star. Diplomate Am. Bd. Surgery, Am. Bd. Abdominal Surgery. Fellow French Soc. Phlebology, Am. Coll. Angiology (pres.); mem. Hawthorne Surg. Soc., Am. Soc. Abdominal Surgeons, N.Y. Acad. Scis., Am. Med. Writers Assn. Author articles in field. Home and Office: 7630 Jeannette Pl New Orleans LA 70118

ENSIGN, GREGORY MOORE, lawyer; b. Cleve., June 3, 1949; s. Gerald Edward and Patricia Mae (Komlos) E.; m. Nancy Beth Udelson, Jan. 9, 1977 (div.); children—Julie Ann, Jennifer Brooke; m. Cathryn Rae Halas, Oct. 24, 1987. B.A., Ohio Wesleyan U., 1971; J.D., Capital U., 1975. Bar: Ohio 1975, U.S. Dist. Ct. (so. dist.) Ohio 1975, U.S. Dist. Ct. (no. dist.) Ohio 1978, U.S. Ct. Appeals (6th cir.) 1984. Mgr. legal sect. Dept. Mental Health and Mental Retardation, Columbus, Ohio, 1972-77, chief counsel, 1977-78; assoc. Weltman, Strachan and Green Co., L.P.A., Cleve., 1978-79; ptnr. Sindell, Sindell & Rubenstein, Cleve., 1979-86; v.p. adminstrn., gen. counsel, sec. Kirkwood Industries, Inc., Cleve., 1986—. Contbr. articles to profl. jours. Mem. Univ. Heights Communications and Devel. Commn., Ohio, 1981-84. Mem. Ohio State Bar Assn., Greater Cleve. Bar Assn. Republican. Club: Shaker Heights (Ohio) Country. Lodge: Rotary. Office: Kirkwood Industries Inc 4855 W 130th St Cleveland OH 44135

ENSIGN, RICHARD PAPWORTH, transportation executive; b. Salt Lake City, Jan. 20, 1919; s. Louis Osborne and Florence May (Papworth) E.; m. Margaret Anne Hinckley, Sept. 5, 1942; children: Judith Ensign Lantz, Mary Jane Ensign Hofmeister, Richard L., James R., Margaret Ensign Aronson. B.S., U. Utah, 1941. With Western Air Lines, 1941-70, v.p. in-flight service, 1963-70, v.p. passenger service, 1970; v.p. passenger service Pan Am. World Airways, 1971, sr. v.p. field mgmt., 1973-74, sr. v.p. mktg., 1974-79; exec. v.p. Western Airlines, 1980-82; pres. R.P. Ensign & Assocs., 1982—; spl. asst. to exec. v.p. Marriott Corp.; Chmn. U. Utah Nat. Adv. Council, 1984-86; bd. dirs. Western Airlines; dir. Pacific Area Travel Assos. Nat. fund raising chmn. U. Utah, 1982-83, 83-84. Recipient Disting. Service award Fla. Internat. U., 1973; named Disting. Alumnus U. Utah, 1976, 86, recipient merit award of honor, 1985. Mem. Am. Soc. Travel Agts., U.S.-Mex. C. of C., Nat. Aeros. Assn. Republican. Mormon. Club: Lochinvar. Home: 3848 Malibu Country Dr Malibu CA 90265 Office: PO Box 566 Malibu CA 90265

ENSTROM, JAMES EUGENE, cancer epidemiologist; b. Alhambra, Calif., June 20, 1943; s. Elmer Melvin, Jr. and Klea Elizabeth (Bissell) E.; B.S., Harvey Mudd Coll., Claremont, Calif., 1965; M.S., Stanford U., 1967, Ph.D. in Physics, 1970; M.P.H., UCLA, 1976; m. Marta Eugenia Villanea, Sept. 3, 1978. Research asso. Stanford Linear Accelerator Center, 1970-71; research physicist, cons. Lawrence Berkeley Lab., U. Calif., 1971-75; Celeste Durand Rogers cancer research fellow Sch. Pub. Health, UCLA, 1973-75, Nat. Cancer Inst. postdoctoral trainee, 1975-76, cancer epidemiology researcher, 1976-81, assoc. research prof., 1981—; program dir. for cancer control epidemiology Jonsson Comprehensive Cancer Center, 1978—, sci. dir. tumor registry, 1984-87, mem. dean's council, 1976—; cons. epidemiologist Linus Pauling Inst. Sci. and Medicine, 1976—; cons. physicist Rand Corp., 1969-73, R&D Assos., 1971-75; mem. sci. bd. Am. Council on Sci. and Health, 1984—. NSF predoctoral trainee, 1965-66; grantee Am. Cancer Soc., 1973—, Nat. Cancer Inst., 1979—; Preventive Oncology Acad. award, 1981-87. Fellow Am. Coll. Epidemiology; mem. Soc. Epidemiologic Research, Am. Heart Assn., Am. Pub. Health Assn., Am. Phys. Soc., AAAS, N.Y. Acad. Scis., Galileo Soc. Author papers in field. Office: U Calif Sch Pub Health Los Angeles CA 90024

ENSTROM, RONALD EDWARD, electronics executive; b. N.Y.C., Mar. 22, 1935; s. Sixtus Nathanial and Mary (Kroboth) E.; S.B., M.I.T., 1957, S.M., 1962, Sc.D., 1963; postgrad. Eidgenössische Tech. Hochschule, Zurich, Switzerland, 1973-74; m. Daly Hirsch, Sept. 6, 1958; children—Lars, Birgit. Research asst. Union Carbide Corp., Niagara Falls, N.Y., 1957-58; materials engr. Nuclear Metals, Inc., Concord, Mass., 1958-60; research asst. M.I.T., 1960-63; mem. tech. staff David Sarnoff Research Ctr. formerly RCA Labs., Princeton, N.J., 1963—, research leader, 1969—; chmn. Princeton area, ednl. council M.I.T., 1979—. Pres. Luth. Ch. of Messiah, Princeton, 1968, fin. sec., 1976-78; v.p. Montgomery Twp. League, 1969-71; pres. Ocean Course Regime, Hilton Head, S.C., 1982-84. Served as 2d lt. Ordnance Corps, AUS, 1958. Recipient award RCA Labs., 1966, 72, 83, David Sarnoff medal, 1967. Sr. mem. IEEE; mem. Electrochem. Soc. (chmn. electronics div. 1981-83, dir., soc. v.p. 1983-86, soc. pres. 1986-87), Am. Phys. Soc., AIME, Am. Assn. Crystal Growth, Sigma Xi. Clubs: M.I.T. (pres. Princeton 1977-79, dir. N.Y.C. 1976—, a founder Switzerland 1973), Bedens Brook. Author, patentee in field. Home: 67 Colfax Rd Skillman NJ 08558 Office: David Sarnoff Research Ctr Princeton NJ 08543-5300

ENTMAN, BARBARA SUE, broadcaster, writer, photographer; b. Glen Cove, N.Y., Sept. 24, 1954; d. Bernard Entman and Rose (Jacobson) Entman Pachter; B.A., U. Conn., 1976. Freelance writer/photographer, 1975—; announcer, publicity dir. Sta. WHUS-FM, Storrs, Conn., 1975-76; announcer, copywriter Sta. WKAJ-AM-FM, Saratoga Springs, N.Y., 1976-77; traffic coordinator Sta. WMHT-FM, Schenectady, 1977-79; ops. dir. Sta. WNIU-FM, Dekalb, Ill., 1980-82; ops. mgr. Sta. KUHF, Houston, 1982-86, announcer, 1987-88, membership dir., 1988—; media cons. Ill. Heart Assn., DeKalb, 1982, Sojourner Women's Bookstore, DeKalb, 1980-81; exhibited photographs in galleries and univs., 1970—; contbr. articles and poetry to mags. and newspapers. Newsletter editor Congregation Aytz Chayim, Houston, 1983-84; founder DeKalb Area Women's Network, 1981; bd. dirs., newsletter editor Art Resources Open to Women, 1977-79; mem. Chgo. Artists Coalition, 1981-82; mem. adv. bd. Houston Women's Caucus for Art, 1985-88, chairperson publicity nat. conf., 1988; del. Tex. Dem. Conv., 1984, 86. Mem. Houston Ctr. Photography, Assn. Vol. Adminstrs., Cultural Arts Council Houston. Home: 1909 Colquitt Suite 4 Houston TX 77098 Office: Sta KUHF U Houston Houston TX 77204-4061

ENTREMONT, PHILIPPE, conductor, pianist; b. Rheims, France, June 7, 1934; s. Jean and Renée (Monchamps) E.; m. Andree Ragot, Dec. 21, 1955; children: Félicia, Alexandre. Student, Conservatoire National Superieur de Musique, Paris, Jean Doyen. Profl. debut at 17, in Barcelona, Spain, Am. debut at 19, at Nat. Gallery, Washington, 1953, performs throughout world; pianist-condr. debut at, Mostly Mozart Festival, Lincoln Center, N.Y.C., 1971; rec. artist, CBS, Teldec, EMI, Schwann and ProArte records, guest condr. Pitts. Symphony, Royal Philharm., Orch. Nat. de France, Montreal Symphony, San Francisco Symphony, Phila. Orch., Detroit Symphony, numerous others; lifetime mus. dir. Vienna Chamber Orch., 1975—; mus. dir. New Orleans Symphony Orch., 1981-85; music dir. Denver Symphony, 1986—; mus. dir. l'Orchestre Colonne de Paris, 1988—. Decorated Knight, Legion of Honor, Officer de l'Order National du Merite; Austrian First Class Cross of Honor for the Arts and Scis.; A finalist Queen Elizabeth of Belgium Internat. Concours, 1952; Grand Prix Marguerite Long-Jacques Thibaud Competition, 1953; Harriet Cohen Piano medal, 1953; 1st prize Jeunesses Musicales; Grand Prix du Disque, 1967, 68, 69, 70; Edison award, 1968; Nominee Grammy award, 1972. Former mem. Academie Internationale de Musique Maurice Ravel (pres. 1975-80). Office: Denver Symphony Orch 910 15th St Suite 330 Denver CO 80202

ENTRIKEN, ROBERT KERSEY, management educator; b. McPherson, Kans., Jan. 15, 1913; s. Frederick Kersey and Opal (Birch) E.; m. Elizabeth Freeman, May 26, 1940 (div. Nov. 1951); children—Robert Kersey, Jr., Edward Livingston Freeman, Richard Davis; m. Jean Finch, June 5, 1954; 1 child, Birch Nelson. B.A., U. Kans. 1934; M.B.A., Golden Gate U., 1961; postgrad. City Univ. Grad. Bus. Sch., London, 1971-73. C.P.C.U. Ins. broker, Houston, Tex. and McPherson, Kans., 1935-39; asst. mgr. Cravens, Dargan & Co., Houston, 1939-42; br. mgr. Nat. Surety Corp., Memphis and San Francisco, 1942-54; v.p. Fireman's Fund Ins. Co., San Francisco. 1954-73; adj. prof. Golden Gate U., San Francisco, 1953-73, prof. mgmt., 1974—; resident dean Asia Programs, Singapore, 1987-88; underwriting mem. Lloyd's of London, 1985—. Contbr. articles to trade and profl. jours. Bd. dirs., sec., treas. Northstar Property Owners Assn., Calif., 1982-86. Served to capt. USNR, 1944-73, ret., 1973. Mem. Ins. Forum San Francisco (pres. 1965, trustee 1975-78, 84—), Surety Underwriters Assn. No. Calif. (pres. 1956), CPCU Soc. (pres. No. Calif. chpt. 1957, named Ins. Profl. of Yr., San Francisco chpt. 1981), Chartered Ins. Inst., Ins. Inst. London, Musicians' Union Local No. 6 life), Acad. Polit. Sci., U.S. Naval Inst., Phi Delta Theta. Republican. Episcopalian. Clubs: University, Marines' Meml. (San Francisco); Commonwealth. Lodge: Naval Order U.S. Office: Golden Gate U 536 Mission St San Francisco CA 94105

ENVALL, MARKKU SAKARI, Finnish literature educator; b. Hämeenlinna, Finland, July 28, 1944; s. Eero Alfred and Siiri Maria (Mäkinen) E. PhD, U. Helsinki, Finland, 1987. Asst. Finnish lit. U. Helsinki, 1982—. Author: Rakeita, 1983, Kirjailijoiden Kentät ja Kasarmit, 1984, Nasaretin Miehen Pitkä Marssi, 1985, Pahojen Henkien Historia, 1986, Suomalainen Aforismi, 1987. Home: Nervanderink 5 E 57, 00100 Helsinki Finland

ENZENSBERGER, HANS MAGNUS, poet, author; b. Kaufbeuren, Nov. 11, 1929; m. Maria Aleksandrovna Makarova (div.); 1 child, Katharina Bonitz. Ed. U. Erlangen, U. Freiburg im Breisgau, U. Hamburg, U. Paris; Dr. Phil. Third program editor Stuttgart Radio (Germany), 1955-57; lectr. Hochschule fur Gestaltung, Ulm, Germany, 1956-57; lit. cons. Shrkamp Verlag, Frankfurt/Main, Germany, 1960—; mem. Group 47, editor Kursbuch rev., 1965-75, pub., 1970—, DIe Andere Bibliothek, 1985— . Author: (poetry) Verteidigung der Wölfe, 1957, Landessprache, 1960, Blindenschrift, 1964, Poems for People Who Don't Read Poems, 1968, Gedichte 1955-1980, 1971, Mausoleum, 1975, Der Untergang der Titanic, 1978, Die Furie des Verschwindens, 1980; (essays) Clemens Brentanos Poetik, 1961, Einzelheiten, 1962, Politik und Verbrechen, 1964; Deutschland, Deutschland unter Anderm, 1967; (play) Das Verhör von Habana, 1970; Der Menschen Freund, 1984; Freisprüche, 1970; (novel) Der Kurze Sommer der Anarchie, 1972; Gespräche mit Marx und Engels, 1973; Palaver, 1974, Ach Europa , 1987, Mittelmass Und Wahn, 1988, Requiem fü einc romantisdie Frau, 1988; editor: Museum der Modernen Poesie, 1960; Allerleirauh, 1961; Andreas Gryphius Gedichte, 1962; Edward Lears kompletter Nonsense, 1977; Raids and Reconstructions; Politische Brosamen, 1982; Critical Essays, 1982; editor TransAtlantik mag., 1980-82. Recipient Hugo Jacobi prize, 1956, Kritiker prize, 1962, Georg Buchner prize, 1963, Premio Pasolini, 1982. Office: care Suhrkamp Verlag, Postfach 101945, D-6000 Frankfurt/Main Federal Republic of Germany

EÖRSI, ANNA, art historian; b. Budapest, Hungary, Nov. 9, 1950; d. Gyula and Marianna (Hajdu) E.; m. János Körner, July 17, 1971 (div. 1987); 1 child, Julia. BA, U. Budapest, 1974. Sr. researcher dept. art history Faculty of Letters, U. Budapest, 1974—. Author: Cosimo Tura, 1976, International Gothic Style in Painting, 1986. Mem. Hungarian Soc. for Art History. Home: Lóránt Utca 8/A, 1025 Budapest Hungary Office: Elte Btk Müvészettort, Pesti Barnabàs v 1-3, 1052 Budapest Hungary

EPLER, VENETIA, painter, muralist, sculptor; b. Linwood, W.Va., Mar. 7; d. Franklin and Anne (Farrer) E. Student of painting Slades Sch. Art, London, Ecole de Louvre, Paris, London Sch. Arts and Crafts. Motion picture illustrator, layout and background artist M.G.M., Hanna-Barbera, Wexler Documentary Films, Filmation, Cathedral Films, 1963-78; muralist Forest Lawn, Glendale, Calif., 1965-70, (with Daphne Huntington) painted original oil on canvas mural Life of Christ, recreated in tesserie as world's largest religious mosaic fascade at Christian Heritage Mausoleum, West Covina, Calif.;, designed 12 stained glass windows Science of Mind Ch., Beverly Hills, Calif., 1974; painted altar mural and (with D. Huntington) designed alter windows St. Augustine Ch., East Los Angeles, 1985; painted portraits of Pres. Dwight D. Eisenhower at White House, His Excellency Peter J. Velez for Embassy of Malta to Guatemala, 1971; represented in permanent collections; San Bernardino County Mus., Redlands, Calif., De Saisset Gallery of Santa Clara (Calif.) Mus., Phiffer Hall, Claremont (Calif.) Coll., Occidental Coll., Los Angeles, Am. embassy, London, others; contbr. poems to Secrets of the Poetic Vision, 1986. Recipient Nat. First award Smithsonian Ins Instn., 1967; Gold medal Council Traditional Artists Socs., 1969; numerous others. Fellow Am. Inst. Fine Arts (Gold medal 1969), Am. Artists Profl. League; mem. San Gabriel Fine Arts Assn. (Gold medal 1971, 72), Accademia Italia delle Arti e de Lavoro (Gold medal 1979), Artists of S.W. (Lillian Prest Ferguson award 1982, Duncan Gleason Meml. award, 1986). Address: 1835 Outpost Dr Hollywood CA 90068

EPLEY, MARION JAY, oil company executive; b. Hattiesburg, Miss., June 17, 1907; s. Marion Jay and Eva (Quin) E.; m. Dorris Glenn Ervin, Feb. 12, 1934; children: Marion Jay III, Sara Perry (Mrs. Richard H. Davis). LL.B., Tulane U., 1930. Bar: La. 1930. Practiced in New Orleans, 1930-42, 45-47; gen. atty. Texaco, Inc., New Orleans, N.Y.C., 1948-58; v.p., asst. to chmn. bd. Texaco, Inc., N.Y.C., 1958-60; sr. v.p. Texaco, Inc., 1960-61, exec. v.p., 1961-64, pres., 1964-70, chmn. bd., 1970-71; also dir.; pres., dir. Dormar Ltd., 1986—. Served as lt. USNR, 1942-45. Decorated officer Ordre de la Couronne, Belgium. Mem. ABA, La. Bar Assn. Clubs: Boston (New Orleans); Everglades, Bath and Tennis, Seminole Golf (Palm Beach, Fla.); Governors (West Palm Beach, Fla.); Roaring Gap (N.C.). Address: 340 S Ocean Blvd Palm Beach FL 33480

EPP, ARTHUR JACOB, Canadian government official; b. St. Boniface, Man., Can., Sept. 1, 1939; s. Jacob Peter and Margaretha (Toews) E.; m. Lydia Martens, Aug. 17, 1961; 1 child, Lisa Dawn. B.A., U. Man., 1961, B.Ed., 1965. Councillor Town of Steinbach, 1970-72; mem. Ho. of Commons, Ottawa, Ont., Can., 1972—, minister Indian and No. Affairs, 1979, minister nat. health and welfare, 1984—. Progressive Conservative. Mem. Evangelical Ch. Office: House of Commons, Ottawa, ON Canada K1A 0A6 *

EPP, ELDON JAY, religion educator; b. Mountain Lake, Minn., Nov. 1, 1930; s. Jacob Jay and Louise (Kintzi) E.; m. ElDoris Balzer, June 13, 1951; children: Gregory Thomas, Jennifer Elizabeth. A.B. magna cum laude, Wheaton Coll., 1952; B.D. magna cum laude, Fuller Theol Sem., 1955; S.T.M., Harvard U., 1956, Ph.D., 1961. Spl. research asst. Princeton Theol. Sem., 1961-62; vis. instr. Drew U. Theol. Sch., 1962; asst. prof. religion U. So. Calif. Grad. Sch. Religion, 1962-65, assoc. prof., 1965-67, assoc. prof. classics, 1966-68; assoc. prof. religion Case Western Res. U., Cleve., 1968-71; prof. religion, Harkness prof. bibl. lit. Case Western Res. U., 1971—, dean humanities and social scis., 1977-85; acting dean Western Res. Coll., 1984, chmn. dept. religion, 1982—; Mem. Am. exec. com. Internat. Greek New Testament Project, 1968—; commr.-at-large, Commn. on Insts. Higher Edn., North Cen. Assn., 1986—; Kenneth W. Clark lectr. Duke U., 1986. Author: The Theological Tendency of Codex Bezae Cantabrigiensis in Acts, 1966; co-editor: New Testament Textual Criticism: Its Significance for Exegesis, 1981, The New Testament and Its Modern Interpreters, 1988; assoc. editor Jour. Bibl. Lit, 1971—; mem. editorial bd. Soc. Bibl. Lit. Monograph Series, 1969-72, Soc. Bibl. Lit. Centennial Publs, 1975—, Studies and Documents, 1971—, Critical Review of Books in Religion, 1987—; exec. sec.: Hermeneia: A Critical and Historical Commentary on the Bible, 1962—; mem. editorial bd., 1966—. Contbr. articles, reviews to publs. Active Boy Scouts Am., 1975-78; Bd. mgrs. St. Paul's Episcopal Cathedral, Los Angeles, 1964-68, clk., 1967-68. Harvard Faculty Arts and Scis. fellow, 1958-59, Rockefeller doctoral fellow in religion, 1959-60; postdoctoral fellow Claremont Grad. Sch., 1966-68; Guggenheim fellow, 1974-75. Mem. Am. Acad. Religion (sect. pres. 1965-66), Soc. Bibl. Lit. (chmn. textual criticism seminar 1966, 71-84, mem. permanent Centennial com. 1975-80, mem. council 1980-82, 85-87, del. Council on Study of Religion 1980-82), Studiorum Novi Testamenti Societas, Cath. Bibl. Assn., New Testament Colloquium (chmn. 1974), Soc. Mithraic Studies, AAUP (chpt. exec. com. 1970-72), Inst. Antiquity and Christianity, Phi Beta Kappa. Office: Dept Religion Case Western Res Univ Cleveland OH 44106

EPP, MARY ELIZABETH, software engineer; b. Buffalo, Aug. 7, 1941; d. John Conrad and Gertrude Marie (Murphy) Winkelman; m. Harry Francis Epp, Aug. 31, 1963. BA in Math., D'Youville Coll., 1963; MS in Math., Xavier U., 1974, MBA in Fin., 1981, MBA in Mktg., 1987. Systems analyst Gen. Electric, Evendale, Ohio, 1965-71; techniques and ops. mgr. Palm Beach Co., Cin., 1972-73; hardware systems engr. Procter & Gamble, Cin., 1973-76; systems engr. CalComp Inc., Anaheim, Calif., 1980-84; software engr. SDRC Inc., Cin., 1984-86; advanced systems project mgr. SAMI/Burke Mktg., Cin., 1986—; cons. Shelley & Sands, Zanesville, Ohio, 1983-85. Contbr. articles to profl. jours. Mem. Fairfield Charter Rev. Commn., 1981-83. Mem. AAUW (br. treas. 1975-79, state women's chair 1979-80, state treas. 1980-82), Assn. Computing Machinery (treas. Cin. chpt. 1987-88, pres. 1988—), Nat. Computer Graphics Assn., Nat. Assn. Female Execs., Nat. Fedn. Music (Ohio fedn. music parade chair 1979-81.). Republican. Roman Catholic. Clubs: Mercy Hosp. Aux. (treas. 1978-79), Musical Arts. Avocations: bridge, skiing, music, fishing, travel. Home: 4900 Pleasant Ave Fairfield OH 45014 Office: SAMI/Burke Mktg 800 Broadway Cincinnati OH 45202

EPP, MELVIN DAVID, plant geneticist, tissue culture specialist; b. Newton, Kans., June 16, 1942; s. John, Jr. and Marie (Harder) E.; m. Sylvia K. Rieger, June 26, 1964; children—David S., J. Terry. B.S., Wheaton (Ill.) Coll., 1964; M.S., U. Conn., 1967; Ph.D., Cornell U., 1972; NIH genetics trainee Cornell U., Ithaca, N.Y., 1967-71; Hort. trainee Pan Am. Seed Co., Paonia, Colo., 1964-65; Damon Runyon fellow Brookhaven Nat. Lab., Upton, N.Y., 1972-74; sr. research biologist Monsanto Co., St. Louis, 1974-77; research supt. Philippine Packing Corp. subs. Del Monte Corp., Manila, 1977-82; mgr. plant propagation and tissue culture research parent co., San Leandro, Calif., 1982-84; prin. scientist ARCO-PCRI, Dublin, Calif., 1984-86; prin. scientist PCRI, Dublin, Calif., 1987—. Contbr. articles to sci. jours. Mem. Genetics Soc. Am., Bot. Soc. Am., AAAS, Calif. Acad. Sci. Office: 6560 Trinity Ct Dublin CA 94566

EPPERSON, ERIC ROBERT, international tax consultant; b. Oregon City, Oreg., Dec. 10, 1949; s. Robert Max and Margaret Joan (Crawford) E.; B.S., Brigham Young U., 1973, M.Acctg., 1974; M.B.A., Golden Gate U., 1977, J.D., 1981; m. Lyla Gene Harris, Aug. 21, 1969; 1 dau., Marcie. Instr. acctg. Brigham Young U., Provo, Utah, 1973-74; supr. domestic taxation Bechtel Corp., San Francisco, 1974-78; supr. internat. taxation Bechtel Power Corp., San Francisco, 1978-80; mgr. internat. tax planning Del Monte Corp., San Francisco, 1980-82, mgr. internat. taxes, 1982-85; internat. tax specialist Touche Ross & Co., San Francisco, 1985-87; dir. internat. tax Coopers & Lybrand, Portland, 1987—. Eagle Scout, 1965; scoutmaster, Boy Scouts Am., Provo, 1971-73, troop committeeman, 1973-74, 83—; mem. IRS Vol. Income Tax Assistance Program, 1972-75; pres. Mut. Improvement Assn., Ch. Jesus Christ of Latter-day Saints, 1972-74, pres. Sunday sch., 1977-79, tchr., 1974-80, ward clk., 1980-83, bishopric, 1983-87 . Mem. Am. Acctg. Assn., Tax Assn. Am., World Affairs Council, Japan/Am. Soc., Internat. Tax Planning Assn., Internat. Fiscal Assn., Beta Alpha Psi. Republican. Clubs: Commonwealth, Masters of Accountancy Brigham Young U. Author: (with T. Gilbert) Interfacing of the Securities and Exchange Commission with the Accounting Profession: 1968 to 1973, 1974. Office: Coopers & Lybrand 2700 First Interstate Tower Portland OR 97201

EPPERSON, VAUGHN ELMO, civil engineer; b. Provo, Utah, July 20, 1917; s. Lawrence Theophilus and Mary Loretta (Pritchett) E.; m. Margaret Ann Stewart Hewlett, Mar. 4, 1946; children: Margaret Ann (Mrs. Eric V.K. Hill), Vaughn Hewlett, David Hewlett, Katherine (Mrs. Franz S. Amussen), Lawrence Stewart. BS, U. Utah, 1953. With Pritchett Bros. Constrn. Co., Provo, 1949-50; road design engr. Utah State Road Commn., Salt Lake City, 1951-53, bridge design engr., 1953-54; design engr. Kennecott Copper Corp., Salt Lake City, 1954-60, office engr., 1960-62, sr. engr., 1962, assigned concentrator plant engr., 1969-73, assigned concentrator project engr., 1973-78; cons. engr. Vaughn Epperson Engrng. Service, Salt Lake City, 1978-87; project engr. Newbery-State Inc., Salt Lake City, 1980, geneal. extraction and research programs, 1983—. Scoutmaster Troop 190, Salt Lake City, 1949-51. Served to capt. AUS, 1941-45; maj. N.G., 1951; col. Utah State Guard, 1952-70. Decorated Army Commendation medal; recipient Service award Boy Scouts Am., 1949, Community Service award United Fund, 1961, Service award VA Hosp., Salt Lake City, 1977. Mem. ASCE, Am. Soc. Mil. Engrs., Sons of Utah Pioneers. Republican. Mormon. Home: 1537 E Laird Ave Salt Lake City UT 84105 Office: PO Box 8769 Salt Lake City UT 84108

EPPINETTE, SHIRLEY LYNN, educator, journalist; b. New Orleans; d. Woodie Trevillion and Thelma Elizabeth (Axline) E.; A.A. (Journalism Alumni Assn. scholar), East Los Angeles, Coll., 1967; B.A. (Arthur J. Baum journalism scholar), Calif. State U., Los Angeles, 1969, postgrad., 1969-70; postgrad. U. Santa Clara, 1981, U. So. Calif., 1982, Chapman Coll., 1983, Loyola Marymount U., Los Angeles, 1986-87. Elem. tchr. Covina-Valley Unified Sch. Dist., 1970-74, San Gabriel (Calif.) Sch. Dist., 1974-75, Alhambra (Calif.) City Sch. Dist., 1976-78, Los Angeles City Unified Sch. Dist., 1978—; rewrite editor, staff writer San Gabriel Valley Newspaper Publs., 1975-76; mem. membership adv. group Automobile Club So. Calif. Contbr. articles to newspapers and profl. publs. Recipient TAP award Alhambra-San Gabriel dist. Soroptimist Club, 1975; Calif. State PTA scholar, 1981. Mem. NEA, Calif. Tchrs. Assn., Los Angeles City Tchrs. Math. Assn., United Tchrs. Los Angeles, Women in Communications, Nat. Press Women, AAUW (com. internat. relations 1977-78, chmn. ednl. com. 1978-79), Humane Soc. U.S., Nat. Rifle Assn., Sigma Delta Chi. Club: Pacific Coast Press. Home: 7318 W 91st St Los Angeles CA 90045

EPPLEY, ROLAND RAYMOND, JR., financial services executive; b. Balt., Apr. 1, 1932; s. Roland and Verna (Garrettson) E.; m. LeVerne Pittman, June 20, 1953; children: Kimberly, Kent, Todd. B.A., Johns Hopkins U., 1952, M.A., 1953; D.C.S. (hon.), St. John's U., 1984. Pres., chief exec. officer Comm. Credit Computer, Balt., 1962-68; pres., chief exec. officer CIPC, Balt., 1968-77; vice chmn. Eastern States Monetary, Lake Success, N.Y., 1982—; pres., chief exec. officer, dir. Affiliated Financial, Wilmington, Del., 1983-85, Eastern States Bankcard, Lake Success, N.Y., 1971—; adj. prof. St. John's U., 1973—; dir. Eastern States Monetary. Chmn. bd. trustees Calgary Bapt. Ch., Balt., 1969-71; chmn. investment com. Community Ch., Manhasset, N.Y., 1983—; bd. advisers St. John's U., 1973—. Recipient Disting. Service award St. John's U., 1981, 84 Laucheimer grantee, 1952-53. Mem. Am. Bankers Assn., Data Processing Mgmt. Assn., Am. Mgmt. Assn. Pres. Assn., Electronic Funds Transfer Assn., Mensa, Phi Beta kappa, Omicron Delta Epsilon, Beta Gamma Sigma, Sigma Phi. Epsilon (citation). Republican. Mem. Reformed Ch. Am. Clubs: Madison Square Garden, Meadowbrook, Plandome Country (dir. 1977-86), Hillendale. Lodges: Masons, Shrine. Home: 77 Westgate Blvd Plandome NY 11030 Office: 4 Ohio Dr Lake Success NY 11042

EPSTEEN, CASPER MORLEY, physician, educator; b. East Chicago, Ind., May 6, 1902; s. Hyman and Sarah Ida (Goodman) E.; m. Aline Gertrude Grossman, Sept. 26, 1934; children: Lynn, Robert. B.Sc., U. Ill., 1923, M.D., 1925; D.D.S., Loyola U. Chgo., 1930. Diplomate: Internat. Bd. Surgery. Intern Michael Reese Hosp. and Med. Center, Chgo., 1925-26; now sr. attending surgeon; preceptorship with Dr. Truman W. Brophy, 1926-29; practice medicine specializing maxillofacial and plastic surgery Chgo., 1926—; cons. Weiss Meml. Hosp., Jackson Park Community Hosp. and Med. Center, Central Community Hosp.; clin. prof. maxillofacial and plastic surgery Chgo. Med. Sch., 1960-84, clin. prof. emeritus, 1984—. Author: Tice's Practice of Medicine, 1948; Guest editor: Am. Jour. Surgery, Dec. 1952; editorial asso.: Internat. Jour. Surgery. Served to lt. col. AUS, 1942-46. Guest of honor 1st Internat. Congress Maxillofacial Surgeons, Venice, Italy, 1971; recipient hon. mention for research salivary glands Am. Soc. Plastic and Reconstructive Surgeons, 1953; Honor award Michael Reese Hosp. and Med. Ctr., 1955; Honor award Louis A. Weiss Meml. Hosp., 1960; Internat. Book Honor Hall of Fame Am. Biographical Inst., 1986. Fellow Ill. Soc. for Med. Research, Ednl. and Sci. Found. Ill. Med. Soc.; mem. Am. Soc. Maxillofacial Surgeons (founder mem.; pres. 1960, Leadership award 1960, Distinguished award 1966, Presdl. Achievement award 1982), Chgo. Med. Soc. (pres. 1962-63, award merit 1963, founder ann. clin. conf., Testimonial of Appreciation 1978, Biog. Roll of Honor award 1983), Ill. Med. Soc. (1st v.p. 1968), AMA, Am., Internat. colls. surgeons, World Med. Assn., Internat. Assn. Burn Injuries, Chgo. Natural History Mus. (life), Am. Burn Assn., Art Inst. Chgo. Clubs: Quadrangle (Chgo.), Executive (Chgo.). Home: 5750 S Kenwood Ave Chicago IL 60637

EPSTEIN, BEE J., consultant, professional speaker; b. Tubingen, Fed. Republic Germany, July 14, 1937; came to U.S., 1940, naturalized, 1945; d. Paul and Milly (Stern) Singer; student Reed Coll., 1954-57; m. Leonard Epstein, June 14, 1959 (div. 1982); children—Bettina, Nicole, Seth. BA, U. Calif., Berkeley, 1958; MA, Goddard Coll., 1976; PhD, Internat. Coll., 1982. Bus. instr. Monterey Peninsula Coll., 1975-85; owner, mgr. Bee Epstein Assos., cons. to mgmt., Carmel, Calif., 1977—; pres. Success Tours Inc., Carmel, 1981—; founder, prin. Monterey Profl. Speakers, 1982; instr. Monterey Peninsula Coll., Golden Gate U., U. Calif., Santa Cruz, Am. Inst. Banking, Inst. Ednl. Leadership, Calif. State Fire Acad. Monterey Peninsula Coll., U. Calif., Berkeley, Foothill Coll., U. Alaska. Author: The Working Woman's Stress First Aid Handbook, How to Create Balance at Work, at Home, in Your Life; contbr. articles to newspapers and trade mags. Research grantee, 1976. Mem. Nat. Speakers' Assn., Am. Soc. Tng. and Devel., Nat. Assn. Female Execs., Peninsula Profl. Women's Network, Calif. Tchrs. Assn. Democrat. Jewish. Office: PO Box 221383 Carmel CA 93922

EPSTEIN, BENJAMIN ROSS, electrical engineer; b. Phila., Nov. 21, 1955; s. Donald Morris and Nancy Lea (Hyman) E. B.S.E.E., U. Rochester, 1978; M.S. in Bioengrng., U. Pa., 1980, Ph.D. in Bioengrng., 1982. Postdoctoral fellow Centre Nat. de la Recherche Scientifique, Paris, 1982-83; mem. tech. staff RCA Labs., Princeton, N.J., 1983—; instr. U. Pa., Phila., 1984; adj. prof. elec. engrng. Drexel U., 1986-87. Contbr. articles to engrng. jours. Postdoctoral fellow French Govt., 1982-83; Ashton scholar, U. Pa., 1978-82; NIH assistantship, U. Pa., 1979-82. Mem. IEEE, N.Y. Acad. of Scis., AAAS, Bioelectromagnetics Soc., Microwave Theory and Technique Soc. (chmn.), Electronic Devices Soc. (chmn.), Antennas and Propogation Soc., Automatic RF Techniques Group, Curtis Organ Restoration Soc., Tau Beta Pi, Sigma Xi. Home: 1610 Aspen Dr Plainsboro NJ 08536

EPSTEIN, DAVID STANLEY, educator, consultant; b. N.Y.C., Apr. 17, 1948; s. Mortimer and Shirley Ruth (Silver) E. B.A., Adelphi U., 1970, M.S., 1972; Ph.D., St. John's U., Jamaica, N.Y., 1979. Cert. tchr., N.Y. Research scientist N.Y. State Inst. Basic Research, S.I., 1979-80; tchr. N.Y.C. Bd. Edn., 1981—; ednl. cons. Contbr. articles, mainly on invertebrate and vertebrate neurobiology, to profl. jours., 1972-81. Mem. Am. Soc. Microbiologists, Am. Soc. Zoologists, Chemistry Tchr.'s Club N.Y., Sigma Xi. Democrat. Jewish. Avocation: collecting books. Home: 88-05 171st St Apt 3E Jamaica NY 11432

EPSTEIN, EDNA SELAN, lawyer; b. Yugoslavia, July 26, d. Carl and Lotte (Eisner) Selan; came to U.S., 1944, naturalized, 1951; A.B. cum laude, Barnard Coll., 1960; M.A. (AAUW fellow), Johns Hopkins U., 1961; Ph.D., Harvard U., 1967; J.D. cum laude (Law Rev.), U. Chgo., 1973; m. Wolfgang Epstein, June 12, 1961; children—Matthew, Ezra, Tanya. Asst. prof. French, U. Ill., Chgo. Circle, 1967-70; Bar: Ill. 1973; with Cook County State's Atty., 1973-75; ptnr. Sidley & Austin, Chgo., 1976—; mem. faculty Nat. Inst. Trial Advocacy, 1979-86; vis. lectr. U. Chgo. Sch. Law, 1979-81; vis. lectr. NITA programs Hofstra U., Emory U., 1980-86. Bd. govs. Hyde Park-Kenwood Community Conf., 1974-77, Chgo. Fin. Exchange, 1985-86, Jefferson Found., Ill. Humanities Council, 1982-86; bd. dirs. Friends of Parks, 1978-80 ; mem. Citizens Com. for Victim Assistance, 1976-78, Cook County State's Atty.'s Profl. Adv. Com., 1981-84 Mayor Byrne's Transition Task Force, 1979, Chgo. Econ. Club, Chgo. Execs. Club; del. Dem. Nat. Conv., 1980, also mem. rules com., Credentials Com., 1988. Mem. Internat. Bar Assn., ABA (chmn. trial evidence com. 1979-83, mem. litigation sect. council 1984-87), Chgo. Bar Assn., Chgo. Council Lawyers (bd. govs. 1975-77), Phi Beta Kappa, Order of Coif. Author: Client Privilege; Conflicts of Interest; Sanctions; contbr. articles to learned jours. Office: Sidley & Austin 1 First Nat Plaza Suite 4800 Chicago IL 60603

EPSTEIN, HYMAN DAVID, lawyer, lecturer; b. Bklyn., Jan. 2, 1910; s. Samuel and Jennie (Winning) E.; m. Bertha Goncharow, Oct. 21, 1934; children—Robert Joseph, Jonathan Edward. B.S. in Commerce, NYU, 1932, LL.M., 1949; LL.B., Bklyn. Law Sch., 1936, J.D., 1967, J.S.D., 1949. Bar: N.Y. 1937, U.S. Ct. Internat. Trade 1939, U.S. Tax Ct. 1939, U.S. dist. ct. (ea. and so. dists.) N.Y. 1954, U.S. Supreme Ct. 1972, U.S. Ct. Mil. Appeals 1978. Sole practice Staten Island, N.Y., 1937—; with tax adminstrn. Kuhn, Loeb & Co., N.Y.C., 1946-54; account exec. Schweickart & Co., N.Y.C., 1957-74; staff lectr. N.Y. Stock Exchange, N.Y.C., 1956-68; lectr. Community Coll., Staten Island, 1960, 62, New Sch., N.Y.C., 1968. Author article in legal publ. Chmn. workshop Assn. for Brain Injured Children, Wagner Coll., Staten Island, 1968; committeeman Democratic Party Richmond County, Staten Island, 1959-61; advisors Richmondtown Prep. Sch., 1966—; v.p. Staten Island Council Boy Scouts Am., 1957-68; pres. Temple Tifereth Israel, Staten Island, 1952-55. Served with USAAF, 1944-46. Recipient Silver Beaver award Boy Scouts Am., 1961, Shofar award, Nat. Jewish Com. on Scouting, 1963. Mem. ABA, Richmond County Bar Assn., Am. Legion. Lodges: B'nai B'rith, K.P., Masons. Home: 14 Grand Ave Staten Island NY 10301 Office: 14 Grand Ave Staten Island NY 10301

EPSTEIN, JUDITH ANN, lawyer; b. Los Angeles, Dec. 23, 1942; d. Gerald Elliot and Harriet (Hirsch) Rubens; m. Joseph I. Epstein, Oct. 4, 1964; children: Mark Douglas, Laura Ann. AB, U. Calif., Berkeley, 1964; MA, U. San Francisco, 1974, JD, 1977. Bar: Calif. 1978, U.S. Dist. Ct. (no. dist.) Calif 1978, U.S. Supreme Ct. 1983, U.S. Ct. Appeals (9th cir.) 1984. With social services dept. Sutter County, Yuba City, Calif., 1964-66; bus. devel. assoc. Yuba County C. of C., Marysville, Calif., 1968-70; research clk. Calif. Supreme Ct., San Fransisco, 1977; ptnr. Crosby, Heafey, Roach & May, Oakland, Calif., 1978—; lectr. U. Calif. Grad. Sch. of Journalism in Media Law, Berkeley, 1987—; bd. dirs. Sierra Pacific Steel, Hayward, Calif. Bd. dirs., v.p. Oakland Ballet, 1980—. Recipient Pres.'s award Oakland Ballet. Mem. Calif. Women Lawyers Assn., Alameda Bar Assn. Club: Berkeley Tennis. Office: Crosby Heafey Roach & May 1999 Harrison Oakland CA 94612

EPSTEIN, SHERWIN LEWIS, lawyer; b. N.Y.C., Sept. 29, 1930; s. Theodore H. and Tillie (Gitelis) E.; m. Ruby Lee Snider, Apr. 2, 1966; 1 son, Mark Harold; m. 2d, Johanna Mary Rose, May 31, 1979. A.B., U. Mo., Columbia, 1955, J.D., 1957; postgrad. U. Wis., 1955, 56. Bar: Mo., 1957, U.S. Ct. Apls. (8th cir.) 1957, U.S. Sup. Ct. 1976. Assoc., Achtenberg, Sandler & Balkin, Kansas City, Mo., 1957-59; title atty. Kansas City Title Ins. Co., 1959-62; assoc. city atty. City of Kansas City (Mo.), 1962-68; sole practice, Kansas City, 1968-70, 76-86 ; ptnr. Stubbs, Epstein and Mann, Kansas City, 1970-76; sr. mem.k Sherwin Epstein & Assocs.; adj. prof. U. Mo., Kansas City, 1960-76; lectr. Rockhurst Coll., Tex. A & M U. Served to 1st lt. USAF, 1952-54. Recpient Mo. Resolution Outstanding Legal Service, City Council Kansas City. Mem. ABA, Mo. Bar Assn., Kansas City Bar Assn., Lawyers Assn., C. of C. Democrat. Jewish. Club: B'nai B'rith. Office: 1006 Grand Ave Suite 1700 Kansas City MO 64106

EPTON, BERNARD EDWARD, lawyer; b. Chgo., Aug. 25, 1921; s. Arthur I. and Rose (Goldstein) E.; m. Audrey Issett, June 8, 1945; children: Teri Lynn, Jeffrey David, Mark Richard, Dale Susan. Student, U. Chgo., 1938-39, Northwestern U., 1939-40, DePaul U., 1947. Bar: Ill. 1947. Since practiced in Chgo.; ptnr. firm A.I. Epton & Sons, 1941-47, Epton, Mullin & Druth, Ltd., 1947-87; mem. Ill. Gen. Assembly from 24th Dist., 1969-82; chmn. ins. com.; dir. Pemcor, Inc.; mem. Ill. Ins. Exchange, 1982-87, sec., 1985-87, chmn., 1986-87. Mem. South Shore O'Keefe Conservation Community Council, 1960-66; mem. Jewish Bd. Edn., 1965-70; past pres. Nat. Conf. Ins. Legislators; chmn. Ill. Ins. Study Commn., 1972-82; mem. Lloyds of London; v.p. Jane Dent Home Aged Negros, 1961-87, also bd. dirs.; bd. dirs. Jewish Community Ctrs. Chgo.; trustee Coll. Jewish Studies; mem. pres.'s council St. Xavier Coll.; mem. estate planning council DePaul U., Republican candidate for mayor, Chgo., 1983. Served to capt. USAAF, 1942-45, ETO. Decorated D.F.C. with oak leaf cluster, Air medal with three oak leaf clusters. Mem. Ill., Chgo. bar assns., Decalogue Soc. Lawyers (bd. dirs. 1949, pres. 1961-62), Fedn. Ins. Counsel, Trial Lawyers Club, Am. Legion, Air Force Assn. (bd. dirs. 1947-50), South Shore C. of C. (dir., counsel 1953—, pres. 1959-61), Mil. Order World Wars (vice comdr.), Chgo. Hist. Soc. (life), U. Chgo. Alumni Assn. (life). Clubs: Standard (Chgo.); Idlewild Country (Flossmoor, Ill.) (dir. 1964-67, dir., v.p. 1986-87). Office: 140 S Dearborn St Chicago IL 60603 *Died Dec. 13, 1987.*

ERB, RICHARD LOUIS LUNDIN, resort and hotel executive; b. Chgo., Dec. 23, 1929; s. Louis Henry and Miriam (Lundin) E.; m. Jean Elizabeth Easton, Mar. 14, 1959; children: John Richard, Elizabeth Anne, James Easton, Richard Louis. BA, U. Calif.-Berkeley, 1951, postgrad., 1952; student San Francisco Art Inst., 1956. Cert. hotel adminstr. Asst. gen. mgr. Grand Teton Lodge Co., Jackson Hole, Wyo., 1954-62; mgr. Colter Bay Village, Grand Teton Nat. Park, Wyo., 1962-64, Mauna Kea Beach Hotel, Hawaii, 1964-66; v.p., gen. mgr. Caneel Bay Plantation, Inc., St. John, V.I., 1966-75; gen. mgr. Williamsburg (Va.) Inn, 1975-78; exec. v.p., gen. mgr. Seabrook Island Co., Johns Island, S.C., 1978-80; v.p., dir. hotels Sands Hotel and Casino, Inc., Atlantic City, 1980-81; v.p., gen. mgr. Disneyland Hotel, Anaheim, Calif., 1981-82; chief operating officer Grand Traverse Resort, Grand Traverse Village, Mich., 1982—; v.p. Spruce Devel. Co., 1986—. Contbr. articles to trade jours. V.p. V.I. Montessori Sch., 1969-71, bd. dirs., 1968-76; bd. dirs. Coll. of V.I., 1976-79; mem. adv. bd. U. S.C., 1978-82, Calif. State Poly. Inst., 1981-82, Orange Coast Community Coll., 1981-82, Northwestern Mich. Coll., 1983—; trustee Munson Med. Ctr., Traverse City, 1985—; vice chmn. Charleston (S.C.) Tourism Council, 1979-81; bd. dirs. Anaheim Visitors and Conv. Bur., 1981-82, Grand Traverse Conv. and Visitors Bur., 1985—, N.A. Vasa, 1987—, US 131 Area Devel. Assn., 1983—, Traverse Symphony Orch., 1984—, N.A. Vasa, 1987—; mem. adv. panel Mich. Communities of Econ. Excellence Program, 1984—. Served to lt., arty. U.S. Army, 1952-54. Mem. Am. Hotel and Motel Assn. (dir. 1975-77, Service Merit award 1976; trustee Ednl. Inst. 1977-83, mktg. com., exec. com. 1978-83, chmn. projects and programs com. 1982-83, AH & MA resort com. 1986—, AH & MA condominium com. 1985—, Ambassador award 1986), Caribbean Hotel Assn. (1st v.p. 1972-74, dir. 1970-76, hon. life mem., Extraordinary Service Merit award 1974), V.I. Hotel Assn. (pres. chmn. bd. 1971-76, Merit award 1973), Calif. Hotel Assn. (dir. 1981-82), Caribbean Travel Assn. (dir. 1972-74), Internat. Hotel Assn. (dir. 1971-73), S.C. Hotel Assn. (dir. 1978-82), Am. Hotel Assn. Inst., (Lamp of Knowledge award 1988), Va. Hotel Assn., Williamsburg Hotel Assn. (dir. 1975-78), Atlantic City Hotel Assn. (v.p. 1981-82), Mich. Lodging Assn. (dir. 1983—, treas. 1986, sec. 1987, v.p. 1988, mktg. com. 1986—, govtl. affairs com. 1986—, chmn. edn. com. 1983-84), Mich. Gov.'s Task Force on Tourism, 1986-87, Grand Traverse C. of C. (bd. dirs. 1984—), Nat. Restaurant Assn., Beta Theta Pi. Congregationalist. Clubs: Tavern, Golden Horseshoe, German, Greate Bay, Seabrook Island, Kiawah Island, Grand Traverse Resort. Lodge: Rotary. Address: Grand Traverse Resort Grand Traverse Village MI 49610-0404

ERBACHER, KATHRYN ANNE, writer, editor; b. Kansas City, Mo., Dec. 11, 1947; d. Philip Joseph and Thelma Lillian (Hines) E. BS in English, U. Kans., 1970; BA magna cum laude in Art, Metro State Coll., Denver, 1983. Reporter, Kansas City Star (Mo.), 1970-71; newswriter Washington U., St. Louis, 1972-76; copy editor Kansas City Star-Times (Mo.), 1976-79; editor Petro-Lewis Corp., Denver, 1979-82; assoc. Artours, Inc., Denver, 1983-84; assoc. editor arts and travel editor Denver Mag., 1984-86; freelance writer, editor, 1986—; internat. editor Gates Rubber Co., Denver, 1987—. Creative dir. TV shorts for contemporary art collection Denver Art Mus., 1983. Mem. Metro State Coll. Alumni Bd. Dirs., 1986-87, co-chair 1987 Metro State Coll. Alumni Awards Dinner, Denver; bd. govs. Metro State Coll. Found., 1986-87. Recipient award for arts writing Denver Partnership, 1986. Mem. Women in Communications (jobs chmn. Denver 1981-82). Home: 1539 Platte St Denver CO 80202

ERBE, GARY THOMAS, artist; b. Union City, N.J., Sept. 2, 1944; s. Herman Charles and Florance (Bertone) E.; student public schs., Union City; children—Kim, Chantell. One man shows: Pace Gallery, Houston, 1970, Veldman Gallery, Milw., 1971, New Britain Mus. Am. Art, 1976, Summit (N.J.) Art Center, 1976, Bergen Community Mus., Paramus, N.J., 1979, Alexander Gallery, N.Y.C., 1982, 85, N.J. State Mus., Trenton, 1983, Butler Inst. Am. Art, Youngstown, Ohio, 1985, Sordon; Art Gallery, Wilkes Barre, Pa., 1985, Montclair Art Mus., N.J., 1988, Westmoreland (Pa.) Mus. Art, 1988, Canton (Ohio) Art Inst., 1988, Woodmere Art Mus., Phila., 1988; exhibited in group shows: Newark Mus., 1971, Rutgers U., 1971, Heritage Gallery, N.Y.C., 1972, N.J. State Mus., 1972, 75; represented in permanent collections: Butler Inst. Am. Art, N.J. State Mus., New Britain Mus. Am. Art, Montclair Art Mus. Recipient Julius Hallgarten award NAD, 1975, Gold medal honor Allied Artists Am., N.Y.C., 1975, 1st award Salmagundi Club, N.Y.C., 1975, John Young-Hunter Meml. award Allied Artis Am., 1982; Gold medal of Honor, Allied Artists Am., 1984. Mem. Allied Artists Am. (John Young-Hunter Meml. award 1985), Assoc. Artists N.J., Audubon Artists, Salmagundi Club. Developed contemporary approach to Am. Trompe l'oeil called Levitational Realism, and extended this sch. to 3 dimensional compositions, oil on bronze. Office: 539 42d St Union City NJ 07087

ERBE, YVONNE MARY, marketing specialist, educator; b. Wausau, Wis., Nov. 18, 1947; d. Rudolph Anton and Lucille Virginia (Andrew) Karlen; m. Drake H. Erbe, June 26, 1971; children—Daniel, Heather. B.Mus.Edn., U. Wis., Madison, 1969; postgrad. U. Wis.-Milw. Lic. music educator, Wis. Ky. Music-vocal tchr. Bayport Jr. High Sch., Greenbay, Wis., 1969-70; tchr. bassoon, oboe U. Wis.-Greenbay, 1969-70; jr. high choral dir. Kenosha Unified Schs., Wis., 1970-76; univ. supr.-edn. U. Wis.-Parkside, Kenosha, 1976-78; parent adv. com. mem. Northern Hills Sch. and Onalaska Mid. Sch., 1981-88; mktg. specialist Metro Prodns., La Crosse, Wis., 1984-85; tchr. music elem., jr. high sch., LaCrosse, Wis., 1987-88, Lexington, Ky., 1988—. Parent vol. coordinator Fauver Hill Sch., 1983-84; sec. exec. bd. Great River Festival of Arts, La Crosse, 1982-83, 1st v.p. exec. bd., chmn. adult choral workshop and performance, chmn. swing choir workshop, 1983-84, pres. bd. dirs., 1984-85; pres. La Crosse Area Newcomers Club, 1982-83; tchr. Confraternity of Christian Doctrine, 1985-88, bd. dirs. La Crosse Boy Choir, 1985-88. Roman Catholic. Avocations: tennis, cross-country skiing, aerobic exercises, needlecrafts, gourmet cooking. Home: 484 Marble Rock Way Lexington KY 40503

ERCKLENTZ, ENNO WILHELM, JR., lawyer; b. N.Y.C., Jan. 27, 1931; s. Enno Wilhelm and Hildegard (Schlubach) E.; m. Mai A. Vilms, Sept. 20, 1969; children: Cornelia, Stephanie. AB, Columbia U., 1954; JD, Harvard U., 1957. Bar: N.Y. 1958. Assoc. Curtis, Mallet-Prevost, Colt & Mosle, N.Y.C., 1957-60; sec., gen. counsel Channing Fin. Corp., N.Y.C., 1960-69; v.p., sec., gen. counsel Inverness Mgmt. Corp., N.Y.C., 1969-75; sole practice, N.Y.C., 1975-78; ptnr. Whitman & Ransom, N.Y.C., 1978-87, Greeven & Ercklentz, N.Y.C., 1987—. Author: Modern German Corporation Law, 1979. Mem. ABA, N.Y. State Bar Assn., Assn. of Bar City of N.Y., Am. Soc. Internat. Law, Am. Fgn. Law Assn. Republican. Roman Catholic. Clubs: Mid-Atlantic, Knickerbocker (N.Y.C.). Office: Greeven & Ercklentz 30 Rockefeller Plaza Suite 3030 New York NY 10112

ERDELYI, MIKLOS, conductor; b. Budapest, Hungary, Feb. 9, 1928; s. Ernö and Ida (Friedrich) E.; m. Katalin Miklós. Student, Music Acad. Budapest. Condr. Hungarian State Opera, Budapest, 1951—. Condr. concerts with Berlin Philharm. Orch., 1974-75, 78, Bamberg Symphony orch., 1976, 78; toured throughout Europe, also concerts in San Antonio, 1972, Japan, 196-88; guest condr. Holland Nat. Orch., 1982-86, Finland Nat. Opera, 1986-88; author: Franz Schubert, 1963. Recipient Liszt prize, 1960, Merited Artist award, 1967, Kossuth prize, 1975, Outstanding Artist award, 1985. Roman Catholic. Home: Tetenyi-Ut 7/A, 1115 Budapest Hungary

ERDEM, ISMET KAYA, minister of state, deputy prime minister of Turkey; b. Safranbolu-Kastamonu, Turkey, Sept. 10, 1928; s. Ahmet Hilmi and Pakize E.; BA, Marmara U., 1951; m. Sevil Sibay, June 23, 1956; children: Deniz, Tuna. Asst. gen. dir. Turkish Sugar Factories Corp., Ankara, 1952-61; dir. gen. Turkish Treasury, 1966; fin. attache Turkish embassy, London, 1966-69; dir. gen. Treasury, 1973; fin. counselor Turkish embassy, London, 1973-76; gen. dir. Social Security, 1976-77; gen. mgr. WATT Electronics Co., Istanbul, 1977-78; sec.-gen. Treasury, 1978-80, minister of fin., 1980-82; mem. Higher Edn. Council, 1982-83; mem. Parliament, minister state, dep. prime minister, 1983—; instr. Anadolu U., 1959-66. Served to lt. arty., Turkish Army, 1950-51. Office: Deputy Prime Minister, Bakanliklar, Ankara Turkey

ERDIM, ESIM, English language and literature educator; b. Izmir, Turkey, July 24, 1944; d. Mustafa and Aliye Zisan (Dágüstü) Bozoklar; m. Mehmet Murat Erdim, Oct. 27, 1967; children: Burak, Firat. Student, Carleton Coll., 1963-65; BA, Ankara (Turkey) U., 1968, PhD, 1973. Instr. Ankara (Turkey) U., 1968-74; english faculty Ege U., Bornova, Izmir, Turkey, 1974-78, asst. prof., 1978-82, head English dept., 1982-84, assoc. prof., 1986—. Contbr. articles to profl. jours. Mem. local exec. council Am. Bd. Sch., Izmir, 1986—. Brit. Council scholar Leeds U., 1977; Fulbright fellow U. Miss., Oxford, 1984-86. Mem. Nat. Assn. Am. Studies, European Assn. Am. Studies, Turkish-Am. Assn. (culture com. 1986—, acad. com. 1986—). Home: 1743 Sok 7/9, 35530 Karsiyaka, Izmir Turkey Office: Ege U Faculty of Letters, Dept of English, Bornova Izmir Turkey

ERDMAN, PAUL EMIL, author; b. Stratford, Ont., Can., May 19, 1932; s. Horace Herman and Helen E.; m. Helly Elizabeth Boeglin, Sept. 11, 1954; children: Constance Anne Catherine, Jennifer Michele. Student, Concordia Coll., Ft. Wayne, Ind., 1950-51, Concordia Sem., St. Louis, 1952-53; B.A., Concordia Coll., St. Louis, 1954; B.Sc., Sch. Fgn. Service, Georgetown U., 1956; M.A., Ph.D., U. Basel, Switzerland, 1958. Econ. cons. European Coal and Steel Community, Luxembourg, Luxembourg, 1958; internat. economist Stanford Research Inst., Menlo Park, Calif., 1958-61; exec. v.p. Electronics Internat. Capital Ltd., Hamilton, Bermuda, 1962-64; vice chmn. United California Bank in Basel A.G., 1965-70; Cons. RAI Corp., TV corp., Italy.; host Moneytalk Sta. KGO, ABC, San Francisco, 1983-86, commentator, 1987—. Author: Swiss-American Economic Relations, 1959, Die Europaeische Wirtschaftsgemeinschaft und die Drittlaender, 1960, The Billion Dollar Sure Thing, 1973, The Silver Bears, 1974, The Crash of '79, 1976, The Last Days of America, 1981, Paul Erdman's Money Book: An Investor's Guide to Economics and Finance, 1984, The Panic of '89, 1987; contbg. editor, columnist Manhattan Inc. mag., 1987—; columnist The Nikon Keizai Shimbun, 1987-88, The Palace, 1988, What's Next?, 1988; contbr. articles, revs. to popular mags. Mem. bd. advisors program in internat. bus. diplomacy Sch. fgn. Service, Georgetown U., Washington, 1980—, faculty mem. Georgetown leadership seminar, 1982—. Recipient Champion Media award for econ. understanding Amos Tuck Sch. Bus. Administrn., Dartmouth Coll., 1984. Mem. Authors Guild, Mystery Writers Am. (Edgar award 1974). Lutheran. Address: 1817 Lytton Springs Rd Healdsburg CA 95448

ERDMAN, WILLIAM JAMES, II, physician, educator; b. Phila., Apr. 8, 1921; s. Frederick and Mary (Hickok) E.; B.A. in Econs., Swarthmore Coll., 1943; M.D., U. Pa., 1950, M.S., 1954, M.A., 1971; m. Betty Jane Frick, June 30, 1956; children—Mary Belle, Jane Elizabeth. Intern Presbyn. Hosp., Phila., 1950-51; asst. instr. phys. medicine and rehab. U. Pa. Sch. Medicine, 1951-53, instr., 1953-54, asst. prof., chmn. dept., 1954-56, assoc. prof., chmn. dept., 1956-60, prof., chmn., 1960-87, prof. emeritus, 1987—; also with Grad. Sch. Medicine, 1951—, asst. instr., 1951-53, instr., 1953-54, asso., 1954-55, asst. prof., 1955-56, assoc. prof., 1956-60, prof., 1960—, chmn. dept., 1955—, asst. dean, 1968-74, dir. dept. phys. medicine and rehab. Hosp. U. Pa., chmn. med. staff, 1965-67, med. dir., 1968-78; nat. rehab. cons. Internat. Rehab. Assoc., 1971—; mem. spl. med. adv. group VA, Washington; cons. Lebanon, Wilmington VA hosps.; chmn. dept. phys. medicine and rehab. Phila. Gen. Hosp.; cons. Presbyn. Hosp., Phila., VA Hosp. Vice pres., med. dir. Presbyn. Ministers Fund. Served with AUS, 1943-46. Decorated Bronze Star, Purple Heart. Diplomate Am. Bd. Phys. Medicine and Rehab. Fellow ACP; mem. AMA (chmn. sect. phys. medicine and rehab. 1967-68, del. 1978—), Am. Congress Phys. Medicine and Rehab. (pres. 1964-65, treas. 1970—), Internat. Fedn. Phys. Medicine and Rehab. (hon. treas. 1980—), Internat. Rehab. Medicine Assn. (treas. 1969-77), Am., Pa. (pres. 1958-59) acads. phys. medicine and rehab., Assn. Acad. Psychiatrists (pres. 1970), Coll. Physicians Phila., Gold Key. Presbyterian. (elder) Home: 3803 The Oak Rd Philadelphia PA 19129 Office: 3400 Spruce St Philadelphia PA 19104

ERDMANN, JAMES BERNARD, educational psychologist; b. Springfield, Ill., Oct. 27, 1937; s. George C. and Emma (Hiltebrand) E.; cum laude, Pontifical Coll. Josephinum, 1959; M.A., Loyola U., Chgo., 1964, Ph.D., 1966; m. Rebecca Susan Lindsay; children—Theodore Michael, Carolyn Louise, Christopher Joseph, Timothy James. Research asst. Psychometric Lab., Loyola U., Chgo., 1960-63, research asso., project dir., 1963-65, acting dir., 1965-66, asso. dir., 1967-69, instr. dept. psychology, 1964-66, asst. prof. measurement program, 1966-69; assoc. prof. Sch. Edn. and Sch. Human Medicine, evaluation coordinator Office Med. Edn., Research and Devel., Mich. State U., 1969-70; dir. div. ednl. measurement and research Assn. Am. Med. Colls., Washington, 1970-87; clin. assoc. prof. psychiatry and behavioral scis. George Washington U. Sch. Medicine and Health Scis., 1973-87; assoc. dean adminstrn. and spl. projects Jefferson Med. Coll. Thomas Jefferson U., Phila., 1987—. Mem. Am. Psychol. Assn., Psychometric Soc., AAAS, Am. Ednl. Research Assn., Nat. Council Measurement in Edn. Roman Catholic. Contbr. articles to profl. publs. Home: 408 Bickmore Dr Wallingford PA 19086 Office: 1025 Walnut St Philadelphia PA 19107

EREZ, MIRIAM, industrial psychology educator; b. Haifa, Israel, June 23, 1943; d. Matityahu and Naomi (Ribatsky) Markel; m. Haim Lipa Erez, Aug. 18, 1964; children: Mor., Mattan. BA in Psychology, Hebrew U., Jerusalem, 1966; MSc in Behavioral Scis., Technion, Israel, 1969, DSc in Behavioral Scis., 1972. Lectr. Technion-Israel Inst. Tech., 1972-79; sr. lectr. Technion, 1980-87, assoc. prof. indsl. and orginizational psychology, 1987—; vis. assoc. prof. U. Ill, Champaign, 1980-81, U. Md., College Park, 1985-86; acting head personnel orgn. Raphael Armament Devel. Authority, Haifa, 1983-84, also cons.; research assoc. acting head Lab. Inds. Psychology, Haifa, 1972-78; mem. profl. forum Nat. Inst. Testing and Evaluation, Jerusalem, 1987—. Co-author: Psychology of Work, 1968, Incentives, Values and Risk-Taking, 1974; contbr. articles to profl. publs. Research fellow U. Md., 1975-76; fellow Yad-Avi Hayishuv, Israel, 1975, Japan Found., 1987, Japan Soc. Promotion of Sci., 1987. Mem. Am. Psychol. Assn., Acad. Mgmt., Internat. Assn. Applied Psycholgy, Israel Assn. Psychologists (chairperson div. ind. psychologists 1985-87). Jewish. Office: Faculty Indsl Engring and, Mgmt Technicion, Technion City, Haifa 32000, Israel

ERICHSEN, CARL, corporate executive; b. Jan. 8, 1932; s. Christian Gottlieb Leberecht and Claudia Petrea (Nielsen) E.; m. Bende Jespersen, Feb. 19, 1961; children: Hans Carsten, Jan Christian. Officer EAC's Vessels, Worldwide, 1958-64; officer, master EAC's Devel. Dept., Copenhagen, 1964-76; mgr. EAC's Container Dept., Copenhagen, 1977; project leader EAC's People's Republic of China Ports, Beijing, Tientsin, Shanghai, 1978-80, EAC's Fremantle Western Australia-Container Terminal, 1981-82; v.p. EAC's Trans Pacific Service Ops., Pasadena, Calif., 1983-84; mgr. EAC's Tech. Services EDP Devel., Copenhagen, 1985-88; tech. dir. Global Equipment Mgmt., London, 1988—; Denmark rep. IMO/UNCTAD London Container Safety Conv., ISO TC IOH Container Com., 1973-78; chmn. Danish Standard Ins. Container Com., 1975-78. Served to 1st lt. Royal Danish Navy, 1956-58. Home: Soelystparken 1, 2990 Nivaa Denmark Office: Global Equipment Mgmt, 2 Jubilee Pl, London SW2, England

ERICKSON, ARTHUR CHARLES, architect; b. Vancouver, B.C., Can., June 14, 1924; s. Oscar and Myrtle (Chatterson) E. Student, U. B.C., Vancouver, 1942-44; B.Arch., McGill U., Montreal, Que., Can., 1950; LL.D. (hon.), Simon Fraser U., Vancouver, 1973, U. Man., Winnipeg, Can., 1978, Lethbridge U., 1981; D.Eng. (hon.), Novia Scotia Tech. Coll., McGill U., 1971; Litt.D. (hon.), U. B.C., 1985. Asst. prof. U. Oreg., Eugene, 1955-56; assoc. prof. U. B.C., 1956-63; ptnr. Erickson-Massey Architects, Vancouver, 1963-72; prin. Arthur Erickson Architects, Vancouver and Toronto, 1972—, Los Angeles, 1981—; dir. Campus Planning Assocs., Toronto. Prin. works include Can. Pavilion at Expo '70, Osaka (recipient first prize in nat. competition, Archtl. Inst. of Japan award for best pavilion), Robson Square/The Law Courts (honor award), Mus. of Anthropology (honor award), Eppich Residence (honor award), Habitat Pavilion (honor award), Sikh Temple (award of merit), Champlain Heights Community Sch. (award of merit); contbr. articles to profl. publs. Mem. com. on urban devel. Council of Can., 1971; bd. dirs. Can. Conf. of Arts, 1972; mem. design adv. council Portland Devel. Commn., Can. Council Urban Research; trustee Inst. Research on Pub. Policy. Served to capt. Can. Intelligence Corps, 1945-46. Recipient Molson prize Can. Council for Arts, 1967, Triangle award Nat. Soc. Interior Design, Royal Bank of Can. award, 1971, Gold medal Tau Sigma Delta, 1973, residential design award Can. Housing Council, 1975, August Perret award Internat. Union of Architects' Congress, 1975, Chgo. Architecture award, 1984, Gold medal French Acad. Architecture, 1984, Pres.' award Excellence, Am. Soc. Landscape Architects, 1979; named Officer, Order of Can., 1973, Companion, Order of Can., 1981; McLennan Travelling scholar; Can. Council fellow, 1961. Fellow AIA (hon., Pan Pacific citation Hawaiian chpt. 1963, Gold medal 1986), Royal Archtl. Inst. Can. (recipient award 1980, Gold medal 1984); mem. Archtl. Inst. B.C., Ont. Assn. Architects, Royal Can. Acad. Arts (academician), Am. Soc. Interior Designers, Ordre des Architectes du Quebec, Am. Soc. Planning Officials, Community Planning Assn. Can., Heritage Can., Planning Inst. B.C., Urban Land Inst. Clubs: Vancouver, U. B.C. Faculty, Univ. Office: Arthur Erickson Architects Inc, 80 Bloor St W, 16th Floor, Toronto, ON Canada M5S 2V1 also: 2412 Laurel St, Vancouver, BC Canada V5Z 3T2 also: 125 N Robertson Los Angeles CA 90048 *

ERICKSON, CAROL ANN, psychotherapist; b. Worcester, Mass., Dec. 26, 1933; d. Milton Hyland and Helen (Hutton) E.; m. Jean LaRue Barnes, Mar. 20, 1952 (div. Sept. 1962); children: Stephanie Free, Suzanne Hackett, Paul, Sandra Smith, Larry, Cynthia Baker. BS, Ariz. State U., 1964; MSW, Calif. State U., Fresno, 1977. Social worker Los Angeles County, 1964-83; pvt. practice psychotherapy Berkeley, Calif., 1977—; exec. dir. Erickson Inst., Berkeley, 1981—; adj. faculty U. Calif., Berkeley; adj. faculty Vermont Coll. San Francisco, 1986—. Co-writer, composer Deep Self Appreciation, 1983, Self-Hypnosis, A Relaxing Time Out, 1984, Natural Self Confidence, 1985. Bd. dirs. YWCA, Torrance, Calif., 1981-83. Mem. Internat. Soc. Hypnosis, No. Calif. Soc. Clin. Hypnosis, So. Calif. Soc. Clin. Hypnosis, Calif. Assn. Marriage and Family Therapists (cert.), Soc. Clin. and Exptl. Hypnosis, Soc. Clin. Social Workers, Nat. Assn. Social Workers (cert.), AAUW, NOW, Phi Kappa Phi. Democrat. Office: Erickson Inst PO Box 739 Berkeley CA 94701

ERICKSON, RALPH ERNEST, lawyer; b. Jamestown, N.Y., Oct. 3, 1928; s. Lawrence Harold and Myrtle (Jespersen) E.; m. Janet Cass, June 6, 1953; children: Sandra Lynne, John Cass. B.S., Cornell U., 1952; J.D., Harvard U., 1955. Bar: Calif. 1956, U.S. Supreme Ct. 1968, D.C. 1973. Ptnr. Musick, Peeler & Garrett, Los Angeles, 1962-70; asst. atty. gen. U.S. Dept. Justice, 1971-72, dep. atty. gen., 1972-73; ptnr. Erickson, Zerfas & Adams, Los Angeles, 1974-79, Jones, Day, Reavis & Pogue, Los Angeles, 1979—; spl rep. of U.S. for Am. Indian Movement Wounded Knee negotiations, 1973; mem. steering com. Am. Businessmen of Riyadh, Saudi Arabia, 1986—. Founding mem., trustee Victor Gruen Found. Environ Planning; chmn. legal adv. com. San Marino Sch. Dist., Calif., 1979-81; mem. Investment Commn., 1979—, Los Angeles Citizens Olympics Commn., Los Angeles World Affairs Council, 1984—. Fellow Huntington Library and Gallery, San Marino, Calif., 1984—. Mem. ABA (ho. of dels. 1972-73), Calif. State Bar, D.C. Bar. Republican. Episcopalian. Clubs: Calif. (Los Angeles); Met. (Washington); Springs (Rancho Mirage, Calif.); Annandale Golf (Pasadena, Calif.); Town Hall (Los Angeles) (life mem.). Office: Jones Day Reavis & Pogue 355 S Grand Ave Suite 3000 Los Angeles CA 90071

ERICSON, RICHARD CHARLES, social service agency executive, consultant; b. St. Paul, June 21, 1933; s. Rolph Christopher and Sonia Margaret (Carlson) E.; m. Carol Joy Turnwall, Jan. 1, 1955; children: Lynn Ericson Starr, David Alan. BA, Roosevelt U., 1959; MA, U. Chgo., 1961. U.S. probation officer U.S. Probation Office, Chgo., 1960-61; juvenile probation officer Hennepin County Ct. Services, Mpls., 1961-62; asst. supr. Hennepin County Juvenile Detention Center, Mpls., 1962-63; asst. dir. Pres.'s Com. on Youth Crime, Charleston, W.Va., 1963-64; project coordinator parolee rehab. project Mpls. Rehab. Center, 1964-67; pres. Minn. Citizens Council on Crime and Justice, 1967—; trustee Klingberg Family Centers, New Britain, Conn., Sunny Ridge Family Center, Wheaton, Ill.; mem. Minn. Crime Victim and Witness Adv. Council; pres. Ericson Properties, Inc. Active Mpls. Soc. Fine Arts, Walker Art Ctr. Served with C.E., U.S. Army, 1954-56. Grantee in field. Mem. Nat. Council on Crime and Delinquency, Am. Correctional Assn. Lodge: Rotary of Mpls. Contbr. articles on crime and justice to profl. jours. Office: 822 3rd St S #101 Minneapolis MN 55415

ERICSON, ROGER DELWIN, timber resource company executive; b. Moline, Ill, Dec. 21, 1934; s. Carl D. and Linnea E. (Challman) E.; m. Norma F. Brown, Aug. 1, 1957; children: Catherine Lynn, David. A.B., Stetson U., DeLand, Fla., 1958; J.D., Stetson U., 1958; M.B.A., U. Chgo., 1971. Bar: Fla. 1958, Ill. 1959, Ind. 1974. Atty. Brunswick Corp., Skokie, Ill., 1959-62; asst. sec., asst. gen. counsel Chemetron Corp., Chgo., 1962-73; asst. v.p. Inland Container Corp., Indpls., 1973-75, v.p., gen. counsel, sec., 1975-83; gen. counsel, sec. Temple-Inland Inc., 1983—; v.p., sec., bd. dirs. Inland-Rome Inc. (formerly Ga. Kraft Co.); bd. dirs. Inland Container Corp., Inland-Orange, Inc., Temple-Eastex Inc., Inland Real Estate Investments, Inc. Trustee Chgo. Homes for Children, 1971-74; mem. alumni council U. Chgo., 1972-76; mem. Palatine Twp. Youth Commn., 1969-72; sect. chmn. Chgo. Heart Assn., 1972, 73; alumni bd. dirs. Stetson U. Mem. ABA, Chgo. Bar Assn., Ill. State Bar Assn., Ind. Bar Assn., Fla. Bar Assn., Indpls. Bar Assn. (chmn. corp. counsel sect., mem. profl. responsibility com. 1982), Am. Soc. Corp. Secs., Am. Paper Inst. (past mem. govt. affairs com.), Indpls. C. of C. (mem. govt. affairs com.), Omicron Delta Kappa, Phi Delta Phi. Clubs: Plum Grove (Chgo.) (pres. 1969); Crown Colony Country (Lufkin, Tex.). Home: 4 Cypress Point Lufkin TX 75901 Office: Temple-Inland Inc Drawer N Diboll TX 75941

ERICSON, RUTH ANN, psychiatrist; b. Assaria, Kans., May 15; d. William Albert and Anna Mathilda (Almquist) E.; student So. Meth. U., 1945-47; B.S., Bethany Coll.; M.D., U. Tex., 1951. Intern, Calif. Hosp., Los Angeles, 1951-52; resident in psychiatry U. Tex. Med. Br., Galveston, 1952-55; psychiatrist Child Guidance Clinic, Dallas, 1955-63; clin. instr. Southwestern Med. Sch., Dallas, 1955-72; practice medicine specializing in psychiatry, Dallas, 1955—; cons. Dallas Intertribal Council Clinic, 1974-81, Dallas Ind. Sch. Dist., U.S. Army, Welfare Dept., Tribal Concerns, alcoholism, Adv. Bd. Intertribal Council. Fellow Am. Geriatrics Assn.; mem. So., Tex., Dallas med. assns., Am. (life), Tex., North Tex. psychiat. assns., Am. Med. Women's Assn., Dallas Area Women Psychiatrists, Alumni Assn. U. Tex. (Med. Br.), Navy League (life), Air Force Assn., Tex. (life mem.), Dallas (life mem., pres. 1972-73, 82-84) archaeol. socs., C., South Tex. Archaeol. Soc., N. Mex. Archaeol. Soc., Paleopathology Soc., Alpha Omega Alpha, Delta Psi Omega, Alpha Psi Omega, Pi Gamma Mu, Lambda Sigma, Alpha Epsilon Iota. Lutheran. Home: 4007 Shady Hill Dr Dallas TX 75229 Office: Internat Psych Assn 2915 LBJ Freeway Suite 135 Dallas TX 75234

ERIKSEN, GARY L(YNN), sculptor, medallist; b. Jackson, Mich., Sept. 11, 1943; s. Kristen Berg and Evelyn (Jensen) E.; m. Eloise Christiansen, Sept. 3, 1963 (div. 1971); 1 child, Grant. B.A., Oberlin Coll., 1966; M.A., Kent State U., 1968; postgrad. U. Chgo., 1971-73, Accademia Delle Belle Arti (Italy), 1973-77; diploma Scuola dell Arte Della Medaglia (Italy), 1977. Instr. econs. U. Akron, Ohio, 1969-71; lectr. econs. U. Ill.-Chgo., 1971-73; free lance sculptor, 1977—; commns. include: Bishop O. M. Kelly, Ch. of God in Christ, N.Y.C. and Memphis, 1980, Thirty Bas Reliefs, Nat. Basketball Hall of Fame, Springfield, Mass., 1985, Erasmus Hall High Sch. Seal, Bklyn., 1987; cons. Sculpture House, Inc., N.Y.C., 1980-81. Author: This Book Is Long Past Due, 1973. Steering com. Democratic Nat. Com., Italy, 1976-77; vol. Deaf Contact-Helpline, Marble Collegiate Ch., N.Y.C., 1981-86. Recipient N.Y. State Council on Arts grantee 1983; 1st prize Salmagundi Club, 1983. Mem. Am. Medallic Sculpture Assn. (co-founder, pres. 1982-83, bd. dirs. 1983-87), Visual Artists and Galleries Assn. Home: PO Box 7222 New York NY 10163

ERIKSEN, LARS HENRIK, literature educator; b. Hammel, Denmark, Apr. 26, 1957; s. Poul and Nina E. Degree in Philosophy, U. Aarhus, Denmark, 1982; Degree in Law, U. Bayreuth, Fed. Republic Germany, 1987. Lectr. Danish lang., lit. U. Bayreuth, 1980-88. Office: Univ Bayreuth, Postfach 101251, 8580 Bayreuth Federal Republic of Germany

ERIKSEN, POUL JAKOB, civil engineer; b. Landet, Denmark, Jan. 10, 1925; s. Carl Martin and Hansine (With) E.; M.S. in Civil and Structural Engring., Tech. U. Denmark, 1951; m. Birgit Sigrun Johansen, May 3, 1952; children—Dan Birger, Jens Henning, Jorn Ditlev. Partner, Axel Hansen and Partners, Cons. Engrs. and Architects, Copenhagen, 1961-78; owner, mgr. Dan-Project ApS, Copenhagen, 1978—; FAO del. to Kenya, Somalia, Tanzania and Nigeria, 1975; lectr. in field. Mem. Danish Instn. Civil Engrs., Danish Assn. Cons. Engrs., Fedn. Internat. des Ingenieurs-Conseils. Author: Slaughterhouse and Slaughterslab, Design and Construction (in English, French and Spanish), 1978; The Opager-Saga, 1984; contbr. travel articles to Danish newspapers. Home: 30 Tukshojen, DK2710 Herlev Denmark Office: 21 Gladsaxe Mollevej, DK-2860 Copenhagen, Soborg Denmark

ERIKSON, GEORGE EMIL, anatomist, archivist, historian; b. Palmer, Mass., May 3, 1920; s. Emil and Sofia (Gustafson) E.; m. Suzanne J. Henderson, Apr. 23, 1950; children: Ann, David, John, Thomas. BS, Mass. State Coll. (now U. Mass.), 1941; MA, Harvard U., 1946, PhD, 1948. Reader in history of sci. and learning Harvard U., 1943-45, asst. prof. gen. edn. in biology, 1949-52; instr. anatomy Harvard Med. Sch., 1947-49, assoc. in anatomy, 1952-55, asst. prof. anatomy, 1955-65, assoc. curator Warren Anat. Mus., 1961-65; prof. med. sci. Brown U., Providence, 1965—, chmn. sect. morphology, 1968-85, co-chmn. sect. population biology, morphology & genetics and chmn. for anatomy; anatomist various Boston hosps., 1952-82; anatomist depts. surgery, orthopedics & rehab., and neurosurgery R.I. Hosp.; cons. anatomist Surg. Techniques Illus., 1976-80; cons. Dorlands Illus. Med. Dictionary; Rockefeller Found. cons. medicine and pub. health, S. Am., 1959; specialist State Dept., Brazil, 1962. Sheldon traveling fellow, Cen. Am., 1946; Guggenheim fellow, S. Am., 1949. Mem. AAAS, Am. Assn. Phys. Anthropologists (archivist and co-historian 1980—), Am. Soc. Mammalogists, History Sci. Soc., Am. Soc. Zoologists, Am. Assn. Anatomists (historian, archivist 1972-86, archivist 1986—), Am. Assn. History Medicine (council 1972-74), Anat. Soc. Gt. Britain and Ireland, Oral Hist. Assn., Anatomische Gesellschaft, Sigma Xi. Home: 153 Bay Rd Norton MA 02766 Office: Div Biology and Medicine Brown U Providence RI 02912

ERIKSSON, PER OLOF, corporate executive; b. Seglora, Sweden, Mar. 1, 1938; s. Herbert and Gunhild (Nyman) E.; m. Helena Joachimsson, Dec. 28, 1962; children: Katarina, Joachim, Henrik. Degree in Tech. Physics, Royal Inst. Tech., Stockholm, 1961. With Research Inst. Swedish Nat. Def., Stockholm, 1961-62, Uddeholm AB, Stockholm, 1963-65, Sandvik AB, various locations, 1966-75; pres., chief exec. officer Sandvik AB, Sandviken, Sweden, 1984—; also bd. dirs. Sandvik AB, Sandviken; mng. dir. Seco Tools AB, Fagersta, Sweden, 1976-83; bd. dirs. Svenska Handelsbanken, AB SKF, SSAB Swedish Steel Corp., Sandvik AB. Mem. Fedn. Swedish Industires (bd. dirs.). Home: Hedasvagen 57, S-81161 Sandviken Sweden Office: Sandvik AB, S-811 81 Sandviken Sweden

ERIM, KENAN TEVFIK, classicist, educator; b. Istanbul, Turkey, Feb. 13, 1929; came to U.S., 1947; s. Kerim Tevfik and Fahime (Osan) E. Student, Coll. de Geneve, 1941-46; B.A., NYU, 1953; M.A., Princeton U., 1955, Ph.D., 1958; Vis. instr., Ind. U., 1957-58. Asst. prof. NYU, N.Y.C., 1958-62; assoc. prof. classics NYU, 1962-71, prof., 1971—; field dir. research project 1961, now dir. excavation archeol. discovery Aphrodisias in Turkey. Research and publs. in field. Recipient Franklin L. Burr prize Nat. Geog. Soc., 1973, Liberty medal Mayor Ed Koch of N.Y., 1986, Centennial award Nat. Geog. Soc., 1988; named Commendatore dell' Ordine al Merito, Italy, 1988; Guggenheim fellow, 1961-62. Mem. Archaeol. Inst. Am. (Charles Eliot Norton lectr. 1985-86), Royal Numis. Soc., Turk Tarih Kurumu (corr.), Phi Beta Kappa. Home: 182 Nassau St Princeton NJ 08542

ERKELENS, SIMON, chemical company executive, marketing professional; b. Amstelveen, The Netherlands, Jan. 10, 1951; s. Leendert and Gerritje-Beertje (De Groot) E.; m. Hendrika Cornelia Janssen, Nov. 17, 1972; children: Otto, Joppe. Degree in Chem. Engring., Polytech. Bur. Nederland Arnhem U., 1972. Registered profl. engr., The Netherlands. Analyst, lab. asst. Shell Research, Amsterdam, 1968-74, with tech. service, 1975-83, research chemist, 1983-84; with tech. service Mobil Polymers Internat., Brussels, 1984-86, sales rep., 1986-87; asst. mktg. mgr., sales rep. Mobil Polymers Benelux, Brussels, 1987-88; comml. dir. High Tech Plastics, Ede, The Netherlands, 1988—. Chmn., City Found. Soc. Cultural Work, Hilversum, The Netherlands, 1981ú. Served with Air Force of Netherlands, 1971-72. Mem. Greenpeace party. Office: High Tech Plastics, Lorentzstraat 6, 6716-AD Ede The Netherlands

ERKKO, AATOS JUHO, publishing company executive; b. Helsinki, Finland, Sept. 16, 1932; s. Juho Eljas and Violet Eugenie (Sutcliffe) E.; m. Jane Tulikki Marianna Airola, 1959. MS in Journalism, Columbia U., 1952. Editor-in-chief weekly news mag. Viikkosanomat, Helsinki, 1953-61; editor-in-chief newspaper Helsingin Sanomat, Helsinki, 1961-70, pub., 1965—; exec. v.p. Samona Corp., Helsinki, 1961-65, pres., 1965-76, chief exec. officer, 1965—, chmn., 1972—; pres. Sanoma Inc., N.Y.C., 1981—; chmn. Eurocable Oy, Helsinki, 1987—, ECI Communications AG, Zug, Switzerland, 1987—; chmn. bd. Effoa-Finnish S.S. Co., Helsinki, 1985—; chmn. supervisory bd. Kansallis-Osake-Pankki Bank, Helsinki, 1985—; bd. dirs. Kymmene Corp., Finnair Oy, Helsinki. Bd. govs. European Cultural Found., Amsterdam. 1972—; overseas trustee Am.-Scandinavian Found., N.Y.C., 1983—. Mem. English Speaking Union (hon. rep. 1982—). Office: Sanoma Corp, PO Box 17, 01771 Vantaa Finland

ERKUTAY, KAYA, civil engineer; b. Zonguldak, Turkey, Apr. 27, 1944; s. Abdurrahmann and Behire (Gecmez) E.; m. Inci Karaca, Sept. 29, 1975; children: Ugur, Pinar. BS, 1st Tech U., Turkey, 1969, MS, 1971. Registered profl. engr., Turkey. Office engr. Engring. Office, Bonn, Fed. Republic Germany, 1971-72; site engr. Enka Insaat Ve Sanayi A.S., Iskenderun, Turkey, 1974-75, Benghazi, Libya, 1975-77, Yatan, Turkey, 1977-79; project mgr. Enka Insaat Ve Sanayi A.S., Riyadh, Saudi Arabia, 1979-81; project mgr., site agt. Enka Insaat Ve Sanayi A.S., Amman, Jordan, 1981-83, br. mgr., site agt., 1983—; advisor Enka Insaat Ve Sanayi A.S., Istanbul, Turkey, 1981—. Served with Turkish Air Force, 1972-74. Muslim. Lodge: Lions. Home: PO Box 19277 Sportcity, Amman Jordan Office: Enka Insaat Ve Sanayi, Balmumucu Mah, Istanbul Turkey

ERLANDER, SVEN BERTIL, academic administrator, educator; b. Halmstad, Sweden, May 25, 1934; s. Tage and Aina (Andersson) E.; m. Lillemor Sandahl; children: Charles, Kim, Gunnel, Inger. Licentiate, Stockholm U., 1964, Doctor of Philosophy, 1968. Asst. to prof. Stockholm U., 1959-68, docent, 1969-70; prof. Linköping U., Sweden, 1971—, pres., 1983—. Mem. Royal Swedish Acad. Engring. Scis., Math. Programming Soc., Ops. Research Soc. Am., Internat. Statis. Inst., Inst. Math. Stats., Am. Math. Soc. Home: Hedborns Gata 13, 58249 Linköping Sweden Office: Linköping U, 58381 Linköping Sweden

ERLANDSON, RAY SANFORD, SR., retired former business educator; b. Wausau, Wis., May 3, 1893; s. Paul and Torgine (Olson) E.; m. Margery McKillop, Aug. 22, 1919; children: Paul McKillop, Ray Sanford, William. A.B., U. Wis., 1918; M.A., George Washington U., 1921. Sch. adminstr. Chippewa Falls, Wis., 1913-16; asst. sec., bus. mgr. NEA, 1919-24; bus. mgr. Internat. Council Religious Edn., 1924-27; sales exec. John Rudin & Co., 1927-29, Grigsby Grunow Co., 1929-32, Zenith Radio Corp., 1932-35; v.p. Rudolph Wurlizer Co., 1935-45; v.p. San Antonio Music Co., 1945-50, pres., 1950-53; pres. Bledsoe Furniture Co., 1950-53; dir. 1st Fed. Savs. & Loan Assn., San Antonio, 1952-84; hon. life dir. 1st Fed. Savs. & Loan Assn., 1984—; chmn. dept. bus. adminstrn. Trinity U., 1953-64, prof. emeritus, 1980—. Pres., chief exec. officer Children's Fund, San Antonio, 1964-70; pres. Am. Inst. Character Edn., 1970-74, chmn. bd., chief exec. officer, 1970-86, emeritus, 1986—; bd. dirs. SW Research Center, 1954—; founder Am. Sch. of Air, 1929; pres. Am. Music War Council, 1942-44; chmn. nat. trade practice code com., music industry, 1944-53; Nat. vice chmn. ARC, 1959-60; past bd. dirs. San Antonio chpt., San Antonio Symphony Soc., Taxpayers League, Community Welfare Council; bd. dirs., exec. com. S.W. Research Inst., chmn. bd. of control, 1961-64. Served as lt. F.A. U.S. Army, World War I; cons. joint Army-Navy com. on welfare, recreation World War II. Named Father of Year San Antonio, 1951; Distinguished Alumnus award Wis. State U., 1969. Mem. NEA (life), San Antonio Chamber Music Soc. (pres. 1950-56), Research and Planning Council (pres. 1957), San Antonio Council Presidents (pres. 1951), Nat. Assn. Music Mchts. (pres. 1950-52, hon. life). Republican. Presbyterian. Clubs: Masons, Rotary (gov. dist. 584 internat. 1958-59, hon. life mem., pres. 1954, 50 Year award 1987), Knife and Fork (pres. 1954), Breakfast (pres. 1953), San Antonio; Kiwanis Internat. (hon. life). Home: 401 Shook Ave San Antonio TX 78212 Office: 342 W Woodlawn Ave San Antonio TX 78212

ERLICHMAN, STANTON ROY, industrial consultant, psychotherapist; b. Detroit, Mar. 24, 1939; s. William Isaiah and Lydia (Bloom) E.; B.A., Franklin and Marshall Coll., Pa., 1961; M.A., Goddard Coll., Vt., 1975; Ph.D., Union Grad. Sch., Ohio, 1977; postgrad. Eastern Pa. Psychiat. Inst., Phila. Sch. Psychoanalysis, Family Inst. Phila.; children—Karen, Daniel, William. Pres., Richards Mfg. Co., Phila., 1962-73; ptnr. G.T. Mfg. Corp., San Juan, P.R., 1973—, Erlichman Assocs., Bala Cynwyd, Pa., 1973—; co-dir. ERE Health Systems, Bala Cynwyd, 1980—, South Miami, Fla.; mem. field faculty Goddard Coll.; mem. bd. dirs., v.p. Compugen Corp., Malvern, Pa.; speaker in field. Mem. Lower Merion (Pa.) Twp. Recycling Com., 1969-72. Fellow, diplomate Am. Bd. Med. Psychotherapists; mem. Am. Assn. Marriage and Family Therapists, Am. Psychol. Assn., Nat. Assn. Accreditation Psychoanalysis, Assn. Applied Psychoanalysis, Am. Orthopsychiat. Assn., Acad. Family Psychology, Phi Beta Kappa, Zeta Beta Tau. Author articles in field.

ERMA, REINO MAURI, lawyer, university chancellor; b. Tampere, Finland, Apr. 8, 1922; s. Edvin Eugen and Ida Irene (Haapala) E.; m. Hilkka Marjatta Ahjo, Jan. 5, 1946; children: Juhani, Sinikka, Anneli, Tapio. LLM, Helsinki U., 1944, Licentiate in Laws, 1948, LLD, 1955. With KOP Bank, Helsinki, 1947-70, dir., 1960-70; prof. bus. law Faculty Econs. and Adminstrn. U. Tampere, 1970—; chmn. supervisory bd. United Paper Mills Ltd., Tampereen Kirjapaino Oy (Tamprint), Wihuri-yhtymä; bd. dirs. YIT Corp. (Constrn.). Author: Contract of Work, 1955, General Conditions for The Building Contracts, 1974, Legal Aspects of Subcontracting, 1975, General Conditions for the Delivery of Goods between Finland and CMEA Countries, 1980, Banking Laws, 1986. Served with Finnish Army, 1940-44. Decorated Comdr. Order Finnish White Rose, Cross of Freedom, Medal of Freedom. Mem. Internat. Law Assn., Am. Arbitration Assn., Arbitrators of European Internat. Contractors, Finland Arbitration of the Cen. C. of C. (chmn. bd.). Lodge: Rotary (past pres.). Home: Mustanlahdenkatu 1 B 87, Tampere 21 Finland Office: U Tampere, Kalevantie 4, Tampere 10 Finland

ERNI, HANS, painter; b. Lucerne, Switzerland, Feb. 21, 1909; m. Doris Kessler, 1949; 3 children. Ed. Academie Julien, Paris, and Vereinigte Staatsschulen fur freie und angewandte Kunst, Berlin. Exhibited in Lucerne, Paris, Basel, Switzerland, Oxford, Eng., Liverpool, Eng., London, Cambridge, Eng., Leicester, Eng., Zurich, Switzerland, Milan, Italy, Rotterdam, Netherlands, Prague, Czechoslovakia, Stockholm, Chgo., N.Y.C., Rome, Copenhagen, Tokyo, San Francisco, Los Angeles, Washington, Mannheim, Germany, Cologne, Germany, Japan and Australia, 1963, 64, Chgo., N.Y.C. and Geneva, 1966-68; works include: abstract mural Swiss sect. Triennale Milan; frescoes, Lucerne, great mural for Swiss Nat. exhbn., Zurich, 1939; mural for Gt. Murals Expn. internationale de l'Urbanisme et de l'Habitation, Paris, 1947; mural in Bernese hospital Montana; murals for Internat. Exhbn., Brussels, 1958; mosaics for Abbey St. Maurice, 1961, for Swiss TV and Radio Bldg., Berne, 1964, in Rolex Found., Union de Banques Suisses, Sion, 1966, for Swissair Zurich and La Placette Geneva, 1957; illustrator bibliophile edits. of classics by Plato, Pindar, Sophocles, Virgil, Buffon, Renard, Valery, Paul Eluard, others; illustrator; Odyssey; La Paix; Candide; engraved glass panels Day and Night, and Towards a Humanistic Future for Societe des Banques Suisses, Geneva, 1963; author: Wo Steht der Maler in der Genenwart?, 1947; Ernie en Valais, 1967; Israel Sketchbook, 1968. Recipient Internat. prize Biennale del Mare, 1953. Mem. Groupe Abstraction-Creation, Alliance Graphique Internationale. Address: 6045 Meggen, Lucerne Switzerland *

ERNST, CHADWICK ELLSWORTH, fastener company executive; b. Oakland, Calif., Mar. 19, 1933; s. Archibald Ellsworth and Beatrice Jessie (Ort) E.; B.A., U. Calif., Berkeley, 1958. Gen. mgr. Cee Mdse. Co., Oakland, Calif., 1948-67; v.p. F.W. Aurich & Co., Inc., Seattle, 1967-68; exec. v.p. Aimsco Inc., Seattle, 1969-75; pres., dir. Cheler Corp., Seattle, 1976—; dir. Beacon Wholesale, Seattle, Amalgamated Counseling Services, Inc., Vaughn. Wash.; dir., chmn. bd., pres. Aurich, Inc., Aimsco, Inc. Active CD, Berkeley, 1955-62; deacon Presby. Ch. Fellow Internat. Biographers Assn; mem. Internat. Mail Dealers Assn., Mfrs. Agts. Nat. Assn., Nat. Assn. Credit Mgmt., Gideons Internat., Nat. Assn. Notaries (life), Seattle Opera Assn., Seattle Symphony Assn. Clubs: Steel, Lake of the Woods Country. Home: 18210 92d Ave NE Bothell WA 98011 also: #6 Lake of Woods Gig Harbor WA 98335 Office: 4024 22d Ave W Seattle WA 98199

ERNST, JOHN LOUIS, television programming executive; b. Pine Bluff, Ark., Dec. 24, 1932; s. Albert C. and Christine (Vinent) E.; m. Lois R. Geraci, June 12, 1971; children: Ann Marie, Catherine Teresa, Laura Elizabeth, Christine Margaret. BS, Spring Hill Coll., Mobile, Ala., 1954; postgrad., Georgetown U. Law Sch., 1957. Stockbroker Washington Planning Co., 1957-58; sales exec. Am. Airlines, Washington, Phila. and N.Y.C., 1958-62; account exec. Ted Bates Advt. Agy., N.Y.C., 1962-65; sr. v.p., mgmt. dir. Marschalk Advt. Agy., N.Y.C., 1965-68; dir. Interpub. Service Corp., 1967-69; sr. v.p., mng. dir. McCann-Erickson Advt. Agy., N.Y.C., 1969-70; pres. Ernst-Van Praag, N.Y.C., 1970-75; chmn. bd. A.V.E. Corp., N.Y.C., 1974-75, Advt. to Women, Inc., N.Y.C., 1975-86; pres. Bellvinent Communications, Inc., N.Y.C., 1986—. Served to capt. USMC, 1954-57. Address: 20 Monroe Ave Spring Lake NJ 07762

ERNST, ULRICH ROBERT, textile executive; b. Zürich, Switzerland, Mar. 26, 1947; s. Richard Alfred and Berthe (Bolleter) E.; m. Elisabeth Franziska Hiller, Aug. 22, 1987; 1 child, Tiffany Chantal Jacqueline. MBA, U. Zürich, 1972. Owner, dir. ETU Mgmt. Cons., Zürich, 1973-80; pres., bd. dirs. Tiffanys Socimex Group, Zürich, 1975—.

ERON, LEONARD DAVID, psychology educator; b. Newark, Apr. 22, 1920; s. Joseph I. and Sarah (Hilfman) E.; m. Madeline Marcus, Mar. 21, 1950; children—Joan Hobson, Don, Barbara. B.S., CCNY, 1941; M.A., Columbia U., 1946; Ph.D., U. Wis., 1949. Diplomate Am. Bd. Profl. Psychology. Asst. prof. psychology and psychiatry Yale U., New Haven, 1948-55; dir. research Rip Van Winkle Found., 1955-62; prof. psychology U. Iowa, Iowa City, 1962-69; research prof. U. Ill.-Chgo., 1969—. Author 7 books; editor Jour. Abnormal Psychology, 1973-80; assoc. editor Am. Psychologist, 1986—; contbr. numerous articles to profl. jours. Served to 1st lt. AUS, 1942-45. Fulbright lectr., U. Amsterdam, 1967-68; recipient Fulbright Sr. Scholar award, Queensland U., Australia, 1976-77, James McKeen Cattell Sabbatical award, U. Rome, 1984-85. Fellow Am. Psychol. Assn. (Disting. Contbns. to Knowledge award 1980), Am. Orthopsychiat. Assn., AAAS; mem. Midwestern Psychol. Assn. (pres. 1985-86), Internat. Soc. for Research in Aggression (pres. 1988—). Office: U Ill Dept Psychology Chicago IL 60680

ERREY, JOHN RICHARD, photographic business executive; b. Camperdown, Victoria, Australia, Dec. 2, 1944; arrived in Japan, 1987.; s. Reginald Gilbert and Nancy (Duke) E.; m. Renate Karin Preussler, Dec. 9, 1967; children: Craig Steffen, Jason Cameron. BS, Melbourne U., 1965; PhD, Monash U., Melbourne, 1969. So. region mgr. Kodak (Australasia) Pty Ltd., Melbourne, 1976-79, processing labs. mgr., 1979-83, regional ops. mgr., 1983-85; chief exec. officer Pacific Photofinishing Pty Ltd., Sydney, 1985-87; v.p. Kodak Imagica KK, Tokyo, 1987—; Mem. Nat. Photographic Mktg. (bd. dirs. Queensland area,1983—), Fotographics North Queensland (bd. dirs. 1983—), Photo Mktg. Assn., Australian Inst. Mktg. Club: Tokyo Am. Office: Kodak Imagica KK Gotanda NT Bldg, 1-18-9 Nishigotanda, Shinagawa-Ku 141 Tokyo, Japan

ERRICKSON, BARBARA BAUER, electronic equipment company executive; b. Pitts., Apr. 5, 1944; d. Edward Ewing Bauer and Margaret J. McConnell; m. James Jay Burcham, June 30, 1966 (div. May 1972); children: James Jay II, Linda Lee; m. William Newel Errickson, Apr. 9, 1976 (div. Feb. 1987); children: David Reid, Amy Beth. BA, U. Ill., 1966; MBA, So. Meth. U., 1981. Programming trainee Allstate Ins. Co., Northbrook, Ill., 1973; programmer, team leader Motorola, Inc., Chgo., 1974-78; supr. systems Tex. Instruments, Inc., Dallas, 1978-81, product line mgr. worldwide shipping systems, 1981-83, product line mgr. shipping, inventory systems, 1983-84, mgr. mktg. info. systems, 1985, mgr. benefit systems, 1986—; dir., billing and software developer Spring Park Home Owners, Garland-Richardson, Tex., 1984—, pres. and chmn. fin., 1985, v.p. legal, 1986; active Dallas Women's Ctr., 1984—; mem. bus. adv. council So. Meth U. Bus. Adv. Program; United Way chmn. mktg. systems Tex. Instruments, 1985. Recipient Women in Leadership cert. YWCA Met. Chgo., 1977. Mem. Am. Mgmt. Assn., Am. Women in Computing (bd. dirs. 1987—), Community Assns. Inst., So. Meth. U. MBA Soc., Beta Gamma Sigma. Republican. Presbyterian. Club: Spring Park Racqette. Avocations: sailing, horseback riding, reading, oil painting. Home: 6702 Lakeshore Dr Garland TX 75042 Office: Tex Instruments Inc 6500 Chase Oaks Blvd PO Box 869305 Plano TX 75086

ERROLL, FREDERICK JAMES, container manufacturing company executive; b. May 27, 1914; s. George Murison and Kathleen Donovan Edington E.; m. Elizabeth Erroll, 1950. Student Trinity Coll., Cambridge, Eng. Engr., Met.-Vickers Elec. Co. Ltd., Manchester, Eng., 1936-38; commd. 4th County of London Yeomanry, 1939; tech appointments in connection with tank constrn. and testing, 1940-43; service in India and Burma, 1944-45, col., 1945; with Altrincham and Sale, 1945-64; parliamentary sec. Ministry of Supply, 1955-56; econ. sec to the Treasury, 1958-59; minister of State, 1959-61; minister of Power, 1963-64; chmn. Bowater Corp., London, 1973-84; chmn. Consol. Gold Fields, 1976-82, pres., 1982—; chmn. Flakt Ltd., 1971-85, Whessoe Ltd., 1970-87. Pres. Hispanic and Luso-Brazilian Councils, 1969-73; dep. chmn. Decimal Currency Bd., 1966-71; chmn. Com. on Liquor Licensing, 1971-72; trustee Westminster Abbey Trust, 1978—. Mem. Council Inst. Dirs. (chmn. 1973-76, pres. 1976—), London C. of C. (pres. 1966-69), U.K.-South Africa Trade Assn., Elec. Research Assn. Office: House of Lords, London SW1A 0PW, England also: Consol Gold Fields PLC, 31 Charles II St, London SW1Y 4AG, England *

ERSHAD, HUSSAIN MUHAMMAD, president of People's Republic of Bangladesh; b. Rangpur, Pakistan, Feb. 1, 1930; grad. U. Dacca, 1950, student Nat. Def. Coll., New Delhi, 1975. Commd. Pakistan Army, 1952, advanced through grades to lt. col., 1969; comdr. 3d East Bengal Regiment, 1969-70, 7th East Bengal Regiment, 1971-72; adj. gen. Bangladesh Army upon repatriation from Pakistan, advanced through grades to lt. gen., 1979; dep. chief Army Staff, 1975-78, chief of Army Staff, 1978; led mil. takeover in Bangladesh, 1982, ret., 1986; chief of state Bangladesh, 1982—; pres. Council of Ministers, 1982—; supreme commdr. Bangladesh Armed Forces, pres., 1984—; first chmn. South Asian Assn. Regional Cooperation. Author 2 books poetry. Chmn. Nat. Sports Control Bd.; pres. Bangladesh Lawn Tennis Fedn.; chief adv. Bangladesh Muktijoddha Sangshad; chmn. coordination and control cell for Nat. Security; chmn. governing bodies Cadet Colls.; bd. trustees Sena Kalyan Sangstha. Recipient UN Population award, 1987. Office: President's House (Bangabhaban), Dhaka Bangladesh

ERSKINE, RALPH, architect and town planner; b. London, Feb. 24, 1914; came to Sweden, 1939; s. George and Mildred (Gough) E.; m. Ruth Monica Francis, Aug. 29, 1939; children—Jane Kristina, Karin Elizabeth, Patrick Jon. RIBA, Regent St. Poly., London, 1937, MRIPI, 1938; postgrad. Royal Acad. Arts, Stockholm; Dr.Tech. (hon.), U. Lund, 1975; Dr. Litt. (hon.), Heriot-Watt U., Edinburgh, Scotland, 1982. Cert. architect, town planner. Pvt. practice architecture, Drottningholm, Sweden, 1940—. Decorated comdr. Brit. Empire, 1978; recipient Kasper Salin prize, 1970, 81; Swedish Ytong prize, 1974; Litteris et Artibus medal, Sweden, 1980; Guld Kanga award, Stockholm, 1983; Gold medal Royal Architecture Inst. of Can., 1982; Wolf Found. Internat. prize, 1984; Royal Gold medal Royal Inst. Brit. Architects, 1987. *

ERTEGUN, AHMET MUNIR, record company executive; b. Istanbul, Turkey, 1923; s. M. Munir and Hayrunisa Rustem (Temel) E.; m. Ioana Maria Banu, Apr. 6, 1961. B.A., St. John's Coll., Annapolis, Md., 1944; postgrad., Georgetown U., 1944-46. Co-founder Atlantic Records, N.Y.C., 1947; chmn. bd., chief exec. officer Atlantic Records, 1947—; co-founder Cosmos Soccer Club, N.Y.C., 1971; pres. Cosmos Soccer Club, 1971-83; chmn. Am. Turkish Soc., Rock and Roll Hall Fame Found., Am. br. Nordoff-Robbins Music Therapy Ctr.; trustee Parrish Art Mus.; mem. adv. council Dept. Near Eastern Studies Princeton U. Producer various Grammy-Award-winning records; writer various award-winning songs. Recipient Humanitarian award Conf. Personal Mgrs., 1977, Humanitarian of Yr. award T.J. Martell Found. Leukemia Research, 1978, Humanitarian award Nat. Conf. Christians and Jews, 1987, TTV Turkish Presl. award, 1987, Golden Plate Am. Acad. award, 1988 Achievement; named Man of Yr. United Jewish Appeal, 1970, Turkish Am. Yr., Am. by Choice, 1986; inductee Rock and Roll Hall Fame, 1987, Best Dressed Hall Fame, 1987. Mem. Rec. Industry Assn. Am. (dir.), Black Music Assn. (dir.), Nat. Assn. Record Merchandisers (Presdl. award 1977), Nat. Acad. Rec. Arts and Scis., ASCAP, Broadcast Music Industry. Office: Atlantic Records 75 Rockefeller Plaza New York NY 10019

ERUMSELE, ANDREW AKHIGBE, development policy analyst; b. Auchi, Nigeria, Nov. 18, 1944; came to U.S., 1966, naturalized, 1971; s. Erumsele Bello and Itete (Isadoh) Iyoke; m. Mary Catherine Wimbley, Dec. 6, 1969 (div. 1975); 1 child, Uwadia Alexis; m. Laura Ann Stepanski, Jan. 21, 1987; 1 child Ashley Idiagbon. BA magna cum laude, Loyola U., Los Angeles, 1969; MPA (Univ. scholar, Nigerian Govt. scholar), UCLA, 1971; MA, Am. U., 1974, PhD, 1977. Leadership fellow Los Angeles County Planning Commn., 1969-70; research fellow UN Inst. for Tng. and Research, 1970; mem. staff U.S. Congressional Commn. on Reorgn. of D.C. Govt., 1972-73; mgmt. and policy analyst U. D.C., Washington, 1973—, also asst. to dean Coll. Life Scis.; founder, pres. Devel. Analytics, Inc., 1983—; cons. Internat. City Mgmt. Assn., Orgn. of African Unity, Inst. for Public Adminstrn. Recipient Hall of Nations award Am. U., Washington, 1972. Mem. Am. Soc. for Public Adminstrn., Acad. Polit. Sci., Soc. for Internat. Devel., Am. Soc. for Internat. Law, Pi Gamma Mu. Democrat. Moslem. Spl. corr. for various African newspapers. Office: PO Box 39067 Washington DC 20016

ERVERDI, EZEL, editor, builder; b. Erzurum, Turkey, Oct. 22, 1943; s. Osman Nabi and Nihade (Cinisli) E.; m. Nevra Yolac, Oct. 25, 1973; children—Aslihan, Osman Kerim, Asim Onur. PhD, Cerrahpasa Faculty Med., Istanbul, 1973. Founder, owner Hareket Pub. Co., Istanbul, 1966-77, Dergah Pub. Co., Istanbul, 1976—, Dergah Kitapcilik, Istanbul, 1975—, Emek Matbaacilik, Istanbul, 1978—. Editor books and encys. Turk Dili Encyclopedia Islami Bilgiler Ans., 1976. Islam. Office: Dergah Yayinlari, Nuruosmaniye Cad, Istanbul, Cagaloglu Turkey

ERWIN, CHESLEY PARA, JR., utility company executive, lawyer; b. Milw., Apr. 6, 1953; s. Chesley Para and Constance June (Raab) E.; student Occidental Coll., 1971-72; A.B., Stanford U., 1974; M.A. in Public Policy and Adminstrn., U. Wis., Madison, 1976, M.S. in Bus., 1976, J.D./M.B.A., U. Wis., 1987; m. Karen Jane Leonard, Dec. 27, 1974. Bar: Wis. 1987, U.S. Dist. Ct. (ea. and we. dists) Wis. 1987. Intern, Bur. Fiscal Policy Planning and Analysis, Wis. Dept. Revenue, 1976; energy researcher energy systems and policy research group Inst. Environ. Studies, U. Wis., Madison, 1974-76; health planning analyst Wis. Dept. Health and Social Services, Madison, 1976-77; energy analyst Office State Planning and Energy, Wis. Dept. Adminstrn., Madison, 1977-78; govt. relations specialist Wis. Power & Light Co., Madison, 1978-81; regulatory affairs advisor, 1981-85, coordinator environ. regulation, 1985-88. Mem. New Republican Conf. Wis., 1976—; coordinator Anderson for Pres., Dane County, Wis., 1979-80; moderator, pres. First Congl. United Ch. of Christ, Oconomowoc, Wis., 1986; alt. del. Rep. Nat. Conv., 1980; mem. Waukesha County Solid Waste Mgmt. Bd., 1982-85. Mem. ABA, Am. Soc. Public Adminstrn., Chgo. Council Fgn. Relations. Republican. Home: 820 Old Tower Rd Oconomowoc WI 53066

ERZINGER, DENNIS EUGENE, SR., factory automation executive; b. Elkins, W.Va., Feb. 21, 1951; s. Vincent Joseph and Jacqueline (James) E.; m. Kathy Parneace McClam, June 22, 1974; children: Amberlyn Marie, Dennis E. Jr. AA, Charles County Community Coll., La Plata, Md., 1971; BS in Acctg., Carson-Newman Coll., 1973. Sales rep. Skil Corp., Miami, Fla. and Atlanta, 1973-75, Black & Decker Corp., Atlanta, 1975-78; internat. mktg. mgr. Black & Decker Corp., Towson, Md., 1978-80, mktg. mgr. research and devel., 1980-83; product mgr. robotic and vision systems dept. Gen. Electric Corp., Orlando, Fla., 1983-86; mktg. mgr. Vistronic, Honeywell Inc., Denver, 1986-87, Advanced Indsl. Sensors Microswitch div. of Honeywell, Denver, 1988—; cons. Johns Hopkins Univ., Balt., 1981; instr. Goucher Coll., Towson, 1982-84. Named Cons. of Yr. Jr. Achievement, Balt., 1982. Mem. Am. Mktg. Assn., Licensing Exec. Soc., Soc. Mfg. Engrs., AAAS. Republican. Baptist. Office: Honeywell Inc 4800 E Dry Creek Rd Littleton CO 80122

ESAKI, LEO, physicist; b. Osaka, Japan, Mar. 12, 1925; came to U.S., 1960; s. Soichiro and Niyoko (Ito) E.; m. Masako Kondo, May, 31, 1986; children from previous marriage: Nina Yvonne, Anna Eileen, Eugene Leo. B.S., U. Tokyo, 1947, Ph.D., 1959. With Sony Corp., Japan, 1956-60; with Thomas J. Watson Research Center, IBM, Yorktown Heights, N.Y., 1960—; IBM fellow Thomas J. Watson Research Center, IBM, 1967—, mgr. device research, 1965—; dir. IBM-Japan. Recipient Morris N. Liebmann Meml. prize I.E.E.E., 1961; Stuart Ballantine medal Franklin Inst., 1961; Japan Acad. award, 1965; Nobel Prize in physics, 1973; decorated Order of Culture Govt. of Japan, 1974. Fellow Am. Phys. Soc. (councillor-at-large 1971-74); IEEE; Fellow Japan Phys. Soc., Am. Vacuum Soc. (dir. 1973-74); mem. Am. Acad. Arts and Scis., Nat. Acad. Scis. (fgn. asso.), Nat. Acad. Engring. (fgn. asso.), Academia Nacional de Ingenieria Mex. (corr.), Japan Acad. Home: Rural Rt 4 Box 105 Young Rd Katonah NY 10536 Office: Watson Research Ctr IBM PO Box 218 Yorktown Heights NY 10598

ESCALANTE, ROEL, material management executive; b. Los Angeles, July 16, 1937; s. Angel and Maria (Arellanos) E.; m. Myrna L. Walterscheid, May 3, 1985; 1 son, Anthony Miles. AA, Valley Jr. Coll., 1959. Asst. purchasing agt. Colony Paint & Chem. Co., Los Angeles, 1964-67; buyer Traid Corp., Los Angeles, 1967-69; asst. purchasing mgr. Walt Disney Prodns., Burbank, Calif., 1969-76; dir. purchasing MCA, Inc., Universal City, Calif., 1976-79, corp. dir. material, div. v.p., 1979—. Mem. Los Aneles Purchasing Mgmt. Assn., Am. Mgmt. Assn., Nat. Assn. Purchasing Mgmt. (cert.), So. Calif. Regional Purchasing Council (bd. dirs.). Republican. Roman Catholic. Home: PO Box 8836 Universal City CA 91608 Office: MCA Inc 100 Universal City Plaza Universal City CA 91608

ESCALE, FRANCOIS ALAIN, anesthetist; b. Tourane, Annam, Republic Vietnam, Aug. 2, 1940; arrived in France, 1946; s. Pierre and Hèlene (Guibier) E.; m. Amaya Zabalza, Oct. 1961; 1 child, Francois-Xavier. Diploma in Aeronautic and Space Medicine, U. Bordeaux, France, 1971; Diploma in Anesthesiology, U. Paris, 1971. Anesthetist Univ. Hosp., Bordeaux, 1970-73; practice medicine specializing in anesthesiology Arcachon, France, 1973—. Author articles, research reports in field. Served to maj. Health Ministry French Army Res., 1968—. Mem. Doctors of the World (founder). Mem. R.P.R. Roman Catholic. Office: Clinique d'Arcachon, 109 Blvd de la Plage, 33120 Arcachon Gironde, France

ESCHENBACH, CHRISTOPH, conductor, pianist; b. Breslau, Silesia, Fed. Republic Germany, Feb. 20, 1940. Attended, Hamburg (Fed. Republic Germany) Conservatory, State Conservatory Music, Cologne, Fed. Republic Germany. Performed with leading orchs., including Concertgebouw, Amsterdam, The Netherlands, Paris Orch., London Symphony, Berlin Philharm., Cleve. Orch., London Philharm., Orchestre National de France; soloist with Cleve. Orch. during European Festival Tour, 1967; N.Am. debut Expo '67, Montreal, Que., Can., 1967; soloist with Cleve. Orch., 1969; Carnegie Hall debut with Cleve. Orch., 1969; toured Europe, North and South Am., Israel, Japan; appeared at festivals including Salzburg, Austria, Lucerne, Switzerland, Bonn, W. Ger., Aix-en-Provence, France; chief condr. Staatsphilharmonie Rheinland-Pfalz, Fed. Republic Germany, 1979; first prin. guest condr. Tonhalle Orch., Switzerland, 1981, chief condr., 1982; rec. artist, Deutsche Grammophon, Polydor, EMI; music dir. Houston Symphony Orch., 1988—. Office: care Columbia Artists Mgmt Inc 165 W 57th St New York NY 10019 also: Houston Symphony Orch Jesse H Jones Hall 615 Louisiana St Houston TX 77002 *

ESCHENMOSER, ALBERT, chemist; b. Erstfeld, Aug. 5, 1925; s. Alfons and Johanna (Oesch) E.; m. Elizabeth Baschnonga, 1954; 3 children. Dr.Nat.Sci., Swiss Fed. Inst. Tech., 1956; student Collegium Altdorf,

Kantonsschule St. Gallen, ETH Zurich; Dr. rer.nat. (hon.), U. Fribourg, 1966; D.Sc. (hon.), U. Chgo., 1970, U. Edinburgh, 1979. Privatdozent organic chemistry Swiss Fed. Inst. Tech., 1956, assoc. prof. 1960, prof. organic chemistry, 1965. Fgn. hon. mem. Am. Acad. Arts and Scis., 1966; fgn. assoc. Nat. Acad. Scis. U.S.A., 1973; corr. mem. Akademie der Wissenschaften, Göttingen, 1986—. Recipient Kern award Swiss Fed. Inst. Tech., 1949, Werner award Swiss Chem. Soc., 1956, Ruzicka award Swiss Fed. Inst. Tech., 1958, Fritzsche award Am. Chem. Soc., 1966, Marcel Benoist prize, Switzerland, 1973, R.A. Welch award in Chemistry, Houston, 1974, Kirkwood medal Yale, 1976, A.W.V. Hofmann-Denkmunze, GDCh., 1976, Dannie Heinemann prize Akademie der Wissenschaften Göttingen, 1977, Davy medal Royal Soc. London, 1978, Tetrahedron prize Pergamon Press, 1981, G. Kenner award U. Liverpool, 1982, Arthur C. Cope award Am. Chem. Soc., 1984, Wolf prize for chemistry, 1986. Contbr. articles to profl. jours. Mem. Deutsche Akademie der Naturforscher Leopoldina (Halle), Royal Soc. Chemistry (hon.). Address: Bergstrasse 9, 8700 Kusnacht (ZH) Switzerland *

ESCOLIER, JEAN-CLAUDE, psychiatrist; b. Auxerre, Yonne, France; s. Marc and Josette (Roques) E.; m. Jacqueline Peck; children: Alexandre, Olivier. D of Medicnie, U. Paris, 1966. Pvt. practice psychiatrist Paris, 1969—; dept. head Hosp. St. Jean au Dieu, Lyon, France, 1974—. Mem. Syndicate of Psychiatrists (nat. sec.). Office: Hosp St Jean au Dieu, 290 Rt de Vienne, 69008 Lyon France

ESCUDERO, LAUREANO FERNANDO, mathematician, educator, researcher; b. Palazuelo, Valladolid, Spain, Sept. 23, 1942; s. Andres Escudero and Laura Bueno; m. Adela Aldamiz, July 7, 1967; children: Mar, Enrique, Inigo. MSc in Law, Valladolid, Spain, 1965; MSc in Computer Scis., Polytech. U., Madrid, 1971; PhD, Deusto, Bilbao, Spain, 1974. With IBM, Bilbao, 1965-71; advisor IBM Sci. Ctr., Madrid, 1972-75; mgr. edn. sci. programs IBM, Madrid, 1976-77; sci. advisor IBM Sci. Ctr., Palo alto, Calif., 1978-80; sci. sr. IBM Sci. Ctr., Madrid, 1981-85, IBM GMTC, Sindelfingen, Fed. Republic Germany, 1986—; prof. Ad Honorem Scis. Sch. U. Autonoma, Madrid, 1985—. Author: Estadistica Aplicada a la Empresa, 1968 (4 vols.), Teoria de Colas y Simulacion, 1972 (Best Sci. Book award, 1976), Programacion Lineal, 1976, Reconocimiento de Patrones, 1977, Teoria de Grafos, 1978; contbr. numerous articles to profl. jours. Recipient Medalla Merito Aeronautico, Distintivo Blanco, primera clase, Gobierno Espanol, 1985. Mem. N.Y. Acad. Sci., Soc. de Investigacion Operative, Spain, Math. Programming Soc. Roman Catholic. Home: Poniente 51, 28023 Montealina-Pozuelo Madrid Spain Office: IBM Research Ctr PO Box 218 Yorktown NY 10598

ESENWEIN-ROTHE, INGEBORG, economist, statistician; b. Chemnitz, Germany, June 24, 1911; d. Hermann A. and Auguste (Kühl) Rothe; Dr. rer. pol., U. Leipzig (Germany), 1937; Habilitation U. Munster (Germany), 1954; Dr. rer. pol., U. Trier, 1986; m. Hermann O. Esenwein, Mar. 1, 1948. Apprentice to a banking house, 1928-30; with Civil Service, Leipzig, 1938-41, Salzburg, Austria, 1941-45; lectr. polit. econs. and stats. Chemnitz (Germany) Coll., 1947-50; lectr. Coll. Wilhelmshaven (Germany), 1950-61, prof., 1961-62; prof. U. Göttingen (Germany), 1962, U. Erlangen/Nürnberg, 1962-76, emeritus prof., 1976—. Mem. Gesellschaft fur Wirtschafts-und Sozialwissenschaften, Deutsche Statische Gesellschaft, Deutsche Gesellschaft für Bevölkerungswissenschaft e. V., Internat. Union for Sci. Study Population, Internat. Stat. Inst., Akademie fur Raumforschung und Landesplanung. Evangelical Lutheran. Author books, including: Die Verkehrs-Effizienz, 1956, Die Wirtschaftsverbände von 1933 bis 1945, 1965; Allgemeine Wirtschaftsstatistik, 1969; Die Methoden der Wirtschaftsstatistik, vols. 1 and 2, 1976; Einführung in die Demographie/Bevölkerungsstruktur und Bevö lkerhgsprozess aus der Sicht der Statistik, 1982; contbr. articles to profl. publs.; editor: Kompendium der Volkswirtschaftslehre, 2 vols., 5th edit., 1972, Verdienst-Orden d Freistaats Bayern, 1984. Home: 1 Am Stadtpark 430 (Augustinum), 8542 Roth bei, Nürnberg Federal Republic of Germany Office: Wirtschafts-und SozialwissenschafthFakultat, der Universitat Erlangen-Nurnberg, 20 Lange Gasse, D-8500 Nurnberg Federal Republic of Germany

ESHØJ, BIRGER, pension company executive; b. Stoense, Denmark, Dec. 13, 1936; s. Peder Grube and Minna (Larsen) E.; m. Rita Larsen, Sept. 2, 1961 (div. July 1971); 1 child, Henriette; m. Ragnhild Jacobsen, Nov. 1972; 1 child, Dorte. Cert. data process systems engr. Data processing systems analyst ATP, HillerØd, Denmark, 1964-69, mgr. data processing, 1969-77, head tech.-adminstrv. dept., 1977-80, mng. dir., 1980—; mng. dir. AER, HillerØd, 1980—, LG, HillerØd, 1980—; also other orgns.; mem. Danish EDP Council, Copenhagen, 1978-86. Decorated knight Order of Dannebrog. Lodge: Rotary. Home: Rordamsvej 2, DK-3400 Hillerod Denmark Office: ATP Kongens Vaenge 8, DK-3400 Hillerod Denmark

ESIN, NUMAN SABIT, export company executive; b. Biga/Canakkale, Turkey, Oct. 18, 1929; s. Ali Sevket and Ayse E.; m. Aynur Yalcin, July 21, 1957; children: Ali Sevket, Hüseyin Tuğrul, Ayse Nur. Student, Army War Coll., Istanbul, Turkey, 1957-59. Commd. 2nd lt. Turkish Army, 1949, advanced through grades to maj., 1960, ret., 1960; prin. Esin Private Cos., Turkey, Italy, Switzerland, 1963—; chmn. bd. Esin Internat. Transport Co. Inc., Istanbul, 1974-86, Esin Tourism Co. Inc., Istanbul, 1977-86, Esin Indsl. and Agr. Products Export Co. Inc., Istanbul, 1978—, Esin Italiana S.R.L., Modena, Italy, 1980—, Esin SA, Geneva, 1981—; cons. Turkish Embassy, Madrid, 1961-63. Editor, owner: Vatan Daily Newspaper, 1975-78. Asst. to pres. Republican Nat. Paysant Party; mem. Nat. Unity Com. Turkish Parliament. Muslim. Clubs: Galatasaray, Anadolu. Office: Esin Turizm AS, Cumhuriyet Caddesi 47/2 Taksim, 80090 Istanbul Turkey

ESLAMI, HOSSEIN HOJATOL, physician; b. Tehran, Iran, July 30, 1927; s. Abul-Hassan and Assieh (Ghafari) E.; M.D., Tehran U., 1952; m. Jean Chinigo, Apr. 27, 1956; children—Darius, Cyrus. Intern, Jersey City Med. Center, 1955-56; resident in surgery Newark Beth Israel Med. Center, 1956-60, fellow in vascular surgery, 1960-61; practice medicine specializing in surgery and kidney transplantation, Newark, 1961-67; mem. faculty U. of Medicine and Dentistry of N.J., 1969—, dir. organ transplantation, 1968—, dir. surg. edn., 1967—, asso. prof. surgery, 1976—; chief surgery Newark Beth Israel Med. Center. Diplomate Am. Bd. Surgery. Fellow ACS, Acad. Medicine N.J.; mem. Essex County Med. Soc., Med. Soc. N.J., AMA, Am. Soc. Abdominal Surgeons Am. Soc. Artificial Internal Organs, Nat. Kidney Found., Transplantation Soc., Am. Soc. Transpolant Surgeons, N.J. Nephrology Soc. Research kidney and liver transplantations. Contbr. articles to profl. jours. Office: 62 Jefferston St Newark NJ 07105

ESLICK, LEONARD JAMES, philosopher, educator; b. Denver, Nov. 8, 1914; s. Theodore Parker and Leila (Van Natta) E.; m. Florence Elizabeth Weber, May 3, 1935. A.B., U. Chgo., 1934; M.A., Tulane U., 1936; Ph.D., U. Va., 1939. Instr. philosophy Drake U., Des Moines, 1939-42; tutor St. John's Coll., Annapolis, Md., 1943-48; asso. prof. St. Louis U., 1948-57, prof., 1957—; vis. prof. U. Va. at Charlottesville, 1961, U. Ill. at Urbana, 1965, U. Notre Dame, 1968. Assoc. editor: Modern Schoolman, 1950—; editorial Bd.: Process Studies, 1970—; Contbr. articles on metaphysics, Plato, A.N. Whitehead to philos. jours., books. Served with AUS, 1942. Mem. Am. Philos. Assn., Mo. Philos. Assn. (pres. 1958-59), Metaphys. Soc. Am., Cath. Commn. Intellectual and Cultural Affairs, Phi Beta Kappa. Home: 4253 Flora Pl Saint Louis MO 63110

ESPARZA, THOMAS, SR., university athletics administrator; b. Edinburg, Tex., May 21, 1921; s. Greg and T.R. (Tirsa) E.; student Allen Mil. Acad., 1943; BS, Tex. A. & I. U., 1948, MS, 1951, PhD, 1977; m. Esther La Madrid, June 1, 1949; children—Tommy Jr., Steven, Teylene. Coach Edinburg (Tex.) Consol. Ind. Sch. Dist., 1948-68, adminstrv. asst., 1963-65, instructional media cons., 1963-65, athletic events mgr., 1957-68, health, phys. edn. cons., 1950-68; dir. intramurals dept. phys. edn., Pan Am. U., Edinburg, 1968—, univ. chmn. steering com. Nat. Phys. Edn. and Sports Week; mem. steering com. Met. Bank, 1973—. Cons. edn. City Park bd., 1968—; coordinator dist. I, Spl. Olympics, 1968-78; workshop cons. health and phys. edn. to various schs., 1968—; lectr. phys. edn. and athletic dirs., Mexico, 1981—; pres. Edinburg Tchrs. Credit Union, 1958-65, Pan Am. U. Credit Union, 1970; mem. selection com. Steering Com. of Rio Grande Valley All-Acad. Football Team, 1985—; pres. Leo Najo Amateur Baseball League, 1985—; co-coordinator Rio Grande Valley Leo Najo Baseball Reunion, Edinburg; founder, v.p. Rio Grande Valley Sports Hall of Fame, 1985—. Bd. dirs. Am. Cancer Soc., 1948-73, v.p. Edinburg unit, 1976, ednl. dir. Edinburg unit, 1977—; founder ann. Panocha Bread Cook-Off, 1979. Served with USNR, 1946-48. Named to Alice (Tex.) Baseball Hall of Fame, 1986, Rio Grande Valley Hall of Fame, 1979, South Tex. Baseball Hall of Fame, 1984, Recreation (emeritus); honoree Rio Grande Valley East-West All-Star Baseball Game, 1985. Mem. NEA, AAHPER, Tex. High Sch. Coaches Assn., Tex. Assn. Health Phys. Edn., Tex. State Tchrs. Assn., Nat. Intramural Assn., Edinburg C. of C., Hidalgo County Hist. Soc. (bd.), Am. Legion (comdr. post 1970-75, 83—, 15th dist. baseball chmn. 1975—, 3d div. baseball chmn. 1975—, state baseball chmn. 1980—, mem. state Americanism, constn. and by-laws, credentials coms. 1976—, nat. exec. com. 1983—, nat. legis. council 1982—, Tex. legis. council 1988—), DAV (life). Author numerous publs. in field. Home: 811 S 16th Ave Edinburg TX 78539

ESPEGARD, SVEND BIRKE, educator, literary critic; b. Alborg, Denmark, Aug. 31, 1941; s. Arne Anders and Carola Czermak (Nielsen) E.; m. Marianne Petersen, Aug. 31, 1968 (div. 1973); 1 child, Torsten; m. Vera Anita Hassel, July 12, 1975; children: Ranva, Nina. MA in Danish and Russian, Arhus (Denmark) U., 1970. Sr. master Risskov Amtsgymnasium, Arhus, 1970—; external examiner Faroese Directorate Edn., Torshavn, Faroe Islands, 1976—; lectr. extension courses U. Denmark, 1984—. Contbr. revs. and articles to profl. publs. Served with Danish Army, 1960-61. Home: Lyngsvinget 31 Tilst, 8381 Mundelstrup Aarhus Denmark Office: Risskov Amtsgymnasium, Tranekaervej 70, 8240 Risskov Aarhus Denmark

ESPELETA, FEDERICO CARPENA, JR., physician, business educator; b. Pasay City, Metro-Manila, Philippines, June 22, 1943; s. Federico Flores and Gaudiosa Mojica (Carpena) E.; m. Trinidad Ison Colon, Feb. 6, 1972; children: Federico C. III, Marita C. BS, U. of East, Manila, 1965; MD, U. East Ramon Magsaysay, Quezon City, The Philippines, 1970; B in Bus. Mgmt., U. of City of Manila, 1977, MBA, 1979. Resident physician Children's Med. Ctr., Quezon City, 1971-73; health ctr. physician Pasay City Health Dept., 1973; family and co. physician United Labs., Inc., Mandaluyong, The Philippines, 1973-78, med. officer, 1978—; adj. faculty business Jose Rizal Coll., Mandaluyong, 1979-86; mem. Main Security and Safety Com., Mandaluyong, 1978—. Mem. Antipolo Valley Homeowners, Rizal, Philippines, 1981—. Recipient Plaque of Appreciation, Makati Host Lions Club, 1980, Plaque of Appreciation, Panday Pira Lions Club, 1983, Presdl. Award Merit, Antipolo Valley Homeowners, 1986. Fellow Philippine Occupational and Indsl. Med. Assn.; mem. Philippine Med. Assn., Mandaluyong Med. Soc., Indsl. Med. Assn. Philippines (assoc. 1975-78), Philippine Acad. Family Physicians, UERMMMC Med. Alumni, Children's Med. Ctr. Alumni, U. of City of Manila BBM-MBA Alumni, Beta Sigma. Roman Catholic. Lodge: Lions. Office: United Labs Inc, 66 United St, Mandaluyong, Metro Manila Philippines

ESPINOSA DE LOS REYES, JORGE, Mexican ambassador to the U.S.; b. Mexico City, June 20, 1920; s. Isidro and Amparo (Sanchez) E.; m. Sofia Davila, Sept. 30, 1949; children—Jorge, Silvia, Pablo, Monica. B.S., Frances Morelos Coll., Mexico City, 1939; M. in Econs., Nat. U., Mexico City, 1944; postgrad., London Sch. Econs., Eng., 1945-47; LL.D. (hon.), U. N.Mex., 1983. Prof. econ. Nat. U., Mexico City, 1948-61; prof. econ. Tech. Inst., Mexico City, 1953-55; dir. industry Ministry of Industry and Commerce, Mexico City, 1959-61, chief mgmt. officer, 1961-64; dep. dir. gen. Petroleos Mexicanos, Mexico City, 1964-76, Banco de Mexico, Mexico City, 1976-77; dir. gen. Nacional Financiera, Mexico City, 1977-82; ambassador to U.S. Govt. of Mexico, Washington, 1983—; dir. gen. Sch. Econ., Nat. Polytech. Inst., Mexico City, 1960-63; Mex.'s rep. in internat. confs. dealing with oil industry and fin. matters. Author: Economic Relations Between Mexico and the U.S.A., 1951. Contbr. articles to profl. jours. Mem., Instnl. Revolutionary Party of Mexico, 1954—. Office: Embassy of Mexico 2829 16th St NW Washington DC 20009

ESPINOZA, DANIEL R., government administrator; b. Johnstown, Pa., Mar. 22, 1933; s. Alfonso P. and Helen (Rushnak) E.; m. LaVerne F. Cernogorsky, Aug. 19, 1955; children—Diane J., David R., Deborah A. A.A. in Printing Mgmt., Montgomery Coll., 1971; A.A. in Bus. Administrn., B.S. in Bus. Administrn., both U. Md. Print specialist print procurement U.S. Govt. Print Office, Washington, 1970-72, asst. chief contracts, paper, material procurement, 1972-76, chief dept. print plant, 1980, asst. supt. field printing, 1977-82, print specialist copy mgmt. HUD, Washington, 1976-77; div. adminstr. Dept. of Transp., Washington, 1982—; bd. dirs. Met. Washington Sch. of Printing, Rockville, Md., 1974-76; program chmn. Copier, Duplicator Group, IRAC, Washington, 1977; v.p. Print House Craftsmen, Washington, 1979-80, 81-82. Served with U.S. Army, 1953-55. Recipient Superior Service award U.S. Govt. Print Office, 1963, 64; Spl. Achievement award U.S. Print Office, 1971, 72. Mem. Franklin Tech. Soc., Washington Lithographic Club, Info. Resources Adv. Council-Copiers-Duplicators Group, Washington Craftsmen Club (v.p. 1979-80, 1981-82) (Outstanding Craftsman of Yr., 1982). Home: 12779 Lost Creek Ct Manassas VA 22111 Office: Dept Transp 7th & D St SW Washington DC 20590

ESPMARK, KJELL, literary historian, poet, novelist; b. Strömsund, Jämtland, Sweden, Feb. 19, 1930; s. Erik and Margit (Christensson) E.; m. Anna Sjögren, June 21, 1959; children: Catharina, Erik. PhD in Comparative Lit., U. Stockholm, 1964. Assoc. prof. comparative lit. U. Stockholm, 1964-78, prof., 1978—. Author: Att Översätta Själen, 1977, Det Litterära Nobelpriset, 1986, Den Motsträviga Skapelsen, 1987, Glömskan, 1987; (poems) Béla Bartók against the Third Reich, 1986. Recipient Övralid prize Stiftelsen Övralid, 1974, Svenska Dagbladet Literary prize Svenska Dagbladet, 1975, Carl Emil Englund prize Stiftelsen Litteraturfrämjandet, 1976, Esselte Literary prize, 1979. Mem. The Swedish Acad. (Schück prize 1980, Bellman prize 1985). Home: Eriksbergsgaten 12 A, 114 30 Stockholm Sweden Office: U Stockholm, Dept History Literature, 106 91 Stockholm Sweden

ESPOSITO, JOHN VINCENT, lawyer; b. Logan, W.Va., Dec. 25, 1946; s. Vito T. and Mary Frances (Lamp) E. B.A. magna cum laude, W.Va. U., 1968, J.D., 1971. Bar: W.Va. 1971, S.C. 1980, U.S. dist. ct. (no. and so. dists.) W.Va., S.C. Legis. aide to Congressman Ken Hechler, 4th Dist. W.Va., 1971; counsel to Hans McCourt, Pres. W.Va. State Senate, 1972; instr. So. W.Va. Community Coll., 1972-74; sr. ptnr. Esposito & Esposito, Logan, W.Va. and Hilton Head Island, S.C., 1972—; arbitrator United Mine Workers Am.-Coal Operators Assn.; spl. judge Cir. Ct. Logan County (W.Va.); commr. in chancery Cir. Ct. Logan County; judge Mcpl. Ct. City of Chapmanville (W.Va.); spl. pros. atty., W. Va. Citizen Ambassador to People's Republic of China and Soviet Union for legal cons. Founder, Citizens Environ. Quality, 1983. Served to 2d lt. U.S. Army. U. Calif. Hastings Coll. Law Coll. Advocacy scholar. Mem. ABA, Assn. Trial Lawyers Am., Am. Judicature Soc., W.Va. State Bar, S.C. Bar, Internat. Platform Assn. Coauthor: Laws for Young Mountaineers, 1973-74. Office: One Saint Augustine PO Box 5705 Hilton Head Island SC 29938 also: 401 Stratton St PO Box 1680 Logan WV 25601

ESQUIVEL, AGERICO LIWAG, research physicist; b. Manila, June 5, 1932; came to U.S., 1957, naturalized, 1971; s. Enrique Frias and Pacita Ramos (Liwag) E. AB, Berchmans Coll., Manila, 1955, MA, 1956; PhD, St. Louis U., 1963. Research assoc. St. Louis U., 1961-63; research scientist Research Inst. Advanced Studies, Balt., 1963, Materials Research Lab., Martin Co., Orlando, Fla., 1964-65; sr. research engr. Materials Tech. Labs., Boeing Co., Seattle, 1965-71; postdoctoral fellow Advanced Research Projects Agy., U. So. Calif., Los Angeles, 1971-73; mem. tech. staff Hughes Aircraft Co., Culver City, Calif., 1973-76, Semiconductor Process and Design Ctr., Tex. Instruments, Inc., Dallas, 1976—. U.S. and Japan patents, issued and pending, nonvolatile memory devices; contbr. papers to jours. and procs. on X-ray, electron diffraction, radiation hardening, cathodoluminescence, deep level transient spectroscopy, electronic materials, nonvolatile memories, trench isolated EPROMs, FLASH EPROMS, submicron CMOS devices; sci. papers presented at internat. symposia in U.S., Japan and Europe. NSF postdoctoral fellow, 1963. Mem. Am. Phys. Soc., IEEE Elec. Devices Soc., Electrochem. Soc., Sigma Xi, Pi Mu Epsilon. Republican. Office: Tex Instruments Inc MS-944 PO Box 655012 Dallas TX 75265

ESQUIVEL, MANUEL, prime minister Belize; b. Belize City, Belize, May 2, 1940; s. John Peter and Laura (Bolton) E.; m. Kathleen Levy; children—David, Laura, Ruth. B.S. in Physics, Loyola U., New Orleans, 1962, L.H.D. (hon.), 1986; cert. physics edn., Bristol U., Eng., 1967. Instr. physics and math. St. John's Coll., Belize, 1963-82; founding mem. United Democratic Party, 1973, party chmn., 1976-82, party leader, 1982, mem., leader opposition bus. in senate, 1979-84, prime minister Belize, 1984—; mem. Her Majesty's Privy Council, 1986—; mem. Belize City Council, 1974-80. Office: Office of Prime Minister,, Belmopan Belize

ESQUIVEL, RODERICK LORENZO, vice president of Panama, gynecologist; b. Gualaca, Chiriqui, Panama, May 12, 1927; s. Lorenzo and Ana (Clement) E.; m. Jean Klein; children: Anita, Juan David, Miguel, Rodrigo Jose. BS, Ripon Coll., 1949, LLD, 1986; MD, U. Chgo., 1953. Resident in ob-gyn Gorgas Hosp., Panama, 1954-57; practice medicine specializing in ob-gyn, Panama City, Panama, 1960-86; chief ob-gyn dept. U. Panama, 1969-78; minister labor and health Republic of Panama, 1964, then v.p.; now underground leader for democracy in Panama against Noriega dictatorship, 1987—; ambassaor O.I.T., Geneva, Panama, 1965; adviser Pan Am Health Orgn., Washington, 1979—; population expert Fedn. Med. Schs. Panama, 1980-83. Mem. polit. commn. Liberal Com. Panama, 1967; pres., 1983; founder Fedn. Liberal Parties Cen. Am. and the Caribbean. Decorated Orden Hipolito Unanue (Peru). Mem. Med. Assn. Panama, Gunecologists and Obs. Assn. Panama. Roman Catholic. Lodge: Rotary (pres. 1983). Avocations: fishing, scuba diving. Office: Palacio Presidencial, Panama City Republic of Panama

ESSBERGER, KARIN LISE-LOTTE MARGARET, publishing executive; b. Cape Town, Republic of South Africa, Dec. 30, 1962; d. Margaret (De Vos) E. BA, U. Witwatersrand, South Africa, 1984. Prodn. asst. Brigadier Film Co., Johannesburg, Republic South Africa, 1984-85; mgr., producer Lynton Stephenson Prodn., Johannesburg, 1985-86; dir. Lynton Stephenson Prodn., 1986-87. Office: Who's Who Southern Africa, PO Box 81284, Parkhurst Republic of South Africa

ESSENWANGER, OSKAR MAXIMILIAN KARL, supervisory research physicist, educator; b. Munich, Bavaria, Germany, Aug. 25, 1920; came to U.S., 1956, naturalized, 1963; s. Oskar and Anna E.; m. Katharina D. Dorfer, June 17, 1947. B.S., U. Danzig, Germany, 1941; M.S., U. Vienna, Austria, 1943; Ph.D., U. Wurzburg, Germany, 1950. Instr., meteorologist German Air Force, 1944-45; research meteorologist German Weather Service, 1946-57; project assoc. dept. meteorology U. Wis., 1956; prin. investigator Nat. Weather Records Center, Asheville, N.C., 1957-60; supervisory research physicist, research dir. U.S. Army Missile Command, Huntsville, Ala., 1961—; adj. prof. earth and environ. sci. U. Ala.-Huntsville, 1970—. Author: Applied Statistics in Atmospheric Science, 1976, Elements of Statistical Analysis, 1986; contbg. author, editor: International Compendium World Survey of Climatology, vol. I, 1984; contbr. numerous articles to profl. jours. Named Profl. of Yr. 1987 Huntsville Assn. Tech. Socs.; recipient Sci. and Engring. Achievement award Missile Command, Redstone Arsenal, Ala., 1965. Fellow AIAA (assoc., Ala.-Miss. div. Hermann Oberth award 1981, v.p. Ala.-Miss. div. 1984-85, pres. 1985-86); mem. Am. Soc. Quality Control (sr.), Am. Meterol. Soc. (profl.), Ala. Acad. Sci. (v.p. 1973), Sigma Xi (v.p. club 1976-77, pres. chpt. 1977-82, Outstanding Researcher 1977). Home: 610 Mountain Gap Dr Huntsville AL 35803

ESSEX, MYRON ELMER, microbiology educator; b. Coventry, R.I., Aug. 17, 1939; s. Myron Elmer and Ruth Hazel (Knight) E.; m. Elizabeth Katherine Jordan, June 19, 1966; children—Holly Anne, Carrie Lisa. B.S., U. R.I., Kingston, 1962; D.V.M., Mich. State U., East Lansing, 1967; M.S., Mich. State U., 1967; Ph.D., U. Calif.-Davis, 1970; M.A. (hon.), Harvard U., 1979; DSc (hon.), U. R.I., 1987, Mich. State U., 1988. Research fellow Karolinska Inst., Stockholm, 1970-72; asst. prof. Harvard U., Cambridge, Mass., 1972-76, assoc. prof., 1976-78, prof., chmn. dept. microbiology, 1978-81; chmn. dept. cancer biology Harvard U., 1981—, assoc. dir. Ctr. Infectious Diseases, 1981-88, chmn. AIDS Inst., 1988—; mem. sci. adv. bd. Cambridge Biosci. Corp., 1981—, ARC, 1985—; chmn. AIDS Inst. Harvard U., 1988—. Editor: Viruses in Cancer, 1980. Co-editor: Human T-cell Leukemia Viruses, 1984. Contbr. articles to profl. jours. Patentee test for human T leukemia virus infection and AIDS blood tests and vaccines. Bd. sci. counselors Nat. Cancer Inst., 1982—; mem. Lasker award jury Albert & Mary Lasker Found., 1982-84; sci. adv. bd. ARC, 1985—. Leukemia Soc. Am. scholar, 1972; Am. Cancer Soc. Nat. Cancer Inst. grantee, 1973—; recipient Bronze medal Am. Cancer Soc., 1978, Ralston Purina research award, 1985, Outstanding Investigator award Nat. Cancer Inst., 1985, Disting. Alumnus award Mich. State U., 1986, Lasker award, 1986, Carnation Research award, 1987, Disting. Alumnus award U. Calif. Davis, 1987. Mem. AAAS, Am. Assn. Cancer Research, Am. Soc. Microbiology, Am. Assn. Immunologists, AVMA, Internat. Assn. Research in Leukemia, Infectious Disease Soc. Am., Am. Soc. Virology, Nat. Acad. Practitioners, Reticuloendothelial Soc., Soc. Gen. Microbiology, Am. Cancer Soc. (research com. Mass. br. 1975—), Leukemia Soc. Am. (adv. bd. 1978-83, 85—, med./sci. adv. com. 1978—). Office: Harvard Sch Pub Health Dept Cancer Biology 665 Huntington Ave Boston MA 02115

ESSIEN, MARTIN EFIONG, metallurgical engineer, engineering and marketing consultant; b. Efa, Etinan, Cross River State, Nigeria, Sept. 22, 1944; s. Efiong Ekong and Iquo Emmanuel (Inyang) E.; m. Alsandyra Lee Jackson, June 12, 1968 (dec. 1977); children: Umana, Iko; m. Justina Ada Chimezie, July 7, 1978. BSc in Metall. Engring., U. Ill., 1968; MSc in Engring. Mechanics, U. Mo., Rolla, 1975; postgrad., Yale U., 1976. Registered profl. engr., Ill., Nigeria, France. Chartered engr., Eng. Metallurgist Olin corp., Stamford, Conn., 1973-76; engr. Michelin et CIE, Clermont Ferrand, France, 1977-78; shop mgr. Michelin Nigeria Ltd., Port Harcourt, 1978-80; vice rector Fed. Poly., Bauchi, Nigeria, 1980-82; rector Fed. Poly., 1982-83; gen. mgr. Sunshine Batteries Ltd., Ikot Ekpene, Nigeria, 1983-86; dir. Delta Steel Co., Warri, Nigeria, 1985-86; prin. ptnr. Martin Essien & Assocs., London, Lagos and N.Y.C., 1986—; chmn. Validback U.K. Ltd., London, 1986—; mem. Nigerian Steel Devel. Authority, Lagos, 1972-73; lectr. metallurgy Ahmadu Bello U., Zaria, 1972; corrosion engr. Shell-BP Nigeria Ltd., Port Harcourt, 1970-77; metallurgist Kennecott Copper Corp., Salt Lake City, 1968-70. Mem. Instn. Metallurgists, Am. Soc. Mech. Engrs., Assoc. of the Inst. Mech. Engrs. Clubs: Ronnie Scott (London), Bauchi (Nigeria). Office: Validback Ltd, 37A Maida Vale, London W91TP, England

ESSIG, WILLIAM JOHN, lawyer; b. South Bend, Ind., July 13, 1938; s. William Frederick and Grace Dorothea (Adelheit) (Hennig) E.; m. Agnes Constance Yodelis, July 13, 1968; children: William Victor, Peter Frederick. B.A., Yale U., 1959; J.D., U. Chgo., 1965. Bar: Ill. 1966, U.S. Dist. Ct. (so. dist.) Ill. 1966, U.S. Dist. Ct. (no dist.) Ill. 1981. CLU, chartered fin. cons. Atty., Lawyers Title Ins. Corp., 1965-67; title officer Pioneer Nat. Title Ins. Corp., Chgo., 1967-69; assoc. Ralph E. Brown, Chgo., 1969-71; asst. gen. counsel Benefit Trust Life Ins. Co., Chgo., 1971-85; sole practice, 1985-86; mem. Ill. State Scholarship Commn., 1986—. Served with USAR, 1961-62. Fellow Life Mgmt. Inst.; mem. Chgo. Bar Assn. Republican. Lutheran.

ESSL, HOWARD CARL, government official; b. Chgo., June 22, 1939; s. Carl Henry and Josephine (Hoffner) E.; m. Mary Griffin Kirkpatrick, June 23, 1962; children—Carl Kirkpatrick, Margaret Josephine. B.A. in Sociology, U. Chgo., 1962; M.S. in Indsl. Relations, U. Wis., 1964. Analyst Nat. Assn. Blue Shield Plans, Chgo., 1964-67; program officer med. programs U.S. Office Econ. Opportunity, Washington, 1967-69; mgr. sch. health programs U.S. Dept. Edn., Washington, 1969-75, evaluator state assistance programs, 1975-82, evaluator elem. and secondary edn., 1982-87; coordinator compensatory edn. evaluation, 1987—. Bd. dirs. St. Andrews Episcopal Sch., Bethesda, Md., 1981-83, pres. PTA, 1979-81. Mem. Am. Ednl. Research Assn., Am. Pub. Health Assn. Democrat. Avocations: horology, horticulture. Home: 5301 Yorktown Rd Bethesda MD 20816 Office: Dept Edn 400 Maryland Ave SW Washington DC 20000

ESSLINGER, ANNA MAE LINTHICUM, realtor; b. Clifton, Tenn., May 29, 1912; d. Wallace Prather and Minnie P. (Bates) Linthicum; student Miss. State Coll. Women, La. State U.; m. William Francis Esslinger, Sept. 29, 1932; children—Ann Lynn (Mrs. James C. Wilcox), Susan Angie (Mrs. Heinz J. Selig). Founder, Esslinger-Wooten-Maxwell Inc., real estate, Coral Gables, Fla., 1968—. Pres. Coral Gables Bd. Realtors, 1975. Mem. Fla. (dir.), Nat. assns. realtors, DAR, Chi Omega. Christian Scientist. Clubs:

Assistance League of Eugene, Am. Contract Bridge League, Eugene Garden, Eugene Symphony Guild. Home: 759 Fair Oaks Dr Eugene OR 97401 Office: 1553 San Ignacio St Coral Gables FL 33146

ESSMYER, MICHAEL MARTIN, lawyer; b. Abilene, Tex., Dec. 6, 1949; s. Lytle Martin Essmyer and Roberta N. Essmyer Nicholson; m. Cynthia Rose Piccolo, Dec. 27, 1970; children: Deanna, Mike, Brent Austin. BS in Geology, Tex. A&M U., 1972; student Tex. Christian U., 1976; JD cum laude, South Tex. Coll. Law, 1980. Bar Tex. 1980, U.S. Ct. appeals (5th cir.) 1981, U.S. Dist. Ct. (no., so., ea., dists.) Tex. 1982 (we. dist.) 1988. Briefing atty. Supreme Ct. Tex., Austin, 1980-81; ptnr. Haynes & Fullenweider, Houston, 1981—. Lead article editor south Tex. Law Jour., 1979. Democratic candidate for state rep., Bryan, Tex., 1972; del. Dem. Party, Houston, 1982, 84; precinct chmn. Harris County Democratic Exec. Com., Houston, 1983-86. Served to capt. USAF, 1972-78. Nat. Merit Scholar, 1968-72. Mem. ABA, Houston Bar Assn., Houston Young Lawyers Assn., Assn. Trial Lawyers Am., Tex. Criminal Def. Lawyers Assn., Harris County Criminal Lawyers Assn. (dir. 1986—). Roman Catholic. Club: Houstonian. Home: 1122 Glourie Houston TX 77055 Office: Haynes & Fullenweider PLC 4300 Scotland Houston TX 77007-7328

ESSRICK, ABRAHAM JOSEPH, judge; b. Phila., Feb. 8, 1914; s. Jacob and Rachel (Pressman) E.; B.A. in Accounting, George Washington U., 1956; J.D. cum laude, Rutgers U., 1940; postgrad. U. Grenoble, France, 1945, Nat. Coll. State Judiciary, U. Nev., 1974, Georgetown U., 1976; m. Riva Krakuzin, Feb. 14, 1943 (dec. Aug. 1959); children—Helene (Mrs. Feldsher), Carol; m. 2d, Pearl Gibel, May 20, 1972 (div. 1983). Admitted to D.C. bar, 1941, U.S. Supreme Ct., 1964; atty. adviser SEC, Washington, 1946-53; atty. advisor ICC, Washington, 1953-59, hearing examiner, 1959-72, adminstrv. law judge, 1972-74; ret., 1974. Mem. Phila. Speakers Council, 1942, Jewish Educators Council, 1958-60. Bd. dirs. govt. div. United Jewish Appeal of Greater Washington, Inc., 1958-74, mem. exec. com., 1964-65, trustee, 1960-61, 64-73, vice chmn. exec. com. govt. div., 1965. Served with Signal Intelligence Div., ETO, 1944-45. Recipient commendation ICC; Merit award United Jewish Appeal Greater Washington, 1977, 78, 80. Mem. Am., Fed., D.C. bar assns., Am. Judicature Soc., Nat. Lawyers Club, Fed. Adminstrv. Law Judges Conf. Smithsonian Assocs., Friends John F. Kennedy Center. Jewish. Mem. B'nai B'rith. Club: Rutgers. Home: 13475 SW 9th St Apt 109 Pembroke FL 33027

ESSUNGER, JAN, finacial executive; b. Lund, Sweden, July 27, 1938; s. Ragnar and Sonja (Bondeson) E.; m. Lillemor Nordahl, July 27, 1961; children: Magnus, Paulina, Henrik. M in Engring., Chalmers U., Gothenburg, Sweden, 1961; MBA, Gothenburg Sch. of Bus. Adminstrn., 1964. Mgr. adminstrv. devel. SKF, Gothenburg, 1965-68; fin. mgr. SKF Norden, Gothenburg, 1968-72; v.p. fin. SKF Industries, Inc., King of Prussia, Pa., 1972-76; chief fin. officer SKF Group Hdqrs., Gothenburg, 1976-81; exec. v.p., chief fin. officer AB SKF, Gothenburg, 1981—. Office: AB SKF, Hornsgatan 1, 41550 Gothenburg Sweden

ESTEB, ADLAI ALBERT, retired clergyman, author; b. La Grande, Oreg., Nov. 17, 1901; s. Lemuel Albert and Addretta (Koger) E.; B.Th., Walla Walla Coll., 1931; M.A., Calif. Coll., Peiping, China, 1953; Ph.D., U. So. Calif., 1944; m. Florence Edna Airey, Feb. 5, 1923; children—Adeline, Lucille. Ordained to ministry Seventh-day Adventist Ch., 1923; missionary to China, 1923-37; pastor Seventh-day Adventist Ch., Long Beach, Calif., 1938-40; sec. home missionary dept. So. Calif. Conf. Seventh-day Adventist Ch., 1940-46, Pacific Union Conf. Seventh-day Adventist Ch., Glendale, Calif., 1946-50; editor Go, Jour. for Adventist Laymen, gen. conf. Seventh-day Adventist Ch., Washington, 1950-70; vis. prof., lectr. Christian ethics Andrews U., Berrien Springs, Mich., 1955-75, ret. Cited as poet laureate of denomination by pres. World Conf., 1966; named Alumnus of Yr., Walla Walla Coll., 1979. Mem. China Soc. of So. Calif. (pres. 1946-50), Oriental Fellowship (pres. 1963), Phi Beta Kappa, Phi Kai Phi, Phi Kappa Phi. Author: Driftwood, 1947; Firewood, 1952; Sandalwood, 1955; Morning Manna, 1962; Rosewood, 1964; Scrapwood, 1967; (poetry) Redwood, 1970; Kindle Kindness, 1971; The Meaning of Christmas, 1972; When Suffering Comes, 1974; Straight Ahead, 1974. Home: 15 Oak Court Candler NC 28715

ESTES, CARL L., II, lawyer; b. Fort Worth, Tex., Feb. 9, 1936; s. Joe E. and Carroll E.; m. Gay Gooch, Aug. 29, 1959; children: Adrienne Virginia, Margaret Ellen. B.S., U. Tex., 1957, LL.B., 1960. Bar: Tex. 1960. Law clk. U.S. Supreme Ct., 1960-61; assoc. firm Vinson & Elkins, Houston, 1961-69; ptnr. Vinson & Elkins, 1970—. Bd. dirs. Houston Grand Opera Assn. Fellow Am Bar Found., Tex. Bar Found.; mem. Am. Law Inst., Am. Coll. Probate Counsel, ABA, Internat. Bar Assn., Tex. Bar Assn., Internat. Fiscal Assn. (v.p.), Internat. Acad. Estate and Trust Law. Clubs: Houston, Ramada, Houston Country, Allegro; Marks (London). Home: 101 Broad Oaks Circle Houston TX 77056 Office: Vinson & Elkins 3300 First City Tower 1001 Fannin Houston TX 77002

ESTES, JOE EWING, judge; b. Commerce, Tex., Oct. 24, 1903; s. Joe Guinn and Della Marshall (Loy) E.; m. Carroll Virginia Cox, Dec. 1, 1931; children: Carl Lewis, Carroll. Student, E. Tex. State Tchrs. Coll., 1923-24; LL.B., U. Tex., 1927; LL.D., E. Tex. State U., 1974. Bar: Tex. 1927. Partner Crosby & Estes, Commerce, 1928-30, Phillips, Trammell, Estes, Edwards & Orn, Ft. Worth, 1930-45, Sanford, King, Estes & Cantwell, Dallas, 1946-52, Estes & Cantwell, 1952-55; U.S. dist. judge Dallas, 1955-60; chief judge U.S. Dist. Ct. No. Dist. Tex., Dallas, 1959-72; sr. judge U.S. Dist. Ct. No. Dist. Tex., 1972—; also judge Temp. Emergency Ct. Appeals U.S., 1972—; mem. adv. com. on rules evidence U.S. Supreme Ct. Contbr. articles to profl. jours.; also to: Handbook of Recommended Procedures for the Trial of Protracted Cases; co-author: Handbook for Newly Appointed U.S. District Judges; editorial bd.: Manual for Complex Litigation. Trustee, mem. exec. com. S.W. Legal Found.; Research fellow, mem. med.-legal com., chmn. Oil and Gas Inst. of S.W. Legal Found.; chmn. exec. com. bd. trustees St. Mark's Sch. of Tex., Dallas, 1951-55. Served as lt. comdr. USNR, 1942-45; mem. Res. Recipient Hatton W. Sumners award S.W. Legal Found., 1972, Citizen of Yr. award Kiwanis Club of Dallas, 1972. Fellow Am. Bar Found.; mem. Nat. Conf. Commrs. on Uniform State Laws, Am. Law Inst., Inter-Am., Fed., ABA (chmn. sect. jud. adminstrn. 1961-62, mem. ho. dels.), Dallas Bar Assn. (past v.p.), Fort Worth Bar Assn. (past dir.), State Bar Tex., Am. Judicature Soc., Jud. Conf. U.S. (chmn. com. on trial practice and technique, mem. exec. com. 1969-71, dist. judge rep.), Nat. Lawyers Club, Inst. Jud. Adminstrn., Philos. Soc. Tex., Newcomen Soc., Am. Legion, Chancellors, Phi Delta Phi, Kappa Sigma, Order of Coif. Methodist. Clubs: Masons (33 deg.), Shriners (hon. insp. gen., Jester). Home: 5846 Desco Dr Dallas TX 75225

ESTES, WILLIAM KAYE, psychologist, educator; b. Mpls., June 17, 1919; s. George D. and Mona; m. Katherine Walker, Sept. 26, 1942; children: George E., Gregory W. Mem. faculty Ind. U., 1946-62, prof. psychology, 1955-60, research prof. psychology, 1960-62; faculty research fellow Social Sci. Research Council, 1952-55; lectr. psychology U. Wis., summer 1949; vis. prof. Northwestern U., spring 1959; fellow Center Advanced Study Behavioral Scis., 1955-56; spl. univ. lectr. U. London, Eng., 1961; prof. psychology, mem. Inst. Math. Studies Social Scis., Stanford, 1962-68; prof. Rockefeller U., 1968-79, Harvard U., 1979—; chmn. Office Sci. and Engring. Personnel NRC, 1982-85, chmn. com. on prevention of nuclear war NRC 1984—. Author: An Experimental Study of Punishment, 1944, Learning Theory and Mental Development, 1970, Models of Learning, Memory, and Choice, 1982; co-author: Modern Learning Theory, 1954; also numerous articles.; Editor: Handbook of Learning and Cognitive Processes, 1975, Jour. Comparative and Physiol. Psychology, 1962-68, Psychol. Rev., 1977-82; assoc. editor: Jour. Exptl. Psychology, 1958-62. Served with AUS, 1944-46. Fellow Am. Psychol. Assn. (pres. div. exptl. psychology 1958-59, Distinguished Sci. Contbn. award 1962), AAAS, Am. Acad. Arts and Scis.; mem. Nat. Acad. Scis., N.Y. Acad. Sci. (hon. life), Soc. Exptl. Psychologists (Warren medal 1963), Psychometric Soc., Midwestern Psychol. Assn. (pres. 1956-57). Home: 95 Irving St Cambridge MA 02138 Office: Harvard U 620 W James Hall 33 Kirkland Cambridge MA 02138

ESTEVES, RUI JORGE FERREIRA, software engineer; b. Lourenço Marques, Mozambique, Portugal, Jan. 31, 1959; s. Octavio Pestana and Maria Adelina Macedo (Ferreira) E.; m. Maria Alice Monteiro Ramos de Ferreira Lopes, Aug. 6, 1983; 1 child, Sergio Alexandre. M.S., Faculdade de Engenharia da Universidade do Porto, Portugal, 1982. Math. tchr. Escola Secundaria de Penafiel, Portugal, 1982-83; software engr. Tex. Instruments, Maia, Portugal, 1983—; practicant Roederstein Electronica, V.N. Famalição, Portugal, 1980; developer Fac. Engenharia Universidade Porto, 1982-83. Mem. Ordem dos Engenheiros, Mensa Internat. Avocations: personal computing; chess, pencil drawing. Home: Rua E #36 2o Esq Urb Bouça, Grande Vila Nova da Telha, 4470 Maia Portugal Office: Texas Instruments, R Eng Frederico Ulrich 2650, 4470 Moreira da Maia Portugal

ESTRADA, FELIX ALISANGCO, pediatrician, educator; b. Manila, June 16, 1917; s. Felix Soria Estrada and Justa Gabat Alisangco; m. Juanita Quizon, Apr. 27, 1946; children: Lourdes, Rosa, Alfonso, Concepcion, Eugenia, Mario. MD, U. St. Tomas, Manila, 1933-38. Adminstrv. officer St. Tomas Hosp., Manila, 1964-77; dean, faculty medicine U. St. Tomas, 1977-78; med. dir. St. Tomas Hosp., 1982-85; prof. U. St. Tomas, 1947-82, lectr., 1982-88; cons. St. Tomas Hosp., Candelaria Charity Clinic, St. Martin Charity Hosp. Editor: (with others) Textbook of Pediatrics and Child Health, 1976, Manual of Infant Nutrition, 1985. Recipient Proecclesia et Pontifice (Vatican), 1987. Fellow Philippine Pediatric Soc. (outstanding pediatrician, 1972). Roman Catholic. Home: 504 Lt Artiaga, San Juan Metro Manila Philippines Office: U St Tomas Hosp, España St, Manila Philippines

ESTRADA-YCAZA, JULIO, historian, author; b. Guayaquil, Ecuador, Nov. 16, 1917; s. Victor Emilio Estrada and Isabel Victoria Ycaza; student M.I.T., 1935, Calif. Inst. Tech., 1936; m. Maria Teresa Sola, Aug. 22, 1940; children—Maria Teresa, Julio Enrique, Isabel, Cecilia. Mgr. Compania General de Construcciones, 1938-43; mgr. Compania Ecuatoriana de Seguros, 1943-52; mgr. Patria C.A. de Seguros, 1952-57; pres. Financiera del Hogar, Guayaquil, 1958—; mgr. Banco Ecuatorianao de la Vivienda, Guayaquil, 1966-68; dir. Archivo Historico, 1971—; asst. mgr. Banco Central, Guayaquil, 1984—; author: El Puerto de Guayaquil, 3 vols., 1972-77, El Hospital de Guayaquil, 1974; La Fundacion de Guayaquil, 1974; Bancos del Siglo XIX, 1976; Migracion y Regionalismo, 1978; La Lucha de Guayaquil por el Estado de Quito, 2 vols., 1984; Catalogo de los billetes del Ecuador, 1984, 89; Andanzas de Cieza por tierras americanas, 1986; prof. ins. and finance U. Guayaquil, 1950-61. Pres. Junta Civica de Guayaquil, 1969—. Mem. C. of C. Roman Catholic. Clubs: de la Union, Yacht. Columnist, El Universo, 1969-81, Expreso, 1984-86, El Telegrafo, 1987—, mem. editorial bd., 1988—. Home: 4141 Seis de Marzo, Guayaquil Ecuador Office: Casilla 1333, Guayaquil Ecuador

ESTRIN, HERMAN ALBERT, English language educator; b. North Plainfield, N.J., June 2, 1915; s. Morris I. and Ida Ruth (Bender) E.; m. Pearl Simon, June 26, 1949; children: Robert Keith, Karen Ruth. A.B., Drew U., 1937; M.A., Columbia U., 1942, Ed.D., 1954. Instr. social sci. South Plainfield, N.J., 1938-42; mem. faculty N.J. Inst. Tech., Newark, 1946—, prof. English, 1958-81; lectr. U. Paris, 1978, 79, 80, 81; lectr. various orgns.; cons. in field. Author: (with Paul Obler) The New Scientist: Essays on the Methods and Values of Science, 1963, Technical and Professional Writing: A Practical Anthology, 1963, (with Delmer Good) College and University Teaching, 1966, (with Arthur Sanderson) Freedom and Censorship of the College Press, 1966, (with Esther Lloyd-Jones) The American Student and His College, 1967, How Many Roads?, The 70's, 1970, (with Donald Mehus) The American Language in the 70's, 1974; editor: (with Donald Cunningham) The Teaching of Technical Writing, 1975, The Best Student Poetry in New Jersey, 1978—, Poetic Engineers, 1983; author brochures and articles. Mem. adv. bd. Donor Estrin scholarships, 1971-88; bd. dirs. N.J. Poetry Contest, 1976, N.J. Lit. Hall of Fame, 1976. Served to capt. U.S. Army, 1942-46. Recipient Alumni Achievement award in arts Drew U., 1958, Gold Key award Columbia Scholastic Press Assn., 1962, Robert Van Houton award N.J. Inst. Tech. Alumni Assn., 1970, Nat. Disting. Newspaper Adviser award Nat. Council Coll. Publs. Advisers, 1970, Western Electric Fund award, 1971, James Robbins award 1979, Disting. Service award N.J. Edn. Assn., 1986, Outstanding Tchr. Tech. Writing award Assn. Tech. Writing Tchrs., 1975, plaque Soc. Collegiate Journalists, 1981; named Outstanding Faculty Mem. N.J. Inst. Tech., 1979-80; recipient citation Div. Continuing Edn., 1981, Silver medal for Outstanding Service to students U. Paris, Mayor of Paris, 1984, Disting. Service award Coll. Media Assn., 1984, Disting. Service to Edn. award N.J. Edn. Assn., 1986, Cullimore award N.J. Inst. Tech., 1987, Disting. Alumnus award Tchrs. Coll., Columbia U., 1988; elected to N.J. Lit. Hall of Fame, 1986 and recipient Michael award. Fellow Assn. Tchrs. Tech. Writing; mem. Nat. Council Tchrs. English (past dir., Disting. Service Award 1980), N.J. Council Tchrs. English (past pres., Disting. Tchrs. Award 1973), N.J. Coll. Press Assn. (founder), Nat. Council Publs. Advisers (past pres., Disting. Service award 1984), Coll. English Assn. (past regional pres.), N.J. Writers Conf. (dir. 1966—), N.J. Authors Luncheons (dir. 1959—), AAUP, Am. Soc. Engring. Edn., Phi Beta Kappa, Omicron Delta Kappa (award for service 1981), Alpha Pi Omega, Phi Delta Kappa (award for service 1980), Kappa Delta Pi, Phi Eta Sigma, Pi Delta Epsilon (past pres.). Home: 315 Henry St Scotch Plains NJ 07076 Office: Alumni Ctr NJ Inst Tech Newark NJ 07102

ESTUAR, FIORELLO DEL ROSARIO, civil engineer; b. Manila, July 27, 1938; s. Bienvenido and Felicidad (del Rosario) E.; m. Flor Lubaton, Oct. 12, 1969; children—Jose Atanacio, Bienvenido, Fiorello, Alfredo, Marie Grace. B.S. in Civil Engring., U. Philippines, 1959; M.S., Lehigh U., 1962, Ph.D., 1965. Design engr. Erectors, Inc., Philippines, 1959-60; structural engr. Rust Engring. Co., 1966-67; treas., mng. prin. structural engring. Engrs. Collaborative Philippines, 1967-69; pres., chmn. bd. computer systems Unisystems Group Corp., Philippines, 1968—; mng. prin. Estuar-Caparros & Assocs., cons. engrs., Philippines, 1970-73; pres. F.R. Estuar & Assocs., cons. engrs., Philippines, 1973-80, Elco Devel. & Constrn. Corp., Philippines, 1975-80; ptnr. Consultech Group Ltd., Philippines, 1974-80; adminstr. Nat. Irrigation Adminstrn., 1980-83; pres. Philippine Nat. Constrn. Corp., 1984-87; under sec. Acctg. Sec. Dept. Pub. Works and Hwys.; presdl. adviser, 1987; mem. of cabinet, 1988; dir. Hotel Mirador, Inc., Planning Resources & Operation System; researcher, mem. faculty Lehigh U., 1960-65; lectr. Grad. Sch. Engring., U. Philippines, 1968-73; cons. in field. Co-author: (textbook) Structural Steel Design, 1964. Contbr. articles and reports to profl. lit. Recipient A.F. Davis Paper award Am. Welding Soc., 1963; named Outstanding Young Man, Philippines Jaycees, 1976. Mem. Philippine Assn. Civil Engrs. (research and scholarship award 1972), Philippine Inst. Civil Engrs., Philippine Contractors Assn. (bd. dirs.), Nat. Research Council Philippines, ASCE, Am. Concrete Inst., Fritz Engring. Research Soc., Assn. Structural Engrs. Philippines, C. of C. Philippines, Aircraft Owners and Pilots Assn., Sigma Xi, Tau Alpha. Clubs: Rotary, Capitol City Sports and Country. Office: Project Facilitation Com, c/o POCB 5th fl, Trade and Industry Ctr, Makati Metro Manila Philippines

ESWEIN, BRUCE JAMES, II, advertising agency executive; b. San Mateo, Calif., Oct. 26, 1951; s. Bruce James and Janet Gordon (Copeland) E.; m. Sarah Anne Shames, Feb. 7, 1981; 1 child, Thomas Jonathan. Student, U. Wash., 1969-71; A.B., U. Calif.-Berkeley, 1973, M.B.A., 1977. Brand asst. Clorox Co., Oakland, Calif., 1977-79, coll. relations mgr., 1979-83; mgr. exec. recruitment and devel. BBDO Worldwide, N.Y.C., 1983-84, v.p., 1984-87, v.p. personnel adminstrn., 1987-88, v.p. human resources, mgr. worldwide tng. and devel., 1988—. Mem. Am. Soc. for Tng. and Devel., U. Calif. at Berkeley Bus. Sch. Alumni Assn. (bd. dirs. 1980-83), Phi Beta Kappa, Chi Psi (v.p. 1972-73, bd. dirs. 1979-82, trustee 1983-84, trustee emeritus 1984—). Republican. Episcopalian. Home: 92 Amber Dr Croton-on-Hudson NY 10520 Office: BBDO Worldwide 1285 Ave of the Americas New York NY 10019-6095

ETCHEGARAY, ROGER CARDINAL, archbishop; b. Espelette, France, Sept. 25, 1922; s. Jean-Baptiste and Aurélie (Dufau) E. Ed. Petit Séminaire, Ustaritz, France, Grand Séminaire, Bayonne, France. Ordained priest Roman Catholic Ch., 1947; served diocese of Bayonne, 1947-60; asst. sec. then sec.-gen. French Episcopal Conf., 1961-70, pres., 1975-81; consecrated archbishop of Marseilles (France), 1970; prelate Mission of France, 1975-81; elevated to Sacred Coll. of Cardinals, 1979; pres. Council European Episcopal Conf., 1971-79; pres. Pontifical Commn. for Justice and Peace, 1984—. Author: Dieu à Marseille, 1976. Decorated Legion of Honor (France). Mem. Congregation of Cath. Edn., Congregation of Christian Unity, Commn. of Social Communication. Address: Piazza San Calisto, Città del Vaticano Vatican Office: Archeveche, 4 Place du Colonel-Edon, 13007 Marseille France *

ETESS, ELAINE GROSSINGER, hospitality industry consultant; b. N.Y.C., Dec. 9, 1927; d. Harry and Jennie Grossinger; student Russell Sage Coll., Troy, N.Y., Syracuse (N.Y.) U.; m. David Etess, Aug. 10, 1947; children—Susan, Mark, Mitchell. Pres., Elaine G. Estess Assoc.; chmn. Internat. Hotel and Motel Show, 1984, 85; mem. adv. bd. Coll. of Boca Raton. Life mem. N.Y. State PTA. Recipient Career award N.Y. State Bus. and Profl. Women's Clubs, 1977; Doris L. Crockett Disting. Service award Russell Sage Coll., 1979; named Sullivan County Bus. and Profl. Woman of Yr., 1985. Mem. N.Y. State Hotel & Motel Assn. (past chmn. bd. 1979-80), Am. Hotel and Motel Assn. (dir., mem. exec. com., v.p., long-range planning com., trustee Ednl. Inst., Lawson Odde award of yr. 1983), Sullivan County Bus. and Profl. Women.

ETHERINGTON, EDWIN DEACON, lawyer, business executive, educator; b. Bayonne, N.J., Dec. 25, 1924; s. Charles K. and Ethel (Bennett) E.; m. Katherine Colean, Sept. 11, 1953; children: Edwin Deacon, Kenneth C., Marion (dec.), Robert. B.A. with honors and distinction, Wesleyan U., 1948; J.D., Yale U., 1952. Bar: D.C 1953, N.Y. 1955. Asst. dean, instr. English, Wesleyan U., 1948-49; asst. instr. Yale Law Sch., 1951-52; law clk. to judge Ct. Appeals, Washington, 1952-53; asso. Wilmer & Broun, Washington, 1953-54, Milbank, Tweed, Hope & Hadley, N.Y.C., 1954-56; sec. N.Y. Stock Exchange, 1956-58, v.p., 1958-61; ptnr. Pershing & Co., 1961-62; pres. Am. Stock Exchange, 1962-66; pres. Wesleyan U., Middletown, Conn., 1966-70, now pres. emeritus; pres. Nat. Center for Voluntary Action, Washington, 1971; chmn. bd. advs. U.S. Trust Co. of Fla.; chmn. Nat. Advt. Adv. Rev. Bd., 1973-74, Conn. Gov.'s Commn. on Services and Expenditures, 1971-72; bd. dirs. Automatic Data Processing Corp. Mem. Commn. on Pvt. Philanthropy and Pub. Needs, 1972-73; mem. nat. adv. council Ariz. Heart Inst., 1972-82; incorporator Nat. Housing Partnership; vice chmn. bd. visitors U.S. Naval Acad., 1966-68; mem. bd. visitors U.S. Mil. Acad., 1969-71; hon. trustee Hammonasset Sch., North Madison, Conn.; trustee Alfred P. Sloan Found., 1969-76, Schumann Found., Coll. of Wooster; hon. chmn. Hobe Sound Child Care Ctr., Fla., Lyme's (Conn.) Youth Services Bd. Served with AUS, 1943-44. Mem. Phi Beta Kappa Assos., Phi Beta Kappa, Kappa Beta Phi, Phi Delta Phi, Order of Coif. Congregationalist. Clubs: Black Hall Golf, Old Lyme (Conn.) Country, Old Lyme Beach, Island, Jupiter Island (Fla.) (v.p.), Hobe Sound (Fla.) Yacht, Seminole Golf North Palm Beach (Fla.). Home: 102 Bassett Creek Trail Hobe Sound FL 33455

ETKIND, EFIM GRIGORIEVICH, educator, author; b. Leningrad, Russia, Feb. 26, 1918; s. Grigori Etkind and Polina Spivak; m. Katherine Zvorykina, 1940; 2 children. Cand. Philol.Sc., Leningrad. U., 1947, Dr.Philol.Sc., 1965; Docteur d'Etat, Sorbonne, U. Paris, 1975. Taught in Faculty Romance Langs., Leningrad. Pedagogical Inst., 1947-74; degrees and title of prof. removed, expelled from USSR Union of Writers for def. of various poets, 1974; left USSR, 1974; now mem. faculty Universite de Paris X. Author: Poetry and Translation, 1963; Russian Poet-Translators from Trediakovsky to Pushkin, 1973; The Substance of Verse and the Problems of the Theory of Translation, 1974; Notes of a non-Conspirator, 1977; Form as Content, 1977; Un art en crise (Essai d'une poetique de la traduction poetique), 1981, Poésie Russe. Anthology 18th-20th Centuries, 1983, Russische Lurik von der Oktoberrevolution bis zur Gegenwart, Versuch einer Darstellung, 1985, Symmetry in the poems of Pushicin, 1988., 323 epigrams of Soviet-Russia, 1988. Served with Soviet Army, World War II. Corr. mem. Bayerischen Akademie der Schonen Kunste, Akademie der Wissenschaften und der Literatur zu Mainz, deutschen Akademie fur Sprache und Dichtung.

ETLIN, MICHEL CLAUDE JULIEN, financial advisor; b. Paris, May 26, 1924; s. Philippe Maurice and Jacqueline Juliette (Bloch) E.; m. Suzana Nogueira Baptista, Aug. 8, 1962; children: Jean-Marc Robert, Patrice Philippe, Christian Michel. Student, Ohio U., 1942; LLD, The Sorbonne, Paris, 1947; postgrad., Polit. Sci. Sch., Paris, 1947. Adjoint dir. Banque de la Cite, Paris, 1948-49; sr. v.p., treas. Dutch-Am. Merc. Corp., N.Y.C., 1949-60; fin. advisor, investment broker in internat. market São Paulo, Brazil, 1960—; advisor CELUSA (CESP), São Paulo, 1966-67, Regie Renault, Paris, 1979-80; coordinator Brazil, Libra Bank, London, 1972; internat. advisor C.D.F. Chimie Internat., France, 1983, mng. dir., São Paulo, 1983-85. Bd. dirs. Mus. Modern Art, São Paulo, 1985—. Served with French Resistance, 1940-41, to lt. French Air Force, 1942-45. Decorated officer Legion of Honor, Croix de Guerre with palme, comdr. Etoile Noire (France). Mem. Franco-Brazil C. of C. (counsellor 1980-83). Clubs: Jockey, Harmonia (São Paulo). Home: Praca das Guianas 103, 01428 Sao Paulo Brazil Office: Ave Angelica 501-Coj 1106, 01227 Sao Paulo Brazil

ETO, FUMIO, physician, lecturer of medical school; b. Tokyo, July 26, 1946; s. Takeo and Chiyoko (Murata) E.; m. Yasuko Yoshimune, Apr. 24, 1974; children: Hiromitsu, Toshinori. MD, U. Tokyo, 1972, D of Med. Sci., 1978. Intern, then resident U. Tokyo Hosp., 1972-75; attending physician Yokufukai Hosp., Tokyo, 1974-75; asst. physician U. Tokyo Hosp., 1975-79; assoc. Faculty of Medicine U. Tokyo, 1979-84, lectr., 1984—; cons. physician Hatsuishi Hosp., Kashiwa, Japan, 1980—; lectr. Kiyose Rehab. Sch., Kiyose, Japan, 1982—. Author: Rehabilitation Medicine, 1984, Aging 2000, 1985; contbr. articles to profl. jours. Mem. Japanese Soc. Internal Medicine, Japanese Geriatrics Soc. (councilor 1985), Life Support Tech. Soc. (councilor 1986), Japanese Soc. Rehab. Medicine (sec. 1986). Home: 3-2-15 Higashinakano, Nakano-ku, Tokyo 164, Japan Office: U Tokyo, 7-3-1 Hongo Bunkyo-ku, Tokyo 113, Japan

ETO, JUN, literary critic, educator; b. Tokyo, Japan, Dec. 25, 1932; s. Takashi and Hiroko (Miyaji) E.; B.A. in English, Keio Gijuku U., Tokyo, 1957; Litt.D. in Comparative Lit., Keio U., 1974; m. Keiko Miura, May 13, 1957. Editor, Mita Bungaku (Mita Rev. Lit.), Tokyo, 1957-62; lit. critic Asahi Shimbun, Tokyo, 1964-66; mng. editor Kikan Geijutsu, art quar., Minatoku, Tokyo, 1967-72; asso. prof. Tokyo Inst. Tech., 1971-73, prof. lit. and comparative culture, 1973—; vis. lectr. Princeton (N.J.) U., 1963-64. Rockefeller Found. fellow Princeton U., 1962-63; recipient Shincho Lit. prize Kobayashi Hideo, 1962; Noma Lit. prize, 1970; Japanese Acad. Art prize, 1976; Yoshida Shigeru prize, 1978; fellow Woodrow Wilson Center, 1979-80. Mem. Japan Writers Assn. (dir.). Author (books) Natsume Soseki, A Critical Study, 1956, rev. edit., 1965; Kobayashi Hideo, A Critical Biography, 1962; Seijuku to Soshitsu (Maturity and Loss), 1967; Soseki and his Times (Kikuchi Kan prize), 1970; Umi wa Yomigaeru (The Sea Reborn) (Bungei Shunju prize), 1983. Home: 1-15-5 Nishimikado, Kamakura 248, Japan Office: Tokyo Kogyo Daigaku, 2-12-1 Ookayama/Meguro-Ku, Tokyo 152, Japan

ETO, TOSHIYA, concert violinist, educator; b. Tokyo, Nov. 9, 1927; s. Toshiaki and Takako (Hoshimo) E.; m. Angela Nudo, Sept. 8, 1955; children—T. Curtis, T. Michael. Student Tokyo U. Music, 1944-48, Curtis Inst. Music, Phila., 1948-52. Debut Carnegie Hall, N.Y.C., 1951; violinist throughout world, 1951—; instr. Curtis Inst. Music, Phila., 1953-61; guest prof. Toho U. Music, 1963—, Ueno U. Music, Tokyo, 1963—. Roman Catholic. Home: 1-7-15 Kihei-machi Kodaira, Tokyo 187 Japan

ETROG, LESLEY SIMONE, physician; b. Montpellier, Herault, France, Dec. 2, 1956; d. Gerard and Barbara Elisabeth (Whittle) Romestan; m. Yehoshua Etrog, July 24, 1981; children: Tiphaine, Teddie, Jonathan. Baccalaureat, Lycee Claude Debussy, 1974; MD, U. Medicine, Montpellier, France, 1982. Gen. practice medicine Voisins Le Bretonneux, France, 1983—; tchr. unalphabet people Assn. de Solidarité pour Travailleurs Immigrés, Marly-Le-Roi, France, 1973. Mem. Marly Tiers-Monde (pres 1983-85), Medecins Sans Frontieres, Amnesty Internat. Home: 27 Rue Des Peupliers, Voisins Le Bretonneux Yvelines 78960, France Office: 13 Rue Lindbergh, Voisins Le Bretonneux Yvelines 78960, France

ETTERS, RONALD MILTON, lawyer, government official; b. San Antonio, Nov. 6, 1948; s. Milton William and Ilse Charlotte (Ostler) E.; m. Anna Colleen Wesson, Feb. 12, 1977; children—William Lawrence, Elizabeth Charlotte, Margaret Lawreen. B.A., Am. U., 1971, J.D., 1975. Bar: Va. 1976, U.S. Ct. Appeals (D.C. cir.) 1977, U.S. Dist. Ct. (ea. dist.) Va. 1978, U.S. Ct. Appeals (4th and 9th cirs.) 1978, U.S. Supreme Ct. 1979, D.C. 1980, U.S. Ct. Appeals (1st and 2d cirs.) 1980, U.S. Ct. Appeals (7th cir.) 1981, U.S. Ct. Appeals (3rd, 11th and Fed. cirs.) 1982, U.S. Ct. Appeals (5th cir.) 1983. Intern to gen. counsel Adminstrv. Office of U.S. Cts., Washington, 1970-71; fed. mgmt. intern IRS, Washington, 1971-72, labor relations officer, 1972-75; ptnr. Nusbaum & Etters, Burke, Va., 1976-80; hearing officer, chief hearing officer Nat. Mediation Bd., Washington, 1975-80, gen. counsel, 1980—; professorial lectr. Am. U., Washington, 1978-83; adj. prof. law Georgetown U., Washington, 1985-88. Contbr. ABA reports. Mem. ABA (co-chmn. com. on railway and airline labor law 1987—), Christian Legal Soc. Republican. Methodist. Home: 5315 Indian Rock Rd Centreville VA 22020 Office: Nat Mediation Bd Office of the Chmn 1425 K St NW Washington DC 20572

ETTINGER, JEAN-CLAUDE GEORGES, university professor; b. Namur, Belgium, July 20, 1947; s. Marcel and Marguerite (Bastin) E.; m. Kathleen Vande Walle, Aug. 30, 1980 (div. May 1985). MBA, U. Brussels, 1970, D of Applied Econs., 1980; cert. in internat. tchrs. program, London Bus. Sch., 1975. Asst. mgr. J. Hegelbach & Cie, Brussels, 1970-73; mgmt. cons. Groupe Ergos, Brussels, 1973-83; teaching and research asst. Solvay Bus. Sch. U. Brussels, 1976-80; pres. Optimum Mgmt., Braine L'Alleud, Belgium, 1983—; 1st v.p. Centre de Technologie et de Gestion des Affaires, Nivelles, Belgium, 1983—; ptnr. Optimum Indsl. Strategies, Brussels, 1986-88; prof. Solvay Bus. Sch. U. Brussels, 1980—; bd. dirs., treas. Groupe Ergos, Brussels, 1974-84; bd. dirs. Centre de Formation et de Recherche Appliquée a L'Enseignement, Brussels. Contbr. articles to profl. jours. Served to lt. Armored Forces of Belgium, 1971-72. Named Officer of the Order of the Crown, Kingdon of Belgium, 1987. Mem. European Acctg. Assn., Internat. Small Bus. Council, Union des Ingenigurs Commerciaux, Fondation Universitaire. Clubs: Waterloo (Belgium) Golf; Officiers du les Guider (Brussels). Home: Rue Grange des Champs 191, 1420 Braine L'Alleud Belgium Office: ULB Ave FD, Roosevelt 19, 1050 Brussels Belgium

ETTINGER, JOSEPH ALAN, lawyer; b. N.Y.C., July 21, 1931; s. Max and Frances E.; B.A., Tulane U., 1954, J.D. with honors, 1956; m. Julie Ann Ettinger; children—Amy Beth, Ellen Jane, Alex William. Admitted to La. bar, 1956, Ill. bar, 1959; asst. corp. counsel City of Chgo., 1959-62; practiced in Chgo., 1962-73, 76—; sr. partner firm Ettinger & Schoenfield, Chgo., 1980—; asso. prof. law Chgo.-Kent Coll., 1973-76; chmn. Village of Olympia Fields (Ill.) Zoning Bd. Appeals, 1969-76; chmn. panel on corrections Welfare Council Met. Chgo., 1969-76. Served to capt., Judge Adv. Gen. Corps, U.S. Army, 1956-59. Recipient Service award Village of Olympia Fields, 1976. Mem. Chgo. Bar Assn., Assn. Criminal Def. Lawyers (gov. 1970-72). Clubs: Ravisloe Country, Carlton Club, Contbr. articles to profl. publs. Office: 415 N LaSalle St Chicago IL 60610

ETTORRE, ELIZABETH MARY, sociology educator; b. Bridgeport, Conn., June 28, 1948; d. James Edward and Helen Anna (Turczi) E. BA in Sociology, Fordham U., 1972; PhD in Sociology, London Sch. Econs. and Polit. Sci., 1978. Research asst. dept. sociology Fordham U., Bronx, N.Y., 1972; research asst. human rights and edn. Inst. Edn. U. London, 1977-78, research sociologist, lectr. in sociology Inst. Psychiatry, 1978-86, research assoc. dept. politics and sociology Birkbeck Coll., 1986—; cons. Open U., Milton Keynes, U.K., 1986-87, Brit. Broadcasting Co., London, 1987. Author: Lesbians, Women and Soc., 1980. Central Research fund grantee, 1976; Soc. for Psychol. Study of Social Problems grantee, 1976; Mental Health Found. grantee, 1986. Mem. Brit. Sociol. Assn. (exec. officer), Assn. of U. Tchrs., Eugenics Soc. Club: U. Women's. Office: U London Birkbeck Coll, Dept Politics and Sociology, Malet St, London WC1E 7HX, England

ETTRICK, MARCO ANTONIO, theoretical physicist; b. Panama City, Panama, July 17, 1945; came to U.S., 1963.; s. Clemente Adolfo and Olga Rosa (Birmingham) E.; m. Ady Marie Hippolyte, Oct. 22, 1966 (div. Mar. 1977); children: Rudolphe Antoine, Mark. BS in Math., Poly. U., Bklyn., 1968; MS in Math., PolyTech. U., 1986; postgrad., MIT. Programmer analyst Citibank, N.Y.C., 1969-71; lic. bacteriologist Lincoln Hosp., N.Y.C., 1975-76; lectr. in math. Queens (N.Y.) Coll., 1980-81, L.I. U., Bklyn., 1981-82, N.Y. Tech. Coll., Bklyn., 1982-84, Huston Community Coll., Bklyn., 1984—, Medgar Evers Coll., Bklyn., 1986—. Contbr. articles to sci. jours. Mem. AAAS, Am. Fedn. Scientists, Am. Phys. Soc. Roman Catholic. Home: 79 Sterling St Brooklyn NY 11225

ETZEL, BARBARA COLEMAN, psychologist, educator; b. Pitts., Sept. 19, 1926; d. Walter T. and Ruth (Coleman) E. A.A., Stephens Coll., 1946; B.S. in Psychology, Denison U., 1948; M.S., U. Miami, Fla., 1950; Ph.D. in Exptl. Child Psychology, State U. Iowa, 1953. Staff psychologist Ohio State Bur. Juvenile Research, Columbus, 1953-54; asst. prof. psychology Fla. State U., Tallahassee, 1954-56; chief psychologist, child psychiatry U. Wash. Med. Sch., Seattle, 1956-61; assoc. prof. psychology Western Wash. State U., Bellingham, 1961-65, dir. grad. program in psychology, 1963-65; spl. fellow sect. early learning and devel. NIMH, Bethesda, Md., 1965-66; assoc. prof. dept. human devel. U. Kans., Lawrence, 1965-69, mem. grad. faculty, 1965—, prof. human devel., 1969—, dir. Edna A. Hill Child Devel. Lab., 1965-72, dir. Kans. Ctr. for Research in Early Childhood Edn., 1968-71, assoc. dean Office of Research Adminstrn. and Grad. Sch., 1972-74, dir. John T. Stewart Children's Ctr., 1975-85; vis. prof. Universidad Central de Venezuela, Caracas, 1981-82; cons. Manchester Sch. Presch. Program, U. Mex., Mexico City, 1973-75, George Peabody Tchrs. Coll., 1978, St. Luke's Hosp., Kansas City, Mo., 1981-83, Anne Sullivan Sch. for Handicapped Children, Lima, Peru, 1982-85. Author: (with J.M. LeBlanc and D.M. Baer) New Developments in Behavioral Research, 1977; contbr. articles to profl. jours.; mem. editorial bd. Behavior Analyst, 1988-90. Bd. dirs. Community Children's Ctr., Inc., 1968-71; trustee Ctr. for Research, Inc., U. Kans., 1975-78. Elected to U. Kans. Women's Hall of Fame, 1975; Japan Soc. Promotion for Sci. fellow, 1981. Fellow Am. Psychol. Assn. (Div. 25 Don Hake award, 1987); mem. Assn. Behavior Analysis (pres. 1987—, pres.-elect 1986-87), Soc. Research in Child Devel., Midwestern Psychol. Assn., Am. Ednl. Research Assn., AAAS, AAUP, Southwestern Soc. Research in Human Devel., Sigma Xi, Psi Chi, Pi Lambda Theta. Home: Woodsong at JB Ranch Route 1 PO Box 82-E Oskaloosa KS 66066 Office: U Kans Dept Human Devel Lawrence KS 66045

EUGSTER, ERNEST, telecommunications company executive; b. Bern, Switzerland, June 7, 1950; came to U.S., 1955; s. Ernest and Betty (Fischlin) E.; m. Suzanne Perrette Rogers, Sept. 22, 1973. B.A., U. Colo., 1972, M.S., 1973; Ph.D., Grad. Inst. Internat. Studies, Geneva, 1981. Mktg. cons. Eurosat Satellite Systems S.A., Geneva, 1978-79; media planner, buyer Burson-Marsteller Internat. S.A., Geneva, 1981-82; advt. dir. Beckman Instruments Internat., Geneva, 1982-86; mktg. dir. Service 800, Nyon, Switzerland, 1986-87; mktg. dir. Hasler Ltd., Bern, 1987—. Author: Cross-Media Ownership: Dangers to the Public Interest, 1973, Television Programming Across National Boundaries: The EBU and OIRT Experience, 1983; contbr. numerous articles on telecommunications to profl. jours.; corr. World Broadcast News, 1986—. Asst. scoutmaster Boy Scouts Am., Geneva, 1982-87. Mem. Internat. Inst. Communications, Inc. Soc. British Advertisers Ltd. Republican. Lutheran. Avocations: reading, skiing, hiking. Home: Chemin de Flonzel 41, 1093 La Conversion Switzerland

EUSTICE, RUSSELL CLIFFORD, consulting company executive; b. Hackensack, N.J., July 11, 1919; s. Russell C. and Ethel (Hutchison) E.; B.A., Colgate U., 1941; M.B.A., Am. U., 1973; m. Veronica B. Dabrowski, Mar. 15, 1946; children—Russell Clifford, David A., Paul M. With Vick Chem. Corp., N.Y.C., 1941-42, 46-47; with Johnson & Johnson, 1947-61, div. sales mgr., 1954-61; nat. sales mgr. Park & Tilford div. Schenley Affiliates, N.Y.C., 1961-62; pres. Mid-Atlantic Assos., Inc., Prospect Harbor, Maine, 1962—; dir. Small Bus. Inst., Husson Coll., Bangor, Maine, 1979—, asst. prof. bus. adminstrn., 1979—; part-time instr. mktg. The Am. U., Washington, 1970-74. Served to capt. AUS, 1942-46. Mem. Assn. Mil. Surgeons, Reserve Officers Assn., Assn. Mktg. Educators, SBA. Republican. Methodist. Home: Lighthouse Rd Prospect Harbor ME 04669 Office: Husson Coll Bangor ME 04401

EUTON, MICHAEL FRED, landscape architect; b. Houston, Aug. 10, 1938; s. William Robert and Lillie Bertha (Wischer) E.; student U. Tex., Austin, 1956-59, Massey Bus. Coll., Houston, 1972. Sales mgr. Civic Reading Club, Houston and San Antonio, 1960-62; designer Davis Landscape Service, Houston, 1962-66; landscape architect Mike Euton Landscape Service, Barker, Tex., 1966—, City of Katy (Tex.), 1975-80; founder, pres. Teutonic Internat., 1985; lectr. in field. Exec. com. Democratic Party Harris County (Tex.), 1966-68; del. Harris County Dem. Conv., 1960-80, 84, Tex. State Dem. Conv., 1960, 64, 68, 72, 74; precinct election judge, 1976; mem. U.S. Senator William A. Blakley's Harris County Campaign Staff, 1961; active campaigns J. Evetts Haley for Gov., 1956, W. Lee O'Daniel for Gov., 1956, Dolph Briscoe for Gov., 1968, 72, 74, Bill Clements for Gov., 1978, George Wallace for Pres., 1968, 72, Lloyd Bentsen for Pres., 1976, Reagan for Pres., 1976, John Connally for Pres., 1980, Dems. for Reagan, 1980; Jesse Jackson for Pres., 1984, Reagan-Bush campaign, 1984; active numerous campaigns for U.S. Senate and Ho. of Reps. from Tex., 1957—; mem. Rep. Presdl. Task Force, 1984, 85; active Dems. for Eisenhower, 1956, Dems. for Goldwater, 1964; mem. U.S. Olympic Com., 1980; ex post facto mem. Katy Horizons Com., 1980, 81; mem. horizons com. Tri County Am. Revolution Bicentennial Commn., 1976; mem. Statue of Liberty-Ellis Island Centennial Commn., 1983; mem. Presdl. Task Force, 1984, 85. Recipient U.S. Presdl. Achievement award, 1983; U.S. Presdl. Achievement award for environ. protection, 1985; cert. of appreciation Vietnam Vets. Meml. Fund, 1983; cert. of recognition Republican Congl. Com., 1985; Presdl. cert. of merit for environ. protection, 1985. Mem. Tex. Soc. Landscape Architects, Tex. Farm Bur., Barker Heritage and Preservation Soc. (charter mem., sec. 1976, pres. 1977-78, chmn. bd. 1979—), Native Plant Soc. Tex. (charter), Teutonic Internat. (founder, pres. 1986—), Katy C. of C., U. Tex. Ex-students Assn., C. of C. (life), Nat. Rifle Assn. Club: One-Hundred (Houston). Died May 4, 1988. Address: 3506 Greenhouse Rd Barker TX 77413

EUZENNAT, MAURICE, archaeologist, consultant; b. Mt. St. Aignan, France, Nov. 15, 1926; s. Gaston and Yvonne (Laveix) E.; m. Marguerite Marie de Coux, Dec. 21, 1960; 1 child, Philippe. Diploma, Le Sorbonne, 1949; grad., Ecole Pratique Hautes Etudes, 1951. Mem. Ecole Francaise d'Archéologie, Rome, 1951-54; dir. Dept. Antiquities Morocco, 1955-62, French Archaeol. Mission, Morocco, 1962-63; asst. dir. Ctr. Recherches sur L'Afrique Méditerranéenne, Aix en Provence, France, 1964; dir. Dept. Antiquities, Provence and Corsica, France, 1965-68, Inst. d'Archeologie Méditerranéenne, Aix en Provence, 1970-78; research dir. Ctr. Nat. Recherche Sci., Aix en Provence, 1976—; cons. UNESCO, Tunisia, 1967; mem. nat. com. Ctr. Nat. Sci. Research, France, 1980—; mem. Conseil Superieur Recherche Archeologique, France, 1985—. Author: Inscriptions Antiques du Maroc, 1982, Recherches sur la Frontière Romaine au Maroc, 1988; contbr. articles to profl. jours. Served to lt. air force, France, 1953-54. Recipient Silver medal Acad. d'Architecture, Paris, 1961; named Knight Legion d'Honneur, France, 1979. Mem. Acad. Inscription et Belles Lettres (corres.), Deutsche Archeologische Inst. Home: 8 Rue Mazarine, 13100 Aix en Provence France

EVA, EHRLICH, economist; b. Budapest, Hungary, June 18, 1932; s. Ehrlich Zolt and Irén (Hermann) E.; m. Saandor Piukovics, Aug. 22, 1957 (div. 1970); m. Gaabor Révésv, Dec. 31, 1971. MA in Econ., Karl Marx U., Budapest, 1958, PhD, 1975. Research scientist Hungarian Nat. Planning Office, Budapest, 1959-79; sr. research scientist Inst. World Econs. of Hungarian Acad. Sci., Budapest, 1979—; dir. UN Econs. Commn. of Europe, Geneva, 1980-82; lectr. Karl Marx U., 1976—, various U.S. univs., 1984, Geneva, 1968; vis. prof. St. Anthony's Coll., Oxford, 1974. Author: International Analyses to be Used in Hungarian Long-Term Planning, 1968, Japan: A Case of Catching Up, 1979; co-author: Infrastructure, 1975. Mem. European Econ. Assn. Home: Felsozo dmoli ut 17, 1025 Budapest Hungary Office: Inst for World Econs, Kolo esperes ut 15, PO Box 36, 1531 Budapest Hungary

EVANS, ANTHONY JOHN, librarian; b. Bristol, Eng., Apr. 1, 1930; s. William John and Marian Audrey (Young) E.; m. Anne Horwell, Aug. 21, 1954; children: Elizabeth Jane, Susan Mary. BPharm, U. London, 1954, Postgrad. Diploma in Librarianship, 1960, PhD in Pharmacy, 1961. Lectr. pharm. engring. Sch. Pharmacy U. London, 1954-58, librarian, 1958-63; librarian Loughborough (Eng.) U., 1964—, dean Sch. Ednl. Studies, 1973-76, prof. dept. library and info. studies, 1973—; cons. Brit. Council, UNIDO, UNESCO, World Bank, 1971—. Author: Education and Training of Users of Scientific and Technical Information, 1977; contbr. articles to profl. jours. Fellow Library Assn. U.K.; mem. Internat. Assn. Technol. Univ. Libraries (hon. life, treas. 1968-70, pres. 1970-75), Internat. Fedn. Library Assns. and Instns. (exec. bd. 1983—, treas. 1985—). Club: Royal Commonwealth Soc. (London). Home: 78 Valley Rd, Loughborough LE11 3QA, England Office: Loughborough U Tech, Pilkington Library, Loughborough LE11 3TU, England

EVANS, BLACKWELL BUGG, pediatric urologist; b. Forksville, Va., Nov. 5, 1927; s. Clarence Meredith and Saluda Ann Rebecca (Bugg) E.; m. June Helen Banks, Oct. 8, 1949; 1 child, Blackwell Bugg. B.A., U. Va., 1955; M.D., Med. Coll. Va., 1959. Diplomate Am. Bd. Urology. Intern, resident in surgery Johnston-Willis Hosp., Richmond, Va., 1959-61; resident in urology, research fellow in urology Tulane U. Med. Center, 1961-65; clin. asst. urology Med. Coll. S.C., 1965-67; mem. faculty Tulane U. Med. Center, 1967—, prof. pediatrics, 1975—, prof. urology, 1974-82, Sobin prof. pediatric urology, 1982—, chief sect. pediatric urology, 1978-82, chmn. dept. urology, 1982—, acting dean, 1988—, dir. urologic edn. Children's Hosp., New Orleans, 1978—; pres. med. staff Children's Hosp., 1981-83; med. adv. bd. La. Kidney Found., 1973-74; med. adv. com. La. Handicapped Children's Service Program, 1976—; cons. in field. Served as officer USAF, 1951-53. Fellow ACS, Am. Acad. Pediatrics, Internat. Coll. Pediatrics; mem. Am. Urol. Assn. (dir., chmn. fin. com. Southeastern sect. 1979-83), Soc. Pediatric Urology, Soc. Univ. Urologists, Royal Soc. Medicine, Societe Internationale d'Urologie, Internat. Soc. Nephrology, AMA, Pan-Am. Med. Assn., So. Med. Assn., Am. Assn. Med. Colls., N.Y. Acad. Scis., So. Soc. Pediatric Research, La. Urol. Assn. (pres. 1977-78), United Ostomy Assn. (profl. adv. bd. 1974-79), Greater New Orleans Ostomy Assn. (med. adv. bd. 1980—), Soc. Nuclear Medicine, Sigma Xi. Address: Tulane U Med Sch 1430 Tulane Ave New Orleans LA 70112

EVANS, CHRISTOPHER HOWARD, biochemist, educator; b. London, Eng., Feb. 11, 1950; came to U.S., 1977; s. Idwal Howard and Edna (Bioletti) E.; m. Melinda Hays, Aug. 15, 1981. B.S., U. Wales, Swansea, 1971, Ph.D., 1974; M.A., U. Pitts., 1983. Research student U. Wales, Swansea, 1971-74; research fellow Free Univ., Brussels, Belgium, 1974-77; research biochemist Foxboro Co., Burlington, Mass., 1978; asst. prof. orthopaedic surgery and biochemistry U. Pitts., 1979-84, assoc. prof., 1984—, tenure, 1986, dir. Orthopaedic Research Labs., 1984—. Contbr. numerous articles to sci. jours. Vice pres. The Bach Choir of Pitts., 1981—. Recipient Kappa Delta award, 1985; research grantee Arthritis Found., Pitts., 1980—, NSF, 1983—, NIH, 1986—. Mem. Biochem. Soc., Royal Soc. Chemistry, Orthopaedic Research Soc., History of Sci. Soc. Congregationalist. Club: Old Colfeians Association (London). Office: Dept Orthopaedic Surgery 986 Scafe Hall Pittsburgh PA 15261

EVANS, DANIEL FRALEY, JR., lawyer; b. Indpls., Apr. 19, 1949; s. Daniel Fraley and Julia (Sloan) E.; m. Marilyn Shultz, Aug. 11, 1973; children: Meredith, Benjamin, Suzannah, Theodore. BA, Ind. U., 1971, JD, 1976. Bar: Ind. 1976, U.S. Dist. Ct. (so. dist.) Ind. 1976, U.S. Ct. Appeals (7th cir.) 1983, U.S. Supreme Ct. 1983. Assoc. Sparrenberger, Duvall, Tabbert & Lalley, Indpls., 1976-77; ptnr. Duvall, Tabbert, Lalley & Newton, Indpls., 1977-81, Bayh, Tabbert & Capehart, Indpls., 1981-85, Baker & Daniels, Indpls., 1985—. Chmn. Ind. Bd. Correction, Indpls., 1976—, Quayle for Senate Com., 1980, 86; mem. Fed. Jud. Merit Selection Com., Indpls., 1981—, Adminstrv. Conf. U.S., 1983—, Indpls. Dist. Fed. Home Loan Bank Bd. Mem. Indpls. Bar Assn., Ind. Bar Assn., ABA. Republican. Methodist. Clubs: University, Woodstock, (Indpls.). Office: Baker & Daniels 810 Fletcher Trust Bldg Indianapolis IN 46204

EVANS, DANIEL JACKSON, U.S. senator; b. Seattle, Oct. 16, 1925; s. Daniel Lester and Irma (Ide) E.; m. Nancy Ann Bell, June 6, 1959; children: Daniel Jackson, Mark L., Bruce M. B.S. in Civil Engring, U. Wash., 1948, M.S., 1949. Registered profl. engr., Wash. With Asso. Gen. Contractors, Seattle, 1953-59; cons. civil engr. Seattle, 1949-51; partner Gray & Evans, structural and civil engrs., Seattle, 1959-65; mem. Wash. Ho. of Reps. from, King County, 1956-65; Republican floor leader Wash. Ho. of Reps. from, 1961-65; gov. State of Wash., 1964-77; pres. Evergreen State Coll., Olympia, 1977-83; mem. U.S. Senate from Wash. State 1983—; mem. Adv. Council on Intergovernmental Relations, 1972-77, Fed. Adv. Commn. Project Independence, 1974, Nat. Commn. on Productivity and Work Quality, 1975, President's Vietnamese Refugee Adv. Com., 1975; chmn. Pacific NW Electric Power and Conservation Planning Council, 1981-83. Keynote speaker Rep. Nat. Conv., 1968; mem. Nat. Gov.'s Conf., chmn., 1973-74; chmn. Western Gov.'s Conf., 1968-69; trustee Carnegie Found. for Advancement of Teaching, Nature Conservancy, 20th Century Fund. Served to lt. USNR, 1943-46, 51-53. Recipient Human Rights award Pacific N.W. chpt. Nat. Assn. Intergroup Relations Ofcls., 1967; Service to the Profession award Cons. Engrs. Council, 1969; Scales of Justice award Nat. Council Crime and Delinquency, 1968; Pub. Ofcl. of Year award Wash. Environmental Council, 1970; Distinguished Eagle, Silver Beaver, Silver Antelope awards Boy Scouts Am.; Distinguished Citizen award Nat. Municipal League, 1977. Congregationalist. Address: US Senate 702 Hart Senate Bldg Washington DC 20510 *

EVANS, EDWARD PARKER, publishing and information services company executive; b. Pitts., Jan. 31, 1942; s. Thomas Mellon and Elizabeth Parker (Kase) E. BA, Yale U., 1964; MBA, Harvard U., 1967. V.p. Evans & Co., Inc., N.Y.C. and Mo., 1975-82; chmn. bd. H.K. Porter Co., Inc., Pitts., 1976-82, Mo. Portland Cement Co., 1975-82, Fansteel, Inc., 1977-82, Evans Broadcasting Corp., Mo., 1968-82; chmn. bd., chief exec. officer Macmillan, Inc., N.Y.C., 1980—, also bd. dirs.; owner Spring Hill Farm, Casanova, Va., 1969—; bd. dirs. Fasig-Tipton Co., Inc. Mem. Andover Devel. Bd. Served with Air N.G., 1965-71. Clubs: Duquesne (Pitts.); River, Harvard Bus. Sch. (N.Y.C.); Round Hill (Greenwich, Conn.); Rolling Rock (Ligonier, Pa.); Blind Brook (Purchase, N.Y.); Spouting Rock Beach Assn. (Newport, R.I.); Lyford Cay (Nassau, Bahamas). Office: Macmillan Inc 866 Third Ave New York NY 10022

EVANS, EVAN, petroleum executive; b. N.Y.C., May 19, 1925; s. John William, Jr. and Therese Rosemary (Guilfoyle) E.; student St. Lawrence U., 1942-43, 46, B.S., 1949; B.S., MIT, 1951; m. Natalie Coe Holbrook, Feb. 20, 1968; children—Megan, Meredith, Rhys, Valerie, Cynthia, David. Engr., Calif. Tex. Oil Corp., N.Y.C., 1951-55, Bahrain, 1955-57, refinery ops. asst., N.Y.C., 1957-60, Rotterdam, 1960-62, refinery plant mgr., Lebanon, 1963, refinery specialist, N.Y.C., 1963-65, refinery project mgr., King Wilkinson, Antwerp, 1966-68; v.p. United Refining Co., Warren, Pa., 1972-81, dir., 1974-81; pres. Kiantone Pipeline, 1970-81; dir. Texoma Pipe Line, 1974-83; v.p. Western Crude Oil, Inc., 1981-83; pres. Wesco Internat., Inc., 1981-83, Holvan Properties, Inc., Madison, Conn., 1983—. Chmn. Am. Sch. Rotterdam, 1961-62. Served with USN, 1943-46. Clubs: N.Y. Athletic; Denver. Address: 331 Old Toll Road Madison CT 06443

EVANS, FRANKLIN BACHELDER, emeritus advertising educator; b. Chgo., Feb. 9, 1922; s. Franklin B. and Arline (Brown) E.; m. Barbara V. Both, Sept. 16, 1943; children: Mary A., Amy B., Geoffrey B., Christopher G. A.A., U. Chgo., 1941, A.B., 1943, M.B.A., 1954, Ph.D., 1959. Asst. prof. mktg. U. Chgo., 1957-64; prof. mktg. U. Hawaii, 1964-69; prof. advt. Northwestern U., 1969-80, prof. emeritus, 1981—; cons. to bus. and industry. Contbr. articles to profl. jours. Served with AUS, 1943-45, CBI. Decorated Bronze Star. Mem. Am. Statis. Assn., Am. Sociol. Assn., Am. Mktg. Assn., Am. Acad. Advt., AAAS, AAUP, Psi Upsilon. Home: Yacht Haven #206 340 Pinellas Bay Way Tierra Verde FL 33715

EVANS, GARY LEE, communications educator; b. Davison, Mich., June 26, 1938; s. Joe Howard and Annie Annette (Colden) E.; children: Gary James, Aimee Lynn. BA, Wayne State U., 1962; MA, U. Mich., 1965, PhD, 1977. Prof. internat. and intercultural communication Eastern Mich. U., Ypsilanti, 1964—; bd. dirs. wilderness edn. program Eastern Mich. U., 1984-88; dir. Summer Inst. for Talented and Gifted Students, Mich. State Bd. Edn., 1984-88; cons. Med. Data Systems, Medtronic, Ann Arbor, Mich., 1980-84, Mich. Pub. Schs., 1982—, Volvo Automated Systems, Sterling Heights, Mich., 1985—, NSK-Hoover, Inc., Ann Arbor, 1985—. Editor Communication Jour., 1979-83. Sec. bd. edn. Pinckney Community Schs., 1980-84; Peace Corps Tng. and Teaching. Mem. Internat. Communication Assn., Speech Communication assn., Mich. Acad. Sci., Arts and Letters (communication chmn. 1982), Mich. Speech Communication Assn. (communication chmn. 1978—), Phi Kappa Phi, Delta Sigma Rho. Home: 8775 Coyle Dr Pinckney MI 48169 Office: Eastern Mich U 121 Quirk Bldg Ypsilanti MI 48197

EVANS, GERAINT LLEWELLYN, opera singer; b. Wales, Feb. 16, 1922; s. William John and Gladys May (Thomas) E.; m. Branda Evans Davies, Mar. 27, 1948; children: Alun Grant, Huw Grant. Student, Guildhall Sch. Music; Mus.D. (hon.), U. Wales, 1963, U. Leicester, 1969, Council Nat. Acad. Awards, 1980, U. London, 1982, Oxford U., 1985. Prin. baritone, Royal Opera House, 1948-84, appearances include, Covent Garden, London, Glyndebourne Festival Opera, 1950—, also, Vienna State Opera, La Scala, Milan, Italy, Met. Opera, N.Y.C., San Francisco Opera, Lyric Opera, Chgo., Salzburg (Germany) Opera, Edinburgh Festival Opera, Paris Opera, Teatro Colon, Buenos Aires, Mexico, City Opera, Welsh Nat. Opera, Scottish Opera, Berlin Opera, Teatr Wielki, Warsaw, Poland. Decorated comdr. Brit. Empire, 1959, knight bachelor, 1969; Fellow Guildhall Sch. Music, 1960; recipient Sir Charles Santley Meml. award Worshipful Co. of Musicians, 1963, Harriet Cohen Internat. Music award, 1967; San Francisco Opera medal, 1980; Fidelio medal, 1980; fellow Royal No. Coll. Music Univ. Coll., Cardiff, 1976; fellow Jesus Coll., Oxford, 1979; fellow Royal Coll. Music, 1981; fellow Royal Soc. Arts; hon. mem. Royal Acad. Music; Freeman of City of London, 1984. Home: Trelawney, Aberaeron, Dyfed Wales SA46 OBD

EVANS, GLEN FREDERICK, author; b. Dallas, Apr. 29, 1921; s. Paris F. and Elga (Hacker) E.; m. Margaret Mary Wanex, Jan. 15, 1961; 1 child, Lisa Glyn. BJ, U. Mo., 1949. With Maytag Co., 1949-60, advt. and sales promotion mgr., Atlanta, 1954-60; freelance journalist-author, editor, 1960—. Author: The Family Circle Guide to Self-Help, 1979, The Encyclopedia of Suicide, 1987; author column Man to Man Answers, True mag., 1970-72; work rep. various anthologies. Editor: The Complete Guide to Writing Non-Fiction, 1983; Market Update Newsletter, 1984-88. Co-chmn. White Mountain Sch. PTA, Littleton, N.H., 1979-80; trustee White Mountain Sch., 1979-80; mem. community relations adv. council Meridian House Found. Served with USN, 1940-46. Recipient Mag. Editing award Iowa Indsl. Editors, 1951, Internat. Council Indsl. Editors, 1951; Health Journalism award Am. Chiropractic Assn., 1978; Odyssey House Nat. Media award, 1981; Sigma Delta Chi scholar, 1949; fellow NEH, 1978. Mem. Writers Digest Criticism Service, Rocky Mountain Writers Guild, Am. Soc. Journalists and Authors (dir. 1982—, exec. v.p. 1986-87, pres. 1987-88, Spl. Service award 1986), Authors Guild, Authors League, Nat. Book Critics Circle, Soc. Profl. Journalists, Acad. Ind. Scholars, Sigma Delta Chi. Methodist. Clubs: Nat. Press, Nat. Writers (Washington); Deadline (N.Y.C.). Home and Office: 122 Cedar Heights Rd Stamford CT 06905

EVANS, HANNAH IMOGENE, psychologist; b. Richmond, Va., Nov. 6, 1945; d. Charles and Ruth (Powell) E.; BA, U. Vt., 1967; MS, Pa. State U., 1970, PhD, 1972; MPA, U. Colo., Denver, 1981; m. Robert F. McKenzie, July 12, 1975. Clin. psychology intern, psychol. cons. II, Denver Dept. Health and Hosps., 1972-77; adj. faculty U. Colo., Denver, summer 1978; resource counselor Regional Transp. Dist., 1978-79; pvt. practice psychotherapy, Denver, 1976—. Mem. community adv. bd. Sch. Profl. Psychology, U. Denver; mem. grievance com. Colo. Supreme Ct., 1982—; staff affiliate Bethesda Hosp., 1979—; clin. assoc. sch. profl. Psychology, U. Denver. Mem. Gov.'s Front Range Task Force, 1980-81; bd. dirs. Denver Sexual Assault Council, 1974-80; founding bd. Colo. Center Women and Work, 1979-81; adv. bd. A Woman's Pl. at Rocky Mountain Hosp., 1987—; mem. Women's Forum of Colo., 1979—, selection com., 1980—; mem. grievance bd. Mental Health Occupations, 1988—; mem. Victims and Witness Assistance and Law Enforcement Bd. 2d Jud. Dist. USPHS fellow, 1968-70; named one of Faces of Colo., Colo. mag., 1976. Mem. Am. Psychol. Assn., Nat. Register of Health Service Providers in Psychology, Colo. State Bd. of Psychologist Examiners, Bd. Psychology Practice. Contbr. articles to profl. jours. and popular mags.

EVANS, JO BURT, TV translator company executive, rancher; b. Kimble County, Tex., Dec. 18, 1928; d. John Fred and Sadie (Oliver) Burt; B.A., Mary Hardin-Baylor Coll., 1948; M.A., Trinity U., 1967; m. Charles Wayne Evans II, Apr. 17, 1949; children—Charles Wayne III, John Burt, Elizabeth Wisart. Owner, mgr. Sta. KMBL, Junction, Tex., 1959-61; real estate broker, Junction, 1965-74; staff economist, adv. on 21st Congl. Dist., polit. campaign Nelson Wolff, 1974-75; asst. mgr., bookkeeper family owned ranches and rent property, Junction, 1948—; gen. mgr. TV Translator Corp., Junction,

1968—, sec.-treas., 1980—. Treas., asst. to coordinator Citizens for Tex., 1972; historian Kimble Hist. Soc.; mem. Com. of Conservation Soc. to Save the Edwards Aquifer, San Antonio, 1973; homecoming chmn. Sesquicentennial Year, Junction; treas., asst. coordinator New Constitution, San Antonio, 1974. AAUW scholarship named in honor, 1973; named an outstanding Texan, Tex. Senate, 1973. Mem. Nat. Translator Assn., AAUW, Daus. Republic Tex., Tex. Sheriffs Assn., Nat. Cattlewomens Assn., Internat. Platform Assn., Bus. and Profl. Women (pres. 1981-82). Democrat. Mem. Unity Ch. Home: PO Box 283 Junction TX 76849 Office: 618 Main St Junction TX 76849

EVANS, JOHANNES SANAO, business executive; b. Tokyo, Mar. 10, 1927; s. Paul Yuzuru Kawai and Vicky Wichgraf-Evans; B.S. in Fgn. Service, Akademie Fuer Welthandel, Frankfurt/Main, Germany, 1954; B.S. in Bus. Adminstrn., Georgetown U., 1964; M.B.A., U. Rochester, 1970; m. Mária Johanna Langer, Mar. 10, 1947; children—Helga, Richard, Alphonse. Positions with internat. trade companies, Germany, 1948-61; jr. acct. Stanton, Minter & Bruner, Alexandria, Va., 1964; with Xerox Corp., various locations, 1964—, sr. policy planner, Stamford, Conn., 1972-77, mgr. corp. cost acctg. policy, 1977—. C.P.A., Conn. Mem. Nat. Assn. Accts., Am. Acctg. Assn., Pvt. Sector Council (U.S. Army Task Force), Am. Inst. C.P.A.'s, Conn. Soc. C.P.A.'s, Mensa. Republican. Home: 9 Fawn Rd Bethel CT 06801 Office: Xerox Corp Stamford CT 06904

EVANS, JOHN COLIN, construction consultant; b. Risca, Wales, June 22, 1945; s. David Trvor and Irene (Griffin) E.; degree constrn. econs. Brit. Inst. Engring. Tech., 1966. Sr. quantity surveyor John Laing Constrn., London, 1962-66, Tillyard & Partners, Lagos, Nigeria, 1966; chief quantity surveyor W.F. Rees, Surrey, Eng., 1967; pres., dir. Tillyard Internat., Inc., Chgo., 1968-74, Tillyard Consultores, Sã o Paulo, Brazil, 1974-84 , Tillyard del Paraguay, Asunció n, 1979-84 ; dir. Colin Evans Associados, Ltd., 1984—. Fellow Royal Inst. Chartered Surveyors; mem. Inst. Arbitrators (asso.), Am. Assn. Cost Engrs. (asso.), Constrn. Specifiers Inst. Baptist. Club: Rotary. Home: Al Casa Branca 1143, Apt 132, São Paulo Brazil Office: Rua José, Maria Lisboa 873 #2, Sao Paulo Brazil

EVANS, JOHN DAVID GEMMILL, philosophy and anthropology educator; b. London, Aug. 27, 1942; s. John Desmond and Alice Fortune (Gemmill) E.; m. Rosemary Ellis. BA, Cambridge U., 1963; PhD, Sidney Sussex Coll., Cambridge, 1969. Fellow, lectr. Sidney Sussex Coll., 1965-78; prof. logic and metaphysics Queen's U., Belfast, No. Ireland, 1978—, dean faculty of arts, 1986—, chmn. sch. philos. and anthropol. studies, 1987—. Author: Aristotle's Concept of Dialectic, 1977, Aristotle, 1987. Craven studentship Cambridge U., 1963-64. Mem. Royal Irish Acad., Aristotelian Soc., Cambridge Philol. Assn., Irish Astron. Assn., British Soc. for History of Philosophy. Office: Queens U, Philosophy Dept, Belfast BT7 1NN, Northern Ireland

EVANS, JOHN DAVIES, archaeologist; b. Jan. 22, 1925; s. Harry and Edith (Haycocks) E.; B.A., U. Cambridge, 1948, M.A., 1950, Ph.D., 1956, Litt.D., 1979; Dr.h.c., U. Lyon, 1983; m. Evelyn Sladdin, 1957. Fellow, Brit. Inst. Archaeology, Ankara, Turkey, 1951-52; research fellow Pembroke Coll., Cambridge, 1953-56; prof. prehistoric archaeology London U., 1956-73, prof. archaeology, dir. Inst. Archaeology, 1973—; pres. Prehistoric Soc., 1974-78; pres. Council Brit. Archaeology, 1979-82; mem. permanent council Internat. Congress Prehistoric and Protohistoric Scis., 1975—, pres., 1982-85; chmn. area archaeol. adv. com. for Southeast Eng., 1975-79. Mem. German Archaeol. Inst., Soc. Antiquaries of London (pres. 1984-87). Author: Malta (Ancient Peoples and Places Series), 1959; (with A.C. Renfrew) Excavations at Saliagos, near Antiparos, 1968; The Prehistoric Antiquities of the Maltese Islands, 1971; contbr. articles to profl. jours. Address: Inst Archaeology, Gordon Sq, London WC1H OPY, England

EVANS, JOHN DERBY, telecommunications company executive; b. Detroit, June 3, 1944; s. Edward Steptoe and Florence (Allington) E.; m. Susan Blair Allan, Apr. 7, 1973 (div. Nov. 1986); children: John Derby, Courtenay Boyd. AB, U. Mich., 1966. Pres. Evans Communications Systems Inc., Charlottesville, Va., 1970-72; v.p., gen. mgr. Capitol Cablevision Corp., Charleston, W.Va., 1972-76; regional mgr. Am. TV & Communications Corp., Denver, 1974-76; exec. v.p., chief ops. officer Arlington (Va.) TeleCommunications Corp., 1976-83; pres. Arlington Cable Ptnrs. Ltd., 1983—, Suburban Cable Ptnrs., Brooklyn Pk., Minn., 1985—, Hauser Communications, N.Y.C., 1985—; pres. Evans Telecommunications Corp., Arlington, 1983—, Montgomery Cablevision (LP), Rockville, Md., 1986—; v.p. North Cen. Cable Comminicaions Co., Roseville, Minn., 1986—; telecommunications cons. to asst. sec. for planning and devel. Dept. HEW, Washington, 1976, N. Cen. Cable Communications Co., Roseville, Minn.; bd. dirs. Cable Satellite Pub. Affairs Network (C-SPAN), 1978—. Served to lt. USN, 1966-70. Mem. Nat. Cable TV Assn. (nat. chmn. awards com. 1981, bd. dirs. 1982—, pres.'s award 1979, Challenger award 1984), Va. Cable Assn. (bd. dirs. 1979—, v.p. 1982, pres. 1983-84, chmn. govtl. relations com. 1985-86), Soc. Motion Picture TV Engrs. Republican. Episcopalian. Clubs: Farmington Country, Boars Head Sports (Charlottesville); Old Dominion Boat (Alexandria, Va.); Wintergreen (Va.) Sports; Washington Golf and Country (Arlington). Home: 1530 N Key Blvd PH 1310 Arlington VA 22209 Office: 2707 Wilson Blvd Arlington VA 22201

EVANS, JOHN GLYNDWR, trade union official, economist; b. London, May 22, 1952; came to France, 1985; s. John Denis and Jessie Pettigrew (McDonald) E.; m. Benedicte Musch, July 1, 1983; children: Jessica, Chloe. MA in Philosophy, Politics and Econs., Oxford U., 1973. Econ. asst. Trades Union Congress, London, 1973-78; trade sect. sec. Internat. Fedn. Comml., Clerical and Tech. Employees, Geneva, 1978-79; research officer European Trade Union Inst., Brussels, 1979-85; gen. sec. Trade Union Adv. Com., Orgn. for Econ. Cooperation, Paris, 1985. Author: (study) Microelectronics and Society, 1982; (with others) New Office Technology, 1983. Office: tuac-OECD, 26 Ave de la Grande Armée, 75017 Paris France

EVANS, LAWRENCE JACK, JR., lawyer; b. Oakland, Calif., Apr. 4, 1921; s. Lawrence Jack and Eva May (Dickinson) E.; m. Marjorie Hisken, Dec. 23, 1944; children—Daryl S. Kleweno, Richard L., Shirley J. Coursey, Donald B. Diplomate Near East Sch. Theology, Beirut, 1951; M.A., Am. U. Beirut, 1951; Ph.D., Brantridge Forest Sch., Sussex, Eng., 1968; J.D., Ariz. State U., 1971; grad. Nat. Jud. Coll., 1974. Bar: Ariz. 1971, U.S. Dist. Ct. Ariz. 1971, U.S. Ct. Claims 1972, U.S. Customs Ct., 1972, U.S. Tax Ct. 1972, U.S. Ct. Customs and Patent Appeals 1972, U.S. Ct. Appeals (9th cir.) 1972, U.S. Supreme Ct. 1975. Served as enlisted man U.S. Navy, 1938-41; enlisted man U.S. Army, 1942-44, commd. 2d lt., 1944, advanced through ranks to lt. col., 1962; war plans officer, G-3 Seventh Army, 1960-62, chief, field ops. and tactics div., U.S. Army Spl. Forces, 1963, chief spl. techniques div., U.S. Army Spl. Forces, 1964, unconventional warfare monitor, U.S. Army Spl. Forces, 1964-65; assigned to Command and Gen. Staff Coll., 1960; ops. staff officer J-3 USEUCOM, 1965-68; mem. Airborne Command Post Study Group, Joint Chiefs of Staff, 1967; ret., 1968; sole practice law, cons. on Near and Middle Eastern affairs, Tempe, Ariz., 1971-72, 76—; v.p., dir. Trojan Investment & Devel. Co., Inc., 1972-75; active Ariz. Tax Conf., 1971-75; mem. adminstrv. law com., labor mgmt. relations com., unauthorized practice of law com. Ariz. State Bar. Author: Legal Aspects of Land Tenure in the Republic of Lebanon, 1951; (with Helen Miller Davis) International Constitutional Law, Electoral Laws and Treaties of the Near and Middle East, 1951. Contbr. articles to mags., chpts. to books. Chmn. legal and legis. com. Phoenix Mayor's Com. To Employ Handicapped, 1971-75; active Tempe Leadership Conf., 1971-75; chmn. Citizens Against Corruption in Govt.; mem. Princeton Council on Fgn. and Internat. Studies. Decorated Silver Star, Legion of Merit, Bronze Star, Purple Heart; named Outstanding Adminstrv. Law Judge for State Service for U.S., 1974; named to U.S. Army Ranger Hall of Fame, 1981. Mem. Ranger Bns. Assn. World War II (life), Tempe Rep. Mens Club (v.p., bd. dirs. 1971-72, U.S. Army Airborne Ranger Assn. (life), Mil. Order Purple Heart (life), Nat. Rifle Assn. (life), Phi Delta Phi, Delta Theta Phi. Episcopalian. Lodges: Masons, SL (past master), YR (past high priest, past thrice illustrious master, past comdr.), SR (32, ritual dir.). Home: 539 E Erie Dr Tempe AZ 85282

EVANS, LOUISE, psychologist; b. San Antonio; d. Henry Daniel and Adela (Pariser) E.; m. Thomas Ross Gambrell, Feb. 23, 1960; B.S., Northwestern U., 1949; M.S. in Psychology, Purdue U., 1952, Ph.D. in Clin. Psychology, 1955; Lic. Marriage, Family and Child Counselor Nat. Register of Health Service Providers in Psychology. Intern clin. psychology Menninger Found., Topeka (Kans.) State Hosp., 1952-53, USPHS-Menninger Found. fellow clin. child psychology, 1955-56; staff psychologist Kankakee (Ill.) State Hosp., 1954; head staff psychologist child guidance clinic Kings County Hosp., Bklyn., 1957-58; dir. psychology clinic, instr. med. psychology Washington U. Sch. Medicine, 1959; clin. research cons. Episcopal City Mission, St. Louis, 1959; pvt. practice clin. psychology, 1960—; approved fellow Internat. Council Sex Edn. and Parenthood, 1984; hon. Research Bd. Advs. nat. div. Am. Biog. Inst., 1985; psychol. cons. Fullerton (Calif.) Community Hosp., 1961-81; staff cons. clin. psychology Martin Luther Hosp., Anaheim, Calif., 1963-70; lectr. clin. psychology schs. and profl. groups, 1950—; participant psychol. symposiums, 1956—; guest speaker clin. psychology civic and community orgns., 1950—. Elected to Hall of Fame, Central High Sch., Ind., 1966; recipient Service award Yuma County Head Start Program, 1972, Statue of Victory Personality of the Yr. award Centro Studi E. Ricerche Delle Nazioni, 1985; named Miss Heritage, Heritage Publs., 1965; lic. psychologist N.Y., Calif.; diplomate Clin. Psychology. Fellow Am. Psychol. Assn., Royal Soc. Health of England, Internat. Council of Psychologists (dir. 1977-79, sec. 1962-64, 73-76), AAAS, Am. Orthopsychiat. Assn., World Wide Acad. of Scholars of N.Z.; mem. AAUP, Los Angeles Soc. Clin. Psychologists (exec. bd. 1966-67), Calif. State Psychol. Assn., Los Angeles County Psychol. Assn., Orange County Psychol. Assn. (exec. bd. 1961-62), Orange County Soc. Clin. Psychologists (exec. bd. 1963-65, pres. 1964-65), Am. Public Health Assn., Rehab. Internat., Internat. Platform Assn., Am. Acad. Polit. and Social Scis., N.Y. Acad. Scis., Purdue U. Alumni Assn. (Citizenship award 1975), Am. Judicature Soc., Center for Study of Presidency, Alumni Assn. Menninger Sch. Psychiatry, Sigma Xi, Pi Sigma Pi. Contbr. articles on clin. psychology to profl. publs. Office: 905-907 W Wilshire Ave Fullerton CA 92632

EVANS, MICHAEL CHRISTOPHER, educator; b. Barnstaple, Devon, Eng., Sept. 12, 1946; came to Australia, 1973; s. John Roy and Enid Mary (Frayn) E.; m. Caro Kaye Duncan, Nov. 22, 1986; 1 child, Tobey Duncan. BA, Oxford U., Eng., 1968, MA, 1971; PhD, Cambridge U., Eng., 1971. Lectr. in classics U. Newcastle, New South Wales, Australia, 1973-77, sr. lectr., 1978-81, assoc. prof. drama, 1982—; vis. prof. U. prof. program Boston U., 1986-87. Author: Janacek's Tragic Operas, 1977 (Yorkshire Post Music Book award 1977), Wagner and Aeschylus, 1982; contbr. articles to profl. jours. Mem. Australasian Langs. Lit. Assn., Australasian Drama Studies Assn., Wagner Soc. Australia. Office: U Newcastle, 2308 Newcastle Australia

EVANS, PAULINE (DAVIDSON), physicist, educator; b. Bklyn., Mar. 24, 1922; d. John A. and Hannah (Brandt) Davidson; B.A., Hofstra Coll., 1942; postgrad. N.Y. U., 1943, 46-47, Cornell U., 1946, Syracuse U., 1947-50; m. Melbourne Griffith Evans, Sept. 6, 1950; children—Lynn Janet Evans Hannemann, Brian Griffith. Jr. physicist Signal Corps Ground Signal Service, Eatontown, N.J., 1942-43; physicist Kellex Corp. (Manhattan Project), N.Y.C., 1944; faculty dept. physics Queens Coll., N.Y.C., 1944-47; teaching asst. Syracuse U., 1947-50; instr. Wheaton Coll., Norton, Mass., 1952; physicist Nat. Bur. Standards, Washington, 1954-55; instr. physics U. Ala., 1955, U. N.Mex., 1955, 57-58; staff mem. Sandia Corp., Albuquerque, 1956-57; physicist Naval Nuclear Ordnance Evaluation Unit, Kirtland AFB, N.Mex., 1958-60; programmer Teaching Machines, Inc., Albuquerque, 1961; mem. faculty dept. physics Coll. St. Joseph on the Rio Grande (name changed to U. Albuquerque 1966), 1961—, assoc. prof., 1965—, chmn. dept., 1961—. Mem. Am. Phys. Soc., Am. Assn. Physics Tchrs., Fedn. Am. Scientists, AAUP, Sigma Pi Sigma, Sigma Delta Epsilon. Patentee in field. Home: 730 Loma Alta Ct NW Albuquerque NM 87105 Office: U of Albuquerque Dept Physics Albuquerque NM 87140

EVANS, ROGER, lawyer; b. Syracuse, N.Y., Apr. 18, 1951; s. David Longfellow and Louise Maude (Crawford) E.; m. Claudia Thérèse Benack, Mar. 27, 1976; children: Jonathan Longfellow, Gillian Crawford. AB, Cornell U., 1974; postgrad., Columbia U., 1976-77; JD, Harvard U., 1977. Bar: Ohio 1977, U.S. Dist. Ct. (no. dist.) Ohio 1978, Tex. 1981, U.S. Dist. Ct. (no. dist.) Tex. 1981, U.S. Ct. Appeals (5th, 6th and 11th cirs.) 1981, U.S. Ct. Appeals (10th cir.) 1982. Assoc. Jones, Day, Reavis & Pogue, Cleve., 1977-81, Dallas, 1981-84; ptnr. Shank, Irwin & Conant, Dallas, 1984-86, Gardner, Carton & Douglas, Dallas, 1986-88, Vinson & Elkins, Dallas, 1988—; Gen. counsel Equest, Inc., Dallas, 1986—. Gen. counsel, bd. dirs. Freedom Ride Found., Dallas, 1985-86; active Dallas Dem. Leadership Council, 1986—. Mem. ABA, State Bar of Tex., Ohio State Bar Assn., Cornell U. Alumni Assn. (class pres. 1984—), Harvard Law Sch. Assn. of No. Ohio (sec. 1978-81). Democrat. Episcopalian. Club: Harvard (Dallas). Home: 11410 Strait Ln Dallas TX 75229 Office: Vinson & Elkins 3700 Trammell Crow Ctr 2001 Ross Ave Dallas TX 75201

EVANS, THOMAS EDGAR, JR., title insurance agency executive; b. Toronto, Ohio, Apr. 17, 1940; s. Thomas Edgar and Sarah Ellen (Bauer) E.; BA, Mt. Union Coll., 1963; m. Cynthia Lee Johnson, Feb. 23; children: Thomas Edgar, Douglas, Melinda, Jennifer. Tchr. Lodi, Ohio, 1963-64; salesman Simpson-Evans Realty, Steubenville, Ohio, 1964-65, Shadron Realty, Tucson, 1965-67; real estate broker, co-owner Double E Realty, Tucson, 1967-69; escrow officer, br. mgr., asst. county mgr., v.p. Ariz. Title Ins., Tucson, 1969-80; pres. Commonwealth Land Title Agy., Tucson, 1980-82, also dir.; pres. Fidelity Nat. Title Agy., 1982—; v.p. Fidelity Nat. Corp.; bd. dirs. Western Fin. Trust Co., Fidelity Nat. Fin. Inc., Fidelity Nat. Title Ins. Co., Fidelity Nat. Title Agy. Pinal, The Griffin Co.; bd. dirs., chmn. bd. Cochise Title Agy., TIPCO; v.p., dir. A.P.C. Corp. Named Boss of Year, El Chaparral chpt. Am. Bus. Women's Assn., 1977. Mem. So. Ariz. Escrow Assn., So. Ariz. Mortgage Bankers Assn. (bd. dirs. 1982-85), Ariz. Mktg. Bankers Assn., Old Pueblo Businessmen's Assn. Tucson, Tucson Bd. Realtors, Ariz. Assn. Real Estate Exchangors (bd. dirs. 1968-69), Land Title Assn. Ariz. (pres. 1984), So. Ariz. Homebuilders Assn., Blue Key, Sigma Nu. Republican. Methodist. Clubs: Old Pueblo Courthouse, La Paloma, Ventana Country, Centre Court, Elks, Pima Jaycees (dir. 1966), Sertoma (charter pres., chmn. bd. Midtown sect. 1968-70); Tucson Real Estate Exchangors (pres. 1968); Sunrise Rotary; Old Pueblo. Home: 5142 E Camino Faja Tucson AZ 85718 Office: 4905 E Broadway Suite 100 Tucson AZ 85711

EVANS, THOMAS PASSMORE, business and product licensing consultant; b. West Grove, Pa., Aug. 19, 1921; s. John and Linda (Zeuner) E.; B.S. in E.E., Swarthmore Coll., 1942; M.Engring., Yale U., 1948; m. Lenore Jane Knuth, June 21, 1947; children—Paula S., Christina L., Bruce A., Carol L. Engr., Atomic Power div. Westinghouse Electric Corp., Pitts., 1948-51; dir. research and devel. AMF, Inc., N.Y.C., 1951-60; dir. research O.M. Scott & Sons Co., Marysville, Ohio, 1960-62; v.p. research and devel. W.A. Sheaffer Pen Co., Ft. Madison, Iowa, 1962-67; dir. research Mich. Tech. U., Houghton, 1967-80; dir. research, mem. faculty Berry Coll., Mt. Berry, Ga., 1980-88; prof. bus. adminstrn., 1980-86. Author, patentee in field. Served to lt. USN, 1943-46. Registered profl. engr., Pa. Mem. Am. Forestry Assn., Am. Def. Preparedness Assn., Am. Phys. Soc., IEEE, Soc. Plastics Engrs., Am. Mgmt. Assn., Yale Sci. and Engring. Assn., Nat. Council Univ. Research Adminstrs., Licensing Execs. Soc., Air Force Assn., Am. Legion, AAAS, Art Inst. Chgo., Community Concert Assn., Ga. Friends of Humanities, High Mus. Art, Hunter Mus. Art, Japan-Am. Soc. Ga., Nat. Trust Hist. Preservation, Nat. Ret. Tchrs. Assn., Am. Assn. Ret. Persons, Assn. Pvt. Enterprise Edn., Yale Club of Ga., Rome Little Theatre, Rome Symphony, VFW, Sigma Xi, Tau Beta Pi. Club: Rotary. Home: 25 Wellington Way SE Rome GA 30161 Office: Berry Coll Dept Research PO Box 97 Mount Berry GA 30149

EVANS, WILLIAM THOMAS, physician; b. Denver, Aug. 21, 1941; s. Alfred Lincoln and Marian Audrey (Biggs) E.; BA, U. Colo., 1963; MD, Baylor U., 1967; grad. Chinese Coll. U.K.; Licentiate Acupuncture, Oxford, Eng., 1976; m. Lucy Fales. Intern, Mary Fletcher Hosp., Burlington, Vt.; physician Villages of Kodiak Island and Lake Iliamna, 1968-70; founder, dir. emergency dept. St. Elizabeth Hosp., Yakima, Wash., 1970-75; practice medicine specializing prevention and conservative treatment of spine injuries, Denver; founder, dir. Colo. Back Sch., Denver, 1979—; Friends of Earth del. Limits to Medicine Congress, 1975. Initiated Colo. Sun Day, 1978. Served to lt. comdr. Indian Health Service, USPHS, 1968-70. Mem. Rocky Mountain Traumatological Soc. (exec. sec., treas.), Denver County Med. Soc., Colo. Med. Soc. (workmen's compensation com.), No. Am. Spine Soc., Am. Occupational Medicine Assn., Rocky Mountain Acad. Occupational Medicine (pres. elect), AMA, Am. Coll. Sports Medicine, Traditional Acupuncture Soc. Office: 1720 S Bellaire Suite 1010 Denver CO 80222

EVDOKIMOVA, EVA, ballerina; b. Geneva, Switzerland, Dec. 1, 1948; m. Michael Gregori, 1982. Student, Munich State Opera Ballet Sch., Royal Ballet Sch., London; studied privately with Maria Fay (London), Vera Volkova (Copenhagen), Natalia Dudinskaya (Leningrad). Debut Royal Danish Ballet, Copenhagen, 1966; Prima Ballerina Assoluta, Deutsche Oper Berlin, 1969—; frequent guest artist with numerous major ballet cos. worldwide including London Festival Ballet, Am. Ballet Theatre, Paris Opera Ballet, La Scala, Kirov Ballet, Tokyo Ballet, Teatro Colon, Nat. Ballet of Can., and all other nat. ballet cos.; most frequent ptnr. of Rudolf Nureyev, 1971—; premiered roles in all Rudolf Nureyev's classical ballet prodns.; repertoire of more than 85 roles includes Swan Lake, Giselle, La Sylphide, Sleeping Beauty, Romeo and Juliet, Don Quixote, La Bayadere, Onegin, Raymonda; created roles in ballets including: Aspects (by Frank Schaufuss), Cinderella, The Idiot (both by Valery Panov), Sphinx (by Glen Tetley), Tristan and Isolde (by Loyce Houlton), Unicorn (by John Neumeier), Medea, A Family Portrait (both by Birgit Cullberg), Carmencita (by Patrice Montagnon), Transfigured Night, Child Harold (both by Hans Spörli), Undine (by Tom Schilling); film appearances include The Nutcracker, La Sylphide, Cinderella, A Family Portrait, The Romantic Era, Invitation to the Dance, Portrait of Eva Evdokimova. Recipient Diploma, Internat. Ballet Competition, Moscow, 1969; winner Gold medal Varna Internat. Ballet competition, 1970; awarded title Prima Ballerina, Berlin Senate, 1973; first fgn. mem. Royal Danish Ballet, first Am. and Westerner to win any internat. ballet competition, first Am. to perform with Kirov Ballet, 1976, first Am. to perform in Peking after the Cultural Revolution, 1978, first and only Am. dancer with portrait in permanent collection, Mus. Drama and Dance, Leningrad, first Am. ballerina to perform as guest artist, Great Theatre, Warsaw, 1988. Office: care Gregori Prodns PO Box 279 FDR Sta New York NY 10150-0279 also: Deutsche Oper Berlin, 1000 Berlin (West) 10 Germany

EVENSEN, BJORN ERLING, artist, sculptor; b. Stockholm, Feb. 8, 1924; s. Alf Erling and Lily (Johnson) E.; m. Margit Olsson, Mar. 3, 1952; children—Per-Erling, Micka, Dan, Butte. Ed. Accademia di Belle Arte, Rome, 1953. One-man shows: Henie Onstad Mus., 1974, Freemantle Gallery, Perth Australia, 1975, Galerie Blanche, Stockholm, 1976, 78, 80, 82, 85, 86 Genesis Gallery, N.Y.C., 1977, Vorpal Gallery, N.Y.C., 1984, 86, 87, 88; group shows include: museums in Sweden, 1974-83, Wards Island Sculpture Gallery, 1977, 78, 79, Vorpal Gallery, 1979, 80, 82, 83, 84, 86; represented in permanent collections: Nat. Mus., Stockholm, Mus. Modern Art, Stockholm, Salec Minc Collection Gallery, Perth, Vorpal Gallery; outdoor sculpture in City of Oslo Collection, City of Stockholm Collection, City of N.Y. Collection, City of Perth Collection. Recipient Culture awards Italy, Swedish Commn. Art and Culture; Cert. of Appreciation, City of N.Y., 1981. Home: Norrviksvagen 18, Lidingo 18162 Sweden

EVENSEN, JAN EVEN, communications executive; b. Bergen, Norway, Oct. 31, 1957; s. Odd and Ingrid Evelyn (Landmark) E.; m. Brit Hunstad, Dec. 28, 1982; 1 child, Solveig Hunstad. Student, Norges Teknishe Hoegskole, Trondheim, Norway; MS, Reinisch Westfallische Technische Hochschule, Aachen, Fed. Republic Germany, 1984. Devel. engr. EB-Nera, Bergen, 1984-85; project leader Micro Design A/S, Selbn, Norway, 1986-87; mng. dir. Sandar Telematics A/S, Trondheim, 1987—. Mem. IEEE, Soc. Motion Picture and TV Engrs. Office: Sandar Telematics A/S, Prof Brochsgt 6, 7030 Trondheim Norway

EVERAERT, PIERRE JEAN, retail executive; b. Aalst, Belgium, June 22, 1939; s. Louis Marcel and Melanie (Van der Vinken) E.; m. Diane Antoinette; children: Filip, Michel, Natalie, Liana. BA in Engring., U. Louvain, Belgium, 1963, MBA, 1964. Pres., chief exec. officer Goodyear of Panama, Panama City, 1972; v.p. sales and mktg. Goodyear, Fulda, Fed. Republic Germany, 1973-77, pres., chief exec. officer, 1978; exec. v.p. Generale Biscuit SA, Paris, 1978-81; pres., chief exec. officer Generale Biscuit Benelux, Herentals, Belgium, 1981-82, General Biscuit Am., Elizabeth, N.J., 1982-85; exec. corporate v.p. Ahold NV, Zaandam, Netherlands, 1985—; chmn., chief exec. officer Ahold USA Inc., Morristown, N.J., 1985—; chmn. Bilo Inc., Mauldin, S.C., 1986—, Giant Food Stores Inc., Carlisle, Pa., 1986—; chmn., chief exec. officer FNS Holding Co. Inc., Cleve., 1988—; pres., chief exec. officer-elect Royal Ahold NV; bd. dirs. Parisbas Bank NV, Amsterdam, Netherlands; trust mgr. CSM USA, N.Y.C. Office: Bi-Lo Inc Industrial Blvd Mauldin SC 29662 also: Royal Ahold NV, 2 Ankersmidlein, Zaandam The Netherlands 1506 CK

EVERALL, JOHN DUDLEY, physician, dermatologist; b. London, Eng., Feb. 2, 1917; s. Jack and Dorothy (Parsons) E.; one child, Mark Andrew. M.R.C.S., Royal Coll. Surgeons, London, 1943; L.R.C.P., Royal Coll. Physicians, 1943, F.R.C.P., 1949. Lic. physician Eng. Research fellow Skin & Cancer Unit, Univ. Hosp., N.Y.U., 1953-54; cons. skin physician Royal Marsden Hosp. & Chester Beatty Inst. for Cancer Research, London, 1960-83; cons. skin physician St. Thomas's Hosp., London, 1960-83; cons. skin physician Cromwell Hosp., Cromwell Rd., London, 1983—. Contbr. articles to profl. jours. Served to 1st lt. Med. Corps, RAF, 1943-46. Mem. British Assn. Dermatologists, Royal Soc. Medicine, Am. Acad. Dermatology, Am. Dermatol. Surg. Soc. Clubs: Royal Automobile, Royal Air Force, Naval, Royal Thames, St. Andrews Lodge. Avocations: farming; sailing. Home and Office: 122 Harley St, London W1N 1AG England

EVERDELL, WILLIAM, lawyer; b. N.Y.C., May 29, 1915; s. William and Rosalind (Romeyn) E.; m. Eleanore Darling, July 2, 1940; children—William Romeyn, Coburn Darling, Preston. B.A., Williams Coll., 1937; L.L.B., Yale U., 1940. Bar: N.Y. 1941. Assoc. Debevoise & Plimpton, N.Y.C., 1940-49, ptnr., 1949-85; of counsel Debevoise & Plimpton, 1986—. Contbr. articles to profl. jours. Trustee Woods Hole Oceanographic Instn., Mass., 1978-86; mem. exec. com., 1981-86, hon. trustee, 1987—; trustee, mem. exec. com. Cold Spring Harbor Lab., N.Y., 1987—. Served to lt. comdr. USN, 1942-45, PTO, ATO. Fellow Am. Bar Found.; mem. Assn. Bar of the City of N.Y. (mem. exec. com. 1960-64), N.Y. State Bar Assn. (chmn. com. corp. law 1971-73), ABA. Episcopalian. Club: The Links (gov. 1959-62) (N.Y.C.). Office: Debevoise & Plimpton 875 3d Ave New York NY 10022

EVERETT, BARBARA, English educator; b. Montreal, Can., Sept. 25, 1932; m. Emrys LLoyd Jones, Sept. 1965; 1 child, Susannah Hester. BA in English with 1st class honours, Oxford U., 1954, MA in English, 1958; MA in English, Cambridge U., 1960. Univ. lectr. English U. Hull (Eng.), 1955-60; fellow Newnham Coll., Univ. lectr. Cambridge U., 1960-65; sr. research fellow Somerville Coll., Univ. lectr. Oxford (Eng.) U., 1965—. Author: Poets in Their Time, 1986; editor: Antony and Cleopatra, 1964, All's Well That Ends Well, 1970; contbr. articles to profl. jours. Office: Somerville Coll, Oxford Univ, Oxford England

EVERETT, CARL NICHOLAS, management consulting executive; b. Ardmore, Okla., June 4, 1926; s. Elmer Edwards and Cecile (Jones) E.; B.S., Columbia U., 1948; M.B.A. with distinction, Harvard U., 1951; m. Susan Blessing Lindstrom, Oct., 1975; children by previous marriages—Carl N., Karen Lee, E. Anthony. With Benton and Bowles, N.Y.C., 1951-54, asso. account exec. Gen. Foods Corp., asst. account exec. Hellmanns and Best Foods Mayonnaise; with Campbell Mithun, Mpls., 1954-56, sr. account exec. Pillsbury Mills, account exec. Pillsbury Refrigerated Products; with McCann Erickson, N.Y.C., 1956-62, bottle sales account exec. Coca Cola Co., sr. account exec. Esso. Standard Oil, accounts supr. Westinghouse Electric Corp., account dir. Liggett and Myers Tobacco, mem. marketing plans bd. and marketing and advt. cons. Coca Cola Co.; sr. v.p., dir. Western region operations Barrington & Co., N.Y.C., 1962-64; founder, pres. Everett Assos., Inc., marketing and mgmt. consultants, N.Y.C., 1964-74; founder, pres. Everett Corp., Scottsdale, Ariz., 1974—; cons. Chrysler Corp., Pepsico Inc., Michelin Tire Corp., Gen. Electric Corp., Can. Dry Corp., Allied Van Lines, Continental Airlines; co-founder, dir. Precision Investment Co., Denver, 1977—; founder, mng. partner Wilmot Properties, Scottsdale, Ariz., 1979—. Chmn. bd. dirs. Phoenix Meml. Hosp. Primary Care; bd. dirs. Phoenix Meml. Health Resources, Inc.; bd. adjustment Town of Paradise Valley, Ariz.; chmn. Commn. on Salaries for Elective Officers; mem. Ariz. Cost Efficiency Commn. Served with USNR, 1944-46. Mem. Am. Mgmt. Assn.,

Sigma Alpha Epsilon. Unitarian. Clubs: Harvard Bus. Sch. (bd. dirs. Ariz.), Harvard (bd. dirs.), Safari Internat. (bd. dirs.), Campfire. Patentee in field. Home: 6722 N 60th St Paradise Valley AZ 85253 Office: 5685 N Scottsdale Rd Suite 100 Scottsdale AZ 85253

EVERETT, KARL MENOHER, JR., health policy administrator, educator; b. Latrobe, Pa., Aug. 13, 1935; s. Karl Menoher and Nell Irene (McCullough) E.; R.N. with honors, div. nursing, Coll. Medicine, N.Y. U., 1958; grad. U.S. Fgn. Service Inst., Washington, 1970-71; B.A. cum laude, U. Md., 1974; M.A., U. Okla., 1982, doctoral studies, 1982—; m. June Kay Lenz, Dec. 10, 1960; children—Dianna Lynn, Christopher Douglas. Instr. clin. urology Coll. Medicine, div. nursing N.Y. U., N.Y.C., 1958-59; mem. staffs N.Y. U.-Bellevue Med. Center, N.Y.C., 1955-59, N.Y. U. Postgrad. Hosp., N.Y.C., 1958-59; commd. 2d. lt. U.S. Army, 1959, advanced through grades to maj., 1967; served Brooke Army Med. Center, San Antonio, 1959, Walter Reed Army Med. Center, Washington, 1959-60; intelligence officer Dept. Def., apptd. mem. ad hoc com. Nat. Security Council, 1968-69; pvt. negotiator UN Command, Korea, with People's Republic of China and Dem. People's Republic Korea, 1971-75; dir. Directorate of Security F.A. Center and Ft. Sill, Okla., 1975-77, ret., 1979; pres., chmn. bd. dirs. Okla. World Cons., Inc., Norman, 1977-78; sr. assoc. Karl M. Everett & Assocs., Norman, 1979—; mem. vis. faculty John F. Kennedy Center, Fayetteville, N.C., 1977-80; bd. dirs. SEC LTD, Rockville, Md., 1974-77. , bd. dirs. Cleveland County Mental Health Assn., 1979-82, chmn. public affairs com., 1979-80, pres., 1981-82; del. Okla. White House Conf. on Aging, 1981, 1986-87; trustee Rep. Presdl. Task Force, 1985-86; mem. exec. com. Cleveland County Rep. Com., 1981, ad hoc com. on capital improvements City of Norman, 1985; presenter paper Mid-Am Congress on Aging, 1981, Gerontological Soc. Am., 1981, Assn. Canadienne de Gerontologis, 1981, 86—. chmn. bd. dirs. Citizens for Honest and Responsive Govt., 1982-84. Decorated Bronze Star, Joint Services Commendation medal; recipient Ogden D. Mills scholarship award, 1958, various U.S. mil. awards, ministerial level awards Govt. Republic of Korea. Mem. N.Y. Acad. Scis., Am. Acad. Polit. and Social Scis., Am. Soc. Pub. Adminstrn., Am. Sociol. Assn., Pi Sigma Alpha, Pi Alpha Alpha, Alpha Kappa Delta. Lodges: Masons, Shriners, Shrine Club of Korea (life). Home: 1305 Spruce Dr Norman OK 73072

EVERETT, RICHARD MERVYN, mechanical engineer, manufacturing company executive; b. Moreton, Gloucestershire, Eng., Feb. 22, 1950; s. Charles Frederick Dawson and Phyllis Joan (Brinsford) E.; m. Carolyn Julia Selley, June 29, 1974; children: Simon Anthony Richard, Melanie Faye, Sophie Nichol. Diploma in mech. engring., Trent Poly. U., 1975. Chartered engr. Devel. engr. Dowty Tech. Devels., Andoversford, Eng., 1974-76; sales engr. Dowty Hydraulic Units, Cheltenham, Eng., 1976-77; export exec. Dowty Seals Ltd., Tewkesbury, Eng., 1977-81; sales mgr. Dowty Seals Ltd., Tewkesbury, 1981-86, bus. mgr., 1986—. Mem. Instn. Mech. Engrs. (sec. Gloucester chpt. 1978-83, com. Estern br. 1984-85). Mem. Ch. Eng. Lodge: Lions (charter pres. Winchcombe club 1977-78). Home: Badgerbank Farm, Bushcombe Ln, Woodmancote GL52 4QL, England Office: Dowty Seals Ltd, Ashchurch, Tewkesbury GL20 8JS, England

EVERETT, WARREN SYLVESTER, consultant, former government official; b. Wichita, Kans., Oct. 19, 1910; s. Carl S. and Effie (Barton) E.; m. Ruthmary Francis, June 13, 1935; children: Mary Margaret (Mrs. R.L. Graham), Judith Ann (Mrs. D.L. McKee), Warren Douglas. BA, U. Wichita, 1932; BS, U.S. Mil. Acad., 1935; MS, Cornell U., 1939; student, Army Engr. Sch., 1939-40, Army Command and Gen. Staff Coll., 1942, Princeton U., 1945, Armed Forces Staff Coll., 1949, Georgetown U., Am. U., 1955, Army War Coll., 1956-57. Registered profl. engr., Wash. Commd. 2d lt. U.S. Army, 1935, advanced through grades to col., 1951; dir. U.S. Army Constrn. Agy., France, 1959-61; dist. engr. Vicksburg, Miss., 1961-63; ret. 1963; chief pub. works div. USOM to Vietnam, 1963-65; chief engr. U.S. AID mission to Nigeria, 1965-66, Vietnam Bur., AID, 1966-67; dir. excess property program AID, 1967-68; cons. Office Emergency Preparedness, Exec. Office Pres., 1968-69; exec. archtl.-engring. firm Saigon, Vietnam, 1969-71; dep. dir. U.S. Property Disposal Agy., Vietnam, 1971-74; dep. dir. Office Planning and Mgmt., chief commodity mgmt. and merchandising divs. Def. Property Disposal Service, Battle Creek, 1974-85; nat. security coordinator/exec. dir., sci. and engring. adv. bd. Internat. Coalition for Strategic Def. Initiative, High Frontier, Washington, 1985—. Contbr. articles to profl. jours. Organizer, dir. nat. fallout shelter survey and marking program, 1961; pres. P.T.A., Am. Sch., Tokyo, 1953-54. Decorated Legion of Merit with oak leaf cluster; recipient Korean Ulchi medal with silver star, Korean Disting. Service medal, Presdl. citation (Korea), Chuong-My Outstanding Service medal (Vietnam), Army Commendation medal. Fellow ASCE, Soc. Am. Mil. Engrs. (past pres. Vicksburg and Saigon); mem. Nat. Soc. Profl. Engrs. Home: 1401 Gower Ct McLean VA 22102 Office: High Frontier 2800 Shirlington Rd Alexandria VA 22206

EVERHART, THOMAS EUGENE, physicist, electrical engineer, educator; b. Kansas City, Mo., Feb. 15, 1932; s. William Elliott and Elizabeth Ann (West) E.; m. Doris Arleen Wentz, June 21, 1953; children—Janet Sue, Nancy Jean, David William, John Thomas. A.B. in Physics magna cum laude, Harvard, 1953; M.Sc., UCLA, 1955; Ph.D. in Engring, Cambridge U., Eng., 1958. Mem. tech. staff Hughes Research Labs., Culver City, Calif., 1953-55; mem. faculty U. Calif.-Berkeley, 1958-78, prof. elec. engring. and computer scis., 1967-78, Miller research prof., 1969-70, chmn. dept., 1972-77; prof. elec. engring., Joseph Silbert dean engring. Cornell U., Ithaca, N.Y., 1979-84; prof. elec. and computer engring., chancellor U. Ill., Champaign-Urbana, 1984-87; pres., prof. electrical engring. Calif. Inst. Tech., Pasadena, 1987—; fellow scientist Westinghouse Research Labs., Pitts., 1962-63; guest prof. Inst. für Angewandte Physik, U. Tuebingen, Fed. Republic Germany, 1966-67, Waseda U., Tokyo, Osaka U., Japan, fall 1974; vis. fellow Clare Hall, Cambridge U., 1975; chmn. Electron, Ion and Photon Beam Symposium, 1977; cons. to industry; mem. sci. and ednl. adv. com. Lawrence Berkeley Lab., 1978-85, chmn., 1980-85; mem. sci. adv. com. Gen. Motors Corp., 1980—, chmn. 1984—; mem. tech. adv. com. R.R. Donnelley & Sons, 1981—. NSF sr. postdoctoral fellow, 1966-67; Guggenheim fellow, 1974-75. Fellow IEEE; mem. AAAS, Nat. Acad. Engring. (ednl. adv. bd. 1984—, membership com. 1984—, chmn. membership com. 1988—), Electron Microscopy Soc. Am. (council 1970-72, pres. 1977), Microbeam Analysis Soc. Am., Deutsche Gesellschaft für Elektronenmikroskopie, Assn. Marshall Scholars and Alumni (pres. 1965-68), Nat. Assn. State Univs. and Land Grant Colls. (chmn. higher edn. and tech. com. 1986-87), Sigma Xi, Eta Kappa Nu. Clubs: Athenaeum, Chgo. Home: 415 S Hill Ave Pasadena CA 91106 Office: Calif Inst Tech Office of Pres 1201 E California Blvd Pasadena CA 91125 *

EVERITT, ALAN MILNER, emeritus history educator, writer; b. Sevenoaks, Kent, Eng., Aug. 17, 1926; s. Robert Arthur and Grace Beryl (Milner) E. MA, U. St. Andrews, Scotland, 1951; PhD, U. London, 1957. Edit. asst. Commonwealth Univs. Assn., London, 1951-54; research asst. dept. English Local History U. Leicester, Eng., 1957-59, research fellow, 1960-65; lectr. U. Leicester, 1965-68; prof., head dept. U. Leicester, Eng., 1968-82, emeritus prof., 1982—, adj. prof., 1982-84. Author: Suffolk and the Great Rebellion, 1640-1660, 1960, The Community of Kent and the Great Rebellion, 1640-1660, 1966, The Pattern of Rural Dissent: The Nineteenth Century, 1972, Perspectives in English Urban History, 1973, Landscape and Community in England, 1985, Continuity and Colonization: The Evolution of Kentish Settlement, 1986; contbr. numerous books and jours. Recipient John Nichols prize U. Leicester, 1956. Fellow Royal Hist. Soc., Soc. Antiquaries; mem. Econ. History Soc., Brit. Agrl. History Soc., Past and Present Soc. Home: Fieldedge, Poultney Ln, Kimcote near Lutterworth, Leicestershire LE17 5RX, England

EVERITT, DEREK, data processing executive; b. Doncaster, Yorkshire, Eng., Feb. 11, 1947; s. Albert Burton and Lily (Johnson) E.; m. Carol Ann Griggs, Sept. 23, 1969; children: Nicholas, Paul, Daniel. BA in Bus. honors, Lanchester Polytechnic U., 1969. Sales exec. Rank Xerox, Birmingham, Eng., 1969-74, Singter Bus. M/C's, Birmingham, 1974-75, No. Telecom, Manchester, Eng., 1975-80; sales exec. Tandem Computers, Birmingham, 1980-81, mgr. br., 1981-82, mgr. dist., 1982-83; dir. sales Tandem Computers, London, 1983-85, mng. dir., 1985—. Mem. Inst. Dirs. Office: Tandem Computers Ltd, Peel House, 32-34 Church Rd, Northolt UB5 5AB, England

EVERITT, SANDRA ROOD, decorator, arts and crafts company executive, writer; b. Mexico, D.F., Mex., May 19, 1948; d. Robert Howe Everitt and Deborah (Morrison) Rood; m. Leopoldo Romo, May 19, 1964 (div. 1972). Decorator, LaSalle U., Chgo., 1966-68; with mktg. dept. Centro de Mercadotecnia y Publicidad, Mexico City, 1969; decorator Mexico City, 1969—; pres. Inca-Mex. Crafts Unltd., Inc., N.Y.C., 1975—; co-owner art gallery, Laguna Beach, Calif., 1988—. Vol. Centro Medico, Mexico City, 1964-67, Hosp. Central de Neurologia, Mexico City, 1967-73; collaborator Pronatura, Mexico City, 1984—. Clubs: Lomas Sporting, Mundet (Mexico City); Cuernavaca Racquet. Avocation: wildlife photography.

EVERS, LA FONDA A., library director; b. Randalia, Iowa, Feb. 13, 1931; d. William Donald and Loretta Caroline (Treager) Bronn; m. Wayne Leonard Evers, Mar. 22, 1949; children—Keith Wayne, Cheri Lynn. B.S., Eastern Ill. U., 1981; studied music with Allen Hancock, Santa Maria, Calif., 1968-70. Cert. social rehab. activity dir., social services dir. Social rehab. dir. Wil-Care Home, Wilmington, Ill., 1971-74; workshop tchr. Assn. Health Care, Chgo., 1974; social rehab. dir. Ill. Knights Templar, Paxton, 1975-79; activity therapist Ford County Home, Paxton, 1979-81; coordinator Ford County Task Force on Early Childhood Devel.; ednl. advocate for State Ill. Children's Family Service; dir. Paxton Carnegie Library, 1981—. Bd. dirs. Paxton Nursery Sch., 1983—; mem. welfare services com. and personnel adv. bd. Ford County (Ill.) Dept. Pub. Aid, 1984—, Ill. Dept. Children and family Services Foster Care Families of Ill., 1987—. Mem. Lincoln Trails Library Assn. (sec. 1981-82, v.p. 1982-83, pres. elect 1985). Lutheran. Lodge: Order Eastern Star (officer Paxton 1978-81). Home: 1001 Park Terr Paxton IL 60957 Office: Paxton Carnegie Library 154 S Market Paxton IL 60957

EVERSON, WILLIAM OLIVER (BROTHER ANTONINUS), poet; b. Sacramento, Sept. 10, 1912; s. Louis Waldemar and Francelia Marie (Herber) E.; m. Edwa Poulson, 1938 (div. 1948); m. Mary Fabilli, 1948 (div. 1960); m. Susanna Rickson, Dec. 13, 1969; 1 stepson, Jude. Student, Fresno State Coll., 1931, 34-35. With Civilian Conservation Corps, 1933-34; with Civilian Public Service, 1943-46; dir. Fine Arts Group, Waldport, Oreg., 1944-46; with U. Calif. Press, 1947-49, Catholic Worker Movement, 1950-51, Dominican Order, Province of West, 1951-69; poet-in-residence Kresge Coll., U. Calif., Santa Cruz, 1971-81; master printer Lime Kiln Press, U. Calif., Santa Cruz, 1971-81. Author: verse The Residual Years, Poems, 1934-48, 1968, Man-Fate, 1974, The Veritable Years, Poems, 1949-1966, 1978, The Masks of Drought, 1980, Renegade Christmas, 1984, In Medias Res, 1984, The Poet is Dead: A Memorial for Robinson Jeffers, 1987; prose Robinson Jeffers Fragments of an Older Fury, 1967, Archetype West, 1976, Earth Poetry: Selected Essays and Interviews, 1980, Birth of a Poet: The Santa Cruz Meditations, 1982, On Writing the Waterbirds, Collected Forewords and Afterwords, The Excesses of God: Robinson Jeffers as a Religious Figure, 1988. Recipient Silver medal Commonwealth Club, 1967; Shelley Meml. award, 1978; Book of Yr. award Conf. on Christianity and Lit., 1978; Guggenheim fellow, 1949; Nat. Endowment Arts grantee, 1981. Home: 705 Big Creek Rd Davenport CA 95017

EVERT, CHRISTINE MARIE (CHRIS EVERT), professional tennis player; b. Ft. Lauderdale, Fla., Dec. 21, 1954; d. James and Colette Evert; m. John Lloyd, Apr. 17, 1979 (div.); m. Andy Mill, July 30, 1988. Amateur tennis player until Dec. 1972, profl. tennis player, 1972—. Recipient Lebair Sportsmanship trophy, 1971; named Female Athlete of Yr. AP, 1974, 75, 77, 80; Athlete of Yr. Sports Illustrated, 1976; Greatest Woman Athlete of Last 25 Years Women's Sports Found., 1985. Mem. U.S. Lawn Tennis Assn. (Top Women's Singles Player award 1974), Nat. Honor Soc. Address: care Internat Mgmt Group 1 Erieview Plaza Cleveland OH 44114 also: Polo Club of Boca Raton 5400 Champion Blvd Boca Raton FL 33496 *

EVERTON, MARTA VE, ophthalmologist; b. Luling, Tex., Nov. 12, 1926; d. T.W. and Nora E. (Eckols) O'Leavy; B.A., Hardin-Simmons U., 1945; M.A., Stanford U., 1947; M.D., Baylor U., 1955; postgrad. N.Y.U.-Bellevue Hosp., 1956-57; m. Robert K. Graham, Oct. 15, 1960; children—Marcia, Christie, Leslie Fox. Intern, Meth. Hosp., Houston, 1955-56; resident in ophthalmology Baylor Affiliated Hosps., Houston, 1957-59; clin. instr. ophthalmology Baylor U., 1959-60; asst. clin. prof. ophthalmology Loma Linda U., 1962-73; practice medicine specializing in ophthalmology, Houston, 1959-60, Pasadena, Calif., 1961-74, Escondido, Calif., 1974—. Mem. AMA, Am. Acad. Ophthalmology, Am. Med. Women's Assn., Alpha Omega Alpha. Home: 3024 Sycamore Ln Escondido CA 92025 Office: 810 E Ohio Ave Escondido CA 92025

EVREN, KENAN, president of Turkey; b. Manisa, Turkey, 1918; grad. War Acad. Turkey, 1938; married; 3 children. Commd. 3rd Lt., Turkish Army, 1938, advanced through grades to gen., 1964; battery comdr., 1940-46; art. bn. comdr., 1949-57; asst. chief ops. 1st Army, 1957-58; chief of staff Turkish Brigade, Korea, 1958-59; comdg. Inf. Regt., 1961-62; chief of staff Army Corps, 1962-63; chief tng. br., 1963-67; comdg. gen. div., 1967-68; army chief of staff, 1968-70; chief insp. bd. and chief of staff Turkish Land Forces Command, 1972-75; dep. chief Turkish Gen. Staff, 1975-76; comdr. Aegean Army and Turkish Land Forces, 1976-78; chief Turkish Gen. Staff, 1978-80; chmn. Nat. Security Council and head of state Republic of Turkey, 1980-82, pres., 1982—. Office: Office Head of State, Ankara Turkey *

EWALDSEN, HANS LORENZ, manufacturing company executive; b. Lunden, Fed. Republic Germany, Sept. 6, 1923; s. Lorenz and Marie (Kröger) E.; m. Marianne Paulsen, 1951; 2 children. Grad., U. Kiel, Fed. Republic Germany. Mng. bd. Deutsche Babcock AG, 1960-67, pres., chief exec. officer, 1967-84, chmn. supervisory bd., 1984-86; chmn. supervisory bd. Balcke-Dürr AG, Ratingen Co., Borsig GmbH, Berlin, Gerling-Konzern Lebensversammlung AG, Cologne, Vereinigte Kesselwerke AG, Dusseldorf; bd. dirs. numerous corps. Office: Deutsche Babcock, Duisburgerstrasse 375, 4200 Oberhausen Federal Republic of Germany *

EWBANK, THOMAS PETERS, banker, lawyer; b. Indpls., Dec. 29, 1943; s. William Curtis and Maxine Stuart (Peters) E.; m. Alice Ann Shelton, June 8, 1968; children—William Curtis, Ann Shelton. Student Stanford U., 1961-62; A.B., Ind. U., 1965, J.D., 1969. Bar: Ind. 1969, U.S. Tax Ct., 1969, U.S. Dist. Ct. (so. dist.) Ind. 1969, U.S. Supreme Ct. 1974. Legis. asst. Ind. Legis. Council, 1966-67; estate and inheritance tax adminstr. Mchts. Nat. Bank, Indpls., 1967-69; assoc. Hilgedag, Johnson, Secrest and Murphy, Indpls., 1969-71; asst. gen. counsel Everett I. Brown Co., Indpls., 1971-72; with Mchts. Nat. Bank & Trust Co., Indpls., 1972—, successively probate adminstr., head probate div., head personal account adminstrn. group in trust div., v.p. and sr. trust officer, sr. v.p., head trust and investment div. Asst. treas. Ruckelshaus for U.S. Senator Com., 1970; candidate for Ind. Legislature, 1970, 74. Fellow Ind. Bar Found. (patron); mem. Estate Planning Council Indpls. (pres. 1982-83), Indpls. Bar Assn., Ind. Bar Assn., Indpls. Bar Found. (treas. 1976-81), Blue Key. Republican. Baptist. Clubs: Meridian Hills Country, Riviera, Masons (Indpls.); Kiwanis Circle K Internat. (internat. trustee 1963-65, pres. 1964-65, George Hixson Diamond fellow), Kiwanis of Indpls. (treas. 1980-81, 84-85 designated a maj. builder 1983). Contbr. articles to profl. jours. Home: 4516 Sylvan Rd Indianapolis IN 46208 Office: One Merchants Plaza Suite 600E Indianapolis IN 46255

EWERS, JAMES BENJAMIN, JR., educational administrator; b. Winston-Salem, N.C., Sept. 29, 1948; s. James Benjamin and Mildred Jane (Holland) E.; B.A., Johnson C. Smith U., 1970; M.A., Catholic U. Am., 1971; Ed.D., U. Mass., 1980; m. Bonita Maria Taylor, Aug. 5, 1978; 1 son, Christopher James. Tchr. history Ballou High Sch., Washington, 1971-75; adminstrv. asst. spl. edn. program U. Mass., Amherst, 1975-76; asst. dir. admissions Stockton State Coll., Pomona, N.J., 1976-78; dir. admissions and registrations U. Md. Eastern Shore, Princess Anne, U. Md.-Eastern Shore, 1978-84; v.p. student affairs Livingstone Coll., Salisbury, N.C., 1984-87, Dillard U., New Orleans, La., 1987—; mem. Mental Health Adv. Bd. Atlantic County (N.J.), 1977-78. Bd. dirs. Pleasantville Day Care Center, N.J., 1977-78, New Orleans Job Corps Center; mem. Salisbury-Rowan Human Relations Council, 1985—. Mem. Am. Assn. Counseling Devel., Nat. Assn. Student Personnel Adminstrs., Nat. Assn. Coll. Admissions Counselors, Council Exceptional Children, Assn. Collegiate Registrars and Officers of Admissions, NAACP, Md. Coll. Personnel Assn. (co-chmn.), Phi Kappa Phi. Baptist. Home: 3644 Virgil Blvd New Orleans LA 70122

EWERT, RUSSELL HOWARD, banker; b. St. Paul, Mar. 7, 1935; s. Russell Howard Ewert and Josephine (Conger) Ewert Murphy; m. Marilyn Norgard, Aug. 30, 1957 (div. 1980); children: Russell III, Ann Brennan, Stephen David; m. Pat. Guyer, Aug. 10, 1985. BSL, U. Minn., 1958, BBA with honors, 1960, JD, 1960. Bar: Minn. 1960, Ill. 1980. Asst. v.p., asst. sec. First Capital Corp., Chgo., 1961-64; asst. cashier First Nat. Bank, Chgo., 1964-68, v.p., loan div. head, 1968-74, v.p., sr. lending officer, 1978-80; v.p., regional mgr. First Nat. Bank, Kansas City, Mo., 1974-78; pres., chief exec. officer Drexel Nat. Bank, Chgo., 1980—; dir. Suburban Trust and Savs. Bank, Oak Park, Ill. Co-author: Obtaining Unsecured Loans, 1976. Gen. chmn. Fighting Fund for Freedom dinner Chgo. Southside NAACP, 1984; Ill. state treas. Jesse Jackson for Pres. Com.; bd. dirs. Chgo. Police Dept.; chmn. investment com. Police Annuity and Benefit Fund, Chgo.; bd. advisors Mercy Hosp. and Med. Ctr., Chgo.; v.p. and dir. Chgo. Crime Commn., Cosmopolitan C. of C., The Hundred Club of Chgo. Recipient Cosmopolitan C. of C. and U.S. SBA award of merit, 1968, Christian Profl. Assn. award for Excellence Life Ctr. Ch., 1988; Talent Assistant Program cert. of appreciation, 1970; Am. Inst. Banking award for outstanding contbns., 1972; Malcolm X Ednl. Found. award for outstanding contbns., 1974; Am. Legion citation of appreciation, 1982; Chgo. South End Jaycees Bus. Person of Month award, 1982; Black Contractors United Spl. award, 1982; Abraham Lincoln Centre Select Four Community Leadership award, 1982; Mt. Olive African Meth. Episc. Ch., Inc. award of honor, 1983; City Colls. of Chgo. cert. of appreciation, 1983. Mem. ABA, Chgo. Bar Assn. Home: 2106 N Magnolia Chicago IL 60614 Office: Drexel Nat Bank 3401 S King Dr Chicago IL 60616

EWING, COLEMAN CLAY, architect; b. San Antonio, Oct. 11, 1944; s. William Thomas and Ina Fay (Talley) E.; student San Antonio Jr. Coll., 1963-65; B.S., U. Houston, 1970; m. Marjorie Glennda Sewell, Aug. 28, 1965; children—Christopher Coleman, Michelle InaMarie. Customer engr. IBM Co, Houston, Tex., 1965-67; draftsman Morton Levy, Houston, 1967-71, Roland Johnson, Denver, 1971-72, DMJM Phillips, Denver, 1972-73, Wheeler/Lewis, Denver, 1973-75, Frank Lundquist, Denver, 1975-76, Oliver, Hellegren, Denver, 1976-77; prin. Coleman C. Ewing Architect & Assocs., Denver, 1977-80, 86—; pres. Ewing Gorman Archtl. Group, Denver, 1980-81, also dir.; pres. Ewing Archtl. Group, P.C., 1981-86; CAD/CAM specialist archtl. dept. Martin Marietta Co., Denver, 1981-86. Republican. Mem. Ch. of Christ. Office: Ewing Architect and Assocs 6634 S Clarkson St Littleton CO 80221

EWING, KY PEPPER, JR., lawyer; b. Victoria, Tex., Jan. 7, 1935; s. Ky Pepper and Sallie (Dixon) E.; m. Almuth Rott, Apr. 6, 1963; children: Kenneth Patrick, Kevin Andrew, Kathryn Diana. B.A. cum laude, Baylor U., 1956; LL.B. cum laude, Harvard U., 1959. Bar: D.C. 1959, U.S. Supreme Ct 1963. Assoc. firm Covington & Burling, Washington, 1959-64; partner firm Prather, Seeger, Doolittle, Farmer & Ewing, Washington, 1964-77; dep. asst. atty. gen. antitrust div. Dept. Justice, Washington, 1978-80; partner firm Vinson & Elkins, Washington, 1980—; dir., sec. Washington Inst. Fgn. Affairs. Pres. Potomac Valley League, 1977, Carderock Springs Citizens Assn., 1975-78. Mem. ABA, D.C. Bar Assn., Fed. Bar Assn., Am. Soc. Internat. Law. Democrat. Episcopalian. Clubs: Metropolitan (Washington), 1925 F Street, City (Washington). Home: 8317 Comanche Ct Bethesda MD 20817 Office: Vinson & Elkins 1455 Pennsylvania Ave NW Washington DC 20004

EWING, RAYMOND PEYTON, educator, management consultant; b. Hannibal, Mo., July 31, 1925; s. Larama Angelo and Winona Fern (Adams) E.; m. Audrey Jane Schulze, May 7, 1949; 1 child, Jane Ann. AA, Hannibal La-Grange Coll., 1948; BA, William Jewell Coll., 1949; MA in Humanities, U. Chgo., 1950. Mktg. mgmt. trainee Montgomery-Wards, Chgo., 1951-52; sr. editor Commerce Clearing House, Chgo., 1952-60; corp. communications dir. Allstate Ins. Cos. & Allstate Enterprises, Northbrook, Ill., 1960-85, issues mgmt. dir., 1979-85, pres. Issues Mgmt. Cons. Group, 1985—; assoc. prof., dir. corp. pub. relations program Medill Sch. Journalism Northwestern U., Evanston, Ill., 1986—; pub. relations dir. Chicago Mag., 1966-67, book columnist, 1968-70; staff Book News Commentator, Sta. WRSV, Skokie, Ill., 1962-70. Author: Mark Twain's Steamboat Years, 1981, Managing the New Bottom Line, 1987; contbr. articles to mags. Mem. Winnetka (Ill.) Library Bd., 1969-70; pres. Skokie Valley United Crusade, 1964-65; bd. dirs. Suburban Community Chest Council, Onward Neighborhood House, Chgo., Kenilworth Inst.; mem. Pvt. Sector Foresight Task Force, 1982-83. Served with AUS, 1943-46, ETO. Mem. Pub. Relations Soc. of Am. (accredited; Silver Anvil awards for pub. affairs, 1970, 72, for fin. relations 1970, for bus. spl. events 1976, chmn. nat. pub. affairs sect. 1984), Publicity Club of Chgo. (v.p. 1967, bd. dirs. 1966-68; Golden Trumpet award for pub. affairs, 1969, 70, 72, 79, for fin. relations 1970), Insurers Public Relations Council (pres. 1980-81), Issues Mgmt. Assn. (founder, pres. 1981-83, chmn. 1983-84), Mensa, World Future Soc., U.S. Assn. for Club of Rome, Chgo. Poets and Writers Found. (pub. relations dir. 1966-67), Club: Union League (Chgo.). Author: Mark Twain's Steamboat Years, 1981, Managing the New Bottom Line, 1987; contbr. articles to mags. Office: Northwestern U Medill Sch Journalism Evanston IL 60208

EWING, ROBERT, lawyer; b. Little Rock, July 18, 1922; s. Esmond and Frances (Howell) E.; m. Elizabeth Smith, May 24, 1947; 1 child, Elizabeth Milbrey. B.A., Washington and Lee U., 1943; LL.B., Yale U., 1945. Bar: Conn. 1945. Assoc. Shipman & Goodwin, Hartford, Conn., 1945-50; partner Shipman & Goodwin, 1950—; asst. pros. atty. West Hartford, Conn., 1953-55; dir., asst. sec. H.W. Steane Co. Inc., Rocktide Inc.; dir., pres. Still Pasture Corp.; asst. sec. Linvar Marwin, Inc. Mem. U.S. Constitution Bicentennial Commn. of Conn.; incorporator Hartford Hosp., Mt. Sinai Hosp.; bd. dirs. Travelers Aid Soc. of Hartford, 1951-57, treas., 1954-57; bd. dirs. Greater Hartford chpt. ARC, 1974—, chmn., 1977-79, mem. blood services com., 1986—, vice chmn., 1987—; bd. dirs. Family Service Soc., 1961-65, Conn. Pub. Expenditure Council, 1986—. Mem. ABA, Conn. Bar Assn. (chmn. fed. practice com. 1976-79, exec. com. corp. sect. 1981-85), Hartford County Bar Assn., Am. Law Inst., Conn. Hist. Soc. (trustee, v.p. 1982—, chmn. personnel com.), Newcomen Soc. N.Am. Congregationalist. (sr. deacon 1972-75). Clubs: Twentieth Century (pres. 1975-76), Hartford (counsel, ex officio bd. govs.), Mory's Assn, Dauntless, Rotary (pres. Hartford 1966-67). Home: 28 Birch Rd West Hartford CT 06119 Office: 799 Main St Hartford CT 06103

EXARCHOS, ANNIVAS BASIL, shipyard company executive; b. Athens, Apr. 18, 1933; s. Basil C. and Konstantina (Kiriazopoulou) E.; m. Alexandra Antonios Papageorgakopoulou; children—Basil, Aristi Constantina. Dipl. Engring. Officer, Naval Acad. Greece, 1954, Dipl. Advance Engring., 1956; cert. antibactirilogic-antiatomic-antichem. warfare Greek Navy Edn. Ctr., 1956. Commd. cadet Greek Navy, 1949, advanced through grades to comdr., 1970, ret. 1975; group maintenance mgr. "Fix" Group of Cos., Greece, 1967-69; field mgr. Hellenic Bottling Co., Greece, 1969-71; gen. mgr./mng. dir. Chandris Shipyards SA, Piraeus, Greece, 1971—; prof. Pythagoras Schs. of Engring., Athens, 1955-65. Author: Fuels and Lubricants, 1962; contbr. articles to profl. jours. Pres., Brotherhood of Kaletziton of Epiros, Athens, 1979—; mem. Assn. of Katsanochoriton of Epiros, Athens, 1970—. Decorated Golden Cross of Phinix Battalion, King Constantin the 2nd, 1964; Medal of Mil. Worthiness, Greek Minister of Def., 1965; Medal of St. Achilleus, Bishop of Larissa, 1981. Fellow Inst. Marine Engrs. (London); mem. Inst. Naval Tech., ASME, Am. Welding Soc., Inst. Marine Engrs., Orgn. Ch. Property (dir. 1980-82, 86-87), Union of Ret. Engring. Officers, Assn. Shipbuilders/Ship Repairers (v.p.). Clubs: Propeller of U.S., Yachting of Greece, Rotary. Home: Victoros Hugo St 6, Psichico, 15452 Athens Greece Office: Chandris Shipyards SA, 95 Auti Miaouli, 18538 Piraeus Greece

EXE, DAVID ALLEN, electrical engineer; b. Brookings, S.D., Jan. 29, 1942; s. Oscar Melvin and Irene Marie (Mattis) E.; m. Lynn Rae Roberts; children: Doreen Lea, Raena Lynn. BSEE, S.D. State U., 1968; MBA, U. S.D., 1980; postgrad. Iowa State U., 1969-70, U. Idaho, 1978-80. Registered profl. engr., Idaho, Oreg., Minn., S.D., Wash., Wyo., Utah. Applications engr. Collins Radio, Cedar Rapids, Iowa, 1969-70; dist. engr. Bonneville Power Adminstrn., Idaho Falls, Idaho, 1970-77; instr. math U. S.D., Vermillion, 1977-78; chief exec. officer EXE Assocs., Idaho Falls, Idaho, 1978-83; agys. mgr. CPT Corp., Eden Prairie, Minn., 1983-85; owner, chief exec. officer Exe Inc., Eden Prairie, 1983—; chmn. bd. Applied Techs. Idaho, Idaho Falls, 1979—, chmn., chief exec. officer Azimuth Cons., Idaho Falls, 1979-81; v.p.

D & B Constrn. Co., Idaho Falls, 1980-83. Mem. Eastern Idaho Council on Industry and Energy, 1979—. Served with USN, 1960-64. Mem. Am. Cons. Engrs., IEEE, Nat. Soc. Profl. Engrs., Nat. Contrcts Mgrs. Assn., IEEE Computer Soc., Mensa, Am. Legion. Lodges: Masons, Elks. Office: 8220 Commonwealth Dr Eden Prairie MN 55344

EXLEY, CHARLES ERROL, JR., manufacturing company executive; b. Detroit, Dec. 14, 1929; s. Charles Errol and Helen Margaret (Greenizen) E.; m. Sara Elizabeth Yates, Feb. 1, 1952; children: Sarah Helen, Evelyn Victoria, Thomas Yates. B.A., Wesleyan U., Middletown, Conn., 1952; M.B.A., Columbia U., 1954. With Burroughs Corp., Detroit, 1954-76; controller Burroughs Corp. (Todd div.), 1960-63, corp. controller, 1963-66, v.p., group exec. office products group, 1966-71, v.p. fin., 1971-73, exec. v.p. fin., 1973-76; pres. NCR Corp., Dayton, Ohio, 1976-88, chief exec. officer, 1983—, chmn. bd., 1984—, also dir., mem. exec. com. Clubs: Grosse Pointe (Grosse Pointe Farms, Mich.); Moraine Country (Dayton); Dayton Racquet; The Brook (N.Y.C.). Home: 3720 Ridgeleigh Rd Dayton OH 45429 Office: NCR Corp 1700 S Patterson Blvd Dayton OH 45479 *

EXON, JOHN JAMES, senator; b. Geddes, S.D., Aug. 9, 1921; s. John James and Luella (Johns) E.; m. Patricia Ann Pros, Sept. 18, 1943; children: Stephen James, Pamela Ann, Candace Lee. Student, U. Omaha, 1939-41. Mgr. Universal Finance Corp., Nebr., 1946-53; pres. Exon's, Inc., Lincoln, Nebr., 1954-71; gov. Nebr., 1971-79; mem. U.S. Senate from Nebr., 1979—. Active state, local, nat. Democratic coms., 1952—; del. Dem. Nat. Conv., 1964-74, Dem. nat. committeeman, 1968—. Served with Signal Corps AUS, 1942-45. Mem. Am. Legion, VFW. Clubs: Masons (32 deg.), Shriners, Elks, Eagles, Optimist Internat. Office: US Senate 330 Hart Senate Bldg Washington DC 20510 *

EXTER, JOHN, monetary consultant; b. Chgo., Sept. 17, 1910; s. Joseph and Edith (Gray) E.; m. Marion Fitch, Dec. 18, 1937; children—John Kempton, Janet Exter Butler, Nancy Exter Downs, George Fitch. B.A., Coll. Wooster, 1932; M.A., Fletcher Sch. Law and Diplomacy, 1934; postgrad. Harvard U., 1939-43. Far East econ., acting chief bd. govs. Fed. Res. System, Washington, 1945-50; gov. Central Bank Ceylon, Colombo, Sri Lanka, 1950-53; chief Middle East div. Internat. Bank for Reconstrn. and Devel., Washington, 1953-54; v.p. Fed. Res. Bank N.Y., N.Y.C., 1954-59; sr. v.p., internat. monetary adviser for internat. banking group First Nat. City Bank (now Citibank), N.Y.C., 1959-72; cons. domestic and internat. money, Mountain Lakes, N.J., 1972—. Contbr. articles to profl. jours. Trustee China Found. Promotion Edn. and Culture, 1973—. Recipient Disting. Alumni award Coll. of Wooster (Ohio), 1981. Mem. Council Fgn. Relations, Com. Monetary Research and Edn. (dir. 1973—), Phi Beta Kappa. Republican. Mem. United Ch. of Christ. Club: University. Home and Office: 290 Boulevard Mountain Lakes NJ 07046

EYADÉMA, ETIENNE GNASSINGBÉ, president of Togo; b. Pyra, Lama-Kara, Dec. 26, 1937; s. Gnassingbe and N'Danida Eyadema. Served with French Army, including service in Indo-China, Dahomey, Niger, Algeria, 1953-61, commd. 1963 army chief-of-staff Togo, 1965—, seized power, 1967, pres. of Togo, minister of def., 1967, 81—.Decorated officer Order Nat. de Mono; chevalier Lé gion d'Honneur (France). Office: Office of Président, Lomé Togo *

EYRE, RICHARD CHARLES HASTINGS, stage director; b. Mar. 28, 1943; m. Susan Elizabeth Birtwistle, July 4, 1973; 1 child, Lucy. Student, Sherborne Sch.; BA, Peterhouse, Cambridge. Asst. dir. Phoenix Theatre, Leicester, 1966; assoc. dir. Lyceum Theatre, Edinburgh, 1967-70, dir. prodns., 1970-72; freelance dir. Liverpool, 7:84 Co., West End; tours for Brit. Council, West Africa, 1971, SE Asia, 1972; artistic dir. Nottingham Playhouse, 1973-78; producer/dir. Play for Today, BBC-TV, 1978-80; assoc. dir. Nat. Theatre, 1981-88, dir., 1988—. Dir. plays including The Churchill Play, Nottingham, 1974, Comedians, Old Vic and Wyndhams, 1976, Touched, Nottingham, 1977, Hamlet, Royal Ct., 1980, Edmond, Royal Ct., 1985; plays for Nat. Theatre include Guys and Dolls (SWET Dir. of Yr. 1982, Standard Best Dir. 1982), The Beggar's Opera, 1982, Schweyk in the Second World War, 1982, The Government Inspector, 1985, Futurists, 1986; dir. films including The Ploughman's Lunch (Evening Standard award for Best Film 1983), Loose Connections, 1983, Laughterhouse, 1984, released as Singleton's Pluck in US, 1985 (TV prize Venice Film Festival); dir. TV films including The Imitation Game, Pasmore, 1980, Country, 1981, The Insurance Man, 1986, Past Caring, 1986; dir. premiers of plays by Trevor Griffiths, David Hare, Howard Brenton, Ken Campbell, John McGrath, Barrie Keeffe, Stephen Lowe, Ann Jellicoe, Charles Wood, Adrian Mitchell, Henry Livings, Ian McEwan, V Tumbledown. Recipient STV awards for Best Prodn., 1969, 70, 71. Mem. Nat. Theater of Gt. Britain (assoc. dir.). Address: care Curtis Brown, 162-168 Regent St, London W1R 5TA, England

EYSENCK, HANS JURGEN, psychology educator; b. Berlin, Mar. 4, 1916; s. Eduard Anton and Ruth (Werner) E.; m. Margaret Davies, 1938 (div. 1950); 1 son, Michael; m. Sybil Giuletta Rostal, Oct. 30, 1950; children: Gary, Connie, Kevin, Darrin. BA, U. London, 1938, PhD, 1940, DSc, 1964. Research psychologist Mill Hill Hosp., London, 1942-48; reader Inst. of Psychiatry, London, 1948-55; prof. U. London, 1955-83, prof. emeritus, 1983—; dir. Personality Investigations, Publs. and Services, London, 1975—; founder Behaviour Research and Therapy. Author 60 books, 900 articles; founder, editor Personality and Individual Differences. Fellow Am. Psychol. Assn., Brit. Psychol. Soc.; mem. Internat. Soc. for Study of Individual Differences (pres. 1983-85). Club: Dulwich Tennis (London). Home: 10 Dorchester Dr, London SE24 England Office: Inst of Psychiatry, Denmark Hill, London SE5 England

EYSENCK, MICHAEL WILLIAM, psychologist, educator; b. London, Feb. 8, 1944; s. Hans Jurgen and Margaret Malcolm (Davies) E.; m. Mary Christine Kabyn, Mar. 22, 1975; children: Fleur Davina Ruth, William James Thomas, Juliet Margaret Maria. BA, U. London, 1965, PhD, 1973. Lectr. Birkbeck Coll., U. London, 1965-81, reader, 1981-87; prof. psychology Royal Holloway and Bedford New Coll., U. London, 1987—. Author: Human Memory: Theory, Research and Individual Differences, 1977, Attention and Arousal: Cognition and Performance, 1982, A Handbook of Cognitive Psychology, 1984, (with others) Personality and Individual Differences, 1985; editor: European Jour. Cognitive Psychology, 1989—. Mem. European Soc. for Cognitive Psychology (mem. adv. bd. 1985—), Brit. Psychol. Soc. (chmn. cognitive psychology sect. 1982-87). Office: U London Royal Holloway and, Bedford New Coll Egham Hill, Egham, Surrey TW20 0EX, England

EYSENCK, SYBIL BIANCA, psychologist; b. Vienna, Austria; arrived in Eng., 1934; d. Max Rostal and Sela Trau-Rostal; m. Hans-Jurgen Eysenck, Sept. 30, 1950; children: Gary, Connie, Kevin, Darrin. BSc in Psychology, U. London, 1952, PhD in Psychology, 1955. Sr. lectr. Inst. Psychiatry, London, 1967—; bd. dirs. Personality, Investigations Pubs. and Services Ltd., London. Co-editor: Personality and Individual Differences jour., 1980. Justice of the peace South Eastern Bench London, 1977. Fellow British Psychol. Soc. Home: 10 Dorchester Dr Herne Hill, London SE24 0DQ, England Office: Inst Psychiatry, De Crespigny Park, London SE5, England

EYSSELEIN, VIKTOR ERNST, gastroenterologist; b. Ansbach, Bavaria, Fed. Republic of Germany, June 16, 1951; s. Ernst and Dorothea (Gross) E.; m. Zoi Anastasopoulou, Sept. 30, 1978. MD, U. Würzburg, Fed. Republic of Germany, 1978; pvt. docent, U. Essen, Fed. Republic of Germany, 1988. Research fellow gastroenterology U. Essen, 1979-81, 83—; research fellow UCLA, 1981-83. Recipient Thannhauser preis, 1987. Mem. Am. Gastroenterological Assn., German Gastroenterological Assn., German Assn. for Internal Medicine. Office: U Essen, Hulelandstrasse 55, 4300 Essen Federal Republic of Germany

EYSSETTE, MICHEL JOSEPH, physician; b. Fraisses, Loire, France, Jan. 10, 1938; s. Raoul Louis and Renee Marie (Peyrol) E.; m. Marie France Leleu, July 14, 1958; children: Carine, Anne France, Sabina, Luc-Olivier. MD, Faculté Lyon, 1969. Tng. Hospices Civils, Lyon, 1965-69, sr. hosp. lectr., 1969-77; prof. U. Claude Bernard, Lyon, 1977-81; head dept. Hospice Civils, Lyon, 1981—; dean Réadaptations Tech. Inst., Lyon, 1982, pres. scientific council, 1982. Contbr. 150 articles to profl. jours. Served to lt. French Mil., 1963-65. Mem. French Soc. Functional Re-eduction and Readaptation (gen. sec.), Internat. French Speaking Urodynamique Soc., Internat. Med. Soc. of Paraplegia, French Soc. of Neuropsychology, Emilion's Guild. Roman Catholic. Club: Patch. Home: Domaine du Castellard, 69370 Saint-Didier au Mont d'Or France Office: Hopital Henry Gabrielle, Route de Vourles, 69320 Saint-Genis Laval France

EZAKI, HARUO, surgeon, retired educator; b. Miyama, Japan, Dec. 7, 1921; s. Jisuke and Fumi (Kunii) E.; m. Kazuko Kato, Oct. 9, 1951; children—Osamu, Mikiyo. M.D., Tokyo U., 1945; Ph.D., Nagoya U. Faculty Medicine (Japan), 1955. Resident in surgery Nagoya U., 1945-49; assoc. prof. Hiroshima U. Sch. Medicine (Japan), 1950-62. prof. research inst. nuclear medicine and biology, 1963-73, prof., 1974-85; advisor Atomic Bomb Casualty Commn., Hiroshima, 1963-75; cons. Radiation Effects Research Found., Hiroshima, 1975—; standing dir. Adult Diseases Prevention Soc., Hiroshima, 1976—. Author: Surgery of Thyroid, 1983. Recipient Hiroshima Med. Assn. award, 1982. Mem. Japan Surg. Soc. (councillor 1964—), Japanese Practical Surgeons Soc. (councillor 1957—, pres. 1982-83), Japan Blood-Transfusion Soc. (dir. 1950—, pres. 1977-78). Buddhist. Home and Office: Yoshijima-Higashi 2-17-38, Naka-ku, Hiroshima 730 Japan

EZEKIEL, NISSIM MOSES, writer, retired English language educator; b. Bombay, India, Dec. 16, 1924; s. Moses and Diana (Jhirad) E.; m. Daisy Jacob, Nov. 20, 1952; children: Kavita, Kalpana, Elkana. MA, Wilson Coll., Bombay, 1947. Prof. Mithibai Coll. Arts and Sci., Bombay, 1961-72; prof. English, U. Bombay, 1972-85. Author: Hymns in Darkness, 1972; Latter-Day Psalms (Nat. Acad. Letters award 1983), 1981; Three Plays, 1971. Hon. sec.-treas. The P.E.N. All-India Centre, 1963-65, 71-74, 79—. Decorated Padma Shree Govt. India, 1988. Home: 18 Kala Niketan 6th Floor, 47-C Bhulabhai Desai Rd, Bombay 400026, India Office: PEN All-India Ctr, Theosophy Hall, 40 New Marine Ln, Bombay 400020, India

EZEUGWA, SAMUEL NWANKWO C., sanitarian, consultant; b. Nanka, Nigeria, Dec. 31, 1933; s. Ezeugwa Ezenachukwu and Abigail Udeji (Ezekwem) Ezeugwa; m. Victoria Aguluka, Dec. 16, 1961; children: Chinwe, Ugochukwu, Nkiru, Udolisa, Chibogwu, Kosi. Diploma in health edn., Am. U., Beirut, 1965. Asst. chief health supt. Ministry of Health, Enugu, Nigeria, 1982-87; mgr. sanitation operation Anambra State Environ. Sanitation Authority, Enugu, 1985-87; chief cons. sanitarian Ezeugwa Assocs. Environ. Sanitation Cons., Enugu, 1987—. Pres. gen. NAnka Patrriotic Union, Aguata, Nigeria. Mem. Profl. Assn. Pub. Health Supts. of Nigeria. Club: Golden of Nigeria (Enugu br. chmn. 1984—). Home and Office: Ezeugwa Assocs, 6 Nise St, Uwani Enugu Anambra, Nigeria

EZEYZA-ALVEAR, CARLOS WILLY, publishing company executive, computer company executive; b. Buenos Aires, Argentina, Mar. 9, 1930; arrived in Sweden, 1960; s. Valentin Ezeyza-Alvear and Desideria Ezeyza; m. Birgitta Ringborg, June 23, 1960; children—Veronica Desiree, Nicolas Rafael. Grad., Sorbonne, Paris, 1955. Mng. dir. Impex Co., Paris, 1958-59, Teknotrans AB, Gothenburg, Sweden, 1973-80, Eurocontac Publisher, Gothenburg, 1978-82, Gustavsgatan 80, Gothenburg; pres. ECPrint AB, Gothenburg, 1982—, Internat. Micro Computer Enterprise AB, Gothenburg, 1982—. Roman Catholic. Office: Internat Micro Computer Enterprise AB, Gibraltargatan 48, Gothenburg Sweden

EZZAT, ALAIN NORBERT, oilfield services executive; b. Cairo, Oct. 29, 1932; m. Boussaina Amin, 1955; children: Ahmed, Aiman, Maissa. BS in Mech. Engring., Cairo U., 1955. Maintenance engr. Suez Refinery, Egypt, 1955-57; engr., then sr. engr. Suez Canal Authority, Egypt, 1957-66, dir. offshore services, 1966-69; v.p. ops. Single Buoy Moorings Inc., Marly, Switzerland, 1969-77; mng. dir. Installation and Services div. Single Buoy Moorings Inc., Monte Carlo, Monaco, 1978-84, exec. v.p., 1984-86, pres., 1986—; bd. mgmt. IHC Caland N.V. (parent co. to Single Buoy Moorings Inc.), Holland, 1984—, mng. dir., 1987—. Office: Single Buoy Moorings Inc, POB 199, Monte Carlo Cedex 98007, Monaco

EZZAT, HAZEM A(HMED), research executive; b. Cairo, July 12, 1942; came to U.S., 1966, naturalized, 1978; s. Ahmed M. and Hanya A. (Safwat) E.; m. Shaza Abdelghaffar, Aug. 2, 1972; children—Jeneen H., Waleed H. B.Sc., U. Cairo, 1963; M.S., U. Wis., 1967, Ph.D., 1971. Project engr. Suez Canal Authority, Egypt, 1963-65; instr. faculty engring. Cairo U., 1965-66; research asst. U. Wis., Madison, 1966-70; with Gen. Motors Research Labs., Warren, Mich., 1970—, asst. head engring. mechanics dept., 1981-84, head power systems research dept., 1984—. Mem. ASME (Henry Hess award 1973), Soc. Automotive Engrs., Am. Acad. Mechanics, Engring. Soc. Detroit, Sigma Xi. Contbr. articles to profl. jours. Club: Econ. (Detroit). Office: Gen Motors Research Labs Warren MI 48090

FABER, CHARLES PHILIP, investment company executive; b. Sheboygan, Wis., Aug. 1, 1941; s. Charles W. and Bernetta P. (Metscher) F.; m. Jane E. Schneider, Dec. 22, 1962; children—Charles R., David R. B.B.A. (Dow-Corning scholar), U. Wis., 1966, M.B.A., 1967. Field rep. Caterpillar Tractor Co., Peoria, Ill., 1967-68; mktg. mgr. Apache Corp., Mpls., 1969-72, sales rep., 1973-74; gen. mgr. Apache Programs, Inc., Mpls., 1974-76, br. mgr., Milw., 1976-77; exec. v.p., dir. Investment Search, Inc., Annapolis, Md., 1978-82; chmn., dir. Samson Securities Co., 1983-86; pres., dir. Samson Properties, Inc., Tulsa, 1984-86; sr. v.p. Heritage Asset Mgmt., Inc., St. Petersburg, Fla., 1986—. dir. Samson Resources Co. Served with U.S. Army, 1961-63. Mem. Internat. Assn. Fin. Planners, Assn. for Continuing Edn. in Bus., Nat. Assn. Securities Dealers (lic. prin.), Beta Gamma Sigma. Home: One Beach Dr #2714 Saint Petersburg FL 33701

FABER, MARSHALL LEE, producer; b. Washington, Aug. 20, 1917; s. Marshall Lee and Margaret (Shaw) F.; grad. high sch.; m. Martha Mogan, Aug. 29, 1941; children—Margaret Louise, Marshall Lee, Marianne Lucretia. Owner, operator Bus. Films, indsl. comml., ednl. motion pictures, Washington, 1934-46; film prodn., Phoenix, 1947-50; with KPHO, Phoenix, 1950-53, McClatchy Broadcasting Co., Sacramento, Fresno, Calif., 1953-55, KBTV, Denver, 1955-63; producer Marshall L. Faber Prodns., motion pictures, Denver, 1963—; tech. rep. Western Cine, Denver-Hollywood, 1975-78; tech. cons. Canon 35 Hearing, Colo. Supreme Ct., 1957; cons. Fedn. Rocky Mountain States Satellite Project, 1973; cons. cadre Ariz. Dept. Edn., 1975—, also to producers of feature films, 1974—; sculptor silver miniatures. Recipient citations Du Pont Found., 1955, Inst. Edn. by Radio, Ohio State U., 1961, Advt. Fedn. Am. 9th dist., 1960, ABC TV Network, 1960; recipient 1st pl. awards TV Radio Mirror, 1960, Omaha Art Dirs., 1958, Broadcast Music Inc., Am. Assn. State and Local History 1960, Cine Golden Eagle, 1964; recipient 4 Chris awards Columbus Film Festival, 1964, Ednl. Film Library Assn. award, 1965, Ad Club award, 1966, Am. Assn. Indsl. Advertisers awards, 1966, 68, award of Excellence Sunset Mag. Travel Film Festival, 1971, award for excellence in editing U.S. TV Commls. Festival, Chgo., 1971, bronze medal Internat. Film and TV Festival of N.Y., 1971, commendation award Denver sect. Soc. Motion Picture and TV Engrs., 1972, award Nat. Ednl. Film Festival, 1972. Mem. Soc. Motion Picture and TV Engrs. (life, chmn. Denver sect. 1971), Soc. Photog. Scientists and Engrs. (bd. govs. 1967-69), Internat. Photographers Motion Picture Industry. Episcopalian. Author: Making Money With Low Budget Features, 1977; pioneer in design TV and film camera booth for use in courtroom photography, 1957, Fasdraw timer, 1958; designer teaching machines, audio visual machines for spl. adaption; mfr. F8 projector. Address: 6412 E Desert Cove Scottsdale AZ 85254

FABERT, JACQUES, artist, educator; b. Paris, Apr. 24, 1925; came to U.S., 1957; m. Bonnie MacLean, Aug. 19, 1981; children: David, Wolodia, Graham. Student, Ecole Natonale Des Beaux Arts-Paris, 1943-47. Prof. fine arts San Francisco Art Acad., 1963-70, Calif. Coll. Arts and Crafts, Oakland, 1963-72, Princeton Art Assn., N.J., 1978—; one man shows at Nordness Gallery, N.Y.C., 1969, E.B. Crocker Mus. Art, Sacramento, 1969, Gilman Gallery, Chgo., 1970, Carroll Reece Mus., E. Tenn. State U., 1974, others; exhibited in group shows at: Calif. Palace Legion of Honor, San Francisco, 1963-65-67; Am. Fedn. of Art, N.Y.C., 1968; San Francisco Mus. Art, 1968-69-70; Nat. Inst. Arts and Letters, N.Y.C., 1970; Expo '70, Osaka, Japan, 1970—; Stedman Gallery, Rutgers U., 1977-79; N.J. State Mus., Trenton, N.J., 1978-79; represented in permanent collections at Butler Inst. Am. Art, Youngstown, Ohio, City of San Francisco Art Commn., Norfolk Mus. Art, Va., City of Phila. Free Library, others. Address: 2682 Rt 413 PO Box 103 Buckingham PA 18912

FABRE, SERGE JEAN, physician; b. Salles-Curan, Aveyron, France, Feb. 28, 1926; s. Albert Léon and Olympe Julienne (Niel) F.; m. Sabine Nelly Husquin, Sept. 14, 1949; children: Raphaël, Marie, François, Anne, Marc, Pierre, Elisabeth. PCB, Faculté des Sciences, Montpellier, France, 1945; MD, Faculté de Médecine, Montpellier, France, 1960. Intern Hosp. Montpellier, 1947; resident Faculté de Médecine, 1953; chef de clinique Faculté de Médecine, Montpellier, 1960-63; prof. Faculté de Médecine, Dakar, Sénégal, 1967-71, Sch. of Med., Constantine, Algeria, 1963-67, Ctr. Hosp. Régional, Montpellier, 1971—. Fullbright grantee, Duke U., 1958-59. Mem. Médecins du Monde. Roman Catholic. Home: Ave des Quakers, 30111 Congénies, Gard France Office: Centre Hosp Régional, 5 rue Hoche, 30005 Nimes, Gard France

FABRICIUS, FINN, industrial consultant; b. Copenhagen, Jan. 10, 1958. MME, Tech. U. Denmark, Lyngby, 1981. Cons. research and devel. Inst. Product Devel., Lyngby, 1981—, group mgr. assembly tech., 1985—; nat. project mgr. resource team Danish EUREKA, 1988—; cons. in field. Contbr. articles to profl. jours. Office: Inst Product Devel, Bygning 423, DK-2800 Lyngby Denmark

FACCINI, ERNEST CARLO, mechanical engineer; b. Livo, Trento, Italy, May 28, 1949; s. Carlo and Elena Agnes (Pancheri) F.; parents Am. citizens; A.A., Western Wyo. Community Coll., 1969; B.S., U. Wyo., 1972, M.S., 1976. Engring. technician Laramie (Wyo.) Energy Research Center, 1968-71; field engr. Mountain Fuel Supply Co., Rock Springs, Wyo., 1972; research engr. Aberdeen (Md.) Proving Grounds, 1972-73; research asst. mech. engring. U. Wyo., Laramie, 1973-76; engring. asst. Bridger Coal Co., Rock Springs, Wyo., 1973; mech. engr. Naval Explosive Ordnance Disposal Facility, Indian Head, Md., 1976-85; sr. scientist TERA/NMIMT, Socorro, N. Mex., 1986—. Registered profl. engr., Wyo., Md. Mem. ASME (chmn. student sect. 1971-72), Am. Phys. Soc., AAAS, Am. Soc. Metals. Roman Catholic. Contbr. articles to profl. jours.; patentee in field. Researcher rapid explosive excavation techniques, underwater non-explosive excavation, surface/subsurface ordnance clearance vehicle design, remote fuse disassembly, multi-fuel combuster design, internal ballistics, blast effects design of shaped charges and of grenades for spl. applications. Home: 1211 Hilton Pl Socorro NM 87801 Office: TERA/NMIMT Socorro NM 87801

FACINOLI, JOHN FRANKLIN, osteopathic physician; b. Pitts., Feb. 20, 1948; s. Bert Winston and Helen Irene (Grubb) F.; m. Sallie Ann Dixon, May 12, 1973 (div.). B.S. in Biology, Morris Harvey Coll., 1974; D.O., W.Va. Sch. Osteo. Medicine, 1978. Diplomate Am. Bd. Emergency Medicine. Intern Richmond Heights Gen. Hosp (Ohio), 1978-79; resident in emergency medicine Mt. Sinai Med. Ctr., Cleve., 1980-83; dir. emergency services Putnam Gen. Hosp., Hurricane, W.Va., 1983—. Fellow Am. Coll. Emergency Physicians; mem. AMA.

FACKELMAN, ROBERT HENRY, newspaper executive; b. Ponca, Nebr., Oct. 19, 1907; s. Herman Carl and Jeanette (Pomeroy) F.; student Midland Coll., 1923-25; B.J., U. Mo., 1927; postgrad. Harvard U., 1941-42; m. Anna Laura Torbert, June 6, 1928; 1 dau., Ann Karen (Mrs. Frank Nixon). Editor, pub. Baxter Springs (Kans.) Citizen, 1927-28, Raymondville (Tex.) Chronicle, 1929-40; editor, gen. mgr. Winter Haven (Fla.) News-Chief, 1943-50; editor, pub. Morristown (Tenn.) Sun, 1950-52; pub. Cleveland (Tenn.) Banner, 1952-54; v.p. So. Newspapers, Inc., 1954-58; pres. Newspaper Service Co., Inc., 1953—, Richmond (Mo.) Daily News, Jennings (La.) Daily News, Crowley (La.) Post-Signal, Inc., Excelsior Springs (Mo.) Daily Standard, interests in Ruston (La.) Daily Leader and 8 Fla. and 3 La. non-daily newspapers; co-owner Madison Channel 3 TV Co. Author: Hijackers Abroad, Publishers Primer, The Walls Connection. Served with USAAF, 1941-42. Mem. Am. Newspaper Pubs. Assn., So. Newspaper Pubs. Assn. (dir. 1970-73). Office: 408 S Bonita Ave Panama City FL 32401

FACTOR, MAX, III, lawyer, investment advisor; b. Los Angeles, Sept. 25, 1945; s. Sidney B. and Dorothy (Levinson) F.; 1 child, Jennifer Lee. B.A. in Econs. magna cum laude, Harvard Coll., 1966; J.D., Yale U., 1969. Bar: Calif. 1970, U.S. Ct. Appeals (6th cir.) 1971, U.S. Dist. Ct. (cen. dist.) Calif. 1971. Law clk. U.S. Ct. Appeals (6th cir.), 1969-71; exec. dir. Calif. Law Ctr., Los Angeles, 1973-74; dir. Consumer Protection Sect., Los Angeles City Atty., 1974-77; pres. MF Capital Ltd., Beverly Hills, Calif., 1978-86; ptnr. Cooper, Epstein & Hurewitz, Beverly Hills, Calif., 1986—; expert witness numerous state and fed. bds., 1974-78; guest lectr. UCLA, U. So. Calif., Los Angeles County Bar Assn., Calif. Dept. Consumer Affairs, 1974-76; hearing examiner City of Los Angeles, 1975. Contbr. articles to profl. jours. Bd. dirs. Western Law Ctr. for the Handicapped, Los Angeles, 1977-79, Beverly Hills Unified Sch. Dist., 1979-83; pres. Beverly Hills Bd. Edn., 1983; bd. councilors U. So. Calif. Law Ctr., Los Angeles, 1983—. Recipient scholarship award Harvard Coll., 1965; Max Factor III Day proclaimed in his honor Beverly Hills City Council, 1979; recipient Disting. Service to Pub. Edn. award Beverly Hills Bd. Edn., 1979. Mem. Los Angeles County Bar Assn. (chmn. various coms. 1976-78), Beverly Hills C. of C. (pres.-elect 1986—), Beverly Hills Edn. Found. (pres. 1977-79). Democrat. Jewish. Office: Cooper Epstein & Hurewitz 345 N Maple Dr Suite 200 Beverly Hills CA 90210

FACUNDO, JOSE R., bank executive; b. Manila, May 8, 1938; s. Jose T. and Rosario (Roco) F.; m. Gerda Kaufmann, May 22, 1963; children: Michael, Juergen. BA, Ateneo U., Manila, 1958; postgrad. in stats., U. Philippines, 1958-60. Prof. Ateneo U., Manila, 1958-60, 63; various exec. positions Citibank, N.A. (formerly 1st Nat. Bank of N.Y.), Manila, 1964-76; pres., chief exec. officer Citytrust Banking Corp., Manila, 1976—; bd. dirs. Telefunken Semiconductors Philippines, Manila, others. Pres. Jr. Achievement Philippines, Manila, 1977; treas. Dasmariñas Village Assn., 1985—; trustee Philippines Bus. for Social Progress, 1985-87, Ballet Philippines, 1987. Mem. Mgmt. Assn. Philippines (pres. 1987), Chaine des Rotisseurs (nat. treas. 1986—). Clubs: Manila Golf, Manila Polo. Lodge: Rotary. Office: Citytrust Banking Corp, 379 Sen Gil Puyat Ave, Makati The Philippines

FACUSSÉ, ALBERT SHUCRY, lawyer; b. Tegucigalpa, Honduras, Feb. 10, 1921; s. Nicholas and Maria (Barjum) F.; m. May Bandak, Dec. 22, 1946 (dec.); children—Vivian Neuwirth, Denise Lentz. J.D. cum laude, Loyola U., New Orleans, 1943. Bar: La. 1957. Sole practice, New Orleans, 1957—; pub. speaker. Mem. La. State Bar Assn., ABA, Internat. Platform Assn. Democrat. Roman Catholic. Comment editor Loyola U. Law Rev., 1943. Home: 6731 Manchester St New Orleans LA 70126 Office: 234 Loyola Ave Suite 832 New Orleans LA 70112

FADELEY, HERBERT JOHN, JR., banker, lawyer; b. Ambler, Pa., Feb. 14, 1922; s. Herbert John and Jennie Miller (Lewis) F.; m. Eleanor A. Battafarano, Feb. 8, 1947; children: Herbert John, Brett Duane, Theresa Jane, Scott Lewis. B.S. in Commerce, Drexel U., 1946; J.D., Temple U., 1953; postgrad., Stonier Sch. Banking, Rutgers U., 1957. Bar: U.S. Supreme Ct. 1957, U.S. Ct. Appeals, U.S. Dist. Ct., U.S. Tax Ct.; registered mortgage underwriter (RMU); cert. rev. appraiser (CRA). Asst. cashier First Nat. Bank, Media, Pa., 1951-57; v.p. Boardwalk Nat. Bank, Atlantic City, N.J., 1957-60, Indsl. Trust Co., Phila., 1960-62; v.p., trust officer County Trust Co., White Plains, N.Y., 1963-68; pres. Troy Savs. Bank, N.Y., 1969-82, chmn. bd., chief exec. officer, 1982-87, also trustee; pres., dir. 32 Second St. Inc., Realty Umbrella Ltd., Corhar Inc., Russtend Realty Corp.; lectr. banking and law Drexel U., 1962, Rockland Community Coll., Suffern, N.Y., 1964-68, Westchester County chpt. Am. Inst. Banking, 1965-68, Hudson Valley Community Coll., Troy, 1970; dir., past chmn. bd. Mut. Thrifts Service Ctr. Chmn. Rensselaer County Am. Cancer Fund Crusade, 1970-73; also v.p., dir. Cancer Soc., 1970-73, pres., 1975-76; bd. dirs. Troy Downtown Devel. Found.; mem. Troy Downtown Devel. Council, Tri-county Fifty Group; bd. dirs. Russell Sage Coll., chmn. fin. com., past treas., gen. chmn. 1972 fund drive; bd. dirs. United Community Services; bd. dirs. Soc. Friendly Sons St. Patrick, pres., 1976-77; bd. dirs. Mary Warren Free Inst., also v.p.; pres., bd. dirs. The Family Agy. Inc.; bd. dirs., v.p. Uncle Sam Mall, Inc., 1971-73. Served to lt. (j.g.) USNR, 1942-43, 48-59; maj. Old Guard City of Phila. Named Outstanding Alumnus Drexel U., 1961; recipient trust div. sch. awards N.Y. State Banker's Assn., 1967, 68. Mem. ABA, Am. Inst. Mgmt. (mem. pres.'s council), Am. Judicature Soc., Nat.

Assn. Rev. Appraisers (sr.), Assn. U.S. Army, Lambda Chi Alpha, Phi Alpha Delta (named outstanding alumnus 1957, chief justice Dr. Elden S. Magaw Alumni chpt. 1955-56), Greater Troy C. of C. (dir. 1969-75, pres. 1973-74). Episcopalian. Club: Troy. Lodges: Shriners, Jesters, Masons (Troy). Home: 2568 Western Ave RD #3 Bldg 8 Apt 9 Altamont NY 12009

FADER, SEYMOUR J., management and engineering consulting company exec.; b. N.Y.C., Feb. 9, 1923; s. Louis and Bertha (Stachel) F.; student CCNY, 1938-42; B.S.E.E., U. Pa., 1949, M.B.A. in Indsl. Mgmt., 1950; m. Shirley Ruth Sloan, June 26, 1951; children—Susan Deborah, Steven Micah. Mgr. prodn. Bogue Electric Mfg. Co., Paterson, N.J., 1950-56; mgr. planning and control Rowe Mfg. Co., Whippany, N.J., 1956-58; cons. Koor Crafts & Industries, Ltd., Tel Aviv, 1958-59; dir. mfg. ops. ESC Electronics Corp., Palisades Park, N.J., 1959-62; mgr. mfg. Artistic Mfg., Sun Chem. Corp., Carlstadt, N.J., 1962-66; mgr. ops. Fairchild Instrumentation, Fairchild Camera & Instrument Corp., Clifton, N.J., 1966-67; v.p. Graphic Products, Inc., Hackensack, N.J., 1967-69; gen. mgr., v.p. Berkey Tech., Berkey Photo, Inc., Woodside, N.Y., 1969-72; pres. Suste Assocs., Paramus, N.J., 1972—; asst. prof. mgmt. Ramapo Coll., Mahwah, N.J., 1972-75, assoc. prof., 1975-80, prof. mgmt. and indsl. relations, 1980—, dir. Study Abroad programs, 1983—; adj. prof. mgmt. Grad. Sch. Bus., Fordham U., 1982—; arbitration panelist Better Bus. Bur. of Bergen, Passaic and Rockland Counties, 1983—. Mem. pub. health study N.J. State Assembly Commn. on Conservation, Natural Resources, Air and Water Pollution, 1972-73; commr. Paramus Environ. Commn., 1973-78, vice chmn., 1977-78, chmn. inventory and land use com., 1974-78. Served with U.S. Army, 1942-45. Mem. Am. Mgmt. Assn. (cert. of achievement 1974), Am. Arbitration Assn. (panelist), Am. Inst. Indsl. Engrs., Soc. Advancement of Mgmt., Nat. Panel Consumer Arbitrators, Am. Prodn. and Inventory Control Soc. Author: Fundamentals of Management for First-Line Supervisors, 1974; The Manufacturing Manager, 1975; co-author: Jobmanship, 1979; contbr. articles to profl. jours. Patentee coreless reeler, desk-top copier, photo-copier. Home: 377 McKinley Blvd Paramus NJ 07652 Office: PO Box 422 Paramus NJ 07652

FADIGA, ABDOULAYE, bank governor; b. Touba, Cote d'Ivoire, Mar. 10, 1935; s. Bambadjan and Bamba Manama F.; m. Matieni Doukoure, Sept. 16, 1960; children—Abou, Manama, Djibril, Nina. Diplome d'etudes superieures Droit Publique, 1959-60, Scis. Economiques, 1958-59, Economie Politique, 1957-58; Licencie en Droit, U. de Dijon Faculty Law, France, 1960. Sec. Gen. de l'Organisation Inter-Africaine du Cafe, 1960-62; dir. gen. ajoint C.S.S.P.A., 1962-67, dir. gen., 1967-75; gov. Banque Centrale des Etats de l'Afrique de L'Ouest, 1975—. Office: Banque Ctr des Etats de l'Afrique, Avenue du Barachiors, Dakar BP 3108 Senegal also: BP 356, Ouagadougou Berkina Faso

FADJAR, FABIANUS SAPUTRA, corporate president; b. Bengkulu, Indonesia, Sept. 18, 1949; s. Fung Lok and Tjie Tong Lan Fadjar. BSci in Biology, Nat. U. Indonesia, 1974. Tchr. Ricci Sr. High Sch., Jakarta, 1971-73; lectr. U. Atamajaya Med. Sch., Jakarta, 1973-75; tech. sales rep. Pt. Setio Harto, Jakarta, 1975-78; rep., pres. Cv. Primaco, Jakarta, 1978—. Recipient Am. Award for Tech. Bus. Initiative Direction, 1987. Office: Cv Primaco, Jl Tanah Abang V/54A, Jakarta 10160, Indonesia

FAES, RALPH REMO, aviation company executive; b. Schiers, Switzerland, Mar. 16, 1945; s. Rolf Emil and Yvonne (Gallino) F. Cand.iur, Zurich U., 1972; Eidg. dipl. PR-Berater, SAWI, Biel, Switzerland, 1983; profl. pilot, Swissair SLS, Zurich, 1977. Journalist, Swiss Highsch. Jour., Zurich, 1969-75, editor, 1976—; pilot, comml. mgr. Air Safety, Zurich, 1977-79, pres., 1980—; pres. CAL Pub. Relations, Zurich, 1980—; pub. relations cons. Swiss Reins. Co., 1978-86; exec. mgr., Inst. for Capital and Econ., Zurich, 1986—. Pres., Aquarius Editions, 1987—, Zurich Coll. Orgn., 1965-69, Herrliberg Social-Liberal Party, 1969-78. Mem. Aviation Owners and Pilots Assn., Swiss Pub. Relations Assn., Inst. Democratic Politics (pres.), others. Liberal. Christian Ch. Clubs: Herrliberg Yacht (pres. 1975-79), Swiss Cruising, Yonian Yacht. Home: Seehof, Seestrasse 127, CH-8704 Herrliberg Switzerland Office: PO Box 174, Zurich CH 8034 Switzerland

FAGERBERG, ROGER RICHARD, lawyer; b. Chgo., Dec. 11, 1935; s. Richard Emil and Evelyn (Thor) F.; m. Virginia Fuller Vaughan, June 20, 1959; children: Steven Roger, Susan Vaughan, James Thor, Laura Craft. B.S. in Bus. Adminstrn., Washington U., St. Louis, 1958, J.D., 1961, postgrad., 1961-62. Bar: Mo. 1961. Grad. teaching asst. Washington U., St. Louis, 1961-62; assoc. firm Rassieur, Long & Yawitz, St. Louis, 1962-64; ptnr. Rassieur, Long, Yawitz & Schneider and predecessor firms, St. Louis, 1965—. Mem. exec. com. Citizens' Adv. Council Pkwy. Sch. Dist., 1974—, pres.-elect, 1976-77, pres., 1977-78; bd. dirs. Parkway Residents Orgn., 1969—, v.p., 1970-73, pres., 1973—; scoutmaster Boy Scouts Am., 1979-83; Presbyn. elder, 1976—, pres. three local congs. 1968-70, 77-78, 83-84. Mem. ABA, Mo. Bar Assn., St. Louis Bar Assn., Christian Bus. Men's Com. (bd. dirs. 1975-78, 87—), Full Gospel Bus. Men's Fellowship, Order of Coif, Omicron Delta Kappa, Beta Gamma Sigma, Pi Sigma Alpha, Phi Eta Sigma, Phi Delta Phi, Kappa Sigma. Republican. Lodges: Kiwanis (past bd. dirs.), Masons, Shriners. Home: 13812 Clayton Rd Town and Country MO 63011 Office: Rassieur Long Yawitz & Schneider 1150 Boatmen's Tower Saint Louis MO 63102

FAGGIN, FEDERICO, electronics executive; b. Vicenza, Italy, Dec. 1, 1941; came to U.S., 1968, naturalized, 1978; s. Giuseppe and Emma (Munari) F.; m. Elvia Sardei, Sept. 2, 1967; children: Marzia, Marc, Eric. Grad., Perito Industriale Instituto A. Rossi, Vicenza, 1960; D.Physics, U. Padua, Italy, 1965. Sect. head Fairchild Camera & Instrument Co., Palo Alto, Calif., 1968-70; dept. mgr. Intel Corp., Santa Clara, Calif., 1970-74; founder, pres. Zilog Inc., Cupertino, Calif., 1974-80; v.p. computer systems group Exxon Enterprises, N.Y.C., 1981; co-founder, pres. Cygnet Technologies, Inc., Sunnyvale, Calif., 1982-86; pres., co founder Synaptics, Inc., San Jose, Calif., 1986—. Recipient Marconi Fellowship award, 1988. Office: Synaptics Inc 2860 Zanker Rd Suite 105 San Jose CA 95134

FAGIN, LEONARD HENRY, psychiatrist; b. Buenos Aires, July 29, 1947; arrived in Eng., 1972; s. Jack Monteflore Fagin and Ray (Rosenberg) Goldschmidt; m. Deirdre Pauline East, 1974; children: Abel, Jessica. MD, U. Buenos Aires, 1971, diploma (hon.), 1972. Sr. house officer Bexley Hosp., Kent, Eng., 1972-73; registrar Napsbury Hosp., St. Albans, Eng., 1974-76; sr. registrar The London Hosp., 1976-77; sr. registrar Claybury Hosp., Essex, Eng., 1977-79, cons., 1979—; clin. tutor Claybury Hosp., 1983-86, chmn. div. psychiatry, 1986—; med. adv. Essex Marital Guidance Counsellors, 1986—. Author: The Forsaken Families, 1984; author, editor: Interdisciplinary Work in Mental Health, 1987. Med. advisor unemployment com. Dept. Health and Social Security, London, 1983-86; advisor Com. in Aid of Refuseniks, Oxford, Eng., 1987. Mem. Royal Coll. Psychiatrists, Assn. Family Therapy, Interdisciplinary Assn. Mental Health Workers (founder, nat. council rep. 1983-86). Home: 9 Womersley Rd, London N8 9AE, England Office: Claybury Hosp, Manor Rd, Woodford Bridge 1G8 8BY, England

FAGNIEZ, PIERRE LOUIS, surgeon, educator; b. Salies de Bearn, Aquitaine, France, Dec. 6, 1939; s. Dominique and Elizabeth Fagniez; children—Nathalie, Antoine, Clotilde Thibaut. M.D., U. Paris XII, 1972. Externe, Assitance Publique, Paris, 1961, intern, 1965; practice medicine, specializing in digestive surgery, Creteil, France, 1972—; prof. U. Paris XII, Creteil, 1981—; surgeon Hop. Henri Mondor, Creteil, 1972—; digestive surgery cons. Hopital Henri Mondor, 1972; teaching chief surgery Faculte de Paris XII, 1972-81; head internat. relations Paris XII U., 1982. Editorial bd. Revue du Praticien, 1979-85. Avocations: jogging; skiing. Home: Cite de Fleurs, 75017 Paris France Office: Hopital Henri Mondor, 94000 Creteil France

FAHD IBN ABDUL AZIZ, HIS MAJESTY, King of Saudi Arabia; b. Riyadh, Saudi Arabia, 1923; s. King Abdulaziz and Hassa Bint Ahmad al-Sudeiri; married. Ed.D. (hon.) King Abdulaziz U., 1976, D. (hon.) Islamic U. of Imam Mohamed Ibn Saud, 1982. First minister of edn., Saudi Arabia, 1953; leader dels. to Arab League in Morocco and Lebanon; minister interior, 1962-75, 2d dep. prime minister, 1967-75, crown prince, dep. prime minister, 1975-82, King of Saudia Arabia, 1982—, also prime minister; chmn. Supreme Council Nat. Security, Supreme Council Ednl. Policy, Supreme Council Saudi Univs., Supreme Council Oil Affairs, Supreme Council Youth Welfare, Supreme Council Pilgrimage; chmn. Saudi dels. internat. confs. Avocations: soccer, camel racing, camping. Office: Embassy of Saudi Arabia 601 New Hampshire Ave NW Washington DC 20037 also: Royal Palace, Jeddah Saudi Arabia *

FAHLIN, BO AXEL HENRY, pulp and paper company executive; b. Stockholm, Dec. 29, 1930; s. Nils G. and Agda M. (Fahlin) Anderson; m. Monica B. Norrefors, May 28, 1931; children—Hans, Lars. Degree Engring., HTL, Stockholm, 1950, KTH, Stockholm, 1956; postgrad. IESE, Barcelona, Spain, 1965. Prodn. mgr. Wargons AB, Vargon, Sweden, 1959-65, Papelera Navarra S.A., Pamplona, Spain, 1965-69; dir. SCA Corrugating, Stockholm, 1969-73; project mgr. KMW, Karlstad, Sweden, 1973-77; v.p. Mo & Domsjoe AB, Ornskoldsvik, Sweden, 1977—; lab. mgr. SCA Newspring Mill, Sundsvall, 1957-59; research engr. STFI, Stockholm, 1956-57; bd. dirs. Norrlandsleraft AB, Stockholm, GideKraft AB, Stockholm, Svenska Handelsbanken AB, Oernskoeldsvik, Papeteries Pont St. Maxene SA, Paris, STFI, Stockholm. Mem. Swedish Pulp and Paper Engrs. Assn. (pres.), European Liaison Com. for Pulp and Paper (pres.). Lutheran. Club: Puttom Golf. Lodge: Rotary. Home: Carlgrensvagen 25, 89200 Domsjo Sweden Office: Mo och Domsjo AB, 89200 Ornskoldsvik Sweden

FAHLMAN, SVEN TORSTEN, physician; b. Stockholm, July 11, 1914; s. Vilhelm Torsten and Helga Iris Augusta (Bergstedt) F.; m. Ann-Margret Flensburg, 1939 (dec.); children—Ingrid, Claes; m. Tatiana von Lichtenfeld, 1955 (div. 1967); children—Diana, Beatrice; m. Elsa Ester Birgitta Tyle-Fahlman, Oct. 2, 1968 (dec. 1981); children—Cecilia, Caroline. Student, Karolinska Inst., Stockholm, 1952-60, medicine candidate, 1954. Med. diplomate. Commd. ensign Swedish Royal Navy, 1936, advanced through grades to capt. 1944; ret., 1952; surgeon, Hsp., Enkoping, 1960-61; gynecologist, Stockholm Hosp., 1961-62; practice gen. medicine, Sollentuna, Sweden, 1962—; physician Inst. for Health Control, Stockholm, 1974-84. Mem. Swedish Nat. Fencing Team, 1939-55, team recipient Silver medal Olympics, 1952, Bronze medal world championship, Stockholm, 1951. Swedish foil-fencing champion, 1950, 55, 56, 59, epee fencing, 1951, also teamcompetition champion. Mem. Stockholm Common Fencing Club, Royal Navies Athletic Assn. Recipient medaille Francaise de l'education Physique. Home: Rudbecksvag 73, 19151 Sollentuna Sweden Office: Skyttevagen 20, 19151 Sollentuna Sweden

FAHMY, HISHAM M. A., oil service company executive; b. Cairo, Nov. 12, 1947; s. Mohamed Aly and Samia (Aboul Kheir) F.; m. Zeinab Mostafa Khalil, May 27, 1972; children: Shereen, Nevine. B.Sc., Faculty of Sci., Alexandria, Egypt, 1967; PhD, Univ. Coll., London, 1976. Chief chemist AMOCO Oil Co., Cairo, 1967-71; researcher Naval Am. Research Unit, Cairo, 1971-73; postgrad. researcher Univ. Coll., London, 1973-76; postdoctoral researcher U. London, 1976-77; area rep. NL Industries Treating Chemicals, Abu Dhabi, United Arab Emirates, 1977-79; dist. rep. Cairo, 1979-81; ptnr., mgr. TAM Oilfield Services, Cairo, 1981—; cons. MTH Techs. and Cons. Group, Cairo, 1983—, Amtrade Inc., Cairo, 1985—. Contbr. articles to profl. jours. Brit. Council fellow, London, 1974. Mem. Soc. Petroleum Engrs., Am. C. of C., Soc. Mining Engrs. Office: TAM Oilfield Services, 4 Ghezira St, Zamalek, Cairo Egypt

FAIDLEY, LEVERN WILLIAM, agricultural engineer; b. Prairie City, Iowa, Dec. 4, 1943; s. Gaylord Franklin and Leona (Beintema) F.; m. Barbara Ann Farmer, Aug. 10, 1968; children—LeAnn, Galen, Eric. B.S., Iowa State U., 1967; M.S., Mich. State U., 1969, Ph.D., 1974. Agrl. engr. Food and Agr. Orgn., UN, Rome, Italy, 1974-82, energy program officer, 1982-83, sr. officer energy, 1984-85, sr. officer program and planning, 1985—. Contbg. author: Energy for World Agriculture, 1979; editorial bd. Energy in Agriculture, 1981—. NDEA fellow, 1967-69; Midwest Univ. Consortium Internat. Activities grantee, 1969-70. Mem. Am. Soc. Agrl. Engrs., Internat. Solar Energy Soc., Sigma Xi. Home: via Tespi 184/5, AXA-Acilia, 00125 Rome Italy Office: Food and Agr Orgn UN, via dell terme di Caracalla, 00100 Rome Italy

FAIR, JAMES MILTON, agricultural cooperative company executive; b. Lloydminster, Alta., Can., Apr. 14, 1934; s. James and Evelyn (Warren) F.; m. Joyce Dennis, Aug. 4, 1956; children: Dennis, Donna Fair Frentz. Student, Harvard U., 1981. Chartered acct. With audit dept. govt. of Alta., Edmonton, 1951-59; with computer devel. div. Govt. of Alta., Edmonton, 1959, sr. systems analyst, 1959-65; systems mgr. Sask. Wheat Pool, Regina, 1965-66, asst. treas., 1966-70, corp. treas., 1970-76, dir. adminstrn., dep. gen. mgr., 1976-79, gen. mgr. ops., 1979-81, chief exec. officer, 1981—; dir. Pacific Elevators Ltd., Vancouver, B.C., Western Pool Terminals Ltd., Vancouver, B.C., CSP Foods Ltd., Winnipeg, Man., Can., XCAN Grain Ltd., Winnipeg, Man., Can., Prince Rupert Grain Ltd., Vancouver, Western Co-op Fertilizers Co., Calgary, Alta. Mem. Sask. Inst. Chartered Accts., Alta. Inst. Charteed Accts. Am. Baptist. Lodge: Rotary. Home: 305 Avon Dr, Regina, SK Canada S4V 1L8 Office: Saskatchewan Wheat Pool, 2625 Victoria Ave, Regina, SK Canada S4T 7T9

FAIRBANKS, DOUGLAS ELTON, JR., actor, producer, writer, corporation director; b. N.Y.C., Dec. 9, 1909; s. Douglas Elton Sr. and Anna Beth (Sully) F.; m. Lucille LeSueur (Joan Crawford), June, 1929 (div. 1933); m. Mary Lee Epling, Apr. 22, 1939; children: Daphne Fairbanks Kay, Victoria Fairbanks Vangerbig, Melissa Fairbanks Morant. Cadet, Bovée and Collegiate Schs., N.Y.; student, Knickerbocker Greys, N.Y., Pasadena Poly., Harvard Mil. Sch., Los Angeles; pvt. tutoring, London and Paris; D.F.A. (hon.), Westminster Coll., 1966, Sr. Churchill fellow; vis. fellow, St. Cross Coll., Oxford U.; M.A., Oxford U., 1971; LL.D. (hon.), Denver U., 1974; fellow, Boston U. Libraries, 1978. Chmn. Dougfair Corp. and subsidiaries, The Fairbanks Co., Calif., 1946, Fairtel Corp., N.Y., 1969, Douglas Fairbanks Ltd., U.K., 1952—, (and asso. cos.), 1952-58; past pres. Boltons Trading Co., Inc.; also past dir. or cons. several internat. bus. corps., U.S., Europe, Asia; gov. Am. Mus. in Britain; trustee Edwina Mountbatten Trust; mem. exec. com., bd. govs. Royal Shakespeare Theatre, Stratford on Avon, U.K.; bd. govs. Ditchley Found.; mem. adv. com. Denver Center for Performing Arts; chmn. Internat. Cultural Center for Youth, Jerusalem.; lectr. attached Joint Chiefs Staff, 1971—. Author (autobiography) The Salad Days, 1988, screen plays, articles, polit. essays, short stories; exhibitor paintings and sculpture; began film career, 1923, stage career, 1927; acted in more than 75 films including 3 in French (produced or co-produced 15 in U.S. and U.K.), and 20 plays both U.S. and U.K.; produced 160 1-act TV plays, 1953-58, films include Stella Dallas, Woman of Affairs, The Barker, Chances, Union Depot, Little Caesar, Dawn Patrol, Catherine the Great, The Little Accident, The Amateur Gentleman, Outward Bound, Morning Glory, The Narrow Corner, The Young in Heart, Having Wonderful Time, The Joy of Living, Prisoner of Zenda, Gunga Din, Rage of Paris, Corsican Brothers, Angels Over Broadway, Lady in Ermine, Sinbad the Sailor, The Exile, The Fighting O'Flynn, State Secret, Ghost Story, others, plays include The Dummy, Toward the Light, Romeo and Juliet, Young Woodley, The Jest, Man in Possession, Saturday's Children, Moonlight is Silver, My Fair Lady, The Pleasure of His Company, The Secretary Bird, Present Laughter, Out on a Limb; numerous TV and radio plays for CBS, NBC, ABC, BBC, TV narrations for symphony orchs. throughout U.S., various song recordings for Columbia, Caedman, others; organized own prodn. co., Criterion Films Corp., U.K., 1934. Nat. vice-chmn. Com. Defend America by Aiding Allies, 1940-41, Franco-British War Relief Assn., 1939-41; Presdl. envoy for spl. S.Am. mission, 1941; spl. advisor to comdr. 6th Fleet, NATO, 1969-70; U.S. naval del. SEATO Conf., London, 1971; Nat. v.p. Am. Assn. For UN, 1946-63; nat. chmn. Com. for CARE, 1946-50; chmn. Am. Relief for Korea, 1950-53. Served to capt. USNR, 1941-52, ETO. Decorated Silver Star, Combat Legion of Merit with valor attachment U.S.; knight comdr. Order Brit. Empire; knight Order St. John of Jerusalem; D.S.C. U.K.; officer Legion of Honor (mil. and civil); Croix de Guerre with palm France; knight comdr. Order George I Greece; comdr. Order Orange-Nassau Netherlands; War Cross for Mil. Valor; comdr. Order of Merit; Star of Italian Solidarity Italy; knight comdr. Order of Merit Chile; officer Order So. Cross Brazil; officer Order of the Crown Belgium; Comdr. Cross Order of Merit, Fed. Rep. Germany; Nat. medal of Korea; Hon. Citizen of Korea; others; recipient Gold Medal of Honor VFW, 1966; Armed Forces award, 1972; Am. Image award, 1976; award for contbn. to arts U. Notre Dame, 1971; award for contbn. to world understanding and peace World Affairs Council, Phila., 1978; Spl. award for internat. artistic achievements New Sch. for Social Research, 1978; Nat. Humanitarian award NCCJ, 1979; Nat. Brotherhood award Salvation Army, 1980; Ann. Nat. Vet.'s Day award, 1981; Illustrious Moderns award, 1981; St. Nicholas Soc. Medal of Merit, 1986; Apptd. spl. post-war missions State Dept. Mem. Council Fgn. Relations (councilor), Brit-Am. Alumni Assn. (pres. 1950-57), Am. Soc. Order St. John Jerusalem (gov. 1970—, dep. vice chancellor), Groupe Navale d'Assaut (hon.), Battalion de Choc (hon.), Assn. des Anciens Combatants (France), Pilgrim's Soc. U.S. (bd. dirs.). Episcopalian. Clubs: Racquet (Chgo.); Brook, Century, Knickerbocker (N.Y.C.); Myopia Hunt (hon.) (Hamilton, Mass.); Metropolitan (Washington); Newport (R.I.) Reading Room; White's, Buck's, Beefsteak, Garrick, Naval and Military, R.A.C., American (London); Traveller's (Paris); Puffin's (Edinburgh). Home: care Kay Hutchins The Vicarage 448 N Lake Way Palm Beach FL 33480 Office: Inverness Corp 545 Madison Ave New York NY 10022

FAIRCHILD, JOHN PHILLIP, physician; b. Washington, Dec. 25, 1918; s. Iler James and Vera Fae (Ward) F.; A.B., George Washington U., Washington, 1940, M.D., 1943; m. Julia Pearl Printz, Sept. 12, 1945; children—Jean Printz Fairchild DeTarnowsky, John Phillip, Jacqueline Patricia Fairchild Auxt, James Patrick, Jerome Paul, Jeffrey Preston. Enlisted U.S. Army, 1944, resigned, 1946, re-enlisted 1948, commd. 1st lt., 1944, advanced through grades to col.; intern Gallinger Mcpl. Hosp., Washington, 1943, resident pediatrics, 1948-50; chief pediatric services U.S. Army Hosp. Ft. Bragg, N.C., 1950-53, Brooke Gen. Hosp., Ft. Sam Houston, Tex., 1953-58, Tripler Gen. Hosp., Honolulu, 1958-62, Walter Reed Gen. Hosp., 1963-66; dir. HEW U.S. Civil Adminstrn. Ryukyu Islands, 1966-69; dep. comdr. Walter Reed Hosp., 1969-71, ret., 1971; gen. practice medicine Garnett, Kans., 1946-48; dir. field services div. Montgomery County (Md.) Health Dept., 1971-75; chief surgeon U.S. Soldiers and Airmen's Home Hosp., Washington, 1975-79; staff dept. pediatrics Regional Med. Clinic/Mountain Health Services, McDowell, Ky., 1979-85, chief of staff, 1986—, active staff McDowell Appalachian Regional Hosp., 1979—; asst. to asso. clin. prof. pediatrics Baylor U., 1954-58; asso. clin. prof. pediatrics Georgetown U., 1963-66, clin. prof., 1973-75; clin. prof. U. Louisville, 1981—; cons. in field. Decorated Legion of Merit; recipient Supreme award Japanese Med. Assn., 1969. Mem. AMA, Med. and Chirurg. Faculty State Md., Ky. Med. Soc., Floyd County Med. Soc., Assn. Mil. Surgeons, Am. Public Health Assn., Sigma Chi. Presbyterian. Contbr. articles to profl. publs. Home: PO Box 239 McDowell KY 41647

FAIRCHILD, RAYMOND FRANCIS, lawyer; b. Springfield, Ill., June 29, 1946; s. Francis M. and Estelle G. Fairchild; m. Ann Louise Templeton, Dec. 28, 1968. BA, U. Ill., 1968; JD, Ind. U., 1971. Bar: Ind. 1971, U.S. Dist. Ct. (so. dist.) Ind. 1971. Sole practice Indpls., 1971—. Mem. Assn. Trial Lawyers Am., N.Y. State Trial Lawyers Assn., Ind. Trial Lawyers Assn. Club: Manor House, Skyline (Indpls.). Office: 246 N College Ave Indianapolis IN 46202

FAIRLEIGH, JAMES PARKINSON, music educator; b. St. Joseph, Mo., Aug. 24, 1938; s. William Macdonald and Mable Emily (Parkinson) F.; m. Marlane Alberta Paxson, June 25, 1960; children: William Paxson, Karen Evelyn. MusB, U. Mich., 1960; MusM, U. So. Calif., 1965; PhD, U. Mich., 1973. Instr., asst. prof. Hanover (Ind.) Coll., 1965-75; assoc. prof. R.I. Coll., Providence, 1975-80; prof., head music dept. Jacksonville (Ala.) State U., 1980—; dir. of music First Presbyn. Ch., Anniston, Ala., 1981—. Contbr. articles profl. mags., jours., 1966-86. Served to 1st lt. U.S. Army, 1960-62. Mem. Am. Musicol. Soc., Ala. Mus. Tchrs. Assn. (cert., treas. 1982-86, 1st v.p. 1986-88, pres. 1988—), Coll. Music Soc., Music Tchrs. Nat. Assn. (cert.), Assn. Ala. Coll. Music Adminstrs. (sec., treas. 1985—), Phi Beta Kappa, Phi Kappa Phi, Pi Kappa Lambda, Phi Eta Sigma, Phi Mu Alpha Sinfonia. Republican. Avocations: waterskiing, swimming, backpacking. Home: 70 Fairway Dr Jacksonville AL 36265 Office: Jacksonville State U Dept Music Jacksonville AL 36265

FAISON, EDMUND WINSTON JORDAN, business educator; b. Rocky Mount, N.C., Oct. 13, 1926; s. Nathan Marcus and Margery Lucille (Jordan) F.; m. Lois Harger Parker; children: Charles Parker, Dorothy Anne, Barbara Jeane, Edmund Jr., Diane, Carol. A.B. in Psychology, George Washington U., 1948, M.A., 1950, Ph.D., 1956. Research asst. NRC, Washington, 1948-49; mgr. exptl. lab. Needham, Louis and Brorby, Chgo., 1955-56; account exec. Leo Burnett Co., 1957-58; v.p. Market Facts, Inc., Chgo., 1959; pres. Visual Research Internat., Zurich, Switzerland, 1960-63; adviser AID, Dept. State. Latin Am., 1963-68; prof. bus. adminstrn. U. Hawaii, Honolulu, 1968—; chmn. mktg. dept. U. Hawaii, 1975-82; chmn. bd. Scandata Hawaii, Inc., East-West Research and Design, Inc.; vis. prof. London Grad. Sch. Bus. Studies, 1974-75. Author: Advertising: A Behavioral Approach for Managers, 1980; editorial bd.: Jour. of Mktg, 1958-63; contbr. articles to profl. jours. Served with USN, 1944-46; Served with USAF, 1950-54. Mem. Am. Psychol. Assn., Soc. Consumer Behavior, Am. Mktg. Assn. (pres. Honolulu chpt. 1973-74), Acad. Mktg. Sci., Acad. Mgmt., Am. Acad. Advt., Am. Assn. Public Opinion, Sales and Mktg. Execs. Internat., Advt. Research Found., Japan-Am. Soc., Honolulu Advt. Fedn., Market Research Soc. (U.K.), C. of C. of Hawaii, Japanese C. of C., Hawaii Visitors Bur., Small Bus. Assn. Hawaii, Honolulu Acad. Arts, All-Industry Packaging Assn. (chmn. 1961), European Packaging Fedn. (U.S. rep. 1961), World Packaging Orgn., Sigma Xi, Pi Sigma Epsilon. Clubs: Pacific, Oahu Country, Kaneohe Yacht, Rotary. Home: 619 Paopua Loop Kailua HI 96734 Office: East West Research Inst 735 Bishop St Suite 235 Honolulu HI 96813 also: U Hawaii Honolulu HI 96822

FAIVRE, JEAN-MARC, physician; b. Tunis, Tunisia, Apr. 9, 1945; arrived in France, 1952; s. Joseph Jules and Elizabeth (Borloz) F.; m. Janet Mary Barton, July 12, 1969; children: Nathalie, Christophe, Patrick. MD, U. Besancon, 1972. Gen. practice medicine L'Isle sur-le-Doubs, France, 1972—. Club: Judo (L'Isle sur-le-Doubs) (sec. 1985-87). Home: 4 Ave Foch, 25250 L'Isle-sur-le-Doubs France

FAJARDO LIEVANO, ERNESTO, energy resources company executive, human resources consultant; b. Bogotá, Colombia, June 4, 1941; s. Ernesto and Alicai (Lievano) Fajardo L.; m. Hildegard Pinto, Dec. 22, 1962; children: Ernesto, Roberto, Alejandro, Carolina. BCE, Ga. Inst. Tech., 1965. Human resources analyst Internat. Petroleum Columbia Ltd. div. Exxon, Bogota, 1960-68; supr. personnel and labor relations Cartagena, Bogota, 1968-70, supr. benefits, 1970-72, head dept. employee relations, 1972-73, mgr. div. compensation and benefits, 1973-74, asst. mgr. employee relations, 1977-80; asst. mgr. employee relations Esso Brasilera de Petroleo div. Exxon, Rio de Janeiro, 1974-77, Intercor div. Exxon, Barranquilla, Albania, Columbia, 1981—; bd. dirs. Sena Apprenticeship Inst., Riochacha. Community coordinator Presdl. Election Co., Bogota, 1974; treas. Bogota Community Support Group, 1978. Roman Catholic. Clubs: Jockey (Bogota); Country (Barranquilla); San Andres Golf. Home: Carrera 4a, #114A-19, Bogota Colombia Office: Intercor Carrera, 54 Calle 72 y 74, Barranquilla Colombia

FAKHOURY, MOHAMAD RACHID, diplomat; b. Beirut, Lebanon, Mar. 6, 1925; s. Raef Fakhoury and Ihsan Tabbara; m. Hind Fakhoury, Sept. 17, 1950; children—Ihsan, Raef. Licencie en Droit, St. Joseph U., Lebanon, 1947, Diplome des Etudes Superieures de Droit Pub., 1948; Diplome des Etudes Superieures d'Econimie Politique, U. Beirut, 1949. Sec. to prime minister Fgn. Ministry, Beirut, 1951; sec. Embassy of Lebanon, Brussels, 1952-54, Jeddah, Saudi Arabia, 1956-60, Athens, Greece, 1960-64, charge d'affaires, Karachi, Pakistan, 1965, Paris, 1966-67; ambassador to Saudi Arabia, Jeddah, 1972-78; dir. Directorate of Internat. Orgns., Congresses, and Cultural Relations, Ministry of Fgn. Affairs, Beirut, 1979-83; ambassador, permanent rep. Mission of Lebanon to UN, N.Y.C., 1983—. Office: Perm Mission of Lebanon to UN 866 UN Plaza Room 531-533 New York NY 10017

FALCK, KARIN ANNA MARGARETA, television producer; b. Saffle, Sweden, Feb. 6, 1932; d. Runo and Margareta (Wistrand) Edstrom; m. Ake Falck, Aug. 17, 1960 (dec. 1974); children—Rolf, Anna, Carolina. Student Stockholm U., 1953-55. Producer, Swedish TV, Stockholm, 1955—; stage dir. music, dance and song shows, Stockholm, Gothenburg, Sweden. Office: Swedish Network Prodn AB, Kungsträdgårdsgatan 20, Box 7820, 10397 Stockholm Sweden

FALCO, JOANN, independent fundraising consultant, educator; b. N.Y.C., Aug. 9, 1953; d. Joseph J. and Mary J. Falco. BA summa cum laude in English, Barry Coll., 1974, MA, 1976; EdD., U. Miami, 1987. Asst. dir. Fla. Pub. Interest Research Group, U. Miami, Fla., 1976-79, adminstrv. aide to asst. v.p. devel., 1980-81; prof. English Dade Community Coll., 1985—; ind. devel. cons., Washington and Miami, 1981—.

FALCON, KAREN GAY, designer, linens manufacturer; b. N.Y.C., Jan. 31, 1949; d. Joseph Albert Falcon and Olcay Kent. AA, Pierce Coll., 1970; BA, Calif. State U., Los Angeles, 1972. Sales mgr. Animan Designs, Los Angeles, 1972-76; pres. Kare-Free, Los Angeles, 1976-79; founder, chief exec. officer Hollywood Nights, Inc., Los Angeles, 1979-87; gen. mgr. Dresher Linens/ Hollywood Nights div. Dresher, Inc., 1987—; cons. European mktg. Magma Heimtex, Friesenheim, Fed. Republic Germany, 1985—; seminar speaker SBA, Los Angeles, 1982—. Sponsor Soc. for Prevention Cruelty to Animals, Los Angeles, since 1980—. Mem. Nat. Bath, Bed and Linen Assn., Waterbed Mfrs. Assn. (speaker 1977—, best trade show exhibit awards 1981, 83, 84, 85, 86), Nichiren Shoshu Am. Democrat. Avocations: travel, music. Office: Hollywood Nights Inc 1930 E 15th St Los Angeles CA 90021

FALCON, RAYMOND JESUS, JR., lawyer; b. N.Y.C., Nov. 17, 1953; m. Debra Mary Bomeisl, June 4, 1977; children: Victoria Marie, Mark Daniel. BA, Columbia U., 1975; JD, Yale U., 1978. Bar: N.Y. 1979, U.S. Dist. Ct. (so. and ea. dist.) N.Y. 1979, U.S. Ct. Appeals (D.C. and 2d cirs.) 1983, Fla. 1987. Assoc. Webster and Sheffield, N.Y.C., 1978-82; ptnr. Falcon and Hom, N.Y.C., 1982-85; atty. Degussa Corp., Teterboro, N.J., 1985—; exec. v.p., bd. dirs., cons. IBG, Ltd., N.Y.C., 1984—; corp. counsel Village of Port Chester, N.Y., 1987-88. Contbr. articles to profl. jours. Dem. candidate Town Justice, Town of Rye, N.Y., 1983; Dem. judicial del., Westchester, N.Y., 1984—. Mem. ABA, N.Y. State Bar Assn., Bar Assn. City of N.Y., Fed. Bar Council, Assn. Trial Lawyers Am. Clubs: Yale (N.Y.C.); Columbia Alumni of Westchester County (v.p., dir. 1983—). Home: 1 Halstead Ave Port Chester NY 10573 Office: Degussa Corp 65 Challenger Rd Ridgefield Park NJ 07660

FALDINI, ROBERTO, automotive parts company executive; b. São Paulo, Brasil, Sept. 9, 1948; s. Nelson and Esther (Lafer) F.; m. Catarina Buck, July 9, 1970; children: Marco Buck, Monica Buck, Mirella Buck. B in Bus. Adminstrn., Fundacão Getulio Vargas, São Paulo. Asst. to adminstv. dir. Cia Fabricadora de Papel (Klabin Group), São Paulo, 1969-71; mgr. Banco Safra de Investimentos S/A, São Paulo, 1971-76; fin. dir. Metal Leve S/A Ind. e Com., São Paulo, 1976—; pres. Assn. Brasileira das Cias Abertas, São Paulo, 1987—; bd. dirs. Assn. Comml. do Est. de São Paulo, 1987—. Office: Metal Leve S/A Ind e Com, Rua Brasilio Luz, 535, Sao Paulo 04746, Brazil

FALEY, ROBERT LAWRENCE, instruments company executive; b. Bklyn., Oct. 13, 1927; s. Eric Lawrence and Anna (Makahon) F.; B.S. cum laude in Chemistry, St. Mary's U., San Antonio, 1956; postgrad. U. Del., 1958-59; m. Mary Virginia Mumme, May 12, 1950; children—Robert Wayne, Nancy Diane. Chemist, E.I. Dupont de Nemours & Co., Inc., Wilmington, Del., 1956-60; sales mgr. F&M Sci., Houston, 1960-62; pres. Faley Assos., Houston, 1962-65; sales mgr. Tech. Inc., Dayton, Ohio, 1965-70; biomed. mkt. mgr. Perkin-Elmer Co., Norwalk, Conn., 1967-69; mktg. dir. Cahn Instruments, Los Angeles, 1970-72; pres. Faley Internat., El Toro, Calif., 1972—. Internat. speaker in field; dir. Whatman Lab. Products Inc., 1981-82, Status Instrument Corp., 1985-87; tech. mktg. cons. Whatman Ltd., Abbott Labs., OCG Tech., Inc., Pacific Biochem., Baker Commodities, Bausch & Lomb Co., Motorola Inc., Whatman Inc., Filtration Scis. Corp., PMC Industries. Mem. adv. com. on Sci., tech., energy and water U.S. 43d Congl. Dist., 1985-87. Served to 1st lt. USAF, 1948-53. Charter mem. Aviation Hall Fame. Fellow Am. Inst. Chemists, AAAS; mem. ASTM, Am. Chem. Soc. (sr.), Instrument Soc. Am. (sr.), Inst. Environ. Scis. (sr.), Aircraft Owners and Pilots Assn., U.S. Power Squadrons, Delta Epsilon Sigma. Club: Masons. Contbr. articles on technique of gas chromatography to profl. jours. Home: 27850 Espinoza Mission Viejo CA 92692 Office: PO Box 669 El Toro CA 92630

FALGER, VINCENT STEPHAN EUGENE, political science educator; b. Zaandam, North-Holland, The Netherlands, Sept. 6, 1946; s. Eugène F.J.H. Falger and Regina M.A. Brom; m. Leonie J. Groeneveld, July 19, 1974; 1 child, Jan-Eloy. MA, U. Amsterdam, The Netherlands, 1975. Asst. researcher Europa Inst., U. Amsterdam, 1976-78; sci. librarian U. Limburg, The Netherlands, 1978-80; univ. lectr. U. Utrecht, The Netherlands, 1981—. Editor: The Sociobiology of Ethnocentrism, 1987; contbr. articles to profl. jours. Mem. Assn. for Politics and the Life Scis. (council 1987—), European Sociobiol. Soc. (treas. 1983—). Home: Groenekanseweg 90, 3731 AJ De Bilt The Netherlands Office: U Utrecht, Dept Internat Relations, Janskerkhof 3, 3512 BK Utrecht The Netherlands

FALK, BERNARD HENRY, trade association executive; b. N.Y.C., Sept. 10, 1926; s. Max and Sadie (Orwin) F.; m. Iris G. Tannenbaum, June 13, 1954; children—Cindy, Amy, David. B.E.E., CCNY, 1950; grad. student, Columbia Sch. Bus., 1954. Field engr. RCA, 1950-52; sales engr. Gen. Precision Corp., 1953-56; exec. sec. Nat. Elec. Mfrs. Assn., 1956-65, v.p. govt. relations, 1966-71, pres., 1972—; Chmn. adv. com. elec. goods Dept. Commerce, 1974—; mem. exec. adv. com. nat. power survey FPC, 1972—; mem. Bus. Adv. Council on Fed. Reports; mem. liaison com. White House Trade Assn., 1981—. Served with USNR, 1944-46. Mem. Am. Nat. Standards Inst. (dir.), Am. Soc. Assn. Execs. (v.p. 1978, dir., chmn. Key industries assn. Council 1985-86), N.Y. State Soc. Assn. Execs. (pres. 1975), U.S. C. of C. (bd. dirs.). Home: Watergate South Washington DC 20037 Office: 2101 L St Washington DC 20037

FALK, FERDIE ARNOLD, distilling and importing company executive; b. New Orleans, Nov. 3, 1928; s. Ferdinand N. and Beatrice (Roseman) F.; m. Ursula Blum, May 8, 1971; children by previous marriage: Lori Rose, Christopher. Student, La. State U., 1946-48. With Seagram and Sons, 1955-71; exec. v.p. Gen. Wine and Spirits Co., 1969-71, Schenley Affiliated Brands Corp., 1971-74; pres., dir. Fleischmann Distilling Corp., 1974-76, New Eng. Distillers, Inc.; sr. v.p., group exec. Nabisco Products, Inc., N.Y.C., 1978-82; chmn., chief exec. officer Julius Wile Sons and Co., Inc., 1978-82; chmn. Ancient Age Distillery Co. Holding Co., Frankfort, Ky., 1983—, Blue Grass Wharehouse Co.; dir. L.J. McGuiness Co., Ltd., Can. and All Brand Importers, Inc.; chmn. com. on econ. devel. Spirits Industry. Bd. dirs. Am. Cancer Soc., Fund for Higher Edn.; chmn. N.Y. council drive Boy Scouts Am., 1983; pres. Sky Ranch for Boys.; chmn. United Negro Coll. Fund Drive, 1983. Recipient Louis Berger Meml. award Am. Cancer Soc., N.Y.C., 1979; Sword of Haganah award State of Israel, 1979. Mem. Nat. Assn. Alcoholic Beverage Importers (past dir.), Brit. Export Mktg. Adv. Com., Brit. Am. C. of C. (past v.p., dir.), French-Am. C. of C. in U.S. (councillor). Clubs: Shelter Rock, Sands Point, Deepdale Golf. Office: 36 Main St Roslyn NY 11570

FALK, JAMES H., lawyer; b. Tucson, Aug. 17, 1938; s. George W. and Elsie L. (Higgins) F.; m. Bobbie Jo Vest, July 8, 1960; children—James H., John Mansfield, Kathryn Colleen. B.S., B.A., U. Ariz., 1960, LL.B., 1965. Bar: Ariz., D.C., U.S. Supreme Ct. Counsel El Paso Natural Gas Co., Tex., 1965-66, The Anaconda Co., Tucson, 1967-68; ptnr. Waterfall Economidas, Falk & Caldwell, Tucson, 1968-71; staff asst. to pres. Office of the Pres., Washington, 1971-73; assoc. dir. Domestic Council, The White House, Washington, 1973-76; with Touche Ross & Co., Washington, 1976-78; ptnr. Coffey, McGovern, Noel & Novogroski, Washington, 1978-81, Larkin, Noel & Falk, Washington, 1981-86, Coffey, McGovern and Noel, Washington, 1987—; rep. of U.S. Pres. to state and local govts., D.C., U.S. territories, 1974-75, Asst. city prosecutor, city atty., Tucson, 1966-67. Pres., chmn. bd. Tucson Transit Authority Inc., 1970-71. Mem. Am. Arbitrators Assn. (mem. nat. panel arbitrators), Nat. Conf. Commrs. on Uniform State Laws. Home: 9430 Cornwell Farm Rd Great Falls VA 22066 Office: Coffey McGovern & Noel Ltd 2445 M St NW Washington DC 20037

FALK, MARSHALL ALLEN, physician, university dean and official; b. Chgo., May 23, 1929; s. Ben and Frances (Kamins) F.; m. Marilyn Joyce Levoff, June 15, 1952; children: Gayle Debra, Ben Scott. B.S., Bradley U., 1950; M.S., U. Ill., 1952; M.D., Chgo. Med. Sch., 1956. Diplomate: Am. Bd. Psychiatry. Intern Cook County Hosp., Chgo., 1956-57; resident Mt. Sinai Hosp., Chgo., 1964-67; gen. practice medicine Chgo., 1959-64; resident in psychiatry, faculty dept. psychiatry Chgo. Med. Sch., 1964-67, prof., acting chmn. dept. psychiatry, 1973-74, dean, 1974—, v.p. med. affairs, 1981-82, exec. v.p., 1982—; med. dir. London Meml. Hosp., 1964-74; mem. cons. com. commr. health, City of Chgo., 1972-82 ; mem. Gov.'s Commn. to Revise Mental Health Code Ill., 1973-77, Chgo. Northside Commn. on Health Planning, 1970-74, Ill. Hosp. Licensing Bd., 1981—. Contbr. articles to profl. jours. Served to capt. AUS, 1957-59. Recipient Bd. Trustees award for research Chgo. Med. Sch., 1963; Distinguished Alumni award Chgo. Med. Sch., 1976. Fellow Am. Psychiat. Assn., Am. Coll. Psychiatrists, Ill. Council Deans (pres. 1981-83), Waukegan/Lake County (Ill.) C. of C. (Bd. dirs. 1984—), 1984—, Sigma Xi, Alpha Omega Alpha. Home: 3860 Mission Hills Rd Northbrook IL 60062 Office: 3333 Green Bay Rd North Chicago IL 60064

FALK, ROBERT HARDY, lawyer; b. Houston, Dec. 27, 1948; s. Arnold Charles and Sara Holmes (Pierce) F.; m. Donna Kay Watts, Aug. 18, 1973; children: Dorian Danielle, Dillon Holmes. BS summa cum laude, U. Tex., 1971; BA cum laude, Austin Coll., 1972; JD, U. Tex., 1975. Bar: Tex. 1975, D.C. 1977, U.S. Dist. Ct. (so. dist. Tex.) 1975, U.S. Patent Office, U.S. Ct. Appeals (5th cir.) 1976, Ct. Customs and Patent Appeals 1976, N.C. 1979, U.S. Dist. Ct. (we. dist. N.C.) 1982, U.S. Dist Ct. (no. dist. Tex.) 1984, U.S. Ct. Appeals (fed. cir.) 1982, U.S. Ct. Appeals (5th cir.) 1983, U.S. Ct. Internat. Trade 1985, U.S. Dist. Ct. (no. dist.) Tex. 1987. Process engr. Exxon Co., USA, Baytown, Tex., 1971-72; atty. Pravel, Wilson & Gambrell, Houston, 1975-77; patent and trademark counsel Organon Inc. div. Akzona, Inc., Asheville, N.C., 1977-84; ptnr. Hubbard, Thurman, Turner & Tucker, Dallas, 1984—; pres. Robert Hardy Falk, P.C. Pres. Haw Creek Vol. Fire Dept., Asheville, 1980-84; deacon Cen. Christian Ch., Dallas, 1985—. Fellow U. Tex., 1972. Mem. ABA, Tex. Bar Assn., N.C. Bar Assn., D.C. Bar Assn., Am. Patent Law Assn., Am. Trial Lawyers Assn., Dallas Patent Law Assn., Dallas Bar Assn., Licensing Execs. Soc. Republican. Club: University (Dallas). Home: 2116 Tiburon Carrollton TX 75006 Office: Hubbard Thurman Turner Tucker 2100 One Galleria Tower Dallas TX 75240

FALK, STUART, management consultant; b. N.Y.C., June 8, 1942; s. Max and Bess (Abbes) F. B.A. cum laude, Tufts U., 1964; J.D., U. Va., 1967. Mgr. fin. advt. The N.Y. Times, N.Y.C., 1969-73, mgr. nat. advt., 1973-79; pres. Internat. C. of C. Publishing Corp., N.Y.C., 1979-81, dir. gen., Paris, 1981—, chmn., 1979—; mktg. and promotion dir. Internat. C. of C., 1985-88; free-lance mgmt. cons., Monte Carlo, Monaco, 1988—; mem. plans bd. Newspaper Advt. Bur., N.Y.C., 1976-77. Served with USPHS, 1967-69. Mem. Republicans Ahroad, Paris, 1982—. Mem. Overseas Press Club of Am., Am. C. of C. in France. Clubs: Princeton (N.Y.C.); Am. (London and Paris). Home and Office: 1 rue des Genets, MC 98000 Monte Carlo Monaco

FALKENBERG, HANS-GEERT, retired broadcaster, media consultant; b. Stettin, Pommerania, Prussia, Germany, July 24, 1919; s. Richard Albert and Vera Hilda (Klein) f.; m. Beata Maria Hartung (div. 1953); children: Gabriel; m. Betty Martin (div. 1972); children: Marc, Lynn Giselle; m. Marcia Holly Lerner; 1 child, Benjamin Philip. Dr Phil., Georgia Augusta U., Fed. Republic Germany, 1952. Chief dramaturg Deutsches Theater, Goettingen, Fed. Republic Germany, 1953-57; editor-in-chief S. Fischer Verlag, Frankfurt, Fed. Republic Germany, 1957-60, Kindler Verlag, Munich, 1960-64; controller cultural programs Westdeutscher Rundfunk, Cologne, Fed. Republic Germany, 1965-80, advisor internat. relations programming, 1980-85; vis. prof. U. Duesseldorf, Fed. Republic Germany, 1982—; Mem. permanent bd. Internat. Pub. TV Screening Conf., 1977—; German editor World U. Library, Munich, 1963; del. exec. com. Coop. Internat. Recherche d'action Matière Communication, Liége, Belgiumm 1975—. Author: Heinz Hilpert das Ende einer Epoche, 1968; editor: In Memoriam S. Fischer, 1960, Seven Deadly Sins, 1964. Mem. PEN Club. Social Democrat. Home: Isidor Caro Strasse 62, D-5000 Cologne 80 Federal Republic of Germany Office: Westdeutscher Rundfunk, Postfach 10 19 50, 5000 Cologne Federal Republic of Germany

FALKOWSKI, ANDRZEJ, psychology educator; b. Bialystock, Poland, Nov. 30, 1953; s. Marian and Aleksandra (Chwojko) F.; m. Ewa Maria Balczewska, July 31, 1977; 1 child, Justin. MA, Cath. U., Lublin, Poland, 1977, PhD, 1981. From instr. dept. psychology to asst. prof. Cath. U., Lublin, 1977-83, assoc. prof. dept. exptl. psychology, 1988—; vis. prof. dept. math. psychology U. Nijmegen, The Netherlands, 1984, Human Performance Ctr., U. Mich., Ann Arbor, 1986-87. Co-author: Psychophysical Judgement and the Process of Perception, 1982; contbr. articles on cognitive processes and ecol. psychology to profl. jours. Fulbright grantee U. Mich., 1986-87. Mem. Internat. Soc. for Ecol. Psychology. Roman Catholic. Home: Tybury 7A m 18, 91-043 Lodz Poland Office: Cath U, Dept Psychology, Al Raclawickie 14, 20-950 Lublin Poland

FALL, IBRAHIMA, minister of foreign affairs for Senegal, educator; b. Tivaouane, Thies, Senegal, 1942; s. Momar Khoudia and Seynabou (Diakhate) F.; m. Déguène Fall; children: Ndeye Salla, Boubacar, Ibou, Ndeye Seynabou. Pub. Law Bachelor's Degree, University, Dakar, Senegal, 1967; diploma Inst. Polit. Sci., Paris, 1971; Doctoral Law, Faculty of Law, Paris, 1972, Agregation, 1974; diploma Acad. Internat. Law, 1973. Dean of faculty of law Univ., Dakar, 1975-81; minister higher edn., Republic of Senegal, 1983-84, minister fgn. affairs, 1984—; adviser Supreme Ct. of Senegal; cons. UNESCO. Contbr. articles to profl. publs. Mem. African Council for Higher Edn. Muslim. Office: Ministry of Fgn Affairs, PO Box 4044, Dakar Senegal *

FALLACI, ORIANA, writer, journalist; b. Florence, Italy, June 29, 1930; d. Edoardo and Tosca (Cantini) F. Grad., Liceo Classico Galileo Galilei, Italy; student, U. Florence Faculty Medicine, 1946-48; Litt.D. (hon.), Columbia Coll., Chgo., 1977. Editor and spl. corr. Europeo Mag., Milan, Italy, 1958-77; collaborator with major publs. throughout world, including Look mag., Life mag., The Washington Post, N.Y. Times, London Times; dir. Rizzoli Pubs. Corp. Author: (essay) The Useless Sex, 1964; The Egotists, 1965; (novel) Penelope at War, 1966; (non-fiction) If the Sun Dies, 1967, Nothing and So Be It, 1972 (non-fiction on Vietnam war, Bancarella award); Interview with History, 1976; (novel) Letter to a Child Never Born, 1977, (novel) A Man, 1979 (2 Viareggio prize awards). Recipient St. Vincent award for Journalism, 1971, 73. Office: 355 Lexington Ave 22d Floor New York NY 10017

FALLENBUCHL, ZBIGNIEW MARIAN, educator; b. Katowice, Poland, Nov. 4, 1924; s. Jan and Maria (Molek) F.; m. Teresa Maria Marszalek, July 12, 1950; children—Robert Jan, Adam Edward. B.Sc. in Econs., U. London, 1951; M.A., U. Montreal, 1957; Ph.D., McGill U., 1961; Docteur hon. causa, U. D'Aix-Marseille, France, 1979. Faculty, U. Windsor, Ont., Can., 1959—, prof. econs., 1966—; dean of social sci., 1986—; econ. advisor Govt. Guyana, Georgetown, 1965-66; coordinator of aid program Can. Internat. Devel. Agy., Guyana, 1970-73. Author: East-West Technology Transfer, 1983. Editor: Economic Development in Soviet Union and Eastern Europe, 2 vols., 1975; (with Carl McMillan) East-West Economic Relations, 1980. Served to lt. Polish Army, 1942-47. Wolfson, Oxford U. vis. fellow, 1979-80; Rockefeller Found. resident scholar, Bellagio, Italy, 1983. Mem. Can. Econs. Assn., Am. Econ. Assn., Am. Assn. for Advancement of Slavic Studies. Roman Catholic. Home: 5878 Dalton, Windsor, ON Canada N9H 1N1 Office: U Windsor, Windsor, ON Canada N9B 3P4

FALLER, DOROTHY ANDERSON, social worker; b. Chgo., July 6, 1939; d. Albert T. and Lillian G. (Chalbeck) Anderson; student Ill. Wesleyan U., 1956-59; A.B., U. Ill., 1959-60; M.S.S.A., Case Western Res. U., 1975; m. Adolph Faller, Sept. 5, 1959; children—Carl, Kurt. Child welfare worker Klamath County Public Welfare Commn., Klamath Falls, Oreg., 1960-67; social services cons. Ind. State Dept. Public Welfare, 1968-72; adminstrv. asst. United Meth. Children's Home, Berea, Ohio, 1974; research asst. Case Western Res. U., Sch. Applied Social Scis., 1975; social services supr. Ohio Dept. Public Welfare, Cleve., 1975-81; exec. dir. Cleve. Internat. Program, 1981—; cons. to Cleve. Found., Am. Sickle Cell Anemia Found., John A. Yankey & Assos.; field instr. Case Western Res. U., 1976-77, lectr., 1981. Bd. dirs. West Shore Unitarian Ch., 1978-81. Mem. Nat. Assn. Social Workers (unit chair state bd., nat. bd. dirs. 1985-88, chmn. Internat. Activities Com. of Nat. Bd. 1986—, del. Internat. Fedn. Social Workers, Sweden, 1988, Cleve. unit Social Worker of Yr. 1986), Internat. Council Social Welfare (mem. U.S. Com.), Case Western Res. U. Sch. Applied Social Scis. Alumni Assn., Sigma Kappa (pres. 1959), Alpha Lambda Delta (pres. 1956). Unitarian. Editor, contbr. Ohio Children's Budget Project: A Public Policy Study, 1975. Home: 17703 Woodbury Ave Cleveland OH 44135 Office: 1148 Euclid Ave Suite 503 Cleveland OH 44115

FALLON, IVAN GREGORY, journalist; b. Wexford, Ireland, June 26, 1944; came to Eng. in 1966.; s. Padraic Joseph and Dorothea Margaret F.; m. Susan Mary Lurring, Jan. 14, 1967; children: Tania Helen, Lara Catherine, Padraic Robert. Student, St. Peter's Coll., Wexford, Ireland; B in Bus. Studies, Trinity Coll., Dublin, Ireland, 1966. Fin. journalist Thomson Orgn., London, 1967-68; Fin. journalist Sunday Telegraph, London, 1968-79, city editor, 1979-84; deputy editor Sunday Times, London, 1984—; bd. govs. Buckingham U., 1980—, Eng., St. Thomas' Hosp., 1984—, London. Author: Delorean: The Rise and Fall of a Dream Maker, 1983, (with James Srodes) Takeovers, 1987, (with James Srodes) The Brothers-The Rise and Rise of Saatchi and Saatchi, 1988, Ivan Fallon. Recipient Wincott award for fin. journalism, 1981. Clubs: RAC, Beefsteak (London).

FALLON, JOHN MICHAEL, wine company executive, marketing professional; b. Melbourne, Victoria, Australia, May 12, 1941; s. John Fallon and Nancy (Burne) Donald; m. Diana Elizabeth Whitelaw, June 10, 1965; children: Kathryn, James, Peter, Thomas. Grad. high school, Melbourne. Mgr. J. Gadsden Can Mfrs., Melbourne, 1962-69, Golling Co. Wine and Spirit, Melbourne, 1969-75, Mildara Wines, Melbourne, 1975-77, Burns Philp Wine and Spirit, Melbourne, 1977-80; mktg. dir. Wolf Blass Wines Internat., Adelaide, Australia, 1980—; chmn. Australian Wine Exporters to Japan, Adelaide, 1986—. Club: Melbourne Cricket. Lodge: Kiwanis. Home: 21 Lutana Grove, S075 Dernancourt Australia Office: Wolf Blass Wines Internat, Level 2, S000 Adelaide Australia

FALLS, ARTHUR GRANDPRÉ, physician, surgeon; b. Chgo., Dec. 25, 1901; s. William Arthur and Santalia Angelica (de GrandPré) F.; m. Lillian Steele Proctor, Dec. 1928; 1 child, Arthur GrandPré. Student Crane Jr. Coll., 1918-20; B.S. in Medicine, Northwestern U., 1924, M.D., 1925; postgrad. U. Chgo., U. Ill.-Chgo., Cook County Postgrad. Sch., NYU. Intern Kansas City Gen. Hosp., Mo., 1924-25; gen. practice surgery, Chgo., 1925—; mem. staff Provident Hosp.; faculty Postgrad. Sch. Tb, Chgo., 1939-44, Sch. Nursing, Provident Hosp., Chgo., 1960-65; founder, pres. Com. to End Discrimination in Chgo.'s Med. Instns.; founder, exec. vice chmn. Council for Equal Med. Opportunity; founder, pres. Council for Bio-Med. Careers; founder, chmn. Chgo. chpt. Med. Com. for Human Rights; mem. pub. health com. Commn. on Human Relations, City of Chgo.; mem. health com. Welfare Council Met. Chgo.; chmn. ann. health campaign Nat. Negro Bus. League. Editor Bull. Cook County Physicians Assn., 1930-32, 35-36; assoc. editor Interracial Rev., 1931-34, Bull. Interracial Commn. of Chgo., 1933-36; Chgo. editor Catholic Worker, 1935-38. Contbr. articles to various publs. Mem. exec. bd. Nat. Cath. Interracial Fedn., 1931-36, pres. Chgo. br., 1933-34; founder Chgo. Cath. Workers Credit Union, 1937, bd. dirs., 1950-53, pres., 1952-53; founder, chmn. Progress Devel. Corp., 1959. Recipient award for service in civil rights and liberties Kenwood-Ellis Community Ctr., 1957, Good Am. award Chgo. Com. of 100, 1963. Fellow Am. Coll. Chest Physicians, Am. Geriatrics Soc.; mem. ACLU, Chgo. Urban League, Nat. Urban League, NAACP, Ams. for Democratic Action, Am. Cath. Sociol. Soc. Roman Catholic. Avocations: gardening; traveling; photography; stamp collecting; coin collecting. Home: 4812 Fair Elms Ave Western Springs IL 60558 Office: 5050 S State St Chicago IL 60009

FALTER, JUERGEN WILFRIED, educator; b. Heppenheim, Hesse, Ger., Jan. 22, 1944; s. Robert and Annemarie (Lehmann) F.; m. Christa Niklas, Dec. 1, 1976; children—Anna Friederike, Christoph Philipp. Diploma, M.A., Free U. Berlin, 1968; Ph.D., U. Saar, 1973, habilitation, 1981. Asst. prof. U. of the Saar, Saarbruecken, 1970-73; assoc. prof. Armed Forces U., Munich, 1973-83; full prof. Free U. Berlin, 1983-86; Kennedy fellow, Harvard U., Cambridge, Mass., 1977-78; vis. prof. Johns Hopkins U., Bologna, Italy, 1980-81; pres. Sect. Polit. Sociology, 1984—. Author: Wahlentscheidung, 1973, Behavioralismusstreit, 1982, Weimarer Wahldaten, 1986. Contbr. articles to profl. jours. Recipient award for best dissertation U. Saar, 1973; award for Best Essay in Social Sci., Thyssen Found., 1983. Mem. Am. Polit. Sci. Assn., Berliner Wissenschaftliche Gesellschaft, Deutsche Vereinigung fuer Politische Wissenschaft, Quantum, Deutsche Vereinigung fuer Parlamentsfragen. Roman Catholic. Office: Free Univ Berlin, ZI 6 Sarrazinstrasse 11-15, D-1000 West Berlin 41, Federal Republic of Germany

FÄLTHAMMAR, CARL-GUNNE SIGVARD CHARLON, physicist, educator; b. Markaryd, Sweden, Dec. 4, 1931; s. Oskar Teodor Fritiof and Ingeborg Tatjana (Jonasson) F.; m. Ann-Marie Ingrid Sjunnesson, Aug. 24, 1957; children—Karin Ingeborg Maria, Nils Gustav Martin. Grad. Engr., Royal Inst. Tech., 1956, Ph.D., 1966. Various research positions Royal Inst. Tech., Stockholm, 1956-60, assoc. prof. plasma physics, 1969-75, prof., chmn. dept., 1975—; mem. Swedish nat. coms. for geodesy and geophysics, radio sci.; mem. Swedish Com. for European Incoherent Scatter Facility. Coauthor: Cosmical Electrodynamics, Fundamental Principles. Contbr. articles to profl. jours. Recipient Public Service Group Achievement award NASA, 1979. Mem. Royal Swedish Acad. Scis., Swedish Geophys. Soc. (chmn. 1975-76), Internat. Assn. Geomagnetism and Aeronomy (exec. com. 1979-83), Internat. Acad. Astronautics, others. Home: 35 Bovägen, 18143 Lidingö Sweden Office: Royal Inst Tech, 10044 Stockholm Sweden

FALTINSEN, ODD MAGNUS, educator; b. Stavanger, Norway, Jan. 9, 1944; s. Paul Georg and Margit Marie (Undem) F.; m. Bente Owren, Apr. 9, 1966; children: Vidar, Ingunn, Stig. Cand.Real, U. Bergen, Norway, 1968; PhD, U. Mich., 1971. Sr. research engr. Det Norske Veritas, Oslo, 1968-74; assoc. prof. Norwegian Inst. Tech., Trondheim, 1974-76, prof. marine hydrodynamics, 1976—, chmn. marine tech. dept., 1982-84; bd. dirs. Marintek, Trondheim; vis. prof. MIT, Cambridge, Mass., 1980-81, 1987-88. Home: Bromstadekra 31A, 7000 Trondheim Norway Office: Norwegian Inst Tech, 7034 Trondheim Norway

FALZONE, JOSEPH SAM, retired airlines company executive; b. Passaic, N.J., June 20, 1917; s. Ross and Concetta (Miada) F.; m. Anna Rand, June 21, 1947; children—Michael Joseph, Connie R. A.A.D., Western Air Coll., 1941. Lead field insp. Transworld Airlines, N.Y.C., 1946-83, ret. Author: Hypothesis of Globing and Matter "The Cold Spot", 1985; Zymomatics of Matter and Gravity, 1985, The Atoms' Constant of Motion I, 1987, The Atoms' Constant of Motion II, 1988. Patentee in field. Served with USN, 1941-43. Recipient Aviation Mechanic citation FAA, 1975. Mem. AAAS, N.Y. Acad. Sci. Roman Catholic. Avocations: astronomy; physical science.

FAMADAS, JOSÉ, educator, journalist, translator; b. Rio de Janeiro, Brazil, April 10, 1908; s. João Famadas and Francisca (Herrera) F.; B.S. and Lit., Colegio S. Vicente de Paulo and Colegio Pedro II; Curso Leon Say and Instituto Comercial; C.P.A., Dept. Bus. Edn., Ministry of Edn.; Sch. English Lang. and Lit.; extension and grad. courses U. Rio de Janeiro, U. Distrito Federal, U. Pa. field course, U. Brasil, Instituto de Psicologia, Ministry Edn.; A.M., U. Mich., 1942; postgrad. courses U. Wis., Columbia U., 1942-55; 1 son, Nelson. Staff, Banco do Brasil, 1928-62; translator-editor United Press, 1938; instr. Tech. Council on Economics and Finance, 1939-40, Instituto Watson de Organização do Trabalho, I.B.M., 1939-40; dir. Instituto Britannia, 1937-42; asso. prof Colegio Pedro II, 1939-44; instr. Am. Council Learned Socs., Inst. Brazilian Studies, U. Vt., 1942, U. Mich. English Lang. Inst., 1942; teacher extension Columbia U., 1943-44, instr. faculty philosophy, 1944-47; dir. bibliography, library and cultural archives Hispanic Inst., 1943-47; translator 20th Century Fox, 1950-56, U.S. Dept. State, 1951-53, USIA, 1953-78, Universal Internat., 1953-74, United Artists, 1956-83, Paramount Pictures, 1971-74, others; instr. CCNY extension div., 1947-58; editor in chief Brazilian edit. The Reader's Digest, 1947-50; press officer Brazilian Mission to UN, 1950-55; radio commentator and mem. weekly round table discussion programs on networks, 1944-54. Recipient Order of Merlin Excalibur, Internat. Brotherhood Magicians; Inst. Internat. Edn. and Rockefeller Found. fellow. Life mem. AAAS, Nat. Acad. Econs. and Polit. Sci., MLA, Associação Brasileira de Imprensa, Linguistic Soc. Am., Acad. Polit. Sci., Am. Assn. Tchrs. Spanish and Portuguese (past v.p. N.Y. chpt.), Am. Econ. Assn., Am. Topical Assn., Soc. Am. Magicians; emeritus mem. N.Y. Acad. Sci., Latin Am. Studies Assn., AAUP; mem. Soc. Lang. Specialists (former pres.), Nat. Geog. Soc., Nat. Travel Club, Am. Mus. Natural

History, Smithsonian Instn., Magicians Guild Am., others. Contbr. Columbia Dictionary of Modern European Lit., Revista de Filología Hispánica, The Romanic Rev., New Century Cyclopedia of Names, others. Address: PO Box 752 Flushing NY 11352

FAN, SUSIE WU, medical technologist; b. Taiwan, Republic of China, Oct. 24, 1938; came to U.S., 1963, naturalized, 1973; d. Fu-Tzu and Yan-Chu (Chang) Wu; m. Hsin-Ya Fan, Nov. 3, 1963; children—Calvin A., Carol E., Cathyn S. B.Ed., Taiwan Normal U., 1963; M. Pub. Health, UCLA., 1966; Cert. City of Hope Med. Technologist Tng. Sch., 1978. Cert. med. technologist, Calif. Teaching asst. UCLA Sch. Pub. Health, 1965-66, biochemist, 1966-69; microbiologist, biochemist GEOMET, Pomona, Calif., 1976-77; med. technologist City of Hope Med. Ctr., Duarte, Calif., 1978-83, chemist, 1978-80, microbiologist, 1980-83; med. technologist Kaiser Hosp., Fontana, Calif., 1983—. Mem. Am. Soc. Microbiology, Am. Soc. Clin. Pathologists, Nat. Certifing Agency. Republican. Methodist. Home: 615 Wellesley Dr Claremont CA 91711 Office: Kaiser Hosp 9961 Sierra Ave Fontana CA 92335

FANCHER, GEORGE H., JR., oil company executive, petroleum engineer; b. Austin, Tex., Apr. 30, 1939; s. George Homer and Mattie (Stanfield) F.; m. Mary Ann Rousos, May 24, 1958 (div. July 1963); children: Lisa Renee Blonkvist, George Homer III; m. Carolyn Jane Keithly, Nov. 27, 1976; children: Michael Ryan, Kelly Christine. Registered profl. engr., Tex. Petroleum engr. Chevron Oil Co., Denver, 1962-66, Ball Bros. Research, Boulder, Colo., 1966-67, King Resources Co., Denver, 1967-69; ptnr. Smith-Fancher, Denver, 1969-80; owner Fancher Oil Co., Denver, 1980—; bd. dirs. Treasor Petroleum, Denver. Mem. Chancellor's Council U. Tex., 1982—, Rep. Party State Fin. Com., 1982-85; dir. InterMountain Polit. Action Com., 1983—; bd. trustees St. Anne's Episcopal Sch., 1986. Mem. Ind. Petroleum Assn. Am. (bd. dirs.), Ind. Petroleum Assn. Mountain States (bd. dirs.), Soc. Petroleum Engrs. Episcopalian. Clubs: Cherry Hills Country (Denver), Castle Pines Country (Castle Rock, Colo.). Office: Fancher Oil Company 1801 Broadway #720 Denver CO 80202

FANFANI, AMINTORE, Italian government official; b. Pieve Santo Stefano, Arezzo, Italy, Feb. 6, 1908; s. Giuseppe and Anita (Leo) F.; m. Biancarosa Provasoli, 1939 (dec. 1968); children: Anna Maria, Maria Grazia, Marina, Alberto, Benedetta, Giorgio, Cecilia; m. Mariapia Tavazzani, 1975. D Econs. and Social Scis., Cath. U. Sacred Heart, Milan, Italy, 1930; various hon. degrees. Mem. nat. exec. com. Christian Dem. Party, 1946—, sec. gen., 1954-58, 73-75, pres., 1976-80; minister labor and social security Italy, Rome, 1947-50, minister agr. and forestry, 1951-53, minister interior, 1953-54, 87-88, minister fgn. affairs, 1958-59, 65-68, prime minister, 1954, 58-59, 60-62, 62-63, 82-83, minister budget and economy, 1988—; mem. Italian Senate, Rome, 1968—, pres., 1968-73, 76-82, from 1985. Home: EVR Piazzale Luigi Sturzo 15, Rome Italy Office: Ministry Budget and Economy, Rome Italy *

FANG, AI NONG, mathematic educator; b. She Xian, People's Republic of China, Oct. 25, 1936; s. Ze Zhou and You Di (Jiao) F.; m. Gu Mei Yun, Aug. 1, 1967; children: Ming, Fang. Grad., Fudan U., 1961. Asst., Hunan U., Changsha, 1961-77, lectr., 1978-80, prof., 1981—. Contbr. articles to profl. jours. Mem. copy editor com. on applied math. textbook edn. dept., 1984—. Mem. Am. Math. Soc., People's Republic China Math Soc. (council mem. 1987—) Home: Hunan U, Changsha, Hunan 83171, People's Republic of China

FANG YI, government official People's Republic of China; b. Xiamen, Fujian Province, 1909; m. Yin Sen. Joined Chinese Communist Party, 1931; editor, Comml. Press, Shanghai, 1930; mem. Communist Party, Hubei Province; dir. Govt. Fin. Dept., Shandong-Anhui, 1946; sec. gen. Fin. Econ. Affairs Com., North China People's Govt., 1948; vice chmn. People's Govt., Shandong, 1949, Fujian, 1949-52; dep. mayor Shanghai, 1952-53; vice chmn. fin. econ. affairs com. East China Adminstrv. Council, 1952-54; vice minister fin., 1953-54; with embassy in Hanoi, 1954-61; alt. mem. 8th Cen. Com., Chinese Communist Party, 1958, 9th Cen. Com., 1969, mem. 10th Cen. Com., 1973, mem. Standing Com., 1977, mem. Politburo, 11th Cen. Com., 1977-82, mem. Secretariat, 1980-82, mem. Presidium, 12th Cen. Com., 1982; dep. dir. fgn. affairs office, dir. Bur. Econ. Relations with Fgn. Countries, State Council, 1961-64, chmn. Commn. Econ. Relations with Fgn. Countries, 1964-68, minister econ. relations with fgn. countries, 1969-77, minister state sci. and tech. commn., 1978-84, vice premier Council of State, 1978-82, state councilor, 1982-88; vice chmn. 7th nat. com. Chinese People's Polit. Consultative Conf., 1988—; v.p. Chinese Acad. Scis., 1977-79, pres. 1979-81; chmn. Nat. Acad. Degrees Com., State Council, 1980-83. Address: care Chinese People's Polit, Consultative Conf, Beijing Peoples Republic of China *

FANSHIER, CHESTER, manufacturing executive; b. Wilson County, Kans., Mar. 2, 1897; s. Thomas J. and Nora Bell (Maxwell) F.; m. Ina Muriel Goens, Apr. 12, 1918; 1 child, Norma Elaine (Mrs. Robert B. Rice). Registered profl. engr., Okla. Gen. mgr. Bart Products Co., 1932-39; pres., gen. mgr. Metal Goods Mfg. Co., Bartlesville, Okla., 1939—. Patentee in field. Commr. from Tulsa Presbytery to 156th Gen. Assembly, Presbyn. Ch. U.S.A., 1944; pres. Sunday Eve. Fedn. chs., 1937-38. Recipient Wisdom award Honor, 1970, Gutenberg Bible award; named to Ring Order of Engrs. Mem. NSPE, Okla. Soc. Profl. Engrs. (charter Bartlesville chpt.), ASTM, ASME (life), Profl. Photographers Am., Nat. Rifle Assn. (life), Okla. Rifle Assn., Am. Def. Preparedness Assn. (life), Bartlesville C. of C., SAR. Presbyterian. Club: Engr. (bd. dirs. 1948-49, 54-55). Lodge: Rotary (pres. 1956-57, Paul Harris fellow). Home: 1328 S Cherokee Ave Bartlesville OK 74003 Office: 309 W Hensley Blvd Bartlesville OK 74003

FANT, MAUREEN BURKE BROWN, editor, writer; b. Bryn Mawr, Pa., Sept. 26, 1947; arrived in Italy, 1979; d. Edward David and Nancy (O'Brien) Brown; m. J. Clayton Fant, Aug. 9, 1969 (div. Jan. 1987). BA, Manhattanville Coll., 1969; MA, U. Mich., 1971, postgrad., 1974. Editorial asst. House Beautiful mag., N.Y.C., 1969; freelance editor, writer Boston and Rome, 1974-79, 79—. Co-author: Women's Life in Greece and Rome, 1982; translator: Pandora's Daughters, 1986; contbg. editor: Ceres mag., Food and Agriculture Orgn. of UN, 1981-88; mem. editorial staff Italy Italy mag., 1986—; contbr. articles and book revs. to jours. Singer Centro Italiano di Musica Antica. Mem. Am. Translators Assn. Home: Via B Peruzzi 11, int 2,, 00153 Rome Italy

FANTZ, RAINETTE EDEN, clinical psychologist; b. Cleve., Dec. 13, 1922; d. Dimitri Dimiter and Anna (Asher) Dobreff; student Cleve. Inst. Art, 1941-43, Flora Stone Mather Coll., 1941-43; B.S. magna cum laude, Western Res. U., 1951, Ph.D., 1962; m. Robert L. Fantz, Nov. 2, 1960 (dec. Dec. 1981); 1 dau., Lorian. Comml. artist Bailey's, Cleve., 1943-44; free-lance artist, 1943-48; actress leading roles Repertory Theatre, Washington, 1952-53; cons. Cleve. Diabetes Assn., 1955; asst. psychologist Highland View Hosp., Cleve., (Ohio) Pub. Schs., 1956-57; asst. psychologist Fairview Park 1957-62; psychologist James R. Hodge, M.D., Akron, Ohio, 1958-63; pvt. practice clin. psychology, Cleve., 1962—; mem. faculty Gestalt Inst. of Cleve., 1968—, chmn. intensive postgrad. program, 1973—, also mem. editorial bd. Mem. Am. Psychol. Assn., Ohio Psychol. Assn., Cleve. Psychol. Assn., Am. Acad. Psychotherapists, Cleve. Acad. Cons. Psychologists (past pres.), Assn. for Advancement of Psychology, Cleve. Inst. Music, Cleve. Inst. Art, Cleve. Mus. Art, Supporters of Cleve. Orchestra, ACLU, Common Cause, Phi Beta Kappa. Contbr. chpts. to books; editor publs. in field. Home: 11 Mornington Ln Cleveland Heights OH 44106 Office: 1588 Hazel Dr Cleveland OH 44106

FARAGE, DONALD J., lawyer. A.B., U. Pa., 1930, LL.B. with 1st honors, 1933; LL.D. hon., Dickinson Sch. Law, 1966. Bar: Pa. 1933. Asst. to prof. Francis H. Bohlen, reporter for Restatement of Torts 1933-36; prof. law Dickinson Sch. Law, 1934-46, 50—, George Washington U. Law Sch., 1948-50; sr. ptnr. firm Farage & McBride; vis. prof. med. jurisprudence Jefferson Med. Coll., Phila., 1948-76. Author: Pennsylvania Annotations to Restatement of Restitution, 1940, Pennsylvania Annotations to Restatement Judgments, 1957; co-editor: Hazards of Medication, 1971, 2d edit., 1978. Fellow Law Sci. Acad.; fellow Internat. Soc. Barristers (dir. 1971-74), Am. Coll. Trial Lawyers, Internat. Acad. Law and Sci., Southwestern Legal Found., Internat. Acad. Trial Lawyers (pres. 1970-71); mem. ABA (council, chmn. com. on rules and procedure, sect. ins., negligence and compensation law 1971-73, mem. council sect. torts and ins. practice law 1977-81, chmn. class actions com. 1981-83, chmn. motions and resolutions com. 1983-84), Pa. Bar Assn. (ho. of dels. 1966-73, 75-78, 82—), Phila. Bar Assn., Assn. Trial Lawyers Am. (v.p. Pa. 1956-58), Am. Law Inst. (life), Scribes, Order of Coif, Phi Alpha Delta. Clubs: Lawyers, Union League (Phila.). Office: 836 Suburban Sta Bldg 1617 John F Kennedy Blvd Philadelphia PA 19103

FARAGO, GEORGE, electrical engineer; b. Budapest, Hungary, Dec. 17, 1903; came to U.S., 1959; s. Joseph and Hermin (Friedmann) Klein; m. Lenke Gyongyi Leon, Apr. 4, 1947. Engr. Cand., Technikum, Germany, 1923; Elec. Engr., Polytechnikum, Oldenburg, Germany, 1926; Dipl.Elec.Engr., Tech. U. Dresden, 1927; postgrad. Tech. U. Budapest, 1952-53. Engr.-in-charge (chief engr.) research and devel. Telecommunications, Budapest, 1929-52; research fellow Acad. Scis., Budapest, 1952-53; dep. chief engr. Tungsram Works, Budapest, 1953-57; v.p. research and devel. Faracon Corp., Englewood, N.J., 1962-65; cons. in research and devel. Premier Microwave, Portchester, N.Y., 1967-72, Elec. Cons., Bklyn., 1973-82; elec. engring. cons., Albany, N.Y., 1983-87. Contbr. articles to profl. jours. Patentee in field. Mem. IEEE, Mfg. Tech. Soc., Biomed. Engring. Soc., Inst. Med. Climatology, N.Y. Acad. Scis. Current work: Electrical cleaning systems for automobile exhaust gas. Subspecialties: Electronics; Telecommunications.

FARAH, BADIE NAIEM, educator, consultant; b. Nazareth, Palestine, Jan. 15, 1946; came to U.S., 1970, naturalized, 1983; s. Naim R. and Afifi (Takla) F. B.S., Damascus U., 1967, M.A., 1968; M.S., Wayne State U., 1973; M.S.I.E., Ohio State U., 1976, Ph.D., 1977. Teaching asst. Wayne State U., Detroit, 1971-73; research assoc. Ohio State U., Columbus, 1973-77; sr. systems analyst Gen. Motors Co., Detroit, 1977-78; asst. prof. Oakland U., Rochester, Mich., 1978-82; asst. prof. info. systems and ops. research Eastern Mich. U., Ypsilanti, 1982-86, assoc. prof., 1986—; advisor to bd. dirs. S & G Grocer Co., Detroit, 1979-81, vis. gen. mgr., 1980-81. ; Co-author: Integrated Case Studies in Accounting Information Systems, 1987; contbr. articles to profl. jours. Mem. Am. Inst. Insl. Engrs., Assn. for Computing Machinery (exec. council Met. Detroit chpt.), Ops. Research Soc. Am., Inst. Mgmt. Scis. (sec. SE Mich. chpt.), Mich. Acad. Sci., Arts and Letters, AAUP, Alpha Pi Mu, Beta Gamma Sigma. Syrian Orthodox (pres. local ch. bd.). Research on data communications and networks of computers, expert systems for microcomputers, management information systems. Home: 37 Foxboro Dr Rochester Hills MI 48309 Office: Eastern Mich U 511 Pray-Harrold Hall Ypsilanti MI 48197

FARAH, CAESAR ELIE, Middle Eastern and Islamic studies educator; b. Portland, Oreg., Mar. 13, 1929; s. Sam Khalil and Lawrice F.; m. Irmgard Jacobsen, Dec. 13, 1987; children by previous marriage: Ronald, Christopher, Ramsey, Laurence, Raymond, Alexandra. Student, Internat. Coll. Beirut, 1941-45; B.A., Stanford U., 1952; M.A., Princeton U., 1955, Ph.D., 1957. Pub. affairs asst., cultural affairs officer ednl. exchanges USIS, New Delhi, 1957-58, Karachi, Pakistan, 1958; asst. to chief Bur. Cultural Affairs, Washington, 1959; asst. prof. history and Semitic langs. Portland State U., 1959-63; asst. prof. history Calif. State U.-Los Angeles, 1963-64; assoc. prof. Near Eastern studies Ind. U., Bloomington, 1964-69; prof. Middle Eastern and Islamic history U. Minn., Mpls., 1969—, chmn. dept. South and SW Asian studies, 1988—; cons. U.S. Army, 1962-63; vis. prof. Harvard U., summers 1964-65; guest lectr. Fgn. Ministry, Spain, Iraq, Lebanon, Ministry Higher Edn., Saudi Arabia, Yemen, Turkey, Kuwait, Qatar, Tunisia, Morocco, Turkey, Syrian Acad. Scis.; vis. scholar Cambridge U., 1974; resource person on Middle East, media and service group Minn., 1977—; dir. Upper Midwest Consortium for Middle East Outreach, 1980—. Author: The Addendum in Medieval Arabic Historiography, 1968, Islam: Beliefs and Observances, 4th edit., 1987, Eternal Message of Muhammad, 1964, 3d edit., 1981, (3 vols.) Ta'rikh Baghdad li-Ibn-al-Najjar, 1980-83, 2d edit., 1986; contbr. articles to profl. jours. Mem. Oreg. Republican Com., 1960-64. Recipient cert. of merit Syrian Ministry Higher Edn.; Fulbright Hayes scholar, 1966-68, 85-86; fellow Am. Council Learned Socs., 1953, Ford Found., 1966, Philos. Soc., 1970-71; Dept. State Am. Participants Program grantee, 1981, 84, Minn. Humanities Commn. grantee, 1981, 85, others. Mem. Stanford U. Alumni Assn. (leadership recognition award), Stanford Club Minn. (dir., pres. 1979), Am. Oriental Soc., Royal Asiatic Soc. Gt. Britain, Am. Hist. Assn., Middle East Studies Assn. N.Am., Am. Assn. Tchrs. Arabic (exec. bd.), Pi Sigma Alpha, Phi Alpha Theta. Greek Orthodox. Club: Princeton. Home: 3847 York Ave S Minneapolis MN 55410 Office: Univ Minn 839 Soc Sci Tower Minneapolis MN 55455

FARAH, MOUMIN BAHDON, minister of foreign affairs and cooperation of Republic of Djibouti; b. Djibouti, Republic of Djibouti, 1939; married; 7 children. Controller Djibouti Postal Services and Telecommunications; v.p. Popular African League for Independence, 1975-76; minister of interior Republic of Djibouti, Djibouti, 1976-77, dep. of Republic of Djibouti, from 1977, then first minister of interior, minister of fgn. affairs and cooperation, 1978—. Founder Action for Justice and Progress polit. party, 1969; sec.-gen. Popular Assembly for Progress party, 1979—. Muslim. Office: Ministry Fgn Affairs, and Cooperation, Djibouti Republic of Djibouti *

FARAHMAND, KAMBIZ, mathematics educator, researcher; b. Tehran, Iran, July 4, 1954; came to Republic of South Africa, 1985.; m. Anne Lois Jameson, Oct. 20, 1984. BSc, Nat. U. Iran, 1979; MSc, King's Coll. U. London, 1980; PhD, Chelsea Coll. U. London, 1984. Tchr. Firoz-Bahram High Sch., Tehran, 1976-79; lectr. U. Bophuthatswana, Mafikeng, Republic of South Africa, 1985-86, U. Natal, Durban, Republic of South Africa, 1986—. Mem. Am. Math. Soc., London Math. Soc., South African Math. Soc., South African Statis. Soc. Office: Univ Natal, King George V Ave, Durban, Natal 4001, Republic of South Africa

FARBER, GERALDINE OSSMAN, civic worker; b. Salt Lake City, May 4, 1929; d. Lawrence N. and Janet (Perkins) Ossman; student Vassar Coll., 1947-49, U. Liege (Belgium), 1951-53, U. Utah, 1955; m. John Val Browning, July 19, 1949 (div. June 1964); 1 son, John Allen; m. Seymour M. Farber, June 5, 1973. Tchrs. aid spl. programs elem. schs., Ogden, Utah, Los Altos and Woodside, Calif., 1962-70; cons. Glasrock Products, Inc., 1979-80. Bd. dirs. Am. Field Service, Ogden, 1960-64, Utah Ballet, Ogden, 1963-64, Christmas Bur., Palo Alto and Los Altos, 1964-66, Jr. League Palo Alto, 1966-69. Community Com. for Internat. Students, Stanford, 1965-67; dir. Ednl. TV Fgn. Student Series, Ogden, 1963-64; bd. dirs. Vol. Bur. No. Santa Clara County (Calif.), 1965-68, exec. v.p., 1967-68; vol. parentis in locus, tubercular refugee children Caritas Catholique, Liege, 1952-55; ways and means chmn. San Francisco Ballet Assn. Aux., 1970, pres., 1974-75, trustee assn., 1974-75; co-founder, pres. bd. dirs. Archives for Performing Arts, 1975-76; bd. dirs. Am. Conservatory Theater, 1975-81; mem. Calif. Public Broadcasting Commn., 1975-85 ; vol., asst. media buyer campaign Supt. Public Instrn. Calif., 1970; mem. exec. planning com. and nat. adv. bd. John Muir Med. Film Festival, 1979—; program com. mem. Kauai Found. Continuing Edn. and Hawaii Med. Assn. Recipient awards of Merit City and County San Francisco, Vol. Bur. No. Santa Clara County. Club: San Francisco Peninsula Vassar Alumnae (pres. 1968-70). Editor: Teilhard de Chardin: In Quest of the Perfection of Man, 1973. Home and Office: 26303 Esperanza Dr Los Altos Hills CA 94022

FARCOT, JEAN-CHRISTIAN, physician, cardiologist; b. Mostaganem, Algeria, Dec. 21, 1946; arrived in France, 1980; s. Roger and Nella (Bassi) F.; m. Gueronick Sophie, June 21, 1974 (div 1980). Bachelors, Lycee de Plein Air, Argeles Gazost, 1967; MD, U. Paris, 1974; Diploma (hon.), U. René Descartes, Paris, 1983. Diplomate, France. Research fellow in cardiovascular research UCLA, 1977; med. asst. Ambroise Paré Hosp., Paris, 1981, med. adjoint, 1984; cardiologist U. Paris, 1982; mem. staff Ambroise Paré Hosp., U. ER Paris-Quest, Boulogne, France,1978; mem. com. Consulatative Med. Hosp. Ambroise Paré, 1982, cardiologist Air France Co., Paris, 1986. Edit. bd. Confs. Cardiologiques Internat., 1979, Echodardiography Futura Pub. Co, Mt. Kisco, N.Y., 1981; author: Comprendre L'echo Cardiographie, 1986; patentee in field. Fellow Am. Coll. Cardiology; mem. Am. Heart Assn., Soc. French Cardiologists, Am. Med. Assn. (cert. of merit 1977), Soc. Argentina de Ultrasonografia en Medicina y Biologia. Roman Catholic. Clubs: St. Cloud, De La Diane. Home: 39 Rue Spontini, 75116 Paris France Office: Ambroise Paré, 9 Ave Charles de Gaulle, 92106 Boulogne France

FAREED, AHMED ALI, university dean; b. Cairo, Sept. 27, 1932, came to U.S. 1961; s. Ali E. and Fayka M. (Yousef) F.; m. Houreya A. Abul-Kheir, Sept. 26, 1957, children—Dahlia, Tony-Khalid. B.A. with honors, Cairo U., 1953; gen. diploma Ein Shams U., Cairo, 1954, spl. diploma, 1959; Ph.D., U. Chgo., 1969. Tchr. Kobba Model Sch., Cairo, 1954-56; curriculum expert Ministry of Edn., Cairo, 1956-61; diagnostician U. Chgo., 1965-68; vis. prof. Northwestern U., Evanston, Ill., 1969; prof., chmn. Northeastern Ill. U., Chgo., 1968-79, dean Coll. Edn., 1979—; cons. sch. dists., Ill., 1967—; speaker, panelist profl. orgns., 1965—; ednl. planning expert Kuwait U., 1978; trustee Am. Islamic Coll., Chgo., 1983—; vice chmn. governing bd. Ednl. Service Ctr., Chgo., 1986; chmn. Internat. Conf. on Bilingual Edn. U. Chgo., 1987 . Author standardized silent reading tests, instructional resource units, resource units for elem. tchrs. Contbr. articles to profl. jours. Recipient Outstanding Dissertations in Reading award Internat. Reading Assn., 1970, Outstanding Contbn. Field of Vision award Coll. Optometrists in Vision Devel., 1974, Outstanding Educator Am. award Outstanding Educators of Am., Washington, 1975, Internat. Understanding in Edn. award Ameer Khusro Soc. Am., 1986, Appreciation award dist. 4 Chgo. Bd. Edn., 1987. Mem. Ill. Assn. Deans of Pub. Colls. Edn. (pres. 1983-84), Am. Assn. Colls. of Tchr. Edn., Am. Ednl. Research Assn., Tchr. Edn. Council State Colls. & Univs., Ill. Assn. Colls. of Tchr. Edn., Internat. Reading Assn. (commendation for excellent service 1981), Assn. Egyptian Am. Scholars, Phi Delta Kappa. Avocations: classical music; poetry. Office: Dean Coll Edn Northeastern Ill U 5500 N St Louis Ave Chicago IL 60625

FARGEAS, JEAN LUCIEN, utilities executive; b. Treignac, Correze, France, Sept. 29, 1902; s. Francois and Antoinette (Dupuy) F.; student Ecole Polytechnique, 1922-24; m. Suzanne Henriette Prevost, Mar. 6, 1928; children—Antoinette, Claude. Tech. dir. Societe industrielle des Telephones, Paris, 1926-39, Societe Electro Cable, Paris, 1945-60; chief exec. officer Societe Francaise CEAT, Paris, 1960-74; Etablissements A. Leblond, Bihorel, France, 1962-82; chmn. Chambre Syndicale de la Metallurgie, Rouen, France, 1954-57. Mayor, Amfreville la Mivoie, France, 1947-50. Served with arty., 1939-45. Decorated Legion d'Honneur. Mem. Chambre Syndicale de la Construction Electrique. Roman Catholic. Club: Cercle Militaire (Paris). Home: 39 rue Joffre, Saint Germain 78100 France

FARGUES, PHILIPPE, demographer; b. Paris, Oct. 17, 1948; s. Paul and Viviane (Fraikin) F.; m. Solange Botella, June 12, 1970 (div. 1981); children: Nicolas, Dominique. Doctorat Sociologie, The Sorbonne, Paris, 1974; Expertise demographie, Paris I Pantheon, 1971. Lectr. U. Paris I, 1970-72; UN expert UNO/DTCD, Beirut, 1972-75, Yaounde, Cameroon, 1975-77; researcher Middle Eastern Studies Ctr., Beirut, 1978-80; sr. tech. asst. French Ministry of Cooperation, Abidjan, Ivory Coast, 1980-83; sr. researcher Inst. Nat. d'Etudes Demographiques, Paris, 1983—; cons. UNO, 1984, 85, 86. Author: (Books) The Population of Lebanon, 1974, Migrants Stocks and Oil Rent, 1980, Migration in Ivory Coast, 1982, Urban Mortality in Sahel, 1988; co-editor: Childhood Mortality in LDC's, 1986; contbr. articles to profl. jours. Me. Internat. Union for Sci. Study of Population, Sci. Council of Internat. Chilcren's Ctr. Home: 71 Richard-Lenoir Blvd, Paris 75011, France Office: Inst National d'Etudes Demographiques, 27 rue du Commandeur, Paris 75014, France

FARHA, WILLIAM FARAH, food company executive; b. Lebanon, Nov. 27, 1908; s. Farah Farris and Nahima (Salamy) F.; m. Victoria Barkett, Apr. 15, 1934; 1 child, William George. Grad., U.S. Indsl. Coll., 1948, Brookings Inst., 1968, Doctorate, Hamilton State U., 1973, Colo. State Christian Coll. With F & E Wholesale Grocery Co., 1929-64; mgr. River Bend Shopping Ctr., Wichita, William F. Farha and Son Enterprises; chmn., chief exec. officer Farah Mfg. Co., Inc., El Paso, Tex. Bd. dirs. NCCJ, Kans. Found. for Blind; trustee Met. Bd., YMCA, also internat. bd. World Service; founder Antiochian Greek Orthodox Dioceses of N.Am.; bd. advisers Salvation Army; internat. bd. YMCA World Service; pres. bd. trustees St. George Ch.; chmn. Wichita Leadership Prayer Breakfast; co-founder, past bd. govs. St. Jude Research Hosp., Memphis; past chmn. Wichita Police and Fireman Pension Plan; past trustee Wichita Symphony Soc.; past bd. dirs. Wichita C. of C., St. Joseph Research Hosp. Ctr.; past nat. bd. Inst. Logopedics; nat. adv. bd. Am. Security Council; mem. Nat. Bd. Small Bus., U.S. Congl. Adv. Bd.; charter mem. Pres. Reagan's Republician Presdl. Task Force; mem. Rep. Nat. Com.; invited to presdl. prayer breakfasts in Eisenhower, Kennedy, Johnson, Nixon and Ford adminstrns. named hon. Okla. col., 1956; mem. Pres. Reagan's Rep. Presdl. Task Force, Rep. Nat. Com. recipient Gold medal for outstanding service to orthodoxy Antiochian Patriarch Alexander of Damascus, 1952, Antonian Gold medal of merit Antiochian Orthodox Christian Archdiocese of N.Y. and N.Am., 1972, Brotherhood award NCCJ. Lodge: Rotary (Paul Harris fellow). Home: 8630 Shannon Way Wichita KS 67206 Office: 8100 E 22d St N Bldg 1700 Wichita KS 67226 also: 8889 Gateway W El Paso TX 79925

FARHI, MUSA MORIS, writer; b. Ankara, Turkey, July 5, 1935; arrived in Eng., 1954; s. Hayim Daniel and Palomba (Cuenca) F.; m. Nina Ruth Gould, July 2, 1978; 1 child, Rachel. BA in Humanities, Robert Coll., Istanbul, Turkey, 1954; diploma, Royal Acad. Dramatic Art, London, 1956. Freelance writer London, 1956—. Author: (play) From the Ashes of Thebes, 1969, The Pleasure of Your Death, 1972, The Last of Days, 1983. Mem. Internat. Pen Soc., Soc. Authors of U.K., Writers Guild of U.K., Authors Guild, Inc. of U.S. Mem. Labour Party. Jewish. Home and Office: 11 North Square, London NW11 7AB, England

FARIDAD, ABBAS, economist; b. Tehran, Iran, Jan. 1, 1929; s. Hasan and Keshvar (Behzadi) Ghezelbash; m. Mary Elizabeth Boyer, Aug. 18, 1956; children: Diane S., Derek J. BS Utah State U., 1953, MS 1954; PhD, Ohio State U., 1957. Head research and stats. br., econ. bur. Planning Orgn. Iran, 1958-63; prof. econs. Nat. U. Iran, 1960-63; econ. affairs officer UN ESCAP, Bangkok, Thailand, 1963-72, econ. affairs officer UN, N.Y.C., 1972-75, sr. econ. affairs officer, 1975-84, chief policy coordination br. PCB/PPDPD/DTCD, 1984-86, chief pub. fin. and enterprise mgmt. br. devel. adminstrn. div. Dept. Tech. Cooperation for Devel., 1987—. Mem. Am. Econ. Assn., Econometric Soc. Home: 218-29 Hartland Ave Bayside NY 11364 Office: UN New York NY 10017

FARIS, MUSTAPHA, economist, bank executive; b. Dec. 17, 1933. Dipl.Ing., Ecole Nationale des Ponts et Chaussees, Paris. Govt. civil engr. Dept. Pub. Works, 1956-61; dir. supply Nat. Irrigation Office, 1961-65, dir.-gen. hydraulic engring., 1965-69; sec. of state for planning attached to Prime Minister's Office, 1969-71; minister of fin., 1971-72; pres., dir-gen. Banque Nationale pour le Developpement Economique, Rabat, Morocco, 1972-77, economist, 1977—; former v.p. Internat. Com. on Large Dams; gov. IBRD, African Devel. Bank; gen. mgr. B.A.I.I., Paris; vice chmn., mng. dir. Banque Arabe et Internationale d'Investissement, to 1981. Decorated Ordre du Trone. Office: Banque Nat pour le Devel Econom, BP 407, Rabat Morocco

FARIS, ROBERT E. LEE, retired sociology educator; b. Waco, Tex., Feb. 2, 1907; s. Ellsworth and Elizabeth (Homan) F.; Ph.B., U. Chgo., 1928, M.A., 1930, Ph.D., 1931; m. Claire Guignard, Aug. 18, 1931; children—William Guignard, John Homan, Roger Stuart. Instr., then asst. prof. sociology Brown U., 1931-38; asst. prof. McGill U., 1938-40; assoc. prof. Bryn Mawr Coll., 1940-43; assoc. prof., then prof. Syracuse U., 1943-48; prof. U. Wash., 1948-72, exec. officer dept. sociology, 1953-66. Mem. Social Sci. Research Council (dir. 1953-60), Am. (pres. 1961), Pacific (pres. 1954) sociol. socs., Social Research Assn. (pres. 1959), San Diego Artists Guild. Club: Seattle Yacht Author: Social Disorganization 1948; Social Psychology, 1952; (with H. W. Dunham) Mental Disorders in Urban Areas, 1939; Chicago Sociology, 1920-32, 1967. Editor Am. Sociol. Review, 1952-54. Editor Handbook of Modern Sociology, 1964. Contbr. articles to sociol. jours., article to Ency. Britannica, 15th edit. Home: 19 Ginger Tree Ln Coronado CA 92118

FARISH, JAMES MATTHEW, accountant; b. Monroe, Va., Dec. 18, 1946; s. Robert Franklin and Josephine Elizabeth (Dudley) F.; m. Martha Ann Sawyers, Aug. 11, 1972; 1 child, Robert Joseph. B.S., Va. Commonwealth U., 1975, M.B.A., 1978. Pres. Farish & Assocs., Richmond, Va., 1975—; v.p. Sovran Fin. Corp., 1987—; sec.-treas. Farish, Dixon, Dalton, Inc., 1987—. Pres. Bethlehem Little League, Richmond, 1976-80; treas. Lakeside Little League, Richmond, 1982-85, v.p., 1986-87. Mem. Va. Soc. Pub. Accts., Va. State Umpires Assn. (treas. 1986-88). Republican. Baptist. Lodge: Lions (treas. 1977-81, 85-88). Avocation: Golf. Home: 9711 Needles Way Glen Allen VA 23060

FARKAS, JAMES PAUL, educator, author; b. Buffalo, Mar. 21, 1947 s. Paul Edward and Marie Edith (Weigel) F. B.S. in Edn., SUNY-Buffalo, 1968, M.A. in Am. History, 1971; M.S. in Ednl. Adminstrn., Niagara U., 1976, Specialist in Ednl. Adminstrn., 1976; Ed.D. in Ednl. Adminstrn., SUNY-Buffalo, 1983; grad. with honors U.S. Army Command and Gen. Staff Coll., 1985. Tchr. Buffalo Pub. Schs., 1968-70; tchr. Amherst Central Schs., 1970—, dir. Fed. Sect. Chpt. I programs, 1976-79; faculty Empire State Mil. Acad., 1979—; guest lectr. SUNY-Buffalo, 1984-85, project cons. office of dean faculty of ednl. studies SUNY-Buffalo, 1985. Contbr. articles to numerous profl. jours on mgmt. leadership and stress; manuscript reviewer Issues in Edn., 1984—. Served to lt. col. Corps. Engrs., N.Y. Army N.G., USAR, 1968—. Decorated Army Commendation medal, Humanitarian Service medal. Mem. Am. Ednl. Research Assn., Assn. U.S. Army, Soc. Am. Mil. Engrs., N.Y. State Council for the Social Studies. Home: 116 Crowley Ave Buffalo NY 14207-1536 Office: 55 Kings Hwy Snyder NY 14226

FARLEY, LLOYD EDWARD, educator; b. Nebr. Sand Hills nr. Broken Bow, Nebr., June 20, 1915; s. Arthur L. and Effie (Tyson) F.; A.B., Kearney State Coll., 1945; M.A., Stanford U., 1947, Ed.D., 1950; postgrad. U. Hawaii, U. Oreg., Princeton U.; Litt.D., William Woods Coll., 1982. Tchr. elem. and secondary schs., also adminstr., 1937-41, 47-51; ednl. specialist U.S. Govt., Washington, Anchorage, Edwards AFB, Calif., 1952-60; prof. edn. U. Alaska, Anchorage, 1960-64; Louis D. Beaumont Distinguished prof. edn., head div. social sci., Marshall faculty William Woods Coll., Fulton, Mo.; chmn. dept. edn. Westminster and William Woods Colls., Fulton, 1964-80, prof. edn. emeritus, 1980—; vis. prof. St. Cloud State U., summers 1968-72, Aeromed. Inst., FAA, 1980—. Served to maj. AUS, 1941-46. Named Hon. Tchr. Korea; recipient Centennial medal William Woods Coll. Mem. Mo. Tchrs. Assn., Nat. Assn. Tchr. Educators, Internat. Council on Edn. for Teaching, Phi Delta Kappa, Kappa Delta Pi (hon. mem., named Outstanding Educator). Methodist. Address: 12 Tucker Ln Fulton MO 65251

FARLEY, RAYMOND FRANCIS, wax and chemical specialty manufacturing executive; b. Montclair, N.J., Nov. 27, 1924; s. John A. and Mabel B. (Kinsey) F.; B.S. in Bus., Northwestern U., 1951; m. Mary Miller, Nov. 27, 1954; 1 dau., Gwen Elizabeth. With S.C. Johnson & Son, Inc., Racine, Wis., 1951—, beginning as indsl. products salesman, successively indsl. products regional sales supr., field sales mgr. indsl. products, Porelon products enterprise mgr., regional dir. Japan and Far East, v.p. and regional dir. Japan and Far East, v.p. corp. planning, exec. v.p. U.S. ops., exec. v.p. overseas consumer products, 1951-80, pres., chief operating officer, 1980—; dir. Hart Schaffner & Marx, Chgo., Heritage Bank & Trust Co., Racine. Bd. dirs. St. Mary's Med. Ctr., trustee Northwestern U.; mem. adv. council J.L. Kellogg Grad. Sch. Mgmt. of Northwestern U.; adv. council Ctr. Study of U.S.-Japan Relations of Northwestern U. Served with AUS, World War II. Decorated Bronze Star; named Man of Yr., Internat. Advt. Assn., 1981. Mem. Pvt. Industry Council S.E. Wis. (chmn.), Nat. Alliance Bus. (dir. S.E. Wis.), Racine Area Mfrs. and Commerce, Inc. (dir.), U.S. C. of C., Conf. Bd. (internat. council). Club: Racine Country (past pres.). Office: S C Johnson & Son Inc 1525 Howe St Racine WI 53403 *

FARMAKIS, GEORGE LEONARD, educator; b. Clarksburg, W.Va., June 30, 1925; s. Michael and Pipitsa (Roussopoulos) F.; B.A., Wayne State U., Detroit, 1949, M.S.Ed., 1950, M.A., 1966, Ph.D., 1971; M.A., U. Mich., 1978; postgrad. Columbia U., Yale U., Queens Coll. Tchr., audio-visual aids dir. Roseville (Mich.) Public Schs., 1951-57; tchr. Birmingham (Mich.) pub. schs., 1957-61; tchr. Highland Park (Mich.) Public Schs., 1961-70, resource specialist, 1971-84; computer sci. specialist, 1984—; instr. Highland Park Community Coll., 1966-68, Wayne County Community Coll., 1969-70; founder Ford Sch. Math. High Intensity Tutoring Program, 1971; chairperson Highland Park Sch. Dist. Curriculum Council and Profl. Staff Devel. Governing Bd., 1979-82; pres. Mich. Council for Social Studies, 1984-86; founder, dir. Mich. Social Studies Olympiad, 1987; founder, editor Mich. Social Studies Jour., 1986; participant ESEA Title I/Nat. Diffusion Network. Served to cpl., USNG, 1948-51. Recipient spl. commendation Office of Edn., 1978, Outstanding Service award Nat. Council Social Studies 1987, Presdl. award Mich. Council Social Studies 1988. Mem. Mich. Assn. Supervision and Curriculum Devel., Am. Hist. Assn., Nat. Council Social Studies, Acad. Polit. Sci., Am. Philol. Assn., Assn. Supervision and Curriculum Devel. (bd. dirs. Mich. 1983—), Internat. Reading Assn., U. Mich. Alumni Assn., Wayne State U. Coll. Edn. Alumni Assn. (bd. dirs. 1985—), Internat. Platform Assn., Modern Greek Studies Assn., Nat. Assn. Adminstrs. State and Fed. Edn. Programs, Mich. Assn. Adminstrs. State and Fed. Edn. Programs Specialists, Mich. Reading Assn., Mich. Tchrs. Math., Phi Delta Kappa (Outstanding Educator;s award 1988). Greek Orthodox. Co-author: Michigan School Finance Curriculum Guide. Contbr. poems to books of poetry, articles to Focus jour. Home: 752 Trombley Rd Grosse Pointe Park MI 48230 Office: 20 Bartlett St Highland Park MI 48230

FARMER, GUY, lawyer; b. Foster Falls, Va., Sept. 13, 1912; s. Harbert and Kate (Bell) F.; m. Helen Joura (dec.); children: Mary, Mark, Jane. B.A., W.Va. U., 1934, LL.B., 1936; Rhodes scholar, Oxford (Eng.) U., 1936-37. Bar: W.Va., D.C., U.S. Supreme Ct. Asso. gen. counsel NLRB, 1943-45, atty., 1945, chmn., 1953-55; assoc. Steptoe & Johnson, 1945-49, ptnr., 1949-60; sr. ptnr. Farmer, Wells, McGuinn, Flood & Sibal, 1960-83; of counsel Vedder, Price, Kaufman & Kamholtz, 1983-86; sole practice Washington, 1986—; lectr. labor law Georgetown U., 1957-59; dir. Bartlett Tree Co., Stamford, Conn. Author articles labor topics. Mem. Am., D.C., W.Va. bar assns., Order of Coif, Phi Beta Kappa, Phi Alpha Delta. Club: Cosmos. Office: 1919 Pennsylvania Ave NW Washington DC 20006

FARNHAM, HARRY JUD, lawyer; b. Lincoln, Nebr., Sept. 20, 1925; s. Harry C. and Grace M. (Binfield) F.; LL.D., U. Colo., 1949; m. Sally Link, June 10, 1946; children—Jeff, Dan, Amy. Admitted to Nebr. bar, 1949, since practiced in Omaha and Elkhorn, Nebr. Mem. Nebr. State Racing Commn., 1961—, chmn., 1963—; pres. Nat. Assn. State Racing Commrs., 1969. Mem. legacy com. Morris Animal Found.; sr. warden St. Augustine Episc. Ch., 1981-85. Served with USMCR, 1943-45. Recipient Racing Man of Year award Jockeys' Guild, 1970; Disting. Service award Am. Horse Council, 1972; Man of Year award Horseman's Benevolent Protective Assn., 1970; named to Nebr. Racing Hall of Fame, 1971, Gt. Plains Amateur Boxing Assn. Hall of Fame, 1975; Horsemans Nat. Hall of Fame, 1987. Fellow Am. Acad. Matrimonial Lawyers; mem. Am., Nebr., Omaha bar assns. Democrat. Mason (33 deg.). Home: Rural Rt 2 Elkhorn NE 68022 Office: 1405 N 204th Elkhorn NE 68022

FARNHAM, JACK EDWIN, allergist, consultant; b. Rutland, Vt. Sept. 26, 1931; s. Edwin John and Irma Louise (Kinney) Farnham; m. Anne Bertha Lyman, Sept. 8, 1956; children—Jean Louise, Carol Anne, James Edwin. A.B., U. Vt., Burlington, 1953, M.D., 1957. Diplomate Am. Bd. Allergy and Immunology. Intern Henry Ford Hosp., Detroit, 1957-58; med. resident Lahey Clin., Boston, 1958-59, U. Vt. Med. Ctr., 1959-60, Henry Ford Hosp., 1962-63; clin. asst. medicine Mass. Gen. Hosp., Boston, 1968—; physician Allergy-Immunology Assocs., Chelmsford, Mass., 1969—; dir. New Eng. Pollen Research, Chelmsford, 1981—; cons. allergist Lowell Gen. Hosp. (Mass.), 1969—; St. John's Hosp., Lowell, 1969—, St. Joseph's Hosp., Lowell, 1969—. Contbr. articles in field to profl. jours. Served to capt. M.C., USAF, 1960-62. Fellow Am. Acad. Allergy, Am. Coll. Allergists; mem. New Eng. Soc. Allergy, Mass. Allergy Soc. (sec. 1982-84, pres. 1987-88), AAAS. Baptist. Office: 9 Village Sq Chelmsford MA 01824

FARNSWORTH, HARRISON EDWARD, retired physicist; b. Green Lake, Wis., Mar. 24, 1896; s. Edward H. and Marion (Fortnum) F.; A.B., Ripon Coll., 1918, D.Sc., 1977; A.M., U. Wis., 1921, Ph.D., 1922; D.Sc., Fairfield U., 1971; m. Gertrude Roming, 1925 (dec.); children—Edward Allan, James Alden (dec.); m. Alice Schultze, 1960 (dec.); m. Margaret Bergeron, 1985. Physicist, Western Electric Research Lab., N.Y., 1918; instr. U. Pitts., 1918-19; Nat. Research fellow U. Wis., 1922-24; assoc. prof. physics U. Maine, 1924-26; asst. prof. physics Brown U., 1926-29, assoc. prof., 1929-46, prof., 1946-60, dir. Barus lab. surface physics, 1946-70, research prof., 1960-70, Annette L.R. Barstow Univ. prof., 1963-70, research prof. physics emeritus, Annette L.R. Barstow Univ. prof. emeritus, 1970—; vis. prof. dept. physics U. Ariz., 1971—; dir. Farnsworth Research Lab., Green Valley, Ariz., 1979-84; exec. sec. panel on electron tubes Research and Devel. Bd., dir. coordinating group on electron tube reliability, N.Y.C., 1952-53 (on leave from Brown U.); mem. Planning div. Office Naval Research, summer 1946; cons., 1946-47; cons. Philips Labs., Inc., 1947-49; research physicist on war project Radiation Lab., M.I.T. (leave of absence from Brown U.), 1941; ofcl. investigator N.D.R.C., on war project, Brown U., 1942-43; chmn. dept. physics Brown U., 1942-43, mem. exec. com. dept. physics, 1954-55, mem. Phys. Scis. Council, 1953-63; cons. Lawrence Radiation Lab., Livermore, Calif., 1962-68, Ultek div. Perkin-Elmer Corp., 1965-69, Yale U., 1966-67, Nat. Phys. Research Lab., Pretoria, South Africa, 1970-71; co-operating expert for Internat. Critical Tables; vis. research prof. Wash. State U., summer 1970. Recipient Alumni citation Ripon Coll., 1947, Medal of Merit, 1984 Medard W. Welch award Am. Vacuum Soc., 1981; past fellow Royal Soc. Arts. Fellow AAAS, Am. Phys. Soc., Am. Acad. Arts and Scis.; mem Am. Chem. Soc., Phi Beta Kappa, Sigma Xi, Gamma Alpha. Contbr. numerous sci. articles on electron emission, reflection and diffraction, atomically clean surfaces, reconstrn. of elemental semicondr. surfaces, surface migration, chemisorption, place exchange, oxidation and catalysis, and related subjects. Home: 3940 E Ina Rd Tucson AZ 85718-1526

FARNSWORTH, T. BROOKE, lawyer; b. Grand Rapids, Mich., Mar. 16, 1945; s. George Llelwyn and Gladys Fern (Kennedy) F.; m. Cherrill Kay Bowers, Aug. 24, 1968; children—Leslie Erin, T Brooke. B.S. in Bus., Ind. U., 1967; J.D., Ind. U.-Indpls., 1971. Bar: Tex. 1971, U.S. Dist. Ct. (so. dist.) Tex. 1972, U.S. Tax Ct. 1972, U.S. Ct. Appeals (5th cir.) 1977, U.S. Ct. Appeals D.C. Cir. 1977, U.S. Sup. Ct. 1978, U.S. Ct. Appeals (11th cir.) 1982. Adminstrv. asst. to treas. of State of Ind., Indpls., 1968-71; assoc. Butler, Binion, Rice, Cook & Knapp, Houston, 1971-74; counsel Damson Oil Corp., Houston, 1974-78; prin. Farnsworth & Assocs., Houston, 1978—; bd. dirs. Air Plus, Inc., Enterprise 2000 Inc., TME, Inc; chmn. bd. TME, Inc.; corp. sec. Lomax Oil & Gas Co. Mem. State Bar of Tex., Houston Bar Assn., ABA, Fed. Bar Assn., Fed. Energy Bar Assn., Comml. Law League of Am. Republican. Mem. Christian Ch. (Disciples of Christ). Clubs: Petroleum of Houston, Champions Golf, Greenspoint (Houston). Contbr. articles on law to profl. jours. Home: 5903 Bermuda Dunes Dr Houston TX 77069 Office: Farnsworth and Assocs 333 N Belt Suite 300 Houston TX 77060

FARNUM, HENRY MERRITT, lawyer; b. Lewiston, Maine, June 19, 1919; s. Samuel Merritt and Florence Natalie (Hardy) F. A.B. magna cum laude, Bates Coll., 1939; J.D., Yale U., 1942. Bar: D.C. 1974, Maine 1974, N.Y. 1976, U.S. Patent Office 1976, U.S. Ct. Appeals (fed. cir.) 1986, U.S. Supreme Ct., 1987. Owner Farnum Industries, Inc., Auburn, Maine, 1942-49; patent designer, N.Y.C., 1952-55; automatic setup staff Kollsman Instrument Co., Elmhurst, N.Y., 1952-59; faculty services staff John Jay Coll. Criminal Justice, N.Y.C., 1972-78; sole practice, N.Y.C., 1966—; patent designer, N.Y.C., 1966—; invited del. U.S./Japan Bilataleral Session, tokyo, 1988 . Author: 725 Years of Magna Carta: 1215--1776--Today; patentee Computer-Human responses for tests, Circumferential Stereo spectacular, universal constrn. elements for stage and film sets, multiple use direct mail graphics; inventor 3-D Spectacular and TV by Natural Vision. Originator, chmn. Bates Liberal Arts Expn., Lewiston, 1939; state chmn. Maine Young Republicans, 1947-48; invited del. U.S./Japan Bilateral Session, Tokyo, 1988; active Give America's Dream To A Child: Jackie With Love. Mem. Maine Bar Assn., D.C. Bar Assn., N.Y. Patent, Trademark and Copyright Law Assn. (fgn. law com.), ABA (patent sect., fgn. law com.), Internat. Patent Club, Phi Beta Kappa, Delta Sigma Rho. Jeffersonian Democrat. Mem. Dutch Reformed Ch. Home: Exec House 225 E 46th St New York NY 10017

FARON, BOLESLAW, historian; b. Czarny Potok, Nowy Sacz, Poland, Feb. 17, 1937; s. Jan and Anna (Pulit) F.; m. Barbara (Rejdych), Mar. 13, 1961; 1 child, Piotr. M in Philolgy, High Sch. Pedagogics, Cracow, Poland, 1958. Tch. Secondary Sch., Cracow, Poland, 1958-64; with High Sch. Pedagogics, Cracow, 1959-81, pro-rector, 1971-75, rector, 1975-81; minister Edn. Ministry Edn., Warsaw, 1981-85; dir. Polish inst. Polish Inst., Vienna, 1986—; chief Ruch Literacki, Cracow, 1977-82, com. mem. Polish Acad. Sci., Warsaw, vice chmn. Cracow Branch Polish Acd. Sci., 1970-76. Editor: Zbigniew Unitowski, 1969, Prozaicy Dwudziestolecia Miedzywojennego, 1972Stefan Konaczkowski Jako Krytykihistoryk Literatury, 1976, Oswiatowe Pizekrge Izblizenia, 1985. Recipient Silver Cross of Merit Council of State, 1966, Nat. Edn. com. medal Minister Edn., 1979, Knights Cross Order of Polomia council of State, 1984, First and Second class award Minister of Sch. Mem. Zwigzek Literatow Polskick, Polish United Workers' Party. Home: ul Dobra 29m16, 00-344 Warsaw Poland Office: Polish Inst, AmGestade 7, 1010 Vienna Austria

FARON, JOHN FRANK, engineering executive; b Chgo., Aug. 27, 1933; s. John Theodore and Mary Rose (Szczecina) F.; m. Martha Darling, Nov. 2, 1957; children—Kathleen, Susan, Sandra, Edward. Student Ohio State U., 1951-53, U. So. Calif., 1962, Fresno State U., 1967-69; AB, U.S. Naval Postgrad. Sch., 1971; postgrad. George Washington U., 1972; MA, Calif. State U.-Dominguez Hills, 1982. Commd. ensign U.S. Navy, 1955; advanced through grades to comdr., 1968; pilot, 1953-78; intelligence officer, 1955-59; flight instr., 1959-61; combat pilot, Vietnam, 1962-64; aviation maintenance officer USS Hancock, 1964-66; dept. head tech. tng. Attack Squadron 125, 1966-69; exec. sec. to chief naval ops. sub-com. command, control and communication, 1971-73; chmn. ops. sub-group R-2508 enhancement program, mgr. USN portion 56M radar enhancement program, test pilot, 1973-78; ret., 1978. sr. engring. tech. writer, Comarco Engring. Inc., Ridgecrest, Calif., 1978-80; head systems effectiveness engring. group, sr. staff cons. PRC Ridgecrest Engring. Co., 1980-83; staff engr. Vitro Corp., Oxnard, Calif., 1984-87; advanced programs mgr. Computer Tech. Assocs., 1988—. Decorated Navy Commendation medal, 1973. Mem. AIAA (chmn. China Lake sect. 1986-87), Nat. Air Racing Group, U.S. Air Racing Assn. (hon.), Assn. Naval Aviation, Tailhook Assn., Assn. Old Crows, Soc. Flight Test Engrs. (pres. China Lake chpt. 1986-88), Delta Chi. Republican. Roman Catholic. Clubs: China Lake Men's Golf, So. Calif. Golf Assn., Calif. Golf Assn. Home: 618 Scott St Ridgecrest CA 93555 Office: 900 Heritage Dr Ridgecrest CA 93555

FAROUQ, FADLULLAH, geophysicist; b. Madinah, Saudi Arabia, Nov. 21, 1934; s. Farouq Ahmed Ali; Mohammed, Amira, Mrs. Hind, Eiman. BS in Chemistry and Geology, Cairo U., 1957; MS in Geophysics, St. Louis U., 1963. Served as officer Saudi Arabian Armed Forces, Riyadh, Saudi Arabia, 1957-66; mng. dir. Arabian Geophys. & Surveying, Jeddah, Saudi Arabia, 1966—, also bd. dirs.; lectr. King Saud U., Riyadh, 1963-70, King Abdul Aziz U., Jeddah, 1970—. Bd. dirs. Arab Petroleum Services Co., Tripoli, Libya, Arab Geophys. Service Co. Office: Arabian Geophys & Surveying, POB 2109, Jeddah 21451, Saudi Arabia

FARR, DENNIS LARRY ASHWELL, art galleries director; b. Apr. 3, 1929; s. Arthur William and Helen Eva (Ashwell) F.; m. Diana Pullein-Thompson, 1959; 2 children. B.A., M.A., Courtauld Inst. Art, London U.; D.Ltt. (hon.), U. Birmingham, 1981. Asst. Witt librarian Courtauld Inst. Art, 1952-54; asst. keeper Tate Gallery, 1954-64; curator Paul Mellon Collection, Washington, 1965-66; sr. lectr. fine art and dep. keeper Univ. Art Collections, U. Glasgow, 1967-69; dir. City Mus. and Art Gallery, Birmingham, 1969-80; dir. Courtauld Inst. Galleries, 1980—; Fred Cook Meml. lecture RSA, 1974; hon. art advisor Calouste Gulbenkian Found., 1969-73; mem. fine arts adv. com. Brit. Council, 1971-80, Wright Com. on Provincial Museums and Galleries, 1971-73, Mus. Assoc. Council, 1971-74, v.p., 1978-79, 80-81, pres., 1979-80; art panel Arts Council, 1972-77; exec. bd. ICOM (UK), 1976-85; com. Victorian Soc., 1980; exec. com. Assn. Art Historians, 1981—, chmn., 1983-86; history of art and design and complementary studies bd. CNAA, 1981-87. Author: William Etty, 1958; Catalogue of the Modern British School Collection, Tate Gallery (with M. Chamot and M. Butlin), 1964, British Sculpture since 1945, 1965, New Painting in Glasgow, 1968, Pittura Inglese, 1660-1840, 1975, English Art, 1870-1940, 1978;contbr. British Sculpture in the Twentieth Century, 1981, In Honor of Paul Mellon: Collector and Benefactor, 1986; (with W. Bradford) The Courtauld Collections, Tokyo, 1984; (with W. Bradford) The Northern Landscape, 1986; (with J. House et al) Impressionist and Post-Impressionist Masterpieces: The Courtauld Collection, 1987; gen. editor The Clarendon Studies in the History of Art, 1985—; contbr. articles to profl. jours. Trustee Birmingham Mus. and Art Gallery Appeal Fund, 1980—, chmn. trustees, 1978-80. Address: Courtauld Inst Galleries, Univ London, Woburn Sq, London WC1H OAA, England

FARR, JAMES FRANCIS, lawyer; b. Ludlow, Mass., Mar. 17, 1911; s. Charles H. and Stella (Greene) F.; A.B., Harvard U., 1933, LL.B., 1936. Admitted to Mass. bar, 1937; practiced in Boston, 1937—; sr. ptnr. Haussermann, Davison & Shattuck, 1948—; dir., clk. Durkee-Mower, Inc., Cape Cod Candle & Gift Shops, Inc., Prien Stone Research Labs., Inc., Camp Namequoit, Inc.; dir. H F G Co., Chgo., Savogran Co., Cape Cod Mgmt. Inc., J.J. Crimmings Co., Babson Bros. Co., Blumberg Co., Inc., Robert McF. Brown & Sons, Inc., Currier Cons., Inc. Bd. dirs., clk. Scottish Rite Mus. and Library, Inc.; former pres. Cambridge YMCA; former chmn. bd. dirs. New Eng. Deaconess Hosp.; treas., bd. dirs. New Eng. Edn. Soc. Served to lt. USCGR, World War II. Methodist (trustee), Mason (33 deg., Shriner, dir. grand lodge). Clubs: Cambridge Economy (past pres.), Cambridge, Harvard (Boston). Author: (with Mayo A. Shattuck) An Estate Planner's Handbook, 1953; Loring, A Trustee's Handbook Farr Revision, 1961; An Estate Planner's Handbook, 1966, co-author 1979 edit., supplement, 1982, 85, 87, 88. Home: 51 Martin St Cambridge MA 02138 Office: 176 Federal St Boston MA 02110

FARR, LEE EDWARD, physician; b. Albuquerque, Oct. 13, 1907; s. Edward and Mabel (Heyn) F.; m. Anne Ritter, Dec. 28, 1936 (dec.); children: Charles E., Susan E., Susan A., Frances A.; m. Miriam Kirk, Jan. 22, 1985. BS, Yale U., 1929, MD, 1933. Asst. pediatrics Sch. Medicine, Yale U., 1933-34; asst. medicine Hosp. of Rockefeller Inst. Med. Research, 1934-37, assoc. medicine, 1937-40; dir. research Alfred I. duPont Inst. of Nemours Found., Wilmington, Del., 1940-49; vis. assoc. prof. pediatrics Sch. Medicine, U. Pa., 1940-49; med. dir. Brookhaven Nat. Lab., 1948-62; prof. nuclear medicine U. Tex. Postgrad. Med. Sch., 1962-64, prof. nuclear and environ. medicine Grad. Sch. Bio-Med. Scis., U. Tex. at Houston, 1965-68; chief sect. nuclear medicine U. Tex.-M.D. Anderson Hosp. and Tumor Inst., 1962-67, prof. environ. health U. Tex. Sch. Pub. Health, Houston, 1967-68; head disaster health services Calif. Dept. Health, 1968, chief emergency health services unit, 1968-70, 1st chief bur. emergency med. services, 1970-73; Lippitt lectr. Marquette U., 1941; Sommers Meml. lectr. U. Oreg. Sch. Med., Portland, 1960; Gordon Wilson lectr. Am. Clin. and Climatol. Assn., 1956; Sigma Xi nat. lectr., 1952-53. Mem. adv. com. on naval med. research NRC, 1953-68, adv. com. on atomic bomb, 1953-78, chmn. 1954-76, adv. com. on medicine and surgery, 1955-56, exec. com., 1962-65; Naval Research Mission to Formosa, 1953; tech. adviser U.S. delegation to Geneva Internat. Conf. for Peaceful Uses Atomic Energy, 1955; mem. N.Y. Adv. Com. Atomic Energy, 1956-59; mem. AMA Com. Nuclear Medicine, 1963-66; mem. com. med. isotopes NASA Manned Spacecraft Ctr., 1966-68; mem. expert adv. panel radiation WHO, 1957-79; mem. Calif. Gov.'s Ad Hoc Com. Emergency Health Service, 1968-69; mem. sci. adv. bd. Gorgas Meml. Inst., 1967-72; mem. Naval Res. Adv. Com., 1970-78, numerous other sci. adv. bds., panels; cons. TRW Systems, Inc., 1966-70, Consol. Petroleum Co., Beverly Hills, Calif., 1946-70. Mem. alumni bd. Yale, 1962-65, mem. alumni fund, 1966-76. Served as lt. comdr. M.C., USNR, 1942-46; capt. (M.C.) USNR, ret. Recipient Mead Johnson award for pediatric research, 1940; decorated Gold Cross Order of Phoenix, Greece; Order of Merit, West Germany; named community leader in Am., 1969. Diplomate Nat. Bd. Med. Examiners, Am. Bd. Pediatrics. Fellow AAAS, Royal Soc. Arts, Am. Acad. Pediatrics, N.Y. Acad. Scis., Royal Soc. Health, Am. Coll. Nuclear Medicine (disting. fellow); mem. Soc. Pediatric Research, Soc. Exptl. Biology and Medicine (chmn. adv. com. atom bomb casualties 1954-76, naval research adv. com. 1970-78), Harvey Soc., Am. Pediatric Soc., Soc. Exptl. Pathology, Am. Soc. Clin. Investigation, Radiation Research Soc., A.M.A. (mem. council on sci. assembly 1960-70, chmn. 1968-70), Houston C. of C. (chmn. subcom. on quality in living 1966-68), Med. Soc. Athens (Greece) (hon.), Alameda County Med. Assn., Sigma Xi, Alpha Omega Alpha, Phi Sigma Kappa, Nu Sigma Nu, Alpha Chi Sigma. Club: Commonwealth (San Francisco). Author articles on nuclear medicine, protein metabolism, emergency med. services, radioactive and chem. environ. contaminants, environ. noise. Home: 2502 Saklan Indian Dr Apt 2 Walnut Creek CA 94595

FARR, LINUS GILBERT, lawyer, writer, researcher; b. Bound Brook, N.J., Aug. 28, 1951; s. Asa Hursey and Norma Ardell (Gilbert) F.; m. Joyce G. Farr, Sept. 11, 1976 (div.). B.A. in Govt. and Sociology, Bates Coll., 1974; J.D., U. Miami, 1977. Bar: N.J., Pa. and Fla. 1977, D.C. 1978. Legal asst. Somerset County Prosecutors Office, Somerville, N.J., 1977-78, asst. prosecutor, 1978-82; sole practice, Somerville, 1982—; tchr. Am. Ednl. Inst., Somerset County Coll. Life gold membership N.J. P.B.A.; 1980. Mem. Assn. Trial Lawyers Am., Nat. Dist. Attys. Assn., N.J. Bar Assn., Fla. Bar Assn., Pa. Bar Assn., D.C. Bar Assn., ABA, Somerset County Bar Assn. Home and Office: PO Box 1098 Somerville NJ 08876

FARR, ROBERT MACLAUGHLIN, psychology educator; b. Belfast, Ireland, Dec. 10, 1935; s. Robert James and Henrietta Williamson (MacLaughlin) F.; m. Ann-Marie Wood, Sept. 3, 1966; children: Angus John, Fiona Kate. BA in Psychology with hons., Queen's U., Belfast, 1957; MSc in Psychology, Queen's U., 1959; Div. Testimonium, Trinity Coll., Dublin, Ireland, 1962; PhD in Occupational Psychology, U. London, 1977. Asst. lectr. Queen's U., Belfast, 1962-64; research officer Ministry Def., London, 1964-66; lectr. Univ. Coll., London, 1966-79; prof. psychology, dept. head U. Glasgow, Scotland, 1979-83; prof. social psychology London Sch. Econs., 1983—, convener dept. social psychology, 1983—; chmn. Library Com. Brit. Library Polit. and Econ. Sci., London, 1987—. Co-editor Social Representations, 1984; contbr. over 50 articles to learned jours.; joint editor LSE Quar. Gov. NE London Poly., 1972-75; mem. psychol. bd. Council Nat. Academic Awards, London, 1980-84; mem. health services research com. Scottish Home and Health Dept., Edinburgh, 1982-83; sr. scholars com. U.S.-U.K. Ednl. Commn., London, 1984—. Fulbright scholar U. Mich., Ann Arbor, 1959-60; professorial fellow Social Sci. Research Council, Ecole des Hautes Etudes, Paris, 1976-77. Fellow Brit. Psychol. Soc. (pres. 1985-86); mem. British Nat. Com. Psychol. Sci. Home: Brownings Down, Warren Rd, Guildford GU1 2HQ, England

FARRALL, LYNDSAY ANDREW, science history educator; b. Melbourne, Australia, June 9, 1940; s. Gustavus Alexander Farrall and Fannie Doris (Olsson) Farrall Harris; m. Stephanie Nicolle Oats, Jan. 16, 1965; children: Jeremy, Reia. BS, U. Melbourne, 1961, BA, 1964; BA (hon.), U. Tasmania, Hobart, Australia, 1965; PhD, Ind. U., 1969. Lectr. English Papuan Med. Coll., Port Moresby, Papua New Guinea, 1966; lectr. history U. Papua New Guinea, Port Moresby, 1970-71, sr. lectr., 1972-76; vis. fellow philosophy U. Leeds, Eng., 1976-77; sr. research fellow U. Melbourne, 1977-79; sr. lectr. Deakin U., Geelong, Australia, 1979-84, dean humanities, 1983—, asst. prof., 1985—; vis. asst. prof. U. Pa., Phila., 1969; chmn. Mill Theater Co., Geelong, 1987—. Author: Origins and Growth of Eugenics Movement, 1985, Unwritten Knowledge, 1979; co-editor Social Studies of Science. Mem. nat. exec. com. Australian Student Christian Movement, 1961-63, co-pres. U. Melbourne group, 1961-62; chmn. organizing com. Australian Council Chs. Conf. on Faith, Sci. and Tech., Melbourne, 1983. Grantee Fulbright Found., 1967-69, Australian Research Grants Commn., 1978-86; Dyason research fellow U. Melbourne, 1977-79. Mem. Australasian Assn. for History, Philosophy and Social Studies of Sci. (sec. 1977-80, pres. 1981-83), Australian Hist. Assn., Soc. for Social Studies of Sci., History of Sci. Soc. Quaker. Office: Deakin U Sch Humanities, Geelong 3217, Australia

FARRAR, ELAINE WILLARDSON, artist; b. Los Angeles, Feb. 27, 1929; d. Eldon and Gladys Elsie (Larsen) Willardson; BA, Ariz. State U., 1967, MA, 1969, now doctoral candidate; children:Steve, Mark, Gregory, Leslie Jean, Monty, Susan. Tchr., Camelback Desert Sch., Paradise Valley, Ariz., 1966-69; mem. faculty Yavapai Coll., Prescott, Ariz., 1970—, chmn. dept. art, 1973-78, instr. art in watercolor and oil and acrylic painting, intaglio, relief and monoprints, 1971—; one-man shows include: R.P. Moffat's, Scottsdale, Ariz., 1969, Art Center, Battle Creek, Mich., 1969, The Woodpeddler, Costa Mesa, Calif., 1979; group show Prescott (Ariz.) Fine Arts Assn., 1982, 84, 86, N.Y. Nat. Am. Watercolorists, 1982; Ariz. State U. Women Images Now, 1986, 87; works rep. local and state exhibits; supt. fine arts dept. County Fair; com. mem., hanging chmn. Scholastic Art Awards; owner studio/gallery Willis Street Artists, Prescott. Mem. Mountain Artists Guild (past pres.), Nat. League Am. Pen Women (Prescott br.), NEA, Ariz. Edn. Assn., Nat. Art Edn. Assn., Ariz. Coll. and Univ. Faculty Assn., AAUW, Verde Valley Art Assn., Ariz. Women's Caucus for Art, Kappa Delta Pi, Phi

Delta Kappa. Republican. Mormon. Home: 635 Copper Basin Rd Prescott AZ 86303 Office: Yavapai Coll Art Dept 1100 E Sheldon Rd Prescott AZ 86301

FARRAR, JOHN EDSON, II, business executive, public relations consultant; b. Williamsport, Pa., Oct. 9, 1938; s. John Edson and Ruth (Price) F.; B.A. in Psychology, Pasadena Coll., 1963; postgrad. U. Calgary (Alta.), 1967, pub. relations certificate; postgrad. Claremont Grad. Sch., 1963-64, U. Calif. at Riverside, 1968-71; m. Judith Elizabeth Brodie, Jan. 23, 1965; 1 son, John Edson III. Evaluating social services dir. Head Start dental research project Loma Linda (Calif.) U. Sch. Dentistry, 1966-67; coordinator Head Start, Riverside County Econ. Opportunity Bd., Riverside, Calif., 1967; dir. community relations San Bernardino County Welfare and Probation Depts., San Bernardino, Calif., 1968-73; publicity and promotions coordinator in charge tourism and indsl. devel. Econ. Devel. Dept. San Bernardino County, 1973; dir. pub. relations Middle East, Boeing Comml. Airplane Co., Seattle, 1973-75; dir. pub. relations Northwest Hosp., Seattle, 1975-77; owner Craig & Farrar Pub. Relations and Advt., 1977-80; exec. v.p. Environ. Research and Devel. Corp., Seattle, 1980-82; owner Aamco Transmissions Ctr. of Bremerton (Wash.), 1982-86; stockbroker Prudential-Bache Securities, Seattle, 1984-86; prime bank note broker, London, 1986-87; ind. fin. cons. and broker, Kent, Wash., 1987—; lectr. pub. relations San Bernardino State Coll., Riverside U., Calif. State Coll., San Bernardino, Chaffee Coll.; chmn. dept. pub. relations and advt. City Coll., Seattle; instr. pub. relations U. Wash.; pub. relations cons. to pvt. bus., govt. Pres. bd. dirs. Frazee Community Center, 1970-71; bd. dirs., pub. relations chmn. Chief Seattle council Boy Scouts Am., promotions chmn. for camping in Southwestern U.S.; exec. bd. Seattle-King County Visitors and Conv. Bur.; mem. Republican Presdl. Task Force, 1982-84. Mem. Pub. Relations Soc. Am. (chpt. pres. 1971, 72, dist. chmn. govt. sect.), Calif. Social Workers Orgn. (v.p. 1970-71), Soc. for Internat. Devel., Nat. Pub. Relations Council Health and Welfare Services, Internat. Pub. Relations Assn., U.S.-Arab C. of C. Lodges: Masons, Rotary. Home: PO Box 603 Mercer Island WA 98040 Office: 25825 104th Ave SE Suite 417 Kent WA 98031

FARRAR, KENNETH LISTER, retired hotel proprietor; b. Menston, Ilkley, U.K., Nov. 13, 1927; s. Norman Hall and Mary (Lister) F.; m. Marion Lewis Ridgway, June 6, 1953; children: Nicholas, Katharine, Jennifer, Jonathan. Diploma in Textiles, Bradford Coll. of Further Edn., 1952. Tchr. textiles Bradford Coll. Further Edn., Yorkshire, 1954-64, Halifax Coll. Further Edn., Yorkshire, 1954-58; mgmt. trainee Farrar Bros Ltd., Halifax, 1952-55, dir., 1956-68; hotel proprietor Langdales Hotel, English Lakes, 1968-86. Hon. treas. Langdale Parochial Ch. Council, Ambleside, Cumbria, 1975-86. Fellow Inst. Mgmt. Services; mem. Companion & Assoc. Textile Inst., West Riding Film Soc., (chmn. 1965), Bradford Jr. C. of C. (pres. 1966-67), Brit. Jr. C. of C. (nat. v.p. 1967, regional group chmn., 1968), English Lakes Hotels and Caterers Assn. (chmn. 1978-79), Lakeland Hotels Tng. Group (chmn. 1980-81), Brit. Hotels, Restaurants and Caterers Assn. (chmn. no. div. 1985-86). Anglican. Home: Moor Farm, Torver, Coniston, Cumbria LA21 8BQ, England

FARRELL, EDGAR HENRY, lawyer, building components manufacturing executive; b. N.Y.C., Aug. 31, 1924; s. Edgar Henry and Lillian Sarah (Lancaster) F.; student Tex. A&M U., 1943, Stanford U., 1943-45, George Washington U. Law Sch., 1948-49; J.D., U. Md., 1950; postgrad., Harvard U. Bus. Sch., 1965; m. Mary Louise Whelan, May 3, 1952; children—Brooke Larkin Cragan, Elizabeth Lancaster, Kimberley Hopkins. Exec. sales asst. A.C. Gilbert Co., N.Y.C., 1950; asst. legal counsel U.S. Senate Crime Com., 1951; zone mgr. Life Mag., N.Y.C., 1951-52; account exec. Time Mag., N.Y.C., 1952-55, Phila., 1955-59, Detroit, 1959-62, nat. automotive sales mgr., Detroit, 1962-64, div. sales mgr., 1964-68, world automotive products sales mgr., 1968; regional mgr. communications/research Machines, Inc., Mich., Ohio, 1968; central advt. dir. Petersen Pub. Co., Detroit, 1969; chief exec., officer Internat. Concrete Bldg. Group, London, 1974-79; asst. to pres. Dillon Co., Akron, Ohio, 1979-80; pres. and chief exec. officer Bldg. Components Group, Akron, 1980—; pres. Motorhome Holidays Internat., U.S. Motorhome Corp., pres. BEK Press, Camp Am., Inc.; housing cons. Saudi Arabia, Nigeria, Sri Lanka. Publicity chmn. Youth for Eisenhower Com., N.Y.C., 1952; trustee Baldwin Library, Birmingham, Mich., 1962-65. Served to lt. U.S. Army, 1945-46; PTO. Recipient Low Cost Housing award Ministry of Housing, Sri Lanka, 1979. Mem. Am. Mktg. Assn., Nat. Assn. Home Builders, Phi Delta Theta, Gamma Eta Gamma, Phi Alpha Sigma. Republican. Episcopalian. Author: Computer Center Construction, 1984. Home and Office: 1 Woodbury Hill Woodbury CT 06798

FARRELL, EDWARD JOSEPH, educator; b. San Francisco, Mar. 28, 1917; s. Christopher Patrick and Ethel Ann (Chesterman) F.; m. Pearl Philomena Rongone, Aug. 21, 1954; children: Paul, Paula. B.Sc., U. San Francisco, 1939; M.A., Stanford U., 1942. Faculty U. San Francisco, 1941—, prof. math., 1968-82, prof. emeritus, 1982—; Guest lectr. regional and nat. meetings Nat. Council Tchrs. Math., 1966, 67, 69; cons. math. text pubs. Mem. adv. panels NSF, 1966—, dir. summer and in-service insts., 1960—, dir. confs. geometry, 1967, 68, 70-75; mem. rev. panel Sci. Books. Author math. reports; editor studies teaching contemporary geometry. Served with AUS, 1944-46. NSF faculty fellow, 1956-57. Mem. AAAS, Am. Assn. Physics Tchrs., Nat. Council Tchrs. Math., Sch. Sci. and Math. Assn. Republican. Roman Catholic. Home: 2526 Gough St San Francisco CA 94123

FARRELL, EDWARD WAGNER, dentist, educator; b. Youngstown, Ohio, Jan. 12, 1921; s. John Edward and Florence Mary (Wagner) F.; B.S., Muskingum Coll., 1943; D.D.S., Western Res. U., 1946; M.S., U. Mich., 1952; M.P.H., U. N.C., 1964; m. Marilyn Mae Quailey, June 7, 1947; children—Sandra Lynn, Scott Lee, Susan Jane, Sherry Lee. Dentist, VA Ohio, 1948-50; pvt. practice dentistry, Youngstown, Ohio, 1952-62; dental cons. Ohio Dept. Health, Cuyahoga Falls and Bowling Green, 1962-65; dental dir. Ariz. Dept. Health, Phoenix, 1965-69, Fla. Dept. Health, Jacksonville, 1969-75; dir. dental aux. edn. Ind. U. Sch. Dentistry, N.W. Campus, Gary, 1975-86 Served with U.S. Army, 1943-45, USN, 1946-48. Mem. ADA, Am. Assn. Public Health Dentists, Am. Public Health Assn., Am. Assn. Dental Schs., Ind. Dental Assn., N.W. Ind. Dental Soc., Chgo. Dental Soc., Delta Sigma Delta, Southlake Dental Study Club. Republican. Club: Rotary (Crown Point, Ind.). Author: Dental Materials Lecture/Study Guide, 1981; Oral Pathology Lecture/Study Guide, 1981; contbr. articles to profl. jours. Home: 907 Seneca Dr Crown Point IN 46307 Office: 3223 Broadway Gary IN 46409

FARRELL, JOHN STANISLAUS, manufacturing company executive; b. County Down, No. Ireland, May 19, 1931; came to Can., 1931, naturalized, 1931; s. George Stanislaus and Agnes Anna (McCartney) F.; m. Vyra June white, Aug. 7, 1959; children—John McCartney, Lizanne Jennifer. B.A.Sc. in Elec. Engring., U. Toronto, 1956. Registered profl. engr., Can. With ITT Can., Ltd., Montreal, Que., Can., 1962-69; dir. avionics and transmission ITT Can., Ltd., 1968-69; mktg. dir. Leigh Instruments, Ltd., Carleton Place, Ont., 1969-70; gen. mgr. Leigh Instruments, Ltd., 1970-73; pres., chief exec. officer Gestalt Internat. Ltd., Vancouver, B.C., Can., 1973-76; v.p. Cornat Industries, Ltd., Vancouver, 1976-78; sr. v.p. Versatile Corp., Vancouver, 1978-86; exec. dir. Rimquest Internat., Vancouver, 1986-88; pres. Versatech Trading and Devel. Corp., Vancouver, 1988—, also bd. dirs.; chmn., dir. Summerland Developments Ltd. Australia, Austoft Industries Ltd. Cyprus, Austoff Inc. USA; bd. dirs. Austoff Pty Ltd. Australia. Served with RCAF, 1950-59. Mem. Profl. Engrs. of Ont. Club: Vancouver Lawn Tennis and Badminton.

FARRELL, PETER CRAIG, health care company executive; b. Sydney, New South Wales, June 9, 1942; s. Leslie Joseph and Thelma Marie (Harrison) F.; m. Rosemary Elizabeth Wolstenholme, Sept. 18, 1965; children: Catherine Ann, Paul Antony, Michael James. BE, U. Sydney, 1964; SM, MIT, 1967; PhD, U. Wash., 1971; D of Sci., U. New South Wales, 1981. Cert. Engr. Research engr. Union Carbide Corp., Sydney, 1964-65, Montreal, 1965-66; research engr. Chevron Corp., San Francisco, 1967-68; indsl. liaison officer MIT, Cambridge, Mass., 1968-70; research asst. prof. U. Wash., Seattle, 1971-72; from lectr. to prof. U. New South Wales, Sydney, 1972—, vis. prof., 1977—; v.p. Baxter World Trade Corp., Chgo., 1984—, with exec. com., 1985—; mng. dir. Baxter Ctr. for Med. Research, Sydney, 1985—; bd. dirs. Baxter Ctr. Med. Research, Bellara Med. Products, Sydney. Author: Continuous Ambulatory Peritoneal Dialysis, 1981, In Search of Health and Fitness, 1985, also numerous revs. and articles to internat. and profl. jours. Chmn. fund raising com. U. New South Wales Sports Assn., Sydney, 1987-88. Fellow Australian Acad. Tech Sci. and Engring.; mem. Med. Engring. Research Assn. (chmn. 1983-86). Roman Catholic. Clubs: City Tattersalls, MIT of Australia, U. New South Wales Sr. COmmon Room. Home: 29D Shirley Rd, 2065 Wollstonecraft Australia Office: Baxter World Trade Corp Lake Cook Rd Northbrook IL 60015

FARRELLY, ALEXANDER, governor; b. St. Croix, V.I., Dec. 29, 1923; s. Patrick and Mary (Hardcastle) F.; widowed; children: Velma, Allyson, Richard, Steve (dec.). BA, St. John's Coll., 1951, LLB, 1954; LLM, Yale U., 1961. Former mem. Dem. Nat. Com., V.I.; now chmn. V.I. Dem. Party; now also gov. V.I. Participant, adminstr. Boy Scouts of Am. and Girl Scouts of Am. Roman Catholic. Address: PO Box 1239 Saint Thomas VI 00801 *

FARRER, WILLIAM CAMERON, lawyer; b. Cleve., Apr. 27, 1922; s. William M. and Jean (Cameron) F.; m. Constance Webb, July 25, 1953; children: William W., Cameron W., Jonathan S., Webb M. A.B., UCLA, 1943; J.D., Duke U., 1949. Bar: Calif. 1950. Practiced in Los Angeles, 1950—; atty. Hill, Farrer & Burrill, 1950—, partner, 1958—; del. Calif. Bar Conf., 1952-71; dir. First Fed. Savs. & Loan Assn. San Gabriel Valley. Mem. Calif. Coordinating Council on Higher Edn., 1970; Bd. dirs. Greater Los Angeles Zoo Assn., 1968-71; regent U. Calif., 1970-71; adv. bd. Orthopaedic Hosp., 1974-78; trustee U. Calif. at Los Angeles Found., 1970-74; bd. counsellors U. So. Calif. Law Center, 1972-77; bd. dirs. Dunn Sch., 1977-80; mem. legal com. Los Angeles Music Ctr., 1982—. Served to capt., inf. AUS, 1943-46. Decorated Bronze Star medal. Fellow Am. Bar Found. (life); mem. Am. Bar Assn. (ho. of dels. 1957-80, mem. council sect. internat. law 1964-72, bd. govs. 1973-76), UCLA Alumni Assn. (pres. 1969-71), Am. Law Inst., Am. Judicature Soc. (dir. 1972-75), Duke Law Alumni Council, Newcomen Soc. N.Am., Bel Air Assn (dir. 1981), Phi Gamma Delta, Phi Alpha Delta. Clubs: California, Beach (dir. 1972-73), Lincoln, Chancery (pres. 1973-74), Chevaliers du Tastevin; Balboa (Mex.). Home: 1047 Moraga Dr Los Angeles CA 90049 Office: 445 S Figueroa St 34th Floor Los Angeles CA 90071

FARRIMOND, GEORGE FRANCIS, JR., business educator; b. Peerless, Utah, Sept. 23, 1932; s. George Francis Sr. and Ruth (Howard) F.; m. Polly Ann Fowler, Mar. 21, 1988; children: George Kenneth, Ronald Kay, Carrie Frances, Holly Jean. BS, U. Utah, 1955; MBA, U. Mo., 1968; postgrad., Portland State U., 1979—. Cert. profl. contracts mgr. Enlisted USAF, 1955, advanced through grades to lt. col., 1971; master navigator USAF, various locations, 1955-71; flight commdr. 360th tactical elec. war squadron USAF, Saigon, Socialist Republic of Vietnam, 1971-72; chief procurement ops. USAF, Wright-Patterson AFB, Ohio, 1972-73, chief pricing ops. div., 1973-76; retired USAF, 1976; asst. prof. bus. So. Oreg. State Coll., Ashland, 1976-82, assoc. prof., 1982—; cons. small bus., Jackson County, Oreg., 1976-88; cons. Japanese mgmt., Jackson County, 1981-88. Author: (computer program) Spanish Verb Conjugation, 1980, (workbook) Pricing Techniques, 1983. Chmn. Wright-Patterson AFB div United Fund, 1973-76; little league coach various teams, Ark. and Mo., 1963-71; Sunday Sch. tchr. Ch. of Latter-day Saints, various states. Decorated Disting. Flying Cross, 5 Air medals; Minuteman Ednl. scholar Air Force Inst. Tech., 1964, Education with Industry scholar Air Force Inst. Tech., 1970. Mem. Am. Prodn. and Inventory Control Soc. (v.p. edn. com. 1982-84), DPMA, Air Force Soc., Soc. Japanese Studies, Beta Gamma Sigma. Republican. Home: PO Box 805 Ashland OR 97520 Office: So Oreg State Coll Sch Bus 1250 Siskiyou Blvd Ashland OR 97520

FARRINGTON, JERRY S., utility holding company executive; b. Burkburnett, Tex., 1934. B.B.A., North Tex. State U., 1955, M.B.A., 1958. With Tex. Electric Service Co., 1957-60; v.p. Tex. Utilities Co. (parent co.), Dallas, 1970-76, pres., 1983—; pres. Dallas Power & Light Co., chief exec. officer, 1976-83; now chmn. Tex. Utilities Electric Co., Dallas; pres. Tex. Utilities Fuel Co., Dallas, Tex. Utilities Co. (parent), Dallas. Office: Tex Utilities Co 2001 Bryan Tower Dallas TX 75201 *

FARRINGTON, WILLIAM BENFORD, investment analyst; b. N.Y.C., Mar. 10, 1921; s. Harold Phillips and Edith C. (Aitken) F.; B.C.E., Cornell U., 1947, M.S., 1949; Ph.D., Mass. Inst. Tech., 1953; m. Frances A. Garratt, 1949 (div. 1955); children: William Benford, Phyllis Ashley, Timothy Colfax; m. Gertrude E. Eby, Jan. 3, 1979. Radio engr. Naval Research Labs., 1942-43; dir. Read Standard Corp., 1948-55; plant engr. Hope's Windows, Inc., 1950-51; instr. geology, geophysics U. Mass., 1953-54; research geophysicist Humble Oil & Refining Co., 1954-56; lectr. U. Houston, 1955-56; sr. investment analyst Continental Research Corp., N.Y.C., 1956-61; pres., dir. Farrington Engring. Corp., 1958-67; partner Farrington & Light Assos., Laguna Beach, Calif., 1967-82, Farrington Assocs., 1982—; v.p. Empire Resources Corp., 1961-62; asst. v.p. Empire Trust Co., 1962-64; dir. Commonwealth Gas Corp., N.Y.C.; sci. dir. Select Com. on Govt. Research, U.S. Ho. of Reps., 1964-65; lectr. U. Calif. at Los Angeles, 1968-72; sr. cons. Trident Engring. Assos., Annapolis, Md., 1965—; corporate asso. Technology Assos. So. Calif., 1971—. Chmn. crusade Am. Cancer Soc., Jamestown, N.Y., 1951. Chartered fin. analyst; registered geologist, Calif. Fellow AAAS, Fin. Analysts Fedn.; mem. Am. Assn. Petroleum Geologists, AIME, Am. Petroleum Inst., Am. Inst. Aeros. and Aeronautics, Geol. Soc. Am., Los Angeles Soc. Fin. Analysts, Sigma Xi. Episcolalian. Author articles in field. Home: 1565 Skyline Dr Laguna Beach CA 92651

FARRIOR, J. REX, JR., lawyer; b. Tampa, Fla., June 5, 1927; s. J. Rex and Lera Spotswood (Finley) F.; m. Mary Lee Nunnally, May 30, 1958; children—J. Rex III, Preston Lee, Hugh Nunnally, Robert Pendleton. Student Auburn U., 1945-46; B.S. in Bus. Adminstrn., U. Fla., 1949, J.D., 1951. Bar: Fla. 1951. Assoc. Shackleford, Farrior, Stallings & Evans, P.A. and predecessors, Tampa, Fla., 1951-55, ptnr., 1955—, sr. ptnr., past pres., also bd. dirs.; permanent guest lectr. U. Fla., Coll. Engring.; lectr. U. Fla., Stetson U.; mem. Fed. Jud. Nominating Comm., 1980—. Pres. Pres. Round Table of Tampa, 1965. Served with USNR, World War II. Named to Hall of Fame, U. Fla., 1951. Fellow Am. Coll. Probate Counsel, Fellows of ABA; mem. ABA (ho. of dels. 1976-81), Fla. Bar (pres. Fla. young lawyers sect. 1958, pres. 1975-76, Most Outstanding Local Bar Pres. 1977), Hillsborough County Bar Assn. (pres. 1966), Acad. Fla. Trial Lawyers, Am. Judicature Soc., Inter-Am. Bar Assn., Am. Counsel Assn. (pres. 1983-84), Assn. Trial Lawyers Am., Greater Tampa C. of C. (bd. govs.), Phi Delta Phi, Kappa Alpha Alumni Assn. (pres. 1957). Episcopalian. Clubs: Rotary, Sertoma (founder club 1952, pres. club 1964) Tampa), Masons, Shriners. Office: PO Box 3324 Tampa FL 33601

FARRIS, MILTON GLENN, oil company executive; b. Rockwood, Tenn., Oct. 13, 1906; s. Oscar Alexander and Myrtle Amy (Derrick) F.; LL.B., Atlanta Law Sch., 1935; m. Elizabeth Herzberg, Nov. 15, 1934; children—Sandra Glyn, Janet Gail, Milton Carl, William, Stuart. Admitted to Ga. Bar, 1935; practiced in Atlanta 1935—; asso. Atlanta div. Gulf Oil Corp., 1927—, mgr. bus analysis, market research, 1954-59, mgr. marketing services, 1960-62, mgr. Atlanta div., 1962-65, v.p. 1965—. Alderman, City Council, Atlanta, 1952-69; county commr. Fulton County, 1971—. Pres. bd. trustees Atlanta Pub. Library, 1940-52, awarded Trustee Citation at ALA Chgo. Conf. 1951. Mem. Am. Bar Assn., Ga. Bar Assn., West End Business Men's Assn. (dir.). Methodist. Mason (past master), Lion (past pres.), Kiwanian. Clubs: Commerce, Capital City, Atlanta City (Atlanta). Home: 580 River Valley Rd NW Atlanta GA 30328 Office: Fulton County Ct House Annex Atlanta GA 30303

FARRUKH, MARWAN OMAR, construction company executive; b. Beirut, July 25, 1946; s. Omar Abdullah and Amneh Amin (Hilmi) F.; m. Kamar Nazih Baalbaki, June 1, 1978; children: Ghina, Mohammad. BS in Structural Engring., Ain Shams U., Cairo, 1970; MS in Structural Engring., U. Calif., Berkeley, 1978. Pvt. practice in structural engring. Beirut, 1971-72; bridge engr. W.S. Atkins & Ptnrs., Epsom, Surrey, Eng., 1972-74; structural engr. Khatib & Alami, Beirut, 1974-75; engr.-in-charge Sogex Contracting & Trading, Muscat, Beruit, Oman, Lebanon, 1975-77; sect. leader Sogex Services, Ltd., London, 1978-79, 1980-81; sect. leader Envirogenics System Co., Los Angeles, 1979-80; dep. project mgr., mgr. engring. and procuring Pegel Arabia, Dammam, Saudi Arabia, 1981—. Mem. Am. Concrete Inst., Prestressed Concrete Inst., Post-tensioning Inst., Concrete Reinforcing Steel Inst., Internat. Assn. Bridge and Structural Engring. Office: Pegel Arabia, PO Box 2364, Dammam 31451, Saudi Arabia

FARSHIDI, ARDESHIR B., cardiologist, educator, cardiac electrophysiologist, researcher; b. Kerman, Iran, June 13, 1945; came to U.S., 1972, naturalized, 1977; s. Jamshid and Farangis F.; m. Katayoon Kavoussi, Jan. 2, 1982. M.D., Tehran U., 1969. Diplomate Am. Bd. Internal Medicine, Am. Bd. Cardiovascular Disease. Intern, Washington, 1972-73; resident U. Pa., Phila., 1973-75, resident in cardiology, 1975-77, electrophysiologist, 1977-78; asst. prof. medicine U. Conn., Farmington, 1978-79, dir. electrophysiology, 1982-84, assoc. prof., 1982-84, attending cardiologist Hosp., 1982-84, dir. electrophysiology, 1982-84; co-dir. electrophysiology Yale U., 1979-82, asst. prof. medicine, 1979-82, attending cardiology Hosp., 1979-82, co-dir. electrophysiology, 1979-82; chief cardiology sect. VA Hosp., Newington, Conn., 1982-84; dir. electrophysiology Los Angeles Heart Assn., 1984—. Mem. editorial bd.: Jour. Am. Coll. Cardiology, 1983; contbr. articles in field to profl. jours. Served to lt. Iran Army, 1969-72. Am. Heart Assn. researcher, 1981. Fellow ACP, Am. Coll. Cardiology, Am. Heart Assn.; mem. Am. Fedn. Clin. Research, Am. Electrophysiologic Soc. Zoroastrian. Research on clin. cardiac electrophysiology and arrhythmia. Home: 1508 Pandora Ave West Los Angeles CA 90024 Office: Los Angeles Heart Inst 2131 W 3d St Los Angeles CA 90057

FARUQUI, MOHAMMED NASEEM ASIM, consulting civil engineer; b. Mount Abu, Rajasthan, India, Jan. 11, 1946; s. Mohammed Kazim Faruqui and Naseema Khatoon; m. Seema Naseem Abdulqadeer, Feb. 1971; children—Omer, Saima. B.E. in Civil Engring., Nadirshaw Eduljee Dinshaw Govt. Engring. Coll., Karachi, Pakistan, 1968. Civil engr. in design Engring. Cons., Karachi, 1968-71; design engr. Babar & Assocs., Karachi, 1972-73; supervising engr. Mannai Engring., Bahrain, 1973-75; resident engr. Pan Arab Cons. Engrs., Safat, Kuwait, 1975—. Mem. Am. Concrete Assn., Soc. Engrs.-Kuwait, Soc. Engrs.-Bahrain. Avocations: stamp collecting, photography. Home: B-258 Block L, Nazimbad Karachi Pakistan Office: Pan Arab Cons Engrs, Salhiya Comml Ctr 4th Fl, Fahd Salem St PO Box 1031, Safat Kuwait

FARWELL, CHARLES, IV, physician; b. New Orleans, Dec. 1, 1926; s. Charles Alphonzo and Edwa (Stewart) F.; student Va. Mil. Inst., 1944-45, U. Pa., 1945; M.D., Tulane U., 1949; m. Josephine Gibert, July 22, 1968; children—Laura Farwell, Samuel Adams III, Pharr Adams. Intern, Charit Hosp., New Orleans, 1949-50; psychiat. resident Springfield Psychiat. Hosp., 1950-51, VA, 1951-52; practice medicine specializing in family practice and psychiatry, Wheaton, Md., 1952—; pres. vis. staff Suburban hosp., Bethesda, Md., 1961. Med. dir. Planned Parenthood of Montgomery County, 1958. Pres., Univ. Bldg. Fund, Montgomery County, 1967-68; mem. Nat. Symphony Assn. Recipient med. econs. awards also awards Wheaton Rescue Squad, Boys Club, Silver Spring, Md. Fellow Am. Acad. Family Practice (charter); mem. Am. Psychiat. Assn. (life assoc.), So. Med. Assn. (life), Montgomery County Med. Soc., Med. and Chirurg. Soc. Med., Md. Med. Soc. (jour. rep. 1960-61), Md. Acad. Family Physicians (treas., dir.), SAR, Nu Sigma Nu. Optimist (pres. 1955, lt. gov. 1956) (So. Md.). Episcopalian (mem. vestry). Club: Wheaton (Md.) Chess (founder 1960). Contbr. articles to med. jours. Address: 11406 Veirs Mill Rd Wheaton MD 20902

FARWELL, HARLEIGH ELLIS, construction consultant executive; b. Palisades, Wash., Sept. 23, 1921; s. Harley Elmer and Cecil Nan (Johnston) F.; student public schs.; m. Suzanne Edwina Boehm, Jan. 8, 1966; children by previous marriage—E. Kay Farwell Gilbertson, Sharon A. Farwell Scriba, Marilyn Z. Farwell Gala, Ellis D., Donovan W., Daniel A. Constrn. supt., gen. supt. Bank Bldg. Corp., St. Louis, 1952-60; constrn. supt., project mgr. Howard S. Wright Constrn. Co., Seattle, 1960-73, v.p., Seattle, 1973-80, sr. v.p., 1980-83; pres. Farwell Constrn. Services, Inc., Redmond, Wash., 1983—; guest lectr. Mem. accessibility design adv. com. Easter Seal Soc. Wash., 1978—. Served with AUS, 1944-45. Decorated Purple Heart. Mem. Am. Soc. Mil. Engrs., Am. Concrete Inst., Am. Arbitration Assn. Research on cost improvement methods, devel. and upgrading of unit price data. Home and Office: 15715 NE 66th Pl Redmond WA 98052

FASCETTA, SALVATORE CHARLES, pharmaceutical company executive; b. N.Y.C., Oct. 14, 1940; s. Nicholas and Anne (Piedevillano) F.; B.S. in Pharmacy, St. John's U., 1963; m. Mary Barbara Aprile, Aug. 8, 1964; children—Christopher, Kevin, Timothy. Devel. pharmacist Wallace Labs., Cranbury, N.J., 1967, group leader pharm. devel., 1968-70, mgr. pharm. devel., 1970-74; dir. pharm. devel. Knoll Pharm. Co., Whippany, N.J., 1974-77, prodn. mgr., 1978-79, plant mgr., 1979-84, v.p. plant ops., 1984—. Pres. East Windsor Rescue Squad, 1969-70. Mem. Am. Pharm. Assn. (Lunson Richardson Pharm. award, 1963), Acad. Pharm. Scis., Pharm. Mfrs. Assn., Soc. Mfg. Engrs., Soc. Chem. Engrs., Parenteral Drug Assn., Nat. Assn. Retail Druggists, Internat. Soc. Pharm. Engrs., Am. Prodn. and Invetory Control Soc., Am. Soc. Quality Control, Am. Assn. Pharm. Scis. Roman Catholic. Home: 13 Dunbar Dr RD 4 Trenton NJ 07691 Office: 30 N Jefferson Rd Whippany NJ 07981

FASCIOTTI, VITTORIO, mechanical engineer; b. Milano, Aug. 1, 1930; s. Luigi and Maria (Chiapello) F. D in Ingegneria Meccanica, Politecnico, Milano, 1956; postgrad., Scuola teologica dei cappuccini, Trento, Italy, 1973. Vice capo reparto produzio ne tubi Falck, Milano, 1956-57; servizio progettazione meccanica Edison Chimica, Milano, 1958-59; progettazione turbine Escher Wyss, Zurich, Switzerland, 1960-61; libero traduttore 1962-69; redattore Neue Stadt Verlag, Munchen, 1969-71, direttore, 1972-80; direttore Citta Nuova Editrice, Roma, 1981—. Roman Cattolica. Office: Citta Nuova Editrice, Via degli Scipioni 265, Rome Italy I-00192

FASIANI, LIVIO, data processing executive; b. Milan, Italy, Apr. 7, 1945; s. Santino and Olga (Pareto) F.; m. Arreghini Annamaria, Sept. 30, 1948; children: Roberto, Stefano. BChemEngring, Politecnico Milan, 1968. System engr. Italsiel, Rome, 1970-72, Sperry Univac, Milan, 1972-75; product mgr. ICL, Milan, 1975-76, br. mgr., 1976-80, mgr. mktg., 1980-81, mgr. sales, 1981-83; mng. dir. Datapoint Italia, Milan, 1983—. Served with Italian Air Force, 1969-70. Office: Datapoint Italia, Via Tazzoli 6, 20154 Milan Italy

FASS, FRED WILLIAM ROBERT, geologist, consultant; b. Milw., Oct. 30, 1951; s. Fred William and Barbara Ann (Schwerdtmann) F. B.S., Mich. Tech. Univ., 1975; M.S. (grad. research asst.), Univ. Mo., Rolla, 1981. Geol. technician Coastal Mining Co., St. Louis, 1977; temp. geologist Amoco Minerals Co., Englewood, Colo., 1978, Asarco, Inc., Knoxville, Tenn., 1979; geologist I Cities Service Co. Tulsa, 1981, geologist II, Oklahoma City, 1981-83; jr. processing geophysicist Digicon Geophys. Corp., Oklahoma City, 1984; cons. geology, Milw., 1984—. Mem. AIME, Am. Assn. Petroleum Geologists, Oklahoma City Geol. Soc., Sigma Xi, Sigma Gamma Epsilon. Avocations: Rock and mineral collecting; singing; camping; canoeing; hiking. Home: 1654 E Newton Ave Milwaukee WI 53211

FASSIO, VIRGIL, newspaper publishing company executive; b. Pitts., Aug. 10, 1927; s. Domenico and Carolina (Pia) F.; m. Shirley DeVirgilis; children—Richard, David, Michael. B.A. with honors, U. Pitts., 1949. Founder, editor, pub. Beechview News, Pitts., 1947-51; reporter Valley Daily News, Tarentum, Pa., 1950, circulation mgr., 1951-58; circulation dir. Morning News and Evening Jour., Wilmington, Del., 1958-65; circulation dir. Detroit Free Press, 1965-71, v.p., bus. mgr., 1971; v.p., circulation dir. Chgo. Tribune, 1972-76; v.p., gen. mgr. Seattle Post-Intelligencer, 1976, pub., 1978—; lectr. Am. Press Inst.; cons., lectr. in field. Contbr. articles to profl. jours. Del. White House Conf. on Children, 1960, 70; bd. dirs. Pacific Mus. Flight, Pacific Sci. Ctr. Found., Corp. Council of Arts; bd. regents Seattle U., Washington Council on Internat. Trade; pres. Seattle-King County Conv. and Visitors Bur., 1982-84; bd. dirs. Seattle Goodwill Industries, Medic 1 Emergency Med. Services Found., Boys and Girls Clubs of King County, Wash. Council of Internat. Trade. Served with USNR, 1945-46, comdr. USNR (ret.). Recipient Frank Thayer award U. Wis., 1972; Varsity Letterman of Distinction award U. Pitts. 1974. Mem. Internat. Circulation Mgrs. Assn. (Man of Yr. award 1964), Inter-State Circulation Mgrs. Assn. (sec.-treas. 1954-65, Outstanding Achievement award 1967), Seattle C. of C. (bd. dirs.), Downtown Seattle Devel. Assn. (treas.), Allied Daily Pubs. Assn., Am. Newspaper Pubs. Assn. (vice chmn. industry affairs com. 1982-86),

Hist. Soc. Seattle and King County (bd. dirs.), Medic One Found. (bd. dirs.). Clubs: Rainier, Wash. Athletic (bd. dirs.). Lodge: Rotary (bd. dirs.). Office: Seattle Post-Intelligencer 101 Elliott Ave West Seattle WA 98111

FASSOULIS, SATIRIS GALAHAD, communications company executive; b. Syracuse, Aug. 19, 1922; s. Peter George and Anastasia P. (Limpert) F. B.A., Syracuse U., 1945. Vice pres. Commerce Internat. Corp., N.Y.C., 1945-48; pres. Commerce Internat. Corp., 1949-75; chmn. Global Communications Co., N.Y.C., 1976—, Global Def. Products Inc., N.Y.C., 1976—; dir Comml. Exports (Overseas) Ltd., U.K., CIC Internat. Ltd., N.Y.C. Mem. U.S. Congl. Adv. Bd.; bd. dirs. Better Life Enterprises for the Blind, Inc.; mem. Rep. Presdl. Task Force. Served to 1st lt., USAAF, 1941-45. Decorated Purple Heart, Air medal with 3 oak leaf clusters. Mem. N.Y. C. of C., Am. Def. Preparedness Assn., Navy League U.S., Armed Forces Communications and Electronics Assn., U.S. Naval Inst., Air Force Assn., Assn. of U.S. Army, Internat. Platform Assn. Republican. Episcopalian. Clubs: N.Y. Athletic, Order of Ahepa. Home: 20 Waterside Plaza New York NY 10010 Office: 10 Waterside Plaza New York NY 10010

FAST, JUDITH ELLEN STEPHENSON, scientist; consultant, researcher; b. Welch, W.Va., May 8, 1942; d. Leslie James and Rosa Ellen (Mullens) Stephenson; children: Carrie Lisa, Randolph Leslie. AA in Nursing, St. Petersburg Jr. Coll., 1971; BS in Biology cum laude, U. Tampa, 1973; MS in Physiology, U. Houston, 1977; DPh in Internat. Health, (traineeship), U. Tex. Sch. Pub. Health, Houston, 1988. RN, Fla., La., Tex.; lic. practical nurse, Calif., Fla., W.Va., Tex.; cert. first aid and CPR instr.; cert juvenile probation officer. Staff nurse Wyoming Gen. Hosp., Mullens, W.Va., 1967-69, St. Anthony's Hosp., St. Petersburg, Fla., 1969-71, team leader, charge nurse telemetry CCU and Med. ICU, 1971-74; teaching fellow in biology U. Houston, 1974-77; staff and charge nurse M.D. Anderson Hosp., Houston, 1974-77, critical care program dir., instr., 1977-79, dir. oncology program, 1979-80, mgmt. analyst, 1980-84; nurse mgmt. info. systems analyst Harris County Hosp. Dist., Houston, 1984-85, mem., chmn., vice chmn. various coms.; nurse clinician Harris County Juvenile Probation Dept., Houston, 1985-87; research faculty assoc. Baylor Coll. Medicine, Houston, 1987—. Creator, author 52 ednl. videotapes on critical care, 1978-79; creator, author hosp. patient classification and staffing systems; researcher in field; speaker profl. groups; author articles. Judge exhibits Houston Sci. Fair, 1983-86; vol. first aid, CPR, ARC Olympic Festival Summer, 1986, Am. Cancer Soc. research survey, 1982. Recipient numerous awards. Mem. Am. Assn. Critical Care Nurses (nat. and Gulf Coast chpts.), Oncology Nursing Soc. (cons.), Am. Pub. Health Assn., Greater Houston Hosp. Mgmt. Systems Soc., Houston Consortium Nurses (charter), Assn. Women in Sci. (Houston, sec. 1983-84), Fedn. Houston Profl. Women (del., affiliate), Houston Area League for IBM Personal Computer Users, Alpha Chi. Office: Baylor Population Program Ob/gyn Dept One Baylor Plaza Houston TX 77030

FATEMI, ALI M.S., economist, educator; b. Isfahan, Iran, May 15, 1935; came to U.S., 1954; s. Farrajollah Mesbah Seifpour Fatemi and Tajelmolook Fatemi; m. Jaleh Amir Tahmasseb, Sept. 26, 1959 (dec. Aug. 1975); children: Johann Kevin, Roxanna; m. Niloufar Moaven, Sept. 21, 1978; 1 child, Alexandre. BS, Fairleigh Dickinson U., 1957; MA, New Sch. for Social Research, 1964, PhD, 1967. Economist UN, N.Y.C., 1958-65; asst. prof. U. Akron, Ohio, 1965-67, assoc. prof., 1967-75, prof., chmn. dept. econs., 1975-80; editor-in-chief Iran va Jahan weekly, Paris, 1980-86; dir. Iran Ctr. for Documentation, Paris, 1980-86; chmn., prof. dept. econs. Am. U., Paris, 1986—; sec.-gen. Front for Liberation Iran, Paris, 1982-85. Author: The Role of OPEC in Economic Development, 1967, Money and Banking in the U.S. U.K. and France, 1987, (with others) The Structure of Iranian Economy, 1978; editor: The Political Economy of the Middle East, 1970. Chmn. bd. Model Cities Devel. Corp., Adron, 1972-74. Fellow Middle East Assn. (hon.); mem. AAUP (past pres. Ohio Conf.), Soc. for Iranian Studies, Am. Econ. Assn., Econometric Soc., ACLU, Omcron Delta Epsilon (advisor). Office: 27 Ave de Bretteville, 92200 Neuilly Sur Seine France Office: Am U of Paris, 31 Ave Bosquet, 75007 Paris France

FATHAUER, THEODORE FREDERICK, meteorologist; b. Oak Park, Ill., June 5, 1946; s. Arthur Theodore and Helen Ann (Mashek) F.; m. Mary Ann Neesan, Aug. 8, 1981. BA, U. Chgo., 1968. Cert. cons. meteorologist. Research aide USDA No. Dev. Labs., Peoria, Ill., 1966, Cloud Physics Lab., Chgo., 1967; meteorologist Sta. WLW radio/TV, Cin., 1967-68, Nat. Meteorol. Ctr., Washington, 1968-70, Nat. Weather Service, Anchorage, 1970-80; meteorologist-in-charge Nat. Weather Service, Fairbanks, Alaska, 1980—; instr. U. Alaska, Fairbanks, 1975-76, USCG aux., Fairbanks and Anchorage, 1974—. Contbr. articles to weather mags. Bd. dirs. Fairbanks Concert Assn., 1988—. Recipient Oustanding Performance award Nat. Weather Service, 1972, 76, 83, 85, 86, Fed. Employee of Yr. award, Fed. Exec. Assn., Anchorage, 1978. Mem. Am. Meteorol. Soc. (TV seal of approval), Am. Geophys. Union, AAAS, Royal Meteorol. Soc., Western Snow Conf. Republican. Lutheran. Office: Nat Weather Service Forecast Office 101 12th Ave Box 21 Fairbanks AK 99701

FATOVIC, JOHN, electrical engineer, consultant; b. Sestrunj, Yugoslavia; s. Ciril and Stosija (Svorinic) F. B.E.S., Stevens Tech. U., 1960, M.S.E.E., 1964. Engr. XLO, Englewood, N.J., 1969-72; engring. cons. Bendix Corp., Teterboro, N.J., 1973-76; engr. Conrac Corp., West Caldwell, N.J., 1976-79, Exxon Enterprises, Florham Park, N.J., 1979-81; engring. cons. Bendix, Conrac Corp., Teterboro, N.J., 1981—; pres. CDF Industries Inc., Teterboro, N.J., 1972—. Patentee in field. Served with U.S. Army, 1954-56; Korea. Mem. IEEE. Home: 94 Passaic Valley Rd Montville NJ 07045

FAUBER, J(OSEPH) EVERETTE, III, architect; b. Lynchburg, Va., Mar. 15, 1938; s. Joseph Everette, Jr. and Ella Whitmore (Williams) F.; m. Mary Graves Conley, Apr. 24, 1965; children: Mary Reed, Elizabeth Alexander. BArch, U. Va., 1963. Registered architect, Va., S.C., Md. With Vosbeck-Ward and Assocs., Architects, Alexandria, Va., 1963-65, Vosbeck, Vosbeck and Assocs., Architects, Alexandria, 1965-67; assoc. Vosbeck Vosbeck Kendrick Redinger, Architecture-Engring.-Planning, Alexandria, 1967-70; assoc. J. Everette Fauber, Jr., AIA, Architect, Lynchburg, 1970-78; architect Fauber Garbee, Inc., Forest, Va., 1978-86, Fauber Architects, P.C., 1986—. Mem. bldg. code and appeals bd. Fairfax County, Va., 1969-70, Bedford County, Va., 1974—; chmn. bd. Fairfax Activity Ctr. for Retarded Adults, 1969-70, Lynchburg Com. on Employment of Handicapped, 1971-72, Archtl. Barriers Com., Lynchburg, 1971-74; bd. dirs. Alexandria unit Am. Cancer Soc., 1968-70, Alexandria Boys Club, 1967-70, United Givers Fund Central Va., 1971-72; pres. Lynchburg Area Assn. Retarded Citizens, 1974-75; chmn. Bedford County Bd. Suprs., 1979; treas. Central Va. Planning Dist. Com., 1976-77, chmn., 1977-78; chmn. Central Va. Transp. Planning Council, 1977-78, Bedford Meml. Found., 1987—, Bedford County Fin. Com., 1979; bd. mgrs. New London Acad., 1985-88, Jr. Achievement of Lynchburg, 1986—. Mem. AIA, Va. Assn. Professions, Bldg Ofcls. Conf. Am., Soc. Archtl. Historians, Nat. Trust for Hist. Preservation, U. Va. Alumni Assn. (pres. Lynchburg chpt. 1988—), Sch. of Architecture Assn., Va. Found. for Archtl. Edn., Bldg. Ofcls. and Code Adminstrs. Internat., Nat. Acad. Code Adminstrn., Va. Assn. Counties, Nat. Assn. Regional Councils, Va. Assn. Planning Dist. Commns., Bedford County C. of C. (pres. 1985, 86), Greater Lynchburg C. of C. (v.p. 1977-78), U. Va. Archtl. Alumni Assn., Va. Assn. Professions. Lodge: (pres. Lynchburg club 1976-77). Home: Glen Mary Farm Route 1 Box 777 Forest VA 24551 Office: Fauber Architects PC Forest Square Forest VA 24551

FAULKNER, DEXTER HAROLD, magazine publishing executive, editor; b. Grand Island, Nebr., Sept. 10, 1937; s. Jack L. and Wanetta May (Howland) F.; student U. Calif.-Fresno, 1956-58, Ambassador Coll., 1958-60; m. Shirley Ann Hume, Jan. 11, 1959; children—Nathan Timothy, Matthew Benjamin. Exec. editor Plain Truth Mag; editor Good News mag., Youth/88 mag. and Worldwide News tabloid internat. div. Ambassador Coll., Sydney, Australia, 1960-66, news research asst. dir. Ambassador Coll. Editorial, Pasadena, Calif., 1966-71, regional editor Plain Truth mag., Washington, 1971-75, asst. mng. editor, Pasadena, 1975-78, mng. editor, 1980-82, exec. editor, 1982—, mng. editor Good News mag., Worldwide News-Tabloid, 1978-85, editor, 1986—; mng. editor Youth/88 mag., 1981-85, editor, 1986—; instr. mass communications Ambassador Coll., 1980—; columnist Just One More Thing . . ., By the Way, Just Between Friends. Mem. Inst. Journalists (London), Profl. Photographers Am. Inc., Bur. Freelance Photographers (London), Nat. Press Club, World Affairs Council (Los Angeles), Internat. Assn. Bus. Communicators, Nat. Press Photographers Assn., Am. Mgmt. Assn., Sigma Delta Chi. Mem. Worldwide Ch. God. Contbr. articles, photos on internat. relations, social issues to Plain Truth mag., Good News mag., Worldwide News Publs. Club: Commonwealth of Calif. Home: 7859 Wentworth St Sunland CA 91040 Office: Plain Truth Mag 300 W Green St Pasadena CA 91129

FAULKNER, EDWIN JEROME, insurance company executive; b. Lincoln, Nebr., July 5, 1911; s. Edwin Jerome and Leah (Meyer) F.; m. Jean Rathburn, Sept. 27, 1933. B.A., U. Nebr., 1932; M.B.A., U. Pa., 1934. With Woodmen Accident & Life Co., Lincoln, 1934—; successively claim auditor, v.p. Woodmen Accident & Life Co., 1934-38, pres., dir., 1938-77, chmn. bd., chief exec. officer, 1977-83, hon. chmn., exec. counsel, 1983—; pres., dir. Comml. Mut. Surety Co., 1938—; dir. Lincoln Telecommunications Inc., Universal Surety Co., Inland Ins. Co.; past dir. 1st Nat. Bank & Trust Co., Lincoln; chmn. Health Ins. Council, 1959-60; mem. adv. council on social security HEW, 1974-75. Author: Accident and Health Insurance, 1940, Health Insurance, 1960; Editor: Man's Quest for Security, 1966. Chmn. Lincoln-Lancaster County Plan Commn., 1948-67; mem. medicare adv. com. Dept. Def., 1957-70; Neb. Republican State Finance chmn., 1968-73; Chmn., trustee Bryan Meml. Hosp.; trustee Doane Coll., 1961-70, Lincoln Found., Am. Coll. Life Underwriters, Cooper Found., Newcomen Soc. N.Am.; chmn. bd. trustees U. Nebr. Found.; bd. dirs. Nebraskans for Pub. TV., Bus. Industry Polit. Action Com., Washington. Served from 2d lt. to lt. col. USAAF, 1942-45. Decorated Legion of Merit; recipient Disting. Service award U. Nebr., 1957; Harold R. Gordon Meml. award Internat. Assn. Health Ins. Underwriters, 1955, Ins. Man of Year award Ins. Field, 1958; Dist. Service award Nebr. Council on Econ. Edn., 1986, Exec. of Yr. award Am. Coll. Hosp. Adminstrs., 1971; Nebr. Builders award, 1979; Disting. Service award Lincoln Kiwanis Club, 1980. Mem. Health Ins. Assn. Am. (1st pres. 1956), Am. Legion, Am. Life Conv. (exec. com. 1961-70, pres. 1966-67), Ins. Econs. Soc. (chmn. 1971-73), Nebr. Hist. Soc. (pres. 1982-84), Ins. Fedn. Nebr. (pres.), Phi Beta Kappa, Phi Kappa Psi, Alpha Kappa Psi (hon.). Republican. Presbyn. Lodges: Masons, Elks. Home: 4100 South St Lincoln NE 68506 Office: 1526 K St Lincoln NE 68508

FAULKNER, MAURICE ERVIN, educator, conductor; b. Fort Scott, Kans., Feb. 2, 1912; s. Ervin Phyletus and Minnie Mae (Munday) F.; m. Ellen Stradal, May 24, 1934 (div. 1951); children: Katherine Sydney, Barbara Ellen; m. Suzanne Somerville, Oct. 18, 1958. BS in Music, Fort Hays State Coll., 1932; postgrad. Interlochen U., 1933; MA in Music, Tchrs. Coll., N.Y.C., 1936; PhD, Stanford U., 1956. Instr. music pub. schs., Kans., 1932-37; assoc. prof. instrumental music Columbia U., summers 1934-40; asst. prof. San Jose (Calif.) State Coll., 1937-40; from asst. prof. to assoc. prof. to prof. emeritus U. Calif., Santa Barbara, 1940—, also chmn. dept.; research papers on Bronze Age musical instruments presented Biennial Archeol. Musicology Symposiums, Congress of Traditional Music of UNESCO, Stockholm, 1984, Hanover, Fed. Republic Germany, 1986; vis. prof. U. Tex., summer 1947; music critic Salzburg (Austria) Festival, 1951— (Reinhardt award 1969, Golden Service award 1981), Santa Barbara Star, 1951-56, Santa Barbara News-Press, 1956-82; research musicologist Inst. for Environ. Stress, U. Calif., Santa Barbara, 1979—; condr. Santa Barbara Symphony Orch., 1941-44, All-Calif. High Sch. Symphony Orch., 1941-73, Kern County Honor Band of Calif.; guest condr. Seoul (Korea) Symphony Orch., 1945-46, officer in charge Seoul Nat. U., 1945-46; mus. dir. Santa Barbara Fiesta Bowl Mus. Show, 1951-53. Contbg. editor The Instrumentalist, 1964-86; contbr. articles and criticisms to Mus. Courier, Sat. Rev., Christian Sci. Monitor. Chmn. Santa Barbara Mayor's Adv. Com. on Arts, 1966-69. Served from lt. (j.g.) to lt. USNR, 1944-46. Fellow Internat. Inst. Arts and Letters (life); mem. Music Acad. West (pres. 1949-85, pres. emeritus 1954—, sustaining dir. 1985—), So. Calif. Sch. Band and Orch. Assn. (hon. life, v.p. 1955), Am. Fedn. Musicians (hon. life), Nat. Music Educators Conf., Internat. Congress Traditional Music (lectr. Stockholm 1984, Hannover 1986), Archeol. Musicol. Work Study Group UNESCO's Congress of Traditional Music, Internat. Trumpet Guild, U. Calif. Emeriti Assn., Phi Mu Alpha (life), Phi Delta Kappa. Republican. Presbyterian. Lodge: Mason. Avocation: world traveling. Home and Office: PO Box 572 Goleta CA 93116

FAULSTICH, ALBERT JOSEPH, banking consultant; b. New Orleans, May 28, 1910; s. Albert and Mary (Balser) F.; m. Anna Emily Collignon, June 30, 1940; children: Albert Joseph, Richard Charles. BS in Acctg. and Econs, Columbus U., Washington, 1938, M.S. in Acctg. and Finance, 1948. With Treasury Dept., 1939-64, asst. to personnel dir., 1939-42, dir. positions evaluation and job analysis, 1942-43, indsl. relations specialist, 1943-45, dir. salary adminstrn., coordinator performance evaluation, also chmn. com. union relations, adminstr. policy and standards of govt. early-age retirement of spl. intelligence agts. from various depts., 1946-60, dir. Office Security, 1961, spl asst. to sec., 1961-64, asst. to comptroller currency, directed issuance and redemption of Fed. Reserve currency, 1962-64, coordinator fed. banking, 1964; dir. FDIC, 1965-66, dep. adminstr. nat. banks, 1965-74, asst. dir., 1973-74; treas., mem. Fed. Personnel Council, 1941; acting dir. personnel mgmt., wage bd. chmn., Treasury Dept., (intermittently) 1953-60; mem. rev. bd., spl. com. on liquidations, loans and purchases assets, FDIC, 1966-74; cons. Fin. Gen. Bankshares, Inc., 1974-76, for banks and govt., 1976—; dir. Am. Nat. Bank of Md., 1975-77. Chmn. comptroller currency orgn. for nation-wide campaign for Kennedy Library Fund, 1964. Served to lt. USNR, 1943-46. Recipient Naval Commendation medal, commendation Treasury Dept., 1962, 3 citations, 1972, Meritorious Service award, 1973, Disting. Service award, 1974, Albert Gallatin award, Am. Flag award, Equal Opportunity award, 1974. Democrat. Roman Catholic. Home and Office: 3004 N Ridge Rd Ellicott City MD 21043

FAUMAN, BRUCE CHARLES, educator, management consultant; b. Toronto, Ont., Can., July 6, 1943; s. Earl A. and Rae Russel (Ross) F.; m. Maureen Elizabeth Morris, Aug. 4, 1971; children: Laura Maureen, Sheila Dorothy. BSc, MSc, MIT, 1966; PhD, Stanford U., 1974. Prof. U. Rochester, N.Y., 1972-79; mgmt. cons. Abbey and Fauman, Vancouver, B.C., Can., 1977—; adminstr., prof. U. B.C., Vancouver, 1979—. Gov. Crofton House Sch., Vancouver, 1985—. Sloan Grad. fellow, MIT, 1964; Stanford Grad. fellow, 1967-70. Mem. Am. Mktg. Assn. (bd. dirs. 1986-88), Inst. Mgmt. Scis., Vancouver Bd. Trade. Club: Vancouver. Home: 6465 McCleery St, Vancouver, BC Canada V6N 1G5 Office: U BC, 2053 Main Mall, Vancouver, BC Canada V6T 1Y8

FAURE, FELIX L., retail executive; b. Pamiers, France, Mar. 31, 1925; s. Jean and Louise (Ibry) F.; m. Annie Medeville (div. 1981); 1 child, Dominique; m. Suzanne Girard; 1 child, Frederic. Degree, Ecole Superior de Commerce, 1945; degree in law, Faculte de Droit, 1946. Pres. UNIMAG Faure, Pamiers, France, 1960—, UNIMAG Midi Pyrenees, Auch, France, 1975, DISTRIMAG, Toulouse, France, 1975—, DEPAMAG, Pamiers, 1981—; cons. Bank of France, Foix, 1960—. Club: France U.S.A. Office: UNIMAG Faure, 10 Place de la Republique, 09100 Pamiers France

FAURE, PAUL, diplomat; b. La Tronche, Dauphiné, France, Sept. 28, 1924; s. Josephe and Marcelle (Cathiard) F.; m. Jeanne Deffarges, Aug. 2, 1956; children: Philippe-Emmanuel, Anne-Caroline. LLB, U. Grenoble, France, 1944; grad., ENFOM, Paris, 1948. Civil servant Ministry of FOM, Indochina, 1948-58; 1st sec. French Embassy, La Paz, Bolivia, 1958-60, Canberra, Australia, 1960-63; consul-gen. San Juan, PR, 1968-70; counsellor Lima, Peru, 1970-73; ambassador Managua, Nicaragua, 1979-82, Lilongwe, Malawi, 1983-87; ambassador to OAS Washington, 1987—. Author: Exterritorialité in China, 1948. Recipient Ordre du Merite, 1967, Legion D'Honneur, 1973 (France). Home: 20 Bd de la République, 92210 Saint Cloud France Office: French Embassy 4041 Reservoir Rd NW Washington DC 20007

FAURE, ROBERT, mathematics educator; b. Yen Bay, Tonkin, Socialist Republic of Vietnam, Nov. 10, 1919; s. Charles Faure and Du Fourmantelle; m. Francoise Castagnez, Aug. 26, 1952; 1 child, Manuel. Doctor es Sciences, U. Paris, 1947. Prof. U. Hanoi, Socialist Republic of Vietnam, 1948-53, U. Saigon, Socialist Republic of Vietnam, 1953-55, U. Rennes, France, 1956-57, U. Dakar, Senegal, 1957-72, U. Lille 1, France, 1972-87. Laureat Acad. Sci., Paris, 1986. Mem. Am. Math. Soc., Soc. Math. France, Soc. Indusl. and Applied Math.

FAUROUX, ROGER, corporate executive; b. Montpellier, France, Nov. 21, 1926; s. Théo and Rose (Ségu) F.; m. Marie LeRoy Laduie, 1953; 6 children. Ed., Ecole Normale Supérieure, Ecole Nationale d'Administration. Asst. Insp. Fin. France, 1956-58, Insp. Fin., 1958-60, Minister of Edn., 1960; adminstrv. dir. Cie Pont-à-Mousson, 1961-64, fin. dir., 1964-69; fin. dir. Cie. de Saint-Gobain-Pont-à-Mousson, 1970-72, asst. dir.-gen., 1972-75, adminstrv. dir.-gen., 1978-80, pres., 1980-86; dir. Ecole Nationale d'Administration, 1986—; bd. dirs. Fabbrica Pisana, Italy, Cristaleria Española, Spain, Cie. Générale des Eaux, Inst. Pasteur, Banque Nationale de Paris, Petrofina (Belgium), Smith Kline-Beckman, Phila., Certain Teed Products Corp.; mem. supervisory bd. Vereinigte Glaswerke, Fed. Republic Germany. Decorated Chevalier Legion d'Honneur, Ordre Nationale du Mérite. Home: 13 rue de l'Epée-de-Bois, 75005 Paris France *

FAURRE, PIERRE LUCIEN, mathematics educator, business executive; b. Paris, Jan. 15, 1942; s. Lucien Marie and Anne Jeanne (Dame) F.; m. Pierrette Claudine Mome, July 24, 1962; children—Pierre, Sylvie. Engr., Ecole Polytechnique, Paris, 1962; Ph.D., Stanford U., 1967; doctorate U. Paris, 1972. Asst. mgr. Centre d'Automatique, Ecoles des Mines, Paris, 1967-71; sci. dir. IRIA, Rocquencourt, France, 1971-72; exec. sec. gen. SAGEM, Paris, 1972-83, exec. v.p., chief operating officer, 1983-87, chmn. bd., chief ops. officer, 1987—; prof. math. Ecole Polytechnique, Paris, 1970—. Author: Navigation inertielle optimale, 1971; Elements d'Automatique, 1974, 2d edit., 1984; Elements of System Theory, 1977; Operateurs rationnels positifs, 1979; also articles. Decorated chevalier Ordre National du Merite; recipient prix Laplace, Academie des Sciences, 1962; prix Constantin de Magny, 1979; prix Science et Défense, 1984. Mem. French Nat. Acad. Scis., IEEE, Am. Math. Assn., Assn. Computing Machinery, Société Mathematique de France. Home: 57 rue du Dr Blanche, 75016 Paris France Office: SAGEM, 6 ave d'Iena, 75116 Paris France

FAUST, NAOMI FLOWE, educator, poet; b. Salisbury, N.C.; d. Christopher Leroy and Ada Luella (Graham) Flowe; A.B., Bennett Coll.; M.A., U. Mich., 1945; Ph.D., N.Y. U., 1963; m. Roy Malcolm Faust, Aug. 16, 1948. Elem. tchr. Public Schs. Gaffney (S.C.); tchr. English, French, phys. edn. Atkins High Sch., Winston-Salem; instr. English, Bennett Coll. and So. U., Scotlandville, La., 1944-46; prof. English, Morgan State Coll., Balt., 1946-48; tchr. English, Greensboro (N.C.) Public Schs., 1948-51, N.Y.C. Public Schs., 1954-63; prof. edn. Queens Coll. of City U. N.Y., Flushing, 1964-82; lectr. in field; writer, lectr., poetry readings, 1982—. Named Tchr.-Author of 1979, Tchr.-Writer; cert. of Merit for poem Cooper Hill Writers Conf., 1970; Achievement award L.I. br. AAUW, 1985. Mem. AAUP, Nat. Council Tchrs. English, Nat. Women's Book Assn., World Poetry Soc. Intercontinental, N.Y. Poetry Forum, NAACP, United Negro Coll. Fund, Alpha Kappa Alpha, Alpha Kappa Mu, Alpha Epsilon. Author: Discipline and the Classroom Teacher, 1977; (poetry) Speaking in Verse, 1974; All Beautiful Things, 1983; contbr. poetry to jours. Home: 112-01 175th St Jamaica NY 11433

FAUST, ROBERT JOSEPH, physician; b. Ft. Worth, Mar. 23, 1938; s. Charles Fredrick and Kathleen (Singler) F.; m. Lynn Griffin, June 14, 1958 (div.); children—Wendy Elizabeth, Allison Marie. B.A. in Biology, Tex. Christian U., 1960; M.D., U. Tex.-Galveston, 1964. Diplomate Am. Bd. Internal Medicine. Resident in internal medicine and cardiology John Sealy Hosp., Galveston, 1964-68; pvt. practice medicine, specializing in internal medicine and cardiology, Lubbock, Tex., 1968—; assoc. clin. prof. internal medicine Tex. Tech. U.; dir. cardiopulmonary labs. South Park Hosp., Inc., Lubbock, also trustee. Mem. Lubbock C. of C., Am. Heart Assn. (chpt. pres. 1975-76), Lubbock, Crosby and Garza Med. Soc., AMA, Tex. Med. Soc., Tex. Club Internists, Alpha Omega Alpha. Republican. Roman Catholic. Clubs: Univ. City, Sports Car of Am., Corvette. Office: 6630 Quaker Ave Lubbock TX 79413

FAUST, THOMAS JAMES, marine transporation and finance executive, business consultant; b. San Francisco; s. Thomas J. Faust; m. Ann Sparkman, Jan. 3, 1985. B.S. in Marine Transp., Tex. A&M U., 1969; M.B.A., Stanford U., 1973. Cons. Marine Transport Lines, N.Y.C., 1973-75; dir. planning Dillingham, Honolulu, 1976-77; pres. Faustug Group Inc., San Francisco, 1978—; gen. ptnr. Tractug, San Francisco, 1980—; dir., v.p. Bay Area Employment Devel., Napa, Calif., 1980—. Served with USN, 1969-82; Vietnam. Mem. Stanford Bus. Sch. Alumni, Engineers Club San Francisco. Home: 60 Collins St San Francisco CA 94118 Office: Faustug Group Inc Pier 15 The Embarcadero San Francisco CA 94111

FAUVEL, LUC DANIEL, agricultural economics educator; b. Coutances, France, Nov. 16, 1913; s. Eugene and Maria (Lelievre) F.; m. Renee Lavedan, Dec. 2, 1952; children—Catherine, Jean-Luc. Licencie en Droit, U. Caen, France, 1935; Diplome, Ecole des Scis. Politiques, Paris, 1937; Ph.D., U. Paris, 1939. Charge de mission Ministere de l'Economie Nationale, Paris, 1946-48; prof. econs. U. Lille, France, 1950-59, U. Paris, 1959-83; prof. emeritus, 1984—. Editor: Marches et Structures Agricoles, 1964-75. Decorated Officier de la Legion d'Honneur, France. Mem. Internat. Economic Assn. (sec. gen. 1960-84, council mem. 1986—).

FAUVET, JACQUES, editor; b. Paris, June 9, 1914; s. Pierre and Andree (Meunier-Pouthot) F.; L.en. D., Faculte de Droit, U. Paris; m. Claude Decroix, 1939; 5 children. An editor L'Est Republicain, Nancy, France, 1937-39; joined Le Monde, Paris, 1945, head domestic politics dept., 1948-58, asst. editor-in-chief, 1958-63, editor-in-chief, 1963—, gen. ed., 1968, dir. gen., 1969-82. Mem. Sci. Com. Documentation Franç aise, UNESCO French Commn.; pres. Nat. Commn. on Informatics and Liberties, 1984—. Decorated comdr. Legion d'honneur, Croix de guerre. Author: Les partis politiques dans la France actuelle, 1947; Les forces politiques en France, 1951; La France dechiree, 1957; La politique et les paysans, 1958; La IVe Republique, 1959; La fronde des generaux, 1961; Histoire du parti communiste francaise, Vol. I, 1964, Vol. II, 1965, combined edit., 1977. Office: Le Monde, 5 rue Louis Boilly, 75016 Paris France

FAVELA, FERNANDO LOZOYA, civil engineer, educator; b. Durango, Mex., Dec. 13, 1927; s. Jesus Favela and Gavina (Lozoya) F.; m. Sonia Vara Melero, June 22, 1956; children: Fernando, Sonia, Jesus, Elia and Alejandra. Civil engr. Nat. Autonoma de Mex., Mexico City, 1952; jefe de frente y de obra ICA Group, Mexico City, 1950-56, supt. y jefe de superintendentes, 1956-64, gerente, 1964, dir., 1965-66, v.p., 1967-77, exec. v.p., 1977-88; prof. Nat. U. Mex., Mexico City, 1966—, mem. tech. council engring. faculty, 1981—; prof. Nat. Autonomus U. Mex., Mexico City, 1966-88. Mem. Nat. Reconstruction Commn., 1985. Named Excellent and Eminent Prof., U. Cauca, Colombia, 1981; recipient Honor medal Engring. Coll. Spain, 1982. Mem. Am. Concrete Inst., ASTM, Engrs. and Architects Mex. Assn., Civil Engring. Mex. Coll., Mex. Soc. Engrs. (v.p. 1983—). Instl. Revolutionary party. Roman Catholic. Home: Creston 336, Pedregal de San Angel, 01900 Mexico City Mexico Office: Grupo ICA, Mineria 145, 11870 Mexico City Mexico

FAVRE, HENRI, sociology educator; b. Marseille, France, Dec. 21, 1937; s. Louis and Madeleine (Peiretti) F.; div.; children: Sébastien, Bénédicte. Lic. in history, U. Paris, 1958, lic. in sociology, 1959, diploma in polit. sci., 1959, doctorate, 1968. Research assoc. Inst. Nat. Indigenista, Mex., 1960-61; researcher Inst. Français d'Etudes Andines, Peru, 1963-65; researcher Ctr. Nat. de la Recherche Sci., France, 1966-80, sr. researcher, 1980—; prof. Inst. des Hautes Etudes de l'Amérique Latine, France, 1966—; v.p. Assn. Française d'Etude Recherche Pays Andins, France, 1973—, European Council Social Research Latin Am., Austria, 1977-85. Author: Changement et Continuité Chez les Mayas du Mexique, 1971, Les Incas, 1972; co-author: La Oligarquia en el Peru, 1969. Mem. Assn. Française Sciences Sociales l'Amérique Latine (sec. gen. 1981-84), Equipe Recherche Socs. Indiennes Paysannes d'Amérique Latine (bd. dirs. 1974-84). Home: 77 B rue des Entrepreneurs, 75015 Paris France Office: CNRS, 27 rue Paul Bert, 94200 Ivry France

FAVRE, MICHEL MAURICE, hotel executive; b. Lausanne, Switzerland, June 13, 1940; s. Gaston and Christine Favre; m. Ursula Mueller, May 28, 1966; children—Nathalie, Isabelle. Diploma High Sch. Commerce, Lausanne, 1956; postgrad. Columbia U., 1975. With Inter-Continental Hotels Corp., 1964-80, gen. mgr. Inter-Continental Hotel, Libreville, Gabon, 1971-73, Portman Inter-continental Hotel, London, 1973-80; chmn. London Central

Hotels Group Tng. Scheme, 1978-79; v.p. div. internat. and div. hotels Mövenpick Enterprises, Zürich, 1980-86, v.p., gen. mgr. Am. Express Inc. Internat. Travel Related Services Switzerland, 1987—; mem. exec. com. Am. Express Europe Ltd., Europe, Middle East and Africa. Decorated comdr. Franco-Brittanique Assn., officer Order Gabon; recipient Silver medal City of Paris, Gold medal Greek Orthodox Ch.; named hon. citizen City of New Orleans. Mem. Brit. Inst. Mgmt., Hotel, Catering and Instl. Mgmt. Assn., Brit. Hotels, Restaurants and Caterers Assn., Confrerie de la Chaine des Rotisseurs (vice chancellor Greater London chpt. 1977-79), Order des Coteaux de Champagne (maitre de relais 1976), Internat. Mgmt. Assn., Swiss Econ. Council, Internat. Hotel Assn., European Mgrs. Assn., La Soc. Suisse des Hoteliers. Clubs: Royal Automobile, Lions, Skal Internat. Address: 106 Zürichstrasse, Adliswil, 8134 Zürich Switzerland

FAVRE, PIERRE-MARCEL, publishing company executive; b. Lausanne, Vaud, Switzerland, Aug. 9, 1943; s. Marcel François and Andrée (Glayre) F.; m. Ingrid Françoise Souren, Apr. 10, 1987; 1 child, Bart Jerome. Grad., U. Lausanne. Registered profl. architect Spain. Prin., pub. Editions Favre, Lausanne, Salon Internat. du Livre et de la Presse, Lausanne. Pub. more than 300 books. Mem. Swiss Assn. Editors. Home and Office: Editions Favre, 29 rue de Bourg, CH-1000 Lausanne Switzerland

FAVREAU, DONALD FRANCIS, management consultant; b. Cohoes, N.Y., Sept. 7, 1919; s. Alphonse Emille and Millie Loretta (Smith) F.; m. Helen Patricia Rafferty, June 2, 1945; 1 dau., Susan Debra. B.A., Knox Coll., 1949; M.A., SUNY, 1954. Prof. mil. sci. LaSalle Inst., Troy, N.Y., 1949-54; mgr. tng. Ford Motor Co., Cleve., 1954-57, Am. Bosch Arma Corp., Garden City, N.Y., 1957-59; asst. to v.p. Royal Metal Corp., N.Y.C., 1959-60; mgr. personnel devel. N.Y. Stock Exchange, N.Y.C., 1960-62; manpower coordinator N.Y. State Dept. Labor, 1962-65; asso. dir. Center for Exec. Devel. SUNY-Albany, 1965-69, dir. Center for Exec. Devel. and Pub. Safety Mgmt., 1969-83, prof. emeritus, 1983—; pres. Don Favreau Assocs., 1983—; adj. instr. Western Res. U., 1952-54; adj. prof. C.W. Post Coll., 1975—; cons. in field. Author: Introduction to Fire Protection, 1972, Criminal Victimization of the Elderly, 1977, Modern Police Administration, 1978. Mem. Saratoga Performing Arts Center; met. bd. dirs. Nat. Alliance Bus., 1979—; vice chmn. Pvt. Industry Council, 1980—; v.p. Northeast Alliance of Bus., 1982—; bd. dirs. Vis. Nurse Assn. of Albany, 1984—. Served to lt. U.S. Army, 1943-46. Named hon. citizen Ville de Lafayette; recipient commendation Pres. Carter, 1978, commendation Pres. Reagan, 1982, cert. of merit State of N.Y., 1983; named hon. fire chief City and County of Denver, 1983. Mem. Internat. Fire Adminstrn. Inst. (exec. dir. 1965-73), Am. Mgmt. Assn., Nat. Fire Protection Assn., Internat. Assn. Chiefs of Police, N.Y. State Assn. Fire Chiefs, AAUP, NEA, Soc. Advancement of Mgmt., Am. Soc. Tng. Dirs., Nat. Assn. 10th Mountain Div. Assn., Friendly Sons St. Patrick (dir. 1984—), VFW, Am. Legion, Sigma Nu. Lodge: Elks. Home: 32 Hemlock Dr Clifton Park NY 12065

FAVREAU, SUSAN DEBRA, management consultant; b. Cleve., Dec. 15, 1955; d. Donald Francis and Helen Patricia (Rafferty) F. Cert., N.Y. State Police Acad., 1974; student, Hudson Valley Community Coll., 1983-85, Cornell U., 1984, SUNY, 1984—. Communications specialist N.Y. State Police, Loudonville, 1974-87; communications specialist div. hdqrs., 1987—; mgmt. cons., sec.-treas., dir. Don Favreau Assocs., Inc., Clifton Park, N.Y., 1983-86, v.p., 1986—; adj. faculty Internat. Assn. Chiefs of Police; NYSPIN coordinator FBI/Nat. Crime Info. Ctr. cert. program, 1986. Author: Teamwork in the Telecommunication Center, 1986, One More Time: How to be a Mature and Successful Telecommunications Manager, 1987; also NYSPIN cert. manuals. Recipient Dirs. commendation N.Y. State Police Acad., 1977, commendation N.Y. State Police, 1978, Supt.'s commendation N.Y. State Police, 1986. Mem. Nat. Assn. Female Execs., N.Y. State Civil Service Assn., Emergency Communicators' Profl. Assn. (mem. adv. bd.), Colonie Police Benevolent Assn. (hon.), Assoc. Pub. Safety Communications Officers (planning commn. mem. Atlantic chpt. 1986, registration chair annual NE conf. 1986), N.Y. State Troopers Police Benevolent Assn. (hon.), Nat. Bus. Women Am., Internat. Assn. Chiefs Police, Am. Horse Shows Assn. Republican. Roman Catholic. Avocations: equestrienne, target shooting, reading, sewing. Home: 4D Hollandale Apts Clifton Park NY 12065 Office: Hdqrs NY State Police State Office Bldg Campus Albany NY 12226

FAW, MELVIN LEE, physician; b. Kansas City, Mo., Dec. 4, 1925; s. Floyd Butler and Ivalee Muriel (Harvey) F.; m. Anna Margaret Rose, July 17, 1948; children—Linda, Gary, David, Nancy. Student, U. Kans., 1943-44, Baylor U., 1945; B.S., Washburn U., 1948; M.D., Washington U., St. Louis, 1951. Intern Washington U. Service St. Louis City Hosp., 1951-52, resident in internal medicine, 1952-54; resident in internal medicine U. Kans. Hosp., Kansas City, 1954-55; practice medicine specializing in internal medicine and cardiology Welborn Clinic, Evansville, Ind., 1955—, mng. ptnr., 1965-78; pres. med. staff Welborn Hosp., 1980, chief medicine, 1958-64, dir. cardiovascular services, 1981—; mem. So. Ind. Health Service Agy., 1976—. Served with Inf. AUS, 1944-45. Decorated Bronze Star medal with V device oak leaf cluster, Purple Heart, Combat Infantryman Badge; recipient Disting. Service award U. Evansville, 1980. Fellow Am. Coll. Chest Physicians; mem. ACP, Am. Soc. Internal Medicine, AMA, Ind. Med. Assn., Vanderburgh County Med. Soc., Phi Kappa Phi. Methodist. Home: 2400 E Chandler St Evansville IN 47714 Office: Welborn Clinic 421 Chestnut St Evansville IN 47713

FAWCETT, HOWARD HOY, chemical health and safety consultant; b. McKeesport, Pa., May 31, 1916; s. Harry Garfield and Ada (Deetz) F.; m. Ruth Allen Bogan, Apr. 7, 1942; children: Ralph Willard, Harry Allen. BS in Indsl. Chemistry, U. Md., 1940; postgrad. U. Del., 1945-47. Registered profl. engr., Calif. Research chemist Manhattan project E.I. DuPont de Nemours & Co., Inc., Chgo., Hanford, Wash., 1944-45, research and devel. chemist organic chemistry div., Deepwater, N.J., 1945-48; cons. engr. Gen. Electric Co., Schenectady, N.Y., 1948-64; tech. sec. com. on hazardous materials Nat. Acad. Scis.-NRC, Washington, 1964-75; staff scientist, project mgr. Tracor Jitco, Inc., Rockville, Md., 1975-78; sr. chem. engr. Equitable Environ. Health, 1978—; pres., sr. engr. Fawcett Consultations, Inc., 1981—; mem. adv. com. study on socio-behavioral preparations for, responses to and recovery from chem. disasters NSF, 1977—; adj. prof. Fed. Emergency Mgmt. Agency Acad., 1983—; cons. to industry and govt. agys. Author Am.-Can. supplement Hazards in Chemical Lab., 1983, Hazardous and Toxic Materials, Safe Handling and Disposal, 1984, 2d edit., 1988; co-editor: Safety and Accident Prevention in Chemical Operations, 2d edit., 1982; mem. editorial adv. bd. Jour. Safety Research, 1968—, Transp. Planning and Tech., 1972—; N. Am. regional editor Jour. Hazardous Materials, 1975—; also book chpt. Chief radiol. sect. Schenectady County CD, 1953-63; bd. dirs. Safety sect. Schenectady C. of C., 1957-64. Recipient Disting. Service to Safety citation Nat. Safety Council, 1966, Cameron award, 1962, 69. Fellow Am. Chem. Soc. (sec. com. chem. safety, chmn. council com. on chem. safety 1974-77, chmn. div. chem. health and safety 1977-79, councilor 1980-82, archivist, 1984—, author audio course on hazards of materials 1977), Am. Inst. Chemists; mem. ASTM (membership sec. 1972—, sub-chmn. D-34 com.), Am. Inst. Chem. Engrs. (com. on occupational health and safety 1977—), Internat. Platform Assn., 1986—, Am. Indsl. Hygiene Assn. (dir. Balt.-Washington chpt. 1975-77). Alpha Chi Sigma. Home and Office: PO Box 9444 12920 Matey Rd Wheaton MD 20906-4053

FAWCETT, JAMES DAVIDSON, herpetologist, educator; b. New Plymouth, N.Z., Jan. 10, 1933; s. James and Edna Lola (Catterick) F.; B.Sc., U. N.Z., 1960; M.Sc., U. Auckland (N.Z.), 1964; Ph.D., U. Colo., 1975; m. Georgene Ellen Tyler, Dec. 21, 1968. Head dept. biology Kings Coll., Auckland, 1960; grad. demonstrator dept. zoology U. Auckland, 1961-62, sr. demonstrator, 1963-64; grad. asst. U. Colo., 1969-72; instr. biology U. Nebr., Omaha, 1972-75, asst. prof., 1975-81, asso. prof., 1981—. Recipient Great Tchr. award U. Nebr., 1981. Mem. Royal Soc. N.Z., N.Z. Assn. Scientists, Am. Soc. Zoologists, Soc. Systematic Zoology, Herpetologists League, Brit. Soc. Herpetologists, AAAS, Nebr. Herpetological Soc. (pres. 1979-80), Sigma Xi (pres. Omaha chpt. 1980-81), Phi Sigma. Contbr. articles to profl. jours. Home: 309 S 56th St Omaha NE 68134 Office: Biology Dept U Nebr Omaha NE 68182

FAWCETT, SHERWOOD LUTHER, research laboratory executive; b. Youngstown, Ohio, Dec. 25, 1919; s. Luther T. and Clara (Sherwood) F.; m. Martha L. Simcox, Feb. 28, 1953; children: Paul, Judith, Tom. BS, Ohio State U., 1941; MS, Case Inst. Tech., 1948, PhD, 1950; hon. degrees, Ohio State U., Gonzaga U., Whitman Coll., Otterbein Coll., Detroit Inst. Tech., Ohio Dominican Coll. Registered profl. engr., Ohio. Mem. staff Columbus Labs. Battelle Meml. Inst., 1950-64, mgr. physics dept., 1959-64; dir. Pacific Northwest Labs., Richland, Wash., 1964-67; exec. v.p. Battelle Meml. Inst., Columbus, Ohio, 1967-68; pres., chief exec. officer Battelle Meml. Inst., 1968-80, chmn., chief exec. officer, 1981-84, chmn. bd. trustees, 1984-87; bd. dirs. Columbia Gas Systems, Inc. Served with the USNR, 1941-46. Decorated Bronze Star. Mem. Am. Phys. Soc., Am. Nuclear Soc., Nat. Soc. Profl. Engrs., Am. Inst. Metall. Engrs., Sigma Xi, Delta Chi, Sigma Pi Sigma, Tau Beta Pi. Home and Office: 2820 Margate Rd Columbus OH 43221

FAY, DARCY HUNT, international training and organizational development consultant, educator; b. Cleve.; d. Horace Byron Jr. and Bette (Berne) Fay; m. Paul L. Bundick. BA in Polit. Sci., Boston Coll., 1970; M. in Internat. Adminstrn., Sch. for Internat. Tng., Brattleboro, Vt., 1979; postgrad. Fielding Inst. Cert. in intercultural tng. Tchr. Internat. Sch. Tokyo (Japan), 1971-74, Am. Sch. of Barcelona (Spain), 1974-75; dir. African/Am. Educators program AAUW Ednl. Found., Washington, 1977-81; cons. Internat. Soc. for Intercultural Edn., Tng. and Research, Washington, 1982-84; cons. Delphi Research Assocs., Washington, 1984-85, World Bank, Washington, 1984-85; cons. various domestic and internat. orgns., Washington, 1986—. Contbr. articles to profl. jours. Recipient Japanese Flower Arrangement award Sogetsu Sch., Tokyo, 1974. Mem. Asia Soc., Assn. for Women in Devel., Capital Press Women, Internat. Organizational Devel. Assn., Internat. Soc. Intercultural Edn., Tng. and Research (1984 conf. steering com., program com., chmn. conf. publs. com.), Nat. Assn. Female Execs., Am. Soc. Tng. and Devel., Assn. for Women in Devel., NOW, Soc. for Internat. Devel./Women in Devel., Nat. Mus. Women in Arts (charter), OD Network. Home: 4545 Connecticut Ave NW #635 Washington DC 20008

FAY, RICHARD JAMES, mechanical engineer, executive, educator; b. St. Joseph, Mo., Apr. 26, 1935; s. Frank James and Marie Jewell (Senger) F.; m. Marilyn Louise Kelsey, Dec. 22, 1962; B.S.M.E., U. Denver, 1959, M.S.M.E., 1970; Registered profl. engr., Colo., Nebr. Design engr. Denver Fire Clay Co., 1957-60; design, project engr. Silver Engring. Works, 1960-63; research engr., lectr. mech. engring. U. Denver, 1963-74, asst. prof. Colo. Sch. of Mines, 1974-75, founder, pres. Fay Engring. Corp., 1971—. Served with Colo. N.G., 1962. Mem. Soc. Automotive Engrs. (past chmn. Colo. sect.), ASME (past chmn. Colo. sect., regional v.p.). Contbr. articles to profl. jours.; patentee in field. Office: 5201 E 48th Ave Denver CO 80216

FAYEZ, SAMIR M.K., engineer; b. Jeddah, Saudi Arabia, Jan. 5, 1947; s. Mohammed Kamel and Fatima (Mahmood) F.; children from previous marriage: Neal Samir, Naef Samir; m. Awatif Aoun; children: Randa, Almohaned, Rana. BS, Ariz State U., 1973; MS, Sam Houston State U., 1975; PhD, Tex. A&M U., 1979. Research assoc. Sam Houston State U., Huntsville, Tex., 1973-75, Tex. A&M U., College Station, 1976-79; asst. prof. Coll. English, Jeddah, Saudi Arabia, 1979-81; constrn. dir. Al Redwan, Jeddah, Saudi Arabia, 1981-82; mng. dir. Almahawer Indsl. Engrs., Jeddah, 1982-84; advisor to gen. mgr. Saudi Amoudi Group, 1984-88; pres., chief exec. officer Advanced Electronics Ltd., 1988—. Mem. ASCE, IEEE, Am. Inst. Indsl. Engrs., Brit. Inst. Mgmt., Brit. Computer Soc., Alpha Pi Mu, Sigma Pi Sigma. Home: PO Box 8561, Jeddah 21492, Saudi Arabia Office: Advanced Electronics Co Ltd, PO Box 85319, Riyadh 11691, Saudi Arabia

FAZIO, ANTHONY LEE, investment company executive; b. Wheeling, W.Va., Jan. 27, 1937; s. Frank G. and Julia Louise (DeFillipo) F.; m. Faye Elizabeth Kelly, Sept. 3, 1964; children: Tracey Lee, Kelly Ann. BSEE, W.Va. U., 1959. Registered investment advisor, real estate syndicator; cert. fin. planner. With computer div. RCA, 1964-72, mgr. product mktg., 1970-71, mgr. systems planning, 1971-72; dir. bus. and product planning Univac, 1972-73, dir. product mktg. and bus./product planning N.Am., 1973-75, regional mgr., 1975-77; v.p. sales Sycor, Inc., Ann Arbor, Mich., 1977-78; v.p. sales No. Telecom Systems Corp., 1978-79, v.p. mktg., 1979-80; pres. Gibbs Irwin Investments Co., 1981-83; product procurement and due diligence officer Midland Mgmt. Corp., 1983-86; regional dir. Fin. Network Investment Corp., 1986—. Served with Signal Corps, U.S. Army, 1959-61. Mem. Internat. Assn. Fin. Planners, Data Processing Mgmt. Assn. (cert. in data processing), Tau Beta Pi, Eta Kappa Nu. Republican. Methodist. Home: 4770 Regents Walk Shorewood MN 55331 Office: 6125 Blue Circle Dr Minneapolis MN 55343

FAZIO, PETER VICTOR, JR., lawyer; b. Chgo., Jan. 22, 1940; s. Peter Victor and Marie Rose (LaMantia) F.; m. Patti Ann Campbell, Jan. 3, 1966; children—Patti-Marie, Catherine, Peter. AB, Holy Cross Coll., Worcester, Mass., 1961; JD, U. Mich., 1964. Bar: Ill. 1964, U.S. Dist. Ct. (no. dist.) Ill. 1965, U.S. Ct. Appeals (7th cir.) 1972, U.S. Ct. Appeals (D.C. cir.) 1981, U.S. Supreme Ct. 1977. Assoc. Schiff, Hardin & Waite, Chgo., 1964-70, ptnr., 1970-82, 84—; exec. v.p. Internat. Capital Equipment, Chgo., 1982-83, also dir., 1982-85, sec., 1982-87; dir. Planmetrics Inc., Chgo., 1984—, Chgo. Lawyers Commn. for Civil Rights Under Law, 1976-82, co-chmn., 1978-80, Seton Health Corp. Northern Ill., 1986—. Trustee Barat Coll., Lake Forest, Ill., 1977-82; mem. exec. adv. bd. St. Joseph's Hosp., Chgo., 1984—, chmn., 1986—. Mem. ABA, Ill. State Bar Assn., Chgo. Bar Assn., Am. Soc. Corp. Secs. Clubs: Saddle & Cycle (sec. 1983-86), Tavern, Metropolitan. (Chgo.). Office: Schiff Hardin & Waite 7200 Sears Tower Chicago IL 60606

FEAGINS, WARREN DOUGLAS, advertising executive; b. Portland, Oreg., Nov. 17, 1945; arrived in Eng., 1948; s. Clairmont Douglas Feagins and Joyce Lilian (Humm) Watts; m. Sara Patricia George, July, 1967 (div. 1974); m. Christine Evelyn Boland, Jan. 20, 1979; children: Lucy Clairmont, Henry Tyrrell. BA with honors, U. East Anglia, Norwich, Eng., 1967. Product mgr. Unilever, London, 1968-71; account exec. Garland Compton, London, 1971, Young & Rubicam, London, 1971-80; mng. dir. Young & Rubicam, Melbourne, Australia, 1981-83; dir. Young & Rubicam, London, 1983-84, Wight, Collins, Rutherford, Scott, Mathews, Marcantonio, London, 1984—. Sec. ward Labour Party, London, 1978, publicity cons., 1979-80; gov. Inner London Edn. Authority Jr. Sch., London, 1978. Fellow Advt. Inst. Australia (diploma 1981). Home: 13 Camden Sq, London NW1, England Office: Wight Collins Rutherford, Scott Mathews Marcantonio, 41-44 Great Queen St, London WC2, England

FEAREY, PORTER, distribution and sales executive, retired; b. Albany, N.Y., June 27, 1918; s. Porter and Elizabeth B.W. (Martin) F.; student Williams Coll., 1938-39, S.W. Tex. State U., 1946-48; m. Mary King Estill, May 14, 1944; 1 child, Mary King Estill (Mrs. John Storie). Began career as salesman Westchester Pubs., Inc., Noel Macy Chain, Yonkers, N.Y., 1940-41; mktg. supr. Gulf Oil Corp., N.Y.C., 1941-45, Tex. Co. (Texaco, Inc.), Houston, 1945-46; owner, pres. Water Service Co., San Antonio, 1948-82; real estate investor, rancher, 1982—; pres., dir. Apartimientos S.A., Monterrey, Mexico, 1958-68; owner, pres. Ice Service, Inc., San Antonio. Mem. central exec. com. Episcopal Diocese West Tex., 1960—, mem. dept. fin., 1963—, mem. exec. bd., 1963-66, 69-72, mem. central exec. com. Episc. Advance Fund; del. Tex. Council Chs., 1968, 69-72, 73-74, 75-76, 77-78, 78-79, 79-80, 80-81, 81-82, 82-83, 83-84, 84-85; del. Tex. State Republican Conv., 1960, 74; del. Comal County (Tex.) Rep. Conv., 1956, 74; bd. dirs. Tex. State Guard Assn., 1975-78. Served with USAAF, World War II; ret. Mem. Comal County (dir.), New Braunfels (dir.), S. Tex. chambers commerce, Good Govt. League (dir.), Episc. Churchmen's Assn., Williams Coll. Alumni Assn., Am. Legion, Mil. Order Loyal Legion U.S. (comdr. Tex. commandery 1965-75), Mil. Order World Wars, Res. Officers Assn. Ret. Officers Assn., Armed Forces Communications and Electronics Assn., Am. Ordnance Assn., San Antonio Zool. Soc., Comal County Hist. Soc. (dir.), New Braunfels Conservation Soc. (dir.), Mil. Order Fgn. Wars U.S., St. Nicholas Soc. N.Y.C., N.Y. So. Soc., St. Georges Soc. N.Y., S.R., Soc. Colonial Wars, SAR, Vets. Assn. 7th Regiment N.Y. N.G., Assos. Engr. Corps 7th Regiment N.Y. N.G., Mil. Order World Wars, Am. Georg. Soc., Nat. Wild Life Fed., Tex. Rangers Assn. Found., Kappa Alpha. Republican. Episcopalian (vestryman, sr. warden; diocesan exec. bd.). Clubs: Rotary (Paul Harris Fellow), Elks; Explorers (N.Y.C.); St. Anthony (San Antonio); Williams (N.Y.C.); Corpus Christi Yacht, Argyle, Ft. Sam Houston Officers. Home: 33 Rue Charles San Antonio TX 78217-5156 Office: Los Angeles Ranch PO Box 633 New Braunfels TX 78130

FEATHER, JOHN PLINY, library science educator, writer; b. Leeds, Eng., Dec. 20, 1947; s. Harold R. and Ethel M. (Barrett) F.; m. Sarah Rees, July 10, 1971. BA, Oxford (Eng.) U., 1968, BLitt, MA, 1972; PhD, Loughborough (Eng.) U., 1986. Asst. librarian Bodleian Library, Oxford, 1972-79; fellow in bibliography Cambridge U. Library, Eng., 1977-78; lectr. library sci. Loughborough U., 1979-84, sr. lectr., 1984-88, prof. library sci., 1988—; vis. prof. UCLA, 1982; cons. Brit. Council, 1983—, UNESCO, 1984-85; mem. Acad. Adv. Bd. 19th Century Short Title Catalogue, 1983—; com. mem. Brit. Book Trade Index, 1984—, Book Trade History Group, 1986—. Author: The English Provincial Book Trade to 1850: A Checklist of Secondary Sources, 1981, English Book Prospectuses: An Illustrated History, 1984, The Provincial Book Trade in Eighteenth-Century England, 1985, A Dictionary of Book History, 1986, A History of British Publishing, 1988; editor: The Collected Works of Robert Armin, 2 vols., 1972, Kemp's Nine Days Wonder, 1972; contbr. articles to profl. jours., chpts to books. Fellow Library Assn. (editor Rare Books Group Newsletter 1974-78, subcom. on conservation and preservation 1984—); mem. Oxford Bibliog. Soc. (gen. editor 1975-88, pres. 1988—), Bibliog. Soc. (council 1982-85), Internat. Fedn. Library Assns. (mem. com. on conservation 1985—, mem. Brit. nat. com. 1985—). Office: Loughborough U, Dept Library and Info Studies, Leicester LE11 3TU, England

FEATHERMAN, BERNARD, steel company executive; b. Phila., May 3, 1929; s. Jacob H. and Eva (Feldman) F.; m. Sandra Green, May 29, 1958; children—Andrew C., John James. B.S., Temple U., 1951, postgrad. Grad. Bus. Sch., 1951-52, Law Sch., 1952-54; postgrad. Wharton Sch., U. Pa., 1965-66. Pres. Bernard Franklin Co., Phila., 1958—, Western Steel Co., Phila., 1961—; chmn. bd. Western Metal Bed Co., Phila., 1978—, JBM Equipment Group, Inc., Phila., 1987—; chmn. bd. dirs. Automated Techs., Phila., 1988—; dir. Pa. Steel and Aluminum Corp., Huntingdon Valley, Pa.; bd. dirs. Material Handling Inst., Pitts., 1978-79. Contbr. articles to profl. jours. Inventor electronics locking locker. Mem. exec. bd. Southeast chpt. Nat. Found. March of Dimes, 1969-82, vice chmn., 1978-80; pres. Phila. Assn. for Retarded Citizens, 1975-77; chmn. Mayor's Adv. Com. on Mental Health-Mental Retardation, Phila., 1979—; co-chmn. Mayor's Small Bus. Adv. Com., Phila., 1979—; del. White House Conf. on Small Bus., 1980, Pa. del., vice chmn., 1986; chmn. small bus. council Democratic Nat. Com., 1982-84; fin. chmn. Pa. Democratic Orgn., 1985-86; mem. adv. bd. Coll. Liberal Arts and Scis., Temple U., 1982-87, West Chester (Pa.) State U. Bus. Sch., 1986-87, Frankford Hosp., 1983—; chmn. 3d Congl. Small Bus. Council, Phila., 1984—; bd. dirs. Phila. Citywide Devel. Corp., 1984—. Recipient award of appreciation Small Bus. Council, Dem. Nat. Com., 1983; Gold medal of Honor Adult Trainees Found., Phila., 1976; citation White House Conf. on Small Bus., 1980. Mem. Assn. of Steel Distbrs. (nat. pres. 1975-76, 87-88, named Steel Distbr. of Yr. 1976), Shelving Mfrs. Assn. (nat. chmn. 1977-78), Pa. Soc. Lodge: B'nai B'rith (pres. 1980-82, Nat. Youth Services award Quaker City lodge 1985), Hunting Park West Bus. Assn. (pres. 1986—), Assn. Steel Distbrs. (nat. pres. 1975-76, 86-87). Home: 2100 Spruce St Philadelphia PA 19103

FEATHERMAN, SANDRA, educator; b. Phila., Apr. 14, 1934; d. Albert N. and Rebe (Burd) Green; B.A., U. Pa., 1955, M.A., 1978, Ph.D., 1978; m. Bernard Featherman, Mar. 29, 1958; children—Andrew Charles, John James. Asst. prof. dept. polit. sci. Temple U., Phila., 1978-84, assoc. prof., 1984—, chmn. grad. program, 1982-84, dir. MPA program, 1984-85. Mem. Sch. Bd. Nominating Panel, Phila., 1969-71, 79-81; bd. dirs. Citizens Com. Public Edn. in Phila., 1977—, pres., 1979-81; pres. Pa. Fedn. Community Coll., faculty senate Temple U., 1985-86, dir. Ctr. for Pub. Policy, 1986—, asst. to pres., 1986—; trustees, 1974-75; trustee Community Coll. Phila., 1970—, chmn. bd. trustees, 1984-86; life trustee Samuel Fels Found.; bd. dirs. United Way S.E. Pa., 1977—, United Way Pa., 1981-84, Concerto Soloists of Phila., 1978-81; mem. commn. jud. selection and evaluation Phila. Bar Assn., 1979-81; nat. bd. dirs. Girls Clubs Am., 1971-74, pres., Phila., 1971-73; mem. Pa. Council on Arts, 1979-83; dir. Women and Founds. Corp. Philanthropy, 1986—; mem. nat. bd. dirs. Women and Founds.-Corp. Philanthropy, 1986—; v.p. Jewish Community Relations Council, 1982—, Phila., bd. dirs. 1986—; speaker Commonwealth of Pa. Humanities Council, 1988. Recipient Brooks Graves award Pa. Polit. Sci. Assn., 1987, City of Phila. Community Service award, 1984, Louise Waterman Wise award Am. Jewish Congress, 1988. Mem. Am. Planning Assn., Am. Polit. Sci. Assn., Am. Soc. Public Adminstrn., AAUW (dir. Phila. chpt. 1975-78, 80—, pres. 1984—, chair internat. fellowships panel 1987—, nat. chair ednl. found. program Internat. Fellows Panel 1988—, Outstanding Woman award 1986). Author: Jews, Black and Ethnics, 1979; also articles. Home: 2100 Spruce St Philadelphia PA 19103 Office: Temple U Broad and Montgomery Sts Philadelphia PA 19122

FEATHERSTONE, JOHN DOUGLAS BERNARD, biochemistry educator; b. Stratford, N.Z., Apr. 26, 1944; came to U.S., 1980; s. Alfred Douglas and Yvonne May (Richmond) F.; B.Sc. in Chemistry and Math., Victoria U., Wellington, N.Z., 1962-64, Ph.D. in Chemistry, 1977; M.Sc. in Phys. Chemistry, U. Manchester, 1975; m. Patricia Helen Price, Jan. 21, 1967; children—Michelle, Mark. Quality control chemist Unilever, N.Z., 1965-66; tech. mgr. Chem Industries, Wellington, N.Z., 1966-72; prodn. mgr. Quinoderm Pharms., Oldham, Eng., 1972-74; lectr. pharm. chemistry Central Inst. Tech., N.Z., 1977-78; sr. research fellow Med. Research Council, N.Z., 1979-80; sr. research assoc. Eastman Dental Center, Rochester, N.Y., 1980—, chmn. dept. oral biology, 1983—; asst. prof. U. Rochester, parttime, 1980-83, assoc. prof., 1983—; cons. dental chemistry and dental products, 1980—. Leader scouts, N.Z., 1962-71, mem. N.Z. Nat. Tng. Team, 1968-71; asst. nat. commr. Venturer Scouts N.Z., 1968-70; mem. N.Z. Outdoor Tng. Adv. Bd., 1978-79, N.Z. Mountain Rescue, 1976-80. Recipient Colgate Research prize N.Z. Internat. Assn. Dental Research, 1976; Colgate Travel award Internat. Assn. Dental Research Australia, 1976; Edward Hatton award World Internat. Assn. Dental Research Meeting, Copenhagen, 1977; Hamilton award Royal Soc. N.Z., 1979. Fellow N.Z. Inst. Chemistry; mem. European Orgn. Caries Research (sr.), Internat. Assn. Dental Research. Contbr. articles to profl. jours. Home: 2119 Clinton Ave Rochester NY 14618 Office: Eastman Dental Ctr 625 Elmwood Ave Rochester NY 14620

FEAVER, JOHN CLAYTON, philosopher, educator; b. Fowler, Calif., June 24, 1911; s. Ernest Albion and Agnes Katherine (Hansen) F.; m. Margaret Storsand, June 21, 1936; children: John Hansen, Katherine Elaine, Margaret Ellen. A.B., Fresno State Coll., 1933; student, San Francisco Theol. Sem., 1934; B.D., Pacific Sch. Religion, 1936; Ph.D., Yale U., 1949. Asst., then assoc. prof. philosophy Berea Coll., 1941-51; Kingfisher Coll. prof. philosophy religion and ethics U. Okla., 1951-81, emeritus, 1981—, David Ross Boyd prof. philosophy, 1959-81, emeritus, 1981—; dist. prof. philosophy U. of Sci. and Arts of Okla., Chickasha, 1988—; chmn. exec. com. Coll. Liberal Studies U. Okla., 1961-73; chmn. exec. com. S.W. Center Human Relations Studies, 1971-81. Co-editor: Religion in Philosophical and Cultural Perspective, 1967. Dir. Scholar-Leadership Enrichment Program, 1977-87. Recipient. Disting. Service citation U. Okla., 1979; Disting. Prof. Philosophy, U. Sci. and Arts of Okla., 1987—. Mem. Am. Philos. Assn., Southwestern Philos. Soc. (pres. 1960), Soc. Philosophy Religion, Am. Acad. Religion, AAUP. Phi Beta Kappa, Omicron Delta Kappa. Home: 900 E Boyd St Norman OK 73071 Office: Univ of Sci and Arts of Oklahoma PO Box 81268 Chickasha OK 73018

FEBRES-CORDERO, LEON, former president of Ecuador; b. Guayaquil, Ecuador, Mar. 9, 1931; m. Eugenia Cordovez; 4 children. Ed. Charlotte Hall Mil. Acad., The Mercerburg Acad.; BEE, Stevens Inst. Tech. Mech. engr. Nat. Brewer Co., Emelec Electric Co.; exec. mgr. Indsl. Flour Mill; exec. gen. mgr. San Luis Co. and San Adolfo Co.; exec. gen. mgr. Ecuadorean Cardboard Industry; exec. mgr. Inter-Am. Textile Co.; pres. Latin-Am. Indsl. Assn., 1975-76; congressman, 1966-67; senator, 1968-70, chmn. Senate Com. on Fin. Economy, 1968-70; dir. Indsl. Chamber of Guayaquil, 1968-70; v.p., 1970-72, pres., 1972-79; pres. Ecuadorean Fedn. Indsl. Chambers, 1973-70; congressman Ho. of Reps., 1979-84; pres. of Ecuador, 1984-88. Social Christian. Roman Catholic. Address: Office of Pres, Quito Ecuador *

FEDDER, DONALD OWEN, pharmacist, educator; b. Balt., Nov. 20, 1926; s. William Samuel and Rose F.; student Western Md. Coll., 1944-47; Pharm. B.S., U. Md., 1950; M.P.H., Johns Hopkins U., 1978, Dr.P.H., 1982; m. Michaeline R. Fedder; children: Debra M. Fedder Goren, Ira Louis. Staff pharmacist Pikesville (Md.) Pharmacy, 1950-51; chief pharmacist, owner Fedder's Pharmacy and Fedder Med. Services, Balt., 1951-74; pres. Med. Equipment & Supply Co., Inc., Balt., 1970-76; assoc. prof., dir. community pharmacy and pharmacy high blood pressure programs U. Md. Sch. Pharmacy, 1974—, assoc. prof. Epidemiology and Preventative med., 1987—; chmn. Md. Commn. on High Blood Pressure and Related Cardiovascular Risk Factors, 1984—; chmn. hypertension com. Md. affiliate Am. Heart Assn., 1984-86, sec. bd. dirs., 1984-86, chmn. health site com., 1987—; chmn., exec. dir. Bd. Orthotist Cert., 1984—; cons. in field. Bd. dirs. Dundalk Concert Assn., 1963-75; candidate Md. Legis., 1970. Served with U.S. Army, 1944-45. Recipient Order Double Star, Alpha Zeta Omega, 1972, 75; Beta chpt. award Phi Alpha, 1950; Bowl of Hygeia award, 1980, Vol. of Yr. award Md. Pub. Health Assn, 1988, Disting. Achievement award Md. Pharmacists Assn., 1988. Fellow Acad. of Pharmacy Practice, Soc. Pub. Health Edn.; mem. Am. (dir., chmn. 1976-77), Md. (President's award 1971) pharm. assns., Am. Assn. Colls. Pharmacy, Acad. Pharmacy Practice (pres. 1973-74), Balt. Met. Pharm. Assn. (pres. 1968), Sigma Xi, Rho Chi. Democrat. Jewish. Club: Optimist (pres. local club 1963-64). Contbr. articles to profl. jours. Home: 136 W Welcome Alley Baltimore MD 21201 Office: 20 N Pine St Baltimore MD 21201

FEDER, ROBERT, lawyer; b. N.Y.C., Nov. 29, 1930; s. Benjamin and Bertha (Bloodstein) F.; m. Marjorie Feder, Dec. 3, 1950; children—Susan E., Judith D., Benjamin D., Jessica R., Abigail M. B.A. cum laude, CCNY, 1953; LL.B., Columbia U., 1953. Bar: N.Y. 1953, U.S. Tax Ct. 1956, U.S. Dist. Ct. (so. dist.) N.Y. 1973. Vice pres., gen. counsel Presdl. Realty Corp., White Plains, N.Y., 1953-71; ptnr. Cuddy & Feder, White Plains, 1971—; bd. dirs. Westchester County (N.Y.) Legal Aid Soc., 1972—, pres., 1974-78; adj. prof. sch. bus. Columbia U., 1988—. Pres., White Plains Community Action Program, 1967-69; bd. dirs. White Plains Hosp. Med. Ctr., 1979—, also vice chmn., sec.; commr. White Plains Housing Authority, 1984—; trustee SUNY-Purchase Coll. Found., 1988—; adj. prof. Pace U. Law Sch., 1985-87. Mem. ABA, N.Y. State Bar Assn., Westchester County Bar Assn., White Plains Bar Assn. Home: 9 Oxford Rd White Plains NY 10605 Office: 90 Maple Ave White Plains NY 10601

FEDER, SAUL E., lawyer; b. Bklyn., Oct. 8, 1943; s. Joseph Robert and Toby Feder; m. Marcia Carrie Weinblatt, Feb. 25, 1968; children: Howard Avram, Tamar Miriam, Michael Elon, David Ben-Zion Aaron. BS, NYU, 1965; JD, Bklyn. Law Sch., 1968. Bar: N.Y. 1969, U.S. Ct. Claims 1970, U.S. Customs Ct. 1972, U.S. Ct. Customs & Patent Appeals 1974, U.S. Ct. Appeals (2nd cir.) 1969, U.S. Supreme Ct. 1972. Mng. lawyer Queens Legal Services, Jamaica, N.Y., 1970-71; ptnr. Previte-Glasser-Feder & Farber, Jackson Heights, N.Y., 1972-73, Hein-Waters-Klein & Feder, Far Rockaway, N.Y., 1973-78, Regosin-Edwards-Stone & Feder, N.Y.C., 1979—; spl. investigator Bur. Election Frauds, Atty. Gen.'s Office, N.Y.C., 1976-77, spl. dep. atty. gen., 1969-70; arbitrator, consumer counsel small claims div. Civil Ct. City of N.Y., 1974—. Pres. Young Israel Briarwood, Queens, N.Y., 1978; chmn. polit. affairs com. Young Israel Staten Island, 1985—; rep. candidate State of N.Y. Assembly, Queens, 1976; chmn. Stat Pac Polit. Action Com., Young Israel Staten Island Pub. Affairs Com. Mem. N.Y. Bar Assn., Queens County Bar Assn. Nassau County Bar Assn., Am. Judges Assn., N.Y. Trial Lawyers Assn., Internat. Acad. Law & Sci., Am. Jud. Soc., Soc. Med. Jurisprudence, Am. Arbitration Assn. Republican. Home: 259 Ardmore Ave Staten Island NY 10314 Office: Regosin Edwards Stone & Feder 225 Broadway New York NY 10007

FEDERMAN, JACOB, cardiologist; b. Ainring, West Germany, Oct. 31, 1946; arrived in Australia, 1947; s. Chaim and Freda (Kagan) F.; m. Rachel Gerczuk, Jan. 23, 1972; children—Dean Elliot, Simone Lisa. M.B.B.S., U. Melbourne, 1970. Diplomate Australian Bd. Cardiology. Med. intern Royal Melbourne (Australia) Hosp., 1971; med. resident, registrar Alfred Hosp., Melbourne, 1972-74, research fellow cardiology, 1975-77; fellow cardiology Mayo Clinic, Rochester, Minn., 1977-79; cardiologist, cardiology service Alfred Hosp., Melbourne, 1979—, resident med. staff, 1979—; tchr. med. students Monash U., 1979—. Contbr. articles to cardiac jours. Nat. Heart Found. Australia travel grantee, 1977. Fellow Royal Australian Coll. Physicians, Am. Coll. Cardiology; mem. Australian Med. Assn., Brit. Med. Assn., Australian and New Zealand Cardiac Soc., Am. Soc. Echocardiography, Australian Soc. Ultrasound in Medicine. Jewish. Avocations: golf, tennis, table tennis, chess. Home: 5 Blossom Ct, Doncaster, Melbourne 3108, Australia Office: Alfred Hosp Cardiology Service, Commercial Rd, Prahran, Melbourne 3181, Australia

FEE, GERARD WAYNE COWLE, professional association executive; b. North Fairfield, Ohio, Feb. 12, 1933; s. Cleland Randolph and Helen Marcella (Cole) F. BA, Washington & Lee U., 1955; LittB, Oxford U., 1959; postgrad., U. Madrid, 1955, 1959-60. Asst. to pres. Lake Erie Coll., Painesville, Ohio, 1964-74; exec. dir. Ohio State Pharm. Assn., Columbus, Ohio, 1974-79; exec. sec. Ohio State Bd. Optometry, Columbus, 1979-80; exec. dir. The Inst. Internal Auditors, Altamonte Springs, Fla., 1980-81; dir. adminstrv. services The Lexington (Ky.) Sch., 1982-84; exec. dir. EDP Auditors Assn., Carol Stream, Ill., 1984—; lectr. various univs. and assns. Editor Ohio Pharmacist jour., 1975-79, EDP Auditor Update, 1984—. Reading clk. Ohio Ho. of Reps., 1961-63, rules clk., 1962-63; sec. treas. Ohio Pharmacy Polit. Action Com., 1975-79; vestry mem. Christ Ch. Anglican, 1979, 82; founder, pres. Blue Grass Assn. Ind. Schs., 1982-84. Fulbright scholar, 1955-57. Mem. Oxford Soc., Am. Soc. Assn. Execs., Wheaton (Ill.) C. of C., Conf. Computer Audit, Phi Beta Kappa, Pi Sigma Alpha. Republican. Clubs: United Oxford & Cambridge (London); Athletic of Columbus. Home: 2557 North Park Cleveland Heights OH 44106 Office: EDP Auditors Assn Found 455 Kehoe Blvd PO Box 88180 Carol Stream IL 60188-0180

FEELY, RICHARD ALAN, physician, surgeon; b. Berwyn, Ill., Jan. 4, 1952; s. Daniel Richard and Donna Jean (LaCount) F.; m. Carol Anne Frieders, June 29, 1974; 1 son, Brad Richard. B.S., N.E. Mo. State U., 1974; D.O., Kirksville Coll. Osteo. Medicine, 1978. Diplomate Nat. Bd. Examiners Osteo. Physicians and Surgeons; cert. Am. Osteopathic Bd. Gen. Practice, 1986. Dir. osteo. manipulative medicine Good Samaritan Hosp., Tampa, Fla., 1979-80; physician Mauer Clinic, Zion, Ill., 1980-81; instr. Chgo. Coll. Osteo. Medicine, 1980-82, asst. prof., 1982-83, clin. asst. prof. osteo. medicine, 1983-86; clin. assoc. prof. family medicine, 1986—; pres. Rhema Med. Assocs. Ltd., Chgo., 1985—. Sci. editor Cranial Acad. Newsletter, 1983—; editor Clinical Cranial Osteopathy: Selected Readings, 1988. Mem. Sutherland Cranial Found. (faculty mem. 1982—), Cranial Acad. (trustee 1983—), Christian Med. Found. (regional v.,p.), Am. Osteo. Assn., North Am. Acad. Manipulative Medicine, Am. Acad. Orthopedic Medicine (trustee 1987—). Republican. Roman Catholic. Office: Rhema Med Assocs Ltd 46 E Oak St Suite 401 Chicago IL 60611

FEENEY, DON JOSEPH, JR., psychologist; b. Greenville, N.C., Jan. 17, 1948; s. Don Joseph Sr. and Louise (Saieed) F.; 1 child, Kelly Lynn. BA, Colgate U., 1971; MA, Gov.'s State U., 1973; PhD, Loyola U., Chgo., 1979, fellow, 1976. Registered psychologist, Ill., Ind.; cert. additions counselor. Clin. dir. Champaign (Ill.) Council on Alcoholism, 1976-79; pvt. practice psychology, hypnotherapy, family services Downers Grove, Ill., 1979—; team chief Dangerous Drugs Com., Chgo., 1979-80; psychologist Tri-City Mental Health Ctr., East Chicago, Ind., 1980-82; psychologist alcohol treatment program Christ Hosp., Oak Lawn, Ill., 1982—; chmn. adv. council on alcoholism Gov.'s State U., University Park, Ill., 1979-82; cons. Psychol. Cons. Services, Downers Grove, 1985—. Contbr. articles to profl. jours. Mem. Am. Psychol. Assn., Ill. Psychol. Assn. Roman Catholic. Office: Psychol Cons Services 6800 S Main St Suite 12 Downers Grove IL 60516

FEES, JAMES RICHARD, entrepreneur, investment banker; b. Fairbury, Nebr., Sept. 21, 1931; s. Robert Anthony and Mildred Pauline (Holtz) F.; 1 dau., Christina Marie. B.A., U. Notre Dame, 1957; diploma Arabic, Georgetown U., 1959; diploma French, Alliance Francaise, Paris, 1965. Diplomat, Dept. State, Washington, Arab countries, Switzerland, 1960-80; chief exec. officer Tradeco Ltd., Geneva, 1980—; bd. dirs. Valentine & Co., San Francisco, Fargo Investment Corp., Brussels; advisor Gulf Internat. Fin. Mgrs., Geneva, 1981-82, Riantel Fin. S.A., Basel, Switzerland, 1981—; pres. Internat. Tech. Group Ltd., 1984—; chmn. Luxembourg Fin. Group, 1982—. Mem. Rep. Senatorial Inner Circle, Washington, 1981—, founder Rep. Presdl. Group, 1982—, internat. chmn. Reps. Abroad, Switzerland, 1982—. Served with AUS, 1953-55. Mem. Swiss-Am. C. of C., Am. C. of C. in Egypt. Roman Catholic. Clubs: American (Brussels); St. James (London). Home: 30 chemin du Pommier, 1218 Geneva Switzerland Office: Tradeco Ltd, World Trade Ctr, 1215 Geneva Switzerland Office: Fargo Investment Corp, Blvd E Jacqmain, 180, 1210 Brussels Belgium

FEFFER, PAUL EVAN, publishing company executive; b. N.Y.C., June 27, 1921; s. Joseph A. and Eve (Max) F.; m. Juliette Fein, July 30, 1964; children: Paula, Hilary, Joseph, Alison, Emily, Nicholas. Student, Cornell U. Sch. Medicine, 1940-42, USCG Acad., 1944; postgrad., NYU, 1963-64. Pres. H.M. Snyder & Co., N.Y.C., 1946-55; founder, pres. Feffer & Simons, Inc.subs. Doubleday & Co., N.Y.C., 1955-86; chmn. Feffer & Simons, Inc. subs. W.R. Grace Co., N.Y.C., 1986-88, Baker & Taylor Co. div. W.R. Grace & Co., N.Y.C., 1986—; Fleetbooks Ltd., Zurich Feffer and Simons, B.V., Holland; dir. Victory Pub., London,, Vakil's Feffer & Simons, Inc., India, Feffer and Simons, Australia, Feffer and Simons, Tokyo; mem. govt. adv. com. Am. Book PUb. Council, 1983—. Chmn. adv. com. USIA, 1982-88. Served to lt. (j.g.) USCGR, 1942-46. Mem. Assn. Am. Pubs. (dir. 1982-83, chmn. internat. div. 1982-83). Home: 60 Sutton Pl New York NY 10022 Office: 100 Park Ave New York NY 10017

FEGAN, DAVID ALBERT, lawyer; b. Washington, July 13, 1918; s. David B. and Elizabeth (Jost) F.; m. Lorraine Coyle, Aug. 14, 1943; children: David, Stephen. Student, Harvard U., 1938; LLB, George Washington U., 1942. Bar: S.C. 1943, D.C. 1943, U.S. Supreme Ct. 1944, Md. 1945. Ptnr. Morris, Pearce, Gardner & Pratt, Washington, 1943-60; sole practice Washington, 1960—; Queen's counsel, U.K., 1969—; bd. dirs. Calvert Bank & Trust Co., Prince Frederick, Md.; bd. dirs., pres. Old Line Brick and Tile Co., Mar-Bar Devel. Corp.; bd. dirs., v.p. Capitol Clay Products Inc., St. Leonard's Devel. Corp. Served with USNR, 1942-43. Mem. ABA, D.C. Bar Assn. Republican. Roman Catholic. Club: Reciprocit (pres. 1987). Home: 8709 Seven Locks Rd Bethesda MD 20817 Office: 1511 K St NW Suite 927 Washington DC 20005

FEHLHAMMER, WOLF PETER, chemistry educator; b. Munich, Fed. Republic Germany, Sept. 9, 1939; s. Georg and Franziska Henriette (Groebmair) F.; m. Elisabeth Monika Donhauser, Oct. 14, 1963; children—Michael Georg, Susan Pat Gail, Manuel Anton. Grad., Ludwigs Oberrealschule, Munich, 1959; cert. in Chemistry, Tech. U. Munich, 1966, Ph.D., 1968. Postdoctoral fellow U. Wis., Madison, 1969-70; faculty mem. and research assoc. U. Munich, 1970-76; assoc. prof. chemistry U. Erlangen-Nuremberg, Fed. Republic Germany, 1976-83; full prof. chemistry Free U. Berlin, 1983—, exec. dir. dept. inorganic chemistry, 1984—; guest prof. U. Rennes, France, 1980, 81. Contbr. numerous articles to profl. jours. Mem. German Chem. Soc. (Carl Duisberg prize 1981), Am. Chem. Soc. Roman Catholic. Home: Westhofener Weg 33, Berlin-Nikolasee, D-1000 Berlin Federal Republic of Germany Office: Inst Anorganische u Analytische Chemie, Free Univ Berlin, Fabeckstrasse 34-36, D-1000 Berlin 33 Federal Republic of Germany

FEHLMANN, PETER ROBERT, engineering company executive; b. Berne, Switzerland, Sept. 19, 1922; s. Johann Kaspar and Marta Gertrud (Frey) F.; m. Susan Melanie Weiss, Oct. 29, 1966; children—Peter Lorenz H., Terry Henry N., Marc Philip St. Graduated University, Geneva, 1943; LL.D., University, Berne, 1948. Sec., Winterthur Ins., Zurich, 1948-51; insp. Am. Casualty Co., Reading, Pa., 1951-53; mng. dir. Fehlmann Hydraulic Engring. Inc., Berne, 1953-60, pres., 1960—; pres. Bernische Erdol AG, Berne, 1975—, Fehlmann Españ a, Madria, 1970, Fehlmann Infilco AG, Berne, 1971, Supec Holding Co., Fribourg, 1972—; mem. Swisspetrol Holding, Zug, 1982—. Contbr. articles to profl. jours. Served to capt. Swiss Army, 1942-77. Mem. Am. Waterworks Assn. Mem. Freisinnige Partei Bern. Club: Round Table (Berne). Lodge: Lions (Berne) Home: Augsburgerstrasse 17, 3052 Zollikofen, Berne Switzerland Office: Fehlmann Hydraulic Engring Inc, Monbijoustrasse 16, 3001 Berne Switzerland

FEHR, PETER J., physicist, consultant; b. Schweinfurt, Bavaria, Fed. Republic Germany, May 27, 1957; s. Karl and Ursula (Schalla) F. Diploma in physics, Bayr J. Maxim. U., Wuerzburg, Fed. Republic Germany, 1983. With tech. control support Altos Computer Systems, Graefelfing, Fed. Republic Germany, 1983-86; mgr. product mktg. Aeni Computer, Starnberg, Fed. Republic Germany, 1986-87; system cons. Sun Microsystems GmbH, Unterfoehring, Fed. Republic Germany, 1988—. Contbr. articles to profl. jours. Mem. adv. bd. Munich Proprietors' Orgn., 1986—. With German Reconnaissance, 1976-77. Grantee German Acad. Exchange Service, Bonn, 1980. Mem. German Phys. Soc., German Mus., Stuttgart Stock Market Club. Roman Catholic. Home: Dachauerstrasse 265, 8000 Munich Federal Republic of Germany Office: Sun Microsystems GmbH, Bahnhofstr 27, 8043 Unterfoehring Federal Republic of Germany

FEHRLE, KLAUS PAUL, business executive; b. Stuttgart, Federal Republic Germany, Aug. 24, 1955; m. Dorothea Schnabel, Jan. 9, 1985. Diploma in Bus. Adminstrn. and Econs., U. Hohenheim, Fed. Republic Germany, 1983. Mktg. mgr. Reinfeldtechnik GmbH, Stuttgart, 1983-84; mgmt. cons. Roland Berger & Ptnrs., Munich, 1984-85; owner, mktg. dir. Falk Mktg. GmbH, Stuttgart, 1985—; cons. Basf AG, 1985—, Siemens AG, 1986—. Contbr. articles on medicine-tech. and mgmt. to profl. publs. Mem. Mktg. Club. Office: Falk Mktg GmbH, Nordwestring 19, D-7024 Filderstadt 1 Federal Republic of Germany

FEHRMAN, CHERIE CHRISTINA, interior designer, writer; b. London, Apr. 13, 1945; came to U.S., 1958, naturalized, 1971; d. James Albert and Lucia Allen; B.A. in English and Creative Writing, San Francisco State U., 1969; postgrad. U. Calif., Berkeley, m. Kenneth R. Fehrman, Apr. 7, 1967. Savs. officer Citizens Savs. & Loan, San Francisco, 1969, asst. br. mgr., to 1974; v.p. Kenneth R. Fehrman Interior Design, Ltd., San Francisco, 1976—; free-lance writer, fiction and non-fiction, San Francisco, 1974—; author: The Complete School Handbook, 1981; The School Secretary's Encyclopedic Dictionary, Postwar Interior Design: 1945-60; Designing Women; (novels) Disc, 1980; Fanatic; Einstein, Christ and David Bowie; Friends and Other Fantasies; Death by Design; contbr. articles to design pubs.; tchr. design seminars. Mem. Authors Guild. Democrat. Office: Curtis Brown Ltd care Clyde Taylor 10 Astor Pl New York NY 10003

FEIGELSON, JEAN GEORGES, pediatrician; b. Petrograd, Ingria, USSR, Feb. 3, 1924; arrived in France, 1929; s. E. and H. (Losner) F.; m. Karin Johansson; children: Christian, Cecile, Annicka, J. Thomas, Eric, Elisabeth, Mathieu. MD, Faculte de Medecine, Paris, 1951, CES pediatrics, 1956. Practice medicine specializing in pediatrics Paris, 1956—. Decorated Croix de Guerre; recipient medal Cystic Fibrosis Assn., 1965. Club: Lions (Paris). Home and Office: 153 rue de Saussure, 75017 Paris France

FEIGEN, RICHARD L., art dealer; b. Chgo., Aug. 8, 1930; s. Arthur P. and Shirley (Bierman) F.; m. Sandra Elizabeth Canning Walker, Feb. 23, 1966 (div. 1978); children: Philippa Canning, Richard Wood Bliss. B.A., Yale U., 1952; M.B.A., Harvard U., 1954. Asst. treas. Beneficial Standard Life Ins. Co., Los Angeles, 1955-56; mem. N.Y. Stock Exchange, 1956-57; pres., dir. Richard L. Feigen & Co., Inc., N.Y.C. and Chgo., 1957—; chmn. bd., treas. Castelli Feigen Corcoran Gallery, Inc.; mem. com. works fine art N.Y. State Office Bldg., Harlem; lectr. in field. Contbr. articles to art publs. Candidate, del. Democratic Nat. Conv., 1972; trustee John Jay Homestead Assn., Katonah, N.Y., 1976—. Fellow Mpls. Soc. Fine Arts, Met. Mus. Art, Art Inst. Chgo.; mem. Art Dealers Assn. Am. (dir. 1972-76, 86—), Harvard Bus. Sch. Assn., Phi Gamma Delta. Clubs: Arts, Tavern (Chgo.). Home: Cantitoe House Cantitoe Rd Katonah NY 10536 also: Cantitoe House Cantitoe Rd Katonah NY 10536 Office: 950 N. Michigan Ave Chicago IL 60611

FEIGIN, RALPH DAVID, pediatrician, educator; b. N.Y.C., Apr. 3, 1938; s. Jack Bernard and Dorothy Phyllis (Strauss) F.; m. Judith Sue Zobel, June 26, 1960; children: Susan M., Michael E., Debra F. A.B., Columbia U., 1958; M.D., Boston U., 1962. Diplomate: Am. Bd. Pediatrics. Pediatric intern Boston City Hosp., 1962-63; pediatric resident Boston City Hosp. and Mass. Gen. Hosp., 1963-65; teaching fellow pediatrics Harvard U. Med. Sch., 1964-65; from asst. prof. to prof. pediatrics Washington U. Med. Sch., St. Louis, 1968-77; dir. div. infectious diseases, dept. pediatrics Washington U. Med. Sch., 1973-77; prof. pediatrics, chmn. dept. Baylor Coll. Medicine, Houston, 1977—; physician-in-chief Tex. Children's Hosp., 1977—, exec. v.p., 1987—; pediatric service Harris County Hosp. Dist., 1977—; pediatrician-in-chief Methodist Hosp., 1980—; adv. ad hoc study group spl. infectious disease problems U.S. Army Med. Research and Devel. Command, 1974-83; vis. prof., cons. in field; pres. Pediatric Research Found., 1982—. Co-editor: Nutrition and the Developing Nervous System, 1975, Textbook of Pediatric Infectious Diseases, 1981, 2d edit. 1987; editorial bd.: Pediatrics, 1978—, Jour. Pediatric Infectious Diseases; assoc. editor: Jour. Infectious Diseases, 1984—; contbr. articles to med. jours., chpts. to books. Served with M.C., USAR, 1965-67. Recipient Research Career Devel. award USPHS, 1970, Founders Day award Washington U. Med. Sch., 1977, Sr. Class Outstanding Tchr. award Baylor Coll. Medicine, 1978, 80, 81, 82, 83, 84, 85, 86, Minnie Stevens Piper Professorial award, 1984, John McGovern Outstanding Clin. Faculty award, Baylor Coll. Medicine, 1986; named to Baylor Coll. Medicine Outstanding Tchr. Hall of Fame, 1984; Alumni Teaching scholar Washington U. Med. Sch., 1975. Mem. Am. Pediatric Soc., Soc. Pediatric Research (pres. 1982-83), Am. Acad. Pediatrics, Infectious Disease Soc. Am., Am. Soc. Microbiology, N.Y. Acad. Scis., AMA, Assn. Med. Sch., Pediatric Dept. Chmn., AAAS, Tex. Med. Assn., Tex. Pediatric Soc., Harris County Med. Soc., Houston Pediatric Soc. Office: Baylor Coll Medicine Dept Pediatrics 1 Baylor Plaza Houston TX 77030

FEILDERS, GEORGE GOLDWIN, science equipment executive; b. Ottawa, Ont., Can., Feb. 13, 1943; s. George McRae and Mauvis Eleanor (Kemp) F.; m. Carol Muriel Sproson, June 26, 1965; children: G. Brent, Teri-Anne L. BS, Concordia U., Montreal, Que., Can., 1964. Sales rep. Fisher Sci. Co. Ltd., Fredericton, N.B., 1965-69; account rep. Fisher Sci. Co. Ltd., Ottawa, 1970-74; sales mgr. Fisher Sci. Co. Ltd., Montreal, 1975, dist. mgr., 1976-77; dist. mgr. Jarrell Ash Co., Montreal, 1977-80; pres., founder Seigniory Chem. Products Ltd., Montreal, 1977—, with solar div., 1977-81, with sci. div., 1980—; mgr. advt. Jour. Can. Spectroscopy, Montreal, 1982-86. Active Beaconsfield Minor Hockey Assn., Montreal, 1975-85. City of Beaconsfield award, 1986, Barbara Van Rees award Beaconsfield Minor Hockey Assn., 1986. Mem. Chem. Inst. Can., Spectroscopy Soc. Can., Am. Foundry Soc. of Can. Dept. Agrl. Office: SCP Sci div, 2367 Guenette, Sainte Laurent, PQ Canada H4R 2E9

FEIN, LEAH GOLD, psychologist; b. Minsk, Russia; d. Jacob Lyon and Sarah Freda (Meltzer) Gold; B.S., Albertus Magnus Coll., 1939; M.A., Yale U., 1942, Ph.D. (Marion Talbot fellow), 1944; m. Alfred Gustave Fein, June 10, 1944; 1 son, Ira Hirsh. Health educator New Haven Schs., 1930-43; instr. psychology Carleton Coll., 1944-45; research asso. Conn. Interracial Commn., 1946; chief psychologist Seattle Psychiat. Clinic, 1947-48; prof. U. Bridgeport, 1946-47, 52-58; ind. clin. practice, specializing in clin., child consultation, Seattle, 1948-52, Stamford, Conn., 1952-67, N.Y.C., 1967-81, West Palm Beach, Fla., 1982-87, Stamford, Conn., 1987—; clin. cons. Conn. Commn. on Alcoholism Clinic, 1952-64; research asso. Soc. for Investigation Human Ecology; therapist Norwalk Psychiat. Clinic, 1952-64; cons. Child Edn. Found., 1953-56; dir. research Sch. Nursing Norwalk Hosp., 1961-64; dir. clin. services cerebral palsy and mental retardation, Waterbury, Conn., 1964-65; assoc. prof. Quinnipiac Coll., Hamden, Conn., 1965-66; cons., instr., med. staff N.Y. Hosp.-Cornell Med. Center, White Plains, 1966-67; dir. psychology Psychiat. Treatment Center, N.Y., 1967-68; research asso. Roosevelt Hosp. Child Psychiatry, 1968-69; supr., cons. research psychologist Bur. Child Guidance, N.Y.C. Board Edn., 1969-72; faculty Greenwich Inst. Psychoanalytic Studies, 1971-79; sr. research scientist Postgrad. Center for Mental Health, N.Y.C., 1980-82; mem. program com. Internat. Congress Social Psychiatry, 1974; research cons. N.Y.C. Mayor's Vol. Action Com., Human Resources Adminstrn., N.Y.C. Study of Delinquency and Study Abused and Neglected Children; cons., inservice trainer Center Group Counseling, Boca Raton, Fla., 1982-84; manuscript reviewer Perceptual Motor Skills. Diplomate clin. psychology Am. Bd. Profl. Psychology. Fellow Soc. Personality Assessment, Am. Psychol. Assn. (council of reps. div. 42, 1983-86), Am. Acad. Psychotherapists, Internat. Council Psychologists (v.p. 1961-62, 71-73, pres. 1973-75), Am. Orthopsychiat. Assn., N.Y. Acad. Sci.; mem. Nat. Assn. Gifted (v.p. 1961-62), Internat. Council Women Psychologists (chmn. profl. relations among psychologists), Psychologists in Pvt. Practice (treas. 1972-78), Am. Psychol. Assn. (sec. div. psychotherapy 1966-69; council of reps. 1982-86), N.Y. State Psychol. Assn., Fla. Psychol Assn., Am. Assn. Group Psychotherapy and Psychodrama (council 1973-75), World Fedn. Mental Health, Nat. Council Jewish Women, Hadassah. Club: Yale (N.Y.C.). Author: The Three Dimensional Personality Test—Reliability, Validity and Clinical Implications, 1960; The Changing School Scene: Challenge to Psychology, 1974; editor Jour. Internat. Understanding, vol. 9-10, 1974; Jour. Psychology Div. Am. Friends Hebrew U.; guest editor Jour. Clin. Child Psychology, 1975; cons. editor Jour. Psychotherapy in Pvt. Practice; others; contbr. Jour. Clin. Psychology, other profl. jours. Address: Newburry Common 1450 Washington Blvd Apt N 706 Stamford CT 06902

FEIN, ROGER G., lawyer; b. St. Louis, Mar. 12, 1940; s. Albert and Fanny (Levinson) F.; m. Susanne M. Cohen, Dec. 18, 1965; children—David I., Lisa J. Student Washington U., St. Louis, 1959, NYU, 1960; B.S., UCLA, 1962; J.D., Northwestern U., 1965; M.B.A., Am. U., 1967. Bar: Ill. 1965, U.S. Dist. Ct. (no. dist.) Ill. 1968, U.S. Ct. Appeals (7th cir.) 1968, U.S. Supreme Ct. 1970. Atty. div. corp. fin. SEC, Washington, 1965-67; ptnr. Arvey, Hodes, Costello & Burman, Chgo., 1967—, mem. exec. com., 1977—; mem. Securities Adv. Com. to Sec. State Ill., 1973—, chmn., 1973-79, 87—, vice chmn., 1983-87; spl. asst. atty. gen. State of Ill., 1974-83, 85—; mem. Appeal Bd., Ill. Law Enforcement Commn., 1980-83; mem. lawyer's adv. bd. So. Ill. Law Jour., 1980-83; mem. adv. bd. securities regulation and law report Bur. Nat. Affairs Inc., 1985—; lectr., author. Mem. Bd. Edn., Sch. Dist. No. 29, Northfield, Ill., 1977-83, pres., 1981-83; mem. Pub. Vehicle Ops. Citizens Adv. council, City Chgo., 1985-86; vice-chmn. Chgo. regional bd. Anti-Defamation League of B'nai B'rith, 1980—; chmn. lawyers' com. for ann. telethon Muscular Dystrophy Assn., 1983; past bd. dirs. Jewish Nat. Fund., Am. Friends Hebrew U., Northfield Community Fund. Recipient Sec. State Ill. Pub. Service award, 1976, Citation of Merit, WAIT Radio, 1976, Sunset Ridge Sch. Community Service award, 1984; City of Chgo. Citizen's award 1986. Fellow Am. Bar Found., Ill. Bar Found. (bd. dirs. 1978—, v.p. 1982-84, pres. 1984-86, chmn. Fellows 1983-84, Cert. of Appreciation 1985, 86), Chgo. Bar Found.; mem. Fed. Bar Assn., Decalogue Soc. Lawyers, Attys. Title Guaranty Fund, ABA (state regulation of securities com. 1982—, Ill. liaison of com.), ho. of dels. 1981-85), Ill. State Bar Assn. (bd. govs. 1976-80, del. assembly 1976-88, sec. 1977-78, cert. of appreciation 1980, chmn. Bench and Bar com. 1982-83, sect. council 1983-84, chmn. bar elections supervision com. 1986-87, chmn. assembly com. on hearings 1987-88, mem. com. on jud. appointments 1987—), Chgo. Bar Assn. (mem. task force delivery legal services 1978-80, cert. of appreciation 1976, chmn. land trusts com. 1978-79, chmn. consumer credit com. 1977-78, chmn. state securities law subcom. 1977-79), Legal Club Chgo., Tau Epsilon Phi, Alpha Kappa Psi, Phi Delta Phi. Clubs: Standard, Legal (Chgo.). Office: Arvey Hodes Costello & Burman 180 N LaSalle St Suite 3800 Chicago IL 60601

FEIN, WILLIAM, ophthalmologist; b. N.Y.C., Nov. 27, 1933; s. Samuel and Beatrice (Lipschitz) F.; B.S., CCNY, 1954; M.D., U. Calif., Irvine, 1962; m. Bonnie Fern Aaronson, Dec. 15, 1963; children—Stephanie Paula, Adam Irving, Gregory Andrew. Intern, Los Angeles County Gen. Hosp., 1962-63, resident in ophthalmology, 1963-66; instr. U. Calif. Med. Sch., Irvine, 1966-69; mem. faculty U. So. Calif. Med. Sch., 1969—, asso. prof. ophthalmology, 1979—; attending physician Cedars-Sinai Med. Center, Los Angeles, 1966—, chief ophthalmology clinic service, 1979—, chmn. div. ophthalmology, 1981—; attending physician Los Angeles County-U. So. Calif. Med. Center, 1969—; chmn. dept. ophthalmology Midway Hosp., 1975-78; dir. Ellis Eye Ctr., Los Angeles, 1984—. Diplomate Am. Bd. Ophthalmology. Mem. Am. Acad. Ophthalmology, Am. Soc. Ophthalmic Plastic and Reconstructive Surgery, AMA, Calif. Med. Assn., Los Angeles Med. Soc. Contbr. articles to med. publs. Home: 718 N Camden Beverly Hills CA 90210 Office: 415 N Crescent Dr Beverly Hills CA 90210

FEINBERG, FRANK NOEL, advertising agency executive; b. Chgo., Dec. 25, 1950; s. Frank Henry and Henrietta (Drolshagen) F.; B.A., U. Chgo., 1973. Asst. analyst Leo Burnett Co., Inc., Chgo., 1973-74, analyst, 1974-75, asso. research supr., 1976-77, research supr., 1978, assoc. research dir., 1979; assoc. research dir. Young & Rubicam, N.Y.C., 1979—, v.p., 1980—, mgr.

new product planning, 1982—, mktg. mgr., 1984-86, strategic planning mgr., 1986—. Mem. Assn. Consumer Research, Phi Beta Kappa. Office: Young & Rubicam 285 Madison Ave New York NY 10017

FEINBERG, RICHARD ALAN, consumer science educator, consultant; b. N.Y.C., June 12, 1950; s. Irving and Belle (Kolkowitz) F.; m. Fran Susan Jaffe, Jan. 21, 1973; 1 son, Seth Jason. B.A., SUNY-Buffalo, 1972; M.S., SUNY-Cortland, 1974; Ph.D., U. Okla., 1976. Asst. prof. psychology Ohio State U., 1976-78, Juniata Coll., Huntington, Pa., 1978-80; asst. prof. consumer scis., retailing and environ. analysis Purdue U., West Lafayette, Ind., 1980-85, assoc. prof. consumer and retailing, 1985—, dir. retail mgmt. internship program; research assoc. Purdue Retail Inst., 1980—. David Ross fellow, 1980; NIMH fellow, 1975; Purdue Agrl. Expt. Sta. grantee, 1981. Mem. Am. Psychol. Assn., AAAS, Assn. Coll. Profs. Textiles and Clothing. Contbr. articles in field to profl. jours. Office: Dept Consumer Scis and Retailing Purdue U West Lafayette IN 47907

FEINBERG, ROBERT S., plastics manufacturing company executive, marketing consultant; b. Newark, May 14, 1934; s. Clarence Jacob and Sabina (Zorn) F.; BA in English, BS in Chemistry, Trinity Coll., Hartford, Conn., 1955; MBA in Mktg., Fairleigh Dickinson U., 1966; advt. diploma Assn. Indsl. Advt., 1967, advt. diploma N.Y. Inst. Advt., 1967; Pres., Trebor Assocs. and Trebor Plastics Co., Teaneck, N.J., 1961—; mktg. cons. computer software Zettler Softwear Co., Burroughs Corp.; sr. council Yankelovich, Skelly and White, Inc.; cons. Greenwich Assocs.; co-chmn., partner Edgeroy Co., Ridgefield and Palisades Park, N.J., 1973—; co-chmn., ptnr. LeMont Sales Co., Teaneck, 1973—; cons. plastic formulations W.R. Grace, Endicott Johnson, Brown Shoe Co., U.S. Shoe Co., Ciba, Uniroyal. Mem. Soc. Plastics Engrs. (sr.), Sporting Goods Mfrs. Assn., Sell Overseas Am., U.S. Profl. Tennis Assn., Bergen County Tennis League (v.p.). Club: Ahdeek Tennis. Author: Olympia Shoe Co., 1966; co-inventor Edgeroy Ball Press; Polymer patentee in field. Home: 81 Edgemont Pl Teaneck NJ 07666

FEINSTEIN, CHARLES HILLIARD, economist; b. Johannesburg, Republic of South Africa, Mar. 18, 1932; s. Ludwig and Rose (Hurwitz) F.; m. Ruth Loshak, June 28, 1958 (div. June 1978); children: Jessica, Naomi, Leon, Judy; m. Anne Porter, Jan. 25, 1980. BS in Commerce, U. Witwatersrand, 1950; PhD, U. Cambridge, Eng., 1958. Chartered acct., Republic of South Africa. Lectr. U. Cambridge, Eng., 1958-78; fellow Clare Coll., Cambridge, 1963-78, sr. tutor, 1969-78; prof. econ. and social history U. York, Eng., 1978-87; vis. scholar Harvard U., Cambridge, Mass., 1986-87; reader in recent econ. and social history U. Oxford, Eng., 1987—; fellow Nuffield Coll., 1987—; Editor Econ. Jour. Royal Econ. Soc., London, 1980-86; chmn. econs. com. Econs. Social Research Council, London, 1985-86. Author: Domestic Capital Formation in the United Kingdom, 1920-1938, 1965, National Income, Expenditure and Output of the United Kingdom, 1855-1965, 1972, (with R.C.O. Matthews and J.C. Odling-Smee) British Economic Growth, 1856-1973, 1982, (with S. Pollard) Studies in Capital Formation in the United Kingdom, 1750-1920, 1988; editor: Socialism, Capitalism and Economic Growth, 1967, York, 1831-1981, 1981, The Managed Economy: Essays in British Economic Policy and Performance since 1929, 1983. Fellow British Acad.; mem. Econ. History Soc. (council mem. 1980-86), Royal Econ. Soc. (exec. mem. 1980—). Home: Treetops, Harberton Mead, Oxford OX3 0DB, England Office: Nuffield Coll, Oxford OX1 1NF, England

FEINSTEIN, JERALD LEE, engineering consulting company executive; b. St. Louis, June 22, 1943; s. Seymour S. and Lenore A. (Miller) F.; m. Dorothy Ellen Squire, Aug. 21, 1966; children: Andrew Morrison, Matthew Duane, Jennifer Squire. BS in Physics, Okla. U., 1965; MS in Engring. Sci., N.J. Inst. Tech., 1970. Sci. advisor Dept. of Def., Washington, 1966-75; v.p. DOT Systems, Inc., Vienna, Va., 1975-77; sr. research engr. Stanford Research Inst., Washington, 1977-79; ops. research analyst U.S. EPA, Washington, 1979-84; sr. assoc. Booz Allen and Hamilton, Bethesda, Md., 1984-86; v.p., ptnr. ICF/ Phase Linear Inc., Washington, 1986—; Organized, chaired internat. conf. on Expert System applications in Bus. and Fin., 1987. Mem. editorial bd. Internat. Jour. Knowledge Engring., 1988—, Expert Systems Jour., 1988—; contbr. articles on mil. research and devel., artificial intelligence and cybernetics to profl. publs. Bd. dirs. Capitol Area Bur. Rehab., Washington, 1976-81, Soc. for Prevention Narcotics, Alcohol and Other Drugs of Abuse, Vienna, 1977-78, McLean (Va.) Soccer Assn., 1978-79, dep. dir., Bowie Coll. Inst. for Advanced Research, 1986 . Recipient Research Assistantship NSF, Brookhaven Nat. Labs., 1964, Appreciation award Army Intelligence, 1975, Outstanding Research award Dept. Def., 1968. Mem. IEEE (chmn. 1971-73), Am. Assn. Artficial Intelligence, Armed Forces Communications Electronics Assn., Mensa, Washington Ops. Research Council. Home: 6826 Dean Dr McLean VA 22101 Office: ICF/ Phase Linear Systems Inc 9300 Lee Hwy Fairfax VA 22031

FEIT, JEROME ANTHONY, chemist; b. Chgo., Aug. 4, 1922; s. Aloysius J. and Barbara (Piper) F.; Student Northwestern U., 1942, Purdue U., 1943; B.S., Northwestern U., 1949; m. Genevieve Trella, June 14, 1947; children—Jerome Jeffrey, Antonia Camille (Mrs. Carl Paul Adducci), Lawrence Anthony. Cons. chemist, 1950; founded Jerome & Co., cosmetics co., 1959-65, pres., chmn. bd. Jerome Labs., Inc., Chgo., 1965—. Served with USAAF, 1942-46; ETO. Fellow Am. Inst. Chemists, Am. Chem. Soc., ASTM, Smithsonian Instn., Audubon Soc.; mem. Chgo. Perfumery, Soap and Extract Assn. (dir.), Soc. Cosmetic Chemists (chmn.), Ill. Mfrs. Assn., Chgo. Drug and Chem. Assn. Club: Variety of Ill. Patentee in field; musical composer under name Jerry Feit. Office: Jerome Laboratories Inc 95 E Bradrock Dr Des Plaines IL 60018

FEIT, RICHARD ALVIN, finance executive; b. N.Y.C., May 11, 1941; s. Herbert Balfour and Sylvia (Kaufman) F.; m. Carole Ann Goldberg, July 5, 1965; children: David Evan, Steven Kenneth. BS in Chem. Engring., U. Pitts., 1963. V.p. Blyth Eastman Dillon Co., N.Y.C., 1975-80; sr. v.p. Dean Witter Reynolds Co., N.Y.C., 1980-86; mng. ptnr. Cohen Feit and Co., N.Y.C., 1986—. Chmn. S. Nassau United Jewish Appeal Fedn. Cabinet, L.I., N.Y., 1984—; mem. bd. S. Nassau Communities Hosp., Oceanside, N.Y., 1983—. Mem. Investment Assn. N.Y., L.I. Anti-Defamation League (regional bd. dirs. 1983—). Clubs: Middle Bay Country (Oceanside), Downtown Athletic (N.Y.). Office: Cohen Feit & Co 39 Broadway New York NY 10006

FELABOM, LOREN WAYNE, SR., college administrator, consultant; b. Mishawaka, Ind., July 9, 1933; s. Alden Merrit and Ida May (Airgood) F.; m. Kathleen Jeanette Anderson, Sept. 7, 1952; children—Loren, Kathleen, Pamela, Julie. B.S. in Bus. Adminstrn., Ind. U.-South Bend, 1968; M.B.A., Mich. State U., 1973; certs. in data processing and computers, IBM, Dept. Def. Cert. vocat. tchr., Ind. Instr., programmer South Bend Comml. Sch., 1963-67; supr. adminstrv. services Bendix Corp., South Bend, 1967-74, 52-60; bus. mgr. Miami Christian Coll., Fla., 1974-78; controller Mercy Coll., Detroit, 1978-79; assoc. dean bus. affairs Prince George's Community Coll., Largo, Md., 1979-82; v.p. for adminstr. Cochise Coll., Douglas, Ariz., 1983—. Deacon, First Baptist Ch., Mishawaka, Ind., 1968-72; cons. Capitol Bapt. Ch., Largo, 1982; chmn., deacon First Bapt. Ch., Bisbee, Ariz., 1984—. Served with USNR, 1951-59. Mem. Nat. Assn. Colls. and Univ. Bus. Officers, Ariz. Assn. Coll., Bus. Ofcls. (sec. 1984-85, v.p. 1985-86, pres. 1986-87, treas. 1986-88), Ariz. Assn. Community Coll. Adminstrn. (treas. 1986-88). Republican. Home: 105 Navajo Dr Bisbee AZ 85603 Office: Cochise Coll Rt 1 PO Box 100 Douglas AZ 85607

FELBER, RENÉ, Swiss government official; b. Biel, Switzerland, Mar. 14, 1933; married; 3 children. Teaching diploma. Tchr. Boudevilliers, Switzerland, 1953-55, Le Locle, Switzerland, 1955-64; mem. La Locle Gen. Council, 1960-64; mayor City of La Locle, 1964-80, indsl. services official, 1964-72, in charge of fin. dept., 1972-80; mem. Neuchâtel Parliament, Switzerland, 1965-76; nat. councillor Switzerland, 1967-81; mem. in charge dept. fin. Govt. Republic and Canton Neuchâtel, 1981-87, pres., 1984; minister fgn. affairs Switzerland Fed. Council, Bern, 1988—. Address: Ministry Fgn Affairs, Bern Switzerland *

FELD, JOSEPH, construction executive; b. N.Y.C., June 25, 1919; s. Morris David and Gussie (London) F.; student CCNY, 1946-47; m. Doris Rabinor, Apr. 10, 1948; 1 dau., Elaine Susan. Builder housing, apt. projects, L.I., N.Y.C., N.J., 1948-54; pres. Kohl and Feld, Inc., builder housing devels., Rockland County, N.Y., 1955-57; pres. Feld Constrn. Corp., New City, N.Y., 1957—, Birchland Constrn. Corp., 1957-70, Ramapo Towers, Inc., 1963-83; dir. Rockland County Citizen Pub. Corp., 1959-60; vice chmn. People's Nat. Bank Rockland County, Nyack, N.Y., 1974-85. Mem. Clarkstown Bldg. Code Com., 1959; mem. indsl. devel. adv. com. Rockland County Bd. Suprs., 1969-71; chmn. housing adv. council Rockland County Legislature, 1976—; chmn. Housing Task Force, 1979-80; mem., past v.p. New City Jewish Center, trustee, past pres. Men's Club; mem. Rockland County council Jewish War Vets., past comdr. New City post. Served to staff sgt. AUS, 1941-45. Mem. Rockland County Assn., Inc. (former dir.), Rockland County Home Builders Assn. (past pres., dir., chmn. rental housing com.), Nat. (past dir.; mem. rental housing com.), N.Y. State (past dir., mem. rental housing com.) assns. home builders, Rockland County Apt. Owners Assn. (pres., dir. 1971—), Rockland County Bd. Realtors, N.Y. State Assn. Realtors (dir.), Nat. Inst. Real Estate Brokers, New City C. of C. Clubs: Masons, Lions (local pres. 1959-60; zone chmn. 1961-62), B'nai B'rith. Home: 9 Woodland Rd New City NY 10956 also: 3821 Environ Blvd Lauderhill FL 33319 Office: 20 S Main St New City NY 10956

FELDBERG, MEYER, university president; b. Johannesburg, South Africa, Mar. 17, 1942; s. Leon and Sarah (Kretzmer) F.; m. Barbara Erlick, Aug. 9, 1965; children: Lewis Robert, Ilana. B.A., Witwatersrand U., Johannesburg, 1962; M.B.A., Columbia U., 1965; Ph.D., Cape Town (South Africa) U., 1969. Product mgr. B.F. Goodrich Co., Akron, Ohio, 1965-67; dean Grad. Sch. Bus., U. Cape Town, 1968-79; assoc. dean J.L. Kellogg Sch. Mgmt., Northwestern U., Evanston, Ill., 1979-81; prof., dean Sch. Bus., Tulane U., New Orleans, 1981-86; pres. Ill. Inst. Tech., Chgo., 1986—, chmn. bd. govs. Research Inst.; bd. dirs. Am. Nat. Bank, Chgo., ICL, South Africa, Hotel Properties Am.; vis. prof. MIT, 1974, Cranfield Inst. Tech., 1970-76; cons. in field. Author: Organizational Behaviour: Text and Cases, 1975, American Universities, Divestment of Stock in South Africa, 1978, also articles. Bd. dirs. Isadore Newman Sch., Touro Hosp. Named Jaycee Young Man of Yr., 1972. Clubs: Internat. House (New Orleans); University (N.Y.C.); Chicago. Home: 950 N Michigan Chicago IL 60611 Office: Ill Inst of Tech Office of Pres 3300 S Federal St Chicago IL 60616

FELDBERG, SUMNER LEE, retail company executive; b. Boston, June 19, 1924; s. Morris and Anna (Marnoy) F.; married; children—Michael S., Ellen R.; stepchildren: Mollye S., Beth, James. B.A., Harvard, 1947, M.B.A., 1949. With New Eng. Trading Corp., 1949-56; treas. Zayre Corp., 1956-73, sr. v.p., 1965-68, exec. v.p., 1969-73, chmn. bd., 1973-87, chmn. exec. com., 1987—, also dir.; trustee Mass. Mut. Corp. Investors. Trustee Beth Israel Hosp., Combined Jewish Philanthropies of Greater Boston. Served to 1st lt. USAAF, 1943-46. Address: Zayre Corp PO Box 910 Framingham MA 01701

FELDHUSEN, JOHN FREDERICK, educational psychology educator; b. Waukesha, Wis., May 5, 1926; s. John C. and Luella Elsie (Gruetzmacher) F.; m. Hazel J. Artz, Dec. 18, 1954; children: Jeanne, Anne. B.A., U. Wis., 1949, M.S., 1955, Ph.D., 1958. Counselor Wis. Sch. for Boys, 1949-51; tchr. Northwestern Acad., Lake Geneva, Wis., 1951-54; instr. Madison Bus. Coll., 1955-58, U. Wis., Madison, 1958-59; asst. prof. U. Wis., Eau Claire, 1959-61, assoc. prof., 1961-62; assoc. prof. ednl. psychology Purdue U., West Lafayette, Ind., 1962-65, prof., 1965—; dir. Gifted Edn. Resource Inst., 1979—. Author: (with W. Krypsin) Writing Behavioral Objectives: A Guide for Planning Instruction, 1974, Analyzing Classroom Dialogue, 1974, Developing Classroom Tests, 1974, (with S.J. Moore, D.J. Treffinger) Global and Componential Evaluation of Creativity Instructional Materials, 1970, (with D.J. Treffinger, P. Pine and others) Teaching Children How to Think, 1975; Creative Thinking and Problem Solving in Gifted Education, 1985. Contbr. numerous articles on ednl. psychology and teaching methods to profl. jours. Mem. editorial bd. Gifted Child Quar, 1976—, editor, 1983—; editor The Ednl. Psychologist, 1966-69, Ednl. Psychology Series, 1976—; editor, contbg. author: Toward Excellence in Gifted Education, 1985; cons. editor: Burgess Pub. Co, 1967-76. Pres. West Lafayette P.T.A., 1969. Served with AUS, 1944-45. Recipient U.S. Office Edn. grants, 1967-71, Lilly Endowment grants, 1985-88, Ind. Dept. Edn. grants, 1981-87. Fellow Am. Psychol. Assn.; mem. Am. Ednl. Research Assn., Nat. Assn. Gifted Children (pres.-elect 1981-83), Council Exceptional Children, Phi Delta Kappa. Home: 2187 Tecumseh Park Ln West Lafayette IN 47906 Office: Purdue U Educational Psychology West Lafayette IN 47906

FELDMAN, AVNER IRWIN, neurosurgeon; b. N.Y.C., Mar. 9, 1927; s. Joseph O. and Lillian (Markowitz) F.; B.S., NYU, 1947; M.D., State U. Coll. Medicine, N.Y.C., 1950; m. Helene West, July 21, 1975; children by previous marriage—Sheri, David. Intern, Beth Israel Hosp., N.Y.C., 1950-51; asst. resident in gen. surgery Maimonides Hosp., Bklyn., 1951-52, in neurology Mt. Sinai Hosp., N.Y.C., 1952; resident neurosurgery Beth Israel Hosp., 1953, Bronx Municipal Hosp., N.Y.C., 1955-56; resident Montefiore Hosp., N.Y.C., 1956-57, chief resident, 1957-58; pvt. practice specializing in neurosurgery, Inglewood, Calif., 1959—; assoc. clin. prof. neurol. surgery UCLA Med. Center. Served with USAF, 1953-55. Diplomate Nat. Bd. Med. Examiners, Am. Bd. Neurosurgery. Recipient William S. Linder Surg. prize, 1950. Fellow A.C.S.; mem. Am. Assn. Neurol. Surgeons, Congress Neurol. Surgeons, So. Calif. Neurosurg. Soc., Los Angeles Soc. Neurology and Psychiatry, Calif., Los Angeles County med. assns., Alpha Omega Alpha. Home: 1130 Maytor Pl Beverly Hills CA 90210 Office: 323 N Prairie Ave Inglewood CA 90301

FELDMAN, DONNA, account executive; b. Chgo., Nov. 15, 1945; d. Nathan and June (Somers) Feldman; m. Paul Ruch. B.S., So. Ill. U., 1966; M.S., Murray State U., 1968. Spl. promotions mgr. 1st Nat. Bank Chgo., 1966-67; asst. prof., dir. forensics Luzerne County Community Coll., Nanticoke, Pa., 1968-75; account exec. Merrill Lynch, Pierce, Fenner & Smith, Chgo., 1975-77; transp. supr. Johnson & Johnson Baby Products, Park Forest, Ill., 1977-78; account exec. Christmas Club a Corp., Easton, Pa., 1979-86; FF & S div. Travelers Express, Inc., 1986—; v.p. Ruch and Feldman Inc., corp. meeting planners, 1988, mktg. rep. Mechem Fin. Inc., Erie, Pa., 1988—. Recipient Nat. Sales award Christmas Club a Corp., 1980. Mem. Network Women Execs., Nat. Network Women in Sales (career devel. chmn.), Nat. Assn. Female Execs., Inst. Gen. Semantics, Internat. Soc. Gen. Semantics, Speech Communications Assn. Home: 2306 Henderson Bethlehem PA 18017

FELDMAN, HARRIS JOSEPH, radiologist, educator; b. Balt., Mar. 4, 1942; s. Charles William and Ruth (Emanuel) F. AB, Western Md. Coll., 1963; MD, U. Md., 1967. Diplomate Am. Bd. Radiology. Intern, Mercy Hosp., Balt., 1967-68; resident in radiology George Washington U. Hosp., Washington, 1968-71; staff radiologist U. Ill. Hosp., Chgo., 1973-77, Bethany Meth. Hosp., Chgo., 1977-87, Walther Meml. Hosp., Chgo., 1977-87, Weiss Meml. Hosp., Chgo., 1987—, Lincoln West Hosp., Chgo., 1987—; cons. radiologist Langley AFB Hosp., 1972-73; asst. prof. Abraham Lincoln Sch. Medicine, U. Ill., Chgo., 1974-77, clin. asst. prof., 1977—. Served with M.C., USN, 1971-73. Mem. AMA, Ill. Med. Soc., Chgo. Med. Soc., Am. Coll. Radiology, Ill. Radiol. Soc., Chgo. Radiol. Soc., Radiol. Soc. N.Am. Home: 1339 N Dearborn Pkwy Chicago IL 60610 Office: Louis D Weiss Meml Hosp Dept Radiology 4646 N Marine Dr Chicago IL 60640

FELDMAN, ROGER DAVID, lawyer; b. N.Y.C., Apr. 7, 1943; s. Louis and Dora (Goldsmith) F.; m. Gail Steg, May 31, 1969; children: Rebecca, Seth. A.B., Brown U., 1962; LL.B., Yale U.; M.B.A., Harvard U. Bar: N.Y. 1966, D.C. 1977. Ops. research analyst Office Asst. Sec. Def., Washington, 1967-68; staff asst. Office of Pres. U. S., Washington, 1968-69; assoc. LeBoeuf Lamb Leiby & MacRae, 1969-75; ptnr. Le Boeuf Lamb Leiby & MacRae, 1977-83; mng. ptnr. Nixon Hargrave Devans & Doyle, Washington, 1983—; dep. asst. adminstr. Fed. Energy Adminstrn., Washington, 1975-77; bd. dirs. Pan Atlantic Group Inc., R.J. Rudden & Assocs. Inc., Cogeneration Inst., Assn. Energy Engrs., Nat. Forum for alternate Energy Devel., Internat. Dist. Heating and Cooling Assn.; mem. bd. advisors Energy Bur. Inc.; vice chmn., dir. Privatization Council, 1983—; exec. sec. Project fin. Coalition. Editor: Cogerneration Journal; mem. bd. editors Yale Law Jour., 1965., Stetson Law Rev., Pub. Utilities Fortnightly, Waste Age; contbr. to profl. jours. Mem. ABA (chmn. energy law com. 1980-83, chmn. alt. energy sources com. 1981-85, spl. com. on energy law 1981-84, chmn. environ. values com. 1983—, chmn. spl. com. on privatization 1985—, vice chmn. energy fin. 1986—), Fed. Energy Bar Assn. (chmn. cogeneration com. 1981-82), Internat. Cogeneration Soc. (bd. dirs. 1982-85), N.Y. Bar Assn., D.C. Bar Assn., Faculty, Inst. Gas Technology, Practicing Law Inst., Phi Beta Kappa. Office: Nixon Hargrave Devans & Doyle 1 Thomas Circle Suite 800 Washington DC 20005

FELDSTEIN, MARTIN STUART, economist, educator; b. N.Y.C., Nov. 25, 1939; s. Meyer and Esther (Gevarter) F.; m. Kathleen Foley, June 19, 1965; children—Margaret, Janet. A.B. summa cum laude, Harvard U., 1961; M.A., Oxford U., 1964, D.Phil., 1967; D.Laws (hon.), Rochester U., 1984, Marquette U., 1985. Research fellow Nuffield Coll., Oxford U., 1964-65, ofcl. fellow, 1965-67, lectr. pub. fin., 1965-67; asst. prof. econs. Harvard U., 1967-68, assoc. prof., 1968-69, prof., 1969—; George F. Baker prof. Harvard U., 1984—; pres. Nat. Bur. Econ. Research, 1977-82, 84—; chmn. Council Econ. Advisers, 1982-84; dir. TRW, Am. Internat. Group, Great Western Fin., Hosp. Corp. Am.; Mag.; mem. internat. adv. council Morgan Guaranty Bank; econ. advisor Dean Witter Reynolds, Data Resources Inc., Bay Banks, Inc., trustee Met-Vest Funds. Fellow Am. Acad. Arts and Scis., Econometric Soc. (council 1977-82), Nat. Assn. Bus. Economists; mem. Am. Econ. Assn. (John Bates Clark medal 1977, mem. exec. com. 1980-82), Inst. Medicine Nat. Acad. Scis., Council on Fgn. Relations, Trilateral Commn. (exec. com. 1987—), Phi Beta Kappa. Home: 147 Clifton St Belmont MA 02178 Office: NBER 1050 Massachusetts Ave Cambridge MA 02138

FELDT, KJELL-OLOF, government official; b. Holmsund, Sweden, Aug. 18, 1931; s. Alex and Irma (Jonsson) F.; m. Birgitta von Otter, 1970; 3 children by previous marriage. B.A., U. Uppsala, Sweden, 1956; PhD, U. Lund, Sweden, 1967. With Swedish Ministry of Fin., Stockholm, 1959—, minister of commerce, 1970-75, minister for wages and salaries and dep. minister fin., 1975-76, minister econ. affairs and budget, 1982, minister of fin., 1983—. M.P., 1971—; mem. exec. bd. Social Democratic Party, 1978—, mem. exec. com., 1981—. Office: Ministry of Finance, Rodbodgatan 6, S-10333 Stockholm Sweden

FELDTMAN, HENRY DOUGLAS, chemist; b. Queenscliff, Victoria, Australia, Nov. 1, 1928; s. Rudolf Charles and Irma Lucille (Longuehaye) F.; m. Sylvia Audrey Cardall, Oct. 17, 1928; children: Clinton, Sally, Jane, Rohan, Virginia. Assoc. diploma in applied chemistry, Gordon Inst. Tech., Victoria, 1962. Cert. chemist. Sr. exptl. scientist Commonwealth Sci. and Indsl. Research Orgn. div. Wool Tech., Geelong, Victoria, 1950—; restaurant owner Pimentos. Contbr. articles to profl. jours.; patentee in field; inventor indsl. processes. Councillor Queenscliff Borough Council, 1962-74; mem. Geelong Regional Planning Authority; chmn. Queenscliff Sewerage Authority, 1971-74. Mem. Ch. of Eng. Home: 54 Glaneuse Rd, Point Lonsdale, Victoria 3225, Australia Office: Commonwealth Sci and Indsl, Research Orgn, Div Wool Tech, PO Box 21, Belmont Victoria, Australia

FELEDY, CHARLES FRANK, electronics company executive; b. Middletown, Ohio, July 12, 1935; s. Charles Frank and Mary Carolyn (Danielson) F.; m. Jeanne Wing, Nov. 28, 1964; children—Anne Marie, Jane Elizabeth. B.M.E., Cornell U., 1958; B.S. in Engring. and Bus. Adminstrn., U. Nebr.-Omaha, 1961; M.B.A., U. Mich., 1962. Cert. energy mgr. Assn. Energy Engrs. Pert analyst Boeing Co., Seattle, 1962-64; mgr. Honeywell Inc., Mpls., 1964-68; sr. assoc. Cresap, McCormick & Paget, Inc., Chgo., 1968-72; v.p., gen. mgr. Gen. Instruments Co., N.Y.C., 1972-76; dir. energy United Techs., Corp., Hartford, Conn., 1976-84; corp. v.p. offshore sourcing Harris Corp., Melbourne, Fla., 1984—. Contbr. articles to profl. jours. Recipient Energy Man of the Year, Modern Indsl. Energy Mag., 1981. Sr. mem. Soc. Mfg. Engrs.; charter mem. Assn. Energy Engrs.; mem. Mensa, Eagle Boy Scout, Phi Kappa Phi, Beta Gamma Sigma. Republican. Episcopalian.

FELFE, PETER FRANZ, lawyer; b. Dresden, Germany, Jan. 8, 1939; came to U.S., 1951; s. Frederick Christian Felfe and Ruth (Haberland) Hayden; m. Margareta K. Lindgren, July 19, 1971 (div. June 1976); m. Jenny Leueen Fishel, June 18, 1982; 1 child, Tess Claudia. B.S. in Chem. Engring., Yale U., 1960; J.D., Fordham U., 1964. Bar: N.Y. 1965, U.S. Patent and Trademark Office 1961, U.S. Dist. Ct. (so. and eas. dists.) N.Y., 1974, U.S. Ct. Appeals (2d cir.) 1975, U.S. Ct. Appeals (D.C.) 1983, U.S. Supreme Ct. 1985, U.S. Dist. Ct. (ea. dist.) Mich. 1985. Staff atty. Union Carbide, N.Y.C., 1964-69; assoc. Burgess & Dinklage, N.Y.C., 1969-77; sr. ptnr. Sprung, Felfe et al, N.Y.C., 1977-81; founding ptnr. Felfe & Lynch, N.Y.C., 1981 ; lectr. in field; cons. German-Am. C. of C., N.Y.C., 1981—. Contbr. articles to profl. jours. Mem. ABA (patent, trademark and copyright law com.), Internat. Assn. Protection Indsl. Property, Am. Intellectual Property Law Assn. (com. on internat. and fgn. law), N.Y. Patent, Trademark and Copyright Law Assn., Bar Assn. City N.Y., Internat. Trade Commn. Trial Lawyers Assn., Fed. Cir. Ct. Bar Assn. (patent appeals from cts. com.), Yale Alumni Assn., Tau Beta Pi. Club: Yale (N.Y.C.). Office: Felfe & Lynch 805 Third Ave New York NY 10022

FELGER, RALPH WILLIAM, retired military officer, educator; b. Hamilton, Ohio, Oct. 14, 1919; s. Edward Lewis and Blanche Esther (House) F.; m. Bernice Regina Moeller, Dec. 28, 1944; 1 child, Mary Karen. BA, Whitworth Coll., 1950; MBA, U. Denver, 1952; MS, Trinity U., 1954. Cert. instr. bus. and psychology, Calif. Commd. 2d lt. U.S. Army, 1942, personnel tng. officer, 1941-46, relieved from active duty, 1946; commd. 1st lt. USAF, 1951, advanced through grades to lt. col., edn. and personnel officer, 1951-67, retired, 1967; asst. prof. Bakersfield (Calif.) Coll., 1967-68; dean continuing edn. Lincoln Land Community Coll., Springfield, Ill., 1968-72; dir. corp. tng. Sangamo Electric Co., West Union, S.C., 1972-74; asst. campus dir. Ohio State U., Marion, 1974-79; asst. to v.p. Ohio State U., Columbus, 1979-83; exec. v.p. Internat. Mgmt. Inst., Westerville, Ohio, 1983-84; dir. continuing edn. N.Mex. Inst. Mining and Tech., Socorro, 1984-85; cons. edn. and mktg. Midwest Human Resource Systems, Columbus, 1985-87, mktg. cons., 1987—. Div. chmn. United Way, Springfield, 1973; mem. Police Human Relations Com., Springfield, 1970-72; bd. dirs. ARC, Oconee, S.C., 1973; edn. chmn. Marion econ. council, edn. chmn. Marion County chpt. Am. Heart Assn. Decorated Legion of Merit, U.S. Joint Chiefs of Staff Badge, 3 USAF Commendation medals; recipient 2 commendations United Way Community Service. Mem. Personnel Mgrs. Club (v.p. 1972-74), U.S. Retired Mil. Officers Assn., Internat. Platform Assn., Internat. Biog. Assn., Am. Biog. Inst's. Research Bd. Advisors, Delta Sigma Pi (life). Republican. Lodges: Lions (chmn. edn. com. Waterville, Maine club. 1958-61). Home and Office: 2153 Olde Sawmill Blvd Dublin OH 43017

FELICE, DOMENICO, philosopher, educator; b. Celenza sul Trigno, Abruzzo, Italy, Sept. 15, 1947; s. Grovanni and Maria Rosa (Di Nocco) F. Philosophy degree, U. Bologna, Italy, 1973. Prof. philosophy U. Bologna, 1980—. Author: Montesquieu in Italia: 1800-1985, 1986, J.J. Rousseau in Italia: 1816-1986, 1987. Office: U Bologna Faculty Letters & Philosophy, Zamboni 38, 40126 Bologna Italy

FELICETTA, CESARE, financial consultant; b. Alexandria, Egypt, Aug. 3, 1930; s. Emanuele and Concetta (Lo Presti) F.; m. Raffaella Agostinelli, Apr. 23, 1956; 1 child, Fabio. Grad. Rome U., 1955. Auditor Price Waterhouse & Co., Rome, 1949-54; chief acct. Squibb SpA, Rome, 1954-58; systems mgr. Arthur Andersen & Co., Milan, 1958-60; controller Bowater Europea SpA, Rome, 1960-64; gen. mgr., mng. dir. Cobeva S.P.A., Rome, Pepsi Cola and Schweppes bottler, 1964-67; dir. finance and adminstrn. Warner Lambert Co. for Italy, 1967-70, for Eastern Hemisphere, 1970-71; pres. Rome Daily Am., Inc., 1964-71; dir. fin. and adminstrn. Merck Sharp & Dohme (Italia) SpA, Rome, 1971-73, Romana Calcestruzzi SpA, Rome, 1974-77; acctg. expert Rome Ct. Revisore Ufficiale Dei Conti, 1957; mem. Collegio dei Ragionieri di Roma, 1956; prof. personnel adminstrn. U. Camerino. Decorated Gentleman to His Holiness the Pope, Knight of Malta, knight comdr. Order of Merit Italy, officer St. Agata of San Marino, marianer knight Teutonic Order, Golden Cross of Lathran, comdr. Order of St. Gregorio Magno, knight comdr. Order Holy Sepulcher of Jerusalem, knight Constantinian Order of St. George, mem. Order do Cruseiro do Sul of Brasil, knight comdr. Order of Merit of Order Holy Sepulcher of Jerusalem; comdr. Order of Merit (W.Ger.). Mem. Nat. Assn. Accts. (emeritus life assoc.). Clubs: Brit. Horse Soc. (London); Nuovo Circolo degli Scacchi, Nuovo Tennis Parioli. Lodge: Rotary Sud (Rome).

FELICI, JORGE OSVALDO, civil engineer; b. Buenos Aires, D.C., Argentina, Oct. 20, 1934; s. Riciero Domingo and Julia (Aldanondo) F.; m. Maria

Mercedes Peycere, May 20, 1960; children—Gustavo Jorge, Guillermo Javier, Graciana Julia. Civil Engr., Buenos Aires U., 1965. Sales engr. Equipos y Materiales, Buenos Airea, 1965-67; comml. mgr. Burgwardt & Cia. S.A., Buenos Aires, 1957-72; tech. dir. Pamar S.A., Buenos Aires, 1972—, pres. bd., 1972—; exec. v.p., tech. dir. Cogasco S.A., Buenos Aires, 1980—, bd. mem., 1980—. Mem. Camara Argentina de Sociedades Anonimas, Club Argentino del Petroleo, Inst. Argentiono de la Energia Gral. Mosconi, Bolsa de Comercio de Buenos Aires, Soc. Rural Argentina. Roman Catholic. Avocations: fishing, computing. Home: Avellaneda 762 Adrogue, 1846 Buenos Aires Argentina Office: Pamar SA, Esmeralda 320, 1343 Buenos Aires Argentina

FELICITA, JAMES THOMAS, aerospace company executive; b. Syracuse, N.Y., May 21, 1947; s. Anthony Nicholas and Ada (Beech) F.; AB, Cornell U., 1969; postgrad. Harvard U., 1969, U. So. Calif., 1970, UCLA, 1975-77. Contracting officer U.S. Naval Regional Contracting Office, Long Beach, Calif., 1974-80; sr. contract negotiator space and communications group Hughes Aircraft Co., El Segundo, Calif., 1980-81, head NASA contracts, 1981-84, mgr. maj. program contracts, 1984—. Recipient cost savs. commendation Pres. Gerald R. Ford, 1976. Mem. Cape Canaveral Missile Space Range Pioneer, Nat. Contract Mgmt. Assn., Cornell Alumni Assn. So. Calif., Planetary Soc. Republican. Club: Nat. Space, Hughes Mgmt. Home: 8541 Kelso Dr Huntington Beach CA 92646 Office: 909 N Sepulveda Blvd Los Angeles CA 90245

FELIX, ALEXIS, architect, urban planner; b. Saltibus, St. Lucia, July 17, 1944; s. Edward Augustus and Doreen Celestin (George) F.; m. Louise Alicia LaFranque, Nov. 10, 1973 (div. July 1987); 1 child, Fayola Celeste. AA, Coll. V.I., St. Thomas, 1965; BArch, Hampton Inst., 1972; postgrad., Morgan State U., 1974-75; MArch, Pratt Inst., 1977. Asst. planner City of Balt. Planning Commn., 1972-73, city planner, 1973-76; urban designer City of N.Y. Dept. City Planning, 1977-82; architect, head archtl. sect. Govt. St. Lucia, Castries, 1982-84; owner, dir., architect Total Design, Castries, 1984—; cons. Caribbean Devel. Bank, Bridgetown, Barbados and Govt. St. Lucia, 1987—. Editor Manual for Developers (OAS), 1986; contbr. articles to profl. jours. Ea. Caribbean scholar Coll. V.I., 1965, Competitive scholar Hampton Inst., 1968. Mem. AIA (assoc.), Am. Planning Assn., St. Lucia Assn. Planners (trustee 1987), St. Lucia Assn. Architects (1st pres. 1988-89). Roman Catholic. Lodge: Kiwanis (chmn. club house design com. 1985-87) (Castries). Home and Office: Total Design, Sunny Acres PO Box 1265, Castries Saint Lucia West Indies

FELIX, JOHN HENRY, investments executive; b. Honolulu, June 14, 1930; s. Henry and Melinda (Pacheco) F.; student Chaminade Coll., 1947, San Mateo Coll., 1950; grad. YPO Advanced Mgmt. Program, Stanford, 1967, Harvard 1971; Ph.D., Walden U., 1975; m. Patricia Berry; children—Laura Marie, Melinda Susan, John Morgan, Jayne Sherry, Annette Sherry. Asst. to pres. AFL-CIO Unity House, 1955-57; exec. v.p. Hotel Operating Co. of Hawaii, 1957-60; v.p. Music Polynesia, Inc.; asst. to Gov. of Hawaii, 1960-62; pres. LaRonde Restaurants, Inc., 1962—, Hotel Assocs., Inc.; dir., mem. exec. com., chmn. personnel com. Hawaii Nat. Bank; pres., chmn. exec. com. Hawaiian Meml. Park. Chmn. ARC, 1961-63, 72; del. League Red Cross Socs.; chmn. Gov.'s Jobs for Vets. Task Force, 1971-76, Honolulu Redevel. Agy., 1971, 72, Honolulu City and County Planning Com., 1959; chmn. Bd. Water Supply, 1973-75; chmn. Honolulu City County Bd. Parks Recreation; mem. City and County Honolulu Police Commn., 1979, chmn., 1984; pres. bd. Hawaii Public Radio, 1979; bd. govs. ARC, also chmn. Pacific div.; nat. trustee March of Dimes Birth Defects Found.; mem. internat. com. Boy Scouts Am., council Commr. Pacific area; chmn. Rep. Nat. Hispanic Assembly, Hawaii, 1987; chmn. redevel. com. Castle Meml. Ctr.; U.S. del. South Pacific Commn., 1985; spl. asst. to pres. League of ARC, Red Crescent Soc., 1985 . Served with AUS, 1952-54. Named Young Man of Year, Hawaii Jr. C. of C., 1959, Distinguished Service award Sales and Marketing Execs. Hawaii, 1968, Harriman award distinguished vol. service A.R.C., 1975, Silver Beaver award Aloha Council Boy Scouts Am., 1983, Disting. Eagle award, 1983; named Salesman of Yr., Sales and Mktg. Execs. of Honolulu, 1981, others. Mem. Young Pres.'s Orgn., Hawaii Restaurant Assn. (pres. 1967), Air Force Assn. (pres. Hawaii), C. of C. of Hawaii (life), Nat. Eagle Scout Assn. (life, vice chmn. Hawaii chpt.), CAP-U.S. Air Force Aux. (comdr. Hawaii Wing 1980). Club: Waikiki Rotary (Honolulu). Home: 700 Bishop St #1012 Honolulu HI 96813 Office: 700 Bishop St Suite 1012 Honolulu HI 96813

FELIX, RICHARD JAMES, engineering executive, consultant; b. Sacramento, Apr. 21, 1944; s. Joseph James and Faye Lola (Thornburg) F.; m. Nancy Tucker Thompson, 1970 (div. 1972). Cert., Electronics Tech. A Sch., Treasure Island, Calif., 1963; student, Am. River Coll., 1968-72, Calif. State U., 1972-74. Ptnr. ADRA, Sacramento, 1971-73, Doggie Domes, Sacramento, 1971-72, Fong and Co., Sacramento, 1976-79; project dir. Dynascan Project, Sacramento, 1976-88; dir. research Omni Gen. Corp., Sacramento, 1988—; ptnr. Am. Omnigraph, Sacramento, 1985—; instr. Calif. State U., Sacramento, 1973-74; cons. KDM Design, 1985—. Creator documentary film American River College Rat Decathlon, 1974; editor publicity manual, 1978; inventor omnigraph, 1967. Vol. Leukemia Soc., Sacramento, 1984; artist Camellia City Ctr., Sacramento, 1983. Served with USN, 1962-66. Mem. Sacramento chpt. Mental Health Assn. (bd. dirs. 1980, Clifford Beers award 1983), Mensa. Republican. Episcopalian. Club: New Horizons (Sacramento) (editor 1977-79). Office: Omni Gen Corp 428 J St Suite 110 Sacramento CA 95814

FELKER, DAVID R., manufacturing company executive; b. Torrance, Calif., Sept. 4, 1957; s. Roy Leon and Colleen Mae (Rowland) F.; m. Joanne Stephanie Feigin, Jan. 23, 1982 (div.); 1 child, Megan Kimberly. BS in Econs., UCLA, 1978. Store mgr. Stereo Plus, Los Angeles, 1977-79; gen. mgr. Bel-Aire Audio, Los Angeles, 1976-77, 79-80; nat. mktg. mgr. Leland Energy Corp., Los Angeles, 1980-83; pres. chief exec. officer Bi-Pro Industries, Inc., El Segundo, Calif., 1983—; mktg. cons., sales trainer for varied customers David Felker and Assoc., 1981—. Patentee trapping method for insects. Mem. Calif. Scholarship Fedn. (life), Mensa, Torrance C. of C. (Appreciation award). Democrat. Roman Catholic. Club: Collie (v.p. 1985-86). Office: Bi-Pro Industries Inc 212 N Eucalyptus Blvd El Segundo CA 90245

FELL, FREDERICK VICTOR, publisher; b. Bklyn., May 21, 1910; s. Samuel and Victoria (Greenhut) F.; m. Selma Shampain, May 18, 1975; children: Linda Fell Firestein, Nancy. Student, NYU, 1928-31; LL.B., Bklyn. Law Sch., 1935. Pres. Frederick Fell Pubs., N.Y.C., 1943-81; prin. Frederick Fell & Assocs., Inc., Literary Agts., Hollywood, Fla., 1981—. Author: (pseudonym Vic Fredericks) Crackers in Bed, 1953, More For Doctors Only, 1953, Jest Married, 1958, For Golfers Only, 1964, Wit and Wisdom of Presidents, 1966, others. Trustee Long Beach (N.Y.) Library, 1948-50; councilman City of Long Beach, 1950-54, pres. city council, 1950-52; pres. Long Beach Hosp. Club, 1949, 59; chmn. book pubs. div. crusades N.Y.C. div. Am. Cancer Soc., 1977-81. Mem. Assn. Am. Pubs., Am. Booksellers Assn., Book Group South Fla. Democrat. Jewish. Clubs: Hillcrest Country, Hollywood (Fla.). Home: 3800 Hillcrest Dr Apt 1120 Hollywood FL 33021

FELLEY, DONALD LOUIS, chemical company executive; b. Memphis, Feb. 7, 1921; s. Alfred and Helen Ruth (Meek) F.; m. June Pack, Oct. 1, 1949; children: James D., Douglas C., Richard B., David L., Mary L. B.S., Ark. State Coll., 1941; M.S., U. Ill., 1947, Ph.D., 1949. With Rohm and Haas Co., 1949-86, v.p., gen. mgr. internat. div., 1970-76, v.p., regional dir. N.Am., 1976-78; pres., dir. Rohm and Haas Co., Phila., 1978-86; chmn. Greater Phila. 1st Corp., 1984-85. Bd. dirs. Phila. World Affairs Council, 1976—, Abington (Pa.) Meml. Hosp., 1978-86, U. Ill. Found. Served to capt. F.A. AUS, 1942-46. Mem. Am. Chem. Soc., Soc. Chem. Industry (bd.), Greater Phila. C. of C. (bd. dirs. 1978-86), Sigma Xi, Alpha Chi Sigma, Phi Lambda Upsilon, Soc. des Amis de la Maison de la Chimie, Pa. Horticultural Soc. (vice chair).

FELLINI, FEDERICO, film director, writer; b. Rimini, Italy, Jan. 20, 1920; s. Urbano and Ida (Barbiani) F.; m. Giulietta Masina, Oct., 1943. Student, U. Rome. Journalist 1937-39, writer radio dramas, 1939-42, screen writer, 1943—, dir., 1952—. Writer: films, including Open City (N.Y. Film Critics Circle award 1946), Paisan, (N.Y. Film Critics Circle award 1948), Ways of Love, 1950 (N.Y. Film Critics Circle award 1950), Senza Pieta, 1950; dir.: films, including The White Sheik, 1952, I Vitelloni, 1953, La Strada, 1954 (Acad. award 1957), Il Bidone, 1955, Notti di Cabiria, 1957 (Acad. award for best fgn. film 1958), La Dolce Vita, 1959 (Cannes Festival Gold Palm award 1960, N.Y. Film Critics Circle award 1961), 8 1/2, 1963 (Acad. award for best fgn. film 1964, N.Y. Film Critics Circle award 1963), Juliet of the Spirits, 1965, Never Bet the Devil Your Head, 1968, Histoires Extraordinaires, 1968, Satyricon, 1969, The Clowns, 1970, Fellini's Roma, 1972, Amarcord, 1974 (Acad. award for best fgn. film 1975), Casanova, 1977, Orchestra Rehearsal, 1979, City of Women, 1981, And the Ship Sails On, 1984, Ginger and Fred, 1986, Interview, 1987; Author: films, including Amarcord, 1974, Quattro Film, 1975, Fellini on Fellini, 1977. Recipient Prix du 40th Anniversaire Cannes Film Festival, award Moscow Film Festival. Office: 141a Via Margutta, 110 Rome Italy Address: Corso d'Italia 356, Rome Italy *

FELLMAN, MALCOLM JAY, university administrator; b. N.Y.C., June 25, 1932; s. Herman and Frances F.; m. Ellen Fellman, July 5, 1970; children—Heather, Stacy, Samantha. B.B.A., Hofstra U., 1958, M.B.A., 1981. Asst. v.p. devel. Hofstra U., Hempstead, N.Y., 1968-72, bookstore mgr., 1972-74, exec. dir. ops., 1974-82, v.p. ops., 1982—; cons. U.S. Dept. Labor, 1965, City of N.Y., 1965; adj. prof. Pratt Inst., 1966-72. Contbr. articles to profl. jours. Bd. dirs. Cherry Lawn Sch., Darien, Conn., 1969-72. Served with USMC, 1951-53. Named Man of the Year, L.I. Coll. and Univ. Consortium, 1983. Mem. Nat. Assn. Coll. and U. Bus. Officers, Assn. of Phys. Plant Adminstrs. of Univs. and Colls., Hempstead C. of C. (pres. 1974-76), Hofstra U. Alumni Assn. (dir. 1970—). Republican. Jewish. Clubs: Hofstra U. (dir.). Lodge: Rotary (v.p. 1971-72). Avocations: jogging; music. Home: 123 E Rogues Path Huntington Station NY 11746 Office: Hofstra Univ Hempstead NY 11550

FELSENTHAL, STEVEN ALTUS, lawyer; b. Chgo., May 21, 1949; s. Jerome and Eve (Altus) F.; m. Carol Judith Greenberg, June 14, 1970; children—Rebecca Elizabeth, Julia Alison. A.B., U. Ill., 1971; J.D., Harvard U., 1974. Bar: Ill. 1974, U.S. Dist. Ct. (no. dist.) Ill. 1974, U.S. Ct. Claims 1975, U.S. Tax Ct. 1975, U.S. Ct. Appeals (7th cir.) 1981. Assoc. Levenfeld & Kanter, Chgo., 1974-78, ptnr., 1978-80; sr. ptnr. Levenfeld, Eisenberg, Janger, Glassberg & Lippitz, Chgo., 1980-84, Sugar, Friedberg & Felsenthal, Chgo., 1984—; lectr. Kent Coll. Law, Ill. Inst. Tech., Chgo., 1978-80. Mem. ABA, Ill. State Bar Assn., Chgo. Bar Assn., Harvard Law Soc. Ill., Phi Beta Kappa. Clubs: Standard, Harvard (Chgo.). Office: Sugar Friedberg & Felsenthal 39 N LaSalle St Suite 2600 Chicago IL 60602

FELTER, JOHN KENNETH, lawyer; b. Monmouth, N.J., May 9, 1950; s. Joseph Harold and Rosanne (Bautz) F. BA magna cum laude, MA in Econs., Boston Coll., 1972; JD cum laude, Harvard U., 1975. Bar: Mass. 1975, U.S. Dist. Ct. Mass. 1976, U.S. Ct. Appeals (1st cir.) 1977, U.S. Supreme Ct. 1982. Assoc. Goodwin, Procter & Hoar, Boston, 1975-83, ptnr., 1983—; spl. asst. atty. gen. Commonwealth of Mass., 1982-84; spl. counsel Town of Plymouth, Mass., 1983—, Town of Salisbury, Mass., 1983-85, Town of Edgartown, Mass., 1985—; active devel. com. Greater Boston Legal Services, 1982—, bd. dirs. 1980—; mem. faculty Mass. Continuing Legal Edn., Inc., Boston, 1984—, Am. Law Inst.-ABA Com. Continuing Edn., 1986—; instr. trial adv. program Harvard Law Sch., 1981—; judge moot ct. competition Harvard Law Sch., 1978—. Mem. adv. com. The Boston Plan for Excellence in Pub. Schs.; VIP panelist Easter Seals Telethon, Boston, 1978-79. Mem. ABA (litigation sect., gen. practice sect., personal rights litigation com.), Mass. Bar Assn., Boston Bar Assn. (bd. dirs. law firm resources project 1985—, coll. and univ. law com. 1986—), Am. Arbitration Assn. (comml. arbitrator 1985—), Greater Boston C. of C. (edn. com., health care com.). Office: Goodwin Procter & Hoar Exchange Pl Boston MA 02109

FELTON, SAMUEL PAGE, biochemist; b. Petersburg, Va., Sept. 7, 1919; s. Samuel S. and Pearl (Williams) F.; m. Helen Florence Martin, Dec. 31, 1955; 1 child, Samuel Page. Degree in pharmacy, U.S. Army, San Francisco, 1942; BS in Chemistry, U. Wash., 1951, postgrad., 1954. Chief technician U. Wash., Seattle, 1952-59, research assoc., 1959-62, sr. research assoc., 1976—, dir. cen. facilities lab. anesthesiology, 1969-73, dir. water quality lab., 1976-83, dir. biochem. lab. sch. of Fisheries, 1983—; asst. mem., asst. to dir. div. biochemistry Scripps Clinic and Research Found., La Jolla, Calif., 1962-66; asst. biochemist Children's Orthopedic Hosp., Seattle, 1966-68; vis. scientist Va. Inst. Marine Scis. at Coll. William and Mary, Williamsburg, 1985. Mem. bd. of adjustments City of Edmonds, Wash. Served to sgt. MC, U.S. Army 1941-45. Fellow Am. Inst. Chemists; mem. Am. Chem. Soc., Am. Inst. Fishery Research Biologists, N.Y. Acad. of Scis., Nat. Oceanic Soc. Office: U Wash Fisheries Research Inst Seattle WA 98195

FENDER, PIERRE, physician; b. Alsace, France, June 6, 1950; s. Pierre Anselme and Anne Marie (Braun) F.; m. Bonnaure Paule, Mar. 1, 1948; children: Pierre Emmanuel, Jean-Sebastian, Marie Catherine. Intern Ctr. Hosp. Louis Pasteur, Colmar, France, 1973-78; pvt. practice medicine Guebwiller, France, 1978—. Home and Office: 15 Rue du Cimetiere Berrwiller, Guebwiller France 68500

FENECH-ADAMI, EDDIE, prime minister of Malta; b. Birkirkara, qalta, Feb. 27, 1934; s. Luigi and Josephine (Pace) F.; m. Mary Sciberras, June 6, 1965; children: John, Joseph, Michael, Maria, Luigi. Began studies at St. Aloysius Coll., Birkirkara, Malta; BA, U. Malta, Valletta, 1955; LLD, U. Malta, 1958. Bar: Malta 1959. Advocate Valletta, 1959—; ptnr. Ganado and Assocs., Valletta, 1961-87; M.P. Valletta, 1969—; opposition spokesman on social services Parliament, Valletta, 1971-77, leader opposition, 1977-87; prime minister Sovereign State Of Malta, 1987—; asst. sec. gen. Nationalist Party, 1962-75, also pres. gen. and administrv. councils, 1975-77, party leader, 1977—; v.p. European Union Christian Democrats, Brussels, 1979—. Mem. Nationalist Party (Christian Democrat). Roman Catholic. Home: 176 Main St, Birkirkara Malta Office: Auberge de Castille, Valletta Malta

FENG, LING-YING, pediatrician, researcher; b. Wuxi, Jiangsu, China, Oct. 25, 1944; d. Yonglin Feng and Zhen-xiu Lu; m. Fan-Ming Zhou, Apr. 25, 1972; 1 child, Ping. MS, Shanghai First Med. Coll., China, 1982. Resident Shuicheng People's Hosp., People's Republic China, 1970-79; resident Children's Hosp. of Shanghai Med. U., 1982-86, vis. physician, 1986—. Contbr. articles to med. jours. Mem. Chinese Med. Assn., Chinese Nutritional Assn., Chinese Psychol. Assn.

FENICHEL, RICHARD LEE, biochemist; b. N.Y.C., July 23, 1925; s. Irving and Dorothy (Rothchild) F.; student Bucknell U., 1941-43; AB, N.Y. U., 1947; MS, Poly. Inst. Bklyn., 1951; PhD, Wayne U., 1956; widowed; children: Gladys, Marilyn. Commonwealth fellow for research Poly. Inst. Bklyn., 1948-50; biochemist med. dept. Chrysler Corp., Highland Park, Mich., 1951-54; grad. teaching asst. Wayne U. Med. Sch., 1954-56; investigator Aviation Med. Acceleration Lab., Johnsville, Pa., 1957-59; group leader Ortho Research Found., Raritan, N.J., 1959-63; prin. scientist biochemistry and pharmocology Wyeth-Ayerst Labs., Radnor, Pa., 1963—; mem. instl. rev. bd. Moss Rehab. Hosp., Phila., 1974—. Served with U.S. Army, 1943-45. Recipient Angus McClean Research award Wayne U., 1956, Superior Accomplishment award USN Med. Lab., 1966; Legion of Honor, Chapel of Four Chaplains, 1982. Mem. Am. Chem. Soc., N.Y. Acad. Sci., AAAS, Am. Soc. Biol. Chemists, Sigma Xi. Contbr. numerous articles to profl. jours.; patentee in field. Home: 777 Germantown Pike Plymouth Meeting PA 19462 Office: Wyeth-Ayerst Labs PO Box 8299 Philadelphia PA 19101

FENN, NICHOLAS M., diplomat; b. London, Feb. 19, 1936; s. J. Eric and Kathleen M. (Harrison) F.; m. Susan Clare Russell, Aug. 8, 1959; children: Robert, Charles, Julia. MA, Cambridge U., Eng., 1958. 3d sec. Brit. Embassy Rangoon, Burma, 1959-63; asst. pvt. sec. to Sec. of State for Fgn. Affairs London, 1963-67; head of chancery Brit. Interests sect. Swiss Embassy, Algiers, Algeria, 1967-69; press spokesman Brit. Mission to the UN, N.Y.C., 1969-72; dep. head Energy Dept., London, 1972-75; counsellor Brit. Embassy, Peking, People's Republic of China, 1975-77; press sec. to Lord Carrington Office of the Fgn. Sec., London, 1979-82; ambassador to Burma Rangoon, 1982-86; ambassador to Republic of Ireland Dublin, Ireland, 1986—. Served as officer RAF, 1954-56. Named Companion Order of St. Michael and St. George by Her Majesty the Queen, London, 1980. Fellow Royal Coll Def. Studies. Club: United Oxford and Cambridge U. Office: Brit Embassy, 33 Merrion Rd, Dublin 4 Republic of Ireland

FENNESSY, EDWARD, SIR, medical computer company executive; b. London, Jan. 17, 1912; s. Edward Patrick and Eleanor (Arkwright) F.; m. Marion Banks, 1937 (dec. 1983); children: Sheila Anne, Patrick Alan; m. Leonora Patricia Birkett, 1984. BSc with honors, U. London, 1934; Doctorate (hon.), U. Surrey, Eng., 1971. Cert. engr. Devel. engr. Standard Telephones, London, 1934-38; tech. officer Air Ministry Research, Bawdsey, Eng., 1938-40; mng. dir. Decca Navigator Co., London, 1946-50, Decca Radar Co., London, 1950-65, Plessey Electronics, London, 1965-69, Brit. Post Office Telecommunications, London, 1969-77; deputy chmn. British Post Office, 1975-77; chmn. LKB Biochrom, Cambridge, Eng., 1978-87, British Med. Data Systems, Basingstoke, Eng., 1978—; cons. in electronics and telecommunications. Served to group capt. with Brit. RAF, 1940-46. Named Officer of the Order Brit. Empire, His Majesty King George VI, 1944, Comdr. Order British Empire Her Majesty Queen Elizabeth, 1957, Knight Bachelor, Her Majesty Queen Elizabeth, 1975. Fellow Inst. Electrical Engrs., Brit. Inst. of Mgmt., The Royal Inst. of Navigation (pres. 1975-78). Clubs: Island Sailing, RAF. Home: Northbrook Littleford Ln, Shamley Green Surrey, England GU5 ORH

FENSTERSTOCK, BLAIR COURTNEY, lawyer; b. N.Y.C., Aug. 20, 1950; s. Nathaniel and Gertrude (Isaacson) F.; m. Joyce Narins, Sept. 16, 1979; children: Michael Bayard, Evan Steele, Laurel Sage. A.B. summa cum laude, Bowdoin Coll., 1972; J.D., Columbia U., 1975. Bar: N.Y. 1976, U.S. Dist. Ct. (so. ea. and no. dists.) N.Y., U.S. Ct. Appeals (2d cir.), Ind., U.S. Customs Ct., U.S. Ct. Internat. Trade, U.S. Supreme Ct. Assoc. firm Simpson, Thacher & Bartlett, N.Y.C., 1975-79, firm Dewey, Ballantine, Bushby, Palmer & Wood, N.Y.C., 1979-83; v.p., assoc. gen. counsel, asst. sec. Reliance Group Holdings, Inc., N.Y.C., 1983—, sr. v.p., gen. counsel, Frank B. Hall & Co., Inc., 1987—. Harlan Fiske Stone scholar Columbia U., 1975. Mem. Assn. Bar City N.Y., N.Y. State Bar Assn., ABA, Council N.Y. Law Assocs. (bd. dirs. 1979-82), Lawyers Com. for Internat. Human Rights (bd. dirs. 1979-80), Am. Arbitration Assn. (panel of arbitrators), Internat. Peace Acad. (sec. 1977-79), Phi Beta Kappa. Republican. Jewish. Clubs: University (N.Y.C.); Aspetuck Valley Country (Weston, Conn.). Home: 120 E 75th St New York NY 10021 Office: Reliance Group Holdings Inc 55 E 52d St New York NY 10055 also: Frank B Hall & Co Inc 549 Pleasantville Rd Briarcliff Manor NY 10510

FENSTERSTOCK, JOYCE NARINS, investment banker; b. N.Y.C., Dec. 30, 1948; d. Charles S. and Frances D. (Kross) Narins; BA in Psychology, Wellesley Coll., 1970; MBA, Harvard U., 1973; m. Blair C. Fensterstock; children: Michael Bayard, Evan Steele, Laurel Sage. Assoc. corp. fin. Warburg Paribas Becker Inc., Chgo., 1974-75, Goldman, Sachs & Co., N.Y.C., 1973-78; sr. v.p. corp. fin., mng. dir. Paine Webber Inc., N.Y.C., 1978—. Mem. Fin. Women's Assn. Club: Harvard (N.Y.C.). Home: 120 E 75th St New York NY 10021 Office: 1285 Ave of Americas New York NY 10019

FENTON, COLIN THOMPSON, mining executive; b. Transvaal, Republic of S. Africa, June 20, 1934; 3 children. BSc in Mining, K.E.S. Official learner Crown Mines, 1950-67; with Goldfields of S. Africa, 1967—, asst. mgr., 1967-69, mgr., 1969-75, cons. engr., 1975-79, gen. mgr., 1979-80, exec. dir., 1980—; bd. dirs. Blyvooruitzicht Gold Mining Co., Ltd.; chmn. Mines Bldg. Ltd., Mines Services (Pvt.) Ltd., Corlab Properties (Pvt.) ltd., Deelkraal Gold Mining Co. Ltd., Doornfontein Gold Mining Co. Ltd., Driefontein Consolidated Ltd., Elandsrand Gold Mining Co. Ltd., Elsburg Gold Mining Co., Ltd., The Employment Bur. of Africa Ltd., The Gold Mine Mus. (Pvt.) Ltd., Gold Fields Mining and Devel. Ltd., Gold Fields Tng. Services (Pvt.) Ltd., Harmony Gold Mining Co. Ltd., Internat. Gold Corp. Ltd., Kloof Gold Mining Co. Ltd., Libanon Gold Mining Co. Ltd., Luipaardsvlei Estates Ltd., Mine Labour Orgn. (N.R.C.) Ltd., Rand Mut. Assurance Co. Ltd., Rand Refinery Ltd., Vellefontein Tin Mining Co. Ltd., Venterspost Gold Mining Co. Ltd., Village Main Reef Gold Mining Co. Ltd., Vlakfontein Gold Mining Co. Ltd., Western Areas Gold Mining Co. Ltd., Western Deep Levels Ltd., West Driefontein Gold Mining Co. Ltd., West Wits. Property Trust (Pvt.) Ltd., Winkelhaak Mines Ltd.; alt. dir. G.F.S.A. Holdings Ltd., Waterval (Rustenburg) Platinum Mining Co. Ltd. Club: Rand. Office: Kloof Gold Mining Co Ltd, 75 Fox St, Johannesburg Republic of South Africa *

FENTON, ROBERT LEONARD, lawyer; b. Detroit, Sept. 14, 1929; s. Ben B. and Stella Frances (Saffir) F.; children: Robert L., Cynthia R. A.B., Syracuse U., 1952; LL.B., U. Mich., 1955. Bar: Mich. 1955. Assoc. Marks, Levi, Thill & Wiseman, Detroit, 1955-60; ptnr. Fenton, Nederlander & Dodge, Detroit, 1960—; Lectr. Flint and Lansing Real Estate Bds., 1966-68; spl. counsel Detroit Fire Dept., 1975—, Mich. Motion Picture and TV Commn., 1979; producer Universal Studios, Calif. Treas. Oakland County Democratic Com., 1960-64; mem. Dem. State Finance Com., 1966-69, Nat. Finance Com., 1962-74, Dem. Pres.'s Club, 1962-74; financial adviser to Mayor Roman S. Gribbs, 1969-73, Mayor Coleman A. Young, 1974—; chmn. State of Mich. Film and TV Commn.; Bd. dirs. Detroit Bi-Centennial Commn., Rivers and Harbour Congress of U.S.; mem. adv. bd. NAACP, U. Mich. Pres.'s Club. Served with USAF, 1950-52. Recipient Distinguished Pub. Service medal City of Detroit, 1973; named Man of the 60's City of Detroit, 1964; decorated Order of St. Johns of Jerusalem, 1980. Mem. Am., Mich., Detroit bar assns., Econs. Club, Acad. Magical Arts, Soc. Preservation Variety Arts. Clubs: Mason, Shriner, Franklin Hills Country, Recess (Detroit). Office: Village Park Bldg 31800 Northwestern Hwy Suite 390 Farmington Hills MI 48018

FENVESSY, STANLEY JOHN, management consultant; b. Rochester, N.Y., Oct. 30, 1918; s. John H.W. and Bessie Ruth (Weber) F.; B.S. in Econs., U. Pa., 1940; LL.B., Georgetown U., 1943; m. Doris Goodman, July 10, 1943; children—Alice Fenvessy Healy, Barbara Fenvessy Kahlow. With Aldens, Inc., Chgo., 1945-50; admitted to Ill. bar, 1947; prin. Cresap, McCormick and Paget, N.Y.C., 1950-55; exec. v.p. Am. Merchandising div. Rapid Am. Corp., N.Y.C., 1955-60; adminstrv. v.p. Ethan Allen, Inc., Danbury, Conn., 1960-65; pres. Fenvessy Assos., Inc., mgmt. cons., N.Y.C., 1965-82; chmn. Fenvessy & Schwab, Inc., N.Y.C., 1982-86; Fenvessy & Silbert, Inc., N.Y.C., 1987—; dir. The Sharper Image. Served to lt. (s.g.) Intelligence Corps, USNR, 1941-45. Mem. Chgo. Bar Assn., Inst. Mgmt. Cons., Direct Mktg. Assn. (dir.), Am. Arbitration Assn. Republican. Club: University (N.Y.C.). Author: Keep Your Customers and Keep Them Happy, 1976, Fenvessy On Fulfillment, 1988; contbr. to Graphic Arts Manual, Mag. Public Mgmt., Direct Mail Advt., Selling for Retailers, Direct Mktg. Handbook, also bus. publs.; patentee addressing methods. Home: 167 E 61st St New York NY 10021 Office: 645 Madison Ave New York NY 10022

FERABOLI, SIMONETTA, classical literature and language educator; b. Cremona, Lombardia, Italy, Dec. 29, 1947; d. Marino and Carla (Vigolini) F. D in Ancient Lit., U. Genoa, Italy, 1970. Lectr. Greek Lit. U. Genoa, 1970-71, ministerial scholar, 1972-74, contract researcher, 1974-81, researcher in Greek and Classical Philology, 1981—; vis. researcher U. St. Andrews, Scotland, 1973, U. London, 1973, U. Paris, 1978, 1980, Hardt Found., Geneva, Switzerland, 1982, U. Urbino, Italy, 1982, U. Budapest, Hungary, 1983. Author: Lisia Avvocato, 1980, Tolomeo--Le Previsioni Astrologiche, 1984; contbr. articles to profl. jours. Roman Catholic. Home: Via Caffaro 13, 16124 Genoa Italy Office: U Genoa, Dept Classics, Via Balbi 4, Genoa Italy

FERCHLAND, WILLIAM THOMAS, lawyer, lecturer; b. Chgo., Jan. 15, 1945; s. William H. and Veronica (August) F.; m. Candace Nilsson, Sept. 8, 1973; children: William, Kyle, Kathleen. BS in Fin., U. Ill., 1970; JD, John Marshall Law Sch., Chgo., 1975. Bar: Calif. 1975, U.S. Dist. Ct. Calif. 1975; cert. specialist in workers compensation law. Assoc. Richens L. Wootton, Santa Rosa, Calif., 1975-79; prin. Ferchland Law Office, Santa Rosa, 1979—; judge pro tem Workers Compensation Appeals Bd. Contbr. articles to legal mags. Bd. dirs. Sonoma County Legal Services Found., Sonoma County Legal Aid. Served with U.S. Army, 1967-69. Mem. Calif. Applicant Atty. Assn., ABA, Calif. Bar Assn., Assn. Trial Lawyers Am., Nat. Orgn. Social Security Claimants Reps., Redwood Empire Trial Lawyers Assn., Indsl. Claims Assn., Calif. Soc. Indsl. Medicine and Surgery, VFW. Roman Catholic. Office: 716 College Ave Santa Rosa CA 95404

FERENC, KARPATI, government official Hungary; b. Putnok, Borsod, Hungary, Oct. 16, 1926; 2 sons. Grad., Mil. Acad., Budapest, Hungary, 1953. 1st sec. com. people Army of Hungarian Socialist Workers' Party, Budapest, 1958-70; dep. minister Hungary Ministry Def., Budapest, 1970-85, minister, 1985—; Mem. Hungary Parliament, Budapest, 1971—. Office: Ministry Defense, Palffy Gyorgy utca 7/11, 1055 Budapest Hungary

FERENCZY, OTO, educator; b. Brezovica, Slovakia, Czechoslovakia, Mar. 30, 1921; s. Gejza and Irene (Husovsky) F.; m. Vera Kotuliak, Dec. 27, 1957; 1 child, Vera. PhD in Philosophy, U. J.A. Komensky, Bratislava, Czechoslovakia, 1945. Dean Acad. Music, Bratislava, Czechoslovakia, 1953-55; dean Acad. Music, Bratislava, 1955-62, rector, 1962-65; prof. Acad. of Music, Bratislava, 1965—. Composer: Music for Four String Instruments (Bartók laureate 1948), Opera An Uncommon Humoresque (State prize, 1971). Pres. Union Slovak Composers, Bratislava, 1970072, 82-87. Recipient Golden medal Acad. Music1971, J.A.Komensky medal Ministry of Edn, 1987. Mem. G.F. Händel Soc., Slovak Ednl. Soc. Home: Matusova 27, 811-04 Bratislava Czechoslovakia Office: Wsoka Skola Muzickych Umeni, Jiraskova 3, Bratislava Czechoslovakia

FERENS, MARCELLA, educator, business executive; b. Pitts.; d. Ignatius and Marcella (Buzas) Slevinskas; student Greensburg Bus. Coll., 1934-35, Maison Frederic Cosmetology, 1936, Kree Inst. Electrolysis, N.Y., 1952; B.S., U. Pitts., 1957; postgrad. Mid-Western U., 1962; M.Ed., Duquesne U., 1964; m. Joseph J. Ferens, Nov. 27, 1937; children—Joseph Ferens, James. Cosmetologist and electrologist, Manor and Darragh, Pa., 1937—; research in hair regrowth, Darragh, 1954—; tchr. cosmetology Uniontown (Pa.) Vocat. High, 1954-55; tchr. algebra, reading and drama dir. Harold Jr. High Sch., Greensburg, Pa., 1958—; pres. Marcella Ferens Inc.; treas. Schumacher Labs. Inc., Darragh. Insp., Chem. Corps, Dept. Army, N.Y., 1951. Mem. Nat. Council Tchrs. Math., Nat., Pa. edn. assns. Patentee in field. Home: Box 84 Daragh PA 15625

FERET, ADAM EDWARD, JR., dentist; b. Newark, Mar. 5, 1942; s. Adam Edward and Bronislawa Anne (Szorc) F.; B.A. (athletic scholar), Seton Hall U., 1963; D.M.D., U. Medicine and Dentistry of N.J., 1967. Pvt. practice dentistry, Westfield, N.J., 1972—. Served with USNR, 1967-70. Fellow Am. Acad. Gen. Dentistry; mem. ADA, N.J. Dental Assn., L.D. Pankey Study Club, Soc. Oral Physiology and Occlusion, Quest Study Club, Internat. Coll. Oral Implantologists, Am. Soc. Oral Implantology, Central Dental Soc., Balloon Fedn. Am., Polish-Am. Guardian Soc., Polish Falcons of Am., Copernicus Soc. Am., Psi Omega. Roman Catholic. Club: Toastmasters. Home and Office: 169 Mountain Ave Westfield NJ 07090

FERGUS, PATRICIA MARGUERITA, educator emeritus, writer, editor; b. Mpls., Oct. 26, 1918; d. Golden Maughan and Mary Adella (Smith) F.; B.S., U. Minn., 1939, M.A., 1941, Ph.D., 1960. Various personnel and editing positions with U.S. Govt., 1943-59; mem. faculty U. Minn., 1964-79, asst. prof. English, 1972-79, coordinator writing program conf. on writing, 1975, dir. writing centre, 1975-77; prof. English and writing, dir. writing ctr., assoc. dean Coll., Mt. St. Mary's Coll., Emmitsburg, Md., 1979-81; dir. writing seminars Mack Truck, Inc., Hagerstown, Md., 1979-81; writer, 1964—; editorial asst. to pres. Met. State U., St. Paul, 1984-85; speaker in field; cons. in field; dir. 510 Groveland Assocs.; bus. mgr. Eitel Hosp. Gift Shop; mem. St. Olaf Ch. Choir, St. Olaf Parish Adv. Bd. Recipient Outstanding Contbn. award U. Minn. Twin Cities Student Assembly, 1975; Horace T. Morse-Amoco Found. award, 1976; Ednl. Devel. grantee U. Minn., 1975-76; Mt. St. Mary's Coll. grantee, 1980; 3d prize vocal-choral category Nat. Music Composition Contest, Nat. League Am. Pen Women, speaker and Bronze Medalist, 13th Internat. Biographical Congress, 1986. Mem. Internat. Biog. Centre Assn., Am. Biog. Research Assn. (dep. gov. hon. research adv. bd.), Am. Biog. Research Assn., AAUW, Nat. (regional judge writing awards program 1974, 76-77, state coordinator 1977-79) Minn. (chmn. career and job opportunities com., mem. spl. com. on tchr. licensure, sec. legis. com.) councils tchrs. English, Nat. League Am. Pen Women (1st pres. Minn. State Assn.), World Lit. Acad., Mpls. Poetry Soc. (pres.; 1st prize Haiku contest 1984, 3d prize poetry contest 1986, 1st prize poetry contest 1987, 3d prize poetry contest 1988), League Minn. Poets (3d prize Nature, 2d prize Humor, Autumn poetry contest 1987), Midwest Fedn. Chaparral Poets (2d prize poetry contest 1987, 3d prize poetry contest 1988), AAUP, Pi Lambda Theta. Roman Catholic. Author: Spelling Improvement, 4th edit., 1983; contbr. to Minn. English Jour., Downtown Cath. Voice, Mpls., Mountaineer Briefing, ABI Digest; contbr. poems Minn. English Jour., Mpls. Muse, The Moccasin, Heartsong, Northstar Gold, The PoetryLetter, IBC Mag. Home and Office: 1770 Bryant Ave S #410 Minneapolis MN 55403

FERGUSON, ALBERT SIDNEY, human resource manager; b. Nassau, Bahamas, Dec. 6, 1950; m. Anetta Wyatt, July 2, 1983; 1 child, Albernie L. BSc in Econs. with honors, U. Detroit, 1973; MBA in Fin., SUNY, Albany, 1975; PhD, Walden U., Naples, Fla., 1980. Chief fiscal officer Coll. of the Bahamas, Nassau, 1975-76; v.p., treas. Tomlinson Coll., Cleveland, Tenn., 1976-81; chief personnel officer Bahamas Electricity Corp., Nassau, 1981—; parttime instr. bus. McKenzie Coll., Chattanooga, 1977-78, Cleveland (Tenn.) State Community Coll., 1978-79, Tomlinson Coll., 1976-80, Coll. of The Bahamas, 1981—, Coll. of St. Benedict, Collegeville, Minn./St. John's U., Nassau Extension, 1982—. Contbr. articles to profl. jours. Mem. Am. Soc. Personnel Adminstrs., Am. Soc. Tng. and Devel. Home: PO Box FH 14-075, Nassau The Bahamas Office: Bahamas Electricity Corp, PO Box N-7509, Nassau The Bahamas

FERGUSON, CHARLES AUSTIN, newspaper editor; b. New Orleans, Mar. 16, 1937; s. Austin and Josephine Hayes (Gessner) F.; m. Jane Pugh, Dec. 21, 1961; children: Elizabeth Hayes, Caroline Pugh. B.A., Tulane U., 1958, LL.B., 1961. Bar: La. bar 1961. From reporter to editor States-Item, New Orleans, 1961-80; editor Times-Picayune/States-Item, New Orleans, 1980—; anchorman TV program City Desk, New Orleans, 1971-78. Trustee Dillard U., New Orleans, 1972—, chmn. exec. com., 1978—; trustee Inst. Politics, Loyola U., New Orleans, 1968-75, pres., 1971-75; co-chmn. Louis Armstrong Meml. Park Com., New Orleans, 1971-79. Recipient Torch of Liberty award Anti-Defamation League of B'nai B'rith, 1981; Nieman fellow, 1965-66. Mem. Am. Soc. Newspaper Editors, La. Bar Assn. Club: New Orleans Lawn Tennis. Home: 1448 Joseph St New Orleans LA 70115 Office: The Times-Picayune Pub Corp 3800 Howard Ave New Orleans LA 70140

FERGUSON, CHARLOTTE BRAINARD, wholesale lumber executive; b. Chicopee, Mass., June 18, 1929; d. Charles Duncan and Gladys (Hamilton) Brainard; B.A., Ohio Wesleyan U., 1950; M.Ed., Boston U., 1956; m. Albert D. Wood, 1957 (div. 1972); children—Jeffrey D., Maribeth L., Jennifer H.; m. Robert Bruce Ferguson, Dec. 28, 1973 (dec. 1983). Traffic mgr. sta. WHDH, Boston, 1951-52; sec. Harold Cabot Advt. Agy., Boston, 1953; copywriter Gabriel Stern Advt. Agy., Boston, 1954-55; tchr. Weston (Mass.) Elem. Sch., 1956-57; dir. Village Sch., Boxford, Mass., 1967-72; tchr. Tuftonboro (N.H.) Central Sch., Gov. Wentworth Regional Sch. Dist., 1973-80; v.p. Wood Dimensions Inc., Tuftonboro, 1980-83, pres., 1983—; pres. Hand Pictured Photography, Ossipee, N.H., 1987—. Friend Tuftonboro Library; patron Torpedo Factory Art Ctr., Alexandria, Va., Decatur House, Washington; mem. Huggins Hosp. Fair Com., 1984—, West Point Fund Com. U.S. Mil. Acad. Mem. DAR, Pi Lambda Theta, Alpha Delta Pi, Alpha Epsilon Rho. Republican. Congregationalist. Club: Lakes Region Women's Republican (v.p. 1985-86). Home and Office: Wood Dimensions RFD 1 Box 144 Tuftonboro Corner Ossipee NH 03864

FERGUSON, E. JAMES, history educator, editor; b. Provo, Utah, Jan. 23, 1917; s. Elmer Joseph Archbold and Rose Marie Ferguson; m. Louise Anna Walker, Nov. 12, 1943; 1 son, Bruce Walker. B.A., U. Wash., 1939, M.A., 1941; Ph.D., U. Wisc., 1951. Instr. U. Md., College Pk., 1947-55, asst. prof., 1955-62, assoc. prof., 1962-64, asst. prof., extension in Europe, 1955-57; prof. Queens Coll., 1964—, prof. on leave, 1980—; vis. editor publs. Inst. Early Am. History and Culture, Williamsburg, Va., 1960-61. Author: The Power of the Purse, 1961 (John H. Dunning prize, 1962); The American Revolution, 1974, 1979. Editor hist. papers The Papers of Robert Morris, 1781-84, 1973-84. Contbr. articles to profl. jours. and anthologies. Served with U.S. Army, 1941-45. Guggenheim fellow, 1963-64; grantee Inst. Early Am. Hist. and Culture, 1950, 53, Am. Philos. Soc., 1960, NEH, 1968—, Donaldson, Lufkin and Jenrette, CUNY. Home: 186-C Avenida Majorca Laguna Hills CA 92653 Office: Queens Coll Papers of Robert Morris Flushing NY 11367

FERGUSON, HARLEY ROBERT, service company executive; b. Windsor, Ont., Can., Aug. 13, 1936; U.S. citizen; s. Robert Clifford and Ruby Mills (Chase) F.; m. Ruth Elizabeth Mann, Oct. 6, 1956 (div. 1970); children—Keith, Elizabeth, Kevin, Kent; m. Joyce Elizabeth Bradley, Dec. 26, 1972; children—Harley Robert Jr., William, John, Ian. Student U. Western Ont., London, 1955-56, U. Windsor (Ont.), 1957-58; B.Sc., Carleton U., Ottawa, Ont., 1968. Cert. in data processing. Systems analyst Ford Motor Co., Windsor, 1956-59; various positions Govt. of Can., Ottawa, 1959-70; dir. data processing Canfarm, Guelph, Ont., 1970-76; dir. support services Bell Can., Toronto Ont., 1976-77; dir. bus. systems Bell No. Software Research, Toronto, 1977-80; v.p. info. services ALLTEL Corp. (formerly Mid-Continent Telephone Corp.), Hudson, Ohio, 1980-85; sr. v.p. mgmt. info. services Kelly Services Inc., Troy, Mich., 1985—; bd. dirs. VIM (Internat. Control Data Users Group), 1973-75. Cons., Beechbrook Children's Home, Beechwood, Ohio, 1983. Served to 2d lt. Can. Army, 1955-56. Mem. Soc. for Info. Mgmt. Lutheran. Office: Kelly Services Inc 999 W Big Beaver Rd Troy MI 48098

FERGUSON, JAMES LARNARD, food company executive; b. Evanston, Ill., Mar. 16, 1926; s. J. Larnard and Justine (Dickson) F.; m. Elizabeth Rich, June 17, 1950; children: Deborah, John Dickson, Douglas. AB, Hamilton Coll., 1949; MBA, Harvard, 1951. Assoc. advt. mgr. Procter & Gamble, Cin., 1951-62; sr. v.p., account supr. Lennon & Newell Advt., N.Y.C., 1962-63; asst. to mktg. mgr., Birds Eye div. Gen. Foods Corp., White Plains, N.Y., 1963-67, gen. mgr., Birds Eye div., 1967-68, corp. v.p., gen. mgr.frozen foods div., 1968-70, corp. group v.p., 1970-72, exec. v.p., 1972; pres. Gen. Foods Corp., White Plains, 1972-77, chief operating officer, 1972-73, chief exec. officer, 1973-86, chmn., 1974-86, chmn. exec. com., 1987—, also bd. dirs.; vice chmn. Philip Morris Cos., Inc. (parent), N.Y.C., 1985-86, also bd. dirs.; bd. dirs. Union Carbide Corp., Sawyer-Ferguson-Walker Co.; bd. dirs., mem. exec. com. and compensation com. Chase Manhattan Bank (N.A.). Mem. audit com. Council Fin. Aid to Edn.; trustee Hamilton Coll.; mem. Outward Bound, Bus. Com. for Arts; bd. dirs. Assocs. Harvard Bus. Sch.; sr. warden Episc. ch., 1971—. Served with C.E. U.S. Army, 1944-46. Mem. Grocery Mfrs. Am. (bd. dirs., chmn., exec. com.), Bus. Roundtable (exec. com., policy com.), SRI Internat. Council, Conf. Bd., Confrerie des Chevaliers du Tastevin. Clubs: Econ.; Wilton Riding, Blind Brook, Clove Valley Rod and Gun; Silver Spring Country (Ridgefield, Conn.); Links, Woodway Gun. Home: 77 Middlebrook Farm Rd Wilton CT 06897 Office: Gen Foods Corp 250 North St White Plains NY 10625

FERGUSON, JOHN PATRICK, medical center executive; b. Weehawken, N.J., Jan. 22, 1949; s. Donald George and Margaret (Rienzo) F.; m. Gene Marie Promersperger, Jan 16, 1970; children: Adam, David, Kate. BS in Econs., St. Peter's Coll., 1970; MBA in Hosp. Adminstrn., George Washington U., 1973. Sr. v.p. St. Vincent's Hosp., N.Y.C., 1972-81; v.p. ops. Hackensack (N.J.) Med. Ctr., 1981-85, sr. v.p., 1985, acting pres., chief exec. officer, 1985-86, pres., chief exec. officer, 1986—; adj. faculty New Sch. for Social Research Grad. Sch. Mgmt. and Urban Professions, N.Y.C., 1978—; pres. Met. Health Adminstrs., N.Y.C., 1977-78. One of twenty-five U.S. Healthcare Execs. abstract presenters for the China/U.S. Conf. on "Managing Hospitals in the 90s"; featured in Modern Healthcare Mag. as one of the top 12 "Up and Coming Healthcare Execs." in the nation. Fellow Am. Coll. of Healthcare Execs., mem. Am. Hosp. Assn., Cath. Hosp. Assn. Office: Hackensack Med Ctr Office of the Chief Exec Officer 30 Prospect Ave Hackensack NJ 07601

FERGUSON, MARK WILLIAM JAMES, biology, dental educator; b. Belfast, Northern Ireland, Oct. 11, 1955; s. James and Elanor Gwendoline (McCoubery) F.; m. Janice Elizabeth Forsythe, June 22, 1984; 1 child; Fleur Marcia. BSc in Anatomy with hons., Queen's U., Belfast, 1976, B in Dental Surgery with hons., 1978, PhD in Anatomy and Embryology, 1982. Registered dental surgeon. Lectr. anatomy Queen's U., Belfast, 1979-84; prof. and head Dept. Basic Dental Scis., dir. Dental Research Labs. U. Manchester, Eng., 1984—, head Dept. Cell and Structural Biology, 1986—; cons. Colgate Palmolive Ltd., Manchester, 1985—. Author: The Structure, Development and Evolution of Reptiles, 1984; contbr. to sci. jours; presenter in field. Recipient SCADA Achievement award Am. Dental Assn., 1981, Colyer prize Royal Soc. Med., 1980; named Darwin Lectr. Brit. Assn. for the Advancement of Sci., 1987; Churchill Travelling fellow Winston Churchill Meml. Trust, 1978. Fellow Zool. Soc. London (sci.), Royal Acad. Medicine in Ireland (Conway medal 1985), Anat. Soc. Great Britain and Ireland (council mem. 1982-83), Royal Micros. Soc., N.Y. Acad. Scis., Internat. Assn. Dental Research (Disting. Scientist award, 1988). Presbyterian. Office: U Manchester, Dept Cell & Structural, Biology, Coupland St, Manchester M13 9PL, England

FERGUSON, ROBERT S., film consulting company executive; b. N.Y.C., May 8, 1915; s. Samuel I. and Augusta H. F.; B.S., N.Y. U., 1936; m. Helene B., Aug. 1, 1940; children—Carole Jane, Sandra Joan. With Scripps-Howard Newspapers, 1936-38, Warner Bros. Pictures, 1938-40; v.p. world-wide mktg. Columbia Pictures, Inc., 1940-73; v.p. corp. relations Columbia Pictures Industries, Inc., 1973-74; v.p. world mktg. Am. Film Theatre, 1974-75; v.p. div. entertainment Rosenfeld, Sirowitz & Lawson Advt., 1975-76; v.p. world mktg. Horizon Pictures, 1976-77; pres. Cinema Think Tank, 1977—; dir. Natco Industries, Inc.; instr. in film Adelphi U.; cons. to chmn. Columbia Pictures Industries, Inc., 1979-83, cons. to chmn. bd., 1983—. Mem. Motion Picture Acad. Arts, Sci., Motion Picture Pioneers, Screen Publicists Guild (pres.), Variety Clubs Internat., Motion Picture Assn. Am. (chmn. com. advt. dirs.). Home: 84 Fulton Ave Atlantic Beach NY 11509

FERGUSON, THOMAS C., diplomat; b. Nov. 27, 1933; s. Thomas C. and Grace (Crooks) F.; m. Linda Bleyle; children: Leslie Mead, Ian Thomas, Jessica Ashley. AB, Vanderbilt U., 1955, JD, 1959; cert., Hague Acad. Internat. Law, 1958. Bd. mem. Mead Johnson Found., 1960-70; mktg. mgr. Pharmaseal Labs., 1962-75; pres. Atlantic Salvage Corp., 1975-78, Brevard Marina, 1977-82; dir. Eastern Caribbean Peace Corps, 1982-84; dep. commr. Immigration and Naturalization Service Dept. Justice, 1984-87; U.S. Ambassador to Brunei Darussalam 1987—. Served with U.S. Army, 1955-56. Mem. Fed. Bar Assn. Clubs: Offshore Cruising of Calif., Eau Gallie Yacht. Office: US Ambassador to Brunei Care Dept of State Washington DC 20520 *

FERGUSON, WILLIAM CHARLES, telecommunications executive; b. Detroit, Oct. 26, 1930; s. William and Bessie F. (Barr) F.; m. Joyce G. Soby, June 14, 1952; children: Laura, Ellen, Joanne. B.A., Albion Coll., 1952. With Mich. Bell Telephone Co., 1952-77, 78-83, dist. mgr., 1961-63, div. mgr., 1963-68, gen. traffic mgr., 1968-72, v.p. ops. staff and engring., 1972-73, v.p. metro, 1973-76, v.p. personnel, 1976-77, exec. v.p., chief operating officer, 1978-82; v.p. N.Y.C. region N.Y. Telephone Co., 1977, pres., chief exec. officer, 1983-86; vice chmn. NYNEX Corp., White Plains, N.Y., 1986—; dir. Marine Midland Bank, Gen. Re Corp, CPC Internat. Corp. Chmn. gen. campaign United Way N.Y.C., 1987—; bd. dirs. Detroit Symphony, 1979-82; trustee Albion Coll., 1980; bd. dirs. N.Y. State Bus. Council; bd. dirs. N.Y.C. Partnership, 1984-86; mem. N.Y. Gov.'s Council on Fiscal and Econ. Priorities. Served with U.S. Army, 1952-54. Home: 5 Dogwood Dr Armonk NY 10504 Office: NYNEX Corp 335 Madison Ave New York NY 10017

FERINO, CHRISTOPHER KENNETH, computer information scientist; b. Chgo., May 25, 1961; s. Natale Ferino and Carol Marie (Anderson) Huckeby; m. Anita Louise Vanderhoof, Oct. 19, 1985. Cons. Lachman Assn., Inc., Westmont, Ill., 1979-80; AS/RS operator W.W. Grainger, Niles, Ill., 1980-82; mem. computer staff Paddock Publs., Arlington Heights, Ill., 1982-84; data processing coordinator Power Systems, Schaumburg, Ill., 1984-85; tech. specialist Follett Software Co., Crystal Lake, Ill., 1985-87; tech. service dir. Follett Software Co., Crystal Lake, 1987—. Mem. Boston Computer Soc. Home: PO Box 239 Cary IL 60013

FERLAND, E. JAMES, electric utility executive; b. Boston, Mar. 19, 1942; s. Ernest James and Muriel (Cassell) F.; m. Eileen Kay Patridge, Mar. 9, 1964; children: E. James, Elizabeth Denise. BS in Mech. Engring., U. Maine, 1964; MBA, U. New Haven, 1979; postgrad. in program mgmt. devel., Harvard U. Grad. Sch. Bus. Adminstrn. Electric utility engr. HELCO, New London, Conn., 1964-67; supt. nuclear ops. NNECO, Waterford, Conn., 1967-78; dir. rate regulation N.E. Utilities, Berlin, Conn., 1978-80, pres., chief operating officer, 1983-86; pres., chief operating officer N.E. Utilities, Conn., Mass., 1986; exec. v.p., chief fin. officer NUSCO, Berlin, 1980-83; pres. Pub. Service Electric & Gas Co. (subs. Pub. Service Enterprise Group, Inc.), Newark, 1986, chmn., pres., chief executive officer, 1986—; chmn., pres., chief exec. officer Pub. Service Enterprise Group, Inc., Newark, 1986—; also bd. dirs. all Pub. Service Enterprise Group subs.; bd. dirs. Conn. Yankee Co., Vt. Yankee Co., Maine Yankee Co., Hartford Steam Boiler Inspection and Ins. Co., 1986—. Office: Pub Service Electric & Gas Co 80 Park Plaza Newark NJ 07101 *

FERMAN, IRVING, lawyer, educator; b. N.Y.C., July 4, 1919; s. Joseph and Sadie (Stein) F.; m. Bertha Paglin, June 12, 1946; children—James Paglin, Susan Paglin. B.S., N.Y.U., 1941; J.D., Harvard, 1948. Bar: La. 1948, D.C. 1974. Partner Provensal, Faris & Ferman, New Orleans, 1948-52; dir. Am. Civil Liberties Union, Washington, 1952-59, Am. Civil Liberties Clearing House, 1952-54; exec. vice chmn. Pres.'s Com. Govt. Contracts, 1959-60; v.p. Internat. Latex Corp., 1960-66; pres. Piedmont Theaters Corp., 1966-69; adj. asso. prof. mgmt. N.Y.U. Grad. Sch. Bus., 1964-68; adj. prof. law Howard U., 1968-69, prof. law, 1969-86, prof. emeritus, 1986—; dir. Project for Legal Policy, 1976—; vis. prof. law Am. U., 1971-72; mem. Am. Com. Cultural Freedom, 1954—; mem. Com. of Arts and Scis. for Eisenhower, 1956; mem. citizens adv. com. U.S. Commn. on Govt. Security, 1957; chmn. Police Complaint Review Bd., 1965-73; mem. Dept. HEW Reviewing Authority, 1969-79; chmn. Interdisco Ltd., London, 1986—; bd. dirs. Control Fluidics, Inc., Greenwich, Conn. Contbr. to books and revs. Mem. bd. dirs. New Orleans Acad. Art, 1948-51. Served from cadet to 1st lt. USAAF, 1942-46. Mem. Am., La., D.C., New Orleans bar assns. Jewish. Clubs: International (Washington); Army-Navy Country (Arlington, Va.); Harvard (N.Y.C.), Caterpillar (N.Y.C.). Home: 3818 Huntington St NW Washington DC 20015 also: Rt 1 Sullivan Harbor ME 04689 Office: 2935 Upton St NW Washington DC 20015

FERNANDES, JOSEPH EDWARD, small business owner; b. Maderias, Portugal, Mar. 12, 1923; came to U.S., 1924; s. Jose and Rosa (Teixerira) F.; m. Annabelle Watson, Apr. 24, 1954; children: Joseph, Marcia, Donna Maria. BS in Bus. Adminstrn., Boston U., 1947; D in Comml. Sci. (hon.), Stonehill Coll., 1964. With Fernandes Super Mkts., Inc., Norton, Mass., 1948—, pres., treas., 1952—, chmn. bd. until 1979; treas. Fernandes Realty Corp., Brockton East Shopping Plaza, Inc., Fernandes Twin-City Realty Corp.; pres. Portuguese Times Newspaper, 1980—, Portuguese Cable TV Network, 1981—, Sta. WRCB, Providence, 1982—; dir. Fall River Line Pier, Mass.; cons. Alliance for Progress, Uruguay, 1962. Pres. Annawon council Boy Scouts Am., 1974—, regional NE Dir., 1971—, also bd. dirs.; former chmn. Portuguese Am. Fedn. U.S. and Can.; bd. dirs. Mass. Blue Sheild, Mass. Easter Seals, U.S.S. Mass. Meml. Com., R.I. Philharm. Orch.; trustees council U. Mass., 1973; former trustee Salve Regina Coll., Newport, R.I.; former pres. Portuguese Cultural Found.; pres. Bristol County Devel. Council, 1980—. Served with AUS, 1943-45. Decorated knight St. Gregory the Great; Order Prince Henry the Navigator (Portugal); recipient Peter Francisco award Portuguese Continental Union, 1966, Silver Beaver, Silver Antelope awards Boy Scouts Am., 1977; named Man of Yr. NCCJ. Mem. Internat. Assn. Chain Stores (pres. 1968-71), Portugal-U.S. C. of C. (dir.). Home: Fernandes Circle Norton MA 02766 Office: 378 S Worcester St Norton MA 02766

FERNANDES LOPES, JOSE LUIS, Cape Verde ambassador to U.S.; b. Praia, Cape Verde, Dec. 20, 1947; s. Fernando Lopes Almeida and Catarina Fernandes Lopes de Almeida; 1 child, Dunia Lopes. B.A. in History, Faculty Humanities, Lisbon, Portugal, 1970; LL.D., Ariz. Coll. Polit. Sci., 1983. Agrl. tech. engr. specializing in hydraulics Portuguese Ministry Pub. Works, 1968-72; mem. council African Party for Independence Cape Verde and Guine-Bissau, 1973; tchr. Domingos Ramos High Sch., Praia, 1974-75; mem. del. which negotiated Cape Verde's independence from Portugal, 1974; rep. Popular Nat. Assembly, mem. commn. in charge elaboration of constn. Republic Cape Verde, 1974; sec. state Republic Cape Verde, 1977-80; Cape Verde ambassador to U.S.A., Washington, 1980—. Recipient cert. of award Brockton chpt. NAACP (Mass.), 1982; Unidade award Cape Verdeans United, Inc., 1982. Office: Embassy of Cape Verde 3415 Massachusetts Ave NW Washington DC 20007

FERNANDEZ, MANUEL O., JR., cosmetic plastic surgeon, dermatologist; b. Manila, Mar. 8, 1945; s. Manuel C. Sr. and Rosita (Ocampo) F.; m. Maria Elena C. Torres, Apr. 21, 1972; children: Melissa Ann, Miguel Antonio. BS, U. Philippines, 1966, MD, 1971. Diplomate Am. Bd. Cosmetic Surgery, Philippines Bd. Dermatology. Resident Philippine Gen. Hosp., 1971-72; resident dermatology and cosmetic surgery Temple U., Phila., 1972-75; intern cosmetic plastic surgery various drs., N.Y., N.J., Phila. and Japan, 1975; instr. U. Philippines, Manila, 1975-80, asst. prof. dermatology, 1980—; cons. cosmetic plastic surgery, dermatology Makati Med. Ctr., Manila, 1975—. Philippine Jaycees scholar, 1962-67. Fellow Internat. Acad. Cosmetic Surgery, Am. Acad. Cosmetic Surgery, Am. Acad. Dermatology, Philippine Dermatological Soc.; mem. Internat. Soc. Aesthetic Surgery, Am. Soc. Cosmetic Surgery, Am. Soc. Liposuction surgery, Philippine Soc. Aesthetic Plastic Surgery, Am. Soc. Dermatologic Surgery, Philippine Med. Assn., Makati Med. Soc. Clubs: Manila Polo, Baguio Country. Home: 12 Urdaneta Ave, Urdaneta Village, Makati Metro Manila, Philippines Office: Makati Med Ctr, 2 Amorsolo St, Makati Metro Manila, Philippines

FERNANDEZ BENLLOCH, JOSE VICENTE CARLOS, engineering and construction company executive; b. Aldaya, Valencia, Spain, Nov. 4, 1944; s. Jose Candido Fernandez and Herminia Benlloch; m. Maria Teresa Martinez Rincon, July 11, 1969; children—Jose Carlos, Marcos Angel. Ph.D., ICAI Engring., Madrid, 1968. Utilities engr. Lummus Espanola, Madrid, 1968-71; engring. coordinator Foster Wheeler Iberia, Madrid, 1971; tech. dir. CETEIN Engrs., Madrid, 1976-77; tech. dir. IPEC-SGI, Tarragona, Spain, 1977-80; project mgr. Foster Wheeler Iberia, Madrid, 1980—. Cons., UNIDO, Vienna, Austria, 1983-84, Tequinsa, Madrid, 1984-85. Served with Spanish Army, 1968—. Mem. ICAI Engring. Assn. Patentee in mech. device to draw ellipses of any axis. Avocations: photography; piano. Home: Manuel Maria Iglesias 3, Madrid 28043 Spain

FERNANDEZ-BOLLO, MARIANO FERMIN, civil engineer; b. Madrid, Feb. 26, 1919; s. Mariano and Josefa (Bollo) Fernandez Toral; m. Sol Maria Martinez Moreno, Dec. 26, 1944; children: Michael, Helen, Alice, Edouard. PhD in Civil Engring, High Tech. Sch. for Civil Engring., Madrid, 1943, D. in Civil Engring., 1967. Prof., group coordinator Rock Mechanics ESTP, Paris. Mem. French Commn. on Large Dams, 1965—. Served with Spanish Army, 1939-43. Decorated comdr. Alphonse X; recipient Montblanc Tunnel medal, 1968; Almendra Dam award, 1971; Atazar award, 1972—, Honor medal Spanish Assn. Civil Engrs., 1987. Mem. Internat. Rock Mechanics Soc., Internat. Soils Mechanics Soc., Internat. Applied Geology Soc., Protection of Castles Assn., Santo Domingo Opera Sponsors Assn. Roman Catholic. Clubs: Royal Automobile of Spain; Internacional Colon at San Jose Costa Rica. Home: Apartado 905 Centro Colon, 1007 San Jose Costa Rica also: 106 Blvd Pereire, 75017 Paris France also: Castle of Castellar, Teruel Spain

FERNÁNDEZ-CHAMIZO, CARMEN, computer science educator; b. Madrid, Nov. 30, 1955; d. Jose Fernandez and Lydia Chamizo; m. Antonio Sanz-Azanon, July 10, 1975; children—Ana, Miguel. B.S. in Physics, Universidad Complutense, 1977, Ph.D. in Physics, 1984. Research fellow Universidad Complutense, Madrid, 1978-80, tutor, 1981-84, asst. prof. computer sci., 1985—. Author: (with Antonio Vaquero) La Informática Aplicada a la Enseñanza, 1987; contbr. articles to profl. jours. Nat. Com. Sci. Research grantee, 1984-86; recipient Citema award for thesis on computer sci., 1985. Home: Avenida de Brasilia 9, 4 6 Madrid 28028, Spain Office: Universidad Complutense, Dept Info Facultad Fisicas, Ciudad Universitaria Madrid 28040, Spain

FERNANDEZ-GUZMAN, CARLOS RAMON, bank executive; b. Havana, Cuba, May 14, 1956; s. Carlos J. Fernandez and Myriam R. (Guzman) Valle; m. Maria Elena Valdes, July 31, 1976; children: Natalie Michele, Carlos Eduardo, Melissa Elena. AA, Miami-Dade Community Coll.; student, Fla. Internat. U.; grad. cert. completion, La. State U. Sr. account exec. S.E. Banking Corp., Miami, 1974-79; sr. v.p. Consol. Bank N.A., Hialeah, Fla., 1979—; bd. dirs. Hispanic Heritage, Inc., Miami, Miami Capital Devel., Inc.,

Miami Citywide Devel., Inc., PACE, Miami. Co-chmn. fund raising United Way of Dade County, Miami, 1984; bd. dirs. Hialeah-Miami Springs C. of C., 1984. Recipient award for Excellence in New Club Bldg., Kiwanis Internat., 1979. Fellow Leadership Miami, Internat. Ctr. (investment com. 1981-83); mem. Fla. Bankers Assn. (mktg. com. 1983—), Greater Miami C. of C. (trustee). Republican. Roman Catholic. Lodge: Kiwanis (sec., treas. 1978-80). Office: Consol Bank NA 900 W 49th St Hialeah FL 33012

FERNANDEZ-MORAN, HUMBERTO, biophysicist; b. Maracaibo, Venezuela, Feb. 18, 1924; s. Luis and Elena (Villalobos) Fernandez-M.; m. Anna Browallius, Dec. 30, 1953; children—Brigida Elena, Veronica. M.D., U. Munich, Germany, 1944, U. Caracas, Venezuela, 1945; M.S., U. Stockholm, Sweden, 1951, Ph.D., 1952. Fellow neurology, neuropath. George Washington U., 1945-46; intern George Washington U. Hosp., 1945-46; resident Serafimerlasarettet, Stockholm, 1946-58; fgn. asst. Neurosurg. Clinic, Stockholm, 1946-48; research fellow Nobel Inst. Physics, Stockholm, 1947-49, Inst. Cell Research & Genetics, Karolinska Institutet, Stockholm, 1948-51; asst. prof. Inst. Cell Research & Genetics, Karolinska Institutet, 1952; prof., chmn. dept. biophysics U. Caracas, 1951-58; dir. Venezuelan Inst. Neurology and Brain Research, Caracas, 1954-58; asso. biophysicist neurosurg. service Mass. Gen. Hosp., Boston, 1958-62; vis. lectr. dept. biology Mass. Inst. Tech., 1958-62; research asso. neuropath. Harvard, 1958-62; prof. biophysics U. Chgo., 1962—, A.N. Pritzker prof. biophysics, now prof. emeritus; sci. and cultural attaché to Venezuelan legations, Sweden, Norway, Denmark, 1947-54; head Venezuelan commn. Atomic Energy Conf., Geneva, 1955; chmn. Venezuelan commn. 1st Inter-Am.-Symposium on Nuclear Energy, Brookhaven, N.Y., 1957; minister of edn., Venezuela, 1958; mem. Orgn. Am. States adv. commn. on sci. devel. in Latin Am., Nat. Acad. Scis., 1958; mem. U.S. Nat. Com. UNESCO, 1957. Author: The Submicroscopic Organization of Vertebrate Nerve Fibres, 1952, The Submicroscopic Organization of the Internode Portion of Vertebrate Myelinated Nerve Fibers, 1953, Cryoelectronmicroscopy; Superconductivity; Diamond Knife Ultramicrotomy, 1955-76; author series publs. in fields molecular biology, nerve ultrastructure, electron and cryo-electron microscopy, electron and x-ray diffraction, cell ultrastructure, neurobiology, superconducting lenses, superconductivity, others.; editorial bd. Jour. of Research & Development. Decorated Knight of Polar Star Sweden; Claude Bernard medal Canada; Medalla Andres Bello Venezuela, 1973; Recipient Gold medal City Maracaibo, 1968, John Scott award for invention of diamond knife, 1967; medal Bolivarian Soc. U.S., 1973. Fellow Am. Acad. Arts and Sci.; mem. Venezuelan Acad. Medicine (hon.), Academia Ciencias Fisicas y Matematicas (Caracas), Am. Acad. Neurology (corr. mem.), Internat. Soc. Cell Biology, Buenos Aires, Santiago, Lima, socs. Neurology, Buenos Aires, Santiago, Lima, Porto Alegre societies surgery, Electron Microscopy Soc. Am. (spl. citation), Am. Nuclear Soc., Pan Am. Med. Assn., Sociedad Bolivárianade Arquitectos (Venezuela) (hon.), Pan Am. Assn. of Anatomy (hon.). Home: 55 Dartmouth Rd University Heights Williams Bay WI 53191 Office: Academia Ciencias, Apto 1421, Caracas 1010-A, Venezuela

FERNANDEZ ORDONEZ, FRANCISCO, Spanish minister foreign affairs; b. Madrid, June 22, 1930; m. Maria Paz Garcia Mayo. LL.B., U. Madrid, 1952; diploma internat. tax program Harvard U., 1967. Bar: Spain 1975. Mem. corps state tax lawyers, Spain, 1954-59, corps state fin. and taxation inspectors, 1959-69; tech. sec.-gen. Ministry of Fin., Spain, 1969-73, under sec. fin. economy, 1973-74; pres. Nat. Inst. Industry, Spain, 1974; founder, pres. Fedn. Social Democrat Parties, 1974-77; minister of Finance, 1977-79, minister of justice, 1980-81; chmn. bd. dirs. Banco Exterior de Espana, 1982-83; founder Democratic Action Party, 1982, mem. Parliament for Madrid, minister fgn. affairs, 1985—; sub-dir. Inst. Fiscal Studies; dir. studies Centre Tax Studies; pres. Spanish del. OCED, 1969-73; Spanish rep. GATT, IMF, EEC, numerous other internat. coms.; mem. Internat. Com. of Twenty for Monetary Reform; mem. Com. of Nine. Author: The Necessary Spain, 1980; Words in Freedom, 1982. Editor Economia Financiera Espanola. Contbr. articles to profl. jours. Address: Ministerio de Asuntos Exteriores, Plaza de la Provincia 1, Madrid Spain

FERNANDO, LIONEL, federal official; b. Kandy, Sri Lanka, Feb. 17, 1936; s. Dickmon and Adelin (Fonseka) F.; m. Somalatha Subasinghe, Sept. 6, 1962; children: Kaushalya, Shyamalika. BA, U. Ceylon, Peradeniya, 1959; diploma in devel. econs., U. Cambridge, Eng., 1972. Gen. mgr. Ceylon Fisheries Corp., Colombo, Sri Lanka, 1974-76; chmn. State Distilleries Corp., Colombo, 1976-77; sr. asst. sec. Ministry of Home Affairs and Pub. Adminstrn., Colombo, 1977-78; govt. agt. Dist. Jaffna, Sri Lanka, 1978-79, Dist. Trincomalee, Sri Lanka, 1982; founder, chmn. Nat. Ins. Corp., Colombo, 1979-82; chmn. Ceylon Shipping Corp., Colombo, 1983-86; sec. Ministry of Civil Security, Colombo, 1986—; councillor U. Jaffna, 1979-83; chmn. Presidential Commn. Compensation Payment, 1982; mem. monitoring com. Resettlement of Refugees, 1987; bd. dirs. Ceylon-Norway Found, 1979. Home: Kumbukagahaduwa, Sri Jeyewardenepura Mawatha Kotte, Sri Lanka Office: Ministry of Civil Security, Republic Bldg, Colombo 1, Sri Lanka

FERNANDO, ROSANNE THERESE, company secretary; b. Colombo, Sri Lanka, Oct. 3, 1954; came to Jamaica, 1982; d. Anthony Frances Tilbert and Cynthia Frances Doris (Ernst) Rasquino; m. Chamankumar Skandha Fernando. Asst. to co. sec. Lloyd Serendib Group, Colombo, Sri Lanka, 1975-79; projects officer Community Devel. Services, Colombo, Sri Lanka, 1979-80; programme officer Asian Am. Free Labour Inst., Colombo, Sri Lanka, 1980-82; co. sec. Serv-Wel Group of Cos., Kingston, Jamaica, 1982—; bd. dirs. Serv-Wel Agro Industries Ltd., Kingston, Hadeed Holdings Ltd., Kingston, Trait Industries Ltd., Kingston. Mem. Inst. of Chartered Secs. and Adminstrs., U.K. (licentiate 1976, assoc. 1982). Club: Interact (Colombo) (sec. 1971-72, dir. 1972-73). Office: Serv-Wel Group of Cos, 8-10 Ashenheim Rd, Kingston 11 Jamaica

FERNG, DOUGLAS MING-HAW, infosystems executive; b. Anshan, Peoples Republic of China, Feb. 27, 1945; came to U.S., 1968; s. Jau-Tarng and Hwei-In (Chu) F.; m. Gloria K. Chao, Oct. 28, 1972; children: Jennifer, Albert. BS, Nat. Taiwan U., Taipei, 1967; M in Forestry, Yale U., 1970; MBA, U. Wash., Seattle, 1979. Sci. programmer Weyerhaeuser Co., Federal Way, Wash., 1970-72, computer analyst, 1972-77, forest economist, 1977-79; mgr. silvicultural econs. Champion Internat., Stamford, Conn., 1979-80, mgr. resource econs., 1980-83; mgr. bus. systems Champion Internat., Hamilton, Ohio, 1983-87, mgr. paper applications, 1987—. Served as 2d lt. Taiwan Army, 1967-68. Fellow Yale Univ., 1968-70. Mem. Paper Industry Mgmt. Assn., Assn. System Mgmt., Cin. Chinese Assn., Chinese Assn. of Fairfield County (v.p. 1981-83). Club: cin. Yale. Office: Champion Internat 101 Knightsbridge Dr Hamilton OH 45020

FERNIE, JOHN, geography educator; b. East Wemyss, Scotland, Mar. 4, 1948; s. James Petrie and Sophia Lindsay Anderson (Sutherland) F.; m. Suzanne Isabel Christie, July 19, 1974; children: Sienna Margaret, Duncan John Allen. MA, Dundee (Scotland) U., 1970; PhD, Edinburg (Scotland) U., 1974; MBA, Bradford (Eng.) U., 1988. Lectr., then sr. lectr. Huddersfield (Eng.) Poly. U., 1973—; sr. lectr. in mgmt. Dundee Coll. Tech., Scotland, 1988—; vis. faculty U. Mann., Winnipeg, Can., 1978, 85, U. Victoria, B.C., Can., 1979, Ariz. State U., Tempe, 1981-82; external examiner Inst. Grocery Distbn., 1987—. Author: A Geography of Energy in the U.K., 1980, (with others) Resources: Environment Policy, 1985, Nuclear Waste in the U.K., 1988; contbr. articles to profl. jours. Mem. Inst. Brit. Geographers, Town and Country Planning Assn. (exec. mem. Yorkshire Planning Forum), Inst. Logistics and Distbn. Mgmt. Home: 7 Priory Acre, Saint Andrews Scotland Office: Dundee Coll Tech Dept Bus Studies, Bell Street, Dundee DD11MG, Scotland

FERNIOT, JEAN, journalist, author; b. Paris, Oct. 10, 1918; s. Paul and Jeanne (Rabu) F.; m. Jeanne Martinod, 1942 (div.); m. Christiane Servan-Schreiber, 1959 (div.); m. Beatrice Lemaitre, 1985; 5 children. Ed. Lycee Louis-le-Grand. Head polit. dept. France-tireur, 1945-57; polit. columnist L'Express, 1957-58, editor, 1963-66; chief polit. corr. France-Soir, 1959-63, polit. commentator, 1967-70, asst. chief editor, 1969-70; mem. staff Radio Luxembourg, 1967—. Author: Les ides de mai, 1958; L'ombre porte, 1961; Pour le pire, 1962; Derriere la fenetre, 1964; De Gaulle et le 13 mai, 1965; Mort d'une revolution, 1968; Paris dans mon assiette, 1969; complainte contre X, 1973; De de Gaulle a Pompidou, 1972; Ca suffit!, 1973; Pierrot et Aline, 1973; La petite legume, 1974; (with Michel Albert) Les vaches maigres, 1975; Les honnetes gens, 1976; C'est ca la France, 1977; Vous en avez braiment assez d'etre Francais, 1979; Carnet de croute, 1980; le Pouvoir et la saintete, 1982; Saint Judas, 1985; Le Chien-loup, 1985; Un mois de mai comme on les aimait, 1986. Decorated Croix de Guerve recipient prix Interallie, 1961. *

FERRACCI, MARIE-ANGELE VINCENTE, pediatrician; b. Nice, France, July 29, 1948; d. Antoine and Paulette (Dumski) Vincenti; m. Jean-Paul Ferracci, Feb. 24, 1977; children: Marie-Pauline, Paul and Antoine (twins). MD, Med. Univ., Marseilles, 1980. Intern Marseilles Hosp., 1974-80; resident in anesthesia Nice; practice medicine specializing in pediatrics Cannes, France, 1984—. Roman Catholic. Home: Au Beau Sejour, 06400 Cannes France Office: Les Iridees, 1 Rue des Phalenes, 06400 Cannes France

FERRAIOLI, ARMANDO, biomedical company executive; b. Foggia, Italy, Mar. 19, 1949; s. Alfonso and Luisa (Taurino) F.; Dr.Ing., U. Naples, 1973; M.Sc. in Bioengring., U. Strathclyde, 1974; Ph.D., U. Southampton, 1981; m. Maria T. Kindjarsky-D'Amato, Aug. 30, 1976; children—Solange A.P., Naike M.L., Anika M.V. Registered profl. engr., Salerno, Italy; chartered engr., Gt. Britain. Regional mgr. Gambro Soxil SpA, Bari, Naples, Italy, 1982-84; founder, gen. dir., A.G.A. Biomedica S.r.l., Cava dei Tirreni, 1985—; cons. Studio di Ingegneria Medica, Cava del Tirreni, 1984—; biomed. researcher, designer hosp. structures, Italy, internat. Brit. Council grantee, 1974-78. Mem. Instn. Elec. Engrs. Gt. Britain, IEEE, Associazione Elettrotecnica Italiana, Biol. Engring. Soc. Gt. Britain, Association for the Advancement of Med. Instrumentation, Biomed. Engring. Soc., Associazione Italiana di Ingegneria Medica e Biologica, Centro Nazionale Edilizia e Tecnica Ospedaliera. Mem. adv. bd. Italian biomed. jours.; contbr. over 30 articles on biomed. engring. to profl. jours.; book review editor for various jours. Home: Via A de Gasperi 5, 84013 Cava dei Tirreni Italy Office: Corso Italia n 232, 84013 Cava dei Tirreni Italy

FERRANDO, RAYMOND, nutrition scientist, educator; b. Constantine, Algeria, Mar. 3, 1912; s. Joseph and Etiennette (Dessens) F.; D.Vet.Sci., D.Sci., Vet. Nat. Sch. and Faculties Scis., Lyon, France, 1937, D.Scis., 1952; m. Raymonde Boulud, Dec. 3, 1943. Maitre-asst. Vet. Sch., Lyon, from 1945; prof. nutrition Ecole Veterinaire Alfort, Paris, 1955—, dir. sch., 1957-64, hon. dir., 1968; chmn. Commission interministerielle alimentation animale France; mem., past chmn. sci. com. Animal Nutrition Econ. Community Europe; expert WHO; cons. FAO. Decorated officer Legion of Honor. Mem. Am. Chem. Soc., N.Y. Acad. Scis., Acad. Nat. Medecine France (vice chmn. 1988), Acad. Agr. (France), Société Française de Therapeutique, Acad. Veterinaire France (chmn. 1987, Acad. Royale Medecine Belgique. Roman Catholic. Club: Rotary (pres. club 1971-72, dist. gov. 1982-83) (Paris). Research, numerous publs. on vitamins, nutrition, antibiotics; editor books. Home: 20 Rue de Boulainvilliers, 75016 Paris France Office: 107 Rue de Reuilly, Bat 1, 75012 Paris France

FERRAO, FRANCISCO MANUEL, data process executive; b. Lisbon, Portugal, Dec. 8, 1947; s. Jose and Fernanda Ferrao; m. Maria Linda, Dec. 19, 1970; children—Luisa Maria, Carlos Jose. Degree in Applied Math., U. Lisbon, 1971. Lectr. Faculty of Scis., U. Lisbon, Portugal, 1971-76; customer application specialist Time-Sharing SARL, Lisbon, 1971-76; EDP mgr. Renault Portugal, Lisbon, 1976-80, cons., 1980-84; EDP mgr. Agenave Ltda., Rio de Janeiro, Brazil, 1985-87 . Contbr. articles to profl. jours. Mem. Portuguese Assn. of Info. Roman Catholic. Avocation: tennis.

FERRAO, VALERIANO INOCENCIO, ambassador; b. Beira, Sofala, Mozambique, Oct. 11, 1939; s. Tomas Antonio and Cristina Joana (Araujo) F.; m. Maria Pia Almeida, Sept. 26, 1976; children—Ana Paula, Tania, Liduva. Student mech. engring., Tech. High Sch, Neuchatel, Switzerland. Cert. mech. engr. Mech. engr. Nat. Rys. Co., Maputo, People's Republic of Mozambique, 1975-76; sec. of cabinet People's Republic of Mozambique, Maputo, 1976-78, sec. gen. Ministry Fgn. Affairs, 1978-81, sec. state Ministry Fgn. Affairs, 1981-83; ambassador to U.S. embassy of People's Republic of Mozambique, Washington, 1983—. M.P., People's Assembly, Maputo, 1977. Decorated medal of Vet. of Nat. Liberation Struggle, medal of Bagamoyo (People's Republic of Mozambique). Mem. Frelimo Party. Office: Embassy of People's Republic of Mozambique 1990 M St NW Suite 570 Washington DC 20036

FERRAR, JOYCE PATRICIA, child advocate, parent aide coordinator; b. Cleve., July 11, 1940; d. Michael L. and Theresa Raye (Potoker) Sabrack; m. Robert L. Ferrar, July 11, 1959; children—Robert Brian, John Paul, Jason Channing, Corey Wayne. Student Ohio U., 1958, Kent State U., 1962, U. Oreg., 1966, Allegheny Coll., 1969, Am. U. in Cairo (Egypt), 1974. Dir., Adoption Listing Service Ohio, 1972-73; instr. Am. U. in Cairo, 1974-75; chairperson N.Am. Adoption Week, U.S. and Can., 1977, 78; attendance officer Cuyahoga County Schs., Cleve., 1975-80; assoc. editor Dayton (Ohio) Mag., 1980-82; cons. childrens placement services Ohio Dept. Human Services 1984-85, mem. social services adv. com., 1984—; parent aide coordinator suspected abuse and neglect program Family Service Assn., 1986—; social services adv. com. Ohio Dept. Human Services, 1984—. Contbr. articles on adoption to newspapers. Chmn. edn. com. NAACP, Meadville, Pa., 1969-71; v.p. Cleve. chpt. Council on Adoptable Children, 1975-80; regional rep. N.Am. Council on Adoptable Children, 1976-80; bd. dirs., sec. exec. council Spaulding for Children, Cleve., 1976-80; presenter, mem. incest treatment team Child Welfare League Am. Confs.; mem. Ohio Legal Rights Adv. Com., Columbus, 1981-86; chmn. Ohio Citizens Coalition for Permanence for Children, 1982-85; mem. task force Ohio Com. for Child Welfare Services, 1983-86; mem. Montgomery County Citizens Rev. Bd., 1983-85. Named Humanitarian of Yr., N.Am. Council on Adoptable Children, 1977; recipient spl. commendation Cuyahoga County Bd. Edn., 1980, Gift of Love award, 1987; named one of Top Ten Women award Dayton Newspapers Corp., 1985. Democrat. Roman Catholic. Home: 3700 Pobst Dr Kettering OH 45420

FERRARA, FABRIZIO MASSIMO, computer consultancy company executive; b. Rome, June 27, 1956; s. Luigi and Maria Teresa (Severi) F.; m. Marina Cioncoloni, June 26, 1985. BS, Pacific Western U., 1982, PhD in Computer Sci., 1984. Collaborator computer sci. ctr., faculty engring. U. Rome, 1978-80, 1980-81; cons. Selenia S.p.A., 1979-84; dir. info. systems div., bd. dirs. Rome, 1981-87, mng. dir., 1987—; prof. computer sci. Mil. Acad. Rome, 1986—; cons. definition and design bus. info. systems to various cos., 1979-81; coordinator European area II Nigerian Conf. Computers Application, Lagos, 1987. Co-author: Complements of Assembly Languages, 1979, Introduction to Programming Methodologies in Fortran, 1981; contbr. articles to Computer World Italia. Mem. Assn. Computing Machinery, IEEE. Home: Viale Val Padana 110, 00141 Rome Italy Office: GESI Srl, Via Rodi 32, 00195 Rome Italy

FERRAR GONZÁLEZ, JOSÉ CHIQUINQUIRÁ, petroleum engineering school director, educator; b. Maracaibo, Zulia, Venezuela, Dec. 31, 1938; s. Rafael and Angela (González) Ferrer; m. Magdalena Beatriz Paris, Sept. 4, 1972; children: José Rafael, Minica Beatriz, Juan Carlos. BS in Engring., U. Zulia, Venezuela, 1964; MS, Pa. State U., 1966, PhD, 1975. Successively chmn., counselor, dean, prof., counselor and sec. petroleum engring. sch. U. Zulia, Maracaibo, Venezuela, 1969-84, pres. petroleum engring. sch., 1984—. Author: Recuperacion Secundaria, 1972 (LUZ award), Recuperacion Mejorada, 1977 (LUZ award). Recipient Jesus Enrique Lossada, LUZ, Maracaibo, Venezuela, 1984, Cruz Fuerzas Armadas award Ministerio de la Def., Venezuela, 1987, Andres Bello award Ministerio de Edn., Venezuela, 1988. Mem. AAAS, Am. Soc. Engring. Edn., Venezuelan Assn. Advancement Sci., Am Inst. Mining, Metallurgy and Petroleum Engring., Venezuela Soc. Petroleum Engring. Home: Urb Los Olivos, Calle 74 #63-77, Maracaibo Venezuela Office: Universidad Del Zulia, Apartado de Correos 526, Maracaibo 4011, Venezuela

FERRARI, JUAN, venture capitalist, real estate developer; b. Madrid, Oct. 19, 1950; s. Angel and María Teresa (Herrero) F. BA, Nuestra, Señora Del Pilar Sch., Madrid, 1967; MBA, Harvard U., 1978; licenciado, U. Complutesse, Madrid, 1979. Account officer Citibank N.A., Madrid, 1979-81; engagement mgr. McKinsey and Co., Madrid and Milan, 1981-85; ptnr. Asfin S.A., Madrid, 1985-86; chief exec. officer Forescal S.A., Madrid, 1986—. Served to sgt. arty. Spanish Army, 1984-85. Clubs: Harvard (Spain); Real Puera Hierro (Madrid); Real Tennis (Oriedo). Office: Nũñez De Balboa 81, 28006 Madrid Spain

FERRARINI, ITALO GIACOMO SIRIO, manufacturing executive; b. Decameré, Eritrea, Ethiopia, Oct. 8, 1948; arrived in Saudi Arabia, 1979, came to U.S., 1987; s. Dante and Jolanda (Scalini) F.; m. Maria Romolo, Jan. 2, 1971; children: Sirio, Sheila, Soleil. MBA, Inst. Tech. Comml., Asmara, Ethiopia, 1966. Acct., then adminstrn. mgr. Industria Scatole Asmara, 1966-72; asst. gen. mgr. Ethiopian Textiles Industries, Asmara, 1972-74; mgr. adminstrn. services Zanussi Climatizzazione Corp., Rovigo, Italy, 1974-76; comptroller, fin. advisor Zanussi Climatizzazione Corp., 1977-78; mgr. fin. and adminstrn. Pucci Carlo Corp., Jeddah, Saudi Arabia, 1976-77; mng. dir. Sayegh-Betonval Co. Ltd, Riyadh, Saudi Arabia, 1979-87; v.p., chief exec. officer Amerival Corp., Houston, Tex., 1987—. Mem. Gruppo Sporivo Asmara (v.p. 1970-74). Office: Amerival Corp 13609 Industrial Rd PO Box 9969 Houston TX 77213-0969

FERRARO, BERNADETTE ANGELA, cytologist educator, biomedical writer; b. Newark, Apr. 19, 1952; d. Dominic A. and Josephine C. (Mossucco) F. B.A., Rutgers U.-Newark, 1974, cert. in cytology magna cum laude U. Medicine and Dentistry N.J., 1977. Clin. cytologist Martland Hosp., Coll. Hosp., Newark, 1978-80; interim cytology program coordinator, dept. pathology Univ. Hosp., Newark, 1982; condr. tutorials in sci. writing for grad. students. Grand Ambassador Achievement Internat., 1987; judge 49th Annual N.Y.C. Wide Sci. Fair, 1987. Author: (documentary) Room for Us All, 1986; contbr. articles to profl. publs. Bd. govs. Am. Biog. Inst., 1987. Recipient Golden Poet award, 1986, Statesman award, 1987, Golden Poet award, 1988, Dep. Gov's. award, 1987; fellow Internat. Biog. Assn., 1987. Mem. Am. Soc. Cytology, Am. Soc. Clin. Pathologists, Nargis Dutt Meml. Found. (life mem.; bd. dirs.), N.Y. Acad. Scis., AAAS, Am. Film Inst., Beta Beta Beta. Home: 77 Povershon Rd Nutley NJ 07110

FERRARO, JOHN FRANCIS, business exec., financier; b. N.Y.C., Jan. 3, 1934; s. John Anthony and Angelina Ferraro; B.S.I.E. with honors and distinction, N.Y. U., 1962; m. Linda Diane Zimmerman, Apr. 26, 1985; 1 stepson, Kenneth; children from previous marriage: Elizabeth Ann, John Robert, Laura Marie, Rosemary. With United Techs. Corp., Windsor Locks, Conn. 1962-66, sr. project engr., 1962-64, chief research and devel. promotion, 1964-66; founding ptnr. P.M.C. Corp., 1966-78; chmn. bd., chief exec. officer Thermodynetics, Inc.; pres. Spectrum Inc., 1966—, also dir.; sec., dir. Advanced Energy Concepts Inc.; dir. Turbotec Products, Inc., Xtec Corp. Chmn. Congl. Com. for Appointees to U.S. Air Force Acad., 1980; commr. Devel. Agy., Enfield, Conn., 1981; trustee Suffield (Conn.) Acad., 1980—, chair budget and fin. com., 1987—; trustee Birth right (Conn.); mem. exec. com. Holy Family Retreat League, 1984—. Served to 1st lt. USAF, 1954-58. Decorated Meritorious Service medal. Mem. Psi Upsilon. Club: Suffield Country. Contbr. numerous articles on bus., fin. and stock market to fin. publs., 1966-81; contbg. editor: Handbook of Wealth Management, 1977. Office: 651 Day Hill Rd Windsor CT 06095

FERRE, ANTONIO LUIS, newspaper publisher; b. Ponce, P.R., Feb. 6, 1934; s. Luis A. and Lorenza (Ramirez de Arellano) F.; A.B. magna cum laude, Amherst Coll., 1955; M.B.A., Harvard U., 1957; Inst. for Sr. Mgmt. and Govt. Execs., Dartmouth Coll., 1978; m. Luisa Rangel, Feb. 23, 1963; children—Maria Luisa, Antonio Luis, Luis Alberto, Maria Eugenia, Maria Lorenza. Vice chmn. Puerto Rican Cement Co. and Banco de Pone,; dir Met. Life Ins. Co., Am. Newspaper Pubs. Assn., ; pres., pub. El Nuevo Dia., 1988—. Author: (essays) Un Alto en el Camino; Pan, Paz y Palabra. Pres., P.R. Council on Higher Edn., 1966-68, Gov.'s Adv. Council, 1968-72; mem. Gov.'s Labor Adv. Council, 1975; bd. dirs., Colegio Puertorriqueñ o de Niñ as; v.p. Com. for Econ. Devel. P.R. Served with U.S. Army, 1958. Recipient Presdl. citation, 1976; named one of Puerto Rico's Top Ten Businessmen by bus. newspaper Caribbean Bus., 1986, 87. Mem. P.R. Mfrs. Assn. (pres. 1965-66), Am. Mgmt. Assn., Inc. (pres.'s assn. 1963—), P.R. C. of C., Phi Beta Kappa. Democrat. Roman Catholic. Clubs: Dorado Beach and Golf; Caribe Hilton Swimming and Tennis; Bankers of P.R.; Ponce Yacht; Club Deportivo de Ponce. Home: Guaynabo PR 00657 Office: GPO Box 4487 San Juan PR 00936

FERRÉ, JACQUES, physician; b. Mauriac, France, May 5, 1945; s. Ferre André and Chambenoit Cecile; children: Ferre Isabelle, Ferre Florence. Gen. practice medicine specializing in nutrition Versailles, France. Home: 9 Rue de Provence, 78000 Versailles France

FERREIRA DE CARVALHO, NARCISO JOSÉ, textile company executive; b. Porto, Portugal, July 7, 1949; s. José Rodrigo and Maria Sylvia (Ferreira) Carvalho; m. Maria do Rosário Rumsey de Noronha e Távora, Dec. 3, 1977; children—Narciso Antonio, Bárbara Rumsey. B.S., Instituto Superior de Economia, Lisbon, 1975. Economist, FC-Sociedade de Comercialização Têxtil, Lda., v.p. Sociedade Industrial de Mindelo, S.A.R.L., Porto, Portugal, 1979—; chmn. TEO, S.A.R.L., 1986—. Served with Portuguese Army, 1972-74. Roman Catholic. Home: Rua de Sáda Bandeira 481-1deg, 4000 Porto Portugal

FERRELL, MILTON MORGAN, JR., lawyer; b. Coral Gables, Fla., Nov. 6, 1951; s. Milton M. Ferrell and Annie (Blanche) Bradley; m. Lori R. Sanders, May 22, 1982; children: Milton Morgan III, Whiteny Connolly. BA, Mercer U., 1973, JD, 1975. Bar: Fla. 1975. Asst. state's atty. State's Atty.'s Office, Miami, 1975-77; ptnr. Ferrell & Ferrell, Miami, 1977-84; sole practice Miami, 1985-87; ptnr. Ferrell & Williams, P.A., Miami, 1987—. Bd. dirs. Mus. Sci. and Space Transit Planetarium, 1977; mem. Ambassadors of Mercy, Mercy Hosp. Found., Inc., 1986—; trustee, mem. legal com., Com. Chairperson U. Miami Project, 1986—. Fellow Nat. Assn. Criminal Def. Lawyers, Am. Bd. Criminal Lawyers (bd. of govs. 1981-82, sec. 1983-84, v.p. 1984-86, pres. 1987—); mem. ABA (grantee 1975), Dade County Bar Assn. (bd. dirs. 1977-80), Fla. Bar Assn. (mem. jury instrns. com., 1987-88, grievance com 11 "L", 1987—). Clubs: The Bath, The Palm Bay, Downtown Athletic (Miami). Home: 610 Sabal Palm Rd Bay Point Miami FL 33137 Office: Ferrell & Williams PA 100 Chopin Plaza Suite 1920 Miami FL 33131

FERRER, EDWIN, architect; b. N.Y.C., Dec. 2, 1928; s. Juan and Rosaura (Lopez) F.; m. Nadene Joan Reinders, Oct. 13, 1961 (div.); 1 child, Andrea; m. Barbara Sue Gibson, May 29, 1979. BS, U. Houston, 1957, BArch, 1958. Designer-project architect firm Rustay Martin & Vale, Houston, 1962-69; project architect Neuhaus & Taylor, Houston, 1969-71, Wyatt C. Hedrick, Houston, 1971-72, Koetter Tharp Cowell & Bartlett, Houston, 1973-76; design supr. C.E. Lummus Co., Houston, 1976-78; prin. Edwin Ferrer AIA, 1978—; instr. residential design and residential constrn. Houston Community Coll. Works include schs., comml., residential, chs. Served with AUS, 1946-48. Mem. AIA (hist. resources com. Houston chpt., mem. residential architecture com. Houston), Tex. Soc. Architects. Home: 10738 Hazen Rd Houston TX 77072 Office: 7887 Katy Freeway Suite 110 Houston TX 77024

FERRER, JESÚS, teacher, mathematics educator; b. Alqueria, Valencia, Spain, Oct. 20, 1952; s. Jesús Ferrer and Teresa Llopis, m. Isabel Santos, Dec. 26, 1981; children: Pablo, Marta. BS, U. Valencia, 1976, PhD, 1984. Math. tchr. Oliva Inst., Valencia, 1978—; prof. algebra U. Denia, Alicante, 1984—; researcher U. Poly., Valencia, 1984—. Contbr. articles to math. jours. Lt. mayor Miramar city council, Valencia, 1979-83. Am. Field Service scholar, 1970. Mem. Math. Assn. Am. Home: Cami Collado, 46780 Oliva Spain Office: Inst Oliva, Carretera de Valencia S/N, 46780 Oliva Spain

FERRERA TORRES, RAÚL, architect; b. Mexico City, Nov. 22, 1942. BArch, Nat. Autonomous U. Mex., 1966. Draftsman various archtl. and constrn. cos., 1961-63; with Archtl. firm Luis Barragán, 1964-72, Legorreta Arquitectos, 1974-76; pvt. practice architecture 1976—; participant ceramic open workshop, 1963; freelance graphic design, archtl. projects. Prin. works include D. Ramiro residence, Chihuahua, Mex., Folke Egerstrom residence, Los Clubes, State of Mexico, monumental entrance to Los Clubes, landscaping, residential suburban areas Mexico State, exterior work 1st sect. Lomas Verdes residential area, project for Alteña parish, monumental fountain, Serrano residence, Christer Beckmann stables, equestrian club and residential area The Bugambilias, Guadalajara, dovecote bldg. El Palomar residential area, Guadalajara, Sánchez y Sánchez residence, Mexico City, Riley residence, Valle de Bravo, Mex., Legorreta residence, Valle de Bravo, Dupuis residence, Mexico City, landscaping, plazas, fountains and shopping mall Rosario project, interior decoration José Luis Carrete penthouse, Mexico City; (with Ricardo Legorreta) America Banamex Office Bldg., Mexico City, exterior work IBM plant, Guadalajara, exterior work Camino Real Hotel, Can-Cun, Mex., Gómex residence, Mexico City, main offices Alfa Group Monterrey, N.L., Mex. Address: Gen Francisco Ramirez 12, 11830 Mexico City Mexico

FERRIER, MICHEL GEORGES, physician; b. Bourgstandeol, Ardeche, France, Sept. 9, 1948; s. Charles Henri and Jaqueline (Espinasse) F.; m. Evelyne Delbourg, Dec. 15, 1973; children: Cecilia, Rodolphe. MD in Exotic Pathology, U. Montpellier, France, 1974. Intern Montpellier Hosp., 1970-75, Diabetic Clinic, Perpignam, France, 1974-75; gen. practice medicine Montpellier, 1975—. Served with French mil. Club: Speleologic Group. Home and Office: 143 bis Ave de Lodève, 34080 Montpellier France

FERRITER, JOHN PIERCE, diplomat; b. Boston, Jan. 26, 1938; s. John Clement and Anna Belle (O'Brien) F.; m. Daniela Calvino, Mar. 17, 1970. B.A., Queens Coll., CUNY, 1960; LL.B., Fordham U., 1963; M.P.A., Harvard U., 1973. Bar: N.Y. Fgn. service officer Dept. State, 1964, ambassador to Djibouti, 1985-87, dep. asst. sec. energy and resources policy, 1987—; chmn. standing group on long-term coop. Internat. Energy Agy., Paris, 1981-83, 87—. Served with USMCR, 1957-62. Recipient Superior Honor award Dept. State, 1980. Lodge: Rotary. Office: Deputy Asst Sec Energy Resources Policy US Dept State Room 3336 Washington DC 20520

FERRY, WILBUR HUGH, foundation consultant; b. Detroit, Dec. 17, 1910; s. Hugh Joseph and Fay (Rutson) F.; m. Jolyne Marie Gillier, Oct. 23, 1937 (div. 1972); children: Lucian (stepson), Denise Lesselroth, Fay Ferry Christiansen, Robin F. Cook; m. Carol Underwood Bernstein, 1973; stepchildren: Katherine, John. A.B., Dartmouth Coll., 1932; L.H.D., Starr King Sch., Berkeley, Calif., 1969. Instr. Choate Sch., 1932-33; newspaperman 1933-35, 37-41; dir. publicity Eastern Air Lines, 1936; chief investigator in N.H. for OPA, 1942-44; cons. ILO, 1940-44; dir. pub. relations CIO-Polit. Action Com., 1944; partner Earl Newsom & Co., 1945-54; v.p. Center Study Democratic Instns., 1954-69, cons., 1969—; U.S. rep. European Nuclear Disarmament, 1981; dir. Exploratory Project on the Conditions of Peace, 1984—. Author: The Corporation and The Economy, 1959, The Economy Under Law, 1961, Caught on the Horn of Plenty, 1962, What Price Peace, 1963, Masscomm as Educator, 1966, Farewell to Integration, 1967, Tonic and Toxic Technology, 1967, The Police State Is Here, 1969, The Zaca Manifesto, 1980; editor: Warming Up for Fifty Years, 1982, Letters from Tom, 1983. Address: PO Box 657 Scarsdale NY 10583

FERSHTMAN, JULIE ILENE, lawyer; b. Detroit, Apr. 3, 1961; d. Sidney and Judith Joyce (Stoll) F. Student, Mich. State U., 1979-81; BA in Philosophy and Polit. Sci., Emory U., 1983, JD, 1986. Bar: Mich. 1986. Summer assoc. Kitch, Saurbier et al, Detroit, 1985; assoc. Miller, Canfield, Paddock and Stone, Detroit, 1986—. Mem. Mich. Women's Hist. Ctr. and Hall Fame, Dem. Nat. Com. Mem. ABA, Am. Trial Lawyers Assn., Common Cause, Women Lawyers Assn. Mich., Mich. Women's Hist. Ctr. and Hall of Fame, Nat. Mus. Women and Arts, NOW, Soc. Coll. Journalists, Planned Parenthood, Phi Alpha Delta, Omicron Delta Kappa, Phi Sigma Tau, Pi Sigma Alpha. Democrat. Home: 31700 Briarcliff Franklin MI 48025 Office: Miller Canfield Paddock & Stone 2500 Comerica Bldg Detroit MI 48226

FERSKO, RAYMOND STUART, lawyer; b. Newark, Dec. 6, 1947; s. Seymoure Arnold and Hannah Judith (Geffner) F.; m. Francine Iris Poses, Aug. 23, 1970; children—Stacey Michelle, Madeline Poses. B.A., Am. U., 1969; J.D., 1972. Bar: N.Y. 1973, U.S. Ct. Appeals (D.C. cir.) 1973, U.S. Dist. Ct. (so., ea. and we. dists.) N.Y. 1975, U.S. Ct. Appeals (2d cir.) 1975, U.S. Supreme Ct. 1982. Trial atty. CAB, Washington, 1972-75; assoc. Demov Morris Levin & Shein, N.Y.C., 1975-76; assoc. Walsh & Levine, N.Y.C., 1976-80, ptnr., 1980-82; ptnr. Shapiro Shiff Beilly Rosenberg and Fox, N.Y.C., 1982-84, Tanner Propp Fersko & Sterner, N.Y.C., 1984—; cons. World Aviation Services, Ltd., London, 1982—, Internat. Joint Ventures, Ltd., London, 1983—; sec. Tradewinds Express Inc., N.Y.C., 1982-86; pres. Cornwell Corp., N.Y.C., 1986-88. Treas., Paine Heights Orgn., New Rochelle, N.Y., 1978 . Mem. Assn. Bar City N.Y. (mem. com. on state legis. 1976-78), N.Y. County Bar Assn., ABA (mem. anti-trust sect. civil practice and procedure com. 1973—, mem. adminstrv. law sect. aviation com. 1973-77), N.Y. State Bar Assn., Internat. Bar Assn., Argentine U.S. C. of C., Spain U.S. C. of C., Phi Alpha Delta. Jewish. Clubs: Harmonie (N.Y.C.); Mamaroneck Yacht and Tennis (N.Y.). Home: 61 Bayeau Rd New Rochelle NY 10804 Office: Tanner Propp Fersko & Sterner 99 Park Ave New York NY 10016

FESHBACH, MURRAY, demographer, educator; b. N.Y.C., Aug. 8, 1929; s. Benjamin and Lilly (Harfenist) F.; m. Muriel Joan Schreiner, Dec. 30, 1956; children—Michael Lee, David Steven. A.B. in History, Syracuse U., 1950; M.A. in History, Columbia U., 1951; Ph.D. in Econs., Am. U., 1974. Research asst. Nat. Bur. Econ. Research, N.Y.C., 1955-56; economist U.S. Bur. Census, Washington, 1957-67, chief USSR population, employment, research and devel. br., 1967-81; sr. research scholar Georgetown U., Washington, 1981-84, research prof. demography, 1984—; cons. Rand Corp., Santa Monica, Calif., 1981—, U.S. Dept. Def., 1981—, U.S. Dept. State 1982-83, NSF, 1987; vis. prof. Columbia U., N.Y.C., 1983-84; Sovietologist-in-residence Office of Sec. Gen., NATO, Brussels, 1986-87, bd. dirs. Internat. Research and Exchanges Bd. Author: Soviet Statistical System, 1960; editor National Security Issues in the USSR, workshop held at NATO, Nov. 6-7, 1986, Brussels, Dordrecht, Nijhoff, 1987; contbr. articles to profl. jours. Committeeman Boy Scouts Am., N.Y.C. and Silver Spring, Md., 1950-75. Served to sgt. U.S. Army, 1951-55. Recipient Silver medal Dept. Commerce, Washington, 1979; Woodrow Wilson Internat. Ctr. for Scholars fellow Smithsonian Instn., 1979. Mem. Assn. Comparative Econ. Studies (pres. 1985), Am. Assn. for Advancement of Slavic Studies (pres. Washington chpt. 1974-78, bd. dirs. 1979-82, v.p. 1984-85; nat. pres. 1985-86), Royal Soc. Asian Affairs, Internat. Union for Sci. Study of Population. Democrat. Jewish. Club: Cosmos (Washington). Home: 11403 Fairoak Dr Silver Springs MD 20902 Office: Georgetown U Dept Demography Washington DC 20057

FESLER, DAVID RICHARD, foundation director; b. Mpls., Sept. 21, 1928; s. John K. and Elsie L. Fesler; m. Elizabeth P.; children—Dael F. Zywiec, Nancy K., Janet C. B.B.A. with distinction, U. Minn., 1950. Pres. Lampert Yards, Inc., 1950-79; pres. Liberty State Bank, St. Paul, 1950-82, chmn. bd., 1982-85; treas. Mason City Builders Supply Co., Inc., 1972-85, The Sussel Co., Inc., 1975-79; pres. Wim Co., St. Paul, 1952-79, Liberty Agy., Inc., 1952-75; bd. dirs. Depot Found., Duluth, Minn., St. Paul Area TVI Found., Stout U. Found., Menomonie, Wis. Past bd. dirs., mem. fin. com., exec. com. Shattuck Sch., Inver Grove Heights (Minn.) Planning Commn., Indian Head Council Boy Scouts Am., St. Croix Valley Girl Scouts Council, St. Paul Area YMCA, Family Service St. Paul Area, Edgcumbe Presbyn. Ch.; bd. dirs. Shattuck-St. Mary's Sch., Faribault, Minn. Club: St. Paul Athletic. Lodge: Rotary. Office: 1573 Selby Ave #246 Liberty Bank Bldg Saint Paul MN 55104

FESS, MARILYNN ELAINE EWING, occupational therapist; b. Casper, Wyo., June 20, 1944; d. Frederick Eugene and Norma Wagner (Jarrett Pence) Ewing; m. Stephen W. Fess, Nov. 26, 1966. BS, Ind. U., 1967, MS, 1977. Staff occupational therapist Marion County Gen. Hosp., Indpls., 1966-70; supr. phys. dysfunction unit, 1970-72; supr. adult occupational therapy Ind. U. Med. Ctr., Indpls., 1972-74, instr. occupational therapy curriculum, 1974-76; hand therapist Strickland & Steichen, M.D.'s, Inc., 1974-79; designer, developer, dir. hand therapy Hand Rehab. Ctr. Ind., 1976-79; cons. hand rehab. and hand research, 1979—; cons. to hand surgeons various hosps. and nursing homes. Author: (with others) Hand Splinting Principles and Methods, 1980, 2d edit., 1987; mem. editorial rev. bd. Occupational Therapy Jour. Research, 1983-84, Am. Jour. Occupational Therapy, 1985-87, Jour. Hand Therapy, 1987—, also articles. Mem. exec. bd. Ind. Cerebral Vascular Accident Com., 1973-76. Mem. Am. Occupational Therapy Assn. (roster of fellows 1983, sec. orgn. affiliate pres. 1976-78), Am. Soc. Hand Therapists (founding, mem. at large exec. bd. 1978-79, sec. 1980-82), Ind. Occupational Therapy Assn. (sec. 1969-71, v.p. 1972-73, pres. 1974-76, hand therapy liaison to exec. bd. 1978—). Office: 635 Eagle Creek Ct Zionsville IN 46077

FETALINO, MANUEL SALVADOR ASINAS, radiologist, educator; b. Odiongan, Romblon, Philippines, Sept. 30, 1930; s. Deogracias Fabella and Felisa Menez (Asinas) F.; m. Evalyn Huggins Itaas, Jan. 18, 1964; children: Eric Paul, Liza Rose, Michelle Helen, Eva Marie. BS, U. Philippines, 1954; MD, U. Philippines, Manila, 1958. Resident physician U. Philippines-Philippine Gen. Hosp. Med. Ctr., 1958-70; from instr. to asst. prof. radiology U. Philippines, 1969-81, assoc. prof., 1981—; chief radiologist U. Philippines Health Service, Quezon City, 1972—; attending radiologist Med. Ctr. of Manila, 1968—; sr. cons. Philippine Gen. Hosp., Manila, 1968—; chmn. Dept. Radiology and Cancer Inst. Med. Ctr., 1988. Contbr. articles to profl. jours. Trustee Romblon State Coll., Odiongan, 1987—. Fellow IAEA/U.S. ACad. Scis./Meml. Hosp. for Cancer, N.Y.C., 1965-66, AEC, 1962. Fellow Radioisotopes Soc. Philippines, Philippine Coll. Radiology (past editor newsletter, bd. examiners, pres.), Philippine Soc. Nuclear Medicine; mem. Philippine Med. Assn., Quezon City Med. Soc. Roman Catholic. Home: 29 Pantaleona St, Don Jose Heights, Quezon City Philippines Office: Med Ctr Manila, 1122 Gen Luna St, Ermita, Manila Philippines

FETKO, PAUL, electronics, real estate and building materials executive; b. Central City, Pa., Apr. 12, 1931; s. Charles and Pearl (Doban) F.; m. Eleanore Salamanchuk, June 7, 1955; children: Linda Louise, Debra Marie, Laura Jean. BS, U.S. Mil. Acad., 1955; MBA, Harvard U., 1959; postgrad. NYU, 1960-63. Engr. Arabian Am. Oil Co., N.Y.C., 1955-59; engring. adminstr. Bendix Corp. (Allied), Teterboro, N.J., 1959-61; project control mgr., fin. adminstrn. mgr. Gen. Precision Corp. (Singer), Little Falls, N.J., 1961-64; with Avion Electronics, Inc. and Cardion Electronics, units Gen. Signal Corp., N.Y.C., 1964-68; adminstrv. mgr., 1964-66, v.p., gen. mgr., 1966, pres., gen. mgr., 1966-68; exec. asst. to pres. Paul Venze Assocs. (GAC), Miami, Fla., 1968-70; exec. asst. to pres. Cavanagh Communities Corp., Miami, 1970-71; v.p. ops. Am. Agronomics, Inc., Miami, 1971; exec. v.p. Transworld Realty Corp., Miami, 1971-75; pres., dir., prin. Preferred Equities Corp., Miami, 1972—, Aerotronics, Inc., Miami, 1981—; gen. mgr. T.I.C. Group, Ltd., Fort Lauderdale, Fla., 1977-81; v.p., dir., prin. Puritan Mills, Inc., Atlanta, 1982—, Maintenance-Free Exteriors, Inc., Marietta, Ga., 1985—; Supply and Apply Corp., Atlanta, 1982—; v.p., chief operating officer TelaMktg. Corp., Miami, 1984-85; cons. Martin Marietta Corp., Orlando, Fla., 1982, Devel. Corp. of Am., Fort Lauderdale, 1982; pres. Gen. Home Services, Inc., Hollywood, Fla., 1986—; v.p., dir., prin. Mastic Corp., Atlanta, 1987—. Served with USAF, 1949-51; with U.S. Army, 1955. Mem. U.S. Mil. Acad. Assn. Grads., Am. Soc. Mil. Engrs., Am. Def. Preparedness Assn., Internat. Platform Assn., Assn. for Unmanned Vehicle Systems, Am. Legion, Mensa, Phi Kappa Phi. Contbr. articles to profl. jours; holder of 2 U.S. patents. Home: 6200 Rivercliffe Dr NW Atlanta GA 30328 Office: 1424 Hills Pl NW Atlanta GA 30318

FETRIDGE, BONNIE-JEAN CLARK (MRS. WILLIAM HARRISON FETRIDGE), civic worker; b. Chgo., Feb. 3, 1915; d. Sheldon and Bonnie (Carrington) Clark; student Girls Latin Sch., Chgo., The Masters Sch., Dobbs Ferry, N.Y., Finch Coll., N.Y.C.; m. William Harrison Fetridge, June 27, 1941; children—Blakely (Mrs. Harvey H. Bundy III), Clark Worthington. Bd. dirs. region VII com. Girl Scouts U.S.A., 1939-43, mem. nat. program com., 1966-69, mem. nat. adv. council, 1972-85, mem. internat. commr.'s adv. panel, 1973-76, mem. Nat. Juliette Low Birthplace Com., 1966-69, region IV selections com., 1968-70; bd. dirs. Girl Scouts Chgo., 1936-51, 59-69, sec., 1936-38, v.p., 1946-49, 61-65, chmn. Juliette Low world friendship com., 1959-67, 71-72; mem. Friends of Our Cabana Com. World Assn. Girl Guides and Girl Scouts, Cuernavaca, Mexico, 1969—, vice chmn., 1982-87; founding mem., pres. Olave Baden-Powell Soc. of World Assn. Girl Guides and Girl Scouts, London, 1984—; asst. sec. Dartnell Corp., Chgo., 1981—; bd. dirs. Jr. League of Chgo., 1937-40, Vis. Nurse Assn. of Chgo., 1951-58, 61-63, asst. treas., 1962-63; women's bd. dirs. Children's Meml. Hosp., 1946-50. Staff aide, ARC and Motor Corps, World War II. Vice pres. Latin Sch. Parents Council, 1952-54; bd. dirs. Latin Sch. Alumni Assn. 1964-69, Fidelitas Soc., 1979; women's bd. U.S.O., 1965-75, treas., 1969-71, v.p., 1971-73; women's service bd. Chgo. Area council Boy Scouts Am., 1964-70, mem.-at-large Nat. council, 1973-76, mem. nat. Exploring com., 1973-76; governing mem. Anti-Cruelty Soc. of Chgo. . Recipient Citation of Merit Sta. WAIT, Chgo., 1971; Baden-Powell fellow World Scout Found., Geneva, 1983. Mem. Nat. Soc. Colonial Dames Am. (Ill. bd. mgrs. 1962-65, 69-76, 78-82, v.p. 1970-72, corr. sec. 1978-80, 1st v.p. 1980-84, state chmn. geneal. info. services com. 1972-76, hist. activities com. 1979-83, mus. house com. 1980-83, house gov. 1981-82), Youth for Understanding (couriers bicentennial project), English-Speaking Union, Chgo. Dobbs Alumnae Assn. (past pres.), Nat. Soc. DAR, Chgo. Geneal. Soc., Conn. Soc. Genealogists, New Eng. Historic Geneal. Soc., N.Y. Geneal. and Biog. Soc., Newberry Library Assos., Chgo. Hist. Soc. Guild. Republican. Episcopalian. Clubs: Casino, Saddle and Cycle, The Racquet of Chgo. Home: 2430 Lakeview Ave Chicago IL 60614

FETRIDGE, WILLIAM HARRISON, publishing company executive; b. Chgo., Aug. 2, 1906; s. Matthew and Clara (Hall) F.; m. Bonnie Jean Clark, June 27, 1941; children: Blakely (Mrs. Harvey H. Bundy III), Clark Worthington. B.S., Northwestern U., 1929; LL.D., Central Mich. U., 1954. Asst. to dean Northwestern U., 1929-30; editor Trade Periodical Co., 1930-31, Chgo. Tribune, 1931-34, H. W. Kastor & Son, 1934-35, Roche, Williams & Cleary, Inc., 1935-42; mng. editor Republican mag., 1939-42; asst. to pres. Popular Mechanics mag., 1945-46, v.p., 1946, exec. v.p., 1953-59; v.p. Diamond T Motor Truck Co., Chgo., 1959-61; exec. v.p. Diamond T div. White Motor Co., 1961-65; pres. Dartnell Corp., Chgo., 1965-77, chmn. bd., 1977—; dir. Bank of Ravenswood, Chgo. Author: With Warm Regards, 1976; editor: The Navy Reader, 1943, The Second Navy Reader, 1944, American Political Almanac, 1950, The Republican Precinct Workers Manual, 1968. Trustee Greater North Michigan Ave. Assn., 1949-58; chmn. Ill. Tollway Dedication com., 1958; pres. United Republican Fund of Ill., 1968-73, 79-80; fin. chmn. Ill. Rep. Party, 1968-73; alt. del.-at-large Rep. Nat. Conv., 1956, del.-at-large, 1968, hon. del.-at-large, 1972; mem. Rep. Nat. Finance Com.; chmn. Midwest Vols. Nixon, 1960, Rep. Forum, 1958-60, Nixon Recount Com.; trustee Jacques Holinger Meml. Assn., Am. Humanics Found.; mem. nat. exec. bd., nat. v.p. Boy Scouts Am., 1958-76, chmn. nat. adv. bd., 1976-77; vice chmn. World Scout Found., Geneva, 1977-88; trustee Lake Forest Coll., 1969-77; pres. U.S. Found. for Internat. Scouting, 1971-79, hon. chmn., 1979—; past pres. trustees Latin Sch. Chgo.; chmn. bd. dirs. Johnston Scout Mus., North Brunswick, N.J.; elected lauriate Lincoln Acad. of Ill., 1985. Served as lt. comdr. USNR, 1942-45. Decorated chevalier Grand Priory of Malta, chevalier Order St. John of Jerusalem; recipient Abraham Lincoln award United Republican Fund, 1980; Silver Antelope, Silver Beaver, Silver Buffalo Boy Scouts Am., 1956, Bronze Wolf award World Scout Conf., 1973, Distinguished Eagle award, 1976. Mem. Navy League U.S. (past regional pres.), Ill. C. of C., Ill. St. Andrew Soc. (Disting. Citizen award 1980), Newcomen Soc., Soc. Midland Authors, Beta Theta Pi. Clubs: The Casino, Chicago, Union League, Saddle and Cycle (Chgo.); Capitol Hill (Washington); Chikaming Country (Lakeside, Mich.). Lodge: Rotary. Office: 4660 Ravenswood Ave Chicago IL 60640

FETT, THOMAS H., petrophysicist, consultant; b. Canton, Ohio, Dec. 1, 1943; s. John Crosby and Marjorie (Hatchett) F.; m. Kristina M. Stephens, Apr. 24, 1965; children—Ralph (dec.), Carol, Neil. B.S. in Engring. Sci., Trinity U., 1966. Registered profl. engr., Tex. Engr. field Schlumberger Well Services, Pharr, Tex., 1966-73, mgr. dist., Graham, Tex., 1973-76, sr. sales engr., Corpus Christi, 1976-80, application devel. engr., 1980-85; asst. vis. prof. Tex. Coll. Arts & Indsl., Kingsville, 1978—; lectr. in field. Mem. Am. Petroleum Inst. (local bd. dirs. 1984—), Am. Assn. Petroleum Geologists, Soc. Econ. Paleontol. & Mineralogists, Soc. Profl. Well Log Analysts (internat. sec. 1983-84, internat. bd. dirs. 1982-83), Corpus Christi Geol. Soc., Houston Geol. Soc., San Antonio Geol. Soc., Soc. Petroleum Engrs. (local bd. dirs. 1978-80). Republican. Presbyterian. Avocations: travel; photography; golf. Home: 4134 Sierra St Corpus Christi TX 78410 Office: Schlumberger Well Services 370 Lantana Corpus Christi TX 78408

FETTEROLF, CHARLES FREDERICK, aluminum company executive; b. Franklin, Pa., July 18, 1928; s. Harry B. and Beryl (Linsey) F.; m. Frances Spang, Apr. 11, 1953; children: Regan J., Scott F. BS in Chemistry, Grove City Coll., 1952. Sales trainee Alcoa Aluminum Co., Pitts., 1952, chemist, gen. salesman, 1953; chemist, gen. salesman Alcoa Aluminum Co., Louisville, 1959; chemist, gen. salesman Alcoa Aluminum Co., San Francisco, 1961, industry asst. flexible packaging, 1965, div. sales mgr., 1965-69; asst. dist. sales mgr. Alcoa Aluminum Co., Los Angeles, 1969; dist. sales mgr. Alcoa Aluminum Co., Phila., 1971, industry mgr. def., 1974, gen. mgr. mktg., 1975, gen. mgr. ops., 1977, v.p., 1977, v.p. Alcoa smelting process project, 1979, v.p. ops., 1979, v.p. sci. and tech., 1981, exec. v.p. mill products, 1981, pres., 1983—, also bd. dirs.; bd. dirs. Mellon Nat. Bank, N.A., Union Carbide Corp., Allegheny Ludlum, Aluminum Co. Am., Provident Life. Mem. vestry St. Stephen's Episcopal Ch., 1974—; bd. dirs. Grove City Coll., Pitts. Ballet Theatre, WQED Pub. Broadcasting; trustee Shadyside Hosp., U. Pitts.; mem. adv. bd. Coalition for Addictive Disease of S.W. Pa., 1982—. Served with USN, 1946-48. Recipient Alumni Achievementaward Grove City Coll., 1978. Clubs: Duquesne, Laurel Valley, Internat, Allegheny Country. Office: Aluminum Co Am 1501 Alcoa Bldg Pittsburgh PA 15219

FETTWEIS, YVONNE CACHÉ, archivist; b. Los Angeles, Nov. 28, 1935; d. Boyd Eugene and Georgette Louisa (Tilmann) Adams; m. Rolland Phillip Fettweis, July 22, 1967; children: Maurice C.B. II, Michele-Yvonne (Mrs. Paul E. Cenzer); m. Maurice Lee Caché, Jan. 8, 1955 (div. 1962). B.A., Wagner Coll., 1954; postgrad Am. U., 1973, Bentley Coll., 1981. Legal sec., asst. Judge, Davis & Stern, and Orfinger & Tindall, Daytona Beach, Fla., 1961-66; head recording sect., bd. dirs. First Ch. Christ, Scientist, Boston, 1969-71, research assoc., 1971-72, adminstrv. archivist, 1972-78, sr. assoc. archivist, 1979-84, records adminstr., 1984—. Exec. sec. Volusia County Goldwater campaign, Daytona Beach, 1964. Mem. Soc. Am. Archivists, Automated Records and Techniques Task Force, Am. Mgmt. Assn., New Eng. Archivists, Assn. Records Mgrs. and Adminstrs. (bd. dirs. 1983—), Assn. Col. and Research Librarians, Bay State Hist. League. Republican. Christian Scientist. Lodges: Order Eastern Star, Order Rainbow (bd. dirs. 1972-77). Home: 42 Edgell Dr Framingham MA 01701 Office: 1st Ch Christian Sci Christian Sci Ctr 175 Huntington Ave Boston MA 02115

FEUCHTWANGER, EDGAR JOSEPH, historian, writer; b. Munich, Sept. 28, 1924; came to Eng., 1939; s. Ludwig and Erna Rosina (Rheinstrom) F.; m. Primrose Mary Essame, June 2, 1962; children: Antonia Mary, Adrian James Ludovic, Judith Amaryllis. MA, Magdalene Coll., Cambridge, Eng., 1947; PhD, Southampton U., 1958. Dep. dir. adult edn. U. Southampton, Eng., 1964—, reader history, 1973—. Author: Disraeli, Democracy and the Tory Party, 1968, Prussia: Myth and Reality, 1970, Gladstone, 1975, Democracy and Empire: Britain 1865-1914, 1985. Fellow Royal Hist. Soc.; mem. Internat. Inst. Strategic Studies, Leo Baeck Inst. (bd. dirs. London Bd.). Home: Highfield House, Dean, Sparsholt SO21 2LP, England Office: Univ of Southampton, Highfield, Southampton SO9 5NH, England

FEUER, JONATHAN PHILIP, venture capitalist, corporate consultant; b. London, July 22, 1962; s. Martin and Angela (Fox) F. BSc with honors, Warwick U., Eng., 1983. Chartered acct. With Ernst & Whinney, London, 1983-87, Baring Bros. & Co. Ltd., London, 1987-88, Citicorp Venture Capital Ltd., London, 1988—. Trustee Pace-U.K. Internat. Affairs, London, 1983—. Mem. Inst. Chartered Accts. in Eng. and Wales, Royal Overseas League, London C. of C., English Speaking Union. Jewish. Home: 120 Crystal Palace Rd, East Dulwich, London SE22 9ER, England Office: Citicorp Venture Capital Ltd, PO Box 199, Cottons Ctr, Hay's Ln, London SE1 2QT, England

FEUERSTEIN, MARIE THÉRÈSE, international health consultant; b. Bournemouth, Dorset, Eng., Nov. 27, 1941; d. Stephen Henry Cramer and Gwendolyn Marie (Parker) Wallbridge; m. Malcolm Feuerstein, Sept. 18, 1970; children: Rachel Gabrielle, Joseph Stefon. Diploma in Community Devel., U. Manchester, 1971; MEd, 1974, PhD in Community Devel. State registered nurse. Grad. nurse St. Thomas Hosp., London; co dir. Global Features Ltd., London, 1978-86; freelance cons. 1977—, internat. health to various orgns. including WHO, Geneva and Manila, FAO, Rome and London, Misereor in Phillipines, Aachen, Fed. Republic Germany; as cons. to WHO, Geneva, major rev. of primary health care devel. in 70 countries, 1981-82; mem. council of mgmt. Resources & Tech. Action Group, London, 1983-87. Author: Partners in Evaluation, 1986; mem. editorial bd. Community Devel. Jour., 1983; contbr. articles to profl. jours. Mem. Internat. Union for Health Edn., Nat. Council for Internat. Health, Royal Coll. Nursing, Devel. Studies Assn., Asian Community Health Action Group, Nightingale Fellowship. Social Democrat. Roman Catholic. Home and Office: 49 Hornton St, London W87NT, England

FEULNER, EDWIN JOHN, JR., research foundation executive; b. Chgo., Aug. 12, 1941; s. Edwin John and Helen J. (Franzen) F.; m. Linda C. Leventhal, Mar. 8, 1969; children: Edwin John III, Emily V. B.Sc., Regis Coll., Denver, 1963; M.B.A., Wharton Sch., U. Pa., 1964; PH.D., U. Edinburgh, 1981; hon. degree, Nichols Coll., Dudley, Mass., 1981, Universidad Francisco Marroquin, Guatemala City, 1982, Hanyang U., Seoul, Korea, 1982, Bellevue Coll., Nebr., 1987. Richard Weaver fellow London Sch. Econs., 1965; pub. affairs fellow Hoover Instn., 1965-67; Confidential asst. to sec. def. Melvin Laird, 1969-70; adminstrv. asst. to U.S. Congressman Philip M. Crane, 1970-74; exec. dir. Republican Study Com., Ho. of Reps., 1974-77; pres. Heritage Found., Washington, 1977—; chmn. Inst. European Def. and Strategic Studies, 1977—, U.S. Adv. Com. Pub. Diplomacy, USIA, 1982—; bd. dirs. Credit Internat. Bank; mem. sci. commn. Ctr. Applied Econ. Research, Rome; ; nat. adv. bd. Ctr. for Edn. and Research in Free Enterprise, Tex. A&M U.; disting. fellow Mobilization Concepts, Devel. Ctr. Nat. Def. U.; mem. Pres. Commn. on White House Fellows, 1981-83, Carlucci Commn. on Fgn. Assistance, 1983; pub. del. UN 2d Spl. Session on Disarmament, 1982; White House cons. domestic policy, 1987. Author: Congress and the New International Economic Order, 1976, Looking Back, 1981, Conservatives Stalk the House, 1983; contbr. articles to profl. jours., chpts. to books. Trustee Lehrman Inst., Intercollegiate Studies Inst., Rockford Inst., 1981-87, Roe Found., Am. Council on Germany, Sarah Scaife Found.; bd. govs., mem. exec. com. Council Nat. Policy, Found. Francisco Marroquin; mem. Citizens for Am., chmn. Citizens for Am. Edn. Found.; mem. disting. adv. com. Sch. Communication Am. U. Recipient Disting. Alumni award Regis Coll., 1985; named Free Enterprise Man of Yr. Tex. A&M U., 1985. Mem. Am. Econs. Assn., Am. Polit. Sci. Assn., Internat. Inst. Strategic Studies, U.S. Strategic Inst., Phila. Soc. (treas. 1964-79, pres. 1982-83), Mont Pelerin Soc. (treas.), Alpha Kappa Psi. Republican. Roman Catholic. Clubs: Belle Haven Country (Alexandria, Va.); Union League (N.Y.C.); University, Metropolitan (Washington); Reform (London), Knights of Malta.

FEUTRE, ALAIN PHILIPPE, hotel executive; b. Asnieres, France, Jan. 2, 1945; s. Andre and Eugenie (Guillaure) F.; m. Pariset Jacqueline, Aug. 1, 1970; children: Eric, Laetitia, Fanny. Cert. Lycée Claude Bernard, Paris, 1958. With Hotel du Nord, Compiegne, France, 1959-61, Savoy and Royal Garden, Londres, Eng., 1961-63, La récolte, London, 1966; restaurant mgr. L'Hotel Rue de Beaux-Arts, Paris, 1968-70, gen. dir., 1970-84; mng. dir. Paris-Reception Paris, 1977-84, Les Jardins d'Edgard, Paris, 1980-81, Club 13 Normandie, 1983-86, Le Bailli de Suffren, 1986—; shareholder Conseils S.A. rue Villersexel, Paris, 1983. Editor, press reviewer AlaCarte, 1983-85. Mem. Syndicat General de l'industrie Hoteliere (v.p. 1981-86, pres. 1986—), Syndicat Français de l'Hoteliere (pres. 1984), Cambre Nat. De La Restauration et de l'Hotellerie (pres. 1988). Roman Catholic. Home: 9 rue Stanislas, 75006 Paris France Office: L'Hotel, 13 rue des Beaux Arts, Paris 75006, France

FEVOLA, MARIO, accountant; b. Milan, Feb. 27, 1937; s. Michele and Anna (Serlenga) F.; m. Annamaria Caviglia, 1970; children; Alessandro, Marco. BA in Acctg., Cavalli & Conti U., Italy, 1956; BS in Econs. and Commerce, U. Catolica, Italy, 1959. CPA, Italy. Adminstrv. dir. Radio Allocchio Bacchini, Milan, 1953-66; controller Soilax, Milan, 1967-68, Vosacec, 1968-75, Cogefar, 1976-77; fin. dir. Metecno, 1977—; mng. dir. Emme Nove, Milan, Vendredi, Milan. Mem. Chartered Accts. Assn. (full, ofcl. nat. auditor). Clubs: Touring; Golf Country (Milan). Home: Via s Anatalone #15, Milan Italy 20147 Office: Metecno SPA, Via Cassino 19, Tribiano Italy 20067

FEYIDE, MESHACH OTOKITI, petroleum executive; b. Ipele, Ondo, Nigeria, Mar. 31, 1926; m. Christiana Oluremi Okuboye, June 2, 1954;

children: Ibironke, Olayinka, Olufemi. Assoc. First Class, Camborne Sch. Mines, Eng., 1953; Diploma, Royal Sch. Mines Imperial Coll., London, 1960. Cert. chartered engr. Eng.; registeded engr. Nigeria. Chief petroleum engr. Ministry Mines and Power, Nigeria, 1964-70, dir. petroleum resources, 1970-74; sec. gen. O.P.E.C., Vienna, Austria, 1975-76; head petroleum inspectorate Petroleum Corp. NNPC, Nigeria, 1977-78; petroleum cons. pvt. practice, Lagos, Nigeria, 1979—; dir. Texaco Nigeria Ltd., 1979—, NRB Drilling Services Ltd., Nigeria, 1983; chmn. Comerint Nigeria Ltd, 1984, Energy Pubs. Ltd., Lagos, Nigeria, 1984—. Editor Jour. Nigerian Petroleum News. Recipient Grand Decoration Honour, Austrian Govt., 1978, Sr. Citizens award, Nigerian Am. C. of C., 1983; named Officer Order Fed. Rep., Nigerian Govt., 1982. Fellow Inst. Mining and Metallurgy, Inst. Petroleum, Nigerian Mining and Geoscis. Soc. (past pres.). Anglican. Office: PO Box 1790, Lagos Nigeria

FEYZIOGLU, TURHAN, lawyer, educator; b. Kayseri, Turkey, Jan. 19, 1922; s. Sait Azmi and Neyyire Feyzioglu; m. Leylâ Firdevs, May 5, 1949; 1 child, Metin. BA in Law, Istanbul (Turkey) U., 1945; JD, Ankara (Turkey) U., 1949; postgrad., Oxford (Eng.) U.; D of Econ. Scis. (hon.), Erciyes U., Kayseri, 1984. Asst. prof. polit. sci. Ankara U., 1945-47, assoc. prof., 1947-54, prof., 1954—, dean faculty polit. sci., 1956; pres. Mid. East Tech. U., 1960; prof., mem. exec. com. Atatürk Research Ctr.; cons. to pres. Turkish Republic of Cypress. Author: Judicial Review of Constitutionality, 1951, The Reforms of the French Higher Civil Service, 1955, Democracy and Dictatorship, 1957, In the Service of the Nation, 1976, Atatürk and Secularism, 1981, Chypre, Mythes et Réalités, 1984, Atatürk and Nationalism, 1985, Kemal Atatürk, Leader de la Libération Nationale et du Développement dans la Paix, 1986, The Crux of the Cyprus Question, 1987; editor: Atatürk's Way, 1981. Mem. parliament Govt. of Turkey, 1957, 61, 65, 69, 73, 77, minister of edn., mem. constituent assembly, 1960, minister of state, 1961, dep. prime minister, 1962-63, 75-76, 78-79; mem. Turkish High Planning Council, 1961-63, 75-76, 78-79; Turkish rep. to parliamentary assembly Council of Europe, 1964-66, 72-73, v.p. parliamentary assembly, 1972-73; leader Rep. Reliance Party, 1967-80. Mem. Found. for Devel. Higher Edn. (pres. Kayseri chpt. 1982—). Clubs: Anatolian (Ankara); Galatasouray (Istanbul). Home: Cevre Sokak, 54/9 Cankaya Turkey Office: Ataturk Research Ctr, Ataturk Bulvari, 217 Ankara Turkey

FEZZI, LUDOVICO, information systems company executive; b. Bergamo, Italy, May 9, 1930; m. Silvana Bellinzoni, Feb. 12, 1934; children: Paolo, Francesca, Jolanda. MEE, U. Genoa, Italy, 1954; gen. mgmt. course, Harvard U., 1969. Gen. mgr. systems group Honeywell Bull Italia SpA, Milan, Italy, 1979—, bd. dirs.; mem. mgmt. com. ANIE, Milan; v.p. Assinform, Milan. Fellow Berkeley Roundtable on Internat. Economy. Office: Honeywell Bull Italia SpA, Via GB Pirelli 32, 20124 Milan Italy

FFORDE, ADAM JEROME, economic consultant; b. London, Jan. 1, 1953; s. John Standish and Marya (Retinger) F.; m. Suki Allen, Apr. 21, 1987. BA in Engring. and Econs., Oxford U., Eng., 1973; MSc in Econs., U. London, 1977; PhD, Cambridge U., 1983. Econ. analyst Henley Centre for Forecasting, London, 1973-75; postdoctoral research fellow Birkbeck Coll., London, 1983-87; freelance econ. cons. London, 1987—. Mem. Royal Econ. Soc., Am. Econ. Assn., Devel. Studies Assn., Assn. Southeast Asian Studies, Royal Inst. Internat. Affairs. Home: 47 Hillmarton Rd, London N7 9JD, England

FFRENCH-DAVIS, RICARDO, economic educator; b. Santiago, Chile, June 27, 1936; s. Harry L. and Graciela (Munoz) F.; B.Econs. and Bus. Adminstrn., Catholic U. Chile, 1962; M.A., U. Chgo., 1961, Ph.D., 1971. Prof. econs. Cath. U. Chile, Santiago, 1962-75, U. Chile, Santiago, 1962-73, Inst. Est. Internat., Santiago, 1984—; dep. dir. Research Dept., Central Bank of Chile, Santiago, 1964-70; dir. Corporacion de Investigaciones Economicas Para Latinoamerica, Santiago, 1976—; vis. prof. Oxford (Eng.) U., 1974, Boston U., 1976, Latin Am. Inst., Stockholm U., 1986; cons. in field. Pres., Econ. Circle, AHC, Santiago, 1978-81; nat. dir. tech. dept. Christian Dem. Party, Chile, 1969-70. Rockefeller fellow, 1966-67; Ford Found. fellow, 1971; Ford Found. grantee, 1976-77; Social Sci. Research Council grantee, 1978. Mem. Am. Econs. Assn., World Assn. Internat. Relations, Colegio de Ingenieros de Chile, Circulo de Economia de Chile. Contbr. numerous articles to profl. jours.; author: Economía Internacional, 1979, 2d edit., 1985; Politicas Economicas en Chile: 1952-70, 1973; editor: (with E. Tironi) Latin America and the International Economic Order, 1982, 2d. edit. 1985, (with R. Feinberg) Development and External Debt in Latin America, 1988; mem. editorial bd. El Trimestre Económico, Latin Am. Research Rev., Estudios Cieplan, Cono Sur. Office: Corp for Latin Am Econ Research, 3494 Colon, Santiago 16496, Chile

FIALA, DAVID MARCUS, lawyer; b. Cleve., Aug. 1, 1946; s. Frank J. and Anna Mae (Phillips) F.; m. Maryanne E. McGowan, Jan. 4, 1969 (div. Mar. 1986); 1 child, D. Michael; m. Lyn McDonald Jones, May 31, 1986. B.B.A., U. Cin., 1969; J.D., Chase Coll., No. Ky. State U., 1974. Bar: Ohio 1974, U.S. Dist. Ct. (so. dist.) Ohio 1974, U.S. Tax Ct. 1974. Assoc. Benesch, Friedlander, Coplan and Aronoff, Cin., 1974-78, ptnr., 1979—; lectr. Southwestern Ohio Tax Inst., 1978-79; bd. dirs. Elkhorn Collieries, Cin. Trustee, sec. Sta. WCET-TV, Cin., 1983-87, auction chmn., 1979, chmn. 1987—; trustee Jr. Achievement Greater Cin., 1979—, Mental Health Services West, 1974-83, Contemporary Dance theatre, 1974-80. Mem. ABA, Ohio State Bar Assn., Cin. Bar Assn., Am. Culinary Fedn. Cin. (trustee 1985—). Home: 3718 Mt Carmel Rd Cincinnati OH 45244 Office: Benesch Friedlander Coplan & Aronoff 1900 Carew Tower Cincinnati OH 45202

FIALKOV, HERMAN, investment banker; b. Bklyn., Mar. 23, 1922; s. Isidore and Pearl (Heinish) F.; m. Elaine Dampf, Nov. 25, 1942; children: Carol Fran, Jay Michael. Student, CCNY, 1938-41; B.Adminstrv. Engring., NYU, 1951. Engr. Emerson Radio Corp., 1941-47, MBS, 1947-49, Tele-Tone Radio Corp., 1949-51; chief engr. Radio Receptor Co., 1951-54; pres. Gen. Transistor Corp. (merged with Gen. Instrument Corp. 1960), 1954-60; v.p., dir. Gen. Instrument Corp., 1960-67, sr. v.p., 1967-68; partner Geiger & Fialkov, 1968-78, Venture Capital Investments, 1978—; dir. Gen. Ceramics, Inc., Haskell, N.J., Geotel, Inc., Microsemi Corp., Santa Ana, Calif., Standard Microsystems Corp., Hauppauge, N.Y., EMS Devel. Corp., Radyne Corp., Telebase Systems, Inc., Control Transaction Corp. Panelist Am. Arbitration Assn.; trustee Adelphi U., Garden City, 1959-70, Poly. U. N.Y., Heinish Found. Served with AUS, 1943-46. Decorated Bronze Star with oak leaf cluster; Conspicuous Service Cross N.Y. Mem. IEEE, Am. Technion Soc. (dir.), Tau Beta Pi, Alpha Pi Mu. Home: One Kensington Gate Great Neck NY 11021 Office: 199 Middle Neck Rd Great Neck NY 11021

FIALKOW, STEVEN, accountant; b. Bklyn., July 24, 1943; s. Irving and Ida (Berglass) F.; B.B.A., City U. N.Y., 1965; M.B.A., 1970; m. Arlene Michele Klein, Oct. 19, 1963 (div. Oct. 1985); children—Cheri Ann, Laura Beth; m. Frances Theresa Miller, Apr. 15, 1986. Profl. staff Price Waterhouse & Co., N.Y.C., 1965-69; asst. treas., controller Anglo Am. Corp., N.Y.C., 1969-72; treas., controller Video Playbacks, Inc., N.Y.C., 1972-75; adminstrv. mgr. Kenneth Leventhal & Co., N.Y.C., 1975-77; instr. N.Y. Inst. Tech., N.Y.C., 1975-79; ptnr. Herzig, Blumenfeld & Fialkow, C.P.A.s, N.Y.C., 1979-81; assoc. dir. nat. acctg. and audit profl. edn. Touche Ross & Co., N.Y.C., 1981-83; mng. ptnr. Steven Fialkow & Co., C.P.A.s, Coram, N.Y., El Paso, Tex., 1983—; cons. Brewster Industries of Mass. and Va., Banis Securities Corps. N.Y. Dir. outreach program YMCA, L.I., N.Y. C.P.A., N.Y. Mem. Am. Inst. C.P.A.s, N.Y. State Soc. C.P.A.s, Mensa. Republican. Lodge: Masons. Home: 368 Woodland Ct Coram NY 11727 Office: Fialkow Bldg 976 Skyline Dr Coram NY 11727 also: 4800 N Stanton Suite 48 El Paso TX 79902

FIALKOWSKI, KONRAD RAFAL, computer scientist, writer; b. Lublin, Poland, Dec. 29, 1939; s. Konrad Michal and Aurelia (Pukasiewicz) F.; m. Maria Danuta Knapik, Dec. 10, 1960; children—Konrad, Jerzy. M.Sc., Tech. U. Warsaw (Poland), 1962, Ph.D., 1964, Habilitation, 1966. Programmer Polish Acad. Sci., Warsaw, 1959-62; faculty mem. Tech. U. Warsaw, 1962-75, dir. computer ctr., 1972-75; dir. Inst. Sci. Tech. and Econ. Info., Warsaw, 1975-82; chief advanced tech. unit Unido, Vienna, Austria, 1982—; pres. nat. com. Internat. Fedn. Documentation, 1975-82; chmn. Diebolds Group, Poland, 1978-81. Author: Maszyna Cyfrowa Zam 2, 1963; Wprowadzenie Do Informatyki, 1978; Homo Divisus, 1979; Adam Einer Von Uns, 1982. Recipient Mistrz Techniki award 1967. Mem. IEEE (sr.).

FIALOWSKI, ALICE, mathematician; b. Budapest, Hungary, Jan. 28, 1951; d. Lajos and Alice F. Diploma, Eötvös Loránd U., Budapest, 1974, M, 1977; PhD, Moscow State U., 1980-83. Research assoc. Pedagogical Inst., Budapest, 1974-79, Inst. Math. Hungarian Acad., Budapest, 1983-84; asst. prof. U. Tech., Budapest, 1984—. Contbr. articles to profl jours. Swiss Nat. Found. fellow, 1985-86, NSF fellow 1986, Alexander von Humboldt fellow, 1986-88. Mem. Bolyai János Math. Soc., Deutsche Math. Vereinigung, Am. Math. Soc., Hungarian Psychol. Assn. Home: Villányi 103, 1118 Budapest Hungary Office: U Pa Dept Math 209 S 33d St Philadelphia PA 19104-6395

FICARRA, BERNARD JOSEPH, retired surgeon, legal medicine and bioethics consultant; b. N.Y.C., Jan. 1, 1914; s. Humphrey and Rose Marie (D'Ambra) F.; B.A. magna cum laude, St. Francis Coll., 1935, Sc.B., 1936; M.D., Georgetown U., 1939; Sc.D., U. Steubenville, 1950; LL.D., St. Francis Coll., N.Y.; Ph.D., Minerva U., Milan, Italy, 1960; m. Jean Alice Augustine, Aug. 31, 1967; 1 son, Bernard Thaddeus. Diplomate Am. Bd. Surgery. Surg. intern Kings County Hosp. Med. Center, Bklyn., 1939-41, resident pathology, 1941-42, resident surgery, 1942-44; fellow surgery Lahey Clinic Found., Boston, 1946-48; practice medicine specializing in surgery, N.Y.C., 1948-60, Greenvale, N.Y., 1953—; mem. vis. surg. staffs Kings County, St. Peters, Holy Family, St. Mary's hosps.; dir. surg. research Ficarra Found., Inc., 1949-69; prof. physiology St. Francis Coll., 1948-51; prof. research physiology St. John's U. Postgrad. Sch., 1951-61; professorial research asso. L.I. U., Postgrad. Sch., 1961-73; dir. Somerset Enterprises, Ltd., Doric Corp. Trustee L.I. Ednl. TV Council Inc., Sta. WLIW. Fellow Am. Coll. Gastroenterology (com. for legal matters), Am. Coll. Legal Medicine (edn. com.), Am. Coll. Angiology (achievement honor award 1964-65); mem. A.M.A., N.Y. State Med. Soc., N.Y. Acad. Medicine, N.Y. Soc. Med Jurisprudence, Acad. Templars (Bologna, Italy), Greenvale C. of C., Lahey Clinic Alumni Assn. (mem. council), Cath. Acad. Scis. (U.S.)(pres.), Alpha Omega Alpha, Pi Alpha, Phi Chi. Lodges: Lions, Knights of Malta, Knights of St. Gregory the Great, Equestrian Order of the Holy Sepulchre of Jerusalem (sect. rep. southeastern lieutenancy Washington, So. Md., No. Va.) . Author: Diagnostic Synopsis of Acute Surgical Abdomen, 1950; Emergency Surgery, 1953; Thyroid and Parathyroid Diseases, 1958; Surgical and Allied Malpractice, 1968; Medicolegal Handbook, 1983; Medicolegal Examination Evaluation and Report, 1986; mem. adv. bd. jour. Med. Malpractice Prevention; mem. editorial bd. Jour. Contemporary Health Law and Policy; contbr. 200 articles to profl. jours. Office: PO Box 9611 Washington DC 20016

FIDDLER, THOMAS ROBERT, retail executive; b. N.Y.C., Mar. 24, 1921; s. Earl Thomas and Margaret (Martsolf) F.; m. Jane Carol Sundlof, Sept. 12, 1942; children: Martha J., Thomas N. (dec.), Kathryn A. A.B., Princeton U., 1942. With Marshall Field and Co., Chgo., 1945-51, buyer, 1950-54; with Rich's Inc., Atlanta, 1954-60; gen. mgr. Rich's Inc., Tenn., 1955-60; with Frederick Atkins, N.Y.C., 1960-67, pres., 1963-67; with D.H. Holmes Co. Ltd., New Orleans, 1967—, pres., 1972-86, chmn., 1986—; dir. Hibernia Nat. Bank, Delchamps, Inc.; tchr. mktg. U. Ga., evenings 1952-54; bd. dirs. Internat. Trade Mart, 1983—; mem. council advisers Tulane U. Grad. Sch. Bus. Bd. dirs., exec. com. New Orleans Econ. Devel. Council, 1974—; chmn. maj. gifts United Way, 1974-75; sr. v.p. Council for a Better La., 1983; bd. dirs. New Orleans Met. Area Com., 1970—, New Orleans Symphony, 1974, 79; bd. dirs. New Orleans Tourist Commn., 1969—, pres., 1977-78, chmn., 1979; trustee King Sch., Stamford, Conn., 1962-66, Low Heywood Sch., Stamford, 1964-67, Xavier U., 1979; bd. dirs., exec. mgmt. com. La. World Expn., 1980—, also v.p.; mem. Pres.'s council Tulane U., 1983—; v.p. Los Angeles World Expn., 1980-83; trustee Gulf South Research Inst., Ochsner Found. Hosp. Served to lt. comdr. USNR, 1942-45. Recipient Weiss Brotherhood award NCCJ, 1985. Mem. Nat. Retail Mchts. Assn. (dir. 1974—), Am. Retail Fedn. (dir. 1981—), New Orleans Retail Mchts. Council (pres. 1972-73), New Orleans C. of C. (dir., exec. com.), World Trade Ctr. (dir., exec. com.). Republican. Episcopalian. Clubs: Univ. (N.Y.C.); New Orleans Country (New Orleans), Boston (New Orleans), Plimsoll (New Orleans); Pass Christian Golf (Miss.), Pass Christian Yacht (Miss.); Diamondhead. Home: 5418 Dayna Ct New Orleans LA 70124 Office: DH Holmes Co Ltd 819 Canal St New Orleans LA 70112

FIECHTER, GEORGES ANDRE, multinational company executive, investment, financial and marketing consultant; b. Alexandria, Egypt, Sept. 12, 1930; s. Jacques Rene and Marie Okhanoff F.; m. Francoise Forest, 1955; children: Benoit, Bettina, Gilles. MA Internat. Relations, U. Geneva, 1956, D.Polit. Sci., 1973; student Internat. Mgmt. Devel. Inst., Lausanne, 1961, 70. Exec. sec. Swiss Polit. Sci. Assn., Geneva, 1955-58; head press and info. depts. Internat. Com. Red Cross, Geneva, 1956-58; sec. gen. Internat. Mgmt. Devel. Inst., Lausanne, 1958-61; with leading watch cos., U.K., U.S., Brazil, Switzerland, 1961-77; cons. to dir. Grad. Inst. Internat. Studies and moderator Latin Am./ study group, Geneva, 1971-73; dir. Isopublic S.A. div. Gallup, Zurich, 1970-77; dir. Atlanticomnium S.A., Geneva, 1972—, MEBCO Bank S.A., Geneva, 1984—, Mahmoud K. Shakarchi S.A., Geneva, 1984—; European dir. Simonsen Associados, Sao Paulo, 1977—/ Fidetra S.A., Geneva, 1987—; cons. in asset mgmt., portfolio mgr., Geneva, Monte Carlo, Brazil 1979—. Author: Brazil Since 1964 - Modernization under a Military Regime, 1975, Les Hommes d'Etat celebres de 1920 a nos jours, 1977, Criteres d'evaluation des investissements prives suisses sur le development, 1969. Contbr. articles to profl. jours. Comdr. Nat. Order Rio Branco, Brazil. Grantee Ford Found., 1973. Fellow Inst. Mktg., London, Mktg. Communications Execs. Internat., Swiss Chpt., Geneva, Inst. Dirs., London; mem. Internat. Mgmt. Devel. Inst. Alumni Assn., ECOLINT Alumni Assn., Swiss Press Assn. Clubs: Jockey (Sao Paulo); German Internat. (Monte-Carlo); Golf, Am. Internat. (Geneva). Home: 8 rue Muzy, CH 1204 Geneva Switzerland Office: 8 Place Camoletti, CH 1207 Geneva Switzerland also: Rue Muzy, CH 1207 Geneva Switzerland

FIEDLER, KLAUS, psychologist; b. Wetzlar, Hessen, Fed. Rep. Germany, Sept. 7, 1951; s. Franz Josef Ernst and Hilde (Hess) F.; m. Christine Pauk, Nov. 9, 1952; children: Vera, Ina. Diploma in Psychology, Giessen U., 1975, PhD in Philosophy, 1979, habilitation, 1984. Research asst. Computers in the Study of Psychology, Giessen, 1975-77; research asst. Giessen U., 1978-80, asst. prof., 1982-87, prof., 1987—; editorial cons. Brit. Jour. Social Psychology, Eng., 1986—. Author: Urteilsbildung als Kognitiver Vorgang, 1980, Kognitive Strukturierung der Sozialen Umwelt, 1985, Affect, Cognition and Social Behavior, 1987. Mem. Deutsche Gesellschaft für Psychologie, European Assn. Exptl. Social Psychology. Office: Giessen U Psychology Dept, Otto Behaghel Strasse 10, 6300 Giessen Federal Republic of Germany

FIEDLER, WALTER, retired zoo director, educator; b. Gross-Harras, Austria, Aug. 8, 1922; s. Hans and Therese (Asperger) F.; Ph.D., U. Vienna, 1950. With Anat. Inst. Frankfurt/Main (W. Ger.), 1950-51, 57-59, Zool. Inst. Fribourg (Switzerland), 1951-53, Zool. Gardens Basel (Switzerland), 1953-54, Zool. Gardens Zurich, 1954-55, City Library, Graz, Austria, 1956-57; collaborator expdn. to Ethiopia of Anat. Inst. Frankfurt-Main, 1955-56; zoo dir. Tiergarten Schönbrunn, Vienna, Austria, 1959-88, ret. 1988; lectr. U. Vienna, 1969-81, prof., 1981—. Served with German Army, 1941-45. Decorated Goldenes Ehrenzeichen and Grofess Ehrenzeichen für Verdienste (Austria), Goldenes Ehrenzeichen (Vienna) ; recipient award Theodor Körner Fond, Vienna, 1955, 57. Mem. Osterreichische Gesellschaft für Vogelkunde (pres. 1976-86), Assn. German Speaking Zoo Dirs. (pres. 1976-78), Internat. Assn. Zoo Dirs., Zool.-Bot. Soc. Austria (pres. 1985—), Zool. Soc. Germany, Zool. Soc. Switzerland, Internat. Primatological Soc., German Mammalogical Soc. (3d pres. 1986—), Am. Mammalogical Soc., German Ornithol. Soc., Anthrop. Soc. Vienna, Anat. Soc. Germany, Brit. Fauna Preservation Soc., Nat. Geog. Soc. Roman Catholic. Contbr. articles on anatomy of vertebrates, primatology and zoobiology to profl. jours., chpts. to books. Home and Office: Schloss Schonbrunn, 1131 Vienna Austria

FIELD, FRANCIS EDWARD, electrical engineer, educator; b. Casper, Wyo., Nov. 20, 1923; s. Jesse Harold and Persis Belle (St. John) F.; m. Margaret Jane O'Bryan, Oct. 13, 1945; children—Gregory A., Christopher B., Sheridan Diane. B.S. in Elec. Engring., U.S. Naval Acad., 1945; M.A. in Internat. Affairs, George Washington U., 1965; A.M.P., Harvard Bus. Sch., 1970. Master cert. graphoanalyst; comml. pilot. Owner Field Lumber Co., Lander, Wyo., 1948-50; commd. ensign, U.S. Navy, 1945, advanced through grades to capt. 1966, ret., 1975; research engr., George Washington U., 1975—, adj. faculty, 1977—; program dir. NSF, Washington, 1982—; pres. EXTANT, cons. firm, McLean, Va., 1981—. Author: Chronicle of a Workshop, 1977. Mem. Internat. Graphoanalysis Soc. (award of merit 1984), Nat. Geneal. Soc., Wyo. Hist. Soc., Sigma Xi. Republican. Club: George Washington U. Lodge: Masons. Home: 8122 Dunsinane Ct McLean VA 22102 Office: NSF 1800 G St NW Washington DC 20550

FIELD, J. V., museum curator, historian; b. Newcastle-on-Tyne, Eng., Feb. 21, 1943; s. E.J. and D. (Krawitz) F. BA in Math., U. Cambridge, Eng., 1964, MA, 1968; MS in Astronomy, U. Sussex, Eng., 1967; PhD in History of Sci., U. London, 1981. Research asst. Cambridge U. Obs., 1964-66, asst. in research, 1970-72; curator Sci. Mus., London, 1972—; vis. research fellow Royal Instn. of Gt. Britain, London, 1982—. Author: Kepler's Geometrical Cosmology, 1988, (with others) Byzantine and Arabic Mathematical Gearing, 1985, The Geometrical Work of Girard Desargues, 1987; contbr. articles on history of math. and math. scis. to profl. jours. Fellow Royal Astron. Soc.; mem. Brit. Soc. for History of Sci., Soc. Renaissance Studies. Office: Sci Mus, Exhibition Rd, London SW7 2DD, England

FIELD, KAREN ANN, real estate broker; b. New Haven, Conn., Jan. 27, 1936; d. Abraham Terry and Ida (Smith) Rogovin; m. Barry S. Crown, June 29, 1954 (div. 1969); children: Laurie Jayne, Donna Lynn, Bruce Alan, Bradley David; m. 2d Michael Lehmann Field, Aug. 10, 1969 (div. 1977). Student Vassar Coll., 1953-54, Harrington Inst. Interior Design, 1973-74, Roosevelt U., 1987—. Owner Karen Field Interiors, Chgo., 1970-86, Karen Field & Assocs., Chgo., 1980-81; now dir. sales La Thomus Realty Group div. La Thomus & Co., Chgo., 1988—; pres., ptnr. Field Pels & Assocs., Chgo., 1981-86. Mem. women's council Camp Henry Horner, Chgo., 1960; bd. dirs., treas. Winnetka Pub. Sch. Nursery (Ill.), 1961-63; mem. exec. com. woman's bd. U. Chgo. Cancer Research Found., 1965-66, pres. jr. aux., 1960-66; bd. dirs., sec. United Charities, Chgo., 1966-68, Victory Gardens Theatre, Chgo., 1979; co-founder, pres. Re-Entry Ctr., Wilmette, Ill., 1978-80; mem. br. Parental Stress Services, Chgo., 1981—, Stop Aids Real Estate Div., 1988. Recipient Servian award Jr. Aux. of U. Chgo. Cancer Research Found., 1966, Margarite Wolf award Women's Bd., U. Chgo. Cancer Research Found., 1967. Mem. Chgo. Real Estate Bd., North Side Real Estate Bd. Condex, Chgo. Council Fgn. Relations, English Speaking Union (jr. bd. 1958-59). Office: La Thomus and Co Inc 15 E Superior Chicago IL 60611

FIELD, MARSHALL, business executive; b. Charlottesville, Va., May 13, 1941; s. Marshall IV and Joanne (Bass) F.; m. Joan Best Connelly, Sept. 5, 1964 (div. 1969); 1 son, Marshall; m. Jamee Beckwith Jacobs, Aug. 19, 1972; children: Jamee Christine, Stephanie Caroline, Abigail Beckwith. B.A., Harvard U., 1963. With N.Y. Herald Tribune, 1964-65; pub. Chgo. Sun-Times, 1969-80, Chgo. Daily News, 1969-78; dir. Field Enterprises, Inc., Chgo., 1965-84; dir., mem. exec. com. Field Enterprises, Inc., 1965-84, chmn. bd., 1972-84; chmn. bd. The Field Corp., 1984—; chmn. bd. Cabot, Cabot & Forbes, 1984-85, chmn. exec. com., 1985—; pub. World Book-Childcraft Internat. Inc., 1973-78, dir., 1965-80; bd. dirs. First Chgo. Corp., First Nat. Bank of Chgo. Mem. Chgo. com. Chgo. Council Fgn. Relations; adv. bd. Broader Urban Involvement and Leadership Devel., Inc., Chgo.; pres., trustee Art Inst. Chgo.; vice chmn., trustee, Field Mus. Natural History, Mus. Sci. and Industry, Rush-Presbyn.-St. Luke's Med. Ctr.; bd. dirs. Chgo. Tourism Council, Field Found. of Ill., Smithsonian Instn., McGraw Wildlife Found., Restoration Atlantic Salmon In Am., Inc., Trout Unltd., Lincoln Park Zool. Soc., hon. bd. dirs. Open Lands Project (CorLands); mem. univ. resources Harvard Coll.; mem. adv. bd. Brookfield Zoo. Mem. Nature Conservancy, Chgo. Zool. Soc. Clubs: River (N.Y.C.); Chicago, Mid-Am., Commercial, Harvard, Hundred of Cook County, Shore Acres, Racquet, Tavern (Chgo.), Onwentsia (Lake Forest, Ill.), Somerset (Boston), Jupiter Island (Hobe Sound, Fla.). Office: The Field Corp 333 W Wacker Dr Chicago IL 60606 also: 401 N Wabash Ave Chicago IL 60611

FIELD, NORMAN GEORGE, marketing executive; b. Vancouver, B.C., Can., June 18, 1944; s. George Henry and Ada (Smith) F.; m. Mary Lynn Lawton, Dec. 30, 1983, 1 child, Kevin Lawton. BS, U. B.C., 1966; MBA, Simon Frazer U., Burnaby, B.C., 1981. Registered profl. chemist. Tech. rep. Fisher Sci., Calgary, Alta., Can., 1966-67; tech. specialist Fisher Sci., Edmonton, Alta., Can., 1967-72; instrument specialist Fisher Sci., Vancouver, 1973-80; dist. mgr. Fisher Sci., Edmonton, 1981-83; mktg. mgr. Fisher Sci., Ottawa, Can., 1984—. Mem. Am. Mktg. Assn., Am. Mgmt. Assn. Home: 8 Cypress Ct, Nepean, ON Canada K2H 8Z8 Office: Fisher Sci Ltd, 112 Colonnade Rd, Nepean, ON Canada K2E 7L6

FIELD, NORMAN J., physicist; b. N.Y.C., Dec. 5, 1922; s. Morris S. and Clara (Edinburg) F.; B.S. cum laude, City U. N.Y., 1942; M.S. in Physics, Poly. Inst. Bklyn., 1959; L.H.D. (hon.), Monmouth Coll., West Long Branch, N.J., 1979; m. Gladys Katz, Nov. 23, 1946; children—Joan, Kenneth, Richard, Elaine. Electronic engr. radar lab. Signal Corps, Ft. Monmouth, N.J., 1942-44, physicist, chief, optical microscopy engring. labs., 1946-54, asst. dir. research, 1954-58; asst. dir. Inst. Exploratory Research, U.S. Army Research and Devel. Lab., Ft. Monmouth, 1958-62, dep. dir. research U.S. Army Electronics Lab., 1962-64, chief applied physics div. U.S. Army Electronics Command, 1964-68, chief office sci. and tech., 1968-70, dir. program mgmt., army area communications system, 1970-74, dir. internat. logistics, 1975-79; adj. prof., lectr. physics Monmouth Coll., 1956—. Pres., Monmouth Regional High Sch. Bd. Edn., 1957—; pres. Friends Monmouth County Library Assn., 1981—. Served with AUS, 1944-46. Decorated Bronze Star with oak leaf cluster, Purple Heart. Mem. Am. Phys. Soc., Optical Soc. Am., Am. Chem. Soc., Am. Assn. Physics Tchrs., N.J. Fedn. Dist. Bds. Edn. (v.p. 1966), Monmouth County Sch. Bds. Assn. (pres. 1972-73), Am. Ordnance Assn., Nat. Sch. Bds. Assn., Assn. U.S. Army (pres. 1978—), N.Y. Acad. Scis. Contbr. articles to sci. jours., books. Home: 726 Sycamore Ave Shrewsbury NJ 07702

FIELD, ROBERT EDWARD, lawyer; b. Chgo., Aug. 21, 1945; s. Robert Edward and Florence Elizabeth (Aiken) F.; m. Jenny Lee Hill, Aug. 5, 1967; children—Jennifer Kay, Kimberly Anne, Amanda Brooke. B.A., Ill. Wesleyan U., 1967; M.A., Northwestern U., 1969, J.D., 1973. Bar: Ill. 1973, U.S. Dist. Ct. (no. dist.) Ill. 1974, U.S. Supreme Ct. 1979. Exec. dir. Winnetka Youth Orgn., Ill., 1969-73; assoc. firm Seyfarth, Shaw, Fairweather & Geraldson, Chgo., 1973-79, ptnr., 1979—; bd. dirs. Gt. Lakes Fin. Resources, Blue Island, Ill.; chmn. bd. dirs. 1st Nat. Bank of Blue Island, Winchester Mfg. Co., Wood Dale, Ill., Comml. Resources Corp., Naperville, Ill.; dir., sec. Ellis Corp., Itasca, Ill.; chmn. bd. dirs. Community Bank of Homewood-Flossmoor, Homewood, Ill. Pres. bd. dirs. Family Service and Mental Health Ctr. S. Cook County, Chgo. Heights, 1979—, treas., 1981-82, pres. 1986—; pres. Lakes of Olympia Condominium Assn.; trustee Village of Olympia Fields, Ill., 1981—. Mem. Ill. Bar Assn., ABA. Republican. Methodist. Club: Calumet Country (Homewood). Home: 3424 Parthenon Way Olympia Fields IL 60461 Office: Seyfarth Shaw Fairweather & Geraldson 55 E Monroe St Chicago IL 60603

FIELD, THOMAS WALTER, JR., drugstore chain executive; b. Alhambra, Calif., Nov. 2, 1933; s. Thomas Walter and Pietje (Slagveld) F.; m. Ruth Inez Oxley, Apr. 10, 1959; children: Julie, Sherry, Cynthia, Thomas Walter, III, James. Student, Stanford U., 1951-53. V.p. retail ops. Alpha Beta Co., La Habra, Calif., 1972-73, sr. v.p., 1973-75, exec. v.p., 1975-76, pres., chief exec. officer, 1976-81; pres. Am. Stores Co., 1981-85; pres., chief exec. officer McKesson Corp., San Francisco, 1986—, also chmn. bd. Bd. dirs. La Habra Boys' Club. Mem. Calif. Retailers Assn. (dir.), Automobile Club So. Calif. (adv. bd.). Republican. Office: McKesson Corp One Post St San Francisco CA 94104 *

FIELD, VICTOR GRAHAM, steel draftsman; b. Oldbury, Worcestershire, Eng., Apr. 28, 1926; s. Edward and Rhoda (Burton) F.; m. Bridget Bernadette Nolan; children: Martin Victor, Shaun Edward. Student, Corby Tech. Toll., Birmingham Coll. Further Edn. Apprentice engr. Chances Glass and Lighthouse Works, Smethwick, Eng., 1942-45, jr. draftsman, 1948-49; design draftsman Midland Tar Distillers, Oldbury, 1949-52, Bakelite Ltd., Tysley, Birmingham, 1952-53; leading draftsman T.I. Investments Co., Oldbury, 1953-59; gas engr. West Midlands Gas Bd., 1959-60; leading draftsman Stewarts & Lloyds Corby, Northants, 1960-64; lectr. Wellingborough Tech. Coll., Northants, 1964-67; sect. leader, draftsman British

Steel Corp., Northants, 1967-85; fin. clk. Community Rural Aid Ltd., Corby Northants, 1985-87; draftsman Euroquip Fabrications, Kettering, Eng., 1988—. Served with submarine fleet, Royal Navy, 1946-48. Home: 10 Knights Clise, Corby, Northants England

FIELDING, DAVID ALAN, accountant, consultant; b. Newcastle upon Tyne, England, June 3, 1953; s. Alfred and Ada (Franklin) F.; m. Pamela Deakins, June 22, 1974 (div. Nov. 1977); m. Christine Elizabeth Brand, Dec. 10, 1977; children: Mark Anthony, Jason Andrew. Grad. high sch., Gateshead, England. Audit clk. Allied Suppliers Ltd., South Shields, Tyne and Wear, England, 1971-73; asst. acct. Cascade Ltd., Cramlington, Northumberland, England, 1973-77; co. acct. Dixon and Spearman Ltd., Gateshead, Tyne and Wear, 1977-79; co. sec. Hartonclean Ltd., Newcastle upon Tyne, 1979-83; prin. D.C.M. Bus. Services, Bedlington, Northumberland, England, 1983—; bd. dirs. North East Bus. Mus. Co. Ltd., Bedlington, Serene Travel Ltd., Bedlington, C.M.C.C. Ltd., Bedlington. Gov. Bedlinton Sta. County First Sch., 1985—. Fellow Inst. Fin. Accts. (sec., chmn. local chpt. 1981—); mem. British Inst. Mgmt., North East Bus. Preservation Soc. (treas. 1983-87). Mem. Conservative Party. Mem. Ch. of England. Lodge: Vanbrugh. Office: DCM Business Services, 86A Front St East, Bedlington Northumberland NE22 5AB, England

FIELDS, BERTRAM HARRIS, lawyer; b. Los Angeles, Mar. 31, 1929; s. H. Maxwell and Mildred Arlyn (Ruben) F.; m. Lydia Ellen Minevitch, Oct. 22, 1960 (dec. Sept. 1986); 1 child, James Eldar. B.A., UCLA, 1949; J.D. magna cum laude, Harvard U., 1952. Bar: Calif. 1953. Practiced in Los Angeles, 1955—; assoc. firm Shearer, Fields, Rohner & Shearer, and predecessor firms, 1955-57, mem. firm, 1957-82; ptnr. Greenberg, Glusker, Fields, Claman & Machtinger, 1982—. Bd. editors Harvard Law Rev, 1953-55; subject of biographical article, California Mag., Nov. 1987, and of descriptive report in Sheresky, "On Trial-Masters of the Courtroom", 1977. Served as 1st. lt. USAF, 1953-55, Korea. Mem. Am., Los Angeles County bar assns., Assn. Comml. Trial Lawyers. Office: Greenberg Glusker Fields Claman & Machtinger 1900 Ave of the Stars Suite 2000 Los Angeles CA 90067

FIELDS, DAVID C., diplomat; b. San Pedro, Calif., Jan. 13, 1937; s. Clark and Claudia (Bacon) F.; m. Frances A. Krusic, Oct. 1, 1960; children: Scott D., Stacy A. Student, Napa Jr. Coll., 1957-58; BS, Armstrong Coll., 1960; postgrad., Cornell U., 1972-73. Export negotiator Internat. div. Wells Fargo Bank, San Francisco, 1960-62; acct. Basalt Rock Co., Napa, Calif., 1962-65; sales rep. Calif.-Western State Life Ins. Co., San Rafael, Calif., 1965; chief acct. Thorsen Mfg. Co., Emeryville, Calif., 1965-67; budget officer Am. Embassy, Libreville, Gabon, 1967-70; adminstrv. officer Am. Embassy, Ouagadougou, Upper Volta, 1970-72; budget officer Office of Budget, Dept. State, Washington, 1973-75; adminstrv. officer Am. Embassy, Tunis, Tunisia, 1975-79; adminstrv. counselor Am. Embassy, Islamabad, Pakistan, 1979-80, London, 1980-84; dep. asst. sec. for security Dept. State, Washington, 1984-86; ambassador Am. Embassy, Bangui, Cen. African Republic, 1986—; chmn. Sec. of State's Overseas Security Policy Group, Washington, 1984-86, Dept. State's Security Adv. Council, Washington, 1985-86. Mem. Am. Soc. Indsl. Security, Internat. Assn. Chiefs Police. Office: care Bengui Dept State Washington DC 20520-2060

FIELDS, DOUGLAS PHILIP, building supply and home furnishings wholesale company executive; b. Jersey City, May 19, 1942; s. Douglas Philip and Priscilla (Wagner) F.; m. Paulette Susan Titko, Dec. 15, 1970; children: Douglas Philip, Priscilla Wagner, Jessica Elizabeth. B.S. summa cum laude, Fordham U., 1964; M.B.A. with distinction, Harvard U., 1966. Investment analyst Lehman Bros., N.Y.C., 1966-67; asst. to pres. Talley Industries, Mesa, Ariz., 1967-69; pres. TDA Industries, Inc., N.Y.C., 1969—; chmn. bd. TDA Industries, Inc., 1970—; founder Unimet Corp., N.Y.C., 1970-73; chmn. bd. Westco Corp., Boston, 1970-79, Cooper Distbrs. Inc., Miami, Fla., 1972—, Eagle Supply, Inc., Tampa, Fla., 1973—; pres., chmn. Westcalind Corp., R.I., 1971-87; cons. U.S. Office Edn., 1973-74, Fed. Energy Adminstrn., 1974-75. Outside dir. NYU Grad. Sch. Bus., Mgmt. Decision Lab., 1973-78; mem. N.Y. State adv. com. U.S. Civil Rights Commn., 1974-85; bd. dirs. YMHA-YWHA of So. Westchester, Mt. Vernon, N.Y., 1981—. Mem. Young Pres.'s Orgn. (chmn. seminars to Val d'Isere, France, 1985, Courchevel, France, 1986, Zurs, Austria, 1987). Clubs: Harvard of N.Y.C, Harvard of Fairfield County (Conn.), Harvard Bus. Sch. of N.Y.C; Midtown Tennis (N.Y.C.) (pres. 1969—). Office: 122 E 42d St New York NY 10168

FIELDS, WILMER CLEMONT, minister; b. Saline, La., Mar. 16, 1922; s. Felder Burkett and Eva Mae (Corbett) F.; B.A., La. Coll., Pineville, 1943; Th.M., So. Bapt. Theol. Sem., Louisville, 1946, Ph.D., 1950; m. Rebecca Elizabeth Hagan, June 22, 1946; children—Randall Hagan, Christy Alderson, Rebecca Elizabeth. Student pastor in La., 1940-43; music and ednl. dir. Carlisle Ave. Bapt. Ch., Louisville, 1943-48; ordained to ministry Bapt. Ch., 1940; pastor in Louisville, 1948-51, Yazoo City, Miss., 1951-56; editor Bapt. Record, jour. for Miss., 1956-59; public relations sec., exec. com. So. Bapt. Conv., 1959-87, also press rep., dir. conv. bull. service; editor Bapt. Program mag., 1959-71; dir. Bapt. Press, SBC News Service; nat. pres. Religious Public Relations Council, 1966-67; pres. Associated Ch. Press, 1967-69. Trustee, Council Religion and Internat. Affairs. Mem. Public Relations Soc. Am., Bapt. Public Relations Assn., Bapt. Press Assn., Evang. Press Assn., Pi Kappa Delta, Alpha Chi, Alpha Psi Omega. Author: The Chains Are Strong, 1963; Trumpets in Dixie, 1968. Editor: Religious Public Relations Handbook, 1976. Home: 2223 Woodmont Blvd Nashville TN 37215 Office: 901 Commerce St Nashville TN 37203

FIEN, JEROME MORRIS, accountant; b. Hartford, Conn., Dec. 26, 1921; s. Martin Herman and Frances (Chernaik) F.; m. Ruth Lee Klein, Apr. 3, 1945; children—Mark Allan, Judith Anne. B.A., Johns Hopkins U., 1943; M.B.A., NYU, 1949. Sr. staff acct. Samuel Klein & Co., Newark, 1946-50, now mng. ptnr.; v.p. N.J. State Bd. C.P.A.s, 1965-67, pres., 1967, 78—, sec., 1968-72, mem., 1976-82. v.p. NE region Nat. Assn. State Bds. Accountancy, 1968, pres., 1969-70, regional dir., 1973—, v.p. nat. assn., 1972-73. Vice Pres. Florence Crittenton League, 1965-66, pres., 1967—; overall chmn. Essex County Bonds for Israel, 1963-64, chmn. N.J. council, 1969-70, labor chmn., 1986; sec. K-F. Charitable Found.; treas. ADL, 1988, Hospice Inc., 1988; trustee Jewish Community Council Essex County, N.J., 1959-65, 70—, v.p., 191967, trustee The Hospice, Inc., 1988, ADL, N.J., 1988; adv. council Seton Hall U. Sch. Bus. Adminstrn.; adv. council acctg. program Rutgers U.; fellow Upsala Coll. Served with USNR, 1944-46. C.P.A., N.J.; registered mcpl. acct. Mem. Am. Inst. C.P.A.s, N.J. Soc. C.P.A.s, N.Y. State Soc. C.P.A.s, Pa. Soc. C.P.A.s, Tax Soc. NYU, Registered Mcpl. Accounts Assn. N.J., C.P.A. Assocs. (chmn. 1978), Nat. Assn. C.P.A. Practitioners (dir.), Greater Newark C. of C. (bd. dirs. 1986), Beta Alpha Psi. Club: Green Brook Country (Caldwell, N.J.). Home: 38 Sullivan Dr West Orange NJ 07052-2260 Office: 1180 Raymond Blvd Newark NJ 07102

FIFER, STEPHEN LAMAR, mfg. co. ofcl.; b. Fresno, Calif., Nov. 11, 1947; s. Karson Kirkland and Alma Christina (Mose) F.; student Calif. State U., Fresno, 1965-67, 71-74, A.B. in Internat. Econs., A.B. in Diplomatic History, 1974, M.Internat. Mgmt. in Internat. Econs. and Fin., Am. Grad. Sch. Internat. Mgmr., 1975; m. Mary Lorraine Joy, June 15, 1974. Export mgr. Reliance Crane and Rigging, Phoenix and Mexico City, Mex., 1975; staff Caterpillar Tractor Co., Peoria, Ill., 1976, staff Caterpillar Overseas S.A., Geneva, Switzerland, 1977, sales rep. Cat Overseas, Rome, Italy, 1978-80; sr. mktg. cons. Caterpillar Overseas S.A., Geneva, 1980-81, commodity mktg. support mgr., 1982-84; dist. mktg. mgr. Caterpillar Far East, Kuala Lumpur, Malaysia, 1984—; SBA cons., 1976. Conservator World Wildlife Found. Served with USN, 1967-71. Recipient award of merit SBA, 1976. Mem. Am. Econs. Assn., M.B.A. Assn. Contbr. papers, reports in field to publs. Office: GPO Box 3069, Caterpillar Far East Ltd, 28th Floor Sun Hung Kai Ctr, 30 Harbor Rd, Wanchai Hong Kong

FIFLIS, TED J., lawyer, educator; b. Chgo., Feb. 20, 1933; s. James P. and Christine (Karakitsos) F.; m. Vasilike Pantelakos, July 3, 1955; children: Christina Eason, Antonia Fowler, Andreanna Lawson. B.S., Northwestern U., 1954; LL.B., Harvard U., 1957. Bar: Ill. 1957, Colo. 1975, U.S. Supreme Ct. 1984. Individual practice law Chgo., 1957-65; mem. faculty U. Colo. Law Sch., Boulder, 1965—; prof. U. Colo. Law Sch., 1968—; vis. prof. N.Y. U., 1968, U. Calif., Davis, 1973, U. Chgo., 1976, U. Va., 1979, Duke U., 1980, Georgetown U., 1982, Am. U., 1983, Harvard U., 1988; cons. Rice U. Author: (with Homer Kripke, Paul Foster) Accounting for Business Lawyers, 1970, 3d edit., 1984; Editor-in-chief: Corp. Law Review, 1977—; Contbr. articles to profl. jours. Mem. Am. Assn. Law Schs. (past chmn. bus. law sect.), Colo. Bar Assn. (council mem. sect. of corp., banking and bus. law 1974-75), Am. Law Inst., ABA. Greek Orthodox. Home: 1636 Columbine Boulder CO 80302 Office: Univ of Colo Law Sch Boulder CO 80309

FIGA, PHILLIP SAM, lawyer; b. Chgo., July 27, 1951; s. Leon and Sarah (Mandelkorn) F.; m. Candace Cole, Aug. 19, 1973; children—Benjamin Todd, Elizabeth Dawn. B.A., Northwestern U., 1973; J.D., Cornell U., 1976. Bar: Colo. 1976, U.S. Dist. Ct. Colo. 1976, U.S. Ct. Appeals (10th cir.) 1980, U.S. Supreme Ct. 1980. Assoc. Sherman & Howard, Denver, 1976-80; ptnr. Burns & Figa, P.C., Denver, 1980—; lectr. U. Denver Law Sch., 1984—; bd. dirs. Colo. Lawyers Com., Denver, 1984—, vice-chair, 1987—; mem. adv. com. on group legal services and advt. Colo. Supreme Ct. 1982—; mem. joint com. on model rules of profl. conduct Colo. Supreme Ct./Colo. Bar, 1987—. Contbr. articles to legal jours.; articles editor Cornell Internat. Law Rev., 1975-76. Bd. trustees Rose Med. Ctr., 1987—; bd. dirs. Rocky Mountain region B'nai B'rith Anti-Defamation League, 1984—; co-chmn. Civil Rights Com., 1988—. Evans scholar, 1969. Mem. Colo. Bar Assn. (chmn. ethics com. 1984-85, bd. of govs. 1986—), ABA, Denver Bar Assn., Am. Judicature Soc., Phi Beta Kappa, Phi Eta Sigma. Democrat. Jewish. Home: 9928 E Ida Ave Englewood CO 80111 Office: 3773 Cherry Creek N Dr Ptarmigan Pl Denver CO 80209

FIGARI, ERNEST EMIL, JR., lawyer, educator; b. Navasota, Tex., Feb. 18, 1939; s. Ernest Emil and Louise (Campbell) F.; 1 child, Alexandra Caroline. BS, Tex. A&M U., 1961; LLB, U. Tex.-Austin, 1964; LLM, So. Meth. U., 1970. Bar: Tex. 1964, U.S. Ct. Appeals (5th cir.) 1965, U.S. Dist. Ct. (no. dist.) Tex. 1964, U.S. Supreme Ct. 1967. Law clerk to judge U.S. Dist. Ct. (no. dist.) Tex., Dallas, 1964-65; assoc. Coke & Coke, Dallas, 1965-70, ptnr., 1970-75; ptnr. Johnson & Swanson, Dallas, 1975-86, Figari & Davenport, Dallas, 1986—; adj. prof. law So. Meth. U., Dallas, 1982-84. Contbr. articles to legal jours. Fellow Tex. Bar Found.; mem. State Bar Tex., ABA. Democrat. Roman Catholic. Office: Figari & Davenport 4800 Inter First Plaza 901 Main St Dallas TX 75202

FIGG, ROBERT MCCORMICK, JR., lawyer; b. Radford, Va., Oct. 22, 1901; s. Robert McCormick and Helen Josephine (Cecil) F.; m. Sallie Alexander Tobias, May 10, 1927; children: Robert McCormick, Emily Figg Dalla Mura, Jefferson Tobias. A.B., Coll. of Charleston, 1920, Litt.D., 1970; law student, Columbia U., 1920-22; LL.D., U. S.C., 1959. Bar: S.C. 1922. Practiced in Charleston, 1922-59; gen. counsel S.C. State Ports Authority, 1942-72; circuit solicitor 9th Jud. Circuit of S.C., 1935-47; spl. circuit judge 1957, 75, 76; dean Law Sch., U. S.C., 1959-70; sr. counsel Robinson, McFadden, Moore, Pope, Williams, Taylor & Brailsford, Columbia, 1970—; dir. Home Fed. Savs. & Loan Assn., Charleston. Co-author: Civil Trial Manual (joint com. Am. Coll. Trial Lawyers-Am. Law Inst.-Am. Bar Assn.), 1974. Mem. S.C. Reorgn. Commn., 1948—, chmn., 1951-55, 71-75; elector Hall Fame for Gt. Americans, 1976; mem. S.C. Ho. of Reps., 1933-35; first pres., now hon. life chmn. Coll. of Charleston Found.; trustee Saul Alexander Found., Columbia Mus. Art. Recipient DuRant award for disting. pub. service S.C. Bar Found., 1982; Founders medal Coll. of Charleston, 1986. Fellow Am. Coll. Trial Lawyers; mem. Am. Soc. Internat. Law, Am. Acad. Polit. Sci., Am. Law Inst. (life), Am. Judicature Soc., Inst. Jud. Adminstrn., World Assn. Lawyers, Inter-Am. Bar Assn., Charleston County Bar Assn. (pres. 1953), ABA (ho. of dels. 1971-72, com. fair trial-free press 1965-69, com. spl. study legal edn. 1974—), S.C. Bar Assn., S.C. State Bar (pres. 1971), Order Coif, Blue Key (hon.), Phi Beta Kappa (hon.), Phi Delta Phi (hon.). Clubs: Forum, Forest Lake, Palmetto U. S.C. Faculty. Lodge: Masons (33 degree, grand master S.C. 1972-74). Home: 1522 Deans Ln Columbia SC 29205 Office: Jefferson Bldg Columbia SC 29201

FIGUEIREDO, ANTONIO MODESTO, finance executive; b. Viseu, Portugal, Apr. 30, 1943; s. Jose Maria and Maria Isabel (Peres) F.; m. Maria Luz Guerra, Mar. 16, 1969; children: Carla Alexandra, Joao Luis. Degree in acctg., Inst. Superior Contabilidade e Adminstn. de Lisbon, Lisbon, Portugal, 1972. Controller Singer Sewing Machines, Lisbon, 1969-70; dir. ops. Johnson & Johnson, Lisbon, 1971-78, Smith Kline & French, Lisbon, 1979-88; exec. dir. Cilag Medicamenta, Lisbon, 1988—; exec. dir. Inst. Luso-Farmaco, Lisbon, 1985-88. Dep. candidate Social Dem. Party, Lisbon, 1975; mem. Mcpl. Assembly, Sintra, 1976-80; pres. Father's Sch. Assn., Amora, Setubal, 1981. Served as lt. Portuguese Army, 1965-68. Fellow Am. Mgmt. Assn., Portuguese Accts. Assn., Portuguese Mgmt. Assn., Consumer Assn.; mem. Industry Pharm. Assn. Roman Catholic. Home: Rua Aroeiras 59, 2840 Amora Seixal Setubal Portugal Office: Cilag-Medicamenta, R Marq Fronteira 9, 1000 Lisbon Portugal

FIJALKOWSKI, DOMINIK, biology educator; b. Huta Borowska, Poland, Mar. 14, 1922; s. Jan and Marianna (Gierej) F.; m. Elzbieta Chojnacka, Apr. 11, 1979; 3 children. Prof. dr. hab., U. Maria Curie-Sklodowska. Dr., Maria Curie-Sklodowska U., Lublin, Poland, 1959—, prof., 1971—, dir. Univ. Botanic Garden, 1965-71, head dept. plant geography and Systematics, 1971—. Recipient Knight Bachelor's Cross Polish Revival, Golden Cross of Merit, Meritorious Tchr. of Poland, Minister's award (3 times), Pub. Service Golden Merit award (12 times). Mem. Polish Bot. Soc., Wild Life Preservation Com., Polish Tourist Country-Lover's Assn., N.Y. Acad. Scis. Roman Catholic. Author sci. textbooks. Home: 244 Paganiniego 9, 20-854 Lublin Poland Office: Akademicka 19, 20-033 Lublin Poland

FIKRE-SELASSIE WOGDERESS, prime minister Ethiopia. Prime minister Ethiopia, Addis Ababa. Address: Office Prime Minister, Addis Ababa Ethiopia *

FILALI, ABDELLATIF, diplomat; b. Fez, Jan. 26, 1928. Grad., U. Paris. Joined Ministry of Fgn. Affairs, Morocco, 1957; perm. rep. UN, 1958-59, 78-80; chief Royal Cabinet, Morocco, 1959-61; chargé d'affaires Embassy to France, 1961-62; ambassador to Belgium, the Netherlands and Luxembourg, 1962-63, People's Republic of China, 1965-67, Algeria, 1967-68, Spain, 1970-71, 72-78; minister higher edn., 1968-70, fgn. affairs, 1971-72; ambassador to U.K., 1980-81; minister fgn. affairs and cooperation, 1985—, info., 1985-86. Perm. sec. Acad. Kingdom of Morocco, 1981. Address: Ministry of Fgn Affairs, Rabat Morocco *

FILELLA, JAIME F., psychologist; b. Barcelona, Spain, July 25, 1927; s. Jaime B. and Ana (Ferrer) F.; B.A. (Phil.), Sacred Heart Coll., 1949-52; M.A., Ph.D., Fordham U., 1952-57. Ordained Jesuit priest. Lectr., Universidad Javeriana, 1955-56; prof. psychology St. Xavier's Coll., Bombay, 1957-81; vis. prof. orgnl. psychology ESADE, Barcelona, 1972—, dir. Xavier Inst. Mgmt., 1971-85; vis. sr. lectr. U. Rochester, 1970-71; prof. U. San Francisco Summer Sch., 1971-86; dir. ESADE, Barcelona, Spain, 1988—. Author: Organizational Climate and Commitment Scales. Trustee, St. Xavier's Coll. Trust Soc., Bombay, 1970-83; cons. indsl. and ednl. instns. Mem. Am. Psychol. Assn., Indian Sci. Assn., Am. Mgmt. Assn., Indian Soc. Applied Behavioural Sci., Indian Soc. Tng. and Devel., Internat. Council Psychologists (dir.-at-large 1984-86). Roman Catholic. Address: ESADE, Avenida de Pedralbes 60-62, 08034 Barcelona Spain

FILES, GORDON LOUIS, lawyer, judge; b. Ft. Dodge, Iowa, Mar. 5, 1912; s. James Ray and Anna (Louis) F.; m. Kathryn Thrift, Nov. 24, 1942; children—Kathryn Allen, James Gordon. A.B. in Polit. Sci. with honors, UCLA, 1934; LL.B., Yale U., 1937. Bar: Calif., U.S. Supreme Ct. Law clk. U.S. Ct. Appeals (8th cir.), 1937-38; enforcement atty. Office Price Adminstrn., 1942; ptnr. Freston & Files, Los Angeles, 1938-59; judge Los Angeles Superior Ct., 1959-62; assoc. justice 2d dist., div. 4 Calif. Ct. Appeal, 1962-64, presiding justice, 1964-82, adminstrv. presiding justice, 1970-82; arbitrator, referee and mediator, 1982-86; mem. Jud. Council Calif., 1964-71, 73-77; mem. governing com. Ctr. for Jud. Edn. and Research, 1981-82; mem. bd. govs. State Bar Calif., 1957-59. Bd. editors Yale Law Jour., 1935-37. Served to lt. USN, 1942-45. Fellow Am. Bar Found.; mem. ABA, Am. Judicature Soc., Inst. Jud. Adminstrn., Los Angeles County Bar Assn. (trustee 1952-56), Calif. Judges Assn. (exec. com. 1971-72), Am. Legion, Order of Coif, Phi Beta Kappa, Phi Delta Phi. Democrat. Clubs: Chancery (pres. 1972-73) (Los Angeles); Valley Hunt (Pasadena). Home: 154 S Arroyo Blvd Pasadena CA 91105

FILIPIAK, JANUSZ, electrical engineering educator; b. Bydgoszcz, Poland, Aug. 3, 1952; s. Tadeusz and Cecylia (Chojnacka) F.; m. Elzbieta Staszak, Aug. 20, 1977; children: Anna, Janusz Jeremiasz. MEE, U. Mining and Metallurgy, Krakow, Poland, 1976, PhD in Elec. Engring., 1979. Asst. prof. elec. engring. U. Mining and Metallurgy, 1979-84, prof., 1985—; vis. fellow Ctr. Nat. Study Telecommunications, Paris, 1984-85; research assoc. dept. applied math. U. Adelaide, Australia, 1987-88; dep. dir. Teletraffic Research Ctr., U. Adelaide, 1988—. Author: Modelling and Control of Dynamic Flows in Communication Networks, 1988; contbr. articles to internat. profl. jours. Home: Ul Wyslouchow 21/28, 30-612 Krakow Poland Office: U Mining and Metallurgy, Al Mickiewicza 30, 30-059 Krakow Poland

FILIPS, NICHOLAS JOSEPH, management consultant; b. Garrett, Ind., June 10, 1925; s. John and Elizabeth (Grigore) F.; children by previous marriage: Steven, Mary Beth, Fred John; m. Kathryn V. McDowell, Apr. 6, 1982. Student, U. Detroit, 1942-45, Ind. U., 1945-47; BS in Biology, Am. U., 1948; postgrad., Ind. U., 1979. V.p., mgr. Wayne Pharmacal Supply Co., Ft. Wayne, Ind., 1949-67, pres., chmn. div. Bendway, Inc., South Bend, Ind., 1955-67; v.p., gen. mgr. Karel First-Aid Supply Co., Chgo., 1967-71; pres., gen. mgr. Amedic Surg. Supply Co., Miami, 1971-78; pres., chief exec. officer Med. Supply Co., Inc., Jacksonville, Fla., 1978-81; pres. KNF Med. Enterprises, Inc., 1985—; chmn. bd., pres. Health Distbrs. Mgmt. and Cons. Co. Ltd., Jacksonville, 1981—. Contbr. articles to profl. jours. Benefactor numerous non-profit hosps. and clinics, Colombia, S.Am. Recipient Am. Legion Leadership award, 1939. Mem. Am. Surg. Trade Assn. (Distinctive Service award 1960), Fla. Sheriffs Assn. Democrat. Roman Catholic. Lodge: Lions. Office: Health Distbrs Mgmt and Cons Co Ltd 1837 Sea Oats Dr Atlantic Beach FL 32233

FILLET, MITCHELL HARRIS, financial services executive; b. N.Y.C., Feb. 28, 1948; s. Robert Earl and Barbara Dee (Auerbach) F. BA in Philosophy and Religion, Boston U., 1970; MBA in Fin., NYU, 1978. Trainee Dillon, Read & Co., N.Y.C., 1971-72; salesman Stone & Webster Securities Corp., N.Y.C., 1972-74; asst. v.p. First Boston Corp., N.Y.C., 1974-76; v.p. Bear, Stearns & Co., N.Y.C., 1976-79; exec. v.p., chief fin. officer Auerbach Bath Robe Corp., N.Y.C., 1979-81; v.p. corp. services Merrill Lynch, N.Y.C., 1981—; adj. prof. fin. Fordham U. Martino Grad. Sch. Bus., N.Y.C., 1981—; lectr. in acctg. NYU, 1980-81. Mem. Citizens for Am., Washington, 1984-86, The Jefferson Circle, Washington, 1985, U.S. Senatorial Bus. Adv. Bd., 1988—; spl. adminstrv. asst. City Planning Commn., City of N.Y., 1969. Mem. Am. Biog. Research Inst. (dep. gov.), Boston U. Alumni Assn., Alumni Assn. Grad. Sch. Bus. NYU. Republican. Club: Union League (N.Y.C.). Home: 155 W 68th St New York NY 10023 Office: Merrill Lynch 1185 6th Ave New York NY 10036

FILOSA, GARY FAIRMONT RANDOLPH DE VIANA, II, private investor; b. Wilder, Vt., Feb. 22, 1931; s. Gary F.R. de Marco de Viana and Rosaline M. (Falzarano) Filosa; divorced; children: Marc Christian Bazire de Villadon, III, Gary Fairmont Randolph de Viana, III. Grad., Mt. Hermon Sch., 1950; PhB, U. Chgo., 1954; BA, U. Americas, Mex., 1967; MA, Calif. Western U., 1968; PhD, U.S. Internat. U., 1970. Sports reporter Claremont Daily Eagle, Rutland Herald, Vt. Informer, 1947-52; pub. The Chicagoan, 1952-54; account exec., editor house publs. Robertson, Buckley & Gotsch, Inc., Chgo., 1953-54; account exec. Fuller, Smith & Ross, Inc., N.Y.C., 1955; editor Apparel Arts mag. (now Gentlemen's Quar.), Esquire, Inc., N.Y.C., 1955-56; pres., chmn. bd. Teenarama Records, Inc., N.Y.C., 1956-62; pres., chmn. bd. Filosa Publs. Internat., N.Y.C., 1956-61, Los Angeles, 1974-83, Palm Beach, Fla., 1983-87; pres. Montclair Sch., 1958-60, Pacific Registry, Inc., Los Angeles, 1959-61, Banana Chip Corp. Am., N.Y.C., 1964-67; producer Desilu Studios, Inc., Hollywood, 1960-61; exec. asst. to Benjamin A. Javits, 1961-62; dean adminstrn. Postgrad. Ctr. for Mental Health, N.Y.C., 1962-64; chmn. bd., pres. Producciones Mexicanes Internationales (S.A.), Mexico City, 1957-68, Filosa Films Internat., Beverly Hills, 1962—; pres. Casa Filosa Corp., Palm Beach, Fla., 1982-87; dir. tng. Community Savings, North Palm Beach, Fla., 1983-86; chmn. bd., pres. Cinematografica Americana Internationale (S.A.), Mexico City, 1964-74; v.p. acad. affairs World Acad., San Francisco, 1967-68; asst. headmaster, instr. Latin Bishop Sch., San Diego, 1968-69; asst. to provost Calif. Western U., San Diego, 1968-69; assoc. prof. philosophy Art Coll., San Francisco, 1969-70; v.p. acad. affairs, dean of faculty Internat. Inst., Phoenix, 1968-73; chmn. bd., pres. Universite Universelle, 1970-73; bd. dirs., v.p. acad. affairs, dean Summer Sch., Internat. Community Coll., Los Angeles, 1970-72; chmn. bd., pres. Social Directory Calif., 1967-75, Am. Assn. Social Registries, Los Angeles, 1970-76; pres. Social Directory U.S., N.Y.C., 1974-76; chmn. bd. Internat. Assn. Social Registers, Paris, 1974—; surfing coach U. Calif. at Irvine, 1975-77; instr. history Coastline Community Coll., Fountain Valley, Calif., 1976-77; v.p. Xerox-Systemic, 1979-80; pres., chief exec. officer Internat. Surfing League, Honolulu, 1987—. Pub.: Teenage, Rustic Rhythm, Teen Life, Talent, Rock & Roll Roundup, Celebrities, Stardust, Personalities, Campus monthly mags., N.Y.C., 1956-61; editor: Sci. Digest, 1961-62. Author: (stage play) Let Me Call Ethel, 1955, Technology Enters 21st Century, 1966, musical Feather Light, 1966, No Public Funds for Nonpublic Schools, 1968, Creative Function of the College President, 1969, The Surfers Almanac, 1977, Payne of Florida (TV series), 1985, The Filosa Newsletter, 1986—. Contbr. numerous articles to mags., and profl. jours. and encys. including Sci. Digest, World Book Ency., Ency. of Sports. Trustee Univ. of the Ams., 1986—; candidate for Los Angeles City Council, 1959; chmn. Educators for Reelection of Ivy Baker Priest, 1970; patron Monterey Peninsula Mus. Art, 1978; mem. So. Calif. Com. for Olympic Games, 1977-84; founder, pres. Am. Cath. Ch., 1978—; Served with AUS, 1954-55. Recipient DAR Citizenship award, 1959; Silver Conquistador award Am. Assn. Social Registers, 1970; Ambassador's Cup U. Ams., 1967; resolution Calif. Legislature, 1977; Duke Kahanamoku Classic surfing trophy, 1977; gold pendant Japan Surfing Assn., 1978. Mem. U.S. Surfing Found. (founder, pres. 1974-76), Am. Surfing Assn. (founder, pres. 1960-78, chmn. exec. com. 1974-78, pres. 1980-86), Internat. Surfing Com. (founder, pres. 1960—), U.S. Surfing Com. (founder, pres. 1960—), Am. Walking Soc. (founder, pres. 1980—), Internat. Walking Soc. (founder, pres. 1987), Am. Assn. UN, Authors League, Alumni Assn. U. Americas (pres. 1967-70), Sierra Club, NAACP, NCAA (bd. dels. 1977-82), AAU (gov. 1978-82), Sigma Omicron Lambda (founder, pres. 1965emocrat. Episcopalian. Clubs: Embajadores (U. of Americas, Puebla, Mex.); Palm Beach Surf (Fla); Coral Reef Soc. (Palm Beach). Address: PO Box 2042 Miami Beach FL 33140 Other: PO Box 1315 Beverly Hills CA 90213

FILSTRUP, SCOTT HOGENSON, marketing consultant; b. Evanston, Ill., Apr. 4, 1942; s. Alvin William, Jr., and Elaine H. (Hogenson) F.; B.S.C.E., Northwestern U., 1965, M.B.A., 1967; m. Margaret McGinnis, Dec. 21, 1967; children—Laura Leigh, Scott Douglas. Comml. devel. supr. Monsanto Co., St. Louis, 1973-74; dir. industry planning Agrico Chem. Co., The Williams Co., Tulsa, 1974-76, mgr. planning Edgcomb Metals Co. div., 1977-78, mgr. bus. and market devel., 1978-80, exec. adminstr. The Williams Cos., 1980-81; mgr. strategic planning MAPCO, Inc., Tulsa, 1981-82; pres., chief exec. officer EPM Industries, Inc., Tulsa, 1982-84; v.p., gen. mgr. Polyvoltac, Inc., 1984-86; pres. Consultants Ltd., Tulsa, 1986—; nat. speaker mkgt., planning, chem. and metals industries. Mem. adv. council mktg. Tulsa U.; bd. dirs. Jr. Achievement of Tulsa, 1979-87, exec., adv. and nat. awards; adv. bd. Tulsa Econ. Devel. Commn., 1978-82; bd. dirs., treas. Community Services of Tulsa, Met. Tulsa Transit Authority; trustee Kirk of the Hills Presbyterian Ch. Recipient Alumni award Northwestern U., 1980. Mem. Am. Mktg. Assn. (pres. Tulsa chpt. 1979-80, nat. v.p. indsl. mktg. 81-83), Automotive Parts and Accessories Assn. (bd. dirs., chmn. mktg. com.), Tulsa Econs. Club (pres. 1977-79), 500 Exec. Assn. Republican. Clubs: Rotary, Univ., Northwestern U. Alumni of Okla. (pres. 1976-84). Contbr. articles to Am. Mktg. Jour., Econs., Tulsa, others. Home: 7412 E 67th Pl Tulsa OK 74133

FINAS, LUCETTE RENÉE, literature educator; b. Grenoble, Isére, France, July 13, 1921; d. René Jean and Louise Augustine (Payen) F. Agrégation, U. Paris, 1947, D in Contemporary Lit., 1977. Prof. U. Paris VIII, St. Denis, 1969—, Coll. Internat. De Philosophie, Paris, 1983—; vis. Fulbright prof. NYU, 1987. Author 6 books. Named officer Palmes Acad., 1978. Home: 56 Blvd Beaumarchais, 75011 Paris France Office: U St Denis, 2 rue de la Liberte, 93526 Paris France

FINCH, CALEB ELLICOTT, neurobiologist, educator; b. London, July 4, 1939; came to U.S., 1939; s. Benjamin F. and Faith (Stratton) Campbell; m. Doris Nossamen, Oct. 11, 1975. B.S., Yale U., 1961; Ph.D., Rockefeller U., 1969. Guest investigator Rockefeller U., N.Y.C., 1969-70; asst. prof. Cornell U. Med. Coll., N.Y.C., 1970-72; asst. prof. biology, gerontology U. So. Calif., Los Angeles, 1972-75, assoc. prof., 1975-78, prof., 1978—; ARCO and William Kieschnick prof. neurobiology of aging U. So. Calif., 1985—; mem. cell biology study sect. NIH, Bethesda, Md., 1975-78; prin. investigator co-dir. Alzheimer Disease Research Ctr. So. Calif.; mem. sci. adv. counsil Nat. Inst. Aging, 1987—, sci. adv. bd. Nat. Inst. Health, 1987—. Editor: Handbook of Biology of Aging, 1977, 85; mem. editorial bd.: Jour. Gerontology, 1979-86, Neurobiology of Aging, 1982—; contbr. 200 articles to sci. jours. Cons. Office of Tech. Assessment, U.S. Congress, Washington, 1982-84. NIH research grantee, 1972—; postdoctoral fellow, 1969-71; recipient Brookdale award 1985, Allied-Signal Inc. award Achievement in Biomed. Aging, 1988. Fellow AAAS, Gerontol. Soc. Am. (Robert W. Kleemeier award 1984); mem. Endocrine Soc., Neurosci. Soc., Neuroendocrine Soc., Psychoneuroendocrine Soc., Soc. Study Reprodn. Home: 2144 Crescent Dr Altadena CA 91001 Office: U So Calif University Park Los Angeles CA 90089-0191

FINCH, MICHAEL PAUL, lawyer; b. Galveston, Tex., Jan. 4, 1946; s. Albert Lynn and Ila Belle (Robertson) F.; m. Rebecca Jean Minnear, Dec. 27, 1969; children: Michael Paul, Rachelle Jean. BEE cum laude, Rice U., 1969, MEE, 1969; JD magna cum laude, U. Houston, 1972. Bar: Tex. 1973. Petroleum engr. Exxon Corp., Houston, 1969-72; assoc. Vinson & Elkins, Houston, 1972-79, ptnr., 1980—. Dir. Houston Pops Orch., 1988—. Mem. ABA, Tex. Bar Assn., Houston Bar Assn., Am. Contact Bridge League (life master 1964—). Republican. Methodist. Clubs: Houston Ctr., Governors (Houston). Rice U. (founder). Home: 12531 Overcup Dr Houston TX 77024 Office: Vinson & Elkins 3300 First City Tower 1001 Fannin Houston TX 77002

FINCH, THOMAS WESLEY, corrosion engineer; b. Alhambra, Calif., Dec. 17, 1946; s. Charles Phillip and Marian Louisa (Bushey) F.; m. Jinx L. Heath, Apr. 1979. Student Colo. Sch. Mines, 1964-68. Assayer, prospector Raymond P. Heon, Inc., Idaho Springs, Colo., 1968; corrosion engr. Cathodic Protection Service, Denver, 1973-80, area mgr., Lafayette, La., 1980-81; area mgr. Corrintec/USA, Farmington, N.Mex., 1981-83; dist. mgr. Cathodic Protection Services Co., Farmington, 1983—. Served with C.E., U.S. Army, 1968-72. Mem. Nat. Assn. Corrosion Engrs., Soc. Am. Mil. Engrs., U.S. Ski Assn., Am. Security Council (nat. adv. bd. 1978—), Kappa Sigma. Republican. Lutheran. Home: 1710 E 22d St Farmington NM 87401 Office: PO Box 388 Farmington NM 87499

FINCH, WALTER GOSS GILCRIST, lawyer, engineer; b. Balt., Jan. 25, 1918; s. Walter G. and Lena May (Koontz) F.; m. Mary Adele Roberts, June 25, 1943; children—Vida Marilena McCarty, Lillian Bonnie Murakoshi, Robin Lee, Ruth Mae; m. Patricia Ann Reed, Feb. 22, 1976. B.Engring., Johns Hopkins U., 1940, M. Engring., 1950; LLB, Temple U., 1949, M.B.A., 1950, J.D., 1969; LL.M., George Washington U., 1949; grad., Command and Gen. Staff Coll., 1953, Nat. War Coll., 1965, Indsl. Coll. Armed Forces, 1965. Bar: Md. 1947, D.C. 1951, U.S. Supreme Ct. 1951; registered profl. engr. D.C.; CPA, Md. Asst. patent counsel Office of Sponsored Research, Johns Hopkins U., Balt., 1951-57, patent counsel, 1957-73; sole practice patent, trademark, copyright and taxation law Balt., 1957—. Co-author: The Romance of Invention of the Eastern and Western Worlds; also numerous publs. on patents. Pres. Md. Crime Investigating Commn., 1963-66, gen. counsel, 1963-75; mem. World Peace Through Law Ctr., 1964—; mem. adv. council Catonsville Community Coll., 1959-76, sec.-treas., 1962-64, pres., 1967-68; mem. exec. bd. Balt. Area council Boy Scouts Am.; del. Md. Constl. Conv., 1967-68; Dem. candidate for U.S. Senate, 1968, 70, 74, 76, for U.S. Congress, 1956, 66, for atty. gen. Md., 1978. Served with AUS, 1941-46, ETO; col. Res. ret. 1973. Decorated Bronze Star. Recipient Silver Beaver award Boy Scouts Am., 1969. Mem. Bar Assn. Balt. City, Md. Bar Assn., Fed. Bar Assn. (bd. dirs. Balt. chpt. 1971-80), Inter-Am. Bar Assn., ABA, Internat. Bar Assn., Am. Patent Law Assn., Internat. Patent and Trademark Assn., Nat. Soc. Profl. Engrs., Md. Soc. Profl. Engrs., Md. Acad. Scis., ASME, Soc. Am. Mil. Engrs., Res. Officers Assn. (pres. Patapsco chpt. 1956-57), Balt. Assn. Commerce, Catonsville Community Assn., Md. Hist. Soc., English Speaking Union. Democrat. Presbyterian. Clubs: Johns Hopkins Faculty and Alumni, Merchants of Balt., Nat. Lawyers, Rolling Rd. Golf, Army and Navy. Lodges: Mason (K.T., Shriner). Office: 1501-1503 Fidelity Bldg Baltimore MD 21201

FINCH, WILLIAM GEORGE HAROLD, radio engineer; b. Birmingham, Eng., June 28, 1897; came to U.S., 1906; s. William Joseph and Amelia (Skelding) F.; m. Elsie Grace George, Nov. 29, 1916 (dec. May 1967); 1 child, Eloise Grace Finch Tholen; m. Helen Stork Ambler, Feb. 1, 1969. Grad., Woodward High Sch., Cin.; elec. engring. course with Allis-Chalmers at U. Cin., Norwood, Ohio, 1915; radio communication course, Marconi Inst., N.Y.C., 1917; completed spl. course radio engring. and patent law, Columbia U., 1923; D.Sc. (hon.), Fla. Inst. Tech., 1983. Registered profl. engr., N.Y. patent atty. Asst. engr. Cleve. Electric Illuminating Co., 1916-17; inspecting engr. Nat. Dist. Telegraph Co., N.Y.C., N.Y. Compensating Rating Bd., 1917-19; elec. engr. Royal Indemnity Co., 1919-21; radio engr. and editor Internat. News Service, 1921—; chief engr. Hearst Radio, 1928-34; asst. chief engr. and chief telephone engring. div. FCC and chief engr. fed. investigation telephone cos., 1934-35; pres. Finch Telecommunications, Inc., N.Y.C., 1935-41, Conn. Indsl. Research Corp., Newtown, 1956—; founder, owner Sta. WGHF-FM, N.Y.C., 1946-49; v.p. Sta. WCAE, Pitts.; dir. communications Rowley Newspapers of Ohio, Ashtabula; dir. Telecommunication Cons. Internat. Inc., Washington; patent atty., U.S. and Can.; cons. profl. engr., electronic, facsimile communications and patent engring.; mem. Internat. Radio Consultive Com., U.S. Congl. Adv. Bd.; mem. tech. com. on radio and cable communication Am. Newspaper Pubs. Assn., 1924—; mem. com. allocation of frequency Fourth Nat. Radio Conf.; del. Internat. Telegraphic and Radio Telegraphic Conf., Madrid, 1932, N.Am. Radio Conf., Mexico City, 1933. Contbr. numerous articles to profl. jours. Mem. 1st F.A., N.Y. N.G., 1917-18; lt. (s.g.) USNR; exec. officer U.S. Navy Communication Res., 3d Naval Dist., 1929—, N.Y.C.; comdr. USN, 1913-45; capt., asst. chief Office Naval Research, 1945-57; ret. Decorated Legion of Merit; recipient Presdl. award; Disting. Alumnus award for outstanding achievement U. Cin. Coll. Engring., 1985; active U.S. Congl. Adv. Bd., 1984—. Fellow IEEE (award 1956, Centennial medal for extraordinary achievement 1984), Radio Club Am. (dir. emeritus, Amstrong medal 1976, Dr. Lee DeForest award 1984); mem. N.Y. Acad. Scis., Armed Forces Communications and Electronics Assn., Mil. Order World Wars, Am. Legion, AAAS, Am. Phys. Soc., Franklin Inst. Episcopalian (vestryman). Clubs: Mason. (N.Y.), Bankers (N.Y.), Army and Navy (N.Y.); Masons (Buffalo); Army and Navy (Washington); Crown Point Country, N.Y. Yacht, N.Y. Athletic; Saint and Sinners Yacht (Port St. Lucie, Fla.) (sec. 1965—, commodore 1978-79); St. Lucie (Stuart, Fla.) (rear commodore); Anchor Line Yacht (Jensen Beach, Fla.). Home: 3025 Morningside Blvd Port Saint Lucie FL 34952

FINCHELL, A. RICHARD, financial marketing executive; b. N.Y.C., Jan. 18, 1927; s. Joseph H. and Henrietta (Fritz) F.; B.S. in Social Scis., CCNY, 1947; Doctorat-es-Lettres, U. Paris, 1951; m. Margherita Iskra, Dec. 21, 1971; 1 dau., Mayra Molne-Finchell. Pres., Greater Miami Savs. Center (Fla.), 1954-68, North Am. Fund Mgmt. Corp., London, 1959—, North Am. Group, London, 1961—, Noram Secured Income N.V., Amsterdam, Netherlands, 1970—, North Am. Mgmt. Corp., London, 1977—, North Am. Assets Trust Ltd., London, 1977—; mng. dir. Noramtrust, London, 1976—; chmn. dir. North Am. Fin. Markets Ltd., London, 1969—. Served with U.S. Army, 1945-46. Nichiren Shoshu Buddhist. Office: 15 Bedford Row, London WC1R 4BX, England

FINCK, KEVIN WILLIAM, lawyer; b. Whittier, Calif., Dec. 14, 1954; s. William Albert and Ester (Gutbub) F. BA, U. Calif., Santa Barbara, 1977; JD, U. Calif., San Francisco, 1980. Bar: Calif. 1980. Assoc. Law Offices of E.O.C. Ord, San Francisco, 1980-85; ptnr. Ord & Finck, San Francisco, 1985-87, Ord and Norman, San Francisco, 1987—. Author: California Corporation Start Up Package and Minute Book, 1982, 5th rev. edit. 1988, Representation of Foreign Investors in the United STates: A Brief Overview, vol. 7 San Francisco Barrister Law Jour. No. 3. Republican Methodist. Office: Ord & Norman 1 Maritime Plaza #1313 San Francisco CA 94111

FINE, DAVID JEFFREY, hospital executive, consultant, lecturer; b. Flushing, N.Y., Oct. 10, 1950; s. Arnold and Phyllis Fine; m. Susan Gory, Dec. 29, 1985; 1 child, Jeffrey Jacob. BA, Tufts U., 1972; MHA, U. Minn., 1974. Asst. to dir. U. Calif. Hosp., San Francisco, 1974-76, asst. dir., 1976-78; sr. assoc. dir. U. Nebr. Hosp. and Clinic, Omaha, 1978-83; adminstr. W.Va. Univ. Hosp., Morgantown, 1983-84; pres. W.Va. Univ. Hosps., Inc., Morgantown, 1984-87; pres., chief operating officer Health Net, Charleston, W.Va, 1985-87; vice provost for health affairs, chief exec. officer U. Cin. Health System, 1987—; prof. pharmacy U. Cin., 1987—; cons. Merck, Sharp & Dohme, West Point, Pa., 1983—, Eli Lilly & Co., Indpls., 1984, DuPont Critical Care, Chgo.; bd. dirs., exec. com. Univ. Hosp. Consortium, Atlanta, 1983—. Mem. editorial bd. Hospital Formulary, 1982-87; contbr. jour. articles, book chpts. and films. Trustee Monongalia Arts Council, 1984-86, Cin. Chamber Orch., 1987—. Recipient James A. Hamilton prize, U. Minn., 1974; W. K. Kellog fellow. Fellow Am. Coll. Hosp. Adminstrs. (Robert S. Hudgens Young Adminstr. of Yr. award 1985), Royal Soc. Medicine, Royal Coll. Medicine; mem. Am. Hosp. Assn. (mem. ho. of dels., mem. governing council sect. on met. hosps.), Omicron Delta Epsilon. Jewish. Club: Cin. Bankers. Lodge: Rotary.

FINE, J(AMES) ALLEN, insurance company executive; b. Albemarle, N.C., May 2, 1934; s. Samuel Lee and Ocie (Loflin) F.; student Pfeiffer Coll., 1957-58; BS, U. N.C., 1961, MBA, 1965; m. Marie Nan Morris, Sept. 1, 1957; children: James A(llen), William Morris. Sr. accountant Haskins & Sells, CPA's Charlotte, N.C., 1961-62, Watson, Penry, & Morgan, Asheboro, N.C., 1962-64; instr. U. N.C., Chapel Hill, 1964-65; asst. prof. Pfeiffer Coll., Misenheimer, N.C., 1965-66; treas., v.p. adminstrn. Nat. Lab. for Higher Edn. (formerly Regional Edn. Lab. Carolinas and Va.), Durham, N.C., 1966-72; organizer, chief exec. officer, treas., dir. Investors Title Ins. Co., Inc., Chapel Hill, 1972—; chief exec. officer, treas., dir. Investors Title Ins. Co., Inc., Columbia, S.C., 1973—; pres., dir. Investors Title Co., Inc., Chapel Hill, 1976—; developer Carolina Forest Subdiv., Chapel Hill, 1970-78, Springhill Forest subdiv., Chapel Hill, 1977-80, Stoneycreek subdiv., 1978—; lectr. accounting U. N.C., Chapel Hill, 1967-70. Area officer ann. alumni giving U. N.C., Chapel Hill, 1968-69, 71-73, 75—. Served with USN, 1953-57. Recipient Haskins & Sells Found. award for excellence in accounting, 1961; N.C. Assn. CPA's award for most outstanding accounting student U. N.C., 1961. Mem. Am. Inst. CPA's, N.C. Assn. CPA's, Am. Accounting Assn., Am. Land Title Assn. (research com. 1983, membership com. 1984-85, exec. com. underwriters sect. 1986), CEDAR Bus. Mgrs. (chmn. nat. exec. com. 1971), Nat. Assn. Ins. Commrs. (liaison com. 1987—), Phi Beta Kappa, Beta Gamma Sigma (treas. 1961). Home: 112 Carolina Forest Chapel Hill NC 27514 Office: Investors Title Bldg Chapel Hill NC 27514

FINE, KENNETH RICHARD, computer software consultant; b. Boston, Sept. 14, 1956; s. Henry Selwyn and Shirley Miriam (Lipof) F. AB, Syracuse U., 1978; MBA, Tulane U., 1984. Acct. exec. Arnold & Co., Boston, 1979; ter. rep. Addison-Wesley Pub., Reading, Mass., 1980; underwriter Gray and Co., Metairie, La., 1982-83; pres. Decision Analysis, New Orleans, 1984-85; software cons. Compumark, Inc., New Orleans, 1985-86; pres. Computer Info., Inc., New Orleans, 1986—, Software Wizardry, Inc., New Orleans, 1986-87; project leader Lewton Technologies Inc., Boston, 1987—; software cons. Canal Street Assocs., New Orleans, 1981—, computer analyst Citta Enterprises, Inc., New Orleans, 1981. Sports corr. Needham (Mass.) Times, 1971-74. Staff worker campaign Jimmy Carter for Pres., Syracuse, 1976, McGovern for Pres., Needham, 1972. Democrat. Jewish.

FINE, RICHARD ISAAC, lawyer; b. Milw., Jan. 22, 1940; s. Jack and Frieda F.; m. Maryellen Olman, Nov. 25, 1982; 1 child, Victoria Elizabeth. B.S., U. Wis., 1961; J.D., U. Chgo., 1964; Ph.D. in Internat. Law, U. London, 1967; cert., Hague (Netherlands) Acad. Internat. Law, 1965, 66; cert. comparative law, Internat. U. Comparative Sci., Luxembourg, 1966; diplome superiere, Faculte Internat. pour l'Ensignment du Droit Compare, Strasbourg, France, 1967. Bar: Ill. 1964, D.C. 1972, Calif. 1973. Trial atty. fgn. commerce sect. antitrust div. Dept. Justice, 1968-72; chief antitrust div. Los Angeles City Atty.'s Office, also spl. counsel gov. efficiency com., 1973-74; prof. internat., comparative and EEC antitrust law U. Syracuse (N.Y.) Law Sch. (overseas program), summers 1970-72; individual practice Richard I. Fine and Assocs., Los Angeles, 1974; mem. antitrust adv. bd. Bur. Nat. Affairs, 1981—. Contbr. articles to legal publs. Mem. ABA (chmn. subcom. internat. antitrust and trade regulations, internat. law sect. 1972-77, co-chmn. com. internat. econ. orgn. 1977-79), Am. Soc. Internat. Law (co-chmn. com. corp. membership 1978-83, mem. exec. council 1984-87), Am. Fgn. Law Assn., Internat. Law Assn., Brit. Inst. Internat. and Comparative Law, State Bar Calif. (chmn. antitrust and trade regulation law sect. 1981-84, exec. com. 1981-87), Retinitis Pigmentosa Internat. (bd. dirs. 1985—), Los Angeles County Bar Assn. (chmn. antitrust sect. 1977-78), Ill. Bar Assn., Am. Friends London Sch. Econs. (bd. dirs. 1984—, co-chmn. So. Calif. chpt. 1984—), Phi Delta Phi. Address: Suite 1000 10100 Santa Monica Blvd Los Angeles CA 90067

FINE, TIMOTHY HERBERT, lawyer; b. Washington, Oct. 11, 1937; s. Nathan and Emily Newhall (Brown) F.; m. Mary Ellen Fox, June 16, 1960; children: Margaret Carol, Susan Emily, Rachel Winslow. B.E.E., U. Va., 1959; M.S. in E.E., U. So. Calif., 1962; LL.B., U. Calif.-Berkeley, 1965. Bar: Calif. 1966, U.S. Dist. Ct. (no., ea., so. and cen. dists.) Calif. 1966, U.S. Ct. Appeals (9th cir.) 1966, U.S. Supreme Ct. 1971. Law clk. to Hon. William T. Sweigert, U.S. Dist. Judge, San Francisco, 1965-67; assoc. G. Joseph Bertain, Jr., San Francisco, 1967-77; prin. Law Offices of Timothy H. Fine, San Francisco, 1977—; del. White House Conf. Small Bus., 1980, chmn. No. Calif. delegation, 1986; del. Calif. State Confs. Small Bus., 1980, 82, 84, 86, 1st v.p., 1984-86; chmn. San Francisco Bay Area Small Bus. Caucus, 1984, Small Bus. Legal Def. Com., 1982—; author, lectr., cons., trial atty. on antitrust, franchise and small bus. legal matters.; mem. nat. adv. council U.S. Senate Small Bus. Com., 1983—; mem. adv. bd. Calif. Senate Select Com. Small Bus., 1983—; mem. Calif. Bd. Registration Profl. Engrs., 1982-86. Bd. dirs. Boalt Hall Law Sch. Alumni Assn., 1983-86, 87—; nat. advisor drafting com. Uniform Franchise and Bus. Oppurtunites Act, 1985—. Served to lt. USAF, 1959-62. Mem. ABA (mem. governing bd., forum com. on franchising 1977-84, chmn. 1983 forum on franchising, mem. gov. bd. standing com. on specialization 1986—, author model standards for franchise law), Internat. Bar Assn., Fed. Bar Assn. (exec. com. San Francisco chpt.), State Bar of Calif., The Bar Assn. San Francisco, Lawyers Club of San Francisco. Clubs: Berkeley Tennis, Calif. Commonwealth. Home: 747 San Diego Rd Berkeley CA 94707 Office: 49 Geary St Suite 450 San Francisco CA 94108

FINE, WILLIAM MICHAEL, corporation counselor; b. N.Y.C., July 1, 1926; s. J. George and Susan (Morse) F.; m. Patricia Purdy, Aug. 22, 1948 (div. Apr. 1967); children: Brewster, Douglas, Timothy; m. Rosaleen Garvey, June 15, 1980; 1 son, Alexander Garvey. B.A., Kenyon Coll., 1950. Pub. dir. Harpers Bazaar and Town & Country, N.Y.C., 1960-67, Hearst Mags., N.Y.C., 1967-69; pres., chief exec. officer Bonwit Teller, N.Y.C., 1969-74; pres., chier exec. officer Wamsutta Mills, N.Y.C., 1974-77; chmn., chief exec. officer Frances Denney Corp., Inc., Phila., 1977-82; pres. Dan River Mills, Inc., Danville, Va., 1982—, N.Y.C., 1982-86; chmn. WMF Fund Inc., U.S. and London, 1986—; dir. Galway Crystal Co., Ireland, 1982—, Morgan Oates, Pentland Industries, PLC, London; Towle Co., Boston, 1983—, Shearson, Lehman Bros, London and N.Y.; cons., dir. Hermes, Paris, 1982—. Author: That Day with God, 1964; contbr. articles to various mags. Mem. Adv. Council of the Arts-Presdl. Commn., Washington, 1982—; U.S.-Ireland Council; trustee Georgian Soc., Ireland; U.S. Dept. State observer Anglo-Irish Accord. Served with inf. AUS, 1944-46, ETO. Decorated Bronze Star. Republican. Clubs: Wee Burn Country (Darien, Conn.); Union League (N.Y.C.), Temple Golf (Hurley, U.K.). Home: 60 Westover Rd Stamford CT 06904 Office: WMF Fund Inc 90 Park Ave New York NY 10016

FINEBERG, DAVID L(EMAN), lawyer; b. Hartford, Conn., Nov. 21, 1931; s. Morris W. and Ida (Leman) F.; m. Barbara E. Gold, Sept. 5, 1955; children—Marcia E., Diane E., Laura E. B.A., Colgate U., 1953; LL.B., Columbia U., 1956. Bar: Conn. 1956, Fla. 1976. With Schatz & Schatz, Hartford, 1956-76; mem. firm Albrecht & Richman, Hartford, 1976-77; ptnr., Moller, Horton & Fineberg, P.C., Hartford, 1978—. Cntbr. to legal jours. Mem. town council Town of Bloomfield, Conn., 1965-67, chmn. charter revision com. 1969-70; v.p., legal counsel Conn. Opera Assn., Hartford, 1972-83. Harlan Fiske Stone scholar 1956. Mem. ABA, Conn. Bar Assn., Fla. Bar Assn., Hartford County Bar Assn. Home: 49 Hurdle Fence Dr Avon CT 06001 Office: 90 Gillett St Hartford CT 06105

FINEDORE, WILLIAM FRANCIS, SR., manufacturing company executive; b. Grand Rapids, Mich., Apr. 11, 1923; s. William and Clara Finedore; m. Grace M. Brush, Apr. 28, 1952; children—William F., Thomas E., James G., Nancy C., Jeffrey P. Student pub. schs., Chgo. With mech. div. Kraft Foods, Morton Grove, Ill., 1945-62; from apprentice sheetmetal layout to leadman Dover div. Groen Mfg. Co., Elk Grove, Ill., 1962-72; from foreman to supt. custom div. Leedal Inc., Chgo., 1972-77; plant mgr. Bloomfield Indsl. div. Beatrice Foods, Chgo., 1977-78; dir. mfg., supt. custom div. Elkay Mfg. Co., Broadview, Ill., 1978—. Served with USMC, 1942-45. Recipient Ill. Swimming Assn. Swimming and Diving Ofcls. award, 1981; North Suburban YMCA Swim Coach award, 1973. Mem. Nat. Skeet Shooting Assn., Nat. Rifle Assn., Boat Owners Assn. U.S., Mfg. Mgrs. Assn. (past pres.), Republican. Roman Catholic. Clubs: Northbrook Sports, Gt. Lakes Cruising, Harbor Lite Yacht, Keymen's (pres. execs. Elkay Mfg. Co.). Home: 1850 Beechnut Rd Northbrook IL 60062 Office: Elkay Mfg Co 2700 S 17th Ave Broadview IL 60153

FINGER, JOHN HOLDEN, lawyer; b. Oakland, Calif., June 29, 1913; s. Clyde P. and Jennie (Miller) F.; m. Dorothy C. Riley, Dec. 30, 1950; children: Catherine, John Jr., David, Carol. A.B., U. Calif., 1933. Bar: Calif. 1937. Pvt. practice of law San Francisco, 1937-42; chief mil. commn. sect. Far East Hdqrs. War Dept., Tokyo, 1946-47; mem. firm Hoberg Finger Brown Cox & Molligan, San Francisco, 1947—; trustee Pacific Sch. Religion, bd. chmn., 1969-78; bd. dirs. Calif. Maritime Acad., San Francisco Legal Aid Soc., 1955-70; bd. visitors Judge Adv. Gen. Sch., Charlottesville, Va., 1964-76, Stanford U. Law Sch., 1969-71. Pres. Laymen's Fellowship, No. Calif. Conf. Congl. Chs., 1951-53, moderator, 1954-55. Served to maj. JAGC AUS, 1942-46; col. Res. ret.; comdg. officer 5th Judge Adv. Gen. Detachment, 1962-64; U.S. Army Judiciary, 1967-68. Decorated Legion of Merit. Fellow Am. Bar Found., Am. Coll. Trial Lawyers; mem. Am. Judicature Soc., Am. Bar Assn. (ho. of dels. 1970-78, council jud. adminstrn. div. 1972-77, standing com. assn. communications), Bar Assn. San Francisco (dir. 1960-62, recipient John A. Sutro award for legal excellence 1980), Judge Adv. Assn. (dir. 1957—, pres. 1964-65), Lawyers Club San Francisco (pres. 1953, dir. 1950—), State Bar Calif. (bd. govs. 1965-68, pres. 1967-68), Sierra Club (exec. com. legal def. fund), Phi Alpha Delta, Sigma Phi Epsilon, Alpha Kappa Phi. Home: 12675 Skyline Blvd Oakland CA 94619 Office: Hoberg Finger et al 703 Market St San Francisco CA 94103

FINIZZI, MARGUERITE H(ELENE), educator; b. Allentown, Pa., Nov. 16, 1934; d. John Michael and Margaret Mary (Havrilla) Martin; BS in Secondary Edn., Kutztown State Coll., 1956; MA in English, Lehigh U., 1973; m. Joseph Anthony Finizzi, Nov. 19, 1954. Tchr. English, Harrison-Morton Jr. High Sch., Allentown, 1956-64, Louis E. Dieruff High Sch., Allentown, 1964-76, Allen High Sch., Allentown, 1976—; adviser pubs. Allen HighSch., 1978—, Quill and Scroll chpt., 1978, intramural bowling, 1985-88; instr. to develop. drug edn. competency for tchrs., Pa. dept. edn. Student Assistance Program and Intervention Team Tng., 1987; mem. in-service council Allentown Sch. Dist., 1987—; discussion leader for jr. classes Jewish Day Sch., 1969-71; v.p. Fearless Ladies Bowling League, 1986-89; judge numerous acad. contests, Tchr. Expectations and Student Achievement (TESA), 1987, Allentown Sch. Dist. coordinator for TESA Program, 1988; lectr., speaker in field; seminar discussion leader Council of Youth, 1980; adviser Student Newspaper Adv. Program. Pres. Lehigh County (Pa.) Coordinating Council, 1967-71; mem. steering com. Allentown Sch. Dist., 1984. Recipient Meritorious award Kutztown State Coll., 1956; Newspaper Fund fellow, 1981; Commonwealth Partnerships fellow for lit. Inst. Secondary Tchrs., 1985. Mem. NEA, AAUW, Nat. Council Tchrs. English (co-chmn. conf. 1985, bd. judges 1987-88), Pa. Council Tchrs. English (bd. judges, 1987-88), Pa. State Edn. Assn. (editor eastern region constn.), Allentown Edn. Assn. (social chairperson 1964-79, exec. sec. 1964-69), Allentown Women Tchrs. Club (editor constn. and by-laws, welfare chmn. 1986-88), Lehigh U. Alumni, Kutztown U. Alumni (pres. Lehigh County 1969-72), Columbia Sch. Press Assn. (bd. judges, 1987-88, adviser Reflector Sci. newsletter, 1979-80), Pa. Sch. Press Assn. Home: 3025 Pearl Ave Allentown PA 18103

FINK, AARON HERMAN, box manufacturing executive; b. Union City, N.J., Apr. 1, 1916; s. Jacob and Tessie (Dubow) F.; m. Roslyn Lamb, Dec. 6, 1942; children: Elliot, Illene. AB, Johns Hopkins U., 1938; PhD in Bus. Adminstrn. (hon.), Hamilton State U., 1977, World U., 1982, Marquis Guiseppe Scichules Univ., 1985. Treas., Associated Mills, 1938-45; now dir.; v.p., gen. mgr. Essex Paper Box Mfg. Co., Newark, 1945-48, pres., 1948—; pres. Internat. Gift Box Co., 1948—; U.S. del. Conf. Mfrs., Paris, 1954, Spl. Econ. Mission to Italy, 1954. Mem. N.J. Paper Box Mfg. Assn. (trustee), N.J. Box Craft Bur. (pres.), Am. Soc. Quality Control, TAPPI, NAM, Am. Mgmt. Assn. (pres.'s assoc.), AIM (fellow pres.'s council, adv. bd.), Nat. Soc. Bus. Budgeting, Confrerie de la Chaine des Rotisseurs, Am. Material Handling Soc., Am. Forestry Assn., Am. Soc. Advancement Mgmt., Nat. Paper Box Assn. (dir., assoc. chmn. met. div., chmn. plant ops. and manpower), AIAA, Am. Geophys. Union, Am. Ordnance Assn., N.Y. Acad. Scis., Nat. Space Inst., Fedn. Aeronautique Internat, Seaview C. of C. Assn. N.J. Clubs: Princeton, World Trade, Johns Hopkins (N.Y.C.); Crestmont Country (gov.) (Great Oak); Newark Athletic, Downtown (Newark); Broken Sound Golf, Boca Raton, Fla.; Le Mirador Country (Lake Geneva, Switzerland); Seaview Country. Home: 20 Crestwood Dr Maplewood NJ 07040 Office: 281 Astor St Newark NJ 07114

FINK, CHARLES AUGUSTIN, behavioral systems scientist; b. McAllen, Tex., Jan. 1, 1929; s. Charles Adolph and Mary Nellie (Bonneau) F.; A.A., Pan-Am. U., 1948; B.S., Marquette U., 1950; postgrad. No. Va. Community Coll., 1973, George Mason U., 1974; M.A., Cath. U. Am., 1979; m. Ann Heslen, June 1, 1955 (dec. June 1981); children—Patricia A., Marianne E., Richard G., Gerard A. Journalist, UP and Ft. Worth Star-Telegram, 1950-52; commd. 2d lt. U.S. Army, 1952, advanced through grades to lt. col., 1966, various positions telecommunications, 1952-56, teaching, 1956-58, exec. project mgmt., 1958-62, def. analysis and research, 1962-65, fgn. mil. relations, 1965-67, def. telecommunications exec., 1967-69, chief planning, budget and program control office Def. Satellite Communications Program, Def. Communications Agy., 1969-72, ret. 1972; pvt. practice cons. managerial behavior Falls Church, Va., 1972-77; Editor, publisher (jour.) Circle, 1988—; pres. Behavioral Systems Sci. Orgn. and predecessor, Falls Church, 1978—; leader family group dynamics, 1958-67. Adv. bd. Holy Redeemer Roman Cath. Ch., Bangkok, Thailand, St. Philip's Ch., Falls Church, Va., 1971-73. Decorated Army Commendation medals, Joint Services Commendation medal; named to Fink Hall of Fame, 1982; recipient Behavior Modeling award Internat. Congress Applied Systems Research and Cybernetics, 1980. Mem. Internat. Soc. Gen. Systems Research, Am. Soc. Cybernetics, Internat. Assn. Cybernetics, Internat. Network for Social Network Analysis, Assn. U.S. Army, Ret. Officers Assn., Finks Internat. (v.p. 1981—). Club: K.C. Developer hierarchial theory of human behavior, 1967—, uses in behavioral, social and biol. sci. and their applications, 1972—, behavioral causal modeling research methodology, 1974—, computer-aided behavior systems coaching for persons and orgns., 1982—, adv. for copyrighting computer graphics displays. Home: 3305 Brandy Ct Falls Church VA 22042 Office: PO Box 2051 Falls Church VA 22042

FINK, DONALD GLEN, engineer, editor; b. Englewood, N.J., Nov. 8, 1911; s. Harold Gardner and Margaret (Glen) F.; m. Alice Marjorie Berry, Apr. 10, 1948; children: Kathleen Marion, Stephen Donald, Susan Carol (Mrs. Daniel J. Ehrlich). B.S., MIT, 1933; M.S., Columbia U., 1942. Research asst. MIT, 1933-34; staff radiation lab. Mass. Inst. Tech., 1941-43, head Loran div., 1943; bd. dirs. McGraw-Hill Book Co., Inc., 1947-52; vice chmn. Nat. TV System Com., 1950-52, panel chmn., 1950-53; chmn. prep. com. TV Dept. State, 1951-55; with Philco Corp., 1952-62, dir. research, 1952-58, dir., gen. mgr. research div., 1959-62, v.p.-research, 1961; exec. dir., gen. mgr. IEEE, N.Y.C., 1963-74; exec. cons. IEEE, 1975-76, dir. emeritus, 1974—; ops. dir. Assn. Coop. Engring., 1975-76; cons., Belgium, 1952; mem. bd. for internat. orgns. and programs Nat. Acad. Scis.; chmn. com. on internat. sci. and tech. info. NRC, 1975-78; chmn. com. UNESCO sci. programs NRC, 1976-81; mem. exec. com. World Fedn. Engring. Orgns., 1973-77; mem. U.S. Commn. for UNESCO, 1976-81; trustee Met. Reference and Research Library Agy., 1974-83; chmn. Study Group High Definition TV Soc. Motion Picture and TV Engrs., 1977-83; expert cons. on radar and electronic nav. Office Sec. War, 1943-45; cons. to comdr. atom bomb tests, Bikini, 1946; mem. Army Sci. Adv. Panel, 1957-69; mem. com. nav. research and devel. bd. Dept. Def., 1948-51. Mem. editorial staff Electronics, 1934-52, editor in chief, 1946-52; author: Engineering Electronics, 1938, Principles of TV Engineering, 1940, Microwave Radar, 1942, Radar Engineering, 1947, TV Engineering, 1952, Color Television Standards, 1955, Television Engineering Handbook, 1957, Physics of Television, 1960, Computers and the Human Mind, 1966, Standard Handbook for Electrical Engineers, 1987, Electronics Engineers' Handbook, 1988, Engineers and Electrons, 1984. Recipient Medal of Freedom, 1946; Presdl. Certificate Merit for wartime service, 1948; plaque for contbns. to TV IRE, 1951; Am. Technologists award N.Y. Inst. Tech., 1958; Outstanding Civilian Service medal U.S. Army, 1969; Citation for Outstanding Service to TV Internat. TV Symposium, Montreux, 1971. Fellow IEEE (editor Proc. IRE 1956-57, pres. IRE 1958, Founders medal 1978, Consumer Electronics award 1978), Soc. Motion Picture and TV Engrs. (jour. award 1956, Progress medal 1979); mem. Nat. Acad. Engring., Radio Club Am. (Sarnoff citation 1979, Batcher Meml. award 1985), Sigma Xi, Tau Beta Pi, Eta Kappa Nu (eminent mem.), Phi Mu Delta. Club: Cosmos (Washington). Home: 103-B Heritage Hills Somers NY 10589 Office: 345 E 47th St New York NY 10017

FINK, ERWIN, manufacturing company executive; b. Grossbottwar, Germany, Dec. 18, 1922; s. Adolf Gustav and Pauline Emilie (Pantle) F.; dipl. engring. U. Stuttgart, 1951; m. Emma Haecker, Sept. 14, 1951; 1 dau., Ursula Magdalene. Mechanician, C.F. Roser Co., Stuttgart, 1945-46; tech. designer C. Kaelble GmbH, Backnang, 1951-55, sect. mgr., 1956-73, technics 1974-81, gen. mgr., 1974—, gen. mgr., 1981—; cons. Author four books on local history and geography. Mem. City Council Grossbottwar, 1966—; mem. com. for supplying water in the region of Baden-Württemberg; mem. supevisory bd. nat. bd. of works. Served to 2d lt. German Navy, 1941-45. Decorated Iron Cross. Mem. Com. European Constrn. Equipment, Max Planck Gesellschaft, Deutsche Gesellschaft fur Wehrtechnik, Deutsche Gesellschaft fur Elektrische Strassenfahrzeuge. Evangelical. Contbr. articles to profl. jours. Home: 3 Keltenstrasse, D-7141 Grossbottwar Federal Republic of Germany

FINK, GONTHIER LOUIS, language educator; b. Karlsruhe, Germany, Mar. 19, 1928; s. Otto and Rose Catherine (Rudinger) F.; m. Antoinette Langlois, June 18, 1952. LittB, U. Nancy, France, 1950; MA, Sorbonne U., Paris, 1952, LittD, 1967. Lectr. U. Dijon, France, 1952-56; attaché Nat. Ctr. Research, Paris, 1956-59; prof. German lit. U. Besancon, France, 1959-66; prof. U. Strasbourg, France, 1966—, dean, v.p., 1968-73, dir. Ctr. for Fgn. Images, 1985—; v.p. Jury d'Agrégation d'Allemand, Paris, 1971-76; v.p. German commn. Council for Higher Univs., 1972-82; assoc. prof. U. Regensburg, Fed. Republic of Germany, 1975. Author: Naissance et Apogée du Conte Merveilleux, 1966 (Strasbourg prize 1967), L'Allemagne Face au Classicisme et à la Révolution, 1972; editor: Goethe et l'Alsace, 1971, Cosmopolitisme, Patriotisme et Xénophobie, 1986. Pres. Convention Républicaine, Besancon, France, 1963-66, Jury for Strasbourg Prize, Strasbourg and Hamburg, France, 1971—, Jury for Oberrheinischer Kulturpreis, Bâle, Switzerland, 1985—; v.p. Jury for Goethe Prize of Europe, Hambourg, 1987—. Named as officer to Nat. Order of Merit, Govt. Paris, 1987, officer Order of Palms, Ministry of Edn., Paris, 1986, Médaille d' Or Robert Schuman, 1988. Mem. Internat. Assn. for Germanic Studies (bd. dirs. 1985—), Commn. for German Lit., Goethe Soc., Lessing Soc. Home: 15 Rue d'Offendorf, 67000 Strasbourg France Office: U Strasbourg Dept Scis Humaines 22 Rue Descartes, 67084 Strasbourg France

FINK, JAMES BREWSTER, consulting geophysicist; b. Los Angeles, Jan. 12, 1943. BS in Geophysics and Geochemistry, U. Ariz., 1969; MS in Geophysics cum laude, U. Witwatersrand, Johannesburg, Transvaal, Republic of South Africa, 1980; PhD in Geol. Engring., Geohydrology, U. Ariz, 1988. Registered profl. engr., Ariz.; registered land surveyor. Geophysicist Geo-Comp Exploration, Inc., Tucson, 1969-70; geophys. cons. IFEX-Geotechnica, S.A., Hermosillo, Sonora, Mex., 1970; chief geophysicist Mining Geophys. Surveys, Tucson, 1971-72; research asst. U. Ariz., Tucson, 1973; cons. geophysics Tucson, 1974-76; sr. minerals geophysicist Esso Minerals Africa, Inc., Johannesburg, 1976-79; sr. research geophysicist Exxon Prodn. Research Co., Houston, 1979-80; pres. Geophynque Internat., Tucson, 1980—; cons. on NSF research U. Ariz., 1984-85, adj. lectr. geol. engring., 1985-86, assoc. instr. geophysics, 1986—, supr. geophysicist, geohydrologist, 1986—, bd. dirs. Lab. Advanced Subsurface Imaging, 1986; lectr. South African Atomic Energy Bd., Pelindaba, 1979. Contbr. articles to profl. jours. Served as sgt. U.S. Air NG, 1965-70. Named Airman of Yr., U.S. Air NG, 1967. Mem. Soc. Exploration Geophysicists (co-chmn. Houston chpt. 1980, Dallas chpt. 1981, co-editor IP monograph), Am. Geophys. Union, European Assn. Exploration Geophysicists, South African Geophys. Assn., Assn. Ground Water Scientists, Nat. Water Well Assn. (reviewer), Mineral and Geotech. Logging Soc., Assn. Petroleum Geochem. Explorationists, Ariz. Geol. Soc., Ariz. Computer Oriented Geol. soc. (bd. dirs., v.p.), Mining Geophysicists Denver, Mensa, Intertel, Internat. Platform Assn. Republican. Home: 5865 S Old Spanish Trail Tucson AZ 85747 Office: U Ariz Dept Mining and Geol Engring Tucson AZ 85721

FINK, NORMAN STILES, lawyer, educational adminstrator; b. Easton, Pa., Aug. 13, 1926; s. Herman and Yetta (Hyman) F.; m. Helen Mullen, Sept. 1, 1956; children—Hayden Michael, Patricia Carol. A.B., Dartmouth Coll., 1947; J.D., Harvard U., 1950. Bar: N.Y. 1951, U.S. Dist. Ct. (ea. and so. dists.) N.Y. 1954, U.S. Supreme Ct. 1964. Mem. legal staff Remington Rand, Inc., N.Y.C., Washington, 1949-54; ptnr. Lans & Fink, N.Y.C., 1954-68; counsel devel. program U. Pa., Phila., 1969-80; v.p. devel. and univ. relations Brandeis U., Waltham, Mass., 1980-81; dep. v.p. devel. and alumni relations, assoc. gen. counsel devel. Columbia U., N.Y.C., 1981—. Served with U.S. Army, 1945-46. Recipient Alice Beeman award for excellence in devel. Writing Council Advancement and Support of Edn., 1984; Lilly Endowment grantee, 1979-80. Mem. ABA (mem. com. on exempt orgns. sect. taxation and com. estate planning and drafting, charitable giving, sect. real property, probate, and trust law)), Council Advancement and Support of Edn. (various coms.), Nat. Assn. Coll. and Univ. Attys. (com. on taxation), Am. Arbitration Assn. (panelist), Nat. Assn. Ind. Colls. and Univs. (com. on taxation), N.Y. County Lawyers Assn., Assn. Bar City N.Y. (com. on tax-exempt orgns. 1987—), Dartmouth Lawyers Assn., Harvard Law Sch. Assn., Nat. Soc. Fund Raising Execs (Contbn. to Knowledge award 1985). Democrat. Jewish. Clubs: Nat. Lawyers (Washington); University (N.Y.C.). Editor: Deferred Giving Handbook, 1977; author: (with Howard C. Metzler) The Costs and Benefits of Deferred Giving, 1982. Home: Valeria #69 Furnace Dock Rd Peekskill NY 10566 Office: Columbia U Cen Mail Room PO Box 400 New York NY 10027

FINK, ROBERT STEVEN, lawyer, writer; b. Bklyn., Dec. 7, 1943; s. Samuel Miles and Helen Leah (Bogen) F.; m. Abby Deutsch, Mar. 20, 1980; children—Juliet Leah, Robin Rachel. Diploma, U. Vienna, 1962; B.A., Bklyn. Coll., 1965; J.D., N.Y. U., 1968, LL.M., 1973. Bar: N.Y. 1969, U.S. Dist. Ct. (so. dist.) N.Y. 1970, U.S. Dist. Ct. (ea. dist.) N.Y. 1970, U.S. Dist. Ct. (we. dist.) N.Y. 1975, U.S. Dist. Ct. (no. dist.) N.Y. 1985, U.S. Tax Ct. 1970, U.S. Ct. Apls. (2d cir.) 1970, U.S. Sup. Ct. 1972, U.S. Ct. Claims 1984. Assoc. Kostelanetz & Ritholz, N.Y.C., 1968-75, ptnr., 1975-87, Kostelanetz, Ritholz, Tigue and Fink, N.Y.C., 1987—; lectr. in field; expert witness IRS; mem. adv. com. tax div. Dept. Justice; adj. prof. law NYU. Mem. ABA (chmn. com. civil and criminal tax penalties 1983-85, chmn. task force for revision of tax penalties 1982), N.Y. State Bar Assn. (chmn. com. criminal and civil tax penalties 1982-85, 88—, chmn. compliance and unreported income 1985-87 , chmn. commodities and fin. futures 1987-88), Fed. Bar Assn., N.Y. County Lawyers Assn. (chmn. com. taxation 1988—), Assn. Bar City N.Y., Am. Arbitration Assn. (arbitrator 1973—). Author: Tax Fraud: Audits, Investigations, Prosecutions, 2 vols., 1980, 6th rev. edit., 1988; Co-author: How to Defend Yourself Against the IRS, 1985, You Can Protect Yourself from the IRS, 1987, 2d rev. edit., 1988; contbr. numerous articles in field to profl. jours. Office: 80 Pine St New York NY 10005

FINKE, JOACHIM, neurologist; b. Liegnitz, Silesia, Feb. 4, 1927; s. Alfred and Elly (Günther) F.; Dipl. psych., U. Halle/Saale, 1950, M.D., 1951; m. Waltraut Hoffmann, Sept. 27, 1952; children—Gudrun, Ortrun, Ingrun. Intern, U. Halle/Saale, 1951-53; resident Charité Hosp., Berlin, 1953-58, Bethesda Hosp., Stuttgart, Germany, 1959, U. Tübingen, 1960-65; lectr. U. Tübingen, 1965-72, asso. prof., 1972—; med. dir. Neurol. Hosp., Bürgerhospital, Stuttgart, 1970—. Mem. Anglo-German Med. Assn., German Assn. Neurology. Author: Ophthalmodynamographie, 1966; Die Neurol. Untersuchung, 1968; (with W. Schulte) Schlafstörungen, 1970, 2d edit., 1979; ODG-Symposium, 1974; Neurol. Untersuchungskurs, 1975; (with R. Tölle) Aktuelle Neurol. and psychiat., 1979; Neurol. Erkrankungen, 1981; Neurol. f. d. Praxis, 1985. Office: 14-16 Tunzhoferstrasse, 7000 Stuttgart Federal Republic of Germany

FINKELDAY, JOHN PAUL, software company executive; b. Pleasantville, N.J., Nov. 20, 1943; s. Charles John Henry and Viola Sybilla (Eastlack) F.; student Glassboro State Coll., 1961-63, Rider Coll., 1965; m. Karen Lynn Mattoon, Nov. 16, 1963; 1 son, John Paul. With McGraw Hill Publ. Co., Hightstown, N.J., 1963-65; asst. controller Exel Wood Products Co., Inc., Lakewood, N.J., 1965-66, office mgr., 1966-82, mgr. data processing, 1970-78, v.p., dir. data processing, 1978-83, v.p. mgmt. info. services, 1983-86, v.p. adminstrn., 1983-84, v.p.Amici Systems, Inc., Brick, N.J., 1986—; mem. Del. Valley Computer Users Group. Third v.p. exec. com. Adm. Farragut Acad. Parents Assn., 1980-81. Mem. Am. Mgmt. Assn., Common, U.S. Golf Assn. (assoc.). Club: Moose. Home: 504 Bounty Ct Toms River NJ 08753 Office: Amici Systems Inc 228 Brick Blvd Brick NJ 08723

FINKELSTEIN, SALUS, architect; b. Porto Alegre, Brazil, Nov. 28, 1937; s. Jose and Cheiva Finkelstein; m. Alla Winogron, May 1, 1965; children—Danni, Suanni. Degree in architecture, UFRGS/Faculdade de Arquitectura, 1960. Interior architect, designer, Porto Alegre, 1960—; architect, Porto Alegre, 1960—. Prin. works include Bank from State of Santa Catarina (first prize 1979). Served with Brazilian Army, 1955-57. Jewish. Avocations: jogging; basketball; soccer; volleyball. Office: Salus Finkelstein Architect, Rua Farias Santos 253, Porto Alegre 90000, Brazil

FINKL, CHARLES WILLIAM, II, geologist; b. Chgo., Sept. 19, 1941; s. Charles William and Marian L. (Hamilton) F.; m. Charlene Bristol, May 16, 1965 (div.); children: Jonathan William Frederick, Amanda Marie. B.Sc., Oreg. State U., 1964, M.Sc., 1966; Ph.D., U. Western Australia, 1971. Instr. natural resources Oreg. State U., 1967; demonstrator U. Western Australia, 1968; staff geochemist for S.E. Asia, Internat. Nickel Australia Pty. Ltd., Perth, 1970-74; chief editor Ency. Earth Sci., N.Y.C., 1974-87; dir. Inst. Coastal Studies, Nova. U., 1979-83; pres. Resource Mgmt. & Mineral Exploration Cons., Inc., Ft. Lauderdale, Fla., 1974-85 Info. Mgmt. Corp. (IMCO), 1985-87; exec. dir., v.p. Coastal Edn. and Research Found., Charlottesville, Va., 1983—; prof. dept. geology Fla. Atlantic U., Boca Raton, 1983-87; corr. mem. Internat. Geog. Union Commn. on Geomorphol. Survey and Mapping and Sub-commn. on Morphotectonics, Internat. Geol. Correl. Program; mem. Internat. Geog. Union Commn. on River and Coastal Plains; corr. mem. Internat. Geog. Union Commn. on Coastal Environment; radio and TV appearances. Mem. Am. Geophys. Union, Am. Geog. Soc., Am. Quaternary Assn. Am. Littoral Soc., Am. Shore and Beach Preservation Assn., Australasian Inst. Mining and Metallurgy, Brit. Geomorphological Research Group, Brit. Soc. Soil Sci., Can. Geophys. Union, Coastal Soc., Deutsche Bodenkundlichen Gesellschaft, Deutsche Geologische Vereininung, European Assn. Earth Sci. Editors, Estuarine and Brackish-Water Scis. Assn., Geol. Assn. Can., Geol. Soc. Am., Geol. Soc. Australia, Geol. Soc. London, Geol. Soc. South Africa, Geologists Assn., Geosci. Info. Soc., Internat. Soil Sci. Soc., Internat. Union Geol. Scis., Mineral. Assn. Can., Nature Conservancy, Nat. Parks and Conservation Assn., Soil Sci. Soc. Am., Société de Belge de Pedologie, Soc. Econ. Paleontologists and Mineralogists, Soc. Scholarly Publ., Soc. Mining Engrs., Am. Inst. Profl. Geologists (cert.), Am. Registry Cert. Profls. in Agronomy, Crops and Soils (cert. profl. soil scientist), Gamma Theta Upsilon. Republican. Presbyterian. Contbr. articles, revs. to profl. publs., newspapers. Author: Soil Classification, 1982. Vol. editor, contbg. author: The Encyclopedia of Soil Science, Part I: Physics, Chemistry, Biology, Fertility, and Technology, 1979. Editor, contbg. author: The Encyclopedia of Applied Geology, 1983, The Encyclopedia of Field & General Geology, 1988; editor-in-chief Jour. Coastal Research: An Internat. Forum for the Littoral Scis., 1984—. Series editor Benchmark Papers in Soil Sci., 1982-86. Editor: Current Titles in Ocean, Coastal, Lake and Waterway Sciences, 1985-88; mng. editor Bulletin of Palcomalacology, 1988—. Home: 630 Tanners Ln Earlysville VA 22936 Office: Coastal Edn and Research Found PO Box 8068 Charlottesville VA 22908

FINKS, ROBERT MELVIN, paleontologist, educator; b. Portland, Maine, May 12, 1927; s. Abraham Joseph and Sarah (Bendette) F. B.S. magna cum laude, Queens Coll., 1947; M.A., Columbia U., 1954, Ph.D., 1959. Lectr. Bklyn. Coll., 1955-58, instr., 1959-61; lectr. Queens Coll., 1961-62, asst. prof., 1962-65, acting chmn., 1963-64, asso. prof. geology, 1966-70, prof., 1971—; geologist U.S. Geol. Survey, 1952-54, 63—; research asso. Am. Mus. Natural History, 1961-77, Smithsonian Instn., 1968—; doctoral faculty CUNY, 1983—; cons. in field. Author: Late Paleozoic Sponge Faunas of the Texas Region, 1960; Editor: Guidebook to Field Excursions, 1968; Contbr. articles profl. jours. Fellow AAAS, Geol. Soc. Am., Explorers Club; mem. Paleontol. Soc. (vice chmn. Northeastern sect. 1977-78, chmn. 1978-79), Paleontol. Assn. Britain, Soc. Econ. Paleontologists and Mineralogists, Internat. Palaeontol. Assn., Geol. Soc. Vt. (charter mem.), Planetary Soc. (charter), Phi Beta Kappa, Sigma Xi. (exec. sec. Queens Coll. chpt. 1982-85). Office: Dept Geology Queens Coll Flushing NY 11367

FINLAY, ROBERT DEREK, food company executive; b. U.K., May 16, 1932; s. William Templeton and Phyllis F.; m. Una Ann Grant, June 30, 1956; children: Fiona, Rory, James. B.A. with honors in Law and Econs, Cambridge (Eng.) U., 1955, M.A., 1959. With Mobil Oil Co. Ltd., U.K., 1955-61; assoc. McKinsey & Co., Inc., 1961-67, prin., 1967-71, dir., 1971-79; mng. dir. H.J. Heinz Co. Ltd., U.K., 1979-81; sr. v.p. corp. devel. world hdqrs. H.J. Heinz Co. Ltd., Pitts., 1981—; Bd. dirs. U.S. China Bus. Council. Mem. London com. Scottish Council Devel. and Industry, 1979—; trustee Mercy Hosp., Pitts. Served to capt. Gordon Highlanders, 1950-61; bd. dirs. Pitts. Pub. Theatre. Mem. Inst. Mktg., Inst. Mgmt. Cons. Clubs: Highland Brigade, Leander, Duquesne, Allegheny, Annabel's. Office: H J Heinz Co 600 Grant St Pittsburgh PA 15219

FINLAYSON, DAVID MUNRO, physics educator; b. Dunnet, Caithness, Scotland, May 2, 1919; s. David and Elizabeth (Coghill) F.; m. Angela Finlayson, Oct. 2, 1946; children: Catriona, Mairi. BSc with honors, St. Andrews U., Scotland, 1947, PhD, 1951. Vis. lectr. Purdue U., Lafayette, Ind., 1951-52; lectr. Aberdeen (Scotland) U., 1952-64; sr. lectr. St. Andrew's U., 1964—, dean of sci., 1979-82, mem. univ. ct., 1973-77, mem. univ. senate, 1973-82. Editor: Proceedings 11th Low Temperature Conference, 1968, Localisation and Interaction, 1986; contbr. numerous articles to profl. jours. Served to capt. Royal Elec. Mech. Engrs., 1940-46. Mem. Inst. Physics (low temperature group com. 1983-86). Office: St Andrews U Dept Physics, North Haugh, Saint Andrews KY16 9SS, Scotland

FINLEY, GEORGE ALVIN, III, hardware distribution company executive; b. Aurora, Ill., Apr. 25, 1938; s. George Alvin, II, and Sally Ann (Lord) F.; B.B.A., So. Meth. U., 1962; postgrad. Coll. Grad. Program, Ford Motor Co., 1963; m. Sue Sellors, June 20, 1962; children—Valerie, George Alvin IV. Rep. for Europe, Finco Internat., 1959-61; trainee Ford Motor Co., Dearborn, Mich., 1962-63; v.p. mktg. Internat. Motor Cars, Oakland, Calif., 1963-64, Sequoia Lincoln lease mgr., 1965; regional mgr. Behlen Mfg. Co., Dallas, 1965-67; pres. C C Hardware Inc., Corpus Christi, Tex., 1967—; guest instr. Sch. Bus., So. Meth. U.; dir. Charter Savs. and Loan. Pres. Nueces River Authority, 1976—; bd. dirs. Coastal Bend Alcoholic Rehab. Cntr. Inc., Tex., 1973—, pres., 1976-77. Mem. Nat. Wholesale Hardware Assn., Nat. Acad. Wholesalers, Am. Supply Assn., Wholesale Distbrs. Assn., Nat. Impact Industries Inc. (chmn. bd.) Sandwich, Ill., Tex. (past v.p.) wholesale hardware assns., Nat. Retail Hardware Assn., So. Hardware Assn., Phi Delta Theta. Democrat. Unitarian. Club: Rotary Internat. Asst. in design, engring., production, mktg. Apollo Automobile, 1963-64.-64. Home: 3360 Ocean Dr Corpus Christi TX 78411 Office: 210 McBride Ln PO Box 9153 Corpus Christi TX 78408

FINLEY, ROBERT VAN EATON, clergyman; b. Charlottesville, Va., May 2, 1922; s. William Walter and Melissa (Hoover) F.; B.A., U. Va., 1944; postgrad. U. Chgo. Div. Sch., 1946-47; Litt.D., Houghton Coll., 1952; m. Ethel Drummond, Dec. 23, 1949; children—Deborah Ann, Ruth Ellen. Evangelist, Youth for Christ Internat., Chgo. and Inter-Varsity Christian Fellowship, Chgo., 1945-46, overseas, 1948-51; pastor Evang. Free Ch., Richmond, Calif., 1951-52; minister to fgn. students 10th Presbyn. Ch., Phila., 1952-55; pastor Temple Bapt. Ch., Washington, 1965-66; founder, gen. dir. Christian Aid Mission, Charlottesville, Va., 1953-70, chmn., pres., 1970—; founder, gen. dir. Overseas Students Mission, Ft. Erie, Ont., Can., 1954-68, pres., 1969—; pres. Bharat Evang. Fellowship, Washington, 1973-87; editor Conquest for Christ, 1954-74, Christian Mission mag., 1974—; founder, pres. Internat. Students, Inc., Washington, 1952-67, chmn., 1968-70; ordained to ministry Bapt. Ch., 1957. Mem. Omicron Delta Kappa. Republican.

FINN, JOHN JOSEPH, JR., physician; b. Boston, Mar. 20, 1915; s. John Joseph and Josephine (Killelea) F.; B.S. in Biology, Tufts U., 1937, M.D., 1941. Intern in internal medicine Boston City Hosp., 1941-42, asst. resident medicine, 1946-47, chief resident, 1947-48, assisting physician, 1952-79; resident Joseph H. Pratt Diagnostic Hosp., 1948-49, asso. staff, 1949-79; pvt. practice internal medicine, 1949-79; med. dir. William Filene's Sons Co., 1954-79, Boston Herald-Traveler, 1962-63, Bentley Coll. Accounting and Finance, 1963-79; courtesy staff Sancta Maria Hosp. (Cambridge), Faulkner Hosp.; sr. clin. instr. medicine med. sch. Tufts U., 1950-79, instr. medicine dental sch., 1953-79; instr. Boston Sch. Occupational Therapy; asst. physician Boston Dispensary; comdr. 351 Gen. Hosp., Boston Army Base; Boston examiner for Life Extension Inst., 1953-79; ret., 1979. Col. U.S. Army Res. Diplomate Am. Bd. Internal Medicine. Fellow A.C.P. (asso.); mem. A.M.A., Mass. Med. Soc. (chmn. sect. indsl. medicine 1964), Am. Fedn. Clin. Research, New England Indsl. Med. Assn. (dir. 1959). Author articles in med. jours. Died Apr. 15, 1988. Home: 30 Stearns Rd Brookline MA 02146

FINN, JOSEPH PATRICK, public servant; b. Ottawa, Ont., Can., Apr. 28, 1936; s. Gordon Francis and Marguerite Mary (Bender) F.; m. Susan Ann Hickey, July 9, 1941; children: Michael, Jennifer. Cert. engring. tech. Engring. technician EMI Ltd, Ottawa, 1958-62; tech. insp. Govt. Can., Ont., 1962-65; engring. technician Ian Martin Assocs., Ottawa, 1965-66; pub. servant Govt. Can., Ont. Alta., Nfld., B.C., N.S., 1966—. Contbr. articles to profl. jours.; composer ballads. Served with RCAF, 1953-58. Mem. Ont. Assn. Cert. Engring. Technicians and Technologists (chmn. Ottawa chpt. 1966). Home: 1168 Sherman Dr, Ottawa, ON Canada K2C 2M6 Office: 101 Colonel By Dr, Ottawa, ON Canada K1A OK2

FINN, WILLIAM FRANCIS, obstetrician, gynecologist; b. Union City, N.J., July 23, 1915; s. Neil and Catherine Marie (Hearn) F.; m. Doris Ida Henderson, Sept. 21, 1943; children: Neil C., Sharon R., David. A.B. summa cum laude, Holy Cross Coll., 1936; M.D., Cornell U., 1940; MA, NYU, 1986; MA in Philosophy, NYU, 1986. Intern, Albany Hosp., 1940-41; resident obstetrics and gynecology N.Y. Hosp., 1941-44, asst. attending obstetrician and gynecologist, 1946-48, asso. attending obstetrician and gynecologist 1948-67; asst. prof. obstetrics and gynecology Cornell Med. Coll., 1948-67, asso. clin. prof., 1967—; attending obstetrics and gynecology North Shore Univ. Hosp., also founder com. medicine, soc. and ethics; cons. obstetrics and gynecology Mercy Hosp. Bd. mgrs. Ch. C Found., Episcopal Diocese of L.I.; trustee Plandome Manor. J. Withridge Williams fellow, 1947. Recipient Bishop's Cross for disting. service. Diplomate Am. Bd. Obstetrics and Gynecology. Fellow A.C.S., AMA, Am. Coll. Obstetricians, Am. Soc. Colposcopy; mem. N.Y. Obstet. Soc., Queens (pres.), Nassau (pres.) obstet. socs., Am. Acad. Obstetrics and Gynecology, N.Y. State, N.Y. County med. socs., Found. of Thanatology Inst. Soc., Ethics and Life Scis., Soc. Health and Human Values. Editor: Women and Loss; contbr. articles on dying, death, bereavement and biomed. ethics to profl. jours. Home: 3 Aspen Gate Manhasset NY 11030

FINNBOGADOTTIR, VIGDIS, president of Iceland; b. Reykjavik, Iceland, Apr. 15, 1930; d. Finnbogi Rutur Thorvaldsson and Sigridur Eiriksdottir; matriculated Menntaskolinn I Reykjavik, 1949; student U. Grenoble, Sorbonne, U. Iceland, also studies in Denmark and Sweden; div.; 1 adopted dau., Astridur. Tchr. French, Menntaskolinn I Reykjavik, later Menntaskolinn Vid Hamrahlid; tour guide, later head cultural public relations dept. Iceland Tourist Bur.; dir. Reykjavik Theatre Co., from 1972; tchr. French drama U. Iceland; tchr. French, Icelandic State TV; former mem. Grima, exptl. theatre group; former chmn. Alliance Francaise; lectr. Icelandic culture in fgn. countries; mem. adv. com. on cultural affairs in Nordic countries, 1976—, chmn., 1978—; pres. of Iceland, 1980—. Office: Office Pres, Reykjavik Iceland *

FINNÉ, JEAN M.H., electrical engineer; b. Brussels, Aug. 3, 1936; s. Valere and Marcelle (Delsemme) F.; m. Claudine Vandenbergen, Jan. 3, 1970; children: Sylvie, Arnaud. MSEE, U. Liege, Belgium, 1958. Dep. mgr. elec. dept. Tractebel, Brussels. Mem. Assn. Exec. Electrobel and Intercom (pres. Belgium chpt. 1980-84), Institut Belge Deregulation et Automatisme (bd. dirs. 1984-86). Lodge: Lions (sec. Rixensart, Belgium chpt. 1980-81, pres. 1986—). Home: Ave d'Ingendael 68, 1641 Alsemberg Belgium Office: Tractebel, Place du Trône 1, Brussels Belgium 1000

FINNEGAN, RUTH HILARY, anthropologist, sociologist; b. Londonderry, Ireland, Dec. 31, 1933; d. Thomas and Lucy Agnes (Campbell) F.; m. David John Murray, Sept. 7, 1963; children: Rachel Clare, Kathleen Anne, Brigid Aileen. BA with honors, Oxford U., Eng., 1956, diploma in anthropology, 1959, BLitt, 1960, DPhil, 1963. Lectr. in social anthropology U. Coll. of Rhodesia, Nyasaland, Zimbabwe, 1963-64; lectr. in sociology U. Ibadan, Nigeria, 1965-67, sr. lectr., 1967-69; lectr. sociology Open U., Milton Keynes, Eng., 1969-72, sr. lectr. in comparative social insts., 1972-75, 78-82, reader in comparative social insts., 1982-88, prof. in comparative social insts., 1988—; reader in sociology U. South Pacific, Suva, Fiji, 1975-78; mem. social anthropology com. S.S.R.C., 1978-82, mem. social affairs com., 1982-86, vice chmn., 1985-86. Author: Oral Literature in Africa, 1970, Oral Poetry, 1977, Literacy and Orality, 1988; joint editor: Modes of Thought, 1973. Fellow Royal Anthrop. Inst. (council mem. 1986—, hon. editor jour. Man 1987—); mem. Assn. Social Anthropologists of Commonwealth (com. mem. 1986—), Brit. Sociol. Soc., Internat. African Inst. Office: Open Univ, Walton Hall, Milton Keynes MK7 6AA, England

FINNEGAN, THOMAS JOSEPH, lawyer; b. Chgo., Aug. 18, 1900; s. Thomas Harrison and Marie (Flanagan) F.; J.D., Chgo. Kent Coll. of Law, 1923; m. Hildreth Millslagel, July 1, 1933 (dec. Mar. 1977). Admitted to Ill. bar, 1923, and since practiced in Chicago; mem. firm Fithian, Spengler & Finnegan, 1935-51; mem. firm Korshak, Oppenheim & Finnegan, 1951-86. Mem. ABA, Fed., Ill., Chgo. bar assns., Chgo. Law Inst., Phi Alpha Delta. Home: 5630 Sheridan Rd Chicago IL 60660 Office: 29 S LaSalle St Chicago IL 60603

FINNEY, ALBERT, actor, director; m. Jane Wenham, 1957 (div.); 1 son; m. 2d Anouk Aimee, 1970 (div.). Litt.D. (hon.), Sussex U., 1965, Salford U., 1979. Assoc. artistic dir. English Stage Co., 1972—; appearances include: The Party, New, London, 1958; Cassio in Othello, and Lysander, Stratford-on-Avon, 1959; The Lily White Boys, Royal Court, 1960; Billy Liar, Cambridge Theatre, 1960; Luther, in Luther, Royal Court Theatre and Phoenix Theatre, 1962-62, N.Y., 1963; Armstrong, in Armstrong's Last Goodnight, Miss Julie and Black Comedy, Chichester, 1965, Old Vic, 1966; A Day in the Death of Joe Egg, N.Y., 1968; Alpha Beta, Royal Court and Appollo, 1972; Krapp's Last Tape, Royal Court, 1973; Cromwell, Royal Court, 1973; Chez Nous, Globe, 1974; Uncle Vanya, and Present Laughter, Royal Exchange, Manchester, Eng., 1977; nat. theatre appearances include: Love for Love, 1965, Much Ado About Nothing, 1965, A Flea in Her Ear, 1966, Hamlet, 1975, Tamburlaine, 1976, The Country Wife, 1977, The Cherry Orchard, Macbeth, Has "Washington" Legs?, 1978; stage dir. The Freedom of the City, Royal Court, 1973; Loot, Royal Court, 1975; films include: The Entertainer, 1959, Saturday Night and Sunday Morning, 1960, Tom Jones, 1963, Night Must Fall, 1963, Two for the Road, 1967, Charlie Bubbles, 1968, Scrooge, 1970, Gumshoe, 1971, Murder on the Orient Express, 1974, Wolfen, 1979, Loophole, 1980, Looker, 1980, Shoot the Moon, 1981, Annie,

1982, The Dresser, 1983, Under the Volcano, 1983, John Paul II (TV film), 1983, Orphans, 1987 *

FINNEY, DAVID JOHN, biometrician; b. Warrington, Eng., Jan. 3, 1917; s. Robert George Stringer and Bessie Evelyn (Whitlow) F.; MA, ScD, Cambridge U.; DSc (hon.), City U., London, Heriot-Watt U.; D es Sc (hon.), U. Gembloux; m. Mary Elizabeth Connolly, Apr. 11, 1950; children: Deborah J.C. Finney Langston, Robert F.J., Katharine A. Asst. statistician Rothamsted Exptl. Sta., 1939-45; lectr. design and analysis sci. expt. Oxford U., 1945-56; reader, then prof. stats. U. Aberdeen (Scotland), 1954-66; prof. stats. U. Edinburgh, 1966-84; dir. stats. unit Agrl. and Food Research Council, 1954-84; dir. Internat. Stats. Inst. Research Centre, 1987-88; frequent cons. UN Food and Agr. Orgn., WHO; vis. prof. Harvard U., 1962-63, vis. scientist Internat. Rice Research Inst., 1984-85. Decorated comdr. Order Brit. Empire. Fellow Royal Soc., Royal Soc. Edinburgh, Royal Statis. Soc. (past pres.), Am. Statis. Assn.; mem. Internat. Statis. Inst., Biometric Soc. (past pres.). Anglican. Author books, articles on stats. and applications biol. sci. Home: 43 Cluny Dr, Edinburgh DH10 6DU, Scotland Office: U Edinburgh, Dept Stats, Edinburgh EH10 6DU, Scotland

FINNEY, ROY PELHAM, SR., urologist, surgeon; b. Gaffney, S.C., Dec. 7, 1924; s. Roy P. Finney and Mary Frances (Cannon) Woodard; m. Kay Harkness, Apr. 5, 1962; children: Wright C., James L., Joella R., Gray, Kevin. MD, Med. U. S.C., 1952. Diplomate: Am. Bd. Urology. Resident in urology Johns Hopkins U., Balt., 1952-57; prof. surg. urology U. South Fla., Tampa, 1972—, dir. div. urology, 1972-82. Designer and inventor implantable prosthese, incontinence device, inflatable penile prostheses treatment impotence, Double Jureteral stent, developer new surg. proceedings treatment impotence, 1982. Fellow ACS; mem. Am. Urology Assn., Soc. Internationale D'Urologie, Internat. Continenece Soc., Urodynamic Soc. Republican. Home: 4382 Aztec Ct Bayport FL 34607 Office: U South Fla PO Box 16 12901 N 30th St Tampa FL 33612

FINNIE, PHILLIP POWELL, aerospace engineer; b. Memphis, Dec. 21, 1933; s. Phillip and Daisy L. (Green) F.; B.S.C.E., Howard U., 1956; postgrad. U. Calif., Los Angeles, U. So. Calif.; M.B.A., Pepperdine U., 1979; m. Mary Bebe Clark, Sept. 14, 1968. Stress analyst N.Am. Aviation Corp., Los Angeles, 1956-59; dynamicist RCA, Van Nuys, Calif., 1959-62, Aerojet Gen. Corp., Azusa, Calif., 1962-64, Philco-Ford Corp., Newport Beach, Calif., 1964-67; dynamicist, analyst of radar observables, TRW Inc., Redondo Beach, Calif., 1967—. Mem. Republican Nat. Com. Mem. AIAA, Air Force Assn. Baptist. Home: 20102 Dalfsen Ave Carson CA 90746

FINSTERWALDER, OTTOKARL FLORIAN, banker; b. Wiesbaden, Germany, Feb. 9, 1936; s. Eberhard and Elisabeth (Zimmermann) F.; student U. Frankfurt, 1956-57; law degree U. Hamburg, 1962, 67; m. Almerie Spannocchi, Feb. 12, 1974; children—Pia, Alena, Isabel, Cecily. Bar admission: 1967. Assoc. Shearman & Sterling, N.Y.C., 1967-70; dir. Hill Samuel & Co. Ltd., Mcht. Bankers, London, 1970-74; mng. bd. dirs. Creditanstalt-Bankverein, Vienna, Austria, 1985—; mem bd. mng. dir., 1985—; dir. European Am. Bank, BEC, S.A., Brussels, Central European Internat. Bank, Budapest; chmn. bd. AWT Internat. Handels und Finanzierungs AG, Vienna; chmn. supervisory bd. ALWA, Güter und Vermögensverwaltungs AG, Vienna; vice chmn. supervisory bd. Leykam-Mürztaler Papier-und Zellstoff AG., Gratkorn; mem. bd. advisors Internat. Income Fund; adv. to bd. Wirtschafts-und Privatbank, Zurich, Switzerland. Roman Catholic. Clubs: Overseas Bankers, Turf. Home: Geweygasse 11, 1180 Vienna Austria Office: 6 Schottengasse, Vienna 1010,, Austria

FINZI, BRUNO VITTORIO, physician, educator; b. Bologna, Italy, June 15, 1918; s. Aldo Oscar and Olga (Friedenberg) F.; m. Paola Guetta, Jan. 19, 1947; children—Sonia, Liana. M.D., Padua U., 1942, Specialist in Chest Diseases, 1947; Specialist in Gastroenterology, Pavia U., 1958. Intern, Ospedali Civili, Venice, Italy, 1946-50, attending physician, 1950-64, chief physician, 1964-65; chief physician Geriatric Hosp., Venice, 1966—; prof. geriatrics U. Pavia, 1972—. Contbr. articles to profl. jours.; author: Le Coliti (Vitali award), 1957; Contributo alla storia della Geriatria a Venezia, 1964; L'influenza dei fattori psicologici, 1974. Decorated Croce al merito di guerra, 1963, Medaglia della Guerra di Liberazione, 1962. Mem. Associazione Nazionale Italiana Medici e Operatori Geriatrici (v.p.), Società Italiana di Gerontologia e Geriatria (dir. 1971-81), Sezione Veneta Geriatria (pres. 1971-74). Ligade Geriatras y Gerontólogos de Langua Latina (dir.), Direttore dell'Università della Terza Età diVenezia Mem. Partito Repubblicano Italiano. Home: Accademia 1056, 30123 Venice Italy Office: Accademia 1023, Venice 30123, Italy

FIORAVANTI, NANCY ELEANOR, banker; b. Gloucester, Mass., Apr. 10, 1935; d. Richard Joseph and Evelyn Grace (Souza) Fioravanti; grad. high sch. Various positions and depts. Bank of New Eng.-North Shore (formerly Cape Ann Bank and Trust Co., successor to Gloucester Safe Deposit & Trust Co.), Gloucester, 1953-—, with trust dept., 1959-86, asst. trust officer, 1970-84, trust officer, 1984-86; trust officer Cape Ann Savs. Bank, 1986—. Treas. art adv. com. Gloucester Lyceum and Sawyer Free Library. Mem. Nat. Assn. Bank Women, Bus. and Profl. Women's Club. Home: PO Box 1638 Gloucester MA 01930 Office: 109 Main St Gloucester MA 01930

FIORE, COSMO DOMINIC, electronics company executive; b. N.Y.C., Aug. 4, 1932; s. Angelo Michael and Louise Marie (Bifano) F.; m. Mary Ann Kinney, Feb. 7, 1953; children—Michael, Christopher, Louise, Peter, Patrick. B.S.Eng., Cooper Union, 1962, M.S. Engring., 1968. Registered profl. engr., N.Y., N.J. Dir. engring. Belock Inst. Applied Devices, College Point, N.Y., 1956-69; pres. Amplitronics, Inc., Netcong, N.J., 1969—; cons. engr., N.Y.C., 1972-78. Patentee particle separator. Republican. Roman Catholic. Office: Amplitronics Inc 23 Railroad Ave Netcong NJ 07857

FIORE, JAMES LOUIS, JR., public accountant, educator, lecturer, public speaker; b. Jersey City, Oct. 7, 1935; s. James Louis and Rose (Perrotta) F.; m. Alberta W. Pope, July 21, 1957; children: Carolyn Leigh, James Louis, Toni Lynn. BS in Acctg., Seton Hall U., 1957; MBA in Acctg. and Statis., Western Colo. U., 1978; PhD, Calif. Western U., 1979. Lic. acct. Pa., N.J.; accredited Accreditation Council for Accountancy, Wash. Field auditor, State of N.J. Trenton, N.J., 1959-60; supr. internal auditing Ronson Corp., Woodbridge, N.J., 1960-64; supr. gen. acctg. Electronic Assocs., West Long Branch, N.J., 1964-65; pvt. practice acctg., 1965—; pres. Bucks County Research Inst. Inc., 1972-79; mem. adj. faculty Allentown Coll. of St. Francis De Sales, Center Valley, Pa., 1979-81, Pa. Coll. Straight Chiropractic, 1986—. Author: (with others) Shareholder Loans, The National Public Accountant, 1988, Non-Absorption of Nitrofurazone from the Urethra in Men, 1976, Comparative Bioavailability of Doxycycline, 1974; contbr. articles to profl. jours. Bd. dirs. Brick Twp. (N.J.) Scholarship Found., 1963-67; mem. adv. council Inst. for Accts., Pa. State U.; trustee Pa. Coll. Straight Chiropractic, 1986—; founder, treas. Cath. Acad. of Sci. in U.S.A., Washington; bd. dirs. Neighborhood Devel. Council, Annapolis, Md. Served to 2d lt. U.S. Army, 1957. Named Jaycee of Year, 1962; recipient Legion of Honor, Chapel of Four Chaplains, 1979. Mem. Pa. Soc. Public Accts., Nat. Soc. Public Accts., Calif. Western U. Alumni Assn., Amateur Artists Assn. Am., Western Colo. U. Alumni Assn., Seton Hall U. Alumni Assn. (Crest and Century Clubs). Roman Catholic. Lodges: K.C., Rosicrucians (traditional martinist order). Home: 265 Thompson Mill Rd Upper Makefield Twp Newtown PA 18940

FIORE, JOAN DE WOLFE, civic leader; b. Detroit, July 15, 1924; d. Richard Perrien and Rachel Elizabeth De Wolfe; m. Pasquale Peter Fiore, Nov. 25, 1949; children—Richard, Jill. Grad. Kingswood Girls Sch., Cranbrook, Mich.; student UCLA. Vice pres. Fitness with Finesse, Inc., Houston; regent, Princeton chpt. DAR, 1974-77, Seimes microfilm chmn., Washington, 1977—; state regent N.J., Nat. Soc. Magna Charta Dames; mem. Assn. of Descs. of Knights of the Garter, Gen. Soc. Mayflower Descs., Elder William Brewster Soc., First Colony of Mayflower Descs., Plantagenet Kings of Eng. Soc., Sovereign Colonial Soc. Americans of Royal Descent, Richard 3d Soc., Nat. Soc. Colonial Dames of XVII Century, Japan Soc. Vol. chmn. Med. Ctr., Princeton, N.J., 1960-77; Natural History Mus., N.Y.C., Nat. Trust Historic Preservation; Princeton Hist. Soc., Friends of Vielles Maisons Fracaises Inc. Republican. Quaker. Home: 18 Sturgis Rd Kendall Park NJ 08824

FIRA, ALEKSANDER, judge constitutional court of Yugoslavia; b. Kragujevac, Yugoslavia, May 4, 1929; s. Djordje and Leposava (Zivanovic) Fira; m. Rahela Konjovic, Apr. 12, 1958; children—Djordje, Boris. B.D., Faculty of Law, Beograd, 1952, Doctors D., 1960. Mem. Fed. Govt. Beograd, Yogoslavia; prof. Faculty of Law, Novi Sad-Yug; now judge Constitutional Ct. Yugoslavia, Belgrade. Author: Ustavno pravo, 1976, 4th edit. 1981; Razvoj socijalistickog samoupravljanja u SFRJ, 1981; Ustavnost i politika, 1984; Moc i nemoc federacije, Novi Sad, 1985. Mem. Acad. Art and Sci. Vojvodina. Home: Pozarevacka 12-16, Beograd Yugoslavia

FIRST, WESLEY, publishing company executive; b. Erie, Pa., Feb. 18, 1920; s. Orson John and Pearle (Unger) F.; m. Margaret Elizabeth Whittlesey, Apr. 3, 1943 (div. June 1967); children: Karen Lee, Michael; m. Dianne Jones, Dec. 1975 (div. Sept. 1981); m. Suzanne Lavenas, Jan. 9, 1982. Student, U. Mich., 1937-40; B.S., Columbia U., 1958; M.A., New Sch. for Social Research, 1963. Reporter Erie Dispatch, 1943-47, asst. city editor, 1947-48, asst. to editor, 1948-50; with N.Y. World-Telegram and Sun, N.Y.C., 1950-63; successively copyreader, night news editor N.Y. World-Telegram and Sun, 1950-57, asst. mng. editor, 1957-60, mng. editor, 1960-63; prof. journalism Ohio State U., 1963-65; dir. univ. relations Columbia, N.Y.C., 1965-67; asst. to pres. Sarah Lawrence Coll., 1967-68, Juilliard School, N.Y.C., 1968-69; editor Travel Weekly, 1969-76; editor-in-chief Psychology Today, 1976-77; Staff v.p. editorial Ziff-Davis Pub. Co., 1977-82, cons., 1982—; guest lectr. newspaper design and makeup Fordham U.; instr. journalism Finch Coll., N.Y.C.; Rep. to newspaper design and makeup seminar Am. Press Inst., 1957. Editor: Columbia Remembered, University on the Heights. Served with USAAF, 1944-46. Woodrow Wilson Fellow, 1959. Mem. U. Mich., Columbia U. alumni assns., Phi Beta Kappa, Kappa Tau Alpha, Sigma Delta Chi. Clubs: Overseas Press, Silurians. Home: 305 E 86th St Apt 20-R W New York NY 10028

FISCH, CHARLES, physician; b. Nesterov (Zolkiew), Poland, May 11, 1921; s. Leon and Janette (Deutscher) F.; m. June Spiegal, May 23, 1943; children—Jonathan, Gary, Bruce. A.B., Ind. U., 1942, M.D., 1944; Dr. Medicine (hon.), U. Utrecht, 1983. Diplomate Am. Bd. Internal Medicine, Am. Bd. Cardiovascular Medicine (mem. 1977-82). Intern St. Vincent's Hosp., Indpls., 1945; resident internal medicine VA Hosp., Indpls., 1948-50; fellow gastroenterology Marion County Gen. Hosp., Indpls., 1950-51; fellow cardiology Marion County Gen. Hosp., 1951-53; asst. prof. medicine Ind. U. Med. Sch., 1953-59, asso. prof., 1959-63, prof., 1963—, Distinguished prof., 1975, dir. cardiovascular div., 1963—; dir. Krannert Inst. Cardiology, 1960—; mem. cardio-renal adv. com. HEW-FDA, 1973-77, 79—; Am. Heart Assn. Connor lectr., 1980; chmn. manpower rev. com. Nat. Heart, Lung and Blood Inst., 1985—. Co-editor: Digitalis, 1969; contbr. articles to med. jours.; mem. editorial bd.: Am. Heart Jour, 1967—, Am. Jour. Electrocardiology, 1967—, Coer et Medicine Interne, 1970—, Am. Jour. Medicine, 1973—, Circulation, 1977—, Am. Jour. Cardiology, 1967—; asso. editor, 1977—. Served to capt. M.C. AUS, 1946-48. Recipient James Herrick award Am. Heart Assn. Fellow ACP, Am. Coll. Cardiology (pres. 1975-77, dir.), World Congress Cardiology (v.p. 1986); mem. Am. Fedn. Clin. Research, Central Soc. Clin. Research, Am. Physiol. Soc., Assn. Univ. Cardiologists, Assn. Am. Physicians. Home: 7901 Morningside Dr Indianapolis IN 46240

FISCHBACH, MARC, Luxembourg government defense official; b. Luxembourg, Feb. 22, 1946; s. Marcel and Marie-Ange (Wagener) F.; m. Sylvie Zenner, July 26, 1975; 3 children. Student, U. Luxembourg, 1965; LL.D., Faculte de Droit Nancy, France, 1969. Practice law Tony Biever, Luxembourg, 1969-74; sec. gen. Christian-Social Parliamentarian Group, 1972-79; mem. Luxembourg City Town Council, 1982; notary, Mersch, Luxembourg, 1982; mem. Nat. and European Parliament, 1979-84; minister pub. force, minister pub. services, minister sports, minister agriculture, 1984—. Office: Ministry of Def, Luxembourg

FISCHER, CARL HAHN, actuary, educator; b. Newark, Aug. 22, 1903; s. Carl H.H. Fischer and Minnie (Hahn) F.; m. Kathleen Kirkpatrick, Sept. 25, 1925; children: Patrick Carl, Michael John. B.S., Washington U., St. Louis, 1923; M.S., U. Iowa, 1930, Ph.D., 1932. Spl. engr. Am. Steel Foundries, 1923-26; instr. math. Beloit (Wis.) Coll., 1926-29; asst. U. Iowa, 1929-32; instr. U. Minn., 1932-33; spl. research asst. Northwestern Nat. Life Ins. Co., 1933-34; mem. faculty Wayne U., 1934-41; mem. faculty U. Mich., 1941—, prof. ins. and actuarial math., 1950-74, prof. emeritus, 1974—; vis. prof. U. Calif., Berkeley, 1951; prof. U. Hawaii, 1955, Hebrew U., Jerusalem, 1965, 67, Netherlands Sch. Econs., Rotterdam, 1966; dir. summer actuarial program John Hancock Mut. Life Ins. Co., 1959, 61, Travelers Ins. Co., 1963; cons., actuary, 1939—. Author: (with P.R. Rider) Mathematics of Investment, 1951, (with W.O. Menge) Mathematics of Life Insurance, 1965, Vesting and Termination Provisions in Private Pension Plans, 1970; contbr. articles to profl. jours. Trustee Ann Arbor Employee Retirement System, 1948-73; actuary Tchrs. Retirement Fund, N.D., 1939-77; cons. Philippine Govt. Service Ins. System, 1956, Social Security System, Philippine Govt., 1956, 62, Nat. Social Security and Welfare Corp., Liberia, 1977; mem. Adv. Council Social Security Financing, 1957-58; chmn. study com. mil. retired pay U.S. Senate, 1960-61; mem. Ann Arbor Bd. Edn., 1957-60. Fellow Soc. Actuaries, Conf. Actuaries in Pub. Practice (v.p. 1970-75); mem. Am. Acad. Actuaries, Am. Risk and Ins. Assn., Am. Statis Assn., Math. Assn. Am.; ; mem. Acacia, Sigma Xi, Beta Gamma Sigma. Club: Mason. Home: 1706 Morton Ave Ann Arbor MI 48104 Office: U Mich Grad Sch Bus Adminstrn Ann Arbor MI 48109

FISCHER, DANIEL EDWARD, psychiatrist; b. New Haven, Apr. 22, 1945; s. Alexander and Miriam (Kramer) F.; m. Linda Lee Bradford, June 12, 1969; children—Meredith Tara, Alexis Anne. B.A., Boston U., 1969, M.D., 1969; J.D., Coll. William and Mary, 1986. Bar: Va. 1986, U.S. Dist. Ct. (ea. dist.) Va. 1986, U.S. Ct. Appeals (4th cir.) 1986; Intern in medicine Baylor Affiliated Hosps., Houston, 1969-70; resident in psychiatry Washington U. Sch. Medicine, St. Louis, 1970-73; practice medicine specializing in psychiatry, Virginia Beach, Va., 1975—; chmn. dept. psychiatry DePaul Hosp., Norfolk, Va., 1978-79, Bayside Hosp., Virginia Beach, 1980-81,88—; pres. Am. Investment Mgmt. Services, Inc. Contbr. articles to profl. jours. Bd. dirs. Tidewater Pastoral Counseling Service, Norfolk, 1976—, Kempsville Conservative Synagogue, Virginia Beach, 1982-86; bd. dirs. Beth Chavarim, 1987—. Served as maj. U.S. Army, 1973-75. Decorated Army Commendation medal. Fellow Acad. Psychosomatic Medicine; mem. AMA, Am. Psychiat. Assn., Va. Med. Soc., Va. Psychiat. Assn., Virginia Beach Med. Soc., Tidewater Acad. Psychiatry. Democrat. Jewish. Avocation: Stamp Collecting. Office: Hearst Fischer & Price Ltd Pembroke 5 Suite 331 Virginia Beach VA 23462

FISCHER, DAVID SEYMOUR, internist; b. Bklyn., May 13, 1930; s. Simon and Charolotte (Ohlbaum) F.; m. Iris Liquerman, June 1, 1958; children: Karen, Louise, Francie. A.B., Williams Coll., 1951; M.D., Harvard U., 1955. Diplomate Am. Bd. Internal Medicine, Am. Bd. Med. Oncology, Am. Bd. Hematology. Intern, Kings County Hosp., 1955-56; resident U. Utah, 1956-57, Montefiore Hosp., Bronx, N.Y., 1957-58; fellow U. Washington, Seattle, 1958-59, Yale U., 1962-64; attending physician Yale New Haven Hosp, Hosp. St. Raphael; cons. Milford Hosp., Conn., 1970—, Griffin Hosp., Derby, Conn., 1970—, VA Hosp., West Haven, Conn., 1974—, Yale Comprehensive Cancer Ctr., New Haven, 1978—; clin. prof. medicine Yale U. Author: Cancer Chemotherapy Treatment and Care, 3d edit., 1988; also articles. Editor, author: Cancer Therapy, 1982. Pres., Conn. div. Am. Cancer Soc., 1981; pres. med. staff Hosp. St. Raphael, New Haven, 1980; pres. med. adv. bd. Jewish Home for Aged, 1983-85; med. adv. bd. Leukemia Soc. South Cen. Conn.; pres. Congregation Bikur Cholim Sheveth Achim, 1983-85. Served to capt. U.S. Army, 1959-61. Recipient Harris award Yale New Haven Hosp., 1974; Bronze medal Am. Cancer Soc., 1982. Fellow ACP; mem. Am. Soc. Clin. Oncology (chmn. pub. issues), Am. Soc. Hematology, Am. Fedn. Clin. Research. Jewish. Office: Hematology-Oncology 60 Temple St New Haven CT 06510

FISCHER, DOUGLAS ARTHUR, electrical engineer; b. Tokyo, Japan, Oct. 31, 1952; came to U.S., 1958; s. Robert Kay and Maryann (Carter) F. BEE, Mont. State U., 1974; MEE, So. Meth. U., 1983. Mem. staff Campus Crusade for Christ, San Bernardino, Calif., 1974-80; sr. engr. Gen. Dynamics, Ft. Worth, 1980-84; project engr. Honeywell Aerospace (formerly Sperry Flight Systems), Albuquerque, 1984-86, sr. project engr. Honeywell Def. Avionics Systems Div., 1986—. Mem. IEEE, Tau Beta Pi. Home: 13404 Auburn NE Albuquerque NM 87112 Office: Honeywell Def Avionics Systems PO Box 9200 Albuquerque NM 87119

FISCHER, ERNST OTTO, chemist, educator; b. Munich, Germany, Nov. 10, 1918; s. Karl T. and Valentine (Danzer) F. Diplom, Munich Tech. U., 1949, Dr. rer. nat., 1952, Habilitation, 1954, Dr. rer. nat. h.c., 1972, D.Sc.h.c., 1975, Dr. rer. nat. h.c., 1977, Dr.h.c., 1983. Assoc. prof. inorganic chemistry U. Munich, 1957, prof., 1959; prof. inorganic chemistry inst. Munich Inst. Tech., 1964—. Author: (with H. Werner) Metall-pi-Komplexe mit di- und oligoolefischen Liganden, 1963; transl. Complexes with di- and oligo-olefinic Ligands, 1966; Contbr. (with H. Werner) numerous articles in field to profl. jours. Recipient ann. prize Göttingen Acad. Scis., 1957, Alfred Stock Meml. prize Soc. German Chemists, 1959, Nobel Prize in Chemistry, 1973; Am. Chem. Soc. Centennial fellow, 1976. Mem. Bavarian Acad. Scis., Soc. German Chemists, German Acad. Scis. Leopoldina, Austrian Acad. Scis. (corr.), Accademia Nazionale dei Lincei, Italy (fgn.), Acad. Scis. Göttingen (corr.), Am. Acad. Arts and Scis. (fgn., hon.), Chem. Soc. (hon.). Address: 16 Sohnckestrasse, 8000 Munich 71, Federal Republic of Germany

FISCHER, FRED WALTER, physicist, engineer, educator; b. Zwickau, Germany, June 26, 1922; s. Fritz and Louiska (Richter) F.; B.S. in Mech. Engring., Columbia U., 1949, M.S., 1950; M.S. in Physics, U. Wash., 1957; Dr.Engr. in Elec. Engring., Tech. U. Munich, 1966; m. Yongja Kim, Oct. 1, 1970. Analyst, Boeing Co., Seattle, Munich, Bonn, W. Ger., 1950-84; cons. Boeing Co., 1984—; owner Fischer Cons.; instr. physics, math., and engring. North Seattle Community Coll., 1973—. Author: Analysis for Physics and Engineering, 1982. Served with AUS, 1943-46. Boeing scholar, Max Planck Inst. Plasma Physics, Munich, 1964-65. Mem. Sigma Xi (life). Office: North Seattle Community Coll 9600 College Way N Seattle WA 98103

FISCHER, IVAN, conductor; b. Budapest, Hungary, Jan. 20, 1951; s. Dandor and Evelyn (Boschan) F. Grad. Bela Bartok Conservatorium, Budapest, 1969; diploma Vienna Acad. Music, 1974. Mus. dir. No. Sinfonia, 1979-82, now Kent Opera, England; founder Budapest Festival Orch., 1983; debut appearance Los Angeles Philharm., 1983; past conductor Chgo. Symphony Orch., Cin. Symphony, Detroit Symphony, New Orleans Symphony Orch., Rochester Philharm., San Francisco Symphony, BBC Symphony, 1976; appearances with London Philharm., English Chamber Orch., Scottish Nat. Orch., Royal Liverpool Philharm. Recipient Premio Firenze, 1974, Rupert Found. Internat. Young Conductors award, BBC, 1976. Address: ICM Artists Ltd 40 W 57th St New York NY 10019 other: Kent Opera, Ashford, Kent TN27 9EN, England *

FISCHER, LEROY HENRY, historian, educator; b. Hoffman, Ill., May 19, 1917; s. Andrew LeRoy and Effie (Risby) F.; m. Martha Gwendolyn Anderson, June 20, 1948; children: Barbara Ann, James LeRoy, John Andrew. B.A., U. Ill., 1939, M.A., 1940, Ph.D., 1943; postgrad., Columbia U., 1941. Grad. asst. history U. Ill., 1940-43; asst. prof. history Ithaca (N.Y.) Coll., 1946; asst. prof. history Okla. State U. at Stillwater, 1946-49, assoc. prof. history, 1949-60, prof. history, 1960-72, Oppenheim Regents prof. history, 1973-78, Oppenheim prof. history, 1978-84, Oppenheim prof. emeritus, 1984—; exec. sec. honors program, 1959-61. Author: Lincoln's Gadfly, Adam Gurowski, 1964, (with Muriel H. Wright) Civil War Sites in Oklahoma, 1967, The Civil War Era in Indian Territory, 1974, The Western States in the Civil War, 1975, Territorial Governors of Oklahoma, 1975, The Western Territories in the Civil War, 1977, Civil War Battles in the West, 1981, Oklahoma's Governors, 1907-1979, 3 vols., 1981-85, Oklahoma State University Historic Old Central, 1988; contbr. articles to profl jours. Vice chmn. Honey Springs Battlefield Park Commn., 1968—; chmn. adv. com. Okla. Historic Preservation Rev. Commn., 1969-78, mem., 1978—, vice-chmn., 1978-81, chmn., 1981-83; bd. dirs. Nat. Indian Hall of Fame, 1969—, YMCA, 1951-54, 83-85. Served with Signal Corps, AUS, 1943-45. Recipient Lit. award Loyal Legion U.S., 1963; named Tchr. of Year, Okla. State U.-Okla. Edn. Assn., 1969. Mem. Am., So. hist. assns., Western History Assn., Am. Assn. State and Local History, AAUP, Okla. (dir. 1966—, treas. 1984-87), Ill. hist. socs., Orgn. Am. Historians, Omicron Delta Kappa, Pi Gamma Mu, Phi Alpha Theta, Alpha Kappa Lambda. Methodist (chmn. various coms. 1946—, adminstrv. bd. 1950-77, chmn. 1976-77, lay leader 1970-71). Home: 1010 W Cantwell Ave Stillwater OK 74075

FISCHER, NORMAN, JR., media broker, appraiser, broadcast consultant; b. Washington, Mar. 14, 1924; s. Norman and Agnes Columbia (May) F.; m. Ela Cecile Ragland, Mar. 28, 1959; 1 child, Norman Terrill. BS, Washington and Lee U., 1949. Lic. real estate broker, Tex. Owner, operator radio stas. KUKA-AM, San Antonio, 1961-67, WEBB-AM, Balt., 1967-70, KBER-AM, Abilene, Tex., 1976-82; account exec. radio stas. KTSA-AM, San Antonio, 1957-60, KONO-AM, San Antonio, 1960-61; ptnr. Holt-Fischer, Austin, Tex., 1970-72; v.p. R. Miller Hicks Co., Austin, 1972-75; pres. Advance Inc., owners KRMH, Austin, 1972-75; pres. Norman Fischer & Assocs., Inc., Austin, 1974—; guest instr. U. Tex. Sch. Communications, 1979. Mem. Bexar County Dem. Com., 1966; active Austin chpt. March of Dimes, 1973-77, chpt. chmn., 1976. Served with Signal Corps, AUS, 1943-46. Mem. Nat. Assn. Broadcasters, Tex. Assn. Broadcasters, La. Assn. Broadcasters, Nat. Radio Broadcasters Assn., Nat. Media Brokers Assn., Austin C. of C. Episcopalian. Clubs: Tarry House, Capitol (Austin). Lodge: Rotary. Office: Norman Fischer & Assocs Inc 1209 Parkway PO Box 5308 Austin TX 78763

FISCHER, OLGA CATHARINA MARIA, linguist, educator; b. Hilversum, The Netherlands, Apr. 5, 1951; d. Herman Gerardus and Cornelia Evrarda (Braakhuis) F.; m. Mark Alexander Janssen; children: Daan, Joost. Grad. in English Lang. and Lit. cum laude, U. Amsterdam, The Netherlands, 1973, MA in English Lang. and Lit. cum laude, 1976; MA in English Linguistics, U. Newcastle-upon-Tyne, Eng., 1975. Lectr. U. Amsterdam, 1976—; vis. lectr. U. Manchester, Eng., 1985-86. Author: Explanation and Linguistic Change, 1987, also co-editor; co-author: The Cambridge History of the English Lang., vol II, 1989; co-editor: Papers form the 4th ICEHL, 1985; contbr. articles to profl. jours. Brit. Council grantee, Amsterdam, 1985. Mem. Internat. Courtly Lit. Soc., Linguistic Assn. Great Britain, Linguistics in the Netherlands. Home: Alexanderplein 9 hs, 1018 CG Amsterdam The Netherlands Office: U Amsterdam, Engels Seminarium, Spuistraat 210, 1012 VT Amsterdam The Netherlands

FISCHER, OSKAR, minister of foreign affairs of German Democratic Republic; b. Asch, Czechoslovakia, Mar. 19, 1923; married; 1 child. Tailor, 1946-47; mem. Socialist Unity Party (SED), 1946—, chmn. Spremberg Dist. Exec., 1947-48, land exec. of Brandenburg, 1949-50; sec. central council Free German Youth, World Fedn. Democratic Youth, 1951-55; mem. World Youth Council, 1952-55; ambassador to Bulgaria, 1955-59, dep. minister of fgn. affairs, 1965-73; state sec. and permanent dep. minister of fgn. affairs, 1973-75; minister of fgn. affairs, 1975—; mem. Central Com. Socialist Unity Party, 1971—, dep. People's Chamber, 1976—. Decorated Karl Marx Order, Banner of Labor, Medal of Merit and other awards. Office: Ministerium für Auswärtige, Angelegenheiten, Berlin German Democratic Republic

FISCHER, PETER-MICHAEL, manager; b. Singen, Baden, Fed. Republic Germany, May 23, 1941; s. Arnold W. and Sophie (Brütsch) F.; m. Renate Fischer-Gross, Aug. 4, 1966; 1 child: Oliver. Student, Textilfachschule, Nagold. Mng. dir. Fischer GmbH., Singen, Germany, 1972—; mng. dir. Modehaus Fischer, Singen, Konstanz; mng. dir. Boutique Flair, Singer. Mem. First in Fashion (sec. 1985—). Free Democratic party. Roman Catholic. Home and Office: Scheffelstr 2 4, D770 Singen Baden, Federal Republic of Germany

FISCHER, PHYLLIS LENORE, animal rights activist, beauty shop executive; b. Parkersburg, W.Va., June 24, 1951; d. Robert Paul and June (Fultz) F.; m. Richard Morgan, May 1975; 1 son, R.G. B.S. summa cum laude, Ohio U., 1973. Founder, Writers for Animal Rights, Jonesboro, Tenn., 1978-83; founder, dir. Mobilization for Animals, Columbus, Ohio, 1981-84; founder Protect Our Earth's Treasures, Columbus, 1984-85; founder, pres. Care about the Strays, New Albany, Ohio, 1985—; speaker, media cons. several orgns., 1985—; mng. dir. Topcuts, Inc., Columbus, 1983—. Author numerous published poems. Editor Black Cat jour., 1975—. Avocations: writing; lecturing; rescuing stray animals. Home: PO Box 474 New Albany OH 43054

FISCHER, ZOE ANN, real estate and property marketing company executive, real estate consultant; b. Los Angeles, Aug. 26, 1939; d. George and Marguerite (Carrasco) Routsos; m. Douglas Clare Fischer, Aug. 6, 1960 (div. 1970); children—Brent Sean Cecil, Tahlia Georgienne Marguerite Bianca. B.F.A. in Design, UCLA, 1964. Pres. Zoe Antiques, Beverly Hills, Calif., 1973—; v.p. Harleigh Sandler Real Estate Corp. (now Merrill Lynch), 1980-81; exec. v.p. Coast to Coast Real Estate & Land Devel. Corp., Century City, Calif., 1981-83; pres. New Market Devel., Inc., Beverly Hills, 1983—; dir. mktg. Mirabella, Los Angeles, 1983, Autumn Pointe, Los Angeles, 1983-84, Desert Hills, Antelope Valley, Calif., 1984-85; cons. Lowe Corp., Los Angeles, 1985. Designer album cover for Clare Fischer Orch. (Grammy award nomination 1962). Soprano Roger Wagner Choir, UCLA, 1963-64. Mem. UCLA Alumni Assn. Democrat. Roman Catholic. Avocations: skiing, designing jewelry, interior design, antique collecting, photography.

FISCHER-APPELT, PETER, university president; b. Berlin, Oct. 28, 1932; s. Hans Fischer and Margret Appelt; Dr.theol., U. Bonn, 1965; L.H.D. (hon.), Temple U., Phila., 1983; m. Hildegard Zeller, Oct. 17, 1959; children—Andreas, Bernhard, Dorothee. Comml. apprentice William Prym, Stolberg, 1951-53; sci. asst. Faculty Protestant Theology, U. Bonn, 1961-70; ordained to ministry Protestant Ch. of Rhinelands, 1966; minister, Cologne-Mülheim, 1964-65; co-founder, chmn. Bundesassistentenkonferenz, Bonn, 1968-69; pres. U. Hamburg, 1970—; chmn. adv. bd. Stiftung Weltweite Wissenschaft; dep. chmn., mng. bd. Univ. Gesellschaft; chmn. trustees Hans-Bredow-Inst. Rundfunk und Fernsehen; dep. chmn. bd. trustees Inst. Friedensforschung und Sicherheitspolitik; chmn. Wissenschaftskommn. Versuch für das Fernstudium im Medienverbund, 1975-80; adv. bd., dept. chmn. Zentrale Vergabestelle Studienplätze; trustee Hochschul Informationssystem GmbH, Deutscher Akad. Austauschdienst; chmn. council Inter-Univ. Centre Postgrad. Studies, Dubrovnik, Yugoslavia; mem. jury DAG-Fernsehpreis; bd. dirs. Found. for Internat. Exchange of Sci. and Cultural Info. by Telecommunication, 1982—. Recipient Gold medal Bulgarian Acad. Scis., 1981, medal Pro Cultura Hungarica, 1988. Author, editor in field. Avocations: chess, music, theater, opera, skiing. Home: 22 Waldweg, D-2085 Quickborn-Heide Federal Republic of Germany Office: U Hamburg, 1 Edmund-Siemers-Allee, D-2000 Hamburg 13 Federal Republic of Germany

FISCHER-DIESKAU, DIETRICH, baritone; b. Berlin, May 28, 1925; s. Albert and Dora (Klingelhoffer) F.-D.; m. Irmgard Poppen, Feb. 10, 1949 (dec. Dec. 1963); children: Mathias, Martin, Manuel. Studied music with, Georg A. Walter, Herman Weissenborn; MusD (hon.), Oxford (Eng.) U., 1978, U. Sorbonne, Paris, 1980. Sang lyrical and title role baritone Mcpl. Opera, Berlin, 1948, extensive concert tours in Europe and U.S.; appearance: (festivals) including Edinburgh, Vienna, London, Paris, Netherlands, Munich, Berlin, Salzburg; mem., Vienna State Opera, 1957—, hon. mem., Deutsche Oper, Berlin, 1978; author: Texte Deutscher Lieder, 1968, Aufden Spuren der Schubert-Lieder, 1971, Wagner und Nietzche-Der Mystagoge and sein Abtrünniger, 1974; Chief roles include Wolfram, Jochanaan, Alamavive, Marquis Posa, Don Giovanni, Dr. Faust, Falstaff, Sachs, others. Served with German Army, World War II. Recipient award Internat. Gramophone Record, 1955, 57-58, 60-61, 64-65, 68, 71, 73, 76-77, Art award Berlin, 1950, Golden Orpheus Mantua, 1955, 1st Class Fed. medal for disting. services, 1958, Naras award, 1962, Mozart-Medaille Wien, 1963, Ehrenmitgliedschaft Konzerthausgesellschaft Wien, 1963, Byerischer Kammersänger, 1959, Berliner, 1963, Edison award, 1962, 64, 67, 71, Sonning award, 1975, Grosser Verdienstorden des Bundesverdienstkreuzes, 1974, Friedrich Rückert award Schweinfurt, 1979, award Siemens-Stiftung, Fed. Republic of Germany, 1980; named Hon. Mem., Deutsche Oper Berlin, 1978. Mem. Acad. Arts, Internat. Mahler Soc. Vienna, Internat. Music Council (German sect.), Royal Acad. Music, London, Royal Acad. Music, Stockholm. Address: care Colbert Artists Mgmt Inc 111 W 57th St New York NY 10019 *

FISCHER FZN, JOHANN FRIEDRICH, international marketing executive, marketing consultant; b. Amsterdam, Netherlands, Oct. 22, 1924; s. Johann Friedrich and Wilhelmina (De Visscher) F.; m. Wilhelmina Welther, Feb. 12, 1945; 1 son, John Frits. Cert. Sch. of Commerce, The Hague, 1940, Higher Sch. Commerce, Rotterdam, 1946. European mktg. dir. Johnson's Wax, The Hague, 1945-62, Ursina S.A., Bern, Switzerland, 1962-70, Nestle, Amsterdam, 1970-75; world mktg. dir. Frisian Flag, The Hague, 1975-78; mng. dir. Trefpunt Exec. search, The Hague, 1978-83, Internat. Mktg. and Exec. Search, The Hague, 1983—. Home and Office: Sportlaan 298, 2566 LM The Hague The Netherlands

FISCHER-HARRIEHAUSEN, HERMANN, social scientist; b. Berlin, June 20, 1932; s. Konrad and Ellen (von Heinemann) H.; m. Eva Waitzmann, Sept. 18, 1964. D Philosophy, U. Goettingen, 1961. Pubs. reader Georg Westermann Verlag, Brunswick, 1962-63; sci. collaborator Max-Planck-Inst. fuer Bildungsforschung, Berlin, 1964-66, Fed. Health Office, Berlin, 1966—. Author: Berliner Neubauquartiere, 1973; co-author: Sozialmedizin, 1977; contbr. articles to profl. jours. Home: Prinz-Friedrich-Leopold-Strasse, #48, D1000 Berlin 38 Federal Republic of Germany

FISCHER SARAVIA, JOSE HERBERT, finance company executive; b. Guatemala City, Guatemala, Dec. 6, 1927; s. Roberto and Otilia (Saravia) Fischer; m. Ileana Pivaral Rodriguez (div.); children: Marta Regina, Lorraine, Madelaine, Karen, Michele; m. Beatriz Isabel Guzmán, Jan. 22, 1948; 1 child, Christian José. AA, Menlo Jr. Coll., 1947; BSME, MIT, 1949; BS Ingeniero Mecanico, U. San Carlos, Guatemala, 1950; grad., Ford Merchandising Sch., 1950. Mgr. parts Fischer y Cia Ltd., Guatemala City, 1950-66, asst. mgr., 1976-82, gen. mgr., 1976-82; dir. sec. Financiera Industrial y Agropecuaria S.A., Guatemala City, 1969—; prof. combustion engines U. San Carlos, 1966, prof. machine kinematics, 1967-68; prof. dynamics U. Landivar, Guatemala City, 1970; pres. Verdufrex, Guatemala City, 1983—; cons. Credisa Fidesa, Guatemala City, 1984—. Councillor of State, Guatemala City, 1978-82; sec. Internat. Road Fedn., 1960-63; pres. Chamber of Industry, 1979-81, pres. com. representations, 1986—; aux. maj. Municipality Zone 9, 1963, Guatemala City. Mem. Colegio Ingenieros Guatemala, Assn. Vecinos Eucaliptos (pres. 1987), Sigma Xi, Pi Tau Sigma. Club: MIT (Guatemala).

FISCHLER, PAMELA FRAN, advertising agency executive; b. Bklyn., Sept. 25, 1951; s. Martin Lee and Gilda Augusta (Gerber) G.; m. Burton Fischler, July 3, 1973. Student Stephens Coll., 1969-71; BA, Hofstra U., 1973. New acct. exec. Unique Security Agy., Great Neck, N.Y., 1973-75; career counselor, acct. exec. Dartmouth Cons., N.Y.C., 1975; acct. liaison MGA, Inc., Advt., Great Neck, N.Y., 1975-76, v.p. pub. relations and media, 1977-80, exec. v.p., 1980—. Bd. dirs. Soc. of Friends of Touro synagogue, Newport, R.I. Democrat. Jewish. Home: Grants Corners North Salem NY 10560 Office: MGA Plaza Westbury NY 11590

FISCHMAN, MYRNA LEAH, accountant, educator; b. N.Y.C.; d. Isidore and Sally (Goldstein) F. BS, Coll. City N.Y., 1960, MS, 1964; PhD, NYU 1976. Asst. to controller Sam Goody, Inc., N.Y.C.; tchr. accounting Central Comml. High Sch., N.Y.C., 1960-63, William Cullen Bryant High Sch., Queens, N.Y., 1963-66, vocat. adviser, 1963-66; instr. acctg. Borough of Manhattan Community Coll., N.Y.C., 1966-69; self employed acct., N.Y.C., 1960—; chief acct. investigator rackets, Office Queens Dist. Atty., 1969-70, community relations coordinator, 1970-71; adj. prof. L.I. U., 1970-79, prof. acctg. taxation and law, 1979—, coordinator grad. capstone courses, 1982—, dir. Sch. Professional Accountancy Bklyn. campus, 1984—; dir. Faculty Acctg. Taxation and Law Bklyn. campus, 1986—. Editor Ea. Bus. Educators Jour., 1988. Research cons. pre-tech. program Bd. Edn., City N.Y.; acct.-adviser Inst. for Advancement of Criminal Justice; acct.-cons. Coalition Devel. Corp., Interracial Council for Bus. Opportunities; treas. Breakfree Inc., Lower East Side Prep. Sch.; mem. edn. task force Am. Jewish Com., 1972—; mem. steering com., youth div. N.Y. Dem. County Com., 1967-68, del. to Nat. Conv., Young Dems. Am., 1967, rep. assigned to women's activities com., 1967; mem. Chancellor Com. Against Discrimination in Edn., 1976—; chmn. supervisory com. Fed. Credit Union #1532, N.Y.C., 1983—; mem. legis. adv. bd. N.Y. State Assemblyman Denis Butler, 1979—; chmn. consumer council Astoria Med. Center, 1980—; mem. subcom. on bus. edn. to the econ. devel. and mktg. com. Bklyn. C. of C., 1984—. Recipient award for meritorious service Community Service Soc., 1969; C.P.A., N.Y. Mem. Jewish Guild for Blind, Jewish Braille Inst., Friends Am. Ballet Theatre, Friends Met. Mus. Art, Community Welfare Com., Assn. Govt. Accts. (bd. dirs. N.Y. chpt. 1984—, dir. research and manuscripts 1985—), Am. Acctg. Assn., Nat., Eastern (co-chmn. ann. meeting 1967) bus. edn. assns., Nat., Eastern (chmn. ann. meeting, 1968) bus. tchrs. assns., Internat. Soc. Bus. Edn., Grad. Students Orgn. NYU (treas. 1971-73, v.p. 1973-74), Nat. Assn. Accts. (dir. N.Y. chpt. 1983—), Assn. Govt. Accts. (dir. N.Y. chpt. 1983—), NEA, AAUP, Doctorate Assn. N.Y. Educators (v.p. 1975—), Am. Assn. Jr. Colls., Young Alumni Assn. ; chmn. supervisory com. Fed. Credit Union #1532, N.Y.C., 1983—; Coll. (mem. council), Emanu-El League Congregation Emanu-El, N.Y. (chmn. community services com. 1967-68), Nat. Assn. Accts. (bd. dirs. N.Y. chpt. 1985—, dir. profl. devel. 1986-87, dir. pub. relations 1987-88), Tax Inst. L.I. U. (dir. Bklyn. chpt. 1984—), Delta Pi Epsilon (treas. 1976). Jewish. Democrat. Club: Women's City (N.Y.C.). Developed new bus. machine course and curriculum Borough Manhattan Bus. Community Coll. Home: PO Box 6241 Astoria NY 11106 Office: LI U Zeckendorf Campus Brooklyn NY 11201

FISCHMAR, RICHARD MAYER, controller, consultant; b. N.Y.C., Apr. 11, 1938; s. John B. and Sylvia (Moosnick) F.; m. Sandra P. Fensin, July 3, 1967; children: Brian, Laura. BS, U. Ill., 1959, MA, 1962. CPA, Ill. Sr. auditor L.K.H.&H., Chgo., 1962-66; controller Lake States Engr., Park Ridge, Ill., 1966-68, New Communities Enterprises, Park Forest South, Ill., 1968-70; dep. dir. Ill. Drug Abuse Program, Chgo., 1970-71; dir. internal audit Ill. Dept. Labor, Chgo., 1971-73; controller Ill. Dept. Employment Security, Chgo., 1973-78, D.L. Pattis Real Estate, Lincolnwood, Ill., 1978-86, Goodman Realty Group, Inc., Chgo., 1986—. Author: (booklet) Bibliography of Management Services, 1972; contbr. articles to profl. jours. Mem. Ill. Soc. CPA's (real estate com., mgmt. adv. services and constrn. com.). Office: Goodman Realty Group Inc 6160 N Cicero Chicago IL 60646

FISH, ANDREW JOSEPH, JR., electrical engineering educator, researcher; b. New Haven, Aug. 15, 1944; s. Andrew Joseph and Katherine Pauline (Frey) F. B.S.E.E., Worcester Poly. Inst., 1966; M.S.E.E., U. Iowa, 1973; M.S. in Math., St. Mary U., San Antonio, 1974; Ph.D., U. Conn. Asst. prof. elec. engring. U. Hartford, West Hartford, Conn., 1979-84, Western New Eng. Coll., Springfield, Mass., 1984-87; assoc. prof. elec. engring. U. New Haven, 1987—; co-chmn. nonlinear systems group Am. Control Conf., 1980. Contbr. articles to profl. pubs. Gate keeper West Suffield Grange, 1982; Fellow Yale U., 1972-73. Mem. IEEE (co-chmn. large scale and nonlinear systems group 22d Conf. on Decision and Control, ASME. Research on modeling, analysis, control of nonlinear systems, particularly Hybrid Analog-Digital Systems.

FISH, LILIAN MANN, lawyer; b. Methuen, Mass., Sept. 6, 1901; d. Samuel Eleazer and Ella Agnes (Hobbs) Mann; m. Charles Melvin Fish, Dec. 25, 1923 (div. 1933). Student U. So. Calif., 1930's-40's; J.D. magna cum laude, Southwestern U., 1932. Bar: Calif. 1932, U.S. Dist. Ct. (so. dist.) Calif. 1932, U.S. Ct. Appeals (9th cir.) 1934, U.S. Supreme Ct. 1936. Sec. Lloyd S. Nix, Atty., San Pedro, Calif., 1926-29, Los Angeles, 1931-32; sec. Office of City Prosecutor (Lloyd S. Nix), Los Angeles, 1929-30, Victor R. Hansen, atty., Los Angeles, 1930-31; assoc. Lloyd S. Nix, Los Angeles, 1932-44, Price, Postel & Parma, Santa Barbara, Calif., 1949-71; sole practice, Los Angeles, 1944—, Santa Barbara, 1971—; editor Ancestors West quar., 1979—. Vice pres. Los Angeles County Young Republicans, 1939-40; bd. dirs. Santa Barbara Trust Hist. Preservation, pres., 1975, also sec.; bd. dirs. Santa Barbara County Geneal. Soc., 1978—, also editor, hon. life mem.; bd. dirs. Santa Barbara Hist. Soc., 1971-76, chmn. library com., 1978-83; pres. Santa Barbara Bus. and Profl. Women, 1955-56, Nat. Bus. and Profl. Women, Los Angeles, 1945-46; registrar Mission Canyon chpt. DAR, Santa Barbara, 1965-80, 85—(Roll of Honor cert. 1978). Recipient Cert. of Recognition for service Calif. Senate, 1980; Cert. of Service, Bicentennial Com., City of Santa Barbara, 1975-77; named Woman of Yr., Mar Vista Bus. and Profl. Women's Assn., 1979. Mem. ABA, State Bar Calif. (mem. probate estate planning sect.) Santa Barbara County Bar Assn. (del. state bar convs. 1950s), Women Lawyers Club Los Angeles (pres. 1940-41), Soc. Genealogists (London), Phi Delta Delta. Republican. Mem. United Ch. of Christ. Home: 2546 Murrell Rd Santa Barbara CA 93109

FISHER, ALLAN CAMPBELL, railway executive; b. Westerly, R.I., Aug. 9, 1943; s. Arthur Chester and Norma Jean (Campbell) F.; m. Ellen Tryon Roop, June 14, 1969; children: Bradford Booth, Katherine Thayer. BA in Econs., St. Lawrence U., 1965; MS in Transp., Northwestern U., 1970. Research economist Gen. Motors Research Labs., Warren, Mich., 1969; mgmt. trainee Penn Central, 1970, asst. trainmaster, Chgo., 1970-71, trainmaster, Toledo, 1971-72, terminal trainmaster, Elkhart, Ind., 1972, trainmaster, Cleve., 1972-74, asst. terminal supt., Cleve., 1974, terminal supt., Balt., 1974-75, asst. div. supt. Chesapeake div., Balt., 1975-76, terminal supt. Conrail, Conway, Pa., 1976, div. supt. N.J. div., Elizabethport, 1977, Lehigh div., Bethlehem, Pa., 1978, regional supt. ops. improvement Central region, Pitts., 1978-80, dir. budget control, 1980-82, regional supt. indsl. engring. So. region, Indpls., 1982-83, system dir. operating rules, Phila., 1983—. Served with U.S. Army, 1966-67, Vietnam. Decorated Bronze Star medal. Urban Transp. fellow, 1969. Mem. Fuel and Operating Officers Assn., Am. Inst. Indsl. Engrs. (sr.), Assn. Am. R.R.'s (operating rules com., chmn. transport spent nuclear fuel com.), Operating Rules Assn., Mayflower Descendents (life), Sigma Chi (life). Unitarian-Universalist. Club: Phila. Boys Choir Men's Chorale (bd. dirs.). Lodge: Masons. Home: 215 Poplar Ave Wayne PA 19087 Office: 6 Penn Ctr Room 310 Philadelphia PA 19103-2959

FISHER, ALTON SELTON, JR., healthcare company executive; b. Lebanon, Tenn., Nov. 20, 1943; s. Alton Selton and Ocie (Jewell) F.; B.S., Middle Tenn. State U., 1970; postgrad. U. Minn., 1979-82; m. Janet Laraine Morgan, Sept. 8, 1967; children—Amy Katherine, Stephanie Laraine. With Ernst & Ernst, Nashville, 1970-73, North Fla. Regional Hosp. and Hosp. Corp. Am., Gainesville, 1973-77; v.p. Alachua Gen. Hosp., Inc., Gainesville, 1977-82; v.p., asst. treas. Santa Fe Healthcare Systems, Inc. and Wellness, Inc., Gainesville, 1982-84; v.p. cost containment/profl. and provider relations Blue Cross-Blue Shield of Fla., 1984-86; sr. v.p. fin. U. Hosp., Jacksonville, Fla., 1986—; lectr., cons. Served in USAF, 1961-65. Recipient Follmer award Healthcare Fin. Mgmt., 1980, Reeves award, 1983, Muncie award, 1986. Mem. Healthcare Fin. Mgmt. Assn. (chpt. pres. 1981-82, MATRIX mem. 1983-85, nat. bd. dirs. 1985-87), Am. Coll. Hosp. Adminstrs., Am. Inst. C.P.A.s, Fla. Inst. CPA's, U.S. Power Squadron. Methodist. Editor: Healthcare Financial Management Handbook, 1981, 82. Home: 2434 Castellon Dr Jacksonville FL 32217 Office: University Hosp Inc 655 W 8th St Jacksonville FL 32209

FISHER, ANITA JEANNE, educator; b. Atlanta, Oct. 22, 1937; d. Paul Benjamin and Cora Ozella (Wadsworth) Chappelear; m. Kirby Lynn Fisher, Aug. 6, 1983; 1 child by previous marriage, Tracy Ann. BA, Bob Jones U., 1959; postgrad. Stetson U., 1961, U. Fla., 1963; M.A.T., Rollins Coll., 1969; Ph.D. in Am. Lit., Fla. State U., 1975; postgrad. Writing Inst., U. Cen. Fla., 1978, NEH Inst., 1979. Cert. English, gifted and adminstn. supr. Chmn. basic learning improvement program, secondary sch. Orange County, Orlando, Fla., 1964-65; chmn. composition Winter Park High Sch., Fla., 1978-80; chmn. English depts. Orange County Pub. Schs., Fla., 1962-71; reading tchr. Woodland Hall Acad., Reading Research Inst. Found., Tallahassee, 1976; instr. edn., journalism, reading, Spanish, thesis writing Bapt. Bible Coll., Springfield, Mo., 1976-77; prof. English, SW Mo. State U., Springfield, 1980-84, instr. continuing edn., courses in music and creative writing, 1981-82, editor LAD Leaf; tchr. English County Schs., Fla., 1984-88, gifted students, 1986—. Contbr. writings to pubs. in field, papers to nat. profl. confs. Vol. Greene County Action Com., 1977, Heart Fund, 1982. Writing Program fellow U. Cen. Fla., 1978. Mem. Fla. Council Tchrs. of English, MLA, Nat. Council Tchrs. of English, Volusia County Council Tchrs. of English, Voice of Youth Advocates (book reviewer), Kappa Delta Pi. Republican. Presbyterian.

FISHER, BART STEVEN, lawyer, lecturer; b. St. Louis, Feb. 16, 1943; s. Irvin and Orene (Moskow) F.; m. Margaret Cottony, Mar. 1, 1969; 1 child, Ross Alan. A.B., Washington U., 1963, M.A., Johns Hopkins Sch. Advanced Internat. Studies, 1967, Ph.D., 1970; J.D., Harvard Law Sch., 1972. Bar: D.C. 1972. Assoc. Patton, Boggs & Blow, Washington, 1972-78, ptnr., 1978—; adj. prof. internat. relations Georgetown Sch. Fgn. Service, Washington, 1974-82; mem. adv. council Johns Hopkins Sch. Advanced Internat. Studies, Washington, also professorial lectr. internat. relations, 1983—. Author: The International Coffee Agreement, 1972; (with John H. Barton) International Trade and Investment: Regulating International Business, 1986. Editor: Regulating the Multinational Enterprise, 1983; Barter in the World Economy, 1985. Treas., adv. com. chmn. Aplastic Anemia Found. Am. Inc., Balt., 1983—; program com. Georgetown Leadership Seminar, Washington, 1981—. Recipient Dean's Cert. Appreciation Georgetown U. Sch. Fgn. Service, Washington, 1984. Mem. ABA, Am. Soc. Internat. Law (rapporteur, panel trade policy and insts. 1974-77), Wash. Fgn. Law Soc., Internat. Platform Assn., Nat. Bone Marrow Donor Registry (bd. dirs.), Parkville Post Am. Legion. Jewish. Clubs: Georgetown, Reston Racquet (Va.), Great Falls Swim and Tennis (Va.). Home: 723 Walker Rd Great Falls VA 22066 Office: Patton Boggs & Blow 2550 M St NW Washington DC 20037

FISHER, CALVIN DAVID, food manufacturing company executive; b. Nerstrand, Minn., June 10, 1926; s. Edward and Sadie (Wolf) F.; m. Patricia Vivian Capriotti, July 28, 1950; children—Cynthia, Nancy Joann, Michael. B.S., U. Minn., 1950. Dairy specialist U.S. Dept. Agr., Mpls., 1950-54; chemist and dairy specialist U.S. Dept. Agr., Omaha, 1954-58; with Roberts Dairy Co., Omaha, 1958-80; sr. v.p., chief operating officer Roberts Dairy Co., 1967-70, pres., chief exec. officer, 1970-80, owner, chief exec. officer, 1975-80; owner, chief exec. officer Fisher Foods Ltd., Lincoln, Nebr., 1980—; pres., dir. Master Dairies, Indpls., 1968—; bd. dirs. Internat. Assn. Ice Cream Mfrs. Milk Industry Found., 1973—. Bd. dirs., v.p. Omaha Safety Council, 1981; bd. dirs. Arthritis Found., 1972-81; mem. adv. council SBA. Served with USN, 1944-47. Mem. Omaha C. of C. (pres.'s council 1976, 78), Internat. Food Scientists Assn., Inst. Food Tech., Nat. Ind. Dairies Assn. Republican. Methodist. Clubs: Rotary, Omaha Country; Univ. (Lincoln. Home: University Towers 128 N 13th St Suite 1001 Lincoln NE 68508 Office: Fisher Foods Ltd/Plasti-Cyc 220 S 20th St Lincoln NE 68510

FISHER, CHARLES HAROLD, chemistry educator; b. Hiawatha, W.Va., Nov. 20, 1906; s. Lawrence D. and Mary (Akers) F.; m. Elizabeth Dye, Nov. 4, 1933 (dec. 1967); m. Lois Carlin, July 1968. B.S., Roanoke Coll., 1928; M.S., U. Ill., 1929, Ph.D., 1932; D.Sc. (hon.), Tulane U., 1953; Sc.D. (hon.), Roanoke Coll., 1963. Teaching asst. in chemistry U. Ill., 1928-32; instr. Harvard U., 1932-35; asso. organic chemist U.S. Bur. Mines, Pitts., 1935-40; head carbohydrate div. East Regional Research Lab. U.S. Dept. Agr., 1946-50; dir. So. mktg. and nutrition research div. So. Regional Research Lab. U.S. Dept. Agr., New Orleans, 1950-72; adj. research prof. Roanoke Coll., 1972—. Pres. New Orleans Sci. Fair, 1967-69. Recipient So. Chemists award, 1956, Herty medal, 1959; Chem. Pioneer award Am. Inst. Chemists, 1966. Mem. Am. Inst. Chemists (hon., pres. 1962-63, chmn. bd. dirs.), Sci. Research Soc. Am., Oil Chem. Soc., Am. Chem. Soc. (dir. region IV), Chemurgic Council (dir.), Am. Assn. Textile Chemists and Colorists, Sigma Xi, Alpha Chi Sigma, Gamma Alpha, Phi Lambda Upsilon. Club: Cosmos (Washington). Office: Chemistry Dept Roanoke College Salem VA 24153

FISHER, DELBERT ARTHUR, physician, educator; b. Placerville, Calif., Aug. 12, 1928; s. Arthur Lloyd and Thelma (Johnson) F.; m. Beverly Carne Fisher, Jan. 28, 1951; children: David Arthur, Thomas Martin, Mary Kathryn. B.A., U. Calif., Berkeley, 1950; M.D., U. Calif., San Francisco, 1953. Diplomate: Am. Bd. Pediatrics (examiner 1971-80, mem. subcom. pediatric endocrinology 1976-79). Intern, then resident in pediatrics U. Calif. Med. Center, San Francisco, 1953-55; resident in pediatrics U. Oreg. Hosp., Portland, 1957-58; Irwin Meml. fellow pediatric endocrinology U. Oreg. Hosp., 1958-60; from asst. prof. to prof. pediatrics U. Ark. Med. Sch., Little Rock, 1960-68; prof. pediatrics UCLA Med. Sch., 1968-73; prof. pediatrics and medicine 1973—; research prof. devel. and perinatal biology Harbor-UCLA Med. Ctr., 1975-85, chmn. pediatrics, 1985—; cons. genetic disease sect. Calif. Dept. Health Services, 1978—; mem. organizing com. Internat. Conf. Newborn Thyroid Screening, 1977-82. Co-editor: 5 books including Pediatric Thyroidology, 1985; editor-in-chief: Jour. Clin. Endocrinology and Metabolism, 1978-83; Pediatric Research, 1984-89; contbr. 350 articles profl. jours., chpts. to 80 books. Served to capt. M.C. USAF, 1955-57. Recipient Career Devel. award NIH, 1964-68. Mem. Am. Acad. Pediatrics (Borden award 1981), Soc. Pediatric Research (v.p. 1973-74), Am. Pediatric Soc., Endocrine Soc. (pres. 1983-84), Am. Thyroid Assn. (pres. 1988—), Am. Soc. Clin. Investigation, Assn. Am. Physicians, Lawson Wilkins Pediatric Endocrine Soc. (pres. 1982-83), Western Soc. Pediatric Research (pres. 1983-84), Phi Beta Kappa, Alpha Omega Alpha. Home: 4 Pear Tree Ln Rolling Hills Estates CA 90274 Office: Dept Pediatrics Harbor-UCLA Med Center 1000 W Carson St Torrance CA 90509

FISHER, EUGENE, marketing executive; b. Chgo., Sept. 30, 1927; s. Morris and Sarah (Edelstein) F.; m. Joline Cobb, July 28, 1956; children—Robin Downing, Amy Homer, Douglas. Ph.B., U. Chgo., 1945, M.B.A., 1948. Product mgr. Brunswick Corp., Skokie, Ill., 1955-59, group product mgr., 1959-63, product mktg. mgr., 1963-67, dir. mktg. planning, 1965-72, dir. corp. mktg. research, 1972-87, corp. mktg. dir., 1987—; mem. mktg. com. Nat. Dowling Council, 1975—, pres. Fisher Mktg. Intelligence, Inc., 1983—; guest lectr. in field Mem. Am. Mktg. Assn., Conf. Bd. (research council), Phi Sigma Delta. Home: 1233 Elder Rd Homewood IL 60430 Office: Brunswick Corp One Brunswick Plaza Skokie IL 60077

FISHER, FENIMORE, manufacturing company executive; b. N.Y.C., 1926; s. Benn and Sadie (Cohan) F.; m. Marcia Obler, Nov. 9, 1952; children: Bennett G., Alan L., Karen Soo. BS in Physics, Columbia U., 1951; MBA, U. Pa. 1952. Staff physicist USN Research Lab., Phila., 1951-52; ops. mgr., chief engr. instrument div. Thomas A. Edison Industries, West Orange, N.J., 1952-60; pres. Analogue Controls Inc., Hicksville, N.Y., 1960-67; corp. v.p. IMC Magnetics Corp., Jericho, N.Y., 1967-77, pres., chief exec. officer, 1977—, also bd. dirs.; chmn. bd. Hansen Mfg. Co. Inc., Princeton Ind., IMC Ariz. Div., Tempe, IMC Fla. Div., Miami Lakes, IMC Tenn. Div., Camden, IMC Tex. Div., Mexia, IMC Western Div., Cerritos, Calif., New Eng. Alloys Inc., Lawrence, Mass., Pacific Propeller Inc., Kent Washington, Universal Magnetics Corp., Cerritos. Contbr. numerous articles on bus. econs., tech. edn., relation with the Far East. Bd. dirs. L.I. Philharm., West Suffolk YM & YWHA, L.I. Forum for Tech., Fedn. Employment and Guidance Service, Suffolk Community Planning Council, Old Westbury Coll. Found.; trustee Dowling Coll. Served to 1st lt. U.S. Army, 1944-46, PTO. Mem. Am. Phys. Soc. Am. Def. Preparedness Assn. Clubs: Pine Hollow Country (East Norwich, N.Y.) (bd. govs., pres.); Turnberry Country (North Miami, Fla.). Office: IMC Magnetics Corp 100 Jericho Quadrangle Suite 221 Jericho NY 11753

FISHER, GLADYS SANDRA, government official; b. Clinton, N.C., May 3, 1941; d. Millard R. and Gladys I. (Bryant) F.; m. Robert M. Sprinkle, Mar. 31, 1967. A.B., Meredith Coll., 1963; M.A. in Teaching, U. N.C., 1964; postgrad. Grad. Sch. Bus. Adminstrn., Harvard U., 1981. Coordinator adult edn. program Craven Operation Progress, Inc., N.C., 1965-66; program officer VISTA/OEO, Washington and N.Y.C., 1966-69; assoc. Leo Kramer, Inc., mgmt. cons., Washington, 1970-71; program devel. specialist Adminstrn. on Aging, HEW, 1971; sr. program specialist Ret. Sr. Vol. Program, ACTION, 1971-74; program mgr. div. research applications and demonstrations Adminstrn. on Aging, HHS, 1974-79, dir. div. continuing edn. and tng., 1979-83, dir. div. program mgmt. and regional ops. Office State and Tribal Programs, 1983-86, dep. dir. Office Mgmt. and Policy, 1986—; mem. Howard County Commn. Aging, 1975-80; cons. in adult edn. Scholar N.C. Bd. Edn., 1959-63, James E. and Mary Z. Bryan Found., 1962; Ford Found. grantee, 1963-64. Mem. Am. Soc. Tng. and Devel., Geront. Soc., Am. Assn. Higher Edn., Am. Soc. Pub. Adminstrn, Internat. Council on Social Welfare. Baptist. Office: Adminstrn on Aging HHS Washington DC 20201

FISHER, HAROLD LEONARD, lawyer, banker; b. N.Y.C., Dec. 10, 1910; s. Jacob and Pauline (Sherman) F.; m. Betty Kahn, July 24, 1934; children: H. Leonard, Alice Fisher Rubin, Stephanie Fisher Cooper, Andrew S., Kenneth K. LL.B. cum laude, St. John's U., 1932. Bar: N.Y. 1935, U.S. Dist. Ct. (ea. dist.) N.Y. 1937, U.S. Dist. Ct. (so. dist.) N.Y. 1938, U.S. Ct. Appeals (2d cir.) 1946. Sole practice, Bklyn., 1935-76; ptnr. Fisher & Fisher, Bklyn., 1976—; mem. adv. council to dean Hofstra U. Law Sch., 1987—; chmn. bd. Dime Savs. Bank of Williamsburgh, 1976-85; Bd. dirs. HIP of Greater N.Y., 1978-87, Nat. Housing Conf.; chmn. bd. Met. Transit Authority, 1977-79, dir., 1968-79; mem. presdl. del. at Mt. Sinai Transfer; chmn. urban transp. del. to People's Republic of China, 1979; bd. dirs. Bklyn. Acad. Music,

Borough Hall Restoration Fund; mem. Nat. Citizens Coalition for the Windfall Profits Tax; treas. Democratic County Com. Kings County, N.Y. Recipient B'nai B'rith Youth Service Am. Traditions award, 1981; Gonen Soc. Man of Year award, 1978; L.I. Rail Road Club Transp. Man of Year award, 1977; named March of Dimes Transit Man of Year, 1978. Mem. Bklyn. Bar Assn. (pres. 1977-78, Ann. award for outstanding achievement in law and pub. service 1983), Fed. Bar Council, ABA, N.Y. State Bar Assn., Bklyn. Criminal Bar Assn., N.Y. State Trial Lawyers Assn. Jewish. Clubs: Bklyn., B'nai B'rith. Office: 189 Montague St Brooklyn NY 11201

FISHER, HENRY, investment banker; b. Pitts., Feb. 17, 1936; s. Henry Clayton and Dorothea T. (Smith) F.; B.A., U. Pitts., 1960; student Wharton Sch. Investment Banking, 1967, 68; m. Ann Yeager, Aug. 6, 1960; children—Andrew Clayton, William Bradford. Gen. partner Singer Deane & Scribner, Pitts., 1961-69; exec. v.p. Chaplin McGuiness & Co., Inc., Pitts., 1969-73; pres., mng. dir. Commonwealth Securities and Investments, Inc., Pitts., 1974—; gen. ptnr. Investment Bldg., Pitts., 1982-84; ptnr. Perrymont Bldg., 1980-85; mem. N.Y. Stock Exchange, 1972-74. Served with USMC, 1954-56. Mem. Pitts. Securities Assn., Nat. Assn. Mcpl. Analysts, Pitts. Mcpl. Analysts Soc., Pa. Boroughs Assn., Pa. League of Cities, Pa. Twp. Assn., Pa. Mcpl. Authorities Assn., Internat. Bridge, Tunnel and Turnpike Assn., Pitts. Builders Exchange, Bond Club Pitts., Sierra Club (founder Pitts. chpt.), Am. Youth Hostels, Inc. (past nat. v.p.), Pa. Soc. of N.Y. Clubs: Duquesne, Pitts., Allegheny, Rivers. Office: 1317 Investment Bldg Pittsburgh PA 15222

FISHER, JAMES W., JR., chemical company official; b. Asheville, N.C., Aug. 14, 1942; s. James W. and Virginia (Gustafson) F.; m. Hannelore Enke, Aug. 15, 1966; children: Julia, Heidi, Michael, Elke. BA cum laude, Princeton U., 1964; MBA, Harvard U., 1966. With Gen. Motors Corp., Detroit, 1970-73, Ford Motor Co., Detroit, 1973-80; dir. compensation and benefits Air Products and Chems., Inc., Allentown, Pa., 1980-87, dir. orgn. planning and human resources devel., 1987—; bd. dirs. Airprochem Inc. Bd. dirs. Good Shepherd Rehab. Wrkshop and Vocat. Services. Mem. Nat. Assn. Corp. Dirs. (chair com. compensation orgn. and mgmt. succession 1984—). Served to capt. USAF, 1966-70. Home: Rt 2 Box 424 Emmaus PA 18049 Office: Air Products and Chems Inc PO Box 538 Allentown PA 18105

FISHER, JOHN COURTNEY, surgical physicist, consultant; b. Wilkinsburg, Pa., Apr. 19, 1922; s. Edwin Henry and Elizabeth (Walden) F.; m. Patricia Kingsbury, Nov. 26, 1942; children: Carolyn Fisher Ellis, John Courtney, Stephen Kingsbury; m. Jane Clauss, July 7, 1976. B.S., Harvard U., 1942, M.S., 1947, Sc.D., 1952. Teaching fellow Harvard U., 1942-52; sonar engr. Submarine Signal Co., Boston, 1945-46; dir. electromech. engring. Calidyne Co., Winchester, Mass., 1952-55; dir. devel. privately funded research project, Maynard, Mass., 1955-60; chmn., treas. Am. Dynamics Corp., Cambridge, Mass., 1960-68; northeastern regional sales mgr. Princeton Applied Research Corp., N.J., 1968-72, cons. in sci. instrumentation, Weston, Mass., 1972—; dir. med. devel. Cavitron Lasersonics div., Stamford, Conn., 1976-81; mem. surg. staff St. Barnabas Med. Center, Livingston, N.J., 1980—; founding mem., sec.-treas. Am. Bd. Laser Surgery, 1984—; vis. assoc. prof. laser medicine and surgery U. Cin., 1985. Contbr. articles to profl. jours. Patentee in field. Mem. Weston Planning Bd., 1974-80. Fellow Am. Soc. Laser Medicine and Surgery; mem. Internat. Soc. Laser Surgery, ASME, IEEE, AAAS, Gynecologic Laser Soc., Midwest Biolaser Inst., N.Y. Acad. Scis., Sigma Xi. Home: 417 Palm Tree Dr Wildewood Springs Bradenton FL 34210

FISHER, JOHN MORRIS, association official, educator; b. Fairhaven, Ohio, Apr. 20, 1922; s. Marion Hays and Bessie (Morris) F.; AB, Miami U., Oxford, Ohio, 1947; postgrad. Bklyn. Law Sch., 1950-51, Northwestern U., 1954-55; LLD (hon.), Nasson Coll., 1972; m. Thelma Ison, Feb. 2, 1947; children: Steven Roger, Linda Lucille. With Belden Mfg. Co., Richmond, Ind., 1941; spl. agt. FBI, 1947-53; exec. trainee Sears Roebuck & Co., Chgo., 1953, exec. staff asst. to v.p. personnel and employee relations, 1953-57, chmn. security com., 1957-61; operating dir. Am. Security Council, 1956-57, pres., chief exec. officer, 1957—; pres. Am. Research Found., 1961—; pres., chief exec. officer Am. Security Council Found., 1962—; pres. Communications Corp. Am., 1972-80, chmn., 1980—; pres. Am. Coalition Patriotic Socs., 1978—; adminstrv. chmn. Coalition for Peace Through Strength, 1978—; dir. Center for Internat. Security Studies, 1977-83; organizer, pres. Fidelifax, Inc., 1956-57; chmn. merc. div. Nat. Safety Council, 1959-60, 1st vice chmn. trades and services sect., 1961—. Chmn. Chgo. Retail Safety Conf., 1959-60; spl. adviser Ill. Supt. Pub. Instrn., 1963-64; cons. to Gov. Fla.; cons. to chmn. com. cold war edn. Nat. Gov.'s Conf., 1962-65, Ill. CD Adv. Council, 1965-68; pres. Am. Council World Freedom, 1971-72; mem. exec. com. Nat. Captive Nations Com., 1968—. Bd. visitors Freedoms Found., 1964-65; bd. dirs. Am. Fgn. Policy Inst., 1975-84, James Monroe Library, 1977-85, Security and Intelligence Fund, 1978-84; pres. Culpepper Meml. Hosp. Found., 1984-86; exec. chmn. U.S. Congl. Adv. Bd., 1982—; adminstrv. chmn. Coalition for Peace Through Strength, 1978—. Served to 1st lt. USAAF, 1943-45. Decorated Air medal with clusters; recipient 10th Anniversary medal and scroll Assembly Captive European Nations, Order Lafayette Freedom award, 1973, others. Mem. Am. Soc. Indsl. Security (dir. 1959-62), Phi Kappa Tau. Republican. Presbyterian. Clubs: Army Navy (Washington); Kingsmill Country (Williamsburg, Va.); Nat. Dem. ; Capitol Hill. Home: 201 Roger Webster Williamsburg VA 23185 Office: Am Security Council Found Boston VA 22713

FISHER, JOHN RICHARD, engineering consultant, former naval officer; b. Columbus, Ohio, Dec. 28, 1924; s. Don Alfred and Katherine Buchanan (Galigher) F.; m. Kitson Overmyer, Oct. 2, 1946; children—Scott Owen, Lani Kitson. B.S., U.S. Naval Acad., 1946; B.Civil Engring., Rensselaer Poly. Inst., Troy, N.Y., 1950, M.Civil Engring., 1950; grad. Advanced Mgmt. Program, Harvard, 1971. Registered profl. engr., S.C. Commd. ensign U.S. Navy, 1946, advanced through grades to rear adm., 1972; service in N.Africa, Cuba, Philippines, Vietnam; dep. comdr. Naval Facilities Engring. Command; also comdr. Chesapeake div. constrn. facilities U.S. Naval Acad. and Omega Nav. System, 1969-73; comdr. Pacific div. Naval Facilities Engring. Command, 1973-77; ret. 1977; v.p. Raymond Internat., Inc., 1977-81, sr. group v.p., 1981-83, exec. v.p., 1983-86. Pres. Community Hosp. Assn. Mid-Am., Columbus, Ohio. Decorated DSM, Legion of Merit with combat V (2). Fellow Soc. Am. Mil. Engrs., ASCE; mem. Navy League of U.S. (nat. dir.), Mil. Order Carabao, Sigma Xi, Tau Beta Pi. Clubs: Outrigger Canoe (Honolulu); Army-Navy Country (Arlington, Va.); Scottsdale (Ariz.) Country. Home: 10615 E Arabian Park Dr Scottsdale AZ 85258 Office: PO Box 5585 Scottsdale AZ 85261

FISHER, KENNETH L., sculptor; b. Tacoma, Apr. 28, 1944; s. Henry John and Anna Mary (Trafford) F. B.S., U. Oreg., 1968, B.F.A., 1969, M.F.A., 1971. Cert. univ. level tchr., Calif. One-man shows include Thelma Pearson Gallery, Lincoln City, Oreg., 1971, Internat. Art Gallery, Pitts., 1971, Jewish Community Ctr., Portland, Oreg., 1971, Howell Street Gallery, Seattle, 1981, Lakewood Ctr. Gallery, Lake Oswego, Oreg., 1983, William Temple House, Portland, 1984, Grants Pass Art Mus., Oreg., 1984, 86, Benton County Hist. Mus., Philomath, Oreg., 1984, Pacific U., Forest Grove, Oreg., 1985, Mondak Hist. & Art Soc., Sidney, Mont., 1986, Umpqua Community Coll., Roseburg, Oreg., 1986, Lower Columbia Coll., Longview, Wash., 1987, Pacific Northwest Art Expo., Seattle, 1987; group shows include Coos Art Mus., Oreg., 1981 (hon. mention), 82, Ga. Inst. Tech., 1982, 83 (cert. of recognition), Painters and Sculptors Soc., N.J., 1982, La. Arts Guild, 1982, Galerie Triangle, Washington, 1982, 83, Alexandria Mus. Arts, La., 1982, Terrance Gallery, N.Y.C., 1982 (hon. mention), Cooperstown Art Assn., N.Y., 1982, Knickerbocker Artists, N.Y.C., 1982, 83, 84, Idaho State U. (1st place award), 1982, Del Mar Coll. (Joseph A. Cain Meml. Purchase award in sculpture), Corpus Christi, Tex., 1982, 83, Goldsboro's 3d Ann. Juried Exhbn., N.C., 1982, Fine Arts League 14th Nat. Show (1st place award), Colo., 1982, Franklin Sq. Gallery (M. Grumbacher Inc. Bronze medallion), N.C., 1982, J.K. Ralston Mus. (1st and 2d Place awards), Mont., 1982, Oreg. State U. (honor award), 1983, Hill Country Arts Found., 11th Ann. Exhbn. (1st place award in sculpture), Tex., 1983, Hill Country Arts Found., Tex., 1983, Art Ann. Four, Okla., 1983, Audubon Artists, N.Y.C., 1983, 86, Salmagundi Club, N.Y.C., 1983, Las Vegas Art Mus., 1984, Nat. Art Appreciation Soc., 1984 (hon. mention), Palm Beach Galleries, La. (grand prize), 1984, NAD, N.Y.C., 1984, Allied Artists Am., N.Y.C., 1984, N.Am. Sculpture Exhbn., Colo., 1986, Audobon Artists Nat. exhbn., 1986, 87; represented in permanent collections Grants Pass Art Mus., Coos Art Mus., U. Oreg. Mus. Art, Oreg. State U., Del Mar Coll., Pacific U., Umpqua Community Coll., U. Portland, also numerous pvt. collections. Mem. Portland Art Assn.

FISHER, LEE ELLIOTT, accountant; b. Spokane, Wash., May 6, 1927; s. Gail T. and Cecilia Mildred (Lee) F.; m. Arlene Mae Hoersch, June 20, 1949 (div. May 1956); 1 child, Rodrick Gail; m. Phyllis Diane Harrington, July 20, 1956; children—Scott Richard, Todd Elliott, Lora Diane. M.B.A., Kinman Bus. U., Spokane, 1951. C.P.A., Alaska. Staff acct. Morris, Lee & Co., C.P.A.s, Spokane, 1949-55; controller Pigeon Hole Parking, Inc., Spokane, 1956-57; sr. acct. Rettig, Scott & Co., C.P.A.s, Anchorage, 1958-61; propr. Fisher & Co., C.P.A.s, Anchorage, 1962-74; mng. ptnr. Coopers & Lybrand, C.P.A.s, Anchorage, 1975—; dir. Alaska Mut. Bancorp, Anchorage, 1962-87; state chmn. guardian adv. council Nat. Fedn. Ind. Bus., 1978—. Founder, past pres. Crime Stoppers of Anchorage, 1981-82; pres. United Way Anchorage, 1979-81; bd. dirs. Resource Devel. Council, Anchorage, 1972—, pres., 1978; del. White House Conf. on Small Bus., 1986; treasurer Am. Bald Eagle Found., 1987—; state chmn. Alaska exhibit Expo 88, Brisbane, Australia. Mem. Anchorage C. of C. (Gold Pan award 1982, pres. 1984-85), , Alaska Soc. C.P.A.s, Am. Inst. C.P.A.s. Served with USN, 1944-46. Republican. Episcopalian. Clubs: Woodhaven Country, Palm Desert (Calif.). Home: 2905 E 20th Ave Anchorage AK 99508 Office: Coopers & Lybrand 550 W 7th Ave Suite 600 Anchorage AK 99501

FISHER, MICHAEL BRUCE, lawyer, corporate executive; b. Montgomery, Ala., Jan. 2, 1945; s. Philip and Rita (Joss) F.; m. Noreen Rene Zidel, June 25, 1967; children—Anne Elizabeth, Alex Nicholas. B.A., U. Minn., 1967; J.D., U. Calif.-Berkeley, 1970. Bar: N.Y. 1971, Minn. 1972, U.S. Dist. Ct. Minn. 1972. Assoc. Rosenman, Colin, et al, N.Y.C., 1970-71, Mullin, Swirnoff & Weinberg, P.A., Mpls., 1972-73; staff atty. Fingerhut Corp., Mpls., 1974, assoc. gen. counsel, 1975-80, gen. counsel, 1980-83, v.p., gen. counsel, sec., 1983—; dir. Mchts. Research Council, Chgo., 1976-80. Exec. com., dir. Big Sisters Mpls., Inc., 1976-83, Big Bros./Big Sisters Mpls., Inc., 1984—; v.p., bd. dirs. Herzl Camp Assn., Inc., Mpls., 1975—; vol. Minn. Pub. TV, St. Paul, 1980—, gen. auction chmn., 1988. Mem. Minn. Bar Assn., ABA, Am. Corp. Counsel Assn. Minn., Minn. Retail Mchts. Assn. (trustee 1983—, exec. com. 1988—), Direct Mktg. Assn. (govt. affairs com. 1980—), 3d Class Mail Assn. (sec., bd. dirs. 1981-86, exec. vice chmn. 1987—), Parcel Shippers Assn. (v.p., bd. dirs. 1980-86, pres. 1987—). Jewish. Club: Calhoun Beach (Mpls.). Office: Fingerhut Cos Inc 4400 Baker Rd Minnetonka MN 55343

FISHER, MICHAEL EDWARD, electrical engineer, consultant; b. Tulsa, Sept. 24, 1949; s. Edward Thomas and Bertha Lynn (Sanders) F.; m. Phyllis Dilworth, Oct. 6, 1979; children—Marsha Nichole, Marc Elliot, Alicia Joy, Sandra Janelle. Student UCLA, 1969, 71; B.S. in Elec. Engring., Washington U., St. Louis, 1971; MSEE, U. So. Calif., 1985. Broadcast engr. Sta. KVOO-TV, Tulsa, 1966-68; elec. design engr. Rockwell Internat., El Segundo, Calif., 1969-73; elec. design engr. Hughes Aircraft, Fullerton, Calif., 1973-78, staff systems engr., 1981-87, sr. staff systems engr., 1985-86; sr. tech. specialist, program mgr. Scientific-Atlanta, San Diego, 1986— ; project engr. Technicolor, Costa Mesa, Calif., 1978-79, Interstate Electronics, Anaheim, Calif., 1979-81. Scholar Washington U., 1968-71; Hughes Masters fellow Hughes Aircraft, 1983-85. Mem. Mu Alpha Theta. Republican. Home: 598 Camino De La Cima San Marcos CA 92069 Office: Scientific-Atlanta 8832 Balboa Ave PO Box 23575 San Diego CA 92123

FISHER, NICHOLAS RALPH EDMUND, ancient history educator; b. Oxford, Eng., July 27, 1944; s. Roderick Charles and Margaret Fletcher (Wright) F.; m. Sarah Julian Dyer, July 2, 1966; children: Kate, Matthew, Rebecca. BA, Oxford U., 1967, MA, 1972, PhD, 1976. Lectr. Sch. History and Archaeology U. Wales, Cardiff, 1970—. Author: Social Values in Classical Athens, 1976; contbr. articles to profl. jours. Mem. Soc. for Promotion Hellenic Studies (council), Joint Assn. Classical Tchrs. Office: U Wales, PO Box 78, Cardiff CF1 1XL, Wales

FISHER, ROBERT WILSON, geologist, consultant; b. Chgo., May 11, 1931; s. Clyde and Mary Hannah (Robb) F.; m.. Martha Sue Johnson, Apr. 5, 1952 (div. 1976); children—Thomas R., Richard W., Andrew D., David C.; m., Lauren Huddleston, Apr. 5, 1976. B.S., U. Ill.-Urbana, 1953, M.S., 1956. Cert. prof. petroleum geologist, geol. scientist. Research analyst Ill. Geol. Survey, Champaign, Ill., 1955-56; project geologist Amoco Prodn. Co., New Orleans, 1956-64; chief geologist Estate of William G. Helis, New Orleans, 1964-81; v.p. Lynx Exploration Co., Denver, 1981-83; pres. Bradden Exploration Co., Denver, 1983-86; founder, chmn. Fisher Energy Group, Denver, 1986—. Author: The Fisher Report, 1986, 87, 88; co-author: Visual Estimates of Grain Size Distribution in Some Chester Sandstones, 1959; map compiler Geol. Map of Ill., 1967; contbr. articles to profl. jours. Active Com. for Responsible Devel. of Bergen Park (Colo.), 1983-84. Served to 1st lt. U.S. Army, 1953-55. Mem. Am. Assn. Petroleum Geologists, Am. Inst. Profl. Geologists, Rocky Mountain Assn. Geologists, Internat. Transactional Analysis Assn. (advanced), Ind. Petroleum Assn. Am. (bd. dirs.), Soc. Ind. Earth Scientists. Home: 127 Sawmill Dr Evergreen CO 80439 Office: Fisher Energy Group 1020 15th St Suite 4-L Denver CO 80202

FISHER, THOMAS GRAHAM, judge; b. Flint, Mich., May 15, 1940; s. John Corwin and Bonnie Decou (Graham) F.; m. Barbara Molnar, June 2, 1963; children—Anne Corwin, Thomas Molnar. A.B., Earlham Coll., 1962; J.D., Ind. U., 1965. Bar: Ind. 1965, U.S. Sup. Ct. 1969. Assoc., John R. Nesbitt, Remington and Rensselaer, Ind., 1965-68; ptnr. Nesbitt & Fisher, Remington and Rensselaer, 1968-73, Nesbitt, Fisher & Daugherty, Rensselaer, Remington, 1973-78, Nesbitt, Fisher, Daugherty & Nesbitt, 1978-82, Nesbitt, Fisher & Nesbitt, 1982-83, Fisher & Nesbitt, 1983-86, judge, Ind. Tax Ct., Indpls., 1986—; pros. atty. Jasper County, Ind., 1967-86; lectr. bus. law St. Joseph's Coll., Rensselaer, 1970-86 . Mem. Ind. Bar Assn., Jasper County Bar Assn. Republican. Presbyterian. Home: 933 Harding Plainfield IN 46168 Office: Ind Tax Ct Merchants Plaza 115 W Washington St 1188 S Tower Chamber 23 Indianapolis IN 46204

FISHGAL, SEMYON IOSIFOVICH, mechanical engineer, consultant; b. Kiev, U.S.S.R., July 1, 1938; arrived Canada, 1976; s. Iosif Shaevich and Ita Avromovna (Portnaya) F.; m. Irina Grigorevna Pass, Feb. 14, 1964; 1 son, Aleksander. B.S. in M.E., Indsl. Coll., Kiev, U.S.S.R., 1958; B.S. in Radio Mech., Aviation Coll., Leningrad, U.S.S.R., 1959; M.S. in M.E., Engring. Inst., Kiev, 1964, Ph.D. in M.E., 1971; M.S. in M.E., U. Toronto, 1977; Ph.D. in M.E., Northwestern Coll., Tulsa, 1978. Design engr. Machine Bldg. Co., Kiev, 1958-60; group design leader Research Devel. Inst., Kiev, 1960-66; project mgr. Machine Bldg. Co., Kiev, 1966-75; dir. research and devel. Internat. Design and Devel. Corp., Cedar Falls, Iowa, 1976-79; supr. research and devel. Joy Mfg. Co., Pitts., 1979-80; head patents, research and devel. Corma Inc., Toronto, Ont., Can., 1984-87; engring. assoc. Chemetics Internat. Co., 1988—; cons. Engring. Inst., Kiev, 1965-75, Ingersoll-Rand Co., Cambridge, Can., 1980, Am. Hoist & Derrick Co., St. Paul, 1981-82, Ontario Hydro, 1981-83. Contbr. numerous articles to sci. jours.; numerous patents in field. Served with USSR Air Force, 1958-60. Recipient Silver medal All-Union Exhbn. of Achievements, Moscow, 1965; recipient 2d prize All-Union Competition, All-Union Inventor's Soc., Moscow, 1966. Mem. Assn. Profl. Engrs. Ont. Address: 1908-35 High Park Ave, Toronto, ON Canada M6P 2R6

FISHMAN, BARRY STUART, lawyer; b. Chgo., June 14, 1943; s. Jacob M. and Anita (Epstein) F.; B.A., U. Wis., 1965; J.D., DePaul U., 1968; m. Meredith Porte, Mar. 27, 1976; 1 child, Janna. Admitted to Ill. bar, 1968, Fla., Calif. bars, 1969; partner firm Fishman & Fishman, Chgo., 1968-72; counsel real estate fin. dept. Baird & Warner, Inc., Chgo., 1972-75; gen. counsel Biscayne Fed. Savs. & Loan Assn., Miami, Fla., 1976-79; mem. firm, Ea. regional council Logs Nationwide Representation of Lenders; mem. firm Pallot, Poppell, Goodman & Slotnick, Miami, 1977-80; sr. ptnr. Shapiro & Fishman, North Miami Beach and Tampa, Fla., 1984—; dir. investment div. Cushman and Wakefield of Fla., 1978—. Mem. big gifts com. Greater Miami Jewish Fedn., 1977—; dir. Neighborhood Housing Services, Dade County, Fla., 1977—. Mem. Fla., Calif., Ill., Chgo., Dade County bar assns., Nat. Assn. Realtors, Real Estate Securities and Syndication Inst., Mortgage Bankers Assn., Fla. Mortgage Bankers Assn., Comml. Law League. Jewish. Clubs: Turnberry Isle Yacht & Racquet, Turnberry Country, Covennant. Home: 1025 NE 203d Ln Miami Beach FL 33179 Office: 1031 Ives Dairy Rd Miami FL 33629

FISHMAN, EDWARD MARC, lawyer; b. Cambridge, Mass., Apr. 28, 1946; s. Eli Manuel and Marian (Goldberg) F.; m. Barbara Ellen Stern, June 29, 1969 (div. Sept. 1982); children: Andrea, Bradley; m. Tracy Ann Lind, July 13, 1985; 1 child, Alison. AB, Bowdoin Coll., 1968; JD, Columbia U., 1972. Bar: Tex. 1972. Assoc. Akin, Gump, Strauss, Hauer & Feld, Dallas, 1972-73, Luce, Hennessy, Smith & Castle, Dallas, 1973-76; corp. counsel Centex Corp., Dallas, 1976-78; from assoc. to ptnr. Brice & Barron, Dallas, 1978-82; v.p. Baker, Smith & Mills, Dallas, 1982-86; pres. Kuhn, Fishman, Jones & Walsh, Dallas, 1986—. Bd. dirs. Space Found. Roundtable, Dallas, 1985-87; officer local pub. TV sta., Dallas, 1976—. Mem. ABA, Tex. Bar Assn., Dallas Bar Assn. Home: 6721 Southpoint Dallas TX 75248 Office: Kuhn Fishman Jones & Walsh RPR Tower 700 Pearl Plaza of the Americas Suite 2000 Dallas TX 75201

FISHMAN, JACOB ROBERT, psychiatrist, educator, corporate executive; b. N.Y.C., Aug. 6, 1930; s. Samuel and Francis (Goldin) F.; A.B., Columbia U., 1952; M.D., Boston U., 1956; m. Tamar Hendel, June 1, 1958; children—Marc Judah, Risa Esther, Zalman Schneur, Rebecca Anne. Intern in medicine Einstein Coll. Medicine, Bronx, N.Y., 1956-57, resident psychiatry, 1957-59; research psychiatrist NIMH, Washington, 1959-62; prof. psychiatry Howard U. Coll. Medicine, Washington, 1962-71; dir. Howard-D.C. Comprehensive Mental Health Center, 1966-68; chmn. bd., pres. Univ. Research Corp., Washington, 1968-78, Am. Health Services, Inc., 1971-78; pres. Ctr. for Human Services, 1968-74, Human Service Group, 1971-78, Horizon Mental Health Group, Inc., 1981-84, Cumberland Psychiat. Hosp., 1979-84; chmn. bd. dirs. Am. Mental Health Group, Inc., Am. Health Group Inc.; chmn. psychiatry So. Md. Hosp. Ctr., 1978-81; cons. fed. agys., U.S. Congress, numerous pvt. corps.; bd. dirs. Create Inc., Entertainment Concepts Inc., First Grafton Corp., Med. Services Corp., various others. Bd. dirs. Webster Coll., Washington, 1971-75, Ctr. for Human Services, 1967-75, DePaul Hosp., New Orleans, 1973-78, St. Elizabeth's Hosp., Richmond, Va., 1971-78, Cin. Mental Health Inst., 1971-78, Nat. Capital Day Care Assn., 1966-68; mem. D.C. Public Health Adv. Council, 1966-68; attending psychiatrist Freedman's Hosp., Washington Vets. Hosp., D.C. Gen. Hosp., 1962-68; dir. Potomac Psychiat. Assocs., 1978—, Am. Health Group, 1985—. Served with USPHS, 1959-61. Recipient Gold medal award Phi Lambda Kappa Med. Soc. Fellow Am. Public Health Assn., Am. Assn. Social Psychiatry; mem. Am. Psychiat. Assn., D.C. Psychiat. Soc., Potomac Psychiat. Assos. (pres. 1978—), AAAS, D.C. Public Health Assn. (Disting. Service award), Am. Med. Soc. on Alcoholism and Other Addictive Drugs, Am. Council on Alcoholism, various others. Author numerous profl. articles and books. Bd. editors Nat. Jour. Research on Crime and Delinquency, 1965-71. Home: 1717 Poplar Ln NW Washington DC 20012

FISHMAN, MARK BRIAN, computer scientist, educator; b. Phila., May 17, 1951; s. Morton Louis and Hilda (Kaplan) F.; m. Alice Faber, Feb. 20, 1977 (div. 1986). AB summa cum laude, Temple U., 1974; postgrad. Northwestern U., 1974-76; MA, U. Tex., 1980. Bilingual tchr. Wilmette Pub. Schs., 1974; research assoc., programmer, asst. instr. U. Tex., Austin, 1976-80; instr. computer and info. scis. U. Fla., Gainesville, 1980-85; asst. prof. computer sci. Eckerd Coll., St. Petersburg, Fla., 1985—; instrnl. cons. to IBM, 1980—; cons. artificial intelligence, Battelle Corp., 1987, USN Naval Tng. Systems Ctr., 1987. Editor: Proceedings of the First Florida Artificial Intelligence Research Symposium, 1988; contbr. articles to profl. jours. U. Tex. univ. fellow, 1978-80; F.C. Austin scholar, 1975; Nat. Def. Fgn. Lang. fellow, 1974. Mem. Assn. Computing Machinery (Tchr. of Yr. award U. Fla. 1984), IEEE Computer Soc., Am. Assn. Artificial Intelligence, Assn. Computational Linguistics, Fla. Artificial Intelligence Research Soc. (proceedings chair, sec. Am.), Soc. Engring. Edn. (faculty research fellow summer 1986), Phi Beta Kappa, Phi Kappa Phi, Upsilon Pi Epsilon. Home: 6166 Lynn Lake Dr S Saint Petersburg FL 33712 Office: Eckerd Coll Computer Sci Dept Saint Petersburg FL 33733

FISHMAN, RICHARD E., investment adviser; b. N.Y.C., July 31, 1933; s. Joseph and Lea (Penzel) F.; m. Harlene Birnbach, Mar. 20, 1955; children—Deborah, Andrew, Susan. B.B.A., CUNY, 1963; Cert. fin. planner Coll. Fin. Planning, 1979. With Merrill Lynch Pierce Fenner & Smith, Inc., N.Y.C. and Miami, 1967-80, v.p., Miami, 1979-80; v.p., fin. cons., Boca Raton, Fla., 1982—; v.p. Oppenheimer & Co., Inc., Miami, 1980-82. Pres., Friends of Boca Pops, 1983. Charter mem., v.p. Boca Raton Estate Planning Council, Fin. Analysts Fedn., Internat. Found. Employee Benefits Plans,Fla. Govt. Fin. Officers Ass., Ednl. Conf. Health, Welfare and Pension Funds, Fla. Assn. Public Employee Pension Trustees. Clubs: Boca West, POlo (Boca Raton); Ocean Reef (Key Largo). Lodge: B'nai B'rith (pres. 1979-80, 84-85). Office: Merrill Lynch 6100 Glades Rd Boca Raton FL 33434

FISHMAN, WILLIAM HAROLD, cancer research foundation executive; biochemist; b. Winnipeg, Man., Can., Mar. 2, 1914; s. Abraham and Goldie (Chmelnitsky) F.; m. Lillian Waterman, Aug. 6, 1939; children—Joel, Nina, Daniel. B.S., U. Sask., Can., Saskatoon, 1935; Ph.D., U. Toronto, Ont., Can., 1939; MDhc U. Umea, Sweden, 1983; Dir. cancer research New Eng. Med. Ctr. Hosp., Boston, 1958-72; research prof. pathology Tufts U. Sch. Medicine, 1961-70, prof. pathology, 1970-77, dir. Cancer Research Ctr., 1972-76, dir., 1981; pres. La Jolla Cancer Research Found., Calif., 1976—; mem. basic sci. programs merit rev. bd. com. VA, 1971-75; mem. pathobiol. chemistry sect. NIH, Bethesda, Md., 1977-81. Author in field. Research Career award NIH, 1962-77; Royal Soc. Can. research fellow, 1939, 17th Internat. Physiol. Congress-U.K. Fedn. fellow, 1947. Fellow AIC; mem. Am. Assn. Cancer Research, Am. Soc. Biol. Chemists, Am. Soc. Cell Biology, Am. Soc. Exptl. Pathology, Histochem. Soc. (pres. 1983-84), Internat. Soc. Clin. Enzymology (hon.). Jewish. Club: University (San Diego). Current work: Basic research on expression of placental genes by cancer cells; monoclonal antibodies; oncodevelopmental markers; immunocytochemistry. Home: 715 Muirlands Vista Way La Jolla CA 92037 Office: La Jolla Cancer Research Found 10901 N Torrey Pines Rd La Jolla CA 92037

FISHWICK, JOHN PALMER, retired railroad executive, lawyer; b. Roanoke, Va., Sept. 29, 1916; s. William and Nellie (Cross) F.; m. Blair Wiley, Jan. 4, 1941; children: Ellen Blair (Mrs. Guyman Martin III), Anne Palmer (Mrs. Wesley Posvar), John Palmer. A.B., Roanoke Coll., 1937; LL.B., Harvard U., 1940. Bar: Va. 1939. Asso. Cravath, Swaine & Moore, N.Y.C., 1940-42; asst. to gen. solicitor N. & W. Ry., Roanoke, Va., 1945-47; asst. gen. solicitor N. & W. Ry., 1947-51, asst. gen. counsel, 1951-54, gen. solicitor, 1954-56, gen. counsel, 1956-58, v.p., gen. counsel, 1958-59, v.p. law, 1959-63, sr. v.p., 1963-70, pres., chief exec. officer, 1970-80, chmn., chief exec. officer, 1980-81, also dir.; ptnr. Windels, Marx, Davies & Ives, N.Y.C., 1981-84; sole practice Roanoke, Va., 1984—; chmn., chief exec. officer Erie Lackawanna Ry. Co., 1968-70; pres., chief exec. officer Del. and Hudson Ry. Co., 1968-70; pres., dir. Dereco, Inc., 1968-81; chmn. investment com., bd. dirs. Norfolk So. Corp. Trustee Roanoke Coll., 1964-72; trustee Va. Theol. Sem. (former chancellor Diocese S.W. Va.); bd. dirs. Va. Found. Humanities; former trustee Va. Mus. Fine Arts, Richmond. Served as lt. comdr. USNR, 1942-45. Episcopalian. Clubs: City Tavern Assn. (Georgetown); Metropolitan (Washington); Hillsboro (Pompano Beach, Fla.). Office: 451 Kimball Ave NE Roanoke VA 24042-0055

FISIAK, JACEK, college administrator; b. Konstantynow, Poland, May 10, 1936; s. Czeslaw and Jadwiga (Pasnicka) F.; m. Jadwiga Nawrocka, Jan. 27, 1966. MA, U. Warsaw, Poland, 1959; PhD, U. Lodz, Poland, 1962; DLitt, A. Mickiewicz U., Poznan, Poland, 1965; DHC (hon.), U. Jyvaskyla, Finland, 1984. Asst. lectr. U. Lodz, 1959-63, adj. prof., 1963-65, docent, 1965-67; docent A. Mickiewicz U., 1965-71, prof., 1971—, head dept. English, 1965—, pres., rector, 1985-90; vis. prof. U. Kans., Lawrence, 1970, U. Fla., Gainesville, 1974, SUNY, 1975, Am. U., Washington, 1979-80, U. Kiel, Fed. Republic Germany, 1979, U. Vienna, 1983, U. Zurich, Switzerland, 1984, U. Tromso, Norway, 1985. Author and editor of over 100 books, including: A Short Grammar of Middle English, 1968, 6th rev. edit., 1986, A Bibliography of Writings for the History of English, 1987, Historical Syntax, 1985, others; editor jours. Folia Linguistica Historica, Studia Anglica, Posnaniensia; contbr. more than 100 articles to profl. jours. Chmn. com. on modern langs. and lit. Ministry Higher Edn., 1974—. Recipient Knight's Cross of Order Polonia Restituta Pres. of Poland, 1979, Comdrs. Cross of Order Lion of Finland Pres. of Finland, 1980, Order of Brit. Empire, Queen of England, 1981; others. Mem. Internat. Assn. Univ. Profs. of English (pres. 1974-77), Internat. Assn. Hist. Linguists (v.p. 1979-81, pres. 1981-83), Soc. Linguistica Europaea (v.p. 1973, 83-84, pres. 1982-83), Polish Acad. Scis. (chmn. com. on modern langs. and lit. 1981—), Internat. Fedn. Modern Lang. Tchrs. (sec. gen. 1980-83). Mem. Polish United Workers Party. Office: A Mickiewicz U, Wieniawskiego 1, 61-712 Poznan Poland

FISK, EDWARD RAY, civil engineer, author; b. Oshkosh, Wis., July 19, 1924; s. Ray Edward and Grace O. (Meyer) Barnes; student Marquette U., 1945-49, Fresno (Calif.) State Coll., 1954, UCLA, 1957-58; B.S., M.B.A., Calif.-Western U.; m. Oct. 28, 1950; children—Jacqueline Mary (Mrs. John Joseph Stamp), Edward Ray II, William John, Robert Paul. Engr., Calif. Div. Hwys., 1952-55; engr. Bechtel Corp., Vernon, Calif., 1955-59; project mgr. Toups Engring Co., Santa Ana, Calif., 1959-61; dept. head Perliter & Soring, Los Angeles, 1961-64; Western rep. Wire Reinforcement Inst., Washington, 1964-65; cons. engr., Anaheim, Calif., 1965; asso. engr. Met. Water Dist. So. Calif., 1966-68; chief specification engr. Koebig & Koebig, Inc., Los Angeles, 1968-71; mgr. constrn. services VTN Consol., Inc., Irvine, Calif., 1971-78; pres. E.R. Fisk Constrn., Orange, Calif., 1978-81; corp. dir. constrn. mgmt. James M. Montgomery Cons. Engrs., Inc., Pasadena, Calif., 1981-83; v.p. Lawrance, Fisk & McFarland, Inc., Santa Barbara and Orange, 1983—; pres. E.R. Fisk & Assocs., Orange, 1983—; v.p. Western region Constrn. Cons. Group, Inc., 1987—; adj. prof. engring., constrn. Calif. State U., Long Beach U., Orange Coast Coll., Costa Mesa, Calif., 1957-78, Calif. Poly. State U., Pomona, 1974; lectr. U. Calif., Berkeley, ITS extension, internationally for ASCE Continuing Edn.; former mem. Calif. Bd. Registered Constrn. Insps. Served with USN, 1942-43, USAF, 1951-52. Registered profl. engr., Ariz., Calif., Colo., Fla., Idaho, La., Mont., Nev., Oreg., Utah, Wash., Wyo.; lic. land surveyor, Oreg., Idaho; lic. gen. engring. contractor, Calif.; cert. abritator Calif. Constrn. Contract Arbitration Com. Fellow ASCE (past chmn. exec. com. constrn. div.; former chmn. nat. com. inspection 1978—); mem. Nat. Acad. Forensic Engrs. (diplomate), Orange County Engring. Council (former pres.), Calif. Soc. Profl. Engrs. (past pres. Orange County), Am. Arbitration Assn. (nat. panel), U.S. Com. Large Dams, Order Founders and Patriots Am. (past gov. Calif.), Soc. Colonial Wars (gov.), S.R. (past dir.), Engring. Edn. Found. (trustee), Tau Beta Pi. Republican. Author: Machine Methods of Survey Computing, 1958, Construction Project Administration, 1978, 82, 88, Construction Engineers Form Book, 1981, Contractor's Project Guide, 1988. Home: PO Box 6448 Orange CA 92613-6448 Office: 1224 E Katella Suite 105 Orange CA 92667

FISZER-SZAFARZ, BERTA (BERTA SAFARS), research scientist; b. Wilno, Poland, Feb. 1, 1928; m. David Szafarz; children—Martine, Michel. M.S., U. Buenos Aires, 1955, Ph.D., 1956. Lab. chief Cancer Inst. Villejuif, France, 1961-67; vis. scientist Nat. Cancer Inst., Bethesda, Md., 1967-68; lab. chief Institut Curie, Orsay, France, 1969—; vis. scientist Inst. Applied Biochemistry, Mitake, Gifu, Japan, 1986. Contbr. articles to profl. jours. Mem. European Assn. Cancer Research, Am. Assn. Cancer Research (corres. mem.), N.Y. Acad. Scis., European Cell Biology Orgn., French Soc. Cell Biology.

FITCH, BRIAN HILL, property company executive, money broker; b. London, May 19, 1930; s. Stanley Hill and Marjorie Winifred (Browne) F.; m. Susan Margaret Edwardes, Mar. 26, 1955; children—Adrian Hill, Judy Susan. Student Haileybury Coll., 1944-47. Ins. broker Lloyds, London, 1950-65; dir. London & Westminster Property Co. Ltd., 1956-65, mng. dir., 1965—; chmn. Caledonian Mcpl. Investments Ltd., 1970-80; chmn., mng. dir. London & Westminster (Sterling Brokers) Ltd., 1972-80; mng. dir. London. Fin. Agy. Ltd., 1980—; underwriting mem. Lloyds of London, 1982—. Fellow Inst. Dirs. (life). Conservative. Anglican. Clubs: Rolls-Royce Enthusiasts. Home: Grayleigh St Huberts Ln, Gerrards Cross, Buckinghamshire SL9 7BW, England

FITCH, EDWARD HAROLD, airline executive; b. Sydney, New South Wales, Australia, May 27, 1929; s. Edward William and Dorothy Alice (Rice) F., m. Gretchen Anne Cole, Aug. 20, 1965; children: Nancy Alice, Lincoln Gray. With Qantas Airways, Sydney, 1946—, mgr. cargo services, 1983—. Com. mem. Australian Nat. Trade Facilitation, Canberra, Australia, 1976—. Mem. Australian Inst. Materials Mgmt., Airfreight Acad. Australia (dir. 1982—), Internat. Air Transport Assn. (com. chmn. 1980—). Club: Royal Motor Yacht. Home: 47 Whale Beach Rd, Avalon Beach, New South Wales 2107, Australia Office: Qantas Airways, GPO Box 489, Sydney, New South Wales 2001, Australia

FITCH, RAYMOND WILLIAM, lawyer, musician; b. Mpls., Apr. 10, 1931; s. Ray W. and Eleanor (Fleetham) F.; m. Antoinette C. Suwalsky, May 31, 1958; children—Albert, Robert, Michael, Anne. B.S.L., U. Minn., 1953, JD, 1955. Bar: Minn. 1955, U.S. Supreme Ct. 1988. Assoc. Tyrrell, Jardine, St. Paul, 1957-65, Robb & Van Eps, Mpls., 1965-68; ptnr. Fitch & Johnson, Mpls., 1968—; advisor Minn. Legislature, 1970—; tchr. legal affairs Mpls. pub. schs., 1975—; tchr., advisor, musician Basilica St. Mary, Mpls., 1968—; owner, operator Arabian horse farm, Shakopee, Minn. Served to 1st lt. U.S. Army, 1955-57. Mem. Minn. Bar Assn., Hennepin County Bar Assn., Am. Arbitration Assn. (arbitrator 1980—), Delta Tau Delta. Roman Catholic. Lodge: Knight of Holy Sepulchre. Office: Fitch & Johnson 15 N 16th St Minneapolis MN 55403

FITCH, VAL LOGSDON, physics educator; b. Merriman, Nebr., Mar. 10, 1923; s. Fred B. and Frances Marion (Logsdon) F.; m. Elise Cunningham, June 11, 1949 (dec. 1972); children: John Craig, Alan Peter; m. Daisy Harper Sharp, Aug. 14, 1976. B.Eng., McGill U., 1948; Ph.D., Columbia U., 1954. Instr. Columbia, 1953; instr. physics Princeton, 1954-56, asst. prof., 1956-59, 1959-60, prof., 1960—, Class 1909 prof. physics, 1968-76, Cyrus Fogg Bracket prof. physics, 1976-84, James S. McDonnel Distinguished Univ. prof. physics, 1984—; Mem. Pres.'s Sci. Adv. Com., 1970-73. Trustee Asso. Univ., Inc., 1961-67. Served with AUS, 1943-46. Recipient Research Corp. award, 1967; E.O. Lawrence award, 1968; Wetherill medal Franklin Inst., 1976; Nobel prize in physics, 1980; Sloan fellow, 1960. Fellow Am. Phys. Soc., Am. Acad. Arts and Sci., A.A.A.S.; mem. Nat. Acad. Sci. Office: Princeton Univ Dept Physics PO Box 708 Princeton NJ 08544

FITOUSSI, JEAN-PAUL SAMUEL, economist; b. La Goulette, Tunisia, Aug. 19, 1942; s. Joseph and Mathilde (Cohen) F.; student U. Paris, 1961-63; licencie in econs. U. Strasbourg, 1966, diplome d'etudes superieures in econs., 1967, Docteur d'Etat in Econs., 1971, Agrege in Econs., 1973; m. Annie Krief, July 11, 1964; children—Lisa, David. Asst., Louis Pasteur U., Strasbourg, 1968-71, chargé de cours, 1971-73, maître de conferences, 1973-75, prof. econs., 1975-82, dean Faculty Econs., 1974-77, hon. dean, 1977—; cons. to EEC, 1978-82, 84-86; prof. European U. Inst., 1979-83, prof.-at-large, 1984—, head dept. econs., 1980-81; dir. Bur. Theoretical and Applied Econs., U. Strasbourg, 1974-82; prof. Institut d'Etudes Politiques de Paris, 1982—; dir. research dept. Observatoire Français des Conjonctures Economiques, 1982—; mem. adv. com. Econ. and Social Scis. Research Council, U.K., 1986; mem. French nat. com. Sci. Research, 1987—. Recipient prize Academie des Sciences Morales et Politiques, 1974. Mem. French Econ. Assn. (prize 1972), Am. Econ. Assn., Internat. Assn. Applied Econometrics, European Econ. Assn., Internat. Econ. Assn. (gen. sec. 1984); dir. Revue Française d'Economie. Author: Inflation, Equilibre et Chomage, 1973; Le Fondement microeconomique de la theorie Keynesienne, 1974, (with E. Phelps) The Slump in Europe, 1988; editor: (with E. Malinvaud) Unemployment in Western Countries, 1980; Modern Macroeconomic Theory, 1984; (with M. de Cecco) Monetary Theory and Economic Institutions, 1986; (with P.A. Muet) Macrodynamique et déséquilibres, 1986. Office: Observatoire Francais des Conjonctures Economiques, 69 quai d'Orsay, 75007 Paris France

FITTON, GARVIN, lawyer; b. Harrison, Ark., Oct. 5, 1918; s. David Edwards and Lulu Vance (Garvin) F.; m. Martha Ann Hamilton, Sept. 21, 1941; children—John Dennis, Thomas Garvin, Ann Fitton Kelly. LL.B., U. Ark., 1941, J.D., 1969. Bar: Ark. 1941, U.S. Dist. Ct. (ea. and we. dists.) Ark. 1949, U.S. Supreme Ct. 1982. Sole practice, Harrison, 1946—, civilian aide to Sec. to U.S. Army, 1982-87; mem. Ark. Bd. Law Examiners, 1971-73. Mem. bd., officer Harrison Sch. Dist. Served to col. U.S. Army, 1940-46, ETO. Mem. Boone County Bar Assn. (pres. 1959), Ark. Bar Assn. (bd. govs. 1981-83), ABA. Democrat. Methodist. Lodges: Rotary (pres. 1970-71), Mason. Home: 921 W Nicleson Harrison AR 72601 Office: PO Box 249 211 W Rush Harrison AR 72601

FITZGERALD, EDITH JACKSON, real estate and farming executive; b. Lumberton, N.C., May 6, 1932; d. Corbett and Blanche (Wilkins) Jackson; m. James Thomas Fitzgerald, June 24, 1972; children—S. Dianne Pridgen, Candi Swinson, Angela Fitzgerald Hanno. Student in Econs., N.C. State U., 1973, postgrad., 1979. Adminstr., N.C. Cancer Inst., Lumberton, 1960-70; instr. Army Edn. Ctr., Fort Bragg, N.C., 1970-78; pres. Shamrock Farms, Hope Mills, N.C., 1985—, Shamrock Isle Estate, Ltd., Raeford, N.C., 1985—, also founder; bd. dirs. Fayetteville Tech. Inst. Founder Shamrock Scholarship, Fayetteville Tech. Coll. Recipient Disting. Leadership award for Outstanding Service to the Field of Econs., U.S. VA recognition award, Vita award. Mem. Am. Biog. Inst. (bd. govs., dep. gov.), Am. Soc. Notaries (charter life). Democrat. Baptist. Avocations: reading, outdoor sports. Office: Shamrock Isle Estate LTD Route 2 Box 177 Raeford NC 28376

FITZGERALD, EDMUND BACON, electronics industry executive; b. Milw., Feb. 5, 1926; s. Edmund and Elizabeth (Bacon) F.; m. Elisabeth McKee Christensen, Sept. 6, 1947; children: Karen, Kathleen, Edmund Greer, Rogers Christensen. BSEE, U. Mich., 1946. With Cutler-Hammer, Inc., Milw., 1946-78, v.p. in charge engring., 1959-61, adminstrv. v.p., 1961-63, pres., 1964-69, chmn., chief exec. officer, 1969-78; vice chmn. Eaton Corp., Cleve., 1978-79; mng. dir. Hampshire Assocs., Milw., 1979-80; pres., dir. No. Telecom Inc., Nashville, 1980-82, chmn., 1985—; chmn. bd. dirs. No. Telecom Ltd., Mississauga, Ont., Can., 1985—, chief exec. officier, 1985—, also bd. dirs.; bd. dirs. No. Telecom Ltd., 1984—, Bell Can. Enterprises Inc. Former chmn., bd. dirs. Milw. Brewers Baseball Club, Inc.; former chmn. Com. for Econ. Devel.; mem. Pres. Reagan's Nat. Security Telecommunications Adv. Com. Served to capt. USMCR, 1943-46, 51-52. Named Man of Yr., Milw. Jr. C. of C., 1956. Mem. Nat. Elec. Mfrs. Assn. (pres. 1968). Office: No Telecom Inc 127 Woodmont Blvd Nashville TN 37205 also: No Telecom Ltd, 3 Robert Speck Pkwy, Mississauga, ON Canada L4Z 2G5

FITZGERALD, ELLA, singer; b. Newport News, Va., Apr. 25, 1918; m. Ray Brown (div. 1953); 1 son, Ray. Began singing with Chick Webb Orch., 1934-39; tours throughout U.S., Japan, Europe; with Jazz at the Philharmonic troupe, 1948-57; rec. artist for Decca, 1936-55, Verve, from 1956, now Pablo Records; appeared in motion picture Pete Kelly's Blues, 1955; nightclub appearances include Sahara Hotel, Caesar's Palace, both Las Vegas, Fairmont Hotel, San Francisco, Ronnie Scott's Club, London; appeared on TV in spls. with Frank Sinatra; also on All Star Swing Festival, 1972, concert with Boston Pops, 1972; later with more than 40 symphony orchs. throughout U.S.; records include At Duke's Place, 1966, Best, 1967, Clap Hands, 1961, Cote d' Azur, (with Ellington), 1967, Ella, Ella Fitzgerald: In Hamburg, 1965, Mack the Knife, Ella in Berlin, 1960, Sunshine of Your Love, Things Ain't What They Used to Be, Tribute to Porter, 1965, Whisper Not, 1966, Watch What Happens, 1972, Take Love Easy, 1975, Ella in London, 1975, Lady Time, 1978, A Perfect Match (with Count Basie), 1979, A Tisket a Tasket, 1985, Montreux Ella, numerous others. Recipient 8 Grammy awards, numerous popularity awards from Down Beat mag., Metronome mag., Musicians Poll, JAY Award Poll; named number 1 female singer 16th Internat. Jazz Critics Poll, 1968, Am. Music award, 1978; recipient Kennedy Center honor, 1979, Grammy award as best female jazz vocalist, 1981, 84; recipient Nat. Medal of the Arts, 1987. Address: care Norman Granz 451 N Canon Dr Beverly Hills CA 90210 *

FITZGERALD, GARRET, former prime minister of Ireland, politician; b. Dublin, Ireland, Feb. 9, 1926; s. Desmond and Mabel (McConnell) FitzG.; Leaving Cert., Belvedere Coll.; B.A. with honors Univ. Coll., Dublin, 1946, Ph.D.; LL.D., Kings Inns, 1947; m. Joan O'Farrell, 1947; 3 children. Called to Irish Bar, 1947 Aer Lingus (Irish Air Lines) 1947-58; Rockefeller research asst. Trinity Coll., Dublin, 1958-59; lectr. dept. polit. economy Univ. Coll. Dublin, 1959-73; mem. Seanad Eireann (Irish Senate), Dublin, 1965-69; mem. Dail (Irish Ho. of Reps.), Dublin, 1969—, Fine Gael opposition frontbench spokesman on edn., 1969-72, mem. Dail Com. on Pub. Accounts, 1969-73, Fine Gael opposition frontbench spokesman on fin., 1972-73, minister for fgn. affairs, 1973-77, Taoiseach (prime minister Ireland), 1981-82, 82-87; leader Fine Gael Party, 1977-87; mem. senate Nat. U. Ireland. Dep. for Dublin S.E. Office: Dail Eireann, Dublin Ireland

FITZGERALD, JAMES FRANCIS, cable television executive; b. Janesville, Wis., Mar. 27, 1926; s. Michael Henry and Chloris Helen (Beiter) F.; m. Marilyn Field Cullen, Aug. 1, 1950; children: Michael Dennis, Brian Nicholas, Marcia O'Loughlin, James Francis, Carolyn Jane, Ellen Putnam. B.S., Notre Dame U., 1947. With Standard Oil Co. (Ind.), Milw., 1947-48; pres. F.-W. Oil Co., Janesville, 1950—, Total TV, Inc. (cable TV Systems), Wis., 1965-86; bd dirs. Milw. Ins. Co. Vintage Club, Bank One, Janesville; chmn. bd. Golden State Warriors-Oakland, Calif., 1986—. Bd. govs., chmn. TV com. NBA; chmn. bd., pres. S.P.A.C.E. Inc. subs. Milw. Buck NBA team, 1976-85; chmn. Greater Milw. Open (PGA Tournament), 1985. Served to lt. (j.g.) USNR, 1944-45, 51-52. Mem. Chief Execs. Forum, World Bus. Council, Wis. Petroleum Assn. (pres. 1961-62). Roman Catholic. Clubs: Janesville Country, Castle Pines Golf, Milw. Athletic; Vintage (Indian Wells, Calif.). Home and Office: PO Box 348 Janesville WI 53547

FITZGERALD, JOHN ARTHUR, social work director; b. London, May 14, 1942; s. Bernard John James and Elsie (Steggell) F.; m. Maureen Grace Gooding, Aug. 20, 1966; children: Marion Kim, Alun John. Cert. social worker. Social worker Ch. Eng. Children's Soc., London, 1971-74; area social work mgr. Ch. Eng. Children's Soc., East Sussex, Eng., 1974-76; exec. dir. Brit. Adoption Resource Exchange, London, 1976-80; exchange dir. Brit. Agys. for Adoption and Fostering, London, 1980-84; dir., sec. The Bridge Child Care Consultancy Service, London, 1984—; tech. advisor reports action series Granada TV, Manchester, 1976-80, bd. dirs. post adoption ctr., 1985—, chmn. Post Adoption Ctr., 1988—, Nat. Council for Vol. Child Care Agys., London, 1982-86. Author: Building New Families Through Adoption and Fostering, 1982, author, editor Understanding Disruption, 1983; contbr. articles. Dept. of Health and Consultancy grantee, London, 1984. Mem. Assn. Child Psychiatry, Psychology and Allied Profesions, Assn. Chief Execs. of Vol. Agys. Baptist. Office: The Bridge, Market Towers 1, Nine Elms Ln, London SW8 5NX, England

FITZGERALD, MICHAEL GARRETT, accountant, author; b. El Dorado, Ark., Dec. 14, 1950; s. Johnny Fotch and Tommye Mae (Murphy) F.; B.B.A., So. State Coll., Magnolia, Ark., 1972. Acct., Southwestern Electric Power Co., Shreveport, La., 1972—; works include: Universal Pictures—A Panoramic History in Words Pictures and Filmographies, 1977; American Movies—The Forties, vol. I, 1940-44, 1980, vol. II, 1945-49, 1981. Democrat. Baptist. Home: 1310 Harold Ellen St El Dorado AR 71730 Office: 428 Travis St Shreveport LA 71104

FITZGERALD, PATRICIA ANN, motivational and management consultant; b. Dallas, Sept. 16, 1937; d. Thomas O'Neil and Minerva Hannah (Gililland) Anderson; student Sawyer Bus. Coll., 1955, Phoenix City Coll., 1960-66, Brigham Young U., Hawaii, 1979, U. Calif.-Irvine, 1979, UCLA, 1979-80; m. Gerald William Fitzgerald, Mar. 6, 1976; children by previous marriage—Vicki Lee Jones Duncan, Gregg Ronald Jones, Randall Thomas Jones, Lori Lynn Jones. Service rep. So. Calif. Gas Co., 1956-60, Ariz. Public Service, 1961; sales rep. Shaw Walker Co., 1967-68; sales mgr. Selective Office Service, 1968-69; communications cons., mktg. mgr. Pacific Telephone Co., Orange, Calif., 1970-80; pres. Fitzgerald & Assocs., Anaheim Hills, Calif. and Denver, 1979—; cons. in field. Recipient awards of appreciation Personnel and Indsl. Relations Assn., Brooks Coll., Pacific Telephone. Mem. Am. Soc. Tng. and Devel. (appreciation award), Am. Mktg. Assn., Women in Mgmt. (appreciation award), Internat. Platform Assn., Nat. Speakers Assn., Relief Soc. Republican. Mormon. Contbr. articles to bus. mags. and newspapers, Long Beach and Los Angeles; various appearances ednl. TV, Orange County. Home and Office: 4 Shetland Ct Highlands Ranch CO 80126

FITZ GERALD, WILLIAM HENRY GERALD, corporation executive; b. Boston, Dec. 23, 1909; s. William Joseph and Mary Ellen (Smith) F.; m. Annelise Petschek, July 2, 1943; children: Desmond, Anne. B.S., U.S. Naval Acad., 1931; student, Harvard Law Sch., 1934-35; D.Sc. (hon.), Adelphi U., 1962. With Borden Co., N.Y.C., 1936-41; personal bus. interests Mexico, 1946-47; organized Metall. Research & Devel. Co., Washington, 1947; v.p., treas. Metall. Research & Devel. Co., 1947-56, pres., 1956-58, 60-82, chmn., 1960-82; chmn. bd. Nat. Metallizing Corp., Trenton, N.J., 1956-58, The Cottages, Ltd., Jamaica, B.W.I., 1960-70, Linden Corp., Washington, 1962-70, N.Am. Housing Corp., Washington, 1971-86; chmn. Supramar, Ltd., Lucerne, Switzerland, 1963-69; dir. Supramar, Ltd., 1970-75; pres. Nat. Media Analysis, Inc., Washington, 1968-70; chmn. Nat. Media Analysis, Inc., 1970-72; partner Hornblower & Weeks, Hemphill-Noyes, Inc., 1970-72, 1st. v.p., 1972-77; vice chmn., dir., exec. com. Fin. Gen. Bankshares, Inc., 1977-82; dir., mem. exec. com. First Am. Bank (N.A.), Washington, 1977-83; dir., mem. exec. com., chmn. investment com. Avemco Corp., Washington, Frederick, Md., 1970—; Cosmadent, Ltd., Zurich, Switzerland, 1964-75, Chase Fund of Boston, Chase Convertible Fund, Income & Capital Shares Inc., 1970-75, Pyrotector, Inc., Hingham, Mass., 1963-76; cons. to dir. ICA, Washington, 1957; dep. dir. for mgmt. ICA, Dept. State, 1958-60; U.S. conciliator Internat. Center for Investment Disputes, 1975-82; dir. Inst. Inter Am. Affairs, 1958-60; mem. President's Adv. Bd. on Internat. Investments, 1976-78; treas. Presdl. Inaugural Com., 1981; trustee Presdl. Inaugural Trust, 1981—; mem. Nat. Adv. Com. Internat. Edn., 1982-85. Trustee Fed. City Council, 1962—, Wash. Inst. fgn. Affairs, 1966—; bd. dirs. Atlantic Council U.S., 1976—, treas., 1979—, mem. exec. com., 1980—; trustee Fgn. Student Service Council, 1963—, Oblate Coll. (Cath. U.), 1966—; trustee Corcoran Gallery Art, 1977—, also mem. exec. com., chmn. devel. com.; pres. Soc. for a More Beautiful Nat. Capital, Inc., 1974-77; bd. dirs., mem. exec. com., sr. v.p. Nat. Tennis Found. and Hall of Fame of Tennis, 1974—; U.S. del. Atlantic Treaty Assembly, Reykjavik, Iceland, 1977, Washington, 1979, Rome, 1983, Istanbul, Turkey, 1987; grand officer Confrérie des Chevaliers du Tastevin, 1979—; grand senechal Sous Commanderie de Washington, 1980—; trustee White House Preservation Fund, 1979—, chmn., 1982—; trustee, mem. nominating com. U.D.C., 1982-87; mem. nat. com. Vatican Judaica Exhibition, 1987—. Served as ensign USN, 1931-34; from lt. (j.g.) to comdr. 1941-46. Decorated Order Militar de Ayacucho Peru, Knight Grand Cross Sovereign Mil. Order Malta; knight grand cross Equestrian Order Holy Sepulchre; Knight grand Cross Sacred Mil. Constantinian Order of St. George. Mem. Newcomen Soc. N.Am. Fed. Assn. in U.S.A., Sovereign Mil. Order of Malta (pres. 1975-79), So. Assn. Roman Catholic. Clubs: Army-Navy Country (Washington), University (Washington), Harvard (Washington), 1925 F St (Washington), International (Washington); River (N.Y.C.); Metropolitan (Washington); Essex County (Manchester, Mass.). Home: 2305 Bancroft Pl NW Washington DC 20008 Office: 1730 M St NW Washington DC 20036

FITZ GERALD-BUSH, FRANK SHEPARD, historian, poet; b. Hialeah, Fla., Oct. 11, 1925; s. Frank Shepard and Lady Irene (Coburg-FitzGerald) Bush; A.B., U. Miami (Fla.), 1953, M.A., 1964. Instr. Ransom Sch., Coconut Grove, Fla., 1957-58, St. Johns Country Day Sch., Orange Park, Fla., 1959-61; instr. in history Homestead AFB Extension, Fla. State U., 1961-64; reference librarian, curator Floridiana, John F. Kennedy Meml. Library, Hialeah, 1966-71; historian City of Opa-locka (Fla.), 1975—; dir. South Fla. Archaeol. Museum, 1975; instr. Vivian Laramore Rader Poetry Group, 1973—; author: (poetry) Native Treasure, 1943, Sonnets In Search of Sequence, 1968, Remembered Spring, 1974; Memories of a Golden Land, 1985; (history) A Dream of Araby: Glenn H. Curtiss and the Founding of Opa-locka, 1976; contbr. numerous articles, revs. and poems to profl. jours. in Gt. Britain, France, U.S., 1942—; trustee Friends of Opa-locka Library, 1976—; mem. bd. advisers South Fla. Poetry Inst., 1975. Served with RCAF, 1943-44, USMCR, 1948-51 Am. Field Service, 1944-45, USAF, 1951-55. Recipient Recognition award Laramore Rader Poetry Group, 1975, 76; named knight comdr. Order Holy Sepulcher, knight Orders Holy Cross Jerusalem, St. Stephen the Martyr, St. Gregory the Illuminator. Mem. Fla. Hist. Soc., Hist. Assn. So. Fla., Dade Heritage Trust, Irish Georgian Soc., County Kildare Archaeol. Soc. (life), Fla. Anthropol. Soc., RAF Assn. (life), Opa-locka C. of C. (asso.), S.R., SAR, Magna Charta Barons, English-Speaking Union, Viscayans, DAV (life). Author: Young Alfred: The Forgotten Prince, 1979. Home: 3030 NW 171st St Opa-locka FL 33056

FITZHUGH, DAVID MICHAEL, lawyer; b. San Francisco, Nov. 24, 1946; s. William DeHart and Betty Jean (Jeffries) F.; m. Jenny Lu Conner, Dec. 22, 1967; children—Ross DeHart, Cameron Hyatt, Michael Jeffries. Student Carleton Coll., 1964-67; B.A., Coll. William and Mary, 1972; J.D., U. Va., 1975. Bar: D.C. 1975, U.S. Dist. Ct. D.C. 1979, U.S. Ct. Claims 1980, U.S. Ct. Appeals (fed. cir.) 1982, U.S. Supreme Ct. 1982. Assoc. McKenna, Conner & Cuneo, Washington, 1975-80, ptnr., 1980—. Mem. editorial bd. Nat. Contract Mgmt. Assn. Jour., 1975—. Contbr. articles to legal publs. Referee Alexandria Soccer Assn., Alexandria, Va., 1984. Served to capt. USMC, 1967-71, Vietnam. Mem. ABA (litigation sect., discovery com. pub. contracts sect.) Club: Army-Navy Country. Home: 3606 Cameron Mills Rd Alexandria VA 22305 Office: McKenna Conner & Cuneo 1575 Eye St NW Suite 800 Washington DC 20005

FITZPATRICK, FRANCIS JAMES, lawyer; b. N.Y.C., Apr. 29, 1916; s. Francis James and Susan Clemens (Tompkins) FitzP.; m. Ethel Marie Peters, Mar. 2, 1956. A.B., Duke U., 1938; postgrad. Harvard U. Grad. Sch. Bus. Adminstrn., 1939-40; J.D., Cornell U., 1947. Bar: Iowa 1951, N.J. 1954. Exec. trainee U.S. Fidelity & Guaranty Co., N.Y., 1940-41; counsellor, Western Electric Co., Kearny, N.J., 1942-45; practice, Orange, N.J., 1954—. Served with M.C., U.S. Army, 1941-42. Mem. ABA, N.J. State Bar Assn., Essex County Bar Assn., Am. Judicature Soc., Cornell Law Student Assn. (sec.-treas.), Cornell U. Law Assn., Duke U. Met. Alumni Assn., Delta Theta Phi (pres.), Am. Legion (former judge adv. Orange), Sigma Alpha Epsilon. Home: 5 Ledgewood Court Warren Township NJ 07060 Office: 308 Main St Orange NJ 07050

FITZPATRICK, HAROLD FRANCIS, lawyer; b. Jersey City, Oct. 16, 1947; s. Harold G. and Anne Marie Fitzpatrick; m. Joanne M. Merry, Sept. 22, 1973; children: Elizabeth, Kevin, Matthew. AB, Boston Coll., 1969; MBA, NYU, 1971; JD, Harvard U., 1974. Bar: N.J. 1974, U.S. Dist. Ct. N.J. 1974, U.S. Ct. Internat. Trade, 1986. Securities analyst Chase Manhattan Bank, N.Y.C., 1970-71, Brown Bros., Harriman & Co., N.Y.C., 1971; staff asst. U.S. Senate, Washington, 1972; law clk. to assoc. justice N.J. Supreme Ct., Trenton, 1974-75; assoc. Cleary, Gottlieb, Steen & Hamilton, N.Y.C., 1975-78; sr. ptnr. Waters, McPherson, McNeill & Fitzpatrick, Secaucus and Bayonne, N.J., 1978—; gen. counsel Housing Authority City of Bayonne, 1976—, Dry Color Mfrs. Assn., Alexandria, Va., 1978—, N.J. Assn. Housing & Redevel. Authorities, Bayonne, 1979—, Housing Authority Town of Secaucus, N.J., 1980—, Rahway Geriatrics Ctr. Inc., N.J., 1981—, Housing Authority City of Englewood, N.J., 1985—, Housing Authority City of Rahway, N.J., 1986—, Edgewater Mcpl. Utilities Authority, 1986—. Mem. ABA, N.J. Ban Assn., Hudson County Bar Assn. (trustee 1984-87, officer 1987—), Nat. Assn. Bond Lawyers, Nat. Health Lawyers Assn., Am Soc. Assn. Execs. (legal sect.), Beta Gamma Sigma. Office: Waters McPherson McNeill Fitzpatrick P A 400 Plaza Dr Secaucus NJ 07094

FITZPATRICK, JOSEPH MARK, patent lawyer; b. Jersey City, May 27, 1925; s. Joseph Francis Stephen and Meave (Wilson) F.; ME, Stevens Inst. Tech., 1945; JD, Georgetown U., 1951; m. Elizabeth Anne Keane, June 18, 1949; children: Elizabeth A., Susan E., Christopher M., Stephen R. Examiner. Bar: Va. 1950, U.S. Patent Office 1950, N.Y. 1954. Trial atty., antitrust div. Dept. Justice, 1951-53; mem. firm Ward, McElhannon, Brooks & Fitzpatrick, N.Y.C., 1954-70, Fitzpatrick, Cella, Harper & Scinto, N.Y.C., 1970— . Served with USNR, 1943-46. Fellow Am. Coll. Trial Lawyers; mem. N.Y., Va. bar assns., Assn. Bar City N.Y., Am., N.Y. patent law assns. Clubs: City Midday; Manasquan River Yacht, Fox Meadow Tennis. Home: 17 Oak Ln Scarsdale NY 10583 Office: 277 Park Ave New York NY 10017

FITZPATRICK, MICHELE ANNE, software manufacturing company executive; b. Forbach, France, Aug. 23, 1958; d. Andre and Christiane (Wohluther) Weisslinger; m. Graham Drayton Fitzpatrick. BA in Linguistics, Lille U., France, 1980. Cert. teaching master, 1981. Tchr. various schs. France, U.K., 1980-82; software translator McCordack & Dodge, Natick, Mass., 1982-83; product mgr. McCordack & Dodge, France, 1984; European product mgr. McCordack & Dodge, France, The Netherlands, 1985; salesman McCordack & Dodge, U.K., 1986; European product mktg. mgr.

Lotus Devel. UK Ltd., Windsor, Eng., 1986; mgr. European mainframe system div. Lotus Devel. UK Ltd., Eng., 1987—; cons. on multiple acquisitions, 1983-88; guest speaker in field. Editor book on microecons., 1986. Office: Lotus Devel UK Ltd, Consort House Victoria St, Windsor SL4 1EX, England

FITZPATRICK, PETER BRYAN, lawyer; b. New Orleans, June 30, 1945; s. William H. and Frances (Westfeldt) F.; m. Anne L. Wallace, Aug. 24, 1968; children—Bryan W.W., Lydia W.C. B.A., Princeton U., 1968; M.A., Stanford U., 1969; J.D., U. Va., 1973; postgrad. St. Antony's Coll. Oxford Univ., 1976. Bar: Va. 1974, N.Y. 1977, D.C. 1978. Assoc. Winthrop, Stimson, Putnam & Roberts, N.Y.C., 1976-80; asst. counsel Newsweek Inc., N.Y.C., 1980-83; counsel Hunton & Williams, Norfolk, Va., 1983—. Contbr. articles to profl. jours. Trustee St. Antony's Coll. Trust, Pembroke Coll. Found., Oxford; bd. advisors Va. Ctr. World Trade, Norfolk, 1984; pres. World Affairs Council Greater Hampton Rds., Norfolk, 1986; communications com. campaign U. Va. Mem. ABA, D.C. Bar Assn., Va. Bar Assn., Assn. Bar City N.Y. (com. human rights). Avocations: tennis, hiking, squash, reading, history. Office: Hunton & Williams 101 St Paul's Blvd Norfolk VA 23510

FITZPATRICK, ROBERT, psychologist; b. Cin., Aug. 26, 1924; s. John Joseph and Helen (Collins) F.; B.S., U. Pitts., 1947, M.S., 1948, Ph.D., 1953; m. Joanne Gehring Knauss, Aug. 12, 1952 (dec. Mar. 1970); children—John R., Janet E. Asbury, Jean A.; m. Dorothy May Gallagher, Jan. 31, 1976; 1 stepson, Matthew A. Kail. Project dir. Am. Inst. for Research, Pitts., 1948-54, program dir., 1954-59, 64-71; human factors unit supr. Boeing Co., Seattle, 1959-61; operational design group supr. System Devel. Corp., Lexington, Mass., 1961-62; mgr. psychol. dept., humetrics div. Thiokol Chem. Corp., Los Angeles, 1963-64; pvt. practice indsl. psychology, Pitts., 1971—; dir. research Psychol. Service, Pitts., 1976-78; lectr. U. Pitts., 1977—; assoc. prof. St. Francis Coll., Pitts., 1979-85; grad. lectr. European div. U. Md., 1985-86. Served with USMC, 1943-46, 51-53. Mem. Nat. Council Measurement in Edn., Am. Ednl. Research Assn., Am. Psychol. Assn., Pa. Psychol. Assn.. Home: 447 Arden Rd Pittsburgh PA 15216

FJÄLLSTRÖM, PER-OLOF ROLF, mathematician; b. Råneå, Sweden, Mar. 7, 1954; s. Rolf Helmer and Birgitta Anna (Hellberg) F.; m. Kari Gill McCall, June 27, 1987. MS, Royal Inst. Tech., Stockholm, 1978, PhD, 1985. Researcher Royal Inst. Tech., 1980-85; cons. IBM Sweden, Stockholm, 1985—. Mem. IEEE, Soc. Indsl. and Applied Math. Office: IBM Sweden, 16392 Stockholm Sweden

FJELDGAARD, KJELD, oil company executive; b. Dronninglund, Denmark, Nov. 4, 1946; s. Gunnar and Elly (Nielsen) F.; m. Kirsten Larsen, Oct. 30, 1971; children: Kristian, Kristopher. BS in Mech. Engring., Aalborg U. Ctr., Denmark, 1971; New Frontiers of Mgmt., Columbia U., 1986. Petroleum engr. Gulf Oil, Denmark, 1972-75, Chevron Research, Los Angeles, 1975; sr. petroleum engr. Shell, Brunei, Indonesia, 1979-81; sr. petroleum engr. Maersk Oil & Gas, Copenhagen, 1976-79, ops. mgr., 1981-84, v.p., 1984-85, sr. v.p., 1985-86, prodn. dir., 1987—; chmn. North Sea Operators Com., Copenhagen, 1985—. Mem. Soc. Petroleum Engrs. Office: Maersk Oil & Gas, Esplanaden 50, 1263 Copenhagen Denmark

FLACH, WERNER, publisher; b. Hof/Saale, Bavaria, Germany, Feb. 2, 1935; s. Karl and Gertrud (Kuenzel) F.; m. Dorette Ebert, Sept. 13, 1958 (div. Jan. 1970); 1 child, Thomas. Pres. Werner Flach, Internat. Sci. Booksellers, Frankfurt, Fed. Republic Germany, 1957—, IDD Verlag Für Internat. Dokumentation Werner Flach KG, Frankfurt, 1973—, Verlag für Humanistische Psychologie Werner Flach KG, Frankfurt, 1978—. Editor Jour. Sensus Kommunikation; contbr. articles to profl. jours. Mem. Börsenverein Deutschen Buchhandels. Office: Internat Sci Booksellers, Heddernheimer Landstr 78 a, 6000 Frankfurt M 50 Hessen Federal Republic of Germany

FLACK, JAMES MONROE, former business executive; b. Baxterville, Miss., Aug. 29, 1913; s. Jesse James and Lenora (Lucas) F.; m. Hertha E. Eisenmenger, Aug. 30, 1941; children: James Monroe, Sonya Karen, Robert Frank, Suzanne Margaret. B.S., Delta State U., 1935; M.Div., Yale U., 1942; postgrad., Harvard U., 1952. Prin. Shaw (Miss.) High Sch., 1935-39; with employee relations dept. Standard Oil Co. of N.J., 1946; officer, dir. subs. Textron, Inc., 1946-53; v.p., dir. Indian Head, Inc., 1953—, vice chmn., 1972-74. Served as lt. comdr. USN, 1942-45. Clubs: N.Y. Athletic, Yale of N.Y.C, Red Fox Country, Tyron (N.C.) Country. Home: 165 Wilderness Rd Tryon NC 28782

FLAGG, E. ALMA WILLIAMS, ednl. adminstr.; b. City Point, Va., Sept. 16, 1918; d. Hannibal Greene and Caroline Ethel (Moody) Williams; B.S., Newark State Coll., 1940, Litt.D. (hon.), 1968; M.A., Montclair (N.J.) State Coll., 1943; Ed.D., Columbia U., 1955; m. J. Thomas Flagg, Jr., June 24, 1942; children—Thomas L., Lois Luisa. Tchr., Washington, 1941-43; with Newark Pub. Schs., 1943-83, vice-prin., 1963-64, prin., 1964-67, asst. supt., 1967-78, dir., 1978-83; cons. edn., 1972—; adj. instr., guest speaker various univs. and colls, poet-in-residence various pub. schs. Mem. Newark Bicentennial Commn. Recipient various profl. awards; E. Alma Flagg Sch. erected, 1984; E. Alma Flagg Scholarship Fund established, 1984. Mem. LWV (pres. Newark 1982-84), N.J. Hist. Soc., AAUW, Assn. Supervision and Curriculum Devel., Nat. Soc. Study of Edn., Nat. Council Tchrs. of English, Nat. Assn. Negro Bus. and Profl. Women's (recipient Truth award, 1985) Nat. Council Tchrs. of Math., NAACP (life), Nat. Alliance Black Sch. Educators, Nat. Council Negro Women (life), Alpha Kappa Alpha (life), Kappa Delta Pi. Presbyterian. Author: (poetry) Lines and Colors, 1979; Feelings, Lines, Colors, 1980; Twenty More with Thought and Feeling, 1981, Bioprosthesis, 1987; editor: Cardiac Valve Bioprosthesis. Home: 44 Stengel Ave Newark NJ 07112

FLAGG, JOHN FERARD, retired manufacturing company executive; b. Wellsville, N.Y., Dec. 30, 1914; s. Emory William and Maude Sarah (Vincent) F.; B.S., U. Rochester (N.Y.), 1936; A.M., Princeton, 1937, Ph.D., 1939; children—George V., Nancy B. Flagg Maxon. Instr., then asst. prof. chemistry U. Rochester Coll. Arts and Sci., 1939-46; research asso. Knolls Atomic Power Lab., Gen. Electric Co., 1946-52; mgr. chem./chem. engring. div., 1951-55, mgr. indsl. atomic products, 1955-57, mgr. materials engring. lab., 1957-61; dir. central research div. Am. Cyanamid Co., 1961-72; pres. Cyanamid European Research Inst., Geneva, 1967-69; v.p., dir. research UOP Inc., Des Plaines, Ill., 1972-80; chemist OSRD, 1941-44, Manhattan Project, 1944-46; U.S. del. Atoms for Peace, Geneva, 1955; lectr. Union Coll., Schenectady, 1950-52; adv. bd. chem. engring. div. Argonne (Ill.) Nat. Lab. Recipient Levy medal Franklin Inst., 1940; McKay fellow, 1938-39. Life fellow Franklin Inst.; mem. Am. Chem. Soc. (chmn. Rochester sect. 1946, Western Conn. sect. 1964), Chem. Soc. London, Soc. Chem. Industry, Am. Nuclear Soc. (charter), AAAS, Indsl. Research Dirs. Assn. Chgo., Dirs. of Indsl. Research, Phi Beta Kappa, Sigma Xi. Club: Cosmos (Washington). Author: A Short Course in Quantitative Analysis, 1944; Semi-micro Qualitative Analysis, 1944; Organic Reagents in Gravimetric and Volumetric Analysis, 1948; Processing of Nuclear Fuels, 1961; also articles; patentee in field.

FLAHERTY, DAVID THOMAS, JR., lawyer; b. Boston, June 17, 1953; S. David Thomas Sr. and Nancy Ann (Hamill) F.; m. Margaret Lynn Hoyle, Oct. 2, 1986; 1 child, Alexandra Lynn. BS in Math., German, U. N.C., 1974, JD, 1978. Bar: Mass. 1979, N.C. 1979, U.S. Dist. Ct. (we. dist.) N.C. 1979, U.S. Dist. Ct. (mid. dist.) N.C. 1981, U.S. Ct. Appeals (4th cir.) 1981, U.S. Tax Ct. 1982, U.S. Supreme Ct., 1987. Assoc. Wilson & Palmer, Lenoir, N.C., 1979-80, Ted West P.A., Lenoir, 1980-82; ptnr. Robbins, Flaherty & Lackey, Lenoir, 1982-85, Robbins & Flaherty, Lenoir, 1985—. Mem. exec. com. Caldwell County Reps., Lenoir, 1985-86, 88—. Mem. N.C. Bar Assn., Assn. Trial Lawyer Am., N.C. Acad. Trial Lawyers, 25th Judicial Dist. Bar Assn. (exec. com.), Reps. Men's Club, Young Reps., Blue Key. Methodist. Home: 228 Pennton Ave SW Lenoir NC 28645 Office: Robbins & Flaherty 204 Main St NW Lenoir NC 28645

FLAHERTY, JOHN JOSEPH, quality assurance company executive; b. Chgo., July 24, 1932; s. Patrick J. and Mary B. F.; BEE, U. Ill., 1959; m. Norrine Grow, Nov. 20, 1954; children: John, Bridgette, George, Eileen, Daniel, Mary, Michael, Amy. Design engr. Admiral Corp., Chgo., 1959-60; project engr. Magnaflux Corp., Chgo., 1960-79, v.p., mgr. research and engring., 1979-84, v.p., mgr. mktg. and sales, 1984-86; v.p., gen. mgr. electronic products, 1986-87; pres. Flare Tech., 1988—. Served with AUS, 1951-53. Mem. Am. Soc. Non-Destructive Testing, IEEE, Am. Soc. Quality Control, Am. Soc. Metals (tech. bd. dirs.). Roman Catholic. Numerous patents, publs. on nondestructive testing, including med. ultrasonic; laser scanning. Home: 671 Grosvenor Ln Elk Grove Village IL 60007 Office: 6140 W Higgins Rd Chicago IL 60630

FLAHERTY, JOHN P., JR., supreme court justice; b. Pitts., Nov. 19, 1931; s. John Paul and Mary G. (McLaughlin) F. B.A. in Philosophy, Duquesne U., Pitts., 1953; J.D., U. Pitts., 1958. Bar: Pa. 1958. Pvt. practice Pitts., 1958-73; mem. faculty Carnegie-Mellon U., 1958-73; judge Ct. Common Pleas Allegheny County, 1973-79, pres. judge civil div., 1978-79; justice Supreme Ct. Pa., 1979—; USIA speaker in Far East, 1985-86. Chmn. Pa. Records Commn. Served as officer AUS, 1953-55. Recipient Medallion of Distinction U. Pitts., 1987; named Man of Yr. in Law and Govt., Greater Pitts. Jaycees, 1978. Mem. Pa. Acad. Sci. (Disting. Alumnus 1977, chmn. hon. exec. bd. 1979—, chmn. Pa. Records Com.), Pa. Soc., Mil. History Soc. Ireland, Irish Soc. Pitts., Friendly Sons St. Patrick, Irish-Am. Cultural Inst., Gaelic Arts Soc., Knights Equity, Ancient Order Hibernians, Am. Legion. Office: Pa Supreme Ct Six Gateway Ctr Pittsburgh PA 15222

FLAHIFF, GEORGE BERNARD CARDINAL, former archbishop of Winnipeg; b. Paris, Ont., Can., Oct. 26, 1905; s. John James and Eleanor Rose (Fleming) F. B.A., St. Michael's Coll., U. Toronto, 1926; student, U. Strasbourg, France, 1930-31; Dipl. Archiviste-Paleographe, Ecole Nat. des Chartes, Paris, 1935; Dipl. hon. degree in law, U. Seattle, 1965, U. Notre Dame, 1969, U. Man., 1969, U. Windsor, 1970, U. Winnipeg, 1972, U. Toronto, 1972, U. St. Francis Xavier, 1973, Laval U., 1974, St. Bonaventure U., 1975, U. St. Thomas, Houston, 1977. Ordained priest Roman Catholic Ch., 1930; prof. medieval history Pontifical Inst. Medieval Studies and U. Toronto, 1935-54, sec. inst., 1943-51; superior-gen. Basilian Fathers, 1954-61; archbishop of Winnipeg, Can., 1961-82; proclaimed cardinal 1969. Mem. Sacred Congregation for Religious. Named to Coll. Cardinals, 1969; Decorated companion Order of Can., 1974. Home: 39 Bishop's Lane, Winnipeg 9, MB Canada R3R 0A8 Office: 50 Stafford St, Winnipeg, MB Canada R3M 2V7 *

FLAMM, DONALD, radio broadcaster, writer, real estate, investments, theatrical producer; b. Pitts., Dec. 11, 1899; s. Louis and Elizabeth (Jason) F.; ed. pub. schs. N.Y., extension courses N.Y. U.; m. Elayne Knee, Dec. 9, 1979. Pub. mags. and books, 1921-30; owner, operator radio sta. WMCA, N.Y., 1925-41, WPCH, N.Y., 1927-32; pres. and operator Intercity Network, 1927-41; co-owner WPAT, Paterson, N.J., 1942-48; former owner, operator Sta. WMMM-AM, WDJF-FM, Westport, Conn., 1959-87; now engaged in theatre, real estate and social welfare activities; theatrical producer, N.Y.C., London, Eng.; pres. Flamm Realty Corp., N.Y.; dir. Oscar Lewestein Plays, Ltd., London, 1959-76. Former mem. N.Y. exec. com. Anti-Defamation League, mem. N.Y. regional bd., hon. life mem. nat. commn.; past chmn. N.J. Civil War Centennial Commn.; charter founder Eleanor Roosevelt Inst. Cancer Research, Denver; bd. dirs., v.p. Hebrew Free Loan Soc. N.Y.; past pres., trustee Mt. Neboh Temple, N.Y.C.; trustee, former officer Manfred Sakel Inst. Served as spl. liaison officer OWI, World War II; formulated plans for Am. Broadcasting Sta. in Eng. and Voice of Am. Mem. Royal TV Soc. (London), Internat. Radio and TV Soc. U.S.A., Drama Desk, United Hunts Racing Assn., Pa. Soc. Clubs: Rockefeller Luncheon, Catholic Actors Guild, Friars, Dutch Treat, Alpine Country; Le Club (N.Y.C.); Annabel's, White Elephant (London). Contbr. articles on theatre, radio and TV to trade publs. in U.S. and Eng. Home: 470 Anderson Ave Closter NJ 07624 Office: 25 Central Park W New York NY 10023

FLAMSON, RICHARD JOSEPH, III, banker; b. Los Angeles, Feb. 2, 1929; s. Richard J. and Mildred (Jones) F.; m. Arden Black, Oct. 5, 1951; children: Richard Joseph IV, Scott Arthur, Michael Jon, Leslie Arden. B.A., Claremont Men's Coll., 1951; cert. Pacific Coast Banking Sch., U. Wash., 1962. With Security Pacific Nat. Bank, Los Angeles, 1955—, v.p., 1962-69, sr. v.p., 1969-70, exec. v.p. corp. banking dept., 1970-73, vice-chmn., 1973-78, pres., chief exec. officer, 1978-81, chmn., chief exec. officer, 1981—, dir., 1981-85; also dir. Security Pacific Corp., Los Angeles; vice-chmn. Security Pacific Corp., 1973-78, pres., 1978-81, chief exec. officer, 1978—, chmn., 1981—; bd. dirs. Northrop Corp., Kaufman and Broad, GTE Calif. Inc. Trustee Claremont Men's Coll. 1st lt. AUS, 1951-53. Mem. Res. City Bankers, Robert Morris Assocs., Town Hall, Stock Exchange Club. Clubs: Caif. Los Angeles Country; Balboa Bay (Newport Beach, Calif.), Balboa Yacht (Newport Beach, Calif.). Office: Security Pacific Corp 333 S Hope St Los Angeles CA 90071 *

FLANAGAN, CHARLES ALLEN, engineering administrator; b. Aultman, Pa., Oct. 14, 1931; s. Paul John and Mabel Celia (Bloomquist) F.; m. Jane Hoyt Pell, Nov. 27, 1959; children: Catherine Anne, William Patrick. B.S. in Physics, Lafayette Coll., 1953; M.B.A., U. Pitts., 1972. Jr. scientist Westinghouse-Bettis, West Mifflin, Pa., 1956-57, assoc. scientist, 1957-58, scientist, 1958-62, sr. scientist, 1962-66, supr., mgr., 1966-75, mgr., Madison, Pa., 1975-80, dep. mgr. Fusion Engring. Design Ctr., Oak Ridge, 1980—; fusion reactor studies participant IAEA, Vienna, 1980-82, 83—; mem. indsl. adv. com. nuclear engring. dept. N.C. State U. Mem. editorial adv. bd. Jour. Fusion Tech., Nat. Research Council Study on Future Engring. Needs of Magnetic Fusion. Served as 1st lt. U.S. Army, 1953-55. Recipient cert. of appreciation Dept. Energy, 1981. Mem. Am. Nuclear Soc. (chmn. fusion energy div., program com. 1977-78, vice-chmn. fusion div. 1982, chmn. div. 1983, cert. of appreciation 1983, cert. of governance 1984). Unitarian. Home: 106 Dana Dr Oak Ridge TN 37830 Office: Westinghouse Fusion Design Engring Ctr PO Box Y Oak Ridge TN 37830

FLANAGAN, JAMES HENRY, JR., lawyer; b. San Francisco, Sept. 11, 1934; s. James Henry Sr. and Mary Patricia (Gleason) F.; m. Charlotte Anne Nevins, June 11, 1960; children: Nancy, Christopher, Christina, Alexis, Victoria, Grace. AB in Polit. Sci., Stanford U., 1956, JD, 1961. Bar: Calif. 1962, U.S. Dist. Ct. (no. dist.) Calif. 1962, U.S. Ct. Appeals (9th cir.) 1962, U.S. Dist. Ct. (so. dist.) Calif. 1964, U.S. Dist. Ct. (ea. dist.) 1967, Oreg. 1984. Assoc. Creede, Dawson & McElrath, Fresno, Calif., 1962-64; ptnr. Pettitt, Blumberg & Sherr and successor firms, Fresno, 1964-75; sole practice Clovis, Calif., 1975—; instr. Humprey's Coll. Law, Fresno, 1964-69, bus. Calif. State U., Fresno, 1986—; judge pro tem Fresno County Superior Ct., 1974-77; gen. counsel Kings River Water Assn., 1976-79. Author: California Water District Laws, 1962. Mem. Fresno County Rep. Cen. Com., 1964-66, exec. com. parish council St. Helen's, 1982-85, chmn. 1985; pres. Fresno Opera Assn., 1965-69, parish council St. John's Cathedral, 1974-82; pres. bd. dirs. 3d Floor, Cen. Calif.; bd. dirs. Fresno Facts Found., 1969-70, Fresno Dance Reperatory Assn., St. Anthony's Retreat Ctr., Three Rivers, Calif. Served to 1st lt. USMC, 1958-61. Recipient President award Fresno Jaycees, 1964. Mem. Calif. Bar Assn., Oreg. Bar Assn., Fresno County Bar Assn. (various coms.), Clovis Bar Assn., Assn. Trial Lawyers Am., Calif. Trial Lawyers Assn. (pres. Fresno chpt. 1975, 83), Oreg. Trial Lawyers Assn., Fresno Trial Lawyers Assn., Stanford Alumni Assn. (life, service award), Fresno Region Stanford Club (pres. 1979-80), Celtic Cultural Soc. Cen. Calif. (pres. 1977-78), Fresno County and City C. of C. (chmn. natural resources com. 1977-78), Clovis Dist. C. of C. (bd. dirs. 1977-87, award of merit 1982), Clovis-Big Dry Creek Hist. Soc. (past vice chmn.), Internat. Platform Assn., Phi Alpha Delta. Republican. Roman Catholic. Club: Fresno Serra (pres. 1980-81, v.p. 1986—). Lodge: Rotary. Home: 1770 Robinwood Clovis CA 93612 Office: PO Box 1048 Clovis CA 93613

FLANAGAN, JOSEPH PATRICK, advertising executive; b. Chgo., Jan. 6, 1938; s. Charles Larkin and Helen Mary (Sullivan) F.; m. Charlotte Mary Stepan, Sept 9, 1961; children: Charlotte Ahern, Joseph P. Jr., Michael S., Larkin S., Brian A. BA, Mich. State U., 1959; MBA, U. Chgo., 1961. Dist. mgr. sales Time mag., Pitts. and Chgo., 1961-69; gen. mgr. Ctr. Advanced Research in Design, Chgo., 1969-75; v.p., dir. client services BBDO, Chgo., 1975-77; sr. v.p. Impact subs. Foote, Cone & Belding Communications Co., Chgo., 1977-85, pres., 1985-88; corp. dir. sales promotion Foote, Cone & Belding Communications Co., Chgo., 1987—, also bd. dirs.; pres. Council on Sales Promotion Agys., 1986—. Mem. governing bd. Chgo. Symphony Orch., 1974-80; v.p. Lyric Opera Guild, Chgo., 1974. Roman Catholic. Club: Exmoor Country (Highland Park, Ill.). Home: 136 Chestnut St Winnetka IL 60093 Office: Impact FCB Ctr 101 E Erie Chicago IL 60611

FLANAGAN, PATRICK ARTHUR, chemical company executive; b. Harrow, Middlesex, Eng., July 26, 1932; s. Cyril Patrick and Doris Edith (Leacey) F.; m. Barbara Phyllis Jones, Jan. 28, 1960. Cert. acct. Asst. auditor Exchequer Audit Dept., London, 1952-53; exec. asst. Smith Mackenzie & Co. Ltd., Kenya, 1953-63, sales mgr., 1963-65; regional sales mgr. Middle East and Africa BDH Chems. Ltd., Poole, Eng., 1966-70, sales mgr. U.K., 1970-74; gen. mgr. diagnostics BDH Chems. Ltd., Poole, 1982—; gen. mgr. Hickman & Kleber (PTY) Ltd., Johannesburg, Republic South Africa, 1975-80, mng. dir., 1980-82. Pres. Sandton (Republic South Africa) C. of C., 1977-78; v.p. Assn. C. of C., South Africa, 1980. Fellow Brit. Inst. Mgmt., Soc. Co. Comml. Accts. Office: BDH Diagnostics, Broom Rd, Poole BH12 4NN, England

FLANDERS, DONALD HARGIS, manufacturing company executive; b. Memphis, Apr. 26, 1924; s. Henry Jackson and Mae (Hargis) F.; m. Phala Kathryn Davis, Dec. 15, 1946; children: Donald Hargis, Dudley Kennedy, Phala Kathyrn. Student, Tex. Christian U., 1943; BBA, Baylor U., 1947. Dir. cost acctg., purchasing agt. McCoy-Couch Furniture Mfg. Co., Benton, Ark., 1947-50, Garrison Furniture Co., Ft. Smith, Ark., 1950-54; pres., founder Flanders Mfg. Co., Ft. Smith, 1954-70, Flanders Industries, Inc., Ft. Smith, 1970—; chmn. bd. Lloyd/Flanders Industries, Menominee, Mich.; dir. 1st Nat. Bank, Ft. Smith, Arkla, Inc., Shreveport, La. Chmn. exec. com. Ft. Smith Freight Bur., 1960-61; chmn. furniture bd. govs. Dallas Mkt. Ctr., 1968; exec. com. Ark. Council on Econ. Edn., 1964-67; mem. Ark. Small Bus. Adv. Council, 1966-68; chmn. Ft. Smith United Fund drive, 1962; dist. chmn. Boy Scouts Am., Ft. SMith, 1960-62, pres. Westark Area council 1963-65, regional exec. com., 1964-72, vice chmn. region 5, 1967-69, chmn. region 5, 1969-72, nat. exec. bd., 1969-77; Com. of 100, 1965—; exec. dir. Ark. Indsl. Devel. Commn., 1981-83; trustee, vice chmn. Sparks Regional Med. Ctr., Hendrix Coll., Westark Coll. Found., North Ark. Conf. Meth. Ch. Served from apprentice seaman to lt. (s.g.) USNR, 1943-46. Recipient Silver Antelope, Silver Beaver, Silver Buffalo, Disting. Eagle Scout awards Boy Scouts Am., Free Enterprise award, 1964; named Industrialist of Yr. Ft. Smith Realtors Bd., 1965. Mem. SW Furniture Mfg. Assn. (pres. 1963), Ft. Smith C. of C. (dir. 1961-63, 73—), Ark. Wood Products Assn. (dir. 1965-68), Delta Sigma Pi. Methodist. Clubs: Masons (33d deg.), Shriners, KT. Home: 20 Berry Hill Rd Fort Smith AR 72903 Office: 1901 Wheeler Ave PO Box 1788 Fort Smith AR 72902-1788

FLANDERS, DWIGHT PRESCOTT, economist; b. Rockford, Ill., Mar. 14, 1909; s. Daniel Bailey and Lulu Iona (Nichol) F.; m. Mildred Margaret Hutchison, Aug. 27, 1939 (dec. Dec. 1978); children—James Prescott, Thomas Addison. BA, U. Ill., 1931, MA, 1937; teaching cert., Beloit (Wis.) Coll., 1934; PhD in Econs., Yale U., 1939. With McLeish, Baxter & Flanders (realtors), Rockford, 1931-33; instr. U.S. history and sci. in secondary schs. Rockford, 1934-36; asst. prof. econs. Coll. Liberal Arts and Scis.; also statistics Maxwell Grad. Sch., Syracuse (N.Y.) U., 1939-42; acad. staff econs. dept. social sci. U.S. Mil. Acad., West Point, N.Y., 1942-46; mem. faculty U. Ill., Urbana, 1946—; prof. econs. U. Ill., 1953-77; prof. emeritus dept. econs. Coll. Commerce and Bus. Adminstrn., 1977—; prof. emeritus dept. family and consumer econs. Coll. Agr., 1980—; chmn. masters research seminar, 1947-74, cons. in field. Author: Science and Social Science, 2d edit, 1962, Status of Military Personnel as Voters, 1942, Collection Rural Real Property Taxes in Illinois, 1938; co-author: Contemporary Foreign Governments, 1946, The Conceptual Framework for a Science of Marketing, 1964; contbr. numerous articles to profl. jours. Pres. Three Lakes (Wis.) Waterfront Homeowners Assn., 1969-71, dir., 1971-75, ofcl. bd., 1975—. Served to lt. col. AUS, 1942-46. Univ. fellow U. Ill., 1936-37; Univ. fellow Yale U., 1937-39; recipient Bronze tablet U. Ill., 1931, Excellence in Teaching award, 1977. Mem. Am., Midwest econs. assns., Royal Econ. Soc., Econometric Soc., Phi Beta Kappa, Beta Gamma Sigma (chpt. pres. 1959-61), Phi Kappa Phi, Alpha Kappa Psi. Methodist (ofcl. bd.). Club: Yale (Chgo.). Home: 719 S Foley Ave Champaign IL 61820

FLANDERS, GILBERT LEE, lawyer; b. San Diego, Sept. 18, 1935; s. James L. and Josephine (Medrano) F.; m. Amy, Dec. 2, 1961; children—Therese, Sean, Patrick. Student U. San Diego, 1954-57; J.D., Southwestern Sch. Law, Los Angeles, 1964. Bar: Calif., 1965, U.S. dist. ct. (cent. dist.) Calif. 1965. Assoc., H. H. Hiestand, Los Angeles, 1965-66, English & MacDowell, Lynwood, Calif., 1966-68; sole practice Downey, Calif., 1968—; csl. Mexican-Am. Polit. Assn., 1965-68; mem. Los Angeles Dist. Atty. Adv. Council, 1967-70; bd. dirs. Legal Services S.E. Dist. Los Angeles 1970—; mem. Calif. Atty. Gen. Adv. Council, 1970-77; gen. csl. United Nat. Italian Charitable Orgns., 1978—. Bd. dirs. Downey YMCA, 1979—; found. bd. mem. Downey Community Hosp., 1980—; pres. Oralingua Found. for the Deaf, 1973-74, trustee, 1974-75; advisor selective service, 1972-76. Served with U.S. Army, 1958-60. Mem. Themis Legal Soc. (founding), Calif. Trial Lawyers Assn., ABA, Am. Trial Lawyers Assn., S.E. Bar Assn., Los Angeles County Bar Assn., Internat. Platform Soc. Republican. Roman Catholic. Office: 11510 S Downey Ave Downey CA 90241

FLANDERS, HENRY JACKSON, JR., religion educator; b. Malvern, Ark., Oct. 2, 1921; s. Henry Jackson and Mae (Hargis) F.; m. Tommie Lou Pardew, Apr. 19, 1943; children: Janet Flanders Mitchell, Jack III. BA, Baylor U., 1943; BD, So. Bapt. Theol. Sem., 1948, PhD, 1950. Diplomate: ordained to ministry Baptist Ch., 1941. Asst. prof., assoc. prof. Furman U., Greenville, S.C., 1950-55, prof., chaplain, chmn. dept. religion, 1955-62; pastor First Bapt. Ch., Waco, Tex., 1962-69; prof. dept. religion Baylor U., Waco, Tex., 1969—, chmn. dept. religion, prof., 1980-83; chmn., trustee Golden Gate Bapt. Theol. Sem., Mill Valley, Calif., 1971-76; chaplain Tex. Ranger Commn., 1965—; mem. exec. com. Bapt. Gen. Conv. Tex., Dallas, 1966-68. Author: (with R.W. Crapps and D.A. Smith) People of the Covenant, 1963, 73, 88, (with Bruce Cresson) Introduction to the Bible, 1973; TV speaker: weekly program Lessons for Living, WFBC-TV, 1957-62. Trustee Baylor U., Waco, Tex., 1964-68; trustee Hillcrest Bapt. Hosp., 1963-64; chmn. Heart of Tex. Red Cross, 1967-68; narrator Waco Colton Palace Pageant, 1970-80; chaplain Tex. Aero Commn., 1986—; pastor emeritus First Bapt. Ch., Waco, 1987. Served to 1st. lt. USAAC, 1943-45, ETO. Named disting. alumnus Baylor U., 1986; grantee Furman U., 1960; grantee Baylor U., 1977, 82. Mem. Assn. Bapt. Profs. Religion (pres. 1958-59), AAUP (chpt. pres. 1973), Soc. Bibl. Lit., Am. Acad. Religion, Inst. Antiquity and Christianity, Waco Bapt. Ministerial Assn. (pres. 1967-68). Lodges: Rotary; Shriners. Home: 3820 Chateau St Waco TX 76710 Office: Baylor U Waco TX 76798

FLANIGAN, JOHN MAURICE, educator, consultant; b. English, Ind., Mar. 27, 1933; s. Maurice Melton and Mary Margaret (Thornbury) F.; m. Anne Leigh Curtis, Sept. 6, 1959; children—Russell Glen, Randall Orr, Leslie Anne. B.A. in Math., Ind. U., 1962, M.A.T. in Math., 1966. Tchr. math. Fia Iloa High Sch., Pago Pago, Am. Samoa, 1967-71, Nova Schs., Davie, Fla., 1974-78; instr. math. Am. Samoa Community Coll., Pago Pago, 1971-74; instr. computer sci., Mapusaga, 1978-84; dir. acad. computing Hawaii Loa Coll., Kaneohe, 1984—; cons. No. Marianas Community Coll., Saipan, 1981, Am. Samoa Govt., Pago Pago, 1979-84, Truk State Hosp., 1986. Author: Earth, Fire and Water A Natural History of Tutuila Island, 1979. Council mem. PEACESAT (Pacific Edn. and Communication Satellite), Pago Pago, 1978-82; terminal mgr., experimenter Experiment by Satellite, 1978—. Served to s/sgt. USAF, 1953-58, to capt. USAFR, 1958-68. Mem. Assn. for Computing Machinery, Am. Math. Assn. Club: Am. Samoa Scuba Divers (pres. 1971-75, 78-80). Avocations: scuba diving, photography, sports, music, dialectic conversation. Home: 45-546 Kapalai Rd Kaneohe HI 96744 Office: Hawaii Loa Coll 45-045 Kamehameha Hwy Kaneohe HI 96744

FLANNAGAN, BENJAMIN COLLINS, IV, lawyer; b. Richmond, Va., Sept. 7, 1927; s. Benjamin Collins and Virginia Carolyn (Gay) F.; B.A., U. Va., 1947, M.A. in Econs., 1948, J.D., 1951; LL.M., Georgetown U., 1956. Admitted to Va. bar, 1951; trial atty. Justice Dept., Washington, 1955—, sr. trial atty. in charge civil litigation unit, appellate and civil litigation sect., internal security div., 1971-73, spl. asst. internal security sect. criminal div., 1973-74, sr. trial atty. spl. litigation sect., 1974-79, sr. legal adv. gen. litigation and legal advice sect., 1979—. Mem. editorial bd. Va. Law Rev., 1949-50, book rev. editor, 1950-51. Served to 1st lt. U.S. Army, 1952-55. Recipient

Sustained Superior Service award Justice Dept., 1964, 74, 82, Spl. Commendation for Outstanding Service award criminal div., 1976, 84. Mem. Va. Bar Assn., Beta Gamma Sigma. Episcopalian. Clubs: Country of Va., Deep Run Hunt (Richmond). Home: 4000 Massachusetts Ave NW Washington DC 20016 also: 210 Nottingham Rd Richmond VA 23221 Office: Dept of Justice 1400 New York Ave Washington DC 20530

FLANNERY, JOHN PHILIP, II, lawyer; b. N.Y.C., May 15, 1946; s. John Philip and Agnes Geraldine (Applegate) F.; m. Bettina Gregory, Nov. 14, 1981. B.S. in Physics, Fordham Coll., 1967; B.S. in Engring., Columbia U., 1969, J.D., 1972; student Art Student League, 1972-73. Bar: N.Y. 1973, U.S. Dist. Ct. (so. dist.) N.Y. 1973, U.S. Ct. Appeals (2d cir.) 1973. Mem. staff Ford Found. Project to Restructure Columbia U., 1968; news rep. nat. press relations IBM, 1970; law clk. Adminstrv. Conf. U.S., 1971; law clk. U.S. Ct. Appeals 2d cir., 1972-74; asst. U.S. atty. Narcotics and Ofcl. Corruption units So. Dist. N.Y., 1974-79; sr. assoc. Poletti Freidin Prashker Feldman & Gartner, N.Y.C., 1979-82; spl. counsel U.S. Senate Judiciary Com., 1982; spl. counsel U.S. Senate Labor Com., 1982-83; Dem. candidate for U.S. Congress from Va. 10th Dist., 1983-84; sole practice in civil and criminal litigation, 1984—; spl. counsel Sen. Howard Metzenbaum, 1985-87; asst. dist. atty., Bronx, N.Y., 1986-87; lectr. in field. Committeeman Dem. Party N.Y. County, 1979-80; mem. legis. commn. Citizen's Union, 1971-72; mem. Arlington Transp. Commn., 1983-85; chmn. bus. council Va. Gov.'s War on Drugs Task Force, 1983-84; committeeman Dem. Party Arlington County, 1983-84; coordinator N.Y. State Lawyers Com. for Senator Edward M. Kennedy, 1979-80; dir. Citizens for Senator M. Kennedy, 1980; pres. Franklin Soc., 1979-80. Recipient U.S. Justice Dept. award for Outstanding Contbns. in the Field of Drug Law Enforcement 1977; U.S. Atty. Gen.'s Spl. Commendation for Outstanding Service, 1979. Mem. ABA, Bar Assn. City N.Y., N.Y. County Lawyers Assn., Arlington County Bar Assn., Loudon County Bar Assn., Acad. Polit. Sci. Democrat. Author: Commercial Information Brokers, 1973; Habeas Corpus Bores Hole in Prisoners' Civil Rights Action, 1975; Pro Se Litigation, 1975; Prison Corruption: A Mockery of Justice, 1980. Home: Shamrock Farm Rt 2 Box 144A Leesburg VA 22075

FLANSBURGH, EARL ROBERT, architect; b. Ithaca, N.Y., Apr. 28, 1931; s. Earl Alvah and Elizabeth (Evans) F.; m. Louise Hospital, Aug. 27, 1955; children: Earl Schuyler, John Conant. B.Arch., Cornell U., 1954; M.Arch., MIT, 1957; S.C.M.P., Harvard U. Sch. Bus., 1982. Job capt., designer The Architects Collaborative, Cambridge, Mass., 1958-62; partner Freeman, Flansburgh & Assos., Cambridge, 1961-63; prin. Earl R. Flansburgh & Assocs., Inc., Cambridge, 1963-69; pres., dir. design Earl R. Flansburgh & Assocs., Inc., 1969—; bd. dirs. Dāka, Inc.; exec. v.p. Environment Systems Internat., Inc.; vis. prof. archtl. design Mass. Inst. Tech., 1965-66; instr. art Wellesley Coll., 1962-65, lectr. art, 1965-69; cons. Arthur D. Little, Inc., Cambridge, 1964—. Archtl. works include Weston (Mass.) High Sch. Addition, 1965-67, Cornell U. Campus Store, 1967-70, Cumnock Hall, Harvard U. Bus. Sch, 1973-75, Acton (Mass.) Elementary schs, 1966-68, 69-71, Wilton (Conn.) High Sch, 1968-71, 14 Story St. Bldg, 1970, Boston Design Ctr., 1985-86, Glenwood Sch., Dallas, 1985-88; exhibited works Light Machine I, IBM Gallery, N.Y.C., 1958, Light Machine II, Carpenter Center, Harvard, 1965, 5 Cambridge Architects, Wellesley Coll., 1969, Work of Earl R. Flansburgh and Assos, Wellesley Coll., 1969, New Architecture in New Eng, DeCordova Mus., 1974-75, Residential Architecture, Mead Art Gallery, Amherst Coll., 1976, works represented in, 50 Ville del Nostro Tempo, 1970, Nuove Ville, New Villas, 1970, Vacation Houses, 1970, Vacation Houses, 2d edit., 1977, Interior Design, 1970, Drawings by American Architects, 1973, Interior Spaces Designed by Architects, 1974, New Architecture in New England, 1974, Great Houses, 1976, Architecture Boston, 1976, Presentation Drawings by American Architects, 1977, Architecture, 1970-1980, A Decade of Change, 1980, Old and New Architecture, A Design Relationship, 1980, 25 Years of Record Houses, 1981; Author: (with others) Techniques of Successful Practice, 1975. Chmn. architecture com. Boston Arts Festival, 1964; chmn. Downtown Boston Design Adv. Com.; Bd. dirs. Cambridge Center Adult Edn.; chmn. bldgs. and properties com., 1976, 78-87; mem. exec. com., academic affairs com., bd. trustees Cornell U., 1972—; class sec. SCMP VII. Served to 1st lt. USAF, 1954-56. Recipient design awards Progressive Architecture, design awards Record Houses, design awards AIA, design awards City of Boston, design awards Mass. Masonry Inst., spl. design citations Am. Assn. Sch. Adminstrs., spl. 1st prize Buffalo-Western N.Y. chpt. AIA Competition., Walter Taylor award Am. Assn. Sch. Adminstrs., 1986; Fulbright research grantee Bldg. Research Sta., Eng., 1957-58. Fellow AIA; mem. Royal Inst. Brit. Architects, Boston Soc. Architects (chmn. program com. 1969-71, commr. pub. affairs 1971-73, commr. design 1973-74, dir. 1971-74, pres. 1980-81), Boston Found. Architecture (treas. 1984—), Cornell U. Council, Quill and Dagger Soc., Tau Beta Pi. Home: 225 Old County Rd Lincoln MA 01773 Office: 77 N Washington St Boston MA 02114

FLASCHEN, STEWARD SAMUEL, corporation executive; b. Berwyn, Ill., May 28, 1926; s. Hyman Herman and Ethel (Leviton) F.; m. Joyce Davies, Apr. 21, 1949; children: John, Sheryl, David, Evan. BS in Chemistry, U. Ill., 1947; MA, Miami U., Oxford, Ohio, 1948; Ph.D. in Geochemistry, Pa. State U., 1953. Supr. research dept. Bell Telephone Labs., Murray Hill, N.J., 1952-59; dir. phys. scis., research and devel. semiconductor products div. Motorola, Inc., Phoenix, 1959-64; sr. v.p., gen. tech. dir., mem. corp. policy bd. ITT Corp., N.Y.C., 1964-86; pres. Flaschen & Davies, N.Y.C. and New Canaan, Conn., 1986—; lectr. Pace U. Grad. Sch. Bus. Author: Search and Research, 1965; also articles. Mem. Phoenix Bd. Edn., 1962-64. Served with USNR, 1944-46. Fellow Am. Inst. Chemists, IEEE; mem. Electromech. Soc. Am., Am. Ceramic Soc., AAAS, Indsl. Research Inst., N.Y. Acad. Scis. Home: 592 Weed St New Canaan CT 06840

FLASTER, RICHARD JOEL, lawyer; b. N.Y.C., Jan. 7, 1943; s. Charles and Sylvia (Moss) F.; m. Esther S. Stomel, Aug. 10, 1945; children—Kiva Moss, Eben Scott. B.S. in Econs., U. Pa., 1963; J.D., Harvard U., 1966. Bar: N.Y. 1967, U.S. Tax Ct. 1971, N.J. 1972, D.C. 1972. Law clk. to judge U.S. Dist. Ct. (ea. dist.) N.Y., 1966-68; Reginald Heber Smith fellow U. Pa., 1968-69; assoc. Stroock, Stroock & Lavan, N.Y.C., 1969-72; v.p. Liebman & Flaster, P.C., Cherry Hill, N.J., 1972-86; pres. Flaster, Greenberg, Mann & Wallenstein, P.C., Marlton, N.J., 1986—; frequent lectr. on various tax subjects ABA, N.J. Inst. Continuing Legal Edn. Mem. Camden County Bar Assn., N.J. State Bar Assn., N.Y. State Bar Assn., ABA, Beta Gamma Sigma, Beta Alpha Psi, Pi Gamma Mu. Author: Basic Federal Tax Aspects of Real Estate Transactions, 1976; Tax Aspects of Separation and Divorce, 1982; tax editor N.J. Family Lawyer. Office: Flaster Greenberg Mann & Wallenstein PC Five Greentree Ctr Suite 200 Rt 73 & Lincoln DrW Marlton NJ 08053

FLAVIER, JUAN MARTIN, rural development executive, physician; b. Manila, Philippines, June 23, 1935; s. Dominador Acosta and Francisca Santi (Martin) F.; m. Alma Susana Dumuk Aguila, Feb. 14, 1960; children—Jonathan, Juanito, James, Jocelyn. B.S., U. Philippines-Manila, 1956, M.D., 1960; M.P.H., Johns Hopkins U., 1969. Intern Philippine Gen. Hosp., 1959-60; tech. expert Philippine Rural Reconstrn. Movement, 1961-67, pres., 1967-68; v.p. Internat. Inst. Rural Reconstrn., Philippines, 1969-78, pres., 1978—; professorial lectr. U. Philippines, Manila, 1970—; dir. Gattaran Rural Bank, Cagayan, Philippines, 1972—. Author: Doctor to the Barrios, 1970; My Friends in the Barrios, 1974; Back to the Barrios, 1978. Past pres. Family Planning Orgn. of Philippines, 1971, Tierra Homeowners Assn., 1977; trustee Silliman U., Dumaguete, Philippines, 1969-79, Nutrition Found., Philippines, 1972—, Communications Found. of Asia, Philippines, 1972—. Republic awardee in rural devel. Civic Assembly of Women in Philippines, Manila, 1978. Mem. Philippine Med. Assn., U. Philippines Med. Alumni Soc. (outstanding alumnus 1973), Philippines Alumni Assn. (Most. Disting. Alumnus 1985), Phi Kappa Phi. Roman Catholic. Home: IIRR Cottage 2, Silang, Cavite 2720, Philippines Office: IIRR 1775 Broadway Suite 619 New York NY 10019

FLECK, MARIANN BERNICE, health scientist; b. San Francisco, June 19, 1922; d. Erwin and Grace B. (Fisher) Kahl; m. Jennings McDaniel, June 1946; m. Jack Donald Fleck, Mar. 28, 1980; children: Gary, Eugene. B of Vocat. Edn., Calif. State U., 1965, BA, 1965, MA, 1968; PhD, U. Santa Barbara, 1975. Prof. life sci. div., adminstr. Fullerton (Calif.) Coll., 1960-75; profl. adminstr. Cypress (Calif.) Coll., 1975-80, prof. emeritus, 1980—; dir., owner Profl. Services Assn. Counseling, Santa Ana, Calif., 1977-80, Hypnosis Ctr., La Mirada, Calif., 1975-80; producer Dr. Mariann Health Program, Sta. KJON, Boonville, Ark., 1980-85; dir. Jack Fleck Golf and Health Acad., Magazine, Ark., 1980—; cons. and lectr. in field. Mem. Am. Guild Hypnotherapists, Am. Personnel and Guidance Assn., Calif. Personnel and Guidance Assn., Am. Running and Fitness Assn. (profl. mem.), Hypnotherapists Speakers Platform. Republican. Presbyterian. Home: Route 1 Box 15A Magazine AR 72943 Office: H&P Internat Magazine AR 72943

FLEISCHAKER, MARTIN, mental health counselor, educator; b. Savannah, Ga., June 25, 1941; s. Jack and Eva (Nathan) F.; m. Laurice Koudsi, Dec. 17, 1967; children: Lara, Natasha, Thomas. AA, Armstrong Coll., 1959-61; BEd, MEd, Ga. So. Coll., 1964; postgrad. Johns Hopkins U., 1971-73, Towson State U., 1972-73, Southeastern Mo. U., 1980-81. Instr. math. Edison Twp., N.J., 1965-68; asst. prof. Embry Riddle U., Daytona Beach, Fla., 1968-71; instr. math. Anne Arundel Co., Annapolis, Md., 1971-79; sch. psychologist Counseling Services, Saint Genevieve, Mo., 1979-82; dir., therapist Ministry for Christ, Mental Health Counseling Services, Ladson, S.C., 1982—; adj. faculty Coll. Charleston, fall 1987. guest speaker edn. Charleston County Rep. Unity Breakfast, 1986, mental health counseling Sta. WQIZ, 1986, Sta. WKQB, 1986; cons. testing Charleston Bd. Edn., S.C., 1983-84. Chmn. Saint Genevieve Mental Health Bd. Trustees, 1981-82. Mem. Am. Assn. Counseling and Devel., Am. Mental Health Counselors Assn., S.C. Assn. Counseling and Devel., S.C. Mental Health Counselors Assn. Republican. Lutheran. Avocations: Christian ministry, creative writing, guitar, tennis, gardening. Office: Ministry for Christ Mental Health Counseling Services 215 Elliot Dr Ladson SC 29456

FLEISCHAUER, KURT, professor of anatomy; b. Dusseldorf, Fed. Republic of Germany, Oct. 14, 1929; m. Sabine neé Waller, 1965; children: Caroline, Johann-Christoph, Marie-Thérèse. AB, Dusseldorf, 1949; MD, U. Kiel, 1954, Habilitation, 1960. Mem. sci. staff Dept. Anatomy U. Kiel, 1954-58; British Council scholar Nat. Inst. Med. Research, London, 1958-60, mem. sci. staff, 1960-62; head neuroanatomy div. Dept. Anatomy U. Hamburg, 1962-68; head Dept. Anatomy U. Bonn, 1968-85, rector, 1985—; mng. editor sci. jour. Anatomy and Embryology. Contbr. articles to profl. jours. Home: Herzogsfreudenweg, D-5300 Bonn Federal Republic of Germany Office: Rheeinische Friedrich-Wilhelms, U Bonn, Regina-Pacis-Weg 3, D-5300 Bonn Federal Republic of Germany

FLEISCHER, CARL AUGUST, legal educator, consultant; b. Oslo, Aug. 26, 1936; s. Carl Johan and Marie (Mathiesen) F.; grad. Vestheim High Sch., Oslo, 1954; legal exam. laudabilis, U. Oslo, 1960, LL.D., 1964; m. Eva Sylvia Funder, Sept. 15, 1967. First sec. legal div. Ministry Fgn. Affairs, 1960-61; spl. cons. internat. law, 1962—; lectr. law U. Oslo Faculty Law, 1961-69, prof., 1969—; adviser in internat. law Ministry Fgn. Affairs, 1986—; lectr., cons., mem. dels. internat. confs. Mem. Internat. Council Environ. Law, Norwegian Petroleum Soc., Norwegian Soc. Int. Law. Author: Jurisdiction on Fisheries, 1963; International Law, 5th edit., 1984; Constitutional Limitations, 1969; The Law on Building and Regulation of Property, 4th edit., 1983; Commentary to the Act of Expropriation and Compensation, 1974; The Economic Zone, 1976; The Law of Expropriation, 1978; Expropriation Procedure, 1980; Application and Interpretation of Judgements, 1981; Petroleum Law, 1983; La pêche (the fisheries), 1985; co-author: Traiteé du Nouveau Droit de la Mer, 1985; Compensation to Fisheries for Offshore Devel. report, 1986, The New Regime of Maritime Fisheries, 1988; also articles, reports. Home: 13 Thomas Heftyes, Oslo 2, Norway Office: 7 Juni Pl, Oslo 1, Norway

FLEISCHMAN, LAWRENCE ARTHUR, art dealer, publisher, consultant; b. Detroit, Feb. 14, 1925; s. Arthur and Stella (Granet) F.; m. Barbara Greenberg, Dec. 18, 1948; children: Rebecca, Arthur, Martha. Student, Purdue U., 1942-43; B.S., U. Detroit, 1948; L.H.D. (hon.), St. John's U., 1978. Pres. Lawrence Investment Co., Detroit, 1949-66, Lawrence Advt. Agy., Detroit, 1950-60; dir. Ind. Newspaper, Inc., Detroit, 1952-60, WITI, Channel 6, Milw., 1952-59; pres., owner Kennedy Galleries, N.Y.C., 1966—; dir. Hartwell Hedge Fund, N.Y.C., 1966-72; founder, pres. Archives Am. Art, 1952-66, dir., 1967—; mem. Fine Arts Commn., USIA, 1956-62; advisor Fine Arts Commn., White House, 1960-62, 64-66; pres Detroit Arts Commn., 1962-66; Treas. Soc. Arts and Crafts Sch., Detroit, 1953-66; bd. dirs. Mannes Coll. Music, N.Y.C., 1967-71, Skowhegan Sch. Painting and Sculpture, Maine and N.Y., 1968-83; v.p. Com. Religion and Art of Am., N.Y.C., 1977—; mem president's council Met. Mus. Art, N.Y.C.; nat. trustee Balt. Mus. Art. Editor Am. Art Jour., 1969—. Served with AUS, 1943-46, ETO. Recipient Spl. Resolution award City of Detroit, 1966, Art award Lotus Club, N.Y.C., 1967; Copley medal Nat. Portrait Gallery, 1978; decorated knight Order of San Silvestre Pope Paul VI, 1978; fellow Morgan Library, N.Y.C., 1968. Mem. Pa. Acad. Fine Arts (life), Pa. Hist. Soc. (life), Art Dealers Assn. Am. (bd. dirs.). Office: Kennedy Galleries Inc 40 W 57th St New York NY 10019

FLEMING, DOUGLAS RILEY, journalist, publisher, public affairs consultant; b. Fairmont, W.Va., Jan. 25, 1922; s. Douglas Riley and Sarilda Artemes (Short) F.; m. Irene Stachowicz, Oct. 28, 1944 (dec. 1979). B.S., Georgetown U., 1953. Commd. ensign U.S. Navy, 1944, advanced through ranks to comdr.; naval aviator; chief protocol NATO, Naples, 1962-67, ret. 1967; with Francis I. DuPont & Co., Investment Banking, Rome, 1968-70; exec. editor, gen. mgr. Daily American, Rome, 1970-75; pres. Stampa Generale, S.R.L., Pubs., Naples, Italy, 1975—; mng. dir. Italo-Am. Assn., Naples; dir. Am. Studies Ctr., Naples, 1975-80; pres. Gen. Press Services, Washington, 1979—; dir. Va. Winery Coop., Inc., Culpeper, 1985—; proprietor, operator Campicello Vineyards, Madison, Va., 1982—. Active Nat. Trust Hist. Preservation, Smithsonian Assocs., Assn. Naval Aviation. Mem. Associazione Della Stampa Estera in Italia, The Cogswell Soc., Georgetown U. Alumni Assn. (pres. Italy 1972-80), Am. C. of C. in Italy, Retired Officers Assn., Navy League of U.S., Nat. Press Club, Vinifera Wine Growers Assn., Jeffersonian Wine Grape Growers Soc., Va. Vineyards Assn. Clubs: Naval and Mil., Steering Wheel, Royal Aero (London); Circolo Canottieri (Naples); N.Y. Athletic; Dist. Yacht (Washington). Home: 515 S Fairfax St Alexandria VA 22314 also: Campicello Box 589 Madison VA 22727

FLEMING, GEORGE ROBERT, psychologist; b. New Haven, July 24, 1947; s. George Robert and Susie Mae F.; B.A., Hillsdale Coll., 1969; M.A., Mich. State U., 1972, Ph.D., 1975; 1 child, Maisha Amirz. Dir., East N.Y. Mental Health Clinic Adult Day Treatment Program, N.Y.C., 1973-77; chmn. psychology dept. Malcolm-King Harlem Coll. Extension, N.Y.C., 1979, adj. prof., 1977-79; staff psychologist Bedford-Stuyvesant Community Mental Health Center, N.Y.C., 1977-79; cons. Detroit Public Schs., 1981-82, Centrax Diversified Services, 1977—, City of Detroit Comprehensive Youth Services Program, 1980-81; dir. Cen. City br. Children's Ctr., Detroit, 1979-81, Sacred Heart Women's Day Treatment Ctr., 1981-84, Total Health Care, Inc., 1982-86; chief psychologist Southwest Detroit Hosp., 1986— , Greater Detroit Life Consultation Ctr., 1982-84, Detroit Osteo. Hosp., 1984—. NIMH fellow, 1974-75. Mem. Nat. Black Child Devel. Inst. (mem. steering com. met. Detroit 1981), Nat. Register Health Service Providers in Psychology, Am. Psychol. Assn., Assn. Black Psychologists, Am. Orthopsychiat. Assn., Internat. Neuropsychol. Soc., Mich. Psychol. Assn., Mich. Assn. Black Psychologists (chmn. 1981-82), Mich. Soc. Clin. Psychologists, Omicron Delta Kappa.

FLEMING, JON HUGH, business executive; b. Dallas, Oct. 8, 1941; s. Durwood and Lurlyn (January) F.; B.A., So. Meth. U., 1963, Th.M., 1966; Rel.D., Sch. Theology at Claremont, 1968; m. Ann Robinson, Apr. 17, 1961; children—Marcus, Phillip, Jon Mark, Mallory, Jonathan Robinson. Exec. asst. to dean, dir. devel. U. Tex. Med. Sch., Houston, 1970-73; dir. devel., exec. dir. health sci. center relations U. Tex. Health Sci. Center, Houston, 1973-76; lectr. dept. psychiatry, 1971-76, adj. prof. psychiatry, 1976-78; exec. v.p., prof. psychology and human devel. Tex. Woman's U., Denton, 1976-78; pres., prof. psychology Tex. Wesleyan Coll., Ft. Worth, 1978-84; pres., chief exec. officer EData, Inc., Dallas, 1984-87 ; pres., chief exec. officer Asset Cons. Inc, exec. v.p. The Unimark Cos., Dallas, 1974—; grad. teaching asst. Sch. Theology at Claremont, Calif., 1966-68; cons. Sadler Clinic and Doctor's Hosp., Conroe, Tex. Telemetrics Internat., 1974-75. Bd. dirs. Edna Gladney Home; state chmn. educators for Reagan-Bush, 1980; mem. chancellor's council, U. Tex. System; mem. Tex. Gov.'s Select Com. on Pub. Edn., chmn. educating the child, vice chmn. teaching profession. Mem. Council Advancement and Support Edn., Philos. Soc. Tex., Assn. Higher Edn. North Tex. (mem. bd.). Republican. Methodist. Clubs: Ft. Worth; Ramada, Doctor's (Houston); Headliners (Austin, Tex.). Office: Asset Consultants Inc & The Unimark Cos 2777 Stemmons Freeway Dallas TX 75207

FLEMING, LOUIS K., performing arts consulting company executive, management and facilities planning consultant; b. London, Eng., Apr. 5, 1925; s. Austin Lloyd and Helen (Hyde) F.; m. Valerie Ann Exton, June 21, 1952; 1 child, Elaine Leslie Fleming Fish. Student Appleby Coll., 1934-36, Lakefield Coll., 1936-41, Jarvis Coll., 1941-44, Ont. Theatre technician MRA Prodns., N.Y.C., 1946-50, tech. dir., 1950-60; prodn. mgr. Westminster Theatre, London, 1960-65, exec. dir., 1965-75; contract cons. Ont. Ministry Culture, Toronto, 1975-76; theatre cons. Louis K. Fleming Assocs., 1976-79; mng. dir., ARTEC Cons., N.Y.C., 1979-82; v.p. Theatre Projects Cons.'s, Inc. N.Am., N.Y., 1982—, also sr. ptnr. Author numerous planning reports for performing arts facility devel. in U.S., Can. Mem. editorial bd. Performing Arts Can., 1977—. Served with Can. Navy, 1944-46. Mem. Actor's Equity Assn., U.S. Inst. for Theatre Tech., Internat. Soc. Performing Arts Adminstrs, Inst. Mgmt. Cons., Inc. Episcopalian. Avocations: sailing; theatre; music. Home: 58 W 85th St New York NY 10024 also: 14 Stafford Pl, London SW1E 6NP, England Office: Theatre Projects Cons Inc 155 W 72d St New York NY 10023

FLEMING, REX JAMES, meteorologist; b. Omaha, Apr. 25, 1940; s. Robert Leonard and Doris Mae (Burrows) F.; m. Kathleen Joyce Ferry, Sept. 3, 1969; children: Thane, Manon, Mark, Noel. B.S., Creighton U., 1963; M.S., U. Mich., 1968, Ph.D., 1970. Commd. lt. U.S. Air Force, 1963, resigned commn. as capt., 1972; research scientist Offutt AFB, Nebr., 1963-67; sci. liaison to Nat. Weather Service for Air Weather Service, Suitland, Md., 1970-72; resigned 1972; mgr. applications mktg. advanced sci. computer Tex. Instruments, Inc., Austin, 1972-75; dir. U.S. Project Office for Global Weather Expt., NOAA, Rockville, Md., 1975-80, Spl. Research Projects Office, 1980-82, Office of Climate and Atmospheric Research, 1983-84, Internat. Tropical Ocean and Global Atmosphere Project Office and Nat. Storm Program Office, 1984-86; pres. Tycho Tech. Inc., Boulder, Colo., 1986-87, Creative Concepts, 1987—; vis. scientist Nat. Ctr. for Atmospheric Research, 1987—. Contbr. articles to profl. jours. Recipient Gold Medal award Dept. Commerce, 1980. Fellow AAAS; Mem. Am. Meteorol. Soc. (chmn. probability and statistics com. 1976-77), The Planetary Soc., Am. Geophys. Union (sec. atmospheric scis. sect. 1984-86), The Ocean Soc. Republican. Home: 4889 Country Club Way Boulder CO 80301 Office: Creative Concepts 4775 Walnut St Boulder CO 80301

FLEMING, WILLIAM SLOAN, energy and mechanical engineering company executive; b. Long Beach, Calif., Aug. 13, 1937; s. William Sloan and Helen Jean (Disler) F.; B.S.M.E., Calif. Martime Acad., 1958; M.B.A., Syracuse U., 1970; m. Jacquline M. Carrio, Mar. 9, 1960; children—Katherine A., Kimberly A. Mech. engr. Carrier Corp., Syracuse, N.Y., 1967-70; regional sales mgr. Rheem Mfg., Atlanta, 1970-71; market devel. supr. Owens Corning, Toledo, 1971-73, pres. W.S. Fleming & Assos., Inc., Syracuse, N.Y., 1975-86, chief exec. officer, 1986—, also dir.; chmn. bd. dirs. Assn. Intelligent System Tech. Served with USN, 1958-67. Mem. ASHRAE (past chmn. tech. com. solar energy utilization , nat. program com., system engring., chmn. sp-52 solar energy design manual), DAV, Am. Legion, Ret. Officers Assn. Roman Catholic. Contbr. articles to profl. jours. Home: 4 E Shore Path Cazenovia NY 13035 Office: W S Fleming Assocs Inc 6308 Fly Rd East Syracuse NY 13057

FLEMINGS, MERTON CORSON, engineer, materials scientist, educator; b. Syracuse, N.Y., Sept. 20, 1929; s. Merton C. and Marion (Dexter) F.; m. Elizabeth Goodridge, Sept. 7, 1956 (div. 1976); children—Anne, Peter; m. R. Elizabeth ten Grothenhius, Feb. 20, 1977; children—Cecily, Elspeth. S.B., MIT, 1951, S.M., 1952, Sc.D., 1954. Mem. faculty MIT, Cambridge, Mass., 1956—, ABEX prof. Metallurgy, 1970-75, Ford prof. engring., 1975-81, dir. materials processing ctr., 1979-82, Toyota prof. materials processing, 1981—, dept. head materials sci. and engring., 1982—; mem. tech. adv. bd. Norton Co.; bd. dirs. Hitchiner Corp., Metal Casting Tech., Inc. Author: Foundry Engineering, 1959; Solidification Processing, 1974. Contbr. numerous articles on metallurgy to profl. jours. Recipient Simpson Gold medal Am. Foundryman's Soc., 1961, Henri Sainte-Claire Deville medal Soc. Francaise de Metallurgie, 1977. Fellow Am. Soc. Metals (Henry Marion Howe medal 1973); mem. Nat. Acad. Engring., Am. Inst. Metall. Engrs. (Matheson Gold medal 1969), Am. Acad. Arts and Scis., Japan Foundrymen's Soc. (hon.), Iron and Steel Inst. Japan (hon., Yukawa meml. lectr. 1985), Italian Metall. Assn. (Luigi Losana Gold medal 1986). Home: 11 Hillside Ave Cambridge MA 02140 Office: MIT Dept Materials Sci and Engring 8-309 Cambridge MA 02139

FLEMMING, JOHN STANTON, economist; b. Reading, Eng., Feb. 6, 1941; s. Gilbert Nicholson and Virginia (Coit) F.; m. Jean Elizabeth Briggs, July 27, 1963; children: Rebecca, Edward, Thomas, William. BA, Oxford U., 1962. Fellow, tutor in econs. Oriel Coll., Oxford U., 1963-65; ofcl. fellow Nuffield Coll., 1965-80; chief adviser econs. Bank of Eng., London, 1980—. Author: Inflation, 1976; editor: Private Saving, Public Debt, 1987; contbr. articles to acad. publs. Mem. Royal Econ. Soc. (jour. editor 1976-80, mem. council 1980—), Inst. Fiscal Studies (mem. council 1981—), European Econ. Assn. (mem. council 1986—). Office: Bank of Eng, Threadneedle St, London EC2 R8AH, England

FLESCHNER, MARCIA HARRIET, marketing executive, personnel consultant; b. Bklyn., Mar. 31, 1947; d. Max and Bettina (Koerner) F.; m. Arthur Mace Teicher, Nov. 23, 1974; 1 son, Craig Morgan. B.A., CUNY, 1967. Sr. vice pres. market research, placement dir. Smith's 5th Ave Agy., Inc., N.Y.C., 1965—. Mem. Am. Mktg. Assn. (2d v.p. 1987-88, dir. N.Y.C. chpt. 1973-87 , cert. 1975, 82), Nat. Assn. Personnel Cons., Advt. Women N.Y., Assn. Personnel Cons. N.Y. (dir. 1979-80). Club: Castaways Yacht (New Rochelle, N.Y.). Office: Smith's 5th Ave Agy Inc 17 E 45th St New York NY 10017

FLETCHER, ALAN JOHN, English and medieval literature educator; b. Staffordshire, Eng., June 30, 1952; came to Ireland, 1978; s. Victor John and Marie (Sharratt) F. BA in English with honors, Leeds (Eng.) U., 1973, MA in Medieval Studies, 1974; BLitt, Oxford (Eng.) U., 1978. Temporary lectr. Leeds U., Eng., 1977-78; lectr. U. Coll. Dublin, Ireland, 1978—. Contbr. articles to profl. jours. Mem. Société Internat. Pour L'étude du Théâtre Médiéval (nat. rep. for Ireland). Anglican. Office: U Coll Dublin, Eng Dept, Dublin 4, Ireland

FLETCHER, BEN (C.), psychology educator; b. Redditch, Eng., Aug. 1, 1952; s. John and Iris (Glover) F.; m. Anita Carola Jackson, Nov. 11, 1984. BA with honors, Keele U., Eng., 1975; D Phil., Oxford U., Eng., 1978. Research fellow Med. Research Council, Sheffield U., Eng., 1978-79; sr. lectr. Hatfield Poly., Hertfordshire, Eng., 1979-87; prin. lectr. 1987-88, reader occupational of health psychology, 1988—; research assoc. Human System Cons. Assocs., London, 1986—; co-dir. Microcomputers in Edn., Hatfield, 1984—; dir. Occupational Stress & Health Ctr., Hatfield, 1987—; cons. various oil cos., 1980—. Author: Psychological Factors in Disease; Occupational Stress, Disease & Life Expectancy. Contbr. articles to profl. jours. Grantee Med. Research Council, 1975, Econ. & Social Research Council, 1984. Fellow Brit. Psychol. Soc., mem. Exptl. Psychology Soc., Brit. Soc. Exptl. and Clin. Hypnosis, Brit. Acad. Mngt. Avocations: sports, modern art, fine wine, fine vegetarian food. Home: 12 Abbey View Rd, Saint Albans AL3 4QL, England Office: Hatfield Poly Psychology Div, PO Box 109, Hatfield AL10 9AB, England

FLETCHER, BRADY JONES, vocational education specialist; b. Natchitoches, La., Apr. 17, 1928; d. Louis Benjamin and Isadore Hannah (Stephens) Jones; BA, Clark Coll., 1950; MA (fellow), Howard U., 1953; postgrad. (NDEA fellow) Ind. U., summer, 1965; EdS in Guidance, George Washington U., 1967, EdD, 1977; m. Donald Greene Fletcher, Aug. 13, 1950; children: Donald Bruce, Nathan Louis, Debra Patrice. Tchr. math. and sci. Fairmont Heights (Md.) High Sch., 1951-54, Douglas High Sch., Upper Marlboro, Md., 1955-57, Prince George's County (Md.) pub. schs., 1951-59, Banneker Jr. High Sch., Washington, 1959-63; chmn. guidance dept. Garnet/Patterson Jr. High Sch., Washington, 1963-67; counselor Lincoln Jr. High Sch., D.C. pub. schs., 1967-69, Kensington (Md.) Jr. High Sch., 1969-73,

Banneker Jr. High Sch., 1975-77; career edn. specialist Montgomery County (Md.) Schs., 1973-75; cons. D.C. pub. schs., 1974, Md. State Dept. Edn., 1973, Balt. City Pub. schs., 1973, Balt. County pub. schs., 1973; mem. adv. com. for spl. needs population Montgomery Coll., Rockville, Md., Am. Coll. Testing Bd., Md., DC, 1987—; project dir. InterAmerica Research Assos., Inc., Rosslyn, Va., 1977—; rep. to Community Action Bd. for Montgomery County Edn. Assn.; dir. D.C. Summer Youth Job Program, 1981. Inst. Ednl. Leadership fellow, summer 1984, Montgomery County Vocat. Assessment Ctr. (recipient dedicated service award 1987). Recipient Educators award Clinton A.M.E. Ch., 1988, Multicultural Counseling award Founders of Orgn., 1987. Mem. Am. (Human Relations Com. award 1974, editor conv. newsletter 1983), Md. (award 1975), Nat. Capital (award 1975-76) personnel and guidance assns., D.C. Assn. Counseling and Devel. (pres. 1986-87, del. to North Atlantic region assembly, recipient award distinguished profl. leadership 1987, award for profl. devel. of assn. 1986), Nat. Vocat. Guidance Assn., Assn. Non-White Concerns, Nat. Assn. Career Edn., Nat. Sch. Counselor Assn., Internat. Platform Assn., Alpha Kappa Alpha. Editor: Career Edn., 1973-75; Increasing Collaboration in Career Education (2 vols.). Home: 1 Waterway Ct Rockville MD 20853 Office: 850 N Hungerford Rockville MD 20850

FLETCHER, LEROY STEVENSON, engineering educator; b. San Antonio, Oct. 10, 1936; s. Robert Holton and Jennie Lee (Adkins) F.; m. Nancy Louise McHenry, Aug. 14, 1966; children: Laura Malee, Daniel Alden. B.S., Tex. A&M U., 1958; M.S., Stanford U., 1963, Engr., 1964; Ph.D., Ariz. State U., 1968. Registered profl. engr., Ariz., N.J., Va., Tex. Research scientist Ames Research Ctr., NASA, Moffett Field, Calif., 1958-62; instr. Ariz. State U., Tempe, 1964-68; prof. aero., engring. Rutgers U., New Brunswick, N.J., 1968-75, assoc. dean, 1974-75; prof., chmn. dept. mech. and aero. engring. U. Va., Charlottesville, 1975-80; dir. Ctr. Energy Analysis, 1979-80; assoc. dean Tex A&M U., College Station, 1980-88, assoc. dir. Tex. Engring. Expt. Sta., 1985-88, Dietz prof. mech. engring., 1988—; hon. prof. Ruhr U.-Bochum, Fed. Republic Germany, 1988—; cons. to various industries; dir. and univs. Accreditation Bd. Engring. and Tech., 1979-82, 83—. Author: Introduction to Engineering Including FORTRAN Programming, 1977, Introduction to Engineering Design with Graphics and Design Projects, 1979; editor: Aerodynamic Heating and Thermal Protection, 1978, Heat Transfer and Thermal Control Systems, 1978. Served to capt. USAF, 1958-61. Recipient Disting. Alumni award Ariz. State U., 1985. Fellow ASME (bd. govs. 1983-87 , pres. 1985-86, Charles Russ Richards award), AAAS (chmn. sect. M-Engring. 1988—), Am. Astron. Soc., Inst. Mech. Engrs. London, Am. Soc. Engring. Edn. (dir. 1978-80 George Westinghouse award 1982, Ralph Coats Roe award 1983, Donald E. Marlowe award 1986), AIAA (dir. 1981-84, Aerospace Edn. Achievement award 1982, Energy Systems award 1984); mem. Internat. Acad. Astronautics (corr. mem.), Sigma Xi, Tau Beta Pi, Pi Tau Sigma, Sigma Gamma Tau, Phi Kappa Phi. Office: Tex A&M Univ Mech Engring College Station TX 77843

FLETCHER, MARY LEE, business exec.; b. Farnborough, Eng.; d. Dugald Angus and Mary Lee (Thurman) F.; B.A., Pembroke Coll., Brown U., 1951. Ops. officer C.I.A., Washington, 1951-53; exec. trainee Gimbels, N.Y.C., 1953-54; head researcher Ed Byron TV Prodns., N.Y.C., 1954; copywriter Benton & Bowles, Inc., N.Y.C., 1955-63; creative dir. Alberto-Culver Co., Melrose Park, Ill., 1964-66; v.p. advt. and publicity Christian Dior Perfumes, N.Y.C., 1967-71; v.p. Christian Dior-N.Y., N.Y.C., 1972-78, exec. v.p., dir., 1978-85; cons. Fletcher & Co., N.Y.C., 1985—. Home: 12 Beekman Pl New York NY 10022 Office: 885 3d Ave New York NY 10022-4082

FLETCHER, PAUL LOUIE, businessman; b. Phila., Apr. 18, 1930; s. James Louie and Pearl (Lawson) F.; diploma mech. and archtl. drawing, McKee Vocat. Trade Sch., S.I., N.Y., 1958; m. Ying-Lun, Apr. 18, 1968; children—James, Raymond, Pearl, Dana, Paul Louie, England. With United Trading & Fletcher Inc., N.Y.C., 1950—, exec. v.p., 1950—, sec., 1950—; salesman Prosperity Laundry Machine Co., 1950-69; exec. v.p., sec. Canbeth Realty Corp., 1950—. Chmn., Chinatown div. March of Dimes, N.Y.C., 1960-64, Mei Wah Day Care Center, N.Y.C., 1977-80, Mei Wah Chinese Sch., 1977-80; pres. Soo Yuen Benevolent Assn., 1977-78; pres., chmn. Chinese Meth. Community Center, N.Y.C., 1977-80. Served with USAF, 1947-50. Recipient numerous community and service awards; Disting. Service award Council of Chs., City of N.Y.; knighted Order of St. Georges, 1986, received the Deputy Comdr. honours. Club: Lions (pres. Chinatown chpt., N.Y.C., 1975-76, charter pres. N.Y.C. Chinese Ams. 1978-80, dist. cabinet sec.-treas. 1980-81, dist. gov. 1982-83; numerous awards 1972—, council chmn. 1982-84, Internat. Pres.'s award 1982-84, 86-87). Home: 77 Lynhurst Ave Staten Island NY 10305 Office: 162 Canal St New York NY 10013

FLETCHER, PHILIP B., food products company executive. Pres., chief operating officer ConAgra Prepared Food Co. subs. ConAgra Inc., Omaha. Office: ConAgra Inc One Central Park Plaza Omaha NE 68102 *

FLETCHER, RILEY EUGENE, lawyer; b. Eddy, Tex., Nov. 29, 1912; s. Riley Jordan and Lelih Etta (Gill) F.; m. Hattie Inez Blackwell, June 11, 1954. B.A., Baylor U., 1950, LL.B., 1950. Bar: Tex. 1950, U.S. Dist. Ct. (no. dist.) Tex. 1958, U.S. Ct. Appeals (5th cir.) 1959, U.S. Ct. Mil. Appeals 1965, U.S. Ct. Appeals (11th cir.) 1981, U.S. Supreme Ct. 1965. Asst. county atty. Navarro County, Corsicana, Tex., 1951-52, county atty., 1952-54; sole practice, Corsicana, 1955-56; asst. atty gen. Atty. Gen. dept., Austin, Tex., 1956-62, chief Law Enforcement div., 1958-61, chief Tax div., 1961-62; asst. gen. counsel Tex. Mcpl. League, Austin, 1962-63, gen. counsel, 1963-78, special counsel, 1978-88, ret., 1988. Served to capt. U.S. Army, 1942-46, New Guinea, Philippines; lt. col. AUS ret. Recipient Disting. Service award Tex. Mcpl. Courts Assn. 1980, Appreciation award Tex. City Atty.'s Assn. 1982, Assn. Mayors, Councilmen & Commrs. Tex. 1984, City Bowie, Tex. 1984, Appreciation Resolution City Round Rock, Tex., 1988. Mem. ABA, State Bar Tex., Travis County Bar Assn., Judge Advocates Assn. Baptist. Home: 7201 Creekside Dr Austin TX 78752

FLETCHER, ROSE MARIE, mortgage banker, consultant; b. Oakland, Calif., Dec. 8, 1940; d. Martin George Maher and Gertrude Elizabeth (Noe) Maher McCarthy; m. Jamie Franklin Fletcher, Aug. 1, 1960; children: Roberta JoAnne, Rebecca Louise, Jamie Suzanne. Student San Jose State U., 1958-60, West Valley Coll., 1972-76. Lic. real estate broker, Calif. Formerly br. mgr. Sutro Mortgage Co., San Jose, Calif., 3 yrs.; sr. v.p. Unified Mortgage Co., Cupertino, Calif., 1981-85; owner, pres., cons. Processing Place, San Jose, 1985—; dir. ops. Mortgage Loans Am., Campbell, Calif., 1986—; cons., lectr., trainer in lending field. Mem. Calif. Assn. Residential Lenders (1st v.p. 1985, pres. 1986), Assn. Profl. Mortgage Women (regional gov. 1980-81, Woman of Yr. 1979). Democrat. Roman Catholic. Avocations: water skiing; swimming; dancing. Home: 3704 Heppner Ln San Jose CA 95136 Office: Mortgage Loans Am 62 San Thomas Rd Campbell CA 95008

FLIEDNER, THEODOR M., university president; b. Hamburg, Germany, Oct. 1, 1929; s. Karl and Henriette (Katterfeld) F.; m. Gisela; children—Karen, Monika, Thilo, Katja. M.D., U. Heidelberg, 1956. Assoc. scientist Brookhaven Nat. Lab., Upton, N.Y., 1961-63; sr. scientist European Atomic Community, Brussels, 1963-67; prof. clin. physiology and occupational medicine U. Ulm, Fed. Republic Germany, 1967—, rector, pres., 1983—. Contbr. articles to profl. jours. Chmn. European Adv. Com. for Med. Research, WHO, Copenhagen, 1983—; pres. Internat. Inst. for Sci. Cooperation, 1969—. Lutheran. Club: Rotary. Office: U Ulm Occupational Medicine, Oberer Eselsberg M-24, D7900 Ulm/Donau Federal Republic of Germany

FLINN, DONAL PATRICK, diversified business executive; b. Cork, Munster, Ireland, Nov. 8, 1923; s. Flinn Hugo and Monica (Wilson) F.; m. Heather Mary Cole, Aug. 19, 1953; children—William Hugo, Richard Donal, Jenniffer Ann. B.Com., U. Coll. Cork, 1943. Ptnr. Kevans & Sons, Dublin, Ireland, 1953-68; mng. ptnr., chmn. bd. Coopers & Lybrand, Dublin, 1968-83; chmn. bd. Barclays Bank, 1978—, DeLaRue Smurfitt, 1978—, PJ Brennan Ltd. dir. AER Lingus, 1970—, Abbey Life Ireland, 1983—, Fitzwilton Ltd., 1983—. Recipient Peal Meml. award U. Coll. Cork, 1943. Fellow Inst. Chartered Accts. Ireland (pres. 1976-77), Irish Mgmt. Inst. (council), U.S. C. of C. Roman Catholic. Clubs: Portmarnock Golf, Royal St. George Yacht. Home: 44 Orwell Park, Rathgar, Dublin 6 Ireland

FLINN, ROBERTA JEANNE, commercial printing executive; b. Twin Falls, Idaho, Dec. 19, 1947; d. Richard H. and Ruth (Johnson) F. Student Colo. State U., 1966-67. Ptnr., Aqua-Star Pools & Spas, Boise, Idaho, 1978—, mng. ptnr., 1981-83; ops. mgr. Polly Pools, Inc., Canby, Oreg., 1983-84, br. mgr. Polly Pools, Inc., A-One Distributing, 1984-85; comptroller, Beaverton Printing, Inc., 1986—. Mem. Nat. Assn. Female Execs., Nat. Appaloosa Horse Club. Republican. Mem. Christian Ch. Home: 24687 S Central Point Rd Canby OR 97013

FLIPO, GEORGES PIERRE, advertising agency executive; b. Marcq-en-B, France, Nov. 1, 1945; s. Georges Henri and Chantal Jacqueline (Piat) F.; m. Mercedes Beatrice Gomez, Nov. 20, 1976; children: Georges-Santiago, Barthelemy, Marine. Diplome d'Etudes Superieurs, ESSEC, Paris, 1968. Jr. exec. Agence Intermerco, Paris, 1970-71; copywriter Doyle Dane & Bernbach, Paris, 1972; chief copywriter De Plas Homsy Delafosse, Paris, 1973-75, Dorland Grey, Paris, 1975-77, NCK, Paris, 1978-79; creative dir. Ted Bates, Paris, 1979-81, Quadrillage, Paris, 1981—. Author several comml. films. Recipient Clio awards 1976, Gold & Minerve award 1981, Grand Pris Acc awards, 1981. Home: 190 Ave Jean Jaures, 92140 Clamart France Office: Groupe Quadrillage, 175-177 rue d'Aguesseau, 92140 Boulogne France

FLOCH, HERVE ALEXANDER, medical biologist; b. Lambezellec, France, Oct. 3, 1908; s. Herve Marie and Jeanne (Le Rouzic) F.; m. Lucie Henry; children—Therese, Herve Henri, Daniele. M.D., Faculté de Medecine de Bordeaux, 1932. Asst. Colonial Hosp., scholar Pasteur Inst., Paris, from 1938; mil. physician, medicin col., until 1956; dir., founder Pasteur Inst. Cayenne, French Guiana (br. Pasteur Inst., Paris), 1940-66; dir. Pasteur Inst. Pointe à Pitre, Guadeloupe, 1969-71; chief Anti-Mosquito Service and Leprosy Service, French Guiana, 1940-66, Guadaloupe, 1969-71; chief lab. Inst. Pasteur, Paris, 1956-73; biologist chief Lab. Service Hosp., Morlaix, France, 1974-79; prof. microbiology Faculty Odontology, Brest, 1978-85; malariologist and pathologist WHO. Author over 900 publs. to profl. jours. Mem. French Acad. Medicine (6 prizes), French Acad. Sci. (Prix Muteau, grand prix Etancelin 1974), French Acad. Overseas Sci., other sci. socs. Research, publs. on leprology, promoter use of D.D.S. in treatment of leprosy, malariology, epidemiology, entomology, acarology parasitology, mycology, virology, bacteriology, biology and tropical pathology; studies on tropical alimentation-nutrition habitat. Home: 45 Ave Camille Desmoulins, 29200 Brest France

FLOCH-BAILLET, DANIELE LUCE, ophthalmologist; b. Brest, France, Jan. 9, 1948; d. Herve Alexandre and Lucie (Henry) Floch; m. Gilles Pierre Baillet, Dec. 6, 1980. MD, Med. U. Brest, 1972. Cert. in ophthalmology, 1975. Med. cons. ophthalmology Brest Hosp., 1976-85; gen. practice ophthalmology Landivisiau, France, 1977—; researcher ophthalmic bacteriology, 1985—. Author: (with P. Francois) Nosological Outlines from Coats, 1975, Exsudation from Coats, 1976. Mem. French Ophthalmologist Soc., European Contact Lenses Soc. Ophthalmologists, Nat. Syndicat French Ophthalmology. Roman Catholic. Home: 11 Rue Creach Joly, 29210 Morlaix France Office: 7 Rue Georges Pompidou, 29230 Landividiau France

FLOHR, DANIEL GEORGE, III, manufacturing company executive; b. Vicksburg, Miss., Oct. 10, 1942; s. Daniel G. and Lillian A. (Buchanan) F. A.A., Hinds Jr. Coll., 1966; B.S. in Bus. Miss. State U., 1968. Acct., Christian Sci. Ctr., Boston, 1968-69; sr. auditor Texaco Inc., N.Y.C., 1969-74; sr. fin. analyst IBM, Toronto, Ont., Can., 1974-77; mgr. internal audit Recognition Equipment, Inc., Dallas, 1977-79; staff auditor Overhead Door Corp. (name now Dallas Corp.), 1979-80, dir. internal audit, 1980-82, corp. sec., dir. internal audit, 1982-83, v.p. auditing, 1983—. Served with USN, 1960-64. Mem. Inst. Internal Auditors (dir. 1979-85, sec. 1981-82, coms. 1980-82). Christian Scientist. Home: 10808 Pinocchio Dr Dallas TX 75229 Office: Dallas Corp 6750 LBJ Freeway Dallas TX 75240

FLOOD, JOAN MOORE, corporate librarian; b. Hampton, Va., Oct. 10, 1941; d. Harold W. and Estalena (Fancher) M.; B.Mus., North Tex. State U., 1963, postgrad., 1977; postgrad. So. Meth. U., 1967-68, Tex. Women's U., 1978-79, U. Dallas, 1985-86; 1 dau. by former marriage, Angelique. Bar: Tex. 1982. Clk. Criminal Dist. Ct. Number 2, Dallas County, Tex., 1972-75; reins. librarian Scor Reins. Co., Dallas, 1975-80, Assocs. Ins. Group, 1980-83; corp./securities legal asst. Akin, Gump, Strauss, Hauer & Feld, 1983—. Mem. ABA, Spl. Libraries Assn., Am. Assn. Law Librarians, Tex. Libraries Assn., S.W. Libraries Assn., Dallas County Library Assn., Dallas Assn. Legal Assts., ABA, State Bar Tex. (charter mem. legal assts. div.), Dallas Assn. Law Librarians, other orgns. Republican. Episcopalian. Home: PO Box 1763 Dallas TX 75221

FLOOD, JOHN LEWIS, Germanic studies educator; b. Leicester, England, Sept. 22, 1938; s. William Henry and Ethel Mary (Daffern) F.; m. Ann Matthews, July 21, 1973; children: Alexander Lewis, Robert Christopher, Adrian John. BA, U. Nottingham, Eng., 1961, MA, 1963; PhD, U. London, 1980. Lectr. German Loughborough (Eng.) Coll. Advanced Tech., 1962-63; lectr. English U. Erlangen-Nuremberg, Fed. Republic Germany, 1963-64; asst. lectr. German U. Nottingham, 1964-65; asst. lectr. German U. London King's Coll., 1965-67, lectr. German, 1967-72, sr. lectr. German, 1972-79; dep. dir., reader in German U. London Inst. Germanic Studies, 1979—. Editor Modern Swiss Literature, 1985, Ein Moment Des Erfahrenen Lebens zur Lyrik der DDR, 1987; contbr. numerous articles to profl. jours. Mem. Conf. Univ. Tchrs. German in Gt. Brit. and Ireland (hon. sec. 1971—), Henry Sweet Soc. for History of Linguistic Ideas (hon. treas. 1984—). Office: Inst Germanic Studies, 29 Russell Sq, London WCIB 5DP, England

FLOOD, LENNART, economist; b. Gothenburg, Sweden, Oct. 19, 1952; s. Otto and Karin (Nicklasson) F.; m. Agneta Johansson, June 1983; children: Mikael, Mattias. BS in Engring., U. Gothenburg, 1973, BSc, 1979, PhD in Econs., 1986. Researcher dept. stats. U. Gothenburg, Sweden, 1979-80, 82-83; researcher dept. econs. U. Gothenburg, 1980-82, 84—; advisor Ministry of Econs., Stockholm, 1980; researcher U. Fla., Gainsville, 1983-84, Inst. Social Research, Ann Arbor, Mich., 1984. Contbr. articles to internat. jours. Fulbright grantee, 1983-84, grantee Royal Acad. Sci., 1984. Mem. Econometric Soc., Nationalekonomiska Foreningen. Home: Nyhagen 23, 42700 Billdal Sweden Office: Dept Econs Univ Gothenburg, Viktoriagaten 30, 41125 Gothenburg Sweden

FLORENCE, KENNETH JAMES, lawyer; b. Hanford, Calif., July 31, 1943; s. Ivy Owen and Louella (Dobson) F.; m. Verena Magdalena Demuth, Dec. 10, 1967. B.A., Whittier Coll., 1965; J.D., Hastings Coll. Law, U. Calif.-San Francisco, 1974. Bar: Calif. 1974, U.S. Dist. Ct. (cen. dist.) Calif. 1974, U.S. Dist. Ct. (ea. and so. dists.) Calif., 1976, U.S. Dist. Ct. (no. dist.) Calif. 1980, U.S. Ct. Appeals (9th cir.) 1975, U.S. Supreme Ct. 1984. Dist. mgr. Pacific T&T, Calif., 1969-71; assoc. Parker, Milliken, et al, Los Angeles, 1974-78; ptnr. Dern, Mason, et al, 1978-84, Swerdlow & Florence, A Law Corp., Beverly Hills, 1984—; pres. Westside Legal Services, Inc., Santa Monica, Calif., 1982-83. Served to lt. USNR, 1966-69, Vietnam. Col. J.G. Boswell scholar, 1961. Mem. ABA (co-chmn. state labor law com. 1988—). Democrat. Home: 1063 Stradella Rd Los Angeles CA 90077 Office: Swerdlow & Florence 9401 Wilshire Blvd Suite 828 Beverly Hills CA 90212

FLORES, FRANK FAUSTO, graphics and communications company executive; b. N.Y.C., Sept. 18, 1930; s. Frank E. and Marie (Navarro) F.; m. Elizabeth L. Weekes, Oct. 2, 1948; children—Donald, Stephen, Allen. Sales mgr. Marsden Offset Printing Co., Inc., N.Y.C., 1955-59, treas., 1959—; pres. Marsden Reprodns., Inc., N.Y.C., 1962—; bd. dirs. Nat. Minority Bus. Council, Cath. Interracial Council; bd. dirs. N.Y.-N.J. Minority Purchasing Council, chmn. vendor input com.; mem. Manhattan adv. council Salvation Army, Affirmative Action Adv. Bd. N.Y. State Dept. Transp. Com., City Coll. Sch. Edn. adv. bd., Hispanic Bus. adv. bd. for N.Y.C.; bd. dirs. Regional Plan Assn. (dir. exec. com.), Amistad MESBIC, Puerto Rican Family Inst., League of United Latin Am. Citizens Found., Private Industry Council, Alliance N.Y.C. Bus., Sch. and Bus. Alliance for N.Y.C.; trustee Blueprinting Union Health & Wealth Fund Local 966 Pension Fund. Named Hispanic Businessman of Yr., League United Latin Am. Citizens, 1981, N.Y. Minority Businessman of Yr., Nat. Minority Bus. Council, 1981, Employer of Yr., Goodwill Industries, 1982, 83, 84, Employer of Yr., Nat. Mental Health Assn. and Pres.'s Com. on Employment of Handicapped, 1983; recipient Small Bus. award N.Y. Chamber Commerce and Industry, 1983, Hispanic Businessman of Yr., Albany Hispanic Coalition, 1986, Wall Street Chpt. of Image, 1986, Minority Purchasing Council, Inc. award in grateful appreciation for outstanding contributions,1988. Mem. Nat. Hispanic Bus. Group (founder, v. chmn. 1984—), Soc. Tech. Communication (past chmn.), Internat. Reprographics Assn., Nat. Assn. Photo Lithographers, Blue Printers Assn. N.Y., IMAGE (chmn. adv. bd. Wall St. chpt.), N.Y. State Hispanic C. of C. (Hispanic businessman of yr. 1985), Latino Commn. for United Way, P.R. Family Inst., Nat. Rifle Assn. Home: 40 Rockwood Ln Greenwich CT 06830 Office: 30 E 33d St New York NY 10016

FLORES MAGON, EDUARDO ENRIQUE, economist; b. Mexico City, May 31, 1946; s. Pedro and Ligia Irma (Lopez) Flores-Magon; diploma U. Autonoma Mex., 1968; MSc, Stanford U., 1970, PhD, 1973; m. Christine Blackard, Feb. 4, 1969. Research leader U. Autonoma Mex., 1973; with Mexican Govt., 1974—; adv. to dir. gen. de Inversiones Publicas, 1974-76; adv. to Secretario de Agricultura y Recursos Hidraulicos, 1976-82; adv. to dir. gen. Soc. Mex. Cré dito Indsl., 1977-78; dir. multi-disciplinary planning group Ministry Energy, 1978-82; lectr. U. Autonoma Mex.; advisor on food supply and demand in future Mexican Congress, 1979-82; dir. energy planning group Uranio Mexicano, 1983; head long range planning group Petroleos Mexicanos, 1984-87; adviser to the Undersec. Mines and Basic Industry, Semip, 1987; dir. gen. Siderurgia y Fertilizantes, Semip, 1988. Fellow Inst. Nat. Investigacion Cientifica, 1968-73, Consejo Nat. Ciencia y Technologi a, 1968-73, Mary S. Jenkins Found., 1969-71, OAS, 1973. Mem. Mex. Fisica Assn. Author govt. reports. Home: Cda Sindicalismo 6, 11800 DF Mexico City Mexico Office: Insurgentes Sur 552 piso 12, 06769 DF Mexico City Mexico

FLORESTANO, DANA JOSEPH, architect; b. Indpls., May 2, 1945; s. Herbert Joseph and Myrtle Mae (Futch) F.; m. Peggy Joy Larsen, June 6, 1969. BArch, U. Notre Dame, 1968. Designer, draftsman Kennedy, Brown & Trueblood, architects, Indpls., 1965-69, Evans Woolen Assn., architects, Indpls., 1966; designer, project capt. James Assos., architects and engrs., Indpls., 1969-71; architect, v.p. comml. projects Multi-Planners Inc., architects and engrs., 1972-73; pvt. practice architecture, Indpls., 1973—; pres. Florestano Corp., constrn. mgmt., Indpls., 1973—; co-founder, pres. Solargenics Natural Energy Corp., Indpls., 1975—; prof. archtl. and constrn. tech. Ind. U.-Purdue U. at Indpls.; instr. in field. Tech. adviser hist. architecture Indpls. Model Cities program, 1969-70; mem. Hist. Landmarks Found. Ind., 1970-72; chmn. Com. to Save Union Sta., 1970-71, founder, pres. Union Sta. Found. Inc., Indpls., 1971—. Dep. commr. and tournament dir. archery Pan-Am. Games, Indpls., 1987. Recipient 2d design award Marble Inst. Am., 1967, 1st design award 19th Ann. Progressive Architecture Design awards, 1972; Design award for excellence in devel. Marriott Inn, Indpls., Met. Devel. Commn.-Office of Mayor, 1977; 1st place award design competition for Visitor's Info. Center, Cave Run, Lake, Ky., 1978; 2d design award 1st Ann. Qualified Remodeler, Nat. Competition for Best Rehab. Existing Structures in Am., 1979. Mem. U. Notre Dame Alumni Assn., Notre Dame Club Indpls., AIA (nat. com. historic resources 1974—, commn. on community services, Speakers Bur. Indpls. chpt. 1976—), Ind. Soc. Architects (chmn. historic architecture com. 1970—), Ind. Archery Assn. (founder, pres. 1985—), No. Archery Assn. (bd. dirs., pres. 1987—), Constrn. Specifications Inst., Constrn. Mgrs. Assn. Ind. (incorporator, dir. 1976—), World Archery Ctr. Home: 5697 N Broadway St Indianapolis IN 46220 Office: 6214 N Carrollton Ave Indianapolis IN 46220

FLORIAN, SHERWOOD LESTER, manufacturing executive; b. Hartford, Conn., June 21, 1920; s. Frank Benjamin and Gertrude Bruce F.; student Hillyer Coll., 1939; m. Shirley Moeller, Sept. 23, 1942; children—John, William, Nanette. Owner, Florian Co., Hartford, 1947-51; partner H.P. Loewenberg Co., 1951-56; co-founder, v.p. Amplex Corp., Bloomfield, Conn., 1956-76, pres., dir., 1976-82, chmn., chief exec. officer, 1982-84; ptnr. Britton Diamond Labs., 1978-84; cons. Florian Assocs., 1984—; dir. Amplex Internat.; partner Britton Assocs., from 1978. Served with USAF, 1942-45. Clubs: U.S. Power Squadren, Sarasota Yacht. Mem. Indsl. Diamond Assn., Diamond Wheel Mfrs. Inst., Wire Assn., Abrasive Engring. Soc., Soc. Mfg. Engr s. Author tech. articles on indsl. diamonds.

FLORY, ROBERT MIKESELL, computer systems analyst, personnel management specialist; b. Bridgewater, Va., Feb. 21, 1912; s. John Samuel and Vinnie (Mikesell) F.; m. Thelma Thomas, Sept. 14, 1942; 1 child, Pamela. B.A., Bridgewater Coll., 1932; M.A., U. Va., 1938; postgrad. U. Chgo., 1946-51. Job/methods analyst United Air Lines, Chgo., 1945-47; job analyst Julian Baer, Chgo., 1948; asst. to v.p. Fairbanks, Morse, Chgo., 1949-60; mgmt. cons. Yarger & Assocs., Falls Church, Va., 1961; computer systems analyst, various fed. agys., Washington, 1962-82; tchr. Roosevelt U., Chgo., 1956-61; seminar leader U. Chgo., 1960-61; cons. Va. Gov.'s Commn. for Reorgn. State Govt., 1961. Served to lt. comdr. USN, 1942-45, PTO. Mem. Inst. Mgmt. Scis. Home: 5501 Seminary Rd Apt 1204-S Falls Church VA 22041

FLØTTUM, KJERSTI, linguist, philologist; b. Frosta, Trøndelag, Norway, July 12, 1953; d. Egil Peder and Anna (Kosberg) F. Candidate philology, Univ., Trondheim and Bergen, 1979. Research asst. Univ., Oslo, 1982; research asst. Univ., Trondheim, 1982-86, instr. romance studies, 1980—; researcher Norwegian Council of Research, Trondheim, 1986-89; mem. Council of Humanities Faculty, Trondheim, 1983-85, Nat. Com. Coordination of Research Edn. in Humanities, 1987-88. Author: Fransk og tysk som fremmedspråk, 1987, Fransk språklaere, 1987. Home: Nedre Møllenberg gt 49a, 7014 Trondheim Norway Office: Univ Trondheim, Dept Romance Studies, 7055 Dragvoll Norway

FLOUD, RODERICK CASTLE, historian, educator; b. London, Apr. 1, 1942; s. Bernard Francis Castle and Ailsa (Craig) F.; m. Cynthia Anne Smith, Aug. 6, 1984; children: Lydia Jane, Sarah Katherine. BA, Oxford U., Eng., 1964, DPhil, 1970. Asst. lectr. U. Coll. London, 1966-69; lectr. U. Cambridge, Eng., 1969-75; prof. Stanford U., Calif., 1980-81; prof. modern history Birkbeck Coll. U. London, 1975-88, senator, 1986-88; provost City of London Poly., 1988—. Author: Introduction to Quantitative Methods for Historians, 1973, The British Machine Tool Industry, 1976; author, editor Econ. History of Britain, 1981. Fellow Royal Hist. Soc. Labor Party. Club: Athenaeum (London). Home: 21 Savernake Rd, London NW3 2JT, England Office: City of London Polytechnic, 117-119 Houndsditch, London EC3A 7BU, England

FLOWERS, AUREATHA WILLIS, educator; b. Albany, Ga., Aug. 22, 1936; d. R.L. and Susie Mae (Miller) Willis; m. Eallie Flowers, July 22, 1959 (dec. Oct. 1969). B.S. in Elem. Edn., Albany State Coll.; M.Ed., Tuskegee Inst., 1968; Ed.S., Atlanta U., 1981. Cert. tchr., Ga. Tchr. LaGrange Bd. Edn., Ga., 1965, Cobb County Bd. Edn., Ga., 1965-69; tchr., dept. chairperson Atlanta Bd. Edn., 1969-81; interrelated spl. edn. specialist Atlanta U., 1981—. Editor activity manual Love Them, 1982. Fundraiser Am. Cancer Soc., Atlanta, 1980-83; tchr. sponsor Spl. Olympics, Atlanta, 1981—; explorer adviser Carver High Sch. council Boy Scouts Am., 1982; tchr. Close Up, Atlanta, 1982. Recipient cert. award George Washington Carver Comprehensive chpt. Jr. Civitan, Atlanta, 1982, Youth Leadership in Am. award Boy Scouts Am., 1983. Mem. AFT (local 1565), Council Exceptional Children (chpt. cert. merit 1973), NEA, Ga. Assn. Educators, Atlanta Tchr.'s Assn., Phi Delta Kappa. Democrat. Baptist. Office: Atlanta City Bd Edn 4 Middle Plantation Rd NW Atlanta GA 30318

FLOWERS, BARON BRIAN HILTON, university vice chancellor; b. Swansea, Eng., Sept. 13, 1924; s. Harold Joseph and Marion V. (Hilton) F.; m. Mary Frances Behrens, Oct. 26, 1951; stepchildren—Peter Buneman, Michael Buneman. MA, Cambridge U., Eng., Oxon U., Eng., 1956; DSc, Birmingham U., Eng.; D.Sc. (hon.), U. Sussex, Eng., U. Wales, U. Manchester, Eng., U. Leicester, Eng., U. Liverpool, Eng., U. Bristol, Eng., U. Oxford, Eng.; ScD, U. Dublin, Ireland; LLD (hon.), Dundee U., Eng., Glasgow U., Eng.; DD (hon.), Glasgow U., Eng., 1987; D in Eng. (hon.), Tech. U. N.S. (Can.), 1983. Researcher in nuclear physics, atomic energy Atomic Energy Research Establishment, Harwell, Eng., 1946-50; lectr. dept. math. physics U. Birmingham, Eng., 1950-52; head theoretical physics Atomic Energy Research Establishment, Harwell, Eng., 1952-58; prof. theoretical physics, Langworthy prof. Manchester U., Harwell, Eng., 1958-72; chmn. Sci. Research Council, London, Eng., 1967-73; rector Imperial Coll. Sci. and Tech., London, Eng., 1973-85; vice chancellor U. London, London,

Eng., 1985—; Chmn. Sci. Research Council, 1967-73, Computer Bd. for Univs. and Research Councils, 1966-70, Royal Commn. on Environ. Pollution, 1973-76, Standing Commn. on Energy and Environment, 1978-81, Univ. London Working Party on Future of Med. and Dental Teaching Resources, 1979-80, Com. Vice-Chancellors and Principals, 1983-85; mem. Select Com. on Sci. and Tech., 1980—; pres. Nat. Soc. for Clean Air, 1977-79. Author: Properties of Matter, 1970; contbr. articles to profl. jours. Life peer House of Lords, SDP mem. (founder); chmn., trustee Nuffield Found. Decorated officier de la Legion d'Honneur, 1981; recipient Rutherford medal and prize IPPS, 1968, Glazebrook medal and prize, IPPS, 1976, Chalmers medal Chalmers Univ. Tech., Sweden, 1980. Fellow Inst. Physics. (pres. 1974-74), Royal Soc., Royal Cambrian Acad., Univ. Manchester Inst. Sci. and Tech.; mem. European Sci. Found. (pres. 1974-80), Swiss Acad. Engring. Scis. Home: 48 Gordon Sq, London England Office: U London Senate House, Malet St, London WC1E 7HU, England also: Imperial Coll, London SW7 2AZ, England

FLOWERS, CHARLES ELY, JR., physician emeritus medical educator; b. Zebulon, N.C., July 20, 1920; s. Charles Ely and Carmen (Poole) F.; m. Juanita Bays, Nov. 23, 1944 (dec.); children: Charles Ely III, Carmen Eva; m. Jaunzetta Shew, Sept. 25, 1972. B.S., The Citadel, 1941; M.D., Johns Hopkins U., 1944. Diplomate: Am. Bd. Ob-Gyn (assoc. examiner). Intern Johns Hopkins Hosp., 1944, resident, 1945-50; instr. SUNY, 1950-51, asst. prof., 1951-53; assoc. prof. U. N.C., 1953-61, prof., 1961-66; prof., chmn. dept. obstetrics and gynecology Baylor U. Med. Sch., 1966-69; prof., chmn. dept. ob-gyn U. Ala. Med. Center, Birmingham, 1969-85; chmn. emeritus U. Ala. Med. Center, 1985—, disting. prof., 1985—; obstetrician and gynecologist in chief U. Ala. Hosp., 1969-85; cons. NIH; mem. adv. com. oral contraceptives Internat. Planned Parenthood; mem. med. services adv. com. Nat. Found.; chmn. 6th World Congress Gynecology and Obstetrics, 1970. Mem. editorial bd.: Obstetrics and Gynecology. Served to capt. M.C., AUS, 1946-48. Recipient Disting. Service award U. N.C., 1970. Mem. AMA, Continental Gynecol. Soc., Am. Gynecol. and Obstet. Soc. (treas. 1981), Am. Assn. Obstetricians and Gynecologists (v.p. 1978-80), Central Assn. Obstetricians and Gynecologists, ACS, Am. Coll. Obstetricians and Gynecologists (chmn. com. obstetrics anesthesia and analgesia, v.p. 1983), Soc. Gynecologic Surgeons (pres. 1986), Internat. Coll. Anesthetists. Home: 3757 Rockhill Rd Birmingham AL 35223

FLOWERS, KENNETH ANTHONY, neuropsychologist, educator; b. London, Aug. 7, 1942; s. Thomas Harold and Eileen Margaret (Green) F.; m. Susan Hilary Pratt, Apr. 6, 1974; children: Catherine, Josephine, Jonathan. BA, U. Cambridge, Eng., 1965, MA, 1967, PhD, 1972. Research asst. Nat. Hosp. Nervous Diseases, London, 1969-70; research assoc. brain and perception lab. Bristol (Eng.) U. Sch. Medicine, 1971-76; lectr. dept. psychology U. Hull, Eng., 1977—. Contbr. articles to profl. jours. Grantee Parkinson's Disease Soc., Hull, 1981-84, Med. Research Council, 1984-86. Mem. Brit. Psychol. Soc., Exptl. Psychology Soc., Brain Research Assn., European Brain and Behavior Soc. Office: U Hull, Hull HU6 7RX, England

FLUEGGE, RONALD MARVIN, nuclear engineer; b. Cape Girardeau, Mo., Nov. 22, 1948; s. Marvin Alvin and Maxine Louise (Hamilton) F.; m. Vicki Sue Oldham, Aug. 9, 1969; children: Terasa Dawn, Jennifer Beth. BS, U. Mo.-Rolla, 1970. Registered profl. engr., Mo., Md., Kans., Tex. Engr. Balt. Gas & Electric Co., 1970-74; reactor engr. Nuclear Regulatory Commn., Bethesda, Md., 1974-76; med. physicist Shoss Radiology Group, Cape Girardeau, Mo., 1976-78; pres. Diagnostic Services Unltd., Jackson, Mo., 1978-79; dir. Mo. Pub. Service Commn., Jefferson City, 1979-83; nuclear cons. analyst UCCEL Corp., Dallas, 1983-86; supv. data, records and report services, Tex. Utilities Generating Co. (name changed to TU Electric), Dallas, 1986—; curriculum adv. U. Mo., Rolla, 1980—; econs. adv. Atomic Indsl. Forum, Washington, 1982—; tech. adv. Gov's. Office, Jefferson City, Mo., 1979-83; radiation cons. Oliver, Oliver, Waltz & Cook/Geo-Log, 1978. Vol. Mo. Nuclear Emergency Team, Jefferson City, 1979-83. Served with Md. Nat. Guard, 1970-71. Mem. Am. Nuclear Soc., ASME, Nat. Soc. Profl. Engrs., Tex. Soc. Profl. Engrs. Republican. Methodist. Home: 5633 N Colony Blvd The Colony TX 75056 Office: TU Electric 400 N Olive St LB 81 Dallas TX 75201

FLÜGELMAN, MÁXIMO ENRIQUE, financier, composer; b. Buenos Aires, Nov. 2, 1945; s. Cirilo and Matilde (Rhein) F. Lic. es Sci. Econ., U. Geneva, 1967; diploma in econ. policy Catholic U., Buenos Aires, 1968; M.B.A., Harvard U., 1972; B.M., Manhattan Sch. Music, 1980; M.Composition, Juilliard Sch., 1981. Fin. mgr. Solex Industrias Quimicas S.A., Buenos Aires, 1967—; credit officer Citibank, Buenos Aires and N.Y.C., 1968-69; investment officer World Bank Group, Internat. Fin. Corp., Washington, 1972-77; internat. mgr., chief external funding, negotiator Nat. Devel. Bank, Buenos Aires, 1981-84; Latin Am. rep. Taha & Al-Kazemi Trading Co., Kuwait; cons. HTC Trading Corp., N.Y.C., 1984—; investment banker 1st Chgo. Internat. Capital Markets Group, Chgo. and N.Y.C., 1985—; mem. ofcl. Argentine del. to IMF/World Bank meetings, 1981, 82, Inter Am. Devel. Bank gen. assemblies 1983, 84; lectr. Buenos Aires Nat. U. Author: Argentina and the Debt Crisis, 1983; contbr. articles on internat. fin. and arts to profl. jours. including La Nacion, Ambito Financiero; musical compositions include Symphonic Variants for orch., 1979, Concertino for woodwinds and orch., 1981, Piano sonata, 1982, Sonatina per corde for string orch., 1984, Sea Sonnets for soprano and orch., 1985, Sonatina for chamber orch., 1987; chamber works performed at Aspen Festival, Latin Am. Chamber Music Festival, Quinteto Rego, Argentina; orchestral works performed Indpls. Symphony, Interam. Festival Orch., Kennedy Ctr., Washington, Northwestern U. Orch., Nat. Argentine Symphony, Buenos Aires Philharm. at Teatro Colon, Conn. Chamber Orch. Trustee, founding mem. Teatro Colon Found. Recipient 14th ann. contemporary orchestral composition award Ind. State U./Indpls. Symphony, 1980; 1st prize LRA Argentine State Radio Chamber Orch. composition contest, 1981; Outstanding Young Musician of Yr. award Argentine Jr. C. of C., 1983; Amigos de la Música composition prize, 1986; winner Pan-Am. composition contest Indpls. Symphony, 1986; Bunge and Born Found. fellow, 1979. Mem. Argentine Council on Fgn. Relations, Teatro Colón Found. (trustee, founding mem.), A. Ginastera Found. (adv.), Sociedad Argentina de Autores y Compositores. Club: Doubles (N.Y.C.); Sociedad Rural Argentina; Nautico San Isidro (Buenos Aires). Office: Reconquista 150, Buenos Aires Argentina also: 153 W 51st St Suite 4200 New York NY 10019

FLUHR, FREDERICK ROBERT, electronics engineer; b. Omaha, Jan. 7, 1922; s. Frederick R. and Ruby (Wright) F.; student U. Omaha, 1946-47; B.S., Iowa State U., 1949, M.S., 1950; m. Mary Annie Rosser, June 7, 1952; 1 dau., Glynis Ann. Elec. engr., head high energy laser staff U.S Naval Research Lab., Washington, 1951-81; sr. research engr. Sachs/Freeman Assocs., Landover, Md., 1981—. Served with USAAF, 1940-45. Recipient Profl. Achievement citation in Engring., Iowa State U., 1983. Mem. IEEE, VFW, AAAS. Patentee in field. Home: 8716 E Ft Foote Terr Oxon Hill MD 20744 Office: 1401 McCormick Ln Landover MD 20785

FLUKE, LYLA SCHRAM, publisher; b. Maddock, N.D.; d. Olaf John and Anne Marie (Rodberg) Schram; m. John M. Fluke, June 5, 1937; children: Virginia Fluke Gabelein, John M. Jr., David Lynd. BS in Zoology and Physiology, U. Wash., Seattle, 1934, diploma teaching, 1935. High sch. tchr., 1935-37; tutor Seattle schs., 1974-75; pub. Portage Quar. mag., Hist. Soc. Seattle and King County, 1980—. Author articles on histroy. Founder N.W. chpt. Myasthenia Gravis Found., 1953, pres., 60-63; obtained N.W. artifacts for destroyer Tender Puget Sound, 1966; mem. Seattle Mayor's Com. for Seattle Beautiful, 1968-69; sponsor Seattle World's Fair, 1962; charter mem. Seattle Youth Symphony Aux., 1974; bd. dirs. Cascade Symphony, Salvation Army, 1985-87; mem. U.S. Congl. Adv. Bd.; benefactor U. Wash., 1982—, nat. chmn. ann. giving campaign, 1983-84; benefactor Sterling Circle Stanford U., 1984, Wash. State Hist. Soc., Pacific Arts Ctr.; mem. condr.'s club Seattle Symphony, 1978—. Fellow Seattle Pacific U., 1972—; mem. Wash. Trust for Hist. Preservation, Nat. Trust for Hist. Preservation, N.W. Ornamental Hort. Soc. (life, hon.), Smithsonian Assocs., Nat. Assn. Parliamentarians (charter mem., pres. N.W. unit 1961), Wash. Parliamentarians Assn. (charter), IEEE Aux. (chpt. charter mem., past pres.), Seattle C. of C. (women's div.), Seattle Symphony Women's Assn. (life, sec. 1982-84, pres. 1985-87), Hist. Soc. Seattle and King County (exec. com. 1975-78, pres. women's mus. league 1975-78, pres. Moritz Thomsen Guild of Hist. Soc., 1978-80, 84-87), Highlands Orthopedic Guild (life), Wash. State Hist. Soc, Antiquarian Soc. (v.p. 1986-88, pres. 1988—). Republican. Lutheran. Clubs: Women's U., Rainier, Seattle Golf, Seattle Tennis, U. Wash. Pres.'s. Address: 1206 NW Culbertson Dr Vendovi Island WY 98177

FLUM, JEROME MICHAEL, architect; b. Detroit, Sept. 30, 1950; s. Lawrence John and Mildred Mary (Selensky) F.; m. Rosa Josefine Pischem, Dec. 24, 1976. BArch, U. Detroit, 1972. Field coordinator Greimel, Malcomson et al, Detroit, 1972-75; constrn. mgr. Area Constrn., Detroit, 1977-80; supr. Belvedere Constrn. Co., Detroit, 1977-80; v.p. F. Lax Inc., Ferndale, Mich., 1980-84; sales dir. Guaranteed Constrn., Farmington Hills, Mich., 1984-87; pres. Jeromen Inc., 1987—; Inventor fireplace/kachelofen, 1983; patentee in field. Assoc. Detroit Symphony Orch., 1983; mem. Founders Soc. Detroit Symphony Orch., Detroit Hist. Soc.; patron Save Orch. Hall, Founders Soc. Detroit Inst. of Art. Mem. Internat. Platform Assn. Home & Office: 29800 Stockton Farmington Hills MI 48024

FLUME, VIOLET BRUCE SIGOLOFF, artist gallery director; b. Huntington, W.Va.; d. Rufus Otho and Rachel (Witt) Bruce; student Huntington Coll., Trinity U., 1964-65; studied with portrait artist David Philip Wilson, 1963-64; m. Samuel Sigoloff, Oct. 20, 1945 (dec.); children—Bruce Myron, Nelson Witt; m. 2d, Lawrence Flume, Jr., Feb. 1, 1979. Owner, Wonderland Gallery, 1966-80, Sigoloff Fine Art Galleries, San Antonio, 1972—; exhibited one-man shows St. Mary's U., 1966, Southwestern Fine Arts Inst., U. Tex., 1967, HemisFair, 1968, Trinity U., 1968; exhibited in group shows at River Art, 1964-68, San Antonio Art League, 1964-70; represented in pvt. collections. Chmn. edn. for family living PTA, 1962, v.p., 1964-65; art judge Hallmark Contest, 1969. Author: Last Mountain: Life of Robert Wood, 1983. Recipient 1st Pl. award in miniatures Composers Authors and Artists Am. Nat. Exhibit, N.Y.C., 1965; named San Antonio's Outstanding Woman in Art, San Antonio Express and San Antonio Evening News, 1967. Mem. Tex. Fine Art Assn., San Antonio Art League, San Antonio River Art Group. Clubs: Acacia (pres. 1961, 64), Zonta (San Antonio). Home: 3806 Mill Ct San Antonio TX 78230 Office: Sigoloff Gallery 7700 Broadway San Antonio TX 78209

FLYCHT, LENNART KNUT SAMUEL, business executive; b. Kristianstad, Sweden, Oct. 14, 1918; s. Albin and Elsa (Fredriksson) F.; m. Britta Dahlin, May 7, 1956. Degree in econs., U. Commerce, Gothenberg, Sweden, 1942. Expert bus. The Price-Control Bus., Swedish Govt., Stockholm, 1943-45; expert orgn. The Orgn. Bur., Swedish Govt., Stockholm, 1946-48, Scandinavian Airlines System, Stockholm, 1948-51; v.p. econs. and fin. AB Germa, Sundbyberg, Sweden, 1952-54, Marieholm (Sweden) Yllefabrik AB, 1954-57; v.p. econs. Cewe AB Group, Nyköping, Sweden, 1958-80; mng. dir. Förvaltnings AB Fruängen, Nyköping, 1980—, also bd. dirs.; mng. dir. Elektriska AB Cewe, Nyköping, 1980—, also bd. dirs.; bd. dirs. Cewe Instrument AB Group, Nyköping. Recipient Gold Medal award Royal Soc. Pro Patria, 1984. Home and Office: Kungsgatan 25, 61132 Nykoping Sweden

FLYNN, JOHN ALLEN, lawyer; b. Riverside, Ill., Jan. 12, 1945; s. William and Marian Rae (Gustafson) F.; children: Judson John, Erin Courtney. AB, Stanford U., 1966; JD, U. Calif., San Francisco, 1969. Bar: Calif. 1970, U.S. Dist. Ct. (no. and ea. dists.) Calif. 1970, U.S. Ct. Appeals (9th cir.) 1970, U.S. Supreme Ct. 1975. Assoc. Graham & James, San Francisco, 1969-75, ptnr., 1976—; lectr. in field. Mem. ABA, Maritime Law Assn. (mem. com. on practice and procedure 1983—), San Francisco Bar Assn. (chmn. admiralty com. 1978—). Roman Catholic. Club: San Francisco Press. Office: Graham & James 1 Maritime Plaza San Francisco CA 94111

FLYNN, RICHARD JAMES, lawyer; b. Omaha, Dec. 6, 1928; s. Richard T. and Eileen (Murphy) F.; m. Kay House Ebert, June 28, 1975; children: Richard McDonnell, William Thomas, Kathryn Eileen Merritt, James Daniel. Student, Cornell U., 1944-46; B.S., Nothwestern U., 1950; J.D., Northwestern U., 1953. Bar: D.C. 1953, Ill. 1954. Law clk. to Chief Justices Vinson and Warren, 1953-54; assoc. Sidley, Austin, Burgess & Smith, Chgo., 1954-63; ptnr. Sidley, Austin, Burgess & Smith, Washington, 1963-66, Sidley & Austin, 1967—. Contbr. articles to profl. jours. Mem. exec. com. Washington Lawyers Com. for Civil Rights Under Law. Served with USN, 1946-48. Fellow Am. Coll. Trial Lawyers, mem. ABA, Fed. Bar Assn., Fed. Energy Bar Assn., Assn. Transp. Practitioners, Nat. Lawyer Club, Chgo. Bar Assn., D.C. Bar Assn., Order of Coif, Phi Beta Kappa, Phi Delta Phi, Sigma Chi. Republican. Presbyterian. Clubs: Economic of Chgo, Legal, Kenwood Golf and Country; Metropolitan (Washington). Home: 2342 S Queen St Arlington VA 22202 Office: Sidley & Austin 1722 Eye St NW Washington DC 20006

FLYNN, ROBERT JAMES, veterinarian; b. Chgo., Jan. 8, 1923; s. James Robert and Rose (Kunz) F.; student Kennedy-King Coll., 1940-41; D.V.M., Mich. State U., 1944; m. Doris Jean Ashe, Dec. 19, 1942; children—Robert J., Jean B., Susan J., Nancy J. (Mrs. James Masters), James R., Betty J. (Mrs. John Zinke). With Argonne Nat. Lab. (Ill.), 1948-81, successively supr. animal quarters, 1948-55, asso. veterinarian, 1948-66, sr. veterinarian, 1966-81, research on care and diseases of lab. animals, 1948-76, asst. dir. for animal facilities, 1962-76, research on biology of aging, 1971-74, on viral carcinogenesis, 1976-77, on environ. impacts, 1977-81; vet. insp. state of Ill., 1944-57; veterinarian, Lake County, Ill., 1957-76, rabies insp., 1970-73, animal control adminstr., 1973-83; veterinarian Lake County Health Dept., 1976-83; mem. NRC, 1967-70, mem. com. vet. med. research and edn., 1968-72. Served with AUS, 1943-44. Diplomate Am. Coll. Lab. Animal Medicine (dir. 1956-64, 73-75, sec.-treas. 1956-62, pres. 1963). Mem. Am. Assn. Lab. Animal Sci. (dir. 1949-65, sec.-treas. 1953-62, pres. 1963-64, Griffin award 1968, R.J. Flynn award 1969). Editor numerous texts, including: Laboratory Animal Science: a review of the literature, 1966; (with W.F. Riley, Jr. and K.W. Smith) The Year Book of Veterinary Medicine, vols. 1, 2 and 3; Parasites of Laboratory Animals, 1973; Laboratory Animal Science, 1976-78. Contbr. numerous articles to profl. jours. Organizer, participant in nat. and internat. symposia. Home: 421 E Westleigh Rd Lake Forest IL 60045

FOBES, JOHN EDWIN, international organization official; b. Chgo., Mar. 16, 1918; s. Wilfred and Mable (Skogsberg) F.; B.S. cum laude (Clarion Dewitt Hardy scholar), Northwestern U., 1939; M.A., Fletcher Sch. Law and Diplomacy, 1940; H.H.D. (hon.), Bucknell U., 1973; m. Hazel Ward Weaver, June 7, 1941; children—Patricia Cleveland, John Geoffrey Weaver. With Bur. Budget, Washington, 1942, 46-48; secretariat prep. commn. of UN, London, 1945; exec. sec. UN advisory group of experts on adminstrn., personnel and budgetary questions, 1946; adviser Pan Am. Union, 1947-48; with ECA, Marshall Plan, 1948-52; attache U.S. del. to NATO and OEEC, Paris, 1952-55; dir. Office Internat. Adminstrn., Dept. State, Washington, 1955-59, spl. asst. to asst. sec. state, 1959-60; asst. dir. Tech. Cooperation Mission to India, 1960-62; dep. dir. AID Mission to India, 1962-64; asst. dir. gen. UNESCO, Paris, 1964-70, dep. dir. gen., 1970-77. Vis. research scholar Ind. U., Harvard, 1970; vis. scholar Duke U., Durham, 1978-82; vis. lectr. U. N.C., Chapel Hill, 1981-82; adj. prof. Western Carolina U., 1983—. Pres. Am. Library in Paris, 1968-70. Mem. advisory com. UN Gen. Assembly, 1955-60; chmn. U.S. Nat. Commn. for UNESCO, 1980-81. Served as maj. USAAF 1942-46. ETO. Mem. Soc. Internat. Devel., Internat. Studies Assn., Internat. Inst. Communications, World Futures Studies Fedn. U.S. Assn. for Club of Rome (chmn. 1982—), Club of Rome (exec. com. internat.), Assn. Promotion of Humor in Internat. Affairs (co-founder), Ams. for Universality of UNESCO (founder, chmn.), Atwater Devel. Found. (chmn.), Phi Beta Kappa. Home: 28 Beaverbrook Rd Asheville NC 28804

FOCSANEANU FOX FOCH, GABRIEL, electrical and mechanical engineer, technological corporation executive; b. Bucharest, Rumania, Aug. 11, 1921; arrived in Can., 1957; s. Paul and Cecilia (Schwatz) F.; widower; children: Raoul, Cornelius, Georges. B in Engring., MBA, U. Bucharest, 1945; PhD in Electronics, Physics, Ecole Poly., Paris, 1952; postgrad., MIT; MBA, 1965. With Titano Engring. Inter-Continental Group of Cos., Montreal, Que., Can., 1948—; now pres., chief exec. officer Titano Engring. Inter-Continental Group of Cos. Author numerous books various engring. fields pub. internationally. Mem. Engring. Inst. Can., Can. Soc. Mech. Engrs., Nat. Soc. Profl. Engrs., ASME, ASHRAE, Air Polution Control Assn., Project Mgmt. Inst., Inst. Power Engrs., AIME, Soc. Petroleum Engrs., Am. Soc. Steel Engrs., Internat. Assn. Hydrogen Energy Eng., Atomic Scientists Inst., Fusion Sci. Tech. Found., Inst. Sci. Info., Planetary Soc. Space Research Inst., Soc. Computer Scientists, Soc. Devel. Sci., Can. C. of C., Montreal C. of C., Can. Inst. Strategic Studies, Hong Kong-Can. Bus. Assn., Can. Club. Mem. Conservative Party. Home and Office: Titano Engring Ltd, 2255 St Mathew St #1006, Montreal, PQ Canada H3H 2J6

FODIMAN, AARON ROSEN, restaurant chain executive; b. Stamford Conn., Oct. 10, 1937; s. Yale J. and Thelma F.; B.S., Tulane U., 1958; LL.B., N.Y. U., 1960, MBA, 1961; grad. L'Academie de Cuisine Canardier, Washington, 1977. Admitted to N.Y. bar, 1960, D.C. bar, 1961, Va. bar, 1965; FTC, Washington, 1961-65; practiced in Arlington, Va., 1965-78; pres. Fast Food Operators, Inc., N.Y.C., 1978-84; pres. Hampton Healthcare, 1984—, Tampa Bay Publs., 1986—; dir. Hayloft Dinner Theatre, Inc., Manassas, Va., Hygolet Inc., Palm Beach, Fla., Tampa Players Inc., Washington Ballet, Manhattan Punch Line Theatre, Dunedin Art Ctr., Pinellas County Arts Council, Golda Mier Ctr.; community advisor Clearwater Dunedin Jr. League.; mem. adv. bd. Am. Film Inst.; chmn. Ford Presdl. Campaign, 1976; cons. spl. services U.S. Dept. State spl. envoy to Iran, Poland, Russia, Senegal, 1964-78; TV host local sports show, Dine Line, Tampa Bay Mag. Participant Leadership Pinellas, Leadership Tampa Bay, Golda Meir Nat. Conf. Christians and Jews. Recipient Miniature Palette award Miniature Art Soc. of Fla., 1987, Hyam Soloman Freedom award, 1974. Mem. Pinellas County Restaurant Assn. (pres.), Fla. Restaurant Assn. (bd. dirs.), Phi Delta Phi. Club: Barrister Inn (pres.) (Washington). Lodge: B'nai Brith (pres. Washington 1988—).

FODOR, ISTVÁN, biochemist; b. Ungvár, Uzhgorod, Hungary, Aug. 22, 1940; arrived in USSR, 1945; s. István and Irén (Iváncsó) F.; m. Nadezhda Saveljeva, June 22, 1968; children: Irena, Christina. BS, Uzhgorod State U., 1962; aspirant, Inst. Molecular Biology, USSR Acad. Scis., 1963-67; PhD, Inst. Biochem. USSR Acad. Sci., Moscow, 1968; DSc, Moscow State U., 1985. Jr. researcher Inst. Botany, Acad. Scis., Kiev, USSR, 1967-69, Inst. Biochemistry and Physiology of Microorganisms, USSR Acad. Sci., Pushchino, 1969-72; sr. researcher Inst. Biochemistry, Physiology and Microorganisms, USSR Acad. Sci., Pushchino, 1972—, head. lab., 1973—; vis. researcher U. Calif. San Francisco, 1975-76, Yale U., New Haven, Conn., 1979; mem. Council on Biotech., USSR Acad. Scis., 1985—. Contbr. over 120 articles to profl. jours. Recipient USSR Council of Ministries prize, 1981, Order of Badge of Honour, Moscow, 1981. Home: AB-5/36, 142292 Pushchino USSR Office: Inst Biochem Physiol Microrgn, 142292 Pushchino USSR

FODOR, MAGDA MARIA, civil engineer; b. Hungary, Sept. 21, 1942; d. Jeno and Edith Gotz; 1 child, Thomas. Ed. Europe. Civil squad leader Am. Cyanamid Co., Wayne, N.J., 1974-76; sr. engr. Merck & Co., Rahway, N.J., 1976-77; project engr. Exxon Research and Engring., Florham Park, N.J., 1977-79; mem. tech. staff TRW Inc., Redondo Beach, Calif., 1980-81; project engr. research and devel. Todd Pacific Shipyards Corp., San Pedro, Calif., 1981-83; aerospace engr. U.S. Air Force, Los Angeles, 1983-85; supervisory gen. engr. U.S. Navy, Long Beach, Calif., U.S. Air Force, Los Angeles, 1985—. Mem. Am. Soc. Naval Engrs.

FOERST, JOHN GEORGE, JR., counselling service executive; b. Queens, N.Y., June 8, 1927; s. John George and Mary Elizabeth (McGinn) F.; m. Marion Theresa Cassidy, June 27, 1953; children—Gerard M.; m. Kathryn J.A. B.A., St. Johns U., Queens, N.Y., 1950. Regional rep. Nat. Found. for Infantile Paralysis, N.Y.C., 1950-52; campaign dir., v.p. Community Counselling Service, N.Y.C., 1952-59, v.p., asst. to pres., 1965-69, pres., 1969—; pres. John G. Foerst, Inc., N.Y.C., 1959-65; dir. 59 Wall St. Fund, N.Y.C. Contbg. author: Complete Guide to Corporate Fund Raising, 1982. Bd. dirs. St. Francis Hosp., Roslyn, N.Y., 1972—, Nassau Ctr. for Disabled, Woodbury, N.Y., 1974—, Human Resources Ctr., Albertson, N.Y., 1988—; chmn. Am. Assn. Fund Raising Counsel, N.Y.C., 1982; mem. Cardinal's Com. of Laity, Roman Catholic Archdiocese N.Y., 1984—. Mem. Am. Irish Cultural Inst., Nat. Council and Civil Bd. Dirs. Soc. Propagation of the Faith. Republican. Club: Union League. Lodge: Knights of Malta. Home: 77 Dover Rd Manhasset NY 11030 Office: Community Counseling Service Co 350 Fifth Ave Suite 7210 New York NY 10118

FOG, RASMUS, psychiatrist, researcher; b. Copenhagen, Oct. 15, 1936; s. Soeren and Else (Kofoed Olsen) F.; m. Lisbeth Regeur, Dec. 4, 1980; children: Soeren, Torben. MD, U. Copenhagen, 1963, Dr. Med., 1972. Trainee in neurology, psychiatry and medicine various Danish hosps., 1963-72; head psychiat. dept. and research lab. St. Hans Hosp., Roskilde, Denmark, 1972—, psychiatrist-in-chief, 1984—; mem. Danish Med. Research Council, 1984—. Author: Stereotypy and Catalepsy, 1972; contbr. over 100 articles on biol. psychiatry and neurology to sci. jours. Served to lt. Danish Army, 1963-64. Recipient research award Lundbeck Found., 1985. Mem. numerous Danish, Scandinavian and internat. psychiat. and neurol. sci. assns. Home: Parcelgaardsvej 6, DK 4000 Roskilde Denmark Office: St Hans Hosp Research Lab, DK-4000 Roskilde Denmark

FOGARASI, GYULA FRIGYES, construction company executive; b. Bucharest, Rumania, July 7, 1937; s. Gyula Geza and Katalin Maria (Resch) F.; m. Esther Maria Molnar, Sept. 17, 1964; children—Miklos, Andras, Fabian. B.Sc. in Engring., Tech. U. Civil Engring., Budapest, Hungary, 1960; Dr.Eng., 1980. Bldg. mgr. Kev-Metro Constrn. Co., Budapest, 1960-61; structural designer Iparterv Constrn. Co., Budapest, 1961-66; constrn. mgr. BVM Prefabrication Co., Budapest, 1966—, v.p. Fedn. Internat. Précontrainte; pres. Hungarian Fedn. Internat. Précontrainte Group; cons. Unido, Libya, Costa Rica; expert in prefabrication UN Indsl., Orgn.; Devel. lectr. prefabrication, design and constrn. Author: Welded Reinforcements, 1976; Joints of Concrete (Book of Year 1977), 1977; Prestressed Concrete Technology, 1986. Patentee concrete prefabrication. Recipient Outstanding Innovator award State Planning Office Ministry Housing, Hungary, 1975, Outstanding Inventor award, 1976, Outstanding Work Ministry Housing, 1979. Roman Catholic. Avocations: painting; skiing; wind surfing. Home: Bakats-utca 1-3 f 2, H-1093 Budapest Hungary Office: BVM Concrete and Reinforced, Concrete Works, Budafoki ut 209, H-1117 Budapest Hungary

FOGARTY, MARGARET MARY, psychologist; b. New Haven, Feb. 17, 1909; d. James Augustine and Grace Marion (Hyland) Fogarty; diploma New Haven Normal Sch., 1928; B.S., New Britain State Tchrs. Coll., 1939; M.A., Yale, 1944. Tchr. West Haven, Conn., 1928-52; sch. psychologist, dir. psychol. services West Haven Schs., 1952-79; pvt. practice, West Haven, 1954—; bd. dirs. Clifford Beers Guidance Clinic, 1975-83; mem. Catchment area 6 Mental Health Adv. Com., 1975—; mem. West Haven Mental Health Bd., 1974-82, v.p., 1975—; hon. bd. mem. Clifford Beers Clinic, 1984—. Mem. adv. com. West Haven Community Devel. Action Plan, Race Relations Com. Mem. Am., Conn. psychol. assns., Conn. Assn. Sch. Psychologists (sec. 1961-63, chmn. role and functions com. 1963-65, Disting. Service award 1983), NEA (life), West Haven Community Service Assn. (sec. 1969-70), West Haven Adminstrs. Assn. Roman Catholic. Editor: Study of Role and Function of School Psychological Personnel Working in the Public Schools of Connecticut, 1965. Home: 487 Washington Ave West Haven CT 06516

FOGEL, IRVING MARTIN, consulting engineer; b. Gloucester, Mass., Apr. 15, 1929; s. Jacob and Ethel (David) F.; B.S., Ind. Inst. Tech., 1954, D.Eng. (hon.), 1982; children: Ethan, Ronit. Civil engr. Ill. Hwy. Dept., Peoria, 1954-55; field engr. Peter Kiewit Sons Co., East Gary, Ind., 1955, field engr., progress engr., cost engr., Ogdensburg, N.Y., 1955-56; supt. grading and paving Merritt, Chapman & Scott, Binghamton, N.Y., 1956; cost engr. Drake-Merritt, Goose Bay, Labrador, 1956-57; constrn. mgmt. engr. Mil. Estimating Corp., Madrid, Spain, also P.I., 1957-58; project mgr. Ministry of Def., State Israel, 1958-59, Frederic R. Harris (Holland) N.V., The Hague, also Tehran, Iran, 1959-61; project mgr. Solel Boneh & Assocs., Addis Ababa, Ethiopia, 1961-63; asst. to tech. dir. Frederic R. Harris, Madrid, 1963-64; chief engr. McKee-Berger-Mansueto, Inc., N.Y.C., 1964-65, v.p. constrn. mgmt., 1965-69; pres. Fogel & Assocs., Inc., N.Y.C., also Detroit, Carmel (Calif.), Ft. Lauderdale (Fla.), 1969—; lectr. Registered profl. engr., 22 states, D.C., Israel. Fellow ASCE; mem. Am. Arbitration Assn., Am. Assn. Cost Engrs., Am. Inst. Constructors, Am. Mgmt. Assn., Constrn. Specifications Inst., Nat. Contract Mgmt. Assn., Nat. Soc. Profl. Engrs., N.Y. Bldg. Congress, Project Mgmt. Inst., Soc. Am. Mil. Engrs. Author guides and handbooks on constrn. bus., latest being: Planning, Financing, and Constructing Health Care Facilities, 1983. Contbr. articles to profl. jours. Home: 525 E 86th St New York NY 10028 Office: 373 Park Ave S New York NY 10016

FOGEL, JERRY, association executive, actor; b. Rochester, N.Y., Jan. 17, 1936; s. Max and Belle (Levy) R.; m. Benda Levison, Mar. 1, 1959 (div. 1969); children—David, Mark; m. Barbara Fromm, Dec. 23, 1978; children—David, Mark, Paige, Ross. Student, Wesleyan U., 1953-55, U.S. Mil. Acad., 1955-57, Mid-Valley Coll. Law, 1975-76; B.A., Pacific Western U., 1984. sr. v.p., bd. dirs. Martin Fromm & Assocs., Kansas City, Mo., 1979—; Pres. JB Productions, Inc., 1982-86; Radio personality, news, talk shows Sta. KCMO Radio; morning team co-host Sta. KCMO, 1982-86. Co-star in TV shows The Mothers-In-Law, 1966-68, The White Shadow, 1978-80, various TV shows, commercials, 3 movies, Los Angeles, 1966-80. Rep. primary candidate for U.S. House Calif. 1976, candidate Kansas City City Council, 1987; bd. overseers West Point Jewish Chapel Fund, N.Y., 1977—; pres. West Point Soc. Los Angeles, 1974-75; sec. West Point Soc. Kansas City, 1983—. Served to lt. U.S. Army, 1955-68; lt. comdr. N.Y. Guard, 1988—. Mem. Screen Actors Guild, (nat. dir. 1976-78), Am. Federation TV and Radio Artists (pres. Rochester, N.Y. 1964), Assn. AUS, Assn. Grads. U.S. Mil. Acad., Assn. USN (pres. Kansas City Chpt.), Am. Assn. Mng. Gen. Agts. (exec. v.p.) State Def. Force Assn. of U.S. a9exec. dir.), Diamond Council of Am. (exec. dir.). Sigma Chi. Lodges: Rotary, Masons, Shriners. Office: Martin Fromm & Assocs 9140 Ward Pkwy Kansas City MO 64114

FOGEL, RICHARD, lawyer; b. Bklyn., Feb. 9, 1932; s. Sam and Anna (Markow) F.; m. Sheila Feldman, Dec. 21, 1957; children—Bruce, Lori Ellen. B.A., York Coll., CUNY, 1971; J.D., N.Y. Law Sch., 1974. Bar: N.J. 1976, U.S. Dist. Ct. N.J. 1976, N.Y. 1981, U.S. Tax Ct. 1977. Tax law specialist IRS, Newark, 1975-77; sr. pension cons., atty. N.Y. Life, N.Y.C., 1977-81; sole practice, Franklin, N.J., 1981-85, Wayne, N.J., 1985—, McAfee, N.J., 1988—; lectr. Inst. for Continuing Legal Edn., Newark, 1977—; mem. adj. faculty Upsala Coll., East Orange, N.J., 1978—. Recipient Certs. of Appreciation, IRS, Newark, 1977, Inst. Continuing Legal Edn., Newark, 1981-82, 84, Cert. in Recognition of Accomplishments, Coop. Extension Cook Coll., Rutgers U., 1982, Disting. Grad. award York Coll., 1984. Mem. N.J. State Bar Assn. (tax sect.). Jewish. Lodge: Masons. Home: RR 7 28 Elizabeth Dr Sussex NJ 07461 Office: Vernon Colonial Plaza PO Box 737 Rt 94 McAfee NJ 07428

FOGEL, STEVEN TEDD, physician; b. St. Louis, July 7, 1950; s. Harry Y. and Evelyn F.; m. Connie Jean Eller, Dec. 21, 1973 (div. Mar. 1980); 1 dau., Melissa Shawn. AB, Washington U., St. Louis, 1973; MD, U. Mo., 1976. Diplomate Am. Bd. Ob-Gyn., Nat. Bd. Med. Examiners. Intern, Kansas City (Mo.) Gen. Hosp., 1976-77; resident dept. ob-gyn U. Mo., Kansas City, 1976-79, chief resident, 1979-80, asst. clin. prof. dept. ob-gyn; practice medicine specializing in ob-gyn, Kansas City, 1980—; coordinator resident physician teaching program in ob-gyn Menorah Med. Ctr., Kansas City. Mem. AMA, Mo. State Med. Assn., Jackson County Med. Soc., Kansas City Gynecol. Soc., Am. Coll. Obstetricians and Gynecologists, Phi Beta Kappa. Jewish. Clubs: K.C. Racquet. Lodge: B'nai B'rith. Home: 3715 Shawnee Mission Pkwy Fairway KS 66205 Office: Plaza Medical Bldg 1000 E 50th St Suite 300 Kansas City MO 64110

FOHRMANN, JÜRGEN ERNST OTTO, German educator; b. Bielefeld, Fed. Republic Germany, Oct. 16, 1953; s. Alfred and Lotte (Karcher) F.; m. Ilona Richter, April 6, 1973; 1 child, Melanie. Staatsexamen, U. Bielefeld, 1977, Dr Phil., 1980. Sci. asst. Fakultät für Linguistik/Literaturwissenschaft U. Bielefeld, 1977-78, research asst. Ctr. for Interdisciplinary Studies, 1979-82, asst. prof., 1983-84; scholar Deutsche Forschungsgemeinschaft U. Bielefeld, Bonn, Fed. Republic Germany, 1985-87; dir. research project on history of philology U. Bielefeld, 1985—, also pvt. dozent für linguistic/literaturwissenschaft. Author: Geschichte der deutschen Robinsonaden, 1981; contbr. articles on utopian lit. and history of philology to profl. jours. Mem. Internat. Vereinigung germanistische Sprach-und Literaturwissenschaft. Mem. Evangelical Ch. Home: Bielefelder Strasse 76, 4806 Werther Federal Republic of Germany Office: U Bielefeld, Universitätstrasse, 4800 Bielefeld 1 Federal Republic of Germany

FOK, THOMAS DSO YUN, civil engineer; b. Canton, China, July 1, 1921; came to U.S., 1947, naturalized, 1956; s D. H. and C. (Tse) F.; m. Maria M.L. Liang, Sept. 18, 1949. B.Eng., Nat. Tung-Chi U., Szechuan, China, 1945; M.S., U. Ill., 1948; M.B.A. Dr. Nadler Money Marketeer scholar, NYU, 1950; Ph.D., Carnegie-Mellon U., 1956. Registered profl. engr., N.Y., Pa., Ohio, Ill., Ky., W.Va., Ind., Md., Fla. Structural designer Lummus Co., N.Y.C., 1951-53; design engr. Richardson, Gordon & Assocs., cons. engrs., Pitts., 1956-58; assoc. prof. engring. Youngstown U., Ohio, 1958-67, dir. computing ctr., 1963-67; ptnr. Cernica, Fok & Assocs., cons. engrs., Youngstown, Ohio, 1958-64; prin. Thomas Fok & Assocs., cons. engrs., Youngstown, Ohio, 1964-65; ptnr. Mosure-Fok & Syrakis Co., Ltd., cons. Engrs., Youngstown, Ohio, 1965-76; cons. engr. to Mahoning County Engr. Ohio, 1960-65; pres. Computing Systems & Tech., Youngstown, Ohio, 1967-72; chmn. Thomas Fok and Assocs., Ltd., cons. engrs., Youngstown, Ohio, 1977—. Contbr. articles to profl. jours. Trustee Pub. Library of Youngstown and Mahoning County, 1973—; trustee Youngstown State U. Found, 1975—; trustee Youngstown State U., 1975-84, chmn., 1981-83. Recipient Walter E. and Caroline H. Watson Found. Disting. Prof.'s award Youngstown U., 1966, Outstanding Person award Mahoning Valley Tech. Socs. Council, 1987. Fellow ASCE; mem. Am. Concrete Inst., Internat. Assn. for Bridge and Structural Engring., Am. Soc. Engring. Edn., Nat. Soc. Profl. Engrs., AAAS, Soc. Am. Mil. Engrs., Ohio Acad. Sci., N.Y. Acad. Sci., Sigma Xi, Beta Gamma Sigma, Sigma Tau, Delta Pi Sigma. Lodge: Rotary. Home: 325 S Canfield-Niles Rd Youngstown OH 44515 Office: 3896 Mahoning Ave Youngstown OH 44515

FOKUO, EMMANUEL ADU, mechanical engineer; b. Mampong-Ashanti, Ghana, Apr. 18, 1954; s. Samuel Kwaku Fokuo and Adwoa Sika; m. Dora Afua Pokuaah, Dec. 31, 1984; children: Ebenezer Adu Dwomoh, Rhoda Adu Fokuo. B. Engring., Sunyani Tech. Inst., 1972; Mech. Engring., Sch. Mines, 1974, Takoradi Poly. Inst., 1976. Maintenance trainee Volta Aluminium Co. Ltd., Tema, Ghana, 1976-78; mech. technician Mim Timber Co. Ltd., Ghana, 1978-79; plant engr. Trasacco Furniture Ltd., Accra, Ghana, 1979; plant and mech. engr. Poku Transport Industries Ltd., Kumasi, Ghana, 1979-85, asst. tech. and prodn. mgr., 1985-88; mech. engr. Ehwia Wood Products Ltd, Ghana, 1988—; tutor mech. engring. dept. Kumasi Poly. Inst., 1982. Designer Dimension-Push Bench, Circular Saw Machine. Methodist. Avocations: reading; writing; riding; photography. Home: RBR 2 Kofiase Rd, Mampong-Ashanti Ghana also: Plot 18 Block U, Asokwa, Kumasi Ghana Mailing Address: PO Box 9004, Ahensan, Kumasi Ghana also: Plot 17 Block Q, Ayigya, Kumasi Ghana

FOL, JEAN-JACQUES, historian, educator, university president; b. Clamecy, France, June 19, 1930; s. Louis Francois and Aimee (Marcelot) F.; m. Edith Evelyn Morael, July 11, 1957 (div. Nov. 1987); children—Emmanuel, Juliette, Nicolas, Camille-Solveig, Jean-Baptists. B.E.P.C., Baccalaureat Moderne et Philosophie-Lettres, Diplome d'eleve brevete de l'E.N.L.O.V. (Finnish-Hungarian Langs.), Licence-es-Lettres; Doctorat de 3eme cycle, Doctorat d'Etat d'Histoire. Writing clk. Ministry of Fin., France, 1949-50; French lang. lectr. Lycee normal de Helsinki & Ecole Suedoise des HEC, 1950, 52; tchr. Centre Psycho-pedagogique, Senlis, France, 1953, 13th dist. of the Seine, France, 1954-59, Lycee franco-finlandais, 1959-62; CEG J. laborde, Mantasoa, Madagascar, 1962-65, CEG Lycee Rabearivelo, Tananarive, Madagascar, 1965-68; asst. instrn. Lycee Rabearivelo, Tananarive, 1968-70; asst. master Univ. du Benin, Lome, Togo, 1970-72; asst. master U. Paris VII, 1972-78, conf. master, 1978-79, prof., 1979, v.p., 1976-81, pres., 1982-87; dir. CIREN, 1978—, French-Can. integrated project of didactic disciplines, 1980—; v.p. Conférence des Présidents d'Université, 1982-83; pres. de la Commn. des Relations Extérievres, 1983-86; mem. du Comité Directeur de la Conférence des Recteurs Européens, 1984—; mem. Social and Econ. Com. of France, 1984—; mem. exec. com. Maison des Cultures du Monde, 1984—. Translator: Souls of Black Folk du Dr. W.E.B. Dubois, 1957; Ici sous l'etoile polaire de V. Linna, 3 vols., 1961-64; author: Petsamo 1920-44, 1968; Accession de la Finlande a l'Independance 1917-1919, 1977; Finlande Hier et Aujourd'hui, 1960; L'Europe du Nord aux XIXene et XXeme siecles, 1978; Finlands-Peuple et civilisation, 1982; Suede, 1982; contbr. articles to profl. jours. Decorated officier Ordre des Palmes Academiques, 1976; chevalier Legion d'honneur, 1983; Svomen Valkotisen Ruusun Komentajan Risti, 1986. Mem. Association des Universités Partiellements au Entièrement de Langue Française (exec. com.), Association linquistique franco-asiatique (pres. 1978—). Office: Univ de Paris VII, 2 Pl Jussieu, 75251 Paris 5 France

FOLCKER, JONAS LARS, airline executive; b. Stockholm, Apr. 4, 1933; s. Jonas Fredrik and Elsa (Olsson) F.; m. Gunilla Gaulitz, May 2, 1957 (div. Oct. 1963); 1 child, Johan; m. Susanne Inger Winbladh, Oct. 1, 1964; children: Frederik, Adam. Student pub. schs., Stockholm. Traffic officer Scandinavian Airlines, Stockholm, 1953-62; officer Swedish UN Contingent, Leopoldville, Kinshasha, 1962-63; sr. traffic officer Linjeflyg, Stockholm, 1963; sr. traffic officer Brit. European Airways, Stockholm, 1963-66, airport mgr., 1966-70; dist. supt. Brit. European Airways, Gothenburg, Sweden, 1970-73; dist. mgr. for West and South Sweden Brit. Airways, Landvetter, 1973—; chmn. Airline Operators Com., Stockholm, 1966-70, Gothenburg, 1970-73. Served to 1st lt. Swedish Army, 1962-63. Mem. Airline Reps. Gothenburg (founder). Clubs: Göta Par Bricole, Skal (Gothenburg); Forsgarden Golf (Kungsbacka, Sweden). Home: Bjornbärsvägen 8, S-434 99 Kungsbacka Sweden Office: Brit Airways, Box 2085, S-438 02 Landvetter Sweden

FÖLDES, CSABA JÁNOS, linguist, educator; b. Bácsalmás, Bács-Kiskun, Hungary, June 8, 1958; parents: János and Margit Katalin (Szekeres) F. Diploma, Lajos Kossuth U., Debrecen, Hungary, 1981, PhD, 1983; PhD, Friedrich Schiller U., Jena, German Dem. Republic, 1987. Language tchr. Tech. Coll. Machine Engring., Kecskemét, Hungary, 1981-85; asst. prof. Tchr. Tng. Coll., Szeged, Hungary, 1985-87; head German dept. Gy. Juhász Tchr. Tng. Coll., Szeged, 1987—; com. pres. Tchr. German Langs. Lit. Hungarian Colls. Author: Magyar-német-orosz beszédfordulatok, 1987; contbr. articles in field. Grantee Hungarian Acad. Scis., 1984. Mem. Soc. Modern Philology Hungarian Acad. Scis. Home: Szivarvany u 25, H-6725 Szeged Hungary Office: Tchr Tng Coll, Haman Kato u 25, H-6701 Szeged Hungary

FOLDES, LUCIEN PAUL, economics educator; b. Vienna, Austria, Nov. 19, 1930; s. Egon and Marta (Landau) F. B in Commerce, U. London, 1950, D in Bus. Adminstrn., 1951, MS, 1952. Asst. lectr. econs. London Sch. Econs., 1951-52, 54-55, lectr. econs., 1955-61, reader econs., 1961-79, prof. econs., 1979—. Author: Optimal Accumulation in a Neo-classical Model with Risk, 1988; contbr. articles to profl. jours. Served to lt. British Army, 1952-54. Rockefeller Travelling fellow, 1962. Fellow Royal Econ. Soc.; mem. Am. Econ. Assn., Inst. Math. Stats., London Math. Soc. Office: London Sch Econs, Houghton St, London WC2A 2AE, England

FOLEY, DANIEL EDMUND, real estate development executive; b. St. Paul, Mar. 1, 1926; s. Edward and Gerry (Fitzgarld) F.; student U. Minn., 1941-43; m. Paula Evans, Apr. 1, 1946. Chmn. bd. Realty Ptnrs. Ltd., Los Angeles; pres. Alpha Property Mgmt. Served with AUS, 1943-46. Office: 523 W 6th St Suite 385 Los Angeles CA 90014

FOLEY, DANIEL JOSEPH, gerontologist, statistician, researcher; b. Alexandria, Va., Dec. 11, 1952; s. Raymond Patrick and Maria Lillian (Trejo) F.; m. Shelby Leland Sotera, Sept. 12, 1981; children: Isaac, Zachary. B.A. in Sociology, George Mason U., 1979; M.S. in Biostats., Georgetown U., 1986. Statistician, Nat. Ctr. for Health Stats., Hyattsville, Md., 1978-81, Nat. Inst. Aging, Bethesda, Md., 1981—. Publ. articles on nursing home care. Mem. Am. Statis. Assn. Home: 1127 N Kentucky St Arlington VA 22205 Office: Nat Inst Aging 7550 Wisconsin Ave Bethesda MD 20814

FOLEY, DANIEL RONALD, personnel executive; b. Chgo., Dec. 13, 1941; s. Daniel Edward and Louise Jean (Connolly) F.; m. Mae Geraldine Muscarello, Jan. 30, 1965; 1 child, Louise Ann. AB in Psychology, Marquette U., 1965; JD, Depaul U., 1971. Bar: Ill 1971, U.S. Dist. Ct. (no. dist.) Ill. 1971, U.S. Supreme Ct. 1975. Personnel recruiter Civil Service Commn. City of Chgo., 1965-66; personnel adminstr. Alberto Culver Co., Melrose Park, Ill., 1966-67; personnel dir. Litton Industries, Des Plaines, Ill., 1967-68; equal oportunity coordinator, mgr. labor relations Canteen Corp., Chgo., 1968-71; mgr. labor relations Internat. Telephone and Telegraph World Headquarters, N.Y.C., 1971-79, dir. employee relations, 1979-81, 1981-85; dir. employee relations, environ. health and safety, group v.p. human resources IBP, Dakota City, Nebr., 1985-88; sr. cons. TSM, Inc., Ann Arbor, Mich., 1988—; speaker labor law and bus. seminars, Wharton Sch. U. Pa., St. Mary's Coll., U. Mich. Mem. ABA. Roman Catholic (deacon). Home: 2025 Winsted Ct Ann Arbor MI 48103 Office: TSM Inc PO Box 985 24 Frank Lloyd Wright Dr Ann Arbor MI 48106

FOLEY, EUGENE ARTHUR, controller; b. San Jose, Calif., May 6, 1953; s. Eugene Frank and Shirley Ann (Merrill) F.; m. Kathleen Anne Welles, May 15, 1976; children: Eugene Welles, Patrick Michael, Brian Ross. BSBA, U. Hartford, 1976; MS in Taxation, Golden Gate U., 1979. CPA, Calif., Conn.; cert. mgmt. acct.; cert. info. systems auditor. Acct. J.K. Lasser et al, San Jose, 1976-79; internal auditor Carter Hawley Hale, Los Angeles, 1979-81; lectr., asst. prof. Calif. State U., Sacramento, 1979-84; owner, cons. E.A. Foley Accountancy, Sacramento, 1981-84; corp. audit mgr. Emhart Corp., Farmington, Conn., 1984-86; controller Powers Mfg. Inc. div. Emhart Corp., Elmira, N.Y., 1986. Sec., treas. and exec. dir. Elmira YMCA, 1986 and 1987; treas. Supreme Ct. Project, Calif., 1985-86; v.p. fin., 1987 and treas., 1988, Sullivan Trail Council Boy Scouts; treas. Calif. Pub. Policy Found., 1987-88. Mem. Am. Inst. CPA's, Calif. Soc. CPA's, Inst. Internal Auditors (cert.), Inst. Mgmt. Accts., EDP Auditors Assn., Inst. Cost Analysts (cert.), Mensa, Am. Numismatic Assn., Am. First Day Cover Soc., Am. Topical Assn. (life), Am. Soc. Personnel Adminstrn., Data Processing Mgmt. Assn. Lodges: Masons, Scottish Rite. Home: 514 Underwood Ave Elmira NY 14905 Office: Powers Mfg Inc 1140 Sullivan St Elmira NY 14901

FOLEY, MICHAEL THOMAS, consulting firm executive; b. Piedmont, S.D., July 21, 1945; s. Peter Francis and Mary Kathryn (Brockhoff) F.; m. Marilyn Kathryn Etten, July 9, 1977; children—Michelle Kathryn, Matthew John. B.A. in Math. and Sociology, Black Hills State Coll., Spearfish, S.D., 1967; B.S. in Computer Sci., Nat. Coll. Bus., Rapid City, S.D., 1971. Instr. data processing Gates Coll., Waterloo, Iowa, 1971-72; systems analyst Blackhawk Broadcast Corp., Waterloo, 1973; systems engr. NCR Corp., Dayton, Ohio, 1974-78; dir. data processing Forward Communications Corp., Wausau, Wis., 1978-80, v.p. data communications, 1980-88; pres. Realtime Computer Cons., Wausau, Wis., 1988—; cons. in field. Served with U.S. Army, 1969-70. Decorated Vietnam Cross Gallentry, Bronze Star, Air medals, and numerous commendations; recipient Letter of Commendation, NCR, 1976. Mem. Fedn. Computer Users, Computer User Group, Nat. Computer Graphics Assn, Nat. Assn. Investors Corp. Roman Catholic. Designer, installer computerized broadcast systems, info. systems, computerized newsroom for various radio and TV stas. Home: 3707 Powers St Schofield WI 54476 Office: 610 Jackson St Suite D Wausau WI 54401

FOLEY, PETER HINMAN, insurance company executive; b. Hanover, N.H., June 17, 1947; s. Robert Joseph and Katherine (Hinman) F.; m. Charlene Anne Harrison, Oct. 12, 1968; children—Kristin A., Peter M., Sara K. B.A. summa cum laude, Franklin Pierce Coll., 1971; M.B.A., Fairleigh Dickinson U., 1974. Underwriter Aetna Life and Casualty, Newark, 1974-76; asst. sec. Gen. Reins. Corp., N.Y.C., 1976-78; v.p. Insco, Ltd., Hamilton, Bermuda, 1978-79; exec. v.p. I.N.A., N.Y.C., 1979-81; mng. dir. British Nat., London, 1981-84, Sedgwick Group Underwriting Services, London, 1984-85, Rivers Group subs. Sedgwick Group, London, 1985—; dir. E.W. Payne Cos. Ltd., mng. dir. N. Am. subs., 1987—. Author: (with others) Executive Insurance, 1980. Contbr. articles to profl. jours. Served with U.S. Army, 1968-70. Republican. Roman Catholic. Club: Union League (N.Y.C.). Avocations: sailing; jogging. Office: Rivers Group Ltd, 150-152 Fenchurch St, London EC3, England

FOLEY, ROBERT DOUGLAS, librarian; b. St. Jean, Que., Can., Feb. 20, 1954. BA with honors, York U., Toronto, Ont., 1977; MLS, U. Western (London) Ont., 1978. Cert. in Ednl. TV London (Ont.) Bd. Edn. Head librarian Banff (Alta.) Centre for Continuing Education, Sch. Fine Arts; reference librarian Architecture and Fine Arts Library, U. Manitoba, Winnipeg; founder Banff Centre Library, 1979; cons. in field. Contrb. articles to profl. jours. Mem. Can. Library Assn., Can. Assn. for Info. Sci., Art Libraries Soc. N. Am., Can. Assn. Music Libraries, Can. Art Libraries Soc., Alta. Assn. Coll. Librarians, Library Assn. Alta. Office: The Banff Centre, Box 1020, Banff, AB Canada T0L 0C0

FOLK, SHARON LYNN, printing company executive; b. Bellefontaine, Ohio, June 13, 1945; d. Emerson Dewey and Berdena Isabelle (Brown) F.; A.A. in Liberal Arts, Sacred Heart Coll., 1965, L.H.D. (hon.), 1985; A.B. in Econs. and Bus. Adminstrn., Belmont Abbey Coll., 1968. Exec. v.p. Nat. Bus. Forms, Inc., Greeneville, Tenn., 1968-73; sec., treas. Nat. Forms Co., Inc., Gastonia, N.C., 1969-73, chairperson, bd. dirs., pres., 1973—, SF Enterprises, Inc., Greeneville, 1987—. Andrew Johnson Golf Club, Inc., Greeneville, 1987—; mem. bus. adv. com. Bus. Ptnrs., Inc., Washington, 1987—; bd. dirs. Andrew Johnson Bank, Greeneville, chairperson employee relations com., Internat. Bus. Forms Industries, Arlington, Va., 1978-83. Mem. fin. com. YMCA, Greeneville, 1977-78, bd. dirs., 1977-80; bd. dirs. United Way, 1980-85, Greeneville, Takoma Hosp. Found., Greeneville, 1987—; mem. presdl. steering com. U.S. Senator Howard Baker, 1979-80; mem. Republican Presdl. Task Force, 1981—; life mem. Rep. Nat. Com., 1981—; mem. Rep. Senatorial Inner Circle, Washington, 1984—; vice-chmn. parish council Notre Dame Cath. Ch., Greeneville, 1984-85, chmn., 1985-87; founding mem. Com. 200, Chgo., 1981—, vice chmn., membership chmn. Southeast region, 1983-84, bd. dirs. 1984-85, v.p., bd. dirs., 1985-86; mem. bd. advisors Belmont Abbey Coll., 1984—, trustee, 1986-89; trustee Sacred Heart Coll., Belmont, N.C., 1985—; 2d lt. CAP, 1984—; maj. Civilian Guard, Middleboro, Ky., 1986—; oblate Order of St. Benedict, Our Lady Help of Christians Abbey, Belmont, 1967—. 1st lt. Search and Rescue Pilot Civil Air Patrol, Aux. USAF, Maxwell Air Force Base, Ala., 1984—. Mem. Nat. Bus. Forms Assn., Forms Mfrs. Credit Interchange, Am. Mgmt. Assn., Tenn. Bus. Roundtable (bd. dirs. 1986), Belmont Abbey Alumni Coll. Assn. (bd. dirs. 1986—), U.S. Tennis Assn. (life), Airplane Owners and Pilots Assn. Avocations: tennis, airplane pilot, photography, golf, reading, music. Home: 1131 Hixon Ave Greeneville TN 37743 Office: Nat Bus Forms Co Inc 100 Pennsylvania Ave Greeneville TN 37743

FOLKS, ROBERT LOGUE, lawyer; b. Amityville, N.Y., Aug. 6, 1947; s. T. John Jr. and Bernice (O'Keefe) F.; m. Rosemary Elizabeth Ruggiero, June 28, 1975; children: Kelly, Shannon, Jennifer. BA, U. Notre Dame, 1969; LLD, St. John's U., Jamaica, N.Y., 1972. Bar: Fla. 1973, N.Y. 1973, U.S. Dist. Ct. (so. dist.) N.Y. 1980, U.S. Ct. Mil. Appeals 1980, U.S. Ct. Appeals (2d cir.) 1980, U.S. Supreme Ct. 1980. Asst. dist. atty. Suffolk County Dist. Atty.'s Office, Riverhead, N.Y., 1972-84; asst. county atty. Suffolk County Atty.'s Office, Hauppauge, N.Y., 1984; asst. atty. so. dist. U.S. Atty.'s Office, N.Y.C., 1984-87; ptnr. Rivkin, Radler, Dunne & Bayh, Uniondale, N.Y., 1987—; v.p. Edn. Assistance Corp., Port. Washington, N.Y., 1984—; pres. Suffolk County Acad. of Law, Ronkontoma, N.Y., 1985-87. 1st v.p. Community Mediation Bd., Coram, N.Y., 1983—, Police Athletic League, Yaphank, N.Y., 1985—. Recipient Recognition award Suffolk County Acad. of Law, 1981-85. Fellow N.Y. State Bar Found. (recognition award 1983); mem. N.Y. State Bar Assn. (chmn., county cts. com. recognition award 1982-85), Criminal Bar Assn. (bd. dirs. 1980-81, sec. 1981-82), Suffolk County Bar Assn. (bd. dirs. 1985-87, recognition award 1985), Suffold County Acad. of law (pres. 1985-87). Republican. Roman Catholic. Clubs: N.Y. Athletic (N.Y.C.); Southward Ho Country (Brentwood, N.Y.); Sayville (N.Y.) Yacht. Home: 150 Kilburn Rd Garden City NY 11530

FOLLANSBEE, DOROTHY LELAND, publisher; b. St. Louis, Mar. 24, 1911; d. Robert Leathan and Minnie Cowden (Yowell) Lund; grad. Sarah Lawrence Coll., 1931; m. Austin Porter Leland, Apr. 24, 1935 (dec. 1975); children—Mary Talbot Leland MacCarthy, Austin Porter Jr. (dec.), Irene Austin Leland Barzantny; m. 2d, Robert Kerr Follansbee, Oct. 20, 1979. Pres., Station List Publ. Co., St. Louis, 1975—; dir. Downtown St. Louis Inc. Hon. chmn. Old Post Office Landmark Com., 1975—; bd. dirs. Services Bur. St. Louis, 1943, pres., 1951; bd. dirs. Robert E. Lee Meml. Assn.; mem. St. Louis County Parks and Recreation Dept., 1969; bd. dirs. Stratford Hall, Va., 1953—, pres., 1967-70, treas., 1970—; bd. dirs. Historic Bldgs. Commn. St. Louis County, 1959-85, Mo. Hist. Soc., 1960-77, Mo. Mansion Preservation Com., 1975-80, Chatillon DeMenil House, 1977-79. Recipient Landmarks award Landmarks Assn. St. Louis, 1974; Pub. Service award GSA, 1978; Crownenshield award Nat. Trust for Hist Preservation, 1979. Mem. Colonial Dames Am., Daus. of Cin. Episcopalian. Clubs: St. Louis Country, Fox Chapel Golf, Princeton of N.Y., St. Louis Jr. League. Home: 35 Pointer Ln Saint Louis MO 63124 also: 1001 River Oaks Dr Pittsburgh PA 15215 Office: 906 Olive St Saint Louis MO 63101

FOLLICK, EDWIN DUANE, chiropractic physician, legal educator, educational administrator; b. Glendale, Calif., Feb. 4, 1935; s. Edwin Fulfford and Esther Agnes (Catherwood) F.; m. Marilyn K. Sherk, Mar. 24, 1986. BA Calif. State U., Los Angeles, 1956, MA, 1961; MA Pepperdine U., 1957, MPA, 1977; ThD St. Andrews Theol. Coll., Sem. of the Free Protestant Episcopal Ch., London, 1958; MS in Library Sci., U. So. Calif., 1963, MEd in Instructional Materials, 1964, AdvMEd in Edn. Adminstrn., 1969; Calif. Coll. Law, 1965; LLB Blackstone Law Sch., 1966, JD, 1967; DC Cleve. Chiropractic Coll., Los Angeles, 1972; PhD, Academia Theatina, Pescara, 1978. Tchr., library adminstr. Los Angeles City Schs., 1957-68; law librarian Glendale U. Coll. Law, 1968-69; coll. librarian Cleveland Chiropractic Coll., Los Angeles, 1969-74, dir. edn. and admissions, 1974-84, prof. jurisprudence, 1975—, dean student affairs, 1976—, chaplain, 1985— ; assoc. prof. Newport U., 1982—; extern prof. St. Andrews Theol. Coll., London, 1961; dir. West Valley Chiropractic Health Ctr., 1972—. Contbr. articles to profl. jours. Served as chaplain's asst. U.S. Army, 1958-60. Decorated Cavaliere Internat. Order legion of Honor of Immacolata (Italy); knight of Malta, Sovereign Order of St. John of Jerusalem; chevalier Ordre Militaire et Hospitalier de St. Lazare de Jerusalem, numerous others. Mem. ALA, NEA, Am. Assn. Sch. Librarians, Los Angeles Sch. Library Assn., Calif. Media and Library Educators Assn., Assn. Coll and Research Librarians, Am. Assn. Law Librarians, Am. Chiropractic Assn., Internat. Chiropractors Assn., Nat. Geog. Soc., Internat. Platform Assn., Phi Delta Kappa, Sigma Chi Psi, Delta Tau Alpha. Democrat. Episcopalian. Home: 6435 Jumilla Ave Woodland Hills CA 91367 Office: 590 N Vermont Ave Los Angeles CA 90004 also: 7022 Owensmouth Ave Canoga Park CA 91303

FOLLINGSTAD, HENRY GEORGE, mathematics educator emeritus, consultant; b. Wanamingo, Minn., Jan. 6, 1922; s. Henry A. and Lottie R. (Johnson) F.; m. Helen Jane Chrislock, May 26, 1945; children—Nancy Ellen, Daniel Mark, Karen Joy, Sharon Ruth, Carl Martin. BEE, U. Minn., 1947, MS, 1971. Mem. tech. staff Bell Telephone Labs., Inc., Murray Hill, N.J., 1948-62; instr. Augsburg Coll., Mpls., 1962-66, asst. prof., 1966-78, assoc. prof., 1978-87, prof. emeritus, 1987—; sci. research cons. Honeywell, Mpls., St. Paul, 1964-81; electronics research cons. North Star Research and Devel. Inst., Mpls., 1965-66. Contbr. numerous articles to profl. jours. Trustee Luther Coll. Bible and Liberal Arts, Teaneck, N.J., 1960-63; Bible lectr. Augsburg Coll., 1983, Central Luth. Ch., Mpls., 1969-71, 81-82. Served in USAAF, 1943-46. Mem. IEEE (sr.), Math. Assn. Am., Tau Beta Pi, Sigma Pi Sigma. Lutheran. Home: 3506 Garfield Ave S Minneapolis MN 55408 Office: 731 21st Ave S Minneapolis MN 55454

FOLSOM, JAMES CANNON, psychiatrist; b. Sweetwater, Ala., Oct. 11, 1921; s. Douglas Lawrence and Lillian (Hart) F.; student Livingston State Coll., 1939-41, U. Ariz., 1941, U. Ala., 1942-44; M.D., Washington U., St. Louis, 1946; postgrad. U. Vienna (Austria), 1948; m. Ruth Elizabeth Becton, Aug. 14, 1947 (div. 1950); 1 dau., Ivy Folsom Simpson; m. 2d, Geneva Rose Scheihing, Dec. 29, 1958 (div. 1977); 1 dau., Lisa Kay; m. 3d, Barbara A. Foster, July 10, 1982. Intern, Jefferson-Hillman Hosp., Birmingham, Ala., 1946-47; psychiatrist Hill Crest Sanitarium, Birmingham, 1949; resident in psychiatry Timberlawn Sanitarium, Dallas, 1950-52, staff psychiatrist, 1952; resident in psychiatry Menninger Sch. Psychiatry, VA Hosp., Topeka, 1952-53; admission physician VA Hosp., Topeka, 1953-55, chief phys. medicine rehab. service, 1955-60; clin. dir. Mental Health Inst., Mt. Pleasant, Iowa, 1960-62; chief of staff VA Hosp., Tuscaloosa, Ala., 1962-66, hosp. dir., 1966-71; dep. commr. for hosps. Ala. Dept. Mental Health, also supt. Bryce Hosp., Tuscaloosa, 1971-72; dir. rehab. medicine service, dept. medicine and surgery VA Central Office, Washington, 1972-76; dir. Internat. Center for Disabled, N.Y.C., 1976-84; assoc. chief staff for extended care VA Med. Ctr., Topeka, 1984-86, chief rehab. medicine service, acting chief intermediate medicine service, 1986—; clin. prof. psychiatry Menninger Sch. Psychiatry,

1953-60, N.Y. U. Med. Center, 1976—; asso. clin. prof. psychiatry U. Ala. Sch. Medicine, 1963-72, adj. prof. health care mgmt., 1972-76; mem. teaching roster Med. Assn. State of Ala., Montgomery, 1968-72; clin. prof. psychiatry and behavioral scis. George Washington U. Sch. Medicine, 1974-76; cons. Ala. Dept. Mental Health and state hosps., 1969-71. Mem. Interagy. bd. U.S. Civil Service Examiners for North Ala., 1966-71; mem. Ala. Gov.'s Com. on Employment of Handicapped, 1967-72; mem. steering com. Comprehensive Mental Health Center Program, Bibb, Pickens and Tuscaloosa counties, 1967-70; mem. adv. council Am. Corrective Therapy Assn., 1972—; mem. regional adv. com. Rehab. Research and Tng. Center, George Washington U., 1974-76; mem. adv. bd. Nat. Rehab. Tng. Inst., 1973-74; chmn. Ala. White House Conf. on Aging, 1971; spl. field rep. Accreditation Council for Psychiat. Facilities, Joint Commn. on Accreditation Hosps., 1973-78; mem. spl. adv. bd. reality orientation tng. project Am. Hosp. Assn., 1973-75, adv. com. for devel. exams. for occupational therapists, 1973-75; mem. med. com. Pres.'s Com. on Employment of Handicapped, 1975-86, vice chmn., 1981-86, mem. exec. com., 1976-86, mem. steering com. of exec. com., 1982-86, mem. med., health and ins. com., 1987—; bd. dirs. Ala. Assn. Mental Health, Tuscaloosa County Assn. Mental Health, Tuscaloosa County Boys Club, United Fund Tuscaloosa County, Alzheimer's Disease and Related Disorders Assn., Topeka, 1986—, Vol. Ctr. of Topeka, 1986—, Huntington's Disease Soc. Am., 1987; nat. project adv. council Boys' Clubs Am., 1977-81; bd. mgmt. Tuscaloosa County YMCA; mem. adv. bd. Tuscaloosa County Salvation Army, Mental Health Bd. Bibb, Pickens and Tuscaloosa counties; mem. bd. advisers Ala. Womens Hall of Fame; trustee Menninger Found., Topeka, 1972—, Wesley Homes Found., Atlanta, 1971-74. Served to capt. M.C., AUS, 1943-46. Recipient Dir.'s Commendation awards VA Hosp., Topeka, 1960, VA Hosp., Tuscaloosa, 1965, Superior Performance award VA Central Office, 1969, Adminstr.'s Commendation medal VA Central Office, 1969, Achievement award Nat. Rehab. Conf., 1973, John E. Davis award Am. Corrective Therapy Assn., 1974, Meritorious Service award Tex. Assn. Homes for Aging, 1974, others; named Boss of Yr., VA Hosp. Secs. Assn., 1970, also Am. Bus. Women's Assn., Tuscaloosa, 1971; diplomate Am. Bd. Psychiatry and Neurology. Fellow Am. Geriatric Soc., Am. Psychiat. Assn. (com. chmn., editor Newsletter Ala. Dist. br., chmn. nat. rehab. com. 1980—, chmn. com. on rehab. N.Y. County dist. br. 1979-81, mem. com. on aging 1978—), Am. Coll. Psychiatrists; mem. AMA, Menninger Sch. Psychiatry Alumni Assn. (editor bull., past pres.; mem. nat. adv. council), Tuscaloosa County Med. Soc., Ala. Acad. Neurology and Psychiatry (past pres.), N.Y. Acad. Medicine (sec. sect. geriatric medicine 1981-82, chmn. 1983-84), N.Y. State Soc. Indsl. Medicine, Assn. Regional Planning Dirs. and Adminstrs., Assn. Med. Supts. Mental Hosps. (pres.-elect 1972), Am. Hosp. Assn. (gov. council psychiat. services sect. 1968, chmn. 1974, del.-at-large to ho. of dels. 1976-80, adv. panel Center for Mental Health and Psychiat. Services 1978-82), Assn. Med. Rehab. Dirs. and Coordinators (hon.), World Psychiat. Assn. (chmn. sect. on psychiat. rehab.), Phi Gamma Delta. Unitarian. Mem. editorial adv. panel Just One Break, 1977; contbr. articles to profl. jours. Office: VA Med Center 2200 Gage Blvd Topeka KS 66622

FOLTZ, MELVYN LEROY, counselor; b. Barstow, Calif., July 21, 1940; s. Raymond Edwin and Ethel Gertrude (Wright) F.; student N.W. Christian Coll., Eugene, Oreg., 1959-60; B.S., U. Oreg., 1964, M.S., 1966; m. Mary Jane Gabriel, June 20, 1964 (dec. Jan. 1971); 1 dau., Melody. Vocat. rehab. counselor Oreg. Div. Vocat. Rehab., Eugene, 1965-66, Calif. Dept. Rehab., Vallejo, 1966-71, Napa, 1971-77, Fairfield, 1977-79; pvt. practice counseling, specializing in hypnosis, Napa, 1980—; pvt. practice group co-counseling, 1976; vocat. rehab. counselor Mirfak Assocs., Santa Rosa, 1986—. Mem. Health Manpower Com., 1973-75, Napa County Comprehensive Health Planning Council, 1975, Napa County Manpower Planning Council, 1974-77; founder, pres. Napa New Age Enterprises; alt. mem. Napa County Democratic Central Com., 1976; bd. dirs. Napa County chpt. Am. Cancer Soc., 1978-80. Lic. marriage, family and child counselor, Calif. Mem. Am. Soc. for Psychical Research, Am. Assn. Counseling and Devel., Am. Rehab. Counselors Assn., Mental Health Assn. of Napa County. Democrat. Club: Single Parents (founder, pres. 1973-79). Home: 1698 San Vicente Napa CA 94558 Office: 2025 Redwood Rd Suite 6A Napa CA 94558

FOLTZ, RICHARD HARRY, business executive; b. Frackville, Pa., Apr. 11, 1924; s. John Boyd and Blanche (Price) F.; m. Margie Alexander, June 6, 1948 (dec.); children—Richard Gary (dec.), Karen Lynn, Terri Nan; m. Ruth M. Capper, Mar. 21, 1980. Student extension center, Pa. State Coll., 1941; B.A., Harding Coll., 1949. Chief inspector's office Glenn L. Martin Co., Balt., 1941-42; adminstrv. insp. Far East Air Forces, 1942-45; writer lectr. dept. nat. edn. Harding Coll., 1945-49; with Freedoms Found., Valley Forge, Pa., 1949—; v.p. pub. relations Freedoms Found., 1952-62, sr. v.p., 1962-65, exec. v.p. Western region, 1965-78; asst. to pres. Hydril Co., Los Angeles, 1978—. Author articles on citizenship. Past pres. Upper Merion Twp. Sch. Bd.; mem. nat. pub. relations com., nat. uniform and insignia com. Boy Scouts Am. Republican. Mem. Ch. of Christ. Club: Jonathan (Los Angeles). Office: 714 W Olympic Blvd Los Angeles CA 90015

FÓNAGY, IVAN, linguist, psychoanalyst; b. Budapest, Hungary, Apr. 8, 1920; came to France, 1967; s. Béla and Ilona (Polonyi) F.; m. Judith Baráth; children: Eva, Peter. PhD, Eötvös Loránd, Budapest, 1949; DSc, Hungarian Acad. Sci., Budapest, 1956; Doctorat d'Etat, U. Paris Sorbonne, 1971. Head phonetic dept. Linguistic Inst. of Hungarian Acad. Scis., Budapest, 1957-67; assoc. prof. U. Paris Sorbonne, 1967-70; research fellow Centre Nat. de la Recherche Scientifique, Paris, 1970-79; research dir. Centre Nat. de la Scientifique Recherche, Paris, 1979—; dir. grad. studies in linguistics, phoneticsU. Société Psychanalytique de Paris, 1986—. Author: Phonetics of poetic language, 1957, Les métaphores en phonétique, 1980, Situation et signification, 1982, La vive voix Pyschophonétique, 1983. Ford Found. grantee, N.Y.C., 1964-65. Mem. Soc. Lingistique de Paris, Soc. Linguisticae Europaeae, Linguistic Soc. Am., N.Y. Acad. Scis. Home: 1 Sq Claude Debussy, 92160 Antony France

FONBERG, ELZBIETA WIKTORIA, neurophysiology scientist, researcher; b. Warsaw, Poland, Aug. 14, 1920; d. Ignacy and Zofia Adela (Luniewska) F.; 1 child, Iva Jasionowska-Blanc. MD, U. Warsaw, 1947; D of Biology, Nencki Inst. Exptl. Biology, 1959, Dr Habilit, 1963. Asst. dept. histology and embryology U. Warsaw, 1947-48; asst. dept. neurophysiology Nencki Inst. Exptl. Biology, Warsaw, 1948-50, from adj. to high prof., 1950—, head higher nervous activity lab., 1966-71, head-in-chief histology lab., 1966-75, head limbic lab., 1971—. Author 2 books, 12 chpts. in books; mem. sci. councils and editorial bds. various jours. including Acta Neurobiologiae Experimentalis, Appetite, Psychology and Behavior; contbr. over 170 articles on mechanisms of neuroses, depression, motivation and emotions to profl. jours. Served with Polish underground army, 1941-44. Decorated Cross Polonia Restituta; recipient Polish Ministry Health award, 1954, Pres. of Polish Acad. Scis. and Minister of Sci., Higher Edn. and Technique award, 1973, Sec. of Polish Acad. Scis. award, 1980, 86; Rockefeller Found. fellow Yale U., 1959-61, Psychiatry fellow Yale U., 1961, 75, UCLA fellow, 1974. Mem. Phronesis-World Conf. Neurosci. (pres. Polish sect.), Polish Physiology Assn., Internat. Brain Research Orgn., Internat. Soc. for Research on Aggression, Internat. Commn. Food and Fluid Intake, Assn. Authors and Composers, European Neurosci. Assn., European Brain and Behavior Soc., Intermozg/Brain Research in Socialist Countries, Pavlovian Soc. Am. (corr.). Office: Nencki Inst Exptl Biology, 3 Pasteur St, 02-093 Warsaw Poland

FONDER, ANDRE, gynecologist/obstetrician; b. Longuyon, France, Jan. 3, 1934; s. Maurice and Lucienne (Lecugy) F.; m. Nicole Formell, Aug. 13, 1959; children: Carole, Isabelle. ME, Faculte of Medicine, Nancy, 1960. Resident Gen. Hosp. Ctr., Nancy, France, 1953-66; practice medicine specializing in ob-gyn Sarreguemines, France, 1966—; chief of service Gen. Hosp. Ctr., Sarreguemines, 1966—. Contbr. articles to profl. jours. Served with French Army, 1960-62. Mem. French Soc. Ob-Gyn. Office: Hosp du Parc, 57200 Sarreguemines France

FONDILLER, SHIRLEY HOPE ALPERIN, nurse, journalist, educator; b. Holyoke, Mass.; d. Samuel and Rose (Sobiloff) Alperin; m. Harvey V. Fondiller, Dec. 27, 1957 (div. June 1984); 1 child, David Stewart. Grad., Beth Israel Hosp. Sch. Nursing, Boston; BE Columbia U., 1962, MA, 1963, MEd, 1971, EdD, 1979. Staff asst. Am. Nurses Assn., N.Y.C., 1963-64, dir. ednl. adminstrs., cons. and tchrs. sect., 1964-66, coordinator careers program Am. Nurses Assn., 1967-70, coordinator clin. sessions, 1971-72, editor Am. Nurse, Kansas City, Mo., 1975-78; assoc. prof., asst. to dean for spl. projects Rush-Presbyn.-St. Luke's Med. Ctr., 1979-86; exec. dir. Mid-Atlantic Regional Nursing Assn., N.Y.C., 1986—; adj. assoc. prof. Columbia U., N.Y.C., 1986—. Contbg. editor: Am. Jour. Nursing, also books and articles in nursing and healthcare edn. Mem. Kappa Delta Pi, Sigma Theta Tau.

FONG, JOSEPH YEE-TUNG, chemist, consultant; b. Canton, China, Mar. 5, 1946; s. Sik Chuen and Oi Ling (Lai) F. B.S., Kans. Newman Coll., 1970; Ph.D., Ohio U., 1978. NSF post-doctoral fellow Tex. Tech. U., Lubbock, 1978-80; tech. mgr. Berec Group Ltd., Hong Kong, 1980-81; Far East regional dir. tech. div. Givaudan Far East Ltd., Hong Kong, 1981—. Mem. Am. Chem. Soc., Royal Soc. Chemistry. Home: 115 Kau Pui Lung Rd, 3-F, Kowloon Hong Kong Office: Givaudan Far East Ltd, 16/F Sunning Plaza 10 Hysan Ave, Causeway Bay Hong Kong

FONSECA, FERNANDO ADÃO DA, economics educator, consultant; b. Lisbon, Portugal, Jan. 29, 1947; s. Aureliano and Zamira (Adão) F.; m. María José de Abreu Castello-Branco, Sept. 20, 1974; children—Luís, María, José, Tomás, Pedro. Licenciatura (engring.), U. do Oporto, 1972; MA, U. Lancaster, Eng., 1975, PhD, 1983. Lectr., U. de Luanda, Angola, 1972-74; lectr. U. Católica Portuguesa, Lisbon, 1980-83, asst. prof., 1983-85, assoc. prof. 1985—, hed dept. econs., 1983—, dir. Centro de Estudos Económicos e Empresariais Aplicados, 1983—; cons. Planning Commn., Govt. Gen. Angola, Luanda, 1972-73. Contbr. article to profl. jour. Recipient Fundação Antonio de Almeida award, 1972; NATO award, 1976-79. Mem. Inst. Econ. Affairs Eng., European Econ. Assn, The Chartered Inst. of Bankers. Roman Catholic. Home: 5 Rua Watts John Garland, S Joao do Estoril, 2765 Estoril Portugal Office: U Católica Portuguesa, Dept Econs, Palma de Cima, 1600 Lisboa Portugal

FONSECA, JOSÉ CARLOS DA, planning company executive; b. Basto, Braga, Minho, Portugal; Dec. 3, 1949; s. José Joaquim and Maria Amélia da F. Bachelor degree Accountancy and Bus. Inst., Lisbon, 1977; Bachelor degree Tech. U., Lisbon, 1979. Chartered acct. Acct., Construtora Tâmega Lda, Amarante, Oporto, 1978-81, fin. controller, Lisbon, 1981-82, ptnr. exec., 1982—. Author: Statistics for Applied Business, 1982; Cash Flow and Inflation, 1983; contbr. articles to profl. jours. Liga Dos Combatentes fellow, 1973; UNICEF fellow, 1983. Mem. Inst. Mgmt. Scis., Am. Acctg. Assn. Roman Catholic.

FONTAINE, BURT CASPAR MARIA, multi-nat. co. exec.; b. Amsterdam, Netherlands, July 15, 1928; s. Franciscus and Lamberta (Kannegieter) F.; came to U.S., 1960; student St. Ignatius Coll., Amsterdam, St. Canisius Coll., Djakarta, Indonesia, 1950-51; grad., Station for Maalderij en Bakkerij, Wageningen, The Netherlands, 1948; m. Elly van der Heijden, Aug. 4, 1958; children: Marc, Patrick (dec.), Christina, Thomas. Officer mgr. Borneo Sumatra Trading Co., Sumatra, Indonesia, 1951-57, div. supr., The Hague, Netherlands, 1957-60, with N.Y.C. office, 1960-61; first asst. to gen. purchase and sales mgr. Ocean Marine Ins., Tuteur and Co., Inc., N.Y.C., 1961-65; import mgr. E. Miltenberg, Inc., N.Y.C., 1965—, mgr. sporting goods and hardward div., 1966—, asst. treas., 1967-68; asst. v.p. fin. Brasil/FCIA/Africa Worldwide, N.Y.C., 1968; with Philipp Bros. div. Engelhard Minerals and Chems., N.Y.C., 1968—, v.p., 1979-81, v.p. Philipp Bros. Inc. Subs. Phibro-Salomon Bros., 1981—, dir. trade financing, v.p., Philipp Bros. div. Salomon Bros., 1986-87; v.p. Trade Fin. Corp. div. Metallgesellschaft Corp., N.Y.; cons. traders, banks. Past mem. steering com. parish council Roman Cath. Ch. Served as platoon comdr., commando Royal Dutch Air Force, 1948-51. Decorated Medal Order and Peace. Home: 1439 E 15th St Brooklyn NY 11230-6601 Office: Metallgesellschaft Corp Trade Fin Corp 520 Madison Ave New York NY 10022

FONTAINE, JEAN-PAUL, physician; b. Versailles, Yvelines, France, Apr. 29, 1943; s. Paul and Jeanne (Coustans) F.; m. Vanina Bonelli, Oct. 12, 1968; children: Anne-Laure, Isabelle, Paul-Vincent, Francois-Xavier. MD, U. Reims, France, 1974, postgrad., 1985—. Mem. group med. practice Reims, 1974-86, gen. practice medicine, 1987—; physician attaché Hosp. Ctr., Reims, 1974-76; adj. instr. physiopathology Tech. High Sch., Reims, 1976—, Coll. Med., U. Reims, 1980—. mem. editorial bd. Revue française de Généalogie, 1982—; editor: Le Bibliophile Rémois, 1985—; contbr. articles to profl. jours. Mem. Order of Physicians, Ethic Bd. Cancer Research, Med. Syndicate (dir. 1976-82), History and Archeology Soc. Brittany, Genealogy and History Ctr. Am.'s Islands, Nat. Acad., Book Research Inst. Roman Catholic. Lodge: Round Table. Home and Office: 19 Blvd Doumer, 51100 Reims Marne France

FONTANA, FRANCO, photographer; b. Modena, Italy, Dec. 9, 1933; s. Anselmo and Anita (Guidetti) F.; m. Fochi Fontana, Mar. 9, 1977; children by previous marriage—Laura, Andrea. Student pub. schs., Modena. One man shows of photographs include: Saletta 70, Modena, Associazione Fotografica Napoletana, Naples, 1971, Palazzo dei Musei, Modena, 1972, Artemide Showroom, Milan, 1972, Sala della Rocca, Vignola, Italy, 1973; Palazzo Strozzi, Florence, 1974, Internat. Cultural Centrum, Antwerp, 1975, The Darkroom, Chgo., 1976, Canon Photo Gallery, Geneva, 1976, Galerie Optica, Montreal, 1976, St. Gallen Photogalerie, Switzerland, 1976, Museu de Arte de Sao Paulo, Brazil, 1976, Galleria Ghelfi, Vicenza, Italy, 1977, Galleria la Citta, Verona, 1977, Photo Art Gallery, Basle, 1977, The Photographers Gallery, London, 1977, Nikon Galley, Zurich, 1978, Photog. Gallery, Dublin, 1979, 80, Galleria Fonte d'Abisso, Modena, 1979, Palazzo Pallavicino Busseto, Italy, 1979, White Gallery, Tel Aviv, 1979, Focus Gallery, San Francisco, 1980, Centro Internacional de Fotografia, Barcelona, 1980, Galleria d'Arte Moderna Rondanini, Rome, 1980, Forum Gallery, Nice, 1981, Rizzoli Gallery, N.Y., 1981, Silver Image Gallery, Seattle, 1981, Nagase Salon, Tokyo, 1981, Chiostro di San Nicolo, Spoleto, Italy, 1981, Galerie Vogt, Zurich, 1981, Nat. Gallery Art, Peking, 1982, Pusckin Mus., Moscow, 1983, City Hall, San Francisco, 1983, Porin Taide Museo, Finland, 1985, Ludwig Mus., Cologne, 1985, Circulo de Bellas Artes, Madrid, 1985, Tower Comml. Bank, Houston, 1986, Fuji Photo Salon, Tokyo, 1986, Biennale di Fotografia, Turin, Italy, 1987, Fondation Vasarely, Aix en Provence, France, Fondation Cartier, Paris, Mus. Ludwig, Cologne, Fed. Republic Germany, Photokema Gallery, Prague, Czechoslovakia, Madrid-Circulo de Bellas Artes, 1985, Houston-Tex. Comml. Tower, 1986, Torino-Chiostro della Juvarra, 1987, Praga-Inerkamera, 1987, Chgo.-Hilton and Towers, 1988, Udine-Torre di Santa Matia, 1988, Tokio-G.I.P., 1988, others.; permanent collections include: Cabinet des Estanpes de la Biblioteque Nationale de Paris, France, Internat. Mus. Photography G. Eastman House, Rochester, N.Y., Art Mus. Albuquerque, U. N.Mex., Mus. Modern Art, N.Y.C., Photog. Mus., Helsinki, Finland, Kunsthus Mus., Zurich, Museum of Modern Art, San Francisco, Nat. Gallery of Peking, China, Nat. Gallery Victori Australia, Stadelijk Museum, Amsterdam, Canadian Ctr. of Photography, Toronto, Fondation nationale de la photographie, Lyon, France, Denver Art Mus., Kyushu Indsl. U., Tokyo, Union Bank of Finland, Helsinki, Musee d'Art Modern, Paris, Pushkin State Mus. Fine Arts, Moscow, Mus. Fine Art, Houston, The Israel Mus., Jerusalem, Mus. Modern Arte, Norman, Okla., other; Author: Modena una citta, 1971, Terra de Leggere, 1974; Bologna il volto della citta, 1975, Franco Fontana, 1976, Laggiu' gli uomini, 1977, Skyline, 1978, Presenze Veneziane, 1980, Paesaggio Urbano, 1980, Landscape Photography, 1984, Emilia Romagna, 1985, Universita Oggi, 1986, Lui Lavorali, 1986, Walt Disney World, 1986, San Marino, Il Gioco Delle Apparenze, 1987, Franco Fontana, Monografia, 1987; Photoedition n.3, Franco Fontana, 1981, Presenzassenza, 1982, Franco Fontana, 1983, Meisterfotos Gestalten, 1983, Fullcolor, 1983, I Primi Dieci Ristoranti e. Alberghi d'Italia, 1983, Piscina, Diapress, Milano, 1984; EU 42, Rondanini, Roma, 1984. Home and Office: Via Benzi No 40, 41010 Cognento Modena Italy

FONTANELLA DE WEINBERG, MARIA BEATRIZ, linguist, educator; b. Bahia Blanca, Buenos Aires, Argentina, Sept. 23, 1939; d. Felix and Carolina (Taverna) Fontanella; m. Felix Weinberg, July 15, 1968; 1 child, Gabriel Felix. Lic. in letters, U. Nac. del Sur, Bahia Blanca, 1961; D in Letters, U. de Buenos Aires, 1975. Asst. prof. U. Nac. del Sur, Bahia Blanca, 1964-68, assoc. prof., 1968-80, prof., 1980—, dir. Gabinete de Linguistica, 1980—; researcher in linguistics Consejo Nac. de Investigaciones Cientificas, Buenos Aires, 1982—, mem. linguistics com., 1987—. Author: Spanish Outside Spain, 1977, Social Dynamics of a Linguistic Change, 1979, Buenos Aires Spanish Linguistic Evolution, 1987; contbr. more than 50 articles to profl. jours. Recipient 2d place Nat. Linguistics award Ministry of Edn., Buenos Aires, 1982; named one of Best Argentine Linguists, Fundacion Konex, Buenos Aires, 1986. Fellow Argentine Acad. Letters; mem. Assn. de Linguistica Y Filologia de América Latina (mem. exec. com. 1981—), Argentine Soc. Linguistics (mem. exec. com. 1980-85), Programa Interam. de Linguistica (del. 1968—), Linguistic Soc. Am. Home: Pasaje Delfino 352, 8000 Bahia Blanca Buenos Aires Argentina Office: U Nac del Sur Humanidades, 12 de Octubre Y Peru, 8000 Bahia Blanca Buenos Aires Argentina

FONTEYN, MARGOT See ARIAS, MARGOT FONTEYN DE

FOO, KAM SO STEPHEN, physician, educator; b. Hong Kong, Oct. 31, 1939; s. Po On Foo and Pui Yung Sin; m. Maria Kit Nor Siu, Dec. 24, 1968; children: Louis H.Y., Veronica W.Y., Marietta Y.Y., Kevin B.Y. MBBS, U. Hong Kong, 1966. Intern Queen Elizabeth Hosp., Hong Kong, 1966-67; resident in surgery Queen Elizabeth Hosp., 1967-68, resident in orthopaedic surgery, 1968; resident in gen. practice, surgery, ob-gyn, pediatrics Our Lady of Maryknoll Hosp., Hong Kong, 1969-70; council mem. St. Luke's Guild, Hong Kong, 1978-84; v.p. Coll. Gen. Practitioners, Hong Kong, 1982-86, chmn. exam. bd., 1984—; gen. practice medicine Hong Kong, 1971—; hon. clin. tutor dept. community medicine, Chinese Univ. Hong Kong; hon. lectr. General Practice Unit Dept. Medicine U. Hong Kong, 1988—; hon. med. advisor Hong Kong Life Guard Club, 1986—. Sub-editor Med. Directory Hong Kong, 1981, 85. Served as med. officer aux. med. services, Hong Kong, 1968-87. Decorated Civil Def. Long Service medal (Hong Kong). Fellow Hong Kong Coll. Gen. Practitioners. Roman Catholic. Home: No 6 Seventh St, Hong Lok Yuen, Tai Po Hong Kong Office: No 9 Tak Ku Ling Rd, Kowloon Hong Kong

FOOKES, PETER GEORGE, engineering geologist, educator; b. Essex, Eng., May 31, 1933; s. George Ernest and Ida Corina Fookes; B.Sc. with honours, Queen Mary Coll., London U., 1960, Ph.D., 1967, D.Sc. in Engring., 1979; m. Edna May Nix, July 25, 1987; children by former marriage: Jennifer, Gregory, Timothy, Anita, Rosemary. Research asst. Brewing Industry Research Found., 1950-54; sr. technician Chelsea Coll., London U., 1956-57; field engring. geologist Binnie and Partners, London, 1960-65; lectr. Imperial Coll., London U., 1966-71; cons. engring. geologist, 1971—; vis. prof. London U., 1979—. Assoc., Instn. Civil Engrs.; chartered engr., U.K. Recipient several awards including Wm. Smith medal geol. Soc., 1985. Fellow Inst. Geology, Geol. Soc., Instn. Mining and Metallurgy; mem. Geologists Assn. Author numerous profl. papers. Avocations: industrial archaeology, canal boats. Address: Lafonia, 11A Edgar Rd Rd,, Winchester, Hampshire S023 9SJ, England

FOONBERG, JAY G., lawyer, accountant; b. Chgo., Oct. 29, 1935; s. Hyman J. and Esther (Leon) F.; m. Lois Alpin, Aug. 31, 1958; children: Alan Marshall, David Jeffrey Steven Mark. B.S., UCLA, 1957, J.D., 1963. Auditor Calif. Bd. Equalization, 1957-59; accountant Seidman & Seidman, C.P.A.s, Beverly Hills, Calif., 1959-60, Lever & Anker, C.P.A.s, 1960-63; pres. law corp. of Foonberg & Frandzel, Beverly Hills, 1970-79; prin. Slavitt, King & Foonberg, Los Angeles, 1979-81, Foonberg, Jampol & Gardner, 1981—; arbitrator Am. Arbitration Assn., 1965—; judge pro tem Beverly Hills Mcpl. Ct., 1970-71, Los Angeles Mcpl. Ct., 1980-81; trustee, pres. Brazil-Calif. Trade Assn.; spl. advisor for Latin Am. to Calif. sec. state, 1983-88; adj. vis. prof. law U. Houston Law Sch., 1986; adj. vis. prof., Kenelm Lectr. Campbell U. Sch .Law, 1986, 87, 88; appointee Spl. Commn. on Interam. Affairs, 1986—. Author: How To Start and Build A Law Practice, 1976, 2d edit., 1984, How To Get and Keep Good Clients, 1986; editor various publs.; contbr. articles to profl. jours.; lectr. in field. Mem. Men's Club of Cedars-Sinai Med. Center; Mem. Speakers Bur., 1966, also dir.; mem. Los Angeles Olympics Adv. Commn., 1981—. Served with USAF, 1958-64. Decorated Order of So. Cross (Brazil), Order of Rio Branco (Brazil); recipient Republic Panama Disting. Visitor award, 1984, Gubernatorial Welcome award Del., 1984, Resolution of Hon. award N.J., 1984, award of merit Govt. of Argentina, 1985, other Certs. of Appreciation; named Ky. Col., Adm. Tex. Navy, Ga. Col., Okla. Marshal, Ark. Traveler, Adm. Nebr. Navy, HGon. Citizen S.D., Hon. Citizen Ariz., 1983, Hon. Lt. Co. Ala., 1986, others. Mem. Am. Assn. Atty.-CPA's (charter sec., pres., dir., Outstanding Achievement and Contbn., award 1987), Calif. Assn. Atty.-CPA's (dir., pres.), Calif. Soc. CPA's, ABA (council econs. of law practice sect. 1975-77, Gold Key award law student div. 1977, Highest Honors award law students div. 1983, mem. commn. interam. affairs 1986, 87, Spl. Recognition award young lawyers div. 1986, spl. commn. on lawyer competency 1986, 87), Beverly Hills Bar Assn. (gov.), Century City Bar Assn. (bd. govs. 1980-81), State Bar Calif. (mem. spl. commn. for assimilation of new lawyers into the profession; chmn. econs. of law practice sect. 1977, 78), Argentine-Calif. Bus. Assn. (founder, pres. 1983), Interam. Bar Assn. (chmn. econs. of law practice com. 1985, 86), Phi Alpha Delta, Phi Epsilon Phi. Home: 716 N Rexford Dr Beverly Hills CA 90210 Office: 8500 Wilshire Blvd Suite 900 Beverly Hills CA 90211

FOOSHEE, MALCOLM, lawyer; b. Charleston, Tenn., Oct. 1, 1898; s. Joseph Crockett and Lillian (Powell) F.; A.B., U. South, 1918, D.C.L., 1983; J.D., Harvard, 1921; B.C.L., Christ Church, Oxford U. (Rhodes scholar), 1924; m. Clare Fraser Murray, 1930 (dec. 1951); children—Joan Murray (Mrs. Shepard A. Spunt) (dec.), Clare Fraser Childres; m. 2d, Wynne Byard Taylor, 1953. Admitted to N.Y. bar, 1922, since practiced in N.Y.C.; with Murray, Aldrich & Roberts, 1921-22, Davis, Polk, Wardwell, Gardiner & Reed, 1925-42; mem. Donovan, Leisure, Newton & Irvine, N.Y.C. and Washington, 1943-81, of counsel, 1981—; legal work, Europe and Japan. 1928, 35, 49, 50; barrister; mem. Inner Temple (Inns of Court), London, 1922—. Mem. legislative com. Citizens Union, N.Y.C., 1926-27; mem. Rye (N.Y.) Planning Commn., 1943-45, Rye Sch. Consolidation Commn., 1943-44; mem. Diocesan Commn. Coll. Work, New York City, 1951-58. Pres. Rye Library, 1950-53, trustee, 1948-59; trustee Rye Country Day Sch., 1947-51, trustee U. of South, 1953-56. Mem. Am. delegation to Atlantic Congress, London, 1959. Mem. Harvard Naval Unit, 1918; Squadron A Cav., N.Y. N.G., 1926-20. Assoc. Knight Order St. John Jerusalem. Mem. Am. (chmn. sect. corp., banking and bus. law 1951-52), Internat., N.Y. State bar assns., Assn. Bar City N.Y., Am. Law Inst., Am. Judicature Soc., Assn. Am. Rhodes Scholars (bd. dirs. 1949-82), Huguenot Soc. Am. (chancellor 1976-79), S.R., Phi Beta Kappa, Kappa Sigma. Democrat. Episcopalian. Clubs: Century, Harvard, Church (N.Y.C.). Contbr. to legal publs. Office: 30 Rockefeller Plaza New York NY 10112

FOOTE, EDWARD THADDEUS, II, university president, lawyer; b. Milw., Dec. 15, 1937; s. William Hamilton and Julia Stevenson (Hardin) F.; m. Roberta Waugh Fulbright, Apr. 18, 1964; children: Julia, William, Thaddeus. B.A., Yale U., 1959; LL.B., Georgetown U., 1966; LL.D. (hon.), Washington U., St. Louis, 1981; hon. degree, Tokai U., Tokyo, 1984. Bar: Mo. 1966. Reporter, Washington Star, 1963-64, Washington Daily News, 1964-65; exec. asst. to chmn. Pa. Ave. Commn., Washington, 1965-66; assoc. Bryan, Cave, McPheeters & McRoberts, St. Louis, 1966-70; vice chancellor, gen. counsel, sec. to bd. trustees Washington U., St. Louis, 1970-73; dean Sch. Law Washington U., 1973-80, spl. adv. to chancellor and bd. trustees, 1980-81; pres. U. Miami, Coral Gables, Fla., 1981—; chmn. citizens com. for sch. desegregation, St. Louis, 1980; chmn. desegregation monitoring and adv. com., St. Louis, 1980-81. Author: An Educational Plan for Voluntary Cooperation Desegregation of School in the St. Louis Met. area, 1981. Mem. Council on Fgn. Relations; founding pres. bd. New City Sch., St. Louis, 1967-73; mem. gov.'s task force on reorganization State of Mo., 1973-74, steering com., chmn. goverance com. Mo. Gov.'s Conf. on Edn., UN Assn. (Greater St. Louis chpt.), 1977-79, adv. com. Naval War Coll., 1979-82, Fla. Council 100, So. Fla. Metro-Miami Action Plan, exec. com. Miami Citizens Against Crime. Served with USMCR, 1959-62. Recipient Order of Sun (Peru). Democrat. Office: Univ of Miami Office of Pres PO Box 248006 Coral Gables FL 33124

FOOTE, PAUL SHELDON, business educator, seminar leader, consultant; b. Lansing, Mich., May 22, 1946; s. Harlon Sheldon and Frances Norene (Rotter) F.; B.B.A., U. Mich., 1967; M.B.A. (Loomis-Sayles fellow), Harvard U., 1971; advanced profl. cert. NYU, 1975; Ph.D., Mich. State U., 1983; m. Badri Seddigheh Hosseinian, Oct. 25, 1968; children—David, Sheila. Br. mgr., divl. mgr. Citibank, N.Y.C., Bombay, India and Beirut, Lebanon, 1972-74; mgr. planning and devel. Singer Co., Africa/Middle East, 1974-75;

instr. U. Mich., Flint, 1978-79; lectr. acctg. Mich. State U., East Lansing, 1977; asst. prof. U. Windsor (Ont., Can.), 1979-81; assoc. prof. Saginaw Valley State Coll., University Ctr., Mich., 1981-82; asst. prof. Oakland U., Rochester, Mich., 1982-83; asst. prof. NYU, 1983-87; assoc. prof. Pepperdine U., Malibu, Calif., 1987—; founder, pres. The Computer Coop., Inc., 1981-82. Served to lt. AUS, 1968-69. Haskins and Sells Doctoral Consortium fellow, 1977. Mem. Am. Accounting Assn., Internat. Assn. Bus. Forecasting (bd. dirs.), Nat. Speakers Assn., EDP Auditors Assn., Internat. Inst. Forecasters, Strategic Mgmt. Soc.

FOOTS, SIR JAMES WILLIAM, Australian business executive and mining engineer; b. July 12, 1916; m. Thora H. Thomas, 1939; 3 children. B.M.E., Melbourne U. Mining engr. North Broken Hill Ltd., 1938-43, Allied Works Council, 1943-44, Lake George Mines, Ltd., 1944-45, Zinc Corp. Ltd., 1946-54; asst. gen. mgr. Zinc Corp. and New Broken Hill Consolidated Ltd., 1952-54; gen. mgr. Mt. Isa Mines, Ltd., 1955-66, dir., 1956-87, mng. dir., 1966-70, chmn., 1970-81; chief exec. M.I.M. Holdings Ltd., 1970-81, chmn., 1970-83, dep. chmn., 1983-87; dir., Westpac Banking Corp., 1971—, chmn., 1987—; dir., Nat. Mutual Life Assn. of Australasia Ltd., 1982-85, Castlemaine Tooheys Ltd., 1983-85, ASARCO Inc., 1985-87; mem. Senate Queensland U., 1970—; chancellor U. Queensland, 1985—; chmn. Queensland U. Found., Ltd., 1982-85, gov., 1985—; pres. Australian Mining Industry Council, 1974, 75. Hon. D.Eng. Mem. Australasian Inst. Mining and Metallurgy (pres. 1974), Council of Mining and Metallurgical Insts. (pres. congress 1986). Address: PO Box 662, Kenmore, Qld 4069, Australia

FORBES, BRYAN, actor, writer, director; b. London, Eng., July 22, 1926; s. William Theobald and Judith Kate Helen (Seaton) F.; m. Constance Smith, Feb. 19, 1951 (div. 1955); m. Nanette Newman, Aug. 27, 1955; children: Sarah Kate Amanda (Lady Leon), Emma Katy (Mrs. Graham Clempson). Student, Royal Acad. Dramatic Art, London, 1941-42; DLitt (hon.), 1987. chief cons. editor King mag.; mem. gen. adv. council BBC, 1965. Debut in The Corn is Green, London, 1942; other stage appearances include Flare Path, 1943, Gathering Storm, 1948, September Tide, 1948, The Holly and The Ivy, 1950, Tobias and The Angel, 1953, A Touch of Fear, 1956; dir. Macbeth for The Old Vic, 1980, Killing Jessica, Savoy Theater, 1986; dir. revival of The Living Room, Royalty Theatre, 1987; actor in films The Baby and the Battleship, 1955, The Wooden Horse, 1948, An Inspector Calls, 1954, The Key, 1957, The League of Gentleman, 1959; dir. films including Whistle Down the Wind, 1961, The L-Shaped Room, 1962, Seance on a Wet Afternoon, 1963, King Rat, 1964, The Wrong Box, 1965, The Whisperers, 1966, Deadfall, 1967, The Madwoman of Chailot, 1968, The Raging Moon (U.S title Long Ago Tomorrow), 1970, The Stepford Wives, 1974; writer, dir. films The Slipper and the Rose, 1975; writer, producer, dir. films International Velvet, 1978; dir. Brit. segment of The Sunday Lovers, 1980; writer, dir. (original screenplay for BBC 1) Jessie, broadcast Dec. 1980; Menage à Trois (U.S. title Better Late Than Never), 1981, The Naked Face, 1983, The Endless Game, 1988; fiction critic: Spectator, 1961-52; screenwriter The Angry Silence, 1959 (Brit. Acad. award), The League of Gentlemen, 1959, Only Two Can Play, 1962 (Brit. Acad. award), The L-Shaped Room, 1962 (UN award), Seance on a Wet Afternoon, 1964 (Edgar award); author (with Brian Garfield) Hopscotch, (short stories) Truth Lies Sleeping, 1951, (autobiography) Notes for a Life, 1974, Ned's Girl, The Biography of Dame Edith Evans, 1977, (novels) The Distant Laughter, 1972, The Slipper and the Rose, 1976, International Velvet, 1978, Familiar Strangers (U.S. title Stranger), 1979, The Rewrite Man, 1983, The Endless Game, 1986, That Despicable Race, 1980. Served with Brit. Army, 1943-48. Mem. Brit. Screenwriters Guild (council treas. 1960-63), Brit. Actors Equity, Screen Actors Guild, Writers Guild Am., Dirs. Guild Am., Assn. Cinema Technicians, Nat. Youth Theatre Gt. Britain (pres. 1984—), Beatrix Potter Soc. (pres.). Office: care Pinewood Studios, Iver Heath, Buckinghamshire England

FORBES, DONALD DAVID, laboratory administrator, consultant; b. Melbourne, Australia, May 30, 1922; s. John William and Mary Ann (Colhoun) F.; m. Betty Eleanor Slatter, Sept. 7, 1946; children: Suzanne Eleanor, Anthony David, Kerri-Lynne. Diploma in Applied Chemistry, Royal Melbourne Inst. Tech., 1952; postgrad., Swinburne Inst. Tech., 1954. Research chemist Australian Paper Mfg., Melbourne, 1938-39, 46-50; analytical chemist Commonwealth Aircraft Corp., Port Melbourne, Australia, 1951-54; lab. mgr., dir. N.K.S. Labs., Melbourne, 1954—. Author: Quality Control Zinc and Alloys, 1963, Electro Polishing Metals, 1974, X-Ray Fluorescence Analysis of Materials, 1977; inventor polyester powder brass coating. Served with Royal Army Air Force-RAF, 1941-45. Fellow Inst. Metal Finishing London; mem. Royal Australian Chem. Inst., Inst. Metals Melbourne, Standards Assn. (chmn. Zn and alloys com. 1970-78, analytical com. 1974—, metals sect. 1962-75), Nat. Assn. Testing Authorities (sr. lab. assessor 1964—). Mem. Ch. of England. Club: Sandringham Yacht. Home: Lot 81, Monbulk-Olinda Rd, Monbulk 3793, Australia Office: NKS Labs Inc, 7 Edward St, Huntingdale Victoria, Australia

FORBES, FRED WILLIAM, architect; b. East Liverpool, Ohio, Aug. 21, 1936; s. Kenneth S. and Phylis C. Forbes; B.S. in Architecture, U. Cin., 1960, postgrad.; m. Carolyn Lee Eleyet, Dec. 27, 1969; children—Tallerie Bliss, Kendall Robert. Material research engr. U.S. Air Force Materials Lab., 1960-61, structural research engr. Flight Accessories Lab., 1961-63, tech. area mgr. Aero Propulsion Lab., 1964-67; prin. Fred W. Forbes, Architect, Xenia, Ohio, 1966-68; br. chief U.S. Air Force Aero Propulsion Lab., Wright Patterson AFB, Ohio, 1967-72, pres. Forbes and Huie, Xenia, 1968-73; pres. Forbes, Huie & Assos., Inc., Xenia, 1973-76; pres. Fred W. Forbes & Assos., Inc., Xenia, 1976—; instr. U. Dayton, 1963-64. Past pres. Xenia Area Living Arts Council. Recipient Exceptional Civilian Service award U.S. Air Force, 1966; Archtl. Award of Excellence for Moraine Civic Center, Masonry Inst., 1976, Archtl. Award of Merit for Xenia br. of 3d Nat. Bank, 1981 Excellence in Masonry, Spl. award for renovation Dayton Area Red Cross Bldg., 1982; Dayton City Beautiful award for Martin Electric Co., 1977; award of merit Greene County Mental Health Facility 1983. Fellow Brit. Interplanetary Soc.; mem. Greene County Profl. Engrs. Soc. (past pres.), Am. Astron. Soc. (past nat. dir.), AIA, Ohio Soc. Profl. Engrs. (Young Engrs. award 1970), Nat. Soc. Profl. Engrs. (top 5 Outstanding Young Engr. award 1972), Nat. Asbestos Contractors Assn. (assoc.), Xenia Area C. of C. (v.p. econ. devel. 1985-86, pres. 1986-87), Theta Chi. Republican. Methodist. Contbr. 24 articles to profl. jours.; patentee in field. Office: 158 E Main St Xenia OH 45385

FORBES, JOHN DOUGLAS, architectural and economic historian; b. San Francisco, Apr. 9, 1910; s. John Franklin and Portia (Ackerman) F.; m. Margaret Funkhouser, Feb. 4, 1937 (dec.); children: Pamela, Peter; m. Mary Elizabeth Lewis, July 26, 1980; 1 child, Michael. A.B., U. Calif.-Berkeley, 1931; M.A., Stanford U., 1932; A.M., Harvard U., 1936, Ph.D., 1937. Accountant J.F. Forbes & Co. (C.P.A.'s), San Francisco, 1937-38, 42-43; asst. to dir. fine arts, curator paintings San Francisco World's Fair, 1938-40; chmn. dept. fine arts U. Kansas City, Mo., 1940-42; faculty history Bennington Coll., 1943-46; asso. prof. history and fine arts Wabash Coll., 1946-50, prof., 1950-54; prof. bus. history U. Va., 1954-80, prof. emeritus, 1980—, lectr. art history Div. Continuing Edn., 1982—; adv. bd. Historic Am. Bldgs. Survey, 1974-78. Author: Israel Thorndike, 1953, Victorian Architect, 1953, Murder in Full View, 1968, Death Warmed Over, 1971, Stettinius, Sr., Portrait of a Morgan Partner, 1974, J.P. Morgan, Jr. (1867-1943), 1981; editor: Jour. Soc. Archtl. Historians, 1953-58; adv. editor industry: Ency. Brit., 1956-58. Served as 2d lt. AUS, 1942. Decorated officier Ordre des Palmes Académiques (France); cavaliere Ordine al Merito (Italy). Mem. Am. Hist. Assn. (life), Coll. Art Assn. (life), Mystery Writers Am., Soc. Archtl. Historians (pres. 1962-64, life), Colonial Soc. Mass. (life), AAUP, AIA (hon.), Audubon Soc., Nat. Trust Historic Preservation, Wilderness Soc. (life), Sierra Club (life), Nature Conservancy (life), Mechanics Inst. (life), Victorian Soc., Victorian Soc. in Am., Calif. Hist. Soc., Soc. Calif. Pioneers (life), Friends of Sea Otter (life), Tamalpais Conservation Club (life), Am. Kitefliers Assn. (life), Am. Soc. Dowsers (life), Phi Beta Kappa. Clubs: Colonnade (Charlottesville) (life), Pacific-Union (San Francisco); Farmington Country (Charlottesville); Cambridge (Mass.) Boat. Home: Box 3607 Charlottesville VA 22903 also: 1250 Jones St San Francisco CA 94109

FORBES, JOHN RIPLEY, naturalist, educator; b. Chelsea, Mass., Aug. 25, 1913; s. Kenneth Ripley and Ellen Elizabeth (Barker) F.; m. Margaret Sanders, Dec. 10, 1951; children: Ripley, Anne. Spl. student, U. Iowa, 1933-34, Bowdoin Coll., 1934-35; LHD (hon.), Bowdoin Coll., 1987. Founder, dir. Stamford (Conn.) Mus., 1935-37; ornithologist, taxidermist Lee Mus. Biology, Bowdoin Coll., MacMillan-Arctic Expdn., Labrador and Baffin Island, 1937; founder, dir. William T. Hornaday Meml. Found., N.Y., 1938-50; organizer, dir. Kansas City (Mo.) Mus., 1939-41; founder Nashville Children's Mus., 1944, acting dir., 1945-46, trustee for life, 1975; exec. dir. Jacksonville (Fla.) Children's Mus., 1945, Fernbank Children's Nature Mus., Atlanta, 1946; organizer, dir. Oreg. Mus. Sci. and Industry, Portland, 1947-49; founder Nat. Found. for Jr. Mus., N.Y., dir., 1951-60; founder Sacramento Jr. Mus., dir., 1951-53; co-founder, dir. ops. Nature Centers for Young Am., 1959-60; founder, pres., chmn. bd. Natural Sci. for Youth Found., Conn., 1961—; founder Big Cypress Nature Center, Naples, Fla., 1959; organizer Ft. Worth's Children's Mus., 1945. Founder, pres. William T. Hornaday Meml. Trust, Conn., 1961-77; founder Mid-Fairfield County Youth Mus., Westport, Conn., 1958, pres., 1963-66, trustee for life, 1966; founder Am. Assn. Youth Mus., 1964, hon. life mem., 1976; co-founder, v.p. Aspetuck Land Trust, Fairfield County; pres. St. John's on the Lake Assn., 1963-64; pres. emeritus, trustee John and Anna Newton Porter Found., 1974; founder Outdoor Activity Ctr., Atlanta, chmn., 1977-80; founder Chattahoochee Nature Ctr., Roswell, Ga., pres., 1977-78; founder Reynolds Arboretum and Nature Preserve Morrow, Ga., 1976; founder, pres. Lakes Region Conservation Trust, Meredith, N.H., 1977; founder Ragged Island Nature Ctr., Lake Winnipesaukee, N.H., 1979, Kimball Castle Arboretum and Wildlife Sanctuary, Gilford, N.H., 1981; trustee Hilla Von Rebay Found., 1968; trustee Milford (Pa.) Reservation 1977, pres. 1977-82 1983; founder, pres. Natural Sci. Solar Ctr., Milford, 1983; founder, trustee Cochran Mill Nature Ctr. and Arboretum, Atlanta, Ga., 1987, Cobb County Nature Rehab. Ctr., Marietta, Ga., 1988 Served with M.C., USAAF, 1942-45. Recipient Am. Motors Conservation award, 1971; William T. Hornaday Gold Medal award, 1977; Founder's award Natural Sci. for Youth Found., 1979. Mem. Am. Assn. Mus. (chmn. children's mus. sec. 1965), Nat. Audubon Soc. (life), Am. Nature Study Soc., Nature Conservancy, Wilderness Soc., Am. Ornithologist Union (life), N.Y. Zool. Soc., Am. Birding Assn. (life), Nat. Wildlife Fedn., Conn. Conservation Assn. (pres. 1969-70), Sierra Club, Audubon Soc. N.H. (pres. 1975). Clubs: Bald Peak Colony (Melvin Village, N.H.); Explorers (N.Y.C.); Mazamas (Portland, Oreg.); Campfire of America. Home: 11 Wildwood Valley NE Atlanta GA 30350 Office: Natural Scis for Youth 130 Azalea Dr Atlanta GA 30075

FORBES, KENNETH ALBERT FAUCHER, urological surgeon; b. Waterford, N.Y., Apr. 28, 1922; s. Joseph Frederick and Adelle Frances (Robitaille) F.; m. Eileen Ruth Gibbons, Aug. 4, 1956; children: Michael, Diane, Kenneth E., Thomas, Maureen, Daniel. BS cum laude, U. Notre Dame, 1943; MD, St. Louis U., 1947. Diplomate Am. Bd. Urology. Intern St. Louis U. Hosp., 1947-48; resident in urol. surgery Barnes Hosp., VA Hosp., Washington U., St. Louis. U. schs. medicine, St. Louis, 1948-52; fellow West Roxbury (Harvard) VA Hosp., Boston, 1955; asst. chief urology VA Hosp., East Orange, N.J., 1955-58; practice medicine specializing in urology Green Bay, Wis., 1958-78, Long Beach, Calif., 1978-85; mem. cons. staff Fairview State Hosp. U. Calif. Med. Ctr., Irvine, VA Hosp., Long Beach; asst. clin. prof. surgery U. Calif., Irvine, 1978-85; cons. Vols. in Tech. Assistance, 1986—. Contbr. articles to profl. jours. Served with USNR, 1944-46; capt. U.S. Army, 1952-54. Named Outstanding Faculty Mem. by students, 1981. Fellow ACS, Internat. Coll. Surgeons; mem. AAAS, AMA, Calif. Med. Assn., Am. Urol. Assn. (exec. com. North Cen. sect. 1972-75, western sect. 1980—), Royal Soc. Medicine (London), N.Y. Acad. Scis., Santa Barbara County Med. Soc., Surg. Alumni Assn. U. Calif. Irvine, Justin J. Cordonnier Soc. of Washington U., Confedn. Americana de Urologia, Urologists Corr. Club, Phi Beta Pi. Republican. Roman Catholic. Clubs: Notre Dame (Los Angeles) (Man Yr. 1965); Great Lakes Cruising; Retired Officers, Channel City, Cosmopolitan of Santa Barbara. Home and Office: 15 Langlo Terr Santa Barbara CA 93105

FORBES, LEONARD, engineering educator; b. Grande Prairie, Alta., Can., Feb. 21, 1940; came to U.S., 1966; s. Frank and Katie (Tschetter) F.; B.Sc. with distinction in Engring. Physics, U. Alta., 1962; M.S. in E.E., U. Ill., 1963, Ph.D., 1970. Staff engr. IBM, Fishkill, N.Y. and Manassas, Va., 1970-72; IBM vis. prof. Howard U., Washington, 1972; asst. prof. U. Ark., Fayetteville, 1972-75; assoc. prof. U. Calif.-Davis, 1976-82; prof. Oreg. State U., Corvallis, 1983—; with Hewlett-Packard Labs., Palo Alto, Calif., 1978; cons. to Telex Computer Products, D.H. Baldwin, Hewlett-Packard, Fairchild, United Epitaxial Tech.; organizer Portland Internat. Conf. and Exposition on Silicon Materials and Tech., 1985-87. Served with Royal Can. Air Force, 1963-66. Mem. IEEE. Contbr. articles to profl. jours. Home: 537 Mountain View Ave Santa Rosa CA 95407 Office: Oreg State U Dept Elec Engring Corvallis OR 97331

FORBES, TIMOTHY CARTER, publisher; b. Morristown, N.J., Oct. 5, 1953; s. Malcolm Stevenson and Roberta (Laidlaw) F.; m. Anne Shepard Harrison, Mar. 4, 1983; 1 child, Isabelle Flowerree. AB with honors, Brown U., 1976. Producer Seven Seas Cinema, N.Y.C., 1977-81; producer, screenwriter N.Y.C., 1981-85; v.p. Forbes Inc., N.Y.C., 1986—; also bd. dirs. FOrbes Inc., N.Y.C.; pres. Am. Heritage Mag., N.Y.C., 1986—. Dir., producer: (films) Some Call It Greed, 1977, Lost to the Revolution, 1979, Golden Age of Toy Boats, 1981. Trustee Anthology Film Archives, N.Y.C., 1981—, vice chmn. bd., 1982—; trustee St. Vincent's Hosp, N.Y.C., 1986—, Am. Assn. for State and Local History, 1987—; comsr. Constitutional Bicentenial Commn., N.J., 1986—, Brown U., 1988—. Mem. Am. Antiquarian Soc. Office: American Heritage Magazine Forbes Bldg 60 Fifth Ave New York NY 10011

FORD, BETTY (ELIZABETH) BLOOMER, wife of former President of United States; b. Chgo., Apr. 8, 1918; d. William Stephenson and Hortence (Neahr) Bloomer; m. Gerald R. Ford (38th Pres. U.S.), Oct. 15, 1948; children: Michael Gerald, John Gardner, Steven Meigs, Susan Elizabeth. Student, Sch. Dance Bennington Coll., 1936, 37; LL.D. hon., U. Mich., 1976. Dancer Martha Graham Concert Group, N.Y.C., 1939-41; model John Powers Agy., N.Y.C., 1939-41; fashion dir. Herpolscheimer's Dept. Store, Grand Rapids, Mich., 1943-48; dance instr. Grand Rapids, 1932-48; pres., bd. dirs. The Betty Ford Ctr., Rancho Mirage, Calif. Author: autobiography The Times of My Life, 1979. Bd. dirs. Nat. Arthritis Found. (hon.); formerly active Cub Scouts Am.; program chmn. Alexandria (Va.) Cancer Fund Drive; chmn. Heart Subday, Washington Heart Assn., 1974; pres. ARC Senate Wives Club; supporter Nat. Endowment Arts; mem. Nat. Commn. Observance Internat. Women's Year, 1977; bd. dirs. League Republican Women, D.C.; trustee Eisenhower Med. Ctr., Rancho Mirage; advisory bd. Rosalind Russell Med. Research Fund; hon. chmn. Palm Springs Desert Mus.; nat. trustee Nat. Symphony Orch.; trustee Nursing Home Advisory and Research Council Inc.; mem. Golden Circle Patrons Ctr. Theatre Performing Arts; bd. dirs. The Lambs, Libertyville, Ill. Episcopalian (tchr. Sunday sch. 1961-64). Home: PO Box 927 Rancho Mirage CA 92270 *

FORD, DAVID CLAYTON, lawyer; b. Hartford City, Ind., Mar. 3, 1949; s. Clayton I. and Barbara J. (McVicker) F.; m. Joyce Ann Bonjour, Aug. 22, 1970; children—Jeffrey David, Andrew Clayton. B.A. in Polit. Sci., Ind. U., 1973; J.D., Ind. U.-Indpls., 1976, MBA Internat. Trade, Ball State U., 1988. Bar: Ind. 1975, U.S. Dist. Ct. (no. dist.) Ind. 1977, U.S. Dist. Ct. (so. dist.) Ind. 1976, U.S. Supreme Ct. 1983. City atty. City of Montpelier, Ind., 1977-79; town atty. Town of Shamrock Lakes, Ind., 1977—; gen. counsel Ind. Farm Bur. Inc., 1988—; chief dep. prosecutor, Blackford County, 1979; pros. atty. 71st Jud. Cir., Blackford County, Hartford City, Ind., 1983—. Republican nominee for 19th Dist. Ind. State Sen., 1986; dir. Blackford County Young Republicans, 1977-82, pres., 1977-78; chmn. Town of Shamrock Lakes Republican Com., 1983; vice-chmn. Blackford County Rep. Central Com., 1978-82; precinct committeeman Blackford County, Licking 7, 1980—; mem. Ind. 10th Congl. Dist. Rep. Caucus, 1978-82; U.S. Edn. Appeals Bd. mem. U.S. Dept. Edn., 1982—; Nat. Def. Execs. Res. 1983—; mem. bus. adv. com. to Congressman Dan Burton; chmn. bus., industries and devel. com. Ptnrs. of Ams., Ind. chpt., 1983—; mem. Blackford County Bd. Aviation Commrs., 1977-83, pres., 1979-83; bd. dirs. Dollars of Scholars, Blackford County, 1977—, v.p., 1977—; mem. St. John's-Riedman Meml. Sch. Bd., 1978-82, pres., 1978-82; mem. Blackford County Sheriff's Merit Bd., 1981-82. Named Man of Yr., Hartford City C. of C., 1978; Sagamore of the Wabash, Gov. Otis Bowen, 1978; Hon. Sec. of State, Edwin J. Simcox, 1981; participant Rotary group study exchange to São Paulo, Brazil, 1981; named Outstanding Young Man of Am., U.S. Jaycees, 1982. Mem. ABA, Assn. Trial Lawyers' Am., Ind. State Bar Assn., Blackford County Bar Assn., World Trade Club Ind., Mensa, Sigma Iota Epsilon. Home: 2776 S Angling Park Hartford City IN 47348 Office: 210 W Main St Hartford City IN 47348

FORD, GERALD RUDOLPH, JR., former President of United States; b. Omaha, July 14, 1913; s. Gerald R. and Dorothy (Gardner) F.; m. Elizabeth Bloomer, Oct. 15, 1948; children: Michael, John, Steven, Susan. A.B., U. Mich., 1935; LL.B., Yale U., 1941; LL.D., Mich. State U., Albion Coll., Aquinas Coll., Spring Arbor Coll. Bar: Mich. 1941. Practiced law at Grand Rapids, 1941-49; mem. law firm Buchen and Ford; mem. 81st-93d Congresses from 5th Mich. Dist., 1949-74, elected minority leader, 1965; v.p. U.S., 1973-74, pres., 1974-77; del. Interparliamentary Union, Warsaw, Poland, 1959, Belgium, 1961; del. Bilderberg Group Conf., 1962; dir. Santa Fe Internat., GK Technologies, Shearson Loeb Rhoades, Pebble Beach Corp., Tiger Internat. Served as lt. comdr. USNR, 1942-46. Recipient Grand Rapids Jr. C. of C. Distinguished Service award, 1948; Distinguished Service Award as one of ten outstanding young men in U.S. by U.S. Jr. C. of C., 1950; Silver Anniversary All-Am. Sports Illustrated, 1959; Distinguished Congressional Service award Am. Polit. Sci. Assn., 1961. Mem. Am., Mich. State, Grand Rapids bar assns., Delta Kappa Epsilon, Phi Delta Phi. Republican. Episcopalian. Clubs: Univiversity (Kent County), Peninsular (Kent County). Lodge: Masons. Home: PO Box 927 Rancho Mirage CA 92262 *

FORD, GORDON BUELL, accountant, real estate executive; b. Greenville, Ky., Sept. 27, 1913; s. Otha and Martha Jane (Newman) F.; B.S., Western Ky. U., Bowling Green, 1934; m. Glenda Lou Cox, Oct. 10, 1974; children: Gregory Newman, Gordon Buell Jr., Gayle Ford Whittenberg; CPA, Ky., Tenn., Ind.; ptnr. Yeager, Ford & Warren, C.P.A.s, Louisville, 1934-60, mng. ptnr., 1960-70; mng. ptnr. Coopers & Lybrand, CPA's, Louisville, 1970-78, ret. mng. ptnr., 1978—; pres., chief exec. officer Southeastern Investment Trust, Inc., Louisville, 1960—; v.p. Vogue Furniture, Inc., Louisville, 1947-51, Sta. WSUA, Inc., Bloomington, Ind., 1946-50; dir. Hubbuch's, Louisville, Broadway Chevrolet Co., 845, Inc. Pres., chief exec. officer Gorjim Found., Inc., Louisville, 1960—; bd. dirs. Louisville Central Area, Inc., 1973-76; trustee, mayor City of Mockingbird Valley (Ky.), 1949-73; trustee, treas. Ky. So. Coll., Louisville, 1963-71; trustee So. Bapt. Theol. Sem., Louisville, 1963-71, Bellarmine Coll., 1979-87. Mem. Am. Inst. CPA's (council 1965-71, v.p. 1972-73), Ky. Soc. CPA's (pres. 1948-49). Presbyterian. Clubs: Louisville Country, Pendennis (Louisville); Harmony Landing Country (Goshen, Ky.); Delray Dunes Country (Delray Beach, Fla.); Rotary. Author: (with L. C. J. Yeager) The History of the Professional Practice of Accounting in Kentucky: 1875-1965, 1967. Home: 5915 Brittany Valley Rd Louisville KY 40222 also: 107 MacFarlane Dr Delray Beach FL 33444 Office: 3600 First National Tower Louisville KY 40202

FORD, GORDON BUELL, JR., educator, author, financial management specialist; b. Louisville, Sept. 22, 1937; s. Gordon Buell and Rubye (Allen) F. AB in Classics, Princeton U., 1959; AM in Classical Philology and Linguistics, Harvard U., 1962, PhD in Linguistics, 1965; postgrad., U. Oslo, 1962-64, U. Sofia, Bulgaria, 1963, U. Uppsala, Sweden, 1963-64, U. Stockholm, 1963-64, U. Madrid, 1963. Asst. prof. Indo-European and Baltic linguistics, Sanskrit and Medieval Latin Northwestern U., Evanston, Ill., 1965-72; assoc. prof. English and linguistics U. No. Iowa, Cedar Falls, 1972-76; fin. specialist Gorgay, Inc., Louisville, 1976-77; reimbursement fin. mgmt. specialist Humana, Inc., The Hosp. Co., Louisville, 1978—; dir. Southeastern Investment Trust Inc., Louisville, 1979—; vis. asst. prof. Medieval Latin, U. Chgo., 1966-67; lectr. linguistics U. Chgo. univ. extension, 1966-67, 70-72; asst. prof. anthropology Northwestern U. evening div., 1971-72. Author: The Ruodlieb: The First Medieval Epic of Chivalry from Eleventh-Century Germany, 1965, The Ruodlieb: Linguistic Introduction, Latin Text, and Glossary, 1966, The Ruodlieb: Facsimile Edition, 1965, 2d edit. 1967, Old Lithuanian Texts of the Sixteenth and Seventeenth Centuries with a Glossary, 1969, The Old Lithuanian Catechism of Baltramiejus Vilentas (1579): A Phonological, Morphological, and Syntactical Investigation, 1969, Isidore of Seville's History of the Goths, Vandals, and Suevi, 1966, 2d edit. 1970, The Letters of Saint Isidore of Seville, 1966, 2d. edit. 1970, The Old Lithuanian Catechism of Martynas Mazvydas (1547), 1971, others; translator: A Concise Elementary Grammar of the Sanskrit Language with Exercises, Reading Selections, and a Glossary (Jan Gonda), 1966, The Comparative Method in Historical Linguistics (Antoine Meillet), 1967, A Sanskrit Grammar (Manfred Mayrhofer), 1972; contbr. numerous articles to many scholarly jours. Named to Hon. Order Ky. Cols. Mem. Linguistic Soc. Am.(life), Internat. Linguistic Assn., Societas Linguistica Europaea, Am. Philol. Assn. (life), Classical Assn. Middle West and South (life), Am. Assn. Tchrs. Slavic and East European Langs., Medieval Acad. Am. (life), MLA (life), Am. Assn. Advancement Slavic Studies, Assn. for Advancement Baltic Studies, Inst. Lithuanian Studies, SAR (life), Princeton Alumni Assn. (Louisville chpt.), Phi Beta Kappa. Baptist. Clubs: Princeton (N.Y.C.); Harvard (Chgo.); Louisville Country; Harvard-Radcliff (Ky.). Home: 3619 Brownsboro Rd Louisville KY 40207

FORD, HUGH, mechanical engineer; b. July 16, 1913; s. Arthur and Constance F.; attended City and Guilds Coll., U. London; D.Sc. in Engring.; Ph.D.; D.Sc. (hon.), Salford, 1976; QUB, 1977, Aston, 1978, Bath, 1978, Sheffield; m. Wynyard Scholfield, 1942; 2 children. Practical trainee GWR Locomotive Works, 1931-36; research into heat transfer, 1936-39; R. and Eng. Imperial Chem. Industries, Northwich, 1939-42; chief engr. tech. dept. Brit. Iron and Steel Fedn., 1942-45, then head mech. working div. Brit. Iron and Steel Research Assn., 1945-47; reader in applied mechanics U. London Imperial Coll. of Sci. and Tech., 1948-51, prof., 1951-69, head dept. mech. engring., 1965-78, prof. mech. engring., 1969-80, prof. emeritus, 1981—, prorector, 1978-80; chmn. Sir Hugh Ford and Assocs., Ltd.; dir. Ricardo Cons. Engrs. Ltd., Air Liquide U.K. Ltd.; tech. dir. Davy-Ashmore Group, 1968-71; dir. Herbert Ltd., 1972-79; SRC, 1968-72 (chmn. engring. bd.); ARC, 1976-82. Created Knight, 1975; recipient James Watt Internat. Gold medal, 1985; Whitworth scholar. Fellow Royal Soc. (council 1973-74), Inst. Mech. Engrs. (council, v.p. 1972, 75, sr. v.p. 1976, pres. 1977-78, Thomas Hawksley gold medal 1948), Fellowship of Engring. (v.p. 1982-84), ICE, CGI; mem. Inst. Metals (pres. 1963, Robertson medal), Welding Inst. (pres. 1983-85), Brit. Assn. (pres. sect. 6, 1975-76), ASME (hon.), New Inst. Medals (pres. 1985-87). Club: Athenaeum. Author: Advanced Mechanics of Materials, 1963; author profl. papers. Office: care Royal Soc, 6 Carlton House Terr, London SW1 5AG, England

FORD, JAMES DAYTON, lawyer, retired moving company executive; b. Harrisburg, Ill., May 31, 1924; s. J. Dayton and Anna (Dorris) F.; m. Alice Maria Evans, June 9, 1944; children—Lynn Alice (Mrs. G. Personius), Katherine Anne (Mrs. Wayne E. Graham), Anna Maria (Mrs. M.S. Rottenstein), Elizabeth Ellen (Mrs. James E. Flores), Jamie LaCene (Mrs. C.C. Carrier). B.B.A., U. Mich., 1948, M.B.A., 1948, J.D., 1951. Bar: Ill. bar 1952, Ariz. bar 1960. Tax. atty. U.S. Steel Corp. subsidiaries in Duluth, Minn. and Pitts., 1951-54; tax mgr. M.W. Kellogg Co., N.Y.C., 1954-58, Comml. Solvents Corp., N.Y.C., 1958-59; partner firm Hull, Terry & Ford, Tucson, 1960-66; gen. counsel Allied Van Lines, Broadview, Ill., 1966-68; exec. v.p. Allied Van Lines, 1968-71, pres., 1971-75; practice law Tucson, 1976—. Served with AUS, 1943-46. Mem. Ariz., Pima County bar assns., Nat. Def. Transp. Assn. (life), Nat. Rifle Assn. (life), Household Goods Carriers Bur. (v.p. 1974-76), Am. Movers Conf. (dir. 1973-76), Delta Sigma Pi. Republican. Presbyterian. Club: Tucson Rod and Gun. Lodges: Masons, Shriners, Elks. Home: 6742 N Los Arboles Circle Tucson AZ 85704 Office: 6985 N Oracle Rd Tucson AZ 85704

FORD, JOHN BATTICE, III, business executive; b. Detroit, July 3, 1924; s. John Battice and Katharine (Tanner) F.; B.S., Yale U., 1949; m. Peggy Powers, July 12, 1980; 1 child, John Battice IV. Adminstrv. asst. Nat. Bank of Detroit, 1950-53; asst. treas. Huron Portland Cement Co., Detroit, 1953-58, treas., 1958-59; owner, pres. TRADCO/DETROIT, Inc., 1960-69; pres. H.M. Robins Co., 1961-67; pres. Gentrex, Inc., 1968-82; pres., owner John Ford & Assocs., Inc., St. Clair Shores, Mich., 1982—. Bd. dirs. United Found., Meals for Millions/Freedom From Hunger Found.; pres., gen. mgr. Detroit Grand Opera Assn.; 1st vice chmn. S.E. Mich. chpt. ARC; pres., mem. exec. com. Harbor Point Assn. Mem. Founders Soc. Detroit Inst. Arts, U.S. C. of C., Detroit Bd. Commerce. Episcopalian. Clubs: Yondotega, Country of Detroit; Grosse Pointe (Mich.); Yale (N.Y.C.); Circumnavigators,

Little Harbor, Mill Reef, Little Traverse Yacht. Home: 39 Waverly Ln Grosse Pointe Farms MI 48236 Office: John Ford & Assocs 20630 Harper Ave Suite 203 Harper Woods MI 48225

FORD, JOHN CHARLES, communications executive; b. Washington, Oct. 8, 1942; s. Edgar Martin and Mary (Crowley) F. BA, U. Md., 1964, postgrad., 1964-65; MA, NYU, 1966; postgrad. N.Y. Inst. Finance, 1967-68, New Sch. for Social Research, 1969, Crowell-Collier Inst., 1969, Friesen-Kaye Inst., 1971, Sterling Inst., 1975, U. Wis., 1977, Colgate-Darden Sch. Bus., U. Va., 1978, Harvard U., 1982. TV prodn. asst. USIA, Washington, 1963-65; instr. U. Md., 1965; acct. exec. Ruder & Finn Inc., N.Y.C., 1965-66; asst. to exec. v.p., mgr. ednl. services Am. Stock Exchange, N.Y.C., 1966-70; mgr. communications and audio visual tng. Merrill Lynch, Pierce, Fenner & Smith Inc., N.Y.C., 1970-74; dir. edn. and tng. CBS Inc., 1974-77, dir. employee devel. and edn., 1977-79; pres. Travel U., v.p. Travel Network Corp. subs. ABC, N.Y.C., 1979-81; dir. human resources Home Box Office, Inc., 1981-84; communications cons., 1984—; mem. faculty N.Y. Inst. Fin., 1971-73, Katherine Gibbs Sch., 1972-74. Bd. dirs., treas. Archeus Found.; trustee U. Md. Found., 1984—; mem. U. Md. Pres.'s Club, bd. dirs., 1984—; chmn. Carnegie Hall concert U. Md. Piano Festival; bd. dirs. Care, Inc., One-to-One; bd. overseers Emerson Coll., Boston, 1978—; mem. bd. advisors corp. and cable communications program Manhattan Community Coll., CUNY; mem. devel. council Neumann Coll., Aston, Pa.; bd. dirs., v.p. 15 W 81st St. Tenants Corp., 1978-80, pres., 1979; mem. Council of West Side Coops., 20th Precinct Community Council, N.Y. Police Dept.; guest speaker Iowa Assn. for Life Long Learning. Mem. Nat. Acad. TV Arts and Scis. (bd. govs., trustee 1969—, sec. 1971—, trustee 1973—), Am. Soc. Tng. and Devel. (award 1978), Fin. Industry Tng. Assn. (pres. 1969-71), AAUP, Speech Communications Assn., Eastern Communication Assn. (area chmn. 1975), N.Y. State Communication Assn. (speaker), West 70th St. Assn., Fedn. West Side Block Assns., W. 82d St. Block Assn., Internat. Radio & TV Soc., Nat. Soc. Programmed Instrn., Nat. Audio-Visual Assn., Wall Street Tng. Dirs.'s Assn., Presidents Assn. of Am. Mgmt. Assns. (seminar leader), U. Md. Alumni Assn. Greater N.Y. (dir. 1966—), N.Y. Personnel Mgrs. Assns., Organizational Devel. Network, Group for Strategic Organizational Effectiveness, N.Y. Human Resource Planners, Organizational Devel. Network, Internat. Platform Assn., Omicron Delta Kappa, Phi Delta Theta. Home: 15 W 81st St New York NY 10024 Office: 485 Fifth Ave Suite 1042 New York NY 10017

FORD, JOHN STEPHEN, treasurer; b. Clinton, Mass., Apr. 27, 1957; s. James Joseph and Rita (Hart) F.; m. Mary Andrejczyk, Apr. 15, 1978; children: Michelle, Amanda, William. BS, Lowell U., 1979. CPA, Mass.; notary pub., Mass. Staff acct. Main, Hurdman, Cranston, CPA's, Worcester, Mass., 1979; sr. acct. William S. Reagan & Co. CPA's, Fitchburg, Mass., 1979-82; treas. Peterborough Oil Co., Inc., Leominster, Mass., 1982—; cons. in field. Treas. Dem. Town Com., Lancaster, Mass., 1982—; v.p. Lancaster Softball Assn., 1982. Fellow Mass. Soc. CPA's; mem. Am. Inst. CPA's (mem. personal fin. planning div.), Internat. Platform Assn. Roman Catholic. Office: Peterborough Oil Co 665 N Main PO Box 787 Leominster MA 01453

FORD, JON ALLAN, psychologist; b. Iowa Falls, Iowa, July 17, 1943; s. Verner Allen and Edna Marie (Huse) F.; B.A. in Math., U. No. Iowa, 1966, M.A. in Psychology, 1968; doctoral candidate Ind. U.; m. Carolyn Kay Stewart; children—Jon, Sara, Christine, Jamie. Tchr. math. and sci., Iowa, 1967-69; teaching asst. U. No. Iowa, 1969-70; psychol. intern Area Edn. Agy. 7, Cedar Falls, Iowa, 1970-71; psychologist Joint County Sch. Dist., Cedar Falls, 1971-72; asso. instr. Ind. U., 1972-73, psychotherapist univ. developmental tng. center, 1972-73; treatment supr. severe emotional disabilities program Area Edn. Agy. 7, Cedar Falls, 1973—; pvt. practice, 1972—; adj. asst. prof. U. No. Iowa, 1975; psycholgist Blackhawk County Sheriff's Dept., 1986—; cons., workshop leader in field. Mem. Am., Iowa psychol. assns., Nat., Iowa edn. assns., Iowa Sch. Psychologists Assn., Internat. Neuropsychol. Soc. Author: Developmental Meaning in the Assessment and Treatment of Emotionally Disturbed Students: A Book About Doing Battle with Psychological Disturbance in Schools. Contbr. articles and chpts. to profl. publs. and textbooks. Home: 1825 Hawthorne Dr Cedar Falls IA 50613 Office: 2315 Falls Ave Suite 4A Waterloo IA 50701

FORD, JOSEPH DILLON, composer, educator; b. Americus, Ga., Feb. 6, 1952; s. William Lamar and Julia King (Dillon) F. B.F.A., Fla. Internat. U., 1975; A.M., Harvard U., 1978. Tchrs. asst. Dade County Pub. Sch. System, Miami, Fla., 1979-80; music prof. Miami-Dade Community Coll., 1980-82; tchr. The Am. Sch. Tangier (Morocco), 1982-83; former mem. acad. music faculty South campus Miami-Dade Community Coll. Bd. dirs., sec. S. Fla. Chamber Ensemble, 1979-80. Variell scholar Harvard U., 1976, 77. Author: Cosmic Strings, 1978; Chromatic-1: A New Technique for Instrumental Speech, 1983; Sidi Mustafa: A Fable, 1984; composer: De l'Ombreterre, Suite en forme d'arabesques, Chromicons, Timbeaux, Thanatopsis, Twelve Ancient Dances, Capricci. Home: 9060 SW 187th Terr Miami FL 33157

FORD, LEE ELLEN, scientist, educator, lawyer; b. Auburn, Ind., June 16, 1917; d. Arthur W. and Geneva (Muhn) Ford; B.A., Wittenberg Coll., 1947; M.S., U. Minn., 1949; Ph.D., Iowa State Coll., 1952; J.D., U. Notre Dame, 1972. CPA auditing, 1934-44; assoc. prof. biology Gustavus Adolphus Coll., 1950-51, Anderson (Ind.) Coll., 1952-55; vis. prof. biology U. Alta. (Can.), Calgary, 1955-56; asso. prof. biology Pacific Luth. U., Parkland, Wash., 1956-62; prof. biology and cytogenetics Miss. State Coll. for Women, 1962-64; chief cytogeneticist Pacific N.W. Research Found., Seattle, 1964-65; dir. Canine Genetics Cons. Service, Parkland, 1963-69. Sponsor Companion Collies for the Adult, Jr. Blind, 1955-65; dir. Genetics Research Lab., Butler, Ind., 1955-75, cons. cytogenetics, 1969-75; legis. cons., 1970-79; dir. chromosome lab. Inst. Basic Research in Mental Retardation, S.I., 1968-69; exec. dir. Legis. Bur. U. Notre Dame Law Sch., also editor New Dimensions in Legislation, 1969-72; editor Butler Record Herald, 1972-76; bd. dirs. Ind. Interreligious Com. on Human Equality, 1976-80; exec. asst. to Gov. Otis R. Bowen, Ind., 1973-75; dir. Ind. Commn. on Status Women, 1973-74; bd. dirs. Ind. Council Chs.; editor Ford Assos. pubs., 1972-86; mem. Pres.'s Adv. Council on Drug Abuse, 1976-77. Admitted to Ind. bar, 1972. Adult counselor Girl Scouts U.S.A., 1934-40; bd. dirs. Ind. Task Force Women's Health, 1976-80; mem. exec. bd., bd. dirs. Ind.-Ky. Synod Lutheran Ch., 1972-78; bd. dirs., mem. council St. Marks Lutheran Ch., Butler, 1970-76; mem. social services personnel bd.; mem. DeKalb County (Ind.) Sheriff's Merit Bd., 1983-87; founder, dir., pres. Ind. Caucus for Animal Legislation and Leadership, 1984-87. Mem. or ex-mem. AAUW, AAAS, Genetics Soc. Am., Am. Human Genetics Soc., Am. Genetic Assn., Am. Inst. Biol. Scis., Am. Soc. Zoologists, La., Miss., Ind., Iowa acads. sci., Bot. Soc. Am., Ecol. Soc. Am., Am. (dir.), Ind. (dir.), DeKalb County (dir.) bar assns., Humane Soc. U.S. (dir. 1970-88), DeKalb County Humane Soc. (founder, dir. 1970-86), Ind. Fedn. Humane Socs. (dir. 1970-84), Nat. Assn. Women Lawyers (dir.), Bus. and Profl. Women's Club, Nat. Assn. Republican Women (dir.), Women's Equity Action League (dir.), Assn. So. Biologists, Phi Kappa Phi. Club: Altrusa. Editor: Breeder's Jour., 1958-63; numerous vols. on dog genetics and breeding, guide dogs for the blind. Contbr. over 2000 sci. and popular publs. on cytogenetics, dog breeding and legal topics; contbr. Am. Kennel Club Gazette, 1970-81, also others. Researcher in field. Home and Office: 824 E 7th St Auburn IN 46706

FORD, WENDELL HAMPTON, U.S. senator; b. Owensboro, Ky., Sept. 8, 1924; s. Ernest M. and Irene (Schenk) F.; m. Jean Neel, Sept. 18, 1943; children: Shirley Jean (Mrs. Dexter), Steven. Student, U. Ky., 1942-43. Ptnr. Gen. Ins. Agy., Owensboro, 1959—; chief asst. to gov. Ky. 1959-61; mem. Ky. Senate, 1966-67; lt. gov. Ky. 1967-71, gov. Ky., 1971-74, U.S. senator from Ky., 1974—; mem. Energy and Resources Com., Rules Com., Commerce, Sci. and Transp. Com., Dem. steering com.; past chmn. Dem. Senatorial Campaign Com., Nat. Dem. Gov.'s Caucus; chmn. Dem. Nat. Campaign Com., 1976. Served with AUS, 1944-46, Ky. N.G., 1949-62. Baptist. Club: Elk. *

FORDHAM, CHRISTOPHER COLUMBUS, III, medical educator, university dean and chancellor; b. Greensboro, N.C., Nov. 28, 1926; s. Christopher Columbus and Frances Long (Clendenin) F.; m. Barbara Byrd, Aug. 16, 1947; children—Pamela Fordham Richey, Susan Fordham Crowell, Betsy Fordham Templeton. Cert. in medicine, U. N.C., 1949; M.D., Harvard U., 1951. Diplomate Am. Bd. Internal Medicine. Intern Georgetown U. Hosp., 1951-52; asst. resident Boston City Hosp., 1952-53; sr. asst. resident N.C. Meml. Hosp., Chapel Hill, 1953-54; fellow in medicine U. N.C. Sch. Medicine, 1954-55, instr. medicine, 1958-60, asst. prof., 1960-64, assoc. prof., asst. dean, Sch. Medicine, 1964-68, prof., assoc. dean, 1968-69; acting asst. sec. for health Dept. HEW, Washington, 1977; prof., dean U. N.C. Sch. Medicine, 1971-79, prof. community medicine and hosp. adminstrn., 1978—, vice chancellor for health affairs, 1977-80, chancellor, 1980-88; prof. medicine, v.p. for medicine, dean Sch. Medicine, Med. Coll. Ga., Augusta, 1969-71; practice medicine, specializing in internal medicine Greensboro, N.C., 1957-58. Served as officer USAF, 1955-57. Fellow ACP, AAAS; mem. AMA, N.C. Med. Soc., So. Soc. Clin. Investigation, Am. Soc. Nephrology, Am. Fedn. Clin. Research, Soc. Health and Human Values, Am. Assn. Med. Colls. (exec. council 1975-78, rep. liaison com. med. edn. 1977-79), Am. Assn. Med. Coll. So. Regional Deans (chmn. 1972-73, 75-76, chmn. council deans 1977), N.Y. Acad. Scis., Inst. Medicine of Nat. Acad. Sci. (council 1985—), Elisha Mitchell Sci. Soc., AAUP, Order Golden Fleece, Sigma Xi, Alpha Omega Alpha. Office: 522 Morgan Creek Rd Chapel Hill NC 27514

FOREMAN, EDWIN FRANCIS, broker; b. Syracuse, N.Y., July 24, 1931; s. Herve Joseph and Ruth Margaret F.; m. Colleen Frances Tapp, July 7, 1962; children—Lisa C., Eric E. BAE in Econs. and Fgn. Trade, U. Fla., 1957; postgrad. in real estate Fla. Internat. U., 1974-75. Owner, prin. Edwin F. Foreman, Mortgage Broker, Hollywood, Fla., 1974—; with Consol. Energy Corp., Hollywood, 1977—, pres., chmn. bd., 1977—; v.p. Ea. State Securities, Inc., 1977—; owner, prin. Edwin F. Foreman, Real Estate Broker, 1978—; pres., chmn. One-Fore-Devel., Inc., 1985, Three-Fore-Devel., Inc., 1985, L&E Communications Inc., 1985; chmn., chief exec. officer Universal Traction, Hollywood, 1988—; gen. ptnr. Four-Fore Devel. Ltd., Five-Fore-Devel. Ltd., Six-Fore Devel., Ltd., 1987—. Econ. cons., dir. v.p. Michael I. Warde de Colombia Ltda. Served with USAF, 1950-53. R.J. Reynolds fellow U. N.C., 1961. Mem. Hollywood C. of C., Ft. Lauderdale World Trade Council. Democrat. Unitarian. Clubs: Jockey, Grove Isle (Miami), Fisher Island. Avocations: camping, fishing, music, photography, travel. Office: PO Box 7570 Suite 840 Hollywood FL 33081-1570

FORETTE, BERNARD PIERRE, physician; b. Paris, Jan. 28, 1937; s. Paul Marie and Jeanne (Corps) F.; m. Anne-Marie Somen, Dec. 1958 (dec. 1967); 1 child, Agnes; m. Françoise Madeleine Bribet, May 24, 1968; 1 child, Pierre. MD, U. Paris, 1968. Chief clin. staff Hosp. de la Pitie, Paris, 1968-78; prof. internal medicine U. Paris VI, 1978-84; prof. U. Rene Descartes, Paris, 1984—; head geriatric dept. Hosp. Ste.-Perine, Paris, 1984—; dir. Research Center at Centre de Gerontologie Claude Bernard, Paris, 1984—. Editor: Modern Trends in Aging Research, 1987; contbr. over 100 articles to profl. jours. Mem. French Soc. Rheumatology, French Soc. Gerontology, Internat. Ctr. Social Gerontology, European Assn. for the Study of Diabetes. Mem. RPR Party. Club: Automobile of France. Home: Boulevard St Michel 127, 75005 Paris France Office: Hosp Sainte-Perine, 11 Rue Chardon-Lagache, 75016 Paris France

FORGACS, JOSEPH, mycotoxicologist; b. Nokomis, Ill., Mar. 20, 1917; s. John and Elizabeth (Hallas) F.; B.S., U. Ill., 1940, M.S., 1942, Ph.D., 1944; m. Lillian Pearl Little, June 1, 1945; children—Theresa Maria, Joseph Alan, Lawrence David, Paul Axel, Lillian Pearl Maria. Dir. mycotoxicoses research Fort Detrick, Frederick, Md., 1944-54; sr. research fellow Am. Cyanamid Corp., Pearl River, N.Y., 1954-57; dir. lab. Spring Valley (N.Y.) Hosp., 1957-61; mycotoxicologist, staff microbiologist Good Samaritan Hosp., Suffern, N.Y., 1961-69; dir. clin. microbiology Ramapo Gen. Hosp. and Automated Biochem. Labs., Spring Valley, 1969-78. Cons. mycotoxicologist Agrl. Research Service, U.S. Dept. Agr., food and feed industries, 1957—; cons. microbiologist N.Y. State Dept. Mental Hygiene, Letchworth Village, Thiells, 1973—. Served with AUS, 1944-46. Diplomate Am. Acad. Microbiology. Fellow Am. Acad. Microbiology, Inst. Food Technologists, AAAS; mem. N.Y. Acad. Scis., Am. Inst. Biol. Scis., N.Y. Med. Mycology Soc., Phi Sigma, Sigma Xi. Contbr. articles to profl. jours. Patentee in field. Home and Office: 302 N Highland Ave Pearl River NY 10965

FORGET, VERDAYLE MARIE, artist, poet; b. Alliance, Nebr., Oct. 29, 1942; d. Walter Dale O'Neal and AlVerda Mae (Shigley) Brosz; m. Francois Leon Forget, Dec. 18, 1964. Cert. recognition, Famous Artists Sch., 1973; student, Dennis Ramsay Studio, Deal, Eng., 1973. One-woman shows include Bon Nat. Gallery, Seattle, 1977, Merchants Nat. Bank Plaza Gallery, Indpls., 1982, The Glass Chimney, Carmel, Ind., 1983, Cystic Fybrosis Found., Anderson, Ind., 1985, The Honeywell Found., Wabash, Ind., 1985; exhibited in group shows at Olde Main Gallery, Bellevue, Wash., 1971-73, Hoosier Salon, Indpls., 1982-86, Indpls. Mus. Art, 1985-86; work includes posters Ind. Pacers, 1985-86, commemorative painting and poster of Julius "Dr.J." Erving of Phila. 76ers playing his final game against Ind. Pacers, 1987, 4 championship covers NCAA, commemorative calendar New Indpls. Zoo, posters 10th anniversary Hoosier Horse Fair and Expo, Woodland Park Zoo, Seattle, Purdue U. football centennial poster and program covers, ofcl. poster Indpls. Zoo, 1988; author numerous poems, 1987—. Named Most Popular Artist Burien (Wash.) Arts Festival, 1971. Mem. Hoosier Salon. Republican. Protestant. Home and Studio: 3431 102d Pl SE Everett WA 98208

FORGETT, VALMORE JOSEPH, JR., arms company executive; b. Worcester, Mass., July 31, 1930; s. Valmore Joseph and Veron Rita (Sawicki) F.; B.S., Clemson U., 1956; m. Heidi Erika Kober, Apr. 28, 1963; children—Diana Lynn, Susan Lee, Valmore Joseph III. Pres., Service Armament Co., 1957—, Navy Arms Co., Inc., 1958—, Great Am. Arms Corp., 1960—, Collectors' Arms, Inc., 1964—(all Ridgefield, N.J.), Service Welding Co., Union City, N.J., 1970—. Cons., Ordnance Corp. Mus., Aberdeen, Md., 1958—, U.S. Arty. Sch. Mus., Ft. Sill, Okla., 1960—; spl. adviser U.S. Marine Corps Mus., 1958—, U.S. Mil. Acad., 1961—. Served with U.S. Army, 1953-55. Decorated cavalieri Order of Merit (Italy). Fellow Co. of Mil. Collectors and Historians; mem. Carolina Gun Collectors Assn. (dir. 1961-62, 74—), Soc. Gun Collectors (hon. mem. Birmingham, Eng.), South African Rifle Assn., U.S. Internat. Muzzle Loading Com. (chmn.). Republican. Club: Rotary (pres. Ridgefield). Author: (with others) Handbook of Small Arms, 1954. Home: Eagle's Roost 60 Pinecrest Dr Woodcliff Lake NJ 07680 also: Cant.,on Hill Farm Box 459 RD 4 Sussex NJ 07461 Office: 689 Bergen Blvd Ridgefield NJ 07657

FORJE, JOHN WILSON, sociologist, political scientist; b. Bali, Mezam, Cameroon; s. Elias Mbaham and Lydia Forje; m. Catherine Lema Fonyonga, Nov. 20, 1971; children: Gert, Ellinor, Paulina. BA in Philosophy, U. Lund, Sweden, 1974; MA, U. Hull, Eng., 1977; PhD, U. Lund, 1981, U. Salford, Eng., 1985. Research asst. Research Policy Inst. U. Lund, Sweden, 1975-82; research dir., founder Centre for Action-Oriented devel. on Africa, Lund, Sweden, 1979—; research assoc. Research Policy Inst., Lund, Sweden, 1982—; researcher Advanced Sch. Mass Communication U. Yaounde, Cameroon, 1985-86; cons. UNESCO, Paris, 1986—; researcher Ministry of Higher Edn. and Sci. Research, Yaounde, Cameroon, 1987—. Author: The One and Indivisible Cameroon, 1981, S&T in Cameroon, 1987, Trends in the Development of S&T, 1987; editor: Third World Development, 1984. Active Swedish Football Referee Assn. Lund Br., 1980—, African Assn. Polit. Sci., 1982—. Mem. African Non-govtl. Environ. Network, Assn. for Advancement of Research and Devel. in Third World, Soc. Internat. Devel. Home: BP 11429, Yaounde Cameroon Office: MESRES, BP 1457, Yaounde Cameroon

FORLANI, ARNALDO, Italian government official and politician; b. Pesaro, Italy, Dec. 8, 1925; s. Luigi and Caterina Forlani; m. Alma Ioni, 1956; 3 children. Ed. U. Urbino. Mem. Chamber of Deputies, 1958—; dep. sec. Christian Democratic Party, 1962-69, leader, 1969-73, now pres.; minister state undertakings, 1969-70; minister def., 1974-76; minister fgn. affairs, 1976-79; prime minister Italy, 1980-81, dep. prime minister, v.p. council of ministers, 1983. Address: Christian Dem Party, Piazza Con Luigi Sturzo 15, 001441 Rome Italy *

FORLINI, FRANK JOHN, JR., cardiologist; b. Newark, Mar. 30, 1941; s. Frank Sr. and Rose Theresa (Parussini) F.; m. Joanne Marie Horch, July 19, 1969; children: Anne Marie, Victoria, Frank III, Anthony. BS in Biology, Villanova (Pa.) U., 1963; MD, George Washington U., 1967. Diplomate Am. Bd. Internal Medicine, Am. Bd. Cardiovascular Disease. Intern Bklyn.-Cumberland Med. Ctr., N.Y., 1967-68, resident in internal medicine, 1968-70; fellow in cardiology Inst. Med. Sci. Pacific Med. Ctr., San Francisco, 1970-72; practice medicine specializing in cardiology Rock Island, Ill., 1974—; sr. ptnr. Forlini Med. Speciality Clinic, Rock Island, 1974—; owner Forlini Farm and Forlini Devel. Enterprises; adj. prof. pharmacy L.I. U., Bklyn., 1970; pres., chief exec. officer U.S. Oil and Transp. Co., Inc., 1966—; pres. Profl. and Execs. Ins. Assocs., 1973—, Profl. Assocs., 1973—; med. and exec. dir. Cardiovascular Inst. Northwestern Ill., 1984—. Contbr. articles to profl jours. Chmn. D.C. Young Reps., 1965-66; mem. exec. com. Rep. Cen. Com., Washington, 1965-66; vice chmn. Rock Island Reps., 1985—, precinct committeeman, 1985—; dep. registrar County of Rock Island, Ill., 1985—; trustee South Rock Island Twp., Rock Island County, 1987—; pres. parish council, extraordinary minister. Served to maj. USAF, 1972-74. Nat. Inst. Heart Disease NIH-USPHS grantee, 1964-66, 70-72. Fellow Am. Coll. Cardiology, N.Am. Soc. Pacing and Electrophysiology. Roman Catholic. Office: 2701 17th St Rock Island IL 61201

FORM, FREDRIC ALLAN, accountant; b. Bklyn., Mar. 2, 1942; s. Milton and Tedde (Bilus) F.; m. Jo Ann August, Aug. 29, 1964; 1 child, Harold. Jr. BBA, Pace U., 1970. Sr. acct. S.P. Cooper & Co., N.Y.C., 1963-69; pvt. practice pub. acctg., Levittown, N.Y., 1969—. Bd. dirs. Wantagh Community Arts Program, Inc., 1980-84; bd. dirs., treas. Cen. Nassau County React, Inc., 1979-82; treas. Your, Ours, Mine Community Ctr., Levittown, N.Y., 1987—; v.p. Reli React, Inc., 1983—. Mem. Nat. Soc. Pub. Accts. (1st v.p.), N.Y. Soc. Ind. Accts. (2d v.p. 1983-85, v.p. 1985-86, pres. 1986-87). Lodge: Kiwanis (treas. Levittown club 1988—). Office: 2900 Hempstead Turnpike Levittown NY 11756

FORMAN, H. CHANDLEE, architect, art educator; b. N.Y.C.; s. Horace Baker, Jr. and Elizabeth (Chandlee) F.; A.B., Princeton U., 1926; M.Arch., U. Pa., 1931, Ph.D. in Fine Arts, 1942; Litt.D., St. Mary's Coll. Md., 1981; m. Caroline Biddle Lippincott, Sept. 28, 1929 (dec. June 5, 1975); children—Elizabeth Forman Harrell, Richard Townsend Turner, Lawrence Thorne; m. 2d, Rebecca Anthony Russell, May 26, 1978. Pvt. practice architecture as H. Chandlee Forman, Easton, Md., specializing residences, chs., hist. restorations, 1931-35, 52-78; chief architect Jamestown (Va.) Archaeol. Project, 1935-36; editor nat. records Historic Am. Bldgs. Survey, 1936-37; lectr. fine arts Haverford Coll., 1937-39; instr. art Rutgers U., 1939-40; lectr. history art U. Pa., 1940-41; Catherine L. Comer prof. fine arts Wesleyan Coll. of Ga., 1941-45; prof. art, head dept. Agnes Scott Coll., 1945-52; cons. architect Ga. Hist. Commn., 1952-60. Adviser Md. St. Mary's City Commn., 1965-69; mem. Md. Archeol. Commn., 1968-77, chmn., 1973; sec. bd. dirs. Soc. Preservation Md. Antiquities, 1952-54; lectr. throughout world for State Dept., 1964; mem. corp. bd. Haverford Coll., 1975-85. Recipient Frederick Barnard White prize Princeton U., 1926, Calvert prize for historic preservation State of Md., 1976, Md. Gov.'s citation for history and archaeology, 1983; Historic Preservation award Assn. for Preservation Va. Antiquities, 1982; U. Center Ga. grantee for archaeology studies in Mex., 1946-47; Carnegie Found. fellow creative painting, 1947. Fellow AIA (charter mem. Chesapeake Bay chpt., exec. com. Balt. chpt. 1955-57, v.p. Chesapeake Bay chpt. 1965-67), Explorers Club; mem. Talbot County (Md.) Hist. Soc. (dir., co-organizer, trustee, librarian, 1st curator), Archaeol. Soc. Md. (hon.), Nantucket Garden Club (hon.), Townsend Soc. Am. (hon.), Soc. Colonial Wars, Robert Gilmore Soc., Princeton U. Alumni Assn. Eastern Shore (pres. 1960-61, 70-72, 77-79), various mus. in U.K. Author numerous books, including: Early Manor and Plantation Houses of Maryland, 1934; Jamestown and St. Mary's: Buried Cities of Romance, 1938; The Architecture of the Old South, The Medieval Style, 1948; Virginia Architecture in the 17th Century, 1957; Early Nantucket and its Whale Houses, 1966; Old Buildings, Gardens and Furniture in Tidewater Maryland, 1967; The Virginia Eastern Shore and its British Origins: History, Gardens & Antiquities, 1975; The Rolling Year on Maryland's Upper Eastern Shore, 1985; exhibited art work Library of Congress, Washington, Balt. Mus. Art, Art Inst. Chgo., others; donor H. Chandlee Forman Nature Preserve to Nantucket Maria Mitchell Assn., 1973, The Ending of Controversie Mus. and Collections to Talbot County Hist. Soc., 1984. Address: PO Box 807 Easton MD 21601

FORMAN, J(OSEPH) CHARLES, chemical engineer, consultant; b. Chgo., Dec. 22, 1931; s. Joseph O. and Marie (Smith) F.; m. Ursula Diane Weston, July 22, 1953; children: Stephen Charles, Diane Brigitte, Mary Erika. S.B., M.I.T., 1953; M.S., Northwestern U., 1957, Ph.D., 1960. Registered profl. engr., Ill. Trainee chem. engring. Dow Chem. Co., Midland, Mich., 1953-54; from sr. chem. engr. to dir. mfg. ops. agrl. vet. div. Abbott Labs., North Chicago, Ill., 1956-77; assoc. exec. dir. Am. Inst. Chem. Engrs., N.Y.C., 1977-78; exec. dir., sec., pub. Jour of Am. Inst. Chem. Engrs., Internat. Chem. Engring., pub. Biotech. Progress, Energy Progress, Environ. Progress; exec. dir., sec. Plant/Ops. Progress, 1978-87; pres. and prin. Forman Assocs. Cons. and Tech. Services, 1987—; cons. in field, accreditation insp. chem. engring. curricula. Mem. ednl. council M.I.T., 1961-74, 78—; mem. Lake Bluff (Ill.) Bd. Edn., 1967-73, pres., 1971-73; pres. Lake County (Ill.) Sch. Bd. Assn., 1969-71; mem. Lake Bluff Plan Commn., 1973-77, chmn., 1976-77; mem. Darien (Conn.) personnel Adv. Commn., 1986—. Served with USAF, 1954-56. Fellow Am. Inst. Chem. Engrs., AAAS; mem. Am. Chem. Soc., Am. Soc. Assn. Execs., Council Engring. and Sci. Soc. Execs. (dir. 1980-83, sec. 1983-84, v.p. 1984-85, pres. 1985-86), Nat. Eagle Scout Assn., Sigma Xi, Tau Beta Pi, Phi Lambda Upsilon, Alpha Tau Omega. Home and Office: 77 Stanton Rd Darien CT 06820

FORMHALS, ROBERT WILLARD YATES (SANGUSZKO), ret. ednl. adminstr.; b. Los Angeles, June 14, 1919; s. Carl Wright and Muriel (Yates) (Sanguszko) Formhals; LLB, JD, Welch Coll. Law, Los Angeles, 1943; cert. pub. adminstrn. Sacramento State Coll., 1959; DCL, Sheffield Coll. of Nat. Univs., Doncaster, 1965; m. Elaine Mary Peters, Apr. 4, 1947; 1 child, Robert Arthur Clinton. Personnel mgr. Warman Steel Casting Co., Vernon, Calif., 1943-47; dep. labor commr. Calif., 1948; adminstrv. asst. to state architect Calif., 1948-59; No. Calif. mgr. William L. Aldrich Co., 1960-61; exec. sec.-treas. Calif. Sch. Bds. Assn., 1961-67; dir. bd. policies services Ednl. Service Bur., 1967; pres. Assos. Mgmt. Service, 1967-70; mcpl. employee relations officer City of San Jose (Calif.), 1970-74; program mgr. West Valley Coll., Saratoga, Calif., 1975-76, also instr. labor relations and mgmt., 1972-75; dir. employer-employee relations Conejo Valley Unified Sch. Dist., 1976-81. Commr. Calif. Commn. Sch. Dist. Orgn., 1961-64; chmn. Gov. Calif. Edn. and Tng. Adv. Com. Civil Def., also mem. Calif. Disaster Council, 1961-67; personnel commr. Pleasant Valley Sch. Dist., 1979-81, trustee, 1981— ; exec. vice chmn. Young Dems. Calif., 1941-44; mem. Nat. Com. Dems. for Dewey, 1944; Calif. chmn. Dems. for Knowland, 1946; vice chmn. Sacramento County Com. for Nixon, 1960. Chmn. bd. Pacific Maritime Acad., 1950-52; trustee St. John Found., 1972—. Served with AUS, 1943-44; maj. USNG, 1960-70; col. JAG Corps Res. 1982-83. Created knight by King Peter II of Yugoslavia; decorated grand officer White Eagle, grand officer Crown (Yugoslavia); grand master, grand cross St. John Jerusalem; grand cross Constantine the Gt.; knight comdr. St. Laszlo (Hungary). Mem. Am. Soc. Safety Engrs. (past nat. exec. bd.), Am. Arbitration Assn. (nat. labor panel), Am. Legion (comdr. PV Post 382 1988—), SAR (pres. Palo Alto chpt., pres. Patton chpt., state exec. sec. 1978-79, state pres. 1979-80 nat. trustee 1980-81, nat. v.p. gen. 1981-82, 84-85), KP, Eagles. Clubs: Commonwealth (San Francisco); Severance (Los Angeles). Author: Handbook of Armed Forces of the World, 1948, Book of Precedence, 1965, White Cross, 1980; also articles. Address: 5609 E Willow View Dr Camarillo CA 93010

FORMICA, GIANNI, space research scientist; b. Milan, Italy, Mar. 23, 1922; s. Aldo and Angioletta (Veggi) F.; m. Emma Saracchi, 1958; 1 dau. Ph.D., Milan Poly. Dir. CGE-Gen. Electric, Milan, 1959-69; dir. Societa Italiana Sistemi Informativi Elettronici, 1969-73, head Milan office, 1970-73; dir. European Space Ops. Centre, Darmstadt, W.Ger., 1973—; prof. hydraulics Faculty Agronomy, Catholic U. Milan, 1962-70, Faculty Engring., U. Ancona, 1971-73. Contbr. articles to profl. publs. Office: European Space Ops Centre, 50 Robert-Bosch-Strasse, 6100 Darmstadt Federal Republic of Germany *

FORNOFF, FRANK, JR., retired chemistry educator; b. Mt. Carmel, Ill., Mar. 29, 1914; s. Frank and Ada (Arnold) F.; A.B., U. Ill., 1936; M.S., Ohio State U., 1937, Ph.D. (Proctor & Gamble fellow), 1939. Asst. prof. Lehigh U., Bethlehem, Pa., 1942-44; chem. engr. Western Electric Co., N.Y.C.,

1944-45; asst. prof. chemistry Lehigh U., 1945-47, asso. prof., 1947-53; asso. prof. Kans. State U., Manhattan, 1953-56; lectr. Rutgers U., New Brunswick, N.J., 1956-84; sr. examiner Ednl. Testing Service, Princeton, N.J., 1956, group head, 1956-83. Active Boy Scouts Am., Princeton, 1957—. NRC fellow U. Calif., Berkeley, 1939-40. Mem. Am. Chem. Soc. (chmn. local sect. assn. publs. 1960-70), AAAS, Am. Soc. Engring. Edn., Nat. Sci. Tchrs. Assn., Nat. Council Measurements in Edn., N.J. Acad. Sci. Methodist. Contbr. articles to profl. jours.; editor AP Chemistry newsletter, 1976—. Home: 338 Franklin St Princeton NJ 08540 Office: Ednl Testing Service Princeton NJ 08541

FORREST, HERBERT EMERSON, lawyer; b. N.Y.C., Sept. 20, 1923; s. Jacob K. and Rose (Fried) F.; m. Marilyn Lefsky, Jan. 12, 1952; children: Glenn Clifford, Andrew Matthew. B.A. with distinction, George Washington U., 1948; J.D. with highest honors, 1952; student, CCNY, 1941, Ohio U., 1943-44. Bar: Va. 1952, D.C. 1952, U.S. Supreme Ct. 1956, Md. 1959. Plate printer Bur. Engraving and Printing, Washington, 1942-43, 1946-52; law clk. to chief judge Bolitha J. Laws U.S. Dist. Ct., Washington, 1952-55; practice in Washington, 1952—; mem. firm Welch & Morgan, 1955-65; mem. firm Steptoe & Johnson, 1965-85, of counsel, 1986-87; trial atty. Fed. Programs Br. Civil div. U.S. Dept. Justice, Washington, 1987—; chmn. adv. bd. D.C. Criminal Justice Act, 1971-74; sec. com. admissions and grievances U.S. Ct. Appeals, D.C., 1973-79; mem. Title-1 audit hearing bd. U.S. Office Edn. HEW, 1976-79; mem. edn. appeals bd. U.S. Dept. Edn., 1979-82; mem. Lawyer's Support Com. for Visitors Service Center, 1975-87. Contbr. articles to legal jours.; advisory bd.: Duke Law Jour, 1969-75. Pres. Whittier Woods PTA, 1970-71. Served with F.A., Signal Corps U.S. Army, 1943-46. Recipient Walsh award in Irish history, 1952, Goddard award in commerce, 1952. Fellow Am. Bar Found.; mem. George Washington Law Assn., Am. Judicature Soc., ABA (council 1972-75, 1981-84, budget officer 1985—, vice chmn. task force on sect. devel. 1987—, chmn. com. on agy. rule making 1968-72, 1976—, chmn. membership com. 1984-85, editor ann. reports 1973—, adminstrv. law sect., mem. communications com. public utilities law sect., vice chmn. industry regulation com. 1985-86, chmn. communications subcom. 1983-85 antitrust law sect., internat. law sect., sec. judicial adminstrn., sect. sci. and tech., communications forum), Va. State Bar Assn., Fed. Bar Assn. (chmn. jud. rev. com. 1981-85, vice chmn. adminstrv. law sect. 1985-87), Fed. Communications Bar Assn. (del. to ABA Ho. Dels. 1979-81, exec. com. 1967-71, 76-84, v.p. 1981-82, pres. 1982-83, chmn. telecommunications com. 1983-87), D.C. Bar Assn. (past sec., exec. com.), NAM, Nat. Assn. Bar Pres., Washington Council Lawyers, Legal Aid and Pub. Defender Assn., Am. Arbitration Assn. (comml. panel 1976-87), D.C. Unified Bar (bd. govs. 1976-79, chmn. com. on employment discrimination complaint service 1973-79, chmn. task force on services to public 1974-78, chmn. com. on appointment counsel in criminal cases 1978—, co-chmn. com. on participation govt. employees in pro bono activities 1977-79), Broadcast Pioneers, Order of Coif, Phi Beta Kappa, Pi Gamma Mu., Artus, Phi Eta Sigma, Phi Delta Phi. Democrat. Lodge: B'nai Brith. Home: 8706 Bellwood Rd Bethesda MD 20817 Office: US Dept Justice 10th & Pennsylvania Ave NW Room 3342 Main Bldg Washington DC 20530

FORRESTAL, MICHAEL VINCENT, lawyer; b. N.Y.C., Nov. 26, 1927; s. James Vincent and Josephine (Ogden) F. Student, Princeton U., 1949; LL.B., Harvard U., 1953. Bar: N.Y. 1954. Since practiced in N.Y.C; partner Shearman & Sterling, 1960—; spl. asst. to Averell Harriman (dir. Marshall Plan), 1948-50; sr. mem. White House Nat. Security Staff, 1962-65; sec. tripartite Naval Commn., Berlin, 1946; asst. U.S. naval attache, Moscow, USSR, 1946-47. Chmn. Met. Opera Guild, 1965-70; bd. dirs., treas. Met. Opera Assn., 1967—, Nat. Opera Inst., 1971-80; exec. sec. adv. com. Kennedy Inst. Politics, Harvard U., 1967-82; trustee Inst. Advanced Study, Princeton, N.J., 1970—; trustee Phillips Exeter Acad., 1979—, pres. bd. trustees, 1981—. Mem. ABA, Assn. Bar City N.Y., Am. Arbitration Assn. (dir. 1980-83), Council Fgn. Relations. Episcopalian. Clubs: Racquet and Tennis (N.Y.C.), Links (N.Y.C.); Metropolitan (Washington); Travellers (Paris, France). Home: 25 Central Park West New York NY 10023 Office: Shearman & Sterling 599 Lexington Ave New York NY 10022

FORRESTER, EUGENE PRIEST, former army officer, management marketing consultant; b. Watertown, Tenn., Apr. 17, 1926; s. Robert L. and Christine Elizabeth (Phillips) F.; B.S., U.S. Mil. Acad., 1948; M.A. in Internat. Relations, George Washington U., 1967; LL.D., Chung Ang U. (Republic of Korea), 1981; grad. Command and Gen. Staff Coll., Armed Forces Staff Coll., Brit. Staff Coll., Nat. War Coll.; m. Mary Louise Wagner, Dec. 28, 1953 (dec. 1971); children—Eugene Priest, II, Pamela Louise, Elizabeth Wagner. Commd. 2d lt. U.S. Army, 1948, advanced through grades to lt. gen., 1978; with Command and Gen. Staff Coll., Ft. Leavenworth, Kans., 1958-59; staff officer Supreme Hdqrs. Allied Powers Europe, 1961-63; dep. battle group comdr. 504th Inf., 82d Airborne Div., later asst. chief of staff for ops. 82d Airborne Div., Ft. Bragg, N.C., 1963-65; mil. asst. to Sec. Army, Washington, 1966; chief forces devel. U.S. Army, Vietnam, 1967-68, comdr. 3d Brigade, 4th Inf. Div., 1968; exec. officer to vice chief of staff Dept. Army, Washington, 1968-70; asst. div. comdr. 1st Cav. Div., Vietnam, 1970; dep. asst. chief of staff Civil Ops. and Rural Devel. Support, Hdqrs. Mil. Assistance Command, Vietnam, 1970-71; dir. officer personnel, later dir. procurement, tng. and distbn., then dir. plans, program and budget, Hdqrs. Dept. Army, 1971-73; comdr. U.S. Army Adminstrn. Center, Ft. Ben Harrison, Ind., 1973-75; comdr. U.S. Army Recruiting Command, Ft. Sheridan, Ill., 1975-78; comdr. 6th U.S. Army, Presidio, San Francisco, 1978-79; comdr. Combined Field Army, Korea, 1979-81; comdr. U.S. Army Western Command, Ft. Shafter, Hawaii, 1981-83; ret., 1983; mgmt. mktg. cons., corp. dir., 1983—. Decorated D.S.M. with oak leaf cluster, Silver Star, Legion of Merit with 3 oak leaf clusters, D.F.C., Bronze Star with 2 oak leaf clusters, Air medal with 18 oak leaf clusters, Joint Service Commendation medal, Combat Inf. badge (2), Nat. Order Vietnam 4th-5th class, Gallantry Cross with 2 palms and gold star (Vietnam), Armed Forces Honor medal 1st class (Vietnam), numerous others. Clubs: Chicago, Bohemian. Address: 1101 S Arlington Rd Arlington VA 22202

FORRESTER, WILLIAM DONALD, public relations executive; b. Port Chester, N.Y., Dec. 20, 1931; s. John J. and Catherine (McDonald) F.; B.S., Columbia U., 1955; m. Margaret A. Ward, Feb. 2, 1952. Vice pres. George Peabody & Assocs., N.Y.C., 1957-64; dir. public relations project Am. Export Isbrandtsen Lines, N.Y.C., 1964-65; account supr. Cunningham & Walsh, N.Y.C., 1965-67; gen. mgr. PR Communications, Clifton, N.J., 1967-69; v.p. Burson-Marsteller, N.Y.C., 1969-74; v.p. adminstrn. and communications U.S.-USSR Trade and Econ. Council, N.Y.C./Washington/Moscow, 1974—. Served with USMC, 1950-52. Mem. Public Relations Soc. Am. Contbr. articles to bus. jours. Home: Overhill Road RD 2 Town of Cortlandt Peekskill NY 10566 Office: 805 Third Ave New York NY 10022

FORRY, JOHN EMERSON, retired aerospace company executive; b. Coweta, Okla., Feb. 13, 1920; s. Fred Emerson and Elizabeth (Ingram) F.; B.S. in Mech. Engring., Okla. State U., 1939; LL.B., George Washington U., 1953; m. Marion Carlotta MacArthur, May 24, 1941; children—John Ingram, Anne Elizabeth. Asst. chief engr. Piper Aricraft Corp., 1939-41; project engr. CAA, Kansas City, Mo., 1942; head aircraft design research br. Bur. Aeros., U.S. Navy, 1946-54; admitted to D.C. bar, 1953, Mo. bar, 1960; asst. dir. Office Aircraft and Marinecraft, Dept. Def., 1954-57; with McDonnell Douglas Corp., St. Louis, 1957—, v.p., controller, 1968-77; exec. v.p. fin. Douglas Aircraft Co., 1977-79; ret., 1979; bus. cons., 1979—. Various offices Protestant Episcopal Diocese Mo.; trustee Maryville Coll.; chmn. Santa Ynez Valley Hosp.; bd. dirs. Santa Barbara Symphony Assn. Served to lt. USNR, 1943-46. Registered profl. engr., D.C. Mem. Sigma Tau, Phi Delta Phi. Home: 3737 Oak Trail Rd Box 855 Santa Ynez CA 93460

FORSBERG, KEVIN JOHN, consulting company executive; b. Oakland, Calif., July 20, 1934; s. Ted Otto and Gladys (Reid) F.; m. Edna Dorles, Apr., 1966 (div. Nov. 1979); m. Cindy Jane Beason, Jan. 1, 1981; children: Ian, Chenoa. BSCE, MIT, 1956; MS in Engring. Mechanics, Stanford U., 1958, PhD in Engring. Mechanics, 1961, postgrad., 1979. Mem. tech. staff Lockheed Missiles & Space Co., Sunnyvale, Calif., 1956-61, program mgr., 1973-84; mgr. solid mech. Lockheed Missiles & Space Co., Palo Alto, Calif., 1963-71, asst. dir., 1971-73; v.p. Consulting Resources, Inc., Santa Clara, Calif., 1984—; lectr. grad. sch. Santa Clara U., 1984—, U. Calif. Santa Cruz, 1985—. Co-author: (handbook) Project Management and Project Leadership, 1985; regional editor Jour. Computers and Structures, Washington, 1970-80; contbr. articles to profl. jours. Chmn. Citizens' Com. on High Sch. Edn., Redwood City, Calif., 1969-70. Served to capt. U.S. Army, 1961-63. Recipient Pub. Service medal NASA, 1981. Fellow ASME; assoc. fellow AIAA. Home: 1225 Vienna Dr #584 Sunnyvale CA 94089 Office: Consulting Resources Inc 5333 Betsy Ross Santa Clara CA 95052

FORSBERG, STEVEN GEORGE, manufacturing executive, consultant; b. Worcester, Mass., Jan. 13, 1954; s. Harold Axel and Dorothy (Smith) F.; m. Helen Cecila Winroth, Sept. 7, 1977; 1 child, Nina Rebekka. AS, Quinsigamond Coll., 1974; BS, U. Mass., 1977; MBA, Anna Maria Coll., 1983; cert. logistics, Cranfield U. Sales mgr. Great Can. Canoe Inc., Worcester, 1977-85; gen. mgr. Elegant Entries Inc., Worcester, 1977-85; sales mgr. DHL Internat., Oslo, 1986-87, sales coordinator Norway, 1988—. Recipient Salesmanship Gold award Elegant Entries, 1982. Republican. Roman Catholic. Clubs: Bogstad Golf (Oslo); Captains Course (Brewater, Mass.). Home: Mellomasvm 122, 1414 Trollasen Norway

FORSEY, (MARGARET) NUALA, sales executive; b. Belfast, No. Ireland, Nov. 10, 1956; d. James and Theresa (Morris) McErlane; m. Frank Forsey (div. 1980); 1 child, Danielle Therese; m. John Edward Conaghan; 1 child, Lauren Nicole. Grad. high sch., Belfast, Northern Ireland. Jr. sales exec. Smiths Food Group, London, 1973-75; negotiator Swindall Pendred and Atkins, Kettering, Eng., 1975-77; sales rep. Buntin and Keyes, Ltd., Kettering, 1977-80; sales exec. Comda Services, Toronto, Ont., Can., 1980-83; dealer, sales mgr. Pegasus Software, Kettering, 1983-84; sales mgr. U.K. Facts Software, Ltd., Bedford, Eng., 1984-86, sales dir., 1987—; sales mgr. U.K. Intuitive Systems, Stevenage, Eng., 1986-87. Roman Catholic. Home: 20 High St, Willingham CB4 5ES, England Office: Facts Software Ltd, Ketwell House Tavistock St, Bedford England

FORSTE, NORMAN LEE, management consultant; b. Carthage, Mo., Aug. 18, 1935; s. John Edward and Lula Mae (Martin) F.; m. Catherine Jean Culver, July 20, 1958; children: Patricia, Diana, John II, Karl. AA, Am. River coll., 1961; BA, Calif. State U., 1964, MA, 1971; MBA, Golden Gate U., 1973; PhD in Higher Edn., U. Wash., 1984. Adminstrv. analyst State of Calif., Sacramento, 1962-64, sr. data processing systems analyst, 1966-67, supr. info. systems devel., 1967-68; sr. adminstrv. analyst County of Sacramento (Calif.), 1964-66, dir. systems and data processing dept., 1968-74; dir. adminstrv. data processing div. U. Wash., Seattle, 1974-76; mgr. mgmt. adv. services Deloitte Haskins & Sells, 1976-81, dir. mgmt. adv. services, 1981-85; pvt. practice mgmt. cons., Carmichael, Calif., 1985—; instr. mgmt. scis. program U. Calif. at Davis, 1968; professorial lectr. mgmt. info. systems Golden Gate U., Sacramento, 1971-74, 79—; instr. info. systems Calif. State U.-Sacramento, 1982-83; instr. systems analysis and introduction to data processing Am. River Coll., Sacramento, 1968-71. Mem. curriculum adv. com. for data processing Am. River Coll., Sacramento, 1969-74, mem. com. to evaluate vocational and tech. edn. program for accreditation, 1972-73. Served with USAF, 1954-57, 62, maj. USAFR, Ret. Mem. Am. Soc. Pub. Adminstrn. (dir. 1969-71, 84-85), Data Processing Mgmt. Assn. (chpt. pres. 1968-69), Methods and Procedure Assn. (pres. 1969), Calif. Assn. County Data Processors (1st v.p. 1973-74), Air Force Res. Officers Assn. (chpt. v.p. 1971-74, 79-82), Air Force Calif. Dept. Res. Officers Assn. (jr. v.p. 1971). Home and Office: 5401 Valhalla Dr Carmichael CA 95608

FORSTER, ALFRED PAUL, advertising executive; b. Reading, Berkshire, Eng., Feb. 19, 1942; s. Alfred G. and Dorothy J. Forster; m. Patricia M. Hammond, Aug. 19, 1966; children: Simone C., Eleanor J. BA in Indsl. Econs. with honors, U. Nottingham, Eng., 1961. Mktg. product mgr. Cadbury Confectionery, Birmingham, Eng., 1961-68, mktg. mgr., 1968-71; ptnr. Lippa Newton, London, 1971-73; mng. dir. PLN Ptnrs., London, 1973-77, Roe Downton, London, 1977-79; mng. dir. Colman RSCG, London, 1979-86, chmn., chief exec. officer, 1986—; cons. Procol Mktg., Buckinghamshire, Eng., 1980—. Mem. Inst. Practitioners in Advt., Inst. Mktg., Mktg. Soc. Office: Colman RSCG & Ptnrs Ltd, 35 Bedford St, London WC2E 9EN, England

FORSTER, GORDON COLIN FAWCETT, historian; b. Tadcaster, Yorks, Eng., Aug. 30, 1928; s. Norman P. and Violet Isabel (Fawcett) F.; m. Judith Mary Duffus Passey. BA in History, U. Leeds, London, 1949. Douglas Knoop fellow U. Sheffield, Eng., 1952-55; asst. lectr., lectr., sr. lectr. U. Leeds, Eng., 1955—, chmn., head Sch. History, 1982-85. Editor: Northern History, 1966—, vols. 1 through 24; contbr. articles to profl. jours., chpts. Vict. Co. Hists. and other hist. vols. Fellow Royal Hist. Soc., Soc. Antiquaries of London; mem. Yorkshire Archeol. Soc. (pres. 1974-79), Thoresby Soc. (pres. 1980-85), Surtees Soc. (v.p. 1986—), Conf. Tchrs. Regional and Local History (pres. 1978-81). Home: 187 Adel Ln, Leeds LS16 8BY, England Office: Univ of Leeds, Sch History, Leeds LS2 9JT, England

FORSTING, LUCY THEILER, family counselor; b. Indianapolis, Oct. 29, 1945; d. John Paul and Jane (Fry) Baker; m. Allen John Theiler, Oct. 20, 1967 (div. Feb. 1977); 1 child, Nicholas Andrew; m. James Edward Roberts, Nov. 4, 1977 (div. Jan. 1987); m. Jack L. Forsting, Aug. 1, 1987. BA in Psychology, Lindenwood Coll., St. Charles, Mo., 1967, MA in Child Psychology, 1977; postgrad., Washington U., St. Louis, Mo., 1979. Tchr. St. Ferdinand Elem. Sch., Florissant, Mo., 1967-68, Our Lady of Loretto Sch., Spanish Lake, Mo., 1968-70, St. Peters Sch., St. Charles, Mo., 1971-72, Duchesne High Sch., St. Charles, Mo., 1976; intern psychology Malcolm Bliss Mental Health Ctr., St. Louis, Mo., 1976-77, Child Ctr. of Our Lady of Grace, Normandy, Mo., 1976-77; cons. counselor Christian Psychol. and Family Services, Bridgeton, Mo., 1977-79; instr. psychology Lindenwood Coll., St. Charles, 1980-81; therapeutical counselor O'Fallon (Ill.) Med. Ctr., 1980-85; grief counselor Baue Funeral Home, St. Charles, 1984-87; cons. Wentzville (Mo.) Sch. Dist., 1984-87; grief counselor Blaney Funeral Home, Green Bay, Wis., 1988—; family therapist Edward J. Johnson M.D. and Assocs., Green Bay, 1988—; founder Coping and Living Life widow/widower's orgn. Baue Funeral Homes, 1985—. Speaker numerous symposiums and workshops in field; developer newsletter for widow/widowers group, 1986. Chmn. publicity "Chemin de Fer" Acad. Sacred Heart, St. Charles, 1985; bd. dirs. St. Charles div. Am. Heart Assn. 1986—. Grantee "Thinkers Edge" Program Monsanto Corp., 1983. Mem. Am. Assn. Marriage and Family Therapists (clinical). Democrat. Roman Catholic. Home: 846 W Saint Francis Depere WI 54115 Office: Blaney Funeral Home Shawano Ave Green Bay WI 54305 also: Edward D Johnson & Assocs 333 Main St Suite 501 Green Bay WI 54301

FORSTMOSER, PETER BRUNO, lawyer, educator; b. Zurich, Switzerland, Jan. 22, 1943; s, Alois and Ida (Locher) F.; divorced; children—Marco, Stefan. Lic. Juris, Zurich Law Sch., 1967, J.D., 1970; LL.M., Harvard U., 1972. Asst. prof. Zurich Law Sch., 1971-74, prof., 1974—; assoc., Zurich, 1970-74; chief editor Swiss Lawyers Rev., 1973—; ptnr. Niederer Kraft & Frey, Zurich, 1974—; dir. IBM, Zurich, 1977, Mikron Holding AG, Biel, Switzerland, 1976, Charles Jourdan Holding AG, Glarus, Switzerland, 1979, Credit Suisse First Boston, 1987; chmn. Commn. Inquiry on Misuse Inside Info., 1982—. Author: Schweiz. Genossenschaftsrecht, 1972-74, Schweiz. Aktienrecht, 1981; contbr. articles to profl. jours. Pres. Liberales Inst., Zurich, 1979. Served to maj. Swiss Inf., 1981—. Mem. Zivilrechtslehrervereinigung, Schweiz. Anwaltsverband. Office: Niederer Kraft & Frey, Bahnhofstrasse 13, 8001 Zurich Switzerland

FORSTNER, HELMUT ALOIS, economist; b. Linz, Austria, Nov. 14, 1947; s. Karl and Hedwig (Miedl) F.; m. Anneliese Bousek, Sept. 19, 1975; children: Susanne, Martina. Mag.rer.nat., U. Vienna, 1973; diploma, Inst. Advanced Studies, Vienna, 1976; PhD, Tech. U., Vienna, 1977. Research asst. Inst. Advanced Studies, Vienna, 1974-76; economist UN Indsl. Devel Orgn., Vienna, 1976—. Contbr. articles to profl. jours. Mem. European Econ. Assn. Avocation: classical music. Home: Glasergasse 10/25, A-1090 Vienna Austria Office: UN Indsl Devel Orgn, Vienna Internat Ctr, A-1400 Vienna Austria

FORSYTH, FREDERICK, author; b. Ashford, Kent, Eng., 1938; m. Carrie Forsyth; 2 sons. Student Tonbridge Sch., Kent., Eng. Journalist, Eastern Daily Press, Norwich and later in King's Lynn, Norfolk, 1958-61; reporter Reuters, London, Paris, Berlin, 1961-62; reporter BBC Radio, London, 1965-67; asst. diplomatic corr. BBC TV, 1967; free lance journalist, Africa, 1967-69; novelist, 1969—; author: The Day of the Jackal, 1971, The Odessa File, 1972, The Dogs of War, 1974, The Shepherd, 1975, The Devils Alternative, 1979, Forsyth's Three, 1980, No Comebacks, 1983, The Fourth Protocol, 1984; screenwriter, co-exec. producer film: The Fourth Protocol, 1987. Served with RAF. Recipient Edgar Allan Poe award, Mystery Writers Am., 1971. Address: care Hutchinson Pub Group Ltd, 3 Fitzroy Sq, London W1P 6JD England *

FORSYTHE, PATRICIA HAYS, foundation executive; b. Curtis, Ark.; d. John Chambers and Flora Jane (Eby) Hays; m. Kurt G. Pahl, Dec. 15, 1962 (div. Dec. 1980); children: Thomas Walter, Susan Clara; m. Robert E. Forsythe, June 20, 1981; 1 child, Nathaniel Ryan. BA, Calif. State U., Los Angeles, 1974; MSLS, U. So. Calif., 1976. Asst. to dir. devel. office The Assocs., Calif. Inst. Tech., Pasadena, 1978-81; exec. dir. Iowa City Pub. Library Found., 1982—. Mem. LWV (editor 1985-87), Eastern Iowa Nat. Soc. for Fund Raising Execs. (pres. 1988), Am. Library Assn., Iowa City C. of C. Congregationalist. Club: Hancher Guild (Iowa City) (audience devel. 1981-85, pres. 1985-86). Home: 1806 E Court St Iowa City IA 52240 Office: Iowa City Pub Library Found 123 S Linn Iowa City IA 52240

FORT, ARTHUR TOMLINSON, III, physician; b. Lumpkin, Ga., Sept. 24, 1931; s. Thomas Morton and Gladys (Davis) F.; m. Jane Wilmer McClelland, June 15, 1957; children: Abby Lucinda, Arthur Tomlinson, Jr., Juliana Melody, Ernest Arlington, II. B.B.A., U. Ga., 1952; M.D., U. Tenn., 1962. Diplomate: Am. Bd. Ob-Gyn, Am. Bd. Family Practice. Intern, then resident in ob-gyn U. Tenn.-City of Memphis Hosp., 1962-66; asst. prof. U. Tenn. Med. Sch., 1966-70; prof. ob-gyn, head dept. La. State U. Med. Sch., Shreveport, 1970-73; prof. maternal-child health and family planning, head program family health Tulane U. Sch. Public Health, 1973-74; practice medicine specializing in rural family medicine Vacharie, La., 1974-79; prof. ob-gyn and family medicine, head dept. family medicine and comprehensive care La. State U. Med. Sch., Shreveport, 1980—. Author articles in field. Adv. bd. mem. State of La. Dept. Health and Human Resources, 1986—. Served with USAF, 1952-57. Recipient Golden Apple Teaching award Student AMA, 1969, Golden Apple Teaching award Western Interstate Commn. on Higher Edn., 1973. Fellow Am. Coll. Ob-Gyn, Am. Acad. Family Practice; mem. AMA. Office: PO Box 33932 Shreveport LA 71130

FORTE, SIR CHARLES (BARON FORTE), hotel and catering company executive; b. Nov. 26, 1908; m. Irene Mary Chierico, 1943; 6 children. Ed. Alloa Acad., Dumfries Coll., Mamiani, Rome. Dep. chmn. Trust Houses Forte PLC, 1970-78, chief exec., 1971-78, exec. chmn., 1978-81, chmn., 1982—; mem. small consultative adv. com. to Ministry Food, 1946; mem. London Tourist Bd.; pres. Italian C. of C. for Gt. Britain from 1952, Westminster C. of C. from 1983—; contbr. articles to catering trade papers. Hon. consul gen. for Republic San Marino. Decorated grand officier Ordine al Merito dell Repubblica Italiana, cavaliere di Gran Croce della Repubblica Italiana; decorated knight, 1970. Fellow Catering Inst. (exec. com.), Brit. Inst. Mgmt., Royal Soc. Arts. Clubs: Carlton, Caledonian, Royal Thames Yacht, Nat. Sporting (pres.) Office: Trusthouse Forte Ltd, 1 Hanover Sq, London W1, England *

FORTENBAUGH, SAMUEL BYROD, III, lawyer; b. Phila., Nov. 6, 1933; s. Samuel Byrod and Katherine Francesca (Wall) F.; m. Patricia Lee Dooley, June 7, 1975; children: Samuel Byrod IV, Cristina Carlson, Katherine Dooley, Francessa Cowden. BA, Williams Coll., 1955; LLB, Harvard U., 1960. Assoc. Kelley, Drye & Warren, N.Y.C., 1960-69, ptnr., 1970-79; ptnr. Morgan, Lewis & Bockius, N.Y.C., 1980—; bd. dirs. Thomson McKinnon Bank & Trust Co., N.Y.C., Esmark, Inc., N.Y.C., Baldwin Tech. Co., Inc., Stamford, Conn.; bd. dirs., sec. Goodman Equipment Corp., Chgo., Goodman Conveyor Co., Inc., Belton, S.C., Furgueson Capital Mgmt. Inc., N.Y.C.; chmn. bd. dirs., sec., Knight Textile Corp., Wall Industries, Inc.; gen. ptnr. Palmetto Restoration Assocs., Columbia, S.C., 1981—; trustee Patroni Scholastici, New Brunswick, N.J., 1978—, sec. 1985—. Contbr. articles to profl. jours. Mem. ABA, Assn. of the Bar of City of N.Y. (mem. Young Lawyers com. 1962-65, corp. law com. 1976-79, com. on securities regulation 1982-85, chmn. issue an distbn. of securities 1984-85), Phi Beta Kappa. Clubs: Racquet & Tennis, University (N.Y.C.); Bay Head (N.J.) Yacht. Office: Morgan Lewis & Bockius 101 Park Ave New York NY 10178

FORTES, MAURICIO, physics educator; b. Mexico City, Jan. 29, 1946; s. Abraham Fortes and Beba Besprosvani; m. Marcia Chachamowitz, Jan. 11, 1969 (div. 1973); m. Magdalena Acosta Urquidi, Nov. 27, 1979; children: Mara, Elena. BSc, Nat. U. Mex., 1967; PhD, SUNY, Stony Brook, 1973. Assoc. researcher Niels Bohr Inst., Copenhagen, 1971-73, U. Paris VI, 1973-74; assoc prof. Inst. Physics Nat. U. Mex.s, Mexico City, 1975-80, prof., 1980—; gen. editor Ciencia y Desarrollo, Mexico City, 1983—. Editor: Recent Progress in Many Body Theories, 1981; contbr. articles to internat. sci. jours. Mem. European Assn. Sci. Editors, AM. Phys. Soc., N.Y. Acad. Scis., Acad. de la Investigacion Cientifica (editorial dir. 1987), Friends of Weizmann Inst. of Sci. (pres. sci. com. 1987). Home: Cjon Escondida 39, Coyoacan, 04000 Mexico DF Mexico Office: Inst de Fisica Unam, PO Box 20-364, 01000 Mexico City Mexico

FORTNEY, ANNE PRICE, lawyer; b. Miami Beach, Fla., June 9, 1944; d. Camden Page and Margery (Shaut) F.; m. Richard A. Riddell, May 10, 1986. B.A., Mary Washington Coll., 1966; J.D., Georgetown U., 1969; postgrad. sr. mgrs. in govt. program Harvard U., 1985. Bar: D.C. 1969, Hawaii, 1987. Assoc. Cleary, Gottlieb, Steen & Hamilton, Washington, 1969-71; atty. FTC, Washington, 1971-76, adv. to commr., 1972-73; atty. Bur. Consumer Protection, 1972-76; atty. Washington Legal Office, J.C. Penney Co., Inc., 1976-82; assoc. dir. (credit practices) Bur. Consumer Protection, FTC, Washington, 1982-86; of counsel Carlsmith, Wichman, Case, Mukai & Ichiki, Honolulu, 1987—. Bd. visitors Mary Washington Coll. Found., 1982-84, bd. dirs. Mary Washington Found., 1985—, alumni bd. dirs., 1980-82, mem. regional scholarship com., 1974-78, chmn., 1974-76, 1st v.p. alumni bd. dirs., 1972-74, Bowfin Meml. Scholarship Com., 1987—. Recipient Sr. Exec. Service award, 1983. Mem. ABA, Hawaii Bar Assn., D.C. Bar Assn., Submarine Officers Wives Club (chmn. 1986—),

FORTUNE, JAMES MICHAEL, marketing, editorial executive; b. Providence, Sept. 6, 1947; s. Thomas Henry and Olive Elizabeth (Duby) F.; m. G. Suzanne Hein, July 14, 1973. Student, Pikes Peak Community Coll., 1983, Regis Coll., 1987—. Owner Fortune Fin. Services, Colorado Springs, Colo., 1975-79; ptnr. Robert James and Assocs., Colorado Springs, 1979-81; pres. Fortune & Co., Colorado Springs, 1981-88; v.p. mktg. Phoenix Mgmt. Ltd. (name changed to Phoenix Communications Group, Ltd.), 1988—; bd. dirs. Colorado Springs Computer Systems, Perfect Printer Inc., Colorado Springs, Am. Discount Securities, Inc., Phoenix Communications Group, Ltd.; radio talk show host Sta. KRCC; fin. commentator Wall Street Report Sta. KKHT, 1983-84. Editor Fortune newsletter, 1981-85, The Can. Market News, 1981-83; editor, pub. Penny Fortune newsletter, 1981—, The Low Priced Investment newsletter, 1986-87, Women's Investment Newsletter, 1987—; editor, pub. Can. Market Confidential, 1988—, Spl. Option Situations, 1988—; contbr. articles to profl. jours. Cons. Jr. Achievement bus. project, Colorado Springs, 1985. Served as sgt. U.S. Army, 1968-70, Vietnam. Mem. Internat. Assn. Fin. Planners (pres. 1977-78), Newsletter Assn. Lodge: Elks. Office: Phoenix Communications Group, Ltd. PO Box 670 Suite 2B Colorado Springs CO 80901

FORTUNE, ROBERT RUSSELL, business executive; b. Collingswood, N.J., Nov. 22, 1916; s. Colin C. and Minnie M. (Brown) F.; m. Christine E. Dent, Nov. 10, 1956. B.S. in Econs., U. Pa., 1940. C.P.A., Pa. With Haskins & Sells (C.P.A.s), 1940-42, 46-48; with Pa. Power & Light Co., Allentown, 1948-84; v.p. fin. Pa. Power & Light Co., 1966-75, exec. v.p. fin., dir., 1975-84; chmn., chief exec. officer Associated Electric and Gas Ins. Services Ltd., 1984—, Dirs. and Officers Liability Ins., Ltd., 1985—; dir. Ind. Sq. Income Securities, Inc., Temp. Investment Fund, Inc., Chestnut St. Exchange Fund, Prudential-Bache Utility Fund, Inc., Municipal Fund for Temporary Investment, Trust for Short-Term Fed. Securities, Chestnut St. Cash Fund, Portfolios for Diversified Investment, Prudential-Bache Income Vertible Plus Fund ; mem. tech. adv. com. fin. FPC, 1974-75. Treas. Allentown Sch. Dist. Authority, 1963-85, Lehigh-Northampton Airport Authority, 1985—. Served in USN, 1942-46. Mem. Fin. Execs. Inst., Am., Pa. insts. C.P.A.s. Republican. Club: Lehigh Country. Home: 2920 Ritter

Ln Allentown PA 18104 Office: Harborside Fin Ctr 700 Plaza Two Jersey City NJ 07311-3994 also: Prudential Bache Utility Inc 34 Exchange Plaza Jersey City NJ 07303

FORTUNE, WILLIAM LEMCKE, journalist; b. Indpls., Dec. 6, 1912; s. Russell and Elinor (Lemcke) F.; m. Jane Hennessy, Nov. 26, 1938; children: Janie, Pamela, William Lemcke, Richard Hennessy. A.B., Princeton U., 1935. Reporter Ft. Wayne (Ind.) Jour. Gazette, 1936; reporter, polit. writer Indpls. Times, 1937-38; pub. Dunkirk (Ind.) News, 1938-40, Waveland (Ind.) Independent, 1941; acct. Mem. Ind. Gen. Assembly, 1947-48; treas. State of Ind., 1951-53; revenue commr. Ind., 1965-69; Spl. legis. corr. for 48 newspapers; lectr. state tax problems. Author: The Moment, 1979; Contbr. articles on state taxes and internat. trade to newspapers and mags. Campaign dir. Marion County March of Dimes, 1961-62; Bd. dirs. Indpls. Mus. Art, Indpls. Symphony Orch., Butler U., all Indpls. Served from pvt. to sgt. AUS, 1942-46. Office: 7990 Hillcrest Rd Indianapolis IN 46240

FOSBROKE, L. LINDLEY POWERS, theatre arts educator; b. Albany, N.Y., Aug. 19, 1926; d. William Tibbits and Winifred Lispenard (Robb) Powers; A.B., Smith Coll., 1948; M.A. in Speech, U. Wis., 1963, M.F.A. in Theater Directing, 1963, Ph.D. in Theatre (E.B. Fred fellow), 1968; postdoctoral Episcopal Theol. Sch., 1972-74, Weston Coll. Sch. Theology, 1974-75; m. Davis Spencer, Mar. 5, 1949 (div. 1961); children—Eleanor Tibbits Spencer Tupper, Joseph Allen Powers Spencer; m. 2d, Gerald E. Fosbroke, Dec. 17, 1976. Children's librarian N.Y.C. Public Library, 1948-49; tchr., Racine, Wis., 1959-61; dir. Wis. 4-H Drama Program, also research asst. U. Wis., 1961-64; instr. U. Wis., 1964-65, 66-67, teaching asst. Sch. Music, 1965-66; asst. prof. drama Bridgewater (Mass.) State Coll., 1968-69; assoc. prof., dir. grad. study theatre edn. Emerson Coll., Boston, 1969-71, assoc. prof. fine arts, 1971-76, prof., 1977-79, founder, adviser creative service interdisciplinary program, 1974-79. Condr. community and conv. workshops in theatre arts; lectr. to clergy and parishes on liturgical experience of myth and symbol; also active in ch. renovation and conducting classes for lay lectors and clergy Dioceses of N.J. and Mass. Vice pres. bd. dirs. Ch. Home Soc., Boston; sec. Iona Community New World Found.; founder, sec., bd. dirs. Iona Cornerstone Found., Inc., 1981—, Iona Cornerstone Found. Ltd., 1982—; mem. Diocesan Ecumenical Commn., 1980-84, sec., 1980-82; mem. Mass. Council Chs. Jewish Community Council Dialogues, 1982-84. Mem. AAUP, Iona Community (asso.), Soc. St. John the Evangelist (asso.), Dobbs (dir., mem. exec. com. 1949-57, editor Bull., 1949-57), Smith alumnae assns., Shakespeare Club Boston, Conservation Law Found. Author: Proclaim the Word, 1980, also drama ednl. materials. Episcopalian (lay lector). Home: 70 Carey Ln Quissett Harbor Falmouth MA 02540

FOSHER, DONALD H., advertising company executive, inventor; b. St. Louis Mo., Jan. 6, 1935; s. Hobart L. and Alby U. (Andrews) F.; m. Charlotte B. Reich, Oct. 6, 1956 (div. Dec. 1976); 1 child, Carey B.; Janet L. Leiber, Dec. 31, 1977. B.S., in Bus. Adminstrn., Washington U., St. Louis Mo., 1956. Copywriter Gen. Am., St. Louis, Mo., 1956-59; art dir. Artcraft, St. Louis, 1959-67; creative dir. Frank Block Assocs., St. Louis, 1967-69; account exec. Vangard/Wells, Rich, Green, St. Louis, 1969-74; ptnr., v.p. Vinyard & Lee, St. Louis, 1974-77; sr. v.p., creative dir. Hughes Advt., St. Louis, 1977—; pres., owner Don Fosher, Inc., St. Louis, 1974—; co-owner Freelance Studios, Clayton, Mo., 1979—, BrandBank div. Don Fosher Inc., 1986—. Author: Art for Secondary Education, 1962. Contbr. articles on cuisine to popular mags. Patentee sports, medicine, mech. design. Advisor, St. Louis County Spl. Sch. Dist., 1966-76; bd. dirs. Vocat. Schs., St. Louis, 1969-88; campaign designer St. Louis Better Bus. Bur., 1975, St. Louis Arts & Edn. Fund, 1984. Recipient Art Dir. of Yr. award Soc. Communications Arts, 1967; Venice Biennial, Internat. Congress Designers, 1966, Package Design award Am. Fishing Tackle Mfrs. Assn., 1981, numerous Creative awards Art Directors, 1959-1988. Mem. Internat. Congress Designers, Soc. Communications Arts (pres. 1966-67), Direct Mail Mktg. Assn., SAR. Mem. Christian Ch. Club: Glen Echo Country. Avocations: inventing, cooking, collecting primative art. Home: 7266 Creveling Dr University City MO 63130 Office: Hughes Advt Inc 130 S Bemiston Clayton MO 63105

FOSKETT, DOUGLAS JOHN, librarian; b. London, June 27, 1918; s. John Henry and Amy Florence (Lugg) F.; m. Joy McCann, June 2, 1948; children: Penelope, Rosalind, Trevor. BA, Queen Mary Coll., England, 1939; MA, Birkbeck Coll., England, 1954. Asst. librarian Ilford Mcpl. Libraries, Essex, Eng., 1939-48; librarian Metal Box Co. London, 1948-57, Inst. Edn., London, 1957-78; dir. cen. library services U. London, 1978-83; acting dir. library and info. services Aston U., Birmingham, Eng., 1985. Author: Assistance to Readers, 1952, Information Service in Libraries, 1958, 2d edition, 1967, Classification and Indexing in the Social Sciences, 1963, 2d edition, 1974, Pathways for Communication, 1984; contbr. articles to profl. publs. Officer, Order Brit. Empire, 1977. Home: 1 Dale Side, Gerrards Cross SL9 7JF, England

FOSS, CHARLES R., government agency buyer; b. Chgo., Nov. 1, 1945; s. Raymond C. and Marilyn (Halas) F. Assoc. in Transp., Davenport Coll., 1973, B in Mktg., 1985, postgrad., 1985-87. Yardmaster Chesapeake and Ohio Ry., Benton Harbor, Mich., 1963-66; ticket agt. Chesapeake and Ohio Ry., Holland, Mich., 1969-71; freight agt., train dispatcher Penn Cen. Ry., Ft. Wayne, Ind., 1971-76; sales rep. Foss Police Equipment and Communications, Battle Creek, Mich., 1976-85; customer service rep. Superior Brand Produce, Hudsonville, Mich., 1985; purchasing buyer U.S. Dept. Def., Dayton, Ohio, 1986—. Author: Evening Before The Diesel, 1980. Coordinator Susquicentennial Commemorative Winchester Carbine, Byron Twp., Byron Ctr., Mich., 1985. Served with U.S. Army, 1966-69, Vietnam. Mem. R.R. Mus. (hon. life), Chgo. and Northwestern Hist. Soc. (contbr.), So. Mich. R.R. Soc. Inc. (contbr.), Am. Truck Hist. Soc. (life), Nat. Rifle Assn. (life). Republican.

FOSS, LUKAS, composer, conductor, pianist; b. Berlin, Germany, Aug. 15, 1922; came to U.S. from Paris, 1937, naturalized, 1942; s. Martin and Hilde (Schindler) F.; (m); 2 children. Student, Paris Lycée Pasteur, 1932-37; grad., Curtis Inst. Music, 1940; spl. study, Yale, 1940-41; pupil of, Paul Hindemith, Julius Herford, Serge Koussevitzky, Fritz Reiner, Isabelle Vengerova; recipient of 6 hon. doctorates. Former prof. UCLA (in charge orch. and advanced composition); faculty Harvard U., 1970-71; Founder Center Creative and Performing Arts, Buffalo U.; vis. prof. Carnegie Mellon U., Pitts., 1987-88. Former condr., music dir., Buffalo Philharmonic, mus. dir., condr., Bklyn. Philharmonic, 1971—, music dir., condr., Milw. Symphony Orch., 1981-86, condr. laureate, 1986—; orchestral compositions performed by many major orchs.; best known works include (opera) Griffelkin, Baroque Variations (orch.), Echoi (4 instruments); orch., chamber music, ballets, works commd. by, League of Composers, Nat. Endowment for Arts, N.Y. Arts Council, NBC opera on TV, Am. Choral Condrs. Assn., Ind. U., 1979 Olympics, others.; (recipient N.Y. Critic Circle citation for Prairie 1944, Soc. for Pub. Am. Music award for String Quartet in G 1948, Rome prize 1950, Horblit award for Piano concerto No. 2 1951, Naumburg Rec. award for Song of Songs 1957, Creative Music grant Inst. Arts and Letters 1957, N.Y. Music Critics Circle award for Time-Cycle orch. songs 1961, for Echoi 1963, Ditson award for condr. who has done the most for Am. music 1973, N.Y.C. award for spl. contbn. to arts 1976, ASCAP award for adventurous programming 1979, CRI rec. award for Thirteen Ways of Looking at a Blackbird 1979). Guggenheim fellow, 1945; Creative arts award Brandeis U., 1983; Laurel leaf award Am. Composers Alliance, 1983. Mem. Nat. Acad. and Inst. Arts and Letters. Address: 17 E 96th St New York NY 10128

FOSSEEN, NEAL RANDOLPH, business executive; former banker, former mayor; b. Yakima, Wash., Nov. 27, 1908; s. Arthur Benjamin and Florence (Neal) F.; A.B., U. Wash., 1930; LL.D. (hon.), Whitworth Coll., 1967; m. Helen Witherspoon, Sept. 26, 1936; children—Neal Randolph, William Roger. With Wash. Brick, Lime & Sewer Pipe Co., 1923-32, v.p., 1932-38; pres. Wash. Brick & Lime Co., 1938-58; v.p. Old Nat. Bank Wash., 1958-68; v.p. Wash Bancshares, 1968-71, vice chmn., 1971-72, chmn. bd., pres., 1972-73; chmn. emeritus Old Nat. Bancorp., 1973-77; pres. 420 Investment Co., 1982-84 ; mem. enlish adv. bd. Washington State U. Coll., 1949-79, past chmn., emeritus, 1979—; ptnr. Villa 90 Assocs., West Riverside Investment dir. Day Mines, Inc., 1968-81. Vice chmn. Expo '74. Mayor, City of Spokane, 1960-67, mayor emeritus, 1967—. Past chmn. adv. bd. Wash. State Inst. Tech.; hon. trustee St. Luke's Hosp.; regent emeritus, past chmn. Gonzaga U.; bd. dirs., past pres. council Boy Scouts Am.; bd. dirs. Wash. Research Council, sec., 1968-74; bd. dirs. YMCA, 1969-80, Pacific Sci. Found., 1970-73, Mountain States Legal Found., 1979-85, Deaconess Hosp. Found.; mem. adv. bd. Grad. Sch. Bus., U. Wash., 1974-81, emeritus, 1981—. Served as lt. col. USMCR, 1942-45; col. Res. ret. Recipient Disting. Eagle Scout award Boy Scouts Am., 1976, Silver Beaver, Silver Antelope awards; Non Sibi, Sed Patriae award Marine Corps Res. Officers Assn.; Outstanding Service awards Fairchild AFB, Spokane Mcpl. League; Forward Spokane award Spokane County Hotel and Restaurant Council; Liberty Bell award Spokane County Bar Assn.; Book of Golden Deeds, Exchange Club; Sister City Outstanding Service award Town Affiliation Assn.; Disting. Citizen award Eastern Wash U., 1982; named hon. citizen, Nishinomiya, Japan; Honor Patriot '75, Spokane Percussionauts. Mem. Assn. Wash. Bus. (past pres.), Spokane C. of C. (v.p. 1946-51), Spokane-Nishinoniya Sister City Soc. (pres.), Srs. N.W. Golf Assn., Beta Theta Pi. Episcopalian. Clubs: Balboa de Mazatlan (Mex); Spokane, Spokane Country, University, Prosperity. Home: W 1224 Riverside Ave Spokane WA 99201 Office: Old Nat Bank Bldg Spokane WA 99201

FOSTER, CATHERINE RIERSON, metal components manufacturing company executive; b. Balt., Mar. 14, 1935; d. William Harman and Ella Fredericka (Magsamen) Rierson; m. Morgan Lawrence Foster, Nov. 17, 1957; children: Diana Kay, Susan Ann, Morgan Lawrence, Heather Lynne. Student Balt. City Coll., 1955, Johns Hopkins U., 1956-57, Glendale Coll., 1962-63. Sec., Martin Co., Balt., 1956-57, adminstrv. sec., 1957-58; v.p., corp. sec. Fostermation, Inc., Meadville, Pa., 1971—, also dir.; mem. adv. com. Vocat./Tech. Sch., Meadville, 1982-86. Pres. La Crescents, La Crescenta, Calif., 1962; active City Hosp. Aux., Meadville, 1969-86; active Republican Women's Workshop, Glendale, Calif., 1966-68, Com. to Elect Ronald Reagan, Glendale, 1967; bd. dirs. YWCA, Meadville, 1988—, also chmn. fin. com., 1988—. Mem. Nat. Assn. Female Execs., Daus. Am. Revolution. Lutheran. Lodge: Order Eastern Star. Avocations: genealogy, history, bridge. Home: 1121 Lakemont Dr Meadville PA 16335 Office: Fostermation Inc 200 Valleyview Dr Meadville PA 16335

FOSTER, DAVID RAMSEY, soap company executive; b. London, Eng., May 24, 1920 (parents Am. citizens); s. Robert Bagley and Josephine (Ramsey) F.; student econs. Gonville and Caius Coll., Cambridge (Eng.) U., 1938; m. Anne Firth, Aug. 2, 1957; children—Sarah, Victoria. With Colgate-Palmolive Co. and affiliates, 1946-79, v.p., gen. mgr. Europe, Colgate-Palmolive Internat., 1961-65, v.p., gen. mgr. household products div. parent co., N.Y.C., 1965-68, exec. v.p., 1968-70, pres., 1970-75, chief exec. officer, 1971-79, chmn., 1975-79. Trustee, Woman's Sport Found.Served to lt. comdr. Royal Naval Vol. Res., 1940-46. Decorated Disting. Service Order, D.S.C. with bar, Mentioned in Despatches (2); recipient Victor award City of Hope, 1974, Herbert Hoover Meml. award, 1976, Adam award, 1977, Harriman award Boys Club N.Y., 1977, Charter award St. Francis Coll., 1978, Walter Hagen award, 1978, Patty Berg award, 1986. Mem. Soc. Mayflower Descs. Clubs: Am. (London); Hawks (Cambridge U.); Royal Ancient Golf (St. Andrews, Scotland); Royal St. Georges Golf, Royal Cinque Ports Golf (life), Sunningdale Golf, Swinley Forest Golf (U.K.); Sankaty Head Golf; Racquet and Tennis (N.Y.C.); Baltusrol Golf, Mission Hills Country, Bally Bunion Golf. Home: 540 Desert West Dr Rancho Mirage CA 92270 also: High Time Wauwinet Nantucket MA 02554

FOSTER, DUDLEY EDWARDS, JR., musician, educator; b. Orange, N.J., Oct. 5, 1935; s. Dudley Edwards and Margaret (DePoy) F.; student Occidental Coll., 1953-56; A.B., UCLA, 1957, M.A., 1958; postgrad. U. So. Calif., 1961-73. Lectr. music Immaculate Heart Coll., Los Angeles, 1960-63; dir. music Holy Faith Episcopal Ch., Inglewood, Calif., 1964-67; lectr. music Calif. State U., Los Angeles, 1968-71; assoc. prof. music Los Angeles Mission Coll., 1975-83, prof., 1983—, also chmn. dept. music, 1977—; dir. music First Lutheran Ch., Los Angeles, 1968-72; organist, pianist, harpsichordist; numerous recitals; composer O Sacrum Convivium for Trumpet and Organ, 1973, Passacaglia for Brass Instruments, 1969, Introduction, Arioso & Fugue for Cello and Piano, 1974. Fellow Trinity Coll. Music, London, 1960. Mem. Am. Guild Organists, Am. Musicol. Soc., Town Hall Calif., Los Angeles Coll. Tchrs. Assn. (pres. Mission Coll. chpt. 1976-77, v.p., exec. com. 1982-84), Mediaeval Acad. Am. Republican. Anglican. Office: Los Angeles Mission Coll Dept Music 1212 San Fernando Dr San Fernando CA 91340

FOSTER, GEORGE WILLIAM, JR., lawyer, educator; b. Boston, Nov. 23, 1919; s. George William and Marguerite (Werner) F.; m. Jeanette Raymond, May 26, 1950; children—Susan, Bill, Fred. Student, Antioch Coll., 1937-40; B.S. in Chemistry, Stanford U., 1947; LL.B., Georgetown U., 1951; LL.M., Yale U., 1952. Bar: Wis. bar 1972. Exec. asst. to U.S. Senator, 1949-50; spl. asst. to Sec. of State Dean Acheson, 1951; asst. prof. law U. Wis., Madison, 1952-56; assoc. prof. U. Wis., 1956-59, prof., 1959-86, assoc. dean, 1969-72, prof. emeritus, 1986—; reporter Wis. Long-Arm Process Statute, 1955-59; cons. sch. desegregation guidelines HEW, 1965; legal advisor Ministry of Justice, Kabul, Afghanistan, 1976. Served to lt. (j.g.) USN, 1942-46. Mem. Am. Bar Assn., Am. Ornithologists Union, State Bar Wis., Am. Law Inst. Democrat. Home: 5616 Lake Mendota Dr Madison WI 53705 Office: U Wis L438 Law Bldg Madison WI 53706

FOSTER, JUDITH CHRISTINE, lawyer, writer; b. Columbus, Ohio, Nov. 25, 1952; d. Paul Marvel and Jean Harper (Uhland) F.; m. Sabah Amin Wali, Dec. 28, 1973; children: Samed Michel Sabah, Russeen Paul Sabah. BS in Natural Sci. and BA in Linguistics, Pa. State U., 1973; JD, Coll. William & Mary, 1979. Bar: Va. 1979, U.S. Ct. Appeals (4th cir.) 1979, U.S. Supreme Ct. 1984. Sole practice Fairfax, Va., 1980—; of counsel U.S. Justice Found., Escondido, Calif., 1982—; judge Internat. Moot Ct. Competition Assn. of Student Internat. Law Soc., 1984, 86. Author: (with Erich Pratt) Sanctuary: A People's Primer, 1986. Del. Va. Reps., Fairfax, 1981, 85. Mem. Am. Immigration Lawyers Assn. (legis. com. 1985, D.C. chpt. 1980—), Washington Foreign Law Soc., Fairfax County Bar Assn. (continuing legal edn. com. 1983-86). Republican. Lutheran. Office: 4021 University Dr Fairfax VA 22030

FOSTER, LAWRENCE, concert and opera conductor; b. Los Angeles, 1941. Student, Bayreuth Festival Masterclasses; studied with, Fritz Zweig. Debut as condr., Young Musicians' Found., Debut Orch., 1960; condr., mus. dir., 1960-64, condr., San Francisco Ballet, 1961-65, asst. condr., Los Angeles Philharmonic Orch., 1965-68, chief guest condr., Royal Philharmonic Orch., Eng., 1969-75, guest condr., Houston Symphony, 1970-71, condr. in chief, 1971-72, music dir., 1972-78, Orch. Philharmonique of Monte Carlo, 1979—, gen. music dir., Duisburg & Dusseldorf Opera (Ger.), 1982-86, music dir. Lausanne Chamber Orch., 1985—, guest condr. orchs. in, U.S. and Europe. (Recipient Koussevitsky Meml. Conducting prize 1966, Eleanor R. Crane Meml. prize Berkshire Festival, Tanglewood, Mass. 1966). Office: care Harrison/Parrott, 12 Penzance, London England W11 also: Orchestre Philharmonique de, Monte Carlo Casino, Monte Carlo Monaco

FOSTER, LLOYD BENNETT, lawyer, musician; b. Wellman, Iowa, May 6, 1911; s. George Elliott and Lulu Nettie (Bennett) F.; m. Rowene Stevens, Sept. 1, 1940. BA cum laude in Commerce and Fin., Coe Coll., 1937; MS in Econs., Iowa State U., 1939; JD, De Paul U., 1952. Bar: Ill. 1952, U.S. Supreme Ct. 1980. Instr. Shenandoah Coll., Va., 1939-41; acct. McGladrey, Hansen, Dunn and Co., Cedar Rapids, Iowa, 1941-42; agt. Office of Dist. Dir., IRS, Chgo., 1946-52, pension plan reviewer, 1952-53, tech. advisor Appellate div., 1953-60; atty. Office of Chief Counsel, Washington, 1961-67; dep. asst. chief counsel Bur. of Pub. Debt, Chgo., 1967-71, atty., Washington, 1967; atty., income tax hearing officer, supr. regulations legis. rulings sect., litigation counsel, adminstrv. law judge Ill. Dept. Revenue, Chgo., 1971-87; with tax counsel McDermott, Will & Emery, Chgo., 1988—. Mem., Chgo. Met. Symphony Orch., 1969—, Deerfield Park Dist. Community Band, 1968—. Served to comdr. USN, 1942-46. Mem. Fed. Bar Assn., Ill. Bar Assn., Chgo. Fedn. Musicians, D.C. Fedn. Musicians, Naval Res. Assn., Retired Officers Assn. Office: McDermott Will Emery 111 W Monroe St Chicago IL 60603

FOSTER, LOWELL WALTER, engineer, consultant; b. Mpls., Oct. 22, 1919; s. Walter James and Ferne Constance (Edmunds) F.; grad. USCG Acad., 1944; student U. Minn., 1950, Mpls. Inst. Arts, 1953; m. Marion Jane Bjorklund, Feb. 5, 1944; children—Michael Lowell, Janette Marie, John Edward. With Honeywell, Inc., Mpls., 1946-77, successively tool designer, lead tool designer, asst. supr. tool design, lead standardization engr., sr. standardization engr., prin. standardization engr., project adminstr., sr. project adminstr., dir. corp. standardization services, dir. corp. standardization, 1974-77, dir. industry standards, 1977; pres. Tech. Concepts and Engring. Internat., 1977—, Lowell W. Foster Assos., Inc., seminars and videotape programs; adviser drafting curriculum Mpls. Public Schs., 1973—; engring. cons.; tech. adviser Ferris State Coll., Big Rapids, Mich., 1970—. Active Viking council Boy Scouts Am., 1956-59, 73-77; v.p. John Ericsson Sch. PTA, 1971—. Bd. dirs. Am. Nat. Standards Inst. Served with USCG, 1941-46; PTO. Recipient Centennial award ASME, 1980. Fellow Standards Engrs. Soc. (Leo B. Moore award 1973, Disting. Service award Minn. sect. 1970, spl. service citation 1981); mem. Internat. Standards Orgn., Soc. Mfg. Engrs., Air Conditioning and Refrigeration Inst., Soc. Advancement of Mgmt., Honeywell Engrs. Club (past pres.), Am. Legion. Author 30 books, numerous articles. Home: 3120 E 45th St Minneapolis MN 55406 Office: Foster Assocs Inc Minneapolis MN 55406

FOSTER, MARK EDWARD, lawyer, consultant, international lobbyist; b. Detroit, May 12, 1948; s. Herbert Edward and Joyce Mary (Campbell) F.; m. Miyoko Katabami, Apr. 20, 1974; children—Lorissa Chieko. B.A., Alma Coll., 1970; M.A., U. Calif.-Berkeley, 1973, Japanese lang. cert., 1982, J.D., 1981. Bar: Calif. 1981. Grantee, Rockefeller Found., Geneva and Tokyo, 1973-74; law clk. U.S. Dist. Ct., San Francisco, 1980-81; atty. Hetland & Hansen, Berkeley, Calif., 1981-82; cons. Foster Assocs. Internat., 1982—; atty. Braun Moriya Hoashi, Tokyo, 1982-84; ptnr. Lindsay, Hart, Neil & Weigler, Portland, 1985—; Spl. Counsel U.S. Embassy, Tokyo, 1983-85; Japan Counsel U.S. Electronic Industries Assn., 1985-86; lectr., cons. on internat. tech. standards, tech. transfer, product compliance, engring. to Internat. Standards Orgn., U.S. Dept. Commerce. Author articles, books in internat. law and tech. Mem. ABA, Internat. Bar Assn., State Bar Calif., Am. C. of C. in Japan,World Trade (Tokyo, Portland, Oreg.), World Affairs Council. Presbyterian. Office: ABS Bldg 2-4-16, 3-F, Kudan Minami Tokyo 102, Japan also: 222 SW Columbia Ave Suite 1800 Portland OR 97201

FOSTER, NORMAN ROBERT, architect; b. Reddish, Eng., June 1, 1935; s. Robert and Lilian (Smith) F.; m. Wendy Ann Cheesman, 1964; 2 children. Dip.Arch., Manchester U.; M.Arch., Yale U.; Litt.D. (hon.), East Anglia, 1980; D.Sc. (hon.) Bath, 1986. Cons. urban renewal and city planning, 1962-63; prin. Team 4 Architects, London, 1963—, Foster Assocs., London, 1967—; collaborator with Buckminster Fuller, from 1968; cons. architect U. East Anglia, 1978—; former external examiner R.I.B.A.; former mem. Archtl. Assn. Council, v.p., 1968; former tchr. U. Pa., Archtl. Assn., London, London Poly., Bath Acad. Arts; mem. council R.C.A., 1981. Archtl. works include: Pilot Head Office, IBM, Hampshire, 1970; Tech. Park, IBM, Greenford, 1975; Sainsbury Centre for Visual Arts, Norwich, 1977; Head Office, Willis, Faber and Dumas, Ipswich (R.S. Reynolds Internat. Meml. award 1976), 1979; devel. project Whitney Gallery, N.Y.C., 1979; students union project Univ. Coll., London U., 1979; Salisbury Centre for Visual Arts (R.S. Reynolds Internat. Meml. award 1979); Third London Airport Terminal and Master Planning Studies, 1980; Centre for Renault Car Co. U.K., 1980; Hong Kong and Shanghai Banking Corp. Hdqrs; Nat. German Indoor Athletics Stadium, Frankfurt; Radio Centre for BBC, London; exhbns.: Mus. Modern Art, N.Y.C., 1979; also in Barcelona, Spain, 1976, London, 1979, Parma, Italy, 1979, Copenhagen, 1979; represented in permanent collection: Mus. Modern Art, N.Y.C.; contbr. articles to archtl. and tech. publs. Recipient Archtl. Design Projects award, 1964, 65, 66; Fin. Times Indsl. Architecture award, 1967, 74, citations, 1970, 71; R.I.B.A. award, 1969, 72, 77, 78, commendation, 1981; R.S.A. Bus. and Industry award, 1978; Internat. Design award, 1976, 80, Finniston award, 1978; Structural Steel award, 1972, 78, citation, 1980; Ambrose Congreve award, 1980; Royal Gold Medal for Architecture, 1986; winner numerous internat. competitions; IBM fellow Aspen Design Conf., 1980. Fellow S.I.A.D., AIA (hon.). Office: Foster Assocs, 172-182 Great Portland St, London W1N 5TB England *

FOSTER, WALTER HERBERT, JR., real estate company executive; b. Belmont, Mass., Nov. 2, 1919; s. Walter Herbert and Gertrude (Sullivan) F.; m. Hazel Campbell, Aug. 7, 1942 (div. July 1981); children: Katherine D., Walter H. III, Stephen C., Banton T.; m . Nedra Ann Thompson, July 3, 1981; 1 child, Timothy John. Student, Harvard U., 1937-38; BS, U. Maine, 1947; grad. in real estate, Tri-State Inst., 1968-70. Cert. appraiser and real estate broker. Owner, mgr. Foster Bros., Lyndeborough, N.H., 1947-56; ter. sales mgr. Beacon Milling Co., Oakland, Maine, 1956-64; v.p. Sherwood & Foster, Inc., Old Town, Maine, 1964-67; sales rep. Bangor (Maine) Real Estate, 1967-73; chief appraiser James W. Sewall Co., Old Town, 1970-73; mgr. J.F. Singleton Co., Bangor, 1973-80; pres. Coldwell Banker Am. Heritage, Bangor, 1980—; dean Tri-State Inst., 1981; mem. Maine Real Estate Commn., 1987. Mem. Rep. Nat. Com., Washington, 1980, Assessment Bd. Appeals, Old Town, Maine. Served to capt. USAF, 1941-46. Mem. Nat. Assn. Realtors (bd. dirs. 1980-81), Maine Assn. Realtors (bd. dirs. 1976-80, pres. 1980; Realtor of Yr. 1976 and 1984), Bangor Bd. Realtors (bd. dirs. 1973-74, pres. 1976; Realtor of Yr. 1984), Nat. Assn. Rev. Appraisers, Am. Assn. Cert. Appraisers, Res. Officers Assn., Soc. Real Estate Appraisers (assoc.). Episcopalian. Clubs: Tarratine (Bangor); Harvard (Maine). Lodge: Rotary. Home: Mistover Dole Hill Rd RFD 2 Box 692 East Holden ME 04429 Office: Coldwell Banker Am Heritage 510 Broadway Bangor ME 04401

FOSTER, WALTON ARTHUR, broadcasting executive; b. San Angelo, Tex., Aug. 26, 1927; s. Arthur Rambo and Katie Pearl (Walton) F.; m. Arla Vee Bishop, Feb. 17, 1950; 1 son, Walton Arthur II. AA, San Angelo Coll., 1948. Mem. staff Sta. KGKL, San Angelo, 1944-46; gen. mgr. Stas. KTXL-AM-FM and KTXL-TV, San Angelo, 1947-54; mem. staff Stas. KGKO, KLIF, Dallas, 1954-56, Sta. KTRK-TV, Houston, 1954-56; founder, pres. Stas. KWFR-AM-FM, KIXY-AM-FM, Solar Broadcasting Co., San Angelo, 1954-78; founder, chief exec. officer Stas. KHOS-AM-FM, KYXX-AM-FM, The Foster Broadcasters, Inc., 1974—, Stas. KIXY-FM and KAYJ-AM, Foster Communications Co., Inc., San Angelo, 1984—. 1st violin San Angelo Symphony Orch., 1947; bd. dirs. United Blood Services, chmn. Concho Valley chpt. ARC, 1988—, Ret. Srs. Vol. Program, San Angelo Civic Theatre; Ct. Appointed Special Advocate. Mem. SAR, Phi Theta Kappa. Home: 3002 Oak Mountain Trail San Angelo TX 76904 Office: Foster Communications Co Inc Stas KIXY-FM/KAYJ #1 City Hall Plaza San Angelo TX 76903

FOSTER, WANELL BAIZE, oncology social worker; b. Hartford, Ky., May 7, 1928; d. Charles Ellis and Viola (Simpson) Baize; children: Charles Keaton, Don Franklin, Susan Kay. AA, U. Ky., 1975; MS in Social Work, U. Louisville, 1977. Tchr. Jefferson County Pub. Schs., Louisville, 1978-79; social worker Dept. Human Services, Louisville, 1979-80, VA Med. Ctr., Long Beach, Calif., 1980—; adj. prof. Calif. State U., Long Beach, 1986—; cons. at large, 1981—. Author: Health & Social Work Jour., 1981. Named to Hon. Order of Ky. Cols. Mem. Nat. Assn. Social Workers, Nat. Assn. Oncology Social Workers. Home: PO Box 90031 Long Beach CA 90809 Office: VA Med Ctr 5901 E 7th St Long Beach CA 90822

FOTINOS, KATHERINE, educator; b. San Francisco, Apr. 12, 1926; d. Christ Anastasios and Ageliki George (Pilarinos) F. B.A., San Francisco State Coll., 1948; M.A., Stanford U., 1955. Life diploma tchr. Calif. Tchr. Excelsior Sch., San Francisco, 1948-53, Ridgepoint III, San Francisco, 1953-54, Jedediah Smith Sch., San Francisco, 1954-55; head tchr. Washington Irving Sch., San Francisco, 1955-60, Jean Parker Sch., San Francisco, 1960—; curriculum designer 1951—; cons. Calif. Geog. Alliance. Co-author: Curriculum Guide for Language Arts, Curriculum Guide for Music, Curriculum Guide for Social Studies and Science (all for grades K-6 in San Francisco Unified Sch. Dist.). Designer Deaf Scrabball, 1981. Vol. Assn. for Deaf and Blind, 1980—; docent Calif. Hist. Soc., Sonoma; festival decoration chmn. Greek Orthodox Ch., Solono County 1982; vol. Sonoma Rep. Com., 1982; U.S. senatorial candidate campaign chmn. Sonoma County, 1986; scholarship chmn. Northern Div. Calif. Fedn. Rep. Women, 1987-88. Mem. AAUW, Calif. PTA (hon. life), Calif. Tchrs. Assn., Stanford Edn. Club (sec. 1972-74), Sonoma Valley Chorale, Sonoma County Ballet Guild, Am. Chorale Dirs. Assn., European Touring Concert Group, Sonoma Valley Rep. Women (charter mem.), Nat. Fedn. Rep. Women (fed. regent), Alpha Delta Kappa (life; pres. 1962-64). Clubs: Jack Anderson, Etude Music (scholarship chmn.). Lodge: Daus. Penelope (v.p. 1974-76). Avocations: travel, archaeology, dance, art, gardening. Home: 150 El Portola Dr Sonoma CA 95476

FOTTNER, GÜNTHER RUDOLF, scientist, technical business executive; b. Munich, Mar. 15, 1948. MS in Physics, U. Munich, Fed. Republic Germany, 1974; PhD in Physics, Tech. U. Munich, Fed. Republic Germany; Maitrise, U. Grenoble, France. With subs. Bayer AG, Munich, 1974-77, Swiss Inst. Nuclear Research and Tech. U. Munich, Villigen, 1977-82, McKinsey & Co. Inc., Düsseldorf, Federal Republic of Germany, 1982-84; dir. ops. strategy and tech. cons. PA Tech., Frankfurt, Fed. Republic Germany, 1984—. Office: PA Technology, Wiesenau 27-29, D-6000 Frankfurt Federal Republic of Germany

FOULKES, BERNARD VINCENT, plastics company executive; b. Stoke-on-Trent, Eng., July 30, 1937; s. Vincent James and Isabella (Clarke) F.; children—Simon Edward, Caroline Ann. D.P.M., Aston U., 1976. Gen. mgr. Plastics Coating Ltd., Farnham, Eng., 1979-82; mng. dir. Jarzon Plastics Ltd., Hayes, Eng., 1982—; dir. BVF Enterprises Ltd., Hayes, 1982—. Chmn. Guilford Engring. Tng. Assn., Eng., 1979-83; chmn. govs. Farnborough Coll. Tech., 1982—. Served with Royal Air Force, 1957-75. Recipient Gen. Service medal, 1964. Fellow Brit. Inst. Mgmt. Home: Woodacre, Sandy Ln Tilford, Farnham England Office: Jarzon Plastics Ltd, Golden Crescent, Hayes England

FOURTOU, JEAN-RENÉ, chemical company executive; b. Libourne, Gironde, France, June 20, 1939; s. Rene an Inés (Stinus) F.; m. Janelly Harrburger, July 20, 1963; children: Jean-Francois, Xavier, Julien. Student, Ecole Polytech., France. Orgn. engr. Orgn. Bossard Michel, 1963-72; dir. gen. Bossard Groupe, 1972-76; pres. Bossards Cons., 1977-83; pres., dir.-gen. Groupe Bossard S.A., 1979—; now chmn. Rhone-Poulenc S.A., Coubevoie, Cedex, France. Club: Racing. Office: Rhone-Paulenc S A, 25 Quai Paul Daumer, 92408 Courbevoie Cedex France *

FOUSSE, JEAN-LOUIS MICHEL, management executive; b. Paris, Jan. 14, 1938; s. Henri and Odette (Petit) F.; m. Marianne Peloille, June 27, 1961 (div. 1987); children: Valery, Ciril, Pascaline. MBA, Stanford U., 1962; HEC, Paris U. V.p., fin. Peloille (div. of Johnson & Johnson), Champigny, France, 1966-68, BN (div. Gen. Mills Co.), Nantes, France, 1966-68, Corning France, Levallois, 1973-76; asst. to chmn. Ratier Forest G&P, Paris, 1976-79; gerant Nordatron, Cergy, France, 1978—; mgmt. cons., gen. mgr. Wooddwave, Argenteuil, France, 1987—; prof. ISSEC/ESSEC, Cergy, 1977—. Author: How to Install a Management Information System, 1972, Dictionary Finance, 1979. Mem. Nat. Assn. Accts., Dirs. Financiers and Cntrollers of Gestion. Home: 37 Rue de Chezy, 92200 Neuilly France Office: I D Cons, 37 Rue de Chezy, 99220 Neuilly France

FOUST, RICHARD DUANE, JR., academic administrator; b. Windber, Pa., Dec. 3, 1945; s. Richard Duane and Edna Larue (Pebley) F.; m. Lorraine Beverly Felt, June 24, 1967 (div. Oct. 1983); children: Richard Duane III, Barbara Anne, Cynthia Marie; m. Glenda Earle Swanner, Oct. 29, 1983. BS, Pa. State U., 1967; PhD, U. Calif., Santa Barbara, 1971. Chemist Westvaco, Luke, Md., 1966-67; asst. prof. No. Ariz. U., Flagstaff, 1972-75, assoc. prof., 1975-87, prof., 1987—, dir. Bilby Research Ctr., 1981—; state dir. Am. Energy Week, Washington, 1982. Author: Arizona Energy Education Activities, 1982; mem. edit. bd. Jour. Coll. Sci. Teaching, 1983—; contbr. articles to profl. jours. Bd. dirs. Arizonans for Jobs and Energy, Pheonix, 1977-82; mem. Ariz. Adv. Council on Energy Edn., Pheonix, 1977—; mem. The Ariz. Acad., 1981—. Recipient Excellence in Coll. Teaching award Danforth Found., St. Louis, 1980. Mem. Internat. Soc. Chem. Ecology, Soc. Applied Spectroscopy, NSF (peer rev. psnel 1977—), Nat. Sci. Teachers Assn. (Search for Excellence in Sci. Edn. award 1984), Am. Chem. Soc., Ariz. Sci. Teachers Assn. (pres. 1982-83), Sigma Xi (pres. 1982-83). Democrat. Methodist. Home: 3430 Fox Lair Flagstaff AZ 86004 Office: No Ariz U Ralph M Bilby Research Ctr Flagstaff AZ 86011

FOUTS, JAMES FREMONT, mining company executive; b. Port Arthur, Tex., June 3, 1918; s. Horace Arthur and Willie E. (Edwards) F.; m. Elizabeth Hanna Browne, June 19, 1948; children: Elizabeth, Donovan, Alan, James. B Chem Engring., Tex. A&M U., 1940. Div. supt. Baroid div. N.L. Industries, U.S. Rocky Mountain area and Can., 1948-60; pres. Riley-Utah Co., Salt Lake City, 1960-67, Fremont Corp., Monroe, La., 1967—, Auric Metals Corp., Salt Lake City, 1972—; bd. dirs. La Fonda Hotel, Santa Fe, N.Mex., High Plains Natural Gas Co., Canadian, Tex. Hon. asst. sec. of State of La. Served to lt. col. arty U.S. Army, 1942-46. Mem. Wyo. Geol. Assn. (v.p. 1958), Rocky Mountain Oil & Gas Assn. (bd. dirs. 1959), Res. Officers Assn. Wyo. (pres. 1948), Am. Assn. Petroleum Geologists, Internat. Geol. Assn., Mont. Geol. Assn., Ind. Petroleum Producers Assn. Republican. Episcopalian. Club: Univ. Lodge: Elks. Home: 4002 Bon Aire Dr Monroe LA 71203 Office: Fremont Corp PO Box 7070 Monroe LA 71211 also: Auric Metals Corp 2220 Wilson Ave Salt Lake City UT 84108

FOUTZ, HOMER EZRA, endodontist; b. Kansas City, Mo., Mar. 1, 1932; s. Homer Sylvanus and Margurite Saylor (Mohler) F.; m. Shirley Ann Rosenau, June 12, 1956 (dec. 1968); m. Cleo Elaine Cook, May 8, 1969; children—Kris Diane, Homer Paul. B.A., U. Kans., 1955; D.D.S., U. of Mo., 1960; postgrad. endodontia Loyola U., Temple U. and U. of Boston, 1965-71. Gen. practice dentistry, Colby, Kans. 1960-73; practice dentistry specializing in endodontics, Hays, Kans., 1973—; cons. Kans. Dental Bd., Topeka, 1978—; mem. exec. com. combined med.-dental staff St. Anthony and Hadley Hosps., Hays, 1983—; mem. dental adv. bd. Kans. Blue Cross-Blue Shield, Topeka, 1983—. Scoutmaster Coronado council Boy Scouts Am., Colby, 1961-71, Hays, 1979—, mem. exec. com., Salina, Kans., 1982—, recipient Silver Beaver award, 1987 ; elder Presbyterian Ch., Hays, 1972—. Mem. ADA, Kans. Dental Soc., Golden Belt Dental Soc. (past pres.), NW Dental Soc. (past pres.), Fed. Dental Int., Am. Endodontics Assn., Am. Soc. Dentists for Children. Republican. Club: Smokey Hill Country (Hays) (pres. 1979-80). Lodge: Masons. Avocations: raising quarter horses; camping; fishing. Home: 3008 Tam O'Shanter Hays KS 67601 Office: PO Box 994 2501 Canterbury Rd Hays KS 67601

FOWKES, ANTHONY STANLEY, academic researcher, educator; b. Leicester, East Midlands, Eng., June 16, 1950; s. Stanley and Margaret (Allen) F. BA, Leeds U., 1971, PhD, 1978. Research asst. Sch. Econs. Leeds U., 1973-74, lectr. econs., 1974-76, research fellow, 1982-83; research officer Inst. Transport Studies Leeds U., 1976-82, research fellow, 1983-87, sr. research fellow, 1987—. Co-author: Car Ownership Modelling and Forecasting, 1982; contbr. articles to profl. jours. Office: U Leeds, Inst Transport Studies, Leeds LS2 9JT, England

FOWLER, CHARLES ALLISON EUGENE, architectural engineer; b. Halifax, N.S., Can., Jan. 24, 1921; s. Charles Allison and Mildred (Crosby) F.; m. Dorothy Christine Graham, Aug. 30, 1947; children: Graham Allison, Beverly Anne. B.Sc., Dalhousie U., 1942; B.Eng., McGill U., 1944; B.Arch., U. Man., 1948; D.Eng. (hon.), N.S. Tech. Coll., 1975. With C.A. Fowler, Bauld & Mitchell, Ltd. (and predecessor firms), Halifax, 1946-80; sr. partner C.A. Fowler, Bauld & Mitchell, Ltd. (and predecessor firms), 1950-70, pres., 1970-80, chmn., 1980-81; pres. C.A. Fowler & Co., 1981—; dir. Tidal Power Corp.; mem. standing com. energy conservation in bldgs. NRC; mem. Energy Sector and Constrn. Sector Voluntary Planning N.S.; chmn. N.S. chpt. Can. Construction Research Bd. Prin. works include Miners Mus., Glace Bay, N.S., Dalhousie U. Fine Arts Center, 1970, univ. center Acadia U., Acad. Center at Mt. St. Vincent U., Halifax Law Cts., Canadian Martyrs Ch., Can. Permanent Bldg. Hfy, Halifax Metro Center, Stadacona Hosp., Victoria Gen. Hosp., Centre 200, Sydney, N.S. Gov. N.S. Coll. Art and Design. Served with Can. Army, 1943-45. Fellow AIA (hon.), Royal Archtl. Inst. Can. (pres. 1965); mem. Engring. Inst. Can., Assn. Profl. Engrs. N.S., N.S. Assn. Architects (past pres.), N.S. Mus. Fine Art (pres. 1971, 72, 74), Royal United Service Inst. Mem. United Ch. Clubs: Halifax (Halifax); Royal N.S. Yacht Squadron. Home and Office: 2 Hall's Rd, Halifax, NS Canada B3P 1P3

FOWLER, DONALD RAYMOND, lawyer, educator; b. Raton, N.Mex., June 2, 1926; s. Homer F. and Grace B. (Honeyfield) F.; m. Anna M. Averyt, Feb. 6, 1960; children—Mark D., Kelly A. B.A., U. N.Mex., 1950; J.D., 1951; M.A., Claremont Grad. Sch., 1979, Ph.D., 1983. Bar: N.Mex. 1951, Calif. 1964, U.S. Supreme Ct. 1980. Atty. AEC, Los Alamos and Albuquerque, 1951-61, chief counsel Nev. Ops., 1962-63; pvt. practice, Albuquerque, 1961-62; asst., then dep. staff counsel Calif. Inst. Tech., Pasadena, 1963-72, staff counsel, 1972-75, gen. counsel, 1975—; lectr. exec. mgmt. program Claremont Grad. Sch., Calif., 1981-84. Contbr. articles to profl. publs. Served with USAAF, 1944-46. Recipient NASA Pub. Service award, 1981. Mem. ABA, Calif. State Bar Assn., N.Mex. State Bar Assn., Fed. Bar Assn., Los Angeles County Bar Assn., Nat. Assn. Coll. and Univ. Attys. (exec. bd. 1979-82, 84—, chmn. publs. com. 1982-84, pres. 1987-88). Office: Calif Inst Tech 4800 Oak Grove Dr Bldg 180 Suite 305 Pasadena CA 91109

FOWLER, EARL BEALLE, electrical engineer, consultant; b. Jacksonville, Fla., Sept. 29, 1925; s. Earl Beall and Veva May (Carpenter) F.; m. Helen Marie Jorgenson, Feb. 2, 1948; children: Mary Helen, Joan Ann. B.S. in Mech. Engring., Ga. Inst. Tech. 1946; BEE, MIT, 1949; postgrad. Harvard U., 1971. Commd. ensign U.S. Navy, 1943, advanced through grades to vice admiral, ret., 1985, project mgr. Naval Ships Systems Command, Washington, 1967-71, dep. comdr. Naval Electronic Systems Command, Washington, 1972-75, vice comdr., 1975-76, comdr., 1976-80; comdr. Naval Sea Systems Command, Washington, 1980-85; cons., Washington, 1985—; pres. Fowler Internat. Corp., 1980—. Decorated Legion of Merit, Meritorious Service medal, Disting. Service medal. Mem. IEEE, Am. Soc. Naval Engrs., Soc. Naval Architects and Marine Engrs. Democrat. Episcopalian. Clubs: N.Y. Yacht; Army Navy Country (Arlington, Va.); Cosmos (Washington). Avocation: golf. Home: 4916 Hidden Oak Trail Sarasota FL 34232 Office: 1800 Diagonal Rd Suite 600 Alexandria VA 22314

FOWLER, GEORGE SELTON, JR., architect; b. Chgo., Jan. 20, 1920; s. George Selton and Mabel Helena (Overton) F.; m. Yvonne Fern Grammer, Nov. 25, 1945; 1 child, Kim Ellyn. Cert. Hamilton Coll., 1944; B.S., Ill. Inst. Tech., 1949, postgrad. 1968; cert. Elec. Assn. Ill., 1976. Registered architect, Ill., Ohio. Urban planner Chgo. Land Clearance Commn., 1949-50; liaison architect Chgo. Housing Authority, 1950-68, chief design-tech. div., 1968-80, dir. dept. engring., 1980-84; prin. George S. Fowler, Architect, Chgo., 1984—; architect, planner and cons. Interconco., 1965-66; cons. in field. Author: (text book study guide) Reinforced Concrete Design, 1959. Patentee in field. Mem. Mayor's Adv. Commn. to Revise the Bldg. Code, 1986—. Served with C.E., U.S. Army, 1942-46. Recipient Citation for Residential Devel., Mayor Richard J. Daley, Chgo., 1960, Black Achievers of Industry Recognition award YMCA, Chgo., 1977; Kappa Alpha Psi grantee, 1936. Mem. Architects in Industry, Nat. Assn. Housing and Redevelopment Officials, Inventors Council of Chgo. Avocations: classic cars; classical music; jazz. Home and Office: 8209 S Rhodes Ave Chicago IL 60619

FOWLER, HENRY HAMILL, investment banker; b. Roanoke, Va., Sept. 5, 1908; s. Mack Johnson and Bertha (Browning) F.; m. Trudye Pamela Hathcote, Oct. 19, 1938; children: Mary Anne Fowler Smith, Susan Fowler-Gallagher, Henry Hamill (dec.). A.B., Roanoke Coll., 1929, LL.D., 1962; LL.B., Yale U., 1932, J.S.D., 1933; LL.D., William and Mary U., 1966, Wesleyan U., 1966. Bar: Va. 1933, D.C. 1946. Counsel TVA, 1934-38, asst. gen. counsel, 1939; spl. asst. to atty. gen. as chief counsel subcom. Senate Com. Edn. and Labor, 1939-40; spl. counsel Fed. Power Commn., 1941; asst. gen. counsel O.P.M., 1941, W.P.B., 1942-44; econ. advisor U.S. Mission Econ. Affairs, London, 1944; spl. asst. to adminstr. Fgn. Econ. Adminstrn., 1945; dep. adminstr. N.P.A., 1951, adminstr., 1952; adminstr. Def. Prodn. Adminstrn., 1952-53; dir. Office Def. Moblzn., mem. NSC, 1952-53; sr. mem. firm Fowler, Leva Hawes & Symington, Washington, 1946-51, 1953-61, 64-65; undersec. Treasury 1961-64, sec. Treasury, 1965-68; gen. partner Goldman, Sachs & Co., N.Y.C., 1969-81, ltd. ptnr., 1981—; chmn. Goldman, Sachs Internat. Corp., N.Y.C., 1969-84. Trustee Lyndon B. Johnson Found., Atlantic Council U.S. (vice chmn., 1972-78); co-chmn. Citizens Network for Fgn. Affairs, 1987—, Com. on the Present Danger, 1976—, Bretton Woods Commn., 1985—; chmn. bd. trustees Roanoke Coll., 1974-81; chmn. Atlantic Council of U.S., 1973-78; chmn. bd. trustees Inst. Internat. Edn., 1972-77; mem. council Miller Ctr. for Pub. Affairs U. Va., 1980—; bd. dirs. Alfred E. Sloan Found, 1971-81, Carnegie Found for Peace, 1974-80. Mem. Conf. Bd. (councilor), Yale Law Sch. Assn. Washington (pres. 1955), Pi Kappa Phi, Phi Delta Phi. Democrat. Episcopalian. Clubs: River (N.Y.C.), Links (N.Y.C.); Metropolitan (Washington); Bohemian (San Francisco). Home: 209 S Fairfax St Alexandria VA 22314 also: 200 E 66th St New York NY 10021 Office: Goldman Sachs 85 Broad St New York NY 10004

FOWLER, H(ORATIO) SEYMOUR, educator; b. Detroit, Mar. 1, 1919; s. Horatio Seymour and Bessie Liona (Ladd) F.; m. Kathleen M. Marshall, Nov. 21, 1945 (dec.); 1 dau., Kathleen Marie Fowler Barto. B.S., Cornell U., 1941, M.S., 1946, Ph.D., 1951. Tchr. sci. McLean (N.Y.) Central Sch., 1946-47, Dryden (N.Y.) Freeville Central Sch., 1947-49; asst. prof. sci. edn. So. Oreg. Coll., Ashland, 1951-52; asst. prof. biology U. No. Iowa, Cedar Falls; also dir. Iowa Tchrs. Conservation Camp, 1952-57; prof. edn., dir. Pa. Conservation Lab. for Tchrs., Pa. State U., University Park, 1957-83, chmn. sci. edn. faculty, 1969-83, coordinator div. acad. curriculum and instrn., 1974-76, prof. nature and sci. edn. emeritus, 1983—; dir. Pa. Gov.'s Sch. for Scis., 1978-79; sci. advisor Nat. Jr. Sci. and Humanities Symposium, Program U.S. Army Research Office, Acad. Applied Sci. Author: Secondary School Science Teaching Practices, 1964, Las Ciencias en la Esquelas Secundarias, 1968, Fieldbook of Natural History, 1974; contbr. articles to profl. jours. Served with 9th inf. div. AUS, 1942-45, ETO. Fulbright lectr. Korea, 1968-69; recipient citation Pa. Dept. Edn., 1970, 83, Centre County (Pa.) Conservation award, 1973, Faculty Service award Nat. Univ. Continuing Edn. Assn., 1983, citation Pa. Ho. of Reps., 1983, Service award U.S. Army Office of Research, 1983; Paul Harris fellow Rotary Club, 1983. Fellow AAAS, Iowa Acad. Sci., Explorers Club; mem. Am. Nature Study Soc. (pres. 1967), Nat. Assn. Biology Tchrs. (v.p. 1956, dir. region II 1971-74, hon. mem. 1974), Nat. Assn. Research in Sci. Teaching, Nat. Sci. Tchrs. Assn. (Disting. Service citation 1976), Pa. Sci. Tchrs. Assn. (dir. 1971—, v.p. 1975, pres. 1976, meritorious service to sci. teaching citation 1975), Korean Sci. Tchrs. Assn., Royal Asiatic Soc., Sigma Xi, Phi Kappa Phi, Phi Delta Kappa (chpt. v.p. 1973, pres. 1974-75, Leadership award 1983), Beta Beta Beta, Phi Sigma. Clubs: Masons, Shriners, Rotary (1st v.p. 1981, pres. 1982, gov. dist. 735 1988—), Elks. Home: 1342 Park Hills Ave W State College PA 16803 Office: Pa State U Sci Edn Dept University Park PA 16802

FOWLER, JAMES ARTHUR, JR., dentist; b. Balt., July 27, 1934; s. James Arthur and Margaret Dorothy (Frank) F.; B.S., U. Md., 1957, D.D.S., 1959; M.S., U. Tex., Houston, 1968; m. Nancy Houston, Aug. 16, 1958; children—James Scott, Keith Houston. Commd. 1st lt. Dental Corps, USAF, 1959, advanced through grades to col., 1975; service in Eng., Hawaii, Colo., Ohio, Tex.; ret., 1979; assoc. prof. dentistry U. Tex. Dental Sch., San Antonio, 1979—. Decorated Commendation medal with oak leaf cluster; diplomate Am. Bd. Prosthodontics. Fellow Am. Coll. Dentists; mem. ADA, Am. Prosthodontic Soc., Am. Coll. Prosthodontists, Gorgas Odontological Soc., U. Tex. Alumni Assn., Omicron Kappa Upsilon, Psi Omega. Methodist. Author: (with others) Essentials of Dental Technology; contbr. articles to profl. publs.; co-inventor mouth mounted accelerometer. Office: U Tex Sch Dentistry 7703 Floyd Curl Dr San Antonio TX 78284

FOWLER, JAMES WILEY, III, minister, educator; b. Reidsville, N.C., Oct. 12, 1940; s. James Wiley and Lucile May (Haworth) F.; m. Lurline Locklair, July 7, 1962; children—Joan S., Margaret. B.A., Duke U., 1962; B.D., Drew U., 1965; Ph.D., Harvard U., 1971. Ordained to ministry Methodist Ch., 1968. Assoc. dir. Interpreters House, Lake Junaluska, N.C., 1968-69; minister United Meth. Ch., 1968—; asst. prof. to assoc. prof. Harvard U. Div. Sch., Cambridge, Mass., 1969-76; assoc. prof. Boston Coll., Chestnut Hill, Mass., 1976-77; prof. theology and human devel. Emory U., Atlanta, 1977—, founder, dir. Ctr. Faith Devel., 1980—, Charles Howard Candler prof., 1987—; bd. dirs. Nat. Cath. Reporter, Zygon, 1988. Author: To See the Kingdom, 1974; (with Sam Keen) Life Maps, 1978; (with others) Trajectories in Faith, 1980; (with others) Toward Moral and Religious Maturity, 1980; Stages of Faith, 1981; Becoming Adult, Becoming Christian, 1984; (with others) Faith Development and Fowler, 1986, Faith Development and Pastoral Care, 1987. Mem. Am. Acad. Religion, Religious Edn. Assn., Assn. Profs. and Researchers in Religious Edn., Soc. Scientific Study Religion. Democrat. Home: 2740 Janellen Dr NE Atlanta GA 30345 Office: Emory U Sch of Theology Atlanta GA 30322

FOWLER, NANCY CROWLEY, government economist; b. Newton, Mass., Aug. 8, 1922; d. Ralph Elmer and Margaret Bright (Tinkham) Crowley; m. Gordon Robert Fowler, Sept. 11, 1949; children—Gordon R., Nancy P., Betty Kainani, Diane Kuulei. A.B. cum laude, Radcliffe Coll., 1943; Grad. Cert., Harvard-Radcliffe Mgmt. Tng. Program, 1946; postgrad. U. Hawaii, 1971-76. Econ. research analyst Dept. Planning & Econ. Devel., Honolulu, 1963-69; assoc. chief research Regional Med. Program, Honolulu, 1969-70; economist V and VI, Dept. Planning and Econ. Devel., Honolulu, 1970-78, chief policy analysis br., 1978-85, tech. info. services officer, 1985—; staff rep. State Energy Functional Plan Adv. Com., Honolulu, 1983—, Hawaii Integrated Energy Assessment, 1978-81. Contbr. articles to profl. jours. Com. mem. Kailua Com. to Re-elect Mayor Eileen Anderson, 1984. Recipient Employee of Yr. award Dept. Planning and Econ. Devel., Honolulu, 1977, others. Mem. Hawaii Econs. Assn. (various offices). Democrat. Clubs: Radcliffe of Hawaii, Propeller of Port of Honolulu (pres.). Avocations: gardening; surfing. Home: 203 Aumoe Rd Kailua HI 96734

FOWLER, THOMAS JAMES, pharmacist, hospital executive; b. Pitts., Jan. 6, 1933; s. Charles T. and Clara Theresa (Zahren) F.; B.S. in Pharmacy, Duquesne U., 1955; m. Joan A. Craig, Sept. 2, 1961; children—Thomas M., John P., Michael C., Julie Ann. Pharmacist in community pharmacy, Pitts. and Kensington, Md., 1957-62; staff pharmacist Mercy Hosp., Pitts., 1962-66, chief pharmacist, 1964-66; dir. of pharmacy services Sewickley Valley Hosp., Pa., 1966—; pharmacist cons. D.T. Watson Rehab. Hosp., 1970—; adj. instr. intern program Duquesne U. Sch. Pharmacy, Pitts., 1976—; lectr. Sewickley Valley Hosp. Sch. of Nursing, 1966—; vice chmn. pharmacy adv. com. Hosp. Council Western Pa., 1978-80, chmn., 1981-82, chmn. intravenous sub-com., 1980-81, mem. value analysis steering com., 1982-83; mem. pharmacy com. Voluntary Hosps. Am., 1985—. Counselor, Allegheny Trails council Boy Scouts Am. Served with USN, 1955-57. Recipient Sister M. Gonzales award for outstanding mgmt. Hosp. Council of Western Pa., 1982; Merck, Sharp and Dohme Corp. Pharmacy Achievement award for mgmt., 1983; diplomate Am. Bd. Diplomates in Pharmacy (charter). Fellow Am. Coll. Apothecaries; mem. Am. Soc. Cons. Pharmacists, Am., Western Pa. (pres. 1970-71), Pa. socs. hosp. pharmacists, Am., Pa. pharm. assns. Republican. Roman Catholic. Club: KC. Author: Incompatibilities of Some Intravenous Additives, 1971. contbr. articles on pharmacy to profl. publs. Home: 104 Connie Dr Pittsburgh PA 15214 Office: Sewickley Valley Hosp Blackburn Rd Sewickley PA 15143

FOWLER, WILLIAM ALFRED, physicist, educator; b. Pitts., Aug. 9, 1911; s. John McLeod and Jennie Summers (Watson) F.; m. Ardiane Olmsted, Aug. 24, 1940; children: Mary Emily, Martha Summers Fowler Schoenemann. B of Engring. Physics, Ohio State U., 1933, DSc (hon.), 1978; PhD, Calif. Inst. Tech., 1936; DSc (hon.), U. Chgo., 1976, Denison U., 1982, Ariz. State U., 1985, Georgetown U., 1986, U. Mass., 1987, Williams Coll., 1988; Doctorat hc, U. Liège (Belgium), 1981, Observatoire de Paris, 1981. Research fellow Calif. Inst. Tech., Pasadena, 1936-39; asst. prof. physics Calif. Inst. Tech., 1939-42, asso. prof., 1942-46, prof. physics, 1946-70, Inst. prof. physics, 1970—; Recipient Sullivant medal Ohio State U., 1985; Fulbright lectr. Cavendish lab. U. Cambridge, 1954-55; Guggenheim fellow, 1954-55; Guggenheim fellow St. John's Coll. and dept. applied math. and theoretical physics U. Cambridge, 1961-62; vis. fellow Inst. Theoretical Astronomy, summers 1967-72; vis. scholar program Phi Beta Kappa, 1980-81; asst. dir. research, sect. L NDRC, 1941-45; tech. observer, office of field service OSRD, South Pacific Theatre, 1944; sci. dir., project VISTA, Dept. Def., 1951-52; mem. nat. sci. bd. NSF, 1968-74; mem. space sci. bd. Nat. Acad. Scis., 1970-73, 77-80; chmn. Office of Phys. Scis., 1981-84; mem. space program adv. council NASA, 1971-73; mem. nuclear sci. adv. com. Dept. Energy/NSF, 1977-80; Phi Beta Kappa Vis. scholar, 1980-81; E.A. Milne Lectr. Milne Soc., 1986; named lectr. univs., colls. Contbr. numerous articles to profl. jours. Bd. dirs. Am. Friends of Cambridge U., 1970-78. Recipient Naval Ordnance Devel. award U.S. Navy, 1945, Medal of Merit, 1948; Lammé medal Ohio State U., 1952; Liège medal U. Liège, 1955; Calif. Co-Scientist of Yr. award, 1958; Barnard medal for contbn. to sci. Columbia, 1965; Apollo Achievement award NASA, 1969; Vetlesen prize, 1973; Nat. medal of Sci., 1974; Bruce gold medal Astron. Soc. Pacific, 1979; Nobel prize for physics, 1983; Benjamin Franklin fellow Royal Soc. Arts. Fellow Am. Phys. Soc. (Tom W. Bonner prize 1970, pres. 1976, 1st recipient William A. Fowler award for excellence in physics So. Ohio sect. 1986), Am. Acad. Arts and Scis., Royal Astron. Soc. (assoc., Eddington medal 1978); mem. Nat. Acad. Scis. (council 1974-77), AAAS, Am. Astron. Soc., Am. Inst. Physics (governing bd. 1974-80), AAUP, Am. Philos. Soc., Soc. Royal Sci. Liège (corr. mem.), Brit. Assn. Advancement Sci., Soc. Am. Baseball Research, Mark Twain Soc. (hon.), Naturvetenskapliga Foreiningen (hon.), Sigma Xi, Tau Beta Pi, Tau Kappa Epsilon. Democrat. Clubs: Athenaeum (Pasadena); Cosmos (Washington). Office: Calif Inst Tech Kellogg 106-38 Pasadena CA 91125

FOWLER, WILLIAM DIX, construction company executive; b. Glendale, Calif., Jan. 29, 1940; s. H. Dix and Bertha Grace (Graveling) F.; m. Sheila Antonia Sandstrom, Feb. 7, 1964; children—Kurtis Walter Dix, Kara Antonia Grace, Kevin William Victor, Keir Andrew Bexar. B.B.A., Tex. Christian U., 1964, M.P.A., 1967. C.P.A., Alaska, Tex. Sr. v.p., mgr. J.L. Cox & Son, Inc., Kansas City, Mo., 1973-74; project adminstrn. mgr. Perini Arctic Assn., Delta Junction, Alaska, 1974-77; Alaska div. mgr. Majestic Wiley Contractor, Fairbanks, Alaska, 1974-77; v.p., treas. Frank Moolin & Assocs., Anchorage, 1977-78; sr. v.p., gen. mgr. Alaska Internat. Constrn. Inc., Fairbanks, 1978-80; pres. Alaska Internat. Constrn. Inc., 1980-85. FANCO Engring. & Constrn., 1986—, Southeast Pipeline Contractors, Inc., Ariz. and Alaska, 1987-88. U. Alaska Found. fellow. Mem. Am. Inst. CPA's, Alaska Soc. CPA's, Tex. Soc. CPA's, Associated Gen. Contractors (bd. dirs. Fairbanks 1984—), Beta Alpha Psi. Republican. Episcopalian. Lodge: Rotary. Home: PO Box 82010 Fairbanks AK 99708 Office: FANCO Engring & Constrn PO Box 60288 Fairbanks AK 99706 also: 8711 E Pinnacle Peak Rd #237 Scottsdale AZ 85260

FOWLER, WILLIAM WYCHE, JR., U.S. senator, former congressman; b. Atlanta, Oct. 6, 1940; s. William Wyche and Emelyn (Barbre) F.; 1 dau., Katherine Wyche. B.A., Davidson Coll., 1962; J.D., Emory U., 1969. Bar: Ga. 1970. Chief asst. to Congressman Charles Weltner, 1965; mem. Atlanta Bd. Aldermen, 1969-73; pres. Atlanta City Council, 1973-77; mem. 95th-99th Congresses from 5th Ga. Dist., 1977-87; U.S. Senator from Ga. Washington, 1987—; asso. firm Smith Cohen Ringel Kohler & Martin, Atlanta. Served in U.S. Army. Recipient Myrtle Wreath award, 1972; named Outstanding Young Man Atlanta Jaycees, 1972, Outstanding Young Man Ga. Jaycees, 1973. Mem. ABA, State Bar Ga. Democrat. Office: US Senate 204 Russell Senate Bldg Washington DC 20510 *

FOWLES, JOHN, author; b. Essex, Eng., Mar. 31, 1926; s. Robert and Gladys (Richards) F.; m. Elizabeth Whitton, Apr. 2, 1954. Honours degree in French, Oxford U., 1950; D.Litt., Exeter U., 1983. Author: The Collector, 1963, The Aristos, 1964, The Magus, 1966, The French Lieutenant's Woman, 1969, Poems, 1973, The Ebony Tower, 1974, Shipwreck, 1977, Daniel Martin, 1977, Islands, 1978, The Tree, 1979, Mantissa, 1982, A Maggot, 1985. Office: care Anthony Sheil Assocs, 43 Daughty St, London WC1N 2LF, England *

FOWLKES, NANCY LANETTA PINKARD, social worker; b. Athens, Ga.; d. Amos Malone and Nettie (Barnett) Pinkard; m. Vester Guy Fowlkes, June 4, 1955 (dec. 1965); 1 dau., Wendy Denise. BA, Bennett Coll., 1946; MA, Syracuse U., 1952; MSW, Smith Coll., 1963; MPA, Pace U., 1982. Dir. publicity Bennett Coll., Greensboro, N.C., 1946-47, 49-50; asst. editor Va. Edn. Bull. ofcl. organ Va. State Tchrs. Assn., Richmond, 1950-52; asst. office mgr. Community Service Soc., N.Y.C., 1952-55; social caseworker, asst. supr. Dept. Social Services, Westchester County, White Plains, N.Y., 1959-67, supr. adoption services, 1967-77, supr. adoption and foster care, 1977—; mem. adv. bd. White Plains Adult Edn. Sch. First v.p. Eastview Jr. High Sch., 1970-71; area chmn. White Plains Community Chest, 1964; sec. Mt. Vernon Concert Group, 1952-54; fund raising co-chmn. Urban League Guild of Westchester, 1967; pres. White Plains Interfaith Council, 1972-74, northeastern jurisdiction United Meth. Ch., 1988—; chmn. adminstrv. bd. Methodist Ch., 1970-72, 82-83, vice chmn., 1978-80, vice chmn. trustees, 1973-77, treas., 1978-83; lay speaker, v.p. Met. dist. United Meth. Women, 1977-79, exec. bd. N.Y. conf., N.Y. conf. rep. Upper Atlantic Regional Sch., 1981-83, mem. nominating com., 1982-83, trustee N.Y. conf., 1982-88, pres.

N.Y. conf., 1983-87; bd. dirs. Family Service of Westchester, Bethel Meth. Home, Ossining, N.Y.; bd dirs. White Plains YWCA, 1985—. Mem. Nat. Assn. Social Workers, Acad. Cert. Social Workers, Jack and Jill of Am. Inc. (chpt. pres. 1954-56, regional sec.-treas 1967-71), Nat. Bus. and Profl. Women's Club (chpt. sec. 1954-56), Internat. Platform Assn., Theta Sigma Phi (Sec.-Treas.), Zeta Nu Omega, Alpha Kappa Alpha (pres. 1960-64, treas. 1975-78). Club: Regency Bridge (pres. 1963-65). Home: 107 Valley Rd White Plains NY 10604 Office: 112 E Post Rd White Plains NY 10601

FOX, BYRON EVANS, lawyer, educator; b. N.Y.C., Aug. 30, 1931; s. Samuel and Evelyn (Leader) V.; m. Eleanor Mae Cohen, Mar. 31, 1957; children—Douglas, Margot, Randall. B.A., NYU, 1952; LL.B., U. Va., 1955. Bar: Va. 1955, N.Y. 1963. Assoc. Davis Polk & Wardwell, 1955-58, Stein, Stein & Engel, 1958-66, Hay, Fales & Co., Inc., 1966-80; ptnr. Bushkin, Gaims, Gaines, Jonas & Stream, N.Y.C., 1980-84; counsel Kaufman, Caffey, Gildin, Rosenblum & Schaeffer, N.Y.C., 1984—; adj. prof. law Fordham U., N.Y.C., 1976—; lectr. in law U. Va., also legal seminars. Named Man of Yr. YMCA of Greater N.Y., 1983. Mem. ABA (governing council forum com. on franchising), N.Y. State Bar Assn., Va. State Bar Assn., Internat. Bar Assn. Republican. Jewish. Club: Univ., Princeton of N.Y. Co-author: (with Eleanor M. Fox) Corporate Acquisitions and Mergers, 4 vols., 1968, 70, 72, 84, with quar. supplements, 1970—; contbr. numerous articles to legal jours. Office: Kaufman Caffey Gildin et al 777 3d Ave 24th Floor New York NY 10017

FOX, GERALD LYNN, oral surgeon; b. Asheboro, N.C., Mar. 4, 1942; s. Clarence William and Jane Marie (Brock) F.; B.S., U. Tenn., 1964, D.D.S., 1967; m. Ellen Carol Smith, Mar. 18, 1961; children—Angela Carol, Michael Lynn, Lisa Elaine. Rotating intern Wilford Hall USAF Hosp., San Antonio, 1968-69; intern and resident in oral surgery U. Tex. Med. Sch., San Antonio, 1974; mem. teaching staff U. Tex. Sch. Dentistry and VA Hosp., San Antonio; practice dentistry specializing in oral and maxillofacial surgery; mem. staff Holston Valley Hosp. and Med. Center, Indian Path Hosp., Tenn.; apptd. by gov. to Mal-Practice Rev. Bd., Tenn., 1975-81; pres. Sullivan County Chpt. Am. Cancer Soc., 1975-77; med. missionary, Honduras, 1980, 83, 85; People-to-People ambassador to Japan, Malaysia and Korea, 1985—. Served to capt. USAF, 1968-72. Recipient Marion Fuller award, 1967; award Am. Cancer Soc., 1977; award So. Bapt. Missionary Bd., 1980; diplomate Am. Bd. Oral & Maxillofacial Surgery. Fellow Am. Coll. Oral and Maxillofacial Surgeons (a founder); mem. ADA, Am. Assn. Oral and Maxillofacial Surgeons, Internat. Assn. Oral Surgeons, Tenn. Dental Assn., Tenn. Assn. Oral and Maxillofacial Surgeons, Am. Assn. Hosp. Dentists, 1st Dist. Dental Soc., Kingsport Dental Soc. & Study Club, Flying Dentists Assn., Tex. Bd. Dentistry, Fla. Bd. Dentistry, Airplane Owners and Pilots Assn., Xi Psi Phi. Methodist. Clubs: LeConte (Knoxville, Tenn.), Ridgefield Country. Contbr. articles to profl. jours. Home: 2525 Essex Dr Kingsport TN 37660 Office: 2008 Brookside Rd Kingsport TN 37660

FOX, JUDITH ELLEN, personnel executive; b. N.Y.C., Aug. 2, 1941; d. Murray A. and Harriette Schneider; student Pa. State U., 1959-60; m. Jerry Fox, Aug. 16, 1964; children: Brian Spencer, Jennifer Leslie. Asst. personnel dir. Miles Shoe Co., N.Y.C., 1961-63; freelance writer, photographer Coronet, The Progressive, U.S. Catholic, numerous local and state periodicals, 1962-77; asst. personnel dir. Wallachs, Inc., N.Y.C., 1963-64; co-owner, photographer J. Fox Photographers, Stony Brook, N.Y., 1968-72; mgr. Forbes Temporaries, Richmond, Va., 1975-78; pres. Fox-Huber Cos., Inc., Richmond, 1978—, Rosemary Scott Temps., N.Y.C., 1983—, Fox-Huber Temps., Inc., 1978—; adv. bd., chmn. women in bus. com. Women's Bank, 1981-83; chmn. customer adv. bd. Va. Electric Power Co., 1981-84, chmn. task force 12th Street Hydroelectric Plant Project, 1983-84, mem. communications customer cons. group, 1985—; cons. to pvt. industry, 1980—. Dist. chmn. Va. gubernatorial campaign, 1977; charter mem. Businesses Who Care; bd. dirs. Sci. Mus. of Va., 1985—, Multiple Sclerosis Soc., Central Va. chpt., 1979-80; active Pres. Roundtable James Madison Univ., 1987—, Local Corp. Gifts Com. The Campaign for Va. Commonwealth Univ., 1987; mem. exec. com. Gov's Adv. Com. Small Bus.; 1982-86; co-chair Industrialist of Yr. Awards Com. Sci. Mus. of Va., 1987—; bd. dirs. Met. Richmond YMCA, 1982-86, Pvt. Industry Council, 1983-86; vice-chmn. Richmond area U.S. Olympic Com., 1983-86; mem. fundraising com. Hampton Inst. Named Richmond Small Bus. Women of Yr., 1987, one of Richmond' 100 Most Influential People, 1986. Mem. Profl. Orgn. of Temporary Services, Va. C. of C. (small bus. com. 1983-85), Richmond C. of C. (chmn. small bus. council 1982-84, dir. 1983—, exec. bd. 1984—, mem legis affairs com. 1981—), Va. Assn. Temp. Services (v.p. 1981—), Nat. Assn. Female Execs., Richmond Assn. Women Bus. Owners. Office: 7301 Forest Ave Suite 200 Richmond VA 23226-3766 also: 200 W 57th St Suite 810 New York NY 10019

FOX, KARL AUGUST, economist, educator; b. Salt Lake City, July 14, 1917; s. Feramorz Young and Anna Teresa (Wilcken) F.; m. Sylvia Olive Cate, July 29, 1940; children: Karl Richard, Karen Frances Anne. B.A., U. Utah, 1937, M.A., 1938; Ph.D., U. Calif., 1954. Economist USDA, 1942-54; head div. statis. and hist. research Bur. Agrl. Econs., 1951-54; economist Council Econ. Advisers, Washington, 1954-55; head dept. econs. and sociology Iowa State U., Ames, 1955-66; head dept. econs. Iowa State U., 1966-72, Distinguished prof. scis. and humanities, 1968-87, prof. emeritus, 1987—; Vis. prof. Harvard, 1960-61, U. Calif., Santa Barbara, 1971-72, 78, vis. scholar, Berkeley, 1972-73; William Evans vis. prof. U. Otago, N.Z., 1981; Bd. dirs. Social Sci. Research Council, 1963-67, mem. com. econ. stability, 1963-66, chmn. com. areas for social and econ. statistics, 1964-67; mem. Com. Reg. Accounts, 1963-68. Author: Econometric Analysis for Public Policy, 1958, (with M. Ezekiel) Methods of Correlation and Regression Analysis, 1959, (with others) The Theory of Quantitative Economic Policy, 1966, rev. edit., 1973, Intermediate Economic Statistics, 1968, rev. edit, (with T.K. Kaul), 1980, (with J. K. Sengupta) Economic Analysis and Operations Research, 1969, (with W.C. Merrill) Introduction to Economic Statistics, 1970, Social Indicators and Social Theory, 1974, Social System Accounts, 1985; author-editor: Economic Analysis for Educational Planning, 1972; Co-editor: Readings in the Economics of Agriculture, 1969, Economic Models Estimation and Risk Programming (essays in honor of Gerhard Tintner), 1969, Systems Economics, 1987; contbr. articles to profl. jours. Recipient superior service medal USDA, 1948, award for outstanding pub. research Am. Agrl. Econs. Assn., 1952, 54, 57, for outstanding doctoral dissertation, 1953. Fellow Econometric Soc., Am. Statis. Assn. (Census Research fellow 1980-81), Am. Agrl. Econs. Assn. (v.p. 1955-56, award for publ. of enduring quality 1977), AAAS; mem. Am. Econs. Assn. (research and publs. com. 1963-67), Regional Sci. Assn., Ops. Research Soc. Am., Am. Ednl. Research Assn., Phi Beta Kappa, Phi Kappa Phi. Home: 234 Parkridge Circle Ames IA 50010 Office: Iowa State U Ames IA 50011

FOX, LAWRENCE MARTIN, veterinarian; b. Chgo., Feb. 26, 1946; s. Alexander Louis and Annette (Singer) F.; B.S., U. Ill., 1966, D.V.M., 1968; m. Carlina Mary Renzy, Mar. 18, 1967; children—Kevin Lawrence, Brandon Douglas, Robin Christopher. Practice vet. medicine, Chgo., 1970-72, River Grove, Ill., 1972—; dir. Elmwood-Grove Animal Hosp., Ltd., River Grove, 1972—;treas., dir. Oak Park (Ill.) Village Humane Soc., 1974-76. Sec., Willard Sch. PTA, River Forest, Ill., 1978-79, v.p., 1979-80, pres., 1980-81; sec. River Forest Parental Music Assn., 1983-85, pres., 1986-87; bd. mgrs. River Forest Schs., 1980; cubmaster Boy Scouts Am., River Forest, 1979-83, also Webelos leader, 1979-81. Served as capt. Vet. Corps, U.S. Army, 1968-70. Diplomate Am. Bd. Vet. Practitioners (chmn. Midwest cluster, pub. relations, continuing edn. coms.). Mem. AVMA, Ill. State, Chgo. (edn. com. 1981-86 , chmn. 1983-86, installation dinner dance com. 1986-87, bd. dirs. 1986—, membership com. 1987-88, St. Charles Spring Clinic com. 1988-89) vet. med. assns., Am. Animal Hosp. Assn., Vet. Inst. for Practitioners, Vet. Cancer Soc., Am. Assn. Feline Practitioners, Chgo. Zool. Soc., Chgo. Area Runners, Ground-Zero, Greenpeace, Mensa. Contbr. articles to profl. jours. Home: 1200 Franklin Ave River Forest IL 60305 Office: 8035 Grand Ave River Grove IL 60171

FOX, MICHAEL DAVID, art educator, visual imagist artist; b. Cortland, N.Y., Dec. 29, 1937; s. Donald F. Fox and Ethel (Allen) Sullivan; m. Carol Ann Hampston, Nov. 5, 1967; 1 child, Kathryn Gabrielle. B.S., SUNY-Buffalo, 1962, M.S., 1969; cert. in sculpture Bklyn. Mus. Sch., 1964. Tchr. art City Schs., Rochester, N.Y., 1962-63, 64-65; prof. art. Morehead State Univ., Ky., 1965-67, SUNY, Oswego, 1967—; speaker in field; vis. artist univs. and art ctrs., U.S.A., Can.; dir. Popular Image Gallery, Oswego, 1967—. Work featured on CBS-TV, 1976, 78, 80, also featured in N.Y. Times, Look, Evergreen Review, Nat. Lampoon, others, 1970—; represented in pvt. and pub. collections U.S.A., Can., Japan, Africa, Asia, Europe, S.Am. Recipient Outstanding Teaching award Morehead State Univ., 1967; Chancellors award for Excellence in Teaching, SUNY, 1981; numerous awards for drawing, painting, and sculpture, 1962—. Mem. United Univ. Profs. (v.p., del.). Home: 7 West End Ave Oswego NY 13126 Office: Tyler Hall SUNY Oswego NY 13126

FOX, PETER KENDREW, librarian; b. Beverley, Yorkshire, Eng., Mar. 23, 1949; came to Ireland, 1979; s. Thomas Kendrew and Dorothy (Wildbore) F.; m. Isobel McConnell, Mar. 28, 1983; 1 child, Louise Catherine. BA, King's Coll., London, 1971; MA, U. Sheffield, 1973. Asst. library officer U. Library, Cambridge, Eng., 1973-77, asst. under-librarian, 1977-78, under-librarian, 1978-79; dep. librarian Trinity Coll., Dublin, Ireland, 1979-84, librarian, 1984—; council mem. An Chomhairle Leabharlanna, Dublin, 1982—; mem. Nat. Preservation Adv. Com., London, 1984—; chmn. Sconul Adv. Com. on Info. Services, London, 1987—. Author: Reader Instruction Methods in Academic Libraries, 1974; editor: International Conferences on Library User Education Proceedings, 1980, 82, 84, Treasures of the Library: Trinity College, Dublin; editor An Leabharlann: The Irish Library, 1982-87. Mem. Library Assn. Ireland, Library Assn. U.K. (assoc.). Club: Oxford and Cambridge (London). Office: Trinity Coll Library, College St, Dublin 2 Ireland

FOX, RICHARD PAUL, lawyer; b. N.Y.C.; m. Joan Thompson, Mar. 23, 1962 (div. Feb. 1988); children—Joseph, Paul, Jonathan, Jeffrey. B.A., UCLA, 1966; J.D., Loyola U., Los Angeles, 1969; M.A. in Ethics, Pepperdine U., 1981. Bar: Calif. 1970, U.S. Supreme Ct., 1974, U.S. Ct. Claims 1973, U.S. Ct. Mil. Appeals 1973, U.S. Ct. Appeals (5th cir.) 1979, U.S. Ct. Appeals (6th cir.) 1980, U.S. Ct. Appeals (7th cir.) 1977, U.S. Ct. Appeals (9th cir.) 1971, U.S. Ct. Appeals (10th cir.) 1977, U.S. Ct. Appeals (D.C. cir.) 1983. Ptnr. firm Richard P. Fox & Max Gest, P.C., Los Angeles, 1970—. Mem. staff Loyola U. Law Rev., 1968-69. Contbr. articles to profl. jours. Served to maj. U.S. Army, 1951-63. Mem. Nat. Lawyers Guild, Christian Legal Soc. Lutheran. Office: Richard P Fox & Max Gest PC 9911 W Pico Blvd Suite 1030 Los Angeles CA 90035

FOX, VERNON BRITTAIN, emeritus criminology educator; b. Boyne Falls, Mich., Apr. 25, 1916; s. John Lorenzo and Ethel (Hamilton) F.; m. Laura Grace Ellerby, Mar. 22, 1941; children: Karen, Vernon, Loraine. AB in Sociology, Mich. State U., 1940, cert. in social work, 1941, MA in Sociology, 1943, PhD in Sociology, 1949. Caseworker, athletic dir. Starr Commonwealth for Boys, Albion, Mich., 1941-42; psychologist Dept. Corrections, State Prison So. Mich., Jackson, Mich., 1942-46, dep. warden, 1949-52; psychologist Cassidy Lake Tech. Sch., Mich. Dept. Corrections, 1946-49; prof. criminology Fla. State U., Tallahassee, 1952-86; prof. emeritus Fla. State U., 1986—, chmn. dept. criminology, 1952-71. Author: Violence Behind Bars, 1956, reprinted, 1974, Guidelines for Corrections Programs in Community and Junior Colleges, 1969, Crime and Law Enforcement, 1971, Introduction to Corrections, 1972, 2d edit., 1977, 3d edit., 1985, A Handbook for Volunteers in Juvenile Court, 1973; co-author, editor: Crime and Law Enforcement, 1971; co-author: Introduction to Criminal Justice, 1975, 2d edit., 1979, Introduction to Criminology, 1976, 2d edit., 1985, Russian edit., 1980, 85, Community-Based Corrections, 1977, (with Burton Wright) Criminal Justice and the Social Sciences, 1978, Correctional Institutions, 1983; internat. bd. editors: Abstracts in Criminology, 1959-71; asso. editor: Criminal Justice, 1971—, Jour. Humanics, 1973—; mem. adv. bd. dirs.: Criminal Justice Rev., 1975—; bd. advisors Internat. Jour. Comparative and Applied Criminal Justice, 1976—; mem. internat. bd. cons. Crimcare, 1985—; abstractor Abstracts for Social Workers, Fed. Probation. Mem. Tallahassee Com. of 99. Served with AUS, 1945-46. Named Alumni Prof. of Year, Fla. State U., 1970, Outstanding Prof., Tally-Ho, 1960, 68; Outstanding Criminal Justice Educator award So. Assn. Criminal Justice Educators, 1979; Social Sci. award Delta Tau Kappa, 1963. Mem. Am. Correctional Assn., Am. Sociol. Soc., Fla. Psychol. Assn., Omicron Delta Kappa, Delta Tau Kappa (chancellor Southeastern U.S.). Clubs: Capital City-Country, Exchange (Tallahassee). Home: 644 Voncile Ave Tallahassee FL 32303

FOXEN, GENE LOUIS, insurance executive; b. Chgo., Mar. 28, 1936; adopted son Henry and Mary Foxen; student public schs.; m. Diane E. Young, 1986; children from previous marriage: Dan, Kathleen, Michael, Patricia, James, Karen, Ellen. With New Eng. Life Ins. Co., 1957—, assoc. gen. agt., 1970-73, gen. agt., Chgo., 1973—. Cubmaster DuPage council Boy Scouts Am., 1963; Midwest regional dir. Adoptees Liberty Movement Assn. Served with USMC, 1954-57. Recipient life membership award Gen. Agents and Mgrs. Conf.; named as life mem. Hall of Fame, New Eng. Life Ins. Co., 1972, life mem. Million Dollar Round Table. C.L.U. Mem. Nat. Assn. Life Underwriters, Execs. Club Chgo., Gen. Agents and Mgrs. Assn., Am. Soc. C.L.U.'s (pres. Chgo. chpt. 1977-78, v.p. Midwest region 1981-82), Chgo. Estate Planning Council (pres. 1981-82), Am. Soc. Life Underwriters. Republican. Roman Catholic. Club: Metropolitan. Home: 2247 Hidden Creek Ct Lisle IL 60532 Office: Foxen Fin 120 S Riverside Plaza Chicago IL 60606

FOXEN, RICHARD WILLIAM, manufacturing company executive; b. N.Y.C., Nov. 12, 1927; s. William Aloysius and Mae Dorothea (Scully) F.; m. Hilda Duran-Ballen, Feb. 11, 1956; children—Richard, Theresa, Thomas, Patricia, Anthony. B.M.E., Bklyn. Poly. Inst., 1950. V.p. corp. staffs Westinghouse Air Brake Co., Pitts., 1961-69; pres. European indsl. group Am. Standard, Brussels, 1969-73; v.p. Europe bus. div. Gen. Electric, Brussels, 1973-78, sr. v.p. Rockwell Internat., 1978-88; adj. prof. bus. adminstrn. Carnegie Mellon U., U. Pitts. Chmn. Western Pa. Family Ctr., Pitts.; vice chmn. Pitts. Mercy Health Systems Inc., Pitts.; bd. fellows N.Y. Poly. U. Bd. dirs. Pitts. Mercy Health Corp., 1978—. Served with U.S. Army, 1946-48. Mem. Tau Beta Pi, Pi Tau Sigma. Roman Catholic. Club: Duquesne. Home: 5529 Dunmoyle St Pittsburgh PA 15217

FOXHOVEN, MICHAEL JOHN, retail/wholesale company executive, retail merchant; b. Sterling, Colo., Mar. 2, 1949; s. Mark John and Mary Kathryn (Hagerty) F.; m. Catherine Marie Carricaburu, Feb. 16, 1980; children—Patrick Michael, Rachel Marie. Student U. Colo., 1967-70, U. San Francisco, 1971-72, postgrad. Columbia Pacific U., 1987—. Comml. sales mgr. Goodyear Tire & Rubber Co., Denver, 1978-80, area sales mgr., 1980-81, store mgr., 1981-83, wholesale mgr., 1983-84, appeared in TV commls., 1972; v.p. Foxhovens, Inc., Sterling, 1984—; cons. Foxhoven Bros., Inc., Sterling, 1984—; participant dealer mgmt. seminar, Akron, Ohio, 1973, 85. Mem. mgmt. adv. com. Northeastern Jr. Coll., Sterling, 1976-78; sec. Highland Park Sanitation Dist., Sterling, 1984—. Mem. Logan County C. of C. Republican. Roman Catholic. Club: Sterling Country. Lodges: Elks, Kiwanis. Home: 107 Highland Ave Sterling CO 80751 Office: Foxhovens Inc 1100 W Main St Sterling CO 80751

FOY, THOMAS PATRICK, lawyer, state legislator; b. Camden, N.J., Mar. 13, 1951; s. Dennis A. and Sarah R. Foy; m. Janice A. Mullin, June 30, 1978; children: Brian, Alexandra. B.A. magna cum laude, Duke U., 1973, postgrad., 1974; J.D., Rutgers U., 1977. Bar: N.J. 1977, D.C. 1977, U.S. Ct. Appeals (D.C. cir.) 1978, U.S. Supreme Ct. 1981, U.S. Ct. Appeals (3d cir.) 1983, U.S. Tax Ct., U.S. Dist. Ct. N.J. Sole practice, Burlington, N.J., 1977-80; ptnr. Schlesinger, Schlosser, Foy, & Harrington, Mt. Holly, N.J., 1980—, also dir.; mem. N.J. Gen. Assembly, 1984—, mem. labor and govt. oversight coms., minority parliamentarian, 1986-87, asst. minority leader, 1988—. Mem. Commr.'s Task Force on Econ. Devel.; bd. dirs. Century of Service-Burlington County Meml. Hosp., Natural Resources Edn. Found. N.J., 1987—; mem. Gov.'s Task Force on Inmate and Ex-Offenders Edn., 1976-77; mem. Burlington County Manpower Adv. Council, 1973-76, Burlington County Commn. on Aging, 1974-79; chmn. Burlington Twp. Heart Fund Dr., 1973-76; active N.J. Arthritis Found., 1974-75; chmn. Burlington Twp. Bd. Assessors, 1975; mem. Deborah Hosp. Humanitarian Award Dinner Com., 1981. Active Burlington County Young Dems., 1972-75, mem. Dem. Com., 1970—; mem. Burlington County Dem. Com. Exec. Bd., 1976—, Dem. state com., N.J., 1981-85; mem. Burlington Twp. Council, 1976. OEO fellow, 1974; mem. panel comml. arbitrators Am. Arbitration Assn., 1977. Mem. ABA, D.C. Bar Assn., N.J. State Bar Assn., Burlington County Bar Assn., Assn. Trial Lawyers Am. (chmn. lawyer directory com.), N.J. Assn. Trial Lawyers, N.J. Inst. Mcpl. Lawyers (chmn. labor law sect.), L.E.G.A.L., Pi Sigma Alpha. Roman Catholic. Clubs: Vesper, Duke (Phila.); Oneida Boat, Elks, Roma (Burlington); South Jersey Irish Soc., Sons of Italy, Riverside. Office: 129 High St Mount Holly NJ 08060

FOZZATI, ALDO, automobile manufacturing company executive; b. Italy, Mar. 10, 1950; s. Danilo and Piera (Bretto) F.; m. Ana Maria Ruiz, June 7, 1977; children: Giacomo, Hugo, Daniel. PhD in Aero. Engring., Poly. U. of Turin, Italy, 1975. Registered profl. engr., Europe, U.S. and Can. Project mgr. Fiat Aerospace, Turin, 1975-78; U.S. rep. Fiat Corp., N.Y.C. and Detroit, 1978-82; ind. internat. bus. cons. Los Angeles, Paris and N.Y.C., 1982-84; program dir. Gen. Motors Corp., Detroit, 1984-87; dir. new bus. devel. Gen. Motors Europe, Zurich, Switzerland, 1987—. Mem. Soc. Automotive Engrs., Am. Security Council. Republican. Roman Catholic. Home: 250 Marlboro Bloomfield Hills MI 48013 Office: Gen Motors Corp 3044 W Grand Blvd Detroit MI 48126

FRACCI, CARLA, classical ballerina; b. Milan, Italy, Aug. 20, 1936. Student, La Scala Ballet Sch., 1958; advanced tng. in London, Paris and N.Y. With Am. Ballet Theatre, 1974—. Danced in classical and modern ballets, including La Sylphide, Coppelia, Francesca da Rimini, Giselle, Il Lago dei Cigni, Romeo e Guilietta, Concerto Barocco, Les Demoiselles de La Nuit, Il Gabbiano, Palleas et Melisande, Il Fiore di Pietra, Bilitis e le Faune, Bergkristall, Dalla Taglioni a Diaghilev; in TV movie The Ballerinas, 1984. Address: Via Santo Spirito 5, 20121 Milan Italy *

FRACKER, ROBERT GRANGER, librarian; b. Spout Spring, Va., Sept. 29, 1928; s. Dudley Granger and Ruby Walker (Page) F.; m. Sandra Elizabeth Snyder, June 5, 1965; 1 child, Mary Susan. Student Va. Poly. Inst. and State U., 1946-49, Roanoke Coll., 1948; BS, E. Tenn. State U., 1954; MA, Appalachian State U., 1957; postgrad. U. Ill., 1957-59, Duke U., 1962-65, U. N.C., Chapel Hill, 1977, N.C. Central U., 1978. Coach, tchr. English, social studies Beaver Creek High Sch., West Jefferson, N.C., 1954-56; counselor Univ. Council on Tchr. Edn., U. Ill., Urbana, 1957-59; mem. faculty Meredith Coll., Raleigh, N.C., 1962—, reference librarian, media coordinator Carlyle Campbell Library, 1977—. Campus chmn. United Way of Wake County, 1976. Served with U.S. Army, 1951-53. Mem. N.C. Assn. Tchr. Educators (pres. 1975-76), Internat. Phenomenological Soc., Assn. Tchr. Edn., Philosophy of Edn. Soc., Am. Soc. Mil. Insignia Collectors, Kami Kaze, Kappa Komma Kappa, Kappa Delta Pi, Phi Delta Kappa, Order Silver Sunset. Democrat. Presbyterian. Home: 307 Oak Ridge Rd Cary NC 27511-4515 Office: Meredith Coll Carlyle Campbell Library Raleigh NC 27611-5298

FRADE, PETER DANIEL, chemist; b. Highland Park, Mich., Sept. 3, 1946; s. Peter Nunes and Dorathea Grace (Gehrke) F. B.S. in Chemistry, Wayne State U., 1968, M.S., 1971, Ph.D., 1978. Chemist Henry Ford Hosp., Detroit, 1968-75; analytical chemist, toxicologist dept. pathology, div. pharmacology and toxicology Henry Ford Hosp., 1975-86, sr. clin. lab. scientist dept. pathology div. clin. chemistry and pharmacology, 1987—; research assoc. in chemistry Wayne State U., Detroit, 1978-79; vis. scholar U. Mich., Ann Arbor, 1980—; vis. scientist dept. Hypertension Research, Henry Ford Hosp., Detroit, 1986-88. Contbr. sci. articles to profl. jours. Mem. Republican Presd. Task Force, 1984—. Recipient David F. Boltz Meml. award Wayne State U., 1977. Fellow Am. Inst. Chemists, Nat. Acad. Clin. Biochemistry, Assn. Clin. Scientists; mem. European Acad. Arts, Scis. and Humanities, Fedn. Am. Scientists, Am. Chem. Soc., AAAS, IntraSci. Research Found., Soc. Applied Spectroscopy, Am. Assn. Clin. Chemistry, Assn. Analytical Chemists, N.Y. Acad. Scis., Detroit Hist. Soc., Mich. Humane Soc., Am. Coll. Toxicology, Royal Soc. Chemistry (London), Titanic Hist. Soc., Bibl. Archaeology Soc., Virgil Fox Soc., Founders Soc., Detroit Inst. Arts, Sigma Xi, Phi Lambda Upsilon, Alpha Chi Sigma. Lutheran. Club: U.S. Senatorial (Washington). Home: 20200 Orleans Detroit MI 48203 Office: Henry Ford Hosp 2799 W Grand Blvd Detroit MI 48202

FRAGALA, GUY ANDREW, safety engineer; b. Lawrence, Mass., Sept. 28, 1947; s. Andrew F. and Margaret (Hyder) F.; B.S., U. New Hampshire, 1969; M.S., U. Mass., Amherst, 1971, M.Ed., 1974, Ph.D., 1982; m. Susan Fucarile, Sept. 9, 1972; children—Matt, Maren, Michael. Loss prevention rep. Comml. Union Assurance Co., Boston, 1972-74; mem. corp. risk mgmt. and safety staff E. I. DuPont de Nemours & Co., Inc., Wilmington, Del., 1974-76; instr. U. Wis.-Stout, Memomonie, 1976-77; campus safety and fire prevention engr. U. Mass., Amherst, 1977-78; dir. risk mgmt. and safety assurance, asst. prof. U. Mass. Med. Center, Worcester, 1978—; adj. faculty Inst. Safety and Systems Mgmt., U. So. Calif., Eastern region, 1982—; adj. faculty dept. indsl. engring. and ops. research U. Mass., Amherst, 1983—; adj. faculty dept. mgmt. Worcester Polytechnic Inst., 1986— ; cons., lectr. in field. Mem. City of Worcester Loaned Exec. Council., 1979-80. Mem. Am. Soc. Safety Engrs., Am. Soc. Hosp. Risk Mgmt. (dir. 1984—), Nat Fire Protection Assn., Nat. Safety Council (mem. exec. com. health care sect. 1981—). Contbr. indsl. safety articles in field to profl. publs. Home: 9 Coram Farm Rd Northborough MA 01532 Office: 55 Lake Ave N Worcester MA 01605

FRAGNER, BERWYN N., business development executive; b. Uniontown, Pa., Aug. 5, 1927; s. Rudolph and Rose (Lebowitz) F.; B.A. with distinction, U. Del., 1950; M.A., Harvard U., 1952; m. Marcia Ruth Salkind, June 11, 1950; children—Robin Beth, Matthew Charles, Lisa Rachel. Vice pres. Royer & Roger, Inc., N.Y.C., 1952-62; dir. Western div. Goodway Printing Co., Los Angeles, 1962; v.p., dir. indsl. relations TRW Def. and Space Systems Group, Redondo Beach, Calif., 1963-77, v.p. human relations TRW Systems and Energy, Redondo Beach, 1977-81, TRW Electronics and Def., 1981-87; v.p. strategic bus. devel. TRW Space and Def., 1988—; mem. adv. bd. 1st Women's Bank of Calif. Chmn. Los Angeles City Pvt. Industry Council, 1979-81; mem. Calif. Ednl. Mgmt. and Evaluation Commn., 1974-82; chmn. bd. trustees Calif. Acad. Decathalon, 1980-81; mem. bus. execs. adv. com. So. Calif. Research Council, 1979—; USAR mem. Res. Forces Policy Bd., 1981-84; mem.-at-large U.S. Army Res. Forces Policies Com., 1979-82. Bd. dirs. Ind. Coll. So. Calif., 1982-86; bd. govs. U. So. Calif. Sch. Pharmacy, 1982—; chmn. Los Angeles County Pvt. Industry Council, 1983-88. Served with AUS, 1944-47. Decorated Meritorious Service medal with 2 oak leaf clusters, Legion of Merit, D.S.M.; recipient Presdl. citation, 1981; Calif. Medal of Merit. Mem. Assn. U.S. Army, Res. Officers Assn., Internat. Assn. Applied Social Scientists (cert.). Clubs: Army and Navy (Washington); Los Angeles Athletic. Contbr. to New World of Managing Human Resources, 1979. Office: One Space Park E2 11092 Redondo Beach CA 90278

FRAIDIN, STEPHEN, lawyer; b. Boston, July 29, 1939; s. Morris and Freda (Rozeff) F.; m. Susan Greene, July 4, 1963; children—Matthew, Sam, Sarah. A.B., Tufts U., 1961; J.D., Yale U., 1964. Bar: N.Y. Ptnr. Fried, Frank, Harris, Shriver & Jacobson, N.Y.C., 1964—; lectr. Practising Law Inst.; vis. lectr. Yale U. Law Sch., spring 1988. Contbr. numerous articles to profl. jours. Mem. Assn. Bar City N.Y., ABA. Office: Fried Frank Harris Shriver Jacobson 1 New York Plaza New York NY 10004

FRAIN, ERNEST GEORGE CURRIE, sales executive; b. Edinburgh, Scotland, Oct. 10, 1954; s. Robert Currie and Marion (Wright) F. Degree in mech. engring., Stevenson Coll., 1971, degree in elec. engring., 1974; degree in elec. engring., Stevenson Coll., 1976. Trainee engr. Brit. Railways, Edinburgh, 1970-74; supr. prodn. Racal Security, Edinburgh, 1974-77, tech. buyer, 1977-81; buyer electronics Keltek Electronics, Kelso, Scotland, 1981-83, TMC, Malmesbury, Eng., 1983-84; mgr. sales Jermyn Distbn., Kent, Eng., 1984—. Mem. Ch. of Scotland. Home: 172 Partridge Way, Cirencester GL7 1BQ, England Office: Jermyw Distbn, Vestry Estate, Sevenoaks TN14 5EV, England

FRAIR, WAYNE FRANKLIN, biologist, educator; b. Pitts., May 23, 1926; s. Herbert E. and Elizabeth M. (Greenawald) Gfroerer. BA, Houghton Coll., 1950; BS, Wheaton (Ill.) Coll., 1951; MA, U. Mass., 1955; PhD, Rutgers U., 1962. Tchr. sci. Ben Lippen Sch., Asheville, N.C., 1951-52; mem. faculty King's Coll., Briarcliff, N.Y., 1955—, prof. biology, 1967—. Chmn. Heart Club, Phelps Meml. Hosp., Tarrytown, N.Y., 1979-80. Served with USN, 1944-46, PTO. Author: A Case for Creation, 3d edit., 1983;

contbr. articles to profl. jours. Fellow AAAS, Am. Sci. Affiliation, Creation Research Soc. (sec. 1974-84, v.p. 1985-86, pres. 1987—); mem. Am. Inst. Biol. Sci., Am. Soc. Zoology, Evang. Theol. Soc., Sigma Xi (life). Baptist. Club: Saw Mill River Audubon Soc. (bd. dirs. 1963-66). Home: 34 Piping Rock Dr Ossining NY 10562 Office: King's College Briarcliff Manor NY 10510

FRAME, SIR ALISTAIR (GILCHRIST), metal products company executive; b. Dalmuir, Dunbartonshire, Eng., Apr. 3, 1929; s. Alexander and Mary (Fraser) F.; m. Sheila Mathieson, 1953; 1 daughter. BSc, Glasgow (Scotland) U.; MA, U. Cambridge, Eng. Dir. Reactor and Research Groups U.K. Atomic Energy Authority, 1964-68; with Rio Tinto-Zinc Corp., 1968—, bd. dirs., 1973—, chief exec., dep. chmn., 1978-85, chmn., 1985—; bd. dirs. Plessey Co. Ltd., Toronto Dominion Bank, Glaxo; past dir. Britoil; mem. NEB, 1978-79, engring. council, 1982—; chmn. Council of Mining and Metall. Instns., 1983—. Decorated Knight, 1981. Home: Pine Cottage, Holmbury St Mary, Dorking, Surrey England *

FRAME, ANNE PARSONS, civic worker; b. Berkeley, Calif., Jan. 3, 1904; d. Reginald Hascall and Maude (Bemis) Parsons; A.B., Mills Coll., 1924; postgrad. Columbia, 1924-25; m. Frederic D. Tootell, Apr. 3, 1926 (div. July 1935); children—Geoffrey H., Natalie (Mrs. Oliver); m. Jasper Ewing Brady, July 31, 1935; (dec. Dec. 1944); 1 son, Hugh Parsons; m. Howard Andres Frame, Mar. 29, 1948. Dir. Parsons, Hart & Co., Seattle, Hillcrest Orchard Co., Seattle. Mem. bd. mgmt. Palo Alto br. A.R.C., 1955-61; trustee Children's Hosp. & Med. Ctr., Seattle, 1942-48; bd. dirs. Children's Health Council, Palo Alto, Calif., 1953-63, 64-76, pres., 1954-58; sponsor Nat. Recreation Assn., 1942-66, trustee, 1948-66; sponsor Nat. Recreation and Park Assn., 1966—, trustee, 1966-73; trustee Nat. Recreation Found., 1964—; 1st v.p. Children's Hosp. at Stanford Sr. Aux., 1965-85, bd. dirs. Hosp., 1967-81; former mem. adv. com. Holbrook-Palmer Park; trustee Mills Coll., 1952-62; bd. dirs. Holbrook-Palmer Recreation Park Found., 1968-86; bd. govs. San Francisco Symphony Assn., 1949-79; mem. Atherton (Calif.) Park and Recreation Commn., 1968-81. Mem. LWV, Bowne House Hist. Soc., San Mateo County, Seattle, Chgo., Calif. hist. socs., Calif. Heritage Council, San Francisco Mus. Art, Seattle Art Mus., Museum Soc., Nat. Trust for Historic Preservation, Nat. Soc. Colonial Dames Am. Episcopalian. Clubs: Sunset, Tennis (Seattle); Woodside-Atherton Garden (dir. 1966-68); Francisca (San Francisco).

FRAME, CLARENCE GEORGE, former banker; b. Dakota County, Minn., July 26, 1918; s. George and Helen (Hunter) F. AB, U. Minn., 1941; JD, Harvard U., 1947. Bar: Minn. 1947. With First Nat. Bank, St. Paul, 1947-80, asst. cashier, 1953-54, cashier, 1954-57, v.p., cashier, 1957-59, v.p., 1959-61, sr. v.p., 1961-68, exec. v.p., 1968-72, pres., 1972-80; vice-chmn. First Bank System, Inc., St. Paul, 1980-83; chmn. bd. dirs., chief exec. officer Tosco Corp., St. Paul, 1986—, also bd. dirs.; bd. dirs. Northland Co., Mpls., Opus Corp., Mpls., Genmar Industries, Inc., Mpls., Morisow Asset Allocation Fund, Mpls., Voyageur Asset Mgmt. Group, Inc., Mpls., Chgo. Milw. Corp., Chgo., Courier Dispatch Group, Atlanta, TG Friday's Inc., Dallas. Trustee Walker Art Ctr., Mpls., Breck Sch., Mpls. Served to lt. comdr. USNR, 1942-46, to comdr. 1951-53. Clubs: Somerset Country, St. Paul; Mpls. Office: Tosco Corp W-3070 1st Bank Bldg 332 Minnesota St Saint Paul MN 55101 *

FRAMPTON, DAVID RODMELL, health science facility administrator; b. Manchester, Lancashire, Eng., Sept. 12, 1940; s. William Rodmell and Irene Mary (Frost) F.; m. Priscilla Rosemary Anne Chappell; children: Andrew Marcus, Daniel Paul, Ruth Elizabeth. MBBS, Univ. Coll. Hosp., London, 1963; diploma, Royal Coll. Ob-Gyn, 1965; diploma in child health, 1967. House surgeon Princess Alexandra Hosp., Eastbourne, Eng., 1963; house physician St Andrew's Hosp., London, 1964; sr. house officer in obstetrics, then pediatrics North Middlesex Hosp., London, 1964-67; gen. practice medicine Ongar, Eng., 1967-83; cons. physician St. Joseph's Hospice, London, 1983-87; med. dir. Chelmsford (Eng.) Hospice, 1987—; chmn. arts com. Help the Hospices, 1986-88. Former dir., chmn. Pilgrims Hall Fellowship Ltd., Brentwood/Essex, Eng., 1970-88. Mem. Royal Coll. Gen. Practitioners, Royal Coll. Ob-Gyn, Assn. Palliative Care Physicians. Home: Old Bake House, 315 Main Rd, Broomfield/Chelmsford, Essex England Office: Chelmsford Hospice, 212 London Rd, Chelmsford, Essex CM2 9AE, England

FRAMPTON, PAUL HOWARD, physics educator, researcher; b. Kidderminster, Eng., Oct. 31, 1943; came to U.S., 1968; s. Harold Albert and Grace Elizabeth (Howard) F. B.A., U. Oxford, Eng., 1965, M.A., 1968, D. Phil., 1968, D.Sc. (hon.), 1984. Research assoc. U. Chgo., 1968-70; fellow CERN, Geneva, 1970-72; vis. assoc. prof. Syracuse U., 1972-75, UCLA, 1975-77; vis. scholar Harvard U., Cambridge, Mass., 1978-80; Asst. prof. physics U. N.C., Chapel Hill, 1981-83, assoc. prof., 1983-85, prof., 1985—; vis. prof. Boston U., 1986-87, U. Tex., fall 1983; chmn. streering com. for Workshops on Grand Unification, 1980—, chmn. organizing com. 1st workshop U. N.H., 1980, 3d workshop U. N.C. Chapel Hill, 1982; project dir. Super Collider in N.C., 1987. Author: Dual Resonance Models, 1974; Gauge Field Theories, 1986; editor books in field; contbr. over 100 articles to profl. jours. Fellow Am. Phys. Soc., Inst. Physics, Sigma Xi. Home: 32 Fearrington Post Pittsboro NC 27312 Office: U NC Dept Physics and Astronomy Chapel Hill NC 27514

FRANCA, JOSE-AUGUSTO, art historian, educator, author; b. Tomar, Portugal, Nov. 16, 1922; s. Jose M. and Carmen (Rodrigues) F.; diplome sociology of art Ecole Hautes Etudes, Paris, France, 1962; D.History, U. Paris, 1962. Doctor es Lettres, 1969; remarried Marie-Therese Mandroux, 1972; 1 dau., Manuela. Art critic, publs. including Art d'Aujourd'hui, Paris, Goya, Madrid, Estado de Sao Paulo (Brazil), others, 1946—; cinema critic, 1948—; prof. sociology art, history modern art Curso de Formacao Artistica, Lisbon, 1964-70; prof. modern culture and art, head dept. U. N. Lisbon, 1974—; dir. Ctr. Culturel Portuguesa, 1983—; C. Gulbenkian Found., Paris. City councilor, Lisbon, 1974-75; pres. Instituto de Cultura Portuguesa, 1976-80. Decorated officier Ordre National du Merite; Chevalier Ordre des Arts et Lettres (France); comdr. Orden Rio Branco (Brazil). Mem. Academia das Ciencias, Academia Nacional de Belas Artes (v.p. 1975-77, pres. 1977-80), Academia Portuguesa de Historia, Internat. Com. Art History, European Acad. Scis. et Lettres (v.p. 1985—), Internat. Assn. Art Critics (v.p. 1970-73, pres. 1984-87, hon. pres. 1987—); World Acad. Scis. and Arts (v.p. 1985—); Acad. Nat. Lettres ex des Arts de Bordeaux (pres. 1984-87, hon. pres. 1987—); Société Européenne de Culture. Author: (novel) Natureza Morta, 1949; (play) Azazel, 1957; (short stories) Despedida Breve, 1958; (essays) Charles Chaplin, the self-made-myth, 1953; Situacao da Arte Ocidental, 1959, Une Ville des Lumieres; la Lisbonne de Pombal, 1965, Oito Ensaios sobre arte Contemporanea, 1967, A Arte em Portugal no seculo XIX, 2 vols., 1967, A Arte em Portugal no Seculo XX, 1974, Le Romantisme au Portugal, 1975, Rafael Bordalo Pinheiro, 1980, Amadeo e Almada, 1986, Historia da Arte Ocidental: 1780-1980, 87. Editor Unicornio, 1955-56; Cadernos de Poesia, 1952-53; Pintura e Nao, 1969-71; Coloquio Artes, 1970—. Home: Fundacao C Gulbenkian, Ave Berne, 49/A Rue Escola Politecnica, Lisbon Portugal also: 51 ave d'Iena, 75116 Paris France

FRANCAVIGLIA, MAURO, mathematical physics educator, researcher; b. Torino, Italy, June 22, 1953; s. Giovanni and Lucia (dePalma) F.; m. Annamaria Vercesi, June 7, 1979; 1 child, Gianpiero. Dr. Math., U. Torino, 1975. CNR Consiglio Nazionale delle Ricerche fellow U. Torino, 1975-78, asst. prof., 1978-79, assoc. prof., 1979-80, prof. math. physics, 1980—; nat. coordinator Research Project, Geometry and Physics, Italy, 1980—; mem. council Group for Math. Physics, CNR, Italy, 1984—; mem. Internat. Com. on Gen. Relativity and Gravitation, 1986—; dir. CIME Centro Internat. Math. Estiva course, 1988. Editor: Modern Developments in Analytical Mechanics, 1983, Journées Relativistes 1983, 1985; mng. editor Jour. Geometry and Physics, 1984—. Recipient Premio Bonavera, Acad. Scis., Torino, 1977. Mem. Am. Math. Soc., Unione Matematica Italiana, Gen. Relativity and Gravitation Soc., Associazione Italiana Meccanica Teorica e Applicata, Acad. Tiberina (corr.). Roman Catholic. Club: Torino Host (counselor 1985-87, v.p. 1987-88). Avocation: philately. Home: Via E Torricelli 5, Torino Italy Office: Istituto di Fisica Matematica, J L Lagrange, Via C Alberto 10, 10123 Torino Italy

FRANCE, JOSEPH DAVID, securities analyst; b. Smithville, Mo., July 24, 1953; s. Raymond Hughes France and Bonnie Lee (Cavin) Vinzant; m. Judith Ann Tehel, May 29, 1976. BS in Pharmacy, U. Kans., 1977, MBA, 1980. Registered pharmacist; chartered fin. analyst. Staff pharmacist U. Kans. Med. Ctr., Kansas City, 1977-80; securities analyst First Nat. Bank of Chgo., 1980-82; securities analyst Smith Barney, Harris Upham & Co., Inc., N.Y.C., 1982—, mng. dir., 1986—. Mem. Am. Soc. Hosp. Pharmacists, Healthcare Fin. Mgmt. Assn., N.Y. Soc. Securities Analysts, Fin. Analysts Fedn., Inst. Chartered Fin. Analysts. Democrat. Roman Catholic. Office: Smith Barney Harris Upham & Co 1345 Ave of the Americas New York NY 10105

FRANCES, ROBERT, psychologist; b. Bursa, Turkey, Dec. 12, 1919; s. Isaac and Allegra (Rousseau) F.; m. Simone Pesle (dec.); children: Michel, Laurent. PhB, Sorbonne U., Paris, 1941. Dir. research C.N.R.S., Paris, 1959-65; prof. psychology U. Paris, 1965—, dir. lab. exptl. psychology, 1967—; dir. lab. psychology of culture U. Paris, 1964-85, dean's asst. for research, 1968-70; mem. nat. com. C.N.R.S., Paris, 1962-66. Author: The Perception of Music, 1958, Perceptual Development, 1963, The Psychology of Aesthetics, 1969; ten other books on psychology and 50 papers on psychology. Active French Resistance, Paris, 1942-43. Served to lt. French Interior Forces, 1943. Decorated Croix de Guerre, Knight Order of Merit, Resistance medal (France); recipient Dagnan-Bouveret prize Acad. Social and Polit. Sci., 1973. Mem. French Psychol. Soc. (pres. 1972-73), Internat. Soc. Empirical Aesthetics (pres., founder 1964-70). Roman Catholic. Home: 59 rue Brillat Savarin, 75013 Paris France Office: Univ de Paris-X, 2 rue de Rouen, 92000 Nanterre France

FRANCESCHI, ERNEST JOSEPH, JR., lawyer; b. Los Angeles, Feb. 1, 1957; s. Ernest Joseph and Doris Cecilia (Beluche) F.; m. Jeannean Lee Baker, Oct. 27, 1983. BS, U. So. Calif., 1978; JD, Southwestern U., Los Angeles, 1980. Bar: Calif. 1984, U.S. Dist. Ct. (cen. dist.) Calif. 1984, U.S. Dist. Ct. (ea. dist.) Calif. 1986, U.S. Dist. Ct. (no. dist.) Calif. 1987, U.S. Ct. Appeals (9th cir.) 1984, U.S. Dist. Ct. (so. dist.) Calif. 1987. Sole practice Seal Beach, Calif., 1984—. Mem. Assn. Trial Lawyers Am., Calif. Trial Lawyers Assn., Los Angeles Trial Lawyers Assn. Republican. Roman Catholic. Office: 500 Pacific Coast Hwy Suite 212 Seal Beach CA 90740

FRANCFORT, ALFRED JOHN, JR., educator; b. Washington, June 28, 1939; s. Alfred John and Lucille Joan (Wall) F.; m. Elisabeth A. Dey, Aug. 5, 1968. BS, Monmouth Coll., 1964; M.A., U. Pitts., 1969, Ph.D., 1972. Instr. econs. Chatham Coll., Pitts., 1970-72; teaching fellow U. Pitts., 1966-70, asst. prof. econs., 1972-77, assoc. prof., 1977-83; prof. fin. James Madison U., Harrisonburg, Va., 1983—; cons. on electric utility rate cases and regulation, 1977—; lectr. corp. mgmt. tng. programs, 1973—; mem. U. Pitts. Steering Com. on Regional Econ. Devel., 1973-75. Mem. editorial bd. Jour. Econ. Lit., 1970-83. Contbr. articles to profl. jours. MIT scholar, 1974; fellow Univ. Chgo., 1977; faculty fellow U.S. Gen. Acctg. office, Washington, 1979-80; Fulbright prof., 1987. Mem. Am. Econ. Assn. (transp. and pub. utility group), Am. Fin. Assn., Eastern Fin. Assn., Fin. Mgmt. Assn. So. Fin. Assn. Home: 1115 Chestnut Dr Harrisonburg VA 22801 Office: James Madison Univ Dept Fin Harrisonburg VA 22807

FRANCIOSA, JOSEPH ANTHONY, cardiologist, researcher; b. Easton, Pa., Apr. 24, 1936; s. Joseph and Letizia Beatrice (Cascioli) F.; m. Antonietta Battistoni, Feb. 8, 1964 (div. 1972); m. Barbara Ann Neilan, Aug. 3, 1973; 1 son, Christopher David. B.A., U. Pa., 1958; M.D., U. Rome, 1963. Diplomate; Am. Bd. Internal Medicine. Intern USPHS Hosp., S.I., N.Y., 1964-65; resident Washington Hosp. Ctr., 1967-69; cardiology fellow VA Hosp.-Georgetown U., Washington, 1969-71; chief ICU, VA Hosp., Washington, 1971-73; assoc. dir. cardiac research Georgetown U., 1973-74; dir. CCU VA Hosp., Mpls., 1974-76, cardiac research, 1976-79; chief cardiology VA Hosp., Phila., 1979-82; dir. cardiology div. U. Ark., Little Rock, 1982-86; asst. prof. medicine Georgetown U., 1973-74, U. Minn., Mpls., 1974-77, assoc. prof., 1977-79, U. Pa., Phila., 1979-82, adj. prof., 1987—; prof. U. Ark., 1982-86; dir. cardio-renal drugs ICI Americas Inc., Wilmington, Del., 1986—. Contbr. numerous articles to med. jours. Mem. med. research com. Am. Heart Assn., Mpls., 1976-79 Mem. med. research com. Am. Heart Assn., Phila., 1981-82. Served to lt. comdr. USPHS, 1964-67. VA grantee, 1974-84; U. Ark. grantee, 1982-83. Fellow ACP, Am. Coll. Cardiology, Am. Coll. Chest Physicians (chmn. hypertension com. 1981-83, gov. Ark. 1984-86), Am. Heart Assn. (circulation council 1978—, council high blood pressure research 1982—, clin. cardiology council 1984); mem. Am. Soc. Clin. Pharmacology and Therapeutics (vice chmn. cardiopulmonary com. 1981—, Assn. Univ. Cardiologists. Roman Catholic. Home: 1037 Radley Dr West Chester PA 19382 Office: Stuart Pharms ICI Americas Inc Wilmington DE 19897

FRANCIS, JOSEPH ROBERT, design engineer; b. Gateshead, Tyne and Wear, Eng., Mar. 13, 1943; s. Frank and Mary (Davis) F.; m. Eileen Steanson, Sept. 12, 1964; children—Debarah Marie, Garry Joseph. Student St. Joan of Arc Gateshead Tech. Coll., Newcastle Poly. Coll. Chief engr. B.T. Rolatruc, Mercury Maintenance Ltd., Gateshead, Tyne and Wear, Eng.; dir. Hercules Security, Quality Pipework Services Ltd. Designer cacti rotary antivandal climbing unit. Named Innovator of Yr., Cacti Unit, 1985. Avocation: football referee. Home: 15 Arisaig, Ouston England Office: Hercules Security Fabrications, Kingsway, Gateshead England

FRANCIS, MARK, university lecturer; b. Toronto, Ont., Can., Sept. 24, 1944; s. Peter and Audrey (Cecil) F.; m. Linda Jane Murison, May 23, 1969 (div. Dec. 1976); 1 dau., Hypatia; m. 2d, Debra Jane Parsons, Jan. 19, 1982; 1 dau., Clio. B.A. with honors, U. B.C., Vancouver, 1968; M.A., U. Toronto, Ont., 1969; Ph.D., Cambridge (Eng.) U., 1973. Lectr. U. Canterbury, Christchurch, N.Z., 1973-77, sr. lectr., 1977—; vis. fellow Research Sch. Social Scis., Australian Nat. U., Canberra, 1982-83, 85; departmental visitor London Sch. Econs., 1979. Area gov. Conf. for Study Polit. Thought, 1980—. William Lyon Mackenzie King travelling scholar Cambridge U., 1969-70; Can. Council doctoral fellow, 1970-73. Mem. Am. Soc. Legal and Polit. Philosophy, Australasian Polit. Sci. Assn., Australian Soc. Legal Philosophy. Contbr. articles and revs. to polit. sci. and history jours. Home: 32 Greers Rd, Christchurch New Zealand Office: Polit Sci Dept, Univ Canterbury, Christchurch New Zealand

FRANCIS, PETER ROBERT, tropical agriculturalist, educator; b. London, Apr. 18, 1922; s. William Holland and Florence Mary (Tomlinson) F.; m. Monique Doris Bleynie, Sept. 9, 1950; children—Solveig, Anthony, Christine, Bernadette, Godfrey, Margaret. Diplomate Agr., U. Nottingham, Eng., 1951; M.Degree, U. Reading, 1975. Cert. biologist. Faculty, Coll. Agr., Writtle, Eng., 1951-55; farm exec. Luela Farms, Kitwe, Zambia, 1956-59; poultry officer Dept. Agr., Harare, Zimbabwe, 1959-63; chief poultry officer Govt. Rep. Zambia, Lusaka, 1964-74; faculty Sch. Vet. Sci., Khartoum, Sudan, 1976-81; gen. mgr. Oman Farms, Ruwi, Sultanate of Oman, 1982-85; gen. mgr. agrl. project Ominvest, Ruwi, Sultanate of Oman, 1986—; cons. in field; examiner Nat. Agr. Coll., Lusaka, Zambia, 1968-74, U. Zambia, 1972-74; ofcl. judge Agr. Show Soc., Zambia, Kenya, Zimbabwe, Sudan, 1961—; mem. Farmers Union Com., Lusaka, 1959-74. Contbr. articles to profl. jours. Mem. Parent/Tech. Com., Lusaka, 1965-70. Served with Royal Air Force, 1942-47. Commonwealth fellow, Carnegie Found., 1965. Mem. Inst. Biology London, World's Poultry Sci. Assn. Clubs: Royal Overseas, Zambia Soc. Avocations: gardening; walking; classical music; reading. Home: PO Box 6886, Ruwi Oman Office: Ominvest, PO Box 6886, Ruwi Sultanate of Oman also: Melville Rd, Croxton Thetford, Norfolk IP24 1NG, England

FRANCIS, PETER WYER, oil company official, counselor; b. Mauritius, June 26, 1921; s. Bertram Alexander and Minnie Ada (Wyer) F.; m. Frances Rosemary Walton, Mar. 30, 1951; children: Philip, Molly, David. Various personnel and mktg. mgmt. positions Shell Internat. Petroleum Co., Far East and Africa, 1947-71; mng. dir. Lion Emulsions Ltd. subs. Shell Co., Hereford, England, 1971-76; career counselor Ind. Schs. Careers Orgn., Perryfield, Eng., 1976—. Served to maj. Indian Army, 1940-46, CBI. Mem. Ch. of England. Club: Travellers (London). Home and Office: Perryfield, Sollers, Hope HR1 5RN, England

FRANCIS, THERESA P., medical record administrator, nursing home administrator; b. Thodupuzha, India, Mar. 20, 1938; came to U.S., 1976; naturalized, 1984; d. Frenchu (Francis) Aleykutty Nallanirappel; m. Francis Palayan Vargheese, May 10, 1970; 1 child, Bobby Francis; Diploma nursing Cama and Albless Hosp., 1967, diploma midwifery, 1968; B.S. in Health Adminstrn., St. Joseph's Coll., Bklyn., 1986; D of Naturopathy, Naturopathic Coll. Am., Birmingham, Ala. Staff nurse Breach Candy Hosp. and Nursing Home, Bombay, India, 1968-76; dir. Panvel Mcpl. Hosp., Bombay, 1975-76; nurse's aide, lic. practical nurse Meth. Med. Ctr., Des Moines, 1976-78; staff nurse Ahn-Wyckoff Heights Hosp., Bklyn., 1978-81; supr. Willoughby Nursing Home, River Manor, Parkshore Manor, 1981-84; med. record adminstr. State Univ. Hosp., Bklyn., 1984—; yoga, aerobic instr. Bklyn. Coll. Author: (plays) This is Amerika, 1983; Slaughtered Sheeps; 1982; Barbed Wire, 1983. Mem. Indian Nat. Congress, Bombay, 1964-70, Kerala, 1953-59. Recipient awards Bombay Nursing State Bd., 1965, 67. Mem. N.Y. Assn. Quality Assurance Profls., Nat Assn. Female Execs., United Univ. Profls., Am. Nursing Assn., Kerala Samagam of Greater New York (sec. 1983-84). Roman Catholic. Lodge: Lionesses (Bklyn.). Avocations: reading; writing; cooking; dancing; teaching; yoga. Home: 262 Saint Nicholas Ave Brooklyn NY 11237

FRANCISCO, JUAN RODRIGO, foundation administrator; b. Pangasinan, Philippines, Mar. 8, 1929; s. Rosendo I. Ramos Sr. and Eulalia Laureta (Rodrigo) F.; m. Beatriz Sumulong Reyes, Mar. 18, 1961; 1 child, Caesar Cecilio Rajan R. BA, Wesleyan U., Philippines, 1951, BE, 1952; MA, Philippine Christian U., Philippines, 1954; PhD, U. Madras, India, 1964. Instr. Philippine Christian U., Manila, 1956-57; from instr. indology to prof. U. Philippines, Diliman, Quezon City, 1961—; exec. dir. Philippine-Am. Ednl. Found., Makati (Philippines), Manila, 1974—; dean U. Philippines Coll., Tarlac, 1969-71, Clark Air Base, 1974; v.p. acad. affairs Mindanao State U., Marawi City, Philippines, 1972-73;. Author: (books) Indian Influences in the Philippines, 1964, Maharadia Lawana, 1969, The Philippines and India, 1971, (monograph) Philippine Palaeography, 1973. Chmn. Council for Living Traditions, Manila, 1979-83. Fulbright grantee, 1954-56, Govt. of India grantee, 1957-61. Fellow Philippine Assn. for Advancement of Sci.; Nat. Research Council Philippines, Phi Kappa Phi. Home: 13 J Luna St Area 2, U Philippines Campus Diliman, Quezon City Philippines 1101 Office: Philippine Am Ednl Found, 395 Sen Gil Puyat Ave, Makati Metro Manila Philippines 1200

FRANCK, HEINZ-GERHARD, chemist; b. Jan. 3, 1923. D in Chemistry. Mng. dir. Ges fur Teerverwertung mbH, Duisburg-Meiderich; bd. dirs. Rütgerswerke AG, 1964, chmn. bd., 1972—; chmn. supervising bd. Ruberoidwerke AG, Hamburg, Teerbau Strassenbau GmbH, Essen; mem. adv. and supervising bds. of other firms. Contbr. articles to profl. jours. Home: Mainzer Landstr 217, D-6000 Frankfurt Federal Republic of Germany *

FRANCOIS-PONCET, JEAN ANDRE, business executive; b. Paris, Dec. 8, 1928; s. Andre and Jacqueline Constance Henriette (Dillais) Francois-P.; B.A., Wesleyan U., Middletown, Conn., 1947; M.A., Fletcher Sch. Law and Diplomacy, Tufts U., 1948; M.A., U. Paris, 1949, Ph.D., 1952; postgrad. Nat. Sch. Pub. Adminstrn., 1955, Stanford U., 1971; m. Marie Therese de Mitry, Apr. 18, 1959; children—Philippe, Jacques, Florence. Joined French Ministry for Fgn. Affairs, 1955; with Bur. of Sec. State, 1956-58; sec. gen. French Del. charge negotiating treaties of Common Market and Euratom, 1956-57, charge European instns. at Ministry Fgn. Affairs, 1958-61, head French Assistance and Coop. Mission in Morocco, 1961-63, charge African affairs Ministry Fgn. Affairs, 1963-68, counsellor French embassy, Tehran, Iran, 1968-70; chmn. bd., pres., chief exec. officer Ets J.J. Carnaud & Forges de Basse-Indre, 1973—; minister of state for fgn. affairs, chief coordinator Presidency of French Republic, 1976-78, minister fgn. affairs, 1978-81; mem. French Senate, chmn. Council Gen., vice chmn. Region Aquitaine; chmn. econ. com. French Senate. Decorated chevalier Legion of Honor; Ordre Nat. du Mérite. Home: 6 Blvd Suchet, 75016 Paris France

FRÄNDBERG, KNUT ÅKE, legal educator; b. Gothenburg, Sweden, Dec. 15, 1937; s. Knut and Annie Christina (Carlson) F.; m. Viveca Margareta Geijer, Jan. 5, 1977; children: Peter, Louise. LLB, Uppsala U., Sweden, 1965, BA, 1967, LLD, 1973. Researcher Uppsala U., 1973-76, asst. prof., 1976—. Author: On Analogical Use of Legal Norms, 1973, The Concept Legal Rule and Choices of Law, 1984; contbr. articles to profl. jours. Mem. Royal Acad. Arts and Scis. Uppsala, Värmlands Student Nation (hon., inspector 1987—). Home: Säves Väg 11, S-75263 Uppsala Sweden Office: Uppsala U Faculty Law, Box 512, S-75120 Uppsala Sweden

FRANGOS, VASSILIOS, agricultural department administrator; b. Lamia, Fthiotis, Greece, May 4, 1942; s. Dimitrios and Ioanna (Pilali) F.; m. Paraskevi Nakratza, June 28, 1970; children: Dimitrios, Andreas. Degree in Forestry Econs., U. Thessaloniki, Greece, 1974; MSc, U. Coll. North Wales, Bangor, Wales, 1978. Cert. forest economist. Regional forester Ministry Agriculture, Lamie-Katerina, Greece, 1968-78; cons. ECG subjects, Athens, 1978-81, chief internat. relations dept., 1984—; first sec. at Permanent Rep. of Greece of EEC Ministry Foreign Affairs, Brussels, 1981-84. Author: EEC-Greece Forestry, 1978; contbr. articles to profl. jours. Mem. Union of Spartians, Lamia, 1975. Greek Govt. scholar, Athens, 1976. Mem. Union Foresters, Chamber Agrotechnique. Christian Orthodox. Home: 12 Deligianni Str, Kifissia, 14561 Athens Greece

FRANK, ALAN I. W., manufacturing company executive; b. Pitts., Mar. 6, 1932; s. Robert Jay and Cecelia (Moreell) F.; children: Darcy Mackay, Kimberly deVou. AB cum laude, Harvard U., 1954; LLB, Columbia U., 1960. Pres., chmn. bd. AIWF Corp., 1962—; bd. dirs. numerous corps. Patentee in field. Gen. chmn. $200 million campaign Pitts. area, Columbia U., N.Y.C., 1968-70, mem. nat. devel. bd., 1974—; mem. Rensselaer council Rensselaer Poly. Inst., 1974-83. Served with Counter Intelligence Corps, Spl. Agt. U.S. Army, 1955-57. Mem. N.Y. Bar, Pa. Bar. Clubs: Harvard-Yale-Princeton; Mid-Ocean (Bermuda). Address: 96 E Woodland Rd Pittsburgh PA 15232

FRANK, BARRY H., lawyer; b. Norristown, Pa., Nov. 19, 1938; s. David and Rose (Pearl) F.; divorced; children—Toby L., S. Kenneth, Gary A.; m. 2d Carole A. Factor, June 26, 1983. B.S., Pa. State U., 1960; LL.B., Temple U., 1963. Bar: Pa. 1964. Staff atty. IRS, Phila., 1963-66; tax mgr. Ernst & Whinney, Phila., 1966-74; exec. v.p., gen. counsel Nat. Freight, Inc., Vineland, N.J., 1974-75; ptnr. Pechner, Dorfman, Wolffe, Rounick & Cabot, Phila., 1975-87, Mesirov, Gelman, Jaffe, Cramer & Jamieson, Phila., 1987; instr. Ctr. for Profl. Devel., Temple U., Phila., 1976—. Co-author: Alimony, Child Support and Counsel Fees; contbg. editor The Tax Times; contbr. articles to profl. jours. Exec. com. Mayor's Small Bus. Adv. Council, Phila., 1981-83. Mem. ABA, Phila. Bar Assn., Am. Inst. C.P.A.s, Pa. Inst. C.P.A.s, (chmn. small bus. council 1977-78, chmn. emeritus 1981-83, bd. dirs. 1977-78, 80-81). Republican. Jewish. Office: Mesirov Gelman Jaffe Cramer & Jamieson The Fidelity Bldg Philadelphia PA 19109

FRANK, BERNARD, lawyer; b. Wilkes-Barre, Pa., June 11, 1913; s. Abraham and Fanny F.; m. Muriel I. Levy, June 19, 1938; children: Roberta R. Frank Penn, Allan R. Ph.B., Muhlenberg Coll., Allentown, Pa., 1935, LHD, 1987; J.D., U. Pa., 1938; postgrad., N.Y. U., 1940-42. Bar: Pa. 1939. Since practiced in Allentown; asst. U.S. atty. Eastern Dist. Pa., 1950-51; asst. city solicitor Allentown, 1956-60. Author articles on ombudsmen in profl. jours. Vice chmn. B'nai B'rith Nat. Commn. Adult Jewish Edn., 1959-61, chmn., 1961-63; bd. dirs. Muhlenberg Coll., 1987—. Served with F.A. AUS, 1943-46. Decorated comdr. Order of North Star Sweden; recipient Disting. Service award Internat. Ombudsman Inst., 1980. Mem. Internat. Bar Assn. (chmn. com. ombudsman 1973-80), ABA (chmn. com. ombudsman 1970-76), Fed. Bar Assn. (chmn. com. ombudsman 1971-74), Pa. Bar Assn., Lehigh Bar Assn., Inter-Am. Bar Assn., World Assn. Lawyers, U.S. Assn. Ombudsmen (hon.), Internat. Ombudsman Inst. (dir. 1978—, pres. 1984—), Jewish Publ. Soc. Am. (dir. 1982—, v.p. 1986—), 94th Inf. Div. (pres. 1953-54). Home: 3203 W Cedar St Allentown PA 18104 Office: 931 Hamilton Mall Allentown PA 18105

FRANK, EDWARD, editor; b. Binghamton, N.Y., Aug. 30, 1924; s. Leon H. and Frances (Parnagian) F.; m. Doris K. Lyon, May 16, 1959; 1 son, Stephen. B.S., Am. U., 1952. Feature writer USIA, Washington, 1951-53; reporter Binghamton Sun, 1953-59; asst. news editor Syracuse (N.Y.) Post-Standard, 1960-62, Rochester (N.Y.) Democrat and Chronicle, 1962-66; news editor Cocoa (Fla.) Today, 1966-73; news editor Phila. Inquirer, 1973-85, asst. mng. editor, 1985—. Served with U.S. Army, 1943-46. Office: Phila Inquirer Newspapers Inc 400 N Broad St Philadelphia PA 19101

FRANK, GEROLD, writer; b. Cleve., Aug. 2, 1907; s. Samuel and Lillian (Frank) Lefkowitz; m. Lillian Cogen, Sept. 1, 1932; children: Amy (Mrs. William Rosenblum), John Lewis. B.A., Ohio State U., 1929; M.A., Western Res. U., 1933. With Cleve. News, 1933-37; with N.Y. Jour. Am., 1937-43; U.S. war corr. Overseas News Agy., Middle East, 1943-45; Europe and Middle East corr. Overseas News Agy., 1946-50; sr. editor Coronet mag., 1952-58; screen writer Warner Bros., 1960; lectr. non-fiction writing Ind. U. Summer Writers Workshop, 1968, 71, Santa Barbara Writers Workshop, 1982; bd. dirs. Copyright Clearance Ctr.; juror Am. Book Awards, 1981. Author: Out in the Boondocks, 1943, (with James D. Horan) U.S.S. Seawolf, 1945, (with Lillian Roth and Mike Connolly) I'll Cry Tomorrow, 1954 (Christophers award), (with Diana Barrymore) Too Much Too Soon, 1957, (with Sheilah Graham) Beloved Infidel, 1958, Zsa Zsa Gabor: My Story, 1960, The Deed, 1963 (Edgar Allan Poe award), The Boston Strangler, 1966 (Edgar Allan Poe award), An American Death: The True Story of the Assassination of Dr. Martin Luther King Jr., 1972, Judy (biography of Judy Garland), 1975; contbg. author: Headlining America, 1937, The Road to Victory, 1946, Deadline Delayed, 1947, 100 Best True Stories of World War II, 1947, Men Who Make Your World, 1949, Readings in Twentieth Century European History, 1950, Battle Stations, 1953, Sudden Endings, 1964, Israel: A Reader, 1968; panelist: Harper's Dictionary of Contemporary Usage, 1975, 83; contbr. to Grolier Ency., nat. mags. Mem. chancellor's council U. Tex.; trustee Carnegie Fund for Authors. Mem. Authors Guild (sec. 1970—, council 1971—), P.E.N., Authors League (treas. 1973-76, 85—, council 1971—), Am. Soc. Journalists and Authors. Clubs: Dutch Treat (N.Y.C.); Overseas Press (past gov.). Home: 930 Fifth Ave New York NY 10021 Office: care William Morris Agy 1350 Ave of Americas New York NY 10019

FRANK, HARVEY, lawyer, author; b. N.Y.C., Aug. 24, 1930; s. Leon and Hannah (Lehr) F.; m. Judith Ellen Lewis, Nov. 29, 1959; 1 child, David L. A.B., NYU, 1951, LL.M., 1961; J.D., Harvard U., 1954. Bar: N.Y. 1954, Va. 1977, Md. 1981, Ohio 1982. Ptnr. Hays Feuer Porter & Spanier, N.Y.C., 1963-69, Burns, Summit, Rovins & Feldesman, N.Y.C., 1970-74; prof. law Coll. William and Mary, Williamsburg, Va., 1974-80; adj. prof. Johns Hopkins U., Balt., 1981; ptnr. Benesch Friedlander, Coplan & Aronoff, Cleve., 1982—. Author: The ERC Closely Held Corporation Guide, 1981, 2d edit., 1984; contbr. articles to legal jours. Mem. ABA, Ohio Bar Assn. Home: 1701 E 12th St Apt 5TW Cleveland OH 44114 Office: Benesch Friedlander Coplan & Aronoff 1100 Citizens Bldg Cleveland OH 44114

FRANK, HELMAR GUNTER, educational cyberneticist; b. Waiblingen, Baden Württemberg, Fed. Republic Germany, Feb. 19, 1933; s. Manfred Helmut and Erna Hedwig (Glocker) F.; m. Brigitte Christine Böhringer, June 30, 1970; children: Ines Ute, Tilo Ingmar. M in Math., Tech. U., Stuttgart, Fed. Republic Germany, 1956, PhD, 1959; Universitätsdozent, Johann Kepler U., Linz, Austria, 1970; Prof. in Cybernetics (hon.), Pedagogical U., West Berlin, 1972. Tchr. math., physics gymanasiums Bad Württemberg, 1958-61; sci. collaborator Tech. U. Karslruhe, 1961-63; assoc. prof. cybernetics Pedagogical U., West Berlin, 1963-70, prof., 1971-72; prof. U. Paderborn, North Rhine Westphalia, Fed. Republic Germany, 1972—; Pres. Soc. Programmed Instruction, 1964-70, Internat. Acad. Scis., Republic of San Marino, 1987—; unlimited vis. prof. U. Nat. Rosario, Argentina, 1984, South China Normal U., Guangzhou, Peoples Republic China, 1986. Author: Cybernetic Foundation of Education Science, 1962, 2d edit., 1969, Cybernetics and Philosophy, 1966. Mem. Internat. Assn. Cybernetics Namur (bd. dirs.), World Assn. Cybernetics, Informatics and Systems Theory (v.p.). Mem. Free Dem. Party. Club: European (pres. 1978-80). Office: U Paderborn, Cybernetics Inst, KleinenbergerWeg 16B, D-4790 Paderborn Federal Republic of Germany

FRANK, ILYA MIKHAILOVICH, physicist; b. Leningrad, Oct. 23, 1908; ed. Moscow U. Asst. to prof. S.I. Vavilov, 1928; with Leningrad Optical Inst., 1930-34; with Lebedev Inst. Physics, USSR Acad. Scis., 1934-70; prof. physics Moscow U., 1944—; head lab. of neutron physics, Joint Inst. for Nuclear Research, 1957—; corr. mem. USSR Acad. Scis., 1946-48, academician, 1968—. Recipient Nobel prize for physics (with Tamm and Cherenkov), 1958; State Prize, 1946, 54, 71; Order of Lenin (3); Order of Red Banner of Labor; Order of October Revolution 1978; Varilov Gold medal, 1979. Author: Function of Excitement and Curve of Absorption in Optic Dissociation of Tallium Ioclate, 1933; Coherent Radiation of Fast Electron in a Medium, 1937; Pare Formation in Krypton under Gamma Rays, 1938; Doppler Effect in Refracting Medium, 1942; Radiation of a Uniformly Moving Electron Due to Its Transition from One Medium into Another, 1945; Neutron Multiplication in Uranium-Graphite System, 1955; On Group Velocity of Light in Radiation in Refracting Medium, 1958; Optics of Light Sources Moving in Refracting Media, 1960; On Some Peculiarities of Vavilov- Cherenkov Radiation, 1986. Office: Joint Inst Nuclear Research, Lab of Neutron Physics, 141980 Dubna USSR

FRANK, JUDIT, chemical engineer; b. Pécs, Hungary, Dec. 5, 1942; d. Kálmán and Veronica (Radich) F. MS, Technical U., Budapest, Hungary, 1966, PhD, 1974. Chem. researcher CHINOIN Pharm. Chem. Works, Budapest, Hungary, 1966-69, research group leader, 1969-74; vis. scientist U. East Anglia, Norwich, Eng., 1974-75; head research group CHINOIN Pharm. Chem. Works, Budapest, Hungary, 1976-86, head semisynthetic antibiotics devel., 1987—. Contbr. articles to profl. jours.; Patentee (17) patents in field. Fellow Hungarian Acad. Scis. (head research group Ctr. Research Inst. Chemistry, 1976—, heterocyclic chem. com.1987—). Home: Szőlő-köz 2, H-1032 Budapest Hungary Office: CHINOIN Pharm Chem Works, Tó u 1-5, H-1045 Budapest Hungary

FRANK, LEONID SIMON, mathematician, scientist, educator; b. Moscow, Apr. 25, 1934; s. Simon Iliahu and Tzila (Tabachnik) F. B.A., Moscow State U., 1953, M.A., 1958, Ph.D., 1964. Asst. prof. math., assoc. prof. Moscow State U., 1958-68; head scientist fluid dynamics dept., Soviet Acad. Sci., Inst. of Space Research, Moscow, 1968-71; vis. prof. Ecole Poly., Paris, 1972-73, U. Pavia, Italy, 1973; assoc. prof. Hebrew U., Jerusalem, 1976-77; vis. full prof. U. Paris, Lexington, 1986-87; full prof. U. Ky., The Netherlands, 1987— . Author: Coercive Singular Pertubations. Editor: Analytical and Numerical Approaches to Asymptotic Problems in Analysis, 1981; editor-in-chief jour. Asymptotic Analysus, 1988. Contbr. articles to profl. jours. Mem. Am. Math. Soc., Moscow Math. Soc., Israeli Math. Soc., French Mat. Soc., Dutch Math. Soc. Home: Pompweg 13, Ubbergen The Netherlands Office: Catholic U of Nijmegen, Toernooiveld, Nijmegen The Netherlands

FRANK, LUDWIG MATHIAS, psychiatrist; b. Phila., Apr. 16, 1920; s. Ludwig and Eleanore Emily (Saverwald) F.; A.B. maxima cum laude, LaSalle Coll., 1942; M.D., U. Pa., 1945; m. Marie T. Johnson, Sept. 21, 1946; children—Ludwig Matthew, Terri Frank Terni, Mary Ellen Frank Willsey; m. 2d, Hallie E. Moore, June 2, 1979. Intern, Fitzgerald Mercy Hosp., Darby, Pa., 1945-46; resident in psychiatry Mayo Found., Rochester, Minn., 1948-51; 1st asst. in psychiatry Mayo Clinic, 1948-52; clin. dir. Inst. Living, Hartford, 1952-55; pvt. practice medicine, specializing in psychiatry, West Hartford, 1955-—; chief psychiatry St. Francis Hosp., 1955-75; clin. asso. U. Conn. Med. Sch., 1975-—; cons. USAF, San Antonio, 1947—, Met. Tribunal, Hartford, St. Francis Hosp., 1987—; v.p., dir. Swiss Meadows Inc.; v.p., dir. Hatchetts Improvement Co. Mem. Sch. Bd. Archdiocese Hartford, 1969-74. Served to capt., M.C., AUS, 1946-48. Diplomate Am. Bd. Psychiatry. Fellow Am. Psychiat. Assn. (life), ACP; mem. Hartford Psychiat. Soc. (dir.; past pres.), AMA, Conn., Hartford County med. socs., Conn., Hartford psychiat. socs., Assn. Am. Med. Colls., N.Y. Acad. Sci., Piersol Anat. Soc., Mayo Clinic, Inst. Living, U. Pa. alumni assns. Contbr. to profl. jours. Home: 21 Walbridge Rd West Hartford CT 06119 Office: 801 Farmington Ave W Hartford CT 06119

FRANK, MARJORIE HOFHELMER (MRS. CHRISTOPHER GABLE), health consultant, educator; b. N.Y.C., Feb. 25, 1906; d. Arthur and Helen (Milius) Hofhelmer; student Columbia Sch. Bus. Adminstrn., 1924; m. Harry Frank, Jr., Oct. 14, 1926 (dec. Mar. 1963); m. Christopher Gable, Dec. 29, 1969. Dir. service in VA hosps. North Atlantic area ARC, 1945-49; asst. exec. dir. Nat. Assn. Mental Health, N.Y.C., 1949-59; asso. adminstrv. sec. Nat. Family Life Found., 1959-61; assoc. adminstrv. dir. Jewish Guild for Blind, N.Y.C., 1961-63; N.Y.C. regional planning rep. N.Y. Dept. Mental Hygiene, 1963-65; asst. to commr. Mental Health Services, N.Y.C. 1965-68; instr. Adminstrv. Sch. Pub. Health, 1968-73; instr. dept. psychiatry Coll. Physicians and Surgeons, Columbia U., 1968—, adminstrv. assoc. to chmn. dept. psychiatry, 1968-75; spl. cons. N.Y.C. Comprehensive Health Planning Agy., 1973-74; cons. New Sch. for Social Research, 1974-76, faculty, 1976-80; assoc. dir. mental health services Gouverneur Hosp., N.Y.C. Health and Hosp. Corp., 1973-76; rehab. cons. N.Y. State Dept. Mental Hygiene, N.Y.C., 1976-78; cons. Health Systems Agy. N.Y.C., 1978-79; dir. grants devel. and mgmt. Met. Hosp., N.Y.C. Health and Hosp. Corp., 1979-83; cons. Fountain House, N.Y.C., 1985—. Dep. comdr. Warren Twp. (N.J.) CD, 1940-45; bd. mem. at large Plainfield Council Social Agys., 1944-47; founder, pres. Union County Mental Hygiene Soc., 1944-49; mem. adv. council on citizen participation Community Chests and Councils of Am., 1951-57; alt. pres. Nathan Hofheimer Found., 1959-75; bd. dirs. 1155 Park Ave. Coop., 1980—. Fellow Am. Pub. Health Assn., Am. Orthopsychiat. Assn.; mem. N.Y. Acad. Scis. Unitarian. Home: 1155 Park Ave New York NY 10128

FRANK, MILTON, diplomat; b. Reno, Dec. 18, 1919; One child. BA, U. Calif., Berkeley, 1941; MS, Boston U., 1958. Commd. U.S. Air Force, 1946, advanced through grades to col., ret., 1968; dir. pub. affairs Calif. State U. System, Long Beach, 1969-83; pub. relations and pub. affairs cons. Santa Monica, Calif., 1983-86; asst. to pres. Adelphi U., Garden City, N.Y., 1985-86; ambassador Nepal, 1988—; mem. Presdl. del. to the coronation of His Majesty the King of Swaziland, 1986-87; vice-chmn. bd. dirs. African Devel. Found. Served with U.S. Army Air Corps, 1942-45. Office: American Embassy, Pani Pokhari, Kathmandu Nepal *

FRANK, MORTON, newspaper executive; b. Pitcairn, Pa., June 14, 1912; s. Abraham and Goldie (Friedenberg) F.; m. Agnes Dodds, June 2, 1944 (div. 1957); children: Allan Dodds, Michael Robert, Marilyn Morton; m. Elizabeth Welt Pope, Dec. 31, 1963. A.B., U. Mich., 1933; postgrad., Carnegie Inst. Tech., U. Pitts., Duquesne U.; LL.D., Alfred U., 1979. Advt. mgr. Braddock (Pa.) Daily News-Herald, 1933-34; editor Braddock Free Press, 1934-35; advt. salesman, entertainment writer 1935-37; rotogravure mgr. Pitts. Press, 1937-42; writer, commentator Pitts. radio stas., corr. trade mags. 1935-42; v.p., bus. mgr. Ariz. Times, Phoenix, 1946; editor, pub. Canton (Ohio) Economist, 1946-58, Lorain (Ohio) Sun News, 1949-50, Inter-County Gazette, Strasburg, Ohio, 1950, Stark County Times Canton, 1950-58, Farm and Dairy, Salem, Ohio, 1952-53; pres. Tri-Cities Telecasting, Canton, 1953-61, Printype, 1956-58, Property Devel. Corp., 1956-58; dir. publisher relations, v.p. Family Weekly and Suburbia Today, N.Y.C., 1958-65; pub., exec. v.p. Family Weekly, 1966-71, pres., pub., 1971-75, 76-80, chmn., 1976, chmn., pub., 1980-82, chmn. emeritus, 1982-85; cons. CBS, 1982-88; cons. USA Weekend/Family Weekly, CBS, Gannett Co., 1985—; chmn. emeritus USA Weekend, 1985—; dir. Horizon Communications, Inc., 1984—; dir. Am. Jour. of Nursing Co., 1984—, chmn. fin. com., 1986—; cons. Greenhow Newspapers, 1982-86. Chmn. Commn. Corr. Ind. Higher Edn. N.Y., 1976-79, exec. com., 1980-82; trustee Alfred U., 1968—, Mus. Cartoon Art, 1980—; exec. com. Council Governing Bds., 1982—; bd. dirs. Cancer Care, Nat. Cancer Found., 1985—, Canton Symphony Orch., 1950-56. Served from ensign to lt. USNR, 1942-45. Recipient 1st prize for feature writing N.E.A., 1954; community service award Accredited Hometown Newspapers Am., 1954. Mem. Tri-State Fedn. Non-Comml. Theatres (pres. 1936-38), Controlled Circulation Newspapers Am. (dir. 1948-56), Pitts. Fgn. Policy Assn. (dir. 1940-42), Newspaper Advt. Bur. (plans com. 1974-82), Am., So., Inland, Tex., Calif., N.Y. newspaper pubs. assns., Internat. Press Inst., Interam. Press Assn., Internat. Circulation Mgrs. Assn., Internat. Newspaper Promotion Assn., Internat. Newspaper Advt. Execs. Assn., Sigma Alpha Mu, Sigma Delta Chi. Clubs: Canton Advt, Players, N.Y.C. Sales Execs, Overseas Press (dir. 1983-87, found. trustee 1983—), Deadline (pres. 1974-75, chmn. 1975-76, bd. dirs. 1977—, N.Y. Journalism Hall of Fame 1985); Silurians (dir. 1985-86, v.p. 1986-87, pres. 1987-88). Home: 105 Rock House Rd Easton CT 06612 also: 115 E 67th St New York NY 10021 Office: 502 Park Ave New York NY 10022

FRANK, ROBERT ALLEN, advertising executive; b. Albany, N.Y., Sept. 26, 1932; s. Edward and Marian (Kostelanetz) F.; m. Cynthia Tull, Aug., 1984; children: David, Chelsea, Alison. B.A., Colby Coll., 1954; M.B.A., Amos Tuck Sch. Bus. Adminstrn., Dartmouth Coll., 1958. Cost control adminstr. ABC-TV, N.Y.C., 1958-59, corp. auditor CBS, Inc., N.Y.C., 1959-60, TV sales service account exec., 1961, account exec. radio network sales, 1962-69; exec. v.p., co-founder SFM Media Corp., N.Y.C., 1969—, pres. Media Service div., 1981. Radio-TV cons. Nat Kidney Fund., 1974. Active radio TV for various polit. campaigns including Robert Kennedy for Senator, 1964, Richard Nixon for Pres., 1972, Ford for Pres., 1976, Bush for Pres., 1980, Reagan for Pres., 1980, Du Pont for Pres., 1988; mem. Leadership Council Nat Rep. Congl. Com., Rep. Nat. Com., 1980—, Pres.' Club, 1984—, Rep. Nat. Senatorial Com. Inner Circle, 1985—, Citizens for Rep. Pres. Com., 1984—; trustee Nat. Child Labor Com., Myasthenia Gravis Found., 1984—; Served to capt. USAF, 1954-56. Mem. Internat. Radio-TV Soc., Amos Tuck Alumni Assn. N.Y. (pres. 1976-77, dir. 1979—), Internat. Platform Assn., Pi Gamma Mu. Club: Dartmouth (N.Y.C.). Home: 35 Lounsbury Rd Ridgefield CT 06877 Office: SFM Media Corp 1180 Ave of Americas New York NY 10036

FRANK, RONALD EDWARD, marketing educator; b. Chgo., Sept. 15, 1933; s. Raymond and Ethel (Lundquist) F.; m. Iris Donner, June 18, 1958; children: Linda, Lauren, Kimberly. B.S. in Bus. Adminstrn, Northwestern U., 1955, M.B.A., 1957; Ph.D., U. Chgo., 1960. Instr. bus. statistics Northwestern U., Evanston, Ill., 1956-57; asst. prof. bus. adminstrn. Harvard U., Boston, 1960-63, Stanford U., 1963-65; assoc. prof. mktg. Wharton Sch., U. Pa., 1965-68, prof., 1968-84, chmn. dept. mktg., 1971-74, vice dean, dir. research and Ph.D. programs, 1974-76, assoc. dean, 1981-83; dean, prof. mktg. Krannert Grad. Sch. Mgmt., Purdue U., 1984—; bd. dirs. Lafayette Life Ins. Co., The MAC Group, Home Hosp. Lafayette (Ind.); cons. to industry. Author: (with Massy and Kuehn) Quantitative Techniques in Marketing Analysis, 1962, (with Matthews, Buzzell and Levitt) Marketing: an Introductory Analysis, 1964, (with William Massy) Computer Programs for the Analysis of Consumer Panel Data, 1964, An Econometric Approach to a Marketing Decision Model, 1971, (with Paul Green) Manager's Guide to Marketing Research, 1967, Quantative Methods in Marketing, 1967, (with Massy and Lodahl) Purchasing Behavior and Personal Attributes, 1968, (with Massy and Wind) Market Segmentation, 1972, (with Marshall Greenberg) Audience Segmentation Analysis for Public Television Program Development, Evaluation and Promotion, 1976, The Public's Use of Television, 1980, Audiences for Public Television, 1982. Bd. dirs., fin. com. Home Hosp. of Lafayette, 1985—. Recipient pub. TV research grants John and Mary R. Markle Found., 1975-82. Mem. Am. Mktg. Assn. (dir. 1968-70, v.p. mktg. edn. 1972-73), Inst. Mgmt. Sci., Assn. Consumer Research, Am. Assn. Pub. Opinion Research. Home: 144 Creighton Rd West Lafayette IN 47906 Office: Purdue U Grad Sch Mgmt West Lafayette IN 47907

FRANK, SANDRA KAYE, mathematics educator; b. Springfield Twp., Mich., June 11, 1941; d. Virgil Euleas and Dorothy Arliene (Wells) Noble; m. Joseph Frederic Frank, Aug. 1, 1970; 1 child, Joseph Lindbergh. B.A., Central Mich. U., 1963; M.A., U. Mont., 1967. Tchr. math. Dearborn Pub. Sch., Mich., 1963—, Edsel Ford High Sch., 1978—. Mem. Mich. Council Tchrs. Math., Mich. Assn. Computer Users and Learners, Nat. Council Teachers of Math., Math. Assn. Am. Clubs: Mich. Flyers, Ninety-Nines. Home: 21222 Audette St Dearborn MI 48124

FRANK, VICTOR H., JR., international banker; b. Apr. 4, 1927; married; three children. BA, Yale U., 1950, LLB, 1953; LLM in Taxation, NYU, 1960. Pvt. practice law N.Y.C. and Phila., 1953-66; tax counsel CPC Internat., Englewood Cliffs, N.J., 1966-73, v.p. fin., adminstrn. Best Foods div., 1973-77, v.p. diversified unit ops., 1977-79, spl. asst. to chief exec. officer, 1979-82, v.p. for info. resources, 1982-85, v.p. for govt. relations, 1986-87; U.S. dir., ambassador Asian Devel. Bank, Manila, 1987—; former mem. Nat. Adv. Bd. to U.S. Sec. Edn. on Internat. Programs. Contbr. articles to Harvard Bus. Rev. Office: Asian Devel Bank, PO Box 789, 1099 Manila The Philippines

FRANK, WILLIAM NELSON, financial marketing executive; b. Cin., June 3, 1953; s. Nelson A. and Marion A. (Kirbert) F. Student, Capital U., 1971-74; BS in Edn., Bowling Green State U., 1975; JD, U. Toledo, 1978; postgrad., U. Cin., 1980-82. Bar: Ohio, 1978; CPA, Ohio; cert. tchr., Ohio.. Asst. city prosecutor City of Columbus, Ohio, 1978-80; asst. pub. defender Hamilton (Ohio) County, 1981-84; sole practice William N. Frank, Columbus, 1978-85; regional fin. mktg. mgr. A.L. Williams, Columbus, 1984—; auditor Phillip Willeke, Inc., Columbus, 1985-87; securities rep. First Am. Nat. Securities, Columbus, 1985—. Mem. Hamilton County Rep. Club, Cin., 1981—. Named Ky. Colonel Commonwealth of Ky., 1978, One of Outstanding Yount Men in Am., 1987. Mem. ABA, Cin. Bar Assn., Ohio Soc. CPA's, Delta Tau Upsilon, Phi Alpha Delta Law Fraternity. Republican. Mem. Ch. of Christ. Lodges: Masons (32 degree), Shriners, Order of DeMolay (Chevalier degree 1972). Home: 2087 E Lake Club Terr Columbus OH 43232 Office: 2101 S Hamilton Suite 112 Columbus OH 43232

FRANKE, ALOIS JOSEF, aluminum company executive; b. Quedlinburg, Germany, May 31, 1940; s. Karl R. and Hildegard (Theobald) F.; m. Margrit Biesle, Apr. 23, 1966; children: Erika, Ruediger. BS in Physics, Saarbrucken U. (Germany), 1961, MS in Materials Sci., 1964, PhD, 1966. Research assoc. Saarbrucken U., 1964-67; sect. head research and devel. Rasselstein AG, Neuwied, W.Ger., 1967-70; head dept. prodn. Leichtmetallgesellschaft, Essen, W.Ger., 1970-79; plant mgr. Icelandic Aluminium Co., Hafnafjordur (Iceland), 1979-82; mem. exec. com. Aluminium-Rheinfelden (W.Ger.), 1982—. Mem. econ. adv. bd. Christlich Demokratische Union. Mem. AIME, Gesellschaft Deutscher Metallhuetten und Bergleute, Verein Deutscher Eisenhuettenleute, Deutsche Gesellschaft fuer Keramik. Office: Aluminium-Rheinfelden GmbH, Friedrichstrasse 80, 7888 Rheinfelden Federal Republic of Germany

FRANKE, ARNOLD GENE, business management educator, arbitrator; b. Mount Olive, Ill., Nov. 3, 1932; s. Bernard and Hannah (Scheiter) F.; m. Roseanne Moruskey, June 19, 1954; children: Cara Lyn, Lisa Kay, Jenny Jo, Susan Jean. BS, Eastern Ill. U., 1955; MS, Purdue U., 1960; PhD, Sussex Coll., England, 1968. Cert. arbitrator. Analyst Shell Oil Co., Wood River, Ill., 1960-65; instr. So. Ill. U., Edwardsville, 1965-67, asst. v.p., 1968-77, dir. small bus. devel. ctr., 1984—; mem. small bus. investment com., Ill. S. Conf., Springfield, 1980—; rep. White House Small Bus. Conf., Washington, 1985-86. Pres. Ill. Ctr. for Autism, Fairview Hts., Ill., 1976-78; local chmn. United Way, 1984—; facilitator Spirit of St. Louis. Served to lt. USN, 1955-60. Mem. Am. Arbitration Assn. (arbitrator), Fed. Mediation and Conciliation Service (arbitrator), Atlantic Econ. Assn., Acad. of Mgmt. (assoc.), Am. Legion. Club: Sunset Hill Country (Edwardsville). Lodge: Moose. Home: 730 Saint Louis St Edwardsville IL 62025 Office: Southwestern Ill Small Bus Devel Ctr Box 1107 SIUE Edwardsville IL 62026

FRANKE, BRUNO HENRI VICTOR, advertising executive; b. Utrecht, The Netherlands, July 20, 1941; s. Anton Bruno and Catherine Marie L. (Smits) F.; m. Köster Edith Marie Theresia; children: Victor Anton, Fleur Sophie Catrien, Myrtle Maryn. MBS-b, Ryks HBS, 1962; SIOO, SIOO, 1972. Asst. dir. Techniscl Mandelsbureau van Grootel, Utrecht, 1964-65; mem. mgmt. team Mgmt. Cons. Wage 8 U., de Bilt, The Netherlands, 1965-76, van der Torn & Baningh, Mgmt. Cons., Utrecht, 1976-85; mng. dir. Dutch Advertisers Assn., Amsterdam, The Netherlands, 1985—; bd. dirs. Planeta 8 V. Print Group, 1984—, Beheersmaatschappy Waanders 8 V., Zwolle, 1978-82, B.V. Timmervabrick de Concurrent, Bergambccll, 1977-82 (pres.); cons. in field. Editor: Handbook on Personal Selling, 1974-81; author/editor: de Vennootsclap Nederland, 1977; co-editor: Handbook on Sales Training Policy and Organisation, 1982. Served in Dutch infantry, 1962-64. Mem. Dutch Assn. Mgmt. Cons. (pres. 1973-85), Assn. Mng. Dirs., Internat. AdvertisersAssn., Internat. C. of C. V V.D. Roman Catholic. Clubs: Oud Roest, Oud London. Lodge: K.W.V.L. Home: Jacobus Pennweg 42, 1217 JH Hilversum The Netherlands Office: Bond ven Adverteerders, Koningslaan 34, 1075 Amsterdam The Netherlands

FRANKE, FREDERICK RAHDE, physician; b. Pitts., Oct. 14, 1918; s. Frederick Ferdin and Louise Anna (Rahde) F.; m. Nancy Olive Digby, Mar. 22, 1943; children—Suzanne, Paula, Frederick Rahde, Paul D., John C., Virginia N. B.S., U. Pitts., 1941, M.D., 1943; M.S., U. Pa., 1950, D.Sc., 1952. Diplomate: Am. Bd. Internal Medicine (cardiovascular diseases). Intern, then resident St. Francis Hosp., Pitts., 1943-45; research asso. physiology St. Francis Hosp., 1947-52, physician-in-chief charge therapeutics, 1953-56; pvt. practice Pitts., 1952—; asst. prof. medicine Sch. Medicine U. Pitts., 1953-56; chief medicine St. Clair, South Side, St. Margaret hosps., 1955-63; mem. faculty Sch. Medicine Johns Hopkins U., 1960-61; sr. cardiologist charge cardiovascular-pulmonary lab., chief div. medicine Western Pa Hosp., 1963-69, med. dir., 1967-73; clin. prof. pharmacology U. Pitts. Sch. Pharmacy, 1972—; Bd. dirs. Health Research Services Found.; governing com. Pa. Comprehensive Health Planning Com. Contbr. articles, chpts. in books. Served with M.C. USNR, 1945-46. Fellow A.C.P., Council Clin. Cardiology, Am. Heart Assn.; mem. Pa. Heart Assn. (past pres., com. chmn., Meritorious Service award 1962), Soc. Exptl. Biology and Medicine, Am. Therapeutic Soc., Am. Soc. Human Genetics, AMA, Sigma Xi. Republican. Presbyterian. Club: Rolling Rock (Ligonier, Pa.). Home: 19 Glen Ridge Ln Pittsburgh PA 15243 Office: 4815 Liberty Ave Pittsburgh PA 15224

FRANKE, HERBERT MAX WOLFGANG, sinologist; b. Cologne, Germany, Sept. 27, 1914; s. Max and Berta (Maase) F.; m. Ruth Freiin von Reck, Apr. 3, 1945; 1 child, Michael. LLD, U. Cologne, 1938, PhD, 1947. Reader U. Cologne, 1949-52; prof. East Asian studies U. Munich, 1952—; German consul in Hong Kong, 1953-54; vis. prof. U. Wash., Seattle, 1964-65, 69-70; v.p. German Research Council, 1974-80; mem. com. study Chinese civilization Am. Council Learned Socs., 1967-77. Author, contbr. to books and articles on Chinese and Inner Asian history. Served with German Army, 1937-45. Recipient Prix Stanislas Julien, Acad. des Inscriptions et Balles-Lettres, Paris, 1953; Fed. Order of Merit, Fed. Republic Germany, 1978; Brit. Council fellow, 1951-52; hon. fellow Jesus Coll. Mem. German Oriental Soc. (hon.) (pres. 1960-65), Royal Asiatic Soc. Great Britain and Ireland, Mongolia Soc., Royal Irish Acad. (hon.), Soc. Asiatique. Home: 23 Fliederstrasse, 8035 Gauting Federal Republic of Germany Office: Kaulbachstrasse 51a, 8000 Munich 22, Federal Republic of Germany

FRANKEL, GEORGE JOSEPH, aerospace engineer; b. N.Y.C., Jan. 3, 1923; s. Joseph and Celia (Simon) F.; B.M.E., CCNY, 1944; grad. Poly. Inst. Bklyn., 1968; m. Miriam Josephson, Apr. 15, 1945; children—Paul Jay, Alice Frankel Pratt, Lee Jeffrey. Product test engr. Arma Corp., 1944-45; chief engr. Metaplast Process, Inc., 1945-60, sec., 1953-60; prodn. mgr. Brillium Metals Corp., Hollis, N.Y., 1960-62; chief space environment Republic Aviation Corp., Farmingdale, N.Y., 1962-65; prin. engr. Grumman Corp., Bethpage, N.Y., 1965—, corporate metrication officer, 1977—; cons. vacuum metalizing, 1960-—; gen. chmn. space simulation conf. AIAA/ASTM/Inst. Environ. Scis., 1973, tech. program chmn., 1975. Assoc. fellow AIAA (chmn. L.I. sect. 1976-77; tech. com. on ground testing and Simulation 1970-73; tech. com. on life scis. 1975-78, public policy officer region I, 1978-81, chmn. regional public policy officers com. 1978-81; dir. region I 1981-84; Disting. Service award 1981, v.p. mem. services 1985—); sr. mem. Inst. Environ. Scis.; mem. Nat. Fire Protection Assn. (chmn. tech. com. fire hazards in oxygen-enriched atmospheres 1966-—), Am. Nat. Metric Council (bd. dirs. 1986—, chmn. aerospace sector com. 1976—), U.S. Metric Assn. (cert. advanced metrication specialist), Pi Tau Sigma. Contbr. to profl. jours. Office: Grumman Corp S Oyster Bay Rd Bethpage NY 11714

FRANKEL, JAMES BURTON, lawyer; b. Chgo., Feb. 25, 1924; s. Louis and Thelma (Cohn) F.; m. Louise Untermyer, Jan. 22, 1956; children—Nina, Sara, Simon. Student U. Chgo., 1940-42; B.S., U.S. Naval Acad., 1945; LL.B., Yale U., 1952. Bar: Calif. 1953. Mem. Steinhart, Goldberg, Feigenbaum & Ladar, San Francisco, 1954-72; of counsel Cooper, White & Cooper, San Francisco, 1972—; sr. fellow, lectr. in law Yale U., 1971-72; lectr. Stanford U. Law Sch., 1973-75; vis. prof. U. Calif. Law Sch., 1975-76. Pres. Council Civic Unity of San Francisco Bay Area, 1964-66; chmn. San Francisco Citizens Charter Revision Com., 1968-70; mem. San Francisco Pub. Schs. Commn., 1975-76; trustee Natural Resources Def. Council, 1972-77, 79—, staff atty., 1977-79; chmn. San Francisco Citizens Energy Policy Adv. Com., 1981-82. Mem. ABA, Calif. Bar Assn., San Francisco Bar Assn. Democrat. Office: 101 California St 16th Floor San Francisco CA 94111

FRANKEL, KENNETH MARK, thoracic surgeon; b. Bklyn., July 29, 1940; s. Clarence Bernard and Ruth (Rutes) F.; m. Felice Cala Oringel, Dec. 10, 1967; children—Matthew David, Michael Jacob. B.A., Cornell U., 1961;

M.D., SUNY-Bklyn., 1965. Diplomate Am. Bd. Surgery, Am. Bd. Thoracic Surgery. Intern in surgery Yale New Haven Hosp., 1965-66; resident in surgery Kings County-SUNY Med. Ctr., Bklyn., 1966-67, 69-71, chief resident in gen. surgery, 1971-72, resident in thoracic surgery 1972-73, chief resident thoracic and cardiovascular surgery, 1973-74; att. thoracic surgeon Mercy Hosp., Springfield, Mass., Holyoke (Mass.) Hosp., Providence Hosp., Holyoke, 1974—; cons. in thoracic surgery Ludlow (Mass.) Hosp., Noble Hosp., Westfield, Mass., 1976—; practice medicine specializing in thoracic surgery, Springfield, Mass., 1974—; chief thoracic surgery Baystate Med. Center, Springfield, Mass., 1977—; assoc. clin. prof. cardiothoracic surgery Tufts U. Sch. Medicine, 1978—; alt. del. to interspity. med. adv. com. Blue Shield-Blue Cross of Mass. Contbr. articles to profl. jours. Corporator Springfield (Mass.) Symphony Orch., Stage West, Springfield. Cons. Hosp. for Crippled Children, Springfield, 1986—; corporator Symphony Orch., Springfield, Regional Repertory Theater Co. Served to capt. U.S. Army, 1967-69. Decorated Bronze Star, Gallantry Cross (Republic of Vietnam). Fellow ACS, Am. Coll. Chest Physicians; mem. Soc. Thoracic Surgeons, Am. Thoracic Soc., Springfield Acad. Medicine (past pres), AMA, Mass. Med. Soc. (councilor 1981-83), Hampden Dist. Med. Soc., Physicians for Social Responsibility (chpt. treas.), Amnesty Internat., ACLU, Internat. Physicians for Prevention Nuclear War, Union Concerned Scientists. Democrat. Jewish. Clubs: Cornell of Western Mass., Porsche of Am., Maimonides Med. Club (past pres.). Home: 202 Ellington Rd Longmeadow MA 01106 Office: Baystate Med Ctr 2 Bdlg Ctr Dr Med Office Bldg Suite 304 Springfield MA 01107

FRANKEL, LINDA DAIGNAULT, economic development administrator; b. Springfield, Mass., Aug. 12, 1945; d. Alfred Philip and Jeane (Lacine) Daignault; m. James Melton Howell, Sept. 24, 1983. BA, Wellesley Coll., 1967; MA in Teaching, Brown U., 1969. Sr. copy editor Wall St. Transcript, N.Y.C., 1970-74; dir. econ. devel. program New Eng. Regional Commn., Boston, 1974-75; spl. asst. to sr. v.p., fin. U. Mass. System, Boston, 1975-76; pres. Council for Econ. Action, Inc., Boston, 1976—, dir., 1980—; cons. urban affairs Bank of Boston, 1978—. Fundraiser, French Library, Boston, 1981; bd. dirs. New Eng. Congl. Inst., Washington, 1980—. Mem. Council Urban Econ. Devel., Wellesley Coll. Alumni Assn. Episcopalian. Home: 73 Beacon St Boston MA 02108 Office: Council Econ Action Inc 17th Floor 100 Federal St Boston MA 02110

FRANKEL, MARTIN RICHARD, statistician, educator, consultant; b. Washington, June 16, 1943; s. Lester R. and Vera B. Frankel; m. Jean L. Kaiser, Mar. 24, 1970; children: Jennifer, Margaux. AB, U. N.C., 1965; MA, U. Mich., 1967, PhD, 1971. Asst. prof. stats. U. Chgo., 1971-73, assoc. prof., 1974-76; prof. stats. Baruch Coll., CUNY, 1977—; tech. dir. Nat. Opinion Research Center, U. Chgo., 1972—; chnm. Quality Research Council, Advtg. Research Found., 1988—; cons. statis. methods and quality control, 1965—; mem. panel on occupational and health stats. Nat. Acad. Scis. Author: Inference from Complex Samples, 1971, Total Survey Error, 1979; also articles; mem. editorial bd. Jour. Am. Statis. Assn., Pub. Opinion Quar., Ency. Statis. Scis., Sociol. Research and Methods. Fellow Am. Statis. Assn. (chmn. census adv. com. 1981, chmn. sect. survey research methods 1975-76), Royal Statis. Soc.; mem. Am. Assn. Pub. Opinion Research (chmn. standards com.), Internat. Statis. Inst. Home: 14 Patricia Ln Cos Cob CT 06807 Office: 17 Lexington Ave New York NY 10010

FRANKEL, PETER, export company executive; b. Berlin, Feb. 4, 1921; s. Kurt and Steffi (Ausnit) F.; m. Edith Eva Mariella Kennedy, Dec. 28, 1948; children—Roger Charles, Anthony Michael. Student Theresianische Akademie, Vienna, Austria. Mng. dir. Intimex Ltd., Rio de Janeiro, Brazil, 1942-60; chmn. Keys Trading Internat. Party Ltd, Caulfield South, Victoria, Australia, 1964—; cons. on agrl. policy EEC, 1967—; cons. Minister of Trade, 1985-86; speaker in field. Contbr. articles to profl. jours. World pres. Jr. C. of C., 1961; chmn. Defend Australia Com., 1966-75; pres. Melbourne (Australia) C. of C., 1977-79; mem. exec. com. Liberal Party Victoria, 1971-77, 79—; chmn. Australian C. of C. Export Council, 1983-86, Victoria Exporters Assn., 1984-86; mem. Trade Devel. Council. Fellow Inst. Mgmt., Inst. Dirs. (Exporter award, 1984, 87). Jewish. Club: Victorian Amateur Turf, Lodge of Commerce, Royal Automobile Club of Victoria. Home: Caixa Postal 1081, Marginal-Cascais, 2751 Cascais Codex Portugal

FRANKEL, STANLEY ARTHUR, public relations executive; b. Dayton, Ohio, Dec. 8, 1918; s. Mandel and Olive (Margolis) F.; m. Irene Baskin, Feb. 20, 1946; children—Stephen, Thomas, Nancy. B.S. with high honors, Northwestern U., 1940; student, Columbia U., 1940, U. Chgo., 1946-49. Reporter Chgo. News Bur., 1940; publicist CBS, 1941; asst. to pres. Esquire and Coronet mags., N.Y.C., 1946-56; pres. Esquire Club, 1956-58; with McCall Corp., N.Y.C., 1958-61; asst. to pres. and pub. McCall Corp., 1958-61, v.p., 1959-61; v.p., dir. corporate devel. Ogden Corp., 1961—, cons., 1988—; cons. Manning, Selvage & Lee Pub. Relations Corp., N.Y.C., 1961—; dir. Michaelis Prodns., Inc., Rockwood Corp., Careful Office Service Inc., Western Calif. Canners Corp., Internat. Terminal Operating Co., Inc., Ogden Am. Corp.; adj. prof. Baruch Coll., CUNY, 1974—, Pace U., 1983—; bd. dirs. Baruch Coll. Ctr. of Mgmt., 1986—; bd. visitors PhD Program Baruch Coll., 1986—; guest lectr. N.Y. U., 1974; mem. Pres.'s Adv. Council on Peace Corps, 1965, Pres.'s Adv. Council on Youth Opportunity.; Mem. chancellor's panel State U. N.Y., 1970—; mem. N.Y. State Task Force on Higher Edn., 1974—; bd. mem., exec. com. Nat. Council Crime and Delinquency; bd. mem., vice chmn. Nat. Businessmen's Council; bd. dirs., officer Scarsdale Adult Sch. Author: History of 37th Division, 1947; contbr. articles to popular mags. Exec. bd. Writers for Stevenson, 1952, 56, for Kennedy, 1960, McGovern for Pres., 1972; pub. relations dir. Stevenson-for-Pres., 1956; chmn. Writers for Senator Humphrey Vice-Presdl. campaign, 1964; exec. bd. Businessmen for Humphrey-Muskie, 1968; chmn. N.Y. Writers for Humphrey-Muskie, 1968; mem. nat. exec. com. McGovern for Pres., 1972; vice chmn. N.Y. State McGovern for Pres. Com., 1972; bd. overseers Rutgers U., 1977—; chancellor's external relations com. City U. N.Y., 1977—; bd. dirs., v.p., mem. exec. com. YMCA of Greater N.Y.; founder Public Relations Bd., Inc., N.Y. and Chgo., Bedford Stuyvesant Project (T.R.Y.); mem. Vice President's Task Force on Youth Unemployment, 1979—. Served to maj. AUS, 1940-46. Decorated 2 Presdl. Citations, 3 Bronze Stars; recipient Peabody award for TV Series Adlai Stevenson Reports, 1961-63; Northwestern U. Alumni Merit award, 1964. Mem. Am. Mgmt. Assn. (chmn. pub. relations course 1971), Phi Beta Kappa, Phi Beta Kappa Assocs. (pres., trustee), Phi Beta Kappa Assn., Scarsdale-Westchester (pres. 1980—). Clubs: Northwestern U. of N.Y. (pres. 1964); Overseas Press (N.Y.C.); Scarsdale (N.Y.) Town (bd. govs.), Sunningdale; County. Home: 109 Brewster Rd Scarsdale NY 10583 Office: Ogden Corp 2 Pennsylvania Plaza New York NY 10121

FRANKISH, PATRICIA, psychologist; b. Cleethorpes, Humberside, Eng., Nov. 12, 1947; d. Herbert Alan and Ada Peggy (Lamming) F.; m. Edward Kenneth Brock, Apr. 2, 1966 (div. May 1979); children: Alan James Brock, Amanda Jane Brock, Talitha Jo Brock; m. William David John Eldridge, May 7, 1982. BA, Open U., Buckinghamshire, Eng., 1982; BSc in Psychology with honors, U. Hull, Eng., 1982; M of Clin. Psychology, Liverpool (Eng.) U., 1985. Programmer Ruston & Hornsby, Lincoln, 1965-66; registrar births and deaths Lincolnshire (Eng.) County Council, 1976-79; psychologist Nat. Health Service, Liverpool, 1983-85; sr. clin. psychologist Grimsby, Eng., 1985—; chair Div. Clin. Psychology, Yorkshire, Eng., 1986—. Councillor Town of Brigg, Eng., 1983—; organizer Constituency Assn., Brigg and Cleethorpes Liberals, Eng., 1987—. Mem. Brit. Psychol. Soc. Anglican. Clubs: Brigg Arts (dept. chair), Brigg Youth Ctr. (com. mem.). Home: 61 Grammar School Rd, Brigg DN20 8AY, England Office: Grimsby Health Authority, Dist Gen Hosp, Grimsby DN33 2BA, England

FRANKL, WILLIAM STEWART, cardiologist, educator; b. Phila., July 15, 1928; s. Louis and Vera (Simkin) F.; m. Razelle Sherr, June 17, 1951; children: Victor S. (dec.), Brian A. B.A. in Biology, Temple U., 1951, M.D., 1955, M.S. in Medicine, 1961. Diplomate: Am. Bd. Internal Medicine, Am. Bd. Cardiovascular Disease. Intern Buffalo Gen. Hosp., 1955-56; resident in medicine Temple U., Phila., 1956-57, 59-61; mem. faculty Temple U. (Sch. Medicine), 1962-68, dir. EKG sect. dept. cardiology, 1966-68, dir. cardiac care unit, 1967-68; research fellow U. Pa., Phila., 1961-62; prof. medicine, dir. div. cardiology Med. Coll. Pa., Phila., 1970-79; prof. medicine, assoc. dir. cardiology div. Thomas Jefferson U., Phila., 1979-84; physician-in-chief Springfield (Mass.) Hosp., 1968-70; practice medicine specializing in cardiology Phila., 1962-68, 70—; prof. medicine, co-dir. William Likoff Cardiovascular Inst. Hahnemann U., Phila., 1984-86, dir. William Likoff Cardiovascular Inst., dir. div. cardiology, 1986—, Thomas J. Vischer Prof. medicine, chmn. dept. medicine, 1987—; cons. cardiology Phila. Va Hosp., 1970-79; Fogarty Sr. Internat. fellow Cardiothoracic Inst., U. London, 1978-79; pres. Pa. affiliate Am. Heart Assn., 1985-86. Contbr. articles to profl. jours. Served with M.C. U.S. Army, 1957-59. Recipient Golden Apple award Temple U. Sch. Medicine, 1967; award Med. Coll. Pa., 1972; Lindback award for distinguished teaching, 1975. Fellow A.C.P., Am. Coll. Cardiology (gov. Eastern Pa. 1986-89), Phila. Coll. Physicians, Am. Coll. Clin. Pharmacology (regent 1980-85), Council Clin. Cardiology, Am. Heart Assn. (council on arteriosclerosis); mem. N.Y. Acad. Scis., Am. Fedn. Clin. Research, AAUP, AAAS, Assn. Am. Med. Colls., Am. Heart Assn. (bd. govs. S.E. Pa. chpt. 1972—, pres. 1976), Am. Soc. Clin. Pharmacology and Therapeutic Therapeutics. Home: 536 Moreno Rd Wynnewood PA 19096 Office: William Likoff Cardiovascular Inst 230 N Broad St Philadelphia PA 19102

FRANKLE, ALLAN HENRY, psychologist; b. Des Moines, Nov. 5, 1921; s. Harry Raymond and Ruth (Cohen) F.; m. Esther Alpern, June 22, 1947; children: Katherine, Jonathan. Student U. Chgo., 1939, Ph.D., 1953; student U. Minn., 1943. Dir. Des Moines Child Guidance Ctr., 1947-52; pvt. practice clin. psychology, Des Moines, 1952-85, clin. research, 1985—; Univ. fellow Drake U., 1970—; vis. clin. assoc. prof. psychology U. Iowa, 1969-70; cons. clin. psychology Broadlawns Polk County Hosp., 1967-81; cons. VA Hosp., Knoxville, Iowa, 1976-81; supervising psychologist N.Am. Mensa, 1966-78. Served with U.S. Army, 1943-45. Decorated Bronze Star. Diplomate Am. Bd. Profl. Psychology. Contbr. articles to profl. jours. Fellow Am. Orthopsychiat. Assn.,; mem. Am. Psychol. Assn., Iowa Psychol. Assn. (pres. 1960-61, Disting. Service award 1973), Am. Acad. Psychotherapists, Internat. Neuropsychology Soc., Brit. Psychol. Soc. (fgn. mem.), Sigma Xi, Psi Chi, Mensa. Democrat. Jewish. Home: 7931 Caminito Del Cid La Jolla CA 92037

FRANKLIN, ALAN JAMES, pediatrician, allergist; b. London, Aug. 21, 1933; s. Leonard James and Violet May (Puddifoot) F.; m. Ursula Rosemary Mileson, Apr. 1, 1959; children—Rebecca, Merrill, Daniel. L.R.C.P., M.R.C.S., West London U., 1960; D. Obstetrics R.C.O.G., Coll. Ob-Gyn., D.C.H., London, 1962. House surgeon West London Hosp., 1960; sr. house officer in pediatrics Hillingdon Hosp., Middlesex, Eng., 1961-62; sr. house officer, registrar medicine Wigan and Leigh Hosps., Lancashire, 1962-66; registrar in pediatrics Royal Free Hosp., London, 1967-69, sr. registrar, 1969-72; cons. pediatrician Mid Essex Health Authority, Chelmsford, Essex, 1972—. Contbr. articles to profl. jours. Fellow Royal Coll. Physicians London, Royal Coll. Physicians Edinburgh, Royal Soc. Medicine; mem. Brit. Pediatric Assn. (mem. council 1985-88), Brit. Soc. Allergy and Clin. Immunology, Brit. Soc. Allergy and Environ. Medicine. Baptist. Avocations: model railways; steam preservation; photography; music. Home: Lyndale, 11 Braemar Ave, Chelmsford CM2 9PN, England Office: St John's Hosp, Wood St, Chelmsford CM2 9BG, England

FRANKLIN, ARLEY FRANCIS, education official; b. Mountain Grove, Mo., June 5, 1938; d. Arley Columbus and Hazel Irene (Francis) F.; m. Linda Lee Hayman, Dec. 29, 1963; children—James Kirk, John Kent, Kellee Michelle. B.S., S.W. Mo. State U., 1959; M.S., George Washington U., 1978; cert. Columbia U., 1980. Cert. internal auditor. Auditor, GAO, Frankfurt, W.Ger., mgr., Washington, 1972-74, dep. dir. staff devel., 1974-77, dep. dir. orgn. analysis and planning, 1977-80, dir. orgn. and human devel., 1980-85; spl. asst. to dean Coll. Edn., U. Md., 1985-87, dir. devel. 1987—; assoc. dir. mgmt. program Council Gt. City Schs., Washington, 1985-86, sr. cons. human resources, 1986—. Deacon Calvery Hill Bapt. Ch., Fairfax, Va., 1977—. Served to 1st lt. U.S. Army, 1959-63. Recipient Comptroller Gen.'s award GAO, 1979, Disting. Service award, 1983. Mem. Am. Mgmt. Assn. (human resources council), Am. Soc. for Tng. and Devel. Republican. Home: 7410 Willowbrook Rd Fairfax Station VA 22039 Office: U Md Coll Edn College Park MD 20742

FRANKLIN, CARTHEL FLOYD, real estate broker; b. Rittman, Ohio, Aug. 26, 1920; s. William Frederick and Queen Rebecca (Dickerson) F.; student Purdue U., 1939-40; 1 dau., Catherine F. Real estate broker, Chgo., 1946-54; gen. sales mgr. Swift Homes, Inc., Pitts., 1954-62; v.p. sales Gen. Homes subs. Koppers Co., Ft. Wayne, Ind., 1962-64; pres. C.F. Franklin & Co., Inc., Ft. Wayne, 1964—. Pres., Allied Real Estate Bd., Chgo., 1954. Served with USCGR, 1942-45. Mem. Ft. Wayne Bd. Realtors, Nat. Assn. Flight Instrs., Am. Legion, Soaring Soc. Am., Quiet Birdmen, Aircraft Owners and Pilots Assn. Clubs: Masons, Shriner, K.T., Royal Order Jesters, Elks, Kiwanis. Address: 9622 Aboite Center Rd Fort Wayne IN 46802

FRANKLIN, DELANCE FLOURNOY, horticulture educator; b. Yakima County, Wash., Apr. 9, 1909; s. Watson Miller Taylor and Hattie Belle (Flournoy) F.; m. Florence Rebecca Kooser, Sept. 3, 1935; children: DeLance Flournoy Jr., Eleanor Gay. BS in Agriculture, U. Idaho, 1942, MS in Agriculture, 1955. Food products inspector Idaho State Dept. Agriculture, 1928-39; asst. horticulturist U. Idaho, Parma, 1942-45, assoc. horticulturist, 1945-50; supr. Agricultural Research and Extension Ctr., Parma, 1942-74; research prof. horticulture U. Idaho, Parma, 1950-74, research prof. emeritus, 1974—; collaborator USDA, 1942-74, cons. 1974—; cons. to U.N., Cairo, 1974; chmn., co-founder Nat. Carrot and Onion Improvement Program, 1960; originator numerous F, hybrid onions and carrots; sec. Idaho Seed Council, 1955-73; cons. Vegetable Seed Prodn. and Breeding, 1974—. Contbr. numerous articles to profl. jours. Trustee Parma Devel. Corp., 1955-60, Sch. Bd., Parma, 1945-50, Idaho State Redevel. Bd., Boise, 1968-74. Named Disting. Citizen, Idaho Statesman Newspaper, 1968, Man-of-Yr., Pacific Seedsmen's Assn., 1968; recipient Disting. Service award Idaho-Eastern Oreg. Seed Assn., 1971, U. Idaho Gold and Silver award, 1985. Mem. Idaho Seed Council (hon.), Idaho Seed Assn. (hon.), Parma C. of C. (pres. 1943-45), Nat. Carrot and Onion Confs., SW Idaho-Eastern Oreg. Onion Assn. (Hall of Fame 1987), Am. Hort. Sci., Nat. Soc. Horticulturists, Entomologists and Plant Pathologists (pres. 1958-59), Sigma Xi, Alpha Zeta (Chancellor 1941—), Phi Gamma Delta, Gamma Sigma Delta. Republican. Lodge: Shriners, Lions (pres. Parma club 1949—). Home: 227 N 10th St Parma ID 83660

FRANKLIN, FREDERICK RUSSELL, legal association executive; b. Berlin, Germany, Mar. 20, 1929; s. Ernest James and Frances (Price) F.; A.B., Ind. U., 1951, J.D. with high distinction, 1956; m. Barbara Ann Donovan, Jan. 26, 1952; children—Katherine Elizabeth, Frederick Russell. Bar: Ind. 1956. Trial atty. criminal div. and ct. of claims sect., civil div. U.S. Dept. Justice, Washington, 1956-60; gen. counsel Ind. State Bar Assn., Indpls., 1960-67; dir. continuing legal edn. for Ind., adj. prof. law Ind. U., Indpls., 1965-68; staff dir. profl. standards Am. Bar Assn., Chgo., 1968-70; exec. v.p. Nat. Attys. Title Assurance Fund, Inc., Indpls., 1970-72; staff dir. legal edn. and admissions to the bar Am. Bar Assn., Chgo., 1972—. Trustee, Olympia Fields (Ill.) United Methodist Ch., 1980-84; treas. bd. dirs. Olympia Fields Pub. Library, 1984—; mem. Olympia Fields Police Bd., 1983—. Served to capt. USAF, 1951-53. Mem. Am., Ind., Ill. bar assns., Fed. Bar Assn. (officer, found. bd. dirs. 1974—, historian 1979—, nat. council 1965—, nat. v.p. 1967-69, chpt. pres. 1965-66, chmn. admission to practice and recert. com. 1980-82, bd. dirs. Chgo. chpt. 1984—), Nat. Orgn. Bar Counsel (pres. 1967), Order of Coif, Phi Delta Phi. Kiwanian, Elk. Home: 3617 Parthenon Way Olympia Fields IL 60461 Office: 750 N Lake Shore Dr Chicago IL 60611

FRANKLIN, GEORGE S., private commission executive; b. N.Y.C., Mar. 23, 1913; s. George Small and Elizabeth (Jennings) F.; m. Helena Edgell, June 24, 1950; children: Helena, George III, Cynthia, Sheila. Student, U. Grenoble, 1931-32; A.B., Harvard, 1936; LL.B., Yale, 1939. Law clk. Davis, Polk, Wardwell, Gardiner & Reed, 1939; asst. Nelson A. Rockefeller, 1940; div. world trade intelligence Dept. State, 1941-44; assoc. Council on Fgn. Relations, 1945-71, asst. exec. dir., 1951-53, exec. dir., 1953-71; N.Am. sec. Trilateral Commn., 1972-76, coordinator, 1977-82; pres. Trilateral Commn. N. Am., 1982-85, vice-chmn., 1985-88, sr. advisor, 1988—. Life trustee Internat. House, N.Y.C.; former trustee Brearley Sch., N.Y. Soc. Library, Boys Brotherhood Republic, N.Y.C., Robert Coll., Istanbul, Turkey, Council on Fgn. Relations; trustee Atlantic Council U.S., Commn. United World Colls., Salzburg Seminar Am. Studies, French Am. Found.; hon. trustee American Ditchley Found.; hon. chmn. Mid-Atlantic Club; past sec., trustee Am. Com. on United Europe; chmn. bd. Erick Hawkins Dance Co. Presbyterian. Clubs: Century (N.Y.C.), River N.Y.C.), Seawanhaka (Oyster Bay). Home: 1220 Park Ave New York NY 10128 also: 63 Cove Neck Rd Osyter Bay NY 11771 Office: Trilateral Commn 345 E 46th St New York NY 10017

FRANKLIN, MARGARET LAVONA BARNUM (MRS. C. BENJAMIN FRANKLIN), civic leader; b. Caldwell, Kans., June 19, 1905; d. LeGrand Husted and Elva (Biddinger) Barnum; B.A., Washburn U., 1952; student Iowa State Tchrs. Coll., 1923-25, U. Iowa, 1937-38; m. C. Benjamin Franklin, Jan. 20, 1940 (dec. 1983); children—Margaret Lee (Mrs. Michael J. Felso), Benjamin Barnum. Tchr. pub. schs., Union, Iowa, 1925-27, Kearney, Nebr., 1927-28, Marshalltown, Iowa, 1928-40; advance rep. Chautauqua, summers 1926-30. Mem. Citizens Adv. Com., 1965-69; mem. Stormont-Vail Regional Ctr. Hosp. Aux.; bd. dirs. Topeka Pub. Library Found., 1984—. Recipient Waldo B. Heywood award Topeka Civic Theatre, 1967; named Outstanding Alpha Delta Pi Mother of Kans., 1971; Topeka Public Library award, 1977. Mem. DAR (state chmn. Museum 1968-71), AAUW (mem. 50 yrs.), Gemini Group of Topeka, Topeka Geneal. Soc., Topeka Art Guild, Topeka Civic Symphony Soc. (dir. 1952-57, Service Honor citation 1960), Doll Collectors Am., Marshalltown Community Theatre (pres. 1938-40), Topeka Pub. Library Bd. (trustee 1961-70, treas., 1962-65, chmn. 1965-67), Shawnee County Hist. Soc. (dir. 1963-75, sec. 1964-66), Nat. Multiple Sclerosis Soc. (dir. Kans. chpt. 1963-66), Stevengraph Collectors Assn., Friends of Topeka Public Library (dir. 1970-79, Disting. Service award 1980), P.E.O. (pres. chpt. 1956-57, coop. bd. pres. 1964-65, chpt. honoree 1969), Native Sons and Daus. Kans. (life), Topeka Stamp Club, Alpha Beta Gamma, Nonoso. Republican. Mem. Christian Ch. Clubs: Western Sorosis (pres. 1960-61), Minerva (2d v.p. 1984-85), Woman's (1st v.p. 1952-54), Knife and Fork.

FRANKLIN, RAOUL NORMAN, university administrator; b. Hamilton, Auckland, New Zealand, June 3, 1935; s. Norman George and Thelma Brinley (Davis) F.; m. Faith Ivens, July 29, 1961; children: Robert, Nicholas. BSc, B Engring., Auckland U., 1956, MSc, M Engring., 1957; PhD, Oxford (Eng.) U., 1961, DSc, 1978. Sr. research fellow Royal Mil. Coll. Sci. Shrivenham, Swindon, Eng., 1961-63; fellow, tutor Keble Coll., Oxford, 1963-78; lectr. Oxford U., 1966-78, vice chmn. gen. bd. faculties, 1971-74; vice chancellor, prin. City Univ., London, 1978—; chmn. City Tech. Ltd., London, 1978—; cons. U.K. Atomic Energy Authority, 1968—, assessor, 1985—; advisor Dept. Energy, London, 1987—. Author: Plasma Phenomena in Gas Discharges, 1976; editor: Physical Kinetics, 1981, Interaction of Intense Electromagnetic Fields with Plasmas, 1981. Trustee Ruskin Sch. Art, Oxford, 1974-78. Served to capt. U.K. Def. Sci. Corps., 1957-69. Hon. fellow Keble Coll., 1980. Fellow Inst. of Physics, Inst. Math. and Applications, Instn. Elec. Engrs.; mem. Brit. Inst. Mgmt. (companion), Bus. in the Community. Mem. Ch. of Eng. Club: Athenaeum (London). Office: City Univ, Northampton Sq, London EC1V 0HB, England

FRANKLIN, RONALD DAVID, psychologist; b. Pinehurst, N.C., Jan. 1, 1946; s. Carl David and Cletus (Lassiter) F.; B.A., East Carolina U., Greenville, N.C., 1975, M.A., 1978; Ph.D., N.C. State U., 1986; m. Charlene Landis, Dec. 31, 1978; children—Leslie Irene, Alyssa Ward. pres. Am. Atrax, Inc., Raleigh, N.C., 1972—; Mem. Am. Psychol. Assn., N.C. Psychol. Assn., Phi Kappa Phi. Office: Psychol Program Mgr NC Dept Correction Caledonia-Odom Complex Tillery NC 27837

FRANKLIN, WILLIAM DONALD, government official; b. Dacula, Ga., Nov. 26, 1933; s. Thomas Kimsey and Lora Claudia (Martin) F.; m. Carole Lynn McCullough, 1959 (div. 1969); m. Elizabeth Ann Giles, Nov. 25, 1970; children: Braden, Kimette, Laura, Thomas, Amy, Holly. B.S., Austin Peay State U., 1961; M.S., Tex. A&M U., 1963; Sc.D. (hon.), London Research Inst., 1972; Ph.D., U.S. Univ., 1973; A.M.P., Harvard U., 1973; grad. Indsl. Coll. Armed Forces, 1971; grad., Command and Gen. Staff Coll., 1975, Air U., 1977, Nat. Def. U., 1978. Data processing mgr. Boillin-Harrison, Inc., Clarksville, Tenn., 1959-61; economist Tex. A&M U., 1961-63; asst. prof. bus. Upper Iowa U., 1963-64; economist Tex. A&M U., 1964-69; head dept. econs., dir. mgmt. devel. Tenn. Weseleyan Coll., Athens, 1969-75; pres. Econotec Research Co., Athens, Tenn., 1969-75; dep. div. dir. trade and industry analysis div. Bur. Internat. Econ. Affairs, Dept. Labor, Washington, 1975-77; industry economist Fed. R.R. Adminstrn., Dept. Transp., Washington, 1977; div. tech. assessment Fed. Hwy. Traffic Safety Adminstrn., Dept. Transp., Washington, 1977-78; chief airport and consumer affairs br. Office Noise Control and Abatement, EPA, Washington, 1978-81, dir. plans and programs staff, 1981-82; sr. economist Office of Asst. Adminstr. for Air, Noise and Radiation, EPA, Washington, 1982-83; spl. asst. to asst. adminstr. Office of Policy, Planning and Evaluation, EPA, Washington, 1983-84; sr. economist Office of Asst. Adminstr. for Air and Radiation, EPA, 1984-86, dir. EPA Noise Program, Office Fed. Activities, 1986—; fed. coordinator Emergency Transp. for State of Tenn., 1973-76; adj. prof. bus. Nova U., Annandale Campus, 1976—. Author: (with Doyle) Federal Emergency Transportation Preparedness, 1968, Management: Theory and Practice, 1972, Civil Affairs Personnel Survey, 1973, (with Hutson and Ryberg) Community Leadership Developement, 1975; contbr. numerous articles to profl. publs. Chmn. Christian edn. com. Vienna Bapt. Ch., 1985-87; bd. dirs. Statewide Council Community Leadership Tenn., 1973-75, Tenn. Alcohol and Drug Abuse Higher Edn. Planning Council, 1973, Ctr. Govt. Tng. Tenn., 1973-75; mem. Presdl. Exec. Res., Office Pres. U.S., 1966-75; fed. coordinator for emergency transp. State of Tenn., 1973-76; deacon Vienna Bapt. Ch., 1988—. Served with U.S. Army, 1953-58, col. Res. ret. Decorated Army Achievement medal; recipient cert. of acheivement Dept. Def., 1958, Outstanding Achievement award Dept. Def., 1967, Presdl. commendation Pres. of U.S., 1983, Spl. Achievement award EPA, 1982, 87; Woodrow Wilson fellow, 1961; univ. fellow Tex. A&M U., 1961-63; grad. acad. fellow Harvard U., 1971-72. Mem. Harvard U. Bus. Sch. Alumni Assn., Internat. Platform Assn., Res. Officers Assn., Assn. U.S. Army, Phi Sigma Kappa, Phi Alpha Theta. Clubs: Harvard, Harvard Bus. Sch, Capitol Yacht, Officers of Mil. Dist. Washington, Nat. Aviation. Lodges: Lions; Rotary. Home: 509 Lewis St Vienna VA 22180 Office: Office Fed Activities (A-104) Washington DC 20460

FRANKS, HERBERT HOOVER, lawyer; b. Joliet, Ill., Jan. 25, 1934; s. Carol and Lottie (Dermer) F.; m. Eileen Pepper, June 22, 1957; children—David, Jack, Eli. B.S., Roosevelt U., 1954. Bar: Ill. 1961, U.S. Dist. Ct. (no. dist.) Ill. 1961, U.S. Supreme Ct. 1967. Ptnr. Franks & Filler, 1985—; chmn. Wonder Lake State Bank, Ill., 1979—; chmn. First Nat. Bank, Marengo, Ill., 1976-81, mem. exec. com., 1976—. Bus. editor Am. U. Law Rev. 1959, 60. State pres. Young Democrats of Ill., 1970-72; trustee Hebrew Theol. Coll., Skokie, Ill., 1974—; trustee, sec. Forest Inst. Profl. Psychology, Des Plaines, Ill., 1979—; chmn. Forest Hosp., Des Plaines, 1980—. Served with U.S. Army, 1956-58. Fellow Ill. State Bar; mem. Ill. Trial Lawyers (mng. bd. 1975—, treas. 1985-87, 88—), Sigma Nu Phi (pres. 1980-82). Lodges: Masons, Shriners. Home: 19324 E Grant Hwy Marengo IL 60152 Office: Franks & Filler 19333 E Grant Hwy Marengo IL 60152

FRANKS, HERSCHEL PICKENS, judge; b. Savannah, Tenn., May 28, 1930; s. Herschel R. and Vada (Pickens) F.; m. Joan Loope, June 2, 1935; 1 dau., Ramona. Student U. Tenn.-Martin, U. Md.; J.D., U. Tenn.-Knoxville; grad. Nat. Jud. Coll. of U. Nev. Bar: Tenn. 1959, U.S. Supreme Ct. 1968. Claims atty. U.S. Fidelity & Guaranty Co., Knoxville, 1958; ptnr. Harris, Moon, Meacham & Franks, Chattanooga, 1959-70; chancellor 3d Chancery div. of Hamilton County, 1970-78; judge Tenn. Ct. Appeals, Chattanooga, 1978—; spl. justice Tenn. Supreme Ct., 1979, 86, 87; presiding judge Hamilton County Trial Cts., 1977-78. Served with USNG, 1949-50, USAF, 1950-54. Mem. Tenn. Bar Assn. (award of merit 1968-69), Chattanooga Bar Assn. (pres. 1968-69, Founds. of Freedom award 1986), ABA (award of merit), Am. Judicature Soc., Inst. Jud. Adminstrn., Phi Alpha Delta. Mem. United Ch. of Christ. Clubs: Optimist (pres. 1965-66), Community Service award 1971), Mountain City, LeConte, City Farmers, Torch. Address: 540 McCallie Ave Chattanooga TN 37402

FRANSSENS, CONSTANT, banker; b. Tienen, Belgium, Dec. 14, 1922; s. Louis and Valentine Marie (Gilis) F.; m. Marie-louise Picard, Oct. 26, 1963; 1 child, Johanna. MA in Econs., Cath.U. Louvain, Belgium, 1944. Analyst Kredietbank N.V., Brussels, 1944-49; insp. Accountex N.V., Brussels, 1949; holder of procura Kredietbank S.A. Luxembourgeoise, Luxembourg, 1949-

53, asst. mgr., 1953-59, joint mgr., 1959-63, mgr., 1963-68, exec. dir., 1968-69, mng. dir., 1969-87, pres., mng. dir., 1987—; chmn. Henkel Belgium S.A., Egidio Galbani, S.p.A., Italy, Kredietbank (Suisse) S.A.; bd. dirs. numerous banks, holding cos., fin., real estate and mfg. cos. worldwide. Officier de l'Ordre de Léopold; Comdr. de L'Ordre Grand-Ducal de la Couronne de Chêne, Luxembourg; Comdre. de l'Ordre du Mérite Civil et Militaire d'Adolphe de Nassau. Mem. Assn. des Banques et Banquiers Luxembourgeois (pres. 1979-80), Internat. Bankers Assn. Inc. Roman Catholic. Clubs: Cercle Munster (Luxembourg); Cercle Royal Gaulois (Brussels). Home: rue Laach 47, 6945 Niederanven Luxembourg Office: Kredietbank SA Luxembourg, 43 Blvd Royal, 6945 Luxembourg Luxembourg

FRANSSENS, DOUWE HIJLKE, land use planner; b. Aduard, Groningen, Netherlands, Apr. 9, 1924; s. Engelbertus Lodewijk and Grietje (Gerber) F.; m. Susanna Elisabeth de Nies, Mar. 29, 1950; children—Susanna Henriette Margriet Gezina, Engelbertus Lodewijk. Doctorandus Social Geography, U. Amsterdam, 1950. Research asst. Agrl. U., Wageningen, Netherlands, 1949-53; dep. insp. State Domain Bd., The Hague, Netherlands, 1953-56; dep. sec. Landbouwschap, The Hague, 1956-66, sec., 1968-87; head planning dept. Rijnmond-Council, Rotterdam and Schiedam, Netherlands, 1966-68; mem. Nat. Council Phys. Planning, 1965-66, 69-87, coms. Nat. Council of Waterstaat, 1968-87; mem. P.T.T. Council, 1983-87; cons. landed property; mem. adv. com. Initiative Group Markerwaard, 1987—. Author: (with others) Boer en Cooperatie in Zelhem, 1953; contbr. articles on land use planning to profl. jours. Supervisory council Nat. Tourist Orgn. A.N.W.B., 1976-87; v.p. Soc. Waterstaat en Landinrichting, 1979-87. Mem. Netherlands Inst. Phys. Planning and Housing, Royal Soc. Agrl. Scis. (past pres. sect. agrl. economy). Liberal. Lodge: Rotary, Ordre van Oranje Nassau (officer 1987). Home and Office: Frankenstraat 53, 2582 SG The Hague The Netherlands

FRANTSVE, DENNIS JOHN, graphics company executive, educator, columnist; b. Chgo., Mar. 14, 1938; s. Carl Henning and Elizabeth Dorothy (Waldock) F.; m. Julieta Maria Chacon, Oct. 26, 1967; children—Lisa, Julie, Dennis. B.S. in Commerce, DePaul U., 1969, MBA in Mktg., 1988. Cost acct. R.R. Donnelley & Sons Inc. Chgo., 1956-60; supr. Gregg Moore Co., Chgo., 1965-69; prodn. coordinator Regensteiner Press, Chgo., 1969-70; supr. Acme Press, Chgo., 1970-72; print buyer Beslow Assocs., Inc., Chgo., 1972-74; exec. v.p. Darby Graphics, Chgo., 1974—. Tchr., Printing Industry Ill. Assn., 1973—. Served with USAR, 1957-63. Honored at testimonial Internat. San. Supply Assn., 1979; recipient cert. of appreciation Printing Industry Ill. Assn., 1980. Mem. Am. Mktg. Assn., Internat. Assn. Bus. Communicators, Publ. Club Chgo., Soc. Nat. Assn. Publs., Pan Am. Council, Park Ridge C. of C. (dir. 1980—; cert. of appreciation 1981). Clubs: Toastmasters (treas.) (Des Plaines, Ill.); N.W. Press, PII Sales (Chgo.). Author: Printing Production Management, 1983; columnist Am. Printer mag., 1976—. Home: 215 N Chester Ave Park Ridge IL 60068 Office: 4015 N Rockwell St Chicago IL 60618

FRANZ, JERRY LOUIS, cardiac surgeon; b. Decatur, Ind., Aug. 5, 1943; s. Lyle D. and Helen J. (Martin) F.; B.S. in Chemistry, Ohio No. U., 1965; M.S. in Bacteriology, U. Fla., 1967; M.D., U. Ky., 1971; m. Jennie Rose Heim, June 20, 1970. Intern surgery U. Ky. Hosps., Lexington, 1971-72; jr. asst. resident surgery Bexar County Hosp., San Antonio, 1972-73, resident surgery, 1973-76, adminstrv. resident surgery, 1975-76, resident cardiothoracic surgery, 1976-78. Diplomate Am. Bd. Surgery, Am. Bd. Thoracic Surgery. Fellow Am. Coll. Surgeons; mem. Am. Coll. Chest Physicians, Bexar County Med. Soc., AMA, Tex. Med. Assn., Assn. for Acad. Surgery, J. Bradly Anst Surg. Soc. (pres. 1983-84), Cooley Cardiovascular Soc., Soc. Thoracic Surgery, So. Thoracic Soc., Contbr. articles to profl. jours. Home: 920 Holston Ave Bristol TN 37620 Office: 350 Blountville Hwy #201 Bristol TN 37620

FRANZ, WOLFGANG, economics educator; b. Nassau, Fed. Republic Germany, Jan. 7, 1944. Diploma Volkswirt, U. Mannheim, Fed. Republic Germany, 1970, Dr. Rer. Pol., 1974, Dr. Habil., 1981. Prof. econs. U. Mannheim, 1982-83, U. Mainz, Fed. Republic Germany, 1984, U. Stuttgart, Fed. Republic Germany, 1984—. Author: Econometric Model, 1974, Youth Unemployment, 1982. Mem. Gesellschaft für Wirtschafts und Sozialwissenschaften, Am. Econ. Assn. Home: Birkenwaldstrasse 185A, 7000 Stuttgart Federal Republic of Germany Office: U Stuttgart, Friedrichstrasse 10, 7000 Stuttgart Federal Republic of Germany

FRANZEN, CHARLES KUGLER, educator, actor; b. Bloomington, Ind., Jan. 7, 1926; s. Carl Gustave Frederick and Florence Josephine (Buker) F.; B.S., Western N.Mex. U., 1949; M.S., Ind. U., 1953; Ed.D., Duke U., 1961; m. Nancy Morris Edwards, Aug. 14, 1951; children—Stephen Edwards, Timothy Charles. Secondary sch. tchr., coach, public schs., Tex., Va., 1949-57; prin. elem. sch., Martinsville, Va., 1957-59; instr. Duke U., 1960-61; asst. prof. elem. edn. Furman U., 1961-66; asso. dir. Multi-State Tchr. Edn. Project, Balt., 1966-68; dir. Atlanta Area Tchr. Edn. Service, Emory U., 1968—; assoc. prof. curriculum and supervision U. Ga., 1968—; ednl. cons. to Atlanta area sch. systems; actor TV commls. and feature films. Active Onstage Atlanta. Served with USAAF, 1944-45. Mem. Am. Ednl. Research Assn., Assn. Supervision and Curriculum Devel., Assn. Tchr. Educators, Ga. Assn. Tchr. Educators, (pres. 1978-79), S.E. Regional Assn. Tchr. Educators (pres. 1978-79), Ga. Assn. Curriculum and Instructional Supervision (exec. sec. 1984—), Screen Actors Guild (v.p. Ga. br. 1986-88, pres. Ga. br. 1987—), AFTRA. Episcopalian. Author: (with E.L. Dambruch) Governance of Teacher Centers, 1975. Home: 988 Viscount Ct Avondale Estates GA 30002 Office: Coll Edn U Ga Athens GA 30602

FRANZÉN, LARS OLOF, literary critic, novelist; b. Vryd, Östergötland, Sweden, June 21, 1936; s. Sven and Gun (Holmberger) F.; m. Inger Maria Alfvén, June 28, 1985; children: Mattias, Kristofer. Student, Göteborgs U., Sweden, 1960. Literary critic, editor Dagens Nyheter, Stockholm, 1965—. Author: (essays) Omskrivninger, 1968, Danska Bilder, 1971; (novels) Instrumentmakarna, 1981, De Rätta Älskarna, 1983, Konrad, 1986, Fikonträdet, 1988. Recipient award Djerassi Found., Woodside, Calif., 1986. Mem. Svenska Journalistför Bundet, Sveriges forfattarforbund, PEN Internat. Home: Gillsätragränd 96, S-12756 Skärholmen Sweden Office: Dagens Nyheter, S-10515 Stockholm Sweden

FRANZ JOSEF, II, Prince of Liechtenstein; b. Frauenthal, Aug. 16, 1906; s. Alois and Elisabeth, Archduchess of Austria; student Schottengymnasium Wien, forest engring. U. Wien; m. Georgine, countess Wilczek, Mar. 7, 1943; children—Hans-Adam, Philipp, Nikolaus, Nora, F.J. Wenzel. Succeeded grand-uncle Prince Francis I, as reigning prince of Liechtenstein, 1938—. Address: Office of Head of State, Vaduz Liechtenstein *

FRANZKE, HERMANN ROBERT, business executive, architect; b. Essen, Fed. Republic Germany, June 21, 1930; s. Hermann and Mia (Roettger) F.; m. Elisabeth Daey Ouwens; children: Dominique, Nicholas. Diploma in architecture, Rheinisch Westfalische Tech. Hochschule, Aachen, Fed. Republic Germany, 1956. Architect designer Suter & Suter Architects, Basel, Switzerland, 1957-61; project mgr. Lathrop Douglass FAIA, N.Y.C., 1961-66; architect H.H. Franzke, Essen, 1966-68; mgr., gen. contractor Kufus Constrn. Co., Recklinghausen, Fed. Republic Germany, 1968-75; dir. Robert Bosch GmbH, Stuttgart, Fed. Republic Germany, 1975—; instr. facility planning, U. Stuttgart, 1984—. Contbr. articles to profl. jours. Recipient awards numerous archtl. competitions. Mem. Architekten Kammer BW. Club: Rowing (Stuttgart-Cannstatt). Lodge: Lions. Home: Hainbuchenweg 5, D 7000 Stuttgart 70 Federal Republic of Germany Office: Robert Bosch GmbH, PO Box 50, 1 Stuttgart Federal Republic of Germany

FRANZKOWSKI, RAINER, association executive; b. Berlin, Apr. 8, 1935; s. Karl and Johanna (Robbert) R.; m. Hanna Maria Doring, Jan. 11, 1963; children—Johannes, Cornelia. Diplom-Ingenieur, Tech. U. Berlin, 1966. Factory engring. mgr. electron tube div. AEG-Telefunken, Berlin, 1966-70, Ulm, Fed. Republic Germany, 1970-79; factory engring. mgr. Videocolor GMBH, color picture tube prodn., Ulm, 1979-80; edn. and tng. mgr. German Soc. Quality, Frankfurt, 1980—; lectr. quality tech., 1977—; chmn. com. statis. methods European Orgn. for Quality Control, 1983—; mem. tech. com. statis. methods Internat. Orgn. Standardization and Deutsches Instituta Normung, 1980—. Mem. Deutsche Physikalische Gesellschaft, Verein Deutscher Ingenieure, Deutsche Statistische Gesellschaft, European Orgn. Quality Control, Deutsche Gesellschaft Qualitat, Am. Soc. Quality Control, Am. Statis. Assn. Home: 18 An Der Eiskaut, D 6390 Usingen Federal Republic Germany Office: 95 Kurhessenstrasse, D-6000 Frankfurt-Main Federal Republic of Germany

FRANZ-WILLING, GEORG, scientist, historian; b. Bad Aibling, Germany, Mar. 11, 1915; s. Karl Ludwig and Theresia Franz-Willing; m. Hildegard Suhm Franz, Dec. 2, 1961; children—Siegfried, Ingeborg. Student U. Munich, 1937-39. Collaborator Suedostinstitut, Munich, 1938-52, Institut fuer Kultur-und Sozialforschung, Munich, 1952-55; educator Albertinum, Tegernsee, 1955-58; collaborator Ost-Europa-Institut Munich, 1958-59; tchr. Marine-Offiziersschule, Flensburg-Muerwik, 1960-63; collaborator Militaergeschichtliches Forschungs amt, Freiburg, 1963-78. Contbr. articles to profl. jours. Mem. Gesellschaft fuer Religions und Geistesgeschichte, Ranke-Gesellschaft, Gesellschaft fuer Wehrforschung. Roman Catholic. Avocations: astronomy, ornithology. Address: Seehaldenstrasse 3, B-7770 Ueberlingen/Bodensee Federal Republic of Germany

FRAPPE, THIERRY ANDRÉ MARIE JOSEPH, physician; b. Forest/Marque, North, France, May 23, 1952; s. Joseph Camille and Madeleine Henriette (Regent) F.; m. Monique Marie Logez, Dec. 29, 1981; children: Quentin, Anaïs. MD, U. Lille (France), 1981. Physician Arras, France, 1979-81; gen. practitioner Bruay en Artois, France, 1982—. Lodge: Rotary (Bruay en Artois). Office: Rue de Bourgogne 12, 62700 Bruay France

FRASER, JOHN GILLIES, retired minister; b. Glasgow, Scotland, July 5, 1914; s. John and Catherine Boyd (Gillies) F.; m. Jessie MacKenzie Mayer, June 29, 1949; children: Elizabeth Goddes, Catherine Gillies, Alexander Mayer, Janet MacKenzie. Student, Shawlands Acad., Glasgow, 1931; diploma in Pub. Adminstrn., Glasgow U., 1934; diploma in Soc. Studies, Glascow U., 1936; degree, Ch. of Scotland Trinity Coll., 1950. Pub. asst., poor law insp. City of Glasgow, 1931-48; exec. officer Ministry Nat. Ins., Glasgow, 1948; ordained missionary Ch. of Scotland, Kitwe, N. Rhodesia, 1951-54, Lubwa, Rhodesia, 1955-59; minister Ch. of Scotland Elderpark MacGregor Meml. Ch., Glasgow, 1960-86. Joint chmn. Ch. of Scotland Livingstonia Fellowship, Edinburgh, 1985—; chmn. Ch. of Scotland Total Abstainers Assn., 1980—. Mem. Nat. Ch. Assn. (vice chmn. 1986), Scottis Assn. (chmn. Lord's Day Observance Soc. 1983—). Home: 17 Beaufort Gardens, Bishopbriggs, Glasgow G64 2DJ, Scotland

FRASER, ROBIN, pathology educator; b. Melbourne, Australia, Dec. 20, 1933; came to N.Z. 1974; s. Malcolm and Kathlen Elizabeth (Gault) F.; m. Isabel Emily Gidney, Aug. 14, 1957 (div. 1976); children: Elizabeth Jean, Jane Caroling, Simon Hugh, Sarah Anne; m. Linda Marjorie Bowler, May 5, 1979; children: Kate Victoria, Rachel Lucille. BSc, U. Sydney, 1956, MB, BS, 1958; PhD, Australian Nat. U., 1968; MD, U. Otago, 1987. Registered med. practitioner N.Z. Resident Royal Prince Alfred Hosp., Sydney, 1958-59, sr. resident, 1959-60, registrar, 1960-61; gen. practice physician Coonabarabran, Australia, 1961-66; postgrad. scholar John Curtin Sch. Med. Research, Canberra, Australia, 1966-68; USPHS fellow in pathology U. Chgo., 1969-70; sr. lectr. pathology U. Sydney, 1970-74; assoc. prof. pathology Christchurch (N.Z.) Sch. Medicine, 1974-78; acting chmn. dept. pathology U. Otago, Christchurch, 1987—; dir. project grants N.Z. Med. Research Council, 1974-87. Contbr. articles to internat. jours. Fellow Royal Coll. Pathologists Australia; mem. Sigma Xi. Home: 45 Kidson Terr, Christchurch 2, New Zealand Office: Christchurch Sch Medicine, Christchurch Hosp, Christchurch New Zealand

FRATER, ROBERT WILLIAM MAYO, surgeon, educator; b. Cape Town, South Africa, Nov. 12, 1928; came to U.S., 1964, naturalized, 1974; s. Kenneth and Ethel (Barrow) F.; m. Elaine Glynn Nagle, Aug. 27, 1954; children: Hugh R., Dirk A., Phillipa. M.B., B.Chir. (Jagger Scholar, Medalist, Anatomy, Surgery, Pathology), U. Cape Town Med. Sch., 1952; M.S. in Surgery (Minn. Heart Assn. fellow), U. Minn., 1961. Intern medicine and surgery Groote Schuur Hosp., Cape Town, 1953; resident casualty officer Lewisham Hosp., London, 1955; fellow in gen. and thoracic surgery Mayo Clinic, Rochester, Minn., 1955-61; sr. lectr. cardiothoracic surgery U. Cape Town, 1962-64; asst. prof. surgery Albert Einstein Coll. Medicine, N.Y.C., 1964-68; assoc. prof. Albert Einstein Coll. Medicine, 1968-72, prof. surgery, 1972—, chief cardiothoracic surgery, 1968—, acting chmn. dept. surgery, 1971-75; mem. Albert Einstein Coll. Medicine (Senate Council), 1971-74; chief cardiothoracic surgery Montefiore Hosp. and Med. Center, 1975—; mem. staff, exec. council Bronx Mcpl. Hosp. Center, Albert Einstein Coll. Hosp., 1969—; mem. staff Lawrence Hosp., Bronxville, N.Y.; mem. organizing com. Internat. Symposium on Cardiac Bioprostheses, 1985, 88, honored guest, 1985. Mem. editorial bd. Cardiac chronicle, Jour. Cardiac Surgery, 1987—. Mem. Concern for Dying Council, 1982—; active sci. com. Internat. Symposium onBioprosthesis, 1982, 85,88. Recipient award Noble Found., 1961; NIH grantee, 1965-70, 68-70, 74-78, 79-81, 82-84; Am. Heart Assn. grantee, 1966, 71. Fellow Royal Coll. Surgeons, A.C.S., Am. Coll. Cardiology; mem. Am. Assn. Thoracic Surgery, Soc. Thoracic Surgeons (postgrad. edn. com. 1978—, chmn. postgrad. program 1981), N.Y. Soc. Thoracic Surgery (pres. 1978), N.Y. Surg. Soc. (mem. council 1975-80), Thoracic Surgery Dirs. Assn. (exec. council 1982-85), Assn. Acad. Surgeons, Am. Heart Assn. (exec. com. Council on Cardiovascular Surgery 1979-84, program com. 1979-82), Sigma Xi, Alpha Omega Alpha. Club: Bronxville Field (Squash capt., bd. govs. 1987—). Home: 17 Gladwin Pl Bronxville NY 10708 Office: 1300 Morris Park Ave Bronx NY 10461

FRAZIER, HENRY BOWEN, III, government official, lawyer; b. Bluefield, W.Va., Aug. 9, 1934; s. Henry Bowen and Margaret Beale (West) F.; m. Joan McIntosh, Dec. 30, 1959. B.A. with honors, U. Va., 1956; J.D. with honors, George Washington U., 1967; LL.M. in Labor Law, Georgetown U., 1969, M.L.T., 1985. Bar: Va. 1967, D.C. 1980. Personnel adminstr. Army Dept. Washington, 1959-63, spl. projects officer, 1963-67; dep. for civilian personnel policy and civil rights Office Sec. Army, 1967-70; chief program div. Fed. Labor Relations Council, Exec. Office Pres., 1970-71, dep. exec. dir., 1971-72, exec. dir., 1973-78; mem. Fed. Labor Relations Authority, Washington, 1979-87, acting chmn., 1984-85; adminstrv. law judge EPA, Washington, 1987—; chmn. Employee Relations Commn., U.S. Fgn. Service, 1979-81; acting chmn. Fgn. Service Labor Relations Bd., 1984-85. Served with USAF, 1961-62. Recipient W.H. Kushnick award Sec. Army, 1968, Exceptional Civilian Service award, 1970, spl. commendation award Dir. OMB, 1978. Mem. ABA, Soc. Fed. Labor Relations Profs., Soc. Profs. in Dispute Resolution, Jefferson Soc., Indsl. Relations Research Assn., SAR, U. Va. Alumni Assn. (nat. v.p. 1984-85; nat. pres. 1985-86, bd. mgrs. 1980-87), Raven Soc., Order of Coif, Phi Beta Kappa, Omicron Delta Kappa, Phi Kappa Psi. Office: US EPA 401 M St SW A110 Washington DC 20460

FRAZIER, WALTER RONALD, real estate investment company executive; b. Dallas, Mar. 3, 1939; s. Walter and Gracie Neydene (Bowers) F.; m. Bertina Jan Simpson, May 10, 1963; children—Ronald Blake, Stephen Bertram. B.S. in Civil Engring., Tex. A&M U., 1962, B.S. in Archtl. Constrn., 1962. Tech. dir. Marble Inst., Washington, 1965-68; dir. mktg. Yeonas Co., Vienna, Va., 1969-72; pres. McCarthy Co., Anaheim, Calif., 1972-76, The Frazier Group, Annandale, Va., 1977-79; chmn. Equity Programs Investment Corp., Falls Church, Va., 1980-85; pres., dir. Community Constrn. Co., Falls Church, 1982-85; pres. Palestrina Corp., Falls Church, 1986—; bd. dirs. Annandale Jaycees, 1967-69, Annandale Nat. Little League, 1983-85. Served to 1st lt. U.S. Army, 1963-65. Named to Outstanding Young Men Am., U.S. Jaycees, 1973. Republican. Methodist. Avocations: golf; boating. Home: 4203 Elizabeth Ln Annandale VA 22003 Office: Palestrina Corp 5119A Leesburg Pike Suite 249 Falls Church VA 22041

FREBERG, STAN(LEY) (VICTOR), satirist; b. Los Angeles, Calif., Aug. 7, 1926; s. Victor Richard and Evelyn Dorothy (Conner) F.; m. Donna Andresen; children: Donna Jean, Donavan Stanley. Recording artist Capitol Records, Hollywood; pres. Freberg Ltd., 1958. Author: It Only Hurts When I Laugh, 1988; comedy albums include Stan Freberg Presents The U.S.A., Child's Garden of Freberg, St. George and the Dragonet; actor, writer; children's TV show Time for Beany (Winner 3 Emmys). Mem. founding bd. of govs. Nat. Acad. of Recording Arts and Scis. Recipient Best Written Comedy Radio Show, CBS, 1957, Grammy award 1958, Gold Medal N.Y. Art Dirs., 21 Clios, Cannes Film Festival, Grand Prize, Venice Film Festival; star Hollywood Walk of Fame. Mem. ASCAP, Songwriters Hall of Fame, Composers and Lyricists Guild, Writers Guild of Am., Dirs. Guild of Am. Home: 911 N Beverly Dr Beverly Hills CA 90210

FREDENBURG, DAVID MARSHALL, SR., data processing executive, consultant, system designer; b. Fargo, N.D., Apr. 16, 1932; s. David Ralph and Mary Elizabeth (Davies) F.; m. Audrey Frances Brown, Apr. 11, 1959; children: David Marshall Jr., Dane Michael, Debra Michelle. B.S.E.E., U. Wash., 1954. Mem. tech. staff reliability Aerospace Corp., El Segundo, Calif., 1965-69; mgr. project control Computer Scis., Corp., El Segundo, 1969-73; mgr. product assurance data systems Lear Siegler, Grand Rapids, Mich., 1973-80, Northrop DSD, Rolling Meadows, Ill., 1980-83, Simmonds Precision, Vergennes, Vt., 1983—, also project leader, cons.; cons. Nat. Ski Patrol, Denver; ind. product assurance cons., Torrance, Calif., 1968-73. Contbr. articles to profl. publs. Nat. adviser Nat. Ski Patrol System, Denver, 1959-65, regional officer, Wash., Colo., Calif. and Mich., 1954-82. Named Outstanding Ski Patroller, 1978, also recipient 3 Gold Star Service awards Nat. Ski Patrol System, 1955, 64, 82; named Outstanding Profl. Engr. Northrop Def. System Div., 1982. Mem. Astron. Soc. (v.p. 1955-58), Hunting Beach C. of C. (chmn. polit. action 1970-73), Huntington Beach C. of C. (v.p. 1971-75). Republican. Baptist. Lodge: Rotary. Home: Box 2933 RD 2 Charlotte VT 05445 Office: Simmonds Precision Panton Rd Vergennes VT 05491

FREDERICKS, CARLTON, nutritionist, researcher, author, educator; b. N.Y.C., Oct. 23, 1910; s. David Charles Caplan and Blanche Goldsmith; m. Betty Shachter, Oct. 26, 1946; children: Alice, April, Dana, Spencer, Rhonda. B.A., U. Ala., 1931; M.A., NYU, 1949, Ph.D., 1955. Dir. edn. Casimir Funk Lab., N.Y.C., 1939-44; nat. broadcaster local and network radio N.Y.C., 1941-83; dir. nutrition services Atkins Med. Ctr., N.Y.C., 1982—; nutrition cons. Dr. Paul Rosch, Yonkers, N.Y., 1983—; vis. prof. edn. Fairleigh Dickinson U., Rutherford, N.J., 1974-82; bd. dirs. Am. Inst. Stress, Yonkers, N.Y., 1982—; founding fellow Internat. Coll. Applied Nutrition, La Habra, Calif., 1955—. Author: Low Blood Sugar and You, 1969 (ABA award 1970), Nutrition Guide, 1982, Program for Living Longer, 1983. Recipient Rachel Carson Found. award, 1982; recipient citations Huxley Inst., N.Y.C., 1980, citations Internat. Acad. Metabology, Los Angeles, 1980, Disting. Achievement award Fairleigh Dickinson U., 1984. Fellow Internat. Acad. Preventive Medicine (hon. pres.), Internat. Acad. Metabology (hon. pres.), Royal Soc. Health, Price-Pottenger Found., Internat. Acad. Orthomolecular Medicine ((hon. mem.)); mem. Phi Beta Kappa. Home: 5 Patricia Dr New York NY 10956 Office: Atkins Center for Alternate Therapy 400 E 56th St New York NY 10022

FREDERICKS, DAVID MICHAEL, venture capitalist; b. Balt., Sept. 17, 1950; s. John Leonard and Emily F.; 1 dau., Marcy Lee. B.S. in Mgmt., Indiana U. of Pa., 1972. C.P.A., N.Y. State. Owner, ptnr. K & F Constrn., L.I., N.Y., 1967-69, ICW, Ltd., L.I., 1969-71; staff acct. Price Waterhouse & Co., L.I., 1972-75; ptnr. Touche Ross & Co., N.Y.C., 1975-85; mng. dir. Fredericks Michael & Co., N.Y.C., 1985—; chmn. Circle C Trucking, Inc., 1986—; bd. dirs. Hobart McIntosh Inc. Contbr. in field. Mem. Concerned Citizens of Montauk (N.Y.), 1976—; bd. dirs. N.Y. Gilbert & Sullivan Players, N.Y.C., 1982-86; mem. Democratic Bus. Council N.Y., 1984-85; mem. nat. steering com. Alan Cranston's Bid for Presidency. Mem. Am. Inst. C.P.A.s, N.Y. State Soc. C.P.A.s (chmn. acctg. and auditing com. Suffolk County chpt. 1980-81), Nat. Venture Capital Assn. Roman Catholic. Clubs: India House, N.Y. Athletic (N.Y.C.). Home: Dogwood St PO Box 520 Montauk NY 11954 Office: One World Trade Ctr 15th Floor Suite 1509 New York NY 10048

FREDERICKS, HENRY JACOB, lawyer; b. St. Louis, Dec. 1, 1925; s. Henry Jacob III and Mary Elizabeth (Pieron) F.; m. Marjorie Helen Kiely, 1951 (div. 1962); children: Joseph Henry, James Andrew, Elizabeth Ann.; m. Susan Kay Brennecke, 1971; 1 child, William Michael. JD, St. Louis U., 1950; postgrad., Sch. Commerce and Fin., 1945-47. Bar: Mo. 1950, U.S. Dist. Ct. (ea. and so. dists.) Mo. 1951, U.S. Ct. Appeals (8th cir.) 1978, U.S. Supreme Ct. 1986. Sole practice St. Louis County, 1950-80; assoc. Mark D. Eagleton, St. Louis, 1960, Goldenhersh Fredericks & Newman, St. Louis, 1961-69, Friedman and Fredericks, St. Louis, 1969-81; chief trial atty for cir. atty. St. Louis, 1955, 1st asst. to cir. atty., 1957, spl. asst to cir atty., 1960-81; asst. atty. U.S. Dist. Ct. (ea. dist.) Mo.; lectr. in field. Mem. Mo. Athletic Commn., 1974-76, boxing chmn. Mo. Athletic Commn. and AAU, 1977. Served with USAAF, 1943-46, ETO. Decorated Air medal with 4 battle stars. Mem. ABA, Mo. Bar Assn., St. Louis County Bar Assn., Am. Trial Lawyers Assn., Internat. Platform Assn., Delta Theta Phi. Home: 2243 Whitby Rd Clarkson Valley MO 63017 Office: US Ct and Custom House Office US Atty Saint Louis MO 63101

FREDERICKS, MARSHALL MAYNARD, sculptor; b. Rock Island, Ill., Jan. 31, 1908; s. Frank A. and Frances Margaret (Bragg) F.; m. Rosalind Bell Cooke, Sept. 9, 1943; children: Carl Marshall and Christopher Matzen (twins), Frances Karen Bell, Rosalind Cooke, Suzanne Pelletreau. Student, John Huntington Poly. Inst., Cleve.; grad., Cleve. Sch. Art, 1930; student, Heimann Schule, Schwegerle Schule, Munich, Germany, Academie Scandinav, Paris, France; pvt. studies, Copenhagen, Rome and London, Carl Milles' Studio, Stockholm, Sweden; student, Cranbrook Acad. Art; 3 hon. doctorate degrees in fine arts. Faculty Cleve. Sch. Art, 1931, Cranbrook Sch., Bloomfield Hills, Mich., 1932-38; Kingswood Sch., Cranbrook, 1932-42, Cranbrook Acad. Art, Bloomfield Hills, Mich., 1932-42; Royal Danish consul. for, Mich. Local, nat., internat. exhbns. art since 1928 include, Carnegie Inst., Pitts., Cleve. Mus., Pa. Acad., Chgo. Art Inst., Whitney Mus Am. Art Nat. Invitational, Detroit Art Inst., Denver Mus., Phila. Internat. Invitational, N.Y. World's Fair Am. art exhbn., Modern Sculpture Internat. Exhbn. Detroit, Internat. Sculpture Show Cranbrook Mus., AIA, Nat. Sculpture Soc., Archtl. League of N. Y., Mich. Acad., Brussels, Belgium, Port of History Mus. Phila. Nat. Sculpture Soc. Exhbn.; others; commns. include Vets. Meml. Bldg, Detroit, adminstrn. bldg. war meml., U. Mich., Louisville Courier-Jour. Bldg, Jefferson Sch., Wyandotte, Mich., Holy Ghost Sem., Ann Arbor, Mich.; State Dept. Fountain, Washington, Cleve. War Meml. Fountain, Milw. Pub. Mus. Sculpture, N.Y. World's Fair permanent sculpture, Fed. Bldg. sculpture, Cin., Community Nat. Bank, Pontiac, Mich., Sir Winston Churchill Meml., Freeport, Bahamas; union bldg., Freeport, Bahamas; J.L. Hudson's Eastland, Northland, and Flint (Mich.) Mall, Two Sister fountain, Cranbrook, Michigan, Dallas Library sculpture, Henry Ford Meml., Dearborn, Mich., Oakland U., Saints and Sinners Fountain, Midland Center for Arts, Crittenton Hosp., Rochester, Fgn. Ministry Copenhagen, Freedom of the Human Spirit, Shain Park, Birmingham, Mich., 1986, Wings of the Morning, Kirk-in-the-Hills, Bloomfield Hills, Mich., 1986, many others; portrait commns. include Willard Dow, Midland, Mich., George G. Booth Meml., Cranbrook, Mrs. Horace Rackham Meml, Pres. John F. Kennedy, Yoshita, others; works included numerous museums, pvt., civic collections. Mem. Pres.'s Com. for Employment of Handicapped; mem. Gov.'s State Capitol Com.; co-founder, dir. DIADEM Program for Internat. Exchange of Handicapped.; Trustee Am.-Scandinavian Found., People-to-People Program, Inc. Served with C.E. U.S. Army, 1942-44; lt. col. 20th bomber command; 8th Air Force 1944-45, Okinawa. Decorated knight Order of Dannebrog, also officer 1st class, comdr. Order Dannebrog (Denmark); knights cross 1st class Order of St. Olav (Norway); recipient of 1st prize Cleve. Mus. Art, 1931; Anna Scripps Whitcomb prize Detroit Inst. Arts, 1938; 1st prize internat. exhbn. Dance Internat., Rockefeller Center, N.Y.C.; 1st prize Barbour Meml. nat. competition; medal Mich. Inst. Architects; gold medal Achtl. League of N.Y.; Golden Plate award Am. Acad Achievement; citation Mich. Assn. Professions; citation Nat. Soc. Interior Designers; citation Internat. Com. of Internat. Ctr. Disabled; citation U. Detroit; President's Cabinet award U. Detroit, 1973, 1st prize NAD 160th Ann. Exhbn., 1985, Am. Soc. Landscape Architects award, 1987; Marshall M. Fredericks Sculpture Gallery named in his honor Saginaw Valley State U.; other Am. and fgn. awards and decorations. Fellow Internat. Inst. Arts and Letters, Royal Soc. Arts, Nat. Sculpture Soc. (Henry Heriog medal, Herbert Adams Medal, Medal of Honor 1985, bd. dirs., 1st v.p. Brookgreen Gardens); mem. Mich. Soc. Architects (hon.), Federation Internationale de la Medaille, AIA (fine arts gold medal 1952, Gold Medal), St. Dunstans Dramatic Guild, Mich. Acad. Sci., Arts and Letters (gold medal honor 1953), Nat. Acad. Design (academician, Agop Agopoff award 1987), C. of C., Am. Soc. Interior Designers, Mich. Assn. Professions, Nat. Soc. Interior Designers, Beta Sigma Phi, Alpha Beta Delta. Clubs: Royal Swedish Yacht, Orchard Lake Country; Architectural League N.Y. (N.Y.C.); Prismatic (Detroit); Royal Norwegian Yacht, Royal Danish Yacht. Studio: 4113 N Woodward Ave Royal Oak MI 48053 also: East Long Lake Road Bloomfield Hills MI 48013

FREDERICKS, WARD ARTHUR, internal technology executive; b. Tarrytown, N.Y., Dec. 24, 1939; s. Arthur George and Evelyn (Smith) F.; BS cum laude, Mich. State U., 1962, M.B.A., 1963; m. Patricia A. Sexton, June 12, 1960; children—Corrine E., Lorrine L., Ward A. Assoc. dir. Technics Group, Grand Rapids, Mich., 1964-68; gen. mgr. logistics systems Massey-Ferguson Inc., Toronto, 1968-69, v.p. mgmt. services, comptroller, 1969-73, sr. v.p. fin., dir. fin. Americas, 1975—; comptroller Massey-Ferguson Ltd., Toronto, Ont., Can., 1973-75; cons. W.B. Saunders & Co., Washington, 1962—; sr. v.p. mktg. Massey/Ferguson, Inc., 1975-80, also sr. v.p., gen. mgr. Tractor div., 1978-80; v.p. ops., Rockwell Internat., Pitts., 1980-84; v.p. Fed. MOG., 1983-84; pres. MIXTEC Corp., 1984—, also dir., chmn.; dir. Badger Northland Inc., Tech-Mark Group Inc., MIXTEC Corp., Compu-Kore Ltd., Unicorn Corp., Harry Ferguson Inc., M.F. Credit Corp., M.F. Credit Co. Can. Ltd. Bd. dirs., mem. exec. com. Des Moines Symphony, 1975-79; exec. com. Conejo Symphony,pres. 1988—; mem. exec. com. Alliance for Arts.; mem. Constn. Bicentennial Com., 1987-88, v.p. Com. Leaders Club, 1988, Gov.'s Task Force on Tech., Am. Transp. Assn. fellow, 1962-63; Ramlose fellow, 1962-63. Mem. Am. Mktg. Assn., Nat. Council Phys. Distbn. Mgmt. (exec. com. 1974), IEEE, Soc. Automotive Engrs., U.S. Strategic Inst., Toronto Bd. Trade, Westlake Village C. of C., Community Leaders Club, Pres.'s Club Mich. State U., Beta Gamma Sigma. Rotarian. Author: (with Edward W. Smykay) Physical Distribution Management, 1974, Management Vision, 1988. Contbr. articles to profl. jours. Home: 1640 Aspenwall Rd Westlake Village CA 91361 Office: 32123 Lindero Canyon Rd Westlake Village CA 91361 also: 625 I St Washington DC 11111

FREDERICKS, WESLEY CHARLES, JR., businessman, lawyer; b. N.Y.C., Mar. 31, 1948; s. Wesley Charles and Dionysia W. (Bitsanis) F.; m. Jeanne Maria Judson, May 19, 1973; children: Carolyn Anne, Wesley C. III. BA Johns Hopkins U., 1970; JD, Columbia U., 1973. Bar: N.Y. 1974, Conn. 1976, U.S. Supreme Ct. 1979. Assoc. Shearman & Sterling, N.Y.C., 1973-76, 76-83, Cummings & Lockwood, Stamford, Conn., 1976; dir. Automobile Importers Am., Inc., Washington, 1983-87, British Performance Car Imports, Inc., Norwood, N.J., 1982-86, Carbodies N. Am., Inc., Dover, Del., 1983-84; chmn. bd. Lotus Performance Cars, L.P., Norwood, 1983-86, chief exec. officer, 1986-87; group exec. cons. Group Lotus PLC, 1987—. Honors judge Columbia U. Law Sch. Stone Moot Ct. Honors Program, 1980—; mem. Johns Hopkins U. Alumni Schs. Com.; trustee Wilton Hist. Soc., 1986—. Served with USMC, 1968-69. Mem. Blue Key Soc., Sigma Phi Epsilon. Republican. Congregationalist. Clubs: India House (N.Y.C.); Steering Wheel (London), Sandanona, Campfire Am. (N.Y.); Weston Gun (Conn.). Home: 221 Benedict Hill Rd New Canaan CT 06840 Office: Lotus Cars USA 530 Walnut St Norwood NJ 07648

FREDETTE, RICHARD C., computer specialist; b. Springfield, Mass., June 14, 1934; s. Chester Edward and Lucille Clara (Douillard) F.; A.B. in Econs., Brown U., 1956; grad. cert. in mgmt. info. systems Am. U., 1977; m. Terry G. Schwarzenboeck, Mar. 23, 1959; children—Steven R., Gregory R., Karin I. Br. chief ADP Systems, Naval Air Command, Washington, 1965-67; mgr. naval programming lang. standards Office of Sec. Navy, Washington, 1967-71; dep. dir. naval programming langs. sect. Navy Mgmt. Info. Systems, Washington, 1971-76; dir. tech. transfer, command plans and career mgmt. dept. Naval Data Automation Command, Washington, 1977-86, chmn. fed. ADP users spl. interest group on software, Washington, 1975-81; lectr. Moore Sch. Electronics, U. Pa., Phila., 1968-71, George Washington U. Grad. Sch., 1972-73. Served to lt. USN, 1956-60. Mem. Assn. Computing Machinery, Data Processing Mgmt. Assn., IEEE, Zeta Psi. Republican. Roman Catholic. Contbr. articles to profl. jours. Home: 11605 Sourwood Ln Reston VA 22091 Office: Washington Navy Yard Bldg 166 Washington DC 20374

FREDRIKSSON, KURT BERTIL, software engineer; b. Ostersund, Jamtland, Sweden, Jan. 5, 1932; s. Georg F. and Margareta I. (Karlsson) F.; m. Ragnhild G. Johansson, Nov. 7, 1961; 1 child, Kerstin Gun Maria. BEE, Tech. Inst. of Gothenburg, Sweden, 1968. With L.M. Ericsson, Molndal, Sweden, 1963-68; programmer L.M. Ericsson, Molndal, 1968-69, asst. mgr., 1969-76, dep. mgr., 1976-1984; staff engr. Ericsson Radar Electronics, Molndal, 1984—; Mem. Ericsson Group Tech. Com. for Software. Sec. Liberal Party; served on several civic coms. Served with the Swedish Navy, 1952-53. Mem. Assn. for Computing Machinery, IEEE, Swedish Soc. for Info. Processing. Club: Players Theatre (London). Home: Ringleken 7, S-43169 Molndal Sweden

FREE, ANN COTTRELL, writer; b. Richmond, Va.; d. Emmett Drewry and Emily (Blake) Cottrell; grad. Collegiate Sch. for Girls, Richmond, 1934; student Richmond div. Coll. William and Mary, 1934-36; A.B., Barnard Coll., Columbia, 1938; m. James Stillman Free, Feb. 24, 1950; 1 dau., Elissa. Reporter Richmond Times Dispatch, 1938-40; Washington corr., Newsweek, 1940-41, Chgo. Sun, 1941-43, N.Y. Herald Tribune, 1943-46; pub. information dir. UNRRA China Mission, Shanghai, 1946-47; corr. Middle and Nr. East and Europe, 1947-48; writer-photographer Marshall Plan, Washington and Western Europe, 1949-50; contbr. editor Between the Species; contbr. newspapers and mags.; Washington editor EnviroSouth Quar., 1977-82. Mem. Friends of the Rachel Carson Nat. Wildlife Refuge (hon. founding mem.); chmn. Mrs. Roosevelt's Press Conf. Assn., 1943; cons. expert Rachel Carson Council; chmn. Vieguec Puerto Rico Animal Emergency Fund; coordinator Albert Schweitzer Summer Fellows Program. Recipient Dodd Mead-Boys' Life Writing award, 1963, Albert Schweitzer medal, Animal Welfare Inst., 1963, Jr. Book award certificate Boys Clubs of Am., 1964; Humanitarian of Yr. awards Washington Animal Rescue League, 1971, Montgomery County Humane Soc., 1971, Washington Humane Soc., 1983, News Writing award Dog Writers Assn. Am., 1975, 78, Rachel Carson Legacy award, 1987; recognition Dept. Interior, 1969. Mem. Soc. Woman Geographers. Club: Washington Press, Am. Newswomen's (bd. dirs.). Author: Forever the Wild Mare, 1963; Animals, Nature and Albert Schweitzer, 1982, No Room, Save in the Heart, 1987. Home: 4700 Jamestown Rd Bethesda MD 20816

FREEBORN, (IRENE) SALLY, educator; b. Leeds, Eng., June 22, 1941; d. Benjamin and Bertha (Korn) Bell; children: Richard S., Jason O. BSc, London U., 1975; M in Philosophy, Council Nat. Acad. Awards, 1987. Sr. lectr. Cornwall (Eng.) Coll. Further and Higher Edn., Pool, Redruth, 1969—; originator, co-ordinator implementer program on equal opportunities initiative, 1985. Recipient Fawcett Soc. award for program, 1986. Fellow Royal Micros. Soc.; mem. Nat. Assn. Tchrs. in Further and Higher Edn. (nat. council 1983—). Home: Annesley, Carnon Downs, Truro TR3 6HH, England Office: Cornwall Coll Further &, Higher Edn, Pool, Redruth TR16 3RD, England

FREED, ARTHUR, civil engineer; b. Paris, Dec. 11, 1930 (parents Am. citizens); s. Harry and Mollie (Feinberg) F.; B.C.E., CCNY, 1953; m. Judith Lois Kaplan, July 31, 1960; children: Lisa Anne, Andrew Scott. Jr. civil engr. Westchester County (N.Y.) Dept. Public Works, 1953-58, asst. civil engr., 1958-60, sr. civil engr., 1960-62, traffic engr., 1962-79, dir. traffic engring. and hwy. safety, 1979-86; dep. commr. pub. works, 1986-87, chief of ops., 1987—; exec. dir. Traffic Safety Bd., 1971—. Mem. N.Y. State traffic engring. adv. com. to Dept. Motor Vehicles, 1959-68; mem. Nat. Adv. Com. on Uniform Traffic Control Devices, 1972-79, chmn. Nat. Assn. Counties del.; rep. Pres.'s Com. on Traffic Safety; mem. Hwy. Research Bd. Commn. on Motor Vehicle and Traffic Law, 1965-76; v.p. N.Y. State Assn. Traffic Safety Bds., 1972-79, pres., 1979-81; mem. tech. transfer adv. com. Cornell U.; Westchester Community Coll., 1971—; mem. adv. bd. on tech. transfer Cornell U.; instr. N.Y. State Police Acad.; mem. Gov.'s Youth Safety Com., Gov.'s Task Force on Alcohol and Hwy. Safety; mem. traffic engring. adv. com. N.Y. State Dept. Transp., 1978—. Served with U.S. Army, 1953-55. Recipient award of merit State Traffic Safety Council, 1964; Engr. of Yr. award Internat. Inst. Transp., 1978; award for pub. service Nat. Hwy. Traffic Safety Adminstrn., 1985. Mem. Inst. Transp. Engrs. (pres. N.Y.-N.J. 1965-66, chmn. student activities activities), ASCE, N.Y. Soc. Profl. Engrs. (chmn. career guidance com. Westchester county, state scholastic coordinator, Outstanding Engr. in Community Service award 1982, Outstanding Engr. in Service to the Profession award 1984, Engr. Yr. 1988), Nat. Soc. Profl. Engrs. (pre-coll. guidance com.), Nat. Acad. Sci., N.Y. State Safety Council, Greater N.Y. Safety Council, Hwy. Users Fedn., Am. Pub. Works Assn., Nat. Soc. of Profl. Engrs. (chmn. pre-coll. guidance com.), Am. Rd. and Transp. Builders Assn., Physicians for Auto Safety, Nat. Assn. Counties (chmn. traffic adv. com. 1974—, County Achievement award 1977, 81, 85, 87, award for Initiative in Mgmt.), Nat. Hwy. Traffic Safety Adminstrn. award for Pub. Service, Nat. Assn. County Info. Officers (award of excellence 1981). Registered profl. engr., N.Y. Contbr. articles to profl. jours. Home: 6 Patricia Ln White Plains NY 10605 Office: County Office Bldg White Plains NY 10601

FREEDEN, MICHAEL STEPHEN, political theorist, educator; b. London, Apr. 30, 1944; s. Herbert Hermann and Marianne (Hochdorf) F.; m. Irene Gerszzon, 1968; children: Jonathan, Daniella. BA, Hebrew U. of Jerusalem, 1966; D.Phil., Oxford U., Eng., 1972. Sr. lectr. Haifa U.-Israel, 1972-77; fellow, tutor Mansfield Coll., Oxford U., 1978—. Author: The New Liberalism, 1978, Liberalism Divided, 1986; editor: J.A. Hobson: A Reader, 1988. Fellow Royal Hist. Soc. Office: Mansfield Coll, Oxford Mansfield Rd, Oxford OX1 3TF, England

FREEDMAN, HOWARD JOEL, lawyer; b. Cleve., Jan. 30, 1945; s. Samuel Brooks and Marian (Kirschner) F.; m. Terry Jay Greene, Dec. 22, 1966; children—Randall Greene, Jonathan Jay; m. 2d, Rita Bialosky, June 20, 1981. B.A., Tulane U., 1967; J.D., Case-Western Res. U., 1970. Bar: Ohio 1970. Assoc. Benesch, Friedlander, Coplan & Aronoff and predecessors, Cleve., 1970-75; founding ptnr. Friedman, Freedman & Kurland, and predecessors, Cleve., 1975-85, Goodman Weiss Freedman, Cleve., 1986—. Mem. ABA, Ohio Bar Assn., Bar Assn. Greater Cleve. Club: Cleve. Racquet (Pepper Pike, Ohio). Home: 2951 Montgomery Rd Shaker Heights OH 44122 Office: 100 Erieview Plaza 27th Floor Cleveland OH 44114

FREEDMAN, JAMES OLIVER, lawyer, university president; b. Manchester, N.H., Sept. 21, 1935; s. Louis A. and Sophie (Gottesman) F. AB, Harvard U., 1957; LLB, Yale U., 1962; LLD (hon.), Cornell Coll., 1982; LHD (hon.), St. Ambrose Coll., 1984. Bar: N.H. 1962, Pa. 1971, Iowa 1982. Prof. law U. Pa., 1964-82, assoc. provost, 1978, dean, 1979-82, also univ. ombudsman, 1973-76; pres., disting. prof. law and polit. sci. U. Iowa, 1982-87; pres. Dartmouth Coll., Hanover, 1987—. Author: Crisis and Legitimacy: The Administrative Process and American Government, 1978; editorial bd.: U. Pa. Press, 1974-81; chmn., 1979-82; contbr. articles to profl. jours. Mem. Phila. Bd. Ethics, 1981-82; chmn. Pa. Legis. Reapportionment Commn., 1981; chmn. Iowa Gov.'s Task Force on Fgn. Lang. Studies and Internat. Edn., 1982-83; trustee Jewish Pub. Soc., 1979—; mem. Salzburg Seminar Am. Studies, 1979, 83; bd. dirs. Am. Council on Edn., 1986—. Recipient Scholarship award Pa. chpt. Order of the Coif, 1981; NEH fellow and research vis. fellow Clare Hall Cambridge (Eng.) U., 1976-77; 8th ann. Roy R. Ray lectr. So. Meth. U. Sch. Law, 1985. Mem. Am. Law Inst. Office: Dartmouth Coll Office of Pres 207 Parkhurst Hall Hanover NH 03755

FREEDMAN, KENNETH DAVID, lawyer; b. N.Y.C., Dec. 25, 1947; s. Samuel and Ethel Roberta (Myers) F.; m. Maxine Lantin, July 25, 1976; children—Jill Rose-Sophia, Robert Lantin. B.S., Ariz. State U., 1970; M.Ed., U. Ariz., 1973; J.D., Calif. Western Sch. Law, San Diego, 1979. Bar: Ariz. 1980, D.C. 1985, U.S. Dist. Ct. Ariz. 1980, U.S. Ct. Internat. Trade, 1980, U.S. Ct. Mil. Appeals 1980, U.S. Ct. Appeals (9th cir.) 1980, U.S. Tax Ct. 1981, U.S. Supreme Ct. 1983, D.C. 1985. Grad. asst. U. Ariz., Tucson, 1972-73; adminstr. So. Colo. State Coll., Pueblo, 1973-74; adult probation officer Maricopa County Superior Ct., Phoenix, 1974-76, judge pro tem, 1986—, law clk. to Hon. Robert C. Broomfield, 1979-80; assoc. Hocker, Yarbrough & Gilcrease, Tempe, Ariz., 1980-81; sole practice, Phoenix, 1981—; commr. pro tempore mental health involuntary commitments Juvenile div. Maricopa County Superior Ct., 1980—, commr. mental health, 1988—; instr. Park Coll., Williams AFB, 1976, Phoenix Coll., 1981—, U. Phoenix, 1985—; adj. prof. Ariz. State U., 1988—; mem. disciplinary panel Ariz. State Bar, def. rep. exec. counsel criminal justice sect., mem. coms. legal edn., criminal and continuing legal edn. Served to 1st lt. U.S. Army, 1970-72. Mem. Nat. Assn. Criminal Def. Lawyers, Am. Arbitration Assn. (arbitration panel, 1986—), Ariz. State Univ. Greater Phoenix Alumni Assn. (bd. dirs.), State Bar of Ariz. (cert. specialist criminal law) Maricopa County Bar Assn. (chmn. com. on continuing legal edn. 1983-84, speakers bur.), Phi Alpha Delta. Republican. Jewish. Office: 11 W Jefferson St Suite 810 Phoenix AZ 85003

FREEDMAN, MONROE HENRY, lawyer, educator; b. Mount Vernon, N.Y., Apr. 10, 1928; s. Chauncey and Dorothea (Kornblum) F.; m. Audrey Willock, Sept. 24, 1950; children: Alice Freedman Korngold, Sarah Freedman Izquierdo, Caleb, Judah. AB cum laude, Harvard U., 1951, LLB, 1954, LLM, 1956. Bar: Mass. 1954, Pa. 1957, D.C. 1960, U.S. Ct. Appeals (D.C. cir.) 1960, U.S. Supreme Ct. 1960, U.S. Ct. Appeals (2d cir.) 1968, N.Y. 1978, U.S. Ct. Appeals (9th cir.) 1982, U.S. Ct. Appeals (11th cir.) 1986, U.S. Ct. Appeals (Fed. cir.) 1987. Assoc. Wolf, Block, Schorr & Solis-Cohen, Phila., 1956-58; ptnr. Freedman & Temple, Washington, 1969-73; dir. Stern Community Law Firm, Washington, 1970-71; prof. law George Washington U., 1958-73; dean Hofstra Law Sch., Hempstead, N.Y., 1973-77, prof. law, 1973—; faculty asst. Harvard U. Law Sch., 1954-56, instr. trial advocacy, 1978—; exec. dir. U.S. Holocaust Meml. Council, 1980-82, gen. counsel, 1982-83, sr. adviser to chmn., 1982-87; cons. U.S. Commn. on Civil Rights, 1960-64, Neighborhood Legal Services Program, 1970; legis. cons. to Senator John L. McClellan, 1959; spl. com. on courtroom conduct N.Y.C. Bar Assn., 1972; exec. dir. Criminal Trial Inst., 1965-66; expert witness on legal ethics state and fed. ct. proceedings, U.S. Senate and House Coms., U.S. Dept. Justice; reporter Am. Lawyer's Code of Conduct, 1979-81; mem. Arbitration panel U.S. Dist. Ct. (ea. dist.) N.Y., 1986—; lectr. numerous profl. confs. Author: Contracts, 1973, Lawyers' Ethics in an Adversary System, 1975 (ABA gaval award cert. of merit 1976), Teacher's Manual Contracts, 1978, American Lawyer's Code of Conduct, 1981; vice chmn. editorial bd. ABA Human Rights; reviewing editor Georgetown Jour. Legal Ethics, 1986—; contbr. articles to profl. jours. Recipient Martin Luther King Jr. Humanitarian award, 1987. Fellow Am. Bar Found.; mem. ACLU (nat. bd. dirs. 1970-80, nat. adv. council 1980—, spl. Litigation counsel, 1971-73), Soc. Am. Law Tchrs. (gov. bd. 1974-79, exec. com. 1976-79, chmn. com. on profl. responsibility 1974-79, 87—), ABA (vice chmn. ethical considerations com. criminal justice sect.), N.Y. State Bar Assn. (com. on legal edn. and admission to bar 1987—), D.C. Bar Assn. (chmn. legal ethics com. 1974-76, award of merit 1980, spl. com. on model rules profl. conduct 1983-86), Fed. Bar Assn. (chmn. com. on profl. disciplinary standards and procedures 1970-71), Am. Law Inst., Am. Jewish Congress (nat. governing council 1984—), Am. Arbitration Assn. (arbitrator, nat. panel arbitrators 1964—, cert. service award 1986, arbitration panel, U.S. Dist. Ct. Ea. Dist. N.Y., 1986—), Nat. Network on Right to Counsel (exec. bd., exec. com. 1986—), N.Y. Lawyers Against Death Penalty, Assn. of Bar of City of N.Y. (com. on profl. responsibility 1987—), Internat. Assn. Jewish Lawyers and Jurists (chmn. acad. adv. com. Project Casaz 1987—), Suffolk County Bar Assn. (ethics com. 1987—), Nat. Prison Project (steering com. 1970—). Democrat. Jewish. Office: Law Bldg 1000 Fulton Ave Hempstead NY 11550

FREEMAN, ALAN HUGH, diagnostic radiologist; b. Bath, Eng., Jan. 21, 1945; s. William John and Violet Cissie (Head) F.; m. Jacqueline Mary Burns, June 28, 1975; children—Christopher, Nicholas. M.B., B.S., Westminster Hosp., U. London, 1968, D.M.R.D., 1972. Intern, Westminster Hosp., London, 1968-69, Kingston Hosp., Surrey, 1969-70; resident in radiology Westminster Hosp., 1970-73, Addenbrookes Hosp., Cambridge, 1973-75; cons. radiologist Addenbrookes Hosp., 1975—. Asst. editor Brit. Jour. Radiology, 1985—. Author papers on diagnostic radiology, contbr. chpt. to textbook. Fellow Royal Coll. Radiologists (Kodak scholar U. Calif.-San Francisco 1975); mem. Brit. Inst. Radiology, Brit. Soc. Gastroenterology (sec. radiologists group, London 1984). Conservative. Anglican. Avocations: reading, cycling, hill walking. Home: Victoria Cottage, 16 Main St, Hardwick CB3 7QS, England Office: Addenbrookes Hosp, Hills Rd, Cambridge CB2 2QQ, England

FREEMAN, ANTOINETTE ROSEFELDT, lawyer; b. Atlantic City, Oct. 7, 1937; d. Bernard Paul and Fannie (Levin) Rosefeldt; m. Alan Richard Freeman, June 22, 1958 (div. Apr. 1979); children—Barry David, Robin Lisa. BA, Rutgers U., 1972; JD, Ind. U., 1975; LLM, Temple U., 1979. Bar: Pa. 1975, U.S. Dist. Ct. (ea. dist.) Pa. 1976, U.S. Ct. Appeals (3d cir.) 1982. Substitute tchr. Washington Twp. Sch. Dist., Indpls., 1972; dep. prosecutor intern Marion County Prosecutor, Indpls., 1974-75; asst. dist. atty. City of Phila., 1975-76; mgr. EEO, Wyeth Labs., Radnor, Pa., 1976-80, SmithKline & French Labs., Phila., 1980-82; atty. SmithKline Beckman Corp., Phila., 1982—; arbitrator Am. Arbitration Assn., 1976—. Counsel Regional Interests Developing Efficient Transp., 1983-85; adv. bd. Family Service Phila., 1980-81, Greater Phila. C. of C., 1983; pres. Croskey Ct. Condominium Assn., 1983-87; bd. dirs. Logan Sq. Neighborhood Assn., 1983—, pres., 1985-87; v.p., sec. Friends of Logan Sq. Found., counsel Hapoel Games USA; chairperson Ctr. City Coalition for Quality of Life; atty. Vol. Lawyers fot the Arts, Phila., 1985—. Mem. ABA, Pa. Bar Assn., Phila. Bar Assn., Merit Employers Council (1st v.p. 1978-79), Phila. Women's Network, Phila. Lawyers Club, Phila. Vol. Lawyers for Arts. Democrat. Jewish. Office: Smith Kline Beckman Corp One Franklin Plaza Philadelphia PA 19101

FREEMAN, CHRISTOPHER PAUL, psychiatrist; b. York, Eng., Apr. 21, 1967; s. Aleck Frederick and Elizabeth (Wing) F.; m. Heather, July 26, 1968; children: Paul, Robin. BS in Med. Sci., Edinburgh U., Scotland, 1968; MB, Edinburugh U., 1971, M in Philosophy, 1975. Registrar Edinburgh U., 1972-78, lectr., 1976-79, sr. lectr., 1980-84; cons. psychiatrist Royal Edinburgh Hosp., 1984—; examiner Royal Coll. Psychiatrists, London, 1982—; sec. Royal Coll. Research Com., London, 1984—. Contbr. articles to profl. jours. Mem. Brit. Psychol. Assn., Brit. Assn. Behavioral Psychotherapists, Gold Medal Royal Coll. Psychiatrists. Office: Royal Edinburgh Hosp, Morningside Terr, Edinburgh Scotland EH10 5HF

FREEMAN, DONALD WILFORD, real estate developer, Arabian horse breeder; b. Brooksville, Fla., Sept. 25, 1929; s. Fred Maxwell and Dovie (Keef) F.; B.S., U. Ala., 1953, LL.B., 1953; LL.M., N.Y. U., 1957; m. Ruby Jane Lewis, Feb. 25, 1956; children—Clifton Lewis, Susan Anne. Acct., Ernst & Ernst, Atlanta, 1953-55; tax atty. Office Chief Counsel, U.S. Treasury Dept., N.Y.C., 1955-57, West Point Mfg. Co. (Ga.), 1957-58; asst. treas. Ryder System, Inc., Miami, Fla., 1958-61; v.p., dir. Henderson's Portion Pak, Inc., 1961-63; pres. Biscayne Capital Corp., Miami, Fla., 1964-66; sr. asso. Lazard Freres & Co., N.Y.C., 1967-69; pres. James A. Ryder Corp., Miami, 1969-78; owner Kiyara Arabians, 1978—. Served with AUS, 1946-48; PTO. C.P.A., Ga. Mem. Fla. Inst. C.P.A.s, Phi Kappa Sigma, Beta Gamma Sigma. Episcopalian. Home: Route 1 Box 239 AA Reddick FL 32686

FREEMAN, GEORGE CLEMON, JR., lawyer; b. Birmingham, Ala., Jan. 3, 1929; s. George Clemon and Annie Laura (Gill) F.; m. Anne Colston Hobson, Dec. 6, 1958; children: Anne Colston, George Clemon III, Joseph Reid Anderson. B.A., Vanderbilt U., 1950; LL.B., Yale U., 1956. Bar: Ala. 1956, Va. 1958, D.C. 1974. Law clk. Justice Hugo L. Black, U.S. Supreme Ct., 1956; practiced in Richmond, Va., 1957—; mem. firm Hunton & Williams, 1957—, partner, 1963—. Contbr. articles to profl. jours. Pres. Va. chpt. Nature Conservancy, 1962-63; mem. sect. 301 Superfund Act Study Group Congl. Adv. Com., 1981-82; mem. Falls of James Com., 1973—; chmn. Richmond City Democratic Com., 1969-71; chmn. adv. council Energy Policy Studies Ctr., U. Va., 1981—; chmn. legal adv. com. to Va. Commn. on Transp. in the 21st Century, 1986-87; mem. Va. Gov.'s Commn. to Study Historic Preservation, 1987—; councilor The Atlantic Council, 1986—; sec., bd. dirs. Richmond Symphony, 1960-63. Served to lt. (j.g.) USNR, 1951-54. Fellow Am. Bar Found. (chmn. Va. chpt. 1986—); mem. ABA (bus. (formerly corp. banking and bus.) law sect.; chmn. ad hoc on Fed. Criminal Code 1979-81, chmn. program com. 1981-82, mem. coordinating group on regulatory reform 1981-85; chmn. ad hoc com. on tart law reform, 1986-87, sec., del. to ho. of dels. 1983-87, 87-88, editor The Business Lawyer, 1988— , nominating com. 1984-87;chmn. standing com. on facilities of Law Library of Congress 1967-73), Richmond Bar Assn., Va. Bar Assn., Am. Law Inst. (council 1980—, advisor to council on project on compensation and liability for product and process injuries, 1986—), Am. Judicature Soc., Phi Beta Kappa, Phi Delta Phi, Omicron Delta Kappa, Alpha Tau Omega. Episcopalian. Clubs: Country of Virginia (Richmond); Knickerbocker (N.Y.C.); Metropolitan (Washington). Home: 10 Paxton Rd Richmond VA 23226 Office: 707 E Main St Richmond VA 23212 also: 2000 Pennsylvania Ave Washington DC 20036

FREEMAN, GEORGE THOMAS, space designer; b. London, Mar. 7, 1930; s. Richard Edward and Florence Elizabeth (Quickenden) F.; m. Adelheid Simon, May 1962 (Feb. 1975); children: Richard Edward, James Thomas; m. Ann Elizabeth Piggott, June 2, 1979; stepchildren: Joanna Lucy, Sarah Jane, James William. Diploma 1st class, Royal Coll. Art, London, 1956. Prin. Freeman Robertson Leese, London and Hong Kong, 1958—; lectr. Royal Coll. Art, Kingston Poly. U., London; chmn. interior design com. Council for Nat. Acad. Awards, London, 1972-82; external assessor for degree course Council for Nat. Acad. Awards, London, 1978—. Gov. Kingston Poly., London, 1982—. Fellow Chartered Soc. Designers (council mem. 1970, chmn. profl. practice bd. 1976-78, pres. 1979-81, trustee 1986—). Clubs: Arts, Marylebone Cricket (London). Office: Freeman Robertson Leese, 33 Drayton Park, London N5 1NT, England also: Freeman Robertson Leese, Aberdeen Marina Tower #1-4, 1st Floor, 8 Shum Wan Rd, Aberdeen Hong Kong

FREEMAN, JAMES DARCY CARDINAL, archbishop; b. Sydney, Australia, Nov. 19, 1907; s. Robert and Margaret (Smith) F.; grad. St. Columba's Coll., Springwood, 1924, St. Patrick's Coll., Manly, 1927. Ordained priest Roman Catholic Ch., 1930; asst. priest in country and city parishes, 1930-37; mem. cathedral staff, Sydney, 1938-41; pvt. sec. to Archbishop of Sydney, 1941-46; dir. Cath. Info. Bur. Australia, 1946-49; pastor, Haymarket, 1949-54; parish priest, Stanmore, 1954-68; named domestic prelate, 1949, aux. bishop, 1957; bishop of Armidale, 1968-71; archbishop of Sydney, 1971-83; elevated to Sacred Coll. of Cardinals, 1973. Decorated knight Order Brit. Empire, 1977. Office: St Mary's Cathedral, Sydney NSW 2000, Australia *

FREEMAN, MILTON VICTOR, lawyer; b. N.Y.C., Nov. 16, 1911; s. Samuel and Celia (Gelfand) F.; m. Phyllis Young, Dec. 19, 1937; children: Nancy Lois (Mrs. Gans), Daniel Martin, Andrew Samuel, Amy Martha (Mrs. Malone). A.B., Coll. City N.Y., 1931; LL.B., Columbia U., 1934. Bar: N.Y. 1934, D.C. 1946, U.S. Supreme Ct. 1943. With gen. counsel's office SEC, 1934-42, asst. solicitor, 1942-46; staff securities div. FTC, 1934; with firm Arnold & Porter and predecessor firms, Washington, 1946—; adj. prof. Yale U., 1947, Georgetown U. Law Sch., 1952; vis. scholar various univs., 1978-79; mem. adv. bd. Bur. Nat. Affairs, Securities Regulation and Law Report, Washington, Nat. Law Jour., N.Y., Internat. Fin. Law Rev., London. Contbr. articles to profl. jours.; bd. editors Columbia Law Rev., 1933-34 (Ordronaux prize 1934). Mem. exec. com. Securities Regulation Inst., U. Calif., San Diego; bd. visitors U. San Diego Law Sch. Mem. ABA (chmn. subcom. on SEC practice and enforcement 1972-83, exec. com. fed. regulation of securities com. 1983—, ad hoc com. on corp. governance project, ad hoc com. on insider trading), Fed. bar Assn., D.C. Bar Assn., Internat. Law Inst. (hon. chmn. 1977—, trustee 1955—). Club: International (Washington). Home: 3405 Woolsey Dr Chevy Chase MD 20815 Office: 1200 New Hampshire Ave NW Washington DC 20036

FREEMAN, PATRICIA ELIZABETH, library and education specialist; b. El Dorado, Ark., Nov. 30, 1924; d. Herbert A. and M. Elizabeth (Pryor) Harper; m. Jack Freeman, June 15, 1949; 3 children. B.A., Centenary Coll., 1943; postgrad. Fine Arts Ctr., 1942-46, Art Students League, 1944-45; B.S.L.S., La. State U., 1946; postgrad. Calif. State U., 1959-61, U. N.Mex., 1964-74; Ed.S., Peabody Coll., Vanderbilt U., 1975. Librarian, U. Calif.-Berkeley, 1946-47, U.S. Air Force, Barksdale AFB, 1948-49, Albuquerque Pub. Schs., 1964-67; ind. sch. library media ctr. cons., 1967—. Painter lithographer; one-person show La. State Exhibit Bldg., 1948; author: Pathfinder: An Operational Guide for the School Librarian, 1975; compiler, editor: Elizabeth Pryor Harper's Twenty-One Southern Families, 1985. Mem. task force Goals for Dallas-Environ., 1977-82; pres. Friends of Sch. Libraries, Dallas, 1979-83. Honoree AAUW Ednl. Found., 1979; vol. award for outstanding service Dallas Ind. Sch. Dist., 1978; AAUW Pub. Service grantee 1980. Mem. ALA, AAUW (dir. Dallas 1976-82, Albuquerque 1983-85), LWV (sec. Dallas 1982-83, editor Albuquerque 1984—), Nat. Trust Historic Preservation, Friends of Albuquerque Pub. Library, N.Mex. Symphony Guild, Alpha Xi Delta. Home: 3016 Santa Clara SE Albuquerque NM 87106

FREEMAN, RONALD RAY, engineer; b. Lincoln, Ill., Aug. 19, 1940; s. Raymond L. and Mary E. (Conley) F.; m. Barbara A. Lueke, Sept. 19, 1964;

children—Aimee, Michelle. Student Mich. Tech. U., 1964-66, U. Nebr., 1968, Met. Tech. Community Coll., 1983-84. Mgr. Northwestern Bell, Omaha, 1969-77; staff mgr. AT&T Corp. Hdqrs., Basking Ridge, N.J., 1977-79; sr. engr. U.S. West Communications, Inc. (formerly Northwestern Bell Corp.) Staff, Omaha, 1979-86, mgr. network planning, Omaha, 1986— cons. Personal Computer Support Group, Omaha, 1983—. Pres. Brandon Park Owners Assn. Inc., 1987—, chmn. bd. dirs. Served with USAF, 1963-67. Mem. Telephone Pioneers Am., Am. Radio Relay League (life). Roman Catholic. Avocations: amateur radio; antique radio collecting. Office: U S West Communications Inc 1314 Douglas on the Mall Omaha NE 68102

FREEMAN, STANLEY ROGER, accountant; b. Cheltenham, Gloucestershire, Eng.; s. Lawrence Sam and Margaret (Miller) F.; m. Lee Lewis, Aug. 3, 1969; children: Helen, Graham. BA with honors, Leicester U., 1966; MS in Econs., London Sch. Econs., 1968. Cert. acct. Ops. research asst. Unilever, London, 1968-69, 1968-69; ops. research mgr. Purfleet, Essex, Eng., 1969-72, project cost. acct., 1972-73; asst. comml. mgr. London and Burgess Hill, Sussex, 1973-76; co. mgmt. account internat. specialities London and Burgess Hill, Rotterdam, The Netherlands, 1976-80; group acct. London and Burgess Hill, Europe, 1980-86; acctg. officer head office London and Burgess Hill, London, 1986—. Chmn. Hertfordshire Swimming League, 1987—. Mem. Chartered Inst. Mgmt. Accts. Jewish. Club: Commonwealth of The Netherlands (sec. 1982-83, chmn. 1983-85). Office: Unilever PLC Unilever House, PO Box 68, London EC4P 4BQ, England

FREER, JOHN RICHARD, computer executive; b. Yorkshire, Eng., Dec. 15, 1947; married, Sept. 15, 1972; 2 children. BS in Electronics, U. Salford, Lancashire, Eng., 1971; diploma in mgmt. studies, Coll. Tech., Southampton, Eng., 1977. Chartered engr. Devel. engr. Ferranti Digital Systems, Ltd., Bracknell, Berks, Eng., 1971-72, Marconi Space and Def. Systems, Ltd., Portsmouth, Eng., 1972-73; project engr. electronics and instruments div. Bell and Howell, Basingstoke, Eng., 1973-75; prin. analyst electronic systems research div. Plessey Radar, Ltd., Addlestone, Eng., 1975-78; prin. cons. Software Scis., Ltd., Farnborough, Eng., 1978—; tech. group exec. networks Software Scis., Ltd., Farnborough, 1985—; cons. series editor Pitman Pub., Ltd., London, 1986—. Author: Systems Design With Advanced Microprocessors, 1986, Computer Communications and Networks, 1987; patentee self tuning inductive sensor, 1976; contbr. articles to profl. jours. Fellow Instn. Elec. Engrs. Office: Software Scis Ltd, Farnborough GU14 7NB, England

FREERKSEN, ENNO, educator; b. Emden, Germany, Sept. 9, 1910; m. Edith Prussas; children: Edith, Renate, Jens-Peter. PhD, U. Rostock, 1933, MD, 1936. Asst. prof. U. Giessen, 1939-40; prof. exptl. medicine U. Kiel, 1940; dir. Forschungsinstitut Borstel, Fed. Republic Germany, 1946-78. Home: Sterleyerstrasse 44, D-2410 Molln Federal Republic of Germany

FREERKSEN, GREGORY NATHAN, lawyer; b. Washington, Iowa, June 4, 1951; s. Floyd and Betty Jo (Frederick) F.; m. Patricia A. Menges, Mar. 21, 1981; children: Suzanna Lynn, Andrea Elizabeth. B.S., No. Ill. U., 1973; J.D., DePaul U., 1976. Bar: Ill. 1976, U.S. Dist. Ct. (no. dist.) Ill. 1976, U.S. Supreme Ct. 1980, U.S. Ct. Appeals (D.C. cir.) 1983. Law clk. Ill. Appellate Ct., Waukegan, Ill., 1976-78; assoc. Law Offices of A.E. Botti, Wheaton, Ill., 1978-79; assoc. DeJong, Poltrock & Giampietro, Chgo., 1979-86; mem. Poltrock & Giampietro, 1986-87, ptnr. Witwer, Burlage, Poltrock & Giampietro, 1987—. Author: (annotated bibliography) Children in the Legal Literature, 1976; Non-Salary Provisions in Negotiated Teacher Agreements, 1975. Editor Ill. law issue DePaul U. Law Rev., 1975-76. Dem. candidate for State Senate, 1986; committeeman 26th precinct Downers Grove Twp. Mem. ABA, Ill. State Bar Assn., Chgo. Bar Assn., Appellate Lawyers Assn., DuPage Bar Assn. Democrat. Home: 5224 Fairmount Ave Downers Grove IL 60515 Office: Witwer Burlage Poltrock & Giampietro 125 S Wacker Dr Suite 2700 Chicago IL 60606

FREI, FELIX WILHELM, psychologist, consultant; b. Solothurn, Switzerland, Nov. 3, 1952; s. Theo and Margrit (von Deschwanden) F.; m. José Elfring, Dec. 30, 1977 (div. Sept. 1980); children: Carole, Dana, Saskia. Lic. phil., U. Bern, Zurich, Switzerland, 1976, PhD, 1982. Asst. U. Zurich, 1974-77; sr. researcher Swiss Fed. Inst. Tech., Zurich, 1977-87; vis. prof. U. Bremen, Fed. Republic Germany, 1984-85; chief exec. officer a&o consearch, Zurich, 1987—. Author: Qualification in Work, 1980, Competence Development, 1984.

FREIBERGER, WALTER FREDERICK, mathematics educator; b. Vienna, Austria, Feb. 20, 1924; came to U.S., 1955, naturalized, 1962; s. Felix and Irene (Tagany) F.; m. Christine Mildred Holmberg, Oct. 6, 1956; children: Christopher Allan, Andrew James, Nils H. B.A., U. Melbourne, 1947, M.A., 1949; Ph.D., U. Cambridge, Eng., 1953. Research officer Aero. Research Lab. Australian Dept. Supply, 1947-49, sr. sci. research officer, 1953-55; tutor U. Melbourne, 1947-49, 53-55; asst. prof. div. applied math. Brown U., 1956-58, asso. prof., 1958-64, prof., 1964—, dir. Computing Center, 1963-69; dir. Center for Computer and Info. Scis., 1969-76, chmn. div. applied math., 1976-82, chmn. grad. com., 1985-88, assoc. chmn., 1988—; mem. fellowship selection panel NSF, Fulbright fellowship selection panel. Author: (with U. Grenander) A Short Course in Computational Probability and Statistics, 1971; Editor: The International Dictionary of Applied Mathematics, 1960, (with others) Applications of Digital Computers, 1963, Advances in Computers, Volume 10, 1970, Statistical Computer Performance Evaluation, 1972; Mng. editor: Quarterly of Applied Mathematics, 1965—; Contbr. numerous articles to profl. jours. Served with Australian Army, 1943-45. Fulbright fellow, 1955-56; Guggenheim fellow, 1962-63; NSF Office Naval Research grantee in field. Mem. Am. Math. Soc. (asso. editor Math. Reviews 1957-62), Soc. for Indsl. and Applied Math., Am. Statis. Assn., Inst. Math. Stats., Assn. Computing Machinery. Republican. Episcopalian. Club: Univ. (Providence). Home: 24 Alumni Ave Providence RI 02906 Office: 182 George St Providence RI 02912

FREIDAY, DEAN, church official; b. Irvington, N.J., June 20, 1915; s. William Sidney and Ethel (Deane) F.; B.A., U. Rochester (N.Y.), 1936; m. Esther Dorothea Selke, June 27, 1946; children—Gail Freiday Crockett, William Arthur. Mem. Christian and interfaith com. Friends Gen. Conf., Phila., 1958—, chmn., 1966-72; del. 4th World Conf. on Faith and Order, World Council Chs., Montreal, 1963, mem. consultation on baptism, eucharist and ministry, Switzerland, 1977, mem. Nat. Faith and Order Colloquium, 1967—, FGC del. to 6th Gen. Assembly, Vancouver, B.C., 1983; observer-cons. 3d World Congress of Lay Apostolate, Vatican, Rome, 1967; ann. conf. cons. Christian World Communions Geneva, 1968, 69, 72, 73, 74, London, 1976, 86, Rome, 1977; pres. Council Chs., Greater Red Bank (N.J.) Area, 1965-67; mem. central and exec. coms. Friends Gen. Conf., 1966-72; mem. exec. com. U.S. Conf. World Council Chs., 1967-72, 83-87; sponsor Cath. and Quaker Studies, 1971—; mem. Faith and Order Commn., Nat. Council of Chs. of Christ-U.S.A., 1983—.Served with USNR, 1942-45. Mem. Delta Upsilon. Club: Masons (32 deg.). Author: The Bible—Its Criticism, Interpretation and Use—In 16th and 17th Century England, 1979; Nothing Without Christ, 1984; editor: Barclay's Apology in Modern English, 1967, 3d printing, 1980; The Day of the Lord, 1981; co-editor: Quaker Religious Thought, 1980-83, editor, 1984—. Home: 1110 Wildwood Ave Manasquan NJ 08736

FREIDBERG, SIDNEY, lawyer, real estate development company executive, author; b. N.Y.C., Jan. 20, 1914; s. David and Tillie (Friedman) F.; children: David, Emily. B.S., NYU, 1933; LL.B., Yale U., 1936. Bar: N.Y. 1936, D.C. 1945. Assoc. Phillips, Nizer, Benjamin, Krim, 1936-42; practice law N.Y.C., 45-68; ptnr. firm Freidberg, Rich & Blue, N.Y.C., 1945-62, Posner, Fox, Arent & Freidberg, Washington, 1945-54; research and analysis div. OSS, 1942-43; counsel printing and pub. div. WPB, Washington, 1943-45; counsel Ho. of Reps. select com. on newsprint and paper supply, Washington, 1948-49; commr. Fgn. Claims Settlement Commn. U.S., Washington, 1968-70; exec. v.p., gen. counsel Nat. Corp. for Housing Partnerships, Washington, 1970-77; counsel firm Arent, Fox, Kintner, Plotkin & Kahn, Washington, 1977-84; pres. Morningside Heights Property Assn., 1960-62. Contbr. articles to legal jours., also to Washingtonian, Esquire, Holiday, Modern Photography. Modern Maturity. Mem. alumni bd. visitors N.Y. U., 1959-61; bd. dirs. Nat. Housing Conf., Inc., 1979-83, Planned Parenthood of Met. Washington, Inc., 1979-86, Preterm, Inc., 1983-85; bd. dirs., sec.-treas. Nat. Minority Purchasing Council, Inc., 1977-81. Mem. Am., Fed., D.C., N.Y. State, City N.Y. bar assns., Am. Soc. Internat. Law, World Assembly Judges, World Peace Through Law Center, D.C. C. of C. (dir., counsel 1979-80), Phi Beta Kappa. Democrat. Clubs: Fed. City, Nat. Lawyers, Nat. Press, Army and Navy (Washington); Yale (N.Y.C. and Washington). Home: 1832 24th St NW Washington DC 20008

FREIHA, ISSAM, publishing executive; b. Salhié, Lebanon, Nov. 2, 1936; s. Saöd and Hassiba (Cookhy) F.; m. Asma Albert Lattouf; children: Saöd, Amale, Zeina. BA in Journalism, Am. U. Cairo, 1959. Editor in chief al Anwar newspaper Darassayad, Beirut, 1959-84, chmn. bd., 1978—. Office: Darassayad, Saödfreiha Ave, Hazmieh Lebanon

FREIHERR VON VILLIEZ, HANSJÜRGEN, aeronautical engineer; b. Berlin, Nov. 20, 1927; arrived in The Netherlands, 1970; s. Franz and Margarethe (Schwarze) Freiherr von Villiez; m. Anneliese Stückrath, Aug. 13, 1956; children: Christian, Gabriele. Diploma in engring., Tech. U. Berlin, 1958, D of Engring., 1962. Chief engr. Aviation Inst., Tech. U. Berlin, 1960-62; prin. expert Assn. Eurocontrol, Paris, 1962-63; head div. Eurocontrol Agy., Brussels, 1963-70; dir. Eurocontrol Agy., Beek, The Netherlands, 1970—. Author various books and pubs. Mem. German Inst. Navigation (chmn. aviation commn. 1981—). Lodge: Rotary (chmn. internat. com. 1976-79). Home: Wolfhaag 62, 6291 NB Vaals, Limburg The Netherlands Office: Eurocontrol Agy, Horsterweg 11, 6191 RX Beek, Limburg The Netherlands

FREIMAN, ALVIN HENRY, cardiologist; b. N.Y.C., Jan. 26, 1927; s. Maurice and Beatrice (Freeman) F.; B.A., N.Y. U., 1947, M.D., 1953; M.S., U. Ill., 1949; m. Nadine Roehr, June 12, 1959; children—Audrey L., Gail L., Marshall. Intern, Montefiore Hosp., N.Y.C., 1953-54; resident in medicine and cardiology Beth Israel Hosp., Boston 1954-56; fellow in cardiology Meml. Hosp., N.Y.C., 1956-58; individual practice medicine specializing in internal medicine and cardiology, N.Y.C., 1954—; asso. physician Sloan-Kettering Inst., N.Y.C., 1960—; asso. prof. Cornell U. Med. Coll., N.Y.C., 1967—; attending staff cardiology Meml. Hosp., N.Y.C., 1971—, dept. medicine Meml. Sloan-Kettering Cancer Center, N.Y.C., 1971—, dir. clin. info. center, 1974—. Served with USNR, 1945-46. Diplomate Am. Bd. Internal Medicine. Mem. Nat. Cancer Inst., A.C.P., Am. Coll. Cardiology, Am. Coll. Chest Physicians, Am. Coll. Angiology, AAAS, Am. Heart Assn., N.Y. Acad. Sci., Internat. Coll. Angiology, Alpha Omega Alpha, Sigma Xi. Contbr. articles to profl. jours. Home: 74 Homestead Rd Tenafly NJ 07670 Office: 178 East End Ave New York NY 10128

FREIMAN, DAVID BURL, radiology educator; b. Phila., Apr. 1, 1947; s. Henry David and Rose (Specter) F.; m. Arlene Cathy Olanoff, June 15, 1969; children—Michael, Lesley, Daniel. A.B., U. Pa., 1969, M.D., 1973. Diplomate Am. Bd. Radiology. Intern Hosp. of U. Pa., Phila., 1972-73, resident, 1973-77; asst. prof. radiology U. Pa., Phila., 1977-81, assoc. prof., 1981-83, assoc. clin. prof. radiology, 1983—; chief radiology Presbyn.-U. Pa. Med. Ctr., Phila., 1983—. Contbr. numerous articles, chpts. and revs. to lit. on angiography. Fellow Am. Heart Assn., Am. Coll. Angiology; mem. Radiol. Soc. N. Am., Am. Coll. Radiology, AMA. Democrat. Jewish. Avocations: racing catamarans, windsurfing. Office: Presbyn-U Pa Med Ctr 39th and Market Sts Philadelphia PA 19104

FREIRE, GLORIA MEDONIS, social worker; b. Pitts., Apr. 19, 1929; d. Vincent X. and Anastasia T. (Puida) Medonis; B.A. in Polit. Sci. and Econs., Carlow Coll., 1950; M.S.S.A., Case-Western Res. U., 1955; M.P.A., Cleve. State U., 1986; m. Luis Francis Freire, Aug. 30, 1958; children—Michael, Charles. Teen-age dir. Merrick House, Cleve., 1955-62; group psychotherapist Cleve. Psychiat. Inst., 1966-73; lectr. Sch. Applied Social Scis., Case-Western Res. U., Cleve., 1973-75; cluster dir. Golden Age Centers, Cleve., 1975-76; specialist Community Guidance and Human Services, Cleve., 1976, staff tng. and devel. coordinator, 1977, dir. consultation and edn., 1978-84; coordinator psychiat. emergency services systems Lake County Mental Health Bd. (Ohio), 1984-86; adminstr. hispanic office Cath. Counseling Ctr., Cleve., 1986—. Chmn. steering com. East Community Task Force on Desegregation; chmn. subcouncil of Ohio Community Mental Health Ctrs. Consultation and Edn.; chmn. Consultation and Edn. Council Cleve.; coordinator Christian Formation Community of St. Malachi, 1975-77, coordinator liturgy commn., 1978-80, coordinator social concerns com., 1982-84; mem. Diocesan Commn. on Cath. Community Action, 1982-88, vice chmn., 1986-87; mem. Urban League Edn. Adv. and Task Force on Minimum Competency, 1978-80. Recipient Disting. Leadership award Alumnae Assn. Carlow Coll., 1982. Mem. Nat. Assn. Social Workers (task force on desegregation 1974-83, co-chmn. 1981-83, coordinator polit. action com. 1977, dir. Cleve. chpt. 1975-77, sec.-treas. Ohio council of chpts. 1975-76, steering com. Cleve. chpt. 1987), Acad. Cert. Social Workers, Am. Soc. Pub. Adminstrn. (trustee Cleve. chpt. 1987—), Am. Soc. Profl. and Exec. Women (exec. bd.), Nat. and Cuyahoga County Women's Polit. Caucus, Am. Group Psychotherapy Assn., Tri-State Group Psychotherapy Soc. Democrat. Roman Catholic. Editor: SASS mag., Case-Western Res. U. Alumni, 1973-79. Home: 5001 Tuxedo Ave Cleveland OH 44134 Office: Hispanic Office Cath Counseling Ctr 2012 W 25th St Cleveland OH 44113

FREISER, LAWRENCE M., lawyer; b. Bklyn., Mar. 3, 1942; m. Frances A., June 7, 1970; children—Jeffrey A., Dana M. BA, NYU, 1963; LLB, Bklyn. Law Sch., 1966. Bar: N.Y. 1966, Calif. 1972, U.S. Dist. Ct. (so. and ea. dists.) N.Y. 1968, U.S. Tax Ct. 1969, U.S. Customs Ct. and Patent Appeals 1969, U.S. Ct. Appeals (2d cir.) 1969, U.S. Ct. Claims 1970, U.S. Supreme Ct. 1970, U.S. Dist. Ct. (no. dist.) Calif. 1973, U.S. Dist. Ct. (cen. dist.) 1976, U.S. Ct. Internat. Trade 1980; cert. instr. law community colls., Calif. Assoc. Kaufman, Taylor, Kimmel and Miller, N.Y.C., 1967-68, Ruben Schwartz, N.Y.C., 1968; sole practice N.Y.C. and Calif., 1968-75, 77-79; atty. Hughes Aircraft Corp., San Mateo, Calif., 1972-73; assoc. Alvin B. Green, Los Angeles, 1975-77; atty. Continuing Edn. of the Bar, State Bar of Calif. and U. Calif. Extension, Berkeley, 1979—; tchr. math. N.Y.C. Bd. Edn., 1966-67; adj. prof. Northrop U. Sch. Law, 1978-79. Mem. staff Bklyn. Law Rev., 1964-66; editor, contbg. author several sects. Calif. Civil Procedure During Trial vol 1, 1982, supp. atty.-editor vol. 2, Calif. Civil Procedure During Trial, 1984; co-atty., editor Calif. Worker's Compensation Practice 3d ed., 1985, Calif. Civil Appellate Practice 2d ed., 1985, Civil Discovery Practice in California, 1987; contbg. author, atty., editor Debt Collection Practice in Calif., 1987, Atty.-editor chpts. 5, 6, Civil Discovery Practice in California, 1987. Mem. ABA, Calif. Bar Assn. Home: 105 Montanya Ct Walnut Creek CA 94596 Office: 2300 Shattuck Ave Berkeley CA 94704

FREITAG, FREDERICK GERALD, osteopathic physician; b. Milw., Feb. 12, 1952; s. Frederick August and Shirley June (Siewert) F.; m. Lynn Nadene Stegner, Sept. 10, 1977. BS in Biochemistry, U. Wis., 1974; DO, Chgo. Coll. Osteopathic Medicine, 1979. Intern Brentwood Hosp., Warrensville Heights, Ohio, 1979-80, resident in family practice, 1980-81; dir., physician Twinsburg (Ohio) Family Clinic, 1981-83; assoc. prof. family medicine Coll. Osteo. Medicine, Ohio U., Warrensville Heights, 1982-83; mem. staff Diamond Headache Clinic, Chgo., 1983-86, assoc. dir., 1986—; attending staff mem. Louis A. Weiss Meml. Hosp., Chgo., 1983—; mem. Janssen Research Council; vis. lectr. dept. family medicine Chgo. Coll. Osteo. Medicine, 1985—, others. Contbr. articles and abstracts to profl. jours. and chpts. to books. Mem. AMA, Am. Assn. Study Headache, Am. Coll. Gen. Practitioners in Osteo. Medicine, Am. Osteo. Assn., Am. Soc. Clin. Pharmacology and Therapeutics, Ill. Assn. Osteo. Physicians and Surgeons, Ill. Med. Soc., Internat. Assn. Study Pain, Nat. Headache Found, Chgo. Med. Soc. (speaker's bur.), German Wine Soc., U. Wis. Alumni Assn. Lutheran. Home: 920 W Carmen Unit 2E Chicago IL 60640 Office: The Diamond Headache Clinic 5252 N Western Ave Chicago IL 60625

FREIWALD, JOYCE GROSS, electronics company executive; b. Fulton, Mo., June 22, 1944; d. Fred Alfred and Susan (Kist) Gross; B.S. in Math. (scholar), U. N.Mex., 1966; postgrad. in math. and physics, 1967-68, M.Arch. (scholar), 1976; m. David Allen Freiwald, Apr. 3, 1976; children—Wesley, Todd, Christopher. Mathematician, Air Force Weapons Lab., Albuquerque, 1963-65, Sandia Nat. Lab., Albuquerque, 1966-69; owner, mgr. Costello Cons. Co., Albuquerque, 1970-72; scientist Sci. Applications, Inc., Albuquerque, 1973-75; pres. Phoenix Forth, Inc., Albuquerque, 1975-76; mem. staff Los Alamos Nat. Lab., 1976-81; Republican staff dir. U.S. Ho. Reps. Com. on Sci. and Tech., Washington, 1981-86; mgr. bus. devel. Gen. Atomics, San Diego, 1986—. Candidate for Albuquerque City Commn., 1970, N.Mex. Senate, 1971; chairwoman N.Mex. Equal Rights Legis. Com., 1972, Citizen's Coalition for Land Use Planning, 1975; former mem. various state and county bds. and commns. Mem. Assn. Women in Sci., N.Mex. Women in Sci., Am. Nuclear Soc., Am. Astron. Soc., Women in Aerospace, AAUW, AAAS, Nat. Assn. Female Execs., Phi Kappa Pi, Kappa Mu Epsilon, Alpha Delta Pi. Republican. Contbr. numerous articles on energy, environ. and tech. issues to profl. jours. Home: 10574 Livewood Way San Diego CA 92131 Office: PO Box 85608 San Diego CA 92138-5608

FREIZER, LOUIS A., radio news producer; b. N.Y.C., Oct. 10, 1931; s. Morris and Celia (Lassersohn) F.; m. Michèle Suzanne Orban, July 6, 1968; children: Sabine, Eric. BS, U. Wis., 1953; postgrad., U. Heidelberg, Fed. Republic Germany, 1956; MA, Columbia U., 1964, postgrad., 1966—. Corr. UPI, Madison, Wis., 1953-54; desk asst. CBS News, N.Y.C., 1956-59, newswriter, 1959-60; newswriter Sta. WCBS, N.Y.C., 1960-62, news editor, 1963-68, sr. news producer, 1968-73, sr. exec. news producer, 1973—; adj. prof. communications Fordham U.; lectr., cons. journalism and internat. relations. Producer: (pub. affairs series) Let's Find Out, 1966, International Briefing series, 1968-72. Served to 1st lt. U.S. Army, 1954-56; capt. USAR. Recipient Am. Legion medal; Radio Journalism award AMA, Radio Journalism award Nat. Headliners Club, Radio Journalism Nat. award for Outstanding Newscast UPI, 1st place award for Best Regularly Scheduled Local News Program N.Y. State AP Broadcasters Assn., spl. mention for Best One Day News Effort N.Y. State AP Broadcasters Assn.; fellow CBS News Found. Mem. Am. Polit. Sci. Assn., Acad. Polit. Sci., Am. Acad. Polit. and Social Scis., Radio-TV News Dirs. Assn., Broadcast Pioneers, Sigma Delta Chi. Home: 1619 3d Ave New York NY 10128 Office: Sta WCBS 51 W 52d St New York NY 10019

FREMON, RICHARD C., college administrator, educator; b. St. Louis, May 28, 1918; s. Richard Horatio and Hazel Pauline (Rhea) F.; m. Virginia Isabelle Moore, Sept. 7, 1940; children—Carolyn E. Fremon Maycher, Richard L., James N., Nancy I. Fremon Fullem. A.B., Columbia U., 1939; B.S. in Elec. Engring., 1940, M.S. in Elec. Engring., 1944. With personnel Bell Telephones, N.Y.C., 1941-54, dir. salary adminstrn., Murray Hill, N.J., 1954-73, dir. adminstrv. systems, 1973-81; dir. computer ctr. Centenary Coll., Hackettstown, N.J., 1981—. Contbr. chpt. to book. Trustee Sea Cliff Sch. Bd., N.Y., 1950-52; past chmn. Engring. Manpower Commn., N.Y.C., 1965. Mem. Data Processing Mgmt. Assn.; mem. Inst. Indsl. Engrs. (sr.). Democrat. Presbyterian. Club: Panther Valley. Home: 32 Barn Owl Dr Hackettstown NJ 07840 Office: Centenary Coll 400 Jefferson St Hackettstown NJ 07840

FRENCH, BRUCE COMLY, lawyer, educator; b. Phila., June 22, 1947; s. Paul Comly French and Dorothy (Felten) Boothertone; m. Diane Wortman, July 19, 1987. B.A., Am. U., 1969, M.A., 1970; J.D., Antioch Sch. Law, 1975. Bar: Pa. 1975, D.C. 1976, Ohio 1985, U.S. Tax Ct. 1984, U.S. Dist. Ct. D.C. 1976, (ea. dist.) Pa. 1976, (no. dist.) Ohio 1979, U.S. Supreme Ct. 1979, U.S. Ct. Appeals (D.C. cir.) 1976, (fed. cir. 1984), (6th cir. 1985). Campus coordinator CARE, Washington, 1966-69; community relations dir. Met. Washington Planning and Housing Assn., 1969-70; research assoc., pres. adv. council on exec. orgns., White House, 1970; project dir. Inst. for Study Health and Soc., Washington, 1970-72; staff dir., counsel D.C. Council, 1975-78, legis. counsel, 1979-83; asst. prof. law Ohio No. U., Ada, 1978-79, assoc. prof. law, 1983-87, prof. law 1987—; assoc. mem. Nat. Conf. Commrs. on Uniform State Laws, Washington, 1981-84; mem. D.C. Law Revision Com., Washington, 1980-85; hearing examiner D.C. Com. on Human Rights, 1980-83; acting genl. counsel, D.C. Taxicab Commn., 1987; neutral, Ohio State Employees Relations Bd. Contbr. articles to profl. jours. Treas. Neighbors, Inc., Washington, 1982-83. Democrat. Mem. Society of Friends. Office: Ohio Northern Coll Law Ada OH 45810

FRENCH, HAROLD S., food company executive; b. Bklyn., Oct. 2, 1921; s. Morris and Fay (Kaufman) F.; m. Claire E. Weingart, Oct. 3, 1943 (dec. Mar. 1983); children: Madelaine Diane, Janet Gail; m. Gloria Rosario, June 2, 1984. BA, L.I. U., 1942; postgrad., NYU, 1950, Columbia U., 1960. Asst. buyer R.H. Macy Co., N.Y.C., 1949-52; group mgr. Abraham & Straus Co., Hempstead, N.Y., 1952-54; mdse. mgr. Popular Club Plan, Passaic, N.J., 1954-60, Nat. Silver Co., N.Y.C., 1964-69; mktg. dir. Waverly Products Co., Phila., 1970-74; pres. Pet Food Industries, Inc., N.Y.C., 1974—, Harold French & Co., Inc., N.Y.C., 1974—; chmn. Rosario Homes, Inc., P.R.; pres. King Agro-Indsl. Corp., 1986, King Agro-Shellfish (Nigeria) Ltd., 1988—, King Agro-Cattle Ranching (Nigeria) Ltd., 1988—. Patentee in field. Served with M.I., U.S. Army, 1943-45. Decorated Bronze Star. Home: 60 E 8th St New York NY 10003 Office: 432 Park Ave S New York NY 10016

FRENCH, HENRY PIERSON, JR., historian, educator; b. Rochester, N.Y., Nov. 21, 1934; s. Henry Pierson and Genevieve Lynn (Johnson) F.; AB, U. Del., 1960; MA, U. Rochester, 1961, MA in Edn., 1962, EdD, 1968; m. Beverly Anne Bauernschmidt, Aug. 22, 1959; children—Henry Pierson III, Donna Lynn (dec.), William Dean, Susan Gayle, John Douglas. Tchr. Pittsford (N.Y.) Cen. High Sch., 1962-66; field service asso. U. Rochester, N.Y., 1962-66, asso. lectr., 1967-68, vis. asst. prof. Coll. Edn. and E. Asian Ctr., 1968-69; adj. asst. prof. history SUNY-Monroe Community Coll., 1964-67, asst. prof. history, 1967-70, assoc. prof., 1970-74, prof., 1974—, chmn. dept. history and polit. sci., 1979-85, chmn. tenure, promotion com., sabbatical leave, 1986; asst. prof. edn. U. Rochester, 1969-70, assoc. prof., 1970-72, lectr. East Asian studies East Asian Ctr., 1972-74, sr. lectr., 1974—; prof. Canisius Coll., summers 1968, 69, 71, 73, Rochester Inst. Tech., 1969-70, spring 1977, SUNY, Brockport, summer 1971; adj. mentor State U. N.Y.-Empire State Coll., 1976; dir. polit. insts. Robert A. Taft Inst. for Govt., 1962-65; co-dir., adminstr. NDEA insts., 1965-69; bd. dirs. Rochester Assn. UN, 1972-83, 85—, chmn. policy com., 1972-74, v.p., 1975-77, pres., 1977-78, chmn. bd., 1978-79, chmn. nominating com., 1983-84; panelist 10th conf. Internat. Assn. Historians of Asia, Singapore, 1986. Vestryman St. Thomas Episcopal Ch., Rochester, 1965-68; vestryman Christ Episc. Ch., Pittsford, 1976-79, jr. warden, 1979-80, sr. warden, 1980-81, chmn. rector selection com., 1982; mem. com. on Ministry, Episcopal Diocese of Rochester (N.Y.), 1988; trustee Friends of Rochester Pub. Library, 1983—, v.p., 1986-88, pres., 1988—; chmn., presenter Rochester Literary Award to James Baldwin, 1986. Served with AUS, 1955-57. Ctr. for Internat. Programs and Comparative Studies grantee, 1970. Mem. Assn. Asian Studies, Am. Acad. Polit. and Social Scis., Chinese Lang. Tchrs. Assn., AAUP, Torch Clubs Internat. (dir. Rochester chpt. 1973-76, v.p. 1973-74, pres. 1974-75), Rochester Com. on Fgn. Relations, Delta Tau Delta. Episcopalian. Club: University (dir. 1973-76, 87-90, v.p. 1975-76, sec. 1988—, chmn. nominating com. for bd. dirs. 1977) (Rochester). Moderator, permanent panelist Fgn. Policy Assn. and Rochester Assn. for UN Great Decisions-1973, 77, 78 series Channel 21 Ednl. TV, Rochester; cons., panelist Great Decisions TV series, 1982, 84; moderator, host Disciplines Within the Social Sciences series, 1968. Contbr. articles to profl. jours. Home: 78 Smith Rd Pittsford NY 14534 Office: U Rochester Asian Studies Faculty Ctr for Spl Degree Programs Rochester NY 14627 also: SUNY-Monroe Community Coll Rochester NY 14623

FRENCH, JOHN, III, lawyer; b. Boston, July 12, 1932; s. John and Rhoda (Walker) F.; m. Leslie Ten Eyck, Jan. 11, 1957 (div. 1961) children: John B., Lawrence C.; m. Ann Hubbell, Jan. 9, 1965; children: Daniel J., Susanna H. BA, Dartmouth Coll., 1955; JD, Harvard U., 1958. Bar: N.Y. 1959. Assoc. Milbank, Tweed, Hadley & McCloy, N.Y.C., 1961-68, Satterlee & Stephens, N.Y.C., 1968-73; asst. gen. counsel Continental Group, Inc., Stamford, Conn., 1973-81; v.p., gen. counsel, sec. Peabody Internat. Corp., Stamford, Conn., 1981-82; ptnr. Appleton, Rice & Perrin, N.Y.C., 1982-84, Beveridge and Diamond, N.Y.C., 1985—; lectr. Practising Law Inst., 1979-83, Am. Law Inst., 1978; bd. dirs. Resorts Mgmt., Inc., U.S Tel. Inc., N.Y.C. Contbr. articles to profl. jours. Trustee Hudson River Found., 1982—, YM-YWCA Camping Services of Greater N.Y., Inc., 1983—; bd. dirs. Third St. Music Sch. Settlement House, Inc., N.Y.C., Internat. House, Inc., N.Y.C., Young Concert Artists, Inc., 1980—; mem. Westchester County Planning Bd., 1974-85; mem. N.Y. State Environ. Bd., 1976—. Served to capt. JAGC, USAF, 1958-61. Mem. ABA, N.Y. State Bar Assn. (lectr.), Assn. Bar City N.Y. (lectr.), Environ. Law Inst., Am. Soc. Corp. Secs. Republican. Clubs: River, Harvard, Knickerbocker (N.Y.C.). Home: 33 E 70th St New York NY 10021 Office: Beveridge & Diamond 101 Park Ave Suite 1202 New York NY 10178

FRENCH, JOHN DWYER, lawyer; b. Berkeley, Calif., June 26, 1933; s. Horton Irving and Gertrude Margery (Ritzen) F.; m. Annette Richard, 1955; m. Berna Jo Mahling, 1986. B.A. summa cum laude, U. Minn., 1955; postgrad, Oxford U., Eng., 1955-56; LL.B. magna cum laude, Harvard U., 1960. Bar: D.C. bar 1960, Minn. bar 1963. Law clk. Justice Felix Frankfurter, U.S. Supreme Ct., 1960-61; legal asst. to commr. FTC, 1961-62; assoc. Ropes & Gray, Boston, 1962-63; assoc. Faegre & Benson, Mpls., 1963-66, ptnr., 1967-75, mng. ptnr., 1975—; adj. faculty mem. Law Sch. U. Minn., 1965-70; mem. exec. com. Lawyers Com. for Civil Rights under Law, 1978—; co-chmn. U.S. Dist. Judge Nominating Commn., 1979; vice chmn. adv. com., mem. dir. search com., chmn. devel. office search com. Hubert Humphrey Inst., 1979-87. Contbr. numerous articles and revs. to legal jours. Chmn. or co-chmn. Minn. State Democratic Farm Labor Party Conv., 1970, 72, 74, 78, 80, 82, 84, 86, 88, chmn. Mondale Vol. Com., 1972, treas., 1974; assoc. chmn. Minn. Dem.-Farmer-Labor Party, 1985-86; mem. Dem. Nat. Com., 1985-86; del. Democratic Nat. Conv., 1976, 78, 80, 84, 88; trustee Twin Cities Public TV, Inc., 1980-86, mem. overseers com. to visit Harvard U. Law Sch., 1970-75, 77-82; chmn. Minn. steering com. Dukakis for Pres., 1987-88. Served with U.S. Army, 1955-56. Rotary Found. fellow, 1955-56. Mem. ABA (mem. editorial bd. jour. 1976-79), Minn. Bar Assn., Hennepin County Bar Assn., Jud. Council Minn., Lawyers Alliance for Nuclear Arms Control (nat. bd. dirs. 1982-84), U. Minn. Alumni Assn. (mem. exec. com. 1985-87), Phi Beta Kappa. Episcopalian. Office: 2300 Multifoods Tower Minneapolis MN 55402

FREND, WILLIAM HUGH CLIFFORD, emeritus educator, clergyman; b. Shotterhill, Surrey, England, Jan. 11, 1916; s. Edwin George Clifford Frend and Edith Bacon; m. Mary Grace Crook, June 2, 1951; children: Sarah Anne, Simon William Clifford. BA, U. Oxford, Eng., 1937, D in Philosophy, 1940, MA, 1951, DD, 1966; BD, Cambridge U., Eng., 1964; DD (hon.), Edinburgh U., 1974. Asst. prin. War Office, London, 1940-41, War Cabinet Office, London, 1941-42; intelligence officer Polit. Warfare Exec. Office, 1942-45; info. officer British Mil. Govt., Austria, 1945-46; with editorial bd. German War Document Project, 1942-51; commd. 2d lt. British Army, 1947, advanced through grades to capt., ret., 1967; research fellow U. Nottingham, Eng., 1951-52; Bye fellow Gonville and Caius Coll., Cambridge, Eng., 1952-54; lectr. faculty of div. U. Cambridge, 1954-69; fellow Gonville and Caius Coll., Cambridge, 1956-69; prof. eccles. history U. Glasgow, Scotland, 1969-84; priest-in-charge Barnwell Rectory, Peterborough, Eng., 1984—; hon. pres. Eccles. Comparée, 1983—; sr. fellow Dumbarton Oaks, Washington, 1984; vis. prof. Rhodes U., Republic of S. Africa, 1964—, U. S. Africa, 1976—, John Carroll U., Cleve., 1981—. Author: The Donatist Church, 1952, Martyrdom and Persecution in Early Christianity, 1965, Rise of Monophysite Movement, 1972, Rise of Christianity, 1984, Saints and Sinners in the Early Church, 1985. Chmn. Assn. Univ. Tchrs., Scotland, 1976-78; vice chmn. Community Council, Buchanan, Scotland, 1980-84. Recipient Territorial Efficiency Decoration War Office, 1959, 67. Fellow The British Acad. (elected mem. 1983), Royal Soc. Edinburgh, Royal Hist.Soc.; mem. Eccles. History Soc. (pres. 1979—). Conservative. Anglican. Club: Arts & Authors (London). Home: Barnwell Rectory, Peterborough PE8 5PG, England

FRENDO, ANTHONY JOSEPH, religious educator; b. Valletta, Malta, Mar. 10, 1950; s. Anthony and Lydia (Dimech) F. Baccalaureate in Philosophy, Aloisianum Inst. of Philosophy, Gallarate, 1972; Licentiate in Ancient Near Ea. Studies, Pontifical Bibl. Inst., Rome, 1975, Licentiate in Sacred Scripture, 1981; Dottore in Lettere, State U. Rome, 1976; Baccalaureate in Theology, Hochschule Sankt Georgen, Fed. Republic Germany, 1979; PhD in Syro-Palestinian Archaeology, Inst. Archaeology, U. London, 1986. Ordained priest, Roman Catholic Ch., 1979. Lectr. Sacred Scripture and N.T. Greek Mill Hill Missionary Inst., London, 1986-87; lectr. Bibl. Archaeology and Bibl. Geography Pontifical Bibl. Inst., Rome, 1987—. Contbr. articles to profl. jours. Diocese of Bamberg, West Germany scholar, 1972; recipient Overseas Research Students award, U.K. Univ.'s Prins. 1981-82, 82-83, 84-85; Brit. Sch. Archaeology travel grantee, 1983, Margary Gift Fund grantee, 1983, Anglo-Israel Archaeol. Soc. grantee, 1984, Gordon Childe and Margary Bequest Fund grantee, 1986. Address: Pontifical Bibl Inst, Via Della Pilotta 25, Rome Italy

FRENGER, PAUL FRED, medical computer consultant, physician; b. Houston, May 9, 1946; s. Fred Paul and Frances Mae (Mitchell) F.; m. Sandra Lee Van Schreeven, Aug. 17, 1979; 1 child, Kirk Austin. BA in Biology, Rice U., 1968; MD, U. Tex.-San Antonio, 1974. Lic. physician, Tex., Colo. Pediatric intern Keesler USAF Med. Ctr., Biloxi, Miss., 1974-75; course dir. U.S. Air Force Physician Assistant Sch., Sheppard AFB, Tex., 1976-78; spl. projects cons. Med. Networks, Inc., Houston, 1979-81; dir. med. products Microprocessor Labs., Inc., Houston, 1983; chief med. officer, dir. Mediclinic, Inc., Houston, 1984-85; pres., cons. Working Hypothesis, Inc., Houston, 1981-83, 85-86.; project leader Telescan, Inc., Houston, 1987-88. Contbr. numerous articles to profl. jours.; patentee life raft test device. Served to lt. col. USAF, 1969-78. Decorated Air Force Commendation medal. Mem. Am. Assn. Med. Dirs., Am. Assn. Med. Systems and Informatics, Nat. Model R.R. Assn., Mensa. Episcopalian. Avocations: model engineering, railroading. Home: 12502 Boheme Dr Houston TX 77024

FRENI, MIRELLA, soprano; b. Modena, Italy, Feb. 27, 1935; d. Ennio and Gianna F.; m. Leone Magiera, 1955; 1 dau., Micaela. Debut as Micaela in Carmen, Modena, 1955, since has appeared in maj. opera houses throughout world including Covent Garden, 1961, La Scala, 1962, Royal Opera House, Met. Opera, 1965, Vienna State Opera, Paris Opera, Salzburg Festival, Glyndebourne Festival; appeared in film Madame Butterfly and U.S. pub. TV broadcast of The Marriage of Figaro; maj. roles include: Zerlina in Don Giovanni, Nanette in Falstaff, Mimi in La Boheme, Violetta in La Traviata, Desdemona in Otello; numerous operatic recs., including Carmen (Grammy award for best opera rec. 1964). Office: care Herbert H Breslin Inc 119 W 57th St New York NY 10019 also: care John Coast Concerts, 1 Park Close, London SW1 England *

FRENOIS, MICHEL ALBERT, transportation executive; b. Rouen, France, Mar. 4, 1939; s. Pierre Emile and Genevieve (Dufetelle) F.; m. Sylvie Heidmann, Apr. 3, 1964; children: Jean, Eric. Baccalaureat, Lycee Corneille, Rouen, 1956; Ingenieur E.P., Ecole Poly., Paris, 1960; Desge, U. Lyon II, France, 1975. Engr., plant mgr. Shell France, 1962-75; crude oil trader Shell Europe, The Hague, 1969-71; regional mgr. Transexel, Paris, 1976-79; asst. mng. dir. Transports en Commun, Lyonnais, Lyon, France, 1979-85; mng. dir. Progemar-Transports Terrestres, Paris, 1986-88, Transcet, Paris, 1988—; prof. Ecole Superieure Transports, Paris, 1979-84. Contbr. articles to profl. jours. Pres. Polytechs. Lyonnais, Lyon, 1984-87; v.p. Union Des Ingenieurs, Lyon, 1984-87; com. pour la Def. Civile, Lyon, 1985—. Served to lt. French mil., 1960-62. Mem. Commn. Economie Union Transports PUbs. (pres. 1979-85). Home: 30 Rue Jean Broquin, 69006 Lyon France Office: Transcet, Tow Maine-Montparnasse, 33 Ave du Maine, 75015 Paris France

FRENTZEL-ZAGÓRSKA, JANINA ZOFIA, sociology educator; b. Warsaw, Poland, Nov. 27, 1931; d. Boleslaw and Zofia (Dutkiewicz) Frentzel; m. Janusz Szpotanski (div.); m. Krzysztof Zagórski, July 2, 1966; 1 child, Natalia. BA, Warsaw U., 1953, MA, 1962, PhD, 1973. Research fellow Polish Acad. Scis., Warsaw, 1964-65; asst. lectr. sociology Warsaw U., 1965-69; head sect. Ctr. for Pub. Opinion Research and Broadcasting Studies Polish Radio and TV, Warsaw, 1969-75, Inst. Culture, Warsaw, 1975—; sr. research fellow Austrian Nat. U., Canberra, 1988—; vis. fellow Australian Nat. U., Canberra, 1984-87; lectr. Macquarie U., Sydney, Australia, 1986. Author: (in Polish) Works of Symbolic Art as Vehicles for Social Communication; contbr. numerous articles on social and polit. psychology and sociology of culture to profl. jours. Instl. exec. mem., advisor Warsaw br. Solidarnosc, 1980-83. Mem. Internat. Sociol. Assn., Australasian Polit. Studies Assn., Polish Sociol. Assn. Office: Australian Nat U-RSSS, Canberra 2601, Australia

FRENYÓ, ZOLTÁN, philosopher, researcher, educator; b. Budapest, Hungary, Dec. 30, 1955. Diploma, Eötvös Lóránd U. Arts and Scis., Budapest, 1980. Cert. tchr. history and philosphy. Researcher Inst. Philosophy Hungarian Acad. of Scis., Budapest, 1980—. Contbr. articles to profl. jours. Mem. Hungarian Soc. Philosophy. Home: Kárpát 7/a, 1133 Budapest Hungary Office: Inst Philo, Hungarian Acad Sci, V Szemere u 10, Budapest Hungary

FRERE, PAUL, journalist; b. LeHavre, France, July 30, 1917; s. Maurice Paul and Germaine Ernestine (Schimp) F.; m. Suzanne Juliette Millo; children: Marianne, Martine, Nicole. Ingeneur Commercial, U. Libre, Brussels, Belgium, 1940. Sec. Ucobelwag & Ucobelloc, Brussels, 1941-45; service mgr. Auto Import Co., Brussels, 1948-52; auto racing driver 1952-60; v.p. tech. commn. FISA, 1972-84; freelance auto journalist Vence, France, 1946—; European editor Road & Track Mag., 1970-75, 80—; pres. European "Car of the Year" award, 1970-85, hon. pres., 1985—. Author several books on driving technique and auto. devel., 1960-86. Recipient Prix Charles Faroux, Societe des Ing; Automobile, Paris, 1964, Pemberton Trophy, Guild of Motoring Writers, London, 1974; winner Le Mans 24 hour race and South African Grande Prix, 1960. Mem. Brit. Racing Drivers Club (hon. mem.ú, club Internat. Anciens Pilotes de Grand Prix, Societe des Ingenieurs Belges del'Automobile. Home and Office: 684 Chemin Ste Elisabeth, Vence 06140, France

FRESCHI, BRUNO BASILIO, architect; b. Trail, B.C., Can., Apr. 18, 1937; s. Giovanni and Irma (Pagotto) F.; m. Vaune Ainsworth, Dec. 13, 1986; children from previous marriage: Dea Rachelle, Anna Nadine, Aaron Basilio, Reuben Alessandro. BArch with honors, U. B.C., 1961; Cert. Royal Can. Acad. Art, 1973. Assoc., Erickson Massey Architects, Vancouver, B.C., 1964-70; prin. Keith, King, Freschi, Vancouver, 1970-74; prin., owner Bruno Freschi, Architects, Vancouver, 1974—, Urbanisma Designs Ltd., Vancouver, 1975—, Bruno Freschi Architect, Inc., 1986; prof. architecture U. B.C., Vancouver, 1969-79; chief architect Expo '86. Prin. works include: Jamatkhana Mosque, Expo '86 Master Plan, Expo Centre, Burnaby Mcpl. Hall, Cathedral Sq. and Ga. Place; cons. Teleport, Van, B.C.; lectr. in field. Chmn., Italian Heritage Plaza, Vancouver, 1985; past mem. numerous civic and cultural orgns. Recipient Man of Yr. award Confratellanza Italo-Canadese, 1983; Gov. Gen. medal, 1984; First prize Wheel-Expo Symbol Competition, 1984; Sweney award CKVU-Vancouver, 1985. Fellow Royal Archtl. Inst. Can. (medal 1961); mem. Archtl. Inst. B.C., Royal Can. Acad. Arts (academician). Lodge: Christopher Columbus. Avocations: painting; hiking; bike riding. Home and Office: 1575 W 7th Ave, Vancouver, BC Canada V6J 1S1

FRESCO-KAUTSKY, EDITH JAKOBINE, writer; b. Vienna, Austria, Feb. 22, 1925; arrived in The Netherlands, 1938; d. Benedict and Gerda (Brunn) Kautsky; m. Jacob Fresco, Sept. 19, 1959; 1 child, Karin Elisabeth. MD, U. Zürich, Switzerland, 1954, PhD in Medicine, 1956; BS in Polit. Sci., U. Amsterdam, The Netherlands, 1974, MS in Polit. Sci., 1977; PhD in Polit. Sci., U. Leiden, The Netherlands, 1982. Gen. practitioner in medicine. Physician Tuberculosis Sanitarium, Davos, Switzerland, 1956-57; asst. prof. dept. pharmacology U. Bâle, Switzerland, 1957-58; research asst. CIBA, Bâle, 1958-59; assoc. dept. polit. sci. U. Leiden, 1978—. Author: Henry A. Kissinger, Historian and Statesman, 1983. U. Leiden grantee, 1978. Home: Vinkenlaan 3, 5104 PD Dongen The Netherlands

FRESE, MICHAEL, industrial psychologist; b. Munich, Bavaria, Fed. Republic of Germany, Aug. 9, 1949; s. Frank and Margarete Frese. Diploma, Free U., Berlin, 1976; PhD, Tech. U. of Berlin, 1978. Sci. asst. Tech. U., Berlin, Fed. Republic of Germany, 1976-80; assoc. prof. U. Pa., Phila., 1981-83; prof. U. Munich, Fed. Republic of Germany, 1984—; vis. prof. U. Bremen, Fed. Republic of Germany, 1980; adj. assoc. prof. U. Pa., Phila., 1984—. Author: Psychological Disturbances in Workers, 1977; editor: Industrial Psychopathology, 1978, Goal Directed Behavior, 1985, Psychological Issues of Human-Computer Interaction in the Workplace, 1987. Grantee Biomed. Fund, Phila., 1982, Deutsche Forschungsgemeinschaft, 1984-85, German Minister of Tech., 1987—. Office: Leopoldstrasse 13, D-8000 Munich Federal Republic of Germany

FRETER, MICHAEL CHARLES FRANKLIN, advertising executive; b. Surrey, Eng., Oct. 29, 1947; s. Leslie Charles and Myra (Wilkinson) F.; m. m. Jan Wilson, June 2, 1979. BA with honors, Oxford U., 1970. Sr. brand mgr. Unilever Co., London, 1970-76; account dir. Batton, Barton, Durstine & Osborn, London, 1976-78; bd. dirs. McCann-Erickson, London, 1978—.

FRETES-DAVALOS, MARLOS JORGE, former Paraguayan army officer, foreign service officer; b. Asuncion, Paraguay, Apr. 23, 1924; s. Cesar and Irene Conuelo (Davalos) Fretes-Ayala; m. Elsa Beatriz Flecha Alzamora, Apr. 30, 1970; children: Jorge Nicolas, Cesar Augusto, Carlos Gustavo. Inf. officer Mil Acad. Mariscal F.S. Lopez, Asuncion, 1940-45; commd. officer Paraguayan Army; comdr. Presdl. Guard, Asuncion, 1954-66, 3rd Ing. Div. Misiones, 1967-69; mil. attache Washington, 1970-78; ambassador to South Africa 1980—. Contbr. articles to mil. jours. Recipient Order of Condor of the Andes (Bolivia), Order of Mil. Merit (Brazil), Legion Merit (U.S.A.). Mem. Centenary Club (dir. 1956-66). Roman Catholic. Clubs: Touring and Automobile of Paraguay, Club Libertad (Asuncion). Office: Embassy of Paraguay, PO Box 3646, Pretoria 0001, Republic of South Africa

FREUDENBERG, HERMANN, company executive; b. Berlin, Aug. 18, 1924; m. Gisela Dumur, 1923; children—Eva, Dorothee, Klaus, Maria. Lic.sc.chim, U. Geneva, 1950. With Freudenberg & Co. and Carl Freudenburg, Weinheim, W. Ger., 1950—, gen. ptnr., 1959—. Office: Carl Freudenberg, PO Box 1369, D-6940 Weinheim Federal Republic of Germany

FREUDENBERG, REINHART, lawyer, business executive; b. Berlin, July 22, 1932; s. Adolf and Elsa (Liefmann) F.; m. Annegret Bartholome, 1959; children: Anna-Katharina, Sebastian, Martin, Monica, Hans. D of Law, U. Bonn, 1957. Lawyer, Mannheim, Fed. Republic of Germany, 1959-61; gen. mgr. Teneria Temola S.A., Mexico City, 1962-69; gen. ptnr. Freudenberg & Co., Weinheim, Fed. Republic of Germany, 1972—. Office: Carl Freudenberg, PO Box 1369, D-6940 Weinheim Federal Republic of Germany also: Freudenberg NAm Inc 401 Andover St North Andover MA 01845 also: Freudenberg & Co, Zwischen Dammen Weilheim AD Teck, 6940 Bad-Wuertt Federal Republic of Germany

FREUND, CAROL LOUISE, social service agency administrator; b. Mineola, N.Y., Feb. 21, 1933; d. Warren Edwin and Dorothy Geraldine (Gilbrech) Darnell; m. Curtis B. Bennett, Jr., July 17, 1954 (dec. 1959); m. William O.H. Freund, Jr., Sept. 16, 1960; children: Carol Burnam, William O.H. III. BA, Allegheny Coll., 1954; MA, John Carroll U., 1982. Tchr. South Euclid Lyndhurst City Schs., Ohio, 1955-57; trainer Episcopal Diocese of Ohio, Cleve., 1972—; exec. dir. Hitchcock House, Cleve., 1983-87. Mem. adv. com. Women and Alcohol Project, Cleve., 1983-87; mem. council agy. execs. United Way Services, Cleve., 1983-87; mem., v.p. Children's Services, Cleve., 1965-75; pres. Shaker Heights PTA, 1975-76, Cleve. Internat. Program, 1980-83; 1st v.p. Council Internat. Programs, 1984-88; pres. Council Internat. Programs, Cleve., 1988—. Recipient Outstanding Vol. Service award Cleve. Internat. Program, 1983, Founding Trustee award Edn. for Freedom of Choice in Ohio, 1982, cert. of recognition Council Internat. Programs, 1981. Episcopalian. Avocation: flower arranging. Home: 699 High St PO Box 1366 Coshocton OH 43812

FREUND, EMMA FRANCES, medical technologist; b. Washington; d. Walter R. and Mabel W. (Loveland) Ervin; B.S., Wilson Tchrs. Coll., Washington, 1944; M.S. in Biology, Catholic U., Washington, 1953; cert. in mgmt. devel. Va. Commonwealth U., 1975; student SUNY, New Paltz, 1977, J. Sargeant Reynolds Community Coll., 1978; m. Frederic Reinert Freund, Mar. 4, 1953; children—Frances, Daphne, Fern, Frederic. Tchr. math. and sci. D.C. Sch. System, 1944-45; technician in parasitology lab., zool. div., U.S. Dept. Agr., Beltsville, Md., 1945-48; histologic technician dept. pathology Georgetown U. Med. Sch., Washington, 1948-49; clin. lab. technician Kent and Queen Anne's County Gen. Hosp., Chestertown, Md., 1949-51; histotechnologist surg. pathology dept. Med. Coll. Va. Hosp., Richmond, 1951—, supr. histology lab., 1970—; mem. exam. council Nat. Cert. Agy. Med. Lab. Personnel. Asst. cub scout den leader Robert E. Lee council Boy Scouts Am., 1967-68, den leader, 1968-70. Co-author (mini-course): Instrumentation in Cytology and Histology, 1985. Cert. Nat. Cert. Agy. for Clin. Lab. Personnel. Mem. Am. Soc. Med. Technology (rep. to sci. assembly histology sect. 1977-78, chmn. histology sect. 1983-85), Va. Soc. Med. Technology, Richmond Soc. Med. Technologists (corr. sec. 1977-78, dir. 1981-82, pres. 1984-85), Va. Soc. Histology Technicians (dir. 1979—, pres. 1982-88), Nat. Certification Agy. (clin. lab. specialist in histotech.), N.Y. Acad. Scis., Am. Soc. Clin. Pathologists (cert. histology technician), Nat. Geog. Soc., Va. Govtl. Employees Assn., AAAS, Nat. Soc. Histotech. (by-laws com. 1981—; C.E.U. com. 1981—, program com. regional meeting 1984, 85, chmn. regional meeting 1987), Am. Mus. Natural History, Smithsonian Instn., Am. Mgmt. Assn., Clin. Lab. Mgmt. Assn., Nat. Soc. Historic Preservation, Am. Biog. Inst. Research Assn. (life; recipient Commemorative medal of Honor 1986), Sigma Xi, Phi Beta Rho, Kappa Delta Pi, Phi Lambda Theta. Home: 1315 Asbury Rd Richmond VA 23229 Office: Surgical Pathology Dept Med Coll VA Hosp PO Box 240 Richmond VA 23298-0240

FREVERT, JAMES WILMOT, financial planner; b. Richland Twp., Iowa, Dec. 19, 1922; s. Wesley Clarence and Grace Lotta (Maw) F.; m. Jean Emily Sunderlin, Feb. 12, 1949; children—Douglas James, Thomas Jeffrey, Kimberly Ann. B.S. in Gen. Engrg., MIT, 1948. Prodn. mgr. Air Reduction Chem. Co., Calvert City, Ky., 1955-61; plant mgr. Air Products & Chems., West Palm Beach, Fla., 1961-62; pres. Young World HWD, Ft. Lauderdale, Fla., 1962-66; v.p. Shareholders Mgmt. Co., Los Angeles, 1966-73; v.p. cert. fin. planner Thomson McKinnon Securities, Inc., North Palm Beach, Fla., 1973—. Founder, past pres. MIT Club Palm Beach County, dir., 1976—, ednl. council mem., 1977-81. Served to 1st lt. USAF, 1943-46. Mem. Internat. Assn. Fin. Planning (dir. Gold Coast chpt. 1968-87), Inst. Cert. Fin. Planners (cert. 1975, registry fin. planners 1983—). Republican. Presbyterian. Club: Palm Beach Pundits. Home: 883 Country Club Dr North Palm Beach FL 33408 Office: Thomson McKinnon 713 US Hwy 1 North Palm Beach FL 33408

FREY, BRUNO S., economics educator; b. Basel, Switzerland, May 4, 1941; s. Leo and Julia (Bach) F. Licentiatus, U. Basel, 1964, Dr. rerum politicarum, 1965; habilitation, 1969. Assoc. prof. econs. U. Basel, 1969—; prof. econs. U. Zurich, Switzerland, 1977—; vis. lectr. Wharton Sch. U. Pa., Phila., 1967-68; ofcl. visitor Nuffield Coll. Oxford U., Eng., 1975; vis. prof. U. Stockholm, 1982; vis. fellow All Souls Coll. Oxford U., 1983; fellow Wissenschaftskolleg, Berlin, 1984, 85. Author: Modern Political Economy, 1978, Democratic Economic Policy, 1983, International Political Economy, 1984, Umweltoekonomie, 1985. Office: Inst Empirical Econ Research, Kleinstrasse 15, CH-8008 Zurich Switzerland

FREY, CHARLES FREDERICK, surgeon, educator; b. N.Y.C., Nov. 15, 1929; s. Charles N. and Julia (Leary) F.; m. Jane Louise Tower, July 20, 1957; children: Jane Elizabeth, Susan Ann, Charles Frederick, Robert Tower, Nancy Louise. BA, Amherst Coll., 1951; MD, Cornell U., 1955. Diplomate Am. Bd. Surgery. Intern Cornell Med. Ctr., N.Y.C., 1955-56, asst. resident, 1956-57, 59-61, 1st asst. resident, 1962, chief resident, 1963; instr. surgery U. Mich., Ann Arbor, 1964-65, asst. prof. surgery, 1965-68, assoc. prof., 1968-72, prof., 1972-76; prof. U. Calif., Davis, 1976—, vice. chmn. dept. surgery, 1976-81, exec. vice-chmn. dept., 1981—; mem. staff VA Hosp., Martinez, Calif., chief surg. service, 1976-80; surg. cons. U. Mich., 1966-76, VA, 1971—, Highway Safety Research Inst., 1973-76. Assoc. editor: The Pancreas; contbr. numerous articles to profl. jours. Served to capt. USAF, 1957-59. Fellow ACS (chief regional com. on trauma 1976—, disaster preparedness com. 1978—, med. motion pictures com. 1981—, allied health com. 1981-82, program com. No. Calif. chpt. 1981—, credentials com. No. Calif. chpt. 1982—), Am. Assn. Surgery Trauma; mem. AMA, Calif. Med. Assn., Contra Costa Med. Assn., Am. Fedn. Clin. Research, Am. Assn. Automotive Medicine (bd. dirs. 1970-74), Internat. Assn. Accident and Traffic Medicine, Am. Trauma Soc. (founding, standards devel. com. 1978—, v.p. Calif. div. 1979—, bd. dirs. 1980—), Calif. Trauma Soc. (trustee 1977—), Nat. Trauma Com. of ACS (chmn. membership com. 1980-84, exec. com. 1981-85) Assn. Acad. Surgery, Am. Surg. Assn., Brazilian Surg. Soc., Western Surg. Assn., Cen. Surg. Assn. (membership com. 1971-73), Pacific Coast Surg. Assn., Sacramento Surg. Soc., Assn. VA Surgeons (publs., program coms. 1981—), Soc. Univ. Surgeons, Soc. Surgery Alimentary Tract (constn. and by-laws com. 1969—, chmn. 1972-76), Internat. Assn. Pancreatology (mem. editorial bd. 1986, steering com.), Internat. Biliary Assn., Am. Gastroenterology Assn., Pancreas Club (chmn. 1975—). Home: 52 Charles Hill Rd Orinda CA 94563 Office: U Calif Med Ctr Dept Surgery 4301 X St Sacramento CA 95817

FREY, H. GARRETT, stockbroker; b. Cin., Dec. 2, 1938; s. John H. and Mary G. (Grever) F.; student U. Detroit, 1956-57, U. Cin., 1957-59, U. Miami, 1960-61; m. Mary Knollman, July 23, 1960; children—John, Robert, Meg, Amy, Brad, Julie. Salesman, Verkamp Corp., Cin., 1958-60, Formica Corp., Cin., Miami, Fla., and Hartford, Conn., 1960-62; stockbroker Westheimer & Hayden Stone, Cin., 1962-64; stockbroker Harrison & Co., 1964-66, gen. partner, 1966-73, mng. partner, 1972-77; v.p. Bache Halsey Stuart Shields Inc., Cin., 1977-79; chmn. bd. Queen City Securities Corp., Cin., 1979—, Queen City Group Cos., 1979—. Mem. investment com. Sisters of Charity, Cin., 1970; chmn. Ursuline Acad., 1986—, Ursuline Found.; pres. Springer Ednl. Found. Served with AUS, 1959. Named Big Brother of the Year, 1968. Mem. Cin. Stock Exchange (v.p. 1970-72, trustee 1979—), N.Y. Stock Exchange, Am. Stock Exchange, Purcell High Sch. Alumni (pres. 1972-73), Chgo. Bd. Options Exchange, Cath. Big Bros. Cin. (pres. 1966-67). Roman Catholic (council pres. 1971-72). Clubs: Cincinnati Stock and Bond (pres. 1969), Buckeye (pres. 1968-69). Home: 3660 Kroger Ave Cincinnati OH 45226 Office: 1500 Merc Ctr Cincinnati OH 45202

FREY, HERMAN S., publishing company executive; b. Murfreesboro, Tenn., Apr. 19, 1920; s. Saleem McCool and Minnie May (Felts) F.; m. Daisy Rook Corlew, Apr. 3, 1946; 1 child, Pamela Anne. Cert. commerce, U. Va., 1958; cert., Internat. Ct. Justice, The Netherlands, 1959; BA, Am. U., 1964; MBA, George Washington U., 1965; cert. constl. history, Oxford U., 1974, cert. fgn. and imperial policy, 1975. Commd. navigator USN, 1937-61; advanced through grades to lt. comdr., 1955; with navigation dept. USS Quincy, 1937-41, navigator USS Sagamore, 1941-42, asst. navigator USS Iowa, 1942-44, with Naval Schs., Norfolk, Va., N.Y.C., Miami, 1944-45, navigation and gunnery officer USS Zuni, 1945-46, exec. officer USS Chickasaw, 1946-47, comdg. officer, 1947-48; instr. Naval Sch., Boston, 1948-51; comdg. officer USS Sisken, 1951-52; comdr. mine div., task unit, 1952-54; exec. officer USS McClellan, 1954-55; officer detailer Bur. Naval Personnel, Washington, 1955-58; advisor, liaison Am. Embassy, The Netherlands, 1958-61; stock broker Auchincloss, Parker & Redpath, Arlington, Va., 1966-67; asst. prof. Georgetown U., Washington, 1967, U. Va., Charlottesville, 1967-69; freelance journalist Europe, U.S., 1972-76; pres. Frey Enterprises, 1976—; faculty U. Md., College Park, 1978; mem. bd. govs. Am. Sch. of Hague, Netherlands, 1959-61; cons. State of Tenn., 1969-70. Author: Jefferson Davis, 1977. Ran for U.S. Senate, Tenn., 1970, 72; bd. govs. Meth. Ch., Arlington, 1962-64; mem. U.S. Hist. Soc.; research bd. advisors Am. Biog. Inst., Inc. Mem. Am. Bus. Men's Assn., The Hague, 1958-61. Fellow Internat. Biog. Ctr., Am. Biog. Inst. Research Assn. (life); mem. World Inst. Achievement, Soc. Advancement Mgmt. (pres. 1964), Am. Assn. Univ. Profs., Internat. Platform Assn., U.S. Naval Inst. (life), Tenn. Hist. Soc., Tenn. Sheriff's Assn., Ret. Officers Assn. (life), Nat. Assn. Uniformed Services (life), Am. Legion, VFW (life), Veteran's Assn., Navy League of U.S., Phi Alpha Theta. Democrat. Club: Mil. Dist. Officer's (Washington). Avocations: history, literature, collecting rare books, travel, amateur cooking. Office: Frey Enterprises 2120 Crestmoor Rd Nashville TN 37215

FREY, MARC ALEXANDER, business executive; b. Zurich, May 2, 1956; s. Max and Yvonne (Forster) F.; m. Anuška Stariha, Apr. 11, 1987. Bachelor's, Paris, 1979; MBA, Monterey, Calif., 1981. With Jean Frey Group, Zurich, 1982—, chief exec. officer, 1987—, also bd. dirs.

FREY, PETER, editor, publisher; b. Baden, Switzerland, Jan. 16, 1923; s. Friedrich Wilhelm and Hedwig (Heusser) F.; m. Edith Zust, Sept. 9, 1952; 1 child, Anne-Catherine Chantal. Dipl. Ing. agr., Fed. Inst. Tech., 1949; PhD Sociology, U.Geneva, 1970. Editor, Illustrated Die Woche, Zurich, 1953-62; fgn. corr. Tages Anzeiger, Paris, 1963-65, editor in chief, Zurich, 1978-83; co-founder, Tages-Anzeiger Magazin, Zurich, 1970-78, editor, 1984-88 . Mem. exec. bd. Internat. Press Inst., London, 1981—; v.p. Swiss Film Center Found., Zurich, 1979—; pres. Swiss Film Council, 1983-85. Contbr. articles to profl. jours. Mem. Fed. Commn. Peace Research Inst., Bern, 1973. Recipient Press award Press Assn. Zurich, 1973. Mem. Internat. Press Inst., Swiss Assn. Journalists. Roman Catholic.

FREY, RENÉ L., economics educator; b. Basel, Switzerland, Mar. 9, 1939; s. Leo and Julia (Bach) F.; m. Verena Schnurrenberger, May 7, 1965; children: Claudia, Isabel, Miriam. Research dir. Gesellschaft für Bauforschung,

Zurich, Switzerland, 1964-66; asst. prof. econs. U. Basel, 1966-70, prof., 1970—; cons. in field. Author: Infrastruktur, 2d edit., 1972, Wachstumspolitik, 1979, Regionalpolitik, 1985, Wirtschaft, Staat und Wohlfahrt, 5th edit., 1987; mng. editor Kyklos, 1970—. Mem. Schweizerische Gesellschaft für Statistik und Volkswirtschaft (v.p. 1986—), Am. Econ. Assn., Verein für Socialpolitik, List Gesellschaft. Home: Adlerstrasse 38, CH4052 Basel Switzerland Office: Wirtschaftswissenschaftliches, Zentrum, Petersgraben 51, CH4003 Basel Switzerland

FREYINGER, KLAUS CHRISTOPH, real estate developer; b. Augsburg, Federal Republic of Germany, July 9, 1933; came to U.S., 1980; s. Johann Jakob Freyinger and Magdalene Hermine (Amann) Kositz; m. Eva Maria Wilczek, Dec. 16, 1959; children: Claus Christoph, Benjamin Patrick. BArch, Technische Hochschule, Munich, 1956, MArch, 1963. Registered architect, Fed. Republic Germany and Common Mkt. Assoc. architect Scheidle Wörner, Calw, Württemberg, Fed. Republic Germany, 1963-64; pvt. practice architecture Augsburg, 1964-80; pvt. practice real estate investor, developer St. Paul, 1980—; consulting architect Beier/Kraus, Augsburg, 1976-80; real estate cons., St. Paul, 1986; mgmt. cons. K.C.S. Mgmt., Mpls., 1985-86, real estate refinancing cons., 1985-86. Lifeguard Rotes Kreuz, Augsburg, 1974-80. Recipient award for rescuing a swimmer, City of Augsburg, 1959; numerous awards for archtl. competitions in Fed. Republic Germany. Mem. Minn. Soc. of AIA (assoc.), Bavarian Chamber of Architects. Republican. Presbyterian. Clubs: Town and Country (St. Paul).

FREYMAN, LEONARD, speech communication educator; b. Cleve., May 9, 1912; s. Henry Louis and Eva Evelyn (Krohn) F.; B.A., Case-Western Res. U., 1939, M.A., 1940, Ph.D., 1955; student Mich. State U., 1943, Royal Acad. Dramatic Arts, U. London, 1945; m. June Delories Snyder, May 24, 1944. Instr. dept. edn. Edmonton and Calgary, Alta., Can., summers, 1940, 41; tchr. English, Cleveland Heights (Ohio) High Sch., 1948-58, English coordinator, 1958-62, English and library coordinator, 1962-66, dir. edn., 1966-74, curriculum and dir. fine arts, 1974-78; instr. speech Shrivenham (Eng.) Am. U., 1945, Cleve. State U., 1946-48; tchr. English, Glen Oak Sch., Gates Mills, Ohio, 1978-79; asst. prof. speech communication and area adviser div. humanities Bethune-Cookman Coll., 1979—; instr.-trainer, cons. Dale Carnegie and Assos., Inc., Garden City, N.Y., 1947-85, instr. emeritus, 1985—; cons. Silver-Burdett Publishers, Boston, 1966-69. Dir. speech tng. tours, speakers and films div. United Appeal of Greater Cleve., 1962-69; chmn. youth adv. com. Greater Cleve. chpt. ARC, 1965-67; co-chmn. Temples and Schs. div. Jewish Welfare Fund Greater Cleve., 1976, 77; bd. govs. Western Res. U., 1957-61, bd. overseers, 1972-75. Served with AUS, 1942-45. Named Alumnus of Yr., Cleve. Coll., Western Res. U., 1962. Fellow Royal Soc. Arts; mem. Northeastern Ohio Drama Assn. (pres. 1952-54), Greater Cleve. Council Tchrs. English (pres. 1956-58), Nat. Council Tchrs. English (co-chmn. Cleve. conv. 1964), AAUP, Speech Communication Assn., NEA, Assn. for Supervision and Curriculum Devel., Ohio Ret. Tchrs. Assn., Ohio Edn. Assn., Fla. Speech Communication Assn., Ohio PTA, Western Res. Hist. Soc. Jewish. Club: B'nai B'rith. Contbg. author: Books For You, 1964; Improving English Composition, 1965; Language Arts Tests, 1969; contbr. articles to profl. jours. Home: PO Box 4704 South Daytona FL 32021 Office: Bethune-Cookman Coll 640 2d Ave Daytona Beach FL 32015

FREYTAG, SHARON NELSON, lawyer; b. Larned, Kans., May 11, 1943; d. John Seldon and Ruth Marie (Herbel) Nelson; m. Thomas Lee Freytag, June 18, 1966; children: Kurt David, Hillary Lee. BS with highest distinction, U. Kans., Lawrence, 1965; MA, U. Mich., 1966; JD cum laude, So. Meth. U., 1981. Bar: Tex. 1981, U.S. Dist. Ct. (no. dist.) Tex. 1981, U.S. Ct. Appeals (5th cir.) 1982. Tchr. English, Gaithersburg (Md.) High Sch., 1966-70; instr. English, Eastfield Coll., 1974-78; law clk. U.S. Dist. Ct. for No. Dist. Tex., 1981-82, U.S. Ct. Appeals for 5th Circuit, 1982; assoc. in litigation Haynes and Boone, Dallas, 1983—, vis. prof. law Southern Meth. U., 1985-86. Editor-in-chief Southwestern Law Jour., 1980-81; contbr. articles to law jours. Mem. ABA, Tex. Bar Assn., Dallas Bar Assn., Dallas Mus. Art, Dallas Shakespeare Soc., Order of Coif, Barristers, Phi Delta Phi, Phi Beta Kappa. Lutheran. Office: Haynes & Boone 3100 First Republic Plaza Dallas TX 75202

FREZZOTTI, RENATO, ophthalmologist; b. Imperia, Italy, Dec. 19, 1924; s. Giuseppe and Rosa (Pirani) F.; m. Angela Tabanelli, Feb. 9, 1961; children—Maria Luce, Paolo, Guido. Laureate in Medicine and Surgery, U. Perugia, 1949. Asst. and clin. oculist U. Siena, 1950-67, prof. ophthalmology, 1967—. Author: Oftalmologia Essenziale, 1982; Pathologia, Clinica e Terapia delle Malattie dell' Orbita, 1985. Contbr. articles to profl. jours. Recipient Medaglia d'Oro Benemeriti della Scuola, Cultura, Arte, Ministero Pubblica Istruzione, 1982. Lodge: Rotary. Home: Viale XXIV Maggio 23, 53100 Siena Italy Office: Istit di Scienze Oftalmologiche, Univ Siena, 53100 Siena Italy

FRIBERG, LARS TORSTEN, physician, educator; b. Malmo, Sweden, Feb. 25, 1920; s. Otto Lorens and Lydia Elvira (Andrews) F.; m. Britt-Marie Westerberg, Aug. 15, 1951 (div. 1976); children—Bertil, Goran, Jan; m. Monika Lundin Abramson, Apr. 12, 1986. M.D., Karolinska Inst., Stockholm, 1945, D.Med. Sci., 1950. Asst. prof. environ. hygiene Karolinska Inst., 1951-56, prof., 1957-87, chmn. dept. environ. hygiene, 1957-87, prof. emeritus, 1988—; mem. Nobel Assembly, 1957-85; dept. head Nat. Inst. Pub. Health, Stockholm, 1957-71; dir. Nat. Inst. Environ. Medicine, Stockholm, 1980-87; vis. prof. U. Cin., 1967; chmn. sci. com. Toxicology of Metals, 1972—; mem. adv. bd. occupational health WHO, 1975—, dir. Collaborating Ctr. for Environ. Health Effects, Stockholm, 1976-87; mem., chmn. com. potentially harmful substances GESAMP, 1982-86; mem. adv. bd. Swedish Bd. Health and Welfare, Nat. Food Adminstrn.; mem. med. adv. bd. Swedish Armed Forces. Contbr. articles to profl. jours. Bd. dirs. Swedish Nuclear Power Inspectorate; trustee Nobel Found., 1984-85. Recipient prize of Jubilee Swedish Soc. Med. Scis., 1951, William P. Yant award Am. Indsl. Hygiene Assn., 1985; Distinguished Service medal Finnish Inst. Occupational Health, 1987. Mem. N.Y. Acad. Scis. (hon.), Purkinje Soc. (corr.), Finnish Indsl. Med. Soc. (corr.). Home: Kevingeringen 83, 18233 Danderyd Sweden Office: Karolinska Inst, Solnavagen 1, 104 Stockholm Sweden

FRIBOURGH, JAMES HENRY, university official; b. Sioux City, Iowa, June 10, 1926; s. Johan Gunder and Edith Katherine (James) F.; m. Cairdenia Minge, Jan. 29, 1955; children: Cynthia Kaye, Rebecca Jo, Abbie Lynn. Student, Morningside Coll., 1944-47; B.A., U. Iowa, 1949, M.A., 1949, Ph.D., 1957. Instr. Little Rock Jr. Coll., 1949-56; assoc. prof. biology Little Rock U., 1957-60, prof., chmn. div. life scis., 1960-69; vice chancellor U. Ark.-Little Rock, 1969-72, interim chancellor, 1972-73, exec. vice chancellor for acad. affairs, 1973-82, interim chancellor, exec. vice chancellor for acad. affairs, 1982, provost, exec. vice chancellor, 1983—, disting. prof., 1984—; cons. in field; assoc. Marine Biol. Lab., Woods Hole, Mass. Contbr. articles to profl. jours. Mem. Ark. Gov.'s Com. on Sci. and Tech., 1969-71; bd. dirs., mem. nat. adv. bd. Nat. Back Found., 1979; vice chmn. NCCJ, 1981-82; div. rep. United Way of Pulaski County, 1980-82; bd. dirs. Ark. Dance Theatre, Little Rock, 1980-82; vestryman Good Shepherd Episcopal Ch.; del. Episcopal Diocese of Ark.; fellow Ark. Mus. Sci. and History, 1987. NSF fellow Hist. of Sci. Inst., 1959-60. Fellow AAAS, Coll. of Preceptors (London), Am. Inst. Fishery Research Biologists, Ark. Mus. Sci. and History; mem. Am. Fisheries Soc. (chmn. com. on internationalism cert. fisheries scientist), AAUP (pres. Ark. conf.); Electron Microscopy Soc. Am., Ark. Mus. Sci. and History; mem. Am. Soc. Swedish Engrs. (corr. mem.), Ark. Acad. Sci. (pres. 1966), Ark. Dean's Assn. (pres. 1982), Am. Assn. State Colls. and Univs., Am. Swedish Inst., Sigma Xi, Phi Kappa Phi. Democrat. Clubs: Swedish (Chgo.); Vasa Order Am. Lodge: Rotary. Office: U Ark 33d and University Ave Little Rock AR 72204

FRICK, JAMES WILLIAM, university administrator, consultant; b. New Bern, N.C., Aug. 5, 1924; s. Odo Aloysius and Mary Elizabeth (Cox) F.; m. Bonita Charlotte Torbert, Mar. 26, 1951 (div. 1984); children—Michael, Terence, Thomas, Theresa, Kathleen; m. Karen Ann Fogle, Oct. 13, 1984. B.S. in Commerce, U. Notre Dame, 1951, Ph.D. in Edn., 1973, LL.D., 1983. Project dir. U. Notre Dame, Ind., 1951-56, regional dir., 1956-61, exec. dir., 1961-65, v.p., 1965-83, asst. to pres., 1983-87, v.p. emeritus, 1987—; pres. James W. Frick Assocs., Inc., South Bend, Ind., 1983—; chmn. exec. com. St. Joseph Bank and Trust, South Bend, 1968—; dir. W.R. Grace Co., Inc., N.Y.C., Magic Circle Energy Corp., Oklahoma City. Contbr. chpts. to books, articles to profl. jours. Chmn. United Way St. Joseph County, 1970, Project Future, South Bend, 1982; exec. com. Fin. Devel. Council Nat. Urban Coalition, Washington, 1975; nat. devel. council Assn. Am. Colls., Washington, 1978. Served to lt. (j.g.) USN, 1942-46. Recipient James E. Armstrong award U. Notre Dame, 1978; named Knight of Malta, Cath. Ch., 1981. Mem. Council Advancement and Support Edn. (pres. 1971-72, Ashmore award 1982), Assn. Governing Bds. (devel. adv. council 1982—), Phi Delta Kappa. Roman Catholic. Clubs: Marco Polo (N.Y.C.); Pith Helmet (Pomona, Calif.). Avocations: opera; symphonies; reading; historical novels; walking. Office: James W Frick Assocs Inc 1410 Trustcorp Bldg South Bend IN 46601

FRICKE, RICHARD JOHN, lawyer; b. Ithaca, N.Y., Apr. 17, 1945; s. Richard I. and Jeanne L. (Hines) F.; m. Carol A. Borelli, June 17, 1967; children—Laura, Richard, Amanda. B.A., Cornell U., 1967, J.D., 1970. Bar: Conn. 1970. Assoc., Gregory & Adams, Wilton, Conn., 1970-73; ptnr. Crehan & Fricke, Ridgefield, Conn., 1973—; dir. Village Bank & Trust Co.; town atty. Town of Ridgefield, 1973-81. Bd. dirs. Ridgefield Community Ctr., Ridgefield Montessori, Ridgefield Community Kindergarten; founder, pres. Ridgefield Lacrosse League; mem. Conn. Bar Commn. on Women, 1976. Mem. ABA, Conn. Bar Assn., Danbury Bar Assn. Democrat. Roman Catholic. Co-patentee low reactive pressure foam. Home: 94 Main St Ridgefield CT 06877 Office: 181 Main St Ridgefield CT 06877

FRICKER, PETER RACINE, composer, educator; b. London, Sept. 5, 1920; came to U.S., 1964; s. Edward Racine and Deborah (Parr) F.; m. Helen Clench, Apr. 17, 1943. Student, Royal Coll. Music, London, 1937-41; Mus.D. (hon.), U. Leeds, Eng., 1958. Dir. music Morley Coll., London, 1953-64; prof. music Royal Coll. Music, London, 1956-64; prof. music dept. U. Calif. at Santa Barbara, 1964—, Corwin chair, 1987—; condr., lectr., 1948—; pres. Cheltenham Internat. Festival Music, 1983-86. Composer 5 symphonies, 2 oratorios, 2 violin concertos, 2 piano concertos, horn concerto, viola concerto, organ concerto, concerto for orch., chamber music, music for piano and 2 pianos, music for films and radio. Pres. emeritus Cheltenham Internat. Festival, 1987. Served to flight lt. RAF, 1941-46. Decorated Order of Merit (Fed. Republic Germany); recipient Freedom City of London, 1962. Fellow Royal Coll. Organists, asso. Royal Coll. Music; mem. Composer's Guild Gt. Britain (chmn. 1955, v.p. 1986), Royal Philharmonic Soc. London, Soc. Promotion New Music, Am. Music Ctr., AAUP, Am. Soc. Univ. Composers, Royal Acad. Music (hon.). Home: 5423 Throne Ct Santa Barbara CA 93111 Office: U Calif Music Dept Santa Barbara CA 93106

FRICON, TERRI MADELINE, music publisher, producer, consultant; b. Buffalo, July 19, 1943; d. Anthony Edward and Josephine Rose (D'Amico) F.; 1 child, Donelle Jo; student San Jose State U., 1961; MusB, U. Miami, 1963. Asst. to profl. mgr. Screen Gems Music, 1965; asst. w. coast dir. record div. 20th Century Fox, 1966-67; v.p., partner Wednesday's Child Prodns., 1967-72; pres. music group Filmways, also dir. music dept. Filmways TV and Filmways Motion Pictures, 1974-81; pres. Fricon Entertainment Co., Inc., Los Angeles, 1981—. Composer: I Can See it in your Eyes, Bow to Bob; music supr. TV series Cagney & Lacey. Recipient Golden Staff award Music and Arts Found. Am., 1975-86, Profl. Achievement award Soroptimist Club Los Angeles, 1977. Mem. ASCAP (pubs. adv. com. 1977—), Assn. Ind. Music Pubs., Nat. Acad. Rec. Arts and Scis., Nashville Songwriters Assn., Acad. Country Music, Black Music Assn., Nat. Music Pubs. Assn., Broadcast Music, Inc., Women in Film, Acad. TV Arts and Scis., Am. Fedn. Musicians, Calif. Copyright Conf. (pres. 1980-81), Music Pubs. Forum (chmn. 1979-81). Home and Office: 1048 S Ogden Dr Los Angeles CA 90019

FRICS, LASZLO, veterinarian; b. Hungary, Apr. 27, 1909; came to U.S., 1951, naturalized, 1956; s. Gyula and Ida (Honeczy) F.; m. Margit Maria Harto Szokolay, May 19, 1940; children—Laszlo Agoston, Kornelia Frics Smith, Agoston Zsigmond. D.V.M., Royal Hungarian U. Sci. and Agr., Budapest, 1932; Ph.D. cum laude in Physiology, Technicum and Oeconomicum Jozsef Ná dor U. Budapest, 1939. Asst. instr. Sci. and Agr. U. Budapest, 1930-32; practice race horse vet. medicine, Hungary, 1934-39; govt. dist. veterinarian, 1939-45; veterinarian, W. Ger., 1945-51, Cleve. and Akron, Ohio, 1951-54, Emery, S.D., 1954—. Served to capt. Hussar Regt. Life mem. S.D. Vet. Med. Assn. Roman Catholic. Club: K.C. Research on blood, nutrition in animals. Address: 200 Senlac Hills Dr Chagrin Falls OH 44022

FRIDAY, WILLIAM CLYDE, university president emeritus; b. Raphine, Va., July 13, 1920; s. David L. and Mary E. (Rowan) F.; m. Ida Howell, May 13, 1942; children: Frances H., Mary H., Ida E. Student, Wake Forest Coll., 1937, LL.D., 1957; B.S., N.C. State Coll., 1941; LL.B., U. N.C., 1948; LL.D., Belmont Abbey Coll., 1957, Duke U., 1958, Princeton U., 1958, Elon Coll., 1959, Davidson Coll., 1961, U. Ky., 1970, Mercer U., 1977; D.C.L., St. Augustine's Coll., 1986, U. of South, 1976; DPS, U. N.C., Charlotte, 1986; DFA, N.C. Sch. Arts, 1987. Bar: N.C. 1948. Asst. dean student U. N.C., 1948-51, asst. to pres., 1951-55, sec. of univ., 1955-56, acting pres., 1956, pres., 1956-86; Mem. Carnegie Commn. on Higher Edn., Commn. to Study SUNY, So. Regional Edn. Bd.; chmn. President's Task Force on Edn., 1966-67; mem. Commn. White House Fellows, 1965-68. Mem. Nat. Com. for Bicentennial Era., Am. Council Edn., Commn. Natl. Changes Higher Edn., Ctr. Creative Leadership (chmn. 1981), Gov.'s Commn. Literacy (chmn. 1987); trustee Howard U. Served as lt. USNR, World War II. Mem. Assn. Am. Univs. (pres. 1971). Democrat. Baptist. Office: The William R Kenan Jr Fund PO Box 3808 Univ NC Chapel Hill NC 27515-3808

FRIDHOLM, GEORGE H., management consultant; b. Blue Island, Ill., Oct. 24, 1921; s. Oscar and Anna (Bolin) F.; B.E.E., Purdue U., 1949; m. Sheila Mary Malley, May 11, 1957; children—Gregory, Christian, John, Rachel. Test engr. Gen. Electric Co., Phila. also Ft. Wayne, Ind., 1949-50, design engr., 1950-53, mem. advanced product planning team, Lynn, Mass., 1953-54, design engr., Ft. Wayne, 1954-55, design engr., Schenectady, 1955-57, fin. specialist, 1957-59, mfg. engr., 1959-60, mem. corp. staff value cons., 1960-62, value program mgr. value programs for industry, Schenectady, 1962-68; pres. George Fridholm Assocs., Cons. Value Mgmt. Systems, Burnt Hills, N.Y., 1968—; leader, facilitator Creative Problem-Solving Inst., Buffalo. Vice-chmn. Ballston (N.Y.) Zoning Bd. Appeals, 1969-82; troop com. chmn. Schenectady County council Boy Scouts Am., 1970-80. Served with USAAF, 1941-45. Decorated Bronze Star medal. Cert. mgmt. cons., value specialist. Fellow Paul Harris; Mem. Internat. Platform Assn., Soc. Mfg. Engrs. (sr. mem.), Inst. Mgmt. Cons., IEEE, Soc. Am. Value Engrs., Assn. Mgmt. Cons., Eta Kappa Nu. Republican. Lutheran. Club: Burnt Hills-Ballston Lake. Lodge: Rotary. Home: One Fridholm Dr Burnt Hills NY 12027 Office: PO Box 88 Burnt Hills NY 12027

FRIEDE, J(ERZY) GEORGE, business executive; b. Warsaw, Poland, Sept. 12, 1920; came to U.S., 1941, naturalized, 1943; s. Maximilian and Stefania (Anker) F.; m. Fella Pressner, Dec. 28, 1952 (div. 1983); children—Andrew, Stephanie, Margaret, Caroline; m. Adrienne M. Krausz, Mar. 3, 1985. B.S., Cambridge U., 1941. Founder, owner Seaward Commerce Co., Bridgeport, Conn., 1946—; pres. Seaward Mgmt. Corp., Bridgeport, 1976—; dir., treas. KFC Nat. Purchasing Coop., Inc., Louisville, 1978—; pres. Big Apple KFC, Inc., N.Y.C., 1984—; dir. NE. Franchise Assn., Hartford, Conn., 1977—. Mem. Sarasota Opera Assn., Fla., 1980; mem. Hon. Order Ky. Cols., Frankfort, 1978; Am. Jewish Com., N.Y.C., 1961. Served with AUS, 1942-46, ETO, PTO. Recipient Commendation cert. U.S. Dept. Commerce, 1964. Mem. Bridgeport Bus. Industry Council, Nat. Restaurant Assn., U.S. C. of C. Home: 15 Rice's Ln Westport CT 06880 Office: Seaward Mgmt Corp 4301 Main St Bridgeport CT 06606

FRIEDEL, BERNARD, manufacturing company executive; b. N.Y.C., Jan. 26, 1930; s. Joseph and Jeanne (Shoenback) F.; m. Rosalie Gertsenstein, Mar. 17, 1951 (div. 1978); children: Steven, Joyce; m. 2d. Mel Scherzer, 1983 (div. 1986). BS, Hofstra U., 1951, MBA, 1952. Pres. David Allison Co., Inc., Woodbury, N.Y., 1957—, chmn. bd., 1959—; pres., chmn. bd. Daco Internat. Corp., 1959—; pres. Kingsley Brass Co., Ltd., Woodbury, 1963-71, chmn. bd., 1963; mgmt. cons. Patentee hardware. Served to lt. USN, 1952-56. Mem. Mensa, Am. Hardware Mfrs. Assn. Clubs: Turnberry, Williams Island (Miami). Office: 220 Crossways Park W Woodbury NY 11797

FRIEDERICI-HAAG, ANGELA DORKAS, psycholinguist; b. Cologne, Feb. 3, 1952; d. Lothar Karl Wilhelm and Elisabeth Maria Louise (Mannherz) Friederici; m. Arnim Karl Haag, Dec. 21, 1982. D of Philosophy, U. Bonn, Fed. Republic Germany, 1976; Degree in Psychology, U. Bonn, 1980; Habilitation, U. Giessen, 1986, pvt. dozent, 1987. Research fellow Rheinische Landesklinik for Sprachgestorte, Bonn, Fed. Republic Germany, 1974-78, Boston U., MIT, Cambridge, Mass., 1978-79, Max Planck Inst. Psycholinguistik, Nijmegen, Netherlands, 1979-82; mem. staff Max Planck Inst. Psycholinguistik, 1982-87, Heisenberg fellow, 1987—. Author: Neuropsychologie der Sprache, 1984, Kognitive Strukturen des Sprachverstehens, 1987; contbr. articles to internat. jours. Mem. Acad. Aphasia, Internat. Neuropsychol. Soc., Deutsche Gesellschaft fur Psychologie. Office: Max Planck Inst Phycholing, Wundlaan 1, 6525 XD Nijmegen The Netherlands

FRIEDL, RICK, college president, lawyer; b. Berwyn, Ill., Aug. 31, 1947; s. Raymond J. and Ione L. (Anderson) F.; m. Diane Marie Guillies, Sept. 2, 1977; children: Richard, Angela, Ryan. BA, Calif. State U., Northridge, 1969; MA, UCLA, 1976; postgrad. UCLA, 1984; JD Western State U., 1987. Dept. mgr. Calif. Dept Indsl. Relations, 1973-78; mem. faculty dept. polit. sci. U. So. Calif., 1978-80; pres. Pacific Coll. Law, 1981—; bd. dirs. Calif. State U., Northridge, 1979. Author: The Political Economy of Cuban Dependency, 1982; tech. editor Glendale Law Rev., 1984; contbr. articles to profl. jours. Calif. State Grad. fellow, 1970-72. Mem. Calif. State Bar Assn., Los Angeles County Bar Assn., Am. Polit. Sci. Assn., Latin Am. Studies Assn., Acad. Polit. Sci., Pacific Coast Council Latin Am. Studies, L.A. County Bar Assn., Calif. Trial Lawyers Assn. Home: 9760 Kessler Ave Chatsworth CA 91311

FRIEDLANDER, CHARLES DOUGLAS, investment company executive, consultant; b. N.Y.C., Oct. 5, 1928; s. Murray L. and Jeane (Sottosanti) F.; m. Diane Mary Hutchins, May 12, 1951; children: Karen Diane, Lauren Patrice, Joan Elyse. BS, U.S. Mil. Acad., 1950; exec. mgmt. program, NASA, 1965; grad., Command and Staff Coll. USAF, 1965, Air War Coll. USAF, 1966. Commd. 2d lt. U.S. Army, 1950, advanced through grades to 1st lt.; officer inf. U.S. Army, Korea, 1950-51; resigned U.S. Army, 1954; mem. staff UN Forces, Trieste, Italy, 1953-54; chief astronaut support office NASA, Cape Canaveral, Fla., 1963-67; space cons. CBS News, N.Y.C., 1967-69; exec. asst. The White House, Washington, 1969-71; pres. Western Ranchlands Inc., Scottsdale, Ariz., 1971-74; pres. Fairland Co. Inc., Scottsdale, 1974—, also bd. dirs.; bd. dirs. Internat. Aerospace Hall of Fame, San Diego; space program cons., various cos., Boca Raton, Fla., 1967-69; mem. staff First Postwar Fgn. Ministers Conf., Berlin, 1954; radio/TV cons. space program. Author: Buying & Selling Land for Profit, 1961, Last Man at Hungnam Beach, 1952. V.p. West Point Soc., Cape Canaveral, Fla., 1964. Served to lt. col. USAFR. Decorated Bronze Star, Combat Inf. badge; recipient Emmy award CBS TV Apollo Moon Landing, 1969. Mem. Nat. Space Club, Nat. Exec. Service Corps, Explorer's Club, West Point Soc., Chosin Few Survivors Korea.

FRIEDLER, YA'ACOV MEIR, journalist; b. Sterkrade, Fed. Republic Germany, Sept. 24, 1928; arrived in Israel, 1949; s. Gustav and Henny (Kaufmann) F.; m. Malca Shalit, Sept. 21, 1954; children: Daliah, Eran. Matriculation, London U., 1945. Journalist The Jerusalem Post, Haifa, Israel, 1951—, The Israel Broadcasting Authority, Haifa, 1955-78. Served to lt. Israeli Army Res., 1949-84. Mem. Israel Journalists (v.p. 1983-85). Jewish. Home: 16-A Danya St, Haifa 34980, Israel Office: Jerusalem Post, 16 Nordau St, Haifa 31047, Israel

FRIEDLI, BÊAT, pediatric cardiologist, educator; b. Berne, Switzerland, July 24, 1936; s. Louis and Margrit (Hedinger) F.; m. Gillian Mary Day, Sept. 7, 1974; children: Marc, Mathieu. MD, U. Geneva, 1962; MSc, U. Montreal, Que., Can., 1970. Intern, resident Univ. Hosp., Geneva, 1963-68; resident Univ. Hosp., Seattle, 1968-69; fellow Inst. Cardiology, Montreal, 1969-70; fellow in pediatric cardiology Hosp. Ste. Justine, Montreal, 1970-71, Hosp. for Sick Children, Toronto, Que., Can., 1971-73; cons. pediatric cardiology Hosp. Cantonal U., Geneva, 1973-81, head pediatric cardiac unit, 1982—; assoc. prof. pediatric cardiology U. Geneva, 1986—. Contbr. articles to profl. jours, chpts. to books. Fellow Am. Coll. Cardiology; mem. European Soc. Pediatric Cardiology, European Soc. Clin. Investigation, Swiss Cardiac Soc., Swiss Pediatric Soc. Home: 11 Chemin des Ramiers, 1245 Collonge-Bellerive, Geneva Switzerland Office: Hopital Cantonal Univ, Pediatric Clinic, Blvd de la Cluse, 1211 Geneva Switzerland

FRIEDMAN, ALAN HERBERT, ophthalmologist; b. N.Y.C., 1937; B.A. in Chemistry with honors, Cornell U., 1959; M.D. (summer fellow NIH 1960, 62-63), N.Y.U., 1963; m. Sandra Yasser, 1960; children—David, Jonathan, Lisa, Jennifer. Intern in medicine Bellevue Hosp., N.Y.C., 1963-64; resident in ophthalmology N.Y.U. Med. Ctr., 1966-69, fellow ophthalmic pathology, 1969-70; research fellow histochemistry Royal Postgrad. Med. Sch., London, 1972; practice medicine specializing in ophthalmology, N.Y.C., 1970—; attending ophthalmologist and pathologist Mt. Sinai Hosp.; attending ophthalmologist and ophthalmic pathologist Beth Israel Med. Ctr.; clin. prof. ophthalmology and pathology, dir. eye pathology lab. Mt. Sinai Sch. Medicine; assoc. examiner Am. Bd. Ophthalmology; cons. in field. Contbr. numerous articles to profl. publs. Served with M.C., USAR, 1964-66. Diplomate Am. Bd. Ophthalmology. Fellow ACS, Am. Acad. Ophthalmology, N.Y. Acad. Medicine, N.Y. Acad. Scis., Royal Soc. Medicine; mem. Am. Ophthal. Soc., Ophthal. Soc. U.K., French Ophthal. Soc., Assn. Research Vision and Ophthalmology, AMA, Am. Assn. Ophthalmic Pathologists, N.Y. County Med. Soc., Med. Soc. State N.Y., Eastern Ophthalmic Pathology Soc., Pan Am. Assn. Ophthalmology. Address: Mt Sinai Sch Medicine 1 Gustave Levy Pl New York NY 10029 also: 888 Park Ave New York NY 10021

FRIEDMAN, BARBARA SIEGEL, accountant; b. N.Y.C., Jan. 19, 1953; d. Philip and Laura (Gitlen) Siegel; B.S., Fairleigh Dickinson U., 1973, postgrad., 1974—; m. Bennett Friedman, June 1, 1975; children: Erica Brooke, Brett Ross (twins). Sr. auditor Benjamin Nadel & Co., N.Y.C., 1973-76; acctg. mgr. N.Y. Zool. Soc., Bronx, 1976-79; controller Vera Inst. Justice, N.Y.C., 1979-80; sr. acctg. coordinator Salomon Bros., N.Y.C., 1980-81; controller N.Y. Bot. Garden, 1981-83; controller, asst. treas. N.Y. Pub. Library, 1983—. Tech. asst. N.Y. State Council on Arts; bd. dirs. Am. Soc. Preservation of Nature in Israel, N.Y.C., Community Family Planning Council, N.Y.C., Inwood House, N.Y.C.; bd. dirs., treas. Bulova Sch., Woodside, N.Y., Bronx 2000, Ctr. for Preventive Psychiatry, White Plains, N.Y., Westchester Day Sch., Mamoroneck, N.Y. Home: 1 Cricklewood Ln Harrison NY 10528-2809 Office: The NY Pub Library 8 W 40th St 7th Floor New York NY 10018

FRIEDMAN, ELI A., nephrologist; b. N.Y.C., Apr. 9, 1933; s. Israel and Ida (Gutman) F.; m. Mildred Barrett-Lennard, June 16, 1957; children: Amy Louise, Rebecca Alicia, Sara Jo. B.S., Bklyn. Coll., 1953; M.D., SUNY Downstate Med. Center, 1957; D.Sc. (hon.), Maduri Kamaraj U., India, 1985. Intern in medicine Harvard Med. Sch., 1957-58; resident in medicine Peter Bent Brigham Hosp., Boston, 1960-61; Am. Heart Assn. research fellow Harvard U., 1958-60; mem. faculty Downstate Med. Center, Bklyn., 1963—; prof. Health Sci. Ctr. SUNY, Bklyn., 1972—; chief div. renal disease Downstate Med. Center, 1963—; bd. dirs. Am. Bur. Med. Aid to China, 1979—, Cleve. Found., 1979—, Bklyn. Nephrology Found., 1978—. Author: Acute Renal Failure, 1973, Strategy in Renal Failure, 1978, Diabetic Renal-retinal Syndrome, 1980, Diabetic Renal-retinal Syndrome 3 Therapy, 1986, Diabetic Nephropathy, 1986, Diabetic Renal-retinal Syndrome 4: Management Strategy, 1987; editor: Journal of Diabetic Complications, 1986—. Served to lt. comdr. USPHS, 1961-63. Grantee NIH; Grantee USPHS; Grantee N.Y. Kidney Found.; Grantee N.Y. State Kidney Disease Inst.; Grantee Am. Kidney Fund; Alumni medal Downstate Med. Coll.; recipient Hoenig award Nat. Kidney Found., N.Y., 1986. Mem. Am. Soc. Nephrology, Internat. Soc. Nephrology, Am. Soc. Artificial Internal Organs (pres. 1987—, editor Transactions 1985), A.C.P., Am. Soc. Immunology, Transplantation Soc., Assn. Am. Physicians, Internat. Soc. Artificial Organs (pres. 1986),Talion Soc. Nephrology, fellow Explorers Club. Home: 1049 E 17th St Brooklyn NY 11230 Office: 450 Clarkson Ave Brooklyn NY 11203

FRIEDMAN, EMANUEL A., medical educator; b. N.Y.C., June 9, 1926; s. Louis and Pauline (Feldman) F.; m. E. Judith Salomon, June 6, 1948; children: Lynn Alice, Meryl Ruth, Lee Martin. A.B., Bklyn. Coll., 1947; M.D., Columbia U., 1951, Med. Sc.D., 1959; M.A., Harvard U., 1969. Diplomate Am. Bd. Ob-Gyn. Intern Bellevue Hosp., N.Y.C., 1951-52; resident Columbia-Presbyn. Hosp., N.Y.C., 1952-57; instr. Columbia Coll. Physicians and Surgeons, 1957-59, asst. prof., 1960-62, assoc. prof., 1962-63; prof., chmn. dept. ob-gyn Chgo. Med. Sch., 1963-69; chmn. dept. ob-gyn Michael Reese Hosp., Chgo., 1963-69; prof. ob-gyn Harvard U., 1969—; obstetrician-gynecologist-in-chief Beth Israel Hosp., Boston, 1969—; prof. health scis. and tech. MIT, 1985—. Author: Labor: Clinical Evaluation and Management, 1967, 2d edit., 1978, Rh-Isoimmunization and Erythroblastosis Fetalis, 1969, Lymphatic System of Female Genitalia, 1971, Biological Principles and Modern Practice of Obstetrics, 1974, Blood Pressure, Edema and Proteinuria in Pregnancy, 1976, Pregnancy Hypertension, 1977, Uterine Physiology, 1979, Advances in Perinatal Medicine, 1981, 5th edit., 1986, Obstetrical Decision Making, 1982, 2d edit., 1987, Management of Labor, 1983, 2d edit., 1988, Gynecological Decision Making, 1983, 2d edit., 1987, Labor and Delivery Impact on Offspring, 1987, Legal Principles and Practice in Obstetrics and Gynecology, 1988. Served with USNR, 1944-46. Recipient Joseph Mather Smith research prize Columbia U., 1958, Disting. Alumnus award Bklyn Coll., 1964, Bicentennial commemorative silver medallion award Columbia U., 1967. Fellow ACS, Am. Coll. Ob-Gyn, N.Y. Acad. Medicine; mem. N.Y. Acad. Scis., Soc. Exptl. Biology and Medicine, Soc. Gynecologic Investigation, AAUP, AAAS, Alpha Omega Alpha. Home: 260 Beacon St Boston MA 02116 Office: 330 Brookline Ave Boston MA 02215

FRIEDMAN, ERNEST HARVEY, physician, psychiatrist; b. Cleve., Jan. 8, 1931; s. Sol and Ann (Nittskoff) F.; m. Anita Rose Bogdanow, Oct. 26, 1962; children: Rachel Samantha, Sarah Ann, Eric Daniel, Jessica Emily. BS, Case Western Res. U., 1952; MD, Ohio State U., 1956. Diplomate Am. Bd. Psychiatry and Neurology. Intern U. Ill. Hosps., Chgo., 1956-57; psychiat. resident U. Hosps. of Cleve., 1957-60; clin. instr. Case Western Res. U., Cleve., 1974-86, asst. clin. prof., 1983—; vis. psychiatrist Mt. Sinai Hosp., Cleve., 1963-70, sr. vis. psychiatrist, 1970—; med. staff Huron Hosp., East Cleveland, Ohio, 1971—; pvt. practice psychiatry, medicine Cleve., 1962—; owner, computer mfr. Voxaflex Co., East Cleveland, Ohio, 1986—; chmn. ad hoc com. on stress Am. Heart Assn., Cleve., 1977; cons. psychiatrist Nat. Exercise and Heart Disease Study, Washington, 1972-75. Mem. editorial bd. Heart and Lung, 1974-80; patentee computer software and hardware. Served as lt. comdr. M.C., USNR, 1960-62. Grantee-in-aid Am. Heart Assn., Cleve., 1964, 65, 75. Fellow Am. Psychiat. Assn. Democrat. Jewish. Office: Voxaflex Co 1831 Forest Hills Blvd East Cleveland OH 44112-5104

FRIEDMAN, GERALD MANFRED, geologist, educator; b. Berlin, Germany, July 23, 1921; came to U.S., 1946, naturalized, 1950; s. Martin and Frieda (Cohn) F.; m. Sue Tyler, June 27, 1948; children: Judith Fay Friedman Rosen, Sharon Mira Friedman Azaria, Devorah Paula Friedman Zweibach, Eva Jane Friedman Scholle, Wendy Tamar Friedman Spanier. Student, U. Cambridge, Eng., 1938-39; B.Sc., U. London, Eng., 1945, D.Sc., 1977; M.A., Columbia U., 1950, Ph.D., 1952; Dr. rer. nat. (hon.), U. Heidelberg, Germany, 1986. Lectr. Chelsea Coll., London, 1944-45; analytical chemist E.R. Squibb & Sons, New Brunswick, N.J., also J. Lyons & Co., London, 1945-48; asst. geology Columbia, 1950; temporary geologist N.Y. State Geol. Survey, 1950; instr., then asst. prof. geology U. Cin., 1950-54; cons. geologist Sault Ste. Marie, Ont., Can., 1954-56; mem. research dept. Pan Am. Petroleum Corp. (Amoco), Tulsa, 1956-64; sr. research scientist Pan Am. Petroleum Corp. (Amoco), 1956-60, research asso., 1960-62, supr. sedimentological research, 1962-64; Fulbright vis. prof. geology Hebrew U., Jerusalem, Israel, 1964; prof. geology Rensselaer Poly. Inst., 1964-84, prof. emeritus, 1984—; prof. geology Bklyn. Coll., 1985—, Grad. Sch. of CUNY, 1985—; pres. Gerry Exploration Inc., 1982—; research scientist Hudson Labs., Columbia, 1965, 66-69, research assoc. dept. geology, 1968-73; vis. prof. U. Heidelberg, Germany, 1967; cons. scientist Inst. Petroleum Research and Geophysics, Israel, 1967-71; lectr. Oil & Gas Cons. Internat., 1968—; pres. Northeastern Sci. Found. Inc., 1979—;; vis. scientist Geol. Survey of Israel, 1970-73, 78; mem. Com. Sci. Soc. Presidents, 1974-76. Co-author: Principles of Sedimentology, 1978, Exploration for Carbonate Petroleum Reservoirs,, 1982, Exercises in Sedimentology, 1982; pub. Northeastern Environ. Sci., 1982—; editor: Jour. Sedimentary Petrology, 1964-70 (Best Paper award 1961), Northeastern Geology, 1979—, Earth Scis. History, 1982—, Carbonates and Evaporites, 1986—; sect. co-editor: Chem. Abstracts, 1962-69; editorial bd.: Sedimentary Geology, 1967—, Israel Jour. Earth Scis, 1971-76, Jour. of Geology, 1977—, GeoJournal, 1977-83; co-editor, contbr.: Carbonate Sedimentology in Central Europe, 1968, Hypersaline Ecosystems: The Gavish Sabkha, 1985; editor, contbr.: Depositional Environments in Carbonate Rocks, 1969; co-editor: Modern Carbonate Environments, 1983, Lecture Notes in Earth Scis., 1985—. Contbr. articles to profl. jours. Mem. phys. edn. com. Tulsa YMCA, 1958-63; adviser, instr. Judo Club Rensselaer Poly. Inst., 1964-84; bd. dirs. Troy Jewish Community Council, 1966-72, 74-77; v.p. Temple Beth El, 1986—, bd. dirs. 1965-76; bd. dirs. Leo Baeck Inst., N.Y.C., 1986—. Fellow Mineral. Soc. Am. (mem. nominating com. for fellows 1967-69, awards com. 1977-78), Geol. Soc. Am. (life London chpt., chmn. sect. program com. 1969, candidate sect. chmn. 1969, publs. com. 1980-82), AAAS (chmn. geology and geography 1978-79, councillor 1979-80), Geol. Soc. London (life); mem. Am. Chem. Soc. (group leader 1962-63), Am. Assn. Petroleum Geologists (chmn. carbonate rock com. 1965-69, mem. research com. 1965-71, 76-82, lectr. continuing edn. program 1967—, adv. council 1974-75, disting. lectr. 1972-73, mem. disting. lectr. com. 1975-78, ho. of dels. 1977-80, 83-87, sect. sec. 1979-80, sect. treas. 1980-81, sect. v.p. 1981-82; sect. pres 1982-83, nat. v.p. 1984-85, hon. mem. Eastern sect. 1984, Disting. Service award 1988), Soc. Econ. Paleontologists and Mineralogists (nat. v.p. 1970-71, pres. 1974-75, sect. pres. 1967-68, Best Paper award Gulf Coast sect. 1974, hon. mem. 1984), Am. Geol. Inst. (governing bd. 1971-72, 74-75), Internat. Assn. Sedimentologists (v.p. 1971-75, pres. 1975-78, nat. corr. U.S.A. 1971-73, hon. mem. 1982), Geol. Soc. Israel, Geol. Vereinigung, Assn. Geology Tchrs. (nat. treas. 1951-55, pres. Okla. 1962-63, pres. Eastern sect. 1983-84), Assn. Earth Sci. Editors (v.p. 1970-71, pres. 1971-72), N.Y. State Geol. Assn. (pres. 1978-79), U.S. Judo Fedn. (San Dan), Sigma Gamma Epsilon (nat. v.p. 1978-82, nat. pres 1982-86, hon. mem. 1986), Sigma Xi (v.p. Rensselaer chpt. 1969-70). Home: 32 24th St Troy NY 12180

FRIEDMAN, HAROLD IRA, plastic surgeon, educator; b. N.Y.C., Oct. 22, 1946; s. Joseph and Dorothy (Asnin) F.; m. Clarke Emmons, Nov. 24, 1976. BS, Hobart Coll., 1967; PhD, U. Va., 1972, MD, 1974. Diplomate: Nat. Bd. Med. Examiners. Intern surgery U. Va. Med. Center, Charlottesville, 1974-75; cell biologist gen. surgeon Letterman Army Inst. Research, San Francisco, 1975-78; resident gen. surgery U. Ariz. Med. Center, Tucson 1978-82; resident in plastic surgery U. Va. Med. Center, Charlottesville, 1982-84; assoc. prof. dept. surgery Sch. Medicine USC, Columbia, 1984—, adj. assoc. prof. Coll. Health, 1986—; adj. assoc. prof. dept. biomed. engring. Clemson U., 1985—. Contbr. articles to profl. jours. Served to maj., M.C. U.S. Army, 1975-78; lt. col. M.C. USAR. Diplomate Am. Bd. Surgery. Recipient Van Winkle award U. Ariz., 1982; Upjohn Achievement award, 1982; decorated Army Commendation medal; recipient James Kembrough award for outstanding urologic research, 1976. Mem. Am. Inst. Nutrition, Am. Assn. Clin. Nutrition, Am. Soc. Exptl. Biology, Am. Soc. Parenteral and Enteral Nutrition, AMA, Assn. Mil. Surgeons U.S., S.C. Soc. Plastic and Reconstructive Surgeons. Home: 22 Olde Springs Rd Columbia SC 29223 Office: U SC Dept Surgery 3320 Medical Park Rd Suite 300 Columbia SC 29203

FRIEDMAN, HERBERT, physicist; b. N.Y.C., June 21, 1916; s. Samuel and Rebecca (Seligson) F.; m. Gertrude Miller, 1940; children—Paul, Jon. BA, Bklyn. Coll., 1936; PhD in Physics, Johns Hopkins U., 1940; DSc (hon.), U Tübingen, Fed. Republic Germany, 1977, U. Mich., 1979. With U.S. Naval Research Lab., Washington, 1940—, supt. atmosphere and astrophysics div., 1958-63, supt. space sci. div., 1963-80; chief scientist E. O. Hulburt Ctr. Space Research U.S. Naval Research Lab., 1963-80, Emeritus, 1980—; adj. prof. physics U. Md., 1960—, U. Pa., 1974—; vis. prof. Yale U., 1966-68; mem. space sci. bd. Nat. Acad. Scis.-NRC, 1962-75, chmn. com. on solar-terrestrial research, 1968-71; mem. com. sci. and pub. policy Nat. Acad. Scis., 1967-71, mem. geophysics research bd., 1969-71, chmn., 1976-79, mem. adv. com. internat. orgns. and programs, 1969-77; pres. Interunion Com. on Solar-Terrestrial Physics, 1967-74; chmn. COSPAR working group II, Internat. Quiet Sun Yr.; v.p. COSPAR, 1970-75, 86—; mem. Pres.'s Sci. Adv. Com., 1970-73; chmn. commn. on phys. scis., math and resources NRC, 1984-86. Recipient Disting. Service award Dept. Navy, 1945, 80; medal Soc. Applied Spectroscopy, 1957; Disting. Civilian Service award Dept. Def., 1959; Disting. Achievement in Sci. award, 1962; Janssen medal French Photog. Soc., 1962; Presdl. medal for disting. fed. service, 1964; Eddington medal Royal Astron. Soc., 1964; R.D. Conrad medal Dept. Navy, 1964; Rockefeller Pub. Service award, 1967; Nat. Medal Sci., 1969; medal for exceptional sci. achievement NASA, 1970, 78; Michelson medal Franklin Inst., 1972; Dryden Research award, 1973; Wolf Found. prize in physics, 1987. Fellow Am. Phys. Soc., Am. Optical Soc., Am. Geophys. Union (pres. sect. on solar-planetrary relationships 1967-70, Bowie medal 1981), Am. Astron. Soc. (Lovelace award 1973), AIAA (Space Sci. award 1963); mem. AAAS (v.p. 1972), Nat. Acad. Scis. (council 1979-82, chmn. assembly of math. and phys. scis. 1980-83), Am. Acad. Arts and Scis., Internat. Acad. Astronautics, Am. Philos. Soc.; hon. mem. Spl. Com. on Solar-Terrestrial Physics, 1984. Club: Cosmos. Home: 2643 N Upshur St Arlington VA 22207 Office: Naval Research Lab Code 4190 Washington DC 20375 *

FRIEDMAN, HERBERT A., rabbi, educator, fund raising executive; b. New Haven, Sept. 25, 1918; s. Israel and Rae (Aaronson) F.; children from previous marriage: Judith, Daniel Stephen, Joan Michal; m. Francine Bensley, June 28, 1963; children—David Herbert, Charles Edward. B.A., Yale U., 1938; M.H.L., Jewish Inst. Religion, 1943; D.D. (hon.), Hebrew Union Coll., 1969. Ordained rabbi, 1944. Rabbi Temple Emanuel, Denver, 1943-52, Milw., 1952-55; exec. chmn. Nat. United Jewish Appeal, N.Y.C., 1955-75; pres. Am. Friends of Tel Aviv U., N.Y.C., 1982-85; pres. Wexner Heritage Found, 1985—. Author: Collected Speeches, 1971. Served as chaplain (capt.) U.S. Army, 1944-47, ETO. Mem. Central Conf. Am. Rabbis. Club: Yale (N.Y.C.). Home: 500 E 77th St Apt 2519 New York NY 10162 Office: Wexner Heritage Found 551 Madison Ave New York NY 10022

FRIEDMAN, IRA HUGH, surgeon; b. N.Y.C., July 17, 1933; s. Leonard Seymour and Ruth (Binder) F.; m. Erika Berger, Oct. 22, 1961; children—Richard Lawrence, Joanne Beth. B.A., NYU, 1953, M.D., 1957. Diplomate Am. Bd. Surgery, Nat. Bd. Med. Examiners. Intern, resident in surgery Beth Isreal Med. Ctr., N.Y.C., 1957-59, 61-63; surg. resident Bellevue Hosp., N.Y.C., 1959-60; practice medicine specializing in surgery N.Y.C., 1963—; attending surgeon Beth Israel Med. Ctr., pres. med. bd., 1981-82; assoc. clin. prof. surgery Mt. Sinai Sch. Medicine; med. adv. to N.Y.C. dir. SSS, 1968. Contbr. articles to profl. jours. Bd. dirs. Union Orthodox Jewish Congregations Am., Am. Com. for Shaare Zedek Hosp. of Jerusalem, Yeshiva Sha-alvim, Isreal, P'Tach; co-chmn. bd. dirs. Yeshiva Chofetz Chaim, N.Y.C. Recipient Koach award Israel Bond Orgn., 1977; N.Y. Heart Assn. fellow, 1960-61. Fellow A.C.S., Am. Coll. Gastroenterology, Am. Soc. Colon and Rectal Surgeons, Royal Soc. Medicine; mem. AMA, N.Y. Acad. Medicine, N.Y. Surg. Soc., Soc. Surgery of Alimentary Tract, Am. Gastroent. Assn., N.Y. Gastroent. Assn., N.Y. Cancer Soc., N.Y. Soc. Colon and Rectal Surgeons, Collegium Internationale Chirugiae Digestive, N.Y. State Med. Assn., N.Y. County Med. Assn. Home: 1175 Park Ave New York NY 10028

FRIEDMAN, JON GEORGE, lawyer; b. N.Y.C., Sept. 2, 1951; s. George Alexander and Viola Elizabeth (Elson) F. BBA, Adelphi U., 1972; MBA, Golden Gate U., 1972; MPA, NYU, 1974; JD, Hofstra U., 1977; MA, NYU, 1978. Bar: N.Y. 1978, U.S. Dist. Ct. (ea. and so. dists.) N.Y. 1978, U.S. Ct. Appeals (2d cir.) 1981, U.S. Supreme Ct. 1984, U.S. Dist. Ct. P.R. 1982. V.p., gen. counsel Allou Distbrs., Inc., Brentwood, N.Y., 1978-82; bus. cons. internat. trade, fin. Long Island, N.Y., 1982—; v.p., bus. editor Caribbean Bus., San Juan, P.R., 1983-84; sole practice Long Island, P.R., 1984—. Contbr. articles to profl. jours. Mem. ABA, N.Y. State Bar Assn., Assn. of Bar of City of N.Y. Home and Office: 82-46 268th St Floral Park NY 11004

FRIEDMAN, MARION, internist, family physician; b. Onley, Va., Aug. 15, 1918; s. Jacob and Bertha (Bernstein) F.; BS, U. Md., 1938, MD, 1942; m. Esther Lerner, May 29, 1941; 1 son, Barry Howard. Rotating intern U.S. Marine Hosp., Norfolk, Va., 1942-43; asst. health officer Montgomery County (Kans.), 1943-44; health officer Cherokee County (Kans.), 1944-45; asst. health commr. St. Louis County (Mo.), 1945-46; resident internal medicine U.S. Marine Hosp., Balt., 1946-49; fellow medicine Johns Hopkins Sch. Medicine, Balt., 1948-49; individual practice medicine, specializing in family practice internal medicine, Balt., 1949-84; asst. medicine U. Md., Balt., 1954-72; chief dept. gen. practice Doctors Hosp., 1952-54; chief dept. family practice N. Charles Gen. Hosp., Balt., 1972-75, med. dir. ambulatory services, 1972-86, assoc. chief medicine, 1975—, pres. med. staff, 1964, 68, chmn. med. exec. com., 1984-85, trustee, 1984-85, physician advisor, 1984—. Chmn. cultural com. Liberty Jewish Center, 1960-62; mem. Md. High Blood Pressure Coordinating Council, 1980-82; trustee Jimmie Swartz Found., 1982—. Served with USPHS, 1942-49. Diplomate Am. Bd. Family Practice (charter). Fellow Am. Acad. Family Physicians (charter); mem. Balt. City Med. Soc. (alt. del. 1978-82, del. 1982—, profl. edn. com. 1985-87, chmn. 1987—), Med. and Chirurg. Faculty Md., AMA, World Med. Assn., Am. Acad. Family Physicians, Md. Acad. Family Physicians (prodn. editor 1984-86, editor 1986—), Md. Acad. Family Physicians (pres. 1983-84), Pan-Am. Med. Assn., Md. Heart Assn., Md. Thoracic Soc., Am. Thoracic Soc., Am. Heart Assn., Balt. City Med. Soc. (profl. edn. com. 1985-87, chmn. 1987—), Phi Kappa Phi. Democrat. First to suggest use of steroid in subacute deltoid bursitis in world lit., 1952. Home: 7906 Terrapin Ct Baltimore MD 21208

FRIEDMAN, MILTON, economist, educator; b. Bklyn., July 31, 1912; s. Jeno Saul and Sarah Ethel (Landau) F.; m. Rose Director, June 25, 1938; children: Janet, David. AB, Rutgers U., 1932, LLD, 1968; AM, U. Chgo., 1933; PhD, Columbia U., 1946; LLD, St. Paul's (Rikkyo) U., 1963; LLD (hon.), Kalamazoo Coll., 1968, Lehigh U., 1969, Loyola U., 1971, U. N.H., 1975, Harvard U., 1979, Brigham Young U., 1980, Dartmouth Coll., 1980, Gonzaga U., 1981; DSc (hon.), Rochester U., 1971; LHD (hon.), Rockford Coll., 1969, Roosevelt U., 1975, Hebrew Union Coll., Los Angeles, 1981; LittD (hon.), Bethany Coll., 1971; PhD (hon.), Hebrew U., Jerusalem, 1977; DCS (hon.), Francisco Marroquin U., Guatemala, 1978. Assoc. economist Nat. Resources Com., Washington, 1935-37; mem. research staff Nat. Bur. Econ. Research, N.Y.C., 1937-45, 1948-81; vis. prof. econs. U. Wis., Madison, 1940-41; prin. economist, tax research div. U.S. Treasury Dept., Washington, 1941-43; assoc. dir. research, statis. research group, War Research div. Columbia U., N.Y.C., 1943-45; assoc. prof. econs. and statistics U. Minn., Mpls., 1945-46; assoc. prof. econs. U. Chgo., 1946-48, prof. econs., 1948-62, Paul Snowden Russell disting. service prof. econs., 1962-82, prof. emeritus, 1983—; Fulbright lectr. Cambridge U., 1953-54; vis. Wesley Clair Mitchell research prof. econs. Columbia U., N.Y.C., 1964-65; fellow Ctr. for Advanced Study in Behavioral Sci., 1957-58; sr. research fellow Stanford U., 1977—; mem. Pres.'s Commn. All-Vol. Army, 1969-70, Pres.'s Commn. on White House Fellows, 1971-74, Pres.'s Econ. Policy Adv. Bd., 1981—; vis. scholar Fed. Res. Bank, San Francisco, 1977. Author: (with Carl Shoup and Ruth P. Mack) Taxing to Prevent Inflation, 1943, (with Simon S. Kuznets) Income from Independent Professional Practice, 1946, (with Harold A. Freeman, Frederic Mosteller, W. Allen Wallis) Sampling Inspection, 1948, Essays in Positive Economics, 1953, A Theory of the Consumption Function, 1957, A Program for Monetary Stability, 1960, Price Theory: A Provisional Text, 1962, (with Rose D. Friedman) Capitalism and Freedom, 1962, Free To Choose, 1980, Tyranny of the Status Quo, 1984, (with Anna J. Schwartz) A Monetary History of the United States, 1867-1960, 1963, Monetary Statistics of the United States, 1970, (with Anna J. Schwartz) Monetary Trends in the U.S. and the United Kingdom, 1982, Inflation: Causes and Consequences, 1963, (with Robert Roosa) The Balance of Payments: Free vs. Fixed Exchange Rates, 1967, Dollars and Deficits, 1968, The Optimum Quantity of Money and Other Essays, 1969, (with Walter W. Heller) Monetary vs. Fiscal Policy, 1969, A Theoretical Framework for Monetary Analysis, 1972, (with Wilbur J. Cohen) Social Security, 1972, An Economist's Protest, 1972, There's No Such Thing As A Free Lunch, 1975, Price Theory, 1976, Milton Friedman's Monetary Framework, 1974, Tax Limitation, Inflation and the Role of Government, 1978, Bright Promises, Dismal Performance, 1983; editor: Studies in the Quantity Theory of Money, 1956; bd. editors Am. Econ. Rev, 1951-53, Econometrica, 1957-69; adv. bd. Jour. Money, Credit and Banking, 1968—; columnist Newsweek mag, 1966-84, contbg. editor, 1971-84; contbr. articles to profl. jours. Recipient Nobel prize in econs., 1976, Pvt. Enterprise Exemplar medal Freedoms Found., 1978, Grand Cordon of the Sacred Treasure Japanese Govt., 1986; named Chicagoan of Yr. Chgo. Press Club, 1972, Educator of Yr. Chgo. United Jewish Fund, 1973, Nat. Medal of Sci., 1988. Fellow Inst. Math. Stats., Am. Statis. Assn., Econometric Soc.; mem. Nat. Acad. Scis., Am. Econ. Assn. (mem. exec. com. 1955-57, pres. 1967; John Bates Clark medal 1951), Am. Enterprise Inst. (adv. bd. 1956-79), Western Econ. Assn. (pres. 1984-85), Royal Economic Soc., Am. Philos. Soc., Mont Pelerin Soc. (bd. dirs. 1958-61, pres. 1970-72). Club: Quadrangle. Office: Stanford U Hoover Instn Stanford CA 94305-6010

FRIEDMAN, RICHARD NATHAN, lawyer; b. Phila., June 13, 1941; s. Martin Harry Friedman and Caroline (Fruchtman) Shaines; B.A., U. Miami, 1962, J.D., 1965; LL.M. in Taxation, Georgetown U., 1967; m. Catherine Helen Gulotta, Nov. 7, 1970; 1 dau., Melissa Danielle. Bar: Fla. 1965. Staff atty. SEC, Washington, 1965-66; asso. firm Feldman & Warner, Washington, 1966-67; individual practice law, Miami, Fla., 1968—; adj. prof. U. Miami, 1972-76; arbitrator N.Y. Stock Exchange, 1973—, AMEX and NASD, 1988— . Founder, pres. Am. Stockholders Assn., Inc., 1971-74, Stop Transit-Over People, Inc., 1975—; chmn. Sales Taxes Oppressing People, Fla., 1987—; mem. endowment com. U. Miami, 1970—; mem. Soc. Univ. Founders, U. Miami, 1980. Recipient cert. of merit Dade County Bar Assn., 1972-73; numerous certs. of appreciation Rotary Internat., Kiwanis and other service orgns., 1970—; Richard N. Friedman Week held in his honor City of Homestead, Fla., Apr. 1978; named Hon. Citizen, State of Tenn., Citizen of Day, Dade County (Fla.), Radio Sta. WINZ, 1980; recipient Leaders award Sunrisers Community, 1986. Mem. Unified Bar D.C., World Peace Through Law Ctr. Featured performer motion picture Lenny, 1974, other TV and theatrical films. Office: 100 N Biscayne Blvd Miami FL 33132

FRIEDMAN, ROBERT MICHAEL, lawyer; b. Memphis, June 19, 1950; s. Harold Samuel and Margaret (Siegel) F.; m. Elaine Freda Burson, Dec. 21, 1975; children: Daniel Justin, Jonathan Aaron. B.S., U. Tenn., 1973, J.D., 1975; postgrad., Exeter U., Eng., 1974, Nat. Coll. Trial Advocacy, 1985. Bar: Tenn. 1976, U.S. Dist. Ct. (we. dist.) Tenn. 1977, U.S. Dist Ct. (no. dist.) Miss. 1979, U.S. Ct. Appeals (5th cir.) 1979, U.S. Supreme Ct. 1983, U.S. Dist. Ct. (so. dist.) Tex. 1986, U.S. Ct. Appeals (6th cir.) 1986. Assoc., Cassell & Fink, Memphis, 1976-78; pres., sr. ptnr. Friedman & Sissman, P.C., Memphis, 1978—; corp. legal/litigation counsel, dir. Tenn. Interpreting Service for Deaf, Memphis, 1981—, Mid-South Hospitality Mgmt. Ctr., Inc., Memphis, 1984—; legal counsel Moss Hotel Co., Inc., 1986—, Helena Hotel Co., 1986—, Charlestown Hotel Co., 1986—, Jackson Hotel Co., 1986—, Murfreesboro Hotel Co., 1986—, Santee Hotel Co., 1986—, Kingsport Hotel Co., 1986—, Raleigh Hotel Assocs., Ltd., 1986, Ozark Regional Eye Ctr., 1986—, Brookfield Mortgage Co., Inc., 1987—, Mt. Pleasant Hotel Co., 1987—, Hattiesburg Hotel Assocs. Ltd., 1987—, Wright and Assocs. Constrn. Co. Inc., 1987—; legal counsel, pres. Biloxi Hotel Co., Inc., 1986—; litigation counsel Independence Fed. Bank Batesville (Ark.), 1987—. Mem. staff, contbr. Tenn. Law Rev., 1974-75, recipient cert., 1975. Bd. dirs. Project 1st Offenders, Shelby County, Tenn., 1976-78; bd. dirs., legal counsel Memphis Community Ctr. for Deaf & Hearing Impaired, 1980-81; bd. dirs. Eagle Scout Day, Chickasaw council Boy Scouts Am., 1978—. Served with USCG, 1971-72. Recipient Outstanding Service award and Key Alpha Phi Omega, 1972, Am. Jurisprudence award Lawyers Co-op. Pubg. Co. and Bancroft-Whitney Co., 1973-74, Chancellor's Honor award George C. Taylor Sch. Law, U. Tenn., 1975; A.S. Graves Meml. scholar, 1974-75. Mem. ABA, Assn. Trial Lawyers Am., Bar Assn. Tenn., Tenn. Trial Lawyers Assn., Nat. Assn. Criminal Def. Lawyers, Memphis and Shelby County Bar Assn., Fed. Bar Assn., Nat. Criminal Justice Assn. (charter 1984—). Alpha Phi Omega, Delta Theta Phi. Democrat. Jewish. Home: 3303 Spencer Dr Memphis TN 38115 Office: Friedman & Sissman P C 100 N Main St Suite 3010 Memphis TN 38103 also: 1052 Brookfield Memphis TN 38119

FRIEDMAN, RONALD MARVIN, cellular biologist; b. Bklyn., Apr. 26, 1930; s. Joseph and Helen (Plotkin) F.; B.S., Columbia U., 1960; M.S., N.Y.U., 1967, Ph.D., 1976; children—Philip, Joelle. Predoctoral fellow Inst. Microbiology, 1968-72, N.Y.U., 1972-76; postdoctoral fellow Columbia U., 1976, Yale U., 1977-78; vis. fellow Princeton U., 1978-79; vis. scientist N.Y. State Inst. Basic Research, 1979-81; research fellow Albert Einstein Coll. Medicine, 1981-82; sci. advisor Royal Arch Med. Research Found., Riverdale, N.Y., 1982—; research fellow meml. Sloan-Kettering Cancer Center, N.Y.C., N.Y., 1984-85; sr. research assoc. dept. pathology Catholic Med. Cent.1983-84; research assoc. dept. biochemistry U. Medicine and Dentistry N.J., Newark, 1984-85; sr. research assoc. in hematology CUNY, 1985—; research assoc. dept. immunology and biochemistry Roswell Park Meml. Inst., Buffalo, 1986-87. research assoc., infectious disease, Channing Laboratory, Harvard Medical School, Boston, 1987—. Vol. Office of Sec. of Agr., 1970-71; conducted survey of emergency med. home call service, Bronx County, NY., 1971-72. Knights Templar fellow, 1973—; NIH fellow, 1981-82. Mem. Harvey Soc.Am. Soc. for Exptl. Biology, 1973—; Am. Soc. Zoology, Animal Behavior Soc., Am. Soc. Cell Biologists, N.Y. Acad. Scis., AAAS, Sigma Xi, International Platform Assn. Clubs: Columbia U. Faculty, Nippon. Lodges: Masons, Shriners, K.T. Office: Channing Lab 180 Longwood Ave Boston MA 02115 *

FRIEDMAN, SUE TYLER, technical publications executive; b. Nürnberg, Fed. Republic Germany, Feb. 28, 1925; came to U.S., 1938; d. William and Ann (Federlein) Tyler (Theilheimer); m. Gerald Manfred Friedman, June 27, 1948; children—Judith Fay Friedman Rosen, Sharon Mira Friedman Azaria, Devora Paula Friedman Zweibach, Eva Jane Friedman Scholle, Wendy Tamar Friedman Spanier. R.N., Beth Israel Sch. Nursing, 1941-43. Exec. dir. Ventures and Publs. of Gerald M. Friedman, 1964—; owner Tyler Publications, Watervliet and Troy, N.Y., 1978—; treas. Northeastern Sci. Found., Inc., Troy, 1979—; treas. Gerry Exploration, Inc., Troy, N.Y., 1982—; office mgr. Rensselaer Ctr. Applied Geology, Troy, 1983—. Pres. Pioneer Women/ Na'amat, Tulsa, 1961-64, treas., Jerusalem, Israel, 1964, pres., Albany, N.Y., 1968-70; bd. dirs. Temple Beth-El, 1965—, dir. Hebrew Sch., 1965-80. Sue Tyler Friedman medal for distinction in history of geology created in her honor, Geol. Soc. London, 1988. Jewish. Avocation: world travel. Home: 32 24th St Troy NY 12180 Office: Rensselaer Ctr Applied Geology 15 3d St Box 746 Troy NY 12181

FRIEDMANN, PERETZ PETER, aerospace engineer, educator; b. Timisoara, Romania, Nov. 18, 1938; came to U.S., 1969; s. Mauritius and Elisabeth (Gross) F.; m. Esther Sarfati, Dec. 8, 1964. DSc, MIT, 1972. Engring. officer Israel Def. Force, 1961-65; sr. engr. Israel Aircraft Industries, Ben Gurion Airport, Israel, 1965-69; research asst. dept. aeronautics and astronautics MIT, Cambridge, 1969-72; asst. prof. mech., aerospace and nuclear engring. dept. UCLA, 1972-77, assoc. prof., 1977-80, prof., 1980—; chmn. Dept. Mech Aerospace Nuclear Engring., Los Angeles, 1988—. Editor-in-chief Vertica-Internat. Jour. Rotorcraft and Powered Lift Aircraft; contbr. numerous articles to profl. jours. Grantee NASA, U.S. Army Research Office, NSF. Fellow AIAA (assoc.); mem. ASME (Structures and Materials award 1983), Am. Helicopter Soc., Sigma Xi. Jewish. Home: 221 N Bowling Green Way Los Angeles CA 90049 Office: UCLA Dept Mech Aerospace Nuclear Engring Los Angeles CA 90024

FRIEDRICH, PETER, biochemist, researcher; b. Budapest, Hungary, June 15, 1936; s. Árpád and Aranka (Strohmayer) F.; m. Maria Várady-Szabó, Aug. 21, 1969; children: Balázs, Adam. MD, Budapest Med. Sch., 1960; PhD, Hungarian Acad. Sci., Budapest, 1967, DSc, 1982. Intern Miskolc City Hosp., Hungary, 1960-61; grad. student Inst. Biochemistry, Budapest, 1962-67; postdoctoral fellow U. Oxford, Eng., 1967-68; sr. research fellow Inst. Enzymology, Budapest, 1969-75, sci. adviser, 1977-85, dep. dir., 1986—; cons. UNESCO U. Alexandria, Egypt, 1975-76; lectr. Free U., Budapest, 1972-82; lectr. biochemistry Attila József U., Szeged, Hungary, 1978-86, prof. (hon.), 1984;. Author: Supramolecular Enzyme Organization, 1986,(Acad. award 1986) ; contbr. articles to profl. jours. Sec. Trade Union for Civil Servants, Inst. Biochemistry, 1969-71. Budapest. Mem. Hungarian Biochem. Soc. (chmn. fgn. affairs 1979-86, v.p. 1986—), Hungarian Acad. Scis. (chmn. biochem. com. 1985—), FEBS Publs. Com. Home: Matyashegyi ut 15 B, H-1037 Budapest Hungary Office: Inst Enzymology, Karolina ut 29, H-1113 Budapest Hungary

FRIEDRICH, ROSE MARIE, travel agency executive; b. Chgo., May 17, 1941; d. Theodore A. and Ann Bernadine (Coppoth) Dlugosz; m. Gerhard K. Friedrich, Apr. 18, 1964; 1 child, Alan C. Student, Roosevelt U., 1986—. Cert. travel agt. Travel cons. Chgo. Motor Club, 1959, Drake Travel, Chgo., 1960-65; mgr. 1st Nat. Travel, Arlington Heights, Ill., 1969-71, Total Travel, Palatine, Ill., 1971-76; owner, mgr. Travel Bug Ltd., Lake Zurich, Ill., 1977—; advisor Coll. Lake County, Grayslake, Ill., 1985—.

Author: (books) Travel Career Textbook, 1980, Guide to Tour Organizing, 1984, Build Profits Through Group Travel, 1984, Independent Travel Agent, 1986. Mem. Inst. Cert. Travel Cons. (chmn. edn. forum 1981-84, appreciation award 1984), Soc. Travel and Tourism Educators, State of Ill. Council Vocat. Edn. (mem. Career Guidance Consortium, Appreciation award 1986), Lake Zurich C. of C. (pres. 1984-85). Republican. Roman Catholic. Home: 407 E Knob Hill Dr Arlington Heights IL 60004 Office: Travel Bug Ltd 15 S Old Rand Rd Lake Zurich IL 60047

FRIEDT, GLENN HARNER, JR., financial executive; b. Detroit, Nov. 23, 1923; s. Glenn H. and Lucy (Lawrence) F. Student Duke U., 1941-42, Northwestern U., 1942-44; BA in Econs., U. Mich., 1947; JD, Wayne State U., 1950, PhD (hon.), Cleary Coll. Admitted to Mich. bar, 1951; asst. to pres. United Platers, Inc., Detroit, 1950-53, v.p., 1953-59, pres., gen. mgr., 1959-63, chmn., 1963-65; v.p., dir. Metal Finishers, Inc., Cleve., 1959-68; asst. to chmn. Gulf & Western Industries, Inc., N.Y.C., 1965-66; dir. Am. Pres.'s Life Ins. Co., 1965-69, exec. v.p., 1966, pres., treas., 1966-68, chmn. bd., 1968-69; pres., dir. Books By Wire Internat., Inc., 1969—; co-owner AAI Holding Co., Inc.; pres., dir. So. United Industries, Inc.; chmn., dir. Books by Wire Internat., Inc. Mem. ABA, Mich. Bar Assn., Detroit Bar Assn., World Bus. Council, Am. Electroplaters Soc. (exec. bd. Detroit 1959-66), Detroit C. of C. (past com. mem.), Coral Ridge (Fla.) C. of C., Theta Delta Chi. Clubs: Coral Beach and Tennis, Detroit Athletic, N.Y. Athletic, Indian Village Tennis, Tower, One Hundred of Detroit, Otsego Ski, University (Detroit); Grosse Pointe (Mich.) Hunt; Le Club (N.Y.); Coral Ridge Country (Fla.). Lodges: Masons, Shriners. Office: The Friedt Group 4950 N Dixie Hwy Fort Lauderdale FL 33334

FRIENDLY, ED, television producer; b. N.Y.C., Apr. 8, 1922; s. Edwin S. and Henrietta (Steinmeier) F.; m. Natalie Coulson Brooks, Jan. 31, 1952; children—Brooke Friendly-Jones, Edwin S. III. Grad., Manlius Sch., 1941. Radio exec., dir. BBD&O, N.Y.C., 1946-49; sales exec. ABC-TV, N.Y.C., 1949-53; ind. producer and packager N.Y.C., 1953-56; producer, program exec. CBS-TV, N.Y.C., 1956-59; v.p. spl. programs NBC-TV, N.Y.C., 1959-67; pres. Ed Friendly Prodns., Los Angeles, from 1967; co-chmn. steering com. Caucus for Producers, Writers and Dirs. Exec. producer: film Little House on the Prairie; Laugh-In; producer: film Peter Lundy and the Medicine Hat Stallion (Emmy nomination); Young Pioneers; mini-series Backstairs at the White House (11 Emmy nominations); also producer motion pictures and TV spls.; exec. producer/producer: Barbara Cartland's The Flame Is Love. Served with inf. U.S. Army, 1942-45, PTO. Recipient Spl. award Internat. Film and TV Festival N.Y., 1967; Emmy award for Laugh-In, 1968; Producer of Yr. award Producers Guild of Am., 1968; Golden Globe award Hollywood Fgn. Press, 1968; Gold medal of honor Internat. Radio and TV Soc., 1970; Christopher award for motion picture, 1975; Western Heritage award Nat. Cowboy Hall of Fame and Western Heritage Center, for Little House on the Prairie, 1975, for Peter Lundy and the Medicine Hat Stallion, 1978; Scout awards for best weekly series and show of yr. for Laugh-In, 1969. Office: 8501 Wilshire Blvd Suite 250 Beverly Hills CA 90211

FRIES, HELEN SERGEANT HAYNES, civic leader; b. Atlanta; d. Harwood Syme and Alice (Hobson) Haynes; student Coll. William and Mary, 1935-38; m. Stuart G. Fries, May 5, 1938. Bd. mem. Community Ballet Assn., Huntsville, Ala., 1968—; mem. nat. nurses aid com. ARC, 1958-59; dir. ARC Aero Club, Eng., 1943-44; supr. ARC Clubmobile, Europe, 1944-46; mem. women's com. Nat. Symphony Orch., Washington, 1959—, chmn. residential fund drive for apts., 1959; bd. dirs. Madison County Republican Club, 1969-70; mem. nat. council Women's Nat. Rep. Club N.Y., 1963—, chmn. hospitality com., 1963-65; bd. mem. League Rep. Women, 1952-61; patron mem., vol. docent Huntsville Mus. Art; vol. docent Weeden House, Twickenham Hist. Preservation Dist. Assn., Inc., Huntsville. Recipient cert. of merit 84th Div., U.S. Army, 1945. Mem. Nat. Soc. Colonial Dames Am., Daus. Am. Colonists, DAR, Nat. Trust Hist. Preservation, Va., Nat., Valley Forge (Pa.), Eastern Shore Va., Huntsville-Madison County hist. socs., Assn. Preservation Va. Antiquities, Greensboro Soc. Preservation, Tenn. Valley Geneal. Soc., Friends of Ala. Archives, AIM, Nat. Soc. Lit. and Arts, Va. Hist. Soc., English Speaking Union, Turkish-Am. Assn. Clubs: Army-Navy, Washington, Capitol Hill, Army-Navy Country (Washington); Garden (Redstone Arsenal), Redstone (Ala.) Yacht; Huntsville Country, Heritage, Botanical Garden (Huntsville, Ala.). Home: 409 Zandale Dr Huntsville AL 35801

FRIES, HERLUF BECK, rancher, investor; b. Fresno, Calif., Apr. 1, 1915; s. Christian Peterson and Emma (Beck) F.; ed. pub. schs., Fresno; m. Geraldine Wood, Aug. 17, 1954; children—Donna, Doug, Jean, Benta. Farmer, rancher, Oakhurst, Calif., 1980-83; cons. Fgn. Farming Corp., Fidanam, Lugano, Switzerland, 1977-80; state pres. Calif. Young Farmers, 1948. Recipient Calif. State Farmer degree Future Farmers Am., 1949. Mem. Fresno County Farm Bur. (dir.) Republican. Lutheran. Address: 1860-5 Minniwawa Fresno CA 93727

FRIESE, HARRISON LEONARD, city official; b. L.I., N.Y., July 17, 1904; s. Herman A. and Marie Louise (Elcholtz) F.; A.B. in Econs. and Banking, Colgate U., 1927; m. Grace M. Fellows, May 6, 1933 (dec. Oct. 1966); children—Harrison Leonard, John Frank; m. 2d, Bette H. Hinsdale, June 29, 1968. With Fellows Engring. & Constrn., Hollis, N.Y., 1934-37; v.p. Fellows and Friese Constrn., 1938-42; planning Grumman Aircraft, Bethpage, L.I., 1942-47; owner, operator Sunrise Nursery, architect, landscape constrn. and design, Fort Lauderdale, Fla., 1945-68; vice mayor Fort Lauderdale, 1967-69, city commr., 1963-71. Vice chmn. Fort Lauderdale Planning and Zoning Bd., 1961-63; mem. Fort Lauderdale-Hollywood Internat. Airport Zoning Bd., 1965-67; mem. area planning bd. Community Shelter Com. Broward County, 1969-71; mem. Broward County Erosion Prevention Bd., 1967-71; mem. Ft. Lauderdale Little Yankee Stadium Com.; Republican precinct committeeman, Fort Lauderdale, 1961-63; bd. dirs. Fort Lauderdale Mus. Arts, 1967-71, Fort Lauderdale Symphony Orch., 1967-71; bd. dirs. Fla. Dist. 5 Mental Health Bd., 1973-77, sec., mem. exec. com., 1975, treas., 1976; bd. dirs., v.p. Fla. Dist. 3 Mental Health Bd., 1977-84; mem. Fla. Planning Council on Alcohol, Drug Abuse and Mental Health, 1985—; trustee Fort Lauderdale Parker Play House, 1967-69. Recipient V.I.P. award Little League Baseball League, 1970. Mem. Fla. League Municipalities (legis. com. 1967-69), Taxpayers League Broward County (v.p. 1960), Fla. Nurserymen and Growers Assn. (charter), Suwannee River Assn. (v.p. at large), Phi Kappa Psi. Methodist. Clubs: Masons, Shriners, Elks, Rotary, Colgate Gold Coast Alumni (pres. 1962), Harbor Beach Surf (pres. 1963-67). Address: Route 3 Box 562 Trenton FL 32693 also: 150 NE 15th Ave Fort Lauderdale FL 33308

FRIESE, ROBERT CHARLES, lawyer; b. Chgo., Apr. 29, 1943; s. Earl Matthew and Laura Barbara (Mayer) F.; m. Chandra Ullom; 1 child, Matthew Robert. A.B. in Internat. Relations, Stanford U., 1964; J.D., Northwestern U., 1970. Admitted to Calif. bar, 1972; dir. Tutor Applied Linguistics Center, Geneva, Switzerland, 1964-66; atty. Bronson, Bronson & McKinnon, San Francisco, 1970-71, SEC, San Francisco, 1971-75; atty., partner Shartsis, Friese & Ginsburg, San Francisco, 1975—; dir., co-founder Internat. Plant Research Inst., Inc., San Carlos, Calif., 1978-86. Chmn. Bd. Suprs. Task Force on Noise Control, 1972-78; chmn. San Franciscans for Cleaner City, 1977; exec. dir. Nob Hill Neighbors, 1972-81; bd. dirs. Nob Hill Assn., 1976-78, Inst. of Range and the Am. Mustang, Calif. Heritage Council, 1977-78, San Francisco Beautiful, 1986— (pres. 1988—); mem. major gifts com. Stanford U. Mem. Am. Bar Assn., Calif. Bar Assn., Bar Assn. San Francisco, (chmn. bus. litigation com., 1978-79, chmn. state ct. civil litigation com. 1983—), Lawyers Club of San Francisco, Mensa, Calif. Hist. Soc. Clubs: Commonwealth; Swiss-American Friendship League (chmn. 1971-79). Office: Shartsis Friese & Ginsburg 1 Maritime Plaza 18th Floor San Francisco CA 94111-2204

FRIESECKE, RAYMOND FRANCIS, management consultant; b. N.Y.C., Mar. 12, 1937; s. Bernhard P. K. and Josephine (De Tomi) F.; B.S. in Chemistry, Boston Coll., 1959; M.S. in Civil Engring., MIT, 1961. Product specialist Dewey & Almy Chem. div. W. R. Grace & Co., Inc., Cambridge, Mass., 1963-66; market planning specialist USM Corp., Boston, 1966-71; mgmt. cons., Boston, 1971-74; dir. planning and devel. Schweitzer div. Kimberly-Clark Corp., Lee, Mass., 1974-78; v.p. corp. planning Butler Automatic, Inc., Canton, Mass., 1978-80; pres. Butler-Europe Inc., Greenwich, Conn. and Munich, Fed. Republic Germany, 1980; v.p. mktg. and planning Butler Greenwich Inc., 1980-81; pres. Strategic Mgmt. Assocs., San Rafael, Calif., 1981—; bd. dirs. Butler-Europe, Inc., Greenwich, 1980-81; corp. clk., v.p. Bldg. Research & Devel., Inc., Cambridge, 1966-68. State co-chmn. Citizens for Fair Taxation, 1972-73; state co-chmn. Mass. Young Reps., 1967-69; chmn. Ward 7 Rep. Com., Cambridge, 1968-70; vice chmn. Cambridge Rep. City Com., 1966-68; Rep. candidate Mass. Ho. of Reps., 1964, 66; pres. Marin Rep. Council, 1986—; chmn. Kentfield Rehab. Hosp. Found., 1986—, Calif. Acad., 1986-87; sec. Navy League Marin Council, 1984—. Served to 1st lt. U.S. Army, 1961-63. Mem. Am. Chem. Soc., The Planning Forum, Am. Mktg. Assn., Am. Rifle Assn. Author: Management by Relative Product Quality; contbr. articles to profl. jours. Home and Office: 141 Convent Ct San Rafael CA 94901

FRIGERIO, CHARLES STRAITH, lawyer; b. Detroit, Mar. 8, 1957; s. Louie John and LaVern (Straith) F.; m. Annette Angela Russo, Oct. 18, 1985. BA, St. Mary's U., 1979, JD, 1982. Bar: Tex. 1982, U.S. Ct. Appeals (5th cir.) 1987, U.S. Supreme Ct. 1987. Pros. atty. City Attys. Office, San Antonio, 1982-84, trial atty., 1984—. Mem. Dem. Nat. Com., San Antonio, 1976; asst. mgr. local campaigns, San Antonio, 1976-84. Mem. ABA, Tex. Bar Assn., Fed. Bar Assn., San Antonio Bar Assn., Assn. Trial Lawyers Am., Cath. Lawyers Assn., Delta Epsilom Sigma. Democrat. Roman Catholic. Home: 317 Cleveland Ct San Antonio TX 78209 Office: City Attys Office P O Box 839966 San Antonio TX 78285

FRIGGIERI, OLIVER, literary critic, writer; b. Floriana, Malta, Mar. 27, 1947; s. Charles and Mary (Galea) F.; m. Eileen Cassar, Apr. 6, 1972; 1 child, Sara. BA cum laude, U. Malta, 1968, MA, 1976, PhD, 1978; post-grad., Cath. U. Milan, 1977. Lectr. Maltese lit. and lit. theory U. Malta, Msida, 1976—; guest lectr. numerous internat. congresses, various countries. Author: Movimenti letterari e coscienza romantica Maltese, 1980, L-Istramb, 1980, Dun Karm - Il-Poeziji Migbura, 1980, Dun Karm - Il-Bniedem fil-Poeta, 1980, Laz, 1982, Baruhove Zagate, 1982, Stejjer ghal Qabel Jidlam, 1979, 83, Ruzar Briffa - Il-Poeziji Migbura, 1983, L'esperienza leopardiana di un poeta maltese, Karmenu Vassallo, 1983, Il-Gidba, 1977, 2d edit., 1984, Il-Hajja ta' Ruzar Briffa, 1984, Storia della letteratura maltese, 1986, Cross Winds, 1987, Na Raskruscu, 1987, Gesabella, 1987, A Turn of the Wheel, 1987, Il-Ktieb tal-Poezija Maltija, 1987, numerous others; co-founder, co-editor Saghtar, 1971—; editor Jour. Maltese Studies, 1984—; contbr. articles to profl. jours. Mem. Assn. Internat. Des Critiques Litteraires. Roman Catholic. Home: 93 Fleur de Lys Rd, Birkirkara Malta Office: U Malta, Msida Malta

FRIGON, HENRY FREDERICK, diversified company executive; b. Bridgeport, Conn., Nov. 16, 1934; s. Henry Xavier and Veronica Anne (Beloin) F.; m. Anne Marie McCarthy, Sept. 20, 1965; children: Megan, Michele, Henry, Scott, Mark, Stephanie. B.S.C.E., Tufts U., 1957; post-grad., U. Pa., 1958-59; M.B.A., NYU, 1962. With Gen. Foods Corp., 1960-68, various fin. and mktg. positions, 1960-66; chief fin. officer, internat. ops. Gen. Foods Corp., White Plains, N.Y., 1966-68; v.p. fin., sec., treas. Gen. Housewares Corp., N.Y.C., 1968-70; pres. Gen. Housewares Corp. (Giftware Group), Stamford, Conn., 1970-74; also dir. parent co.; group v.p. Masco Corp., Taylor, Mich., 1974-81; exec. v.p., chief fin. and adminstrv. officer Batus Inc., Louisville, 1981-83, pres., 1983-85, pres., chief operating officer, 1985, pres., chief exec. officer, 1985—; bd. dirs. Batus, Inc., B.A.T. Capital Corp., Appleton Papers Inc., Marshall Field & Co., Saks Fifth Ave., First Ky. Nat. Corp., First Nat. Bank Louisville, Joint Council Econ. Edn. Bd. dirs. Ky Econ. Devel. Corp. Served with USNR, 1957-65. Mem. Conf. Bd., The Brookings Inst., World Bus. Council, Bretton Woods Com. Home: 4008 Woodstone Way Louisville KY 40222 Office: Batus Inc 2000 Citizens Plaza Louisville KY 40202

FRIGOUT-BAUSSART, MARIJAN RENEE MONIQUE, physician; b. Roubaix, France, Aug. 4, 1951; d. Jean Desablin and Jacqueline Baussart; m. Fabien Frigout, July 9, 1977; 1 child, Laury. Medical Degree, Faculté de Lille, France, 1981. Practice medicine Wasquehal, France, 1981—. Home and Office: Ave du Roi Albert 1er, 59290 Wasquehal France

FRIHART, BRYANT CLIFFORD, retired oil company executive; b. Richland Center, Wis., June 14, 1928; s. Bryant and Maude (Farley) F.; B.S. in Petroleum Engring., U. Tulsa, 1951; m. Ruth Helen Siegele, Sept. 1, 1956; children—Bryant Curtis, Matthew Christian, James Eric. Various engring positions Cities Service Co., Okla., Tex., N.Y., 1954-63, v.p. Argentina ops., Buenos Aires, 1963-67, pres., gen. mgr. Argentine ops., Buenos Aires, 1967-74, gen. mgr. Latin Am. ops., Houston, 1974-76, gen. mgr. S. Am./Africa, Houston, 1976-79, dir. Joint Ventures, Tulsa, 1979-81, v.p. govt. and industry affairs, energy resources group, Tulsa, 1981-82, v.p. adminstrn., land and human resources, 1982-83, corp. v.p. govt. affairs, 1983-87; ret. 1987. Active Southwestern Art Assn. Served with USMC, 1951-54. Mem. Soc. Petroleum Engrs. of AIME (chmn. N.Y. petroleum sect. 1961-62), Am. Petroleum Inst., Mid-Continent Oil and Gas Assn., Okla.-Kans. Mid-Continent Oil and Gas Assn. (chmn. bd. 1986—). Republican. Methodist. Club: Petroleum (Tulsa). Lodges: Masons (master, 1973-74), York Rite, Consistory, Shrine. Home: 6627 E 89th Pl Tulsa OK 74133

FRIJHOFF, WILLEM THEODORE M., JR., professor cultural history; b. Zutphen, The Netherlands, May 31, 1942; s. Willem Th. M. Sr. and Theodora J. (Elders) F.; m. Sabine F.M. de Mezamat de Lisle, Sept. 22, 1978; 1 child, Laia. M in History, U. Sorbonne, France, 1970; D in Social Scis., Tilburg U., 1981. Research asst. Ecole Hautes Etudes Scis. Sociales, Paris, 1971-77; research officer Inst. Nat. Recherche Pedagogique, Paris, 1977-81; asst. prof. faculty social scis. Tilburg U., The Netherlands, 1981-83; prof. faculty social history Erasmus U., Rotterdam, The Netherlands, 1983—, dean faculty social history, 1986—; chmn. Dutch Com. for Bicentennial French Revolution, The Netherlands, 1984—; mem. sci. bd. P.J. Meertens-Inst., Amsterdam, 1984—; bd. dirs. Cen. Office Genealogy, The Hague, Netherlands. Author: Ecole et Societe dans la France d'Ancien Regime, 1975, La Societe neerlandaise et ses Gradues, 1981, The Supply of Schooling, 1983. Recipient Prince Bernhard Found. award Dutch Soc. Scis., 1983. Mem. Internat. Standing Conf. for History Edn. (bd. dirs., sec. 1985—), Maatschappij der Nederlandse Letterkunde, Assn. Internat. llengua i Literature Catalanes (founder). Roman Catholic. Home: Jan van Ghestellaan 25, NL-3054 CE Rotterdam The Netherlands Office: Erasmus U, PO Box 1738, NL-3000 DR Rotterdam The Netherlands

FRILOT, BERT CLARK, audio recording engineer; b. New Orleans, Apr. 24, 1939; s. Gilbert C. and Rhea (Curry) F.; m. Callie Marie LeBlanc, Dec. 5, 1962 (div. 1971); 1 dau., Lisa. Rec. engr. Cosimo's Rec. Studios, New Orleans, 1961-64, ACA Rec. Studios, Houston, 1964-66; mgr., chief engr. Gilley's Rec. Studios, Pasadena, Tex., 1966—. Served with USN, 1957-61. Recipient Golden Reel award Ampex Tape Corp., 1982, for engring. and mixing platinum album by artist Willie Nelson, Somewhere over the Rainbow. Recorded or produced million seller records on artists: Fats Domino, B.J. Thomas, Jimmy Clanton, Pete Fountain, Dr. John, Archie Bell and the Drells, 8 others. Recorded or produced recordings on country artists: Mickey Gilley, Johnny Lee, Charlie Daniels Band, Floyd Tillman. Recorded portion of sound track of Urban Cowboy with John Travolta from movie by Paramount Pictures. Chief recording and mixing engr. for Gilley's syndicated radio show Live from Gilley's, aired on 450 stations each week, including overseas. Lodges: Elks, Eagles (Pasadena). Home: 4218 Spencer Hwy Pasadena TX 77504 Office: Gilleys Rec Studio 4500 Spencer Hwy Pasadena TX 77504

FRIMML, JAYMEE JO, chiropractor, nurse; b. Watertown, S.D., Oct. 18, 1949; d. Rodney Elsworth and Marie Ruth (Musta) Dale; m. Steven James Frimml, July 1, 1984; 1 child, Richard Mark. AS in Nursing, So. Coll., Collegedale, Tenn., 1970; student U. Ariz., 1979-81; D. Chiropractic, Palmer Coll. Chiropractic, Davenport, Iowa, 1985. Registered nurse, Tenn., Tex., Okla., Mich., Ariz., Iowa, Idaho. Emergency room nurse Madison Hosp., Tenn., 1970-71; nursing supr. Wilson N. Jones Hosp., Sherman, Tex., 1972-74; neonatal nurse specialist Lansing Gen. Hosp., Mich., 1974-78; clin. nurse leader, pediatrics Tucson Med. Ctr., 1978-81, pulmonary nurse specialist, 1981-82; chiropractor Cramer Chiropractic Clinic, Boise, Idaho, 1986; owner, operator, dir. Northwest Health Inst., 1986—. Contbr. biweekly articles Idaho Press Tribune. Bd. dirs. Seventh-day Adventist Better Living Com., Caldwell, Idaho, 1986. Mem. Am. Chiropractic Assn., Internat. Chiropractic Assn., Council on Roentgenology, Idaho Assn. Chiropractice Physicians (mem. polit. action com.), Nampa C. of C., Sigma Phi Chi (legis. com.). Seventh-day Adventist. Lodge: Soroptimists. Home: 3613 Juanita Way Nampa ID 83651 Office: Northwest Health Inst. 1203 10th St S Nampa ID 83651

FRISCH, FRED I., real estate executive; b. Indpls., Oct. 19, 1935; s. Leon and Blanka (Frankovitz) F.; m. Rochelle L. Fein, Sept. 15, 1957; children: Caryn, Susan, Daniel. BBA, U. Miami, Fla., 1957. Lic. real estate broker. Pres. Frisch & Assocs., Indpls., 1976—; pres. Prime Property Investment Group; bd. dirs. Hooverwood Homes, Indpls.; bd. dirs. comml. and indsl. div. Met. Indpls. Bd. Realtors, pres. 1984. Served with USAF, 1960-64. Mem. Real Estate Securities and Syndication Inst. Republican. Jewish. Club: Indpls. Men's (pres. 1966-68). Office: 9302 N Meridian Indianapolis IN 46260

FRISCH, KURT CHARLES, educator, administrator; b. Vienna, Austria, Jan. 15, 1918; came to U.S., 1939; s. Jacob J. and Clara F. (Spondre) F.; m. Sally Sisson, Sept. 14, 1946; children—Leslie Frisch Nickerson, Kurt C. Jr., Robert J. M.A., U. Vienna, 1938; candidate Sc. Chim., U. Brussels, 1939; M.A., Columbia U., 1941, Ph.D., 1944. Project leader Gen. Electric Co., Pittsfield, Mass., 1944-52; acting mgr. research E.F. Houghton & Co., Phila., 1952-56; dir. polymer research and devel. Wyandotte Chems. Corp., Mich., 1956-68; prof., dir. Polymer Inst., U. Detroit, 1968—; v.p., dir. research Polymer Techs. subs. U. Detroit, 1986—; pres. Kurt C. Frisch, Inc., Grosse Ile, Mich., 1982—; cons. various corps. Patentee in field. (52); author, co-author, editor 25 books. Contbr. articles to profl. jours. Recipient medal of merit German Foam Soc., 1981, medal of merit Brit. Rubber and Plastics Group, 1982; named to Polyurethane Hall of Fame, 1984; IR-100 award Indsl. Research Inst. Fellow Am. Inst. Chemists; mem. Soc. Plastics Industry (div. chmn.), Soc. Plastics Engrs.(Outstanding Achievement award 1986), Am. Chem. Soc., Soc. Coating Tech. Republican. Episcopalian. Home: 17986 Parke Ln Grosse Ile MI 48138

FRISCH, MAX RUDOLF, writer; b. Zurich, May 15, 1911; diploma in architecture ETH, 1941; Dr. h.c., Philipps U., Marburg, 1963, Bard Coll., N.Y.C., 1980, CUNY, 1982. Fgn. corr. for newspapers in Europe and Near East, 1931-33; practice architecture, Zurich, 1946-54; lived in Mexico, 1951-52, U.S., 1951-52, 73-74, Rome, 1966; plays and novels include: Blätter aus dem Brotsack, 1941, J'adore ce qui me brule oder Die Schwierigen, 1942, Santa Cruz, 1944, Bin oder Die Reise nach Peking, 1944, Nun singen sie wieder, 1945, Die chinesische Mauer, 1946, Tagebuch mit Marion, 1947, Als der Krieg zu Ende war, 1949, Graf Oederland, 1951, Don Juan oder Die Liebe zur Geometrie, 1953, Stiller, 1955, Homo Faber, 1957, Herr Biedermann und die Brandstifter, 1958, Die grosse Wut des Philipp Hotz, 1958, Andorra, 1961, Mein Name sei Gantenbein, 1964, Biografie: Ein Spiel, 1967, Öffentlichkeit als Partner, 1968, Wilhelm Tell für die Schule, 1971, Tagebuch 1966-71, 1972, Dienstbüchlein, 1974, Montauk, 1975, Werkausgabe, 1976, Triptychon-3 szenische Bilder, 1978, Der Mensch erscheint im Holozän, 1979, Blaubart, 1982. Rockefeller drama grantee, 1951; recipient Conrad Ferdinand Meyer prize, 1951; Georg Büchner prize German Acad. Lang. and Poetry, 1958; Jerusalem prize, Ehrenpreis des Schillergedächtnispreises des Landes Baden-Württemberg, 1965, Grosser Schillerpreis, Zurich, 1975; Peace prize German Book Trade, 1976; decorated comandeur de l'Ordre des Arts et des Lettres (Paris), 1985; recipient Commonwealth award MLA; Neustadt prize for lit., 1986. Mem. Am. Acad. Arts and Letters, Akademie der Künste, Deutsche Akademie für Sprache und Dichtung. Archtl. design includes Zurich Recreation Park. Address: care Suhrkamp-Verlag, Frankfurt/Main Federal Republic of Germany Other: CH-6611 Berzona Switzerland *

FRISCHENSCHLAGER, FRIEDHELM, former government official of Austria; b. Salzburg, Oct. 6, 1943. Dr. Laws, Vienna U., 1969. Reader faculty Vienna U., 1969-71; group leader Ring Freiheitlicher Studenten 1968; dep. chmn. Austrian Students Movement, 1969; founder-mem. FPO's Politico-Sci. Working Group, Mcpl. councillor, 1972; mem. Salzburg City Bd.; Mem. Nationalrat, Austrian Parliament, 1977—, mem. constl. com. and com. sci. and research; fed. minister for nat. def., 1983-86. Mem. Freedom Party, leader parliamentary group. Address: care Freedom Party, Karntnerstn 28, 1010 Vienna I Austria *

FRISCHMUTH, ROBERT ALFRED, landscape planner, filmmaker; b. N.Y.C., Dec. 15, 1940; s. Alfred P. and Emma (Glas) F.; student SUNY, Albany, 1958-60; B.B.A., Pace U., 1973; m. Marlis Lowenhagen, July 15, 1967 (div. 1979); children—Bettina, Malissa. Statis. analyst N.Y. Central System, N.Y.C., 1961-68; landscape planner Rosedale Nurseries, Hawthorne, N.Y., 1969—; founder RAF Prodns., 1980—; producer films: Gardening: A Brief History, 1979, Tree Transplant, 1980, Florida, 1981, Best of the West, 1982; Kenya Safari, 1983; Of Temples and Tombs, 1984. Bd. dirs. Paramount Center for the Arts, 1981-87, pres. 1983-85. Served with U.S. Army, 1963-65. Cert. nurseryman, N.Y. State. Mem. Am. Film Inst., Info. Film Producers Am. Lutheran. Home: 31 Ogden Ave Peekskill NY 10566 Office: Rosedale Nurseries 51 Saw Mill River Rd Hawthorne NY 10532

FRISHMAN, JUDITH, educator, researcher; b. Monsey, N.Y., July 4, 1953; d. Louis and Mimi (Mandel) F.; m. Edward Van Voolen, June 13, 1976. BA, Barnard Coll., 1976; PhD, Rijks U. Leiden, Holland, 1983. Researcher, educator Rijks U. Leiden, Holland, 1984—; cons. Liberal Jewish Tchrs. Tng., Adult Edn. of Netherland, 1982—; guest curator Jewish Hist. Mus. Exhibit on Jewish Women, Amsterdam, 1985-86. Contbr. articles to profl. jours. Treas. Shalom Achshav-Dutch Friends of Peace Now, 1984-88. Clubs: Tamar, Jewish-Christian Feminist Group. Home: Oude Spiegelstraat 7, 1016BM Amsterdam Holland Office: Rijks U Leiden,, M de Vrieshof 4,, 2311 BZ Leiden Holland

FRISINA, ROBERT DANA, sensory neuroscientist; b. Evanston, Ill., Sept. 11, 1955; s. D. Robert and Louise (Boaz) F.; m. Susan Taylor Frisina, July 31, 1982; 1 child, Laurin Taylor. A.B. in Exptl. Psychology summa cum laude, Hamilton Coll., 1977; Ph.D. in Neurosci., Syracuse U., 1983. Research asst. Hamilton Coll., Clinton, N.Y., 1977; recipient Communicative and Neurosensory Disorders First award NIH, 1988; Root fellow in sci. Inst. Sensory Research, Syracuse, N.Y., 1977-78, NSF grad. fellow, 1978-81, grad research assoc., 1981-83; NIH research fellow Ctr. for Brain Research U. Rochester, 1983-85, asst. prof. physiology and otolaryngology, 1985—; mem. staff Nat. Tech. Inst. for Deaf, Rochester, 1975. Author: Hearing, 1988. Contbr. articles to profl. jours. Dir. vols. Hamilton Coll. Aspect of Marcy Psychiat. Ctr. Vols., Marcy, N.Y., 1974-77. NSF fellow, 1978-81; recipient Communicative and Neurosensory Disorders First award NIH, 1988. Mem. Acoustical Soc. Am., Assn. Research in Otolaryngology, Soc. Neurosci., N.Y. Acad. Sci., Phi Beta Kappa, Sigma Xi. Roman Catholic. Avocations: tennis, squash, skiing, martial arts, skating. Office: U Rochester Med Ctr Otolaryngology Div Box 629 Rochester NY 14642

FRISK, TAGE E., data processing executive; b. Tvärån, Sweden, Apr. 3, 1929; s. Albert and Alvina (Seger) F.; children from previous marriage: Karin, Sara, Henrik; m. Mona-Lisa Viola Karlsson, Aug. 2, 1981; children: Thomas, Michael. MS, Yale U., 1958; PhD, Chalmers Inst. Tech., Gothenburg, Sweden, 1961. Project mgr. ASEA, Västeras and Ludvika, Sweden and London, 1955-61; project mgr. IBM Corp., Stockholm, 1961-64, dir. lab, 1964-67, 72-79; dir. labs. Harrison, U.S., 1967; dir. labs Nice (France), 1968-72; dir. internat. edn. Brussels, 1979-83; v.p. sci. and tech. Paris, 1983-88; pres. Europace, Paris, 1988—. Office: IBM Corp, European Div Tour Pascal, Cedex 40, 92075 Paris France

FRITCHEY, JOHN AUGUSTUS, II, physician; b. Harrisburg, Pa., Mar. 15, 1902; s. Elmer Eugene and Bertha Belle (Maurer) F.; Ph.B., Dickinson Coll., 1924; postgrad. Dartmouth, 1925-27; M.D., U. Pa., 1929; m. Dorotha Amy Warren, Nov. 12, 1932; children—Margaret Ann (Mrs. Henry Voltaire Trahan, Jr.), John Warren. Resident, Harrisburg Hosp., 1929-30; practice medicine, Harrisburg; mem. staff Polyclinic Hosp., Harrisburg, med. chief, 1931-48; state med. adminstr. Pa. Bur. Vocat. Rehab., 1948-63; med. cons. Pa. Dept. Pub. Assistance, 1950-54, Cumberland County Bd. Assistance, 1975-86, Dauphin County Bd. Assistance, 1976-86; sec.-treas., dir. San Family Washing Co., Harrisburg, 1943-48; internist Harrisburg Dist. Armed Forces Induction Service, 1942-53; county dep. coroner, 1934-69. Author: Leonard and Clarissa Brown and their Descendants, 1968, Ancestry of

Margaret Ann Trahan, 1969, Ahnenliste Fritschi, Hessische Ahnenlisten, 1972. Chmn. Harrisburg City Democratic Com., 1942-43, chmn. Dauphin County Dem. Com., 1943-46; v.p. Unity Ch. of Harrisburg, 1982-83, pres., 1983-84; Mem. AMA, Dauphin County Med. Soc., Harrisburg Acad. Medicine, Nat. Rehab. Assn. (life), Geneal. Soc. Pa., Gesellschaft fur Familienkunde in Kurhessen und Waldeck, SAR (chpt. pres. 1942-44, state pres. 1948-50, v.p. gen. 1947-49, nat. exec. com. 1949-50, registrar gen. 1950-53, surgeon gen. 1956-57), Palatines to Am. (organizing chmn. Pa. chpt. 1977-78, nat. exec. council 1978-79, nat. v.p. 1979-81, nat. pres. 1981-83; nat. exec. council 1983-84) South Central Pa. Geneal. Soc. (charter), Cumberland County Hist. Soc., Mennonite Hist. Soc., The Perry Historians, Sigma Chi, Phi Chi. Mason (32 deg., Shriner). Home: 1002 King Arthur Ct Camelot Retirement Community Harlingen TX 78550

FRITH, JAMES BURNESS, construction company executive; b. Henry County, Va., Jan. 29, 1916; s. Jacob Ewell and Sally Ada (Nunn) F.; B.S.C., Nat. Bus. Coll., 1937; m. Mary Kathryn Nininger, Aug. 21, 1947; children—Shelley Anne, Jacob Ewell II, James Burness. Gen. bldg. contractor, 1945—; chmn. bd., dir., treas. Frith Constrn. Co., Inc., Martinsville, Va., 1956—; dir. Frith Equipment Corp., Martinsville, Tultex Corp., Martinsville, Piedmont Trust Bank, Piedmont Bank Group, Martinsville, Henry County Plywood, Ridgeway, Va., Hop-In Food Stores, Inc., Roanoke, Va.; co-founder Multitrade Group, Martinsville. Bd. dirs. Martinsville Henry County Econ. Devel. Corp.; founder Patrick Henry Coll. Scholarship Found.; trustee emeritus Averett Coll., Danville, Va. Served with USAAF, 1942-45. Mem. Assoc. Gen. Contractors Am. (state bd. dirs. 1967-72, mem. exec. com. 1971-72), Martinsville-Henry County C. of C. (dir. 1973, sec. 1973, v.p. 1974, Heck Ford award 1983). Elk, K.P., Kiwanian (pres. 1952, lt. gov. 1955). Clubs: Shenandoah (Roanoke, Va.); Chatmoss Country, Forest Park Country (Martinsville, Va.). Home: 1127 Cherokee Trail Martinsville VA 24112 Office: PO Box 5028 Martinsville VA 24112

FRITSCHE, WOLFGANG, association executive; b. Dortmund, Germany, Mar. 11, 1928; s. Gerhard and Marie (Jaeger) F.; diplom-chemiker U. Bonn, 1953, Dr. rer. nat., 1954; m. Gerti Gassen, Aug. 27, 1955; children—Sabine, Johann-Gerhard. Asst. to tech. dir. Vereinigte Ultramarinfabriken AG, 1955-60; head dept., sec. Gesellschaft Deutscher Chemiker, Frankfurt, 1960-71, sec. gen., 1972—; dir. Verlag Chemie GmbH, Weinheim, Germany, Fachinformationszentrum Chemie GmbH, Berlin. Recipient Lavoisier Medal Soc. Française de Chimie, 1987. Fellow Royal Soc. Chemistry London; mem. Max Planck-Gesellschaft, Verein Osterreichischer Chemiker, Am. Chem. Soc., Chem. Soc. Thailand, Assn. Univ. Profs. for Chemistry Fed. Republic Germany (sec.), Deutscher Zentralausschuss für Chemie (sec.), Fedn. European Chem. Socs. (chmn.council, Hon. Medal 1985). Home: Ober den Birken 13, 6233 Kelkheim-Ruppertshain Federal Republic of Germany Office: Gesellschaft Deutscher Chemiker, Varrentrappstrasse 40-42, 6000 Frankfurt Federal Republic of Germany

FRITZ, JOHANN PAUL, newspaper executive; b. Ober-Eggendorf, Austria, Apr. 15, 1940; s. Johann and Amalia (Piringer) F.; m. Brigitte Weick, May 2, 1964; 1 child, Susanne. Student in philosophy, U. Vienna, Austria, 1958-61; student in social scis., Western Res. U., 1961; student, Hochschule fur Welthandel, U. Econs., Vienna, 1962-64. Gen. sec. Österreich Jungarbeiterbewegung, Vienna, 1958-67, v.p., 1967-70; dep. sec. gen. Österreich Wirtschaftsbund, Vienna, 1970-75; dir. exec. Kabel TV Wien GmbH, Vienna, 1975-83; mng. dir. Die Presse (daily newspaper), Vienna, 1975—; lectr. on media Vienna U. Econs., 1979—. Author: Kabelfernsehen in Österreich, 1975; editor in chief (monthly mag.) Der Österreich Jungarbeiter, 1968-72, Jazz Info., 1967-70. Mem. Austrian Newspaper Pub. Assn. (v.p. 1981—), Internat. Fedn. Newspaper Pubs. (chmn. electronic media com. 1982—), Internat. Assn. for Newspaper and Media Tech. (bd. dirs. 1976-80, senator 1980—), Internat. Advt. Assn. (pres. Austrian chpt. 1980-82), Austrian Cable TV Assn. (pres. 1980—), Internat. Press Telecommunication Council (chmn. pub. policy com. 1986—), Austrian Press Agy. (chmn. 1983-85, 88—), Austrian Jazz Fedn. (pres. 1961-71), European Jazz Fedn. (sec.-gen. 1969-72). Club: Mgmt. (Vienna) (mng. dir. 1971-75, mng. editor report 1971-75). Office: Die Presse, Parkring 12a, A-1015 Vienna Austria

FRITZ, RENE EUGENE, JR., manufacturing executive; b. Prineville, Oreg., Feb. 24, 1943; s. Rene and Ruth Pauline (Munson) F.; B.S. in Bus. Adminstrn., Oreg. State U., 1965; m. Sharyn Ann Fife, June 27, 1964; children—Rene Scott, Lanz Eugene, Shay Steven, Case McGarrett. Sales mgr. Renal Corp., Albany, Oreg., 1965-66, Albany Machine and Supply, 1965-66; pres. Albany Internat. Industries, Inc., 1966-85, Wood Yield Tech. Corp., 1972-85, Albany Internat. D.I.S.C., 1972-85, Automation Controls Internat., Inc., Albany, 1975-85; co-founder, chmn. Albany Titanium Inc., 1981—; founder, pres. WY Tech. Corp., 1984—, R. Fritz & Assocs., 1987—; dir. Home Fed. Savs. & Loan, Albany, 1973-87, Sunne Maskiner, Stockholm, 1969. Pres., Oreg. World Trade Council, 1982—; trustee U.S. Naval Acad. Found., Annapolis, Md., 1988—. Mem. Oreg. State Alumni, Forest Prods. Research Soc., Young Pres. Orgn. Presbyterian. Clubs: Rotary, Elks. Patentee sawmill machinery.

FRITZ, TERRENCE LEE, investment banker, strategic consultant; b. Ft. Dodge, Iowa, Mar. 10, 1943; s. George and Julia Evelyn (Katnik) F.; children: Erich, Kevin, Tanya. BS in Indsl. Engring., Iowa State U., 1967. Registered profl. engr., Colo. Mfg. system analyst Martin-Marietta, Denver, 1967-68; system fin. analyst N.Am. Philips, Denver, 1968-69; mgmt. cons. Denver, 1970-74; exec. dir. Met. Transit Authority-Iowa Dept. Transp., Des Moines, 1974-78; sr. v.p. mktg., strategic planning Holiday Inns, Trailways, Dallas, 1978-80; pres. Strategic Actions, Dallas, 1984—. Bd. dirs. Dallas, Ft. Worth Adv. Bd., 1980-84; cons. Dallas, Ft. Worth Transp. Authority, 1980; bd. mem. Govs. Com. on Tech., Austin, 1982-83. Mem. Dallas C. of C. (pres., chief exec. officer 1980-84). Clubs: Tower, Univ. Home: 9347 Briarhurst Dr Dallas TX 75243 Office: Strategic Actions 1700 FirstCity Ctr Dallas TX 75201

FRITZE, JULIUS ARNOLD, marriage counselor; b. Albuquerque, Dec. 30, 1918; s. Martin Herman and Mary (Staerkel) F.; student St. Paul's Jr. Coll., 1937-39; diploma Concordia Sem., 1944; B.A., in Edn., U. N.Mex., 1943; M.S., Central Mo. State Coll., 1969; nat. cert. counselor; m. Marion Caroline Becker, June 4, 1944; children—Christine, Timothy; m. 2d, Anita Carol Dozier, May 18, 1973. Ordained to ministry Lutheran Ch., 1944; pastor in Corpus Christi, Tex., 1944-48, Higginsville, Mo., 1948-57; exec. dir. Marriage and Parenthood Center, Dallas, 1957-59; pvt. practice marriage counseling, Dallas, 1959—; indsl. psychologist N. Am. Mktg., 1975-76; mgmt. cons. Concord Systems, Inc., 1978—. Cons. Mo. Snyod, Luth. Ch., St. Louis, 1961, Tex. dist., 1976—; lectr. to profl. and laymen's insts., 1956—; lectr. Dallas County Jr. Coll. Bd. dirs. Dallas area Am. Lung Assn., 1976—. Lic. profl. counselor, Tex. Mem. Am. Assn. Marriage Counselors, Am. Personnel and Guidance Assn., Nat. Vocat. Guidance Assn., Nat. Council Family Relations, Am., Southwestern, Tex. psychol. assns., Am. Orthopsychiat. Assn., Internat. Platform Assn. Author: The Essence of Marriage, 1969; Mini Manual for Ministers, 1978. Contbr. series of articles to nat. mags. Home: 3118 Royal Gables Dallas TX 75229 Office: 3198 Royal Ln #100 Dallas TX 75229

FRITZHAND, MAREK, philosophy educator; b. Buczacz, Poland, Oct. 12, 1913; s. Schmerl and Frimetta (Sommer) F.; m. Karolina Gruszczynska, 1949; 1 dau., Annete. Bachelor degree, U. Lwow (Poland), 1936; Doctorate, U. Warsaw (Poland), 1950. Mem. faculty U. Warsaw, 1950—, assoc. prof. philosophy, 1954-65, prof., 1965—, dean Faculty Philosophy, 1962-65, dean Faculty Social Scis., 1975-77, head dept. moral sci.; mem. Com. Nat. Edn. Medal, 1979—. Author (in Polish): Young Marx's Ethical Thought, 1961; Man, Humanism, Morals, 1961; Konieczność a Moralnosc, 1961; About Marxist Ethics, 1962; W Kregu Etyki Marksistowskiej, 1966; Main Problems of Metaethics, 1970; O Niektorych Wlasciwosciach Etyki Marksistowskiej, 1975; Facts and Values, 1983; editor-in-chief Etyka, 1966-71, mem. editorial staff, 1973—; contbr. numerous articles on ethics and philosophy to profl. publs. Decorated Gold Cross of Merit (2), Cross of Valour, Cross of Grunwald 3d class, Knight's Cross, Order Polonia Restituta; named Tchr. of Merit, People's Republic of Poland, 1978; Sztandar Pracy 1st class, 1984; state reward, 1984. Mem. Polish Acad. Scis. (chmn. com. philos. scis.), Polish Philos. Soc. Mem. Polish United Workers Party. Office: Al Wyzwolenia 2 m 3, 00-570 Warsaw Poland

FRODSHAM, JOHN DAVID, English and comparative literature educator, university dean; b. Wallasey, Cheshire, Eng., Jan. 5, 1930; s. John Keith and Winifred Elizabeth (Williams) F.; m. Beng Choo Tan, July 12, 1964; children: Simon, Stefan, Jonathan, Myfanwy, Julia. MA, Cambridge U., Eng., 1956; PhD, Australian Nat. U., Canberra, 1960. Lectr. U. Baghdad, Iraq, 1956-58; research fellow Australian Nat. U., 1958-60, reader, 1967-71; lectr. U. Malaya, Kuala Lumpur, 1961-65; sr. lectr. Adelaide (Australia) U., 1965-67; prof. U. Dar es Salaam, Tanzania, 1971-73; Found. prof. English and comparative lit. Murdoch U., Perth, Australia, 1973—, dean of humanities, 1973—; chmn. Council for Welfare of Overseas Students; mem. Nat. Authority for the Accreditation of Translators and Interpretors, 1977-83. Author: An Anthology of Chinese Verse, 1966, Murmuring Stream, 1967, Poems of Li Ho, 1970, First Chinese Embassy, 1974, Goddesses, Ghosts, Demons, 1983; author numerous other publs. Australian Reseach Council grantee, 1966-76. Fellow Australian Acad. of the Humanities, Profs. World Peace Acad. (pres. 1982—); mem. Australasian Soc. Psychical Research (pres. 1978—), World Freedom League (pres. 1985—), Australia-China Council. Mem. Anglo-Cath. Ch. Home: 277 Riverton Dr, 6155 Shelley Australia Office: Murdoch U, South St, 6150 Perth Australia

FROEBEL, WALTER ROBERT, broadcasting electronic engineer; b. Bamberg, Germany, June 28, 1920; s. Wilhelm and Elisabeth (Fritsch) F.; m. Ingeborg Ernestine Rokahr, July 12, 1956; children—Ursula, Ludger. Master of Craft TV-Set, Handwerkskammer, Cologne, Fed. Republic Germany, 1952; cert. engring. Regierungspräsident, Cologne, 1962. Apprentice, Derichsweiler, Uerdingen, Germany, 1937-39; technician, Telefunken, Berlin, 1939-40; cons. Telefunken, France, 1943-44; electronic engr. German Broadcasting, Sta. WDR, Cologne, 1961-85. Club: Kunstverein. Home: Friedrich-Karl-Strasse 119, D-5000 Koln 60, Federal Republic of Germany

FROESSL, HORST WALDEMAR, business executive, data processing developer; b. Mannheim, Baden-Württemberg, Fed. Republic Germany, Apr. 12, 1929; s. Otto and Friederike (Wieder) F.; m. Waltraut Kühnreich, Apr. 26, 1963 (div. Sept. 1971); m. Monika Morgener, Nov. 3, 1972. Student, pvt. schl., Shanghai, People's Republic China, 1945-50, pvt. schl., Mannheim, 1958-60. Interpreter, sect. chief Ordnance Procurement Ctr. U.S. Army, Mannheim, 1951-57; system analyst, mgr. data processing U.S. Army Indsl. Ctr. Europe, Mannheim, 1961-65; systems deliverer AEG-Telefunken, Konstanz, Fed. Republic Germany, 1966-68; mgr. orgn. and data processing Pakistan Machine Tool Factory, Karachi, 1969-71; researcher, inventor Hemsbach, Fed. Republic Germany, 1972-78; inventor, mgr., co-owner Froessl GmbH, Hemsbach, 1979—. Author 13 patents various data processing systems. Home and Office: Froessl GmbH, Gutenberg Strasse 2-4, D 6944 Hemsbach Federal Republic of Germany

FRÖHLICH, JÜRG MARTIN, physicist, educator; b. Schaffhausen, Switzerland, July 4, 1946; s. Walter Werner and Annemarie (Roth) F.; m. Eva Daniela Schubert, Aug. 31, 1972; children: Judith Monica, Sonja Gabriela. Diploma, Eidgenössische Technische Hochschule, Zurich, 1969, PhD in Physics, 1972. Research asst. U. Geneva, 1972-73; research fellow Harvard U., Cambridge, Mass., 1973-74; asst. prof. Princeton (N.J.) U., 1974-77; prof. Inst. Hautes Études Sci., Paris, 1978-82, vis. prof., 1987; full prof. Eidgenössische Technische Hochschule, 1982—, head Ctr. Theoretical Studies, 1985—; vis. mem. Inst. Advanced Study, Princeton, N.J., 1984-85; speaker in field. Author: Progress in Physics, 1983; editor, contbr. Scaling and Self-Similarity in Physics; contbr. more than 100 articles to profl. jours. Recipient Latsis prize Swiss Nat. Sci. Found., 1984; Alfred P. Sloan fellow, 1976; numerous research grants from U.S. and Swiss Nat. Sci. Founds. Mem. Am. Math. Soc., Naturforschende Gesellschaft, Swiss Phys. Soc. Home: Neuhausstrasse 10, 8044 Zurich Switzerland Office: ETH-Z Theoretical Physics, ETH-Honggerberg, 8093 Zurich Switzerland

FROHNEN, RICHARD GENE, educator; b. Omaha, Mar. 26, 1930; s. William P. and Florence E. (Rogers) F.; student U. Nebr., Omaha, Mo. Valley Coll., 1948-52; BA, Calif. State U., 1954; MS, UCLA 1961; EdD, Brigham Young U., 1976; grad. Army War Coll., 1982 m. Harlene Grace LeTourneau, July 4, 1958; children—Karl Edward, Eric Eugene. Bus. mgr. athletics and sports publicity dir. U. Nebr., Omaha, 1951-52; pub. relations dir. First Congl. Ch. Los Angeles, 1953-54, 58-59; writer Los Angeles Mirror News, 1959; gen. assignment reporter, religion editor Los Angeles Times, 1959-61; prof. journalism, dean men Eastern Mont. Coll., Billings, 1961-65; N.W. editor, editorial writer Spokesman-Review, Spokane, 1965-67, also editor Sunday mag.; prof. journalism U. Nev., Reno, 1967-79; exec. dir. devel. Coll. of Desert/Copper Mountain, 1982-85, Ariz. Health Scis. Ctr., Tucson, 1986—; pub. relations devel. officer Sch. Med. Scis. U. Nev., 1969-75; adj. prof. mgmt., dir. grad. pros. in Mgmt. U. Redlands (Calif.), 1979-85; cons. pub. relations. Mem. exec. bd. Nev. area council Boy Scouts Am., 1968-76, council commr., 1973-74, v.p., 1975-76; mem. exec. bd. Yellowstone Valley council Boy Scouts Am., 1961-65, council pres. 1963-64; v.p. Catalina council Boy Scouts Am., 1987—; founder, mng. dir. Gt. Western Expdns., 1958—; adminstrv. asst. to Gov. of Nev., 1985. Served to 1st lt. USMC, 1954-58; now col. Res. Recipient Silver Beaver award Boy Scouts Am., 1974, Pres.' Vol. Action award Coll. Desert/Copper Mountain, 1984, Outstanding Faculty award U. Redlands, 1984. Mem. Assn. Edn. Journalism, Am. Legion, Res. Officers Assn. U.S., Marine Corps Assn., Marine Corps Res. Officers Assn., Am. Humanics Found., Internat. Platform Assn., Nat. Soc. Fund Raising Execs., Planning Execs. Inst., Internat. Communication Assn., Religion Newswriters Assn., Navy League, Semper Fidelis Soc., Kappa Tau Alpha, Alpha Phi Omega, Sigma Delta Chi (sec.-treas. chpt.). Episcopalian. Kiwanian, Lion, Rotarian. Home: 6631 N Cibola Ave Tucson AZ 85718 Office: U Ariz 1501 N Campbell Ave Tucson AZ 85724

FROHNHOFEN, HERBERT, theologian; b. Erkelenz, Fed. Republic Germany, Apr. 23, 1955; s. Hans and Ria (Esser) F. MA, Hochschule für Philosophie of S.J., Munich, Fed. Republic Germany, 1978, D in Philosophy, 1981; Dip. in Theology, U. Munich, 1985, D in Theology, 1986. Sci. asst. U. Munich, Fed. Republic Germany, 1982-86; lectr. Kath. Bibelwerk, Stuttgart, Fed. Republic Germany, 1986; leader of studies Kath. Acad., Wiesbaden, Fed. Republic Germany, 1987—. Author: Structure in Mathematics, 1981, The Apathy of God in the Early Church, 1987. Home: Am Ruhwehr 32, 6200 Wiesbaden Federal Republic of Germany Office: Cath Acad Wilhelm-Kempf-Haus, 6200 Wiesbaden Federal Republic of Germany

FROLUND, HAKON, former chief national Danish forest service; b. Frederiksberg, Denmark, Sept. 10, 1916; s. Thomas and Stella (Fleischer) F.; m. Else Ejbol Rasmussen; children—Bjarke, Thordis, Skjalm, Askil, Karen, Sune. MS in Forestry, Kgl. Vetr. and Landbohojskole, 1941. With Skovstyrelsen, Klampenborg, Denmark, 1942-86, asst. officer, 1942-53, chief comml. div., 1953-58, chief nat. Danish forest service, 1958-86; chmn. Danish Forest Research Comm., 1958-86, FAO/ECE/ILO Study Group Forest Workers, Tng., Health, Safety, 1954-73; mem. Nordic Forest Research Com., 1968—, chmn. 1977-81; mem. Danish FAO Com., 1954-87, Danish Council Nature Conservation, 1959-72, Danish Council Overseas Devel. (Danida), 1972-87 , chief forestry mission FAO/Danida, Nigeria, 1971, ILO/Danida, Tanzania, 1980, 86; forestry adviser Nordic Com. Govt. Ofcls. Agr. and Forestry, Oslo, 1979-87; mem. donor community group forestry advisors Tropical Forestry Action Plan, 1984-87. Decorated kommandor af Dannebrog (Denmark), 1975; commandeur du Merite Agricole (France), 1964; recipient Silver Medal, Sveriges Skogsvardsforbund, 1983, O.M. Pro Silvis Ansioplaketti Suromen Metsäyhdistys, 1986; hon. fellow Det Norske Skogselskap, 1984. Mem. Danish Soc. Forest Engrs. (chmn. 1955-59), Danish Forest Soc. (vice chmn. 1958-67), Nordic Forest Union (bd. 1955-86, chmn. Danish com. 1959-86, pres. 1962-67, 78-82), Internat. Soc. Tropical Foresters. Home: Enghavevej 4, DK-2930 Klampenborg Denmark

FROMM, ERWIN FREDERICK, insurance company executive; b. Kalamazoo, Oct. 24, 1933; s. Erwin Carl and Charlotte Elizabeth (Wilson) F.; student U. Mich., 1951-52, Flint Jr. Coll., 1952-53; B.A., Kalamazoo Coll., 1959; postgrad. Ill. State U., 1970-72. Underwriter, State Farm Ins., 1959-72; cons. Met. Property & Liability Ins. Co., Warwick, R.I., 1972-73, dir. underwriting and policyholders services, 1973, asst. v.p., 1973-74, v.p., 1974—; sr. v.p. Royal Ins. Co., N.Y.C., 1979—; past chmn. All Industry Ins. Com. for Arson Control; chmn. bd. dirs. Nat. Council on Compensation Ins.; bd. dirs. Workers Compensation Research Inst.; mem. adv. com. underwriting program Ins. Inst. Am. Mem. adv. council Bus. Sch., U. R.I; bd. dirs. Charlotte Symphony, N.C. Ins. Edn.; bd. dirs. Workers Compensation Research Inst. Served to 1st lt. U.S. Army, 1953-56. CPCU, CLU. Mem. CPCU Assn. of Charlotte, N.C., English Speaking Union. Clubs: Masons, Shriners. Home: 3601 Sharon Rd Charlotte NC 28211 Office: 9300 Arrowpoint Blvd Charlotte NC 28217

FROMM, GERHARD HERMANN, neurologist, educator; b. Konigsberg, Germany, Sept. 7, 1931; s. Fritz Wilhelm and Ilse (Pflaum) F.; m. Antoinette McKenna, May 26, 1973; children—Allison, Devin BS, U. P.R., Rio Piedras, 1949; MD, Jefferson Med. Coll., Phila., 1953. Diplomate Am. Bd. Psychiatry and Neurology. Instr. neurology Tulane U. Sch. Medicine, New Orleans, 1961-62, asst. prof., 1962-66, assoc. prof., 1966-68; assoc. prof. neurology U. Pitts. Sch. Medicine, 1968-81, prof., 1981—; attending physician Presbyn.-Univ. Hosp., Pitts. Editor: Epilepsy and the Reticular Formation (Alan R. Liss), 1987, Medical and Surgical Management of Trigeminal Neuralgia, 1987; contbr. articles to med. jours. Served to lt., M.C. USNR, 1956-58. NIH fellow, 1959-61; career devel. awardee, 1962-68. Mem. Am. Acad. Neurology, Am. Epilepsy Soc., Soc. Neurosci., Am. EEG Soc., Eastern Assn. EEG (pres. 1985-86), Internat. Assn. for Study of Pain, Am. Pain Soc., Am. Neurol. Assn. Research on neuropharmacology of anticonvulsant drugs, epilepsy, trigeminal neuralgia, pain mechanisms. Home: 1401 N Negley Ave Pittsburgh PA 15206 Office: U Pittsburgh 322 Scaife Hall Pittsburgh PA 15261

FROMM, HANNA, educational administrator; b. Nuremberg, W.Ger., Dec. 20, 1913; d. David and Meta (Stiebel) Gruenbaum; m. Alfred Fromm, July 4, 1936; children—David, Caroline Fromm Lurie. Grad. in choreography and music Folkwang Sch. Dancing and Music, Essen, Gemany, 1934; D.Pub. Service (hon.), U. San Francisco, 1979. Served with ARC, World War II; exec. dir. Fromm Inst. Lifelong Learning, U. San Francisco, 1975—. Cofounder Music in the Vineyards, Saratoga, Calif.; bd. dirs. Amnesty Internat., Nat. Council of Fine Arts Museums; former bd. dirs. Young Audiences, Community Music Ctr., Legal Aid to Elderly, San Francisco Chamber Music Soc.; coordinating com. geriatric curriculum and program U. Calif.-San Francisco; dir. Nat. Council on Aging. Mem. Gerontology Soc. Am., Psychoanalytic Inst. of San Francisco Jewish. Club: Met. (San Francisco). Home: 850 El Camino del Mar San Francisco CA 94121 Office: 538 University Center 2130 Fulton St San Francisco CA 94117

FROMM, JOSEPH L., financial consultant; b. Detroit, May 22, 1930; s. Charles and Elizabeth F.; A.B. cum laude, Princeton U., 1953; M.B.A., Harvard U., 1958; m. Beverly C. Booth, June 18, 1960; children—Charles, Laurence, Kenneth, Lisa, Brian. Research asst. Harvard Bus. Sch., 1959; asst. to pres. Gen. Electronic Labs., Cambridge, Mass., 1960-62; with Chrysler Corp., Highland Park, Mich., 1963-68; treas. Marantette & Co., Detroit, 1969; asst. treas. Am. Motors Corp., Southfield, Mich., 1970-87; pres. Fiduciary Advisors, Inc., Grosse Pointe, Mich., 1988—; instr. U. Detroit Evening Div., 1964-65. Councilman, City of Grosse Pointe Farms, 1973-86, mayor, 1986—; pres. Fiduciary Advisors Inc., Grosse Pointe, 1988—, trustee, Bon Secours Hosp., Grosse Pointe, 1975—. Served with AUS, 1954-56. Mem. Sentinel Pension Inst., Midwest Pension Conf. Republican. Roman Catholic. Club: Grosse Pointe Indoor Tennis, Country of Detroit. Office: Fiduciary Advisors Inc 377 Fisher Rd Suite H Grosse Pointe MI 48230

FROMM, STEFAN H., surgeon; b. Vienna, Austria, Dec. 24, 1936; s. Fritz W. and Ilse (Pflaum) F.; B.S., U. P.R., 1955, M.D., 1959; m. Shirley J. Burgy, June 25, 1960; children—Theresa, Stefan, Richard, Michael, Sandra. Intern, San Francisco Gen. Hosp., 1959-60; resident Wayne State U. program Detroit Gen. Hosp., 1961-62, 64-68; practice medicine specializing in surgery, Detroit, 1968-69, Hato Rey, P.R., 1969-78; asst. prof. surgery Wayne State U., 1968, VA Hosp., San Juan, P.R., 1969-71; attending surgeon Hamilton Meml. Hosp., Dalton, Ga., 1978—, chief surgery, 1982-85; asst. prof. surgery U. P.R. Sch. Medicine, Rio Piedras, 1969-76. Bd. dirs. Pee Wee Football League, 1974-77. Served with AUS, 1962-64. Diplomate Am. Bd. Surgery. Mem. A.C.S. (chmn. com. trauma 1975, sec. P.R. chpt. 1975), Christian Med. Soc., Whitfield-Murray County Med. Soc. (sec. 1985-88, pres. 1988), Med. Assn. Ga. (del. 1987, 88), AMA (del. 1976-78; Physician Recognition Award 1981, 84, 87), So. Med. Assn., Alpha Omega Alpha. Home: 2235 Rocky Face Circle Dalton GA 30720 Office: PO Box 1969 Dalton GA 30720

FROMMER, WILLIAM S., lawyer; b. Bklyn., Sept. 27, 1942; s. Herbert S. and Molly B. (Steigman) F.; m. Karen Beagle, July 31, 1966; 1 dau., Hillary. B.E.E., Cornell U., 1965; J.D., Am. U., 1969. Bar: N.Y. 1970, U.S. Patent Office, 1970, U.S. Ct. Customs and Patent Appeals 1975, U.S. Ct. Appeals (fed. cir.) 82, U.S. Supreme Ct. 1985. Assoc. Marn & Jangarathis, N.Y.C., 1969-73, Curtis, Morris & Safford, P.C., N.Y.C., 1973-76, ptnr., 1976—. Mem. N.Y. Patent Law Assn., ABA, N.Y. State Bar Assn., Internat. Patent and Trade Assn., Internat. Bar Assn. Mem. staff, contbr. Am. U. Law Rev., 1967-69. Office: 530 Fifth Ave New York NY 10036

FROMMHOLD, WALTER, radiologist; b. Geringswalde, Germany, Aug. 28, 1921; s. Arno and Welly (Thalheim) F.; MD, U. Würzburg, 1944; Dr. h.c., U. Bordeaux, 1981, U. Pécs, 1985, U. Poznán, 1986; m. Gabriele Körner, Mar. 17, 1951; children—Anke, Uwe. Resident radiology Karlsruhe Hosp., 1946-50; teaching fellow radiology Harvard Med. Sch., 1957; asst. prof. radiology Free U. Berlin, 1952; radiologist-in-chief Auguste Viktoria Hosp., Berlin, 1956-68; prof. radiology, dir. dept. U. Tübingen Med. Sch., 1968—. Served with German Air Force, 1939-45. Recipient medal Slovakian Med. Soc., Radiol. Soc. Netherlands; C. Wegelius medal Finnish Soc. Radiology; Boris-Rajewsky medal European Soc. Radiology; Röntgen medal City of Würzburg. Mem. Acad. Leopoldina, German Soc. Radiology (pres. 1971-75, H. Rieder medal), IV European Congress Radiology (pres. 1979); hon. mem. Columbian, Indonesian, French. Hungarian, Yugoslavian, Luxembourg, Egyptian, Czechoslovakian, Belgian, Polish, Italian, Austrian, Berlin, Finnish, Swiss radiol. socs.; corr. mem. Soc. Med. Radiology German Democratic Republic, Swedish Soc. Radiology. Lodge: Lions. Editor: Klin-radiol. Seminar, Vols. 1-17, Röntgen-Wie Wann?, Vols. 4-9; co-editor: Fortschritte auf dem Gebiete der Röntgenstrahlen; Lehrbuch der Röntgendiagnostik, 7th edit. Home: 23 Im Rotbad, Tübingen Federal Republic of Germany Office: 11 Röntgenweg, Tubingen Federal Republic of Germany

FROSINI, VITTORIO, lawyer; b. Catania, Italy, Mar. 9, 1922; s. Tommaso and Concettina (Perni) F.; Dr. Phil., Scuola Normale Superiore, Pisa, 1943; LL.D., U. Catania, 1947; postgrad Magdalen Coll. Oxford U., 1950-52; m. Silvia Sardo, June 2, 1958; children—Immacolata, Annalisa, Tommaso Edoardo. Prof. history polit. theories U. Catania, 1954-64, prof. philosophy of law, 1965-71; prof. philosophy of law U. Rome, 1971-86, prof. theory of legal interpretation, 1986—; vis. prof. U. Tokyo, 1978, Harvard U., 1985. Mem. Consiglio Superiore della Magistratura, 1981; Italian del. Info. Computer Communication Policy, OECD, Paris, 1977. Served with Italian Army, 1943. Recipient prize Italian Parliament, 1958, prize Accademia Nazionale dei Lincei, 1963, Gold medal Ministry Public Instrn., 1980. Mem. Institut International de Philophie Politique, Paris, Internat. Commn. for History of Parliamentary Instns., Scienze Lettere Arti Bergamo. Mem. Partito Repubblicano Italiano. Clubs: Oxford and Cambridge (London); Circolo della Corte dei Conti. Author: La struttura deldiritto, 6th edit., 1977; Cibernetica diritto e societa, 4th edit., 1979; Il diritto nella societa tecnologica, 1981; , L'uomo artificiale, 1986. Home: 26 via Giacomo Trevis, 00147 Rome Italy Office: Facoltàdi Giuris Prudenza, Università La Sapienza, Rome Italy

FROSSI, PAOLO, engineer, consultant; b. Verona, Italy, Mar. 30, 1921; s. Luigi and Pina (Bellavite) F.; dottore in ingegneria indsl., Poly. Milan, 1945; M.B.A. (spl. student), Harvard U., 1955; m. Gabriella Crespi, Oct. 27, 1962. With Società Edison, Milan, 1956-59; mng. dir. Edison Page, Rome, 1960-67; dir. Montedel, Rome, 1968-72; bus. cons., Verona and Rome, 1973—. Mem. Assn. Elettrotecnica Italy, Assn. Internat. Ingegneri Telecommunicazioni, Union Cristiana Impreditori e Dirigenti, Roman Catholic. Clubs: Harvard Bus. Italy, MIT Alumni of Italy. Lodge: Verona East Rotary. Author papers in field. Address: Lungadige Matteotti 1,, 37126 Verona Italy

FROST, BRIAN GEORGE, religious organization adminstrator; b. Reigate, Surrey, England, Apr. 4, 1935; s. William Edwin and Ivy Kathleen (Jones) F. MA in English Lang. and Lit., Oxford U., 1958. Dir. London (formerly Notting Hill) Ecumenical Ctr., 1968-77; gen. sec. The Chs. Council for

Health and Healing, 1978-81; staff mem. Christian Aid British Council of Chs., London, 1960-68; dir. Forgiveness and Politics Study Project British Council of Chs., 1983—. Author: Citizen Incognito-Meditations on the City, 1971, Glastonbury Journey-Biography of M. Milne Mowbrays, 1986; editor: The Tactics of Pressure, 1974, Dissent and Descent-Essays on Methodism and Catholicism, 1975, Celebrating Friendship, 1986. Ecumenical work with World and British Councils of Chs. (hosted consultation on racism, World Council 1969) 1969—. Mem. Amnesty Internat., Soc. for Anglo/Chinese Understanding. Anglican/Methodist.

FROST, DAVID (PARADINE), author, producer, columnist; b. Tenderdon, Eng., Apr. 7, 1939; s. W.J. and Paradine F.; m. Lynne Frederick, Jan. 1981 (div. 1982); m. Carina Fitzalan Howard, 1983; 1 child, Miles Paradine. M.A., Gonnville and Caius Coll., U. Cambridge (Eng.). TV appearances include: That Was the Week That Was, 1962-63, Not So Much a Programme, More a Way of Life, 1964-65, The Frost Report, 1966-67, Frost Over England, 1967, David Frost at the Phonograph, 1966, The Frost Programme, 1966-68, David Frost's Night Out in London, 1966-67, The Nixon Interviews, 1977; series Headliners with David Frost, 1978, The Kissinger Interviews, 1979, The Shaw Speaks, 1980, David Frost Presents the International Guinness Book of World Records, ann., 1981—; theatrical appearances include: An Evening with David Frost, 1966, London Weekend TV; chmn., mng. dir. David Paradine Prodns.; exec. producer: James A. Michener's Dynasty, 1976; author: That Was the Week that Was, 1963, How to Live Under Labour, 1964, Talking with Frost, 1967, To England with Love, 1967, The Presidential Debate, 1968, The Americans, 1970, Whitman and Frost, 1974, I Gave Them a Sword, 1978, I Could Have Kicked Myself, 1982, Who Wants to Be a Millionaire?, 1983. Decorated Order Brit. Empire, recipient Golden Rose of Montreaux 1967; TV Soc. silver medal 1967; Richard Dimbleday award, 1967; Emmy award (2); Guild of TV Producers award; named TV Personality of Yr.; recipient Emmy award, 1970, 71; Religious Heritage Am. award, 1971; Albert Einstein award, 1982. Office: David Paradine Ltd, Breakfast TV Ctr, Hawley Crescent, London NW1, England Address: 46 Egerton Crescent, London SW3, England *

FROST, JOHN ELDRIDGE, emeritus librarian; b. Eliot, Maine, Jan. 13, 1917; s. Martin and A. M. (Eldridge) F.; B.A., U. Maine, 1938; S.T. B., Berkeley Divinity Sch., 1941; B.S., Columbia, 1948; M.A., U. N.H., 1948; Ph.D., N.Y.U., 1953. Asst. minister, Worcester, Mass., 1941-42; asso. rector, Westbury, L.I., N.Y., vicar, Carle Place, L.I., 1943-44; asst. librarian Drew U., 1949; asst. librarian N.Y.U. Library, N.Y.C., 1950, librarian, 1955-82, emeritus, 1982. Served with USNR, 1945-46. Mem. ALA, Bibliog. Soc. Am., Newcomen Soc. Eng. Author: Nicholas Frost Family, 1943; Colonial Village, 1948; Sarah Orne Jewett, 1953; Maine Genealogy, 1976. Editor: Portsmouth Record Book, 1946; Soc. for the Libs Bull., 1958—. Contbr. articles to profl. publs. Home: 119 E 60th St New York NY 10022

FROST, JOHN ELLIOTT, minerals company executive; b. Winchester, Mass., May 20, 1924; s. Elliott Putnam and Hazel Lavera (Carley) F.; m. Carolyn Catlin, July 12, 1945 (div. 1969); children—John Crocker, Jeffrey Putnam, Teresa Baird, Virginia Nicholl; m. Martha Hicks, June 6, 1969 (div. 1984); m. Catherine Kearns, July 27, 1985. B.S., Stanford U., 1949, M.S., 1950, Ph.D., 1965. Geologist Asarco, Salt Lake City, 1951-54; chief geologist, surface mines supt. Philippine Iron Mines Inc., Larap, Camarines Norte, 1954-60; chief geologist Duval Corp. (Pennzoil Corp.), Tucson, 1961-67; minerals exploration mgr. Exxon Corp., Houston, 1967-71; minerals mgr. Esso Eastern Inc. div., 1971-80; sr. v.p. Exxon Minerals Co. div., Houston, 1980-86; pres., Frost Minerals Internat., 1986—; bd. dirs., United Engring. Trustees, N.Y.C., 1982—, chmn. real estate com., 1986—. Mem. adv. bd. Sch. Earth Scis., Stanford (Calif.) U., 1983-85; pres. SEG Found., 1984—. Served to 1st lt. USAAF, 1943-45; PTO. Fellow Geol. Soc. Am.; mem. Soc. Econ. Geologists (pres. elect 1988, pres. 1989, councilor 1982-84, program com., nominating com. chmn. 1982), AIME (chmn. edn. com. Soc. Mining Engrs. 1971; Charles F. Rand medal 1984, Disting. Mem. award 1984), Australian Inst. Mining and Metallurgy, Sigma Xi. Republican. Congregationalist. Clubs: Mining (N.Y.C.); Mining of Southwest (Tucson). Home: 602 Sandy Port Houston TX 77079 Office: Exxon Minerals Company 13111 Northwest Freeway Houston TX 77040

FROST, JOHN KINGSBURY, pathologist, educator, author; b. Sioux Falls, S.D., Mar. 12, 1922; s. Roland Curtis and Madeleine (Veale) F.; m. Moira Anne Keane, Aug. 20, 1949; children—Moira Anne, Rosanne Grace, Noreen Anne Regina, Therese Anne Olivia, John Kingsbury, Shiela Anne Maureen, James Keane. B.A., U. Calif.-Berkeley, 1943; M.D., U. Calif.-San Francisco, 1946. Diplomate Am. Bd. Pathology. Intern-fellow U. Calif. Med. Sch., San Francisco, 1946-48; fellow Harvard U. Med. Sch., Cambridge, Mass., 1948; instr. pathology U. Calif. Sch. Medicine, San Francisco, 1953-56; assoc. prof. pathology U. Md. Sch. Medicine, Balt., 1956-59; asst. prof. gynecology Johns Hopkins U. Sch. Medicine, Balt., 1956-59, assoc prof. pathology, 1959-75, joint appointment obstetrics and ob-gyn., 1959—, prof. pathology, 1975—; cons. U.S. Army, 1955—, USPHS, 1959—, WHO, 1965—, AFIP Registry of Cytopathology, Washington, 1968—; dir. Ann. Postgrad. Inst. for Pathologists in Clin. Cytopathology, 1959—. Author: The Cell in Health and Disease, 1969, 86, Concepts Basic to General Cytopathology, 1959, 61, 72, also in fgn. lang. edits.; med. dir., author: (films) Cytology I (Golden Eagle award CINE), 1962, Cytology II (Golden Eagle award CINE), 1962. Served to lt. col. USAR, 1948-53; Korea. Fellow Coll. Am. Pathologists, Am. Soc. Clin. Pathologists (Disting. Achievement award 1977), Internat. Acad. Cytology (Goldblatt award and lectr. 1979); mem. Am. Soc. Cytology (pres. 1964-65, Papanicolaou award and lectr. 1972), Am. Cancer Soc. (Disting. Service award 1976), Phi Beta Kappa. Republican. Roman Catholic. Club: Serra Internat. Home: 1004 Brooklandwood Rd Lutherville MD 21093 Office: Johns Hopkins U Sch Medicine 604 Pathology Bldg Johns Hopkins Hosp Baltimore MD 21205

FROST, MARY KATHERINE, clinic executive; b. Windsor, Ont., Can., Nov. 13, 1928; came to U.S., 1951, naturalized, 1967; d. Philip Francis and Elizabeth Eppert; cert. in acctg. Windsor Bus. Coll., 1946; student Toronto Conservatory Music, 1946-47, Am. Inst. Banking, 1954-57; A.S., Wayne State U., 1967; m. William Max Frost, July 17, 1948; Teller, bookkeeper, asst. acct. Toronto Dominion Bank, Windsor, 1947-51; with Nat. Bank Detroit, 1951-54; mgr., customer relations officer City Nat. Bank Detroit, 1954-62; psychobiology research supr., adminstrv. asst. dept. mental health Lafayette Clinic, Detroit, 1964—; co-founder, coordinator, polysomnographer Lafayette Clinic Sleep Center, 1975—, lectr., 1978—. Mem. citizens adv. council Lafayette Clinic, chmn. membership, 1979-82, vice chmn., 1982—; bd. dirs. Travelers Aid Soc., 1973—, Casa Maria, 1974-81, Casgrain Hall, 1974—; trustee League Catholic Women, 1974—, mem. adv. bd., 1982—; co-founder Windsor Light Opera Co., 1948; mem. Institutional Animal Care and Use Com., 1974—. Named Disting. Employee of 1981, Lafayette Clinic, 1982. Mem. Mich. State Employees Assn. (pres. mental health dept. Lafayette Clinic chpt. 1975-81), Assn. Polysomnography Technologists, Assn. Profl. Sleep Socs., Am. Narcolepsy Assn., Midwest Inst. Alumni, Nat. Assn. Female Execs., Mich. Assn. Govt. Employees, Econ. Club Detroit, Internat. Platform Assn., Mich. Mental Health Soc., Project Hope League, Smithsonian Assocs. Republican. Clubs: Five o'Clock Forum, U. Detroit, U.S. Senatorial. Contbr. articles to profl. jours. Home: 1 Lafayette Plaisance Suite 2115 Detroit MI 48207 Office: Dept Psychobiology Lafayette Clinic 951 E Lafayette St Detroit MI 48207

FROST, S. NEWELL, telecommunications company executive; b. Oklahoma City, Dec. 21, 1935; s. Sterling Johnson and Eula Dove (Whitford) F.; m. Patricia Joyce Rose, Aug. 18, 1957; children: Patricia Diane Wiscarson, Richard Sterling, Lindy Layne Wasilko. BS Indsl. Engring., U. Okla., Norman, 1957; MS Indsl. Engring., Okla. State U., 1966. Registered profl. engr., Okla. Calif. Asst. mgr. acctg. Western Electric, Balt., 1972-73, mgr. indsl. engring., Chgo., 1973-75, mgr. devel. engring., 1975-76, mgr. acct. mgmt., San Francisco, 1976-78, dir. staff, Morristown, N.J., 1978-79; distbn. & repair AT&T Techs., Sunnyvale, Calif., 1979-85, ops. gen. mgr., 1979-85; dir. Contract Office Group, San Jose, Calif., 1983—, chmn., 1984—; with material mgmt. services AT&T, San Francisco, Calif., 1985—, v.p., 1985—. Bd. dirs. Santa Clara County YMCA, San Jose, Calif., 1981-84, Imedia, Los Angeles. Recipient Man of Day citation Sta. WAIT Radio, Chgo. Mem. Nat. Soc. Prof. Engrs. (chmn. edn. com. 1969-70), Am. Inst. Indsl. Engrs. (pres. bd. dirs. 1966-68), Okla. Soc. Profl. Engrs. (v.p. 1968-69), San Jose C. of C. Republican. Baptist. Home: 4144 Paradise Dr Tiburon CA 94920 Office: AT&T 1000 Broadway Oakland CA 94607

FROST, WILLIAM LEE, lawyer; b. Larchmont, N.Y., Nov. 5, 1926; s. Charles and Eva (Rodman) F.; m. Judith Spivak, Oct. 18, 1952 (dec. 1961); children—Rebecca, Hannah; m. Susan Lasersohn, June 16, 1966; children—Abigail, Robert. B.A., Harvard U., 1947, M.P.A., 1958; LL.B., Yale U., 1951. Assoc. Sherman & Goldring, N.Y.C., 1951-52; fgn. service officer Dept. State, Washington, 1952-59; sole practice N.Y.C., 1959—; exec. Lucius N. Littauer Found., N.Y.C., 1978—, pres., 1985—. Contbr. articles to profl. publs. Mem. Pub. Health Council, State of N.Y.; trustee Collegiate Sch., N.Y.C., 1980, 1988, Radcliffe Coll., Cambridge, Mass.; pres. Jewish Telegraphic Agy., N.Y.C., 1985—; chmn. bd. dirs. N.Y. Heart Assn., 1985-87, P.E.F. Israel Endowment Fund. Served with USN, 1945-46, PTO. Hon. curator of Judaica, Harvard Coll. Library. Mem. Assn. Bar City N.Y., N.Y. County Bar Assn., N.Y. State Bar Assn., Harvard Alumni Assn. (bd. dirs. 1985). Jewish. Clubs: Harvard, Yale, Century Assn. (N.Y.C.). Office: Lucius N Littauer Found 60 E 42d St Suite 2910 New York NY 10165

FROW, JOHN, comparative literature educator; b. New South Wales, Australia, Nov. 13, 1948; s. A.G. and Nola (Funnell) F.; m. Mayerlene Engineer, 1978; 1 child, Toby; m. Christine Alavi; 1 child, Eleanor. BA, Australian Nat. U., 1967; MA, Cornell U., 1974, PhD, 1977. Lectr. U. Salvador, Buenos Aires, 1970, Murdoch U., Perth, Australia, 1975—. Author: Marxism and Literary History, 1986; contbr. articles to profl. publs. Home: 20 Wesley St, 6162 South Fremantle Australia Office: Murdoch Univ, South St, 6153 Murdoch Australia

FROWEN, STEPHEN FRANCIS, economist, educator; b. Remscheid, Germany, May 22, 1923; arrived in Eng., 1949; naturalized, 1956; s. Adolf and Anna (Bauer) Frowein; m. Irene Minskers, Mar. 21, 1949; children: Michael Bernard James, Tatiana Mary Anne Frowen Hosburn. Student, U. Cologne, Fed. Republic of Germany, 1944, U. Würzburg, Fed. Republic of Germany, 1944-45, U. Bonn, Fed. Republic of Germany, 1946-48; Diplom-Volkswirt, U. Bonn, 1948. Asst. editor Bankers' Mag., London, 1954-55, editor, 1956-60; econ. advisor Indsl. and Comml. Fin. Corp. Ltd., London, 1959-60; research officer Nat. Inst. Econ. and Social Research, London, 1960-62; lectr. Thames Poly., London, 1962-63, sr. lectr., 1963-67; sr. lectr. in monetary econs. U. Surrey, Eng., 1967-87; prof. econs. U. Frankfurt, Fed. Republic Germany, 1987; Bundesbank prof. monetary econs. Free Univ. Berlin, 1987—. Author: (with H.C. Hillmann) Economic Issues, 1957, (with others) Monetary Policy and Economic Activity in West Germany, 1977; editor: A Framework of International Banking, 1979, Controlling Industrial Economies, 1983, Business, Time and Thought: Selected Papers by G.L.S. Shackle, 1983; translator: Value, Capital and Rent (Knut Wicksell), 1954, The Role of the Economist as Official Adviser (W.A. Jöhr and H.W. Singer), 1955; co-editor: Enzyklopädisches Lexikon für das Geld-, Bank- und Börsenwesen, 2 vols., 1957; editor Woolwich Econ. Papers, 1963-67; Surrey Papers in Econs, 1967; contbg. author Festschrift in Honor of Stphen Frowen: Contemporary Issues in Money and Banking, 1988; contbr. articles to leading profl. jours. Office: Free Univ Berlin, Dept Econs, Boltzmannstrasse 20, D-1000 Berlin, 33 Federal Republic of Germany

FRUCHTMAN, ERIC ZALL, construction management consultant, architect, civil engineer, professional/planner; b. Phila., Mar. 23, 1953; s. Leon and Eda (Greenbaum) F.; m. Vicky Viviane Cohen, Jan. 9, 1977; children—Danielle, Elliot. B.S. in Architecture, Drexel U., 1978, B.S. in Civil Engring., 1975. Registered profl. engr., Pa., N.J., prof. planner, N.J. Project engr., architect Delta Group, Phila., 1974-82; cons. Wagner Hohns Inglis, Mt. Holly, N.J., 1982-84; v.p. Contract Mgmt. Corp., Camden, N.J., 1984; sr. project mgr. O'Brien-Kreitzberg & Assoc., Inc., Merchantville, N.J., 1984-88, asst. v.p., 1988—; cons. Metropolitan Fair and Exposition Authority, Chgo., 1985—, IBM Corp. Headquarters, Armonk, N.Y., 1984, Office of Atty. Gen. of Va., Richmond, 1984, Smithsonian Instn., Washington, 1983—, IBM, Poughkeepsie, N.Y., 1982—, Pratt & Whitney, Hartford, Conn., 1983—, U.S. Postal Service, 1988—. Mem. ASCE, Constrn. Specification Inst., AIA (assocs.), Constrn. Mgmt. Assn. Am.

FRUHBECK DE BURGOS, RAFAEL, conductor; b. Burgos, Spain, Sept. 15, 1933; s. Wilhelm and Stefanie Ochs F.; m. Maria Carmen Martinez, 1959; 2 children. Attended, Bilbao Conservatory, Madrid Conservatory, High Sch. for Music, Munich, Germany, U. Munich, U. Madrid. Formerly chief condr., Mcpl. Orch., Bilbao, music dir. and chief condr., Spanish Nat. Orch., Madrid, music dir., Dusseldorf (W.Ger.) and, chief condr., Dusseldorf Symphony, music dir. and prin. condr., Montreal (Que., Can.) Symphony Orch., now prin. guest condr., Yomiuri Symphony, Tokyo, prin. guest condr., Nat. Symphony, Washington. (Decorated Orden de Alfonso X, Orden de Isabel la Católica, Gran Cruz al Mérito Civil.). Office: care Vitoria Alcala 30, 28014 Madrid Spain also: Shaw Concerts Inc 1900 Broadway New York NY 10023 also: care Harold Holt Ltd, 31 Sinclair Rd, London W14 0NS, England

FRÜHBECK OLMEDO, FEDERICO, lawyer; b. Madrid, Jan. 27, 1955; s. Guillermo Frühbeck and Maria Esperanza Olmedo; m. Maria Teresa Gómez-Arribas, Jan. 7, 1983; 1 child, Federico Frühbeck Gómez. Grad. Faculty of Law, Madrid; licentiate in econs., U. Madrid. Ptnr., Dr. Frühbeck Abogados, Madrid, 1978—; ptnr., exec. dir. FICESA INTERNACIONAL DE REVISIONES, S.A., Madrid, 1981—; dir. numerous cos. Contbr. articles to legal jours. Mem. Madrid Bar, Bilbao Bar, Málaga Bar, Balearic Bar, Swiss Arbitration Assn., German Arbitration Assn., Spanish-German Jurist Assn., Association Européenne des Practiciens des Procedures Collectives, numerous chambers commerce. Roman Catholic. Office: Marqués del Riscal 11, 5, 28010 Madrid Spain

FRUHMANN, KAREN ANNE, laboratory administrator; b. Orange, N.J.; d. Robert Whitin and Anna (Harvey) Mullin; B.A. magna cum laude in Psychology and Biology, William Paterson Coll., 1974; cert. med. tech. St. Mary's Hosp., 1975; M.S. summa cum laude in Med. Tech., Fairleigh Dickinson U., 1977; postgrad. Southeastern U., 1982-85. Cert. bioanalyst, clin. lab. dir. Am. Bd. Bioanalysis. Biochemistry technologist Raritan Valley Hosp., Greenbrook N.J., 1975-76; asst. supr. enzymology, tech. writer quality assurance, diagnostic researcher, chemistry adminstr. Warner Lambert Gen. Diagnostics, Morris Plains, N.J., 1976-78; dir. lab. services Kessler Inst. for Rehab. W. Orange, N.J., 1979—. Mem. Am. Soc. Clin. Pathologists (affiliate mem.), N.Y. Acad. Scis., Am. Soc. Med. Tech., N.J. Soc. Med. Tech., Assn. for Women in Sci., Nat. Certification Agy. (clin. lab. scientist), Alpha Mu Tau. Presbyterian. Contbr. articles on hematology to profl. jours. Office: Kessler Inst 1199 Pleasant Valley Way West Orange NJ 07052

FRUSH, JAMES CARROLL, JR., health services cons.; b. San Francisco, Oct. 18, 1930; s. James Carroll and Edna Mae (Perry) F.; BA, Stanford, 1953; postgrad. U. Calif. at San Francisco, 1957-58; MA, Saybrook Inst., 1981; PhD, 1985; m. Patricia Anne Blake, Oct. 29, 1960 (div. 1977); children—Michael, Gloria; m. 2d, Carolyn Fetter Bell, Aug. 23, 1978; 1 child, Stephen. Partner, James C. Frush Co. San Francisco, 1960-70; v.p., dir. research Retirement Residence, Inc., San Francisco, 1964-70, pres., 1970—; pres. Nat. Retirement Residence, San Francisco, 1971—, Casa Dorinda Corp., 1971—; lectr. Pres., Marin Shakespeare Festival, 1971-73, James C. Frush Found., 1972-78; adj. faculty mem. Spring Hill Coll., Mobile, Ala., 1988—. Bd. dirs. San Francisco Sr. Center, 1973-78, Found. to Assist Calif. Tchrs. Devel. Inc., 1987—. Mem. Gerontol. Soc., Southeastern Psychol. Assn., Assn. for Anthropology and Gerontology, Stanford Alumni Assn. Author (with Benson Eschenbach): The Retirement Residence: An Analysis of the Architecture and Management of Life Care Housing, 1968, Self-Esteem in Older Persons Following a Heart Attack: An Exploration of Contributing Factors, 1985. Contbr. articles to profl. jours.; producer ednl. films. Office: care T Pimsleur 2155 Union St San Francisco CA 94123

FRY, BARBARA ANN, government official; b. St. Charles, Ill., Nov. 10, 1937; d. Robert Nicholas and Marianne Eloise (Earhart) Wilford; B.S., U. Ill., 1959; M.B.A., Roosevelt U., 1976; m. Ronnie Darrel Fry, June 15, 1974; children—Kim Buskirk, Gena Buskirk. Budget analyst, then budget officer Navy Electronics Supply Office, Great Lakes, Ill., 1962-73; regional budget officer IRS, Chgo., 1973-75, Atlanta, 1975-76, regional fiscal mgmt. officer, 1976-83, regional mgmt. analysis officer, 1983—; former mem. adv. com. EEO. Past treas. Loch Lomond Property Owners Assn., PTA. Served with USAF, 1959-61. Mem. AAUW (past treas.), Fed. Employees Credit Union (past mem. credit com., mem. supervisory com.), Federally Employed Women (past co-chmn. Inter-Agy. Council, past pres. Atlanta chpt., past legis. chmn.), Nat. Assn. Female Execs., Atlanta Assn. Fed. Execs. (past treas.), Decatur Bus. and Profl. Women (past pres., past. v.p., past treas.) U. Ill Alumni of Atlanta (treas. 1984-87), Sigma Kappa Alumnae of Atlanta (treas. 1987-87). Lodge: Zonta (pres. 1988—, past v.p., past sec., past bd. dirs.). Home: 1511 Montevallo Circle Decatur GA 30033 Office: 275 Peachtree St NE Atlanta GA 30043

FRY, BERNARD MITCHELL, librarian b. Ind., Oct. 24, 1915; s. Francis Earl and Veva V. (Mitchell) F.; A.B., Ind. U., 1937, M.A., 1939; M.L.S., Catholic U., 1952; postgrad. Am. U., 1963-66; m. June Foster, June 19, 1943; children—David, Richard, Douglas, Donald, Bernard. Librarian, instr. Mary Washington Coll., U. Va., Fredricksburg, 1939-40; chief bibliographer legis. reference service Library of Congress, Washington, 1941-42; mem., dir. tech. info. service AEC, Washington, 1947-58; dir. Clearinghouse for Fed. Sci. and Tech. Info., U.S. Dept. Commerce, 1963-67; dep. head Sci. Info. Service, NSF, Washington, 1959-62; dean, prof. grad. library sch. Ind. U., Bloomington, 1967-80, dir. research center Sch. Library and Info. Scis., 1980-83; publ. cons., 1985—. Active Boy Scouts Am. Served with C.E., U.S. Army, 1942-46. Mem. Am. Soc. Info. Sci. (pres. 1967, gen. conf. chmn. 1977, award of Merit 1986, award of Pioneer 1987), ALA, Spl. Libraries Assn., AAAS, Am. Assn., Civitan, Phi Delta Kappa. Methodist. Editor: Info. Processing and Mgmt., 1967-84; Govt. Publs. Rev., 1974-83; co-author: Publishers and Libraries, 1977; author: Role of Government Publications in National Program, 1979. Home: 3649 E 3d St Bloomington IN 47401 Office: Ind U Sch Library and Info Sci Bloomington IN 47401

FRY, CHARLES GEORGE, theologian, educator; b. Piqua, Ohio, Aug. 15, 1936; s. Sylvan Jack and Lena Freda (Ehle) F.; BA, Capital U., 1958; MA, Ohio State U., 1961, PhD, 1965; BD, Evang. Lutheran Theol. Sem., 1962, MDiv, 1977; DMin, Winebrenner Theol. Sem., 1978. Ordained to ministry Lutheran Ch. U.S.A, 1963; pastor St. Mark's Luth. Ch. and Martin Luther Luth. Ch. (both Columbus, Ohio), 1961-62, 63-66; theologian-in-residence North Community Luth. Ch., Columbus, 1971-73; instr. Wittenberg U., 1962-63; instr. Capital U., 1963-75, asst. prof. history and religion, 1966-69, assoc. prof., 1969-75; assoc. prof. hist. theology, dir. missions edn. Concordia Theol. Sem., Ft. Wayne, Ind., 1975-84; sr. minister First Congl. Ch., Detroit, 1984-85; Protestant chaplain St. Francis Coll., Fort Wayne, 1982—; vis. prof. Damavand Coll., Tehran, Iran, 1973-74, bd. dirs., 1976—; vis. prof. Reformed Bible Coll., 1975-79, Concordia Luth. Sem. at Brock U., summer 1977, St. Francis Coll., 1980—; vis. scholar Al Ain U., United Arab Emirates, 1987; bd. dirs. Samuel Zwemer Inst., 1978—; mem. Luth.-Baptist Dialogue team Luth. Ch. U.S.A.-World Bapt. Alliance, 1978-81; vis. theologian Luth. Ch. Nigeria, 1983, Luth. Ch. Venezuela, 1981, Nat. Presbyterian Ch. Mexico, 1977, 79, First Community Ch., Columbus, 1971-73; mem. N.Am. Laussane Com., 1977-78. Recipient Praestantia award Capital U., 1970, Concordia Hist. Inst. citation, 1977; Regional Council for Internat. Edn. research grantee, 1969; Joseph J. Malone post-doctoral fellow Egypt, 1986. Mem. Am. Hist. Assn., Am. Acad. Religion, Middle East Studies Assn., Middle East Inst., Brit. Interplanetary Soc., Phi Alpha Theta. Democrat. Author books, including: Age of Lutheran Orthodoxy, 1979; Lutheranism in America, 1979; Islam, 1980, 2d edit., 1982; The Way, the Truth, the Life, 1982; Great Asian Religions, 1984, Francis: A Call To Conversion, 1988, The Middle East: A History, 1988. Home: 158 W Union St Circleville OH 43113 Office: St Francis College Protestant Chaplain 2701 Spring St Fort Wayne IN 46808

FRY, MORTON HARRISON, II, communications company executive, lawyer; b. N.Y.C., May 15, 1946; s. George Thomas Clark and Louise Magdalen (Cronin) F.; m. Patricia Laylin Coffin, May 29, 1971. A.B., Princeton U., 1968; J.D., Yale U., 1971. Bar: N.Y. 1973, U.S. Ct. Mil. Appeals 1973, U.S. Dist. Ct. (so. dist.) N.Y. 1975, U.S. Dist. Ct. (ea. dist.) N.Y. 1975, U.S. Ct. Appeals (2d cir.) 1975. Assoc. Cravath, Swaine & Moore, N.Y.C., 1971-72, 75-79; dep. gen. counsel Columbia Pictures Industries, Inc., N.Y.C., 1979-81; v.p., gen. counsel Warner Home Video Inc., N.Y.C., 1982-83; exec. v.p., gen. counsel Warner Electronic Home Services, N.Y.C., 1983-84; acquisitions and divestitures counsel Warner Communications Inc., N.Y.C., 1984-85, pres., chief exec. officer, bd. dirs. The Congress Video Group, Inc., 1985-87, entertainment, communications cons., 1987-88; bd. dirs. Tintoretto, Inc., 1987 88; pres., cons. Fry Assocs., 1987 ; mem. governing bd. Council N.Y. Law Assocs., 1976-78, presiding officer, 1977-78; counsel Hosp. Audiences, Inc., N.Y.C., 1979-82. Served to capt. USMC, 1972-75. AIA grantee, 1970-71. Mem. Assn. of Bar of City of N.Y. Liberal Democrat. Congregationalist. Clubs: University (N.Y.C.), Point O'Woods; Campus (Princeton). Home: 719 Greenwich St New York NY 10014

FRY, ROBERT WILLIAM, orthodontist; b. Independence, Mo., Apr. 23, 1948; s. Stanton and Marie (Jorgensen) F.; m. Mary Louise Stowell, Aug. 15, 1970; children—Jeremy Randall, Mary Whitney. B.S./A.A., Graceland Coll., Lamoni, Iowa, 1970; D.D.S., U. Mo.-Kansas City, 1973; M.S., U. N.C., 1977. Cert. fin. planner Coll. Fin. Planning, Denver, 1979. Gen. practice dentistry, U.S. Army, Fort Hood, Tex., 1973-75; practice dentistry specializing in orthodontics, Overland Park, Kans., 1977—. Mem. Parks and Recreation Bd., Lenexa, Kans., 1979-80; vice chmn. Planning Commn., Lenexa, 1980-84; chmn. Leffel for Congress, Kans., 1984; chmn. bd trustees Johnson County Community Coll., 1987—. Served to capt. USAR, 1973-75. Recipient Leadership Kans. award Kans. Assn. Commerce and Industry, 1984. Mem. ADA (del. 1983-84), Kans. Dental Assn. (del. 1979-82, chmn. publs. 1980-82, treas. 1982-85, pres. 1987—), Am. Assn. Orthodontics, Kans. Orthodontics Soc. (assoc. editor jour. 1982-83), Assn. Fin. Planners, Lenexa C. of C. (pres. 1982). Republican. Mem. Reorganized Ch. Jesus Christ of Latterday Saints. Club: Toastmasters. Home: 12340 Pflumm Rd Olathe KS 66062 Office: 6500 W 95th Overland Park KS 66212

FRYATT, JOHN, ceramic fibre manufacturing company executive; b. Felling, Durham, Eng., Jan. 12, 1944; s. John Robert William and Frances (Hann) F.; m. Meryl Ann O'Donnell, Oct. 2, 1971; 1 child, Martin John. BSc in Applied Sci., U. Newcastle upon Tyne, Eng., 1965. Researcher Clarke Chapman and Co., Ltd., Gateshead, Eng., 1965-69; applications engr., applications engring. mgr., tech. mgr. Morganite Ceramic Fibres, Neston, Eng., 1970-76; U.K. market mgr. Carborundum Co., Rainford, Eng., 1976—; European mktg. mgr. Fiberfrax Carborundum Co., Sale, Eng., 1979-81, distbn. mgr. Fiberfrax, 1981-83, product mgr. Fiberfrax, 1983-85, new bus. mgr. Fiberfrax, 1985—. Contbr. articles to profl. jours. Home: 15 Broadlake, Willaston L64 2XB, England

FRYE, JOHN H., JR., metallurgical engineering educator; b. Birmingham, Ala., Oct. 1, 1908; s. John H. and Helen (Mushat) F.; m. Helen Lewis Johnston, Sept. 21, 1935; children: John H. III, Helen (Mrs. Grant Van Siclen Parr), Kathleen (Mrs. Walter T. Woods, Jr.). BA with honors, Howard Coll., 1930; MS, Lehigh U., 1934; DPhil, Oxford (Eng.) U., 1942. Asst. prof. metallurgy Lehigh U., 1937-40, asso. prof. metallurgy, 1940-44; civilian employee Office Sci. Research and Devel., 1944; research engr. Bethlehem Steel Co., 1944-48; dir. metals and ceramics div. Oak Ridge Nat. Lab., Tenn., 1948-73; lectr. U. Tenn. Grad. Sch., 1950-73; hon. adj. prof. U. Ala. Coll. Engring., 1964-67, prof. metall. engring., 1973—; bd. dirs. Bank Oak Ridge, 1956-74; tech. adviser on U.S. del. to 2d Internat. Conf. on Peaceful Uses Atomic Energy, Geneva, Switzerland, 1958. Editorial adv. bd.: Jour. Less-Common Metals, 1962-78; contbr. articles to profl. jours. Fellow AAAS, Am. Soc. for Metals (mem. handbook com. 1969-72), Metall. Soc. of AIME (exec. com. inst. metals div. 1959-60); mem. Sigma Xi. Episcopalian. Clubs: Indian Hills Country, University. Lodge: Rotary. Home: 1520 High Forest Dr North Tuscaloosa AL 35406

FRYE, JUDITH ELEEN MINOR, editor; b. Seattle; d. George Edward and Eleen G. (Hartelius) Minor; student U. Cal. at Los Angeles, evenings 1947-48, U. So. Calif., 1948-53; m. Vernon Lester Frye, Apr. 1, 1954. Accountant, office mgr. Colony Wholesale Liquor, Culver City, Calif., 1947-48; credit mgr. Western Distbg. Co., Culver City, 1948-53; partner in restaurants, Palm Springs, Los Angeles, 1948, partner in date ranch, La Quinta, Calif., 1949-53; partner, owner Imperial Printing, Huntington Beach, Calif., 1955—; editor New Era Laundry and Cleaning Lines, Huntington Beach, 1962—; registered lobbyist, Calif., 1975-84. Mem. Laundry and Cleaning Allied Trades Assn., Laundry and Dry Cleaning Suppliers Assn., Calif. Coin-op Assn. (exec. dir. 1975-84), Cooperation award 1971, Dedicated Service award 1976), Nat. Automatic Laundry and Cleaning Council (Leadership award 1972), Women in Laundry/Drycleaning (past pres.; Outstanding Service award 1977), Printing Industries Assn., Master Printers Am., Nat. Assn. Printers and Lithographers, Huntington Beach C. of C. Office: 22031 Bushard St Huntington Beach CA 92646

FRYE, NORTHROP, English language educator, writer; b. Sherbrooke, Que., Can., July 14, 1912; s. Herman and Catharine and (Howard) F.; m. Helen Kemp, Aug. 24, 1937 (dec.). B.A., U. Toronto, 1933; M.A., Oxford U., 1940; MA, also 35 hon. degrees. Ordained to ministry United Ch. Can., 1936. Lectr. English Victoria Coll., U. Toronto, 1939—, prof., 1947—, chmn. dept. English, 1952, prin. coll., 1959-67; Univ. prof. U. Toronto, 1967—; chancellor Victoria U., 1978—; adviser curricular planning and English teaching, Can. and U.S.; mem. adv. com. Am. Council Learned Socs., 1965; adv. mem. Can. Radio and TV Commn., 1968-77. Author: Fearful Symmetry, 1947, Anatomy of Criticism, 1957; also 21 other books; editor Canadian Forum, 1948-52. Decorated companion Order Can.; Hon. fellow Merton Coll., Oxford, 1973. Fellow Brit. Acad. (corr.); mem. MLA (exec. council 1958-61, pres. 1976), Am. Acad. Arts and Scis. (hon. fgn.), Am. Acad. and Inst. Arts and Letters (hon.). Office: Univ Toronto, 4 Devonshire Pl, Toronto, ON Canada M5S 2E1

FRYER, APPLETON, publisher, sales exec., lectr.; b. Buffalo, Feb. 25, 1927; s. Livingston and Catherine (Appleton) F.; A.B. cum laude, Princeton U., 1950; m. Angeline Dudley Kenefick, May 16, 1953; children: Appleton, Daniel Kenefick, Robert Livingston, Catherine Appleton. Head interpreter Hewitt-Robins, Inc., Buffalo, 1950-51; advt. dept. Buffalo Evening News, 1953-55; field rep. Ketchum, MacLeod & Grove, Inc., advt., 1955-56; pres. Duo-Fast of Western N.Y., Inc., Buffalo, 1956-84; pub. Buffalo Bus. Jour., 1984-86; hon. consul gen. of Japan, Buffalo, 1979—. Dep. sheriff, Erie County, N.Y., 1954-68; adv. bd. Children's Hosp. of Buffalo; mem. Community Welfare Council Buffalo and Erie County; co-chmn. Corp. Div. Episc. Charities, 1988; mem. bd. Erie County Sesquicentennial Commn., 1970-71; co-chmn. Erie Bicentennial Commn., 1974-76; adviser City Buffalo Environ. Mgmt. Commn., 1973-75; trustee Theodore Roosevelt Inaugural Nat. Historic Site Found., 1969-87; bd. dirs. Zool. Soc. Buffalo, 1972-78, Buffalo Fine Arts Acad., Albright-Knox Art Gallery, 1973-76; chmn. Buffalo-Kanazawa Sister Cities Com., 1978-79; pres. Arboretum of Met. Buffalo, 1977-78; bd. dirs. Maud Gordon Holmes Arboretum, 1974-88, pres., 1976-78; mem. Buffalo Landmark and Preservation Bd., 1978-87, Erie County Preservation Adv. Bd., 1978-82; mem. council Charles Burchfield Center, 1974—; mem. council Central Erie deanery Diocese Western N.Y., 1970; mem. Erie County Sesquicentennial Commn., 1970-71; mem. com. Young Life on Niagara Frontier, 1971-72; chmn. planning com. Venture in Mission, 1979, mem. campaign exec. com., 1979-80; chmn. N.Y. State sect. ann. giving Princeton U., 1979—, chmn. Western N.Y. annual giving regional com., 1978-79, mem. nat. ann. giving com.; mem. adv. bd. Erie County Cultural Resources, 1986—, Concerned Ecumenical Ministry (West Side), 1986—; chmn. devel. com. Crane Cutting Ctr., 1987—. Served with USNR, 1945-46, to 1st lt. AUS, 1951-52. Mem. Niagara Frontier Indsl. Distbrs. Assn., Buffalo Area C. of C. (Buffalo Beautiful Com. 1975—), Am. Assn. Museums (trustee 1978-81), SR (pres. Buffalo Assn. 1966-73), Soc. Mayflower Descs. (regent Buffalo colony 1961-65), Soc. Colonial Wars, Holland Soc. of N.Y. (pres. Niagara Frontier br. 1969-79), Buffalo and Erie County Hist. Soc. (bd. mgrs. 1969—, v.p. 1977-82, pres. 1982-84), Buffalo Soc. Natural Scis., Landmark Soc. Niagara Frontier, Outstanding award 1979 (pres. 1969-73), Old Ft. Niagara Assn. (dir. 1980—), Order Colonial Lords of Manors, Princeton Alumni Assn. (chmn. schs. com. Western N.Y. area 1974-77). Episcopalian (warden, licensed lay reader). Clubs: Masons, Rotary of Buffalo (internat. service com. 1978—, bd. dirs. 1983-86); Princeton (N.Y.C.); Princeton of Western N.Y. (pres. 1960), Saturn (vice dean 1963, 86) (Buffalo); Nassau, University Cottage (Princeton, N.J.); Porcupine (gov. 1969-73) (Nassau). Home: 85 Windsor Ave Buffalo NY 14209 Office: 125 Broadway Buffalo NY 14203

FRYER, FRANK, nursery director; b. England, Apr. 3, 1919; s. Arthur and Pheobe (Barlow) F.; m. Jean Gwendoline Hubbard, Jan. 12, 1943; children: Gareth R., Karen Fryer Rotherham. Student, Edgerton Sch., Eng. Dir. Fryers Nurseries, Ltd., Knutsford, Eng., 1946-87. Served with the British Army, 1939-46. Mem. Rose Growers Assn. (recipient Service to the Rose medal, 1987). Lodge: Rotary (pres. 1957-58). Home and Office: Fryers Nurseries, Manchester Rd, Knutsford Cheshire WA16 0SX, England

FRYER, GLADYS CONSTANCE, nursing home medical director, medical educator; b. London, Mar. 28, 1923; came to U.S., 1967; d. William John and Florence Annie (Dockett) Mercer; m. Donald Wilfred Fryer, Jan. 20, 1944; children: Peter Vivian, Gerard John, Gillian Celia. MB, BS, U. Melbourne, Victoria, Australia, 1956. Resident Box Hill Hosp., 1956-57; cardiologist Assunta Found., Petaling Jaya, Malaysia, 1961-64; clin. research physician U.S. Army Clin. Research Unit, Malaysia, 1964-66; intern Hawaii Permanente Kaiser Found., Honolulu, 1968-73; practice medicine specializing in internal medicine Honolulu, 1973-88; med. dir. Hale Nani Health Ctr., Honolulu, 1975—, Beverly Manor Convalescent Ctr., Honolulu, 1975—; asst. clin. profl. medicine John Burns Sch. Medicine U. Hawaii, 1968—; med. cons. Salvation Army Alcohol Treatment Facility, Honolulu, 1975-81; physician to skilled nursing patients VA, Honolulu, 1984-88; preceptor to geriatric nurse practitioner program U. Colo., Honolulu, 1984-85; lectr. on geriatrics, Alzheimer's disease, gen. medicine, profl. women's problems, and neurosci., 1961—; mem. ad hoc due process bd. Med. Care Evaluation Com., 1982—, Hospice Adv. Com., 1982—; mem. pharmacy com. St. Francis Hosp. Clin. Staff, 1983—, chmn. 1983-84. Contbr. articles to profl. jours. Mem. adv. com. Honolulu Home Care St. Francis Hosp., Honolulu, 1974-87; mem. adv. bd. Honolulu Gerontology Program, 1983—, Straub Home Health Program, Honolulu, 1984-87; mem. sci. adv. bd. Alzheimers Disease and Related Disorders Assn., Honolulu, 1984—; mem. long term care task force Health and Community Services Council Hawaii, 1978-84. Recipient Edgar Rouse Prize in Indsl. Medicine, U. Melbourne, 1955, Outstanding Supporter award Hawaii Assn. Activity Coordinators, 1987. Mem. AAAS, ACP, Hawaii Med. Assn. (councillor 1984—), Honolulu County Med. Soc. (chmn., mem. utilisation rev. com. 1973—), World Med. Assn., Am. Geriatrics Soc., Gerontol. Soc. Am., N.Y. Acad. Scis. Episcopalian. Office: Hale Nani Health Ctr 1677 Pensacola St Honolulu HI 96822-2699

FRYER, ROBERT SHERWOOD, theatrical producer; b. Washington, Nov. 18, 1920; s. Harold and Ruth (Reade) F. B.A., Western Res. U., 1943. Asst. to mng. dir. Theatre Inc., 1946, casting dir., 1946-48; asst. to exec. CBS, 1949-51, casting dir., 1951-52; producer: (Broadway plays) (with others) A Tree Grows in Brooklyn, 1951, (with others) By the Beautiful Sea, 1954, Wonderful Town, 1953, The Desk Set, Shangri-La, Auntie Mame, Redhead, There Was a Little Girl, Advise and Consent, A Passage To India, Hot Spot, Roar Like a Dove, Sweet Charity, Chicago, 1975, The Norman Conquests, 1976, California Suite, 1976, On the Twentieth Century, 1977, Sweeney Todd, 1978, Merrily We Roll Along, The West Side Waltz, 1981, Brighton Beach Memoirs, Noises Off, 1983, Benefactors, 1985, Wild Honey, 1987, (films) The Boston Strangler, 1963, Abdication, 1973, Mame, 1973, Great Expectations, 1974, Voyage of the Damned, 1976, The Boys from Brazil, 1978, Prime of Miss Jean Brodie 1969, Travels with My Aunt, 1973, The Shining 1979 ; artistic dir.: Ahmanson Theatre, Ctr. Theatre Group, Los Angeles; author: Professional Theatrical Management New York City, 1947. Bd. dirs. Kennedy Ctr., Ctr. Theatre Group, Music Ctr., Los Angeles; trustee, exec. com. John F. Kennedy Ctr., Washington. Served as capt. AUS, 1941-46; maj. Res. Decorated Legion of Merit.; Rockefeller Found. fellow. Mem. Episcopal Actors Guild (v.p.), League of N.Y. Theatres (bd. govs.). Office: 135 N Grand Ave Los Angeles CA 90012

FRYMAN, VIRGIL THOMAS, JR., lawyer; b. Maysville, Ky., Apr. 9, 1940; s. Virgil Thomas and Elizabeth Louis (Marshall) F. A.B. cum laude, Harvard U., 1962, LL.B., 1966. Bar: N.Y. 1967, U.S. Ct. Appeals (2d cir.) 1967, U.S. Dist. Ct. (so. and ea. dists.) N.Y. 1968, U.S. Supreme Ct. 1970, U.S. Ct. Appeals (6th cir.) 1988, U.S. Dist. Ct. (ea. and we. dist.) Ky. 1988. Assoc. Cravath, Swaine & Moore, N.Y.C., 1966-73; asst. U.S. atty. U.S. Dist. Ct. (so. dist) N.Y., N.Y.C., 1973-78; assoc. gen. counsel Price Waterhouse, N.Y.C., 1978-86; staff counsel U.S. Ho. of Reps. select com. to investigate covert arms transactions with Iran, 1987; ptnr. Greenebaum Doll & McDonald, Lexington, Ky., 1988—. Mem. ABA, Assn. Bar City of N.Y. Democrat. Episcopalian. Clubs: Harvard, West Side Tennis (N.Y.C.), Idle Hour Country (Lexington, Ky.). Contbr. to Proving Federal Crimes, 6th edit., 1976. Home: Fed Hill Washington KY 41096 Office: Greenebaum Doll & McDonald 1400 Vine Ctr Tower Lexington KY 40508

FU, SHOU-CHENG JOSEPH, biomedicine educator; b. Peking, China, Mar. 19, 1924; came to U.S., 1946; s. W.C. Joseph and W.C. (Tsai) F.; m. Susan B. Guthrie, June 21, 1951; children—Robert W.G., Joseph H.G., James B.G. B.S., M.S., Catholic U., Peking, 1944; Ph.D., Johns Hopkins U., 1949. Gustav Bissing fellow Johns Hopkins U., at Univ. Coll., London, 1955-56; chief Enzyme and Bioorganic Chemistry Lab. Children's Cancer Research Found. (now Dana Farber Cancer Ctr.), 1956-67; research assoc. Harvard U. Med. Sch., Boston, 1956-67; Univ. prof., chmn. bd. chemistry Chinese U., Hong Kong, 1967-70 dean sci. faculty, 1967-69; vis. prof. Coll. Physicians and Surgeons, Columbia U., N.Y.C., 1970-71; prof. biochemistry U. Medicine & Dentistry, Newark, 1971—, asst. dean, 1975-77, acting dean Grad. Sch. Biomed. Scis., 1977-78, Contbr. articles to profl. jours. Served to lt. comdr. USPHS Res., 1959—. Named Hon. Disting. Prof. and Academic Advisor Inner Mongolia Med. Univ., Huthot, Peoples Republic China, 1988. Fellow AAAS, Royal Soc. Chemistry (London); mem. Sigma Xi (chpt. pres. 1976-80, sec. 1974-76, 81-82). Clubs: Royal Hong Kong Jockey, American (Hong Kong). Home: 693 Prospect St Maplewood NJ 07040 Office: NJ Med Sch Med Sci Bldg 185 S Orange Ave Newark NJ 07103

FUA, GIORGIO, economist, educator; b. Ancona, Italy, May 19, 1919; s. Riccardo and Elena (Segre) F.; m. Erika Rosenthal, Sept. 16, 1943; children—Silvano, Daniele, Lorenzo. Laurea in Scienze Politiche, Laws Faculty and Scuola Normale Superiore, Pisa, Dr. en Droit, U. Lausanne; grad. Inst. Internat. Studies, Geneva. Jr. econ. advisor to pres. Olivetti s.p.a., 1941-45; with Istituto Mobilare Italiano, Rome, 1946-47; assoc. prof. econ. stats. U. Pisa (Italy), 1947-50; econ. affairs officer UN Econ. Commn. for Europe, Geneva, 1950-54; chief econ. adviser to pres. Enrico Mattei, Ente Nazionale Idrocarburi, Rome, 1954-60; prof. econs. Universita degli studi di Ancona, 1960—; pres. ISTAO (managerial edn.), Ancona, 1967—. Author: Reddito nazionale e politica economica, 1957; Idee per la programmazione economica, 1963; Lo Stato e il risparmio privato, 1970; Occupazione e capacita produttiva, 1976; Problems of Lagged Development in OECD Europe, 1980; Lo sviluppo economico in Italia: Lavoro e reddito, 1981; Industrializzazione senza fratture, 1983; Troppe Tasse Sui Redditi, 1985; Conseguenze economiche dell'evoluzione demografica, 1986. Office: ISTAO, via delle Grazie 67, 60100 Ancona Italy Other: Faculty of Econs, Universitádegli studi di Ancona, Palazzo degli Anziani, 60100 Ancona Italy

FUCHS, AMNON, hotel manager; b. Nahalal, Israel, May 6, 1940; s. David and Shoshana (Singer) F.; m. Hanne Stenner, May 28, 1967; 1 child, Gabriella. BA, Hebrew U., 1968; MA, U. Copenhagen, 1973. Cert. hotel administr. Personnel dir. Jerusalem Plaza Hotel, 1973-77; exec. asst. Mandarin Hotel, Tel Aviv, 1982; gen. mgr. Knesset Tower Hotel, Jerusalem, 1983-85, Kikar Zion & Eyal Hotels, Jerusalem, 1986; lesee Savoy Hotel, Copenhagen, Denmark, 1987—; lectr. Israel Inst. Tech., 1986; bd. dirs. Elton Constrn. & Hotels Co. Served to col. Israel Liaison, 1977-82. Mem. Israel Hotel Assn. Mem. Labour Party. Club: Tzevet. Home: Havevej 1, DK-2970 Horsholm Denmark Office: Savory Hotel, Vesterbrogade 34, DK-1620 Copenhagen Denmark

FUCHS, HELMUTH HANS, chemist, educator; b. Chgo., Aug. 25, 1931; s. Hans and Alycia F.; B.S., Loyola U., 1962; M.S., N.Mex. State U., 1966; Ph.D., Fordham U., 1974; Copy boy Chgo. Daily News, 1954-55; research asst. Great Lakes Naval Tng. Center, 1960-62; sci. tchr. Franklin High Sch., Somerset, N.J., 1965-67; assoc. prof. chemistry State U. N.Y., Farmingdale, 1970—. Bd. dirs. Germaine Pinault Sch. Music and Performing Arts, N.Y., Ana Sieiro de Trenchi Internat. Piano Competition, N.Y.C. Served with USN, 1952-54. Mem. Am. Chem. Soc., N.Y. Acad. Scis., Sigma Xi, Phi Lambda Upsilon. Composer: Ein Stueck Fuer Susanne, 1976; Lieblichkeit, 1977; Schlummerlied, 1977; Sonata for piano, 1980, 10 Fantases for piano, four impromptus for piano. Contbr. articles to sci. publs. Home: 804 Front St Dunellen NJ 08812

FUCHS, JEROME HERBERT, management consultant; b. N.Y.C., Jan. 7, 1922; s. Berthold and Fannie (Neuschotz) F.; m. Eleanor May DeRoo, May 26, 1945; children—Jerome S. Taylor, Susan Fuchs Decker, Sandra Fuchs Lombino. B.S. cum laude, Syracuse U., 1950, M.B.A., 1951. Systems analyst Carrier Corp., 1951-52; supr. systems and procedures Lukens Steel, Coatesville, Pa., 1952-54; mgr. systems and procedures PennWalt Co., Phila., 1955-57, Amax, Inc., Greenwich, Conn., 1958-60; exec. asst. to pres. Rockbestos Wire & Cable Co., 1960-61; v.p. mfg. United Aircraft Products, Dayton, Ohio, 1970-71; exec. v.p. Bus. Supplies Corp. Am., N.Y.C., 1972; sr. ptnr. Fuchs Assocs., Massapequa, N.Y., 1960—; bd. dirs. Del Electronics Corp., Extended Techs., indsl. research asst., Syracuse U., N.Y.C., 1949-51; lectr. Syracuse U., 1950-52, John Hopkins U., Balt., 1953-54, Drexel Inst., Phila., 1955-57, Queens Coll., N.Y.C., 1963-65, SUNY, Stony Brook, 1987-88; bd. dirs. Del. Electronics Corp. Author: Making the Most of Management Consulting Services, 1975; Managment Consultants in Action, 1975; Computerized Cost Control Systems, 1976; Computerized Inventory Control Systems, 1977; Administering the Quality Control Function, 1979, The Prentice-Hall Illustrated Handbook of Advanced Manufacturing Methods, 1988. Served as 2nd lt. AC, U.S. Army, 1943-46. Mem. Soc. Profl. Mgmt. Cons. (charter, pres. 1977-79), Inst. Mgmt. Cons. (cert., founding mem.). Home and Office: 30 Cabot Rd W Massapequa NY 11758

FUCHS, PATRICK EUGENE, perfume company executive; b. Paris, Apr. 14, 1930; s. Georges and Florence Simone (Campbell) F.; m. Edina Maria de Marffy-Mantuano, June 23, 1960; children—Stephanie, Frederic, Sandrine. B.S., U. Paris, 1946; postgrad. in chem. engring., E.N.S.C.P. (Paris), 1951; M.S., Stevens Inst. Tech., 1952; M.A., Harvard U., 1954, Ph.D., 1956. Tech. dir. S.A. Parfumerie Fragonard, Grasse, France, 1958-74, pres., 1974—; pres. S.A. T.P.L.T., Grasse, 1974—. Contbr. articles to profl. jours. Served with French Navy, 1956-58. Fulbright grantee, 1952-53. Mem. Am. Chem. Soc. Roman Catholic. Clubs: Harvard (N.Y.); M.B.C. (France). Avocations: skiing; tennis; golf. Home: La Petite Campagne, Les Quatre Chemins, 06130 Grasse France Office: SA Parfumerie Fragonard, 20 Blvd Fragonard, 06130 Grasse France

FUCHS, SIR VIVIAN, geologist; b. Isle of Wight, Feb. 11, 1908; s. Ernest and Violet (Watson) F.; student Brighton Coll., 1922-26; M.A., Cambridge U., 1932, Ph.D., 1936, D.Sc. (hon.), 1959; LL.D. (hon.), Edinburgh U., 1958, Birmingham U., 1974; D.Sc. (hon.), Durham U., 1958, Swansea U., 1971, Leicester U., 1972; m. Joyce Connell, 1933; children—Hilary Brooks, Peter E.K. Geologist, Cambridge East Greenland Expdn., 1929, East Africa Expdn. 1930-32; leader Lake Rudolf Rift Valley Expdn., 1934, Lake Rukwa Expdn., 1938, Falkland Islands Dependencies Survey, 1947-50; dir. Brit. Antarctic Survey, 1950-73, leader Trans-Antarctic Expdn., 1955-58. Recipient Founders medal Royal Geog. Soc., 1951, Spl. Gold medal, 1958; Gold medal Royal Scottish Geog. Soc., 1958, Paris Gold medal, 1958; Silver medal Royal Soc. Arts, 1951, Polar medal, 1951, 58; Gold Richthofen medal Berlin Geog. Soc., 1958; Gold Kirchenpauer medal Hamburg Geog. Soc., 1958; Gold Plancius medal Amsterdam Geog. Soc., 1958; Hubbard medal Nat. Geog. Soc., 1959; Gold medal Chgo. Geog. Soc., 1959; Gold medal N.Y. Explorers Club, 1959; Hans Egede Silver medal Copenhagen Geog. Soc., 1959. Fellow Royal Soc., Royal Geog. Soc. (pres. 1982-84), Geol. Soc. London; mem. Internat. Glaciol. Soc. (pres. 1963-66), Brit. Assn. for Advancement Sci. (pres. 1972). Club: Athenaeum (London). Author: Crossing of Antarctica, 1959; Antarctic Adventure, 1959; Of Ice and Men, 1982; editor: Forces of Nature, 1977; author geog., geol. papers. Home: 106 Barton Rd, CB3 9LH Cambridge England Office: 55 Hans Pl, London SW1X OLA, England

FUELLHART, DAVID CLARK, broadcasting executive; b. Pitts., Oct. 16, 1938; s. William Clarke and Katherine Modiset (Marsh) F.; m. Patricia Ann O'Reilley, Sept. 9, 1961 (div.); children: David Clark, Elizabeth Ann; m. Judith Sandra MacFarland, Oct. 31, 1969 (div.); 1 child, Mathew Scott; m. Stephanie Ann Cunningham, Feb. 1, 1985. BS, Ithaca Coll., 1963. Staff announcer Stas. WNAE-WRRN, Warren, Pa., 1958-59; disc jockey, sportscaster Sta. WTKO, Ithaca, N.Y., 1960-61; program dir. N.E. Radio Network, Ithaca, 1961-62; account exec. Cogan Advt., Ithaca, 1962-63; exec. producer Sun Dial Films, Washington, 1967-68; regional sales mgr. Stas. WPIK-WXRA, Alexandria, Va., 1968-70; gen. mgr. Sta. WPST, Trenton, N.J., 1970-74, Sta. WPOC, Balt., 1974—; group mgr. Nationwide Communications Inc, 1985—; instr. sales and mktg. Broadcast Inst. Md., 1979-81; chmn. adv. bd. ABC Radio Direction Network Affiliates; chmn. client adv. bd. Eastman Radio, Inc., 1986-87, Arbitron Radio Adv. Council, 1984, 1988—; mem. adv. council ABC Radio Networks Affiliate, 1988—. Past mem. public relations subcom. Johns Hopkins Children's Center; past bd. dirs. Am. Lung Assn., Trenton, N.J.; past chmn. broadcast skills bank Balt. Urban League; trustee Md. Econ. Edn. Commn. Served with USN, 1963-67. Decorated Armed Forces Expeditionary medal, 1965; recipient ann. award Aviation Adv. Council N.J., 1972-73, citation and Merit award Mayor of Balt., 1982, Silver award Mayor of Balt., 1984. Mem. Broadcast Pioneers, Md., D.C., Del. Broadcasters Assn. (past pres.), Advt. Assn. Balt. (past pres. two terms), Radio Execs. Balt. (v.p. 1987-88, past pres. two terms), Balt. Broadcasters Coalition (past pres.), Greater Trenton Execs. Assn. (past v.p.), Am. Bowling Congress. Presbyterian. Club: Hunt Valley Golf (Balt.). Office: 711 W 40th St Baltimore MD 21211

FUENTES, CARLOS, writer, former ambassador; b. Mexico City, Nov. 11, 1928; s. Rafael Fuentes Boettiger and Berta Macías Rivas; m. Rita Macedo, 1959 (div. 1969); 1 dau., Cecilia; m. Sylvia Lemus, 1973; children: Carlos, Natasha. Ed., U. Mex., Institut des Hautes Etudes Internationales, Geneva; hon. degrees, Columbia Coll., Chgo. State U., Cambridge U., Essex U., Harvard U. Mem. Mexican del. ILO, Geneva, 1950-52; asst. head press sect. Mexican Ministry Fgn. Affairs, 1954; asst. dir. cultural dissemination U. Mex., 1955-56; head dept. cultural relations Mexican Ministry Fgn. Affairs, 1957-59; fellow Woodrow Wilson Internat. Center for Scholars, Washington, 1974; former Mexican ambassador to Franc; Robert F. Kennedy prof. Harvard U.; Simon Bolivar prof. Cambridge U., Robert F. Kennedy prof., Harvard U. Author: Los días enmascarados, 1954, La región más transparente, 1958, Las buenas conciencias, 1959, Aura, 1962, The Death of Artemio Cruz, 1962, Cantar de Ciegos, 1964, Zona sagrada, 1967, Cambio de piel, 1967 (Biblioteca Breve prize Barcelona), La Nueva Novela Hispanoamericana, 1969, Cumpleaños, 1969, Casa con dos puertas, 1970, Todos los Gatos son pardos, 1970, El Tuerto es Rey, 1971, Tiempo Mexicano, 1971, Don Quixote or the Critique of Reading, 1974, Terra Nostra, 1975 (Rómulo Gallegos prize), La cabeza de la hidra, 1982, The Old Gringo, 1985; Una familia lejana, 1980, Agua Quemada, 1981, Distant Relations, 1982; play Orchids in the Moonlight, 1982 (Mex. nat. award for lit. 1984), Cristobal Mex., 1987, Cristobal Nonato, 1987, Myself With Others, 1987; contbr. to mags. and newspapers including Los Angeles Times, N.Y. Times, Newsweek; editor: Rivista Mexicana de Literatura, 1954-58, Siempre and Politica, 1960—; co-editor: El Espectador, 1959-61. Trustee N.Y. Pub. Library. Recipient Miguel de Cervantes Lit. prize Spanish Ministry of Culture, 1987, Medal of Honor for Lit., Nat. Arts Club, N.Y.C., 1988. Mem. Am. Acad. and Inst. Arts and Letters, Nat. Coll. Mex., Interam. Dialogue, Inst. Nat. Strategy (bd. dirs.).

FUENTES, F. JAVIER, distributing company executive; b. Zaragoza, Spain, Oct. 19, 1941; s. Antonio Fuentes and Manuela Solsona; m. Maria Carmen Otero; children: Beatriz, Javier. Diploma in Chem. Scis., U. Zaragoza, 1966; M of Mgmt., Inst. Estudios Superiores de la Empresa, Barcelona, Spain, 1981. Area mgr. for So. Europe, North Africa, Middle East Labs. Hosbon, Barcelona, 1966-69; comml. and mktg. mgr. Quimigranel Corp., Barcelona, 1969-75; mng. dir. Quimigranel Corp., Barcelona and Madrid, 1975—. Mem. Spanish-Afro-Asiatic Inst. Cooperation, Am. C. of C. in Spain (bd. dirs. 1977-80). Home: Calle Eucaliptos 26, Monteclaro, Madrid 23, Spain

FUERSTENAU, DOUGLAS WINSTON, mineral engineering educator; b. Hazel, S.D., Dec. 6, 1928; s. Erwin Arnold and Hazel Pauline (Karterud) F.; m. Margaret Ann Pellett, Aug. 29, 1953; children: Lucy, Sarah, Stephen. B.S., S.D. Sch. Mines and Tech., 1949; M.S., Mont. Sch. Mines, 1950; Sc.D., MIT, 1953; Mineral Engr., Mont. Coll. Mineral Sci. and Tech., 1968. Asst. prof. mineral engring. MIT, 1953-56; sect. leader, metals research lab. Union Carbide Metals Co., Niagara Falls, N.Y., 1956-58; mgr. mineral engring. lab Kaiser Aluminum & Chem. Corp., Permanente, Calif., 1958-59; asso. prof. metallurgy U. Calif.-Berkeley, 1959-62, prof. metallurgy, 1962-86, P. Malozemoff prof. of mineral engring., 1987—, Miller research prof., 1969-70, chmn. dept. materials sci. and mineral engring., 1970-78; dir. Homestake Mining Co.; chmn. Engring. Found. Research Conf. on Comminution, 1963; mem. adv. bd. Sch. Earth Scis., Stanford, 1970-73; mem. Nat. Mineral Bd., 1975-78; Am. rep. Internat. Mineral Processing Congress Com., 1978—. Editor: Froth Flotation-50th Anniversary Vol, 1962; co-editor-in-chief: Internat. Jour. of Mineral Processing, 1972—; Mem. editorial adv. bd.: Jour. of Colloid and Interface Sci, 1968-72, Colloids and Surfaces, 1980—; Contbr. articles to profl. jours. Recipient Disting. Teaching award U. Calif., 1974; Alexander von Humboldt Sr. Am. Scientist award Fed. Republic Germany, 1984. Fellow Instn. Mining and Metallurgy, London. Mem. Nat. Acad. Engring., Am. Inst. Mining and Metall. Engrs. (chmn. mineral processing div. 1967, Robert Lansing Hardy Gold medal 1957, Rossiter W. Raymond award 1961, Robert H. Richards award 1975, Antoine M. Gaudin award 1978, Mineral Industry Edn. award 1983), Soc. Mining Engrs. (dir. 1968-71, Distinguished mem.), Am. Chem. Soc., Am. Inst. Chem. Engrs., Sigma Xi, Theta Tau. Congregationalist. Home: 1440 LeRoy Ave Berkeley CA 94708

FUERSTENBERG, JOACHIM EGON, Fürst (Prince) business executive; b. Schloss Grund, Bohemia, June 28, 1923; s. Max Egon zu and Wilhelmine (Gräfin von Schoenburg-Glauchau) F.; m. Paula Gräfin zu Koenigsegg-Aulendorf, June 25, 1947; 6 children. Owner, Fürstenberg Forest Properties; gen. ptnr. Fuerstlich Fuerstenbergische Brauerei KG; chmn. supervisory bd. Baren-Brauerei AG, Schwenningen; owner Holzindustrie Fürst zu Fürstenberg; owner Autohaus Freiburg, Autohaus Fürst Fürstenberg Baden-Baden. Roman Catholic.

FUGARD, ATHOL HAROLD, playwright, actor, director; b. Middleburg, Republic of South Africa, June 11, 1932; s. Harold David and Elizabeth Magdalene (Potgieter) F.; student U. Cape Town; m. Sheila Meiring, Sept. 22, 1955; 1 child, Lisa Maria. Author: (plays) The Blood Knot, Hello and Goodbye, People Are Living There, The Road to Mecca, Boesman and Lena, Sizwe Banzi is Dead, The Island, Statements After an Arrest Under the Immorality Act, No Good Friday, Nongogo, Dimetos, A Lesson from Aloes (N.Y. Critics award), Master Harold and the Boys (also dir. Broadway prodn.), Notebooks: 1960-77, Tsotsi, 1980, The Killing Fields, 1983; author, actor film Boesman and Lena (Obie award), Marigolds in August (Silver Bear award Berlin Film Festival), 1980; actor films: The Guest, Meetings with Remarkable Men, Gandhi, 1982, The Killing Fields, 1984; appeared in Broadway play Blood Knot, 1986; dir.: Sizwe Banzi is Dead, The Island, Dimetos, A Place with the Pigs, 1987. Recipient Internat. Grand Prix Ernst Artaria award Locarno Film Festival for script and performance in The Guest, 1977. Mem. Dramatists Guild, Mark Twain Soc. Address: PO Box 5090, Walmar, Port Elizabeth Republic of South Africa

FUGATE, WILBUR LINDSAY, lawyer; b. Pulaski, Va., Mar. 27, 1913; s. Jesse Honaker and Elizabeth Gertrude (Brown) F.; m. Barbara Louise Brown, Sept. 19, 1942; m. Cornelia Wolfolk Alfriend, Jan. 2, 1971; children—William, Richard, Barbara, Elizabeth. B.A. cum. laude, Davidson Coll., 1934; LL.B., U. Va., 1937; LL.M., George Washington U., 1951, S.J.D., 1954. Bar: Va. 1937, W.Va. 1938, U.S. Supreme Ct. 1949, D.C. 1971, U.S. Dist. Ct. D.C. 1971, U.S. Ct. Appeals (D.C. cir.) 1971, U.S. Dist. Ct. (ea. dist.) Va. 1979, U.S. Ct. Appeals (5th and 8th cirs.) 1980. Assoc. Campbell & McNeer, Huntington, W.Va., 1937-38; counsel Kanawha Banking & Trust Co., Charleston, W.Va., 1938-42; with antitrust div. Dept. Justice, 1947-73; asst. chief trial sect. Dept. Justice, Washington, 1951-53; chief Honolulu office Dept. Justice, 1960-61; chief fgn. commerce sect. Dept. Justice, Washington, 1962-73; of counsel Glassie, Pewitt, Beebe & Shanks, Washington, 1974-77, Baker & Hostetler, Washington, 1977—; U.S. del. OECD Restrictive Bus. Practices Commn., 1962-73. Author: Foreign Commerce and the Antitrust Laws, 1958, 3d edit., 1982; contbr. articles to legal jours., chpts. to books; bd. advisors Va. Jour. Internat. Law, 1976—. Served to lt. USCG, 1942-45. Mem. ABA (chmn. antitrust com. internat. law sect. 1975-76, chmn. subcoms. in patents, fgn. antitrust laws sect. antitrust law 1971-77), Fed. Bar Assn., Internat. Bar Assn., Inter-Am. Bar Assn. Democrat. Presbyterian. Clubs: Cosmos, Internat. (Washington); Army

Navy Country (Arlington, Va.). Home: 2805 Dartmouth Rd Alexandria VA 22314 Office: Baker & Hostetler 1050 Connecticut Ave NW Washington DC 20036

FUGLEDE, BENT, mathematician; b. Copenhagen, Oct. 8, 1925; s. Albert and Adda (Fjord Pedersen) F.; m. Olafia Einarsdottir, Mar. 6, 1954; 1 child, Einar. MSc, U. Copenhagen, 1948, Dr.Phil., 1960. Teaching asst. Tech. U. Copenhagen, 1952-54; asst. prof. U. Copenhagen, 1954-59, assoc. prof., 1959-60; prof. math. Tech. U. Copenhagen, 1960-64, U. Copenhagen, 1965—. Author: Finely Harmonic Functions, 1972; contbr. articles to profl. jours. Mem. Royal Danish Acad. Scis. and Letters, The Finnish Acad. Scis. and Letters. Home: Trongaardsparken 67, Lyngby Denmark

FUHRER, LARRY, investment banker; b. Ft. Wayne, Ind., Sept. 23, 1939; s. Henry Roland and Wilhelmine Ellen (Kopp) F.; A.B., Taylor U., 1961; postgrad. No. Ill. U., 1965—; MBA, Ill. Benedictine Coll., 1988; m. Linda Larsen, Dec. 31, 1962; 1 son, Lance. Exec. club dir. Youth for Christ, Miami, Fla., 1961; publs. mgr. Campus Life mag. Wheaton, Ill., 1962-65; asst. to pres. then v.p. Youth for Christ Internat., Wheaton, 1965-66; asso. dir. devel. Ill. Inst. Tech., 1966-68; exec. asst. to pres., The Robert Johnston Corp., Los Angeles, Chgo., N.Y.C., 1968; pres. Compro, Inc. now Presdl. Services, Inc., Glen Ellyn, Ill., 1973-85; chmn., pres. The Centre Capital Group Inc., Wheaton; pres. Killian Assocs. Inc., Wheaton, 1973-75; chmn. Family Programming Inc., Rockford Equities Ltd., Rockford Prodns. Inc., Fin. Services Group Ltd., Equity Realty Group Inc., Internat. Telemedia Ltd., Quadrus Media Ministry, Inc.; dir. Gamel Broadcasting, Inc.; pres. Presdl. Services, Inc., Travel Equities and Mgmt. Co. (Teamco), Chgo Sports Prodns. Inc., Royal Travel Services Inc., Family Programming Inc., Fin. Services Centre Inc., ednl. mgmt. cons. numerous pvt. colls. and sems. Bd. dirs. Chicagoland Youth for Christ. Mem. Am. Mgmt. Assn., Am. Inst. Mgmt. Cons.'s, DuPage Bd. Realtors, Nat., Ill. assns. realtors, Am. Mktg. Assn., Mortgage Bankers Assn. Presbyterian. Club: Union League (Chgo.). Home: 521 Iroquois Naperville IL 60540 Office: Box 1077 Lisle IL 60532

FUHRMAN, ROBERT ALEXANDER, aerospace company executive; b. Detroit, Feb. 23, 1925; s. Alexander A. and Elva (Brown) F. B.S., U. Mich., 1945; M.S., U. Md., 1952; postgrad., U. Calif., San Diego, 1958; Exec. Mgmt. Program, Stanford Bus. Sch., 1964. Project engr. Naval Air Test Center, Patuxent River, Md., 1946-53; chief tech. engring. Ryan Aero. Co., San Diego, 1953-58; mgr. Polaris 1958-64, chief engr. MSD, 1964-66; v.p., asst. gen. mgr. missile systems div. Lockheed Missiles & Space Co., Sunnyvale, Calif., 1966-68; v.p., gen. mgr. Lockheed Missiles & Space Co., 1969, v.p., 1973-76, pres., 1976-83, chmn., 1979—; v.p. Lockheed Corp., Burbank, Calif., 1969-76; sr. v.p. Lockheed Corp., 1976-83, group pres. Missiles, Space & Electronics System, 1983-85, pres., chief operating officer, 1986—; also dir., pres. Lockheed Ga. Co., Marietta, 1970-71; pres. Lockheed Calif. Co., Burbank, 1971-73; chmn. bd. Ventura Mfg. Co., 1970-71; bd. dirs. Bank of the West; mem. FBM Steering Task Group, 1966-70. Mem. adv. bd. Sch. Bus., U. Santa Clara; bd. govs. Federated Employees of Bay Area; trustee United Way of Santa Clara County, 1975-85; bd. dirs. Atlanta Jr. Achievement; mem. adv. council Sch. Engring., Stanford U.; mem. adv. bd. Coll. Engring., U. Mich., 1981—; mem. adv. council Coll. Engring. Found. U. Tex.-Austin, 1983-86; mem. Def. Sci. Bd., chmn. task force on indsl. responsiveness, 1980; mem. exec. com. San Jose Mgmt. Task Force; mem. sci. adv. com. Ala. Space and Rocket Center; bd. dirs. Bay Area Council. Served to ensign USNR, 1944-46. Recipient Silver Knight award Nat. Mgmt. Assn., 1969, John J. Montgomery award, 1964; award Soc. Mfg. Engrs., 1973; Disting. Citizen award Boy Scouts Am., 1983; Donald C. Burnham award Soc. Mfg. Engrs., 1983; Recipient Eminent Engr. award Tau Beta Pi, 1983. Fellow AIAA (hon., dir.-at-large, Von Karman 1978), Soc. Mfg. Engrs.; mem. Nat. Acad. Engring., Am. Astron. Soc. (sr.), Nat. Aero. Assn., Ga. C. of C. (dir.), Am. Def. Preparedness Assn. (dir., exec. com.), Navy League U.S. (life), Air Force Assn., Assn. U.S. Army, Soc. Am. Value Engrs. (hon.), Santa Clara County Mfrs. Group (past chmn.), Beta Gamma Sigma. Clubs: Los Altos Country (Calif.),Burning Tree (Bethesda, Md.), N. Ranch Country (Westlake Village). Office: Lockheed Corp 4500 Park Granada Blvd Calabasas CA 91399

FUHS, G(EORG) WOLFGANG, state agency administrator; b. Cologne, Fed. Republic Germany, May 19, 1932; came to U.S., 1964; s. Friedrich Karl and Lisette I. (Stayen) F.; children: Lisette I., H. Georg, Dagmar A. Diploma in biology, D in Nat. Scis., U. Bonn, Germany, 1956; postdoctoral, Tech. U. Delft, The Netherlands, 1956-57. Sci. employee dept. botany U. Frankfurt, Fed. Republic Germany, 1957-58; research assoc. dept. hygiene U. Bonn Sch. Medicine, 1958-63; fellow dept. genetics U. Cologne, 1963-64; sr., prin. research scientist div. labs. and research N.Y. State Dept. Health, Albany, 1964-72, dir. environ. health labs., 1973-85; chief div. labs. Calif. Dept. Health Services, Berkeley, 1985—; vis. prof. U. Wis., Milw., 1973; research assoc. U. Minn. Sch. Pub. Health, Mpls., 1970-74; adj. prof. dept. biology SUNY, Albany, 1984-86; mem. exptl. com. on human health effects of Great Lakes water Quality U.S./Can. Internat. Joint Commn., 1978—, co-chmn. 1983—. Contbr. articles to profl. jours. (Inst. Sci. Info. award 1969); mem. editorial bd. Jour Phycology, 1972-74, Limnology and Oceanography, 1973-76, Microbial Ecology, 1974—. Mem. AAAS, Am. Soc. Microbiol. (past chmn. Eastern N.Y. br.), Internat. Assn. Theoretical Applied Limnology, Am. Pub. Health Assn., Water Pollution Control Fedn., Am. Water Works Assn. Office: Calif Dept Health Services Div Labs 2151 Berkeley Way Berkeley CA 94704

FUJII, KIYO, pharmacist; b. Portland, Oreg., July 1, 1921; s. Kanji and Mitoyo (Kurata) F.; student U. Wash., 1939-42; B.S., St. Louis Coll. Pharmacy, 1943. Pharmacist, C.F. Knight Drug, St. Louis, 1943-48, Sargent Drug, Chgo., 1950-52, Mt. Sinai Hosp., Chgo., 1953-54, Campus Pharmacy, Los Angeles, 1973—; chief pharmacist Evang. Hosp., Chgo., 1948-49, Am. Hosp. Clinic, Los Angeles, 1958-60. Mem. Am., Calif. Pharm. Assns., St. Louis Coll. Pharmacy Alumni Assn., Rho Chi, Sigma Epsilon Sigma. Democrat. Presbyterian. Home: 7913 Kentwood Ave Los Angeles CA 90045

FUJII, KOICHI, ecologist, researcher; b. Kyoto, Japan, June 14, 1942; s. Yasaku and Harue (Takada) F.; m. Isuzu Sano, Jan. 28, 1969; 1 child, Rika. B.A., Kyoto U., 1965, M. Agr., 1967; M.A., SUNY-Stony Brook, 1972; Ph.D., U. Kans., 1972. Research fellow U. B.C., Vancouver, Can., 1971-73; asst. prof. Purdue U., West Lafayette, Ind., 1973-78; assoc. prof. U. Tsukuba, Ibaraki, Japan, 1978-88, prof., 1988—. Author: Recent Advances in Entomology, 1981; Computer Use In Ecology, 1982; translator: Biometry, 1983. David Ross Found. research grantee, 1975; Ministry Edn. (Japan) research grantee, 1979; NSF grantee, 1976. Mem. Soc. Population Ecology (editor 1979—, exec. com. 1983—), Japanese Soc. Ecology (editor 1983—), Am. Soc. Naturalists, Ecolog. Soc. Am., Sigma Xi. Home: 2-815-1 Azuma, Tsukuba, Ibaraki 305 Japan Office: Inst Biol Sci, Univ Tsukuba, Ibaraki 305 Japan

FUJII, TADASHI, medical products company executive; b. Kyoto, Japan, Feb. 28, 1947; s. Eiichi Fujii and Tami Isozaki; m. Youko Dobashi; children: Masakazu, Tomoya. BS, Sci. U. Tokyo, 1969; MS, Tokyo Inst. Tech., 1971. Research and deve. engr. Japan Electron Optics Lab. Ltd., Tokyo, 1972-79; asst. mgr. med. electronics sect. Terumo Corp., Tokyo, 1979—. Patentee in field. Mem. Japan Soc. Ultrasonics in Medicine, Japan Soc. Med. Electronics and Biol. Engring. Office: Terumo Corp, 2656-1 Obuchi, Fuji-shi 417, Japan

FUJIKAWA, YOSHIYUKI, literary critic, educator; b. Okayama City, Japan, Sept. 13, 1938; s. Hideo and Mitsuko (Akazawa) F.; m. Yukiko Muraki, Nov. 15, 1970; children: Takayuki, Miki. BA in Edn., Tokyo U., 1964, MA, 1967. Instr. Kokugakuin U., Tokyo, 1970-72; lectr. Tokyo Met. U., 1972-74, assoc. prof., 1974-87; prof. Tokyo U., 1988—. Author: The Poetics of Landscape, 1983; translator: Pale Fire (Nabokov), 1983, Renaissance (Pater), 1986. Mem. English Lit. Soc. Japan (sec. 1987—). Liberal-Democratic Party. Buddist. Home: 1220 Yamanouchi, 247 Kamakura-shi Japan

FUJIMORI, KAZUO YORIAKI, economics educator; b. Imari, Saga, Japan, Feb. 17, 1946; s. Gihachiro and Harue (Yoshida) F. B.A. in Econs., Yokohama State U., 1968; M.A. in Econs., Hitotsubashi U., Tokyo, 1970; Dr. Econs., Hokkaido U., Sapporo, 1983. Lectr. Kanagawa U., Yokohama, 1973-78, Meiji Gakuin U., Tokyo, 1973-78; assoc. prof. econ. theory Josai U., Saitama, Japan, 1974-84, prof., 1984—, editor Josai U. Press, Saitama, 1985—. Author: Modern Analysis of Value Theory, 1982. Contbr. articles on pure econ. theory to profl. jours. Research grantee Tokyo Club, 1979; research fellow Dutch Govt., Amsterdam U., 1978-79. Mem. Econometric Soc., Royal Econ. Soc., Japan Assn. Econs. and Econometrics, Internat. Assn. Survey Statisticians. Home: 1133-32 Aihara, Machida Tokyo 194-02, Japan Office: Josai U, 1-1 Keyakidai, Sakado Saitama Japan

FUJIMORI, MASAMICHI, metal company executive; b. Osaka, Japan, Dec. 22, 1921; s. Tatsumaro and Kimiko (Ono) F.; m. Yoko Sato, Jan. 8, 1951; children—Izumi, Kaoru. B. Metallurgy, Tokyo Imperial U., 1944, Dr.Engring. Lectr. Tokyo U., 1948-50; with Sumitomo Metal Mining Co. Ltd., Tokyo, 1972—, mng. dir. 1977, sr. mng. dir., 1979, exec. v.p., 1981, pres. 1983—, also dir. Recipient Blue Ribbon medal, 1982. Mem. London Inst. Mining and Metallurgy (hon. fellow); Council of Mining, Mining and Metall. Inst. of Japan (chmn. 1985—), Japan Mining Industry Assn. (pres. 1987-88). Avocation: bonsai. Office: Sumitomo Metal Mining Co Ltd, 5-11-3 Shimbashi, Minato-ku, Tokyo 105 Japan *

FUJIMOTO, HIROSHI, bank executive; b. Tokyo, Mar. 11, 1945; s. Akira and Suma (Ohkubo) F.; m. Mieko Kakiuchi, Nov. 2, 1978; children: Hiroyuki, Akiko. BA, Keio U., Tokyo, 1967. Asst. gen. mgr. Long-Term Credit Bank Japan, Ltd., Tokyo, 1975-79, assoc. gen. mgr. corp. fin. group, 1980-83, dep. gen. mgr. mcht. banking group, 1984—; gen. mgr. corp. planning Teikoku Databank, Ltd., Tokyo, 1986—; advisor Port of Los Angeles, 1983-85, Western Gov.'s Assn., Denver, 1984-85; fin. advisor Burlington No. Inc., Seattle, 1984-85. Mem. com. U.S. Maritime Commn., Washington, 1983-85; mem. alumni com. Inter-Univ. Seminar House, Tokyo, 1983—. U. Mich. scholar, 1971-72. Office: Long-Term Credit Bank Japan Ltd, 1-2-4 Ohtemachi, 100 Chiyoda-ku, Tokyo Japan

FUJIOKA, MASAO, banker; b. Tokyo, Oct. 31, 1924; married; 3 children. LLM, Tokyo U., 1947; postgrad., U. Chgo., 1950-51. Economist IMF, 1960-64; dir. short-term capital div. Internat. Fin. Bur., Ministry of Fin., Tokyo, 1964-66, dep. dir. gen., 1970-75, dir. gen., 1975-77; with ECAFE, Tokyo, 1966; dir. adminstrn. dept. Asian Devel. Bank, Manila, Philippines, 1966; dir. coordination dept. Overseas Econ. Cooperation Fund, Tokyo, 1969; exec. dir. Export-Import Bank of Japan, Tokyo, 1977-81; pres. Asian Devel. Bank, Manila, Philippines, 1981—; advisor to Minister of Fin., 1981. Contbr. articles to profl. jours. Office: Care Asian Devel Bank, 2330 Roxas Blvd, PO Box 789, Manila 2800, Philippines

FUJISAKI, AKIRA, mining company executive; b. Kagoshima City, Kagoshima Pref, Japan, May 1, 1917; s. Kokichi and Misako (Morita) F.; m. Sakae Ishida, Apr. 3, 1951; 1 dau., Youko. LL.B., Tokyo Imperial U., 1941. Controller, Sumitomo Metal Mining, Tokyo, 1964-67, dir., 1967-70, mng. dir., 1970-73, pres., 1973-83, chmn., 1983—. Pres., Japan Mining Industry Assn., Tokyo, 1976-77, 81-82; exec. dir. Fedn. Econ. Orgn., 1977—; trustee Japan Com. Econ. Devel., 1971—. Served to lt. Japanese Navy, 1942-45. Recipient Blue Ribbon medal, Tokyo, 1979, 1st Order of Sacred Treasure, 1987. Lodge: Rotary. Home: 2-7-14 Nishi Kamakura, Kamakura City, Kanagawa Prefecture 248 Japan Office: Sumitomo Metal Mining Co Ltd, 5-11-3 Shimbashi, Minato-Ku, Tokyo 105 Japan *

FUJITA, MASAAKI, politician; b. Hiroshima, Japan, Feb. 3, 1922; s. Sadaichi and Masano Fujita; m. Jun Ohara, 1947; 4 children. Grad., Waseda U. With Fujita Corp.; mem. Japanese Ho. of Councillors, 1965—, then chair fin. com.; parliamentary vice-minister fin; chair Diet Policy Com. Liberal Dem. Party, sec. gen., 1980-83; then assoc. of Masayoshi Ohir, minister of state, dir.-gen. of adminstrv. affairs in Office of Prime Minister; dir.-gen. Okinawa Devel. Agy., 1976-77. Office: 1713 Motoyoyogicho, Shibuyaku, Tokyo 151 Japan *

FUJITA, MASAO, construction company executive; b. Hikone, Shiga, Japan, Jan. 3, 1943; parents: Yoshio and Sato (Nakagawa) F.; married; children: Motoki, Noriko, Tadahira. Degree in architecture, Kyoto U., Japan, 1965. Licensed architect 1st class, civil engring. diplomate;. With Shimizu Corp., Tokyo, 1965—, dep. gen. mgr., 1986—. Office: Shimizu Corp, No 2-16-1 Kyobashi, 104 Chuo-ku Tokyo Japan

FUJITA, OSAMU, electrical engineer; b. Fukuoka, Japan, Feb. 22, 1957; s. Atsuhiko and Keiko F.; m. Sachiko Arima, Oct. 18, 1986. BS, Kyushu U., Fukuoka, 1979, MS, 1981. Engr. elec. communications labs Nippon Telegraph & Telephone Pub. Co., Musashino, Japan, 1981-83; engr. elec. communications labs Nippon Telegraph & Telephone Pub. Co., Atsugi, Japan, 1983-87, research engr. NTT LSI labs, 1987—. Contbr. articles to profl. jours. Mem. Phys. Soc. Japan, Japan Soc. Applied Physics, Inst. Electronics, Info., Communication Engrs., Internat. Neural Network Soc. Office: NTT LSI Labs, 3-1 Morinosato Wakamiya, Atsugi 243, Japan

FUJIWARA, TAKESHI, contracting association executive; b. Tokyo, Apr. 11, 1923; s. Takejiro and Akie Fujiwara; m. Sumiko Munetomo, Nov. 12, 1951; children: Yosuke, Hinako. B of Tech., Hokkaido U., 1948. Chief Tokyo Highway Constrn. Office Ministry of Constrn., 1960-66, chief Yokohama Highway Constrn. Office, 1966-70; chief hwy. sect. Hokuriku Bur. Ministry of Constrn., Nigata, Japan, 1970-72, Kanto Bur. Ministry of Constrn., Tokyo, 1972-75; dir. gen. Chugoku Bur. Ministry of Constrn., Hiroshima, Japan, 1975-77; v.p. Japan Road Contractors Assn., Tokyo, 1977—. Author: Maintenance of Pavement, 1968, Mr. Road, 1970, Mr. Road Continued, 1975, The Story of Roman Road, 1985. Mem. Japan Roads Assn.

FUJIYAMA, RODNEY MICHIO, lawyer; b. Honolulu, Aug. 1, 1945; s. Wallace Sachio Fujiyama and Jean (Osumi) Shin; m. Vicki Ann Yamaguchi, Dec. 28, 1968; children—Christopher, Laurie, Sandra, Jonathan, Shannon. Student Oberlin Coll., 1963-64; B.A. with high honors, U. Hawaii, 1967; J.D., U. Calif.-San Francisco, 1970. Bar: Hawaii 1970, U.S. Dist. Ct. Hawaii 1970, U.S. Ct. Appeals (9th cir.) 1971. Assoc., Chuck & Fujiyama, Honolulu, 1970-74; assoc. Law Offices of Wallace S. Fujiyama, Honolulu, 1974; ptnr. Fujiyama, Duffy, Fujiyama, Honolulu, 1975-78, Fujiyama, Duffy, Fujiyama & Koshiba, Honolulu, 1979, Fujiyama, Duffy & Fujiyama, Honolulu, 1979—; per diem judge Dist. Ct. of 1st Cir., State of Hawaii, Honolulu, 1979-85. Mem. ABA, Hawaii State Bar Assn., Assn. Trial Lawyers Am., Phi Beta Kappa. Office: Fujiyama Duffy & Fujiyama 1001 Bishop St 2700 Pauahi Tower Honolulu HI 96813

FUJIYOSHI, TSUGUHIDE, chemical company executive; b. Fukuoka, Japan, Jan. 24, 1913; s. Kiichi and Haruko F.; m. Yuko, 1941; 5 children. Ed. Tokyo U. Joined Toyo Rayon Co. Ltd. (now Toray Industries Inc.), 1935, with Hamburg office, 1960-61, mgr. Nagoya plant, 1961, dir., 1962-64, mng. dir., 1964-66, exec. v.p., 1966-71, pres., 1971-80, chmn., 1980—. Office: Chuo-ku, Toray Industries Inc, 2-chome, Nihonbasi-Muromachi, Tokyo Japan *

FUKASHI, FUJITA, retired food manufacturing company executive; b. Kobe, Japan, Aug. 9, 1926; s. Motokichi and Kinu (Terajima) F.; m. Yuriko Matsushita, Feb. 28, 1953; children—Keiko, Yutaka. B. Econs., Kobe U., 1950. Asst. office mgr. Marubeni-Iida Am. Inc., Los Angeles, 1957-61, dep. sect. chief, Tokyo, 1961-62; cons. Japan Mgmt. Assn., Tokyo, 1962-65; asst. mgr. Nestle Japan Ltd., Kobe (now Nestle K. K.), 1965-83, exec. officer in-charge personnel, 1983-86; dir. Nestle Health Ins. Soc., Nestle Mut. Relief Fund. Coordinator donors Japan Red Cross, 1979—. Mem. Tea Ceremony Masters Assn. Clubs: Sun Mems., Japan FCI (Nagoya). Avocations: tea ceremony; noh dancing; music; arts. Home: 764-2 Nishiwaki, Ohkubo-cho, Akashi Japan 674 Office: 1-16 Gokoh-dori 7-chome, Chuo-ku, Kobe 651, Japan

FUKUDA, MASAO, plastics company manufacturing executive; b. Utsunomiya-shi, Japan, Sept. 21, 1944; s. Kaiji and Yoshie Fukuda; m. Akemi Mitsuhashi; children—Masahiro, Emi. A.A., Los Angeles Harbor Jr. Coll., 1968; B.S., Calif. Polt. State U., 1972; M.S., 1974; Ph.D., Oreg. State U., 1981. Instr. Oreg. State U., Corvallis, 1980-81; research engr. research and devel. Union Carbide Co., Boundbrook, N.J., 1981-83; mgr. Nuclear Data Co., Tokyo, 1983-84, Engring. Plastics Ltd., Moka, Japan, 1984—; engring. cons. N.W. Geothermal Co., Portland, Oreg., 1978; research asst. dept. edn. Oreg. State U., 1978-79. Contbr. articles to profl. jours. Mem. ASME (assoc.), Japan Soc. Mech. Engrs. (assoc.). Office: Engring Plastics Ltd, 2-2 Kinugaoka, Moka-shi 321 43, Japan

FUKUDA, MINORU, cancer research scientist; b. Hiroshima, Japan, July 6, 1945; came to U.S., 1975, naturalized, 1980; s. Iwao and Sueko (Fujiwara) F.; m. Michiko Nishida, Apr. 8, 1970; children—Ko, Shun. B.S. in Biochemistry, U. Tokyo, 1968, M.S., 1970, Ph.D., 1973. Research assoc. U. Tokyo, 1973-75; postdoctoral assoc. Yale U., 1975-77; assoc. Hutchinson Cancer Research Ctr., Seattle, 1977-81; asst. prof. U. Wash., Seattle, 1980-81; staff scientist La Jolla (Calif.) Cancer Research Found., 1982—, dir. carbohydrate chemistry lab., 1984—, program dir., 1988—. Author: Biology of Glycoproteins, 1984; also chpts. and articles in profl. publs. Nat. Cancer Inst. grantee, 1981—; NSF grantee, 1983. Mem. Am. Soc. Cell Biology, N.Y. Acad. Scis., Am. Soc. Biol. Chemists. Home: 2818 Passy Ave San Diego CA 92122 Office: La Jolla Cancer Research Found 10901 N Torrey Pines Rd La Jolla CA 92037

FUKUI, HATSUAKI, electrical engineer; b. Yokohama, Japan, Dec. 14, 1927; came to U.S., 1962, naturalized, 1973; s. Ushinosuke and Yoshi (Saito) F.; m. Atsuko Inamoto, Apr. 1, 1954 (dec. 1973); children: Mayumi, Naoki; m. Kiku Kato, Dec. 12, 1975. Diploma, Miyakojima Tech. Coll. (now Osaka City U.), 1949; D.Eng., Osaka U., 1961. Research assoc. Osaka City U., 1949-54; engr. Shimada Phys. and Chem. Indsl. Co., Tokyo, 1954-55; sr. engr. to supr. Sony Corp. semi-condr. div., Tokyo, 1955-61; mgr. engring. div. Sony Corp., 1961-62; mem. tech. staff Bell Telephone Labs., Murray Hill, N.J., 1962-69, supr., 1969-73; v.p. Sony Corp. Am., N.Y.C., 1973; asst. to chmn. Sony Corp., Tokyo, 1973; staff mem. Bell Labs., Murray Hill, N.J., 1973-81; supr. Bell Labs., 1981-83, AT&T Bell Labs., 1984—; lectr. Tokyo Met. U. (part-time), 1962. Author: Esaki Diodes, 1963, Solid-State FM Receivers, 1968; contbr. to: Semiconductors Handbook, 1963, GaAs FET Principles and Technologies, 1982; editor: Low-Noise Microwave Transistors and Amplifiers, 1981; contbr. articles to profl. jours.; patentee in field. Fellow IEEE (standardization com. 1976-82, editorial bd. IEEE Transactions on Microwave Theory and Techniques 1980—, com. on U.S. competitiveness 1988—, Microwave prize 1980); mem. Inst. Electronics, Info. and Communication Engrs. Japan (Inada award 1959), IEEE Communications Soc., IEEE Electron Devices Soc., IEEE Lasers and Electro-Optics Soc., IEEE Microwave Theory and Techniques Soc., com. on U.S. Competiveness, Japan Soc. Applied Physics, Inst. TV Engrs. Japan (tech. com. 1973-75), Gakushi-Kai, Internat. House Japan. Home: 53 Drum Hill Dr Summit NJ 07901 Office: Bell Labs 600 Mountain Ave Murray Hill NJ 07974

FUKUI, KENICHI, chemist; b. Nara, Japan, Oct. 4, 1918; s. Ryokichi and Chie Fukui; m. Tomoe Horie, 1947; 2 children. Student, Kyoto Imperial U. Researcher synthetic fuel chemistry Army Fuel Lab., 1941-45; lectr. in fuel chemistry Kyoto Imperial U., 1943, asst. prof., 1945-51, prof., 1951-82; pres. Kyoto Inst. Tech., 1988; dir. Inst. for Fundamental Chemistry, 1988—; councillor Kyoto U., 1970-73, dean faculty engring., 1971-73, pres. indsl. arts and textile fibres, 1982—; chemist U.S.-Japan Eminent Scientist Exchange Programme, 1973; counselor Inst. Molecular Sci., 1976—;. Contbr. articles to profl. jours. Chmn. exec. com. 3d Internat. Congress Quantum Chemistry, Kyoto, 1979; fgn. assoc. Nat. Acad. Sci., 1981. Sr. Fgn. Scientist fellow NSF, 1970; recipient Japan Acad. medal, 1962, Nobel Prize for chemistry, 1981, Order of Culture award, 1981; named Person of Cultural Merits, 1981. Mem. Am. Acad. Arts and Scis. (hon. mem.), European Acad. Arts Scis. and Humanities, Japan Acad., Pontifical Acad. Scis., Chem. Soc. (v.p. 1978-79, pres. 1983-84). Home: 23 Kitashirakawa-Hiraicho, Sakyo-ku, Kyoto 606, Japan Office: Inst Fundamental Chemistry, 34-4 Takano-Nishihiraki-cho, Sakyo-ku, Kyoto 606, Japan

FUKUNAGA, GEORGE JOJI, corporate executive; b. Waialua, Oahu, Hawaii, Apr. 13, 1924; s. Peter H. and Ruth (Hamamura) F.; B.A., U. Hawaii, 1948; cert. Advanced Mgmt. Program Harvard U./U. Hawaii, 1955; HHD (hon.) U. Hawaii, 1954; m. Alice M. Tagawa, Aug. 5, 1950; 1 son, Mark H. Adminstrv. asst., dir. Service Motor Co., Ltd. (named changed to Servco Pacific Inc. 1969), Honolulu, 1948-52, v.p., 1952-60, pres., 1960—; chmn., 1981—, dir. 14 subsidiaries and affiliates, Service Fin., Ltd. (name now Servco Financial Corp.), 1960-81, Servco Services Corp., Am. Ins. Agy. Inc., Servco Securities Corp., Servco Investment Corp., Servco Calif. Inc., Servco Japan, Inc., Servco Fgn. Sales Corp. (Guam), Hawaiiana Advt. Agy., Pacific Internat. Co. Inc. (Guam), Pacific Fin. Corp. (Guam), Pacific Motors Corp. (Guam), Pacific Internat. Marianas Inc., Saipan, Pacific Marshalls Inc., Majuro; dir. Am. Fin. Services Inc., Am. Trust of Hawaii Inc., Island Ins. Ltd., Hawaiian Pacific Resorts, Inc. Bd. govs. Iolani Sch.; trustee Fukunaga Scholarship Found.; trustee Hawaii Pacific Coll., Contemporary Arts Found., U.S. Army Mus.; bd. govs. Pub. Schs. Found., East-West Ctr. Found. Served to 2d lt. AUS, 1945-47, to 1st lt., 1950-52. Mem. Hawaii (v.p. 1970, 83-84, dir. 1970-75, 82—), Honolulu Japanese (pres. 1969, dir. 1963—) chambers commerce, Hawaii Round Table Council (bd. dirs.), Hawaii Econ. Study Club (pres. 1962), Hawaii-Japan Econ. Council, U.S.-Japan Soc. (dir. 1983—, v.p. 1986—). Methodist. Clubs: Pacific, Plaza (dir.), 200 Rotary, Deputies, Oahu Country. Office: Servco Pacific Inc 900 Fort St Mall Honolulu HI 96813

FUKUSHIMA, TATSUHISA, automotive company executive; b. Tokyo, Mar. 10, 1928; s. Chikuhei Nakajima and Hatsu Fukushima; m. Jinko Tezuka, Mar. 23, 1958; children—Tomoko, Daisuke. B.S., Tokyo U., 1952. Cert. cons. engr., Japan. Research engr. Japan Optical Industries Co. (Nikon), Tokyo, 1952-53; research and devel. engr. Fuji Heavy Industries, Ltd., Tokyo, 1953-71; sr. mgr., engring. dept. F.H.I. Ltd., Tokyo, 1971-81, dep. gen. mgr. Subaru engring. div., 1981-83, dir., dep. gen. mgr., 1983-87, mng. dir., gen. mgr. Subaru Product Planning and Mgmt. div., 1987—. Mem. Japan Soc. Automotive Engrs. Home: 1-8-4 Sakuraga-oka, Tama-City Tokyo 206, Japan Office: FHI Ltd, 1-7-2 Nishi Shinjuku, Shinjuku-ku, Tokyo 160, Japan

FUKUWATARI, ISAO, architect; b. Osaka, Japan, Oct. 13, 1931; s. Rokuro and Misako (Kurata) F.; m. Toyoko Saito, Mar. 6, 1962; children: Sayoko, Jun. B in Tech., U. Osaka, 1955, M in Tech., 1957; postgrad., Hochschule Gestaltung, Ulm, Fed. Republic of Germany, 1962-63; student, Inst. Urbanism, Paris, 1963-64. Registered architect, Japan. Architect Obayashi-Gumi Ltd., Osaka, 1957-60, chief architect, 1964-71; with Candilis, Josic, Woods, Paris, 1960-61, SETAP, Paris, 1961-62, Ecochard, Paris, 1963-64; prin. Fukuwatari Archtl. Cons. Ltd., Tokyo, 1971—; cons. Sekisui System House Ltd., Osaka, 1971—, Fujitsu Ltd., Tokyo, 1980—. Winner archtl. competitions, 1960, 81. Mem. Japan Inst. Architects, Archtl. Inst. Japan, Japan Inst. Hosp. Architecture, Bldg. Ctr. Japan, Assn. Promotion Internat. Cooperation. Clubs: Jingu Tennis, Tojoko Country. Office: Fukuwatari Archtl Cons Ltd, 3-10-7 Kita Aoyama Minato, 107 Tokyo Japan

FULBRIGHT, JAMES WILLIAM, former U.S. senator; b. Sumner, Mo., Apr. 9, 1905; s. Jay and Roberta (Waugh) F.; m. Elizabeth Williams, June 15, 1932; children—Elizabeth (Mrs. John Winnacker), Roberta (Mrs. Edward Thaddeus Foote II). A.B., U. Ark., 1925; B.A., Oxford (Eng.) U., 1928, M.A., 1931; LL.B., George Washington U., 1934. Bar: D.C. 1934. Spl. atty. Anti-Trust Div. U.S. Dept. Justice, 1934-35; instr. in law George Washington U., 1935-36; lectr. in law U. Ark., 1936-39, pres., 1939-41; mem. 78th congress from 3d Dist. Ark.; U.S. senator from Ark., 1945-74; mem. com. on fin., mem. joint econ. com., chmn. com. on fgn. relations; of counsel firm Hogan & Hartson, Washington, 1975—; Del. 9th Gen. Assembly UN, 1954. Mem. Sigma Chi. Democrat. Mem. Disciples of Christ Ch. Club: Rotarian. Office: Hogan & Hartson 555 13th St Washington DC 20004-1109

FULBROOK, MARY JEAN ALEXANDRA, educator; b. Cardiff, Wales, Eng., Nov. 28, 1951; d. Arthur James Cochran and Harriett Charlotte (Friedeberg) Wilson; m. Julian George Holder Fulbrook, June 28, 1973; children Conrad Arthur, Carl Howard, Erica Harriett (twins). MA, Cambridge U., 1970-73; AM, Harvard U., 1975, PhD, 1979. Research fellow Cambridge U., Eng., 1979-82, Kings Coll., London, 1982-83; lectr. German History U. Coll., London, 1983—. Author: Piety and Politics, 1983; editor: German History; contbr. articles to profl. jours. Grantee British Acad., London, 1984, 86. Fellow Royal Hist. Soc.; mem. German History Soc. (exec. com. 1981—), Assn. for the Study of German Politics. Labour. Office: Univ Coll London, Gower St, London England

FULCOMER, JAMES JOSEPH, educator; b. Elizabeth, N.J., Nov. 20, 1943; s. James Samuel and Josephine Mary (Decker) F.; m. Katherine Eleanor Harms, Nov. 15, 1967; children: Jennifer Jean, Jacqueline Jayne, Jason James. BE, Kean Coll., 1966; MA in Polit. Sci., NYU, 1972. Cert. high sch. tchr., N.J. Tchr. history and polit. sci. Elizabeth High Sch., 1968—; councilman City of Rahway, N.J., 1977—; moderator Bd. Deacons, 1986-87. Co-editor Union County AFL-CIO News, 1972-73. Mem. solid waste disposal com. Union County, Elizabeth, 1972-74, mem. environ. health com., 1972-76, labor adv. bd., 1986—, liaison for adv. bd. on edn., 1987; chmn. Union County Utilities Authority, 1986-87; liaison adv. bd. Mus. Union County History, 1987-88; alt. del. Nat. Republican Nominating Conv., Miami, Fla., 1972; chmn. Rahway Rep. Com., 1973-77, 78-79, 81—; mem. exec. bd. Young Rep. Nat. Fedn., Washington, 1975-78; chmn. Young Reps. of N.J., Inc., 1977-78; 2d vice chmn. Union County Rep. Com., 1980-81; mem. Union County Bd. Freeholders, 1986—. Recipient Commendation award Union County Bd. Chosen Freeholders, 1976, Most Outstanding Young Rep. in N.J. award Young Reps. of N.J., 1978; named Outstanding Young Man of Am., U.S. Jaycees, 1978. Mem. Elizabeth Tchrs. Union (v.p. 1972-82), Elizabeth Edn. Assn. (council rep. 1969-71), Rahway C. of C. (pub. relations officer 1982-83). Presbyterian. Club: Rahway Rep. (pres. 1972-73). Lodge: Lions (pres. 1980-81). Home: 1142 Midwood Dr Rahway NJ 07065 Office: Elizabeth High Sch Halsey House 600 Pearl St Elizabeth NJ 07202

FULDA, MICHAEL, political science educator, space policy researcher; b. Liverpool, Eng., Apr. 21, 1939; came to U.S., 1962, naturalized, 1966; s. Boris and Catherine (Von Dehn) F.; m. Rosa Bongiorno, July 19, 1970; children—Robert, George. Student Polytechnique, Grenoble, France, 1956-57, Tech. U., West Berlin, Germany, 1957-58, Karl Eberhardt Coll., Tubingen, Germany, 1963-66; M.A., Am. U., 1968, Ph.D. in Internat. Studies, 1970. Prof. polit. sci. Fairmont State Coll., W.Va., 1971—; internat. relations specialist NASA, Washington, summer 1979; fellow NASA Marshall Ctr., Huntsville, Ala., summer 1977, Langley Ctr., Hampton, Va., summer, 1976. Author: Oil and International Relations, 1979; (with others) United States Space Policy, 1985. Contbr. articles to profl. jours. Bd. dirs. Faimont Chamber Music Soc., 1983—; W.Va. state com. chmn., dir. space policy Nat. Unity Campaign for John Anderson, 1980; mem. nat. adv. com. John Glenn Presdl. Com., 1984. Served with U.S. Army, 1962-66. Woodrow Wilson Found. fellow, 1969-70; Humanities Found. W.Va. grantee, 1978-80. Mem. AIAA, Am. Astronautical Soc., Nat. Space Soc., World Future Soc. (pres. W.Va. chpt. 1977-80), Nat. Space Club, Inst. for the Social Sci. Study of Space (pres. 1988—). Home: 1 Timothy Ln Fairmont WV 26554

FULGHUM, JAMES T., management consultant; b. Fla., July 12, 1923; m. Marla Tyrolerin. Diploma Indsl. Engring.; MBA, Harvard U. Various exec. positions with ITT, German-speaking Europe, 1950-64; joined Boyden Assn., Geneva, 1964; established 1st European operation of Eastman-Fulghum Group, 1966; Eastman-Fulghum merged with a North and South Am. group to form Cons. Ptnrs. Inc., Munich, Zurich, Brussels, London, N.Y.C., San Francisco,, Los Angeles, Mexico City, Caracas, Sao Paolo and Buenos Aires, 1972; founded Consilium AG. Home: Weinmanngasse 118, 8700 Kusnacht Switzerland Office: Consilium AG, Seefeldstr 102, CH-8008 Zurich Switzerland

FULKS, ROBERT GRADY, computer executive; b. Kansas City, Mo., Apr. 8, 1936; s. Hilburne Grady and Dora Elouise (Johnson) F.; children—Stephanie, Scott Grady. B.S.E.E., M.I.T., 1958, M.S.E.E., 1959. Engr., chief engr. v.p. engring. and product mktg. GenRad, Inc. (formerly Gen. Radio Co.), Concord, Mass., 1959-73; pres. Mirco Systems, Inc., 1973-75, Omnicomp, Inc., Phoenix, 1975-80, gen. mgr. advanced tech div. (formerly Omnicomp, Inc.) GenRad, Inc., Phoenix, 1980-86, also v.p. parent co.; v.p. engring. Telesis Systems Corp., Chelmsford, Mass., 1986-87; v.p., gen. mgr. Valid Logic Systems PCB CAD div., 1987—; bd. dirs. Cirrus Sigma Ltd., Fareham, Eng., Texcon Corp., Phoenix, Custom Data Mgmt. Inc., Phoenix, Markwood, Inc., Phoenix, Office Tech. Ltd., Boston. Mem. IEEE, Assn. Computing Machinery, Concord C. of C. (former bd. dirs., chmn. fin. com.), Sigma Xi. Contbr. articles tech. jours. Patentee in field. Office: 2 Omni Way Chelmsford MA 01824

FULLBRIGHT, WILBUR D., educator; b. Spearman, Tex., Jan. 19, 1926; s. Ralph Robert and Myrtle Ella (Files) F., m. Lorraine Barker, Jan. 2, 1947; children—Glen Arthur, Karl Robert, Dale Norman. B.A., Okla. State U., 1950; M.F.A., Bob Jones U., 1953; Ph.D., Boston U., 1956. Faculty, Bob Jones U., Greenville, S.C., 1953-56; registrar and asst. prof. music Boston U., 1957-59; asst. dean Sch. for Arts and assoc. prof. Boston U., 1959-66, dir. Sch. Music and prof., 1966-80, prof. music, 1980—, assoc. dean for acad. affairs, 1983—; mem. adv. bd. Internat. Inst. for Advanced Musical Studies, Sion, Switzerland, 1972-75. Mem. Bd. dirs. Greater Boston Youth Symphony Orchestra, 1966—; bd. advisors Walnut Hill Sch., Natick, Mass., 1970—, chmn. cultural exchange Ptnrs. of the Americas, 1971—; bd. govs. Handel and Haydn Soc., Boston, 1976—. Mem. Pi Kappa Lambda (bd. regents 1966—, pres. 1966-70). Home: 1059 Beacon St Brookline MA 02146 Office: Boston Univ Sch for Arts 855 Commonwealth Ave Boston MA 02215

FULLER, HARRY LAURANCE, oil company executive; b. Moline, Ill., Nov. 8, 1938; s. Marlin and Mary Helen (Ilsley) F.; m. Nancy Lawrence, Dec. 27, 1961; children: Kathleen, Laura, Randall. B.S. in Chem. Engring., Cornell U., 1961; J.D., DePaul U., 1965. Bar: Ill. 1965. With Standard Oil Co. (and affiliates), 1961—, sales mgr., 1972-74, gen. mgr. supply, 1974-77; exec. v.p. Standard Oil Co. (Amoco Oil Co. div.), Chgo., 1977-78; pres. Amoco Oil Co., Chgo., 1978-81; exec. v.p. Standard Oil Co. of Ind. (now Amoco Corp.), Chgo., 1981-83, pres., 1983—; bd. dirs. Chase Manhattan Corp., Chase Manhattan Bank N.A., Am. Petroleum Inst. Bd. dirs. Chgo. Rehab. Inst.; trustee Northwestern U., Orchestral Assn., Art Inst. Chgo.; bd. dirs. central area com. Chgo. United. Mem. Ill. Bar Assn. Republican. Presbyterian. Clubs: Mid-Am, Chgo. Golf, Chicago. Office: Amoco Corp 200 E Randolph Dr Chicago IL 60601 *

FULLER, JACQUELINE KAY, university administrator; b. London, May 29, 1939. BA, U. Southampton, Eng., 1960. Exec. sec. Sci. Policy Research Unit, U. Sussex, Brighton, 1966—. Mem. Assn. U. Tchrs., Conf. U. Adminstrs. Office: Sci Policy Research Unit, U Sussex Falmer, Brighton E Sussex BN1 9RF, England

FULLER, LEE DENNISON, nursing educator, therapist; b. Oceana County, Mich., June 7, 1910; s. Arthur Oglethorpe and Georgiana Katrina (Dennison) F. Diploma in nursing, McLean Hosp., 1932; BS, N.Y.U., 1949, MA, 1950; EdD, Ind. U., 1970. RN, Mass., Ind. Staff nurse N.Y. State Psychiat. Inst., N.Y.C., 1944-52; dir. in-service edn. Jacksonville (Ill.) State Hosp., 1953-55; edn. cons. Ind. Dept. Mental Health, Indpls., 1955-60; prof. nursing Ind. U., Indpls., 1955-80, prof. emeritus, 1980—; pvt. practice psychotherapy Bloomington, Ind., 1982—; cons. Reid Meml. Hosp., Richmond, Ind., 1973-74, 77, Ind. State Prison, Mich. City., Ind., 1973, Psychodrama Ind. Meth. Ch., 1979-81, Marion (Ind.) Vets. Hosp., 1977-83; adj. staff therapist South Cen. Community Mental Health Ctr., Bloomington, 1975-85. Leader Boy Scouts U.S., Belmont, Mass., 1932-36, N.Y.C., 1944-48; layreader Trinity Epsicopal Ch., N.Y.C., 1943-52, Jacksonville, 1953-54, Bloomington, 1956-65. Recipient Disting. Service award to Non-Mem. Ind. U. Nurses Alumni Assn., 1981. Mem. Am. Nurses Assn. (pres. dist. 16 1968-72, Lit. award, cert.), Am. Group Psychotherapy Assn., Am. Soc. Group Psychotherapy and Psychodrama, Am. Assn. Marriage and Family Therapy, Tri-State Group Psychotherapy Assn. (pres. 1978-79), Oceana County Hist. Soc. Club: Ruby Creek Conservation (Mich.). Home: 600 E 2d St Bloomington IN 47401

FULLER, MARY FALVEY, management consultant; b. Detroit, Oct. 28, 1941; d. Lawrence C. and Mathilde G. Falvey; m. James W. Fuller, Aug. 22, 1981. BA in Econs. with honors, Cornell U., 1963; MBA, Harvard U., 1967. Systems engr. IBM Corp., N.Y.C., 1963-65; mgmt. cons. McKinsey & Co., Inc., N.Y.C., 1967-75; v.p. Citibank, N.A., N.Y.C., 1975-78, head asset servicing div., 1977-78; sr. v.p., dir., head adminstrn. div., mem. exec. com., mem. operating com. Blyth Eastman Dillon & Co., Inc., N.Y.C., 1978-80; pres. M.C. Falvey Assocs., Inc., N.Y.C., 1980-81; v.p. fin. Shaklee Corp., San Francisco, 1981-82; pres. Falvey Autos, Inc., Troy, Mich., 1978—, also chmn., bd. dirs.; trustee Fed. Hosp. Ins. Trust Fund, Fed. Old Age and Survivors Ins. Trust Fund, Fed. Disability Ins. Trust Fund, 1984—, Williamsburg Charter Found. 1988—; dir. Tech. Funding Inc., 1983—; mem. regional dealer adv. council Toyota Motor Sales Corp. Mem. Com. for N.Y. Philharmonic, 1975-77; mem. 1979 Adv. Council on Social Security, 1979-80, Pres. Reagan's Transition Task Force on Social Security, 1979-80, Nat. Commn. on Social Security Reform, 1982-83; adminstrv. bd. Cornell U. Council, 1984-86; trustee fellow Cornell U., 1988—; mem. adminstrn. and legal processes adv. council Mills Coll., 1982-85; chmn. bd. trustees San Francisco Performances, 1982—. Harvard Bus. Sch. grantee, 1965-67. Republican. Episcopalian. Club: Commonwealth of Calif. (chmn. Asia Pacific study sect., program com. 1983-85, chmn. Asia-Pacific study sect.). Home and Office: 2584 Filbert St San Francisco CA 94123

FULLER, RICHARD JOSEPH, accountant; b. Yonkers, N.Y., Oct. 14, 1945; s. Joseph V. and Catherine (Tracey) F.; B.B.A., Pace U., 1967, postgrad., 1973; M.A., U. Mo., 1968; postgrad. U. Md. in Germany, 1969. With Exxon Corp., N.Y.C., 1967-68, Arthur Young & Co., C.P.A.'s, N.Y.C., Tampa, Fla., 1970-77, Kurt T. Borowsky, C.P.A., Largo, Fla., 1977-80; pres. Richard J. Fuller, C.P.A., P.A., Clearwater, Fla., 1980—; grad. asst. U. Mo., 1967-68; faculty Opportunities Indsl. Council, N.Y., 1971-72. Mem. Pinellas Estate Planning Council, 1978—. Served with U.S. Army, 1968-70. C.P.A., Fla., N.Y. Mem. Am. Inst. C.P.A.'s, N.Y. Soc. C.P.A.'s, Fla. Inst. C.P.A.'s (chmn. com. on membership services), Greater Clearwater C. of C. Republican. Roman Catholic. Club: Civitan. Home: 2576 Laurelwood Dr Clearwater FL 33515 Office: 2240 Belleair Rd Suite 295 Clearwater FL 34624

FULLER, ROBERT L(EANDER), lawyer; b. N.Y.C., Sept. 8, 1943; s. Robert Leander and Elsie Virginia Fuller; m. Barbara Braverman, Dec. 5, 1973. BS cum laude, SUNY, Stony Brook, 1971; MBA, Columbia U., 1972; JD, Cath. U., Washington, 1977; M. Laws in Taxation, Georgetown U., 1981. Bar: Md. 1977, D.C. 1978. Acct. Ernst & Whinney, N.Y.C., 1972-74; controller Warner-Jenkinson East Inc., N.Y.C., 1974-75, Atomic Indsl. Forum, Inc., N.Y.C., Washington, 1975-76; tax analyst So. Rwy. Co., Washington, 1976-78; asst. tax counsel CACI, Inc., Arlington, Va., 1978-84; tax counsel, mgr. VSE Corp., Alexandria, Va., 1984-87, dir. taxes Newmont Mining Corp., N.Y.C., 1987-88, CIBA Corning Diagnostics Corp., Medfield, Mass., 1988—. Served with USN, 1961-67. CPA, N.Y., D.C. Mem. ABA (tax sect.), Tax Execs. Inst. (chpt. dir. and officer 1983-87), Am. Inst. CPA's, Mayflower Descendants, SAR, Sigma Pi Sigma. Home: 4700 Connecticut Ave NW Apt 203 Washington DC 20008-5611 Office: CIBA Corning Diagnostics Corp 63 North St Medfield MA 02052

FULLER, SHARON S., insurance agent; b. Hagerstown, Md., Sept. 6, 1946; d. Gerald Browning and Lillian Dorathy (Lane) Smith. Student schs. Hagerstown. Cert. ins. agt., Fla.; lic. ins. rep., mgr. With Washington Adventist Hosp., Takoma Park, Md., 1968-79; word processing coordinator Fla. Hosp., Orlando, 1979-84; info. systems adminstr. Broad & Cassel, Miami, Fla., 1984-85; ins. agt., Orlando, 1985—; owner, gen. mgr. Fuller Agy., 1987—. Contbr. articles to profl. publ. Active Competency Evaluation Com. Orange County Pub. Schs., Orlando, 1984-85. Mem. Assn. Info. Systems Profls. (v.p. 1985). Seventh-day Adventist. Avocations: reading; travel. Home: 8712 Gopher Ln Orlando FL 32829 Office: Fuller Agy PO Box 720356 Orlando FL 32822

FULLER, WALLACE HAMILTON, research scientist, educator; b. Old Hamilton, Alaska, Apr. 15, 1915; s. Henry Ray and Bessie (Gaines) F.; m. Winifred Elizabeth Dow, Dec. 23, 1939; 1 dau., Pamela Elizabeth. B.S., Wash. State U., 1937, M.S., 1939; Ph.D., Iowa State U., 1942. Research asst. Wash. State U., Pullman, 1937-39; soil surveyor U.S. Dept. Agr., Lancaster, Wis., Neosho, Mo., 1939-40; bacteriologist U.S. Dept. Agr., Beltsville, Md., 1945-47; soil scientist U.S. Dept. Agr., 1947-48; research asso. Iowa State U., Ames, 1940-45; asso. prof., biochemist U. Ariz., Tucson, 1948-56; prof., biochemist, head dept. agrl. chemistry and soils U. Ariz., 1956-72, prof., biochemist soils, water and engring. dept., 1972—, prof. soil and water sci. dept., 1985—, prof. emeritus; cons. in field; poet-in-residence Ariz. State Hist. Soc., 1987—. Fellow Am. Soc. Agronomy and Soil Sci., AAAS, N.Y. Acad. Sci.; mem. Am. Chem. Soc., Am. Soc. Biol. Sci., Am. Soc. Plant Physiologists, Sigma Xi, Phi Kappa Phi, Phi Lambda Upsilon, Gamma Sigma Delta, Alpha Zeta. Presbyterian. Home: 5674 W Flying Circle Tucson AZ 85713

FULLERTON, ROBERT VICTOR, lawyer; b. Lakewood, Ohio, Mar. 30, 1918; s. Victor G. and Gertrude H. (Horsley) F.; B.S. in Bus., Miami U., Oxford, Ohio, 1939; LL.B., Western Res. U., 1941; m. Frances Riebel, Aug. 23, 1941; children—Susan Anne, Thomas George. Admitted to Calif. bar, Ohio bar, U.S. Supreme Ct.; spl. agt. FBI, 1941-46; dep. dist. atty. San Bernardino County (Calif.), 1946, asst. dist. atty., 1946-47; individual practice law, San Bernardino, 1947—; chmn. San Bernardino County U.S. Savs. Bond Com. Dept. Treasury, 1963—; mem. adv. bd. Automobile Club of So. Calif., 1969-80. Pres. United Fund, San Bernardino, 1961-62; trustee Found. for Calif. State U.-San Bernardino, 1981—; bd. dirs. Inland Action, 1974—; Inland Area Symphony Assn., 1983—, v.p. 1986— ; bd. dirs. Estate Planning Council of San Bernadino County, 1984—; chmn. planning div. United Community Services, San Bernardino, 1966-69. Recipient Citizens of Yr. award San Bernardino Realtors, 1967. Mem. Am. Bar Assn., State Bar Calif., Am. Judicature Soc., Air Force Assn. (pres. local chpt. 1969-70), San Bernardino C. of C. (pres. 1968-69). Republican. Clubs: Kiwanis (pres. local club 1959-60), Arrowhead Country, Elks. Home: 3255 N Valencia St San Bernardino CA 92404 Office: 472 N Arrowhead Ave San Bernardino CA 92401

FULLING, KATHARINE PAINTER, educator, writer; b. Dodge City, Kans., Aug. 6; d. William George and Carrie (Lopp) Painter; BA, Northwestern U., 1940; MA, Columbia U., 1947; postgrad. Vassar Coll., 1948, San Marcos U., Lima, Peru, 1948-49, (fellow) Inst. Internat. Edn., U. Madrid, Spain, 1952-53; m. Virgil H. Fulling, Sept. 24, 1948. Asst. dir. Casa Panamericana, Mills Coll., 1944; asst. to dir. Fine Arts Dept., Columbia U., N.Y.C., 1945-47; tchr. public schs. Port Washington, L.I., N.Y., 1953-55; lectr. Global Edn., UN, N.Y.C., 1953-56; public relations dir. Nat. League Am. Pen Women, Washington, 1958-60; Non-Govtl. Orgns. rep. United Women of the Ams., UN, N.Y.C., 1959-62; lectr. Asia and Africa Halls, Smithsonian Inst., Washington, 1965-69; lectr. Folger Shakespeare Library, Washington, 1969-73; art reviewer Wyo., Denver Art Mus., 1974—; mem. nat. adv. bd. for Bob Dole's Presdl. campaign, 1988—, Nat. Trust for Historic Preservation, Washington, 1987—; charter mem. Nat. Mus. Women in Arts, 1987—. Mem. Wyo. Council for Humanities, 1979-80; bd. dirs. Am. Security Council, Washington. Mem. Asia Soc., Inter-Am. Center, AAUW, Nat. League Am. Pen Women (Woman of Achievement award 1973), LWV (pres. 1967-69), Nat. Mus. Women in the Arts (charter), Buffalo Bill Hist. Mus., Mark Twain Soc. (hon. mem.), Sigma Alpha Iota, Kappa Delta. Club: National Press (Washington). Author: The Cradle of American Art, 1948; Mantillas and Silver Spurs, 1952; contbr., columnist numerous jours. and mags. Address: 1295 Race St Apt 312 Denver CO 80206

FULLMAN, JANICE ELAINE, dance adjudicator; b. Welwyn, Hertfordshire, Eng., Aug. 24, 1944; d. Joseph Steward and Doris Rose (Brown) F. A of Dance, The Arts Ednl. Schs., Tring, Herts, 1964; degree in dance, The Arts Ednl. Schs., London, 1965; teaching diploma, London Coll. of Dance and Drama, 1968. Cert. tchr. dance and drama. Dance tchr. The Internat. Dance Tchrs. Assn., Brighton, Eng., 1968, examiner of dancing, 1974; adjudicator of festivals British Fedn. of Music Festivals and All-Eng. Dance Competitions, Macclesfield, Eng., 1975; prin. The Jandor Sch. of Dancing, Cambridge and Loughton, Eng., 1968—. Essex County Council grantee, 1960; recipient Major award Essex County Council, 1965. Fellow and examiner Internat. Dance Tchrs. Assn.; Imperial Soc. of Tchrs. of Dancing (assoc.). Mem. Ch. of Eng. Home and Office: 69 Tower Ct, Westcliff on Sea SS0 7QH, England

FULLMER, HAROLD MILTON, dentist, educator; b. Gary, Ind., July 9, 1918; s. Howard and Rachel Eva (Tiedge) F.; m. Marjorie Lucile Engel, Dec. 31, 1942 (dec. Apr. 1983); children: Angela Sue, Pamela Rose; m. Shirley Ford Davis, Mar. 28, 1987. B.S., Ind. U., 1942, D.D.S., 1944; hon. doctorate, U. Athens (Greece), 1981. Diplomate: Am. Bd. Oral Pathology. Intern Charity Hosp., New Orleans, 1946-47, resident, 1947-48, vis. dental surgeon, 1948-53; instr. Loyola U., New Orleans, 1948-49, asst. prof., 1949-50, assoc. prof. gen. and oral pathology, 1949-53; cons. pathology VA hosps., Biloxi and Gulfport, Miss., 1950-53; asst. dental surgeon Nat. Inst. Dental Research, NIH, Bethesda, Md., 1953-54; dental surgeon Nat. Inst. Dental Research, NIH, 1954-56, sr. dental surgeon, 1956-60, dental dir., 1960-70; chief sect. histochemistry Nat. Inst. Dental Research, 1967-70, chief exptl. pathology, 1969-70, cons. to dir., 1971-72; mem. dental caries program adv. com. HEW, 1975-79, chmn., 1976-79; dir. Inst. Dental Research; prof. pathology, prof. dentistry, assoc. dean Sch. Dentistry, U. Ala. Med. Center, Birmingham, 1970—; sr. scientist cancer research and tng. program, sci. adv. com. Sch. Dentistry, U. Ala. Med. Center (Diabetes Research and Tng. Center), 1977-87; mem. med. research career devel. com. VA, 1977-81; mem. com. grants and allocations Am. Fund for Dental Health, 1977-83. Editor: (with R. D. Lillie) Histopathologic Technic and Practical Histochemistry, 1976, Jour. Oral Pathology, 1972—, Tissue Reactions, 1976-88 ; assoc. editor: Jour. Cutaneous Pathology, 1973-83, Oral Surgery, Oral Medicine, Oral Pathology, 1970. Served to capt. AUS, 1944-46. Recipient Isaac Schour award for outstanding research and teaching in anat. scis. Internat. Assn. Dental Research, 1973, Disting. Alumnus of yr. award Ind. U. Sch. Dentistry, 1978; Disting. Alumnus of yr. award Ind. U., 1981; Fulbright grantee, 1961. Fellow Am. Coll. Dentists, Am. Acad. Oral Pathology (v.p. 1984-85, pres.-elect 1985-86, pres. 1986-87), AAAS (chmn. sect. 1976-78, sec. sect. 1979-87); mem. ADA (cons. Council Dental Research 1973-74), Internat. Assn. Dental Research (v.p. 1974-75, pres. 1976-77, pres. Exptl. Pathology Group 1985-86), Am. Assn. Dental Research (pres. 1976-77), Internat. Assn. Pathologists, Histochem. Soc., Nat. Soc. Med. Research (dir. 1977-79), Biol. Stain Commn. (trustee 1977—), Commd. Officers Assn., Internat. Assn. Oral Pathologists (co-founder, 1st pres. 1979-81, 1st editor 1978—). Club: Exchange (Birmingham) (pres. New Orleans 1952-53). Home: 3514 Bethune Dr Birmingham AL 35223

FULOP, CHRISTINA ROSE, educator, researcher, consultant; b. London, Feb. 6, 1926; d. Christopher John and Rosina (Foster) Harms; m. Walter Fulop, Oct. 11, 1947; children: Ruth Ann, Noami Judith, Mark John. BSc in Econs. with honors, U. London, 1948; PhD in Econs., Brunnel U., Uxbridge, Middlesex, 1980. Asst. editor 'Stores and Shops', London, 1949-55; extra-mural lectr. U. London, 1964-66; lectr. City of London Poly., 1968-74, prin. lectr., 1974-83, prof. mktg., 1983—; vis. lectr. univs. in South Korea, Hongkong, Czechoslovakia, 1985-87; cons., expert witness Registrar Restrictive Trade Practices, London, 1966-68; mem. consumer safeguards com. Ministry of Agriculture and Dept. of Prices and Consumer Protection, London, 1977-80; appointed mem. Milk Mktg. Bd., London, 1976—. Author: Buying by Voluntary Chains, 1962, Competition for Consumers, 1966, Advertising, Competition and Consumer Behaviour, 1980, Retailer Advertising and Retail Competion, 1986; also author of monographs and articles on Retail Distribution, Consumer Protection and Marketing. Office: City of London Poly, 84 Moorgate, London EC2M 6SP, England

FULTON, MICHAEL, language consultant; b. Portsmouth, Hampshire, Eng., Apr. 26, 1938; s. Henry and Norah (Conolly) F.; m. Rosa Leonor Berrios; children: Maria Caroline Fiona, Christopher Javier Michael. BS in Chemistry, U. Birmingham, Eng., 1959, PhD in Chemistry, 1963. Sr. lectr., leader research team U. Chile, Santiago, 1964-66; mktg. exec., devel. chemist Midland Silicones Ltd., Barry, Wales, 1966-70; sr. ptnr. 20th Century Translators and Interpreters, Woodcote, Reading, Eng., 1970—. Contbr. articles to profl. jours.; patentee in field. U. Birmingham research fellow, 1963. Fellow Inst. Linguistics; mem. Inst. Translating and Interpreting, Royal Yachting Assn. (yachtmaster Dept. Trade and Industry). Clubs: Goring Thames Sailing (sec., rear and vice comdr.), Hamble River Sailing.

FULWEILER, SPENCER BIDDLE, photo processing cons.; b. West Chester, Pa., Aug. 26, 1913; s. Walter Herbert and Lydia (Baird) F.; B.S. in Chemistry, Harvard U., 1937; m. Patricia Louise Platt, Oct. 5, 1946; children—Marie-Louise, Pamela Spencer, Hull Platt, Spencer Biddle. Owner, Color Photolab., Phila., 1938-42; technician Product Service Lab. and Film Quality-Control, Ansco, Binghamton, N.Y., 1946-48; dir. research Photo-Finishing Inst., N.Y.C., 1948-54; dir. process control Berkey Photo Service, N.Y.C., 1954-79. Tchr., St. James Ch. Sch., N.Y.C., 1958-69. Served to lt. comdr. USNR, 1942-46; CBI. Mem. Am. Chem. Soc., Soc. Photog. Scientists and Engrs. Republican. Episcopalian. Clubs: Norwalk Yacht, N.Y. Yacht, St. Nicholas Soc. Patentee silver recovery from photog. solutions. Home: 158 E 83d St New York NY 10028

FUMI, FAUSTO GHERARDO, physicist, educator; b. Milan, Italy, Aug. 22, 1924; s. Riccardo and Elfrida (Fischer) F.; m. Lina Buiatti, Jan. 26, 1951; children—Renata, Elena. M.Sc. in Phys. Chemistry, U. Genoa (Italy), 1946, D.Sc. in Physics, 1948; postdoctoral fellow Carnegie Inst. Tech., 1948-49, U. Ill., 1949-51. Lectr. statis. mechanics U. Milan, 1951-54; research fellow Cavendish Lab., U. Cambridge, 1954-55; prof. theoretical physics U. Palermo, 1955-57, U. Pavia, 1957-59; research cons. IBM Research Lab., Yorktown Heights, N.Y., 1959-60; vis. research prof. physics Cornell U., Ithaca, N.Y., 1960; sr. scientist Argonne (Ill.) Nat. Lab., 1961-65; prof. physics Northwestern U., Evanston, Ill., 1962-66; prof. theoretical physics, dir. Inst. Physics, U. Palermo, 1966-69; vis. prof. H. H. Wills Physics Lab., U. Bristol (U.K.), 1974-75; Royal Soc. vis. prof. dept. theoretical physics U. Oxford (U.K.), 1978-79; prof. solid state physics U. Genoa, 1969—; mem. Commn. des Publs. Francaises de Physique, 1973-78; mem. nat. physics com. Italian Research Council, 1974-76; mem. solid state commn. Internat. Union Pure and Applied Physics, 1972-78. Author: Quantochimica, 1951; Lezioni di Fisica dello Stato Solido, 1974; editor; Physics of Semiconductors, 1976; co-editor Highlights of Consenses Matter Theory, 1985; advisory editor Europhysics Letters; mem. editorial adv. bd. Jour. Physics and Chemistry of Solids, Semiconductors and Insulators, Crystal Lattice Defects and Amorphous Solids. Recipient Poma Prize, Accademia dei Lincei, Rome, 1951, Gold medal Italian Ministry Pub. Edn., 1986. Fellow Am. Phys. Soc., British Inst. Physics; mem. European Phys. Soc. (mem. council 1981-84), Académie Européenne Des Scis., Italian Phys. Soc., N.Y. Acad. Scis., Sigma Xi. Republican. Roman Catholic Research on Solid State theory, especially tensor properties, ionic crystals and point defects. Home: Via Solimano 77 Sori, Genoa Italy Office: U Genoa, Dipartimento di Fisica, Via Dodecaneso 33, 16146 Genoa Italy

FUNABA, MASATOMI, political economy educator; b. Wakayama-Ken, Japan, Feb. 20, 1938; s. Masao and Fujiko (Taki) F.; m. Kimiko Komuro, Oct. 7, 1968; children: Hisamichi, Chisumi, Yuki. BA, Kyoto U., 1960, LittM, 1962, M in Econs., 1966, D in Econs., 1974. Assoc. prof. Ryukoku U., Kyoto, Japan, 1969-76; assoc. prof. Hiroshima (Japan) U., 1976-80, prof., 1980; prof. Grad. Sch., 1978—; mem. Com. Local Fin., Osaka, Prefecture, Japan, 1975—, Com. Housing, Osaka, 1980—, Com. Indsl. Policy, Min. of Internat. Trade and Industry of Japan at Hiroshima, 1980—; chmn. Com. on Taxing, Kyoto-shi, Japan, 1976—; vis. prof. U. Lille II, France, 1988. Author: History of British Public Credit, 1971, Local Finance in Japan, 1974, Choice of Environment, 1986; editor: Life of Information Era, 1985. Mem. Internat. Inst. Pub. Fin. Buddhist. Home: 29-9 Ansyu Babahigashi Yamashina, Kyoto-shi 607, Japan Office: Hiroshima U Faculty Integrated Arts and Scis, 1-89 Higashisenda-cho Naka-ku, Hiroshima 730, Japan

FUNG, HO WANG, venereologist; b. Hong Kong, Oct. 17, 1951; s. Ping Kee and Pui Tak (Lui) F.; m. Anita Man Yuen Yue, July, 1983. MBBS, U. Hong Kong, 1975; diploma in venereology, U. Liverpool, Eng., 1979. Venereologist Sexually Transmitted Diseases Clinic, Hong Kong, 1979-85, venereologist in charge, 1985—. Contbr. articles to profl. jours. Queen's Scout award Queen Elizabeth, 1969. Mem. Med. Soc. for Study Venereal Disease, Am. Venereal Disease Assn., Hong Kong Med. Assn. Lodge: Lions (Hong Kong chpt. pres. 1983-84). Office: STD Clinic, 306A Tung Ying Bldg, 100 Nathan Rd, Kowloon Hong Kong

FUNG, KWOK PUI, biochemistry educator; b. Hong Kong, July 11, 1951; s. Moon and Lai (Moong) F.; m. Fung Kuen Leung, Dec. 12, 1976; children: Chi Yan, Chi Hang. BSc, The Chinese U. Hong Kong, 1973, M in Biochemistry, 1975; PhD in Microbiology, U. Hong Kong, 1978. Asst. lectr. dept. biochemistry The Chinese U. Hong Kong, 1978-79, lectr. dept. biochemistry, 1979-87, sr. lectr. dept. biochemistry, 1987—; dean of students United Coll. The Chinese U. Hong Kong, 1982-85, Shaw Coll. The Chinese U. Hong Kong, 1987—. Trustee Shaw Coll. The Chinese U. Hong Kong, 1988—. Mem. Hong Kong Biochemistry Assn. (hon. treas. 1979-81), Hong Kong Soc. Microbiology (hon. sec. 1981-84), United Coll. Alumni Assn. The Chinese U. Hong Kong (v.p. 1986—). Club: The Royal Hong Kong Jockey. Home: The Chinese U Hong Kong, 8A Staff Residence 5, Shatin, NT Hong

Kong Office: The Chinese U Hong Kong, Dept Biochemistry, Shatin Hong Kong

FUNG, RAYMOND SAI-CHEUNG, physician; b. Hong Kong, Jan. 24, 1937; s. Hing Tong and Wai Fong (Ip) F.; m. Yuk Ngan Choy, Dec. 21, 1969; children: Celine, Kaiser, Annette, Pius. MBBS, U. Hong Kong, 1965. Medical and health officer Yaumatei Jockey Club Polyclin., Kowloon, Hong Kong, 1967-68; supr. Li Po Chun Health Ctr., Kowloon, 1968-69; gen. practice medicine Kowloon, 1969—; med. cons. Jr. Police Officers Assn. Royal Hong Kong Police, 1979—. Mem. Brit. Med. Assn., Hong Kong Med. Assn., Hong Kong Coll. Gen. Practitioners. Clubs: Royal Jockey, Kowloon Tong. Office: 442 Nathan Rd 1/F, Kowloon Hong Kong

FUNK, CYRIL REED, JR., agronomist, educator; b. Richmond, Utah, Sept. 20, 1928; s. Cyril Reed and Hazel Marie (Jensen) F.; m. Donna Gwen Buttars, Feb. 2, 1951; children: Bonnie Arlene, David Christopher, Carol Jean. B.S. (Scholarship A 1955), Utah State U., 1952, M.S., 1955; Ph.D., Rutgers U., 1961. Mem. faculty Rutgers U., New Brunswick, N.J., 1956—; research prof. turfgrass breeding soils and crop dept. Rutgers U., 1969—, also instr. grad. faculty. Author, patentee in field. Served to 1st lt. AUS, 1952-54. Recipient Green Sect. award U.S. Golf Assn., 1980, Achievement award Lawn Inst., 1977. Fellow Crop Sci. Soc. Am., Am. Soc. Agronomy (research award N.E. sect. 1979); mem. AAAS, Am. Genetic Assn., Am. Sod Producers Assn. (hon.), Golf Course Supts. Assn. (hon. mem.; Disting. Service award 1979), Internat. Turfgrass Soc., N.J. Turfgrass Assn. (Achievement award 1976, Hall of Fame award 1984), N.J. Golf Course Supts. Assn. (hon.), N.J. Acad. Scis., Sigma Xi, Phi Kappa Phi. Mormon. Home: 4 Delaware Dr East Brunswick NJ 08816 Office: Rutgers U Cook Coll New Brunswick NJ 08903

FUNK, DAVID ALBERT, law educator; b. Wooster, Ohio, Apr. 22, 1927; s. Daniel Coyle and Elizabeth Mary (Reese) F.; children—Beverly Joan, Susan Elizabeth, John Ross, Carolyn Louise; m. Sandra Nadine Henselmeier, Oct. 2, 1976. Student, U. Mo., 1945-46, Harvard Coll., 1946; B.A. in Econs., Coll. of Wooster, 1949; M.A., Ohio State U., 1968; J.D., Case Western Res. U., 1951, LL.M., 1972; LL.M., Columbia U., 1973. Bar: Ohio 1951, U.S. Dist. Ct. (no. dist.) Ohio 1962, U.S. Tax Ct. 1963, U.S. Ct. Appeals (6th cir.) 1970, U.S. Supreme Ct. 1971. Ptnr. Funk, Funk & Eberhart, Wooster, Ohio, 1951-72; assoc. prof. law Ind. U. Sch. Law, Indpls., 1973-76, prof., 1976—; vis. lectr. Coll. of Wooster, 1962-63; dir. Juridical Sci. Inst., Indpls., 1982—. Author: Oriental Jurisprudence, 1974, Group Dynamic Law, 1982; (with others) Rechtsgeschichte und Rechtssoziologie, 1985, Group Dynamic Law: Exposition and Practice, 1988; contbr. articles to profl. jours. Chmn. bd. trustees Wayne County Law Library Assn., 1956-71; mem. Permanent Jud. Commn., Synod of Ohio, United Presbyn. Ch. in the U.S., 1968. Served to seaman 1st class USNR, 1945-46. Harlan Fiske Stone fellow Columbia U., 1973; recipient Am. Jurisprudence award in Comparative Law, Case Western Res. U., 1970. Mem. Assn. Am. Law Schs. (sec. comparative law sect. 1977-79, chmn. law and religion sect. 1977-81, sec., treas. law and soc. sci. sect. 1983-86), Japanese-Am. Soc. Legal Studies, Law and Soc. Assn., Am. Soc. for Legal History, Pi Sigma Alpha. Republican. Office: Ind U Sch Law 735 W New York St Indianapolis IN 46202

FUNK, HARALD FRANZ, chemical engineer; b. Herzogenburg, Austria, Sept. 20, 1917; s. Franz Anton and Anna Maria (Seifried) F.; m. Karin Maria Plank, Dec. 10, 1952; children—Stephan, Christine. Grad. in chem. engring. Fridericiana U., Karlsruhe, Ger., 1940, D. Engring., 1944. Research engr. BASF, Ludwigshafen, BRD, 1940-46; cons. chem. engr., 1946-51; with Gulf Oil Can., 1952-56; N. Am. rep. for Linde A.G., 1956-62; mgr. cryogenics Allied Chem. Co., N.Y.C., 1962-65; pres. Silvichem Corp., Toronto, Ont., Can. and Salzburg, Austria, 1965—; cons. World Bank. Contbr. articles to profl. jours., also chpts. to books in field of solid waste gasification; holder more than 35 patents on sugars from wood, activated carbon, solid waste gasification, and energy recovery, stack gas desulferization, solar energy converter. Mem. Assn. Profl. Engrs. Ont., Am. Inst. Chem. Engrs., Am. Pollution Control Assn., Verein Deutscher Ingenieure, Deutsche Gesellschaft fü r Chem. Apparatewesen, Acad. Scis. N.Y., Explorers Club, N.Y. Acad. Home: Haus Sonnenlehen, 5084 Grossgmain 44, Austria Office: 166 Pearl St, Toronto, ON Canada M5H 1L3

FUNK, WILLIAM HENRY, civil engineer, educator; b. Ephraim, Utah, June 10, 1933; s. William George and Henrietta (Hackwell) F.; m. Ruth Sherry Mellor, Sept. 19, 1964 (dec.); 1 dau., Cynthia Lynn. B.S. in Biol. Sci, U. Utah, 1955, M.S. in Zoology (USPHS trainee), 1963, M.S. in Zoology, 1963, Ph.D. in Limnology, 1966. Tchr. sci., math. Salt Lake City Schs., 1957-60; research asst. U. Utah, Salt Lake City, 1961-63; head sci. dept. N.W. Jr. High Sch., Salt Lake City, 1961-63; mem. faculty Wash. State U., Pullman, 1966—; assoc. prof. environ. engring. Wash. State U., 1971-75, prof., 1975—, chmn. environ. sci./regional planning program, 1979-81; dir. Environ. Research Center, 1980-83, State of Wash. Water Research Ctr., 1981—; cons. Harstad Engrs., Seattle, 1971-72, Boise Cascade Corp., Seattle, 1971-72, U.S. Army C.E., Walla Walla, Wash., 1970-74, ORB Corp., Renton, Wash., 1972-73, State Wash. Dept. Ecology, Olympia, 1971-72, U.S. Civil Service, Seattle, Chgo., 1972-74; mem. High Level Nuclear Waste Bd., State of Wash. Author publs. on water pollution control and lake restoration. Served with USNR, 1955-57. Recipient President's Disting. Faculty award Wash. State U., 1984. Grantee NSF Summer Inst., 1961, Office Water Resources Research, 1971-72, 73-76, EPA, 1980-83, U.S. Geol. Survey, 1983-88, Nat. Parks Service, 1985-87. Mem. Naval Res. Officers Assn. (chpt. pres. 1969), Res Officers Assn. (U.S. Naval Acad. info. officer 1973-76), N.Am. Lake Mgmt. Soc. (pres. 1984-85), Pacific N.W. Pollution Control Assn. (editor 1969-77, pres.-elect 1982-83, pres. 1983-84), Water Pollution Control Fedn. (Arthur S. Bedell award Pacific N.W. assn. 1976, nat. dir. 1978-81), Nat. Assn. Water Inst. Dirs. (chair 1985-87, bd. dirs. Universities council on water resources 1986-88), Wash. Lakes Protection Assn. (co-founder 1986), Am. Water Resources Assn. (v.p. Wash. sect. 1988), Am. Soc. Limnology and Oceanography, Am. Micros. Soc., N.W. Sci. Assn., Sigma Xi, Phi Sigma. Home: SW 330 Kimball Ct Pullman WA 99163

FUNKE, EDMUND HEINRICH, educator; b. Dorsten, Fed. Republic of Germany, June 17, 1940; s. Alois and Ida (Grewe) F.; m. Mária Rácz, Mar. 29, 1985; 1 child, Simon-Árpád. Grad., U. Giessen, 1965; PhD, U. Marburg, 1977. Tchr. various schs. Giessen, Fed. Republic of Germany, 1965-72; prof. ednl. sci. GHK U., Kassel, Fed. Republic of Germany, 1972-73, U. Edn. Heidelberg, 1973—; dir. spl. edn., 1975-76, 85-87; mem. editorial bd. Jour. of Rehab. Research, Heidelberg, 1977—. Author: Grundschulzeugnisse..., 1972, Sein-Erknnen-Handeln, 1981, Lernbehinderung u. Kriminalität, 1979, others. Functionary mem. Sozialdemokr Partei Deutschlands, Giessen, 1963-69; cons. Friedrich-Ebert-Stiftung, Bonn, 1972—. Mem. Amnesty Internat., Deutsche Gesellschaft für Erziehungswissenschaft, Deutsche Gesellschaft für Sozialpädiatre, Verband Deutscher Sonderschulen, Gewerkschaft Erziehung und Wissenschaft. Home: Schillerstrasse 3, 6900 Heidelberg Federal Republic of Germany Office: Pädagogische Hochschule, Kepletstrasse 87, Heidelberg Federal Republic of Germany

FUNT, RICHARD CLAIR, horticulturist; b. Gettysburg, Pa., Feb. 13, 1946; s. Sterling Samuel and Dorothy Mildred (Guise) F.; m. Shirley May Fox, Sept. 6, 1969; children—Elizabeth Anne, Caroline Claire. B.S., Delaware Valley Coll., 1968; M.S., Pa. State U., 1971, Ph.D., 1974; postgrad., Wye Coll., Kent, Eng., 1985. Asst. prof., extension pomologist U. Md.-College Park, 1974-78, assoc. prof., extension pomologist, 1978-86; prof., extension horticulturist Ohio State U., Columbus, 1986—. Mem adminstrv. bd. United Meth. Ch., 1976-77, 81-83, pres. Men's Club, 1976-77, mem. council ministries, 1976-77, com. pastor-parish relations, 1985-87. Served with U.S. Army, 1968-70. Decorated Bronze Star; recipient Shepard award Am. Pomological Soc., 1977, GoOdling Meml. Lecture award, 1986; C. K. Bay grantee, 1979-83, 84, 85, Kellogg grantee, 1985-87. Mem. Sigma Xi, Gamma Sigma Delta, Phi Sigma, Phi Epsilon Phi, Epsilon Sigma Phi. Home: 1877 Stockwell Dr Columbus OH 43220 Office: Ohio State U 2001 Fyffe Ct Columbus OH 43210

FURÅKER, BENGT, sociologist; b. Mariestad, Sweden, Oct. 25, 1943; s. Konrad and Märta (Olausson) F.; m. Carina Kårleman, Mar. 27, 1969; children: Åsa, Torbjörn. BA, U. Lund, Sweden, 1968, PhD, 1977; MA, U. Calif., Santa Barbara, 1970. Lectr., teaching asst. U. Lund, Sweden, 1970-72, 74-79; asst. prof. U. Umeå, Sweden, 1979-84, assoc. prof., 1984—, head dept. sociology, 1981-83, 86. Author: Stat och Arbetsmarknad, 1976, Stat och Offentlig Sektor, 1987; contbr. articles to profl. jours. and chpts. to books. Home: Gökropsvägen 10B, 90237 Umeå Sweden Office: U Umeå, Dept Sociology, 90187 Umeå Sweden

FURBERG, OLLE R(AGNAR), furniture federation executive; b. Byske, Sweden, Feb. 14, 1930; s. Karl Hjalmar and Anna Maria (Lindberg) F.; m. Solvej D., Mar. 2, 1961; children: Suzanne Elizabeth, Eva Maria. Grad., U. Stockholm, 1982. Store mgr. retail family bus., Slottsbron, Sweden, 1947-57; retailing supr. Stop & Shop, New Eng. area, 1957-58; bus. cons. Swedish Textile Retailing Assn., Stockholm, 1959-61; systems cons. Sweda Internat., Solna, Sweden, 1961-68; asst. mktg. mgr. Sweda Internat., 1968-74; industry mktg. mgr. Sweda Internat., London, 1974-75; mng. dir. Scandinavia Kimball Systems, Solna, 1975-83, Swedish Furniture Retailing Assn., Stockholm, 1983—. Office: Sveriges Möbelhandl, Centralförbund, 10561 Stockholm Sweden

FURCON, JOHN EDWARD, management and organizational consultant; b. Chgo., Mar. 17, 1942; s. John F. and Lottie (Janik) F.; m. Carolyn Ann Warden, Aug. 15, 1964; children: Juliana, Annalisa, Diana. BA, DePaul U., 1963, MA, 1965; MBA, U. Chgo., 1970. With Human Resources Ctr. (name formerly Indsl. Relations Ctr.), U. Chgo., 1963-81, project dir., 1966-70, research psychologist, div. dir., 1970-81; with Chgo. div. Harbridge House, Inc., Northbrook, Ill., 1981—, v.p., 1987—; mem. faculty Traffic Inst., Northwestern U., 1969-84, DePaul U. Sch. for New Learning, 1974-82; cons. bus., ednl. and govt. orgns.; lectr. in field. Contbr. articles on personnel mgmt. and human resources planning to profl. jours. Served to lt. AUS, 1963-65. Mem. Am. Psychol. Assn., Indsl. Psychology Assn. Chgo. (chmn. 1973-75), Internat. Assn. Chiefs of Police. Office: Chgo Div Harbridge House Inc 2875 Milwaukee Ave Northbrook IL 60062

FURGIUELE, MARGERY WOOD, educator; b. Munden, Va., Sept. 28, 1919; d. Thomas Jarvis and Helen Godfrey (Ward) Wood; B.S., Mary Washington Coll., 1941; postgrad. U. Ala., 1967-68, Catholic U. Am., 1974-76, 80; m. Albert William Furgiuele, June 19, 1943; children—Martha Jane Furgiuele MacDonald, Harriet Randolph. Advt. and reservations sec. Hilton's Vacation Hide-A Way, Moodus, Conn., 1940; sec. TVA, Knoxville, 1941-43; adminstrv. asst., ct. reporter Moody AFB, Valdosta, Ga., 1943-44; tchr. bus. Edenton (N.C.) High Sch., 1944-45; tchr. bus., coordinator Culpeper (Va.) County High Sch., 1958-82; ret., 1982; tchr. Piedmont Tech. Edn. Center, 1970—. Co-leader Future Bus. Leaders Am., Culpeper, mem. state bd., 1979-82; state advisor 1978-79, Va. Bus. Edn. Assn. Com. chmn., 1978-79. Certified geneal. record Searcher. Mem. Nat., Va. bus. edn. assns., Am., Va. vocat. assns., Smithsonian Assos. Club: Country (Culpeper). Home: 1630 Stonybrook Ln Culpeper VA 22701

FURINO, ANTONIO, economist, educator; b. Rome, Italy, May 7, 1931. J.D., U. Rome, 1955; M.A., U. Houston, 1965, Ph.D., 1972. Asst. prof. to asso. prof. econs. St. Edwards U., Austin, Tex., 1967-70; dir. regional analysis Alamo Area Council Govts., San Antonio, 1970-73; prof. econs. U. Tex., San Antonio, 1973—; dir. Center for Studies in Bus., Econs. and Human Resources, U. Tex., 1973-78, dir. human resource mgmt. and devel. program, 1978-82; sr. partner, dir. Devel. Through Applied Sci., San Antonio, 1972—; prof. econs. U. Tex. Health Sci. Ctr., San Antonio, 1985—, dir. ctr. for studies in health econs., 1987—; sr. research fellow U. Tex. IC 2 Inst., Austin, 1986—; cons. Cattedra di Techniche di Richerche di Mercato, U. Rome, 1972—; econ. cons. others. Mem. Am. Econ. Assn. Home: 8915 Data Point 48-D San Antonio TX 78229

FURLAUD, RICHARD MORTIMER, diversified pharmaceutical company executive, lawyer; b. N.Y.C., Apr. 15, 1923; s. Maxime Hubert and Eleanor (Mortimer) F.; children: Richard Mortimer, Eleanor Jay, Elizabeth Tamsin; m. Isabel Phelps Furlaud. Student, Institut Sillig, Villars, Switzerland; A.B., Princeton, 1944; LL.B., Harvard, 1947. Bar: N.Y. bar 1949. Asso. Root, Ballantine, Harlan, Bushby & Palmer, 1947-51; legal dept. Olin Mathieson Chem. Corp., 1955-56, asst. to exec. v.p. for finance, 1956-57, asst. pres., 1957-59, v.p., 1959-64, gen. counsel, 1957-60, gen. mgr., v.p. internat. div., 1960-64, exec. v.p., 1964-66; now dir.; pres., dir. E. R. Squibb & Sons, Inc., 1966-68; pres., chief exec., dir. Squibb Beech-Nut, Inc. (renamed Squibb Corp. 1971), 1968-74, chmn., chief exec., dir., 1974—; dir. Mut. Benefit Life Ins. Co., Am. Express Co., Shearson Lehman Bros. Holdings, Inc. Mem. profl. staff Ho. of Reps. Com. Ways and Means, 1954; Trustee Rockefeller U.; bd. mgrs. Meml. Sloan-Kettering Cancer Center. Served as 1st lt., Judge Adv. Gen. Corps U.S. Army, 1951-53. Mem. Assn. Bar City N.Y., Pharm. Mfrs. Assn. (dir. 1965—), Council on Fgn. Relations. Clubs: Links (N.Y.C.), River (N.Y.C.). Home: 644 Pretty Brook Rd Princeton NJ 08540 Office: Squibb Corp PO Box 4000 Princeton NJ 08543-4000

FURLONG, PATRICK DAVID, educator, researcher; b. Cleve., Sept. 27, 1948; s. Harold Joseph and Jean Ann (Blair) F.; BS magna cum laude, Lake Erie Coll., Painesville, Ohio, 1975. Staff psychometrist VA Med. Center, North Chicago, Ill., 1975-78; psychometrist Northwestern U. Med. Sch., Chgo., 1978-80; counselor/coordinator vets. affairs Columbia Coll., Chgo., 1980-81; assoc. coordinator internat. edn. Roosevelt U., Chgo., 1981-84; dir. accreditation Nat. Commn. on Correctional Health Care, Chgo., 1984-85; coordinator student support services, United Edn. and Software, Chgo., 1985-87; neuropsychometrist Northwestern U. Med. Sch., Chgo., 1987—. Served with USN, 1967-71; Vietnam. Decorated Navy Achievement medal with combat V. Mem. N.Y. Acad. Scis., Am. Assn. for Counseling and Devel., Am. Psychol. Assn., Nat. Acad. Neuropsychologists, Psi Chi. Home: 1233 W Winnemac Chicago IL 60640

FURMAN, HOWARD, lawyer, federal mediator; b. Newark, Nov. 30, 1938; s. Emanuel and Lilyan (Feldman) F.; m. Elaine Sheitleman, June 12, 1960 (div. 1982); children—Deborah Toby, Naomi N'chama, David Seth; m. 2d Janice Wheeler, Jan. 14, 1984. B.A. in Econs., Rutgers U., 1966; J.D. cum laude, Birmingham Sch. Law, 1985. Designer/draftsman ITT, Nutley, N.J., 1957-61; personnel mgr. Computer Products Inc., Belmar, N.J., 1962-64, Arde Engring. Co., Newark, 1964-66; econs. instr. Rutgers U., New Brunswick, N.J., 1966-74; dir. indsl. relations Harvard Ind. Frequency Engring. Labs. Div., Farmingdale, N.J., 1966-74; commr. Fed. Mediation and Conciliation Service, Birmingham, Ala., 1974—; sole practice, Birmingham, 1974—. Pres. Ocean Twp. Police Res. (N.J.), 1968. Recipient ofcl. commendation Fed. Mediation and Conciliation Service, 1979, 81, 82. Mem. ABA, Ala. Bar Assn., Birmingham Bar Assn., Ala. Trial Lawyers Assn., Soc. Profls. in Dispute Resolution, Fed. Soc. Labor Relations Profls., Sigma Delta Kappa. Jewish. Lodges: Elks, Masons, B'nai B'rith. Home: 900 Kathryne Circle Birmingham AL 35215 Office: Fed Mediation and Conciliation Service 2015 2d Ave N Suite 102 Birmingham AL 35203

FURMAN, SAMUEL ELLIOTT, dentist; b. Jersey City, Dec. 13, 1932; s. Sol T. and Cecilia (Berman) F.; A.B., U. Pa., 1953; D.D.S., 1957; m. Margaret Ann Gilardi, Feb. 27, 1971; children: Laurie, Jill, Sean, Ashley. Diplomate, Am. Bd. Quality Assurance and Utilization Rev. Physicians. Gen. practice dentistry, Tinton Falls, N.J., 1959—; mem. staff Monmouth Med. Center; mem., past pres. N.J. Bd. Dentistry; mem. N.E. Regional Bd. Dental Examiners. Served to capt. USAF, 1957-59. Fellow Acad. Gen. Dentistry, Internat. Coll. Dentists, Am. Coll. Dentists, Internat. Acad. Dentistry; mem. N.J. Soc. Dentistry for Children, Am. Prosthodontic Soc., Am. Assn. Dental Examiners, Pierre Fauchard Acad., ADA, N.J. Dental Assn. (past trustee), Monmouth-Ocean County Dental Soc. (past pres.), Omicron Kappa Upsilon, Alpha Omega. Club: B'nai B'rith. Home: 8 Woods End Rd Rumson NJ 07760 Office: 1029 Sycamore Ave Tinton Falls NJ 07724

FURNAS, DAVID WILLIAM, plastic surgeon; b. Caldwell, Idaho, Apr. 1, 1931; s. John Doan and Esther Bradbury (Hare) F.; m. Mary Lou Heatherly, Feb. 11, 1956; children: Heather Jean, Brent David, Craig Jonathan. AB, U. Calif.-Berkeley, 1952, MS, 1957, MD, 1955. Diplomate: Am. Bd. Surgery, Am. Bd. Plastic Surgery (dir. 1979-85). Intern, U. Calif. Hosp., San Francisco, 1955-56; asst. resident in surgery U. Calif. Hosp., 1956-57; asst. resident in psychiatry, NIMH fellow Langley Porter Neuropsychiat. Inst., U. Calif., San Francisco, 1959-60; resident in gen. surgery Gorgas Hosp., C.Z., 1960-61; asst. resident in plastic surgery N.Y. Hosp., Cornell Med. Center, N.Y.C., 1961-62; chief resident in plastic surgery VA Hosp., Bronx, N.Y., 1962-63; registrar Royal Infirmary and Affiliated Hosps., Glasgow, Scotland, 1963-64; asso. in hand surgery U. Iowa, 1965-68, asst. prof. surgery, 1966-68, asso. prof., 1968-69; asso. prof. surgery, chief div. plastic surgery U. Calif., Irvine, 1969-74; prof., chief div. plastic surgery U. Calif., 1974-80, clin. prof., chief div. plastic surgery, 1980—; surgeon East Africa Flying Doctors Service, African Med. and Research Found., Nairobi, Kenya, 1972-87; plastic surgeon S.S. Hope, Nicaragua, 1966, Ceylon, 1968, Sri Lanka, 1969; mem. Balakbayan med. mission, Mindanao and Sulu, Philippines, 1980, 81, 82. Contbr. chpts. to textbooks, articles to med. jours.; author/editor 4 textbooks; assoc. editor Jour. Hand Surgery, Annals of Plastic Surgery. Expedition leader Explorer's Club Flag 171 Skull Surgeons of the Kisii Tribe, Kenya, 1987. Served to capt. M.C., USAF, 1957-59. Recipient Golden Apple award for teaching excellence U. Calif.-Irvine Sch. Medicine, 1980, Kaiser-Permanente award U. Calif.-Irvine Sch. Medicine, 1981, Humanitarian Service award Black Med. Students, U. Calif. Irvine, 1987, Sr. Research award (Basic Sci.) Plastic Surgery Ednl. Found., 1987; named Orange County Press Club Headliner of Yr., 1982. Fellow ACS, Royal Coll. Surgeons Can., Royal Soc. Medicine, Explorers Club, Royal Geog. Soc.; mem. AMA, Calif., Orange County med. assns., Am. Soc. Plastic and Reconstructive Surgeons, Am. Soc. Reconstructive Microsurgery, Soc. Head and Neck Surgeons, Am. Cleft Palate Assn., Am. Soc. Surgery of Hand, Soc. Univ. Surgeons, Am. Assn. Plastic Surgeons (trustee 1983-86, treas. 1988—), Am. Soc. Aesthetic Plastic Surgery, Am. Soc. Maxillofacial Surgeons, Assn. Acad. Chmn. Plastic Surgery (bd. dirs. 1986—), Assn. Surgeons East Africa, Pacific Coast Surg. Assn., Internat. Soc. Aesthetic Plastic Surgery, Internat. Soc. Reconstructive Microsurgery, Pan African Assn. Neurol. Scis., African Med. and Research Found. (bd. dirs. N.Y. 1987), African Med. and Research Found. N.Y. (bd. dirs. 1987), Phi Beta Kappa, Alpha Omega Alpha. Clubs: Muthaiga, Center, Club 33. Office: U Calif Div Plastic Surgery Irvine Med Ctr 101 City Dr S Orange CA 92625

FURNIVAL, PATRICIA ANNE, social worker; b. Poughkeepsie, N.Y., Feb. 3, 1938; d. Edwin A. and Esther L. Smith; BA, Maryville (Tenn.) Coll., 1960; MA, U. Chgo., 1970; m. George E. Furnival, Feb. 15, 1967. Cert. addiction profl.; lic. marriage and family therapist. Sr. caseworker Dutchess County Dept. Social Services, Poughkeepsie, 1961-67; rural resources dir. OEO, Freeport, Ill., 1967-68; program coordinator H. Douglas Singer Zone Ctr., Rockford, Ill., 1968-72; family therapist Bur. Alcohol Rehab., Avon Park, Fla., 1973-74; dir. Tri-County Alcoholism Rehab. Services, Inc., Avon Park, 1974-80; exec. dir. Tri-County Alcoholism Rehab. Services, Inc., Winter Haven, Fla., 1980—; exec. dir. adult and adolescent programs Tri-County Addictions Rehab. Services, 1986—; field instr. Fla. State U. Sch. Social Work, 1977—; instr. South Fla. Jr. Coll., 1979; pvt. practice psychotherapy, 1973—; bd. dirs. Pride of Polk County and Turnaround, Inc. drug rehab. ctr.; mem. alcohol and drug abuse task force Polk County Sch. Bd.; cons. in field. Mem. Nat. Assn. Social Workers, Acad. Cert. Social Workers, Fla. Alcohol and Drug Abuse Assn. (Bill Snyder meml. award 1986, bd. dirs.), Alcohol and Drug Problems Assn. N.Am., AAUW. Democrat. Mem. United Ch. Christ. Home: PO Box 1761 Avon Park FL 33825 Office: PO Drawer 9306 Winter Haven FL 33880

FURR, O(LIN) FAYRELL, JR., lawyer; b. Clinton, S.C., Jan. 19, 1943; s. Olin Fayrell and Helen Ella (Osborn) F.; m. Ann Longwell, June 10, 1967 (div.); m. Karole Jensen, Apr. 1, 1983; children: Sara Shannon, Karolan Marie, Paul Andrew. B.S., U. S.C., 1965, J.D., 1968. Bars: S.C. 1968, U.S. Dist. Ct. S.C., 1968, U.S. Ct. Appeals (4th cir.) 1982, (5th cir.) 1977, U.S. Supreme Ct. 1977. Mem. Law Offices of Kermit S. King, Columbia, S.C., 1973-77; ptnr. King & Furr, Columbia, 1977-79; sole practice law, Columbia, 1980—; lectr. various univs. Pres. bd. dirs. Contact Help, 1975-76; bd. dirs. Appelate Pub. Defender Orgn., 1980. Served to capt. U.S. Army, 1968-73. Decorated Bronze Star. Mem. S.C. Trial Lawyers Assn. (pres. 1979-80; most valuable mem. 1974), S.C. Bar Assn., Am. Trial Lawyers Assn. (cert. trial adv.), Richland County Bar Assn., Horry County Bar Assn. Democrat. Baptist. Editor, S.C. Trial Lawyers Bull., 1974-77; contbr. articles to profl. jours. Office: 1534 Blanding St Columbia SC 29201 Office: PO Box 2909 Myrtle Beach SC 29577

FURR, QUINT EUGENE, advertising executive; b. Concord, N.C., Sept. 21, 1921; s. Walter Luther and Mary (Barnhardt) F.; m. Helen Wilson, Dec. 30, 1961; children: Tiffany Grantham, Quentin, Robert; stepchildren: Pamela Erickson, Erik Erickson. AA, Belmont Abbey Coll., BA, U. N.C., Chapel Hill, 1943, postgrad. Law Sch., 1946-47. Promotion rep. Sears, Roebuck & Co., Atlanta and Greensboro, N.C., 1947-49; nat. advt. and sales promotion mgr. Western Auto Supply Co., Kansas City, Mo., 1949-61; regional mgr. J.F. Pritchard Co., Charlotte, N.C., 1961-63; gen. mgr. Hogan Rose Advt., High Point, N.C., 1963-65; regional mgr. Top Value Enterprises, Washington, 1965-67; v.p. corp. mktg. Textilease Corp., Beltsville, Md., 1967-85; v.p. sales and mktg. Am. Directory Service Agy., Bethesda, Md., 1985—. Served as lt. USNR, World War II, Korea. Recipient Mktg. award Textile Leasing Industry, 1970-74. Mem. Sales and Mktg. Execs. Internat., Inst. Indsl. Laundries (past chmn. mktg. com.), Am. Legion, VFW, Pi Kappa Alpha. Roman Catholic. Club: AD (Washington). Lodges: Moose, Elks. Home: 9232 Three Oaks Dr Silver Spring MD 20901 Office: 4719 Hampden Ln Bethesda MD 20814

FURRER, JOHN RUDOLF, business executive; b. Milw., Dec. 2, 1927; s. Rudolph and Leona (Peters) F.; m. Annie Louise Waldo, Apr. 24, 1954; children: Blake Waldo, Kimberly Louise. B.A., Harvard U., 1949. Spl. rep. ACF Industries, Madrid, 1949-51; asst. supr. Thermo nuclear Devel. and Test-Los Alamos, Eniwetok Atoll, 1952-53; dir. product devel. ACF Industries, N.Y.C., 1954-59; dir. machinery, systems group, central engring. labs. FMC Corp., San Jose, Calif., 1959-68; gen. mgr. engineered systems div. FMC Corp., San Jose, 1968-70; v.p. in charge planning dept., central engring. labs. an engineered systems div. FMC Corp., Chgo., 1970-71, v.p. material handling group, 1971-77, v.p. corp. devel., 1977-88, sr. v.p., 1988—; bd. dirs. Centocor, Teknowledge, Inc. Patentee in field. Trustee Ravinia Festival, 1986—. Served with USN, 1945-46. Mem. ASME, Council of Planning Execs. (chmn. conference bd. 1986-87). Clubs: Harvard (N.Y.C. and Chgo.); Glen View Country (Golf, Ill.); Economic,, Mid-America, Chgo. Yacht Club. Home: 1242 N Lake Shore Dr Chicago IL 60610 Office: FMC Corp 200 E Randolph St Chicago IL 60601

FURSDON, FRANCIS WILLIAM EDWARD, defense and security consultant; b. London, May 10, 1925; s. George Ellsworth Sydenham and Aline Lucinda (Gastrell) F.; m. Joan Rosemary Worssam, Mar. 25, 1950; children: Edward David, Sabina Mary. LittM, Aberdeen U., Scotland, 1978; LittD, Leiden U., Netherlands, 1979. Enlisted Brit. Army, 1942, advanced through grades to maj. gen., 1977, ret., 1980; def. and mil. corr. The Daily Telegraph, London, 1980-86; ind. def. and security cons. Eng., 1986—. Author: Grains of Sand, 1971, There Are No Frontiers, 1973, The European Defense Community--A History, 1980; contbr. numerous articles to profl. jours. Dir. ceremonies Order of St. John of Jerusalem, London, 1980—. Named Mem. of Order Brit. Empire, 1956, Companion of Order of Bath, 1980, Knight Order of St. John of Jerusalem, 1980, Freeman City of London, 1987. Fellow Inst. Brit. Mgmt.; mem. Inst. Journalists. Anglican. Clubs: St. John House, Spl. Forces (London). Address: care Nat Westminster Bank, 1 St James Square, London SW1Y 4JX, England

FURST, ALEX JULIAN, thoracic and cardiovascular surgeon; b. Augusta, Ga., Dec. 21, 1938; m. George Alex and Ann (Segall) F.; student U. Fla., 1963; M.D., U. Miami, 1967; m. Elayne Kobrin, Aug. 11, 1962; children—James Andrew, Jeffrey Michael, Joseph Robert. Intern, U. Miami Hosp., 1967-68, resident, 1968-72, clin. instr. dept. surgery, 1974—; chief resident in thoracic and cardiovascular surgery Emory U. Hosp., Atlanta, 1972-73; sr. surg. registrar of thoracic unit Hosp. for Sick Children, London, 1973-74; practice medicine specializing in thoracic and cardiovascular surgery, Miami, Fla.; chief thoracic surgery, pres. med. staff Mercy Hosp.; mem. staff Bapt. Hosp., South Miami Hosp., Doctor's Hosp. (all Miami), North Ridge Gen. Hosp., Ft. Lauderdale. Served with U.S. Army, 1958-60. Fellow Am. Coll. Cardiology, Am. Coll. Chest Physicians, A.C.S.; mem. Dade County Med. Assn., Fla. Med. Assn., Heart Assn. Greater Miami, Soc. Thoracic Surgeons, So. Thoracic Surg. Assn. Home: 8802 Arvida Dr Coral Gables FL 33156 also: 8740 N Kendall Dr #215 Miami FL 33176

FURST, ARTHUR, toxicologist, educator; b. Mpls., Dec. 25, 1914; s. Samuel and Doris (Kolochinsky) F.; m. Florence Wolovitch, May 24, 1940; children: Carolyn, Adrianne, David Michael, Timothy Daniel. A.A., Los Angeles City Coll., 1935; A.B., UCLA, 1937, A.M., 1940; Ph.D., Stanford

U., 1948; Sc.D., U. San Francisco, 1983. Mem. faculty, dept. chemistry San Francisco City Coll., 1940-47; asst. prof. chemistry U. San Francisco, 1947-49, asso. prof. chemistry, 1949-52; asso. prof. medicinal chemistry Stanford Sch. Medicine, 1952-57, prof., 1957-61; with U. Calif. War Tng., 1943-45, San Francisco State Coll., 1945; research assoc. Mt. Zion Hosp., 1952-82; clin. prof. pathology Columbia Coll. Physicians and Surgeons, 1969-70; dir. Inst. Chem. Biology; prof. chemistry U. San Francisco, 1961-80, prof. emeritus, 1980—, dean grad. div., 1976-79; Vis. fellow Battelle Seattle Research Center, 1974; Michael vis. prof. Weizmann Inst. Sci., Israel, 1982; cons. toxicology, 1980—; cons. on cancer WHO; mem. com., bd. mineral resources NRC. Contbr. over 225 articles to profl. and ednl. jours. Bd. trustees Pacific Grad. Sch. Psychology. recipient Klaus Schwartz Commemorative medal Internat. Toxological Congress, Tokyo, 1986. Fellow AAAS, N.Y. Acad. Scis.; mem. Am. Soc. Pharmacology and Exptl. Therapeutics, Am. Chem. Soc., Am. Assn. Cancer Research, Soc. Toxicology, Am. Coll. Toxicology (nat. sec., pres. 1985), Sigma Xi, Phi Lambda Upsilon. Home: 3736 La Calle Ct Palo Alto CA 94306 Office: U San Francisco Inst Chem Biology San Francisco CA 94117-1080

FURSTE, WESLEY LEONARD, II, surgeon, educator; b. Cin., Apr. 19, 1915; s. Wesley Leonard and Alma (Deckebach) F.; m. Leone James, Mar. 28, 1942; children—Nancy Dianne, Susan Deanne, Wesley Leonard III. A.B. cum laude (Julius Dexter scholar 1934-35); Harvard Club scholar 1933-35), Harvard U., 1937, M.D., 1941. Diplomate: Am. Bd. Surgery. Intern Ohio State U. Hosp., Columbus, 1941-42; fellow surgery U. Cin., 1945-46; asst. surg. resident Cin. Gen. Hosp., 1946-49; sr. asst. surg. resident Ohio State U. Hosps., 1949-50, chief surg. resident, 1950-51; limited practice medicine specializing in surgery Columbus, 1951—; instr. Ohio State U., 1951-54, clin. asst. prof. surgery, 1954-66, clin. assoc. prof., 1966-74, clin. prof. surgery, 1974-85, clin. prof. emeritus, 1985—; mem. surg. staff Mt. Carmel Med. Center, chmn. dept. surgery, 1981-85, dir. surgery program, 1981-82; mem. surg. staff Children's, Grant Med. Ctr., Univ., Riverside, Meth. hosps., St. Anthony Med. Ctr. (all Columbus); surg. cons. Dayton (Ohio) VA Hosp., Columbus State Sch., Ohio State Penitentiary, Mercy Hosp., Benjamin Franklin Hosp., Columbus; regional adv. com. nat. blood program ARC, 1951-68, chmn., 1958-68; invited participant 2d Internat. Conf. on Tetanus, WHO, Bern, Switzerland, 1966, 3d, São Paulo, Brazil, 1970, 5th, Ronneby Brunn, Sweden, 1978, 6th, Lyon, France, 1981, 7th, Copanello, Italy, 1984, 8th, Leningrad, USSR, 1987; invited guest signing of health services extension amendments act Pres. Johnson, 1965; invited rapporteur 4th Internat. Conf. on Tetanus, Dakar, Sénégal, 1975; mem. med. adv. com. Medic Alert Found. Internat., 1971-73, 76—, bd. dirs., 1973-76; Douglas lectr. Med. Coll. of Ohio, Toledo; founder Digestive Disease Found. Prime author: Tétanos; Tetanus: A Team Disease; contbg. author: Advances in Military Medicine, 1948, Management of the Injured Patient, Immediate Care of the Acutely Ill and Injured, 1978; editor Surgical Monthly Review; contbr. articles to profl. jours. Mem. Ohio Motor Vehicle Med. Rev. Bd., 1965-67; bd. dirs. Am. Cancer Soc. Franklin County, pres., 1964-66. Served to maj., M.C. AUS, 1942-46, CBI. Recipient 2 commendations for surg. service in China U.S. Army; cert. of merit Am. Cancer Soc.; award for outstanding achievement in field clostridial infection dept. surgery Ohio State U. Coll. Medicine, 1984, Outstanding Service award, 1985; award for outstanding and dedicated service Mt. Carmel Med. Ctr., 1985; award for over 25 yrs. service St. Anthony Med. Ctr. Mem. Cen. Surg. Assn., Surgical Infection Soc., Internat. Biliary Assn., Shock Soc., Soc. Am. Gastrointestinal Endoscopic Surgeons (com. on standards of practice and on resident and fellow edn.), Soc. Surgery of Alimentary Tract, AAAS, A.C.S. (gov.-at-large, chmn. Ohio com. trauma; nat. subcom. prophylaxis against tetanus in wound mgmt., Ohio chapter Disting. Service award 1987; regional credentials com.), Am. Assn. Surgery of Trauma, Ohio Surg. Assn., Columbus Surg. Assn. (hon. mem.; pres. 1983), AMA, Am. Trauma Soc. (founding mem., dir.), Ohio Med. Assn., Acad. Medicine Columbus and Franklin County (Award of Merit for 17 yrs. service), Acad. Medicine Cin., Am. Public Health Assn., Am. Med. Writers Assn., Grad. Surg. Soc. U. Cin., Robert M. Zollinger Club, Mont Reid Grad. Surg. Soc., Am. Geriatrics Soc., N.Y. Acad. Scis., Assn. Program Dirs. in Surgery, Assn. Physicians State of Ohio, Collegium Internationale Chirurgiae Digestivae, Assn. Am. Med. Colls., Internat. Soc. Colon and Rectal Surgeons, Soc. Internat. de Chirurgie, Am. Med. Golfing Assn., Internat. Brotherhood Magicians, Soc. Am. Magicians, N.Y. Cen. System Hist. Soc. Presbyterian. Clubs: Scioto Country, Ohio State U. Golf, Ohio State Faculty, Capital (Columbus); University (Cin.); Harvard (Boston). Home: 3125 Bembridge Rd Columbus OH 43221-2203 Office: 3545 Olentangy River Rd Columbus OH 43214-3955

FURTH, ALAN COWAN, corporate director, lawyer; b. Oakland, Calif., Sept. 16, 1922; s. Victor L. and Valance (Cowan) F.; m. Virginia Robinson, Aug. 18, 1946; children: Andrew Robinson, Alison Anne. A.B., U. Calif., Berkeley, 1944, LL.B., 1949; grad., Advanced Mgmt. Program, Harvard U., 1959. Bar: Calif., U.S. Supreme Ct. With So. Pacific Co., San Franciso, 1950-87, gen. counsel, from 1963, v.p., 1966, exec. v.p. law, 1976-79, pres., 1979-87, also dir. and mem. exec. com.; chmn., dir. Fed. Res. Bank; bd. dirs. Indsl. Indemnity Co., Bank of Calif., Gilmore Steel Corp., Am. Home Shield Corp., Flecto Corp. Trustee Merritt Hosp., Oakland, Calif.; trustee Pacific Legal Found.; bd. dirs. U. Calif. at Berkeley Found. Served to capt. USMCR, 1944-46, 51-52. Mem. Am. Bar Assn., Calif. State Bar Assn. Clubs: Bohemian (San Francisco), Pacific-Union (San Francisco), San Francisco Golf (San Francisco). Home: 244 Lakeside Dr Oakland CA 94612 Office: So Pacific Co One Market Plaza Stewart St Tower San Francisco CA 94105 *

FURTH, FREDERICK PAUL, lawyer; b. West Harvey, Ill., Apr. 12, 1934; s. Fred P. and Mamie (Stelmach) F.; children: Alison Darby, Ben Anthony, Megan Louise; m. Peggy Wollerman, July 19, 1986. Student, Drake U., 1952-53; BA, U. Mich., 1956, JD, 1959; postgrad., U. Berlin, 1959, U. Munich, Fed. Republic Germany, 1960. Bar: Mich. 1959, N.Y. 1961, D.C. 1965, U.S. Supreme Ct. 1965, Calif. 1966. Assoc. Cahill, Gordon, Reindel & Ohl, N.Y.C., 1960-64; with Kellogg Co., Battle Creek, Mich., 1964-65; assoc. Joseph L. Alioto, San Francisco, 1965-66; sr. ptnr. Furth, Fahrner, Bluemle, Mason & Wong, San Francisco, 1966—; spl. counsel to Ariz. Atty. Gen., 1968-82; spl. counsel San Francisco Redevel. Agy., 1969-70; speaker in field; vice chmn., bd. dirs. Robert Half Internat., BF Enterprises; chmn. bd., chief exec. officer Chalk Hill Winery, Petro Gen. Corp., Furth-Rader Builders. Mem. Citizens Com. for 25th Anniversary of UN, 1970; mem. Calif. Dem. Party Reform Commn., 1968-71; trustee Furth Found., San Francisco. Mem. ABA, Internat. Bar Assn., N.Y. Bar Assn., San Francisco Bar Assn., State Bar Calif., Assn. Bar City N.Y., San Francisco Criminal Trial Lawyers Assn., UN Assn. San Francisco (pres. 1969-70), NAACP (mem. bd. legal def. fund), Am. Judicature Soc., Sigma Alpha Epsilon. Clubs: Lawyers, St. Francis Yacht, Press, Bankers Commonwealth (San Francisco), Concordia Argonaut. Office: Furth Fahrner Bluemle & Mason Furth Bldg 201 Sansome St Suite 1000 San Francisco CA 94104

FURUMOTO, KOKI, trading company executive; b. Kobe, Hyogo, Japan, Feb. 11, 1933; Kenichi and Aiko (Suzuki) F.; m. Takako Waku, Feb. 3, 1962; children: Takayuki, Noriko, Hinako, Yoshinori. B in Econs., Kyoto (Japan) U., 1956. Pres. Koryu Co., Ltd., Kobe, 1972—; dir. Hyonen Kogyo Co., Ltd., Kobe, 1978-81, mng. dir., 1981-84, rep. exec. dir., 1984—. Home: 3-1 2 chome Sekimori Suma, 654 Kobe Hyogo Japan Office: Hyonen Kogyo Co Ltd, 3-1- 2 chome Kominatodori, 650 Kobe Japan

FURUSAKI, SHINTARO, chemical engineering educator; b. Tokyo, Jan. 20, 1938; s. Hiroshi and Ayako Furusaki; m. Kazuko Watanabe, Apr. 4, 1964; children: Akira, Noriko. BS in Engring., U. Tokyo, 1960, Dr. Engring., 1977; SM, MIT, 1964. Engr. Mitsui Toatsu Chems. Inc., Mobara, Japan, 1960-66, research chemist Yokohama br., 1966-73; research assoc. U. Tokyo, 1973-76, asst. prof., 1976-80, assoc. prof., 1980-82, prof., 1982—. Author: (with T. Miyauchi) Advances in Chemical Engineering, 1979; (Japanese) (with D. Kunii) Theory on Transfer Rates, 1980, Invitation to Chemical Engineering (Japanese), 1987; contbr. articles to profl. jours. Mem. Chem. Soc. Japan, Soc. Chem. Engrs. Japan, Am. Inst. Chem. Engrs., Membrane Soc. Japan. Office: Dept Chem Engring, U Tokyo, 7-3-1 Hongo, Tokyo 113, Japan

FURUYA, ZENBEI, architect; b. Izumo, Shimane-Ken, Japan, May 1, 1931; came to Can., 1962, naturalized, 1974; s. Kenzo and Michiyo (Nagao) F.; m. Natsuko Yoshimura, Mar. 25, 1961; children—Michi, Emi. B.Arch., Waseda U., Tokyo, 1954, M.Arch., 1956; M.S. in City and Regional Planning, Ill. Inst. Tech., 1961. Architect Japan Housing Corp., Tokyo, 1956-59, Mies Van Der Rohe, Chgo., 1961-62; pvt. practice architecture, Toronto, Ont., Can., 1963-68; architect Ont. Dept. Edn., Toronto, 1969-72, Ministry of Colls. and Univs., Toronto, 1973-76; tech. cons. Ont. Devel. Corp., Toronto, 1977—. Univ. scholar Waseda U., 1952, 53; Fulbright scholar, 1959; Internat. House fellow, 1959; inst. scholar Ill. Inst. Tech., Chgo., 1959, 60. Mem. Ont. Assn. Architects, Royal Archtl. Inst. Can. Avocation: world travel. Home: 62 Grandview Ave, Thornhill, ON Canada L3T 1H2

FUSAROLI, MARZIO, semiconductor manufacturing company executive; b. Milan, Oct. 4, 1939; s. Omero and Amalia (Inghingoli) F. Grad. in physics, U. Bologna, Italy, 1964. Engr. Selenia Research and Devel. Labs., Rome, 1965-66, Ates Research and Devel. Labs., Milan, 1967-72; mgr. small signal trnasistors lines SGS-Ates, Milan, 1977-80; mgr. prodn. and engring. Power Transistor Lines and Linear I.C.S. Lines SGS-Ates, Catania, 1973-76; mgr. materials dept. Epitaxy, Milan, 1977-80; mgr. certralized packaging engring sector SGS Microelecttronica SpA, Milan, 1981-85, dir. ops. div. VLSI, 1986—. Patentee linear integrated circuit, U.S., Japan, France and Spain. Home: Via Correggio 3, Milan 20149, Italy

FUSCO, ANDREW G., lawyer; b. Punxsitawney, Pa., Jan. 11, 1948; s. Albert G. and Virginia N. (Whitesell) F.; m. Deborah K. Lucas; children: Matthew, Geoffrey, David. BS in Bus. Adminstrn. and Fin., W.Va. U., 1970, JD, 1973. Bar: W.Va. 1973, U.S. Supreme Ct. 1977, U.S. Ct. Appeals (4th cir.) 1974, U.S. Ct. Appeals (Fed. cir.) 1985. Sole practice, Morgantown, W.Va., 1973-85; ptnr. Fusco & Newbraugh, Morgantown, 1985—; pros. atty. Monongalia County, W.Va., 1977-81; instr. Coll. bus. and Econ., W.Va. U., 1975-76; dir. Pitts. Environ. Systems Inc., 1983—. Author: Antitrust Law (West Virginia Practice Handbook), 1988; editor, contbg. author: Twenty Feet From Glory (John R. Goodwin), 1970, Business Law (John R. Goodwin), 1972, Beyond Baker Street (Michael Harrison), 1976. Bd. dirs. W.Va. Career Colls., 1971-76; mem. profl. adv. bd. Childbirth and Parent Edn. Assn., Rape and Domestic Violence Info. Ctr.; mem. W.Va. Sec. State's Tribunal on Election Reform, 1977-81; chmn. Monongalia County Drug Edn. Task Force, 1978-80. Mem. ABA, Monongalia County Bar Assn., W.Va. Bar, Am. Trial Lawyers Assn., W.Va. Trial Lawyers Assn., Internat. Platform Assn., Baker St. Irregulars of N.Y., W.Va. Dist. Attys. Assn., Nat. Dist. Attys. Assn., Am. Judicature Soc., Sons of Italy, W.Va. Law Sch. Assn., Monongalia Arts Ctr. (pres.-elect, treas., trustee). Recipient Am. Jurisprudence award Bancroft-Whitney Publ. Co. 1971; named Outstanding Young Man of 1979, Morgantown, 1979. Author: Antitrust Law, (West Virginia Practice Handbook), 1988; editor, contbg. author: Twenty Feet From Glory (John R. Goodwin), 1970, Business Law (John R. Goodwin) 1972, Beyond Baker Street (Michael Harrison) 1976. Democrat. Roman Catholic. Home: 20 Harewood Morgantown WV 26505 Office: 220 Pleasant St Morgantown WV 26505

FUSS, WERNER, business executive; b. Witten, Fed. Republic Germany, Apr. 1, 1940. BEE, Profl. Engring. Sch. Dortmund, Fed. Republic Germany, 1963; B. in Commerce, Westfälische Wilhelms-Universität Münster, Fed. Republic Germany, 1970. Research fellow Inst. for Mktg., Westfälische Wilhelms-Univ. Münster, 1970-72; Mgr. sales and mktg. Wildfang Metallwerk GmbH, Gelsenkirchen, Fed. Republic Germany, 1976-81; sales exec. Thiele oHG, Iserlohn, Fed. Republic Germany, 1981-85; mng. dir., speaker Doerrenberg Edelstahl GmbH, Engelskirchen, Fed. Republic Germany, 1985—. Office: Dorrenberg Edelstahl GmbH, Hammerweg, 5250 Engelskrichen Federal Republic of Germany

FUTCH, GRACE BONNER, real estate broker, developer; b. Manchester, Ga., Sept. 24, 1924; d. Warner Augdon and Johnnye Grace (Brown) Bonner Harris; children by previous marriage—Lynda Futch Creed, Carol Futch Bores. Student Ga. State Coll. for Women, 1941-43, Woodrow Wilson Coll. Law, Ga. State U., 1954-55; grad. Realtors Inst. Pres. Realty Ctr. Assocs., Inc., Pensacola, Fla., 1960-85, Pensacola Beach Realty, Inc., 1970—; gen. ptnr. Lake Russell, Ltd., Pensacola, 1976—, Rockdale, Ltd., 1975—; trustee Turtle Lake Land Trust, 1974-87; dir. loan com. Am. Bank and Trust, 1987—; chmn. bd. dirs. Pensacola Beach Realty. Pres., United Cerebral Palsy of Northwest Fla., 1971-73, United Cerebral Palsy, Fla., 1974. Mem. Pensacola Bd. Realtors, Fla. Assn. Realtors, Nat. Assn. Realtors, Pensacola C. of C. Republican. Baptist. Club: Zonta (pres. 1981). Office: Pensacola Beach Realty Inc 649 Pensacola Beach Blvd Pensacola Beach FL 32561

FUTCH, TOMMY RAY, health service corporation executive, pulmonary physiologist; b. Jacksonville, Fla., Dec. 8, 1951; s. Charleton Harris and Barbara Ann (Whidden) F.; m. Virginia Ann Thweatt, Sept. 11, 1976; children: Bradley Allen, Branden Wesley. BS, Fla. Tech. U., 1974; MBA, Nova U., 1981. Registered respiratory therapist, physician asst.; lic. lab. technologist. Dir. cardiopulmonary Fla. Med. Ctr., Ft. Lauderdale, 1976-77, adminstr. profl. services, 1977-82, Southeastern Med. Ctr., North Miami Beach, Fla., 1982; regional adminstr. Rehab. Hosp. Services, Ft. Lauderdale, 1982-85, v.p., 1985-86, sr. v.p., 1986-87; sr. v.p. Continental Med. Systems, Mechanicsburg, Pa., 1987—; chmn. bd. N. La. Rehab. Ctr., Ruston, 1987—, Baton Rouge Rehab. Inst., 1988—, Rocky Mountain Rehab. Hosp., Denver, 1988—, Kansas Rehab. Hosp., Topeka, 1987—, Midwest Rehab. Hosp., Kansas City, Kans., 1988—, Kentfield (Calif.) Rehab. Hosp., 1987—, Lakeview Rehab. Hosp., Elizabethtown, Ky., Braintree (Mass.) Hosp., Coral Gables Rehab. Hosp., Miami, Fla., Sunrise Hosp., Ft. Lauderdale, 1984-86, Pinecrest Hosp., Delray Beach, Fla., 1986, Rehab. Inst. Sarasota (Fla.), 1986-87, Edison Rehab. Hosp., Ft. Myers, Fla., 1986-87, Seacrest Health Corp., Melbourne, Fla., 1987, Montgomery (Ala.) Health Corp., 1987, Kentfield (Ca.) Hosp., 1987; dir. Fla. Assn. Rehab. Facilities, Tallahassee; del. Fla. Renal Adminstrs., Tampa, 1981. Contbr. articles to profl. jours. Trustee Am. Lung Assn., Ft. Lauderdale, 1977-80; mem. adv. council Broward Community Coll., Ft. Lauderdale, 1976-82; mem. Southeast Air Quality Council, Ft. Lauderdale, 1978. Mem. Am. Coll. Hosp. Adminstrs., Am. Health Planning Assn., Am. Hosp. Assn., Internat. Assn. Rehab. Facilities, Nat. Assn. Rehab. Facilities, Broward County C. of C. Democrat. Presbyterian.

FUTRELL, ROBERT FRANK, historian, consultant; b. Waterford, Miss., Dec. 15, 1917; s. James Chester and Sarah Olivia (Brooks) F.; m. Marie Elizabeth Grimes, Oct. 8, 1944 (dec. 1978); m. Jo Ann McGowan Ellis, Dec. 15, 1980. BA with distinction, U. Miss., 1938, MA, 1939; PhD in History, Vanderbilt U., 1950. Spl. cons. U.S. War Dept., Washington, 1946; historian USAF Hist. Office, Washington, 1946-49; assoc. prof. mil. history Air U., Maxwell AFB, Ala., 1950-51, prof., 1951-71, sr. historian, 1971-74, prof. emeritus mil. history, 1974—; professorial lectr. George Washington U., 1963-68; guest lectr. Air U. Squadron Officer Sch., Air Command and Staff Coll., Air War Coll., Air Force Acad., Army War Coll., Militärgeschichtliches Forschungsamt, German Fed. Republic, 1951—; vis. prof. mil. history Airpower Research Inst., Ctr. for Aerospace Doctrine Research and Edn., Air U., 1982-85, hist. advisor to USAF project Corona Harvest, 1969-74; cons. East Aviation Services & Tech., Inc., Chantilly, Va. Author: Ideas, Concepts, Doctrine: A History of Basic Thinking in the United States Air Force, 1907-1964, 1971, rev. edit., 1907-84, 2 vols., 1988, The United States Air Force in Korea, 1950-1953, 1961, rev. edit., 1983, The United States Air Force in Southeast Asia: The Advisory Years to 1965, 1981, (with Wesley Frank Craven, James L. Cate) The Army Air Force in World War II, 1948-1958; contbr. chpts. to hist. books, articles to scholarly publs. Served to capt. USAAF, 1941-45, lt. col. Res., ret. Recipient Meritorious Civilian Service award USAF, 1970, Exceptional Civilian Service decoration Sec. of USAF, 1973. Mem. Ala. Hist. Assn., SAR (pres. Montgomery County chpt. 1971-74), So. Hist. Assn., Air Force Hist. Found. (mem. editorial advisors 1969-81, trustee 1985—), Inst. Mil. Affairs, Phi Eta Sigma, Pi Kappa Pi. Methodist. Address: 908 Lynwood Dr Montgomery AL 36111

FUTTER, VICTOR, corporate executive, lawyer; b. N.Y.C., Jan. 22, 1919; s. Leon Nathan and Merle Caroline (Allison) F.; m. Joan Babette Feinberg, Jan. 26, 1943; children: Jeffrey Leesam, Ellen Victoria Shutkin, Deborah Gail. A.B. with honors in Govt, Columbia U., 1939, J.D., 1942. Bar: N.Y. 1942, U.S. Supreme Ct 1948. Assoc. firm Sullivan & Cromwell, 1946-52; with Allied Corp., Morristown, N.J., 1952-84, assoc. gen. counsel, 1976-78, v.p., sec., 1978-84; dir. Allied Chem. Nuclear Products, 1977-84; gen. counsel, sec. to bd. trustees Fairleigh Dickinson U., 1984-85; sec. Nova Pharm. Corp., 1985—; ptnr. Sills, Beck, Cummis, Zuckerman, Radin, Trschman & Epstein, P.A., 1984-87, of counsel, 1987—; spl. prof. law Hofstra Law Sch., 1976-78, 1988—; lectr., seminar on corp. in modern soc. Columbia U. Law Sch., 1986—. Editor: Columbia Law Rev; contbr. articles to profl. jours. Trustee, dep. mayor Village of Flower Hill, N.Y., 1974-76; mem. senate Columbia U., 1969-75; chmn. bd. dirs. Columbia Coll. Fund, 1970-72; pres. parents and friends com. Mount Holyoke Coll., 1978-80; pres. Flower Hill Assn., 1968-70; bd. dirs. N.Y. Young Democrats, 1946-52; co-chmn. fund drive Port Washington Community Chest, 1965-66, bd. dirs., 1965-75; mem. council of overseers C.W. Post, 1984-85; bd. dirs. Acad. of Polit. Sci., 1986—, Greenwich House, 1985—, sec. 1986—. Served to maj. AUS, 1942-46. Recipient Alumni medal for disting. alumni service Columbia U., 1970; James Kent scholar. Mem. Am. Soc. Corp. Sec. (pres. N.Y. region 1983-84, N.Y. region adv. com. 1984-88, bd. dirs. 1987—), ABA (chmn. sr. corp. lawyers com. sr. lawyers div. 1986—, chmn. N.Y. state membership for sr. lawyers div., 1987-88, sect. on corp. banking and bus. law, com. on long range issues affecting bus. law practice 1986—), Am. Law Inst. (consulative group for restatement of law governing lawyers 1987—), Assn. of Bar of City of N.Y. (com. on internat. human rights 1983-85, com. on 2d century 1985—), N.Y. State Bar Assn. (corp. counsel sect., com. on SEC fin., corp. law and governance), Nat. Assn. Corp. Dirs. (pres. N.Y. chpt. 1988—), Nat. Assn. Coll. Univ. Attys. (sect. on personnel relations, tenure and retirement programs 1984-86), Stockholder Relations Soc. N.Y., Columbia Coll. Alumni Assn. (pres. 1972-74), Am. Philatelic Soc., Phi Beta Kappa. Clubs: Cold Spring Harbor Beach, Collector's. Office: Sills Beck Cummis Zuckerman 450 Park Ave New York NY 10022

FUZES, ENDRE, ethnologist, museum director; b. Dobrokoz, Hungary, Apr. 27, 1932; s. Janos and Irma (Kovacs) F.; m. Erika Pentz, Dec. 18, 1972; children: Gergely, Marton. Grad., Eotvos Lorand U., Budapest, Hungary, 1955. Asst. Mus. of City of Pecs, Hungary, 1955-63; counselor Hungarian Ministry Culture, Budapest, 1964-79; sci. researcher Ethnographical Inst., Hungarian Acad. Sci., Budapest, 1980-86; gen. dir. Open Air Mus. of Szentendre, Hungary, 1986—. Author: A gabona tarolasa a magyar parasztgazdasagokban, 1984. Mem. Hungarian Ethnographical Assn. (treas.), Council Hungarian Mus., Council Hungarian Folk Art. Home: 4 Tornalja, 1124 Budapest Hungary Office: Open Air Mus Szentendre, PO Box 63, 2001 Szentendre Hungary

FYFE, WILLIAM MORTON, pediatrician, consultant; b. Glasgow, Scotland, Apr. 27, 1923; s. James Campbell and Jean (Morton) F.; m. Elizabeth Lydia Millar, Feb. 27, 1926; children: Alan Campbell, Susan Alison, John Morton, Carol Elizabeth. B Medicine, B Surgery, Glasgow U., MD. House officer, registrar posts Stobhill Hosp., Glasgow, 1949-52, cons., 1958—; registrar posts. Royal Hosp. Sick Children, Glasgow, 1952-58, cons., 1958-88. Contbr. articles to profl. jours. Served to maj. Royal Army Med. Corp., 1946-48. Fellow Royal Coll. Physicians (chmn. paediatric com. Glasgow chpt. 1985—); mem. British Paediatric Assn., Scottish Paediatric Assn. Home: 77 Drymen Rd, Bearsden G61 3RL, Scotland Office: Royal Hosp for Sick Children, Yorkhill, Glasgow Scotland

FYLE, CECIL MAGBAILY, social science educator, dean; b. Freetown, Sierra Leone, Aug. 23, 1944; s. Benoni Samuel and Gwendolyn (Johnson) F.; m. Olivette Omolara; children: Cecilia, Omolara, Caiemi, Chinwe, Chima. BA in History, Fourah Bay Coll., Freetown, 1968, diploma in edn., 1969; PhD, Northwestern U., 1976. Research fellow U. Sierra Leone, Freetown, 1973-75, lectr., 1975-80, dir. inst. African studies, 1976—, sr. lectr., 1980-83, prof., 1985—, dean, faculty of arts, 1986—, pub. orator, 1986—; vis. prof. Macalester Coll., St. Paul, 1983-84, 86, U. S.C., Columbia, 1984; cons. Uneca div. Unesco, Addis Ababa, Dakar, Saudi Arabia, 1983. Author: (books) Solima Yalunka Kingdom, 1979, Almamy Sukuku of Sierra Leone, 1979, History of Sierra Leone, 1981. Mem. Sydney Warne Commn. Enquiry, Freetown, 1987, Bicentennary of Sierra Leone Com., Freetown, 1987. Fulbright fellow, 1978. Methodist. Home: Kortright 21, Fourah Bay Coll, Freetown Sierra Leone Office: Fourah Bay Coll, Inst African Studies, Freetown Sierra Leone

GAAR, NORMAN EDWARD, lawyer, former state senator; b. Kansas City, Mo., Sept. 29, 1929; s. William Edward and Lola Eugene (McKain) G.; student Baker U., 1947-49; A.B., U. Mich., 1955, J.D., 1956; children—Anne, James, William, John; m. Marilyn A. Wiegraffe, Apr. 12, 1986. Bar: Mo. 1957, Kans. 1962, U.S. Supreme Ct. 1969. Assoc. Stinson, Mag, Thomson, McEvers & Fizzell, Kansas City, 1956-59; ptnr. Stinson, Mag & Fizzell, Kansas City, 1959-79; mng. ptnr. Gaar & Bell, Kansas City and St. Louis, Mo., Overland Park and Wichita, Kans., 1979-87, ptnr. Burke, Williams, Sorensen & Gaar, Overland Park, Kans., Los Angeles, Ventura, and Costa Mesa, Calif.; mem. Kans. Senate, 1965-84, majority leader, 1976-80; mem. faculty N.Y. Practising Law Inst., 1969-74; adv. dir. Panel Pubs., Inc., N.Y.C. Mcpl. judge City of Westwood, Kans., 1959-63, mayor, 1963-65. Served with U.S. Navy, 1949-53. Decorated Air medal (2); named State of Kans. Disting. Citizen, 1962. Mem. Am. Bar Assn.,Am. Radio Relay League, Antique Airplane Assn., Exptl. Aircraft Assn. Republican. Episcopalian. Clubs: Woodside Racquet, Brookridge Country. Office: Burke William Sorensen & Caar 7300 College Suite 220 Overland Park KS 66210

GAARDEMO, PETER MICHAEL, service executive, psychology consultant; b. Solna, Stockholm, Sweden, Sept. 21, 1956; s. Erik Gunnar Gustav and Margoth Elaine (Gustavsson) G. Degree in psychology, Uppsala U., Sweden, 1981, degree in psycholoanalysis, 1983. Sales mgr. Meta-Consult, Stockholm, 1981-82; chief exec. Meta-Consult/Made-in Cos., Stockholm, 1982-83, chmn. exec., 1984—; investigator Gen. Directorate of Posts, Stockholm, 1983-85, project mgr., 1985-87, chief rural post service, 1987—; pvt. cons. psychology Stockholm, 1984—; Chmn. Banking Commn. Swederate, Stockholm, 1982-85, Skattax, Stockholm, 1984—, Meta-Invest Banking, Stockholm, 1985—. Author: Investigator: The Ground for Personal Evolution, 1986. Pres. local sch. orgn., Solna, Sweden, 1975-76, local bldg. orgn., Solna, 1982-87. Mem. Labour Party. Lutheran. Home: Norrby 5661, S 76200 Skederid Sweden Office: Gen Directorate Posts, Olof Palmes Gata 31 NB, 10500 Stockholm Sweden

GABADOU, ROLAND GEORGES, marketing professional; b. Paris, Nov. 23, 1931; s. Georges Gaston and Marie Therese (Cazin) G.; m. Marie Louise Albert, July 4, 1956; 1 child, Michel Louis. Degree, Soreze (France) Coll.; student in Econs. and Geography, Reading (Eng.) U., 1951. Bd. dirs. Friden, Inc., Belgium, 1954-62, Singer, Inc., France, 1962-67; dir. internat. products Singer Internat., Brussels, 1967-69, dir. internat. graphic arts, 1973-76; founder, bd. dirs. Graphic Systems, Paris, 1976—; dir. Internat. Graphic Systems, 1987—. Home: 6 Parc de Noailles, 78100 Saint Germain En Laye France Office: Graphic Systems, 33 Bld De Latrre De Tassigny, 94123 Fontenay/Bois France

GABALDONI, LUIS EMILIO, writer; b. Lima Peru; m. Gertrude Vanderbilt Whitney Henry, 1946; children—Luis Vicente, Berbara Gertrudes. B.S., Columbia U., 1938, M.A., 1939. Formerly with Consulate Gen. of Peru, N.Y.C. Assoc. Whitney Mus., Manhattan. Author 14 books, numerous works of non-fiction. Fellow Internat. Biog. Assn. Recipient Grand Prix Humanitaire de France, 1968, Croix Chevalier, 1975, Croix Officer, 1981, medal of Honor Acad. Archaeol. Italiana, 1983, Gold Sceptre for Lit. Work Inst. Internat. pour L'Afrique, 1974; named Comdr. Order St. John and Jerusalem (Denmark), 1967, Knight of Justice Inst. Français de Lettres, Arts, and Scis., 1968, Hon. DHL Princedom Anderra, 1967. Clubs: Anteneo Madrid, Lima Golf, Nacional Lima Peru. Address: Gran Hotel Bolivar, Union 958, Plaza San Martin, Lima Peru

GABBAY, MARCEL, management consultant; b. Istanbul, Turkey, June 25, 1923; arrived in Eng., 1944; s. Albert M. and Elise (Roditi) G.; m. Vera Beck, Dec. 23, 1948; children: John, Mark. BA in Commerce, Robert Coll., Istanbul, 1943; BSc in Tech., U. Manchester, Eng., 1948. Chartered textile technologist Textile Inst. Eng. Mgr. mill Makaracilik Tas & Kadiotti, Istanbul, 1950-56, Kraftcord Ltd., Radcliffe, Eng., 1956-58; cons. A.I.C./Inbucon Ltd., London, 1958-63; sr. exec. Friedland, Doggart Ltd., Stockport, Eng., 1963-67; mng. dir. Bias (Mgmt. Cons. Ltd.), Chorley, Eng., 1967-80; indsl. devel. cons. expert UN Indsl. Devel Orgn., Internat. Labor Orgn. and various countries, France, 1970—. Decorated officier Palmes Academiques (France); recipient Disting. Service medal Servicio Nacional de Aprendizaje Nat. Council, Bogota, Colombia, 1976. Fellow Brit. Inst. Mgmt.; mem. Inst. Mgmt. Cons. (council 1971). Lodge: Rotary (pres. Ste.

Maxime/St. Tropez, France club). Home: 5 Ave F Mistral, 83120 La Nartelle, Sainte Maxime Var France

GABBAY, SHLOMO, accountant, educator; b. Bagdad, Iraq, Sept. 19, 1945; s. Eliahu and Rebecca Hananya; came to Israel, 1951; m. Shalom Carmela, Aug. 20, 1972; children—Gali, Shai, Ori. C.P.A. degree, Jerusalem Univ., 1972; computer controller courses, 1975-76, C.P.A.; cert. internal auditor. Sr. Acct. Vaysberg Shechter, Tel-Aviv, Israel, 1966-73; chief acct. Discount Ltd., Tel-Aviv, 1973-86; ptnr. Himmelfarb, Gabbay & Co., 1986—; lectr. in tax planning. Home: Hamatmid 33, Ramat Gan 50251, Israel Office: Himmelfarb Gabbay & Co, Herzel 77, Ramat Gan 50251, Israel

GABEL, GEORGE DESAUSSURE, JR., lawyer; b. Jacksonville, Fla., Feb. 14, 1940; s. George DeSaussure and Juanita (Brittain) G.; m. Judith Kay Adams, July 21, 1962; children: Laura Elizabeth, Meredith Rion. AB, Davidson Coll., 1961; JD, U. Fla., 1964. Bar: Fla. 1964, D.C. 1972. Mem. firm Toole, Taylor, Moseley, Gabel & Milton, Jacksonville, 1966-74, Wahl and Gabel, Jacksonville, 1974-88; Gabel, McDonald and Anderson, 1988—; mem. Fla. Jud. Nominating Commn., 4th Circuit, 1982-86. Pres. Willing Hands, Inc., 1971-72; chmn. N.E. Fla. March of Dimes, 1974-75; mem. budget com. United Way, 1972-74, chmn. rev. com., 1976; bd. dirs. Central and South brs. YMCA, 1973-79, Camp Immokalee, 1982-86; elder Riverside Presbyterian Ch., 1970-77, 80-86, clk. session, 1975-76, 85-86, trustee, 1988—; pres. Riverside Presbyn. Day Sch., 1977-79; chmn. Nat. Eagle Scout Assn., 1974-75; bd. dirs., v.p. adminstrn, chmn. long range planning com. N. Fla. Boy Scouts Am., 1974—, Silver Beaver award, 1978; mem. Jacksonville Council on Citizen Involvement, 1976-79; trustee Davidson Coll., 1984—. Served to capt. U.S. Army, 1964-66. Fellow Am. Coll. Trial Lawyers, Am. Bar Found.; mem. ABA (chmn. admiralty and maritime law com. 1980-81, chmn. defamation torts com. 1988—, tort and ins. practice sect. 1980-81, def. counsel sect., libel def. resource ctr., charter mem.), World Assn. Lawyers (founding mem.), Am. Counsel Assn. (bd. dirs. 1980-82), Assn. Trial Lawyers Am., Am. Judicature Soc., Maritime Law Assn. U.S., Fla. Bar (chmn. grievance com. 1973-75, chmn. admiralty law com. 1978-79), Acad. Fla. Trial Lawyers, Southeastern Admiralty Law Inst. (bd. govs. 1973-75), Duval County Legal Aid Assn. (bd. dirs. 1971-74, 81-84), Am. Inn of Ct. (master of bench). Democrat. Club: Rotary of Jacksonville (bd. mem. 1982-84, 1988—, treas. 1985-86, pres. 1987-88). Home: 1850 Shadowlawn St Jacksonville FL 32205 Office: Gabel McDonald and Anderson PA Suite 920 Barnett Bank Bldg Jacksonville FL 32202

GABLE, EDWARD BRENNAN, JR., lawyer, federal agency administrator; b. Shamokin, Pa., Mar. 15, 1929; s. Edward Brennan and Kathleen (Welsh) G.; B.S., Villanova U., 1953; J.D., Georgetown U., 1957; m. Judy Lipshy July 17, 1981; children by previous marriage—Karen Lynn, Kimberly Ann, Katherine Rebel; stepchildren—Steven H., Karen Sue, Scott Michael. Admitted to D.C. bar, 1957, U.S. Supreme Ct. bar; with U.S. Customs Service, Treasury Dept., Washington, 1958—, chief documentation br., 1965-66, chief carrier rulings br., 1966-76, chief penalties br., 1976-78, spl. asst. to asst. commr. Office of Regulations and Rulings, 1978-82, dir. carriers, drawback and bonds div., 1983—; mem. U.S. del. Intergovtl. Maritime Cons. Orgn., London, 1972-75, U.S. rep., inter-sessional meeting, Hamburg, W.Ger., 1973. Pres., Customs Fed. Credit Union, 1967-69. Recipient Superior Performance award Treasury Dept., 1962, commendation letter from asst. sec. treasury, 1964, Customs Outstanding Performance award, 1983, Customs Cash Performance award, 1984, 85. Mem. Customs Lawyers Assn. (pres. 1965-66), Fed. Bar Assn., Propeller Club U.S., United Seamen's Service (council of trustees 1986—), Delta Theta Phi. Roman Catholic. Clubs: Elks, Nat. Lawyers. Home: 955 26th St NW Washington DC 20037 Office: US Customs Service 1301 Constitution Ave NW Washington DC 20229

GABLE, JAMES G., electrical engineering executive, consultant; b. Phila., Mar. 26, 1918; s. James F. and Stella (Gingrich) G.; m. Ruth Ann Goetz, Oct. 14, 1940; (dec. 1977); children—Suzanne R. Tognazzini, Mary C. Price, James E. BSEE, Carnegie-Mellon U., 1940. Registered profl. engr., Calif. Design engring. mgr. Westinghouse Electric Corp., Buffalo, 1951-54, div. gen. mgr., 1954-62; orgn. devel. mgr. Lockhead Missiles & Space Co., Sunnyvale, Calif., 1962-70; pvt. cons., 1970-74; v.p. Micro Power Systems, Inc., Santa Clara, Calif., 1974-85, ret., 1985. Patentee 4 control systems. Chmn. Town Long Range Fiscal Planning Commn.; engr. mem. Town Drainage Com., Los Altos Hills, Calif. Served to 1st lt. U.S. Army, 1943-45, ETO. Mem. Nat. Soc. Profl. Engrs., Calif. Soc. Profl. Engrs. Lodges: Masons (32 degree), KT (past cmdr.), Shriners, Jesters. Home: 7251 Via Mimosa San Jose CA 95135

GABLE, MARTHA ANNE, educator; b. Phila.; d. James F. and Stella (Gingrich) G. BE, Ind. U., 1942; MEd, Temple U., 1935. Tchr., Phila. Pub. Schs., 1926-41, asst. dir. phys. and health edn., Phila., 1942-48, asst. dir. sch. and community relations, 1948-55, dir. radio-TV edn., 1955-68; editor Am. Assn. Sch. Adminstrs., Washington, 1968-73, cons. Editechnology, 1973—; mem. Pa. Gov.'s Adv. Commn. on Edn., 1956-58, White House Conf. on Edn., 1955; cons. Joint Council Ednl. TV, Washington; chmn. adv. com. Pa. Ednl. TV, 1960-68; del. Internat. Conf. Ednl. TV, London, 1954. Judge, Olympic Games, London, 1948, Helsinki, 1952, Melbourne, 1956, Rome, 1960, Tokyo, 1964; bd. dirs. Phila. Home and Sch. Council, 1950-68; v.p. Women for Greater Phila. Named Disting. Dau. of Pa.; recipient Pres.'s award Phila. C. of C., Silver Medal award Phila. Club Advt. Women, Trustee Service award Pop Warner Little League, Service award Mus. Council Phil. and Del. Valley; named to Pa. Sports Hall of Fame. Mem. Phila. Pub. Relations Assn. (Hall of Fame), Am. Women in Radio and TV, NEA, Pub. Relations Soc. Am., TV-Radio Advt. Club, AAUW, Am. Assn. Sch. Adminstrs., Phila. Mus. Art, Women in Communications, Am. Newswomen's Club. Presbyterian. Club: Cosmopolitan, Nat. Press. Home: 2601 Parkway Philadelphia PA 19130

GABLE, ROBERT ELLEDY, real estate investment company executive; b. N.Y.C., Feb. 20, 1934; s. Gilbert E. and Paulina (Stearns) G.; m. Emily Brinton Thompson, July 5, 1958; children—James, Elizabeth, John. B.S., Stanford U., 1956. John. With The Stearns Co. (formerly Stearns Coal & Lumber Co. Inc.), Lexington, Ky., 1958—, asst. to pres., 1958-60, sec., 1960-70, treas., 1961-62, v.p., 1962-70, chmn. bd., 1970—, pres., 1975-78, also dir.; former chmn. bd., dir. Ky. & Tenn. Ry., Lexington; former chmn. bd. Lumber King Inc., Lexington; former dir., mem. audit com. Kuhn's-Big K Stores Corp., Nashville, 1979-81; dir. emeritus Blue Cross and Blue Shield Ky.; former dir. Bank of McCreary County. Commr. Ky. Dept. Parks, 1967-70; mem. pub. lands com. Interstate Oil Compact Commn., 1968-70; mem. adv. com. Ky. Ednl. TV, 1971-75; former mem. Breaks Interstate Park Commn.; past pres., past dir. McCreary County Indsl. Devel. Corp.; former trustee Stearns Recreational Assn., Inc.; mem. S.E. regional adv. com. Nat. Park Service, 1973-78, sec., 1977-78; former bd. dirs. Ky. Mountain Laurel Festival Assn., v.p., 1974-75; mem. McCreary County Air Bd., 1967-81; mem. adv. bd. U. Ky. for Somerset Community Coll., 1965-73. Republican candidate for U.S. Senate from Ky., 1972; Ky. co-chmn. Finance Com. for Re-election of Pres., 1972; mem. Rep. Nat. Com., 1986—, Rep. Nat. Finance Com., 1971-76; Rep. state finance chmn., 1973-75, 86; mem. Ky. Rep. Central Com., 1974—; state chmn. Rep. Party Ky., 1986—; Rep. nominee for gov. Ky., 1975; trustee George Peabody Coll. for Tchrs., Nashville, 1970-79, mem. exec. com., 1976-79, chmn. bd., 1979; former trustee Capital Day Sch., Frankfort, Ky.; bd. dirs., past chmn., past pres., founder Ky. Council on Econ. Edn., Inc.; bd. dirs. Joint Council Econ. Edn., N.Y.C., 1982—; trustee Ky. State U. Found., 1979-82; trustee Vanderbilt U., Nashville, 1979—, former mem. budget com.; past mem. bd. dirs. Ky. Better Roads Council, Inc., vice chmn., 1976-79; former mem. missions bd. Episcopal Diocese of Lexington; bd. dirs. Lexington Conv. and Tourist Bur., 1982-85, Ky. Opera Assn., 1982—, Rehab. Found., Inc., Louisville, 1982-84, Headley-Whitney Mus., Lexington, 1985—; founding bd. Lexington Fund for the Arts, 1984-86. Served to lt. (j.g.) USNR, 1956-58. Named Ky. Col., Mr. Coal of Ky., 1970. Former mem. Ky. Coal Assn. (dir. 1972—, exec. com. 1974-78, sec. 1979-86), Ky. C. of C. (regional v.p., 1971-72, 76-80, exec. com. 1971-72, 76-80, dir. 1971-80, fin. com. 1978-79), Lexington C. of C. (dir. 1982, 84-87), Urban Land Inst., Tau Beta Pi, Alpha Kappa Lambda (past chpt. pres.). Clubs: Frankfort (Ky.) Country; Keeneland, Lafayette, Bluegrass Auto (dir.) (Lexington); Pendennis, River Valley (Louisville); Capitol Hill (Washington). Home: 1715 Stonehaven Dr Frankfort KY 40601 Office: The Stearns Co 410 W Vine St Lexington KY 40507

GÁBOR, RÉVÉSZ, economist; b. Baja, Hungary, Apr. 14, 1924; s. Bela and Julia (Abonyi) R.; married; children: Gábor, Magda. MS in Econs., Karl Marx U., Budapest, Hungary, 1952; PhD, Hungarian Acad. Sci., Budapest, 1972. Sr. research worker Hungarian Planning Office, Budapest, 1961-67; head dept. research Inst. Econs., Hungarian Acad. Sci., Budapest, 1967—; lectr. econs. Karl Marx U., Budapest, 1971—, Budapest Polit. Acad., 1968—. Author: Problems of Collective Interest in Hungarian Firms, 1971, (with others) The Origins and Development of the Model of Social Economy and Economic Policy, 1985. Mem. European Econ. Assn. Home: Felsozoldmali ut 17, 1025 Budapest Hungary Office: Hungarian Acad Scis Inst Econs, Budaorsi ut 45, 1112 Budapest Hungary

GABRIA, JOANNE BAKAITIS, information processing systems equipment company executive; b. Washington, Pa., Jan. 16, 1945; d. Vincent William and Mary Jo (Cario) Bakaitis. BA in English, U. Dayton, 1965, MA in Mktg. Communications, 1973, MBA, 1979. Advt. writer Dancer-Fitzgerald-Sample, Dayton, Ohio, 1969-72; advt. coordinator Monarch Marking Systems, Dayton, 1972-73; product tech. editor Frigidaire div. GM, Dayton, 1973-77; dir. tech. communications Mead Tech. Lab., Dayton, 1977-79; publs. mgr. NCR Corp., Dayton, 1979-81, internat. product mgr., 1981-86, mgr. internat. market analysis, 1986-87, mgr. Internat. Market Research, 1987—. bd. dirs. Contact-Dayton, 1984-85. Author: Microwave Cooking in 3 Speeds, 1976, Communications Standards, 1978, Retail Operations, 1982; editor: Ivy Jour., 1980-82. Chair numerous coms. St. Leonard Community, Centerville, Ohio, 1978—; telephone vol. Contact-Dayton Crisis Intervention, 1982-86; big sister Big Bros./Big Sisters, Dayton, 1985-86; bd. dirs. Miami Valley chtp. Nat. Kidney Found. of Ohio, 1987—. Recipient Disting. Achievement award Contact-Dayton, 1985, Outstanding Service award Miami Valley chpt. Nat. Kidney Found. of Ohio, 1988. Mem. Nat. Assn. Female Execs., Dayton Soc. Natural History, Marianist Affiliates (co-chmn. 1981-86). Democrat. Roman Catholic. Avocations: gardening, nature, classical music. Home: 7807 Graceland St Dayton OH 45459 Office: NCR Corp World Hdqrs-2 1700 S Patterson Blvd Dayton OH 45479

GABRIEL, EUGENE RICHARD, broadcast engineer, consultant; b. Huntington, W.Va., Dec. 31, 1949; s. Daniel Edmund and Mae Susan (Eskew) G.; m. Cynthia Simms Gardner, Feb. 1, 1981 (div. 1982). Student Emory and Henry Coll., 1966-69. Disc jockey Sta. WSWV, Pennington, Gap, 1965-67, broadcast engr., Lee County, Va., 1967-75; dir. engring. Sta. K92-FM CEBE Investments, Inc., Roanoke, Va., 1975—; founder, pres. Dog Gone Corp., Roanoke, 1984—; cons. in field. Mem. Am. Security Council, 1980—; mem. Republican Presdl. Task Force, 1982—. Served with U.S. Army, 1970-71. Mem. Soc. Broadcast Engrs., MENSA. Methodist. Lodges: Lee Jaycees, Eagles (Pennington Gap, Va.). Home: Rt 1 Box 654 Vinton VA 24179 Office: Dog Gone Corp 2728 Colonial Ave SW Box 1180 Roanoke VA 24006

GABRIEL, JOSEPH MARTIN, entrepreneur; b. Chgo., Jan. 27, 1927; s. Martin Joseph and Anna (Kohl) G.; m. Lillian Joyce Opie, May 8, 1958 (div. 1970); children—Mark John, Russel Knight, Loretta Lynn; m. Diane Lynn Horbacz, Nov. 23, 1972; 1 dau., Kerry Ann. Ph.B., U. Chgo., 1949. Asst. to pres. SMECO Industries, Inc., Chgo., 1958-60, exec. v.p., 1960-66, pres., chmn. bd., Willow Springs, Ill., 1966—; chmn. bd. Lippmann-Milw., Inc., Cudahy, Wis., Vira Corp., Burr Ridge, Ill. Served with inf. U.S. Army, 1945-46. Methodist. Avocations: gardening; reading. Home: PO Box 335 Winthrop Harbor IL 60096 Office: Vira Corp 8695 S Archer Ave Willow Springs IL 60480 Also: PO Box 586 Cudany WI 53110

GABRILOVE, JACQUES LESTER, physician; b. N.Y.C., Sept. 21, 1917; s. Benjamin and Pauline (Levine) G.; m. Hilda R. Weiss, May 19, 1946; children: Sandra Leslie Saltzman, Janice Lynn Gabrilove Dirzulaitis. B.S. magna cum laude, CCNY, 1936; M.D. (Alpha Omega Alpha prize), N.Y.U., 1940. Diplomate: Am. Bd. Internal Medicine. Intern Mt. Sinai Hosp., N.Y.C., 1940-41; rotating intern Mt. Sinai Hosp., 1941-43, vol. radiology, 1943, resident medicine, 1943-44, Blumenthal fellow medicine, 1946-48, research asst. medicine, 1949-51, asst. attending physician, 1952-60, assoc. attending physician, 1960-68, attending physician, 1969—; cons. endocrinology, 1953—; chief endocrine clinic, also clin. prof. medicine Mt. Sinai Sch. Medicine, 1969-82, Baumritter prof. medicine, 1982—, acting dir. div. endocrinology, 1985, assoc. dir., 1986—; Libman fellow medicine Yale, 1945; clin. asst. prof. medicine SUNY Coll. Medicine N.Y.C., 1957-59, clin. assoc. prof., 1959-66, clin. prof., 1966-69, professorial lectr., 1969—; cons. endocrinology VA Hosp., East Orange, N.J., 1958-66, Elizabeth A. Horton Hosp., Middletown, N.Y., 1961—, VA Hosp., Bronx, N.Y., 1969—, Norwalk Hosp., Conn. 1974—, Elmhurst City Hosp., N.Y., St. Francis Hosp., Port Jervis, N.Y.; mem. panel on metabolic and rheumatoid diseases U.S. Pharmacopeia, 1956—; mem. spl. com. research tng. grants in diabetes, endocrinology and metabolism NIH, 1976-79, mem. com. on diabetes research and tng. centers, 1977-79; Saltzman lectr. Mt. Sinai Hosp., Cleve., 1974. Author, contbr. books in field, also articles in med. jours.; mem. editorial bd. jour., Mt. Sinai Hosp. Pres. Mt. Sinai Alumni Assn., 1970. Recipient Jacobi medallion Mt. Sinai Alumni Assn., Globus prize Mt. Sinai Jour. Medicine. Fellow ACP, N.Y. Acad. Medicine; mem. N.Y. County Med. Soc., AMA, N.Y. Acad. Sci., AAAS, N.Y. Diabetes Assn., Endocrine Soc., Am. Diabetes Assn., Harvey Soc., Royal Soc. Medicine, Peruvian Endocrine Soc. (hon.), Pan Am. Med. Assn. (v.p. N.Am. endocrinology), Phi Beta Kappa, Alpha Omega Alpha. Jewish (trustee, v.p. synagogue). Club: Lotos (bd. dirs.). Home: 25 E 86th St New York NY 10028 Office: 79 E 79th St New York NY 10021

GABRINER, PAUL JEFFREY, English and American literature educator; b. Newark, Jan. 21, 1943; s. Abraham and Dorothy (Segal) G.; m. Mariet Dornseiffen, Dec. 31, 1970 (dec. 1978); children: David, Daniel. BA in English Lit., Bard Coll., 1965; MA in English Lit., Johns Hopkins U., 1966; Phd in English Lit., U. Conn., 1979. Lectr. in English Hebrew U., Jerusalem, 1971-75; U. docent in English lit. U. Amsterdam, 1975—. Author: Alexander Pope and the Poetry of Succession, 1989, Benelux, fgn. edit. Scriblerian; contbr. articles to scholarly publs. Leopold Schepp Found. scholar, 1961-65. Home: Dr Koomansstr 28, 1391 XB Abcoude The Netherlands Office: Engels Seminarium U Amsterdam, Spuistr 210, Amsterdam The Netherlands

GADHAFI, MUAMMAR MUHAMMED, Libyan chief of state; b. Sirta, Libya, 1942; s. Mohamed Abdulsalam Abuminiar and Aisha Ben Niran; student U. Libya, Benghazi; grad. mil. acad., Benghazi, 1965; m. 1970; 4 sons, 2 daus. Served with Libyan Army, 1965—; chmn. Revolutionary Command Council, 1969-77; comdr. in chief Armed Forces, 1969—; leader of 1969 Revolution; prime minister, 1970-72; minister of def., 1970-72; pres. of Libya, 1977—; sec. gen. of Gen. Secretariat of Gen. People's Congress, 1977-79; mem. Pres. Council, Fedn. of Arab Reps., 1971—; rank of Maj. Gen., 1976, still keeping title of col. Author: The Green Book (3 vols), Military Strategy and Mobilisation, The Story of the Revolution. Address: Office of Pres, Tripoli Libya *

GADZHIEV, RAUF SOLTANOGLY, composer; b. Baku, Azerbaidzhan, USSR, May 15, 1922; s. Soltan Muchtar ogly and Nana Kurban (Muradova) G.; m. Irina Surenovna; children: Fuad, Natavan, Nana. Grad., Azerbaidzhanian Conservatory, Baku, 1948-53. Mgr., conductor Orch. of Baku, 1944-55, Azerbaidzhanian Orch., Baku, 1955-65; minister of culture State of Azerbaidzhan, Baku, 1964-71, sec. bd. of Composers Union, 1971—; sec. bd. of Composers Union USSR, Moscow, 1985—; tchr. Azerbaidzhanian State Conservatory, Baku, 1954—. Author: (ballets) Three Revolutions, 1973, Flame, 1976, Uria, 1979; (musical comedies) Romeo is My Neighbor, 1960, Don't Hide a Smile, 1969, Mother, I'm Marrying, 1976, Crossroads, 1976, Golden Ship, 1985; also 10 symphonies, 8 oratorio and canata, 100 songs, various music for theater and cinema. Dep. State of Azerbaidzhan; dir., mgr. Azerbaidzhanian Philharmonic Soc., 1963-64. Named People's Artist of Yr. USSR, 1978. Home: S Vurgun St 85, Baku, Azerbaidzhan USSR Office: Composers' Union of Azerbaidzhan, Chaganistr 27, Baku USSR

GAERTNER DORADO, MARIANNE, lawyer; b. Neptune, N.J., May 18, 1956; d. Wolfgang W. and Marianne L. (Weber) Gaertner; m. Richard Manuel Dorado, Oct. 1, 1982. BA, Yale U., 1978; JD, U. Mich., 1981. Bar: N.Y. 1982. Adminstrv. asst. W.W. Gaertner Research, Inc., Norwalk, Conn., 1972-79; assoc. Shearman & Sterling, N.Y.C., 1981—; dir. W.W. Gaertner Research, Inc., 1981—. Contbr. articles to profl. jours.; editor U. Mich. Jour. Law Reform, 1980-81. Externship Office Legal Advisor U.S. Dept. State, 1980. Mem. ABA. Republican. Roman Catholic. Club: Yale. Home: 111 E 30th St New York NY 10016 Office: Shearman & Sterling 599 Lexington Ave New York NY 10022

GAETA, GIUSEPPE, management consultant, educator; b. Nocera Inferiore, Italy, Sept. 13, 1928; s. Michele Gaeta and Elvira della Valle Gaeta; Ph.D., Istituto Universitario Orientale, Naples, 1955; m. Giuseppina Scognamillo, June 29, 1957; children—Michele, Elvira, Giovannimaria. Chief exec. Gabriele Gambardella & Figli, Nocera Inferiore, 1950-67; chief exec. Tradexport S.P.A., Nocera Inferiore, 1967-70; pres. Fermac, s.p.a., Nocera Inferiore, 1968—; spl. cons. Centri Regionali per il Comercio Estero-Union Italiana Camere di Comercio, Rome, 1970—; prof. econs. State Tech. High Schs., 1956-74; prof. modern lits. State Classical High Sch., Nocera Inferiore, 1975—. Roman Catholic. Home: Via a Barbarulo 10, 84014 Nocera Inferiore Italy

GAFFNEY, PATRICK JOSEPH, research scientist; b. Cork, No. Ireland, Aug. 19, 1934; s. Patrick Joseph and Anna Theresa (O'Donovan) G.; m. Dinah Zedora Davis; children: Jane, Anna, Patrick, Timothy, Siobhan, Daniel, Kathleen. BSc, Nat. U. Ireland, 1957, MSc, 1958, DSc, 1976; MSc, Nat. Coll. Food Tech., Weybridge, 1959; PhD, Ohio State U., 1965. Postdoctoral fellow Am. Nat. Red Cross Blood Program, Washington, 1965-67; sr. scientist Med. Research Council, Cambridge, Eng., 1967-69, London, 1969-72; professorial fellow Nat. Int. for Biol. Standards and Control, London, 1972—. Editor: Fibrinolysis, 1978, 87; contbr. articles to profl. jours. Recipient Conway medal, Royal Acad. Medicine-Ireland, 1982; MRC grantee, 1982, 84, 86. Fellow Royal Coll. Pathologists; mem. Internat. Soc. Thrombosis and Hemostasis, European Thrombosis Research Orgn., European Concerted Action on Thrombosis, Haemostasis (founder, sec. 1972-82, chmn. 1982-85). Roman Catholic. Home: 27 Milton Rd, Harpenden AL5 5LA, England Office: Nat Inst Biol Standards Control, South Mimms EN6 3QG, England

GAGGERO, JAMES PETER, corporate executive; b. Gibraltar, Aug. 1, 1959; s. Joseph James and Marilys (Healing) G.; m. Arabella Colvin, Apr. 21, 1983; children: Nicholas James, Alexander Charles. Grad., Royal Mil. Acad. Sandhurst, Eng., 1979. Mng. dir. Bland, Gibraltar, 1983—; bd. dirs. GB Airways, Ltd., Rock Hotel Ltd., Cadogan Travel Ltd., Bland, Ltd., House of Bellingham, Ltd., Gibraltar Airways. Swedish Vice-Consul Gibraltar, 1983—; trustee Gibraltar Heritage Trust, 1987—. Served to lt. inf. Irish Guards, 1979-82. Mem. Gibraltar C. of C. (bd. dirs. 1983—, sec. 1985—). Clubs: Guards and Cavalry, Royal Gibraltar Yacht. Home: 22/3 Witham's Rd, Gibraltar Gibraltar Office: Bland Group Cos, Cloister Building, Irishtown Gibraltar

GAGGERO, JOSEPH JAMES, diversified companies executive; b. Gibraltar, Nov. 20, 1927; s. George and Mabel (Andrews-Speed) G.; m. Marilys Healing, Nov. 8, 1958; children: James, Rosanne. Chmn., mng. dir. Bland Group Cos., Gibraltar; bd. dirs. Gibraltar Trust Bank Ltd. Hon. consul gen. Sweden Gibraltar; head tourist dept. Govt. Gibraltar, 1955-59, also various other coms.; past vice chmn. Gibraltar Soc. for Handicapped Children, Royal Life Saving Assn., Gibraltar. Mem. Gibraltar Hotel Assn. (chmn. 1962-75, 78, 86), Gibraltar Shipping Assn. (chmn. 1970-79), Brit. Travel Assn. (mem. council 1958-69), Brit. Maritime League (pres. Gibraltar chpt. 1983-84). Clubs: Travellers of London; Royal Gibraltar Yacht. Lodges: Rotary (pres. Gibraltar chpt. 1973-74), Knight of Holy Sepulchre, Order of North Star. Office: Bland Group of Cos, Cloister Bldg, Gibraltar Gibraltar

GAGGINI, MURIEL MARGUERITE, calligrapher; b. Le Coteau, Loire, France, Nov. 12, 1951; came to Japan, 1983.; Cert. calligraphy, New Sch. Social Research, 1983. Prof. calligraphy Tokyo YMCA, 1984—; free-lance calligrapher, illuminator; lectr. Internat. Christian U., Tokyo, 1984, Tokyo Internat. Family Y's Mens' Club, 1986—; researcher Biblioteca Medicea-Laurenziana, Firenze, Italy, 1986, Stiftsbibliotek, St. Gall, Switzerland, 1987, U. Miami, Ohio, 1988. Works exhibited at Tokyo Met. Gallery of Art. Recipient award from Japanese Minister of Fgn. Affairs, 1988. Mem. Soc. Scribes N.Y., Soc. Scribes and Illuminators London, Internat. Calligraphers Assn. (Gratianimi Testimonium 1987). Club: Tify's (Tokyo) (pres.). Home: Tomioka 2-10-12-202, Koto-ku, Tokyo 135, Japan

GAGNON, PAUL MICHAEL, lawyer, county attorney; b. Manchester, N.H., July 9, 1949; s. Raymond Charles, Sr. and Mary Elizabeth (Mullen) G.; m. Catherine Mary McBride, June 5, 1976; children—Nicole Marie, Amy Catherine. B.A., U. N.H., 1971; J.D., Suffolk U., 1977. Bar: N.H. 1977, U.S. Dist. Ct. N.H. 1977, U.S. Supreme Ct. 1984. Asst. county atty. Hillsborough County, Manchester, 1977-79, county atty., 1982-86; assoc. Malloy & Sullivan, 1979-81; sole practice, Manchester, 1981—; criminal law instr. St. Anselm's Coll., 1985-86. Bd. dirs. Hillsborough County Task Force Crimes Against Children, 1984-86; advisor Law Explorer post Boy Scouts Am., Manchester, 1981; committeeman Nat. State Democratic Com., 1984-86; Dem. candidate for gov., N.H., 1986. Served to 1st lt. USAF, 1971-74, N.H. Air N.G., 1975—. Mem. N.H. Bar Assn. (chmn. com. 1981-83), Manchester Bar Assn., ABA, Am. Trial Lawyers Assn., N.H. Assn. County Prosecutors. Democrat. Roman Catholic. Office: 795 Elm St Suite 501 Manchester NH 03101

GAHRTON, PER, political party official, author; b. Malmo, Sweden, Feb. 2, 1943; s. Arnold and Asta (De Sharengrad) G.; B.A., U. Lund, 1967; Ph.D. in Sociology, 1983; m. Ulla Lemberg, 1983; children by previous marriage—Petter, Stina. Mem. central bd. Swedish Liberal Youth, 1963-69, pres., 1969-71; mem. council City of Lund, Sweden, 1973-76; M.P., 1976-79; mem. polit. bur. Green Party, 1981-83, ofcl. spokesman, 1984-85; co-sec. European Greens, Brussels, 1985-88. Mem. Swedish Assn. Authors, Swedish Sociol. Assn. Author: Children in Sweden, 1968; Egypt's Revolution, 1968; Liberal Are You Crazy, 1970; The Struggle for Palestine, 1970; Stand Up in Fight, Oldies, 1972; Revolution in Swedish, 1973; What Role for the Liberal Party, 1972; The Arab World Facing the 80's, 1978; The Party Congress, 1978; Open Letter from a Politician, 1979; (novel) Can the Oldies trust us, 1979; The Election Campaign, 1980; Sweden Needs a New Party of the Future, 1980; (thesis) The Swedish Parliament from Within, 1983; Gold or Green Forests, 1985; Our Doubtful Defence, 1985; Egypt--An Arab Democracy, 1987; What do the Greens Want, 1988, Circus Sweden, 1988. Office: Henriksdalsringen 35, S-13132 Nacka Sweden

GAI, PEI, archaeologist; b. Helongjiang, Peoples Republic of China, Nov. 22, 1931; s. Wenhua and Kunfan (Zhao) G.; m. Wei Bai, Feb. 14, 1952; children: Na, Ming, Kedi. BS, U. Helongjiang, 1951. Asst. prof., assoc. research prof. Inst. Vertebrate Paleontology and Paleoanthropology, Academia Sinica, Beijing, 1956-87; vis. prof. Ariz. State U., 1981, U. Tsukuba, Tokyo, 1982, Bern U., Switzerland, 1985. Contbr. articles to profl. jours. Research grantee Smithsonian Instn., 1981. Mem. Archaeol. Soc. of China, Anthrop. Soc. of China. Office: Inst Vertebrate Paleontology, PO Box 643, Beijing Peoples Republic of China

GAILEY, ROBERT ALAN, museum director; b. Galway, Ireland, Oct. 4, 1935; s. Andrew James and Mary (Porter) G.; m. Evelyn McNee Thomson Sclater, Mar. 24, 1961; children: Michael Andrew Thomas, Alan James. BA with honors, Queens U., Belfast U., 1957; PhD, U. Glasgow, Scotland, 1961. Asst. U. Glasgow, 1957-60; research officer Ulster Folk & Transport Mus., Holywood, Ireland, 1960-63, asst. keeper, 1963-73, keeper dept. bldgs., 1973-86, acting dir., 1986-88, dir., 1988—. Author: Irish Folk Drama, 1969, Rural Houses of North of Ireland, 1984; editor Ulster Folklife jour. 1973-86; co-editor: Gold Under the Furze, 1982. Mem. Soc. Folklife Studies (sec. 1974-83, v.p. 1983-86, pres. 1986—). Presbyterian. Office: Ulster Folk & Transport Mus, Cultra Manor, Holywood BT18 0EU, Northern Ireland

GAILLON, ROLAND PIERRE, physician; b. Chatellerault, France, Jan. 7, 1938; s. Leri Goldenberg; children: Claire, Xavier. MD, U. Paris, 1964, diploma in Social Sci. and Econs., 1967. Intern, researcher Ctr. Hayem Hosp. St. Louis, Paris, 1964-65; dir. research and devel. Pharm. Industry,

Paris, 1965-72; gen. practice medicine Chatellerault, 1972—; cons. Direction Dept. l'Action Sanitare et Soc., Chatellerault, 1976—. Contbr. articles to profl. jours. Dep. mayor City of Chatellerault, 1983—. Socialist. Roman Catholic. Home and Office: 37 Ave Du Mal Leclerc, 86100 Chatellerault France

GAINES, IRVING DAVID, lawyer; b. Milw., Oct. 14, 1923; s. Harry and Anna (Finkelman) Ginsburg; m. Ruth Rudolph, May 22, 1947, (dec. Apr. 5, 1979); children—Jeffrey S., Howard R., Mindy S. Gaines Pearce; m. 2d, Lois Shier, Nov. 25, 1979. B.A., U. Wis., Madison, 1943, J.D., 1947; student U. Pa., Phila., 1943-44; Bar: Wis., 1947, Fla., 1971, U.S. Dist. Ct. (ea. dist.) Wis. 1947, U.S. Dist. Ct. (we. dist.) Wis. 1970, U.S. Dist. Ct. (so. dist.) Fla. 1972, U.S. Dist. Ct. (mid. dist.) Fla. 1976, U.S. Ct. Appeals (7th cir.) 1954, U.S. Ct. Appeals (11th cir.) 1981, U.S. Supreme Ct. 1954. Sole practice, Milw., 1947-72; ptnr. Gaines & Saichek, S.C. (and predecessor firm), Milw., 1972-78; sr. ptnr. Irving D. Gaines, S.C., Milw., 1979—. Served with AUS, 1943-46. Mem. Fla. Bar (bd. editors jour. 1973-84), Milw. Bar Assn. (past mem. exec. com., cts. com., econs. law com., past chmn. unauthorized practice of law com., past chmn. negligence sect., lectr. programs, seminars), State Bar Wis. (bd. govs. 1982-85, communications com. 1981-85), ABA (various coms.), 7th Fed. Cir. Bar Assn., Inter-Am. Bar Assn., Mem. Acad. Fla. Trial Lawyers, Wis. Acad. Trial Lawyers (pres. 1958-59, 70-71), Assn. Trial Lawyers Am. (state committeeman 1981-83), Am. Judicature Soc., Am. Soc. Law and Medicine, Am. Coll. Legal Medicine. Cert. civil litigation specialist Nat. Bd. Trial Advocacy. Home: 7821 N Mohawk Rd Milwaukee WI 53217 Office: 735 N Water St Suite 726 Milwaukee WI 53202

GAINES, WILLIAM MAXWELL, publishing executive; b. N.Y.C., Mar. 1, 1922; s. Max C. and Jessie K. (Postlethwaite) G.; m. Hazel Grieb, Oct. 21, 1944 (div. Feb. 9, 1948); m. Nancy Siegel, Nov. 17, 1955 (div. Mar. 1, 1971); children: Cathy, Wendy, Chris; m. Anne Griffiths, Feb. 21, 1987. Student, Poly. Inst. Bklyn., 1939-42; B.S. in Edn, N.Y. U., 1948. Pres. E. C. Publs. Inc. (pub. MAD Mag.), N.Y.C., 1948—. Served with AUS, 1942-46. Mem. Wine and Food Soc., Phi Alpha. Office: 485 Madison Ave New York NY 10022

GAINET, MICHEL EUGENE, physician; b. Hericourt, Haute Saone, France, Nov. 19, 1940; s. André and Mariette (Menetrez) G.; m. Annie Pautot, Oct. 29, 1965; children: Isabelle, Christine, Anne Valerie. MD, U. Besancon, France, 1969. Faculty asst. Faculty of Scis., Besancon, 1960-61; intern St. Jacques Hosp., Besancon, 1964-67; faculty asst. Faculty of Medicine, 5, 1966-69; sole practice Pierre-fontaine Les Varans, France, 1969—. Co-author therapy test, film on pollution of water; contbr. articles to med. and sci. jours. Councillor Municipality of Pierrefontaine Les Varans, 1977—. Served to capt. Mil. Health Service of France, 1968-69. Decorated chevalier Ordre Nat. du Merite, chevalier Palmes Academiques. Mem. French Assn. Gen. Practice. Roman Catholic. Lodge: Lions.

GAINSFORD, IAN DEREK, dental surgeon; b. Twickenham, Middlesex, Eng., June 24, 1930; s. Morris and Anne Freda (Aucken) Ginsberg; m. Carmel Liebster, June 13, 1957; children—Ann, Jeremy, Deborah. FDSRCS King's Coll., London U., 1955; BDS, London U., 1956; DDS with honors, Toronto (Can.) U., 1960; fellow Dental Surgery Royal Coll. Surgeons, Eng., 1968, mem. Gen. Dental Surgery Royal Coll. Surgeons, Eng., 1979. Lectr., King's Coll. Hosp. Med. Sch., London, 1956-57, London Hosp. Med. Coll., 1957-60, sr. lectr., 1960-70; sr. lectr., cons. King's Coll. Med. Sch., London, 1970—, vice-dean dental studies, 1973-77, dean Faculty of Clin. Dentistry, dir. Clin. Dental Services, 1977-87, dean Kings Coll. Sch. Medicine and Dentistry, 1988—; examiner London U., Leeds U., Royal Coll. Surgeons, Hong Kong U. Author: Silver Amalgam in Clinical Practice, 1965; co-author film: Amalgam Restoration, 1967. Fellow Kings Coll., Royal Soc. Medicine (mem. council odontology sect. 1983), Internat. Coll. Dentists; mem. Am. Dental Soc. London (past pres.), Am. Dental Soc. Europe (past pres.), Brit. Soc. Restorative Dentistry (past pres.), Am. Coll. Dentists; hon. mem. ADA. Clubs: Carlton, Athenaeum. Home: 31 York Terr East, London NW1 4PT England Office: King's Coll Sch Med and Dent, Denmark Hill, London SE5 8RX, England

GAISWINKLER, ROBERT SIGFRIED, savings and loan executive; b. Chgo., Jan. 7, 1932; s. Joseph Konrad and Henriette (Amlung) G.; m. Marilyn M. Reissen, Apr. 25, 1953; children: Janet Kay Sondles, Julia Ann Ervin, Robert, Ericka Lyn. BS, U. Ill., 1953. Chief exec. officer Security Savs. & Loan, Belleville, Ill., 1960-74; exec. v.p., chief exec. officer Metro East Fin. Corp., Belleville, 1965-74; exec. v.p., first chief operating officer Fed. Savs. and Loan, Columbus, Ohio, 1974-77; pres., chief exec. officer Nat. Savs. and Loan, Milw., 1977-88; chmn., dir. First Fin. Savs. Assn. and First Fin. Corp., Milw., 1988—; bd. dirs. First Fin. Savs. Assn. and First Fin. Corp.; chmn. bd. Nat. Equity Investments Corp., Nat. Diversified Fin., Inc., Nat Equity Real Estate Corp., Nat. Equity Securities, Venture Corp.; chmn. exec. com. Guaranty Nat. Morgage Corp., Los Angeles and San Francisco; sec. Nat. Council Savs. Instn., Washington; adv. bd. Fed. Savs. & Loan Adv. com.,; dir. rev. bd. Drayton Co., Bermuda, State of Wis. Savs. & Loan. Ill. commr. N.Y. Worlds Fair, 1963-65; Ill. commr. Office Equal Opportunity, 1963-65; bd. dirs. KETC Ednl. TV, St. Louis, WOSU Ednl. TV, Columbus; vice chmn. WMVS Ednl. TV, Milw.; trustee Mo. Mil. Acad. Served with USAF, 1951-52, AUS, 1952-54. Mem. Fed. Nat. Mortgage Assn. (bd. dirs.), Delta Upsilon. Roman Catholic. Clubs: Blue Mound Country; Vantana Country (Tucson). Home: 18465 Surrey Ln Brookfield WI 53005 Office: 2675 N Mayfair Rd Milwaukee WI 53226

GAITHER, GANT, artist, sculptor, designer, producer; b. Hopkinsville, Ky., Aug. 1, 1917; s. Joseph Gant and Jane Eskridge (Lum) G. Student U. Mex., Mexico City, 1933-34; B.A., U. of South, 1938; postgrad. Yale Sch. Architecture, 1938-39. Owner, producer Miami Beach Playhouse, Fla., 1940-43; producer Broadway Theater, N.Y.C., 1947-56; exec. producer Paramount Pictures Corp., Hollywood, Calif., 1960-64; artist-designer, licensor Shedrain Umbrella Co., Portland, Oreg., 1977—, Lilli Ann Corp. Ladieswear, San Francisco, 1986—, Bergquist Imports, Cloquet, Minn., 1981—, Artex-Green Corp., Bklyn., 1976—, Schreter Mens Neckwear, Balt., 1977—, Art Guild Greeting Cards, Glendale, Calif., 1980—. Artist-sculptor The Zoophisticates Collection, New York, Paris, Chgo., Mexico City, other locations. Author: Princess of Monaco, 1957. Author/illustrator: Sally Seal, 1964. Trustee Princess Grace Found.; bd. dirs. Baar & Beards Inc. Scarves, N.Y.C., Jewelmark Originals Ltd., N.Y.C. Served as sgt. USAF, 1943-46, PTO. Decorated Bronze Star; recipient Bronze Sculpture award Loews Monte-Carlo Hotel, Monaco, 1984. Republican. Episcopalian. Club: Yale (N.Y.C.). Home and Studio: The Zoophisticates Collection 1411 Buena Vista Dr Palm Springs CA 92262

GAJDUSEK, DANIEL CARLETON, pediatrician, research virologist; b. Yonkers, N.Y., Sept. 9, 1923; s. Karl A. and Ottilia D. (Dobroczki) G.; children: Ivan Mbagintao, Josede Figirliyong, Jesus Raglmar, Jesus Mororui, Mathias Maradol, Jesus Tamel, Jesus Salalu, John Paul Runman, Yavine Borima, Arthur Yolwa, Joe Yongorimah Kintoki, Thomas Youmog, Toni Wanevi, Toname Ikabala, Magame Prima, Senavayo Anua, Igitava Yoviga, Luwi Ikavara, Iram'bin'ai Undae'mai, Susanna Undapmaina, Steven Malrui, John Fasug Raglmar, Launako Wate, Louise Buwana, Regina Etangthaw Raglmar, Vincent Ayin, Daniel Sumal. BS, U. Rochester, 1943; MD, Harvard U., 1946; NRC fellow, Calif. Inst. Tech., 1948-49; DSc (hon.), U. Rochester, 1977, Med. Coll. Ohio, 1977, Washington & Jefferson Coll., 1980, Harvard U. Med. Sch., 1987, Dental Coll. of N.J., 1987; DHL (hon.), Hamilton Coll., 1977, U. Aix-Marseille, France, 1977, U. Hawaii, 1986; LL.D. (hon.), U. Aberdeen, Scotland, 1980. Diplomate: Am. Bd. Pediatrics. Intern, resident Babies Hosp., Columbia Presbyn. Med. Center, N.Y.C., 1946-47; resident pediatrics Children's Hosp., Cin., 1947-48; pediatric med. mission Germany, 1948; resident, clin. and research fellow Childrens Hosp., Boston, 1949-51; research fellow pediatrics and infectious diseases Harvard U., 1949-52; with Walter Reed Army Inst. Research, Washington, 1952-53, Institut Pasteur, Teheran, Iran and dept. med. U. Md., 1954-55; vis. investigator Nat. Found. Infantile Paralysis, Walter and Eliza Hall Inst. Med. Research, Melbourne, Australia, 1955-57; dir. program for study child growth and devel. and disease patterns in primitive cultures and lab. slow, latent and temperate virus infections Nat. Inst. Neurol. and Communicative Disorders and Stroke, NIH, Bethesda, Md., 1958—; chief Central Nervous System Studies Lab., 1970—; chief scientist research vessel Alpha Helix expdn. to Banks and Torres Islands, New Hebrides, South Solomon Islands, 1972; hon. prof. Hupei Med. Coll., Wuhan, Peoples Rep. of China, 1986; hon. prof. neurology Beijing Med. U., Republic of China, 1987; hon. faculty Med. Sch. U. of Papa New Guinea, Port Moresby, 1980; vis. prof. Royal Soc. of Medicine, 1987;. Author: Hemorrhagic Fevers and Mycotoxicoses in the USSR, 1951, Journals, 40 vols., 1954-85, Hemorrhagic Fevers and Mycotoxicoses, 1959, Slow Latent and Temperate Virus Infections, 1965, Correspondence on the Discovery of Kuru, 1976, (with Judith Farquhar) Kuru, 1980. Recipient E. Meade Johnson award Am. Acad. Pediatrics, 1963, Superior Service award NIH, HEW, 1970, Disting. Service award HEW, 1975, Prof. Lucian Dautrebande prize in pathophysiology Belgium, 1976, Nobel prize in physiology and medicine, 1976; Dyer lectr. NIH, 1974; Heath Clark lectr. U. London, 1974; B.K. Rachford lectr. Children's Hosp. Research Found., Cin., 1975; Langmuir lectr. Center for Disease Control, Atlanta, 1975; Withering lectr. U. Birmingham, Eng., 1976; Cannon Elie lectr. Boston Children's Med. Center, 1976; Zale lectr. U. Tex., Dallas, 1976; Bayne-Jones lectr. Johns Hopkins Med. Sch., Balt., 1976; Harvey lectr. N.Y. Acad. Medicine, 1977; J.E. Smadel lectr. Infectious Disease Soc. Am., 1977; Burnet lectr. Australasian Soc. Infectious Disease, 1978; Mapother lectr. U. London, 1978; Disting. lectr. in medicine Mayo Clinic, 1978; Kaiser Meml. lectr. U. Hawaii, 1979; Eli Lilly lectr. U. Toronto, 1979; Payne lectr. Children's Hosp. D.C., 1981; Ray C. Moon lectr. Angelo State U., Tex., 1981; Silliman lectr. Yale U., 1981; Blackfan lectr. Children's Hosp. Med. Ctr., Boston, 1981; Hitchcock Meml. lectr. U. Calif.-Berkeley, 1982; Nelson lectr. U. Calif.-Davis, 1982; Derick-MacKerres lectr. Queensland Inst. Med. Research, 1982; Bicentennial lectr. Harvard U. Sch. Medicine, 1982; Cartwright lectr. Columbia U., 1982; lectr. Chinese Acad. Med. Sci., 1983; Michelson lectr., prof., U. Tenn., Memphis, 1986; plenary lectr., Chinese Assn. Med. Virology, Yentai, 1986; returned Nobel Laureate, Karolinska Inst., Stockholm and U. Tromsö, Norway, 1986. Mem. Nat. Acad. Scis., Am. Acad. Arts and Scis., Am. Philos. Soc., Deutsche Akademie Naturförschen Leopoldina, Royal Acads. Medicine Belgium, Royal Anthrop. Inst. Gt. Britain and Ireland, Soc. Pediatric Research, Am. Pediatric Soc., Am. Soc. Human Genetics, Am. Acad. Neurology (Cotzias prize 1979), Soc. Neurosci., Am. Epidemiol. Soc., Infectious Diseases Soc. Am., Société des Oceanistes, Paris, Papua and New Guinea Sci. Soc., Slovak Acad. Scis., Academia Nacional de Medicina, Mexico and Colombia, Phi Beta Kappa, Sigma Xi. Home: Prospect Hill 6552 Jefferson Pike Frederick MD 21701 Office: NIH 36-5B21 Bethesda MD 20892

GALANE, IRMA ADELE BERESTON, electronic engineer; b. Balt., Aug. 23, 1921; d. Dr. Arthur and Sarah (Hillman) Bereston; B.A., Goucher Coll., 1940; postgrad. Johns Hopkins, 1940-42, Mass. Inst. Tech., 1943, George Washington U., 1945, 65, 73, 77, 79, U. Md., 1958, Army Mgmt. Sch., 1964; 1 dau., Suzanne Felice Galane Duvall. Physicist, Naval Ordnance Lab., 1942-43; electronic engr. Navy Bur. Ships, 1943-49, Army Office Chief Signal Officer, 1949-51, Navy Bur. Aeros., 1951-56, Air Research and Devel. Command, USAF, 1956-57, FCC, 1957-60, NASA, 1960-62; supervisory electronic engr. USCG Hdqrs., 1962-64; sci. specialist engring. scis. Library of Congress, 1964-65; project engr. Advanced Aerial Fire Support System, Army Materiel Command, 1965-66; engr. Naval Air Systems Command, 1966-71; electronic engr. Spectrum Mgmt. Task Force, FCC, 1971-76, sr. research engr. FCC, 1976—; Judge nat. capitol awards for engrs. and architects, 1975. Registered profl. engr., D.C. Mem. IEEE (sr.), Am. Inst. Aeros. and Astronautics, Nat. Soc. Profl. Engrs. (chmn. publs. com. 1959-60, co-chmn. civil def. com. 1965, spl. asst. to pres. 1965), Soc. Women Engrs. (sr. mem.; nat. membership chmn. 1952, nat. dir. 1953, mem. nat. scholarship com. 1958), Armed Forces Communications and Electronics Assn., Fedn. Profl. Assn., Am. Ordnance Assn., Johns Hopkins Alumni Assn., AAAS, U.S. Naval Inst., Marine Tech. Soc., Internat. Platform Assn., Smithsonian Inst. (assoc.), Mensa. Editor: The Met. Washington Profl. Engr., 1958-60. Home: 4201 Cathedral Ave NW Washington DC 20016

GALANE, MORTON ROBERT, lawyer; b. N.Y.C., Mar. 15, 1926; s. Harry J. and Sylvia (Schenkelbach) G.; m. Rosalind Feldman, Dec. 22, 1957; children: Suzanne Galane Duvall, Jonathan A. B.E.E., CCNY, 1946; LL.B., George Washington U., 1950. Bar: D.C. 1950, Nev. 1955, Calif. 1975. Patent examiner U.S. Patent Office, Washington, 1948-50; spl. partner firm Roberts & McInnis, Washington, 1950-54; practice as Morton R. Galane, P.C., Las Vegas, Nev., 1955—; spl. counsel to Gov. Nev., 1967-70. Contbr. articles to profl. jours. Chmn. Gov.'s Com. on Future of Nev., 1979-80. Fellow Am. Coll. Trial Lawyers; mem. Am. Law Inst., IEEE, Am. Bar Assn. (council litigation sect. 1977-83), State Bar Nev., State Bar Calif., D.C. Bar. Home: 2019 Bannies Ln Las Vegas NV 89102 Office: 302 E Carson Ave Suite 1100 Las Vegas NV 89101

GALANG, JESUS BELTRAN, exploration company executive; b. San Simon, Philippines, Oct. 21, 1943; s. Fernando Galang and Eduviges (Beltran) G.; m. Nectar Laurel, May 2, 1971; 1 child, J. Fernando. B.S. in Geology, U. Philippines, 1965; M.S. in Bus. and Mgmt. with distinction, Asian Inst. Mgmt., 1970. Vice pres. ops. Philippine Oil and Geothermal Co., 1974-78; regional acquisitions mgr. Bow Valley S.E.A., Singapore, 1979; chmn. Kingpin Internat., Philippines, 1981-86; pres. Ionex Corp., Philippines, 1980-81; sr. v.p. ops. Landoil GCSI Basic Co., United Arab Emirates, 1982-84; v.p. Landoil Mgmt. Ltd., Hongkong, 1982-85; petroleum adviser Emirate of Ajman, 1986. Author: (with others) Philppine Petroleum Handbook, 1976. Chmn. Philippine Friendship Soc., United Arab Emirates, 1983-84; Recipient Alumni Assn. award Asian Inst. Mgmt., 1979. Mem. Soc. Petroleum Engrs. (vice chmn. Dubai and No. Emirates chpt. 1985-86), United Arab Emirates Computer Soc., Assn. of Geoscientists for Internat. Devel., Am. Assn. Petroleum Geologists, Soc. Exploration in the Emirates (founder, pres. 1985-86). Roman Catholic. Club: Dubai Country (United Arab Emirates). Lodge: Lions (bd. dirs. Metro Manila 1976-78). Avocations: swimming; computers; golf. Home: PO Box 4288, Sharjah United Arab Emirates Office: Dept Petroleum and. Mineral Resources, Box 739, Ajman United Arab Emirates

GALANOPOULOS, KELLY, biomedical engineer; b. Athens, Greece, Jan. 4, 1952; came to U.S. 1970, naturalized, 1976; d. Panayotis and Catherine (Calas) G.; m. Dale S. Kruchten, Sept. 4, 1982; 1 child, Catherine Roberta Kruchten. B.A., CUNY, 1974; M.S., Poly. Inst. N.Y., 1978, postgrad., 1982—; postgrad. L.I. U., 1982—. Dir. bio-med. engring. Wycoff Heights Hosp., Bklyn., 1980-83, Bronx Lebanon Hosp., N.Y.C., 1983—; cons. Environ. Co., N.Y.C., 1980—, Joint Purchasing, N.Y.C., 1980—. Mem. Assn. Advancement Med. Instrumentation, IEEE, Soc. Women Engrs., N.Y. Acad. Scis.

GALANTE, JANE HOHFELD, pianist, music historian; b. San Francisco, Feb. 14, 1924; d. Edward and Lillian (Devendorf) Hohfeld; A.B., Vassar Coll., 1944; M.A., U. Calif.-Berkeley, 1949; m. Clement Galante, Dec. 26, 1956; children—Edward Elio, John Clement. Instr., U. Calif., Berkeley, 1948-52, Mills Coll., Oakland, Calif., 1950-52; music editor Berkeley, A Jour. of Modern Culture, 1944-52; founder, dir. Composers' Forum of San Francisco, 1946-56; concert pianist German tours for USIS, 1952-54; Young Audience Concerts, San Francisco, 1963-70; now mem. Lyra Chamber Music Ensemble; trustee Morrison Chamber Music Center at San Francisco State U., ; hon. trustee San Francisco Conservatory of Music, 1970—. Transl.: Darius Milhaud (Paul Collaer) including revised and edited catalog Milhaud's Compositions, 1988. Decorated chevalier de l'ordre des arts et des lettres. Mem. Am. Fedn. of Musicians, Women Musicians Club of San Francisco, Chamber Music Am.

GALANTE, MARY THERESE, nurse; b. Albany, N.Y., Nov. 25, 1956; d. Thomas Joseph and Anne Therese (Davis) Dunvar; m. Nicholas Thomas Galante, III, June 10, 1978; children—Elizabeth Nolan, Nicholas Thomas, Katharine Carey, James Davis. B.S. in Nursing, Catholic U. Am., 1978. Nurse pvt. office, Washington, 1975-77; nurse acute CCU, St. Peter Hosp., Albany, N.Y., 1979-80, registered profl. nurse Tri-Cities Nursing Registry, Albany, 1982—, patient care coordinator, 1983—. Vol., mem. fundraising com. Am. Cancer Soc., 1979—, Leukemia Soc., 1978—, M.S. Assn., 1983—; sec., chmn. Jr. League Provisional Com., Troy, N.Y., 1983-85, chmn. ways and means com., 1986-87, mem. ednl. policy and long-range planning com. Emma Willard Children's Sch., 1985-86, bd. dirs., 1984-87, active mem. Jr. League of Albany, 1987—. Author: Hold the Fort, 1984. Mem. Am. Nursing Assn., Nat. League Nursing. Democrat. Roman Catholic. Home: 10 Loudon Heights N Loudonville NY 12211

GALASKO, CHARLES SAMUEL BERNARD, orthopedic surgeon, educator; b. Johannesburg, Republic of South Africa, June 29, 1939; s. David Isaac and Rose (Shames) G.; m. Carole Freyda Lapinsky; children: Deborah, Gavin. MB, BCh with honors, U. Witwatersrand, Republic of South Africa, 1962, MCh, 1970; MSc (hon.), U. Manchester, Salford, Eng., 1980. Fellow Royal Coll. Surgeons. House surgeon Johannesburg Gen. Hosp., 1963-64, sr. house surgeon orthopaedic surgery, 1965, registrar orthopaedic surgery, 1965-66; house surgeon Hammersmith Hosp., London, 1966-67, surg. registrar, 1966-67, dir. orthopaedic surgery, 1973-76; sr. orthopaedic registrar Radcliffe Infirmary, Oxford, Eng., 1970-73; prof. orthopaedic surgery U. Manchester, 1976—; hon. cons. orthopaedic surgery Salford (Eng.) Health Authority; temporary advisor World Health Authority, 1981; lectr. in field. Author: Skeletal Metastases, 1986, Radionuclide Scintigraphy in Orthopaedics, 1984, (with others) Principles of Fracture Management, 1984; editor: Neuromuscular Problems in Orthopaedics, 1987, Recent Developments in Orthopaedics, others; contbr. over 150 articles to profl. jours. U. Witwatersrand scholar; fellow Australian Commonwealth, Internat. Union Against Cancer, SICOT, ABC. Fellow Brit. Orthopaedic Assn., Royal Soc. Medicine, Manchester Med. Soc.; mem. Brit. Orthopaedic Research Soc., Girdlestone Orthopaedic Soc., Internat. Orthopaedic Research Soc. (founder), Surg. Research Soc., Metastasis Research Soc. (founder), South African Surg. Research Soc., Brit. Assn. Surg. Oncology (founder), Brit. Nuclear Medicine Soc., Brit. Rheumatol. Assn. (assoc.), Brit. Med. Assn., Brit. Orthopaedic Travelling Assn., Brit. Children's Orthopaedic Surgery Soc., Brit. Skeletal Dysplasia Group, Rhino, Charles O'Neill Med. Club, Manchester Pediatric, ABC Orthopaedic, Manchester and Salford Med. Engring. (past pres.). Office: U Manchester, Dept Orthopaedic Surgery, Old Eccles Rd, Salford M6 8HD, England

GALBIATI, RODOLFO ENRICO, library director; b. Giussano, Italy, Feb. 4, 1914; s. Arturo and Eugenia (Mazzuchelli) G. Grad., Theol. Faculty, Milan, 1937; grad. in Biblical Scis., Pontif Biblical Inst., Rome, 1954. Ordained priest Roman Cath. Ch., 1937. Prof. Theol. Sem., Milan, 1941-76; Dr. Biblioteca Ambrosiana, Milan, 1953—, dir., 1984—; tchr. Hebrew Univ. Cattolica, Milan, 1965-73. Office: Biblioteca Ambroisiana, Piazza PIO X1 2, 20123 Milan Italy

GALBRAITH, EUGENE KEITH, anthropologist, consultant; b. N.Y.C., Aug. 28, 1952; s. Eugene Xavier and Virginia Marie (Fleming) G.; m. Suzanne Eloise Siskel, June 3, 1978. BA, Johns Hopkins U., 1974, PhD, 1983. Lectr. U. Md., College Park, 1976-77, George Wash. U., Washington, 1980-82; instr. McCoy Coll., Balt., 1982-83; dir. Perhimpunan Persahabatan Indonesia-Am., Surabaya, Indonesia, 1983-84; advisor NTT Provincial Devel. Planning Bd., Kupang, Indonesia, 1984—; examiner U. Diponegoro, Semarang, Indonesia, 1984. Contbr. articles to profl. jours. Observer Contag Third Congress, Brasilia, Brazil, 1979. Mem. Am. Anthropol. Assn., Am. Ethological Assn., Camp Network. Home: Jl Hati Mulia 8, Kupang 85111, Indonesia Office: Bappeda TK 1 NTT, Jl Terate, Kupang 85111, Indonesia

GALBRAITH, JOHN KENNETH, economist; b. Iona Station, Ont., Can., Oct. 15, 1908; s. William Archibald and Catherine (Kendall) G.; m. Catherine Atwater, Sept. 17, 1937; children: Alan, Peter, James. B.S., U. Toronto, 1931; M.S., U. Calif., 1933, Ph.D., 1934; postgrad., Cambridge (Eng.) U., 1937-38; LL.D. (hon.), Bard Coll., U. Calif., Miami U., U. Mass., U. Mysore, Brandeis U., U. Toronto, U. Guelph, U. Sask., U. Mich., U. Durham, R.I. Coll., Boston Coll., Hobart and William Smith Colls., Albion Coll., Tufts U., Adelphi Suffolk Coll., Mich. State U., Louvain U., Cambridge U., U. Paris, Carleton Coll., U. Vt., Queens U., others. Research fellow U. Calif., 1931-34; instr. and tutor Harvard U., 1934-39; asst. prof. econs. Princeton U., 1939-42; econ. adviser Nat. Def. Adv. Commn., 1940-41; asst. adminstr. in charge price div. OPA, 1941-42, dep. adminstr., 1942-43; mem. bd. of editors Fortune Mag., 1943-48; lectr. Harvard U., 1948-49, prof. econs., 1949-75, Paul M. Warburg prof. econs., 1959-75, ret., 1975; fellow Trinity Coll., Cambridge U.; hon. prof. U. Geneva; U.S. ambassador to India, 1961-63. Author: numerous books including American Capitalism, 1952, A Theory of Price Control, 1952, The Great Crash, 1955, The Affluent Society, 1958, The Liberal Hour, 1960, Economic Development, 1963, The Scotch, 1964, The New Industrial State, 1967, Indian Painting, 1968, The Triumph, 1968, Ambassador's Journal, 1969, Economics, Peace and Laughter, 1971, A China Passage, 1973, The Age of Uncertainty, 1977, Economics and the Public Purpose, 1973, Money: Whence It Came, Where It Went, 1975, (with Nicole Salinger) Almost Everyone's Guide to Economics, 1978, Annals of an Abiding Liberal, 1979, The Nature of Mass Poverty, 1979, A Life in Our Times, 1981, The Anatomy of Power, 1983, The Voice of the Poor: Essays in Economic and Political Persuasion, 1983, The Triumph, 1984, Economics in Perspective: A Critical History, 1988; contbr. to econ. and sci. jours. Dir. U.S. Strategic Bombing Survey, 1945; dir. Office of Econ. Security Policy, State Dept., 1946. Fellow Social Sci. Research Council, 1937-38; Recipient Medal Freedom, 1946. Fellow Am. Acad. Arts and Scis. (pres., bd. dirs. 1984-87); mem. Nat. Inst. of Arts and Letters (pres., bd. dirs. 1984—), Am. Econ. Assn. (pres. 1972), Am. Agrl. Econ. Assn., Americans for Democratic Action (chmn. 1967-68). Clubs: Century (N.Y.C.); Federal City (Washington); Saturday (Boston). Home: 30 Francis Ave Cambridge MA 02138 Office: Am Acad & Inst of Arts & Letters 633 W 155th St New York NY 10032-7599 *

GALE, MARLA, clinical social worker; b. Uniontown, Pa., July 20; d. Saul and Sarah (Lisowitz) Krongold; m. Edward Gale, June 12, 1954; children: Jeffrey, Wendy, Lori. AB magna cum laude, U. Miami, 1970; MSW, Barry Coll., 1972. Diplomate in clin. social work. Research social worker VA Hosp., Miami, Fla., 1971; caseworker Jewish Family Service Broward County, Hollywood, Fla., 1971-81, supr. profl. staff, 1981—; mem. clin. faculty Barry U., Miami Shores, Fla.; parent effectiveness instr.; real estate investor and developer; pres. Gold Coast Convenient Food Marts. Mem. Nat. Assn. Social Workers, Acad. Cert. Social Workers, Common Cause, Project Newborn, Met. Mus., Animal Protection Soc., Diabetes Research Inst. Democrat. Jewish. Office: 4517 Hollywood Blvd Hollywood FL 33021

GALE, ROBERT PETER, physician, medical educator, scientist, researcher; b. N.Y.C., Oct. 11, 1945; s. Harvey Thomas and Evelyn (Klein) G.; m. Tamar Tishler, June 2, 1976; children—Tal, Shir, Elan. B.A., Hobart Coll., 1966; M.D., SUNY-Buffalo, 1970; Ph.D., UCLA, 1976. Diplomate Am. Bd. Internal Medicine, Am. Bd. Med. Oncology. Intern, then resident dept. medicine UCLA, 1970-72, resident I and II in hematology and oncology, 1972-74; Postdoctral studies UCLA Med Ctr.; assoc. prof. medicine UCLA, 1974—; chmn. Internat. Bone Marrow Transplant Registry, Milw., 1982—; Meyerhoff vis. prof. Weizmann Inst. Sci., Israel, 1983; vis. prof. Excerpta Medica Found., Amsterdam, 1979; pres. Armand Hammer Ctr. for Advanced Studies in Nuclear Energy and Health. Author 13 books, numerous articles on hematology, oncology and transplantation. Recipient Presdl. award N.Y. Acad. Sci., 1986, Olender Peace Prize, 1986; Leukemia Soc. Am. scholar, 1976-81. Fellow ACP; mem. Transplantation Soc., Am. Soc. Hematology, Am. Assn. Immunologists, Internat. Soc. Hematology, Internat. Soc. Exptl. Hematology, Am. Soc. Clin. Oncology, Am. Assn. Cancer Research. Home: 2316 Donella Circle Bel Air CA 90077 Office: UCLA Sch Medicine Los Angeles CA 90024 *

GALE, STEVEN HERSHEL, college director; b. San Diego, Aug. 18, 1940; s. Norman Arthur and Mary Louise (Wilder) G.; m. Kathy L. L. Johnson, May 20, 1973; children—Shannon Erin, Ashley Alyssa, Kristin Heather. B.A., Duke U., 1963; M.A., UCLA, 1965; Ph.D., U. So. Calif., 1970. Reading asst. English, Los Angeles Met. Coll., 1965-66; teaching asst. U. So. Calif., 1966, instr., 1967-68; assoc. UCLA, 1968-70; asst. prof. U. P.R., Rio Piedras, 1970-73; Fulbright prof. U. Liberia, Monrovia, 1973-74; assoc. prof. U. Fla., Gainesville, 1974-80; prof., head dept. English, Mo. So. State Coll., Joplin, 1980-84, dir. coll. honors program, 1984-87; endowed prof. humanities Ky. State U., Frankfort, 1988—; dir. Univ. Players, Monrovia Players; author lecture series Am. Film History for USIS, Liberia, 1974, Assn. Depts. English Ann. Salary Survey, 1984; spl. advisor Liberian Ministry Edn., 1973-74; cons. NEH, Fla. Fine Arts Council; participant confs., convs., seminars, also NEH Humanities Perspectives on Professions, USIS cultural exchange tour, India, 1964. Author: Butter's Going Up, 1977; Harold Pinter: An Annotated Bibliography, 1978; S. J. Perelman: An Annotated Bibliography, 1985; Harold Pinter: Critical Approaches, 1986, S.J. Perelman: A Critical Study, 1987, Ency. of Am. Humorists, 1988; also short stories, dramas, poetry. Abstractor ann. Internat. Bibliography of the Theatre, Abstracts of English Studies. Series editor: Contemporary American and British Drama and Film, 1983-88. Pacific film editor RIMU. Editor: Readings for Today's Writers, 1980; co-editor: The Pinter Rev.; contbr. articles to profl. jours. Reviewer, Garland Press, John Wiley & Sons, St. Martin's Press, Modern Drama, Pacific Quar., Harcourt, Brace, Jovanovich, Little-Brown, Prentice-Hall, William C. Brown. Referee, Theatre Jour., Publs. of Mo. Philol. Assn., Studies in Am. Humor. Mem. alumni admissions com. Duke U.; judge Joplin Globe Regional Spelling Bee; sideline ofcl. Joplin Boys' Club Girls' Soccer; umpire Joplin Girls Little League softball; v.p. Great Plains Regional Honors Council, 1986; pres., adv. bd. dirs. Joplin-Nat. Affiliation for Literacy Advance, 1982—. Grantee NEH, 1987, U. P.R., 1971, 72, U. Fla. Humanities Council, 1975, 77, Mo. So. State Coll., 1980, 81, 82, 83, 84, 85, 86, 87; Danforth assoc., 1976-84, grantee, 1982. Mem. MLA (dir. session grad. program and curriculum devel., Del. Assembly 1981-83, co-chmn. Assn. Depts. English Job Seekers Workshop 1981), Am. Theatre Assn. (regional del. Univ. and Coll. Theatre Assn.), African Studies Ctr. (U. Fla.), AAUP, Am. Film Inst., So. Assn. Africanists, Fulbright Alumni Assn., Nat. Ret. Tchrs. Assn., Con. on Coll. Composition, Coll. Eng. Assn., Nat. Collegiate Honors Council, Beckett Soc., Harold Pinter Soc. (founder, pres. 1986—), Fla. Track Ofcls. Assn., Mid-Fla. Ofcls. Assn., Fla. High Sch. Activities Assn., Mo. State Tchrs. Assn., Am. Soc. Theatre Research, Chi Delta Pi. Home: Route 5 Box 510 Joplin MO 64804 Office: Ky State Univ Frankfort KY 40601

GALER, BENJAMIN ANDERSON, lawyer, financial executive; b. Mt. Pleasant, Iowa, May 3, 1915; s. Paul B. and Ruth (Anderson) G.; m. Dorothy I. Mathews, Sept. 4, 1939; children—Dorothea Galer Higgins, Ernest L. Student Iowa Wesleyan Coll., Mt. Pleasant, 1931-33; B.A., U. Iowa, 1935, J.D. magna cum laude, 1937. Bar: Iowa 1937, U.S. Dist. Ct. (so. dist.) Iowa 1937, U.S. Supreme Ct. 1972. Ptnr., Galer & Galer, and predecessors, 1937—; county atty., 1942-46; counsel Capitol Savs. and Loan Assn., Mt. Pleasant, 1945-84 , also dir.; v.p. Peoples State Bank, Winfield, Iowa, 1960-72, also dir.; dir. United Service Corp., Mt. Pleasant, 1971-84. Chmn., Henry County (Iowa) Republican Com., 1949-58, dist. chmn. State Central Com., 1958-66, del. Nat. Conv., 1960; mem. Henry County Mental Health Commn., 1958-75. Mem. ABA, Iowa Bar Assn. (gov. 1964-68), Henry County Bar Assn., Order of Coif, Phi Alpha Delta, Beta Theta Pi, Pi Kappa Delta. Methodist. Clubs: Kiwanis (pres. 1940), Masons. Co-editor Iowa Law Rev., 1936-37. Home: 707 Alter Dr Mount Pleasant IA 52641 Office: 211 W Monroe St Mount Pleasant IA 52641

GALIC, PAVAO, librarian, philologist; b. Zadar, Yugoslavia, Jan. 31, 1931; s. Paško and Ester (Pirih) G. Dr Philosophy, U. Zagreb, 1954, PhD, 1960. Librarian-counsellor to sci. counsellor Naučna Biblioteka, Zadar, 1954—. Author: The History of Zadar's Libraries, 1969, The History of Zadar's Printing House, 1979; contbr. over 100 articles on library sci. and philology to profl. jours. Mem. Croatian Library Assn. (Kukuljeviceva povelja award 1979). Roman Catholic. Home: O Price 11, 57000 Zadar Yugoslavia Office: Naučna Biblioteka, 57000 Zadar Yugoslavia

GALICIAN, MARY-LOU, broadcasting educator; b. New Bedford, Mass., Apr. 5, 1946; d. Benn and Evelyn Nancy (Scott) G. BA magna cum laude, L.I. U., 1966; MS, Syracuse U., 1969; EdD, Memphis State U., 1978. Writer, N.Y. corr. Standard Times, New Bedford, 1961-66; producer, dir., talk show host Sta. WCMU-TV, Mt. Pleasant, Mich., 1967-70, dir. programming, 1968-70; v.p., dir. Evelyn-Nancy Cosmetiques, Inc., New Bedford, 1970-73; nat. advt. mgr. Maybelline Co./Schering-Plough, Memphis, 1973-75; pres., creator FUN-dynamics!, Memphis, Little Rock, Phoenix, 1976—; prof. journalism Memphis State U., 1978-80; nat. mktg. mgr. Fedn. Am. Hosps., Little Rock and Washington, 1980-82; prof. broadcasting Ariz. State U., Tempe, 1983—; motivation, communication cons. various nat. pub. and pvt. orgns., 1966—; speaker, performer nat. convs. and co., 1966—; mem. broadcast services subcom. FCC Industry Adv. Com., Grand Rapids, Mich., 1967-70; mem. adv. bd. Cen. Mich. Ednl. Resources Council, Mich., 1967-70; anchor nat. TV fund drives, 1984—. Author: Medical Education and the Physician-Patient Relationship, 1978, The Dr. Galician Prescription for Healthy Media Relations, 1980; writer, producer No Miracles Here, 1967, Witch is it?, 1969-70, Saturday's Child: 20 Years of Network TV Children's Programs, 1969; editor: The Coming Victory, 1980; radio host To Broadway with Love, 1967, TV host Interview with Mary-Lou Galician, 1967-70; scriptwriter, songwriter, presenter FUN-dynamics! The FUN-damentals of DYNAMIC Living, 1976—; writer, performer FUN-dynamics! FUN-notes, 1982; contbr. articles to profl. publs. Charter mem. Symphony League of Cape Cod, Mass., 1972-73; adviser Boy Scout Explorer Post, Cape Cod, 1972-73; mem. exec. bd. Tenn.-Ark.-Miss. Girl Scouts U.S., Memphis, 1973-75; patron Memphis Ballet Co., 1974-75; mem. steering com. Make Today Count, Memphis, 1976; Health Systems Agy. Council mem. MidSouth Med. Ctr. Council, Memphis, 1976-78; chair campaign kick-off Valley of the Sun United Way, Phoenix, 1987; co-chair Ariz. State U. United Way Campaign, 1988-90. Recipient Cert. Achievement, S.W. Edn. Council for Journalism, 1985, 86, 87, Walter Cronkite Sch. Service award, 1988; named Mich.'s Woman of Yr., Outstanding Ams. Found., 1969; Conolly Coll. scholar L.I. U., 1963-66; grantee Ariz. State U., 1984, 85, 87; Syracuse U. fellow, 1966-67. Mem. AAUW (bd. dirs. Mich. and Memphis chpts. 1967-73), Am. Advt. Fedn. (pyramid awards com. 1980), Am. Women in Radio and TV (com. chair Tenn. chpt. 1979), Ariz. State U. Faculty Women's Assn., Assn. Edn. in Journalism and Mass Communication, Broadcast Edn. Assn. (promotion com. 1985, leadership challenge com. 1988—), Pub. Relations Soc. Am. (faculty adviser Ariz. State U. 1983-84), Sales and Mktg. Execs. Internat. (com. chair Ark. chpt. 1981-83), Women in Communications Inc. (founding faculty adviser Cen. Mich. U. 1969-70, Memphis State U. 1979-80, Ariz. State U. 1985—, bd. dirs. Phoenix Profl. chpt., 1985—, mem. Nat. bd. dirs. and v.p. Far West region, 1987—, nat. editorial bd. 1987—, Outstanding Adv. award 1985-86, 87-88), Zeta Tau Alpha (gen. faculty adviser 1968-70, membership adviser 1974-75). Club: Univ. of Ariz. State U. Home: 614 E Diamond Dr Tempe AZ 85283 Office: Ariz State U Walter Cronkite Sch Journalism Tempe AZ 85287-1305

GALIE, LOUIS MICHAEL, electronics company executive; b. Phila., Aug. 10, 1945; s. Adam Michael and Phyllis Anne (Bowers) G.; m. Elizabeth D. Viviano, June 23, 1969 (div. June 1980); 1 child, Kathryn Louise; m. Charlene Mary Gates, Aug. 27, 1983. BS, U. Chgo., 1967, MS, 1968. Prin. researcher System Devel. Corp., Santa Monica, Calif., 1975-80; dir. devel. Burroughs Corp., Danbury, Conn., 1980-82; dir. engring. Timex Corp., Waterbury, Conn., 1982-86, v.p. research and devel., 1986—. Author: Means for Database Search, 1980, Electronic Spelling Correction, 1981; patentee in field. Warden Trinity Episcopal Ch., Newtown, Conn., 1985—. Served to comdr. USN, 1969-75. Mem. IEEE, Soc. for the History of Tech. Republican. Home: 141 Brushy Hill Rd Newtown CT 06470 Office: Timex Corp Waterbury CT 06720

GALIMORE, MICHAEL OLIVER, marketing communications company executive; b. Bloomington, Ind., June 15, 1947; s. Howard Fenwick and Donna (Patterson) G.; m. Kathryn Carol Kaser, Nov. 30, 1975; 1 child, Jonathan Michael. Student, Ind. U., 1966-68; B.A., Ambassador Coll., Pasadena, Calif., 1972. Art dir. White Arts, 1976-79; advt. mgr. Cook, Inc., Bloomington, 1979-80, graphics dir., 1980—; writer, graphics cons. Wyldefyre Communications, 1987—. Graphic artist The Plain Truth mag., 1972. Recipient Recognition award for graphic arts excellence Consol. Papers, Inc., 1983. Mem. Ch. of God Seventh Day. Club: Ambassador Spokesman. Home: Rt 1 Box 752 Spencer IN 47460 Office: Cook Inc 925 S Curry Pike Bloomington IN 47401 also: Wyldefyre Communications PO Box 271 Bloomington IN 47402

GALINIS, NORBERT MICHAEL, educational consultant; b. Detroit, Sept. 9, 1944; s. Charles Joseph and Marie Rita (Wojtczak) G. BS, Western Mich. U., 1967; MA, U. Mich., 1983, postgrad., 1985—. Tchr. history Willow Run Community Schs., Ypsilanti, Mich., 1969-73, tchr. indsl. arts, 1973-80, ednl. asst. House B, Edmonson Middle Sch., 1980-83, tchr. microcomputer edn., 1984-86; ednl. cons., Ypsilanti, 1986—. Dir. field sports Boy Scouts Am., 1968-70, dir. camp, 1971-74. Mem. NEA, Mich. Edn. Assn., Nat. Hist. Soc., Assn. Supervision and Curriculum Devel., Mich. Assn. Middle Sch. Educators, Mich. Assn. Computer Users in Learning, Nat. Council States on Inservice Edn., Internat. Council Computers in Edn., Pi Kappa Alpha (dist. pres. 1971-73, Disting. Service award 1972). Office: 1800 E Forest St Ypsilanti MI 48197

GALITZINE, GEORGES PIERRE, company executive; b. Paris, Dec. 20, 1931; s. Boris and Olga Galitzine; m. Catherine de Schulthess Rechberg; children: Pierre, Cyril. H.E.C., Stanford U. Mgr. Au Printemps, Paris, 1955-75; chmn. bd. AAF La Providence, Paris, 1976—. Lodge: Rotary. Home: 12 rue d'Andigne, 75116 Paris France Office: AAF La Providence SA 14, Blvd de la Chapelle, 75018 Paris France

GALKIN, SAMUEL BERNARD, orthodontist; b. Newark, Feb. 9, 1933; s. Saul J. and Mollie (Kleinberg) G.; student U. Conn., 1951-54; D.D.S., Temple U., 1958; M.S. in Histology, certificate in grad. orthodontics U. Ill., 1963; children from previous marriage: Jamie Michelle, Richard Stewart; m. Gail Beth Elkin, Feb. 26, 1972; children—Scott David, Seth Paul. Group practice orthodontics, Woodbridge, N.J., 1963—; staff orthodontist J.F.K. Community Hosp., Edison, N.J., 1966—, cleft palate com., 1971—, dir. dental dept., 1979—; staff Woodbridge Health Center, 1967—, dental adv. com., 1971—; dir. dept. dentistry John F. Kennedy Med. Center, Edison, 1979-81; staff orthodontist Perth Amboy Gen. Hosp., N.J., 1986—, Rahway Hosp., N.J., 1986—; asst. prof. orthodontics N.J. Coll. Medicine and Dentistry, Jersey City, 1963-73; mem. panel physicians N.J. Crippled Children Program, 1971—. Chmn., Woodbridge Twp. Debutante Ball, 1970; bd. dirs. Woodbridge Twp. YMCA. Served to lt. Dental Corps, USNR, 1958-61. Diplomate Am. Bd. Orthodontics. Mem. Middle Atlantic Soc. Orthondontists (chmn. clinics 1969, 72), N.J., Middlesex County dental socs., ADA, Am. Soc. Dentistry for Children, Am. Assn. Orthodontists, Am. Lingual Orthodontic Assn. (charter), Am. Assn. Dental Schs., Am. Acad. Oral Medicine, Alpha Omega (chpt. v.p. 1969—), Omicron Kappa Upsilon. Home: 3 Dorset Rd Colonia NJ 07067 Office: 711 Amboy Ave PO Box 830 Woodbridge NJ 07095 also: 233 Madison Ave Perth Amboy NJ 08861

GALL, FRANCOIS, TV executive producer; b. St. Germain, Ile de France, France, Nov. 9, 1922; s. Adolphe and Hemon (Suzan) G. Correspondent French Press, Indochina, 1948-50; correspondent freelance, 1951-56; reporter France Soir newspaper, Paris, 1956-68; TV producer French TV, Paris, 1968—; author free lance, 1954—. Author: numerous novels. Served in French Resistance Movement 1942-44, 2nd lt. First French Army, 1944-45, ETO. Roman Catholic. Home: 43 rue St Merri, 75004 Paris France Office: Antenne 2 TV Channel, 22 Ave Montaigne, 75008 Paris France

GALL, LENORE ROSALIE, educational administrator; b. Bklyn., Aug. 9, 1943; d. George W. Gall and Olive Rosalie (Weekes) Gall Bryant. AAS, NYU, 1970, cert. tng. and devel., 1975, BS in Mgmt., 1973, MA in Counselor Edn., 1977; EdM and EdD, Columbia U., 1988. Various positions Ford Found., N.Y.C., 1967-75; dep. dir. career devel. Grad. Sch. Bus., NYU, N.Y.C., 1976-79; dir. career devel. Pace Lubin Sch. Bus., N.Y.C., 1979-82; dir. career devel. Sch. Mgmt., Yale U., New Haven, 1982-85; asst. to assoc. provost Bklyn. Coll., 1985-88, asst. to provost, 1988—; adj. lectr. LaGuardia Community Coll., L.I. City, N.Y., 1981—, Sch. Continuing Edn. NYU, 1983-84; dir., sec. devel. workshop Coll. Placement Services, Bethlehem, Pa., 1978-81. Bd. dirs. Langston Hughes Community Library, Corona, N.Y., 1975-83, 86—, chair, 1975-79, 82-83, 2d v.p., 1986, 1st v.p., 1987-88, chair awards com. Dollars for Scholars, Corona, 1976—. Mem. Assn. Black Women in Higher Edn. (exec. bd., membership chair, pres.-elect 1988), Am. Assn. Univ. Adminstrs., Nat. Assn. Univ. Women (chaplain 1987-88, 2d v.p. 1988), AAUW, Nat. Assn. Women Deans and Adminstrs., Black Faculty and Staff Assn. Bklyn. Coll. (1st vice-chair 1986-87, chair 1987-88), New Haven C. of C. (chmn. women bus. and industry conf. 1984), Nat. Council Negro Women Inc. (1st v.p. North Queens sect. 1986—, life), Phi Delta Kappa, Kappa Delta Pi. Mem. A.M.E. Ch. Office: CUNY Bklyn Coll 3137 Boylan Hall Bedford Ave and Ave H Brooklyn NY 11210

GALL, LOTHAR, historian, educator; b. Lötzen, Fed. Republic Germany, Dec. 3, 1936; s. Franz and Gabriele (Boetticher) G.; m. m. Claudia Eder, July 4, 1973; children: Franziska, Tobias. PhD, U. Munich, 1960. Habilitation U. Cologne, Fed. Republic Germany, 1967; prof. history U. Giessen, Fed. Republic Germany, 1968-72, Free U., Berlin, 1972-75, J.W. Goethe U., Frankfurt/Main, Fed. Republic Germany, 1975—; vis. prof. Oxford U., 1972-73. Author: Benjamin Constant, 1963, Der Liberalismus als regierende Partei, 1968, Bismarck., Der Weisse Revolutionar, 1980 (English, French, Italian, Japanese translations), Europa auf dem Weg in die Moderne, 1850 1890, 1984; editor Historische Zeitschrift, 1975 . Mem. Bayerischen Acad. Wissenschaften (hist. commn.), Kommission für die Geschichte des Parlamentarismus and Politischen Parteien. Lodge: Rotary. Home: Rosselstrasse 7, 6200 Wiesbaden Federal Republic of Germany Office: JW Goethe U, Hist Seminar, Senckenberganlage 31, D-6000 Frankfurt/ Main Federal Republic of Germany

GALLACHER, HUGH PATRICK, sociologist, publisher; b. Voorburg, The Netherlands, Dec. 28, 1946; s. James and Johanna Maria (De Hoog) G.; m. Antonia Jacoba van Servellen, Nov. 26, 1971. Gymnasium alpha, St. Aloysius Coll., The Hague, Netherlands, 1965; sociology State U. Leyden (Netherlands), 1971. Tchr. history Rembrandt Lyceum, Leyden, 1971; asst. prof. sociology State U. Leyden, 1971-82, guest asst. prof. sociology, 1982-84; research coordinator Ministry of Agr., The Hague, 1984-86, head sect. fauna and flora protection, Ministry of Agr., The Hague, 1986; head sect. Info., Communication and Research, Twijnstra Gudde Mgmt. Cons., Deventer, The Netherlands, 1986—; pub. Vogelvreugd Pub. House, Voorhout, 1982—. Author: Vogels Leren Kennen, 1974; De Spreeuw (Jacques P. Thysse award 1980), 1978; Gids voor Vogelonderzoek, 1984. Founder, chmn. Found. Critical Wildlife Mgmt., 1975-82. Fellow Royal Soc. Arts; mem. Philosophy Sci. Assn., Soc. Social Studies Sci., Internat. Soc. Phenomenology and Human Scis. Home: Torenlaan 36, Voorhout 2215 RX The Netherlands Office: Twijnstra Gudde Mgmt Cons, Akkerdistel 18, 7122 MA Deventer The Netherlands

GALLAGHER, ANNE PORTER, business executive; b. Coral Gables, Fla., Mar. 16, 1950; d. William Moring and Anne (Jewett) Porter; m. Matthew Philip Gallagher, Jr., July 31, 1976; children: Jacqueline Anne, Kevin Sharkey. BA in Edn., Stetson U., 1972. Tchr. elem. schs., Atlanta, 1972-74; sales rep. Xerox Corp., Atlanta, 1974-76, Fed. Systems, Rosslyn, Va., 1976-81; sales rep. No. Telecom Inc. Fed. Systems, Vienna, Va., 1981-84, account exec., 1984-85, sales dir., 1985—. Mem. Nat. Assn. Female Execs., Pi Beta Phi. Episcopalian. Avocations: skiing, aerobics, needlepoint. Home: 4052 Seminary Rd Alexandria VA 22304 Office: No Telecom Fed Systems Inc 8614 Westwood Center Dr Vienna VA 22180

GALLAGHER, BERNARD PATRICK, editor, publisher; b. N.Y.C., Feb. 25, 1910; s. Bernard A. and Mary Helen (Fitzsimmons) G.; m. Harriet Denning, Oct. 17, 1942; 1 dau., Jill. Student, Columbia U., 1928-29, Akron U., 1941-44. Single-copy sales mgr. Crowell Pub. Co., 1932-34; sales mgr. charge sales tng. Stenotype Co., Inc., Chgo., 1934-39; pres. Stenotype Co. Ohio, Inc., Cleve., 1939-45, World Wide Publs. Inc., 1945-83, Gallagher Communications, Inc., 1974—; editor-in-chief pub. The Gallagher Report, 1952—, The Gallagher Presidents' Report, 1965—, Gallagher Med. Report, 1983—; pres. Gallagher Found., 1978—. Served with AUS, 1944-45. Mem. Southampton Assocs. Clubs: Canadian, Met. Office: Gallagher Communications Inc 230 Park Ave New York NY 10017

GALLAGHER, DENNIS HUGH, television, film and multi-media writer, producer, director; b. Chgo., May 2, 1936; s. Frederick Hugh and Mildred Agnes (Buescher) G.; student Wright Coll., 1954-56, Ill. Inst. Tech., 1956-57; B.Sc. in Physics, U. Ariz., 1966. Dir., Noble Planetarium and Obs., Ft. Worth Mus. Sci. and History, 1960-64; planetarium dir. Man. Mus. Man and Nature, Winnipeg, Can., 1966-70; pres. Omnitheatre Ltd., Winnipeg, 1970-72; pres. Gallagher & Assocs., Chgo., 1972-78, Internat. Travel Theatres, Chgo., 1978-81, Galaxy Prodns. Ltd., Chgo., 1981—; mem. faculty in astronomy and civil engring. U. Man., 1967-68; cons. edn., theater, 1967—. Served with USAR, 1959-65. Mem. Planetarium Assn. Can. (founding pres. 1968-69), Internat. Council Planetarium Execs., Am. Astron. Soc., Nat. Acad. TV Arts and Scis., Am. Soc. Tng. and Devel., Internat. TV Assn., Assn. Multi-Image, Chgo. Film Council. Author: North American Planetariums, 1966; Planetariums of the World, 1969; contbr. articles to profl. jours.; writer, producer, dir. multi-media road show: The Beginning & End of the World, 1972. Office: 5820 N Oriole St Chicago IL 60631

GALLAGHER, DONALD GERARD, consulting firm executive; b. Cleve., Nov. 1, 1948; s. Frank Henry and Adele Marie (Murray) G.; Asso. Data Processing, Cuyahoga Community Coll., 1964; B.S., Cleve. State U., also postgrad.; cert. in prodn. and inventory mgmt.; m. Anna Marie Vechio, July 6, 1968; children—Sean, Paul, Colleen. Mgr. mfg. systems ATO Systems Mgmt. Group, Inc., Cleve., 1971-79; program mgr. Honeywell Info. Systems, Inc., McLean, Va., 1979-81; prin. Rath & Strong Systems Products, 1981-82; pres. Gallager & Assocs., Inc., 1982—, Serg Internat. Ltd., 1987—. Named Tech. Mgr. of Year, Honeywell, 1981. Mem. Am. Prodn. and Inventory Control Soc., Reston Bd. Commerce. Home: 1507 N Village Rd Reston VA 22094 Office: 11860 Sunrise Valley Dr Reston VA 22091

GALLAGHER, JAMES JOSEPH, career consultant; b. S.I., N.Y., Mar. 12, 1930; s. James Joseph and Edith Louise (O'Brien) G.; B.A., Villanova U., 1952; M.A., NYU, 1971, Ph.D., 1973; LL.D. (hon.), Sacred Heart U., 1985; m. Nicole de Recat; children—Maryanne, Maura Kathleen, MaryBeth, Serena. Vice pres. public relations Palmer, Willson & Worden, Inc., N.Y.C., 1959-64; exec. dir. John LaFarge Inst., N.Y.C., 1964-68; pres. Tombrock Coll., West Paterson, N.J., 1968-70; chmn. J.J. Gallagher Assos., N.Y.C., 1970—; cons. on outplacement human resource devel. to maj. U.S. corps. Adv. bd. multi-nat. corporate studies Upsala Coll., East Orange, N.J., 1977—; chmn. social relations commn. Archdiocese of Newark, 1974-76; adv. bd. corporate internship program Bloomfield (N.J.) Coll., 1981—; co-chmn. Ctr. for Policy Studies, Sacred Heart U., Bridgeport, Conn., 1986—. Served with inf. AUS, 1952-54. Mem. Am. Personnel and Guidance Assn., Human Resource Planning Soc., Employment Mgmt. Assn., Assn. Outplacement Cons. Firms (pres. 1986). Democrat. Roman Catholic. Clubs: N.Y. Athletic, Sixty East. Home: 81 Christopher St Montclair NJ 07042 Office: 60 E 42d St New York NY 10022

GALLAGHER, JOSEPH ANTHONY, computer specialist; b. Enniscorthy, Leinster, Ireland, July 30, 1948; s. James and Margaret (O'Sullivan) G.; m. Elizabeth Anne Maxwell, Feb. 12, 1977; children: Maria Elizabeth, Aine Patricia, James William, Teresa Margaret. Diploma in Pub. Adminstrn., Univ. Coll. Dublin, 1968. EDP specialist Aer Lingus, Dublin, 1966-73, systems analyst, 1982—; project leader CARA Data Processing, Dublin, 1973-78; systems cons. CARA Cons., Dublin, 1978-79; systems coordinator Airmotive Ireland, Dublin, 1979-81; mgmt. cons. PARC, Baghdad, Iraq, 1981-82; lectr. Univ. Coll. Galway (Ireland), 1979-81; cons. Gael Linn, Dublin, 1987—. Designer software. Mem. Aer Lingus Social and Athletic Assn. Roman Catholic. Home: 74 Carrick Ct, Portmarnock, Dublin Leinster, Ireland Office: Aer Lingus, HOB PA8, PO Box 180 Dublin Airport, Dublin Ireland

GALLAGHER, PAUL JOHN, academic administrator; b. Kilkenny, Eire, Eng., June 15, 1939; s. Paul Felix and Ellen (O'Neil) G.; m. June Hanson, Aug. 7, 1965; children: Michelle, Julie. MS in Elec. and Electronic Engring., U. Bradford, Eng., 1971, PhD, 1975; diploma in Further Edn., U. Leeds, Eng., 1972. Chartered engr. Engr. radio and TV Anchor Supply Co., Bradford, 1955-60; engr. systems devel. Richard Sutcliffe Ltd., Wakefield, Eng., 1960-64; prin., lectr. Bradford and Ilkley Community Coll., 1965—; fin. dir. Bradford Ilkley Community Coll. and Bradford Calderdale C. of C. Tng. Services, Bradford, 1984—; cons. elec. safety P.J. Gallagher Cons., Bradford, 1971—; cons. edn., 1987—. Contbr. numerous papers in field. Fellow IEEE, Instn. Electronic and Radio Engrs. Home: 24 Birchdale, Bingley BD16 4SE, England

GALLAGHER, PHIL C., insurance executive; b. Miami, Fla., Nov. 10, 1926; s. Phil J. and Blonda (Burrow) G.; B.B.A., U. Miami, 1949; children—Pamela Robertson, Vivien Elizabeth. With D.R. Mead & Co., Miami, 1949-72, exec. v.p., 1958-72; pres. Gallagher-Cole Assos., Miami, 1972—; dir. Skylake State Bank, North Miami Beach, Fla.; underwriting mem. Lloyd's of London; former instr. Lindsey Hopkins Edn. Center. Bd. dirs. Grand Jury Assn. Fla., J. Edwin Larson Found. for Ins. Edn. Served with USNR, 1944-46. Mem. Ind. Ins. Agts. Am. (past nat. dir., past chmn. agy. mgmt. com.), Nat. Assn. Ins. Brokers, Am. Risk and Ins. Assn., Nat. Assn. Casualty and Surety Agts., Fla. Surplus Lines Assn., Nat., Fla., Miami assns. life underwriters, Fla. Assn. Ins. Agts. (past pres.), Ind. Ins. Agts. Dade County (past pres.), Assn. Internat. Ins. Agts., Profl. Ins. Agts., Profl. Ins. Agts. Fla. and Caribbean, Profl. Ins. Agts. Dade County, Greater Miami C. of C., Econ. Soc. South Fla. Clubs: Palm Bay, Bankers (Miami); La Gorce Country, Bath, Surf, Miami. Home: 1 Palm Bay Ct Miami FL 33138 Office: 1500 Biscayne Blvd Suite 310 Miami FL 33137

GALLAHER, STUART WILLIAM, architect; b. Appleton, Wis., Apr. 11, 1931; s. William U. and Winefred S.(Stuart) G.; student Lawrence U., 1949-50; B.Arch., U. Ill., 1955; m. Emmy Bunks, June 9, 1956; children—Stacia Leigh, William Stuart. Staff, Shattuck & Siewert Assos. Neenah, Wis., 1957-60; architect John J. Flad & Assos., Madison, 1960-64, Fritz & Rosenthal & Assos., Madison, 1964-65; pres. Stuart William Gallaher, Architect, Inc., Madison, 1965—; U.S. rep. Voglauer Mobelwerk, Abtenau, Austria. Mem. City of Madison Bldg. Bd. Examiners and Appeals, 1978—. Served to 1st. lt. C.E., U.S. Army, 1955-57. Allerton Travelling fellow, 1954. Mem. AIA. Conglist. Designer: Garner Park Pavilion, Madison, 1975; Hilton Inn, Lake Geneva, Wis., 1976; Olbrich Bot. Center Complex, Madison, 1977; Office-Store-Factory Avanti Foods Co., Walnut, Ill., 1978; entrance bldg. Swiss Hist. Village, New Glarus, Wis., 1979; Chalet Landhaus Hotel, New Glarus, 1980; Islamic Student Center Complex, Madison, 1981, Senner Chalet, Steamboat Springs, Colo. Office: Stuart W Gallaher Architect Inc 702 N Blackhawk Ave Madison WI 53705

GALLAND, RICHARD I., oil company executive, lawyer; b. Denver, Oct. 13, 1916; s. Raymond F. and Mabel (Wilson) G.; m. Alice Halstead, July 21, 1941; children: Richard I., Holley, John H. A.B., Yale U., 1937, LL.B., 1940. Bar: N.Y. 1940. Asso. Cravath, deGersdorff, Swaine and Wood, N.Y.C., 1940-43, Cravath, Swaine & Moore, 1946-50; chief counsel Mathieson Chem. Corp., 1950-55; v.p., gen. counsel Colo. Oil and Gas Corp., 1955-58; pres. Am. Petrofina Co. of Tex., 1958-76; pres. Am. Petrofina, Inc., 1969-76, chief exec. officer, 1976-83, chmn. bd., 1976-85; of counsel Jones, Day, Reavis & Pogue, Dallas, 1983—; bd. dirs. Tex. Industries, Inc., Am. Petrofina, Inc., Associated Materials, Inc. Served as lt. (j.g.) USNR, 1943-46. Office: PO Box 660623 Dallas TX 75266

GALLANT, SANDRA KIRKHAM, psychologist; b. Dallas, July 15, 1933; d. Eugene Raley and Anita Bernice (Brandenburg) Kirkham; A.B., Hollins Coll., 1954; M.S., Va. Commonwealth U., 1956; m. Wade Miller Gallant, Jr., Sept. 15, 1979. Psychologist aide Lynchburg Tng. Sch. and Hosp., 1954-56, Rehab. Center of Rapides Parrish, 1956; clin. psychologist Bowman Gray Sch. Medicine, Wake Forest U., 1956-64, staff psychologist, acting dir. reading, speech and psychology center, 1962-64; staff psychologist Reading Speech and Psychology Center, part-time 1964-74; sch. psychologist Winston-Salem/Forsyth County Schs., part-time, 1974-75; clin. psychologist Child Guidance Clinic, Winston-Salem, N.C., 1975-82; ptnr. Triad Psychol. Assocs., 1982—; cons. to various community orgns. and agys. Bd. dirs. Family Services, 1964-66; bd. dirs. Little Theatre, 1963-66, pres., 1964-65; trustee to exec. com. Arts Council, 1965-68, v.p., 1967-68; bd. dirs. Mental Health Assn. Forsyth County, 1971-77, 79-85, pres., 1974-75; bd. dirs. Mental Health Assn. N.C., 1975-82, sec., 1977-79, v.p., 1979-81. Named Vol. of Yr., Mental Health Assn. Forsyth County, 1976; co-recipient Forsyth Mental Health Bell award, 1981. Mem. Am. Psychol. Assn., N.C. Psychol. Assn. Episcopalian. Home: 2534 Warwick Rd Winston-Salem NC 27104 Office: Triad Psychol Assocs 840 W 4th St Winston-Salem NC 27101

GALLANT, WADE MILLER, JR., lawyer; b. Raleigh, N.C., Jan. 12, 1930; s. Wade Miller and Sallie Wesley (Jones) G.; m. Sandra Kirkham, Sept. 15, 1979. BA summa cum laude, Wake Forest U., 1952, JD cum laude, 1955. Bar: N.C. 1955. Since practiced in Winston-Salem, N.C.; ptnr. Womble, Carlyle, Sandridge & Rice, 1963—; bd. dirs. EuroCaribe Bank & Trust Co. Ltd., Brenner Cos., Inc., Piece Goods Shops Corp., Trinity Am. Corp.; lectr. continuing edn. N.C. Bar Found., 1966—. Contbr. articles to legal publs. Pres. Forsyth County Legal Aid Soc., 1963-67; assoc. Family and Child Service Agy., Winston-Salem, 1962-65, Winston-Salem Symphony Assn., 1965-66, Forsyth Mental Health Assn., 1972-73, N.C. Mental Health Assn., 1974-75; dir.-at-large Nat. Mental Health Assn., 1978-84, v.p., 1981-82; bd. dirs., exec. com. Blumenthal Jewish Home for the Aged Inc. Fellow Am. Bar Found. (life); mem. Internat. Bar Assn., N.C. Bar Assn., Forsyth County

Bar Assn., Am. Counsel Assn. (hon.), Am. Law Inst., Phi Beta Kappa, Omicron Delta Kappa, Phi Delta Phi. Democrat. Episcopalian. Clubs: Old Town, Twin City, Piedmont (Winston-Salem), Bald Head Island. Home: 2534 Warwick Rd Winston-Salem NC 27104 Office: Womble Carlyle Sandridge & Rice 2400 Wachovia Bldg Winston-Salem NC 27101

GALLAR, JOHN JOSEPH, mechanical engineer, educator; b. Poland, July 3, 1936; came to U.S., 1981; s. Joseph and Sophie (Gallar) Filipecki; m. Christina B. Wilczynski, June 30, 1962; 1 child, Darek A. BSME, State U. Poland, 1957, MSME, 1958; PhD in Tech. Scis., M & M Acad., 1966; professorship, Ahmadu Bello U., Zaria, Nigeria, 1980. Dir., prof. engring. Acad. State U., Poland, 1957-72; dir., prof. engring. Ahmadu Bello U., 1973-81, dir. postgrad. studies, 1976-81; with module design Timex Co., Cupertino, Calif., 1981-82; mgr. mfg. Computer Research Co., Santa Clara, Calif., 1982-84; mgr. hardware devel. Nat. Semiconductor Co., Santa Clara, 1984-85; chief robotics engr. Varian Corp., Palo Alto, Calif., 1986—; dep. vice-chancellor State U., Poland, 1970-71; cons. Enplan Corp., Kaduna, Nigeria, 1980-81, Criticare Tech., Sparks, Nev., 1985-86, also bd. dirs.; mgr. mfg. engring. Retro-Tek Co., Santa Clara, 1986. Contbr. articles to profl. jours.; patentee in field. Trustee, charter mem. Presdl. Task Force, Washington, 1984; mem. Nat. Conservative Polit. Action Com., Washington, 1981. Recipient U.S. Ceremonial Flag Presdl. Task Force; Medal Merit from Pres. Ronald Reagan, Washington, 1985. Mem. Calif. State Sheriff's Assn., Nat. Rifle Assn. Roman Catholic. Home: 5459 Entrada Cedros San Jose CA 95123 Office: Varian Corp 611 Hansen Way Palo Alto CA 95051

GALLARDO, JOSÉ MARÍA, museum director; b. Buenos Aires, Aug. 1, 1925; s. Gallardo Angel León and Demarchi de Gallardo María Luisa; m. Vayo Juana de Jesús; children: Juana María, José María, María Aurelia Trinidad, María del Espíritu Santo. Bachiller, Colegio Champagnat, Buenos Aires, 1943; Licenciado Ciencias Naturales, U. Buenos Aires, 1950, Dr. Ciencias Biológicas, 1982. Investigator, scientist Argentine Mus. Natural Scis., Buenos Aires, 1946-71, dir. cargo, 1971-73, dir. titular, 1973—; prof. Católica U. Argentina, Buenos Aires, 1971-81, U. Buenos Aires. 1981; investigator prin. CONCINET, Buenos Aires, 1961. Author: Anfibios de los Alrededores de Buenos Aires, 1974, Reptiles, 1977, Antibios Argentinos, 1987, Anfibios y Reptiles del Partido de Magdalena, 1987. Sci. fellow N.Y. Zool. Soc., 1975. Mem. Históricas de la Manzana de las Luces (pres. 1984), Acad. del Plata, Soc. Científica Argentina Buenos Aires, Acad. Argentina de Ciencias del Ambiente (v.p.), Acad. Nat. de Geographía, Soc. Herpetólogica Argentina (v.p.). Home: Rodríguez Peña 1616, 1021 Buenos Aires Argentina Office: Argentine Mus Natural Scis, Ave A Gallardo 470, 1405 Buenos Aires Argentina

GALLARINI, LUCIANO, architect; b. Novara, Italy, Oct. 22, 1932; s. Basilio and Giuseppina Maria (Fizzotti) G.; m. Ivana Astori; 1 child, Vittorio. DArch, Politecnico Milan, Italy, 1957. Cert. architect, Italy. Researcher Sch. Architecture Politecnico Milan, 1959-71; prin. Luciano Gallarini Studio Architecture, Novara, 1959—; Italian del. to jury 6th European Architecture Competition, Brussels, 1980; mem. Novara Town Commn. Bldg., 1961-65, 81-86. Author: Cities and Towns in Italy, 1966, (with others) Museo Novarese, 1987. V.p. Major Hosp. Charity, Novara, 1967-69; councillor for scholarships Nobile Coll. Caccia, Novara, 1974-80; mem. Novara Town Commn. Culture, 1985—. Named knight Republic of Italy, 1977. Italian del. United European Architects, Brussels; mem. Nat. Council Architects (cons. fgn. relations 1977—), Provincial Architects' Council (pres. Novara chpt. 1974-78). Mem. Italian Socialist party. Roman Catholic. Lodge: Kiwanis. Home: 18 Sottile St, 28100 Novara Italy Office: Luciano Gallarini Studio, Via Carducci 3, 28100 Novara Piemonte Italy

GALLAWAY, LOWELL EUGENE, economist, educator; b. Toledo, Jan. 9, 1930; s. Leroy and Bessie Marguerite (Hiteshew) G. Means; m. Gladys Elinor McGhee, Dec. 19, 1953; children: Kathleen Elizabeth Gallaway Searles, Michael Scott, Ellen Jane. B.S., Northwestern U., 1951; M.A., Ohio State U., 1955, Ph.D., 1959. Asst. prof. Colo. State U., Fort Collins, 1957-59; asst. prof. San Fernando Valley State Coll., Northridge, Calif., 1959-62; vis. asso. prof. U. Minn., Mpls., 1962-63; chief analytic studies sect. Social Security adminstrn., Balt., 1963-64; asso. prof. U. Pa., Phila., 1964-67; prof. econs. Ohio U., Athens, 1967-74; disting. prof. Ohio U., 1974—; vis. prof. U. Lund, Sweden, 1973, U. Tex., Arlington, 1976, U. New South Wales, Australia, 1978, U. N.C., Chapel Hill, 1980, Mara Inst. Tech., Kuala Lumpur, Malaysia, 1987; staff economist Joint Econ. Com. U.S. Congress, 1982. Author: The Retirement Decision, 1965, Interindustry Labor Mobility in the United States 1957-1960, 1967, Geographic Labor Mobility in the United States 1957-1960, 1969, Manpower Economics, 1971, Poverty in America, 1973, The "Natural Rate" of Unemployment, 1982, Paying People to Be Poor, 1986, Poverty, Income Distribution, The Family and Public Policy, 1986; contbr. articles to profl. jours. Served with USN, 1951-54. Ford Found. faculty fellow, 1960, fellow Gen. Electric Found., 1962, Pacific Inst. for Pub. Policy Research, Liberty Fund fellow Inst Humane Studies, 1983; Ford Rockefeller Population policy research grantee, 1974-75; Fulbright-Hays sr. scholar Australia, 1978. Mem. Manhattan Inst. (assoc.), Phi Beta Kappa, Beta Gamma Sigma. Home: 33 Longview Heights Rd Athens OH 45701

GALLESE, ROBERTO, pharmaceutical company executive; b. Milan, Italy, Oct. 7, 1931; s. Alfredo and Irma (Castagnetti) G.; m. Ornella Puttini, Sept. 23, 1968; 1 child, Roberta. Diploma in Medicine and Surgery, Pavia State U., Italy, 1955. Diplomate Italian Bd. Medicine. Intern, asst. surgery dept. U. Hosp. Medicine, Pavia, 1957-60; med. asst. Niguarda Hôsp., Milan, 1960-63; dir. Social Medicine Provincial Ctr., Como, Italy, 1963-65; dir. med. dept. Italfarmaco Spa, Milan, 1966-68; dir. mktg. dept. Zambon spa, Milan, 1969-73; gen. mgr. Zambon Italy, Milan, 1979-83; corp. mng. dir. Zambon Group Spa, Milan, 1983—. Contbr. articles to profl. jours. Club: Sporting (Monza). Home: Ramazzotti 30, 20052 Monza, Milano Italy Office: Zambon Group Spa, 12 Lillodelduca, 20091 Bresso, Milano Italy

GALLETTA, JOSEPH LEO, physician; b. Bessemer, Pa., Dec. 21, 1935; s. John and Grace (Galletta) G.; student U. Pitts., 1953-56; MD, U. Santo Tomas, Manila, Philippines, 1962; m. Teresita Suarez Soler, Feb. 19, 1961; children: John II, Angela, Eric, Christopher, Robert Francis, Michael Angelo. Intern, St. Elizabeth Hosp., Youngstown, Ohio, 1963-64; family practice medicine, 29 Palms, Calif., 1967-77, Hemet, Calif., 1977—; chief of staff 29 Palms Community Hosp., 1970-71, 73-76; vice chief of staff Hi-Desert Med. Center, Joshua Tree, Calif., 1976-77; chmn. dept. family practice Hemet Valley Hosp., 1981-83; med. dir. chem. dependency dept. Heart Valley Hosp., Hemet, 1985—; pres. Flexisplint, Inc.; founding mem. Hemet Hospice; former cons. Morongo Basin Mental Health Assn. Hon. mem. 29 Palms Sheriff's Search and Rescue, 1971-77. Bd. dirs. 29 Palms Community Hosp. Dist., Morongo Unified Sch. Dist. Served with M.C. USN, 1964-67. Diplomate Am. Bd. Family Practice. Founding fellow West Coast div. Am. Geriatric Soc.; fellow Am. Acad. Family Practice; mem. AMA, Calif. Med. Assn., Riverside County Med. Assn., Am. Holistic Med. Assn. (charter), Am. Med. Soc. on Alcoholism and Other Drug Dependencies, Calif. Soc. Treatment Alcoholism and Drug Dependencies, Am. Acad. Family Practice, Calif. Acad. Family Practice. Roman Catholic. Established St. Anthonys Charity Clinic, Philippines, 1965; inventor Flexisplint armboards. Home: 27691 Pochea Trail Hemet CA 92344 Office: 850 E Latham Ave Suite B Hemet CA 92343

GALLI, GIAMPAOLO, economist, educator; b. Milan, Mar. 13, 1951; s. Pietro and Silvia (Roditi) G.; m. Agnes Kalpagos-Szabo; children: Silvia, Gabriele. Laurea in Econs., U. Bocconi, Milan, 1975, Laude e Dignita di Pubblicazione; PhD in Econs., MIT, 1980. Economist monetary div. Banca D'Italia, Rome, 1980-82, dep. head econometrics, 1982-84, head econometrics, 1984—; prof. econs. U. Bocconi, 1984—; mem. sci. council Ente Einaudi, 1986—; speaker in field. Co-author: A Model of the Italian Economy, 1986; contbr. articles to profl. jours. Grantee Consiglio Nazionale Ricerche, 1976, Banca D'Italia, 1977, Ente Einaudi, 1978, NSF, 1979. Mem. Am. Econ. Assn., European Econ. Assn. Clubs: MIT (Italy), Am. Field Service. Home: Via Urbana 150, 00184 Rome Italy Office: Banca D'Italia, Via Nazionale 91, 00184 Rome Italy

GALLIHER, KEITH EDWIN, JR., lawyer; b. Fond du Lac, Wis., July 29, 1947; s. Keith Edwin and Dolores Mae (Hazen) G.; m. Linda Lee Dessauer, May 18, 1985; children: Patrick, Christy Lyn. B.S, U. Nev. at Las Vegas, 1970; J.D., Ariz. State U., 1974. Bar: Nev. 1974, U.S. Dist. Ct. Nev. 1974, U.S. Ct. Appeals (9th cir.) 1976. Assoc. Lionel, Sawyer & Collins., Las Vegas, 1974-75; atty. Clark County Pub. Defender, Las Vegas, 1975-76; sr. ptnr. Mills, Galliher, Lukens, Gibson, Schwartzer & Shinehouse, Las Vegas, 1976-80, Galliher & Tratos, Las Vegas, 1980-83; pres., sr. ptnr. Keith E. Galliher, Jr., Chartered, Las Vegas, 1983—; instr. hotel law U. Nev.-Las Vegas, 1980: alt. mcpl. judge City Las Vegas, 1983—. Author: Supplement to Comparison Analysis of ABA Criminal Justice Standards to Nevada Law, 1976. State del. Democratic Party, 1976; bd. govs. March of Dimes, Las Vegas, 1978. Mem. Nat. Assn. Trial Lawyers, Nev. Trial Lawyers Assn., ABA, Nev. Bar Assn., Clark County Bar Assn., State Bar Nev. (mem. fee dispute com. 1983), Comml. Law League Am., Real Estate Securities and Syndication Inst., Nat. Coll. Criminal Def. Lawyers and Pub. Defenders. Lutheran. Home: 6855 Stone Dr Las Vegas NV 89110 Office: 1850 E Sahara Ave Suite 100 Las Vegas NV 89104

GALLINARO, NICHOLAS FRANCIS, bus. exec.; b. Somerville, Mass., Feb. 25, 1930; s. Joseph Michael and Mary Marie (Valerio) G.; B.A., Boston Coll., 1952, M.B.A., 1964; B.S. in Mech. Engring., Notre Dame U., 1953; m. Inez Hanken, July 27, 1957; children—Michael J., James J., Stephen P., Robert N. With Clark Equipment Corp., Battle Creek & Benton Harbor, Mich., 1951-53; v.p., Harnischfeger Internat, Corp., Milw., Wis., 1953-63; v.p., dir. McLaughlin Equipment Corp., N.Y.C., 1963-71; v.p., dir. Prudential Internat. Corp., N.Y.C., 1971-72; pres. GAR Internat. Corp., GAR Equipment Corp., South Plainfield, N.J., 1972—; chmn. bd. CIMAT S.r.1., Milan Italy. Trustee, Christian Brothers Acad. Served with USMC, 1949-51. Mem. Soc. Am. Mil. Engrs., N.Y. World Trade Assn., Pan Am. Soc., Am. Mining Congress, Associated Equipment Distbrs. Republican. Roman Catholic. Clubs: K.C., Navesink Country. Home: 31 Esshire Dr Middletown NJ 07748 Office: 3005 Hadley Rd S Plainfield NJ 07080

GALLINER, PETER, publisher; b. Berlin, Sept. 19, 1920; s. Moritz and Hedwig Isaac; m. Edith Marguerite Goldschmidt, 1948; 1 child. Ed. Berlin and London. With Reuters, London, 1942-45; fgn. mgr. Fin. Times, London, 1945-61; chmn. bd., mng. dir. Ullstein Pub. Group, Berlin, 1961-64; vice chmn., mng. dir. Brit. Printing Corp., Pub. Group, London, 1967-70; internat. pub. cons., 1965-67, 70-75; dir. Internat. Press Inst., Zurich/London, 1976—. Decorated Fed. Cross Merit 1st class, Fed. Republic of Germany, Orden de Isabel la Cató lica, Spain. Home: Untere Zäune 15, 8001 Zurich Switzerland

GALLINOT, RUTH MAXINE, educational consultant, educator; b. Carlinville, Ill., Feb. 16, 1925; d. Martin Mike and Augusta (Kumpus) G. BS, Roosevelt U., Chgo., 1971, MA with honors, 1974; PhD, Union for Experimenting Colls. and Univs., Cin., 1978. Adminstrv. asst., exec. sec. Karoll's Inc., Chgo., 1952-66; asst. dean Cen. YMCA Community Coll., Chgo., 1966-81, dir. life planning inst., 1979-80; pres. Gallinot & Assocs., Chgo. and St. Louis, 1980—; mem. task force Office Sr. Citizens and Handicapped, City of Chgo., 1971-79; mem. criteria and guidelines com. Council on Continuing Edn. Unit, 1983-86, survey and research com., 1984-88; mem. nat. adv. council bus. edn. div. Am. Vocat. Assn., 1980-84, sec., 1982-84. Developer leisure time adult edn. time series for elderly Uptown model cities area dept. human resources City of Chgo., 1970; host show Sta. WGCI-FM, Chgo., 1975-81; editor: Certified Professional Secretaries Review, 1983; contbr. articles to profl. jours. Chmn. Commn. Status of Women in State of Ill., 1963-68; del. White House Conf. on Equal Pay, 1963, White House Conf. on Civil Rights, 1965, City of Chgo. White House Conf. on Info. and Library, 1976, State of Ill. White House Conf. Info. Services and Library Services, 1977; life mem. Mus. Lithuanian Culture, Chgo., 1973—; pub. mem. Fgn. Service Selection Bd. U.S. Dept. State, 1984; bd. dirs. Luths. for Chgo., 1978-83, also founding member; member adv. edn. com. Chgo. Commn. Human Relations, 1968-75, Task Force Office Sr. Citizens and Handicapped City of Chgo., 1975-79. Recipient Leadership in Civic, Cultural and Econ. Life of the City award YWCA, Chgo., 1972, Achievement in Field Edn. award Operation P.U.S.H., Chgo., 1975. Mem. Profl. Secs. Internat. (pres. 1961, 62, edn. cons. 1980-84), Edn. Network Older Adults (v.p., sec. 1979-86), Nat. Assn. Parliamentarians (Ill. chpt., Chgo. chpt.), Literacy Council Chgo. (bd. dirs. 1979-86). Club: Zonta of Chgo. (treas. 1965-66). Home and Office: Gallinot & Assocs 11161 Estrada Dr #9 Spanish Lake Saint Louis MO 63138-2278

GALLION, MICHAEL LEWIS, educator, writer, consultant; b. Charleston, W.Va., Sept. 18, 1942; s. John William and Sylvia Elizabeth Gallion; m. Carol V. Vierbuchen, June 23, 1984. B.A., W.Va. State U., 1964; M.A., Marshall U., 1967; Ph.D., Pacific Coll., 1975. Counselor Boys and Girls Club, Montreal, Que., Can., 1964; asst. track coach W.Va. State U., Institute, 1965-66, lab. asst., 1967; counselor Upward Bound Inc., Institute, 1967; tchr. D.C. Pub. Schs., 1967—; cons. Internat. Edn. Assn., Detroit, 1973-75, Aquarian Age, Washington, 1975-77. Author: 13th Street to No Where, 1984. Cons., v.p. Concerned Citizens for Social Improvement, Washington, 1973—; minister Ch. Two Worlds, Washington, 1982—; boxing inspector D.C. Boxing Commn.; election officer Fairfax County, Va. Claude Woungton Bellyton grant 1960. Mem. Washington Ind. Writers, U.S. Friendship Soc. China, Beethoven Soc., Washington Tchrs. Union, Smithsonian Inst. (Cert. Appreciation 1982), Republican. Avocations: coaching; track; travel; photography. Home: PO Box 345 Oakton VA 22124 Office: Cardozo High Sch 13th and Clifton St NW Washington DC 20009

GALLIVAN, GREGORY JOHN, thoracic and laser surgeon, voice care consultant; b. Hartford, Conn., Apr. 25, 1938; s. John Norman and Stella (Chmiel) G.; BS, Tufts U., 1958, MD, 1962; m. Helen Krawski, Apr. 4, 1964; children: Elizabeth Kerry, Kathleen Holly, Gregory John. Intern, Hartford Hosp., 1962-63; resident in gen. surgery USPHS Hosp., S.I., N.Y., 1963-64, resident in gen. and thoracic surgery, 1964-65; jr. resident internal medicine Hartford Hosp., 1965-66, gen. surg. resident, 1966-67; asst. resident in gen. surgery New Britain (Conn.) Gen. Hosp., 1967-68, chief resident, 1968-69; jr. resident thoracic and cardiovascular surgery U. Tex., Southwestern Med. Sch., Dallas, 1969-70, sr. resident, 1970-71; practice medicine, specializing in thoracic and laser surgery, profl. voice care, Springfield, Mass., 1971—; asst. clin. prof. cardiothoracic surgery Tufts U., Boston, 1977—; attending thoracic surgeon Baystate Med. Ctr., Springfield, 1971—, Mercy Hosp., Springfield, 1971—, Holyoke (Mass.) Hosp., 1971—, Providence Hosp., Holyoke, 1971—; cons. in thoracic surgery Noble Hosp., Westfield, 1971—, Holyoke Soldiers Home, 1971—, Ludlow (Mass.) Hosp., 1971—, Wing Meml. Hosp., Palmer, Mass., 1971—, Cooley Dickinson Hosp., Northampton, Mass., 1971—; cons. on surg. Stapler instrument design U.S. Surg. Corp., Auto Suture Co., Norwalk, Conn., 1983—, Am. V. Mueller div. Am. Hosp. Supply Corp., 1983; cons. on cardiac pacemakers Western Mass PSRO, 1983-85. Baritone soloist Project Opera of Mass., 1976—; pianist, composer, also bd. dirs. 1988—; baritone soloist, mem. chorus, mem. chamber chorus, mem. leadership com. Springfield Symphony, 1974-76; baritone soloist Western Mass. Regional Summer Park Concerts, 1977—; baritone soloist, mem. Springfield Tuesday Morning Music Club, 1982—. Served with USPHS, 1963-65. Diplomate Am. Bd. Surgery, Am. Bd. Thoracic Surgery. Fellow ACS (instr. advanced trauma life support 1984), Am. Coll. Chest Physicians; mem. AMA, Mass., Hampden Dist med. socs., Soc. Thoracic Surgeons. Contbr. articles to med. jours. Home: 108 White Oaks Dr Longmeadow MA 01106 Office: 2 Medical Center Dr Suite #204 Springfield MA 01107

GALLO, MARIO MARTIN, clinical psychologist, neuropsychologist; b. Chgo., Sept. 13, 1947; s. Mike Vito and Christina Mary (Serritella) G. B.S., Loyola U., Chgo., 1969; M.A., Roosevelt U., 1972; Ph.D., Miami U., Oxford, Ohio, 1977. Diplomate Am. Bd. Vocat. Experts; lic. psychologist, Ill., Ohio, Ariz., Calif., Fla. Intern Greater Lawn Mental Health Ct., Chgo., 1970-71; trainee Miami U. Psychol. Clinic, Oxford, Ohio, 1972-75; psychiat. ward specialist U.S. Air Force Res., Chgo., 1972-76; intern Good Samaritan Hosp., Dayton, Ohio, 1974-75; resident Northwestern U., 1975-77; clin. dir. Kevin Coleman Mental Health Ctr., Kent, Ohio, 1978-83; pvt. practice psychology, Kent, 1978-83, Evergreen Park, Ill., 1983—; vis. staff psychologist dept. neuroscis. Columbus-Cuneo-Cabrini Med. Ctr., Chgo., 1983—; profl. adv. staff Children with Learning Disabilities, Chgo., 1983—; adj. asst. prof. psychology Kent State U., 1978-83; instr. dept. behavioral scis. Northeastern Ohio U. Coll. Medicine, 1982-83; cons. psychologist various depts. State of Ill., 1983—, Medicare, HHS, Marion, Ill., 1983—, Cath. Family Consultation Service, Blue Island, Ill. and Chgo., 1985—, Beacon Therapeutic Sch., Chgo., 1985—; community adv. council staff Learning Disability and Behavior Disorders Clinic, St. Xavier Coll., Chgo., 1985—; practicum supr. in clin. psychology Ill. Sch. Profl. Psychology, Chgo., 1985—, Chgo. Sch. Profl. Psychology, 1986—. Served with USMC, 1969-70. Nat. Inst. Mental Health fellow. Fellow Masters and Johnson Inst.; mem. Am. Psychol. Assn., Am. Acad. Psychotherapists, Am. Soc. Clin. Hypnosis, Internat. Neuropsychol. Soc., Nat. Acad. Neuropsychologists, Am. Assn. Marriage and Family Therapy (clin.), Am. Assn. Sex Educators, Counselors and Therapists (cert. sex therapist and counselor), Internat. Council Sex Edn. and Parenthood of Am. Univ. (approved fellow in sex therapy and counseling). Current Work: Neuropsychological assessments and rehabilitation; psychotherapy, hypnotherapy and biofeedback. Subspecialties: Neuropsychology; Clinical psychology. Office: 3830 West 95th St Suite 110 Evergreen Park IL 60642

GALLO, ROBERT CHARLES, research scientist; b. Waterbury, Conn., Mar. 23, 1937; s. Francis Anton and Louise Mary (Ciancuilli) G.; m. Mary Jane Hayes, July 1, 1961; children: Robert Charles, Marcus. BA, Providence Coll., 1959, DSc (hon.), 1974; MD, Jefferson Med. Coll., 1963; postgrad., Jefferson U., 1987—. Clin. assoc. med. br. Nat. Cancer Inst. NIH, Bethesda, Md., 1965-68, sr. investigator human tumor cell biology br., 1968-69, head sect. cellular control mechanisms, 1969-72, chief lab. tumor cell biology, 1972—; adj. prof. genetics George Washington U.; adj. prof. microbiology Cornell U.; cons. Georgetown U. Cancer Center; U.S. rep. to world com. Internat. Comparative Leukemia and Lymphoma Assn., 1981—; hon. prof. biology Johns Hopkins U., 1985—; bd. govs. Franco Am. AIDS Found. 1987, World AIDS Found., 1987. Served with USPHS, 1965-68. Recipient Dameshek award Am. Hematol. Soc., 1974, CIBA-GEIGY award in biomed. sci., 1977, 88, Superior Service award USPHS, 1979, Meritorious Service medal, 1983, Stitt award, 1983, Disting. Service medal, 1984, F. Stohlman lecture award, 1979, Lasker award for basic biomed. research, 1982, 86, Abraham white award in biochemistry George Washington U., 1983, 1st Otto Herz award for cancer research Tel Aviv U., 1982, Griffuel prize Assn. for Cancer Research, France, 1983, Gen. Motors award in cancer research, 1984, Gruber prize Am. Soc. Investigative Dermatology, 1984, Lucy Wortham prize in cancer research Soc. for Surg. Oncology, 1984, Gold medal Am. Chem. Soc., 1984, Hammer prize, 1985, Gairdner prize for Biomed. Research from Can., 1987, spl. award Am. Soc. Infectious Disease, 1986, Gold Plate award Am. Acad. Achievement, Lions Humanitarian award, 1987, Japan prize in Preventative Medicine, 1988, others. Mem. Internat. Soc. Hematology, Am. Soc. Clin. Investigation, Am. Soc. Biol. Chemists, Am. Microbiology Soc., Biochem Soc., Am. Assn. Cancer Research (Rosenthal award 1983), Am. Fedn. Clin. Research, Fedn. for Advanced Edn. in Scis., Alpha Omega Alpha.

GALLOGLY, JAMES JOHN, healthcare executive, financier; b. N.Y.C., May 24, 1948; m. Janice Trupiano, July 29, 1966; children: Lori, James, Mike. BBA, Manhattan Coll., 1969. Cost acct. Johnson & Johnson Co., New Brunswick, N.J., 1970-74, mktg. controller, 1974-77; plant controller Johnson & Johnson Co., Athens, Ga., 1977-79; group controller Johnson & Johnson Co., Solon, Ohio, 1979-81; v.p. fin. and mgmt. info. systems Richards Med. Co., Memphis, 1981-83, pres., microsurgery div., 1984-88; pres., chief exec. officer Resound Corp., Palo Alto, Calif., 1988—; bd. dirs. OMNI Hearing Systems, Dallas, Hearing Lab., Inc., N.J. Served with USAR, 1970-75. Mem. Health Industry Mfg. Assn. Home: 1930 Idyllwild Ave Redwood City CA 94061 Office: Resound Corp 220 Saginaw Dr at Seaport Blvd Redwood City CA 94063

GALLOWAY, ALISTAIR, metal processing executive; b. Glasgow, Scotland, Oct. 30, 1940; s. George and Mary Jeannie (French) G.; m. Elizabeth Rosemary Cobain, Jan. 9, 1943; children: William Meiklejohn, Jillian Denise. Dir., sec. Atholl Palace Hotel Pitlochry (Scotland), Ltd., 1964-71, William Thomson and Co. (Kinning Park), Ltd., Glasgow, Scotland, 1963—, The Portable Forge and Engring. Co., Ltd., Glasgow, 1963—, George Galloway and Co., Ltd., Glasgow, 1963—. Elder New Kilpatrick Parish Ch., Bearsden, Scotland, 1987. Mem. Inst. Chartered Accts. Scotland, The Iron Steel and Ironmongers Benevolent Assn. Scotland (pres. 1978-79), The Incorporation of Hammermen. Mem. Ch. of Scotland. Club: Royal Scottish Automobile. Home: 68 Switchback Rd, Bearsden, Glasgow G61 1AF, Scotland Office: George Galloway and Co Ltd, 43 Middlesex St, Glasgow G41 1EB, Scotland

GALLOWAY, DIANE LENOIR, foundation executive; b. Phila., Aug. 24, 1941; d. Howard William and Florence Eleanor (Wagner) Galloway; B.A., Am. U., 1963, postgrad. 1963-64. Staff asst. Mfg. Chemists Assn., Washington, 1963-64; research asst. Federazione Italiana dei Consorzi Agrari, Washington, 1964; asst. Office of the Chief of Protocol, N.Y. World's Fair Corp., Flushing Meadow, N.Y., 1964-65; research asst. Population Office, Ford Found., N.Y.C., 1965-66; sr. staff asst. Office of the Pres., 1966-67, adminstrv. asst. Office of the Sec., 1967-68, exec. asst. Office of Sec. and Gen. Counsel, 1968-72, asst. adminstrv. officer 1972-78, asst. to gen. counsel and adminstrv. officer, 1978-83, asst. sec., 1983—. Mem. Women and Found./Corporate Philanthropy, Am. Soc. Profl. and Exec. Women, Nat. Assn. Female Execs., Alpha Chi Omega, Pi Sigma Alpha. Presbyterian. Clubs: Rockaway River Country, U.S. Senatorial. Home: 327 Morris Ave Boonton NJ 07005 Office: 320 E 43 St New York NY 10017

GALLOWAY, EILENE MARIE, national, international outerspace consultant; b. Kansas City, Mo., May 4, 1906; d. Joseph Locke and Lottie Rose (Harris) Slack; student Washington U., St. Louis, 1923-25; A.B., Swarthmore Coll., 1928; postgrad. Am. U., 1937-38, 43; m. George Barnes Galloway, Dec. 23, 1924; children—David Barnes, Jonathan Fuller. Tchr. polit. sci. Swarthmore Coll., 1928-30; editor Student Service, Washington, 1931; staff mem., edn. div. Fed. Emergency Relief Adminstrn., 1934-35; asst. chief info. sect., div. spl. info. Library of Congress, 1941-43, editor abstracts Legis. Reference Service, 1943-51, nat. def. analyst, 1951-57; specialist in nat. def., 1957-66; sr. specialist internat. relations (nat. security) Congl. Research Service, 1966-75; cons. internat. space activities, 1975—. staff mem. Senate Fgn. Relations Com., 1947; profl. staff mem. U.S. group Interparliamentary Union, 1958-66; cons. Senate Armed Services Com., 1953-74, Ford Found., 1958; spl. cons. spl. Senate Com. on Space and Astronautics, 1958; spl. cons. to Senate Com. on Aero. and Space Sci., 1958-77; cons. to Senate Com. on Commerce, Sci. and Transp., 1977-82; chmn. com. edn. and recreation Washington, 1937-38; forum leader 1976-79; guest Soviet Acad. Sci., 1982, adult edn. U.S. Office Edn., 1938; mem. Internat. Inst. Space Law of Internat. Astronautical Fedn., 1958—, U.S. mem. bd. dirs., v.p., 1967-79, hon. dir., 1979—, Fedn. ofcl. observer at sessions UN Com. on Peaceful Uses Outer Space, 1981-88, mem. com. for relations with internat. orgns., 1979—; mem. Am. Rocket Soc.'s Space Law and Sociology Com., 1959-62; mem. adv. panel Office Gen. Counsel, NASA, 1971; adviser outer space del. U.S. Mission to UN Working Group on Direct Broadcast Satellites, 1973-75, legal subcom., 1976; observer UN Conf. Exploration and Peaceful Uses of Outer Space, Vienna, 1982; lectr. Nat. Acad. Sci., 1973, U.S. CSC, Exec. Seminar Center, Oak Ridge, 1973, 74, 75, 76, 78; ednl. counselor Purdue U., 1974; lectr. Inst. Air and Space Law McGill U., 1975, Inter Am. Def. Coll., 1977, 78, U. Akron, 1984; mem. panel on solar power for satellites and U.S. space policy Office Tech. Assessment, 1979-80, 82-86, cons., 1982; cons. COMSAT, 1983, FCC Commn. on U.S. Telecommunications Policy, 1983-87. Pres., Theodore Von Karman Meml. Found., 1973-84; mem. alumni council Swarthmore Coll., 1976-79; mem. organizing com., author symposium on Conditions Essential For Maintaining Outer Space for Peaceful Uses, Peace Palace, Netherlands, 1984; bd. advisers Students for Exploration and Devel. of Space, 1984—. Rockefeller Found. scholar-in-residence, Bellagio, Italy, 1976. Recipient Andrew G. Haley gold medal Internat. Inst. Space Law, 1968; NASA Gold Medal for Pub. Service, 1984, USAF Space Command plaque, 1984; Internat. Acad. Astronautics' Theodore Von Karman award, 1986, Women in Aerospace Lifetime Achievement award, 1987; Wilton Park fellow, Eng., 1968. Fellow Am. Astronautical Soc.; mem. LWV (chmn. study groups housing, welfare in D.C., 1937-38, mem. tech. com. on law and sociology task force on legal aspects 1979—), AIAA (tech. com. on legal aspects of aeros. and astronautics 1980-84, internat. activities com. 1985—), World Peace Through Law Center, Am. Soc. Internat. Law, Am. Astronautical Soc., Lamar Soc. Internat. Law, Internat. Acad. Astronautics (trustee, chmn. social scis. sect. 1982-88), Internat. Law Assn., Phi Beta Kappa, Delta Sigma Rho, Kappa Alpha Theta. Episcopalian. Author: Atomic Power: Issues Before Congress, 1946; (with Bernard Brodie) The Atomic Bomb and the Armed Services, 1947; History of United States Military Policy on Reserve Forces, 1775-1957, 1957; Guided Missiles in Foreign Countries, 1957; The Community of Law and Science, 1958; United Nations Ad hoc Committee on Peaceful Uses of Outer Space, 1959; Satellites: A Force for World Peace, World (trustee, chmn. social scis. sect. Security and the Peaceful Uses of Outer Space, 1960; International Cooperation and Organization for Outer Space, 1965; Space Treaty Proposals by the United States and U.S.S.R., 1966; Treaty on Principles Governing the Activities of States in the Exploration and Use of Outer Space, Including the Moon and Other Celestial Bodies: Analysis and Background Data, 1967; Remote Sensing of the Earth by Satellites: Legal Problems and Issues, 1973, 75; The Future of Space Law, 1976; Consensus as a Basis for International Space Cooperation, 1977; The Role of the United Nations in Earth Resources Satellites, 1972; Settlement of Space Law Disputes, 1980; Perspectives of Space Law, 1981; Conditions for Success of International Space Institutions, 1982; Space Manufacturing, 1981; U.S. Space Policy and Programs, 1982; Space Station, 1986; U.S. National Space Legislation and Peaceful Uses Of Outer Space, 1987; Expanding Article IV of 1967 Space Treaty, 1982; History and Development of Space Law, 1982; editor: Space Law Symposium, 1958; The Legal Problems of Space Exploration, 1961; United States International Space Programs, 1965; International Cooperation in Outer Space: A Symposium, 1972; assoc. editor Advances in Earth Oriented Applications of Space Tech., 1978-82, Acta Astronautica Jour., Space Technology: Industrial and Commercial Applications; mem. editorial adv. bd. Jour. Space Law, U. Miss. Law Sch., Space Communication and Broadcasting. Home: 4612 29th Pl NW Washington DC 20008

GALLUP, JANET LOUISE, business official; b. Rochester, N.Y., Aug. 11, 1951; d. John Joseph and Mildred Monica (O'Keefe) VerHulst; m. Robert Hicks Gallup, June 26, 1982 (div. Nov. 1985); 1 son, Jason Hicks. B.A., Hofstra U., 1973; M.A. (grad. asst.), Calif. State U.-Long Beach., 1979. Asst. trader E.F. Hutton, N.Y.C., 1973-75, Los Angeles, 1975, instr. Calif. State U.-Long Beach, 1978-79; fin. analyst Rockwell Internat., Seal Beach, Calif., 1979-85, coordinator mgmt. and exec. devel. and succession planning, 1985—. Vol. Cedar House Ctr.-Child Abuse, Long Beach, 1976. Democrat. Roman Catholic. Office: Rockwell Internat 2600 Westminster Blvd Seal Beach CA 90740

GALPIN, BRIAN JOHN FRANCIS, circuit judge; b. London, Mar. 21, 1921; s. Christopher John and Gladys Elizabeth (Souhami) G.; m. Ailsa McConnel (dec. Dec. 1959); 1 child, Mary Frances (dec.); m. Nancy Cecilia Nichols; children: Joseph Dabney Jay, Daniel Kinder. MA, Oxford U., 1947. Barrister London, 1948-78, circuit judge for Western Circuit, 1978—; official referee High Ct. of Justice, 1986—. Author: A Manual of International Law, 1949; editor: Maxwell Interpretation of Statutes, 10th edit., 1953, 11th edit. 1962, Every Man's Own Lawyer, 6th-8th edits., 1962, 71, 81; contbr. Halsbury's Laws of England, 1960. Councillor Met. Borough of Fulham, London, 1950-59; vice-chmn. Fulham Conservative Assn., 1954-60; com. mem. Bach Choir, 1950-61. Served as flight lt. RAF, 1941-45. Harmsworth law scholar, 1947. Mem. Fellowship Makers and Restorers of Hist. Instruments, Galpin Soc. for Study Mus. Instruments (chmn. 1955-72, v.p. 1972—), Hertford Soc. (com. mem.). Mem. Ch. of Eng.Clubs: Travellers', Pratt's (London). Home: St Bruno House, Charters Rd, Sunningdale, Berkshire SL5 9QB, England

GALVIN, MADELINE SHEILA, lawyer; b. N.Y.C., Jan. 31, 1948; d. Rod Sheil and Madeline (Twiss) G. BA cum laude with highest honors, Russell Sage Coll., 1970; JD, Albany Law Sch., 1973. Bar: N.Y. 1974, U.S. Dist. Ct. (no. dist.) N.Y. 1974, U.S. Supreme Ct. 1978; cert. parliamentarian, lic. real estate broker. Atty. N.Y. State Dept. Law, Albany, 1973-74; sr. atty. Dormitory Authority State of N.Y., Elsmere, 1974-78; sole practice, Delmar, N.Y., 1974—. Bd. dirs., mem. endowment com., mem. exec. bd. YMCA, Albany, 1980-86; bd. dirs. Mercy House, 1980-83, v.p., 1981-82; mem. fin. com. Ronald McDonald House, 1981-83; mem. Bethlehem Zoning Bd. Appeals; Rep. committeeman 15th dist. Town of Bethlehem. Kellas scholar, 1967-70. Mem. AAUW (recognition cert. Albany br., pres. 1983-84), Nat. Assn. Parliamentarians, ABA, N.Y. State Bar Assn. (numerous coms.), Albany County Bar Assn., N.Y. State Trial Lawyers Assn., Albany Claims Assn., Women's Bar Assn., Albany Law Sch. Alumni Assn., N.Y. Geneal. and Biog. Soc., Strafford Hist. Soc., Russell Sage Coll. Alumni Assn. (pres. 1983-87, pres. bd. dirs., 1987-88), Albany Inst. History and Art, DAR (regent 1980-82, bd. dirs.), Bethlehem C. of C., Capital Dist. Trial Lawyers Assn., Bus. and Profl. Women Assn., Athenian Honor Soc., Russell Sage Coll. Alumni Assn. (pres. 1983-87, bd. dirs. 1987—, past pres.), Phi Alpha Theta. Roman Catholic. Clubs: NYU; Zonta (Albany), Union U. Outing. Office: 217 Delaware Ave Delmar NY 12054

GALVIN, ROBERT J., lawyer; b. New Haven, Conn., Dec. 10, 1938; s. Herman I. and Freda (Helfand) G.; m. Susan I. Goldstein, Oct. 15, 1960 (div.); children—David B., Peter J. A.B., Union Coll., Schenectady, N.Y., 1961; J.D., Suffolk U., Boston, 1967. Bar: Mass. 1967, U.S. Dist. Ct. Mass. 1967, U.S. Supreme Ct. 1988. Sole practice, Boston, 1967-78; ptnr. firm Lippman & Galvin, Boston, 1978-84; of counsel Gage, Tucker & Vom Baur Boston, 1984-86; ptnr. firm Davis, Malm & D'Agostine, Boston, 1986—; lectr. Boston Ctr. Adult Edn., 1972—, Northeastern U., Boston, 1977-78. Real estate columnist Boston Ledger, 1981. Contbr. numerous articles to profl. jours. Bd. dirs., v.p. Rental Housing Assn. div. Greater Boston Real Estate Bd., 1974, Boston Ctr. Adult Edn., 1979—, chmn. fin. com., 1985-86, pres., 1987—. Mem. Mass. Bar Assn. (council mem. property law sect. 1977-80, chmn. condominium com. 1979—), Mass. Continuing Legal Edn. (real estate curriculum adv. com. 1983-87), Am. Arbitration Assn. (comml. arbitration panel), Mass. Conveyancers Assn., Thoreau Soc. (life, chmn. devel. com. 1985—), Soc. for Censure, Reproof and Arraignment of Pub. Error; fellow Mass. Bar Found. Home: 33 Pond Ave Brookline MA 02146 Office: Davis Malm & D'Agostine One Boston Pl Suite 3900 Boston MA 02108

GALVIN, ROBERT W., electronics executive; b. Marshfield, Wis., Oct. 9, 1922. Student, U. Notre Dame, U. Chgo.; LL.D. (hon.), Quincy Coll., St. Ambrose Coll., DePaul U., Ariz. State U. With Motorola, Inc., Chgo., 1940—, exec. v.p., 1948-56, pres., from 1956, chmn. bd., 1964—, chief exec. officer, 1964-86, also dir. Former mem. Pres.'s Commn. on Internat. Trade and Investment.; chmn. industry policy adv. com. to U.S. Trade Rep.; mem. Pres.'s Pvt. Sector Survey; chmn. Pres.'s Adv. Council on Pvt. Sector Initiatives; chmn. Ill. Inst. Tech., U. Notre Dame; bd. dirs. Jr. Achievement Chgo. Served with Signal Corps, AUS, World War II. Named Decision Maker of Yr. Chgo. Assn. Commerce and Industry-Am. Statis. Assn., 1973; Sword of Loyola award Loyola U., Chgo.; Washington award Western Soc. Engrs., 1984. Mem. Electronic Industries Assn. (pres. 1966, dir., Medal of Honor 1970, Golden Omega award 1981). Office: Motorola Inc 1303 E Algonquin Rd Schaumburg IL 60196 *

GALWAY, JAMES, flutist; b. Belfast, No. Ireland, Dec. 8, 1939; s. James Galway and Ethel Stewart (Clarke) G.; m. Anna Christine Renggli, 1972 (div.); 4 children; m. Jeanne Cinnante, 1984. Student, Royal Coll. Music, Guildhall Sch. Music, London, Conservatoire National Superieur de Musique, Paris; MA (hon.), Open U., Eng., 1979; MusD (hon.), Queen's U., Belfast, 1979, New Eng. Conservatory Music, 1980. Flutist, Wind Band of Royal Shakespeare Theatre, Sadler's Wells Orch., 1960-65, Royal Opera House Orch., BBC Symphony Orch., prin. flutist, London Symphony Orch., 1966, Royal Philharm. Orch., 1967-69, prin. solo flutist, Berlin Philharm. Orch., 1969-75; now solo performer and condr. U.S. debut, 1978; rec. artist. works of C.P.E. Bach, J.S. Bach, Beethovan, Franck, Mozart, Prokofiev, Reinecke, Rodrigo, Stamitz, Telemann, Vivaldi, Khachaturian. Author: James Galway: An Autobiography, 1978, Flute, 1982. Decorated officer Order Brit. Empire; recipient Grand Prix du Disque. Fellow Royal Coll. Music. Office: care London Artists, 73 Baker St, London England W1M 1AH other: care ICM Artists Ltd 40 W 57th St New York NY 10019

GAMA E SILVA, ANTONIO CARLOS DA, civil engineer; b. Sao Paulo, Brazil, July 11, 1949; s. Luis Antonio and Eddy De Mattos (Pimenta) Da G.E.S.; m. Lucia Marina F. Ferreira, Dec. 18, 1979. Degree in Civil Engring., Inst. Superior Tecnico, Lisbon, Portugal, 1972; Degree in Bus. Adminstrn., U. Sao Paulo, 1979. Registered civil engr., mgr., Brazil, Portugal. Civil engr. AC-Trab. Arq. E Construção, Lisbon, 1973-74, Fig. Ferraz Cons. Engr. Projects, São Paulo, 1974-80; dir. GPA Engring. Proj. Avaliaçoes, Sãa Paulo, 1980-87; pres. GPA Grupo De Proj. E. Asses., Sãa Paulo, 1987—; econs. adv. Transbrasil Linhas Aéreas, São Paulo, 1981-83, project mgr. airport, 1983-85, Transbrasil Lin. Aereas, São Paulo; prof. Ibero-Americana São Paulo, 1976-82; cons. in field. Mem. Cons. Reg. Eng. Arq. Agr. S. Paulo, Cons. Reg. Adminstrn. S. Paulo, Ass. Braz. Eng. Econ. e Custos S. Paulo. Roman Catholic. Office: GPA Engenharia, Rua Jacarezinho 234, Cep 01456 São Paulo-SP Brazil

GAMBLE, WILLIAM BELSER, JR., physician; b. Andrews, S.C., Apr. 17, 1925; s. William Belser and Anna (Moyd) G.; B.S., U. S.C., 1945; M.D., Med. Coll. S.C., 1948; M.P.H., U. N.C., 1972; m. Margaret Florence DuBose, June 7, 1947 (dec.); children—William Belser III, Richard Ervin, Heather Moyd; m. Bertie Hemingway Bunch, Mar. 1986. Intern, Roper Hosp., Charleston, S.C., 1948-49; resident pediatrics, teaching fellow Med. Coll. S.C., Charleston, 1953-56, assoc. prof. pediatrics; practice medicine subspecializing in pediatric allergy and immunology, Charleston, 1956—; state epidemiologist State Bd. Health, also dir. div. epidemiology State Dept. Health and Environ. Control, Columbia, S.C., 1972-78, dep. chief bur. disease control, 1978—; chief pediatrics Roper Hosp.; mem. staff Med. Coll., St. Francis hosps., Charleston. Pres., Coastal Carolina Tb. and Health Assn. Dist. dir. S.C. Bd. of Health, 1972. Bd. dirs. Charleston County Mental Health Assn., Charleston County Tb Assn., Charleston. Served with M.C., U.S. Army, 1951-53. Diplomate Am. Bd. Pediatrics, Am. Bd. Allergy and Clin. Immunology, Am. Bd. Epidemiology. Fellow Am. Acad. Allergy, Am. Acad. Pediatrics, Am. Coll. Allergy and Immunology; mem. AMA, Am. Acad. Pediatrics (infectious disease com., Red Book com.), S.C. Soc. Allergy and Clin. Immunology (charter pres.), Southeastern Allergy Assn., Phi Beta Kappa, Alpha Kappa Kappa, Kappa Sigma, Alpha Omega Alpha, Delta Omega. Presbyterian (elder). Club: Rotary (past pres.). Contbr. articles on communicable diseases in U.S., Latin Am. and Can. to profl. jours. Address: 3251 Seabrook Island Rd Johns Island SC 29455

GAMBON, MICHAEL JOHN, actor; b. Oct. 19, 1940; s. Edward and Mary Gambon; m. Anne Miller, 1962. Student, St. Aloysius Sch. for Boys, London. Engring. apprentice 7 yrs.; with Edwards/MacLiammoir Theatre Co., Dublin, Ireland, 1962, Nat. Theatre, Old Vic., 1963-67, Birmingham Rep. and other provincial theatres, 1967-69. Performances include: (with regional theatres) Othello, Macbeth, Coriolanus; Aldwych, 1970-71, Norman Conquests, 1974, Otherwise Engaged, 1976, Just Between Ourselves, 1977, Alice's Boys, 1978, King Lear and Anthony and Cleopatra, 1982-83, Old Times, 1985, Galileo, 1980 (recipient Best Actor award, London Theatre Critics'), Betrayal, 1980, Tales from Hollywood, 1980, Chorus of Disapproval, 1985 (Olivier award, Best Comedy Performance), Tons of Money, 1986, A View form the Bridge, 1987, A Small Family Business, 1987; numerous film and TV appearances including The Singing Detective, 1986 (BAFTA award, Best Actor). Office: care Larry Dalzell Assocs, 126 Kennington Park Rd, London SE11 4D, England *

GAMBRELL, RICHARD DONALD, JR., reproductive endocrinologist, educator; b. St. George, S.C., Oct. 28, 1931; s. Richard Donald and Nettie Anzo (Ellenburg) G.; m. Mary Caroline Stone, Dec. 22, 1956; children—Deborah Christina, Juliet Denise. B.S., Furman U., 1953; M.D., Med. U. S.C., 1957. Diplomate Am. Bd. Obstetrics and Gynecology. Intern Greenville Gen. Hosp., S.C., 1957-58, resident, 1961-64; commd. USAF, 1958, advanced through grades to col.; chmn. dept. ob-gyn, cons. to surgeon gen. USAF Hosp. USAF, Wiesbaden, Germany, 1966-69; chief gynecologic endocrinology Wilford Hall USAF Med. Ctr. USAF, Lackland AFB, Tex., 1971-78; ret. USAF, 1978; clin. prof. ob-gyn and endocrinology Med. Coll. Ga., Augusta, 1978—; practice medicine specializing in reproductive endocrinology Augusta, 1978—; fellow in endocrinology Med. Coll. Ga., 1969-71; mem. staff Westlawn Bapt. Mission Med. Clinic, San Antonio, 1972-78; assoc. clin. prof. U. Tex. Health Sci. Ctr., San Antonio, 1971-78; internat. lectr. Co-author: The Menopause: Indications for Estrogen Therapy, 1979, Sex Steroid Hormones and Cancer, 1984, Unwanted Hair: Its Cause and Treatment, 1985, Estrogen Replacement Therapy, 1987, Estrogen Replacement Therapy Users Guide, 1988; contbr. chpts. to med. books, articles to profl. jours.; mem. editorial bd. Jour. Reproductive Medicine, 1982-85, Maturitas, 1982—, Internat. Jour. Fertility, 1986—, assoc. editor, 1988—. Deacon, Sunday sch. tchr. Baptist Ch., 1971—). Recipient Chmn.'s Best Paper in Clin. Research from Teaching Hosp. award Armed Forces Dist. Am. Coll. Ob-Gyn, 1972, Host award, 1977, Chmn.'s award, 1978, Purdue-Frederick award, 1979, Outstanding Exhibit award Am. Fertility Soc., 1983, Am. Coll. Obstetricians and Gynecologists award, 1983, Thesis award South Atlantic Assn. Ob.-Gyn., Winthrop award Internat. Soc. Reproductive Med., 1985, Chmn.'s Best Paper award Pan Am. Soc. for Fertility, 1986, Outstanding Sci. Exhibit award Am. Acad. Family Practitioners, 1986, 87. Fellow Am. Coll. Obstetricians and Gynecologists (subcom. on endocrinology and infertility 1983-86); mem. So. Med. Assn., Am. Fertility Soc., Tex. Assn. Ob-Gyn., Can. Soc. Obstetricians and Gynecologists (hon.), San Antonio Ob-Gyn. Soc. (v.p. 1975-76), Chilean Soc. Ob-Gyn. (hon.), Soc. Obstetricians and Gynecologists of Can., Internat. Family Planning Research Assn., Internat. Menopause Soc. (exec. com. 1981-84), Internat. Soc. for Reproductive Medicine (program chmn. 1980, pres. 1986-88), Am. Geriatric Soc. (editorial bd. 1981-83), Nat. Geog. Soc., Phi Chi, Am. Philatelic Soc., Alpha Epsilon Delta. Home: 3542 National Ct Augusta GA 30907 Office: 903 15th St Augusta GA 30910

GAMBRELL, SARAH BELK, retail executive; b. Charlotte, N.C., Apr. 12, 1918; d. William Henry and Mary (Irwin) Belk; B.A., Sweet Briar Coll., 1939; D. Humanities, Erskine Coll., 1970, U. N.C.-Asheville, 1986; m. Charles Glenn Gambrell; 1 dau., Sarah Belk. pres., v.p., dir. Belk Stores, various locations, 1947—, pres. 32 stores. Trustee Princeton (N.J.) Theol. Sem., Johnson C. Smith U., Charlotte, N.C., Warren Wilson Coll., Swannanoa, N.C.; trustee nat. bd. YWCA; bd. dirs. Parkinson's Disease Found.; bd. dirs. Opera Carolina, Charlotte, Planned Parenthood, Charlotte, YWCA, Charlotte; hon. trustee Cancer Research Inst., N.Y.C.; hon. bd. dirs. YWCA, N.Y.C., Mem. Fashion Group, Inc., Jr. League N.Y.C., Nat. Soc. Colonial Dames, DAR. Home: 300 Cherokee Rd Charlotte NC 28207 Office: PO Box 31788 Charlotte NC 28231 also: 111 W 40th St New York NY 10018

GAMBRO, MICHAEL S., lawyer; b. N.Y.C., July 15, 1954; s. A. John and Rose A. (Grandinetti) G.; m. Joan L. Thurneyssen, Aug. 9, 1980; children: Dana E., Merrill R. BS summa cum laude, Tufts U., 1976; JD, Columbia U., 1980. Bar: N.Y. 1981, U.S. Dist. Ct. (so. dist.) N.Y. 1981, U.S. Dist. Ct. N.J. 1981, N.J. 1983, Calif. 1988. Assoc. Cadwalader, Wickersham & Taft, N.Y.C., 1980-86, ptnr., 1987—. Harlan Fiske Stone scholar, 1978-79, 1979-80. Mem. ABA, Phi Beta Kappa, Psi Chi. Office: Cadwalader Wickersham & Taft 100 Maiden Ln New York NY 10038

GAME, DAVID AYLWARD, physician; b. Adelaide, Australia, Mar. 31, 1926; s. Tasman Aylward and Clarice Mary (Turner) G.; M.B., B.S., U. Adelaide, 1949; m. Patricia Jean Hamilton, Dec. 8, 1949; children—Ann (Aylward) Philip, Timothy, Ruth. Resident Royal Adelaide Hosp., 1950, Outpatient Registrar, 1951; gen. practice medicine Adelaide, 1953—; officer Order of Australia, 1983—; chmn. Eastern Region Geriatric and Rehab. Adv. Com., 1976-83; chmn. Central Eastern Health Adv. Com., 1983-86. Mem., chmn. social welfare council Diocese of Adelaide; mem. standing com. Synod Diocese Adelaide, Ch. of Eng., 1966-79, 81-84. Fellow Royal Australian Coll. Gen. Practitioners (chmn. fed. council, 1969-72, pres. elec. 1972-74, pres., 1974-76, censor in chief, 1976-80), Hon. Fellow Royal Coll. Gen. Practitioners, Hong Kong Coll. Gen. Practitioners; fellow ad eudem Royal Coll. Gen. Physicians, hon. mem. Coll. Family Physicians of Can.; mem. World Orgn. Nat. Colls. and Acads. and Academic Assns. Gen. Practitioners/Family Physicians (hon. sec. treas. 1972-80, pres. 1983-86), Australian Postgrad. Fedn. Medicine (council), Coll. Family Physicians Can. (hon.), Australian Med. Assn., Australian Geriatric Soc. Club: Adelaide. Home: 50 Lambert Rd, Royston Park 5070, Australia Office: 19 North Terrace, Hackney 5069, Australia

GAMMILL, LEE MORGAN, JR., insurance company executive; b. N.Y.C., Mar. 25, 1934; s. Lee Morgan and Blanche (Reeves) G.; m. Jane Houchin, Apr. 2, 1960; children: Christopher Morgan, Sarah Louise. BA, Dartmouth Coll., 1956. CLU. Mgmt. trainee N.Y. Life Ins. Co., San Francisco, 1957-58, field underwriter, 1958-60, sales mgr., 1960-64, gen. mgr., 1965-71, regional supt., 1971-75, gen. mgr., 1975-86, sr. v.p., 1986—; pres. N.Y. Life and Annuity Corp., N.Y.C., 1987; bd. dirs. N.Y. Life Securities Corp., N.Y.C., N.Y. Life Equity Corp., N.Y.C., N.Y. Life Realty Corp., N.Y.C. Chmn. Town Recreational Adv. Bd., Ross., Calif., 1977; trustee Ross Sch. Dist., 1978-84. Mem. Gen. Agts. and Mgrs. Assn. (pres. San Francisco chpt. 1985), Nat. Assn. Life Underwriters, CLU Assn. Republican. Presbyterian. Clubs: Mill Valley Tennis (pres. 1972-73); Lagunitas Country (Ross); Pacific Union (San Francisco). Office: NY Life Ins Co 51 Madison Ave New York NY 10010

GAMMON, JAMES EDWIN, SR., clergyman; b. San Diego, Jan. 23, 1944; s. Jack Albert and Thalia Gammon; BA, Tex. Christian U., 1970, postgrad., 1970-72; m. Sharon Elaine Head, June 27, 1965; children—John Paul, James Edwin, Jeffrey David. Ordained to ministry Ch. of Christ, 1966; minister Carter Park Ch., Ft. Worth, 1966-69, Scotland Hills Ch., Ft. Worth, 1969-70, Northside Ch., Dallas, 1970-73, Central Ave Ch., Valdosta, Ga., 1973-78; debate coach Christian Coll. S.W., Dallas, 1971-73; pres. So. Bible Inst., Valdosta, 1977-78; minister Trinity Oaks Ch. of Christ, Dallas., 1978-80, Parkview Ch. of Christ, Sherman, Tex., 1980-85; pres. Texoma Bible Inst., 1980-85; minister Eisenhower Ch. of Christ, Odessa, Tex., 1985-86; minister, Cen. Ch. of Christ, McMinnville, Tenn., 1986—. Author: Notes on I, II, Thessalonians; Notes on James; Notes on Romans. Served with U.S. Army, 1963-66. Republican. Home: Rt 11 PO Box 14A McMinnville TN 37110 Office: Court Sq Box 536 McMinnville TN 37110

GAN, FELISA SO, physician; b. Manila, June 29, 1943; d. Victor Ang So and Siok Gee Tan; m. David Jr. Lo Gan, June 30, 1968; children: Jason, Johann, Tanya. BA, U. Santo Tomas, Manila, 1963; postgrad., U. Santo Tomas East, Manila, 1977—. Asst. to med. dir. Met. Gen. Hosp., Manila, 1968—, perceptorship, 1968-79; gen. practice internal medicine Manila, 1968—. Contbr. articles to profl. jours. Pres. Greenhills Christian Women's Fellowship, Manila, 1985-86, v.p. 87—. Fellow Philippines Soc. Gastroenterology (assoc.); mem. Philippines Med. Assn. Office: Met Gen Hosp, 1357 G Masangkay St, Binondo, Manila Philippines

GAN, TIAN HUAT, manufacturing company executive; b. Singapore, Nov. 26, 1944; s. Thiam Hoo and Geok Kheng (Teo) G.; m. Chor Tian Sng/Gan, Jan. 31, 1972; children—Lorraine Su-Shen, Gavin Chuen-Jin. B in Accountancy, Nat. U. Singapore, 1969. Office asst. Internat. Comml. Co., Singapore, 1962-69; credit trainee Bank of Am. NT 7 SA, Singapore, 1969-70; with Eveready Singapore Pte Ltd., 1970—, mgr. planning, materials, purchasing and control, 1984—. Busary, Ministry of Edn., Singapore, 1961. Christian. Clubs: Seletar Country, Jurong Country, Tanah Meruah Country. Home: 4A St Martin's Ct, St Martin's Dr, Singapore 1025, Singapore Office: Union Carbide Singapore Pte Ltd, 25 Gul Way, Jurong, Singapore 2262 Singapore

GAN, WOON SIONG, acoustician; b. Republic of Singapore, Mar. 6, 1943; s. Eng Hwa and Chai Luan (Tan) G.; m. Madam Chiong Siu Hui, Mar. 4, 1973; children—Gan Cheong Kiat, Judy Gan, Gan Cheong Toh. B.Sc. in Physics, Imperial Coll., London, 1965, DIC in Acoustics and Vibration Sci., 1967, Ph.D. in Acoustics, 1969. Assoc. prof. dept. physics Nanyang U., Singapore, 1970-79; dir. Acoustical Services Pte Ltd., Singapore, 1976—; dir. WS Gan Realty & Devel. Pte Ltd., Galaxy Internat. Pte Ltd.; cons. in field. Contbr. numerous articles and papers in acoustical research; assoc. editor Internat. Jour. Acoustical Holography and Imaging. Internat. Centre for Theoretical Physics fellow Trieste, Italy. Fellow Inst. Acoustics U.K., Inst. Elec. Engrs. (U.K.); mem. Acoustical Soc. U.S., Acoustical Soc. France, Acoustical Soc. Japan, Acoustical Soc. Italy, Acoustical Soc. India, Acoustical Soc. South Africa, IEEE (sr.), Inst. Noise Control Engring. (assoc.), N.Y. Acad. Sci. Office: 29 Telok Ayer St, Singapore 0104 Singapore

GANATRA, VALLABHDAS MADHAVJI, accountant; b. Fatana, Gujrat, India, Feb. 11, 1916; arrived in London, 1972.; s. Madharji Vasanji and Zaverben G.; m. July, 1939; children: Kumudini, Tansukh, Chandra, Suvandra. Undergrad., Bahaudin Coll., Junagad, India, 1935. Fin. acct. Madavani Group, Uganda, Africa, 1965-72; asst. acct., fin. mgr. Emile Woolf Group, London, 1979-84; pvt. practice acctg. 1984—. Mem. S.E. Hindu Assn. (exec. com. 1987—), Greenwich Gujrati Samat (exec. com. 1987—).

GANCHROW, JUDITH RUTH, biopsychologist, educator; b. DuQuoin, Ill., Oct. 28, 1941; d. Everett Russell and Bertha Ruth (Halemeyer) Jay; m. Donald Ganchrow, May 28, 1967; children—Dov Amir, Raviv Tal. A.B., Carleton Coll., Northfield, Minn., 1963; M.Sc., Brown U., Providence, 1965; Ph.D., Duke U., Durham, N.C., 1969. Post-doctoral fellow Harvard U., 1969-71; lectr. San Francisco State U., 1973-74; lectr., research fellow dept. oral biology Hebrew U., Jerusalem, Israel, 1975-87, sr. lectr., assoc. prof., 1987—; vis. scientist U. Conn. Health Ctr., Farmington, 1979-81. Editor: (with J.E. Steiner) Determinants of Behavior by Chemical Stimuli, 1982; contbr. articles in field to profl. jours. Grantee NIH, Charles Smith Found. for Psychobiology, Bi-Nat. Sci. Found. Fellow Sigma Xi; mem. N.Y. Acad. Scis., European Chemosensory Research Orgn., Assn. Chemoreception Scis., Israel Physiol. and Pharm. Soc. Home: 29/16 Naveh Sha'anan, Jerusalem Israel Office: Hadassah-Hebrew Univ, Sch Dental Medicine, Dept Oral Biology, Jerusalem Israel

GANDEVIA, BRYAN HARLE, physician; b. Melbourne, Australia, Apr. 5, 1925; s. Eric Neville Harle and Vera Brooking (Hannah) G.; m. Dorothy Virginia Murphy, Aug. 25, 1950; children—Simon Charles, Robin Harle. M.B., B.S., U. Melbourne, 1948, M.D., 1953. Intern, resident, Melbourne and London, Eng., 1950-57; sr. fellow occupational medicine U. Melbourne, 1958-63; assoc. prof. medicine U. New South Wales, Sydney, 1963-85; chmn. dept. respiratory medicine Prince Henry and Prince of Wales Hosps., Sydney, 1963-85; cons. physician sole practice, Sydney, 1985—. Author: Annotated Bibliography of History of Medicine in Australia, 1957; Tears Often Shed: Child Health and Welfare in Australia from 1788, 1978. Co-author: Annotated Bibliography of History of Medicine and Health in Australia, 1984. Chmn. editorial com.: BIBAM (Bibliography of Australian Medicine Project), 1983—. Contbr. articles to profl. and hist. jours. Served to maj. Royal Australian Army Med. Corps, 1949-60. Mem. council Australian War Meml., Canberra, 1967-83. Decorated Order of Australia. Mem. Internat. Commn. Occupational Health, Internat. Soc. History Medicine, Internat. Epidemiological Assn.; fellow Royal Australian Coll. Physicians (history of medicine library com. 1963—, chmn. 1983—), Brit. Thoracic Soc. (hon.), Australian Coll. Occupational Medicine. Club: Univ. & Schs. (Sydney). Avocations: History; wine and food; books. Office: 69 Arthur St, Randwick, Sydney 2031, Australia

GANDHI, BHARAT R., construction company executive; b. India, Oct. 16, 1942; came to U.S., 1971; naturalized, 1979; s. Ramanlal and Shardaben (Sura) G.; m. Purnima Bharat, Dec. 25, 1966; children: Manish, Nisha. BS in Civil and Sanitary Engring., V.J.J. Inst., Bombay, India, 1964; postgrad. constrn. engring., U. Wis., 1971-72. Ptnr., v.p. constrn. co. in India; project mgr. Corbetta Constrn. Co. Des Plaines, Ill., 1972-75; project mgr. Pepper Constrn. Co., Schaumburg, Ill., 1975-81, v.p. healthcare div., 1981-84, exec. v.p., 1984-87; sr. v.p. The Pepper Cos., Inc., 1987—; pres. Pepper West, Inc., 1987—. Contbr. articles to profl. publs. Home: 2333 Sussex St Northbrook IL 60062 Office: 643 N Orleans St Chicago IL 60610

GANDHI, OM PARKASH, electrical engineer; b. Multan, Pakistan, Sept. 23, 1934; came to U.S., 1967, naturalized, 1975; s. Gopal Das and Devi Bai (Patney) G.; m. Santosh Nayar, Oct. 28, 1963; children: Rajesh Timmy, Monica, Lena. B.S. with honors, Delhi U., India, 1952; M.S.E., U. Mich., 1957, Sc.D., 1961. Research specialist Philco Corp., Blue Bell, Pa., 1960-62; asst. dir. Cen. Electronics Engring. Research Inst., Pilani, Rajasthan, India, 1962-65, dep. dir., 1965-67; prof. elec. engring., research prof. bioengring. U. Utah, Salt Lake City, 1967—; cons. U.S. Army Med. Research and Devel. Command, Washington, 1973-77; cons. to industry and govtl. organizations; mem. Internat. URSI Commn. B., 1976—; mem. study sect. on diagnostic radiology NIH, 1978-81; co-chmn. ANSI C 954 Com. on RF Safety Standards, 1988—. Author: Microwave Engineering and Applications, 1981; editor Engineering in Medicine and Biology mag., Mar., 1987; contbr. over 180 articles on biol. effects and med. applications of electromagnetic energy, microwave semicondr. devices and microwave tubes to profl. jours. Recipient Disting. Research award U. Utah, 1979-80; grantee NSF, NIH, EPA, USAF, U.S. Army, USN, N.Y. State Dept. Health, others. Fellow IEEE (editor Procs. of IEEE Spl. Issue, 1980; Tech. Achievement award Utah sect. 1975); mem. Bioelectromagnetics Soc. (dir. 1979-82, 87—). Office: U Utah Elec Engring Dept 3254 Merrill Engineering Salt Lake City UT 84112

GANDHI, RAJIV, prime minister and minister of external affairs of India; b. Bombay, India, Aug. 20, 1944; s. Firoze and Indira G.; m. Sonia Maino, 1968; two children. Grad. mech. engring., Trinity Coll., Cambridge, Eng., 1965; student Imperial Coll., London, 1962-65. Pilot, Indian Airlines, 1972-81; elected to Lok Sabha (Ho. of People of Parliament) from Amethi Uttar Pradesh, 1981, 84; mem. Nat. Exec. of Indian Youth Congress, 1981-83; gen. sec. Indian Nat. Congress, 1983-84, pres., 1984—; prime minister India, 1984—, also minister of program implementation, personnel and adminstrv. reforms, planning, and sci. and tech. Office: Office of Prime Minister, 1 Safdarjung Rd, New Delhi 110011, India *

GANELIUS, TORD HJALMAR, secretary general, educator; b. Stockholm, Sweden, May 23, 1925; s. Hjalmar Gustaf and Ebba Gunhild (Bejbom) G.; m. Aggie Agnes Hemberg, Oct. 6, 1951; children: Per, Truls, Svante, Aggie. Filosophie Magister, U. Stockholm, 1946, Fil. Dr., 1953. Docent U. Lund, Sweden, 1953-56; assoc. prof. U. Lund, 1956-57; prof. U. Göteborg, Sweden, 1957-80; sec. gen. Royal Acad. Scis., Stockholm, 1981—; vis. prof. Cornell U., Ithaca, N.Y., 1967-68, U. Calif., San Diego, 1972-73; bd. dirs. Nobel Found., Stockholm, 1981—. Author: Tauberian Remainder Theorems, 1971, (with others) Lectures on Approximation and Value Distribution, 1982; editor proceedings of Nobel symposium #58 Progress in Science and It's Social Conditions, 1986. Fellow Royal Swedish Acad. Scis. (3d v.p. 1978-80), Finnish Acad. Scis., European Acad. Scis. Arts and Humanites. Home: Bergianska Trädgarden, S-10405 Stockholm Sweden Office: Royal Acad Scis, PO Box 50005, S-104 05 Stockholm Sweden

GANGULY, SUKANTA, accountant, financial consultant; b. Calcutta, India, Oct. 1, 1950; s. Sushil and Mamata G.; m. Bharati Banerjee, Aug. 11, 1979; children: Sukrit, Mekhola. B in Commerce, U. Calcutta, 1972. Sr. auditor Coopers and Lybrand, London, 1972-80; sr. cons., mgr. Talal Abu Ghazaleh Co., Muscat, Oman, 1981—; examiner Cen. Bank Oman. Fellow Middle East Soc. Associated Accts.; assoc. Inst. Chartered Accts. Eng. and Wales, Inst. Arab Certified Accts. Mem. Labour Party. Hindu. Office: Talal Abu Ghazaleh Co, PO Box 5366, Muscat Oman

GANILAU, RATU SIR PENAIA KANATABATU, Fiji government official; b. Fiji, July 28, 1918; student Devonshire course for adminstrn. officers Wadham Coll., Oxford U., 1947; m. Adi Laisa Delaisomosomo, 1949 (dec. 1971); children: Adi Mei Kainona, Ratu Epeli Gavidi, Adi Lusiana Sivo, Ratu Jone Rakuro, Ratu Josefa Sukuna, Ratu Isoa Fugawai, Ratu Jone Rabici; m. 2d, Adi Davila Liliwaimanu, 1975 (dec. 1984); With Colonial Adminstrn. Service, 1947; dist. officer, 1948-53; mem. Commonwealth on Fijian Post Primary Edn. in the Colony, 1953; Fijian econ. devel. officer, Roko Tui Cakaudrove, 1956; tour mgr., govt. rep. Fiji Rugby Football tour, N.Z., 1957; dep. sec. for Fijian affairs, 1961-65, minister for Fijian affairs and local govt., 1965-72, leader govt. bus., minister for communications, works and tourism, from 1972, dep. prime minister of Fiji, minister for Fijian affairs and rural devel., gov.-gen., comdr.-in-chief of Fiji, 1983-87, pres., 1987—; mem. Council of Ministers; ofcl. mem. Legis. Council; chmn. Fijian Affairs Bd.; mem. Fijian Devel. Fund Bd., Native Land Trust Bd., Gt. Council of Chiefs; sr. chief Tovata Confederacy, 1988—. Served with Fiji Inf. Regt., 1940-46, hon. col. 2d bn., 1973, col., 1979; with Fiji Mil. Forces, 1953-56. Decorated knight Order Brit. Empire, Knight grand class St. Michael and St. George, Knight Companion Royal Victorian Order, Disting. Service Order. Home and Office: Office of Governor Gen, Government House, Suva Fiji *

GANNATAL, JOSEPH PAUL, mechanical engineer; b. Ventura, Calif., Sept. 9, 1955; s. Paul and Janet Mae (Carpenter) G.; m. Sandy Jean Lincoln, Jan. 14, 1984; children: Leonard Troy Garcia, Jennfier Lynn Garcia, Sarah Jean Gannatal. BSME, Calif. Polytech. Inst., San Luis Opisbo, 1979; M in Space Systems Tech., Naval Postgrad. Sch., 1987. Indsl. engr. Nat. Semiconductor, Santa Clara, Calif., 1979-81; spl. projects engr. Pacific Missile Test Ctr., Point Mugu, Calif., 1981—, mgr. devel. program, 1986-88. Mem. bldg. com. Camarillo Bapt. Ch., 1984-86. Recipient Spl. Achievement award USN, 1982, 84, Letter of Commendation USN, 1983, Outstanding Service award USN, 1985, 86. Mem. AIAA, ASME. Republican.

GANNON, PETER JOHN, chiropodist, gunsmith; b. London, Dec. 30, 1944; s. Henry John and Mabel (Bradenham) G.; m. Janet Ann Kenny, 1946 (div. 1974); children: Michael Peter, Lynn Ann; m. Shirley Florence Coe, Sept. 27, 1939; 1 stepchild, Lisa Maria Holden. Student, East Herts Coll., Hertford, Eng., 1959-64, London Sch. Chiropody. Apprentice engr. Med. Devel. Co., Enfield, Middlesex, Eng., 1959-65; gunsmith Ministry Def., Enfield, 1965-74; chiropodist English Chiropody Assn., Enfield, 1977—. Patentee in field. Mem. English Chiropody Assn., Irish Chiropody Assn., British Chiropody Assn., Sch. Surg. Chiropody. Clubs: Rifle (Cuffley Herts, Eng.); Clay Pigeon, Veteran Vehicle Soc. (Enfield). Home and Office: 77 Addison Rd, Enfield, Middlesex EN 3 5JX, England

GANS, SAMUEL MYER, temporary employment service exec.; b. Phila., June 10, 1925; s. Arthur and Goldie (Goldhirsh) G.; grad. Peirce Jr. Coll., 1949; m. Ada Zuckerman, Aug. 1, 1948; children—Gary M., Jeffrey R. Public acct., 1949-55; sales exec., 1955-58; franchise owner, pres., chief exec. officer Manpower, Inc. Delaware Valley, Pennsauken, N.J., 1958—; franchise cons.; instr. motivation courses. V.p., exec. bd. United Fund Camden County; v.p., bd. dirs. So. N.J. Devel. Council, Am. Red Cross Camden County, Nat. Conf. of Christian and Jews; bd. mgrs. Am. Cancer Soc. Camden County; active Boy Scouts Am., Employer Legis. Com., Camden County Bicentennial Com., Score and Ace programs, Camden, YMCA, Allied Jewish Appeal, World Affairs Council; mem. N.J. Gov.'s Mgmt. Commn., 1971; trustee Camden County Heart Assn., Camden County Mental Health Assn.; exec. bd., founder Big Bros. Assn. Camden County; public relations com. U.S. Savs. Bonds, Camden and Trenton. Served with USNR, 1943-46. Mem. Nat. Assn. Temp. Services (chpt. relations com. 1973), Nat. Soc. Public Accts., Camden County C. of C., S. Jersey Public Relations Assn. (pres. 1967), S. Jersey Mfg. Assn. (exec. bd., treas.), S. Jersey Personnel Assn. (treas.), Cherry Hill C. of C. (bd. dirs., v.p.), Better Bus. Bur. Camden County, Adminstrv. Mgmt. Soc., N.J. Assn. Temp. Services (pres. 1970-72, bd. dirs.), South Jersey Purchasing Agts. Assn., Assn. of Manpower Franchise Owners, Jewish War Veterans; Jewish (exec. bd. dirs. congregation). Lodges: Masons, Lions (pres. Camden 1972-73, Lion of Year 1977), Shriners, B'Nai B'Rith. Home: 4 N Derby Ln Ventnor NJ 08406 Office: 3720 Marlton Pike Pennsauken NJ 08105

GANSÄUER, KARL-FRIEDRICH, diplomat; b. Perseifen, Fed. Republic Germany, Oct. 29, 1932; s. Gustav and Hedwig Karoline (Klein) G.; m. Gabriele Brigitte Costa, July 9, 1965; children: Andreas, Michael, Tobias. Diplom-Volkswirt, U. Cologne, Fed. Republic Germany, 1957, Dr. rer. pol., 1961. Cert. economist. Asst. prof. U. Cologne, 1959-63; diplomat Fed. Fgn. Office, Bonn, Fed. Republic Germany, 1963—; ambassador Fed. Republic Germany, Port-au-Prince, Haiti, 1985—. Fgn. policy advisor Free Dem. Parliamentary Group of Fed. Parliament, Bonn, 1981-83. Home: Zülpicher Strasse 3, Bonn 5300, Federal Republic of Germany Office: Auswärtiges Amt, Adenauer Allee 99-103, Bonn 5300, Federal Republic of Germany

GANTIN, BERNARDIN CARDINAL, former archbishop of Cotonou; b. Toffo, Dahomey (now Benin), May 8, 1922. Ordained priest Roman Catholic Ch., 1951; titular bishop of Tipasa di Mauritania, also aux. bishop of Cotonou, 1953; archbishop of Cotonou, 1960-71; asso. sec., then sec. Sacred Congregation for Evangelization of Peoples, 1971-75; v.p., then pres. Pontifical Commn. Justice and Peace, 1975-76; elevated to Sacred Coll. Cardinals, 1977; deacon Sacred Heart of Christ the King; pres. Pontifical Commn. Justice; archbishop of Ernakulam of the Chaldean-Malabar Rite; mem. Congregation Oriental Chs., Secretariat of Non-Christians; mem. Commn. Revision Code of Canon Law; pres. Commn. Revision of Oriental Code of Canon Law. Address: Palazzo San Calisto, Vatican City Vatican *

GANZ, DAVID L., lawyer; b. N.Y.C., July 28, 1951; s. Daniel M. and Beverlee (Kaufman) G.; m. Barbara Bondanza, Nov. 3, 1974 (div. 1978); m. Sharon Ruth Lamnin, Oct. 30, 1981; children—Scott Harry, Elyse Toby, Pamela Rebecca. B.S. in Fgn. Service, Georgetown U., 1973; J.D., St. John's U., 1976. Bar: N.Y. 1977, D.C. 1980, N.J. 1985. Assoc. firm Regan, Dorsey & DeRiso, Flushing, N.Y., 1977-79; ptnr. firm Durst & Ganz, P.C., N.Y.C., 1979-80; mng. ptnr. firm Ganz, Hollinger & Towe P.C., N.Y.C., 1981—; cons. FAO, Money Office, Rome, 1975—; cons. to sub-com. on historic preservation and coinage House Banking Com., 94th and 95th Congresses; bd. dirs. Industry Council Tangible Assets, Washington, 1983—. Author: A Legal and Legislative History of 31 USC Sec 324d-324i, 1976; The World of Coins and Coin Collecting, 1980, 2d edit., 1985. Corr., Numis. News Weekly, 1969-73, asst. editor, 1973-74, spl. corr., 1974-75; contbg. editor, columnist COINage Mag., 1974—; columnist Coin World, 1974—, COINS Mag., 1973-83. Contbr. articles to legal publs. Mem. U.S. Assay Commn., 1974; bd. dirs. Georgetown Library Assocs., Washington, 1982—; mem. N.Y. County Draft Bd., 1984, Bergen County, N.J., 1985—; sec., mem. Zoning and Adjustment Bd., Fair Lawn, N.J., 1988—. Mem. Nat. Assn. Coin and Precious Metals Dealers (assoc. mem., gen. counsel 1981-85), Flushing Lawyers Club (pres. 1982-83), N.Y. State Bar Assn. (mem. civil practice com., chmn. sub-com. 1978-84), Am. Soc. Internat. Law, Am. Numis. Assn. (legis. counsel 1978-81, 83—, elected bd. govs. 1985—). Democrat Jewish. Office: Ganz Hollinger & Towe 1394 3d Ave New York NY 10021-0404

GANZARAIN, RAMON CAJIAO, psychoanalyst; b. Iquique, Chile, Apr. 18, 1923; s. Eusebio Gastanaga and Maria Gonzalez G.; m. Matilde Vidal Soto, Oct. 10, 1953; children: Ramon, Mirentxu, Alejandro. BS, St. Ignacio Coll., Santiago, Chile, 1939; MD, U. Chile, Santiago, 1947; postgrad., Chilean Psychoanalytic Inst., 1947-50, cert. tng. analyst, 1953. Assoc. prof. psychiatry U. Chile, Santiago, 1955-68, dir. dept. med. edn., 1962-68; prof. depth psychology, sch. psychology Cath. U., Santiago, 1962-68; dir. Chilean Psychoanalytic Inst., Santiago, 1967-68; tng. analyst Topeka Inst. Psychoanalysis, 1968-87; dir. group psychotherapy services The Menninger Found., Topeka, 1978-87; geog. tng. analyst Columbia U. Ctr. for Psychoanalytic Tng. and Research, Atlanta, 1987; assoc. prof. psychiatry Emory U., Atlanta, 1988—; tng. analyst Atlanta Psychoanalytic Inst., 1988—. Author: Fugitives of Incest, 1988; contbr. articles to profl. jours. Fellow Am. Group Psychotherapy Assn.; mem. Internat. Assn. Group Psychotherapy (bd. dirs., exec. counselor 1986), Am. Group Psychotherapy Assn. (bd. dirs. 1984-87), Internat. Psychoanalytic Assn., Am. Psychoanalytic Assn., AMA, Kans. Med. Soc., Topeka Psychoanalytic Soc. (pres. 1985-87). Roman Catholic. Office: Emory U Dept Psychiatry Psychoanalytic Ctr 1711 Uppergate Atlanta GA 30322

GANZLER, KATALIN, bioengineer, researcher; b. Budapest, Hungary, Mar. 19, 1959; parents László and Klára (Kovách) G.; m. Tibor Baranya, Feb. 5, 1983; children: Peter, Akos. B in ChemE for Food Industry and Biotech., Tech. U. Budapest, 1980, B in Bioengring. for Environment, 1982, PhD, 1987. Research asst. Inst. Enzymology, Hungarian Acad. Sci., Budapest, 1982-85; researcher Cen. Inst. Chemistry, Hungarian Acad. Sci., Budapest, 1985—; cons. engr. Tech. U. Budapest, 1982—. Contbr. articles to profl. jours. Recipient 1st prize Hungarian Sci. Soc. for Food Industry, 1982, 85, 1st prize Students' Sci. Assn., 1985. Mem. Hungarian Biochemists' Soc. Roman Catholic. Home: 21 Keleti Károly, 1024 Budapest Hungary Office: Cen Inst Chemistry Hungarian Acad Sci, 59-67 Pusztaszeri ut, 1025 Budapest Hungary

GANZONI, JOHN JULIAN See BELSTEAD, LORD

GAO, JINGDE, academic administrator; b. Shaanxi, China, Feb. 5, 1922; m. Huiru Jiang, Jan. 1939; 1 child, Ping. BSc, Northwestern Inst. Tech., Xian, China, 1945; D of Tech. Sci., Leningrad (USSR) Inst. Tech., 1956. Prof. elec. engring. Tsinghua U., Beijing, 1956—, v.p., 1978-83, pres., 1983—; head sect. elec. scis. The State Council Acad. Degree Com., Beijing. Author: Basic Theory and Analytical Methods of Transient Behaviors of Electrical Machines, 2 vols., 1982, 83; chief editor: Self Excitation of Induction Motor caused by Series Capacitance, 1978. Fellow IEEE (Centennial award 1984); mem. Chinese Acad. Scis., Chinese Elec. Engring. Soc. (v.p.), Chinese Electrotech. Soc. Address: Tsinghua U, Dept Elec Engring, Tsinghua Yuan, Haidian, Beijing People's Republic of China

GARANCE, DOMINICK (D.G. GARAN), lawyer, author; b. Varaklani, Latvia, Oct. 14, 1912; came to U.S., 1950, naturalized, 1955; s. John and Virginia (Cakuls) Garans. LL.M., U. Riga, Latvia, 1935; J.U.D., U. Freiburg, Germany, 1945; LL.D., U. Paris, France, 1947; Ph.D., U. London, Eng., 1949. Bar: N.Y. 1958. Atty.-at-law, legal counsel Ministry of Welfare, Riga, 1936-42; law sec. French Mil. Govt. in Germany, Freiburg, 1945-46; documentary officer Harvard Law Sch. Internat. Program of Taxation, 1952-57; pvt. practice law N.Y.C., 1958—. Author: The Paradox of Pleasure and Relativity, 1963, Relativity for Psychology, A Causal Law for the Modern Alchemy, 1968, The Key to the Sciences of Man, 1975, Against Ourselves: Disorders from Improvements under the Organic Limitedness of Man, 1979, Our Sciences Ruled by Human Prejudice, 1987. Mem. ABA, N.Y. State Bar Assn., N.Y. State Trial Lawyers Assn., N.Y. Acad. Sci., Philosophy of Sci. Assn., Am. Assn. Advancement Sci., Lacuania. Address: 2926 E 196th St New York NY 10461

GARAVANI, VALENTINO (VALENTINO), fashion designer; b. Voghera, Italy, May 11, 1932; s. Mauro and Virginia (de Biaggi) student Chambre Syndicale de la Couture, Paris. Asst. to designer Jean Desses, Paris, Guy Laroche, Paris; founder Maison de Couture, Rome, 1959, Valentino Boutique, Rome, 1969—, shops Europe, U.S., Japan; designer apparel, accessories, household furniture and accessories, cosmetics; founder Valentino for Men, 1972—. Recipient Nieman Marcus award, 1969, various other awards; decorated grande ufficiale Order Merit Republic of Italy. Roman Catholic. Avocation: skiing. Office: 24 Gregoriana, Rome 00187 Italy

GARAVINI, FAUSTA MARIA, university educator; b. Bologna, Italy, Jan. 15, 1938; d. Costante and Anna (Geminiani) G.; m. Lafont Robert, Apr. 10, 1985. Laurea in Lettere, U. Florence, Italy, 1963. Prof. U. Bologna, 1969-71, U. Florence, 1971—; cons. in field. Author: L'Empèri dóu Souléu, 1967, Gli occhi dei pavoni, 1979 (Mondello prize 1979), La casa dei giochi, 1980, Itinerari a Montaigne, 1983, others; contbr. articles to profl. jours. Recipient literary prize Il Ceppo Proposte, 1978, literary prize L'Inedito. 1978. Mem. Soc. d'Histoire Littéraire de la France, Soc. des Amis de Montaigne, Soc. du Xvie Siècle. Home: Via Bolognese 58, 50139 Florence Italy Office: U Firenze, Piazza Brunelleschi 3, 50121 Florence Italy

GARAYBLAS, GRACIELA MENDOZA, physician, educator; b. Manila, June 15, 1953; s. Victorio Reyes and Juana Sta. Ana (Mendoza) G. BS, U. Santo Tomas, Manila, 1973; MD, U. Santo Tomas, 1977. Diplomate Splty. Bd. Internal Medicine. Intern Makati Med. Ctr., Metro-Manila, 1977-78; resident St. Tomas U. Hosp., Manila, 1979-82; assoc. med. staff St. Tomas U. Hosp., 1987—; mem. faculty medicine and surgery U. Santo Tomas, 1982—; cons. Nat. Econ. Devel. Authority, Pasig, Metro-Manila, 1984—, Med. Missions, Inc., Manila, 1979—, Bukas Palad Found., Manila, 1984—; sec., treas. Com. Postgrad. Course Internal Medicine, 1985—; sec. Dept. Medicine Allied Splty., 1984—. Contbr. articles to profl. jours. U. Santo Tomas scholar, 1969-71. Fellow Philippine Coll. Physicians; mem. U. Santo Tomas Med. Alumni Assn. (life), Philippine Med. Assn. (life, mem. com. booth exhibits 1984—), Cath. Physicians Guild of Philippines (life). Roman Catholic. Club: Focolare Movement (Pasay City, Metro-Manila). Home: Pag-Asa, Obando, Bulacan Philippines Office: Santo Tomas U Hosp Rm 226, Espanña, Manila Philippines

GARBER, SAMUEL B., lawyer, retail company executive; b. Chgo., Aug. 16, 1934; s. Morris and Yetta (Cohen) G.; children: Debra Lee, Diane Lori. J.D., U. Ill., 1958; M.B.A., U. Chgo., 1968. Bar: Ill., 1958; mem. firm Brown, Dashow and Langluttig, Chgo., 1960-62; corporate counsel Walgreen Co., 1962-69; v.p., gen. counsel, exec. asst. to the pres. Carlyle & Co., 1969-73; dir. legal affairs Stop & Shop Co., Inc., 1973-74; gen. counsel Goldblatt Bros., Inc., 1974-76; v.p., sec., gen. counsel Evans, Inc., 1976—; prof. mgmt. DePaul U., 1975—. Served with U.S. Army, 1958-60. Mem. ABA, Nat. Retail Mchts. Assn., Ill. Retail Mchts. Assn. Clubs: Carlton, East Bank. Home: 320 Oakdale Chicago IL 60657 Office: Evans Inc 36 S State St Chicago IL 60603

GARBO, GRETA, actress; b. Stockholm, Sweden, Sept. 18, 1905; came to U.S., 1925, naturalized, 1951; d. Sven and Louvisa Gustaffson. Ed., Royal Dramatic Acad., Stockholm. (Won her first film recognition in Goesta Berling, 1924, through work in Royal Acad.); came to U.S. and appeared in: The Temptress, 1926, The Torrent, 1926, Love, 1927, Flesh and the Devil, 1927, Anna Christie, 1930, Susan Lenox, 1931, Mata Hari, 1931, Grand Hotel, 1932, As You Desire Me, 1932, Queen Christina, 1933, The Painted Veil, Anna Karenina, 1935, Camille, 1936, Conquest, 1937, Ninotchka, 1939, Two Faced Woman, 1941 (Recipient Spl. Acad. award 1954). Office: 450 E 52nd St New York NY 10022 *

GARBRECHT, KURT, electronic company executive; b. Wittstock, Germany, Jan. 26, 1932; s. Kurt and Martha (Falkenthal) G.; m. Eva Schmidt, Jan. 28, 1956; children—Sabine, Oliver. Diplom-Ingenieur, U. Dresden (W.Ger.), 1958; Doctor, U. Munich, 1962. Scientist, U. Dresden, 1958-60; engr. ITT, Stuttgart, W.Ger., 1960-62; with Siemens, Munich, 1962—, mgr. satellite communication, 1970-75, gen. mgr. integrated circuits div., 1975—; exec. dir., gen. mgr. Semiconductor Bus. Groups, Siemens; dir. Doduco, Pforzheim, W.Ger., 1979—. Contbr. articles to profl. jours.; patentee in microwave and microelectronics. Fellow Internat. Radio Union; mem. IEEE (sr.), Verein Deutscher Elektrot. Home: 13 Nussbaumweg, 8012 Ottobrunn Federal Republic of Germany Office: Siemens AG, 73 Balanstr, Munich Federal Republic of Germany

GARCIA, ALVIN B., lawyer, investment banker; b. Cebu City, Philippines, June 29, 1946; s. Jesus P. and Severiana O. (Biaño) G.; m. Trinidad Z. Neri; children: Jess, Jerald, Raymond. BA in Polit. Sci. with honors, Ateneo de Manila, Philippines, 1966, LlB, 1970. Bar: Philippines 1971. Ptnr. J.P. Garcia and Assocs., Cebu City, 1970-73, sr. ptnr., 1984—; v.p. PAIC (former affiliate Chase Manhattan Bank), Cebu City, 1974-83. Vice-mayor Cebu City, Philippines, 1988. Roman Catholic. Home: 101 F R Aboitiz St, Cebu City Philippines Office: JP Garcia & Assocs, Jesever Bldg, Osmeña Blvd, Cebu City Philippines

GARCIA, FERNANDO FLORES, banker, consultant; b. David, Chiriqui, Panama, July 4, 1947; s. Maximo and Adriana (Flores) G.; m. Edilberta Castillo, Feb. 17, 1968; 1 child, Adriana. BA, Francisco Morozon U., Panama, 1971; degree in acctg., U. Panama, 1979. CPA, Panama. Mgr. adminstrn. Cerveceria del Barú, Panama City, 1971-77; comptroller Vereins und West Bank, Panama City, 1977-86; asst. mgr. Banco Alemon-Pandmeño, Panama City, 1986—, treas., 1987—; pres. Cabo Frio S.A., Panama City, 1979—; cons. Proitotira de Finanzas, Panama City, 1984—. Mem. Panamanian Bankers Assn., Assn. CPA's, Nat. Geographic Soc. Democrat. Roman Catholic. Club: de Montana (Panama). Lodge: Lions (bd. dirs. Panama City chpt. 1985). Office: Banco Alemon-Pandmeno, Federico Boyd PO Box 6180, Panama City 5, Republic of Panama

GARCIA, FERNANDO SALCEDO, financial consultant; b. Manila, July 3, 1960; Came to U.S., 1970; s. Dionicio Castillo and Nenita Baquir (Salcedo) G. BBA, Loyola U., Chgo., 1983. Cert. ins. producer, real estate agt., Ill. Dept. mgr. Carson Pirie Scott and Co., Chgo., 1983-84; computer operator Comml. Nat. Bank, Chgo., 1984-85; fin. planner IDS Fin. Services, Des Plaines, Ill., 1985-86, Southmark Fin. Services, Wheaton, Ill., 1986-87; pres., owner First Am. Securities Corp., Wheaton, Ill., 1987—, Integrated Realty and Investment Corp.; prin. Integrated Realty and Investment Corp., Chgo.; fin. cons. Merrill Lynch, Pierce, Fenner & Smith, Inc., Chgo., 1987—. Mem. Internat. Assn. Fin. Planning, Inst. Cert. Fin. Planners, Nat. Futures Assn., Nat. Assn. Securities Dealers (series 3, 7, 8, 24, 27, and 63), Ill. Dept. Ins. (producer), Theta Xi (athletic coordinator 1979-80). Republican. Roman Catholic. Clubs: Kapwa (Chgo.) (pres. 1980-82), Invesment (Chgo.) (pres. 1985—). Home: 2721 W Winnemac Chicago IL 60625 Office: Merrill Lynch Pierce Fenner and Smith Inc One South Wacker Dr Mezzenine Level Chicago IL 60606

GARCIA, LAMBERTO H., physician; b. Cebu, Philippines, Sept. 17, 1944; s. Florentino Atilano and Petra (Hermoso) G.; m. Glenda Manznares, May 11, 1970; children: Lamberto Jr., Janice, Lani. AA, Cebu Inst. Tech., 1963, MD, 1968. Diplomate Am. Bd. Internal Medicine, Philippines Bd. Internal Medicine, Philippines Soc. Gastroenterology. Resident internal medicine Cebu (Velez) Gen. Hosp., 1968-70, St. Josephs Hosp., Chgo., 1971-74; fellow gastroenterology Cook County Hosp., Chgo., 1974-75; cons. Thorek Med. Ctr., Chgo., 1975-78; cons. internal medicine Cebu Doctors Hosp., 1979—, also bd. dirs. GI fellowship, assoc. prof., 1982—; chmn. dept. medicine Cebu Doctors Coll. Medicine, 1982—, sec., bd. dirs, 1984—. Recipient Plaque Merit Cebu Inst. Medicine Alumni Assn. Fellow Philippines Coll. Physicians, Philippines Soc. Gastroenterology; mem. Cebu Med. Soc. (pres., Leadership award 1984, Plaque Merit 1985), Philippine Soc. Microbiology and Infectious Diseases (pres., Plaque of Merit 1983). Roman Catholic. Office: Diaz Bldg Suite #214, Osmeña Blvd, Cebu Philippines

GARCIA, LUIS CESAREO, lawyer; b. Hato Rey, P.R., Apr. 19, 1949; came to U.S., 1965; s. Elena and John B. Amos (foster parents); s. Evelina Maura; m. Kathy Jo Mims, Dec. 4, 1970; children—Joseph Amos, Evelyn Kathleen. Student Columbus Coll., 1967-70; J.D., John Marshall Law U., Atlanta, 1973; postgrad. Harvard U., 1978, 84. Bar: Ga. 1974, U.S. Dist. Ct. (mid. dist.) Ga. 1974, U.S. Ct. Appeals (11th cir.) 1983, U.S. Supreme Ct. 1977. Assoc. Keil, Riley & Fort, Columbus, Ga., 1974-75; sole practice, Columbus, 1975-76; sr. ptnr. Garcia & Hirsch, P.C., Columbus, 1976-79; regional mgr. Am. Family Life Assurance Co., Columbus, 1979-82, exec. v.p., chief counsel, 1982—; sr. v.p. counsel internat. ops., 1986—; legal counsel LMI, Inc., 1979-82; mem. legis. com. Am. Prepaid Legal Inst., Chgo., 1983-86. Bd. dirs. Better Bus. Bur. of W. Ga.-E. Ala., 1984—; mem. bd. adv. council CETA, 1979-83; adv. bd. Ga. Pub. TV, 1979-82. Mem. ABA, Ga. Bar Assn., Columbus Lawyers Club, Younger Lawyers Club, Sigma Delta Kappa. Episcopalian. Clubs: Toastmasters, Country of Columbus. Office: Am Family Life Assurance Co 1932 Wynnton Rd Columbus GA 31999

GARCIA, NORMA PLAZA DE, lawyer, notary public; b. Guayaquil, Guayas, Ecuador, May 8, 1942; d. Carlos Luis Plaza Danin and Maruja (Aray) de Plaza; m. Eduardo Garcia Riera, Feb. 8, 1966; children—Luis Eduardo, Tatiana, Carlos, Andres Martin. M. Comparative Jurisprudence, NYU, 1970; LL.D., Catholic U., Guayaquil, 1970. Pub. notary of Guayaquil, 1970—; sole practice law, Guayaquil; prof. civil law Catholic U., Guayaquil, 1971-75, dean's asst. Law Sch., 1971-72; legal advisor Front of Social Protection, Guayaquil, 1978—; journalist E'Universo. Mem. Pub. Notaries Orgn. (v.p. 1983—), Nat. Fedn. Notaries (bd. dirs. 1984—), Catholic U. Alumni Assn. (pres. 1985), NYU Alumni Assn. Clubs: Catholic Univ. Sport Assn. (Guayaquil). Avocations: traveling; reading; swimming. Home: J Salcedo 206, PO Box 3484, Guayaquil Guayas Ecuador Office: Public Notary N13 Guayaquil, Luque 203-Office 6, First Floor, Guayaquil, Guayas Ecuador

GARCIA-GRANADOS, SERGIO EDUARDO, brokerage house executive; b. Mexico, June 11, 1942 (citizen of Guatemala); s. Jorge and Miriam Garcia-Granados; Licenciado en Ciencias Juridicas y Sociales with honors (scholar 1960-66), U. San Carlos, 1966; postgrad. U. Paris, Inst. Scis. Politiques, Paris, 1966-68; m. Elizabeth Bentley, Apr. 3, 1973; children—Tatiana, Sybil. Admitted to bar, 1966; research assoc. The Hague Acad. Internat. Law, 1969, Internat. Bur. Fiscal Documentation, Amsterdam, 1969-70; partner law firm Saravia y Muñoz, Guatemala City, 1970-77; v.p. sales mgr. Merrill Lynch Capital Market Internat., N.Y.C., 1982-88, v.p. resident mgr. internat. div. Shearson Lehman Hutton, N.Y., 1988—; lectr. tax problems in Central Am. Common Market, U. San Carlos, bus. orgns., U. Landivar; dir. Rawmat Corp., Tucasa S.A., Maprigna S.A.; bd. adminstrn. Gebira Investment Corp., 1977-81; Bd. dirs. Patronato de Bellas Artes, 1977—, Guatemala Nat. Theatre Directorate, 1979-80. Mem. Colegio de Abogados, Internat. Bar Assn., Internat. Fiscal Assn. (gen. council 1972—), Am. Soc. Internat. Law. Contbr. articles to profl. jours. Organizer, 1st editor loose-leaf corporate taxation in Latin Am., 1970. Address: 11 Larchmont Ave Larchmont NY 10538

GARCIA GRANADOS DE VALDES, SYLVIA, performing arts studio owner; b. Guatemala City, Guatemala, Oct. 4, 1946; d. Raul Garcia Granados Quiñonez and Enriqueta (de Garay) Garcia Granados; m. Alvaro Arzu Irigoyen, Mar. 14, 1969 (div. 1981); children: Roberto, Diego, Maria; m. Gregorio Valdes O'Conell, Feb. 19, 1986; 1 child, Sofia. Cert., Assoc. Montessori Internat., Washington, 1965; student in interior design, Washington, 1966-67; student in liberal arts, U. Landivar, Guatemala, 1968-80;

student in clin. psychology, Francisco Marroquin U., Guatemala, 1980-88; studiesin ballet, guitar, modern-jazz dance, singing, and tap dance, Guatemala and USA. Tchr. English Kindergarten/Am. Sch., Guatemala City, 1963-65; founder Montessori sch. Guatemala City, 1969-76; founder, mgr., choreographer, producer, tchr. Performing Arts Studio, Guatemala City, 1984—, artistic rep., 1985—. Mem. Am. Montessori Soc., Tap Tchr. Dance Educators Am., Inc., Singer Assn. Guatemala. Home and Office: 3 Ave 12-48 Zona 9, Guatemala City Guatemala also: 77 Crandon Blvd 2 Miami FL 33149

GARCÍA MÁRQUEZ, GABRIEL JOSÉ, author; b. Aracataca, Magdalena, Colombia, Mar. 6, 1928; s. Gabriel Eligio García and Luisa Santiaga Márquez; ed. U. Bogotá; LL.D. (hon.), Columbia U., 1971; m. Mercedes Barcha; children: Rodrigo, Gonzalo. With daily newspaper El Heraldo, Barranquilla; film critic, reporter El Espactador, Bogotá, also European corr., Rome and Paris; with various periodicals in Venezuela, 1957-59; established Bogotá office Prensa Latina, 1959, later worked in Havana, asst. bur. chief, N.Y.C., 1961; editor, screenwriter, copywriter, Mexico City; author: (novels) La Hojarasca, 1955, El Colonel no tiene quien le escriba, 1958; (stories) Los Funerales de la Mamá Grande; (novels) La Mala Hora, Cien Años de Soledad, 1967, Relato de un náufrago, 1970, Love in the Time of Cholera, 1988; (stories) La Increíble y Triste Historia de la Cándida Eréndira y de su Abuela Desalmada, 1972; (anthology of newspaper articles) Cuando era feliz e indocumentado, 1975; (stories) Todos los cuentos; (novels) El otoño del Patriarca, 1975, Crónica de una muerte anunciada, 1981; Collected Stories, 1985; The Story of a Shipwrecked Sailor, 1986. Recipient Premio Chianciano (Italy), for Cien Añ os de Soledad, 1969; Prix de Meilleur Livre Étranger (France), for Cien Años de Soledad, 1969; Rómulo Gallegos prize, 1972; Neustadt Internat. prize for lit., 1972; Nobel prize, 1982. Address: care Agencia Literaria, Carmen Balcelos, Diagonal 580, Barcelona 21 Spain *

GARCIA PÉREZ, ALAN, president of Peru, lawyer; b. Lima, Peru, May 23, 1949; s. Carlos Garcia Ronceros and Nita Perez de Garcia; m. Pilar Nores Bodereau; children—Carla, Josefina, Gabriela, Luciana. LL.B., Universidad Nacional Mayor de San Marcos; Doctor of Law, Universidad Complutense de Madrid; student La Sorbonne, Paris, Inst. Superior Studies. Mem. Constituent Assembly of Peru, 1979-80, mem. chamber of deputies, 1980-85; pres. Republic of Peru, 1985—; mem. Partido Aprista Peruano, gen. sec. Founder Alianza Popular Revolucionaria Americana. Office: Palacio de Gobierno, Lima Peru *

GARCIA RAMIREZ, SERGIO, lawyer, government official; b. Guadalajara, Mex., Feb. 1, 1938; Student Univ. Nacional de Mex., Ph.D. lectr. in Penal Law. Researcher legal research dept. Univ. Nacional de Mex., 1966-76, Nat. Inst. Penal Scis., pres. 1st bd.; head. com. Social Prevention Fed. Dist. Jail; dir. Jail of State of Mex.; judge Prison for Minors, Mex.; gen. subdir. govt. Ministry of Interior; atty. gen. Fed. Dist.; subsec. Ministries Nat. Patrimony, of Interior, Pub. Edn., and Indsl. Devel.; head Prevention Jail, Mexico City; minister labour and social prevision; univ. lectr; atty. gen. Mex., 1982—. Mem. Mex. Acad. Penal Scis., Mex. Inst. Law, Nat. Inst. Procedure Law, Internat. Assn. Penal Law (Mex. sect.), Prevention of Crimes and Treatment of Delinquents of UN, Directive Council Internat. Soc. Social Def., Mex. Bar Assn., Supreme Council Nat. Assn. Lawyers. Address: Dept of Attorney Gen, Mexico City DF, Mexico *

GARCIA ROBLES, ALFONSO, Mexican diplomat; b. Mar. 20, 1911; s. Quirino and Theresa Robles Garcia; m. Juana Maria de Szyszlo, 1950; 2 children. LL.B., U. Nacional Autonoma de Mexico, 1933; LL.D., U. Paris, 1937; diploma, Acad. Internat. Law, The Hague, 1938. Entered Mex. Fgn. Service, 1939—, head dept. internat. orgns., later dir. gen. of Polit. Affairs and Diplomatic Service, 1941-46, dir. div. polit. affairs UN Secretariat, 1946-57, head dept. for Europe, Asia and Africa, Mexican Ministry of Fgn. Affairs, 1957-61, ambassador to Brazil, 1962-64, under-sec. for Fgn. Affairs, 1964-71, permanent rep. to UN, 1971-75, sec. Fgn. Affairs, 1975-76, pres. Preparatory Com. for the Denuclearization of Latin Am., 1964-67, permanent rep. to Disarmament Conf., Geneva, 1977—; chmn. Mex. Del. to UN Gen. Assembly on disarmament, N.Y.C., 1978. Author: Le Panaméricanisme et la Politique de Bon Voisinage, 1938; La Question du Petrole au Mexique et le Droit International, 1939; La Sorbona Ayer y Hoy, 1943; México en la Postguerra, 1944; La Conferencia de San Francisco y su Obra, 1946; Política Internacional de México, 1946; Ecos del Viejo Mundo, 1946; El Mundo de la Postguerra, 2 Vol., 1946; La Conferencia de Ginebra y la Anchura del Mar Territorial, 1959; La Anchura del Mar Territorial, 1966; The Denuclearization of Latin America, 1967; El Tratado de Tlatelolco.-Génesis, Alcance y Propósitos de la Proscripción de las Armas Nucleares en la América Latina, 1967; México en las Naciones Unidas, 2 Vol., 1970; Mesures de Désarmement dans des Zones Particulières: Le Traité visant l'Interdiction des Armes Nucleaires en Amérique Latine, 1971; La Proscripción de las Armas Nucleares en la América Latina, 1975; Seis Años de la Política Exterior de México, 1970-1976; La Conferencia de Revisión del Tratado sobre la no Proliferación de las Armas Nucleares, 1977; 338 Días de Tlatelolco, 1977; La Asamblea General del Desarme, 1979; El Comité de Desarme, 1980. Shared Nobel Peace Prize, 1982. Office: 13 Ave de Bude, Geneva Switzerland *

GARCIA-SANZ, RAUL, animator, filmmaker; b. Madrid, Jan. 16, 1958; s. Ricardo Garcia Maroto and Milagros (Sanz) De Benito. BA, Complutense U., Madrid, 1980. Animator TV series for Hanna-Barbera Prodns., Madrid, 1980-82; co-dir. Woman Waiting in a Hotel, Madrid, 1982; co-dir. Night Gallery, Metropolis P.C., Madrid, 1983; dir. Animarathon, Olympic Art Festival, Los Angeles and Madrid, 1984; animator Asterix and Cesar's Surprise, Gaumont, Paris, 1984-85, animator Asterix in Britain, 1985; supr. The Chipmunks Great Adventure, Bagdasarian, Los Angeles and Korea, 1986-87; animator Land Before Time Began, Amblin-Bluth, Dublin, Ireland, 1987; animator Who Framed Roger Rabbit Amblin-Disney, London, 1988; dir. live action film Delirium for El Regador Prodns., Madrid, 1982. Author: (screenplays) Teveo, 1981, Lapsus, 1981; editor film Expresión Fantastica, 1980. Recipient Best Animated Film award Bilbao (Spain) Film Festival, 1982. Mem. Assn. Internat. du Film de Animation (sec. Madrid delegation 1983-84). Home and Office: Valleguerra 1, Madrid 28017, Spain

GARCIA TERRES, JAIME, writer, publisher, lawyer; b. Mexico City, May 15, 1924; s. Trinidad and Elisa (Terres) Garcia; m. Celia Chavez, May 4, 1960; children: Alonso, Ana Ximena, Ruy Martin. Student, Colegio Frances, Mex., 1940-41; grad. in law, U. Nacional Autónoma de Mex., 1946; postgrad. estética, U. Paris, 1950; postgrad. medieval philosophy, Coll. de France, 1950. Licenciado en Derecho. Gen. subdirector Inst. Nacional de Bellas Artes, Mexico City, 1948-49; dir. difusion cultural U. Nacional Autonoma de Mex., Mexico City, 1953-65; dir. Revista de la Univ. de Mex., Mexico City, 1953-65; ambassador to Greece Athens, 1965-68; dir. library and archives Sec. de Relaciones Exteriores, Mexico City, 1968-71; subdirector Fondo de Cultura Económica, Mexico City, 1972-74, dir., 1982—; dir. La Gaceta, Mexico City, 1971—; cons. Nat. Radio and TV, 1986-87; juror Neustadt Internat. Prize for Lit., 1981; invited speaker various symposia and orgns. N.Y., Paris, London, Dublin, Ireland, Montevideo, Uruguay. Author: Los reinos combatientes, 1961, Los infiernos del pensamiento, 1967, 100 imágenes del mar, 1962, Grecia 60, 1962, Todo lo más por decir, 1971, Reloj de Atenas, 1977, Letanias Profanas, 1980, Poesia y Alquimia, 1980, Corre La Voz, others; collaborator numerous other scholarly publs. Recipient (first prize) Magda Donato, Mex., 1978. Mem. El Collegio Nacional, PEN. Home: Paseo de la Reforma #1310, 11000 Mexico City Mexico Office: Fondo de Cultura Economica, Ave Universidad #975, 03100 Mexico City Mexico

GARD, PHILIP LEONARD, manufacturing executive; b. Evansville, Ind., Nov. 18, 1931; s. Russell G. and Ora G.; B.A. in Prodn. Mgmt., Evansville U., 1958; m. Gwendolyn M. Gard, Sept. 26, 1974; children—Philip K., Catherine M.; 1 stepdau., Tracy Gillum. Prodn. planner Mead Johnson, Evansville, Ind., 1962-68, mgr. prodn. planning, 1968-73; dir. materials control E.R. Squibb, Montreal, Que., Can., 1973-75; v.p. ops. William T. Thompson Co., Carson, Calif., 1975-86, Nat. Patent Devel. Corp., 1986—. Served with USN, 1950-55. Mem. Am. Mgmt. Assn., Purchasing Mgmt. Assn., Prodn. Control Soc. Lutheran. Home: 276 Moosup Pond Rd Moosup CT 06354 Office: 23529 S Figueroa St Carson CA 90745

GARD, RICHARD ABBOTT, religious institute executive, educator; b. Vancouver, B.C., Can., May 29, 1914; parents U.S. citizens; s. Charles Ned and Clara Edna (Abbott) G.; m. Tatiana Ruzena Kristina Moravec, Nov. 1, 1952; children—Alan Moravec, Anita Nadine. B.A., U. Wash., 1937; M.A., U. Hawaii, 1940; postgrad. U. Pa., 1945-47; Ph.D., Claremont Grad. Sch., 1951; postgrad. Otani U. and Ryukoku U., Kyoto, Japan, 1953-54; D.H.L. (hon.), Monmouth Coll., 1963. Spl. adviser to pres. Asia Found., San Francisco and Tokyo, 1956-63; cultural affairs officer USIA, Washington, 1963-64; Buddhist affairs officer Dept. State, Washington and Hong Kong, 1964-69; librarian Inst. for Advanced Studies of World Religions, SUNY-Stony Brook, 1971-73, dir. inst. services, 1971-84, pres., 1985—; v.p. for U.S., World Fellowship of Buddhists, Bangkok, Thailand, 1961-64, asst. sec. gen., 1971-75; vis. assoc. prof. Yale U., New Haven, 1959-63; vis. prof. Asian studies Wittenberg U., Springfield, Ohio, 1970; adj. prof. Asian studies St. John's U., Jamaica, N.Y., 1974-78; vis. prof. Inst. Sino-Indian Buddhist Studies, Taipei, Taiwan, Republic of China, 1981—. Editor-in-chief series: Great Religions of Modern Man, 1961; editor, contbg. author: Buddhism, 1961; editor Buddhist Text Info., 1974—, Buddhist Research Info., 1979-84. Contbr. articles to acad., religious jours, Asia, U.S. Sec. 3 Village Men's Garden Club, Setauket, N.Y., 1980-84; bd. dirs. plans dept. Asia Found., San Francisco, 1954-56, cons., 1959-63, Buddhist Affairs, 1957-59. Served to lt. col. USMCR, 1941-46; PTO. Japanese Buddhist okesa Jodo-shu, Phila., 1946, Japanese Buddhist okesa Shingon-shu, Los Angeles, 1950; recipient Thai Buddhist Theravada award Mahamakuta Found., Bangkok, 1956, Burmese Buddhist Theravada award Shwedagon, Rangoon, 1957, Korean Buddhist Mahayana award Cho-gye-jong, Pom-o-sa, Republic of Korea, 1965; Rockefeller Found. research fellow U. Pa., Phila., 1946-47; Ford Found. grantee Wittenberg U., 1970. Mem. Assn. Asian Studies (pres. Mid-Atlantic region 1974-75), Tibet Soc. (bd. dirs. 1978-83, 87), Internat. Assn. Buddhist Studies (bd. dirs. 1982-86, 87—), Am. Soc. for Study Religion (exec. com. 1983-86). Buddhist. Avocations: landscape gardening; mountain hiking; chamber music. Office: Inst Advanced Studies of World Religions SUNY Melville Meml Library Stony Brook NY 11794-3383

GARDEN, DOMNERN, lawyer; b. N.Y.C., Nov. 3, 1928; arrived in Thailand, 1952; m. Rareun Netrayon; children: Sansang, Po. AB, Kenyon Coll., Gambier, Ohio, 1948; JD, Harvard U., 1952. Bar: Thailand, 1954. Assoc. Somnuk & Sutee, Bangkok, 1954-57; ptnr. Jorgensen & Co., Bangkok, 1957-85, Domnern Somgiat & Boonma, Bangkok, 1985—. Founder Trademark, Patent & Copyright Assn. Thailand, Bangkok, 1971. Mem. Inst. Trademark Agts. U.K., Fedn. Internat. Conseils en Propriete Industrielle, Am. Intellectual Property Law Assn., U.S. Trademark Assn., Asian Patent Attys. Assn., Lawyers' Assn. Thailand. Buddhist.

GARDENER, EDWARD PATRICK MONTGOMERY, banking educator, consultant; b. Dublin, Mar. 27, 1947; s. Edward Kitchener Maurice and Ethnea Maev (Kennedy) G.; m. Anne Christine Price-Smith, Oct. 15, 1973;. MSc, U. Coll. North Wales, 1973, PhD, 1979. Sr. fin. asst. Shell-Mex and BP Ltd., Manchester, Eng., 1966-71; lectr. U. Coll. North Wales, Bangor, 1975-80, 1980-83, sr. lectr. banking, 1983-86, prof. banking, 1986—; dep. dir. Inst. European Fin., Bangor 1981-85, dir. 1985—; non-exec. dir. DC Gardner and Group plc, London, 1984—. Author: Capital Adequacy and Banking Supervision, 1981; editor: u.K. Banking Supervision, 1986; contbr. articles to profl. jours. Mem. Inst. Chartered Secs. and Adminstrs. (assoc.), JW Slack prize, 1967). Roman Catholic. Office: Inst European Finance, Univ Wales, Bangor LL57 2DG, Wales

GARDENIER, TURKAN KUMBARACI, statistical company executive, researcher; b. Istanbul, Turkey, Nov. 10, 1941; d. Celal and Aysel (Triandafilidu) K.; m. Harry M. Peyser, Nov. 24, 1966 (div. Aug. 1968); m. John Stark Gardenier, June 18, 1977; children: Pamela Lee, George Bonneval, Jason Stark. AB, Vassar Coll., 1961; MA, Columbia U., 1962, PhD, 1966. Ops. research scientist IIT Research Inst., Chgo., 1966-68; asst. prof., chmn. Middle East Tech. U., Ankara, Turkey, 1968-70; vis. scientist Brookhaven Nat. Labs., Upton, L.I., N.Y., 1970-71; assoc. dir. Pfizer Pharms., N.Y.C., 1971-73; asst. prof. N.Y. State Maritime Coll., Bronx, N.Y., 1973-78; health scientist U.S. EPA, Washington, 1978-81; assoc. prof. Am. U., Washington, 1982-84; pres. TKG Cons. Ltd., Vienna, Va., 1982—; tech. cons. Analytic Services Corp., Arlington, Va., 1982—; expert U.S. Energy Info. Adminstrn., Washington, 1982-84; statis. cons. Engring. Computer Optecnomics, Annapolis, Md., 1977—; cons. C.R. Cushing Co., Marine Engring., N.Y.C., 1974-77. Corp. mem. Am. Friends of Turkey, Mclean, Va., 1983—; com. mem. World Mut. Service Com., N.Y.C., 1982—, D.C. parents rep. Foxcroft Sch., Middleburg, Va., 1981-84. Grantee, NSF, 1980, CENTO, 1969. Mem. Am. Statis. Assn. (audio-visual graphics com. 1979), Ops. Research Soc. Am. (fin. com. 1980), Soc. Computer Simulation (assoc. editor jour. 1980-84), (fin. com. 1980), AAAS (symposium organizer 1979-82). Club: Skyline Racquet & Health (Falls Church, Va.). Lodge: Fairfield Williamsburg, Lake of the Woods. Home: 115 St Andrews Dr Vienna VA 22180 Office: TKG Cons Ltd 301 Maple Ave W Suite 100 Vienna VA 22180

GARDINE, JUANITA CONSTANTIA FORBES, educator; b. St. Croix, V.I., Aug. 6, 1912; d. Alphonso Sebastian and Petrina (Actien) Forbes; B.A., Hunter Coll., 1934; M.A., Columbia U., 1940; postgrad. U. Chgo., 1949, NYU, 1960-66, Cheyney Coll., 1967; M.Ed., U. Ill.-Chgo., 1985; m. Cyprian A. Gardine, Apr. 23, 1942; children—Cyprian A., Vicki Maria Camilla, Letitia Theresa, Richard Whittington. Tchr. elementary schs., 1934-35; tchr. math. high sch., 1935-41, 48-49; acting asst. high sch. prin., 1941; jr. high sch. prin., 1941-47; substitute tchr. English, math., physics, Montclair, N.J., 1947-48; asst. supt. edn., 1949-55; assoc. dean Community Colls., supr. elem. schs., 1955-57; high sch. prin., 1957-58; supr. ednl. stats., 1958-62; social worker Dept. Welfare, 1962-63; prin. Christiansted (St. Croix) Pub. Grammar Sch., 1963-74; tchr. math. evening session extension classes Cath. U. P.R., 1960-61; asst. dir. and tutor St. Croix Tutorial Sch., 1974-82; part-time instr. math. Coll. V.I., 1974-75, 80-81. Past sec. bd. dirs. St. Croix Fed. chpt. ARC; mem. bd., chmn. supervisory com. St. Croix Fed. Credit Union; past sec. St. Croix Sch. Health Com., Girl Scout Com., Fredericksted Hosp. Aux.; past mem. and pres. St. Croix (V.I.) Mental Health Assn. Pres., Tchrs. Assn., 1940, Municipal Employees Assn., 1942. Sch. named in her honor, 1974; honoree P.R. Friendship Day Com., 1979, St. John's Ch., 1981. Mem. Am. Statis. Assn., NAESP, V.I. Fedn. Bus. and Profl. Women's Clubs (past sec.), Episcopal Ch. Women of V.I. (past chmn. world affairs com.), Christiansted Bus. and Profl. Women's Club (past pres.; Woman of Year 1966), Daus. King (sec.), Christiansted Bus. and Profl. Club (past parliamentarian, past pres.). Episcopalian (past pres. women's group). Home: 142 Whim Estate Frederiksted Saint Croix VI 00840 Mailing address: Box 1505 Christiansted Saint Croix VI 00820

GARDINER, LESTER RAYMOND, JR., lawyer; b. Salt Lake City, Aug. 20, 1931; s. Lester Raymond and Sarah Lucille (Kener) G.; m. Janet Ruth Thatcher, Apr. 11, 1955; children—Allison Gardiner Bigelow, Annette Gardiner Weed, John Alfred, Leslie Gardiner Crandall, Robert Thatcher, Lisa Gardiner West, James Raymond, Elizabeth, David William, Sarah Janet. BS with honors, U. Utah, 1954; JD, U. Mich., 1959. Bar: Utah 1959, U.S. Dist. Ct. Utah 1959, U.S. Ct. Apls. (10th cir.) 1960. Law clk., U.S. Dist. Ct., 1959; assoc. then ptnr. Van Cott, Bagley, Cornwall & McCarthy, Salt Lake City, 1960-67; ptnr. ptnr. Gardiner & Johnson, Salt Lake City, 1967-72; ptnr. Christensen, Gardiner, Jensen & Evans, 1972-78; ptnr. Fox, Edwards, Gardiner & Brown, Salt Lake City, 1978-87, ptnr. Chapman & Cutler, 1987—; reporter, mem. Utah Sup. Ct. Com. on Adoption of Uniform Rules of Evidence, 1970-73, mem. com. on revision of cirminal code, 1975-78; master of the bench Am. Inn of Ct. I, 1980—; mem. com. bar examiners Utah State Bar, 1973; instr. bus. law U. Utah, 1965-66; adj. prof. law Brigham Young U., 1984-85. Mem. Republican State Central Com. Utah, 1967-72, mem. exec. com. Utah Rep. Party, 1975-78, chmn. state convs., 1980, 81; mem. Salt Lake City Bd. Edn., 1971-72; mem. bd. dirs. Salt Lake City Pub. Library, 1974-75. Served to 1st lt. USAF, 1954-56. Mem. ABA, Utah State Bar Assn., Salt Lake County Bar Assn. (mem. exec. com. 1967-68). Mormon. Clubs: Ft. Douglas Hidden Valley Country, Sons of Utah Pioneers, Bonneville Knife & Fork (Salt Lake City). Lodge: Rotary. Office: 50 S Main St Salt Lake City UT 84144

GARDIS, GILDA J., quality analyst; b. Jersey City, Jan. 16, 1944; d. William Patrick and Gilda Esther (Weber) Cornett; m. David Richard Gardis, Oct. 8, 1966 (div. 1981). Student, Oceanside-Carlsbad Jr. Coll., Santa Monica City Coll. Prin. typist clk. UCLA, 1966-69, adminstrv. asst., 1969-73, acctg. asst., 1973-75, mgmt. services officer, UCLA, 1975-79; mgmt. services officer U. Calif., San Diego, La Jolla, 1979-85; quality analyst Teledyne Kinetics, Solana Beach, Calif., 1986—; part-time sales rep. Mervyn's, Oceanside, Calif., 1986—. Active Oceanside High Sch. Booster Club, 1980-83. Recipient Tiffany award Manpower, Inc., Carlsbad, Calif., 1985. Mem. Am. Mgmt. Assn. (assoc.), Nat. Assn. Female Execs., Network Exec. Women, Teledyne Kinetics Recreation Assn. (sec. 1987, chairperson 1988). Roman Catholic. Avocations: tennis, bicycling, art, bowling. Home: 3559 Guava Way Oceanside CA 92054 Office: Teledyne Kinetics 410 S Cedros Solana Beach CA 92075 also: PO Box 1401 Oceanside CA 92054

GARDNER, ALAN JOEL, lawyer; b. Los Angeles, July 18, 1945; s. Leonard and Charlotte M. (Cohen) G.; m. Trudi York; children: Jordan Casey, Andrew Ryan. B.A. cum laude, UCLA, 1967; J.D., U. Calif.-Berkeley, 1970. Bar: Oreg. 1970, U.S. Ct. Appeals (9th cir.) 1970, U.S. Dist. Ct. Oreg. 1971, Wash. 1971, U.S. Ct. Appeals (4th cir.) 1975, U.S. Ct. Appeals (D.C. cir.) 1975, D.C. 1976, U.S. Supreme Ct. 1976, U.S. Dist. Ct. (we. dist.) Wash. 1979. Law clk. U.S. Ct. Appeals (9th cir.), Seattle, 1970-71; assoc. McColloch, Dezendorf, Spears & Lubersky, Portland, Oreg., 1971-72; corp. atty. Pacific N.W. Bell Telephone Co., 1972-75, 77-78, Oreg. area, Portland, 1978-81, hdqrs., Seattle, 1981-83, Wash.-Idaho-Oreg. area, Seattle, 1983-84; head civil litigation, 1984-86, leagal head directory and op. services, 1984—, legal head mktg. services, 1986—; corp. atty. AT&T, N.Y.C., 1975-77; judge pro tempore Bellevue Dist. Ct.; instr. Nat. Inst. Trial Advocacy, 1979—. Active United Way, 1979—; bd. dirs. Wash. State Film Council, 1986—, v.p., 1987—; bd. dirs. Pacific Northwest Studio, 1986—. Mem. ABA (litigation com., trial advocacy subcom.), Oreg. State Bar Assn., Wash. State Bar Assn., D.C. Bar Assn., Seattle-King County Bar Assn., FCC Bar Assn., Phi Beta Kappa. Clubs: Bellevue Athletic (Wash.) Seattle Skeet and Trap (past bd. dirs., treas., v.p.). Address: 3206 Bell Plaza Seattle WA 98191

GARDNER, BOOTH, governor of Washington; b. Tacoma, Aug. 21, 1936; m. Jean Gardner; children—Doug, Gail. B.A. in Bus., U. Wash., 1958; M.B.A., Harvard U., 1963. Asst. to dean Sch. Bus. Adminstrn., Harvard U., Cambridge, Mass., 1966; dir. Sch. Bus. and Econs., U. Puget Sound, Tacoma, 1967-72; pres. Laird Norton County, 1972-80; mem. Wash. Senate, 1970-73; county exec. Pierce County, Tacoma, 1981-84; gov. State of Wash., 1985—. Co-founder Central Area Youth Assn. Seattle; trustee U. Puget Sound. Office: Legislative Bldg AS-13 Olympia WA 98504 *

GARDNER, BRENDA ANN ELLEN, publishing executive; b. Vancouver, B.C., Can., June 1, 1949; d. Michael Peter and Flora (Gibb) Sweedish. BA, EdB, U. Sask., Can., 1970; postgrad., Washington U., St. Louis, 1970-72. Editorial asst. Penguin Books, London, 1972-77; editor W.H. Allen, London, 1977-79; editorial dir. Pepper Press/E.J. Arnold, London, 1979-83; mng. dir., chmn., owner Piccadilly Press, London, 1983—; chmn. Children's Book Circle, London, 1981-82. Mem. Inst. Dirs. London. Club: Groucho (London). Office: Piccadilly Press, 5 Canfield Pl, London NW6 3BT, England

GARDNER, DAVID CHAMBERS, educator, psychologist, bus. exec., writer; b. Charlotte, N.C., Mar. 22, 1934; s. James Raymond and Jessica Mary (Chambers) Bumgardner; B.A., Northeastern U., 1960; M.Ed., (U.S. Office Edn. fellow), Boston U., 1970, Ed.D. (U.S. Office Edn.-univ. research fellow), 1974; Ph.D., Columbia Pacific U., 1984; m. Grace Joely Beatty, 1984; children—Joshua Avery, Jessica Sarah. Diplomate Am. Bd. Med. Psychotherapists. Mgr. market devel. N.J. Zinc Co., N.Y.C., 1961-66, COMINCO, Ltd., Montreal, Que., Can., 1966-68; dir. Alumni Ann. Giving Program, Northeastern U., Boston, 1968-69; dir. career and spl. edn. Stoneham (Mass.) Public Schs., 1970-72; asso. prof. div. instructional devel. and adminstrn. Boston U., 1974—, coordinator program career vocat. tng. for handicapped, 1974-82, chmn. dept. career and bus. edn., 1974-79, also dir. fed. grants, 1975-77, 77-79; co-founder Am. Tng. and Research Assocs., Inc., chmn. bd., 1979-83, pres., chief exec. officer, 1984—; dir. La Costa Inst. Lifestyle Mgmt., 1986-87. Served with AUS, 1954-56. Recipient Am. Profl. Teaching and Research award Region X, Am. Assn. Mental Deficiency, 1979. Fellow Am. Assn. Mental Deficiency (nat. ethics com); mem. Nat. Assn. Career Edn. (dir., past pres.), Council Exceptional Children, Eastern Ednl. Research Assn. (founding dir.), Am. Vocat. Assn., Phi Delta Kappa, Delta Pi Epsilon. Author: Careers and Disabilities: a career education approach, 1978; Dissertation Proposal Guidebook: how to prepare a research proposal and get it accepted, 1980; Career and Vocational Education for the Mildly Learning Handicapped and Disadvantaged, 1984; Stop Stress and Aging Now, 1985; Never Be Tired Again, 1988; editor Career Education Quar., 1975-81; contbr. articles to profl. jours. Home: 265 Via del Cerrito Encinitas CA 92056 Office: Boston U Sch Edn 605 Commonwealth Ave Boston MA 02215

GARDNER, DAVID EDWARD, baking company executive; b. Portsmouth, Ohio, Dec. 5, 1923; s. David Edward and Mary Petrea (Gableman) G.; m. Marie Emma Nickles, Oct. 17, 1948; children: David Alfred, Ernest Edward, Philip Gableman, Mary Emma. Student, U. Mich., 1941-43, U. Ill., 1944, Shrivenham (Am.) U., Eng., 1945; BA, Ohio Wesleyan U., 1948; grad., Am. Inst. Baking, 1962. With Alfred Nickles Bakery, Inc., Navarre, Ohio, 1948—, sec., 1956—, v.p. adminstrn., 1967-80, pres., 1980—, also bd. dirs.; bd. dirs. W.E. Long Ind. Bakers Coop., Chgo. Mem. Blue Cross Community Resource Bd., 1976-82; bd. dirs. Massillon (Ohio) Community Hosp., 1978-82. Served with USAAF, Signal Corps. U.S. Army, 1943-46. Mem. Am. Soc. Bakery Engrs., Am. Inst. Baking Alumni Assn., Phi Kappa Psi, Omicron Delta Kappa, Pi Delta Epsilon, Pi Sigma Alpha. Republican. Mem. United CH. of Christ. Office: 26 Main St Navarre OH 44662

GARDNER, FREDERICK BOYCE, library administrator; b. Hopkinsville, Ky., Mar. 12, 1942; s. Boyce and Alleen Louise (Brown) G. BA, U. Ky., 1964; MA, Ind. U., 1966; postgrad., CUNY, 1970-71, Calif. State U., Northridge, 1973-76, UCLA, 1982-85. Head librarian U. Ky. Hopkinsville Community Coll., 1966-69; head, reader's services Manhattan Community Coll. CUNY, N.Y.C., 1969-71; reference librarian Calif. Inst. Arts, Valencia, 1971-74, head pub. services, 1974-85, dir. computer services, 1984-87, dean of library, 1988—; cons. Total Interlibrary Exchange, Ventura, Calif., 1984-85, v.p. 1980-81, pres. 1981-82, chmn. tech. task force 1983—. Sec. Sequoia String Quartet Found., Los Angeles, Calif., 1977—. Served to capt. USAF, 1968-69. Mem. Calif. Conf. on Networking (del. 1985), ALA, Calif. Library Assn. Office: Calif Inst Arts 24700 McBean Pkwy Valencia CA 91355

GARDNER, GARY VAN, equipment manufacturing company official; b. Fort Wayne, Ind., Jan. 29, 1946; s. Van Watt and Margaret Joann (Little) G.; m. Barbara Rose Lapadot, Sept. 16, 1967; children—Monica Lynn, Gregory Ryan. B.A., St. Francis Coll., 1968, M.S., 1973, JD, 1988. Sales coordinator Mobil Aerial Towers, Inc., Fort Wayne, Ind., 1969-75; ops. mgr. Internat. Trade Services, Fort Wayne, 1975-77; internat. bus. cons. Free Trade Resources, Orlando, Fla., 1977-79; mgr. internat. mktg. adminstrn. Altec Industries, Inc., Birmingham, Ala., 1979—; cons. Africa, Europe Free Trade Resources, Orlando, 1977-79. Del., Nat. Catholic Congress. Mem. Jaycees, Orlando C. of C., Ala. World Trade Assn., Sigma Lambda, Sigma Delta Kappa. Club: Letterman's (Ft. Wayne). Home: 5199 Redfern Way Birmingham AL 35243 Office: ALTEC Industries Inc 210 Inverness Center Dr Birmingham AL 35243

GARDNER, JAMES RICHARD, pharmaceutical company executive; b. Wellsville, N.Y., Nov. 18, 1944; s. James Myers and Adelaide (Stockman) G.; m. Linda Marie Cuomo, Oct. 14, 1967; children: Alexandra K., Mindy M. BS in Engring., U.S. Mil. Acad., 1966; M in Pub. Adminstrn., Princeton U., 1968, PhD, 1977; MBA, Long Island U., 1977. Commd. U.S. Army, 1966, advanced through grades to maj., resigned, 1977; staff asst. Office of U.S. Atty. Gen., 1973; asst. prof. U.S. Mil. Acad., West Point, N.Y., 1974-77; dir. agrl. planning Pfizer, Inc., N.Y.C., 1977-81, dir. corp. strategic planning, 1981—; v.p. Pfizer Found., N.Y.C., 1985—; faculty U.S. Army Command and Gen. Staff Coll., 1986—, U.S. Army War Coll., 1987—; adv. council Ctr. of Internat. Studies, Princeton U., 1987—. Author: (with others) American National Security, 1981, Business Competitor Intelligence, 1984; editor: Handbook of Strategic Planning, 1986; contbr. articles to profl. jours. Strategic planning com. United Way of Tri-State, N.Y.C., 1984-87; dir. adminstrn. Pfizer Inc. United Way Campaign, N.Y.C., 1985-87; dir. Greater N.Y. Councils Boy Scouts Am, 1988—. Served to lt. col. USAR, 1977—. Decorated Five Bronze Stars; recipient George Washington medal

The Freedoms Found., Valley Forge, Pa., 1970. Mem. Planning Forum (pres. N.Y.C. chpt. 1985-86), N. Am. Soc. Corp. Planning (nat. v.p. 1984-85), West Point Soc. N.Y. (bd. dirs. 1984—, v.p. 1986-88, pres. 1988—), Phi Kappa Phi. Republican. Roman Catholic. Home: 250 Mamaroneck Rd Scarsdale NY 10583 Office: Pfizer Inc 235 E 42nd St New York NY 10017

GARDNER, JOHN DARRELL, mining engineering educator; b. San Francisco, Mar. 16, 1929; s. Darrell and Mary Canice (Sullivan) G.; m. Ruth Ann Richmond; children: Shannon, Jean. BS in Mining Engring., U. Ariz., 1956, (hon.) Mining Engr. degree, 1968; MBA, Harvard U., 1961; PhD in Mining Engring., U. Utah, 1981. V.p. Howmet Corp., N.Y.C., 1961-70; pres. Mgmt. Vectors, Blue Bell, Pa., 1970-76, Tintic Western Mining, Salt Lake City, 1978-88; gen. mgr. Mullen Engring., Casper, Wyo., 1976-79; asst. prof. mining engring. U. Wyo., Laramie, 1981-83, assoc prof., 1984—; cons. Benchmark Engrs., Laramie, 1979—. Author: Mine Evaluation and Design Opti., 1981; contbr. articles to profl. publs. Served to 1st lt. U.S. Army, 1951-53. Mem. N.W. Mining Assn., Soc. Mining Engrs., Sigma Xi, Tau Beta Pi, Theta Tau. Republican. Club: Harvard (N.Y.). Home: Box 3101 University Station Laramie WY 82071 Office: U Wyo Dept Mining Engring Laramie WY 82071

GARDNER, JULIAN RICHARD, art history educator; b. Dumfries, Scotland, May 6, 1940; s. John Vincent and Jessie Lamb (Walker) G.; m. Ann Margaret Stoves, Sept. 28, 1967 (dec. 1968); m. Christa Freiin Teuffel von Birkensee, Jan. 5, 1973; children: Jocasta Helen, Corinna Julia. BA, Oxford U., 1961, MA, 1966; diploma in art history, London U., 1964, PhD, 1969. Lectr. Courtauld Inst., London U., 1966-74; Found. prof. history of art Warwick U., Coventry, Eng., 1974—; vis. research prof. Bibliotheca Hertziana, Max-Planck-Gesellschaft, Rome, 1983-85; chmn. library standing com. on art documentation Brit. Library, 1985—. Mem. editorial consultative com. Burlington Mag., 1975—, Arte Cristiana, 1980—; contbr. articles to learned jours. Rivoira fellow in medieval archaeology Brit. Sch. at Rome, 1965-66; state studentship Dept. Edn., London, 1965-67. Fellow Soc. Antiquaries London; mem. Comité Internat. Histoire Art. Club: Vincents (Oxford, Eng.). Office: Warwick U Dept History of Art, Coventry, Warwickshire CV4 7AL, England

GARDNER, LELA MARSHALL, speech pathologist; b. Wymore, Nebr., 1908; d. Virgil Ralph and Jeanie Mae (Warriner) Marshall; m. John Hall Gardner, June 7, 1932; 1 child, Marvel Jean. BS in Edn., U. Nebr., 1930; MS in Pub. Adminstrn., Washington U., St. Louis, 1932; postgrad., Columbia U., 1958-59, 60-61. Cert. tchr., N.J., profl. in speech and hearing. Speech pathologist Toledo Hearing League, 1959-60, Newark Bd. Edn., 1960-63, Johnstone Tng. Sch., Bordentown, N.J., 1963-66, Frederick County (Md.) Bd. Edn., 1966-76, Western Md. Ctr., Hagerstown, 1976-77; freelance writer weekly letters on nat. and internat. affairs, 1976—; cons. speech pathology State Home for Boys, Jamesburg, N.J., 1964-67. Mem. nat. adv. bd. Am. Security Council, 1973; life mem. Am. Conservation Union, 1973, John Birch Soc., 1973; founder Ctr. for Internat. Securities Studies, 1977; sponsor Am. Council for World Freedom, 1972, Young Ams. for Freedom, 1982—; pres. W.Va. Panhandle chpt. Eagle Forum, 1977; mem. Nat. Conservative Polit. Action Com., 1982—, U.S. Justice Found., Com. for a Free Afghanistan, Heritage Found.; active Coalition for Peace through Strength, Found. of Law and Soc., 1978; bd. dirs. Com. to Restore the Constn., 1982; bd. dirs. Northampton County (Pa.) Soc. for Crippled Children and Adults, 1951-55, dir. pub. relations, 1953-55; coordinator for 2d Congl. dist. Conservative Caucus, 1983; nat. sr. adv. bd. Coll. Reps.; corr. sec. Women's Rep. Club, 1981-83; pub. relations staff Make Today Count, 1982—. Mem. Am. Speech and Hearing Assn. (life mem., cert. clin. competence), AAUW (arts chmn. Easton, Pa. br., bd. dirs.), Internat. Platform Assn., Internat. Soc. Philos. Enquiry, Gun Owners Am., Second Amendment Found., Ch. League Am. Intertel, Triple Nine Soc., Mensa, Citizen's Fire Company (hon.), Council InterAm. Security (sustaining mem.), Moral Majority, Black Silent Majority (hon. sustaining mem.), Citizens for Republic, Ctr. for Free Enterprise, Pi Lambda Theta. Clubs: Nat. Congl. (sponsor 1982—), Women's (music chmn. Easton chpt.). Home: Rt 3 Box 1350 Harpers Ferry WV 25425

GARDNER, LEONARD BURTON, II, industrial automation engineer; b. Lansing, Mich., Feb. 16, 1927; s. Leonard Burton and Lillian Marvin (Frost) G.; m. Barbara Jean Zivi, June 23, 1950; children: Karen Sue, Jeffrey Frank. B.Sc. in Physics, UCLA, 1951; M.Sc., Golden State U., 1953, Sc.D. in Engring, 1954; M.Sc. in Computer Sci, Augustana Coll., Rock Island, Ill., 1977. Registered profl. engr.; cert. mfg. engr. Instrumentation engr. govt. and pvt. industry 1951—; prin. engr. computerized systems Naval Electronic Systems Engring. Center, San Diego, 1980-82; founder, dir. Automated Integrated Mfg., San Diego, 1982—; prof. and dir. Center for Automated Integrated Mfg.; cons. govt. agys. and industry, lectr., adj. prof. vaious univs. and colls., sci. advisor state and nat. legislators, 1980—, speaker in field. Author: Computer Aided Robotics Center; editor: Automated Manufacturing. Contbg. author: Instrumentation Handbook, 1981; contbr. numerous articles to tech. jours. Recipient award U.S. Army. Fellow IEEE; sr. mem. Soc. Mfg. Engrs. (Pres.'s award 1984); mem. ASTM, Nat. Soc. Profl. Engrs., Calif. Soc. Profl. Engrs., Sigma Xi. Office: PO Box 1523 Spring Valley CA 92077

GARDNER, MARJORIE HYER, science administrator; b. Logan, Utah, Apr. 25, 1923; d. Saul Edward and Gladys Ledingham (Christiansen) Hyer; B.S., Utah State U., 1946, Ph.D. (hon.), 1975; M.A., Ohio State U., 1958, Ph.D., 1960; cert. Ednl. Mgmt. Inst., Harvard U., 1975; m. Paul Leon Gardner, June 6, 1947; children—Pamela Jean, Mary Elizabeth. Tchr. sci., journalism and English high schs., Utah, Nev., Ohio, 1947-56; instr. Ohio State U., Columbus, 1957-60; asst. exec. dir. Nat. Sci. Tchrs. Assn., 1961-64; vis. prof. Australia, India, Yugoslavia, Nigeria, Thailand, Peoples Republic of China, 1965-82; assoc. dean, dir. Bur. Ednl. Research and Field Service, College Park, Md., 1975-76; dir. Sci. Teaching Center, U. Md., College Park, 1976-77, prof. chemistry, 1964-84; dir. Lawrence Hall Sci., U. Calif.-Berkeley, 1984—; div. dir. NSF, 1979-81; cons. UNESCO, 1970—; NSF grantee, 1964—; recipient Catalyst medal Chem. Mfrs. Assn., 1980, Nyholm medal Royal Soc. Can., 1987, U.S.U. Centennial award, 1987, ACS Chemical Edn. award, 1988. Fellow AAAS (council), Am. Inst. Chemistry; mem. Am. Chem. Soc., Chemistry Assn. Md. (pres.), Internat. Union of Pure and Applied Chemistry (exec. com.), Internat. Orgn. Chemistry in Devel. (edn. panel), Assn. Edn. of Tchrs. of Sci., Nat. Assn. Research in Sci. Teaching, Nat. Sci. Tchrs. Assn., Am. Assn. Higher Edn., Soc. Coll. Sci. Tchrs. (pres.), Fulbright Alumni Assn. (pres., dir.), Phi Delta Kappa, Phi Kappa Phi. Author: Chemistry in the Space Age, 1965; editor: Theory in Action, 1964, Vistas of Sci. Series, 1961-63; Investigating the Earth, 1968, Interdisciplinary Approaches to Chemistry, 1973, 1978-79; Under Roof, Dome and Sky, 1974, Toward Continuous Professional Development: Designs and Directions, 1976; contbr. articles in on chemistry and sci. edn. to profl. jours. Home: 517 Vista Height Rd Richmond CA 94805 Office: U Calif Lawrence Hall of Sci Centennial Dr Berkeley CA 94720

GARDNER, RALPH DAVID, advertising executive; b. N.Y.C., Apr. 16, 1923; s. Benjamin and Myra (Berman) G.; m. Nellie Jaglom, Apr. 9, 1952; children: Ralph David, John Jaglom, Peter Jaglom, James Jaglom. Diploma in journalism, NYU, 1942; diploma in mil. adminstrn., Colo. State Coll., 1943. With N.Y. Times, 1942-55; copy boy, city desk, fgn. corr., started internat. edit. N.Y. Times, Paris, 1949; bur. mgr. for Germany and Austria, Frankfurt N.Y. Times, 1950, resigned, 1955; pres. Ralph D. Gardner Advt., N.Y.C., 1955—; dir. Gardner Internat. Corp.; Quality Irish Food Export (Dublin) Ltd.; dir. various other U.S. and fgn. corps.; writer, book reviewer, lectr., bibliographer 19th Century Am. lit.; Mary C. Richardson lectr. SUNY-Geneseo, 1974; vis. prof. U. Wyo., others; mem. faculty Georgetown U. Writers Conf., 1976, 80; Hess research fellow U. Minn., 1979; book reviewer, host Ralph Gardner's Bookshelf, WVNJ-N.Y., other radio stas. Author: Horatio Alger, or The American Hero Era, 1964, 78, Road to Success: The Bibliography of the Works of Horatio Alger, 1971, Introduction to Silas Snobden's Office Boy, 1973, Introduction to Cast Upon the Breakers, 1974, History of Street & Smith, in Publishers for Mass Entertainment in 19th Century America, 1980, Introduction to a Fancy of Hers, 1981, The Disagreeable Woman, 1981, Struggling Upward, 1984, Writers Talk to Ralph D. Gardner, 1988, others; contbr. to: N.Y. Times Book Rev., Sat. Eve. Post, 1st Printings of Am. Authors, vol. 5, 1987, other newspapers and nat. mags. Mem.-at-large Greater N.Y. council Boy Scouts Am., 1950-60; bd. dirs. Fresh Air Council, 1964-66; mem. hon. exec. com. Nat. Citizens for Public Libraries. Served as newswriter with inf. AUS, 1943-46, ETO.; field Corr. Yank Mag. Recipient award for lit. Horatio Alger Soc., 1964, 72, 81, 85; spl. citation scroll Horatio Alger Awards Com., 1978. Mem. Manuscript Soc., Bibliog. Soc. Am., Childrens Lit. Assn., Friends of Princeton U. Library, Syracuse U. Library Assocs. (hon.), Brandeis U. Bibliophiles (hon.), Overseas Press Club of Am. (assoc. editor OPC Bulletin, best book on fgn. affairs selection awards com.), Frankfurt Press Club (Germany), Nat. Book Critics Circle, Soc. of Silurians, PEN, Alpha Epsilon Pi. Clubs: Grolier; Baker St. Irregulars (N.Y.C.). Home: 135 Central Park West Apt 5N New York NY 10023 Office: 745 Fifth Ave New York NY 10151

GARDNER, RICHARD CALVIN, educator, librarian; b. Indpls., Sept. 21, 1931; s. Selby A. and Mary E. (Armstrong) G.; B.S., Butler U., 1951; M.A., East Tenn. U., 1955; postgrad. U. Del., 1959, U. Tenn., 1960, 72, U. Wis., 1965; m. Dorothy Faye Fleenor, Aug. 25, 1951; children—Sylvia Jeannine, Kirby Hunter, Trevor Christian. Tchr. elem. sch. Kingsport Pub. Schs., Tenn., 1951-55; asst. prof. edn. SUNY, Oneonta, 1955-57; elem. sch. supr. Kingsport City Schs., 1957-61, asst. supt. schs., 1961-65, 69-71; supr. curriculum devel. Tenn. Dept. Edn., Nashville, 1966-67, coordinator div. instrn., 1972; supt. schs. Norton (Va.) City Schs., 1972-79; supr. elem. edn. Wise County Pub. Schs., Va., 1979-80; tchr.-librarian Hamilton Elem. Sch., Mendota, Va., 1980-83, tchr., 1983-85, prin., 1985—; extension instr. E. Tenn. State U., Johnson City, 1959-65, U. Va., Charlottesville, 1967—, U. Tenn., Knoxville, 1967-72, Va. Poly. Inst. and State U., Blacksburg, 1973-80; vis. prof. St. Mary of the Plains Coll., Dodge City, Kans., summer 1971; mem. tchr. edn. adv. council Clinch Valley Coll., U. Va., 1974-76; mem. adv. council Wise Speech and Hearing Clinic, 1975; cons. to Day Care Services, Tenn. Dept. Public Welfare, 1959-71. Bd. dirs. Regional Child Devel. Ctr., 1974-79, Appalachian Regional Lab., 1971-72, Kingsport Community Chest; bd. dirs. Dilenowisco Ednl. Co-op, chmn., 1972-73. Recipient Good Citizenship award Jaycees, 1962. Mem. NEA, Va., Washington County edn. assns., Nat. Soc. Study of Edn., Am. Assn. Sch. Adminstrs., Phi Delta Kappa, Kappa Delta Pi, Phi Kappa Phi. Mem. Universalist Ch. (trustee 1955-57, ch. sch. dir. 1955-57). Club: Kiwanis (dir. 1972-75, v.p. local chpt. 1974-75). Home: Hunter's Oak Route 6 Box 306 Abingdon VA 24210 Office: PO Box 67 Mendota VA 24270

GARDNER, RUSSELL MENESE, lawyer; b. High Point, N.C., July 14, 1920; s. Joseph Hayes and Clara Emma-Lee (Flynn) G.; m. Joyce Thresher, Mar. 7, 1946; children—Winthrop G., Page Stansbury, June Thresher. AB, Duke U., 1942, JD, 1948. Bar: Fla. 1948, U.S. Ct. Appeals (5th cir.) 1949, U.S. Tax Ct. 1949. Mem. McCune, Hiaasen, Crum Ferris & Gardner and predecessor firms, Ft. Lauderdale, Fla., 1948-50, mem., 1950—; bd. govs. Nova Ctr. for Study of Law. Trustee Mus. of Art, Inc., Ft. Lauderdale, pres., 1964-67; bd. dirs. Stranahan House, Inc., 1981—, pres. 1983-85; bd. dirs. Ft. Laud Hist. Soc., 1962—, pres. 1975-85, pres. emeritus, 1985—; pres. Ft. Lauderdale Hist. Soc., 1975—; mem. estate planning council, Duke U. Sch. Law; bd. dirs., vice chmn. Broward Performing Arts Found., Inc., 1985—. Served to lt. USNR, 1943-49. Fellow Am. Coll. Probate counsel; mem. Am. Judicature Soc., ABA (real property, probate, trust sect.), Fla. Bar Assn. (probate, guardianship rules com.), Broward County Bar Assn. (estate planning council). Democrat. Presbyterian. Clubs: Coral Ridge Country, Lauderdale Yacht, Tower (Ft. Lauderdale). Office: McCune Hiaasen Crum Ferris Gardner PO Box 14636 Fort Lauderdale FL 33302

GARDNER, WILLIAM ALBERT, JR., pathologist; b. Sumter, S.C., Aug. 2, 1939; s. William A. and Betty Lee (Kennedy) G.; m. Kathryn Ann Medlin, June 30, 1960; children: Mary Elizabeth, Kathryn Lee, William Dylan. B.S., Wofford Coll., 1960; M.S. in Anatomy, Med. Coll. S.C., 1963, M.D., 1965. Diplomate: Am. Bd. Pathology. Intern Johns Hopkins Hosp., Balt., 1965-66, asst. resident, 1966-67, fellow in pathology, 1965-67; asst. resident Duke U., Durham, N.C., 1967-68, chief resident, 1968-69, instr. pathology, 1968-69; chief lab. service VA Hosp., Charleston, S.C., 1969; asst. prof. pathology Med. U. S.C., 1969-72, assoc. prof., 1972-76; prof. pathology Vanderbilt U., Nashville, 1976-81, vice chmn. dept. pathology; chief lab. service VA Hosp., Nashville, 1976-81; prof., chmn. dept. pathology U. South Ala., Mobile, 1981—. Contbr. articles on oncology, urology, parasitology and pathology to profl. jours. Recipient Outstanding Teaching award Med. U. S.C., 1975, Disting. Alumnus award Med. U. S.C., 1988. Fellow Am. Soc. Clin. Pathologists, Coll. Am. Pathologists (del. for govtl. pathology); mem. Internat. Acad. Pathology (U.S. and Can. Acad. Pathology Council), Acad. Clin. Lab. Physicians and Scientists, AMA, Ala. Med. Assn., Assn. Pathology Chmn. Council, Alpha Omega Alpha. Methodist. Home: 1565 Fearnway Mobile AL 36604 Office: U South Ala 2451 Fillingim St Mobile AL 36617

GARDNER-CHLOROS, PENELOPE HELEN, linguist, educator; b. Aberystwyth, Wales, Nov. 14, 1954; d. Alexander George and Helen (Comninos) Chloros; m. James Piers Gardner, Dec. 16, 1978; children: Alexander, Nicholas, Zoe. BA in English, Somerville Coll., Oxford, Eng., 1976; MA in Applied Linguistics, Birkbeck Coll., London, 1981; Dr. in Psychology, Strasbourg (France) U., 1985. Conf. interpreter EEC, Brussels, 1977-78; research asst. Ealing Coll. Higher Edn., London, 1979-81; researcher, lectr. Strasbourg U., 1982-88; freelance interpreter Council Europe, Strasbourg, 1979—. Author: Language Selection and Switching in Strasbourg, 1989; contbr. articles to profl. jours. Sec. Young European Federalists, Oxford, 1975-76. Brti. Acad. Research fellow, 1988-91. Mem. Assn. Internat. des Interprétes de Conf. Home: 8 Royal Crescent, London W11, England Office: Dept Lang and Linguistics, U of Essex Wivenhoe Park, Colchester, Essex CO4 3SQ, England

GAREY, DONALD LEE, pipeline executive; b. Ft. Worth, Sept. 9, 1931; s. Leo James and Jessie (McNatt) G.; B.S. in Geol. Engring., Tex. A. and M. U., 1953; m. Elizabeth Patricia Martin, Aug. 1, 1953; children—Deborah Anne, Elizabeth Laird. Reservoir geologist Gulf Oil Corp., 1953-54, sr. geologist, 1956-65; v.p., mng. dir. Indsl. Devel. Corp. Lea County, Hobbs, N.Mex., 1965-72, dir., 1972-86, pres., 1978-86; v.p., dir. Minerals, Inc., Hobbs, 1966-72, pres., dir., 1972-86, chief exec. officer, 1978-82; mng. dir. Hobbs Indsl. Found. Corp., 1965-72, dir., 1965-76; v.p. Llano, Inc., 1972-74, exec. v.p., chief operating officer, 1974-75, pres., 1975-86, chief exec. officer, 1978-82, also dir.; pres., chief exec. officer, Pollution Control, Inc., 1969-81; pres. NMESCO Fuels, Inc., 1982-86; chmn., pres., chief exec. officer Estacado Inc., 1986—; pres. Llano Co2, Inc., 1984-86; cons. geologist, geol. engr., Hobbs, 1965-72. Chmn., Hobbs Manpower Devel. Tng. Adv. Com., 1965-72; mem. Hobbs Adv. Com. for Mental Health, 1965-67; chmn. N.Mex. Mapping Adv. Com., 1968-69; mem. Hobbs adv. bd. Salvation Army, 1967-78, chmn., 1970-72; mem. exec. bd. Conquistador council Boy Scouts Am., Hobbs, 1965-75; vice chmn. N.Mex. Gov.'s Com. for Econ. Devel., 1968-70; bd. regents Coll. Southwest, 1982-85. Served to capt. USAF, 1954-56. Registered profl. engr., Tex. Mem. Am. Inst. Profl. Geologists, Am. Assn. Petroleum Geologists, AIME, N.Mex., Roswell geol. socs., N.Mex. Amigos. Club: Rotary. Home: 315 E Alto Dr Hobbs NM 88240 Office: Broadmoor Bldg PO Box 5587 Hobbs NM 88241

GARFIELD, LESLIE JEROME, real estate executive; b. N.Y.C., Mar. 23, 1932; s. Jack and Anne (Weinert) G.; m. Johanna Rosengarten, Sept. 28, 1960; children: Clare Louisa, Jed Herbert, Cory Alexander. BA, U. Wis., Madison, 1953; MA, Harvard U., 1956; MBA, Columbia U., 1958. V.p. Pease & Elliman, Inc., N.Y.C., 1965-68, William A. White & Sons, Inc., N.Y.C., 1968-78; pres. Leslie J. Garfield & Co., Inc., N.Y.C., 1978—. Chmn. bd. N.Y. Youth Symphony, 1986, pres. bd., 1975-86; bd. dirs. Carnegie Hill Neighbors, N.Y.C., 1985-88. Served as cpl. U.S. Army, 1954-55. Mem. Real Estate Bd. N.Y. (chmn. sales brokers com. 1985-86), The Drawing Soc. (bd. dirs.). Clubs: Century Assn., Nat. Arts, Harvard, Grolier. Office: 654 Madison Ave New York NY 10021

GARFINKEL, LAWRENCE SAUL, university administrator; b. N.Y.C., Mar. 9, 1932; s. Benjamin and Rose (Rochkind) G.; m. Adrienne Rederer, June 26, 1960; children—Andrew, Rodger, Craig. B.S. in Art Edn., NYU, 1953, M.A. in Higher Edn., 1955, Ed.D. Studies, 1975. Tchr., supr. art, prin. high schs. West Hempstead Pub. Schs., N.Y., 1954-56, dir. related arts, 1957-69, dir. community relations, 1961-71; prof. edn. adminstrn. and communication, dir. instrnl. communications program Hofstra U., Hempstead, N.Y., 1969-76; dir. gifted programs Sachem Pub. Schs., Lake Ronkonkoma, N.Y., 1978-79; dir. ednl. communications NYU Dental Ctr., N.Y.C., 1979—; adj. prof. Speech Dept. Baruch Coll., Adelphi U., C.W. Post U., St. Johns U., Temple U.; adj. assoc. prof. Nassau Community Coll.; cons. bd. regents N.Y. State Edn. Dept., Ctr. Urban Edn., N.Y.C. Editor: Restorative Dentistry, 1985. Illustrator: Classroom Television, 1970. Producer numerous ednl. video tapes; asst. producer WPIX-TV. Contbr. articles to profl. jours.; pub. Garson Assocs. Bd. dirs. Hist. Soc. Merricks, 1983—, Higher Edn. Assn. T.V., 1972; v.p. Health Equities, N.Y.C.; oral historian Bi Centennial Commn., 1975; illustrator N.Y. Times, John Huston Prodns., Century Theatres, Nat. Audio Visual Assoc., numerous publs. Recipient Grad. Medal award NYU; numerous awards Nat. Com. Sch. Public Relations; Fulbright scholar, alternate; grad. fellow NYU, Woodrow Wilson fellow nominee. Mem. N.Y. Acad. Sci., L.I. Art Tchrs. Assn. (pres. 1967-68), Nat. Com. Art Edn. (co-pres. 1967). Avocations: illustrating; lecturing on communications theory; arts. Home: 172 Babylon Turnpike Merrick NY 11566 Office: NYU Dental Ctr 345 E 24th St New York NY 10010

GARGALLO, JUAN, agricultural company executive; b. Barcelona, Spain, June 17, 1953; arrived in Republic of Korea, 1985; s. Salvador and Maria (Costa) G.; m. Maria Antonia Margarit, June 20, 1981; children: Agustin, Alberto. DVM, U. Zaragoza, Spain, 1975; PhD, Iowa State U., 1980. Mgr. product devel. Am. Cynamid Co., Wayne, N.J., 1980-81; mgr. agrl. mktg. Cynamid de Mexico S.A. de C.V., Mexico City, 1981-82, dir. agrl. div., 1982-84; asst. mng. dir. Gallina Blanca Purina S.A., Barcelona, 1984-85; rep. dir. Purina Korea, Inc., Seoul, 1985—. Contbr. articles to profl. jours. Served with Spanish cavalry, 1976-77. Fullbright-Hays Found. scholar, 1977. Mem. Am. C. of C. in Korea. Roman Catholic. Club: Seoul. Home: Lavosier 26, Terrassa, Barcelona Spain Office: Purina Korea Inc, CPO Box 5112, Seoul Republic of Korea

GARGAN, THOMAS JOSEPH, plastic surgeon; b. Denver, Sept. 28, 1952; s. Thomas Joseph and Maria Augusta (Casagranda) G.; m. Nancy Lee Hall, Jan. 20, 1979; children: Daniel Thomas, John William. BA summa cum laude, Colo. Coll., 1974; MD, U. Colo., 1978. Diplomate Am. Bd. Plastic Surgery. Intern Presbyn. Med. Ctr., Denver, 1978-79, resident in surgery, 1978-79; resident in surgery Beth Israel Hosp., Boston, 1979-81, instr. gen. surgery, 1979-82, sr. resident in surgery, 1981-82, chief resident in plastic surgery, 1983-84; sr. resident in plastic surgery Cambridge (Mass.) City Hosp., 1982-83; resident in plastic surgery Children's Hosp. and Brigham and Women's Hosp., Boston, 1983, Newton-Wellesley Hosp., Mass., 1983; clin. fellow in surgery Harvard U. Med. Sch., Boston, 1979-84; clin. instr. plastic surgery U. Colo. Sch. Med., Denver, 1984; chief plastic surgery div. Rose Med. Ctr., 1987—; instr. plastic surgery Cambridge Hosp., Children's Hosp., and Beth Israel Hosp., Boston, 1982-84, Harvard Med. Sch., Boston, 1984. Contbr. articles to profl. jours. Bd. dirs. Rocky Mt. Adoption Exchange. Recipient George B. Packard award for excellence in surgery U. Colo. Med. Ctr., 1978; Eagle Scout; Barnes Chemistry scholar Colo. Coll. Fellow ACS; mem. AMA, Denver Med. Soc. (Pres. Gold Star award), Colo. Med. Soc., Am. Soc. Plastic and Reconstructive Surgeons, Colo. State Soc. Plastic and Reconstructive Surgeons, Rocky Mountain Hand Surgery Soc., Rocky Mountain Soc. of Reconstructive Plastic Surgeons. Lodge: Ancient Order Hibernians in Am. Home: 10 Blackmer Rd Englewood CO 80110 Office: 4545 E 9th Ave Denver CO 80220

GARGANO, FRANCESCO, accountant; b. Rome, July 31, 1943; s. Aldo and Rossane (Bersani) G.; m. Emma Enriquez, Feb. 25, 1965; children: Francesco, Fabrizio, Giorgia. Degree in Acctg., U. Rio de Janeiro, 1966; Degree in Economy and Commerce, U. Rome, 1978. Audit staff Arthur Andersen & Co., Rio de Janeiro, 1963-66, Rome, 1967-68; audit staff Arthur Andersen & Co., Lisbon, Portugal, 1969-71, audit mgr., 1971-74; audit mgr. Arthur Andersen & Co., Milan, Italy, 1975-78; mng. ptnr. Arthur Andersen & Co., Treviso, Italy, 1979-87, Bologna, Italy, 1987—. Club: Bologna Golf. Lodge: Rotary.

GARGIULO, ROSALYN MANDO, architect; b. Chgo., Sept. 12, 1924; d. Samuel J. and Emily (Greco) Mando; m. Francis Foley (div. 1963); m. Gerardo Gargiulo, Sept. 9, 1964; 1 child, Emy. BS, Ill. Inst. Tech., 1954. Graphic designer Marshall Field and Co., Chgo., 1946-53; pvt. practice interior and architecture design Sorrento, Italy, 1967—. Home: via Correale 20, 80067 Sorrento Italy

GARGOUR, RAMZI ALLENBY, tourism company executive; b. Cairo, July 23, 1955; s. Allenby Toufic and Charlotte John (Jellad) Gargour; m. Katrin Wegelius, Sept. 6, 1956; children: Charlotte, Danielle. Degree in Acct., LaSalle Coll., Lebanon, 1976; BS, U. So. Calif., 1980; MBA, Century U., 1988. Mktg. mgr. Lecico, Lebanon, 1980-83; asst. gen. mgr. Lecico, 1983-85; mng. dir. Sunshine Tours & Services, Cairo, 1985—; mktg. cons. Indsl. Bank Kuwait, 1984. Mem. Tourism Chamber Egypt, Am. Soc. Travel Agts., Internat. Assn. Travel Agts., Internat. Assn. Travel Agents, Indsl. C. of C. and Industries in Lebanon (pres. 1982-84). Club: Hunting (Cairo), Gezira.

GARIBAY-GUTIERREZ, LUIS, physician, educator; b. Zamora, Mexico, Sept. 28, 1916; s. Ignacio Garibay Zamora and Sara Gutierrez Macias; children: Luis, Jorge, Bertha (Mrs. Oscar Soria), Teresa (Mrs. Antonio Rivero), Gabriela (Mrs. Ramón Escobar), Martha (Mrs. Fernando Torres), Cristina (Mrs. Vicente Deméneghi), Patricia, Fernando; m. Bertha Bagnis Flores, Jan. 20, 1940 (dec. 1965); m. Rita Sawicki, Sept. 9, 1966 (dec. 1982); m. Annie Pemberton McNeill, Feb. 20, 1984. B.A., Inst. Scis., Guadalajara, 1931; med. studies U. Guadalajara, 1932-33; Dr. Surgery and Obstetrics, Nat. Autonomous U. Mexico, 1934; Dr. Surgery and Obstetrics Autonomous U. Guadalajara, 1940; pediatrician, Hosp. Infantil de Mexico, 1946; M.Ed., Autonomous U. Guadalajara/U. Houston, 1977; 13 hon. doctorates. Intern Ramón Garibay Hosp., 1938-40; resident in pediatrics Children's Hosp. of Mexico, 1945-46; prof. Sch. Nursing, Uruapan, 1942-45; founder, dir., prof. Secondary Sch., Uruapan, 1942; prof. pediatrics, head dept. Autonomous U. Guadalajara, 1949-62, sec. faculty medicine, 1947-49, dean faculty medicine, 1949-52, bd. dirs., 1948—, sec. gen., 1952-55, vice rector, 1955-57, rector, 1957—; founder, pres. Exam. Bd. Pediatrics, 1961-62; adviser Ministry Edn. and Culture Brazil, 1970; dir. Nat. Inquiry into Nutrition, Nat. Inquiry into Infantile Diarrhea; adviser Council Rectors Brazilian U., 1966; lectr. univ. adminstrn., Ecuador, 1968, Brazil, 1966, others; founder, bd. dirs. Mexican Pvt. Higher Edn. Instns. Fedn., 1981; v.p. Inter Am. Council Econ. and Social Devel., 1982—; trustee Internat. Council Ednl. Devel., 1982—; pres. Ajijic Ctr. to Help Improve Higher Edn. in the Americas, 1977-83; ex-officio mem. Ajijic Inst. Internat. Edn., 1978—; trustee Internat. Council for Ednl. Devel., 1982—. Author: La Trampa, 1972, Reforma Universitaria, 1972, Financiamiento de la Universidad, 1973, Juventude em Trance, 1973, Programas de Educación en la Comunidad, 1979, System of Higher Education in Mexico, 1975, others; contbr. articles to med. and ednl. jours. Dir. U.S. Seminar on Improvement Univ. Curriculum, 1972; co-organizer Conf. Edn. Nutrition, UNICEF, 1962; pres. 4th Congress Pediatricians Latin Nations, 1968; 1st pres. Congress Latin Am. Pediatricians, 1966; ex officio mem. Ajijic Inst. Internat. Edn., 1978—; pres. Jalisco Inst. Spanish Culture, 1950-52. Decorated Knight Order Isabel the Catholic; comdr. Nat. Order Cruzeiro do Sul; grand officer Nat. Order Ednl. Merit, Brazil; Order Andres Bello Venezuela; medal Koeler Brazil, 1975, Order of the Sacred Treasure, Japan, 1987; medal of Honor, IAUP, 1981; Disting. Son and Guest of Honor, City of Zamora (Mex.), 1981; medal of Honor, Kyung Hee U., Korea, 1983, Order Francisco Miranda 1st Class, Venezuela, 1984; Univ. medal Hankuk U. Fgn. Studies, Korea, 1985; Order of Sacred Treasure, Gold and Silver Star, Japan, 1987; presdl. fellow Aspen Inst. Humanistic Studies, 1979. Fellow Aspen Inst. of Humanistic Studies (pres. 1979); mem. Soc. Profls. Uruapan (pres.), Internat. Assn. U. Pres. (v.p. 1981, pres. elect 1984, pres. 1987—), Jalisco Soc Pediatrics (pres. 1958), Nat. Assn. Pediatrics Mexico (pres. 1959-63), Latin Am. Assn. Pediatrics (pres. 1963-66), Latin Am. Study Group for Improvement and Reform of Edn. (founder, pres. 1965-67, v.p. 1977, pres. emeritus 1982), numerous others. Club: Rotary (pres. Uruapan 1944-45). Home: 5016 Paseo de Loma Larga, Guadalajara, 45110 Jalisco Mexico Office: 1201 Avenida Patria, Guadalajara, 44100 Jalisco Mexico

GARIBOLDI, FRANCO, food products executive; b. Binasco, Italy, June 10, 1926; s. Attilio and Rosa (Galbiati) G.; diploma mech. engring., U. Milan, 1949. Engaged in rice industry, 1955—; owner Riseria Gariboldi S.p.A., Milan, 1935—, Gariboldi Engring. Co. S.p.A., Carugate, Milan, 1973—; Finrice S.p.A. Milan; leader and/or del. numerous FAO rice processing commns., 1958—. Author bulls., papers in field. Address: Riseria Gariboldi, 20 Via Pienza, 20142 Milan Italy

GARIN, EUGENE, artist; b. Odessa, USSR, Nov. 30, 1922; came to U.S., 1959; s. Vasilij and Martha (Drokov) G.; m. Raisa Peredelsky, Mar. 24, 1958 (dec. Aug. 1977); m. Rita Seljavin, Dec. 27, 1978; children: Irene, Tanja, Stella. Art student, Novomoskowsk, USSR, 1936-39, Comml. Coll., Odessa, 1940-41; cert., Chgo. Tech. Coll., 1962. Freelance artist Buenos Aires, 1948-59. Exhibited at H. Morseburg Galleries, Los Angeles, 1962-78, G. Livingston Galleries, Monterey, Calif., 1965-80, Old Main Gold Gallery, Bellevue, Wash., 1970-82, Lyon Gallery, San Francisco, 1970-83, Simic Galleries, Carmel, Calif., 1982. Editor in chief (newspaper) Our Days, 1974—; editor Golden Weath, 1984—. Sec. Slavic Bapt. Assn., Sacramento, 1976-84. Home: 1002 La Jolla Ct Roseville CA 95678 Office: care Simic Galleries Attention Jessica Haynes PO Box 5687 Carmel CA 93921

GARLAND, SYLVIA DILLOF, lawyer; b. N.Y.C., June 4, 1919; d. Morris and Frieda (Gassner) Dillof; m. Albert Garland, May 4, 1942; children—Margaret Garland Clunie, Paul B. B.A., Bklyn. Coll., 1939; J.D. cum laude, N.Y. Law Sch., 1960. Bar: N.Y., 1960, U.S. Ct. Appeals (2d cir.), 1965, U.S. Ct. Claims, 1965, U.S. Supreme Ct., 1967, U.S. Customs Ct., 1972, U.S. Ct. Appeals (5th cir.), 1979. Assoc. firm Borden, Skidell, Fleck and Steindler, Jamaica, N.Y., 1960-61, Fields, Zimmerman, Skodnick & Segall, Jamaica, 1961-65, Marshall, Brater, Greene, Allison & Tucker, N.Y.C., 1965-68; law sec. to N.Y. Supreme Ct. justice, Suffolk County, 1968-70; ptnr. firm Hofheimer, Gartlir, Gottlieb & Gross, N.Y.C., 1970—; asst. adj. prof. N.Y. Law Sch., 1974-79; mem. com. on character and fitness N.Y. State Supreme Ct., 1st Jud. Dept., 1985—. Author: Workman's Compensation, 1957; Wills, 1959; Labor Law, 1962; contbg. author: Guardians and Custodians, 1970; editor-in-chief Law Rev. Jour., N.Y. Law Forum, 1959-60 (service award 1960); contbr. article to mag. Trustee N.Y. Law Sch., 1979—; pres. Oakland chpt. B'nai B'rith, Bayside, N.Y., 1955-57. Recipient Disting. Alumnus award, N.Y. Law Sch., 1978. Mem. ABA (litigation sect.), N.Y. State Bar Assn., Queen's County Bar Assn. (sec. civil practice 1960-79), N.Y. Law Sch. Alumni Assn. (pres. 1976-77), N.Y. Law Forum Alumni Assn. (pres. 1963-65). Jewish. Home: 425 E 58th St New York NY 10022

GARLOCK, JOHN ALAN, child psychologist, consultant; b. Bklyn., Dec. 16, 1946; s. Leon Mantis and Catherine (Belden) G. AA, Eastfield Coll., 1972; BS, U. Tex.-Dallas, 1973; MS, East Tex. State U., 1975, 77, EdD, 1980; PhD, U. So. Miss., 1984. Cert. eating disorder therapist, nat. cert. sch. psychologist, assoc. psychologist, employee assistance profl., counselor, sch. psychologist, devel. examiner, alcohol and drug abuse counselor. Acct. J.W. Bateson Co., Dallas, 1967-70; work study coordinator East Tex. State U., Commerce, 1974-77; asst. dir. student services/fin. aid U. Houston, 1978-81; psychologist intern Hattiesburg Pub. Schs., Miss., 1981-82; psychologist Jefferson Parish Schs., Metairie, La., 1982-84, Associated Counseling, Harker Heights, Tex., 1984-86, Patrick Counseling and Psychotherapy Ctr., Inc., Houston, 1986-88, Laurelwood Psychiatric. Hosp., The Woodlands, Tex., 1987-88; Ctr. for Psychiat. Services of the Woodlands, The Woodlands, Tex., 1988—;. pvt. practice psychology, Metairie, 1982-84, Hattiesburg, 1981-82, Spring, Tex. 1986—; pvt. practice ednl. cons., Houston, 1978-81. Author articles. Active polit. campaign, Dallas, 1979. Served with USAR, 1966-72. Recipient Outstanding Service award Nat. Assn. Student Fin. Aid Adminstrs., 1980, Cert. of Profl. Recognition Tex. Assn. of Alcoholism and Drug Abuse Counselors, 1988, Profl. Service award; Eddie Estes scholar, 1977. Mem. Am. Psychol. Assn., Am. Assn. Counseling Devel., Nat. Assn. Sch. Psychologists, Nat. Assn. Alcoholism and Drug Abuse Counselors, Tex. Assn. Alcoholism and Drug Abuse Counselors, La. Sch. Psychologist Assn., La. Psychol. Assn., Kappa Delta Pi, Phi Delta Kappa. Republican. Baptist. Club: Apple Computer. Avocations: computers; fishing; sailing. Home: 4210 Tylergate Dr Spring TX 77373 Office: Ctr Psychiat Services Woodlands 77380 Groogins Mill Rd The Woodlands TX 77387 also: Laurelwood Psychiat Hosp PO Box 7695 The Woodlands TX 77387

GARLOUGH, WILLIAM GLENN, marketing executive; b. Syracuse, N.Y., Mar. 27, 1924; s. Henry James and Gladys (Killam) G.; m. Charlotte M. Tanzer, June 15, 1947; children: Jennifer, William, Robert. BEE, Clarkson U., 1949. With Knowlton Bros., Watertown, N.Y., 1949-67, mgr. mfg. services, 1966-67; v.p. planning, equipment systems div. Vare Corp., Englewood Cliffs, N.J., 1967-69; mgr. mktg. Valley Mould div. Microdot Inc., Hubbard, Ohio, 1969-70; dir. corp. devel. Microdot Inc., Greenwich, Conn., 1970-73, v.p. corp. devel., 1973-76, v.p. adminstrn., 1976-77, v.p. corp. devel., 1977-78; v.p. corp. devel. Am. Bldg. Maintenance Industries, San Francisco, 1979-83; pres. The Change Agts., Inc., Walnut Creek, Calif., 1983—; mem. citizens adv. com. to Watertown Bd. Edn., 1957. Bd. dirs. Watertown Community Chest, 1958-61; ruling elder Presbyn. ch. Served with USMCR, 1942-46. Mem. Am. Mgmt. Assn., Bldg. Service Contractors Assn., Internat. Sanitary Supply Assn., Mensa, Am. Mktg. Assn., TAPPI, Assn. Corp. Growth (pres. San Francisco chpt. 1984-85, v.p. chpts. west 1985-88), Lincoln League (pres. 1958), Am. Contract Bridge League (life master), Clarkson Alumni Assn. (Watertown sect. pres. 1955), Tau Beta Pi. Clubs: Olympic; No. N.Y. Contract (pres. 1959), No. N.Y. Transp. Home: 2557 Via Verde Walnut Creek CA 94598 Office: The Change Agts Inc 1990 N California Blvd Walnut Creek CA 94596

GARMON, FREDRIC DAVID, marketing company executive; b. Boston, Sept. 13, 1921; s. Samuel Leo and Bertha (Fishman) G.; grad. Sch. Mgmt., Boston U., 1947; m. Vivienne Claire Robinson, Dec. 30, 1956; children—Paul Dana, Linda Beth. Pres., Fred Garmon Mktg. Corp., 1953—; exec. dir. Inst. Mass Mktg., 1970—; pub. Inside Mass Mktg. Newsletter; mktg. columnist Modern Retailer; guest lectr. Harvard U., U. Mass., Northeastern U., NYU; continuing edn. prof. mktg. Mass. Bay Community Coll. Served with USCGR, 1942-44. Mem. New Eng. Newsletter Assn., Am. Mgmt. Assn., Housewares Club New Eng. (bd. dirs., program chmn.). Lodge: B'nai B'rith (past pres. housewares-hardware-toy lodge). Home: 16 Ashmont Rd Wellesley Hills MA 02181 Office: 200 Boylston St Chestnut Hill MA 02167

GARN, EDWIN JACOB (JAKE), senator; b. Richfield, Utah, Oct. 12, 1932; s. Jacob Edwin and Fern (Christensen) G.; m. Hazel Rhae Thompson, Feb. 2, 1957 (dec. 1976); children: Jacob Wayne, Susan Rhae, Ellen Marie, Jeffrey Paul; m. Kathleen Brewerton, Apr. 8, 1977; children: Matthew Spencer, Christopher Brook, Jennifer Kathleen. B.S., U. Utah, 1955. Spl. agt. John Hancock Mut. Life Ins. Co., Salt Lake City, 1960-61; asst. mgr. Home Life Ins. Co. N.Y., Salt Lake City, 1961-66; gen. agt. Mut. Trust Life Ins. Co., Salt Lake City, 1966-68; city commr. Salt Lake City, 1968-72, mayor, 1972-74; dir. Met. Water Dist., 1968-72; mem. U.S. Senate from Utah, 1974—. Chmn. joint bd. commrs. Salt Lake Model Cities Agy., 1973—; Bd. dirs. Salt Lake Community Action Program, 1968—; pres. Salt Lake County unit Am. Cancer Soc., 1970-72, chmn. county crusade, 1967, bd. dirs. Utah div., 1968—; mem. advisory bd. Salvation Army; bd. dirs. Utahns for Effective Govt., Columbus Community Center; mem. Utah Republican party fin. com., 1965-68; chmn. Rep. voting dist., 1960-64, Rep. legis. dist., 1962-66; bd. dirs. Salt Lake County Young Reps., 1960-66; co-chmn. Coalition Peace Through Strength. Served to lt. (s.g.) USNR, 1956-60; col. Utah Air N.G., 1963-79; payload specialist, space shuttle mission 51D, 1985. Recipient Tom McCoy award Utah League Cities and Towns, 1972. Mem. Utah League Cities and Towns (pres. 1971-72, dir. 1968—), Nat. League Cities (1st v.p. 1973-74, hon. pres. 1975), Sigma Chi. Mormon. Club: Kiwanian. Office: 505 Dirksen Senate Bldg Washington DC 20510 *

GARNER, ROBERT EDWARD LEE, lawyer; b. Bowling Green, Ky., Sept. 26, 1946; s. Alto Luther and Katie Mae (Sanders) G.; m. Suzanne Marie Searles, Aug. 22, 1981; children: Jessica Marie, Abigail Lee. B.A., U. Ala.-Tuscaloosa, 1968; J.D., Harvard U., 1971. Bar: Ga. 1971, Ala. 1982, U.S. Dist. Ct. (no. dist.) Ga. 1974, U.S. Ct. Appeals (5th cir.) 1974, U.S. Ct. Appeals (11th cir.) 1981. Assoc., Gambrell, Russell & Forbes, Atlanta, 1972-76, ptnr., 1976-80; ptnr. Haskell, Slaughter & Young and predecessor firms, Birmingham, Ala., 1981—; sec., gen. counsel, dir. Builders Transport, Inc. Charter mem. Meadow Brook Bapt. Ch.; mem. Shelby County Rep. Com. Served to 1st lt. JAGC, USAF, 1971-72. Mem. ABA, Ga. Bar Assn., Ala. State Bar, Birmingham Bar Assn., U. Ala. Alumni Assn., Harvard U. Alumni Assn., Phi Alpha Theta, Pi Sigma Alpha. Republican. Clubs: Relay House, Cahaba Valley Lions (charter). Home: 5204 Meadow Brook Rd Birmingham AL 35243 Office: Haskell Slaughter & Young 1st Nat Southern Natural Bldg Suite 800 Birmingham AL 35203

GARNES, RONALD VINCENT, computer co. exec., fin. broker, cons.; b. Washington, Mar. 7, 1947; s. Ernest W. Love and Vauda Hall Love G.; student U. Dayton, 1965-68; B.S., U. Md., 1975; postgrad. Am. U., 1980. Adminstrv. mgr. Western Union Electronic Mail, Inc., McLean, Va., 1976; dir. mktg. Communications Cons., Inc., Silver Spring, Md., 1977; partner CAC, Washington, 1977; account mgr. PRC Computer Center, Inc., McLean, Va., 1978-79, sr. account mgr., 1979—; mktg. exec. Dun and Bradstreet Corp.; prin. Ronald V. Garnes Assos. Cons. Mem. Fairfax County Republican Com. Mem. Nat. Council Tech. Service Industries, Nat. Assn. Market Developers, Am. Entrepreneurs Assn., Internat. Assn. Bus. and Fin. Cons., Mortgage Bankers Assn. Am., Greater Washington Bd. Trade, Fairfax County C. of C. Republican. Roman Catholic. Clubs: Lincoln; U.S. Senatorial. Office: PO Box PP McLean VA 22101

GARNET, ROBERT IRA, podiatrist; b. Jersey City, Sept. 10, 1944; s. Morris Louis and Perle (Ruberman) G.; m. Avis Lorraine Polikoff, Aug. 3, 1974; children—Jenna, Michael, Jonathan. Student Bucknell U., 1962-65; D.P.M., N.Y. Coll. Podiatric Medicine, 1969. Externship, Beth Israel Hosp., N.Y.C., 1968-69; practice podiatry, Cutler Ridge, Fla., 1970—; cons. podiatrist Fusion Dance Co., Miami, Super Stars-ABC Sports, Dade County Jail and Stockade, and others; mem. staff Westchester Gen. Hosp., Miami, Jackson Meml. Hosp., Miami, Larkin Gen. Hosp., South Miami, South Dade Community Health Center, Goulds, Fla., Ambulatory Ctr., Miami, Coral Reef Gen. Hop., Miami, Bapt. Hosp., Miami, Am. Hosp., Miami; clin. assoc. prof. dept. family medicine U. Miami Med. Sch., 1972—; co-dir. Miami Runner-Road Runners Club Am., Miami, 1978—. Fellow Am. Coll. Foot Surgeons, Acad. Podiatric Sports Medicine, Acad. Ambulatory Foot Surgeons; mem. Dade County Podiatry Assn. (pres. 1976-77), Am. Podiatry Assn., Fla. Podiatry Assn., Am. Public Health Assn., Fla. Public Health Assn., Dade-Monroe Profl. Standard Rev. Orgn. Diplomate Am. Bd. Podiatric Surgery. Home: 10620 SW 127th St Miami FL 33176 Office: 18430 S Dixie Hwy Miami FL 33157

GARNIER, PHILIPPE-PIERRE, psychiatrist, psychoanalyst, educator; b. Montreuil, France, May 20, 1935; s. Jacques Jean and Pauline Adrienne (Bourgeois) G.; m. Marie-Chantal Singer, Nov. 20, 1964 (div. Apr. 1978); children: Catherine, Veronique, Karin, Brice, Violaine, Raphaele; m. Carinais Appavoupoulle, Jan. 2, 1984; 1 child, Mohini. BS in Math. and Philosophy, Paris, 1952; MD, Univ. Med. Sch., Paris, 1966. Resident various hosps., Paris, 1958-64; lectr. psychiatry, psychoanalysis Broussais Medical Sch., Paris, 1981-87; practice medicine specializing in psychiatry Paris. Contbr. Analyse Psychodrama, 1980, articles to profl. jours. Served to capt. French Air Force, 1962-64. Mem. Cartels Constituants l'Anolyse Freudienne, Soc. d'Etudes Psychodrame Freudien. Club: Soc. Hippique du Hurepoix (pres. 1986-88). Home: 2 Grand St-Villeconin, 91-580 Etrechy France Office: 205 Blvd Vincent Auriol, 75013 Paris France

GARNIER, ROBERT CHARLES, management consultant; b. Gary, Ind., June 6, 1916; s. Edward Jacob and Rose (Peters) G.; m. Katherine Mary Sulich, Aug. 17, 1940; children: Robert Charles, Katherine Rosa Garnier Kavemeier, Elizabeth Ann Garnier Moschea, John Edward. B.S. in Pub. Service Engring., Purdue U., 1939; postgrad., U. Chgo., 1940. Cert. accredited exec. in personnel Personnel Accreditation Inst. Life. Mem. staff Am. Pub. Works Assn., Chgo., 1939-41; classification officer, personnel staff officer TVA, Knoxville, Tenn., 1941-46; 1st classification examiner, then 1st chief labor negotiator City of Milw., 1946-65; city personnel dir., sec. City Service Commn., 1958-81; mgmt. cons. 1982—; pres. Fastback Ltd.; mem. Wis. Statutory Joint Study Com. Civil Service, 1965-66. Author articles, chpt. in book. Mem. Am. Pub. Works Assn. (life; exec. council Inst. Adminstrv. Mgmt. 1978-83), Internat. Personnel Mgmt. Assn. (pres. 1977; hon. life), Indsl. Relations Research Assn. (pres. Wis. 1965-66, sec.-treas. 1971-81; life), Internat. City Mgmt. Assn., Am. Soc. Personnel Adminstrn., Mcpl. Employers Assn. Wis. (hon., life), Milw. Area Soc. Pub. Adminstrn. (pres. 1954-55), Purdue U. Alumni Assn. Roman Catholic. Home: 9611 W Lorraine Pl Milwaukee WI 53222

GARON, OLIVIER MARIE, broadcast executive; b. Lyon, France, Jan. 21, 1946; s. Fernand and Medeleine (Emery) G.; m. Edith Marmonier, July 18, 1970; children: Charlotte, Antoine, Philippe. Lic. en droit, U. Clermont-Ferrand, 1970. Tax inspector Direction des Services Fiscaux, Basse Terre, Guadeloupe, 1970-72; sec. gen. Assocanne-Coderum, Pointe a Pitre, Guadeloupe, 1972-77; attaché direction Reynoird S.A., Fort de France, Martinique, 1977-80; gen. mgr. Radio Caribbean 1978 Ltd., Fort de France, 1980-82, Radio Caribbean 1982 Ltd., Fort de France, 1982—. Clubs: Union des Anciens des Impôts (Paris). Home: La Ferme Redoute, 97200 Fort de France Martinique Office: Radio Caraibes Internat, B P 1111, 97248 Fort de France Martinique

GARRETT, CHARLES GEOFFREY BLYTHE, physicist, communications development administrator; b. Ashford, Kent, Eng., Sept. 15, 1925; s. Charles Alfred Blythe and Laura Mary (Lotinga) G. B.A. in Natural Scis., Trinity Coll., Cambridge U., Eng., 1946; M.A. in Natural Scis., Ph.D. in Physics, Cambridge U., 1950. Instr. physics Harvard U., 1950-52; mem. tech. staff Bell Labs., Murray Hill, N.J., 1952-54; supr. Bell Labs., 1955-56, dept. head, 1960-69; dir. AT&T Bell Labs., Murray Hill-Morristown, N.J., 1969—; chmn. Gordon Conf. on non-linear optics, 1964. Author: Magnetic Cooling, 1954, Gas Lasers, 1963; contbr. articles to profl. jours.; patentee in field. Named knight of Sovereign Order St. John of Jerusalem (Orthodox). Fellow Am. Phys. Soc., IEEE; mem. Guild of Carillonneurs in N.Am. Episcopalian. Home: 41 Elm St Morristown NJ 07960 Office: AT&T Bell Labs 600 Mountain Ave Murray Hill NJ 07974

GARRETT, DAVID CLYDE, JR., airline executive; b. Norris, S.C., July 0, 1922; s. David Clyde and Mary H. G.; m. Lu Thomasson, Sept. 11, 1947; children: David, Virginia, Charles. BA, Furman U., 1942; MS, Ga. Inst. Tech., 1955. With Delta Air Lines, Inc., Atlanta, 1946-87, pres., from 1971, chief exec. officer, 1978-87, chmn., 1984-87, now chmn. exec. com., 1987—, also dir.; dir. Travelers Corp., U.S. Steel, Nat. Service Ind. Served with USAAF, 1943-46. Office: Delta Air Lines Inc Hartsfield Atlanta Internat Airport Atlanta GA 30320

GARRETT, GEORGE PALMER, JR., language professional, educator, writer; b. Orlando, Fla., June 11, 1929; s. George Palmer and Rosalie (Toomer) G.; m. Susan Parrish Jackson, June 14, 1952; children: William, George, Rosalie. Grad., Hill Sch., 1947; A.B., Princeton U., 1952, M.A., 1956, Ph.D., 1985. Asst. prof. English Wesleyan U.; writer-in-residence, resident fellow in creative writing Princeton U., 1964-65; former assoc. prof. U. Va.; prof. English Hollins Coll. Va., 1967-71; prof. U. S.C., Columbia, 1971-73, Princeton U., 1974-78, U. Mich., 1979-80, 83-84; Hoyns prof. creative writing U. Va., Charlottesville, 1984—; prof. Bennington Coll., 1980. Author: The Reverend Ghost: Poems (Poets of Today IV), 1957, King of the Mountain, 1958, The Sleeping Gypsy and Other Poems, 1958, The Finished Man, 1959, Which Ones Are the Enemy, 1961; poems Abraham's Knife, 1961; In the Briar Patch, 1961; play Sir Slob and the Princess, 1962; Cold Ground Was My Bed Last Night, 1964; screenplay The Young Lovers, 1964; Do, Lord, Remember Me, 1965, For a Bitter Season, 1967, A Wreath for Garibaldi, 1969, Death of the Fox, 1971, The Magic Striptease, 1973, Welcome to the Medicine Show, Postcards/Flashcards/Snapshots, 1978, To Recollect a Cloud of Ghosts: Christmas in England 1602-03, 1979, Luck's Shining Child: Poems, 1981, The Succession: A Novel of Elizabeth and James, 1983, The Collected Poems of George Garrett, 1984, James Jones, 1984; An Evening Performance: New and Selected Short Stories, 1985; Poison Pen, 1986, Understanding Mary Lee Settle, 1988; editor: The Girl in The Black Raincoat, 1966, The Sounder Few, 1971, The Writer's Voice, 1973, Botteghe Oscure Reader, 1975, Intro 8: The Liar's Craft, 1977, Intro 9: Close to Home, 1978. Served in occupation of Trieste, Austria and Germany. Recipient Rome prize Am. Acad. Arts and Letters, 1958-59, Sewanee Rev. fellow poetry, 1958-59, Am. Acad. and Inst. of Letters award, 1985; named Cultural Laureate of Va., 1986; Ford Found. grantee in drama, 1960; Nat. Found. of Arts grantee, 1966; Guggenheim fellow, 1974. Fellow Am. Acad. in Rome; mem. MLA, Author's League, Writers Guild Am. East, Poetry Soc. Am., PEN. Democrat. Episcopalian. Home: 1845 Wayside Pl Charlottesville VA 22903 Office: Dept English Univ Virginia Charlottesville VA 22903

GARRETT, PAMELA DENISE, educator; b. Los Angeles, Nov. 2, 1954; d. Travis and Bette Jean (Perkins) G. B.A. in Child Devel. Calif. State U.-Los Angeles, 1976; A.A. in Psychology, West Los Angeles Coll., 1974. Tchrs. credential, Calif. Tchr.'s aide Los Angeles Unified Sch. Dist., 1975-76, tchr. Children's Ctr., 1977-79; tchr. Marcus Garvey Pre-Sch., Los Angeles, 1976-77; tchr. Compton Unified Sch. Dist. (Calif.), 1979—, Stephen C. Foster Elem. Sch., 1981-87, George Washington Carver Elem. Sch. 1987—; cons. Mary Kay Cosmetics, Inc., 1975—; asst. dir., mem. bd. Creative Learning Inst., Compton, Calif., 1983—; travel cons. L.A. By Pam, sight seeing tours. Mem. Nat. Council Negro Women, Calif. Tchrs. Assn., Internat. Platform Assn., Research Council of Scripps Clinic and Research Found., Nat. Assn. Female Entrepreneurs, Tau Gamma Delta, Phi Delta Kappa. Democrat. Baptist. Home: 847 E 116th Pl Los Angeles CA 90059

GARRETT, ROBERT STEPHENS, public relations executive; b. Bell, Calif., July 12, 1937; s. Sammie Jacob and Martha Ethelwynn (Dench) G.; m. Mary Lynn Harris, Sept. 9, 1955 (div. July 1972); children: Lisa, Julie, Kim; m. Camille Ann Priestley, Feb. 15, 1975; children: Lee Ann, Nikki, Grant. Grad. high sch., Downey, Calif. From machinist to head shipping dept. Axelson Mfg. Co., Vernon, Calif., 1955-60; prodn. control planner, methods analyst autonetics div. Rockwell Internat., Downey, Compton and Anaheim, Calif., 1960-70; pub. relations mgr., property mgr., clinic coordinator, investigator, property researcher and chief adminstr. bd. UMEDCO Inc., Long Beach, Calif., 1970-77; dir. ops. Regency Mgmt. Service, Anaheim, 1977-78; cons. med. pub. relations Garden Grove, Calif., 1978—. Bd. dirs. Boys Club of Garden Grove, 1978—, Girls Club of Garden Grove, 1980—, treas. 1983-84, v.p. 1984-86, pres. 1986; traffic commr. City of Garden Grove, 1981—; vice chmn. traffic commn., 1988—. Republican. Lodges: Rotary (bd. dirs. Paramount 1975-76, Garden Grove club 1978-79), Elks. Office: PO Box 1221 Garden Grove CA 92642

GARRETTO, LEONARD ANTHONY, JR., insurance company executive; b. N.Y.C., Apr. 13, 1925; s. Leonard and Evenia (Egidio) G.; B.E.E., Manhattan Coll., 1951; m. Theresa Cennamo, Aug. 6, 1949; children—Deborah, Mark, Michael, Paula, David. Engr., Gen. Precision Lab. Inc., Pleasantville, N.Y., 1951-53, project adminstr., 1953-55, project mgr., 1955-58, subcontracts mgr., 1958-59; adminstrv. engr. Sperry Systems Mgmt. div. Sperry Rand Corp., Great Neck, N.Y., 1959-61, mgmt. services adminstr., 1961-63, mgmt. services mgr., 1963-65, fin. planning mgr., 1965-66, planning mgr., 1966-68, dir. adminstrn., 1968; agt. First Investors Corp., N.Y.C., 1966-69, dist. mgr., 1969-70; gen. mgr. David Gracer Co., N.Y.C., 1970-72; v.p. regional sales Somerset Capital Corp., N.Y.C., 1972-75; regional dir. Wis. Nat. Life Ins. Co., Oshkosh, 1975-77, regional sales v.p., Englewood Cliffs, N.J., 1977-84, sr. regional sales v.p., 1984-86, area sales v.p., Stroudsburg, Pa., 1986—. Served with U.S. Army, 1943-45; ETO. Mem. Am. Soc. Nataries, Nat. Assn. Life Underwriters. Democrat. Roman Catholic. Office: Wis Nat Life Ins Co 804 Sarah St Suite 103 Stroudsburg PA 18360

GARRIDO ATENAS, JORGE, surgeon, surgical educator; b. Santiago, Chile, Apr. 15, 1940; s. Jorge Garrido and Mariá Atenas; m. Isabela Beiztegui Saracibar, Jan. 14, 1972; children—Beatriz, Julio, Eduardo. M.D., U. Madrid, Spain, 1968, Specialist in cardiovascular surgery U. Madrid, 1971; specialist in pulmonary surgery, U. Zaragoza, 1974, specialist in caridology, 1977; physician Chilean Consulate, Madrid, 1968-71; physician LAN-Chile Airline, Madrid, 1970-72; resident cardiovascular diseases and cardiovascular surgery Fundación Jiménez Díaz, Madrid, 1967-71; assoc. prof. cardiovascular surgery U. Navarra, 1980—; mem. Red Cross Confs., Pamplona, 1980-83; participant 34 nat. and internat. congresses, 1976-83. Contbr. articles to profl. jours. Inst. de Cultura Hispanica grantee, 1963-66. Mem. Soc. Española de Cirugía Cardiovascular, Soc. Española de Cardiologia, Soc. European de Cirugia Cardiovascular, Internat. Cardiovascular Soc. Roman Catholic. Clubs: Pamplona Tennis; Pamplona Golf. Avocation: classical music.

GARRIGLE, WILLIAM ALOYSIUS, lawyer; b. Camden, N.J. Aug. 6, 1941; s. John Michael and Catherine Agnes (Ebeling) G.; m. Jeannette R. Regan, Aug. 15, 1965 (div.); children—Maeve Regan, Emily Way; m. Rosalind Chadwick, Feb. 17, 1984; 1 child, Susan Chadwick. B.S., LaSalle Coll., 1963; LL.B., Boston Coll., 1966. Bar: N.J. 1966, U.S. Dist. Ct. N.J. 1966, U.S. Ct. Appeals (3d cir.) 1973, U.S. Supreme Ct. 1973; cert. civil trial atty. Assoc. Taylor, Bischoff, Neutze & Williams, Camden 1966-67; assoc. Moss & Powell Camden 1967-70; ptnr. Garrigle & Palm and predecessors Cherry Hill, N.J. 1970—. Served with USAR, 1959-67. Mem. ABA, N.J. State Bar Assn., Burlington County Bar Assn., Camden County Bar Assn., Internat. Assn. Ins. Csl., Def. Research Inst., Fedn. of Ins. and Corp. Counsel, Trial Attys. N.J., Camden County Inn of Ct. (sr.). Clubs: Moorestown (N.J.) Field; Atlantic City Country (Northfield, N.J.); Downtown (Phila.); Tavistock Country (Haddonfield, N.J.). Home: 223 E Main St Moorestown NJ 08057 Office: 2 W Evesham Ave Cherry Hill NJ 08003

GARRISON, RAY HARLAN, lawyer; b. Allen County, Ky., Aug. 6, 1922; s. Emmett Washington and Ollie Irene (Keen) G.; m. Eunice Anne Bolz, Oct. 7, 1961. B.A., Western Ky. U., 1942; M.A., U. Ky., 1944; postgrad., Northwestern U., 1945-46; J.D., U. Chgo., 1949. Bar: Ky. 1951, Ill. 1962, U.S. Ct. Appeals 1962, U.S. Tax Ct. 1962, U.S. Ct. Internat. Trade 1968, U.S. Supreme Ct. 1980. Tax acct. Ky. Dept. Revenue, Frankfort, 1943, supr. escheats, 1944-45, fiscal analyst, 1945; research asst. Bur. Bus. Research, U. Ky., Lexington, 1943-44; research assoc. Fedn. Tax Adminstrs., Chgo., 1946-52; spl. atty. U.S. Dept. Treasury, St. Louis, 1952-57; spl. asst. U.S. Dept. Treasury, 1957-59, asst. regional counsel, 1959-61; sr. counsel Internat. Harvester Co., Chgo., 1961-86; gen. tax atty. Navistar Internat. Corp., Chgo., 1986—; lectr. Loyola U., Chgo., 1949-51. Contbr. articles to various publs. Mem. Ill. Racing Bd., 1975—; mem. adv. bd. Ill. Thoroughbred Breeders Fund, 1976-80. Mem. NAM (taxation com. 1969—), Ill. Mfrs. Assn. (taxation com. 1969—), Motor Vehicle Mfrs. Assn. (taxation com. 1963—), ABA, Ill. Bar Assn., Ky. Bar Assn., Chgo. Bar Assn., Nat. Assn. State Racing Commrs., Chgo. Tax Club, South Suburban Geneal. and Hist. Soc. (bd. dirs. 1973-77), Ky. Hist. Soc., Mecklenburg Hist. Assn., Beta Gamma Sigma. Club: Filson. Home: 2625-F Hawthorne Ln Flossmoor IL 60422 Office: 401 N Michigan Ave Chicago IL 60611

GARRISON, WILLIAM LLOYD, cemeterian; b. Ridgway, Pa., Dec. 26, 1939; s. Lloyd and Mary Rebecca (Morrow) G.; m. Mary Jo Florio, May 30, 1964; children: David, Mark. BA in Psychology, Ohio Wesleyan U., 1962; postgrad. Garrett Theol. Sem., 1962-63; MSW, Fla. State U., 1967; MS in Mgmt., Case Western Res. U., 1976. Caseworker Mpls. Ct. Chgo., 1963-64, United Cerebral Palsy Assn., Phila., 1964-65; psychiat. social worker Bellefaire, Shaker Heights, Ohio, 1967-74; dir. personnel and tng. Ctr. Human Services, Cleve., 1974-81, dir. resource devel., 1981-83; exec. dir. Cleve. Soc. for the Blind, 1983-85, Cleve. Eye Bank, 1983-85; exec. v.p. Lake View Cemetery Assn., Cleve., 1985-87, pres., 1987—; v.p. Lake View Cemetery Found., Cleve., 1988—; adj. prof. Sch. Applied Social Sci., Case Western Res. U., 1974-80; v.p. E.A. Mabry Inc., Akron, Ohio, 1970—. Dist. chmn. Cub Scouts, 1978-81, dist. chmn. Boy Scouts Am., 1981-84, scoutmaster, 1983-87, mem. exec. bd. council, 1981—, asst. council commr., 1984-87; v.p. Boy Scouting, 1987—; active personnel com. Lake Erie council Girl Scouts U.S.; mem. Big Bros. Cleve., 1968-73; pres. Mayfield Heights Homeowners Assn., 1974-84; bd. dirs. Garfield Meml. United Meth. Ch., 1979-81; bd. dirs. Cuyahoga County Reach Out Services, 1977—; mem. United Way Services of Cleve. Assembly, 1987—. Recipient Merit award Boy Scouts Am., 1980, Silver Beaver award, 1984; Menninger Found. fellow. Mem. Acad Cert. Social Workers, Nat. Assn. Social Workers, Am. Soc. Personnel Administrs., Personnel Accreditation Inst., Am. Cemetery Assn., Ohio Assn. Cemetery Supts. and Ofcls., Greater Cleve. Cemetery Assn. (pres. 1987—), Nat. Eagle Scout Assn., Greater Cleve. Personnel Council, Social Agys. Employees Union (pres. 1970-73), Greater Cleve. Growth Assn., St. Luke's Hosp. Assn., Delta Tau Delta, Phi Mu Alpha. Lodge: Rotary. Clubs: Cleveland, Univ. Circle Inc., Am. Field Service, Cleve. Play House. Office: Lake View Cemetery Assn 12316 Euclid Ave Cleveland OH 44106

GARRITY, RODMAN FOX, psychologist, educator; b. Los Angeles, June 10, 1922; s. Lawrence Hitchcock and Margery Fox (Pugh) G.; m. Juanita Daphne Mullan, Mar. 5, 1948; children—Diana Daphne, Ronald Fox. Student, Los Angeles City Coll., 1946-47; B.A., Calif. State U., Los Angeles, 1950; M.A., So. Meth. U., Dallas, 1955; Ed.D., U. So. Calif., 1963. Tchr. elem. sch. Palmdale (Calif.) Sch. Dist., 1952-54; psychologist, prin. Redondo Beach (Calif.) City Schs., 1954-60; asst. dir. ednl. placement lectr., ednl. adviser U. So. Calif., 1960-62; asso. prof., coordinator credentials programs Calif. State Poly. U., Pomona, 1962-66; chmn. social sci. dept. Calif. State Poly. U., 1966-68, dir. tchr. preparation center, 1968-71, coordinator grad. program, 1971-73, prof. tchr. preparation center, 1968—, coordinator spl. edn. programs, 1979—; cons. psychologist, lectr. in field. Pres. Redondo Beach Coordinating Council, 1958-60; mem. univ. rep. Calif. Faculty Assns., 1974-76. Served with Engr. Combat Bn. AUS, 1942-45. Mem. Prins. Assn. Redondo Beach (chmn. 1958-60), Nat. Congress Parents and Tchrs. (hon. life), Am. Psychol. Assn., Calif. Tchrs. Assn. Democrat. Office: Calif State U Pomona CA 91768

GARRŌN DE DORYAN, VICTORIA, government official, educator; b. Oct. 8, 1920; d. Stanislao Garrōn Lermitte and Claudia Oroxco Casorla; m. Edward Doryan, Mar. 1, 1951 (dec.); 1 child, Eduardo. Prof. Escuela Nornal de Heredia, 1942, N. Am.—Costa Rican Cultural Ctr., 1946-48, U. Costa Rica, 1946-55; dir. Liceo Anastasia Alfaro, 1956-72; now 2d v.p. Republic of Costa Rica; pres. Coll. Bachelors in Letters and Philosophy, 1951-53, 55-57, 63-65; treas. Inst. Infantile Lit., 1983-85; sec. Pro Edn. Assn. of Young and Blind, 1980-85; v.p. Ateneo de Costa Rica, 1983-85; permanent sec. Costa Rican Commn. of Coop., UNESCO, Paris, 1960-75; del. XII World Conf. Edn., Geneva, 1949. Contbr. articles to profl. publs. Decorated Order of Bright Star (Republic of China); recipient Honor of Merit award Union of Am. Women, 1979, 86; gymnasium dedicated to her name Colegio Anastasio Alfaro, 1973. Mem. Costa Rican Assn. Univ. Women (pres. 1974, 75, 77), Costa Rican Assn. Authors (v.p. 1962, 63, 74, 75, sec. 1969-70). Democrat. Roman Catholic. Home: PO Box 2233, 1000 San Jose Costa Rica Office: PO Box 520, 2050 Zapote, Casa Presidencial, San Jose Costa Rica *

GARRONE, GABRIEL MARIE CARDINAL, former archbishop of Toulouse; b. Aix-les-Bains, France, Oct. 12, 1901; s. Jean and Josephine (Mathieu) G.; Diploma Advanced Studies in Philosophy; Doctorate Scholastic Philosophy and Theology; licence ès lettres in Philosophie, certificat d'etudes Supérieures de Philosophie. Ordained priest Roman Catholic Ch., 1925; prof., superior Grand Sem. Chambery; archbishop-coadjutor Toulouse, 1947; archbishop of Toulouse and Narbonne, primate Gaule narbonnaise, 1956-66; v.p. Permanent Council Plenary Assembly French Episcopate, 1964-66; pro-prefect Congregation for Cath. Edn. Rome, 1966, prefect, 1968; chargé des Rapports de L'Eglise avec la Culture, 1980; created cardinal, 1967. Decorated grand cross Legion of Honor, Croix de Guerre. Author: Psalms and Prayers; Invitation to Prayer; Lessons on Faith; The Credo's Moral; The Door to Scriptures; Holy Church Out Mother; The Credo's Panorama; There is Your Mother; Catholic Action; Faith and Pedagogy; The Eucharist; Why Pray?; The Nun, Sign of God in the World; Psalms, Prayer for Today; Offers to God and to the World; Lord, Tell Me Your Name; Christian Morals and Human Values; What Must One Believe?; Le Concile, Orientations; Lumen Gentium; Gaudium et spes; Qu'est-ce que Dieu? L'Eucharistie au secours de la foi; Religieuse aujourd'hui? Oui, mais..., 1969; translations: What God Is; What Theresa of Lisieux Believed; Eucharistic and Belief; Que faut-il faire? Ce que croyait Pascal; L'Eglise 1965-72; la Foi en 1973; la Foi au fil des jours; Le Credo lu dans l'histoire; Pour vous qui sus-je? Allerjusqu'à Dieu; Le Prêtre; Marie, hier et aujourd'hui; Parole et Eucharistie; La Foi tout entiè re; Je suis le Chemin; Ceque croyait Jeanne Jugan; Ce que croyait Anne-Marie Javouhey; 50 ans de vie d'Eglise; Synode 85; La Communion fraternelle "dernière volontē" du Seigneur: Pour une prēsentation sommaire et ordonnē de la foi. Address: Largo del Colonnato 3, 00193 Rome Italy

GARRY, JACQUELYNN LEE, holding corporation executive; b. Salem, N.J., Mar. 11, 1957; d. Henry Edward Klingler and Josephine Sarah (Poulson) Parker. Student, Delcastle Vocat. Tech. Inst., 1975; AA, AS, Fort Steilacoom Community Coll., AS in Bus., AS in Broadcasting; student, L.H. Bates Vocat. Tech. Inst., 1979-80. Mgr. inventory control, pub. relations McDonalds of Wilmington, Del., 1974-77; sales account rep. Rainbow of Tacoma/Auburn, Wash., 1977-80; mgmt. trainee Agy. Rent-A-Car, Wash., 1980; sales mgr. Puget (Wash.) Mobilex Inc., 1980-82; planning specialist Bus. Ins. Assocs., 1982, Target Ins. Bus. Service, 1982-84; chief exec. officer Just Like Gold, Inc., San Diego, 1983—. Dir. TV including The Music Hour, Meet the Candidates; co-dir. film The Great Am. Masacare; producer TV The Fashinable Female, (co-producer) Condomania; author newspaper columns The Fashionable Female, 1984-85. Served with USAF, 1974-77. Mem. Ch. Religious Sci.

GARSON, ROBERT ANTHONY, historian, educator; b. London, Mar. 25, 1946; s. Gustav and Selma Rachel (Meinbach) G.; m. Yvonne Garson, Sept. 25, 1967 (div. 1981); children: Sonia, Adrian; m. Victoria Alexandra Webster. BA, U. Sussex, Eng., 1967; PhD, London Sch. Econs., 1971. Lectr. U.S. History U. Keele, Knutsford, Eng., 1970—. Author: Democratic Party and the Politics of Sectionalism, 1974; contbr. articles to profl. jours. Fulbright scholar, 1968. Jewish. Office: U Keele, Keele England

GARSON, WILLIAM DONALD, publishing company executive; b. Phila., May 25, 1927; s. William Roy and Anne (Reilly) G.; B.S., Temple U., 1950; postgrad. N.Y. U., 1963-64; m. Mildred L. Baughman, Sept. 11, 1965; 1 son, Graham Donald. Office and personnel mgr. Ward Wheelock Co., Phila., 1950-54; gen. mgr. Met. Reporting, N.Y.C., 1954-57; asst. to pres. Willard Alexander, Inc., N.Y.C., 1957-60; promotion copy chief N.Y. Mirror, 1960-63; promotion mgr. Saturday Rev. mag., N.Y.C., 1963-66; dir. sales promotion, research and public relations, Forbes Inc., N.Y.C., 1966-78, dir. corp. communications, 1978—; dir. corp. communications Sangre de Cristo Ranches Inc., 1978—, Fiji Forbes, 1978—; mem. exec. com. Pub. Hall of Fame, 1986. Served with USNR, 1945-46. Recipient Ace award for advt. communications excellence Bus. and Profl. Advt. Assn., 1978. Mem. Mag. promotion Group (v.p., dir. 1971-72), Media Research Dirs. Assn. (v.p. 1971-72 pres. 1972-73), Am. Mktg. Assn. Home: 19 Kempster Rd Scarsdale NY 10583 Office: 60 Fifth Ave New York NY 10011

GARSON, WILLIAM J., writer, editor, historian; b. Hammond, Ind., May 1, 1917; s. John Soteriou and Helen Glenn (McKennan) G.; B.A., Milton Coll., 1939; postgrad. Grad. Sch. Bank Mktg., Northwestern U., 1968; m. Florence Rebecca Penstone, Sept. 21, 1974; children—Geneva Garson Swing, Gary William. Mng. editor, reporter, columnist Rockford (Ill.) Register-Republic, 1939-55; pub. relations dir. Sundstrand Corp., Rockford, 1956-65; community info. officer Rockford C. of C., 1965-66; mktg. dir. City Nat. Bank & Trust Co. Rockford, 1966-82; pub. relations cons. imagination plus, Rockford, 1955—. Bd. dirs. Tb Assn., Heart Assn., ARC, 1952-54; Recipient George Washington Honor medals Freedoms Found., 1965-66. Mem. Am. Interprofl. Inst. (local pres.), Rockford C. of C. (Community Service award 1952, dir.), Am. Inst. Banking, Bank Mktg. Assn., Internat. Assn. Bus. Communicators, Internat. Word Processing Assn., Rockford Hist. Soc. (pres., treas.). Methodist. Author: Daddy Wore An Apron, 1974; Brother Earth, 1975; The Knight on Broadway, 1978; Rockford-The Pet Food Story, 1923-87 (One Chapter in the History of the Quaker Oats Company), 1987; also numerous short stories and articles; co-author: Political Primer, 1960; We The People..., 1976; Forest City Firelog, 1982; hist. cons. Wordprints in the Sands of Time, 1984—. Home: 3516 Meadow Ln Rockford IL 61107 Office: Box 3126 Rockford IL 61106

GARTEL, LAURENCE MAURY, video computer photographer, artist; b. N.Y.C., June 5, 1956; s. Henry and Carol (Rosenblum) G. B.F.A., Sch. Visual Arts, 1977. Computer cover artist Computer Design mag., Littleton, Mass., 1981-82; instr. creative photography workshop Sch. Visual Arts, N.Y.C., 1978-83; computer cover illustrator Nikkei Computer mag., Tokyo, 1982, 83, 84, 85; computer illustrator Scholastic Publishing, N.Y.C., 1984—, Psychology Today mag., Washington, 1983, 84, 85, Zoommag, 1986, School Arts mag., New Orleans, 1986; prof. computer graphics Sch. Visual Arts, N.Y.C., 1983—; judge Pan Pacific Computer Art Competition, Melbourne, Australia, 1985. Exhibits include Nikon House Gallery, N.Y.C., 1980, ACM Siggraph, Detroit, 1983, San Francisco, 1985, Dallas, 1986, computer art Mus. Art U. Okla., Norman, 1982, Long Beach Mus. Art (Calif.), 1983, Princeton U. Art Mus., 1983, Bronx Mus. Art, N.Y., 1987-88, Fine Arts Mus. of L.I., N.Y., 1988 and touring; art work in lending collection Mus. Modern Art, N.Y.C., 1981, Bibliotheque Nationale, Paris, 1985, Long Beach (Calif.) Mus., 1986; contbr. articles to profl. jours. Recipient N.J. Art Dirs. Club award, 1985. Exptl. TV Ctr. grantee, 1978-88; Polaroid Corp. grantee, 1985-88; Intermedia Art Center grantee, 1984; Film and Video Arts residency Grantee, 1987. Address: 270-16B Grand Central Pkwy Floral Park NY 11005

GARTENBERG, SEYMOUR LEE, recording company executive; b. N.Y.C., May 27, 1931; s. Morris and Anna (Banner) G.; m. Anna Stassi, Feb. 18, 1956; children: Leslie, Karen, Mark. BBA cum laude, CCNY, 1952. Asst. controller Finlay Straus, Inc., N.Y.C., 1950-56; controller Tappin's Inc., Newark, 1956; exec. v.p. Columbia House div. CBS, N.Y.C., 1956-73; pres. CBS Toys Div., Cranbury, N.J., 1973-78; v.p. CBS/Columbia Group, N.Y.C., 1978—; sr. group v.p. CBS Records Group, 1979-87; exec. v.p. CBS Records Inc., 1987—. V.p., bd. dirs. City Coll. Fund; treas., bd. dirs. T.J. Martell Found. Leukemia Research. Mem. Mill Island Civic Assn., Nat. Assn. Accts., Am. Mgmt. Assn. Office: 51 W 52d St New York NY 10019

GARTNER, LLOYD PHILIP, historian, educator; b. N.Y.C., June 3, 1927; s. Hyman and Betty P. (Miller) G.; m. Ruth S. Hagler, Oct. 8, 1961; children: Moshe Reuben, Eva Miriam. BA, Bklyn. Coll., 1948; MA, U. Pa., 1949; PhD, Columbia U., 1957. Successively research assoc., instr., asst. prof. history Jewish Theol. Sem. Am., N.Y.C., 1958-67; assoc. prof. history CCNY, 1967-73; grad. faculty CUNY, 1967-73; prof. modern Jewish history Tel-Aviv U., Ramat-Aviv, Israel, 1973—, Spiegel Family Found. prof. European Jewish history, 1978—; vis. prof. Hebrew U., Jerusalem, 1970-72, Yale U., 1976, U. Cape Town (Rep. of South Africa), 1984, Yeshiva U., N.Y.C., 1985. Author 7 books and numerous articles in modern Jewish history; mem. editorial bd. 5 profl. jours. Served with U.S. Army, 1946-47. Fellow Am. Acad. Jewish Research; mem. World Union Jewish Studies, Hist. Soc. Israel (exec. council), Jewish Hist. Soc. Eng., Israel Assn. Am. Studies (founder, pres. 1977-81). Home: 40 Shimoni St, Jerusalem Israel Office: Tel-Aviv U, Ramat-Aviv Israel

GARUTTI FERRACUTI, MIRELLA ANNA, psychologist, educator; b. Torre Pellice, Turin, Italy, Mar. 8, 1931; d. Guido and Giulia Margherita (Salomon) Garutti; m. Franco Ferracuti, Jan. 26, 1955; children: Stefano, Daniele. MA in Journalism, U. Social Studies, Rome, 1955; PhD in Psychology, U. Rome, 1987. Asst. prof. U. P.R., San Juan, 1956-57, 59-60; translator various books and articles, 1956—. Editor criminological textbooks. Roman Catholic. Home: Via G Marchi 3, 00161 Rome Italy

GARVIN, THOMAS CHRISTOPHER, educator, researcher; b. Dublin, Ireland, July 7, 1943; s. John and Kathleen (Daly) G.; m. Maire Treasa Tuomey, July 23, 1969; children: Cliona, Anna, John. BA, Univ. Coll., Dublin, 1964, MA, 1966; PhD, U. Ga., 1974. Lectr. Univ. Coll. Dublin, 1967—; fellow Wilson Ctr. Smithsonian Instn., 1983-84; Fulbright prof. in comparative politics Mt. Holyoke Coll., South Hadley, Mass., 1987-88. Author: Evolution of Irish Nationalist Politics, 1981, Nationalist Revolutionaries in Ireland, 1987; contbr. articles to profl. jours. Home: Ardeevin, Upper Kilmacud Rd, Dundrum Dublin 14 Ireland Office: Univ Coll, Belfield, Dublin 4 Ireland

GARY, JAMES FREDERICK, business executive; b. Chgo., Dec. 28, 1920; s. Rex Inglis and Mary Naomi (Roller) G.; m. Helen Elizabeth Gellert, Sept. 3, 1947; children: David Frederick, John William, James Scott, Mary Anne. BS, Haverford (Pa.) Coll., 1942. With Wash. Energy Co. and predecessors, Seattle, 1947-67; v.p. Wash. Energy Co., 1956-67; pres., chief exec. officer Pacific Resources Inc., Honolulu, 1967-79, chmn., chief exec. officer, 1979-84, chmn., 1985, chmn. emeritus, 1986—; bd. dirs. Bancorp. Hawaii, Inc., Bank of Hawaii, Castle & Cooke, Inc., Wash. Energy Co., Seattle, Wash. Nat. Gas Co., Airborne Freight Corp., Seattle, GDC, Inc., Chgo., Petroleum Industry Research Found., Inc., N.Y. Pres. Chief Seattle council Boy Scouts Am., 1966-67, Aloha council, 1973-74; mem. Nat. Council, 1964—, v.p. western region, 1978-85, pres., 1985—, also bd. dirs.; chmn. Aloha United Way, 1978, pres., 1979, chmn., pres., 1980; bd. regents U. Hawaii, 1981—; trustee Linfield Coll., McMinnville, Oreg.; bd. mgrs. Haverford Coll.; adv. bd. Kamehameha Schs., Honolulu; bd. dirs. Research Corp. of U. Hawaii, 1971-77, chmn., 1974-77; bd. dirs., officer and trustee Oahu Devel. Conf., Hawaii Employers Council, Hawaii Loa Coll., Friends of East-West Ctr., Honolulu Symphony Soc., East-West Ctr. Internat. Found.; chmn. The Hawaii Community Found. Served to capt. AUS, 1942-46. Recipient Distinguished Eagle award Boy Scouts Am., 1972, Silver Beaver award Boy Scouts Am., 1966, Silver Antelope award Boy Scouts Am., 1976, Silver Buffalo award Boy Scouts Am., 1988. Mem. Am. Gas Assn. (bd. dirs. 1970-74), Pacific Gas Assn. (pres. 1974; Basford trophy 1960), Nat. LP-Gas Assn. (bd. dirs. 1967-70), Am. Petroleum Inst., Inst. Gas Tech. (trustee 1975-86), Hawaii Econ. Council, Nat. Petroleum Council, Hawaii Dist. Export Council, Japan-Western Assn., Japan-Hawaii Econ. Council, U.S Nat. Com. Pacific Econ. Cooperation, Pacific Basin Econ. Council (chmn. U.S. com. 1985-86), Japan-Am. Soc. Honolulu, Pacific Forum, Honolulu Commn. on Fgn. Relations, Hawaii C. of C. (chmn. 1979). Episcopalian. Clubs: Pacific Union (San Francisco); Oahu Country, Waialae Country, Outrigger Canoe, Pacific, Plaza (Honolulu); Seattle Tennis, Wash. Athletic (Seattle), Rainier. Office: Pacific Resources Inc 733 Bishop St PO Box 3379 Honolulu HI 96842

GARZONETTI, JEFFREY ROCCO, probation officer; b. Chgo., June 25, 1953; s. Angelo Rocco and Emily Mary (Schmidt) G.; A.S. in Police Adminstrn., Triton Coll., 1974; student U. Ill., Chgo., 1975; B.A. in Polit. Sci., DePaul U., 1976, M.S. in Pub. Adminstrn./Mgmt. Scis., 1982. Desk officer Triton Coll. Police Dept., 1972-74; ramp service Flying Tiger Cargo Line, Chgo., 1974-75; clk., messenger Kirkland & Ellis, Chgo., 1975-76; bus operator Chgo. Transit Authority, summers 1975-76; adult probation officer Cook County, Chgo., 1977—; personal probation officer, investigator for Presiding Judge Dist. 4, Frank Barbaro, Criminal and Civil Div.; supr. Criminal Div. for Chief Judge Richard Fitzgerald, Supr. Dist. 4 Mcpl. Div. Founder Creative Impressions, 1982; part-time in-house plain clothes security officer and investigator Marriott O'Hare, Chgo. Chmn. social com. young adult div. Joint Civic Com. of Italian Americans, 1977-78, pres., 1978—; precinct capt. 36th Ward Regular Democratic Orgn., 1972—. Served to comdr., 1st lt. CAP/USAF Aux. Lic. pilot. Mem. Ill. Probation and Court Services Assn., Airplane Owners and Pilots Assn., DePaul U. Alumni Assn., Amateur Trapman's Assn. Roman Catholic (mem. Holy Cross Council). Lodge: K.C.

GASBARRO, LOUIS DONALD, safety director; b. Tampa, Fla., Nov. 23, 1937; s. Ernest A. and Rose M. (Iasa) G.; children: Mark, Glen, David, Donald. BS, U. Nebr., 1970; AS, Hillsborough Community Coll., 1983; MS in Criminal Justice, Nova U., 1981. Cert. risk mgr., Fla. Enlisted airman USAF, 1956, advanced through grades to capt., 1980, spl. agt. Office Spl. Investigation, 1970-80, resigned, 1980; tchr. Hillsborough County Sch. System, Tampa, Fla., 1980-81; coordinator safety and security County Hosp. Authority, Tampa, 1981-83, dir. safety and security, 1983—; pres., cons. Loss Prevention Inc., Fla., 1988—; also lectr.; pres. Loss Prevention Inc. Cons. Services. Contbr. articles to profl. jours. Soccer coach Tampa County Soccer League, 1977; pres., bd. dirs. Community Swim and Tennis Club, 1981-83. Decorated U.S. Air Force Commendation medal, Vietnam Honor medal. Mem. Internat. Assn. Hosp. Security (pres. Bay Area chpt. 1984-86), Fla. Hosp. Assn. (pres.), Soc. Health Care Security Profls. (v.p. 1984-87, pres. 1985, cert. healthcare protection adminstr.), Am. Soc. Safety Engrs. (program dir. West Fla. chpt. 1984-87), Am. Indsl. Hygiene Assn., Nat. Fire Protection Assn., Tampa Area Safety Council, Fla. Affiliate of Nat. Assn. to Prevent Blindness (bd. dirs.), Hazardous Materials Response Com. for S.E. Fla., Nat. Mgmt. Assn. (program dir. hosp. chpt.). Roman Catholic. Avocations: scuba diving, golfing, tennis, writing. Home: 19111 Vista Bay Dr Indian Shores FL 33535 Office: Tampa Gen Hosp Hillsborough County Hosp Authority Devils Island Tampa FL 33606

GASCHE, PAUL, mechanical engineer; b. London, July 23, 1926; s. Walter and Rose (Enzler) G.; m. Sybil Jessie Dunstan, June 28, 1952; children: Stephen, Philip, Joseph, Thomas, Isabel. Ordinary nat. cert., Sch. of Engring.; diploma in mech. engring., Regent St. Polytech., London, 1947; higher nat. cert., S.E. Tech. Coll., London, 1952, endorsements, 1954. Registered profl. engr. Spl. apprentice Sulzer Bros. Ltd., Leeds, Yorkshire, London, 1947-50; asst. engr. Met. Water Bd., London, 1950-56; design engr. English Electric Co. Ltd., London, 1956-66; project engr. Great London Council, then transferred to Thames Water Authority, London, 1966-84; mech. electrical engr. Lewin, Fryer and Ptnrs., London, 1986—; asst. engr. Met. Water Bd. Ashford Common Pumping Sta., London, 1950-56; design engr. E.E.C. Flyingdales Early Warning Power Sta., Yorkshire, 1958-61; project engr. G.L.C./TWA, Beckton Sewage Treatment Works, London, 1966-71; on loan by TWA to Taylor/Binnie Cons. for Cairo Waste Water Project Egypt, 1977; lectr. on sewage pumping sta. design Westminster Coll., London, 1983. Mem. Inst. Mech. Engrs., Inst. Water Environ. Mgmt. Conservative. Roman Catholic. Home: 2 Lynsted Close, Bexleyheath DA6 7PR, England

GASH, JOHN MERVYN, art history educator; b. London, Feb. 15, 1948; s. Arthur Mervyn and Helene Victoria Maria Luisa (Capella) G. BA in Modern History, Oxford U., 1969; MAin History of Art, Courtauld Inst., London U., 1972; MA in Modern History, Magdalen Coll., Oxford, 1987. Lectr. in the history of art Aberdeen U., Scotland, 1972—. Author: Caravaggio, 1980; contbr. articles to profl. jours. Brit. Acad. grantee; Carnegie Trust for the U. Scotland grantee. Mem. Assn. of Art Historians, Soc. for Renaissance Studies, Soc. for Mediterranean Studies, Assn. of U. Tchrs. Mem. Ch. of Eng. Office: Dept of History of Art, Kings Coll, Aberdeen AB9 2UB, Scotland

GASKIN, SYDNEY, retail business owner; b. Enfield, Middlesex, Eng., Jan. 2, 1947; s. Sidney and Mizellay (Douglas) G.; m. Rosie Finney, June 5, 1968; children: Rosie, Sydney. Student pub. schs., Eng. Prin. Gaskin Carpets, Rhyl, Wales. Conservative. Mem. Ch. of Eng. Lodges: United Grand of Eng., Waltham Abbey, St. Asaph. Home: 44 Vale Rd, Rhyl Clwyd LL18 2BU, England Office: Gaskins Carpets, 44 46 Vale Rd, Rhyl Clwyd LL18 2BU, England

GASPARRO, FRANK, sculptor; b. Phila., Aug. 26, 1909; s. Bernard and Rosa G.; m. Julia Florence Johnston, Nov. 11, 1939; 1 dau., Christina Julia. Ed., Phila. Indsl. Arts, Pa. Acad. Fine Arts. With U.S. Mint, Phila., 1942—; asst. chief engraver-sculptor U.S. Mint, 1962-65, chief-sculptor engraver, 1965-81; instr. sculpture Fleisher Art Meml., Phila., Pa. Acad. Fine Arts, 1981. Designer: Am. coinage including Lincoln Meml. cent reverse, 1959, John F. Kennedy half-dollar reverse, 1964, Eisenhower dollar, 1972, Susan B. Anthony dollar, 1979, Phila. Medal of Honor, 1955; FAO medals Lillian Carter and Shirley Temple Black; Presdl. medals Congl. Medal of Honor; George Washington bicentennial medal; Statue of Liberty Commemorative Medal series, 1986; fgn. coinage including Guatemala, 1943, Philippine Islands, 1967, Panama, 1971, 75, $2500 proof gold coin (reverse design Isabella and Columbus) The Bahamas, 1987. Recipient Order of Merit Italian Republic, 1973, United Vets. Am. Distinguished Citizen award of Phila., 1975, Outstanding Achievement award Da Vinci Art Alliance, 1967, Commemorative Medal George Washington 250th Ann., 1982, Pres.'s Day Celebration Medal Washington and Lincoln, 1983; Cresson Traveling scholar, 1930, 31. Fellow Pa. Acad. Fine Arts (Percy Owens award 1979); mem. Le Club Francais de la Medaille of Paris. Home: 216 Westwood Park Dr Havertown PA 19083

GASPER, JO ANN, government official; b. Providence, Sept. 25, 1946; d. Joseph Siegleman and Jeanne Van Matre Shoaf; m. Louis Clement Gasper, Sept. 21, 1974; children: Stephen Gregory, Jeanne Marie, Monica Elizabeth, Michelle Bernadette (dec.), Phyllis Anastasia, Clare Genevieve. B.A., U. Dallas, 1967, M.B.A., 1969. Adminstrv. asst. U. Dallas, 1964-68; asst. dir. adminstrn. Britian Convalescent Ctr., Irving, Tex., 1964-68; pres. Medicare Ctrs., Inc., Dallas, 1968-69; bus. mgr., treas. U. Plano, Tex., 1969-72; ins. agt. John Hancock Ins. Co., Dallas, 1972-73; systems analyst Tex. Instrument, Richardson, 1973-75; pvt. practice acctg., bus. cons. McLean, Va., 1976-81; editor, pub. Congl. News for Women and the Family, McLean, Va., 1978-81, Register Report, McLean, Va., 1980-81; dep. asst. sec. for social services policy HHS, Washington, 1981-85; exec. dir. White House Conf. on Families, HHS, Washington, 1982-85; dep. asst. sec. for population affairs HHS, Washington, 1985-87; policy advisor to under sec. U.S. Dept. Edn., Washington, 1987-88, cons., 1988—. Co-chmn. St. John's Refugee Resettlement Commn., Va., 1977; bd. dirs., treas. Council Inter-Am. Security, Washington, 1978-80; active Fairfax County Citizens Coalition for Quality Child Care, Va., 1979-80; del. White House Conf. on Families, Va., 1979-80; active Franklin Area Citizens Neighborhood Watch, McLean, Va.; mem. U.S. adv. Inter-Am. Commn. on Women, OAS, 1982-85; U.S. del. XVI Pan Am. Child Congress, Washington, 1984; mem. nat. family policy adv. bd. Reagan/Bush Campaign, 1980. Recipient Eagle Forum award, 1979, Wanderer Found. award, 1980, Bronze medal HHS, 1982; named Outstanding Conservative Woman, Conservative Digest, 1980, 81. Mem. Exec. Women in Gov. (treas. 1985, sec. 1986). Roman Catholic. Home: 6235 Park Rd McLean VA 22101 Office: 115-228 1350 Berexly Rd McClean VA 22101

GASPER, JULIA MARGARET, educator; b. Poona, India, July 6, 1954; d. Thomas Ronald and June Margaret (Cocksedge) G.; m. Marcus John Andrew Watney, Aug. 4, 1984. BA in English with honors, Reading U., Eng., 1976; MA in Shakespeare Studies, Birmingham U., Eng., 1978; D. Phila. in English Lit., Oxford U., Eng., 1987. Pvt. tutor English Parma, Italy, 1976-77; lect. English lit. Shimer Coll., Chgo., Oxford, 1982-84; lectr. English lit. Stanford U. Ctr. in Oxford, 1986—; examiner U. of London G.C.E. Bd., 1987—, Oxford and Cambridge (Eng.) G.C.E. Bd., 1982-86. Contbr. articles to Review of English Studies, Durham U. Jour., Notes and Queries, and other profl. jours. Clubs: Friends of The Earth U.K. Ltd., Devon Trust for Nature Conservation.

GASPERONI, ELLEN JEAN LIAS (MRS. EMIL GASPERONI), interior designer; b. Rural Valley, Pa.; d. Dale S. and Ruth (Harris) Lias; student Youngstown U., 1952-54, John Carrol U., 1953-54, Westminster Coll., 1951-52; grad. Am. Inst. Banking; m. Emil Gasperoni, May 28, 1955; children—Sam, Emil, Jean Ellen. Mem. Coeurde Coeur Heart Assn., Orlando Opera Guild, Orlando Symphony Guild. Mem. Jr. Bus. Women's Club (dir. 1962-64). Presbyterian. Clubs: Sweetwater Country (owner, pres.) (Longwood, Fla.); Lake Toxaway Golf and Country (N.C.). Home: 1126 Brownshine Ct Longwood FL 32779

GASPERONI, EMIL, SR., real estate developer; b. Hillsville, Pa., Nov. 13, 1926; s. Attico and Rose Mary (Sarnicola) G.; m. Ellen Jean Lias, May 28, 1955; children: Samuel Dale, Emil Attico, Jean Ellen. Diploma real estate U. Pitts., 1957. Owner, pres. Gasperoni Real Estate, New Castle, Pa., 1956-63, Ft. Lauderdale, Fla., 1965—; founder, chmn. bd. Fill-R-Up Auto Wash Systems Inc., Ft. Lauderdale, 1967-70; pres., owner Sweetwater Golf and Country, Orlando, Fla., 1975—. Served with U.S. Army, 1945-46, ETO. Mem. Nat. Inst. Real Estate Brokers, Internat. Real Estate Fedn., Nat. Soc. Fee Appraisers, Fla. Assn. Mortgage Brokers. Club: Lake Toxaway (N.C.) Country Home: 1126 Brownshire Ct Longwood FL 32779 Office: 505 Wekiva Springs Rd Suite 800 Longwood FL 32779

GASQUE, (ALLARD) HARRISON, radio announcer, entertainer; b. Richmond, Va., Oct. 10, 1958; s. Thomas Nelson and Susan (Folline) G. Student, U. S.C., 1978-80; degree, Columbia Sch. Broadcasting, Washington, 1982. Announcer, disc jockey Sta. WKDK-AM, Newberry, S.C., 1982-84, Sta. WEEL-AM, Washington, 1984-85, Sta. WDCT-AM, 1985, Dynalectron Corp., McLean, Va.,1985; night-club entertainer, Washington, 1985—; announcer Sta. WWGO-FM, Columbia, S.C., 1986-87, Sta. WNOK-AM, 1987—; v.p. transp., Folline Vision Ctrs., 1986—. Mem. U. S.C. Alumni Assn., Columbia Sch. Broadcasting Alumni Assn., Columbia Jaycees, Sierra Club, Greenpeace, Handgun Control, Inc., World Wildlife Fund, John Buchanan Group, Phi Kappa Psi. Episcopalian. Avocations: singing, coin collecting, stamp collecting, record collecting. Home: 938 Broad River Rd Columbia SC 29210

GASS, ERNST, electronics executive; b. Jenoe, Hungary, June 11, 1932; arrived in Fed. Republic Germany, 1946.; s. Josef and Margit (Szep) G.; m. Maria E. Schäfer, Mar. 20, 1966; children: Miriam, Sebastian, Janka. Diploma Engring., Technische Hochschule, Stuttgart, Fed. Republic Germany, 1958. Cert. engr. Research engr. Rechen Inst. Technische Hochshule, Stuttgart, 1958-62; devel. engr. Novotechnik GmbH, Ruit, Fed.

Republic Germany, 1962-68, tech. dir., 1972-78; pres. Novotechnik GmbH, Ostfildern, Fed. Republic Germany, 1978-88; chief engr. Sick Optik Eleckronik, Munich, 1968-72; gen. mgr. Balluff GmbH, Neuhausen, Fed. Republic Germany, 1988—. Contbr. articles to tech. publs.; patentee in field. Home: Walterflexstrasse 36A, D7000 Stuttgart Federal Republic of Germany

GASS, ROBERT LOUIS, JR., furniture company executive; b. Murray, Ky., Jan. 8, 1943; s. Robert Louis and Mildred (Childers) G.; student Murray U., 1972-73, Broward Community Coll., 1971-72, Am. Inst. Banking, 1967-72; m. Victoria Fuhrer, Aug. 21, 1965; children—Kimberly Ann, Kelly Elizabeth. With finance div. Gen. Electric Co., West Palm Beach, Fla., 1965-66; trust officer Landmark First Nat. Bank, Ft. Lauderdale, Fla., 1967-72; pres. Mar-Tec Corp., Ft. Lauderdale, 1972—; pres., chmn. Kalp-Son Rattan div., Santa Fe Springs, Calif.; pres., chmn. bd. Internat. Cushion Co., Ft. Lauderdale; chmn. bd. Wudlite, Inc., Phoenix; dir. Am. Nat. Bank, Ft. Lauderdale. Group leader United Fund of Broward County, 1973; mem. Broward Citizens Commn. Mem. South Fla. Mfg. Assn. (chmn.), Ft. Lauderdale C. of C. Lodge: Kiwanis. Home: 541 San Marco Dr Fort Lauderdale FL 33301 Office: 900 SW 20th Way Fort Lauderdale FL 33312

GASSLER, FRANK HENRY, lawyer; b. N.Y.C., Apr. 21, 1951; s. Frank and Frieda (Grupe) G.; m. Pamela Kay Tedder, June 16, 1984; 1 child, Loren Nicole. BA, Villanova U., 1973; JD, Columbia U., 1976. Bar: Fla. 1976, U.S. Dist. Ct. (mid. dist.) Fla. 1976, U.S. Ct. Appeals (5th and 11th cirs.) 1983, U.S. Supreme Ct. 1983. Shareholder Fowler, White, Gillen, boggs, Villareal and Banker, Tampa, Fla., 1976—. Mem. ABA, Fla. Bar Assn., Hillsborough County Bar Assn., Def. Research Inst. Roman Catholic. Home: 4907 W Bay Way Dr Tampa FL 33629 Office: Fowler White Gillen Boggs Villareal Banker 501 E Kennedy Blvd Tampa FL 33602

GASSMAN, VITTORIO, actor, director, writer; b. Genoa, Italy, Sept. 1, 1922; s. Enrico Gassmann and Luisa Ambron; m. Nora Ricci; 1 son, Paola; m. 2d, Shelley Winters; 1 son, Vittoria; m. 3d, Diletta D'Andrea; 1 son, Alessandro-jacopo. Ed. U. of Law, Rome, Accademia D'Arte Drammatica, Rome. Dir. theater prodns., 1951—; appeared in numerous plays, 1943—, including: Hamlet; Othello; As You Like It; Troilus and Cressida; Oedipus Rex; Prometheus Bound; Ghosts; Peery Gynt; Orestes; Rosencrantz and Guildenstern are Dead; Richard III; actor films, including: Bitter Rice, Anna, Rhapsody, War and Peace, The Miracle, I Soliti Ignoti, I Mostri, 1968; Brancaleone, Profume di Donna, 1975, Sharkey's Machine, Tempest; dir. films, including: Kean 1956 and the Great War (Venice Festival winner), dir. plays, including: (musical) Irma La Douce; dir., played Agamemnon in Oresteia, Syracuse, 1960; creator Teatro Popolare Italiano; author: Un Grande Avvenire Dietro le Spalle (Sel Bahcarella award), 1982. Recipient 7 Davide Di Donatello awards for films, 4 Best Italian Theatre Actor of Yr. awards, 4 Best Film Actor awards, Best Actor award for I Mostri, Buenos Aires Festival, 1968, for Brancaleone, San Sebastian Festival, for Profumo Di Donna, Canne Festival, 1975. Office: Piazza S Alessio 32, 00191 Rome Italy *

GASSON, ANTHONY GILBERT, biotechnologist; b. London, Jan. 1, 1937; s. William Reginald and Mary Winifred (Ridgley) G.; m. Gillian Mary Lissenden; children: Mark William, Sara Louise. BS in Physiology with honors, King's Coll., London, 1961; BA, Open U., Eng., 1977; MS in Analytical Chemistry, Thames Poly., London, 1981, MA in Mgmt., 1988. Chartered biologist, chemist. With Wellcome Research Labs., Beckenham, Kent, Eng., 1962-80; sci. tech. adv. Wellcome Biotech Ltd., Beckenham, Kent, Eng., 1981-84, prodn. mgr., 1985-87, chief auditing/validation, 1987—; trustee Wellcome Pension Fund, London. Instr. Royal Life Saving Soc., London, 1963—; chmn. West Wickham council Boy Scouts Eng., 1981-83. Mem. Internat. Assn. Biol. Standardisation, Soc. Applied Bacteriology (com. mem., editorial bd. jour. 1976—), Inst. Biology, Royal Soc. Chemistry Biotech. Group (founder, sec.). Mem. Ch. of England. Clubs: King's Coll. (com. 1983—), Biosep Harwell. Office: Wellcome Biotech Ltd, Langley Ct, Beckenham Kent BR3 3BS, England

GASTAMBIDE, DANIEL, orthopedic surgeon; b. France, Sept. 7, 1942; s. Jean and Francine (Leenhardt) G.; m. Alice Jay Gastambide, Jan. 17, 1969; children: Isabelle, Florence, Claire, François, Sylvie. Surg. fellow, U. Paris, 1973; asst. unit d'enseignment et de recherche, Paris Hosp., 1975. Extern Assistance Publique, Paris, 1963, intern, 1967; gen. practice medicine U. Paris Med. Sch., 1973, fellow in surgery, 1973-75; chief dept. surgery Hosp. Nemours, France, 1975-78; chief dept. orthopedic surgery Hosp. Blois, France, 1978—; dir. dept. teaching U. Tours (France) Med. Sch., 1978—. Contbr. articles to profl. jours. Mem. Soc. Française de Chirurgie Orthopedique, Coll. Française de Chirurgie Orthopedique, Percutaneous Nucleotomy (gen. sec.). Home: Rue Beauvoir, 41000 Blois France Office: Blois Hosp, Service Chirurgie, Nouvel Hosp, 41000 Blois France

GASTEL, BARBARA JEAN, medical writer; b. Washington, Sept. 26, 1952; d. Joseph P. and Sophie (Bergman) G. BA, Yale, 1974; MD, Johns Hopkins, 1978, MPH, 1978. Spl. asst. office of dir. Nat. Inst. Aging, Bethesda, Md., 1978-80; spl. asst. to dir. Nat. Ctr. for Health Care Tech., Rockville, Md., 1980-81; asst. prof. sci. writing MIT, Cambridge, 1981-84; vis. prof. tech. communication Beijing (People's Republic of China) Med. U., 1983-85; asst. adj. prof. epidemiology internat. health U. Calif. Sch. Med., San Francisco, 1985—, asst. dean teaching and teaching evaluation, 1985—; lectr., cons. Chinese Med. Jour., Beijing, 1983-85. Author: Presenting Science to the Public, 1983; asst. editor: Johns Hopkins Medical Journal, 1976-82; contbr. articles to profl. and popular jours. AAAS mass media internship Newsweek, N.Y.C., 1978. Mem. AAAS, Assn. Tchrs. Preventive Medicine, Council Biology Editors, Am. Med. Writers Assn., Phi Beta Kappa. Office: Office of Dean U Calif Sch Med 513 Parnassus Ave Room S-224 San Francisco CA 94143-0410

GASTEYER, CARLIN EVANS, cultural center administrator; b. Jackson, Mich., Mar. 30, 1917; d. Frank Howard and Marian (Spencer) Evans; student Barnard Coll., 1934-35; B.A., CUNY, 1983; m. Harry A. Gasteyer, Jan. 8, 1944; 1 dau., Nancy Catherine. Clk., First Nat. City Bank, 1939-42; statistician Bell Telephone Labs., 1942-45; dir. asst. S.I. Mus., 1956-61; bus. mgr. Mus. of the City of N.Y., 1961-63; mus. adminstr., 1963-66; asst. dir. Monmouth (N.J.) Mus., 1966-67, Mus. of City of N.Y., 1967-70; vice dir. adminstrn. Bklyn. Mus., 1970-74; dir. planning Snug Harbor Cultural Center, S.I., N.Y., 1975-79; cable TV Cons., 1980—; adj. lectr. mus. studies Coll. S.I. CUNY, 1985—. Active Girl Scouts. Co-founder, pres. Jr. Mus. Guild, S.I. Mus., 1956-58. Mem. N.Y.C. Local Sch. Bd. 54, 1960-61. Mem. Am. Assn. Mus., Mus. Council of N.Y.C. Club: Cosmopolitan. Home: 50 Fort Pl Staten Island NY 10301

GASTEYGER, CURT WALTER, international relations educator, consultant; b. Zurich, Switzerland, Mar. 20, 1929; s. Carl J. and Gertrud (Lauser) G.; m. Doris Anna Asmuth, 1975; children—Christoph, Stephan. Dr. in Law, U. Zurich, 1954; postgrad. Coll. of Europe, Bruges, Belgium, 1954-55, Free U., Berlin, 1955-56. Research fellow German Council for Relations, Frankfurt, W.Ger., 1955-59; legal officer Internat. Commn. of Jurists, Geneva, Switzerland, 1959-61; dir. programmes Internat. Inst. for Strategic Studies, London, 1964-68; dep. dir. Atlantic Inst., Paris, 1968-74; prof. internat. relations Grad. Inst. Internat. Studies, Geneva, Switzerland, 1974—; dir. Programme for Strategic and Internat. Security Studies, Geneva, 1979—; adviser, cons. to various govts., firms. Mem. found. bd. European Mgmt. Forum, Geneva, 1979-83; mem. exec. com. European Cultural Found., Amsterdam, 1982—; mem. research bd. various instns. in U.S., Europe, 1972—; Served to capt. Swiss Army, 1978—. Ford Found. fellow, 1975, Thyssen Found. fellow, 1981, 88. Mem. Swiss Officers Assn., Swiss Soc. Protection Environment, Swiss Assn. Fgn. Policy (bd. dirs. 1980—), Internat. Inst. Strategic Studies (council 1969-77), German Council Fgn. Affairs, Inst. for East-West Security Studies (bd. dirs. 1983—), Société Littéraire of Geneva. Presbyterian. Clubs: Garrick (London); Bonmont Golf. Author: Two Germanies in World Politics, 1976; Searching for World Security, 1985. Home: 9 Rue Henry Spiess, 1208 Geneva Switzerland Office: Grad Inst Internat Studies, 132 Rue du Lausanne, 1211 Geneva 21, Switzerland

GASTON, HUGH PHILIP, marriage counselor, educator; b. St. Paul, Sept. 12, 1910; s. Hugh Philander and Gertrude (Heine) G.; B.A., U. Mich., 1937, M.A., 1941; postgrad. summers Northwestern U., 1938, Yale U., 1959; m. Charlotte E. Clarke, Oct. 1, 1945 (dec. 1960); children—Trudy E. Gaston Crippen, George Hugh. Counselor, U. Mich., Ann Arbor, 1936; tchr., counselor W. K. Kellogg Found., Battle Creek, Mich., 1937-41; tchr. spl. edn., Detroit, 1941; instr. airplane wing constrn. Briggs Mfrs. Co., Detroit, 1942; psychologist VA, 1946-51; sr. staff asso. Sci. Research Asso., Chgo., 1951-55; marriage counselor Circuit Ct., Ann Arbor, 1955-60; pvt. practice marriage counseling, Ann Arbor, 1955—; former chief Guidance Center, U. Mich. and Mich. State U.; lectr., Eastern Mich. U., Ypsilanti, 1964-67, asst. prof., 1967-81; mem. Study Group for Health Care of Elderly, China, USSR, 1983, Profl. Study Group on Family Affairs, USSR, 1986. Acting postmaster, Ann Arbor, 1960-61. Chmn. Wolverine Boys State, Am. Legion, 1957-86; chmn. com. on Christian marriage Presbyn. So. Mich., 1962-69; mem. exec. com., legis. agt., chmn. legis. com. Mich. Council Family Relations, 1972-74; bd. dirs. Internat. Parents Without Partners, 1968-69, 1st pres. Mich. chpt., 1961; bd. dirs. Ann Arbor Sr. Citizens, 1982-85, Washtenaw County Council Alcoholism, 1982-84. Served with U.S. Army, 1943-46. Decorated Purple Heart (2), Bronze Star; Medallion of Nice (France); named Citizen of Year, Am. Legion, 1968, Single Parent of Yr., 1978, Patriot of Yr. State of Mich., Mil. Order of Purple Heart, 1987-88. Mem. Am. Assn. Marriage Counselors, Circumnavigators Club, Am. Personnel and Guidance Assn., Nat. Vocat. Guidance Assn., D.A.V. (past comdr.), Am. Soc. Tng. Dirs., Mich. Indsl. Tng. Council (charter), SAR (past pres.), U. Mich. Band Alumni Assn. (pres. 1957-58), Mil. Order Purple Heart (nat. exec. com. 1977-82, 1st comdr. chpt. 459 Mich., state comdr. Mich. 1984-85, nat. historian 1981-85), Phi Delta Kappa (past pres. U. Mich.). Lodge: Rotary. Address: 513 4th St Ann Arbor MI 48103

GATENBEE, ELIZABETH ROBBINS, bearings company executive; b. Louisville, Feb. 24, 1916; d. Orlando Douglass and Elizabeth (Holtzhauer) Robbins; spl. student Tarkio Coll., 1955-56; m. Robert James Gatenbee, Sept. 11, 1934; children—Robert James, John Douglass. Sec., Ky. Bearings Service, Inc., Louisville, 1934-48, 57-60, exec. v.p., 1973-80, chmn. bd., 1980—, also dir.; sec., dir. So. Bearings Service, Inc., Knoxville/Kingsport, Tenn., 1976-82, 1976-84. Mem. DAR (Mo. chpt.), Daus. Founders and Patriots (Lexington chpt.). Home: PO Box 336 Pewee Valley KY 40056

GATERE, GEORGE GACHARA, banker; b. Dist. Nyeri, Kenya, Sept. 29, 1941; s. Gideon and Ruth (Wangeci) G.; m. Margaret Njeri, Oct. 4, 1969; children: Caroline, Janet, Gideon, Fredrick. BA in Econs, Haile Sellasie U., 1967. Statis. officer Kenya Ministry Econ. Planning, Nairobi, 1967-69; trainee Grindlays Bank, London, 1970-71; officer Nat. Bank Kenya Ltd., Nairobi, 1971-72, br. acct., 1973, insp., 1973; br. mgr. Nat. Bank Kenya Ltd., Kisumu, Nakuru, Mombasa, 1974-78; dep. supt. Nat. Bank Kenya Ltd., Nairobi, 1978-80, staff mgr., 1980-86, sr. mgr., 1986—; alt. dir. Indsl. Devel. Bank, Nairobi, 1978-81, Ins. Co. East Africa Ltd., Nairobi, 1978-81, Estates Services Ltd., Nairobi, 1978-80. Mem. Kenya Inst. Bankers (hon. sec. 1983-85). Mem. Kenya African Nat. Union. Clubs: Muthaiga Golf (chmn. 1981), Kenya Golf Union (chmn. 1987-88) (Nairobi). Home: PO Box 61271, Nairobi Kenya Office: Nat Bank of Kenya, PO Box 41862, Nairobi Kenya

GATES, EDGAR DAY, personnel executive; b. Warren, Ohio, Dec. 1, 1925; s. Edgar Pier and Dorothy (Day) G.; m. Patricia McCarty, Sept. 9, 1949; children: Philip, Karen Gates Moore. AB, Miami U., Oxford, Ohio, 1948; MA, Ohio U., Athens, 1949; postgrad. Tulane U., New Orleans, 1950, U. Md.-College Park, 1951. Cert. psychologist, Md. Dir. personnel The City Baking Co., Balt., 1951-56; v.p. New Haven Board & Carton, New Haven, 1957-61; orgn. devel. cons. Birds Eye div. Gen. Foods, White Plains, N.Y., 1961-63, personnel mgr. food service, 1963-65, personnel mgr Jello div., 1965-68, corp. personnel dir., 1968-70; v.p. personnel Graybar Electric, N.Y.C., 1970-79; v.p. personnel and adminstrn. Am. Maize Products, Stamford, Conn., 1979-87; pvt. investor Gates Assocs., Inc., Greenwich, Conn., 1987—. Served with USNR, 1943-46. Mem. Am. Psychol. Assn., Sigma Xi. Republican. Congregationalist. Home: 2600 Marion Dr Fort Lauderdale FL 33316 Office: Gates Assocs Inc 543 Stanwich Rd Greenwich CT 06831

GATES, HENRY LOUIS, JR., English educator; b. Keyser, W.Va., Sept. 16, 1950; s. Henry-Louis and Pauline Augusta (Coleman) G.; m. Sharon Lynn Adams, Sept. 1, 1979; children: Maude Augusta Adams, Elizabeth Helen-Claire. BA summa cum laude, Yale U., 1973; MA, Cambridge (Eng.) U., 1974, PhD, 1979. Lectr. English Yale U., New Haven, 1976-79, asst. prof. English and Afro-Am. studies, 1979-84, assoc. prof., 1984-85; prof. English, comparative lit. and Africana studies, Cornell U., Ithaca, N.Y., 1985—, W.E.B. DuBois prof. lit., 1988—; pres. Afro-Am. Acad., 1984—. Author: Figures in Black, 1987, Signifying Monkey, 1988; editor: Our Nig, 1983, The Slave's Narrative, 1985, Black Literature and Literary Theory, 1985, Race, Writing, and Difference, 1986, The Classic Slave Narratives, 1987; series editor: Oxford-Schomburg Library of 19th Century Black Women, 1988; mem. editorial bd.: Black Am. Lit. Forum, 1981—, Am. Quar., 1981, Studies in Am. Fiction, 1981, Proteus, 1984—, Diacritics, 1985—, Publs. of MLA, 1987, Critical Inquiry, 1987, Cultural Critique A/B. Recipient MacArthur prize MacArthur Found., 1981—, Faculty prize Yale Afro-Am. Cultural Ctr., 1984. Mem. Zora Neale Hurston Soc. (award for creative scholar 1986), African Lit. Assn., Am. Studies Assn., MLA, Assn. for Study of Afro-Am. Life and History, Coll. Lang. Assn., PEN, Caribbean Studies Assn., Phi Beta Kappa. Democrat. Episcopalian. Avocations: jazz, pocket billiards. Home: 503 Triphammer Rd Ithaca NY 14850 Office: Cornell U 347 Rockefeller Hall Ithaca NY 14853

GATEWOOD, ROBERT PAYNE, financial planning exec.; b. Nebr., Mar. 4, 1923; s. Robert Harvey and Bess (Payne) G.; B.S., U.S. Naval Acad., 1946; postgrad. La. State U., 1974; m. Marilyn Wengert, June 6, 1946; children—Robert, Lottie, Traber, Cy, Marilyn, Bess, John, Anthony, Judemarie, Anne, Tressa, Joseph, Ruth. Estate planner J.D. Marsh & Assos., 1959-56; pres. estate planning Fin. Corp. Am., 1956-61; pres. Robert P. Gatewood & Co., specialists in tax and estate planning, 1961—; internat. lectr.; mem. sales execs. adv. bd. Inst. Ins. Mktg., La. State U., 1970-79, bd. dirs. Found. Served with USN, 1946-50. Recipient Bernard L. Wilner Meml. award; C.L.U. Mem. Nat. Assn. Life Underwriters (past pres.), Assn. Advanced Life Underwriting, Million Dollar Round Table, Am. Soc. C.L.U.s (exec. com. 1972-77, pres. 1975-76), Five Million Dollar Internat. Forum (founder). Republican. Roman Catholic. Contbr. articles to profl. jours. Home: 3838 52d St NW Washington DC 20016 Office: 905 16th St NW Washington DC 20006

GATHMAN, JAMES DENIS, real estate investment company executive; b. Chgo., Dec. 23, 1941; s. James Arthur and Helen Mary (Konkolitz) B.; m. Julianne Clare Thompson; children—Alaina, Joseph, Matthew, Michael, Justin, Christopher. B.B.A. in Fin., Loyola u., 1963. Real estate appraiser Talman Fed. Savs. and Loan, Chgo., 1963-74; v.p., dir. Real Estate Research Corp., Chgo., 1974-83; sr. v.p. VMS Realty, Inc., Chgo., 1983—. Contbr. articles to profl. publs., chpts. to books. Mem. Am. Inst. Real Estate Appraisers, Soc. Real Estate Appraisers, Am. Arbitration Assn., Lambda Alpha. Roman Catholic. Home: 13 Willet Way Trout Valley Cary IL 60013 Office: VMS Realty Inc 8700 W Bryn Mawr St Chicago IL 60631

GATRAD, ABDUL RASHID, pediatrician, educator; b. Blantyre, Malawi, Nov. 27, 1946; arrived in Eng., 1964; s. Mahomed and Jubaida Gatrad; m. Valerie Barraclough, Sept. 13, 1975; children: Sabina, Adam. MB, ChB with honours in Anatomy, U. Leeds, Eng., 1971. House officer in gen. medicine Nat. Health Service, Wakefield, Eng., 1971-72, house officer in gen. surgery, 1972-73; sr. house officer in obstetrics Doncaster (Eng.) Royal Infirmary, 1973-74; registrar child health Pontefract (Eng.) Infirmary, 1975-77; registrar Royal Manchester (Eng.) Children's Hosp., 1977-79, Booth Hall Hosp., N.W. Ctr. for Perinatal Medicine, Manchester, 1983-84; med. dir. Dutch Missionary Hosp., Blantyre, 1980-82; cons. pediatrician Manor Hosp., Walsall, Eng., 1984—; hon. sr. lectr. dept. child health U. Birmingham, Eng., 1984—; med. adviser World Fedn. Khoja Shia Ithna-Asheri Muslim Communities, 1985—. Contbr. articles to med. jours. Recipient award of merit U. Salford/Manchester, 1983. Mem. Royal Coll. Physicians, Royal Coll. Surgeons, Royal Coll. Obstetricians and Gynecologists (diploma), Brit. Pediatric Assn., Brit. Acupuncture Soc., Brit. Med. Assn. Moslem. Lodge: Rotary (coordinator polio and eye camp project Walsall 1985—, Paul Harris fellow 1988). Home: 5 Lowercroft Way, Sutton, Coldfield, Birmingham West Midlands B74 4XF, England

GATTAZ, WAGNER FARID, psychiatry educator; b. Rio Preto, Sao Paulo, Brazil, Feb. 10, 1951; s. Farid and Laila Gattaz; m. Kathrin Zalenga, Nov. 4, 1983. Medical degree, Faculty Medicine Found. ABC, Sao Paulo, 1975; MD, U. Heidelberg, Fed. Republic Germany, 1979, habilitation in psychiatry, 1983. Resident in psychiatry U. Sao Paulo, 1976-77; vis. scientist Cen. Inst. Mental Health, Mannheim, Fed. Republic Germany, 1978-80, vis. prof., 1981-83, prof. psychiatry, 1984—. Co-editor: Search for the Causes of Schizophrenia; (jour.) European Archives Psychiatry and Neurol. Scis.; mem. editorial bd. European Jour. Psychiatry. Mem. Soc. Biol. Psychiatry, World Psychiatric Assn., Internat. Soc. Human Biologists. Home: Gaisbergstr 27, 6900 Heidelberg 1 Federal Republic of Germany Office: Cen Inst Mental Health, PO BOX 5970, 6800 Mannheim Federal Republic of Germany

GATTI PERER, MARIA LUISA, art historian; b. Turin, Italy, Nov. 3, 1928; d. Guido and Maria (Fantino) Perer; diploma piano, Verdi Conservatory, 1947; Laurea in lettere, U. Degil Studi, Milan; m. Virginio Gatti, June 4, 1960. Tchr. art history in various schs., 1951-62; mem. faculty U. Degli Studi, 1954-63, asst. prof. medieval history, 1958-63; mem. faculty U. Cattolica, Milan, 1963—, prof. history of art criticism, 1967—, prof. Storia dell'Arte Lombarda, 1978—, dir. Scuola di Perfezionamento in Archeologia e Storia dell'Arte, 1981—; editor Arte Lombarda, 1958—; dir. Inst. History Lombard Art, 1967-85; internat. adv. com. Internat. Repertory Musical Iconography; mem. exec. com. Accademia di S. Carlo, 1978—. Scholar Ministry Pub. Instrn., 1951; recipient S. Vincent award, 1952; Gold medal Milan City Hall, 1970. Author: Carlo Giuseppe Merlo, architetto, 1966; La Chiesa e il convento di S. Ambrogio della Vittoria a Parabiago, 1966; Umanesino a Milano, L'Osservanza agostiniana dell Incoronata, 1980; also articles. Home: 4 Lovanio, Milan 20121 Italy Office: Univ Cattolica di Storia, Dept Studi Medioevali Rinascimentali, largo Gemelli 1, 20123 Milan Italy

GATTUNG, ERWIN ADOLF, utilities executive; b. Ladenburg, Fed. Republic of Germany, Sept. 16, 1941; s. Jean and Maria (Taufertshoefer) G.; m. Monika E. Feuerstein, Mar. 12, 1966; children: Armin, Diana. MBA, Verwaltungs U. Wirtsch. Acad., Mannheim, Fed. Republic of Germany, 1967. With Brown Boveri & Cie AG, Mannheim, 1957-69; with Brown Boveri-York Kaelte- und Klimatechnik GmbH, Mannheim, 1970—, controller, 1970-81, mgr. div., 1981-87, mng. dir., 1987—. Roman Catholic. Club: Tennis. Office: Brown Boveri-York, Gottlieb-Daimler-Str 6, 6800 Mannheim Federal Republic of Germany

GAUBERT, LLOYD FRANCIS, shipboard and industrial cable distribution company executive; b. Thibodaux, La., Jan. 6, 1921; s. Camille J. and Leonise (Henry) G.; children—Lloyd Francis, Leonise, Bruce, Blane, Gwen, Greg. Student Southwestern La. Inst., 1941, U.So. Calif., 1942-43, Tex. Christian U., 1946-47. Tool engr. Consol.-Vultee Aircraft Corp., San Diego, 1941-45; tool project engr. Fort Worth plant Convair, 1946-47; founder, owner, pres. L.F. Gaubert & Co., Inc., New Orleans, 1947—; pres. Michoud Indsl. Complex, Inc., Marine Indsl. Cable Corp., Carmel Devel. Corp.; dir. First Nat. Bank Commerce, New Orleans; pres. Holiday Inn Thibodaux. Chmn. regional planning commn. New Orleans Mayor's Coordinating Com. for NASA, 1961-63, chmn. mfrs. com., 1961-63; bd. dirs. Better Bus. Bur., New Orleans, Met. New Orleans Safety Council, New Orleans Pub. Belt R.R., New Orleans Port Com., New Orleans Traffic and Transp. Bur., USCG Acad., New Orleans Opera House Assn., Christian Bros., New Orleans; trustee Sta. WYES-TV, New Orleans; exec. com. Sugar Bowl Football; founder, chmn. Greatest Bands in Dixie; pres. Holiday Inn of Thibodaux; dir., USCG Acad. Served with USAAF, 1942-45. Mem. Am. Soc. Tooling and Mfg. Engrs. (pres. 1948-49), Soc. Naval Architects and Marine Engrs., Am. Soc. Naval Engrs., La. Engring. Soc., Navy League (past pres. New Orleans council, nat. rep., state pres. La.), New Orleans Petroleum Club, Sugar Bowl (exec. com.), Los Angeles Navy Leage of U.S. (nat. dir., pres., past pres. New Orleans council), Am. Legion. Democrat. Roman Catholic. Clubs: Plimsoll, Bd. of Trade, New Orleans Petroleum, Internat. House. Lodges: Optimists (pres. 1957-58, lt. gov. 1959-70), K.C. Home: 5668 Bancroft Dr New Orleans LA 70122 Office: LF Gaubert & Co Inc 700 S Broad St New Orleans LA 70119

GAUBICHER, MICHEL, gastroenterologist; b. Saint-Herve, France, Mar. 30, 1947; s. Maurice Jean-Marie and Josephine Therese (Helard) G.; m. Jacqueline Blondet, June 20, 1970 (div. 1986); children: Solenn, Morgane, Anne-Gaelle; m. Laurence Gaultier. MD, U. Rennes, France, 1974. Intern and resident in gastroenterology Hosp. Pontchaillou, Rennes, 1973-77; practice medicine specializing in gastroenterology Chateaubriant, France, 1978—. Author: La Poudriere, 1974; founder Eskalibor Jour., 1982; designer, patentee Celtic Union Flag and Keltia Symbol. Pres. Brittany Team Supporters Club. Served to 1st lt. French Armed Forces, 1974-75. Club: Araok Vreizh (pres. 1982—). Home: Sav Heol, 44110 Chateaubriant France Office: Centre Med Kastell Uhel, Rue du Prievre de Bere, 44110 Chateaubriant France

GAUCI, COUNT CHARLES ANTHONY, anaesthetist, therapist; b. Malta, Oct. 19, 1947; s. Carmelo and Carmen (Zarb) Gauci; m. Marie Josette Sammut-Alessi dei Marchesi della Taflia, Nov. 28, 1971; children: Camilla Louise Gauci-Alessi. MD, Royal U. of Malta, 1971; fellow in faculty of anaesthetists, Royal Coll. Surgeons of Eng., 1975. Commd. Royal Army Med. Corps, 1976, advanced through grades to lt. col., 1983; cons.-in-charge Pain Relief Clinic Queen Elizabeth Mil. Hosp., Woolwich, Eng., 1983—; hon. cons. pain relief Guy's Hosp., London, 1988—. Author (book): The Genealogy and Heraldry of the Noble Families of Malta, 1981, The Palaeologos Family-A Genealogical Review, 1985, A Guide to the Maltese Nobility, 1986, A Key to Maltese Coats of Arms, 1988; contbr. numerous articles to jours., incl. Burke's Peerage. Created Knight Equestrian Order of Holy Sepulchre Holy See, Rome, 1974. Fellow Soc. of Antiquaries of Scotland; mem. Council of Intractable Pain Soc. of Gt. Britain and Ireland, Brit. Med. Assn. (Armed Forces com. 1984—, council of Brit. Med. Assn. 1986—) Com. of Privileges of Maltese Nobility (hon. overseas sec. 1982—), Accademia Tiberina di Roma (named academician 1984), Assn. Anaesthetists of Gt. Britian and Ireland, Soc. for Back Pain Research, Internat. Back Pain Soc., and others. Roman Catholic. Office: Queen Elizabeth Mil Hosp, Stadium Rd Woolwich, London SE18, England

GAUDINO, MARIO, physician, pharmaceutical company executive; b. Buenos Aires, Argentina, May 22, 1918; came to U.S., 1946, naturalized, 1966; s. Nicolas M. and Maria Teresa (Ferrari) G.; B.A., U. Buenos Aires, 1934, M.D., 1944; Ph.D., N.Y. U., 1950; m. Ann Murray, Sept. 24, 1947 (div. Jan. 1983); children—David, Brian; m. 2d, Judith A. Jenkins, May 19, 1984. Asst., Inst. Histology and Embryology, U. Buenos Aires, 1936, asst., research asst. Inst. Physiology, 1937-42, chief of lab. biol. physics, 1944; resident, chief resident Ramos Mejia Hosp., Buenos Aires, 1941-44; Millet and Roux fellow Argentine Assn. for Advancement Sci., 1943; asst., attending physician Inst. Semiology, Nat. Clin. Hosp., Buenos Aires, 1944-46; fellow Argentine Nat. Cultural Commn., 1945; Sauberan fellow Argentine Assn. Advancement Sci., 1946; physiol. research fellow N.Y. U., U.S. State Dept., Dazian Found. Med. Research, 1946-49; asst. prof. Tex. U., 1949; chmn. dept. biol. physics U. La Plata, Argentina, 1950-51; attending physician Central Inst. Cardiology, Buenos Aires, 1950-51; asso. dir. med. writing and advt. Lederle Labs. div. Am. Cyanamid Co., N.Y.C., 1951-52; research asso., prof. dept. surgery N.Y. U., 1952-55, adj. asso. prof. surgery, 1955-57; established investigator Am. Heart Assn., N.Y.C., 1954-57; med. dir. Abbott Labs. Internat. Co., Abbott Universal Ltd., Chgo., 1957-61; asso. dept. medicine Northwestern U., 1959-61; asso. med. dir. Pfizer Internat., Inc., N.Y.C., 1962-67; asso. dir. advanced clin. research Internat. Merck Sharp & Dohme Research Labs., Rahway, N.J., 1967-70, dir., 1970-71, sr. dir. clin. research internat. med. affairs area, 1971-74; dir. med. compliance drug regulatory affairs CIBA-GEIGY Pharms., Summit, N.J., 1974-80, asso. dir. med. services med. affairs dept., 1980—; clin. asst. prof. medicine Cornell U., N.Y.C., 1971-77. Fellow N.Y. Acad. Scis.; mem. Am. Physiol. Soc., Am. Acad. Clin. Toxicology, AMA, Am. Soc. Clin. Pharmacology and Therapeutics, Acad. Medicine N.J., Summit Med. Soc., Soc. for Exptl. Biology and Medicine, Am. Fedn. Clin. Research, Harvey Soc., Am., Internat. socs. nephrology, Microcirculatory Soc. Clubs: Jockey,

Argentine Yacht., University, Buenos Aires Rowing. Home: 3 Brainerd Rd Summit NJ 07901 Office: 556 Morris Ave Summit NJ 07901

GAUFFENIC, ARMELLE ELISABETH, educator, consultant; b. Drancy, France, Feb. 9, 1954. Student Ecole des Hautes Etudes Scis. Sociales, Paris, 1976-83; EdB, Universite Vincennes, France, 1979; MA, Universite Paris VIII, 1980, D.A., Universite, 1983. Lectr. Ecole Superieure des Lettres, Liban, 1974-76; research asst. Universite Paris XII, Paris, 1976-81; lectr. internat. relations Ecole Superieure Commerce, Paris, 1981—; assoc. research worker Centre National de la Recherche Scientifique, Paris, 1983-85; lectr. internat. relations Institut Supèrieur des Affaires, Jouy en Josas, 1982-84; prof. doctorate program Ecole des Hautes Etudes Commerciales, Paris, 1983—; cons., 1982—; radio producer Radio France, 1984—; cons. internat. orgns., 1982—. Contbr. articles to profl. jours. Producer radio program. Mem. Mondial Council Edn., Comparative Edn. Soc. in Europe, Internat. Sociol. Assn., Institut Français de Relations Internationales, World Assn. for Ednl. Research, Internat. Sociol. Assn., Internat. Fedn. Social Sci. Orgns., Trigone Cons. (pres.), Centre d'Etudes et de Recherches Interculturelles (cofounder). Avocation: psychoanalyst. Home: 3 rue des Patures, 75016 Paris France Office: 95 rue de Charenton, 75012 Paris France

GAUGHAN, EUGENE FRANCIS, accountant; b. Paterson, N.J., Aug. 31, 1945; s. Eugene Francis and Ruth Mae (Webster) G.; m. Arlene Barber, July 8, 1972 (dec. May 1981); m. 2d Margaret Duffy, Jan. 2, 1983. A.B., Coll. Holy Cross, 1967; M.B.A., Rutgers U., 1968. C.P.A., N.Y., N.J. and Conn. Staff acct., Price Waterhouse, 1968-70, sr. acct., 1970-72, mgr., The Hague, Netherlands, 1972-75, mgr., N.Y.C., 1975-78, sr. mgr., 1978-79, ptnr., 1979—; World Firm Council Ptnrs., 1987—; adv. assoc. Rutgers Grad. Sch. Mgmt. Trustee, treas. Lenox Hill Hosp., N.Y.C., 1981—. Mem. Am. Inst. C.P.A.s, N.Y. State Soc. C.P.A.'s (bd. dirs. 1986-89), Am. Acctg. Assn., The Netherlands/Am. Community Assn. (bd. dirs.), Hosp. Trustees of N.Y., Internat. Newspaper Fin. Execs., Philippine Am. C. of C., The Netherlands C. of C. in U.S. Roman Catholic. Clubs: Netherlands of N.Y., N.Y. Athletic, Hampton Hills Country. Lodges: K.C., Elks. Home: 333 E 66th St New York NY 10021 also: Box 485 Quogue NY 11959 Office: Price Waterhouse 153 E 53d St New York NY 10022

GAUGHAN, PEARL MARY, former public health nurse, consultant; b. Reading, Pa., Apr. 9, 1921; d. Raymond Bucher and Lillian May (Fields) Fichthorn; m. Michael J. Gaughan, Jr., Feb. 14, 1946 (dec. 1985); children—Michael J., Patricia Ann. R.N., Reading Hosp. Sch. Nursing, 1943; student UCLA, 1965-83, U. So. Calif., 1965-83, Calif. State U.-San Bernardino, 1965—. Pvt. duty nurse, Reading, Pa., 1943-45; charge nurse U.S. Army Hosp., Richmond, Va., 1945-47; pvt. duty nurse, Roswell, N.M., 1947-48; charge nurse U.S. Indian Hosp., Winslow, Ariz., 1948-51; pvt. duty nurse, San Bernardino, Calif., 1951-62; asst. dir. Vis. Nurse Assn., San Bernardino, Calif., 1963-70; pub. health nurse San Bernardino County Health Dept., 1970-83; now ret.; student nurse cons. Calif. State U., others, 1965—. Author: Home Nursing Care Procedure, 1974. Instr. San Bernardino chpt. ARC, 1957-59; sec. Am. Lung Assn., 1975-86, bd. dirs., 1987—; chmn. children and youth commn. Calif. dept. Am. Legion, 1983-87, vice chmn., 1988—; chmn. stroke com. Am. Heart Assn., 1977—; pres. Arrowhead Republican Women, 1958; active Boy Scouts Am., Girl Scouts U.S.A., 1955-67; comdr. Am. Legion Post 14, San Bernardino, Calif., 1974. Served as lt. Army Nurse Corps, 1945-47. Named Citizen of Yr. San Bernardino LWV, 1986. Mem. Calif. Nurses Assn., So. Calif. Pub. Health Assn., Hosp. Discharge Planners Assn., Am. Assn. Continuity of Care, Bus. and Profl. Women of San Bernardino (committeewoman), Reading Hosp. Alumni Assn., Am. Nurses Assn., Nat. Orgn. World War Nurses, Internat. Platform Assn. Republican. Roman Catholic. Lodge: Elks Wives Orgn. (sec. 1960-63). Home: 2870 Serrano Rd San Bernardino CA 92405

GAUHAR, HUMAYUN ALTAF, publishing company executive; b. Karachi, Sindh, Pakistan, Apr. 13, 1949; arrived in Eng., 1980; s. Altaf Hussain and Bilquis Azmat (Razzaq) g.; m. Manizeh Khan, Aug. 29, 1975; children: Saniyya, Mashaal, Fazila, Ali. BA in Econs., U. Punjab, Rawalpindi, Pakistan, 1969; MA in Social and Polit. Sci., U. Cambridge, Eng., 1972. Market research trainee Nasiruddeen & Assocs., Karachi, 1973-74; chmn. Micas Assocs. Ltd., Karachi, 1974-79, Micas Food Insustries Ltd., Karachi, 1974-79; mng. dir. Third World Found. for Social and Econ. Change, London, 1980—, Third World Media Ltd., London, 1980—; pres., pub. South Pubs. Ltd., London, 1980—; vice chmn. South-North Bus. Forum, London, 1985—; co-chmn. Third World Advt. and Mktg. Congress, 1985—. Co-editor: (with Bruno Kreisky) Decolonisation and After: The Future of the Third World, 1987. Info. sec. Tehrik-I-Istiqlal Party, Sindh, 1978-82; chmn. South-Save the Children Fund, London, 1986—. Mem. Interaction Council of Vienna (communication com.). Muslim. Clubs: Sindh (Karachi), Royal Automobile and Inst. Dirs. (London). Home: 21 D Cadogan Gardens, London SW3, England Office: South Pubs Ltd, 13th Floor New Zealand House, London SW1Y 4TS, England

GAULIN, JEAN, gas distribution company executive; b. Montreal, July 9, 1942; s. Paul and Berthe (Lariviere) G.; m. Andrée LeBoeuf; children: Marie-Claude, Philippe, Mathieu. Student, St.-Jean Royal Mil. Coll.; chem. Engr. and B.A.Sc., Ecole Polytechnique Montreal U., 1967. Dir. Que. Refinery of Canadian Ultramar Ltd., 1976-79; v.p. Golden Eagle Can., Montreal, 1977-79; v.p. supply and refining Ultramar Can. Inc., Toronto, 1979-80, pres., 1985—; also bd. dirs. Ultramar Can. Ltd., Toronto; pres. Nouveler Inc., Montreal, 1980-82; pres., chief operating officer Gaz Métropolitain, Inc., Montreal, 1982-85; bd. dirs. Scepter Resources Ltd, Ultramar PLC London, Quebec Telephone, Ultramar Can., Inc. Bd. dirs. Internat. Centre for Research and Studies in Mgmt., Montreal, 1982—; bd. dirs. Foundation de l'Universite du Quebec a Montreal, 1982—, Institut de Cardiologie de Montreal, 1983—; pres. Telethon for Quebec Soc. for Disabled Children, 1986. Served with Canadian Navy, 1958-62. Mem. Canadian Gas Assn. (dir. 1982—), Am. Gas Assn., Ordre des Ingénieurs du Que. Club: St. Denis. Office: Ultramar Canada Inc, 2020 Rue University, Montreal, PQ Canada H3A 2L4 also: Can Ultramar Ltd, 1 Valleybrook Dr, Don Mills, ON Canada M3B 2S8

GAULKE, MARY FLORENCE, library administrator; b. Johnson City, Tenn., Sept. 24, 1923; d. Gustus Thomas and Mary Belle (Bennett) Erickson; m. James Wymond Crowley, Dec. 1, 1939; 1 son, Grady Gaulke (name legally changed); m. 2d, Bud Gaulke, Sept. 1, 1945 (dec. Jan. 1978); m. 3d, Richard Lewis McNaughton, Mar. 21, 1983. B.S. in Home Econs., Oreg. State U., 1963; M.S. in L.S., U. Oreg., 1968, Ph.D. in Spl. Edn., 1970. Cert. standard personnel supr., standard handicapped learner, Oreg. Head dept. home econs. Riddle Sch. Dist. (Oreg.), 1963-66; library cons. Douglas County Intermediate Edn. Dist., Roseburg, Oreg., 1966-67; head resident, head counselor Prometheus Project, So. Oreg. Coll., Ashland, summers 1966-68; supr. librarians Medford Sch. Dist. (Oreg.), 1970-73; instr. in psychology So. Oreg. Coll., Ashland, 1970-73; library supr. Roseburg Sch. Dist., 1974—; resident psychologist Black Oaks Boys Sch., Medford, 1970-75; mem. Oreg. Gov.'s Council on Libraries, 1979. Author: Vo-Ed Course for Junior High, 1965; Library Handbook, 1967; Instructions for Preparation of Cards For All Materials Cataloged for Libraries, 1971; Handbook for Training Library Aides, 1972. Coordinator Laubach Lit. Workshops for High Sch. Tutors, Medford, 1972. Mem. So. Oreg. Library Fedn. (sec. 1971-73), ALA, Oreg. Library Assn., Pacific N.W. Library Assn., Delta Kappa Gamma (pres. 1980-82), Phi Delta Kappa (historian, research rep.). Republican. Methodist. Clubs: Lodge: Order Eastern Star (worthy matron 1956-57). Home: 1625 Days Creek Rd Days Creek OR 97429 Office: Roseburg Pub Schs 1419 Valley View Dr Roseburg OR 97470

GAULTNEY, JOHN ORTON, life insurance agent, consultant; b. Pulaski, Tenn., Nov. 7, 1915; s. Bert Hood and Grace (Orton) G.; m. Elizabethine Mullette, Mar. 30, 1941; children: Elizabethine (Mrs. Donald H. McClure), John Mullette, Walker Orton, Harlow Denny. Student, Am. Inst. Banking, 1936; diploma, Life Ins. Agy. Mgmt. Assn., 1948, Little Rock Jr. Coll., 1950; Mgmt. C.L.U. diploma, 1952; grad. sales mgmt. and mktg., Rutgers U., 1957. CLU. With N.Y. Life Ins. Co., 1935—; regional v.p. N.Y. Life Ins. Co., Atlanta, 1956-64; v.p. N.Y. Life Ins. Co., N.Y.C., 1964-67; v.p. in charge group sales N.Y. Life Ins. Co., 1967-68, v.p. mktg., 1969-80, agt., 1980—; life ins. cons. 1981—; v.p. N.Y. Life Variable Contracts Corp., 1969-80; hon. dir. Bank of Frankewing (Tenn.), 1984—. Elder Presbyn. Ch.; chmn. Downtown YMCA, Atlanta, 1963-65; mem. Bd. Zoning Appeals Bronxville, N.Y., 1970-80; mem. pub. relations com. Nat. Council YMCAs, 1965-80; mem. internat. world service com. YMCA, 1968-80; chmn. Vanderbilt YMCA, 1974-76, Bd. dirs., N.Y.C., 1966-76; Bd. dirs. Memphis YMCA, 1939-40, Little Rock YMCA, 1941-55, Atlanta YMCA, 1959-65, Greater N.Y. YMCA, 1975-80, Nashville YMCA, 1981—. Served to capt., inf. AUS, 1942-45, MTO. Decorated Silver Star, Bronze Star with 3 clusters, Purple Heart with 2 clusters.; recipient Devereux C. Josephs award N.Y. Life Ins. Co., 1954; named Ark. traveler, 1955; hon. citizen Tenn., 1956; Tenn. ambassador, 1981-88; Ky. col., 1963. Mem. Am., Tenn. socs. CLU's, Nat., Tenn. assns. life underwriters, Sales and Mktg. Execs. Internat., Am. Risk and Ins. Assn., Heritage Found., Carnton Assn. (bd. dirs. 1981—, pres. 1987-88), N.Y. So. Soc. (trustee 1965-80), Williamson County Hist. Soc. (pres. 1983-85), 361st Inf. Assn. World War II (pres. 1967-70), SAR (N.Y. state dir. 1970-80), St. Nicholas Soc. City N.Y., Soc. Colonial Wars, Descendants of Colonial Clergy, Tenn. Sons of Revolution, Assn. Preservation Tenn. Antiquities (trustee), Tenn. Soc. in N.Y. (pres. 1971-74, trustee 1980—), Newcomen Soc. in Am. Clubs: Capital City (Atlanta); Siwanoy (Bronxville, N.Y.); Md. Farms Racquet and Country (Brentwood, Tenn.); Nashville City. Lodges: Rotary, Masons, Shriners, Sojourners, Temple of Jerusalem. Home: 6109 Johnson Chapel Rd Brentwood TN 37027 Office: One Nashville Pl Suite 1610 Nashville TN 37219

GAUTHIER, LINDA KATHERINE, aerospace and electronics company executive; b. N.Y.C., Oct. 4, 1947; d. Norman Leonard and Catherine (Layer) G.; student Pan Am. Art Sch., 1966-69, Dutchess Community Coll., 1980—. Clk., Samberg Bros., Maspeth, N.Y., 1964; statis. clk. N.Y. Telephone Co., Bklyn., 1964-65; sec. Govt. Employees Ins. Co., 1965-66; adminstrv. asst. Rheingold Breweries, Bklyn., 1966-69; partner ARTvertising Agy., N.Y.C., 1969-71; reprographic services mgr. Singer Co., Stamford, Conn., 1971-85, reprographic services mgr., 1985—. Mem. Union Vale Park Commn., 1977-78, Union Vale Bicentennial Com., 1975-76; chmn. publicity Union Vale Republican Club, 1977-78. Recipient citation of appreciation Am. Legion, 1967; award of merit Union Vale Bicentennial Com., 1976, cert. of merit Dutchess Community Coll.; Mgmt. award The Singer Co., 1983. Mem. Bus. Forms Mgmt. Assn. (sec. N.Y. chpt.), Mgmt. Books Inst., Nat. Assn. Female Execs., Am. Soc. Exec. Women, Exec. Program. Roman Catholic. Club: All Sport Fitness and Racquetball. Office: Singer Co 8 Stamford Forum Stamford CT 06904

GAUTIER-DALCHÉ, JEAN JACQUES, history educator; b. Podensac, Gironde, France, Mar. 31, 1913; s. Gabriel Francois and Marie Jeanne (Dalché) Gautier; m. Lydie Arbaudie, Aug. 14, 1939; children—Alain, Patrick. B.A., U. Bordeaux, 1931; M.A., U. Sorbonne, 1936, Ph.D., 1971. Prof., Lycee, Oujda, Rabat, Morocco, 1940-43; resident Casa de Velá zquez, Madrid, 1946-49; prof. Lycé e, Casablanca, Morocco, 1949-58, U. Rabat, Morocco, 1958-65; prof. history U. Nice, France, 1965-81, prof. emeritus, 1981—. Author: Histoire économique et sociale de l'Espagne chrétienne au Moyen Age, 1976; Historia urbana de Leon y Castille en la Edad Media (Siglos IX-XIII), 1979; Economie et societé dans les pays de la Couronne de Castille, 1982. Contbr. numerous articles to profl. jours. Served to lt. French Navy, 1939-40, 43-45. Recipient Presdl. Unit citation Pres. U.S., 1945; Croix du Cumbattant, 1945, caballero Orden de Isabel la Católica, King of Spain, 1979. Fellow Real Academia de la Historia. Home: Parc Vigier 5, 23 bd F Pilatte, 06300 Nice France Office: U Nice, Faculty Lettres, 98 Bd Edouard-Herriot, 06007 Nice Cedex France

GAUZON, ZORAYDA AIDA BENJAMIN, physician, obstetrician, gynecologist; b. Biñan, Laguna, Philippines, Nov. 26, 1943; d. Domingo Salandanan and Elena Guico (Lim) Benjamin; m. Antonio mondragon Gauzon, Jan. 5, 1969; children: Jocelyn, Antonio Jr., Maria Virginia Regina. MD, U. of the E., 1968. Resident ob.-gyn. Philippine Gen. Hosp., Manila, 1968-70; instr. obstetrics U. of the Philippines, Manila, 1969-70; prof. family planning U. of Negros Occidental and Riverside Med. City, Bacolod City, Philippines, 1972-74; cons. ob.-gyn. Bacolod Doctor's Hosp. and Riverside Med. Ctr., Bacolod City, 1972—. Mem. REACH Found. for Drug Abuse, Bacolod City, 1984—, Days With the Lord, Bacolod City, 1980—. Recipient Disting. Citizen award Biñan Disaster Rehab. Council, 1972, Disting. Mem. award Rotary, 1983. Mem. Philippine Ob.-Gyn. Soc., Philippine Med. Women's Assn. (bd. dirs. Negros chpt., Med. Assistance award 1982, Negros Occidental Med. Soc. (life), Philippine Med. Assn. (life, Med. Assistance award 1980, 81, 82). Lodge: Rotary (bd. dirs. Bacolod City club 1977-81). Home: #1 Margarita Rd, Capitolville Subdivision, Bacolod City Negros Occidental, Philippines 6001 Office: Riverside Med Ctr, North Dr, Bacolod City Negros Occidental, Philippines 6001

GAVA, ANTONIO, Italian government official; b. Castellamare di Stabia, Italy, July 30, 1930. Chair Union Provinices Italy, 1968, provincial sec. Naples, 1969; chair 1st Regional Assn. Campania, Christian Dem. Group, Campania; M.P. Italy, Rome, 1972—, minister posts and telecommunications, from 1986, minister interior, 1988—. Address: Camera del Deputati, Rome Italy *

GAVALÁS, ALEXANDER BEARY, artist; b. Limerick, Ireland, Jan. 6, 1945; came to U.S., 1946; s. Emmanuel Zenon and Mary (Beary) G. Diploma, Sch. Art & Design, N.Y.C., 1963; student Manhattanville Coll., 1969-70, Guilmant Organ Sch., 1970, Kerpel Sch. Dental Tech., 1972. Cert. 20th Century Hudson River Artist. One man shows at Krasl Art Ctr., St. Joseph Mich., 1980, The Tweed Mus. Art, U. Minn., Duluth, 1980, Fine Arts Center of Clinton, Ill., 1980, Western Ill. U. Library Gallery, Macomb, 1981, Ft. Wayne Mus. Art, Ind., 1982, Mary crest Coll., Eberdt Art Gallery, Davenport, Iowa, 1982, Arnot Art Mus., Elmira, N.Y., 1982, Queens Coll. Art Ctr., Flushing, N.Y., 1983; exhibited in group shows Taft Hotel, N.Y.C., 1964, J. Walter Thompson Art Gallery, N.Y.C., 1964, Hudson River Mus., Yonkers, N.Y., 1974-75, Far Gallery, N.Y.C., 1976-79, Eric Galleires, N.Y.C., 1981-82. Contbr. articles to profl. jours. Honorable mention Congl. record 88th congres for cultural contbr. to Life or Nation, 1964, award for work on spl. file Smithsonian Inst. from Harry Rand. Address: 65 Horton St Malverne NY 11565

GAVAZZI, ALADINO A., medical center administrator; b. Exeter, Pa., July 24, 1922; s. Guido and Ambrozina (Santoni-O'Brien) G.; m. Nancylee Ray, June 21, 1958; children—William A., Ann Marie, Lisa Kathryn, Alan Lee, Michael J. B.S., Columbia, 1953, M.S., 1955; Ph.D., U. Chgo., 1959. Adminstrv. officer VA br.-dist. office, N.Y.C., 1946-50; med. adminstrv. officer VA hosps., Bklyn., Bronx, N.Y., 1950-53; hosp. adminstrv. resident Bronx, Beth Israel and Presbyn. hosps., N.Y.C., 1953-54; hosp. adminstr. VA Hosps., Hampton, Va., 1955-57; hosp. adminstr. Chgo. Research Hosp., 1957-59, Dwight, Ill., 1960-62; hosp. adminstr. Mt. Alto VA Hosp., Washington, 1963-64; dir. VA Med. Ctr., Martinsburg, W.Va., 1964-68; exec. asst. to Chief Med. Dir. and Dir. for Adminstrn., Washington, 1968-71; dir. med. dist. and med. ctr. VA Med. Ctr., Washington, 1971-86; mem. State Health Coordinating Council, Washington, 1971-86; health care cons., lectr. 1986—; guest lectr. hosp. adminstrn. Med. Coll. Va., Richmond, Northwestern U., Chgo., U. Fla., U. Ala., Duke U., Cornell U., Columbia U., U. Sao Paulo, Brazil; adj. prof. in internat. health Georgetown U.; bd. dirs. Vinson Hall Corp., McLean, Va.;. Dist. chmn. Boy Scouts Am., W.Va., 1967-68; chmn. Combined Fed. Campaign for W.Va. for all fed. agys., 1966-68; mem. citizens bd. Providence Med. Ctr., Washington, 1976-87; bd. dirs., trustee U.S. Navy and Marine Coast Guard Residence Found., McLean, 1986—; bd. dirs. Vinson Hall Found., McLean, Va., 1986—, Navy-Marine-Coast Guard Found., Washington, 1986—. Served to 1st lt. Armored Div. AUS, 1940-45; ret. Col. USAR, 1981—. Recipient Outstanding Performance awards VA, 1952, 56, 59, 63, 65, 70, 74, 80, Exceptional Service award, 1981; Disting. Career award 1986, Nat. Civil Servant of Year-Silver Helmet award Amvets, 1974. Fellow Am. Coll. Hosp. Adminstrs. (regent for D.C. 1965-69, mem. various commns.), Royal Soc. Health (London), Am. Hosp. Assn.; mem. Fed. Exec. Inst. Alumni Assn. (pres. 1974-75). Home: 1541 Dahlia Ct McLean VA 22101

GAVELIS, JONAS RIMVYDAS, dentist, educator; b. Boston, Jan. 11, 1950; s. Mykolas and Janina (Povydis) G.; m. Bonnie Sylvester; children—Gregory, Nikolas. B.S., U. Mass., Amherst, 1971; D.M.D., U. Conn., 1975. Resident in dentistry Cabrini Health Care Center, N.Y.C., 1975-76; fellow in prosthetic dentistry Harvard U. Sch. Dental Medicine, Boston, 1976-78, instr., 1978-79; asst. prof. U. Conn. Sch. Dental Medicine, Farmington, 1979-82; practice dentistry specializing in prosthodontics Harvard Community Health Plan, Boston, 1982—; asst. prof. Harvard Sch. Dental Medicine, 1982—. Contbr. articles on prosthetic dentistry to profl. jours. Fellow Acad. Gen. Dentistry (Vernon S. Johnson award 1981). Recipient Health Care for the Homeless Program Diamond award, 1988. Mem. ADA, Northeast Prosthodontic Soc., Internat. Assn. Dental Research, Am. Assn. Dental Schs., Harvard Odontological Soc., Am. Acad. Crown and Bridge Prosthodontics. Roman Catholic. Clubs: Southboro (Mass.), Rod and Gun, New Eng. Aquarium Dive (Boston), Southboro Rod and Gun. Home: 1238 Washington St Gloucester MA 01930 Office: Harvard Community Health Plan 2 Fenway Plaza Boston MA 02215

GAVEY, JAMES E., real estate investment and construction company executive; b. Buffalo, June 6, 1942; s. George W. and Clara E. (Hanley) G.; m. Joan M. Moran, June 6, 1964; children: Philip W., Peter J., John P. BS, LeMoyne Coll., 1964; MBA, Columbia U., 1965. Acct. Peat, Marwick, Mitchell & Co., Buffalo, 1960-64; bus. cons. Arthur Andersen & Co., N.Y.C., 1965-73; pres. Gavey & Company, Inc., N.Y.C., 1973-87; founder, 1988—. Contbr. articles to profl. jours. Chmn. com. United Fund, Bronxville, N.Y., 1970—; commr. Tuckahoe (N.Y.) Housing Authority, 1974-76, chmn., 1976-81; capt. N.Y. ann. fund Fordham Prep. Sch., 1980-83. Recipient various achievement awards. Mem. Am. Inst. CPA's, N.Y. State Soc. CPA's, Fla. Soc. CPA's, Fla. Inst. CPA's, Nat. Assn. Rev. Appraisers, Internat. Inst. Valuers, Nat. Apt. Assn., Nat. Assn. Home Builders, Newcomen Soc. N.Am. Republican. Roman Catholic. Clubs: Union League, Cooperstown Country. Home and Office: PO Box 2158 Marco Island FL 33969

GAVIN, T. EDWARD, investor; b. Jersey City, Aug. 20, 1922; s. Thomas P. and Josephine E. (Groves) G.; B.S., St. Peter's Coll., 1945; M.S., Stevens Inst. Tech., 1955; postgrad. N.Y. U., 1955-59; Ph.D. (hon.), 1980; m. Allene Helen Scheithauer, Aug. 18, 1951. Asst. sales mgr. B.T. Babbitt Co., N.Y.C., 1951-53; sales mgr. Gallawhau Chem. Co., N.Y.C., 1953-55; mktg. research account exec. Batten, Barton, Durstine & Osborn, N.Y.C., 1955-58; dir. research Lennen Newell Co., N.Y.C., 1958-61; dir. corp. research for devel. Am. Cyanamide Co., Wayne, N.J., 1958-63; mgr. comml. research and intelligence Cyanamide Internat., 1963-66; investor, real estate developer, farm operator, 1966-81. Mem. bd. regents St. Peter's Coll., pres. bd., 1980-81, trustee, 1982—; chief exec. officer World Trade Industries, 1985—; dir. ARDA, 1987—; active Mental Health Assn. Hudson County (N.J.). Mem. Am. Chem. Assn., Chem. Industry Assn., Chem. Market Research Assn., Assn. Governing Bds. Univs. and Colls., Nat. Time Sharing Assocs. Am. Land Devel. Assn., Nature Conservancy. Clubs: Hudson County University, Chemists, Towanda Hunt, Bergen Carteret, Ducks Unlimited, Nags Head Woods. Home: 201 St Pauls Ave Jersey City NJ 07306 also: SR 275 Kitty Hawk NC 27949

GAVLOCK, EUGENE HARLAN, retail drinking water equipment co. exec.; b. Rockford, Ill., Mar. 28, 1925; s. Paul G. and Melvina C. (Smith) G.; master barber degree Cedar Rapids Barber Coll., 1955; m. Margaret Berneice Andersen, Feb. 15, 1952; children—Gregory Douglas, Sheryl Lynn, Carol Jean, Sharon Kay, Peggy Ann, Karla Raye, Kary Kaye. Drummer, bandleader various nat. bands, Gene Harlan Orch., 1942-54; barber, Waterloo, Iowa, 1954-60; owner, mgr. Violet Ray Coin Laundry, Waterloo, 1960-65; pres. Locktow Products, Inc., Waterloo, 1965-70; auto. salesman Simpson Dodge, Waterloo, 1967-70; pres. Pure Water Assos., Waterloo, 1974-79, Pure Water Assos., Internat., Inc., Waterloo, 1979—; pres., founder Distillerland Discount Centers, Inc., Cedar Falls, Iowa, 1979—; pres. Midwest Distilled Water Bottlers, Inc., Inc., Cedar Falls, 1983—. Pres. Blackhawk Village Mchts. Assn., 1982—. Named Outstanding Sales Individual for Yr., Pure Water, Inc., 1979. Mem. Nat. Assn. Self-Employed, Nat. Fedn. Ind. Bus., Internat. Platform Assn., C. of C., Family Motor Coach Assn. Home: 132 Hampshire Rd Waterloo IA 50701 Office: 600 State St Cedar Falls IA 50613

GAY, SERGE DELMAS, artist; b. Port-au-Prince, Haiti, Aug. 28, 1953; s. Jules and Mercilia Marie (Delmas) G.; m. Marie Micerose, Dec. 29, 1977; children: Stephael, Sebastien, Serge Jr. Grad. in fine art, Fines Art Conalyt, Mexico City, 1978; degree in conservation and restoration of ceramics, I.N.A.C., Panama City, Panama, 1982. Founder Gay Pottery, Port-au-Prince, 1973—, mgr., 1976-85; tchr. Nat. Sch. Fine Art, Port-au-Prince, 1983-85, Montessori Sch. d'Haiti, Port-au-Prince, 1983-85. Exhbtr. sculpture and ceramics, 1974—. Studio: 657 Van Siclen Ave Brooklyn NY 11207

GAYA, HAROLD, medical microbiologist; b. Glasgow, Scotland, Oct. 15, 1940; s. Ralph and Anne (Salamon) G.; M.B., Ch.B., Glasgow U., 1963; m. Celia Jeffries, June 1, 1969; children—Andrew, David, Richard. Lectr. microbiology St. Bartholomew's Hosp. Med. Coll., U. London, 1965-71, cons. microbiologist Royal Postgrad. Med. Sch., Hammersmith Hosp., 1971-74, reader microbiology St. Mary's Hosp. Med. Sch., 1974-80, hon. sr. lectr. Cardiothoracic Inst., 1980—; cons., dir. depts. microbiology Nat. Heart and Chest Hosps., Brompton Hosp., London, 1980—; found. pres. Internat. Antimicrobial Therapy Group, European Orgn. Research on Treatment of Cancer, 1973-78, sec., 1978—. Fellow Royal Coll. Pathologists, Royal Soc. Medicine; mem. Brit. Med. Assn., Brit. Soc. Antimicrobial Chemotherapy, Hosp. Infection Soc., Am. Soc. Microbiology, Infectious Diseases Soc. Am. (corr. fellow). Contbr. numerous articles to profl. jours. Office: Nat Heart and Chest Hosps, Brompton Hosp Fulham Rd, London SW3 6HP, England

GAYLORD, EDWARD LEWIS, publishing company executive; b. Denver, May 28, 1919; s. Edward King and Inez (Kinney) G.; m. Thelma Feragen, Aug. 30, 1950; children: Christine Elizabeth, Mary Inez, Edward King II, Thelma Louise. A.B., Stanford U., 1941; LL.D., Oklahoma City U., Okla. Christian Coll., Pepperdine U., 1984. Chmn., chief exec. officer Gaylord Broadcasting Co., Oklahoma City, also bd. dirs.; chmn., chief exec. officer Sta. WSM-AM-FM, Nashville, also bd. dirs.; chmn., chief exec. officer Sta. KTVT, Dallas and Ft. Worth, also bd. dirs.; chmn., chief exec. officer Sta. KHTV, Houston, also bd. dirs.; chmn., chief exec. officer Sta. WVTV, Milw., also bd. dirs.; chmn., chief exec. officer Sta. KSTW-TV, Seattle and Tacoma, also bd. dirs.; chmn., chief exec. officer Sta. WUAB-TV, Cleve. and Lorain, Ohio, also bd. dirs.; pres., gen. mgr. Okla. Pub. Co., also bd. dirs.; editor, pub. Daily Oklahoman, Sunday Oklahoman; pres. Sun Resources, Inc., Greenland (Colo.) Ranch, OPUBCO Resources, Inc., OPUBCO Devel. Co.; chmn. Opryland U.S.A., Inc., Nashville; chmn. bd. Gayno, Inc., Colorado Springs, ptnr. Cimarron Coal Co., Denver, Lazy E Ranch, St. Jo, Tex., Westwind Ranch, San Saba, Tex.; bd. dirs. Telerate, Inc., N.Y.C. Chmn., trustee Okla. Industries Authority; hon. chmn. bd. govs. Okla. Christian Coll.; bd. dirs. Okla. State Fair, pres., 1961-71; chmn. bd. dirs. Nat. Cowboy Hall of Fame and Western Heritage Ctr.; vice chmn. bd. govs. Am. Citizenship Ctr.; chmn. Okla. Med. Research Found., 1983—; past trustee Casady Sch., Oklahoma City U. Served with AUS, 1942-46. Recipient Brotherhood award NCCJ named to Okla. Hall of Fame, 1974; first recipient Spirit of Am. award U.S. Olympic Com., 1984; Disting. Service award U. Okla., 1981; Golden Plate award Am. Acad. Achievement, 1985. Mem. Oklahoma City C. of C. (dir., past pres.), So. Newspaper Pubs. Assn. (past pres.). Conglist. Home: 1506 Dorchester Dr Oklahoma City OK 73120 Office: Gaylord Broadcasting Co PO Box 25125 Oklahoma City OK 73125

GAYMAN, PATRICIA GYNETH, chiropractor; b. San Pedro, Calif., Aug. 16, 1938; d. Norman Alan and Olive Delone (Jensen) Smith; m. Robert Dale May, Jan. 13, 1956 (div. Nov. 1968); children: Cheryl, Robert, Karla, Kym, Leland, Deirdre, Stacy; m. Merrill Gene Gayman, Mar. 29, 1969. Student Monterey Peninsula Coll., 1958-59, Shasta Coll., 1971-73; D.C., Palmer Coll. of Chiropractic, 1964. Chiropractor, Monterey, Calif., 1964; assoc. in chiropractic practice, Hayward, Calif., 1968-69, Redding, Calif., 1974-87; owner, operator Gayman Chiropractice Ctr., Redding, 1979-87; owner, operator The Whole Approach, Redding, 1987-88; founder Metaphys. Exploration Ctr., Redding, 1973-83; dir. Wellness Resource Ctr., Redding, 1979-87; founder, sponsor Holistic Health Fair, 1979-86; speaker. Contbr. articles to profl. jours. Personnel chmn. Family Planning Inc., Redding, 1972-77; regent Pacific States Chiropractic Coll., San Leandro, 1979-81; team tchr. Parker Chiropractic Resource Found.; sec. Jazz Soc., Redding, 1985-86. Named Dr. of Yr., Parker Chiropractic Resource Found., 1987. Mem. Nat. Assn. Female Execs., Bus. and Profl. Women's Club (Woman of Yr. 1987), C. of C. (bd. dirs. 1987-88, Bus. Woman of Yr. 1985). Avocations: continuing education, metaphysical studies. Home: 2146 Stillspring Pl Martinez CA 94553

GAYNOR, LEE, media service co. exec.; b. N.Y.C., Dec. 9, 1927; B.S., N.Y.U., 1949; m. Martha Freidler, July 5, 1952; children—Steven, Eric, Robert. Media dir. William G. Seidenbaum, N.Y.C., 1949-50; sr. time buyer Doherty, Clifford, Steers and Shenfield, N.Y.C., 1950-56; media supr. Dancer, Fitzgerald-Sample, N.Y.C., 1956-58; nat. sales mgr. Rust Craft Broadcasting Co., N.Y.C., 1958-67; pres. Colonial Records, N.Y.C., 1967-69, Cornwall Posters Inc., N.Y.C., 1967-69; Cornwall Records Inc., 1967-69; exec. v.p. Video Girls Cosmetics, N.Y.C., 1967-69; chmn. bd. Media Partners, Inc., N.Y.C., 1969-73; pres. Gaynor Media Corp., N.Y.C., 1974—. Bd. dirs. New Orch. of Westchester, Hartsdale, N.Y., 1987—. Mem. Internat. Radio and TV Soc., Advt. Club N.Y., N.Y.U. Alumni Assn., Alpha Delta Sigma (past. chmn., dir., pres.). Club: Friars. Contbr. articles to profl. jours. Home: 120 Central Park S New York NY 10019 Office: 555 5th Ave New York NY 10017 Other: 120 Central Park South New York NY 10019

GAYOOM, MAUMOON ABDUL, president Maldives; b. Dec. 16, 1939; m. Nasreena Ibrahim; 4 children; ed. Al-Ahzar U., Cairo, Am. U. Cairo. D. Litt. (hon.), Algarh Muslim U. India, 1983. Lectr. in Islamic studies Abdullahi Bayero Coll., Ahmadu Bello U., Nigeria, 1969-71; tchr. Aminiyo Sch., 1971; entered Govt. service Maldives, 1971, dir. telephone dept.; mgr. govt. shipping dept., 1972-73, dir., 1973-74; spl. undersec. Office Prime Minister, 1974-75; dep. ambassador to Sri Lanka, 1975-76; permanent rep. to UN, 1976-77, head del. Gen. Assembly, 1976; minister of transport, 1977-78; pres. Republic of Maldives, 1978—, also responsible for home affairs, edn., provincial affairs, public safety, and agr., 1978-80, minister if Def. and nat. security; gov. Cen. Bank. Office: Office of Pres, Male Maldives *

GAYRARD, PIERRE JEAN, pneumologist; b. Marseille, France, Dec. 17, 1934; s. Andre and France (Senequier) G.; children: Delphine, Julien. MD, U. Marseille, 1965. Intern Hosp. Marseille, 1963-67; resident NYU, 1966; chef de clinique Faculte de Medecine, Marseille, 1967-72; practice medicine specializing in pneumology Draguignan, 1972—; chief of service in pneumology Draguignan Hosp., 1975—. Contbr. articles to profl. jours. Pres. Amis de Saint Hermentaire, 1984. Served with French Army, 1962. Roman Catholic. Home: 64 Ave Carnot, 83300 Draguignan France Office: General Hosp, Route de Montferrat, 83300 Draguignan France

GAZALE, MIDHAT JOSEPH, communications company executive; b. Alexandria, Egypt, July 22, 1929; s. Joseph H. and Adele Georgette (Debs) G.; m. Marielle Stamm (div. 1971); children: Stephane, Valerie, Olivia. BEE, Cairo U., Egypt, 1951; MEE, Ecole Supérieure d'Electricité, Paris, 1953; DS, Sorbonne U., France, 1959. Registered profl. engr. Egypt. Dir. product mktg. IBM, 1956-66; dir. corp. product strategy Co. Internat. pour l'Info., 1966-74; pres. Inforex France, 1975, Inforex Internat., 1976-79; chmn. bd. I.C.L. France, 1979, v.p., 1979-83; chmn. bd. Sperry France, 1983, v.p. internat. div., 1984; v.p. European div. AT&T, 1985-87, pres. directorate, 1987; prof. mgmt. Sorbonne U., 1982—. Decorated De l'Ordre Du Merite Pres. the Republic of France, 1981. Clubs: Automobile, Cercle Interallie Racing (Paris). Home: 9 Rue du Centre, 92200 Neuilly France Office: AT&T France, 2 Quai De dion Bouton, 92800 Puteaux France

GAZIS, DENOS CONSTANTINOS, electrical engineer; b. Salonica, Greece, Sept. 15, 1930; s. Evangelos George and Lila Constantine (Veniamin) G.; came to U.S., 1953, naturalized, 1960; BS, Tech. U. Athens (Greece), 1952; MS, Stanford U., 1954; PhD in Engring. Mechs., Columbia U., 1957; m. Jean Ellen Ryniker, Sept. 15, 1974; children—Paul, Jean, Lynn, Andrew, Carey, Jessie, Alexander, James, Kyle. Sr. research scientist Gen. Motors Co., Warren, Mich., 1957-61; with IBM, 1961—, dir. gen. scis. dept., 1970-74, tech. adv. to v.p., chief scientist, Armonk, N.Y., 1975-77, cons. to v.p., dir. research, Yorktown Heights, N.Y., 1977-79, asst. dir. computer scis. dept., 1979-82, asst. dir. semicondr. sci. and tech. dept., 1982—; vis. prof. Yale U., 1969-70; cons. to govt. agys.; mem. transp. research bd. NRC-Nat. Acad. Scis., mem. Commn. Engring. and Tech. Systems, mem. Bldg. Research Bd. Recipient Lanchester prize Johns Hopkins U.-Ops. Research Soc. Am., 1959. Mem. Ops. Research Soc. Am., Soc. Natural Philosophy, AAAS, N.Y. Acad. Scis. Author: Free Vibrations of Circular Cylindrical Shells, 1969; Traffic Science, 1974; asso. editor Transp. Sci., 1970-82, editor, 1983-86; assoc. editor Networks, 1971-81, adv. editor, 1981—; asso. editor Computing, 1969-76; contbr. articles on physics, engring. and ops. research to profl. jours. Home: RR 4 Lake Rd Katonah NY 10536 Office: IBM Research Ctr Box 218 Yorktown Heights NY 10598

GBEHO, JAMES VICTOR, Ghanaian diplomat; b. Keta, Ghana, Jan. 12, 1935; s. Philip and Louise Gbeho; B.A., U. Ghana, 1959; m. Edith Wuta-Ofei, Aug. 14, 1961; children—Eric, Anita, Kenneth. With Fgn. Service of Ghana, 1959—; 2d sec., Peking, 1960-61, New Delhi, 1961-63; 1st sec., Lagos, 1963-64; counselor Permanent Mission to UN, N.Y.C., 1964-67; minister, counselor, Bonn, 1969-71; dep. high commr., London, 1972-76; supervising dir. Internat. Orgns. and Confs. Bur., Ministry of Fgn. Affairs, Accra, Ghana, 1976-78; ambassador to UN, Geneva, 1978-80, permanent rep. UN, N.Y.C., 1980—; chmn. com. econ. cooperation among developing countries UNCTAD V., 1979; chmn. Prep. Commn. Common Fund for Commodities, 1980—; chmn. 1st com. (pol. and security), 37th sesssion of Gen. Assembly (1982); chmn. United Nations Disarmament Commn. (1984); chmn. 4th com. (decolonisation) 41st session Gen. Assembly (1986); mem. Security Council (1986-87). Roman Catholic. Office: Ghana Mission to UN 19 E 47th St New York NY 10017

GBEWONYO, SYLVESTRE KWADZO, financial manager; b. Sekondi, Ghana, Mar. 16, 1942; s. James Constance Awovor and Dorothea Aku (Sedode) G.; m. Gifty Esi Ribeiro, June 28, 1969; children: Sylvestre Jerry, Hugh Fifi, Theophile Edem, Rene Dela. Degree in hosp. adminstrn., U. Ghana, Legon, 1967; MSc in Fin. Mgmt., U. Southampton, Eng., 1985. Hosp. adminstr. Ministry of Health, Accra, Ghana, 1967-70, Volta River Authority, Ghana, 1970-75; chief acct. motors div. UTC Ghana Ltd., Accra, 1975-79; chief acct., adminstrv. mgr. Jos Hansen & Soehne Ghana, Ltd., Accra, 1979-81; fin. mgr. World Vision Internat., Accra, 1981-87; regional fin. mgr. World Vision Internat., Western Africa, 1987—; lectr. acctg. Accra Poly., 1975-77, U. Ghana, 1986—; lectr. bus. fin. Inst. Profl. Studies, Accra, 1987—. Recipient Norman Griffiths prize Corp. Cert. Secs., London, 1967. Mem. Inst. Chartered Secs. and Adminstrs., Brit. Inst. Mgmt., Soc. Strategic and Long Range Planning. Lodge: Rotary. Home: 3 Bamboo St, Teshie/ Nugua Estates, Accra Ghana Office: World Vision Internat, Pvt Mail Bag, Accra North Ghana

GE, WUJUE, writer; b. Zhe Jiang, People's Republic of China, Sept. 12, 1937; s. Luyang Ge and Wecang Zhang; m. Zhao Baoqing, Feb. 1, 1962; 1 child, Cong. Student, Beijing U., 1955-58, People's U. Beijing, 1958-59. Journalist Ningxia (People's Republic of China) Daily, 1959-83; writer Fedn. Art and Lit. Ningxia, 1983—, chmn., 1988—; del. to Sixth Internat. Writers Conf., 1986. Author: A Journalist and Her Story, 1982, (short story) An Experience in the Summer, 1982, adapted for TV, 1985, (short story) She and Her Girl Friend, 1984, Four Days in All of Life, 1988, adapted for TV. Vice leader Fedn. Polit. Party Ningxia, 1982. Mem. Union of Journalists, The Union of Writers (vice chmn.). Mem. The Communist Party of China. Home: Culture St, Yichuan, Ningxia People's Republic of China Office: Fedn Art and Lit, Culture St, Ningxia People's Republic of China

GEADA, EDUARDO MANUEL C.F., film director; b. Lisbon, Portugal, May 21, 1945; s. Antonio Fernandes and Maria Piedade (Carvalho) G.; divorced; children: Rossana, Apolloni. PhD in Letters, Faculdade Letras, Lisbon, 1975; D in Film, U. London, 1978; M in Media, U. Nova, Lisbon, 1985. Journalist A Capital, Lisbon, 1968-74; free lance film maker Lisbon, 1974—, free lance TV producer, 1974—; tchr. Conservatory of Arts, Lisbon, 1979—; film, letter critic A Capital, Lisbon, 1986—. Author: Imperialism and Fascism in Cinema, 1977, Cinema and Transfiguration, 1978, The Power of Cinema, 1985, The Aesthetics of Cinema, 1985, Cinema As Spectacle, 1987; dir., producer feature films Sofia and the Sexual Education, 1973, The Holly Alliance, 1976, Mariana Alcoforado, 1979, Greetings To D. Genciana, 1983-85; (TV films) Lisboa, The Right To The City, 1974, He Boss's Funeral, 1975; (TV series) Feastime, 1976, Risk and Drawing, 1978-79, Lisbon: The Anonymous Society, 1981-82, The Form of Things, 1986. Gulbenkian fellow, 1977-78; scholar U. Nova, 1984-85. Fellow Portuguese Film Makers Assn.; mem. Portuguese Authors Soc. Home: R Prof Hernani Cidade 3-5A, 1600 Lisbon Portugal

GEALY, WALFORD LLOYD, philosopher, educator; b. Llanelli, Wales, Sept. 18, 1938; s. Gwilym and Sarah Jane (Owen) G.; m. Marlene Norah Squires, Dec. 24, 1960; children: Ioan, Catrin, Steffan. BA in Philosophy, U. Wales, 1962; BLitt in Philosophy of Religion, U. Oxford, Eng., 1966; MLitt, U. Oxford, 1982. Tutor in philosophy dept. extra mural studies Univ. Coll. Wales, Aberystwyth, 1979-87, sr. tutor in philosophy, 1987—; named J.R. Jones Meml. Lectr., Univ. Coll., Wales. Author: Wittgenstein; co-editor Efrydiau Athronyddol. Home: Awelon Queens Ave, Aberystwyth, Dyfed SY23 2EG, England Office: Univ Coll Wales, Dept Extra Mural Studies, 9 Marine Terr, Aberystwyth, Dyfed SY23 2AX, Wales

GEAR, ANTHONY RALPH EDWARD, corporation executive, analyst; b. Coventry, England, July 25, 1938; s. Ralph Douglas and Grace Emily (Pritchard) G.; m. Jillian Turney, Aug. 1, 1966; children: Andrew Edward, Sarah Jane. BSc in Physics, Queen Mary Coll., 1961; PhD in Astro Physics, U. London, 1965. Research officer Steel Co. of Wales, Port Talbot, Eng., 1965-66; prin. engr. Plessey, Hants, Eng., 1966-68; sr. research fellow Manchester (Eng.) Bus. Sch., 1968-72; sr. lectr. Open U., Milton Keynes, Eng., 1972-75; assoc. prof. U. Auckland, New Zealand, 1975-80; prof. bus. studies Trent Poly Tech., Nottingham, Eng., 1980-85; mgr., head ctr. for mgmt. studies Royal Ordnance PLC, Chorley, Eng., 1985—; bd. dirs. Corp. Mgmt. Cons., Ltd., London, Decision Dynamics Ltd., Wigan, Okla.; exec. officer U.S. New Zealsnd Sci. Program, Auckland, 1978-80; mem. CNAA Com., London, 1982-85. Author: (with others) Management in Education, 1975, (with others) A Second Guide to Operational Research, 1977. Mem. Operational Research Soc., Inst. Mgmt. Sci., Inst. Physics. Office: Royal Ordnance PLC, Euxton Ln, Chorley, Lancs England

GEARY, DAVID LESLIE, military officer, educator, communication executive; b. Connellsville, Pa., Sept. 30, 1947; s. Harry and Edith Marie (Halterman) G.; B.A., Otterbein Coll., 1969; M.S.J., W.Va. U., 1971; postgrad. U. Denver, 1974-75; diploma Defense Info. Sch., 1971, Def. Dept. Sr. Pub. Affairs Officers Course, 1984, Nat. Def. U., 1986. Foreign Service Inst., US Dept. State, 1984. Admissions counselor Otterbein Coll., 1968-69; instr. English, staff counselor Office of Student Ednl. Services, W.Va. U., Morgantown, 1969-71; dir. info. Luke AFB, Ariz., 1971-72; course dir. English and communications U.S. Air Force Acad., Colo., 1972-76; dir. public affairs Loring AFB, Maine, 1976-79, spl. asst. pub. affairs, Seymour Johnson AFB, N.C., 1980: U.S. Air Force Engring. and Services Center, Tyndall AFB, Fla., 1980-84, U.S. Air Forces, Korea, 1984-85; assoc. prof. aerospace studies U. Ala., 1985-88; dir. community relations USAFR, 1988—; guest lectr. U. Maine, 1976-79, U.S. Air Force Inst. Tech., 1981-82, Fla. State U., 1982-83, U. Md., 1984-85, U. So. Calif., 1984-85, Seoul (Korea) Nat. U., 1985. Decorated 3 Meritorious Service medals, 2 Air Force commendation medals, Air Force Achievement medal, Armed Forces Reserve medal, Humanitarian Service medal, Nat. Def. Service medal, various others; Reader's Digest Found. grantee, 1970; recipient Pres.'s Extraordinary Service award Otterbein Coll., 1969, Nat. Disting. Service medal Arnold Air Soc., 1986; nominee U. Ala. Outstanding Commitment to Teaching award, 1987. Mem. Nat. Acad. TV Arts and Scis., Am. Assn. Public Opinion Research, Public Relations Soc. Am., Internat. Assn. Bus. Communicators. Republican. Episcopalian. Home: 4C Springhill Lake Tuscaloosa AL 35405-4750 Office: USAFR Office Pub Affairs Robins AFB GA 31098

GECKELER, HORST FRITZ, university professor; b. Sulz, Württemberg, Fed. Republic Germany, Oct. 4, 1935; s. Ernst Wilhelm and Hedwig Johanna (Beilharz) G.; m. Armelle Jeanne Pilven, Oct. 16, 1964; children: Tilmann, Eleonor, Alba. Student, U. Paris and U. Leicester (Eng.); staatsexamen, U. Tübingen, 1964, PhD, 1969, habilitation, 1973. Asst. prof. U. Tübingen, 1965-69, temp. prof., 1973-74; temp. prof. U. Merida, Venezuela, 1970-71, U. Pamplona, Spain, 1972, U. Göttingen, 1973; univ. prof. U. Münster, 1974—; dean faculty of Romance and Slavonic philologies U. Münster, 1977-78, 87—; expert Deutsche Forschungsgemeinschaft (Romance Linguistics), 1984—. Author: Zur Wortfelddiskussion, 1971, Strukturelle Semantik des Französischen, 1973, Strukturelle Semantik und Wordfeldtheorie (translations into Spanish and Italian), 1983, (with D. Kattenbusch) Einführung in die italienische Sprachwissenschaft, 1987. Mem. Deutscher Romanistenverband, Deutscher Hispanistenverband, Deutscher Italianistenverband, Soc. de Linguistique Romane, Deutscher Hochschulverband. Home: Westring 10, 4409 Havixbeck, Westfalia Federal Republic of Germany Office: Romanisches Seminar Univ, Bispinghof 3/A, 4400 Münster, Westfalia Federal Republic of Germany

GEDDA, NICOLAI H. G. (NICOLAI H. G. USTINOV), tenor; b. Stockholm, July 11, 1925; s. Michael and Olga (Gedda) Ustinov; m. Anastasia Caraviotis, Feb. 21, 1965; children: Tatiana, Dimitri. Studied with, Karl-Martin Oehman, Stockholm; attended opera sch., Stockholm Conservatory. Opera debut in Le Postillon de Longjumea, Stockholm Opera, 1952; La Scala debut in Trionfo di Afrodite, 1953; Paris Opera debut in Faust, 1954; Covent Garden debut in Rigoletto, 1954, Am. debut with Pitts. Opera in Faust, 1957, Met. Opera debut in 1957; roles include: Dimitri in Boris Godunov, Rodolpho in La Boheme, Hoffman in Les Contes d'Hoffenski in Eugene Onegin; appeared with opera cos. in Europe and N.Am., including Vienna State Opera, Hamburg (W. Ger.) Opera, Munich (W. Ger.) Opera, Budapest (Hungary) Opera, Rome Opera, Monte Carlo (Monaco) Opera, Edinburgh (Scotland) Festival, Met. Opera, La Scala, Paris Opera; rec. artist, beginning with EMI, 1952, apptd. royal ct. singer of Sweden. Decorated Order of Vasa Litteris et Artibus (Sweden), comdr. Order Daneborg (Denmark); winner Christine Nilsson award. Mem. Royal Acad. Stockholm (hon. mem.). Office: care Les Askonas, 19 A Air St, London W1, England *

GEDDES, JOHN STAFFORD, cardiologist; b. Belfast, No. Ireland, June 10, 1939; s. Stafford and Rachel Olive (Semple) G.; m. Florence Anne Hughes, May 5, 1969; children: Stephen William, John Stafford. BSc with honors, Queen's U., Belfast, 1960; MB, Queen's U., 1963, MD, 1966. House physician Royal Victoria Hosp., Belfast, 1963-64, registrar and sr. registrar in cardiology, 1964-71, cons. clin. physiologist, 1971-77, cons. cardiologist, 1977-87; assoc. prof. medicine (cardiology) U. Manitoba, Winnipeg, 1987—; vis. scientist depts. cardiology and biophysics U. Utah, Salt Lake City, 1969-70; spl. tchr. Queen's U., 1983-87. Co-author: The Acute Coronary Attack, 1975; editor: The Management of the Acute Coronary Attack, 1986; mem. editorial com. Brit. Heart Jour., 1984-87; contbr. numerous articles to med. jours. R.R. Leathem traveling scholar, 1969-70, Mackay Wilson traveling scholar, 1969-70. Fellow Am. Coll. Cardiology, Royal Coll. Physicians (London); mem. Brit. Cardiology Soc., Brit. Pacing Electrophysiology Group. Presbyterian. Home: 100 Lamont Blvd, Winnipeg, MB Canada R3P OE6 Office: Health Scis Ctr, 700 William Ave, Winnipeg, MB Canada R3E OZ3

GEDER, LASZLO, neurologist, educator; b. Debrecen, Hungary, Aug. 11, 1932; came to U.S., 1974, naturalized, 1982; s. Joseph and Irene (Kardoss) G.; M.D., U. Debrecen, 1956, Ph.D., 1969; m. Julianna Toth, Sept. 22, 1956; children—Judith, Martha, Laszlo. Assoc. prof. dept. microbiology Med. Sch., U. Debrecen, Hungary, 1956-72; research assoc. Children's Hosp., Cin., 1964-65; Welcome research fellow dept. virology Med. Sch., U. Birmingham, Eng., 1970-71; acting head dept. microbiology, Ahmadu Bello U., Zaria, Nigeria, 1972-74; assoc. prof. dept. microbiology Coll. of Medicine, Pa. State U., Hershey, 1974-80; physician in neurology, dept. medicine Milton S. Hershey Med. Center, 1980-85, asst. prof. neurology dept. medicine, 1985—; mem. Nat. Prostatic Cancer Project. Mem. Am. Soc. Microbiology, Am. Acad. Neurology, AAAS, N.Y. Acad. Scis., Sigma Xi. Presbyterian. Contbr. numerous articles on viral oncology to profl. jours. Home: RD 1 Box 58 Valley Rd Hummelstown PA 17036 Office: Pa State U Milton S Hershey Med Ctr Div Neurology Hershey PA 17033

GEDGE, TIMOTHY JOHN HENRY, military officer; b. London, Mar. 1, 1943; s. Henry Francis Sydney and Eleanor Catherine (Lea) G.; m. Monika Eva, Dec. 17, 1976; children: Philippa Eleanor, Mary. Grad. pub. sch., Harpenden, Hertfordshire, Eng. Commd. sub lt. Royal Navy, 1963, advanced through grades to comdr.; comdg. officer 800 Naval Air Squadron, 1980-82, 809 Naval Air Squadron, 1982—. Mem. Royal Aero. Soc., British Inst. Mgmt. Club: Army and Navy (London).

GEELHAAR, CHRISTIAN WALTHER, museum administrator, art historian; b. Bern, Switzerland, Aug. 24, 1939; s. Wilhelm Heinrich and Alice Marie (Burgi) G. Dr.phil.hist., Universitat Bern, 1972. Designer Bally of Switzerland, 1959-64; freelance art historian, 1972-75; asst. curator Staatliche Graphische Sammlung Munchen, Munich, Fed. Republic Germany, 1976; curator Kunstmuseum Basel, 1977-80; dir. Oeffentliche Kunstsammlung, Basel, 1981—. Author monographs on Paul Klee, Jasper Johns, Frank Stella, others. Served to 1st lt. Swiss Army. Mem. Internat. Assn. Art Critics, Internat. Council Mus. Lodge: Rotary. Office: Oeffentliche Kunstsammlung, Saint Albangraben 16, 4010 Basel Switzerland

GEENTIENS, GASTON PETRUS, JR., former constrn. mgmt. cons. co. exec.; b. Garfield, N.J., Apr. 6, 1935; s. Gaston Petrus and Margaret (Piros) G.; B.S. in Civil Engring., The Citadel, 1956; m. Barbara Ann Chamberlain, Oct. 14, 1960; children—Mercedes Frith, Faith Piros. Plant engr. Western Elec. Co., Inc., Kearny, N.J., 1956-58, owner's rep., N.Y.C., 1960-64; v.p. Gentyne Motors, Inc., Passaic, N.J., 1958-60; project engr. Ethyl Corp., Baton Rouge, La., 1964-65; mgr. Timothy McCarthy Constrn. Co., Atlanta, 1965; asst. to v.p. A.R. Abrams, Inc. and Columbia Engring., Inc., Atlanta, 1965-66; supr. engring. and constrn. Litton Industries, N.Y.C., 1966-71; pres. G.P. Geentiens Jr., Inc., Charleston, S.C., 1971-82; gen. partner Engineered Enterprises Co., Charleston, 1973-76; dir. Cayman Broadcasting Assos., Cayman Islands, B.W.I., 1977-82. Mem. Ramapo (N.Y.) Republican Com., 1961-64. Served to 1st lt. C.E., AUS, 1956-58. Registered profl. engr., 13 states. Mem. ASCE, S.C. Indsl. Developers Assn. Club: Charleston Yacht. Home: 1219 Pembroke Dr Charleston SC 29407

GEERTINGER, PREBEN GERT, forensic pathologist; b. Copenhagen, Feb. 3, 1923; grad. Copenhagen U. Med. Sch., 1956; M.D.Sc., U. Copenhagen, 1966; m. Lilan Woldum, Sept. 22, 1966; 1 dau., Felicia. Intern, Falkenberg lazaret, Sweden, 1955-56; gen. practice medicine, 1957-59; practice forensic pathology, 1959—; dir. Govt. Inst. Forensic Medicine, U. Umea and U. Gothenburg (Sweden), 1964-70; asst. prof. forensic medicine U. Copenhagen, 1970—; sec. Danish Medico-Legal Bd. Recipient award His Majesty King Christian X's Found., 1962, 64, Danish Heart Found., 1971, 77. Author: Sudden Death in Infancy, 1968. Contbr. articles to med. jours. Home: 65A Strandvejen, 2100 Copenhagen Denmark Office: 11 Frederik den Femtes Vej, Copenhagen 2100,, Denmark

GEERTS, LEO (MIKE ADAMS), writer; b. Doel, Antwerp, Belgium, Feb. 18, 1935; s. Gerard and Anna (Huygen), G.; m. Rika Heymans, 1962; children: Hank, Ina. Licentiate in Philosophy, Catholic U., Louvain, Belgium, 1958. Literary critic De Nieuwe Mag., Brussels, 1964-84; TV presenter Flemish TV, Belgium, 1970-75; editor Streven Mag., Belgium, 1975—; Tchr. Catholic Schs., Belgium, 1964—. Author: Loeders, 1975, Pagadders, 1982, Dada-ders, 1984; plays Ballad of Blood and Tears, 1977, Free Belgium, 1980, The Fair of Blood, 1982; opera Ulrike an Antique Tragedy, 1979. Named Knight in Leopold's order, 1987. Mem. P.E.N. Club.

GEERTZ, ARMIN WILBERT, religious writer, educator; b. Elmhurst, Ill., Feb. 25, 1948; s. Armin Martin Geertz and Audrey Grace (Blum) Jedinak. Magistrate of Art, Aarhus (Denmark) U., 1978. Asst. prof. Aarhus U., 1979-82; research fellow Aarhus U., 1983-84, assoc. prof., 1984—, head dept. history of religions, 1985-87. Author: Hopi Indian Altar Iconography, 1987, Children of Cottonwood, 1988; editor: Og Da Blev Jeg En Sky, 1986, Religionsvidenskabeligt Tidsskrift mag., 1982-87; assoc. editor: Temenos: Studies in Comparative Religion mag., 1986—, European Review of Native Am. Studies mag., 1986—; contbr. articles to profl. jours. Research grantee Danish Research Council, 1978, 82, Aarhus U. Research Fund, 1986-88. Mem. Danish Assn. of History Religions (chmn. 1982—), Nordic Commn. of History Religions (chmn. 1988—), Soc. Study Indigenous Langs. Ams., Am. Indian Workshop, Soc. for Study Native Am. Religious Traditions (bd. dirs. 1987—). Office: Aarhus U Dept History Religions, Hovedbygningen, Aarhus C Denmark

GEERY, MICHAEL JAMES, electronics company executive; b. Missoula, Mont., July 15, 1937; s. Glenn Leroy and Rhye (Ward) G.; B.S. in Aero. Engring., Northrop U., 1960; m. Michelle A. Decrow, July 9, 1983; children—Laura Lynn, Angela, Jill, Holly, Michelle, Laura, Melanie, Jeff, Coleen. Electronic design engr. N. Am. Aviation, Los Angeles, 1960-62; electronic project engr. Lockheed Electronics, Los Angeles, 1962-64; biomed. electronic design engr. Space Labs Inc., Chattsworth, Calif., 1964-65; mktg. staff exec. TRW, Los Angeles, 1965-73; western area mgr. Gates Energy Products Co., Los Angeles, 1973-78; chief exec. officer Xenotronix Inc., Valencia, Calif., 1978—; cons. Mem. Ch. of Scientology. Home: 23544 Maple St Newhall CA 91351 Office: 26074 Ave Hall #10 Valencia CA 91355

GEFFNER, DONNA SUE, speech pathologist, audiologist, educator; b. N.Y.C.; d. Louis and Sally (Weiner) G.; B.A. magna cum laude, Bklyn. Coll., 1967; M.A., N.Y. U., 1968, Ph.D. (NDEA fellow), 1970, postgrad. student Advanced Inst. Analytic Psychotherapy, 1973-75. Asst. prof. Lehman Coll., 1971-76; asso. prof. dept. speech St. John's U., 1976-81, prof., 1982—, dir. Speech and Hearing Center, 1976—, chmn. dept. speech communication scis. and theater, 1983—, developer M.A. program in speech pathology and audiology; pvt. practice, 1980—; cons. to corp. execs.; TV producer and hostess NBC, 1977-78, CBS, 1978-79. Emmy nominee for Outstanding Instrnl. Program, 1978; recipient award Pres.'s Com. on Employment of Handicapped, Pres's. medal for Outstanding Faculty Achievement St. Johns U., 1987; N.Y. State Edn. Dept. grantee, 1976-78; City U. N.Y. Research Found. grantee, 1972. Fellow Am. Speech, Lang. and Hearing Assn. (legis. councillor 1978-87); mem. N.Y. State Speech and Hearing Assn. (pres. 1978-80), Audiology Study Group N.Y., Contbr. articles to profl. jours. and textbooks; issue editor Jour. Topics in Lang. Disorders, 1980; editor ASHA monograph, 1987. Office: St John's U Speech and Hearing Ctr Grand Central Pkwy Jamaica NY 11439

GEFFROY, JEAN-PHILIPPE, international management consultant; b. Paris, May 16, 1937; s. Pierre and Gisele (Feral) G.; m. Isabelle Dessevre, Aug. 18, 1962; children—Jacques, Celine. Dipl., Ecole Polytechnique, Paris, 1960; MSc Nuclear Engring., U. Calif., 1963; student Harvard Bus. Sch., 1970. Physicist UKAEA, Winfrith, UK Eng., 1964-66; mgmt. cons. McKinsey & Co., Paris, Toronto, 1966-73; physicist AEA, Winfrith, Eng., 1964-66; chief fin. officer J. Borel Internat., Paris, 1973-75; corp. controller and planning dir. Creusot Loire, Paris, 1975-79; chief fin. officer Serete Engring., Paris, 1979-80; internat. dir. Gan, Paris, 1980-83; v.p. Europe-Bendix Automation, Paris, 1983-84; internat. mgmt. cons., Paris, 1984—. Contbr. articles to profl. jours. Served to lt. Cavalry, 1960-62, Algeria. Recipient Croix de la Valeur Militaire, 1961. Expert auprès du Tribunal de Commerce. Fellow Inst. Dirs.-London; mem. X-Banque-Paris, Chambre Nationale des Conseillers Financiers, Cour d'Appel Aix (expert judiciaire). Home: 17 Rue Alphonse de Neuville, 75017 Paris France Office: Conseil en Gestion, 22 Rue de Chaillot, 75016 Chaillot France

GEGIOS, EVAN, computer company executive; b. Athens, Greece, May 1, 1946; s. Elias E. and Eugenia (Mitilineou) G.; m. Chrisanthi Soula M., July 11, 1971; 1 child, Eugenia (Venia). B.S. in Bus. Adminstrn. with high distinction, Deree Coll., 1981. Acct. Comml. Bank of Greece, Salonica, 1966-70; fin. acct. Citibank, Salonica, 1970; fin. acct. Bank of Greece, Athens, 1970-72; fin. planning and analysis mgr. Rank Xerox Greece, Athens, 1972-77, mktg. dir., 1977-82, mng. dir., gen. mgr., 1982—. Mem. Greek Mgmt. Assn., Greek Mktg. Inst., Am./Hellenic C. of C. (bd. dirs. 1982—). Club: Ekali (Athens). Avocation: tennis. Home: 1-3 Rodon St, Drosia, Athens 14565, Greece Office: Rank Xerox Greece SA, 154 Sygrou Ave, Athens 17671 Greece

GEH, CHENG HOOI, accountant; b. Georgetown, Malaysia, Sept. 6, 1934; s. Hun Kheng Geh and Siew Hwa Lim; m. Teh Moh Lee; children: Ju Ian, Li Dah. CPA, Malaysia; FCA. Qualified asst. Price Waterhouse, London, 1960-61; chmn. Kewangan Usahasama Makmur Bhd; dir. Star Publs. Bhd, Malaysia, 1988—. Treas. Council Chs. Malaysia and Singapore, Kuala Lumpur, 1969. Mem. Malaysian Assn. CPA's (chmn. tech. com., council 1972—). Methodist. Clubs: Royal Selangor Golf, Selangor (Kuala Lumpur). Lodge: Read Lodge No. 2337 EC (past master). Home: 46 Jalan Batai, Damansara Heights, 50490 Kuala Lumpur Malaysia Office: Peat Marwick, Wisma Perdana Jalan Dungun, Damansara Heights, 50490 Kuala Lumpur Malaysia

GEHA, ALEXANDER SALIM, cardiothoracic surgeon, educator; b. Beirut, June 18, 1936; came to U.S., 1963; s. Salim M. and Alice I. (Hayek) G.; m. Diane L. Redalen, Nov. 25, 1967; children—Samia, Rula, Nada. B.S. in Biology, Am. U. Beirut, 1955, M.D., 1959; M.S. in Surgery and Physiology, U. Minn.-Rochester, 1967, Yale U., 1978. Asst. prof. U. Vt., Burlington, 1967-69; asst. prof. Washington U., St. Louis, 1969-73, assoc. prof., 1973-75; assoc. prof. Yale U., New Haven, 1975-78, prof., chief cardiothoracic surgery, 1978-86; prof., chief cardiothoracic surgery Case Western Res. U. and U. Hosp. of Cleve., 1986—; cons. VA Hosp., West Haven, Conn., 1975-86, VA Hosp., Cleve., 1986—, Cleve. Met. Gen. Hosp., 1986—, Waterbury Hosp., 1976-86, Sharon Hosp., 1981-86; mem. study sect. Nat. Heart Lung and Blood Inst., 1981-85. Editor: Thoracic and Cardio-vascular Surgery, 1983; editor Basic Surgery, 1984. Bd. dirs. New Haven Heart Assn., 1981-85. Mem. Assn. Clin. Cardiac Surgery (chmn. membership com. 1978-80, sec.-treas. 1980-83), Am. Heart Assn. (bd. dirs. 1981-85, council on cardiovascular surgery), Am. Coll. Chest Physicians (steering com. 1980-84), Am. Assn. Thoracic Surgery, Am. Coll. Cardiology, ACS (coordinating com. on edn. in thoracic surgery), AMA, Am. Physiol. Soc., Am. Surg. Assn., Am. Thoracic Soc., Assn. Acad. Surgery, Central Surg. Assn., Internat. Soc. Cardiovascular Surgery, Lebanese Order Physicians, New Eng. Surg. Soc., Pan Am. Med. Assn., Halsted Soc., Soc. Thoracic Surgeons (govt. relations com., manpower com., program com.), also others. Home: 17050 South Park Blvd Shaker Heights OH 44120 Office: Case Western Res U Sch Medicine 2074 Abington Rd Cleveland OH 44106

GEHA, ANDRE GEORGES, financial executive; b. Beirut, Lebanon, May 9, 1925; came to France, 1976;; s. Georges Jacques and Malake Catherine (Nassif) G.; m. Dedee Maria Haddad, Feb. 12, 1953; children: George, Elie, May. Lic. in Bus. Adminstrn., St. Joseph U., Beirut, 1961; Diploma Etudes Suterieures in Econs. and Fin., U. Paris, 1969. Staff accts. dept. Mobil Oil Co., Beirut, 1943-63, chief auditor, systems mgr., 1964-73; comptroller fin. CAT/Mothercat Group, Beirut, Paris, London, 1976-80; chief exec. fin. and adminstrn. CAT/Mothercat Group, Paris, 1981—; sworn-in-expert in acctg., Lebanon; chmn. bd. dirs. Family Bookshop Holdings Ltd.; bd. dirs. Francat S.a.l., Mothercat Saudi Arabia s.l.l., Mothercat Ltd. Author: Aspects du raffinage Petrolier au Liban, 1969; contbr. articles to profl. jours. Bd. dirs. Eccumenical Devel. Coop. Soc., Amersfoort, Holland, 1977-82; mem. fin. com. Holy Sinod Orthodox Ch. Antioch., Damascus, 1981—, Middle East Council of Churches, Beirut. 1981—. Decorated Cross of St. Peter and St. Paul Orthodox Patriarch of Antioch and all the East, 1983. Mem. Lebanese Mgmt. Assn., Expert Accts. Soc., Cenacle Libanais, Icons Restauration Assn., Mus. France, French Lebanese Cultural Assn. Home: 3 rue des Lacs, Grigny 91350, France also: 8 Ave Charles Floquet, Paris 75007, France Office: Eurocat, 50 rue Boissiere, Paris 75116, France

GEHLMANN, TIMOTHY SHAWN, controller; b. Washington, Feb. 16, 1960; s. Donald Eugene and Barbara Ann (Elder) G. AA, Lorain County (Ohio) Community Coll., 1980; BBA in Acctg., Ohio U., 1982; postgrad., Cleve.-Marshall Coll. of Law, 1985, Golden Gate U., 1986. CPA, Calif., Ohio. Asst. mgr., tng. coordinator McDonald's Corp., Amherst, Ohio, 1978-80; acct. Gen. Motors Corp., Flint, Mich., 1981; audit and tax specialist Ernst & Whinney, Cleve., 1982-84; CPA, tax cons. Deloitte Haskins & Sells, Cleve., 1985; CPA, sr. tax cons. Deloitte Haskins & Sells, San Francisco, 1985-86; controller Lincoln Property Co., Foster City, Calif., 1986-88. Contbr. articles to company publs. Mem. judiciary candidate evaluation com. Citizens League of Greater Cleve., 1985, current affairs com. Commonwealth Club of Calif., San Francisco, 1985—. Mem. Am. Inst. CPA's, Ohio Soc. CPA's (Congl. Key Person, 1985—), Calif. Soc. CPA's, Real Estate Securities and Syndication Inst. (nat. budget com., regulatory-legis. com.). Club: City (Cleve.) (trustee 1984-85). Office: Source Fin 345 California St San Francisco CA 94104

GEIGER, LOUIS GEORGE, historian; b. Boonville, Mo., Mar. 21, 1913; s. George Victor and Dorothea Elizabeth (Hoflander) G.; m. Helen Margery Watson, Dec. 20, 1946; 1 son, Mark Watson. Student, Elmhurst Coll., 1929-30; B.S., Central Mo. State U., 1934; M.A., U. Mo., 1940, Ph.D., 1948, L.H.D. (hon.), 1985. Tchr. pub. sch. Mo., 1930-31, 34-39; grad. asst., instr. U. Mo., 1939-42; asst. prof. history U. N.D., 1946-55, assoc. prof., 1955-58, prof., 1958-60; prof. history, chmn. dept. Colo. Coll., 1960-70, prof., 1971-72; prof. history Iowa State U., Ames, 1972-79; prof. emeritus Iowa State U., 1979—, chmn. dept., 1972-77; vis. prof. U. Mo., 1960, Jadavpur U., 1963-64, Miami U., Ohio, 1967, Ariz. State U., 1970-71; Fulbright lectr. U. Leningrad, 1978-79; chmn. N.D. Com. Social Sci. Curricular Revision, 1959-60. Author: From Apennines to Po, 1948, Joseph W. Folk of Missouri, 1953, University of the Northern Plains, 1958, Higher Education in a Maturing Democracy, 1963, Voluntary Accreditation: History of North Central Association, 1970; Contbr.: Muckrakers and American Society, 1968; author articles and revs. Served to 1st lt. AUS, 1942-46. Fellow Fund for Advancement Edn. Harvard and Stanford, 1953-54; Fulbright lectr. U. Helsinki, 1954-55; recipient research award Social Sci. Research Council, 1963. Mem. Western Social Sci. Assn. (v.p. 1965-66, v.p. 68-69), N.D. Social Sci. Assn. (pres. 1959-60), AAUP, Am. Hist. Assn., Am. Studies Assn., History Edn. Soc., Agr. History Soc., Orgn. Am. Historians. Club: Rotarian. Home: 19A E Burnam Rd Columbia MO 65203

GEIKEN, ALAN RICHARD, contractor; b. Toledo, Aug. 24, 1923; s. Martin Herman and Herta Regina G.; B.S. in Engring., Iowa State U., 1950. Engr., sec. Hot Spot Detector, Inc., Des Moines, 1950-53, sales engr., asst. gen. mgr., 1953-60; pres., owner Alan Geiken Inc., Sacramento, 1960—; cons. on grain storage. Served with USAAF, 1943-45. Mem. Am. Soc. Agrl. Engrs., Council for Agrl. Sci. and Tech., Calif. Warehousemens Assn., Calif. Grain and Feed Assn., Grain Elevator and Processing Soc. Clubs: Sacramento Engrs., Sacramento 50/50 (bd. dirs.). Lutheran. Developed electronic system to maintain healthful condition of stored grain and bulk foods. Address: PO Box 214505 Sacramento, CA 95821

GEIL, JOHN CLINTON, lawyer; b. San Antonio, Oct. 27, 1951; s. William Clinton and Frances E. (Coverdale) G. B.A., Occidental Coll., 1972; J.D., Lewis and Clark Coll., 1976. Bar: Oreg. 1976, U.S. Dist. Ct. Oreg. 1977, U.S. Ct. Appeals (9th cir.) 1977, U.S. Supreme Ct. 1981. Sole practice, Portland, Oreg., 1976-78; ptnr. Rieke, Geil & Savage, P.C., and predecessor Portland, 1978—. Mem. Multnomah County Corrections Classifications System Adv. Commn., Oreg., 1982. Named to Outstanding Young Men Am., U.S. Jaycees, 1979, 81. Mem. Oreg. Young Attys. Assn. (pres. 1983-84), ABA (bd. dirs. law student div. 1975-76, exec. council young lawyers div. 1981-82, dir. young lawyers div. 1984-85, assembly speaker young lawyers div. 1987-88), Multnomah Bar Assn. (chmn. corrections com. 1981-83, chmn. legis. com. 1984-86, Recognition award 1983), Cornelius Honor Soc. Office: Rieke Geil & Savage PC 820 SW 2d St Suite 200 Portland OR 97204

GEIS, ROBERT HENRY, advertising agency executive; b. N.Y.C., May 14, 1937; s. Henry and Eileen Marion (Kelly) G.; m. Loretta De Luca, Oct. 27, 1962; children: Christina, Jeffrey, Lori, Steven. BBA, CCNY, 1962. Mgr. media, Warner-Lambert, Morris Plains, N.J., 1966-74; sr. v.p., corp. dir. media Wells, Rich, Greene, N.Y.C., 1974—. Contbr. articles in field to profl. jours. Chmn. bus. adv. council Easter Seals Soc., N.Y.C., 1986—, chmn. media com. Juvenile Diabetes Found., N.Y.C., 1983-84; mem. twp. council, Mine Hill, N.J., 1969-72; trustee, pres. Lord Stirling Sch., Basking Ridge, N.J., 1983-86. Served with U.S. Navy, 1955-59. Recipient service awards Easter Seal Soc., 1981-87; named Media Person of Yr., Juvenile Diabetes Found., 1983. Mem. Alpha Delta Sigma. Office: Wells Rich Greene Inc 9 W 57th St New York NY 10019

GEISE, HARRY FREMONT, ret. meteorologist; b. Oak Park, Ill., Jan. 8, 1920; student U. Chgo., 1938-39, Meterorol. Service Sch., Lakehurst, N.J., 1943-44; m. Juanita Calmer, 1974; children—Barry, Gary, Harry (triplets); children by previous marriage—Marian Frances, Gloria Tara. Pioneered in extending pvt. weather services in Chgo., 1937; chief meteorologist Kingsbury Ordnance, 1943; meteorologist radio sta. WLS, and Prairie Farmer Newspaper, 1941, 42, 46; asso. Dr. Irving P. Krick, metorol. cons., 1947-49; Army Air Corps research, 1948-49, developed new temperature forecasting technique; condr. weather and travel shows WBKB-TV, Chgo., also radio sta. WOPA, Oak Park, 1950-51; developed radio and television shows, San Francisco and San Jose, Cal., 1954-55; dir. media div. Irving P. Krick Assos., 1955-59; produced, appeared on weather programs Columbia Pacific Radio and TV Networks, also weatherman KNXT, Hollywood, Calif., 1957-58; comml. weather service, 1962-80; instr. meteorology Santa Rosa Jr. Coll., 1964-66, Sonoma State Coll., 1967-68; weather dir. WCBS-TV, 1966-67, established weather center for CBS, N.Y., 1966-67. Research relationship between specified solar emission and major change in earth's weather patterns, tornado forecasting and long-range forecasting up to 4 years in advance. Meteorologist, Nat. Def. Exec. Res., 1968-74. Served with USMC, 1944-45. Mem. Royal Meterol. Soc. (life fgn. mem.). Author articles in field, contbr. to newspapers and mags. Contbr. long range forecasts. Mailing Address: 49975 Avenida Obregon La Quinta CA 92253 Home: 4585 Brighton Pl Santa Maria CA 93455

GEISENDORFER, JAMES VERNON, author; b. Brewster, Minn., Apr. 22, 1929; s. Victor H. and Anne B. (Johnson) G.; student Augustana Coll., 1950-51, Augsburg Coll., 1951-54, Orthodox Luth. Sem., 1954-55; B.A., U. Minn., 1960; LL.D., Burton Coll. and Sem., 1961; m. Esther Lillian Walker, Sept. 23, 1949; children—Jane, Karen, Lois. Grain buyer Pillsbury Mills, Inc., Worthington, Minn., 1947-48; hatchery acct., Worthington, 1949-50; night supr. Strutwear, Inc., Mpls., 1951-52; dispatcher Chgo. and North Western Ry., 1953-54; office mgr. Froedtert Malt Corp., Mpls., 1955-56, Nat. Automotive Parts Assn., 1957-60; sr. creative writer Brown & Bigelow, St. Paul, 1960-72; religious researcher, writer, 1972—; research cons. Inst. for the Study of Am. Religion; mem. panel of reference Chelston Bible Coll., New Milton, Eng.; mem. U.S. Congl. Adv. Bd., 1985. Recipient Amicus Poloniae medal Polish Ministry of Culture and Edn., 1969. Mem. Am. Acad. Religion, Acad. Ind. Scholars, Wis. Evang. Luth. Synod Hist. Inst., Augustana Hist. Soc., Wis. Acad. Scis., Arts and Letters, Can. Soc. Study of Religion, Aristotelian Soc., Hegel Soc. Am., Acad. Polit. Sci. Lutheran. Author: (with J. Gordon Melton) A Directory of Religious Bodies in the United States, 1977; Religion in America, 1983; mem. editorial bd. Biog. Dictionary of American Cult and Sect Leaders; contbr. articles to books and periodicals; cons. editor Directory of Religious Organizations in the United States, 1977. Address: 1001 Shawano Ave Green Bay WI 54303

GEISSLER, HEINER, West German government official, political leader; b. Oberndorf/Neckar, Baden-Wü rttemberg, Germany, Mar. 3, 1930; m. Susanne Geissler; children: Dominik, Michael, Nikolai. Student philosophy and law univs. Munich and Tübingen, 1st State Law Exam., 1957, 2d, Stuttgart, 1962. Judge; head office Minister Labor and Social Affairs, Baden-Württenberg, 1962-65; mem. Bundestag (W.German Parliament), 1965-67, 80—; mem. Rheinland-Pfälz State Parliament, 1971-79; minister social affairs, health and sport Rheinland-Pfä lz, 1967-77; minister of youth, family and health Fed. Republic Germany, from 1982. Mem. fed. bd. Christian Democratic Union, 1967-77, gen. sec., from 1970, also mem. Rheinland-Pfalz regional bd., mem. fed. bd. of social coms. Author: Die Neue Soziale Frage, 1976; Der Weg in die Gewalt, 1978; Sicherheit für unsere Freiheit, 1978; Recht sichert die Freiheit, 1978; Verwaltete Bürger-Gesellschaft in Fesseln, 1978; Grundwerte in der Politk, 1979; Zukunftschancen der Jugend, 1979; Optionen auf eine lebenswerte Zukunft, 1979; Sport-Geschäft ohne Illusionen'9, 1980; Mut zur Alternative, 1981. Decorated Grand Fed. Cross of Merit. Roman Catholic. Office: Demokratische Union K Aden Haus, Friedrich-Ebert-Allee 73-75, 5300 Bonn 1 Federal Republic of Germany *

GEISTFELD, RONALD ELWOOD, dental educator; b. St. James, Minn., Nov. 9, 1933; s. Victor E. and Viola (Becker) G.; m. Lois N. Tolzman Wilkens, June 15, 1955 (div. June 1974); m. Annette L. Swenson, Jan. 14, 1977; children: Shari, Mark, Steven, Ann, Leah, Erik. AA, Bethany Jr. Coll., 1952; BS, U. Minn., 1954, DDS, 1957. Gen. practice dentistry Northfield, Minn., 1959-72; clin. asst. prof. dentistry U. Minn. Sch. Dentistry, Mpls., 1969-72, assoc. prof., 1972-77, chmn. dept. operative dentistry, 1978-87, prof., 1982—; dental cons. Hennepin County Med. Ctr., Mpls., 1975—, Vets. Hosp., Mpls., 1977—, Vets. Hosp., St. Cloud, Minn., 1978—. Pres. PTA, Northfield, 1965, Arts Guild, Northfield, 1968; bd. dirs., chairperson Rice County Health and Sanitation Bd., Faribault, Minn., 1966-74; bd. dirs. Northfield Bd. Edn., 1969-74; pres. Roseville Luth. Ch., 1987-88. Served to capt. U.S. Army, 1957-59. Am. Coll. Dentists fellow, 1972. Mem. Am. Dental Assn. (chairperson operative dentistry sect. 1979-80, curriculum cons. 1981—), Minn. Dental Assn. (ethics com. 1969-76, chairperson sci. and ann. sessions com. 1984-86), Mpls. Dist. Dental Soc. (program chairperson 1978-79), Minn. Acad. Restorative Dentistry (pres. 1979-80), Minn. Acad. Gnathological Research (pres. 1986-87), Am. Assn. Dental Schs. (chairperson operative dentistry sect. 1984-85, edit. rev. bd. 1984—), Acad. Operative Dentistry (exec. council 1978-81, research com. 1987—), Am. Acad. Gold Foil Operators, Northfield C. of C. (treas. and chairperson 1968-70), Delta Sigma Delta, Omicron Kappa Upsilon (Theta chpt.). Lodge: Rotary (pres. Northfield 1972-73). Home: 2173 Folwell Ave Saint Paul MN 55108 Office: U Minn Sch Dentistry 515 Delaware St SE 8-450 Moos Tower Minneapolis MN 55455

GELAS, JACQUES HUBERT, chemistry educator; b. Vichy, France, Aug. 30, 1940; s. Louis and Yvonne (Cheval) G.; m. Yvonne Mialhe, June 29, 1970; children—Pauline, Hélène. Baccalaureat, Coll. Cusset, 1958; Licence es Scis., U. Clermont-Ferrand, 1963, 3d Cycle Doctorat, 1967, Doctorat d'Etat, 1970. Asst., U. Clermont-Ferrand, Aubière, France, 1965-70, maitre-asst., 1970-78, maitre confs., 1978-79, prof. chemistry, 1979—, vice chmn. Nat. Sch. Chemistry, 1980-86, chmn., 1986—; vis. research assoc. Ohio State U., Columbus, 1973—; chmn. French Carbohydrate Group, 1984-86; cons. various chem. and pharm. cos.; organizer internat. meetings. Contbr. articles to profl. jours., chpt. to book. Editorial adv. bd. Internat. Jour. Carbohydrate Research, 1984—. Served with Sci. Corps, French Armed Forces, 1967-68. Mem. Soc. Chimique de France, Am. Chem. Soc., Sigma Xi. Roman Catholic. Home: 17 Ave du Puy de Gravenoire, Domaine de Gravenoire, 63122 Ceyrat France Office: U Clermont-Ferrand, BP45, 63170 Aubiere France

GELB, JOSEPH DONALD, lawyer; b. Wilkes-Barre, Pa., Dec. 13, 1923; s. Edward and Esther (Fierman) G.; student Pa. State Coll., 1943; B.S., U. Scranton, 1950; LL.B., George Washington U., 1952; m. Anne Mirman, July 3, 1955; children—Adam, Roger. Adjudicator, War Claims Commn., 1952-54; admitted to D.C. bar, 1954, Md. bar, 1963; practiced in Washington, Md., 1954—; partner Gelb & Pitsenberger, Washington, 1969-74; prin. Joseph D. Gelb Chartered, 1974-80, Gelb, Abelson & Siegel, P.C., 1980-82, Gelb & Siegel, P.C., 1982-85; prin. Joseph D. Gelb, Chartered, 1985-85; prin. Jeseph D. Gelb, Chartered, 1985—. Served with USAAF, 1943-46. Mem. Am. Bar Assn., Md. Bar Assn., D.C. Bar, Assn. Trial Lawyers Am. Bar Assn. D.C., Assn. Plaintiff's Trial Attys. Clubs: Bethesda Country, Masons, B'nai B'rith. Home: 9620 Annlee Terr Bethesda MD 20817 also: 525 N Ocean Blvd Pompano Beach FL 33062 Office: 1120 Connecticut Ave NW Washington DC 20036

GELB, JUDITH ANNE, lawyer; b. N.Y.C., Apr. 5, 1935; d. Joseph and Sarah (Stein) G.; m. Howard S. Vogel, June 30, 1962; 1 child, Michael S. B.A., Bklyn. Coll., 1955; J.D., Columbia U., 1958. Bar: N.Y. 1959, U.S. Dist. Ct. (so. dist. and ea. dist.) N.Y. 1960, U.S. Ct. Appeals (2d cir.) 1960, U.S. Ct. Mil. Appeals 1962. Asst. to editor N.Y. Law Jour., N.Y.C., 1958-59; confidential asst. to U.S. atty. ea. dist. N.Y., Bklyn., 1959-61; assoc. Whitman & Ransom, N.Y.C., 1961-70, ptnr., 1971—. Mem. ABA (individual rights sect.), Fed. Bar Counsel, N.Y. State Bar Assn. (trusts and estates com.), N.Y. State Dist. Attys. Assn., Assn. Bar City N.Y. Clubs: Princeton, Assn. Ex-mem. Squadron A. Home: 169 E 69th St New York NY 10021 Office: Whitman & Ransom 200 Park Ave New York NY 10166

GELBART, ABE, mathematician, educator; b. Paterson, N.J., Dec. 22, 1911; s. Wolf and Pauline (Landau) G.; m. Sara Goodman, July 2, 1939; children: Carol Marie (Mrs. Ivan P. Auer), Judith Sylvia (dec.), William Michael, Stephen Samuel. B.Sc., Dalhousie U., 1938, LL.D. honoris causa, 1972; Ph.D. in Math, MIT, 1940; D.Sc. (h.c.), Bar-Ilan U., Israel, 1985. Asst. MIT, 1939-40; instr. math. N.C. State Coll., 1940-42; research asso. Brown U., 1942; asso. physicist NACA, Langley Field, Va., 1942-43; asst. prof. to prof. math. Syracuse U., 1943-58; dir. Inst. Math., Yeshiva U., 1958-59; dean Belfer Grad. Sch. Sci., 1959-70, dean emeritus, 1970—, disting. univ. prof. math., 1968—; vis. disting. prof. math. Bard Coll. and fellow Bard Coll. Center, 1979—, David and Rosalie Rose Disting. prof. natural sci. and math., 1983—; lectr., Sorbonne, Paris, 1949; vis. prof. U. So. Calif., 1951; Mem. Inst. Advanced Study, Princeton, 1947-48, 77—; Fulbright lectr., Norway, 1951-52; Mem. directorate math. scis. USAF Office Sci. Research.; vice chmn. bd. dirs., chmn. sci. adv. bd. Daltex Med. Scis., Inc., 1983—; mem. adv. bd. Inst. for Thinking and Learning, Pace U., 1982—. Editor: Scripta Mathematica, 1957—. Trustee, chmn. acad. sci. com. Bar-Ilan U., Israel, 1982—. Recipient Bard medal, 1981; spl. award of recognition U. Pa. Sch. Nursing; chair in math. named in his honor Bar-Ilan U., 1983. Mem. Am. Math. Soc., Math. Assn. Am., Acad. Ind. Scholars (trustee 1982—), Xi. Home: 140 West End Ave New York NY 10023

GELBART, STEPHEN SAMUEL, mathematician educator; b. Syracuse, N.Y., June 12, 1946; s. Abe and Sara (Goodman) G.; m. Mary Rae Glick, June 16, 1968; children—Ben, Ruth, Daniel. B.A., Cornell U., 1967; M.A., Princeton U., 1968, Ph.D., 1970. Instr. math. Rutgers U., Newark, 1968-70, Princeton U., 1970-71; from asst. prof. to prof. math. Cornell U., Ithaca, N.Y., 1971-85; prof. math. Tel Aviv U., 1983-84, Weizmann Inst. Sci., Rehovot, Israel, 1984—; vis. mem. Inst. Advanced Study, Princeton, N.J., 1972-73; vis. assoc. prof. Hebrew U. Jerusalem, 1977-78, vis. prof., 1981-82. Author: Automorphic Forms on Adele Groups, 1975; Weil's Representation and the Spectrum of the Metaplectic Group, 1976; Explicit Constructions of Automorphic L-functions, 1987—; also numerous articles. Chmn., United Jewish Appeal, Tompkins County, N.Y., 1982-83. Sloan fellow, 1977-79. Mem. Am. Math. Soc., Israeli Math. Union. Office: Weizmann Inst Sci, Rehovot 76100, Israel

GELBEIN, JAY JOEL, accountant; b. Bklyn., Sept. 11, 1949; s. Leo and Sara (Eskolsky) G.; B.S., Bklyn. Coll., 1972; M.S. with distinction, L.I. U., 1978; m. Marilyn Stern, Dec. 8, 1974; children—Moshe, Avi, Danielle. Appellate conferee IRS, N.Y.C., 1971-79; tech. mgr. Am. Inst. C.P.A.s, N.Y.C., 1979-81; pvt. practice acctg. and tax cons., Staten Island, N.Y., 1979—; assoc. prof. bus. Kingsborough Community Coll., Bklyn., 1981—; nat. tax lectr. C.P.A., N.Y. Mem. Am. Inst. C.P.A.s, N.Y. State Soc. C.P.A.s (mem. profl. service corp. com.). Co-author: Accounting Demonstration Problems Workbook. Home and Office: 13 President St Staten Island NY 10314

GELBER, DON JEFFREY, lawyer; b. Los Angeles, Mar. 10, 1940; s. Oscar and Betty Sheila (Chernitsky) G.; m. Jessica Jeasun Song, May 15, 1967; children: Victoria, Jonathan, Rebecca, Robert. Student UCLA, 1957-58, Reed Coll., 1958-59; AB, Stanford U., 1961, JD, 1963. Bar: Calif. 1964, Hawaii 1964, U.S. Dist. Ct. (cen. and no. dists. Calif.) 1964, U.S. Dist. Ct. Hawaii 1964, U.S. Ct. Appeals (9th cir.) 1964. Assoc. Greenstein, Yamane & Cowan, Honolulu, 1964-67; reporter Penal Law Revision Project, Hawaii Jud. Council, Honolulu, 1967-69; assoc. H. William Burgess, Honolulu, 1969-72; ptnr. Burgess & Gelber, Honolulu, 1972-73; prin. Law Offices of Don Jeffrey Gelber, Honolulu, 1974-77; prin., pres. Gelber & Wagner, Honolulu, 1978-83; prin., pres. Gelber & Gelber, Honolulu, 1984—; legal counsel Hawaii State Senate Judiciary Com., 1965; adminstrv. asst. to majority floor leader Hawaii Senate, 1966, legal csl. Edn. Com., 1967, 68; majority counsel Hawaii Ho. of Reps., 1974; spl. counsel Hawaii State Senate, 1983. Contbr. articles to legal publs. Mem. State Bar Calif., ABA (sect. bus. law), Am. Bankruptcy Inst., Hawaii Bar Assn. (sect. corps. and securities). Clubs: Pacific, Plaza. (Honolulu). Office: Gelber & Gelber 745 Fort St Suite 1400 Honolulu HI 96813

GELDMACHER, ERWIN HELMUT, communication executive; b. Cologne, Germany, June 20, 1923; s. Erwin and Paula (Justen) G.; m. Elizabeth Klosges, Apr. 6, 1955; children: Wolf, Britta, Bernd, Karin. Student, U. Cologne, 1942-44, 51-52, U. Frankfurt, 1953-56. Owner, mgr. Zeit im Ton, Cologne, 1950-52, Townstudio, Frankfurt, Fed. Republic Germany, 1952-72, Comml. Film, Frankfurt, 1956-68; comml. cons. Frankfurt, 1968-72; gen. mgr. Comunicaon AG, Teufen, Switzerland, 1972—; guest prof. Hochschule der Kunste, Berlin, 1983-87, hon. prof., 1988—; kuratorium mem. Acad. Communication, Frankfurt. Contbr. articles on communication and mktg. to profl. jours; author films on econ. problems; author, kproducer advt. films and radio spots; patentee in field. Named hon. pres. BierConvent Internat., Munich, 1987. Mem. Internat. Advt. Assn. Office: Comunicon AG, Hauptstr 111, CH 9052 Niederteufen Switzerland

GELDOF, BOB, musician; b. Dublin, Ireland, Oct. 5, 1954; m. Paula Yates, 1986; 1 daughter. Student, Black Rock Coll. journalist Georgia Straight, Vancouver, Can., New Musical Express, Melody Maker; joint founder rock band Boomtown Rats, 1975; organizer Band Aid concert to raise money for famine relief in Ethiopia, 1984, Live Aid concerts London and Phila., 1985, Sport Aid, 1986; films include: Pink Floyd- The Wall, 1982, Number One, 1985; TV films include The Price of Progress, 1987; author: (autobiography) Is That It?, 1986. Founder Live Aid Found., 1985—. Decorated KBE (hon.), 1986; named Freeman Borough of Swale, 1985. Home: Davington Priory, near Faversham, Kent England Office: Bank Aid Trust, PO Box 4TX, London W1, England *

GELFAND, IVAN, investment advisor, columnist; b. Cleve., Mar. 29, 1927; s. Samuel and Sarah (Kruglin) G.; m. Suzanne Frank, Sept. 23, 1956; children: Dennis Scott, Andrew Steven. B.S., Miami U., Oxford, Ohio, 1950; postgrad., Case-Western Res. U., 1951; grad., Columbia U. Bank Mgmt. Program, 1968; certs., Am. Inst. Banking, 1952-57. Acct. Central Nat. Bank Cleve., 1950-53, v.p., mgr. bank and corp. investments, 1957-75; chief acct. Stars & Stripes newspaper, Darmstadt, Germany, 1953-55; account exec. Merrill, Lynch, Pierce, Fenner & Smith, Inc., Cleve., 1955-57; chmn., chief exec. officer Gelfand, Quinn & Assos., Inc., Cleve., 1975-83; v.p., mng. dir. Prudential-Bache Securities, Inc., 1983-85; pres. Lindow, Gelfand and Quinn, Inc., 1976-83; co-editor Gelfand-Quinn/Liquidity Portfolio Mgr. Newsletter, 1978-81, Gelfand-Quinn Analysis/Money Market Techniques, 1981-84; money market columnist Nat. Thrift News, 1976-78, guest money market columnist, 1982-85; pres. Ivan Gelfand & Assocs., Inc., 1985-88; sr. v.p. Prescott, Ball & Turben, Inc., 1986—; v.p., dir. fixed income investments Rowlston & Co., 1988—; instr. investments adult div. Cleve. Bd. Edn., 1956-58, Am. Inst. Banking, 1958-68; guest lectr., speaker nat. and local TV and radio stas.; lectr. in econs., fin. instn. portfolio mgmt., cash mgmt., 1972—. Mem. investment com. United Torch Cleve., 1972-74; study-rev. team capt. Lake Erie Regional Transp. Authority, 1973-77; trustee Mt. Sinai Med. Ctr., Cleve., 1983—, treas., 1986—, trustee Jewish Community Fedn., 1986—, Cleve. Coll. Jewish Studies, 1988—; mem. bond com. Jewish Community Fedn., Cleve., 1979—, mem. fin. com., 1981-85; mem. Cuyahoga County Republican Fin. Com., 1978-82; mem. exec. com. Cuyahoga County Rep. Orgn., 1982—. Served with AUS, 1945-47. Mem. Greater Cleve. Growth Assn., Cleve. Soc. Security Analysts, Les Politiques. Republican. Clubs: Mid-day (Cleve.), Commerce (Cleve.), Oakwood, Union, Univ. Lodge: Masons. Home: 2900 Alvord Pl Pepper Pike OH 44124 Office: 4000 Chester Ave Cleveland OH 44103

GELIN, PATRICK, bank executive; b. Meersburg, Fed. Republic Germany, Dec. 16, 1945; s. Charles and Genevieve (Wattez) G.; m. Janick Farcot; children: Sophie, Chloé. Diplôme, Inst. Etudes Polit., Paris, 1966. Head of syndication Société Générale, Paris, 1979-83; asst. gen. mgr. Société Générale, London, 1983-86; gen. mgr. Société Générale, Amsterdam, The Netherlands, 1986—. Office: Societe Generale, Banque Francse, Fndee 1864, Museumplein 17, Amsterdam The Netherlands

GÉLINAS, GRATIEN, medical librarian; b. Ste.-Flore, Que., Can., Feb. 1, 1937; s. Alfred and Annette (Lavergne) G. B in Pedagogy, Laval U., Que. City, 1966; Baccalaureate ès Art, U. Trois-Rivières, Que., 1968; B in Library Sci., U. Ottawa, 1969. Chief librarian Commn. Scolaire Regionale de la Mauricie, Shawinigan, Que., 1966-68; librarian, cataloger Coll. d'Enseignement Gen. et Profl. de Trois-Rivières, 1970-71; med. librarian Hosp. Christ-Roi, Quebec City, 1971—. Mem. Assn. Pour Advancement des Scis. et Techniques de Documentation, Corp. des Bibliothécaires Profls. du Que. Home: 177 Bernatchez St, Ville de Vanier, PQ Canada G1M 2A3 Office: Hosp Christ-Roi, 300 Blvd W Hamel, Ville de Vanier, PQ Canada G1M 2R9

GELINAS, JOHN GERALD, public relations and public affairs consultant; b. Stroudsburg, Pa., Feb. 24, 1929; s. Anthony J. F. and Margaret E. (Morris) G.; m. Barbara Ann Link, Sept. 6, 1958; children: Cynthia A., John Gerald, Amy Elizabeth, Gregory J., Garrick M. A.A., Keystone Jr. Coll., 1951; B.S. in Public Communication, Boston U., 1953, M.S. (fellow), 1954. Public relations intern Alleghany-Young-Kirby Ownership Bd., N.Y.C., 1954; public relations staff asst. N.Y. Central R.R., 1955-56, Mobil Corp., 1956-58; public relations advisor Mobil Oil Nigeria Ltd. and Mobil Exploration Nigeria, Inc., Lagos, 1958-62; sr. public relations advisor Mobil Internat., 1962; account exec. Thomas J. Deegan Co., Inc., 1962-65, asst. v.p., 1965, v.p., 1965-67; dir. corp. communication Nat. Union Electric Corp., 1967-68, exec. asst. to chief exec. officer, cons. public relations, 1968-71; exec. v.p., chief ops. officer Thomas J. Deegan Co., Inc., 1971-73, vice chmn., 1973; sr. v.p., dir. fin. services Edward Gottlieb & Assos., N.Y.C., 1973-76; internat. public affairs cons., pres. John G. Gelinas Assos., Inc., N.Y.C., 1976—; adv. and asst. in various capacities to Pres. and Govt. of Guyana, several internat. confs., 1981, 82, 83, 84, 85, 86, 87; program dir. communication arts grad. sch., Coll. New Rochelle, N.Y., 1986—. Contbr. articles to profl. jours. Mem. planning bd. Town of Eastchester, N.Y., 1975-78; exec. bd. Westchester-Putnam council Boy Scouts Am., 1977—, chmn. quality program com. of long range planning com., 1978; mem. exec. council Greater N.Y. Councils, chmn. public relations com., 1967-72; mem. adv. bd. Save Our Sound, White Plains, N.Y.; mem. nat. alumni council Boston U., 1971—. Served with U.S. Army, 1947-48. Recipient Robert R. Young-Boston U. award, 1954; PR News Gold Key award, 1970; first American to receive Republic of Guyana's Order of Arrow Nat. award, presented by pres. H. Desmond Hoyte, 1987; one of first 5 recipients of first Pres.'s award Keystone Jr. Coll., 1987. Mem. Internat. Inst. Communications, Nat. Press Club Nigeria (life), Soc. Internat. Devel. (past v.p., exec. bd. N.Y. chpt.), Explorers Club, Classic Car Club Am. (former dir.), Tau Mu Epsilon. Home: 96 Puritan Dr Scarsdale NY 10583 Office: 576 Fifth Ave New York NY 10036

GELLER, ROBERT DENNIS, internist; b. N.Y.C., Apr. 5, 1941; s. Martin Max and Elvira Joan (Reich) G.; B.Met.E. cum laude, N.Y. U., 1962; M.D., Cornell U., 1966; m. Karen Hannk Greshes, Feb. 7, 1974; children—Meredith Anne, Evan Scott. Intern, Bellevue Hosp., N.Y.C., 1966-67, resident in medicine, 1967-68; resident in medicine North Shore U. Hosp., 1968-70; practice medicine specializing in internal medicine, cons. infectious disease, Manhasset, N.Y., 1972-77; practice medicine specializing in internal medicine, cons. infectious disease Freeport (Ill.) Clinic, S.C., 1977—, pres., chmn. bd., 1981—; cons. infectious disease. Theda Clark Regional Med. Ctr., Neenah, Wis., 1980—; pres. med. staff Freeport Meml. Hosp., 1982—, chief medicine, 1986—; clin. asst. prof. medicine Cornell U., U. Ill., 1986—; mem. med. malpractice panel N.Y. State Supreme Ct., Mineola, 1976; peer rev. com., bd. dirs. No. Ill. Profl. Standards Rev. Orgn., Rockford, 1978; mem. Freeport Bd. Health, 1984—. Served with USPHS, 1970-72. Diplomate Am. Bd. Internal Medicine. Fellow A.C.P.; mem. Am. Heart Assn., Am. Soc. Microbiology, Am. Fedn. Clin. Research, AMA, Ill., Stephenson County med. socs. Contbr. articles on Coccidioidin skin test sensitivity to Am. Rev. Respiratory Diseases, 1972-73. Office: 1036 W Stephenson St Freeport IL 61032

GELLER, ROBERT JAMES, advertising agency executive; b. N.Y.C., May 5, 1937; s. Jerome and Pearl (Klein) G.; B.S., CCNY, 1958; m. Lois Dee Fromkin, June 9, 1968; children—Richard Evan, Stephen Laurence. Account exec. Furman, Feiner & Co., N.Y.C., 1958-62; media supr. Interpublic Group of Cos., N.Y.C., 1962-64; asst. media dir. Foote, Cone & Belding, N.Y.C., 1964-69; pres. Adforce Inc., N.Y.C., 1970—. Mem. Assn. Nat. Advertisers (mgmt. policy com.), Am. Advt. Fedn. (bd. dirs.). Republican. Contbr. numerous articles to profl. jours. Home: 155 E 76th St New York NY 10021 also: Ocean Rd Bridgehampton NY 11932 Office: Adforce Inc 235 E 42d St New York NY 10017

GELLERSTEDT, MARIE ADA, manufacturing company executive; b. Davenport, Iowa, Oct. 19, 1926; d. Charles Beecher and Marie Elizabeth (Pasvogel) Kaufmann; m. Keith Orval Gellerstedt, Mar. 16, 1957; children: Lori Beth Doroba, Keith Todd, Jon Erik, Cory Andrew. BBA, Augustana Coll., 1950. Gen. mgr., pres. Nixalite Co. Am., East Moline, Ill., 1957—. Life mem. Moline St. High Sch. PTA, also bd. dirs., 1973-76. Mem. Ill. Mfrs. Assn., Nat. Trade Show Exhibitors Assn., Internat. Exhibitors Assn., Nat. Pest Control Assn., Nat. Animal Damage Control Assn., Nat. Assn. Women Bus. Owners, Nat. Assn. Ind. Bus., East Moline Bus. Assn., Constrn. Specifier Inst. Republican. Lutheran. Clubs: Daus. of Mokanna, Zal Caldron, Daus. of the Nile. Lodge: Zonta.

GELLINEK, CHRISTIAN JOHANN GEORG, educator; b. Potsdam, Germany, May 11, 1930; came to U.S., 1961, naturalized, 1966; s. Christian Johann Michael, and Margaretha C. (Lorenzen) G.; BA, U. Toronto, 1959; MA, Yale U., 1963, PhD, 1964; Dr. Phil. Habil., U. Basel (Switzerland), 1975; m. Josepha E. Schellekens, June 27, 1975; children—Else and Saskia (twins), Torsten, Jens. Instr. German, Yale U., 1964-66, asst. prof., 1966-68, asso. prof., 1968-70; prof. German, chmn. dept. Conn. Coll., 1970-71; prof. German and culture of cities U. Fla., Gainesville, 1971-87; guest prof. Inst. Vergleichende Stadtgeschichte, Münster, Fed. Republic Germany, 1987—; guest prof. Salt Lake City, Basel, Poznan, Poland, Münster, Westphalia, The Hague, Netherlands, UCLA. Bushnell fellow Yale U., 1962-63, Morse fellow, 1965-66; Deutscher Akadem. Austauschdienst fellow U. Fla., 1980; Fulbright fellow, 1980-81. Mem. MLA, Grotiana (corr. mem.). Calvinist. Author: König Rother, 1968; Kaiserchronik, 1971; Einführung in die Linguistik, 1980; Herrschaft im Hochmittelalter, 1980; Friedenssaal, 1982; Hugo Grotius, 1983; Pax Optima Rerum: Grotius und Goethe, 1984. Office: Inst für Vergleichende Stadtgeschichte, Syndikatplatz 4/5, D-44 Münster Federal Republic of Germany

GELL-MANN, MURRAY, theoretical physicist; b. N.Y.C., Sept. 15, 1929; s. Arthur and Pauline (Reichstein) Gell-M.; m. J. Margaret Dow, Apr. 19, 1955 (dec. 1981); children: Elizabeth, Nicholas. BS, Yale U., 1948; PhD, Mass. Inst. Tech., 1951; ScD (hon.), Yale U., 1959, U. Chgo., 1967, U. Ill., 1968, Wesleyan U., 1968, U. Turin, Italy, 1969, U. Utah, 1970, Columbia U., 1977, Cambridge U., 1980. Mem. Inst. for Advanced Study, 1951, 55, 67-68; instr. U. Chgo., 1952-53, asst. prof., 1953-54, assoc. prof., 1954; assoc. prof. Calif. Inst. Tech., Pasadena, 1955-56; prof. Calif. Inst. Tech., 1956—, now R.A. Millikan prof. physics.; vis. prof. MIT, spring 1963, CERN, Geneva, 1971-72, 79-80; Mem. Pres.'s Sci. Adv. Com., 1969-72; mem. sci. and grants com. Leakey Found., 1977—; chmn. bd. trustees Aspen Ctr. for Physics, 1973-79. Author: (with Y. Ne'eman) Eightfold Way. Regent Smithsonian Instn., 1974—; bd. dirs. J.D. and C.T. MacArthur Found., 1979—. NSF post doctoral fellow, vis. prof. Coll. de France and U. Paris, 1959-60; recipient Dannie Heineman prize Am. Phys. Soc., 1959; E.O. Lawrence Meml. award AEC, 1966; Overseas fellow Churchill Coll., Cambridge, Eng., 1966; Franklin medal, 1967; Carty medal Nat. Acad. Scis., 1968; Research Corp. award, 1969; Nobel prize in physics, 1969. Fellow Am. Phys. Soc.; mem. Nat. Acad. Scis., Royal Soc. (fgn.), Am. Acad. Arts and Scis. (v.p., chmn. Western ctr. 1970-76), Council on Fgn. Relations, French Phys. Soc. (hon.). Clubs: Cosmos (Washington); Century Assn., Explorers (N.Y.C.); Athenaeum (Pasadena). Office: Calif Inst Tech Dept Physics Pasadena CA 91125

GELLNER, ERNEST ANDRE, social sciences and philosophy educator, writer; b. Paris, Dec. 9, 1925; arrived in Eng., 1939; s. Rudolf and Anna (Fantl) G.; m. Susan Ryan, Sept. 1954; children: David, Sarah, Deborah, Benjamin. BA, MA, U. Oxford, 1947; PhD, London U., 1961; DSc (hon.), Bristol U., Eng., 1986. Lectr. London Sch. Econs., 1949-62, prof., 1962-84; prof. Social Anthropology King's Coll. Cambridge U., Eng., 1984—. Author: Words and Things, 1959, Thought and Change, 1965, Saints of the Atlas, 1969, Muslim Society, 1981, Culture, Identity and Politics, 1987, Nations and Nationalism, 1983, The Psychoanalytical Movement, 1985, State and Society in Soviet Thought, 1988. Served with Czech. Army in exile, 1944-45. Fellow Brit. Acad., Royal Anthropol. Inst., Am. Acad. Arts and Scis. (hon.). Office: King's College, Cambridge England

GELVEN, MICHAEL PAUL, retail company executive; b. Boston, June 4, 1946; s. Abraham and Sarah Rebecca (Glick) G.; student Boston State Coll., 1964-66, Northeastern U., 1969-71; cert. Southeastern Mass. U., 1978; m. Wendy Ellen Tanzer, Oct. 20, 1968; children—Marc Ian, Shana Lee. Mgr. trainee Contan Liquors, Inc., Somerville, Mass., 1967-68, mgr., 1968-73; mgr. Tanza Liquors, Inc., Somerville, 1973-74; pres., chief exec. officer Perry's Liquor Inc., North Dartmouth, Mass., 1974-82 ; pres. GTC Assos. Inc., North Easton, Mass., 1978-85; pres., chief operating officer MPG Mktg. Inc., 1985—; pres. DeRoy's Package Store, Chicopee, Mass., 1979-80; pres. Computer 'N Things, Inc., North Dartmouth, 1982-85 ; pres. Medi-Save Cos., North Dartmouth, 1987—; instr. Bristol Community Coll., 1979—. Served with Army N.G., 1966. Mem. Mass. Beverage Assn., Soc. Wine Educators, Les Amis DuVin, La Confrerie Saint-Etienne d'Alsace, Assn. Better Computer Dealers, Mensa. Democrat. Jewish (pres. temple 1978-80, dir. 1980-84, 87—). Lodges: Lions, Masons, KP, B'nai B'rith (pres. 1973-74). Home: 41 William Bradford Rd North Dartmouth MA 02747 Office: Box 9518 North Dartmouth MA 02747

GEMAYEL, AMIN, President of Lebanon; b. Bikfaya, Lebanon, Jan. 22, 1942; s. Pierre and Genevieve G.; m. Joyce Tyan, Dec. 1967; children: Nicole, Pierre, Sami. M.A. in Polit. Scis., LL.B., St. Joseph U., Beirut, 1966. Mem. Lebanese Parliament, 1970—; Pres. of Lebanon, Beirut, 1982-88; founder Le Reveil newspaper, 1977, Panorama de l'Actualite mag., 1977; former mgr. family shipping and ins. bus. Gen. sec. Inst. Strategic Studies for Peace. Mem. Phalangist Party. Avocations: music, reading, art, theatre. Office: Presidence de la Republique, Palais de Baabda, Beirut Lebanon *

GEMMER, H. ROBERT, civic worker, clergyman; b. Indpls., Apr. 4, 1923; s. Hiram Conrad and Edith May (Miller) G.; m. Myrna Jean Flory, June 11, 1949; children: David Robert, Jean Annalee Gemmer McCutchan. BS, Ind. U., 1944; cert. Yale Sch. Alcohol Studies, 1945; BD, Chgo. Theol. Sem., also U. Chgo., 1947; postgrad. Christian Theol. Sem., 1950; MA, Western Res. U., 1960. Ordained to ministry Christian Ch. (Disciples of Christ), 1947; asst. minister, dir. youth activities First Friends Ch., Indpls., 1948-49; pastor First Ch. of Brethren, Cleve., 1951-55, interim co-pastor, 1978-79; asst. to dir. student activities and guidance Fenn Coll. (now Cleve. State U.), 1955-56, acting dir. student activities, 1956-57; dir. social welfare dept. Cleve. Area Ch. Fedn., 1957-63; rep. local councils of chs. World Migration Conf. World Council Chs., Leysin, Switzerland, 1960; exec. dir. Council Chs. Mohawk Valley Area, Utica, N.Y., 1963-67, Council Chs. Greater St. Petersburg (Fla.), 1967-70; sales rep. Wholesale Tours Internat. N.Y., 1972—, Ednl. Opportunities, Inc., 1977—; dir. Dean Mohr Plaza Apts., Inc., St. Petersburg, 1976-81 , sec., 1979-81; dean Bapt. Disciples Brethren Sch. Christian Living, Cleve., 1954, 55; mem. adv. com. Sta. WLCY-TV, 1968-74, commentator, 1967-70, corr. at World Council Chs. Assembly, Nairobi, 1975. Bd. dirs. Ludlow Community Assn., 1956-63; mem. nat. council Fellowship of Reconciliation, 1955-65; mem. bd. social welfare and dept. ednl. devel. Nat. Council Chs., 1961-67; sec. Downtown Neighborhood Center, Goodrich House Bd., Cleve., 1962-63; chmn. Adirondack-Mohawk Regional Planning Commn., 1965-67, Utica Area Interreligious Commn. on Religion and Race, 1964-66; pres. Council Human Relations of Greater St. Petersburg, 1968-80, 1985-87, 1st v.p. 1987—, chmn. edn., 1980—; sec. Religions United in Action for Community, 1968-69, mem. exec. com., 1969-70, observor Pinellas County (Fla.) Sch. Bd., 1971-76; mem. Minority Relations Goals Com., City of St. Petersburg, 1970-73; mem. adv. com. Pinellas County Charter Commn., 1971-72; chmn. Public Health Council, Utica, 1966-67; treas. Suncoast Progress, 1968, Pinellas Opportunity Council, 1969; v.p. Lakewood Property Owners (now Lakewood Civic) Assn., 1972, pres., 1974, 75, 81, 85, bd. dirs., 1976—, sec., 1979, pres., 1981-85; mem. Nat. Ch. Commn. on Scouting, 1963-70; pres. H.C. Gemmer Family Christian Found., Indpls., 1956—; edn. chmn., bd. dirs. St. Petersburg br. NAACP, 1969—, treas., 1974-76, 2nd v.p., 1976-83, 1st v.p., 1983—, edn. chmn. Fla. state conf., 1976-78; mem. Shalom Task Force, Dist. of Fla. and P.R., Ch. of Brethren, 1977-82, chmn., 1977-78; mem. UN Day Com., St. Petersburg, 1969—; bd. dirs. Tampa Bay chpt. UN Assn. U.S.A., 1969—, 1st v.p., 1980-82, pres., 1982-86, treas. Fla. div., 1987—; active numerous other orgns.; Republican candidate Pinellas County Sch. Bd., 1968, chmn. bi-racial adv. com., 1969-70, 80-81, sec.-treas., 1970-71, alt., 1971-75, voting mem., 1975—, vice-chmn., 1977-80, 86—, chmn., 1980-82, chmn. zoning com., 1976-78, 1985—, mem. 1982—, vice chmn. Sch. Facilities Task Force, 1977-78, Middle Sch. Task Force, 1983, Stabilization of High Schs. Task Force, 1986-87; non-partisan candidate St. Petersburg City Council, 1970; bd. dirs. Found. Religious Studies Indpls., 1973—, N.Y. Council Chs., 1963-67, Baptist Children's Home, Oneida, N.Y., 1965-67, Suncoast Goodwill Industries, 1969-72, Nat. Neighbors, Washington, 1978-80; bd. dirs. Urban Devel. Corp., St. Petersburg, 1976—, sec., 1979—, Pinellas County Latch Key; bd. dirs. Services to Children, Habitat for Humanity, Internat., Inc., 1976—, program devel. and evaluation com. 1976-86, 1st v.p. and chmn. program devel. and evaluation com., 1980-86, chmn. recognition com., 1986, bd. dirs. Habitat for Humanity Immokalee affiliate , 1980-86, bd. dirs. Habitate for Humanity Com. Pinellas County affiliate, 1984-88, site chmn. 1984—, fin. com. chmn. 1985-86; mem. Nat. Farm Workers Support Com., 1969—; del. World Religious Leaders Conf. on Gen. and Nuclear Disarmament, Tokyo, 1981; exec. bd. Pinellas Suncoast Urban League, 1976-80, sec., 1977-78; Dem. precinct commiteeman, 1982—; candidate Pinellas County Sch. Bd., 1982, 86; chaplain Pinellas County Dem. Com., 1982-87. Recipient citation U.S. Sec. HEW, 1962 and many other awards. Mem. Acacia. Contbg. editor Peace Action, 1955-68. Contbr. articles to mags. Address: 1863 Lakewood Dr S Saint Petersburg FL 33712

GENCHEV, MINCHO SEMOV, sociologist, educator; b. Todorcheto, Gabrovo, Bulgaria, Dec. 7, 1935; s. Semo Genchev Nikolova and Iova (Ivanova) Nikolova; m. Donka Hristova Nenkova, Jan. 31, 1935; children: Simeon Minchev, Negina Mincheva. PhD, Sofia U., Bulgaria. Editor in chief Mladez mag., Sofia, Bulgaria, 1963-66; head Ctr. Sociol. Studies on Youth, Sofia, 1966-72; assoc. prof. High Economical Inst. Karl Marx, Sofia, 1972-81; prof. Sofia U., 1981-86, rector, 1986—. Author: The Propaganda in the System of Social Life, 1975, The Bulgarian Contribution in the Socio-Political Life, 1982, The Politics Theory and History, 1985. Mem. I.P.S.A. Communist. Home: Biser No 3, Sofia Bulgaria 1000 Office: Sofia U Kliment Ohridski, boul Ruski 15, Sofia 1000 Bulgaria 1000

GENEL, MYRON, pediatrician, educator; b. York, Pa., Jan. 6, 1936; s. Victor and Florence (Mowitz) G.; m. Phyllis Norma Berkman, Aug. 25, 1968; children: Elizabeth, Jennifer, Abby. Grad., Moravian Coll., 1957; M.D., U. Pa., 1961; M.A. hon., Yale U., 1983. Diplomate: Am. Bd. Pediatrics. Intern Mt. Sinai Hosp., N.Y.C., 1961-62; resident in pediatrics Children's Hosp. Phila., 1962-64; trainee pediatric endocrinology Johns Hopkins Hosp., Balt., 1966-67; instr. pediatrics U. Pa. Sch. Medicine, 1967-69, assoc. in pediatrics, 1969-71; trainee in genetics, inherited metabolic diseases Children's Hosp. Phila., 1967-69, spl. postdoctoral fellow NIH, trainee in genetics and inherited metabolic diseases NIH, 1967-69; assoc. physician, 1969-71; mem. faculty Yale U. Sch. Medicine, New Haven, 1971—, prof., 1981—; program dir. Children's Clin. Research Ctr. Yale U. Sch. Medicine, 1971-86, dir. pediatric endocrinology, 1971-85, assoc. dean, 1985—, dir. Office Govt. and Community Affairs, 1985—; attending physician Yale-New Haven Hosp., 1971—; cons. Newington Children's Hosp., Hosp. St. Raphael, also Milford, Norwalk, Stamford hosps.; Robert Wood Johnson Health Policy fellow Inst. Medicine, Nat. Acad. Scis., Washington, 1982-83; mem. genetic adv. bd. State of Conn., 1979-82; mem. med. adv. bd. New Eng. Congenital Hypothyroidism Collaborative; cons. subcom. investigations and oversight com. sci. and tech. U.S. Ho. of Reps., 1982-84; chmn. transplant adv. com. Office of Commr., Conn. Dept. Income Maintenance, 1984—. Contbr. articles to profl. jours. Served as capt. U.S. Army, 1964-66. Recipient ann. award Conn. Campaign Against Cooley's Anemia, 1979. Mem. AAAS, Am. Acad. Pediatrics (task force organ transplants, council on govt. affairs), Am. Coll. Nutrition, Am. Diabetes Assn. (co-recipient Jonathan May award 1979), Am. Fedn. Clin. Research, Am. Pub. Health Assn., Am. Pediatric Soc., Am. Soc. Bone and Mineral Research, Assn. Am. Med. Colls. (mem. adminstrv. bd. council acad. socs. 1987—), Assn. Program Dirs. (pres. elect 1980-81, pres. 1981-82), Children's Transplant Assn. (bd. dirs. 1984—), Am. Council Transplantation, Conn. Endocrine Soc., Endocrine Soc. (pub. affairs com.), Lawson Wilkins Pediatric Endocrine Soc., Soc. Pediatric Research, Sigma Xi. Democrat. Jewish. Home: 30 Richard Sweet Dr Woodbridge CT 06525 Office: PO Box 3333 New Haven CT 06510

GENER, JOSEP, banker; b. Barcelona, Spain, July 11, 1941; s. Josep Gener and Josefa Tarré s. B.Econs., Central Barcelona Univ., 1972; B. Automation, Autonomous Barcelona Univ., 1976; C.P.A., Auditing Inst. (Barcelona), 1976. Adminstr. Banco Comml. Transatlántico, Barcelona, 1956-61; computer programmer, analyst La Caixa, Barcelona, 1961-76, gen. auditor, 1976-79, asst. gen. mgr., 1979—contbr. Internat. Savings Bank Inst., Geneva, 1972—, Savings Bank Group European Econ, European Council for Payment Systems, 1987—. Community, Brussels, 1982—, Confederación Española de Cajas de Ahorros, Madrid, 1972—. Mem. Col·l. Economistes Catalunya, Inst. de Censors de Comptes, Am. Mgmt. Assn. Internat. Roman Catholic. Club: Natació Barcelona. Avocations: running; swimming. Home: Copèrnic 47-49, Barcelona 08021 Spain Office: La Caixa, Via Laietana 60, Barcelona 08003, Spain

GENGE, HARALD WALTER, communication company executive; b. Essen, Fed. Republic Germany, Apr. 13, 1953; s. Walter and Else (Vershoven) G. M in Econs., U. Essen, 1976. Asst. to tax advisor Vehling and Ptnr., Essen, 1977; asst. to cons. System Mgmt. and Ptnr., Heiligenhaus, Fed. Republic Germany, 1978; exec. mem. Vershoven Elektrotechnik, Essen, 1979—; mng. dir. Vershoven GmnH and Co. KG, Essen, Vershoven Stahlbau, Borken, Fed. Republic Germany, Vershoven and Steenhans Communication Co., Essen and Horten, Norway. Mem. Bundesverband Junger Unternehmer, Wirtshaftsjunioren Essen (bd. dirs. 1981-84). Lodge: Round Table 26. Office: Vershoven and Steenhans Co, Riedingerstr 10, Essen 1 NRW Federal Republic of Germany

GENICOT, ANDRÉ GUSTAVE LÉON, accountant, consultant; b. Tienen, Belgium, July 18, 1947; s. Pierre and Octavia (Paenhuysen) G.; m. Paula Vanthienen, Dec. 18, 1968; children: Günther, Fabienne. Degree in Acountancy, Belgische Vereniging van Beroeps, Brussels, 1976; degree in Personnel Mgmt., Hogere Secundaire Avondleergang, Antwerp, Belgium, 1979; degree in Personnel Psychology, Inst. Voor Psychologische Vormingen, Antwerp, 1980. Adminstrv. med. supr. U. Hosp., St. Raphael, Leuven, Belgium, 1972-75; asst. mgr., dir. ELGB, Gent, Tienen, Belgium, 1975-78; adminstr., fin. mgr. VDB Compton, Brussels, 1978-84; pvt. practice accountancy Tienen, 1978-84; chief acct. Peat Marwick Continental Europe, Paris, 1984; chief acct., controller Peat Marwick Continental Europe, Brussels, 1984-85, European controller, 1985-87; dir. adminstrn. and fin., controller KPMC Continental Europe, Brussels, 1988—. Author: Administrative Organizations, 1980, Accounting Small and Medium Enterprises, 1983. Fellow Inst. Der Accts. ven Belgie. Roman Catholic. Clubs: Tennis d l Cure (Jodoigne); Executive (Ghent, Belgium). Home: Swinnenstraat 12, 3300 Tienen Belgium Office: KPMG Continental Europe, Av Louize 54, 1050 Brussels Belgium

GENILLARD, ROBERT LOUIS, financier; b. Lausanne, Switzerland, June 15, 1929; s. André Edmond and Mildred M. (Cornish) G. Ed. Coll. and Gymnase Scientifique, Lausanne, U. Lausanne, NYU, 1948-53. Vice chmn. supervisory bd., chmn. supervisory bd. TGB Holdings N.V., Netherlands; chmn. Clariden Bank, Switzerland, Transatlantic Ventures N.V., N.A.; dir. Corning Glass Works, N.Y.; financière, Crédit Suisse First Boston, Switzerland, Swiss Aluminum Ltd., Switzerland, Sandoz S.A., Switzerland. Clubs: Links (N.Y.C.); Cercle de la Terrasse (Geneva); Monte Carlo Country (Monaco). Contbr. articles to profl. jours. Office: 3 rue Louis Aureglia, MC 9800 Monaco Monaco Other: 1 Quai du Mont Blanc, 1211 Geneva 1,, Switzerland

GENN, NANCY, artist; b. San Francisco; d. Morley P. and Ruth W. Thompson; m. Vernon Chathburton Genn; children: Cynthia, Sarah, Peter. Student, San Francisco Art Inst., U. Calif., Berkeley. lectr. on art and papermaking Am. Centers in, Osaka, Japan, Nagoya, Japan, Kyoto, Japan, 1979-80; guest lectr. various univs. and art museums in U.S., 1975—. One woman shows of sculpture, paintings include, De Young Mus., San Francisco, 1955, 63, Gumps Gallery, San Francisco, 1955, 57, 59, San Francisco Mus. Art, 1961, U. Calif., Santa Cruz, 1966-68, Richmond (Calif.) Art Center, 1970, Oakland (Calif.) Mus., 1971, Linda/Farris Gallery, Seattle, 1974, 76, 78, 81, Los Angeles Inst. Contemporary Art, 1976, Susan Caldwell Gallery, N.Y.C., 1976, 77, 79, 81, Nina Freudenheim Gallery, Buffalo, 1977, 81, Annely Juda Fine Art, London, 1978, Inoue Gallery, Tokyo, 1980, Toni Birckhead Gallery, Cin., 1982, Kala Inst. Gallery, Berkeley, Calif., 1983, Ivory/Kimpton Gallery, San Francisco, 1984, 86, Eve Mannes Gallery, Atlanta, 1985, group exhbns. include, San Francisco Mus. Art, 1971, Aldrich Mus., Ridgefield, Conn., 1972-73, Santa Barbara (Calif.) Mus., 1974, 75, Oakland (Calif.) Mus. Art, 1975, Susan Caldwell, Inc., N.Y.C., 1974, 75, Mus. Modern Art, N.Y.C., 1976, traveling exhbn. Arts Council Gt. Britain, 1983-84, Inst. Contemporary Arts, Boston, 1977; represented in permanent collections, Mus. Modern Art, N.Y.C., Albright-Knox Art Gallery, Buffalo, Nat. Collection Fine Arts, Smithsonian, Washington, McCrory Corp., N.Y.C., Mus. Art, Auckland, N.Z., Aldrich Mus., Ridgefield, Conn., (collection) Bklyn. Mus., (collection) U. Tex., El Paso, Internat. Center Aesthetic Research, Torino, Italy, Cin. Art Mus., San Francisco Mus. Modern Art, Oakland Art Mus., City of San Francisco Hall of Justice, Harris Bank, Chgo., Chase Manhattan Bank, N.Y.C., various mfg. cos., also numerous pvt. collections; commd. works include, Bronze lectern and 5 bronze sculptures for chancel table, 1st Unitarian Ch., Berkeley, Calif., 1961, 64, bronze fountain, Cowell Coll., U. Calif., Santa Cruz, bronze menorah, Temple Beth Am, Los Altos Hills, Calif., 1981, 17, murals and 2 bronze fountain sculptures, Sterling Vineyards, Calistoga, Calif., 1972, 73, fountain sculpture, Expo 1974, Spokane, Wash. U.S./Japan Creative Arts fellow, 1978-79; recipient Ellen Branston award, 1952; Phelan award De Young Mus., 1963; honor award HUD, 1968. Home: 1515 La Loma Ave Berkeley CA 94708

GENNADIOS, HIS GRACE BISHOP (HIS GRACE BISHOP GENNADIOS CHRYSOULAKIS), Bishop of Buenos Aires; b. Crete, Greece, Mar. 9, 1924; s. John and Evantia (Katanxsakis) Chrysoulakis. Grad. in Theology, U. Aristontelion, 1952, LL.D. Ordained priest Greek Orthodox Church, 1944, ordained bishop, 1979. Diacono, Sitia, Crete, 1944-46, presbitero, 1946-79; obispo, N.Y., 1979; bishop of Buenos Aires (Argentina), Greek Orthodox Archdiocese of N. and S. Am., 1979—; prof. theology, Greek Church, Venezuela. Author: La Liberacion de Chipre, 1958; Sincronismo del Cristianismo, 1960; Los Contenidos de los Valores, 1962; Pedagogia y Moral, 1964. Served to lt., chaplain Greek Army, 1948-51. Decorated by Gen. Alexander for merit and valor, World War II, 1943. Office: Avda Figueroa Alcorta 3187, Buenos Aires 1425, Argentina *

GENS, RICHARD HOWARD, lawyer, consultant; b. Lynn, Mass., Jan. 29, 1929; s. Aaron Leonard and Doris L. (Damsky) G.; m. Helen Diane Pransky, June 10, 1952; children—William, Sara Lee, Julie Ann, James, Cory, Noah. B.A., Ohio State, 1949; J.D. cum laude, Boston U., 1952. Bar: Mass. 1952, U.S. Dist. Ct. Mass. 1953, U.S. Ct. Claims 1953, U.S. Ct. Appeals (1st cir.) 1954, U.S. Ct. Appeals (5th cir.) 1975, U.S. Ct. Appeals (7th cir.) 1980, U.S. Supreme Ct. 1956. Atty., Isadore H.Y. Muchnick, Boston, 1952-54; mem. firm Sheff & Gens, Boston, 1954-58, Richard H. Gens, Boston, 1958-73, Leppo & Gens, Boston, 1973-77, Gens & Gens, Sherborn, Mass., 1978—; dir. Voice, Inc., Bellingham; asst. atty. gen. Commonwealth of Mass., 1958-61. Bd. dirs. of pub. charities Commonwealth of Mass., 1959-61. Republican. Jewish. Home: 381 Old Jail Ln Barnstable MA 02630

GENSCHER, HANS-DIETRICH, vice chancellor of West Germany; b. Reideburg, Mar. 21, 1927; s. Kurt G. and Hilde (Kreime) G.; ed. Leipzig U., Hamburg U.; m. Barbara Schmidt; 1 dau., Martina. Lawyer, then parliamentarian, 1965—; minister interior Fed. Republic of Germany, Bonn, 1969-74, vice chancellor, minister fgn. affairs, 1974—. Vice chmn. Free Dem. Party, 1968-74, chmn., 1974-85. Address: Office of Vice Chancellor, Bonn Federal Republic of Germany *

GENSERT, RICHARD MICHAEL, structural engineer, consultant; b. Cleve., Oct. 10, 1922; s. Lewis Michael and Coletta Louise (Waldeisen) G.; m. Ruth Bernice Hersko, May 30, 1980; children: Stuart, Clyde, Laurel, Christopher, Kurt. BS, Case Western Res. U., 1944; MS, Ohio State U., 1947. Designer, draftsman J. Gordan Turnbull, Cleve., 1947-48; designer, draftsman Jules Schwartz Assoc., Cleve., 1948-50; designer Dalton & Dalton, Cleve., 1950-52; cons. engr. R.M. Gensert Assocs., Cleve., 1952-80, Gensert Bretnall Bobel Inc, Cleve., 1980—; prof. Fenn Coll., Cleve., 1946-47, Case Western Res. U., Cleve., 1960-68; Andrew J. Mellon vis. prof., Pitts., 1968-79; mem. Nat. Archtl. Accreditation Bd., Washington, 1971-73; mem. Masonry Research Adv. Bd., Washington, 1979—; spl. advisor NSF, Washington, 1980—. Author: (with others) Building Design Handbook, 1960, Design of Prestressed Concrete Apartment Buildings, 1972; also articles. Arbitrator, Am. Arbitration Bd., Cuyahoga County, Ohio, 1974-80. Served to lt. (j.g.) USN, 1944-46; PTO. Recipient Martin P. Korn award Prestressed Concrete Inst., 1975. Fellow Am. Concrete Inst. and ASCE (past chmn. masonry com. 1982-85, joint masonry com. 1985-88), ASTM (Alfred E. Lindau award 1982), Internat. Assn. Bridge and Structural Engrs. Home: PO Box 36 Point Chautaugua Dewittville NY 14728 Office: Gensert Bretnall Bobel 718 The Arcade Cleveland OH 44114

GENSTER, HELGE GOTFRED, surgeon; b. Copenhagen, May 24, 1932; s. Jens Gotfred and Anna (Lotz) Jensen; m. Hanne Arkil, Feb. 8, 1958; children: Lene, Annemarie, Birgitte. MD, U. Arhus, 1958. Resident, VA Hosp., Madison, Wis., 1968; chief urologist Arhus U. Hosp. (Denmark), 1969-78; chief surgeon Sonderborg Hosp. (Denmark), 1978—; asst. prof. U. Arhus Med. Sch., 1976-78, bd. dirs. Faculty of Medicine, 1971-78. Contbr. articles on urology and surgery to profl. jours. Served to 1st lt. Danish Army, 1962. Recipient prize Am. Urol. Assn., 1969. Fellow Danish Surg. Soc.; mem. Scandinavian Urol. Assn. (bd. dirs. 1977-79), Soc. Internat. d'Urologie. Lodge: Rotary (pres. 1986-87) (Sonderborg, Denmark). Office: Sonderborg Hosp Dept Surgery, DK-6400 Sonderborg Denmark

GENTILE, ANTHONY, coal company executive; b. Aquila, Italy, Nov. 1, 1920; s. Gregorio and Antonietta (Duronio) G.; m. Nina Angela DiScipio, Mar. 4, 1943; children: Robert Henry, Anita Marie, Rita Ann, Thomas Gregory. Student Youngstown Coll., 1939-42; LHD (hon.), U. of Steubenville, 1977, DHL (hon.). Co-owner Pike Inn-Restaurant, Bloomingdale, Ohio, 1946-52; asst. to owner Huberta Coal Co., Steubenville, Ohio, 1952-55; gen. mgr. Half Moon Coal Co., Weirton, W.Va., 1955-57; gen. mgr. Ohio River Collieries Co., Columbus, 1957-59, pres., 1959—; pres. Lafferty Coal Mining Co., Eastern Ohio Coal Co., 1959—; v.p. Big Mountain Coals, Inc., Prenter, W.Va., 1962—, chmn. bd., 1962—; pres. Bither Mining Co. W.Va.; v.p. N & G Constrn., Bannock Land Co.; now chmn., pres. Bannock Coal Co., Lafferty, Ohio, 1985—; chmn. bd. dirs. Mining and Reclamation Council Am., Washington; bd. dirs. Union Bank, Steubenville. Mem. 1st Ohio Trade Commn. to Europe, 1965; mem. adv. bd. St. John Med. Ctr., Steubenville; trustee Coll. Steubenville, Ohio Valley Hosp., Steubenville. Served to 1st lt AUS, 1942-45, capt. Res. ret. Decorated Purple Heart, Silver Star; recipient Citizen of Yr. award Wintersville C. of C., 1976, Conservation award for Ohio River Collieries from Gov. Ohio, 1977, Humanitarian award Jeffersonian Lodge, Jefferson County, Ohio, 1979. Mem. Am. Mining Congress (mem. adv. council coal div. 1965). Home: 4 Normandy Dr Wintersville OH 43952 Office: Ohio River Collieries Co Box 128 Bannock OH 43972

GENTILE, JACK VITO, corporate and commercial jet aircraft specialist, internat. trading company executive; b. Flushing, N.Y., Aug. 14, 1950; s. Vito and Angela (Tandoi) G.; grad. Manhattan Sch. Printing, 1970. Asst. prodn. mgr. Frank Orlandi Printers, N.Y.C., 1970-75; electronic technician Hobart Corp., Troy, Ohio, 1975-76; mgmt. position Reliance Electric Co., Cleve., 1976; pres., chief exec. officer Giacomo Internat. Trading Co., Bayside, N.Y., 1977—; cons. to fgn. govts. on trading raw materials and aircraft. Served with U.S. Army, 1969-73. Mem. Smithsonian Assos. Roman Catholic. Club: Internat. Lions, U.S. Senatorial.

GENTRY, WILLIAM NORTON, safety consultant; b. Greenwood, Ark., May 29, 1908; s. William Fred and Lola (Caudle) G.; m. Margaret Sue Whaley, May 25, 1938 (dec.); children: Susan Margaret, William David. BS in Bus. Adminstrn., U. Ark., 1929; BA, U. Ark.-Little Rock, 1984. Wire chief SW Bell Telephone Co., Hope, Ark., 1932-34, constrn. foreman, 1935-40, exchange engr., 1940-42, 46-50, plant tng. supr., 1950-57, plant personnel and tng. supr., 1958-67, plant tng. and employment supr., 1967-73; safety cons. Little Rock Mcpl. Water Works, 1974-85; safety cons. Hiway Safety Corp., Ft. Smith, Ark., 1986-87. Div. leader Community Chest, Little Rock, 1949-52; pres., del. from Ark., Pres.'s Conf. on Occupational Safety, 1958; organizing pres. United Cerebral Palsy of Central Ark., 1959-60; chmn. Little Rock Safety Commn., 1970-71, mem., 1966-85, vol. instr., 1985—; registered instr. Nat. Safety Council's driver improvement program bd. dirs. Little Rock Central YMCA, 1972-74; worker, mem. organizing bd. Contact Inc., Crisis Prevention Center, Little Rock, 1968-76; mem. Gov.'s Com. on Employment of Handicapped, Ark., 1973-80; del. to Pres.'s Conf. on Employment of Handicapped, Washington, 1977; chmn. work area on evangelism First United Meth. Ch., Little Rock, 1980, lay speaker, 1980-82, del. internat. conf., London, 1981. Served with Signal Corps, U.S. Army 1942-46. Recipient W.H. Sadler trophy Community Chest of Little Rock, 1950-51, Service award United Cerebral Palsy of Central Ark., 1969, Safety award of commendation Ark. Dept. Labor, 1973; Cert. of Service First United Meth. Ch., Little Rock, 1983. Mem. Am. Soc. Safety Engrs. (charter mem. Ark. chpt., sec. 1974-80, vice chmn. 1959-60, gen. chmn. 1960-61, chmn. ann. safety inst. 1972-76), So. Safety Conf. (pres. 1968-69, exec. dir. 1969-72, dir. 1962-86), Reserve Officers Assn. (life), Telephone Pioneers Am. (life), The Order of Bookfellows (treas. 1987-88), Phi Alpha Theta. Democrat. Club: Order of Bookfellows (treas. 1987-88). Address: #3 Shepherd's Cove apt 319 Little Rock AR 72205-7068

GEOFFREY, IQBAL (SAYYID MOHAMMED JAWAID IQBAL JAFREE), reformer, artist, lawyer; b. Chiniot, Pakistan, Jan. 1, 1939; s. Syed Iqbal Hussain and Shahzadi Mumtazjehan Shah; m. Regina Wai-ling Cheng, 1967 (div. 1978); children: Syed Hussain Haider, Shahzadi Zohra Elinoi; m. Sayyeda Farzaana Nuccwe, Mar. 3, 1988. BA with distinction, Govt. Coll., Lahore, 1957; LLB summa cum laude, Punjab U., Lahore, 1959; LLM with honors, Harvard U., 1966; A.I.C.E.A., London, 1961, A.M.B.I.M., 1969; PhD, Read Coll., 1970; also LLD; MA, Sangamon State U., 1973. Bar: Pakistan 1959, U.S. Supreme Ct. 1975. Ptnr., sr. counsel firm Geoffrey & Khitran (internat. lawyers), 1960—; lectr., art critic, cons. urban affairs and aesthetics; human rights officer UN, 1966-67; drafted Establishment of Office Of Ombudsman Order, Pakistan, 1983; spl. advisor to the Pres. of Pakistan, 1980-84. Author: Qose-Qizah, 1957, Justice is the Absence of Dictatorial Prerogative, 1965, Human Rights in Pakistan, 1966, A Critical Study of Moral Dilemmas, Iconographical Confusions and complicated Politics of XX Century Art, 1967, The Concept of Human Rights in Islam, 1981; editor: Law Rev., 1958-59; grad. editor: Harvard Art Rev., 1965-66; one-man shows include Hyde Park, London, 1960-62, Hull (Eng.) U., Birmingham (Eng.) U., Queens U., Arts Council No. Ireland, Los Angeles Mcpl. Art Gallery, PakistaN Arts Council, Lahore, Grand Central Moderns, Lahore, Henri Gallery, Washington, St. Mary's Coll., Ind., Franklin Coll., Miami Mus. Modern Art, Herbert Johnson Art Mus. Cornell U., Everson Art Mus., Syracuse, N.Y., Indus Gallery, Karachi, 1988, other exhbns. include kinetic reliefs, supersculptures, supraconceptuals; biennials, Paris, Sao Paolo, Brazil, Tokyo, Ljubljana, Yugoslavia, Arts Council Gt. Britain touring exhibits, N.Y.C., Montreal, Tokyo; represented in permanent collections Herbert Johnson Mus. Cornell U., Philips Collection, Washington, Boston Mus. Fine Arts, Pasadena Mus. Art, Arts Council Gt. Britain, Tate Gallery, London, Eng., Brit. Mus., London, Chase Manhattan Bank, N.Y.C., also pvt. collections. Recipient Paris Biennial award, 1965; pub. tribute by Pakistan Pres. Sir Ayub Khan, 1964; Sir Philip Hendy and Lord Goodman award, Arts Council Gt. Britain, 1969; Disting. Community Service award L.A.W., 1970; Huntington Hartford II and John D. Rockefeller III fellow, 1962-65; Aug. 14 designated Syed Iqbal Jafree Day by Gov. Ill., 1977; Outstanding New Citizen award Citizenship Council Met. Chgo., 1979. Fellow Royal Soc. Arts, London, 1961. Home: 13651 Peacock Farm Rd Saint Louis MO 63131 also: 128 E 1 Main Blvd, Gukberg 3, Lahore 54662, Pakistan

GEORGE, ALEXANDER ANDREW, lawyer; b. Missoula, Mont., Apr. 26, 1938; s. Andrew Miltiadin and Eleni (Efstathiou) G.; m. Penelope Mitchell, Sept. 29, 1968; children—Andrew A., Stephen A. BBA honors, U. Mont., 1960, JD, 1962; postgrad. John Marshall U., 1964-66. Bar: Mont. 1962, U.S. Ct. Mil. Apls. 1964, U.S. Tax Ct. 1970. Sole practice, Missoula, 1966—; mem. adv. com. U. Mont. Tax Inst., 1973-76; lectr. in field. Pres., Missoula Civic Symphony, 1973; nat. dir. Assn. Urban and Community Symphony Orch., 1974. Served to capt JAG U.S. Army, 1962-66. Recipient Jaycee Disting. Service award, 1973. Mem. State Bar Mont. (pres. 1981), Western Mont. Bar Assn. (pres. 1971), Mont. Law Found. (treas. 1986—), Mont. Soc. C.P.A., Phi Delta Phi, Alpha Kappa Psi, Sigma Nu (alumni trustee 1966-71). Greek Orthodox (pres. 1978). Lodges: Rotary (pres. 1972, state chmn. found. 1977, membership com. chmn. 1978), Ahepa (pres. 1967, state gov. 1968). Home: 4 Greenbrier Ct Missoula MT 59802 Office: 127 E Front St Suite 201 Missoula MT 59802

GEORGE, JAMES, research physicist; b. Lynn, Mass., Dec. 29, 1922; s. John Jeanto and Thalia Anne (Pappas) Zorzy; m. Winifred Rose Nazzaro, Mar. 8, 1952; children—James Kevin, Carolyn Anne. B.S., Northeastern U., 1948; postgrad., Georgetown U., 1951-55. Physicist high energy radiation physics div. NIH, Nuclear Radiation Physics Lab., Bethesda, Md., 1948-53; physicist Mass Spectrometry Lab., U.S. Naval Med. Research Inst., Bethesda, 1953-55; sr. physicist dept. physics Cesium atomic beams Nat. Co., Melrose, Mass., 1955-66; dir. atomic research Frequency Electronics Inc., New Hyde Park, N.Y., 1973-78; research physicist JG Research & Tech., Salem, Mass., 1969—; dir. Electronautics Corp., Maynard, Mass., 1964-66; pres., treas. Frequency Control Corp., Topsfield, Mass., 1966-69. Contbr. articles to profl. jours. Mem. Am. Phys. Soc., N.Y. Acad. Sci. Investigations in the hyperfine energy transitions of cesium, surface ionization of atoms, atomic collisions with surfaces, atomic and ionic impact phenomena on metal surfaces; secondary electron emissions. Patentee in field. Home: 15 Oakledge Rd Swampscott MA 01907 Office: One Southside Rd Danvers MA 01923

GEORGE, JOHN ANTHONY, health corporation executive; b. New Kensington, Pa., July 11, 1948; s. Moses and Veronica (Raymond) G.; B.S., Duquesne U., Pitts., 1970; M.B.A., U. Pitts., 1973; M.S. in Taxation, Robert Morris Coll., Pitts.; cert. fin. planner; m. Leah Diane Vota, Oct. 30, 1971; children—Jessica, Cara, John. Asst. adminstr. mental health and mental retardation program Western Psychiat. Inst. and Clinic, Pitts., 1971-72; asst. dir. Latrobe Area Hosp., Latrobe, Pa., 1973-76; asst. dir. Presbyn. Univ. Hosp., Pitts., 1976-80; owner, prin. George-Anstey Food Distributing Corp., Pitts., 1978-81; mgmt. cons. Arthur Young & Co., Pitts., 1980-82; exec. dir. Eastern Allegheny County Health Corp., 1982-85; pres. Alpha Health Network, 1985—; sr. v.p. Intergroup Service Corp.; lectr. in field. Contbr. articles to profl. jours. Chmn. environ. adv. com., Forest Hills, Pa. Mem. Am. Coll. Health Care Execs., Am. Hosp. Assn., Healthcare Fin. Mgmt. Assn., IACFP, Pitts. Assn. Fin. Planners, Nat. Assn. Life Underwriters, AAPPU (adv. bd. dirs.). Roman Catholic. Home: 107 Cherry Valley Rd Pittsburgh PA 15221 Office: 201 Penn Center Blvd Suite 400 Pittsburgh PA 15235

GEORGE, NORMAN, foreign minister, parliamentarian; b. Areora, Atiu, Cook Islands, Feb. 7, 1946; s. Raita and Tungane (Ambridge) G.; m. Nane Florry Hosking; children: Norman Anthony, Kevin Clifford, Brett, Alexander, Leon. LLB, U. Auckland, New Zealand, 1982. Sr. sgt. New Zealand Police, Auckland, 1969-79; officer consular affairs Auckland, 1979-82; m.p. from Areora/Tengatangi/Ngatiarua dist. 1983—, minister fgn. affairs, 1983—. Mem. Parliamentary Assn. Cook Islands (exec. com. 1986—). Mem. Cook Islands Democratic Party. Home: Avaria, Barotonga Cook Islands Office: Ministry Fgn Affairs, Atiu Cook Islands

GEORGE, YVES MARTIN, physician; b. Nantes, Loire Atlantique, France, July 14, 1942; s. Maurice Fernand and Marie Antoinette (Chevrolet) G.; m. Manneveau Marie-Thérese, July 6, 1966 (div.); children: Claire, Nathalie, Isabelle. BEPC, Externat des Enfants Nantais, Nantes, 1958, 1st Baccalaureat, 1960; MD, CHU, Nantes, 1968; ca. Asst. U. Nantes, France, 1966-72, chief de travous, 1972-76; asst. in biology Ctr. Hosp. Regional, France, 1968-76, attache-asst., 1986—; omnipraticien liberal The Rue du Calvaire, Nantes, 1976—; cons. au triangle d'or 6 Triangle d'Or, Nantes, 1980—; cons. Foyers d'Aide a L'Enfance, 1980—; cons. in field. Author: Atlas d'Ultrastructure Oculaire Humaine, 1973, Influence de la Thyroxine, 1968; contbr. articles to profl. jours. Decorated Crox de Bronze, 1975. Mem. Medecine Generale et Recherche en Pharmacologie Clin. (pres. 1986). Office: 24 Rue du Calvaire, 44000 Nantes France

GEORGEL, PIERRE, museum executive, educator; b. Safi, Morocco, Jan. 14, 1943; s. Lucien and Santia Maria (Santini) G. Ancien eleve diplome de la section sup., Ecole du Louvre, Paris, 1965; Doctorat en litterature francaise, U. Lille, 1971. Curator, Musee du Louvre, Paris, 1966-70; detached researcher C.N.R.S., Paris, 1970-74; curator Musee National d'art Moderne, Paris, 1974-79; dir. Musee des Beaux-Arts, Dijon, 1980-86; dir. Musee Picasso, Paris, 1986—; prof. history of French painting Ecole du Louvre, 1980-86. Author: Jean Cocteau et son temps, 1965; Jean Cassou, 1967; Dessins de Victor Hugo, 1971, La Gloire de Victor Hugo, 1985, La Peinture dans la Peinture, 1987, others. Office: Musee Picasso, 3 Rue de Thorigny, 75004 Paris France

GEORGES, JOHN A., paper company executive; b. El Paso, Feb. 24, 1931; s. John A. and Opal (Biffle) G.; m. Zephera M. Givas, June 15, 1952; children: Mark, Andrew, Elizabeth. B.S., U. Ill., 1951; M.S. in Bus. Adminstrn, Drexel U., 1957. Exec. v.p. internat. and wood products and resources Internat. Paper Co., N.Y.C., 1979, vice chmn., 1980, pres., chief operating officer, 1981-85, chmn., chief exec. officer, 1985—, also dir.; bd. dirs. Warner Lambert Co., N.Y. Stock Exchange, Fed. Res. Bank N.Y. Mem. Joint Council Econ. Edn.; dir. Bus. Council N.Y. State. Served with U.S. Army, 1953-55. Club: N.Y. Yacht. Office: Internat Paper Two Manhattanville Rd Purchase NY 10577

GEORGES, PETER JOHN, lawyer; b. Wilmington, Del., Sept. 8, 1940; s. John Peter and Olga Demetrius (Kazitoris) G.; m. Joan Markessini, Jan. 29, 1981. BS in Chemistry, U. Del., 1962; JD, John Marshall Law Sch., 1970; LLM in Patent and Trade Regulations, George Washington U., 1973. Bar: Ill. 1970, U.S. Ct. Appeals (fed. cir.) 1972, D.C. 1973, U.S. Supreme Ct. 1973, Del. 1978. Chemist engring. labs Bell & Howell Co., Chgo., 1966; patent coordinator Armour & Co., Chgo., 1967; patent agt., atty. UOP Inc., Chgo., 1968-71; Washington counsel UOP Inc., Arlington, Va., 1972-77; ptnr. Kile, Gholz, Bernstein & Georges, Arlington, 1977-78; assoc., then ptnr. Law Office Sidney W. Russell, Arlington, 1978-83; mng. officer Russell, Georges & Breneman and predecessor firm Russell, Georges, Breneman, Hellwege & Yee, Arlington, 1983—. Served to 1st lt. USMC, 1963-65, Vietnam. Mem. ABA, Ill. Bar Assn., D.C. Bar Assn., Del. Bar Assn., Fed. Cir. Bar Assn., Assn. Trial Lawyers Am., Am. Intellectual Property Law Assn., Am. Hellenic Lawyers Soc., Internat. Platform Assn. Home: 2331 9th St S Arlington VA 22204 Office: Russell Georges Breneman et al 745 S 23d St Suite 304 Arlington VA 22202

GEORGES, RICHARD MARTIN, lawyer, educator; b. St. Louis, Nov. 17, 1947; s. Martin Mahlon Georges and Josephine (Cipolla) Rice. AB cum laude, Loyola U., New Orleans, 1969; JD cum laude, Stetson Coll. Law, 1972. Bar: 1972, U.S. Dist. Ct. (mid. dist.) Fla. 1973, U.S. Ct. Appeals (11th cir.) 1981, U.S. Supreme Ct. 1982. Ptnr. Kieffer & Georges, St. Petersburg, Fla., 1973-80, Kieffer, Georges & Rahter, St. Petersburg, 1980-85; sole practice St. Petersburg, 1985—; adj. prof. Fla. Inst. Tech., Melbourne, 1977-86, Stetson Coll. Law, 1985—; adj. prof. Eckerd Coll., St. Petersburg, 1986—. Contbg. author: Florida Law of Trusts, 1983. Arbitrator, United Steelworkers Union, Continental Can Co., 1975—; hearing examiner City of St. Petersburg, 1982—; mem. citizen's adv. com. Pinellas County Met. Planning Orgn., 1986-87; exec. committeeman Pinellas County Rep. Party, Clearwater, Fla., 1981-82. Served to 1st lt. U.S. Army, 1972. Recipient Rafael Steinhardt award Stetson Coll. Law, 1972, Clint Green award, 1972. Mem. ABA, Fla. Bar, St. Petersburg Bar Assn. (chmn. legal check-up course), Pinellas County Trial Lawyers Assn., Fla. Camera Club Council (pres. 1985), Phi Alpha Delta. Roman Catholic. Clubs: Feather Sound Country, Suncoast Camera (Clearwater) (v.p. 1982-84; pres. 1985). Office: 3656 First Ave N Saint Petersburg FL 33713

GEORGESCU, ADELINA C., mathematics educator; b. Turnu Severin, Romania, Apr. 25, 1942; d. Constantin C. and Berindei G.; m. Mihnea Moroianu, Apr. 25, 1969 (div. 1979); children: Andrei, Sergiu. Grad., Coll. Math. and Mechanics, Bucarest, Romania, 1965. Mathematician Inst. Fluid Mechanics, Bucarest, 1965-70; head researcher Inst. Math., Bucarest, 1970-75, Nat. Inst. Scientific and Tech. Creation, Bucarest, 1975—. Author: Teoria Stabilitătii Hidrodinamice, 1976 (Prze of the Acad. 1978), Hydrodynamic Stability Theory, 1985, Sinergetica, 1987; co-author: Cercetari Matematice în Teonia Modernö, 1982; contbr. more than 65 articles to profl. jours. Recipient Gheorge Lazăr prize Acad. Sci. Romania, 1978. Mem. Soc. Matematicö, Am. Math. Soc. Home: Baneasa 2-6, bl 7/1 ap 33, 71547 Bucarest Romania

GEORGI, RUDOLF, publisher; b. Dresden, Fed. Republic of Germany, Aug. 23, 1943; s. Friedrich and Rosemarie (Olbricht) G.; m. Joana Maria Sanllehy Espinas, Sept. 30, 1983; 1 child, Maria Ifigenia. D of Nat. Research, Free U. Berlin, 1961. Owner, pub. Paul Parey Sci. Pubs., N.Y.C., Berlin and Hamburg, Fed. Republic of Germany, 1961; mem. exec. com. Berlin Verleger und Buchhändlervereinigung, 1974-85; mem. dif. com. Börsenverein des Deutschen Buchhandels Frankfurt, Fed. Republic of Germany, 1980—; mem. Steuerausschuss der Industrie und Handelskammer, Berlin, 1986—. Mem. exec. com. Forschungsgemeinschaft 20.Juli, Berlin, 1974—; mem. Berlin Kommission gegen Antisemitismus, 1986—. Mem. Deutsche Zoologische Gesellschaft, Deutsche Botanische Gesellschaft, Deutsche Ornithologen Gesellschaft, Ethologen Gesellschaft. Lutheran. Club: Internat. Flying Dutchman Class Orgn. (hon. treas., mem. exec. com.). Lodge: Rotary. Home: Finkenstrasse 13B, 1000 Berlin 33 Federal Republic of Germany Office: Paul Parey Sci Pubs, Spitalerstrasse 12, 2000 Hamburg Federal Republic of Germany

GEORGIADES, WILLIAM DEN HARTOG, university dean; b. Chgo., May 30, 1925; s. George and Alice (Den Hartog) G.; m. Ruth Taylor Long, Oct. 29, 1983; children from previous marriage—Sheldon Franklin, Beverly Jo. A.B., Upland (Calif.) Coll., 1946; M.A., Claremont (Calif.) Grad. Sch., 1949; Ed.D., U. Calif. at Los Angeles, 1956. Tchr. Whittier (Calif.) High Sch., 1947-49; teaching asst. UCLA, 1950-51; dean Upland Coll., 1951-53; chmn. dept. English Whittier High Sch., 1953-56; prof. edn., chmn. dept. curriculum and instrn. U. So. Calif., 1956-79, asso. dean edn. program devel., 1973-74; dean Coll. Edn., U. Houston, 1979—; Fulbright lectr., Cyprus and Greece, 1962, vis. lectr. in, U.S., Eng., Netherlands, Iraq, Pakistan, India, Iran, Japan, Saudi Arabia, Indonesia, Nigeria, Costa Rica; asso. dir. Danforth Found.-Nat. Assn. Secondary Sch.; Prins. model sch. project, 1968—, cons. in field. Author: Models for Individualized Instruction, 1974, New Schools for a New Age, 1977, How Good Is Your School? Program Evaluation for Secondary Schools, 1978, How to Change Your School, 1978, Take Five: A Methodology for the Humane School, 1979; Editor bulls.; Contbr. to research and edn. jours. Pres. La Cresta PTA, 1966, Sr. Danforth asso., 1962. Mem. AAUP, Assn. Higher Edn., Assn. Supervision and Curriculum Devel. (bd. dirs.), Nat. Soc. Study Edn., World Curriculum Council, Doctoral Alumni Assn. (Disting. Leadership award 1982), Phi Delta Kappa (Research award 1978). Presbyn. (elder 1959—). Home: 204 Sugarberry Circle Houston TX 77024 Office: Coll Edn U Houston Houston TX 77004

GEORGIOU, JOHN CHRYSOSTOM, mathematician; b. Vovousa, Epirus, Greece, Aug. 1, 1946; s. Chrysostom John Georgiou and Aglaia Gourgoulis. BS in Math. with distinction, Athens U., 1970; MS in Math., Mich. State U., 1971; postgrad., U. Calif., Berkeley, 1979—. Teaching asst. Mich. State U., East Lansing, 1972-73; researcher Metsovo, Epirus, 1978-79, 86—; teaching asst. U. Calif., Berkeley, 1979-83; prof. U. So. Calif., Los Angeles, 1983; lectr. Calif. State U., Hayward, 1983-86. Contbr. articles to profl. jours. Served to lt. Greek Army, 1975-78. Fellow Onassis Found., U. Calif., Berkeley, 1979-81, Found. Baron Michael Tositsa, Mich. State U., 1970-79, Athens U., 1965-70. Mem. AAUP, Math. Assn. Am. Greek Orthodox. Home: 44200 Metsovo, Epirus Greece

GERAETS, LUC HENRY, mechanical engineer; b. Uccle, Belgium, Sept. 14, 1946; s. Marcel A. and Agnes P. (Florent) G.; m. Denise G. Jooris, Aug. 2, 1969; children—Anne, Eric, David, Claude. M.E., U. Louvain, 1969, Ph.D., 1974. Research asst. U. Louvain, Belgium, 1969-74; structural analyst Tractionel, Brussels, Belgium, 1974-77, supr. structural analysis, 1978-86; mgr. piping and engring. sect. Tractebel Corp., Brussels, 1986—; invited assoc. prof. U. Louvain, 1976-82; AI project mgr. Tractionel, Belgium, 1984-86; mgr. structural mechanics, Belgatom, Belgium, 1982—. Contbr. articles to profl. jours. Mem. ASME, Belgian Nuclear Soc., Assn. Belge Pour l'Emploi des Materiaux, Belgian Assn. Artificial Intelligence, Internat. Tube Assn., Soc. Belge des Mecaniciens. Home: Rue Joseph Bens 75, B-1180 Brussels Belgium Office: Tractebel, Blvd du Regent 8, B-1000 Brussels Belgium

GERARD, ALAIN PIERRE, rheumatologist; b. Avesnes, France, Mar. 8, 1945; s. Paul Louis and Solange (Lipkowski) G.; m. Anne Gauntlett, Nov. 24, 1972; 1 child, Nicolai. MD, Faculté de Médecine, Paris, 1969. Externe Faculté de Médecine, Paris, 1965-69, intern, 1970-74, rheumatology asst., 1975—; tchr. AMENAB, Paris, 1978-80, Ecole de Podologie, 1978—. Patentee in field; contbr. articles to profl. jours. Recipient Chargé d'Enseignement à la Faculté, Paris, 1983. Mem. French Soc. Rheumatology. Roman Catholic. Home: 11 Blvd de la Porte Verte, 78000 Versailles France Office: Clinique des Maussins, 67 Rue de Romainvlle, 75019 Paris France

GERARD, BARBARA, educator, visual artist; b. N.Y.C., Apr. 21, 1943; d. Arthur and Edith (Perrone) De Bernarda; BS, NYU, 1963, MA, 1966, postgrad., 1972; profl. diploma, City Coll. of CUNY, 1975; postgrad. Columbia U., 1977-79; m. Marvin Hartenstein, Sept. 18, 1976; 1 son by previous marriage, David Gerard. Graphic designer C. A. Parshall Advt. Agy., N.Y.C., 1962; art tchr. Herman Ridder Jr. High Sch., N.Y.C., 1963-65; free lance designer Sam Muggeo Advt. Inc., N.Y.C., 1965-67; art chmn. Herman Ridder Jr. High Sch., 1967-70; program counselor recruitment and tng. of Spanish-speaking tchrs., N.Y.C. Bd. Edn., 1970-72, program coordinator bilingual pupil services Ctr. for Bilingual Edn., 1972-75, dir. bilingual tchr.-intern program, 1975-79, dir. Ctr. for Dissemination, 1979-81; owner, v.p. George Gerard Assocs., Inc., Port Washington, N.Y., 1981-83; cons. Yeshiva U., Pace U., 1973, Aspiria of N.Y., 1974, Children's TV Workshop - Sesame St., 1975; adj. lectr. CCNY, 1973-74, N.Y.U., 1974-75, Coll. New Rochelle, 1974-75; cons., participant WNBC-TV, 1970, 75, 79; project dir. N.Y.C. Bd. Edn., 1983—. One woman shows: Lincoln Inst. Gallery, N.Y., 1968, Henry Hicks Gallery, Bklyn., 1976, Second Story Spring St. Gallery, N.Y., 1976, Viridian Gallery, N.Y., 1977, 79; exhibited in group shows Loeb Student Center Gallery, N.Y.C., 1962, 63, Riverdale Community Gallery, N.Y., 1965, Environment Gallery, N.Y.C., 1969, Metamorphosis, N.Y., 1970, Concepts II, N.Y.C., 1971, Union Carbide, N.Y., 1972, Lever House, 1973, Westchester Arts Soc., White Plains, N.Y., 1973, Gillary Gallery, Jericho, L.I., 1974, Manhattan Savs. Bank, 1976, Bklyn. Acad. Music, 1976, Pvt. Viewings/The Erlichs, The Colins, 1976, Gallery 91, Bklyn., 1976, Henry Hicks Gallery, Bklyn., 1975, 76, 77, Lincoln Center, Avery Fisher Hall N.Y., 1976, Second Story Spring St. Gallery, 1976, Bergdorf Goodman, White Plains, 1976, First Women's Bank, 1976, 80, Viridian Gallery, 1976, 77, 80, Womanart Gallery, 1976, Norman Kramer Gallery, Danbury, Conn., 1976, Mfrs. Hanover Bank, N.Y., 1977, Guild Hall Mus., East Hampton, N.Y., 1977, 80, Union of Maine Artists, Portland, 1977, Northeastern U., Boston, 1978, Vered Internat. Gallery, East Hampton, 1978, Women in the Arts Gallery, 1979, Rensselaer Inst., Troy, 1979, Marie Pellicone Gallery, 1981, N.Y. Tech. Coll., 1982, Guild Hall Mus., 1983, 84, Gov. of N.Y.-World Trade Ctr., 1985, Marte Previti Gallery, 1986, South Street Gallery, Guild Hall Mus., 1987; represented in permanent collections Mus. Contemporary Crafts, N.Y.C., BBD&O Advt., Inc., N.Y.C.; also pvt. collections. Chmn., Pres.' Task Force on Bilingual Edn., 1972; v.p. Viridian Gallery, 1976-77; bd. dirs. Nat. Assn. Italian-Am. Dirs., 1982; v.p. Italian Bilingual Bicultural Educators Assn., 1982. HEW/Fed. Govt. ESEA Title VII grantee, 1975-79; recipient Nat. Scene Award for Achievement in Arts and Culture, 1979. Mem. NEA, Nat. Assn. Bilingual Edn., N.Y. State Assn. Bilingual Edn., Council Supervisory Adminstrs., NOW, Am. Council for Arts, Coalition of Women Artists Orgn., Assn. of Artist-Run Galleries, Women in the Arts, Advt. Women N.Y., Women Bus. Owners of N.Y. Contbr. articles to profl. jours. Home: 30 Waterside Plaza Apt 29F New York NY 10012 Office: 131 Livingston St Brooklyn NY 11201

GERARD, JAMES WILSON, book distributor; b. Chgo., May 16, 1935; s. Ralph Waldo and Margaret (Wilson) G.; student U. Vt., 1955, Roosevelt U., 1955-59. Ptnr. UNIPUB, N.Y.C., 1962-77; pres. Brookfield Pub. Co., Vt., 1977-87, Gower Pub. Co., Brookfield, 1987—; pres. Gregg Internat. N.A. Mem. Brookfield Hist. Soc., Assn. Scholarly Pub. Instn. Democrat. Club: Les Ambassadeurs. Home: 333 E 34 St New York NY 10016 Office: Gower Pub Co Old Post Rd Brookfield VT 05036

GERARD, JEAN BROWARD SHEVLIN, ambassador, lawyer; b. Portland, Oreg., Mar. 9, 1938; d. Edwin Leonard and Ella (Broward) Shevlin; m. James Watson Gerard, June 20, 1959 (dec. 1987); children: James W., Harriet C. AB, Vassar Coll., 1959; JD, Fordham U., 1977; LLD (hon.), U. S.C., 1983. Bar: N.Y. 1978, Fla. 1978, D.C. 1979, U.S. Dist. Ct. (ea. and so. dists.) N.Y. 1978. Atty. Cadawalader, Wickersham & Taft, N.Y.C., 1977-81; ambassador, permanent rep. of U.S. to UNESCO, Paris, 1981-85; U.S. ambassador to Luxembourg, 1985—. Editor: Fordham Internat. Law Forum, 1977. Bd. govs. Women's Nat. Rep. Club, 1967-73, 74-80, pres., 1971-73; hon. del. Rep. Nat. Conv., N.Y.C., 1972; alt. del. 18th Congl. Dist. N.Y., N.Y.C., 1980. Recipient SAR medal, 1970, medal of honor VFW, 1982. Mem. N.Y. County Lawyers Assn., Assn. Bar City of N.Y. Presbyterian. Clubs: Colony; City Midday (N.Y.C.); Capitol Hill (D.C.); Cercle de l'Union Interalliee (Paris); Cercle Munster (Luxembourg). Office: US Ambassador to Luxembourg care US State Dept Washington DC 20520 also: 22 blvd Emmanuel Servais, 2535 Luxembourg Luxembourg

GERARD, STEPHEN STANLEY, lawyer; b. N.Y.C., June 2, 1936; m. Nancy Mercer Keith, Apr. 25, 1969; children: Robert, Lillian, Stephen. BS, NYU, 1958, JD, 1963; cert. in employee relations law, Inst. for Applied Mgmt. and Law, Newport Beach, Calif., 1983. Bar: N.Y. 1964, U.S. Dist. Ct. (so. and ea. dists.) N.Y. 1967, U.S. Ct. Appeals (2d cir.) 1968. Commd. 2d lt. U.S. Army, 1954, advanced through grades to capt. M.I. Corps, 1966, ret., 1974; assoc. Haight, Gardner, Poor & Havens, N.Y.C., 1965-72; counsel Am. Hoechst Corp., Somerville, N.J., 1972-77, asst. sec., sr. counsel, 1977-87, assoc. gen. counsel, 1987—. Patron N.J. Youth Symphony, 1986, Colonial Symphony, 1988-89. Mem. ABA, Am. Corp. Counsel Assn., Am. Counsel Internat. Personnel, N.J. World Trade Council, N.J. Assn. Corp. Counsel, N.Y. Zool. Soc., Smithsonian Inst. Nat. Assocs., Morris Mus. Astron. Soc. Office: Hoechst Celanese Corp Rt 202-206 N Somerville NJ 08876

GERBA, CHARLES PETER, microbiologist, educator; b. Blue Island, Ill., Sept. 10, 1945; s. Peter and Virginia (Roulo) G.; m. Peggy Louise Scheitlin, June 9, 1970; children: Peter, Phillip. BS in Microbiology, Ariz. State U., 1969; PhD in Microbiology, U. Miami, 1973. Postdoctoral fellow Baylor Coll. Medicine, Houston, 1973-74, asst. prof. microbiology, 1974-81; assoc. prof. U. Ariz., Tucson, 1981-85, prof., 1985—; cons. EPA, Tucson, 1980—; advisor CRC Press, Boca Ratan, Fla., 1981—. Editor: Methods in Environmental Virology, 1982, Groundwater Pollution Microbiology, 1984, Phage Ecology, 1987; contbr. numerous articles to profl. and sci. jours. Mem. Pima County Bd. Health, 1986—; mem. sci. adv. bd. EPA, 1987—. Named Outstanding Research Scientist U. Ariz., 1984; environ. science and engrng. fellow AAAS, 1984. Mem. Am. Soc. Microbiology (div. chmn. 1982-83, 87-88, pres. Ariz. br. 1984-85, councilor 1985-88), Inst. Food Technologists, Internat. Assn. Water Pollution Research (sr. del. 1985—). Home: 1980 W Paseo Monserrat Tucson AZ 85704 Office: U Ariz Dept Microbiology and Immunology Tucson AZ 85721

GERBER, ABRAHAM, economic consultant, executive; b. N.Y.C., Dec. 19, 1925; s. Morris and Rose (Levy) G.; m. Beverly Kulkin, Dec. 23, 1948 (dec. 1966); children—Douglas K., Judith E.; m. Ilene Pomerantz, Sept. 28, 1967; children—Barbara J. Nakazawa, Gary L. A.B., Columbia Coll., 1948; M.A., Columbia U., 1950; postgrad. New Sch. for Social Research, 1950-51. Economist U.S. Dept Commerce, Washington, 1951, U.S. Dept. Interior, Washington, 1951-53; economist, asst. to pres., sec. system devel. com. Am. Electric Power Service Corp., N.Y.C., 1953-67; sr. v.p. Nat. Econ. Research Assoc., White Plains, N.Y., Palm Beach, Fla., 1967—; bd. dirs. Regent Bank, Davie, Fla.; cons. Pres.'s Cabinet Com. Energy, Washington, 1953; mem. adv. com. U.S. Dept. Interior Office Coal Research, Washington, 1961-69; chmn. com. Energy Econ. Growth, Nat. Acad. Engring. Com. on Power Plant Siting, Washington, 1971-72. Contbr. articles to profl. jours. Mem. exec. com. Pub. Utility Research Ctr. U. Fla., Gainesville, 1982—; panel mem. Nuclear Regulatory Commn. State Regulatory Activity, Washington, 1977. Served with USAAF, 1943-45. Mem. IEEE (sr.), Am. Econ. Assn., AAAS, Am. Nuclear Soc. Internat. Conf. Large High Voltage Electric Systems. Jewish. Club: Governors. Avocations: tennis; swimming; theater; opera. Office: Nat Econ Research Assocs 350 Royal Palm Way Palm Beach FL 33480

GERBER, JOHN CHRISTIAN, English language educator; b. New Waterford, Ohio, Jan. 31, 1908; s. Christian G. and Leonora (Hauptmann) G.; m. Margaret E. Wilbourn, Sept. 3, 1941; children: Barbara Page Barrett, Ann Wilbourn Gerber Sakaguchi. A.B., U. Pitts., 1929, M.A., 1932; Ph.D., U. Chgo., 1941; D.Letters (hon.), Morningside Coll., 1979. Instr. English U. Pitts., 1931-36; instr. English U. Chgo., 1938-42, pre-meteorology, 1942-44; asst. prof. English U. Iowa, 1944-47, asso. prof., 1947-49, prof., 1949-76, Carpenter prof. emeritus, 1976—, chmn. dept. English, 1961-76, dir. Sch. Letters, 1967-76, coordinator fine arts, 1984-86; prof. English State U. N.Y. at Albany, 1976-84, chmn. dept., 1976-81, acad. Laureate, 1984; vis. asso. prof. English U. So. Calif., summer 1949; vis. prof. U. N.Mex., summers 1952, 57, Trinity Coll., summers 1960, 63, U. Calif. at Berkeley, 1960-61, U. Colo., summer 1965, U. Philippines, 1969, Am. U. at Cairo, 1970, Korean univs., summers; 1972, 1984 Chinese univs., summer 1979; cons. English U.S. Office Edn., 1964-65. Author: (with Walter Blair) Factual Prose, 1945, Literature, 1948, Writers Resource Book, 1953, (with Fleece and Wylder) Toward Better Writing, 1958, (with Arnold and Ehninger) Repertory, 1960, Twentieth Century Interpretations of the Scarlet Letter, 1968, Studies in Huckleberry Finn, 1971, Mark Twain, 1988; (with Brown, Kaufmann and Lindberg) Pictorial History of the University of Iowa, 1988; also chpts. in Toward General Education, 1948; editorial bd.: Coll. English, 1947-48, 65-71, Am. Quar, 1963-68; editorial adviser: Philol Quar, 1951-57; editorial adv. bd.: Resources for American Literary Study, 1971—; chmn. editorial bd.: Windhover Press, 1968-72; mem. editorial bd.: U. Iowa Press, 1963-67; chmn. editorial bd.: Iowa-California Edit. of the Works of Mark Twain, 1965-83; hist. editor: Tom Sawyer vol., 1980; editor: Teaching Coll. English, 1965, Scott-Foresman Key Edits; contbr. articles to profl. jours.; author intros. several books. Recipient Distinguished Service award Iowa Council Tchrs. English, 1972, Academic Laureate Disting. and Sustained Service SUNY Albany, 1984, Resolution of Commendation N.Y. Legis., 1984, Citation, State of N.Y. Gov. Cuomo, 1984. Mem. Nat. Council Tchrs. English (Hatfield award 1964, Exec. Com. award 1974, trustee of research found. 1962-65, pres. 1955, Disting. Lectr. award 1966), Conf. Coll. Composition and Communication (chmn. 1950, Founders award 1976), Modern Lang. Assn. (chmn. Am. lit. sect. 1969, mem. exec. council 1972-75, mem. nominating com. 1981-83), Midwest Modern Lang. Assn. (pres. 1966), N.E. Modern Lang. Assn., Assn. Depts. English (chmn. 1964), Phi Beta Kappa. Address: 359 Magowan Ave Iowa City IA 52246

GERBER, RENE, musician, composer; b. Travers, Switzerland, June 29, 1908; s. Ernest and Anna (Pellaton) G.; m. Ruth MAtthey Doret, June 15, 1934. MD, U. Zurich, Switzerland, 1929; postgrad., Zurich Conservatory, 1930-33. Dir. Neuchatel (Switzerland) Conservatory, 1947-51, prof. music, condr. orchs., 1933—. Composer 19 works for orch., 14 concertos and concertinos, 41 works of chamber music, 31 works of vocal music, 59 works for piano, 1 organ piece, 2 operas. Mem. Assn. Musiciens Suisse (pres. sect. Neuchateloise de la Soc. Suisse Pedagogie Musicale, 1968-82), Soc. Belles'Lettres (hon.), Amicale des Arts, Soc. des Amis des Arts. Home: 22 Rue de Neuchatel, 2022 Bevaix Neuchatel Switzerland

GERBERDING, WILLIAM PASSAVANT, university president; b. Fargo, N.D., Sept. 9, 1929; s. William Passavant and Esther Elizabeth Ann (Habighorst) G.; m. Ruth Alice Albrecht, Mar. 25, 1952; children: David Michael, Steven Henry, Elizabeth Ann, John Martin. B.A., Macalester Coll., 1951; M.A., U. Chgo., 1956, Ph.D., 1959. Congl. fellow Am. Polit. Sci. Assn., Washington, 1958-59; instr. Colgate U., Hamilton, N.Y., 1959-60; research asst. Senator E.J. McCarthy, Washington, 1960-61; staff Rep. Frank Thompson, Jr., Washington, 1961; faculty UCLA, 1961-72, prof., chmn. dept. polit. sci., 1970-72; dean faculty, v.p. for acad. affairs Occidental Coll., Los Angeles, 1972-75; exec. vice chancellor ULCA, 1975-77; chancellor U. Ill., Urbana-Champaign, 1978-79; pres. U. Wash., Seattle, 1979—; dir. Wash. Mut. Savs. Bank, Pacific Northwest Bell, Safeco Corp., Seattle; cons. Def. Dept., 1962, Calif. Assembly, 1965. Author: United States Foreign Policy: Perspectives and Analysis, 1966; co-editor, contbg. author: The Radical Left: The Abuse of Discontent, 1970. Trustee Macalester Coll., 1980-83. Served with USN, 1951-55. Recipient Distinguished Teaching award U. Calif., Los Angeles, 1966; Ford Found. grantee, 1967-68. Mem. Am. Polit. Sci. Assn. Office: U Wash Pres Office 301 Administrn Bldg AH-30 Seattle WA 98195 *

GERBERG, EUGENE JORDAN, entomologist; b. N.Y.C., June 1, 1919; s. Morris and Bessie (Ehrlich) G.; B.S., Cornell U., 1939, M.S., 1941; Ph.D., U. Md., 1954; m. Josephine Elizabeth Vick, June 21, 1941; children: Gary V., Jordan V., Jon A., Glen G., Gail M. Pres. Insect Contrl & Research, Inc., Balt., 1946—; pres. Cornell Chem. & Equipment Co., Inc., Balt., 1946-79; dir. Nat. City Bank of Balt., 1966-71; mem. U.S. Trade & Investment Mission to Nigeria, W. Africa, 1961, Pakistan, 1968; cons. World Health Orgn. UN, 1969, 70, project leader East African Aedes Research Unit, Tanzania; cons. Pan Am. Health Orgn., 1975, AID, Sri Lanka, 1978, Thailand, 1979; sci. cooperator U.S. Dept. Agr., 1954—; adj. prof. Sch. Public Health U. S.C., 1982-85, Uniformed Services U. Health Scis., 1986—. Served to col. USAR. Mem. Entomol. Soc. Am., Am. Registry Profl. Entomologists (Med./Vet. Entomologist of Yr. award), Am. Mosquito Control Assn. (Meritorious Service award), Royal Soc. Tropical Medicine & Hygiene, Am. Soc. Tropical Medicine & Hygiene, Inst. Food Technologists, Biol. Research Inst. Am. (pres.). Clubs: Explorers, Cosmos. Lodge: Masons. Contbr. numerous articles to profl. jours. Office: 1330 Dillon Heights Ave Baltimore MD 21228

GERDES, NEIL WAYNE, library director; b. Moline, Ill., Oct. 19, 1943; s. John Edward and Della Marie (Ferguson) G. A.B., U. Ill., 1965; B.D., Harvard U., 1968; M.A., Columbia U., 1971; M.A. in L.S., U. Chgo., 1975. Diplomate: Ordained to ministry Unitarian Universalist Assn., 1975. Copy chief Little, Brown, 1968-69; instr. Tuskegee Inst., 1969-71; library asst. Augustana Coll., 1972-73; editorial asst. Library Quar., 1973-74; librarian, prof. Meadville Theol. Schs., Chgo., 1973—; library program dir. Chgo. Cluster Theol. Schs., 1977-80; dir. Hammond Library, 1980—; prof. Chgo. Theol Sem., 1980—. Mem. ALA, Am. Theol. Library Assn., Chgo. Area Theol. Library Assn., Phi Beta Kappa. Office: Chgo Theological Seminary Hammond Library 5757 S University Ave Chicago IL 60637

GERDES, PETER RENE, communications educator; b. Zurich, Switzerland, Sept. 26, 1941; s. Karl and Friedel (Bertschinger) G.; m. Dagmar Steinemann, July, 1986; 1 child, Alana Mara. PhD, U. Basel, Switzerland, 1970. Registered journalist. Tchr. Basel, 1966-70; freelance journalist Switzerland; freelance theatre dir. Switzerland, Ireland, 1965-70; editor in chief Swiss Newsreel Co., Geneva, 1970-75; instr. U. New South Wales, Sydney, Australia, 1975—; fgn. correspondent Neue Zürcher Zeitung, Switzerland, 1983—; media cons. Friedrich Naumann Found., Bonn, 1982-83; film cons. Pro Helvetia, Zurich, 1985. Author: Major Works of Brendan Behan, 1973. Mem. Assn. Swiss Journalists, Australian Screen Studies Assn. (founder), Australian Drama Studies Assn. (founder), Swiss-Australian C. of C. (bd. dirs. 1986—).

GERDES, RALPH DONALD, fire safety consultant; b. Cin., Aug. 11, 1951; s. Paul Donald and Jo Ann Dorothy (Meyer) G. BArch, Ill. Inst. Tech., 1975. Registered architect, Ill. Architect Schiller & Frank, Wheeling, Ill., 1976; sr. assoc. Rolf Jensen & Assocs., Inc., Chgo., 1976-84; pres. Ralph Gerdes & Assocs., Inc., Indpls., 1986—; Lectr. Purdue U., Ind. U., Ill. Inst. Tech., Butler U. Co-author: Planning and Designing the Office Environment, 1981. Recipient Joel Polsky prize Am. Soc. Interior Designers, 1983. Mem. ASHRAE, Soc. of Fire Protection Engring. (assoc.), Nat. Fire Protection Assn., AIA, Bldg. Ofcls. and Code Adminstrs., Internat. Conf. of Bldg. Officials, Ind. Fire Safety Assn. (exec. com. 1986-88). Roman Catholic. Club: Columbia (Indpls.). Home: 556 Lockerbie Circle N Indianapolis IN 46202 Office: 127 E Michigan St Indianapolis IN 46204

GERENTZ, SVEN THURE, news agency executive; b. Visby, Sweden, Sept. 3, 1921; s. Thure and Elin (Hemstrom) G.; m. Kerstin Blix, Sept. 14, 1945; children: Martin, Anna. Licentiate in Econs., Stockholm Sch. Econs., 1956. Sec. Swedish Bd. of Trade, Stockholm, 1945-52; sec. Stockholm C. of C., Stockholm, 1952-57; gen. mgr. Assn. Swedish Automobile Mfrs., Stockholm, 1957-59; dep. gen. mgr. Svenska Dagbladet, Stockholm, 1960-62, gen. mgr., 1962-73, editor-in-chief, 1969-73; gen. mgr. Tidningarnas Telegrambyrå, Stockholm, 1974-86; chmn. Nat. Swedish Rd. Adminstrn., Borlange, 1982—. Author: The Stockholm Mercantile Marine Office 1748-1948, 1948. Decorated knight comdr. Cross of the Vasa Order (Sweden), comdr. Finnish Order of Lion. Mem. Stockholm Club of Merchants (chmn. 1980-85), Stockholm C. of C. (vice chmn., 1982—). Office: Tidningarnas Telegrambyrå, Kungsholmstorg 5, 10512 Stockholm Sweden

GERHARD, HARRY E., JR., management consultant; b. Phila., Aug. 7, 1925; s. Harry E. and Frances Jane (Edwards) G.; children: Marjorie Chasteen, Jane Tehan, Susan Jillson, John, Nancy, Barbara Thomas. Student Muhlenberg Coll., 1943-44; AB, George Washington U., 1968; MA, 1969. Commd. ensign U.S. Navy, 1943, advanced through grades to rear admiral, 1971; exptl. test pilot, 1955-57; ret., 1976; exec. v.p., chief operating officer Costa Line Cargo Services, Inc., N.Y.C., 1976-80; gen. mgr. Olayan Transp. Group, Dammam, Saudi Arabia, 1980-82; pres., owner Domestic & Overseas Countertrade & Cons. Services, Ltd., Pa., N.Y., Washington, 1983—; pres., Research and Locating Assocs., Ltd., 1986—. Active Boy Scouts Am. Decorated Silver Star, D.F.C. (2), Meritorious Service medal (2), Air medals (16), Navy Commendation medals with combat V (2), Ground Combat Action Ribbon, Navy Unit Citation. Mem. Assn. Naval Aviation, Air Force Assn., Am. Def. Preparedness Assn., Navy League U.S., Nat. Aero. Assn., Ret. Officers Assn., Order of Daedalians, Tailhook Assn., Cousteau Soc., Four C's, Fleet Res. Assn., Maritime and Environ. Cons., Mil. Order World Wars, Nat. War Coll. Alumni Assn., Soc. Maritime Arbitrators, Soc. Marine Cons., U.S. Def. Com., Am. Security Council, Internat. Platform Assn., Greater Pitts. C. of C., Smaller Mfrs. Council. Republican. Lutheran. Clubs: Wings, N.Y. Yacht, Army Navy, London #1. Lodge: Masons, Shriners. Address: Gateway Towers 17N Pittsburgh PA 15222

GERLE, LADISLAV, Czechoslovakian government official; b. Kozlovice, Novy Jicin Dist., Czechoslovakia, Nov. 26, 1936. Ed. Mining Coll., Ostrava. Various positions in metall. plant Novăhut Klementa Gottwalda, Ostrava, 1959-66, prodn. mgr. Karvinăplant, 1966-70; 2d dep. dir., later dep. dir. for tech. devel. and investments, Ostrava, 1970-75; tech. dir. gen. directorate Hutnictvizeleza (ferrous metallurgy), Prague, 1975-78; dep. minister metallurgy and heavy engring. Govt. Czechoslovakia, 1979-81, dep. prime minister, 1981-88, dep. to Ho. of Nations, Fed. Assembly, 1981—, minister metallurgy, engring., and electrotech. industry, 1988—. Mem. central com. Communist Party Czechoslovakia, 1981—. Address: Office of Deputy Premier, Prague 1 Czechoslovakia *

GERMAN, EDWARD CECIL, lawyer; b. Phila., Dec. 28, 1921; s. Samuel Edward and Reba (Trimble) G.; m. Jane Harlos, Sept. 2, 1950; 1 child, Jeffrey Neal. JD, Temple U., 1950. Bar: Pa. 1951. Assoc. LaBrum & Doak, Phila., 1953-80; ptnr. German, Gallagher & Murtagh, Phila., 1980—; cons., lectr. to law schools including Harvard U., U. Pa., Syracuse U., others; bd. dirs., mem. products liability, def. research coms. Def. Research Inst., Def. Research Regional Library Inst.; instr. Practicing Law Inst. Contbr. chpts. to books, articles to profl. jours. Dist. dir. United Fund Campaign, 1960; solicitor-counsel Civic Assns. Delaware County, 1955-60; sec. Haven Beach Assn., 1962-63, v.p., 1963-64; trustee Pop Warner's Little Scholars, 1968—; sec., treas. Henryville Conservation Club. Served with USAAF, 1942-46, with USAF, 1950-51. Mem. ABA (chmn. trial techniques com. 1969, mem. profl. and officers and dirs. liability law com. ins. sect. 1974—, pvt. antitrust litigation com. litigation sect. 1974—, subcom. miscellaneous malpractice re accts., bankers, etc. 1976—), Urban Club (pres. 1987-88), Pa. Bar Assn. (com. unauthorized practice 1976—), Phila. Bar Assn. (mem. Pa. rules of civil procedure com. 1963-71, unauthorized practice law com. 1965—, common pleas ct. com. 1964-71, com. antitrust laws corp. sect., mem. Federal bench-bar conf.), Am. Law Firm Assn. (chmn. bd. 1985—), Fedn. Ins. Counsel (bd. govs. 1960-62, v.p. 1962-63, sec.-treas. 1963-65, exec. v.p. 1965-66, pres. 1966-67, chmn. bd. 1967-68), Maritime Law Assn., U.S. Am. Legion, 40 and 8, Internat. Assn. Ins. Counsel (def. research com., profl. liability and malpractice com.), Internat. Assn. Humble Humbugs, Pa. C. of C., Phila. Def. Counsel Assn., Scribes, Phi Delta Phi. Lodges: Masons, Shriners. Clubs: Union League, Down Town, Maxwell Meml. Football, Union (pres. 1987—) (Phila.); Beach Haven (N.J.) Yacht; Little Egg Harbor Yacht; Seaview Country (Absecon, N.J.); Little Mill Country; Belleplain Farms Shooting Preserve; India House. Home: 129 The Mews Haddonfield NJ 08033 Office: Suite 3100 1818 Market St Philadelphia PA 19103

GERMANN, J. GARY, lawyer; b. Ventura, Calif., Dec. 13, 1946; s. Otto A. and Frances W. (Crawford) G.; m. Virginia Ann Vermeulen, May 10, 1975; 1 child, Vanessa Charlene. B.A. magna cum laude, Calif. State U.-Fresno, 1968; J.D., U. San Francisco, 1973. Bar: Calif. 1973, U.S. Dist. Ct. (no. dist.) Calif. 1973, U.S. Ct. Appeals (9th cir.) 1977, U.S. Dist. Ct. (cen. dist.) Calif. 1978, U.S. Dist Ct. (so. dist.) Calif. 1984. Assoc., Barfield, Barfield, Dryden & Ruane, San Francisco, 1974-76, Hunt, Liljestrom & Wentworth, Santa Ana, Calif., 1976-78; sole practice, Newport Beach, Calif., 1978-82; ptnr. Germann & Welputt, Irvine, Calif., 1982—. Chmn. Woodbridge Homeowners Assn. Legal and Fin. Com., Irvine, 1977. Mem. Calif. Young Lawyers Assn. (bd. dirs. 1978-81), Orange County Young Lawyers Assn. (bd. dirs. 1979-81), Orange County Bar Assn., Profl. Ski Instrs. Am., Calif Trial Lawyers Assn., Pi Gamma Mu. Republican. Roman Catholic. Office: Germann & Welputt 19762 Mac Arthur Blvd Suite 100 Irvine CA 92715

GERMANN, RICHARD P(AUL), chemist, business executive; b. Ithaca, N.Y., Apr. 3, 1918; s. Frank E.E. and Martha Mina Marie (Knechtel) G.; m. Malinda Jane Plietz, Dec. 11, 1942; 1 child, Cheranne Lee. Student (lab. asst.), U. N.Mex., summers 1938, 39; student, Calif. Inst. Tech., 1939; B.A., Colo. U., 1939, postgrad., 1940-41; student, Western Res. U. (Naval Research fellow), 1941-43, Brown U., 1954. Chief analytical chemist Taylor Refining Co., Corpus Christi, 1943-44; research devel. chemist Calco Chem. div. Am. Cyanamid Co., 1944-52; devel. chemist charge pilot plant Alrose Chem. Co. div. Geigy Chem. Corp., 1952-55; new product devel. chemist, research div. W.R. Grace & Co., Clarkesville, Md., 1955-60; chief chemist soap-cosmetic div. G.H. Packwood Mfg. Co., St. Louis, 1960-61; coordinator, promoter chem. product devel. Abbott Labs., North Chicago, Ill., 1961-71; internat. chem. cons. to mgmt. 1971-73; pres. Germann Internat. Ltd., 1973-82, Ramtek Internat. Ltd., 1973—; real estate broker, 1972—. Author: Science's Ultimate Challenge—The Re-Evaluation of Ancient Occult Knowledge, Decomtamination of PLant Wastes-An Overview; patentee in U.S. and fgn. countries on sulfonamides, vitamins, detergent-softeners and biocides. Rep. Am. Inst. Chemists to Joint Com. on Employment Practices, 1969-72; vestryman St. Paul's Episcopal Ch., Norwalk, Ohio, 1978-81, also chmn. adminstrn. and long-range planning commn., 1980-81; trustee Services for the Aging, Inc., 1982—; chmn. nutritional council Ohio Dist. Five Area Agy. on Aging, 1983-84; sr. adv. Ohio Assn. Ctrs. for Sr. Citizens, Inc., 1982—; pres. Huron county Firelands chpt. Am. Assn. Retired Persons #4110, 1986-88; bd. dirs. Christie Lane Workshop, 1981—; mem. com. Huron County Disaster Services Agy., 1987—. Fellow AAAS, Am. Inst. Chemists (chmn. com. employment relations 1969-72), Chem. Soc. (London), AAAS, Am. Assn. Ret. Persons; mem. Am. Chem. Soc. (councilor 1971-73, chmn. membership com. chem. mktg. and econs. div. 1966-68, chmn. program com. 1968-69, del. at large for local sects. 1970-71, chmn. 1972-73, chmn. Chgo. program com. 1966-67, chmn. Chgo. endowment com. 1967-68, dir. Chgo. sect. 1968-72, chmn. awards com. 1972-73, sec. chem. mktg. and econs. group Chgo. sect. 1964-66, chmn. 1967-68), Internat. Sci. Found., Sci. Research Soc. Am., Comml. Chem. Devel. Assn. (chmn. program com. Chgo. conv. 1966, mem. fin. com. 1966-67, ad hoc com. of Comml. Chem. Devel. Assn.-Chem. Market Research Assn. 1968-69, co-chmn. pub. relations Denver conv. 1968, chmn. membership com. 1969-70), Chem. Market Research Assn. (mem. directory com. 1967-68, employment com. 1969-70), Midwest Planning Assn., Nat. Security Indsl. Assn. (com. rep. ocean sci. tech. com., maintenance adv. com., tng. ad. com. 1962-70), Midwest Fedn., Midwest Planning Assn., Am. Assn. Textile Chemists and Colorists, Am. Pharm. Assn., Midwest Chem. Mktg. Assn., Am. Pharm. Assn., N.Y. Acad. Scis., Internat. Platform Assn., Water Pollution Control Fedn., Lake County Bd. Realtors, World Future Soc., Midwest Planning Assn. Am., Sigma Xi, Alpha Chi Sigma (chmn. profl. activities com. 1968-70, pres. Chgo. chpt. 1968-70). Clubs: Chemists (N.Y.C., Chgo.); Torch, Toastmasters. Lodges: Lions (sec. Allview, Md. 1956-57), Kiwanis, Masons (32 degree), Knights Templar, Rotary. Home and Office: 6 Vinewood Dr Norwalk OH 44857

GERMANN-AUDEOUD, HÉLÈNE-LISE, language professional; b. Paris, Mar. 25, 1937; arrived in Switzerland, 1960; d. Pierre and Ida Amelie (Méchin) A.; m. Paul Germann, Nov. 7, 1960; children: Edgar Pierre, Caroline Sandra. Student, Lycée Racine, Paris, 1946-53; diploma in interpreting, Ecole d'Interprete, Paris, 1959, diploma in translating, 1959. Cert. interpreter, translator. Interpreter Adia-Interim, Basel, 1960-77; translator Consulado del Perú, Basel, 1964-66. Translator numerous books and articles. Home: Breitestrasse 141, 4132 Muttenz Switzerland

GERNER, JAN KRISTIAN, history researcher, journalist; b. Piteå, Sweden, May 25, 1942; s. Göran Krister Tore and Gullan (Rock) G.; m. Ingrid Kerstin Birgitta Nyström, Dec. 19, 1975; children: Annika Marianne, Max Hyung-Taek. MA in Russian, History and Philosophy, U. Lund, Sweden, 1969, PhD in History, 1984. Research asst. U. Lund, Sweden, 1969-78, asst. prof. history, 1978-84, assoc. prof., 1984—; research fellow Swedish Council for Humanities and Social Scis., Sweden, 1987—; guest researcher Swedish Inst. Internat. Affairs, Stockholm, 1982, 85, 86-87. Author: (in Swedish) The Heritage of the Past, 1980, The Soviet Union and Central Europe, 1985 (Swedish Acad. Learning 1985); co-author: Planned Economy and Environmental Problems, 1978. Mem. Swedish Hist. Soc., Nordic Com. for Soviet and East European Studies. Home: Nyckelkroken 42, S-22247 Lund Sweden Office: U Lund Dept History, Magle Lilla Kyrkogata 9A, S-22351 Lund Sweden

GERNSHEIM, HELMUT ERICH ROBERT, photohistorian, writer; b. Munich, Fed. Republic Germany, Mar. 1, 1913; arrived in Eng., 1937, naturalized, 1946; s. Karl-Theodor and Hermine (Scholz) G.; m. Alison Eames, Mar. 1942 (dec. Mar. 1969); m. Irene Guenin, Oct. 1971. Student art history, U. Munich, 1933-34; Dip., Bavarian State Sch. Photography, Munich, 1936; MSc (hon.), Brooks Inst., Santa Barbara, Calif., 1984. Photographer Warburg Inst. Art, London, 1942-45; founder Gernsheim Collection Photography London, 1945-64, U. Tex., 1964—; lectr. history of photography Franklin coll., Lugano, Switzerland, 1971-72; disting. guest prof. history of art U. Tex., Austin, 1979, Ariz. State U., Tempe, 1982; Regents prof. history of art U. Calif., Riverside, 1984 and Santa Barbara, 1985; curator exhbns., London, Lucerne, Goteborg, Stockholm, Amsterdam, Milan, Essen, Cologne, Frankfurt, Munich, N.Y.C., Rochester, N.Y., Detroit, Austin, Numerous others, 1951-84; advisor to the editor Encyclopaedia Britannica, 1968—; trustee Swiss Found. Photography, Zurich, 1975, Alinari Mus. Photography, Florence, Italy, 1985—. Author: Julia Margaret Cameron, 1948, 75, Lewis Carroll-Photographer, 1949, 68, Roger Fenton, Photographer of Crimean War, 1954, 73, The History of Photography, 1955, 69, 83, and twenty other books; contbr. overt 260 articles to newspapers, jours. and art mags. Decorated Cross of Merit (Fed. Republic Germany); recipient Gold medal Italian Acad. Art, 1980, D.O. Hill medal German Acad. Photography, 1983, Assn. Internat. Photog. Art Dealers award, 1984. Fellow Am. Photohistory Soc. (hon.), German Photog. Soc. (Kulturpreis 1959). Club: Daguerre (Frankfurt) (hon.). Home: Via Tamporiva 28, 6976 Castagnola Switzerland

GERNYX, OLE, marine executive; b. Copenhagen, Aug. 31, 1937; s. Julius and Poula (Rasmussen) G.; m. Inger Holland, Nov. 28, 1964; 1 child, Flemming. Grad., Shipmaster Naval Coll., Copenhagen, 1962; MBA, Copenhagen Comml. Sch., 1985. With Norden Steamship Co., Copenhagen, 1962-79, marine supt., 1979—; judge sea Ct. Justice, Copenhagen, 1986—; commr. mem. tech. com. Norske Veritas, Oslo, 1987—; mem. governing body Kogtved Seaman Sch., 1982—. Served as jr. officer Royal Danish Navy, 1954-60. Mem. Copenhagen Shipmasters Soc. (bd. dirs. 1987—), Danish Shipowners Assn. (commr. 1979—). Home: Skansoerevej 10, 3000 Helsingoer Denmark Office: ssco Norden A/S, 49 Amaliegade, 1256 Copenhagen Denmark

GERO, JOHN STEVEN, architectural and engineering educator; b. Budapest, Hungary, Dec. 21, 1943; arrived in Australia, 1948; s. Emery Imre and Helene Gero; m. Annette Marie Angyal, Jan. 23, 1974. B in Engring., U. New South Wales, Sydney, Australia, 1965; M of Bldg. Scis., U. Sydney, 1966, PhD, 1974. Chartered profl. engr., Australia. From lectr. to assoc. prof. engring. U. Sydney, Australia, 1966-84; prof. U. Sydney, 1985—; vis. assoc. prof. Columbia U., N.Y.C., 1970-71; research fellow MIT, 1973-74, U. Calif., Berkeley, 1974-75; vis. prof. Harvard U., Cambridge, Mass., 1974-75, Strathclyde U., Glasgow, Scotland, 1979-80, Nat. Inst. Applied Sci., Lyon, France, 1981, UCLA, 1983, Carnegie Mellon U., Pitts., 1987, Loughborough U., Loughborough, 1987; adj. prof. Carnegie Mellon U., 1987-89. Author, editor 13 books; contbr. chpts. to other books; author numerous research papers in field. Fulbright scholar, 1970-71; Harkness fellow, 1974-75; recipient Silver Core Internat. Fedn. Info. Processing, Switzerland, 1986; Sr. Fulbright scholar, 1987. Fellow Instn. Australian Engrs., Royal Soc. Arts; mem. numerous profl. orgns. Club: Mosman Rowing (Sydney). Office: Univ Sydney, Sydney New South Wales Australia 2006

GERONEMUS, DIANN FOX, social work consultant; b. Chgo., July 4, 1947; d. Herbert J. and Edith (Robbins) Fox; B.A. with high honors, Mich. State U., 1969; M.S.W., U. Ill., 1971; 1 dau., Heather Eileen. Lic. clin. social worker, marriage and family therapist, Fla. Social worker neurology, neurosurgery and medicine Hosp. of Albert Einstein Coll. Medicine, 1971-74; prin. social worker ob-gyn and newborn infant service Rush-Presbyn.-St. Luke's Med. Center, Chgo., 1974-75; social worker neurology, adminstr. Multiple Sclerosis Treatment Center, St. Barnabas Hosp., Bronx, N.Y., 1975-

77, socio-med. researcher (Nat. Multiple Sclerosis Soc. grantee), dept. neurology and psychiatry, 1977-79, dir. social service, 1979-80; field work instr. Fordham U. Grad. Sch. Social Service, 1979-80; preceptor, social work program Fla. Atlantic U., Fla. Internat. U.; mem. edn. com., med. adv. bd., program cons. Nat. Multiple Sclerosis Soc., 1980-83, area service cons., 1983-86 ; pvt. practice psychotherapy; social work cons.; cons. in gerontology, rehab. and supervision. Mem. Acad. Cert. Social Workers, Nat. Assn. Social Workers (diplomate), Registered Clin. Soc. Hosp. Social Work Dirs., Am. Orthopsychiat. Assn. Jewish. Contbr. articles to profl. jours. Home: 833 NW 81st Way Plantation FL 33324

GEROYANNIS, NICHOLAS EVANGELOS, automotive sales executive; b. Volos, Greece, May 16, 1934; s. Evangelos Nicholas and Dimitra Nicholas (Tsanaka) G.; m. Anastasia Xenofon Michelopoulos, Aug. 21, 1965; children: Evangelos, Xenofon. Diploma Mech./Elec. Engring., Tech. U., Athens, Greece, 1958, Dr. of Mech./Elec. Engring., 1972. Asst. prof. internal combustion engines Tech. U., 1960-77; prof. Air Force Acad., Athens, 1961-63, 71-74; products engr. BP of Greece Ltd., Athens, 1962-67, tech. sales mgr., 1967-75, mgr. new ventures, 1975-82; mng. dir. Dynamotors S.A., Athens, 1982—; dep. gov. Pub. Power Corp., 1984-85; speaker various meetings, confs. Editor Applied Thermodynamics, 1965. Served with Tech. Corps Greek Army, 1958-60. Recipient Math. award Math. Soc. Greece, 1952. Mem. Tech. C. of C., Comml. and Indsl. Chamber Greece, Assn. Greek Car Distbrs. Christian Orthodox. Home: 17 Thalias Str Ekali, Attica Greece 145 65 Office: Dynamotors SA, Kifisias & Distomou, Maroussi Greece 151 25

GERPOTT, TORSTEN JÖRG, personnel researcher, educator, consultant; b. Bremen, Fed. Republic Germany, Aug. 11, 1958; s. H.-Jörg and Karin B.H. (Rode) G. Diplom-Kaufmann, U. Bundeswehr, 1982, Dr. rer. pol., 1987. Research asst. U. Bundeswehr, Hamburg, Fed. Republic Germany, 1983, research fellow, 1983-86; sr. research fellow U. Bundewehr, Fed. Republic Germany, 1986-88; assoc. Booz, Allen & Hamilton, Düsseldorf, Fed. Republic Germany, 1988—; cons. various West German corps.; lectr. Manchester Bus. Sch., U. Wash., Seattle, Acad. Mgmt., Boston, San Diego, New Orleans, 1983—. Contbr. articles and revs. to profl. publs., chpts. to books. Served to lt. West German Air Force, 1977-83. Mem. Acad. Mgmt. Office: Booz Allen & Hamilton Inc, Königsallee 98a, D-4000 Düsseldorf 1, Federal Republic of Germany

GERRETSEN, JOHANNES CORNELIS, cinematographer; b. Groningen, The Netherlands, Sept. 17, 1945; s. Johannes Cornelis and Clasina Helena (Willemse) G.; m. Didy Han, Aug. 8, 1969; children: Marcella, John. Dir. audio visual dept. State U., Groningen, The Netherlands, 1963—. Dir. The Donor, 1986, Limb Salvage in Osteosarcoma, 1986. Home: Slangenborg 7, Roden Drenthe The Netherlands 9301 VC Office: State U, Audio Visual Dept, Blauwborgje 2 c, 9747 AC Groningen The Netherlands

GERRINGER-BUSENBARK, ELIZABETH JACQUELINE, systems analyst, consultant; b. Edmund, Wis., Jan. 7, 1934; d. Clyde Elroy and Evangeline Matilda Knapp; student Madison Bus. Coll., 1952, San Francisco State Coll., 1953-54, Vivian Rich Sch. Fashion Design, 1955, Dale Carnegie Sch., 1956, Murray Sch. Modern Dance, 1956, Biscayne Acad. Music, 1957, Los Angeles City Coll., 1960-62, Santa Monica (Calif.) Jr. Coll., 1963; Hastings Coll. of Law, 1973, Wharton Sch., U.Pa., 1977, London Art Coll., 1979; Ph.D., 1979; m. Roe Devon Gerringer-Busenbark, Sept. 30, 1968 (dec. Dec. 1972). Actress, Actors Workshop San Francisco, 1959, 65, Theatre of Arts Beverly Hills (Calif.), 1963, also radio; cons. and systems analyst for banks and pub. accounting agys.; artist, singer, songwriter, playwright, dress designer. Pres., tchr. Environ Improvement, Originals by Elizabeth, Dometrik's, JIT-MAP, San Francisco, 1973—; ordained ministerUnitarian Ch., 1978. Author: New Highways, 1967; Happening - Impact-Mald, 1971; Seven Day Rainbow, 1972; Zachary's Adversaries, 1974; Fifteen from Wisconsin, 1977; Bart's White Elephant, 1978; Skid Row Minister, 1978; Points in Time, 1979; Special Appointment, A Clown in Town, 1979; Happenings, 1980, Votes from the Closet, 1984, Wait for Me, 1984, The Stairway, 1984, The River is a Rock, 1985, Happenings Revisted, 1986, Comparative Religion in the United States, 1986, Lumber in the Skies, 1986, The Fifth Season, 1987, Summer Thoughts, 1987, Toast Thoughts, 1988. Club: Toastmasters. Address: PO Box 1640 7th and Mission Station San Francisco CA 94101

GERRISH, HOLLIS G., confectionery co. exec.; b. Berwick, Maine, June 23, 1907; s. Perley G. and Grace (Guptill) G.; A.B., Harvard U., 1930, postgrad. Bus. Sch., 1930-31; m. Catherine G. Ruggles, Sept. 10, 1946. With Squirrel Brand Co., mfg. confectioners, 1931—, pres., 1939-42, 46—. Bd. dirs. Middlesex-Cambridge (Mass.) Lung Assn., Cambridge YMCA, East End House, Cambridge Home for the Aged; trustee Lesley Coll., Cambridge; corp. mem. New Eng. Deaconess Hosp. Served as lt. comdr. USNR, 1942-46; capt. Res. Mem. Am. Soc. Candy Technologists, Cambridge Hist. Soc., Nat. Tax Assn., Mass. Audubon Soc. Episcopalian (trustee). Clubs: Harvard, Faculty, New England Confectioners, Norfolk Trout, Flycasters, Cambridge, Economy. Lodge: Rotary. Home: 207 Grove St Cambridge MA 02138 Office: 10-12 Boardman St Cambridge MA 02139

GERRY, ROGER GOODMAN, retired oral surgeon; b. Far Rockaway, N.Y., Feb. 26, 1916; s. Bernard Abraham and Edith Rose (Goodman) G.; A.B., U. N.C., 1936; D.M.D., U. Louisville, 1940; m. Peggy Newbauer, Nov. 6, 1944. Diplomate Am. Bd. Oral and Maxillofacial Surgery. Commd. lt. (j.g.) Dental Corps, USN, 1941, advanced through grades to capt., 1955; ret., 1965; dir. dental and oral surgery service Mt. Sinai Hosp. Services, City Hosp. Center, Elmhurst, N.Y., 1965-81; attending oral surgeon, head div. oral surgery Mt. Sinai Hosp., N.Y.C. Prof. oral surgery Mt. Sinai Sch. Medicine, City U. N.Y. Chmn., Planning Bd Roslyn, N.Y. 1960-72; pres. Roslyn Landmark Soc., Roslyn Preservation Corp., 1964—. Trustee Bryant Library. Trustee inc. Village Roslyn, N.Y. Recipient Howard C. Sherwood award Soc. for Preservation L.I. Antiquities, 1976, award Nat. Trust Historic Preservation, 1982, Ann. award Victorian Soc. in Am., 1985. Fellow Internat., Am. colls. dentists, Internat. Assn. Oral Surgeons, Met. Mus. Art (life), Brit. Assn. Oral and Maxillofacial Surgeons (hon.); mem. Am. Assn. Oral and Maxillofacial Surgeons, Am. Acad. Oral Pathology (emeritus), Am. Dental Assn. (hon.), Soc. Archtl. Historians, Japan Soc. Author: Catalogue of Japanese Ceramics, 1961. Contbr. articles to profl. jours., Dictionary of Art. Office: George Allen House 20 Main St Roslyn NY 11576

GERSON, NOEL BERTRAM, writer; b. Chgo., Nov. 6, 1914; s. Samuel Philip and Rosa Anna (Noel) G.; children: Noel Anne (Mrs. Brennan), Michele (Mrs. Schechter), Margot (Mrs. Burgett), Paul; m. Marilyn A. Hammond. A.B., U. Chgo., 1934, M.A., 1935. Reporter, rewriteman Chgo. Herald-Examiner, 1931-36; exec. Sta. WGN, Chgo., 1936-41. Radio and TV scriptwriter over 10,000 scripts for nat. networks, 1936-51; Author numerous fiction and non-fiction books under own name and various pseudyonyms; books include The Golden Lyre, 1961, The Land is Bright, 1961, The Naked Maja, 1962, Queen of Caprice, 1963, The Slender Reed, 1964, Old Hickory, 1963, Sex and the Mature Man, 1964, Kit Carson, 1964, Lady of France, 1965, Yankee Doodle Dandy, 1965, Give Me Liberty, 1966, Sex and the Adult Woman, 1965, Light-Horse Harry Lee, 1966, The Swamp Fox, The Anthem, 1967, Sam Houston, 1968, Jefferson Square, 1968, The Golden Ghetto, 1969, P.J., My Friend, 1969, TR, 1969, Mirror, Mirror, 1970, Warhead, 1970, The Divine Mistress, 1970, Because I Loved Him, 1971, Island in the Wind, 1971, Victor Hugo, 1971, Double Vision, 1972, The Prodigal Genius, 1972, George Sand, 1972, Daughter of Earth and Water, 1973, State Trooper, 1973, Peter Paul Rubens, 1973, Rebel-Thomas Paine, 1974, The Exploiters, 1974, All That Glitters, 1975, The Caves of Guernica, 1975, Special Agent, 1976, Harriet Beecher Stowe, 1976, Liner, 1977, The Vidocq Dossier, 1977, The Smugglers, 1977, Trelawny's World, 1977, Wagons West, 1979, White Indian, 1980; also numerous articles. Fellow Internat. Inst. Arts and Letters; mem. Authors Guild Am., Mystery Writers Am., Am., Miss. Valley hist. assns., Am. Acad. Polit. and Social Sci., Centro Studi E Scambi Internat., Phi Beta Kappa, Kappa Alpha. Clubs: Boca Del Mar Country, Bankers.

GERSON, RALPH JOSEPH, business executive; b. Detroit, Nov. 30, 1949; s. Byron Hayden and Dorothy Mary (Davidson) G.; m. Erica Ann Ward, May 20, 1979. BA, Yale U., 1971; MSc, London Sch. Econs., 1972; JD, U. Mich., 1975. Bar: Mich. 1975, D.C. 1976, U.S. Dist. Ct. D.C. 1976, U.S. Ct. Appeals (D.C. cir.) 1976. Counsel Dem. Nat. Com., Washington, 1975-77; spl. asst. U.S. Spl. Trade Rep., Washington, 1978-79; counselor Pres. Spl. Middle East Negotiator, Washington, 1979-80; ptnr. Akin, Gump, Strauss, Hauer & Feld, Washington, 1981-83, 85-87; dir. Mich. Dept. Commerce, Lansing, 1983-85; exec. v.p. Guardian Industries Corp., Northville, Mich., 1988—, also bd. dirs. Mem. ABA, Mich. Bar Assn., D.C. Bar Assn. Clubs: Royal Automobile (London); Yale (N.Y.C.); Franklin (Mich.) Hills Country; Detroit. Home: 1719 Hoban Rd NW Washington DC 20007 Office: Guardian Industries Corp 43043 W Nine Mile Rd Northville MI 48167

GERST, ELIZABETH CARLSEN (MRS. PAUL H. GERST), university dean, researcher, educator; b. N.Y.C., June 10, 1929; d. Rolf and Gudrun (Wiborg) Carlsen; A.B. magna cum laude, Mt. Holyoke Coll., 1951; Ph.D., U. Pa., 1957; m. Paul H. Gerst, Aug. 3, 1957; children—Steven Richard, Jeffrey Carlton, Andrew Leigh. Instr. physiology Grad. Sch. Medicine, U. Pa., 1955-57, Cornell U. Med. Coll., N.Y.C., 1957-58; instr. Columbia Coll. Physicians and Surgeons, N.Y.C., 1959-61, asst. prof., 1961—, dir. Center Continuing Edn. in Health Scis., 1978-87, asst. dean continuing edn., 1984-87, dir. Office Med. Edn., N.Y. Acad. Med., 1987—; Authors: (with others) The Lung, Clinical Physiology and Pulmonary Function Tests, 1955, rev. edit., 1962. Pres. Citizen's Ednl. Council Tenafly, 1972-73; vice chmn. Tenafly Environ. Commn., 1972-77; mem. Citizens Long-Range Planning Com., Tenafly Bd. Edn., 1973-77, chmn. supt. search, edn., tchr. hiring, personnel coms.; vice chmn. Tenafly Environ. Commn., 1972-77; trustee Tenafly Nature Center, 1972-80; bd. dirs., chmn. environ. quality Tenafly LWV, 1971-78; v.p. Bergen County LWV, 1973-75. Porter fellow Am. Physiol. Soc., 1956-57. Mem. Middle States Assn. Colls. and Schs. (team Commn. on higher edn., 1984—), Soc. Med. Coll. Dirs. of Continuing Med. Edn., Am. Physiol. Soc. (task force Women in Physiology 1973-75), N.Y. County Med. Soc. (com. on continuing med. edn. 1978—), Physiol. Soc. Phila., Harvey Soc., Biophys. Soc., Alliance Continuing Med. Edn., N.Y. Acad. Scis., AAAS, Phi Beta Kappa, Sigma Xi, Sigma Delta Epsilon. Unitarian. Home: 141 Tekening Dr Tenafly NJ 07670 Office: Office Med Edn NY Acad Med 2 E 103d St New York NY 10029

GERSTEIN, DAVID BROWN, hardware manufacturing company executive; b. N.Y.C., Jan. 30, 1936; s. Frank and May G.; m. Jane Ellen Bender, May 4, 1963; children: Mark, James. Student, Columbia U., 1951-54, postgrad., 1954-58; B.S., Seton Hall U., 1958. With Thermwell Products Co., Paterson, N.J., 1958—; sales mgr. Thermwell Products Co., 1965-68, v.p., 1968-74, pres., 1974—; prin. owner N. J. Nets NBA franchise, 1978—; v.p. Lever Mfg. Co., Paterson; pres. Woodlowe Realty, Paterson, Wait Assocs., Paterson, Dim Assocs., Mahwah, N.J. Chmn. adv. council energy and conservation State of N.J.; co-chmn. athletic program Seton Hall U. Home: 432 Long Hill Dr Short Hills NJ 07078

GERSTEN, HARRY ROBERT, real estate executive; b. Reno, Nev., Apr. 10, 1946; s. Milton and Mary (Uzekevich) G.; B.S., San Diego State U., 1973; m. Cynthia Kathryn Greek, May 2, 1969; children—Andrew, Matthew, Christina. Lic. real estate broker, Calif. Property mgr. The Gersten Cos., Beverly Hills and San Diego, 1967-80; sr. real estate officer Calif. First Bank-Trust Dept., San Diego, 1980—. Active Chula Vista Assn. Gifted Children, 1979—. Mem. Nat. Assn. Rev. Appraisers and Mortgage Underwriters (cert. rev. appraiser, registered mortgage underwriter), Inst. Real Estate Mgmt. of Nat. Assn. Realtors (cert. property mgr.), Mensa. Home: 893 Mesa Pl Chula Vista CA 92010 Office: 530 B St Suite 700 San Diego CA 92101

GERSTNER, LOUIS VINCENT, JR., financial services executive; b. N.Y.C., Mar. 1, 1942; s. Louis Vincent and Marjorie (Rutan) G.; m. Elizabeth Robins Link, Nov. 30, 1968; children—Louis, Elizabeth. B.A., Dartmouth Coll., 1963; M.B.A., Harvard U., 1965. Dir. McKinsey & Co., N.Y.C., 1965-78; exec. v.p. Am. Express Co., N.Y.C., 1978-81; vice chmn. bd. Am. Express Co., 1981-83, chmn. exec. com., 1983-85, pres., 1985—, also bd. dirs.; bd. dirs. Caterpillar Inc., Squibb Corp., The New York Times Co. Bd. mgrs. Meml. Sloan Kettering Hosp., 1978—; trustee Joint Council on Econ. Edn., 1975-87, chmn. 1983-85; bd. dirs. Greenwich Boys' Club Assn., Lincoln Ctr. for Performing Arts, Internat. Mgmt. Inst. Found., Geneva; mem. vis. com. Harvard U.; mem. Bus. Com. for Arts, Nat. Cancer Adv. Bd.; mem. bd. trustees Ctr. for Strategic and Internat. Studies, Inc., bd. dirs. Am-China Soc. Mem. Council Fgn. Relations. Office: Am Express Co Am Express Tower World Fin Ctr New York NY 10285-5120

GERTLER, MENARD M., physician, educator; b. Saskatoon, Sask., Can., May 21, 1919; came to U.S., 1947, naturalized, 1953; s. Frank and Clara (Handelman) G.; m. Anna Paull, Sept. 4, 1943; children—Barbara Lynn, Stephanie Jocelyn, Jonathan Paull. B.A., U. Sask., 1940; M.D., McGill U., 1943, M.Sc., 1946; D.Sc., N.Y. U., 1959. Intern Royal Victoria Hosp., Montreal, Que., Can., 1943-44; resident Mass. Gen. Hosp., Boston, 1947-50; also research fellow in medicine Mass. Gen. Hosp., Harvard Med. Sch., 1947-50; dir. cardiology Francis Delafield div. Columbia Presbyn. Med. Ctr., N.Y.C., 1950-54; spl. research fellow NIH, NYU Dept. Biochemistry, 1954-56; prof. Sch. Medicine, dir. cardiovascular research Rusk Inst. NYU Med. Ctr., 1958-71; sr. med. examiner FAA, 1975; med. dir. Sinclair Oil Corp., 1958-68; dir. Washington Fed. Savs. & Loan Assn., 1972-83; internat. cons. cardiovascular diseases, social and rehab. services HEW, Washington, 1968—. Author: Coronary Heart Disease in Young Adults, 1954, Coronary Heart Disease, 1974; Contbr. articles to profl. jours. Pres. Friends of McGill Univ. Served with M.C. Royal Canadian Army, 1940-43. Recipient Founders Day award N.Y. U., 1959. Clubs: Cosmos (Washington); Harvard (Boston); University (N.Y.C.). Home: 1000 Park Ave Apt 2C New York NY 10028 Office: NYU Med Ctr Rusk Inst 400 E 34th St New York NY 10016

GERTLER, NORBERT FRANK, financial executive; b. Vienna, Apr. 6, 1937; arrived in Can., 1956; s. Joseph and Maria (Menzler) G.; m. Margaret Rose Schyle, June 27, 1964; children: Peter Johann, Elisabeth Helen. B in Commerce, Sch. Econs., Vienna, 1972. Cert. mgmt. acct. Accet. Popular Auto, Montreal, Can., 1956-58; acctg. mgr. Steinberg Ltd., Montreal, 1959-67; controller Computer Sales and Service, Vienna, 1969-70; v.p., controller advt. agy., Vienna, 1971-72; controller Steinberg Inc., Montreal, 1973-74; v.p., controller, treas. M Stores div. Aligro Inc., Montreal, 1975—; program dir. Planning Exec. Inst., Montreal, 1976-77. Mem. Corp. Mgmt. Accts., Planning Forum. Office: M Stores Inc, 5151 Thimens, Saint Laurent, PQ Canada H4R 2C8

GERTSEN, WILLY BERG, marketing executive; b. Horsens, Denmark, May 5, 1933; s. Ejgil and Henny (Andersen) G.; m. Vivi Elsa Troing, Jan. 28, 1956; children—Hanne Lis, Nils Gert (dec.). M.Sc. in Chem. Engring., Tech. U. Denmark, 1957; H.D. in Bus. Econs. and Mktg., Handelshojskolen, Denmark, 1960. Sales mgr. W.R. Grace A/S, Denmark, 1959-65; mgmt. trainee W.R. Grace & Co., Cambridge, Mass., 1963, product mgr., N.Y.C., 1965-68; W.R. Grace Ltd., London, 1969-70; mktg. dir. Grace Internat. Chems., Lausanne, Switzerland, 1970-77; mktg. dir. Mercomed Sarl, Lausanne, 1977—, also chmn. bd.; also chmn. bd. Engelsk-Dansk Hosps.-forsyning A/S, Denmark, Bio Mktg. A/S Denmark. Served to lt. Danish Army, 1957-59. Mem. Assn. Danish Bus. Econs. Home: Chemin de la Possession 10, CH-1066 Epalinges Switzerland Office: Mercomed Sàrl, PO Box 34, CH-1066 Epalinges Switzerland

GERTZBERG, MOSHE (SASCHA), management consultant, foundation executive; b. Bershade, Russia, Apr. 3, 1913; came to Israel, 1934; s. Levy and Shoshana-Rosa (Gincher) G.; m. Aliza Yaritz, May 8, 1966; 1 child, Lihee. Degree in Indsl. Engring. and Mgmt., Columbia U., 1957. Acting dir.-gen. Ministry Food and Industry, Jerusalem, 1950-51; chief exec. Nat. Labor Exchange Network, Tel Aviv, 1951-52; founder, 1st dir. Israel Productivity Inst., Tel Aviv, 1952-55; productivity expert ILO, Guatemala, San Salvador, Nicaragua, Honduras, Costa Rica, 1956; founder, pres. Israeli Mgmt. Sch., Shefaim, 1960-61; mgmt. cons., pres. Gertzberg & Co., Tel Aviv, 1958-76; founder, pres. found. in memory of son IRA Meml. Found. for Devel. Human Engring. and Quality of Work Life in Israel, 1973—; lectr. and cons. in field. Founder., chief editor Ramaaraha Hamikzoit, mag., 1948-50, Hamifal, 1952-55. Contbr. numerous articles on mgmt. productivity, human resources devel., social and polit. problems to Israeli and internat. profl. jours. and daily media. Sec.-gen. Labor Council, Rishon le Zion, Israel, 1939-41; chief of trade union policy, human resources and party orgn. divs. Central Exec. Council of Labor Party, Palestine and Israel, 1942-51; mem. Kibutz Nir Haim, Kirayat Bialik, Palestine, 1937-41. Served with Brit. Army, 1941-42. Recipient Nat. Kaplan award for outstanding contbn. to devel. of productivity and sci. mgmt. in Israel, Minister of Labor, 1955. Mem. Israel Mgmt. Cons. Assn. (past pres.). Labor Party. Jewish. Home and Office: Ira Meml Found, 5 Shderat Haoranim, Ramat Efal 52960, Israel

GERVAIS, MICHEL, academic administrator; b. Levis, Que., Can., May 27, 1944; s. Paul and Ghislaine (Gosselin) G. BA, Coll. Levis, 1962; LTh, U. Laval, Can., 1966, LPh, 1968; DTh, Pontifical U. of St. Thomas Aquinas, Rome, 1973. Ordained priest Roman Cath. Ch., 1966. Mem. faculty theology, now prof. U. Laval, also rector. Office: Universite Laval, Office of the Recteur, Cite Universitaire, PQ Canada G1K 7P4 *

GERY, PIERRE MARIE, civil engineer, educator; b. St. Marcel, Ardeche, France, May 25, 1918; s. Seraphin Jean and Aline Augustine (Mounier) G.; m. Jeanne-Marie Cussac, Apr. 12, 1944; children—Chantal, Marie-Pierre Gery Acheson, Philippe. Cons. civil engr., 1944—; prof. applied mechanics Ecole Nat. Superieure des Mines, 1955—; prof. civil engring. Conservatoire Nat. des Arts et Metiers, 1965—. Author: Matrix Transfers in Structural Calculations; also articles. Served as officer French Army, 1939-41. Decorated officer Legion of Honor, Merite Maritime, comdr. Order Merit, officer Palmes Academiques. Mem. Internat. Assn. Bridge and Structural Engrs., Internat. Assn. Soil Mechanics. Roman Catholic. Address: Ave du Fort, 06230 Villefranche-Sur-Mer France

GESAMAN, ROSE MARIE, nurse; b. Marion, Ind., Sept. 16, 1944; d. George Paul and Joan Marceille (Cary) Wiegand; R.N., St. Joseph's Sch. Nursing, 1965; m. Steven Ray Gesaman, Dec. 6, 1969; children—Stephanie Louise, Dustan Ray. Staff nurse Whitley County Hosp., Columbia City, Ind., 1965; head nurse orthopedic unit Darnall Army Hosp., Ft. Hood, Tex., 1967; staff nurse Murphey Med. Center, Warsaw, Ind., 1968, ho. mgr., 1968-69, operating room supr., 1969-70; staff nurse Whitley County Hosp., Columbia City, Ind., 1974, ho. mgr., 1975-77; dir. nursing Miller's Merry Manor, Warsaw, Ind., 1977-81; ho. mgr. Whitley County Meml. Hosp., Columbia City, Ind., 1981-85; self-employed, 1985—. Served to 1st lt., Nurse Corps, U.S. Army, 1966-67. Recipient Kosciusko County Med. Aux. Scholarship award, 1962; Scottish Rite Scholarship award, 1962; Outstanding Cath. Youth Kosciusko County award, 1962. Mem. Whitley County Meml. Hosp. Nurses Assn., Am. Legion, ARC, Beta Sigma Phi. Democrat. Roman Catholic. Home: Box 191 North Webster IN 46555 Office: PO Box 337 Syracuse IN 46567

GESLANI, FRANCISCO TAMAYO, hospital administrator, surgeon; b. Malasiqui, Philippines, Jan. 29, 1920; s. Ildefonso Mamaril Geslani and Juana (Geslani) Tamayo; m. Esther Same-Geslani, Nov. 14, 1948; Alexis, Ladelle, Bevan Ali. Premed degree, Philippines Union Coll., Manila, 1940; MD, Manila Cen. U., 1946; med. degree (hon.), Loma Linda U., 1965. Founder, 1st. med. dir. Mindanao Sanitarium and Hosp., Iligan City, Philippines, 1952-56, Miller Sanitarium and Hosp., Cebu City, Philippines, 1956-70; pres., med. dir. Bacolod (City) Sanitarium and Hosp., Philippines, 1971—; asst. prof. surgery Southwestern U. Sch. Medicine, Cebu City, 1965-69. Vice-chmn, bd. dirs. YMCA. Named Outstanding Alumnus Philippines Union Coll., 1967, 86. Fellow Philippines Coll. Surgeons (pres. Negros Occidental Chpt., 1988), Internat. Coll. Surgeons; mem. Lanao Med. Soc. (pres. 1946), Cen. Philippines Union of Seventh Day Adventists (med. sec. 1956-69), Assn. Southeast Asia Surgeons, Philippines Med. Assn. Seventh Day Adventist. Lodge: Rotary (officer Cebu West, Bacolod chpts.). Home: Taculing, Bacolod City 6100, Philippines Office: Bacolod Sanitarium and Hosp, Taculing, Bacolod City Negros 6001, Philippines

GESTETNER, DAVID, office equipment company executive; b. London, June 1, 1937; s. Sigmund and Henny (Lang) G.; m. Alice Floretta Sebag-Montefiore, Oct. 16, 1961; children—Geoffrey, Emily, Rachel, Sarah. M.A. with honors, Oxford U., 1960. With Gestetner Holdings Ltd., London, 1960—, joint chmn., 1971—, chief exec. officer, 1981-86, pres., 1987—. Served with Royal Engrs., 1955-57. Avocations: sailing; tennis.

GESTETNER, JONATHAN, financial executive; b. Mar. 11, 1940; s. Sigmund and Henny Gestetner; m. Jacqueline Margaret Strasmore, 1965; 3 children. BSc in Mech. Engring., MIT. With Gestetner Ltd., 1962—; joint chmn. Gestetner Holdings Ltd., 1972-87, joint pres., 1987—; bd. dirs. Ctr. for Policy Studies; mem. ednl. council, MIT, 1973—. Mem. Maplin Devel. Authority, 1973-74, SSRC, 1979-82. Mem. Engring. Employers' London Assn. (mem. exec. council 1972-77, v.p. 1975-77). Clubs: Brooks, MCC. Home: 7 Oakhill Ave, London NW3 7RD, England *

GETREU, SANFORD, city planner; b. Cleve., Mar. 9, 1930; s. Isadore and Tillie (Kuchinsky) G.; B.A. in Architecture, Ohio State U., 1953; M.A. in Regional Planning, Cornell U., 1955; m. Gara Eileen Smith, Dec. 8, 1952 (div. Feb. 1983); children—David Bruce, Gary Benjamin, Allen Dana, Kelly Heim. Resident planner Mackesey & Reps., consultants, Rome, N.Y., 1955-56; planning dir., Rome, 1956-57; dir. gen. planning, Syracuse, N.Y., 1957-59, dep. commr. planning, 1959-62, commr. planning, 1962-65; planning dir. San Jose, Calif., 1965-74; urban planning cons., 1974—; pres. Sanford Getreu, AICP, Inc., vis. lectr., critic Cornell U., 1960-65, Syracuse U., 1962-65, Stanford, 1965—, San Jose State Coll., 1965—, Santa Clara U., Calif. State Poly. Coll., DeAnza Coll., San Jose City Coll., U. Calif. at Berkeley; pres. planning dept. League of Calif. Cities, 1973-74; advisor State of Calif. Office of Planning and Research. Past bd. dirs. Theater Guild, San Jose, Triton Mus., San Jose. Mem. Am. Soc. Cons. Planners, Am. Planning Assn., Am. Inst. Cert. Planners, Bay Area Planning Dirs. Assn. (v.p. 1965-74, mem. exec. com. 1973-74), Assn. Bay Area Govts. (regional planning com. 1967-74). Club: Rotary. Home: 105 Coronado Ave Los Altos CA 94022 Office: 399 Main St Los Altos CA 94022

GETTIG, MARTIN WINTHROP, mechanical engineer; b. South Bend, Ind., Nov. 8, 1939; s. Joseph H. and Esther (Scheppele) G.; m. Nancy Caroline Buchannan, June 25, 1960 (dec. 1965). Student Pa. State U., 1957-60. Process engr. Gettig Techs., Inc., Spring Mills, Pa. 1960—. Inventor ultralight non-solid state miniature ignition systems for model aircraft employing small two cycle spark ignition engines. Served to staff sgt. USNG, 1961-67. Mem. Nat. Rifle Assn., Model Engine Collectors Assn., Soc. Antique Modelers and Model Airplanes, Delta Phi. Republican. Lutheran. Clubs: University (University Park, Pa.); Acad. Model Aeronautics (Reston, Va.). Home: Box 85 Boalsburg PA 16827

GETTINGS, FRED, writer, photographer; b. Dewsbury, Yorkshire, Eng., May 13, 1937; s. Alfred and Lily (Owen) G.; div.; 1 child, Tiffany. MA, Sussex U., Eng., 1969. Author: Techniques of Drawing, 1971, Hidden Art, 1978, Dictionary of Occult, Hermetric and Alchemical Sigils, 1981, Dictionary of Astrology, 1985, Secret Zodiac: The Hidden Art in Mediaeval Astrology, 1987, Dictionary of Demons, 1988 and numerous other books; contbr. numerous articles. Served with RAF, 1955-57. studio: 24 Haincliffe Rd, BD21 5BU Keighley, West Yorkshire England

GETTLE, MICHAEL JAMES, training researcher; b. Ancon, Canal Zone, May 17, 1955; s. Jesse Richard and Olga (Maransky) G.; m. Catherine A. Gettle, Aug. 11, 1979; 1 child, Jennifer Michelle. B.S. in Edn., Millersville State Coll., 1977; M.Ed., Ga. State U., 1986. Tng. analyst Ala. Power Co., Birmingham, 1978-80; project engr. Inst. Nuclear Power Ops., Atlanta, 1981—, sr. project engr., 1984-88, project mgr., 1988—. Mem. Am. Soc. Tng. and Devel., MENSA. Baptist. Contbr. articles to profl. jours. Office: 1100 Circle 75 Pkwy Suite 1500 Atlanta GA 30339

GETTLER, BENJAMIN, lawyer, manufacturing company executive; b. Louisville, Ky., Sept. 16, 1925; s. Herbert and Gertrude (Cohen) G.; m. Deliaan Angel, Mar. 1972; children: Jorian, Thomas, Gail, John, Benjamin. B.A. with high honors, U. Cin., 1945; J.D. (Frankfurter scholar), Harvard U., 1948. Bar: Ohio 1949, U.S. Supreme Ct. 1973. Partner firm Brown & Gettler, Cin., 1951-73, Gettler, Katz & Buckley, Cin., 1973—; chmn. bd., dir., sec. Cin. Transit Inc., 1957-73; chmn. bd. Am. Controlled Industries Inc., Cin., 1973-86; v.p., chmn. exec. com. Vulcan Corp., Cin., 1976—; chmn. bd. Colorpac Inc., Cin., 1973-86; chmn. exec. com. Valley Industries, Inc., Cin., 1973-86; spl. counsel U. Cin., 1975-77. Mem. Ohio, Ky. and Ind. Mass Transit Policy Com., 1970-75; pres. Cin. Jewish Community Relations Council, 1978-80; chmn. bd. trustees Jewish Hosp. of Cin., 1985-87; chmn. Midwest Health Systems, Inc., 1987—; chmn. Cin. Coalition for Reagan, 1980; co-chmn. Hamilton County Reagan Campaign, Ohio, 1984. Served to capt. U.S. Army, 1955-56. Mem. Am., Cin. bar assns., Shoe Last Mfrs. Assn. (pres. 1984-85), Phi Beta Kappa, Omicron Delta Kappa. Club: Coldstream Country. Office: 6 E 4th St Suite 1500 Cincinnati OH 45202

GEVERS, JAN KAREL MARIA, educational organization executive; b. Valkenswaard, Netherlands, June 10, 1944; s. Johan Jozef and Maria Clara (Gijselhart) G.; m. Margareth Louise Breusers, June 6, 1967. PhD, U. Leiden, Netherlands, 1968. Instr. sociology U. Leiden, 1967-78, v.p., 1972-78; cons. nat. policy Netherlands Acad. Council, The Hague, 1978-84; chmn. World Conf. on Coop. Edn., London, 1987—; pres. U. Amsterdam, 1988—. Author books on sociology; columnist 2 newspapers, 1983—; contbr. articles on sociology, policy andd edn. Chmn. Leiden Sch. Bd., 1978—; bd. dirs. Netherlands Theatrical Inst., Amsterdam, 1985—; pres. Netherland Council for Higer Profl. Edns., 1984-88. Mem. Am. Polit. Sci. Assn., Soc. Francaise 18th Siecle. Mem. Labor Party. Club: Amicitia (Leiden). Home: Carel Fabritiuslaan 29, 2343 SE Oegstgeest The Netherlands Office: U Amsterdam, PO Box 19268, 1000 GG Amsterdam The Netherlands

GEWEILY, SAID M.H., police officer; b. Cairo, Nov. 13, 1938; s. Mahmoud Hammad Geweily and Ahssan Mahmed Amaira; 2 daus. Grad. secondary sch., Cairo. Police officer Alexandria, Egypt, 1961-86, Cairo, 1986—. Club: El Trsana. Home: 99 Omer Ebn El Kattab, Cairo Arab Republic of Egypt

GEWIRTZ, GERRY, editor; b. N.Y.C., Dec. 22, 1920; d. Max and Minnie (Weiss) G.; m. Eugene W. Friedman, Nov. 11, 1945; children: John Henry, Robert James. B.A., Vassar Coll., 1941. Editor Package Store Mgmt., 1942-44, Jewelry Mag., 1945-53; freelance editor promotion dept. McCall's Mag., Esquire, 1953-56; free-lance fashion and gifts editor Jewelers Circular Keystone, N.Y.C., 1955-71; editor, pub. The Fashionables, 1971-74, The Forecast, 1974—, Nat. Jeweler, Ann. Fashion Guide, 1976-80; editor, assoc. pub. Exec. Jeweler, 1980-83; editor The Gerry Gewirtz Report, N.Y.C., 1983—, The Fashion Source (formerly Internat. Fashion Index), N.Y.C., 1984—. Mem. exec. com. Inner City Council of Cardinal Cooke, N.Y.; chairperson women's task force United Jewish Appeal Fedn.; former bd. govs. Israel Bonds; former trustee Israel Cancer Research Fund, Central Synagogue; bd. dirs. Double Image Theater; former pres. women's aux. Brandeis U. Honored guest Am. Jewish Com., 1978; Israel Cancer Research Fund, 1978-81; recipient Disting. Community Service award Brandeis U., 1987; named to Jewellry Hall Fame, 1988. Mem. N.Y. Fashion Group, Nat. Home Fashions League, Women's Jewelry Assn. (pres. 1983-87 , named editor who has contbd. most to jewelry industry 1984), Phi Delta Epsilon. Clubs: N.Y, Vassar, Overseas Press. Home: 45 Sutton Pl S New York NY 10022 Office: Gerry Gerwitz Report 310 Madison Ave Suite 824 New York NY 10017

GEWIRTZ, JACOB, social science researcher; b. N.Y.C., Apr. 11, 1926; arrived in Eng., 1961; s. Joseph Chaim and Frieda (Horowitz) G.; m. Agathe Hajnal-Konyi, Sept. 18, 1958; children: Deborah, Jonathan, Sharon. BA, Syracuse U., 1949; JD, U. Pa., 1952. Bar: N.Y., 1953. Official Jewish Agy. for Israel, Jerusalem, 1957-59; lit., features editor The Jewish Chronicle, London, 1964-71; exec. dir. Jewish def. and group relations com. Bd. of Deps. of British Jews, London, 1974-86; sr. research fellow The City Univ., London, 1987—; mem. exec. bd. Trades Adv. Council, Eng., 1976, Joint Com. Against Racism, Eng., 1979, Friends of Tel Aviv Univ., Eng., 1987—; cons. Bd. of Deps. of British Jews, 1987—. Served with U.S. Army, 1945-47. Office: The City Univ, Northampton Sq, London EC1 VOHB, England

GEWIRTZ, MORRIS, city official; b. Bklyn., July 18, 1915; s. Henry and Lena (Wilner) G.; m. Frances Yvonne Wigler, Oct. 7, 1939; children: Joan Susan Gewirtz Zweiback, Lawrence Herbert. BA, Bklyn. Coll., 1937; post-grad., 1937-41; B in Engring., NYU, 1962, postgrad., 1942-43, 46-48. Registered profl. engr., Mass. With U.S. Navy, 1948-73; dep. head program support dept. U.S. Naval Tng. Device Ctr., Port Washington, N.Y., 1955-56, asst. planning officer, 1957-58; dir. mgmt. analysis div. Dist. Pub. Works Office, 3d Naval Dist., N.Y.C., 1959-62; facilities mgmt. coordinator Third Naval Dist., Eastern Div., Naval Facilities Engring. Command, N.Y.C., 1963-66, dir. mgmt. services div. U.S. Naval Facilities Engring. Command, Alexandria, Va., 1966-73; chief human resources adminstrn. revenue sect. Office of Budget and Fiscal Affairs N.Y.C. Human Resources Adminstrn., 1979-87, dep. dir. div. revenue control and analysis Office of Fin. Mgmt., 1987—. Vice chmn. local sch. bd. Dist. 14 Bklyn., 1963-64, chmn., 1965; chmn. subcom. on budget N.Y.C. Bd. Edn., 1965; councilor mem. Atlantic Council; benefactor Bklyn. Ctr. for Performing Arts. Served with U.S. Army, 1943-45. N.Y. State War Service Scholar, 1946. Mem. Inst. Mgmt. Scis., Am. Inst. Indsl. Engrs. (sr.), Soc. Am. Mil. Engrs., Bklyn. Engrs. Club (corp. mem.), Am. Technion Soc., World Future Soc., Am. Assn. Individual Investors, Bklyn. Coll. Alumni Assn. (life), N.Y. Poly. Alumni Assn. (assoc. dir.), Weizmann Inst. Sci. (assoc.), Navy League, U.S. Naval Inst. Home: 1311 Brightwater Ave Apt 5D Brooklyn NY 11235 Office: NYC Human Resources Adminstrn 155 W Broadway Room 709 New York NY 10013

GEWIRTZMAN, GARRY BRUCE, dermatologist; b. Albany, N.Y., Mar. 26, 1947; s. Benjamin Joseph and Mary (Leibowitz) G.; m. Sheila Ellen Cuba, July 4, 1971; children—Beth Lauren, Aron Jeffrey. B.A., Rutgers U., 1969; M.D., Albany Med. Coll., 1973. Diplomate Am. Bd. Dermatology. Intern, U. Miami (Fla.), 1973-74; resident in dermatology SUNY-Buffalo, 1974-77; practice medicine specializing in dermatology; mem. staffs Humana Hosp., Plantation Gen. Hosp.; pres. Arbet Enterprises Inc. Author: Smooth as a Baby's Bottom. Fellow Am. Acad. Dermatology; mem. AMA, Fla. Med. Assn., Broward County Med. Assn., Fla. Soc. Dermatology, Soc. Dermatol. Genetics, Broward Bus. and Profl. Assn. (pres.), Broward County Dermatol. Soc. Contbr. articles to profl. jours. Office: Bennett Med Park 201 NW 82d Ave Plantation FL 33324

GEYMAN, JOHN PAYNE, physician, educator; b. Santa Barbara, Calif., Feb. 9, 1931; s. Milton John and Betsy (Payne) G.; m. Emogene Clark Deichler, June 9, 1956; children: John Matthew, James Caleb, William Sabin. A.B. in Geology, Princeton U., 1952; M.D., U. Calif., San Francisco, 1960. Diplomate: Am. Bd. Family Practice. Intern Los Angeles County Gen. Hosp., 1960-61; resident in gen. practice Sonoma County Hosp., Santa Rosa, Calif., 1961-63; practice medicine specializing in family practice Mt. Shasta, Calif., 1963-69; dir. family practice residency program Community Hosp. Sonoma County, Santa Rosa, 1969-71; asso. prof. family practice, chmn. div. family practice U. Utah, 1971-72; prof., vice chmn. dept. family practice U. Calif., Davis, 1972-77; prof., chmn. dept. family medicine U. Wash., 1977—. Author: The Modern Family Doctor and Changing Medical Practice, 1971, Family Practice: Foundation of Changing Health Care, 1980, 2d edit., 1985; editor: Content of Family Practice, 1976, Family Practice in the Medical School, 1977, Research in Family Practice, 1978, Preventive Medicine in Family Practice, 1979, Profile of the Residency Trained Family Physician in the U.S. 1970-79, Funding of Patient Care, Education and Research in Family Practice, 1981, The Content of Family Practice: Current Status and Future Trends, 1982, Archives of Family Practice, 1980, 81, 82; founding editor: Jour. Family Practice, 1973—; co-editor: Behavioral Science in Family Practice, 1980; editor: Family Practice: An International Perspective in Developed Countries, 1983. Served to lt. (j.g.) USN, 1952-55, PTO. Recipient Gold-headed Cane award U. Calif. Sch. Medicine, 1960. Mem. Am. Acad. Family Physicians, AMA, Soc. Tchrs. Family Medicine, Inst. Medicine of Nat. Acad. Scis. Republican. Unitarian. Home: 2325 92d Ave NE Bellevue WA 98004 Office: Dept Family Medicine RF 30 U Wash Sch Medicine Seattle WA 98195

GEZAW, TESEMA, shipping executive; b. Harar, Ethopia, Apr. 30, 1936; s. Gezaw Aredo and Etagegnehu Workie; m. Menen Betre, June 10, 1973; children: Hirut, Helen. BS in Marine Engring., Maritime Coll., Rijeka, Yugoslavia. Marine engr. Dept. Marine, Addis Ababa, Ethiopia, 1954-64; marine supt. Ethopian Shipping Lines, Addis Ababa, 1968-74, overseas mgr., 1974-81, gen. mgr., 1981—; shipbuilding contracts negotiator. Mem. Inst. Marine Engrs., Inst. Chartered Engrs. Mem. Coptic Christian Ch. Lodge: Rotary. Home: Gruttosingel 22, 2903 EG Capelle A/D Ijssel The Netherlands Office: PO Box 23118, 3001 KC Rotterdam The Netherlands

GHAFAR BABA, ABDUL, government official; b. Kuala Pilah, Negri Sembilan, Malaysia, Feb. 18, 1925; m. Puan Asmah Binti Alang; 10 children. Grad., Sultan Idris Tchrs. Tng. Coll. Mem. Fed. Legis. Council, Malaysia, 1955-59; chief minister of Malacca Malaysia, 1959-67; chmn. Majlis Amanah Rakyat, Malaysia, 1967; minister Govt. of Malaysia, minister nat. and rural devel., 1969, 86—, minister agr. and rural devel., 1974-76, dep. prime minister, 1986—; sec. Malacca div. United Malay Nat. Orgn., 1951-55, then chmn., then v.p., chmn. econ. bur.; chmn. Fed. Agrl. Mktg. Authority; sec.-gen. Nat. Front, 1974; chmn. Majlis Amanah Rakyat Shares Trust and Edn. Fund; com. chmn. Aid Algerian Independence Struggle; dir. Dunlop Holdings Ltd., 1983—. Club: Ayer Kroh Country (chmn.). Office: Office of Dep Prime Minister, Kuala Lumpur Malaysia *

GHAFFAR, HUSSEIN ABDEL, international arbitrator; b. Cairo, June 10, 1940; came to Belgium, 1984; BBA, Victoria Coll., 1964, MBA, 1970, PhD in Bus. Adminstrn., 1974, PhD in Internat. Law, 1984. Arbitrator Internat. Arbitrator Adv. Services, Cairo, 1970, London, 1974-83; pres. Brussels, 1983—; advisor Investment Authority, Egypt, 1970-74, Arab Monetary Fund, Belgium, 1984, others; mem. European Council of London Ct. for Internat. Arbitration, 1988—; cons. authority on internat. arbitration, resolution of disputes by arbitration, mediation or conciliation. Author: International Law and Islam, 1980, Who is What-The Arab Mind-A Question Mark, 1987, The Shortcomings of International Law, 1988. Recipient Nile award Egyptian Govt., Cairo, 1980. Mem. Am. Arbitration Assn., ABA, Profl. Mgrs. Assn., Inst. Fin. Advisors, Chartered Inst. of Arbitrators London. Moslem. Office: Internat Arbitration Services, PO Box 3, Forest 3, Brussels 1190, Belgium

GHAI, OM PARKASH, publishing company executive; b. Bedian, Punjab, India, Oct. 1, 1919; s. Bishen Das and Lakshmi G.; m. Vimia, Feb. 22, 1941; children—Kamlesh, Surinder. B.A., Hindu Coll., Amritsar, India, 1938; B.T., Govt. Coll., Lahore, India, 1941. Mng. ptnr. Univ. Publishers, Punjab, India, 1948-68; chmn., mng. dir. Sterling Publishers (P) Ltd., Delhi, India, 1969—. Editor: International Publishing Today: Problems and Prospects and Unity In Diversity, 1986. Sec., Family Planning Assn., Lahore, 1944-46. Mem. Punjab Publishers Assn. (sec. 1949-68), Fedn. Pubs. and Booksellers Assns. in India (pres. 1972-73), Fedn. Indian Publishers (pres. 1978-79, 83—). Clubs: India Internat Ctr., Book Man's (Delhi). Home: A-1/256 Safadarjand Enclave, New Delhi 110029, India Office: Sterling Publishers (P) Ltd, L-10 Green Park Ext, New Delhi 110016, India

GHALI, ANWAR YOUSSEF, psychiatrist, educator; b. Cairo, May 30, 1944; came to U.S., 1974, naturalized, 1980; s. Youssef and Insaf Wahba (Soliman) G.; m. Violette Fouad Saleh, May 23, 1968; 1 child, Susie. MD, Cairo U., 1966, DPM, 1970, DM, 1971. Cert., Am. Bd. Psychiatry and Neurology; cert. adminstrv. psychiatry. Registrar in psychiatry Woodilee Hosp., Glasgow, Scotland, 1973-74; resident in psychiatry N.J. Med. Sch., Newark, 1974-77, instr., 1977-78, clin. asst. prof., 1978-79, asst. prof., 1979-83, clin. assoc. prof., 1983—; chief Outpatient Dept.-Community Mental Health Ctr., N.J. Med. Sch., 1978-86; dir. Emergency Psychiatric Services, Univ. Hosp., U. Medicine and Dentistry of N.J., 1986-87; med. dir. Profl. Counsel Ctr., Westfield, N.J., 1984-87; med. chief ambulatory psychiat. services Elizabeth (N.J.) Gen. Hosp., 1987—. Contbr. articles to profl. jours. Recipient Exceptional Merit award Coll. Medicine & Dentistry, Newark, 1981. Mem. Christian Med. Soc., Am. Psychiat. Assn., AMA, N.J. Psychiat. Assn., N.Y. Acad. Scis. Republican. Presbyterian. Home: 22 Benvenue Ave West Orange NJ 07052

GHAMBIR, RAMESH CHANDER, gynecologist; b. Campbellpur, Pakistan, Aug. 28, 1938; s. Gobind Ram and Savitri Devi (Kasturi) G.; m. Michele Renee Gintz, May 15, 1964; children: Christophe, Anne-Marie. BS, U. Delhi, India, 1959; MD, U. Heidelberg, Fed. Republic Germany, 1967; specialist diploma, U. Stuttgart, Fed. Republic of Germany, 1973; MD, U. Angers, France, 1975. Intern various hosps., Stuttgart, Cologne, Fed. Republic Germany, 1967-69; fgn. asst. Maternity of Port Royal, Paris, 1969-71; med. asst. Maternity of Margariten Hosp., Schwabisch, Fed. Republic Germany, 1972-74; med. officer Ob-Gyn dept. 2d Gen. U.S. Army Hosp., Landstuhl, Fed. Republic Germany, 1974-75; practice medicine specializing in ob-gyn, Laval, France, 1975—. Contbr. articles to profl. jours., various case studies. Mem. France-German Soc. Gynecology, German Soc. Ob-Gyn, French Soc. Gynecology, French Nat. Soc. Ob-Gyn, Bombay's Gynecol. and Obstet. Soc. Hindu. Home: #19 Carrefour aux Toiles, 53000 Laval France Office: Cabinet Med, #20 Carrefour aux Toiles, 53000 Laval France

GHANÉ, IRAJ, manufacturing company executive; b. Asfahan, Iran, June 1, 1943; s. Manouchehr and Heshmat Almolouk (Doulat Shahi) G.; married; 2 children. BS, Utah State U., 1968; MS in Mgmt. Sci., Calif. Western U., 1969; postgrad., Ariz State U. Mng. dir. Isfahan Pasteurized Milk Plant, 1969-70, Isfahan Bag Producing Co., Inc., 1972-76, Computer & Mechanized Systems Co. subs. Behshahr Indsl. Group, 1976-78; chmn., mng. dir., chief exec. officer Electric Storage Battery Iran Co. subs. ESB Internat., mfrs. Ray-O-Vak batteries, 1979—, B.G. Trading Co. Ltd., 1979—; mng. dir., chief exec. officer Iran Med. Equipment Mfg. Co., 1980—; Pres. GTS Universal GmbH, Hamburg, Fed. Republic Germany, 1981; chmn. chief exec. officer Iran Valves Industry Corp., 1983—; chmn., pres., chief exec. officer Calif. Oil and Investment Corp., Beverly Hills, Calif., 1985—. Moslem. Home: Yousef Abad ASP Bldg Tower B, Apt 2022, Tehran Iran Office: Calif Oil and Investment Corp 8530 Wilshire Blvd #404 Beverly Hills CA 90211

GHANI, ASHRAF MUHAMMAD, mechanical engineer, consultant; b. Wazirabad, Pakistan, Oct. 12, 1931; emigrated to Saudi Arabia, 1967; s. Abdul and Alam (Bibi) G.; m. Yasmeen Elahi, Nov. 15, 1964; children—Faiza, Saad, Farha. B.S. in Mech. Engring., Ind. Inst. Tech., 1962; M.S. in Mech. Engring., Columbia U., 1963; Ph.D. in Mgmt., Franklin U., 1977. Tech. dir. Engring. Controls, Karachi, Pakistan, 1963-67; asst. prof. Riyadh U., Saudi Arabia, 1967-76; tech. expert Saudi Fund for Devel., Riyadh, 1976-86; cons. dir. Poly Engring. Co., Riyadh, 1979-87, Polyconsult, Riyadh, 1979—; chmn. Inter-Services Corp., Metuchen, N.J., 1982—; chmn. Vols. Orgn. for Tech. Assistance to Underdeveloped Countries, U.K., 1985—; convener Internat. Solidarity for Peace, U.K., 1986—; sec. Internat. Vols. for Human Relief, Vienna, 1986—. Author: Management of Complex Development Projects, 1979. Hon. sec. Pakistan Red Crescent Soc., Lahore, 1965. Recipient William Henry Caswell award Ind. Inst. Tech., 1961. Fellow Pakistan Assn. Mgmt. Cons. (Achievement award 1981); mem. Soc. Am. Mil. Engrs., mem. Brit. Inst. Mgmt. (assoc.), Soc. Internat. Devel., Internat. Journalists Assn. London, Am. Soc. for Tng. and Devel. Moslem. Club: Gymkhana (Lahore, Pakistan). Home: 11-H Gulberg Three, Lahore Pakistan

GHARAGOZLOU-HAMADANI, HOUSHANG, psychiatrist; b. Tehran, Iran, Oct. 14, 1936; s. Ali and Malak (Moghadam) G.-H.; came to U.S., 1963; M.D., Tehran U., 1963; diploma in psychiatry McGill U., 1970; m. Aug. 1966; children—Jasmine, Roya. Intern, Deaconess Hosp., Buffalo, 1963; resident in psychiatry Binghamton (N.Y.) State Hosp., Queen Mary VA Hosp., Montreal Children's Hosp., 1964-70; clin. dir. Hawaii State Hosp., Honolulu, 1972; asso. prof. psychiatry Pahlavi U., Shiraz, Iran, 1975-79, chmn. dept., 1975-79; vis. prof. U. Pa., 1979—; mem. staff Allentown (Pa.) Hosp. Diplomate Am. Bd. Psychiatry and Neurology. Fellow Am. Psychiat. Assn., Internat. Assn. Social Psychiatry (council), Brit. Assn. Social Psychiatry; mem. Lehigh Valley Med. Soc. Mem. adv. bd. Ency. Psychiatry, Psychology, Psychoanalysis and Neurology, 1974. Home: 4001 Lilac Rd Allentown PA 18103 Office: 2895 Hamilton Blvd Suite 103 Allentown PA 18104

GHATALIA, SHATISCHCHANDRA VIRCHAND, accountant; b. Vijapur, Gujarat, India, Jan. 26, 1920; parents: Virchand Damji and Chhabalben (Virchand) G.; married; children: Dilip, Nanak, Devan, Swati. BA in Commerce, Sydenham Coll. Commerce and Econs., Bombay, 1941. Pvt. practice acctg. Bombay, 1947—; ptnr. S.V. Ghatalia and Assocs., Bombay, 1978—; prof. acctg., bus. mgmt. Sydenham Coll. Commerce and Econs., 1952-79; bd. dirs. Aegis Chem. Industries Ltd., Beco Engring. Co. Ltd., Jay Electric Wire Corp. Ltd., Tranasia Carpets Ltd., Khatau Junker Ltd.chmn. program and pub. subcom. 4th Conf. Asian and Pacific Accts., 1965; del. 5th Conf. Asian and Pacific Accts., New Zealand, 1968; ofcl. del. 10th Internat. Congress Accts., Australia, 1972. Author: Indian Edition of Spicer and Pegler's Practical Auditing, 1962, The Law and Practice of Super Profits Tax, 1964. Mem. senate U. Bombay, 1954-82, exec. council, dean faculty commerce; mem. law adv. com. Govt. India; mem. All India Bd. Tech. Studies in Mgmt. Fellow Inst. Chartered Accts. India (mem. acctg. standards bd. com.), Inst. Chartered Accts. in Eng. and Wales. Mem. Jain religion. Clubs: United Services, Western India Automobile Assn., Mahablewhwar. Office: 23 Advent, 12A Gen Bhonsale Marg, Bombay 400021, India

GHEBREHIWET, BERHANE, immunologist, educator; b. Asmara, Ethiopia, Sept. 28, 1946. D.V.M., Sch. Vet. Medicine, Warsaw, Poland, 1971; M.V.Sc., Ecole Nationale Vétérinaire D'Alfort, France, 1973; D.Sc., U. Paris VII, 1974. Research assoc. dept. molecular immunology Scripps Clinic and Research Found., La Jolla, Calif., 1974-79; asst. prof. medicine SUNY, Stony Brook, 1979-85, asst. prof. pathology, 1983-85, assoc. prof. medicine and pathology, 1985—. Contbr. articles to profl. jours. Mem. Am. Assn. Immunology, Am. Tissue Culture Assn., Am. Fedn. Clin. Research, N.Y. Acad. Sci., Am. Chem. Soc., AAAS., Am. Assn. Vet. Immunology, Reticuloendothelial Soc., The Planetary Soc., Sigma Xi. Coptic Orthodox. Office: SUNY Stony Brook HSC T-16 Room 040 New York NY 11794

GHEDINI, ROLANDO, business executive; b. Milan, Italy; s. Giorgio and Franca (Dalmonte) G.; m. Gloria Schenck, Dec. 5, 1969; children—Marco, Roberto, Silvia. B.S. in Elec. Engring. ETH, Zurich, 1965, M.S. in Indsl. Engring., 1966; M.S. in Indsl. Adminstrn., Purdue U., 1967. Trainee, W.R. Grace Co., N.Y.C., 1967-68, Milw., 1968-69, fin. analyst, N.Y.C., 1969-70, Paris, 1970, asst. to pres., Paris, 1971-73, dir. acquisitions, 1973-74; internat. fin. advisor, Lugano, Switzerland and N.Y.C., 1975-79; v.p. fin. ICOS Corp. Am., N.Y.C., 1980-82; exec. v.p., chief fin. officer, dir. Nanco Environ. Services, Inc., 1985—; dir. Transworld Ventures Ltd., 1983—, Allira Inc., 1975-80. Pres. 314 Tenantowners Corp., 1981-86. Home: Route 3 Box 493, Pleasant Valley, NY 12569 Office: Nanco Labs Robinson Ln Rd 6 Wappingers Falls NY 12590

GHEKIERE, GABRIEL JOSEPH, software company personnel executive; b. Mechelen, Belgium, Apr. 14, 1940; s. Gerard and Barbara (Potemans) G.; m. Lieve Van Mol, May 27, 1967; children—Anne, Geert. Acct. Hertsens, Mechelen, 1962-64; supr. Singer, Mechelen, 1964-69; personnel mgr. Europe, S.C.M. Corp., N.Y.C., 1969-77; dir. personnel and adminstrn. for Europe, Accuray Corp., Columbus, Ohio, 1977-83; mgr. human resources for Europe, Cincom Systems Inc., Brussels, 1983—. Grad. examination com. HHT Bus. Sch., Mechelen, Belgium, 1982—; bd. dirs. Found. Autistic Children, Hever, Belgium. Mem. Personnel Execs. Europe, Am. Mgmt. Assn., Mechelen Jaycees (senator). Avocation: piano playing. Office: Cincom Systems Internat, Ave Louise 489, 1050 Brussels Belgium

GHELARDI, RAYMOND EUSEBIUS, financial analyst, urban planner; b. Bloomsburg, Pa., July 26, 1951; m. Lourdes M. Frau, Apr. 30, 1984. B.S. in Community Devel., Pa. State U., 1973; M.C.P., (EPA fellow), Harvard U., 1975; M.B.A. (Merit scholar), Emory U., 1985. Planning asst. Centre Regional Planning Commn., State College, Pa., 1972; land use planner Conn. Dept. Environ. Protection, Hartford, Conn., 1974; assoc. planner Mass. Exec. Office Environ. Affairs, Boston, 1975-79; policy analyst Environ. Research & Tech., Inc., Concord, Mass., 1979-80, sr. analyst policy and planning, 1980-82; pres. R. Ghelardi, Inc., 1982; sr. planner EG & G Inc., Waltham, Mass., 1982-83; cons. city planner in pvt. practice, 1983; fin. analyst Laventhol & Horwath, Phila., 1985, subs. Valuation Counselors, Inc., Princeton, N.J., 1986, mgr. Mergers and Acquisitions Group; guest lectr. Harvard Grad. Sch. Design, Lowell (Mass.) Technol. Inst. Chmn. urban policy com. N.E. Sierra Club, 1978-79; mem. exec. com. Greater Boston Group, Sierra Club. Mem. Am. Inst. Cert. Planners (charter), Am. Planning Assn. (charter), Am. Mktg. Assn., Air Pollution Control Assn. Home: 11 Theresa Dr Lawrenceville NJ 08648 Office: Princeton Pike Office Park CN30 Princeton NJ 08543

GHEORGHIU, MIHNEA MIHAIL, writer, educator; b. Bucharest, Romania, May 5, 1919; s. Dumitru and Alexandrina G.; m. Anda Boldur, 1953; 1 child, Manuela. BA, Fratii Buzesti Coll., Craiova, Romania, 1937; MA, Faculty of Letters and Philosophy, Bucharest, 1941; PhD, U. Bucharest, 1961, DSc, 1966. Journalist, editor-in-chief Scinteia Tineretului, 1944-45; prof. Acad. Econ. Studies, Bucharest, 1946-48, U. Bucharest, 1948-64, Inst. Theatre and Film Arts, 1953-73; founder and editor Secolul 20, 1960-64; pres. Acad. Social and Polit. Scis., Bucharest, 1972—, Nat. Ctr. for Promotion of Cooperation and Friendship with Other Peoples, Bucharest, 1978—. Author: Orientations in World Literature, 1957, Scenes of Shakespeare's Life, 1964, Dionysos, 1969, Letters from Neighbourhood, 1971, Scenes of Public Life, 1972, Five Worlds as Spectacle, 1980; (poems) The Last Landscape, 1974; (essays) Tobacco Flowers, Justice Economique Internationale, 1986, Breve Historia de Rumania, 1983, Les Educateurs, les Decideurs et les Sciences Sociales dans un Monde a Changer, 1984; (plays) Sign of Taurus, The Head, Patetica '77 (laureate)Zodia Taurului (acad. award); (film scripts) Tudor (state prize, spl. internat. film fesitval prize), Iron and Gold, Virgo (spl. internat. film festival prize); translator works from Shakespeare, Jonson, Whitman, Lorca, Garcia Marquez, others. Pres. Council fo Cinematography, 1962-65, v.p. State Com. for Culture and Arts, 1965-67; 1st v.p. Romanian Inst. for Cultural Relations with Fgn. Countries, 1967-72; pres. numerous internat. juries of film festivals including Cannes, Mar del Plata, Monte Carlo, San Sebastian, Cork, 1963-69; chmn. Free Tribune of World Population Conf., 1974, pres. organizing com. 15th Internat. Congress of Hist. Scis., Bucharest, 1980; advisor UNESCO European Ctr. Higher Edn., 1980-88. Named to Cultural Merit Order of Romania 1st class, Order des Arts et des Lettres, France, Ordine al Merito, Italy, Order Orange and Nassau, The Netherlands; recipient Grande Croix des Verdienstorder, Fed. Republic of Germany, Apararea Patriei 1st class award, Romania. Mem. Acad. Socialist Republic Romania, Acad. Social and Polit. Scis., Writers Union (prize for play Capul), Film Makers Assn. (prize for script Cantemire), Club of Rome, Societe Europeenne de Culture, N.Y. Acad. Scis., Acad. Mondiale de Prospective Sociale, Acad. Internat. di Pontzen. Home: 74 Dionisie Lupu, Bucharest Romania Office: Acad Stiinte Sociale si Polit, 11 Onesti Str, 70119 Bucharest Romania

GHETTI, BERNARDINO FRANCESCO, neuropathologist, neurobiology researcher; b. Pisa, Italy, Mar. 28, 1941; s. Getulio and Iris (Mugnetti) G.; m. Caterina Genovese, Oct. 8, 1966; children—Chiara, Simone. M.D. cum laude, U. Pisa, 1966, specialist in mental and nervous diseases, 1969. Lic. physician, Italy; cert. Edn. Council for Fgn. Med. Grads.; diplomate Am. Bd. Pathology. Postdoctoral fellow U. Pisa, 1966-70; research fellow in neuropathology Albert Einstein Coll. Medicine, Bronx, N.Y., 1970-73, resident, clin. fellow in pathology, 1973-75, resident in neuropathology, 1975-76; asst. prof. pathology Ind. U., Indpls., 1976-77, asst. prof. pathology and psychiatry, 1977-78, assoc. prof. pathology and psychiatry, 1978-83, prof., 1983—; mem. Nat. Inst. Neurol. and Communicative Disorders and Stroke rev. com. NIH, 1985-89. Contbr. articles and abstracts to profl. jours. Mem. Am. Assn. Neuropathologists, Soc. Neurosci., Assn. Research in Nervous and Mental Diseases, Internat. Brain Research Orgn., Am. Soc. Cell Biology, Italian Soc. Psychiatry, Italian Soc. Neurology, Sigma Xi. Roman Catholic. Home: 1124 Frederick Dr S Indianapolis IN 46260 Office: Ind U 635 Barnhill Dr Room 157 Indianapolis IN 46223

GHIAUROV, NICOLAI, opera singer; b. Velingrad, Bulgaria, Sept. 13, 1929; m. Zlatina Ghiaurov; 2 children. Student, Acad. Music, Sofia, Bulgaria, Moscow Conservatory. Debut at Sofia Opera House in Barber of Seville, 1955; roles include Don Basilia in The Barber of Seville, King Philip in Don Carlo, Ramfis in Aida, Varlaanin Boris Godunov; appearances in maj. opera houses include La Scala, Lyric Opera Chgo., Met. Opera, Phila. Lyric Opera, London Royal Opera, Bolshoi Opera. Recipient 1st prize Internat. Singin Contest Paris, 1955. Office: care John Coast, Manfield House 376/9 Strand, Covent Garden, London WC2R OLR, England *

GHIBU, CĂLIN GHEORGE, director of photography, lecturer; b. Bucharest, Romania, Apr. 23, 1939; s. Ghibu V. Ioan and Florica (Tiron) G.; m. Cătălina Victoria, June 7, 1986. Grad., Sch. Drama and Filmmaking, Bucharest, 1972. guest lectr. Sch. Drama and Filmmaking, Bucharest, 1974—; tech. councillor Amateur Filmmakers, Bucharest, 1978—; contbr. to specialized mags., 1974—. Dir. photography 14 feature films including 7 Days, 1974, Beyond the Bridge, 1976, Between Facing Mirrors, 1978, Fox

Hunting, 1981, Luchian, 1982, Glissando, 1984, Călifar's Mill, 1985, Winter Romance, 1987. Recipient 5 awards Romanian Filmmaker's Assn., 1974, 76, 78, 82, 84; award of art film Karlovy Vary Film Festival, 1983. Fellow Internat. Visitor Programme of USIA; mem. Romanian Filmmakers' Assn., Profl. Commn. of Bucharest Film Studio. Home: Str Maxim Gorki, no 20 Sec 1, Bucharest Romania

GHIRALDINI, JOAN, financial executive; b. Bklyn., Mar. 31, 1951; d. Robert and Anne (Centineo) G.; B.A., Smith Coll., 1972; M.B.A., U. Pa., 1975. Intern, N.Y.C. Econ. Devel. Adminstrn., 1971; econ. specialist Western Electric Co., N.Y.C., 1975-76; sr. fin. analyst Internat. Paper Co., N.Y.C., 1976-78, mgr. strategic planning, 1978-81; dir. fin. planning Executone Inc., Jericho, N.Y., 1981-82, dir. strategic bus. planning, 1982-83; dir. corporate analysis Equitable Life Assurance, N.Y.C., 1983-84; asst. v.p. First Boston Corp., N.Y.C., 1985—. Mem. Am. Fin. Assn., N.Am. Soc. for Corp. Planning, Fin. Women's Assn. N.Y. Clubs: Wharton Bus. Sch. (past v.p.), Smith Coll. N.Y. (bd. dirs.). Home: 155 E 38th St New York NY 10016 Office: First Boston Corp 5 World Trade Ctr New York NY 10048

GHISE, DUMITRU, philosopher, educator; b. Pestisul, Romania, May 18, 1930; s. Gheorghe and Galenia (Harau) G.; m. Ana Cristodulo, 1955; children: Lucian, Andrei. PhD in Philosophy, U. Cluj-Napoca, Romania, 1960. Asst. lectr. philosophy U. Cluj-Napoca, 1952-61, lectr., 1961-63, sr. lectr., 1963-67; univ. prof., pres. philos. div. Acad. for Social and Polit. Research, Bucharest, Romania, 1981—; dir. Editura Politica, Bucharest, 1984—; pres. Roamnian Nat. Com. Philosophy, 1984—. Author: French Existentialism and the Problem of Ethics, 1967, Enlightened Fragmentarism, 1972, Counterpoint, 1972, Dimension of the Human Being, 1979. Mem. Central Com. Romanian Communist Party, 1970—; dep. Gt. Nat.Assembly, 1985—; v.p. Council and Socialist Edn., 1971-77. Decorated Order Cultural Merit 2d and 4th class, Star of Socialist Rep. Romania 3d class, Order Tudor Vladimirescu 3d class. Office: Editura Politica, Piata Scinteii 1, Bucharest Romania

GHOSH, ASHOKE KUMAR, German language educator, consultant; b. Jamshedpur, Bihar, India, Mar. 26, 1949; s. Nilmoni and Gita (Mittra) G. Diploma in German Lang., Lessing Kolleg, Marburg, W.Ga., 1979. Head German lang., prof. in charge, lectr. French lang. Karimia Sch. Langs., Jamshedpur, India, 1976 ; head lang. dept. Internat. Communication Wing, Jamshedpur, 1980—; prof. German langs. Mgmt. Inst., Jamshedpur, 1982-83; dir. Ghosh Inc., Jamshedpur, 1980—. Editor: Unser Blatt, 1980—. Joint sec. Indo-German Assn., Jamshedpur, 1980—. Mem. Assn. Tchrs. German, Indian Assn. Tech. Translators, Institut Fur Anslandsbeziehungen, Fgn. Lang. Tchrs. Assn., Bombay Natural Hist. Soc., Deutscher Autoren Verband e.v., Assn. Fgn. Lang. Lovers of India (v.p.). Hindu. Club: Barisha Sporting. Avocation: photography. Home: E/479 A/B Block,, Sonari New Lay Out,, Jameshedpur, Bihar, India 831011

GHOSH, RABINDRA NATH, economics educator, research economist; b. New Delhi, India, Dec. 6, 1932; s. Suresh Chandra and Sudhangsu Bala (Mitra) G.; m. Surekha Mukhopadhyay, July 3, 1958; children—Jaya, Ratna. B.A. with honours in Econs., U. Delhi, 1951, M.S. in Econs., 1953; Ph.D., Birmingham U., Eng., 1962. Lectr. in econs. Delhi Coll., 1953-63; reader in econs. Visva-Bharati, Santiniketan, West Bengal, 1963-65; research dir. Indian C. of C., Calcutta, 1965-68; sr. lectr. U. Western Australia, Nedlands, 1968-81, head econs. dept., 1981—; chmn. New Internat. Econ. Order, UN Assn. of Australia, 1981. Author: Classical Macroeconomics, 1967; Agriculture in Economic Development, 1977. Editor: Problems of Economic Growth, 1960. Editor Econ. Activity jour., 1971-77. Mem. Austcare/Freedom from Hunger, 1971-75. Smith-Mundt/Fulbright scholar, 1960, Commonwealth scholar Brit. Govt., 1960-63. Mem. Am. Econ. Assn., Internat. Union for Sci. Study of Population, Australian and N.Z. Econ. Soc. Office: U Western Australia, 6009 Nedland, Perth Western Australia, Australia

GHOUGASSIAN, JOSEPH, ambassador; b. Cairo, Mar. 6, 1944; s. Antoine Hagop and Marie Antoinette (Wazir) G.; m. Zena Yasmine, 1970; children—Yasmine, Samara, Jihan, Joseph. M.A., U. Gregorian, Rome, 1965; Ph.D., U. Louvain, Belgium, 1969; M.A., U. San Diego, 1977, J.D., 1980. Assoc. prof. U. San Diego, 1966-86; mem. Office Policy Devel., White House, 1981; dir. Peace Corps, Sanaa, YAR, 1982-85; U.S. Ambassador to Qatar Doha, 1985—; cons. Immigration and Naturalization Service, U.S. Dept. Justice, Washington, 1982. Contbr. articles to profl. jours. Founding mem. UNESCO Forum. NSF grantee, 1978-79. Mem. Sociedade de Psicanalise Integral (hon.), Phi Sigma Tau, Phi Dleta Phi. Republican. Address: Am Embassy, Doha State of Qatar Office: Dept of State US Ambassador to Qatar Washington DC 20520

GHUBRIL, FOUAD ADIB, engineer; b. Alexandria, Egypt, July 9, 1944; s. Adib Assaad and Adele (Kashami) G.; m. Miriam Ghubril, May 30, 1970; children: Bahi, Rima, Noradele, Rosa-Lynn. MSEE, Loughborough (Eng.) U., 1967. Inspector Mid. East Airlines, Beirut, 1968-69; site engr. Lahoud Engrng. Co., Dubai, United Arab Emirates, 1970-71, site mgr., 1972-74, project mgr., 1975-76, area mgr., 1977, dir. ops., 1978—; rep. London, 1986—. Home: 54 Campden Hill Gate, London W8 7QJ, England Office: Lahoud Engring Co, PO Box 10111, Dubai United Arab Emirates

GIACCO, ALEXANDER FORTUNATUS, diversified plastics company executive; b. St. John, Italy, Aug. 24, 1919; s. Salvatore J. and Maria Concetta (de Maria) G.; m. Edith Brown, Feb. 16, 1946; children: Alexander Fortunatus, Richard John, Mary P. Giacco Walsh, Elizabeth B. Giacco Brown, Marissa A. Giacco Rath. B.S. in Chem. Engring, Va. Poly. Inst., 1942; postgrad. in mgmt., Harvard U., 1965; D.B.A. (hon.), William Carey Coll., Hattiesburg, Miss., 1980; D.Bus. (hon.), Goldey Beacom Coll., 1984; LL.D. (hon.), Widener U., 1984. With Hercules Inc., Wilmington, Del., 1942-87, gen. mgr. polymers dept., 1968-73, dir., 1970-87, gen. mgr. operating dept. (Hercules Europe), 1973, v.p. parent co., 1974-76, mem. exec. com., 1974-87, exec. v.p., 1976-77, pres., chief exec. officer, chmn. exec. com., 1977-87, chmn. bd., 1980-87; chmn. bd. HIMONT Inc., Wilmington, Del., 1983—, chief exec. officer, 1987—; vice chmn., chief exec. officer Montedison SpA, Milan, 1988—; dir. Montedison S.p.A.; mem. U.S. Com. on New Initiatives in East-West Co-op., 1976—. Trustee, bd. dirs., mem. exec. com. Med. Ctr. of Del., 1975—, rector, 1984-87; trustee, bd. visitors Va. Poly. Inst. and State U., 1980-87; chmn. bd. dirs. Grand Opera House, Wilmington, 1980—; bd. dirs. WHYY, Inc., 1983—. Named One of Ten Outstanding Chief Exec. Officers Fin. World, 1980, 87, Best Chief Exec. Officer in Chem. Industry Fin. World, 1984, Outstanding Chief Exec. Officer in the Chem. Industry Wall Street Transcript, 1983, 84, 85, 87; Commendatore Order Merit (Italy). Mem. Am. Assn. of the Sovereign Mil. Order of Malta, Soc. Plastics Industry, Soc. Chem. Industry, Soc. Automotive Engrs., Nat. Acad. Engrs., Am. Ordnance Assn. (past dep. chmn.), Del. Roundtable (chmn. econ. devel. com.). Clubs: Wilmington, Wilmington Country (bd. dirs.), Vicmead Hunt, Hercules Country, Rehoboth Beach Country, Rodney Sq. (bd. dirs.), Jonathan's Landing Country (Fla.). Lodge: Knights of Malta. Office: Himont Inc 3 Little Falls Ctr 2801 Centerville Rd Wilmington DE 19850-5439 *

GIACCONI, RICCARDO, astrophysicist; b. Genoa, Italy, Oct. 6, 1931; came to U.S., 1956, naturalized, 1967; s. Antonio and Elsa (Canni) G.; m. Mirella Manaira, Feb. 15, 1957; children: Guia Giacconi Chmiel, Anna Lee, Marc A. Ph.D., U. Milan, Italy, 1954; Sc.D. (hon.), U. Chgo., 1983; laurea ad honorem in astronomy, U. Padua, 1984. Asst. prof. physics U. Milan, 1954-56; research assoc. Ind. U., 1956-58, Princeton U., 1958-59; exec. v.p., dir. Am. Sci. & Engring. Co., Cambridge, Mass., 1959-73; prof. astronomy Harvard U.; also assoc. dir. high energy astrophysics div. Center Astrophysics, Smithsonian Astrophys. Obs./Harvard Coll. Obs., Cambridge, 1973-81; dir. Space Telescope Sci. Inst., Balt., 1981—; prof. astrophysics Johns Hopkins U.; mem. space sci. adv. com. NASA, 1978-79, mem. adv. com. innovation study, 1979—; mem. NASA Astrophysics Council; mem. adv. com. innovation study astronomy adv. com., 1979—; mem. high energy astronomy survey panel Nat. Acad. Scis., 1979-80, mem. Space Sci. Bd., 1980-84; mem. adv. com. Max-Planck Inst. für Physik und Astrophysik; chmn. bd. dirs. Instituto Guido Donegani, Gruppo Montedison; mem. vis. com. to div. of phys. scis. U. Chgo., U. Padova. Co-editor: X-ray Astronomy, 1974, The X-Ray Universe, 1985; author numerous articles, papers in field. Fulbright fellow, 1956-58; recipient Röntgen prize astrophysics Physikalish-Medizinische Gesellschaft, Wurzburg, Germany, 1971; Exceptional Sci. Achievement medal NASA, 1971, 80; Disting. Public Service award, 1972; Space Sci. award AIAA, 1976; Elliott Cresson medal Franklin Inst., 1980; Gold medal Royal Astron. Soc., 1982; A. Cressy Morrison award N.Y. Acad. Sci., 1982; Bruce medal; Heinneman award, Wolf Prize in Physics, 1987; Russell lectr. Mem. Am. Astron. Soc. (Helen B. Warner award 1966, chmn. high energy astrophysics div. 1976-77, councilor 1979-82, task group on directions in space sci. 1995-2015), Italian Phys. Soc. (Como prize 1967), AAAS, Internat. Astron. Union (Nat. Acad. Scis. astron. rep. 1979-82), Nat. Acad. Scis., Am. Acad. Arts and Scis., Md. Acad. Sci. (sci. council 1982—), Accademia Nazionale dei Lincei (fgn.), Italian Phys. Soc., Am. Phys. Soc. Club: Cosmos (Washington). Home: 203 Lambeth Rd Baltimore MD 21218 Office: Space Telescope Sci Inst 3700 San Martin Dr Baltimore MD 21218

GIACONA, CORRADO ANTHONY II, container company executive; b. New Orleans, Dec. 14, 1942; s. Louis Joseph and Claire (LaRocca) G.; m. Patricia Ellen Nunez, July 25, 1964; children: Gina Lisa, Corrado Anthony, Louis. BA, U. New Orleans, 1965. Plant mgr. Amos C. Harris Can Co., New Orleans, 1962-64; ter. mgr. Ross Labs., New Orleans, 1964-72; pres. Giacona Container div. Giacona Group, New Orleans, 1972—. Bd. dirs. La. Maritime Mus., Sci. Ctr., La. Sci. Ctr., Family Services of La.; pres. La. Maritime Mus.; officer Krewe of Alla. Mem. Phi Kappa Theta. Republican. Roman Catholic. Club: Timberlane Country. Home: 704 Fairfield Ave Gretna LA 70053 Office: Giacona Container 121 Industrial Ave New Orleans LA 70121

GIAEVER, IVAR, physicist; b. Bergen, Norway, Apr. 5, 1929; came to U.S., 1957, naturalized, 1963; s. John A. and Gudrun (Skaarud) G.; m. Inger Skramstad, Nov. 8, 1952; children: John, Anne Kari, Guri, Trine. Siv. Ing., Norwegian Inst. Tech., Trondheim, 1952; Ph.D., Rensselaer Poly. Inst., 1964. Patent examiner Norwegian Patent Office, Oslo, 1953-54; mech. engr. Can. Gen. Electric Co., Peterborough, Ont., 1954-56; applied mathematician Gen. Electric Co., Schenectady, 1956-58, physicist Research and Devel. Ctr., 1958—. Served with Norwegian Army, 1952-53. Recipient Nobel Prize for Physics, 1973; Guggenheim fellow, 1970. Fellow Am. Phys. Soc. (Oliver E. Buckley prize 1965); mem. IEEE, Norwegian Profl. Engrs., Nat. Acad. Sci., Nat. Acad. Engring. (V.K. Zworykin award 1974), Am. Acad. Arts and Scis., Norwegian Acad. Sci., Norwegian Acad. Tech. Office: Gen Electric Co Research and Devel Ctr PO Box 8 K1 Room 3C Schenectady NY 12301 *

GIALANELLA, PHILIP THOMAS, newspaper publisher; b. Binghamton, N.Y., June 6, 1930; s. Felix and Frances (Demuro) G.; 1 son, Thomas Davis. B.A., Harpur Coll., 1952; M.A., State U. N.Y., 1955. Promotion dir. Evening Press and Sta. WINR-TV, Binghamton, 1957-62; v.p., gen. mgr. Daily Advance, Dover, N.J., 1962-66; v.p. Hartford (Conn.) Times, 1966-70; pres., pub. Newburgh (N.Y.) News, 1970-71; exec. v.p. Hawaii Newspaper Agy., Honolulu, 1971-73, pres., 1974-86; pub. Honolulu Star-Bull., 1975-86; pres. USA Today, 1982-83, pub., 1983; exec. v.p., pub. Honolulu Advertiser, 1986—; exec. v.p., chief operating officer Persis Corp., Honolulu, 1986—, pres. Persis Media div., 1986—; v.p., chief exec. officer Longview Pub. Co., Bellevue, Wash., 1986—; bd. dirs. Capital Investment Co., Hawaii Newspaper Agy., Inc., Waterhouse Properties, Persis Corp., Honolulu Advertiser Inc., Longview Pub. Co.; v.p., bd. dirs. ASA Properties, Inc., Bay-Area Steuart, Inc., Shiny Rock Mining Corp. Past chmn., exec. com. mem. Nat. Alliance Businessmen for Hawaii and Micronesia; v.p. Hawaii Newspaper Agy. Found.; bd. dirs. Aloha United Way, AP Assn., Calif., Ariz., Hawaii and Nev.; mem. Japan Hawaii Econ. Council; bd. govs. Pacific Asian Affairs Council; bd. dirs. Hawaii Theatre Ctr., Honolulu Boy Choir, Honolulu Symphony; mem. adv. group Western Command U.S. Army. Served with U.S. Army, 1952-54. Mem. Am. Newspaper Pubs. Assn., Hawaii Pubs. Assn., AP Assn. Calif., AP Assn. Ariz., AP Assn. Hawaii, AP Assn. Nev., Sigma Delta Chi. Roman Catholic. Office: The Honolulu Advertiser Honolulu HI 96802

GIAMATTI, A. BARTLETT, sports executive, former university president; b. Boston, Apr. 4, 1938; married; 3 children. BA, Yale U., 1960, PhD in Comparative Lit., 1964; LLD, Princeton U., 1978, Harvard U., 1978, Notre Dame U., 1982, Coll. of New Rochelle, 1982, Dartmouth Coll., 1982; LittD, Am. Internat. Coll., 1979, Jewish Theol. Sem. Am., 1980, Atlanta U., 1981; HHD, Oberlin Coll., 1983. Instr. Italian and comparative lit. Princeton (N.J.) U., 1964-65, asst. prof., 1965-66; asst. prof. English Yale U., New Haven, 1966-69, assoc. prof. English and comparative lit., 1969-71, prof. English and comparative lit., 1971-86, master Ezra Stiles Coll., 1970-72, Frederick Clifford Ford prof. English and comparative lit., 1976-77, John Hay Whitney prof. English and comparative lit., 1977-78, pres. univ., 1978-86; pres. Nat. League, N.Y.C., 1986—, now also treas.; vis. prof. comparative lit. NYU, N.Y.C., summer 1966; mem. faculty Bread Loaf Sch. English, summers 1972-74. Author: The Earthly Paradise and the Renaissance Epic, 1966, Play of Double Senses: Spenser's Faerie Queene, 1975, History of Scroll and Key, 1942-1972, 1978, The University and the Public Interest, 1981, Exile and Change in Renaissance Literature, 1984; editor: (with others) The Songs of Bernart de Ventadorn, 1962, rev. edit., 1965, Ludovico Ariosto's Orlando Furioso, 1968, A, Variorum Commentary On the Poems of John Milton, Western Literature, 3 vols, 1971, 6 vols., 1972, Dante in America: The First Two Centuries, 1983. Trustee The Ford Found., Mt. Holyoke Coll.; bd. dirs. Baxter Travenol Labs. Inc., Coca-Cola Enterprises Inc. Decorated comdr. Order of Merit Italian Republic, 1979, comdr. Cross of Fed. Order Merit, Republic Germany, 1985, comdr. l'Ordre Nat. des Arts et des Lettres, Republic France, 1985; J.S. Guggenheim fellow, 1969-70; recipient Outstanding Contribution to Higher Edn. award Brown U., 1985, Liberty Bell award New Haven County Bar Assn., 1985; Americanism award Anti-Defamation League of B'nai B'rith, 1986, Ellis Island Medal of Honor, 1986, Leonardo da Vinci award, 1986. Fellow Am. Acad. Arts and Scis.; mem. Am. Philos. Soc., Council on Fgn. Relations. Office: Office of Pres Nat League Profl Baseball Clubs 350 Park Ave New York NY 10022 *

GIAMPIETRO, WAYNE BRUCE, lawyer; b. Chgo., Jan. 20, 1942; s. Joseph Anthony and Jeannette Marie (Zeller) G.; B.A., Purdue U., 1963; J.D., Northwestern U., 1966; m. Mary E. Fordeck, June 15, 1963; children—Joseph, Anthony, Marcus. Bar: Ill. 1966. Since practiced in Chgo.; assoc. Elmer Gertz, 1966-73; mem. firm Gertz & Giampietro, 1974-75; sole practice, 1975-76; ptnr. Poltrock & Giampietro, 1976-87, ptnr. Witwer, Burlage, Poltrock and Giampietro, 1988— . Cons. atty. Looking Glass div. Traveler's Aid Soc. Pres. Chgo. 47th Ward Young Republicans, 1968. Bd. dirs. Ravenswood Conservation Commn. Mem. ABA, Ill. Bar Assn. (chmn. sect. on Individual Rights and Responsibilities, 1986-87, 2d pl. Lincoln award 1975), Chgo. Bar Assn., Assn. Trial Lawyers Am., Ill. Trial Lawyers Assn., First Amendment Lawyers Assn. (sec. 1982, treas. 1983, pres. 1986), Order of Coif, Phi Alpha Delta. Lutheran. Contbr. articles to profl. jours. Home: 23 Windsor Dr Lincolnshire IL 60015 Office: 125 S Wacker Dr Suite 2700 Chicago IL 60606

GIANCARLO, VAJ, industrialist; b. Milan, Italy, Sept. 23, 1922; s. Angelo and Maria (Ferrari) V.; m. Carla Chiappini, Apr. 28, 1949; children—Daniela, Maria Sole. Grad. in Econ. Scis., U. Bologna, 1946. Mgr., Vaj Angelo Firm, Piacenza, Italy, 1942-58; joint owner Vaj F.lli S.n.c., Piacenza, 1958-71; pres. Vaj S.p.A., Piacenza, 1972—; mng. councillor Unispray S.r.l., Cologno M. (Milan), 1983—. Served with Italian Army, 1943-45. Decorated cavaliere della Republica La Primogenita Gold medal, 1981. Mem. Italian Chem. and Cosmetic Scis. Assn. Roman Catholic. Club: Lions (pres. 1965-66). Home: Via V Veneto 65, Piacenza 29100, Italy Office: Vaj Spa, VV Veneto 67, Piacenza Italy 29100

GIANNINI, A. JAMES, psychiatrist, educator, researcher; b. Youngstown, Ohio, June 11, 1947; s. Matthew and Grace Carla (Nistri) G.; m. Judith Ludvik, Apr. 26, 1975; children—Juliette Nicole, Jocelyn Danielle. B.S., Youngstown State U., Ohio, 1970; M.D., U. Pitts., 1974; postgrad., Yale U., 1974-78. Diplomate: Nat. Bd. Med. Examiners. Intern St. Elizabeth Med. Ctr., Youngstown, 1974; resident dept. psychiatry Yale U., New Haven, 1975-78, chief resident, 1977-78; assoc. psychiatrist Elmcrest Psychiat. Inst., Portland, Conn., 1976-78; acting ward chief Conn. Mental Health Center, New Haven, 1977; assoc. dir. family medicine, psychiatry St. Elizabeth Med. Ctr., Youngstown, 1978-80; chmn, depts. psychiatry and toxicology Western Reserve Care System Hosps., Youngstown, 1985—; assoc. prof. dept. psychiatry Northeast Ohio Med. Coll., 1978-84, prof., 1984—, program dir., 1980—, vice chmn., 1985—; assoc. clin. prof. dept psychiatry Ohio State U., 1983-87, clin. prof. 1987—; sr. cons. Fair Oaks Hosp., Summit, N.J., 1980—, Regent Hosp., N.Y.C., 1981—, chmn. Nat. Adv. Council Prevention and Control of Rape, NIMH, Rockville, Md., 1984-85; mem. drug abuse clin., behavioral and research rev. com. Nat. Inst. Drug Abuse, Rockville, Md., 1987—; cons. Smith-Kline Labs., McNeil Labs., Excerpta Medica Pubs., Amino Labs., Fund for Am. Renaissance; dir. clin. research Princeton Diagnostic Labs., South Plainfield, N.J., 1987—. Author: (with Henry Black) Psychiatric, Psychogenic, Somatopsychic Disorders, 1978; (with Robert Gilliland) Neurologic, Neurogenic and Neuropsychiatric Disorders, 1982; (with Andrew Slaby) Overdose and Detoxification Emergencies, 1983; Clinical Foundation of Biological Psychiatry, 1985, (with Andrew Slaby and Mark Gold) Drugs of Abuse, 1987, Comprehensive Laboratory Services in Psychiatry, 1987; contbr. numerous articles to profl. jours. Vice chmn. Mahoning County (Ohio) Mental Health Bd., 1982-84, chmn. 1984-87; councilor Nat. Italian Am. Found. Recipient James Earley award U. Pitts., 1974, Upjohn Research prize Upjohn Co., 1974; recipient Fair Oaks Research award Fair Oaks Hosp., 1979, Bronze award Brit. Med. Assn, 1983, Outstanding Leadership award Mahoning County Mental Health Bd., 1986. Fellow N.J. Acad. Medicine, Am. Coll. Clin. Pharmacology; mem. Soc. Neurosci. Brit. Brain Soc., Brit. Brain Soc., European Neurosci. Soc., N.Y. Acad. Scis., Am. Psychiat. Assn., Acad. Clin. Psychiatry, Youngstown C. of C. (vice chmn. health com.), Sigma Xi. Roman Catholic. Club: Youngstown, Atrium (Warren, Ohio).

GIANNOPOULOS, GEORGE ANASTOSIOS, civil engineer, educator; b. Megara, Attica, Greece, Nov. 26, 1946; s. Anastasios George and Irene (Kiousi) G.; m. Artemis Vadoka, Dec. 18, 1982; 1 child, Anastasios. Dip. in Civil Engring., Tech. U., Athens, Greece, 1968; D.I.C., Imperial Coll., London, 1969; MS in Engring., U. London, 1970, PhD, 1973. Spl. scientist U. Patras, Greece, 1975-76; counsellor Dept. of Transport, Athens, 1976-81; assoc. prof. engring. U. Thessaloniki, Salonika, Greece, 1978-82, prof., 1982—, dir. transport research unit, 1981—; dep., Office Greek Sec. Transport at ECMT/OECD, Paris, 1977; cons. EEC, Brussels, 1981—. Author books; contbr. articles to profl. jours.; mem. editorial bd. Jour. Transport Tevs., 1987—. Mem. Hellenic Red Cross, Athens, 1982—. Grantee Schilitsi Found., 1970, Anglo-Hellenic League, 1971; scholar Fulbright Found., 1986. Mem. Hellenic Inst. Transport Engrs. (chmn. 1984-86), U.S. Inst. Traffic Engrs. (assoc.), U.S. Transp. Research Bd. (com.), Tech. Chamber of Greece. Mem. Democratic Solidarity Party. Greek Orthodox. Office: U Augsburg Art History Dept, Universitatstrasse 10, D-8900 Augsburg Federal Republic of Germany

GIANNOTTI, DAVID ALLEN, lawyer; b. Rome, N.Y., May 27, 1947; s. Dominick and Florence Mary (Wilkinson) G.; m. Kathy Ann Hanna, June 5, 1982. B.A. in Polit. Sci., Ithaca Coll., 1969; J.D., Emory U., 1971. Bar: Ga. 1972, Tenn. 1972, N.Y. 1976, Calif. 1981. Assoc., Stophel, Caldwell & Heggie, Chattanooga, 1972-75; assoc. gen. counsel Hooker Chems. & Plastics Corp., Niagara Falls, N.Y., 1975-78; counsel environ. affairs Occidental Chem. Corp., Houston, 1978-81; counsel environ. health and safety Occidental Petroleum Corp., Los Angeles, 1981-84; ptnr. McKenna, Conner & Cuneo, Los Angeles, 1984—; lectr. in field. Contbr. in field. Mem. ABA, Am. Petroleum Inst., Chem. Mfrs. Assn., State Bar Calif. (com. on the environment). Republican. Home: 4251 Parva Ave Los Angeles CA 90027 Office: McKenna Conner & Cuneo 3435 Wilshire Blvd Los Angeles CA 90071

GIARINI, ORIO, economist; b. Trieste, Italy, Jan. 31, 1936; s. Mario and Bianca (Contini) G.; Liceo Scientifico Oberdan, Trieste; postgrad. (Fulbright scholar), U. Tex., 1955-56; Ph.D. in Polit. Sci., U. Trieste; children—Sabine Anne, Francesca Therese. Mem. sales promotion staff Montecatini Co., Milan and Basle, 1959-62, Nitrex Co., Zurich, 1962-65; dir. indsl. econs. and services div. Battelle Inst., Geneva, 1965-73; European sec. gen. European Federalist Movement, Paris, 1962-69; sec. gen., adminstr. Internat. Assn. Ins. Econs. Research, 1973—; prof. service economics Univ. Inst. European Studies, Geneva, 1971—; founder, dir. Institut de la Duree, Geneva, 1983—. Mem. Club of Rome, List Gesellschaft, Centre Europeen de la Culture, others. Clubs: Ocean Inst., Sailing, Tennis. Author: L'Europe et l'Espace, 1968; Les ressources de la mer et l'Europe, 1977; The Diminishing Returns of Technology, 1978; Dialogue on Wealth and Welfare, 1980; Cycles, Value and Employment, 1984; The Limits to Certainty, 1988; editor: Rassegna Europea, 1959-63, Geneva Papers on Risk and Insurance, 1976—, The Emerging Service Economy. Home: 30c Rt Du Preiur, CH-1257, Landecy-Geneva Switzerland Office: 18 chemin Rieu, CH-1208 Geneva Switzerland

GIBARA, GERMAINE, aluminum company executive; b. Cairo, Sept. 20, 1944; came to Can., 1966; parents: Antoine Gibara and Odette Turcomani. BA, American U., Cairo, 1966; MA, Dalhousie U., Halifax, N.S., 1968; CFD, U. Va., 1983; PMD, Harvard U. Bus. Sch., 1984. Chartered fin. analyst, Can. Fin. analyst Exec. Fund of Can., Montreal, Que., 1969-70; portfolio mgr. Lombard Odier Can., Montreal, Que., 1970-75; dir. investor relations Alcan Aluminum, Ltd., Montreal, 1975-84, leader diversification study, 1985-86, dir. adhesive systems, 1986-88; pres. Alcan Automotive Structures, Montreal, 1988—. Mem. Montreal Soc. Fin. Analyst, Harvard Alumni Soc. Office: Alcan Aluminum Ltd, 1188 Sherbrooke St W, Montreal, PQ Canada H3A 3G2

GIBAUD, HENRI ANDRE, retired English language educator, magazine executive, clergyman; b. Auzay, Vendee, France, Aug. 27, 1920; s. Henri Gabriel and Marie-Egyptienne (Merlaud) G. Licence d'Anglais, Universite Catholique de l'Ouest, Angers, France, 1946; D.E.S. d'Anglais, Centre d'Etudes Supé rieures de la Renaissance, Tours, France, 1967, Doctorat es Lettres, 1982. Ordained priest, Roman Catholic Ch., 1944. Tchr., St. Joseph Secondary Sch., Fontenay-le-Comte, France, 1944-59, Notre Dame Secondary Sch., Lucon, France, 1959-66; univ. asst. Universite Catholique Ouest, Angers, 1966-82, assoc. prof. English, 1982-84, prof., 1984-85; adminstr. Moreana mag., Angers, 1967—. Author: Un Inedit d'Erasme-Premiè re Version du Nouveau Testament, (Institut de Recherche Fondamentale et Appliqué e award) (1982). Recipient Erasmus medal Centre d'Etudes Superieures de la Renaissance, Tours, 1982, Palmes Academiques, 1987. Mem. Internat. Assn. Neolatin Studies, Societe des Seiziemistes de France, Amici Thomae Mori (life). Home: 56 Rue Blaise-Pascal, 49000 Angers, Anjou France Office: Univ Catholique de l'Ouest, BP 808, 49005 Angers Anjou France

GIBBERD, FREDERICK BRIAN, neurologist; b. London, July 7, 1931; s. George Frederick and Margaret Erica (Taffs) G.; m. Margaret Clare Sidey, Sept. 3, 1960; children: Ruth, Judith, Lucy, Penelope. BA, Cambridge U., Eng., 1954, MD, 1974; MB, BChir., Westminster Med. Sch., London, 1957. Cons. neurologist Westminster Hosp., London, 1965—, chmn. med. com., 1983-85; chmn. dist. med. com. Riverside, London, 1985—; recognized tchr., examiner London U., 1969—. Contbr. articles to profl. jours. Served to lt. Royal Arty., 1950-51. Fellow Royal Coll. Physicians (examiner 1973—); mem. Royal Soc. Medicine (hon. librarian 1975-79), Worshipful Soc. Apothecaries of London (ct. of assts. 1986—). Home: 7A Alleyn Pk, London SE21 8AV, England Office: Westminster Hosp, Horseferry Rd, London SW1, England

GIBBINS, GEORGE CHARLES, management consultant, accountant; b. London, May 6, 1938; s. William George Robert and Emily Lilian Louisa (King) G.; m. Nectar Dagher, Feb. 28, 1970; 1 child, Andrew David George. Student, Snaresbrook, Eng. Articled clk. G.H. Attenborough & Co., London, 1956-58, Tansley Witt & Co., London, 1958-61; dir., chief acct. Boyd Gibbins Ltd., Bishops Stortford, Eng., 1962-67; co. sec., chief acct. GKN Internat. Trading Ltd., London, 1967-69; fin. controller Trafalger House Group Trollope & Colls (City) Ltd., 1969-71; mng. dir. Jebsens (U.K.) Ltd., London, Ruislip (Eng.), France, 1971-87; prin. George C. Gibbins Mgmt. Cons., London, France, 1987—; mng. dir. Escala Property Investment Ltd., London, 1956—, Passerelle Ltd., London, 1970—, Listerdale Fin. Services Ltd., Fast Consumer Sales Ltd.; comml. dir. Altnacraig Shipping PLC, 1988—. Contbr. articles to various publs. Chmn., v.p. Ruislip Conservative Assn. Fellow Inst. Chartered Accts. Eng., Wales; mem. Baltic Exchange, Inst. Dirs., London Dist. Soc. Chartered Accts. Mem. Conservative Party. Anglican. Club: Moor Park Golf. Home and Office: 23 Kingsend, Ruislip Middlesex HA4 7DD, England

GIBBONS, HARRY LAWRENCE, JR., limnologist, consultant, researcher; b. Spokane, Wash., Sept. 21, 1950; s. Harry Lawrence and Jackie Ann (Payne) G.; m. Maribeth Vivian Hanussak, Aug. 4, 1973; children—Ryan Holt, Michael Harrisons; B.S., Gonzaga U., 1973; M.S., Wash. State U., 1976, Ph.D., 1981. Research asst. Wash. State U., Pullman, 1973-81, postdoctoral research assoc., 1981-85; chief limnologist KCM, Inc., Seattle, 1985—; pres. Water, Pullman, 1983-84; bd. dirs. EnviroScan, Inc., 1987—, Gibbons and Davis, Inc. 1985—; mem. Wash. State Water Quality Commn. for Dept. Ecology. Contbr. articles to profl. jours. Grantee Dept. Ecology, 1981-85, U.S. Army C.E., 1981-85, Dept. Interior, 1982-83, local govts., 1982-85. Mem. N.Am. Lake Mgmt. Soc. (program chmn. 1984, co-chmn. scholarship com. 1987), Pacific N.W. Pollution Control Assn. (chmn. water resources 1984-85), Am. Soc. Limnology and Oceanography, Aquatic Plant Mgmt. Soc., Wash. State Lake Protection Assn. (bd. dirs. 1986—), Mountain Meadows Homeowners Assn. (bd. dirs. 1987—, pres.) Sigma Xi. Roman Catholic. Home: 9515 Wind Song Loop NE Bainbridge Island WA 98110

GIBBONS, JOHN DAVID, bank executive; b. Pembroke, Bermuda, June 15, 1927; s. Edmund and Winifred (Robinson) G.; m. Jean Hook Garrison, Jan. 9, 1954 (div. Aug. 1957); 1 child, Edith Gibbons Conyers; m. Lully Lorentzen, Mar. 7, 1958; children: William T., John D., James L. BA, Harvard U., 1948. Chief exec. officer Family Businesses, Hamilton, Bermuda, 1972—; chmn. The Bank of N.T. Butterfield & Son, Ltd., Hamilton, 1986—, also bd. dirs. Mem. Parliament United Bermuda Party, Pembroke West, 1972-84; parliamentary sec. Govt. of Bermuda, 1974, minister of health and welfare, 1974, minister of fin., 1975-84, premier, 1977-82; chmn. Bermuda Monetary Authority, 1984-86. Knighted Order of Brit. Empire, The Queen of Eng., 1985; recipient Justice of Peace award Govt. of Bermuda, 1985. Mem. Companion Brit. Inst. Mgmt., Bermuda Athletic Assn. Mem. Ch. of Eng. Clubs: Harvard (N.Y.C.); Phoenix S.K. (Cambridge, Mass.); R.B.Y.C. (Bermuda); Royal Hamilton Amateur Dinghy; Mid Ocean; Riddell's Bay Golf; Spanish Point Boat; Lyford Cay. Home: Leeward, 5 Leeside Dr, Point Shares HM 05, Bermuda Office: Gibbons Co Ltd, PO Box HM 454, Hamilton Bermuda

GIBBONS, JOSEPH JOHN, builders supply company financial executive; b. Wheatland, Wyo., Mar. 18, 1906; s. Michael and Edith (D'Arcy) G.; m. Hazel M. Bisson, Jan. 1, 1930; children: Betty Louise (Mrs. Donald G. Smith), Albert J., Robert J. Ph.B., U. Chgo., 1930; student, Northwestern U., 1931-33, DePaul U. Law Sch., 1933-35. C.P.A., Ill. Office mgr. George Hardin Constrn. Co., Chgo., 1927-35; exam. agt. IRS, 1935-40; sr. tax accountant Arthur Andersen and Co. (C.P.A.'s), Chgo., 1941; tax supr. U.S. Steel Corp., Duluth, Minn. and Pitts., 1941-50; mgr. tax and ins. dept. Mine Safety Appliances Co., 1950-52; with Blaw-Knox Co., 1952-69, treas., 1967-68, v.p. finance, 1968-69; pres. Corde Co., 1967-69; treas. Blaw Knox Can. Ltd., 1967-69; controller Cleve. Builders Supply Co., 1969-71. Mem. Am. Inst. C.P.A.s, Tau Kappa Epsilon, Alpha Kappa Psi. Presbyn. (elder). Club: Deerfield Country. Home: Apt 303 1161 Ocean Blvd Hillsboro Beach FL 33062

GIBBONS, MICHAEL JOSEPH, social services administrator; b. Fredericksburg, Va., Aug. 13, 1954; s. John Patrick and Emma Theresa (Euba) G.; m. Karen Louise Leban, May 10, 1986. BA, Williams Coll., 1976. Agrl. vol. Peace Corps, Sierra Leone, 1976-79; tng. dir. Peace Corps, Penn Ctr., USA, 1981-83; assoc. dir. Indochina Resource Action Ctr., Washington, 1984; field office dir. Save the Children USA, Westport, Conn., 1986—; tng. cons. Peace Corps, Washington, 1984, League for Internat. Food Edn., Honduras, Jamaica, Gambia, 1985; rural devel. cons. CARE, Bolivia, 1985. Author: (manual) Extension Training Guide, 1978, (book) Agricultural Extension, 1983; co-author, editor series Agricultural Development Workers Training Manuals, 1983. Vol., mem. Glencree Reconciliation Ctr., Belfast, No. Ireland, 1980, Nat. Peace Acad. Campaign/Nat. Peace Inst., Washington, 1980—, Penn Community Services, Inc., Frogmore, S.C., 1981-83. Recipient Conn. State Poetry Contest award, 1981. Club: Williams (N.Y.C.). Office: Save the Children 54 Wilton Rd Westport CT 06880

GIBBONS, ROBERT JOSEPH, educator; b. Pitts., Jan. 1, 1945; s. Joseph J. and Hazel (Bisson) G.; AB, Kenyon Coll., 1967; MPhil, Yale U., 1969, PhD, 1972; children: Michael L., Jean G.; m. Mary Harrison, Jan. 1, 1984; stepchildren: Mary Jo, Caroline Wells. Mem. faculty St. Joseph's Coll., Phila., 1970-77, asst. prof. history, 1973-77; dir. adminstrv. research and devel. Am. Inst. Property and Liability Underwriters, Malvern, Pa., 1977-78, dir. premium auditing edn., 1978-83, v.p., 1983—. Mem. vestry Trinity Ch., Gulph Mills, Pa., 1974-77. Nat. Merit scholar, 1963-67; NDEA fellow, 1967-70; Yale Internat. Relations Council fellow, 1970. Mem. Am. Econ. Assn., Am. Hist. Assn., Econ. History Assn., Soc. CPCUs. Episcopalian. Author: Economics for the Accountant, 1981; contbg. author works in field. Home: 760 Red Oak Terr Wayne PA 19087 Office: 720 Providence Rd Malvern PA 19355

GIBBS, ALONZO LAWRENCE, aircraft engineer, author; b. Bklyn., Feb. 17, 1915; s. Alonzo Lawrence and Annie (Keteltas) G.; student Hofstra U., 1938; Certificate in Aircraft Structural Layout, Columbia U., 1941; m. Iris Ebisch, June 17, 1939; 1 son, Geoffrey. With Grumman Aerospace Corp., Bethpage, N.Y., 1934-73, sect. chief engr., 1965-73; freelance writer, 1935—; pres. Kinsman Pubs., Inc., 1961-64. Mem. Authors Guild. Contbg. editor: L.I. Forum, 1964—; poetry reviewer Voices Mag., 1953-64; editor, pub. The Kinsman lit. quar., 1961-63; author: Weather-House, 1959; The Fields Breathe Sweet, 1963; Monhegan, 1963; The Least Likely One, 1964; Dolphin off Hippo (libretto), 1965; A Man's Calling, 1966; By a Sea-Coal Fire, 1969; Drift South, 1969; One More Day, 1971; Sir Urian's Letters Home, 1974; The Rumble of Time Through Town, 1980; others. Address: HC 60 Box 20 Waldoboro ME 04572

GIBBS, DORSIE JOE, botanist, executive; b. Ashland, Ky., Feb. 19, 1940; s. Dorsie Wilson and Frances Susan (Simpson) G.; m. Madalyn Jeanne Wiegman, Mar. 23, 1963; children: Kayla Dawn, April Renae. BS in Biology, Bethany Nazarene Coll., 1965. Ops. mgr. Stemen Labs., Visalia, Calif., 1965-67; botanist Internat. Biologicals Inc., Oklahoma City, 1967-72; owner, founder Aero-Allergen Labs., Carthage, Mo., 1972-80, exec. v.p., chief ops. officer Allergon Inc., subs. Pharmaç ia Diagnostics, Uppsala, Sweden, 1980-85; owner, founder Interstate Flor-All, Joplin, Mo., 1985-87. Recipient Outstanding Alumni award Bethany Nazarene Coll., 1981. Republican. Inventor field vacuum for collecting pollens in large quantities; inventor methods for particle sizing and separation of pollens.

GIBBS, GRAHAM JOHN, electronics executive; b. Chelmsford, Essex, Eng., Aug. 29, 1945; s. Frederick Earnest and Ivy Maud (Tokely) G.; m. Christina Ann Greenwood, May 20, 1973; children: Zanna, Amy. Student, Mid Essex, Chelmsford, 1967. Engr. The Marconi Co., Basildon, Essex, 1967-72; applications engr. Can. Marconi Co., Montreal, 1972-77, mktg. mgr., 1977-78, product mgr. navigation, 1978-82, product mgr. avionics, 1982-83, group mgr. avionics, 1983-86, sr. group mgr., 1986—. Contbr. articles to profl. jours. Mem. Internat. Omega Assn. (bd. dirs. 1974-87, pres. 1985-87), Inst. Electronic Radio Engrs. (chartered 1967), Aerospace Industries Assn. Can. Anglican. Club: Aquadyne Scuba (bd. dirs. 1973-76). Home: 495 Grosvenor, Westmount, PQ Canada H3Y 2S5 Office: Can Marconi Co, 2442 Trenton Ave, Montreal, PQ Canada H3P 1Y9

GIBBS, JAMES ALANSON, geologist; b. Wichita Falls, Tex., June 18, 1935; s. James Ford and Clovis (Robinson) G.; m. Judith Walker, June 18, 1966; children: Ford W., John A. BS, U. Okla., 1957, MS, 1962. Cert. profl. geologist. Geologist Calif. Co., New Orleans, 1961-63, Lafayette, La., 1963-64; cons. geologist, oil producer, Dallas, 1964—; owner, chief exec. officer Five States Energy Co., 1987—. Served with USNR, 1957-59. Mem. Geol. Soc. Am., Dallas Geol. Soc. (past pres.), Am. Assn. Petroleum Geologists (past sec.), Am. Inst. Profl. Geol. Am., Ind. Petroleum Assn. Am., Tex. Ind. Producers and Royalty Owners Assn., Dallas Geophys. Soc., Geol. Info. Library of Dallas (v.p.), Soc. Ind. Profl. Earth Scientists (past pres. Dallas chpt.), Sigma Xi, Sigma Gamma Epsilon, Phi Delta Theta, Petroleum Engrs. Clubs: Dallas Petroleum, Explorers. Republican. Methodist. Home: 3514 Caruth Blvd Dallas TX 75225 Office: 1106 One Energy Sq Dallas TX 75206

GIBBS, JAMES WENRICH, retired glass company executive; b. Canton, Ohio, Dec. 12, 1915; s. Alvin J. and Eva A. (Wenrich) G.; m. Mary Jewel Hellwig, Apr. 12, 1941; children: Sandra Ann Gibbs Chambers, Stephen V., David S. (dec.). BA, Yale U., 1938; postgrad. U. Mich., 1938-39, U. Pa., 1939-40; D of Horological History, Clayton (Mo.) U., 1980. Asst. to pres. Safetee Glass Co., Inc., Phila., 1940-41, v.p., 1942-67, pres. 1967-71, vice chmn. bd., 1971, also bd. dirs. Mem. adv. com. Med. Coll. Pa.; trustee Am. Clock and Watch Mus., Bristol, Conn. Author: The Dueber-Hampden Story, 1954, The Life and Death of the Ithaca Calendar Clock Company, 1960, Buckeye Horology, 1970, Shaker Clockmakers, Dixie Clockmakers, Pennsylvania Clocks and Watches: Antique Timepieces and Their Makers, From Springfield to Moscow: The Complete Dueber Hampden Story, 1986; also articles. Fellow Royal Soc. Arts, Nat. Assn. Watch and Clock Collectors (Silver Star fellow); mem. Colonial Soc. Pa., Colonial Soc. Mass., Soc. of Mayflower Descs., St. Nicholas Soc., Pa. Soc. Colonial Wars, Cleve. Grays, Colonial Order of Acorn, Dutch Colonial Soc. Del., Ky. Cols., Order of Lafayette, Sovereign Mil. Order Temple Jerusalem, SR, SAR, Vet. Corps Arty., Royal Soc. St. George, Nat. Soc. Sons Colonial New Eng., Newcomen Soc., Nat. Soc. Old Plymouth Colony Descs., Am. Def. Preparedness Assn., Huguenot Soc. Pa., Pa. Hist. Soc., Pilgrim John Howland Soc., Sons St. George, Sons Union Vets. N.J., Valley Forge Hist. Soc., Penn Club, Sons Daus. of Pilgrim Soc., Order Ams. of Armorial Ancestry, Hereditary Order Descs. of Colonial Govs., Order of Descs. Colonial Physicians Chirugiens. Address: 3201 W Coulter St Philadelphia PA 19129

GIBBS, L(IPPMAN) MARTIN, lawyer; b. N.Y.C., Feb. 27, 1938; s. Harold and Shirley (Marks) G.; m. Dona Lynn Fagg, May 3, 1968; 1 child, Bradford. AB, Brown U., 1959; JD, Columbia U., 1962. Bar: N.Y. 1963, D.C. 1963. Atty. Port of N.Y. Authority, N.Y.C., 1963-64; assoc. Weiner, Neuberger & Sive, N.Y.C., 1964-65, Spear & Hill, N.Y.C., 1966-69; assoc. Finley, Kumble, Wagner, Heine & Underberg, N.Y.C., 1969-72, ptnr., 1972-80; pres. L. Martin Gibbs, P.C., 1981-87; ptnr. Rogers and Wells, N.Y.C., 1987—; arbitrator Am. Arbitration Assn., 1967—; bd. dirs. 1st Repub. Bancorp. Inc., Fin. Security Assurance of Iowa, Inc., Fin. Security Assurance of Okla., Inc. Regional dir. United Fund Drive of Rye, 1979. Served with USAR, 1962-63. Mem. ABA, Assn. Bar City of N.Y., N.Y. State Bar Assn. Unitarian. Clubs: N.Y. Yacht, Univ., Fishers Island Yacht, Hay Harbor. Home: 8 Woodland Dr Rye NY 10580 Office: Rogers & Wells 200 Park Ave Pan Am Bldg New York NY 10166

GIBBY, MABEL ENID KUNCE, psychologist; b. St. Louis, Mar. 30, 1926; d. Ralph Waldo and Mabel Enid (Warren) Kunce; student Washington U., St. Louis, 1943-44, postgrad., 1955-56; B.A., Park Coll., 1945; M.A., McCormick Theol. Sem., 1947; postgrad. Columbia U., 1948, U. Kansas City, 1949, George Washington U., 1953; M.Ed., U. Mo., 1951, Ed.D., 1952; m. John Francis Gibby, Aug. 27, 1948; children—Janet Marie (Mrs. Kim Williams), Harold Steven, Helen Elizabeth, Diane Louise, John Andrew, Keith Sherridan, Daniel Jay. Dir. religious edn. Westport Presbyn. Ch. Kansas City, Mo., 1947-49; tchr. elementary schs., Kansas City, 1949-50; high sch. counselor Arlington (Va.) Pub. Schs., 1952-54; counselor adult counseling services Washington U., 1955-56; counseling psychologist Coral Gables (Fla.) VA Hosp., 1956—; counseling psychologist Miami (Fla.) VA Hosp., 1956—, chief counseling psychology sect., 1982-86; sr. psychologist Office Disability Determination Fla. Hdqrs., 1987—. Sec. bd. dirs. Fla. Vocat. Rehab. Found. Recipient Meritorious Service citation Fla. C. of C., 1965, President's Com. on Employment of Handicapped, 1965; commendation for meritorious service Com. on Employment of Physically Handicapped Dade County, 1965, 81, named outstanding rehab. profl., 1966, 81; named Profl. Fed. Employee of Year, Greater Miami Fed. Exec. Council, 1966; Outstanding Fed. Service award Greater Miami Fed. Exec. Council, 1966; Fed. Woman's award U.S. Civil Service Commn., 1968, Community Headliner award Theta Sigma Phi, 1968, Outstanding Alumni award Park Coll., 1968, Freedom award The Chosen Few, Korean War Vets. Assn., 1986; certificate of appreciation Bur. Customs, U.S. Treasury Dept., 1969, Fla. Dept. Health and Rehab. Services, 1970. Mem. Am., Dade County (past sec.) psychol. assns., Nat., Fla. (past dir. Dade County chpt.) rehab. assns., Nat. Rehab. Counseling Assn. (past sec.). Patentee in field. Home: 10260 SW 56th St Miami FL 33165

GIBNEY, FRANK BRAY, publisher, editor, writer, foundation executive; b. Scranton, Pa., Sept. 21, 1924; s. Joseph James and Edna May (Wetter) G.; m. Harriet Harvey, Dec. 10, 1948 (div. 1957); children: Alex, Margot; m. Harriet C. Suydam, Dec. 14, 1957 (div. 1971); children: Frank, James, Thomas; m. Hiroko Doi, Oct. 5, 1972; children: Elise, Josephine. BA, Yale U., 1945; DLitt (hon.), Kyung Hee U., Seoul, Korea, 1974. Corr., assoc. editor Time mag., N.Y.C., Tokyo and London, 1947-54; sr. editor Newsweek, N.Y.C., 1954-57; staff writer, editorial writer Life mag., N.Y.C., 1957-61; pub., pres. SHOW mag., N.Y.C., 1961-64; pres. Ency. Brit. (Japan), Tokyo, 1965-69; pres. TBS-Brit., Tokyo, 1969-75, vice chmn., 1976—; v.p. Ency. Brit., Inc., Chgo., 1975-79; vice chmn., bd. editors Ency. Brit., Chgo., 1978—; pres. Pacific Basin Inst., Santa Barbara, Calif., 1979; adj. prof. Far Eastern studies U. Calif., Santa Barbara, 1986—; bd. dirs. Hudson Reports Internat., Paris, 1981—; cons. Com. on Space and Aero Ho. of Reps., Washington, 1957-59; vice chmn. Japan-U.S. Friendship Commn., 1984—, U.S.-Japan Com. on Edn. and Cultural Interchange, 1984—. Author: Five Gentlemen of Japan, 1953, The Frozen Revolution, 1959, (with Peter Deriabin) The Secret World, 1960, The Operators, 1961, The Khrushchev Pattern, 1961, The Reluctant Space Farers, 1965, Japan: The Fragile Super-Power, 1975, Miracle by Design, 1983; editor: The Penkovskiy Papers, 1965; Presdl. speech writer, 1964. Served to lt. USNR, 1942-46. Decorated Order of the Rising Sun 3d Class Japan, Order of Sacred Treasure 2d Class Japan. Mem. Council on Fgn. Relations, Tokyo Fgn. Corr. Club, Am. C.of C. (Tokyo), Japan-Am. Soc., Japan Soc. Roman Catholic. Clubs: Century Assn., Yale (N.Y.C.); Tokyo; Tavern, The Arts (Chgo.). Home: 1901 E Las Tunas Rd Santa Barbara CA 93103

GIBSON, ELISABETH JANE, principal; b. Salina, Kans., Apr. 28, 1937; d. Cloyce Wesley and Margaret Mae (Yost) Kasson; m. William Douglas Miles, Jr., Aug. 20, 1959; m. Harry Benton Gibson, Jr., July 1, 1970. A.B., Colo. State Coll., 1954-57; M.A. (fellow), San Francisco State Coll., 1967-68; Ed.D., U. No. Colo., 1978; postgrad. U. Denver, 1982. Cert. tchr., prin., Colo. Tchr. elem. schs., Santa Paula, Calif., 1957-58, Salina, Kans., 1958-63, Goose Bay, Labrador, 1963-64, Jefferson County, Colo., 1965-66, Topeka, 1966-67; diagnostic tchr. Cen. Kans. Diagnostic Remedial Edn. Ctr., Salina, 1968-70; instr. Loretto Heights Coll., Denver, 1970-72; co-owner Ednl. Cons. Enterprises, Inc., Greeley, Colo., 1974-77; resource coordinator Region VIII Resource Access Project Head Start Mile High Consortium, Denver, 1976-77; exec. dir. Colo. Fedn. Council Exceptional Children, Denver, 1976-77; asst. prof. Met. State Coll., Denver, 1979; dir. spl. edn. Northeast Colo. Bd. Coop. Edn. Services, Haxtun, Colo., 1979-82; prin. elem. jr. high sch., Elizabeth, Colo., 1982-84; prin., spl. projects coordinator Summit County Schs., Frisco, Colo., 1985—; prin. Frisco Elem. Sch., 1985—; cons. Colo. Dept. Edn., 1984-85; cons. Colo. Dept. Edn., 1984-85, Montana Dept. Edn., 1978-79, Love Pub. Co., 1976-78, Colo. Dept. Inst., 1974-75; pres. Found. Exceptional Children, 1980-81; pres. bd. dirs. Northeast Colo. Services Handicapped, 1981-82; bd. dirs. Dept. Ednl. Specialists, Colo. Assn. Sch. Execs., 1982-84; mem. Colo. Title IV Adv. Council, 1980-82; mem. Mellon Found. grant steering com. Colo. Dept. Edn., 1984-85. Mem. Colo. Dept. Edn. Data Acquisition Reporting and Utilization Com., 1983, Denver City County Commn. for Disabled, 1978-81; chmn. regional edn. com. 1970 White House Conf. Children and Youth; bd. dirs. Advocates for Victims of Assault, 1986—; mem. adv. bd. Alpine Counseling Ctr., 1986—; mem. placement alternatives commn. Dept. of Social Services, 1986—; mem. adv. com. Colo. North Cen. Assn., 1988—. Recipient Ann. Service award Colo. Fedn. Council Exceptional Children, 1981. Mem. Colo. Assn. Retarded Citizens, Assn. Supervision Curriculum Devel., Nat. Assn. Elem. Sch. Prins., Kappa Delta Pi, Pi Lambda Theta, Phi Delta Kappa. Republican. Methodist. Club: Order Eastern Star. Author: (with H. Padzensky) Goal Guide: A minicourse in writing goals and behavioral objectives for special education, 1975; (with H. Padzensky and S. Sporn) Assaying Student Behavior: A minicourse in student assessment techniques, 1974. Contbr. articles to profl. jours. Home: 2443 S Colorado Blvd Denver CO 80222 Office: Frisco Elem Sch PO Box 7 Frisco CO 80443

GIBSON, FRANCES, nurse; b. Junction, Tex., Sept. 28, 1936; d. August and Juanita (Corpus-Garcia) Rehwoldt; m. Richard Gibson, July 4, 1954 (dec. July 25, 1962); childreN; Kenneth, René, Allison. AA, East Los Angeles Coll. Lic. vocat. nurse, 1969; registered nurse 1976, operating room technician, 1971; cert. adult edn. tchr. Instr., profl. expert East Los Angeles Coll., Monterey Park, Calif., 1971-74; hostess talk show (in Spanish) Sta. KMEX-TV, Los Angeles, 1970-76; tchr. adult edn. Garvey Sch. Bd., Rosemead, Calif., 1976-77; clinical nurse Los Angeles County/U. So. Calif. Med. Ctr., 1981—; vol. nurse Lung Assn., Los Angeles, 1970-76, ARC, Los Angeles, 1969—; instr. health classes, ARC, also instr. Spanish to ARC personnel, mgr. info. booths at health fairs and conventions, provide first aid at various gatherings, immunization clinics, etc., chmn. adv. bd., 1971-72, bd. dirs., 1972-75, 80-82; med. review/legal asst. Ivie & McNeill, Los Angeles, 1986—. Author: Spanish for English-Speaking Personnel, 1972. Recipient Spotlight award ARC, 1972, Clara Barton award, 1976; named one of Ten Prettiest Chicanas in East Los Angeles, 1970. Mem. Nursing Edn. Associates, Chicana Nurses Assn., AFL CIO, ACLU, Alpha Gamma Sigma. Democrat. Roman Catholic. Home: 2241 Charlotte Ave Rosemead CA 91770

GIBSON, GERALD JOHN, physician; b. Wetherby, Yorkshire, Eng., Apr. 3, 1944; s. Maurice and Margaret (Cronin) G.; m. Mary Teresa Cunningham, Feb. 12, 1977; children: Paul Daniel, Michael John, David James. Student, St. Michaels Coll., Leeds, Eng., 1954-61; BSc in Physiology, U. London, 1965, MBBS, 1968, MD, 1976. House physician Guys Hosp., London, 1968; house surgeon neurosurgery Leeds Gen. Infirmary, 1969; house physician Hammersmith Hosp., London, 1969-70; casualty med. officer Middlesex Hosp., London, 1970; resident physician McMaster U., Hamilton, Can., 1970-71; registrar respiratory and gen. medicine Hammersmith Hosp., London, 1971-73, sr. registrar respiratory and gen. medicine, 1973-77; cons. physician, hon. clin. lectr. Freeman Hosp., Newcastle Upon Tyne, 1978—. Author: Clinical Tests of Respiratory Function, 1984, also articles to profl. and scientific jours.; co-editor: Respiratory Medicine, 1989. Fellow Royal Coll. Physicians; mem. Brit. Thoracic Soc. (hon. sec., 1986-88), Am. Thoracic Soc., Med. Research Soc., European Study for Clin. Respiratory Physiology, European Soc. Pneumology. Roman Catholic. Home: 36 High St Gosforth, Newcastle upon Tyne Ne3 1LX, England Office: Freeman Hosp, Newcastle Upon Tyne NE7 7DN, England

GIBSON, GLENN VENNING, retired government official; b. Youngstown, Ohio, May 26, 1913; s. Clair Ellis and Bessie Katherine (Blair) G.; m. Helen Marie Frederick, Sept. 3, 1938; children—Donald Wade, Carol Virginia, June Pauline. B.S., U. Ala., 1938; M.S., U. Denver, 1941. Asst. to maintenance officer USN, Fleet Air Base, Pearl Harbor, 1931-35; asst. dean men U. Ala., 1938; research asst. Chgo. Civic Fedn. and Bur. Pub. Efficiency, 1941; asst. to dep. dir. gen. for field ops. WPB, 1942; dir. program analysis div. Office Naval Fiscal Dir., 1946, chief budget estimates div. Navy Dept., 1947-49; asst. budget dir. Dept. Def., 1950-54, dep. comptroller, budget dir., 1954-55, spl. asst. sec. def., 1956, dir. planning and requirements policy Office Asst. Sec. Def., Supply and Logistics, 1957-60, prin. dep. asst. sec. def. for installations and logistics, 1963-72; U.S. coordinator logistics planning NATO, 1964-75; dir. internat. logistics planning U.S. Def., 1970-72, ret., 1972; treas., dir. R.E. Grimm Co., 1975-77; cons. Dept. Def., 1972—, Nat. Bur. Standards, 1976-77; guest lectr. Maxwell Sch., U. Syracuse Grad. Sch. Bus. Adminstrn., 1958-63, George Washington U., 1958-61; dir. Vets. Coop. Housing Assn., 1948-54, pres., chmn., 1949-51; expert exam. budget adminstrs. U.S. CSC, 1949; charter mem. Pres.' Oil Policy Com. Austin Cup scholar U. Ala., 1938; Alfred P. Sloan fellow U. Denver, 1941. Author: (with M.A. Leonard) Aspects of Financial Management, City of Chicago, 1941; also fin. mgmt. chpt. to Report on Chicago Government, 1954. Served from ensign to lt. USNR, 1943-46; lt. comdr. Res. Recipient Distinguished Service award, 1961, 1st Bronze Palm, 1972. Mem. Am. Inst. CPAs, Md. Assn. CPAs, Fla. Inst. CPAs, Am. Soc. Pub. Adminstrn. (sr. adviser Washington 1958-60), Phi Eta Sigma, Beta Gamma Sigma. Presbyterian (deacon 1952—, elder).

GIBSON, JOSEPH LEE, lawyer, lecturer; b. Lufkin, Tex., Mar. 12, 1940; s. Mitchell Osler and W. Christine (Bennett) Gibson; m. Bethanna Bunn, May 27, 1983; 1 child, Mark Corbett. BA, Baylor U., 1962; LLB, Harvard U., 1965. Bar: Tex. 1965, D.C. 1967. Legis. counsel Maritime Adminstrn., Washington, 1965-66; counsel govt. activities subcom. U.S. Ho. of Reps., Washington, 1966-68; assoc. Kirkland & Ellis, and predecessor, Washington, 1968-69; ptnr. Gibson, Branham & Farmer, Washington, 1969-73; counsel Montgomery Ward & Co., Washington, 1974-78; gen. counsel Credit Union Nat. Assn., Washington, 1978-79; counsel Diplomat Nat. Bank, Washington, 1979-80, also dir.; asst. solicitor Econ. Regulatory Adminstrn., Dept. Energy, Washington, 1980 ; lectr. on equal employment in broadcasting, 1971-77, on consumer credit, privacy, electronic fund transfers, 1975—; atty. for mem. Nat. Commn. on Electronic Fund Transfers, Washington, 1976-78. Mem. various campaign and conv. staffs Democratic Party, Young Democrats, Tex. and Washington, 1965-80. Recipient Disting. Service award Maritime Adminstrn., 1966, Disting. Service award Dept. Energy, 1983. Methodist. also: 966 Towlston Rd McLean VA 22102 Office: Dept Energy Econ Regulatory Adminstrn 1000 Independence Ave NW Washington DC 20585

GIBSON, KEIKO MATSUI, writer, educator; b. Kyoto, Japan, Sept. 4, 1953; d. Yoshinobu and Masako (Katayama) Matsui; m. Morgan Gibson, Sept. 14, 1978; 1 child, Christopher So. BA, Kwansei Gakuin U., Japan, 1976; MA, U. Ill., 1983; postgrad., Ind. U., 1983-86. Instr. English ECC Lang. Inst., Osaka, Japan, 1973-79; instr. Japanese Northwestern Mich. Coll., Traverse City, 1980; assoc. instr. comparative lit. Ind. U., Bloomington, 1984-85; research asst. Krannert Art Mus. U. Ill., Champaign, 1981-83; lectr. in English Chukyo U., Nagoya and Toyota, Japan, 1987—. Author: (poems) Tremble of Morning, 1979, (with Morgan Gibson) Kokoro, 1981, Stir Up the Precipitable World, 1983; contbr. poetry and prose to profl. jours. in Japan and U.S. Speaker Peace Edn. Forum, Frankfort, Mich., 1986. Recipient Kenneth Rexroth award for poetry, 1982. Mem. Internat. Comparative Lit. Assn., Am. Comparative Lit. Assn., Japan Comparative Lit. Assn. Buddhist. Home: Shiraume-so 202, 92 Ishida Yamashita Kaizu-cho, Toyota-shi Aichi-ken 470-03, Japan

GIBSON, MELVIN ROY, pharmacognosy educator; b. St. Paul, Nebr., June 11, 1920; s. John and Jennie Irene (Harvey) G. B.S., U. Nebr., 1942, M.S., 1947, D.Sc. (hon.), 1985; Ph.D., U. Ill., 1949. Asst. prof. pharmacognosy Wash. State U., Pullman, 1949-52; assoc. prof. Wash. State U., 1952-55, prof., 1955-85, prof. emeritus, 1985—. Editor: Am. Jour. Pharm. Edn, 1956-61; editorial bd., co-author: Remington's Pharm. Sci, 1970, 75, 80, 85; editor, co-author: Studies of a Pharm. Curriculum, 1967; author over 100 articles. Served as arty. officer AUS, 1942-46. Decorated Bronze star, Purple Heart; sr. vis. fellow Orgn. for Econ. Cooperation and Devel., Royal Pharm. Inst., Stockholm, Sweden and U. Leiden (Holland), 1962; recipient Rufus A. Lyman award, 1972, Wash. State U. Faculty Library award, 1984; named Wash. State U. Faculty Mem. of Yr., 1985. Founder, charter mem. Am. Diplomates in Pharmacy.; fellow AAAS; assoc. fellow Am. Coll. Apothecaries; mem. N.Y. Acad. Sci., Am. Pharm. Assn., Am. Soc. Pharmacognosy (pres. 1964-65), Am. Assn. Coll. Pharmacy (exec. com. 1961-63, bd. dirs. 1977-79, chmn. council of faculties 1975-76, pres. 1979-80, Disting. Educator award 1984), U.S. Pharmacopeia (revision com. 1970-75), Am. Found. Pharm. Edn. (hon. life, bd. dirs. 1980-85, exec. com. 1981-85, vice chmn. 1982-85), AAUP, Acad. Pharm. Sci., Am. Public Health Assn., Fedn. Internat. Pharm., Am. Inst. History of Pharmacy, Am. Acad. Polit. and Social Sci., Sigma Xi, Kappa Psi (Nat. Service citation 1961), Rho Chi, Phi Kappa Phi, Omicron Delta Kappa. Democrat. Presbyterian. Club: Spokane. Home: W 707 6th Ave Apt 41 Spokane WA 99204

GIBSON, MICHAEL FRANCIS, writer, art critic; b. Brussels, Belgium, July 18, 1929; arrived in France, 1958; s. Hugh Simons and Ynès (Reyntiens) G.; m. Odile Geoffroy, Mar. 22, 1969 (div. 1976); children: Emmanuel, Marguerite; m. Monika Truszkowska, Apr. 23, 1977; children: Matthew, Olivia. MA, U. Louvain, Belgium, 1951; PhD, U. Paris, 1987. Founder, dir. Coll. Musical Trie, Trie-la-Ville, France, 1963-68; art critic Internat. Herald-Tribune, Paris, 1969—; lectr. Am. Ctr. Students Artists, Paris; producer Radio-Can., Paris, 1969-79, France-Culture, Paris, 1980—. Author: Pieter Bruegel, 1980, Les Symbolistes, 1984, Les Horizons du Possible, 1984, The Symbolists, 1988, Alexander Calder, 1988; contbr. articles to profl. jours. Active UNESCO (program coordinator for project financed by Internat. Fund Devel. Culture, 1986—). Served with U.S. Army 1951-53. Mem. NAACP (life), Internat. Assn. Art Critics (program coordinator 1986—). Democrat. Home: 34 Rue de Flandre, 75019 Paris France

GIBSON, MORGAN, writer, educator; b. Cleve., June 6, 1929; came to Japan, 1987; s. George Miles and Elizabeth (Leeper) G.; m. Barbara Ann Brown, Sept. 1, 1950 (div. 1972); children: Julia Mary, Lucy Alice; m. Keiko Matsui, Sept. 14, 1978; 1 child, Christopher So. BA, Oberlin (Ohio) Coll., 1950; MA, U. Iowa, 1952, PhD, 1959. Ind. author 1950—; asst. prof. English, humanities Wayne State U., Detroit, 1954-58; asst. prof. English Am. Internat. Coll., Springfield, Mass., 1959-61; asst. to assoc. prof. U. Wis., Milw., 1961-72; chmn. grad. faculty Goddard Coll., 1972-75; prof. English Chukyo U., Nagoya and Toyota, Japan, 1987—; vis. prof. English, Am. lit. Osaka (Japan) U., 1975-79, Ehime U., Matsuyama, Japan, 1976; vis. prof. creative writing Mich. State U. Extension, Traverse City, 1979; vis. prof. Am. lit. Matsuyama U., 1983; vis. prof. comparative lit. U. Ill., 1982. Poetry editor Arts in Soc., 1965-72; pub. Great Lakes Books, Milw., 1967-68; author: (with Barbara Gibson) Our Bedroom's Underground, 1962, Mayors of Marble, 1966, Stones Glow Like Lovers' Eyes, 1970, Crystal Sunlake, 1971, Kenneth Rexroth, 1972, Dark Summer, 1977, Wakeup, 1978, Speaking of Light, 1979, (with Keiko Matsui Gibson) Kokoro: Heart-Mind, 1980, The Great Brook Book, 1981, (with Hiroshi Murakami) Tantric Poetry of Kukai (Kobo Daishi) Japan's Buddhist Saint, 1987, Revolutionary Rexroth: Poet of East-West Wisdom, 1986, Among Buddhas in Japan, 1988; contbr. poems, essays, articles, autobiographies, revs. and plays to anthologies, profl. jours. worldwide. Grantee U. Wis., 1967-69, U. Ill. Ctr. for Advanced Study, 1982. Mem. PEN Am. Ctr., MLA, Japan Comparative Lit. Assn., Poetry Soc. Am., Buddhist Peace Fellowship. Office: Chukyo U 9 Bldg Kyoyobu, 101 Tokotate Kaiuzu-cho, Toyota-shi Aichi-ken 470-03, Japan

GIBSON, PAUL RAYMOND, international trade and investment development executive; b. Cathay, Calif., Apr. 10, 1924; s. Otto and Louella (Vestal) G.; m. Janice Elizabeth Carter, Dec. 19, 1952; children—Scott C., Paula S. B.S. in Internat. Commerce, Sch. Fgn. Service Georgetown U., 1956. Export mgr. Asia Philip Morris Co., San Francisco, 1952-54; founder, v.p., gen. mgr. McGregor and Werner Internat. Corp., Washington, 1954-62, v.p., dir. McGregor and Werner Corp., 1955-62; v.p. fin. Parsons & Whittemore, Inc., N.Y.C., 1962-65; founder, pres. Paul R. Gibson and Assocs., Washington, 1965-70; mng. dir. Black Clawson Pacific Co., Sydney, Australia, 1970-72; pres. Envirotech Asia Pacific, Sydney, 1972-74, pres. Envirotech Internat., Menlo Park, Calif., 1975-80; founder, pres. INTERACT, Burlingame, Calif., 1980—; pres. The Manchester Group, Ltd., Washington, 1987—. dir. Eimco K.C.P., Ltd., India. Mem. Pacific Basin Econ. Council v.p. program and vice chmn. govt. liaison U.S. Sect., 1976—; trustee World Affairs Council No. Calif., 1978—; mem. San Francisco Com. Foreign Relations, 1980—. Served to sgt. USMC, 1941-45. Mem. U.S. C. of C. (chmn. Asia-Pacific council Am. C. of C. 1974, mem. adv. com. 1975—). Clubs: Internat. (Washington); Am. Nat. (Sydney, Australia); Sharon Heights Golf and Country (Menlo Park, Calif.). Home: #9 Brent Ct Menlo Park CA 94025 Office: INTERACT 1350 Old Bayshore Hwy Suite 750 Burlingame CA 94010

GIBSON, RAY ALLEN, obstetrician and gynecologist; b. Webster County, Ky., Jan. 15, 1941; s. Curtis Ray and Mildred J. (Allen) G.; B.S., Berea Coll., 1962; M.D., U. Louisville, 1968; m. Nancy Sue Bailey, Nov. 28, 1963; 1 dau., Rachel Janel. Intern, U. Louisville Hosps., 1968-69, resident in obstetrics and gynecology, 1969-72; sr. obstetrician-gynecologist Howard Clinic, Glasgow, Ky., 1974-82; chief of staff T.J. Samson Hosp., Glasgow, 1976, dir. med. edn., 1976-82. Deacon, Glasgow Bapt. Ch.; bd. dirs. Ky. div. Am. Cancer Soc., 1983-84. Served with U.S. Army, 1972-74. Diplomate Am. Bd. Obstetrics and Gynecology. Mem. Ky. Med. Assn., Barren County Med. Soc., Am. Coll. Obstetricians and Gynecologists, Am. Fertility Soc., So. Seminar Obstetrics and Gynecology, Ky. Ob-Gyn Soc. (pres. 1983-84), Glasgow C. of C. Club: Masons (32 deg). Home: 530 Horton Rigdon Rd Cave City KY 42127 Office: 120 State Ave Glasgow KY 42141

GIBSON, RICHARD WILLIAM, agriculturalist; b. Wisbech, Cambridgeshire, Eng., May 27, 1947; s. Arthur William and Margaret Bowerman (Moore) G.; m. Penelope Anne; 1 child, Thomas, William. BS in zoology, U. Bristol, Eng., 1968, PhD in Agriculture, 1971. Research scientist Rothamsted Exptl. Sta., Harpenden, Hertsfordshire, Eng., 1971—. Mem. Assn. Applied Biologists (convener of virology group). Office: Rothamsted Exptl Sta, Harpenden, Hertsfordshire AL5 2JQ, England

GIBSON, ROBERT RODNEY, finance executive, bank consultant; b. Athens, Ohio, Feb. 6, 1945; s. Robert Bradbury and Frances (Gilkey) G.; m. Anne Reed, Aug. 22, 1970; 1 child, Robin Elise. Student Ohio U., 1963-65, Franklin U., 1978. Regional dir. St. Jude Children's Hosp., Memphis, 1972-76; with Graham Ford Leasing, Columbus, Ohio, 1976-78; dir. leasing services Hills Leasing, Columbus, 1978-81; pres., founder Gibson Leasing Corp., Columbus, 1981-86, BancNet Corp., Columbus, 1984-86; asst. v.p., regional sales mgr. Huntington Nat. Bank, Columbus, 1987—; bank cons. Deacon, trustee Overbrook Presbyterian Ch., Columbus, 1981-84. Served with USN, 1965-69. Recipient meritorious service award City of Columbus Div. Fire, 1978. Mem. Cen. Ohio Sch. Diving (instr.). Republican. Avocations: scuba diving, power boating. Home: 4210 Reed Rd Upper Arlington OH 43220

GIBSON, SAM THOMPSON, internist, educator; b. Covington, Ga., Jan. 1, 1916; s. Count Dillon and Julia (Thompson) G.; m. Alice Chase, Oct. 31, 1942 (dec. Jan. 1971); children: Lena S., Stephen C., Judith Gibson Hammer, Lucy F.; m. Madge L. Crouch, Sept. 20, 1986. B.S. in Chemistry, Ga. Inst. Tech., 1936; M.D., Emory U., 1940. Diplomate: Am. Bd. Internal Medicine. Med. house officer Peter Bent Brigham Hosp., Boston, 1940-41, asst. resident medicine, 1946-47, asst. medicine, 1947-49; research fellow medicine Harvard Med. Sch., 1941-42, spl. research asso., 1943, Milton fellow medicine, 1947-49; asso. medicine George Washington U. Med. Sch., also George Washington U. Hosp., 1949-63, asst. clin. prof. medicine, 1963—; clin. asst. prof. medicine Uniformed Services U. Health Scis., 1980—; asst. med. dir. ARC Blood Program, 1949-51, asso. med. dir., 1951-53, asso. dir., 1953-56, dir., 1956-66; sr. med. officer ARC, 1957-67; asst. dir. div. biologics standards NIH, 1967-72; asst. dir. Bur. of Biologics, FDA, Bethesda, Md., 1972-74; asst. to dir. Bur. Biologics, FDA, Bethesda, Md., 1974-77, dir. div. biologics evaluation, 1977-83; dir. div. biol. product compliance Ctr. for Drugs and Biologics, 1983-85; assoc. dir. sci. and tech. Office of Compliance, Ctr. Drugs and Biologics, FDA, 1985—; cons. blood Naval Med. Sch., Nat. Naval Med. Center, Bethesda, 1950-63; mem. med. adv. bd. CARE-Medico, 1962-70, cons., 1970—; chmn. U.S. com. for tranfusion equipment for med. use Am. Standards Assn., 1954-66, tech. adv. group transfusion equipment for med. use Nat. Commn. Clin. Lab. Standards/Am. Nat. Standards Inst., 1975—; adviser orgn. blood transfusion services League Red Cross Socs., 1955-66. Contbg. editor: Vox Sanguinis Jour. Blood Transfusion, 1956-65; mem. adv. bd., 1965-76. Served from lt. (j.g.) to comdr., M.C. USNR, 1941-46; capt. Res. ret. Mem. AMA, AAAS, Internat., Am. socs. hematology, Nat. Health Council (dir. 1957-60, 61-64), Internat. Soc. Blood Transfusion (regional counselor 1962-66), Am. Fedn. Clin. Research, N.Y. Acad. Scis., Delta Tau Delta, Alpha Kappa Kappa, Alpha Chi Sigma, Tau Beta Pi, Phi Kappa Phi, Omicron Delta Kappa, Alpha Omega Alpha. Home: 5801 Rossmore Dr Bethesda MD 20814 Office: Ctr Drugs and Biologics FDA Rockville MD 20857

GIBSON, WILLIAM CHARLES, county government parks and recreation official; b. Midland, Mich., July 26, 1944; s. Harold David Gibson and Erma Elizabeth (Emrich) Westfall; m. Karen Marie Jarmol, Oct. 5, 1974. Student Mich. Technol. U., 1962-63, U. Mich., 1963-65; B.S. with high honors, Mich. State U., 1972. Registered parks and recreation profl., Mich. Dir. parks and recreation City of Mason, Mich., 1972-74; supt. parks County of Midland, 1974-78, dept. dir. parks and recreation, 1978-83, dir. parks and recreation, 1983—. Chmn., County of Midland Employees Safety Com., 1983, 84; mem. Midland Found., 1984—, chmn. various coms., 1985—. Mich. Recreation and Parks Assn. scholar, 1971, 72; trustee Midland Found., 1987—. Mem. Nat. Recreation and Parks Assn. (cert. profl.), Mich. Assn. County Park and Recreation Ofcls., Mich. Recreation and Parks Assn. (park resources com. 1980—, chmn. 1982-83, bd. dirs. 1982-83, long-range planning com. 1983-86), Midland Area C. of C., Mich. State U. Coll. Agr. and Natural Resources Alumni Assn. (bd. dirs. 1985—), Alpha Zeta. Presbyterian. Lodge: Elks. Avocations: golf, scuba diving, tennis, listening to music, woodworking. Home: 5708 Drake St Midland MI 48640 Office: Midland County Dept County Devel 1270 James Savage Rd Midland MI 48640

GIBSON, WILLIAM EDWIN, mining engineer; b. Weeksbury, Ky., Sept. 16, 1930; s. Edwin Joseph and Irene (Depew) G.; B.S. in Mining Engring., Va. Poly. Inst., 1955; m. Gwenda Jean Wicker, Dec. 15, 1954; children—James Edwin, Barbara Ann, Deborah Irene. Indsl. engr. U.S. Steel Co., Lynch, Ky., 1956-62; mining engr. Evans Elkhorn Coal Corp., Wayland, Ky., 1964-66; indsl. engr. Eastern Coal Corp., Stone, Ky., 1962-64, mining engr., 1966-70; mining engr. Ky. Carbon Corp., Phelps, 1970-74, Beth Elkhorn Corp., Jenkins, Ky., 1974-77, Va. Iron, Coal & Coke Co., Coeburn, 1978-82, Branham and Baker Coal Co., Prestonsburg, Ky., 1982-85, William E. Gibson and Assocs., 1985—. Registered profl. engr. Mem. Nat., Ky., Va., W.Va. socs. profl. engrs., AIME. Club: Masons. Office: 596 Elkhorn Ave PO Box 179 Jenkins KY 41537

GIBSON, WILLIAM LEE, manufacturing company executive; b. Newark, Dec. 1, 1949; s. Joseph Wilton Gibson and Margaret (Reynolds) Gibson Leavens; stepson William Barry Leavens, Jr.; BA in Chemistry, Bucknell U., 1972, BS in Chem. Engring., 1972; postgrad. Harvard Bus. Sch., 1977; MBA NYU, 1987; m. Lorraine Wrightson Besch, July 10, 1982. With Bur. Solid Waste Mgmt., EPA, Cin., 1970-71; chemist Dow Chem. Co., Midland, Mich., 1972-75; mktg. cons. Westvaco, Charleston, S.C., 1976; sales rep. Diamond Shamrock Co., Cleve., 1977-79; market devel. specialist strategic planning and ventures operation, plastics bus. div. Gen. Electric Co., Pittsfield, Mass., 1979-81; mktg. programs mgr. Allied-Signal Corp., Morristown, N.J., 1981-86, mgr. tech. and bus. devel., 1986—. Trustee Hartford Family Found. Mem. Soc. Automotive Engrs., Soc. Plastic Engrs., Harvard Bus. Sch. Club N.Y., Mensa, Kappa Sigma (pres. Alpha Phi chpt.). Club: Toastmasters (exec. officer). Home: 8 Lone Oak Rd Basking Ridge NJ 07920 Office: Box 2332 R Morristown NJ 07960

GICHON, MORDECHAI, archaeologist, historian, educator; b. Berlin, Aug. 16, 1922; arrived in Israel, 1934; s. Nahum and Charlotte (Salomon) Gichermann; m. Chava Renate Goldberg, June 27, 1948; children: Eran Zeev, Arion Ramit, Eyal Nahum. Grad., Ben Yehuda Coll., Tel Aviv, 1941; MA, Hebrew U., Jerusalem, 1956, PhD, 1975; grad., Israel Staff Command Coll., Gelilot, 1959. Asst. dir. intelligence, research Israeli Armed Forces, Jerusalem, 1949-55, dir. sch. strategic intelligence, 1955-57; head chair mil. history Tel Aviv U., 1962-65, sr. lectr. archaeology, 1965-71, assoc. prof., 1971-80, prof., 1980—; chmn. Israel Roman Milestone Com., Tel Aviv, 1970—; vis. fellow Archeology Inst. Oxford U., Wolfson Coll., Oxford, Eng., Birmingham U., Eng., Inst. Jewish Studies, Oxford, 1968-87. Author: Carta's Atlas of the Military History of Israel, 1969, 2d rev. edit., 1975, (with H. Herzog) Battles of the Bible, 1978; contbr. articles to profl. jours. Bd. dirs. The Israel Germany Assn., Tel Aviv. Served to lt. col. Israeli Armed Forces, 1947-62. Recipient Sukenik Prize for Archaeology, Hebrew U., 1956. Fellow Soc. Antiquaries; mem. Israel Exploration Soc. (council mem.), Israel Soc. Mil. History (bd. dirs. 1986—), Israel Assn. for Classical Studies, Deutsches Archaeologisches Inst. Club: Explorer. Lodge: Rotary. Home: Zahala, Tel Aviv 69083, Israel Office: Tel Aviv U, Ramat Aviv, Tel Aviv Israel

GIDAL, NACHUM TIM, picture historian, photographer; b. Munich, Germany, 1909; came to Israel, 1970; s. Abraham and Pauline (Eiba) G.; m. Sonia Epstein, July 4, 1944 (div.); 1 child, Peter Emmanuel; m. 2d, Pia Lis, Sept. 4, 1980. Ph.D. in History, Internat. Law and Econs. Free-lance photographer, 1929-70; lectr. New Sch. for Social Research, N.Y.C., 1954-58; sr. lectr. social scis. Hebrew U., Jerusalem, 1971-73, research sr. lectr., 1973-77, vis. prof., 1986-87; guest prof., Germany and Eng.; hon. cons. Israel Mus., Jerusalem, 1972—; adv. bd. History of Photography, Pa. State U., 1979—. Co-author and photographer: My Village Series, 1956-70; author: Origin and Development of Modern Photojournalism, 1973; Eternal Jerusalem, 19th Century, 1980; Land of Promise, 1984; Jews in Germany from Roman Times to 1933, 1988; and others. Served to capt. Brit. Army, 1942-45. Recipient Kavlin prize for Creative Photography, Writing and Lecturing Israel Mus., 1979; Dr. Erich Salomon prize for Outstanding Achievements and Pioneering Work in Photojournalism Deutsche Gesellschaft fur Photography, 1983. Fellow Royal Photographic Soc.; corr. mem. Deutsche Gesellschaft fur Photographie. Pioneer in modern photojournalism.

GIDCUMB, LANCE EDWARD, lawyer; b. Harrisburg, Ill., Oct. 5, 1950; s. Charles F. and Barbara A. (Bigelow) G.; m. Candice Harper, Jan. 29, 1972; children—Kelly, Shaun. B.S. in Edn., Ill. State U., 1972; J.D., Baylor U., 1975. Bar: Tex. 1975, U.S. Mil. Appeals 1975, Alaska 1978, U.S. Ct. Appeals (9th cir.) 1979, U.S. Supreme Ct. 1979. Assoc. Groh, Eggers, Anchorage, 1979-81, ptnr., 1981—; guest lectr. Anchorage Sch. Dist., 1983-84. Negotiator, gen. counsel Kenai Natives Assn., Inc., Alaska, 1983—; lobbyist Tesoro Alaska Petroleum Corp., Alaska Land Title Assn., 1983—. Served to capt. JAGC, USAF, 1975-79. Mem. ABA (mil. law com. 1975-79, litigation, tort and ins. practice sects.), Assn. Trial Lawyers Am., Nat. Assn. R.R. Trial Counsel, Tex. Bar Assn., Alaska Bar Assn., Anchorage Bar Assn. Lodge: Masons. Home: 2530 Brittany Dr Anchorage AK 99504 Office: Groh Eggers & Price 550 W 7th St Suite 1250 Anchorage AK 99501

GIDDINGS, PHILIP GEORGE HERBERT, electrical engineer; b. Montreal, Que., Can., Sept. 7, 1955; s. George Herbert and Juliette (Girard) G.; m. Nicole Hugente Filiatrault, July 10, 1982. BEE, McGill U., Montreal, 1979. Registered profl. eng. Jr. engr. Strand Century Ltd., Toronto, Ont., Can., 1979-80; project engr. Intercontinental Communication Services, St. Catarines, Ont., 1980-81, Engineered Sound Systems, Toronto, 1981-83; chief engr. Gerr Electro Acoustics Ltd., Toronto, 1983-88; pvt. practice cons. engr. 1988—. Mem. Audio Engr. Soc. (chmn. Toronto 1984, treas. 1985), Soc. Motion Picture & TV Engrs., Can. Acoustical Soc. Home and Office: 16 Wilkins Ave, Toronto, ON Canada M5A-3C3

GIDLEY, (GUSTAVUS) MICK, American literature educator; b. Southhampton, Eng., Mar. 1, 1941; s. Gustavus and Doris (Boulton) G.; m. Nancy Rebecca Gordon, Oct. 17, 1964; children: Ruth Mayen, Benjamin Peter. BA, U. Manchester, Eng., 1963; MA, U. Chgo., 1966; PhD, U. Sussex, Eng., 1976. Sr. English tchr. Vol. Service Overseas Agy. Meml. Coll., Arochuku, Nigeria, 1963-65; fellow Am. studies U. Sussex, 1969-70; from lectr. to sr. lectr. Am. lit. U. Exeter, Eng., 1971—; dir. Ctr. for Am. and Commonwealth Arts and Studies, Exeter, 1984—; vis. prof. San Diego State U., 1985. Author: With One Sky Above Us, 1979, Kopet, 1981, American Photography, 1983; editor: The Vanishing Race, 1976. Am. studies fellow Am. Council Learned Socs., 1976. British Labor Party. Office: U Exeter, Queens Bldg, Exeter EX4 4QH, England

GIELEN, MICHAEL ANDREAS, conductor; b. Dresden, Germany, July 20, 1927; s. Josef and Rose (Steuermann) G.; m. Helga Augsten, May 20, 1957; children: Claudia, Lucas. Student, U. Dresden, 1936, U. Berlin, 1937, U. Vienna, 1940, Buenos Aires U., 1950. Coach, Teatro Colón, Buenos Aires, 1947-50; condr., Vienna State Opera, 1950-60, Stockholm Royal Opera, 1960-65; free lance condr., Cologne, Germany, 1965-68; mus. dir., Belgian Nat. Orch., Brussels, 1969-73; chief comdr., Netherlands Opera, 1973-75; music dir., gen. mgr., Frankfurt (Germany) Opera House, 1977-87; music dir., Cin. Symphony Orch., 1980-86; prin. guest condr., BBC Symphony Orch., London; guest condr., Washington Nat. Symphony, Chgo. Symphony, Pitts. Symphony, Minn. Orch., Detroit Symphony, others; chief condr. SWF Radio Orch., Baden-Baden, Fed. Republic of Germany, 1986—. Composer: 4 Gedichte von Stefan George, 1958, Variations for 40 Instruments, 1959, Un dia Sobresale, 1963, die glocken sind auffalscher spur, 1969, Mitbestimmunes Modell, 1974. also: care SW German Radio, D-7570 Baden-Baden Federal Republic of Germany Address: care Ingpen & Williams Ltd, 14 Kensington Ct, London W8 5DN, England *

GIELGUD, SIR (ARTHUR) JOHN, actor, director; b. London, Apr. 14, 1904; s. Frank and Kate (Terry-Lewis) G. Student, Hillside Godalming, 1913-18, Westminster Sch., 1918-20, Lady Benson, 1920-21, Royal Acad. Dramatic Art, 1922-23; LLD (hon.), U. St. Andrews, 1950, U. London, 1977; LittD (hon.), Oxford (Eng.) U., 1953. Established repertory theater in London, 1938, Haymarket, 1943-44. Shakespearean roles include Hamlet, 1929, 30, 34, 36, 37, 39, 44, Richard II, 1929, 38, Macbeth, 1929, 42, Mark Antony in Julius Caesar, 1929, Hotspur in Henry IV, 1930, Malvolio in Twelfth Night, 1930, Shylock in The Merchant of Venice, 1938; achieved first London success as Lewis Dodd in The Constant Nymph, 1926, other stage appearances in The Good Companions, 1930, Musical Chairs, 1931, Richard of Bordeaux, 1932, School for Scandal, 1938, Dear Octopus, 1939, The Importance of Being Earnest, 1930, 39-40, 43, Love for Love, Eng. and U.S.A., 1942-44, 47, The Duchess of Malfi, 1944, Crime and Punishment, London, 1946, Medea, U.S.A., 1947-48, The Return of the Prodigal, 1948, Much Ado About Nothing, 1949, 52, 55, N.Y.C. and Boston, 1959, Ages of Man, 1959, 63, Australia and New Zealand, 1963-64, Othello, 1961, as Gaev in Cherry Orchard, Broadway, 1961, Aldwych, London, 1962, as Julian in Tiny Alice, N.Y.C., 1964-65 (Della Austrian medal Drama League of N.Y. 1965), at Stratford-On-Avon Festival in Measure for Measure, Julius Ceasar, Much Ado About Nothing, King Lear, 1950, A Winter's Tale, 1951, The Best of Friends, 1988; also toured in King Lear with Stratford-On-Avon Co., London and other locations, 1955; dir., actor in Nude With a Violin, 1956-57, The Tempest, 1957, 58, Joseph Surface in School for Scandal, Broadway, 1963, Ages of Man, Lyceum Theater, N.Y.C., 1963, Australia and New Zealand, 1963-64, Julian in Tiny Alice, Broadway, 1964-65, Hamlet, Broadway, Boston and Can., 1974; dir. plays Lady Windemere's Fan, 1946, The Glass Menagerie starring Helen Hayes, 1948, Medea, 1948, The Heiress, 1949; producer, dir. Berlioz's The Trojans, Broadway, 1958, Britten's A Midsummer Nights Dream, Royal Opera House, Covent Garden, London, 1961, Big Fish, Little Fish, Broadway, 1961 (Tony award), Dazzling Prospect, 1961, The School for Scandal, Haymarket Theatre, 1962; film appearances include Diary for Timothy, The Good Companions, 1932, The Secret Agent, 1937, The Prime Minister, 1940, Julius Caesar, 1952, A Day By The Sea (also dir.), 1953, The Cherry Orchard (also dir.), 1954, Richard III, 1955, The Barretts of Wimpole Street, 1957, St. Joan, 1957, Becket, 1964, The Loved One, 1964, Chimes at Midnight, 1966, Mister Sebastian, 1967, The Charge of the Light Brigade, 1968, The Shoes of the Fisherman, 1968, Oh! What a Lovely War, 1968, Julius Caesar, 1970, Lost Horizon, 1972, Eagle in a Cage, 1973, Murder on the Orient Express, 1974, 11 Harrowhouse, 1974, Gold, 1974, Aces High, 1976, Joseph Andrews, 1977, Providence, 1977, Portrait of a Young Man, 1977, Caligula, 1977, The Elephant Man, 1979, The Human Factor, 1979, The Conductor, 1980, Murder by Decree, 1980, The Formula, 1980, Chariots of Fire, 1981, Arthur, 1981, Sphinx, 1981, Lion of the Desert, 1981, Priest of Love, 1982, Gandhi, 1982, Wagner, 1983, Invitation to the Wedding, 1983, Scandalous, 1983, The Wicked Lady, 1983, Camille, 1984, The Shooting Party, 1985, Plenty, 1985, Leave All Fair, 1985, The Whistle Blower, 1987, Appointment With Death, 1988, Arthur 2, 1988; TV appearances include Probe, 1972, QB VII, 1973, Frankenstein: The True Story, 1973, Les Miserables, 1978, Richard II, 1979, Brideshead Revisited, 1981, Marco Polo, 1982, Inside the Third Reich, 1982, The Hunchback of Notre Dame, 1982, Neck, 1983, The Scarlet and the Black, 1983, The Master of Ballantrae, 1984, The Far Pavillions, 1984; author: (autobiography) Early Stages, 1938, Stage Directions, 1964, Distinguished Company, 1972, Gielgud: An Actor and His Time, 1980. Decorated Knight Order Brit. Empire, Companion of Honor, chevalier Legion of Honor; recipient Antoinette Perry award Ages of Man, 1958, spl. award, 1959, Best Actor award Providence N.Y. Film Critics, 1977; named Brandeis University Companion, 1960. Mem. Shakespeare Reading Soc. (pres. 1958—), Royal Acad. Dramatic Art (pres. 1977—). Clubs: Garrick, Players (N.Y.C.). Office: care Internat Famous Agy, 22 Grafron St, London W1, England

GIELGUD, MAINA, ballerina; b. London, Jan. 14, 1945; d. Lewis and Elisabeth (Grussner) Gielgud. B.E.P.C. (French); studied ballet in France with Tamara Karsavina, Stanislas Idzikowsky, Lubov Egorova, Rosella Hightower. Dancer, Ballet du Marquis de Cuevas, 1962-63, Ballet Classique de France, 1965-67, Ballet of the 20th Century, Maurice Bejart, Brussels, 1967-72, London Festival Ballet, 1972-77, Royal Ballet London, 1977-78; guest dancer numerous cos. worldwide, 1978—; rehearsal dir. London City Ballet, 1981-82; artistic dir. Australian Ballet, 1983—; producer, dir. show: Steps, Notes and Squeaks, 1978. Address: Australian Ballet, 2 Kavanaugh St, 3205 South Melbourne Australia

GIEM, ROSS NYE, JR., physician, surgeon; b. Corvallis, Oreg., May 23, 1923; s. Ross Nye and Goldie Marie (Falk) G.; student U. Redlands, Walla Walla Coll.; B.A., M.D., Loma Linda U.; children—John, David, Paul, James, Ross Nye, Matthew, Julie. Intern, Sacramento Gen. Hosp., 1952-53; resident in ob-gyn, Kern County Gen. Hosp., Bakersfield, Calif., 1956-57, in gen. surgery, 1957-61; practice medicine specializing in gen. surgery, Sullivan, Mo., 1961-70; staff emergency dept. Hollywood Presbyn. Med. Center, 1971-73, Meml. Hosp., Belleville, Ill., 1973-85, St. Elizabeth Hosp., Belleville, Ill., 1985—; St. Luke Hosp., Pasadena, Calif., 1973—; instr. nurses, physicians, paramedics, emergency med. technicians, 1973—. Served with AUS, 1943-46. Diplomate Am. Bd. Surgery. Fellow ACS, Am. Coll. Emergency Physicians; mem. AMA, Ill. Med. Assn., Pan Am. Med. Assn., Pan Pacific Surg. Assn., Royal Coll. Physicians (Eng.)

GIERE, FREDERIC ARTHUR, biologist, educator; b. Galesville, Wis., Dec. 10, 1923; s. Arthur F. and Agnes (Peterson) G.; A.B., Luther Coll., 1947, M.S., Syracuse U., 1951; Ph.D., U. N.Mex., 1953; m. Hazel Marie Teien, June 11, 1955; children—Nils, John, Martha. Instr. to asso. prof. biology Luther Coll., Decorah, Iowa, 1947-62; asso. prof. Lake Forest (Ill.) Coll., 1962-70, prof., 1970—, chmn. biology dept., 1964—; cons. Argonne Nat. Labs., 1967—, Abbott Labs., 1978—, Nat. Bur. Standards, 1983. Bd. dirs. Iowa div. Am. Cancer Soc., 1958-62, Ill. div., 1973—. Served with USNR, 1943-46. Recipient Disting. Service medal Am. Cancer Soc., 1983; USPHS fellow, Arbeidsfysiologisk Institutt, Oslo, 1968-69. Mem. AAAS, AAUP, Am. Physiol. Soc., Am. Soc. Zoology, Soc. Exptl. Biology and Medicine, Sigma Xi, Beta Beta Beta, Phi Sigma. Home: 321 E Washington St Lake Bluff IL 60044 Office: Lake Forest Coll Lake Forest IL 60045

GIERING, RICHARD HERBERT, information systems executive; b. Emmaus, Pa., Nov. 27, 1929; s. Harold Augustus and Marguerite (Bruder) G.; BS in Engring. and Math., U. Ariz., 1962; m. Carol Alice Scott, Aug. 16, 1959; children: Richard Herbert, Scott K. Enlisted U.S. Army, 1947, commd. 2d lt., 1963, advanced through grades to capt., 1965; sect. chief data processing Def. Intelligence Agy., Washington, 1965-67; ret., 1967; with Data Corp. (name changed to Mead Tech. Labs. 1968), Dayton, Ohio, 1967-77, v.p. tech. ops., 1970-71, dir. info. systems, 1971-77; pres., chief exec. officer DG Assos., Inc., 1974—; pres. Infotex Assos., 1977-86, mgr. Product Systems, Commerce Clearing House, Inc., 1986—; instr. data processing U. Ariz., Tucson, 1962-63. Mem. Assn. Computing Machinery, Am. Soc. Info. Scis. Inventor Data/Cen. (used to establish electronic newspaper libraries). Home: 906 Red Top Dr Libertyville IL 60048 Office: 4025 Peterson Chicago IL 60648

GIEROWSKI, JÓZEF ANDRZEJ, historian; b. Czestochowa, Poland, Mar. 19, 1922; s. Jó zef and Stefania (Wasilewska) G.; m. Danuta Wolniak, Dec. 27, 1945; children—Józef Krzysztof, Elzbieta Pluta; m. Maria Przetacznik, Jan. 19, 1985. M.A., Jagellonian U., Krakow, Poland, 1945, Ph.D., 1947; Doctorate (hon.), U. Uppsala (Sweden), 1983, U. Conn., 1986. Asst., U. Wroclaw (Poland), 1946-54, prof., 1954-65, prorector, 1958-61, dean historico-philos. faculty, 1964-65; prof. Inst. History, Polish Acad. Sci., 1953-68; prof. modern history Jagellonian U., 1965—, rector, 1981-87, dir. Ctr. for Research on History and Culture of Polish Jews, 1986—. Author: Sejmik Generalny Mazowiecki, 1948; Dzieje Wroclawia 1618-1741, 1958; Historia Polski 1505-1864, 1978, Historia Wloch, 1986; contbr. articles in field to profl. jours. Sec., Polish-German Commn. Historians, 1957-63; mem. Polish Parliament, 1985—. Mem. Wroclawskie Towarzystwo Naukowe (v.p. 1963-65), Polskie Towarzystwo Historyczne, Komitet Nauk Historycznych. Roman Catholic. Home: Lokietka 1 m 2, 30-010 Krakow Poland Office: Jagiellonian Univ, Golebia 24, 31-007 Krakow Poland

GIERSCH, HERBERT HERMANN, economist, educator; b. Reichenbach, Germany, May 11, 1921; s. Hermann and Helene (Kleinert) G.; m. Friederike Koppelmann; 3 children. Dr. rer. pol., U. Munster; Dr. (hon.), U. Erlangen, F U. Basle. Asst. to prof. U. Munster, 1948, 50, privatdozent, 1950-52; Brit. Council fellow London Sch. Econs., 1948-49; adminstr. econs. directorate OEEC, 1950-52, counsellor, head div. trade and fin. directorate, 1953-54; in charge econs. chair Technische Hochschule, Brunswick, W.Ger., 1954; prof. econs. U. Saarbrucken (W.Ger.), 1955-69; prof. econs. U. Kiel (W.Ger.), 1969—, pres. Inst. World Econs., 1969—; vis. prof. econs. Yale U., 1962-63, 77-78; mem. German Econ. Expert Council, 1964-70; chmn. Assn. German Econ. Research Insts., 1970-82. Author: Acceleration Principle and Propensity to Import, 1953; The Trade Optimum, 1957; Allgemeine Wirtschaftstumspolitik, 1977; Growth, Cycles and Exchange Rates—The Experience of West Germany (Wicksell Lecture), 1970; Kontroverse Fragen der

Wirtschaftspolitik, 1971; Indexation and the Fight against Inflation, 1973-74; The European Community and the World German Economy, AEI, 1976; Im Brennpunkt: Wirtschaftspolitik-kitische Beitrage von 1967-77, 1978; A European Look at the World Economy (MacInally Lecture), 1978; Deutsche Wirtschaft wohin, 1980; Aspects of Growth, Structural Change and Employment—A Schumpeterian Perspective, 1979; Die Rolle der reichen Lander in der wachsenden Weltwirtschaft, 1980; Problems of Adjustment to Imports from Less-Developed countries, 1981; Rationality in Political Economy, 1981; Wachstum durch dynamischen Wettbewerb, 1982; Schumpeter and the Current and Future Development of the world Economy, 1982; Arbeit, Lohn und Produktivitat, 1983. Hon. fellow London Sch. Econs. Mem. Internat. Econ. Assn. (council 1971—, exec. com. 1971—, treas. 1974—, hon. pres. 1983—), Am. Econ. Assn. (hon.). Office: Kiel Inst World Econs, Duesternbrooker Weg 120, PO Box 4309, D-2300 Kiel Federal Republic of Germany

GIERSING, MORTEN STIG OLE, international agency official; b. Copenhagen, June 30, 1945; s. Franz Edmund and Mille (Frederiksen) G.; m. Benedicte Helly-Hansen, July 15, 1967; children: Matias, Jonas, Pil, Ida. PhD, U. Copenhagen, 1972. Asst. prof. U. Copenhagen, 1972-76, assoc. prof., 1976-84; head sect. free flow of info. UNESCO, Paris, 1984—; cons. Denmarks Radio and TV, Copenhagen, 1978-84, Nordic Council of Ministers, Oslo, 1981-84; mem. adv. council Inst. Internat. Media Communication, 1986—. Author: The Future of Television, 1979, Television in the United States, 1982, Consumer Information in Radion and TV, 1983; editor/author several books on lit. criticism, 1970-79. Personal mem. Govtl. Media Com. Copenhagen, 1981-84. Mem. Internat. Assn. Mass Communication Researchers, Danish Writer's Assn. Office: UNESCO, 7 Place de Fontenoy, 75007 Paris France

GIERTZ, MAGNUS, mathematics educator; b. Stockholm, Sept. 23, 1932; s. Lars Magnus and Brita (Deutgen) G.; m. Marie-Luoise Folkesson, May 15, 1955 (div. 1976); children—Caroline, Lars; m. Monica Blom, July 17, 1977; children—Mattias, Maria. B.S., Alleghany Coll., Meadville, Pa., 1954; Civil Engr., Royal Inst. Tech., Stockholm, 1959, Tekn. Lic., Tekn. Dr., 1969, Bergsman (hon.), 1970. Lectr. Royal Inst. Tech., 1965—, prefekt math. dept., 1972—; vis. prof. UCLA, 1965-66, U. Calif.-Dundee, 1968, 74, U. So. Calif., 1970-71, U. Toronto, Ont. Can., 1976; cons. Swedish Defense Research, Stockholm, 1960-66, Industrimatematik, Stockholm, 1967—. Author: Algebra och Geometri, 1983, Om tal och matriser, 1984. Contbr. research papers to profl. publs. Served to fanrik Swedish Armed Forces, 1954-55. Recipient Galostipendiat, Galostiftelsen, 1956, Stipendium Allegheny Coll., 1952-54, Royal Inst. Tech., 1955-59. Mem. Swedish Math. Soc., Am. Math. Soc., Swedish Assn. for Congressmen and Research Scientists, Nat. Sci. Research Council (rep.). Clubs: Saltsjobadens Golf; Gastronomiska Sallskapet. Lodge: Masons. Home: Ringv 24, Saltsjobaden 13300, Sweden Office: Royal Inst Tech, Dept Math, 10044 Stockholm 70, Sweden

GIESBERS, JOHANNES HENDRIUKUS, university professor; b. Nypmegen, The Netherlands, June 11, 1932; s. Hendrikus Johannes and Maria Johanna (Nillesen) G.; m. Edith Carla de Jong, July 27, 1963; children: Esther, Sharon, Michael, Jan. MA, Cath. U. Nymegen, 1969, PhD, 1970. Tchr. primary and secondary schs., The Netherlands, 1950-57; univ. tchr. Cath. U. Nymegen, 1972-78, prof. edn., 1978—, dean of faculty social scis., 1978-82, rector magnificus, 1982-87. Contbr. articles on ednl. orgn. and mgmt. to profl. jours. Served to 1st lt. Cavalry of The Netherlands, 1953-55. Christian Democrat. Roman Catholic. Office: Cath Univ Nypmegen, Erasmusplein 1, 6500 HD Nymegen The Netherlands

GIESCHEN, MARTIN JOHN, artist, art historian; b. N.Y.C., Apr. 5, 1918; s. John Christian and Bertha Wilhelmina (Christopher) G.; A.B., Antioch Coll., 1941; m. Elizabeth Hutchinson, Aug. 5, 1940; children—Jenifer Jean, Paul Allen. B.F.A., Syracuse U., 1966, M.F.A., 1967. Ednl. dir. Ohio Farm Bur., 1943-44, 46-54; pres., sec. JGG & Sons Enterprises, Inc. and Elmira Market Place Corp., 1954-64; mem. faculty dept. art Jr. Coll. Albany div. Russell Sage Coll., 1967-86, prof. art history, 1967-86, prof. emeritus, 1986—, prof. art history, 1988—, chmn. dept., 1967-78. Author: Art History of Elmira, 1967; Theories of Color, A Small Digest, 1981. Served with AUS, 1944-46. Decorated Bronze Star. Mem. Pastel Soc. Am., Coll. Art Assn., Nat. Assn. Schs. Art and Design, ACLU, Common Cause, Pub. Citizen, Sierra Club, Nat. Art Edn. Assn., Internat. Soc. Marine Painters, Albany Inst. Art. Democrat. Home: 74 Woodlawn Ave Albany NY 12208 Office: 140 New Scotland Ave Albany NY 12208

GIESE, HEINER, lawyer, real estate investor; b. Passau, Germany, Apr. 16, 1944; came to U.S., 1950, naturalized, 1957; s. Heinz Emil and Wilma Maria (Dunner) G.; m. Barbara Ann Kent, June 28, 1969; children: Anna, Peter. BS in Internat. Affairs, Georgetown U., 1966; JD, U. Wis., 1969. Bar: Wis. 1969, U.S. Dist. Ct. (ea. and we. dists.) Wis. 1969, U.S. Ct. Appeals (7th cir.) 1974, U.S. Supreme Ct. 1974. Law clk. U.S. Dist. Ct., Madison, 1969-70; assoc. Cannon, McLaughlin, Herbon & Staudenmeier, Milw., 1969-74; ptnr. Levin & Giese, Milw., 1974-85, Giese & Weden Law Offices, Milw., 1985—. Bd. dirs. German Fest Milw., 1981-84, legal counsel, 1981—; sec., bd. dirs. Grafton Dells, 1981—; bd. dirs. German Lang. and Sch. Soc., 1976—, Goethe House, Milw.; mem. adv. council Milw. World Festival, 1981-84; legal counsel United Festivals of Milw., Inc., 1984—; Wis. gov.'s rep. Presdl. Commn. for German-Am. Tricentennial, 1983. Recipient Outstanding Young Lawyer award, 1979. Mem. ABA (young lawyers div. affiliate outreach team 1979-80, regional vice chmn. membership com. 1979-81), Wis. Bar Assn., Milw. Bar Assn. (chmn. lawyer referral service 1980-83), Milw. Young Lawyers Assn. (pres. 1978-79), Milw. Bar Found. (bd. dirs. 1979—, v.p. 1986—), Income Property Owners Assn. Democrat. Lutheran. Home: 2022 N 72d St Wauwatosa WI 53213 Office: 1216 N Prospect Ave Milwaukee WI 53202

GIESE, ROBERT JOSEPH, corporate executive; b. N.Y.C., June 16, 1934; s. Emil Joseph and Noreen (Black) G.; m. Dolores J. Moran, Nov. 19, 1960; 1 child, Lara. Student, Bklyn. Coll., 1952-57, NYU, 1968-69. Archtl. draftsman Ebasco Services, Inc., N.Y.C., 1952-53, adminstrv. asst. to supt. design, 1953-56, engring. coordinator on pulp and paper projects, 1956-57, adminstrv. asst. to engring. mgr., 1957-60, mgr. advt. and publicity, 1960-73, mgr. corp. communications, 1973-78, dir. mktg. and corp. communications, 1973-78, 1978-80, dir. govtl. relations, 1980-85; pres., chmn. bd. CDI cons. Developers Energy Systems Corp., Franklinville, N.J., 1985—; spl. investigator N.Y. Atty. Gen.'s Office, N.Y.C., 1959-61; bd. dirs. Britten Plastics Inc., Am. Guarantee and Credit Corp.; chmn. bd. dirs. Developers Energy Systems Corp. Caribbean Inc., P.R. Elected judicial del. City of N.Y., 1960; liaison officer Dep. Mayor's Office of Econ. Devel. of N.Y.C. Served with USNR, 1951-59. Mem. Advt. Club, N.Y. Alumni Assn., N.Y. Chamber Commerce and Industry, U.S. C. of C. Roman Catholic. Clubs: World Trade Ctr., Forsgate. Home: 314 Pinebrook Rd Englishtown NJ 07726 Office: 452 Coles Mill Rd Franklinville NJ 08322 also: 117 Eleanor Roosevelt Blvd Hato Rey PR 00918

GIESEN, DIETER JOSEPH HEINRICH KONRAD, lawyer; b. Dessau, Germany, Nov. 20, 1936; s. Josef and Anna (Weck) G.; Dr. iur., U. Bonn., 1962; M.A. status Oxford U., 1976; m. Angelika Cottmann, July 28, 1966; children—Katrin, Cornelia, Christiane, Barbara. Mem. faculty Ruhr U., Bochum, 1966-73, sr. lectr. 1971, prof. law, 1972-73; prof. comparative law, pvt. law and legal history Free U. Berlin, 1973—, also dir. Inst. Internat., Fgn. and Comparative Law and head Working Ctr. Studies in German and Internat. Med. Malpractice Law; subdean law, 1974-76; vis. fellow Pembroke Coll., Oxford (Eng.) U., 1976-77, 83—; vis. prof. Melbourne U. Law Sch., 1981; Fulbright vis. prof. U. Ill., 1982; mem. Commn. on Rights of Women in Soc., German Fed. Parliament, 1974-80. Mem. Internat. Soc. Family Law (exec. council 1973, v.p. 1975, pres. 1977-79), Soc. Comparative Law, Soc. Public Tchrs. Law U.K. Author: Die kuenstliche Insemination als ethisches u. rechtliches Problem, 1962; Aktuelle Probleme einer Reform des Scheidungsrechts, 1971; Grundlagen u. Entwicklung des englischen Eherechts in der Neuzeit, 1973; Zur Problematik der Einführung einer Familiengerichtsbarkeit in der Bundesrepublik Deutschland, 1975; Civil Liability of Physicians With Regard to New Methods of Treatment and Experiments, 1976; Ehe, Familie und Erwerbsleben, 1977; Kindesmisshandlung?, 1979; Medical Malpractice Law—A Comparative Law Study of Civil Responsibility Arising from Medical Care, 1981; Wandlungen des Arzthaftungsrechts, 1983, 2d edit., 1984; International Medical Malpractice Law, 1988; contbr. articles to profl. jours. Mem. Christian Dem. Union. Clubs: The Athenaeum, United Oxford and Cambridge Univ. (London). Home: 38 Ihnestrasse, D-1000, Berlin 33 Federal Republic of Germany Office: 3 Boltzmannstrasse, D-1000 Berlin 33 Federal Republic of Germany

GIFFEN, LAWRENCE EVERETT, SR., family physician, anesthesiologist, historian; b. Jefferson City, Mo., Jan. 30, 1923; s. Fred Lemon and Angeline Henrietta (Patterson) G.; m. Mary Opal McKnight, Oct. 15, 1947 (div. Mar. 1950); 1 child, Lawrence Everett Jr.; m. Jerena East, June 17, 1955; children: Michael Gregory, Jerena Ann. DO, Kirksville Coll. Osteo Medicine, 1945; BS in Biology, Lincoln U., 1960; BA in History, U. Md., 1981; MS in Criminal Justice, Cen. Mo. State U., 1980; MA in History, Lincoln U., 1987. Diplomate Am. Osteo. Bd. Anesthesiology, Am. Bd. Family Practice. Intern Osteo. Hosp. Maine, Portland, 1945-46; practice gen. medicine Chamois, Mo., 1946-50; resident in anesthesiology Art Ctr. Hosp., Detroit, 1950-51; practice gen. medicine and anesthesiology Jefferson City, Mo., 1951-80, 83—; med. examiner Jefferson City, 1968-80. Contbr. articles to profl. jour. Served to comdr. USNR, 1980-83. Fellow Am. Osteo. Coll. Anesthesiologists (pres. 1962), Am. Osteo. Coll. Surgeons (hon.), Am. Acad. Family Physicians; mem. AMA, Mo. State Med. Soc., U.S. Naval Inst., Am. Assn. Mil. Surgeons, Am. Assn. History Medicine. Republican. Presbyterian. Lodge: Masons, Shriners, Rotary. Home: 1915 Hayselton Dr Jefferson City MO 65101 Office: 420 E High St Jefferson City MO 65101

GIFFIN, MARGARET ETHEL (PEGGY), management consultant; b. Cleve., Aug. 27, 1949; d. Arch Kenneth and Jeanne (Eggleton) G.; m. Robert Alan Wyman, Aug. 20, 1988. BA in Psychology, U. Pacific, Stockton, Calif., 1971; MA in Psychology, Calif. State U., Long Beach, 1973; PhD in Quantitative Psychology, U. So. Calif., 1984. Psychometrist Auto Club So. Calif., Los Angeles, 1973-74; cons. Psychol. Services, Inc., Glendale, Calif., 1975-76, mgr., 1977-78, dir., 1979—; researcher Social Sci. Research Inst., U. So. Calif., Los Angeles, 1981; mem. tech. adv. com. on testing Calif. Fair Employment and Housing Commn., 1974—, mem. steering com., 1978—. Mem. Internat. Personnel Mgmt. Assn. Assessment Council, Am. Psychol. Assn., Western Psychol. Assn., Personnel Testing Council So. Calif. (pres. 1980, exec. dir. 1982, 88, bd. dirs. 1980—). Club: Athletic (Los Angeles). Home: 330 S Westmoreland Ave Los Angeles CA 90020 Office: 100 W Broadway #1100 Glendale CA 91210

GIFFORD, GEOFFREY L., lawyer; b. Kirksville, Mo., Nov. 26, 1946; s. Robert M. and Elnora Frances (Overstreet) G.; m. Jerrilyn A. Randall; children—Andrew, Katie. B.A., U. Mo., 1968; J.D., U. Mich., 1971. Bar: Mo. 1971, Mich. 1972, U.S. Dist. Ct. (we. dist.) Mo. 1973, Ill. 1977, U.S. Dist. Ct. (no. dist.) Ill. 1978. Assoc. firm Forsythe, Campbell, Vandenberg & Clevenger, Ann Arbor, Mich., 1972; ptnr. firm Gifford & Gifford, Green City, Mo., 1973-77; of counsel Gifford & Richardson, Green City; adj. prof. law Ill. Inst. Tech.-Chgo. Kent Coll. Law, 1977-78; prin. firm Asher, Pavalon, Gittler & Greenfield, Chgo., 1978—; lectr. in field; speaker IICLE Automobile Products Liability Seminar, Chgo., 1986—. Contbr. articles to profl. jours. Fellow The Roscoe Pound Am. Trial Lawyers Found. (patron); mem. ABA, Ill. Trial Lawyers Assn. (assoc. editor 1980-82, editor 1982-86, bd. mgrs. 1982—, chmn. products liability com. 1984-86, chmn. seminar planning com. 1984-86, chmn. med. malpractice com., 1985-87, mem. numerous coms.), Assn. Trial Lawyers Am. (lectr. U. Wis., vice chmn. reorganization com.), Tenn. Trial Lawyers Assn. (guest lectr. 1986), W.Va. Trial Lawyers Assn. (guest lectr. 1986), Ill. Inst. Continuing Legal Edn. (author and lectr.), Soc. Trial Lawyers, Ill. Bar Assn., Trial Lawyers Club Chgo., Phi Beta Kappa, Phi Alpha Delta. Democrat. Home: 834 W George St Chicago IL 60657 Office: Asher Pavalon Gittler & Greenfield Ltd 2 N LaSalle St Chicago IL 60602

GIFFORD, NELSON SAGE, manufacturing company executive; b. Newton, Mass., May 3, 1930; s. Gordon Babcock and Hariette Rose (Dooley) G.; m. Elizabeth B. Brow, Nov. 12, 1955; children: Susan Helen, Ian Christopher, Diane Brow. A.B., Tufts Coll., 1952. With Dennison Mfg. Co., Framingham, Mass., 1954—, mem. acctg. staff, 1954-63, controller, 1964-65, gen. mgr., 1965-67, v.p., 1967-72; pres. Dennison Mfg. Co., Framingham, 1972-86, chmn., 1986—; bd. dirs. Reed & Barton, John Hancock Mut. Life Ins. Co., Boston, Boston Edison Co., Bank of Boston, M/A Com, Burlington, Mass. Bd. dirs. New Eng. Colls. Fund; trustee Newton Wellesley Hosp., Mass. Gen. Hosp.; past chmn. Wellesley Personnel Bd.; mem. Woods Hole Oceanographic Inst., Mass. Served to lt. comdr. USNR, 1952-54. Mem. Silvanus Packard Soc., Mass. Bus. Roundtable (bd. dirs., vice-chmn.), Associated Industries Mass. (bd. dirs.). Clubs: Kittansett (Marion), Brae Burn Country (Newton). Home: 14 Windsor Rd Wellesley MA 02181 Office: Dennison Mfg Co 275 Wyman St Waltham MA 02254

GIFFORD, RAY WALLACE, JR., physician, educator; b. Westerville, Ohio, Aug. 13, 1923; s. Ray Wallace and Alma Marie (Wagoner) G.; m. Frances Anne Moore, Jan. 13, 1973; 1 son, Graydon; children by previous marriage: Peggy, Cynthia, Susan. B.S., Otterbein Coll., 1941, ScD (hon.), 1986; M.D., Ohio State U., 1947; M.Sc., U. Minn., 1952. Diplomate: Am. Bd. Internal Medicine. Intern Colo. Gen. Hosp., Denver, 1947-48; resident in internal medicine Mayo Clinic, Rochester, Minn., 1949-52; practice medicine specializing in hypertension and nephrology; asst. prof. medicine, cons. sect. medicine Mayo Clinic, Mayo Found., 1953-61; staff mem. dept. hypertension and nephrology Cleve. Clinic Found., 1961-67, head dept. hypertension and nephrology, 1967-85, sr. physician dept. hypertension and nephrology, 1985—, bd. govs., 1973-78, vice chmn., 1977-78, vice chmn. div. medicine, 1978—, dir. regional health affairs, 1986—; mem. commn. on stroke Nat. Inst. Neurol. Disease and Stroke, 1972-74; chmn. Nat. Council on Drugs, 1976-78; chmn. hypertension task force Intersoc. Commn. on Heart Disease Resources, 1979-81; mem. nat. high blood pressure coordinating com. Nat. Heart, Lung and Blood Inst., 1978—; mem. 2d, 3d and 4th joint nat. coms. on detection, evaluation and treatment of high blood pressure, 1979-80, 83-84, 87-88; mem. Congl. Commn. on Drug Approval Process, 1981-82; mem. adv. com. to dir. NIH, 1982-86. Author: (with William Manger) Pheochromocytoma, 1977; contbr. numerous papers to med. jours.; editorial bd.: Stroke Jour, 1971-74, Am. Jour. Cardiology, 1973-78, Geriatrics, 1974—. Mem. Rochester (Minn.) City Council, 1960-61, Republican precinct committeeman, Cleveland Heights, Ohio, 1966-70. Served as lt. comdr. MC USNR, 1954-56. Recipient Alumni Achievement award Ohio State U., 1962, Disting. Sci. Achievement award Otterbein Coll., 1970, Oscar B. Hunter Meml. award in therapeutics Am. Soc. for Clin. Pharmacology and Therapeutics, 1979. Fellow Am. Coll. Cardiology (bd. trustees 1969-70, gov. Ohio 1970-73), A.C.P., Am. Coll. Chest Physicians (chmn. com. on hypertension 1970-72, Simon Rodbard Meml. award 1982); mem. Am. Heart Assn. (bd. dirs. 1969-72, chmn. stroke council 1970-72), AMA (mem. council on sci. affairs 1976-85, vice chmn. council on sci. affairs 1981-83, chmn. council on sci. affairs 1983-85, trustee 1986—), Am. Soc. Clin. Pharmacology and Therapeutics (pres. 1976-77), Am. Soc. Nephrology, Central Soc. Clin. Research, Internat. Soc. Hypertension, Internat. Soc. Nephrology, Interstate Postgrad. Med. Assn. (pres. 1976-77). Methodist. Home: 3479 Glen Allen Dr Cleveland Heights OH 44121 Office: 9500 Euclid Ave One Clinic Ctr Cleveland OH 44195

GIGANTE, HUGH ANTHONEY, marketing executive; b. N.Y.C., Oct. 12, 1947; s. Hugh Anthoney and Gilda Katheryn (Raccioppo) G.; m. Lorraine Bedell, Sept. 11, 1971; children—Hugh M., Richard P., Alexandria L., Victoria K., Nicholas J. B.B.A., St. John's U., 1969, M.B.A., 1974. Market research analyst Am. Airlines, N.Y.C., 1969-70; market devel. mgr. L.I. Lighting Co., Mineola, N.Y., 1970-73; new products mgr. European Am. Bank, Westbury, N.Y., 1973-75, sales promotion mgr., 1975-77; new products mgr. Citicorp., Melville, N.Y., 1977-78, mktg. mgr., 1978-79, edn./communication dir., 1979-80; dir. mktg. and public affairs Periphonics div. Exxon Corp., Bohemia, N.Y., 1980-83; dir. mktg. and devel. IDR Inc., subs. Reuters Ltd., 1983-87; dir. Edn. Services Festo U.S.A., Hauppauge, N.Y., 1987—; adj. prof. econs. Dowling Coll., Oakdale, N.Y. Pres., fin. trustee St. Pius X Sch. Bd.; v. chmn. St. Pius X Parish Council. Mem. Am. Mgmt. Assn., Public Relations Soc. Am. Roman Catholic. Home: 31 Oxford Rd Old Bethpage NY 11804 Office: Festo Corp 395 Moveland Rd Hauppauge NY 11788

GILASHVILI, PAVEL GEORGIYEVICH, Soviet government official; b. Georgia, 1918. Ed. Party High Sch. Communist Party Soviet Union Central Com. Mem. CPSU, 1939—; locksmith 1934-38; head of a dept. of Central Com. of Georgian Komsomol, First Sec. of a Reg. Com. of Georgian Communist Party, Sec. of Tblilisi City Com. of Georgian CP, 1945-58, First Sec., 1972-76; mem. staff Georgian CP, 1958-67, mem. Central Com., 1956-58, 1971—, mem. Politburo of Central Com., 1972—; chmn. Council of Ministers of Abkhazian A.S.S.R., 1967-72; chmn. Presidium of Supreme Soviet of Georgian S.S.R., 1976—; mem. Central Auditing Com. of CPSU, 1976—; vice chmn. and mem. Presidium Supreme Soviet of U.S.S.R., 1977—. Served with Soviet Army, 1939-45. Office: Office of Deputy Chmn, Moscow USSR *

GILBERT, ARTHUR CHARLES FRANCIS, psychologist; b. N.Y.C., Feb. 8, 1929; s. Arthur Charles and Rose Anne (Gallagher) G.; B.Sc., U. Nebr., 1950, M.A., 1954, Ph.D., 1957; postgrad. U. Chgo., 1961, Indsl. Coll. Armed Forces, 1976; m. Mary Louise Doran, June 23, 1951; 1 dau., Jane Marcina (dec.). Project dir. Ednl. Research Corp., Cambridge, Mass., 1956-57; dir. counseling service, lectr. Princeton (N.J.) U., 1957-59; clin. psychologist USAF, 1959-64; coordinator research, clin. psychologist Mental Hygiene Clinic, VA Hosp., Washington, 1965-71; pvt. practice, Silver Spring, Md., 1967—; research psychologist Naval Personnel Research and Devel. Lab., Washington, 1971-73; sr. research psychologist U.S. Army Research Inst., Alexandria, Va., 1973—; staff asst. for tng. and personnel systems tech. Office of Undersec. Def., 1986; professorial lectr. Am. U., Washington, 1967-69, adj. prof., 1969-71; assoc. professorial lectr. George Washington U., Washington, 1967-74; lectr. U. Md., College Park, 1974—; cons. Princeton Family Service Clinic, N.J., 1958-59, Hamilton Psychiat. Hosp., Ont., Can., 1968, NIMH, 1970. Served with U.S. Army, 1946-48, USAF, 1951-53. Recipient Nat. Commanders award DAV, 1971. Fellow Am. Psychol. Assn., AAAS, Inter-Univ. Seminar Armed Forces and Soc.; mem. Mil. Testing Assn. (co-chmn. program com. 1980-81), Southeastern Soc. Multivariate Exptl. Psychology (exec. officer 1980-81, 82-83, 85-87), Eastern Psychol. Assn., Southeastern Psychol. Assn., Psi Chi, Phi Delta Kappa. Roman Catholic. Lodge: Elks. Contbr. articles to profl. jours. Home: 8708 1st Ave Silver Spring MD 20910

GILBERT, CREIGHTON EDDY, art historian; b. Durham, N.C., June 6, 1924; s. Allan H. and Katharine (Everett) G. B.A., N.Y. U., 1942, Ph.D., 1955. Jr. appts. Emory U., Louisville U., Ind. U., Ringling Mus., 1946-61; assoc. prof. Brandeis U., 1961-65, Sidney and Ellen Wien prof. history of art, 1965-69, chmn. dept., 1963-66, 68-69; prof. Queens Coll. City U. N.Y., 1969-77, chmn. dept., 1969-72; Jacob Gould Schurman prof. history of art Cornell U., 1977-81; prof. Yale U., 1981—; Fulbright sr. lectr. U. Rome, 1951-52; Kress fellow Harvard Center for Italian Renaissance Studies, Florence, Italy, 1967-68; fellow Netherlands Inst. for Advanced Study, 1972-73; vis. prof. U. Leiden, 1974-75; Robert Sterling Clark vis. prof. Williams Coll., 1976; Zacks Found. vis. prof. Hebrew U. Jerusalem, 1985. Author: Michelangelo, 1967, Change in Piero della Francesca, 1968, History of Renaissance Art, 1972, The Works of Girolamo Savoldo, 1986 Editor: Renaissance Art: Contemporary Essays, 1970, Italian Art 1400-1500, Sources and Documents, 1979; editor-in-chief: The Art Bull, 1980-85; Translator: Complete Poems and Selected Letters of Michelangelo, 1963, 3d edit., 1979; contbr. entry on Michelangelo to Encyclopedia Britannica, 1987. Recipient Mather award Coll. Art Assn., 1964. Fellow Am. Acad. Arts and Scis.; mem. Istituto per la Storia dell'Arte Lombarda (dir. 1983-88). Office: Dept History of Art 56 High St Yale U New Haven CT 06520

GILBERT, GENE SANDRA (SOGLIERO), mathematical statistician, educator; b. Pawtucket, R.I.; d. Frank T. and Sarah Agnes (Taggart) Cianfarani; Ed.B., R.I. Coll., 1947; A.M., Brown U., 1954; Ph.D., U. Conn., 1970; m. June 28, 1951 (div. July 1982); m. James Dwight Gilbert, Apr. 11, 1986; children—Stephen William, Christine Marie. Sr. math. specialist United Techs. Research Center, East Hartford, Conn., 1974-75, sr. research engr., 1975-77; math. statistician USCG Research and Devel. Center, Groton, Conn., 1979-82; sr. research scientist/statistician Pfizer Central Research, Groton, 1982-86, supr. biostats., 1986—; prof. applied math. U. Lovanium, Zaire, 1971-74; asst. prof. math and stats. U. Conn., Trinity Coll., Hartford; speaker in field. Recipient spl. achievement award for plasma emission studies U.S. Coast Guard Research and Devel. Center, 1980; NASA summer faculty fellow, 1979. Mem. Am. Statis. Assn., AIAA, AAAS, N.Y. Acad. Sci. Contbr. articles to profl. jours. Home: 134 Scotland Rd Rt #97 Sprague CT 06300 Office: Dept Clin Research Pfizer Cen Research Groton CT 06340

GILBERT, HEATHER CAMPBELL, manufacturing company executive; b. Mt. Vernon, N.Y., Nov. 20, 1944; d. Ronald Ogston and Mary Lodivia (Campbell) G.; BS in Math. (Nat. Merit scholar), Stanford U., 1967; MS in Computer Sci. (NSF fellow), U. Wis., 1969. With Burroughs Corp., 1969-82, sr. mgmt. systems analyst, Detroit, 1975-77, mgr. mgmt. systems activity, Pasadena, Calif., 1977-82; mgr. software product mgmt. Logical Data Mgmt. Inc., Covina, Calif., 1982-83, dir. mktg., 1983, v.p. bus. devel., 1983-84; v.p. profl. services, 1984-85; mgr. software devel. Unisys Corp., Irvine, Calif., 1985—. Mem. Assn. Computing Machinery, Am. Prodn. and Inventory Control Soc., Stanford U. Alumni Assn. (life), Stanford Profl. Women Los Angeles County (pres. 1982-83), Nat. Assn. Female Execs., Town Hall. Republican. Home: 21113 Calle de Paseo El Toro CA 92630 Office: Unisys Corp 19 Morgan Irvine CA 92718

GILBERT, LEWIS, film director; b. London, Mar. 6, 1920; m. Hylda Henrietta Tafler, 2 sons. Performed as child actor; asst. dir. to William Keighley on Target for Today, 1939; with G.B. Internat., from 1944, writer, dir. The Ten Year Plan, Sailors Do Care, Arctic Harvest, The Little Ballerina, 1947-48; producer, dir. Internationalist Realist, 1948, Paul and Michelle, 1973; dir. films: the Little Ballerina, 1947, Once a Sinner, 1950, Scarlet Thread, 1951, There is Another Sun, 1951, Time Gentlemen Please, 1952, Emergency Call, 1952, Cosh Boy, Johnny on the Run, 1963, Albert R.N., 1953, The Good Die Young, 1954, The Sea Shall Not Have Them, 1954, Cast a Dark Shadow, 1955, Reach for the Sky, 1956, The Admirable Crichton, 1957, Carve Her Name With Pride, 1957, A Cry from the Streets, 1958, Ferry to Hong Kong, 1959, Sink the Bismarck, 1960, Light Up The Sky, 1960, The Greengage Summer, 1961, H.M.S. Defiant, 1962, The Seventh Dawn, 1964, Alfie, 1966, You Only Live Twice, 1967, Seven Men at Daybreak, 1975, Seven Nights in Japan, 1976, The Spy Who Loved Me, 1977, Moonraker, 1978, Educating Rita, 1982; producer Spare The Rod, 1959-60. Served with RAF. Address: 19 Blvd de Suisse, Monaco Monaco also: Baker Rooke Clement House, 99 Aldwych, London WC2 BJY, England *

GILBERT, PETER HUMPHREY, advertising executive; b. Livingstone, Zambia, June 27, 1939; s. Francis Walter and Muriel Margaret (Toulson) G.; m. Jean Mildred Green, Aug. 21, 1961; children: Patricia Anne, Christopher Michael. Diploma, Marist Bros. Coll., Johannesburg, Republic of South Africa, 1957. Layout clk. Cen. African Post (Argus Newspaper), Lusaka, Zambia, 1959; sales rep. Northern News(Argus Newspaper), Ndola and Kitwe, 1960-61; admag exec. Rhodesia TV Ltd., Kitwe, 1961-63; comml. mgr. Rhodesia TV Ltd. (later Zambia TV Ltd.), Kitwe, 1964-65; advt. mgr. Times Newpapaers Zambia Ltd., Ndola, 1965-69; account exec. Barker McCormac (Zambia) Ltd., Ndola, 1969-70, gen. mgr., 1970; chmn. bd., chief shareholder Gilbert Advt. Ltd., Ndola, 1971—; chmn. bd. Owen's Motors Ltd., Ndola, 1971-80, W.L. Cherry Ltd., Ndola, 1971—. Author, photographer mag. Lake Lure (The Fishing Mag.) 1980—. Fellow Inst. of Dirs., British Inst. of Mgmt.; mem. Internat. Advt. Assn., Nat. Geog. Soc., Kitwe Jaycees (com. chmn. 1963). Roman Catholic. Club: Ndola Boating and Sailing (bd. dirs. 1975-78, commodore 1978-80, 82-85, pres. 1987—). Lodge: Lions. Home: 18 Bupingulo Ave, Ndola Zambia Office: Gilbert Advt Ltd, Meridien House Moffat Rd, PO Box 71077, Ndola Zambia

GILBERT, PHIL EDWARD, JR., lawyer; b. Chgo., Jan. 31, 1915; s. Phil Edward and Florence (Miller) G.; m. Nancy Thompson Merrick, June 24, 1939 (div. 1967); children: Mary Randolph, John Sale, Clinton Merrick; m. Joan Stulman, Oct. 6, 1968. AB magna cum laude, Dartmouth Coll., 1936; LLB, Harvard U., 1939. Bar: N.Y. 1941. Practiced in N.Y.C. 1941—; atty. Donovan, Leisure, Newton & Lumbard, 1939-41, Debevoise, Stevenson, Plimpton & Page, 1941; ptnr. Gilbert, Segall & Young (and predecessor), 1946—; pres. Rolls-Royce, Inc., N.Y.C., 1957-71, dir., 1957-85; dep. chmn. Magnesium Elektron, Inc. Mem. council Salk Inst., 1976-83, trustee, 1983—. Served to maj. inf. AUS, 1941-46, ETO. Decorated Bronze Star, Croix de Guerre. Fellow Am. Bar Found.; mem. Am., Fed., Westchester bar assns., Bar Assn. City N.Y., Phi Beta Kappa. Baptist. Home: The Croft

Spring Valley Rd Ossining NY 10562 Office: 430 Park Ave New York NY 10022

GILBERT, WALTER, molecular biologist; b. Boston, Mar. 21, 1932; s. Richard V. and Emma (Cohen) G.; m. Celia Stone, Dec. 29, 1953; children: John Richard, Kate. AB, Harvard U., 1953, AM, 1954; PhD, Cambridge U., 1957; DSc (hon.), U. Chgo., 1978, Columbia U., 1978, U. Rochester, 1979, Yeshiva U., 1981. NSF postdoctoral fellow Harvard U., Cambridge, Mass., 1957-58, lectr. physics, 1958-59, asst. prof. physics, 1959-64, assoc. prof. biophysics, 1964-68, prof. biochemistry, 1968-72, Am. Cancer Soc. prof. molecular biology, 1972-81, prof. biology, 1985-86, H.H. Timken prof. sci., 1986-87, Carl M. Loeb Univ. prof., chair dept cellular and devel. biology, 1987—; chmn. bd., scientist Biogen N.V., Dutch Antilles, 1978-83, co-chmn., supervisory bd., 1979-81, chmn. supervisory bd., chief exec. officer, 1981-84; V.D. Mattia lectr. Roche Inst. Molecular Biology, 1976. Guggenheim fellow, 1968-69; recipient U.S. Steel Found. Nat. Acad. Sci., 1968, Ledlie prize Harvard U., 1969, Warren trienneal prize Mass. Gen. Hosp., 1977, Louis and Bert Freedman Found. N.Y. Acad. Scis., 1977, Prix Charles-Leopold Mayer Academie des Scis., Inst. de France, 1977, Nobel prize in chemistry, 1980; co-winner Louisa Gross Horwitz prize Columbia U., 1979, Gairdner prize, 1979, Albert Lasker Basic Sci., 1979. Mem. Am. Phys. Soc., Nat. Acad. Scis., Am. Soc. Biol. Chemists, Am. Acad. Arts and Scis.; fgn. mem. Royal Soc. Office: Harvard U Dept Biology Cambridge MA 02138

GILBERT, XAVIER FRANCOIS, business administration educator, consultant; b. Chambery, France, Dec. 16, 1943; came to Switzerland, 1971; s. Philippe and Marthe (de Trudon) G. Diploma, ESSEC, Paris, 1967; DBA, Harvard U., 1972. Prof. bus. adminstrn. IMEDE, Internat. Mgmt. Devel. Inst., Lausanne, Switzerland, 1971—; cons. various internat. cos., U.S., Europe and Asia, 1971—. Contbr. articles to profl. jours. Mem. Strategic Mgmt. Soc., European Found. for Mgmt. Devel., SAR (French br.). Office: IMEDE, 23 chemin de Bellerive, 1001 Lausanne Switzerland

GILCHRIST, WILLIAM RISQUE, JR., economist; b. Lexington, Ky., July 16, 1944; s. William Risque and Susan (McLemore) G.; B.B.A., U. Miami, 1966, M.B.A., 1970; postgrad. Northwestern U., 1973—; m. Peggy Linder Gardner, Mar. 20, 1968; children—William Risque, Shannon Linder, Heather Susan. Asso. dir. conf. services div. continuing edn. U. Miami, Coral Gables, Fla., 1966-71; asst. dir. edn. and tng. Mortgage Bankers Assn. Am., Washington, 1971-73; pres. Ventura Fin. Corp., Fort Lauderdale, Fla., 1973-76; pres. Gilchrist and Assos., Pompano Beach., Fla., London, Basel, Switzerland and Santiago, Chile, 1976—; pres. Intervault, Inc., Ft. Lauderdale and Basel, Switzerland, Orlando, Houston; cons. in field. Recipient Cert. of Achievement, Savs. and Loan Execs. Seminar, 1971. Mem. Broward County (Fla.) C. of C., NAB, Econ. Soc. South Fla., Mortgage Bankers Assn., Nat. Assn. Pvt. Security Vaults (pres. 1986—), Senatorial Inner Circle. Republican. Episcopalian. Clubs: Kiwanis. Marina Bay, Mutiny. Author: International Monetary Systems—Alternatives, 1969; Eurodollar Outlook-OPEC and the LDC's, 1978. Home: 1341 SE 9th Ave Pompano Beach FL 33060

GILDRED, THEODORE EDMONDS, JR., ambassador; b. Mexico City, Oct. 18, 1935; s. Theodore Edmonds Sr. and Maxine (Edmonds) G.; m. Suzanne Gail Green (div. 1975); children: Theodore Edmonds III, Jennifer Lynn, Edward Ames, John Taylor; m. Stephanie Ann Gildred, Nov. 18, 1978; 1 child, Tory B. BA, Stanford U., 1959; cert., U. Paris Sorbonne, 1960, U. Heidelberg, Fed. Republic of Germany, 1960. Project supr. Investors Marine, Inc., Newport Beach, Calif., 1961; owner, pres., chief exec. officer Costa Pacifica, Inc., Newport Beach, 1961-65; adminstr. Grupo Lindavista, S.A., Mexico City, 1965-68; owner, pres., chief exec. officer The Lomas Sante Fe Cos., Solana Beach, Calif., 1968-86; chmn. bd. Torrey Pines Bank, Solana Beach, 1979-86, Inst. Ams., La Jolla, Calif., 1984-86; U.S. ambassador to Argentina, 1986—; founder, chmn. bd. Torrey Pines Bank; mem. adv. bd. 1st Nat. Bank San Diego, U. Calif. at San Diego Ctr. for U.S.-Mex. Studies. Founding chmn. bd. govs. Inst. of Ams.; pres., trustee Gildred Found.; spl. dep. search and rescue San Diego County Sheriff's Aero Squadron; mem. adv. bd. dirs. Scripps Clinic and Research Found., Scripps Meml. Hosp.; founding mem., bd. dirs. San Dieguito Boys and Girls Club; bd. dirs. Am. Brit. Cowdray Hosp. Found., Mexico City, Salk Inst., San Diego Aerospace Mus., U. Ams. Found., Puebla, Mex. Served with U.S. Army, 1955-57, USAFR, 1957-69. Recipient Gold Medal award for leadership Chgo. Tribune, 1959, Golden Boy award San Dieguito Boys' Club of Am., 1972, Friend of Distinction award Mex. and Am. Found., 1981, Master Key award for spirit of goodwill Panama Canal Commn., 1981, Guest of Honor award for spirit of goodwill Dist. of Panama, 1981, San Diego Aerospace Mus. award, 1982, Hon. Command Pilot award Ecuadorian Ministry of Def., 1984, Hon. keys City of Hermosillo, Mex., Mazatlan, Mex., Mexico City, Guatemala City, Guatemala, San Jose, Costa Rica, Managua, Nicaragua, Panama City, Panama, Colon, Panama, Esmeraldas, Ecuador, Quito, Ecuador; named to Salk Inst. Soc. of Hon. Mems., 1984. Mem. Am. Mgmt. Assn., Young Pres.'s Orgn., U. Calif. at San Diego Chancellor's Assocs. (award 1983), Stanford Alumni Assn., Stanford Alumni Assn. Mexico City (founder), Airplane Owners and Pilots Assn., Internat. Motor Sprots Assn., So. Calif. Automobile Assn. (mem. adv. bd.), Sports Car Club Am., Sports Car Club Calif., Sports Car Club San Diego, Sigma Nu. Republican. Presbyterian. Club: Jockey (Buenos Aires); Fairbanks Polo (Rancho Santa Fe, Calif.); Lomas Santa Fe Country (founder, former pres.). Lodge: Rotary. Home: 16056 El Camino Real PO Box 271 Solana Beach CA 92075 Office: US Embassy Buenos Aires APO Miami FL 34034

GILES, CONRAD LESLIE, ophthalmic surgeon; b. N.Y.C., July 14, 1934; s. Irving Samuel Giles and Victoria Ampole; m. Marilyn Toby Schwartz, June 20, 1955 (div. 1978); children—Keith Martin, Suzanne Speer, Kevin William, Brian Alan; m. Lynda Fern Schenk, Nov. 26, 1978; stepchildren—Jared Schenk, Jamie Schenk. M.D., U. Mich., 1957, M.S., 1961. Diplomate Am. Bd. Ophthalmology. Clin. assoc. NIH, Bethesda, Md., 1961-63; clin. asst. prof. Wayne State U. Sch. Medicine, Detroit, 1965-72, clin. assoc. prof. ophthalmology, 1973—. Contbr. articles to med. jours. Vice Pres. Jewish Welfare Fedn., Detroit, 1981-86, pres. 1986—. Fellow Am. Acad. Ophthalmology; mem. AMA, Mich. State Ophthal. Soc. Avocations: golf; tennis. Home: 6300 Westmoor St Birmingham MI 48010 Office: 4400 Town Ctr Southfield MI 48075

GILES, GERALD LYNN, mathematics, psychology, computer educator; b. Manti, Utah, Jan. 2, 1943; s. Bert Thorne and Sarah Jenett (Carlen) G.; m. Sharon Ruth Bleak, June 12, 1967; children: Kim, David, Kristie, Becky, Michael, Andrew, Brent. BA, U. Utah, 1968, MA, 1971. Tchr. Granite Sch. Dist., Salt Lake City, 1968-72; prof. Utah Tech. Coll. (now Salt Lake Community Coll.), Salt Lake City, 1972—; adj. prof. U. Utah, 1985—; cons. QUE Enterprises, Salt Lake City, 1976—; mem. faculty U. Phoenix, Salt Lake City, 1986—. Author: The Vicious Circle of Life, 1986, The Computer Productivity Planner, 1988. Chmn. Rep. voting dist., Salt Lake City, 1984-86; bishop Mormon Ch. Recipient Teaching Excellence award, 1986; named Outstanding Tchr. of Yr., 1986. Mem. Am. Math. Assn. Two Yr. Colls., Assn. Coll. Unions Internat. Home: 4342 Beechwood Rd Salt Lake City UT 84123 Office: Utah Tech Coll PO Box 30808 Salt Lake City UT 84130-0808

GILES, HOMER WAYNE, lawyer; b. Noble, Ohio, Nov. 9, 1919; s. Edwin Jay and Nola Blanche (Tillison) G.; m. Marcia Ellen Hurt, Oct. 3, 1987; children: Jay, Janice, Keith, Tim, Gregory. A.B., Adelbert Coll., 1940; LL.B., Western Res. Law Sch., 1943, LL.M., 1959. Bar: Ohio bar 1943. Mem. firm Davis & Young, Cleve., 1942-43, William I. Moon, Port Clinton, Ohio, 1946-48; pres. Strabley Baking Co., Cleve., 1948-53; v.p. French Baking Co., Cleve., 1953-55; law clk. 8th Dist Ct. Appeals, Cleve., 1955-58; ptnr. Kuth & Giles, Cleve., 1958-68, Walter, Haverfield, Buescher & Chockley, Cleve., 1968—; pres. Clinton Franklin Realty Co., Cleve., 1958—, Concepts Devel., Inc., 1980—; sec. Holiday Designs, Inc., Sebring, Ohio, 1964—; trustee Teamster Local 52 Health and Welfare Fund, 1950-53; mem. Bakers Negotiating Exec. Com., 1951-53. Contbr. articles to profl. publs.; editor: Banks Baldwin Ohio Legal Forms, 1962. Troop com. chmn. Skyline council Boy Scouts Am., 1961-63; adviser Am. Security Council; trustee Hiram House Camp, Florence Crittenton Home, 1965; chmn. bd. trustees Am. Econ. Found., N.Y.C., 1973-80, chmn. exec. com., 1973-80. Served with AUS, 1943-46, ETO. Mem. Am. Bar Assn., World Law Assn. (founding), Am. Arbitration Assn. (nat. panel), Com. on Econ. Reform and Edn. (life), Inst. Money and Inflation, Speakers Bur. Cleve. Sch. Levy, Citizens League, Pacific Inst., Phila. Soc., Aircraft Owners and Pilots Assn., Cleve. Hist. Soc., Mus. Modern Art, Met. Mus., Mercantile Library, Delta Tau Delta, Delta Theta Phi. Club: The City. Unitarian. Clubs: Cleve. Skating, Cleve. Econ., Harvard Bus., The City. Home: 2588 S Green Rd University Heights OH 44122 Office: Am Econ Found 1215 Terminal Tower Cleveland OH 44113

GILES, JEAN HALL, corporate exececutive; b. Dallas, Mar. 30, 1908; d. C. D. and Ida (McIntyre) Overton; m. Alonzo Russell Hall, II, Jan. 23, 1923 (dec.); children—Marjorie (Mrs. Kenneth C. Hodges, Jr.), Alonzo Russell III; m. 2d, Harry E. Giles, Apr. 24, 1928 (div. 1937); 1 dau., Janice Ruth; 1 adopted dau., Marjean Giles. Capt., comdg. officer S.W. Los Angeles Women's Ambulance and Def. Corps., 1941-43; maj., nat. exec. officer Women's Ambulance and Def. Corps, 1944-45; capt., dir. field ops. Communications Corps of the U.S. Nat. Staff, 1951-52; dir. Recipe of the Month Club. Active Children's Hosp. Benefit, 1946; coordinator War Chest Motor Corps, 1943-44; dir. Los Angeles Area War Chest Vol. Corps and Motor Corps, 1945-46; realtor Los Angeles Real Estate Exchange, 1948—, now ret.; also partner Tech. Contractors, Los Angeles. Bd. dirs. Tchr. Remembrance Day Found. Inc. Mem. Los Angeles C. of C. (women's div.), A.I.M., Los Angeles Art Assn., Hist. Soc. So. Calif., Opera Guild So. Calif., Assistance League So. Calif., Needlework Guild Am. (sect. pres. Los Angeles), First Century Families Calif., Internat. Platform Assn. Clubs: Athletic; Town Hall, The Garden (Los Angles); Pacific Coast. Home: 616 Magnolia Long Beach CA 90802

GILFORD, LEON, research company executive; b. Warsaw, Poland, Feb. 14, 1917; came to U.S., 1922, naturalized, 1928; m. Dorothy Jeanne Morrow, Mar. 31, 1950. B.A., Bklyn. Coll., 1939; M.A., George Washington U., 1949. Prin. scientist Ops. Research Inc., Silver Spring, Md., 1960-71; chief statistician and dir. automatic data processing U.S. Tariff Commn., Washington, 1971-74; spl. asst. for reliability AEC, Germantown, Md., 1974-76; spl. asst. office of dir. U.S. Census Bur., Washington, 1977-81; v.p. research and devel. COBRO Corp., Wheaton, Md., 1982—, also bd. dirs.; bd. dirs. Planning Scis. Inc.; mem. panel quality control nat. welfare program Nat. Acad. Scis., 1986-87; mem. adv. com. Dept. Energy, Washington, 1981-84, mem. adv. council Nat. Ctr. for Edn. Statistics, 1979; expert witness (testimony to U.S. Congress and Fed. Cir. Ct.). Contbr. articles to profl. jours. Served to capt., arty., U.S. Army, 1942-46. Recipient Silver medal Dept. Commerce, 1956. Fellow Am. Statis. Assn. (council 1968-70), AAAS; mem. Washington Statis. Soc. (pres., v.p. 1963-65). Club: Cosmos (Washington). Avocation: microcomputers.

GILHUUS-MOE, CARL CHRISTIAN, pharmaceutical company executive, clinical biochemist; b. Oslo, July 22, 1944; s. Bjarne and Vesla (Blom) Gilhuus-M.; m. Kari Edwardsen, Aug. 9, 1968; children—Bjarne, Christian, Nikolai. M.Sc., Oslo U., 1967, Ph.D., 1971, MBA Stockholm Sch. of Mgmt., 1983. Researcher, Nyegaard & Co., Oslo, 1971-74, mgr. diagnostics, 1974-81; dir., pres. Nyegaard Diagnostics, Oslo, 1982-85; mng. dir. Dynal A.S., 1986—. Mem. Norwegian Biochem. Soc. (gen. sec. 1977-79), Biochem. Soc. Eng., Norwegian Soc. Clin. Chemistry, German Soc. Clin. Chemistry, Royal Soc. Medicine, Internat. Pharm. Mgrs. Assn., Nat. Acad. Clinical Biochemists, European Com. Clin. Lab. Standards (pres. council 1979-84, chmn. 1986—). Lodge: Rotary (Bekkestua, Norway). Home: Lindhaugsvingen 11, 1322 Hoevik Norway Office: Dynal AS PO Box 158, Skoeyen N-0212, Oslo Norway

GILKEY, GORDON WAVERLY, curator, artist; b. Albany, Oreg., Mar. 10, 1912; s. Leonard Ernest and Edna Isabel (Smith) G.; m. Vivian Malone, Oct. 17, 1938; 1 son, Gordon Spencer. B.S., Albany Coll., 1933; M.F.A., U. Oreg., 1936; Arts D. (hon.), Lewis and Clark Coll., 1957. Mem. art staff Stephens Coll., Mo., 1939-42; prof. art, head dept. Oreg. State U., 1947-64; dean Oreg. State U. (Sch. Humanities and Social Scis.), 1963-73, Oreg. State U. (Coll. Liberal Arts), 1973-77; curator prints and drawings, printmaker-in-resident Portland (Oreg.) Art Mus. and Coll., 1978—; dir. Internat. Exchange Print Exhibits, 1956—; U.S. adviser IV Bordighera Biennale, Italy, 1957; Chmn. Gov.'s Planning Council for Arts and Humanities in, Oreg., 1965-67; mem. Gov.'s Commn. on Fgn. Lang. and Internat. Studies. Ofcl. etcher, New York World's Fair, 1939, 1937-39, etcher, Nat. Broadcasting Co., Radio City, N.Y.C., 1937-39; Artist-author: Etchings: New York World's Fair, 1939; Author articles on art.; major work in permanent collection, Met. Mus. Art, others. Bd. overseers Lewis and Clark Coll.; trustee Oreg. State U. Found.; chmn. exec. bd. Oreg. French Study Center, Oreg. German Study Center, Oreg. Japan Study Center, Oreg. Latin Am. Study Center, 1966-77. Entered U.S. Army; active duty July 1942; combat intelligence officer, head of War Dept. spl. staff art projects in Europe and chief of Joint-Chiefs-of-Staff Study in Europe of German Psychol. Warfare 1946-47; collected War Dept. Hist. Properties collection of Nazi and German war art discharged to Res. as maj. USAF, Oct. 1947; col. Res. ret. AIA-Carnegie Corp. fellow, summer 1930, 32; decorated officer with decoration Palmes Academiques (France); officer's cross; comdr.'s cross Order of Merit W. Ger.; Order Star of Solidarity Italy; comdr. Order of Merit Italy; officer Order Acad. Palms (France); chevalier Legion of Honor France; Grand Cross Order St. Gregory the Illuminator; comdr. Order Polonia Restituta; comdr. Order Holy Cross of Jerusalem; comdr. Order St. Stephan the Marytr: King Carl XVI Gustaf's Gold Commemorative medal in art Sweden, German-Am. Friendship award. Mem. Oreg. Art Inst., Soc. Am. Graphic Artists, Calif. Soc. Printmakers, Coll. Art Assn., UN Assn. Oreg. (past pres.), Oreg. Internat. Council (bd. dirs.), Print Council of Am., Phi Kappa Phi, Kappa Pi. Home: 1500 SW 5th Ave Portland OR 97201 Office: 1219 SW Park Ave Portland OR 97205

GILL, EVALYN PIERPOINT, editor, publisher; b. Boulder, Colo.; d. Walter Lawrence and Lou Octavia Pierpoint; student Lindenwood Coll., B.A., U. Colo.; postgrad. U. Nebr., U. Alaska, M.A., Central Mich. U., 1968; m. John Glanville Gill, Nov. 10, 1943; children—Susan Pierpoint, Mary Louise Glanville. Lectr. humanities Saginaw Valley State Coll., University Center, Mich., 1968-72; mem. English faculty U. N.C., Greensboro, 1973-74; editor Internat. Poetry Rev., Greensboro, 1975—; pres. TransVerse Press, Greensboro, 1981—. Bd. dirs. Eastern Music Festival, Greensboro, 1981—, Greensboro Symphony, 1982—, Greensboro Opera Co., 1982—, Weatherspoon Assn.; chmn. O. Henry Festival, 1985. Mem. Am. Lit. Translators Assn., MLA, N.C. Poetry Soc., Phi Beta Kappa. Author: Poetry By French Women 1930-1980, 1980, Dialogue, 1985, Southeast of Here: Northwest of Now, 1986; contbr. poetry to numerous mags. Home: 1501 Kirkpatrick St Greensboro NC 27408 Office: PO Box 2047 Greensboro NC 27402

GILL, GERALD LAWSON, librarian; b. Montgomery, Ala., Nov. 13, 1947; s. George Ernest and Marjorie (Hackett) G.; m. Nancy Argroves, Mar. 5, 1977 (div. 1982). AB, U. Ga., 1971; MA, U. Wis., 1973. Cataloger, James Madison U., Harrisonburg, Va., 1974-76, reference librarian, asst. prof., 1976—. Mem. library adv. com. State Council for Higher Edn. in Va., 1986-87. Mem. editorial bd. James Madison Jour., 1977-80. Mem. Am. Soc. for Info. Sci., Assoc. Info. Mgrs., Va. Library Assn. (council 1986-87, parliamentarian 1979, 81), Spl. Libraries Assn. (treas. Va. chpt. 1983-85, pres. elect 1985-86, pres. 1986-87), ALA (chmn. bus. reference services com. 1984-86; sec. law and polit. sci. sect. 1982-85, chmn. bus. reference services discussion group 1986-87), Am. Mgmt. Assn., Harrisonburg C. of C. Democrat. Home: 1379 Devon Ln Harrisonburg VA 22801 Office: James Madison U Harrisonburg VA 22807

GILL, JAMES KENNETH, advertising executive; b. Sept. 27, 1920; s. Alfred Charles and Isabel Gill; m. Anne Bridgewater, 1948; 1 son. Student, Highgate Sch. Copywriter S.T. Garland Advt. Service, 1938-39; chmn. Garland-Compton Ltd., 1970-76; chmn. Saatchi and Saatchi Co. plc, 1976-85, pres., 1985—. Served RAC, 1939-45. Clubs: Royal Automobile, MCC. Office: Davenport House, Duntisbourne Abbots, Cirencester, Glos GL7 7JN, England *

GILL, JOHN ANTHONY, investment banker; b. Lincolnshire, Eng., June 17, 1953; s. Anthony Mary and Millicent Anne (Hancock) G. BA with honors, Oxford (Eng.) U., 1975, MA, 1981. With Sheppards and Chase, London, 1977-82, Cazenove and Co., London, 1982-85, Scrimgeour Vickers, London, 1985-87; v.p. Citicorp Investment Bank, London, 1987—; mem. London Stock Exchange. Mem. Inst. Econ. Affairs. Clubs: City of London Stags (pres.), Am. Football, Chelsea Conservative, Selsdon Group, Stock Exchange Rowing (capt. 1979—). Roman Catholic. Home: The Castle, Benson, Oxfordshire OX9 6SD, England Office: Citicorp Investment Bank, 335 Strand, London WC2R ILS, England

GILL, REBECCA LALOSH, aerospace engineer; b. Brownsboro, Tex., Sept. 17, 1944; d. Milton and Dona Mildred (Magee) La Losh; m. Peter Mohammed Sharma, Sept. 1, 1965 (div.); m. James Fredrick Gill, Mar. 9, 1985; children: Erin, Melissa, Ben. BS in Physics, U. Mich., 1965; MBA, Calif. State U., Northridge, 1980. Tchr., Derby, Kans., 1966; weight analyst Beech Aircraft, Wichita, Kans., 1966; weight engr. Ewing Tech. Design, assigned Boeing-Vertol, Phila., 1966-67, Bell Aerosystems, Buffalo, 1967; design specialist Lockheed-Calif. Co., Burbank, 1968-79; sr. staff engr. Hughes Aircraft Missile Systems, Canoga Park, Calif., 1979-82, project mgr. AMRAAM spl. test and tng. equipment, 1982-85, project mgr. GBU-15 guidance sect., Navy IR Maverick Missile, Tucson, 1985—; sec. Nat. Cinema Corp. Com. chmn. Orgn. for Rehab. through Tng., 1971-75; speaker ednl. and civic groups. Pres. Briarcliffe East Homeowners Assn. Recipient Lockheed award of achievement, 1977. Mem. Soc. Allied Weight Engrs. (dir., sr. v.p., chmn. pub. relations com.), Aerospace Elec. Soc. (dir.), Nat. Assn. Female Execs, Hughes Mgmt. Club (bd. dirs., chmn. spl. events, chmn. programs, 1st v.p.). Republican. Club: Tucson Racquet. Office: Hughes Aircraft Missile Systems Bldg 805 MS L5A Tucson AZ 85734

GILL, RULAND J., JR., lawyer; b. Roosevelt, Utah, Aug. 18, 1945; s. Ruland Jay and LeNore (Merkley) G.; m. Karen Morris Westergard, Sept. 27, 1974; children—Mary Elizabeth, Erin Lindsey, Jennifer Elise, David Paul. B.S. in Acctg., U. Utah, 1970, J.D., 1973. Bar: Utah 1973, U.S. Dist. Ct. Utah 1973, U.S. Ct. Appeals (10th cir.) 1976. Staff atty. Mountain Fuel Supply Co., Salt Lake City, 1973-79, Wexpro Co., Salt Lake City, 1979-82; staff atty. Celsius Energy Co., Salt Lake City, 1982-84; mng. atty., 1984—; trustee Rocky Mountain Mineral Law Found., 1982—. Author: Intergovernmental Restraints on Oil and Gas Development, 1981. Mem. editorial bd. Law of Federal Oil and Gas Leases, 2 vols., 1982—. Bd. dirs. Utah State Fair Found., 1983—; mem. Utah Gov's. Blue Ribbon Task Force on Oil and Gas Regulation, 1986—; bd. mem. Utah State Land Bd. Served to lt. col. JAGC, Med. Service Corps, USAR, 1963—. Named Lawyer of the Yr., 1986-87. Mem. Rocky Mountain Oil and Gas Assn. (vice chmn. legal com. 1982-85), Utah State Bar (chmn. energy and natural resources sect. 1983-84), Utah State Rifle and Pistol Assn. (bd. dirs. 1978—), mem. nat. champion service rifle team 1983, 84, Sigma Nu. Republican. Mormon. Home: 532 Heritage Dr Bountiful UT 84010 Office: Celsius Energy Co 79 S State St Salt Lake City UT 84111

GILL, THOMAS JAMES, III, physician, educator; b. Malden, Mass., July 2, 1932; s. Thomas James and Marguerite (Capobianco) G.; m. Faith Libbie Etoll, July 8, 1961; children: Elizabeth Ruth, Thomas James IV, Christopher Gregory. A.B. summa cum laude, Harvard U., 1953, M.A. in Chemistry, 1957, M.D., 1957. Diplomate Am. Bd. Pathology (trustee 1981—). Asst. in pathology Peter Bent Brigham Hosp., Boston, 1957-58; intern N.Y. Hosp.-Cornell Med. Center, 1958-59; jr. fellow Soc. Fellows Harvard U., 1959-62; mem. faculty Harvard U. Med Sch., 1962-71, asso. prof. pathology, 1970-71; prof. pathology, chmn. dept. U. Pitts. Med. Sch., 1971—; pathologist-in-chief Univ. Health Center Pitts., 1971—; cons. to govt. and industry; mem. sci. adv. bd. St. Jude Children's Research Hosp., Memphis, 1969-77, chmn., 1974-76; mem. allergy and immunology research com. Nat. Inst. Allergy and Infectious Diseases, 1973-76; mem. med. research service merit rev. bd. in immunology VA, 1976-79, chmn., 1977-79; mem. sci. adv. com. Damon Runyon-Walter Winchell Cancer Fund, 1978-81; mem. com. on animal models and genetic stocks NRC, 1978—, chmn. com., 1983—, mem. com. on rabbit genetic resources, 1979-80; mem. surgery, anesthesiology and trauma study sect. NIH, 1983—; sci. adv. com. on Immunology and Immunotherapy of the Am. Cancer Soc., 1986—; mem. Armed Forces Epidemiol. Bd., 1966-72; prof. human genetics Grad. Sch. Pub. Health, 1984. Mem. editorial bd. several sci. and med. jours.; contbr. articles to profl. jours. Bd. dirs. Easter Seal Soc., Allegheny County, 1972-77, Univs. Assn. for Research and Edn. in Pathology, 1979—. Recipient Lederle med. faculty award, 1962-65, research career devel. award NIH, 1965-71; cert. of appreciation for patriotic civilian service Dept. Army, 1973; Spl. Qualification in Pathology: Immunology, 1983; Disting. Scientist award in genetics S.W. Found. for Biomed. Research, 1986; named George H. Fetterman Lectr. U. Pitts., 1981, George Hoyt Whipple lectr. U. Rochester, N.Y., 1984. Fellow Am. Soc. Clin. Pathologists, Am. Acad. Allergy, Assn. Pathology Chairmen (pres. 1978); mem. Am. Assn. Immunologists, Am. Assn. Pathologists, Am. Soc. Biol. Chemists, Internat. Acad. Pathology, Am. Soc. Human Genetics, Transplantation Soc. (v.p. 1982-84), Internat. Soc. for Immunology of Reprodn. (sec.-gen. 1983—), Am. Chem. Soc., Am. Soc. Cell Biology, Am. Soc. Human Genetics, Internat. Soc. Reprodn. (sec.-gen. 1983—), Genetics Soc. Am., Internat. Soc. Immunology of Reproduction (sec.-gen. 1983—), AMA, Nat. Research Council, Council of the Inst. of Lab. Animal Resources. Clubs: Harvard (Western Pa.); Harvard (Boston); Fox Chapel Racquet (Pitts.); Pitts. Athletic Assn, Harvard Varsity. Home: 117 Crofton Dr Pittsburgh PA 15238 Office: U Pitts Sch Medicine Pittsburgh PA 15261

GILL, ZAFAR ULLAH, health science facility administrator; b. Sialkot, Punjab, Pakistan, Mar. 15, 1947; s. Ch. Samuel and Begum Bibi G.; m. Jeena Zafar Gill, Mar. 11, 1971; children: Suneel, Aneel. MBBS, Nishtar Med. Coll., Multan, 1971; MPH, Columbia U., N.Y.C., 1978, San Diego State U., Calif., 1984. Med. officer Meml. Christian Hosp., Sialkot, 1972, dep. med. supr., 1975-85, dir. rural health care project, 1978-87, med. supt., 1985-87; bd. dirs. Christian Hosp., Tank, Delhi Gate Clinic, Lahore, United Christian Hosp., Lahore. Contbr. articles and papers to profl. jours. Trustee Presbyn. Found., U.S., 1986-87; sec. United Presbyn. Med. Bd., 1987-88; bd. dirs. Adult Basic Edn. Soc., Lahore, Gujranwala, 1986-87. Mem. Am. Pub. Health Assn., Christian Med. Soc., Pub. Health Assn. Pakistan, Nat. Council Internat. Health, Christian Hosp. Assn. Pakistan (chmn. 1988—). Mem. Ch. Pakistan. Home: Chak # 2 G/D, Bethalhem Disst Okara Pakistan Office: Meml Christian Hosp, Paris Rd, Sialkot-1 Punjab Pakistan

GILLAHAN, ROBERT DUGAN, dentistry educator; b. Lawson, Mo., Sept. 25, 1926; s. William and Georgia (Roper) G.; m. Marjorie Louise Mossman, June 1, 1953; children—Sally, Sara, Susan. D.D.S., U. Mo.-Kansas City, 1952; diploma U. Mex., 1977, U. Paraguay, 1979. Licensed dentist, Kans., Mo. Gen. practice dentistry Lawrence, Kans., 1952-74; assoc. prof. U. Mo., Kansas City, 1974—, chmn. dept. occlusion, co-chmn. Tempro Mandibular Joint Clinic, 1979-85, dir. occlusion, 1979-85; lectr. U. Mex. Ptnrs. Am., Mexico City, Pueblo and Guadalahara, Mex., 1977-78, Paraguay, 1979, 81, 83; cons. Truman Hosp., Kansas City, 1980-85, Mercy Hosp., Kansas City, 1981-85. Author manual on occlusion, 1981. Contbr. articles to profl. jours. Chmn. bd. dirs. Achievement Place for Boys, Lawrence, 1966. Served with USAAF, 1944-46. Mem. Ortho-occlusal Study Club (lectr., sec. 1979-80), 1st Dist. Dental Soc. (pres. 1961), Lawrence Dental Study Club (pres.), Oku (pres. 1982-83, Tchr. of Yr. 1962), Am. Equilibration Soc. (life). Republican. Clubs: Lawrence Country (pres. 1956-57), Kansas U. Downtown Quarterback (pres. 1960-61) (Lawrence), Cosmopolitan (v.p. 1964-65). Avocations: woodworking, fishing, shooting, swimming.

GILLAN, ROGER BENNETT, humanities educator; b. Pitts., Dec. 21, 1943; s. Gilbert Sherman and Virginia Lilian (Bennett) G. A.B. in English, Bucknell U., 1965, A.M. in English, 1967; m. Emilie Anne Schier, June 17, 1967; children—Douglas Scott, Susan Marie. Mem. depts. humanities and communications Robert Morris Coll., Coraopolis, Pa., 1966—, assoc. prof. humanities, 1977—, active coll. coms. including chmn. scholarship com., 1969-75. Vice chmn. parent adv. council for Title I program Moon Twp. Sch. Dist., 1980-82; mem. Christian Missionary and Alliance Ch. (asst. Sunday Sch. supt., youth worker; active various civic and religious groups. Mem. AAUP (chpt. treas.), Assn. Supervision and Curriculum Devel., Nat. Council Tchrs. of English, Coll. Conf. on Composition and Communication, Pa. Council Tchrs. of English, Am. Fedn. Tchrs. (various chpt. offices, pres. 1979-81). Republican. Commencement speaker Robert Morris Coll., 1980. Home: 102 Cherry Tree Pl Coraopolis PA 15108 Office: Narrows Run Rd Coraopolis PA 15108

GILLANI, NOOR VELSHI, mechanical engineering and atmospheric sciences educator, researcher; b. Arusha, Tanzania, Mar. 8, 1944; came to U.S., 1963, naturalized, 1976; s. Noormohamed Velshi and Sherbanu (Kassam) G.; m. Mira Teresa Pershe, Aug. 13, 1971; children: Michael, Michelle,

Nicole. GCE (Ordinary Level Div. I), U. Cambridge, 1960, (Advanced Level), U. London, 1963; AB cum laude, Harvard U., 1967; MS in Mech. Engring., Washington U., St. Louis, 1969, DSc, 1974. Vis. scientist Stockholm U., 1977; research assoc. Washington U., 1975-76, research scientist, 1976-77, asst. prof., 1977-80, assoc. prof. 1981-84, prof. mech. engring., 1985—, faculty assoc. CAPITA, 1979—, dir. air quality spl. studies data ctr., 1981-88, mech. engring research computing facility, 1988—; organizer NATO CCMS 15th internat. tech. meeting on air pollution modeling and its applications, St. Louis, Apr. 1985; mem. Sci. Bd. NATO/CCMS Air Pollution Pilot Study, 1986-94. Author 2 chpts. in EPA Critical Assessment Document on Acid Deposition, 1984; editor: Air Pollution Modeling and Its Applications V, vol. 10, 1986; contbr. articles on superconductivity, bioengring., atmospheric scis. and air pollution to nat. and internat. profl. jours. Dir. nat. program for parental involvement in children's edn. program Aga Khan Bd. Edn. for U.S.A.; dir. program parental involvement Childrens' Edn.; Aga Khan scholar and travel grantee, 1961-63; Harvard Coll. scholar, 1963-67; Washington U. Grad. Engring. fellow, 1967-69; research assistantships NIH, EPA, 1971-74; EPA Research grantee, 1978—. Mem. N.Y. Acad. Scis., Air Pollution Control Assn., Am. Meteorol. Soc., Am. Chem. Soc., ASME, Nat. Assn. for Edn. Young Children. Club: Harvard (St. Louis). Avocations: music, racquetball, tennis, early childhood education, computers. Home: 1455 Sycamore Manor Dr Chesterfield MO 63017 Office: Washington U Dept Mech Engring Box 1185 Saint Louis MO 63130

GILLEN, WILLIAM ALBERT, lawyer; b. Sanford, Fla., May 26, 1914; s. William D. and Marie Carolyn (Holt) G.; m. Lillian Stevens Thornton, Aug. 19, 1939 (dec. May 1981); children: William Albert, Susan Marie Gillen Casper; m. Anita Thomas Hapner, Mar. 19, 1988. Student U. Tampa, 1932-33, LL.D., 1983; J.D., U. Fla., 1936. Bar: Fla. 1936, U.S. Dist. Ct. (mid. and so. dists.) Fla. 1937, U.S. Supreme Ct. 1950, U.S. Ct. Appeals (5th and 11th cirs.) 1981. Practice law Tampa, Fla., 1936—; mem. Fowler, White, Gillen, Boggs, Villareal and Banker, P.A., 1946—, chmn. bd., pres., 1970-86; mem. Hillsborough County Home Rule Charter Com., 1969-70, 13th Circuit Jud. Nominating Com., 1972-76, Fla. Supreme Ct. Jud. Nominating Commn., 1979-83; bd. dirs. Freedom Savs. and Loan Assn., Tampa, 1972-84, chmn., 1978-84. Asso. editor: Am. Maritime Cases, 1948—. Bd. dirs. U. South Fla. Found., 1965-68, pres., 1967-68; pres. Gulf Ridge council Boy Scouts Am., 1959; bd. dirs. United Fund Tampa, 1956-64, Greater Tampa Citizens Safety Council, 1966-69. Served to maj., inf. AUS, 1942-46. Fellow Am. Coll. Trial Lawyers, Am. Bar Found., Fla. Bar Found.; mem. Hillsborough County Bar Assn. (pres. 1953), Fla. Bar Assn. (gov. 1951-57), Fedn. Ins. Counsel (pres. 1960-61, chmn. bd. dirs. 1961-62), Internat. Assn. Def. Counsel, Def. Research Inst. (v.p. 1961-62), Maritime Law Assn. U.S., ABA (co-chmn. conf. lawyers, ins. cos. and adjusters 1975-78), Com. of 100, Tampa C. of C. (pres. 1968-69), Am. Legion, Gasparilla Krewe (capt. 1968-70, King LVII 1970-71), Phi Delta Phi, Sigma Alpha Epsilon, Sigma Alpha Epsilon Found., Rotary Internat. Found. Democrat. Episcopalian. Clubs: Tampa Yacht and Country (bd. dirs. 1962-64), Univ. (bd. dirs. 1976-79, pres. 1978-79), Merrymakers, Palma Ceia Golf and Country (Tampa). Lodges: Rotary (pres. Tampa chpt. 1959-60), Masons. Home: 3109 Sunset Dr Tampa FL 33629 Office: Fowler White Gillen Boggs et al 501 E Kennedy Blvd Suite 1700 Tampa FL 33602

GILLER, ROBERT MAYNARD, physician; b. Chgo., Sept. 14, 1942; s. Edward M. and Lillian (Katz) G.; student U. Ill., 1960-63; M.D., 1967; postgrad. Columbia U. Sch. Pub. Health, 1979—. Intern, U. Ill., 1967-68; resident in internal medicine Cornell (N.Y.) Hosp., 1968-69; practice medicine specializing in preventive medicine, N.Y.C., 1974—; faculty New Sch. Social Research, 1975—. Served with M.C., U.S. Army, 1969-71. Fellow Am. Coll. Preventive Medicine, Internat. Acad. Preventive Medicine. Am. Acad. Family Physicians; mem. AMA (Physician's Recognition award 1987). Author: A Guide for Health, 1982; Medical Makeover, 1986. Office: 960 Park Ave New York NY 10028

GILLESPIE, CHARLES A., JR., U.S. ambassador; b. Long Beach, Calif., Mar. 22, 1935; m. Vivian Havens; 2 children. B.A., U. Calif., 1958; postgrad., Syracuse U., 1975-76, Nat. War Coll., 1980-81. With U.S. Fgn. Service, 1965—; regional security officer Manila, Philippines, 1965-66, Brussels, Belgium, 1966-68; adminstrv. officer U.S. NATO Mission 1968-70; with U.S. Dept. State, 1970—, spl. asst. Bur. Adminstrn., 1970-72, gen. services officer, Mexico, 1972-75; adminstrv. officer, Managua U.S. Dept. State, Nicaragua, 1976-78, assoc. dir. mgmt. ops. U.S. Dept. State, 1978-80, exec. asst., 1981-83, dep. asst. Sec. State for Caribbean, Bur. Inter-Am. Affairs, 1983-85; U.S. ambassador Colombia, 1985—. Office: Dept State US Embassy to Colombia Washington DC 20520 *

GILLESPIE, DOUGLAS GRANT, food supplement manufacturer; b. Tulsa, Sept. 19, 1946; s. Francis Aiken and Martha Allen (Grant) G.; B.A., Diablo Valley Coll., 1967; postgrad. San Francisco State Coll., 1967-68; children—Jo Ann, Alexander Ryan; m. Melinda Ann Sellers, Apr. 9, 1977. Sales clk. Sports Unltd., Orinda, Calif., 1964-67; loan officer, mgr. United Calif. Bank, Oakland, 1967-69; pres., chief exec. officer Natural Formulas, Inc., Hayward, Calif., 1970-81; pres., chief exec. officer Doug Gillespie & Assocs., Inc., Oakland; founder, pres. GCH Corp., Oakland; founder, chmn. Waterpacu Co., Hayward. Pres. Nat. Protein Council, 1978-79. Mem. Inst. Food Technologists, Council for Responsible Nutrition (vice-chmn. bd. dirs.), Drug Chemicals and Allied Trades Assn. Clubs: Orinda Country, Tahoe Yacht. Home: 11 Vista Del Mar Orinda CA 94563 Office: Gillespie & Assocs Inc 1946 Embarcadero Oakland CA 94606

GILLESPIE, HARRY ROBINSON, management consultant; b. Oak Park, Ill., May 24, 1922; s. Harry Robinson and Margaret Louise (Weisskirchen) G.; m. Shirley Hodek, June 21, 1944; children: Anne Louise, Andrew Scott, Douglas Robinson. BSME, Ill. Inst. Tech., 1944; student exec. program, U. Chgo., 1954-55; postgrad., Claremont Coll., 1960; MBA, Pepperdine U., 1975; D Bus. Adminstrn., U.S. Internat. U., 1980. Registered profl. engr., Ill. Engr., engring. mgr. then div. mgr. Cinch Mfg. Corp., Chgo., 1947-58; div. mgr. Edcliff Instruments, Inc., Monrovia, Calif., 1958-62; pres., gen. mgr. Robinson Components Co., Temple City, Calif., 1962-70; gen. mgr. Los Angeles div. Virco Mfg. Co., 1970-75; v.p. adminstrn. B.P. John Co., Santa Ana, Calif., 1975-76; pres., gen. mgr. Hancock Mfg. Co. subs. Samsonite Corp., San Diego, 1977-81; cons. gen. mgmt. and telecommunications Mgmt. Analysis Co., San Diego, 1981—; adj. prof. Mgmt. Nat. U., San Diego, 1981—. Author: Advanced Mathematics and an Introduction to Calculus, 1947; co-author Telecommunications Challenges for the Electric Utility Industry, 1987; contbr. chpt. The Seven Phases of Strategic Planning, 1986; contbr. articles to profl. jours. Served with USN, 1945-47. Mem. IEEE, Acad. Mgmt., Stategic Mgmt. Soc. Republican. Presbyterian. Home: 7960 Via Capri La Jolla CA 92037 Office: Mgmt Analysis Co 12671 High Bluff Dr San Diego CA 92130

GILLESPIE, JAMES DAVIS, lawyer; b. Elkin, N.C., Apr. 30, 1955; s. John Banner and Jerry Sue (Swaim) G.; m. Tommie Lee Johnson, Aug. 13, 1977; 1 child, John Foster. BA, U. N.C., 1977; JD, Samford U., 1980. Bar: N.C. 1980, U.S. Dist. Ct. (mid. dist.) 1982, U.S. Ct. Appeals (4th cir.) 1983, U.S. Dist. Ct. (we. dist.) N.C. 1984. Ptnr. Neaves & Gillespie, Elkin, 1980—. Bb. editors: Cumberland Law Rev., 1978-80. Commr. Town of Jonesville, N.C., 1983-85, mayor, 1985—; mem. exec. com. NW Piedmont Council Govts., 1987, sec., 1988; active Surry-Yadkin Mental Health, Mental Retardation and Substance Abuse Authority, 1981—, vice-chmn., 1987—; bd. dirs. Foothills Art Council, 1987. Mem. ABA, Assn. Trial Lawyers Am., N.C. Bar Assn., N.C. Trial Lawyers Assn., Surry and Yadkin Counties Bar Assn., Elkin Jaycees (bd. dirs. 1981-83, v.p. 1983-84), N.C. Acad. Trial Lawyers, Greater Elkin-Jonesville C. of C. (charter, bd. dirs. 1987—), Phi Alpha Delta, Soc. Curia Honoris. Democrat. Baptist. Home: 371 Wagoner St Jonesville NC 28642 Office: Neaves & Gillespie 112 A Church St Elkin NC 28621

GILLESPIE, THOMAS WILLIAM, theological seminary administrator, religion educator; b. Los Angeles, July 18, 1928; s. William A. and Estella (Beers) G.; m. Barbara A. Lugenbill, July 31, 1953; children: Robyn C., William T., Dayle E. B.A., George Pepperdine Coll., 1951; B.D., Princeton Theol. Seminary, 1954; Ph.D., Claremont Grad. Sch., 1971; D.D., Grove City Coll., 1984. Ordained to ministry Presbyterian Ch., 1954. Pastor 1st Presby. Ch., Garden Grove, Calif., 1954-66, Burlingame, Calif., 1966-83; pres., prof. N.T. Princeton Theol. Sem., N.J., 1983—. Served with USMC, 1946-47. Recipient A.A. Hodge prize in systematic theology Princeton Theol. Sem., 1953; Disting. Alumnus award Claremont Grad. Sch., 1984; Disting. Alumnus award Pepperdine U., 1986. Mem. Soc. Bibl. Lit. Republican. Lodge: Rotary Internat. (Burlingame). Home: Springdale 86 Mercer St Princeton NJ 08540 Office: Princeton Theol Sem CN821 Princeton NJ 08542

GILLESPIE, WILLIAM TYRONE, judge; b. Great Falls, Mont., Mar. 7, 1916; s. William G. and Alma (McBride) G.; A.B., J.D., D.C.L., Willamette U., 1939; LL.D., Hillsdale Coll., 1957; m. Eleanor Johnson, Aug. 31, 1941; 1 son, William Tyrone. Admitted to Oreg., Wash. bars, 1939, Mich. bar, 1948; spl. agt. FBI, 1939-42; partner Pope & Gillespie, Salem, Oreg., 1946-48; mem. legal dept. Dow Chem. Co., Midland, Mich., 1948-54, asst. to pres., 1954-66; partner firm Gillespie, Riecker & George, Midland, Mich., 1966-76; judge Mich. 42d Jud. Circuit, 1977—. Trustee Hillsdale Coll., 1957-72, chmn., 1972-75, chmn. emeritus, 1975—. Served from 2d lt. to lt. col. AUS, 1942-46. Mem. State Bar Mich., Oreg., Wash., Midland County (past pres.) bar assns., Am. Legion, Michigan C. of C. (v.p.), 40 and 8, Blue Key, Beta Theta Pi. Republican. Methodist. Clubs: Masons (33 deg.), Rotary. Home: 1200 W Sugnet Rd Midland MI 48640 Office: Courthouse Midland MI 48640

GILLETT, CHARLES, travel executive; b. Newport, Ky., Sept. 9, 1915; s. Louis B. and Sarah (Maller) G.; m. Virginia Margaret Littmann, June 11, 1949; children: Valerie, David, Brian Paul, Peter Guy. B.A., U. Cin., 1938. Pub. relations dir. Netherland Plaza Hotel, Cin., 1938-39; account exec. Swafford & Koehl Advt. Agy., N.Y.C., 1939-40; advt. and sales promotion dir. Hotel Gibson, Cin., 1940-41; promotion and pub. relations dir. N.Y. Conv. and Visitors Bur., N.Y.C., 1946-62; v.p. N.Y. Conv. and Visitors Bur., 1962-65, exec. v.p., 1966-74, pres., 1974—; Mem. travel adv. com. U.S. Dept. Commerce, 1963-65, 77—, nat. adv. com. on hwy. beautification, 1965-66; del. White House Conf. Natural Beauty, 1965; spl. adviser to Discover Am. Travel Orgns., 1967-68, dir., 1968—; mem. N.Y. State Bd. Tourist Commrs., 1977—; chmn. Nat. Urban Tourism Council, 1977—; mem. U.S. Congressional Travel and Tourism Caucus.; mem. adv. bd., exec. com. Travel and Tourism Govt. Affairs, Policy Council, 1982—. Editor: The Bridge, 1946; Writer, lectr. on travel bus. subjects. Mem. pub. affairs com. U.S. Air Force Acad., 1968-71. Served from pvt. to maj. AUS, 1941-46. Decorated Bronze Star.; recipient Most Original Travel Idea award Midwest Travel Writers Assn., 1964; Golden Horseshoe award Discover Am. Travel Orgns., 1972; Golden Scroll award Broadway Assn., 1977; installed Order of Corte, 1972; medal of Amity France, 1980; Am. Traditions award B'nai B'rith Youth Services, 1981; award of excellence U. Cin., 1981; N.Y. Gov.'s award for long and disting. service; elected to Hall of Leaders of Conv. Liaison Council, 1985. Mem. Nat. Assn. Travel Orgns. (dir. 1960-62, pres. 1963-65, chmn. bd. 1965-67, award of merit 1966), Internat. Festivals Assn. (dir. 1957-59, sec. 1959-61, sec.-treas. 1966-67), Am. Soc. Travel Agts., Soc. Am. Travel Writers, N.Y. State Travel Council, Nat. Tour Brokers Assn., Hotel Sales Mgrs. Assn., Nat. Indsl. Recreation Assn., Pub. Relations Soc. Am., Sales Promotion Execs. Assn., Internat. Assn. Conv. Burs. (dir. 1968-71, v.p. 1971-72, pres. 1973-74), Travel Industry Assn. Am. (life dir., mem. exec. com., Nat. Travel Mktg. award 1981). Club: Overseas Press (N.Y.C.). Home: 8 Ridge Dr E Great Neck NY 11021 Office: Two Columbus Circle New York NY 10019

GILLETT, VICTOR WILLIAM, JR., title insurance company executive; b. El Paso, Tex., Feb. 4, 1932; s. Victor William and Alice Cecelia (Kemper) G.; B.B.A., Tex. A&M U., 1953; m. Anita Johanne Dexter, Mar. 1, 1975; children—Victor William, III, Blake Andrew. Vice pres., dist. mgr. Stewart Title Guaranty Co., Corpus Christi, Tex., 1955-61; pres., chief exec. officer Stewart Title & Trust Co., Phoenix, 1961-77, dir., 1965-77; sr. v.p., nat. mktg. dir. Stewart Title Guaranty Co., Houston, 1977—, dir., 1981—; dir. Stewart Info. Services Corp. Bd. dirs. Ariz. Heart Assn., 1970-73; bd. dirs., sec. Phoenix Civic Improvement Corp., 1974-76. Served with AUS, 1953-55. Mem. Am. Land Title Assn. (gov. 1969-71), Tex. Land Title Assn., Nat. Assn. Corp. Real Estate Execs., Mortgage Bankers Assn. Am., Nat. Assn. Indsl. and Office Parks, Internat. Council Shopping Centers, Assn. U.S. Army (pres., dir. 1968), Navy League, Newcomen Soc. N.Am., Former Students Assn. Tex. A&M U. Episcopalian. Clubs: Houstonian; Aggie (Tex. A&M U.). Home: 2803 Fairway Dr Sugar Land TX 77478 Office: 2200 W Loop S Houston TX 77027

GILLETTE, HALBERT SCRANTON, publisher; b. Chgo., June 29, 1922; s. Edward Scranton and Claribel (Thornton) G.; B.S., M.I.T., 1944; m. Mary Livingston, Feb. 12, 1949 (dec. Jan. 1962); children—Anne Livingston, Susan L.; m. Karla Ann McCall, June 8, 1963; children—James McCall, Halbert G., Edward S. II. Space buyer Andrews Agy., 1946-48; advt. mgr. Good Roads Mach. Co., Minerva, Ohio, 1948; exec. v.p. Gillette Pub. Co., Chgo., 1949-72, Scranton Pub. Co., Chgo., 1972-77, Ins. News, Inc., Phoenix; pres. Scranton Gillette Communications, Inc., 1977—, chmn. bd., pres. Doctor's Tax Letter, Inc., Publisher's Paper Co., Inc., Ednl. Screen Inc., Diapason, Inc., Piano Trade Mag., Florist and Nursery Exchange, 1972-77; chmn. bd. Occidental Life Ins. Co. N.C., 1973-74, McMillen Co., Jacksonville, Fla., 1974-77; dir. Occidental Fire & Casualty Co., Denver. Mem. Lake Forest City Council. Served to ensign USNR, World War II. Mem. Phi Gamma Delta. Club: Onwentsia (Lake Forest, Ill.). Home: 255 Foster Pl Lake Forest IL 60045 Office: 380 NW Hwy Des Plaines IL 60016

GILLIBRAND, MICHAEL GRAY, development planner; b. Hastings, Sussex, Eng., Feb. 26, 1948; s. Patrick Arundell and Kathleen (MacMahon) G. B.A. in Anthropology, U. Sussex, 1970; M.A. in African Devel. Studies, U. London, 1971; postgrad. (Sloan fellow), London Bus. Sch., 1981. Research assoc. U. Nairobi (Kenya), 1972-73; cons. Economist Intelligence Unit, London, 1974-75, I.C.I. Ltd., Billingham, Eng., 1975-76; devel. adviser Ministry of Planning, Kingdom of Saudi Arabia, 1976-80, now sr. adviser Ministry of Industry; sr. cons. Stanford Research Inst., Menlo Park, Calif., 1976-81; v.p. Arthur D. Little Inc., Cambridge, Mass., 1981—; ptnr. Social Analysis Assocs., Oxford, Eng. Contbr. articles to profl. jours. Fellow Royal Anthrop. Inst.; mem. Royal Soc. Asian Affairs, Soc. Bus. Economists, English Speaking Union. Roman Catholic. Office: Arthur D Little Internat Inc, Ministry of Industry, PO Box 3266, Riyadh 11471, Saudi Arabia

GILLIES, DONALD ALLASTAIR, lawyer; b. Evanston, Ill., Sept. 15, 1931; s. Allastair and Alice (Brown) G.; m. Judith Bonnie Seepe, Aug. 19, 1961; 1 dau., Elizabeth Anne. B.A., Denison U., 1953; J.D., Northwestern U., 1956. Bar: Ill. 1956, U.S. Dist. Ct. (no. dist.) Ill., U.S. Ct. Appeals (7th cir.), U.S. Tax Ct. Assoc. Winston & Strawn, Chgo., 1956-61; assoc. Altheimer & Gray, Chgo., 1961-66, ptnr., 1966—. Contbr. articles to profl. jours. Trustee U. Chgo., 1977-83; trustee Bapt. Theol. Union, 1965—, pres., 1974—; bd. govs. Ill. St. Andrew Soc., 1978-88, pres., 1986-88; bd. dirs. Bapt. Retirement Home, 1964—. Served with U.S. Army, 1956-58. Mem. ABA, Ill. Bar Assn. (mem. bus. advice and fin. planning council and estate planning, probate and trust law council, 1987—), Am. Coll. Probate Counsel (Ill. chmn. 1983-88), Chgo. Bar Assn. (chmn. fed. tax com. 1978-79, com. profl. standards). Republican. Baptist. Clubs: University (Chgo.); Skokie Country (Glencoe, Ill.). Office: 333 W Wacker Dr Chicago IL 60606

GILLILAND, WILLIAM ELTON, lawyer; b. Hood County, Tex., May 8, 1919; s. Albert Floyd and Rosa Lee (Wood) G.; m. Frances Esmond; children: Chloe Ella (Mrs. Tipton Cole), John Marshall. Student, Tex. Tech. Coll., 1937-39, U. Tex., 1939-41; LL.B., U. Tex., 1947. Bar: Tex. 1947. County atty. Martin County, Tex., 1947-48, Howard County, Tex., 1948-49; dist. atty. 118th Jud. Dist., Tex., 1949-54; mem. firm Little & Gilliland, Big Spring, Tex., 1954-59; firm McDonald, Shafer & Gilliland, Odessa, Tex., 1959-62, Shafer, Gilliland, Davis, McCollum & Ashley, Odessa, 1962-85. Served to capt. Signal Corps AUS, 1942-46. Mem. Am. Coll. Trial Lawyers, Am. Law Inst., Tex. Bar Found., State Bar Tex. žBA, Internat. Assn. Ins. Counsel, Am. Judicature Soc., Tex. Assn. Def. Counsel. Home: 11 Chimney Hollow Odessa TX 79762 Office: PO Drawer 1552 Odessa TX 79760

GILLIS, EILEEN FLEMING, educator; b. Boston, Dec. 9, 1930; d. James Joseph and Anna Theresa (Brosnahan) Fleming; m. Joseph L. Gillis, June 17, 1948; children: Kathleen Gillis Sayre, Joseph Leo, Julie Anne G. Dutcher, Daniel Edward, Michael Kerby, F. Brian. AB, Emmanuel Coll., 1946; MEd, Boston U., 1972. Math. researcher MIT, Cambridge, 1946-49; reading specialist Milton (Mass.) Pub. Schs., 1972-79, core evalution chmn., 1979-82, resource tchr., 1982—, dir. inservice tng. program for secondary tchrs. in reading, 1978-79; pres. Gillis Cons., 1988—. Mem. Milton Town Meeting, 1975—; trustee Milton Library, 1976-85, rec. sec., 1981-82, chmn. computer study com., 1982-85; dir. Coll. Entrance Exam. Bd., Milton High Sch., 1980; chmn. Ann. Charity Ball, 1980; bd. dirs. Notre Dame Acad., 1988—, Friends of the Boston Symphony Orch., Friends of Boston Ballet. Mem. Internat. Reading Assn., New Eng. Reading Assn., Mass. Reading Assn., Nat. Tchrs. Assn., Mass. Tchrs. Assn., Mass. Assn. Children with Learning Disabilities, Friends of Milton Library, Milton Hist. Soc., Mus. Fine Arts Boston, LWV, AAUW (pres. Milton area br. 1982-84, rec. sec. Mass. div. 1984-85). Club: Milton Hoosic. Home: 1278 Canton Ave Milton MA 02186 Office: Milton Pub Schs Milton MA 02186

GILLMOR, JOHN EDWARD, lawyer; b. Phila., Oct. 26, 1937; s. John Edward and Louise Ann (Porter) G.; m. Allis Dale Brannon, Aug. 17, 1968; children: Sarah, Abigail, Susan, Eleanor, John, Matthew. B.A., Swarthmore Coll., 1959; LL.B., U. Pa., 1962. Bar: N.Y. 1963, Tenn. 1972, Pa. 1980, D.C. 1962. Asso. Dewey Ballantine Bushby Palmer & Wood, 1962-63, 66-71; v.p., corp. counsel Hosp. Affiliates Internat., Nashville, 1971-78; sr. v.p., gen. counsel Hosp. Affiliates Internat., 1978-79; staff v.p., asst. gen. counsel INA Corp., Phila., 1980; sr. v.p., gen. counsel INA Health Care Group, 1981; partner Gillmor, Mills & Gillmor, 1981-83; dir., exec. v.p. Health Am. Corp., 1983-86; ptnr. Gillmor, Anderson & Gillmor, 1986—. Served with USMC, 1963-66. Mem. Am. Bar Assn., Bar Assn. City N.Y. Republican. Clubs: World Trade (N.Y.C.). Home: 1700 Graybar Lane Nashville TN 37215 Office: Gillmor, Anderson and Gillmor 3322 W End Ave Suite 414 Nashville TN 37203

GILLOW, GEORGE BRACEY, electrical engineer; b. Potrerillos, Chile, Oct. 27, 1945; s. Joseph Robert and Annie Rachel (Taylor) G.; came to U.S., 1957; B.S. in Elec. Engring., San Diego State U., 1970, M.S. in Elec. Engring., 1973; m. Pamela Jean Kennedy, Sept. 24, 1982. Project leader, design central processing units for computer, advanced devel. dept. Data Processing div. NCR Corp., San Diego, 1970-78; group mgr., design of large central processing units for computer Nat. Semi-condr. Corp., San Diego, 1978-80; with JRS Industries, San Diego, 1980-82; mgr. engring. DDG Corp., San Diego, 1982—; v.p. Digidyne Corp., San Diego, 1983—; dir. engring. Questron Corp., 1984-86; instr. Southwestern Coll., evenings, 1974, 75. Chmn. Environ. Control Commn. Chula Vista, 1975-78, chmn. Hist. Sites Bd., 1975-78; mem. Chula Vista City Council, 1978-82, vice mayor, 1979-80. Mem. Tau Beta Pi. Democrat. Home: 250 Camino Del Cerro Grande Bonita CA 92002 Office: 3910 Sorrento Valley Blvd San Diego CA 92121

GILLULY, C(HRISTOPHER) W(ILLIAM), computer systems company executive, consultant, former naval officer; b. London, Dec. 18, 1945; came to U.S., 1946; s. John William and Carol Miriam (Carroll) G. B.S.M.E., Marquette U., 1967; M.A. in Adminstrn., Chapman Coll., 1974; Ed.D. in Ednl. Adminstrn., Catholic U. Am., 1982; grad. Naval War Coll., 1976. Commd. ensign U.S. Navy, 1967, advanced through grades to lt. comdr., 1976; naval aviator Vietnam, 1970-71; resigned, 1980; pres. chmn. bd. Micro Research, Industries, Falls Church, Va.; bd. dirs. Century Nat. Bank, Washington, Congrl. Mgmt. Found., Washington; bd. dirs. Columbia Nat. Bank, Congressional Mgmt. Found. Pres. Cyrandall Valley Homeowners Assn., 1982-83. Decorated Air Medal (12). Mem. D.C. Bd. Trade, Greater Washington Soc. Assn. Execs. Republican. Roman Catholic. Office: 3027 Rosemary Ln Falls Church VA 22042

GILMAN, ESTHER, artist, illustrator, set designer; b. Cleve., Aug. 13, 1925; d. Joseph and Bertha (Tenenbaum) Morgenstern; m. Richard M. Gilman, Sept. 1, 1949 (div. 1964); 1 son; Nicholas Alexander. B.S. in Design, U. Mich., 1961; M.A., NYU, 1981. Stage designer The Open Theater La Mama, N.Y.C., 1964-68; freelance illustrator, N.Y.C., 1964—; dir. Designers Workshop, N.Y.C., 1971—; visual cons. The Open Theater, 1964-68; bd. dirs., cons. The Feminist Press, Old Westbury, L.I., 1970-75; one person exhbn. U. Wis., Madison, 1987; one woman shows at Razor Gallery, N.Y., 1978, Washington Sq. E. Gallery, N.Y.C., 1981, Americana in Soho, 1981, Salle Polyvalente, St. Amand Montrond, France, 1983, Symposium on Women in Arts , U. Wis., 1987, Jewish Community Ctr., 1988; exhibited in group shows at Mus. Modern Art Young Printmakers, N.Y.C., 1956, Riverside Mus., N.Y.C., 1962, Nat. Acad. N.Y., 1965, Am. Water Color Soc., 1966; Illustrator books: Little Girl and Her Mother, 1964; Nothing But a Dog, 1972 Little Boat, 1974; I've Considered My Days, 1964; designer stage sets: Viet Rock, 1966; Keep Tightly Closed, 1966; It's Almost Like Being, 1964, Miss Nefertitti Regrets, 1965. Recipient medal of honor for watercolor, Painters and Sculptors Soc. N.J., 1958; first prize Robert Boardman award Painter Soc. N.J., 1956; Am. Inst. Graphic Art award, 1970. Fellow Va. Ctr. for Creative Arts, Cummington Community for the Arts; mem. Art Students League N.Y. Address: 160 Riverside Dr New York NY 10024

GILMAN, JOHN RICHARD, JR., marketing professional; b. Malden, Mass., July 6, 1925; s. John Richard and Philomene (Gradie) G.; A.B., Harvard, 1945; postgrad. Georgetown U., 1945-46; M.S.W., NYU, 1983; m. Julia Streeter, Feb. 6, 1960; children—Derek, Susan. Cert., N.Y., R.I. Dir. publicity John H. Breck, Inc., Springfield, Mass., 1949-53, asst. advt. mgr., 1950-53, dir. new products, 1955-56, tech. dir., 1956-63; dir. new products Acco Labs., Am. Cyanamid Co., Wayne, N.J., 1963; treas., exec. v.p. August Sauter of Am., Inc., N.Y.C., 1964, pres., 1965-79, also chief exec. officer; pres. John R. Gilman Inc., N.Y.C., 1980—; dir. Slee Internat., Inc., N.Y.C., Finex Mining Co., Reno; asso., Fisher Cons. Internat. Inc. N.Y.C., 1980—, assoc. C.M. Oppenheim & Co. Inc. N.Y.C., 1981-86; cons. Right Assocs., Inc., Providence, 1986—. Trustee, Sculpture Center, N.Y.C., 1977—, mem. exhibition com., 1980-82, v.p., 1983-86. Augustus St. Gaudens Meml., Cornish, N.H., 1982; budget com. Town of Tiverton (R.I.), 1977-79. Served with USNR, 1943-46. Mem. Soc. Cosmetic Chemists, N.Y. Acad. Scis., Am. Pharm. Assn., Am. Orthopsychiatric Assn., Soc. Photog. Scientists and Engrs., Profl. Photographers Am., Art Students League. Clubs: Chemists; Harvard, Nat. Arts (N.Y.C.). Film maker: Water, 1950; Dear Nancy, 1953; co-pub. Arcadia Press, N.Y.C., 1979—. Home: 395 Punkateest Neck Rd Tiverton RI 02878 Office: 1 Richmond Square Providence RI 02906

GILMAN, SHELDON G., lawyer; b. Cleve., July 20, 1943. B.B.A., Ohio U., 1965; J.D., Case Western Res. U., 1967. Bar: Ohio 1967, Ky. 1971, Ind. 1982, Fla. 1984, D.C. 1985, Tenn. 1985, U.S. Supreme Ct., 1987. Mem. staff accts. tax dept. Arthur Andersen & Co., Cleve., 1967-68; assoc. Handmaker, Weber & Meyer, Louisville, 1971-74, ptnr., 1974-78; ptnr. Barnett & Alagia, Louisville, 1984-87; ptnr. Lynch, Cox & Gilman, 1987—; gen. counsel Louisville Assn. Life Underwriters, 1977, 78. Bd. dirs., chmn. Louisville Minority Bus. Resource Ctr., 1975—; pres. Congregation Adath Jeshurun, 1986—; bd. dirs., v.p., sec. Louisville Orch., 1982-85; bd. dirs. City of Devondale (Ky.), 1976. Served with JAGC, AUS, 1968-71. Mem. Ky. Bar Assn. (ethics com. 1982-86), Louisville Employee Benefit Council (pres. 1980). Office: 1800 Meidinger Tower Louisville KY 40202

GILMER, B. VON HALLER, retired educator, industrial psychologist; b. Draper, Va., June 15, 1909; s. Beverly Tucker and Willie Sue (Graham) G.; m. Ellen Conduff, Aug. 23, 1934; 1 child, Nancy Tucker. B.S., King Coll., 1930; M.S., U. Va., 1932, Ph.D., 1934. Instr. psychology King Coll., Bristol, Tenn., 1934-36; asst. prof. psychology Carnegie Inst. Tech. (now Carnegie-Mellon U.), 1936-42, prof. psychology, dept. head, 1947-76; prof. psychology Va. Poly. Inst. and State U., 1976-84; asso. prof. psychology U. Va., 1946-47; vis. prof. U. Calif-Berkeley, 1964-65; adviser U.S. Office Edn., 1949-51; cons. USAF, 1950-51. Author: 18 books on psychology, including Industrial and Organizational Psychology, 4th edit, 1977, Applied Psychology, 1975; also numerous research publs.; edited family genealogy book. Bd. dirs. Pitts. Child Guidance Center, Inc., 1952—, Mental Health Soc. Allegheny County, 1954—; bd. visitors King Coll., 1970-76. Served from 1st lt. to maj. USAAF, 1942-46. Recipient Nat. Author award Am. Soc. Tng. and Devel., 1966. Fellow Am. Psychol. Assn. (mem. edn. and tng. bd. 1955-57), Eastern Psychol. Assn.; mem. So. Soc. Philosophy and Psychology (pres. 1948), Va. Psychol. Assn. (award for disting. contbns. to applied psychology 1986), Pitts. Psychol. Assn. (dir. 1950-51), Sigma Xi, Phi Kappa Phi, Phi Sigma Pi. Presbyn. Home: RD Box 134 Draper VA 24324

GILMORE, EDWARD JOHN, mechanical engineer; b. Ballywalter Newtownands, County Down, No. Ireland, June 27, 1945; s. William and Ann Jane (Patterson) G.; m. Marjorie Watson, Sept. 13, 1944; 1 child,

Stephen. Higher nat. cert., Ashby Inst., Belfast, 1968. Investigation engr. Rolls Royce Aero Engine, Dundonald, No. Ireland, 1967-69; project engr. Norton Abrasives Ltd., Belfast, 1969-76; product mgr. J. Hind and Sons, Belfast, 1976-88; designer, inventor Entec Industries Ltd., Bangor, No. Ireland, 1988—. Inventor spl. purpose machines. Recipient Discus Throwing medal No. Ireland Sports Assn, 1966. Home: 28 Springvale Rd, Ballywalter Newtownands County Down BT22RS, Nothern Ireland Office: Entec Industries Ltd, Old Belfast Rd, Bangor BT191LT, Northern Ireland

GILMORE, JAMES STANLEY, JR., broadcasting company executive; b. Kalamazoo, June 14, 1926; s. James Stanley and Ruth (McNair) G.; m. Diana Holdenreide Fell, May 21, 1949 (dec.); children: Bethany, Sydney, James Stanley III, Elizabeth, Ruth; m. Susan Chitty Maggio, Sept. 13, 1980. Student, Culver Mil. Acad., Western Mich. U., Kalamazoo Coll., 1945; Litt.D. (hon.), Nazareth Coll. Owner, chmn., pres., chief exec. officer Jim Gilmore Enterprises, Kalamazoo, 1960—; chmn., chief exec. officer Gilmore Broadcasting Corp.; owner Jim Gilmore Cadillac-Pontiac Nissan Inc.; pres. Gilmore Racing Team, Inc. (A.J. Foyt, driver); v.p., dir. Continental Corp. Mich.; asst. sec., dir. Fabri-Kal Plastics Corp., Kalamazoo; partner Hotel Investment Realty Corp., Greater Kalamazoo Sports, Inc. (hockey franchise); owner Anthony Abraham Chevrolet, Miami, Fla., GEC Life Ins. Co., Miami, Jim Gilmore Lincoln Mercury, Hialeah, Fla.; ptnr. Kalamazoo Stadium Co.; dir., mem. trust com. First Am. Bank-Mich. N.A.; dir. First Am. Bank Corp.; Mem. Pres.' Citizens Adv. Com. on Environ. Quality; former dir. Fed. Home Loan Bank Bd., Indpls.; mem., past chmn. Mich. Water Resources Commn.; mem. Mich. Gov.'s Forum, Alexander Graham Bell Bd., Washington, Pres.'s Commn. Health Phys. Edn. Sports; mem. nat. adv. cancer council HEW; mem. Nat. Assn. Broadcasters' adv. com. to Corp. for Pub. Broadcasting.; pres. Kalamazoo County Young Rep. Club, 1947-49; mayor Kalamazoo, 1959-61; past mem. Kalamazoo County Bd. Suprs.; past chmn. Kalamazoo County Rep. Exec. Com.; del. Rep. Nat. Conv. Asso. bd. dirs. Boys Clubs Am.; bd. dirs., past chmn. Kalamazoo County chpt. A.R.C.; former chmn. bd. trustees Nazareth Coll.; trustee, mem. finance com. Greater Mich. Devel. Found.; mem., chmn. bldg. com. fund dr. Constance Brown Speech and Hearing Center; past trustee Kalamazoo Coll.; mem. adv. group Center Urban Studies and Community Services; trustee past vice chmn. Kalamazoo Nature Center; mem. bldg. and exec. coms. Bronson Hosp., also chmn. ad hoc legis. com.; past trustee, past v.p. Mich. Found. for Arts, Detroit; founder bd. dirs. Martin Luther King Meml. Fund; life dir. Family Service Center Kalamazoo; mem. Mich. bd. dirs. Radio Free Europe, Novi Motorsports Mus.; nat. sponsor Ducks Unltd.; life mem. March Dimes; chmn. spl. reorganizational com. United Fund: mem. fund raising com. Pres. Ford Library/Mus.; mem. Pres.'s Council Phys. Fitness and Sports; hon. trustee Mich. Alvin Bentley Charitable Found. Served with USAAF, 1943-46. Named Kalamazoo Young Man of 1960, One of Mich.'s 5 Young Men of 1960, hon. citizen of Houston and Indpls.; recipient Ann. Service to Mankind award Sertoma Club, Man of Yr. award Mich. Auto Racing Fan Club, Auto Racing Found. Frat., honors Hoosier Racing Assn., Auto Racing Frat. Found., Inc., Milw. Mem. Kalamazoo County C. of C. (past pres., past dir., mem. exec. com. of indsl. devel. com.), Mich. C. of C. (mem. law and order com.), N.A.M., Mich. Acad. Sci., Arts and Letters. Episcopalian (mem. bd. diocese Western Mich., chmn. cathedral drive, mem. com. Bishop Whittemore Found.). Clubs: Capitol Hill (Washington); Park (Kalamazoo, Mich.) (past dir.); Mid-America (Chgo.); Otsego Ski (Gaylord, Mich.); Ocean Reef (Key Largo, Fla.). Office: Jim Gilmore Enterprises 202 Mich Bldg Kalamazoo MI 49007

GILMORE, JUNE ELLEN, psychologist; b. Middletown, Ohio, Oct. 22, 1927; d. Linley Lawrence and Elizabeth Kathleen (Barker) Wetzel; m. John Lester Gilmore, July 6, 1945; children: John Lester Jr., Michael Edward. BS, Miami U., Oxford, 1961; MS, Miami U., 1964. Lic. psychologist, Ohio. Intern in psychology Hamilton (Ohio) City Schs., 1963-64; psychologist Talawanda, Shiloh, Trenton Schs., Butler County, Ohio, 1964-66, Franklin (Ohio) City Schs., 1966-72, Wapakoneta (Ohio) City Schs., 1972-76, Cin. City Schs., 1978-86; pvt. practice psychology 1975—; planner, evaluator Warren/Clinton Counties Mental Health Bd., Ohio, 1986—. Co-author: Summer Children-Ready or not for School, 1986. Sec. Tri County Drug Council, Lima, Ohio, 1974; chmn. Auglaize County Social Services, Wapakoneta, Ohio, 1973-75. Mem. Ohio Sch. Psychologists Assn. (exec. bd. 1982-86), Southwestern Ohio Sch. Psychologist Assn. (pres.), Southwest Council Exceptional Children (Pres.), Nat. Assn. Sch. Psychologists, Ohio Psychol. Assn., Butler County 648 Mental Health Bd. (bd. dirs. 1978-86, pres. 1983-84). Republican. United Methodist. Home and Office: 6120 Michael Rd Middletown OH 45042

GILSON, ARNOLD LESLIE, engring. co. exec.; b. Perrysburg, Ohio, Apr. 10, 1931; s. Leslie Clair and Velma Lillian (Hennen) G.; B.S. in Mech. Engring., U. Toledo, 1962; m. Phyllis Mary Seiling, Sept. 15, 1951 (dec. May 1982); children—David, Jeffrey, Luann, Suzanne. Engr., Miller, Tillman & Zamis engrs., Toledo, 1962-67, regional mgr., Phoenix br., 1967-69; owner, mgr. A B S Tech. Services, Phoenix, 1969—. Served with U.S. Army, 1952; Korea. Decorated Bronze Star. Mem. Nat. Mil. Intelligence Assn. Republican. Roman Catholic. Commd. extraordinary minister, 1975. Patentee in several fields. Home: 8226 E Meadowbrook Ave Scottsdale AZ 85251 Office: PO Box 2440 Scottsdale AZ 85252

GILSTRAP, JOE JACKSON, insurance executive; b. Pickens, S.C., Apr. 21, 1923; s. Luther Hubbard and Ethel Bulah (Massey) G.; B.A., Furman U., Greenville, S.C., 1948; m. Esterlene Burroughs, Dec. 22, 1945; children—Carol, Donald. Asst. treas. Liberty Life Ins. Co., Greenville, 1948—; v.p. Hampton Ins. Agency, 1969; ins. mgr. Liberty Corp., Greenville, 1970-75, asst. v.p., risk mgr., 1975—. Served with USNR, 1943-46. Fellow Life Office Mgmt. Assn., Risk and Ins. Mgmt. Soc. (former v.p. Carolinas chpt., sec.-treas. Western Carolina chpt.). Methodist (chmn. coms., tchr.). Lodges: Masons, Shriners. Home: 34 Lockwood Ave Greenville SC 29607 Office: PO Box 789 Greenville SC 29602

GIMORO, NEHEMIAH FELIX, economist; b. Ragem, Junam, Nebbi, Uganda, Feb. 15, 1946; came to Italy, 1978; s. Benjamin Duka and Susan (Ojoko) Loka; m. Joyce Ayuleru Ajule, Dec. 31, 1971; children—Edmond, Michael, Andrew, Winifred. B.S. with honors, Makerere U., Uganda, 1972; M.A. Econs., U. Dar Es Salaam, Tanzania, 1977. Research/statis. officer E.A. Community Harbours Corp., Dar es Sallam, Tanzania, 1972-76; lectr. E. African Community UDSM, 1976-77; project analyst Nat. Food and Agr. Corp., Dar Es Salaam, 1977; economist FAO of UN, Rome, 1978, commodity specialist, 1979-86; project analyst, 1987—; dir. Nile Devel. Corp., Kampala, 1980—. Contbr. articles to profl. jours. Prefect, Goli Jr. Secondary Sch., Nebbi Dist., 1963; monitor/prefect King's Coll. Budo, Kampala, 1968; minister Livingstone Hall Govt., Makerere, Uganda, 1971; mem. Uganda Polit. Discussion Group, 1972-79. W. Nile Dist. scholar, 1962-66; Uganda State scholar, 1964-66. Mem. Am. Econs. Assn., Am. Agrl. Econs. Assn., Uganda Inst. Mgmt. Mem. Uganda Peoples Congress. Office: Food and Agr Orgn, Via Terme Di Caracalla 100, Rome 00153, Italy

GIN, KENNETH YING DOON, civil engineer, consultant; b. Dec. 3, 1924. BSCE, Melbourne (Australia) U., 1945. Cons. engr. Scott & Furphy Cons. Engrs., Melbourne, 1946-55; project engr. Hume Industries (Far East) Ltd., Singapore, 1956-59; dep. dir. pub. works Govt. of Singapore, 1959-63, acting dir. pub. works, 1963-66; gen. mgr. Singapore Pub. Utilities Bd., 1966-69; group gen. mgr. Singapore Land and Investment Co. Ltd., 1970-72; gen. mgr. Sentosa Devel. Corp., Singapore, 1973-75; project dir. Kuttner Collins Internat., Kuala Lampur, Malaysia, 1978; pvt. practice cons. engr. Singapore, 1978—; bd. dirs. Internat. Mapping Co., Singapore; cons. Singapore Poly. Inst., 1976-77; chmn. Singapore delegation to World Power Conf., Tokyo, 1967. Mem. Indsl. Facilities Com. of Singapore Econ. Devel. Bd., 1964-66, Singapore People's Assn., 1964-67; sr. v.p. Singapore Met. YMCA, 1975. Fellow Inst. Civil Engrs. U.K. (chmn. adv. com. Singapore chpt. 1972—), Inst. Engrs. Australia (convenor mem. com. Singapore chpt. 1968—), Inst. Engrs. Singapore, Chartered Inst. Arbitrators (pres. 1987).

GIN, WEE KIT, general practitioner; b. Singapore; d. Chuck and Yee Hing (Boey) Lee; m. Kenneth Ying Doon Gin; children: Kevin, Karina, Karolyn. BS, U. Melbourne, Australia, 1951, MBA, 1954. Asst. lectr. U. Singapore, 1956-59; med. officer St. Andrew's Hosp. for Children, Singapore, 1959-60; gen. practice medicine Singapore, 1960—. Address: care Internat Mapping Co, Singapore City Singapore

GINADER, GEORGE HALL, business executive; b. Buffalo, Apr. 5, 1933; s. George Edward and Meredith (Hall) G. B.A., Allegheny Coll., 1955; M.S. in Library Sci, Drexel U., 1964. Asst. Buyer Lord & Taylor, N.Y.C., 1957-59; job analyst Ins. Co. N.Am., Phila., 1959-60; asst. buyer John Wanamaker, Phila., 61960-61; acting curator Automobile Reference Collection, Free Library Phila., 1961-63; librarian N.Y. C. of C., N.Y.C., 1964-66; chief librarian N.Y. Stock Exchange, N.Y.C., 1966-67; exec. dir. Spl. Libraries Assn., N.Y.C., 1967-70; chmn. bus. and fin. div. Spl. Libraries Assn., 1974-75, pres., 1981-82; mgr. research library Morgan Stanley & Co., N.Y.C., 1970-79; cons. to spl. libraries and info. centers 1979-82; dir. ops. Internat. Creative Mgmt., N.Y.C., 1982-86; pres. Info/Tech Planning Service, Inc., Cranbury, N.J., 1986—. Mem. N.Y. Geneal. and Biog. Soc., Internat. Platform Assn., Am. Records Mgmt. Assn. (treas. N.Y. chpt. 1975-76), Adminstrv. Mgmt. Soc., Nat. Microfilm Assn., Nat. Trust for Historic Preservation, N.Y. C. of C., S.A.R., Phi Delta Theta (asst. sec. chpt. 1967-68, pres. N.Y. alumni club 1970—). Republican. Episcopalian. Home and Office: 45 S Main St Cranbury NJ 08512

GINDER, MICHAEL FRANCIS, osteopath, cardiovascular thoracic surgeon; b. Trenton, N.J., Sept. 26, 1936; s. Michael and Caroline (Duacsek) G.; m. Bonnie Braff, Dec. 16, 1964 (div. Dec. 1976); m. Gwendolyn Irene Sopris, Mar. 6, 1977; children: Heather Oona, Heidi Oona, Elizabeth. BA, Seton Hall U., South Orange, N.J., 1958; DO, Phila. Coll. Osteo. Medicine, 1964. Diplomate Am. Bd. Osteopathic Surgery. Intern Flint (Mich.) Osteo. Hosp., 1964-65; resident in gen. surgery Phila. Coll. Osteo. Medicine, 1965-67, Met. Hosp., Phila., 1967-68; resident in thoracic and cardiovascular surgery Detroit Osteo. Hosp., 1970-71, Chgo. Osteo. Hosp., 1971-72; surgeon Tucson Gen. Hosp., 1971-77, Met. Hosp., Grand Rapids, Mich., 1977—; practice medicine specializing in cardiovascular thoracic surgery Grand Rapids, 1977—; sec. dept. surgery Met. Hosp., 1982-83, program chmn. surgical update, 1983-87. Mem. Am. Osteo. Assn., Mich. Assn. Osteo. Physicians and Surgeons, Kent County Assn. Osteo. Physicians and Surgeons, Am. Coll. Osteo. Surgeons (program chmn. thoracic cardiovascular sect. 1985). Mem. Disciples of Christ. Home: 2814 Burrwick SE Grand Rapids MI 49506 Office: 2355 E Paris SE Grand Rapids MI 49506

GINDIN, WILLIAM HOWARD, lawyer, judge; b. Perth Amboy, N.J., Sept. 1, 1931; s. Jac Paul and Belle Ruth (Steinberg) G.; m. Jane Hersh, June 24, 1954; m. Emily Shimkin, Dec. 25, 1965; children—Thomas L., Janine Drucker Gordon, Suzanne B., Geoffrey A. Drucker. A.B., Brown U., 1953; J.D., Yale U., 1956. Bar: N.J. 1956, U.S. Supreme Ct. 1965, U.S. Ct. Appeals (3d cir.) 1980. Assoc., Gindin & Gindin, Plainfield, N.J., 1956-62, ptnr., Plainfield and Bridgewater, N.J., 1962-82; adminstrv. law judge, Newark, 1982-85; U.S. bankruptcy judge, Trenton, 1985—; adj. prof. Rutgers Camden Law Sch., 1988—; lectr. Inst. Continuing Legal Edn., Profl. Edn. Systems, Inc. Mem. Plainfield (N.J.) Human Relations Commn., 1965-72, chmn., 1968-72; pres. Temple Sholom, Plainfield, 1979-81; regional v.p. Union Am. Hebrew Congregations, 1983-86. Mem. Plainfield Bar Assn., Union County Bar Assn., Mercer County Bar Assn., N.J. Bar Assn., ABA. Club: Plainfield Rotary (pres. 1974-75). Bd. editors N.J. Bar Assn. Jour., 1962-72. Home: 30 James Ct Princeton NJ 08540 Office: US Bankruptcy Ct 402 E State St PO Box 1568 Trenton NJ 08607

GINGOLD, DENNIS MARC, lawyer; b. Plainfield, N.J., June 23, 1949; s. Michael Richard and Sally (Weiss) G.; m. Anne Carol Pearson, Sept. 4, 1970; children: Stacy Michele, Samantha Anne. BA, Rollins Coll., 1971; JD, Seton Hall U., 1974; LLM in Internat. Legal Studies, NYU, 1975; postgrad. Joint Program, Princeton U. Bar: N.J. 1974, U.S. Dist. Ct. N.J. 1974, Colo. 1981, U.S. Dist. Ct. Colo. 1981, U.S. Ct. Appeals (10th cir.) 1984, U.S. Supreme Ct. 1985. Atty.-advisor U.S. Comptroller Currency, Washington, 1976-79; regional counsel 12th Nat. Bank Region U.S. Comptroller Currency, Denver, 1979-80; ptnr. Gorsuch, Kirgis, Campbell, Walker & Grover, Denver, 1980-82, Kirkland & Ellis, Denver and Washington, 1982-85; lead banking ptnr. Squire, Sanders & Dempsey, Washington, 1985—; adj. prof. law U. Denver, 1981-82. Sr. mem. Seton Hall U. Law Rev. Named one of the Top 20 Banking Lawyers in U.S. Nat. Law Jour., 1983; Reginald Heber Smith fellow, 1975-76. Mem. Colo. Bar Assn., N.J. Bar Assn., Denver Bar Assn., Banking Law Inst. (adv. council 1983-86). Democrat. Jewish. Clubs: Denver Athletic; Bethesda (Md.) Country. Home: 8712 Crider Brook Way Potomac MD 20854 Office: Squire Sanders & Dempsey 1201 Pennsylvania Ave NW PO Box 407 Washington DC 20044

GINIGER, KENNETH SEEMAN, publisher; b. N.Y.C., Feb. 18, 1919; s. Maurice Aaron and Pearl (Triester) G.; m. Carol Virginia Wilkins, Sept. 27, 1952 (dec. Aug. 1985). Student, U. Va., 1935-39, N.Y. Law Sch., 1940-41. Ptnr. Signet Press 1939-40; assoc. editor Arts and Decoration and The Spur, 1940-41; dir. pub. relations Prentice-Hall, Inc., 1946-49, editor-in-chief trade book div., 1949-52; v.p., gen. mgr. Hawthorn Books div., 1952-61; pres. Hawthorn Books, Inc., N.Y.C., 1961-65, K.S. Giniger Co., Inc., N.Y.C., 1965—, Consol. Book Pubs. div. Processing & Books, Inc., Chgo., 1969-74, Tradewinds Group div. IPC Ltd., Sydney, Australia, 1974-76; lectr. New Sch. Social Research, 1948-49, NYU, 1979-81, adj. asst. prof., 1981-83, adj. assoc. prof., 1983-85. Author: The Compact Treasury of Inspiration, 1955 (NCCJ Brotherhood Week citation), America, America, America, 1957, A Treasury of Golden Memories, 1958, What Is Protestantism?, 1965, A Little Treasury of Hope, A Little Treasury of Comfort, A Little Treasury of Healing, A Little Treasury of Christmas, The Sayings of Jesus, all 1968, Heroes for Our Times, 1969, The Family Advent Book, 1979, Pope John Paul II: Pilgrim of Faith, 1987; Editor: Internat. Pub. Newsletter, 1983—. Mem. editorial bd.: RAM Reports, 1977-83, Communications and the Law, 1978—. Sec. Com. Collective Security, 1952-65; nat. adv. bd. Found. Religious Action, 1956—; dir. Laymen's Nat. Bible Com., 1957—, pres., 1963-71, chmn., 1987—. Served to capt. AUS, 1941-45; asst. to dir. CIA, 1951-52. Decorated chevalier French Legion of Honor. Mem. P.E.N., Phi Delta Phi. Republican. Episcopalian. Clubs: Garrick (London), Authors (London); Nat. Press, Army and Navy (Washington); Overseas Press, Players, Dutch Treat (N.Y.C.). Home: 1045 Park Ave New York NY 10028 Office: 1133 Broadway New York NY 10010

GINN, JOHN CHARLES, newspaper publisher, communications company executive; b. Longview, Tex., Jan. 1, 1937; s. Paul S. and Bernice Louise (Coomer) G.; m. Diane Kelly, Jan. 2, 1976; children—John Paul, Mark Charles, William Stanfield. B.J., U. Mo., 1959; M.B.A., Harvard U., 1972. Successively reporter, copy editor, chief copy desk Charlotte (N.C.) Observer, 1959-62; editor Kingsport (Tenn.) Times-News, 1962-63; city editor Charlotte News, 1963-66; mgr. advt., pub. relations Celanese Corp., 1967-70; dir. corp. devel. Des Moines Register & Tribune, 1972-73; editor, pub. Jackson (Tenn.) Sun, 1973-74; pres., pub. Anderson (S.C.) Ind.- Mail, 1974-77; v.p. Harte-Hanks Communications, Inc., 1978—, pres. S.E. region, 1977-86; dir. Anderson Nat. Bank; dir., mem. exec. com. Anderson Meml. Hosp.; mem. Pulitzer Prize jury, 1977-79; adj. prof. Northwestern U., 1985; frequent lectr. Am. Press Inst. Chmn. Anderson County Civic Ctr. Authority, 1985—, Anderson Cancer Treatment Ctr. Fund Drive; pres. Anderson Area C. of C., 1977, 85, Anderson YMCA, 1975-76; mem. adv. council Anderson Coll.; bd. dirs. So. Newspaper Pubs. Assn. Found., U. Ga. Red and Black; mem. pres.'s adv. council Winthrop Coll., 1985; chmn. bd. dirs. Columbia Missourian. Served with USAFR, 1959-61. R.H. Macy Retail fellow Harvard U., 1972; recipient award for best editorial of year Tenn. Press Assn., 1964, 73,74. Mem. Am. Newspaper Pubs. Assn., So. Newspaper Pubs. Assn. (dir.), S.C. Press Assn. (exec. com.), Sigma Delta Chi. Club: U. Ga.'s Red and Black. Home: 2835 Old Williamston Rd Anderson SC 29621 Office: 1000 Williamston Rd Anderson SC 29621

GINOS, JAMES ZISSIS, research chemist; b. Hillsboro, Ill., Feb. 1, 1923; s. Zissis and Nicoletta M. (Sakellaris) G.; m. Chrisilla Paul Katsas, June 13, 1947; children—Geoffrey, Milton. B.A., Columbia U., 1954; M.S. in Chem. Engring., Stevens Inst. Tech., 1962; Ph.D. in Organic Chemistry, Stevens Inst. Tech., 1964. Chemist, Colgate Palmolive Co., Jersey City, 1953-57; chief chemist Diamond Shamrock Corp., Newark, 1957-58; project coordinator Nopco Chem. Co., Harrison, N.J., 1959-64; asst. scientist Brookhaven Nat. Labs., Upton, N.Y., 1964-68; research asst. prof. Mt. Sinai Sch. Medicine, N.Y.C., 1968-70; assoc. scientist Brookhaven Nat. Labs., 1970-74, scientist, 1974-75; research assoc. prof. Cornell U., 1975—; sr. research assoc. neuro-oncology Lab. Meml. Sloan-Ketting Cancer Center, N.Y.C., 1980-84, assoc. lab. mem., 1984—. Contbr. articles to profl. jours. Mem. Am. Chem. Soc., AAAS, Harvey Soc., Am. Soc. Pharmacology and Exptl. Therapeutics, N.Y. Acad. Sci., Soc. Nuclear Medicine. Research on synthesis of radiopharmaceuticals labelled with shortlived positron emitting radioisotopes used in positron emission tomography. Patentee in field. Home: 200 Winston Dr Cliffside Park NJ 07010 Office: 1275 York Ave New York NY 10021

GINSBERG, ALLEN, poet; b. Newark, June 3, 1926; s. Louis and Naomi (Levy) G. A.B., Columbia U., 1948. With various cargo ships 1945-56; dir. Com. on Poetry Found., 1971—, Kerouac Sch. Poetics, Naropa Inst., Boulder, Colo.; vis. prof. Columbia U., 1986-87. Assoc. with early Beat Generation prose-poets, 1945—; actor: motion picture Pull My Daisy, 1961, Guns of the Trees, 1962, Wholly Communion, 1965, Chappaqua, 1966, Renaldo and Clara, 1978; narrator: film Kaddish, NET, 1977; Author: Howl and Other Poems, 1955, Empty Mirror, 1960, Kaddish and Other Poems, 1960, Reality Sandwiches, 1963, Planet News, Poems, 1961-67, 1968, Indian Journals, 1970, The Fall of America: Poems of these States, 1973 (Nat. Book award 1974), The Gates of Wrath: Early Rhymed Poems 1948-51, 1973, Allen Verbatim, 1974, First Blues, 1975, Journals Early 50's Early 60's, 1977, Contest of Bards, 1977, Mind Breaths, Poems 1972-1977, 1978, As Ever: Correspondence A.G. and Neal Cassady 1948-68, 1978, Poems All Over the Place, 1978, Mostly Sitting Haiku, 1978, Composed on the Tongue, Literary Conversations, 1967-77, 1980, Straight Hearts Delight: Love Poems and Selected Letters, 1980; author: Plutonium Ode, Poems 1977-1980, 1982, Collected Poems, 1947-80, 1984; White Shroed, poems, 1980-85, 1986; recs. include: Songs of Innocence and of Experience by William Blake Tuned by Allen Ginsberg, 1970, Two Evenings with Allen Ginsberg, 1980, First Blues: Songs, 1982, Birdbrain, 1981, Allen Ginsberg First Blues, 1981. Guggenheim fellow in poetry, 1965-66. Mem. Am. Inst. Arts and Letters. Buddhist. Office: care City Lights 261 Columbus Ave San Francisco CA 94133 *

GINSBERG, DAVID LAWRENCE, architect; b. N.Y.C., Sept. 21, 1932; s. Harry Seaman and Zena (Sagal) G.; m. Emily Boor, Dec. 29, 1969; children: Stuart Samuel, Daniel Paul, Laura Ruth. B.Arch., Cornell U., 1955. Pntr. charge N.Y. offices Perkins & Will, 1957-78; exec. v.p. Perkins & Will, Chgo., 1978-79; exec. v.p. planning and program devel. Presbyn. Hosp., N.Y.C., 1979; 2d v.p. Presby. Health Services, Inc., N.Y.C.; asst. clin. prof. pub. health, Columbia U., N.Y.C.; asst. sec. Vol. Hosp. Am./Metro N.Y. Mem. Planning Bd., Scarsdale, N.Y. Served with AUS, 1955-57. Recipient medal N.Y. Soc. Architects, 1955. Fellow AIA; mem. Am. Hosp. Assn., Assn. Am. Med. Colls., Soc. Hosp. Planning, Am. Public Health Assn., Regional Planning Assn., Gargoyle Soc. Club: Town (Scarsdale). Office: Presbyn Hosp Office Planning 161 Fort Washington St New York NY 10032

GINSBERG, EDWARD, lawyer; b. N.Y.C., May 30, 1917; s. Charles and Rose G.; m. Rosalie Sinek, Aug. 11, 1941; children—William, Robert. B.A. with honors, U. Mich., 1938; J.D., Harvard, 1941; D.H.L., Hebrew Union Coll., 1972. Bar: Ohio bar 1941. Former sr. partner law firm Ginsberg, Guren & Merritt; former exec. v.p. and trustee U.S. Realty Investments; past partner N.Y. Yankees Am. League baseball club; past dir. El Al Israel Air Lines, Chgo. Bulls Nat. Basketball Assn., First Israel Bank & Trust Co. N.Y.; now of counsel firm McCarthy, Lebit, et al. Pres., mem. exec. com., nat. campaign cabinet United Jewish Appeal, formerly gen. chmn; v.p. Jewish Telegraphic Agy.; former chmn. Am. Jewish Joint Distbn. Com., now hon. pres.; v.p. Hebrew Sheltering and Immigrant Aid Soc.; Trustee United Israel Appeal, Jewish Community Fedn. Cleve. (life), Mt. Sinai Hosp., Jewish Convalescent Home Cleve. Served with USAAF. Hon. fellow Hebrew U., Jerusalem. Mem. Cleve., Ohio State bar assns., Phi Kappa Phi, Phi Sigma Delta. Jewish religion (pres. temple). Home: 2112 Acacia Park Dr Lyndhurst OH 44124 Office: 900 Illuminating Bldg Cleveland OH 44113

GINSBERG, JERRY HAL, mechanical engineer, educator; b. N.Y.C., Sept. 18, 1944; s. David and Rae Ginsberg, B.C.E., Cooper Union, 1965; M.S. (NASA trainee), Columbia U., 1966, E.Sc.D. (NASA trainee), 1970; m. Rona Lynn Axelrod, June 8, 1968; children—Mitchell Robert, Daniel Brian. Asst. prof. engring. sci. Purdue U., 1969-73, asst. prof. mech. engring., 1973-74, asso. prof. mech. engring., 1974-80; prof. mech. engring. Ga. Inst. Tech., 1980—; pres. JHG Research, Inc.; cons. in field. Fulbright-Hays advanced research fellow, 1975-76; NSF grantee, 1973-75, 75-77, 78-80, 80-83, 86—, Office Naval Research grantee, 1982—. Mem. Acoustical Soc. Am., ASME, Am. Acad. Mechanics, Am. Soc. Engring. Edn., Sigma Xi, Chi Epsilon. Author: (with J. Genin) Statics and Dynamics, 1977, 2d edit., 1984, Advanced Engring. Dynamics, 1987; research and publs. on acoustics, dynamics, vibrations; reviewer for research jours. and publs. Home: 5661 Woodsong Dr Dunwoody GA 30338 Office: Ga Inst Tech Sch Mech Engring Atlanta GA 30332

GINSBERG, LINDA GARTNER, lawyer, author, lecturer; b. Jacksonville, Fla., Sept. 12, 1942; d. Samuel and Clara (Morgenstern) Gartner; m. Murray T. Ginsberg, June 27, 1965 (dec. 1976); children—Leslie, Marc, Tracy. B.S., Jacksonville U., 1963; J.D., John Marshall Law Sch., Atlanta, 1980. Bar: Ind. 1982, U.S. Dist. Ct. (no. and so. dists.) Ind. 1982. Sole practice, Indpls., 1982—; pres. Am. Practice Appraisers, Inc., Savannah, Ga., 1982—; lectr. seminars in field. Author: Family Financial Survival, 1980; How to Succeed in Your Professional Practice, 1984; estate planning editor Dental Practice Mag., 1981-82; contbr. articles to publs. including Dental Mgmt. Mag., Dental Econs. Mag., Dental Student Mag., Podiatry Mgmt., Optometric Mgmt., ADA Jour., Ophthology Mgmt, Prentice Hall Inc. Pres. Aux. to Ga. Dental Assn., Savannah, 1975-76. Recipient Good Samaritan award 1st Ch. Latter Day Saints, Savannah, 1977, Outstanding Woman award Savannah Bus. and Profl. Women, 1980, award Telethon for St. Jude's Children's Hosp., 1980; Disting. Alumni award Jacksonville U., 1985. Mem. ABA, Ind. Bar Assn., Indpls. Bar Assn., Internat. Platform Assn., Ga. Bar Assn. (assoc.). Republican. Jewish. Home: 125 E 45th St Savannah GA 31405 Office: 125 E 45th St Savannah GA 31405

GINSBERG, NORMAN ARTHUR, physician; b. Chgo., May 28, 1946; B.A., So. Ill. U., 1968; postgrad. Ill. Coll. Pharmacy, 1968-69, U. Guadalerjara, 1969-72; M.D., Chgo. Med. Sch., 1974; m. Denise Ginsberg; children—Melinda, Sara. Diplomate Am. Bd. Ob-Gyn. Intern, Michael Reese Hosp. and Med. Center, Chgo., 1974-75, resident in obs-gyn., 1975-79, staff mem., 1979—; practice medicine specializing in obs-gyn., Chgo.; assoc. clin. prof. Northwestern U.; staff mem. Northwestern Hosp. and Med. Ctr., 1984—; investigator 1st trimester diagnosis of inheritable diseases WHO. Bd. dirs. Nat. Abortion Rights League Ill. Fellow Am. Coll. Obs-Gyn.; fellow Am. Soc. Human Genetics; mem. Am. Fertility Soc., AMA, Chgo. Med. Soc. Pioneer chorionic villi sampling in U.S. Home: 1520 Eastwood Highland Park IL 60035 Office: Assn for Women's Health Care Ltd 30 N Michigan Ave Suite 607 Chicago IL 60602

GINSBURG, CHARLES DAVID, lawyer; b. N.Y.C., Apr. 20, 1912; s. Nathan and Rae (Lewis) G.; m. Marianne Laïs; children by previous marriage: Jonathan, Susan, Mark. A.B., W.Va. U., 1932; LL.B., Harvard U., 1935. Atty. for public utilities div. and office of gen. counsel SEC, 1935-39; law sec. to Justice William O. Douglas, 1939; asst. to commr. SEC, 1939-40; legal adviser Price Stblzn. Div., Nat. Def. Adv. Com., 1940-41; gen. counsel Office Price Adminstrn. and Civilian Supply, 1941-42, OPA, 1942-43; pvt. practice law Washington, 1946—; partner firm Ginsburg, Feldman & Bress; adminstrv. asst. to Senator M.M. Neely, W.Va., 1950; adj. prof. internat. law Georgetown U. (Grad. Sch. Law), 1959-67; Dep. commr. U.S. del. Austrian Treaty Commn., Vienna, 1947; adviser U.S. del. Council Fgn. Ministers, London, 1947; Mem. Presdl. Emergency Bd. 166 (Airlines), 1966; mem. Pres.'s Commn. on Postal Orgn., 1967; chmn. Presdl. Emergency Bd. 169 (Railroads), 1969; exec. dir. Nat. Adv. Commn. Civil Disorders, 1967. Author: The Future of German Reparations; Contbr. to legal jours. Bd. mem., chmn. exec. com. Nat. Symphony Orch. Assn., 1960-69; bd. govs. Weizmann Inst., 1965 (hon. fellow 1972); mem. vis. com. Harvard-Mass. Inst. Tech. Joint Center on Urban Studies, 1969; trustee St. John's Coll., 1969-75, chmn. bd., 1974-76; overseers com. Kennedy Sch. Govt. Harvard, 1971—; mem. council Nat. Harvard Law Sch. Assn., 1972—. Served from pvt. to capt. AUS, 1943-46; dep. dir. econs. div. Office Mil. Govt., 1945-46, Germany. Decorated Bronze Star medal, Legion of Merit; recipient Presdl. Certificate of Merit. Mem. Am. Law Inst., Council on Fgn. Relations, Phi Beta Kappa. Democrat. Clubs: Metropolitan, Federal City, Army and Navy. Home: 619 S Lee St Alexandria VA 22314 Office: 1250 Connecticut Ave NW Washington DC 20036

GINZLER, EDWARD RICHARD, chemist, researcher; b. N.Y.C., May 20, 1950; s. Robert Morton and Alice Rhoda (Tolmach) G. B.A. in Chemistry, Kalamazoo Coll., 1972; M.S., in Biochemistry, U. Ill., 1975. Researcher, NIH, Bethesda, Md., 1970-72; teaching asst. U. Ill., Urbana, 1972-75; sr. chemist Mo. Analytical Labs., Inc., St. Louis, 1976-86; chemist Merck & Co. Inc., St. Louis, 1986—. Contbr. articles to profl. jours. Mem. Am. Chem. Soc., N.Y. Acad. Scis., AAAS, Sierra Club. Democrat.

GINZTON, EDWARD LEONARD, engineering corporation executive; b. Dnepropetrovsk, Ukraine, Dec. 27, 1915; came to U.S., 1929; s. Leonard Louis and Natalie P. (Philipova) G.; m. Artemas A. McCann; children: Anne, Leonard, Nancy, David. BS, U. Calif., 1936, MS, 1937; EE, Stanford U., 1938, PhD, 1940. Research engr. Sperry Gyroscope Co., N.Y.C., 1940-46; asst. prof. applied physics and elec. engring. Stanford U., 1946-47, assoc. prof., 1947-50, prof., 1951-68; dir. Microwave Lab., 1949-59; with Varian Assocs., Palo Alto, Calif., 1948—, chmn. bd. dirs., 1959-84, chief exec. officer, 1959-72, pres., 1964-68, chmn. exec. com., 1984—, also bd. dirs.; dir. project M Stanford Linear Accelerator Ctr., 1957-60; mem. commn. 1 U.S. nat. com. Internat. Sci. Radio Union, 1958-68; mem. Lawrence Berkeley Lab. Sci. and Adv. Com., 1972-79; chmn. adv. bd. Sch. Engring., Stanford, 1968-70; bd. dirs., mem. exec. com. co-chmn. Stanford Mid-Peninsula Urban Coalition, 1968-72; bd. dirs. Nat. Bur. Econ. Research, 1981—; mem. com. on animal research NRC; mem. sci. policy bd. Stanford Synchrotron Radiation Lab., 1985—. Author: Microwave Measurements, 1957; contbr. articles to tech. jours. Bd. dirs. Mid-Peninsula Housing Devel. Corp., 1970—, Stanford Hosp., 1975-80; trustee Stanford U., 1977-86. Recipient Morris Liebmann Meml. prize I.R.E., 1958, Calif. Manufacturer of Yr. award, 1974. Fellow IEEE (bd. dirs. 1971-72, chmn. awards bd. 1971-72, medal of Honor 1969); mem. Nat. Acad. Scis. (chmn. com. on motor vehicle emissions 1971-74, co-chmn. com. nuclear energy study 1975-80, com. on sci. and nat. security 1982-84, com. on use of lab. animals in biomed. and behavioral research 1985—), Am. Acad. Arts and Scis. (mem. exec. com. Western Ctr. 1985—), Nat. Acad. Engring. (mem. council 1974-80), Sigma Xi, Eta Kappa Nu, Tau Beta Pi. Home: 28014 Natoma Rd Los Altos Hills CA 94022 Office: Varian Assocs 611 Hansen Way Palo Alto CA 94303

GIOIOSO, JOSEPH VINCENT, psychologist; b. Chgo., Mar. 6, 1939; s. Vincent James and Mary (Bonadonna) G.; B.A., DePaul U., 1962, M.A., 1963; Ph.D. summa cum laude, Ill. Inst. Tech., 1971; m. Gay Powers, Dec. 28, 1963; children—Joseph, Randy Marie, Danielle. Psychologist, Sch. Assn. for Spl. Edn. in DuPage County, Wheaton, Ill., 1964-67; pvt. practice as clin. psychologist, Chgo. and Downers Grove, Ill., 1966—; clin. psychologist J.J. McLaughlin, M.D., Profl. Corp., Chgo., 1970—. Founder dept. psychology Ill. Benedictine Coll., Lisle, 1968, chmn. dept. psychology, prof., dir. testing, 1968-71; cons. psychologist Chicago Ridge (Ill.) Sch. Dist. 127 1/2, 1973-76, Cath. Charities Counseling Service, Chgo., 1963-66, St. Laurence High Sch., Oak Lawn, Ill., 1963-64, Oak Lawn-Hometown Sch. Dist. No. 123, 1967-68, Addison (Ill.) Sch. Dist. 4, 1969-72; vis. prof. psychology Inst. Mgmt., Lisle, 1968-69, George Williams Coll., Downers Grove, 1970-71; chief psychologist Valley View Sch. Dist. 365U, Bolingbrook, Ill., 1971-73; dir. Pub. Program for Exceptional Children, Lisle, 1969-71; mem. Nat. Register Health Service Providers in Psychology, 1975—. Bd. dirs. Ray Graham Assn. for Handicapped, DuPage County, Ill., 1970-73; adv. bd. Care and Counseling Center DuPage County, 1977—. DePaul U. publ. grantee, 1959-61, Fitzgerald Bros. Found. grantee, 1969-71. Mem. Am., Midwestern, Ill. psychol. assns., Soc. Pediatric Psychology, AAAS, Alpha Phi Delta. Clubs: Lakeside Country (Downers Grove); Racquet (Hinsdale, Ill.). Author: Completion Intelligence Test, 1963; Children's Emotional Symptoms Inventory, 1979. Contbr. articles to profl. jours. Home and Office: 6800 S Main St Downers Grove IL 60516

GIOK, SAN ANG, chest physician; b. Amoy, Fukien, Peoples Republic China, Dec. 25, 1916; came to Philippines, 1932; s. Chin Po and Choo (Teo) A.; m. Paz Ty Ang, Oct. 25, 1942; children: Evelina Ty, Andrew Ty. MD, U. Philippines, 1944; postgrad. in Cardiology, Harvard U., 1953; Diplomate, Philippine Coll., 1944; postgras., Mass. Gen. Hosp., 1953. Intern, resident Philippine Gen. Hosp., Manila, 1943; med. examiner Sun Life Can., Manila, Philippines, 1950—; vis. physician Manilla Sanatarium Hosp., 1969—; sr. cons. Chinese Gen. Hosp., Manilla, 1967—; practice medicine specializing in cardiology Manila. Fellow Am. Coll. Chest Physicians, Internat. Acad. Chest Physicans and Surgeons, Philippine Coll. Cardiology, Philippine Coll. Chest Physicians. Home and Office: 441 Juan Luna Binondo, Manilla Philippines

GIOKA, TINA P., sociologist; b. Pyrgos, Ilias, Greece, June 23, 1936; d. Panayiotis C. and Barbara S. (Zarkou) Giokas; BA, Rockford (Ill.) Coll., 1957; MA (Talcott fellow), U. Chgo., 1959; m. Evangelos G. Katsaros, July 6, 1971. Research assoc. Research Center Econ. Devel. and Cultural Change, U. Chgo. at Social Scis. Center, Athens, Greece, 1961-64; research dir. Social Scis. Center, Athens, 1964-67; sci. assoc. Comml. Bank of Greece, Athens, 1968—; lectr. sociology, social pathology; cons. research projects. Sill scholar, 1957; Ford Found. research grantee, Athens, 1968; Fulbright scholar. Mem. Am. Sociol. Assn., N.Y. Acad. Scis., Centre Internat. D'Etudes de Philosophie Du Droit (founding). Research on migration, urban community, family, internal mobility, conflicting systems of values; contbr. articles, book revs. to profl. jours. Home: 12 Ploutarchou St, Athens 140 Greece Office: 9 Karneadou St, Athens 10675, Greece

GIONFRIDDO, MARIO, mathematics educator; b. Messina, Sicily, Italy, Nov. 6, 1946; s. Giuseppe Gionfriddo and Lucia Caruso; m. Maria Ferro; children: Lucia, Giuseppe. Grad., U. Messina, 1970. Asst. prof. math, stable prof. U. Messina, 1973; master prof. U. Catania, Italy, 1981—; chmn., pres., founder sci. com., chmn. organizing com. 1st Catania combinatorial Conf. Author: Istituzioni di Matematiche, 1985, Esercitazioni di Matematiche, 1985; referee many internat. sci. mags., 1981—; assoc. editor Jour. Info. Optimization Scis., 1987—; editor spl. issue Ars. comb., 1987; contbr. articles to profl. jours. Served to lt. U.S. Army, 1971-72. Mem. Am. Math. Soc., Unione Matematica Italiana, Assn. Italiana Scienze Economiche Sociali, Sci. Com. Jour. Le Matematiche, Sci. Com. Conf. Combinatorics, Acc. Pelontane, Acc Gioiemia. Home: Corso Delle Province 50, 95127 Catania Italy Office: Univ Catania, Departimento Matematica, Viale A Doria 6, 95125 Catania, Sicily Italy

GIORDANO, ANTHONY BRUNO, college dean; b. N.Y.C., Feb. 1, 1915; s. Sabino and Natalina (Amato) G.; m. Peggy Cozzi, Dec. 23, 1939; 1 son, Clyde Anton. B.E.E., Poly. Inst. Bklyn., 1937, M.Elec. Engring., 1939, D.Elec. Engring., 1946. Faculty Poly. Inst. N.Y., 1939—, prof. elec. engring., 1953—; dean Poly. Inst. N.Y. (Grad. Sch.), 1960—, acting dean engring., 1978-79; scientist OSRD, 1942-45; research supr. Microwave Research Inst., Bklyn., 1945-65; dir. Northeast Radio Astronomy Council, 1970—; chmn. engring. adv. com. Bd. Edn. City N.Y., 1958-60. Co-author: Network Theory, 1964; author articles in field; assoc. editor: Jour. Radio Sci, 1967-73. Recipient Meritorious award IEEE Communications Soc., 1976. Fellow IRE (chmn. N.Y. sect. 1954-55, regional dir. 1960-62, nat. dir. 1960-62), IEEE (chmn. basic scis. com. 1967-71, chmn. 1967, internat. conv., mem. awards bd. 1972—, fund com. for life 1986—, rep., achievement award edn. soc. 1982, Centennial medal 1984), Engring Found. of United Engring. (trustee 1968—, chmn. projects com. 1973-76, chmn. bd. 1979-80, sec. communications soc. 1963-75, chmn. external awards com. 1975-77, chmn. Edison medal awards com. 1978, chmn. Edn. medal awards com. 1981-83), AAAS, Am. Inst. E.E. (chmn. basic sci. div. 1955-56, rep. Hoover medal awards com. 1976-84); mem. Am. Soc. Engring. Edn. (chmn. meetings com. Middle Atlantic States sect. 1969-71, chmn. sect. 1971-72, chmn. sr. research award com. 1979-81, dir. zone 1 1973-75, v.p. at large 1974-75, v.p. member affairs 1984-86, chmn. grad. studies div. 1979-80, quality engring. edn. project 1985-87, Western Electric Fund award 1981, Charter Fellow award 1983, pres.-elect 1988-89), W. Leighton Collins award Disting. and Unusual Service 1987, Internat. Sci. Radio Union, Sigma Xi, Tau Beta Pi, Eta Kappa Nu. Home: 35-46 74th St Jackson Heights NY 11372 Office: Poly Inst NY 333 Jay St Brooklyn NY 11201

GIORDANO, RICHARD VINCENT, chemical executive; b. N.Y.C., Mar. 24, 1934; s. Vincent and Cynthia (Cardetta) G.; m. Barbara Claire Beckett, June 16, 1956; children: Susan, Anita, Richard. B.A., Harvard U., 1956; LL.B., Columbia U., 1959; D.Comml. Sci., St. John's U., 1975. Bar: N.Y. 1961. Assoc. Shearman & Sterling, N.Y.C., 1960-63; asst. sec. Air Reduction Co. Inc., N.Y.C., 1963-64; v.p. distbr. products div. Air Reduction Co. Inc., 1964-65, exec. v.p., 1965-67; group v.p. Airco, Inc. (now the BOC Group, Inc.), 1967-71, pres., chief operating officer, 1971—, chief exec. officer, 1977—, vice chmn., from 1979; mng. dir., chief exec. officer BOC Internat. Ltd., 1979-85; chmn., chief exec. officer BOC Group, 1985—, also bd. dirs.; dir. Ga. Pacific Corp., Grand Met. Plc.; bd. dirs. Cen. Electricity Generating Bd. Mem. Assn. Bar City N.Y., Am. Iron and Steel Inst. Club: The Links (N.Y.C.). Office: BOC Group, Chertsey Rd, Windlesham Surrey GU20 6HJ, England also: BOC Group Inc 85 Chestnut Ridge Rd Montvale NJ 07645 *

GIOVETTI, ALFRED CHARLES, accountant, consultant, lecturer; b. Alexandria, Va., Sept. 24, 1948; s. Alfred and Alice Jean (McKee) G.; m. Christine Kraft Chandler, Mar. 19, 1977; children—Allison, Catherine, Amanda, Michael. B.A., LaSalle U., 1970, postgrad., 1985; Ph.M., George Washington U., 1979. Cert. fed. taxation Accreditation Council Accountancy. Sr. acct., sr. ptnr. Giovetti and Giovetti, Pub. Accts., Balt., 1968—; owner Computer Wizards, Catonsville, Md., 1983—; mem. credit faculty Catonsville Community Coll., 1987—; food and drug officer FDA, Rockville, Md., 1971-72, Washington, 1972-77; research coordinator dept. medicine U. Md., Balt., 1977-81; supervisory research officer VA Hosp., Balt., 1977-81; mem. mgmt. bd., dir. research and devel., tng. coordinator, quality control supr. Md. Med. Lab., Inc., Balt., 1981; sr. ptnr. World Divers Co., 1962-77, Eagles Internat., 1977-85; instr. and research asst. George Mason Coll., U. Va., Fairfax, 1970-71; supr., sr. ptnr. Am., Eastern, World Aquatics Cos., 1966-77; cons. and project mgr. Hazleton Labs., Vienna, Va., 1972; cons. in counselling Randolph-Macon Women's Coll., Lynchburg, Va., 1975-76; cons. in research mgmt. Royal Iranian Govt., Tehran, 1978; dir. various small cos.; lectr. George Mason U., Catonsville Community Coll., U. Md. and various profl. orgns. Author research papers and abstracts Mem. editorial Com. Free State Acct. jour. Active polit. campaigns; mem. Republican Nat. Com. Presdl. scholar, LaSalle Coll., 1966. Mem. Nat. Soc. Pub. Accts. (mem. by-laws com., IRS liaison com.), Nat. Assn. Enrolled Agts. (mem. inaugural class Nat. Tax Practice Inst. 1986—), Md. Soc. Accts., Mensa. Roman Catholic. Home and Office: Giovetti and Giovetti 1615 Frederick Rd Catonsville MD 21212

GIRARD, CHARLES MARTIN, management, research and training executive; b. Detroit, Feb. 3, 1943; s. Charles G. and Meta Ann (Geschwend) G.; B.A., Park Coll., 1965; M.Govtl. Adminstrn., Wharton Sch., U. Pa., 1967; Ph.D., Wayne State U., 1971; m. Roberta C. Jeorse, June 6, 1965; 1 son, Charles John. Analyst personnel and labor relations Ford Motor Co., 1965-66; asst. to city mgr. City of Port Huron (Mich.), 1966-67; instr., tng. coordinator dept. polit. sci. Wayne State U., Detroit, 1967-69; asst. dir. S.E. Mich. Council of Govt., Detroit, 1969-71; chmn. bd. pres. Internat. Tng., Research and Evaluation Council, Fairfax, Va., 1971—; assoc. dir. resource mgmt. and adminstrn. Fed. Emergency Mgmt. Agy., Washington, 1981-84; sr. mgr. Arthur Andersen & Co., Washington, 1984—. Trustee Stephen B. Sweeney Scholarship Fund, U. Pa., 1982—; bd. dirs., treas., Reagan Presdl. Appointees Alumni Assn., 1986—; curriculum advisor to Commn. on Police Officer Standards and Tng., State of Calif., 1975-79; adj. prof. Am. U., 1977-78; mem. Nat. Crime Prevention Inst.; adv. bd. U. Louisville, 1975-77; reviewer Nat. Criminal Justice Reference Service, Law Enforcement Assistance Adminstrn., Washington, 1978—. Chmn. budget and fin. com. Villa-Lee Community Assn., 1973—, chmn. archtl. com., 1974—. Recipient 1st Disting. Service award Mass. Crime Prevention Officers Assn., 1978; named Hon. Col., Salt Lake City Police Dept., 1978; Fels scholar, 1965-67. Mem. Am. Soc. Public Adminstrn., Am. Polit. Sci. Assn., Am. Mgmt. Assn., Internat. Soc. Law Enforcement and Criminal Justice Instrs., Am. Soc. Tng. and Devel., Nat. Assn. Dirs. Law Enforcement Tng., Nat. Assn. Clock and Watch Collectors, Wilsonian Assn., Nat. Geog. Soc., Internat. Assn. Chiefs Police, Phi Sigma Alpha. Author: A Short Course in Crime Prevention, 1975; contbr. articles profl. publs. Home: 2928 Espana Ct Fairfax VA 22031 Office: 1666 K St NW Washington DC 20006

GIRARD, NETTABELL, lawyer; b. Riverton, Wyo., Feb. 24, 1938; d. George and Arranetta (Bell) Girard. Student, Idaho State U., 1957-58; B.S., U. Wyo., 1959, LL.B., 1961. Bar: Wyo. 1961, U.S. Supreme Ct. 1969, D.C. 1969. Practiced in Riverton, 1963-69; atty.-adviser on gen. counsel's staff HUD; assigned Office Interstate Land Sales Registration, Washington, 1969-70; sect. chief interstate land sales Office Gen. Counsel, 1970-73; ptnr. Larson & Larson, Riverton, 1973-85; sole practice Riverton, 1985 ; guest lectr. at high schs.; condr. seminar on law for layman Riverton br. A.A.U.W., 1965; condr. course on women and law; lectr. equal rights, job discrimination, land use planning. Editor: Wyoming Clubwoman, 1966-68; bd. editors Wyo. Law Jour, 1959-61; writer Obiter Dictum column Women Lawyers Jour; also articles in legal jours. Chmn. fund drive Wind River chpt. ARC, 1965; chmn. Citizens Com. for Better Hosp. Improvement., 1965; chmn. sub-com. on polit., legal rights and responsibilities Gov.'s Commn. on Status Women, 1965-69, adv. mem., 1973—; rep. Nat. Conf. Govs. Commn., Washington, 1966; local chmn. Law Day, 1966, 67; mem. state bd. Wyo. Girl Scouts U.S.A., sec., 1974—, mem. nat. bd., 1978-81 ; state vol. adviser Nat. Found., March of Dimes, 1967-69; legal counsel Wyo. Women's Conf., 1977; pres. Riverton Civic League, 1987-88. Recipient Spl. Achievement award HUD, 1972, Disting. Leadership award Girl Scouts U.S.A., 1973, Franklin D. Roosevelt award Wyo. chpt. March of Dimes, 1985, Thanks Badge award Girl Scout Council, 1987; named outstanding woman Wonder Woman and Girl Scouts U.S.A., 1982. Mem. Wyo., Fremont County, D.C. bar assns., Women's Bar Assn. for D.C., Internat. Fedn. Women Lawyers, Am. Judicature Soc., Am. Trial Lawyers Assn., Nat. Assn. Women Lawyers (del. Wyo., nat. sec. 1969-70, v.p. 1970-71, pres. 1972-73), AAUW (br. pres.), Wyo. Fedn. Womens Clubs (state editor, pres. elect 1968-69, treas. 1974-76), Progressive Women's Club, Kappa Delta, Delta Kappa Gamma (hon. mem. state chpt.). Club: Riverton Chautauqua (pres. 1965-67). Home: 224 W Sunset St PO Box 687 Riverton WY 82501 Office: 513 E Main St Riverton WY 82501

GIRARD, RAPHAELLE ANDRÉE, hygienist; b. Lyon, France, Feb. 13, 1953; s. Pierre Charles and Marguerite Leonie (Mouchet) G.; children: Andeol Ayzac, Camille Ayzac. Grad. high sch., Lyon. Med. Diplomate pub. health studies epidemiologie 2d statis. studies. Med. hygienist Ctr. Hosp., Lyon-Sud, 1980, Hospices Civils, De Lyon, 1982—; tchr. Nurses Schs., Lyon, 1970—. Contbr. articles to profl. jours. Mem. Assn. Francaise D'hygiene Hosp. Office: United Hygiene Epidemology, Pavillon 1 G Ctr Hospitalier, Lyon Sud, 69310 Pierre Benite France

GIRARD, RENÉ MICHEL, psychiatrist; b. Paris, Nov. 20, 1935; s. André G.; m. Jeannine Brun, May 31, 1958; children: Fabienne, Pascale, Pierre-André. MD, Lyon, France, 1962; Neuropsychiatre, U. Caen, France, 1969. Intern Hosp. Psychiatriques Seine, Paris, 1960-64, asst., 1964-68; chief medicine Hosp. Psychiatrique, Caen, 1969—. Editor Jour. Confrontations Psychiatriques, 1968—. Home: 14 Promenade Sévigné, 14000 Caen France Office: Ctr Hosp Spécialisé, 93 rue Caponiè, 14000 Caen France

GIRAUD, ANDRÉ LOUIS YVES, former French minister of defense; b. Bordeaux, France, Apr. 3, 1925; s. Rene and Marie Thérèse (Gamet) G.; m. Claudine Mathurin-Edme, July 1, 1949; children: Francois, Christophe, Sophie. Ed., Lycee de Bordeaux, l'Ecole Polytechnique, l'Ecole nat. supérieure du pétrole et des moteurs. Engr., Ministry of Industry, France, from 1949, head dept. Inst. Francais du pétrole, from 1951, tech. dir., from 1955, dep. gen. dir., 1958-64, mem. consultative com. for scientific and tech. research, 1960-64; dir. fuels Ministry of Industry, 1964-69; v.p. Régie nat. des Usines Renault, 1965-71; bd. dirs. Nat. Centre for Exploitation of Oceans, France, 1967-69, Dept. Edn., 1969-70; adminstrv. gen. govt. del. Commissariat for Atomic Energy, 1970-78; minister of industry, 1978-81; assoc. prof. U. Paris-Dauphine, 1981—; minister of defense, France, 1986-88; bd. dirs. Electricite de France, 1970-78; gen. engr. of mines, 1973-86. Pres. adminstrv. council l'Ecole Polytechnique, 1974; pres. Cie. Generale des Matieres Nucleaires, 1976-78. Decorated Officier Legion d'honneur, Officier Ordre nat. du Merite; Comdr. des Palmes academiques. Address: Ministere de la Defense, 14 rue Saint-Dominique, 75007 Paris France

GIRAULT, LAWRENCE JOSEPH, aircraft engineer; b. Washington, Aug. 27, 1915; s. Alexandre Arsene and Elizabeth Jeanette (Pilcher) G.; m. Lenora Josephine Keahey, Jan. 19, 1946 (dec. 1981); m. 2d, Lois Ione Rasmussen, Aug. 5, 1984. Ground engr. Q.A.N.T.A.S., Brisbane, Queensland, Australia, 1932-41; engring. test operator Commonwealth Aircraft, Port Melbourne, Australia, 1941-42; aircraft insp. Douglas Aircraft Corp., Park Ridge, Ill., 1944; design engr. Belmont Radio Corp., Chgo., 1944-45; engr.-in-charge liaison engring. dept. Aeronca Aircraft Corp., Middletown, Ohio, 1945-46; designer Waco Aircraft Corp., Troy, Ohio, 1946; self-employed airplane and power plant mechanic, Williams, Calif., 1946-47; asst. mech. engr. Phelps Dodge Corp., Ajo, Ariz., 1947-48; designer Fairchild Aircraft Corp., Hagerstown, Md., 1948-50; lead designer Chance Vought Aircraft Corp., Dallas, 1950-60; lead designer The Boeing Co., Renton, Wash., 1960-63, sr. engr., 1967-71; mem. staff N.Mex. State U., Las Cruces, 1963-67, 84-86, YOH, Inc., 1986-87; self-employed gen. aviation aircraft mechanics insp., Las Cruces, 1971—; broker O'Donnell Realty, Las Cruces, 1971-83; owner, founder Shoestring Airport Realty, 1983-87; inspection authorization gen. aviation aircraft, 1987. Served with USAAF, 1942-44. Lic. ground engr., Australia; lic. pilot; real estate broker, N.Mex.; lic. aircraft mechanic. Mem. U.S. Naval Inst., Aircraft Owners and Pilots Assn. Adventist. Inventor main landing gear uplock, outer panel-wing and wing fold prototype, other inventions in field of aircraft mechanics. Home: Courtney Rd PO Box 666 Bingen WA 98605

GIRDEN, EUGENE LAWRENCE, lawyer; b. N.Y.C., Oct. 17, 1930; s. Jules and Freda (Mannes) G.; m. Charlene Margot Tobin, July 4, 1958; children: Lisa Jan, Steven Scott. B.A., U. Md., 1951, LL.B., 1953. Bar: Md. 1953, N.Y. 1957, U.S. Supreme Ct. 1963, U.S. Ct. Mil. Appeals 1954, U.S. Customs Ct., U.S. Ct. Customs and Patent Appeal 1958. Atty. Barnes, Richardson & Colburn, N.Y.C., 1957-58; ptnr. Coudert Bros., N.Y.C., 1959-82, Patterson Belknap Webb & Tyler, N.Y.C., 1982—; guest lectr. NYU Law Sch., 1965—, Columbia Law Sch., 1975—, Cornell Law Sch., 1973—, Practicing Law Inst., 1965—; counsel Am. Theatre Wing, 1985—. State v.p. Conn. Young Dems., Hartford, 1959. Served to lt. USN, 1953-57. Mem. Copyright Soc. U.S.A. (trustee, exec. com. 1967-70, 81-83, 87), Assn. Bar City N.Y., ABA, N.Y. Bar Assn., Libel Def. Resource Ctr. (co-chmn. law firm sect. 1987—). Democrat. Club: Rockrimmon Country (gov. 1978-86, ct. sec. 1978-86). Home: Brookdale Dr Stamford CT 06903

GIRDNER, ALWIN JAMES, credit union executive; b. Albuquerque, Oct. 10, 1923; s. Glen Clark and Marie Ellen (Holcomb) G.; B.S. in Bus. Adminstrn., U. Ariz., 1948, M.A., 1950; m. Marjorie Jo Wilson, Sept. 1, 1946; children—Allen James, Sharon Lynn, Kennan Eugene, Mari Jo. Sales adminstrn. RCA Victor, Camden, N.J., 1952-53; asst. purchasing Temco Aircraft Co., Dallas, 1954-58; asst. dir. edn, Tex. Credit Union League, 1958-61; asst. mng. dir. N.Mex. Credit Union League, 1961-64, mng. dir., 1964-73; treas. N.Mex. Central Credit Union, 1963-73; pres. NMCUL Service Corp., 1971-73; pres. Tenn. Credit Union League, 1973—, TCUL Service Corp., 1973—; chmn. Tenn. Central Credit Union, 1978-79; lectr. in field. Chmn. Credit Union Legislative Action Council, 1972-73; mem. liaison com., chmn. fin. Middle Tenn. State U., 1985—. Mem. Internat. Assn. Mng. Dirs. (sec.), Credit Union Nat. Assn. Internat. (Founders Club award 1962, world extension com. 1967—), Am. Soc. Assn. Execs., Internat. Platform Assn. Republican. Methodist. Author: Navaho-U.S. Relations, 1950; Chapter Leader's Handbook, 1959; Credit Union Informational Manual, 1960. Home: 7829 Parkshore Circle Chattanooga TN 37343 Office: Box 21550 1317 Hickory Valley Rd Chattanooga TN 37421

GIRELLI-ELLINWOOD, ELENA MADDALENA, art collaborator, researcher; b. Bussolengo, Italy, Feb. 15, 1957; d. Giovanni Battista and Maria Girelli; m. Donald Ellinwood, June 25, 1976 (div. Feb. 1980); m. Sakis Papelexiou, Apr. 10, 1980 (div. Aug. 1981). Degree Fgn. Lang., Istituto Seghetti, Verona, Italy, 1976; BLS, Bowling Green State U., 1979; MA in Italian Lit., Ohio State U., 1982. Instr. Ohio State U., Columbus, 1979-82, U. Mich., Ann Arbor, 1982-84, U. Calif., Riverside, 1985-86; governess Ballew Enterprises, Chgo., 1986—. Author poems. Prison ministry corrs. 700 Club, Virginia Beach, 1984-87; mem. Prisioner of War Family Orgns., 1985-87. Served with U.S. Army 1984-85. Recipient Ohio State U. fellow, 1979-82, U. Mich. fellow, 1982-84, U. Calif. Riverside fellow, 1985-86, UCLA fellow, 1987. Home: Lec Canova 36, Bussolengo 37012, Italy

GIROU, MICHAEL, computer systems executive; b. St. Louis, July 2, 1947; s. Jack J. and Patricia S. (Sittner) G.; m. Lynn R. Fessler, Apr. 16, 1965 (div. 1974); 1 child, Beverly; m. Theodora L. Dygert, Dec. 13, 1974; 1 child, Jim. BA in Math., U. Mo., 1969; PhD in Math, 1985. Tech. analyst McDonnell Aircraft Co., St. Louis, 1965-67; sr. systems programmer U. Mo., 1967-69; prin. systems analyst Honeywell, Mpls., 1969-73; pres. SSM, Inc., 1973-79, M.F.D., Inc., 1979-84; program dir. Presearch, Inc., Aiken. S.C., 1984-86; pres. MT Systems Co., Tampa, Fla., 1986—. Designer computer system. Bd. dirs. Amicus, 1978. Curators scholar U. Mo., 1964. Mem. Soc. Indsl. and Applied Math. Am. Math. Soc., IEEE, Assn. Computing Machinery, U. Mo. Alumni Arts and Scis. (trustee 1982—); Pi Mu Epsilon. Republican. Club: Carrollwood Village Golf and Tennis. Home: 13578 Avista Dr Tampa FL 33624

GIRVIN, RICHARD ALLEN, film executive; b. Chgo., Feb. 10, 1926; s. Harry J. and Esther (Easter) G.; Mus.B., Chgo. Music Coll., 1950, Mus.M., 1954; D.F.A., Ga. Tchrs. Coll., 1954; m. Sharon Hillertz, June 9, 1968; children—Gregory, Kimberly, Scott. Instr. in music Bob Jones U., 1950-52; tchr. music Chgo. Public High Schs., 1954-56; dir. radio and TV, NBC, Chgo., 1956-57; asst. prodn. dir. Coronet Instructional Films, Chgo., 1957-62; producer, editor Gilbert Altschul Prodns., Chgo., 1962-64; free-lance producer, writer, Chgo. and Hollywood, Calif., 1964-65; instr. Columbia Coll., 1970-85; author (screenplays) Wine of Morning, 1957 (Cannes Film Festival award 1957), Point of Law, 1986, (book) To See the Stars, 1982, Death Penalty, Burrow, 1988; v.p. Zenith Cinema Service (now div. Dick Girvin Prodns.), Chgo., 1965-73, owner, 1973—, pres. Dick Girvin Prodns. Inc., Chgo., 1967—, owner numerous subs. including Timbrewood Prodn. Music, Timbrewood Pub., Sharilda Pub., Zenith Camera, Typing Unltd., Phase 5 Prodns., db Studios. Served to lt. USAAF, 1943-45. Recipient Indsl. Arts award, 1964, 74, Cine Golden Eagle award USIA, 1964, 67, Atlanta Silver award, 1971, Freedom's Found. award, 1961. Fellow Brit. Internat. Audio Soc.; mem. Audio Engring. Soc., Nat. Assn. TV Arts and Scis., Nat. Assn. Rec. Arts and Scis., Soc. Motion Picture Technicians and Engrs., Aircraft Owners and Pilots Assn., Internat. Brotherhood Magicians. Composer: The Seventh Psalm, 1953; composer film scores: Macbeth, 1951, Pound of Flesh, 1952; composer music for Wild Kingdom TV show, 1973-87, also composer indsl. and ednl. film scores, film library program music scores.

GISCARD D'ESTAING, VALÉRY, 13th president of France; b. Koblenz, Germany, Feb. 2, 1926; s. Edmond Giscard and May (Bardoux) d'E.; grad. Ecole Poly., also Ecole Nat. d'Adminstrn.; m. Anne Aymone de Brantes, 1952; 2 sons, 2 daus. With Fin. Ministry, 1952-54; dep. dir. cabinet of Pres. du Conseil, 1954-56; dep. to Nat. Assembly from Puy-de-Dôme, 1956-58, from Clermont, 1958; mem. gen. council Canton of Rochefort-Montagne from Puy-de-Dôme, 1958; mem. French del. 11th-13th sessions UN; sec. of state, 1959-62; minister of fin. and econ. affairs, 1962-66; minister of economy and fin. 1969-74; leader French del. ann. meetings bd. govs. IMF; pres. of France, 1974-81; conseiller général Puy de Dome Dept., from 1982, dep. 1984-86; pres. Regional Assembly of Auvergne, 1986—; pres. Com. des Finances de l'Econ. Gen. et du plan, 1967-68. Founder, pres. Fedn. Nat. des Republicains Independants, 1966. Mem. Resistance, 1939-44; served with French Army, 1944-45. Decorated Croix de Guerre, Grand Croix de la Lé gion d'Honneur; Grand Croix de l'Ordre National du Merite; Croix de Guerre 39-45; Bronze Star medal. Office: 11 rue Benouville, Paris 16 France *

GISH, EDWARD RUTLEDGE, physician; b. St. Louis, Sept. 5, 1908; s. Edward C. and Bessie (Rutledge) G.; A.B., Westminster Coll., 1930; M.D., St. Louis U., 1935, M.S., 1939; m. Miriam Schlicker, July 8, 1938; children—Ann Rutledge, Mary Priscilla. Intern, St. Louis U. Hosps., 1935-36; resident in surgery St. Mary's Group Hosps., St. Louis, 1936-39; pvt. practice medicine specializing in surgery, Fulton, Mo., 1946—; staff mem. Callaway Meml. Hosp., Fulton. Bd. dirs. Mo. Symphony Soc., pres., 1981; med. dir. Callaway County CD. Served from maj. to lt. col., AUS, 1943-46; lt. col. ret. Res. Hon. col. Gov.'s Staff Mo. Fellow ACS; mem. Royal Soc. London (affiliate), Internat. Coll. Surgeons, AMA, Mo., Callaway County med. socs., Mo. Red Poll Breeders Assn. (pres.), Am. Law Enforcement Officers Assn., Delta Tau Delta, Alpha Omega Alpha. Contbr. articles to profl. jours. Cocapt. U.S. team World Masters Cross-Country Ski Assn., 1985. Home: 7 W 10th St Fulton MO 65251 Office: 5 E 5th St Fulton MO 65251

GISLER, GEORGE LOUIS, lawyer; b. Indpls., Aug. 28, 1909; s. Benjamin Harrison and Anna Marie (Twente) S.; m. m. Georgia Helenanna Umscheid, Apr. 21, 1946; children—John Case, James Robert. A.B., Butler U., 1930; J.D., U. Mich., 1933. Bar: Ind. 1933, Mo. 1934, U.S. Dist. Ct. (we. dist.) Mo. 1934, U.S. Ct. Appeals (8th cir.) 1950, U.S. Supreme Ct. 1950. Assoc., Michaels, Blackmar, Newkirk, Eager & Swanson, 1933-39; ptnr. Sebree, Shook & Gisler, Kansas City, Mo., 1939-42; regional atty. War Prodn. Bd., 1942-43; ptnr. Reeder, Gisler, Griffin & Dysart, Kansas City, Mo., 1947-58; sole practice, Kansas City, 1958—; dir. Dean Research Corp. Bd. dirs. Don Bosco Community Ctr., Kansas City, 1963-85; bd. dirs., sec. corp. Park Lane Med. Ctr., 1980-88; chmn. Ind. Voters Assn., 1960; v.p. Kansas City Philharm. Assn., 1960-65; pres. Kansas City Careers Found., 1959-64; trustee Kansas City Conservatory Music, 1957-59; trustee Kansas City Lyric Opera, 1957-72. Served to lt. USNR, 1943-46 Mem. ABA, Mo. Bar Assn., Kansas City Bar Assn., Lawyers Assn. Kansas City. Clubs: Arrowhead Yacht, Carriage (pres. 1960-61). Contbr. articles to profl. jours. Address: 420 Winnebago Dr Lake Winnebago MO 64034

GISMONOI, PAUL ARTHUR, finance company executive; b. Cleve., Nov. 8, 1955; s. Arthur Anthony and Rena (Scipione) G. BA cum laude, Williams Coll., 1977. Asst. treas. Bank of N.Y., N.Y.C., 1977-81; v.p. Mfrs. Hanover Trust, N.Y.C., 1981-86; group exec. dir. Mfrs. Hanover, Ltd., London, 1986—. Fellow Morgan Library, Guggenheim Mus. (assoc.). Home: 4 South Eaton Pl, London SwlW9JA, England Office: Manufacturers Hanover Ltd, 7 Princes St, London EC2, England

GISOLFI, ANTHONY M., emeritus foreign language educator; b. San Felice a Cancello, Italy, Nov. 13, 1909; s. Ernest E. and Vincenza (Prisco) G.; came to U.S., 1910, naturalized, 1924; AB, CCNY, 1930; MA, Columbia, 1931, PhD in Italian Lit., 1959; m. Eleanor Hayes, June 29, 1935; children: Miriam Gisolfi D'Aponte, Diana Gisolfi Pechukas, Peter, Laura Gisolfi Gilbert. Tchr. Spanish and Italian, High Sch. of Music and Art, N.Y.C., 1937-64; assoc. prof. Spanish and Italian, SUNY, Albany, 1964-76, emeritus 1976—; lectr. Italian lang. and lit. Bronxville Adults Sch., 1980-88; regional specialist overseas br. Office of War Info., Eng. and Mediterranean, 1944-45; lectr. Italian, Sch. Gen. Studies, CCNY, 1947-63, Columbia, summers 1933, 58, 60-63. Mem. Am. Assn. Tchrs. Italian (v.p. 1959-60), MLA, Dante Soc. Am. Author: On Classic Ground, 1962; The Essential Matilde Serao, 1968; Caudine Country: The Old World and an American Childhood, 1985; (with C. Coleman) Classical Italian Songs, 1955. Contbr. to Columbia University Dictionary of Modern European Literature, 1947, 2d edit., 1980; contbr. to A Concordance to Divine Comedy of Dante Alighieri, 1965; also contbr. articles, book revs., poetry translations to profl. jours. Home: PO Box 225 Bronxville NY 10708

GISSEL, HANS, corporate executive, director; b. Rostock, Germany, July 12, 1931. Diploma Ingenieur, Rheinisch Westfälische, 1955; Doktor Ingenieur, Technische Hochschule, Aachen, Fed. Republic Germany, 1960. Chmn. bd. dirs. AEG Aktiengesellschaft, Frankfurt, Fed. Republic Germany. Office: AEG Aktiengesellschaft, Theodor-Stern-Kai 1, 6000 Frankfurt au Main 70 Federal Republic of Germany

GITELSON, SUSAN AURELIA, business executive, civic leader; b. N.Y.C.; d. Moses Leo and Miriam Evelyn (Silverman) G. BA, Barnard Coll.; MIA, Columbia Sch. Internat. Affairs; PhD, Columbia U. Trainee Rockefeller Found.; asst. prof. internat. relations Hebrew U., Jerusalem; research assoc. Columbia U., N.Y.C.; dir. internat. affairs and third world Jewish Congress, N.Y.C.; pres. Internat. Cons., Inc., N.Y.C.; v.p. mktg. and sales Keter Plastic (USA), N.Y.C.; pres., S.J. Internat. Corp., N.Y.C. Author: Multilateral Aid for National Development and Self-Reliance; editor, author: Israel in the Third World; contbr. articles to profl. jours.; mem. editorial com. Jerusalem Papers on Peace Problems. Mem. nat. adv. council Center for Study Presidency, N.Y.C.; mem. Columbia U. seminars; sponsor Gitelson Lecture on Human Rights and U.S. Fgn. Policy, Columbia U., Gitelson Award for human values in internat. affairs Sch. Internat. and Pub. Affairs. Recipient Outstanding Service award Columbia Sch. Internat. and Public Affairs; Alumni medal for conspicuous service Columbia U., 1984. Mem. Columbia Sch. Internat. and Public Affairs Alumni Assn. (pres. 1980-84), Soc. Internat. Devel. (pres.), Columbia U. Alumni Fedn. (exec. com.), Internat. Studies Assn., Am. Polit. Sci. Assn., African Studies Assn., Am. Friends of Hebrew U. (exec. council Greater N.Y.), Am. Jewish Com. (internat. relations commn.), UN Assn. of N.Y. (adv. council). Jewish. Office: Internat Cons Inc 303 E 83d St New York NY 10028

GITLOW, ABRAHAM LEO, retired university dean; b. N.Y.C., Oct. 10, 1918; s. Samuel and Esther (Boolhack) G.; m. Beatrice Alpert, Dec. 12, 1940; children: Allan Michael, Howard Seth. BA, U. Pa., 1939; MA, Columbia U., 1940, PhD, 1947. Substitute instr. Bklyn. Coll., 1946-47; instr. NYU, N.Y.C., 1947-50, asst. prof., 1950-54, assoc. prof., 1954-59, prof. econs., 1959—; acting dean NYU Coll. Bus. and Pub. Adminstrn., 1965-66, dean, 1966-85; pres. Servi-Clean Industries, Inc., Youngstown, Ohio, 1970—; bd. dirs. Macmillan, Inc., Bank Leumi Trust Co. N.Y., Welbilt Inc.; pres. bd. edn. Ramapo (N.J.) Cen. Sch. Dist. 2, 1963-66; pres., sec. Samuel and Esther Gitlow Found., N.Y.C. Author: Economics, 1962, Labor and Manpower Economics, 1971; co-editor: General Economics: A Book of Readings, 1963; contbr. articles to profl. jours. Served to 1st lt. USAAF, 1943-46, PTO. Recipient Univ. medal Luigi Bocconi U., 1983. Mem. Am. Arbitration Assn. (mem. nat. panel 1948—), Am. Econ. Assn., Royal Econ. Soc., Indsl. Relations Research Assn. Home: 9 Island Ave Miami Beach FL 33139 Office: NYU Coll Bus and Pub Adminstrn Washington Sq New York NY 10003

GITTELSON, BERNARD, public relations consultant, author, lecturer; b. N.Y.C., June 13, 1918; s. Sam and Gussie (Lef) G.; m. Rosalind Weinstein, Mar. 1, 1945; children—Louise Barbara, Steven Henry. B.A., St. John's U., 1939. Cons. on race relations N.Y. State War Council, 1939-41, N.Y. Com. on Industry and Labor Relations, 1941-42; dir. N.Y. State Legis. Com. on Discrimination, 1943-45; asso. coordinator Com. on Community Inter-relations, 1945-46; pres. Roy Bernard Co., Inc., 1946-65; chmn. Roy Bernard Co. Ltd., London, 1955-65; pres. Biorhythm Computers, Inc., Med. News. Service, Formulated Health Products, Fairfield Mktg. Corp., Advanced Health Research Products Inc.; chmn. bd. Time Pattern Research Inst., N.Y.C., U.S. Commemoratives Inc., Bernard Gittelson Cons. Inc.; cons. to govts., corps., instns. Author: Gittelson Biorhythm Code Book, Biorhythm, A Personal Science, How to Make Your Own Luck, Intangible Evidence; Syndicated writer column on biorhythm, 1978—; pub.: Med. Hot Line. Mem. Am. Journalists and Authors, Authors Guild. Home: 96 Division Ave Summit NJ 07901 Office: 347 W 57th St New York NY 10019

GITTESS, RONALD MARVIN, dentist; b. Nyack, N.Y., Nov. 10, 1937; s. David and Mildred (Levin) G.; B.S., Columbia, 1959, D.D.S., 1963; postgrad. U. Pa., 1964-66; m. Carol May Block, Apr. 6, 1963; children—Robert Andrew, Leslie Ellen. Intern, Mt. Sinai Hosp., Miami, Fla., 1963-64, now attending dental surgeon; pvt. practice dentistry specializing in endodontics, Miami, 1966—; mem. staff Variety Children's Hosp., VA Hosp., Miami, Mt. Sinai Hosp.; cons. Dade County Dental Research Clinic; ann. guest lectr. dental div. Pan Am. Med. Conf., 1983—. Asst. coordinator dental div. United Fund Campaign, 1968. Recipient certificate of recognition Jarvie Honor Soc., 1961. USPHS fellow, 1962-63. Diplomate Am. Bd. Endodontics. Mem. ADA, Am. Assn. Endodontics, AAAS, Fedn. Dentaire Internationale, Fla., Miami, Miami Beach, South Dade, East Coast dental socs., So. Endodontic Study Group, Alpha Omega. Home: 14520 SW 84th Ave Miami FL 33158 Office: 7400 N Kendall Dr Miami FL 33156

GITTLEMAN, ALLAN MORRIS, investment company executive; b. Providence, June 23, 1942; s. Sidney Allan and Dorothy Foster (Green) G.; student Brown U., 1964; B.S., Northeastern U., 1968; m. Ellen Kaplan, May 28, 1966; children—Danielle, Rachel. Vice pres. Michael Investment Co., Providence, 1966-68, pres., 1968-73; v.p. F.L. Putnam & Co., Inc., Boston, 1973-81, chmn. bd., 1981-82; chmn. bd. Gen. Magnaplate Co., Linden, N.J., 1970-71; pres. Foster, Brown & Ballou, Inc., Providence, 1974—; v.p. Burgess & Leith, Inc., Providence, 1981-84; sr. v.p., dir. N.Am. InvCorp, East Hartford, Conn., 1984-87; v.p. Janney Montgomery Scott, Providence, 1988—; dir. Astro-Med Inc., West Warwick, R.I. Mem. R.I. Public Expenditure Council. Mem. Am. Numis. Assn., Newcomen Soc., Nat., Boston securities traders assns., Soc. Paper Money Collectors, Bond and Share Soc. Clubs: Faculty, Brown. Author: Scripophily-A Guide to Collecting Antique Stock and Bond Certificates, 1980. Office: 98 Main St East Greenwich RI 02818

GITTLEMAN, MORRIS, consulting metallurgist; b. Zhidkovitz, Minsk, Russia, Nov. 2, 1912; came to U.S., 1920, naturalized; s. Louis and Ida (Gorodietsky) G.; B.S. cum laude, Bklyn. Coll., 1934; postgrad. Manhattan Coll., 1941, Pratt Inst., 1943, Bklyn. Poly. Inst., 1946-47; m. Clara Konefsky, Apr. 7, 1937; children—Arthur Paul, Michael Jay. Metall. engr. N.Y. Naval Shipyard, 1942-47; chief metallurgist, chemist Pacific Cast Iron Pipe & Fitting Co., South Gate, Calif., 1948-54, tech. mgr., 1954-57, tech. and prodn. mgr., 1957-58; cons. Valley Brass, Inc., El Monte Calif., 1958-61, Vulcan Foundry, Ltd., Haifa, Israel, 1958-65, Anaheim Foundry Co. (Calif.), 1958-63, Hollywood Alloy Casting Co. (Calif.), 1960-70, Spartan Casting Co., El Monte, 1961-62; Overton Foundry, South Gate, Calif., 1962-70, cons., gen. mgr., 1970-71; cons. Familian Pipe & Supply Co., Van Nuys, Calif., 1962-72, Comml. Enameling Co., Los Angeles, 1963-68, Universal Cast Iron Mfg. Co., South Gate, 1965-71; pres. MG Coupling Co., 1972-79; instr. physics Los Angeles Harbor Coll., 1958-59; instr. chemistry Western States Coll. Engring., Inglewood, Calif., 1961-68. Registered profl. engr., Calif. Mem. Am. Foundrymen's Soc., Am. Foundrymen's Soc. So. Calif. (dir. 1955-57), AAAS, Am. Soc. Metals, N.Y. Acad. Scis., Internat. Solar Energy Soc. (Am. sect.). Contbr. to tech. jours.; inventor MG coupling, patents worldwide. Home: 17635 San Diego Circle Fountain Valley CA 92708 Office: 17044 Montanero St Carson CA 90746

GITTLIN, A. SAM, industrialist, banker; b. Newark, Nov. 21, 1914; s. Benjamin and Ethel (Bernstein) G.; m. Fay Lerner, Sept. 18, 1938; children: Carol (Mrs. Alan H. Franklin), Regina (Mrs. Peter Gross), Bruce David, Steven Robert. B.C.S., Rutgers U., 1938. Ptnr. Gittlin Bag Co. (name now changed to Gittlin Cos. Inc.), Livingston, N.J., No. Miami, Fla., N.Y.C., 1935-40; v.p., dir. Gittlin Bag Co., 1954—, chmn. bd., 1963—; v.p., dir. Abbey Record Mfg. Co., Newark, 1958-60; chmn., treas. Packaging Products & Design Co. (now PPD Corp.), Newark and Glendale, Calif., 1959-71, chmn. exec. com., treas., 1972—; chmn. Pines Shirt & Pajama Co., N.Y.C., 1960-85, Pottsville Shirt & Pajama Co. (Pa.), 1960—, Barrington Industries, N.Y.C., 1963-72, First Peninsula Calif. Corp., N.Y.C., 1964-68, Wall-co Imperial, Miami, Fla., 1965-87, Levin & Hecht, Inc., N.Y.C., 1966-72, Wallco of San Juan (P.R.), Brunswick Shirt Co., N.Y.C., 1966-72, Fleetline Industries, Garland, N.C., 1966-72, All State Auto Leasing & Rental Corp., Beverly Hills, Calif., 1968-72, Packaging Ltd., Newark, 1970-76, Kans. Plastics, Inc., Garden City, 1970-76, Bob Cushman Distbrs., Inc. (now Wallpapers Inc.), Phoenix, 1972-87, Wallpaper Supermarkets, Phoenix, 1976-80, Wallco Internat. Inc., Miami, 1976, Overwrap Equipment Corp., Fairfield, 1978-86, GCI Ala. Inc., Birmingham, 1981—; chmn. Wallpapers Inc., Oakland, Calif., 1982-86, Portland, Oreg., Honolulu, Denver, Los Angeles and Phoenix, 1982-86; pres. Covington Funding Co., N.Y.C., 1963—; vice chmn. bd. Peninsula Savs. and Loan Assn., San Mateo and San Francisco, 1964-67, chmn., 1967-68; chmn. bd., treas. Bob Cushman Painting & Decorating Co. (now Wallco West), Phoenix, 1972-86; treas., dir. Flex Pak Industries, Inc., Atlanta, 1973-76, Ploy Plax Films, Inc., Santa Ana, Calif., 1973-76; sec., chmn. exec. com. Zins Wallcoverings, Newark; ptnr. Benjamin Co., N.Y.C., Laurel Assocs. (Md.), Seaboard Realty Assocs., Miami, 1980—, GHG Realty Assocs., N.Y.C., 1980, Parkway Assocs., Miami, 1987—; ptnr., investors cons. Mission Pack, Inc., Los Angeles; vice chmn., dir., chmn. exec. com. Falmouth Supply, Ltd., Montreal, Que., Can., Ascher Trading Corp., Newark, Aptex, Inc., Newark; dir., fin. cos. Ramada Inns, Phoenix; bd. dirs., fin. cons. Ramada Inns Realty Equities Corp. N.Y., N.Y.C.; bd. dirs. Harris Paint & Wall Covering Super Marts, Miami, Morgan Hill Mfg. Co., Reading, Pa. Chmn. N.C. com. B'nai B'rith, 1940; treas. N.C. Fedn. B'nai B'rith Lodges, 1941-43, v.p., 1943-44, pres., 1944-47; mem. com. to rev. dept. banking and ins. N.J. Commn. on Efficiency and Economy in State Govt., 1967—; trustee Benjamin Gittlin Charity Found., Newark, BAMA Master Retirement Program, Hillel Found. at Rutgers U., Temple Emanuel, Miami; bd. visitors Franklin & Marshall U., Allentown, Pa; founders bd. Miami Gardens Home Aged. Jewish (pres., trustee B'nai Abraham, Livingston N.J., trustee Temple Emanuel, Miami, 1987—). Clubs: Greenbrook Country (Caldwell, N.J.), Turnberry Yacht and Golf (Turnberry Isle, Fla.), Westview Country (Miami, Fla.). Lodge: B'nai B'rith. Home: 59 Glenview Rd South Orange NJ 07079 also: 9801 Collins Ave Miami Beach FL 33154 Office: 21 Penn Plaza New York NY 10001 also: 20801 Biscayne Blvd Suite 400 North Miami Beach FL 33180

GIUFFRIDA, GIUSEPPE, cardiologist, educator; b. Catania, Sicily, Italy, Nov. 4, 1933; s. Carmelo and Giuseppina (Spampinato) G. MD, U. Med. Sch., Catania, 1959. Intern then resident U. Rome, 1959-64; researcher Nat. Research Council, Rome, 1962-63; assoc. prof. internal medicine U. Med. Sch., Rome, 1966-72; assoc. prof. cardiology U. Med. Sch., Naples, Italy, 1972-80; prof. cardiology, dept chief U. Med. Sch., Catania, 1980—, dir. postgrad. sch. cardiology, 1980—. Editor: Cardiology Update: 1985; contbr. articles to profl. jours. Fellow Am. Coll. Cardiology. Lodge: Rotary. Home: Ofelia 35D, Catania Italy 95124 Office: Inst Cardiology, Citelli, Catania Italy 95124

GIULIANO, ROBERT PAUL, pharmacist; b. N.Y.C., Mar. 7, 1943; s. Salvatore Anthony and Marie Rita (LoScalzo) G.; BS in Pharmacy, Fordham U., 1965; MS in Hosp. Pharmacy Adminstrn., L.I. U., 1970; m. Maja Hreljanovic, July 2, 1966; children—Christopher Robert, Kenneth Paul. Clin. pharmacist Columbia-Presbyterian Med. Center, N.Y.C., 1965-70; dir. pharmacy dept. St. Barnabas Hosp., N.Y.C., 1970-71; dir. dept. pharm. scis. Misericordia Hosp. Med. Center, N.Y.C., 1971-78, adminstrv. dir. materiel mgmt., 1978-79, asst. adminstr. Misericordia Hosp. Med. Center, 1979-81; pres. Apotheke Assos. Ltd., N.Y.C., 1980-81; pres., dir., chief exec. officer U.S. Home Health Care Corp. and Steri-Pharm subs., 1981—; affiliated instr. St. John's U., 1971-81; home health care cons. Am. Cancer Soc., 1988—, Robert Wood Johnson Found., 1985; mem. clin. pharmacy adv. bd., 1971-81; mem. exec. com., Bronx Emergency Med. Services Council, 1975-80, chmn. tng. com., 1975-79, chmn. council, 1979-80; sr. emergency med. technician instr./coordinator N.Y. State Dept. Health, Bur. Emergency Med. Services, 1975-81; speaker's bur., CPR instr. Am. Heart Assn., 1975-81; CPR instr. Westchester Heart Assn., 1977-80; speaker's bur. Misericordia Hosp. Med. Center, Westchester County Soc. Hosp. Pharmacists. Asst. Cub Scout master, Eastchester, N.Y., 1976-78; coach youth baseball T.Y.A., Eastchester, 1975-83. Certified Am. Bd. Diplomates in Pharmacy, Nat. Registry Emergency Med. Technicians. Mem. Am. Pharm. Assn., Italian Pharm. Assn., Am. Soc. Hosp. Pharmacists, N.Y. State Council Hosp. Pharmacists, Nat. Assn. Sr. Emergency Med. Technician Instrs., Nat. Assn. Emergency Med. Technicians (founding), Am. Soc. Parenteral-Enteral Nutrition, League IV Therapists, Nat. IV Therapy Assn., Fordham U. Pharmacy Alumni Assn. (dir. 1982—). Republican. Roman Catholic. Club: N.Y. Athletic. Editor Misericordia Hosp. Pharmacy Newsletter, 1971-78. Home: 157 Oakland Ave Eastchester NY 10707 Office: US Home Health Care Corp 670 White Plains Rd Scarsdale NY 10583

GIULINI, CARLO ENRICO, manufacturing company executive; b. Tübingen, Germany, May 19, 1918; naturalized Italian citizen; s. N.H. Guglielmo Paolo and Aenne Caterina (Grohé) G.; m. Leda Geneva, July 1, 1945; children—Jantra, Gabriele, Paolo, Michele. Degree polit. sci. Lausanne U., Switzerland, 1946. Dir., SIGEM, Milan, 1948, Giulini Enea, 1949-53; pres. C.E. Giulini & C. S.r.l., Milan, 1953—; bd. dirs. Mineraria Silius S.p.A., Milan, 1958—, Fluorsid S.p.A., Cagliari, 1970—; chmn., mng. dir. C.E. Giulini (Derbyshire) Ltd., Hopton, Eng., 1970-75; pres. s.a. Pour la Fabrication du Magnesium, Martigny, Switzerland, 1974—, I.C.I.B. S.p.A., Milan, 1976—. Served with Savoy Cav., 1940-44. Roman Catholic. Home: 3 Via dei Foscari, 20151 Milan Italy Office: 1 Via Correggio, 20149 Milan Italy

GIURGEA, CORNELIU EDMOND, neurophysiologist, pharmacologist, educator; b. Bucharest, Romania, Jan. 6, 1923; s. Max and Beatrice (Benvenisti) Geisler; m. Michaela David, June 10, 1950; children: Sanda, Dina, Livia. MD, Faculty of Medicine, Bucharest, 1949, PhD, 1952. Prof. of physiology Faculty of Medicine, Bucarest, 1953-58; chmn. physiology dept. Acad. Inst. of Physiology, Bucharest, 1953-58; chmn. dept. pharmacology UCB, Brussels, 1962-82, scientific advisor, 1983—; prof. psychopharmacology U. Louvain (Belgium), 1969—; head of psychobiology unit U. Louvain, Louvain la Neuve, 1983—. Author: Nootropic Concept, 1972, Pharmacology Mind, 1981, Psychopharmacology, 1985, Pavlovian's Inherit, 1986. Mem. Belgian Coll. of Neuropharmacology and Biol. Psychiatry, Collegium Internat. Activitatis Nervosae Superioris (exec. com. 1979—), Collegium Internat. Neuro-Psycho Pharmacologicum, Belgian Soc. of Physiology and Pharmacology, European Coll. of Neuro-Psycho Pharmacology. Home: Ave de la Jonction N 5, 1060 Brussels Belgium Office: U Louvain, 1 Place Croix du Sud, 1348 Louvain-la-Neuve Belgium

GIUSTINIANI, VITO ROCCO, retired language educator; b. Lucca, Tuscany, Italy, June 25, 1916; s. Francesco and Giovanna (Dell'Osso) G.; m. Doris Ziegler, Jan. 30, 1945 (dec. July 1986); children: Giovanna, Franco. Laurea in lettere, U. Pisa, Italy, 1938; diploma, Scuola Norm. Sup., Pisa, 1939; libera docenza, Ministero Pubblica Istruzione, Rome, 1968. Lectr. U. Freiburg, Fed. Republic of Germany, 1941-55, docent, 1955-69, prof. Italian, 1969-74, prof. emeritus, 1974—; vis. prof. Italian U. Columbia, U. Toronto, Boston Coll., U. Mass., 1958—. Author: Lettere ed Orazioni di A. Rinuccini 1426-1499, 1953, A. Rinuccini: Materialien und Forschungen zur Geschichte des Florentinischen Humanismus, 1965, Il Testo della Nencia e della Beca Secondo le Più Antiche Stampe, 1976, Neulateinisch Dichtung in Italien 1850-1950, 1979, Adam von Rottweils Deutsch-Italienischer Sprachführer, 1986; contbr. articles to profl. jours. and book reviews. Mem. Am. Assn. Italian Tchrs., Am. Dante Soc., Deutsche Dante Gesellschaft. Home: Johanniterstrasse 9, 7800 Freiburg Federal Republic of Germany

GIVANT, PHILIP JOACHIM, mathematics professor, real estate investment executive; b. Mannheim, Fed. Republic of Germany, Dec. 5, 1935; s. Paul and Irmy (Dinse) G.; m. Kathleen Joan Porter, Sept. 3, 1960; children: Philip Paul, Julie Kathleen, Laura Grace. BA in Math., San Francisco State U., 1957, MA in Math., 1960. Prof. math. San Francisco State U., 1958-60, Am. River Coll., Sacramento, 1960—; pres. Grove Enterprises, Sacramento, 1961—; pres. Am. River Coll. Acad. Senate, Sacramento, 1966-69; v.p. Acad. Senate for Calif. Community Colls., 1974-77; mem. State Chancellor's Acad. Calendar Com., Sacramento, 1977-79. Founder, producer Annual Sacramento Blues Music Festival, 1976—; producer Sta. KVMR weekly Blues music program, 1978—, music festivals Folsom Prison, 1979-81, Vacaville Prison, 1985. Pres. Sacramento Blues Festival, Inc., 1985—; mem. Lake Tahoe Keys Homeowners Assn., 1983—, Sea Ranch Homeowners Assn., 1977—. Recipient Spl. Service Commendation, Acad. Senate Calif. Community Colls., 1977, Spl. Human Rights award Human Rights-Fair Housing Commn., Sacramento, 1985. Mem. Faculty Assn. Calif. Community Colls., Am. Soc. Psychical Research, Nat. Blues Found. (adv. com., W.C. Handy Blues Promoter of Yr. 1987). Home and Office: 3809 Garfield Ave Carmichael CA 95608

GIVENCHY See DE GIVENCHY, HUBERT JAMES MARCEL TAFFIN

GIVENS, ROBERT ALLEN, management consulting company director; b. Gary, Ind., Jan. 11, 1946; came to France, 1977; s. William Philip and Madelyn (Rardon) G.; m. Estelle Jeanne Meurice, July 27, 1979; children: Olivia Estelle, Antoine Raphael, Muriel Florence. BS in Fin. and Banking, Miami U., 1967; MBA in Internat. Bus., Columbia U., 1968. Fin. analyst Ford Motor Co., Dearborn, Mich., 1968-70; mgr. fin. analysis Smith, Kline, Beckman, Phila., 1970-72; mgr. corp. treasury Fairchild Camera and Instrument Corp, Mountain View, Calif., 1972-73, fin. dir., Wiesbaden, Germany, 1973-76; European controller Corning Glass Works, Paris, 1976-77; corp. controller Pricel/Groupe Chargeurs, Paris, 1977-82; dir. Givens Profit Devel., Paris, 1982—. Valedictorian, recipient Internat. Bus. award Columbia U., 1968. Mem. Am. C. of C., Assn. Ams. Resident Overseas, Phi Eta Sigma, Beta Gamma Sigma, Phi Beta Kappa. Republican. Club: Am. of Paris. Avocations: sailing, tennis, skiing, cycling, swimming. Home: 37 Ave de Lowendal, 75015 Paris France Office: 19 rue d'anjou, 75008 Paris France

GIVI, PEYMAN, research science educator; b. Tehran, Iran, June 26, 1958; came to U.S., 1977; s. Ali and Aghdas (Gheblehgahi) G.; m. Suzanne Pellarin, July 2, 1983. BE, Youngstown State U., 1980; ME, Carnegie Mellon U., 1982, PhD, 1984. Research asst. Carnegie Mellon U., Pitts., 1980-84, teaching asst., 1984; research scientist Flow Research Inc., Kent, Wash., 1985-87; asst. prof. SUNY, Buffalo, 1988—. Contbr. articles to profl. combustion and fluid mechanics jours. Mem. ASME, AIAA Combustion Inst., Sigma Xi, Phi Kappa Phi, Tau Beta Pi. Home: 123 Hollybrook Dr Buffalo NY 14221 Office: SUNY MEA Dept Buffalo NY 14260

GIVOT, STEVEN IRA, commodities trader; b. Chgo., Feb. 18, 1950; s. Martin Lionel and Elyse Sue (Abrams) G.; children: Brian Lamond, Susan Elizabeth, Sarah Elyse. SB, MIT, 1971; MS with distinction, London Sch. Econs., 1973; MBA with honors, U. Chgo., 1974. Pres. Tech. Enterprises Inc., Barrington Hills, Ill., 1975-86, 88—; head market maker, J. Aron & Co., 1986-87; mem. Chgo. Bd. Options Exchange, 1974-87, chmn. facilities com., 1979-83, chmn. securities and new product com., 1979-80, mem. exec. com., 1980-82, 84-86, chmn. systems com., 1985-86; mem. Chgo. Bd. Trade, 1977-87, Midwest Stock Exchange, 1978-81, N.Y. Futures Exchange, 1980-82, Chgo. Merc. Exchange, 1986—; head market maker J. Aron & Co., Chgo., 1986-87; dir. Chgo. Options Exchange Bldg. Corp., 1980-86. Treas. campaign Armstrong-Libertarian for gov. of Ill. 1982; Libertarian Party candidate for U.S. Senate from Ill., 1984, for Ill. sec. state, 1986; mem. nat. com. Libertarian Party, 1985-86. Jewish. Home and Office: Rt 2 1 Middlebury Rd Barrington Hills IL 60010

GIZELIS, GREGORY, cultural anthropologist; b. Athens, Greece, Aug. 23, 1935; s. Christos and Theodora (Konidaris) G.; m. Helen Throuvalas, July 1, 1965; 1 child, Theodora-Ismene. Diploma in Philosophy, Athens U., 1959; postgrad. in Sociology, Colgate U., 1967; MA, U. Pa., 1970, PhD, 1972. Prof. Athens Coll., 1962-68; research assoc. Ctr. for Urban Ethnography U. Pa., Phila., 1970-72; research dir. Nat. Ctr. for Social Research, Athens, 1973-79; dir. Research Ctr. for Greek Soc.-Acad. Athens, 1979—; prof. sociology Evangelismos Sch. Nursing, Athens, 1975-81; prof. ethnography U. Crete, Greece, 1981-84; Greek com. mem. UNESCO, 1980-83. Author: Narrative Rhetorical Devices of Persuasion, 1974, The Rhetoric of Dress, 1974, The Ethnography of Health, 1977, Culture: Its Semiotic and Communicational Character, 1980, Changing Patterns of Cultural Activity Within the Greek Family, 1983, The Problems of the Greek Book, 1986, 7 others; contbr. articles to profl. jours. Fulbright scholar, 1968-72, Rockefeller Found. scholar, 1968, Ford Found. scholar, 1968; grantee NIMH, 1970. Mem. Am. Folklore Soc., Greek Folklore Soc., Greek Semiotic Soc., Am. Ethnol. Soc., Council on Edn. and Anthropology, Internat. Sociol. Assn. (Greek del. 1974—), Greek Sociol. Soc. (editor jour.). Greek Orthodox. Home: 29 Miaoule, Pefki 15121, Greece Office: Research Ctr for Greek Soc, 84 Solonos, Athens 10680, Greece

GLACEL, BARBARA PATE, management consultant; b. Balt., Sept. 15, 1948; d. Jason Thomas Pate and Sarah Virginia (Forwood) Wetter; m. Robert Allan Glacel, Dec. 21, 1969; children—Jennifer Warren, Sarah Allane, Ashley Virginia. A.B., Coll. William and Mary, 1970; M.A., U. Okla., 1973, Ph.D., 1978. Tchr. Harford County (Md.) Schs., 1970-71; tchr. Dept. Def. Schs., W.Ger., 1971-73; ednl. counselor U.S. Army, W.Ger., 1973-74; lectr. U. Md., W.Ger., 1973-74; adj. prof. Suffolk U., Boston, 1975-77, C.W. Post Ctr., L.I. U., John Jay Coll. Criminal Justice, N.Y.C., 1979-80, St. Thomas Aquinas Coll., N.Y.C., 1981; acad. adviser Central Mich. U. 1981-82; adj. prof. St. Mary's Coll., Leavenworth, Kans., 1981, Anchorage Community Coll., 1982; asst. prof. U. Alaska-Anchorage, 1983-85; mgmt. cons. Barbara Glacel & Assocs., Anchorage, 1980-86, Washington, 1986-88; ptnr., founder Pace Cons. Group, Burke, Va., 1988—; gen. mgr. mgmt. programs Hay Systems Inc., Washington, 1986-88; founder and prin. Pace Cons. Group, Burke, Va., 1988—; ptnr. Pracel Prints, Williamsburg, Va., 1981-85; sr. mgmt. tng. specialist ARCO Alaska, Inc., 1984-85; 2d v.p. Chesapeake Broadcasting Corp. Md.; guest lectr. U.S. Mil. Acad. Chmn. 172d Inf. Brigade Family Council; mem. U.S. Army Sci. Bd., 1986—. Recipient Comdr.'s award for pub. service U.S. Dept. Army, 1984. AAUW grantee, 1977-78. Mem. Am. Soc. Tng. and Devel. (bd. dirs. Anchorage chpt.), Am. Psychol. Assn., Am. Soc. Pub. Adminstrn., Am. Polit. Sci. Assn. Pi Sigma Alpha. Author: Regional Transit Authorities, 1983; (with others) 1000 Army Families, 1983. Home: 5617 Tilia Ct Burke VA 22015 Office: Pace Cons Group 8996 Burke Lake Rd Suite 305 Burke VA 22015

GLADSON, GUY ALLEN, JR., lawyer; b. Chgo., May 14, 1928; s. Guy Allen and Martha Gertrude (Huffman) G.; m. Nancy McDonald Gladson, Jan. 7, 1956; children—Nancy, Guy, Kathryn, Carolyn, Patricia, William. B.A., Northwestern U., 1949; LL.B., U. Mich., 1952. Bar: Ill. 1952, Fla. 1956. Assoc., Winston, Strawn & Shaw, Chgo., 1952-56, Dixon, DeJarnette, Bradford, Williams, McKay & Kimbrell, Miami 1956-62; ptnr. Gladson and Sullivan, and predecessors, Miami, 1963—. Mem. ABA, Fla. Bar Assn., Dade County Bar Assn. Roman Catholic. Clubs: Coral Gables Country. Home: 5395 SW 80th St Miami FL 33143 Office: 7600 Southwest 57th Ave Suite 309 Miami FL 33143

GLAMANN, KRISTOF, foundation executive, author; b. Kerteminde, Denmark, Aug. 26, 1923; s. Kai Kristof and Ebba (Madsen) G.; Dr.Phil., U. Copenhagen, 1958; Fil. dr. h.c., U. Gothenbourg, Sweden, 1974; m. Kirsten Lise Jantzen, Mar. 1954; children—Joakim Jakob, Martin Mikael. Prof. history U. Copenhagen, 1960-80; dir. Carlsberg Brewery Ltd., Fredericia Brewery Ltd., Politiken Publishers Ltd., Royal Copenhagen Investor-Reinvest Group, Ltd.; pres. Internat. Assn. Econ. History, 1970-74; pres. Carlsberg Found., Copenhagen, 1976—; chmn. bd. dirs. United Breweries Ltd., Copenhagen, 1978—; vis. prof. U. Pa., 1960, U. Wis., 1961, London Sch. Econs. and Polit. Scis., 1966; vis. overseas fellow Churchill Coll., Cambridge, U.K., 1971-72, Toho Gakkai Tokyo, 1977. Hon. fellow Brit. Acad.; mem. Royal Danish Acad., Swedish Acad., Royal Hist. Soc. (U.K.), Danish Soc., Econ. Hist. Soc. (chmn.). Author: Dutch Asiatic Trade, 1958, 2d edit., 1982; History Danish Brewing Industry, 1963; The Carlsberg Foundation, 1976, Cambridge Economic History of Europe, Vol. 5, 1977; Studies in Mercantilism, 1984. Office: Carlsberg Foundation, H C Andersens Blvd 35, 1553 Copenhagen K Denmark

GLASBERG, H. MARK, psychiatrist; b. N.Y.C., Oct. 11, 1939; s. Joseph and Elsa (Haber) G.; BA, Yeshiva U., 1953; MS, Columbia U., 1954; MD, SUNY, 1958; m. Paula Drillman, June 19, 1960; children: Scot Bradley, Hilary Jennifer. Intern, Maimonides Hosp. N.Y.C., 1958-59; resident in psychiatry Kings County Hosp., N.Y.C., 1959-60; resident in internal medicine Kingsbridge VA Hosp., N.Y.C., 1960-61; resident Payne Whitney Psychiat. Clin., N.Y. Hosp., 1963-65, fellow, 1965-66; spl. research fellow Nat. Inst. Mental Health, 1966-68; practice medicine specializing in psychiatry, N.Y.C., 1968—; instr. Cornell U. Med. Sch., 1966-68; asst. prof. psychiatry Mt. Sinai Sch. Medicine, 1968—; dir. psychiat. outpatient services Beth Israel Hosp., N.Y.C., 1968-74, asso. attending physician, 1968-74; attending psychiatrist St. Vincent's Hosp., N.Y.C., 1974—, chief psychiat. emergency and cons. services, 1974-75. Cons. mem. panel of ind. psychiatrists N.Y.C. Mental Health Info. Service, 1968—. Mem. Manhattan physicians com. United Jewish Appeal, 1970—; mem. com. admission selection Cornell U. Med. Coll., Ctr. Alumni Assn. Served to lt. col., M.C., AUS, 1961-63. Fellow ACP, Am. Psychiat. Assn. (internat. platform com. 1980—), N.Y. Acad. Scis., N.Y. Acad. Medicine; mem. AAAS, Am. Psychosomatic Soc., Soc. for Adolescent Psychiatry, Internat. Platform Assn. Home and Office: 14 E 73d St New York NY 10021

GLASBERG, LAURENCE BRIAN, finance executive; b. N.Y.C., Apr. 28, 1943; s. William and Tillie (Liebowitz) G.; m. Lana Lucille Pollack, Aug. 10, 1963; children: Jeffrey, Scott, Glenn, David. BBA, CUNY, 1964, MBA, 1968. Mgr. bus. affairs Sta. WCBS-TV, N.Y.C., 1970-72, dir. planning and adminstrn., 1972-74; gen. auditor Eastern ops. CBS Inc., N.Y.C., 1975-76, v.p., gen. auditor, 1982-88; sr. v.p. fin. and adminstrn. N.Am. ops. AEG Corp., 1988—. Served with inf., U.S. Army, 1964-65. Mem. Fin. Execs. Inst. (nat. com. on govt. liaison, local bd. dirs. 1987). Republican. Jewish. Club: Econo. (N.Y.C.). Avocations: physical fitness, outdoor and environmental activities, reading. Office: AEG Corp Orr Dr and Route 22 Somerville NJ 08540 also: 333 Meadowlands Pkwy Secaucus NJ 07094

GLASBERG, PAULA DRILLMAN, advertising executive; b. Dusseldorf, Germany, Nov. 22, 1939; came to U.S., 1940, naturalized, 1942; d. Solomon and Regina (Rubin) Drillman; m. H. Mark Glasberg, June 19, 1960; children: Scot Bradley, Hilary Jennifer. B.A., Bklyn. Coll., 1957; M.A., New Sch. Social Research, 1959, Ph.D., 1962. Research asst. McCann Erickson, N.Y.C., 1962-64; v.p. Marplan, Inc., N.Y.C., 1964-70, Tinker/Pritchard Wood, Inc., N.Y.C., 1970-72; exec. v.p., chmn. exec. com. Rosenfeld, Sirowitz & Lawson, Inc., N.Y.C., 1972-78; exec. v.p., chmn. exec. com., dir. Marschalk Co. div. Interpublic Group of Cos., N.Y.C., 1978-1982; exec. v.p., dir., dir. strategic planning McCann-Erickson World Wide, Inc., 1983—; bd. dirs. Stern Coll. for Women; sponsor mem. Yeshiva U. Women's Orgn., 1985—. Mem. Am. Assn. Advt. Agys., Am. Mktg. Assn., Advt. Research Found., AAAS, Am. Psychol. Assn., Internat. Platform Assn.; fellow N.Y. Acad. Scis., N.Y. Assn. Psychologists, 1975—. Home: 14 E 73d St New York NY 10021 Office: 485 Lexington Ave New York NY 10017

GLASER, ALVIN, mfg. co. exec.; b. New Bedford, Mass., Jan. 8, 1932; s. Morris and Jennie (Brody) G.; student public schs., New Bedford; m. Rosalyn S.F. Clasky, Jan. 20, 1963; children—Iris, Linda, Marjorie, Jeffrey. Mgr., Morris Glaser Glass Co., New Bedford, 1949—; treas. Glaser Inc., 1964—, pres. Glaser Glass Corp., 1985—; corporator New Bedford Five Cents Savs. Bank. Mem. Dartmouth (Mass.) Youth Commn. Mem. Nat. Glass Assn., New Bedford C. of C. Lodges: Masons, Order Eastern Star, Shriners, B'nai B'rith, Moose. Home: 2 Ann Ave North Dartmouth MA 02747 Office: 1265 Purchase St New Bedford MA 02740

GLASER, DONALD A(RTHUR), physicist; b. Cleve., Sept. 21, 1926; s. William Joseph Glaser. B.S., Case Inst. Tech., 1946, Sc.D., 1959; Ph.D., Cal. Inst. Tech., 1949. Prof. physics U. Mich., 1949-59; prof. physics U. Calif. at Berkeley, 1959—, prof. physics and molecular biology, 1964—. Recipient Henry Russel award U. Mich., 1955; Charles V. Boys prize Phys. Soc., London, 1958; Nobel prize in physics, 1960; NSF fellow, 1961; Guggenheim fellow, 1961-62. Fellow Am. Physics Soc. (prize 1959); mem. Nat. Acad. Scis., Sigma Xi, Tau Kappa Alpha, Theta Tau. Office: Molecular Biology Dept Univ of Calif Berkeley CA 94720 *

GLASER, THOMAS WILLIAM, educational administrator; b. Chgo., May 2, 1952; s. Thomas Harry and Cecelia Martha (Hirsch) G.; m. Nancy Lee Poole, Mar. 16, 1983. B.A., Tex. Christian U., 1974; m. Internat. Mgmt., Am. Grad. Sch. Internat. Mgmt., 1975; postgrad. Tex. State U., 1980. Gun dept. mgr. Zales Corp., Cullum & Boren Sporting Goods, Ft. Worth, 1971-75; family security analyst Met. Life Ins. Co., Arlington, Tex., 1975-76; telephone sales coordinator Stocksill Shooters Supply, Grapevine, Tex., 1976-79; coordinator customer service/cost control Greif Bros. Co., Ft. Worth, 1979-82; v.p. mktg. Holloway Arms Co., Ft. Worth, 1982-84; asst. curator exhibits DeGolver Library So. Meth. U., Dallas, 1984-85; dean of students, tchr. The Oakridge Sch., Arlington, Tex., 1985-86; dir. edn. Mansfield BUs. Sch., Dallas, 1986—. Served as maj. Tex. State Guard Mem. Nat. Rifle Assn. (life), Internat. Mil. Arms Soc., Nat. Guard Assn. Tex. (life), Tex. State Rifle Assn. (life.), Civil War Round Table Tex. (treas. 1979-81), Am. Def. Preparedness Assn. (life), Tex. State Guard Assn. (life), Dallas Arms Collectors Assn. (life), So. Hist. Assn., Soc. Historians of Early Am. Republic, Orgn. Am. Historians, Res. Officers Assn., Assn. U.S. Army, Am. Mgmt. Assn., Mensa (nat. coordinator Civil War spl. interest group 1976-80, sec. Ft. Worth 1976-80), Am. Hist. Assn., U.S. Naval Inst., Société Internationale des Officers, Alpha Phi Omega, Phi Alpha Theta (pres. Alpha Lambda chpt. 1983-84). Office: Mansfield Bus Sch 740 Wynnewood Village Dallas TX 75224

GLASHOW, SHELDON LEE, physicist, educator; b. N.Y.C., Dec. 5, 1932; s. Lewis and Bella (Rubin) G.; m. Joan Glashow; children: Jason David, Jordan, Brian Lewis, Rebecca Lee. A.B., Cornell U., 1954; A.M., Harvard U., 1955, Ph.D., 1958; D.Sc. (hon.), Yeshiva U., 1978, U. Marseille, 1982. NSF fellow U. Copenhagen, Denmark, 1958-60; research fellow Calif. Inst. Tech., 1960-61; asst. prof. Stanford U., 1961-62; asst. prof., asso. prof. U. Calif. at Berkeley, 1962-66; faculty Harvard U., 1966—, prof. physics, 1967—, Higgins prof. physics, 1979—; disting. vis. scientist Boston U., 1984—; cons. Brookhaven Nat. Lab., 1966-73, 75—; mem. sci. policy com. CERN, 1979-84; vis. prof. U. Marseille, 1971, MIT, 1974, 80, Boston U., 1983; affiliated sr. scientist U. Houston, 1983—; univ. scholar Tex. A & M U., 1983—. Contbr. articles to profl. jours. and popular mags. Pres. Andrei Sakharov Inst., 1980-85, Nat. Com. for Excellence in Edn., 1985—. Recipient J.R. Oppenheimer Meml. prize, 1977; George Ledlie prize, 1978; Nobel prize in physics, 1979; Castiglione di Sicilia prize, 1983; NSF fellow, 1955-60; Sloan fellow, 1962-66; CERN vis. fellow, 1968. Fellow Am. Phys. Soc., AAAS; mem. Am. Acad. Arts and Scis., Nat. Acad. Scis., Sigma Xi. *

GLASPIE, APRIL CATHERINE, diplomat; b. Vancouver, B.C., Can., Apr. 26, 1942. BA, Mills Coll., 1963; MA, Johns Hopkins U., 1965. With Foreign Service U.S. Dept. of State, 1966—; polit. officer U.S. Embassy, Cairo, 1973-77; asst. to Asst. Sec. State for Near Ea., S. Asian Affairs Washington, 1977-78; polit. officer U.S. Embassy, London, 1978-80, U.S. Mission to UN, N.Y.C., 1980-81; dir. lang. inst. U.S. Embassy, Tunis, Tunisia, 1981-83; polit. officer, dep. chief of mission U.S. Embassy, Damascus, Syria, 1983-85; dir., Office of Jordan, Lebanon, and Syrian Affairs U.S. Dept. of State, Washington, 1985-87; ambassador to Iraq 1987—. Address: U S Ambassador to Iraq care State Dept Washington DC 20520 *

GLASS, CARSON MCELYEA, lawyer; b. Farmersville, Tex., Oct. 8, 1915; s. Emery Carson and Chassie Victoria (McElyea) G.; m. Miriam Celeste Mollberg, Oct. 8, 1938 (div.); 1 son, Christopher C.; m. Lois Adair Felder, Dec. 29, 1960 (dec. 1973); m. Rhoda Swegles Price, Feb. 2, 1979. B.A., U. Tex., 1941, LL.B., 1938. Bar: Tex. 1937. Atty. Justice Dept., 1938-39, Dept. Labor, 1939; spl. atty. antitrust div. Justice Dept., 1939-47; spl. asst. to atty. gen. U.S., 1947-48; partner firm Fischer, Wood, Burney & Glass, Corpus Christi, Tex., 1949-50; mem. firm Clifford & Miller, Washington, 1950-68; partner firm Clifford, Warnke, Glass, McIlwain & Finney, Washington, 1968-77, Clifford, Glass, McIlwain & Finney, Washington, from 1977; partner Clifford & Warnke, to 1980; lectr. econs. U. Corpus Christi, 1948-50. Contbr. articles to profl. jours. Served to lt. (j.g.) USNR, 1943-46. Mem. ABA, Fed. Bar Assn. (nat. council 1961-69), D.C. Bar, State Bar Tex., White House Hist. Assn. (atty.-advisor 1961—, dir. 1975—), Sat. Morning Coffee Soc. (Corpus Christi); founding mem. Nat. Lawyers Club, U.S. Supreme Ct. Hist. Soc. Presbyterian. Home: 3719 63d Dr Lubbock TX 79413 Office: 815 Connecticut Ave NW Washington DC 20006

GLASS, DAVID D., department store company executive; b. Liberty, Mo., 1935; married. Gen. mgr. Crank Drug Co., 1957-67; v.p. Consumers Markets Inc., 1967-76; exec. v.p. fin. Wal-Mart Stores Inc., Bentonville, Ark., to 1976, vice chmn., chief fin. officer, 1976-84, pres., 1984—, chief operating officer, 1984-88, chief exec. officer, 1988—, also bd. dirs. Office: Wal-Mart Stores Inc 702 SW 8th St Bentonville AR 72712

GLASS, ELLIOTT MICHAEL, architect; b. N.Y.C., Nov. 11, 1934; s. M. Milton and Ruth M. (Goodman) G.; m. Paula Denner, Feb. 23, 1974. B.Arch., Cornell U., 1957; Fulbright scholar Finnish Inst. Tech., Helsinki, Finland, 1957-58. Registered architect, N.Y., N.J., Conn.; cert. Nat. Council Arctl. Registration Bds. Draftsman Mayer, Whittlesey & Glass, Architects, N.Y.C., 1958-61; designer, draftsman M. Milton Glass, AIA, Architect, N.Y.C., 1961-66; ptnr. Glass & Glass, Architects, N.Y.C., 1966—. Mem. Nat. Inst. Archtl. Edn., N.Y.C.; Citizens Housing and Planning Council N.Y.C., 1968—; bd. dirs. Gramercy Neighborhood Assn., N.Y.C., 1978—; founder, pres. Washington Irving Community Assn., N.Y.C., 1974-76; past adj. assoc. prof. architecture N.Y. Inst. Tech., 1980-85. Recipient Annual award for design of Cadman Towers, Concrete Industry Bd. N.Y., 1973. Mem. AIA, Nat. Arts Club, N.Y. State Assn. Architects, N.Y. Soc. Architects. Democrat. Jewish. Home: 112 E 17th St New York NY 10003 Office: Glass & Glass Architects 200 Park Ave S New York NY 10003

GLASS, FREDERICK MARION, financial corporation executive; b. Miss., Aug. 15, 1913; s. Frederick Marion and Carolyn Woodson (Hunter) G.; m. Betsy Sunderland Keller, June 28, 1941 (dec. Apr. 17, 1979); children—Frederick Marion, Barbara Richardson, William Keller; m. Marcia J. Hubbard, Nov. 29, 1980. B.A., U. Miss., 1934; J.D., , 1935, LL.M., Northwestern U., 1936. Chief atty. CAB, 1937-39; counsel Am. Airlines, Inc., 1939-42; v.p. Capital Airlines, pres. Air Cargo, Inc., 1946-49; dir. aviation Port of N.Y. Authority, 1949-55; vice chmn. bd., chief exec. officer Empire State Bldg. Corp., 1955-60, dir., 1955-60; exec. v.p., dir. Hertz Corp., 1960-63; pres., chief exec. officer, dir. Nat. Car Rental System, Inc., 1962-65; chmn., dir. Cosmos Am. Corp., 1965-70; vice chmn. Cosmos Bank, Zurich, Switzerland, 1965-73; pres. Cosmos Equities Corp., 1967-70, also dir.; pres., chief exec. officer, dir. Prudential Group, Inc., 1970-75; vice chmn., chief fin. officer The Thinc Group Inc., 1975-78, also dir.; dir. Avemco Corp., Gencor Industries Inc., Internat. Banknote Corp., The Wackenhut Corp., Thermal Profiles Inc. Mem. Nat. Aviation Facilities Study Group, 1955, Com. Mil. Air Transport Policy, 1959; chmn. Task Force Nat. Aviation Goals, 1961, pres. Airport Operators Council, 1955. Bd. govs. Flight Safety Found., 1956-72; trustee Coll. of Aeros., N.Y.C., 1972—, chmn. bd. trustees, 1987—. Served to col. USAAF, 1942-46; col. Res. Decorated Legion of Merit, Bronze Star. Mem. Am. Bar Assn., Am. Assn. Airport Execs., Phi Delta Theta, Phi Delta Phi. Masons. Clubs: Wings (pres. 1953), Racquet and Tennis (N.Y.C.); Metropolitan, Burning Tree (Washington); Wee Burn (Darien); Coral Beach and Tennis (Bermuda). Home: 201 E 62d St New York NY 10021 Office: $S1370 Park Ave New York NY 10022

GLASSELL, ALFRED CURRY, JR., oil and gas investor; b. Cuba Plantation, La., Mar. 31, 1914; s. Alfred Curry and Frances (Lee) G.; m. Clare Attwell; children: Jean Curry, Alfred Curry III. B.A., La. State U., 1934. Ind. oil and gas investor 1936—; cons. Glassell Producing Co., Inc., 1938—; past bd. dirs. Transco Cos., El Paso Nat. Gas, First City Bancorp. Trustee Houston Mus. Natural Sci., Internat. Oceanographic Found., Houston Fine Arts Mus., Kinkaid Sch., Tex. Children's Hosp.; asso. trustee Smithsonian Instn. Assos. Recipient Marine Sci. ann. award Internat. Oceanographic Found., 1971. Mem. Am. Geog. Soc., Am. Mus. Natural History, Tex. Angus Assn., Can. Chianini Assn., Houston Horse Show Assn., Tex. Cattle Feeders Assn., Am. Nat. Cattlemen's Assn., Tex. and Southwestern Cattle Raisers Assn., Mil. and Hospitaller Order St. Lazarus of Jerusalem. Clubs: Atlantic Tuna (Providence), Boston (New Orleans), Cabo Blanco Fishing (Peru), Tex. Game Fishing (Dallas), Tex. Corinthian Yacht (Kemah), Bay of Islands Swordfish and Mako Shark (New Zealand), L.I. Wyandanch, Anglers of N.Y, Houston, Petroleum, Ramada, Bayou, Houston Country, River Oaks Country (Houston), Coronado, Explorers. Office: 2300 First City Nat Bank Bldg 1021 Main St Houston TX 77002

GLASSER, DAVID BENJAMIN, retail executive; b. Lusaka, Zambia, Jan. 2, 1942; s. Goodman and Lilah (Leatherman) G.; divorced; children—Philip, Alan. Trainee mgr. Woolworths Pty. Ltd., Cape Town, South Africa, 1964-65, deptl. mgr., 1965-66, merchandiser, 1966-70, mdse. mgr., 1970-75, exec., 1975-78, dir., 1978—; dir. Bonwit Co., Cape Town, 1981—. Mem. Clothing Inst. (com. 1980-81), South African Inst. Mgmt. (com. 1979-80), Jaycees South Africa (nat. pres. 1981-82, Presdl. award of honor 1968, Jaycee Internat. Senator 1974), S.A. Univ. Judo Assn. (pres. 1962-63). Jewish. Club: Varsity Old Boys Hockey. Office: Woolworths Pty Ltd, 93 Longmarket St, Cape Town 8000, Republic of South Africa

GLASSER, DAVID JEREMY, retail company director; b. Glassow, Scotland, Sept. 10, 1952; s. Abraham Iaaac and Erna Ceila (Leishton) G.; m. Susan DeRose, Feb. 20, 1977; 1 child, Sarah Louise. Postgrad. mgmt. courses, Ashridge Mgmt. Coll., Eng., 1979. Gen. mgr. Marks and Spencer Plc., London, Eng., 1970-85; bus. devel. controller Halford's div. Ward White Plc., Wellingborough, 1985-86; dir. mktg. and bus. devel. Zodiac div. Ward White Plc., Wellingborough, Eng., 1986—. Contbr. articles to newspapers. Mem. Inst. Dirs. Jewish. Home: 33 Hampstead Ln, London N6 4RJ, England

GLASSER, PATRICIA COLLINS, educational administrator; b. Akron, Ohio, Nov. 14, 1927; d. Robert Lee and Mildred Jessie (Nied) Collins; B.S., U. Ga., 1948; M.Ed., Fla. Atlantic U., 1966; Ed.D., U. Miami, 1976; student Oglethorpe U., 1957-58, Emory U., 1958-59; m. Joseph Griffith Glasser, Sept. 7, 1973; children—Clarence Webb Jackson III, Robin Leanne Jackson Gresh. Tchr., DeKalb County, Ga., 1956-59, Broward County, Fla., 1963-68; adminstr. Howard County (Md.) Schs., 1971-73; adminstr. Charlotte County (Fla.) Schs., 1973-77; adminstr. Duval County (Fla.) Public Schs., Jacksonville, 1977—; cons. schs., Ohio, Fla., Md., N.Y., Ky., La., Tex., Washington, Va., Switzerland, N.S. Triple T fellow U. Miami, 1969-70. Mem. Assn. Supervision and Curriculum Devel., Fla. Assn. Sch. Adminstrs., DAR, Jacksonville Panhellenic Assn., Jacksonville Rose Soc., Phi Delta Kappa, Kappa Delta Pi, Delta Kappa Gamma, Kappa Delta. Methodist. Club: San Jose Country. Home: 847 Granada Blvd S Jacksonville FL 32207 Office: 4412 Barnes Rd Jacksonville FL 32207

GLASSMAN, ARMAND BARRY, physician, scientist, educator, administrator; b. Paterson, N.J., Sept. 9, 1938; s. Paul and Rosa (Ackerman) G.; m. Alberta C. Macri, Aug. 30, 1958; children—Armand P., Steven B., Brian A. B.A., Rutgers U., N.J., 1960; M.D. magna cum laude, Georgetown U., Washington, 1964. Diplomate: Am. Bd. Pathology, Am. Bd. Nuclear Medicine. Lic. physician S.C., Ga., Fla., Conn., Va., Calif., N.Y. Intern Georgetown U. Hosp., Washington, 1964-65; resident Yale-New Haven Hosp., West Haven VA Hosp., 1965-69; asst. prof. pathology U. Fla. Coll. Medicine; chief radioimmunoassary lab. Gainesville VA Hosp.; practice lab. and nuclear medicine 1969-71; dir. clin. labs. Med. Coll. Ga., Augusta, 1971-76; cons. physician in pathology VA Hosp., Augusta, 1973-76; cons. physician in nuclear medicine Univ. Hosp., Augusta, 1973-76; med. dir. clin. labs. Med. U. Hosp., Charleston, 1976-87; med. dir. clin. labs. Med. U. S.C., Charleston, 1976-87, attending physician in lab. and nuclear medicine, 1976-87, assoc. med. dir. Med. U. Hosp. and Clinics, 1982-86; med. dir. clin. labs. Charleston Meml. Hosp., S.C., 1976-87; cons. VA Hosp., Charleston, 1976-87; prof., chmn. dept. lab. medicine Med. U. S.C., 1976-87, med. dir. MT and MLT programs, 1976-87, acting chmn. dept. immunology and microbiology, 1985-87, assoc. dean Coll. Medicine, 1979-85, asst. and assoc. dean Coll. Allied Health Sci., 1984-87, chmn. hosp. exec. com., 1985-86, acting med. dir. Univ. Hosp. and Clinics, 1985-86; sr. v.p. med. affairs, prof. lab. medicine and nuclear medicine Montefiore Med. Ctr. and Albert Einstein Coll. Medicine, Bronx, N.Y., 1987—; prof. depts. of nuclear medicine and lab. medicine Albert Einstein Coll. of Medicine; Adv. council Trident Tech. Coll., 1976-87; bd. dirs. Fetter Family Health Ctr., 1976-79; trustee Coll. Prep. Sch., 1979-84, chmn. bd., 1983-84. Contbr. articles in medicine to profl. jours. Trustee, bd. dirs., v.p. Mason Prep. Sch., 1984-87; bd. dirs. United Way, 1983-87, Am. Cancer Soc., 1984-87. Served with USMCR, 1956-64. Johnson and Avalon Found. scholar Georgetown U., 1964. Fellow Coll. Am. Patholgists (numerous coms. including edn. com. 1983—), ACP, Assn. Clin. Scientists, Am. Soc. Clin. Pathology (council immunochem. and blood banking 1983—), Am. Bd. Pathology (blood bank test com. 1984-88), Am. Coll. Nuclear Medicine; mem. Internat. Acad. Pathology, Am. Assn. Pathologists, Soc. Nuclear Medicine (chmn. edn. com. 1973-77, acad. council 1979—), AMA (Physician's Recognition award, instnl. rep. to sect. on med. schs.), Ga. Radiol. Soc., So. Med. Assn., Am. Geriatric Soc. (founding fellow So. div.), Am. Soc. Microbiology, Ga. Heart Assn., Am. Assn. Blood Banks (chmn. cryobiology com. 1974-83, edn. com. 1978-85, sci. program com. 1981-84, autologous transfusion com. 1979-83, bd. dirs. 1984-87), Assn. Schs. Allied Health Professions (bd. editors jour. 1979-83), Soc. Cryobiology (treas., bd. dirs. 1978-80), AAAS, N.Y. Acad. Scis., Acad. Clin. Lab. Physicians and Scientists (exec. council 1978-85, pres. 1982-83), S.E. Area Blood Bankers (pres. 1979-81, exec. council 1980-85), Sigma Xi, Alpha Eta, Alpha Omega Alpha. Club: Charleston Tennis. Office: Montefiore Med Ctr 111 E 210th St Bronx NY 10467

GLASSMAN, EDWARD, biochemistry educator, creativity and leadership consultant; b. N.Y.C., Mar. 18, 1929; s. Jacob S. and Riesa (Bronfman) F.; children—Lyn Judith, Susan Fiona, Ellen Ruth, Marjorie Riesa. A.B., NYU, 1949, M.S., 1951; Ph.D., Johns Hopkins U., 1955. Mem. staff City of Hope Med. Center, Duarte, Calif., 1959-60; faculty biochemistry dept. U. N.C. Med. Sch., Chapel Hill, 1960—; prof. U. N.C. Med. Sch., 1967—; mem. grants rev. study sect. NIMH, 1966-69; vis. prof. Stanford U. Med. Sch., 1968-69, U. Calif., Irvine, 1978; head Program for Team Effectiveness and Creativity, U. N.C., 1981—; vis. fellow Ctr. Creative Leadership, Greensboro, N.C., 1983; vis. scientist Stanford Research Ctr., Menlo Park, Calif., 1986. Author: Molecular Approaches to Neurobiology, 1967; Mem. editorial bd.: Behavior Genetics, 1970-71; mem. editorial adv. bd.: Behavioral Biology, 1971-78, Pharmacology, Biochemistry and Behavior, 1973—; mem. bd. advs.: Neurochem. Research, 1975-78; contbr. 95 articles to profl. jours. Adam T. Bruce fellow, 1954-55; Am. Cancer Soc. fellow, 1955-57; NIH fellow, 1958-59; NIH Career Devel. award, 1961-71; Guggenheim fellow, 1968-69. Fellow AAAS, Royal Soc. Edinburgh; mem. Soc. Neurosci. (pres. N.C. chpt. 1974-75), Elisha Mitchell Sci. Soc. (v.p. 1965-66). Democrat. Home: 112 Kenan St Chapel Hill NC 27516 Office: Dept Biochemistry U NC Med Sch Chapel Hill NC 27599-7260

GLASSMAN, GERALD SEYMOUR, metal finishing company executive; b. Hartford, Conn., July 6, 1932; s. Abram and Lena (Rulnick) G.; B.S., U. Vt., 1954; m. Edwina Wellins, Dec. 1, 1963; children—Cynthia Anne, Barbara Diane, Richard Philip. Exec., Bland Co., Hartford, Conn., 1954-63, Coleco Industries, Hartford, 1963-75; pres. Stanley Plating Co., Forestville, Conn., 1977-82; chmn. CBR Industries, Plainville, Conn., 1977-82, pres. Plainville Electro Plating Co., 1975—, Plainville West doing bus. as Marro Plating, 1986—, Internat. Metal Finishing, Inc., 1986—; mem. regional adv. bd. Bank of Boston Ct., Plainville, 1979—. Pres., Tunxis Community Coll. Found., 1978—; trustee Wheeler Clinic, 1979—, Plainville YMCA, 1980—; mem. Assocs. U. Hartford; active Simsbury Little League. Mem. Nat. Assn. Metal Finishers, Conn. Assn. Metal Finishers (v.p.), Metal Finishers Assn. Conn. (pres.), NAM, Am. Electroplaters Soc., Plainville C. of C. Jewish. Lodge: Masons. Home: 129 Westledge Rd West Simsbury CT 06092 Office: 21 Forestville Ave Plainville CT 06062

GLASSMAN, HARRY, real estate developer; b. Montreal, Que., Can., Aug. 23, 1928; s. Morris and Malka (Milgram) G.; m. Anne Pearl Glait, Aug. 17, 1958; children—Marla, Morrie Leonard. B.Arch., McGill U., Montreal, 1965. Registered architect, Que. Dir., chief operating officer Renomme Inc., Trois-Rivieres, Que., 1948-58; dir., chief exec. officer Frego Constrn. and Related Corps., Montreal., 1958-80; pres. Glomar Inc. and Related Corps., Montreal, 1980—. Recipient Award of Merit McGill U. Alma Mater Fund, 1979. Named hon. alumnus Israel Inst. Tech., Haifa, 1981. Mem. Order Architects Que., Royal Archtl. Inst. Can., Can. Technion Soc. (dir. 1978-87). Jewish. Avocations: skiing, tennis, bridge, windsurfing, boating, skating. Office: Glomar Inc, 8375 Mayrand St, Montreal, PQ Canada H4P 2E2

GLASSMEYER, JAMES MILTON, aerospace and electronics engineer; b. Cin., Mar. 31, 1928; s. Howard Jerome and Ethel Marie (Nieman) G.; m. Anita Mary Tschida, Apr. 21, 1979. Student U. Cin., 1947-49; BSEE with spl. honors, U. Colo., Boulder, 1958, MS in Aeronautics and Astronautics, MIT, 1960. Commd. 2d lt. U.S. Air Force, 1950, advanced through grades to lt. col., 1971; astron. engr. Air Force Space Systems Div. Hdqrs., Los Angeles, 1960-64, astronautical engr. and astronautics tech. intelligence analyst Air Force Rocket Propulsion Lab., Edwards AFB, Calif., 1967-73; ret., 1973; pvt. practice aerospace and electronics research and analysis, 1973—. Contbr. articles to jours. in field. Recipient Air Force Inst. Tech. scholarship, U. Colo., 1956-58, MIT, 1958-60, USAF Master Missileman badge, Air Force Rocket Propulsion Lab., 1970. Mem. AIAA, Air Force Assn., Planetary Soc., Ret. Officers Assn., Tau Beta Pi (1st grand prize Greater Interest in Govt. Nat. Essay Contest 1957), Eta Kappa Nu, Sigma Tau, Sigma Gamma Tau, Sigma Xi. Roman Catholic. Home: 5801 E North Wilshire Dr Tucson AZ 85711 Office: 5610-B E Glenn St Tucson AZ 85712

GLASSMOYER, THOMAS PARVIN, lawyer; b. Reading, Pa., Sept. 4, 1915; s. James Arthur and Margaretha (Parvin) G.; m. Frances Helen Thierolf, May 9, 1942; children—Deborah Jane Beck, Nancy Parvin Brittingham, Wendy Jean Barber. A.B., Ursinus Coll., 1936, LL.D. (hon.), 1972; LL.B., U. Pa., 1939. Bar: Pa. 1940. Law clk. Common Pleas Ct. 6, Phila., 1939-40; assoc. Murdoch, Paxson, Kalish & Green, Phila., 1940-42; atty. Dept. Justice and Office Price Adminstrn., 1942-43; assoc. Schnader, Harrison, Segal & Lewis, Phila., 1946-50, ptnr., 1950-87, of counsel, 1988—, chmn. pension com., 1969-84, chmn. tax dept., 1972-84, chmn. investment com., 1984-86, chmn. bd. trustees of Retirement Trust, 1986—; lectr. NYU Inst. Fed. Taxation; adv. bd. U. Pa. Tax Conf. Author: (with Sherwin T. McDowell) Legal Problems in Tax Returns, 1949; editor-in-chief U. Pa. Law Rev., 1938-39. Past pres. Upper Dublin Twp. PTA Council; mem. Zoning Bd. Adjustment Upper Dublin Twp., Montgomery County, Pa., 1957-59, bd. commrs., 1959-71, pres., 1968-69; mem. Upper Dublin Environ. Control Bd., 1972-82; bd. dirs. Ursinus Coll., Collegeville, Pa., 1956—, 1st v.p., 1978-81, pres., 1981—; bd. dirs. Wissahickon Valley Watershed Assn., 1974-76; trustee Bernard G. Segal Found., Phila., 1969—, Charlotte W. Newcombe Found., Princeton, N.J., 1982—. Served to 1st lt. JAG Dept., AUS, 1943-46. Recipient Eagle Scout award, Boy Scouts Am. Fellow Pa. Bar Found. (life); mem. Lawyers Club, Am. Arbitration Assn., ABA, Pa. Bar Assn. (ho. of dels. 1982—, council sect. taxation), Phila. Bar Assn. (sect. taxation), Fed. Bar Assn., Judge Advs. Assn., Am. Judicature Soc., Assn. Governing Bds. Colls. Univs., Pa. Folklife Soc. (bd. dirs., sec.), Nat. Assn. Coll. and Univ. Attys., Assn. Governing Bds. of Univs. and Colls., Acad. Polit. Sci., Nat.

Audubon Soc., Bucks County Hist. Assn., Quakertown (Pa.) Hist. Soc., U.S. Golf Assn., Order of Coif. Republican. Lutheran. Clubs: Manorlu (pres. 1963-65) (Oreland, Pa.); Mfrs. Golf and Country; Union League (Phila.). Home: 1648 North Hills Ave Willow Grove PA 19090 Office: Schnader Harrison Segal & Lewis 1600 Market St Suite 3600 Philadelphia PA 19103

GLASSPOLE, FLORIZEL AUGUSTUS, governor general Jamaica; b. Kingston, Jamaica, Sept. 25, 1909; s. Theophilus G. and Florence (Baxter) G.; m. Ina Josephine Kinlocke, 1934; 1 child. ed. (Brit. Trade Union Congress scholar 1946-47), Ruskin Coll., Oxford (Eng.) U. Practicing acct., 1932-34; gen. sec. Jamaica United Clks. Assn., 1937-48, Jamaica Trades Union Congress, 1939-52; pres. Jamaica Printers and Allied Workers Union, 1942-48; gen. sec. Water Commn. and Manual Workers Assn., 1941-48; workers rep. numerous govt. bds., 1942—; pres. Macahado Employees Union, 1952-55; mem. Ho. of Reps. for Kingston Eastern and Port Royal, 1944-73; minister of labour, 1955-57, of Edn., 1957-62, 72-73; leader Ho. of Reps., 1955-62, 72-73; mem. del. agreeing constn. with Brit. Govt., 1962; gov.-gen. of Jamaica, 1973—. Bd. govs. Inst. Jamaica, 1944-57; mem. Kingston Sch. Bd., 1944—; v.p. Peoples' Nat. Party; rep. standing com. W.I. Fedn., 1953—. Address: Govenor General's House, Kingston Jamaica *

GLAUBINGER, LAWRENCE DAVID, manufacturing company executive, consultant; b. Newark, Nov. 26, 1925; s. Samuel I. and Pauline (Sandler) G.; B.S. with honors, Ind. U., 1949; M.B.A., Columbia U., 1977; m. Lucienne Lefebvre, Nov. 11, 1967. Adminstrv. asst. to pres. Ronson Inc., Newark, 1949-51; mdse. mgr. United Mchts., N.Y.C., 1951-65; v.p. Marietta Silk Mills (Pa.), 1965-66; pres., chief exec. officer Channel Textile Co. Inc., Bradford, Vt., 1966-75; chmn. bd., chief exec. officer Stern & Stern Industries, Inc., N.Y.C., 1977—, also dir. & pres. Lawrence Econ. Cons. Inc., Hallandale, Fla., 1977—; dir. Leucadia Nat. Corp., Marisa Christina, Inc., House of Ronnie, Inc. Chmn. ann. funds campaigns Columbia U. Sch. Bus., 1980-82. Served with USCGR, 1943-46. Mem. Hoosier Hundred, Ind. U. Dean's Assos., Columbia U. Bus. Assos., Campaign for Columbia (co-chmn. bus. sch.), Am. Arbitration Assn., Beta Gamma Sigma. Republican. Jewish. Clubs: Princeton (N.Y.); Green Brook Country. Home: 437 Golden Isle Dr Hallandale FL 33009 Office: Stern & Stern Industries Inc 708 3rd Ave New York NY 10017

GLAUSER, JUERG, philologist, researcher; b. Zurich, Switzerland, Dec. 7, 1951; s. Jakob and Edith Lola (Kunz) G.; m. Paula Schickel, July 17, 1981. Lic. in philosophy, U. Zurich, 1979, PhD summa cum laude, 1981. Asst. U. Zurich, 1980-86, researcher Swiss Nat. Sci. Found., 1986—. Author: Islaendische Maerchensagas, 1983; co-editor: (series) Beitraege sur Nordischen Philologie, 1980—; literary critic Swiss newspapers; translator various books and articles; contbr. articles and revs. to profl. jours. Various grants. Mem. Swiss Soc. for Scandinavian Studies (hon. sec. 1980-86, bd. dirs.). Home: Reutlenring 20, 8302 Kloten Switzerland Office: U Zurich, Raemistrasse 74, 8001 Zurich Switzerland

GLAVIANO, VINCENT VALENTINO, educator, physiologist; b. Frankford, N.Y., July 19, 1920; s. Salvatore and Josephine (Manzo) G.; m. Eleanor Spargimino, July 18, 1943; children: Joan J., Vincent S. B.S., CCNY, 1950; Ph.D., Columbia U., 1954; M.D., Chgo. Med. Sch., 1982. Faculty Columbia U., 1951-53; fellow Columbia, 1954-56; instr. Hunter Coll., N.Y.C., 1952-54; asst. prof. physiology U. Ill. Coll. Medicine, Chgo., 1956-60; assoc. prof. physiology Loyola U. Sch. Medicine, Chgo., 1960-64; prof. Loyola U. Sch. Medicine, 1964-70; prof., chmn. Chgo. Med. Sch., 1970-85; dir. Biotech. Research Assocs., Glen Ellyn, Ill., 1986—; cons. Cook County Hosp. Cardiopulmonary Lab., Abbot Labs.; cons./physicist in therapeutic radiobiology Hines (Ill.) VA Hosp. Editorial bd.: Circulatory Shock, 1975-85. Postdoctoral research fellow N.Y. Heart Assn., 1954-56; travel awards Nat. Acad. Scis., 1962, 65, 67, 77. Fellow AAAS, N.Y. Acad. Scis.; mem. Am. Physiol. Soc., Soc. Exptl. Biology and Medicine, Am., Chgo. heart assns., Harvey Soc., Am. Soc. Pharmacology and Exptl. therapeutics, Internat. Soc. Heart Research, Sigma Xi, Alpha Omega Alpha. Home: 517 Carlisle Ct Glen Ellyn IL 60137 Office: Biotech Research Assocs PO Box 3181 Glen Ellyn IL 60138

GLAZER, DONALD WAYNE, lawyer, educator; b. Cleve., July 26, 1944; s. Julius and Ethel (Goldstein) G.; m. Ellen S. Sarasohn, July 11, 1968; children: Elizabeth M., Mollie S. A.B. summa cum laude, Dartmouth Coll., 1966; J.D. magna cum laude, Harvard U., 1969; LL.M., U. Pa., 1970. Bar: Mass. 1970. Assoc. Ropes & Gray, Boston, 1970-78, ptnr., 1978—; instr. corp. fin. Boston U. Law Sch., 1975; lectr. law Harvard U., Cambridge, Mass., 1978—. Co-editor First Ann. Inst. on Securities Regulation, 1970; contbr. articles to legal jours. Trustee, treas. Hillel Found. Greater Boston; trustee Cowen Found., Santa Fe Neurol. Scis. Inst. Fellow Salzburg Seminar in Am. Studies, 1975. Mem. Am. Law Inst., ABA (co-chmn. subcom. on employee benefits and exec. compensation fed. securities law com.), Boston Bar Assn. (chmn. corp. sect., past chmn. securities law com.). Jewish. Home: 55 Farlow Rd Newton MA 02158 Office: Ropes & Gray 225 Franklin St Boston MA 02110

GLAZER, GEORGE, corporate executive; b. Phila., Nov. 5, 1930. B.A. in Journalism, Pa. State U.-University Park, 1952. Editor, reporter WCAU-TV and AM, Phila., 1952; account exec. Adelphia Assoc. Pub. Relations, Phila., 1954-56; dir. pub. relations Gresh & Kramer, Inc., Phila., 1956-58; v.p., dir. pub. relations Don Kemper Co., N.Y.C., 1958-60; pres. A.A. Schechter Assocs., N.Y.C., 1960-73; sr. v.p. Hill & Knowlton, Inc., N.Y.C., 1973-84, exec. dir. Worldwide Broadcast and Satellite Services, 1984—, mem. Radio TV News Dirs. Assn., Soc. Satellite Profls. Office: Hill and Knowlton 420 Lexington Ave New York NY 10017

GLAZER, STANFORD PAUL FRANK, restauranteur; b. Kansas City, Mo., Jan. 1, 1932; s. Jack and Ella (Gitterman) G.; m. Rita Ann Studna, July 1, 1951 (div. June 1968); children—Craig, Jeffery, Jack; m. Cheryl Anne Hurley Sheehan, Feb. 12, 1978. Grad. Kemper Mil. Sch., 1949. Pres., Royal Automotive Parts Co., 1958-61, Sav-On Stores, Inc., 1960-62, Mid-West Automobile Auction Corp., 1962-65; exec. v.p. Allied Material Equipment Corp., 1965-70; pres. Kansas City Arena, Ltd., 1970-74, Stanford Glazer & Assocs., 1978-81; chief exec. officer Stanford & Sons, Inc., Kansas City, Mo., 1976—, Stanford & Sons of St. Louis. Fellow Harry S. Truman Library. Served with M.C., U.S. Army, 1952-54. Recipient Epicurean award Carte Blanche, 1976, 77; Good Dining award Am. Diners Soc., 1977, 78; Mobil Fine Dining award; Silver Spoon award Outlook Mag., 1980; rated "Top 1200 Restaurants in Am." in Jacques Pepin book. Mem. Nat. Restaurant Assn., Mo. Restaurant Assn. Jewish. Lodges: Masons, Shriners. Office: 504 Westport Rd Kansas City MO 64111

GLAZIER, ROBERT CARL, publishing executive; b. Brandsville, Mo., Mar. 26, 1927; s. Vernie A. and Mildred F. (Beu) G.; m. Harriette Hubbard, June 5, 1949; children: Gregory Kent, Jeffrey Robert. Student, Drury Coll., 1944-46; B.A., U. Wichita, 1949. Reporter Springfield (Mo.) Daily News, 1944-46; asst. city editor Wichita Eagle, 1946-49; journalism instr. U. Wichita, 1949-53; dir. pub. relations Springfield (Mo.) Pub. Schs., 1953-59; asso. dir. dept. radio and TV The Methodist Ch., Nashville, 1959-61; gen. mgr. WDCN-TV (Channel 2), Nashville, 1961-65, KETC (Channel 9), St. Louis, 1965-76; also exec. dir. St. Louis Ednl. TV Commn.; pres. So. Ednl. Communications Assn., 1976-80, Springfield Communications, Inc., Mo., 1980—. Bd. dirs. Adult Edn. Council Greater St. Louis, 1965-76, United Meth. Communications, 1980-86, Springfield Area Council of Chs., 1980-86, Lester E. Cox Med. Ctrs., 1988—. Served with AUS, 1945-46. Mem. Nat. Sch. Public Relations Assn. (past regional dir.), Nat. Acad. TV Arts and Scis. (gov.), Mo. Instructional TV Council, Ill. Instructional TV Commn., Nat. Assn. Ednl. Broadcasters. Methodist. Club: Rotary Internat. Home: 2305 E Meadow St Springfield MO 65804 Office: 520 South Union Springfield MO 65802

GLEASON, RALPH NEWTON, economic development consultant; b. Townville, S.C., Jan. 5, 1922; s. Arthur Bryan and Clara Belle (McAdams) G.; m. Marjorie Nelle Little, Apr. 4, 1942; children—Ralph Newton Jr., Delno Rex, Charles Stanley, Edward Dean, Cindy Ann. B.S. with honors, Clemson Coll., 1942; certificate, Internat. Corr. Schs., 1957, U.S. Dept. Agr. Grad. Sch., 1957; M.S., Ohio State U., 1963. Statis. adviser to South Korean interim govt., 1947-48; food and econ. adviser ECA, Seoul, Korea, 1949-50; chief food and fertilizer div. Sino-Am. Joint Commn. Rural Reconstrn., Taipei, Taiwan, 1950-56; agrl. programs officer Near East South Asia FOA, Washington, 1957-58; dep. chief agriculturist Tech. Cooperation Mission to India, New Delhi, 1958-62; chief food and agr. div. Econ. Mission to Turkey, 1963-68; dep. dir. Agr. and Rural Devel. Service Office War on Hunger, Washington, 1968-70; dep. asso. dir. food and agr. AID, South Vietnam, 1970-75; econ. devel. cons. 1975—. Mem. dels. UN Food and Agr. Agy. Confs.; Bd. dirs., treas. Taipei Am. Sch., 1950-56; bd. dirs. Ponderosa Parks-Lake Hartwell, 1974—. Served to maj. AUS, 1942-47, ETO, Korea. Decorated Silver Star, Bronze Star. Mem. Am. Fgn. Service Assn., Farm Bur. Fedn., Blue Ridge Rural Electric Co-op, Phi Kappa Phi, Alpha Zeta. Lodge: Mason. Home: 505 Phil Watson Rd Anderson SC 29621

GLEASON, STEPHEN CHARLES, physician; b. Leon, Iowa, June 30, 1946; s. Charles Gerald and Ferne Louise (Pollard) G.; B.S., Iowa State U., 1971; D.Osteopathy with highest honors, Coll. Osteo. Medicine and Surgery, 1974; m. Lisa Ann Corcoran, Aug. 22, 1981; children—Michael John, Timothy Charles, Christian Kelly, Sean Patrick, Keriann Louise. Resident in family practice, Meml. Med. Center, Corpus Christi, Tex., 1974-75; family practice medicine, West Des Moines, Iowa, 1975—; chmn. dept. family practice Mercy Hosp. Med. Center, Des Moines, 1979-82, dir. Mercy Health and Human Services, chief med. officer Mercy Clinic System, 1984; adj. clin. prof. family practice Coll. Osteo. Medicine and Surgery, Des Moines, 1979-86; physician adv. Iowa Found. Med. Care, Profl. Standards Review Orgn., West Des Moines, 1978—; mem. Iowa Legislature's Interim Com. on Health; toxicology cons. Adolescent Detoxification Ctr., Mercy Hosp. Med. Ctr., 1986; bd. dirs. Mercy Health Ctr. of Cen. Iowa, Our Primary Purpose, Inc.; chmn. bd., pres. Valley Med. Services P.C.; mem. papal med. security team Pope John Paul's Am. Pilgrimage, 1979. Chmn. Iowa CARES Med. Found., 1985, Dem. Nat. Health Policy Conf., 1987, Iowa Dem. Health Legislation Com., 1987; mem. Nat. Dem. Platform Com.; bd. dirs. Family Health Plan, Health Maintenance Orgn., 1985. Recipient Outstanding Young Iowan, 1982. Diplomate Am. Bd. Family Practice. Mem. Am. Acad. Med. Dirs., Am. Acad. Clin. Toxicology, Assn. Med. Educators and Researchers in Abuse, AMA, Am. Acad. Med. Dirs., Assn. Med. Educators and Researchers in Substance Abuse, Iowa Med. Soc., Polk County Med. Soc., Sigma Alpha Epsilon, Sigma Sigma Phi. Democrat. Office: Valley West Mall Suite 106 West Des Moines IA 50265

GLEIBER, STUART ANDER, lumber executive; b. Bklyn., July 20, 1942; s. Ira and Anita Jean (Ander) G.; B.B.A., NYU, 1964; m. Jill Ann Fairberg, Aug. 30, 1964; children—Joshua Daniel, Gary Stephen, Douglas Ross. Vice pres., sales dir. Am. Metal Spinning & Stamping Co., N.Y.C., 1964-70; pres., chmn. bd. Abbot & Abbot Box Corp., Long Island City, N.Y., 1970—; pres., dir. Simglib Realty Corp., Long Island City, F. Box Co., Inc., Long Island City; past pres., dir. Ander Lumber Industries, Inc., N.Y.C.; cons. in packaging. Chmn. com. N.Y. State Head Injury Assn., regional dir. L.I. div. Mem. N.Y. State Police Chiefs Assn. Contbr. article to profl. jour. Home: 5 Kristi Ct, Greenlawn, NY 11740 Office: 37-11 10th St Long Island City NY 11101 Other: 32-02 Queens Blvd, Long Island City, NY 11101

GLEICHMAN, JOHN ALAN, safety and security executive; b. Anthoney, Kans., Feb. 11, 1944; s. Charles William and Caroline Elizabeth (Emch) G.; m. Martha Jean Cannon, July 1, 1966; 1 son, John Alan Jr. B.S. in Bus. Mgmt., Kans. State Tchrs. Coll., 1966. Cert. hazard control mgr.; cert. safety profl.; cert. safety exec. Office mgr. to asst. supt. Barton-Malow Co., Detroit, 1967-72, safety coordinator, 1972-76, corp. mgr. safety and security, 1976—; instr. U. Mich., Wayne State U., 1977-81; mem. constrn. safety standards commn. adv. com. for concrete constrn. and steel erection Bur. of Safety and Regulations, Mich. Dept. Labor, 1977—. Instr. multi media first aid ARC, 1976—; past trustee Apostolic Christian Ch., Livonia, Mich. Recipient Safety Achievement awards Mich. Mut. Ins. Co., 1979-83; Cameron award Constrn. sect. Indsl. div. Nat. Safety Conf., 1982, 1987. Mem. Mich. Safety Council (pres. 1984-85), Am. Soc. Safety Engrs. (pres. Detroit chpt. 1982, nat. adminstr. constrn div. 1988, bd. dirs. 198—, Safety Prof. of Yr. chpt. 1984) Nat. Safety Council (chmn. tech. rev. constrn. sect. indsl. div. 1980-84, chmn. standards com. indsl. div. 1983-85, chmn. assn. com. indsl. div. 1985-86, dir. tech. support com. indsl. div. 1986-87, bd. dirs. 1987-88, rep. Am. Nat. Standards Inst.), Am. Arbitration Assn. (panel arbitrators 1985). Author: (with others) You, The National Safety Council, and Voluntary Standards, 1981. Office: PO Box 5200 Detroit MI 48235

GLEISS, HENRY WESTON, lawyer; b. Detroit, Nov. 22, 1928; s. George Herman and Mary Elizabeth (Weston) G.; m. Joan Bette Christopher, July 23, 1955; children—Kent G., Keith W. B.A., Denison U., 1951; J.D., U. Mich., 1954. Bar: Mich. 1955, U.S. Dist. Ct. (ea. dist.) Mich. 1955, U.S. Dist. Ct. (we. dist.) Mich. 1960, U.S. Ct. Appeals (6th cir.) 1964, U.S. Supreme Ct. 1967. Sole practice, Benton Harbor, Mich., 1957-61; ptnr. Globensky, Gleiss & Bittner, St. Joseph, 1961—; spl. asst. atty. gen. Mich., 1960—. Officer Jaycees, Mich.; bd. dirs. United Fund. Served with U.S. Army, 1955-57. Mem. ABA, Mich. Bar Assn., Berrien County Bar Assn. (pres. 1974), Assn. Trial Lawyers Am., Twin Cities C. of C. (v.p. 1975). Congregationalist. Clubs: Kiwanis, Moose (Benton Harbor); Economic of S.W. Mich.; Elks (St. Joseph). Home: 1224 Miami Benton Harbor MI 49022 Office: 610 Ship St PO Box 290 Saint Joseph MI 49085

GLEMP, JOZEF, archbishop; b. Inowroclaw, Poland, Dec. 18, 1929; s. Kazimierz and Salomea (Kosmicka) G.; grad. Priests Sem. Gniezno, 1956; D. Canon and Roman Law, Lateran U., Rome, 1964. Ordained priest Roman Catholic Ch., 1956; sec. to Cardinal Primate Stefan Wyszynski, from 1967; bishop of Warmia, 1979-81; archbishop of Gniezno and Warsaw, 1981—, also primate of Poland; pres. Polish Episcopal Conf.; mem. Cong. for the Eastern Ch. Author: De conceptu fictionis iuris apud Romanos, 1964, Lexiculum iuris romani, 1974, Through Justice in Charity, 1982, Czlowiek wielkiej wiary, 1983, Kosciol na drogach Ojczyzny, 1985, Chcemy z tego sprawdzianu wyjsc prawdomowni i wiarygodni, 1985, Kosciol i Polonia, 1986, W teczy Frankow orzel i krzyz, 1987. Address: 17 Miodowa, 00-246 Warsaw Poland also: ul Kanclerza Jana Laskiego 7, 62-200 Gniezno Poland

GLENDENNING, FRANCIS JOHN, educational gerontologist; b. St. Helens, Eng., Feb. 7, 1921; s. John William and Frances (Varley) G.; m. Marjorie Angela Shears, Oct. 9, 1971. BA with honors, U. Liverpool, 1942; MA, U. Sheffield, 1949; PhD, U. Keele, 1975. Counsellor Student Christian Movement, Yorkshire, Eng., 1949-58; high schs. sec. World Student Christian Fedn., Geneva, 1957-62; warden Student Movement House, London, 1958-64; assoc. dir. Christian Aid Brit. Council Chs., London, 1964-68; sec. adult and continuing edn. U. Keele, Eng., 1968-87, hon. sr. research fellow, 1987—; mem. com. Forum on Rights of Elderly People to Edn., London, 1980—. Author, editor: The Church and the Arts, 1969, Educational Gerontology, 1985; author: Health Needs of Black and Ethnic Minority Elders in Britain, 1988; contbg. editor Beth Johnson Found. Publs., 1976—; joint editor Jour. Ednl. Gerontology, 1985—; mem. editorial bd. Ednl. Gerontology, 1988—. Mem. Staffordshire Retirement Council (chmn. 1978-82), Beth Johnson Found. (chmn. 1980-84), Brit. Soc. Gerontology, Pre-retirement Assn. Gt. Britain and No. Ireland (dep. chmn. 1986—), North Staffordshire Assn. Mental Health (chmn. 1987—), Brit. Assn. Ednl. Gerontology (hon. sec. 1985—). Mem. Labour Party. Home: 32 Dartmouth Ave, Newcastle upon Lyne ST5 3NY, England Office: Ctr Social Gerontology, U Keele, Keele ST5 5BG, England

GLENDINNING, OLIVER NIGEL VALENTINE, language educator; b. East Sheen, Surrey, Eng., Oct. 16, 1929; s. Alexander James Glendinning and Olive Margaret Ledward; m. Victoria Seebohm (div. 1981); children: Paul, Hugo, Matthew, Simon. BA, Cambridge (Eng.) U., 1953, MA, 1957, PhD, 1959; MA, Oxford (Eng.) U., 1958, U. Dublin, Ireland, 1970. Research fellow Trinity Hall, Cambridge U., 1957-58; lectr. Spanish Oxford U., 1958-62; prof. Spanish U. Southampton, Eng., 1962-70; prof. Trinity Coll., Dublin, 1970-74, Queen Mary Coll., U. London, 1974—. Author: Vida y Obra de Cadalso, 1962, A Literary History of Spain, The Eighteenth Century, 1972, Goya and His Critics, 1977, also articles. Named to Order de Isabel la Católica, 1986. Mem. Real Acad. Bellas Artes San Fernando (corr.), The Hispanic Soc. Am. (corr.). Home: 32 Aberavon Rd Bow, London E3 5AR, England Office: U London Queen Mary Coll, Dept Spanish Mile End Rd, London E1 4NS, England

GLENN, CLETA MAE, lawyer; b. Clinton, Ill., Sept. 24, 1921; d. John and Mattie Sylvester (Anderson) Glenn; B.S., U. Ill., 1947; J.D., DePaul U. Coll. Law, 1976; m. Rex Eugene Loggans, Sept. 3, 1948 (div.); 1 dau., Susan. Real estate builder, developer, 1959-69; communications dir. Transp. Research Center, Northwestern U., Evanston, Ill., 1969-72; admitted to Ill. bar, 1977; practice law, Chgo., 1977—; lectr. Assn. Trial Lawyers Am., John Marshall Law Sch. Served with USN, 1943-59. Recipient Real Estate Humanitarian award Kislak Co., Miami, Fla., 1962. Mem. ABA, Ill. Bar Assn. (assembly rep., mem. standing com. on traffic laws and cts., family law sect. council), Chgo. Bar Assn., Assn. Trial Lawyers Am., Ill. Trial Lawyers Assn., Lex Leggio, Phi Alpha Delta. Editor: Collective Bargaining and Technological Change in American Transportation, 1979; contbr. articles to profl. publs. Home: 200 E Delaware Pl Chicago IL 60611 Office: Glenn Law Offices Loggans Bldg 615 N Wabash Ave Chicago IL 60611

GLENN, GUY CHARLES, physician; b. Parma, Ohio, May 13, 1930; s. Joseph Frank and Helen (Rupple) G.; B.S., Denison U., 1953; M.D., U. Cin., 1957; m. Lucia Ann Howarth, June 13, 1953; children—Kathryn Holly, Carolyn Helen, Cynthia Marie. Intern, Walter Reed Army Med. Center, Washington, 1957-58; resident in pathology Fitzsimons Army Med. Center, Denver, 1959-63; commd. 2d lt. U.S. Army, 1956, advanced through grades to col., 1977; demonstrator pathology Royal Army Med. Coll., London, 1970-72; chief dept. pathology Fitzsimons Army Med. Center, Denver, 1972-77; pres. med. staff St. Vincent Hosp.; mem. governing bd. Mont. Health Systems Agy. Diplomate Am. Bd. Pathology. Fellow Coll. Am. Pathologists (chmn. chemistry resources com., chmn. sci. resources com., mem. budget program and review com., council on quality assurance), Am. Soc. Clin. Pathology, Soc. Med. Cons. to Armed Forces, Colo. Assn. Continuing Lab. Edn., Midland Empire Health Assn. (past pres.). Contbr. to profl. jours. Home: 3225 Jack Burke Ln Billings MT 59102 Office: St Vincent Hosp Billings MT 59102

GLENN, JAMES FRANCIS, urologist, educator; b. Lexington, Ky., May 10, 1928; s. Cambridge Francis and Martha (Morrow) G.; m. Gale Brooke Morrison, Dec. 29, 1948; children: Cambridge Francis II, Sara Brooke, Nancy Carrick, James Morrison Woodworth. Student (Yale Regional scholar), Univ. Sch., Lexington, 1946; B.A. in Gen. Sci. (Bausch and Lomb Nat. Sci. scholar), U. Rochester, 1949; M.D., Duke U., 1952. Diplomate: Am. Bd. Urology (mem.), Nat. Bd. Med. Examiners. Intern Peter Bent Brigham Hosp., Boston, 1952-54; asst. resident urology Duke U. Med. Ctr., 1956-58, resident, 1958-59; instr. urology Duke U., 1958-59, prof., chief div. urology, 1963-80; prof. Yale U., 1959-61; asso. prof. Bowman Gray Sch. Medicine, Wake Forest Coll., 1961-63; practice medicine specializing in urology New Haven, 1959-61, Winston-Salem, N.C., 1961-63, Durham, N.C., 1963-80; prof. surgery, dean Med. Sch., Emory U., 1980-83; pres. Mt. Sinai Med. Ctr., 1983-87; prof. surgery U. Ky. Coll. Medicine, Lexington, 1987—; sci. dir. Council for Tobacco Research USA, 1987—; nat. cons. USAF Med. Service, 1971-80. Contbg. author: Renal Neoplasia, 1967, Urodynamics, 1971, Textbook of Surgery, 1972, Plastic and Reconstructive Surgery of The Genital Area, 1973, Current Operative Urology, 1975, Campbell's Urology, 1977; author, editor: Diagnostic Urology, 1964, Ureteral Reflux in Children, 1966, Urologic Surgery, 1969, rev. edit., 1975, 84; contbr. numerous articles to profl. jours. Served to capt. M.C., USAF, 1954-56. Mem. Am. Assn. Genitourinary Surgeons, Am. Surg. Assn., ACS, AMA (sec. sect. urology 1972-73, chmn. 1975-77), Assn. Am. Med. Colls., Internat. Urol Soc., Clin. Soc. Genito-Urinary Surgeons, N.Y. Acad. Scis., Soc. Pediatric Urology, Soc. Pelvic Surgeons (pres. 1980-81), Soc. Univ. Surgeons, Soc. Univ. Urologists (pres. 1971-72), Royal Coll. Surgeons (hon. fellow 1987), German Urol. Assn. (hon.), Royal Soc. Medicine, Am. Assn. Clin. Urologists, Australasian Urologic Soc. (hon.), Brit. Assn. Urologic Surgeons (corres.). Home: PO Box 1 Pine Grove KY 40470 Office: U Ky Med Ctr Div Urology 800 Rose St Room MS-269 Lexington KY 40536

GLENN, JOHN HERSCHEL, JR., U.S. senator; b. Cambridge, Ohio, July 18, 1921; s. John Herschel and Clara (Sproat) G.; m. Anna Margaret Castor, Apr. 1943; children: Carolyn Ann, John David. Student, Muskingum Coll., 1939-42, B.Sc., 1962; naval aviation cadet, U. Iowa, 1942; grad. flight sch., Naval Air Tng. Center, Corpus Christi, Tex., 1943, Navy Test Pilot Tng. Sch., Patuxent River, Md., 1954. Commd. 2d lt. USMC, 1943, assigned 4th Marine Aircraft Wing, Marshall Islands campaign, 1944, assigned 9th Marine Aircraft Wing, 1945-46; with 1st Marine Aircraft Wing, North China Patrol, also Guam, 1947-48; flight instr. advanced flight tng. Corpus Christi, 1949-51; asst. G-2/G-3 Amphibious Warfare Sch., Quantico, Va., 1951; with Marine Fighter Squadron 311, exchange pilot 25th Fighter Squadron USAF, Korea, 1953; project officer fighter design br. Navy Bur. Aero. Washington, 1956-69; astronaut Project Mercury, Manned Spacecraft Center NASA, 1959-64; pilot Mercury-Atlas 6 orbital space flight launched from Cape Canaveral, Fla., Feb., 1962; ret. as col. 1965; v.p. corp. devel. and dir. Royal Crown Cola Co., 1966-74; U.S. Senator from, Ohio, 1975—. Co-author: We Seven, 1962; Author: P.S., I Listened to Your Heart Beat. Trustee Muskingum Coll. Decorated D.F.C. (six), Air medal (18), Astronaut medal USMC, Navy unit commendation; Korean Presidential unit citation; Distinguished Merit award Muskingum Coll.; Medal of Honor N.Y.C.; Congl. Space Medal of Honor, 1978. Mem. Soc. Exptl. Test Pilots, Internat. Acad. of Astronautics (hon.). Democrat. Presbyn. Office: US Senate 503 Hart Senate Bldg Washington DC 20510

GLENN, NORMAN ROBERT, publisher, editor; b. Chicago Heights, Ill., Sept. 3, 1909; s. Max and Jennie (Wechsler) Goldman; student U. Chgo., 1927-30; m. Elaine Lee Couper, June 14, 1945 (dec.); children—Robin Day, Geoffrey Merrit; m. 2d, Roberta Hope Brewster, Oct. 27, 1972. Promotion mgr. radio sta. WLS, Chgo., 1932-36; bus. mgr. Broadcasting mag., Washington, 1937-43; pres., pub. Sponsor mag., N.Y.C., 1946-65; pres., pub., editor Media Decisions mag., N.Y.C., 1966-85, also Encyclomedia, 6-vol. ann. media library; chmn. Decisions Publ. Inc., N.Y.C.; chmn. Mktg. and Media Edn., 1982—, Am. Values (community action network), 1980—; vis. lectr. Syracuse U., 1961; dir. ComCor Publs., Green Mountain Enterprises, Inc. Chmn. Am. Values, 1980—. Served to 1st lt. USAAF, 1943-45. Decorated Army Commendation ribbon; recipient Polk award for distinguished journalism. Mem. Radio and TV Execs. Soc. (v.p.), Broadcast Pioneers, Mag. Pubs. Assn. Christian Scientist. Clubs: Yale; Canadian. Author: (with Irving Settel) Television Advertising and Production, 1953. Home: Forest Rd North Haven NY 11963 Office: 211 E 43d St New York NY 10017

GLENN, ROY JOHNSON, manufactured housing executive; b. Birmingham, Ala., Dec. 23, 1920; s. Willis and Maggie (Johnson) G.; student acctg. Massey Bus. Coll., 1938-39; student engring. Auburn U., 1941-42; m. Sammie Lee Spradling, Feb. 14, 1941; children: Ellen Glenn Andersen, Jerry Alan. Mold loftsman, Higgins Industries, New Orleans, 1943-44; ptnr. Glenn Constrn. Co., Birmingham, Ala., 1946-50; profl. golfer, 1950-57; pres. Crab Orchard Golf Club, Inc., Carterville, Ill., 1958-63; sec., treas. Cavaness-Glenn-Storme, Inc., Carterville, 1964-75; pres. Glenn & Co., Inc., Carterville, 1963-76; sec. Component Building Systems, Inc., Carbondale, Ill., 1976—; ptnr. Roydon & Assocs., Carbondale, 1982—; owner Crest Builders Assocs., 1977-86, Design Cons., 1983—; cons. various golf and country clubs; designer golf courses and bldgs. Bd. trustees John A. Logan Coll., 1968-70; mem. govs. task force on Future of Rural Ill., 1986. Served with USN, 1944-46. Republican. Baptist. Home and Office: Route 2 Carbondale IL 62901

GLENNER, RICHARD ALLEN, dentist, dental historian; b. Chgo., Apr. 14, 1934; s. Robert Joseph and Vivian (Prosk) G.; B.S., Roosevelt U., 1955; B.S. in Dentistry, U. Ill., 1958, D.D.S., 1959; m. Dorothy Chapman, July 13, 1957; children—Mark Steven, Alison. Gen. practice dentistry, Chgo., 1962—; cons. on dental history to Smithsonian Instn., ADA, various corps., libraries, univs., museums, dental jours.; lectr. in field. Served to capt. AUS, 1960-62. Mem. Am., Ill. Dental Assns., Chgo. Dental Soc., Assn. Mil. Surgeons U.S., Am. Acad. History of Dentistry (historian 1984, chmn. Smithsonian Instn. adv. group 1987, Hayden-Harris award 1983), Fed. Dentaire Internationale, Ill. State Dental Soc. (history com.), Am. Med. Writers Assn., Sci. Instrument Soc., Alpha Omega. Author: The Dental Office: A Pictorial History; co-author The American Dentist: A Pictorial and Social History; cons. editor A Bicentennial Salute to Am. Dentistry, 1976; contbr. articles on dental history to profl. jours. Club: Lindsay. Home: 6715 N Lawndale Ave Lincolnwood IL 60645 Office: 3414 W Peterson Ave Chicago IL 60659

GLEYZAL, ANDRE, retired mathematics educator; b. Lake Charles, La., Nov. 23, 1908; s. Noel Eugene and Virginia (Espitalier) G.; m. V. Gene, July

21, 1962. B.A., Ohio State U., 1931, M.A., 1933, Ph.D., 1936. Prof. physics Boston Coll., 1937-38; prof. math. St. Michael's Coll. Burlington, Vt., 1938-41; mathematician U.S. Navy Dept., Washington, 1941-51, Bur. Standards, Washington, 1951-53, U.S. Naval Surface Weapons Lab., Washington, 1953-72; ret., 1972. Discovered math. electron, 1980; contbr. articles to profl. jours. Recipient scholarships Ohio State U., 1930, Princeton U., 1936. Mem. Am. Math. Soc., Phi Beta Kappa, Phi Mu Epsilon. Avocations: riding motorcycles, writing mathematical and physics papers, stock mkt. and real estate research. Home: 300 NE 44th St Boca Raton FL 33431

GLICKENHAUS, SARAH BRODY, speech therapist; b. Mpls., Mar. 8, 1919; d. Morris and Ethel (Silin) Brody; B.S., U. Minn., 1940, M.S., 1945; m. Seth Morton Glickenhaus, Oct. 23, 1944; children—James Morris, Nancy Pier. Speech therapist, Davison Sch. Speech Correction, Atlanta, 1940-42; speech pathologist U. Minn., Mpls., 1945-46; speech therapist Queens Coll., N.Y.C., 1946-48; speech therapist VA, N.Y.C., 1949-50; pvt. practice, New Rochelle, N.Y., 1950-71; speech therapist Abbott Sch. United Free Sch. Dist. 13, Irvinton, N.Y., 1971—; tutor learning disabled children New Rochelle Public Schs., 1968-71. Mem. Am. Speech Hearing And Lang. Assn., N.Y. State Speech and Hearing Assn., Westchester Speech and Hearing Assn., AAAS. Club: Harvard (N.Y.C.). Jewish. Home and Office: 100 Dorchester Rd Scarsdale NY 10583

GLICKSMAN, ARVIN S(IGMUND), physician; b. Bklyn., Mar. 14, 1924; s. Charles and Myrtle (Fetner) G.; m. Bernice R. Grobstein, Jan. 30, 1956; children: Jonathan, Jane Ellen, Merrylee, Caroline, Jeanette. M.B., M.D., Chgo. Med. Sch., 1949. Intern Kings County Hosp., Bklyn., 1948-50; AEC postdoctoral research fellow Duke U., 1950-51; postgrad. research fellow Brookhaven Nat. Labs., Upton, N.Y., 1951-52; resident in medicine Meml. Hosp., N.Y.C., 1952-54; clin. asst. physician in medicine Meml. Hosp., 1955-64, asst. attending radiation therapist, 1964-65; research fellow Sloan-Kettering Inst., N.Y.C., 1954-60; asso. Sloan-Kettering Inst., 1960-65; mem. med. research inst. Michael Reese Hosp., Chgo., 1964-65; asso. chmn. dept. radiation therapy Michael Reese Hosp., 1965-67; dep. dir. radiotherapy Mount Sinai Hosp., N.Y.C., 1967-73; prof. radiotherapy Mount Sinai Sch. Medicine, 1971-73; dir. radiation oncology R.I. Hosp., Providence, 1973—, chmn. dept. modern medicine and biol. research, 1984—; prof. med. scis., chmn. radiation medicine Brown U., 1973-84; practice medicine specializing in radiation oncology; hon. med. cons. NIH, Royal Marsden Hosp.; mem. cancer clin., investigation rev. com. Nat. Cancer Inst., 1975-79, mem. radiation oncology com., 1976—. Editor: (with others) Computers in Radiotherapy, 1970, 73; contbr.: numerous articles to profl. jours. Mem. exec. com. R.I., Am. Cancer Soc., pres., 1987—; chmn. radiotherapy com. Cancer and Acute Leukemia Group B; chmn. task force info. systems R.I. Cancer Control Bd., also mem. exec. com. Dillon fellow Royal Marsden Hosp., Surrey, Eng., 1961-62; Research Career Devel. awardee NIH, 1962-64; Fulbright sr. scholar, 1986-87. Fellow Am. Coll. Radiology; mem. New Eng. Soc. Radiation Oncologists (pres. 1975-76), N.Y. Roentgen Ray Soc. (chmn. sect. therapeutic radiology 1972-73), Am. Soc. Clin. Oncology, Am. Assn. Cancer Edn., Am. Assn. Cancer Research, Am. Radium Soc., Am. Soc. Therapeutic Radiologists, Brit. Inst. Radiology. Home: Old Blackstone Rd Uxbridge MA 01569 Office: Rhode Island Hosp Providence RI 02902

GLIDDEN, DAVID ERIC, marketing executive; b. Phila., May 29, 1951; s. Thomas Evans and Loraine Grace (Fitzwater) G.; m. Terri Pat Wixon, Aug. 11, 1979 (div. July 1987); children—Jonathan, Kevin. B.S. in Speech, Northwestern U., 1972; M.P.A., U. Nebr., 1979; M.B.A., Ariz. State U., 1983. Radio announcer sta.-WGAC, Augusta, Ga., 1973-74; asst. mgr. KYNE-TV, Omaha, 1976-80; mktg. communications mgr. ADR Ultrasound, Tempe, Ariz., 1980-83; western area merchandising mgr. GenRad, Inc., Phoenix, 1983-87; exec. v.p. MarCom, Inc., Lowell, Mass., 1987—. Program dir. Met. Omaha Ednl. Broadcasting Assn., 1978-80; panel mem. Mesa Sch. Dist. Accreditation Rev., Ariz., 1983. Served with U.S. Army, 1972-76 Mem. Bus.-Profl. Advt. Assn., Nat. Assn. Ednl. Broadcasters, Beta Gamma Sigma, Theta Chi. Home: 11 Royal Crest Dr #9 Nashua NH 03060 Office: MarCom Inc 77 E Merrimack St Lowell MA 01852

GLIHA, JOHN LEE, management information consultant, researcher; b. Sidney, N.Y., Feb. 18, 1953; s. Edward Richard and Agnes (Bennett) G. BA, SUNY, Oswego, 1976; postgrad., Ariz. State U., 1977—. Grad. asst. Boulton Collection Mus. Instruments, Ariz. State U., 1977-78; supr. research info. ctr. music library Ariz. State U., 1979-83, cataloger music library, 1979-83, project coordinator collection devel. univ. library, 1983-84, dir. devel. research devel. office, 1984—; cons. AT&T, Phoenix, 1985—. Contbr. book reviews to library jour. Mem. Grievance com. Ariz. State U., 1983-84, ombudsman, chmn. staff personnel com., 1980-84, adv. bd. aux. services, 1981-82, also platform speaker univ. inauguration commn., 1981-82. Mem. Am. Mgmt. Assn., Assoc. Records Mgrs. and Adminstrs., Am. Prospect Research Assn., Ariz. State Library Assn., Ariz. State U. Friends Music, Ariz. State U. Library Assn., Friends KAET. Republican. Club: University (charter) (Tempe). Home: PO Box 1009 Tempe AZ 85280-1009 Office: Ariz State U Devel Office Tempe AZ 85287

GLIMET, THADÉ JOSEPH, rheumatologist; b. Lodz, Poland, Nov. 17, 1930; s. Hilaire and Helene (Landau) G.; m. Colette Galine, Sept. 26, 1964; 1 child, Emmanuel-Hilaire. MD, U. Paris, 1962. Resident various Paris Hosps., 1955-62; practice medicine specializing in rheumatology Paris, 1962—; attending cons. Lariboisiere Hosp., Paris, 1966—; asst. prof. rheumatology Faculté Lariboisiere, Paris, 1972—. Editor: Diagnostic en Rhumatologie, 1978; co-editor, co-author: Actualitié Rhumatologique, 1973, 76, 80, 83, 87. Mem. Soc. Française Rhumatologie. Home and Office: 97 Blvd Malesherbes, F75008 Paris France

GLINES, ALAN CLAIR EDWIN, space systems manager, consultant; b. Independence, Kans., Jan. 1, 1943; s. Lewis Clair and Mary Ellen (Patty) G. B.S. in Elec. Engring., U. Kans., 1966 M.S. in Systems Mgmt., U. So. Calif., 1983. With NASA Johnson Space Ctr., Houston, 1966-79, asst. flight dir. mission control Apollo-Soyuz test project, Apollo and Skylab programs, astronaut rep. Space Shuttle mfg., approach and landing test, Palmdale, Calif., 1976-79; sub-project mgr. payload integration TRW Space and Tech. Group, Redondo Beach, Calif., 1979-84, subproject mgr. space shuttle payload integration orbital maneuvering vehicle and gamma ray obs. projects, 1984-85 ; subproject mgr. Space Station Ops., 1985-88; part-time prof. U. So. Calif. Grad. Sch. in Systems Mgmt., 1986-88; instr. space shuttle/sta. integration and ops. TRW After Hours Program, 1988—; manned space flight engring. and ops. contract mgr. to European Spike Agy. on Columbus and Hermes programs. Recipient Presdl. Medal of Freedom for contbns. to NASA Apollo 13, NASA spl. award Shuttle ALT, 1978, NASA achievement award, 1975, NASA Skylab Flight Crew award, 1975, NASA Apollo achievement award, 1969. Mem. Am. Space Found., Planetary Soc. Nat. Space Council. Republican. Home: Apt Hotel Prinz-Heinrich, Am SchwimmBhd 12-16, 6103 Griesheim Federal Republic of Germany Office: AM Bachwimkel 12A, 6104 Seeheim-Jugenheim Federal Republic of Germany

GLINN, FRANKLYN BARRY, lawyer; b. Newark, Oct. 22, 1943; s. Dave and Gertrude (Weinstein) G.; m. Sandra Lee Scales, Nov. 3, 1943; children—MacAdam Jordan, Dara Elisabeth, Daniel Garrett. B.A.E., U. Fla., 1965, J.D., 1968. Bar: Fla. 1969, U.S. Ct. Appeals (5th cir.) 1969, U.S. Dist. Ct. (so. dist.) Fla. 1970. Assoc. Ser, Greenspahn & Keyfetz, Miami, Fla., 1969-70, Ser & Keyfetz, Miami, 1970-72, Rabin, Sassoon, & Ratiner, Miami, 1972-74; ptnr. Ratiner & Glinn, Miami, 1974—. Mem. ABA, Am. Judicature Soc., Am. Trial Lawyers Assn., Acad. Fla. Trial Lawyers, Am. Arbitration Assn. Democrat. Jewish. Office: Ratiner & Glinn 60 SW 13th St Miami FL 33130

GLOOR, CHRISTOPHER BARTA, corporate professional; b. San Diego, May 6, 1949; s. Fred Gloor and Clarice Barta; m. Agathe Maria Gobertina Winter , Nov. 28, 1987. Student, U. Calif., San Diego, 1969-71. Ptnr. Middlearth, San Diego, 1969-72; pres. Middlearth Internat. Inc., San Diego, 1972—, Middlearth Internat. Inc. dba Corp. Services Internat., San Diego, 1985—; bd. dirs. Antak Proprietary Ltd., Queensland, Australia, 1983—; ptnr. Australia Day, 1986; dir. Australia House, San Diego, 1987—. Dir. Australian House, San Diego, 1987—. Mem. Inventors Assn. Australia, Australian-Am. C. of C. Republican. Office: Corp Services Internat 4009 S Hempstead Circle San Diego CA 92116

GLOSSNER, DAVID CHARLES, psychologist; b. Rochester, N.Y., May 27, 1938; s. Edward N. and Mary Louise (Ceniglis) G.; B.S., St. John Fisher Coll., 1960; M.A., U. Rochester, 1961, postgrad., 1961-73, State U. N.Y., 1963-72; m. Linda May Wiegand, June 22, 1963; children—Heather Ann, David Charles. Tchr. social studies Benjamin Franklin High Sch., Rochester, 1961-68; counselor Frederick Douglass Jr. High Sch., Rochester, 1968-79; dean students Charlotte High Sch., Rochester, 1979—; adj. prof. psychology Monroe Community Coll., Rochester, 1973—; guest lectr. Nozareth Coll., 1983—; adj. lectr. psychology St. John Fisher Coll., Rochester, 1974—, chmn. athletic bd; guest lectr. Nazareth Coll., 1983—. Mem. counselors adv. com. City Sch. Dist., Rochester, 1969-70; co-chairperson Tchr. Unity Com. N.Y. State, 1972-73; bd. dirs. Rochester Sch. Employees Credit Union, 1974—, 2d v.p., 1976—; vice mayor, bd. trustees Village of Fairport (N.Y.). Mem. Am. Assn. Counseling and Devel., N.Y. State Assn. Counseling and Devel., N.Y. State Mental Health Counselors Assn., Assn. Measurement and Evaluation in Guidance, Rochester Tchrs. Assn. (pres. 1971-73), Profl. Counselors Assn., Nat. Vocat. Guidance Assn., N.Y. State United Tchrs. (fin. com. 1972-73, del. 1968-79), Am. Fed. Tchrs. (del. 1971-73), Monroe County Health Assn., Monroe County Mental Health Assn., Genessee Valley Psychol. Assn., Nat. Assn. Sch. Psychologists, Sch. Adminstrs. Assn. N.Y. State, Nat. Assn. Secondary Sch. Prins., Nat. Assn. Sch. Psychologists, N.Y. Assn. Sch. Psychologists, Phi Delta Kappa, Pi Gamma Mu. Roman Catholic. Home: 166 S Main St Fairport NY 14450 Office: 4115 Lake Ave Rochester NY 14612

GLOVER, EDWIN EUGENE, ret. university administrator; b. Stillwater, Okla., Mar. 29, 1922; s. William Earl and Grace Althea (Andrews) G.; B.S., Okla. State U., 1947; m. Mary L. Hall, Jan. 18, 1941; children—Linda Glover Mahar, Thomas E. Acct., Okla. State U., 1947-50, asst. chief acct., 1950-58, internal auditor, instl. rep. for grants and contracts, 1958-65, asst. bus. mgr., internal auditor, instl. rep. for grants and contracts, 1965-69, dir. internal audits, instl. rep. for grants and contracts, 1969-78, dir. internal audit, 1978-88. Sec., treas. Scabbard and Blade Endowment and Resources, Inc., 1965-75, Pleasant Valley Sch. Found., Inc.; chmn. Assn. Coll. and Univs. Midyear Seminars. Served with AUS, 1943-46. Decorated Purple Heart, Bronze Star; recipient citations Inst. Internal Auditors, 1972, Oklahoma City chpt. Inst. Internal Auditors, 1975, Cross of Valor State Okla. Cert. internal auditor. Mem. Inst. Internal Auditors (past pres. Oklahoma City chpt. 1965-71, 75—, gov., 2nd v.p. Tulsa chpt.; Disting. Service award Oklahoma City chpt. 1982), Assn. Coll. and Univ. Auditors (nat. pres. 1976, Stanley C. Smith award 1979, Disting. Service award 1982-83), Okla. State U. Alumni Assn. (life), Ret. Officers Assn., Am. Ex-P.O.W.s (life), Disabled Am. Veterans (life), Am. Legion, Scabbard and Blade (past nat. comdr.). Democrat. Lion (past pres. Stillwater). Club: Red Red Rose. Home: 1111 W Knapp St Stillwater OK 74074 Office: Oklahoma State U Stillwater OK 74078

GLOVER, JAMES EDWARD, physician; b. Bolton, Eng., Jan. 16, 1925; s. Adam and Lois (Tither) G.; m. Patricia May Entwistle, Aug. 25, 1951; children: Edward Peter, Jonathan Richard, Ruth Elizabeth. MB, BChir, U. Manchester, Eng., 1949. cert. in family planning, 1980; licentiate Royal Coll Physicians. Gen. practice medicine Birmingham, Eng., 1952-54, Manchester, Eng., 1954-83; house surgeon (orthopaedics) Manchester Royal Infirmary, 1949-50. Justice of Peace City of Manchester, 1981; contbr. Friends of Collingwood, Mt. Vernon, Va., 1981. Served as flight lt. med. br. RAF, 1950-52; maj. Royal Army Med. Corps, 1963-88; serving officer Army Cadet Force. Mem. Royal Coll. Surgeons Eng., Royal Coll. Gen. Practitioners, Magistrates Assn., Inland Waterways Assn. Mem. Ch. of Eng. Home: Stanycliffe, 553 Rochdale Rd, Middleton, Manchester England M24 2GM Office: 23 Wilvere Ct, Queens Promenade, Blackpool, Lancashire England F45 1PG

GLOVER, RICHARD ELTON, mortgage banker; b. Weatherford, Tex., Jan. 8, 1939; s. Elton William and Mattie Carmen (Shaw) G.; m. Eva Jo Addison, June 25, 1958; children—Jana Kay, Richard Elton, Jeffrey Brian. B.B.A. in Acctg., Tex. Christian U., 1964; D.B.A., Western States U. Lic. real estate broker, Tex.; life ins. broker; cert. property appraiser. Draftsman, Tex. Hwy. Dept., Fort Worth, 1959-64; comptroller Reid & Co., Fort Worth, 1964-66; exec. v.p. So. Mortgage Corp., Fort Worth, 1966-68; real estate appraiser HUD, Fort Worth, 1979-82; owner R.E.G. Realty, Fort Worth, 1968—, Glover Ins. Agy., Fort Worth, 1968—; sec.-treas. Security Bankers Investment Co., Fort Worth, 1978—; pres., chmn. bd. Citizens Nat. Mortgage Corp., Fort Worth, 1968—. Mem. Pres. Reagan's Task Force, 1982—; mem. Fort Worth Community Devel. Council, 1973-75; sec. City of Aledo, 1964-69. Served with Air N.G., 1962-70. Mem. Fort Worth Mortgage Bankers (pres. 1975-76), Tex. Mortgage Bankers Assn., Greater Fort Worth Bd. Realtors, Tex. Assn. Realtors, Nat. Assn. Realtors, Tex. Ind. Producers and Royalty Owners, Assn. Govt. Appraisers, Internat. Orgn. Real Estate Appraisers, Nat. Assn. Cert. Real Property. Baptist. Clubs: Colonial Country, Petroleum, Century II (Fort Worth). Home: 3813 Lawndale Ave Fort Worth TX 76133 Office: 5049B Old Granbury Rd PO Box 16339 Fort Worth TX 76133

GLOYD, LAWRENCE EUGENE, diversified manufacturing company executive; b. Milan, Ind., Nov. 5, 1932; s. Oran C. and Ruth (Baylor) G.; m. Delma Lear, Sept. 10, 1955; children—Sheryl, Julia, Susan. B.A., Hanover Coll., 1954. Salesman Shapleigh Hdwe., St. Louis, 1956-60, W. Bingham Co., Cleve., 1960-61; salesman Amerock Corp., Rockford, Ill., 1961-68, regional sales mgr., 1968-69, dir. consumer products mktg., 1969-71, dir. merchandising, 1971-72, dir. mktg. and sales, 1972-73, v.p. mktg. and sales, 1973-81, exec. v.p., 1981-82, pres., gen. mgr., 1982-86; v.p. Hardware Products Group, Anchor Hocking Corp., Lancaster, Ohio, 1983-86; pres., chief operating officer CLARCOR, Rockford, Ill., 1986-88, pres., chief exec. officer, 1988—, also bd. dirs.; bd. dirs. AMcore Fin. Inc., Rockford, Thomas Industries Inc.; mem. Middle West adv. bd. Liberty Mut. Ins. Co. Bd. dirs. Council of 100; trustee SwedishAmerican Corp. Served with AUS, 1954-56. Mem. Am. Hardware Mfrs. Assn. (bd. dirs.), Presidents Assn. Republican. Lodge: Masons. Home: 4979 Crofton Dr Rockford IL 61111 Office: CLARCOR 2323 6th St PO Box 7007 Rockford IL 61125

GLUBRECHT, HELLMUT, biophysics educator; b. Neise, Poland, Schlesien, Germany, July 9, 1917; s. Rudolf and Eva (Reiners) G.; m. Annaliese Guckeisen, Jan. 10, 1940 (dec. Mar. 1945); m. Jutta Garbe, Oct. 10, 1958; children—Johannes-Michael, Hanna, Tania, Matthias. Diplomphysiker, U. Hannover, Niedersachsen, 1939, Dr.rer.nat., 1943, Dr.habil., 1951. Leading researcher Lab. Feuerstein, Ebermannstadt, Bayern, 1939-45; univ. docent Tech. Hochschule, Hannover, Niedersachsen, 1945-59; prof. Tech. U., Hannover, 1959-73; dep. dir. gen. Internat. Atomic Energy Agy., Vienna, Austria, 1973-77; prof. Inst. Biophysics, U. Hannover, Niedersachsen, W.Ger., 1977—; dir. Inst. Radiation Botany, Gesellschaft fü r Strahlenund Umweltforschung, Munchen, Neuherberg/Bayern, 1968-82, sci. advisor, 1982—; advisor on German/Korean cooperation in sci. Fed. Ministry Research and Tech., Bonn, 1981—; com. dir. Inst. Solar Energy Research, Hameln/Emmerthal, 1986-87, chmn. bd., 1988—. Author books and articles on biophysics, radiation biology and philosophy of sci. to profl. jours. Mem. council Pugwash Conf. on Sci. and World Affairs, London, 1978-87. Recipient Oscar Mahr-Preis, Vereinigung Deutscher Wissenschaftler, 1973; Bundesverdienstkreuz 1.Kl., Fed. Govt. Germany, 1977 Medal of Civil Merit, Republic of Korea, 1984, Niedersächsisches Verdienstkrenz 1.Kl. 1985, Niedersachsenpreis, 1988. Mem. Deutsche Gesellschaft fü r Biophysik (chmn. 1970-73), European Soc. Nuclear Methods in Agr. (chmn. 1969-73, hon. chmn. 1973—), Deutsche Physikal Gesellschaft. Evangelical Lutheran. Lodge: Rotary. Home: Suerser Weg 29, 3015 Wennigsen/Deister, Niedersachsen Federal Republic of Germany Office: Inst für Solarenergie forschung, Sokelant Strasse 5, D-3000 Hannover Niedersachsen Federal Republic of Germany

GLYNN, LEONARD ELEAZAR, pathologist, consultant; b. London, Apr. 29, 1910; s. Lewis and Rebecca (Kanaan) G.; m. Dorothy Evelyn Harding, June 29, 1956 (dec. Feb. 1975); m. Doreen Pitson, Apr. 13, 1976. BSc, U. London, 1931, MB BS, 1934, MD, 1945. House surgeon univ. coll. U. London, 1934-35, lectr. med. sch., 1937-47; house physician Royal Berkshire Hosp., Reading, Eng., 1935-36; dir. pathology Can. Red Cross Meml. Hosp., Taplow, Bucks, Eng., 1947-75; dep. dir. rheumatism research unit Med. Research Council, Taplow, 1958-75; dir. Kennedy Inst. Rheumatology, London, 1972-77, hon. research advisor div. cell biology, 1977—; hon. cons. immunologist Oxford Regional Health Authority, Slough, Eng., 1982—. Co-author: Autoimmunity and Disease, 1965, Immunological Investigation of Connective Tissue Diseases, 1981; editor Immunology, 1963-83. Served to maj. Brit. Army, 1940-45. Fellow Royal Coll. Physicians, Royal Coll. Pathologists (founder, Sir Roy Cameron lectr. 1972), Royal Soc. Medicine, Am. Coll. Allergists (hon.); mem. Heberden Soc. (medal, orator 1967, pres. 1971—), Am. Rheumatism (hon.), Italian Soc. Rheumatology (hon.). Jewish. Home and Office: Four Winds Hammersley Ln, Penn Bucks HP10 8HG, England

GMÜR, PETER, diversified company executive; b. Amden, St. Gallen, Switzerland, May 25, 1939; s. Albert and Anna-Margaretha (Oestreich) G.; m. Rita Monica Kreienbühl; children: Tina, Anina, Selina, Ladina. Mech. Engring. degree, Fed. Inst. Tech., Zurich, Switzerland, 1965; MBA, St. Gall Grad. Sch. Econs., 1967. Cons. McKinsey & Co., Zurich, 1968-74; mem. mng. bd. Schlatter AG, Schlieren, Switzerland, 1974-77; pres., chief exec. officer Distral Holding AG, Zurich, 1978—; several Swiss and European directorships. Contbr. articles to profl. jours. Served to capt. Swiss Anti-Aircraft Corps, 1961—.

GOANS, JUDY WINEGAR, lawyer; b. Knoxville, Tenn., Sept. 27, 1949; d. Robert Henry and Lula Mae (Myers) Winegar; m. Ronald Earl Goans, June 18, 1971; children: Robert Henson, Ronald Earl Jr. Student, Sam Houston State U., 1967-68; BS in Engring. Physics, U. Tenn., 1971, postgrad., 1971-74, JD, 1978. Bar: Tenn. 1978, U.S. Dist. Ct. (ea. dist.) Tenn. 1979, U.S. Patent Office 1980, U.S. Ct. Appeals (Fed. cir.) 1980, U.S. Supreme Ct. 1983. Instr. legal rights Knoxville Women's Ctr., 1977-78; patent analyst nuclear div. Union Carbide Corp., Oak Ridge, Tenn., 1978-79; patent atty. U.S. Dept. Energy, Washington, 1979-82; legis. and internat. intellectual property specialist Patent and Trademark Office, Washington, 1982—; judge Moot Ct. competition, Washington, 1984. Del. Nat. Women's Conf., Houston, 1977; bd. dirs. Nat. Orgn. for Women, Washington, 1977-79, Good Shepherd Kingergarten, 1987; mem. Knox County Rep. Exec. Com., Tenn., 1978-79, legal adv. bd. Knoxville Rape Crisis Ctr., 1979. Mem. ABA, Tenn. Bar Assn., Am. Intellectual Property Law Assn., Patent Lawyers Assn. (sec. 1981-83, gov.). Methodist. Home: 2233 Pinefield Rd Waldorf MD 20601 Office: Patent and Trademark Office Office Legis and Internat Affairs Washington DC 20231

GOBAR, ALFRED JULIAN, economic consultant, educator; b. Lucerne Valley, Calif., July 12, 1932; s. Julian Smith and Hilda (Millbank) G.; B.A. in Econs., Whittier Coll., 1953, M.A. in History, 1955; postgrad. Claremont Grad. Sch., 1953-54; Ph.D. in Econs., U. So. Calif., 1963; m. Sally Ann Randall, June 17, 1957; children—Wendy Lee, Curtis Julian, Joseph Julian. Asst. pres. Microdot Inc., Pasadena, 1953-57; regional sales mgr. Sutorbilt Corp., Los Angeles, 1957-59; market research assoc. Beckman Instrument Inc., Fullerton, 1959-64; sr. marketing cons. Western Mgmt. Consultants Inc., Phoenix, Los Angeles, 1964-66; ptnr., prin., chmn. bd. Darley/Gobar Assocs., Inc., 1966-73; pres., chmn. bd. Alfred Gobar Assocs., Inc., Brea, Calif., 1973—; asst. prof. finance U. So. Calif., Los Angeles, 1963-64; assoc. prof. bus. Calif. State U.-Los Angeles, 1963-68, 70-79, assoc. prof. Calif. State U.-Fullerton, 1968-69; mktg., fin. adviser 1957—; pub. speaker seminars and convs. Contbr. articles to profl. publs. Home: 1100 W Valencia Mesa Dr Fullerton CA 92633 Office: 201 S Brea Blvd Brea CA 92621

GOBER COSGROVE, RITAMAE ADELE, lawyer; b. New Britain, Conn., Oct. 7, 1950; d. Anthony William and Adele (Rita) Akronas) Gober; m. Gerald Paul Cosgrove, Sept. 10, 1982; 1 child, Sarah Adele. AS in Acctg., Greater Hartford Community Coll., 1970; BA in Econs., U. Hartford, 1977; MA in Econs., 1978; JD, U. Tulsa, 1981. Bar: Conn. 1981. Prodn. and broadcast dir. Chirurg & Cairns, Farmington, Conn., 1968-71; media dir. Knudsen & Moore, Stamford, Conn., 1971-72; retail buyer G. Fox & Co., Hartford, Conn., 1972-76; prodn. analyst Conn. Dept. Transp., Wethersfield, 1977-78; hearing examiner Ct. Dept. Pub. Utilities, Hartford, 1979-81; atty. land dept. Arco Oil & Gas Co., Houston, 1981—; research asst. Nat. Energy Law and Policy Inst., Tulsa, 1979-81; adj. prof. U. Midland (Tex.), 1981-82, U. Houston-Downtown Campus, 1983—, Bates Coll. Law, U. Houston, 1984—; dir. and pres. Northwest Mcpl. Utility Dist. 9, Cypress/Houston, Tex., Tchr., cons. Project Bus./Jr. Achievement, Midland, 1981-82. Mem. ABA, Conn. Bar Assn., Nat. Soc. for Econs. Democrat. Roman Catholic.

GODARD, JEAN-LUC, motion picture director; b. Paris, Dec. 3, 1930; s. Paul and Odile Godard m. Anna Karina, Mar. 2, 1961 (div.); m. Anne Wiasemsky, 1967. Ed., Lycée Buffon, Paris. Journalist, film critic Cahiers du Cinema. Dir. motion pictures including: Opération Béton, 1954, Une Femme Coquette, 1955, Tous les garçons s'appelent Patrick, 1957; author screenplay, dir. Charlotte et son Jules, 1958; dir. A Bout de Souffle, 1959 (prix Jean Vigo), Le sept peches captiaux, 1961, The Little Soldier, The Carabiniers, 1963, Une Femme est une Femme, 1961, Vivre et sa Vie, 1962, Weekend, 1967 (diploma of merit Edinburgh Film Festival 1968), La Chinoise, 1967, Les plus belles escroqueries du Monde, 1963, Une femme marieée, 1964, Alphaville, 1965, Pierrot le fou, 1965, Sympathy for the Devil, Lion du Vietnam, 1967, Le plus vieux metier du monde, 1967, Vangelo '70, 1967, Un film comme les autres, 1968, British Sounds, 1969, Made in U.S.A., 1966, Masculine-Feminine, 1966, One Plus One, 1968, One American Movie: 1 A.M., 1969, Le Vent d'est, 1969, Lotte in Italia, 1970, Vladmir et Rosa, 1971, Tout va bien, 1972, Numero deux, 1975, Ici et ailleurs, 1976, Bugsy, 1979, Sauve qui peut, 1980, Every Man for Himself, 1980; author screenplay, dir. Passion, 1982, dir. First Name: Carmen, 1984, Hail Mary, 1985, Detective, 1985, King Lear, 1988. Recipient spl. prize Festival of Venice, 1962; Prix Pasinetti, 1962; Best Picture award Berlin Film Festival. Address: 15 rue du Nord, 1180 Rouille Switzerland •

GODBOLD, WILFORD DARRINGTON, JR., enclosure manufacturing company executive, lawyer; b. Honolulu, Apr. 3, 1938; s. Wilford Darrington and Virginia Mae (Ehlert) G.; m. Shari Gene Coburn, Feb. 7, 1961; children: Sheila Tiari, Bryan Darrington, Lauri Fairchild. AB, Stanford U., 1960; JD, UCLA, 1966, grad. exec. mgmt. course, UCLA Grad. Sch. Bus, 1983. Bar: Calif., 1967. Ptnr. Gibson, Dunn, & Crutcher, Los Angeles, 1967-82; exec. v.p. Zero Corp., Los Angeles, 1982-84, pres., chief exec. officer, 1984—, mem. exec. com., 1982—, also bd. dirs.; instr. securities law U. West Los Angeles, 1976-1982; chmn. Samuel Groves & Co., Birmingham, Eng., 1984—; bd. dirs. Winchell's Donut Houses, 1986-87; bd. advisors Paul-Munroe Hydraulics Co., Inc., 1982-86; trustee Marlborough Sch., Los Angeles, 1985—; lectr. in field. Formerly bd. dirs. Ctr. Theater Group, Los Angeles Music Ctr.; mem. Los Angeles Adv. Olympic Com. Served to lt. (j.g.) USN, 1960-63. Mem. Los Angeles County Bar Assn. (exec. com.), State Bar of Calif., ABA, Order of Coif, Calif. C. of C. (bd. dirs. 1987—), Phi Delta Phi, Delta Upsilon. Republican. Clubs: Jonathan (Los Angeles); Outrigger Canoe (Honolulu). Office: Zero Corp 444 S Flower St Los Angeles CA 90071

GODEAU, HENRY FRANCOIS FERNAND, educational administrator; b. Marchienne-au-Pont, Belgium, June 6, 1920; s. Fernand Ghislain and Leona (Godefroid) G.; m. Raymonde Favart, July 27, 1947 (div.); children: Jacques, Micheline; m. Marie-Brigitte Schils, June 23, 1976. MEd, U. Liege, Belgium, 1944; Audio-visual cert., U. Zagreb, Yugoslavia, 1963. Instr. State Higher Secondary Sch., Charleroi, Belgium, 1944-45, Tournai, Belgium, 1945-46, Binche, Belgium, 1946-55; instr. State Tchr. Tng. Sch., Mons, Belgium, 1955-65; with spl. mission SHAPE, Paris, 1965; prin. State Tech. Inst., Erquelinnes, Belgium, 1965-66; chmn. State Higher Tech. Inst., Brussels, 1966, Mons, 1966-77; chmn. State Higher Indsl. Inst., Mons, 1977-80, hon. chmn., 1980—; instr. Anderlecht, Brussels; served on state missions throughout Europe and in West Chester, Pa. Author: Quick to English, 1959, To Business English, 1960, Technical and Conversational English, 1969, English Through the Black Island, 1985, Het Nederlands door het zwarte Goud, 1986, English Through the Black Island: Méthode autodidactique d'anglais par la bande dessinée avec TINTIN, 1988; contbr. articles to profl. jours. Served with Belgian Army, 1945, Brit. Army, 1945. Decorated 1st Class Civic Cross and medal Officer Order of Leopold.

GODEAUX, JEAN, banker; b. Jemeppe s/Meuse, Belgium, July 3, 1922; s. Leon and Claire (de Barsy) G.; m. Therese Ceron, Sept. 15, 1950; children—Helene, Bernard, Dominique, Francoise, Olivier. LL.D., U. Louvain (Belgium), 1944, Licenciate in Econs., 1946. Attache, Nat. Bank Belgium, Brussels, 1947-49, gov., 1982—; alt. exec. dir., then exec. dir. IMF, Washington, 1949-54; mgr.-ptnr., then pres. Banque Lambert, Brussels, 1955-74; pres. Banking Commn., Brussels, 1974-82. Chmn. bd. Universite Catholique de Louvain, 1974-82. Home: Rue de la Loi 235, Boite 3, B-1040 Brussels Belgium Office: Nat Bank Belgium, Bvd de Berlaimont 5, 1000 Brussels Belgium

GODECHOT, JACQUES, historian, educator; b. Luneville, France, Jan. 3, 1907; s. Georges and Therese (Lazard) G.; m. Arlette Lambert, Sept. 13, 1933; children: Didier, Thierry, Yves, Eveline. Student, U. Nancy, 1924-26; Agrégation d'Histoire, Sorbonne U., 1928, Doctorat és-Lettres, 1938. Prof. history U. Lycee, Aix-en-Provence, France, 1928-29, Bordeaux, France, 1930, Lycee Kleber, Strasbourg, France, 1933-35, Ecole Navale, Brest, France, 1935-39; prof. history U. Toulouse, 1945-80, prof. emeritus, 1980—. Author: Les Institutions, 1951, La Grande Nation, 1956, La Contre-Revolution, 1961, numerous others. Served to capt. French infantry, 1939-45. Recipient award Acad. Francaise, 1938, 73, 77, 78; named Officer de la Legion d'Honneur, 1978. Mem. Commn. Inst. Revolution, Acad. Scis. Morals and Politics. Home: 17 Rue A Mercie, 31000 Toulouse France

GODEMENT, FRANCOIS LEON, Asian history educator, international relations consultant; b. Nancy, France, June 14, 1949; s. Roger and Sonia (Kogon) G.; m. Ning Wang, June 7, 1986. Student, Ecole Normale Superieure Rue d'Ulm, 1968-72; Agregation Histoire, U. Paris, 1972, PhD in History, 1977; postgrad., Harvard U., 1972-73. Cons. OECD, 1975-78; research assoc. Cen. Nat. Research Scientific, 1978-80; asst. prof. Nat. Oriental Langs. and Civilization Sch., Paris, 1981-83, assoc. prof., 1984—; dir. Cen. Preparation Echanges Internationaux, Paris, 1986—; research assoc. French Inst. Internat. Relations, Paris, 1986—. Office: French Inst Internat Relations, 6 Rue Ferrus, 75014 Paris France

GODFREY, GEORGE CHEESEMAN, II, surgeon; b. Atlantic City, Oct. 15, 1926; s. William M. and Elizabeth (Uzzell) G.; student St. Bonaventure Coll., 1944, U. Ky., 1945; A.B., Colgate U., 1948; M.D., Jefferson Med. Coll., 1952; m. Evelyn Fry, Sept. 20, 1952; children—Cheryl Lynn, George Cheeseman III. Intern, Atlantic City Hosp., 1952-53; resident in gen. surgery U.S. VA Hosp., Ft. Howard, Balt., 1953-57; practice medicine specializing in surgery, Somers Point, N.J., 1957—; chief gen. and trauma surgery, dir. dept. surgery Shore Meml. Hosp., Somers Point, 1973-76, dir. surgery, 1982-87; instr. surgery Jefferson Med. Coll., Phila., 1958-84; cons. in orthopedics and neurology N.J. Div. Disability Determinations, N.J. Rehab. Program, 1960—; physician FAA Tech. Center, part-time, 1977—, med. mgr., 1982-85; pres. Shore Surg. P.A., Atlantic Indsl. Med. Assocs. Pres., Bd. Edn., Linwood, N.J., 1972-73; mem. Atlantic County United Way, Atlantic County YMCA, Atlantic Performing Arts. Served with U.S. Army, 1944-46. Recipient Disting. Service award N.J. Jr. C. of C., 1960, Maroon Citation, Colgate U. Diplomate Am. Bd. Surgery, Nat. Bd. Med. Examiners. Fellow ACS; mem. AMA, Am. Trauma Soc., Am. Soc. Abdominal Surgeons, Aerospace Med. Assn., Am. Occupational Med. Soc., N.J., Atlantic County Med. Socs., Atlantic Indsl. Med. Physicians (pres.), Chainede Rotesseurs, Phi Kappa Tau, Phi Beta Pi. Methodist. Clubs: Atlantic City Country, Marriott Seaview Country, Resorts Internat. Racquet, Kiwanis, Masons, (Shriner), K.T. Contbr. articles to profl. jours. Home: 112 Glenside Ave Linwood NJ 08221 also: 5550 N Ocean Dr Singer Island FL also: 674 Shore Rd Somers Point NJ 08244 also: 1616 Pacific Ave Atlantic City NJ also: 705 White Horse Pike Absecon NJ 08201

GODFREY, ROBERT R., financial services executive; b. Sweetwater, Tex., May 22, 1947; s. Ross R. and Lillian L. (Bradford) G.; B.B.A., Tex. Tech. U., 1969, postgrad. in bus. adminstrn., 1969-71; m. Diane M. Kalinowski, June 30, 1972. Underwriter, Aetna Life and Casualty Co., Lubbock, Tex. and Hartford, Conn., 1969-72; teaching fellow Tex. Tech. U., 1969-71, Central Conn. State Coll., 1972; asst. mgr. Gulf Ins. Group, Dallas, 1972-76; asst. v.p. Scor Reins. Co., Dallas, 1976-79; pres. Rollins Burdick Hunter Mgmt. Co., N.Y.C., 1979-81; founder, pres., dir. St. Regis Ins. Group/Drum Fin. Corp., 1981-85; exec. v.p. MBIA/MISC, 1985—. bd. dirs. Fairfield & Southern Corp. Served U.S. Army, 1970. Club: Union League (N.Y.C.). Also: MBIA/MISC 445 Hamilton Ave White Plains NY 10602

GODFREY, SIMON, pediatrician; b. London, Mar. 5, 1939; arrived in Israel, 1977; s. Mark and Nettie (Steinberg) G.; m. Carole Marion Sharp, June 2, 1965; children: Joanne Yael, Joseph, Alisa, Charlotte Sarit, Avigail. MB, BS, U. London, 1962, PhD, 1966, MD, 1971, MRCP, 1964, FRCP, 1976. Intern, resident London, Brompton and Hammersmith Hosps., London, 1962-68; sr. lectr. dept. pediatrics Brompton Hosp., 1968-73, Hammersmith Hosp., 1973-77; chmn. dept. pediatrics Hadassah U. Hosp., Jerusalem, 1977—; prof. pediatrics Hadassah Hebrew U., Jerusalem, 1977—. Author/editor several books; contbr. numerous articles to profl. jours., chpts. to books. Fellow Royal Coll. Physicians (Gulstonian lectr. 1976); mem. N.Y. Acad. Scis., Am. Acad. Allergy, Brit. Thoracic Soc. Office: Hadassah U Hosp Dept Pediatrics, Mount Scopus, Jerusalem 91240, Israel

GODFREY, WILLIAM ASHLEY, ophthalmologist; b. Arkansas City, Kans., May 19, 1938; B.A., U. Kans.-Lawrence, 1961; M.D., U. Kans. Sch. Medicine, Kansas City, 1965. Diplomate Am. Bd. Ophthalmology. Intern, Tulane U., New Orleans, 1965-66; resident U. Kans. Sch. Medicine, 1968-71; research fellow U. Calif.-San Francisco, 1971-73; asst. prof., then assoc. prof. U. Kans. Sch. Medicine, 1973-84, prof. ophthalmology, 1984—; mem. staff St. Luke's Hosp., Kansas City, Mo., 1973—, Kansas U. Med. Ctr., Kansas City, 1973—; cons. Kansas City Vets Hosp., Mo., 1973—. Contbr. articles to profl. publs. Served with USAF, 1966-68. NIH fellow, 1971-73; fellow Am. Acad. Ophthalmology, (honor ward 1983), Am. Uveitis Soc., Am. Coll. Physicians. Mem. AMA, Am. Fedn. Clin. Research, Am. Rheumatism Assn., Assn. Research in Vision and Ophthalmology, Am. Math. Soc., Ocular Immunology and Microbiology Soc., Kansas City Soc. Ophthalmology, Kans. Med. Soc., Mo. Ophthalmology Soc., Jackson County Med. Soc., Am. Ophthalmological Soc., Wyandotte County Med. Soc., Johnson County Med Soc., Alpha Omega Alpha. Office: Curts Wurster & Godfrey 4320 Wornall Rd Kansas City MO 64111

GODINHO, LICIO DA SILVEIRA, chemistry educator, consultant; b. Beja, Alentejo, Portugal, Mar. 19, 1935; s. Virgolino da Costa and Ermezinda Margarida (da Silveira) G.; m. Maria Edith Marcal, Feb. 19, 1960; children: Elgar, Filipe. Bachelor, Escola de Farmacia, U. Lisboa, 1955; Licentiate, Faculdade De Farmacia, U. Porto, 1957; Ph.D., Imperial Coll., U. London, 1964; Diploma of Membership, Imperial Coll. Sci. and Tech., London, 1964. Assoc. prof. Escola de Farmacia, U. Lisboa, 1966-72, prof. Faculdade de Farmacia, 1972-74; head dept. chemistry Faculdade de Ciencias e Tecnologia, U. Nova, Lisboa, 1974-77, pres., 1977-80, prof. chemistry, 1974—; research fellow Research Inst. Medicine and Chemistry, Cambridge, Mass., 1966-67; tech. dir. Labs. Pfizer, Lisboa, 1967-80; v.p. Soc. Ind. Farmaceutica, Lisboa, 1981-83; gen. mgr. Timsa, Gabinete técnico, Lisboa, 1983—. Contbr. sci. articles to profl. jours. Fulbright-Hays fellow Conf. Bd. Assoc. Councils, 1966. Mem. Ordem dos Farmaceuticos, Chem. Soc., Am. Chem. Soc., Sociedade Portuguesa de Quimica. Club: Internacional de Futebol (Lisboa). Lodge: Rotary. Avocations: reading; sports; travel. Office: TIMSA Gabinete Tecnico, R Manuel Correia Gomes 4 1E, 1, 500 Lisboa Portugal

GODSEY, WILLIAM COLE, physician; b. Memphis, Dec. 11, 1933; s. Monroe Dowe and Margaret Pauline (Cole) G.; B.S., Rhodes Coll., 1955; M.D., U. Tenn., 1958; m. Norma Jean Wilkinson, June 18, 1958; children—William Cole, John Edward, Robert Dowe. Intern, John Gaston Hosp., Memphis, 1958-59; resident in psychiatry Gailor Meml. Hosp., Memphis, 1960-63; practice medicine specializing in psychiatry and neurology; mem. staffs Bapt. Meml. Hosp., Lakeside Hosp., St. Joseph Hosp.; asst. supt. Memphis Mental Health Inst., 1965-74; supt. Central State Hosp., Nashville, 1974-75; med. dir. Whitehaven Mental Health Center, Memphis, 1975-84, St. Joseph Hosp. Life Ctr., 1984—; asst. prof. U. Tenn. Coll. Medicine, 1965-74, Coll. Pharmacy, 1972-75; chief of staff Lakeside Hosp., Memphis, 1976-77; Songwriter, pub.; pres. Memphis Country Music, Inc. Diplomate Am. Bd. Psychiatry and Neurology. Fellow Am. Psychiatric Assn. (past pres. West Tenn. chpt.); mem. Tenn. Psychiat. Assn. (exec. council, pres.-elect 1987-88, pres. 1988—), Tenn. Med. Assn., Memphis and Shelby County Med. Soc., Nat. Rifle Assn. Methodist. Club: Moose. Office: 210 Jackson Ave Suite 401 Memphis TN 38105

GODT, PAUL JAY, political science educator; b. Rockville Centre, N.Y., Oct. 21, 1943; arrived in France, 1970; s. Albert and Rita (Weidenfeld) G.; m. Sonia Solange Baldoni, Aug. 6, 1965; children: Sandrine, Nicolas Robin. BA, Bowdoin Coll., 1965; MA, New Sch. for Social Research, 1967, PhD, 1972. Prof. U. Grenoble (France), 1970-74; prof. polit. sci. Am. U., Paris, 1972—. Contbr. articles to profl. jours. Recipient Disting. Tchr. award Am. U., Paris, 1985; Fulbright scholar, Grenoble, 1970-71. Mem. Am. Polit. Sci. Assn., Internat. Polit. Sci. Assn., Conf. Group French Politics and Soc., Tocqueville Soc., Assn. Française Sci. Politique. Home: 32 rue d'Yerres, 91800 Brunoy France Office: Am U, 31 Ave Bosquet, 75007 Paris France

GODWIN, PETER GEOFFREY, insurance company executive; b. London, Nov. 20, 1937; s. James and Lily (Riddiford) G.; m. Margery Farr (div. 1980); children: Ralph, Laura; m. Jennifer Jane Kerr-Bate, Mar. 8, 1986. Grad., City of London Coll., 1959. Mem. exec. staff various Lloyd's brokers, London, 1959-69; mng. dir. Osyr SA, Madrid, 1969-73; bd. dirs. Bain Dawes, div. Lloyd's, London, Madrid, 1973-78; chief exec. for Spain Legal and Gen. Assurance Co., Madrid, 1978-81; mng. dir. Gesinter SA, Madrid, 1982-84; gen. mgr. Switzerland Ins., London, 1984—; bd. dirs. Creative Ins. Services, Reading, Eng.; mem. U.K. Ins. Brokers Com., EEC Legislation, London, 1975-78. Mem. Chartered Ins. Inst. (cert.), Brit. C. of C. (com. mem. Madrid 1980-81). Anglican. Club: City U. (London). Office: Switzerland Ins Co UK Ltd, 169 Kings Rd, Brentwood, Essex CM14 4EF, England

GOEDHUIS, DANIEL, professional association administrator, lawyer, educator; b. Deventer, Netherlands, Jan. 31, 1905; m. Daphne Henderson (dec. 1973); children: Michael, Diana, Jonathon; m. Pamela Miles, 1974. LLD, Leyden (Holland) U., 1933; LLD (hon.), U. Aix Marseille, 1968. Sec.-gen. Internat. Air Transport Assn., Netherlands, 1938-46; counsellor Netherlands Embassy, London, 1946-77; prof. air and space law Leyden U., 1938-77; pres. diplomatic conf. at Peace Palace, The Hague for revision of Warsaw Conv., 1955; head delegation appointed by Netherlands Govt. for negotiations of numerous bilateral air agreements; lectr. Council on Fgn. Relations, N.Y., Harvard U., Columbia U., Northwestern U., U. Pa., William and Mary Coll., the sci. com. of both houses of Parliament, Oxford U., Cambridge U., U. Coll. London, Edinburgh, U. Paris, U. Aix-en-Provence, also Madrid, Rome, Genoa, Istanbul, Ankara, Geneva, The Netherlands; chmn. space law com. World Peace Through Law Ctr. Author 3 books on air and space law; contbr. numerous articles to profl. publs. Served with cav. Dutch Army, 1938-46. Decorated knight in the order of Netherlands Lion; Officer in the Order of Orange Nassau; Cross of Merit; Resistance Commemoration Cross; Comdr. in Order of Dom Enrique of Portugal. Mem. Internat. Law Assn. (chmn. space law com., reporting to confs. worldwide 1958-87). Clubs: White's, Pratt's, Buck's, Beefsteak (London). Home: Ossington House Near Newark, Nottinghamshire NL23 6LY, England

GOEHR, ALEXANDER, composer; b. Berlin, Aug. 10, 1932; s. Walter Goehr. Student, Royal Manchester (Eng.) Sch. Music, 1952-55. Concert planner BBC, London, 1960-68; instr. music New Eng. Conservatory, Boston, 1968-70, Yale U., New Haven, 1970-71, Leeds (Eng.) U., 1971-75, Cambridge U., 1975—. Operas include La Belle Dame sans Merci, 1958, Arden Must Die, 1967, Naboth's Vineyard, 1968, Shadowplay, 1970, / Sonata About Jerusalem, 1971, Behold the Sun, 1985; orchestral works include Fantasia, 1956, Hecuba's Lament, 1961, Concerto for Violin and Orchestra, 1962, Little Symphony, 1963, Pastorals, 1965, /romanza, 1968, Konzertstuck, 1969, Symphony in One Movement, 1970, Concerto for Piano and Orchestra, 1972, Metamorphosis/Dance, 1974, Simfonia, 1980, Deux Etudes, 1981, A Musical Offering, 1985; also numerous choral and vocal works, and numerous works for keyboard and wind instruments. Address: U Cambridge, Dept Music, Cambridge England

GOEI, ING LIAT (JULIUS HADINATA), production and technical director; b. Kudus, Central Java, Indonesia, Aug. 30, 1928; s. Po Liong and Bertha (Oei) G.; m. Kiem Hwa Liem, Sept. 14, 1959; children: Fang Lan, Bing Swan. M.Engring., Tech. Faculty Delft-Holland, 1956. Asst. tech. mgr. N.V. Tiedeman & Van Kerchem, Surabaya, East Java, 1957; tech. mgr. Pusat Perkebunan Negara, Surabaya, 1957-63; with Cigarette Factory P.T. "Djarum", Kudus, Indonesia, 1967—, prodn. and tech. dir., 1974—. Mem. Gereja Kristen Indonesia Peterongan Ch. Club: Semarang Bojong. Lodge: Rotary. Avocations: collecting and planting tropical trees. Home: Jl Kawi II/9, Semarang Cen Java 50231, Indonesia Office: Kudus Central Java, Cigarette Factory PT Djarum, Jl Jen A Yani 28, Indonesia

GOEKJIAN, SAMUEL VAHRAM, lawyer; b. Syra, Greece, Aug. 22, 1927; s. Vahram K. and Aznive (Bagdassarian) G.; came to U.S., 1948, naturalized, 1954; B.A. (scholar), Syracuse U., 1952; J.D. (scholar), Harvard U., 1957; m. Jean Alison MacLeod, July 6, 1957; children—Kenneth Samuel, Christopher Allan, Peter Gregory, Lisa Dorothy. Admitted to N.Y. bar, 1958, D.C. bar, 1960; practiced in N.Y.C., 1957-58, Washington, 1958-68, Beirut, 1968-70, Paris, 1970-78, Washington, 1978-83; assoc. atty. Chase Manhattan Bank, N.Y.C., 1957-58; counsel Devel. Loan Fund, Dept. State, Washington, 1958-60; asso. firm Surrey, Karasik, Gould and Greene, Washington, 1960-62, mng. partner, 1962-68; sr. resident partner firm Surrey, Karasik and Greene, Beirut, 1968-70; sr. resident partner firm Surrey, Karasik, Morse & Goekjian, Paris, 1970-78; sr. partner firm Surrey & Morse, 1978-83; chmn., chief exec. officer Consol. Westway Group Inc., Englewood Cliffs, N.J., 1983-88; counsel Kirkpatrick and Lockhart, Washington, 1988—; cons. UN, 1962, 78—, AID, 1963; professorial lectr. Grad. Sch. Pub. Law, George Washington U., 1963-68; lectr. Internat. Law Inst., Georgetown U. Law Sch., Washington, 1974-83, adj. prof. law, 1979-83; counsel, mem. exec. com. Egypt-U.S. Bus. Council; mem. Council Fgn. Relations. Served with AUS, 1953-55. Mem. Am. (vice chmn. com. on African law 1966-67, chmn. 1967-68), Fed. (vice chmn. com. on internat. devel. 1964-67), Inter-Am., D.C. bar assns., Am. Law Inst. (spl. adv. com. on law governing internat. transactions 1960-62), Phi Beta Kappa. Author articles and book chpts. on internat. law and fin. Home: 4910 Loughboro Rd NW Washington DC 20016 Office: 1800 M St NW Washington DC 20036

GOEL, KEWAL KRISHAN, biology, physics educator; b. Moga, Panjab, India, Sept. 6, 1945; s. Sh. Lachman Das and Tara Wanti Goel; m. Nirmala Devi, Dec. 25, 1977; children: Amit, Anika. BSc in Zoology with honors, Panjab U., India, 1966; MSc in Zoology with honors, Panjab U., 1967; MSc in Biomolecular Organization, Birkbeck Coll. U. London, 1984. Cert. tchr. Lectr. in zoology Arya Coll., Ludhiana, Panjab, 1967-68, D.A.V. Coll., Jullundur, Panjab, 1968-78; sci. tchr. acting head biology Mark Hall Mixed Comp. Sch., Harlow, Essex, Eng., 1979-86; sci. support tchr. Borough of Hounslow, London, 1986—, adv. sci. tchr., 1988—; mem. edn. staff Birkbeck Coll., London, 1984, Brunel U., London, 1987—. Author: Introduction to Zoology for Pre-University Classes in India, 1971. Organized Punjabi Soc., Harlow, 1981-86. Mem. Zool. Soc. Panjab U. (life mem.), Nat. Union Tchrs. Hindu. Lodge: Devon. Home: 12 Grasmere Ave, Hounslow Middx, London England TW3 2JQ

GOENAWAN, HAJI SARWONO, physician; b. Jakarta, Indonesia, Feb. 3, 1942; s. Raden Haji and Soeratni G.; m. Sri Susilowati, Dec. 19, 1964; children: Harry, Uki, Visca, Yuli. MD, U. Indonesia, Jakarta, 1967. Chief physician Health Dept. Lanuma Husein Sastranegar AFB, Bandung, West Java, Indonesia, 1967-83, Air Force Family Planning, West Java, 1978-83, First Air Force Areal Command Health Dept, Medan, North Sumatra, Indonesia, 1983-85, Preventive Sect. at the Airforce Head Quarters, Jakarta, 1985-87, Lanud Sulaeman Airforce Hosp., Margahayu, West Java, 1987—. Served to maj. Indonesian Air Force, 1978—. Moslem. Home: Parakan Resik St 8 Bypass, Soekarno Hatta, Bandung West Java, Indonesia Office: Lanud Sulaeman AF Hosp, Margahayu, Bandung, West Java Indonesia

GOERGEN, JAN ROGER, financier; b. Caledonia, Minn., Dec. 11, 1935; s. Cass Leon and Flavia Joyce (Evans) G.; m. Karen Rolli, June 25, 1977. B.A., U. Minn., 1957; postgrad. Harvard U. Extension, 1958-59, London Sch. Econs., 1968-69, U. Caracas, Venezuela, 1977-82. With Merrill Lynch & Assocs. Investment Corp., N.Y.C., Boston and Denver, 1959-62; v.p. fin., sr. v.p., exec. v.p., pres., pres./chief operating officer, chmn./chief exec. officer Intercap, and its affiliates, Mpls., 1962-82. Mem. Congl. Adv. Council, U.S. Senatorial Bus. Adv. Bd., Am. Econ. Council Found., Nat. Found. for Philanthropy, Big Bros., Little League Football. Served to lt. U.S. Army, 1951-52. Decorated Purple Heart, Silver Star; Order of Bolivar (Venezuela), 1980; named Eagle Scout, Boy Scouts Am., 1950; One of Minn.'s Outstanding Jaycees, 1967; John Sargeant-Pillsbury fellow U. Minn. Found., 1964. Mem. Am. Soc. Profl. Cons., Internat. Assn. Tax Advisors, U. Minn. Found., Eagle Scout Alumni Assn. Club: Fairbanks Ranch Country. Office: PO Box 607 Rancho Santa Fe CA 92067

GOETTELMANN, LOUIS HEYER, II, architect; b. Camden, N.J., Oct. 13, 1929; s. Louis Heyer and Martha McKnight (Kerr) G.; m. Katherine Fretz, Sept. 18, 1954; children—Martha, Katharine, Heyer, Charles, Ann; m. Claudia Brown, Feb. 16, 1980. B.Arch., U. Pa., 1954. Draftsman, Trautwein & Howard, Architects, Phila., 1957-59; job capt. Vincent King, Architect, Phila., 1959-60; project architect Martin, Stewart, Noble, Phila., 1960-63, architect Louis H. Goettelmann II, Phila., 1963-70; pres. Goettelmann Assocs., P.A., Haddonfield, N.J., 1970—. Mem. archtl. examining com. Nat. Council Archtl. Registration Bds., 1983-86; mem. N.J. Bd. planners, 1972-79, pres., 1975-76, 78-79; mem. N.J. Bd. Architects, 1980-84, v.p., 1983-84; co-founder bldg. constrn. tech. course Spring Garden Coll., 1962-68; founder bldg. constrn. tech. cert. program Rutgers U., 1969-80; founder bldg. constrn. tech. assoc. degree program Burlington City Coll., 1988. Contbg. artist This Is Haddonfield, 1962 (Freedoms Found. award 1963). Pres. bd. govs. Haddonfield Civic Assn., 1974; bd. dirs. Family Services of Burlington County, 1980, Camden Econ. Devel. Com., 1984. Recipient design excellence award Camden County Freeholders, 1980, Mazarell award, 1981. Mem. Pa. Soc., West Jersey Soc. Architects, Pa. Soc. Architects, AIA, Phila. Art Alliance, N.J. Soc. Architects., Sons Revolution (N.J. chpt., Pa. chpt.), Swenkfeldian Exiles Pa. (N.J. chpt.). Republican. Office: Goettelmann Architects PC 89 N Main St Medford NJ 08055

GOETZ, FRANK, industrial chemist; b. Hoboken, N.J., Mar. 23, 1949; s. Ludwig and Jennie (Alasio) G.; B.A. cum laude, Alfred U., 1971; M.S., Marquette U., 1974; Ph.D., U. Del., 1978. Research chemist U. Dayton Research Inst. at Air Force Rocket Propulsion Lab., Edwards AFB, Calif., 1978-80; sr. chemist Morton-Thiokol, Elkton, Md., 1980-85, scientist, supr. Propellant Devel. Group, 1985—. Contbr. articles to profl. jours. Mem. Am. Chem. Soc., Soc. Applied Spectroscopy, Royal Soc. Chemistry, Phi Kappa Phi. Republican. Home: 34 Highland Ave Elkton MD 21921

GOETZKE, GLORIA LOUISE, medical social worker; b. Monticello, Minn.; d. Wesley and Marvel (Kreidler) G. BA, U. Minn., 1964; MSW, U. Denver, 1966; MBA, Coll. St. Thomas, 1977. Med. social worker VA Med. Ctr., Los Angeles, 1980—; income tax cons. and instr. H&R Block, Santa Monica, Calif., 1980—; preceptor for grad. social work students at UCLA and U. So. Calif. Mem. Nat. Assn. Social Workers (cert.; dip.), Nat. Assn. of Enrolled Agts. Lutheran.

GOFF, MARTYN, book company executive; b. London, July 6, 1923; s. Jacob and Janey (Levy) G. Student, Clifton Coll., Bristol, Eng., 1933-39. Various positions as bookseller, author, broadcaster, lecturer Eng., 1948-70; dir. Nat. Book League, London, 1970-86; chief exec. Book Trust (formerly Nat. Book League), London, 1986-88; chmn. Henry J. Sotheran Ltd., London, 1988—; fiction reviewer The Daily Telegraph, London, 1975—. Author 8 novels, 4 books on music, 4 others, 1956—. Mem. exec. bd., lit. panel Greater London Arts Council; mem. Sch. Bookshop Assn., 1977—. Named to Order Brit. Empire, 1977. Fellow Royal Soc. Arts; mem. Soc. Bookmen (chmn. 1982-84). Clubs: Athenaeum (London), Savilqe (London). Home: 95 Sisters Ave, London SW11 5SW, England Office: Henry J Sotheran Ltd, 2 Sackville St, 45 East Hill, London W1X 2DP, England

GOFFIN, SUMNER, lawyer, arbitrator, mediator; b. Portland, Maine, June 15, 1919; s. Mitchell and Tena (Agger) G.; m. Dorothy M. Maxcy, Oct. 27, 1953; children: David, Sally, Peter. Student, U. Iowa, 1937-39; grad., Peabody Law Sch., 1942. Bar: Maine, 1942, U.S. Dist. Ct. Maine, U.S. Tax Ct., U.S. Ct. Claims, U.S. Customs Ct. Sole practice Portland, Maine, 1942-73, 85—; price atty. OPA, Augusta, Maine, 1943-45; justice Maine Superior Ct., Portland, Maine, 1973-84; self-employed arbitrator Maine Superior Ct., Portland, New Eng., 1985—; mem. faculty Portland Law Sch., 1949-57, com. Harness Racing, 1985—. Chmn., mem. Yarmouth Town Council, Maine, 1966-67; chmn. State Employees Appeals Bd., Augusta, Maine, 1967-73; mem. State Panel Mediators, Augusta, 1956-73; mem. Harness Racing Commn., Augusta, 1985-88; mem. Maine State Library Com., 1986—; life dir. Maine Sight Commn.; trustee Blind Children's Resource, Portland, Leisure Ctr. for Handicapped, Portland. Mem. Nat. Acad. Arbitrators, Am. Acad. Polit. and Social Sci., Am. Acad. Polit. Sci., Indsl. Relations Research Assn. Lodge: Lions (chmn. council govs. 1965-69, presidential award 1970), Masons. Home: 8 Edgecomb Ct Portland ME 04103 Office: 449 Forest Ave Suite 20 Portland ME 04101

GOFFMAN, JERRY M., psychologist, publisher; b. Bklyn., Feb. 6, 1940; s. Ben and Esther (Bregman) G.; m. Patricia S. Akers, June 10, 1964 (div. May 1972); 1 child, David M.; m. Dora E. Casas, Dec. 29, 1983 (div. 1986). B.A., San Diego State Coll., 1964, M.S. 1969; Ph.D., U.S. Internat. U., San Diego, 1972. Lic. psychologist, marriage, family and child counselor, Calif. Research psychologist med. Neuropsychiat. research unit U.S. Navy, San Diego, 1963-69; research dir. Ctr. for P.O.W. Studies, San Diego, 1970-73; head psychiat. epidemiology br. Naval Health Research Ctr., San Diego, 1973-75; program mgr. San Bernardino County Mental Health Dept., Calif., 1977-82; pvt. practice clin. psychology, San Bernardino, 1980—; founder, coordinator Batterers/Molesters Anonymous, San Bernardino, 1980—, Molesters Anonymous, San Bernardino, 1986—; pub. B.A. Press, San Bernardino, 1982—. Author: (manual) Mutual Support Counseling for Women Batterers, 1980; Self-Help Counseling for Men Who Batter Women, 1984; Self-Help Counseling for Men Who Molest Children, 1986. Contbr. articles to profl. jours. Chmn., San Bernardino County Sch. Attendance Rev. Bd., 1980. Served with U.S. Army, 1963-69. Mem. Inland Psychol. Assn. Jewish. Lodge: Elks. Office: Lawrence Psychological Ctr 407 E Gilbert St Suite 6 San Bernardino CA 92404

GOFFSTEIN, JOHN HOWARD, lawyer; b. St. Louis, Aug. 25, 1942; s. Harry and Naomi (Schreiber) G.; m. Margaret Ann Michael, Jan. 26, 1966; children—Adam, Ann. B.A., U. Mo., 1964, J.D., 1966. Bar: Mo. 1966, U.S. Dist. Ct. (ea. dist.) Mo. 1967, U.S. Ct. Appeals (7th and 8th cirs.) 1968, U.S. Supreme Ct. 1975. Assoc., John H. Martin Law Offices, 1967-68, Levin & Weinhaus, 1968-69; ptnr. Bartley & Goffstein, 1970-71; ptnr. Bartley, Goffstein, Bollato and Lange, and predecessor, St. Louis, 1971—; mem. LCC adv. bd. AFL-CIO. Bd. dirs. Legal Aid Soc. St. Louis, 1972. Mem. St. Louis Met. Bar, St. Louis Bar Assn. (chmn. labor law com. 1977-78, mem. exec. com. 1979), ABA, Mo. Bar, Lawyers Assn. St. Louis, St. Louis County Bar Assn. (chmn. group legal services com. 1972-75, pres. 1980-81; (Outstanding Young Lawyer of St. Louis County, Essen award 1977), Sigma Rho Sigma, Phi Delta Phi. Assoc. editor Developing Labor Law, 1970-86. Office: Suite 604 130 S Bemiston Saint Louis MO 63105

GOFRANK, FRANK LOUIS, retired machine tool company executive; b. Detroit, Dec. 23, 1918; s. Louis and Katherine E. (Schweninger) G.; m. Helen J. Rzeznik, Dec. 27, 1945; children: Shirley, Catherine, Ronald. B.A., Walsh Coll., 1950, LL.B. (hon.), 1982. C.P.A., Mich. Staff acct. Parker & Elsholz (C.P.A.s), 1947-48; staff acct. Lyons & Teetzel (C.P.A.s), 1949-50, partner, 1951-58; partner Coopers & Lybrand (C.P.A.s), Detroit, 1959-67; pres. Wilson Automation Co., Warren, Mich., 1967-73; chmn. bd., chief exec. officer Newcor, Inc., Warren, 1973-87; dir. Newcor, Inc., Mfrs. Nat. Trust Co. Mem. Mich. Assn. C.P.A.s. Clubs: Country of Detroit, Renaissance; Royal Palm Yacht and Country (Boca Raton, Fla.). also: 28 Windemere Ln Grosse Pointe Farms MI 48236

GOGA, MARIAN, economist, educator; b. Topolcany, Westslovakia, Czechoslovakia, Dec. 8, 1950; s. Gejza and Rozalia (Gero) G.; m. Anna Valkovic, Oct. 29, 1977; children: Monika, Lenka. Diploma in engring., Vysoka Sch. Econs., Bratislava, Czechoslovakia, 1976, postgrad., 1983. Asst. Vysoka Sch. Econs., 1976-79, spl. asst. optimal programming, 1979—. Recipient Czechoslovakian Acad. Sci. Honor award, 1984, Slovak Acad. Sci. Honor award, 1986. Mem. Czechoslovakian Sci. and Tech. Soc. Office: Vysoka Skola Ekonomicka, Odbojarov 10, 83220 Bratislava Czechoslovakia

GOH, KOK HWA (ROLAND), personnel manager; b. Singapore, May 30, 1945; s. Woon Biow and Seok Tin (Yap) G; m. Lim Soo Khim, Nov. 28, 1971; children: Yun Lin, Jia Lin, Hong Jin. BSc, U. Singapore, 1966; cert. in edn., Inst. Edn., Singapore, 1967; postgrad., U. Singapore, 1975, Inst. Mktg., Eng., 1976, Inst. Personnel Mgmt., 1979. Tchr. Ministry Edn., Singapore, 1966-68; unit mgr. China Underwriters Life & Ins. Co. Ltd., Singapore, 1968-69; mfg. supt. Tex. Instrument Singapore, 1969-76, sr. cost acct., 1976-78, fin. planning mgr., 1978-79; mktg. engr. Demetron Pte Ltd., Singapore; materials mgnr. Hewlett-Packard Singapore Co. Pte Ltd, Singapore, 1981-83, compensation and benefits mgr., 1983-86; personnel mgr. China Hewlett-Packard Co. Ltd., Beijing, 1986-88, AMD Spore Pte Ltd. Mem. Block Resident Com., Singapore, 1981-82. Mem. British Inst. Mgmt., Singapore Inst. Mgmt., Singapore Inst. Personnel Mgmt., Nat. Productivity Assn., Singapore Quality and Releability Assn. Home: 10 Begonia Terr, 2880 Singapore Singapore Office: AMD Spore Pte Ltd, 512 Chai Cheelane, 07-01--07-15 Bedok Indl Estates 1646, Singapore

GOH CHOK TONG, Minister of Defense and Second Minister of Health of the Republic of Singapore; b. Singapore, May 20, 1941; s. Goh Kah Khoon and Quah Kwee Hwa; m. Tan Choo Leng, 1965; children: Goh Jin Theng and Goh Jin Hian (twins). B.A. with 1st class honors in Econs., U. Singapore, 1964; M.A. in Devel. Econs., Williams Coll., 1967. With Singapore Adminstrv. Service, 1964-69, Neptune Orient Lines Ltd., 1969-77; M.P., 1976—, sr. minister of state, Ministry of Fin., Singapore, 1977-79, minister for trade and industry, 1979-81, minister for health and 2d minister of def., 1981-82, minister of def. 1982—; 2d minister for health, 1982-85; first dep. prime minister, 1985—; chmn. Singapore Labour Found.; chmn. bd. trustees NTUC Fairprice Co-operative, First organizing sec. People's Action Party, 1979—. Mem. Econ. Soc. Singapore. Clubs: Singapore Island Country, Tanah Merah Country, Keppel. *

GOHLKE, REINER MARIA, transportation executive; b. Beuthen, Fed. Republic Germany, July 29, 1934; m. Christa Bechtel; children: Frank, Oliver, Iris. Diploma in engring., U. Aachen, Fed. Republic Germany, 1960, diploma, 1964, D in Engring., 1965. Mgr. mktg. IBM Corp., Fed. Republic Germany, 1969-71, br. mgr., 1971-75, gen. mgr. bus. group, 1978; dir. French industry IBM Corp., France, 1975-78; with Deutsche Bundesbahn, Frankfurt, France. Recipient Graf-Maximilian-Montgelas prize Peutinger Inst., 1987. Office: Deutsche Bundesbahn, Friedrich Ebert Anlage 43, Frankfurt-Main Hesse 6000, Federal Republic of Germany

GOHSHI, YOHICHI, chemistry educator; b. Tokyo, May 9, 1937; s. Kazuo and Toshi (Wada) G.; m. Yasuko Utsumi, Mar. 15, 1974; children: Yuki, Yoichiro, Aya, Tae. B in Engring., U. Tokyo, 1961, DEng, 1977. Researcher Toshiba Research and Devel Ctr., Kawasaki, Japan, 1969-74; sr. mem. research staff Toshiba Research and Devel Ctr., Kawasaki, 1974-77; assoc. prof. engring. U. Tokyo, 1977-81. Mem. Chem. Soc. Japan (award 1986), Japan Soc. Analytical Chemistry (award 1972), Spectroscopical Soc. Japan (v.p.), Japan Soc. Applied Physics, Japan Soc. Surface Scis. (bd. dirs.). Home: 9-14-8-301 Konandai, Konan, Yokohama 233, Japan Office: U Tokyo, Dept Indsl Chemistry, 7-3-1 Hongo, Bunkyo, Tokyo 113, Japan

GOICO CASTRO, MANUEL DE JESUS, lawyer, historian; b. Seibo, Dominican Republic, Sept. 6, 1916. Lic. in Philosophy and Letters, U. Santo Domingo, Dominican Republic, 1947, JD, 1951. Rep. Dominican Nat. Cong., Santo Domingo, 1959-61; dir. stats., asst. sec. state Govt. Dominican Republic, Santo Domingo, 1966-78; pres. Nat. Council of Frontiers, Santo Domingo, 1986—. Author: En Torno a Pedro Santana, 1970, Miranda: El Procer Mas Erudito y Arrogante de America, 1971, Apologia a Jose Marti, 1980, La Prosa Artistica en Santo Domingo, 1982, Pedro Henriquez Urena, 1987. Sec. pub. relations Reformist Party, Santo Domingo, 1964. Decorated Heraldic Order of Merit of Duarte, Sanchez, and Mella Govt. of Dominican Republic, 1973, Order of Francisco de Miranda, 1st class Govt. of Venezuela, 1981, Order of Andres Bello, Great Ribbon of Honor, 1982, Order of Knights of Concord Govt. of Brazil, 1982; named Honourable Ambassador Sec. of State of Fgn. Affairs, 1988. Mem. Dominican-Mex. Cultural Inst. (pres. 1984—), Dominican Acad. of History (librarian 1980—), Dominican Acad. Lang. (sec. 1980—), Dominican Acad. Letters (pres.). Home: Avenida Tiradentes 66, Santo Domingo 5, Dominican Republic

GOIJBERG REIN, NORMAN, architect, consultant; b. Puerto Montt, Llanquihue, Chile, July 4, 1935; s. Issac and Dina (Rein) G.; m. Maria Alicia Benavides, Mar. 12, 1960; children: Pamela, Andrés. Architect, Faculty Architecture, U. Chile, 1960. Ind. architect, Puerto Montt, Chile, 1960-62, Santiago, Chile, 1962-64; exec. dir. Campaña Nacional Reparación Escuelas, Santiago, 1964-68, Fundación Progreso Económico Social, Santiago, 1969-70, Pan. Am. Devel. Found., Washington, 1970-77; ptnr. Inversiones SBG Ltda, Santiago, Chile, 1977—, SBG Consultores, Santiago, 1977—; dir. C.I.D. Chile Ltda, S Santiago, 1980—, C.I.T.U.R. Ltda, Santiago, 1980—, Constructora Ralun Ltda, Santiago, 1977—; cons. UN, N.Y.C., 1978. Bd. dirs. Pvt. Agys. Collaborating Together, N.Y.C., 1974-77, Chol-Chol Found. Human Devel., Washington, 1974, Corporación Desarrollo Metropolitano, Santiago, 1983; treas. Inter-Am. Mus. Festival, Washington, 1974-77. Mem. Colegio de Arquitectos de Chile. Club: Bretton Woods. Office: El Alcalde 15, Oficina 41, Santiago Chile

GOIN, MICHEL, physician; b. Aulnay-Sous-Bois, Seine St. Denis, France, May 30, 1951; s. Jean Etienne and Gisele (Baudrion) G.; m. Francoise Jeanne Gribiot, July 28, 1973; children: Vincent, Ludivine. D of medicine, Rene Descartes U., Paris, 1977. Chief doctor clin. medicine "Les Sources" Nursing Home, Ville d'Avray, France, 1978-80; gen. practice medicine Saint-Cloud, France, 1980—. Mem. Saint-Cloud and Garches Gen. Practitioners Friendly Mtg. Home and office: 9 Rue Pasteur, 92210 Saint-Cloud France

GOINES, LEONARD, music educator, consultant; b. Jacksonville, Fla., Apr. 22, 1934; s. Buford and Willie Mae (Lamar) G.; m. Margaretta Bobo (div.); 1 child, Lisan Lynette. BMus Manhattan Sch. of Music, N.Y.C., 1955, MMus, 1956; MA, Columbia U., 1960, profl. diploma, 1961; EdD, 1963; BA, New Sch. Social Research, N.Y.C., 1980; MA, NYU, 1980; CAS, Harvard U., 1984. Lectr. music Queens Coll., CUNY, N.Y.C., 1969, York Coll., CUNY, 1969, NYU, N.Y.C., 1970—; trumpeter Symphony New World, N.Y.C., 1965-7i6; assoc. prof. music Morgan State Coll., Balt., 1966-68, Howard U., Washington, 1970-72; prof. Manhattan Community Coll., CUNY, N.Y.C., 1970—; freelance musician Broadway shows, theare, orchestras, recording ensembles, jazz groups 1959—; vis. prof. Williams Coll., Williamstown, Mass., 1984, Vassar Coll., Poughkeepsie, N.Y., 1985; Disting. vis. prof. Lafayette Coll., Easton, Pa., 1986; postdoctoral fellow Harvard U., Cambridge, Mass., 1982-85; ptnr. Shepard & Goines Organizational and Ednl. Arts cons., Jazz research cons. Nat. Endowment Arts, 1983, cons. in field. Contbr. articles to profl. publs. Folklore cons., field researcher, African Diaspora, Smithsonian Instn., 1972-76; trustee Nat. Assn. Community Schs. of Arts, N.Y.C., 1982-85; chmn. spl. arts section panel N.Y. State Council on Arts, N.Y.C., 1982-85; music panelist Arts Connection, N.Y.C., 1985. Recipient Pub. Service award U.S. Dept. Labor, 1980, Scholar Incentive award CUNY, 1983-84; Named Hon. Citizen City of Winnipeg, Can., 1958; Coll. Tchrs. fellow NEH, 1982-83; Faculty Research grantee Howard U., CUNY, NYU, 1971-73. Mem. Local 802 of Am. Fedn. Musicians, AAUP, Nat. Acad. Rec. Arts and Scis., Phi Delta Kappa, Phi Mu Alpha. Democrat. Episcopalian. Avocations: running, photography, travel. Home: 221 W 131st St New York NY 10027 Office: CUNY Manhattan Community Coll 199 Chambers New York NY 10007

GOIZUETA, ROBERTO CRISPULO, food and beverage company executive; b. Havana, Cuba, Nov. 18, 1931; came to U.S., 1961; s. Crispulo D. and Aida (Cantera) G.; m. Olga T. Casteleiro, June 14, 1953; children: Roberto S., Olga M., Javier C. BS, BChemE, Yale U., 1953. Process engr. Indsl. Corp. Tropics, Havana, 1953-54; tech. dir. Coca-Cola Co., Havana, 1954-60; asst. to sr. v.p. Coca-Cola Co., Nassau, Bahamas, 1960-64; asst. to v.p. research and devel. Coca-Cola Co., Atlanta, 1964-66, v.p. engring., 1966-74, sr. v.p., 1974-75, exec. v.p., 1975-79, mem. corp. operating com., from 1975, mem. exec. office, mem. office of chmn., mem. retirement plan and thrift coms., from 1978, vice chmn., 1979-80, pres., chief operating officer, 1980-81, chmn. bd., chief exec. officer, 1980—, also bd. dirs.; dir., mem. exec. com. Coca-Cola Export Corp., from 1980; dir. Trust Co. of Ga., So. Natural Resources, Inc., Ford Motor Co., Sonat Inc. Bd. visitors Emory U., 1979—; bd. govs. Lauder Inst.; trustee Emory U., 1980—, The Am. Assembly, 1979—, Engring. Found. Ga., 1979—; mem. Bus. Council, Trilateral Commn. Mem. Tau Beta Pi. Clubs: Capital City (Atlanta) (bd. govs.); Piedmont Driving. Office: The Coca-Cola Co PO Drawer 1734 Atlanta GA 30301 *

GOKEL, GEORGE WILLIAM, organic chemist, educator; b. N.Y.C., June 27, 1946; s. George William and Ruth Mildred G.; B.S. in Chemistry, Tulane U., 1968; Ph.D. in Organic Chemistry, U. So. Calif., 1971; m. Kathryn Smiegocki, June 2, 1978; 1 child, Michael Robert. Postdoctoral fellow UCLA, 1972-74; chemist central research dept. E.I. Du Pont de Nemours & Co., Wilmington, Del., summer 1974; asst. prof. chemistry Pa. State U., University Park, 1974-78; asso. prof. chemistry U. Md., College Park, 1978-82, prof. chemistry, 1982-85, U. Miami, Coral Gables, Fla., 1985—; assoc. chmn., cons. W.R. Grace Co., 1977—; cons. Lion Detergent Co., Tokyo, 1985—, Seal Sands Chem. Co., Stockton-on-Tees, Eng., 1983—; lectr. in field. Recipient Allan C. Davis medal Md. Acad. Sci., 1979; Leo Schubert award Washington Acad. Scis., 1980; Petroleum Research Fund grantee, 1976-78; NIH grantee, 1979—. Mem. Am. Chem. Soc., Chem. Soc. (London), Sigma Xi, Alpha Chi Sigma. Republican. Methodist. Author: Phase Transfer Catalysis in Organic Synthesis, 1977; Experimental Organic Chemistry, 1980; Macrocyclic Polyether Syntheses, 1982; contbr. numerous articles to profl. jours. Home: 15560 SW 54th St Miami FL 33185 Office: U Miami Dept Chemistry Coral Gables FL 33124

GOKHARU, SURENDRA SIHNA, microcomputer consultant; b. Banera, Rajasthan, India, Sept. 24, 1935; s. Phool Chand and Chandra Kumari Gokharu; m. Ratan Ranka, May 10, 1959; children: Priti, Seema, Darpan. BSME, Birla Coll. Engring., Pilani, India, 1960. Scientist, officer Atomic Energy Establishment, Bombay, 1959-66; planning mgr. Assoc. Bearing Co. unit SKF Corp., Poona, India, 1966-73; project mgr. Parrys Bearings, Ltd., Bombay, 1974-77; gen. mgr. Sri Riken Wiguna unit Riken Corp., Surabaya, Indonesia, 1977-81, Dynamatic Hydraulics Co. unit Dowty Corp., Banglore, India, 1981; mgmt. cons. Pembangunan Jaya, Jakarta, Indonesia, 1982-84; microcomputer specialist Harlan Bekti Corp., Jakarta, 1984—. Author: Centreless Grinding, 1967; developer Grinding of Nuclear Materials tech., 1963; designer extended bore grinding tools. Home: 15 Vishwa Mahal, C Rd, Churchgate, Bombay 400020, India Office: Harlan Bekti Corp, Panin Bank Centre 8th Floor, Jl Jend Sudirman 1, Jakarta 10270, Indonesia

GOL, JEAN, vice prime minister, minister justice and institutional reform Belgium; b. Hammersmith, London, Feb. 8, 1942; s. Stanislas and Lea (Karny) G.; m. Rosita Winkler, Sept. 2, 1967; 1 child, Deborah. LLD, U. Leige, Belgium, 1964, LLB, 1969. Mem. Liege Bar, 1964—, Provincial Council Liege, 1968-71, City Council Liege, 1977—; M.P. Belgium, 1977—; asst. minister Ministry Regional Economy for Wallonia, 1974-77; dep. prime minister, minister justice and instl. reform 1981-88, minister fgn. trade, 1985; dep. pres. Liberal Internat., 1980—; mem. exec. bur. European Liberals and Dems.; chmn. Parti Reformateur Liberal, 1979-81. Author: Le Monde de la Presse en Belgique, 1970, Le Redressement Wallon, 1977, L'optimisme de la Volonté, 1985. Decorated Officer Ordre de Leopold, Grand Officier de la Legion d'Honneur. Office: Ministry of Justice, Place Poelaert 3, 1000 Brussels Belgium *

GOLAND, MARTIN, research institute executive; b. N.Y.C., July 12, 1919; s. Herman and Josephine (Bloch) G.; m. Charlotte Nelson, Oct. 16, 1948; children—Claudia, Lawrence, Nelson. M.E., Cornell U., 1940; LL.D. (hon.), St. Mary's U., San Antonio. Instr. mech. engring. Cornell U., 1940-42; sect. head structures dept. research lab., airplane div. Curtiss-Wright Corp., Buffalo, 1942-46; chmn. div. engring. Midwest Research Inst., Kansas City, Mo., 1946-50; dir. for engring. scis. Midwest Research Inst., 1950-55; v.p. Southwest Research Inst., San Antonio, 1955-57; dir. Southwest Research Inst., 1957-59, pres., 1959—; pres. S.W. Found. Research and Edn., San Antonio, 1972-82; dir. Nat. Bancshares Corp. Tex.; chmn. subcom. vibration and flutter NACA, 1952-60; chmn. research adv. com. on aircraft structures NASA, 1960-68, chmn. materials and structures group, aeros. adv. com., 1979-82; sci. adv. com. Harry Diamond Labs., U.S. Army Materiel Command, 1955-75; adv. panel com. sci. and astronautics Ho. of Reps., 1960-73; mem. state tech. services evaluation com., 1967-69; mem. adv. bd. on undersea warfare Dept. Navy, 1968-70, chmn., 1970-73; mem. spl. aviation fire reduction com. FAA, 1979-80; sci. adv. panel Dept. Army, 1966-77; chmn. U.S. Army Weapons Command Adv. Group, 1966-72; mem. materials adv. bd. NRC, 1969-74; vice-chmn. Naval Research Adv. Com., 1974-77, chmn., 1977; dir. Nat. Bank Commerce, San Antonio; dir. Engrs. Joint Council, 1966-69; mem. adv. group U.S. Armament Command, 1972-76; mem. sci. adv. com. Gen. Motors, 1971-81; mem. Nat. Commn. on Libraries and Info. Scis., 1971-78; chmn. NRC Bd. Army Sci. and Tech., 1982—; chmn. Commn. Engring. and Tech. Systems, NRC, 1980-86. Editor: Applied Mechanics Review, 1952-59; editorial adviser, 1959-84. Bd. govs. St. Mary's U., San Antonio, 1970-76, 85—; pres. San Antonio Symphony, 1968-70, chmn. bd., 1970-71; bd. dirs. So. Meth. U. Found. Sci. and Engring., Dallas, 1979—; trustee Univs. Research Assos., Inc., 1979-84. Recipient Spirit of St. Louis jr. award ASME, 1945, jr. award, 1946, Alfred E. Noble prize ASCE, 1947, Outstanding Civilian Service award U.S. Army, 1972, Nat. Engring. award, 1985, W.W. McAllister Patriotism award, 1986, Herbert Hoover medal, 1987. Fellow AAAS, Am. Inst. Aeros. and Astronautics (pres. 1971); hon. mem. ASME (dir., mem. bd. tech., mem. tech. devel. com., v.p. communications); mem. C. of C. (dir.), Nat. Acad. Engring., Sigma Xi, Tau Beta Pi. Home: 306 Country Ln San Antonio TX 78209 Office: SW Research Inst 6220 Culebra Rd San Antonio TX 78284

GOLANGCO, GARY J., industrial engineering consultant; b. Manila, May 15, 1938; s. Juan Golangco and Kim Kaw; m. Catherine Young Yu, June 4, 1967; children: Karen Kim, jan Gary, Quent Garett, Edbert Garry. BS in Indsl. Engring., Adamson U., Manila, 1962, BS in Elec. Engring., Mech. Engring., 1963. Cert. indsl. control procedures system indsl. mgmt. engr. Treas., asst. mgr. Tanduay Lumber, Inc., Manila, 1962-72; engring. faculty Adamson U., Manila, 1965—; pres. Tradeton Corp., Manila, 1972—; pres., gen. mgr. Yuyitung Publs., Inc., Manila, 1970—; pres. Fairdeal Resources Devel. Corp., Makati, Philippines, 1970—; dir. Citichem Indsl., Inc., Manila, 1970—; cons. Mercury Indsl. Philippines, Inc., Manila, 1972—, Apollo Mining Corp., Manila, 1968-72, Astra Devel. Corp., Manila, 1967-68; chmn. Cinese Comml. News, Manila, 1988—. Editor: Chinese Weekly, 1970-72. Mem. Philippines Liong Tek Fraternity, Manila, 1981—; advisor Philippines Tiok Lim Grand Mason, Inc., Manila, 1982-85. Mem. Manila Overseas Press Club, Nat. Press Club, Adamson U. Faculty Employee Assn., Adamson U. Ednl. Found., Assn. Mgmt. and Indsl. Engring. of Philippines, Philippines C. of C. Club: Casion Español (Manila). Lodge: Lions. Home: 416 J Nepomuceno St, Manila Philippines Office: Tradeton Corp, 420 J Nepomuceno St, Manila Philippines

GOLASINSKI, MAREK, mathematician, educator; b. Rzadka Wola, Poland, Apr. 22, 1949; s. Anna Andrzejewska; m. Laczkowska-Golasinski, Aug. 16, 1975; 1 child, Zofia. Grad., U. Torun, Poland, 1971, PhD in Math., 1978. Asst. prof. math. U. M. Kopernika, Torun, 1971-78, adj. prof. math., 1978—; lectr. Ife U., Nigeria, 1982-83; researcher Bangor U., Eng., 1986-87. Author various math. papers. Home: Lyskowskiego 25E/56, 87-100 Torun Poland Office: U M Kopernika, Inst Math, Chopina 12/18, 87-100 Torun Poland

GOLASKI, WALTER MICHAEL, machinery company executive; b. Torrington, Conn., Aug. 12, 1913; s. Paul and Helen (Kulesza) Golaszewski; M.E., Drexel Inst., 1946, completing B.S. degree: D.Sc., Alliance Coll., 1968; m. Helen D. Ambrose, Sept. 5, 1942 (dec. Aug. 1968); 1 dau., Michelle; m. 2d, Alexandra Budna, Oct. 25, 1969; children—Alexandra Maria, John Paul, Edmund Walter. With The Torrington Co., 1928-45; partner Bearing Products Co., Phila., design and manufacture spl. machinery, 1945-47, owner-mgr., 1947-63, pres., mgr., 1963—; pres., treas., Overbrook Knitting Corp., Phila., 1956—; pres. Golaski Labs., Inc., 1967—; former chmn. bd. Nowy Swiat newspaper; dir. 3d Fed. Savs. & Loan Assn. Nat. chmn. bd. trustees Kosciuszko Found. Ball, 1960, 76, co-chmn., 1980. Chmn. bd. trustees Kosciuszko Found., 1973-82; mem. adv. bd. Holy Family Coll., 1958-76 Recipient medal Drexel Inst. Tech., 1953, alumni citation, 1961; George Washington medal, 1972. Mem. Pa. Soc., AAAS, N.Y. Acad. Scis., Am. Soc. Artificial Internal Organs, Am. Ordnance Assn., Pa. Soc., Pa. Mfrs. Assn., Sigma Delta. Clubs: Polish Intercollegiate (alumni pres.), Germantown Cricket. Contbr. papers to profl. lit. Patentee in field. Invented processes converting hosiery machinery to finer gauges, and for making neckties and sweaters, machinery for mfr. blood vessels. Home: 6452 Woodbine Ave Philadelphia PA 19151 Office: 4567 Wayne Ave Philadelphia PA 19144

GOLD, ALBERT, artist; b. Phila., Oct. 31, 1916; s. Rubin and Dora (Sklar) G.; m. Aurora Mary Vanelli, Mar. 3, 1953; children: Madelaine, Robert. Grad., Pa. Mus. Sch. Indsl. Art, 1938. Tchr. pictoral expression Pa. Mus. Sch., Phila., 1945-48; dir. dept. illustration Phila. Mus. Coll. Arts; prof. emeritus Phila. Coll. Art; tchr. art centers, pvt. classes. Exhibited at maj. ann. shows including, Pa. Acad. Fine Arts, Corcoran Gallery, Met. Mus., Art Inst., Chgo., Carnegie Inst., World's Fair, N.Y.C., 1939, Nat. Gallery, London, 1943, Musee Galliera, Paris, La Tausca exhbn., Burlington Acad. Galleries, 1962, Phila. (Alumni grant) Coll. Art, 1968, one-man shows at, Pa. Acad. Fine Arts; Phila. Art Alliance, Hahn Gallery, Chestnut Hill, Pa.; represented in collections, Library of Congress, Soc. Illustrators, N.Y.C., N.Y. Pub. Library, Phila. Mus. Art, War Dept., Pentagon Bldg., U. Pa., Phila., U. Del., Newark, U. Minn., Smithsonian Instn., Atwater-Kent Mus., Phila., New Britain (Conn.) Mus. Am. Art, Forbes Collection, Ford Collection, Pa. Acad. Fine Arts, Soc. Illustrators, N.Y.C., Fogg Mus., U. Pa., Harvard U., Gimbel Pa. collection, Free Library Phila.; numerous pvt. collections; commd. to paint various documentary series; illustrator various mags.; (book) The Commodore (Robert L. Abrahams), 1954; Illus.: book This Was Our War (Frank Brookhouser), 1961, The Court Factor, 1964, The Captive Rabbi (Lillian S. Freehof). Decorated Order Brit. Empire; recipient John Gribbel Meml. prize Phila. Print Club, 1939; Prix de Rome, Am. Acad. in Rome, 1942; Geizel award Phila. Sketch Club, 1982, 83; Tiffany Found. grant, 1947-48; Jennie Sesnan Gold medal, 1950; Dorothy Kohl prize Phila. Art Alliance, 1953; Am. Artist citation Am. Water Color Soc., 1954; Am. Artists Guild award Am. Water Color Soc., 1955; Regional Water Color prize Phila. Art Alliance, 1955; Wm. W. Esty prize Am. Water Color Soc. Ann., 1961; award for series of illustrations Brandywine Ohio State U. Sch. Journalism; prize Phila. Watercolor Club, 1977; Silver Star award Phila. Coll. Art, 1979; Woodmere Endowment Fund grantee, 1968; Tiffany Found. grantee, 1946 and 47. Mem. Artists Equity (dir.), AAUP. Home: 6814 McCallum St Philadelphia PA 19119 Office: D Wigmore Fine Arts Inc 22 E 76th St New York NY 10021

GOLD, BELA, educator, economist; b. Kolozsvar, Hungary, Jan. 30, 1915; came to U.S., 1920, naturalized, 1927; s. Leo and Esther (Ludwig) G.; m. Sonia Steinman, July 5, 1938; 1 son, Robert. B.S. in Mech. Engring, NYU, 1934; Ph.D. (Univ. fellow 1936-37), Columbia U., 1948. Research cons. Life Ins. Sales Research Bur., Hartford, Conn., 1938-39; asst. head div. program surveys Bur. Agr. Econs., 1939-42; econ. cons. subcom. war mblzn. U.S. Senate, 1943-44; econ. adviser FEA and Dept. Commerce, 1944-46; prof. indsl. econs. U. Pitts. Grad. Sch. Bus., 1947-66; Timken prof. and William E. Umstattd prof. indsl. econs., dir. research program indsl. econs. Case Western Res. U., 1966-83, chmn. dept. econs., 1967-73; Fletcher Jones prof. tech. and mgmt. Claremont Grad. Sch. (Calif.), 1983—; pres. Indsl. Econs. and Mgmt. Assocs., Inc., 1980—; vis. professorial fellow Nuffield Coll., Oxford (Eng.) U., 1964; vis. prof. Imperial Coll. Scis. and Tech., London, Eng., 1967, 73; cons. to industry and ednl. instns., 1950—; Mem. com. on steel industry Nat. Acad. Scis.-Nat. Materials Adv. Bd., 1977-78; mem. assembly of engring. com. on computer-aided mfg. NRC, 1978-82, mem. mfg. studies bd., 1982-86, mem. com. on machine tool industry, 1982-84; mem. Interdepartmental Adv. Com. on Fed. Policy on Indsl. Innovation, 1978-79; mem. ferrous metals panel Nat. Acad. Engring., 1980-84, panel on improving the competitiveness of U.S. industries, 1985. Author: Wartime Economic Planning in Agriculture, 2d edit, 1969, How is Higher Education Financed, 1959, Foundations of Productivity Analysis, 1955, Explorations in Managerial Economics, 1971, Japanese edit., 1977, Technological Change: Economics, Management and Environment, 1975, 80, Applied Productivity Analysis for Industry, 1976, Russian edit., 1981, Chinese edit., 1982, Research, Technological Change and Economic Analysis, 1977, Productivity, Technology and Capital, 1979, 2d edit., 1982, Evaluating the Effects of Technological Innovations, 1980, Technological Progress and Industrial Leadership, 1984, 85, Appraising and Stimulating Technological Advances in Industry, 1980; Editorial bd.: Acad. Mgmt. Jour, 1962-73, Omega: Internat. Jour. Mgmt. Scis, 1972—, Jour. Product Innovation Mgmt., 1983—; corr. mem. editorial bd.: Revue d'Économie Industrielle, 1978—; mem. adv. editorial bd.: Jour. Computer Integrated Mfg., 1985—, Transactions in Engring. Mgmt., 1986—contbr. numerous articles to profl. jours., chpts. in books. Social Sci. Research Council fellow, 1937-38, 77, 83; Ford Found. fellow, 1961-62, 66-67, 72. Mem. Am. Econ. Assn., Inst. Mgmt. Scis. (chmn. Coll. on Mgmt. of Technol. Change 1970-85), Soc. Mfg. Engrs., Nat. Assn. Accountants (subcom. on productivity measurement 1977-79), AAUP. Home: 641 Hood Dr Claremont CA 91711

GOLD, I. RANDALL, lawyer; b. Chgo., Nov. 2, 1951; s. Albert Samuel and Lois (Rodrick) G.; m. Marcey Dale Miller, Nov. 18, 1978; children: Eric Matthew, Brian David. BS with high honors, U. Ill., 1973, JD, 1976. Bar: Ill. 1976, U.S. Dist. Ct. (no. dist.) Ill. 1976, Fla. 1979, U.S. Dist. Ct. (so. dist.) Fla. 1979, U.S. Ct. Appeals (5th and 7th cirs.) 1979, U.S. Tax Ct. 1979, U.S. Ct. Appeals (11th cir.) 1981, U.S. Supreme Ct. 1982, U.S. Dist. Ct. (middle dist.) Fla. 1987; CPA, Ill., Fla. Tax staff Ernst & Ernst, Chgo., 1976-77; asst. state atty. Cook County, Ill., 1977-78, Dade County, Miami, Fla., 1978-82; spl. atty. Miami Strike Force, U.S. Dept. Justice, Fla., 1982-87; sole practice, Miami, 1987—; lectr. Roosevelt U., Chgo., 1976-77; vice chmn. fed. practice com. on criminal sect. Fla. Bar 1986-88. Adviser Jr. Achievement, Chgo., 1976-78, Miami, 1982-84; coach, judge Nat. Trial Competition, U. Miami Law Sch., 1983-86, legal project Dade County Sch. System, 1985—. Mem. ABA (govt. litigation counsel com.), Ill. Bar Assn., Chgo. Bar Assn., Dade County Bar Assn. (mem. fed. ct. com., mem. criminal ct. com.), Decalogue Soc. Lawyers, Fed. Bar Assn., Assn. Trial Lawyers Am., Am. Inst. CPA's, Ill. Soc. CPA's, Fla. Inst. CPA's (com. on relations with Fla. Bar 1985-86, bd. dirs. South Dade chpt. 1987—), Am. Assn. Atty.-CPA's, Internat. Platform Assn., Delta Sigma Pi. Jewish. Club: Tiger Bay. Office: 1401 Brickell Ave Suite 910 Miami FL 33131

GOLD, MARK STEPHEN, psychopharmacologist, physician; b. N.Y.C., May 6, 1949; s. Meyer M. and Helene (Levy) G.; m. Janice Finn, June 19, 1971; 4 children. BA, Washington U., 1967; MD, U. Fla., 1975. Neurobehavior fellow Yale U. Sch. Medicine, 1975-78, lectr., 1978-80; v.p. basic research. Psychiat. Inst. Am., Summit, N.J., 1978-80; dir. research Fair Oaks Hosp., Summit, N.J., 1978—, Psychiat. Diagnostic Labs. Am., Summit, 1979-84; Regent Hosp., N.Y.C., 1982—; cons. substance abuse unit Yale U. Sch. Medicine, 1979—; founder Nat. Cocaine Hotline 800-COCAINE, 1983; cons. Office Drug Abuse Policy White House, 1984-86; presdl. appointee White House Conf. for Drug Free Am., 1988, mem. adv. bd., Am. Council Drug Edn. Co-editor Internat. Jour. Psychiatry in Medicine, Advances in Substance and Alcohol Abuse, Jour. Substance Abuse Treatment, Psychiatry Letter, Am. Jour. Drug and Alcohol; contbr. articles to profl. jours.; author: 800-Cocaine, 1984, Stop Drugs at Work, 1986, Wonder Drugs, 1987, The Good News About Depression, 1987, The Facts About Drugs and Alcohol, 1987; patentee in field. Recipient Seymour F. Lustman award for research Yale U. Sch. Medicine, 1978, Founds Fund prize for research in psychiatry Am. Psychiat. Assn. Found., 1981, Presdl. award for Disting. Leadership in Psychiat. Research Nat. Assn. Pvt. Psychiat. Hosps., 1982, Silver Anvil award Am. Council Drug Edn., 1984, Nat. Fedn. Parents award, 1986; named one of Today's Most Valuable Persons, USA Today, 1986, one of People of Yr., 1987; NIMH grantee. Mem. Soc. Neurosci., Am. Psychiat. Assn., Endocrine I Soc., Internat. Soc. Psychoneuroendocrinology, Nat. Assn. Pvt. Psychiat. Hosps., AAAS. Office: 1 Prospect St Summit NJ 07901

GOLD, MARTIN ELLIOT, lawyer, educator; b. N.Y.C., Jan. 6, 1946; s. Herman and Rose (Zippin) G.; 1 dau., Ariane. B.A., Cornell U., 1967; J.D., Harvard U., 1970, M.P.A., 1971. Bar: N.Y. 1972, U.S. Dist. Ct. (so. and ea. dists.) N.Y. 1974, U.S. Ct. Appeals (2d cir.) 1974. Assoc. Freshfields, London, 1969, Operation Crossroads Africa, The Gambia, 1965; research fellow Ctr. Law and Devel. Sri Lanka, Cambridge, Mass., 1971-73; assoc. Debevoise & Plimpton, N.Y.C., 1973-78; chief econ. devel. div. N.Y.C. Law Dept., 1978-85, dir. corp. law, 1980-85; cons. U.S. Dept. Justice, 1968; dir. N.Y.C. Indsl. Devel. Agy., 1979-85; ptnr. Brown & Wood, 1985—. adj. prof. Columbia U., 1987—; guest lectr. Fordham U., Yale U., U.S. Conf. of Mayors. Author: Law and Social Change: A Study of Land Reform in Sri

Lanka, 1977. Contbr. articles to profl. jours. Mem. Legal Aid Soc., 1974—; mem. Sri Lanka council Asia Soc., 1975-81, Cornell Real Estate council, 1988—. Recipient awards Rockefeller Bros. Fund, 1979, 80, Fund for City N.Y. 1981. Mem. ABA, Am. Econ. Assn., Am. Soc. Internat. Law , Lawyers Com. for Internat. Human Rights, Common Cause, Bar Assn. City N.Y. (environ. and energy and real property and housing law coms.), Sierra Club. Club: Harvard, Windows on the World (N.Y.C.). Home: 90 Riverside Dr New York NY 10024 Office: Brown & Wood One World Trade Ctr New York NY 10048

GOLD, MICHAEL NATHAN, technology and finance executive, biomedical engineer; b. Chgo., May 3, 1952; s. Julius and Sarah (Blitzblau) G.; m. Cynthia Bilicki, June 19, 1976; 1 child, Aaron Michael. BA, Kalamazoo Coll., 1976. Research fellow Sinai Hosp., Detroit, 1976; research assoc. Molecular Biological Inst., UCLA, Los Angeles, 1976-77; lab mgr., adminstr. Biomed. Engring. Ctr., U. So. Calif., Los Angeles, 1977-80; asst. dir. Crump Inst., UCLA, 1980-84, assoc. dir., exec. officer Crump Inst. for Med. Engring., UCLA, Los Angeles, 1984—. Mem. IEEE, Assn. for Advancement of Med. Instrumentation, Clin. Ligand Assay Soc., Am. Assn. for Med. Systems and Informatics, Sea Edn. Assn., Biomed. Engring. Soc., Internat. Soc. for Optical Engring. Office: UCLA 1950 Sawtelle Blvd Suite 330 Los Angeles CA 90025-7014

GOLD, NED COOPER, JR., lawyer; b. Santa Fe, N.Mex., July 23, 1941; s. Ned Cooper and Dora Margaret (Hall) G.; divorced; children: Gregory Albert, Marianne Dora; m. Deborah Ann Bemis, Jan 10, 1987; stepchild, Angela Phelps. B.S., St. Louis U., 1963, J.D., 1966; postgrad. Wichita State U., 1967-68, U. Alaska, 1968-69. Bar: Ohio 1966, Mo. 1966, U.S. Ct. Mil. Appeals 1966, U.S. Dist. Ct. (no. dist.) Ohio 1971, U.S. Tax Ct. 1971, U.S. Ct. Appeals (6th cir.) 1980. Assoc., Hoppe, Day & Ford, Warren, Ohio, 1966; assoc. Hoppe, Frey, Hewitt & Milligan, Warren, 1971-76, ptnr., 1976—. Vice pres. area 5 E. Central region Boy Scouts Am., v.p. Western Res. council; bd. dirs. Trumbull County chpt. Am. Red Cross, Vis. Nurse Assn. Trumbull County, Animal Welfare League Trumbull County, Trumbull Art Guild; mem. exec. com. John Carroll U. Parents Assn. Served to capt. USAF, 1966-71. Mem. ABA (corp. law and labor law sects.), Ohio State Bar Assn., Ohio Bar, Trumbull County Bar Assn., Midwest Pension Conf. Roman Catholic. Clubs: Trumbull Country, Buckeye. General corporate, Labor, Pension, profit-sharing, and employee benefits. Home: 8616 Bayberry Dr NE Warren OH 44484 Office: 2d Nat Bank Bldg Suite 500 Warren OH 44481

GOLD, RICHARD N., management consultant; b. Chgo., May 27, 1945; s. Irving Louis and Victoria (Saltzman) G.; m. Renee Bonnie Rein, Nov. 3, 1968; children: Jedd Steven, Amanda Caryn. BSI, U. Wis., 1967; MBA with honors, Columbia U., 1971; MA with honors, NYU, 1971. Tchr., supr. Ocean-Hill Brownsville, N.Y.C. pub. schs., 1968-71; brand mgr. packaged soap and detergent div. Procter & Gamble Co., Cin., 1971-76; exec. v.p. Glendinning Assocs., Westport, Conn., 1976-81; pres. R.N. Gold & Co., 1981—. Producer, ptnr. Enterplan, N.Y.C., 1983-85; dir. mktg. Downtown Council, Cin., 1975-77. Mem. Pres. Assn., Am. Mgmt. Assn. Avocations: sports, theatre, collecting antique electronic musical devices. Office: RN Gold & Co 3 Indian Point Ln Westport CT 06880

GOLDANSKII, VITALII IOSIFOVICH, chemist, physicist; b. Vitebsk, USSR, June 18, 1923; s. Iosif Efimovich and Yudif' (Melamed) G.; m. Lyudmila Nikolaevna Semenova; children: Dmitrii, Andrei. Grad. in Chemistry, Moscow U., 1944, M of Chemistry, 1947, DSc in Physics, 1954. Scientist Inst. Chem. Physics-USSR Acad. Scis., Moscow, 1942-52, from div. head to dep. dir., 1961—; sr. scientist P.N. Lebedev Phys. Inst.-USSR Acad. Scis., Moscow, 1952-61; asst. prof. Phys.-Tech. Inst., Moscow, 1947-51; asst. prof., then prof. Inst. Phys. Engring., Moscow, 1951—. Author: Kinematics of Nuclear Reactions, 1959, Mössbauer Effect and its Applications in Chemistry, 1963, Physical Chemistry of Positron and Positronium, 1968, Tunneling Phenomena in Chemical Physics, 1986, many others; contbr. numerous articles and revs. to profl. jours.; patentee (numerous) in field. Chmn. Soviet Pugwash Com., Moscow, 1987—. Recipient Lenin Prize, 1980, 83, Golden Mendeleev Medal USSR Acad. Scis., 1975, Karpinsky Prize Friedrich von Schiller Found., Hamburg, Fed. Republic Germany, 1983, Order of the October Revolution, 1975, many other awards and decorations. Fellow Am. Chem. Soc. (hon.), Am. Acad. Arts and Scis., Acad. Scis. German Dem. Republic; mem. Royal Danish Acad. Scis. and Letters, Deutsche Akademie der Naturforscher "Leopoldina", USSR Acad. Scis. Mem. Communist Party. Home: Ulitsa Kosygina 6, Apt 49, Moscow 117334, USSR Office: USSR Acad of Scis, Inst Chem Physics, Ulitsa Kosygina 4, Moscow 117334, USSR

GOLDBERG, ALAN JOEL, lawyer, commercial real estate developer; b. Bklyn, Jan. 22, 1943; s. Ralph and Dorothy (Rolnick) G.; 1 child, Cary Adam. BA, U. Miami, 1965, JD, 1968. Bar: Fla. 1968, U.S. Supreme Ct., U.S. Ct. Appeals (4th cir.). Ptnr. Goldberg, Young, Goldberg & Borkson, P.A., Ft. Lauderdale, Fla., 1968-82; atty. City of Margate (Fla.), 1969-70, City of Tamarac (Fla.), 1970-71; sole practice, Ft. Lauderdale, 1982—; pres. Property Systems, Inc. Mem. Citizen's Task Force on Transp., State of Fla.; chmn. Broward County Planning Council. Mem. ABA, Fla. Bar Assn. Republican. Office: 5100 N Federal Hwy Suite 412 Fort Lauderdale FL 33308

GOLDBERG, ARTHUR ABBA, lawyer, investment banker; b. Jersey City, Nov. 25, 1940; s. Jack Geddy and Ida (Steinberg) G.: A.B. with honors, Am. U., 1962; J.D., Cornell U., 1965; m. Jane Elizabeth Gottlieb, Aug. 10, 1968; children—Ari Matthew, Shoshana Eve, Benjamin Saul, Talia Akiva. Bar: N.J. 1965, Conn. 1966. Intern, staff mem. to senator, 1962; law clk. DeSevo & Cerutti, Jersey City, 1964; practiced in Jersey City, 1965—; asst. prof. law U. Conn. Sch. Law., 1965-67; cooperating atty. NAACP Legal Def. Fund, 1965—; adminstrv. asst. to congressman Ohio, 1966-75; dep. atty. gen. N.J., counsel Dept. Community Affairs and Housing Finance Agy., 1967-70; exec. v.p., dir., mgr. mcpl. fin. dept. Matthews & Wright, Inc., N.Y.C., 1970—; exec. v.p., dir. Landamatic Systems Corp., 1982-85, vice chmn., Matthews & Wright Realty, 1986—, Matthews & Wright Pacific, 1986—; pres. New Am. Fed. Credit Union, 1981—; v.p. Alfus Corp., 1958—, Basow Corp., 1965—; partner Shayna Enterprises, 1978—, York Builders, Hudson Mgmt. Services; mng. partner Bank Bldg. Assos., Inst. Profl. and Exec. Devel.; vis. lectr. Rutgers U., 1971-80, Practising Law Inst. 1969-76; mem. exec. com. N.J. Commn. Discrimination in Housing, 1975-80; mem. urban adv. council Anti-Defamation League, 1965-72; spl. cons. exclusionary zoning Nat. Com. Discrimination in Housing, 1965-70; cons. scholarship edn. Def. Fund for Racial Equality, 1965-72; gen. counsel N.J. chpt. Mcpl. Fin. Officers Assn., N.J. chpt. Nat. Assn. Housing and Redevel. Ofcls., 1966-74, chmn. Com. for Absorption of Soviet Emigrees (CASE), 1974—; pres. CASE-UNA Community Devel. Corp., 1976. Co-pres. New Synagogue, Jersey City, 1974-80; bd. dirs. Jersey City Hebrew Free Loan Assn., 1976—; pres. Met. N.Y. Coordinating Com. for Resettlement of Soviet Jewry, 1978—; treas. Hebrew Free Loan N.J., 1977-86 ; Hillel Acad., 1985—; dir. Jewish Community Ctr., 1987, United Jewish Appeal, 1984—; bd. dirs. South Bronx Community Housing Inc., 1977-81; adv. bd. Housing and Devel. Reporter, 1975—; chmn. Novy Americanitz, 1980—; bd. dirs. Citizens Housing and Planning Council; pres. Case Mus. Russian Contemporary Art in Exile, 1980—; pres. Freedom Synagogue, 1982—; bd. dirs. Boys Club of Jersey City, 1975—; mem. Settlement House Fund; treas. Council Jewish Orgns., Jersey City, 1977. mem. bd. edn. Yeshiva of Hudson County, 1977—. Mem. Conn. Assn. Mcpl. Attys. (exec. com., editor newsletter 1965-68), Nat. Housing Conf., ABA, N.J. (chmn. com. housing and urban renewal), Conn., Hudson County bar assns., Am. Polit. Sci. Assn., Nat. Acad. Polit. and Social Sci., Nat. Leased Housing Assn. (nat. pres. 1972-74, chmn. emeritus 1975—), Public Securities Assn. (legis. com. 1978), Nat. Housing Rehab. Assn. (dir. 1982—, v.p. 1985), Omicron Delta Kappa, Pi Gamma Mu, Pi Sigma Alpha, Pi Delta Epsilon. Author: Financing Housing and Urban Development, 1975; Zoning and Land Use, 1972; adv. bd. Housing and Devel. Reporter; contbr. articles to law revs. Home: 83 Montgomery St Jersey City NJ 07302 Office: Matthews & Wright Inc 14 Wall St New York NY 10005

GOLDBERG, ARTHUR JOSEPH, lawyer; b. Chgo., Aug. 8, 1908; s. Joseph and Rebecca (Perlstein) G.; m. Dorothy Kurgans, July 18, 1931; children—Barbara L. Goldberg Cramer, Robert M. B.S.L., Northwestern U., 1929, J.D. summa cum laude, 1930. Bar: Ill. 1929, D.C., N.Y., Va., U.S. Supreme Ct. 1937. Practiced in Chgo., 1929-48; sr. partner firm Goldberg, Devoe, Shadur & Mikva, Chgo., 1945-61, Goldberg, Feller & Bredhoff, Washington, 1952-61; gen. counsel CIO, 1948-55, United Steelworkers Am., 1948-61; spl. counsel, gen. counsel indsl. union dept. AFL-CIO, 1955-61; spl. counsel indsl. union dept. also numerous other internat. unions; sec. labor 1961-62; asso. justice U.S. Supreme Ct., Washington, 1962-65; U.S. rep. to UN, 1965-68, ambassador-at-large, 1977-78; sr. partner Paul, Weiss, Goldberg, Rifkind, Wharton & Garrison, N.Y.C., 1968-71; practice law Washington, 1971—; Charles Evans Hughes prof. Princeton U., 1968-69; distinguished prof. Columbia, 1969-70; prof. law and diplomacy Am. U., Washington, 1972-73; vis. disting. prof. Hastings Coll. Law, San Francisco, 1974—, Santa Clara U., 1980, Nova Law Ctr., 1980, Ala. U., 1985, Okla. U., Boston U., Akron U., No. Ky. U., also several other univs.; chmn. Center for Law and Social Policy, 1968-78, hon. chmn., 1978—; Former chmn. Pres.'s Com. on Migratory Labor, Pres.'s Missile Sites Labor Commn., Pres.'s Com. on Youth Employment, Pres.'s Temporary Com. on Implementation of Fed. Employee-Mgmt. Relations Program, Workers' Adv. Com. on U.S., Pres.'s Adv. Com. on Labor-Mgmt. Policy, Pres.'s Com. on Equal Employment Opportunity; former mem. numerous other Presdl. and federal coms. and councils, including SEC com. on tender offers, Commn. on Wartime Relocation and Internment of Civilians; former ex-officio mem. and ad hoc participant Nat. Security Council; former pres. Internat. Edn. Assn.; U.S. rep., chmn. U.S. del. Conf. on Security and Cooperation in Europe with rank amb.-at-large; spl. asst. to dir. OSS. Author: AFL-CIO; Labor United, 1956, Defenses of Freedom, 1966, Equal Justice: the Warren Era of the Supreme Court, 1972; editor-in-chief Ill. Law Rev, 1929-30; contbr. articles to profl. jours. and jours. of opinion. Past pres., now hon. chmn. Am. Jewish Com.; past chmn., pres. Synagogue Council of Am., Jewish Theol. Sem., Internat. Assn. Jewish Lawyers. Served as civilian, then from capt. to maj. OSS; Served from capt. to maj. U.S. Army, 1942-44, ETO; col. USAF Res. ret. Recipient numerous awards and hon. degrees; Medal of Freedom Pres. Carter, 1978; Order of Lincoln; Northwestern U. Alumnus medal. Mem. Am., Ill., Chgo., D.C. bar assns., Assn. Bar City N.Y., UN Assn. (hon. chmn.), Order of Coif. Address: 2801 New Mexico Ave NW Washington DC 20007 also: Southwood Farm Marshall VA 05602

GOLDBERG, DAVID P., professor of psychiatry, consultant; b. London, Jan. 28, 1934; s. Paul and Ruby Dora (Brandes) G.; m. Ilfra Joy Pink, Apr. 30, 1966; children: Paul Wilfred, Ilfra Charlotte, Katherine Anna, Emma Alexandra. MA, U. Oxford, Eng., 1957; BM, U. Oxford, 1962, DM, 1969; MSc, U. Manchester, 1973; FRC Psychiatry, Royal Coll. Psychiatrists, 1974; student, Hertford Coll., Oxford, Eng., St. Thomas' Hosp., London, 1962, Maudsley Hosp. Lectr. in psychiatry U. London, 1968-69; asst. prof. U. Pa., Phila., 1969-70; sr. lectr. U. Manchester, 1967-72, prof. psychiatry, 1972—; vis. prof. Med. U. S.C.. Charleston, 1978, U. West Australia, Perth, 1987; sci. adviser to chief scientist Dept. Health Social Security, London, 1972-83; cons. WHO, 1976—; chmn. gen. psychiatry Joint Com. Higher Psychiatric Tng., 1982—. Author: Detection of Psychiatric Illness by Questionaire, 1972, Mental Illness in the Community, 1979, Psychiatric Illness in Medical Practice, 1987, User's Guide to General Health Questionaire, 1988. Recipient Doris Odlum Prize, British Med. Assn. Fellow Royal Coll. Physicians of London, Royal Coll. Psychiatrists (Gaskell Gold medal 1968). Office: Withington Hosp, West Disbury, Manchester M20 8LR, England

GOLDBERG, EDWIN, rehabilitation specialist; b. Bklyn., 1937; s. Mary and Daniel Goldberg; m. June Light, June 21, 1972; children—Paul, Joseph, Robert. Diploma X-Ray, Columbia Inst. Chiropractic, 1960; postgrad. Columbia U., Am. Inst. Psychoanalysis ; cert. of study Alfred Adler Inst., Fordham U., 1970; M.A. in Edn., Hebrew Union Coll., 1971; profl. diploma rehab. mgmt., Cornell U., 1973; diploma Sch. of Hygiene, Sussex Tng. Coll., Eng., 1976; cert. assessment in aging U. Pa., 1987. Cert. med. rehab. coordinator, rehab. therapist, rehab. counselor, master therapeutic recreation specialist. Exec. Greater N.Y. councils Boy Scouts Am., 1960-63; supr. Charles Pfizer & Co., N.Y.C., 1963-64; assoc. dir. Western Mediterranean ops. USO, Nice, France, 1964-65; coordinator rehab. skills Jewish Guild Blind, N.Y.C., 1965-68, asst. dir., 1968-77; dir. rehab. services, sect. chief Trenton (N.J.) Psychiat. Hosp., 1977-78; dir. Work Adjustment Center, Jewish Employment and Vocat. Service, Phila., 1979-80; dir. S.I. (N.Y.) Aid for Retarded Children Rehab. Center, 1980-82; sr. rehab. counselor/acting dir. Vocat. Rehab. dept. Ancora Hosp., Hammonton, N.J., 1982-87; habilitation plan coordinator State of N.J. Div. Developmental Disabilities, Hammonton, 1988—; rehab. cons. Beth Israel Hosp., N.Y.C., Goldwater Meml. Hosp., N.Y.C., Montefirore Med. Ctr., Bronx, N.Y., Harlem Med. Ctr., Bronx, Kingsbrook Jewish Med. Ctr., Bklyn., Jewish Home and Hosp. for Aged, N.Y.C., Inst. Rehab. Medicine, NYU, HIllside Med. Ctr.;mobility specialist for severely disabled blind State of N.Y., 1968—; coordinator corrective therapy, internship program VA-Hunter Coll., 1971-77; adj. asst. prof. adapted phys. edn. Hunter Coll., 1970-77; rehab. tng. specialist multiple disabled blind in N.Y. area, 1970-77; lectr. in field, 1970—; legis. rep. N.Y. State Fedn. Workers for Blind, 1973-76, program chmn., 1974. Bd. dirs. Temple Micah, Lawrenceville, N.J., 1987—; mem. Nat. Eagle Scout Assn. Boy Scouts Am. Recipient Dr. Frank E. Dean Meml. award for outstanding contbns. to sci. edn., 1976, Thomas E. Watson Silver award citation Citizenship in Action medal SAR. Fellow N.Y. Acad. Scis., Royal Soc. Promotion Health; mem. Am. Congress Rehab. Medicine, Royal Soc. Health, Royal Inst. Public Health and Hygiene, Nat. Rehab. Counseling Assn., Am. Assn. Workers Blind, Am. Public Health Assn., Am. Assn. Rehab. Therapy, Am. Anthrop. Assn.Jewish. Author: Mobility Training Manual for Teachers of Visually Impaired Children, 1969; Adapted and Corrective Physical Education Curriculum Handicapped, 1972, Rehabilitation Assessment in Psychiatric Facilitities, 1984, Overcoming Feelings of Inferiority: The Role of Mobility Training for the Blind, 1986. Office: 11 Royal Oak Rd Lawrenceville NJ 08648

GOLDBERG, GERALDINE ELIZABETH, psychotherapist; b. Neptune, N.J., Mar. 22, 1939; d. Albert Voorhees and Katherine Irene (Mulholland) McCormick; BS cum laude, East Stroudsburg U., 1967; MA in Psychology, Fairleigh Dickinson U., 1971; m. Arthur Goldberg, July 1, 1961. Staff clin. psychologist Youth Devel. Clinic, Newark, 1971-75; psychotherapist in clin. psychology Mental Health Cons. Center, N.Y.C., 1975—; human resources specialist AGE Corp., Livingston, N.J., 1979—, sec. bd. dirs., 1977—, v.p., 1980—. Mem. N.J. Assn. Profl. Psychologists (past pres.), Am. Psychol. Assn. (asso.), N.J. Psychol. Assn. (asso.).

GOLDBERG, LEE WINICKI, furniture co. exec.; b. Laredo, Tex., Nov. 20, 1932; d. Frank and Goldie (Ostrowiak) Winicki; student San Diego State U., 1951-52; m. Frank M. Goldberg, Aug. 17, 1952; children—Susan Arlene, Edward Lewis, Anne Carri. With United Furniture Co., Inc., San Diego, 1953-83, corp. sec., dir., 1963-83, dir. environ. interiors, 1970-83; founder Drexel-Heritage store Edwards Interiors, subs. United Furniture, 1975; founding ptnr., v.p. FLJB Corp., 1976—, founding ptnr., sec. treas., Sea Fin., Inc., 1980, founding ptnr., First Nat. Bank San Diego, 1982. Den mother Boy Scouts Am., San Diego, 1965; vol. Am. Cancer Soc., San Diego, 1964-69; chmn. jr. matrons United Jewish Fedn., San Diego, 1958; del. So. Pacific Coast region Hadassah Conv., 1960, pres. Galilee group San Diego chpt., 1960-61; supporter Marc Chagall Nat. Mus., Nice, France, Smithsonian Instn., Los Angeles County Mus., La Jolla (Calif.) Mus. Contemporary Art, San Diego Mus. Art. Recipient Hadassah Service award San Diego chpt., 1958-59. Democrat. Jewish.

GOLDBERG, MICHEL ELIE, biophysics educator; b. Neuilly, France, Sept. 28, 1938; s. Szlama Zeev and Esther (Rottenberg) G.; m. Cecile Spiro, July 7, 1963; children: Marc, Muriel. Degree in engring., Ecole Polytechnique, Paris, 1961; PhD, Faculte des Sciences, Paris, 1967. Research assoc. Délégation Générale Recherche Scientifique et Technique, Paris, 1967, Centre National pour Recherche Scientifique, Paris, 1967-68; assoc. prof. U. Paris 7, 1968-74; prof., chmn. dept. biochemistry U. Paris, 1974—; chief of lab. Institut Pasteur, Paris, 1972-86, sci. dir., 1976-79, chmn. sci. council, 1985-87, prof., 1985—. Contbr. articles to profl. jours. Served to lt. French Air Force, 1961-62. Mem. European Molecular Biology Orgn., Societé Française de Chimie Biologique, Cercle Franç Microscopie Quantitative. Office: Institut Pasteur, 28 Rue dr Roux, Paris France

GOLDBERG, PAUL JOSEPH, lawyer; b. N.Y.C., July 18, 1937; s. Simon and Grace (Feder) G.; m. Susan M. Gutman, June 16, 1968; 1 son, Scott Barry. A.B., Brown U. 1959; LL.B., Columbia U., 1962. Bar: N.Y. 1963, U.S. Dist. Ct. (so. and ea. dists.) N.Y. 1964, U.S. Tax Ct. 1964, U.S. Ct. Appeals (2d cir.) 1964, U.S. Ct. Appeals (9th cir.) 1985. Assoc. Chester C. Davis, N.Y.C., 1962-68; ptnr. Davis & Cox, N.Y.C., 1968-71, Lea, Goldberg & Spellun, P.C., N.Y.C., 1971-77, Kissam, Halpin & Genovese, N.Y.C., 1977-84, Golenbock and Barell, 1984—; mem. departmental disciplinary com. 1st Jud. Dept. 1979-81, chmn. hearing panel 1980-81. Mem. ABA (com. on depreciation and investment tax credit tax sect.), N.Y. State Bar Assn. (com. on continuing legal edn.). Home: 28 W Horseshoe Dr East Hills NY 11577 Office: 645 5th Ave New York NY 10022

GOLDBERG, RAY ALLAN, agribusiness educator; b. Fargo, N.D., Oct. 19, 1926; s. Max and Anne G.; m. Thelma R. Englander, May 20, 1956; children: Marc E., Jennifer E., Jeffrey L. A.B., Harvard U., 1948, M.B.A., 1950; Ph.D., U. Minn., 1952. Officer, dir. Moorhead Seed & Grain Co., Minn., 1952-62; dir. Experience, Inc., Mpls., 1963-78; chmn. bd. Agribus. Assocs., 1978—; dir. Internat. Basic Economy Corp., N.Y.C., H.K. Webster Co.; mem. faculty Harvard U. Grad. Bus. Sch., 1955—, Moffett prof. agr. and bus., 1970—, also dir. continuing edn. programs, participant seminars; dir. Pioneer Hi-Bred Internat., Inc., Sporto, All-Flow, Inc., PLM Internat. Inc., Farms of Tex.; vis. prof. U. Minn. Grad. Sch., summer 1960; adv. council Foods Multinat., Inc., 1972-77; mem. agrl. investment com. John Hancock Ins. Co., 1971—; cons. in field, 1955—; adviser Instituto Centroamericano de Administracion de Empresa, Managua, Nicaragua, 1973—, Instituto Panamericano de Alta Direccion de Empressa, Mexico City, 1973—, U.S. Comptroller of Currency, 1975—, Food and Agr. Policy Project, Ctr. Nat. Policy, 1984—; mem. study team, subgroup chmn. world food and nutrition study NRC-Nat. Acad. Scis., 1975—; mem. com. tech. factor contbg. to nation's fgn. trade positions Nat. Acad. Engring., 1976—; chmn. agribus. adv. com. on Caribbean Basin U.S. Dept. Agr., 1982—; mem. com. on indsl. policy for developing countries Commn. on Engring. and Tech. Systems, NRC, 1982—; mem. task force on agr. Fowler-McCracken Commn., 1984—; avd. bd. The First Mercantile Currency Fund Inc., 1985—; internat. adv. bd. Atlantic Exchange Program, 1987—; mem. V.I. Lenin All-Union Acad. of Agrl. Scis. of the Soviet Union, 1988—. Author numerous books, 1948—; Agribusiness Management for Developing Countries-Latin America, 1974, (with Lee F. Schrader) Farmers' Cooperatives and Federal Income Taxes, 1974, (with John T. Dunlop et. al.) The Lessons of Wage and Price Controls—The Food Sector, 1977, (with Richard C. McGinity et. al.) Agribusiness Management for Developing Countries—Southeast Asian Corn Study, 1979; editor: Research in Domestic and International Agribusiness Management, Vol. 1, 1980, Vol. 2, 1981, Vol. 3, 1982, Vol. 4, 1983, Vol. 5, 1984, Vol. 6, 1986, Vol. 7, 1987, Vol. 8, 1988; also numerous articles.; chmn. editorial adv. bd.: Jour. Agribus., 1983—. Bd. govs. Internat. Devel. Research Center, Govt. of Can., 1978—; trustee Roxbury Latin Sch., Boston, 1973-76; trustee Beth Israel Hosp., Boston, 1978—, mem. com. on patents and tech. transfer, 1982—; mem. adv. com. to prep. sch. New Eng. Conservatory Music, 1974—, assoc. trustee, 1978—. Mem. Am. Agrl. Econs. Assn. (editorial council 1974-78, agribus. com. 1982—), Am. Mktg. Assn., Am. Dairy Sci. Assn., Food Distbn. Research Soc. Club: Harvard (Boston and N.Y.C.). Address: 975 Meml Dr Apt 701 Cambridge MA 02138

GOLDBERG, SID, editor; b. N.Y.C., Mar. 1, 1931; s. Emanuel and Florence (Fischbein) G.; m. Lucianne S. Cummings, April 10, 1966; children: Joshua John, Jonah Jacob. B.A., U. Mich., 1950, M.A., 1952; student, N.Y. U., 1952-53. Editorial asst. Washington Post & Times Herald, 1955-56; fgn. affairs editor World Week mag., N.Y.C., 1955-57; asst. editor North Am. Newspaper Alliance, 1957-58, news editor, 1958-60, editor, 1960—, gen. mgr., v.p., 1964—; editor Women's News Service, 1964-81; pres. N.Am. Newspaper Alliance, Inc., Bell-McClure Syndicate, 1972, exec. editor, 1973-81; gen. exec. United Feature Syndicate, 1973, mng. editor, 1974-78, v.p., exec. editor, 1978—; v.p., exec. editor Newspaper Enterprise Assn., 1979—; exec. editor Ind. News Alliance, 1980-84; dir. internat. newspaper ops. United Media, 1984—. Served with AUS, 1953-55. Mem. Nat. Cartoonists Soc., Internat. Press Inst., Interam. Press Assn. Soc. of Silurians, Sigma Delta Chi. Clubs: Overseas Press Am. (N.Y.C.), Dutch Treat (N.Y.C.), Hudson Harbor Yacht (N.Y.C.). Home: 255 W 84th St New York NY 10024 Office: United Media 200 Park Ave New York NY 10166

GOLDBERG, STANLEY ZELIG, lawyer, banker; b. Pitts., May 22, 1937; s. Emanuel and Jeannette C. (Rosenbloom) G.; m. Marlou Synder, June 15, 1960; children—Jennifer J., David C. A.B., U. Pitts., 1959; J.D., Harvard U., 1962; postgrad. U. Paris, 1962-63. Bar: Pa. 1964, U.S. Dist. Ct. (we. dist.) Pa. 1964, U.S. Supreme Ct. 1967. Ptnr., Markel, Markel, Levenson & Schafer, Pitts., 1964-76; v.p. Pitts. Nat. Bank, 1976-87; v.p., PNC Fin. Corp, 1987—. Pres. bd. dirs. Craig House-Technoma Workshop, Pitts., 1979-81. Mem. Internat. Bar Assn., ABA, Pa. Bar Assn., Allegheny County Bar Assn., U. Pitts. Coll. Alumni Assn. (pres. 1980-81). Democrat. Unitarian. Home: 1869 Swallow Hill Rd Pittsburgh PA 15220 Office: Pitts Nat Bank Pitts Nat Bldg 5th Ave and Wood St Pittsburgh PA 15265

GOLDBERG, WILLIAM JEFFREY, accountant; b. Chgo., Jan. 18, 1950; s. Harry and Bernice Dorothy (Benson) G. m. Brenda Liebling; children—Leslie Claire, Hollis Melissa. B.A., Knox Coll., 1971; J.D., Cornell U., 1974; postgrad. U. Chgo., 1976-78. Bar: Ill. 1974, U.S. Dist. Ct. (no. dist.) Ill. 1974. Fin. counseling officer Continental Ill. Nat. Bank, Chgo., 1974-79; supr. Peat Marwick Main & Co., Houston, 1979-80, mgr., 1980-82, ptnr., 1982—; nat. dir. Personal Fin. Planning Services, 1984—; instr. law Ill. Inst. Tech. Chgo. Kent Coll. Law, 1977-78. Chmn. deferred giving Mus. Fine Arts, Houston, 1984—; com. chmn. United Jewish Campaign, 1984; trustee Jewish Fedn. of Greater Houston, 1985—; trustee, chmn. profl. edn. com. Endowment Fund of Jewish Community of Houston, 1987—. Mem. Am. Inst. C.P.A.s (personal fin. planning div., exec. com.), Tex. Soc. C.P.A.s, Houston Estate and Fin. Forum, Houston Bus. and Estate Planning Council, Knox Coll. Club Houston (pres. 1981-82). Clubs: Plaza (gov. 1984-86), Westwood Country. Office: Peat Marwick Main & Co PO Box 4545 Houston TX 77210

GOLDBERGER, MARVIN L., educator, physicist, institute technology president; b. Chgo., Oct. 22, 1922; s. Joseph and Mildred (Sedwitz) G.; m. Mildred Ginsburg, Nov. 25, 1945; children: Samuel M., Joel S. B.S., Carnegie Inst. Tech., 1943; Ph.D., U. Chgo., 1948. Research assoc. Radiation Lab., U. Calif., 1948-49; research assoc. Mass. Inst. Tech., 1949-50; asst.-assoc. prof. U. Chgo., 1950-55, prof., 1955-57; Higgins prof. physics Princeton U., 1953-54, 57-78, chmn. dept., 1970-76, Joseph Henry prof. physics, 1977-78; pres. Calif. Inst. Tech., Pasadena, 1978-87; dir. Inst. Advanced Study, Princeton U., N.J., 1987—; Mem. President's Sci. Adv. Com., 1965-69; Chmn. Fedn. Am. Scientists, 1971-73; dir. Gen. Motors Corp., Haskel, Inc. Fellow Am. Phys. Soc., Am. Acad. Arts and Scis.; mem. Nat. Acad. Scis., Am. Philos. Soc., Council on Fgn. Relations. Club: Princeton (N.Y.C.).

GOLDBLAT, JOZEF, political scientist, researcher; b. Lwow, Poland, Jan. 7, 1923; arrived in Sweden, 1969; s. Adolf and Renata (Kohl) G.; m. Claire Alder; children: Bernard, Fernand. Student various univs. in Poland and USSR, 1948, 49, 54. Editor Polish Press Agy., Warsaw, 1951-54; inspector Neutral Nations Supervisory Commn., Korea, 1954; head commr. Internat. Commn. for Supervision and Control, Vietnam, 1955-57; advisor to Minister and head UN div. Ministry Fgn. Affairs, Warsaw, 1958-61, 64-68; 1st polit. officer UN Secretariat Disarmament Div., N.Y.C., 1961-63; chief arms control program Internat. Peace Research Inst., Stockholm, 1969—; chief Polish del. Conf. of the Com. on Disarmament, Geneva, Switzerland, 1967; bd. Geneva Internat. Peace Research Inst., 1988. Author several books in field including Arms Control Agreements, 1983 (Choice mag. award 1983); contbr. reports and articles to profl. jours. Recipient Pomerance Disarmament award, N.Y.C., 1984. Lodge: Rotary. Home: 2, avenue de Sécheron, 1202 Geneva Switzerland Office: Internat Peace Research Inst, Pipers Väg 28, S-171 73 Solna Sweden

GOLDBLATT, BARRY LANCE, manufacturing company executive; b. Palo Alto, Calif., July 29, 1945; s. Samuel and Joan Charlotte (Morton) G.; B.S., U. So. Calif., 1967, M.B.A., 1968. Supr. market research for brands Procter & Gamble Co., Cin., 1968-71; mgr. market research Personal Products Co. subs. Johnson & Johnson, 1971-74; asso. dir. consumer research Johnson & Johnson Baby Products Co., Skillman, N.J., 1974-87; dir. market research Johnson and Johnson Dental Care Co., New Brunswick, N.J., 1987—. Bd. dirs. New Brunswick Hot Line, 1973; vol. Urban Cons.

Group, 1977—. Mem. U. So. Calif. M.B.A.s, U. So. Calif. Commerce Assos., Am. Mktg. Assn., Assn. M.B.A. Execs., Am. Philatel. Soc., U. So. Calif. Assocs., Skull and Dagger, Zeta Beta Tau. Republican. Club: U. So. Calif. Alumni of N.J. (pres.). Home: 20 Andrews Ln Princeton NJ 08540 Office: Johnson & Johnson Dental Care Co 501 George St New Brunswick NJ 08903

GOLDBLITH, SAMUEL ABRAHAM, food science educator; b. Lawrence, Mass., May 5, 1919; s. Abraham and Fannie (Rubin) G.; m. Diana Greenberg, Apr. 27, 1941; children: Errol (dec.), Judith Ann, Jonathan Mark. S.B., MIT, 1940, S.M., 1947, Ph.D., 1949. Research Arthur D. Little Co., Cambridge, Mass., 1940-41; faculty MIT, 1949—, prof. food tech., 1959-74, Underwood Prescott prof. food sci., 1974-78, acting head dept., 1959-61, exec. officer dept., 1961-66, dep. dept. head, 1967-72, assoc. dept. head, 1972-74, dir. indsl. liaison, 1974-78, prof. food sci., 1978—, v.p., 1978-86, sr. advisor to pres., 1986—; mem. coms. radiation preservation and radionuclides in foods, chmn. com. radiation preservation of foods NRC-Nat. Acad. Scis.; dir. Penicillin Assays, Inc., Florasynth Co., Ionics, Inc. Author: An Introduction to Thermal Processing of Foods, 1961, Milestones in Nutrition, 1964—, Annotated Bibliography on Microwaves In Food Preservations, Freeze Drying and Advanced Food Technology, 1975; also numerous sci. papers. Pub. trustee ILSI-Nutrition Found. Served to capt. AUS, 1941-46, PTO. Decorated Silver Star medal, Bronze Star with oak leaf cluster, Order of Sacred Treasure 2d class (Japan); named One of Ten Outstanding Young Men of Greater Boston, 1953; recipient Babcock-Hart award, 1969; Nicholas Appert medal, 1970. Fellow Inst. Food Technologists (chmn. N.E. sect. 1958, Monsanto Presentation award 1953, Disting. Food Scientist award N.Y. sect. 1969, Phila. sect. 1976), Inst. Food Sci. and Tech. (U.K.), AAAS; mem. Am. Chem. Soc., Royal Swedish Acad. Engring. Scis. (fgn. mem.), Swiss Acad. Engring. Scis. (corr. mem.), Am. Inst. Nutrition, Sigma Xi, Phi Tau Sigma (pres. 1958). Clubs: Cosmos (Washington); St. Botolph, New Century (Boston) (pres. 1962-63). Lodge: Masons. Home: 6 Meadowview Rd Melrose MA 02176 Office: MIT 77 Massachusetts Ave Cambridge MA 02139

GOLDEN, BALFOUR HENRY, private investor; b. Bangor, Maine, Aug. 23, 1922; s. Samuel Henry and Helen (Rybier) G.; A.B. cum laude, Bowdoin Coll., 1944; postgrad. Columbia U., 1945-47; m. Emma Jane Krakauer, June 22, 1956; children—Peter Balfour, Betsy Jane, Robert Henry. Pres., Golden Food Services Corp. of N.Y., 1951-70, of N.J., 1951-70, of Iowa, 1951-70, Golden Co. of Maine, 1952-70, Golden Base Services Corp., 1952-70, Plaza Eats, Inc., 1958-70, Dubonnet Restaurant Corp., 1960-70; food service cons., 1970-74; pres. Guardian Food Service Corp., N.Y.C., 1974-85, Ropes Tremblay, Inc., 1986—. Served with AUS, 1943-45. Mem. New Eng. Soc. in N.Y.C., N.Y. Restaurant Assn. (dir.), Phi Beta Kappa. Club: Williams. Home: 325 Beechwood Rd Ridgewood NJ 07450 Office: 60 W Ridgewood Ave Ridgewood NJ 07450

GOLDEN, CONSTANCE JEAN, aerospace engineer; b. Highland Park, Ill., June 8, 1939; d. Herman William and Chrystle O'Linda Leuer; BS in Math, Physics, Beloit Coll. summa cum laude, 1961; AM in Math., Harvard, 1962; PhD in Math., Stanford U., 1966, MS in Ops. research Engring., 1970; m. Charles Joseph Golden, June 13, 1962; 1 dau., Kerri Lynn. Scientist/engr. research and devel. div. Lockheed Missiles & Space Co., Sunnyvale, Calif., 1962-68, sr. scientist/engr. Palo Alto research labs., 1968-74, mgr. planning requirements and mgmt. control, missile systems div., Sunnyvale, 1975-78; program mgr. manned space ops. studies Ford Aerospace, Palo Alto, 1978-79, corp. strategy mgr., Detroit, 1980-81, mgr. mission ops. and tech. devel., Sunnyvale, Calif., 1982-84, mgr. adv. programs, 1984—; mem. comml. satellite survivability task force. Nat. Security Telecommunications Adv. Com., 1982-84; mem. Nat. Def. Exec. Res.-Fed. Emergency Mgmt. Agy.; mem. adv. council for sci. and math. Mills Coll., 1976-80. NSF fellow, 1961-62; recipient Tribute to Women in Industry award, 1985-86; named Disting. Woman of Yr. Lockheed, 1976. Mem. AIAA (space systems tech. panel 1982-83), Armed Forces Communications and Electronic Assn. (sect. dir. 1979-80), Am. Astronautical Soc. (chmn. San Francisco Bay Area sect. 1984), Soc. Women Engrs. (fellow 1982, past pres. San Francisco Bay Area sect., past nat. scholarship chmn.), Jr. Achievement, Phi Beta Kappa (award 1960-61). Club: Toastmasters (past pres., ATM). Contbg. author: Second Careers for Women, 1975. Office: Ford Aerospace 1260 Crossman Ave Sunnyvale CA 94089

GOLDEN, EDWARD SCOTT, lawyer; b. Miami, Fla., Sept. 25, 1955; s. Alvan Leonard and Fay Betty (Gray) G.; m. Jane Eileen DeKlavon, June 9, 1979; children: Daniel Bryan, Kimberly Michelle. Student, So. Fla. Christian Coll., 1975-76; BS, MIT, 1978; JD, Harvard U., 1981. Bar: Fla. 1981, U.S. Dist. Ct. (so. dist.) Fla. 1982, U.S. Tax Ct. 1982. Assoc. Roberts and Holland, Miami, 1981-82, Valdes-Fauli, Richardson, Cobb & Petrey, P.A., Miami, 1982-83; v.p. Buck and Golden, P.A., Ft. Lauderdale, Fla., 1983-88; sole practice 1988—. Editor-in-chief Harvard Jour. of Law and Pub. Policy, 1980-81; contbr. articles to profl. jours. Chmn. deacons West Lauderdale Bapt. Ch., Broward County, Fla., 1984-86, 87-88, legal cons., 1983—; del. Fla. Rep. Conv., 1987; mem. Rep. Exec. Com., Broward County, 1984—; legal cons. Organizational Model for Elimination of Genocide in Am., Ft. Lauderdale, 1983—. Named one of Outstanding Young Men of Am., 1986; Western Electric grantee, 1972-74. Mem. ABA, Broward County Bar Assn., Christian Lawyers Assn. (pres. 1985-86), Christian Legal Soc., Order of Silver Knight, Zeta Beta Tau. Lodge: Optimists (treas. Dade County Carol City High Sch., 1971-72). Home: 5410 Buchanan St Hollywood FL 33021 Office: 644 SE 4th Ave Fort Lauderdale FL 33301

GOLDEN, LEON, classicist, educator; b. Jersey City, Dec. 25, 1930; s. Nathan and Regina (Okun) G. B.A., U. Chgo., 1950, M.A., 1953, Ph.D., 1958. Instr. ancient langs. Coll. William and Mary, 1958-60, asst. prof. ancient langs., 1960- 65; assoc. prof. classical langs. Fla. State U., 1965-68, prof., 1968—, dir. program in humanities, 1976—, chmn. dept. classics, 1986—; bd. dirs. Fla. Endowment for Humanities, 1983-87. Author: In Praise of Prometheus: Humanism and Rationalism in Aeschylean Thought, 1966, (with O.B. Hardison Jr.) Aristotle's Poetics, 1968. Served with AUS, 1953-55. Fellow coop. program humanities U.N.C. and Duke, 1964-65; Fellow coop. program humanities Soc. for Religion in Higher Edn., 1971-72. Mem. Am. Philol. Assn., Archeol. Inst. Am., Classical Assn. Middle West and South (pres. So. sect. 1972-74), Am. Soc. Aesthetics, Phi Beta Kappa. Office: Dept of Classics Florida State U Tallahassee FL 32306

GOLDEN, MARC ALAN, investment banker; b. Phila., Dec. 26, 1953; s. Mano Robert and Sue E. (Aronsohn) G. B.A., Yale Coll., 1975; M.B.A., J.D., Harvard U., 1980. Bar: N.Y. 1981, U.S. Dist. Ct. (so. and ea. dists.) N.Y. 1984, U.S. Supreme Ct. 1985. Legis. asst. U.S. Senator Richard Stone (Fla.), Washington, 1975; legis. aide, issues analyst U.S. Rep. William Green (Pa.), Washington, 1975-76; legis. counsel U.S. Senate Com. on Vets. Affairs, Washington, 1976; asst. to dep. dir. Fed. Jud. Ctr., Washington, 1978; assoc. Cravath, Swaine & Moore, N.Y.C., 1981-86; v.p. Goldman, Sachs & Co., N.Y.C., 1986—. Active N.Y. chpt. Lawyers' Alliance for Nuclear Arms Control, 1983—. Mem. ABA, N.Y. State Bar Assn., Assn. Bar City N.Y. Office: Goldman Sachs & Co 85 Broad St New York NY 10004

GOLDENBERG, SILVIA SICHTMAN, textile company executive; b. Bucharest, Romania, July 21, 1932; arrived in Venezuela, 1967.; d. Samuel and Fanny (Cohen) Sichtman; 1 child, Mordejai. Grad., Superior Inst. Econ. Studies and Planification, Romania, 1958. Economist Ministry of Commerce and Industry, Romania, 1950-63; adminstrv. mgr. Hilanderias Venezolanas, Venezuela, 1963-83; mgr. Sudamtex de Venezuela, Caracas, 1983—; bd. dirs. TEX 27, C.A. Venezuela, VEL 28, C.A. Venezuela. Club: Puerto Azul. Home: Sudamtex de Venezuela, Av Urdaneta - Edif Karam, Caracas 1010-A, Venezuela

GÖLDENBOOG, CHRISTIAN, freelance journalist; b. Marburg, Fed. Republic of Germany, Aug. 13, 1953; s. Hans and Rheingard (Grüner) G. Student, Higher Econ. Bus. Sch., Düsseldorf, Fed. Republic Germany, 1974. Mng. editor Filmfaust Mag., Frankfurt, Fed. Republic Germany, 1975-85; free-lance journalist Frankfurt, 1985—. Mem. Fédération Internat. de la Presse Cinématographique. Home and Office: Marienkirchgasse 3, 6474 Ortenberg Federal Republic of Germany

GOLDFARB, BERNARD SANFORD, lawyer; b. Cleve., Apr. 15, 1917; s. Harry and Esther (Lenson) G.; m. Barbara Brofman, Jan. 4, 1966; children—Meredith Stacey, Lauren Beth. A.B., Case Western Res. U., 1938, J.D., 1940. Bar: Ohio bar 1940. Since practiced in Cleve.; sr. partner firm Goldfarb & Reznick, 1967—; spl. counsel to atty. gen. Ohio, 1950, 71-74; mem. Ohio Commn. Uniform Traffic Rules, 1973—. Contbr. legal jours. Served with USAAF, 1942-45. Mem. Am., Ohio, Greater Cleve. bar assns. Home: 39 Pepper Creek Dr Pepper Pike OH 44124 Office: 1800 Illuminating Bldg Cleveland OH 44113

GOLDFARB, MURIEL BERNICE, marketing and advertising consultant; b. Bklyn., Mar. 29, 1920; d. Barnett Goldfarb and May (Steinberg) Goldfarb Oshman; B.A., U. Miami, Coral Gables, Fla., 1942; postgrad. CCNY, 1950. Advt. mgr. Majestic Specialities Co., N.Y.C., 1942-43; pub. info. asst. UNESCO, Paris, 1946-47; retail promotion mgr. Glamour Mag., 1955-61; advt. dir. Country Tweeds Co., N.Y.C., 1961-65; advt. dir. S. Augstein & Co., N.Y.C., 1966-72, Feature Ring Co., Inc., Gotham Ring Co., Inc., Fidco Inc., N.Y.C., 1972-79; dir. advt. and promotion Wasko Gold Products Corp., N.Y.C., 1979-81; advt. and mktg. cons., 1981—; advt. prodn. dir. N.E.I. Enterprises, Inc., 1984-85 . Served to lt. WAVES, 1943-46. Mem. Fashion Group N.Y. Inc., Women's Jewelry Assn. (corr. sec. 1983-85). Jewish.

GOLDFIELD, EMILY DAWSON, finance company executive, artist; b. Bklyn., May 31, 1947; d. Martin and Renee (Solow) Dawson; m. Stephen Gary Goldfield, June 17, 1973; children—Stacy Rose, Daniel James. B.S., U. Mich., 1969; M.Ed., Pa. State U., 1971; Ph.D., U. So. Calif., 1977. Chmn. bd. Provident Mut. Escrow, Encino, Calif., 1982—; exec. v.p. Hanover Investment Services, Encino, 1982—; v.p. Rancho Campo el Oro; dir. Hanover Funding, 1985—; dir. Investors Resale Services, Hanover Funding Corp., Encino, Real Estate Trustee Services, Encino, Bell Canyon Leasing. Author: The Value of Creative Dance, 1971; Development of Creative Dance, 1977. Minister Ch. of Scientology. U. Mich. scholar, 1969; Pa. State U. fellow, 1970, U. So. Calif. fellow, 1972. Mem. Mortgage Brokers Inst., Calif. Consumer Fin., Am. Technion Soc., Encino C. of C., San Fernando Valley Bd. Realtors , Calif. Escrow Assn., Nat. Assn. Realtors, Calif. Assn. Realtors, Visual Arts Assn., Am. Horse Show Assn., Paso Fino Horse Assn., Sierra Club, Bell Canyon Homeowners Assn. Club: Ferrari Owners. Office: Provident Mutual Escrow Suite 832 15760 Ventura Blvd Encino CA 91436

GOLDFINGER, CHARLES GERARD, financial company executive; b. Paris, Jan. 29, 1946; s. Elie Abe and Glita (Junghause) G.; m. Eva Maria Piewcewicz, Apr. 19, 1969; 1 child, Alexander Elie. Diploma in architecture, Nat. Fine Arts Sch., Paris, 1969; MArch, U. Calif., Berkeley, 1971, PhD, 1979. Research assoc. French Regional Planning Agy., Paris, 1969-70; project officer World Bank, Washington, 1975-80; dir. SEMA-METRA, Paris, 1980-83, S.W.I.F.T. s.c., Brussels, 1983-87; mng. dir. Global Electronic Fin. S.A., Brussels, 1987—. Author: La geofinance, 1986; monthly columnist Dynasteurs, 1987—. Founding mem. CEPS-PROMETHEE, Paris, 1983; mem. ThinkNet Commn., N.Y.C., 1987. Served with French armed forces, 1973-74. Mem. Internat. Fin. Club Paris, Advanced Fin. Inst. Paris. Home and Office: Global Electronic Fin SA, Av du Marquis de Villalobar 102, 1150 Brussels Belgium

GOLDFRANK, MRS. HERBERT J. See KAY, HELEN

GOLDHURST, WILLIAM, humanities and English educator, writer; b. N.Y.C., Aug. 8, 1929; s. Harry Golden and Genevieve (Gallagher) G.; m. Ellen Eiseman.; children: Barney, Rex. B.A., Kenyon Coll., 1953; M.A., Columbia U., 1956; Ph.D., Tulane U., 1962. Asst. instr. English Ohio State U., 1955-56; teaching fellow Tulane U. and Newcomb Coll., 1956-59; assoc. prof. English U. P.R., 1960-63; prof. humanities and English U. Fla., 1964—; Fulbright prof. Am. lit. univs. Buenos Aires, and La Plata, Argentina, fall 1969; lectr. Am. lit. to Peace Corps U. P.R., 1963; Edgar Allan Poe Meml. lectr., Richmond, Va., 1973; lectr. Santa Fe Community Coll. Author: F. Scott Fitzgerald and His Contemporaries, 1963, Our Own Confidence Man, 1979, also articles, photo—stories in nat. and internat. mags.; book reviewer lit. jours.; editor: Contours of Experience, 1967. Recipient Broome Lit. Agt. award for short fiction, 1979; local awards for poetry and photography; So. fellow, 1959-60; grantee Humanities Council and Faculty Devel., Grad. Sch. Research U. Fla., 1970-71, 72; Presdl. scholar U. Fla., 1975-76. Mem. Poe Soc. (Balt., Richmond), Popular Culture Assn. of South. Home: 3927 NW 21st St Gainesville FL 32605

GOLDIE, RAY ROBERT, lawyer; b. Dayton, Ohio, Apr. 1, 1920; s. Albert S. and Lillian (Hayman) G.; student U. So. Calif., 1943-44, J.D., 1957; student San Bernardino Valley Coll., 1950-51; JD U. So. Calif., 1957; m. Dorothy Roberta Zafman, Dec. 2, 1941; children—Marilyn, Deanne, Dayle, Ron R. Elec. appliance dealer, 1944-54; teaching asst. U. So. Calif. Law Sch., 1956-57; admitted to Calif. bar, 1957; dep. atty. gen. State of Calif., 1957-58; sole practice, San Bernardino, 1958-87. Pres., Trinity Acceptance Corp., 1948-53. Mem. World Peace Through Law Center, 1962—; regional dir. Legion Lex, U. So. Calif. Sch. Law, 1959-75; chmn. San Bernardino United Jewish Appeal, 1963; v.p. United Jewish Welfare Fund San Bernardino, 1964-66, Santa Anita Hosp., Lake Arrowhead, 1966-69. Bd. dirs. San Bernardino Med. Arts Corp. Served with AUS, 1942-43. Fellow Internat. Acad. Law and Sci.; mem. ABA, San Bernardino County Bar Assn., Riverside County Bar Assn., State Bar Calif., Am. Judicature Soc., Am. Soc. Hosp. Attys., Calif. Trial Lawyers Assn. (v.p. chpt. 1965-67, pres. 1967-68), Am. Arbitration Assn. (nat. panel arbitrators), Order of Coif, Nu Beta Epsilon (pres. 1956-57). Club: Lake Arrowhead Country (pres. 1972-73, 80-81), Lake Arrowhead Yacht, Club at Morningside. Home: 1 Hampton Ct Rancho Mirage CA 92270 Office: 44-100 Monterey Ave Palm Desert CA 92260

GOLDIE, RON ROBERT, lawyer; b. San Bernardino, Calif., Apr. 6, 1951; s. Ray R. and Dorothy R. (Zafman) G.; m. Betty J. Cooper, June 13, 1983; children: Meghan Ann, Rand R. Diploma, U. Paris, 1970; BA, U. So. Calif., 1972, MBA, JD, 1975. Bar: Calif. 1975, U.S. Dist. Ct. (cen., no. and so. dists.) Calif., U.S. Tax Ct., U.S. Ct. Appeals (2d, 9th and 11th cirs.). Atty. Goldie Law Corp., Los Angeles and San Bernardino, 1975-82; sole practice Los Angeles, 1982-86; prin. Law Offices of Ron R. Goldie, Los Angeles, 1986-88; sr. ptnr. Rosen, Wachtell & Gilbert, Los Angeles, 1988—. Republican. Jewish. Home: 762 Latimer Rd Rustic Canyon CA 90402 Office: Rosen Wachtell & Gilbert 1888 Century Park E Suite 2100 Los Angeles CA 90067

GOLDING, SIR WILLIAM GERALD, author; b. St. Columb, Cornwall, Eng., Sept. 19, 1911; s. Alec A. and Mildred A. G.; m. Ann Brookfield, 1939; children: David, Judith. B.A., Brasenose Coll., Oxford, Eng., 1935; M.A. hon. fellow, 1966; D. Litt. (hon.), U. Sussex, 1970, U. Kent, 1974, U. Warwick, 1981, Sorbonne, 1981, Oxford U., 1982. Tchr. Bishop Wordsworth's Sch., Wiltshire, Eng., 1940, 45-61. Settlement house work, dir., actor, writer, 1935-39, writer-in-residence, Hollins Coll., 1961-62; author: Poems, 1934, Lord of the Flies, 1954, The Inheritors, 1955, Pincher Martin, 1956, Free Fall, 1959, The Spire, 1964, The Hot Gates, 1965, The Pyramid, 1967, The Scorpion God, 1971, Darkness Visible, 1979 (James Tait Black Meml. prize), Rites of Passage, 1980 (Booker McConnel prize), A Moving Target, 1982, The Paper Men, 1984, An Egyptian Jour., 1985, Close Quarters, 1987; play Brass Butterfly, 1958. Served to lt. Royal Navy, 1940-45. Fellow Royal Soc. Lit., 1955, Companion of Lit., 1981; recipient Nobel prize for lit., 1983; created knight by Queen Elizabeth II, 1988. Address: care Faber & Faber, 3 Queen Sq, London WC1N 3AU, England *

GOLDMAN, BERNARD, leasing company executive; b. Boston, Apr. 16, 1928; s. Samuel and Edith E. (Feister) G.; children: Adria Lee Frenzel, Risa Joy Tajima, Gerald Scott, Jami Sue. A.S., Cambridge Jr. Coll., 1946; student, E.C.C., Boston U., 1947-54. With Bankers Leasing and Fin. Corp. subs. Sante Fe So. Pacific Corp., Chgo., 1955—; v.p. Bankers Leasing and Fin. Corp. subs. Sante Fe So. Pacific Corp., 1955-64, sr. v.p., controller, 1964-68, pres., dir., chief operating officer, 1969—, chief exec. officer, 1975—. Past trustee Temple Beth Shalom, Needham, Mass., Peninsula Temple Beth El, San Mateo; bd. dirs. Peninsula YMCA, San Mateo, Calif.; vice chmn. Calif. Draft Appeal Bd. Mem. Am. Assn. Equipment Lessors (acctg. com.), Western Assn. Equipment Lessors (tax com.), Am. Automotive Leasing Assn. (bd. dirs.), World Affairs Council. Republican. Club: Peninsula Golf and Country (San Mateo), The Commonwealth. Home: 1123 Royal Ln San Carlos CA 94070 Office: 2655 Campus Dr Suite 200 San Mateo CA 94403

GOLDMAN, EMANUEL, microbiology educator, film critic, pianist; b. N.Y.C., Feb. 19, 1945; s. Yehuda and Anne (Slochower) G.; m. Joan Wendy Millner, May 29, 1966 (div. 1975); m. Jill Katherine Brannis, Mar. 14, 1986. BA cum laude, Brandeis U., 1966; PhD in Biochemistry, MIT, 1972. Fellow in viral oncology Pub. Health Research Inst., N.Y.C., 1972-73; research fellow in pathology Harvard U. Med. Sch., Boston, 1973-75; assoc. in med. microbiology U. Calif., Irvine, 1975-77, asst. research microbiologist, 1977-79; asst. prof. microbiology N.J. Med. Sch., Newark, 1979-83, assoc. prof. microbiology, 1983—; cons. in pathology Harvard Med. Sch., 1976; coordinator N.Y. Area Research Club, Columbia U., 1982-85; piano player cocktail lounges. Author film critiques New U., Irvine, 1975-79; asst. editor, author film critiques, Boston, Phoenix, 1969-70; assoc. editor, author Boston Rev. of Arts, 1970-72; author sci. research papers. Active ACLU, Sierra Club, NOW. Damon Runyon fellow, 1973-75; Lievre sr. fellow, Calif. div. Am. Cancer Soc., 1977-79; research career devel. awardee Nat. Cancer Inst., NIH, 1983-88; recipient Faculty Exceptional Merit awards, U. Medicine and Dentistry N.J., 1980, 82. Mem. N.Y. Acad. Scis., Am. Soc. for Microbiology, N.Y./N.J. Molecular Biology Club, Roche Inst. (v.p. , mem. of organizing com. 1985—), N. Am. Vegetarian Soc. Democrat. Jewish. Home: 19 Garrison Ave Jersey City NJ 07306 Office: Dept Microbiology NJ Med Sch Newark NJ 07103

GOLDMAN, JOEL J., lawyer, oil and gas drilling company executive; b. N.Y.C., Sept. 7, 1940; s. Myron and Pearl (Jacobs) G.; m. Jane I. Stalker, July 23, 1973; children: Elizabeth Ann, Rebecca Lynn. BS, U. Va., 1962, JD, Syracuse U., 1965. Bar: N.Y. 1966, U.S. Dist. Ct. (we. dist.) N.Y. 1966. Law clk. Myron Goldman, N.Y.C., 1965; staff atty., chief trial counsel Legal Aid Soc. Rochester, N.Y., 1966-73; ptnr. Kaman, Berlove, Marafioti, Jacobstein & Goldman, Rochester, 1973—; lectr. family law; spl. investigator N.Y. State Spl. Commn. on Attica, 1972; mem. panel arbitrators Am. Arbitration Assn.; mem. faculty Nat. Bus. Inst., 1985—. Referee, Eastern Assn. Inter-Collegiate Football Ofcls., 1974—. Fellow Am. Acad. Matrimonial Lawyers; mem. ABA, N.Y. State Bar Assn. (exec. com. family law sect. 1982, mem. exec. com. 1981-86), Monroe County Bar Assn. (chmn. family law sect. 1982, exec. com. 1981—), Assn. Trial Lawyers Am. Jewish. Author continuing edn. materials. Contbg. editor Bender's Forms for Civil Practice, 1986, Medina's Bostwick, 1986. Home: 67 Mountain Rd Rochester NY 14625 Office: 13 S Fitzhugh St Suite 400 Rochester NY 14614

GOLDMAN, JOSEPH LAWRENCE, otolaryngologist, emeritus medical educator; b. N.Y.C., Jan. 16, 1904; s. Louis and Anna (Sapir) G.; A.B., Columbia U., 1924; M.D., L.I. Coll. Hosp. Med. Sch., 1927; m. Florence A. Green, Nov. 16, 1941 (dec.); children—Elizabeth Anne Goldman Sevin, Barbara Jane Goldman Steinbach, James Lawrence; m. Selma K. Jaffe, June 7, 1981. Intern, Jewish Hosp., Bklyn., 1927-29; resident otolaryngology Mt. Sinai Hosp., N.Y.C., 1929-31, fellow bacteriology, 1931-32, mem. staff, 1933—, dir. dept. otolaryngology, 1954-72, dir. emeritus, 1972—; asst. surgeon otolaryngology, then assoc. surgeon Bellevue Hosp., N.Y.C., 1935-54; practice medicine specializing in otolaryngology, 1932—; from asst. clin. prof. to assoc. prof. NYU Sch. Medicine, 1946-55; clin. prof. Columbia Coll. Physicians and Surgeons, 1955-67; prof. otolaryngology, chmn. dept. Mt. Sinai Sch. Medicine, 1966-72, emeritus, 1972—; prin. investigator research and tng. grants NIH, 1961—. Served to col., M.C., AUS, 1942-46. Diplomate Am. Bd. Otolaryngology. Recipient Disting. Service award Manhattan Eye, Ear and Throat Hosp., 1987. Mem. Am. Acad. Ophthalmology and Otolaryngology (v.p. 1964, Honor Key award and Cert. award 1959), Am. Laryngol., Rhinol. and Otol. Soc. (pres. 1969-70), Am. Broncho-esophagol. Assn., Am. Otol. Soc., Am. Laryngol. Assn. (Newcomb award 1976, award of merit 1985), Am. Soc. Head and Neck Surgery, Am. Soc. Ophthal. and Otolaryngol. Allergy, Am. Acad. Facial Plastic and Reconstructive Surgery (guest of honor 1985), N.Y. Acad. Medicine, AMA (chmn. sect. laryngology, otology and rhinology 1963, Hektoen Bronze medal 1969), Soc. Univ. Otolaryngologists, Alpha Omega Alpha, Sigma Alpha Mu. Editor: The Principles and Practice of Rhinology; contbr. articles to jours., chpts. to books; differentiated vasomotor rhinitis and sinusitis from infectious rhinitis and sinusitis by microbiologic and cytologic methods; introduced concept of combined high dosage preoperative radiation and surgery in treatment of advanced cancer of larynx and laryngopharynx. Home: 737 Park Ave New York NY 10021 Office: 55 E 87th St New York NY 10128

GOLDMAN, LEE, physician, educator, researcher; b. Phila., Jan. 6, 1948; s. Marvin and Kathryn (Schwartz) G.; m. Jill Steinhardt, Mar. 21, 1971; children—Jeff, Daniel, Robyn Sue. B.A., Yale U., 1969, M.D., 1973, M.P.H., 1973. Diplomate: Am. Bd. Internal Medicine. Intern U. Calif.-San Francisco, 1973-74, resident in med., 1974-75, Mass. Gen. Hosp., Boston, 1975-76; fellow in cardiology Yale-New Haven Hosp., 1976-78; asst. prof. medicine Harvard Med. Sch., 1978-83, assoc. prof., 1983—; asst. physician-in-chief dept. med. Brigham and Women's Hosp., Boston, 1983; dir. div. clin. epidemiology Joint Dept. Medicine, Brigham and Women's and Beth Israel Hosps. Contbr. numerous articles to profl. jours. Bd. dirs. Temple Shir Tikva, Wayland, Mass., 1982-84, v.p. 1985-86, pres. 1986-88. ACP teaching and research scholar, 1980-83; Henry J. Kaiser Family Found. scholar, 1982-87. Fellow ACP and Am. Coll. Cardiology; mem. Am. Soc. Clin. Investigation, Am. Fedn. Clin. Research, Soc. Med. Decision Making, Soc. Gen. Medicine (sec.-treas. 1986-88). Office: Brigham and Women's Hosp Dept of Medicine 75 Francis St Boston MA 02115

GOLDMAN, LEON, dermatologist, laser surgeon, hospital administrator; b. Cin., Dec. 7, 1905; s. Abraham and Fannie (Friedman) G.; m. Belle Hurwitz, Aug. 23, 1936; children—John, Steve, Carol. M.D., U. Cin., 1929. Intern, U. Cin. Hosp., 1929-30, resident, 1930-36, chief resident, 1933-36; asst. prof. dermatology U. Cin., 1949-50, assoc. prof., 1950-51, prof., 1951-76, prof. emeritus, 1976—, dir. dermatology U. Cin. Med. Center, 1951-76, dir. laser lab., 1971-76; dir. Laser Treatment Ctr., Jewish Hosp. Cin., 1980—; laser cons. dept. dermatology Naval Hosp., San Diego, 1988—. Served with M.C., USAR, 1943. Recipient award for devel. laser medicine Internat. Soc. Laser Surgery, Tokyo, 1981, Finnerud award Dermatology Found., 1984, Xanar Gold medal, 1985, Leon Goldman medal Am. Soc. Dermatol. Surgery, 1985, Daniel Drake medal Coll. Medicine U. Cin., 1988; named Father of Laser Medicine, Opto-Elektronic Conf., Munich, W.Ger., 1979; named honored citizen Cin. Bicentennial, 1988. Mem. Am. Dermatol. Assn., Am. Soc. Laser Medicine and Surgery (pres. 1979-80, editor newsletter 1980—) W. D. Mark medal 1982), Soc. Investigative Dermatology, Am. Soc. Dermatol. Surgery, Internat. Confedn. Council Laser Medicine (pres. 1982-86), Laser Inst. Am. (formerly Laser Industry Assn., award for valuable service 1977, Schawlow medal 1985), Sigma Xi, Alpha Omega Alpha. Jewish. Club: Losantiville. Author books, including: The Biomedical Laser; Applications of the Laser; Laser Medicine and Surgery in Dermatology; Laser Medicine; contbr. numerous articles on dermatology and laser tech. to profl. jours., articles on history and art to sci. jours. Avocations: sculpture, photography, laser art. Office: US Naval Hosp Dept Dermatology Code 43 San Diego CA 92134

GOLDMAN, MAYNARD, lawyer, financial consultant, retail company executive; b. Boston, Aug. 8, 1937; s. Sumner S. and Harriette F. Goldman; m. Margery Loewenberg, June 12, 1967 (div.); 1 child, Derek Anthony. BA, U. Mich., 1959; LLB, Harvard U., 1962. Bar: Mass. 1962. Sr. cons. Harbridge House, Inc., Boston, 1963-67, Arthur D. Little Inc., Cambridge, Mass., 1968-69; asst. to pres. ITT Sheraton Corp. Am., Boston, 1970-71; chmn., treas. Goldman Del Rossi & Co., Inc., Boston, 1973-79; pres. Hurok Concerts Inc., 1976-77; prin., gen. mgr. Charles Sumner, Inc., Boston, 1977-84; pres. Maynard Goldman and Assocs., Boston, 1985—; dir., treas. Suzanne Inc. 1986—; dir. various cos.; fin. cons., 1963—; exec. dir. Nat. Def. Edn. Inst., 1965-67; chmn. Commonwealth Mass. Outdoor Advt. Bd. Bd. mgrs. Mass. Eye and Ear Infirmary; bd. dirs. Boston Zool. Soc., Crime and Justice Found.; bd. trustees Wang Ctr.; bd. visitors Sch. Theatre Arts, Boston U. Mem. Am. Bar Assn., Am. Arbitration Assn. Clubs: Belmont (Mass.) Country; Harvard (Boston), Algonquin. Home: 375 Beacon St Boston MA 02116 Office: 27 State St Boston MA 02109

GOLDMAN, ROBERT HURON, lawyer; b. Boston, Nov. 24, 1918; s. Frank and Rose (Sydeman) G.; m. Charlotte R. Rubens, July 5, 1945; children: Wendy Eve, Randolph Rubens. A.B., Harvard U., 1939, LL.B.,

1943. Bar: N.Y. State 1945, Mass. 1951. Practiced in N.Y.C., 1945-50, Lowell, Mass., 1951—; law clk. Judge Learned Hand, U.S. Ct. Appeals, 1943-44; partner firm Goldman and Curtis (and predecessor firms), 1951—; columnist Lowell Sunday Sun Daily, 1954-78; v.p., asso. pub. Malden (Mass.) Evening News, 1969-86, Medford (Mass.) Daily Mercury, 1969-86, Melrose (Mass.) Evening News, 1969-86; mem. adv. bd. Baybank Middlesex., 1966-84; Radio commentator on internat. affairs, 1954-86. Author: A Newspaperman's Handbook of the Libel Law of Massachusetts, 1966, rev., 1974, The Law of Libel—Present and Future, 1969; Editor: Harvard Law Review, 1943. Chmn. Greater Lowell Civic Com., 1952-55, Lowell Hist. Soc., 1957-60, Lowell Devel. and Indsl. Commn., 1959-60; Del. Republican State Conv., 1960-62; Bd. dirs. Boston World Affairs Council, 1960-82. Named Citizen of Year Greater Lowell Civic Com., 1956. Mem. ABA (mem. nat. com. on consumer protection 1972-73, Sherman Act com. 1973—), Mass. Bar Assn. (chmn. bar-press com. 1973-76), Middlesex County Bar Assn., Lowell Bar Assn., Boston Bar Assn., Phi Beta Kappa. Club: Harvard (dir. Lowell 1968—). Home: 8 Rolling Ridge Rd Andover MA 01810 Office: 4th Floor 144 Merrimack St Lowell MA 01852

GOLDMAN, ROBERT JOSEPH, life insurance company executive; b. Bronx, N.Y., Jan. 18, 1939; s. Jacob and Gertrude (Sussman) G.; m. Brenda Chasen, July 11, 1965. BA, Queens Coll., 1960; MPA, Golden Gate U., 1976. CLU. Field underwriter N.Y. Life Ins. Co., Boston, 1977-81; sr. sales tng. asst. Sun Life Assurance Co. of Can., Wellesley Hills, MA, 1981-83, mktg. legislation coordinator, 1983-86, sr. quality bus. cons., 1986-87, disability income adminstr., 1987—. Contbr. articles to profl. jours. Prin. bassoonist and soloist Brookline (Mass.) Symphony Orch., 1982—. Served to capt. USAF. Recipient 1981, Ann. Pub. Speaking Contest winner, 1977-78, 80, 85, 87. Mem. Nat. Assn. Life Underwriters, Mass. Assn. Life Underwriters (editor 1981-82), Boston Life Underwriters Assn. (bd. dirs. chpt. 1982-85, editorial bd), Am. Soc. Chartered Life Underwriters, FLMI Soc. Greater Boston (v.p. 1987-88, pres. 1988—). Democrat. Club: Toastmasters Internat. (Portsmouth, N.H.) (pres. 1980, area gov. 1981-82, founder, 1st pres. Wellesley Hills, Mass. 1985), Toastmaster of Yr. award 1981). Home: 18 Mayflower Rd Winchester MA 01890 Office: Sun Life Assurance Co of Can One Sun Life Exec Pk Wellesley Hills MA 02181

GOLDMANN, ROLF LENNART, communication company executive; b. Stockholm, Sweden, Feb. 20, 1951; arrived in Switzerland, 1955.; s. Heinz and Gullevi (Andersson) G.; m. Jette Damgaard, 1971; children: Mattias, Alexander. BA in Psychology, U. Lund, Sweden, 1987. Pres. Profl. Communication Tng. PLT, Ltd., Geneva, Switzerland, 1975—. Home: 14 Chemin Sous-Cherre, CH-1245 Lollonge-Bellerive Switzerland Office: Profl Communications Tng PCT Ltd, 7 Robert-De-Traz, CH-1206 Geneva Switzerland

GOLDNEY, ROBERT DONALD, psychiatrist, educator; b. Adelaide, Australia, Dec. 2, 1943; s. Murray Rufus and Nance (Panton) G.; m. Helen Christine Parsons, May 13, 1967; children—Katherine Ann, Jane Louise, Timothy Robert. M.B.B.S., Adelaide U., 1967, M.D., 1979. Intern Launceston Hosp. (Tasmania), 1968; resident Repatriation Hosp., South Australia, 1969; resident Glenside Hosp. (South Australia), 1970-72, psychiatrist, 1973-74, dir. Dibden research unit, 1981-85; sr. lectr. U. Adelaide (South Australia), 1974-81; clin. assoc. prof. Flinders U. (South Australia), 1981—; sr. vis. cons. Royal Adelaide Hosp., 1981—. Contbr. articles on suicidal behavior and psychiat. edn. to profl. jours. Fellow Royal Australian and N.Z. Coll. Psychiatrists, Royal Coll. Psychiatrists. Office: Suite 3, 142 Ward St, North Adelaide 5600, Australia

GOLDSCHEIDER, SIDNEY, lawyer; b. Balt., Mar. 27, 1920; s. Harry and Esther Goldscheider; m. Sylvia Glick, June 13, 1943; children: Judith, Alan, Eileen (dec.). JD summa cum laude, U. Balt., 1942. Bar: Md. 1942, U.S. Ct. Appeals (4th cir.) 1942. Sole practice Balt., 1942—; with enforcement div. Office of Price Adminstrn., Balt., 1943-45; bd. dirs. Budget Rent-a-Car of N.Y.C. Mem. Balt. Mus. of Art, Save-a-Heart Found, Am. Jewish Congress, Shaarei Tfiloh Conngregation, Shaarei Tfiloh Congregation, Ohel Yaacov Congregation, Beth Tfiloh Brotherhood, Beth Jacob Brotherhood; bd. dirs. Beth Jacob Congregation, Balt., Safety First Club of Md.; sec. One Slade Condominium Council of Co-owners, Balt.; co-chmn. Shaare Zedek Med. Ctr. in Jerusalem, com. mem. Israel Bonds Ambassador's Ball; mem. Met. Civic Assn. Honoree, Beth Jacob Congregation, 1973, 86, State of Israel Bonds, 1976; recipient citations Gov. Md., 1982, 86; City of Balt., 1982; Sidney Goldscheider Day proclaimed by Baltimore County and by City of Balt., Jan. 29, 1986; Disting. Service resolution Md. Ho. of Dels., 1986. Mem. Balt. City Bar Assn., Md. State Bar Assn., Md. Trial Lawyers Assn., U. Balt. Alumni Assn., Balt. C. of C., Jewish Hist. Soc., Zionist Orgn. Am., Hebrew Orthodox Meml. Soc., Associated Jewish Charities and Welfare Fund (lawyer's div.), Israel Prime Minister's Club, Am. Philatelic Soc., Heuisler Honor Soc., Phi Delta Tau. Lodge: Schreter B'nai B'rith (Outstanding Citizen award 1982). Home: 1 Slade Ave Baltimore MD 21208 Office: 218 E Lexington St Baltimore MD 21202

GOLDSCHMID, HARVEY JEROME, legal educator; b. N.Y.C., May 6, 1940; s. Bernard and Rose (Braiker) G.; m. Mary Tait Seibert, Dec. 22, 1973; children: Charles Maxwell, Paul MacNeil, Joseph Tait. A.B., Columbia U., 1962, J.D., 1965. Bar: N.Y. 1965, U.S. Supreme Ct. 1970. Law clk. to judge 2d Circuit Ct. Appeals, N.Y.C., 1965-66; assoc. firm Debevoise & Plimpton, N.Y.C., 1966-70; asst. prof. law Columbia U., 1970-71, assoc. prof., 1971-73, prof., 1973-84, Dwight prof. law, 1984—, dir. Center for Law and Econ. Studies, 1975-78; cons. in field to public and pvt. orgns.; mem. planning and program com. 2d Cir. Jud. Conf., 1982-85; reporter 2d cir. Jud. Conf. Evaluation com., 1980-82, 88—. Author: (with others) Cases and Materials on Trade Regulation, 1975, 2d edit., 1983; editor: (with others) Industrial Concentration: The New Learning, 1974, Business Disclosure: Government's Need to Know, 1979, (with others) The Impact of the Modern Corporation, 1984. Mem. ABA, Am. Law Inst. (dep. chief reporter 1980-84, reporter part IV corp. governance project), N.Y. State Bar Assn., Assn. Bar City N.Y. (v.p. 1985-86, chmn. exec. com. 1984-85, chmn. com. on antitrust and trade regulation 1971-74, nominating com., com. on the second century, chmn. audit com. 1988—), Assn. Am. Law Schs. (chmn. sect. antitrust and econ. regulation 1976-78), Am. Assn. Internat. Commn. Jurists (bd. dirs.), Phi Beta Kappa. Clubs: Century Assn., Riverdale Yacht (bd. govs. 1987—). Office: Columbia U 435 W 116th St New York NY 10027

GOLDSCHMIDT, NEIL EDWARD, governor of Oregon; b. Eugene, Oreg., June 16, 1940; s. Lester H. and Annette (Levin) G.; m. Margaret Wood; children: Joshua, Rebecca. A.B. in Polit. Sci., U. Oreg., 1963; LL.B., U. Calif., 1967. Atty. Legal Aid Oreg., 1967-70; commr. City of Portland, 1971-72, mayor, 1973-79; sec. transp. Washington, 1979-81; v.p. internat. mktg. NIKE/BRS, Inc., Beaverton, Oreg., from 1981; gov. State of Oreg., 1987—; dir. Nat. Semi-Condr. Corp., Gelco Corp. Civil rights worker, Miss., 1964; Former chmn. transp. com. U.S. Conf. Mayors, also chmn. housing and community devel. com.; former co-chmn. energy task force Nat. League Cities; bd. dirs. Kaiser Permanente Found. Health Plan, 1981—. Named Outstanding Young Man Am., 1972. Address: 3900 SW Murray Blvd Beaverton OR 97005 Office: Govs Office 254 State Capitol Bldg Salem OR 97310 *

GOLDSCHMIDT, RICHARD, oil company executive; b. Luanda, Portugal, Dec. 31, 1932; s. Louis and Hertha Helene (Heinemann) G.; m. Maria Emilia Claro, July 19, 1958; children: Maria Helena Claro, Maria Teresa Claro. Student, Coll. Econs., Lisbon, Portugal, 1951; student, Spartan Sch. Aeros., Tulsa, 1952-54. Flight simulator instr. Angola Airlines, Luanda, 1956-61, Civil Aviation Authority, Lisbon, 1961-64; aviation supt. Sacor-Nat. Oil Co., Lisbon, 1965-71; mgr. export dept. Sacor-Nat. Oil Co., 1971-81; export mgr. Petrogal-Nat. Oil Co., 1981-83; mgr. adminstrv. services Petrogal-Nat. Oil Co., Lisbon, 1983—. Contbr. articles to profl. jours. Served to 2d. lt. Portugal Air Force, 1954-56. Mem. bd. dirs. Aero Club Portugal. Home: Rua Pascoal de Melo, 62-40 ESQ, 1000 Lisbon Portugal Office: Petroleos de Portugal EP, Petrogal, Rua das Flores 7, 1200 Lisbon Portugal

GOLDSMITH, LOWELL ALAN, medical educator; b. Bklyn., Mar. 29, 1938; s. Isidore Alexander and Ida (Kaplan) G.; m. Carol Amreich, June 11, 1960; children: Meredith, Eileen. AB, Columbia Coll., 1959; MD, SUNY, Bklyn., 1963. Intern, then resident in medicine UCLA Med. Ctr., 1963-65; resident in dermatology Harvard Med. Sch., Boston, 1967-69; asst. prof. dermatology Harvard U. Med. Sch., Boston, 1970-73; asst. in dermatology Mass. Gen. Hosp., Boston, 1970-71, asst. dermatologist, 1971-73; assoc. prof. medicine Duke U. Med. Ctr., Durham, N.C., 1973-78, prof., 1978-81; James H. Sterner prof. dermatology Sch. Medicine and Dentistry, U. Rochester, N.Y., 1981—, chief dermatology unit, 1981-87, acting chmn. dept. medicine, 1985-87, chmn. dept. dermatology, 1987—; bd. dirs. Monroe Community Hosp., Rochester, Ctr. Alternatives Animal Testing, Balt.;. Author, editor Biochemistry and Physiology of the Skin, 1983. Served with USPHS, 1965-67. Recipient Research Career Devel. award USPHS, 1975-80; Macy Found. fellow, 1978-79, Carl Herzog fellow Am. Dermatol. Assn. Mem. Assn. Am. Physicians, Soc. Investigative Dermatology (bd. dirs.), N.Y. State Soc. Dermatology (pres. 1986—), Buffalo-Rochester Dermatology Soc. (pres. 1987), Rochester Dermatology Soc., Rochester Acad. Medicine, Alpha Omega Alpha. Democrat. Jewish. Office: Univ of Rochester Dept Dermatology 601 Elmwood Ave Box 697 Rochester NY 14642

GOLDSMITH, STANLEY JOSEPH, nuclear medicine physician, educator; b. Bklyn., Aug. 17, 1937; s. Jack and Mae (Greenzweig) G.; m. Miriam Schulman, June 6, 1959; children—Ira, Arthur, Beth, Mark. B.A., Columbia U., 1958; M.D., SUNY-Downstate Med. Ctr., 1962. Diplomate: Am. Bd. Internal Medicine, Am. Bd. Nuclear Medicine. Intern SUNY-Kings County Med. Center, Bklyn., 1962-63, resident, 1965-66, chief resident, 1966-67; fellow in endocrinology Mt. Sinai Hosp., N.Y.C., 1967-68, dir., 1973—; research assoc. radioisotope service Bronx (N.Y.) VA Hosp., 1968-69; dir. nuclear medicine, asst. dir. endocrine dept. Nassau County Med. Ctr., East Meadow, N.Y., 1969-73; asst. prof. medicine radiology SUNY-Stony Brook Health Sci. Ctr., 1971-73, asst. prof. medicine Mt. Sinai Sch. Medicine, 1973-76, assoc. prof., 1976-84, prof. clin. medicine, 1985—; research collborator Brookhaven Nat. Labs., Upton, N.Y., 1971-75; cons. nuclear medicine; cons. dept. health State of N.Y., 1973-77, Health Services Adminstrn., N.Y.C., 1976; radiopharm. adv. com. low level waste diposal site commn. FDA, N.Y., 1987—. Editor-in-chief: Newsline; assoc. Jour. Nuclear Medicine; mem. editorial bds.: Am. Jour. Cardiology, 1978-82, Picker Jour. Nuclear Medicine Instrumentation, 1980; reviewer: Israeli Jour. Med. Scis., 1979, Jour. AMA, 1983—, Jour. Am. Coll. Cardiology, 1984—. Served to capt. U.S. Army, 1963-65. Fellow Am. Coll. Cardiology, ACP, Am. Coll. Nuclear Physicians (chmn. nuclear med. tech. affairs); mem. AAAS, Am. Fedn. Clin. Research, Endocrine Soc., N.Y. Acad. Scis., Radiol. Soc. N.Am. Soc. Nuclear Medicine trustee 1982-84, pres.-elect 1984-85, pres. 1985-86, sec. Greater N.Y. chpt. 1975-78, pres. 1979-80, mem. nuclear med. tech. cert. bd. 1979-81). Home: 72 Ivy Way Port Washington NY 11050 Office: Mt Sinai Sch of Medicine Dept of Nuclear Medicine New York NY 10029

GOLDSMITH, WILLIAM ALEE, environmental engineer; b. Memphis, Nov. 5, 1941; s. Jack Gene and Louise Elizabeth (Alston) G.; m. LaVance Davis, June 1, 1965; children—Jack Gregory, William Vance, Lara Ellen. B.S., Miss. State U., 1964, M.S., 1966; Ph.D., U. Fla., 1968. San. engr. U.S. EPA, Dallas, 1971-73; asst. prof. U. So. Miss., Hattiesburg, 1973-74; staff mem. Los Alamos Sci. Lab., 1974-75; research staff mem. Oak Ridge Nat. Lab., 1975-81; remedial action survey and certification activities program mgr., 1981-82; engring. specialist Bechtel Nat., Inc., Oak Ridge, 1982-86; sr. project mgr. Lee Wan and Assocs., Inc., Oak Ridge, Tenn., 1986-87, dir. for Oak Ridge office, 1987—. Treas. Covenant Presbyn. Ch., Oak Ridge, 1978; stewardship chmn. First United Meth. Ch., Oak Ridge, 1981-87. Served to capt. AUS, 1969-71. Mem. Am. Chem. Soc., Am. Nuclear Soc., AAAS, Health Physics Soc. (councilman East Tenn. chpt. 1979-82), N.Y. Acad. Scis., Sigma Xi, Tau Beta Pi, Phi Kappa Phi. Office: Lee Wan and Assocs Inc 700 S Illinois Ave Suite A-202 Oak Ridge TN 37830

GOLDSMITH, WILLIS JAY, lawyer; b. Paris, Feb. 21, 1947; came to U.S., 1949; s. Irving and Alice (Rosenfeld) G.; m. Marilynn Jacobson, Aug. 12, 1973; children—Andrew Edward, Helene Sara. A.B., Brown U., 1969; J.D., NYU, 1972. Bar: N.Y. 1973, U.S. Ct. Appeals (2d cir.) 1975, D.C. 1978, U.S. Ct. Appeals (4th cir.) 1979, U.S. Ct. Appeals (D.C. cir.) 1979, U.S. Supreme Ct. 1980, U.S. Ct. Appeals (6th. cir.) 1985. Att. Dept. Labor, Washington, 1972-74; assoc. Guggenheimer & Untermyer, N.Y.C., 1974-77; assoc. Seyfarth, Shaw, Fairweather & Geraldson, Washington, 1977-79, ptnr., 1979-83; ptnr. Jones, Day, Reavis & Pogue, Washington, 1983—; adjunct prof. law Georgetown U., 1988—. Contbg. editor Employee Relations Law Jour., 1983—; assoc. editor Occupational Safety and Health Law. Mem. ABA (sect. labor and employment law, com. on occupational safety and health law 1978—), D.C. Bar Assn. Democrat. Jewish. Clubs: University (Washington); Kenwood Golf and Country (Bethesda, Md.). Home: 6409 Elmwood Rd Chevy Chase MD 20815 Office: Jones Day Reavis & Pogue 1450 G St NW Suite 600 Washington DC 20005

GOLDSTEIN, ALLAN LEONARD, biochemist, educator; b. Bronx, N.Y., Nov. 8, 1937; s. Morris and Miriam (Siegel) G.; m. Linda Jo Tish, Dec. 23, 1975; children: Jennifer Joy, Dawn Eden, Adam Lee. B.S., Wagner Coll., 1959; M.S., Rutgers U., 1961, Ph.D., 1964. Teaching asst. Rutgers U., New Brunswick, N.J., 1959-61; asst. instr. biology 1961-63, instr. physiology, 1963-64; research fellow Albert Einstein Coll. Medicine, 1964-66, instr. biochemistry, 1966-67, asst. prof., 1967-71, asso. prof., 1971-72; prof., dir. div. biochemistry U. Tex. Med. Br., Galveston, 1972-78; acting dir. multidisciplinary research program in mental health U. Tex. Med. Br., 1973-78; prof., chmn. dept. biochemistry George Washington U. Sch. Medicine, Washington, 1978—, pres., sci. dir. Inst. for Advanced Studies in Immunology and Aging,, 1985—; chmn. bd. Alpha 1 Biomeds.; cons. Syntex Research, 1972-74, Hoffmann-LaRoche, 1974-82; spl. cons. bd. sci. counselors Nat. Inst. Allergy and Infectious Diseases, 1975-80; mem. med. research service rev. bd. in oncology VA, 1977-80; cons. mem. decisive network com. Biol. Response Modifiers Program, Div. Cancer Treatment, Nat. Cancer Inst., 1982—; mem. sci. adv. com. to pres. Papanicolaou Cancer Research Inst. Miami, Inc., 1981-84 ; mem. AIDS task force adv. com. Nat. Cancer Inst., 1983-84, sci. bd. Alliance for Aging Research, 1986—. Recipient Career Scientist award Health Research Council, City of N.Y., 1967; Alumni Achievement award Wagner Coll., 1974; Gordon Wilson medal Am. Clin. and Climatol. Soc., 1976; Distinguished Faculty Research award U. Tex. Sch. Biomed. Scis., 1976; Van Dyke award in pharmacology Columbia Coll. Phys. and Surgs., 1984; Vis. Prof. award Burroughs Wellcome Found., FASEB, 1986. Mem. Internat. Soc. Exptl. Hematology, AAAS, Endocrine Soc., Am. Soc. Biol. Chemists, Am. Assn. Immunologists, N.Y. Acad. Scis., Reticuloendothelial Soc., Internat. Soc. Immunopharmacology (council mem. 1985—), Assn. Med. Sch. Chmn. of Depts. Biochemistry, AAUP, Sigma Xi. Club: Toastmasters Internat. (pres. N.Y. chpt. 1971). Home: 6800 Glenbrook Rd Bethesda MD 20814

GOLDSTEIN, BERNARD HERBERT, lawyer; b. N.Y.C., June 7, 1907; s. Joseph D. and Gesela (Jerchower) G.; m. Edith I. Spivack, Dec. 22, 1933; children—Rita (Mrs. Robert Christopher), Amy (Mrs. Geoffrey Bass). B.S.S., CCNY, 1927; LL.B., Columbia U., 1930. Bar: N.Y. bar 1932, U.S. Supreme Ct. bar 1964. Asso. gen. counsel Liggett Drug Co., Inc., N.Y.C., 1933-44; partner Roy M. Sterne & Bernard H. Goldstein, N.Y.C., 1944-48, Gettner, Simon & Asher, 1948-59, Tenzer, Greenblatt, Fallon & Kaplan, 1959—; lectr. joint com. Am. Law Inst.-Am. Bar Assn., 1969—. Contbr. articles to profl. jours. Mem. World Peace Through Law Center, Washington, 1969—; mem. Citizens Adv. Com. to Dept. Housing Preservation and Devel., N.Y.C., 1969—; Bd. dirs. Conf. Jewish Social Studies, 1948—. Mem. Assn. Bar City N.Y. (com. chmn. 1971-82), N.Y. County Lawyers Assn. (dir. 1971-78), ABA. Club: Princeton. Home: 21 Colonial Rd Port Washington NY 11050 Office: Chrysler Bldg 405 Lexington Ave New York NY 10174

GOLDSTEIN, BURTON JACK, psychiatrist; b. Balt., Sept. 23, 1930; s. Maurice and Roz (Levin) G.; children: Howard, Herbert, Brian. B.S. in Pharmacy, U. Md., 1953, M.D., 1960. Diplomate Am. Bd. Psychiatry and Neurology (bd. examiner). Intern Jackson Meml. Hosp., Miami, Fla., 1960-61; NIMH fellow in psychiatry Jackson Meml. Hosp., 1961-63, chief resident, 1963-64; dir. div. clin. psychopharmacology, dept. psychiatry U. Miami, 1964—, chief div. research, 1964-71, prof. pharmacology, 1973—, prof. psychiatry, 1973—, acting chmn. dept. psychiatry, 1983-85; bd. advs. Fla. Mental Health Inst. U. S. Fla.; cons. in psychiat. research South Fla. State Hosp., West Hollywood; cons. indsl. security program Dept. Def.; cons. VA Psychiatry Service, Miami; chmn. panel on neuropharmacologic drugs U.S. Pharmacopeial Conv., Inc. Mem. editorial bd. Miami Medicine, Clin. Advancement in Treatment of Depression; contbr. chpts. to books, articles to profl. publs. Served to capt. AUS, 1953-55. Fellow Am. Psychiat. Assn., Am. Coll. Psychiatrists, Am. Coll. Pharmacology; mem. Fla., Dade County med. assns., Am. Coll. Neuropsychopharmacology, Royal Soc. Health, Am. Assn. Clin. Pharmacology and Chemotherapy, Collegium Internationale Neuropsychopharmacologium, South Fla. Psychiat. Soc. Office: U Miami Sch Medicine Dept Psychiatry D4-12 1500 NW 12th Ave Suite 1103 Miami FL 33136

GOLDSTEIN, HOWARD BERNARD, investment banker, advertising and marketing executive, artist, photographer; b. Bronx, N.Y., Dec. 4, 1943; s. Maurice and Matilda Goldstein; B.F.A., Pratt Inst., 1970; m. Susan Nadine Goldberg, June 25, 1967; children—Jill Alecya, Brett Adam. Art dir. Fairfax Advt. div. Ogilvy & Mather, Inc., N.Y.C., 1968-72; creative dir. Hoffman Advt., N.Y.C., 1972-80, Miller, Addison, Steele, Inc., N.Y.C., 1980-82; pres. Gould Advt., Cliffside Park, N.J., 1969—; registered securities broker,1969, br. officer tax shelter coordinator E.F. Hutton & Co., Inc., 1983-85; registered security broker, sr. v.p. Lehman Bros. Shearson Lehman Bros., Inc., 1985—. Vice pres., bd. dirs. Winston Tower 200, Condominium Assn.; Mem. Internat. Assn. Fin. Planning, Inst. Cert. Fin. Planners, Coll. Cert. Fin. Planners, Denver Grad. Police & Fire Acad. of Bergen County, N.J., June 12, 1986. Fin. officer N.J. State Police Office of Emergency Mgmt., Cliffside Park, 1986; spl. police officer Cliffside Park Police Dept., N.J. State Police Benevolent Assn., 1986—; mem. Graphic Artists Guild, 1976-80, Bronx Coutny Hist. Soc., 1968-71, Cliffside Park Baseball Assn., 1979—, coach, 1981, 83; sponsor Project High Frontier, U.S. Govt., 1986, sustaining mem. Rep. Nat. Com., 1981—; preferred mem. U.S. Senatorial Club, 1984—; Sachs art scholar, 1955; Exhibited Bronx Hist. Soc. photo show, N.Y.C., 1970; paintings at Soc. of Illustrators show, 1971-72; numerous other shows. Recipient medal for art service Youth Friends Assn., 1961, Ga. Pacific award, 1978. Mem. Tenafly Rifle and Pistol Club Inc., Nat. Rifle Assn. Jewish. Clubs: Fort Lee Racquetball. Lodge: Bnai Brith. Address: 200 Winston Dr Cliffside Park NJ 07010

GOLDSTEIN, IRVING ROBERT, mechanical engineer, educator, consultant; b. Jersey City, N.J., Apr. 28, 1916; s. David and Anna (Krug) G.; m. Natalie Evelyn Glattstein, Jan. 30, 1949; children—Barbara Joy, David Lee. B.S.M.E., Newark Coll. Engring., 1939; M.S.M.E., Stevens Inst. Tech., 1947. Registered profl. engr., N.J., Calif. Field worker, N.J. Dept. Edn., 1938-39, indsl. engr., Maidenform Co., 1939-40, cost analyst, William Bal Corp., 1940-41, resident insp. N.Y. Ordnance Dist., 1941-43, sales rep., Eagle Hosiery Co., 1946-47, instr. dept. indsl. and mgmt. engring. N.J. Inst. Tech., 1947-50, asst. prof., 1950-55, assoc. prof., 1955-70, prof., 1970-81, prof. emeritus, 1981—; cons. engr. I. R. Goldstein, P.E., Springfield, N.J., 1967—; lectr. in field, rep. Am. Nat. Studies Inst., 1970-73, Engr. Joint Council Com. for Am. Bicentennial, 1975-78, dir. work measures and method engring div. Inst. Indsl. Engrs., 1970-73, conf. chmn., 1973-81. Contbr. articles to profl. jours. Served with U.S. Army, 1943-46, ETO. Fellow Inst. Indsl. Engrs. (rep. 1970-82, Phil Carroll Achievement award 1975, Disting. Service award Met. N.J. chpt. 1970, 76, 85); mem. ASME (life), Ops. Research Soc. Am., Inst. Mgmt. Scis., Nat. Soc. Profl. Engrs. (meeting coordinator 1970-81, vice chmn. 1981-83, treas. 1983-86, mem. N.J. com. for student guidance), N.Y. Acad. Scis., Order of Engr., Alpha Pi Mu, Pi Tau Sigma. Address: 21 Janet Ln Springfield NJ 07081

GOLDSTEIN, JOSEPH LEONARD, physician, genetics educator; b. Sumter, S.C., Apr. 18, 1940; s. Isadore E. and Fannie A. Goldstein. B.S., Washington and Lee U., Lexington, Va., 1962; M.D., U. Tex., Dallas, 1966; D.Sc. (hon.), U. Chgo., 1982, Rensselaer Poly. Inst., 1982, Washington and Lee U., 1986. Intern, then resident in medicine Mass. Gen. Hosp., Boston, 1966-68; clin. assoc. NIH, 1968-70; postdoctoral fellow U. Wash., Seattle, 1970-72; mem. faculty U. Tex. Health Scis. Ctr., Dallas, 1972—, Paul J. Thomas prof. medicine, chmn. dept. molecular genetics, 1977—, regental prof., 1985—; Harvey Soc. lectr., 1977; mem. sci. rev. bd. Howard Hughes Med. Inst., 1978-84, med. adv. bd., 1985—; non-resident fellow The Salk Inst., 1983—. Co-author: The Metabolic Basis of Inherited Disease, 5th edit., 1983; editorial bd. Jour. Biol. Chemistry, 1981-85, Cell, 1983—, Jour. Clin. Investigation, 1977-82, Ann. Rev. Genetics, 1980-85, Arteriosclerosis, 1981-87, Sci. 1985-87. Sci. adv. bd. Welch Found., 1986—; bd. dirs. Passano Found., 1985—. Recipient Heinrich-Wieland prize, 1974, Pfizer award in enzyme chemistry Am. Chem. Soc., 1976; Passano award Johns Hopkins U., 1978; Gairdner Found. award, 1981; award in biol. and med. scis. N.Y. Acad. Scis., 1981; Lita Annenberg Hazen award, 1982; Research Achievement reward Am. Heart Assn., 1984; Louisa Gross Horwitz award, 1984; 3M Life Scis. award, 1984, Albert Lasker award in Basic Med. Research, 1985; Nobel Prize in Physiology or Medicine, 1985, Trustees' medal Mass. Gen. Hosp., 1986. Mem. Nat. Acad. Scis. (Lounsbery award 1979), Assn. Am. Physicians, Am. Soc. Clin. Investigation (pres. 1985-86), Am. Soc. Human Genetics, Amer. Acad. Arts and Scis., Am. Soc. Biol. Chemists, A.C.P. (award 1986), Am. Fedn. Clin. Research, Am. Philos. Soc., Phi Beta Kappa, Alpha Omega Alpha. Home: 3831 Turtle Creek Blvd Apt #22-B Dallas TX 75219 Office: Univ of Texas Health Sci Ctr 5323 Harry Hines Blvd Dallas TX 75235

GOLDSTEIN, MANFRED, consultant; b. Vienna, Austria, Jan. 30, 1927; came to U.S., 1939, naturalized, 1945; s. Isadore and Anna (Hahn) G.; m. Shirley Marie Lavine, Aug. 27, 1950; children—Cindy Marie, Lynn Alyse. Student Manhattan Trade Center, 1947; E.E., Capitol Radio Engring. Inst., 1963; student L.I. U., 1961, Indsl. Coll. Armed Forces, 1967-68. Sr. technician Bklyn. Radio, 1953-55, Budd Stanley, Inc., Long Island City, N.Y., 1955; lead engr. telephone equipment Precision Indsl. Design Newark, 1955-57; project engr., contract adminstr., sales mgr. Lieco, Inc., Syossett, N.Y. 1957-65, v.p., 1964-65; mgmt. and engring. cons., 1965—; pres. Positive Cons.'s Inc., Bellmore, N.Y., 1967—. Owner Lake Luzerne (N.Y.) Seaplane Base, 1969—; mem. small bus. adv. com. to Congressman Thomas J. Downey; mem. small bus. adv. council L.I. Assn. Commerce. Served with AUS, 1945-46. Fellow Nat. Contract Mgmt. Assn. (bd. dirs. L.I. chpt., v.p. 1983-85), IEEE (sr.); mem. Soc. Plastics Engrs., Am. Indsl. Preparedness Assn. (exec. bd. mgmt. div.), Air Force Assn., Capitol Radio Engring. Inst. Alumni (sr.), Nat. Pilots Assn., Aircraft Owners and Pilots Assn., Internat. Platform Assn., Lake Luzerne C. of C. (chmn. indsl. devel. com.). Inventor torpedo fire control cable and connector for Polaris, high pressure seals for Polaris submarine antennae. Address: 1998 Bay Rd PO Box 430 Lake Luzerne NY 12846

GOLDSTEIN, MARK DAVID, advertising agency executive; b. Baltimore, Md., Sept. 24, 1947; s. Sol A. and Jean (Turk) G.; m. Linda Ellen Mouque, Nov. 27, 1974; 1 child, Jenna Elizabeth. BS in Journalism, Northwestern U., 1969, MS in Journalism, 1970. Copywriter Gerson, Howe & Johnson, Chgo., 1970-71; copy supr. Leo Burnett Co., Chgo., 1971-75; exec. v.p., corp. creative dir. Earle Palmer Brown Cos., Bethesda, Md., 1975-86, pres., chief creative officer, 1986—. Bd. dirs. Montgomery Edn. Connection, Md., Arthritis Found., Washington. Recipient Clio awards as lyricist for Song of Yr., 1979, 81, numerous other awards N.Y. Advt. Club, 1976—, Advt. Club Washington, 1976—, Adweek Mag., 1982; named one of Top 100 Young People in Advt., Ad Age, 1985. Mem. Assn. Am. Advt. Agys. (mem. com. 1983-84), ASCAP. Democrat. Clubs: Medill Alumni (class alumni rep.) (Washington), John Evans (Northwestern U.). Office: Earle Palmer Brown Cos 6935 Arlington Rd Bethesda MD 20814

GOLDSTEIN, MARK KINGSTON LEVIN, high technology executive, researcher; b. Burlington, Vt., Aug. 22, 1941; s. Harold Meyer Levin and Roberta (Butterfield) G.; m. Kyoko Matsubara, Mar. 8, 1985. B.S. in Chemistry, U. Vt., 1964, Ph.D., U. Miami-Coral Gables, 1971. Pres. IBR, Inc., Coral Gables, Fla., 1970-74; group leader Brookhaven Nat. Lab., Upton, N.Y., 1974-77; sr. researcher East-West Ctr., Honolulu, 1977-79; sr. tech. advisor JGC Corp., Tokyo, 1979-81; pres., chmn. bd. Quantum Group, Inc., La Jolla, Calif., 1981—; exec. dir. Magnatek, Inc., Brotas, Brazil, 1982—. Contbr. articles to profl. jours.; contbr. poetry to mag. NSF fellow, 1964, 65. Mem. Am. Chem. Soc., AAAS. Club: Hawaii Yacht (Honolulu). Patentee, inventor devices including gas safety valve. Home: 2500 Torrey Pines Rd Apt 805 La Jolla CA 92037 Office: Quantum Group Inc 11211 Sorrento Valley Rd San Diego CA 92121

GOLDSTEIN, MICHAEL ROSS, finance and insurance marketing firm executive; b. Newark, June 26, 1942; s. George and Mildred G.; B.A.,

Fairleigh Dickinson U., 1964; children—Jill, Steven. Acct., Puder & Puder, Newark, 1962-64; pvt. practice acctg., Union, N.J., 1964-76; with First Am. Group, Maplewood, N.J., 1976-83, pres., 1980-83; pres. Protection Adminstrs., Inc., 1984—. C.P.A., N.J. Mem. Am. Inst. C.P.A.s, N.J. Soc. C.P.A.s, Profl. Ins. Agts. Assn. Club: Masons. Home: 245A Scituate Ave Cranston RI 02921 Office: Protection Adminstrs Inc 1280 Park Ave Cranston RI 02910

GOLDSTEIN, SANDRA, consumer products importing company executive, designer and importer; b. Chgo., Dec. 7; d. Jack Julius and Esther Judith (Glickman) Gilbert; student U. Wis., U. Ill.; m. Seymour Leo Goldstein, Aug. 12, 1951; 1 child, Jennie S. Co-founder, sr. v.p., sales mgr. Jennie G. Sales Co., Inc., Lincolnwood, Ill., 1961—. Bd. dirs. Ill. Found. Dentistry for Handicapped. Mem. Nat. Assn. Convenience Stores, Nat. Oil Jobbers Assn., Ill. Petroleum Assn., Tex. Oil Marketers Assn., Intermountain Oil Jobbers Assn., Wis. Oil Jobbers Assn., Ind. Oil Jobbers Assn., Mich. Oil Jobbers Assn., Mo. Oil Jobbers Assn., Iowa Oil Jobbers Assn. Clubs: Carleton (Chgo.); Springs Country (Rancho Mirage, Calif.). Home: 6400 N Cicero Ave Lincolnwood IL 60646 Office: Jennie G Sales Co 3770 W Pratt Ave Lincolnwood IL 60645 Other: The Springs 23 Cornell Rancho Mirage CA 72290

GOLDSTEIN, STANLEY P., retail company executive; b. 1934; married. Grad., Wharton Sch., U. Pa., 1955. V.p. Mark Seven, Inc., 1955-61, Francis I. DuPont, 1961-63; exec. v.p. Consumer Value Stores, 1963-69; pres. CVS div. Melville Corp., Harrison, N.Y., 1969-71, corp. v.p., pres. CVS div., from 1971, then corp. exec. v.p., pres., 1986—, chmn., chief exec. officer, 1987—, also bd. dirs. Office: Melville Corp 3000 Westchester Ave Harrison NY 10528 *

GOLDSTINE, SANDRA DAWN, school administrator; b. Albany, N.Y., July 29, 1940; d. Lyle Laden and Marguerite Arlene (Vrooman) Rulison; m. James Robert Goldstine, July 6, 1957; children: Christopher Mark, Shara Lynn. AA, Suffolk Community Coll., 1972; BA, SUNY, Stony Brook, 1973; MS, C.W. Post Coll., LIU, 1975; profl. diploma, Bank Street Coll., 1979, MEd, 1986; EdD, Columbia U., 1985. Specialist edn. communications Mid. City Schs., Centereach, N.Y., 1973-75; library media specialist Shoreham (N.Y.)/Wading River Schs., 1975-80, prin., 1980-81; prin. Robbins Lane Sch., Syosset, N.Y., 1981-85; asst. supt. instrn. Wantagh (N.Y.) Schs., 1985—. Author: Mentoring, Adult Development and the Career Advancement of Women Leaders, 1985. Mem. Nat. Council Adminstrv. Women in Edn. (research grantee 1985), Nat. Assn. for Supervision and Curriculum Devel., L.I. Assn. Supervision and Curriculum Devel. (pres.), Nassau/Suffolk Council Adminstrv. Women in Edn. (pres.), Phi Delta Kappa. Avocation: stained glass art. Home: 14 Spyglass Ln East Setauket NY 11733 Office: Wantagh Pub Schs Wantagh NY 11793

GOLDWYN, RALPH NORMAN, financial company executive; b. Chgo., Jan. 24, 1925; s. Herman and Rissie F. Goldwyn; B.S., U. Calif. at Los Angeles, 1948; m. Joan J. Snyder, Dec. 25, 1954; children—Bob, Greg, Lisa. Partner, Arc Loan Co., Los Angeles, 1948-52; v.p. Arc Discount Co., Los Angeles, 1952-73; pres. Arc Investment Co., Los Angeles, 1952-73; partner First Factors, Los Angeles, 1960-78; pres. First Comml. Fin., Los Angeles, 1978—; dir. Roy J. Maier, Inc.; trustee UCLA Found. Served to lt. (j.g.) USN, 1943-46. Mem. World Affairs Council, U. Calif. at Los Angeles Chancellor Assos., Anti-Defamation League. Jewish. Clubs: Town Hall of Calif. (life), Brentwood Country, Los Angeles. Office: First Comml Fin 4221 Wilshire Blvd Suite 470 Los Angeles CA 90010

GÖLLNER, THEODOR, musicologist, educator; b. Bielefeld, Fed. Republic Germany, Nov. 25, 1929; Friedrich and Paula (Brinkmann) G.; m. Marie-Louise Martinez, Sept. 30, 1959; Katharina, Philipp. PhD, U. Heidelberg, Fed. Republic Germany, 1957; Habilitation in Musicology, U. Munich, Fed. Republic Germany, 1967. Lectr. U. Munich, 1958-62, from asst. prof. to assoc. prof., 1962-67, prof., chmn. Musicology, 1973—; assoc. prof., then prof. U. Calif., Santa Barbara, 1967-73; mem., dir Commn. Music History, Bavarian Acad. Scis., 1982—. Author: Formen früher Mehrstimmigkeit, 1961, Die mehrstimmigen liturg Lesungen, 1969, Die Sieben Worte am Kreuz, 1986; editor (book series) Münchner Veröffentlichungen zur Musikgeschichte, 1977—. Mem. Soc. Bavarian Music History (pres. 1981—), Soc. for Music Research, Internat. Musicological Soc. Home: Bahnweg 9, 8031 Seefeld 2 Federal Republic of Germany Office: U Munich Inst Musicology, Geschwister-Scholl-Platz 1, 8000 Munich 22 Federal Republic of Germany

GOLLOBIN, LEONARD PAUL, chemical engineer; b. N.Y.C., July 2, 1928; s. Morris and Jennie (Levine) G.; m. Charlotte Weissman, Jan. 21, 1951; children: Michael L., Susan D. BS in Chem. Engring., CUNY, 1951; MS, Kans. State U.-Manhattan, 1952; OMP, Harvard U., 1975. Design engr. Foster Wheeler Corp., N.Y.C., 1952-55; mfg. engr. Gen. Electric Co., Waterford, N.Y., 1955-58; program dir. ORI, Inc., Silver Spring, Md., 1958-63; pres., chief exec. officer Presearch, Inc., Fairfax, Va., 1963—. Bd. dirs. Cultural Alliance Greater Washington, 1980-88; trustee Washington Opera, 1988—. Recipient NSIA Adrm. Charles Weakley award, 1986, Meritorious Pub. Service awardU.S. Dept. Navy, 1987. Mem. Nat. Security Indsl. Assn. (exec. com. 1986—, chmn. antisubmarine warfare com. 1982-84), chmn. amphibious warfare com. 1986—), Naval Undersea Warfare Found. Mus. (v.p. 1982—). Club: Kenwood (Bethesda, Md.). Home: 6710 Bradley Blvd Bethesda MD 20817 Office: Presearch Inc 8500 Executive Park Ave Fairfax VA 22031

GOLLONG, PAUL BERNHARD WERNER, consulting engineer; b. Berlin, Germany, May 24, 1916; came to U.S., 1925, naturalized, 1938; s. Richard Julius and Margaret (Hietzig) G.; m. Mildred Brannan, May 13, 1944 (dec. 1978); m. Marianna Jennings Wofford, Nov. 2, 1978. I.E., B.S., U. Cin., 1941. Registered profl. engr., Wash., Ohio, Pa., Ill. Signaling systems engr. Holtzer-Cabot Co., Ill., 1941-42; research engr. Celotex Corp., Chgo., 1942-43; project engr. Armstrong Cork Co., Lancaster, Pa., 1943-46; cons. engr. Griffenhagen & Assos., Chgo., 1947-50; prin. asso. Griffenhagen & Assos., 1950-51; research engr. IIT Research Inst. (formerly Armour Research Found.), Chgo., 1951-52; chief Asia and Far East ops. IIT Research Inst., 1952-54, mgr. internat. dept., 1954-58, dir. internat. div., 1958-62; internat. adminstr. Boeing Asso. Products, The Boeing Co., 1961-63; spl. indsl. devel. adviser to UN, 1963-66; UN project mgr. Center Indsl. Research, Haifa, Israel, 1966-69; sr. sci. affairs officer Center Indsl. Research, 1970-77; internat. research and devel. cons. 1977—; cons. on research and devel. to govts., Syria, Turkey, Portugal, Nigeria, Cyprus, Trinidad & Tobago; dir. Applied Tech., Ltd., U.K.; mem. Internat. Exec. adv. Council; chmn. Archtl. Rev. Bd.; bd. dirs. Bayou Sound Assoc. Author papers, lectr. on tech. devel. Asian, African and Latin Am. countries. Mem. Vestry All Angels Episcopal Ch. Mem. AAAS, Am. Inst. Indsl. Engrs., Am. Mgmt. Assn., U.S. C. of C., Nat., N.Y., Ill. socs. profl. engrs., Chgo. Hist. Soc., Asia Soc., Soc. Internat. Devel., Library Internat. Relations. Home: 3140 Bayou Sound Bay Isles Longboat Key FL 34228

GOLOMB, FREDERICK MARTIN, surgeon, educator; b. N.Y.C., Dec. 18, 1924; s. Jacob J. and Hannah (Loewy) G.; m. Joan E. Schneider, Nov. 28, 1954; children: James Bradley, Susan Lynn. B.S., Yale U., 1945; M.D., U. Rochester, 1949. Diplomate: Am. Bd. Surgery. Intern Johns Hopkins Hosp., 1949-50; resident NYU Hosp., 1950-56; practice medicine specializing in surgery N.Y.C.; mem. staff N.Y. U. Med. Center, 1950—, dir. chemoimmunotherapy div. tumor service dept. surgery, 1967—; dep. div. dir., chief patient research unit div. II, clin. research div., chief chemotherapy unit div. IV N.Y. U. Cancer Center, 1975-79; attending surgeon Univ., Drs. hosps.; cons. in gen. surgery Manhattan VA Hosp.; cons. surgeon Cabrini Health Care Center; vis. surgeon Bellevue Hosp.; mem. faculty N.Y. U. Sch. Medicine, 1956—, prof., clin. surgery, 1977—; cons. N.Y.C. div. Am. Cancer Soc., 1968—; mem. clin. trials rev. com. Nat. Cancer Inst., 1976-79; chmn. melanoma com. Eastern Coop. Oncology Group, 1978-80; prin. investigator Central Oncology Group, 1969-77, exec. com., 1976-77; mem. met. med. com. Chemotherapy Found.; co-prin. investigator Eastern Coop. Oncology Group NYU, 1978—. Editorial adv. bd., contbg. editor Oncology News; contbr. articles to profl. jours. Served with M.C. AUS, 1953-54, Korea. Fellow A.C.S.; mem. Soc. Head and Neck Surgeons, Soc. Surgery Alimentary Tract, Am. Assn. Cancer Research, Am. Soc. Clin. Oncology (a founder), AMA, N.Y. Cancer Soc. (pres. 1974-75), N.Y. Surg. Soc., N.Y. State, N.Y. County med. socs., Soc. Surg. Oncology, George Hoyt Whipple Soc., Brit. Assn. Surg. Oncology (editorial adv. panel 1980-85), Pan Am. Med. Soc., Sigma Xi. Clubs: Am. Alpine, Explorers. Office: NYU Sch Medicine 530 1st Ave New York NY 10016

GOLOMB, HERBERT STANLEY, dermatologist; b. N.Y.C., Sept. 6, 1933; s. Morris and Ida (Schwartz) G.; AB, U. Pa., 1955; MD, State U. N.Y., Bklyn., 1960; m. Suzanne Nazer, Dec. 20, 1964; children: Meredith, Valerie. Intern, Ohio State U. Hosp., Columbus, 1960-61; resident in dermatology State U. N.Y.-Kings County Med. Center, 1961-62, N.Y. U. Skin and Cancer Unit and Bellevue Hosp., N.Y.C., 1962-64; pres. Falls Church Med. Ctr., 1963-64; practice medicine specializing in dermatology, Falls Church, Va., 1964-66, 68—; mem. staff George Washington U., S.E. Community, Fairfax (Va.), Arlington hosps.; instr., then clin. asst. prof. dermatology George Washington U. Sch. Medicine, 1964—; cons. USPHS Dermatology Clinic, 1964-66; chmn. Atlantic Dermatol. Conf., 1978. Pres. Dermatology Found. No. Va., 1962-64, bd. dirs., 1978-79. Served with USPHS, 1966-68. Diplomate Am. Bd. Dermatology. Fellow Am. Acad. Dermatology; mem. AMA, Soc. Investigative Dermatology, Internat. Soc. Tropical Dermatology, Med. Soc. Va., D.C., Fairfax County med. socs., D.C. (pres. 1977-78), Va. dermatol. socs. Clubs: Tuckahoe Swim and Tennis. Home: 1910 Woodgate Ln McLean VA 22101 Office: 6060 Arlington Blvd Falls Church VA 22044

GOLTZ, ROBERT WILLIAM, physician, educator; b. St. Paul, Sept. 21, 1923; s. Edward Victor and Clare (O'Neill) G.; m. Patricia Ann Sweeney, Sept. 27, 1945; children: Leni, Paul Robert. B.S., U. Minn., 1943, M.D., 1945. Diplomate: Am. Bd. Dermatology (pres. 1975-76). Intern Ancker Hosp., St. Paul, 1944-45; resident in dermatology Mpls. Gen. Hosp., 1945-46, 48-49, U. Minn. Hosp., 1949-50; practice medicine specializing in dermatology Mpls., 1950-65; clin. instr. U. Minn. Grad. Sch., 1950-58, clin. asst. prof., 1958-60, clin. assoc. prof., 1960-65, prof., head dept. dermatology, 1971-85; prof. medicine/dermatology U. Calif.-San Diego,, 1985—; prof. dermatology, head div. dermatology U. Colo. Med. Sch., Denver, 1965-71. Former editorial bd.: Archives of Dermatology; editor: Dermatology Digest. Served from 1st lt. to capt., M.C. U.S. Army, 1946-48. Mem. Am. Dermatol. Assn. (dir. 1976-79, pres. 1985-86), Am. Soc. Dermatopathology (pres. 1981), Am. Dermatologic Soc. Allergy and Immunology (pres. 1981) AMA (chmn. sect. on dermatology 1973-75), Dermatology Found. (past dir.), Minn. Dermatol. Soc., Soc. Investigative Dermatology (pres. 1972-73), Histochem. Soc., Am. Acad. Dermatology (pres. 1978-79, past dir.), Brit. Assn. Dermatology (hon.), Chilean Dermatology Soc. (hon.), Colombian Dermatol. Soc. (corr. mem.), Can. Dermatol. Soc. (hon. mem.), Pacific Dermatol. Soc. (hon.-mem.), S. African Dermatol. Soc. (hon. mem.), N.Am. Clin. Dermatol. Soc., Assn. Profs. Dermatology (sec.-treas. 1970-72, pres. 1973-74). Home: 6097 Avenida Chamnez La Jolla CA 92037 Office: U Calif-San Diego Med Ctr Div Dermatology H-811-J 225 Dickinson St San Diego CA 92103

GOLVERS, LUC FRANÇOIS, business data processing consultant, educator; b. Ixelles, Belgium, July 20, 1949; s. Roger G. Golvers and Lucienne H. Van Geel. BCE, U. Brussels, 1971; MBA, Cranfield Sch. Mgmt., Eng., 1973. Project leader Siemens, Brussels, 1973-76; bus. data processing cons. Brussels, 1978—; lectr. U. Brussels, 1983—; expert witness to the Belgian cts. Contbr. articles to profl. jours. Served as instr. Belgian Navy, 1971-72. Mem. Belgian Assn. Experts, Royal Belgian Soc. Engrs. and Indsls., Brit. Inst. Mgmt. Home and Office: Baron de Vironlaan 31, 1710 DilBeek Belgium

GOLZADEH, MOHAMMAD MEHDI, manufacturing company executive; b. Ghom, Iran, Dec. 20, 1949; s. Ali Golzadeh and Batool Omidvar; m. Zahra Golzadeh, July 3, 1969; children: Nasim, Sepideh. BSEE, MSEE, Tehran U., Iran, 1973; postgrad., Iran Electronic Co., 1974. Chief elec. engr. Abyek Cement Plant, Tehran, 1971-74; mem. planning and program dept. Iran Electronic Industries, Tehran, 1974-75; mng. dir. Iran Indsl. Carbon Co., Tehran, 1975—; dir. cement industry bd. Nat. Iranian Industries Orgn., Tehran, 1981-84, cons., 1982—; chmn. Iran Cement Engring. Ctr., 1982-84, Pars Otu Co., Tehran, 1984—; sec. Research & Self-Sufficiency Ctr. for Carbon Industries, Tehran, 1985—; cons. Ministry of Industries, Iran, 1985—. Editor: Report of Iran Cement Industry, 1981, Report of Iran Asbestos Industry, 1982. Dep. gov. Provience of Khuzestan, Ahwaz, Iran, 1980-81. Served to lt. Iranian mil., 1973-75. Mem. Research Ctr. for Indsl. Carbon. Office: Iran Indsl Carbon Co 166 Ghaemmagham Farahani Ave, Tehran 15869, Iran

GOMBRICH, SIR ERNST (HANS JOSEF), art historian, educator; b. Vienna, Austria, Mar. 30, 1909; s. Karl and Leonie (Hock) G.; m. Ilse Heller, 1936; 1 son, Richard Francis. Ed. Theresianum, Vienna, and Vienna U.; PhD; LittD (hon.), Queen's U., Belfast, No. Ireland, 1963; LLD (hon.), U. St. Andrews, 1965; LittD (hon.), Leeds U., 1965, Oxford U., 1969, Harvard U., London U., 1976; LittD (hon.), U. Cambridge, 1970, Manchester U., 1974; DHumLitt (hon.), U. Chgo., 1975, U. Pa., 1977; DUniv (hon.), U. Essex, 1977; LHD (hon.), Brandeis U., 1981. Research asst. Warburg Inst., U. London, 1936-39, sr. research fellow, 1946-48, lectr., 1948-54, reader, 1954-56, spl. lectr., 1956-59, dir., 1959-76; with BBC Monitoring Service, World War II; prof. history of classical tradition U. London, 1959-76, prof. emeritus, 1976— ; Slade prof. fine art U. Oxford, 1950-53; Durning-Lawrence prof. history of art Univ. Coll., London U., 1956-59; vis. prof. Harvard U., 1959; Slade prof. fine art U. Cambridge, 1961-63; prof. at large Cornell U., 1970-76; trustee Brit. Mus., 1974-79; mem. Standing Commn. on Mus. and Galleries, 1976-82. Author: (with E. Kris) Caricature, 1940; The Story of Art, 1950 (14 edits.); Art and Illusion, 1959; Meditations on a Hobby Horse, 1963; Norm and Form, 1966; In Search of Cultural History, 1969; Aby Warburg, 1970; Symbolic Images, 1972; Art History and the Social Sciences, 1974; The Heritage of Apelles, 1976; The Sense of Order, 1979; Ideals and Idols, 1979; The Image and the Eye, 1982; Tributes, 1984; New Light on Old Masters, 1986; Reflections on the History of Art, 1987; editor: (with R.L. Gregory) Illusion in Nature and Art, 1973. Decorated comdr. Order Brit. Empire, 1966, knighted, 1972, Internat. Balzan prize, 1985, Cross of Honor 1st class (Austria), Pour le Merite, Order of Merit, 1988; recipient W.H. Smith and Son Ann. Lit. award, 1964, medal NYU, 1970, Erasmus prize, 1975, Hegel prize City of Stuttgart (W.Ger.), 1977; Ehrenzeichen für Wissenschaft und Kunst, Austria, 1984, Kulturpreis, Vienna, 1986, Ludwig Wittgenstein prize Österriechische Forschungsgemeinschaft, 1988; hon. fellow Jesus Coll., Cambridge U., 1963, Göttingen Acad. Scis., 1986, FBA, FSA, FRSL, R.I.B.A.; corr. mem. Turin Acad., Uppsala Acad., Netherlands Acad., Bavarian Acad., Acad. dei Lincei, Swedish Acad.; hon. mem. Am. Acad. and Inst. Arts and Letters, Am. Acad. Arts and Scis.; fgn. mem. Am. Philos. Soc.

GOMEL, ABE ABRAHAM, dairy company executive; b. Izmir, Turkey, Jan. 28, 1945; arrived in Can., 1973; s. Richard and Renée (Pessah) G.; m. Rachel DeCiaves, Sept. 1, 1968; children: Rona, Richard, David. BS in Chemistry, Fairleigh Dickinson U., 1969; MS in Organic Chemistry, U. Minn., 1971; MBA, Cornell U., 1973. Sales rep. Internat. Paper Sales, Montreal, Que., Can., 1973-74; mgr. Bamag Trading, Montreal, 1974-77; pres. Liberty Brand Products, Montreal, 1977—. Chairperson gazette com. Council on Aging, Allied Jewish Community Services, Montreal, 1986-87. Mem. Liberal Party. Home: 431 Mount Stephen, Westmount, PQ Canada H3Y 2Y8 Office: Liberty Brand Products, 1 Ave Liberté, Candiac, PQ Canada

GOMERSALL, EARL RAYMOND, business executive; b. Mpls., Dec. 4, 1930; s. John Raymond and Florence Judith (Olson) G.; 1 child, Earl Raymond. B.S. in Bus. Adminstrn., Northwestern U., 1952, M.B.A., 1957. Project engr. Elgin Watch Co., Ill., 1952-57; ops. mgr. Texas Instruments, Dallas, 1957-71; corp. v.p. Motorola, Inc., Schaumburg, Ill., 1971-83; cons. Research Components, Inverness, Ill., 1983—; v.p., dir. tech. devel. A.C. Nielsen Co., Northbrook, Ill., 1985—; ptnr. Thomas Group, Inc., 1986—; dir. Sweeney-Todd, London, 1975—, On Tyme Products, Morton Grove, Ill., 1983—, Licron Corp., Santa Clara, Calif., 1983—, Diamond Circuits, Houston, 1983—. Contbg. author: Manufacturing Man and His Job; inventor on-line real-time pricing; patentee method for operating mfg. line, over-the-air electronics substitution system. Serrved as spl. agt. U.S. Army, 1952-54. Recipient Best Methods Improvement of Yr. awards Indsl. Mgmt. Soc., 1952, 58, 59. Mem. Am. Mgmt. Assn. (planning council 1978—), Am. Mktg. Assn., Am. Legion, Nat. Rifle Assn., Delta Sigma Pi (life), Delta Mu Delta. Republican. Episcopalian. Club: Northwestern U. John Evans. Home: 132 West Wood Palatine IL 60067 Office: Thomas Group 5215 N O'Connor Rd Irving TX 75039-3714

GOMES, NORMAN VINCENT, industrial engineer, business broker; b. New Bedford, Mass., Nov. 7, 1914; s. John Vincent and Georgianna (Sylvia) G.; grad. U.S. Army Command and Gen. Staff Coll., 1944; B.S. in Indsl. Engring. and Mgmt., Okla. State U., 1950; M.B.A. in Mgmt., Xavier U., 1955; m. Carolyn Moore, June 6, 1942 (dec. Apr. 1983). Asst. chief engr. Leschen div. H.K. Porter Co., St. Louis, 1950-52; staff mfg. cons. Gen. Electric Co., Cin., 1952-57; lectr. indsl. mgmt. U. Cin., 1955-56; vis. lectr. indsl. mgmt. Xavier U. Sch. Bus. Adminstrn., 1956-57; staff indsl. engr. Gen. Dynamics, Ft. Worth, 1957-60; chief ops. analysis Ryan Electronics, San Diego, 1960-64; sr. engr., jet propulsion lab. Calif. Inst. Tech., Pasadena, 1964-67, mem. tech. staff, 1967, mgr. mgmt. systems, 1967-71; industry rep. and cons. U.S. Commn. on Govt. Procurement, Washington, 1970-72; adminstrv. officer GSA, Washington, 1973-78, program dir., 1979; now engaged in bus. brokerage; vis. lectr. mgmt. San Antonio Coll., 1982-85. Served as 2d lt. to maj. C.E., AUS, 1941-46; engring. adviser to War Manpower Bd., 1945. Decorated Army Commendation medal; recipient Apollo Achievement award, 1969; Outstanding Performance award GSA, 1974- 75, 76, 77, 79. Registered profl. engr., Calif., Tex.; lic. real estate broker, Tex. Mem. Am. Inst. Indsl. Engrs. (nat. chmn. prodn. control research com., 1951-57; bd. dirs. Cin., Fort Worth, San Diego, Los Angeles, San Antonio chpts. 1954-84, pres. Cin. chpt. 1956-57, pres. Los Angeles 1970-71, nat. dir. community services 1969-73), Nat. Calif. socs. profl. engrs., Soc. Am. Mil. Engrs., Nat. Mgmt. Assn., Ret. Officers Assn. U.S. (chpt. pres. 1968-69, recipient Nat. Pres. certificate Merit 1969), Mil. Order World Wars, Nat. Security Indsl. Assn. (mgmt. systems subcom. 1967-69), Freedoms Found at Valley Forge. Republican. Roman Catholic. Club: K.C. (4th deg.). Home: 2719 Knoll Tree San Antonio TX 78247 Office: 7330 San Pedro Ave Suite 376 San Antonio TX 78216

GOMES DE MATOS, FRANCISCO CARDOSO, linguist; b. Crato, Brazil, Sept. 3, 1933; s. Vicente Roque and Adalgisa Cardoso (Xavier) G.D.M.; m. Helen Herta Brüning, July 14, 1962; children: Patrícia, Maria Regina, Daniel. LLB, U. Fed., Brazil, 1958; M, U. Mich., 1960; PhD, U. Católica, São Paulo, Brazil, 1973. Cert. in applied linguistics. Assoc. prof. U. Católica, São Paulo, Brazil, 1966-79; prof. U. Fed., Recife, Brazil, 1980—; dir. Centro de Linguística Aplicada, São Paulo, 1966-79; vis. prof. Mus. Antropologia, Mexico City, 1968, U. São Paulo, 1969, U. Ottawa, Can., 1971; pres. Interam. Linguistics Program, São Paulo, 1978-81; Fulbright prof. U. Ga., Athens, 1985-86; vis. researcher, U. Tex., Austin. Contbg. author: Let's Have Fun, 1971. Active presdl. coms., Brasília (Brazil), Rio de Janeiro, 1985. Fulbright fellow U. Mich., 1959-60; Ford Found. fellow Ind. U., Bloomington, 1964; recipient Oscar Nobling award Soc. Lang. and Lit., 1977; recognized by U.S. Info. Service, 1976. Mem. Internat. Network on Lang. Rights, Tchrs. of English to Speakers of Other Langs. (internat. concerns com. 1985), Brazilian Linguistics Assn. (pres. 1981-83), Internat. Assn. Crosscultural Communication (v.p. 1984—), Internat. Reading Assn. (chair Latin Am. 1985—), Nat. Collegiate Fgn. Lang. Honor Soc. Roman Catholic. Home: Rua Setubal 860-B, Apt 604, Recife Pernambuco, Brazil 51021 Office: U Federal de Pernambuco, Recife Pernambuco, Brazil 50.000

GÓMEZ, LUIS CARLOS, engineer; b. San José, Costa Rica, July 24, 1915; s. Eduardo and Gertrudis (Portuguéz) G.; m. Virginia Diaz (div. Dec. 1959); children: Virginia, Carlos, Willy, Ana, Randall; m. Rosa Amalia Chinchilla, Aug. 10, 1959; children: Oscar, Carlos, Patricia, Doris, Catalina, David, Anna. Degree in engring., Universidad, San José, 1937; degree in electronics, Nat. Schs., Los Angeles, 1951. Maintenance engr. Tropical Radio and Telegraph Co., Golfito, Costa Rica, 1939-47; engr., installer Compañia de FuerzavLuz, San José, 1951-52, USA Bur. Pub. Roads Adminstrn., San José, 1952-55, Electronic Service Co., San Pedro Sula, Honduras, 1955—; cons. Audio Video S.A., Tegucigalpa, Honduras, 1957-70, Radio Cultura, 1962, Radio El Mundo, San Pedro Sula, 1960—, Radio Internat., 1986—. Recipient Spl. Services diploma Juntade Gobierno, 1979. Lodge: Mason. Office: Electronic Service Co, PO Box 1175, 2d St 9-10 Ave NO, San Pedro Sula Honduras

GOMEZ LOPEZ-EGEA, JOSE LUIS, business school administrator; b. Valencia, Spain, Feb. 6, 1933; arrived in Argentina, 1951; s. Sandalio and Maria Del Carmen (Lopez-Egea) Gomez. BA, Nuestra Señora Del Pilar, Spain, 1950. Acct. U. Del Litoral, Argentina, 1956, Samider SA, Buenos Aires, 1953-58; sr. auditor Price Waterhouse and Co., Buenos Aires, 1958-61; fin. cons. Buenos Aires, 1961-78; treas. Assn. Fumento Cultura, Buenos Aires, 1961-78; dean Inst. de Altos Estudios Empresariales, Buenos Aires, 1978—; dir. Wagon-Lits Cook, 1984—. Contbr. articles to profl. jours. Office: Inst de Altos Estudios F, Aguero 2373, Buenos Aires Argentina

GOMEZ-RUIZ, FRANCISCO, mathematics educator; b. Malaga, Spain, Aug. 20, 1945; s. Custodio Gomez-Mengibar and Maria Victoria Ruiz-Medina; m. Erika Zehntner, Jan. 3, 1979; children: Maria Cristina, Helena. BS in Math., U. Barcelona, Spain, 1967; MSc, U. Toronto, Can., 1975, PhD, 1978. Asst. prof. U. Barcelona, 1967-74; assoc. prof. U. Barcelona and U. Santander, Spain, 1978-81; prof. U. Málaga, Spain, 1981—; reviewer Zentralblatt für Mathematik, Fed. Republic Germany; Extracta Mathematicae, Spain. Author: Grupos de Lie y Clases Caracteristicas, 1983; contbr. articles to profl. jours. Grantee Nat. Research Council Can., 1975-76, 76-77. Mem. Soc. Catalana de Math., Am. Math. Soc. Office: U Malaga, Dept Algebra Geom y Topology, Fac-Ciencias, Campus Teatinos, 29071 Malaga Spain

GOMULKA, STANISLAW, economist, educator; b. Krezoly, Poland, Sept. 10, 1940; s. Wladyslaw and Zofia (Kucharzyk) G.; m. Joanna Majerczyk, Jan. 26, 1964; 1 child, Michael. MSc in Physics, Warsaw U., 1962, PhD in Econs., 1966. Asst. lectr. Warsaw U., 1962-65; research fellow Aarhus (Denmark) U., 1970; lectr., then sr. lectr. in econs. London Sch. Econs., 1970-87, reader in econs., 1987—; fellow Netherlands Inst. Advanced Study, Wassenaar, 1980-81; vis. prof. U. Pa., Phila., 1984-85; scholar Stanford (Calif.) U.-Hoover Inst., 1985; sr. fellow Columbia U.-Harriman Inst., N.Y.C., 1986; cons. Internat. Monetary Fund, Washington, 1985, joint econ. com., U.S. Congress, Washington, 1988—. Author: Inventive Activity, Diffusion and the Stages of Economic Growth, 1971, Growth, Innovation and Reform in Eastern Europe, 1986. Mem. Royal Econ. Soc., European Econ. Soc. Home: 4 Woodfield Way, London N11 2PH, England Office: London Sch Econs, Houghton St, London WC2A 2AE, England

GONCALVES, KAREN PIERCE, marketing and strategic planning consultant, educator; b. St. Johnsbury, Vt., Feb. 5, 1950; d. Ralph Wallace and Betty (Tilton) Pierce; BS with honors, Northeastern U., 1973, MBA with honors, 1975, EdD in Higher Edn. Adminstrn., 1988; m. Humberto F. Goncalves, Apr. 15, 1970; children—Michelle Pierce-Ferreira, Michael David Pierce-Ferreira. Asst. dir. Inst. for New Enterprise Devel., Belmont, Mass., 1974-78; sr. staff cons. Arthur D. Little, Inc., Cambridge, Mass., 1978-81; pres. K.P. Goncalves & Assos., Inc., 1981—; v.p. mktg. Luso Ceramics Corp., Arlington, Mass., 1982-86; instr. Northeastern U., Bentley Coll., Babson Coll.; speaker on mktg. and strategic planning to numerous profl. and ednl. groups, 1975—. Mem. MFA council Boston Mus. Fine Arts, exec. com. of bd. dirs.; life mem. Northeastern U. Pres.'s Club. Mem. Beta Gamma Sigma. Methodist. Office: 42 Temple St Arlington. MA 02174

GONCHARENKO, NICKOLAJ VASILIEVICH, philosopher, sociologist; b. Vasilkovka, Ukraine, USSR, Dec. 2, 1924; s. Vasilij Egorovich Goncharenko and Orina Evtikhievna (Zabashta) Kudina; m. Nadežda Nickolajevna Forman, Jan. 15, 1946; 1 child, Alexander. BS, State U., Kharkov, 1944-49; DSc in Philosophy, Inst. Philosophy, Acad. Sci. Ukraine, Kiev, 1963. Sr. researcher Inst. Philosophy, Acad. Sci. Ukraine, Kiev, USSR, 1949-62, dep. dir., chief aesthetics and ethics dept., 1962-68; prof. philosophy State U., Kiev, 1968-73; chief theory of art dept. Inst. Art, Folkore and Ethnography, Acad. Sci. Ukraine, Kiev, 1973—, dep. academician-sec., dept. lit. lang. and study art, 1979—; participant Internat. Congress Aesthetics, 1964, 68, 72, 76, 80, 84, World Congress Sociology, 1966, 70, 74, 78, 82. Author: Art and Aesthetics Education, 1963, Progress in Art, 1968, Culture: Origin and Factors of Progress, 1980, Dialectics of Culture Progress, 1987. V.p. Ukrainian-French Friendship Soc., Kiev, 1970—. Named to Order Red Banner Labour, Presidium of Supreme Soviet USSR, 1982, Order Patriotic

War, 1985. Communist. Office: Inst Art Folkore and Ethnography, Kirova 4, 252001 Kiev USSR

GÖNNER, WINFRIED K, mechanical engineer; b. Konstanz, Germany, Oct. 24, 1938; s. Karl and Emma (Egle) G.; m. Heidi Karin Mack, May 21, 1964; children: Christian, Susan. Diplom Engenieur Fachhochschule, U. Ulm, 1964. Engr. Robert Bosch GmbH, 1964-66; engr. Bodenseewerk-Gerätetechnik, 1966-70, proj. engr., 1979-80; engr. Bodenseewerk Perkin-Elmer, 1970-79, 1980-86; project engr., small lab. mgr. Bodenseewerk Perkin-Elmer, 1987—. Patentee in field. Mem. German Assn. Engrs. Roman Catholic. Address: Magnolienweg 6, D-7770 Uberlingen Federal Republic of Germany

GONSON, S. DONALD, lawyer; b. Buffalo, June 13, 1936; s. Samuel and Laura Rose (Greenspan) G.; m. Dorothy Rose, Aug. 28, 1960; children—Julia, Claudia. A.B., Columbia U., 1958; J.D., Harvard U., 1961; postgrad., U. Bombay, India, 1961-62. Bar: Mass. 1962. With Hale and Dorr, Boston, 1962—, sr. ptnr., 1972—; lectr. Fin. Times (U.K.), Instl. Investors, New Eng. Law Inst., Mass. Soc. C.P.A.s; co-chmn. Speech-Tech., N.Y.C., 1987; instr. in law Boston U., 1963-65, bd. trustees Boston Five Cents Savs. Bank, 1973-83, bd. advisors 1983—; bd. dirs. Colonial Penn Group, Inc., 1982-86. Chmn. Mass. Community Devel. Fin. Corp., 1976-82; pres. Cambridge Ctr. for Adult Edn., 1985-88. Fulbright scholar, 1961-62. Mem. Internat. Bar Assn., ABA, Mass. Bar Assn., Boston Bar Assn. Clubs: Bay (Boston); Harvard Faculty, Cambridge Tennis (Cambridge). Home: 32 Hubbard Park Cambridge MA 02138

GONZALES, BROTHER ALEXIS (JOSEPH M. GONZALES), theater and communications educator; b. Santa Fe, Oct. 1, 1931. BA, Coll. Santa Fe, 1957; MEd, U. SW La., 1960; PhD candidate, U. Santo Tomas, Manilla, The Phillipines; postgrad, Fordham U., St. Mary's U., San Antonio. mem. teaching order Christian Bros. Acad. dean Cath. Coll., Negros Occidental, Phillipines, 1960-66; tchr. Eng. and religion, drama coach Antonian High Sch., San Antonio, 1967-70; prof. theater and communications, Film Buff Inst. Loyola U., New Orleans, 1970—; participant Christian Bros. Internat. Symposium, Rome, 1978, Cannes (France) Film Festival, 1970-88, USIS Arts in Am. program, Asuncion, Paraguay, 1985-86; organizer internat. festival HemisFair, San Antonio, 1967, seminar on media Ctr. Social Communications, San Antonio, 1968; dir. Creative Arts Festival, San Antonio, Arts in Am. TV and Theatre Project, Paraguay, 1986, Tennessee Williams Fest, Paraguay, 1985-86, film festivals in Hungary, France, Israel, Brazil, Spain, Federal Republic of Germany, Latin Am., Eastern European countries; mem. planning council Coll.-Community Creative Arts Ctr., Model Cities, San Antonio, 1969; bd. cons. Mexican-Am. Social Communications Inst., San Antonio, 1971-72; vis. prof. theatre U. Mex., 1971-72, lectr. communications, 1975-76; vis. prof. U. Monterrey, Mex.; vis. lectr. Latin Am. Ctr. Inst. Latinoamericano de Investigaciones Pedagogicas y Antropologicas, Mexico City, 1971-72; lectr., dir. in Mex., Colombia, Brazil, Italy, France, 1971-88; founder Exptl. Theatre, Loyola U., 1970; dir., coordinator OEO Summer Impact Poverty Program for Disadvantaged Youth; lectr., cons. Project 8 children, Orlean Parish Sch. Bd.; asst. dir. SCOPE program, Loyola U.; jury mem. 3d World Cinema Festival, Brazil, 1974-77, Gramado Brazilian Film Festival, 1975-78, Berlin Internat. Film Festival, 1985, San Sebastian Internat. Film Festival, 1985; Paraguay, 1986; Fullbright sr. lectr., Cath. U. Am., Paraguay, 1988—; cons., lectr. numerous other schs., community and theater related projects. Producer, dir. Antonian Creative Theatre, San Antonio, 1967-70; dir. (Latin Am.premiere) The Serpent, Mexico City, 1970, Black Medea, New Orleans, 1976 and 1st Spoleto-USA Arts Fesitval, Charleston, S.C., 1977, (four casts) Suddenly, Last Summer and Streetcar Named Desire, USIS Theatre Project, Paraguey, 1985, Our Town, Hay Que Deshacer la Casa, (anti-drug video) Desde el Tejado, Centro Paraguayo-Americano, 1986; film archivist, cons. Film Collection Archdiocese of San Antonio; editor at large New Orleans Rev.; contbr. articles to newspapers, mags. Decorated Palmes Academique, France, 1978; named Chevalier des Arts et Lettres, France, 1986; recipient Outstanding Educator awards, 1970, 73, 75, 78, 83, 85, U.S. State Dept. award, 1988-89; Syracuse U. fellow; John D. Rockefeller grantee, 1966-67; Fulbright prof., South Am., 1987-88. Mem. ANTA, Am. Ednl. Theater Assn., Internat. Theater Assn., Nat. Cultural Theater Conf., Assn. Ednl. Communications and Tech of NEA, Internat. Fine Arts Council, Inst. Latinoamericano de Archeologica y Pedagogia, Univ. Film Inst. Office: Loyola U Film Buff Inst 6363 St Charles Ave New Orleans LA 70118

GONZALES, FROILAN TAYAG, fashion designer; b. Manila, Mar. 23, 1944; s. Francisco and Josefina Paras (Tayag) G. Designer with R. T. Paras, Manila, Pierre Cardin, Paris, 1964-70; asst. modeliste Cerruti, Paris, 1972-73; modelist Jean Patou, Paris, 1973-77, art dir., 1977-82; modeliste-styliste Dorothée Bis, Paris, 1982; modeliste-designer Lecoanet Hemant, Paris, 1984—; fashion cons. Bloch Pub. House, Brazil, 1968. Recipient 1st place award Chambre Syndicale de la Couture Parisienne, 1963-64. Roman Catholic. Office: 5 Rue Lamennais, 75008 Paris France

GONZALEZ, EUGENE ROBERT, investment banker. s. Eugenio Tomas and Alice Marie (Macdonald) Gonzalez-Mandiola. B.A. in Internat. Relations, Yale U., 1952; postgrad. in advanced mgmt, L'Institut pour l'Etude des Methodes de Direction de l'Enterprise, Lausanne, Switzerland, 1967. Civil engr. Dept. Pub. Works Commonwealth Mass., Boston, 1952; econ. officer Dept. Defense, Washington, 1954-57; project fin. officer Devel. Loan Fund (now AID), Washington, 1957-58; fin. mgr. RCA Internat., N.Y.C., 1958-61; fin. instns. specialist Interam. Devel. Bank, Washington, 1961-62; fin. officer Interam. Devel. Bank, 1962-63; dep. regional rep. for Europe Interam. Devel. Bank, Paris, 1964; pres., chief exec. officer Adelatec Mgmt. Cons. Co., 1969-72; exec. v.p. Adela Investment Co., Luxembourg, 1964-74; mng. dir. Adela Investment Co., 1974-75, pres., chief exec. officer, 1975-76; adviser, regional coordinator for Ibero Am. Morgan Stanley Internat., N.Y.C., 1977—. Author: International Sources of Financing, 1961. Served with U.S. Army, 1952-54. Fellow Internat. Bankers Assn. (disting.); mem. Am. Enterprise Inst. Nat. Com. on Am. Fgn. Policy, Accion Internat. (dir.), Internat. Assn. Fin. Planners, Pan Am. Soc. U.S. (dir.), Am. Soc. Profl. Cons., Presidents Assn., Center for Interam. Relations, Spanish Inst., Club de Banqueros de Mex., Club de Industriales de Mex. (Mexico City). Clubs: Met. (Washington), City Tavern (Washington); Brook (N.Y.C.), River (N.Y.C.), Racquet and Tennis (N.Y.C.); Meadow (Southampton, N.Y.); Union (Santiago, Chile); Pacific Union (San Francisco). Home: 137 E 66th St Apt #1-B New York NY 10021 Office: Morgan Stanley Co 1251 Ave Americas New York NY 10020

GONZALEZ, JOE MANUEL, lawyer; b. N.Y.C., Aug. 18, 1950; s. Reinaldo Fabregas and Mary Louise (Cermeno) G.; m. Ruia Jane Whiteside, Dec. 30, 1977; children—Matthew Ray, Jane Marie, Jeffrey Joseph. B.A., U. South Fla., 1972; J.D., Gonzaga U., 1980; LL.M. in Taxation, Georgetown U., 1981. Bar: Fla. 1981, U.S. Tax Ct. 1983, U.S. Dist. Ct. (mid. dist.) Fla. 1984, U.S. Ct. Appeals (11th cir.) 1984, U.S. Supreme Ct. 1985. Atty., Gonzaga U. Legal Services, Spokane, Wash., 1980; mng. ptnr. Cotterill, Gonzalez, Hayes & Grantham, Fla., 1981-88; atty. Hispanic Def. League, Tampa, Fla., 1982-88. Assoc. editor Gonzaga Law Rev. Spl. Report: Pub. Sector Labor Law, 1980. Mem. Sheriff's Hispanic Adv. Council, Hillsborough County, Fla., 1982-88 , City of Tampa Hispanic Adv. Council, 1983-88; mem. Hisslborough County Planning commn., citizens adv. com., 1988—; pres. Tampa Hispanic Heritage, Inc., 1985-87; founder Carnavale En Tampa, Inc., 1986-87; master of ceremonies Gasparilla Sidewalk Art Festival, 1988; chief Hispanic adv. com. for Tampa Police Dept., 1988. Mem. ABA, Hillsborough County Bar Assn., Assn. Trial Lawyers Am., Nat. Inst. for Trial Advocacy, Phi Delta Phi. Democrat. Presbyterian. Lodge: Rotary. Home: 1708 Richardson Pl Tampa FL 33606 Office: Cotterill Gonzalez Hayes & Grantham Northfork Profl Ctr 1519 N Dale Mabry Hwy Suite 100 Lutz FL 33549

GONZALEZ, MELESIO, food company executive; b. Monterrey, Nuevo Leon, Mex., Oct. 22, 1941; s. Melesio G. and Hortencia (Cantu) G.; m. Maricela Martinez, Oct. 6, 1967; children: Melesio Alberto, Monica Lucia, Marcela Eugenia. BSME, Inst. Tech. y de Estudio Superiores y de Monterrey, Mex., 1963, B in Indsl. Engring., 1966; MBA, U. Pa., 1969; postgrad. in Strategic Planning and Control, MIT, 1975. Registered profl. engr., Nuevo Leon. Systems mgr. Hylsa, Monterrey, 1973-76; dir. planning and devel. Gentor Group, Monterrey, 1976-78; dir. new bus. Visa Group, Monterrey, 1978-82, dir. corp. planning, 1982-84; dir. planning logistics Cuauhtemoc Brewery, Monterrey, 1984-86; dir. ops. devel. Visa Distbrs., Monterrey, 1986—; tchr. info. systems grad. sch. mgmt. I.T.E.S.M., Monterrey, 1971-74, 85-86. Fellow Data Processing Mgmt. Assn., Inst. Planning Strategies. Roman Catholic. Club: Indsl. Home: Faraday #784, 67170 Guadalupe Nuevo Leon Mexico Office: Visa Distribucion SA DE CV, Juarez #2440 NTE, 64580 Monterrey Nuevo Leon Mexico

GONZALEZ, WENCESLAO JOSE, philosopher, educator; b. Ferrol, Spain, Sept. 21, 1957; s. Jose-Manuel and Maria-Paz (Fernandez) G. BA in Philosophy, U. Salamanca, Spain, 1979; PhD, U. Murcia, Spain, 1983. Lectr. U. Murcia, 1979-82, sr. lectr., 1983-87, titular prof. philosophy and logic, 1987—; mem. governing bd. U. Murcia, 1985-87. Author: La Teoria de la Referencia. Strawson y la Filosofia Analitica, 1986, also articles. Home: Edif Captesa, Alfonso x el Sabio, 30008 Murcia Spain Office: U Murcia, Dept Filosofia y Logica, 30071 Murcia Spain

GONZALEZ-ALLER, CRISTOBAL, engineering company executive; b. Madrid, May 19, 1948; s. Alberto Gonzalez-Aller and Luisa De La Mota; m. Nieves Fontana. Grad. in Indsl. Engring., Escuela Técnica Superior de Ingenieros Industriales, Madrid, 1974. Mktg. engr. Westinghouse Proyectos Electricos, Madrid, 1974-76; tng. engr. Tecnatom, S.A., Madrid, 1976-80, tng. mgr. fossil power plants, 1981-85, mgr. quality assurance, 1986—. Served to 2d lt. Spanish Army, 1971-73. Mem. Sociedad Nuclear Espanola. Roman Catholic. Club: Madrid Country. Home: Concha Espina 18, 28016 Madrid Spain Office: Tecnatom SA, Km 19 CN-Madrid-Irun, 2809 SS Reyes Madrid Spain

GONZÁLEZ AVELAR, MIGUEL, government official; b. Durango, Mex., Mar. 19, 1937. Student, Nat. Autonomous U. of Mex. Sch. Law. Dep. gen. dir. for Coll. Edn. and Sci. Research, Ministry Pub. Edn., Mexico City, 1964-66; gen. dir. profs. and planning commn. Nat. Autonomous U. of Mex., 1966-70; aide Fed. Electoral Commn., Washington, 1970-71; advisor, undersec. Sec. Interior, Washington, 1970; pvt. sec. Sec. of Labor and Social Foresight, Mex., 1971-72; apptd. gen. dir. Social Foresight, Mex., 1971-72; dep. legal dir. Inst. Nat. Workers' Housing Fund, Mex., 1972-76; dep. dir. gen. Nat. Inst. for Devel. Rural Communities and Popular Housing, Mex., 1976-79; apptd. gen. dir. info. Ministry Planning and Budget, Mex., 1979—; elected senator State of Durango, Mex., 1982-85; sec. pub. edn. Mex., 1985—; rep. Permanent Tech. Com. for Labor Affairs of Orgn. of Am. States; prof. Tchr.'s Sch., Mex., 1962-65, Nat. Sch. Econs. Autonomous U. of Mex., 1962-67; resident prof. Autonomous U. of Mex. Sch. Law, 1967—, faculty examine Constitutional Law, Individual Rights and Theory of State, 1976—. Contbr. numerous articles on Mexican politics to profl. jours. Active Instl. Revolutionary Party, 1962—. Mem. Mex. Nat. Coll. Lawyers, Assn. Profls. State of Durango, Nat. Fedn. Pub. Sector Lawyers. Office: Ministry of Edn, Mexico City DF, Mexico *

GONZALEZ CALVILLO, MAYO RAFAEL, finance executive; b. Mexico City, Mar. 8, 1948; s. Rafael and Luz Esperanza (Calvillo) Gonzalez Lamadrid; m. Alda Carrasco, Dec., 1972 (div. Nov. 1980); children: Pablo Ignacio, Santiago Gonzalez Carrasco. BBA, U. Iberoam, Mexico City, 1971; MBA, U. Tex., 1974. Investment advisor Financiera Banamex, S.A., Mexico City, 1970; stock analyst Banco Nal. Mexico S.A., Mexico City, 1970-71; asst. v.p. Citibank, N.A., Mexico City, 1974-77; fin. dir. Industrias Pando Group, Mexico City, 1977-79; chief fin. officer Grupo Seguros la Comercial, Mexico City, 1979-81; sr. exec. v.p. Multibanco Comermex S. N. C., Mexico City, 1981—. Home: Cofre De Perote 280-301, Mexico City 11000, Mexico Office: Multibanco Comermex SNC, Piso 16 Col Polanco Blvd, M Avila Comacho No 1, Mexico City 11560, Mexico

GONZALEZ CASANOVA, PABLO, researcher, educator; b. Toluca, Mexico, Feb. 11, 1922; s. Pablo Gonzalez Casanova and Concepcion del Valle; m. Natalia Henriquez Urena, 1947; 3 children. Ed. El Colegio de Mexico, Escuela Nacional de Antropologia, Universidad Nacional Autonoma de Mexico, U. Paris. Asst. researcher Inst. de Investigaciones Sociales, Universidad Nacional Autonoma de Mexico, 1944-50, researcher, 1950-52, 73-78, titular prof. Mexican sociology Escuela Nacional de Ciencias Politicas y Sociales, 1952-66, titular prof. gen. sociology, 1954-58, dir. Escuela Nacional de Ciencias Politicas y Sociales, 1957-65, titular prof., 1964-65, titular prof. research planning, 1967—, dir. Inst. Investigaciones Sociales, 1966-70, univ. rector, 1970-72; researcher El Colegio de Mexico, 1950-54; sec. gen. Assn. Univs., 1953-54; pres. adminstrv. com. Facultad Latinoamericana de Ciencias Sociales, San Diago and Centro Latinoamericano de Investigaciones Sociales, Rio de Janeiro, Brazil, UNESCO, 1959-65; prof. Cambridge U., 1981-82; cons. United Nations U., 1983-87; dir. Centro Interdisciplimatio Universidad Nacional Autonoma de Mexico, 1986—. Author: El misoneismo y la modernidad cristiana, 1948; (with Jose Miranda) Satira del Siglo XVIII, 1953; Una utopia de America, 1953; La literatura perseguida en la crisis de la Colonia, 1958; La ideologia norteamericana sobre inversiones extranjeras, 1955; Estudio de la tecnica social, 1958; La Democracia en Mexico, 1965; Las catagorias del desarrollo economico y la investigacion en ciencias sociales, 1967; Sociologia de la explotacion, 1969; Historia del Movimiento Obrero en America Latina, Siglo XX, 1981; El Estado y los Partidos Politicos en Mexico, 1981; editor: America Latina; Historia de Medio Siglo 1925-1975, 2 vols., 1977. Mem. Assn. Internationale de Sociologues de Langue Francaise, Comite Internationale pour la Documentation des Sciences Sociales, Academia de la Investigacion Cientifica, Asociacion Latinoamericana de Sociologia (pres. 1969-72).

GONZALEZ DE RIVERA, JOSE LUIS, psychiatrist, educator; b. Bilbao, Spain, Nov. 12, 1944; s. Francisco and Ana Maria (Revuelta) Gonzalez de R.; m. Laura Outomuro; children: Laura, Lydia, Jose Luis, Javier; m. Ana Luisa Monterrey; 1 child, Leonor. BSc, Santiago Apostal, Bilbao, 1961; MD, U. Navarra, Pamplona, Spain, 1969; DSc, U. Pais Vasco, Bilbao, 1976. Lic. Med. Council Can., 1973. Clin. instr. McGill U., Montreal, Can., 1975-76; asst. clin. prof. Autonomous U., Madrid, 1976-80; prof., acting chmn. dept. psychiatry U. La Laguna, Tenerife, Spain, 1980-84; assoc. dean med. sch. U. La. Laguna, 1987; prof., chmn. dept. psychiatry U. La Laguna, 1986—; prof. psychiatry McMaster U., Hamilton, Ont., Can., 1984-86; chief psychiatry Hamilton Civic Hosps., 1984-86; dir. dept. psychiatry U. Hosp. Canary, Tenerife, 1986—. Editor Handbook of Psychiatry, 1980; editor in chief jour. PSIQUIS, Revista de Psiquiatria, 1977—; author monograph, over 70 sci. papers and chpts. in books. Served to 2d lt. Spanish Cavalry, 1967-69. Fellow Royal Coll. Physicians Can., Royal Soc. Medicine Eng., Royal Acad. Medicine Canary; mem. Am. Psychiatric Assn. (corr.), Canarian Soc. Psychiatry (founding mem., pres. 1987). Clubs: Ateneo (Madrid); Aero (Tenerife). Office: U La Laguna Med Sch, Carretera Cuesta Taco s/n, LaCuesta Ofra Tenerife Spain

GONZALEZ HERMOSILLO, MIGUEL JOSE, export-import company executive, international barter and shipping consultant; b. Mazatlan, Sinaloa, Mexico, Apr. 7, 1950; s. Jesus Gonzalez Hermosillo and Maria Emilia Gonzalez-Watkins. LL.M., London Sch. Econs., Eng., 1977; diploma in internat. and nat. develop studies Institute Social Studies, The Hague, Netherlands, 1974. Bar: Mex., 1975. Atty. Goodrich, Riquelme & Assos., Mexico City, Mexico, 1970-73, London, Eng., 1976-77; internat. dir. Belbec S.A., Mexico City, 1978-80; dir. Marc Rich Internat., Ltd., Mexico City, 1980-83; chmn. bd., mng. dir. Intercambio Compensado, S.A. De C.V., Distrito Federal, Mexico, 1983—; rep. in Mex. of Boliden Intertraclé A.B., Stockholm. Sec. gen. Asociacion De Residentes Del Pedregal De San Angel, Mexico City, Mexico, 1983. Mem. Sociedad De Ex-Alumnos De La London Sch. Econs. and Polit. Sci. Clubs: Club De Raqueta El Yaqui, Estado Mayor Presidencial (Mexico City). Advocations: horse-back riding; tennis; skiing; shooting. Home: Bosques de Quiroga #138, Bosques de la Herradura, Mexico City, 53920 Mexico Office: Bosques de Ciruelos N-140-1002, Bosques de las Lomas, Mexico City, 11700 Mexico

GONZALEZ MARQUEZ, FELIPE, prime minister Spain, lawyer; b. Seville, Mar. 5, 1942; m. Carmen Romero; 3 children. Student in law U. Seville, in econs. U. Louvain (Belgium). Mem. provincial com. Spanish Socialist Workers Party, Seville, 1965-70, exec. com., 1970-74, sec.-gen., 1974-76, 76-77, dep. for Madrid, Cortes, 1977-79, 79-81; sec.-gen., 1981-82; v.p. Socialist Internat., after 1981; Prime Minister of Spain, 1982—. Author: What Is Socialism?, 1976; P.S.O.E., 1977. Address: Office of the Prime Minister, Palacio de la Moncola, Madrid Spain *

GONZÁLEZ MARTÍN, MARCELO CARDINAL, archbishop of Toledo (Spain); b. Villanubla, Spain, Jan. 16, 1918; ordained priest Roman Catholic Ch., 1941; formerly tchr. theology and sociology Valladolid Diocesan Sem.; founder orgn. for constrn. houses for poor; consecrated bishop of Astorga, 1961; titular archbishop of Case Medinae, also coadjutor of Barcelona, 1966; archbishop of Barcelona, 1967-71, of Toledo, 1971—; elevated to Sacred Coll. Cardinals, 1973; mem. Congregation of Evangelization of Peoples. Address: Arco de Palacio 1, Toledo Spain *

GONZÁLEZ-OLLÉ, FERNANDO, university educator; b. Madrid, Spain, Feb. 4, 1929; s. Fernando and Pilar G-O. PhD, U. Madrid; Diplomate, Internat. Inst. Bibliography, Boston. Asst. prof. U. Madrid; prof. U. Murcia, Spain, U. Granada, Spain; prof. history Spanish lang. U. Pamplona, Spain, chmn. Spanish linguistics dept.; dir. Spanish lang. Culture Inst. for Foreigners, Pamplona, Spain; vis. prof. France, Fed. Republic Germany, Latin-Am., Japan. Menéndez Pelayo of Research, Higher Counsil of Sci. Research, 1959; Rivadeneira Research, Royal Spanish Acad., 1960, 63. Mem. Royal Spanish Acad., Asociatión de Historia de la Lengua Española. Office: Dept Linguistica Histórica, Facultad de Filologia, U Navarra, Pamplona 31080, Spain

GONZALO, JOSE MARIA AGUIRRE, civil engineer, banker; b. San Sebastian, Spain, Aug. 12, 1897; s. Jose Maria Aguirre and Hilaria (Gonzalo) Sagastume; m. Francisca Gonzalez, Nov. 21, 1925 (dec. 1978); children—Carmen (dec.), Jose Maria, Pilar, Beatriz. Civil Engring. degree, Tech. Superior Coll. Rds., Canals and Harbours, Madrid, 1921. Founder, chmn., mgr. Agroman Empresa Constructora S.A., Madrid, 1927-84; chmn. bd. Bank Guipuzcoano, San Sebastian, 1941—; dir., chmn. bd. Bank Espanol de Credito, Madrid, 1942-84; dir. Cia. Sevillana Electricidad, Madrid and Sevilla, Spain, 1951—; chmn. bd. Acerinox, Algeciras, Spain, 1969—; cofounder, chmn. Inst. Eduardo Torroja Constrn. and Cement, Madrid, 1934-84; chmn. Patronato Colegio Univ. est Financieros, Madrid, 1973—; participant tech., constrn. and fin. confs. Patentee in field. Mem. Spanish Congress, v.p. com., 1968. Decorated Gt. Cross Merito Civil, Gt. Cross Isabel la Catolica, Gt. Cross Cisneros, Gt. Cross Alfonso x el Sabio, Gt. Cross Carlos III; recipient Golden medal Govt. of Spain, 1967. Mem. Assn. Progress Mgmt. (bd. dirs.), Found. European Culture (bd. govs.). Clubs: Casino Circulo Labrado, Golf, Sociedad Hipica. Avocations: music; theatre; literature. Home: Almagro 27, Madrid 28010 Spain Office: Agroman Empresa Constructora SA, Raimundo Fernandez Villaverde 45, Madrid 28003, Spain

GONZENBACH, HANS RUDOLF, surgeon; b. Zurich, Apr. 18, 1946; s. Fritz and Edith Gonzenbach; m. Ursula Elisabeth Stamm, Apr. 15, 1972; children—Martin, Christina, Urs. M.D., U. Zurich, 1972. Resident, Hospital Uster, Switzerland, 1972-74, Virginia Mason Hosp., Seattle, 1974-75, Hosp. St. Gallen, Switzerland, 1975-77, attending surgeon, 1978-82; resident U. Zurich, 1983; attending surgeon Hosp. Herisau, Switzerland, 1983-85; pvt. surg. practice St. Gallen, Switzerland, 1986-88; chief surgeon, Hosp. sursee, Switzerland, 1989—. Contbr. articles to profl. jours. Vice pres. Health Commn., Eggersriet, 1982-85. Served to maj. M.C., Swiss Army, 1966-85. Mem. Swiss Surg. Soc., Paul Ehrlich Soc. Club: Tennis (Eggersriet). Home: Kirchweg 7, 9034 Eggersriet Switzerland

GOOCH, JAMES OLIVER, physician; b. Indian Gap, Tex., Nov. 27, 1913; s. James Walter and Ora Ellen (Oliver) G.; m. Feb. 5, 1935; children—Jon David, Joel Phillips. Student So. Meth. U., 1931-33, U. Tex., 1934-35; M.D., Tulane U., 1939; M.Sc. in Otorhinolaryngology, U. Minn., 1949. Diplomate Am. Bd. Otolaryngology. Intern, Shreveport (La.) Charity Hosp., 1939-40; fellow Mayo Found., Rochester, Minn., 1946-49; asst. prof. otolaryngology Baylor Med. Sch., 1949-51; practice otolaryngology and allergy, Midland, Tex., 1951—; mem. staff Midland Meml. Hosp. Served to col. M.C., U.S. Army, 1940-46. Decorated Purple Heart. Mem. Am. Acad. Ophthalmology and Otolaryngology, AMA, Tex. Med. Assn., Allergy Soc., Am. Acad. Otolaryngic Allergy, Quiet Birdman. Republican. Clubs: Austin Country, Midland Country, Horseshoe Bay Country. Lodges: Masons, Shriners. Home: 1600 W Golf Course Rd Midland TX 79701 Office: 401 N Garfield St Midland TX 79704

GOOD, LEONARD PHELPS, artist; b. Chickasha, Okla., June 25, 1907; s. Jacob Calvin and Belle (Leonard) G.; m. Nancye Dooley, July 15, 1932 (dec. May 1969); 1 son, Leonard Jacob; m. Yoshie Tobe, Nov. 26, 1970. B.F.A., U. Okla., 1927; student, Art Students' League, N.Y.C., 1930, Clarence White Sch. Photography, N.Y.C., 1937, State U. Iowa, 1940. Tchr. pub. sch. art depts. Tex. and Okla., 1927-30; mem. faculty U. Okla. Sch. Art, 1930-50, U. Wis., 1950-52; prof., head dept. art Drake U., 1952-77, emeritus prof., 1977—; curator paintings Mus. Art, U. Okla., 1935-50; vis. artist-in residence Iowa State U., Ames, 1966, Shenandoah (Iowa) Community High Sch. for Nat. Endowment for Arts, 1970-71, Central Coll., Pella, Iowa, 1984. Exhibited: paintings nat. exhbns. Am. Art, 1936, 37, Am. Painters in Paris, France, 1975-76, traveling exhbns., Am. Fedn. Art, 1940-41; rep. permanent collections, Okla. Art Center, Okla. Art Mus., Okla. Hist. Mus., Philbook Art Center, Tulsa, Kans. Fedn. Arts, Brunnier Mus., Iowa State U., Ames, Iowa, Milw. Art Center, Des Moines Art Center, Mabee-Gerrer Mus. Art, Shawnee, Okla., Iowa Hist. Mus., Springville (Utah) Mus. Art, Urasenke Internat. Found., Kyoto, Japan; juror nat. exhbns. Trustee Mabee-Gerrer Mus. Art, Shawnee, Okla. Mem. Omicron Delta Kappa (hon.), Delta Phi Delta (nat. pres. 1958-60). Home: 1320 Oregon Ave Chickasha OK 73018

GOOD, MILTON SHENK, physician, sculptor; b. Morgantown, Pa., Oct. 10, 1932; s. Noah Gehman and Ella Kaufman (Shenk) G.; B.S., Franklin and Marshall Coll., 1954; M.D., Hahnemann Med. Coll., 1958; m. Ann Augsburger, June 11, 1956; children—Sonja Jeanne, Erika Joan, Don Milton, Judith Annette. Intern, Lancaster (Pa.) Gen. Hosp., 1958-59; gen. practice medicine, Elizabethtown, Pa., 1959—; partner Dr. John Barr, 1959-63; pvt. practice, 1963-71; pres. med. corp., 1971—; mem. faculty dept. family practice Pa. State U., Hershey Med. Center. Bd. dirs. Philhaven Hosp., Mt. Gretna, Pa. Recipient various awards for sculpture in juried and non-juried competition, 1967—. Diplomate Am. Bd. Family Practice. Fellow Am. Acad. Family Practice; mem. Am., Mennonite, N.W. Lancaster County (dir. 1973—) med. assns., Pa., Lancaster County med. socs., Am. Physicians Art Assn. (treas. 1976-82, pres. 1982-85), Elizabethtown C. of C. (dir. 1963). Republican. Mem. Ch. of Brethren. Home and Office: 610 Highlawn Ave Elizabethtown PA 17022

GOOD, ROY SHELDON, financial executive; b. Cleve., Dec. 13, 1924; s. Julius and Sally (Sharpe) G.; m. Wendy Rae Polasky, Sept. 12, 1982; children by previous marriage—Jeri Good Dansky, Michael. B.B.A., Western Res. U., 1948, M.B.A., 1951. With tax dept. Touche, Ross & Co., Detroit, 1952-57, supr., 1957-59, mgr., 1959-61; adminstrv. asst. to controller Am. Motors Corp., Detroit, 1961-63, asst. controller, 1963-68; mgr. employee benefits fin. adminstrn. Chrysler Corp., Detroit, 1968-77, mgr. investment rev., 1977-78; mgr. investment rev. and spl. financing, 1978-80; v.p. Alexander & Alexander Inc., Detroit, 1981—; lectr., author employee benefits and pension fund investment mgmt., 1970—; bd. dirs. Health Alliance Plan, 1982-86. Served with U.S. Army, 1943-46; ETO. C.P.A., Mich., Ohio. Mem. Am. Inst. C.P.A.s, Mich. Assn. C.P.A.s, Midwest Pension Conf., Beta Alpha Psi. Democrat. Jewish. Club: Birmingham Athletic. Home: 31462 Hunters Circle Farmington Hills MI 48018 Office: 600 Fisher Bldg Detroit MI 48202

GOOD, SUSAN PAULINE, banker; b. Sanger, Calif., Aug. 17, 1953; d. Alfred Anton and Elsbeth (Grimm) Good; AA, Reedley Coll., 1973; BA summa cum laude, Calif. State U., Fresno, 1975. Advt. asst. Bell Pub. Relations Agy., Fresno, Calif., 1976-77; account exec. Meeker Advt., Fresno, Calif., 1977-78; dir. advt. Coast Savs. and Loan, Fresno, Calif., 1978-81, asst. v.p., br. promotions mgr., br. mgr., 1981-84, br. mgr., 1984—. Mem. mktg. com. U.S. League Savs. Assn., 1980-81; chmn. Fresno City-County Commn. on Status Women, 1979; chmn. Fresno County Dem. Cen. Com., 1985-86; pres. Calif. State U. Fresno Alumni Assn., 1981; regional dir. Calif. Dem. Party; pres. Leadership Fresno Alumni Exec. Bd., 1987; mem. Charter Leadership Fresno Class, 1985; parliamentarian Jr. League of Fresno. Recipient cert. of achievement Inst. Fin. Edn., 1982, Silver medal Am. Advt. Fedn., 1982. Mem. Fresno Advt. Fedn. (pres. 1982), Inst. Fin. Edn., C. of C. (past chmn. ambassadors, Calif. State U. Fresno Alumni). Roman Catholic.

GOODE, RICHARD HARRIS, investment banker; b. Chgo., Sept. 13, 1939; s. William Richard and Lois May (Harris) G.; S.B. in Chem. Engring. and Indsl. Mgmt., MIT, 1961, S.M. in Chem. Engring. and Indsl. Mgmt. (Pullman-Kellogg Inc. scholar), 1965; m. Eleanor Louise, June 26, 1965; 1 son, James Scott. Mgt. internat. sales Pullman-Kellogg Inc., N.Y.C., 1961-69; v.p., mgr. sales Davy Internat. Inc., N.Y.C., 1969-73; internat. sales mgr. Mitchell, Hutchins Inc., N.Y.C., 1973-75; v.p., mgr. internat. dept. Spencer Trask Inc., N.Y.C., 1975-77; sr. v.p.-mgr. internat. Sales dept. Lehman Bros. Kuhn Loeb Inc., N.Y.C., 1977-84; exec. v.p. internat div., Alex. Brown & Sons Inc., 1984-87; pres. Pacific Div. First Manhattan C., 1987— . Mem. task force on energy crisis and alt. fuels FPC, 1970-73; admissions officer MIT Alumni Ednl. Council; mem. Vol. Urban Cons. Group, Harvard U.-MIT, N.Y.C. Mem. MIT Alumni Center. Home: 81 White Oak Ridge Rd Lincroft NJ 07738 Office: 437 Madison Ave New York NY 10022

GOODENOUGH, JOHN, advertising executive; b. Oldham, Lancashire, Eng., Feb. 7, 1940; s. Harold Henry and Nina Daphne (Harris) G.; m. Margaret Ann West, June 24, 1961 (div. 1987); children: Fiona Mary, Alan Mark. Grad., Leeds (Eng.) Poly., 1959. Guardsman H.M. Coldstream Guards, York, Eng., 1959-62; insp. Royal Soc. for Prevention of Cruelty to Animals, Luton, Eng., 1962-64; ptnr. Lance Studios Photography, Peterborough, Eng., 1964-87; mng. dir. Lance Studios Advt. Ltd., Peterborough, 1982—; ptnr. Knights Armoury, Petersborough, 1987—; cons. St. Francis Animal Clinic, Petersborough, 1987—. Served to col. Royal Marines Res., 1968-88. Fellow Inst. Sales and Mktg. Mgmt.; mem. Master Photographers Assn. (lic. 1972). Club: City and Country (Petersborough) (bd. dirs. 1981-84). Lodges: Vine (master 1968-69), Apollo (master 1981-82). Home: 101 Eye Rd, Peterborough PE1 4SG, England Office: Lance Studios Advt Ltd, 212 Lincoln Rd, Petersborough PE1 2NE, England

GOODES, MELVIN RUSSELL, manufacturing company executive; b. Hamilton, Ont., Can., Apr. 11, 1935; s. Cedric Percy and Mary Melba (Lewis) G.; m. Arlene Marie Bourne, Feb. 23, 1963; children: Melanie, Michelle, David. B in Commerce, Queen's U., Kingston, Ont., Can., 1957; MBA, U. Chgo., 1960. Research assoc. Can. Econ. Research Assocs., Toronto, Ont., 1957-58; market planning coordinator Ford Motor Co. Can., Oakville, Ont., 1960-64; asst. to v.p. O'Keefe Breweries, Toronto, 1964-65; mgr. new product devel. Adams Brands div. Warner-Lambert Can., Scarborough, Ont., 1965-68; area mgr. Warner-Lambert Internat., Toronto, 1968-69; regional dir. confectionary ops. Warner-Lambert Europe, Brussels, 1969-70; pres. Warner-Lambert Mex., 1970-76; pres. Pan-Am. zone Warner-Lambert Internat., Morris Plains, N.J., 1976-77, pres. Pan-Am. and Asian zone, 1977-79; pres. consumer products div. Warner-Lambert Co., Morris Plains, N.J., 1979-81, sr. v.p., pres. consumer products group, 1981-83, exec. v.p., pres. U.S. ops., 1984-85, pres., chief operating officer, 1985—, also bd. dirs.; bd. dirs. Chem. N.Y. Corp., Chem. Bank, Unisys; mem. exec. adv. council Nat. Ctr. Ind. Retail Pharmacy, 1984-85. Bd. dirs. Council on Family Health, N.Y.C., 1981-86; mem. fin. com. Joint Council on Econ. Edn., 1984—, trustee, mem. exec. com., 1986—; mem. adv. council Sch. of Bus., Queen's U., 1980-84; trustee Drew U., Madison, N.J., 1985—, Queen's U., Can., 1988. Fellow Ford Found., 1958, Sears, Roebuck Found., 1959. Mem. Nat. Wholesale Druggists Assn. (assoc. adv. com.), Nat. Assn. Retail Druggists (exec. adv. council 1983-85), Proprietary Assn. (v.p. 1983-88, bd. dirs., mem. exec. com. 1981-88), Nat. Alliance Bus. (bd. dirs. 1984-86). Unitarian. Clubs: Plainfield Country (N.J.); Econ. (N.Y.C.). Office: Warner-Lambert Co 201 Tabor Rd Morris Plains NJ 07950

GOODEY, BRIAN, urban design educator; b. Chelmsford, England, July 6, 1941; s. Reginald Rolf and Mirrell (Rolf) Goodey; m. Kathleen Mary Bloom, Feb. 4, 1967; children: Sarah Nicole, Carl Rolf. BA, U. Nottingham, Eng., 1963; MA, Ind. U., 1967. Assoc. fac. mem. Ind. U., Bloomington, Ind., U.S.A., 1964-67; asst. prof. U. N.D., Grand Forks, 1967-69; tutor U. Birmingham, Eng., 1969-75; sr. lectr. Joint Ctr. Urban Design, Oxford (Eng.) Poly., 1975-79, reader, 1979—, assoc., First Interpreters, 1987—; bd. dirs. Landscape Research Group Ltd., London; cons. Dept. Edn. and Sci., London, 1980, Council of Europe, Strasbourg, France, 1972—. Author: Perception of the Enviroment, 1971, A Participatory Culture in the Built Environment, 1981, Urban Culture at a Turining Point, 1983; editor: Urban Cultural Life in the 1980's, 1983. Councillor Middleton Parish Council, Northamptonshire, Eng., 1981—; trustee Clerkenwell Trust, London, 1979—. Recipient Fulbright award Fulbright Found., 1983, Leverhulme Research award Leverhulme Trust, 1972. Fellow Royal Geog. Soc., Royal Soc. Arts; mem. Inst. Brit. Geographers, Soc. for the Interpretation of Britain's Heritage. Home: 14 Queen St, Middleton Cheney, Banbury OX17 2NP, England Office: Oxford Poly Joint Ctr Urban Design, Headington, Oxford OX3 OBp, England

GOODFELLOW, HOWARD DOUGLAS, environmental consultant, educator; b. Brighton, Can., Apr. 21, 1942; s. Douglas Cecil and Bertha Ermina (Nelson) G.; m. Karen Elizabeth Fabian, June 10, 1966; children: Geoffrey Howard, Jennifer Jane. B of Applied Sci. in Chem. Engring., U. Toronto, 1964, M of Applied Sci. in Chem. Engring., 1965, PhD in Chem. Engring., 1968. Environ. mgr. Hatch Assocs. Ltd., Toronto, 1970-85; assoc. prof. U. Toronto, 1980—; pres. Goodfellow Cons. Inc., Toronto, 1985—; lectr. in field; chmn. Ventilation '85 Symposium, 1985. Author: Advanced Design of Ventilation Systems for Contaminant Control, 1985; contbr. over 30 tech. papers in environ. control and occupational health and safety. Mem. Profl. Engrs. Ont., Ministry of Environment (liaison com.), Occupational Hygiene Assn. Ont. (pres.-elect, occupational health issues com.), Profl. Engrs. Ontario (reconsideration com. 1983-87), Air Pollution Control Assn. (iron and steel com.). Office: 2000 Argentia Rd, Plaza III Suite 301, Mississauga, ON Canada L5N 1V9

GOODFELLOW, MARK AUBREY, diplomat; b. London, Apr. 7, 1931; s. Alfred Edward and Lucy Emily (Potter) G.; m. Madelyn Susan Scammell; children: Venetia Katherine, Adam Simeon Nicholas. Third sec. Fgn. and Commonwealth Office, London, 1952-54, 2d sec., 1959-63, 1st sec., 1971-74; 3d sec. Brit. Mil. Govt., Berlin, Fed. Republic Germany, 1954-56; 2d sec. Brit. Embassy, Khartoum, Sudan, 1956-59, Yaounde, Cameroon, 1963-66; 1st sec. Brit. Embassy, Ankara, Turkey, 1974-78; Brit. trade commr. Hong Kong, 1966-71; Her Majesty's consul Atlanta, Ga., 1978-82; counsellor Brit. Embassy, Washington, 1982-84, High Commn., Lagos, Nigeria, 1984-86; Her Majesty's ambassador Embassy, Libreville, Gabon, 1986—. Anglican. Club: Traveller's, Hong Kong, Ikoyi, Nigeria, Hong Kong. Home and Office: Brit Embassy, BP 476, Libreville Gabon

GOODFELLOW, ROBIN IRENE, surgeon; b. Xenia, Ohio, Apr. 14, 1945; d. Willis Douglas and Irene Linna (Kirkland) G. B.A. summa cum laude, Western Res. U., Cleve., 1967; M.D. cum laude, Harvard U., 1971. Diplomate Am. Bd. Surgery. Intern, resident Peter Bent Brigham Hosp., Boston, 1971-76; staff surgeon Boston U., 1976-80, asst. prof. surgery, 1977-80; practice medicine specializing in surgery, Jonesboro, La., 1980-81, Albion, Mich., 1984-87, Coldwater, Mich., 1987—. Bd. Overseers Case Western Res. U., 1977-82. Fellow AAUW, 1970; mem. AMA, Phi Beta Kappa. Republican. Methodist.

GOODHARTZ, GERALD, law librarian; b. N.Y.C., Oct. 23, 1938; s. Jack and Anna (Sperling) G.; student CCNY, 1957-61; m. Carol Scialli, Aug. 18, 1969; children—Joanna, Allison. Night reference asst. Assn. Bar City N.Y., 1956-61; library asst. firm Cravath, Swaine & Moore, N.Y.C., 1961-65; head librarian firm Rosenman Colin Freund Lewis & Cohen, N.Y.C., 1965-69, Keatinge & Sterling, Los Angeles, 1969-70, Kaye, Scholer, Fierman, Hays & Handler, N.Y.C., 1970—. Mem. Am. Assn. Law Libraries (cert.), Law Library Assn. Greater N.Y., Assn. Law Librarians of Upstate N.Y., Spl. Libraries Assn., ALA, Am. Soc. Info. Sci., Assn. Info. Mgrs., Nat. Micrographics Assn. Office: 425 Park Ave New York NY 10022

GOODHUE, WILLIAM WALTER, JR., physician, army officer; b. St. Louis, Feb. 5, 1945; s. William W. and Rose Marie (Vahousek) G.; B.S. cum laude with honors, Georgetown U., 1966; M.D., Cornell U., 1970. Intern anat. pathology N.Y. Hosp.-Cornell Med. Center, N.Y.C., 1970-71, resident anat. pathology, 1971-74; chief resident pediatric anat. pathology Columbia-Presbyn. Med. Center, N.Y.C., 1974-75; resident clin. pathology Tripler Army Med. Center, Honolulu, 1976-78, chief resident, 1978; practice medicine specializing in pathology, 1975—; instr. pathology U. Hawaii Sch. Medicine, Honolulu, 1975-76; chief dept. pathology U.S. Army Hosp., Ft. Campbell, Ky., 1978-80; chief dept. pathology, med. dir. Sch. Med. Tech., dir. pathology residency tng. Gorgas Army Hosp., C.Z. and asso. prof. med. tech. Panama Canal Coll., 1980-82; resident officer U.S. Army Command and Gen. Staff Coll., Ft. Leavenworth, Kans., 1982-83, div. surgeon 2d Inf. Div., 1983-84; dep. comdr. clin. services, chief dept. primary care and community medicine, staff pathologist, acting comdr. Bayne-Jones Army Hosp., Ft. Polk, La., 1984-85; chief dept. pathology and area lab. services, dir. pathology residency tng. Dwight David Eisenhower Army Med. Ctr., Ft. Gordon, Ga., 1985—; clin. asst. prof. pathology Med. Coll. Ga., Augusta, 1986—, also cons. in pathology Eisenhower health service region to comdg. gen.; cons. ARC, 1978-80. Served to col., M.C., U.S. Army, 1975-86. USPHS research fellow, 1971-74. Diplomate Am. Bd. Pathology. Fellow Am. Soc. Clin. Pathologists, Internat. Acad. Pathology, Coll. Am. Pathologists, Am. Soc. Abdominal Surgeons; mem. Soc. for Pediatric Pathology, Med. Assn. Isthmian C.Z. (v.p. 1980-81), Assn. Mil. Surgeons U.S., Am. Assn. Blood Banks, Nashville Pathology Soc., Hawaii Soc. Pathologists, AAAS, N.Y. Acad. Scis., Soc. Armed Forces Med. Lab. Scientists, Assn. Practitioners in Infection Control, Clin. Lab. Mgrs. Assn., Central Savannah River Area Assn. Med. Lab. Personnel, Assn. U.S. Army, AMA (Physician's Recognition award 1976, 78, 80, 82, 86), Sigma Xi, Phi Beta Kappa. Republican. Roman Catholic. Clubs: Cornell of N.Y.; Kauai Yacht. Contbr. articles on pathology to profl. jours.; research in clin. pathology. Home: 421 Halifax Dr Martinez GA 30907-2727 Office: DDEAMC, DPALS Fort Gordon GA 30905-5650

GOODINE, ISAAC THOMAS, bank executive, educator; b. Hazeldean, N.B., Can., Apr. 11, 1932; s. Lewis Ambrose and Beatrice Ann (Babineau) G.; m. Sandra Jean Campbell, May 3, 1958 (div. 1981); children: Darlene Lynn, Sharon Ann, Catherine Elizabeth; m. Gloria Ann Whiting, Aug. 3, 1981; 1 child, Claudia Ann. BS, Mt. Allison U., Sackville, N.B., 1956, Cert. in Engring., 1957, BE, 1960. Instr. N.B. Inst. Tech., Moncton, 1961-65, vice prin., 1965-66, prin., 1966-70; prin. Zambia Inst. Tech., Kitwe, 1970-72; dep. dir. Dept. Tech. Edn. and Vocat. Tng., Lusaka, Zambia, 1973-74; policy analyst N.B. Community Coll., Fredericton, 1974-75; dir. Kenya Tech. Tch's. Coll., Nairobi, 1975-78; sr. tech. educator The World Bank, Washington, 1978—. Sec. Nat. Com. on Physics for Insts. Tech. in Can., 1965-58, Coordinating Com. on Tech. Tchr. Edn. for Eastern Africa, Nairobi, 1975-78; co-chmn. Working Party on Council for Higher Edn. in Zambia, Lusaka, 1973-74; bd. dirs. Greater Moncton Community Chest, 1968-69, Moncton Family YMCA, 1966-69. Served to lt. Can. Army, 1956-59. Mem. Internat. Vocat. Edn. and Tng. Assn., Am. Vocat. Assn., Can. Vocat. Assn., Royal Can. Armoured Corps Assn. Mem. United Ch. Lodge: Rotary (Moncton, Kitwe, Nairobi clubs). Home: 211 Owaissa Ct Vienna VA 22180 Office: The World Bank 1818 H St NW Washington DC 20433

GOODISON, NICHOLAS PROCTOR, stockbroker; b. Radlett, Eng., May. 16, 1934; s. Edmund Harold and Eileen Mary Carrington (Proctor) G.; m. Judith Abel Smith, 1960; children: Katharine, Adam, Rachel. student Marlborough Coll.; BA in Classics King's Coll., 1958, MA; PhD Architecture, History of Art Cambridge U., 1981; LittD (hon.) City U.; Mem. of the stock exchange H.E. Goodison & Co. (named changed to Quilter Goodison Co. and now Quilter Goodison Goodison Co. Ltd.), ptnr., 1962, chnm., 1975-88; elected to the Council of Stock Exchange, 1968; chmn. of the Stock Exchange, 1976-86, Internat. Stock Exchanges (FIBV), 1985-86; chmn. TSB Group plc, 1988— ; dir. Banque Paribas Capital Markets, 1986-88, banque Paribas (Luxembourg) SA 1986-88, Gen. Accident Fire and Life Assurance Corp., 1987—, Ottoman Bank, 1988—, Burlington Magazine, Ltd.; chmn. Paribas French Investment Trust; chmn., 1976—; mem. exec. com. Nat. Art Collections Fund, 1976—, chmn. 1986—; chmn. mgmt. com. Courtauld Inst. of Art, 1982—; dir. English Nat. Opera, 1977, vice-chmn., 1980; hon. keeper of furniture Fitzwilliam Mus., Cambridge ; dir. City Art Trust; gov. Marlborough Coll. Fellow Royal Acad. of Arts in London, Royal Soc. of Arts, Antiquaries;mem. Antiquarian Horological Soc. (pres.), Furniture History Soc. (hon., treas.). Author: English Barometers 1680-1860, 1968, rev. edit., 1977; Ormolu: The Work of Matthew Boulton, 1974; also articles, papers. Clubs: Arts, Atheneaum, Beefsteak. Avocations: study the history of furniture and decorative arts, opera, walking, fishing. Home: 25 Milk St, EC2V 8LU London England Office: The Stock Exchange, Old Broad St, EC2 London England

GOODLAD, CHARLES ALEXANDER, fisheries, acquaculture company executive; b. Shetland, Scotland, Sept. 19, 1943; s. Henry and Willamina (Guthrie) G.; m. Myrtha Magloire, Dec. 17, 1973; children: Natalie, Alexandra. MA in Geography with honors, Aberdeen U., 1965, PhD, 1968. Cert. deep sea fishing capt. Technologist fisheries dept. FAO, Rome, 1971-74; sr. v.p. Arabco Ltd., Auckland, New Zealand, 1975-80; chief ops. officer Saudi Fisheries Co., Dammam, Saudi Arabia, 1980-82; chmn. Shetland Sea Farms Ltd., 1983—; cons. numerous internat. orgns. Author: Shetland Fishing Saga, 1970, North Atlantic Fisherman, 1971. Home: Trondra, Shetland ZE1 0Xl, Scotland Office: Shetland Sea Farms Ltd, Trondra ZE1 0XL, Scotland

GOODMAN, DAVID MICHAEL, marketing company executive; b. Stamford, Conn., Feb. 26, 1948; s. Russell Edgar and Mildred (Rosenberg) G.; m. Suzanne Pesin, Oct. 11, 1975; children: Emily Blaine, Rachel Megan. BS with honors, Phila. Coll. Textiles and Sci., 1971. Sales mgr. to dir. mfg. Alfred Angelo, Inc., Willow Grove, Pa., 1971-75; divisional sales mgr., dist. v.p., founding dir. of govt. contracts div. YKK (USA), Inc., Bristol, Pa., 1975-86; pres., founder Diversified Mktg. Group, Pa., 1986—; lectr. U. Pa., Drexel U., Phila. Coll. Textiles and Sci.; sales rep., cons. to mil. clothing and equipment contractors; mem. Pa. Senate Com. Textile Imports. Contbr. articles to profl. jours. Mem. Phila. Bd. Apparel Mfrs., Am. Apparel Mfrs. Assn., Am. Clothing Designers Guild, Phila. Men's and Boy's Clothing Mfrs., Phila. Textile Salesman's Assn., Nat. Bd. USA Bus. Leaders, Bus. Leaders of Am. Clubs: President's, Frankford Radio. Home: 1236 Greentree Ln Penn Valley PA 19072 Office: 7 Neshaminy Interplex Suite 209 Trevose PA 19047

GOODMAN, G.D. WATSON, publisher; b. Cin., Jan. 22, 1920; s. William Preston and Myrtie Viola (Martt) G.; m. Rose Amelia Stair, Aug. 30, 1943; children: Victoria Raye, Donald Watson, Ruth Estelle, Harry Woodrow. ThB, Marion (Ind.) Coll., 1942, BA, 1943. Pastor Friend's Ch., Fiat, Ind., 1941-43, Pilgrim Holiness Ch., Milton, Del., 1944; dist. supr. Pilgrim Holiness Ch., Mt. Frere, Republic of South Africa, 1945-48; pres. Union Bible Coll., Brakpan, South Africa, 1948-50; dir. Gospel Centre Work, Germiston, South Africa, 1951-61; pres., founder World Missionary Press, Inc., New Paris, Ind., 1961-87; chief exec. officer Enterprises for Emmanuel, Elkhart, Ind., 1985—; founder, pres. Distinctive Products, Inc., Elkhart, 1987—. Author: Look-Out Everybody; numerous booklets. Home: PO Box 1773 Elkhart IN 46515 Office: Distinctive Products Inc 53038 Faith Ave Elkhart IN 46514

GOODMAN, JULIUS, nuclear engineer, consultant, researcher; b. Odessa, USSR, July 19, 1935; came to U.S., 1979, naturalized, 1986; s. Isaac and Eugenia (Lusher) Guttmann; m. Rachel Bezpalko, July 4, 1959; 1 dau., Marina. M.S. in Theoretical Physics, State U., Odessa, 1958, Ph.D., Inst. Nuclear Physics, Tashkent, USSR, 1962. Inst. Tech. Odessa, 1965. Sr. researcher Inst. Nuclear Physics, Tashkent, Acad. Sci., USSR, 1958-63; prof. Inst. Tech., Odessa, 1963-70, Poly U., 1970-76; sr. engr. Bechtel Power Corp., Norwalk, Calif., 1980-86; prof. Calif. State U. Long Beach, 1986—. Author: Professional Education, 1975, (with P.U. Arifov) Positron Diagnostic, 1978; contbr. numerous articles to profl. jours. Pres. Hatchiya (Revival), Orange County, Calif., 1982—. Mem. Am. Nuclear Soc., Internat. Soc. Reliability Engrs., Internat. Platform Assn., Com. on Internat. Freedom of Scientists, AAAS, N.Y. Acad. Scis., Los Angeles Council Engrs. and Scientists (publicity chmn. 1983-84). Club: Toastmasters (Fullerton, Calif.). Lodge: B'nai B'rith. Research on probabilistic risk assessment, reliability, statistics, artificial intelligence, simulation; gen. relativity, atomic and nuclear physics, physics of space nuclear reactors. Patentee nuclear reactor with UF-6. Home: 1630 Via Linda Fullerton CA 92633 Office: Calif State U Sch Engring 1250 Bellflower Blvd Long Beach CA 90840

GOODMAN, LEONARD, personal products company executive; b. N.Y.C., Dec. 13, 1926; s. Abraham Isaac and Mollie (Frishberg) G.; m. Constance Schulman, Mar. 22, 1953; children: Stanley David, Joyce Elsa. BBA, U. Miami, Coral Gables, 1948. Exec. Goody Products, Inc. (formerly H. Goodman & Sons), N.Y.C., 1948-56, v.p. ops., 1962-77; pres., chmn., chief exec. officer Goody Products, Inc. (formerly H. Goodman & Sons), Kearny, N.J., 1977—; div. mgr. Foster Grant Co., Leominster, Mass., 1956-62. Exec. com., trustee Hebrew Arts Sch., N.Y.C., 1973—, v.p., 1982-85; trustee North Shore Child & Family Guidance Assn., Inc., Manhasset, N.Y., 1977—; trustee Temple Israel of Gt. Neck (N.Y.), 1970-80, treas., 1971-77; bd. dirs., exec. com. Jewish Theol. Sem., N.Y.C., 1976-79, overseer, 1980—. Served with USN, 1944-46. Club: Harmonie (N.Y.C.). Office: Goody Products Inc 969 Newark Turnpike Kearny NJ 07032

GOODMAN, LINDA, author; b. Richmond, Va.; d. Robert Stratton and Mazie (McBee) Kemery; grad. high sch.; m. William Herbert Snyder (dec. Oct. 1970); children—Melissa Anne, James, John Anthony, Sarah Elizabeth, William Dana; m. 2d, Sam O. Goodman (dec. Nov. 1983); children—Jill Kemery, Michael Aaron. Writer-broadcaster Letter From Linda radio shows WAMP (NBC), Pitts.; writer Emphasis and Monitor for NBC network radio; continuity chief WHN Radio, N.Y.C. Author: Sun Signs, 1968; Venus Trines at Midnight, 1970; Love Signs, 1978; Love Poems, 1979; Star Signs, 1987. Mem. Assn. for Research and Enlightenment, Virginia Beach, Va. Speech writer for Whitney Young and Nat. Urban League. Named Dau. of Year, W.Va. Soc. Washington, 1971. Mem. AFTRA, Authors League Am., Writers Guild N.Y. Address: care Press Relations Mannu Unltd 137 Hayden St Cripple Creek CO 80813

GOODMAN, MARK N., lawyer; b. Phoenix, Jan. 16, 1952; s. Daniel H. and Joanne G.; m. Gwendolyn A. Langfeldt, Oct. 24, 1982; 1 child, Zachary A. BA, Prescott Coll., 1973; JD summa cum laude, Calif. Western Sch. Law, 1977; LL.M., U. Calif.-Berkeley, 1978. Bar: Ariz. 1977, Calif. 1977 U.S. Dist. Ct. (no. dist.) Calif. 1977, U.S. Dist. Ct. Ariz. 1978, U.S. Ct. Appeals (9th cir.) 1978, U.S. Dist. Ct. (so. dist.) Calif. 1981, U.S. Supreme Ct. 1981, U.S. Dist. Ct. (ce. dist.) Calif., 1982, Nebr. 1983, U.S. Dist. Ct. Nebr. 1983. Practice Law Offices Mark N. Goodman, Prescott, Ariz., 1978-79, 81-83, Mark N. Goodman, Ltd., Prescott, 1983-86; ptnr. Alward and Goodman, Ltd., Prescott, 1979-81; ptnr. Perry, Goodman, Drutz & Musgrove, Prescott, 1986-87, Goodman, Drutz & Musgrove, 1987—. Author: The Ninth Amendment, 1981. Contbr. articles to profl. jours. Bd. dirs. Yavapai Symphony Assn., Prescott, 1981-84. Notes and comments editor Calif. Western Law Review, 1976. Mem. ABA, Am. Trial Lawyers Assn. Yavapai County Bar Assn. (v.p. 1981-82). Office: Goodman Drutz & Musgrove PO Box 2489 Prescott AZ 86302-2489

GOODMAN, PHILIP, computer company executive; b. LaCrosse, Wis., May 14, 1937; s. William and Lilian Goodman; B.A., Miami U., Oxford, Ohio, 1958; 1 son, Charles Daniel. Eastern regional mgr. Gen. Automation Co., Stamford, Conn., 1971-73; v.p. Digital Computer Controls Inc., Fairfield, N.J., 1973-77; v.p. Digi-Log Systems Inc., Horsham, Pa., 1977-79; v.p., dir. Control Transaction Corp., Fairfield, 1979-80; chmn. bd. Data Safe, Inc. (name changed to Fastcomm Data, Inc.), McLean, Va., 1981-85; dir. sales Internat. Robomation/Intelligence, Princeton, N.J., 1985-86, v.p., 1986—; dir. Transidyne Gen. Corp., Ann Arbor, Mich. Mem. Phi Beta Kappa. Home: 4F Brookline Ct Princeton NJ 08540 Office: Internat Robomation-Intelligence 100 Thanet Dr Princeton NJ 08540

GOODMAN, ROBERT LAWRENCE, lawyer, management consultant; b. N.Y.C., May 15, 1953; s. Daniel and Ruth (Miller) G.; m. Wendy Faith Ehrenkranz, Apr. 17, 1983 (div. Dec. 1986). BA, Swarthmore (Pa.) Coll., 1975; MA, Harvard U., 1976, JD, 1980. Bar: D.C. 1981, N.Y. 1982. Law clk. to Judge U.S. Ct. Appeals (D.C. cir.), 1980-81; atty. Davis, Polk and Wardwell, Paris and N.Y.C., 1981-83, Arnold and Porter, Washington, 1983-85; mgmt. cons. McKinsey & Co., Inc., New York and Copenhagen, 1985—. Mem. Harvard Law Review (bd. editors 1978-80). Club: Harvard (N.Y.C.). Office: McKinsey & Co Inc, Ved Stranden 14, DK-1061 Copenhagen Denmark

GOODMAN, STANLEY ERWIN, surgeon; b. Norwalk, Conn., May 4, 1926; s. Robert M. and Francine (Cotler) G.; B.S., Trinity Coll., Hartford, 1947; M.A., U. Pa., 1949; M.D., Cornell U., 1953; m. Alice Marie Vanderbecq, June 20, 1962; m. 2d, Francine Joan. Intern, Strong Meml. Hosp., Rochester, N.Y., 1953-54; asst. resident surgery Mt. Sinai Hosp., N.Y.C., 1954-55; asst. resident surgery Kings County Hosp., Bklyn., 1955-58, chief resident surgery, 1958-59, attending surgeon vascular service and breast tumor bd., 1959 ; research asst. State U. N.Y. Med. Sch., Bklyn., 1956-57; gen. surgery practice, Norwalk, 1959-—; sr. attending surg. staff Norwalk Hosp., also chief sect. neoplastic diseases; asst. instr. SUNY Med. Sch., 1956-57, instr. clin. surgery, 1959—; bd. regional advisors People's Bank Bridgeport, Conn. Bd. dirs. So. Fairfield County unit Am. Cancer Soc.; bd. regional advs. Norwalk Tech. Coll.; bd. dirs. Greater Norwalk Community Council. Served with USNR, 1944-46, Diplomate Am. Bd. Surgery. Fellow ACS; mem. AAAS, Royal Soc. Health, Pan Am. Med. Assn., Norwalk Med. Soc. (past pres.), N.Y. Acad. Medicine, Am. Heart Assn. Home: 40 Pequot Trail Westport CT 06880

GOODRICH, JAMES TAIT, neuroscientist, pediatric neurosurgeon; b. Portland, Ore., Apr. 16, 1946; s. Richard and Gail (Josselyn) G.; m. Judy Loudin, Dec. 27, 1970. Student, Golden West Coll., 1971-72; A.A., Orange Coast Coll., 1972; B.S. cum laude, U. Calif.-Irvine, 1974; M.Phil., Columbia U., 1979, Ph.D., 1970 M.D., 1980. Neuroscientist, pediatric neurosurgeon N.Y. Neurol. Inst., N.Y.C., 1981-86; dir. div. pediatric neurosurgery Albert Einstein Coll. Medicine, N.Y.C., 1986—. Contbr. articles to profl. jours. Recipient Roche Labs. award in neuroscis., 1978, Mead-Johnson award, 1978, Bronze medal Alumni Assn. Coll. Physicians and Surgeons, 1980, Sandoz award for outstanding research, 1980; Willamette Industries scholar; NIH grantee. Fellow Royal Soc. Medicine (London); mem. Worshipful Soc. Apothecaries (London), N.Y. Acad. Medicine (Melicow award 1980), Am. Assn. History of Medicine (Sir William Osler medal 1977-78), AMA, Brit. Brain Research Assn., European Brain Research Assn., Friends of Columbia U. Libraries, Friends of Osler Library of McGill U., N.Y. Acad. Scis., Am. Assn. Neurol. Surgeons, Congress Neurol. Surgeons, Med. History Soc. N.J., ISIS History of Sci. Soc., Soc. for Bibliography of Natural History (London), Columbia Presbyn. Med. Soc., U. Calif. Alumni Assn., Soc. Ancient Medicine, AAAS, Am. Osler Soc., Les Amis du Vin, South Coast Wine Explorers Club (past chmn.), Friends of Bacchus Wine Club (past chmn.), Dionysius Council of Presbyn. Hosp. of N.Y.C., Sigma Xi, Alpha Gamma Sigma. Research on neuronal regeneration, brain reconstruction and craniofacial reconstruction. Home: 214 Everett Pl Englewood NJ 07631 Office: Albert Einstein Coll Medicine Div Pediatric Neurosurgery Bronx NY 10467

GOODSON, WALTER KENNETH, retired clergyman; b. Salisbury, N.C., Sept. 25, 1912; s. Daniel Washington and Sarah (Peeler) G.; m. Martha Ann Ogburn, July 12, 1937; children: Sara Ann (Mrs. Larry M. Faust), Walter Kenneth, Nancy Craven Richey. AB, Catawba Coll., 1934, LHD; student, Duke Div. Sch., 1934-37, D.D., 1960; D.D., High Point (N.C.) Coll., 1951, Birmingham-So. Coll., Athens Coll., Shenandoah Coll., Campbell U., 1985; L.H.D., St. Bernard Coll.; LL.D., U. Ala. Ordained to ministry Methodist Ch., 1939; pastor in Western N.C. Conf., 1935-64; bishop Birmingham area, 1964-72, Richmond area, 1972-80; ret. 1980; now bishop-in-residence Duke U. Divinity Sch., Durham, N.C.; Del. World Conf. Meth. Ch., Oxford, Eng., 1951, Lake Junaluska, N.C., 1956, London, 1966, Denver, 1971, Dublin, 1977; mem. Meth. World Council; bd. dirs. Meth. Com. Overseas Relief, 1964-72; mem. (Mission Team to Gt. Britain), 1962, study team to, France and Berlin, 1962; chmn. finance com. bd. missions United Meth. Ch., 1968-72, pres. commn. on religion and race, 1968-72, pres. gen. bd. discipleship, 1972-80; also pres. council bishops United Meth. Ch., Southeastern Jurisdiction, 1976, pres. council on ministries, 1976. Pres. J.B. Cornelius Found., 1946-64; Trustee Duke Endowment, Brevard Coll., Duke U., Shenandoah Coll. Clubs: Rotarian, Mason (32 deg.). Home: 2116 Front St Apt D-2 Durham NC 27705 Office: Duke U Divinity Sch Durham NC 27706

GOODSTEIN, DANIEL BELA, oral and maxillofacial surgeon; b. Bklyn., Oct. 27, 1937; s. Charles Benjamin and Florence Ann (Apfel) G.; B.A., U. Conn., 1959; D.M.D., Tufts U., 1963; postgrad. in oral surgery N.Y. U., 1964-65; children—Kimberly Joy, Kara Hope, Lauren Faith. Intern in oral surgery Queens Hosp. Center, 1963-64, resident, 1965-66, attending oral and maxillofacial surgeon, 1968—, mem. med. bd.; practice dentistry, specializing in oral and maxillofacial surgery, Hempstead, N.Y., 1969-—; staff oral surgeon L.I. Jewish Hillside Med. Center, 1968-—; assoc. prof. clin. oral and maxillofacial surgery Sch. Dental Medicine, SUNY-Stony Brook. Served with AUS, 1966-68. Decorated Army Commendation medal. Diplomate Am. Bd. Oral and Maxillofacial Surgery. Fellow Internat. Assn. Oral and Maxillofacial Surgeons; mem. Am., N.Y. State (chmn. advanced and continuing edn. com.) socs. oral and maxillofacial surgeons, Am. Assn. Dental Schs., ADA, N.Y. State 10th Dist. (bd. dels.) dental socs., Alpha Omega, Phi Epsilon Pi. Club: Masons. Contbr. articles to profl. jours. Research on effect of surg. correction of facial deformities on speech. Office: 131 Fulton Ave Hempstead NY 11550

GOODSTEIN, SANDERS ABRAHAM, scrap iron company executive; b. N.Y.C., Oct. 3, 1981; s. Samuel G. and Katie (Lipson) G.; m. Rose Laro, June 29, 1942; children: Peter, Esther, Jack, Rachel. Student, Wayne State U., 1934-36; AB, U. Mich., 1938, MBA, 1939, JD, 1946; postgrad., Harvard, 1943. Bar: Mich., 1946. Sec. Laro Coal & Iron Co., Flint, Mich., 1946-60, pres., 1960—; owner, operator Paterson Mfg. Co., Flint, 1953—; gen. ptnr. Indianhead Co., Pontiac, Mich., 1955-70, pres., 1965-70; sec. Amatac Corp., Erie, Pa., until 1969; chmn. bd. Gen. Foundry & Mfg. Co., Flint., Mich., 1968—, pres. 1970—; pres. Lacron Steel Co., Providence, 1975—, ETL Corp., Flint, 1983—; mem. corp. body Mich. Blue Shield, 1970-76. Served to lt. comdr.USNR, 1942-46. Mem. Fed. Bar Assn., Am. Bar Assn., Bar Mich., Am. Pub. Works Assn., Am. Foundrymen's Soc., Order of Coif, Beta Gamma Sigma, Phi Kappa Phi. Jewish. Home: 2602 Parkside Dr Flint MI 48503 Office: G-4296 W Pierson Rd Flint MI 48504

GOODWIN, BERNARD, lawyer, executive, educator; b. N.Y.C., Dec. 19, 1907; s. Mayer and Hannah (Wald) G.; children: Charles Stewart, Wendy Melinda, Nadine Antonia. Sc.B. cum laude, N.Y.U., 1928; J.D. cum laude, Harvard U., 1931. Lawyer Seattle, 1931-34, N.Y.C., 1935—; lawyer, exec. Paramount Pictures Corp., 1934-57; sec., dir. Allen B. Dumont Labs., Inc., Clifton, N.J., 1938-55; pres., dir. Metro Media, Inc., N.Y.C., 1955-59; chmn. bd. Sunrise Broadcasting Corp., Ft. Lauderdale, Fla., 1965-77; guest lectr. U. Mich. Law Sch., 1965-68, U. Bologna, Italy, 1971-80; prof. ospite U. Padua, Italy, 1970; adj. prof. N.Y. Law Sch., N.Y.C., 1981—; Trustee emeritus U. Detroit, 1966—. Author books and articles on legal and govtl. subjects. Mem. Am., Wash. State bar assns., Assn. Bar City N.Y., A.S.C.A.P. (dir.), Acad. Motion Picture Arts and Scis., Am. Soc. Internat. Law, Am. Fgn. Law Assn., Broadcast Pioneers, Copyright Soc. U.S.A., Am. Arbitration Assn. (nat. labor panel), Union Internationale des Avocats, Phi Beta Kappa. Club: Harvard (N.Y.C.). Home and Office: 225 E 49th St New York NY 10017

GOODWIN, DELLA MCGRAW, nurse, educator; b. Claremore, Okla., Nov. 21, 1931; d. James Edward and Allie Mae (Meadows) McGraw; m. Jesse F. Goodwin, Dec. 26, 1959; children—Gordon Francis, Paula Therese, Jesse Stephen. M.S. in Nursing, Wayne State U., 1962. R.N., Mich. Dir. nursing Blvd. Gen., Detroit, 1964-69; cons. Paramed., Detroit, 1969-72; dean nursing and health Wayne County Community Coll., Detroit, 1970-86; pres., cons. Della Goodwin & Co., 1986—; chmn. Detroit Substance Abuse Council, 1982—; pres. Health Systems Agy., Southeast Mich., 1979-81; lectr. in field. Author column. Mem. State Health Coordinating Council, Lansing, Mich., 1979; mem. Detroit Health Commn., 1982; mem. Drunk Driving Task Force, Lansing, 1982; dean emeritus Wayne County Community Coll., 1986; mem. Women's Conf. Concerns, Detroit, 1984, bd. chairperson Nat. Ctr. for the Advancement of Blacks in the Health Professions, 1988. Recipient Health Law award Detroit Coll. Law, 1980, Senate Concurrent resolution, Mich., 1982, cert. of recognition Detroit Common Council, 1973, Headliners award Wayne State U., 1973, Spirit of Detroit award Detroit City Council, 1985; testimonial resolution Detroit City Council, 1985. Mem. Am. Nurses Assn. (cabinet nursing edn. 1984—), Mich. Nurses Assn. (congl. dist. coordinator, Bertha Lee Culp Human Rights award 1985), Nat. League Nursing, United Community Services (v.p. 1983—), Delta Sigma Theta, Sigma Theta Tau. Democrat. Roman Catholic. Avocations: swimming, golf, photography. Home: 19214 Appoline St Detroit MI 48235 Office: PO Box 21121 Detroit MI 48221

GOODWIN, KENNETH LESLIE, English educator, literary critic; b. Sydney, Australia, Sept. 29, 1934; s. Arch Langley and Vera (Haswell) G.; m. Agnes Elizabeth Shannon, July 2, 1971; children: Catherine Celia, Geoffrey Philip, Helen Margaret. BA, U. Sydney, 1956, DipEd, 1957, MA, 1963; PhD, Oxford (Eng.) U., 1970. Tchr. secondary schs. New South Wales (Australia) Dept. Edn., 1957; lectr. English Tchr.'s Coll., Wagga Wagga, New South Wales, 1958; lectr. English U. Queensland, Brisbane, Australia, 1959-67, sr. lectr., 1967-69, reader in English, 1970-71, prof., 1971—; vis. prof. U. Calif., Berkeley, 1967; mem. lit. bd. Australia Council, 1981-84; chmn. edn. com. Bd. Advanced Edn., Brisbane, 1983; chmn. acquisitions com. Queensland Art Gallery, 1983—. Author: The Influence of Ezra Pound, 1966, Understanding African Poetry, 1982, Manuscripts of William Morris, 1983, A History of Australian Literature, 1986. Josiah Symon scholar U. Sydney, 1952; brit. Council travel grant, Oxford, Eng., 1965; Can. Commonwealth research fellow, Guelph, Ont., 1985-86. Mem. Assn. for Can. Studies, Assn. for Study Australian Lit., Australian Univs. Lang. and Lit. Assn. (editorial bd.), Assn. for commonwealth Lit. and Lang. Studies (chmn. 1977-80). Home: 76 Orchard Ter Saint Lucia, Queensland 4067, Australia Office: U Queensland, Dept English, Saint Lucia Queensland 4067, Australia

GOODWIN, REX DEAN, clergyman; b. Martinsville, Mo., Nov. 30, 1909; s. Charles Morgan and Grace Leola (Pyle) G.; A.B., U. Nebr., 1932; B.D., Andover Newton Theol. Sch., 1934; D.D., Sioux Falls Coll., 1957; m. Almira Drew Wallace, June 24, 1933 (dec. Oct. 1964); 1 son, John Charles; m. Loree Presnell, June 18, 1966. Ordained to ministry Bapt. Ch., 1934; pastor chs., Oxford, Nebr., 1934-36, Oakland, Calif., 1936-37, Boston, 1941-44; dir. Christian edn. First Bapt. Ch., Oakland, 1937-38; asst. pastor Central Bapt. Ch., Hartford, Conn., 1938-41; dir. public relations Am. Bapt. Home Mission Soc., N.Y.C., 1944-51; dir. publicity Am. Bapt. Conv., N.Y.C., 1951-58, exec. dir. conv. div. communication, Valley Forge, Pa., 1958-72; public liaison exec. Am. Bapt. Chs. Bd. Ednl. Ministries, Valley Forge, 1972-74; dir. devel. Cushing Jr. Coll., Bryn Mawr, Pa., 1975-77; pastor Pughtown (Pa.) Bapt. Ch., 1977—; chmn. communications com. Bapt. World Alliance, 1972-75, mem., 1970-76; mem. communications com. Nat. Council Chs., 1961-72; v.p. Main Line Ministerium; host TV series The Making of a Protestant, 1972. Trustee Andover Newton Theol. Sch. Mem. Religious Pub. Relations Council (pres. 1961-62), Phi Alpha. Republican. Author: Man-Living Soul, 1952; There Is No End, 1956; editor Cushing Way, 1977-78; contbr. articles to ch. jours. Home: 3307 Windsor Dr Norristown PA 19403 Office: Box 340 RD 1 Spring City PA 19475

GOOKIN, THOMAS ALLEN JAUDON, civil engineer; b. Tulsa, Aug. 5, 1951; s. William Scudder and Mildred (Hartman) G.; m. Leigh Anne Johnson, June 13, 1975 (div. Dec. 1977); m. Sandra Jean Andrews, July 23, 1983. BS with distinction, Ariz. State U., 1975. Registered profl. engr., Calif., Ariz. Civil engr., treas. W.S. Gookin & Assocs., Scottsdale, Ariz., 1968—. Chmn. Ariz. State Bd. Tech. Registration Engring. adv. com., 1984—. Mem. NSPE, Ariz. Soc. Profl. Engrs. (sec. Papago chpt. 1979-81, v.p. 1981-84, pres. 1984-85, named Young Engr. of Yr. 1979), Ariz. Congress on Surveying and Mapping, Am. Soc. Civil Engrs., Ariz. Water Works Assn., Tau Beta Pi, Delta Chi (Tempe chpt. treas. 1970-71, sec. 1970, v.p. 1971), Phi Kappa Delta (pres. 1971-73). Republican. Episcopalian. Home: 10760 E Becker Ln Scottsdale AZ 85259 Office: W S Gookin & Assocs 4203 N Brown Ave Scottsdale AZ 85251

GOOKIN, WILLIAM SCUDDER, hydrologist, consultant; b. Atlanta, Sept. 8, 1914; s. William Cleveland and Susie (Jaudon) G.; m. Mildred Hartman, Sept. 4, 1937; children: William Scudder Jr., Thomas Allen Jaudon. BSCE, Pa. State U., 1937. Registered profl. engr. and hydrologist. Engr. U.S. Geol. Survey, Tucson, 1937-38; inspector City of Tucson, 1938-39; steel designer Allison Steel Mfg. Co., Phoenix, 1939-40; engr. Bur. Reclamation, various locations, 1940-53; chief engr. San Carlos Irrigation and Drainage Dist., Coolidge, Ariz., 1953-58; chief engr. Ariz. Interstate Stream Commn., Phoenix, 1956-62, state water engr., 1961-68; adminstr. Ariz. Power Authority, Phoenix, 1958-60; cons. engr. Scottsdale, Ariz., 1968—; bd. dirs. Cen. Ariz. Project Assn., Phoenix, 1985—. Contbr. articles to profl. jours. Dem. committeeman State of Ariz., 1979-84. Served to 2d lt. C.E., U.S. Army, 1938-42. Fellow Am. Soc. Civil Engrs.; mem. NSPE (bd. dirs.), Nat. Water Resources Assn. (small projects com.), Colo. River Water Users' Assn., State Bar Ariz. (assoc., environ. natural resources sect.), Culver Legion, Order of the Engr., Chi Epsilon. Home: 9 Casa Blanca Estates Paradise Valley AZ 85253

GOOTZEIT, JACK MICHAEL, rehabilitation institute executive; b. N.Y.C., Sept. 27, 1924; s. Morris and Pauline (Genn) G.; B.S. in Phys. Therapy, N.Y. U., 1955, M.A. in Psychology, 1956, Ed.D., 1963; m. Rose Weiss, Mar. 21, 1948; children—Sholom Martin, Elias Steven. Research asst. N.Y. U. Sch. Edn., N.Y.C., 1954; phys. therapy adviser Vis. Nurse Service N.Y., 1957-58; asso. dir. sheltered workshop and tng. center Westchester Assn. Retarded Children, White Plains, N.Y., 1958-65; dir. habilitation services N.Y.C. Assn. for Help Retarded Children, 1959-67; exec. dir. Insts. Applied Human Dynamics, Bronx, N.Y., 1957—, Insts. Applied Human Dynamics St. Jude Habilitation Inst., 1966—; cons. Chapman & Garber, architects state schs. for retarded, 1965-66; cons. N.Y. State Dept. Mental Hygiene; Bronx chpt. Assn. Brain Injured Children, 1965-66; cons. psychologist Operation Headstart, Ringwood, N.J., 1967; adj. asso. prof. Hunter Coll., 1968-76, Pace U., 1979. Instr. water safety ARC, 1941—, staff instr. rehab. swimming, 1950—. Served with AUS, 1942-45; MTO. Decorated Bronze Star, Purple Heart; recipient Disting. Service award N.Y. chpt. Nat. Rehab. Assn., 1965, Exceptional Service award N.E. region, 1978, Profl. of Yr. award Met. N.Y. chpt., 1977. Fellow Am. Assn. Mental Deficiency, Am. Soc. Group Psychotherapy and Psychoanalysis; mem. Am. Psychol. Assn., Rehab. Counseling Assn., Am. Phys. Therapy Assn., Am. Acad. Psychotherapy, AAAS, N.Y. Acad. Scis. Author: Situational Diagnosis and Therapy, 1960; Handbook on Personal Adjustment Training, 1965; Effecting Communication and Interaction in the Mentally Retarded; The Development of Behavior and Its Modification, 1975; Foundations for Serving the Severe and Multihandicapped; The Multihandicapped: Serving the Severely Disabled, 1981; media presentation series in neuro and sensory psychology. contbr. articles to mags. Home: 120-31 DeKrulf Pl Bronx NY 10475 Office: 3625 Bainbridge Ave Bronx NY 10467 also: 40 Wilson Park Dr Tarrytown NY 10591

GOPAL, SARVEPALLI, history educator; b. Madras, India, Apr. 23, 1923; s. Sir Sarvepalli Radhakrishnan (former President of India). Ed. U. Madras, Oxford U.; M.A., D.Phil., D.Litt.; D.Litt. (hon.), Andhra U., 1975, Sri Venkateswara U., Tirupati, 1979. Lectr., reader in history Andhra U., Waltair, India, 1948-52; asst. dir. Nat. Archives, New Delhi, 1952-54; dir. hist. div. Ministry External Affairs, New Delhi, 1954-66; reader in South Asian history Oxford U. (Eng.), 1966-71; prof. contemporary history Jawaharlal Nehru U., New Delhi, 1971-83, prof. emeritus, 1983—; chmn. Nat. Book Trust of India, 1973-76; mem. exec. bd. UNESCO, 1976-80. Author: The Viceroyalty of Lord Ripon; The Viceroyalty of Lord Irwin; British Policy in India; Jawaharlal Nehru, 2 vols. Recipient Sahitya Akademi award, 1976. Fellow Royal Hist. Soc. (corr.). Office: Centre for Hist Studies, Jawaharlal Nehru U, New Delhi 110067 India Address: 97 Radhakridhma Salai, Myladore, Madras 600004 India *

GORAK, JAN, English educator; b. Blackburn, Lancashire, Eng., Oct. 12, 1952; s. Jozef and Mary (Niland) G.; m. Irene Elizabeth Mannion, 1984. BA, U. Warwick, Eng., 1975; postgrad., U. Leeds, Eng., 1975-77; MA, U. So. Calif., 1981, PhD, 1983. Lectr. U. Witwatersrand, Republic of South Africa, 1984-87, sr. lectr., 1988; vis. assoc. prof. U. Denver, 1988-89. Author: God the Artist: American Novelists in a Post-Realist Age, 1987, Critic of Crisis: A Study of Frank Kermode, 1987, The Alien Mind of Raymond Williams, 1988. Recipient Thomas Pringle award English Acad. Southern Africa, 1986. Home: 2500 S York St Apt J-3 Denver CO 80210 Office: U Denver Dept of English University Park Denver CO 80208

GORBACHEV, MIKHAIL SERGEYEVICH, Soviet political leader; b. Privolnoye, Krasnogvardeisky Dist., USSR, Mar. 2, 1931; Grad. Faculty of Law, Moscow State U., 1955, Stavropol Agrl. Inst., 1967. Active Komsomol and Party work, 1st sec. Stavropol city Komosol com, dep. head Propaganda dept., 2nd and 1st sec. Stavropol Krai Komsomel Com., 1955-62; party organizer Stavropol Territorial Prodn. Bd. Collective and State Farms, then head dept. parties Stavropol, Krai Party Com., 1962-66; 1st sec. Stavropol city CPSU Com., 1966-68, 2nd sec., 1968-70 1st sec., 1970-78; mem. Central Com. Communist Party Soviet Union, 1971, sec., 1978, alternate mem. Central Com. Politburo, 1979, mem. 1980—, gen. sec. Cen. Com., 1985—; dep. USSR Supreme Soviet, 1970—; head fgn. affairs commn., after 1984. Author: Perestroika: New Thinking for Our Country and the World, 1987. Decorated Order of Lenin (USSR); recipient Indira Gandhi award, 1987. Address: Cen Com Communist Party, Kremlin, Moscow USSR

GORBACHEV, RAISA MAXIMOVNA, wife of Soviet leader, author, teacher; b. Rubtsovsk, USSR, Jan. 5; d. Maxim Titorenko; m. Mikhail S. Gorbachev, 1954; 1 dau., Irina. Grad., Moscow State U., 1955; PhD, Moscow Pedagogical Inst., 1967. Instr. polit. philosophy Moscow U., from 1978; sociologist Stavropol. Mem. presidium Soviet Cultural Fund, 1986—, dir., 1987—. Address: Kremlin, Moscow USSR *

GORDEVITCH, IGOR, publishing company executive; b. Kaunas, Lithuania, Dec. 17, 1924; s. Alexander Michael and Militsa (de Nikitin) G.; came to U.S., 1950, naturalized, 1955; ed. Institut Sillig, Vevey, Switzerland, 1937-39, Royal U., Rome, 1939-40; m. Margaret Boomer; children—Alexandra, Tatiana; m. 2d, Carin Roechling, Oct. 7, 1960. Sr. adminstrv. asst. Allied Mil. Govt., Europe, 1944-45; corr. N.Y. Herald Tribune, 1945-50; Washington bur. chief Vision Inc., N.Y.C., 1950-56, editor, 1957-64, chief exec. officer, Latin Am. ops., Sao Paulo, Brazil, 1964-67, pub., exec. v.p., dir. Vision Group of Cos., N.Y.C., 1967-76, pres., 1973-77, mng. dir., chmn. Vision/Europe, Paris, 1970-76; pres. Publi-Communications Inc., N.Y.C., 1976-83; exec. v.p., dir. Gruner & Jahr USA, Inc., N.Y.C., 1979-83; also pub. dir. GEO mag. 1979-81; pres. U.S. Investment Pub., 1983—; publishing cons.; lectr. in field. Mem. Pan Am. Soc. U.S., Council of Ams., Akin Hall Assn. Republican. Eastern Orthodox. Club: Knickerbocker (N.Y.C.); Quaker Hill Country (Pawling, N.Y.); Coral Beach and Tennis (Bermuda); Nat. Press (Washington). Home: Quaker Hill Pawling NY 12564 Office: 61 E 82nd St New York NY 10028

GORDIMER, NADINE, author; b. S. Africa, Nov. 20, 1923; d. Isidore and Nan (Myers) Gordimer; ed. Convent Sch., Srpings, S. Africa; m. Reinhold Cassirer, Jan. 29, 1954; children: Oriane, Hugo. Author: (story collections) Soft Voice of the Serpent, 1953, Six Feet of the Country, 1956, Friday's Footprint, 1961, Not for Publication, 1965, Livingstone's Companions, 1971, Selected Stories, 1976, Some Monday for Sure, 1976; (polit. and lit. essays) The Essential Gesture, 1988; (novels) The Lying Days, 1953, A World of Strangers, 1958, Occasion for Loving, 1963. The Late Bourgeois World, 1966, A Guest of Honour, 1970, The Conservationist, 1974; (literary criticisms) The Black Interpreters, 1973; (stories) A Soldier's Embrace, 1980; (novel) Burger's Daughter, 1979; July's People, 1981, A Sport of Nature, 1987; (stories and a novella) Something Out There, 1984. Recipient W.H. Smith award for Commonwealth Writers, 1961; Thomas Pringle award English Acad. S. Africa, 1969; James Tait Black Meml. award, 1972; Booker prize, 1974; CNA award, 1975, 80, 82; Grand Aigle d'Or, 1975, MLA award, 1982, Nelly Sachs prize (Germany), 1985, Malaparte award (Italy), 1986, Bennet award (U.S.), 1987; named Officier de l'Ordre des Arts et des Lettres (France), 1987. Fellow Royal Soc. Lit.; mem. Com. European Authors, Am. Acad. (hon.), Inst. Arts and Letters (hon.), PEN (v.p). Address: 7 Frere Rd/Parktown West, Johannesburg Republic of South Africa

GORDON, BARON JACK, stock broker; s. George M. and Rose (Salsbury) G.; midshipman U.S. Naval Acad., 1946; B.S., Lynchburg Coll., 1953; m. Ellin Bachrach, Aug. 20, 1954; children—Jonathan Ross, Rose Patricia, Alison. Vice pres. Consol. Ins. Agy., Norfolk, 1948-55; asst. treas. Henry Montor Assos., Inc., N.Y.C., 1956; v.p., sec. Propp & Co., Inc., N.Y.C., 1957-58; partner Koerner, Gordon & Co., N.Y.C., 1959-62; sr. partner Gordon, Kulman Perry, and predecessor firm, N.Y.C., 1962-71, pres., chmn. bd., 1971-74; pres., chmn. bd. Palison, Inc., mems. N.Y. Stock Exchange, White Plains, N.Y., 1974—; chmn. bd. Rojon, Inc., real estate and investments, Williamsburg, Va., 1979—. Mem. Harrison (N.Y.) Archtl. Rev. Bd., 1970-72, Harrison Planning Bd., 1975-77; bd. dirs. Montefiore Hosp. Assn., YM-YWHA, Lafayette Ednl. Fund., Inc., 1986—. Served to lt. in U.S.S. Midway, USNR, 1953-55. Mem. Folk Art soc. (bd. dirs. 1987—), U.S. Naval Acad. Alumni Assn. (life). Clubs: Stock Exchange Luncheon (N.Y.C.), Poinciana (Palm Beach, Fla.), Town Point (Norfolk, Va.), Kingsmill Golf (Williamsburg, Va.). Home: 113 Elizabeth Meriwether Williamsburg VA 23185 Office: Drawer JG Williamsburg VA 23187

GORDON, GILBERT, chemist, educator; b. Chgo., Nov. 11, 1933; s. Walter and Catherine Gordon; m. Joyce Elaine Masura; children: Thomas, Susan. B.S., Bradley U., 1955; Ph.D., Mich. State U., 1959. Postdoctoral research asso. U. Chgo., 1959-60; asst. prof. U. Md., College Park, 1960-64; asso. prof. U. Md., 1964-67, prof., 1967; prof. chemistry U. Iowa, Iowa City, 1967-73; prof., chmn. dept. Miami U., Oxford, Ohio, 1973-84; Volwiler Disting. Research prof. Miami U., 1984—; vis. prof. Japanese Soc. Promotion Sci., 1969, 84; cons. Nat. Bur. Standards, Chem Link, Bioxy Internat., John Langdon Enterprises. Editor: catalysis kinetics sect. Chem. Abstracts, 1970—; editorial bd. synthesis inorganic metal, organic chemistry: catalysis kinetics sect. Ohio Jour. Sci, 1971—; contbr. articles to chem. jours. Named Cin. Chemist of Yr., 1981. Mem. Am. Chem. Soc., Chgo. Soc. London, Faraday Soc., Sigma Xi, Phi Kappa Phi. Home: 190 Shadowy Hills Dr Oxford OH 45056 Office: Dept Chemistry Miami U Oxford OH 45056

GORDON, HAROLD PHILIP, lawyer; b. Montreal, Que., Can., Apr. 1937; s. Isaac and Rebecca (Bregman) G.; B. Commerce, McGill U., Montreal, 1958, B. Civil Law, 1964; postgrad. Wharton Sch., U. Pa., 1959-60; B.A., Sir George Williams U., Montreal, 1961. Bar: Que., Yukon Ter. Spl. asst. Ministry Forestry and Rural Devel., Govt. Can., Ottawa, Ont., 1965-67; ptnr. Stikeman, Elliott, Montreal; bd. dirs. Anglo Am. Clays Ltd., Ariola-Eurodisc Inc., Auscan Closures Canada, Inc., Avant Garde Optics Ltd., Berkley Wallcoverings Inc., Burns, Philp & Co. Ltd., Butler Services Group Canada Inc., Casimcan Holdings Inc., DWS/Hines Holdings Ltd., Dersingham Holdings Ltd., Fleischmann's Yeast Ltd., Hasbro Canada Inc., Hasbro Inc., Hayes Microcomputer Products (Can.) Ltd., Henry J. Kaiser Co. (Can.) Ltd., Jordan Petroleum Ltd., LIG Canada Inc., Lombard Odier Trust Co., Luxottica Canada Inc., MacGregor-Navire Canada Ltd., Mercury Asset Mgmt. Corp., Raymond Concrete Pile Co., Ltd., Rentokil (Can.) Ltd., RWI Holdings Ltd., RWI Properties Ltd., Toyoda Gosei Holdings Co. Inc., Waterville (TG) Inc. Bd. dirs. Can. Guild Crafts Que., Montreal, 1979—, Centaur Theatre Co., Montreal, 1983-84. Mem. Quebec Bar Assn., Yukon Bar Assn., Internat. Bar Assn., Internat. Fiscal Assn., Inst. Corp. Dirs. Can., Can. Inst. for Adminstrn. Justice, Can. Bar Assn., ABA (assoc.). Home: 1321 Sherbrooke St W, Apt A-81, Montreal, PQ Canada H3G 1J4 Office: Stikeman Elliott, 1155 Dorchester Blvd W, Suite 3900, Montreal, PQ Canada H3B 3V2

GORDON, HOWARD LYON, advertising and marketing executive; b. Chgo., Oct. 8, 1930; s. Milton Arthur and Betty Z. (Ginsburg) G.; B.S., U. Ill., 1953; M.S., Northwestern U., 1954, M.B.A., 1962; m. Lois Jean Kaufman, Aug. 21, 1955; children—Carolyn Ann, Leslie Meredith. Mktg. research mgr. Marsteller Inc., advt., Chgo., 1960-68, v.p. mktg. services, 1969-76; dir. client service Britt and Frerichs Inc., mktg. research and advt. cons., Chgo., 1977—, sr. v.p., 1978—, prin., 1979—, ptnr., 1986—; lectr. advt. and mktg. Northwestern U., 1963—, vis. prof. Medill grad. studies in advt., 1981—; lectr., seminar leader Am. Mgmt. Assn., 1965-72; chmn. Life Style Research Com. Advt. Research Found., 1985—, alumni awards com. Medill Sch., Northwestern U., 1986, Fundraising Com. Kellogg Grad. Sch. Northwestern U., 1986—. Regional chmn. Crusade of Mercy, Evanston, Ill., 1969; founding dir. Alumni Assn. Medill Sch., 1984—; adv. council athletic dept., Northwestern U., 1985—. Served with AUS, 1954-56. Recipient award Dept. Def., 1956. Mem. Am. Mktg. Assn. (dir., v.p. mktg. mgmt.), Sigma Delta Chi. Club: Northwestern U. Faculty. Contbr. articles to profl. publs. and mktg. texts. Home: 2025 Sherman Ave Evanston IL 60201 Office: 505 N Lake Shore Dr Chicago IL 60611 also: Fisk Hall Northwestern U 1845 Sheridan Rd Evanston IL 60201

GORDON, LEWIS ALEXANDER, electronics executive; b. Milw., Aug. 4; s. Lewis Alexander and Verna Alma (Stocker) G.; B.S. in Mech. Engring., Purdue U., 1959; postgrad. RCA Insts., 1962, No. Ill. U., 1967-68; m. Frances Rita Dziadzio, June 4, 1960; children—Robert Alan, Richard Alan, Pamela Ann. Process engr. Ill. Tool Works, Elgin, 1959-63; chief engr. Norcon Electronics, Elgin, 1963-65; v.p. Midland Standard, Inc., Elgin, 1964-78, chmn. bd., 1967-78; pres., chief exec. officer Gt. Lakes Industries, Elgin, 1978—; del. Joint Electronics Industry Conf.; mem. adv. bd. Electronics mag., 1976—. Vice pres. bd. trustees Gail Borden Pub. Library Dist., 1971—, pres., bd. dirs. North Suburban Library System, 1971-74; mem. automation com. Ill. State Library, 1982—; bd. advisers Easter Seal Assn., Elgin, 1971-74; adv. bd. Elgin Community Coll., 1977—. Registered profl. engr., Ill., Mich., Wis. Mem. Ill. C. of C., Elgin Assn. Commerce, ALA, Ill. Library Assn. (automation com. 1975—), Ill. Council Library Systems Presidents (pres.), Ill. Library Trustee Assn. (bd. dirs. 1983—, pres. 1985-87), Future Ill. Libraries Com., Exptl. Aircraft Assn., Future Ill. Libraries Com., Exptl. Soc. Profl. Engrs., Nat. Brit. Horological Inst., Kane County Farm Bur., Ill. Mfrs. Assn., Assn. Watch and Clock Collectors, Mensa, Agent-Aeronca Champion Club, Pi Tau Sigma. Lutheran. Contbr. articles to profl. jours. Patentee in field. Home: 705 Diane Ave Elgin IL 60123 Office: PO Box 783 Elgin IL 60121

GORDON, LONNY JOSEPH, choreographer, dance and fine arts educator; b. Sept. 21, 1942, Edinburg, Tex.; s. Floyd Charles and Ruth Rebecca (Lee) G. BFA, U. Tex., 1965; MFA, U. Wis., 1967; DFA, Nishikawa Sch. of Classical Japanese Dance, Tokyo, 1980. dir. Kinetic Art Theater, N.Y.C., 1970, Tokyo, 1971-72; dir. modern dance Jacobs Pillow, Lee, Mass., 1970; dir. So. Repertory Dance Theater, So. Ill. U., Carbondale, 1972-76; artist-in-residence Smith Coll., Northampton, Mass., 1975; grad. dir. dance U. Wis., Madison, 1976—, prof. dance, 1985—; choreographer numerous dance works including Fleetings; cons. and lectr. in dance and fine arts to numerous profl. dance cos. and ednl. instns. Contbr. articles to profl. jours. including Japan Modern Dance Quarterly, Okura Lantern, Dance Scope; columnist Capital Times; subject of numerous books and profl. works in dance. One man exhbn. watercolor paintings, collage and mixed media works. Grantee numerous profl. and ednl. instns., fellow Fulbright-Hays, 1967-69, 83, NEA Choreographers, 1982-83, Japan Found. profl., 1979, Mobile Found., 1971-72. Mem. Asian Dance Assn. (bd. dirs.), Am. Coll. Dance Festival (bd. dirs. 1987—), Fulbright Alumni Assn. Club: Univ. (U. Wis.). Avocations: painting; writing; swimming; bodybuilding; gardening. Office: U Wis Lathrop Hall 1050 University Ave Madison WI 53706

GORDON, MICHAEL HERBERT, rheumatologist; b. N.Y.C., Oct. 4, 1941; s. Robert J. and Charlotte J. (Goldstein) G.; m. Beth W. Aisley, June 19, 1966; children—Jill, Stephanie, Craig. B.A., Boston U., 1963; M.D., Chgo. Med. Sch., 1967. Diplomate Am. Bd. Internal Medicine, Am. Bd. Rheumatology. Intern, Cedars-Sinai Hosp., 1967-68; resident Jackson Meml., Miami, 1968-69, 71-72; fellow Albert Einstein No., Phila., 1972-74; practice medicine specializing in rheumatology, Ft. Lauderdale, Fla., 1974—. Served to capt. USAF, 1969-71. Mem. Am. Rheumatism Assn., ACP, AMA, Fla. Med. Assn., Fla. Rheumatology Soc., Broward County Med. Soc. Jewish. Office: 2001 NE 48th Ct Fort Lauderdale FL 33308

GORDON, MILDRED HARRIET GROSS, hospital executive; b. Phila., Mar. 13, 1934; d. Nathan and Kate (Segal) Gross; m. Ivan H. Gordon, June 13, 1954; 1 dau., Radene Lara. Student U. Pa., 1952-56; B.S., Kutztown State U. Pa., 1960; M.S. (Falk Found. fellow), Med. Coll. Pa., 1970, Ph.D. in Psychiatry (fellow), 1972. Tchr. sci. public schs., 1961-66; with Family Guidance Center, 1966-70; dir. dept. psychiatry Mental Health Treatment Center, Reading Hosp., West Reading, 1972—; chief operating officer Ctr. for Mental Health-Reading Hosp. and Med. Ctr.; clin. instr. dept. psychiatry Med. Coll. Pa., Phila., 1972-78; clin. asst. prof. dept. psychiatry Temple U. Med. Sch.; pvt. practice DGR Assos., Wyomissing, Pa.; mem. Pa. Gov.'s Council on Drug and Alcohol Abuse, 1972-78. Bd. dirs. Confront, 1971-73, Council on Chem. Abuse, 1971-73. Mem. Am. Psychol. Assn. Home: 1850 Oak Ln Reading PA 19604 Office: Reading Hosp K Bldg Reading PA 19603 also: 560 Van Reed Rd Wyomissing PA 19610

GORDON, MINITA ELMIRA, governor general of Belize; diploma in teaching Govt. Tng. Coll., Belize City, 1957; diploma in child psychology U. Birmingham (Eng.), 1963; B.Ed. in English, U. Calgary (Can.), 1967, M.S. in Ednl. Psychology, 1969; Ph.D. in Applied Psychology, U. Toronto, 1980. Tchr., Anglican schs., Belize, 1946-58; lectr. ednl. psychology methodology arts and visual aids Belize Tng. Coll., 1959-69; govt. edn. officer Ministry of Edn., Belize, 1969—; justice of the peace, Belize, 1974—; gov. gen. of Belize,

1981; cons. and lectr. in govt. and edn. Patron Belize Red Cross, Rifle Club, Hosp. Aux., Boy Scouts, Girl Guides. Mem. Anglican Ch. Address: Governor General's Office, Belmopan Belize

GORDON, ROBERT THOMAS, surgeon, educator; b. Chgo., Feb. 13, 1950; s. David and Eunice (Wienshienk) G. B.S. in Medicine with highest distinction, Northwestern U., M.D., 1972. Diplomate Am. Bd. Surgery, Am. Bd. Thoracic Surgery; lic. pilot. Resident in gen. surgery Northwestern U. Hosp., Chgo., 1972-77, resident in cardiac surgery, 1977-79; clin. asst. prof. surgery U. Ill., Chgo., 1979—; mem. attending staff, chief dept. cardiac surgery Lutheran Gen. Hosp., Park Ridge, Ill., 1979—, also chief cardiac surgery resident and nurses tng. program; dir. heart transplantation program Edgewater Hosp., Chgo.; mem. attending staff Highland Park (Ill.) Hosp., Mt. Sinai Hosp., Holy Family Hosp., Des Plaines, Ill., North Suburban Med. Center, Schaumburg, Ill., Good Shepherd Hosp., John F. Kennedy Hosp.; instr. gen. and thoracic surgery Northwestern U.; staff assoc. HEW, Bethesda, Md. Contbr. articles to profl. jours. Chmn. Ill. Commn. Conservation, 1966-67. Recipient awards Hoffmann-LaRoche, NASA, Am. Chem. Soc.; Med. Scientists Life Ins. fellow, 1969; G.D. Searle fellow; Macy Found. Research fellow. Fellow Am. Soc. Contemporary Medicine and Surgery, Am. Thoracic Soc., Am. Coll. Thoracic Surgeons, Am. Internat. Coll. of Surgeons, ACS; mem. Internat. Bio-Electro Magnetic Soc., Internat. Coll. Surgeons, Royal Soc. Medicine, Flying Physicians Assn., Internat. Platform Assn., AMA, Internat. Heart Transplantation Soc., Chgo. Thoracic Soc., Am. Coll. Chest Physicians, Chgo. Med. Assn., Ill. Med. Assn., Soc. Contemporary Medicine and Surgery, Ill. Jr. Acad. Scis. (pres., hon. life mem.), Alpha Omega Alpha, Phi Beta Pi, Phi Eta Sigma. Research on cardiac surgery and related research; also research and innovations in biophysics (cancer diagnosis, treatment and prevention; also heart disease and other diseases); genetic engineering and instrumentation; patentee in field. Office: 1775 Dempster St Park Ridge IL 60068 Other: 9301 Golf Rd Des Plaines IL 60016

GORDON-SMITH, NIGEL, publishing company executive; b. London, Feb. 28, 1950; s. Alan Arthur and Myrtle Kathleen (Vaughan) G.-S.; m. Samantha Jill, Dec. 2, 1972; children: Emma, Jane. Degree in History, Eastbourne Coll., Eng., 1967-70. Jr. mgr. Vachon Industries, Brighton, 1970-77; co-founder, chmn. Adams Arts and Cartoona, Gosport, Eng., 1970—; bd. dirs. Peter George Publs., David Jones, E&D Services. Author of 4 poetry books. Chmn. Conservative Com. Hillhead, 1985, 87, Forton Found., 1987. Named Fundraiser of Yr., Hampshire Charity Assn., Portsmouth, 1986. Mem. Hampshire Poetry Assn. (Creative Poetry award 1983), Hampshire Bus. Assn. Mem. Ch. of Eng. Clubs: Hill Head Football (bd. dirs. 1979—), The Connuta, Hill Head Conservative. Home: 31 Solent Rd, Hill Head Fareham, Hants PO 14 3LB, England Office: Adams Arts and Cartoona, Sanderson Ctr, Gosport Hampshire PO12 3LU, England

GORDON-SMITH, RALPH, manufacturing company executive; b. May 22, 1905; s. Sir Allan Gordon-Smith and Hilda Beatrice Cave; m. Beryl Mavis Cundy, 1932. Student, Bradfield Coll. With Smiths Industries, 1927—, bd. dirs., 1933—, chmn., 1951-73, pres., 1973—; past bd. dirs. EMI Ltd. Club: Bosham Sailing. Home: Brook House, Bosham, West Sussex England Office: 23 Kingston House East, Princes Gate, London SW7, England *

GORDONSON, ROBERT MARTIN, retail executive; b. N.Y.C., July 23, 1935; s. Julius and Mildred (Ettinger0 G.; m. Pearl Wunder, Apr. 4, 1965; children; Gary Scott, Judi Michelle, Suzanne Lynn. BS in Acctg., Bklyn. Coll., 1958; postgrad., CCNY, 1965. Accountant Webb and Knapp Inc., N.Y.C., 1955-57, N.Y. and N.J. Lubricant Co., N.Y.C., 1957-58, Lewyt Corp., N.Y.C., 1960-61; chief accountant Masters Inc., Westbury, N.Y., 1961-63, asst. controller, 1963-64, controller, 1964-72, treas., chief fin. officer, 1972—. Served to lt. U.S. Army, 1958-60. Mem. Nat. Assn. Corp. Treas., Fin. Exec. Inst., Met. Retail Fin. Execs. Assn. Lodge: KP. Home: 47 Hazelwood Dr Jericho NY 11753 Office: Masters Inc 725 Summa Ave Westbury NY 11590

GORE, ALBERT, JR., senator; b. Mar. 31, 1948; s. Albert and Pauline (LaFon) G.; m. Mary Elizabeth Aitcheson, May 19, 1970; children: Karenna, Kristin, Sarah, Albert III. B.A. cum laude (Univ. scholar), Harvard U., 1969; postgrad., Grad. Sch. of Religion, Vanderbilt U., 1971-72, Law Sch., 1974-76. Investigative reporter, editorial writer The Tennessean, 1971-76; mem. 95th-98th Congresses from Tenn., 1977-85; U.S. senator from Tenn. 1985—; homebuilder and land developer Tanglewood Home Builders Co., 1971-76; livestock and tobacco farmer from 1973. Served with U.S. Army, 1969-71, Vietnam. Mem. Farm Bur., Tenn. Jaycees. Democrat. Baptist. Clubs: Am. Legion, VFW. Office: Office of the Senate 393 Russell Senate Bldg Washington DC 20515 *

GORE, GEORGE JOSEPH, educator; b. Chgo., Mar. 9, 1926; s. Joseph and Agnes Gore; B.S. in Elec. Engring., U. Ill., 1949, M.S. in Mgmt., 1950; M.B.A. (teaching fellow 1954-57), U. Mich., 1956, Ph.D. in Mgmt., 1961; m. Bette Jeanne Iles, July 28, 1949. With Gen. Electric Co., 1950, DuPont Co., 1950-54; lectr. U. Mich., 1957-59; mem. faculty U. Cin., 1959—, prof. mgmt., 1965—; pres. George J. Gore & Assocs., mgmt. cons., 1958—. Served with USNR, 1944-46. Fellow Nat. Acad. Mgmt. (gov. 1970-73, v.p. 1971-73, chmn. div. managerial cons. 1977, chmn. div. prodn./ops. mgmt. 1975, prof.-in-charge U. Cin. prodn. unit 1959-76, originator various acad. publs. 1971-84, presenter research papers); mem. Mensa, Intertel, Theta Delta Chi (Most Promising Grad. award 1949), Beta Gamma Sigma, Sigma Iota Epsilon, Eta Kappa Nu, Sigma Tau. Republican. Presbyterian. Club: Shriners. Author: Survey of Industrial Relations in Leading Road Construction Firms, 1961; co-author: The Academic/Consultant Connection, 1979; Consultants Manual, 1980; author numerous research papers and articles; lectr. in field. Home: 610 Terrace Ave Cincinnati OH 45220 Office: Coll Bus Adminstrn U Cin Cincinnati OH 45221

GORHAM, MICHAEL JAMES VICTOR, banker; b. Parry Sound, Ont., Can., Dec. 27, 1943; s. Michael Vincent and Mary Maude (Higginbotham) G.; m. Carol Anne Rapp, June 4, 1966. Student pub. schs. Motor vehicle technician D.C. Govt., 1962-66; word processor Herner & Co., Washington, 1966-70; word processing sect. chief World Bank, Washington, 1970—; pres., chief exec. officer MediaTech Ltd.; dir. Dunrovin Typing Service, Alexandria, Va. Campaign vol. R.F. Kennedy presdl. campaign, 1968; active United Givers Fund, World Bank, 1979. Named Pub. Relations Officer of Yr., Probe, 1986. Mem. Internat. Word Processing Assn., World Bank Staff Assn., World Bank Micom Users Group (exec. bd. 1983—), World Bank Wang Users Group (exec. bd. 1983—), World Bank, NBI Users Group (exec. bd. 1983—), Soc. for Preservation and Encouragement Barbershop Singing in Am. (Spl. Media Communications award 1979, award Mid-Atlantic dist. 1985, Barbershopper of Yr.-Arlington chpt. 1979, 85, chpt. bull. editor 1978—, chpt. pres. 1982, sr. area counselor so. div. dist. pub. relations officer so. div./bull. editor 1983-85, ann. show chmn. 1979-85, dist. v.p. so. div., coeditor Mid. Atlantic newsletter, dist. v.p. for so. div.). Republican. Roman Catholic. Home: 2111 Golf Course Dr Reston VA 22091-3803 Office: World Bank 1818 H St NW Washington DC 20433

GORIA, GIOVANNI, Italian government official; b. Asti, Piedmont, Italy, July 31, 1943; m. Eugenia Goria; 2 children. Grad. in econs., U. Turin, Italy. Mem. Christian Dem. Party, 1960—; M.P. Italy, Rome, 1976—, econ. advisor to prime minister, 1978-79, sec. budget and econ. planning, 1981-82, minister treasury, 1982-87, prime minister, 1987-88. Address: Camera del Deputati, Rome Italy *

GORIN, LEONARD JOSEPH, dentist; b. N.Y.C., Dec. 16, 1917; s. Louis and Anna (Hottenstien) G.; B.A., NYU, 1939, D.D.S., 1943; cert. Tokyo Dental Coll., 1983, Med. Dental Coll., Peoples Republic China, 1983. Clin. dir. dental service N.Y.C. Fire Dept., 1952-76; attending dentist Mt. Sinai Hosp., N.Y.C., 1965-76; chief dental research Cabrini Health Care Center, N.Y.C., 1970-76; research fellow N.Y.U. Coll. Dentistry, 1974-76; pvt. dental practice, N.Y.C., 1947—; lectr., clinician micro bio quantum physics of human tissue. Democratic county committeeman, 1960's. Served with USPHS, 1944-47. Recipient commendation sci. contbrn. Faculte de Medicine de Paris, 1969. Knight of Malta. Fellow Royal Soc. Medicine, Royal Soc. Health, Acad. Gen. Dentistry, Collegium Internat. Oris Implantatorum, Internat. Coll. Dentists; mem. ADA, Assn. Mil. Surgeons, Am. Acad. Implant Dentistry (commendation), Am. Assn. Hosp. Dentists, Northeastern Soc. Periodontists, Phila. Soc. Periodontology, N. Am., Internat. assns. dental research, Spanish Soc. Stomatology (v.p.), Italian Group for Implant Study, Am. Soc. Microbiology. Contbr. articles to profl. jours.

GORIN, NORBERT CLAUDE, hematologist, educator, hospital administrator; b. Paris, Feb. 24, 1946; m. Isabelle Claire Jeannin, Sept. 12, 1974; children: Thomas, Laurent-Marc, Claire. MD, U. Paris, 1972. Resident in hematology Paris Hosps., 1968-72; chef de clinique Hosp. St. Antoine, Paris, 1972-79; guest worker Nat. Cancer Inst., Bethesda, Md., 1974-75; prof. hematology U. Paris, 1979—; dir. bone marrow transplant unit Hosp. St. Antoine, cryobiology unit Centre Nat. de Transfusions Sanguine, Paris, 1979—; party pres. Internat. Registry Autologous Bone Marrow Transplantation, 1987— (working on autologous bone marrow transplantation of the European bone marrow transplantation group, 1988—). Author: Technique de l'autogreffe de Moelle, 1987; also numerous articles. Mem. Am. Soc. Hematology, Internat. Soc. Exptl. Hematology. Lodge: Lions. Office: Hosp Saint-Antoine, Dept Hematology, 184 rue du Faubourg, 75012 Paris France

GORINOVITEH-GREENWICH, JURGE JOAN, interior designer, palace and museum designer and restorer; b. Kuokkala, USSR, Sept. 29, 1938; came to U.S. 1979, naturalized, s. Serge Nicolas and Aleutina Joan (Gorinoviteh-Greenwich) Philipow. Student Sch. Restorers, The Hermitage, Leningrad; Cert. The Art Sch., Leningrad, 1960; MA, State Coll. Applied and Indsl. Arts, Leningrad, 1966; numerous hon. doctorate degrees. Ordained bishop, 1987. Asst prof. art State Coll. Indsl. and Applied Arts, Leningrad, 1966-70; prof. art composition Art Coll. V. Serov, Leningrad, 1967-70; chief design dir. State Art Found., Leningrad., 1970-79; archtl. asst. exec. dir. Met. Hosp., N.Y.C., 1981; project mgr. SKM Architects & Ptnrs., N.Y.C., 1981-84; free lance restoration and design cons., 1984—. Chmn., chief Design Council Frunzensky Borough, Leningrad, 1975-77; mem. council Archtl. Council October's Borough, Leningrad, 1974-77. Interiors, restorations include: The Hermitage, Nat. Pushkin Mus., 1974-76, Cameron Gallery, Pushkin, 1975, Petersburg Leningrad City Mus. Jubilee Halls, 1975, Nat. Pub. Library, Leningrad, 1978, Navy Acad., Leningrad, 1977, State Inst. Theatre, Music and Cinematography, Leningrad, 1976, Met. Hosp., N.Y.C., 1981, Chem. Bank, Mfrs. Hanover Trust, Morgan Trust, Ross Jewelry Ctr., N.Y.C., 1984-88, World Trade Ctr. Mem. Creative Group, State Art Found., 1970-79. Recipient Jubilee medal Leningrad, 1975, 75. Mem. Am. Soc. Interior Designers (assoc.), N.Y. Soc. Architects, Archtl. Council N.Y. Home: 363 Ocean Pkwy Apt C-11 Brooklyn NY 11218

GORLAS, FRANCIS LAURENT, crystalware manufacturing company executive, chemist; b. Houdain, Pas de Calais, France, Apr. 18, 1943; s. Laurent and Stephanie (Kicinska) G.; m. Annie De Paoli, Dec. 24, 1965; 1 child, Paul Antoine. License es Sci. in Chemistry, U. Lille, France, 1967, Maitrise es Scis. in Chemistry, 1968. Engr. Verrerie Cristallerie d' Arques, Arques, France, 1969-82; tech. mgr. Verrerie Cristallerie d'Arques, Arques, 1982—. Roman Catholic. Home: 10 Rue de Strasbourg, 62510 Arques France Office: Verrerie Cristallerie d'Arques, Ave Gen de Gaulle, 62510 Arques France

GORLIN, CATHY ELLEN, lawyer; b. Shields Twp., Ill., July 25, 1953; d. Robert James and Marilyn (Alpern) G.; m. Marshall Howard Tanick, Feb. 20, 1982; 1 child, Lauren Gorlin. B.A. magna cum laude, Wesleyan U., 1975; J.D., U. Minn., 1978. Bar: Minn. 1978. Law clk. Minn. Atty. Gen.'s Office, St. Paul, summer 1976, Mpls. and Bloomington City Atty.'s Office, 1977-78; assoc. Mullin, Weinberg & Daly, Mpls., 1978; law clk. to judges Hennepin County Family Ct., Mpls., 1979-80, temp. referee, summer 1980; assoc. Larkin, Hoffman, Daly & Lindgren, Ltd., Mpls., 1980-84; ptnr. Best & Flanagan, 1984—; chairperson family law dept.; sec. Hennepin Lawyer Mag., 1983-85; chmn. Minn. Women Lawyers Appointments Com., Mpls., 1983—; mem. Supreme Ct. Task Force on Gender Fairness in the Cts., 1987; Supreme Ct. Legal Cert. Bd., 1986—. Contbr. articles to legal publs.; guest appearances radio. Advance person Vice-Pres. Mondale, 1979, vol. various polit. candidates; del. 3d dist. conv., Minn., 1980-84. Named Atty. of Month, Larkin, Hoffman, Daly & Lindgren, Ltd., 1983. Mem. ABA, Minn. Bar Assn. (chmn. 1985-86), Hennepin County Bar Assn. (rep. to child support task force 1982, chmn. exec. com. family law sect., chmn. sect. 1982-84), Minn. Trial Lawyers Assn., Jewish Bus. and Profl. Women's Group (dir., support group coordinator), Minn. Women's Network (dir.), Jewish Family and Children Service Counseling Com., West Suburban C. of C. Democrat. Jewish. Home: 1230 Angelo Dr Golden Valley MN 55422 Office: Best & Flanagan 3500 IDS Tower Minneapolis MN 55402

GORMAN, GARY EUGENE, educator, clergyman, author; b. Carmel-By-The-Sea, Calif., Oct. 8, 1944; s. Eugene Wesley and Alma Gertrude (Falt) G.; m. Lynette Chaffey, June 6, 1980; 1 dau., Caroline Theresa Holmes. B.A. cum laude, Boston U., 1967; M.Div., Luth. Theol. Seminary, 1970; S.T.B., Trinity Coll. (Toronto, Can.), 1971; diploma in librarianship Univ. Coll., London, 1975; M.A., U. London, 1977. Chaplain, St. Hugh's Coll., Oxford, Eng., 1972-74; warden Namibia Peace Ctr., Sutton Courtenay, Berkshire, Eng., 1974-75; internat. orgns. librarian Inst. Devel. Studies, Brighton, Sussex, Eng., 1975-83; founding dir. Library Info. and Pub. Cons., Lewes, Eng. and Coolamon, N.S.W., Australia, 1982—; lectr. dept. librarianship Ballarat Coll. Advanced Edn., Victoria, Australia, 1984-86; lectr. Sch. Info. Studies, Riverina-Murray Inst. Higher Edn., New South Wales, Australia, 1986—; cons. UNIDO, Univ. South Africa, IBM (France), World Vision of Australia, others, 1978, 80, 82, 86—; hon. chaplain Anglican Bishop of Ballarat, 1984—; mem. post-ordination edn. com. Diocese of Ballarat, 1986—; priest Anglican Diocese of the Riverina. Author: South African Novel in English, 1978; Guide to Third World National Bibliographies, 1983, 2nd ed., 1987; Theological and Religious Reference Materials (3 vols.), 1984-86, Collection Development for Australian Libraries, 1988; editor: (book series) Topics in Religion, 1982—; (serial) Index of Development Studies Literature, 1983-85; (book series) Development Studies, 1976-83; assoc. editor Jour. Library Acquisitions: Practice and Theory, 1983—; joint editor Riverina Library Rev., 1987—; book rev. editor Jour. African Book Pub. Record, 1977—; editor ANZTLA Newsletter, 1986—; contbr. numerous articles in field to various profl. jours. Eliza Smith fellow Luth. Ch. in Am., 1971, 72; travel grantee Univ. South Africa, 1978. Fellow Library Assn. Eng.; mem. Am. Theol. Library Assn., African Studies Assn. Australia and Pacific, Internat. Assn. Agrl. Librarians and Documentalists, Library Assn. Australia (conv. Distance in Edn. Spl. Interest Group 1985-88, sec. Edn. for Librarianship nat. com. 1986-88, sec. edn. librarianship NSW com., 1989—); exec. Ctr. for Library Studies; Standing Conf. on Library Materials on Africa, Assn. Brit. Theol. and Philos. Libraries, Am. Theol. Library Assn., Australian and N.Z. Theol. Library Assn., Delta Mu, Phi Alpha Theta. Anglican. Office: Riverina-Murray Inst Higher Edn, Sch Info Studies PO Box 588, Wagga Wagga NSW 2650, Australia

GORMAN, JOSEPH TOLLE, corporate executive; b. Rising Sun, Ind., 1937; m. Bettyann Gorman. B.A., Kent State U., 1959; LL.B., Yale U., 1962. Assoc. Baker, Hostetler & Patterson, Cleve., 1962-67; with legal dept. TRW Inc., Cleve., 1968-69, asst. sec., 1969-70, sec., 1970-72, v.p. sr. counsel automotive worldwide ops., 1972-73, v.p., asst. gen. counsel, 1973-76, v.p., gen. counsel, 1976-80, acting head communications function, 1978, exec. v.p. indsl. and energy sector, 1980-84, exec. v.p., asst. pres., 1984-85, pres., chief operating officer, 1985—, mem. policy group, 1975—, also bd. dirs.; bd. dirs. Soc. Corp., Soc. Nat. Bank Cleve., Standard Oil Co. Trustee Univ. Circle, Inc., Cleve. Play House, Cleve. Inst. Art, Leadership Cleve., United Way Services, Cleve. Council on World Affairs, Musical Arts Assn., Denison U.; past trustee Cleve. Fedn. Community Planning, Govtl. Research Inst.; past mem. exec. com. Ctr. of Pub. Resources Project on Dispute Resolution; bd. advisors Yale Law Sch. Urgent Issues Program. Mem. ABA, Assn. Gen. Counsel (emeritus), Ohio Bar Assn., Cleve. Bar Assn., Yale Law Sch. Assn. (exec. com.), Greater Cleve. Growth Assn. (trustee, exec. com.), U.S. C. of C. (past chmn. corp. governance and policy com.), Council on Fgn. Relations. Office: TRW Inc 1900 Richmond Rd Cleveland OH 44124

GORMAN, LYNN RAY, truck rental company executive; b. Des Moines, Iowa, Feb. 13, 1942; s. Raymond Vernon and Virginia (Foote) G.; m. Judy Kay Howard; children—Shannon L., Shelly K. B.B.A., North Tex. State U., 1964. With Ryder Truck Rental, Inc., Dallas, 1957-64, with maintenance dept., Miami, Fla., 1968, dir. warranty, 1973-82, group dir. maintenance, 1982-83, officer of co., v.p. maintenance, 1983—; sales mgr. Internat. Harvester, Dallas, 1964-68. Served with USAF, 1964-71. Mem. Am. Mgmt. Assn., Am. Truck Assn. (truck maintenance council), Soc. Automotive Engrs., Sigma Phi Epsilon. Republican. Baptist. Home: 15831 SW 99th Pl Miami FL 33157 Office: Ryder Truck Rental Inc 3600 NW 82nd Ave Miami FL 33166

GORMAN, MARCIE SOTHERN, franchise executive; b. N.Y.C., Feb. 25, 1949; d. Jerry R. and Carole Edith (Frendel) Sothern; m. N. Scott Gorman, June 14, 1969 (div.); children: Michael Stephen, Mark Jason. A.A., U. Fla., 1968; B.S., Memphis State U., 1970. Tchr., Memphis City Sch. System, 1970-73; tng. dir. Weight Watchers of Palm Beach County and Weight Watchers So. Ala., Inc., West Palm Beach, Fla., 1973—, area dir., then pres., 1977—; pres. Markel Ads, Inc. Cubmaster Troop 130. Hon. lt. col. a.d.c. Ala. Militia. Mem. Women' Am. ORT (program chmn. 1975), Optometric Soc. (sec. 1973), Weight Watchers Franchise Assn. (chair mktg. com., mem. advt./mktg. council, chairperson region IV bd. dirs.), Nat. Orgn. Women, Exec. Women of the Palm Beaches, Am. Bus. Women's Assn., Nat. Assn. Female Execs. Lodge: Zonta. Home: 429 N Country Club Dr Atlantis FL 33462 Office: 7597 Lake Worth Rd Lake Worth FL 33467

GORMAN, ROBERT SAUL, architect; b. N.Y.C., June 28, 1933; s. Philip and Lillian (Weiss) G.; B.Arch., M.Arch., Yale U., 1966; m. Judith Alice Albaum, July 2, 1965; children—Melissa, Sasha William Shannon. Apprentice to Frank Lloyd Wright, 1953-56; designer Eero Saarinen, Hamden, Conn., 1961-67; architect, planner Victor Gruen Assos., N.Y.C., 1967-69, Juster/Pope, Architects, Shelburne Falls, Mass., 1977-78; architect Robert Gorman Assos., Architects, Planners, Solar Energy Cons., Richmond, N.H., 1969-80; founder, prin. Rawson Pl. Architects, 1980—; cons. Bklyn. Coll., 1967-69. Served with AUS, 1956-58. Frank Lloyd Wright Found. fellow, 1953-56. Mem. AIA (Design award 1972). Pioneer in solar energy archtl. applications; architect, planner several projects. Home: Richmond Rd Richmond NH 03470 Office: Green River Architects Green River VT

GORMAN, THOMAS FRANCIS (MIKE), writer, association executive; b. N.Y.C., Dec. 7, 1913; s. Frank and Mary (Naughton) G.; m. Ernestine Brown, June 3, 1946 (dec. June 1958); children—Michael, Patricia; m. Patricia Lea Vierling, Nov. 30, 1979; 1 stepson, Douglas. A.B., NYU, 1934, postgrad., 1934-36. Freelance writer 1936-41; reporter Daily Oklahoman, 1945; writer numerous news stories and editorials in mental hosp. campaig, pioneered establishment of mental hygiene clinic in Okla., also mental hygiene orgn.; chief writer, dir. pub. hearings Pres.'s Commn. on Health Needs of the Nation, 1950-53; exec. dir. Nat. Com. Against Mental Illness, Washington, 1953—; mem. Menninger Found.; mem. Joint Commn. Mental Health of Children, 1966—; mem. nat. adv. mental health council USPHS, 1961—; mem. 1st U.S. Mental Health Del. to USSR, 1967; mem. World Fedn. Mental Health; exec. dir. Citizens for Treatment High Blood Pressure, 1977—; mem. Citizens for Pub. Action on Cholesterol, 1985. Author: Oklahoma Attacks Its Snake Pits, 1948, Every Other Bed, 1956, Psychiatry in the Soviet Union, 1969, Community Mental Health: The Search for Identity, 1970; contbr. articles on psychiat. and med. subjects to mags. Exec. dir. Citizens for Pub. Action on Cholesterol, 1985—. Served with USAAF, 1942-45. Recipient Spl. Lasker award Nat. Com. Mental Hygiene, 1948; Edward A. Strecker Meml. award, 1962; William C. Menninger award, 1971; 1st Dr. Benjamin Rush award, 1976; 1st Disting. Service award Nat. Council Community Mental Health Ctrs., 1973, Mental Health Service medallion Nat. Mus. Am. History, 1986; named one of ten Outstanding Young Men in Am. U.S. Jaycees, 1949. •Fellow Am. Pub. Health Assn., Am. Psychiat. Assn. (hon.), Royal Soc. Health (Eng.), N.Y. Acad. Scis.; mem. Nature Conservancy, Nat. Press Club (med. writing award 1972), Phi Beta Kappa.. Clubs: Federal City, City Tavern (Washington). Office: 1101 17th St NW Washington DC 20036

GORMĚZANO, KEITH STEPHEN, publisher; b. Madison, Wis., Nov. 22, 1955; s. Isadore and Miriam (Fox) G.; BS U. Iowa, 1977, BGS Yeshiva Aish Ha-Torah, 1977; postgrad. in law U. Puget Sound, 1984—. Pub. relations dir. Hillel Found., Iowa City, Iowa; pub. Le Beacon Presse, Seattle, 1980—; owner Keith Gormezano, Effective PR, 1983-86; arbitrator Better Bus. Bur. Greater Seattle, 1987—. Op. Improvement Found., 1980-81; pub. info. officer chmn. Iowa City Young Ams. for Freedom, 1979-81; vol. VISTA, 1982-83; dir. ACJS, Inc., 1981-82. Vice chmn. Resource Conservation Commn., Iowa City, 1979-80; chmn. Iowa City Young Ams. for Freedom, 1979-81; bd. dirs. Seattle Mental Health Inst., 1981-83, Youth Advocates, Seattle, 1984, Atlantic St. Ctr., 1984; mem. City of Seattle Animal Control Commn., 1984-86, vice chmn., 1985-86, chmn. 1986; mem. Selective Service System, 1982—, vice chmn. civilan rev. bd. 742, 1985—. Served to 2d lt. U.S. Army, 1973-77. Mem. Mcpl. League, Com. of Small Mag. Editors and Pubs., League United Latin Am. Citizens Amigos (chair 1984-86), U. Iowa Alumni Assn. (life), Sigma Delta Chi. Republican. Jewish. Editor, M'godolim, 1986-88. Home: PO Box 15945-WO Seattle WA 98115-0945 Office: 2921 E Madison St Suite 7WWW Seattle WA 98112-4242

GORMLEY, DAVID FRANK, marketing executive; b. Swampscott, Mass., Feb. 10, 1934; s. Ernest Raymond and Cathrine (Maitland) G.; m. Mary Lou Carroll, Aug. 22, 1954; children—Kathleen, David, John, Nancy, Robert, Patrick. BA, U. Mass., 1956. CLU. With Sentry Ins. Cos., 1958-75, v.p. sales, 1970-73, v.p. sales and mktg., 1973-75; v.p., sr. mktg. officer United Am. Life Ins., Denver, 1975-78; pres., chief exec. officer Am. Health and Life Ins. Co., Balt., 1978-82; sr. v.p. Bankers Security Life, Washington, after 1982; sr. v.p. mktg. Provident Indemnity; instr. U. Wis. Alumni trustee U. Mass. Served to capt. USMCR, 1956-58. Mem. Am. Soc. Life Underwriters, Nat. Assn. Life Underwriters, Md. Life Underwriters, Nat. Assn. Health Underwriters, Kappa Sigma. Clubs: Balt. Mchts., Balt. Ctr., Lodges: Elks, KC. Home: 372 S Corona St Denver CO 80209 Office: 1600 Market St Philadelphia PA 19101

GORMLY, WILLIAM MOWRY, financial consultant; b. Pitts., Mar. 15, 1941; s. Thomas Wilson and Lourene (Blaine) G.; m. Barbara Diesner, Aug. 21, 1965; children: Kirsten Eve, Kellie Blaine. BA in Econs., Dickinson Coll., Carlisle, Pa., 1963; postgrad. Northwestern U., 1967, DePaul U., 1968; grad. banking degree Stonier Grad. Sch. Banking Rutgers U., 1978. Regional mgr. Harris Bank, Chgo., 1967-69; corp. banking officer Wells Fargo Bank N.A., San Francisco, 1969-73; v.p. 4th Nat. Bank of Wichita, 1973-74, Union Nat. Bank of Pitts., 1974-79; v.p., sr. nat. accts. officer Ariz. Bank, Phoenix, 1979-82; pres. Cons. in Pub. Fin., Ltd., Scottsdale, Ariz., 1982—. Mem. Dickinson Coll. Alumni Council, 1975-80; bd. dirs. Ariz. Theatre Co., Phoenix, 1980-83; trustee Northland Pub. Library, Pitts., 1975-79. Served to 1st lt. U.S. Army, 1963-65. Mem. Assn. Corp. Growth, Am. Hosp. Assn., Phi Delta Theta. Republican. Methodist. Office: Cons in Pub Fin Ltd 23150 N Pima Rd Suite 1 Scottsdale AZ 85255

GÓRNIAK-KOCIKOWSKA, KRYSTYNA STEFANIA, philosopher; b. Polczyn Zdrój, Poland, Oct. 10, 1947; d. Kazimierz and Stefania Wiktoria (Jagielska) G.; m. Andrzej Kocikowski, Aug. 3, 1974; 1 child, Mikolaj. MA in German philology, A. Mickiewicz U., Poznań, Poland, 1973, PhD in philosophy, 1976. Asst. A. Mickiewicz U., 1976-81, sr. lectr., 1981. Coauthor: From The History of German Mental Culture, 1985 (award Minister Higher Edn. 1986). Mem. Polish Philos. Soc. Office: Inst Filozofii UAM, Szamarzewskiego 91C, 60-569 Poznan Poland

GORNICK, ALAN LEWIS, lawyer; b. Leadville, Colo., Sept. 23, 1908; s. Mark and Anne (Grayhack) G.; m. Ruth L. Willcockson, 1940 (dec. May 1959); children: Alan Lewis, Diana Willcockson (Mrs. Lawrence J. Richard, Jr.), Keith Hardin; m. Pauline Martoi, 1972. AB, Columbia U., 1935, JD, 1937. Bar: N.Y. 1937, Mich. 1948. Assoc. Baldwin, Todd & Young, N.Y.C., 1937-41, Milbank, Tweed, Hope & Hadley, 1941-47; asso. counsel charge tax matters Ford Motor Co., Dearborn, Mich., 1947-49; dir. tax affairs, chmn. tax com., tax counsel Ford Motor Co., 1949-64; lectr. tax matters NYU, Inst. Fed. Taxation, 1947-49, ABA and Practicing Law Inst. (courses on fundamentals in fed. taxation), 1946-55, Am. Law Inst. (courses in continuing legal edn.), 1950; spl. lectr. sch. bus. adminstrn. U. Mich., 1949, 53. Author: Estate Tax Handbook, 1952, Arrangements for Separation or Divorce, Handbook of Tax Techniques, 1952, Taxation of Partnerships, Estates and Trusts, rev. edit, 1952; adv. editor Nat. Tax Jour., 1952-55; contbr. articles on tax matters to profl. jours. Exec. bd. Detroit area council Boy Scouts Am., chmn. fin. com., 1960; pres. Mich. Assn. Emotionally Disturbed Children, 1962-65; v.p. Archives of Am. Art; mem. Mich.

Heart Assn., Columbia Coll. council Columbia U., N.Y.C., Founder's Soc. Detroit Inst. Art; trustee Council on World Affairs, Detroit; trustee, past pres. Detroit Hist. Soc.; mem. Bd. Zoning Appeals City Bloomfield Hills, 1980—. Recipient Gov.'s Spl. award State Colo., 1952. Mem. World Bar Assn. for Peace through Law, ABA (council tax sect. 1957-58), Detroit Bar Assn., N.Y. City Bar Assn. (chmn. subcom. estate and gift taxes 1943-47), Am. Law Inst., Tax Inst. Inc. (pres. 1954-55), U.S. C. of C., Empire State C. of C., Council on Fgn. Relations, Nat. Tax Assn. (exec. com.), Internat. Fiscal Assn. (council, nat. reporter 6th Internat. Congress Fiscal Law, Brussels 1952), Internat. Law Assn., Assn. Ex-Mems. Squadron A, Nat. Fgn. Trade Council (mem. com. taxes 1950), Automobile Mfrs. Assn. (chmn. com. on taxation 1960-62), Tax Execs. Inst. (pres. 1956-57), Fedn. Alumni Columbia (bd. dirs. 1946), Class 1935 Columbia Coll. (pres.), N.Y. Adult Edn. Council (bd. dirs. 1939-45), Detroit Hist. Soc. (trustee, pres. 1083-85), Phi Delta Phi. Clubs: Bloomfield Hills (Mich.) Country, Detroit, Detroit Athletic, Columbia U., Church (N.Y.C.); Lawyers of U. of Mich., Columbia U. Alumni of Mich. (pres. 1950—), Otsego Ski (Gaylord, Mich.); Little (Gulfstream, Fla.). Home: 150 Lowell Ct Bloomfield Hills MI 48013 Office: 1565 Woodward Ave Suite 8 PO Box 957 Bloomfield Hills MI 48013

GÓRNIEWICZ, LECH, mathematician, educator; b. Budków, Poland, Jan. 4, 1941; s. Zygmunt and Henryka Górniewicz; m. Maria Wlodarkiewicz; 1 child, Grzegorz. MA, U. Gdansk (Poland), 1965, DSc, 1975; postgrad., Inst. Math. Polish Acad. Sci., Warsaw, Poland, 1972. adj. prof. Inst. Math. of Polish Acad. Sci, Warsaw, 1971-75. Assoc. prof. U. Gdansk, 1965-68, 75-84; prof. U. Torun (Poland), 1984—. Home: Sz Szeregow 7/9, 87200 Torun Poland Office: U Nicholas Copernicus, Dept Math, Chopina 12/18, 87100 Torun Poland

GOROSTIZA, GUILLERMO JORGE, money exchange company executive; b. Buenos Aires, Apr. 7, 1943; s. Gonzalo Guillermo and Maria Elena (Olivero) G.; m. Nora Cecilia Krimer, July 7, 1982. Bachelor degree, Cardenal Newman, Buenos Aires, 1960, U. Cambridge, Eng., 1963. With La Agricola Ins. Co., Buenos Aires, 1958-64; mgr. Elevece SRL, Buenos Aires, 1964-67; pres. Casa de Turismo de Buenos Aires, 1967-77, Cambio Italia, Buenos Aires, 1978—; cons. Six Fortunes Internat. Corp., Buenos Aires, 1982—, Halo SA, Buenos Aires, 1978-87. Roman Catholic. Club: Cardenal Newman. Home: Guemes 1212, Acassuso, 1640 Buenos Aires Argentina Office: Cambio Italia, Tucuman 553, 1049 Buenos Aires Argentina

GORSKI, STANLEY FRANCIS, weed scientist, educator; b. Indpls., Feb. 26, 1949; s. Stanley F. and Ruth A. (Fulmer) G.; m. Mary Jo Dowling, Apr. 18, 1970; children: Stanley Bryce, Jonathin Josef. BS Purdue U., 1973; MS U. Ill., 1975, PhD 1978. Grad. research asst. U. Ill., Urbana, 1974-77; asst. prof. soils and crops Rutgers U., 1978-79; asst. prof. horticulture Ohio State U., 1979-83, assoc. prof., 1984—. Contbr. numerous articles to profl. jours. Grantee in field. Mem. Am. Soc. Hort. Sci., Weed Sci. Soc. Am., Northeastern Weed Sci. Soc., North Central Weed Sci. Soc., Gamma Sigma Delta. Roman Catholic. Home: 960 Lambeth Dr Columbus OH 43220 Office: Ohio State University Department of Horticulture Fyffe Ct 2001 Columbus OH 43210

GORSKI, WILLIAM EDWARD, missionary; b. Chgo., Sept. 2, 1950; s. Arthur William and Lois Ann (Lundell) G.; m. Cynthia Helen Witt, Sept. 22, 1973; children—Amanda Elizabeth, Rebecca Christine. B.A., Augustana Coll., 1972; M.Div., Luth. Sch. Theology, Chgo., 1976. Ordained to ministry, 1976. Pastor, Christ the Lord Luth. Ch., Elgin, Ill., 1976-78; pastor/missionary Luth. Ch. Am., Santiago, Chile, 1978—; bd. dirs., treas. Evang. Theol. Community, Santiago, 1985—, prof. liturgics, 1978—; bd. dirs. Clinica Alemana, Santiago, 1987; sec. of ch. Evang. Luth. Ch. in Chile, 1980, bishop, pres., 1986; dir. Fundacion Ayuda Social Cristiana, Chile, 1978—. Mem. Omicron Delta Kappa. Democrat. Address: Casilla 15167, Santiago Chile

GORSON, JAMES ROY, association official; b. Phila., Sept. 25, 1924; s. Harry Amos and Merle Evelyn G. B.A., Temple U., 1948. Dir. facilitation Air Transport Assn., Washington, 1960—. Served with USN, 1944-46; PTO. Republican. Baptist. Avocation: fishing. Home: 1600 Eads Arlington VA 22202 Office: Air Transport Assn 1709 New York Ave NW Washington DC 20006

GORSUCH, GEORGE EDWARD, former naval officer, physician; b. Toledo, May 9, 1929; s. George Albert and Esther Elizabeth (Smith) G.; B.S. with honors, U. Toledo, 1951; M.D., U. Cin., 1954; postgrad. Naval Med. Sch., Bethesda, Md., 1959; m. Martha Jean Sheard, June 8, 1954 (div. 1970); children—Geoffrey George, Gregory Mark, Gretchen Gene; m. 2d, Jean Ury Turner Evans, Mar. 19, 1970; children—Emily Lovelace, Abby Kate. Commd. lt. (j.g.) U.S. Navy, 1954, advanced through grades to rear adm., 1977; rotating intern Naval Hosp., Phila., 1954-55; resident in internal medicine Naval Hosp., San Diego, 1955-57; resident in cardiology Naval Hosp., Bethesda, 1957-58; head br. cardiology, dept. internal medicine Naval Hosp., Oakland, Calif., 1959-63, chmn. dept. internal medicine, 1970-73; mem. staff med. dept. Naval Activities, London, 1963-65; head cardiovascular sect. Naval Hosp., Nat. Naval Med. Center, Bethesda, 1965-68; chief med. service U.S.S. Repose, South Vietnam, 1969-70; dep. comdg. officer, dir. clin. services Naval Regional Med. Center, Oakland, 1973-75; comdg. officer U.S. Naval Regional Med. Center, Yokosuka, Japan, 1975-77; fleet surgeon, Comdr. in Chief U.S. Pacific Fleet, sr. med. officer Comdr. in Chief Joint Mil. Command, Pacific and sr. med. officer Comdr. Pacific Logistic Command, 1977-78; comdg. officer Naval Regional Med. Center, Portsmouth, Va., dist. med. officer Fifth Naval Dist., Norfolk, Va., 1978-81; prof. medicine Eastern Va. Med. Sch., 1979-81; dep. surgeon gen. U.S. Navy, 1981-82; ret. 1982; asso. v.p. for membership ACP, 1982—. Decorated Legion of Merit with gold star, Navy Commendation medal with gold star, Navy Unit Commendation, Meritorious Unit Commendation; diplomate Am. Bd. Internal Medicine recert. 1974. Fellow A.C.P. (gov. 1980-81), Am. Coll. Cardiology (asso. fellow); mem. Assn. Mil. Surgeons. Office: ACP 4200 Pine St Philadelphia PA 19104

GORUP, GREGORY JAMES, marketing executive; b. Kansas City, Kans., Mar. 27, 1948; s. Mike and Helen F. Gorup; m. Kathleen Susan Grogan, Apr. 12, 1986; 1 child, Michael Thomas. B.A. in Econs., St. Benedict Coll., 1970; M.B.A., U. Pa., 1972. Market analyst product planning and devel. dept. Citibank, N.Y.C., 1972-73, market planning officer corp. product mgmt. div., 1973-74, product mgr. securities services, 1974-75; v.p., dir. product devel. Irving Trust Co. N.Y.C., 1975-80, mgr. product mgmt. dept., 1980-81; v.p. mktg. Credit Suisse, U.S. area, 1981-84; sr. cons. Wesley, Brown and Bartle, N.Y.C., 1985-86; bank mktg. mgr. Digital Equipment Corp., N.Y.C., 1986-87; money mktg. mgr. Reuters N.Am., 1987—. Mem. fund raising com. Big Bros. of N.Y., 1975—. Mem. Am. Mgmt. Assn., Ducks Unltd. Republican. Roman Catholic. Club: Wharton Bus. Sch., Princeton of N.Y. (N.Y.C.). Home: 47 Kingsbury Rd New Rochelle NY 10804 Office: Reuters Info Services 1700 Broadway New York NY 10019

GOSALVEZ, MARIO, cancer pharmacology biochemist, educator; b. Madrid, Sept. 11, 1940; s. Fernando and Concepcion G.; m. Maria Flor Blanco, Oct. 2, 1964; children—Mario, David, Elena. Licenciate in medicine and surgery U. Complutense, Madrid, 1963, Dr. Medicine and Surgery, 1967; postgrad. Karolinska Inst., Stockholm, 1967, U. Pa., Asst. and lecturing prof. U. Complutense, 1964-67; 1968-69. research assoc. Fels Research Inst. Sch. Medicine, Phila., 1969-70; prof. asociado Sch. Medicine, U. Autonoma, Madrid, 1971-73, prof. agregado, 1974-77; head research biochemistry sector Clinica Puerta de Hierro, Madrid, 1974—; prof. titular biochemistry and molecular biology Spanish U. System, 1985—; pres. Internat. Found. Advancement of Knowledge, 1976; v.p. Spanish Assn. for Cancer Research, Madrid, 1982—. Contbr. numerous articles to med. jours. Patentee in field. Painter. Writer poetry and fiction. Recipient Extraordinary award Univ. Complutense, 1968, Nat. prize in Biochemistry Social Security (Ministry of Health), 1977, 79; Premio Rodriguez Pascual, 1979. Mem. Am. Assn. Cancer Research (corr.), Biochem. Soc. Gt. Brit., Spanish Biochem. Soc., European Assn. Cancer Research, Internat. Soc. Oxygen Transport to Tissue, Spanish Acad. Surgery. Liberal. Roman Catholic. Current work: Biochemical Pharmacology of cancer, leading to reversal of cancer to normality, tumor-reduct-targetted cytotoxic drugs carcinogenesis, cell sociology, femtomolar biochemistry, in vivo fluorometry. Subspecialties: Cancer research (medicine); Drug design.

GOSE, RICHARD VERNIE, lawyer; b. Hot Springs, S.D., Aug. 3, 1927; s. Vernie O. and Mame K. (Thompson) G.; B.S., U. Wyo., 1950; M.S. in Engring., Northwestern U., 1955; LL.B., George Washington U., 1967; J.D., George Washington U., 1968; children—Beverly Marie, Donald Paul, Celeste Marlene. Bar: N.Mex. 1967, U.S. Supreme Ct. 1976, Wyo. 1979. Exec. asst. to U.S. Senator Hickey, Washington, 1960-62; mgr. E.G. & G., Inc., Washington, 1964-66; asst. atty. gen. State of N.Mex., Santa Fe, 1967-70; sole practice law, Santa Fe, 1967—; assoc. prof. engring. U. Wyo., 1957-60; owner, mgr. Gose & Assocs., Santa Fe, 1967-78; sole practice law, Casper, Wyo., 1978-83; co-chmn. Henry Jackson for Pres., M.Mex., 1976, Wyo. Johnson for Pres., 1960. Served with U.S. Army, 1950-52. Registered profl. engr., N.Mex., Wyo.; Mem. 1st Jud. Dist. Bar Assn. (past pres.), N.Mex. Bar Assn., Wyo. Bar Assn., Phi Delta Theta, Pi Tau Sigma, Sigma Tau. Methodist. Lodge: Masons. Home and Office: PO Box 8301 Santa Fe NM 87504

GOSNELL, CHARLES FRANCIS, librarian, publicist; b. Rochester, N.Y., July 7, 1909; s. James Francis and Alameda (Whipple) G.; m. Patria Aran-Soler, Mar. 31, 1934; children: Alice, Rita; m. Helen Louise Kuhlman, Dec. 29, 1951; children: Marsh Kuhlman, Deborah, Susan, Catherine. A.B., U. Rochester, 1930; B.S., Columbia, 1932, M.S., 1937; Ph.D., N.Y. U., 1943; certificate, Centro de Estudios Históricos, Madrid, Spain, 1934. Asst. U. Rochester Library, 1927-31; corr. Rochester Democrat and Chronicle, 1928-30; reference asst. N.Y. Pub. Library, 1931-37; librarian, asso. prof. Queens Coll., 1937-45; asso. Sch. Library Service, Columbia, 1943-47; asst. commr. edn. N.Y., 1949-62; state librarian N.Y. State, 1945-62; dir. libraries, prof. library adminstrn. N.Y. U., 1962-74, emeritus, 1974—; adviser to U.S. Gen. Services Adminstrn. on archives and records centers, 1974— ; chmn. Pub. Affairs Info. Service, 1976—; spl. cons., library orgns., and assns., library mus. and historic bldgs. for fire protection, library lighting. U.S. del. to UNESCO Conf. on Libraries, Sao Paulo, Brazil, 1951; head UNESCO survey pub. library services in, Colombia, S.Am., 1959; cons. to Ford Found. and U. Brasilia, Brazil, 1963—; cons. Inter-Am. Devel. Bank, 1966-67. Author: several books latest being New York State's Freedom Train, 1948; Copyright: Grab-bag, 1968, Spanish Personal Names, 1971, Obsolescence of Books, 1978; Contbr. articles to profl. jours. Sec. N.Y. State Freedom Train Commn., N.Y. Cultural Heritage Found.; trustee Center for Study Presidency, Mohawk-Caughnawaga Mus., Fonda, N.Y., Skidmore Coll., Saratoga Springs, N.Y.; chmn. Council Nat. Library Assns., 1956-57; past pres. Nat. Assn. State Libraries; pres. Chancellor Robert R. Livingston Masonic Library; bd. dirs. Library Assn. Rockland County. Recipient Grand Cross Eloy Alfaro Internat. Found., 1968; comdr. Order Jacques Ignace Fresnel Haiti; Good Citizenship gold medal S.A.R.; Lafayette medal Merit, 1977; Benjamin Franklin fellow Royal Soc. Arts, London. Mem. A.L.A. (mem. exec. bd. 1953-57, pres. library adminstrn. div. 1966-67), N.Y. Library Assn. (pres. 1968-69, Moore award 1978), Middle Atlantic Regional Library Council (bd. dirs.), various spl. library assns., nat., state and local bibliog. and library assns., and also assns. in related fields, such as statis., archivist and hist. socs. Clubs: Mason (N.Y.C.) (33 deg., grand historian, grand master N.Y., chmn. Empire State Mason mag., chmn. conf. grand masters N.Am. 1968-69, hon. grand master Guanabara, Rio de Janeiro, hon. mem. supreme council Brazil, hon. past grand master York grand lodge Mexico, Henry Price medalist grand lodge Mass., hon. grand warden grand lodge nat. France, hon. past grand master grand lodge of Okla.), Grolier (N.Y.C.), N.Y. University (N.Y.C.); Rotary; University (Albany). Home: 11 Orchard Circle Suffern NY 10901 Office: 71 W 23d St Room 1700 New York NY 10010

GOSNELL, F. LAURENCE, electronics company sales executive; b. Auburn, N.Y., July 5, 1925; s. Frank L. and (Helen) Evelyn (Conard) G.; BS in Engring. with highest honors, Princeton U., 1946; MBA, Harvard U. Grad. Sch. Bus. Adminstrn., 1954; m. Marilyn J. Zneimer, Oct. 11, 1952; children: James L., Elizabeth M., Peter W., Andrew C. Mgmt. analyst aircraft nuclear propulsion dept. Gen. Electric Co., Evendale, Ohio, 1954-56; sr. sales engr. Weston Instruments, Wellesley, Mass., 1956-60; v.p. sales and market devel. Wang Labs., Tewksbury, Mass., 1960-68; dir. mktg. Bolt, Beranek & Newman, Cambridge, Mass., 1968-69; regional mgr. Measurement Instruments, Inc., Wellesley, Mass., 1969-73; v.p. corp. devel. Tranti Systems, Inc., North Billerica, Mass., 1973—; staff instr. engring. and oceanology Naval Res. Officers Sch., Boston, 1956-66; dir. Auto Veyor, Inc., Boston, 1982—. Trustee, New Eng. Bapt. Hosp., Boston, 1969—, chmn. Sch. Nursing com., 1971—, devel. com., 1985-87; bd. govs. Vol. Trustees of Not-for-Profit Hosps., Washington, 1982—; bd. dirs. Christian Community Found., 1982—; vestryman Trinity Ch., Boston, 1964-70. lay reader St. Andrews Episcopal Ch., Wellesley, 1980—, vestryman, 1984-87; vice chmn. for West Suburban Boston, Princeton U. Alumni Schs. Com., 1975-85, chmn., 1985-87. Served to lt. comdr. USNR, 1943-46, 51-53. Mem. IEEE, Instrument Soc. Am. (sr.; pres. Boston sect. 1964-65), Diploma Nurses Assn., Harvard Bus. Sch. Assn. Boston, Princeton Assn. New Eng. (dir. 1980-87), Tau Beta Pi. Republican. Clubs: Nehoiden Golf; Princeton of New York; Wellesley Coll. Office: E K Shriver Ctr 200 Trapelo Rd Waltham MA 02254

GOSS, BARRY ANDREW, economics educator, researcher, consultant; b. Melbourne, Victoria, Australia, Jan. 13, 1939; s. Andrew Rupert and Audrey Margaret (Martin) G.; m. Shirley May Quinlan, 1972; children—Matthew Barry, Dominic Paul. B.Com. with honors, Melbourne Univ., 1961; Ph.D., London Sch. Econs., Univ. London, 1967. Tutor econs. Melbourne Univ., 1962-63; lectr. econs. Manchester Univ., Eng., 1965-68, Monash Univ., Melbourne, 1969-71, sr. lectr. econs., 1972-86, reader in econs., 1987—; vis. prof. Univ. Louvain, Belgium, 1976-77, Univ. Bologna, Italy, 1976, 81-82; cons. Wheelock Marden, Hong Kong, 1974, World Bank, Washington, 1982; vis. scholar U. Cambridge, Eng., 1985. Author: Theory of Futures Trading, 1972 (with Yamey) Economia dei Mercati a Termini, 1981; editor: (with Yamey) Economics of Futures Trading, 1978; Futures Markets: Their Establishment and Performance, 1986; contbr. articles to profl. jours. Recipient Aitchison-Myer scholarship Univ. Melbourne, 1963-65; Res. Bank Australia grantee, 1970-71; Italian Govt. scholarship, 1981-82; Australian Research grantee, 1979-82; Australian Wool Corp. grantee, 1983-88. Mem. Am. Econ. Assn., Econ. Soc. Australia (convenor 1980-81). Methodist. Avocations: antiques; automobiles. Office: Monash Univ, Dept Econs, Clayton, Victoria 3168, Australia

GOSS, JEFFERY ALAN, lawyer; b. Sydney, N.S.W., Australia, July 31, 1953; s. Henry George and Marjorie Edna (Gaughan) G.; m. Christine Joan Tebb, Feb. 22, 1975; children: Mathew Alan, Adam Eric. LL.B., Sydney U., 1975. Articled clk. Dunhill, Morgan & Macready, Sydney, N.S.W., Australia, 1974-76, solicitor, 1976-77; solicitor Moore & Bevins, Sydney, N.S.W., 1977-80, assoc. ptnr., 1980-82, ptnr., 1982—, resident ptnr., Hong Kong, 1982-83; hon. chmn. Australian Interest Rate Swap Terms Legal Com., 1985-86. Legal asst. Sydney U. Legal Aid Scheme, 1975. Mem. Banking Law Assn., Law Soc. N.S.W., Taxation Inst. Australia. Anglican. Club: Am. Nat. (Sydney). Office: Moore & Bevins, 60 Martin Pl, Sydney New South Wales 2000, Australia

GOSS, JEROME ELDON, cardiologist; b. Dodge City, Kans., Nov. 30, 1935; s. Horton Maurice and Mary Alice (Mountain) G.; m. Lorraine Ann Sanchez, Apr. 20, 1986. BA, U. Kans., 1957; MD, Northwestern U., 1961. Diplomate Am. Bd. Internal Medicine, Am. Bd. Cardiology (fellow, bd. govs. 1981-84). Intern Met. Gen. Hosp., Cleve., 1961-62; resident Northwestern U. Med. Ctr., Chgo., 1962-64; fellow in cardiology U. Colo., Denver, 1964-66; asst. prof. medicine U. N.Mex., Albuquerque, 1968-70; practice medicine specializing in cardiology N.Mex. Heart Clinic, 1970—; mem. bd. alumni counsellors Northwestern U. Med. Sch., 1977—; chief dept. medicine Presbyn. Hosp., Albuquerque, 1978-80, mem. exec. com. 1980-82, bd. dirs. cardiac diagnostic services; cons., cardio-pace med. lectr., Marion Labs., Kansas City (Mo.) and Mpls.; lectr. Winthrope Labs., N.Y.C. Contbr. articles to profl. jours. Bd. dirs. Presbyn. Heart Inst., Ballet West N.Mex., N.Mex. Symphony Orch. Served to lt. comdr. USN, 1966-68. Nat. Heart Inst. research fellow, 1965-66; named one of Outstanding Young Men Am., Jaycees, 1970; recipient Alumni Service award Northwestern U. Med. Sch., 1986. Fellow ACP, Council Clin. Cardiology of Am. Heart Assn., Soc. Cardiac Angiography; mem. Albuquerque-Bernalillo County Med. Soc. (sec. 1972, treas. 1975, v.p. 1980), Alpha Omega Alpha. Republican. Methodist. Lodge: Rotary. Office: NMex Heart Clinic 1001 Coal SE Albuquerque NM 87106

GOSSAN, BRIAN WESLEY, clergyman; b. Escanaba, Mich., Feb. 18, 1954; s. Alfred Anthony and Virginia Anne (Abraham) G.; m. Janice Diane Phillips, Feb. 5, 1983; children: Brijan Kahla, Kristopher Ryan, Phillip Geymayel. AA, Bay De Noc Community Coll., 1978; BS, Andrews U., 1980; postgrad., Grand Valley State Coll. Ordained to ministry United Pentecostal Ch. Internat., 1984. Lay worker and evangelist United Pentecostal Ch., Escanaba, 1975-77; youth minister Bethel Apostolic Tabernacle, Buchanan, Mich., 1978-80; sec. Mich. United Pentecostal Ch. Internat. Conquerors, Holland, Mich., 1979-80, pres., 1979-85; pastor Holland Abundant Life Fellowship, 1980—; dir. Christian edn., youth leader sect. 6 Upper Peninsula United Pentecostal Chs., Mich., 1974-76; camp dir. jr. and sr. high sch. camps, Albion, Mich., 1980—; tchr., evangelist Fishermen's Workshop, Jackson, Miss., 1982—; bible tchr. Beirut, Lebanon, Seoul, Korea, 1973, 88. Contbg. editor Mich. Dist. News, 1980—; contbr. articles to Life, others. Bd. dirs. Cen. Ave. Group Home of the Mich. West Shore chpt. Mich. Soc. for Autistic Children. Recipient Youth Leader Honor award sect. 4 S.W. Mich. United Pentecostal Ch. chs., 1980, sect. 5, 1982, Fishermen's Workshop award Pentecostal Ch. Kingston, Jamaica, 1983, Camp Dir. Honors award Mich. dist. Pentecostal Ch., 1983—, Outstanding Service award World Evangelism Ctr. United Pentecostal Ch. Internat., 1984. Mem Nat. Fedn. Decency, Christian Action Council (promoter, anti-abortion com. 1984—), Travelers Protection Assn., The Attending Clergy Assn. (speaker 1986—), Moral Majority (pubs. com. 1984—). Home: 501 Central Ave Holland MI 49423 Office: Holland Abundant Life Fellowship 20th and Central Holland MI 49423

GOSSET, HUGUES VINCENT, electronics company executive; b. Paris, May 22, 1943; s. Albert and Anik (Dastakian) G.; m. m. Mai Vuthi, May 29, 1971; children: André, Hubert, Bernard. Lic ès Sci Economiques, U. Grenoble, 1970; Diploma, Inst. Contrôle de Gestion, Paris, 1982. Bank attache Société Générale, Paris, 1970-71; asst. to comptroller Parfums Rochas, Paris, 1972-73; fin. exec. Jaz, clocks and watches, Paris, 1974-77; mng. dir. Paris-Dallas Electronique, Paris, 1977—; pres. Voyages du Monde, Paris, 1980-87; ptnr. Cosmose data base, 1988—. Editor, sec. Union for French Democracy, Paris, 1977—. Served with French Army, 1969-70. Mem. Am. C. of C. in France. Roman Catholic. Club: Mozart (Paris). Office: Paris-Dallas Electronique, 15 Rue de Franqueville, 75116 Paris France

GOSSETT, PHILIP, musicologist; b. N.Y.C., Sept. 27, 1941; s. Harold and Pearl (Lenkowsky) G.; m. Suzanne Solomon, Aug. 4, 1963; children—David, Jeffrey. B.A. summa cum laude, Amherst Coll., 1963; student, Columbia U., 1961-62; M.F.A., Princeton U., 1965, Ph.D., 1970. Asst. prof. music and humanities U. Chgo., 1968-73, assoc. prof., 1973-77, prof., 1977-84, Robert W. Reneker disting. service prof. music, 1984—; vis. asso. prof. Columbia U., 1975; cons. in field. Gen. editor: The Works of Giuseppe Verdi, Opera Omnia di Gioachino Rossini; mem. editorial bd. Jour. Am. Musicol. Soc, 1972-78; cons. editor: Critical Inquiry, 1974—, Nineteenth-century Music, 1976—; translator Treatise on Harmony (Jean-Philippe Rameau), (with Charles Rosen) Early Romantic Opera, Anna Bolena and the Maturity of Gaetano Donizetti, 1985, also numerous critical edits.; prepared vocal ornamentation for operas in Rome, Pesaro, Chgo., Miami, St. Louis. Panelist Ill. Arts Council, 1977-80. Decorated Gold medal 1st class (Italy), 1985; Woodrow Wilson fellow, 1963-64, 66-67; Fulbright scholar Paris, 1965-66; Martha Baird Rockefeller fellow, 1967-68; Guggenheim fellow, 1971-72; NEH sr. scholar, 1982-83; Deems Taylor award of ASCAP, 1986. Mem. Am. Musicol. Soc. (council 1972-74, dir. 1974-76, v.p. 1986—, Alfred Einstein award 1969), Internat. Musicol. Soc., Am. Inst. Verdi Studies (dir.), Societa Italiana di Musicologia, Soc. for Textual Scholarship. Home: 5509 S Kenwood Ave Chicago IL 60637 Office: U Chgo Dept of Music Chicago IL 60637

GOSWAMI, MANOJ KUMAR, cardiologist, consultant; b. Bagbahara, India, Feb. 1, 1943; came to U.S., 1967; s. nalini kanta and Satadal (Majumder) G.; m. Mili Sanyal, Nov. 30, 1972. Diploma in Intermediate Sci., Surendranath Coll., Calcutta, India, 1960; MBBS, Calcutta Nat. Med. Coll., 1965. Cert. Am. Bd. Internal Medicine. Intern Norwalk (Conn.) Hosp., 1967-68; resident St. Vincent Hosp., S.I., N.Y., 1968-69; resident Misericordia Hosp., Bronx, N.Y., 1969-71, cardiology fellow, 1971-73; tchr. Bronx Med. Group, 1973-83; practice medicine specializing in cardiology Calcutta, 1983—; cons. in cardiology, Woodlands Nursing Home, Calcutta, 1984-86. Contbr. articles to profl. jours. Home: BG-48 Sector II, Salt Lake City, Calcutta 700091, India Office: Castle Corner, 3A Albert Rd, Calcutta 700017, India

GÓTH, MIKLÓS, internist, educator; b. Budapest, Hungary, Oct. 27, 1944; s. Endre Góth and Klára Erdélyi; m. Edit Rencz, June 27, 1976; children: Mátyás, Gabriella. Dr. medicine, Med. U., Budapest, 1968; Spl. exam. in internal medicine, Postgrad. Med. Sch., Budapest, 1973, Spl. exam. in endocrinology, 1982, PhD, 1986. Intern Postgrad. Med. Sch., Budapest, 1968-69, resident in internal medicine, 1969-73, demonstrator, 1973-83, 1972-83, asst. prof., 1983—. Contbr. articles to profl. jours. Mem. Hungarian Soc. Endocrinology and Metabolism. Home: Fodor St 1, 1126 Budapest Hungary Office: Postgrad Med Sch, Szabolcs St 33 PO Box 112, 1389 Budapest Hungary

GOTHONI, RENE REINHOLD, comparative religion educator; b. Helsinki, Finland, Apr. 10, 1950; s. Guido Danilo and Ulla-Britt (Carlander) G.; m. Raili Tellervo Liukku, June 2, 1973; children—Anthony, Annette, Andre. Cand. theol., U. Helsinki, 1973, Lic. theol., 1976, Th.D., 1983. Asst. researcher Acad. of Finland, Helsinki, 1974-79; jr. researcher Acad. of Finland, 1984; sr. lectr. comparative religion U. Helsinki, 1980—, acting prof., 1985—. Author: Modes of Life of Theravada Monks, 1982, Patimokkha i strukturanalytisk belysning, 1985, Paradise Winthin Reach, 1988. Editor: (with Mikael Tenzin Donden) Bodhipuun Juurella, 1984, (with Mahapanna) Buddhalaista viisautta, 1987, (with Juha Pentikäinen) Mythology and Cosmic Order, 1987. Dir., producer: (film) Buddhism in Sinhalese Culture, 1975; contbr. articles and monographs to profl. jours. Scholar World Council Chs., 1974, Acad. of Finland, 1974-79, 84, 85; sr. scientist grantee Acad. of Finland, 1988-89. Mem. Finnish Soc. Anthropology (dir. 1984—), Finnish Soc. for Study of Comparative Religion (dir. 1985—), Scandinavian Inst. Asian Studies, Donnerska Inst., The Finnish Ministry of Edn. Avocations: music; film-making. Office: U Helsinki Dept Comparative Religion, Luotsikatu 4 A 1, SF-00160 Helsinki 16, Finland

GOTIMER, HARRY ALBERT, lawyer, educator; b. N.Y.C., May 20, 1947; s. John Cornelius and Catherine Agnes (McDermott) G.; children—Susan Eileen, Kevin Patrick, Matthew Brendan. B.S., U.S. Mcht. Marine Acad., 1969; J.D., Georgetown U., 1973. Bar: N.Y. 1974, U.S. Dist. Ct. (so. dist.) N.Y. 1974, U.S. Dist. Ct. (ea. dist.) N.Y. 1974, U.S. Ct. Appeals (2d cir.) 1975, U.S. Ct. Claims 1975, U.S. Ct. Internat. Trade 1984, U.S. Supreme Ct. 1983. Atty. Gen. Counsel's Office, Maritime Adminstrn., U.S. Dept. Commerce, Washington, 1973-74; assoc. Kirlin, Campbell & Keating, N.Y.C., 1974-78, ptnr., 1978—; adj. asst. prof. law N.Y. Law Sch. Mem. sch. bd. Borough of Hopatcong, N.J., 1978-80, v.p., 1980-82; councilman Borough of Hopatcong, 1983-85; recruiting rep. U.S. Mcht. Marine Acad., 1979—. Served to comdr. USNR. Mem. ABA, Maritime Law Assn. U.S. Democrat. Roman Catholic. Clubs: West Shore Democratic (pres. 1983, exec. bd. 1984-85), Whitehall. Home: 8209 Langdale St New Hyde Park NJ 11040 Office: Kirlin Campbell & Keating 14 Wall St New York NY 10005

GOTO, GEORGE, pedodontist; b. Tokyo, Jan. 2, 1937; s. Shohei and Nobuko (Nishiguchi) G.; m. Keiko Goto; children: Shigeru, Wakako, Kanako, Osamu. DDS, Tokyo Dental Coll., 1963; PhD, Tokyo Grad. Sch. Dental Coll., 1967. Asst. prof. Tokyo Dental Coll., 1967-70; prof. dentistry, vis. asst. U. Western Ont., London, Ont., Can., 1970-72; assoc. prof. Tokyo Dental Coll., 1972-83; prof. Nagasaki U. Sch. Dentistry, Nagaski, Japan, 1983—. Author: Dentistry for Handicapped Children, 1979; translator: Dentistry for Adolescent, 1983; patentee restrainer dental device, 1977. Fellow Tokyo Dental Coll. Soc.; mem. Japanese Soc. Dentistry for Children (bd. dirs.), Internat. Assn. Dental Research. Home: 3-19-3 Himonya, Meguro-Ku, Tokyo Japan Office: Nagaski U Dept Pediatric Dentistry, 7-1 Sakamoto-machi, Nagasaki Japan

GOTO, NOBUO, architect, furniture designer; b. Hiroshima, Japan, Aug. 24, 1938; s. Fumihiko and Kazue (Sato) G.; m. Tsuneko Abe, Aug. 20, 1975; 1 child, Arata. Diploma, Tokyo Inst. Tech., 1961. Architect 1st class,

Japan. Asst. to UN expert Cambodian Ministry Pub. Works, Phnom-Peng, 1962-63; architect, planner Office of Michel Ecochard, Damascus, Syria, 1964-67, Paris, 1967-75; ptnr. Kenzo Tange & Urtec, Tokyo, 1975-84; pres. Nissho Planning, Tokyo, 1986—. Editorial bd. World-Wide Interior, 1987; patentee knock-down furniture system; furniture designs exhibited Tokyo, 1987. Recipient 1st place Furniture Design Competition Mitsukoshi Manu Co., Tokyo, 1985. Mem. Japan Interior Designers Assn.

GOTO, SHIGERU, trading company executive; b. Kyoto, Japan, May 6, 1931; came to U.S., 1981; s. Kosaburo and Ieko (Adachi) G.; m. Yukiko Sugiyama, Oct. 23, 1954; children: Shigeyuki, Yasuyuki. B.A. in Econs., Keio U., Tokyo, 1954. Gen. mgr. electronics, elec. machinery div. C. Itoh & Co., Ltd., Tokyo, 1954-69; exec. v.p. C. Itoh & Co. (Am.), Inc., N.Y.C., 1981-82, pres., 1983-86, former chief exec. officer; now mng. dir. C. Itoh & Co., Ltd., Tokyo. Clubs: Nippon; Board Room; Princeton (N.Y.C.). Home: 425 E 58th St New York NY 10022 Office: C Itoh & Co Ltd, 5-1 Kita Aoyama, 2-chome, Minato-ku, Tokyo Japan *

GOTODA, MASAHARU, Japanese politician; b. Aug. 9, 1914. Ed., Tokyo U. With Ministry of Home Affairs, Japan, from 1939, chief sec. Home Affairs Ministry, from 1959, dir. Local Tax Bur., 1959-62, sec.-gen. Nat. Police Agy., 1962-63, dir. Security Bur., 1963-65, dir.-gen., 1969-72, dep. chief cabinet sec., 1972-73, dir.-gen. Nat. Pub. Safety Commn., 1979-80, Hokkaido Devel. Agy., 1979-80, minister of home affairs, 1979-80, chief cabinet sec., 1982-83, 1986—, dir.-gen. Adminstrv. Mgmt. Agy., 1983-84. Address: care House of Representatives, Tokyo Japan *

GOTOH, NOBORU, construction executive; b. Aug. 21, 1916; m. Yoko Gotoh. Grad., Tokyo U., 1940. Pres. Tokyo Corp.; chmn. Tokyo Constrn. Co., Ltd.; bd. dirs. Odakyu Electric Railway Co., Ltd., Japan Airlines. Home: 8-27 Kaminoge, 3-chome Setagaya-ku, Tokyo 158, Japan *

GOTT, WESLEY ATLAS, art educator; b. Buffalo, Mar. 6, 1942; s. Raymond and Rowena (Pettitt) G.; m. Alice Blalock, May 26, 1972; children—Andrew, Deidre. BS, S.W. Mo. State U., 1965; M of Ch. Music, Southwestern Theol. Sem., 1969; MFA, George Washington U., 1975; postgrad. Nova U. Tchr. ceramic classes Springfield Art Mus., Mo., 1964-66; minister of music Terrace Acres Bapt. Ch., Ft. Worth, Tex., 1966-70; minister music and youth First Bapt. Ch. Wheaton, Md., 1970-75; asst. prof. art S.W. Bapt. U., Bolivar, Mo., 1975-79, assoc. prof., chmn. dept. art, 1979—; judge art contests, 1978-84. Artist sculpture with lights, 1981-84. Mem. Coll. Art Assn. Am., Mid-Am. Coll. Art Assn., Smithsonian Assocs., Nat. Trust for Historic Preservation, Community Concert Assn., Alpha Gamma Theta, Phi Mu Alpha. Baptist. Avocations: hunting; fishing; boating; tennis; golf. Home: 127 W Maupin Bolivar MO 65613 Office: Southwest Bapt Univ 623 S Pike Bolivar MO 65613

GOTTA, ALEXANDER WALTER, anesthesiologist, educator; b. Bklyn., Apr. 10, 1935; s. A. Walter and Helen C. (Bruskewic) G.; m. Colleen A. Sullivan, July 17, 1965; 1 child, Nancy C. B.S., St. John's U., 1956; M.D., NYU, 1960. Diplomate Am. Bd. Anesthesiology, Am. Bd. Med. Examiners. Intern, U. Chgo., 1960-61; resident Boston City Hosp., 1961-62, N.Y. Hosp.-Cornell U., N.Y.C., 1962-64; instr. anesthesiology Cornell U., 1964-66, asst. prof., 1978-79; dir. anesthesia St. Mary's Hosp., Bklyn., 1968-78; asst. prof. SUNY-Bklyn., 1968-78, assoc. prof., 1978-85, prof., 1985—; dir. anesthesia L.I. Coll. Hosp., Bklyn., 1983—; speaker in field. Contbr. articles to profl. jours. Served to capt. U.S. Army, 1966-68, Vietnam. Fellow Am. Coll. Angiology, N.Y. Acad. Medicine, Am. Coll. Anesthesiologists; mem. N.Y. Soc. Anesthesiologists (bd. dirs. 1983—), N.Y. Soc. Critical Care Medicine (pres. 1985). Republican. Roman Catholic. Club: Brooklyn. Avocation: History. Home: 29 Ascot Ridge Great Neck NY 11021 Office: LI Coll Hosp Dept Anesthesia 340 Henry St Brooklyn NY 11201

GÖTTE, KLAUS H. W., corporate executive; b. Diepholz, Germany, Apr. 22, 1932; s. Heinrich and Anneliese (Engel) G.; m. Michaela Grazia Elsaesser, 1958; 3 children. Dr. jur., U. Goettingen, 1954. Mgmt. Bankhaus C.G. Trinkaus, Dusseldorf, 1955-68, Fried. Krupp Gmbh, Essen, 1968-72; bd. mgmt. Allianz Versicherungs AG, Munchen, 1972-80; mng. ptnr. Friedr. Flick Industrieverwaltung, Dusseldorf, 1980-82; pres., chief exec. officer MAN Aktiengesellschaft (formerly Gutehoffnungshutte Aktienverein), Oberhausen, 1983—. Office: MAN Aktiensgesellschaft, Ungererstrasse 69, 8000 Munich Federal Republic of Germany Other: Bayerische Hypotheken und Wechel Bank AG, Theatinerstr 11, Pf 200527, D-8000 Munich 2 Federal Republic of Germany

GOTTFRIED, EUGENE LESLIE, physician, educator; b. Passaic, N.J., Feb. 26, 1929; s. David Robert and Rose (Chill) G.; m. Phyllis Doris Swain, Aug. 16, 1957. AB, Columbia Coll., 1950, MD, 1954. Cert. Nat. Bd. Med. Examiners, Am. Bd. Internal Medicine. Intern Presbyn. Hosp., N.Y.C., 1954-55, asst. resident in medicine, 1957-58; resident Bronx (N.Y.) Mcpl. Hosp. Ctr., 1958-59, fellow in medicine, 1959-60; asst. instr. medicine Albert Einstein Coll. Medicine Yeshiva U., N.Y.C., 1959-60, instr., 1960-61, assoc., 1961-65, asst. prof., 1965-69; assoc. prof. medicine Cornell U. Med. Coll., N.Y.C., 1969-81, assoc. prof. pathology, 1975-81; clin. prof. dept. lab. medicine U. Calif., San Francisco, 1981—, vice chmn. dept. lab. medicine, 1981—; hosp. appointments include asst. vis. physician Bronx Mcpl. Hosp. Ctr., 1960-66, assoc. attending physician, 1966-69; assoc. attending physician N.Y. Hosp., N.Y.C., 1969-81, assoc. attending pathologist, 1975-81, dir. lab. clin. hematology, 1969-81; chief lab. medicine San Francisco Gen. Hosp. Med. Ctr., 1981—, dir. clin. labs., 1981—. Assoc. editor Jour. Lipid Research, 1971-72, 75-77; mem. editorial bd. Jour. Lipid Research, 1972-77. Served to lt. comdr. USNR, 1955-57. Recipient Career Scientist award Health Research Council City of N.Y., 1964-72. Fellow Am. Soc. Hematology (com. clin. lab. standards 1984-86), Internat. Soc. hematology, ACP, Acad. Clin. Lab. Physicians and Scientists; mem. AAAS, Phi Beta Kappa, Alpha Omega Alpha. Office: San Francisco Gen Hosp Clin Labs 1001 Potrero Ave San Francisco CA 94110

GOTTFRIED, MAX, medical equipment manufacturing executive; b. Toledo, Aug. 27, 1921; s. Morris and Gussie (Yerzy) G.; student Toledo U., 1939-40, 46-48; children—Brent Morris, Mark Ellis. Sales mgr. Columbus Hosp. Supply Co., Toledo, 1951-60; v.p. Jobst Inst., Toledo, 1960-78; pres. Gottfried Med., Inc., 1981—. Served with AUS, 1940-45. Mem. Aerospace Med. Assn., Assn. for Advancement Med. Instrumentation, Health Care Exhibitors Assn. (dir.). Patentee med. products. Home: 10145 Avienda Del Rio Delray Beach FL 33446 Office: 3350 W Laskey Red Unit 10 Toledo OH 43623

GOTTFRIED, SAMUEL, physicist, investment banker; b. Lampertheim, Germany, July 16, 1946; s. Isadore and Bronia (Engelmaier) G.; came to U.S., 1949; BS, Cornell U., 1967, MEE, 1968; MEE, NYU, 1972; PhD, Poly. Inst. N.Y., 1977; m. Anna Kreiner, Nov. 17, 1973. Mem. tech. staff Bell Telephone Labs., Holmdel, N.J., 1967-79; trader in stocks and options, 1979—; gen. ptnr., GW Ptnrs., Prin. Wellmont Securities, L.P., 1986—; mem. Am. Stock Exchange, 1979—; lectr. profl. seminars on fiber optics. Mem. Cornell U. Secondary Schs. Com., 1968—. Mem. IEEE, Optical Soc. Am., Am. Inst. Physics, Sigma Xi, Tau Beta Pi, Phi Eta Sigma, Eta Kappa Nu, Tau Epsilon Phi. Lodge: B'nai B'rith. Office: Wellmont Sec LP 2 Rector St Suite 1509 New York NY 10006

GOTTHILF, DANIEL LAWRENCE, accountant; b. N.Y.C., Jan. 7, 1924; s. Morris Harris and Rose (Gold) G.; B.B.A., U. Mich., 1948; postgrad. Mgmt. Inst., N.Y.U., 1968. CPA, N.Y.; 1 dau., Marcy. Pvt. practice pub. acctg., N.Y.C., 1948-57; asst. to pres. The Mautner Co., N.Y.C., 1957-62; treas., controller Tech. Tape Corp., Yonkers, N.Y., 1962-65; sr. v.p. fin. Savin Corp., Valhalla, N.Y., 1965-83, also dir.; pres. Columbia Bus. Systems, Inc., 1983-87; pvt. practice acctg., 1987—; mem. Westchester County adv. bd. Chem. Bank; lectr. Am. Mgmt. Assn. Served with USAF, 1942-45. Mem. Am. Inst. C.P.A.s, N.Y. State Soc. C.P.A.s, Nat. Assn. Accts., Fin. Execs. Inst., Beta Gamma Sigma, Phi Eta Sigma. Republican. Clubs: Princeton, Michigan, Lotos. Author: Treasurers and Controllers Desk Book, 1977; Financial Analysis for Decision Making, 1979.

GOTTLIEB, JULIUS JUDAH, podiatrist; b. Jersey City, N.J., May 27, 1919; s. Joseph Uziel and Gussie (Farber) G.; m. Charlotte Papernik, Oct. 18, 1942; children: Sheldon, Cynthia, Lorinda, David, Jonathan. Student NYU, 1938-39, Ill. Coll. Podiatric Medicine, 1940-42; DPM, Ohio Coll. Podiatric Medicine, 1943. Diplomate Am. Inst. Foot Medicine. Pvt. practice podiatric medicine, Washington, 1943—; cons. Army Footwear Clinic. Co-inventor fiberglass foot for prosthetics. Chmn. troop com. troop Nat. Capital area council Boy Scouts Am., 1969-73; pres. Franklin Knolls Citizens Assn., 1963. Recipient Shofar award, Boy Scouts Am.; named Man of the Yr. Columbia Heights Bus. Men's Assn., 1963-64. Fellow Acad. Ambulatory Foot Surgeons (sci. chmn. region 8 1987—), Nat. Coll. Foot Surgeons (founding); mem. Am. Podiatric Med. Assn., Am. Pub. Health Assn., Am. Coll. Podopediatrics, Am. Podiatric Circulatory Soc., Am. Bd. Foot Surgeons (founding diplomate), D.C. Podiatric Med. Soc. (past pres.), Am. Assn. Foot Specialists (past pres., Foot Specialist of the Yr. 1973), Am. Assn. Individual Investors, Internat. Platform Assn., Am. Physicians Fellowship, Inc. for Medicine in Israel, Chevy Chase Citizens Assn. Republican. Jewish. Lodge: B'nai B'rith. Home: 15812 Ancient Oak Dr Darnestown MD 20878 Office: 3900 McKinley St NW Washington DC 20015

GOTTLIEB, LESTER M., real estate and securities company executive; b. N.Y.C., May 3, 1932; s. Samuel and Eva (Schoenfeld) G.; B.A., CCNY, 1954; postgrad. NYU; m. Sarah Dean Tompkins, Dec. 4, 1967; children—Cynthia Anne, Curtis Tompkins; children by previous marriage—Mark Albert, Alyssa Beth, Adine Julia. With IBM, 1956-69, mgr. bus. planning for systems devel. div., 1967-69; pres. CAMAC Equities, Ltd. and CAMAC Securities, Ltd., Riverside, Conn., 1981—; vice chmn. Data Dimensions, Inc., Los Angeles, 1984—; adj. asst. prof. econs. U. Bridgeport; nat. lectr. Assn. Computing Machinery. Pres., Woodlands-Worthington Taxpayers Assn., 1962-68; bd. dirs. North Greenwich Assn., 1973-74, Center for Internat. Mgmt. Studies, Nat. Bd. YMCA's 1972—, Greater N.Y. YMCA. Served with AUS, 1954-56. Fellow Am. Sociol. Soc.; mem. Acad. Polit. Sci., Am. Arbitration Assn. (comml. arbitrator 1981—), CCNY Alumni Assn. (bd. dirs. 1983—, pres. alumni varsity assn. 1987-88). Republican. Club: Landmark (charter mem.). Lodge: Masons. Mem. editorial bd. Jour. Computer Ops., 1965-69, Mgmt. Tech. mag., 1983-84. Home: 21 Calhoun Dr Greenwich CT 06831 Office: 1212 E Putnam Ave Riverside CT 06878

GOTTLIEB, MICHAEL STEVEN, restaurateur, columnist; b. Regensburg, Fed. Republic Germany, June 3, 1947; arrived in Eng., 1970; s. Aaron and Regina (Rudner) G.; m. Ulla Maria Malmberg; children: Oliver, Zachary. BA, Hofstra U., 1969; postgrad., London Bus. Sch., 1970-71. Sales mgr. Vistajet Holidays, London, 1971-72, Peltour Holidays, London, 1972-74; pres. Interscope Travel, London and Tokyo, 1974-76; comml. mgr. Thomson Vacations, London, 1976-78; European mktg. mgr. Hertz Rent-A-Car System, London, 1978-80; ops. dir. My Kinda Town, Ltd., London, 1980-84; pres. The Mood's A Balloon Restaurants, Ltd., London, 1984—. Columnist (monthly) Caterer and Motel Keeper mag., 1986—. Mem. Restaurant Assn. Great Britain. Office: The Mood's A Balloon Ltd, 1 Dover St, London W1X3PJ, England

GOTTSCHALK, ALFRED, college president; b. Oberwesel, Fed. Republic Germany, Mar. 7, 1930; came to U.S., 1939, naturalized, 1945; s. Max and Erna (Trum-Gerson) G.; m. Deanna Zeff Frank, 1978; children by previous marriage: Marc Hillel, Rachel Lisa. A.B., Bklyn. Coll., 1952; B.H.Lit., Hebrew Union Coll.-Jewish Inst. Religion, 1957, M.A. with honors, 1957; Ph.D., U. So. Calif., 1965, LL.D., 1976, S.T.D. (hon.), 1968; D.H.L. (hon.), U. Judaism, 1971; D.Litt. (hon.), Dropsie U., 1974; LLD (hon.), U. Cin., 1976; D.Religious Edn. (hon.), Loyola-Marymount U., 1977; LL.D. (hon.), Xavier U., 1981; Litt.D. (hon.), St. Thomas Inst., 1982; D.D. (hon.), NYU, 1985; DHL (hon.), Jewish Theol. Sem., 1986; hon. fellow, Hebrew U. Jerusalem. Rabbi 1957; dean Hebrew Union Coll.-Jewish Inst. Religion, Los Angeles, 1959-71, prof. Bible and Jewish intellectual history, 1965—, pres., 1971—. Author: Your Future as a Rabbi-A Calling that Counts, 1967, The Future of Human Community, 1967, The Man Must be the Message, 1968, Jewish Ecumenism and Jewish Survival, 1968, Ahad Ha-Am, Maimonides and Spinoza, 1969, Ahad Ha-Am as Bible Critic, 1971, A Jubilee of the Spirit, 1972, Israel and the Diaspora: A New Look, 1974, Limits of Ecumenicity, 1979, Israel and Reform Judaism: A Zionist Perspective, 1979, Ahad Ha-Am and Leopold Zunz: Two Perspectives on the Wissenschaft Des Judentums, 1980, Hebrew Union College and Its Impact on World Progressive Judaism, 1980, Diaspora Zionism: Achievements and Problems, 1980, What Ecumenism Means to a Jew, 1981, A Laudatio for Gershom G. Scholem, 1981, Introduction. Religion in a Post-Holocaust World, 1982, Tribute to Judaism, 1982, Some Jewish Perspectives on Ecumenism, 1982, Problematics in the Future of American Jewish Community, 1982, Introduction to The American Synagogue in the Nineteenth Century, 1982, A Strategy for Non-Orthodox Judaism in Israel, Our Problems and Our Future: Jews and America, 1983, The Making of a Contemporary Reform Rabbi, 1984, Is Yom Kippur Obsolete, 1985, Nostra Aetate, 1985, Ahad Ha-Am: Confronting the Plight of Judaism, 1987, To Learn and To Teach, Your Future as a Rabbi, 1988; translator. Heard in the Bible, 1967, From the Kingdom of Night to the Kingdom of God: Jewish Christian Relations and the Search for Religious Authenticity after the Holocaust, 1983; contbr. to: Studies in Jewish Bibliography, History, and Literature, 1971, The Yom Kippur War: Israel and the Jewish People, 1974, The Image of Man in Genesis and the Ancient Near East, 1976, The Public Function of the Jewish Scholar, 1978, The Reform Movement and Israel: A New Perspective, 1978, also numerous articles to profl. pubs. Mem. Pres.'s Com. on Equal Employment Opportunity, 1964-66, Gov.'s Poverty Support Corps Program, 1964-66, Pres.'s Commn. on Holocaust, 1979, U.S. Holocaust Meml. Council, 1980—, co-chmn. exec. com. U.S. Holocaust Meml. Council, 1980—, chmn. edn. com.; chmn. N.Am. adv. com. Internat. Center Univ. Teaching of Jewish Civilization, 1982; trustee Cin. United Appeal, Am. Sch. Oriental Research, Albright Inst. Archaeol. Research; mem. Pres.'s Council Near Eastern Studies N.Y.U. State Dept. research grantee, 1963; Smithsonian Instn. research grantee, 1967; Guggenheim fellow, 1967, 69; recipient award for contbns. to edn. Los Angeles City Council, 1971, Tower of David award for Cultural Contbn. to Israel and Am., 1972, Gold medallion award Jewish Nat. Fund, 1972, Myrtle Wreath award Hadassah, 1977, Brandeis award, 1977, Nat. Brotherhood award NCCJ, 1979; Alfred Gottschalk Chair in Jewish Communal Service Hebrew Union Coll., 1979; Gottschalk Dept. Judaica named in his honor; Kfar Silver Israel, 1979; named Israel Bonds Man of Yr., 1982. Mem. Union Am. Hebrew Congregations and Central Conf. Am-Rabbis (exec. com.), AAUP, NEA, Soc. Study Religion, Am. Acad. Religion, Soc-Bibl. Lit and Exegesis, Internat. Conf. Jewish Communal Service, Israel Exploration Soc., So. Calif. Assn. Liberal Rabbis (past pres.), So. Calif. Jewish Hist. Soc. (hon. pres.), World Union Jewish Studies, Synagogue Council Am. (inst. research and planning), Am. Jewish Com. (exec. com., Human Relations award 1971), World Union Progressive Judaism (v.p.), Phi Beta Kappa. Home: 17 Belsaw Pl Cincinnati OH 45220

GOTTSCHALK, CHARLES MAX, United Nations administrator; b. Bochum, Germany, Feb. 2, 1928; emigrated to U.S., 1941, naturalized, 1949; s. Josef and Elsbeth (Ermeler) G.; m. Marianne Ida Besser, Dec. 24, 1948; children: Diane Linda, Leslie Anne. B.E.S. in Physics, Cleve. State U., 1950; M.A., Pa. State U., 1951; M.S. in L.S, Catholic U., 1966. Research analyst Library of Congress, 1951-54, phys. sci. adminstr., head reference sect., sci. and tech. div., 1956-62, chief stack and reader div., 1962, head systems identification and analysis sect., 1962-63; instrumentation physicist Nat. Bur. Standards, 1954-56; information systems specialist AEC, 1963-66, dir. libraries, 1966-69; sr. officer Internat. Atomic Energy Agy., Vienna, Austria, 1969-73, Energy Research and Devel. Adminstrn., Washington, 1973-77, Dept. Energy, 1977-79; sr. ofcl. UNESCO, Paris, 1979—; lectr. Dept. Agr. Grad. Sch., 1964-66; cons. Arctic Inst. N.Am., 1954-59; research asst. Ohio State U., 1958-59; exec. sec. operating com. Fed. Council Sci. and Tech. Com. on Sci. and Tech. Information, 1965, exec. sec. panel edn. and tng., 1965-66, mem. panel information scis. and tech., 1966-68, mem. nuclear cross sect. adv. group, 1965-69; mem. com. on terminology World Energy Conf., 1980—. Author articles, monographs. Served with AUS, 1946-47; Served with USMCR, 1947-49. NSF grantee, 1961-62. Mem. Am. Nuclear Soc., Am. Phys. Soc., AAAS, Am. Soc. Metals, Mensa, Beta Phi Mu. Office: UNESCO SC/TER, F-75700 Paris France

GOTTSCHALK, FRANK KLAUS, real estate company executive; b. Berlin, Jan. 25, 1932; came to U.S. 1947, naturalized 1953; s. Richard and Grete Johanna (Singer) G.; m. Ellen Ruth Meinhardt, June 16, 1957. Student N.Y. Inst. Banking & Fin., N.Y.C., 1952-53, NYU, 1955-56. Trainee, investment securities Newborg & Co. mem. N.Y. Stock Exchange, N.Y.C., 1951-52; fin. analyst Bendix Luitweiler & Co. Investment Bankers, N.Y.C., 1952-53; assoc. broker, v.p., dir. Peter F. Pasbjerg & Co., Inc., mortgage banker Newark, N.J., 1955-62; v.p., dir. Baldwin Bros., Inc. Real Estate Investors, Erie, Pa., 1962—; v.p., treas., dir. Baldwin-Gottschalk, Inc. Real Estate and Mortgage Financing, N.Y.C., Erie, Charleston, W.Va., 1962—; v.p., treas., dir. Baldwin Gottschalk Properties, Erie, 1967—, Balgot Realty Corp., Erie, 1963—, Balgot Bldg. Corp., Erie, 1967—; pres., dir. Kanawha Realty & Devel. Corp., Charleston, W.Va., 1959—, Assoc. Properties Holdings, Charleston, 1962—; trustee Assoc. Properties Holding Retirement Trust, Charleston, 1982—; mng. ptnr. Kanawha-Monarch Holdings, Erie, 1980—. Trustee, Erie Philharm., 1971—; corporator Gannon U., 1980—. Served with U.S. Army, 1953-55, ETO. Clubs: Erie, Aviation Country of Erie. Office: Baldwin Gottschalk Inc 5 W 10th St Erie PA 16501

GOTTSCHALK, KLAUS-DIETER, linguistics educator; b. Krefeld, Rhineland, Germany, July 22, 1934; s. Julius Karl and Ingeborg (Croon) G.; m. Anneliese Uhlmann; children—Frank, Annette. Tchrs. diploma, Marburg U., 1962, Dr.Phil., 1962. Acad. liaison officer British Council, Germany, 1964-69; lectr. English dept. U. Bochum, W.Ger., 1969-71; sr. lectr. English dept. U. Tubingen, W.Ger., 1971—, akademischer oberrat, 1973—, dep. on acad. senate, 1980-82, 84-86; examiner English, linguistics State Exam. Bd. for Secondary Sch. Tchrs., Baden-Wurttemberg, 1972—; vis. prof. Calif. State U., Los Angeles, 1986-87. Author: Shaw's Saint Joan, 1972; Idiomatik im Englisch unterricht, 1973, How to Describe Idiomatic English Within the Framework of Universal Grammar, 1982, others. Translator: The Queen's Lectures, 1968, 70, Higher and Secondary Educational Federal Planning Reports, 1970, 73. With adult edn. activities Inter Nationes, Bonn, Fed. Republic of Germany, 1963—; govt. visitors' escort, 1966-69; mem. supervisory bd. Mutual Benefit Volksbank, Tubingen, 1984—; screening officer Amity Inst., De la Mar, Calif., 1972—. Fulbright Commn. scholar Amherst Coll., Mass., 1957-58, Volkswagen Found. acad. grantee Edinburgh U., 1974-75. Avocations: higher edn. planning, teaching English for spl. purposes. Office: English Dept Tuebingen U, Wilhelmstr 50, 74 Tuebingen Federal Republic of Germany

GOTTSTEIN, BARNARD JACOB, retail and wholesale food company executive, real estate executive; b. Des Moines, Dec. 30, 1925; s. Jacob B. and Anna (Jacobs) G.; children—Sandra, James, Ruth Anne, David, Robert; m. Rachel Landau, July, 1986. B.A. in Econs. and Bus., U. Wash., 1949. Pres. J.B. Gottstein, Anchorage, 1953—; chmn. bd. Carr Gottstein Co., Anchorage, 1974—; dir. United Bank Alaska, Anchorage, 1975-86. Commr. Alaska State Human Rights Commn, 1963-68; del. Democratic Nat. Conv., 1964, 68, 76; committeeman Dem. Nat. Com., 1976-80; v.p. State Bd. Edn., Alaska, 1983-87, pres., 1987—. Served with USAF, 1944-45. Jewish. Office: JB Gottstein & Co 6411 A St Anchorage AK 99502

GÖTZ, WIENOLD, linguist, educator; b. Grosspostwitz, Germany, July 15, 1938; s. J.K. and Mary A. (Hansen) W. Student, U. Munich, 1957-58, U. Gottingen, 1958, U. Berlin, 1958-59, U. Münster, 1959-60; PhD, U. Münster, 1964. Habilitation in English philology U. Münster, Fed. Republic Germany, 1969, sci asst., 1966-70; dozent U. Münster, 1970; instr. U. Ill., Urbana, 1964-65, asst. profl., 1965-66; prof. linguistics U. Konstanz, Fed. Republic Germany, 1970—. Author: Genus und Semantik, 1967, Formulierungstheorie, Poetik, Strukturelle Literaturgeschichte, 1971, Semiotik der Literatur, 1972, Die Erlernbarkeit der Sprachen, 1973, Über das Arbeiten an einer Theorie des Zweisprachenerwerbs, 1974; co-author: Lehren und Lernen im Fremdsprachen-unterricht, 1975, Lernmaterial in institutionalisierten Lehr-Lern-Prozessen--Am Beispiel des Englischanfangsunterrichts, 1985. Stiftung Volkswagenwerk acad. stipend, Japan, 1980-81, 85-86. Mem. Deutsche Gesellschaft für Asienkunde, Linguistic Soc. Am., MLA, Gesellschaft fü Angewandte Linguistik, Deutscher Anglistentag, Beiratsmitglied Japonicum Bochum. Home: Gaissbergstrasse 50, CH-8280 Kreuzlingen Switzerland Office: U Constance, Constance Federal Republic of Germany

GOTZE, HEINZ, publisher; b. Dresden, Aug. 8, 1912; student Univs. Leipzig, Munich, Naples; Dr. med. honoris causa, U. Heidelberg, 1972; Dr.med. honoris causa, U. Erlangen, 1972. Ptnr., co-proprietor Springer-Verlag, Berlin, Heidelberg, N.Y.C., London, Paris, Tokyo, Hong Kong, 1957—, J.F. Bergmann Verlagsbuchhandlung, Munich, 1957—, Lange & Springer, Sci. Bookshop, Berlin, 1957—; pres. Springer Verlag N.Y., Inc., 1964—; dir. Universitatsdruckerei H. Sturtz A.G., Wurzburg, 1965—. Mem. German Archaeol. Inst. (corr.). Home: Ludolf-Krehl-Strasse 41, Heidelberg D-69, Federal Republic of Germany Office: Springer-Verlag, Heidelberg, Tiergartenstrasse 17 D-69, Federal Republic of Germany

GOTZOYANNIS, STAVROS ELEUTHERIOS, cardiologist; b. Piraeus, Greece, June 18, 1933; s. Eleutherios G. and Irene Stavros (Nikitaki) G.; M.D. (Greek Govt. scholar), U. Salonica, 1957; Doctorate, U. Athens, 1968; m. Ourania Cavoulacou, Nov. 20, 1969. Intern, 401 Army Gen. Hosp., Athens, 1957-58; resident in internal medicine Army Pansion Share Hosp., Athens, 1960-63; fellow in cardiology Hellenic Red Cross Hosp., Athens, 1964-65; commd. 2d lt. M.C., Greek Army, 1957, advanced through grades to brig. gen., 1984; dir. internal medicine 403 Army Gen. Hosp., Kozani, 1963-64; research asso., div. cardiology Phila. Gen. Hosp., 1970-71; asst. attending physician Georgetown U. Hosp., Washington, 1971-72; asso. CCU, 401 Army Gen. Hosp., Athens, 1972-75, dir. cardiac catheterization lab., 1975-76; dir. cardiology dept. 409 Army Gen. Hosp., Patras, 1976-78; cardiology cons. to chief Hellenic Nat. Def. Gen. Staff, 1978-80; mem. staff cardiology dept. Army Pansion Share Hosp., Athens, 1980-81; dir. div. cardiology dept. 401st Army Gen. Hosp., Athens, 1981-83; cons. cardiology Hellenic Red Cross Hosp., Athens, 1965-69; instr. Army Nursing Sch., Athens, 1976. Fellow Fedn. Internat. Sport Medicine, Am. Coll. Cardiology; mem. Athens Med. Assn., Hellenic Cardiologic Soc., Greek Assn. Sports. Greek Orthodox. Contbr. papers, abstracts to med. books, jours. Home: 3 Evrou St, GR 115 28 Athens Greece

GOUBEAU, JACQUES ETIENNE, oil company executive; b. Boulogne, France, May 25, 1927; s. Fernand and Jane (Groslard) G.; m. Genevieve Laroudie, Feb. 15, 1949; children: Marie, Catherine. Diplome, Inst. d'Etudes Politiques, Paris, 1946. Ingénieur, Kodak Pathe, Vincennes, France, 1949-52, Thomson Houston, Gennevilliers, France, 1952-55; secretaire gen. Total Afrique, Paris, 1955-72, Total CFD, Levallois, 1972-80; managing dir. Total Afrique, Paris, 1980—; chmn. Total Subsidiaires, West Africa, Indian Ocean, Carribean, Pacific Islands, 1980—. Mcpl. conseiller, Poce sur Cisse, France. Mem. Club de Dakar. Roman Catholic. Office: Total Afrique, 26 Rue de la Pepiniere, 75 008 Paris France

GOUDE, CHARLES REUBEN, lawyer, public defender; b. Hemingway, S.C., Apr. 17, 1950; s. Bethel Oliver and Miriam Helena (Joye) G. BA in History magna cum laude, U. S.C., 1975, JD, 1979. Bar: S.C. 1979, U.S. Ct. Mil. Appeals 1980, U.S. Dist. Ct. S.C. 1984. Sole practice Georgetown, S.C., 1984—; dep. pub. defender Georgetown County, 1984-85, pub. defender, 1985—; adj. faculty Horry Georgetown Tech. Coll., 1986—. Served to sgt. USMC, 1968-72; served to capt. JAG USAF, 1980-84. Mem. Am. Trial Lawyers Assn., S.C. Bar Assn., Georgetown County Bar Assn., Phi Beta Kappa. Home: Route 3 Box 269A Hemingway SC 29554 Office: PO Box 706 Georgetown SC 29442

GOUGÉ, SUSAN CORNELIA JONES, microbiologist; b. Chgo., Apr. 18, 1924; d. Harry LeRoy and Gladys (Moon) Jones; student Am. U., Washington, 1942-43, La. Coll., 1944-45; BS, George Washington U., 1948; postgrad. Georgetown U., 1956-58, 66-69, Vt. Coll. of Norwich U., M.A. in Pub. Health, 1984; m. John Oscar Gougé, Aug. 7, 1943; children: John Ronald, Richard Michael (dec.), Claudia Renée Gougé Carr. Med. technician Children's Hosp. Research Lab., Washington, 1948-49; bacteriologist George Washington U. Research Lab., D.C. Gen. Hosp., 1950-53; med. microbiologist Walter Reed Army Inst. Research, Washington, 1953-61; research asst. Dental Research, Walter Reed Army Med. Ctr., 1961-62; microbiologist antibiotics div. FDA, 1962-63; supr. quality control John D. Copanos Co., Pharms., Balt., 1963-64; research tng. asst. infectious diseases and tropical medicine Howard U. Med. Sch., 1964-65; research assoc. Georgetown U. Lab. Infectious Diseases, D.C. Gen. Hosp., 1966-69; mycologist Georgetown U. Hosp. Lab., 1969-70; microbiologist Research Found. of Washington Hosp. Ctr., 1971-73; dir. quality control Bio-Medium Corp., Silver Spring, Md., 1973-76; microbiologist Alcolac, Inc., Balt., 1976-77; microbiologist div. labs., dept. human resources Community Health and Hosps. Adminstrn., Washington, 1978-79; microbiologist div. ophthalmic devices, Office Device Evaluation Ctr. for Devices and Radiol. Health, FDA, Silver Spring, Md., 1979—. Sec. to exec. bd. Bethesda Project Awareness, 1970-71; vol. lead poisoning detection testing project, D.C. Office Vols. Internat. Tech. Assistance, 1970-71; vol. Zacchaeus Free Clinic, Washington, 1979-84. Mem. Nat. Capital Harp Ensemble, 1941-65; mem. parish social concerns com. Roman Cath. Ch. Recipient medal community service; registered microbiologist Nat. Registry Microbiologists; specialist microbiologist Am. Acad. Microbiology. Mem. AAAS, Am. Soc. for Microbiology, Am. Inst. Biol. Scis., Am. Chem. Soc., Internat. Union Pure and Applied Chemistry, N.Y. Acad. Scis., Am. Pub. Heath Assn., Albertus Magnus Guild, Capital Bus. and Profl. Women's Club (rec. sec. 1973-74, 1st v.p. 1974-75, pres. 1975-76), Winchester Bus. and Profl. Women, World Affairs Council of Washington D.C., Pi Kappa Delta. Roman Catholic. Club: Toastmasters (sec. 1979-80). Office: FDA Div Ophthalmic Devices Office Device Evaluation 8757 Georgia Ave Silver Spring MD 20910

GOUGH, HARRISON GOULD, psychologist, educator; b. Buffalo, Minn., Feb. 25, 1921; s. Harry B. and Aelfreda (Gould) G.; m. Kathryn H. Whittier, Jan. 23, 1943; 1 dau., Jane Kathryn Gough Rhodes. A.B. summa cum laude, U. Minn., 1942, A.M. (Social Sci. Research Council fellow 1946-47), 1947, Ph.D., 1949. Asst. prof. psychology U. Minn., 1948-49; asst. prof. U. Calif.-Berkeley, 1949-54, assoc. prof., 1954-60, prof., 1960—, assoc. dir. Inst. Personality Assessment and Research, 1964-67, dir., 1973-83, chmn. dept. psychology, 1967-72; cons. VA, 1951—; dir. cons. Psychologists Press, Inc., 1956—; mem. research adv. com. Calif. Dept. Corrections, 1958-64, Calif. Dept. Mental Hygiene, 1964-69, Gov.'s Calif. Adv. Com. Mental Health, 1968-74, citizens adv. council Calif. Dept. Mental Hygiene, 1968-71; clin. projects research review com. NIMH, 1968-72. Served to 1st lt. AUS, 1942-46. Recipient U. Calif. the Berkeley citation, 1986, Bruno Klopfer Disting. Contbn. award, Soc. Personality Assessment, 1987; Fulbright research scholar, Italy, 1958-59, 65-66; Guggenheim fellow, 1965-66. Mem. Am., Western psychol. assns., Soc. Personality Assessment, Internat. Assn. Cross-Cultural Psychology, Académie National de Psychologie, Soc. Mayflower Desc., Phi Beta Kappa, Sigma Xi. Club: Commonwealth (San Francisco). Author: Adjective Check List, California Psychological Inventory, other psychol. tests; chmn. bd. editors U. Calif. Publs. in Psychology, 1956-58; cons. editor Jour. Cons. and Clin. Psychology, 1956-74, 77-84, Jour. Abnormal Psychology, 1964-74, Jour. Personality and Social Psychology, 1981-84, Med. Tchr., 1978-84, Cahiers d'Anthropologie, 1978-86, Population and Environment: Behavioral and Social Issues, 1977-80; Current Psychol. Research and Revs., 1985—, Pakistan Jour. Psychol. Research, 1985—, Jour. Personality Assessment, 1986—; assoc. editor Jour. Cross-Cultural Psychology, 1969-81. Home: PO Box 909 Pebble Beach CA 93953 Office: U Calif Dept Psychology Berkeley CA 94720

GOUGHER, RONALD LEE, educator; b. Allentown, Pa., July 27, 1939; s. Samuel Franklin and Beatrice Dorothy (Shanaberger) G.; B.A., Muhlenberg Coll., 1961; M.A., Lehigh U., 1964; postgrad. Stanford U., 1963, Harvard U., 1964, U. Pa., 1964-75; advanced cert. Goethe Inst., Munich, W.Ger., 1969; 1 son, Robert. Chmn. fgn. lang. dept. Parkland High Sch., Allentown, Pa., 1961-65; instr. German, Lehigh U., 1965-69; asso. prof. German, West Chester U., Pa., 1969—, dir. internat. edn., 1974-83, chmn. dept. fgn. langs., 1977—; campus dir. Expt. in Internat. Living 1972—; treas. Pa. Consortium Internat. Edn., 1978-83, pres., 1983—; coordinator-chairperson Assn. Depts. Fgn. Languages, State System Higher Edn., Pa., 1984—; lectr. in field. Bd. dirs. Peters Valley Crafts Ctr.; active Congress-Bundestag Youth Exchange Program, 1988. Fulbright travel grantee, 1963, 69; recipient Chapel of Four Chaplains award, 1981, numerous grants for fgn. langs. and internat. studies, programs of Nat. Endowment for the Humanities, Rockefeller Found.; recipient Chapel of Four Chaplins award, 1981. Mem. Am. Assn. Tchrs. German, Am. Council Teaching Fgn. Langs., NE Conf. Teaching Fgn. Lang., Smithsonian Instn. Republican. Lutheran. Author numerous publs. in German lang. and lit., individualizing instrn. in fgn. langs. Co-editor, Individualization Fgn. Lang. Learning in Am., 1970-75. Home: 3309 Windsor Ln Thorndale PA 19372 Office: Dept Fgn Langs West Chester U West Chester PA 19380

GOULD, ALVIN R., international business executive; b. Seattle, May 16, 1922; s. Charlie I. and Laura (Klos) G.; m. Ruth Nelson, May 25, 1946; children: Stephen Charles, Jon Patrick. Grad. pub. schs. Mem. engring. dept. Pacific Car & Foundry Co., Renton, Wash., 1943-45, asst. mgr. indsl. sales, 1945-48, mgr. indsl. sales, 1948-55, gen. sales mgr., 1956-60; gen. sales mgr. Peterbilt Motors Co., Newark, Calif., 1961-64; v.p., dir., gen. sales mgr. Honolulu Iron Works Co., 1964-66, exec. v.p., dir., chief operating officer, 1966, pres., dir., chief exec. officer, 1966-71; group pres. Food Equipment Group Ward Foods Inc., N.Y.C., 1970-71; v.p. merchandising Dillingham Corp., Honolulu, 1972-75, v.p. mining and merchandising, 1973-74, group v.p. mining and merchandising, mem. exec. mgmt. com., 1975-76; pres. T.C.C. Corp., Seattle, 1978—; dir. Haleakala Storage & Transfer Inc., Kahului, Maui, Hawaii, Canmore Mines Ltd., Alta., Can., Honiron Philippines, Inc. (Manila), J&L Engring. Co., Inc., Jeanerette, La., Tweedy Holdings Ltd., Burnley, Eng., Holsum Hawaii Baking, Inc., Honolulu. Mem. nat. export expansion Council Dept. Commerce, 1969-74, chmn. regional export expansion council, 1969-74; mem. Western Regional Export Council; chmn. Honolulu Export Council, 1975-77; Chmn. bd. trustees Hawaii Pacific Coll., 1973-77; bd. dirs. Center for Internat. Bus. Mem. Hawaii C. of C. (chmn. trade com. 1968-69), Hawaii World Trade Assn. (mem. exec. com. 1968-69), Hawaii Assn. Industries (v.p., dir. 1975-76), Navy League (dir.). Clubs: Rotary, Meridian Country, Outrigger Canoe, Rainier. Home: 8464 W Mercer Way Mercer Island WA 98040

GOULD, CHARLES PERRY, lawyer; b. Los Angeles, Mar. 11, 1909; s. Thomas Charles and Viola Frank (Keeney) G.; m. Mary Dalrymple, Sept. 1, 1932; children—Thomas Charles, Mary (Mrs. Robert Lancefield), Anne (Mrs. Thomason). Student, Pomona Coll., 1926-28; Ph.B., U. Chgo., 1930; LL.B., U. So. Calif., 1932. Bar: Calif. bar 1932. Asso. firm Frankley & Spray, Los Angeles, 1932- 35; mem. firm Spray, Gould & Bowers, 1935—; dir. Gould Music Co. Served to lt. comdr. USNR, 1942-45. Mem. Am. Bar Assn., Internat. Assn. Ins. Counsel, Am. Judicature Soc. (dir. 1979), Nat. Club Assn. (pres. 1962, dir.), World Affairs Council, Navy League U.S., Legion Lex, Delta Theta Phi. Republican. Episcopalian. Clubs: Elk. (Los Angeles), Jonathan (Los Angeles), Town Hall (Los Angeles), Los Angeles (Los Angeles); Balboa Bay (Balboa, Calif.); Calif. Book (San Francisco). Home: 1200 Old Mill Rd San Marino CA 91108 Office: 3530 Wilshire Blvd Los Angeles CA 90010

GOULD, DONALD EVERETT, chemicals company executive; b. Concord, N.H., May 19, 1932; s. Everett Luther and Gladys (Wilcox) G.; B.S. in Chem. Engring., U. N.H. 1954; postgrad. math. Rutgers U., 1955-59; m. Marilyn Bachelder, June 13, 1953; children—Barbara, Allen, Douglas. Devel. chem. engr. plastics div. Union Carbide Co., Bound Brook, N.J., 1954-59, tech. service engr., Bound Brook and Wayne, N.J. 1959-64, mgr. tech. service indsl. bag dept., Wayne, 1964-66, mgr. tech. services indsl. fabricated products dept. 1966-67, mktg., mgr. indsl. bags, 1967-69, sr. packaging engr., 1969-72, mgr. packaging, 1972-74, mgr. distbn. safety and regulations, 1974-79, staff engr. for packaging, 1980-85, sr. staff engr., 1985—. Mem. Packaging Inst. (vice chmn. films, foils and laminations com. 1962-64, chmn. 1964-66, sect. leader bottle containers, chmn. bag com. 1975-78, 85—), Am. Soc. Quality Control, Chem. Mfrs. Assn. (chmn. distbn. work group), Am. Council for Chem. Labeling, Alpha Chi Sigma. Club: Packanack Lake Country. Contbr. articles profl. jours., also to Ency. Engring. Materials and Processes. Home: 98 Lake Dr E Wayne NJ 07470 Office: River Rd PO Box 670 Bound Brook NJ 08805

GOULD, HARRY EDWARD, JR., industrialist; b. N.Y.C., Sept. 24, 1938; s. Harry E. and Lucille (Quartucy) G.; m. Barbara Clement, Apr. 26, 1975; children: Harry Edward, III, Katharine Elizabeth. Student, Oxford U., 1958; B.A. cum laude, Colgate U., 1960; postgrad., Harvard Bus. Sch., 1960-61; M.B.A., Columbia U., 1964. Asso. in corporate fin. dept. Goldman, Sachs & Co., N.Y.C., 1961-62; exec. asst. to sr. v.p. ops. Universal Am., N.Y.C., 1964-65; sec., treas. Young Spring & Wire Corp., Detroit, 1965-67, exec. v.p., chief operating officer, 1967-69, also dir.; v.p. adminstrn. and fin. Universal Am. Corp., 1968-69; mem. exec. com., v.p., sec.-treas. Daybrook-Ottawa Corp., Bowling Green, Ohio, 1967-69; dir., mem. exec. com. Am. Med. Ins. Co., N.Y.C., 1966-74; pres., chmn., chief exec. officer, dir. Gould Paper Corp., N.Y.C., 1969—; chmn. bd., dir. Samuel Porritt & Co., East Peoria, Ill., 1969—, Computer Copies Corp., N.Y.C., 1970-73, Ingalls Mfg., Inc., Ceres, Calif., 1971—, McNair Mfg., Inc., Chico, Calif., 1972—, Hawthorne Paper Co., Kalamazoo, 1974—, Weiss Mfg., Inc., Chico, 1974—, Vrisimo Mfg., Inc., Ceres, 1974—; chmn. bd. Lewis & Gould Paper Co., Inc., Northfield, Ill., 1975-78; pres., dir. Carlyle Internat. Sales Corp., N.Y.C., 1975—; chmn., pres., chief exec. officer Signature Communications Ltd., Los Angeles and N.Y.C., 1986—; dir. Reinhold-Gould GmbH, Hamburg, Germany, 1969—; ltd. ptnr. Hardy & Co. (mem. N.Y. Stock Exchange), N.Y.C., 1973-78. Co-chmn. Pacesetter's com. Boy Scouts Am., 1966-69; participant as U.S. Pres.'s rep. UN E-W Trade Devel. Commn., 1967; mem. N.Y. Gov.'s Task Force on N.Y. State Cultural Life and Arts, 1975—; Pres. Harry E. Gould Found., N.Y.C., 1971—; mem. nat. council Colgate U., 1973-76, trustee, mem. budget, devel., fin. and student affairs coms., 1976—; mem. adv. bd. Columbia U. Grad. Sch. Bus., 1980—; bd. dirs. United Cerebral Palsy Research and Ednl. Found., 1976—, Nat. Multiple Sclerosis Soc., 1977—, N.Y.C. Housing Devel. Corp., 1977—, vice chmn., 1987—, USO of Met. N.Y., 1981; bd. dirs. Housing N.Y. Corp., 1986—, vice chmn., 1987—; bd. dirs., chmn. exec. com. Cinema Group, Inc., Los Angeles, 1979-86, chmn., pres., 1982-86; mem. Democratic Nat. Fin. Council, 1974—, also vice chmn. exec. com., chmn. budget and audit coms.; treas. N.Y. State Dem. Com., 1976-77; mem. mayor's citizens com. Dem. Nat. Conv., 1976; mem. U.S. Pres.'s Export Council (exec. com., chmn. export expansion subcom., mem. export promotion subcom.), 1979-82; mem. exec. br. Acad. Motion Picture Arts and Scis., 1985—; nat. trustee, mem. exec. com. Nat. Symphony Orch., Washington, 1978—. Mem. Nat. Paper Trade Assn. (dir., mem. printing paper com. 1973—), Paper Mchts. Assn. N.Y. (dir. 1972—), Young Pres. Orgn., Paper Club N.Y., Fin. Execs. Inst., Columbia U. Grad. Sch. Bus. Alumni Assn. (dir. 1980—), Phi Kappa Tau. Clubs: Pres.'s N.Y. (co-chmn. assocs. div. 1964-68), City Athletic, Harvard, Harvard Business, Friars, Marco Polo (N.Y.C.); Les Ambassadeurs (London); Rockrimmon Country (Stamford, Conn.). Home: 25 Sutton Pl S New York NY 10022 also: Cherry Hill Farm 429 Taconic Rd Greenwich CT 06830 Office: Gould Paper Corp 315 Park Ave S New York NY 10010

GOULD, JAMES SPENCER, financial consultant; b. Albany, N.Y., Oct. 18, 1922; s. James Spencer and Elsie May (Spiegel) G.; m. Shirley Joan Burrett, June 12, 1948 (div. Oct. 1985); children: Deborah Ann, Jeffrey George, Douglas Spencer; m. Mary White Tredennick, Sept. 6, 1986. BS cum laude, Syracuse U., 1944; grad. advanced mgmt. program, Harvard U., 1958. C.P.A., N.Y., Calif. Ptnr. Arthur Young & Co., Buffalo and Los Angeles, 1949-65, N.Y.C., 1966-82; chief fin. officer, v.p. fin. Stanley Works, New Britain, Conn., 1982-87, v.p., 1987; free-lance cons. 1987—; dir. Imo Delaval Inc., Arrow Electronics, Inc. Served to 1st lt. inf. U.S. Army, 1943-46, ETO, 1st lt. Fin. Corps, 1951-52, Korea. Recipient Disting. Merit award Syracuse U. Sch. Mgmt., 1982, Alumnus of Yr. award, Syracuse U., 1987. Mem. Am. Inst. C.P.A.s, Fin. Execs. Inst. Clubs: Manchester Country (Vt.); Farmington Woods Golf. Home: 46 Applewood Ln Farmington Woods Avon CT 06001

GOULD, MAXINE LUBOW, lawyer, marketing professional, consultant; b. Bridgeton, N.J., Feb. 28, 1942; d. Louis A. and Bernice L. (Goldberg) Lubow; B.S., Temple U., 1962, J.D., 1968; m. Sam C. Gould, June 17, 1962 (div. Dec. 1984); children—Jack, Herman, David. Head resident dept. student personnel Temple U., 1962-66; dir., treas. Hilltop Interest Program, Inc., Los Angeles, 1973-74; law clk. law firms, Los Angeles, 1975-77; with Buffalo Resources Corp., Los Angeles, 1978-82, corp. sec., 1979-82; corp. sec., securities prin. Buffalo Securities Corp., Los Angeles, 1979-82; corp. sec. LaMaur Devel. Corp., Los Angeles, 1979-82; contracts analyst, land dept. Texaco Inc., Los Angeles, 1982-83; exec. dir. Sinai Temple, West Los Angeles, 1983-85; pres. Cutting Edge, Los Angeles, 1986; adminstr. law firm Robinson, Wolas & Diamant, Century City, 1986, acctg. firm Roth, Bookstein & Zaslow, Los Angeles, 1986-87; project coordinator Cipher, 1987; mktg. dir. Am. Bus. Capital, Beverly Hills, Calif., 1988—. Mem. Roscomare Valley Assn. Edn. Com., Bel Air, Calif., 1975-76; subcom. chmn. Roscomare Rd. Sch. Citizens Adv. Council, Bel Air; active various community drives. Recipient Joseph B. Wagner Oratory award B'nai B'rith, 1959, Voice of Democracy award, 1958-59, award Commentator Club, 1959. Mem. ABA (law office econs. sect.), Los Angeles Bar Assn. (assoc., law office econs. sect.), Nat. Assn. Legal Adminstrs. (Beverly Hills chpt.), Nat. Assn. Female Execs. (network dir.), Nat. Assn. Law Firm Mktg. Adminstrs., Calif. Women Lawyers, Women in Bus. (co-chmn. membership com.), Calif. CPA Soc. (adminstr. com.), Nat. Assn. Synagogue Adminstrs., Am. Assn. Petroleum Landmen, Los Angeles Assn. Petroleum Landmen, Textile Profl. Soc., Phi Alpha Theta, Alpha Lambda Delta. Jewish. Home: 4101 Knob Hill Dr Sherman Oaks CA 91403

GOULD, SYD S., publisher; b. Boston, Dec. 16, 1912; s. Charles M. and Cecelia (Duke) G.; student Coll. William and Mary, 1934; m. Grace Leich, May 22, 1938; 1 dau., Nancy Hamilton (Mrs. Lucien M. Gex, Jr.). Radio bus., Buenos Aires, Argentina, 1934, 36; advt. dept. Call-Chronicle Newspapers, Allentown, Pa., 1936-42; v.p. adv. dir. Baytown Sun, Tex. 1943-55; pub.-owner Cleveland Daily Banner, Tenn., 1955—; pres. Cleveland Newspapers, Inc., 1956-67; exec. v.p. So. Newspapers, Inc., 1963-69; pres. Syd S. Gould Assocs., 1966—, Bolivar Newspapers, Inc., 1967—, Ironton Tribune Corp. Ohio, Franklin Newspapers, Inc., La., Comet-Press Newspapers, Thibodaux, La., Milton Newspapers, Inc., Fla. Mem. Regional Small Bus. Adv. Council. Sec., Bradley County (Tenn.) Indsl. Devel. Bd., 1961—; bd. dirs. Providence Hosp.; pres. Bradley County Heart Assn., 1960-61. Served with USNR, World War II. Recipient Disting. Eagle Scout award Boy Scouts Am., 1983. Mem. Newspaper Advt. Execs. Assn., Tenn. Press Assn., Bur. Advt., Am. Newspaper Pubs. Assn., So. Newspapers Pubs. Assn., Gulf Coast Conservation Assn., USCG Aux., U.S. Power Squadron, U.S. Naval Inst., Navy League, Eagle Scout Assn., Sigma Delta Chi. Episcopalian. Clubs: Bayou Country, Mobile Big Game Fishing, Isle Dauphine Country, Capitol Hill, Yachting of Am., Internat. Trade, Bienville, Athelstan, Commodore, Bay Point Yacht, Inc. Home: Box 28449 Bay Point Panama City FL 32407 Office: 2111 Thomas Dr Panama City FL 32407

GOULDING, CHARLES EDWIN, consulting engineer; b. Tampa, Fla., Nov. 23, 1916; s. Charles Edwin and Eugenia (Hoy) G.; B.S., U. Tampa, 1939, cert. in civil and chem. engring., 1941; M.S., U. Fla., 1944, Ph.D., 1946; postgrad. U. Pa., 1966-68; DSc in Chem. Engring. (hon.), 1987 Marquis Giuseppe Scicluna Internat. Univ. Found.; m. Germaine Fonteix, Jan. 30, 1950 (dec.); m. 2d, Meta Isabella Hyslop, Nov. 25, 1973 (dec.). Engr., U.S. Phosphric div. Tenn. Corp., East Tampa, Fla., 1939-41; instr. U. Fla., Gainesville, 1941-46; cons. engr. Venezuelan Govt. Ministries Public Works, Caracas, 1946-49; tech. dir. Consultec, Caracas, 1946-51; tech. coordinator Industries Fontura, Sao Paulo, Brazil, 1951-54; chief engr., project dir. Bioquimica, Mexico City, 1954-57; nuclear tng. dir. N.Y. Shipbuilders Corp., Camden, N.J., 1963-64; instr. chemistry Temple U., Phila., 1964-65; vis. lectr. physics and earth sci. U. Tenn., Chattanooga, 1968-69; sr. engr. E.H. Richardson Assos., Newark, Del., 1971-72; prin. environ. engr. Nassaux-Hemsley, Chambersburg, Pa., 1973-77; chief engr. Twin City Engring. Assos., Bristol, Tenn., 1977—; pres. T&M Machining Div., Bristol, 1978-85; pres. Bristol Research Corp., 1985—; cons. chem. processes, 1957-68. Communication engr. CD, Chambersburg, 1973-77; res. dep. sheriff, Sullivan County, Tenn., 1977—; mem. Republican Nat. Com., Am. Security Council, U.S. Congl. Adv. Bd. hon. mayor Boy's Town. Registered profl. engr., Del., Pa., Md., N.J., Ohio, Ky., W.Va., Va., N.C., S.C., Tenn., La., Venezuela. Recipient Albert Einstein medal of honor Albert Einstein Internat. Found., 1986. Mem. Am. Inst. Chem. Engrs., Am. Chem. Soc., IEEE, Am. Ordnance Assn., Nat. Soc. Profl. Engrs., N.Y. Acad. Scis., AAAS, Water Pollution Control Fedn. Profl. Engrs., Am. Assn. Ret. Persons, Nat. Environ. Tng. Assn. Sigma Xi, Phi Sigma. Clubs: Kettlefoot Rod and Gun; Moose (Bristol). Contbr. articles to tech. jours.; patentee (4); inventor energy healing. Office: 2569 Volunteer Pkwy Bristol TN 37620

GOULDING, MERRILL KEITH, engineer, consultant; b. Erie, Pa., Jan. 21, 1933; s. Forest Clute and Felicita Clara (Johnson) G.; BS, UCLA, 1968, PhD, 1979; children: Merrill, Robert, Nida, Gina, Asst. to v.p. Internat. Controls Corp., 1963-69; chmn. bd. Village Verde Corp., 1963-64; pres. Merrill K. Goulding & Assocs., Inc., Los Angeles, 1974—; chief exec. officer Coin Cop Electronics Co., 1975-88; bd. dirs. Mid City Travel Industry; cons. FAA, DOT, DNA. Bd. dirs. Rio Hondo Area Action Com., 1970; guiding counselor Inst. Cultural Affairs; past pres. Request Computer Users Group. Served with USMC, 1953. Registered profl. engr., N.Y., Calif. Mem. ASME, IEEE, AIAA, NSPE, Calif. Soc. Profl. Engrs., Am. Soc. Metals, Constrn. Specifications Inst., Soc. Material and Process Engrs., Vols. in Tech. Assistance, Mensa, Am. Legion, Blue and Gold Circle Alumni Assn. UCLA. Republican. Clubs: Calif. Yacht. Lodges: Shriners, Los Angeles Consistory. Address: PO Box 577 Glendale CA 91209

GOULED APTIDON, HASSAN See APTIDON, HASSAN GOULED

GOULEMOT, JEAN MARIE, language educator; b. Granville, Manche, France, July 20, 1937; m. Maria Maeso Ducloux, June 3, 1961; children: Pablo Aurelio, Paloma. M of French Lit., U. Sorbonne, Paris, 1961, B of Spanish Lit., 1963, PhD, 1973. Asst. prof. French lit. U. Sorbonne, 1965-68, assoc. prof., 1969-70; assoc. prof. U. Tours, France, 1971-73, prof., 1974—; vis. prof. U. São Paolo, Brazil, 1975, Rutgers U., New Brunswick, N.J., 1977, Queen's U., Can., 1983, 85. Author: Discours, Histoire, Révolutions, 1976, Le Clairon de Staline, 1983; editor: Memoires J. Duval, 1981, Traité des Superstitions, 1984. Recipient Martin prize French Acad., 1984; named Officer of Palmes Acad. Roman Catholic. Office: U Tours, 3 Rue des Tanneurs, 37000 Tours France

GOUPIL ROUSSEAU, FRANÇOISE MARIE, gynecologist; b. Rennes, France, June 14, 1947; d. Jacques and Jeanine (Guitton) Gouffault; m. Alain Goupil, Sept. 11, 1970 (div. 1978); 1 child, Julien; m. Danick Jean Rousseau, Oct. 30, 1982; stepchildren: Axel, Robin, Fabrice. MD, U. Rennes, 1972, cert. gynecology, 1976. Intern Rennes (France) Hosp., 1967-70; resident Hosp. Cochin, Paris, 1971, 73, Hosp. Necker, Paris, 1972; med. researcher Nat. Inst. Sci. and Med. Research, Paris, 1972-77; mem. staff Hosp. Cochin, Paris, 1976—; practice medicine specializing in gynecology 1977—; med. columnist Marie Claire mag., France, 1982—; producer, host daily med. program, Luxemurg Radio and TV, Paris, 1986—. Mem. Ordre des Médecins. Club: Racing of France (Paris). Home: 65 Rue la Fontaine, 75016 Paris 16 France Office: 7 Rue T de Banville, 75017 Paris 17 France

GOURAD HAMADOU, BARKAT See HAMADOU, BARKAT GOURAD

GOURGAND, PIERRE, industrial consultant; s. Eugene and Suzanne (Delacquis) G.; m. Helene Pagliano, Dec. 16, 1950. Baccalaureat Philosophie, Diplomé, Ecole Practique des Sciences Sociales, Paris, 1952. Sec. gen. Centre Culturel Internat. de Royaumont, Viarmes, France, 1949; insp. adjoint Banque L. Dupont et cie, Paris, 1951-54; sec. gen. Centre de Synthese Organisation Formation, Paris, 1954-63; chmn. Euroformation, Paris, 1963—. Contbr. numerous articles to profl. jours. Mem. Internat. Cons. Found. (v.p. Europe-Africa; bd. dirs.). Home: 108 Rue du Ranelagh, 75016 Paris France Office: Euroformation, 139 Rue du Ranelagh, 75016 Paris France

GOURLEY, JAMES LELAND, editor, publisher, business executive; b. Mounds, Okla., Jan. 29, 1919; s. Samuel O. and Lodema (Scott) G.; B.Liberal Studies, U. Okla., 1963; m. Vicki Graham Clark, Nov. 24, 1976; children—James Leland II, Janna Lynn Chancellor, Kelly Clark, Brandon Clark. Editor, pub., pres. Daily Free-Lance, Henryetta, Okla., 1946-73; editor Friday, 1974—; chmn. Nichols Hills Pub. Co., 1974—; v.p. Suburban Grphics, Inc., 1987—; pres. Central Okla. Newspaper Group, 1987; pres. radio sta. KHEN, KHEN-TV, Henryetta, 1955-71; pres. Hugo (Okla.) Daily News, 1953-63; chief of staff gov. Okla., 1959-63; chmn., pres. State Capitol Bank, 1962-69; v.p. radio sta. KXOJ Sapulpa, 1972-75; treas. Okla. Radio Co., Inc., 1962-67. Mem. Pres. Nat. Pub. Advisory Com. to sec. commerce, 1963-66; exec. dir. Gov's Comm. Higher Edn., 1960-61; Democratic candidate for gov. Okla., 1966. Bd. dirs. So. Regional Edn. Bd., 1959-67, Okla. Symphony Soc., 1976-88, Oklahoma City Crimestoppers, 1982—, Salvation Army, Oklahoma City, 1985-87; mem. Gov.'s Reform Com., 1984. Served to maj. AUS, 1942-46. Recipient Best Large City Weekly newspaper awards, 1977, 78, 79, 80, 83, 84, 85; inducted Okla. Journalism Hall of Fame, 1980. Mem. UP Internat. Editors Okla. (pres. 1958-59), Okla. Disciples of Christ Laymen (pres. 1964-65), Suburban Newspapers Am. (dir.), Okla. Press Assn. (v.p., pres. 1988-89), Oklahoma City C. of C. (dir.), Okla. State C. of C. (bd. dirs.), Pi Kappa Alpha. Republican. Clubs: Oklahoma City Golf and Country, Econ. (Oklahama City), Men's Dinner (Oklahoma City); Lodge; Rotary (dir.). Home: 1605 W Wilshire Oklahoma City OK 73116 Office: 10801 N Quail Plaza Dr Oklahoma City OK 73156

GOURVISH, TERENCE RICHARD, economics and social studies educator, researcher; b. Leicester, Eng., Mar. 13, 1943; s. Assir and Catherine Mercy (Lond) G.; m. Susan Phillips, Sept. 9, 1967; children: Peter, Matthew. BA with honors 1st class in history, U. London, 1964, PhD in Econ. History, 1967. Asst. lectr. U. Glasgow, 1967-70; lectr. U. East Anglia, Norwich, Eng., 1971-74, sr. lectr., 1974—, dean Sch. Econ. and Social Studies, 1986—; commd. historian Brit. Rwys. Bd., 1979-86; hist. cons., 1987—. Author: Mark Huish, 1972, Railways and the British Economy, 1980, British Railways 1948-73, 1986, Norfolk Beers From English Barley, 1987. Mem. Norfolk County Council Adoption Panel, Norwich, 1985—; mem. Nat. Council Inland Transport, London, 1971-77; sec. Scottish Assn. Pub. Transport, Glasgow, 1968-70. Recipient First Prize in Bus. History Newcomen S. N.Am., 1974. Office: U East Anglia, University Plain, Norwich, Norfolk NR4 7TJ, England

GOUTALLIER, PHILIPE BERNARD, surgeon; b. Paris, Feb. 14, 1931; s. Paul and Andree (Poitou) G.; m. Denise Beilin Goutallier; children: Jerome, Anne-Sophie. MD, Paris, 1963. Intern Paris Hosp., 1959-63; chef de clinique, asst. des hosp. Faculte de Medecine, Paris, 1963-65; surgeon Centre Hosp., Orleans, France, 1965—, Clinique de l'Archette, Olivet, France, 1965—; gen. dir. Clinique de l'Archette, Olivet, 1983—; founding mem. Coll. Internat. Chirurgiae Digestivae, 1971; asst. mem. Acad. de Chirurgie, 1983—. Contbr. numerous articles to profl. jours. Lodge: Rotary. Home: 12 Rue St Marc, 45000 Orleans France Office: Clinique de Archette, 504 Ave du Loiret, 45160 Olivet France

GOUYON, PAUL CARDINAL, archbishop; b. Bordeaux, France, Oct. 24, 1910; s. Jean-Baptiste Louis and Jeanne (Chassaing) G.; ed. in France. Ordained priest Roman Catholic Ch., 1937, consecrated bishop, 1957; bishop of Bayonne, 1957, titular archbishop of Pessinonte, 1963, archbishop of Rennes, 1964—; elevated to Sacred Coll. Cardinals, 1969. Decorated Croix de Guerre, officer Legion of Honor, comdr. Nat. Order Merit. Mem. Pax Christi (past pres. French sect.). Author several books. Address: Ma Maison, 181 rue Jadaique, 33081 Bordeaux Cedex France

GOW, DAVID WHITCOMB, school administrator; b. South Wales, N.Y., Feb. 19, 1924; s. Peter and Mabel Rebecca (Whitcomb) G.; B.A., Yale U., 1945; m. Alice Roberts, June 27, 1960; children—Peter, Persis Gow Whalley, Alexander R., David W., Philip R. Tchr., The Gow Sch., South Wales, 1947—, asst. headmaster, 1953-58, asso. headmaster, 1958-76, headmaster, 1976—, also trustee. Trustee Peter Gow Found., South Wales. Served with USAAF, 1942-44. Mem. Orton Dyslexia Soc., Assn. Children with Learning Disabilities, N.Y. State Personnel and Guidance Assn. Episcopalian. Contbr. in field. Office: Emery Rd South Wales NY 14139

GOW, ROBERT HAIGH, business executive; b. Paris, Apr. 26, 1933; s. Ralph Fredrick and Eleanore (Haigh) G.; m. Patricia Lawson, July 20, 1957 (div. 1972); m. Bebe Lord, Jan. 26, 1974; children—Larua Lawson, David Fredrick, Heather Haigh. Student, Groton Sch., 1946-50; B.S., Yale U., 1955. Supr. indsl. engring. Norton Co., Worchester, Mass., 1955-61; pres., exec. v.p. Zapata Corp., Houston, 1962-70; chmn., chief exec. Stratford of Tex., Houston, 1970-76; pres. Vilelta China Co., Houston, 1977-79; v.p. Gulf Resources & Chem. Co., Houston, 1979-81; pres., chief exec. Enterprise Tech., Houston, 1982-84; pres. LDHG Inc., Houston, 1985—; guest lectr. Harvard Bus. Sch., Cambridge, Mass., 1971-75, Coll. Bus. Adminstrn. U. Houston, 1976; adj. prof. Rice U. Coll. Bus. Adminstrn., 1987—. Served to lt. USAF, 1956-58. Republican. Episcopalian. Clubs: Coronado, University. Home: 11911 McLeod Houston TX 77024 Office: LDHG Inc 955 Dairy Ashford Suite 222 Houston TX 77079

GOWAN, JOSEPH PATRICK, JR., communications equipment manufacturing company executive; b. Bklyn., Sept. 30, 1939; s. Joseph Patrick and Elizabeth C. (Murphy) G.; m. Donna J. DiCostanzo; children—Sheri, Nicole; children by previous marriage—Joseph Patrick III, Thomas, Patricia, Daniel,

Sean, Timothy. Student Villanova U., 1961; B.S., Fordham U., 1965. Dir., CBS, N.Y.C., 1964-67; v.p. Metro Media Records Co., N.Y.C., 1967-69, GRT Record Group, N.Y.C., 1969-71; v.p., chief exec. officer NEC Telephones Inc., Melville, N.Y., 1971-77, pres., dir., 1977-80; v.p. NEC Am. Inc., 1977-80; v.p. Telecom Equipment Corp., Long Island City, N.Y., 1982, chief fin. officer, 1984—, treas., 1986—; exec. v.p., dir., chief fin. officer, treas. TPI Enterprises Inc. (formerly Telecom Plus Internat.), 1982—; pres. Telecom Plus Rental Systems, 1984-87, dir. ELP, various subs., 1984-87; dir. Maxcell Telecom Plus and subs., 1984—; sec., dir. Acctel Telecommunications Systems Inc., Tel Logic Communications Inc., Pactel Communications Inc., Compath Nat. Inc., 1985-88, TPI Restaurants, Inc., 1988—; dir. Shoney's South, Inc. Bd. dirs. Flushing (N.Y.) Community Vol. Ambulance Corps., 1968-73, v.p., 1968-70, treas., 1971-73. Mem. Am. Acad. Scis., Am. Mgmt. Assn., N.Am. Telephone Assns. (dir.). Roman Catholic. Clubs: K.C., Kiwanis. , 1968-70, treas., 1971-73. Mem. Am. Acad. Scis., Am. Mgmt. Assn., North Am. Telephone Assns. (dir.). Roman Catholic. Clubs: KC, Kiwanis. Home: 2921 NW 26th Ct Boca Raton FL 33434 Office: TPI Enterprises Inc 7300 N Fed Hwy Boca Raton FL 33431 also: 885 3d Ave New York NY 10022

GOWER, MARK ALLEN, oil company executive; b. Denver, Dec. 20, 1953; s. Frank Herbert Jr. and Marie Patricia (Pedersen) G.; m. Helen Kathleen Dunn, Apr. 23, 1975; children—Jeffrey Bryan, Jill Elizabeth. Student Santa Barbara City Coll., 1972-74, U. Calif.-San Diego, 1974-75, Scripps Inst., 1974-75; B.S. in Geology, San Diego State U., 1977. Exploration geologist ECHO Oil Co., Casper, Wyo., 1977-80; exploration geologist Gower Oil Co., Denver, 1980-81, exploration mgr., pres., 1981—; owner Mark Gower Oil Properties, Denver, 1983—; v.p. Garske Energy Corp., Denver, 1984—. Mem. Wyo. Geol. Assn., Am. Assn. Petroleum Geologists, Am. Inst. Profl. Geologists, Rocky Mountain Oil and Gas Assn., Internat. Oceanographic Found. Republican. Roman Catholic. Clubs: Metropolitan (founding mem. 1983-84) (Englewood, Colo.); Denver Petroleum, Mt. Vernon Country, Las Verdes Golf (Denver). Office: Gower Oil Co 5600 S Quebec Suite 315-A Englewood CO 80111

GOWERS, SIMON GEOFFREY, psychiatrist; b. London, Jan. 8, 1956; s. John Derek and Gillian (Bieri) G.; m. Gillian Halliday, Mar 17, 1979; 1 child, Imogen. BSc in Psychology, U. London, 1977, M in Philosophy, 1987; B of Medicine and Surgery, St. Georges Med. Sch., London, 1980. Sr. house officer, registrar in psychiatry St. Georges Hosp., London, 1981-85; lectr. psychiatry St. Georges Hosp. Med. Sch., London, 1985-87; hon. sr. registrar Atkinson Morley's Hosp., London, 1985-87, sr. registrar in child psychiatry, Manchester, 1987—. Contbr. articles on anorexia nervosa to profl. jours. Mem. Royal Coll. Psychiatrists, Brit. Med. Assn. Office: Royal Manchester Childrens Hosp, Pendlebury, Manchester M27 1HA, England

GOWLETT, JOHN ANTHONY JAMYS, archaeologist; b. Douglas, Isle of Man, June 1, 1950; s. James A. and Kathleen (Vedmore) G.; m. Catherine Anne Struthers, Aug. 30, 1986. BA, U. Cambridge, Eng., 1972, MA, 1976, PhD, 1980. Lectr. U. Khartoum, Sudan, 1974-77; co-leader Chesowanja Research Expedition, Kenya, 1978; sr. archaeologist radiocarbon accelerator unit, archaeology research lab. U. Oxford, Eng., 1980-87; dep. dir. Inst. Prehistoric Scis. and Archaeology U. Liverpool, Eng., 1987—. Author: Ascent to Civilization, 1984; co-editor: Archaeological Results from Accelerator Dating, 1986; mem. editorial bd. World Archaeology, 1986—; contbr. articles to profl. jours. Mem. Prehistoric Soc. Office: U Liverpool, Inst Prehistoric Scis and Archaeology, PO Box 147, Liverpool L69 3BX, England

GOYAL, ANIL KUMAR, airline executive; b. Muzaffarnagar, Uttar Pradesh, India, Apr. 8, 1948; s. Ashok Chandra and Nirmala (Aron) G.; m. Pavanjeet Chowdhury, Dec. 30, 1973; children: Sameer, Jaya. BE, Allahabad (Uttar Pradesh) U., 1969, MBA, 1971. Mgmt. scis. analyst Indian Airlines, New Delhi, 1971-74, traffic officer, 1974-80, asst. comml. mgr., 1980-83, dep. comml. mgr., 1983-86, sr. dep. comml. mgr., 1986—. Home: C-1/1 SFS Flats, Saket, New Delhi 110017, India Office: Indian Airlines, Airlines House, New Delhi 110001, India

GRABARZ, DONALD FRANCIS, health care industry consultant; b. Jersey City, Sept. 18, 1841; s. Joseph and Frances (Zotynia) G.; m. Joan Isoldi, Aug. 13, 1966; children: Christine, Robert, Danielle. BPharm, St. Johns U., N.Y.C., 1964. Lic. pharmacist, N.Y., Vt. Dir. qualtiy control and assurance Johnson and Johnson Co., New Brunswick, N.J., 1965-72; dir. quality assurance and regulatory affairs Bard Parker div. Becton Dickinson, Franklin Lakes, N.J., 1972-80; asst. corp. dir. regulatory affairs Becton Dickinson, 1972-80; corp. dir. regulatory affairs C.R. Bard Inc., Murray Hill, N.J., 1980-85; v.p. regulatory affairs, qualtiy assurance Symbion Inc., Salt Lake City, 1985-86; cons. DFG & Assocs., Salt Lake City, 1986—; lectr. Inst. for Applied Tech. Author, editor Inspection and Recall Film. Bd. dirs. v.p., asst. treas. Am. Lung Assn., N.J., 1972-75; chmn. Drug Edn., DuPage County, Ill., 1968. Mem. Health Industry Mfg. Assn. (chmn. Legal and Regulatory commn. 1983), Regulatory Affairs Profl. Soc., Am. Soc. Quality Control, Am. Mfr. Med. Instrumentation Assn., Am. Pharm. Assn. Office: DFG & Assocs PO Box 17801 Salt Lake City UT 84117-0801

GRABBE, KARL HUBERT, building, development executive; b. Oldenburg, Germany, Mar. 23, 1936; s. Hubert and Maria (Herzog) G.; m. Madelet P. Reyal, May 29, 1963; 1 child, Yasemin. Diploma Engring., HFT Bremen, 1959, Baumeister, 1965 Dipl. Ing. HFT Brenen, 1980. Architect various locations, 1960-68; pres. Plusbau GmbH, Bremen, Fed. Republic of Germany, 1965-68; pres. Interhomes, Bremen, 1968—, dir. Brussells, 1973-82; bd. dirs. Bremen Overseas Research and Devel. Assn., 1978—, v.p., 1983—. Contbr. numerous articles to profl. jours. on housing. Bd. dirs. Commune of Duensen, Fed. Republic of Germany, 1965-69, Harpstedt, 1967-69; mem. Adminstrv. Bldg. Council Commune of Duensen, 1965-69. Mem. Urban Land Inst. (exec. group council 1979-82), Nat. Assn. Homebuilders, German Socs. (pres.), Bremen Homebuilder Assn. (v.p.), Lower Saxony Bremen Homebuilder Assn. (bd dirs.), Bremen C. of C. (planning council 1982—). Clubs: Vahr, Bremen. Lodge: Rotary (hon.).

GRABER, HARRIS DAVID, sales executive; b. Bronx, N.Y., Mar. 31, 1939; s. Charles and Ella (Shapiro) G.; A.S., Queensborough Community Coll., 1973; B.S. cum laude, CUNY, 1975; M.B.A., St. Johns U., 1979; m. Esther Estelle Feldman, Dec. 28, 1957; children—Donald Irwin, Gregory Stuart, Monique Cheryl, Roy Scott. Draftsman, Paramount Designs Co., N.Y.C., 1956-58; design draftsman Milgo Electronic Co., Miami, Fla., 1961-62; design engr. Cons. and Designers Co., N.Y.C., 1958-61, 62-64; with engring. and engring. mgmt. depts. Grumman Aerospace Co., Bethpage, N.Y., 1964-74, mktg. and sales engr., 1974-75, group head customer engring. tech. requirements, 1975-78, internat. bus. analyst, 1978; govt. sales mgr. Systems-East div. Conrac Corp., West Caldwell, N.J., 1978-80; dir. govt. mktg. Telephonics Corp., Huntington, N.Y., 1980-82; regional sales mgr. Measurement Systems div. Gould Inc., Oxnard, Calif., 1982-83; sales mgr. govt. bus. Servonic div. Gulton Industries Inc., Costa Mesa, Calif., 1983-84; systems mktg. mgr. ILC Data Device Corp., 1984—. Mem. Tech. Mktg. Soc. Am., Assn. M.B.A. Execs., Navy League U.S., Armed Forces Communications and Electronics Assn. Home: 80-51 249th St Bellerose NY 11426 Office: 105 Wilbur Pl Bohemia NY 11716

GRABES, HERBERT, English literature educator; b. Krefeld, Fed. Republic Germany, June 8, 1936; s. Adolf and Elisabeth (Giesen) G.; m. Hannelore Koch, Mar. 2, 1962; children: Arnd, Oliver, Irene. PhD, U. Cologne, Fed. Republic Germany, 1963. Habilitation U. Mannheim, Fed. Republic Germany, 1969. Instr. English U. Detroit, 1959-60; research asst. U. Cologne, 1962-65; research asst. U. Mannheim, 1966-69, dozent, 1969-70; prof. English U. Giessen, Fed. Republic Germany, 1970—, v.p., 1979-81; dir. Inst. für Anglistik und Amerikanistik, Giessen, 1970—. Author: Fictitious Biographies, 1977, Fiktion Imitation Ästhetik, 1981, The Mutable Glass, 1982; editor: Real Yearbook, 1982. Mem. Internat. Assn. Univ. Profs. English, Assn. for Commonwealth Lit. and Lang. Studies, Anglistenstag, Deutsche Gesellschaft für Amerikanstudien, Deutsche Shakespeare Assn. Roman Catholic. Office: U Giessen, Anglistik, Otto-Behaghel St 10, 6300 Giessen Federal Republic of Germany

GRABINSKI, LAWRENCE AUGUST, data processing executive, designer; b. Chgo., Aug. 10, 1929; s. August Jerome and Pearl Josephine (Wanat) G.; (div.); children—Martin, Thomas. Student U. Md., 1950-52, Ill. Inst. Tech., 1952-54, Morraine Valley Coll., 1980. Quality control engr. Foote Bros., Chgo., 1952-55; designer W.L. Stennsgaard, Chgo., 1955-57; chief draftsman Klemp Corp., Chgo., 1957-65; structural designer Rippel Archt. Metals, Chgo., 1965-74; asst. div. mgr. Pullman Sheet Metal Co., Chgo., 1974-77; computer systems specialist Castle Engring. Co., Chgo., 1977—. Served with USAF, 1948-52, ETO. Mem. Am. Fedn. Musicians. Home: 7801 S Lotus Burbank IL 60459 Office: Castle Engring Co 3579 W Columbus Ave Chicago IL 60652

GRABLE, R(EGINALD) HAROLD, psychologist; b. Putnam County, Ind., Sept. 22, 1917; s. Reginald R. and Cecil Ruth (Jones) G.; A.B., U. Kans., 1938, tchr.'s diploma, 1940; M.A., U. Minn., 1949; m. Elizabeth Hannah Baird, Aug. 17, 1946; children—Celia, Nancy, Daniel. Group leader occupational coders Nat. Roster Sci. and Specialized Personnel, Washington, 1940-42; vocat. counselor U. Minn., Mpls., 1947; clin. psychologist trainee VA Hosp., St. Paul, 1947-49; chief clin. psychologist Willmar (Minn.) State Hosp., 1949-51, Winnebago (Wis.) State Hosp., 1951-61; clin. psychologist West Shore Mental Health Clinic (formerly Hackley Adult Mental Health Clinic), Muskegon, Mich., 1961-82; clin. psychologist Kalamazoo Regional Psychiat. Hosp., 1983-85; pvt. practice psychology, Willmar, Minn., 1949-51, Oshkosh, Wis., 1951-61, Spring Lake, Mich., 1961—; instr. extension div. U. Wis., 1956-61; mem. profl. adv. bd. Wis. Council Mentally Retarded Children, 1956-61. Contbr. articles to profl. jours. First aid instr. ARC, 1963-79; exec. bd. Grand Valley council (name now West Mich. Shores council) Boy Scouts Am., 1966-76, dist. chmn., 1968-70, commr., 1972—; various offices PTA, 1953-78, Vols. in Probation; elder, chmn. bd. Muskegon Christian Ch. (Disciples of Christ), 1970-73. Served with AUS, 1942-46. Recipient Silver Beaver award Boy Scouts Am., 1981, Dist. award of Merit, 1977; lic. psychologist, Mich. Mem. Am. Psychol. Assn., Mich. Assn. Children with Learning Disabilities. Lodge: Rotary. Home and Office: 717 Summer St Spring Lake MI 49456

GRABOWSKI, JOZEF, computer science educator, researcher; b. Sokolniki, Poland, July 30, 1938; s. Stanislaw and Stefaniai (Bajor) G.; m. Romana Krupicka, Sept. 22, 1961; children—Malgorzata, Anetta. M. Tech. Sci., Tech. U., Wroclaw, Poland, 1961, Dr. Tech. Sci., 1973; M. Math. Sci., U. Wroclaw, 1970, Diplomate engring. and math. Gen. designer computer systems Computer Ctr., Elwro, Wroclaw, 1963-74; asst. prof. computer sci. Tech. U., Wroclaw, 1974-80, assoc. prof., 1980-85, prof., 1985—, chief sci. group, 1974—, head dept., 1980—; vis. prof. erasmus U. Rotterdam, 1986; vis. prof., U. Osnabruck, Fed. Republic Germany, 1987; dep. dean of faculty electronics and computer sci. Tech. U. Wrocklaw, 1986; lectr. Inst. Math., Wroclaw, 1976-79, Inst. Computer Sci., Krakow, Poland, 1978-81. Author: Methods of Disjunctive Graphs in Optimization Algorithms for the Control of Discrete Production Systems, 1977; Generalized Problems of Operations Sequencing Optimization in the Discrete Production Systems, 1979. Contbr. articles to profl. jours.; inventor of Universal Block Method for solving scheduling problems. Recipient prizes Ministry Edn., 1973, 79, 84, Tech. U., 1973-85. Mem. Am. Math. Soc., Polish Math. Soc. Roman Catholic. Home: Jastrzebia 6/8 m 4, Wroclaw 53-148 Poland Office: Tech U of Wroclaw, Inst Engring Cybernetics, Janiszews, kiego 11/17, Wroclaw 50-372, Poland

GRABSCHEID, WILLIAM HENRY, insolvency and reorganization specialist; b. N.Y.C., May 18, 1931; s. Sidney Oswald and Jeannette (Derdiger) G.; m. Barbara Lee Blam, Dec. 21, 1952 (div. Nov. 1964); children: Paul, Steven, Michael, Karen; m. Carol Sue Birenholtz, Nov. 17, 1964; children: Peter, James, Elizabeth, William Jr. BA in Econs., Lafayette Coll., 1953; MS in Administrv. Mgmt., Columbia U., 1954. Pres. Modern Industries, Inc., N.Y.C., 1954-75, Humphrey's Leather Goodsdiv. Scott & Fetzer, Chgo., 1975-78, E.R. Moore subs. Beatrice Foods, Chgo., 1978-79; mng. dir. William H. Grabscheid and Assocs., Highland Park, Ill., 1979-83; mgr. troubled businesses Friedman, Eisenstein, Raemer & Schwartz, Chgo., 1983-85; mng. dir. midwest region, reorgn. and insolvency div. Arthur Young & Co., Chgo., 1985—; examiner, panel trustee chpts. 7, 11; alt. del. to Insol. Mem. Am. Arbitration Assn., Am. Bankruptcy Inst., Assn. Insolvency Accts., Assn. Bankruptcy Trustees, Assn. for Corp. Growth. Democrat. Jewish. Clubs: Metropolitan, Chgo., Willy's. Home: 3500 University Ave Highland Park IL 60035 Office: Arthur Young & Co One IBM Plaza Chicago IL 60611

GRABSKA, STANISLAWA HALINA, theologian; b. Lwòw, Tolomqise, Poland, Nov. 20, 1922; d. Stanislaw Grabski and Zotia (Smolik) Grabska. MA, Acad. Fine Arts, Warsaw, Poland, 1955; grad., Cath. U. Lublin, Poland, 1969; MSc, D of Theology, Cath. U. Lovanium, Belgium, 1973. Designer Gothern-Lesing Office, Warsaw, 1960-64; specialist theology Club Cath. Intellectuals, Warsaw, 1964-70, v.p., 1973—; lectr. various parishes and priesthoods, Poland, 1973—. Author: The Liberty Christian, 1972, The Hope that Lies Within, 1980, Prayer in the Bible, 1983. Served as officer with Polish Army, 1942-45. Mem. Soc. Theologigue Louvain. Roman Catholic. Home: Al Niepodlegliosci, 71 m 86, 02 626 Warsaw Poland Office: Club Cath Intellectuals, Ropernika 34, 00 336 Warsaw Poland

GRABSKE, WILLIAM JOHN, management consulting company executive; b. Chgo., Jan. 31, 1943; s. Edward Walter and Helen Julia G.; m. Judith Elaine Benz, Apr. 12, 1969; children—Gretchen, Bradford, Lindsay. B.S. in Civil Engring., U. Ill., 1965; postgrad. Columbia U. Sch. of Bus. Operating mgmt. trainee, N.Y. Central System, N.Y.C., 1965-66, asst. supt. shops, E. Rochester, N.Y., 1966-67, prodn. mgr. Beech Grove Works, Indpls., 1967-68; gen. supt. Harmon Diesel and Elec. Shops, Penn. Central Transo. Co., Croton-on-Hudson, N.Y., 1968-69, system mgr. planning and devel., Phila., 1969-70, dir. intermodal ops., Phila., 1970-71; sr. assoc. dir. transp. ops. Booz, Allen and Hamilton, Phila., 1971-73; dir. bicentennial transp. programs City of Phila., 1973-74, dep. mayor, 1974-76; v.p. Boston and Maine Corp., Boston, 1976-83; v.p. Delaware and Hudson Ry., Boston and Maine Corp., Maine Central R.R. Co., 1983-85; corporate v.p. Guilford Industries, 1983-85; corporate sec. Guilford Aviation Corp., 1983-85; group pres. Hill Internat., Inc., 1985-88; pres., chief exec. officer Gibbs & Hill, Inc., N.Y.C., 1988—, also bd. dirs.; chmn. Hill Mgmt. Services; chmn. Candeal Flessig & Assocs., N.Y.C., 1988—; dir. Springfield Terminal Co. Chmn. Mayor's task force for transp. quality, Phila., 1974-76; mem. Market St. East Council, 1974-76, Delaware Valley Council, 1974-76; Delaware Valley Regional Planning Commn., 1974-76. Recipient spl. recognition award for bicentennial planning, Phila., 1976. Mem. ASCE, ASME, Assn. Am. Railroads (gen. com. 1981—), Constrn. Mgmt. Assn., Am. Pub. Transit Assn., Transp. Research Forum, World Affairs Council Phila., U. Ill. Alumni Assn. (life), Illini Club Phila. (v.p.). Republican. Home: Holly Hill Dr Amherst NH 03031 Office: Gibbs & Hill 11 Penn Plaza New York NY 10001

GRACE, J. PETER, business executive; b. Manhasset, N.Y., May 25, 1913; s. Joseph and Janet (Macdonald) G.; m. Margaret Fennelly, May 24, 1941. Student, St. Paul's Sch., Concord, N.H., 1927-32; B.A., Yale U., 1936; LLD (hon.), Mt. St. Mary's Coll., Manhattan Coll., Fordham U., Boston Coll., U. Notre Dame, Belmont Abbey, Stonehill Coll., Christian Bros. Coll., Adelphi U., Furman U., Rider Coll., Mt. St. Vincent Coll.; Dr. Latin Am. Relations, St. Joseph's Coll.; D.Sc., Clarkson Coll.; D.C.S., St. John's U.; L.H.D., Fairleigh Dickinson U., Assumption Coll., The Citadel, Stevens Inst. Tech. With W.R. Grace & Co., N.Y.C., 1936—, sec., 1942, dir., 1943—, v.p., 1945, pres., chief exec. officer, 1945-81, chmn., chief exec. officer, 1981—, pres., 1986—; chmn. bd. dirs. Chemed Corp., Taco Villa, Inc., Restaurant Enterprises Group, Inc., Centennial Ins. Co.; hon. dir. Brascan Ltd.; dir. emeritus Ingersoll-Rand Co.; dir. Stone & Webster, Inc., Omnicare, Inc., Roto-Rooter, Inc., Universal Furniture Ltd., Milliken & Co., Atlantic Reins. Co., Nat. Sanitary SUpply Co.; trustee Atlantic Mut. Ins. Co. Bd. dirs., pres. Cath. Youth Orgn. of Archdiocese of N.Y.; bd. dirs. Boys Clubs Am.; chmn. Radio Free Europe/Radio Liberty Fund, Inc.; pres., trustee Grace Inst.; mem. pres.'s com. Greater N.Y., corp. grants com., emeritus trustee com., Notre Dame U.; chmn. council nat. trustees Nat. Jewish Ctr. for Immunology and Respiratory Medicine, Denver; chmn. Pres.'s Pvt. Sector Survey on Cost Control in Fed. Govt., 1982-84; co-chmn. Citizens Against Govt. Waste; trustee U.S. Council for Internat. Bus.; bd. govs. Thomas Aquinas Coll.; chmn., dir. Amerishares Found., Inc.; bd. dirs. Americares Found. Recipient Sovereign Milit. Order Malta, Knight Grand Cross, Equestrian Order Holy Sepulchre of Jerusalem, Knights of Malta; decorated by govts. of Colombia, Chile, Ecuador, Panama, Peru. Mem. Newcomen Soc., Council on Fgn. Relations. Clubs: Madison Square Garden (gov.), Links, Meadow Brook, Pacific Union (San Francisco), Everglades, Lotus, Lost Tree, River, Deepdale. Office: W R Grace & Co Grace Plaza 1114 Ave of Americas New York NY 10036-7794

GRACE, MICHAEL EDWARD, corporate executive; b. Sydney, New South Wales, Australia, Feb. 20, 1943; s. Bert Augustus and Vera Jean (Miller) G.; m. Carole Anita Proper, June 19, 1967; children: Andrew, Nicholas, Theodore. B Commerce, U. New South Wales, 1964; MBA, Stanford U., 1967. Mng. dir. Grace Bros. Pty. Ltd., Sydney, 1974-84, chmn., 1982—; mng. dir. Paynter Dixon Pty. Ltd., Sydney, 1986-87; chmn. Paynter Dixon Holdings Ltd., Sydney, 1987—; dep. mng. dir. Myer Emporium Ltd., Melbourne, Victoria, Australia, 1983-86; bd. dirs. Advance Bank of Australia, Ltd., Sydney, Sigma Data, Sydney, RF Tech Pty., Ltd., Sydney. Councillor U. New South Wales, Sydney; gov. Youth Bus. Initiative. Fellow Austrialian Inst. Mgmt., Retail Mgmt. Inst. (chmn.). Club: Royal Sydney Golf. Office: Paynter Dixon Pty Ltd, 320 Liverpool Rd, 2131 Ashfield New South Wales, Australia

GRADIN, ANITA, Swedish politician; b. Hornefors, Vasterbotten, Sweden, Aug. 12, 1933; d. Ossian and Alfhild (Englund) G.; m. Bertil Kersfelt; one child, Catherine. Grad., Coll. Social Work and Pub. Adminstrn., Stockholm, 1960. Journalist, Vasterbottens Folkblad, 1950, Arbetarbladet, Gavle, Sweden, 1956-58, Central Orgn. of Salaried Employees, Sweden, 1960-63; mem. staff Social-Welfare Planning Com., Stockholm, 1963-67; sr. adminstrv. officer Cabinet Office, Sweden, 1967-68, mem. Swedish Parliament, standing coms. on edn. and fin., del. Council of Europe, since 1968, minister for migrant and equality affairs, 1982-86; minister for fgn. trade, 1986—. Sec. com. women's affairs Stockholm Central Bd. Adminstrn., 1963-67; mem. Stockholm City Council, 1966-68; chmn. dist. br. Fedn. Social Democratic Women, Stockholm, 1968-82, vice-chmn. Nat. Fedn. Social Democratic Women in Sweden, 1975—; vice chmn. Socialist Internat., 1986; chmn. Socialist Internat. Women, 1986—; chmn. migration, refugees and demographic questions com. Council of Europe, 1978-82; chmn. Swedish Assn. of Graduates from Schs. of Social Work and Pub. Adminstrn., Union Socionomists, 1978-82; chmn. Council Internat., Adoptions, 1973-80. Address: Ministry for Fgn Affairs, Trade Dept, Stockholm Sweden

GRAEF, LUTHER WILLIAM, civil engineer; b. Milw., Aug. 14, 1931; s. John and Pearl (Luther) G.; B.C.E., Marquette U., 1952; M.C.E., U. Wis., 1961; m. Lorraine Linnerud, Sept. 18, 1954; children—Ronald, Sharon, Gerald. Engr., C.W. Yoder & Assos., cons. engrs., Milw., 1956-61; partner Graef-Anhalt-Schloemer, cons. engrs., Milw., 1961—; chmn. bd., pres. Graef Anhalt Schloemer Assos., Inc., Milw., 1967-—; chmn. engr. adv. com. U. Wis., Milw., also U. Wis. extensions. Active Boy Scouts Am. Chmn. bd. assessment, City of Milw., 1962-—. Served to 1st lt. AUS, 1953-56. Named Disting Marquette U. alumnus, 1982, Wis. Profl. Engr. of Yr., 1983. Mem. ASCE (sect. pres. 1968), Nat., Wis. socs. profl. engrs., Cons. Engrs. Council Wis. (pres. 1973-75), Engrs. Scientists Milw. (pres. 1975), Marquette U. Alumni Assn., Tau Beta Pi, Pi Mu Epsilon, Chi Epsilon. Lutheran (pres. ch. council 1969). Home: 3788 S Massachusetts St Milwaukee WI 53220 Office: 345 N 95 St Milwaukee WI 53226

GRAEFF, DAVID WAYNE, maintenance executive, consultant; b. West Reading, Pa., Oct. 24, 1946; s. Wayne Samuel and Sara (Spohn) G.; m. Linda Ruth Lohrke, Aug. 17, 1968; children—Hether, Rebecca, Matthew. B.S.M.E., Ind. Inst. Tech., 1969. Lic. in sewage treatment plant and waterworks, Pa. Maintenance engr. Central Soya, Decatur, Ind., 1969-71; mfg. engr. Nat. Seal div. Fed. Mogul, Van Wert, Ohio, 1971-73; facilities engr. Kawecki Berylco div. Cabot, Reading, Pa., 1973-76; plant engr. Willson Products div. E.S.B., Reading, 1976-78; maintenance supt. Brush-Wellman Inc., Reading, 1978—; maintenance cons. Maintenance Inc., Fleetwood, Pa., 1976—. Vice comr. USCG Aux., Reading, 1983-84, cert. marine examiner, 1982—, info. system officer, 1984. Mem. Soc. Mfg. Engrs., Am. Water Works Assn., Am. Inst. Plant Engrs., Am. Inst. Chem. Engrs., Theta Xi, Ducks Unlimited. Republican. Lutheran. Lodge: Moose. Avocations: boating; woodworking. Home: 815 Forest St Fleetwood PA 19522 Office: Brush-Wellman Inc Shoemakersville Rd Shoemakersville PA 19555

GRAESER, ANDREAS, philosophy educator; b. Greiz, Germany, Nov. 7, 1942; s. Ernst and Edith (Thalmann) G.; m. Eva Marie Isele, Nov. 7, 1980; 1 dau., Isabelle. Student U. Berne, 1965-66; Dr.Phil., Justus Liebig U., 1967; postgrad. Goethe U., 1967-68; M.A., Princeton U., 1969, Ph.D., 1970. Faculty, U. Berne (Switzerland), 1970—, asst., 1970-72, sr. lectr., 1972-78, prof. dept. philosophy, 1979—, dir. dept., 1979— , dean of faculty, 1984-85; vis. prof. U. Zurich, 1978-79, U. Fribourg, 1982-83, 83-84, U. Tex., Austin, 1986. Author: Probleme der Platonischen Seelenteilungslehre, 1969; Plotinus and the Stoics, 1972; Die logischen Fragmente des Theophrast, 1973; Zenon von Kition, 1975; Platons Ideenlehre, 1975; Philosophie der Antike: Sophistik, Sokratik, Platon und Aristoteles, 1983; Kommentar zur Einleitung von Hegels Phänomenologie des Geistes, 1986. Editor 3 books. Contbr. articles to books and jours. Mem. Inst. Advanced Study (Princeton), Philos. Soc. Switzerland (sec. 1976-85). Lutheran. Home: Wasserwerkgasse 33,, CH-3011 Berne, Switzerland Office: Philosophisches Institut, Falkenplatz 16, 3012 Berne,, Switzerland

GRAF, ERVIN DONALD, municipal administrator; b. Crow Rock, Mont., Mar. 9, 1930; s. Emanuel and Lydia (Bitz) G.; m. Carolyn Sue Robinson, Mar. 15, 1956 (div. 1958); m. Eleanor Mahlein, Apr. 13, 1959; children: Debra, Belinda, Corrina, Melanie, Ervin Jr. Enlisted U.S. Army, 1948; served two tours of duty in Vietna; ret. U.S. Army, 1972; with office and maintenance staff Greenfields Irrigation Dist., Fairfield, Mont., 1972-77, sec. to Bd. Commrs., 1977—. Decorated Bronze star with oak leaf cluster. Mem. Am. Legion (all offices Post #80 and Dist. 8 incl. dist. comdr.). Democrat. Lutheran. Home: 211 6th St N Fairfield MT 59436 Office: Greenfields Irrigation Dist Central Ave W Fairfield MT 59436

GRAF, KARL-HEINZ GUENTER, electronics company executive, consultant; b. Vienna, Austria, Dec. 8, 1941; came to U.S., 1954, naturalized, 1960; s. Ignaz Gunter Graf and Hildegard (Kuhfusz) Lutz; m. Edith Martha Guddat, Feb. 28, 1969 (div. Jan. 1986); children: Stephen, Thomas, Monika. Student, Colo. State U., 1961. Communications specialist AT&T Long Lines, Tucson, 1961-63; communications engr. Herman Kaets TS Co, Frankfurt, Germany, 1968-72; customer service rep. Magnavox System Inc., Denver, 1972-73; customer service specialist 3M BPSI, Denver, 1973-74; field engr. Rapicom, Denver, 1974-84; advanced product specialist Rapicom/Ricoh Corp., Denver, 1984-85; internat. tech. mgr. mgr. Ricoh Corp., Denver, 1985—; communication cons., Denver, 1972—; product tchr. Rapicom/Ricoh, Worldwide, 1978—. Developer product test equipment Protocol Decoder, 1983. Exec. officer CAP, Tucson, 1963; active PTA, Denver, 1984. Served with U.S. Army, 1964-68. Recipient Disting. Service award Rapicom Inc., 1983. Mem. Denver Amateur Computer Soc., Amateur Radio Soc., Denver Kaypro Assn. (bd. dirs. 1986-87). Republican. Home: 1356 S Tennyson St Denver CO 80219 Office: Ricoh Corp Box 19388 Denver CO 80219

GRAF, OTTO WALTER, JR., retired entomologist, acarologist, biologist, educator; b. San Francisco, May 26, 1925; s. Otto Walter and and Mildred Ilyne (Morrison) G.; m. Anne Marie Minaker, Mar. 7, 1953; children—Catherine, David, Paul, Lloyd, John, Walter, Matthew, Robert. A.B., San Francisco State Coll., 1952; M.A., U. San Francisco, 1979; postgrad. Stanford U., Duke U., U. Calif.-Berkeley, Calif. State U.-Hayward. Secondary teaching credential, Calif. Profl. asst. San Francisco State Coll., 1950-51; film librarian, supr. student sect. Calif. Acad. Scis., 1954-62; instr. U. Calif.-Berkeley, 1956-61, Washington High Sch., Fremont, Calif. 1955-84. Active Boy Scouts Am., Republican Party. Served with USN, 1943-46; to 1st lt., U.S. Army, 1951-54. Decorated Pacific Theatre ribbon, Am. Theatre ribbon, Korean ribbon, 2 Presidential Unit citations, Presidential citation, Korean Merit citation; recipient Silver Beaver award, Boy Scouts Am., 1971; Outstanding Secondary Tchr. award, 1974; NSF grantee; Biol. Scis. Curriculum Studies grantee. Mem. Pan Pacific Entomol. Soc., Nat. Sci. Tchrs. Assn., Korean War Vets. Assn., Nat. Assn. Biology Tchrs., E. Africa Wild Life Soc., Internat. Wildlife Fedn., Nat. Wildlife Fedn., VFW, Am. Legion. Roman Catholic. Author: Key to the Mosquitos of Korea, 1951, Flies of Medical and Veternary Importance of Japan & Korea, 1952; Nature Games for the Secondary School, 1979; designed trap for live mice in Korea. Home: 5151 Tenaya Ave Newark CA 94560-2653

GRAF, PETER GUSTAV, accountant, lawyer; b. Vienna, Austria, June 19, 1936; came to U.S. 1940, naturalized, 1945; m. Rosalie Greenbaum, Apr. 6, 1963; 1 child, Paul Evan. B.S. in Econs., U. Pa., 1957; LL.B., NYU, 1960, LL.M., 1962. Bar: N.Y. 1960; C.P.A., N.Y. Tax acct. J.K. Lasser & Co., N.Y.C., 1961-62; with Joseph Graf & Co., N.Y.C., 1962—, ptnr., 1966—; v.p., founder, dir. AGS Computers Inc., N.J., 1967—; ptnr., founder, treas., dir. Nardin Gallery, Inc., Cross River, N.Y.; founder Cable Systems USA Assocs., W.Va., Pa. and Ohio; founder USA Mobile Communications, Inc. Mem. Am. Inst. C.P.A.s, N.Y. State Soc. C.P.A.s, N.Y. State Bar Assn. Home: 87 Holly Place Briarcliff Manor NY 10510 Office: Joseph Graf and Co 6 E 43rd St New York NY 10017

GRAFF, HAROLD, psychiatrist, psychoanalyst, hospital administrator; b. Phila., Apr. 11, 1932; s. Joseph and Blanche (Katz) G.; m. Diane Goldblum; children: David, Caron, Robert. BA, U. Pa., 1954, MD, 1958. Intern Phila. Gen. Hosp., 1958-59; resident Inst. Pa. Hosp., Phila., 1959-62; postdoctoral fellow Inst. Neurol. Sci., U. Pa., 1959-62; psychoanalytic trainee Inst. of Phila. Assn. for Psychoanalysis, Bala Cynwyd, Pa., 1962-67; research scientist, dept. clin. sci. Eastern Pa. Psychiat. Inst., Phila., 1963-74; dir. div. psychoanalytic studies, dept. clin. research and tng. Eastern Pa. Psychiat. Inst., 1974-79; dir. adolescent psychiatry Pa. Dept. Pub. Welfare, 1977-79; chmn. research and publs. com. Inst. of the Pa. Hosp., Phila., 1968-78; chmn. psychoanalytic research group 1968-78; clin. assoc. prof. psychiatry Health Scis. Center Temple U., 1974-77; research asst. prof. psychiatry Hahnemann Med. Coll., Phila., 1963-70; assoc. prof. Hahnemann Med. Coll., 1970-74; vis. prof., psychiat. cons. Inst. for Human Resource Devel., 1974-76; clin. prof. psychiatry and human behavior Jefferson Med. Coll., 1977—; vis. faculty Inst. of Phila. Assn. for Psychoanalysis, 1971-86; pres., research dir. Psychiat. Services, Inc., Wynnewood, Pa., 1969-81; chief of psychiatry St. Francis Hosp., 1980-88, adolescent clin. dir.; staff Inst. of Pa. Hosp., Wilmington Med. Center, Phila. Psychiatry, Rockford Center, clin. dir. Adolescent Psychiatry, 1987—; spl. cons. Spl. Action Office for Drug Abuse Prevention, Washington, 1973-74; cons. psychiatry Republic of Panama, 1980. Contbr. articles to profl. jours. Fellow Am. Pa. psychiat. assns., Phila. Coll. Physicians; mem. Del. Psychiat. Soc. (counsellor 1981-83, treas. 1983, sec. 1985-86, pres. 1987-88), Am. Soc. Adolescent Psychiatry (chmn. Eastern States liaison com. 1977-78, cluster chmn. internal affairs 1979-81), Phila. Soc. Adolescent Psychiatry (pres. 1978-79), AMA, Del., New Castle County med. assns., Internat., Am., Phila. psychoanalytic assns., AAUP, Med. Club Phila., Phila. Coll. Physicians, Del. Assn. Child and Adolescent Psychiatry (pres. 1984-86), Dirs. of Psychiatry in Del. (chmn. 1982-87), N.Y. Acad. Sci., AAAS, Mensa, Phi Beta Kappa. Clubs: Rodney Square, University and Whist. Home: 4101 Pyles Ford Rd Greenville DE 19807 also: Trolley Sq Suite 22B Wilmington DE 19806

GRAFF, HENRY FRANKLIN, historian, educator; b. N.Y.C., Aug. 11, 1921; s. Samuel F. and Florence Babette (Morris) G.; m. Edith Krantz, June 16, 1946; children: Iris Joan (Mrs. Andrew R. Morse), Ellen Toby. B.S.S., Coll. City N.Y., 1941; M.A., Columbia, 1942, Ph.D., 1949. Fellow history Coll. City N.Y., 1941-42, tutor history, 1946; lectr. history Columbia, 1946-47; instr. to asso. prof. 1946-61, prof. history, 1961—, chmn. dept. history, 1961-64; lectr. Vassar Coll., 1953; chmn. advanced placement com. Am. history Coll. Entrance Exam. Bd., 1959-63; mem. Nat. Hist. Publs. Commn., 1965-71; mem. hist. adv. com. to sec. Air Force, 1972-80; acad. cons. Gen. Learning Corp., Time-Life Books; cons. editor Alfred A. Knopf, Inc.; hist. adviser to CBS for Bicentennial TV series The American Parade, 1973-76; hist. adviser to ABC for TV series Our World, 1986-87, to CBS for Presidential Portraits, 1987—; dir. Rand McNally Co., trustee Columbia U. Press, 1987—. Author: Bluejackets with Perry in Japan, 1952, (with Jacques Barzun) The Modern Researcher, 1962, rev. edit., 1970, 3d edit., 1977, 4th edit., 1985, (with Clifford Lord) American Themes, 1963, (with John A. Krout) The Adventure of the American People, 3d edit, 1973, The Free and the Brave, 4th edit, 1980, Thomas Jefferson, 1968, American Imperialism and the Philippine Insurrection, 1969, The Tuesday Cabinet, 1970, (with Paul J. Bohannan) The Call of Freedom, 1978, The Promise of Democracy, 1978, This Great Nation, 1983, The Presidents: a Reference History, 1984, America: the Glorious Republic, 1985, rev. edit. 1988. Cons. editor: Life's History of the United States, 1963-64; Contbr. articles to profl. jours. Served to 1st lt. AUS, 1942-46. Recipient citation War Dept.; Am. Council Learned Socs. fellow, 1942; Townsend Harris medal CCNY, 1966; Mark Van Doren award Columbia U., 1981; Gt. Tchr. award Columbia U., 1982. Mem. Orgn. Am. Historians, Am. Hist. Assn., Council Fgn. Relations, Author's Guild, P.E.N., Nat. Council Social Studies, Soc. Am. Historians, Soc. Historians Am. Fgn. Relations, Phi Beta Kappa. Club: Century Assn. (N.Y.C.). Home: 47 Andrea Ln Scarsdale NY 10583 Office: Fayerweather Hall Columbia U New York NY 10027

GRAFFEO, EMILY EARLE, mechanical engineer; b. Birmingham, Ala., Nov. 2, 1955; d. Harry U. and Frankie (Bloodworth) E.; B.S.M.E., Auburn U., 1979; m. Anthony C. Graffeo, Nov. 25, 1979; 1 dau., Amber. Project engr. Square D Co., Leeds, Ala., 1979—; engr., warranty reduction team leader Chrysler Corp., Huntsville, Ala., 1987—. Trustee, Aldersgate United Meth. Ch., 1983-84. Mem. ASME (treas. 1982-84, chmn. 1984). Home: 1209 Todd Mill Circle Huntsville AL 35803 Office: 102 Wynn Dr Plant 1 Huntsville AL 35805

GRAF PFEIL, ENZIO ALEXANDER, economist; b. Windhoek, Namibia, Sept. 7, 1953; s. Friedrich Karl and Helena Paulina (Botha) G.P. PhD in Econs., U. Freiburg, Fed. Republic Germany, 1980. Asst. prof. econs. U. Freiburg, 1978-80; trainee, treas. Morgan Guaranty Trust, Frankfurt, Fed. Republic Germany, N.Y.C., 1980-82; currency risk advisor, asst. mgr. J. Henry Schroder Wagg, London, 1982-84; investment counselor, asst. v.p. Am. Express Bank, London, 1984-86; chief economist Smith New Ct. Far East, London, 1986—; lectr., sr. vis. fellow City U. Bus. Sch., London, 1986—. Author: German Direct Investment In The USA, 1986, Effective Control of Currency Risks, 1988; contbr. articles to profl. jours. Named Eagle Scout Boy Scouts Am., 1968; Studienstiftung Des Deutschen Volkes, 1975, Friedrich Naumann Stifting, 1979. Mem. The Soc. Authors. Home: 3 Weller Ct, 66-68 Ladbroke Rd, London W11 3NT, England Office: Smith New Ct Far East, Chetwynd House, 24 St Swithin's Ln, London EC4N 8AE, England

GRAHAM, ARNOLD HAROLD, lawyer, educator; b. N.Y.C., Dec. 29, 1917; s. Julius E. and Rose Goldstein; m. Roselle Lesser, Dec. 23, 1939; children: Stuart R., Joel M., Jul E. B.S. with honors, NYU, 1945; LL.B., J.D. with honors, N.Y. Law Sch., 1952. Bar: N.Y. 1952, U.S. Supreme Ct. 1959, also U.S. Internat. Trade 1959, U.S. Tax Ct. 1959, U.S. Ct. Appeals for 2d Circuit 1959, U.S. Dist. Ct. for Hawaii 1959; C.P.A., N.Y. Practice pub. acctg. N.Y.C., 1945-52, individual practice law, 1952-76; dep. atty. gen. N.Y., 1952-54; cons. N.Y. Law Sch., N.Y.C., 1952-76; asst. dean, prof., treas. N.Y. Law Sch., 1976-77, vice dean, prof., treas., 1977-85, cons., 1985—; cons., arbitrator Am. Arbitration Assn., 1952—; examiner of attys., N.Y.C.; law cons. exam. div. Am. Inst. C.P.A.s, 1976—; bd. visitors Appellate div., 1st dept. Supreme Ct. N.Y.; mem. jud. screening panel bankruptcy div. U.S. Dist. Ct. for So. Dist. N.Y., 1983-84; numerous guardianship appointments N.Y. State Supreme Ct., Surrogate's Ct.; mem. ind. screening panel Civil Ct. of City of N.Y., 1984. Trustee Ave R Temple, Kings Hwy. Bd. Trade; bd. advisers United Jewish Appeal; mem. exec. com. trusts and estates div. United Jewish Appeal-Fedn. Jewish Philanthropies. Recipient Ira Stone award for prof. of yr. N.Y. Law Sch., 1981. Fellow Am. Bar Found.; mem. ABA, Am. Law Inst., Am. Assn. Attys.-C.P.A.s (founder), Am. Trial Lawyers Assn., N.Y. Trial Lawyers Assn., Consular Law Soc., Fed. Bar Assn., Am. Bar Assn., Inst. Jud. Adminstrn., N.Y. State C.P.A. Soc., Fed. Bar Council, N.Y. County Lawyers Assn., Am. Arbitration Assn., Jewish Lawyers' Guild, Phi Delta Phi (hon., Disting. Alumnus award Dwight Inn). Jewish. Club: Merchants. Office: 2223 Ave T Brooklyn NY 11229

GRAHAM, D. ROBERT (BOB GRAHAM), U.S. senator, former governor; b. Coral Gables, Fla., Nov. 9, 1936; m. Adele Khoury; children: Gwendolyn Patricia, Glynn Adele, Arva Suzanne, Kendall Elizabeth. B.A., U. Fla., 1959; LL.B., Harvard U., 1962. Atty.; cattle and dairy farmer; real estate develope; mem. Fla. Ho. of Reps., 1966-70, Fla. Senate, 1971-78; gov. State of Fla., Tallahassee, 1979-87; U.S. Senator from Fla. Washington, 1987—; chmn. Edn. Commn. of the States, 1980-81, Caribbean/Central Am. Action, 1980-81, U.S. intergovtl. adv. council on edn.; mem. So. Growth Policies Bd., chmn., 1982-83; chmn. So. Govs.' Assn.; chmn. com. trade and fgn. affairs Nat. Govs.' Assn. Active 4-H Youth Found., Nat. Commn. on Reform Secondary Edn., Nat. Found. Improvement Edn., Nat. Com. for Citizens in Edn., Sr. Centers of Dade County, Fla.; chmn. So. Regional Edn. Bd., 1979-81. Named one of 5 Most Outstanding Young Men in Fla. Fla. Jaycees, 1971; recipient Allen Morris award for outstanding 1st term mem. senate, 1972, Allen Morris award for most valuable mem. senate, 1973, Allen Morris award for 2d most effective senator, 1976. Mem. Fla. Bar Assn. Democrat. Mem. United Ch. of Christ. Office: US Senate 241 Dirksen Senate Bldg Washington DC 20510 *

GRAHAM, HERBERT BAXTER, computer systems company executive, consultant systems integration; b. Louisville, Sept. 8, 1935; s. Herbert Montgomery and Gladys Marie (Graham) G.; m. Carol Margarette Kinsinger, June 14, 1958 (dec. Jan. 1979); children: Herbert, Brenda, Krista, Linda. B in Mech. Engring., U. Louisville, 1959, M in Mech. Engring., 1961; postgrad. U. St. Louis, 1960. Indsl. engr. Eastman Kodak Co., Rochester, N.Y., 1962-65; founder, pres. Data Scis. Engring., Silver Spring, Md., 1965-73; exec. dir. Nat. Ctr. for Prosecution Mgmt., Washington, 1973-77; founder, pres. Precision Media Corp., Silver Spring, Md., 1977-83; pres. Graham Assoc., Silver Spring, Md., 1983—; cons. Planning Research Corp., McLean, Va., 1985—. Patentee disposable culture device; developer Trac-it and Grasp Computer Software. Vice pres. PTA, Silver Spring, 1973. Served to capt. USAF, 1959-62. Republican. Avocation: flying. Home: 9212 Woodland Dr Silver Spring MD 20910 Office: 9009 Rhode Island Ave College Park MD 20740

GRAHAM, JAMES HERBERT, dermatologist; b. Calexico, Calif., Apr. 25, 1921; s. August K. and Esther (Choudoin) G.; m. Anna Kathryn Luiken, June 30, 1950 (dec. May 1987); children: James Herbert, John A., Angela Joann. Student, Brawley Jr. Coll., 1941-42; A.B., Emory U., 1945; M.D., Med. Coll. Ala., 1949. Diplomate: Am. Bd. Dermatology (dir. 1977-87, v.p. 1985-86, pres. 1986-87, Disting. Service medal 1987); diplomate in dermatopathology Am. Bd. Dermatology and Am. Bd. Pathology. Intern Jefferson-Hillman Hosp., Birmingham, Ala., 1949-50; resident in dermatology VA Center and UCLA Med. Center, 1953-56; clin. asst. instr. in medicine UCLA, 1954-56; Osborne fellow and NRC fellow in dermal pathology Armed Forces Inst. Pathology, Washington, 1956-58; vis. scientist Armed Forces Inst. Pathology, 1958-69, chmn. dept. dermatopathology, 1980-88; registrar Registry of Dermatopathology, Armed Forces Inst. Pathology, 1980-88, also program dir. dermatopathology, 1979-88; program dir. dermatopathology Walter Reed Army Med. Center, Washington, 1979-88; asst. prof. dermatology and pathology Temple U., 1958-61, asso. prof., 1961-65, prof. dermatology, 1965-69, asso. prof. pathology, 1965-67, prof. pathology, 1967-69; prof. medicine, chief div. dermatology, prof. pathology, dir. sect. dermal pathology and histochemistry U. Calif., Irvine, 1969-78; chief dermatology U. Calif. Med. Ctr., Irvine, 1977-78; prof. emeritus Coll. Medicine, U. Calif., 1978—; head sect. dermatology Orange County (Calif.) Med. Center, 1969-73; cons. dermatology VA Hosp., Long Beach, Calif., 1969-73; chief dermatology sect. VA Hosp., 1973-78, acting chief med. service, 1976; cons. dermatology, dermal pathology Regional Naval Med. Center, San Diego, 1969-82, Long Beach, 1969-78, Camp Pendleton, Calif., 1972-78; cons. dermatology, dermal pathology Meml. Hosp. Med. Center, Long Beach, 1972-86, Fairview State Hosp., Costa Mesa, Calif., 1969-78; cons. for career devel. for rev. clin. investigator applications VA Central Office, Washington, 1973-78; Disting. Eminent physician VA physician and dentist-in-residence program, 1980-88; mem. organizational com. Am. Registry Pathology, Armed Forces Inst. Pathology, Washington, 1976-77; mem. exec. com. Am. Registry Pathology, Armed Forces Inst. Pathology, 1977-78; prof. dermatology, clin. prof. pathology Uniformed Services U. of Health Scis., Bethesda, Md., 1979-88, prof. emeritus, 1989—. Sr. author: Dermal Pathology, 1972; contbr. articles to profl. publs. Served with M.C. USNR, 1949-53. Mem. AMA and Accreditation Council for Grad. Med. Edn. (residency rev. subcom. for dermatopathology 1974-87, mem. residency rev. com. dermatology 1977-87, chmn. 1984-87, cert. of merit 1960), Assn. Profs. Dermatology, Soc. Investigative Dermatology, U.S. and Can. Acad. Pathology, Am. Assn. Pathologists, Am. Dermatol. Assn. (essay award 1958, v.p. 1986-87), Am. Soc. Dermatopathology (pres. 1975-76), Dermatopathology Club (pres. 1980-81), Assn. Mil. Dermatologists, Am. Acad. Dermatology (dir. 1974-77, 82, v.p. 1980-81, rep. to bd. mems. Am. Registry Pathology 1977-78), Pa. Acad. Dermatology, Pacific Dermatologic Assn. (dir. 1972-75, hon. mem. 1981), Dermatology Found., Phila. Dermatol. Soc. (pres. 1967-68), Alpha Omega Alpha. Club: Cosmos (Washington).

GRAHAM, JOHN BORDEN, medical educator; b. Goldsboro, N.C., Jan. 26, 1918; s. Ernest Heap and Mary (Borden) G.; m. Ruby Barrett, Mar. 23, 1943; children: Charles Barrett, Virginia Borden, Thomas Wentworth. B.S., Davidson Coll., 1938, D.Sc. (hon.), 1984; M.D., Cornell U., 1942. Asst. Cornell U., 1943-44; mem. faculty U. N.C., Chapel Hill, 1946—; Alumni Disting. prof. pathology U. N.C., 1966—, chmn. genetics curriculum, 1963-85, assoc. dean medicine for basic scis., 1968-70, coordinator interdisciplinary grad. programs in biology, 1968—, dir. hemostasis program, 1974-87; vis. prof. haematology St. Thomas's Hosp. Med. Sch., London, 1972; vis. prof. Teikyo U. Med. Sch., Tokyo, 1976; mem. selection com. NIH research career awards, 1959-62; genetics tng. com. USPHS, 1962-66, chmn., 1967-71; mem. genetic basis of disease com. Nat. Inst. Gen. Med. Scis., 1977-80; mem. pathology test com. Nat. Bd. Med. Examiners, 1963-67; mem. research adv. com. U. Colo. Inst. Behavioral Genetics, 1967-71; mem. Internat. Com. Haemostasis and Thrombosis, 1963-67; chmn. bd. U. N.C. Population Program, 1964-67; sec. policy bd. Carolina Population Center, 1972-78; cons. Environ. Health Center, USPHS, WHO; Bolt, Beranek & Newman, Inc.; mem. med. and sci. adv. council Nat. Hemophilia Found., 1972-76; hon. cons. in genetics Margaret Pyke Centre, London, 1972—. Mem. editorial bd.: N.C. Med. Jour., 1949-66, Am. Jour. Human Genetics, 1958-61, Soc. Exptl. Biology and Medicine, 1959-62, Human Genetics Abstracts, 1962-72, Haemostasis, 1975-80, Christian Scholar, 1958-60. Markle scholar in med. sci., 1949-54; Recipient O. Max Gardner award U. N.C., 1968. Mem. AMA, AAAS, Elisha Mitchell Sci. Soc. (pres. 1963), AAUP, Soc. Exptl. Biology and Medicine, Am. Soc. Exptl. Pathology, Assn. Univ. Pathologists, Am. Assn. Pathologists and Bacteriologists, Am. Soc. Human Genetics (sec. 1964-67, pres. 1972), Genetics Soc. Am., Internat. Soc. Hematology, Am. Inst. Biol. Sci., Royal Soc. Medicine (London), Med. Soc. N.C., Mayflower Soc., Sigma Xi. Democrat. Presbyterian. Home: 108 Glendale Dr Chapel Hill NC 27514

GRAHAM, JUL ELIOT, lawyer, educator; b. Bklyn., June 14, 1953; s. Arnold Harold and Roselle (Lesser) G.; m. Sherry Robin Goldberg, Nov. 2, 1980. B.A. in Polit. Sci. cum laude, NYU, 1975; J.D. magna cum laude, N.Y. Law Sch., 1978. Bar: N.Y. 1979, U.S. Supreme Ct. 1984. Cons. Consumer Law Tng. Ctr., N.Y. Law Sch., 1976, mem. adj. faculty, 1980—; appellate law research asst. appellate div. 1st Dept., Supreme Ct. of State of N.Y., N.Y.C., 1978-79, staff atty., 1979-82, assoc. atty., 1982-83, law asst. to the justices, 1983—, exec. sec. deptl. adv. com. to family ct., 1979-82, editor criminal trial advocacy handbook, 1980—. Assoc. editor N.Y. Law Sch. Law Rev., 1976-78, contbg. author, 1975. Guest lectr. Joe Franklin Show, WOR-TV, 1982—. Mem. N.Y. County Lawyers Assn. (com. on communications and entertainment law 1980—, com. on penal and correctional reform 1980—, spl. com. on practical legal edn. 1979—), Am. Arbitration Assn. (arbitrator 1985—), Internat. Radio and TV Soc., Am. Film Inst., Phi Delta Phi, Phi Sigma Alpha. Home: 249 Adelaide Ave Staten Island NY 10306 Office: NY State Supreme Ct Appellate Div 1st Jud Dept 41 Madison Ave New York NY 10010

GRAHAM, KATHARINE, newspaper executive; b. N.Y.C., June 16, 1917; d. Eugene and Agnes (Ernst) Meyer; m. Philip L. Graham, June 5, 1940 (dec. 1963); children: Elizabeth Morris Graham Weymouth, Donald Edward, William Welsh, Stephen Meyer. Student, Vassar Coll., 1934-36; AB, U. Chgo., 1938. Reporter San Francisco News, 1938-39; mem. editorial staff Washington Post, 1939-45, mem. Sunday, circulation and editorial depts., pub., 1968-79; pres. Washington Post Co., 1963-73, 77, chmn. bd., 1973—; bd. dirs. Bowater Mersey Paper Co., Ltd., Urban Inst., Fed. City Council, Council for Aid to Edn.; hon. conf. trustee, U. Chgo.; trustee George Washington U.; mem. sr. adv. bd. of the Joan Shorenstein Barone Ctr. on the Press, Politics and Pub. Policy, Harvard U. Fellow Am. Acad. Arts and Scis.; mem. Am. Soc. Newspaper Editors, Nat. Press Club, Sigma Delta Chi. Clubs: Cosmopolitan (N.Y.C.); 1925 F Street. Office: Washington Post Co 1150 15th St NW Washington DC 20071

GRAHAM, LAURA MARGARET (LAURA GRAHAM FORBES), artist; b. Washington, Ind.; d. Ray Austin and Eugenia Bruce (Winston) Graham; student Sacred Heart Convents (Grosse Pointe, Mich., Noroton, Conn., N.Y.C.) Westover and Nightingale Schs.; studied art Art Students League, with Bridgman and Frank du Mond; Grand Central Art Sch.; Traphagen Art Sch.; pvt. study with Mead Schaeffer, Henry Rittenberg, N.A. and Edward Dufner, N.A.; grad. Sch. Adult Edn., N.Y. U., 1965; m. Clifford Lee Forbes, May 4, 1940 (div.); 1 son. Exhibited paintings John Herron Art Mus., Indpls., N.Y. Water Color Club, Am. Water Color Soc., N.A.D. (youngest artist exhibiting Nov. 1932), Pa. Acad. Boston Art Club, Montclair Art Mus., World's Fair 1940, Contemporary Art Bldg., Conn. Acad. Fine Arts Exhibit, Allied Arts of Am., Ogunquit (Maine) Art Center, 50th Anniversary Celebration Westover Sch., Newport Art Assn., Nat. Arts Club. A sponsor N.Y. U. Chamber Music Concert, 1954—, concerts in Washington Sq. Park, 1954-55. Recipient Alexander Wall prize, 1943, Allied Artists Am. exhbn., N.Y. Nat. Arts Club, 1st prize for painting, 1939; 2d prize, 1940, 41, hon. mention, 1947, 48, 72; hon. mention Allied Artists, 1948, Art Assn. Ogunquit, Maine, 1947, 49; hon. mention and war bond, Terry Art Exhbn., Miami, Fla., 1952. Mem. Nat. Assn. Women Artists, Allied Artists of Am. (hon. artist mem.), Conn. Acad. Fine Arts (artist mem.), N.Y. U. Alumni Assn., N.Y. Hist. Soc., Museum City N.Y., Nat. Trust Historic Preservation, Victorian Soc. Am., English Speaking Union, Friends of the Philharmonic, Am. Artists Profl. League, Art Students League (life). Clubs: Nat. Arts, Pen and Brush, Women's Nat. Republican (N.Y.C.). Address: 10 Washington Sq N New York NY 10003

GRAHAM, LOLA AMANDA (BEALL) (MRS. JOHN JACKSON GRAHAM), photographer, author; b. nr. Bremen, Ga., Nov. 12, 1896; d. John Gainer and Nancy Caroline Idella (Reid) Beall; student Florence Normal Sch., 1914; m. John Jackson Graham, Aug. 3, 1917 (dec.); children—Billy Duane, John Thomas, Helen (Mrs. D. Hall), Donald, Beverly (Mrs. Bob Forson). Tchr. elem. public sch., Centerdale, Ala., 1914, Eva, Ala., 1915; free lance photographer and writer, 1950—; editor poetry column Mobile Home News, 1968-69; designer jacket cover for Reader's Digest book Our Amazing World of Nature. Recipient numerous nat. prizes, 1950—; Crossroads of Tex. grand nat. in poetry for For Every Monkey Child, 1980; executed prize-winning Sioux Indian and heirloom photog. quilts. Mem. Nat. Poetry Soc. Ina Coolbrith Poetry Soc., Chapparal Poets. Author: (booklet) How to Recycle Ancestors and Grandcestors, (poetry) Recycling Center, 1988. Contbr. photographs to Ency. Brit., also numerous mags. and books. Address: 225-93 Mount Hermon Rd Scotts Valley CA 95066

GRAHAM, MARTHA, dancer, choreographer; b. Pitts., May 11, 1894. Studied with Ruth St. Denis and Ted Shawn; LL.D., Mills Coll., Brandeis U., Smith Coll., Harvard, 1966, also numerous others. Faculty Eastman Sch., 1925. Soloist, Denishawn Co., 1920, Greenwich Village Follies, 1923, debut as choreographer-dancer, 48th St. Theatre, N.Y.C., 1926; founder, artistic dir., Martha Graham Dance Co., 1926—, also Martha Graham Sch. Contemporary Dance; choreographer with music composed by Aaron Copland, Paul Hindemith, Carlos Chavez, Samuel Barber, Gian-Carlo Menotti, William Schuman, others of more than 170 works including Appalachian Spring, Cave of the Heart, Errand into the Maze, Clytemnestra, Frontier, Phaedra, Herodiade, Primitive Mysteries, Night Journey, Seraphic Dialogue, Lamentation, Acts of Light, Rite of Spring, Judith, Heretic, Diversion of Angels, Witch of Endor, Cortege of Eagles, A Time of Snow, Plain of Prayer, Lady of the House of Sleep, Archaic Hours, Mendicants of Evening, Myth of a Voyage, Holy Jungle, Dream, Chronique, Lucifer, Scarlet Letter, Adorations, Point of Crossing; guest soloist leading U.S. orchs. in solos Judith, Triumph of St. Joan; fgn. tours with Martha Graham Dance Co., 1950, 54, 55-56, 60, 62-63, 67, 68; some under auspices U.S. Dept State; collaborated in over 25 set designs with Isamu Naguchi, also Alexander Calder; also designed costumes for many of her dances; Author: Notebooks of Martha Graham, 1973. Recipient Aspen award, 1965, Creative Arts award, Brandeis U., 1968, Disting. Service to the Arts award, Nat. Inst. Arts and Letters, 1970, Handel medallion, City of N.Y., 1970, N.Y. State Council on Arts award, 1973, Presdl. Medal of Freedom, 1976, Kennedy Center honor, 1979, Samuel H. Scripps Am. Dance Festival award, 1981, Meadows award, So. Meth. U., 1982, Gold Florin, City of Florence, 1983, Paris Medal of Honor, 1985, Arnold Gingrich Memorial award, N.Y. Arts and Bus. Council, 1985, Nat. Medal for Arts, 1985, Decorated knight Legion of Honor (France), 1983; Guggenheim fellow, 1932. Office: Martha Graham Dance Co 316 E 63d St New York NY 10021

GRAHAM, MARTHA JANE, association executive; b. Otterbein, Ind., Dec. 18, 1913; d. Wade Smith and Katherine (Switzer) Bolt; B.S., Purdue U., 1935; m. Gareth Wayne Bussell, Jan. 1, 1936 (dec. 1947); children—Barbara Sue Bussell Campbell, Jerry Wayne; m. Thomas Garland Graham, Nov. 23, 1949 (dec. 1951). Various civic and vol. positions; sec. bd. dirs. Lafayette Home Hosp., 1959-63; province pres. Alpha Chi Omega, 1956-57, nat. collegiate v.p., 1957-64, membership dir., 1964-66; pres. Atlanta Alumnae Panhellenic, 1980-81; treas. Atlanta Alpha Chi Omega Mothers Club, 1973-80, program chmn., 1980-86, 1st v.p., 1986-87, co-pres., 1987, 88, 89; treas. Atlanta Mortar Bd. Alumnae Club, 1979-81, program chmn., 1981-85, v.p., 1988; treas. Wesley Chapel Woman's Club, 1978-81, auditor, 1981-82, pres., 1983-85; auditor Atlata Bus. Womens Assn., 1988; sec. Panthersville Presbyn. Ch. Republican. Home: 572 Tahoe Circle Stone Mountain GA 30083

GRAHAM, PAMELA SMITH, distributing company executive, artist; b. Winona, Miss., Jan. 18, 1944; d. Douglas LaRue and Dorothy Jean (Hefty) Smith; m. Robert William Graham, Mar. 6, 1965 (div.); children—Jennifer, Eric; m. Thomas Paul Harley, Dec. 4, 1976; stepchildren—Tom, Janice. Student U. Colo., 1962-65, U. Cin., 1974-76. Cert. notary pub., Colo. Profl. artist, craft tchr., art exhibitor Colo., N.J., Ohio, 1968-73; property mgmt. and investor Cin., 1972-77; acct., word processor Borden Chem. Co. div. Borden, Inc., Cin., 1974-78; owner, pres. Hargram Enterprises, Cin., 1977-81; owner, pres. Graham & Harley Enterprises. Morrison, Colo., 1981—; tchr.; cons. County committeewoman Bergen County, N.J., 1972, clk. of session, 1975-79, conv. chmn., 1981; campaign chmn. United Appeal, 1977; lifeline telephone counselor Suicide Hotline, 1985—. Recipient numerous awards for art exhibits, bus. achievements, 1962—. Mem. Nat. Assn. Female Execs., United Sales Leaders Assn., Nat. Museum of Women in Arts, Colo. Artists Assn., Evergreen Artists Assn., Colo. Calligraphers Guild, Foothills Art Ctr., Alpha Gamma Chi, Kappa Kappa Gamma. Republican. Club: Queen City Racquet. Office: Graham & Harley Enterprises 4303 S Taft St Morrison CO 80465

GRAHAM, ROBERT KLARK, lens manufacturer; b. Harbor Springs, Mich., June 9, 1906; s. Frank A. and Ellen Fern (Klark) G.; A.B., Mich. State U., 1933; B.Sc. in Optics, Ohio State U., 1937; O.D. (hon.), 1987; hon. Dr. Ocular Sci., So. Calif. Coll. Optometry, 1988; children (by previous marriage)-David, Gregory, Robin, Robert K., Janis, Wesley; m. Marta Ve Everton; children: Marcia, Christie. With Bausch & Lomb, 1937-40; Western mgr. Univis Lens Co., 1940-44, sales mgr., 1945-46; v.p., dir. research Plastic Optics Co., 1946-47; pres., chmn. bd. Armorlite, Inc., 1947-78; lectr. optics Loma Linda U.; assoc. prof. So. Calif. Coll. Optometry, 1948-60. Co-founder (with Hermann J. Muller) Repository for Germinal Choice; trustee Found. Advancement of Man; bd. dirs. Inst. for Research on Morality; bd. dirs. Intra-Sci. Research Found., v.p., 1980. Recipient Herschel Gold medal Germany, Feinbloom award Am. Acad. Optometry, 1987. Fellow AAAS; mem. Am. Inst. Physics Profs., Optical Soc. Am., Am. Acad. Optometry, N.Y. Acad. Scis., Rotary Club, Mensa, Sigma Xi. Republican. Author: The Evolution of Corneal Contact Lenses; The Future of Man; also articles in sci. publs. Inventor variable focus lens, hybrid corneal lens; directed devel. hard resin lenses. Home: 3024 Sycamore Ln Escondido CA 92025 Office: Suite 300 Graham Internat Plaza 2141 Palomar Airport Rd Carlsbad CA 92009

GRAHAM, STEPHEN MICHAEL, lawyer; b. Houston, May 1, 1951; s. Frederick Mitchell and Lillian Louise (Miller) G.; m. Joanne Marie Sealock, Aug. 24, 1974; children: Aimee Elizabeth, Joseph Sealock, Jessica Anne. BS, Iowa State U., 1973; JD, Yale U., 1976. Bar: Wash. 1977. Assoc. Perkins Coie, Seattle, 1976-83, ptnr., 1983—. Bd. dirs. Wash. Spl. Olympics, Seattle,

1979-83, pres., 1983; mem. Seattle Bd. Ethics, 1982-88, chmn., 1983-88, Seattle Fair Campaign Practices Commn., 1982-88; trustee Cornish Coll. of the Arts, 1986—, exec. com., 1988—; trustee Epiphany Sch., 1987—; bd. dirs. Perkins-Coie Community Service Found. Mem. ABA, Wash. State Bar Assn., Seattle-King County Bar Assn. Episcopalian. Clubs: Wash. Athletic, Columbia Tower. Office: Perkins Coie 1201 Third Ave 40th Floor Seattle WA 98101-3099

GRAHAM, WARREN KIRKLAND, dentist; b. Albuquerque, July 22, 1938; s. Warren Reno and Alice Barbara (Eller) G.; m. Nancy Lou White, Apr. 2, 1966; children—John Warren, Jason Kirkland. B.S., U. N.Mex., 1960; D.D.S., Baylor U., 1964. Pvt. practice dentistry, Albuquerque, 1965—; clin. instr. dental programs U. N.Mex., 1968-73. Bd. dirs. N.Mex. Council on Smoking and Health, 1969-71; mem. N.Mex. Medicaid Adv. Bd., 1972-77, Mid Rio-Grande Health Planning Council, 1972-76; chmn. N.Mex. Health System Agy. Subarea Council, Dist. II, 1977-78. Served as capt. USAF, 1964-65. Fellow Am. Coll. Dentists, Acad. Gen. Dentistry (pres. Albuquerque chpt. 1976); mem. ADA, N.Mex. Dental Assn. (sec.-treas. 1982-86, v.p. 1986-87, pres. 1988—), Albuquerque Dist. Dental Soc. (pres. 1976), Pierre Fouchard Acad., Sigma Chi, Delta Sigma Delta. Republican. Mem. Ch. of Jesus Christ of Latter-day Saints. Home: 8216 Delwood NE Albuquerque NM 87111 Office: 7520 D-11 Montgomery NE Albuquerque NM 87109

GRAHAM, WILLIAM B., pharmaceutical company executive; b. Chgo., July 14, 1911; s. William and Elizabeth (Burden) G.; m. Edna Kanaley, June 15, 1940 (dec.); children: William J., Elizabeth Anne, Margaret, Robert B.; m. Catherine Van Duzer, July 23, 1984. S.B. cum laude, U. Chgo., 1932, J.D. cum laude, 1936; LL.D., Carthage Coll., 1974, Lake Forest Coll., 1983; L.H.D., St. Xavier Coll. and Nat. Coll. Edn., 1983; DLaw (hon.), U. Ill., 1988. Bar: Ill. 1936. Patent lawyer Dyrenforth, Lee, Chritton & Wiles, 1936-40; mem. Dawson & Ooms, 1940-45; v.p., mgr. Baxter Travenol Labs., Inc., Deerfield, Ill., 1945-53; pres., chief exec. officer Baxter Travenol Labs., Inc., 1953-71, chmn. bd., chief exec. officer, 1971-80, chmn. bd., 1980-85, sr. chmn., 1985—, also dir.; dir., mem. exec. com. 1st Nat. Bank, Chgo.; dir. Deere & Co.; prof., chairperson Weizmann Inst. Sci., Rehoboth, Israel, 1978. Bd. dirs., pres. Lyric Opera Chgo.; vice chmn. bd. dirs. Nat. Park Fedn.; bd. dirs. Chgo. Hort. Soc., Nat. Council U.S.-China Trade; trustee Orchestral Assn., U. Chgo., Evanston (Ill.) Hosp. Recipient V.I.P. award Lewis Found., 1963, Disting. Citizen award Ill. St. Andrew Soc., 1974, Decision Maker of Yr. award Am. Statis. Assn., 1974, Marketer of Yr. award AMA, 1976, Found. award Kidney Found., 1981, Chicagoan of Yr. Chgo. Boys Club, 1981, Bus. Statesman of Yr. award Harvard Bus. Sch. Club Chgo., 1983, Achievement award Med. Tech. Services, 1983, Disting. Fellows award Internat. Ctr. for Artificial Organs and Transplantations, 1982, Chgo. Civic award DePaul U., 1986, Internat. Visitors Golden Medallion award DePaul U., 1988; recognized for pioneering work Health Industry Mfrs. Assn., 1981; inducted Jr. Achievement Chgo. Bus. Hall of Fame, 1986;. Mem. Am. Pharm. Mfrs. Assn. (past pres.), Ill. Mfrs. Assn. (past pres.), Pharm. Mfrs. Assn. (past chmn., award for spl. distinction leadership 1981), Phi Beta Kappa, Sigma Xi, Phi Delta Phi. Clubs: Chicago (past pres.), Commonwealth, Mid-Am., Commercial, Indian Hill, Casino (Chgo.); Old Elm (Lake Forest, Ill.); Seminole, Everglades, Bath & Tennis (Fla.); University, Links (N.Y.C.). Home: 40 Devonshire Ln Kenilworth IL 60043 Office: Baxter Travenol Labs Inc 1 Baxter Pkwy Deerfield IL 60015

GRAHAM, WILLIAM GORDON, publisher; b. Glasgow, Scotland, July 17, 1920; s. Thomas and Marion (Hutcheson) G.; m. Margaret Milne, 1943 (dec.); 1 dau., Fiona; m. 2d, Friedel Gramm, Feb. 17, 1948; 1 dau., Sylvia. M.A., Glasgow U., 1940. Fgn. corr. throughout Southeast Asia, U.S., 1948-56; internat. sales mgr., v.p., mng. dir. McGraw-Hill Book Co., N.Y.C., 1956-74; chmn., chief exec. Butterworth & Co. Publishers Ltd., London, 1975-86; chmn. R.R. Bowker Co., N.Y.C., 1985—. Contbr. numerous articles to profl. jours. Bd. dirs. The British Library, London, 1980-86; v.p., pres. The Publishers Assn., London, 1985-87. Served to maj. with British Armed Forces, 1941-46, India, Burma. Decorated Mil. Cross, British Army, 1944, Bar to Mil. Cross, 1945. Fellow Royal Soc. Arts. Home: 5 Beechwood Dr, Marlow SL7 2DH, England Office: Butterworth & Co Ltd, 88 Kingsway, London WC2B 6AB, England

GRAHAM, WILLIAM HARDIN, chemist, researcher; b. Birmingham, Ala., Apr. 27, 1932; s. David Franklin and Roberta Lee (Hardin) G.; m. Anna Montalbano, June 9, 1956; children—Carol Anne, Michael David, Janet Lee, Patrick Hardin, Alan Gleason. B.S., La. State U., 1953, M.S., 1955; Ph.D., Fla. State U., 1958; postgrad. Calif. Inst. Tech., 1958-59; research chemist Rohm & Haas Co., Huntsville, Ala., 1959-70, group supr., 1970, Bristol, Pa., 1970-72; sr. research chemist Morton Thiokol, Huntsville, 1972-83, group supr., 1983-87, chief research, 1987— . Contbr. articles to Jour. Am. Chem. Soc., Jour. Organic Chemistry, Jour. Phys. Chemistry, also others. Patentee in field. Pres., Internat. Little League, Huntsville, 1981; chmn. Madison County Republican Com., Huntsville, 1966-68, 1975-80; elector Ala. Rep. Com., 1968, del., mem. rules com. Rep. Nat. Conv., 1976, alternate del. 1984; chmn. 5th Congl. Dist. Rep. Com., 1982-86 ; Ala. state exec. com., 1966-70, 74-86; precinct chmn. Upper Dublin Twp., Ambler, Pa., 1971-72; NSF fellow, 1957-58; Arthur Ames Noyes research fellow, 1958-59. Mem. Am. Chem. Soc. (no. Ala. chpt. chmn. elect 1987), Assn. U.S. Army, Huntsville Assn. Tech. Socs. (treas. 1978). Roman Catholic. Club: Rohm & Haas Employees Assn. (pres. 1967). Current work: Solid propellant chemistry; energetic materials; isocyanate cure chemistry; nitrogen-flourine compounds, diazirines; nitrate esters. Subspecialties: Organic chemistry; Polymer chemistry. Office: Morton Thiokol Inc Redstone Arsenal Huntsville AL 35807

GRAHAM, WILLIAM PIERSON, investment banker, entrepreneur; b. East St. Louis, Ill., Feb. 19, 1935; s. William Schley and Opal Elizabeth (Gray) G.; m. Margaret Newton McDowell, Sept. 30, 1961; children: Lisa, Heather, Jennifer. BS, U. Ill., 1956. With IBM Corp., 1956-69, asst. to pres., 1967-68, dir. mktg. comml. industries data processing div., 1968-69; exec. v.p. EDP Tech., Inc., Washington, 1969-71, pres., chief exec. officer, 1971-73; pres. Washington Profl. Group, 1973-81; pres. SRC Corps., Equisource Corps.; mng. dir. Pierce Investment Banking, Inc. Asst. for domestic programs White House, Washington, 1966-67; chmn. bd. dirs. Congl. Mgmt. Found.; mem. fgn. service profl. devel. rev. group Dept. State, 1976; mem. U.S. Adv. Com. Vocat. Edn., 1968-69, U.S. Fed. Adv. Com. Employment Security, 1968-71, Com. for Excellence in Govt.; panel cons. Edn. Profl. Devel. Act, HEW, 1969-71; del. German Am. Forum, Bonn, Berlin, 1975; chmn. parents assn. Sidwell Friends Sch., Washington, 1976-78; vice chmn. fin. adv. com. Nat. Com. for Effective Congress, 1976-77. Served with AUS, 1957. White House fellow, 1966-67. Mem. White House Fellows Assn. (pres. Found. 1973-74). Home: 1306 27th St NW Washington DC 20007 Office: 1910 K St NW Washington DC 20006

GRAHAM, WILLIS SPRAGINS, entertainment exec.; b. Florence, Ala., Oct. 29, 1919; s. Willis Ramey and Edna Bibb (Spragins) G.; m. Katherine Rowena Dinkins, May 2, 1942. With Memphis Comml. Appeal-Press Scimitar, 1940-42; free-lance writer, 1946; with radio sta. WSM, Nashville, 1946-48; v.p. Noble-Dury & Assos., Inc., Nashville, 1948-55, pres., 1956-63, chmn. bd., 1963-66; chmn. bd. Show Biz, Inc., Nashville, 1966-81; pres. Show Biz Music, Inc. Served with AUS, 1942-46; CBI. Mem. Broadcast Music. Clubs: Belle Meade, City, Cumberland (Nashville). Composer popular songs; contbr. fiction and non-fiction to various nat. mags. Home: 4410 Chickering Ln, Nashville, TN 37215 Office: Show Biz Music Inc Hobbs Bldg Nashville TN 37215

GRAHL-MADSEN, ATLE, law educator, attorney; b. Bergen, Norway, Aug. 31, 1922; s. Mads Madsen and Ragnhild Marie (Grahl-Nielsen) Grahl-Madsen; m. Aasa E. Skurtveit, 1955; 4 children; m. Elisabeth Kjaergaard, 1987. Ed. U. Oslo, and Acad. Internat. Law, The Hague; Dr.Jur. Asst. judge city cts., Oslo and Drammen, Norway, 1947-48; resettlement officer Internat. Refugee Orgn., Brit. Zone of Germany, 1948-49; asst. judge county cts., Idd og Marker and Onsoy, Norway, 1949-50; assoc. Holm, Rode & Christophersen, Oslo, 1951-52; practice law, Oslo, 1952-53, Bergen, 1953-72; prin. lectr. in law Norwegian Sch. Econs. and Bus. Adminstrn., 1967-76; prof. internat. law Uppsala U. (Sweden), 1976-81; prof. law U. Bergen, 1980—; spl. cons. to UN High Commr. for Refugees, Geneva, 1962-63; dir. Swedish Inst. Internat. Law, Uppsala, 1976-81; mem. UN Commn. of Inquiry on Reported Massacres in Mozambique, 1974. Author: Menneskerett og sunt vett, 1959; The Status of Refugees in International Law, vol. I, 1966, vol. II, 1972; Europeisk Fellesskap, 1972; Territorial Asylum, 1980; Norsk fremmedrett i stopeskjen, 1985, The Emergent International Law relating to Refugees, 1985, Ny utlendingslov, 1987; contbr. numerous articles to various publs.; editor: The Spirit of Uppsala, 1983, Bergen i verden, 1985. Decorated Royal Order of North Star (Sweden), comdr. pro Merito Melitensi, Sovereign Mil. Order of Malta, others; recipient Plaquette of Honor, Norwegian Refugee Council, Golden Fridtjof Nansen Ring; research fellow Norwegian Research Council for Sci. and Humanities, 1960-67. Office: Bergen-Universitet, Dept Pub and Internat Law, N-5007 Bergen Norway

GRAMAJO MORALES, HECTOR ALEJANDRO, government official; b. Ostuncalco, Quetzaltenango, Guatemala, Aug. 11, 1940; s. Hector Gramajo y Gramajo and Lucila (de Gramajo) Morales; m. Maria Rosa Salazar Galvez, Nov. 21, 1963 (dec. 1979); children: Hector Antonio, Carmen Lucia, Alejandro Jose.; m. Ligia Castro de Gramajo, Apr. 24, 1982; 1 child, Juan Pablo. Diploma, Escuela Politécnica de Guatemala, Guatemala City, 1959, Interam. Def. Coll., Ft. Leavenworth, Kans., 1976. Commd. 2d lt. Guatemalan Army, advanced through grades to div. gen., 1984; dep. comdr. Zona Militar Aquilar Santa Maria, Jutiapa, 1978-79; prof. strategic studies Ctr. Mil. Studies, Guatemala City, 1979-80; minister counselor Guatemalan Embassy, Washington, 1980-81; mil. attaché Guatemalan Embassy, San Salvador, El Salvador, 1982-83; vice-chief staff Estado Mayor de la Defensa Nacional, Guatemala City, 1984-85, chief of staff, 1986-87; commdr. Mil. Zone #1, Guatemala City, 1984-85; min. def. Ministry Nat. Def., Guatemala City, 1987—; educator Adolfo V. Hall Inst., Guatemala City, 1962-63, Escuela Politécnica, 1976, Guatemala City, 1965-66, dean cadets, 1973-74. Author: Puntos Calientes de la Guerra Fria en el Continte Americano (Medalla de Mérito Intelectual 1976); (with others) Air Mobility and War Against Subversives; promoter The Civil Affairs Doctrine in Guatemalan Army. Decorated commdr. Legion Merit Cross. Roman Catholic. Home: Ave de la Reforma, 2-43 Zone 10, Guatemala City Guatemala Office: Ministry Nat Def, Nat Palace, Guatemala City Guatemala

GRAMM, WILLIAM PHILIP, senator, economist; b. Fort Benning, Ga., July 8, 1942; s. Kenneth Marsh and Florence (Scroggins) G.; m. Wendy Lee, Nov. 2, 1970; children: Marshall Kenneth, Jefferson Philip. B.A., U. Ga., 1964, Ph.D., 1967. Mem. faculty dept. econs. Tex. A.&M. U., College Station, 1967-78, prof., 1973-78; ptnr. Gramm & Assocs., 1971-78; mem. 96th-98th Congresses from 6th Tex. Dist.; U.S. senator from Tex. 1985—; cons. NSF, U.S. Bur. Mines, USPHS, Arms Control and Disarmament Agy. Contbr. articles to profl. jours., periodicals. Recipient Freedom Found. award, 1975. Mem. Am. Econs. Assn. Republican. Episcopalian. Home: 1201 Munson College Station TX 77840 Office: Office of Senate Members 370 Senate Russell Bldg Washington DC 20510 *

GRANA, NICOLA MARIO LUIGI GIOVANNI, philosophy educator, researcher; b. Peschici, Foggia, Italy, June 21, 1949; s. Antonio and Elisabetta (della Torre) G.; m. Isabella Lucchese, June 9, 1979; 1 child, Grad. U. Naples, 1972. Instr. philosophy Scuola Militare Nunziatella, Naples, Italy, 1975-77; researcher U. Naples, 1975—; collaborator Istituto Universitario di Magistero, Naples, 1983—. Author: Filosofia della Logica, 1982; Sentieri della Logica, 1982; Logica Paraconsistente, 1983. Served with Italian Army, 1972-73. Istituto Teoretica scholar, 1975-77. Mem. Assn. for Symbolic Logic, Sociedade Paranaense de Matematica, Am. Math. Soc., Società Filosofica Italiana. Avocations: tennis; soccer. Home: Corso Vitt Emanuele 297, Naples 80135 Italy Office: Dipartimento di Filosofia, Naples Italy

GRANDEMANGE, MICHEL CLAUDE, agricultural equipment company executive; b. Ronchin, Nord, France, July 16, 1926; s. Pierre and Madeleine (Mentien) G.; m. Nicole Besse, June 30, 1952; children: Marie Christine, Olivier. B in Agronomy Engring., Inst. Nat. Agronomique, Paris, 1949. Engr. Comptoir Francais Azote, Paris, 1949-53; comml. mgr. Rigot Stalars, Paris, 1953-61; v.p. Co. Continentale Bemis Rigot, Paris, 1961-67; chmn., mng. dir. Bemis France, Paris, 1967-76; mng. dir. Kongskilde France, Orleans, 1977-86; group advisor Kongskilde Koncern Danemark, Orleans, 1986—. Named Officier Merite Agricole, Minister Agriculture, 1967, Chevalier Legion Honneur, Pres. Republic, 1975, Officer Order Leopold II, King of Belgium. Mem. Inst. Nat. Agronomique Alumni Assn. (chmn. 1970-74, 75-77), Agr. Machinery Importers Assn. (chmn. 1986—), Nat. Fedn. Mechs. Metallurgy Electronics Importers Assns. (chmn. 1987), Salon Internat. Machine Agricole (vice chmn. internat. agrl. machinery show 1986—). Home: Ave Fontenelle 20, 92330 Sceaux France Office: Kongskilde France, BP 57, 45802 Saint Jean de Braye France

GRANDERSON, GEORGE, science teacher; b. Arlington, Tenn., Apr. 25, 1937; s. Willie and Minnie Lee (Davis) G.; m. Marie Nadine Majors, Oct. 2, 1959; children: George, Michael, Gerald, Mark. BS, Tenn. State U., Nashville, 1960, MS, 1965; AS, Lawrence Inst. Tech., 1974; PhD, U. Mich., 1978. Tchr. sci. Durfee Jr. High Sch., Detroit, 1964-68, Cen. High Sch., Detroit, 1968-73; tchr. sci., head dept. Southwestern High Sch., Detroit, 1973—; instr. chemistry Community Coll., Wayne County, Mich., 1978—. Served with U.S. Army, 1960-63, Korea. Recipient Centennial Tchr. award NIH, Bethesda, Mass., 1987, Honor Roll Tchr. award 1987, Prism award Detroit Sci. Ctr., 1987, Cert. of Appreciation for Outstanding Commitment to Edn. Detroit Bd. of Edn., 1986-88; named Michiganian Yr. Detroit News, 1988, Disting. Alumnus U. Mich. Sch. of Edn., 1988. Fellow AAAS, Nat. Sci. Tchrs. Assn., Am. Chem. Soc., Mich. Sci. Tchrs. Assn., Metro Detroit Sci. Tchrs. Assn., Phi Delta Kappa; mem. Alpha Kappa Mu. Democrat. Home: 607 Susan Ann Arbor MI 48103 Office: Southwestern High Sch 6921 W Fort St Detroit MI 48209

GRANDMONT, JEAN-MICHEL, economist, researcher; b. Toulouse, France, Dec. 22, 1939; s. Jancu Wladimir and Paule (Cassou) Grunberg; m. Annick Duriez, Dec. 23, 1967 (div. May 1978); children: Celine, Juliette; m. Josselyne Bitan, 1979. Degree in engring., Ponts et Chaussées, Paris, 1963, Polytechnique U., Paris, 1965; PhD in Econs., U. Calif., Berkeley, 1971. Research assoc. Cermap, Paris, 1965-68; research assoc. then dir. research Centre D' Etudes Prospectives Et De Recherches En Economie Mathematique Appliquees A la Planification, Paris, 1970—; dir. Sci Group ADRES, Paris, 1986—. Author: Money and Value, 1983; editor: Nonlinear Economic Dynamics, 1987, Temporary Equilibrium, 1988; contbr. articles to sci. jours.; assoc. editor various profl. jours. including Econometrica, Jour. Econ. Theory, Jour. Math. Econs., 1973—. Served to lt. with French mil., 1960-63. Named Clarendon lectr. Oxford U., 1987. Fellow The Econometric Soc. (Walras-Bowley lectr. 1984, v.p. 1988); mem. European Econ. Assn., Fondation de France (sci. com. 1984—). Office: Cepremap, 140 Rue De Chevaleret, Paris France 75013

GRANDOFF, ANTHONY BERNARD, SR., investment company executive; b. Tampa, Fla., June 13, 1911; s. John Baptiste and Theresa Agnes (Cantwell) Gandolfo; grad. Jesuit high sch., Tampa; m. Frances Evelyn Kidd, Mar. 4, 1930; children—Elizabeth Joan, Anthony Bernard. Gen. mgr. parcel delivery service, 1928-33; pres. taxicab and city bus. cos., 1933-42; pres. Rent-A-Car Service in 15 cities in 3 states, 1942-57; v.p., Southeastern mgr. Hertz Corp., Tampa, 1957-60, dir., 1960-67; pres., dir. Grandoff Investments Inc., Tampa, 1944—; pres. Grandoff Mortgage Investors Inc., 1979—; owner, chmn., organizer Tri-County Bank, Trenton, Fla., 1987—; dir. Hertz Corp., Landmark Bank Tampa. Bd. dirs. Tampa Port Authority, Jesuit High Sch. Found., St. Leo Coll.; owner, pres., chmn., organizer Tri-County Hosp. Authority, Trenton, Fla., 1987. Recipient award for services on Port Authority, Propeller Club Tampa, 1967; award for contbns. to transp. Sales and Mktg. Execs., 1965. Mem. Tampa C. of C. (chmn. taxation com., chmn. downtown art show com.; recipient Pres.'s award 1965), So., Fla. seniors golf assns. Roman Catholic. Democrat. Clubs: Waynesville (N.C.) Golf, Palma Ceia Golf and Country (Tampa), Univ. (Tampa). Home: Box 90 Route 1 Trenton FL 32693 Other: 409 Country Club Dr Waynesville NC 28786 Office: 412 Madison St Tampa FL 33602

GRANERO, JONAS, air conditioning company executive; b. Madrid, Sept. 22, 1927; s. Marceliano and Adoracion (Medina) G.; m. Manuela Velasco, Sept. 15, 1954; children: Gonzalo, Antonio. Asst. Engr., Engring. Sch., Madrid. Lab. analyst Standard Electrica, Madrid, 1945-54; sr. draftsman Brown-Raymond-Walsh, Madrid, 1954-59; prodn. mgr. Burner, S.A., Maroc, Iran and Spain, 1959-79; gen. mgr. J.G. Granero, Madrid, 1979—. Mem. Asociacion Technica Española De Cliniatizacion y Refrigeracion. Office: J G Granero, Jazmin No 8, Madrid Spain

GRANGE, JEAN-DANIEL, physician, educator; b. Lyon, France, Dec. 29, 1944; s. Jean-Pierre and Monique-Josèphe (Haour) G.; m. Marie-Laure Brosset; children: Thomas, Luc. Student, Ecole Ozanam, Lyon, France, 1952-62, Faculté de Medecine, U. Lyon, 1962-69. Resident Lyon, France, 1969-74, asst., 1974-81, assoc. prof., 1981—. Author: Diabetic Retinopathy and Light Coagulation, 1975. Roman Catholic. Home: 71 Route de Lyon, 69450 Saint-Cyr Au Mont D'or France Office: Hopital Croix-Rousse, 93 Grande rue, 69004 Lyon France

GRANGER, CHARLES R., plant physiologist, science educator; b. Marshalltown, Iowa, Sept. 4, 1939; s. Earl B. and Verna M. (Zhorne) G.; 1 child, Cheryl L. B.S., Iowa State U., 1962; M.S. in Sci. Edn., U. Pa., 1966, M.S. in Biology, 1967; Ph.D., U. Iowa, 1970. Sci. tchr. South Tama County Community Sch., Tama, Iowa, 1962-65; research asst. U. Iowa Hosps., Iowa City, 1964-65; instr. U. Iowa, 1968-70; asst. for acad. affairs Cornell U., Ithaca, N.Y., 1970-71; asst. prof. biology and edn. U. Mo., St. Louis, 1971-76, asso. prof. biology and edn., 1977-81, prof., 1986—, assoc. chmn. dept. biology, 1974-78, chmn., 1981-87; dir. Mo. Jr. Acad., 1972-77; dir. Summer Sci. Research Inst., 1975-77; dir. Jr. Sci., Engring. and Humanities Symposium, 1974—; pres. Granger Ednl. Engring. and Research, 1971—; bd. dirs Geo. Engelmann Inst., 1987—. Author: The Pitch, 1976; editor newspaper series Sci. in Mo.; patents, publs. in field. Recipient Excellence in Teaching award U. Mo., 1975, Burlington No. Found. Faculty Achievement award, 1985, Mo. Acad. Sci. Golden Eagle Service award, 1987. Mem. Am. Inst. Biol. Sci., Assn. for Edn. Tchrs. in Sci., Nat. Assn. Biology Tchrs., Nat. Assn. Research in Sci. Teaching, Nat. Sci. Tchrs. Assn., Assn. Midwest Coll. Biology Tchrs., Sci. Tchrs. Mo. (Outstanding Mo. Sci. Educator award 1981), Mo. Acad. Sci. (pres. 1978-79), Phi Kappa Phi, Phi Delta Kappa. Office: U Mo 8001 Natural Bridge Saint Louis MO 63121

GRANGER, DAVID, investment banker; b. N.Y.C., June 26, 1903; s. David and Felicia (Newton) G.; m. Lee Mason, May 5, 1950; 1 son, Mason. Student, Phillips Exeter Acad., 1917-19; Ph.B., Yale, 1924; student, Christ's Coll., Cambridge (Eng.) U., 1924-25, U. Caen, 1926. Partner Granger & Co., N.Y.C., 1926—; sr. partner Granger & Co., 1946-81; chmn. Granger div. Seligman Securities, 1981-86; vice chmn. Seligman Securities, Inc., 1986—; Mem. N.Y. Stock Exchange, 1926—. Trustee St. Luke's Hosp., Cathedral Ch. of St. John the Divine; v.p. Museum City N.Y.; adv. council Victoria Home for Aged, Ossining, N.Y.; bd. govs. Order St. John; bd. dirs. Hort. Soc. N.Y., Barker Welfare Found. Served from 1st lt. to maj. USAAF, 1942-45. Decorated officer Order Brit. Empire. Mem. English-Speaking Union (nat. v.p.), St. George's Soc. (past v.p.), World Affairs Council L.I. (dir.), Pilgrims U.S. Episcopalian (past mem. vestry). Clubs: Union, Knickerbocker, Down Town Assn., Southampton, Church (past trustee, v.p.), Yale; Century Assn.; Bucks (London); Nat. Golf Links Am; Meadow, Southampton (Southampton, N.Y.); Travellers (Paris). Home: 640 Park Ave New York NY 10021 Office: One Bankers Trust Plaza 111 Broadway 22d Floor New York NY 10006

GRANICK, LOIS WAYNE, association administrator; b. Weatherford, Okla., Mar. 5, 1932; d. Johnny Wayne and Lois Bernice (Wells) Cox; m. Robert Eugene Granick, June 6, 1951; children—Bruce, Leslie Granick Knipling, Jeffrey, Andrea. Student, U. N.Mex., 1949-51. Programmer, systems analyst Documentation, Inc., Bethesda, Md., 1961-66; cons. Mexican Govt., Mexico City, 1966-69; info. specialist Autocomp, Inc., Bethesda, 1970-72; dir. Autocode div. of Autocomp, Inc., Bethesda, 1972-73; exec. editor Psychol. Abstracts Am. Psychol. Assn., Washington, 1974—; dir., PsycINFO Am. Psychol. Assn., 1977—. Mem. Nat. Fedn. Abstracting and Info. Services (bd. dirs. 1977-82, pres. 1980-81), Info. Sci. Abstracts (bd. dirs. 1978-79), Info. Industry Assn. (bd. dirs. 1982—, chmn. 1988—), Assn. Info. and Dissemination Ctrs., Internat. Council Sci. and Tech. Info. (gen. sec. 1986—), Am. Soc. Info. Sci. Home: 5414 Center St Chevy Chase MD 20815 Office: Am Psychol Assn 1200 17th St NW Washington DC 20036

GRANIER, FRANCOIS GEORGES MARIE, psychiatrist; b. Paris, Apr. 24, 1949; s. Marcel and Suzanne (Privat) G.; m. Martine M'Girard; children: Olivier, Florian. MD, Faculty of Medicine, Toulouse, France, 1980. Intern Centre Hosp. Regional, Toulouse, 1974-80, Fondation Vallée, Paris and Gentilly, 1978; practice medicine specializing in psychiatry Toulouse, France, 1980—; staff psychiatrist Cen. Hosp. U., Toulouse, 1984—; researcher U. Paris V Sorbonne Scis. Humaines, 1987—. Editor Review on Art-Therapy, Mediations, 1987; contbr. articles to profl. jours. Mem. Soc. Francaise Psychothologie de l'Expression, Assn. Francaise Toxicologie et Pharmacologie Clin., Soc. Medico-psychologique, Assn. Francaise Psychiat. Biologique. Home: 16 rue Falguiere, 31000 Toulouse Cedex France Office: Hosp Purpan-Casselardit, Service Psychiatry, 31059 Toulouse Cedex France

GRANIT, RAGNAR ARTHUR, neurophysiologist; b. Finland, Oct. 30, 1900; m. Baroness Marguerite (Daisy) Bruun; 1 child, Michael. Grad., Swedish Normallyceum, Helsinki, Finland, 1919; Mag. phil., Helsinki U., M.D., 1927, D.Sc. (hon.); D.Sc. (hon.), U. Oslo, U. Oxford, Loyola U., U. Pisa, U. Göttingen, others. Docent Helsinki U., 1932-37, prof. physiology, 1937-40; fellow med. physics Eldridge Reeves Johnson Research Found., U. Pa., 1929-31; mem. staff Royal Caroline Inst., Stockholm, 1940-67; emeritus mem. Royal Caroline Inst., 1967—, prof. neurophysiology, 1946-67; Thomas Young orator Phys. Soc. London, Eng., 1945; Silliman lectr. Yale U., 1954; Sherrington lectr. London, 1967, Liverpool, 1970; Murlin lectr. Rochester, N.Y., 1973; Jackson lectr. McGill U., 1975; vis. prof. Rockefeller U., N.Y.C., 1956-66, St. Catherine's Coll., Oxford, 1967, Smith-Kettlewell Inst. Med. Sci., San Francisco, 1969, Fogarty Internat. Center, NIH, Bethesda, Md., 1971-72, 75, Düsseldorf U., 1974, Max-Planck Inst., Bad Nauheim, W.Ger., 1976. Author: Ung Mans Vägtill Minerva, 1941, Sensory Mechanisms of the Retina, 1947, Receptors and Sensory Perception, 1955, Charles Scott Sherrington, An Appraisal, 1966, Basis of Motor Control, 1970, Regulation of the Discharge of Motoneurons, 1971, The Purposive Brain, 1977, Hur Det Kom Sig (autobiography), 1983. Co-recipient Nobel prize in medicine, 1967; recipient Donders, Retzius, Sherrington, Purkinje, Tigerstedt medals; 3d Internat. St. Vincent prize, 1961; Jahre prize Oslo U., 1961. Mem. Royal Swedish Acad. Sci. (pres. 1963-65, v.p. 1965-69), Royal Soc. London (fgn. mem.), Nat. Acad. Sci. (U.S.), Am. Philos. Soc., Indian Acad. Sci. (hon.), Acad. di Med. (hon.) (Turin), Acad. Nat. d. Lincei (Rome), Physiol. Soc. Eng. (hon.), Physiol. Soc. U.S. (hon.), Am. Acad. Arts and Scis. (hon.), Societas Scientiarum Fennicae (hon.), Royal Danish Acad., Acad. Finland (fgn. mem.). Address: 14 Eriksbergsgatan, 11430 Stockholm Sweden

GRANÖ, OLAVI JOHANNES, geography educator; b. Helsinki, Finland, May 27, 1925; s. J. Gabriel and Hilma (Ekholm) G.; m. Eeva Kaleva, 1953; 2 children. Student Turku, Helsinki and Copenhagen Univs., PhD (hon.) Torun, Poland. Asst. prof. geography Helsinki U. and Helsinki Sch. Econs., 1948-57; assoc. prof. geography Turku U., 1958-61, prof., 1962-88, chancellor, 1984—; pres. Archipelago Research Inst., 1965-84; pres. Finnish Nat. Research Council for Scis., 1964-69; pres. Central Bd. Research Councils, Acad. Finland, 1970-73; mem. Sci. Policy Council, 1964-74; pres. Adv. Com. for Research Nordic Council Ministers, 1976-82; academician Acad. Finland, 1980; mem. Finnish Acad. Sci. and Letters, 1970; mem. Royal Swedish Acad. Sci.; vis. fellow Clare Hall, Cambridge U., 1982; hon. corr. mem. Royal Geog. Soc. (London); hon. mem. Geog. Soc. South Sweden. Address: Dept Geography, Turku Univ, 20500 Turku Finland Address: Sirppitie 1A, 20540 Turku Finland

GRANQVIST, RAOUL, English literature educator; b. Karleby, Finland, Jan. 11, 1940; arrived in Sweden, 1967; s. Duvald J. and Karin (Wentus) G.; children: Johanna, Tina. MA, Åbo Acad., Finland, 1966; Diploma in Tchr's. Tng., Helsinki U., Finland, 1967; PhD, Uppsala (Sweden) U., 1975. Lectr. in English, French Haparanda (Sweden) Upper Secondary, 1966-76; sr. lectr. English U. Luleå, Sweden, 1976-80; research asst. English lit. Umeå (Sweden) U., 1980-84, assoc. prof., 1984—; vis. scholar Harvard U., Cambridge, Mass., 1987-88. Author: The Reputation of John Donne 1779-1873, 1975, Stereotypes in Western Fiction on Africa, 1984, African Voices: Interviews With Twelve African Writers, 1988; editor: Distorted Perspectives: Five Papers on the Image of Africa, 1987; contbr. articles to scholarly jours. Dep. Swedish bd. Amnesty Internat., Stockholm, 1979-82, Swedish relief fund, 1986-88. Mem. European Assn. Commonwealth Lit. and Lang. Studies, African Lit. Assn., European Assn. Am. Studies. Home: Gustav Garvares gata 3A, S-902 38 Umea Sweden

GRANSTON, DAVID WILFRED, publishing company exec.; b. Schenectady, N.Y., Dec. 5, 1939; s. Arnold Andrew and Edna (Nickerson) G.; B.A., Colgate U., 1958; M.B.A., Syracuse U., 1960; m. Priscilla Day, June 10, 1961; 1 son, David Wilfred. Supr. E.I. DuPont De Nemours & Co., Inc., Parlin, N.J., 1961-62; sr. fin. analyst Bendix Corp., N.Y.C., 1963-69; controller Allied Chem. Corp., N.Y.C., 1969-71; v.p. finance Thomas Borthwick Sons, Ltd., N.Y.C., 1972-78; v.p., chief fin. officer N.Y. Times Syndication Sales Corp., N.Y.C., 1978-82; chief fin. officer, assoc. dir. Consumers Union, Mt. Vernon, N.Y., 1983—. Served with USCGR, 1960. Colgate U. War Meml. scholar, 1954-58. Clubs: Colgate U. Alumni (L.I.) (Pres. 1975-76); Creek (Locust Valley, N.Y.) (bd. govs.); Northport (Maine) Yacht (vice commodore), Windham (N.Y.) Mountain. Home: PO Box 368 Piping Rock Rd Locust Valley NY 11560 Office: Consumers Union Corp 256 Washington St Mount Vernon NY 10553

GRANT, ALAN J., business executive; b. Chgo., Dec. 18, 1925; s. Hugo Bernard and May (Gardner) G.; m. Margaret Stewart, Dec. 21, 1946; children: Pamela Rose, Deborah May, Bruce David. B.S., Ill. Inst. Tech., 1946, M.S., 1948; grad., Inst. Mgmt., Northwestern U., 1961. Instr. elec. engring. Ill. Inst. Tech., Chgo., 1946-49; with N.Am. Aviation, Inc. (Autonetics), Anaheim, Calif., 1949-64; v.p., gen. mgr. computer and data systems div. N.Am. Aviation, Inc. (Autonetics), 1962-64; pres. Lockheed Electronics Co. div. Lockheed Aircraft Corp., Plainfield, N.J., 1965-69; also v.p. parent co.; exec. v.p. Aerojet-Gen. Corp., El Monte, Calif., 1970-74; chmn., pres. Wavecom Industries, Sunnyvale, Calif., 1974-78, Primark Corp., San Mateo, Calif., 1975-80; chmn., chief exec. officer Internat. Rotex, Inc., Reno, Nev., 1980-86; dir. UNC Resources Inc, Falls Church, Va., 1974-81; chmn. Atasi Corp., San Jose, Calif., 1982-85; gen. ptnr. EMC Venture Ptnrs., San Diego, 1984-86; pres. Grant Venture Mgmt. Co., Coronado, Calif., 1986—; chmn. A-B Auto Supply Inc., Fremont, Calif., 1986—; dir. Linear Instruments Corp., Reno, 1984-86; adj. prof. managerial scis. U. Nev., Reno, 1976-87; adj. prof. mgmt. San Diego State U., 1986—; pres. Grant Venture Mgmt. Co., Coronado, Calif., 1986—. Trustee Sierra Arts Found., Reno., 1981-85. Served with USNR, 1944-46. Mem. Am. Electronics Assn. (chmn. 1973, dir. 1970-74), Sigma Xi, Tau Beta Pi, Eta Kappa Nu, Pi Delta Epsilon. Office: PO Box 520 Coronado CA 92118

GRANT, DANIEL GORDON, computer consulting company executive; b. Taplow, Bucks, Eng., June 28, 1957; came to U.S., 1981; s. Victor Daniel and Annie (McKeown) G.; m. Gaynor Kerry Swainson, Aug. 8, 1981; 1 child, Andrew Douglas. BS in Computer Sci. with commendation, Portsmouth (Eng.) Polytech., 1979. Cons. in computers London, 1979-80; applications cons. Tymshare, U.K., London, 1980-81; from cons. to mgr. to internat. mgr. to group div. mgr. Tangent Internat., N.Y.C., 1981—, also bd. dirs. Contbr. articles to profl. jours. Named Chevalier, Conte de Poznan, 1986, Hon. Col. U.S. Army, 1986. Mem. British Computer Soc. Roman Catholic. Club: Franklin Lakes Rangers (N.J.) (capt. 1981). Office: Tangent Internat 30 Broad St New York NY 10004

GRANT, EDWARD, employment services executive; b. Bklyn., Apr. 10, 1936; s. David and Deborah (Jablow) Gorenstein; m. Helene Clarke, Mar. 12, 1961; children—Robin, Fran, Andrew. BBA in Mktg., Hofstra U., 1958. Pres., chief exec. officer Career Employment Services, Inc., Westbury, N.Y., 1960—. Contbr. articles to bus. jours. Bd. trustees Temple Emanu-el, East Meadow, 1980—; mem. L.I. Com. for Soviet Jewry, Carle Place, N.Y., 1983—; chmn. Nassau Community Coll. Adv. Council, Garden City, N.Y., 1983—; program chmn. Dist. Citizen award dinner Nassau County Council Boy Scouts Am., 1985. Served with USAFR, 1958-64. Recipient Service award, L.I. Employment Agy. Council, 1977, Ohio Assn. of Personnel Cons., 1980, Outstanding Contbn. award, N.J. Assn. of Personnel Cons., 1982. Mem. Nat. Assn. Personnel Cons. (mem. Speakers Bur. 1977—, bd. dirs. 1968—), Assn. of Personnel Cons. (N.Y. Bd. dirs. 1968—, Service award 1983), Nat. Assn. of Temporary Services, Cert. Personnel Cons. Soc., Hofstra U. Alumni Assn., L.I. Assn., East Meadow C. of C., Am. Diabetes Assn. L.I. Home: 260 Fox Hunt Crescent So Oyster Bay Cove NY 11791 Office: Career Employment Services Inc 1600 Stewart Ave Westbury NY 11590

GRANT, EDWARD HECTOR, experimental physics educator, consultant; b. Croydon, Eng., Oct. 15, 1931; s. Alfred Edward and Dorothy Winifred (Brookes) G.; m. Kathleen Margaret Stear, Apr. 30, 1955; children—Susan Mary, Paul Andrew, Julian Michael. B.Sc. in Physics, King's Coll., London, 1953; Ph.D. in Physics, Middlesex Hosp. Med. Sch., London, 1956. Asst. lectr. Middlesex Hosp. Med. Sch., 1956-58; sr. asst. physicist King's Coll. Hosp., London, 1958-59; lectr. Guy's Hosp. Med. Sch., London, 1959-64, sr. lectr., 1964-66; reader in exptl. physics U. London, 1966-74; prof. exptl. physics Queen Elizabeth Coll. (now King's Coll.), London, 1974—; cons. Gen. Electric Co., London, 1982—. Author: Dielectric Behaviour of Biological Molecules in Solution, 1978; editor book series on med. physics; contbr. articles to profl. jours. Grantee U.S. Army, U.S. Navy, USAF, Med. Research Council, Nat. Radiol. Protection Bd., Cancer Research Campaign. Fellow Inst. Physics; mem. N.Y. Acad. Scis., Sigma Xi. Anglican. Home: Copsley Mews, Gayhouse Ln, Outwood, Surrey RH1 5PP, England Office: Kings Coll Univ London, Strand, London WC2R 2LS, England

GRANT, EDWARD VINCENT, hospital consultant; b. Jersey City, May 20, 1918; s. John Joseph and Honoriah (Cody) G.; student parochial schs.; m. Helen Joan Grabowski, Apr. 19, 1942; children—Edward, Richard, Robert, Martin, John, Mary Ellen. Barker, Worlds Fair N.Y., 1939; with Lenox Hill Hosp., N.Y.C., 1939-42, 45-55; adminstr. Hunterdon Med. Center, Flemington, N.J., 1955-67; exec. dir. N.Y. Infirmary, N.Y.C., 1967-79; exec. v.p., chief exec. officer N.Y. Infirmary-Beekman Downtown Hosp., from 1979; now hosp. cons.; lectr. Columbia Sch. Public Health and Adminstrv. Medicine, 1958; dir. Hosp. Bur. N.Y.C., 1950-68; preceptor dept. epidemiology and public health Yale U., 1960-65; med. coordinator Hunterdon County (N.J.) CD, 1957-67; preceptor hosp. adminstrn. program Wagner Coll., N.Y.C., 1970-72; guest lectr. Northwood Inst., Midland, Mich. Mem. planning bd. Town of Clinton, 1962-67; chmn. Clinton Citizens Com., 1965-67. Trustee George K. Large Found., Flemington. Served from 2d lt. to maj. AUS, 1942-45. Mem. Am. Coll. Hosp. Adminstrs., Am. (com. home and ambulatory care 1963-66), N.J. (trustee) hosp. assns., Council Hosp. Adminstrs., N.J. Hosp. Adminstrs. Soc., Adminstr. Conf. Group, Adminstrs. Club. Roman Catholic (trustee parish). Mem. adv. bd. Health Instns. Purchasing Mag. Home and Office: 1869 Sea Oats Dr Atlantic Beach FL 32233

GRANT, GERALDINE HUGHES, retired government official; b. Warren, Ark., June 27, 1923; d. Willie and Daisy (Hunter) Hughes; student Ark. Bapt. Coll., 1940-41, 44-46, Ark. State Coll., summer 1947, Los Angeles Jr. Coll. Bus., 1957, Los Angeles City Coll., 1958-60; M.Sci. of Adminstrn., Calif. State U., 1979; m. Joseph Grant, Jan. 12, 1962; 1 son, William Thomas; stepchildren—Kenneth, Phyllis Mary. Tchr. elem. public schs., Ark., 1944-47; posting machine operator, Kansas City, Mo., 1952-53; file clk. Immigration and Naturalization Service, Dept. Justice, Los Angeles, 1954-56, info. clk., 1956-62, supervisory contact rep., 1962-70, immigration insp., 1970-75, immigration examiner, 1975-78, acting immigration examiner supr., 1978, supervisory immigration examiner, 1978-83. Minister of music children's dept. Sunday sch. Victory Bapt. Ch., 1955-61, adult Sunday sch. tchr., 1962—, mem. Voices of Victory Choir, 1953—. Recipient Cert. of Appreciation, Shelley Sch. Child Devel. Center, Raleigh, N.C., 1979. Mem. Nat. Council Negro Women (life, Spl. Recognition award 1979, 81), Am. Inst. Parliamentarians (pres. local chpt. 1977-78, 80-81), Eta Phi Beta (pres. local chpt. 1973-74, 80-82, rec. sec. 1965-66, western regional dir. 1969-73, grand dir. edn. 1974-78, 2d nat. v.p. 1982-86), Black Women's Forum, Alpha Kappa Alpha (chmn. com. Mu Beta Omega chpt. 1984). Democrat. Club: Toastmistress (council del. 1979-80). Home: 3010 S Bronson Ave Los Angeles CA 90018

GRANT, JAMES PINEO, international organization executive; b. Peking, China, May 12, 1922; s. John Black and Charlotte (Hill) G.; m. Ethel Henck, Dec. 30, 1943; children: John Putnam, James Dickinson, William Joseph. AB U. Calif., 1943; LL.B., J.D., Harvard U., 1951; hon. degrees Notre Dame U., 1980, Hacetteppe U., 1980, Maryville Coll., 1981, Denison U., 1983, U. Md., 1986, Clark U., 1987. Rep. UNRRA in North China, 1946-47; cons., spl. asst. to dir. U.S. Econ. Aid Mission to China, 1948-49, 50; asso. Covington & Burling, Washington, 1951-54; regional legal counsel for U.S. Econ. Aid Missions in South Asia, 1954-56; dir. U.S. Econ. Aid Mission to Ceylon, 1956-58; spl. asst. to dir. Internat. Cooperation Adminstrn., 1958, dep. dir. ICA, Washington, 1958-61; dep. asst. sec. state for Near Eastern and South Asian affairs, 1962-64; dir. U.S. Econ. Aid Mission to Turkey, 1964-67; asst. adminstr. AID, Washington, 1967-69; pres. Overseas Devel. Council, 1969-79; exec. dir. UNICEF, 1980—; hon. prof. Capital Med. Coll. China, 1983. Bd. dirs., trustee Rockefeller Found., 1980-87; bd. dirs. Internat. Vol. Services, Johns Hopkins U. (emeritus), Overseas Devel. Council; trustee, mem. vis. com. Sch. Nutrition, Tufts U. Served as capt. AUS, 1943-45, CBI. Decorated Bronze Star with cluster; Breast Order of Yun Hui (China); recipient Disting. Public Service award AID, 1961; Rockefeller Public Service award, 1980. Mem. Soc. Internat. Devel. (pres. 1978-82), Council Fgn. Relations, Bar Assn. D.C., North-South Round Table. Clubs: Metropolitan, Cosmos (Washington); U.S. of Rome. Office: UNICEF 866 UN Plaza New York NY 10017

GRANT, MERWIN DARWIN, lawyer; b. Safford, Ariz., May 7, 1944; s. Darwin Dewey and Erma (Whiting) G.; m. Charlotte Richey, June 27, 1969; children: Brandon, Taggart, Christian. BA in Econs., Brigham Young U., 1968; JD, Duke U., 1971. Bar: Ariz. 1971, U.S. Dist. Ct. Ariz., U.S. Dist. Ct. (we. dist.) Tex., U.S. Ct. Appeals (5th, 8th, 9th and 10th cir.), U.S. Tax Ct., U.S. Supreme Ct. Sole practice Phoenix, 1977—; ptnr. Beus, Gilbert, Wake & Morrill, Phoenix, 1984—. Founding mem. Ronald Reagan Republican Task Force, Washington, 1984—; pres., bd. dirs. Golden Gate Settlement, Phoenix, 1975—. Mem. ABA (tax section), Assn. Trial Lawyers Am. Club: U.S. Senatorial Club. Lodge: Kiwanis (bd. dirs. Phoenix chpt. 1972-79). Home: 4950 E Red Rock Phoenix AZ 85018 Office: Beus Gilbert Wake & Morrill 3200 N Central Ave Phoenix AZ 85012

GRANT, RUBY JAYNE JOHNSON, insurance executive; b. Glen Cove, N.Y., June 28; d. Alfred Lloyd and Ora Mae (Gibson) Pendleton; m. Nolan Eugene Floyd Grant; 1 child, Kristale Michelle. Grad. high sch., Glen Cove. Telephone operator N.Y. Phone Co., Roslyn, 1958-60; bookkeeper Town and Country, Roslyn, 1961-65; real estate sales agt. Parkview Realty, Westbury, N.Y.; salesperson Parkview Realty, Westbury, N.Y., 1965-66; teller Meadowbrook Bank, Jericho, N.Y., 1966-67; cons. Met. Life Ins. Co., Hicksville, N.Y., 1968-73; agt. AllState Ins. Co., Glen Cove, 1973—. Chmn. election dist., bd. inspector New Cassel Rep. Club, Westbury, N.Y., 1985—; pres. Glen Cove Youth Club, 1980-85, advisor, 1986—; chmn. insps. Nassau County Election Bd., 1987—. Mem. Nat. Assn. Negro Bus. and Profl. Women (life; rec. sec. 1985-87, chaplain 1987—), 100 Black Women L.I., Inc. Mem. Ch. of God in Christ. Avocations: interior decorating, bicycling, roller skating. Home: 261 Brook St Westbury NY 11590 Office: Allstate Ins Co 75 Forest Ave Glen Cove NY 11542

GRANT, STEPHEN ALLEN, lawyer; b. N.Y.C., Nov. 4, 1938; s. Benton H. and Irene A. Grant; m. Anne. B. Grant, Feb. 11, 1961 (div. Nov. 1975); children: Stephen, Katharine, Michael; m. Anne-Marie Laignel, Dec. 8, 1975; children: Natalie, Elizabeth, Alexandra. AB, Yale U., 1960; LLB, Columbia U., 1965. Bar: N.Y. 1965, U.S. Supreme Ct. 1969. Law clk. to judge U.S. Ct. Appeals (2d cir.), N.Y.C., 1965-66; assoc. Sullivan & Cromwell, N.Y.C., 1966-73; ptnr. Sulliavan & Cromwell, N.Y.C., 1973—. Served to lt. USN, 1960-62. Mem. ABA, N.Y. State Bar Assn., Assn. of Bar of City of N.Y., Council Fgn. Relations. Clubs: Down Town, Links. Home: 1021 Park Ave New York NY 10028 Office: Sullivan & Cromwell 125 Broad St New York NY 10004

GRANT-FERRIS, PIERS HENRY MICHAEL, priest; b. Birmingham, Midlands, Gt. Britain, Apr. 9, 1933; s. Robert Grant and Florence (De Vine) Harvington. Diploma edn., Strawberry Hill, Middlesex, 1960. Novice Monastic Order St. Benedict, Ampleforth Abbey, Yorkshire, Eng., 1955, solem profession, 1959, priest, 1964; asst. priest Parish of Workington (Cumbria, Eng.), 1977—; form master Gilling Castle Prep Sch. Yorkshire, 1965-75; sch. chaplain St. Joseph's Roman Cath. Comprehensive Sch., Cumbria, Workington, 1979—. Mem. sch. gov. St. Joseph's Comprehensive Sch., Workington, Cumbria, 1979—. Served to lt. Irish Guards, 1951-54. Recipient Gold award British Amateur Swimming Assn., 1967. Conservative. Roman Catholic. Clubs: Kandahar Ski (Silver K award 1954), Alpine Ski, Achille Ratti Climbing, Alpine. Home: The Priory, Banklands, Workington, Cumbria England CA14 3EP Office: Monastery of St Laurence, Ampleforth Abbey, York, East Yorks England YO6 4EN

GRANTHAM, CHARLES EDWARD, broadcast engineer; b. Andalusia, Ala., Mar. 15, 1950; s. J.C. and Geraldine (Brooks) G.; student Enterprise State Jr. Coll., 1968-69; A.A., Lurleen B. Wallace Coll., 1979; m. Sandra J. Mosley, Mar. 9, 1973; 1 son, Christopher Charles. Sales engr., draftsman S.E. Ala. Gas Co., Andalusia, 1968-70; asst. mgr., engr. Sta. WAAO, Andalusia, 1972-78; engr. Ala. Public TV, WDIQ-TV, Dozier, Ala., also chief technician Sta. WAAO, Andalusia, 1978—; South Ala. microwave engr. APTV, 1980—. Notary public, Ala.; bd. dirs. Carolina Vol. Fire Dept.; pres. Andalusia Men's Ch. Softball, 1985-86; youth dir. Cedar Grove Ch., 1987—. Served with inf. U.S. Army, 1970-72. Named Civitan Outstanding Young Am., 1967. Mem. Internat. Soc. Cert. Electronic Technicians, Am. Film Inst., Nat. Rifle Assn., Ala. State Employees Assn. (bd. dirs.), Country Music Assn., Nat. Assn. Bus. and Ednl. Radio, Soc. Broadcast Engrs., Country Music Disc Jockey Assn., Phi Theta Kappa. Mem. Ch. of Christ. Home: Route 5 Box 48 W Andalusia AL 36420 Office: WDIQ TV Route 2 Dozier AL 36028

GRANTS, VALDIS, engineering manager; b. Liepaja, Latvia, Mar. 5, 1942; came to U.S., 1949, naturalized, 1955; s. Karlis Valdemars and Meta Mudite (Greenvalds) G.; m. Yvette Marie Guhl, June 18, 1966; children: Kristine Marie, Carl Raymond. BS in Sci. Engring., U. Mich., 1964, BS in Engring. Math., 1965, MSEE, 1967. Research engr. U. Mich., Ann Arbor, 1965-70; sr. design engr. Info. Instrn., Inc., Ann Arbor, 1970-71; sr. design engr. Allen-Bradley Co., Highland Heights, Ohio, 1971-76, engring. supr., 1976-77, engr. mgr., 1977—. Patentee in field. Mem. IEEE, Tau Beta Pi, Eta Kappa Nu, Phi Kappa Phi. Office: Allen-Bradley Co 747 Alpha Dr Highland Heights OH 44143

GRASS, GUNTER (WILHELM), writer; b. Danzig, Oct. 16, 1927; studied sculpture with Sepp Magesh, painting with Otto Pankok, Kunstakademie (Dusseldorf), 1949; Acad. Fine Arts (Berlin), 1953; D.H.C. (hon.), Kenyon Coll., 1965, Harvard U., 1976; m. Anna Margareta Grass, 1954; children: Franz, Raoul, Laura, Bruno; m. Utte Grunert, 1979. Began as a writer of poems, dramatic scenes, also worked as a drummer and washboard accompanist with jazz band; lectr., reader Harvard U., Yale U., Smith Coll., Goethe House, Poetry Center YM-YWHA, 1964. Served with German Mil. Service, 1943-45. Recipient lit. prize, Gruppe 47; Lyric prize Suddeutscher Rundfunk, 1955; Lit. prize Assn. German Critics, 1960; French award for best fgn. lang. book The Tin Drum, 1962; Georg-Buchner prize, 1965. Mem. Berlin Acad. Fine Arts. Roman Catholic. Author: The Tin Drum (pub. German, other langs.), 1959; (plays) Die bosen Koche, Noch zehn Minuten bis Buffalo, Hochwasser, 1957, Onkel, Onkel, 1965; (poetry) Gleisdreeck, 1960, Die Vorzuge der Windhuhner, 1965; Cat and Mouse, 1961; The Dog Years, 1963; Selected Poems, 1966; Ausgefragt, 1967; Beforehand, 1968; Ortlich Betäubt, 1969; Ausdem Tagebush einer Schnecke, 1972; Dokumente zur Politischen Wirkung, 1972; Der Butt, 1976; Das Treffen in Telgte, 1979; Headbirths: Or the Germans Are Dying Out, 1982; Kinderlied, 1983; Widerstand lernen-Politische, Gegenreden, 1980-83, 1984, The Rat, 1987. *

GRASSIA, THOMAS C., lawyer; b. Westfield, Mass., Aug. 26, 1946; s. Thomas C. and Assunta (Abatiell) G.; m. Judith Chace Cranshaw, Aug. 15, 1970; children—Susan C., Joseph C. B.A., Boston U., 1968; J.D., Suffolk U., 1974. Bar: Mass. 1974, U.S. Dist. Ct. Mass. 1976, U.S. Supreme Ct. 1980. Asst. v.p. Plymouth Rubber Co., Canton, Mass., 1969-71; ptnr., P.T.S. Computer Services, Waltham, Mass., 1971-81; ptnr. D'Angio & Grassia, Waltham, 1974-85, Grassia & Mariolis, Wellesley, Mass., 1985—; agt. Indsl. Valley Title Ins. Co., Phila., 1980—, 1st Am. Title Ins. Co., N.Y.C., 1980—, Lawyers Title Ins. Co., Richmond, Va., Am. Title Ins. Co., Miami, Fla.; dir. of many regional corps. including Sytron Corp., Mepl. Guard Rail Corp., Framingham, Mass., Fortune Guaranty Savs. Bank, Windham, N.H.; dir., asst. treas. Granite Subaru, Milford, Mass.; pres., treas., dir. Lender's Title & Abstract Co., Ltd., Wellesley; Contbr. articles to profl. publs., lectr. on law, pub. interest subjects. Mem. Bd. Health, Sherborn, Mass., 1976-81, Bd. Selectmen, Sherborn, 1981-85; trustee Leonard Morse Hosp., Natick, Mass., 1981-84; mem. Met. Boston Hosp. Council, Burlington, Mass., 1983-84; mem., team leader Sherborn Fire and Rescue Dept., 1974—; former mem. Sherborn Sch. Bd. Long Range Planning com., Sherborn Land Maintenance Study com., Sherborn Police Chief Selection com., Sherborn Emergency Med. Study com. Mem. ABA, Mass. Bar Assn., Mass. Conveyances Assn., Am. Arbitration Assn. (comml. arbitration bd.), Nat. Registry Emergency Med. Technicians. Home: 75 Nason Hill Rd PO Box 178 Sherborn MA 01770 Office: Grassia & Mariolis 40 Grove St Wellesley MA 02181

GRASSLEY, CHARLES E., senator; b. New Hartford, Iowa, Sept. 17, 1933; m. Barbara Ann Speicher; children: Lee, Wendy, Robin Lynn, Michele Marie, Jay Charles. B.A., U. No. Iowa, 1955, M.A., 1956; postgrad., U. Iowa, 1957-58. Farmer; instr. polit. sci. Drake U., 1962, Charles City Community Coll., 1967-68; mem. Iowa Ho. of Reps., 1959-75, 94th-96th Congresses from 3d Iowa Dist., U.S. Senate from Iowa, 1981—. Mem. Am. Farm Bur., Iowa Hist. Soc., Pi Gamma Mu, Kappa Delta Pi. Baptist. Lodges: Masons, Order of Eastern Star. Office: US Senate 135 Hart Senate Bldg Washington DC 20510

GRASSO, ANTHONY ROBERT, priest, educator; b. Boston, Feb. 23, 1951; s. Leonard Joseph and Nancy Antoinette (Solazzo) G. B.A. in English Lit., U. Notre Dame, 1973, M.Th., 1977; M.A., U. Toronto, Ont., Can., 1980, Ph.D. in English, 1985—. Joined Congregation Holy Cross, ordained priest Roman Catholic Ch., 1978. Tchr. English, Notre Dame Cath. High Sch., Fairfield, Conn., 1973-74; teaching asst. theology U. Notre Dame, South Bend, Ind., 1975-76; tchr. English, St. Mark's High Sch., Wilmington, Del., 1978-79; asst. Most Holy Trinity Ch., Saco, Maine, 1977-78; teaching asst. English, Erindale Coll. U. Toronto, 1981-82; dir. Holy Cross Sem., Toronto, 1982-85; pastoral asst., cons. St. Ann's Ch., Toronto, 1979-85; asst. prof. English, King's Coll., Wilkes Barre, Pa., 1985—, humanities rep. Faculty Council, chmn. Bd. Student Communications Media, moderator The Crown student newspaper, writing cons. ACT 101 program, dir. honors program. Author poems. Contbr. Energy Probe, Toronto, 1983-84, Amnesty Internat., Ottawa, Ont., 1983-84. Fellow Sch. Grad. Studies, U. Toronto, 1981-82, 82-83; Charles Gordon Heyd fellow, 1984-85. Mem. MLA, Tennyson Soc., Nat. Council Tchrs. English (Conf. on Christianity and Lit.).

GRASSO, DORIS TENEYCK, artist; b. Sullivan County, N.Y., May 3, 1914; d. Eugene Oscar and Elsie (TenEyck) Teschner; student Ednl. Alliance, N.Y.C., 1957-57; student art centers and pvt. art tng.; m. Dominic Lawrence Grasso, Nov. 29, 1933; children—Robert Eugene, Virginia Ann. Art dir., instr. Doris Grasso Sch. Fine Arts, Bayonne, N.J., 1952-61; exhibited in numerous group shows, including Thomson Gallery, N.Y.C., Pen and Brush Club, N.Y.C., Terry Art Inst., Miami, Fla., Newark Art Mus., Montclair (N.J.) Art Mus., Lever House, N.Y.C., Nat. Arts Club, N.Y.C., Nat. Arts Club, N.Y.C., Salamugundi Club, N.Y.C., North Shore Art & Assoc., others; pvt. collections U.S., Can., N.S., Europe, Bahamas; one man shows Burr Gallery, N.Y.C., Bennett Coll., Bayonne Pub. Library, others; represented in Paul Whitener Meml. Collection, Hickory (N.C.) Mus. Art, Jersey City Mus. Arts, George B. Burr Permanent Collection, N.Y.C., Bambergers Collection Famous People N.J., Jersey City Art Mus. Trustee, Jersey City Mus. Art, 1955-57. Recipient Pauline Wick award, 1961, Windsor Newton awards, 1958, 61, Jersey City Mus. award, 1958, Anna B. Vining award (oil), 1962; gold medallion Jersey Jour. award, gold medal Woman's Club, 1963; Stevens Inst. award, 1964; award for nat. achievement in art Amita, Inc., 1966; Patrons award N.J. Painters and Sculpture Soc., 1968; 1st award for sculpture Fedn. Women's Clubs, Ridgewood, N.J., 1971; 1st sculpture award Womens Club, Atlantic City, N.J., 1971; others. Fellow Am. Artists Profl. League, Internat. Arts and Letters (Switzerland); mem. Burr Artists, Hudson Artists (pres. 1960-62), Jersey City Mus. Assn., N.J. Painters and Sculptors Soc. (dir., rec. sec.), Trailside Art Mus. (permanent mem.), Essex Watercolor Soc. Bayonne Mus. Arts, Whistler Art Soc., Burr Galleries, Village Art Center Galleries, Sarasota Mus. Art Assn., Hunterdon Art Center Assn., Newark Art Center, Hudson Artists (dir.), Gotham Painters Rutherford, Plainfield art assns., Rockport Artists Assn. (asso.), Elks Aux. (pres. 1950-52), Ch. Guild (pres. 1950-52). Club: Bayonne Women's (art. chmn.). Address: Doris TenEyck Grasso Gallery 15 Langsford St Lanesville Gloucester MA 01930

GRATHOFF, RICHARD HELMUT, sociologist; b. Unna, Westphalia, Germany, Aug. 30, 1934; s. Hans and Hilde (Engelke) G.; m. Ruth Ann Blessman, July 29, 1961; children: Georg, Philip. B.S., U. Gottingen, 1961; M.A., New Sch. for Social Research, 1966, Ph.D., 1969; Habilitation, U. Konstanz, 1975. Instr. math. No. Ill. U., DeKalb, 1961-63; instr. math. Seton Hall U., South Orange, N.J., 1963-65; asst. prof. sociology U. Frankfurt (W.Ger.), 1965-70; pvt. dozent sociology U. Konstanz (W.Ger.), 1970-77; assoc. prof. sociology U. Toronto (Ont., Can.), 1977-78; prof. sociology U. Bielefeld (W.Ger.), 1978—; research cons. various countries, 1978—. Author: The Structure of Social Inconsistencies, 1970; editor The Theory of Social Action: Schutz and Parsons, 1978; (series) Uebergaenge, 1983—; contbr. articles to profl. jours. Am. Council Learned Socs. fellow, 1978; various research grants, 1972—. Mem. Internat. Sociol. Assn. (research com. bd. 1974-82), Deutsche Gesellschaft fur Soziologie, Japanese Soc. for Phenomenology and Social Science, Deutsche Gesellschaft für Phaenomenologische Forschung. Office: U Bielefeld, Postfach 8640, D-48 Bielefeld Federal Republic of Germany

GRATTAN-GUINNESS, IVOR OWEN, mathematics educator; b. Bakewell, England, June 23, 1941; s. Gerald Henry and Mary Helena (Brown) G.-G.; m. Enid Beatrice Neville, Jan. 9, 1965. BA, Oxford U., 1962, MA, 1967; MSc in Econs., London U., 1966, PhD, 1969, DSc, 1978. Math. instr. various instns. 1964—; now reader in math. Middlesex Poly., Enfield, Eng. Author: The Development of the Foundations of Mathematical Analysis, 1970, Dear Russell-Dear Jourdain, 1977; co-author: Joseph Fourier 1768-1830, 1972; editor, contbr. From the Calculus to Set Theory, 1980, History in Mathematics Education, 1987; editor Annals of Sci. jour., 1974-81; founder, editor History and Philosophy of Logic, 1979; contbr. numerous articles to profl. publs. Mem. Brit. Soc. History of Math. (pres. 1985—), Brit. Soc. History of Sci., Soc. for Physical Research. Office: Middlesex Poly at Enfield, Enfield Middlesex EN3 4SF, England

GRATTON, PATRICK JOHN FRANCIS, oil company executive; b. Denver, Aug. 28, 1933; s. Patrick Henry and Lorene Jean (Johnson) G.; m. Jean Marie McKinney, June 10, 1955; children: Sara, Vivian, Patrick, Lizabeth. BS in Geology, U. N.Mex., 1955, MS in Geology, 1958. Geologist Westvaco Mineral Devel. Corp., Grants, N.Mex., 1955; mining engr. Utah Internat., Denver, 1956; geologist Shell Oil Co., Roswell, N.Mex. and Tyler, Tex., 1957-62; adminstrv. asst. Delhi-Taylor Oil Corp., Dallas, 1962-64; exploration mgr. Eugene E. Nearburg, Dallas, 1965-70; pres. Patrick J.F. Gratton, Inc., Dallas, 1970—. Contbr. articles to profl. jours. Served with USCG, 1951-53, U.S. Army, 1956-57. Mem. Am. Assn. Petroleum Geologists (v.p. SW sect. 1976-77, del. 1978-81, pres.-elect, dir. profl. affairs 1988-89), Soc. Ind. Profl. Earth Scientists (v.p. 1976-77, pres. 1977-78), Tex. Ind. Producers and Royalty Owners Assn. (exec. com. 1985—), Dallas Geol. Soc. (pub. service award 1985). Roman Catholic. Clubs: Petroleum (Dallas), Explorers (N.Y.C.) (Tex.) (chmn.). Office: 2403 Thomas Ave Dallas TX 75201

GRAU, JAMES JOHN, brokerage house executive; b. Cin., July 9, 1949; s. John Conrad Jr. and Gloria Viven (Cowalsh) G.; m. Linda Lee Seats, Mar. 31, 1974 (div. Apr. 13, 1983); children: Jennifer, Christopher. Grad. high sch., Pitts., 1967. Sales mgr. various corps., 1971-74; pres., chief exec. officer Woods Music and Conservatory, Shawnee, Kans., 1975-79, Kope Food Products Inc., Lenexa, Kans., 1980—, Internat. Leasing Co., Lenexa, 1982—, Internat. Fin. Brokerage Inc., Lenexa, 1982—, Internat. Pub. and Communications Inc., 1988—; cons. in field. Served with USN, 1967-73. Republican. Methodist. Office: Internat Fin Brokerage Inc PO Box 14631 Lenexa KS 66215

GRAU, MARCY BEINISH, investment banker; b. Bklyn., Aug. 7, 1950; d. Joseph Beinish and Gloria (Rosenbaum) Bennett; m. Bennett Grau, Nov. 19,

1978; 2 children. A.B. with high honors, U. Mich., 1971; postgrad. Columbia U., 1972, N.Y. Inst. Fin., 1973. Asst. to chmn. Bancroft Convertible Fund, N.Y.C., 1973-75; precious metals trader J. Aron & Co., N.Y.C., 1975-81, mgr. metals mktg., 1981-83; v.p. Goldman, Sachs & Co/J. Aron, N.Y.C., 1983—; bus.-related translator Augustus Clothiers, N.Y.C., 1979—. Editor, contbr. Precious Metals Rev. and Outlook, 1980—. Vol. worker, pediatrics dept. Lenox Hill Hosp., N.Y.C., 1978-79; asst. The Holiday Project, The Hunger Project, N.Y.C., 1978-83; vol. Yorkville Common Pantry, N.Y.C., 1984; tutor Yorkville Neighborhood Assn., N.Y.C., 1984; assoc. Child Devel. Ctr., N.Y.C. Mem. Phi Beta Kappa. Democrat. Jewish. Avocations: interior design, fashion, cooking, swimming. Home: 300 West End Ave New York NY 10023 Office: Goldman Sachs & Co 85 Broad St New York NY 10004

GRAUZAM, ROLAND, plastic surgeon; b. Perigueux, France, Dec. 13, 1943; s. Andre and Solange (Gross) G.; m. Claudine B. Wiener, Jan. 28, 1979; children—Aline, Arnaud, Elizabeth. M.D., U. Strasbourg, 1972. Resident, asst. surgeon U. Strasbourg Med. Sch. Hosp., France, 1966-68, 71-74; resident plastic surgery Wilmington Med. Ctr., Del., 1974-76; teaching fellow S. Sacrement Hosp. Laval U., Quebec, 1969-70; plastic surgeon Adassa Hosp., Strasbourg, 1976—; expert at the Appelate Ct., Colmar, France, 1988— . Contbr. articles to profl. jours. Recipient 1st prize award Univ. Strasbourg, 1963. Fellow Royal Coll. Surgeons Can.; mem. Am. Soc. Plastic and Reconstructive Surgery.

GRAVEL, CLIFFORD RICHARD-HILAIRE, educator, writer; b. Passaic, N.J., Mar. 5, 1939; s. Raoul Donat and Edith (Shaw) G.; grad. various tax, sales, and ins. schools; BS in Phys. Sci. Teaching, N.Mex., 1986; 1 child, Genevieve. Chemist various cos., 1959-72; sales rep. Benjamin Moore Co., Los Angeles, 1973-81; sales mgr. Western Auto, 1981-82; terr. mgr. Pitts. Paints, 1987—. Editor: Menzia, Touchups, Turning Point, Cliffs Clippings; contbr. articles to various pubs. Fellow Internat. Soc. Philos. Inquiry; mem. Intertel, Fragile Philos. Instruments of Sherlock Holmes, Cincinnatus Soc., Mensa Internat. (news service rep. 1982-83), Internat. Platform Assn., Golden Key, Sigma Pi Sigma, Kappa Delta Pi, Pi Lambda Theta, Phi Eta Sigma. Office: 5800 Osuna Rd NE #307 Albuquerque NM 87110

GRAVES, JAMES HENRY, psychiatrist, educator, physician, administrator; b. Herrin, Ill., Sept. 29, 1924; s. James Henry and Anna Joyce (Keaster) G.; m. Helen A. Mataya, June 26, 1949 (div. June 1984); children—Christina Adrienne, James Willis, John David Nicholas. B.S., Northwestern U., 1946, M.B., M.S., 1949, M.D., 1950. Diplomate Am. Bd. Psychiatry and Neurology. Intern, Charity Hosp., New Orleans, 1949-50; resident in psychiatry U.S. Air Force Med. Corp., 1950-53; chief women's div. Ypsilanti State Hosp., Mich., 1953-55; chief male service-psychiatry Detroit Receiving Hosp., 1955-58, dir. psychiatry, 1958-64; med. dir. Oakland County Community Mental Health Services Bd., 1985—; clin. assoc. prof. psychiatry Wayne State U. Coll. Medicine, Detroit, 1963—; practice medicine specializing in psychiatry, Ann Arbor, Mich., 1954-55, Detroit, 1955-85, Franklin Village, Mich., 1985—; commr. mental health State of Mich., 1959-63; chmn. Pub. Policy Task Force on Mental Health, 1983-84. Mem. Med. Adv. Com. to Pres. Kennedy, 1960-61, Physicians for Social Responsibility, Detroit, 1983—; pres. Oakland County Interagency Council on Children and Youth; bd. dirs. Comprehensive Health Planning Council of Southeastern Mich., Alliance for Mental Health Services. Served to capt. USAF, 1950-53. Fellow Am. Psychiat. Assn. (life), Am. Pub. Health Assn., Am. Orthopsychiat. Assn.; mem. AMA, Mich. State Med. Soc., Oakland County Med. Soc., Mich. Psychiat. Soc. (councillor 1960-63, v.p. 1984-85, pres. 1986-87). Club: Cajal (Montreal, Que., Can.). Avocations: tennis; distance swimming; sailing; skiing. Home: 254 Lewiston Grosse Pointe Farms MI 48236 Office: Oakland County Community Mental Health Services Bd 1200 N Telegraph Pontiac MI 48053

GRAVES, PIRKKO MAIJA-LEENA, clinical psychologist, psychoanalyst; b. Tampere, Finland, Jan. 20, 1930; came to U.S., 1957; d. Frans Vilho and Bertta Katariina (Katajisto) Lahtinen; Mag.Phil. (Finnish State scholar 1949-52), 1954; French Govt. scholar, U. Paris, 1954-55; Ph.D. (Fulbright scholar 1957-58, Lucy E. Elliott scholar 1958-59), U. Mich., 1964; postgrad. Washington Psychoanalytic Inst.; m. Irving Lawrence Graves, Dec. 31, 1969. Psychologist, U. Mich. Psychol. Clinic, 1960-63, asst. study dir. Survey Research Center, 1961-63, instr. psychology, 1964-70; asst. prof. Johns Hopkins U., 1970-76, prin. investigator under-nutrition and infant devel. Internat. Ctr. for Research, Calcutta, India and Kathmandu, Nepal, 1970-73, lectr., sr. research psychologist Precursors Study Med. Sch., 1979—; assoc. clin. prof. U. Md. Med. Sch.; dir. research Mental Health Study Center, NIMH, 1976-79; cons. in field. Fellow Md. Psychol. Assn.; mem. Am. Psychol. Assn., Am. Psychoanalytic Assn. Author articles in field, chpts. in books. Home: 2235 Kentucky Ave Baltimore MD 21213 Office: 550 N Broadway Baltimore MD 21205

GRAVES, SUSAN L. AKERS, marketing specialist; b. Garden City, Kans., Feb. 4, 1948; d. Riley D. and Clara F. (Pallissard) Akers. Student Ariz. State U., 1982-83; BS, U. Calif.-San Diego, 1972; post-grad. in bus. Loyola Marymount U., 1977-80. Pub. info. dir. Coll. Medicine, U. Calif.-Irvine, 1974-77; dir. pub. relations and publs. Loyola Marymount U., Los Angeles, 1977-80; v.p. Ralph Jackson Assocs., Beverly Hills, Calif., 1980-82; dir. pub. affairs Ramada Inns, Inc., Phoenix, 1982-83; pub. relations dir. Am. Med. Internat., Brea, Calif., 1983-84; mktg. dir. Irvine Office & Indsl. Cos. divs. The Irvine Co., Newport Beach, Calif., 1984—; prin. The Creative Consortium, mktg. firm. Active Scottsdale Arts Ctr. Assn., 1982-83, No. Ariz. Hist. Mus., Flagstaff, 1982, Los Angeles County Art Mus.; cons. LWV, Jr. Achievement, Phoenix, 1983; bd. dirs. Irvine Symphony, 1984-87, adv. bd. U. Calif., Irvine; bd. govs. Irvine Valley Coll. Found.; chmn. adv. com. on mktg. Calif. Community Coll., 1985-87; mem. adv. bd. Irvine Sci. Edn. Inst., U. Calif., Irvine. Council for Advancement and Support of Edn. grantee, 1976. Mem. Women in Communications, Inc. (Best Communications Student of Yr. 1970; editor regional newsletter 1970-72, regional student dir. 1970-72, v.p. 1982), Pub. Relations Soc. Am. (co-recipient Silver Anvil award 1973), Profl. Journalists Soc., Sigma Delta Chi. Democrat. Home: 20612 Reef Ln Huntington Beach CA 92646 Office: Irvine Co Newport Beach CA 92660

GRAY, ALLEN GIBBS, metallurgist, materials engineer, editor; b. Birmingham, Ala., July 28, 1915; s. Crawford H. and Marie (Gibbs) G.; m. Jean Breckenridge, Apr. 5, 1948; children: Alice, James. M.S., Vanderbilt U., 1938; Ph.D., U. Wis., 1940. Chemist, metallurgist E.I. du Pont de Nemours & Co., 1940-52; tech. work Manhattan Atomic Bomb Project, 1943-45; tech. editor Steel mag., 1952-58; editor Metal Progress mag., Am. Soc. Metals, 1958-72, pub., 1972-81; dir. periodical publs. Am. Soc. Metals, 1963-81, tech. dir., 1974-83, now cons.; adj. prof. metallurgy and mgmt. of tech. Vanderbilt U., Nashville, 1983—; advisor on strategic materials to industry and govt.; mgr. of govt. program on assessment of Nat. Def. Stockpile Materials, 1982—; lectr. to NATO nations on chromium conservation, Portugal, 1983; presenter of strategic materials, Inst. of Nat. Defense, Portugal, 1983; organizer strategic materials workshops; adv. com. on indsl. info. AEC, 1952—; chmn. spl. com. tech. aspects critical and strategic materials nat. materials bd. Nat. Acad. Scis., 1969—; Disting. Fishel lectr. Vanderbilt U., 1976; gave Congl. testimony on nat. materials policy and substitution, 1979; adv., speaker on materials substitution, raw materials planning and resources mgmt., 1980; mem. Ohio Gov.'s Council on Atomic Energy, 1956-58; gen. chmn. Nat. Conf. on Materials Availability and Utilization, 1975; chmn. 7th Biennial Conf. on Nat. Materials Policy, 1982; mem. adv. bd. Fedn. Materials Socs., 1975-83, Welding Research Council, 1970-82; mem. tech. adv. com. Metal Properties Council, 1975—. Author: Modern Electroplating, 1953; contbr.: sect. steel tech. Ency. Americana; sect. alloy steels Ency. Brit. Fellow Am. Soc. Metals, Am. Inst. Chemists; mem. Am. socs. testing materials, Assn. Technique de Traitement Thermique (hon.), Sigma Xi. Home: 4301 Esteswood Dr Nashville TN 37215 Office: Engring Sch Vanderbilt U Nashville TN 37235

GRAY, BASIL, museum curator, Orientalist; b. July 21, 1904; s. Charles and Florence (Elworthy) G.; M.A., Oxford U.; m. Nicolete Binyon, 1933; 2 sons, 2 daus. (1 dec.). Mem. Brit. Acad. excavations in Constantinople, 1928; with Brit. Mus., from 1928, in charge Oriental antiquities, from 1938, dep. keeper, 1940-46, keeper, 1946-69, acting dir. and prin. librarian, 1968; pres. 6th Internat. Congress Iranian Art and Archeology, Oxford, 1972; mem. Reviewing Com. on Export of Works of Art, 1971-79; chmn. exhbn. com. The Arts of Islam, Hayward Gallery, 1976. Mem. vis. com. Ashmolean Mus., Oxford, 1969-79. Recipient Sir Percy Sykes Meml. medal, 1978. Fellow Brit. Acad.; mem. Oriental Ceramic Soc. (pres. 1962-65, 71-74, 77-78), Soc. South Asian Studies (pres. Soc. Afghan Studies 1979—), Societas Iranologica Europaea (pres. 1983—). Author: Persian Painting, 1930; (with others) Persian Miniature Painting, 1933; (with Leigh Ashton) Chinese Art, 1935; The English Print, 1937; Persian Painting, New York, 1940; Rajput Painting, 1948; (with others) Commemorative Catalogue of the Exhibition of the Art of India and Pakistan, 1947-48, 1950; Treasures of Indian Miniatures in the Bikanir Palace Collection, 1951; Early Chinese Poettery and Porcelain, 1953; Japanese Screen-paintings, 1955; Buddhist Cave Paintings at Tun-huang, 1959; Treasures of Asia: Persian Painting, 1961; (with D.E. Barrett) Paintings of India, 1963; An Album of Miniatures and Illuminations from the Baysonhori Manuscript of the Shahnameh of Ferdowsi, 1971; The World History of Rashid al-Din, a study of the RAS manuscript, 1979; Sung Porcelain and Stoneware, 1983; Studies in Chinese and Islamic Art, 2 vols., 1985-86; author/editor: The Arts of the Book in Central Asia 1370-1506, 1979; The Arts of India, 1981; editor: Faber Gallery of Oriental Art and Arts of the East Series. Address: Dawber's House, Long Wittenham, Oxford OX14 4QQ, England *

GRAY, CHARLES AUGUSTUS, banker; b. Syracuse, N.Y., Sept. 16, 1928; s. Charles William and Elizabeth Marie (Koch) G.; cert. Am. Inst. Banking, 1958, Sch. Bank Adminstrn., 1961. With Mchts. Nat. Bank & Trust Co. of Syracuse, 1946-77, auditor, 1959-77, v.p., 1970-77; N.Y. State dir. Bank Adminstrn. Inst., 1970-72; regional auditor Central N.Y. region Irving Bank Corp., 1977-82, v.p., 1982—. Treas., Upper N.Y. Synod Luth. Ch. in Am., 1966-87, Upstate N.Y. Synod of Evang. Luth. Ch. in Am., 1988—; treas. Luth. Found. Upstate N.Y., 1972-79, bd. dirs., 1980—; pres. Interfrat. Alumni Council, Syracuse U., 1980-83. Cert. internal auditor. Mem. Bank Adminstrn. Inst. (pres. central N.Y. chpt. 1970-72), Inst. Internal Auditors (treas. central N.Y. chpt. 1974-76, pres. 1985-86). Republican. Clubs: Lions (pres. local club 1973-75), Masons, Shriners. Home: 1321 Westmoreland Ave Syracuse NY 13210 Office: 220 S Warren St Syracuse NY 13201

GRAY, CHRISTOPHER DONALD, software researcher, author, consultant; b. Brookville, Pa., May 18, 1951; s. Donald Garrison and Patricia Lee (Huffman) G.; m. Allison Selby Farragher, Oct. 12, 1974; children: Patrick Xanthe, Colin Christopher. BA in Math., Washington and Jefferson Coll., 1973; MS in Math., Carnegie-Mellon U., 1975. Mfg. systems analyst Ohaus Scale Corp., Florham Park, N.J., 1974-76; systems rep. Software Internat. Corp., 1976-77, cons. mfg. systems, 1977-78, mktg. rep., 1978-79; v.p. Mfg. Software Systems, Inc., Essex Junction, Vt., 1979-85, pres., 1985; pres. Oliver Wight Software Research, Inc., 1985—; assoc. Oliver Wight Edn. Assocs., Newbury, N.H., 1982—; cons. Oliver Wight Video Prodns., Essex Junction, 1980-84; advisor mfg. applications, Software News, Sentry Pub. Co., Hudson, Mass., 1983—. Author: The Right Choice: The Complete Guide to Evaluating, Selecting and Installing MRP II Software, 1987; co-author MRP II Standard System, 1983, MRP II/JIT Standard System, 1988; contbr. research reports, articles and conf. papers to tech. lit. Fellow Am. Prodn. and Inventory Control Soc. (cert. fellow prodn. and inventory mgmt.; chpt. program chmn. 1978-79, v.p. 1979-80, pres. 1980-81); mem. Data Processing Mgmt. Assn., Phi Beta Kappa. Republican. Presbyterian. Avocations: gardening, landscaping, house restoration, furniture building. Home: Piscassic Rd PO Box 199 Newfields NH 03856 Office: Oliver Wight Software Research Inc 5 Oliver Wight Dr Essex Junction VT 05452

GRAY, CLARENCE JONES, educator, dean emeritus; b. Red Bank, N.J., June 21, 1908; s. Clarence J. Sr. and Elsie (Megill) G.; B.A., U. Richmond, 1933, LL.D., 1979; M.A., Columbia U., 1934; postgrad. Centro de Estudios Historicos, Madrid, summer 1935; Ed.D., U. Va., 1962; m. Jane Love Little, Aug. 25, 1934; children—Frances Gray Adams, Kenneth Stewart. Underwriter Aetna Life and Casualty, 1925-30; instr. Spanish, Columbia U., 1934-38; gen. sec., mem. exec. council Instituto de las Espanas en los Estados Unidos, 1934-39; instr., sec. dept. Romance langs. Queens Coll., N.Y.C., 1938-46 (on mil. leave 1943-46); dean students U. Richmond (Va.), 1946-68, assoc. prof. modern langs., 1946-62, prof., 1962-79, emeritus, 1979—, dean adminstrv. services, 1968-73, dean adminstrn., 1973-79, emeritus, 1979—, spl. cons. to pres., 1979—, editor bull., 1968-74, moderator U. Richmond-WRNL Radio Scholarship Quiz Program, mem. bd. Univ. Assos. Cons., Commn. on Colls., So. Assn. Colls. and Schs. Trustee' Inst. Mediterranean Studies. Served from lt. to lt. comdr., USNR, 1943-46. Recipient Nat. Alumni award for disting. service U. Richmond. Mem. MLA, NEA, Am. Assn. Tchrs. Spanish, Am. Assn. for Higher Edn., Newcomen Soc. N.Am., Inst. Internat. Edn. (cert. meritorius service), Phi Beta Kappa (sec. emeritus), Phi Delta Kappa, Kappa Delta Pi, Omicron Delta Kappa (nat. sec. gen. council 1966-72, Distinguished Service key 1968, nat. chmn. scholarship awards 1972-78), Alpha Psi Omega, Phi Gamma Delta (award for disting. and exceptional service), Alpha Phi Omega, Phi Beta Kappa (life). Baptist. Mem. Legion of Honor, Order of De Molay. Clubs: Country of Va., Colonnade. Lodges: Masons, Rotary. Contbr. to profl. jours. Home: 2956 Hathaway Rd #611 Richmond VA 23225

GRAY, DAHLI, accounting educator; b. Grand Junction, Colo., Dec. 28, 1948; d. Forrest Walter and Mary (Crockett) G.; m. Paul Victor Konka, Jan. 23, 1981. BS, Ea. Oreg. State U., 1971; MBA, Portland (Oreg.) State U., 1976; D of Bus. Adminstrn., George Washington U., 1984. Instr. acctg. Portland State U., 1976-79, George Mason U., Fairfax, Va., 1980, George Washington U., Washington, 1981-82; asst. prof. Oreg. State U., Corvallis, 1983-86; research fellow U. Notre Dame, South Bend, Ind., 1986-88; assoc. prof. Am. U., Washington, 1988—. Contbr. articles to profl. jours. Named Tchr. of Yr., Alpha Lambda Delta, 1986; Peat Marwick Mitchell & Co. fellow, 1986. Mem. Internat. Assn. Acctg. Research and Edn., Am. Inst. CPA's, Nat. Assn. Accts. (Andrew Barr award 1982, 84, Cert. Merit 1982), Am. Acctg. Assn., Inst. Cert. Mgmt. Accts. Democrat. Home: 5564 Burnside Dr Rockville MD 20853-2457 Office: Am U Kogod Coll of Bus 4400 Massachusetts Ave NW Washington DC 20016

GRAY, DWIGHT ELDER, retired physicist; b. Knoxville, Ohio, July 6, 1903; s. Lorenzo Lackey and Mary Emma (Elder) G.; m. Helen Baldwin, Sept. 5, 1931 (dec. Feb. 1984). A.B., Muskingum Coll., 1925; M.A., Ohio State U., 1929, Ph.D., 1932. Instr. physics U. Akron, 1932-43; tech. reports supr. Underwater Sound Lab., Harvard U., Cambridge, Mass., 1944-45; tech. reports supr. Applied Physics Lab., Johns Hopkins U., Silver Spring, Md., 1945-50; chief tech. info. div. Library Congress, Washington, 1950-55, 63-68; tech. info. specialist NSF, Washington 1955-63; Washington rep. Am. Inst. Physics, 1969-70. Co-author: Man and His Physical World, 1942, Radiation Monitoring in Atomic Defense, 1951; author So You Have to Write A Technical Report, 1970; coordinating editor Am. Inst. of Physics Handbook, 1957, 63, 72. Mem. Am. Phys. Soc., Sigma Xi, Sigma Pi Sigma. Club: Cosmos (sec. 1976-82), (disting. service award, 1982), (Washington). Home: Cole Spring Plaza 1001 Spring St #1105 Silver Spring MD 20910

GRAY, FESTUS GAIL, electrical engineering educator, researcher; b. Moundsville, W.Va., Aug. 16, 1943; s. Festus P. and Elsie V. (Rine) G.; m. Caryl Evelyn Anderson, Aug. 24, 1968; children—David, Andrew, Daniel. B.S.E.E., W.Va. U., 1965, M.S.E.E., 1967; Ph.D., U. Mich., 1971. Instr. W.Va. U., Morgantown, 1966-67; teaching fellow U. Mich., 1967-70; asst. prof. Va. Poly. Inst. and State U., Blacksburg, 1971-77, assoc. prof., 1977-82, prof., 1983—; vis. scientist Research Triangle Inst., N.C., 1984-85; faculty fellow NASA, 1975; cons. Inland Motors, Radford, Va., 1980, Research Triangle Inst., 1987—; researcher Rome Air Devel. Ctr., N.Y., 1980-81, Naval Surface Weapons Ctr., Dahlgren, Va., 1982-83, Army Research Office, 1983-86; publs. chmn. Internat. Symposium on Fault Tolerant Computing, Ann Arbor, Mich., 1985; assoc. treas., Northside Presbyn. Ch., Blacksburg, 1986—. Contbr. articles to sci. jours. Bd. deacons Northside Presbyn. Ch., Blacksburg, 1980-83; coach S.W. Va. Soccer Assn., Blacksburg, 1980-86. Grantee NSF, Office Naval Research, NASA. Mem. IEEE (chpt. chmn. 1979-80), Assn. Computing Machinery, Heath Users Group, Sigma Xi. Democrat. Research on fault tolerance, diagnosis, testing, and reliability issues for VLSI; distributed and multiprocessor computer architectures. Home: 304 Fincastle Dr Blacksburg VA 24060 Office: Va Poly Inst and State U Blacksburg VA 24061

GRAY, GEORGE, mural painter; b. Harrisburg, Pa., Dec. 23, 1907; s. George Zacharias and Anna Margaret (Barger) G. Ed., Harrisburg Tech. High Sch., Sch. Indsl. Art, Phila., 1927-30, Acad. Fine Arts, Wilmington, Del., 1931-33, Art Students League, N.Y.C., Howard Pyle Sch. Illustration, Wilmington. Designer stage scenery, N.Y.C., 1926; invited to sketch scenes of army life in various forts and camps; tchr. anatomy and figure constrn. while attending art classes, Phila., Wilmington, later staff artist, U.S. Inf. Jour., U.S. Cav. Jour., Washington, N.Y. Nat. Guardsmen, Pa. N.G. Mag., mural painter patron, Gen. J. Leslie Kincaid, pres., Am. Hotels Corp., N.Y.C., 1934—; murals exhibited in hotels throughout U.S., including MacArthur of Battan, Hotel Jefferson-Clinton, Syracuse, N.Y.; Gen. George Rogers Clark, Louisville; 3 murals Hist. L.I, Suffolk County Savs. and Loan Bank, Babylon, L.I.; mural painting Brooklyn Bridge, Seamen's Ch. Inst., N.Y.C.; hist. picture map, Hotel Huntington, L.I., portraits and paintings in pvt. collections, U.S. and abroad; mil. artist, Engring. Bd., Ft. Belvoir, Va., combat artist, U.S. Coast Guard Hdqrs., Washington, originator, chmn., Navy Art Cooperation and Liaison Com. of Salmagundi Club. Founder, chmn. Coast Guard Art Program Salmagundi Club. Recipient Meritorious Pub. Service citation Dept. Navy, 1964; Louis E. Seley NACAL award, 1970; medal of honor Salmagundi Club, 1973; George Gray award U.S. Coast Guard, 1983. Life fellow Royal Soc. Arts (London); mem. Soc. Illustrators, Am. Mil. Inst., Co. Mil. Collectors and Historians, Nat. Soc. Mural Painters, Am. Vets. Soc. Artists, Am. Artists Profl. League, Nat. Hist. Soc. (founding mem.), Assn. Mil. Surgeons U.S., Navy League U.S. (Commodore Club), U.S. Naval Inst., Armed Forces Mgmt. Inst., Artists Fellowship. Clubs: Arts (Washington); Salmagundi (N.Y.C.) (orginator, chmn. COGAP, Coast Guard art program of club). Address: Salmagundi Club 47 Fifth Ave New York NY 10003

GRAY, GORDON JOSEPH CARDINAL, emeritus archbishop of St. Andrews and Edinburgh; b. Edinburgh, Aug. 10, 1910; s. Francis William and Angela Gray; student St. John's Sem., Wonerish; M.A. with honours, St. Andrews U., D.D. (hon.); D. Univ., Heriot-Watt U. Ordained priest Roman Catholic Ch., consecrated bishop, elevated to cardinal, 1969; asst. priest, St. Andrews, 1935-41; parish priest, Hawick, 1941-47; rector Blairs' Coll., Aberdeen, Scotland, 1947-51; archbishop of St. Andrews and Edinburgh, 1951-85, cardinal, 1969—. Mem. Congregation for Evangelization of Peoples, Congregation of the Sacraments, Congregation of Clerics. Hon. fellow Ednl. Inst. Scotland. Office: St Bennets, 42 Greenhill Gardens, Edinburgh 10 Scotland

GRAY, HANNA HOLBORN, university president; b. Heidelberg, Germany, Oct. 25, 1930; d. Hajo and Annemarie (Bettmann) Holborn; m. Charles Montgomery Gray, June 19, 1954. AB, Bryn Mawr Coll., 1950; PhD, Harvard U., 1957; MA, Yale U., 1971, LLD, 1978; LittD (hon.), St. Lawrence U., 1974; HHD (hon.), St. Mary's Coll., 1974; LHD (hon.), Grinnell (Iowa) Coll., 1974, Lawrence U., 1974, Denison U., 1974; LLD (hon.), Union Coll., 1975, Regis Coll., 1976; LHD (hon.), Wheaton Coll., 1976; LLD (hon.), Dartmouth Coll., 1978, Trinity Coll., 1978, U. Bridgeport, 1978, Dickinson Coll., 1979, Brown U., 1979, Wittenburg U., 1979; LHD (hon.), Marlboro Coll., 1979, Rikkyo (Japan) U., 1979; LittD (hon.), Oxford (Eng.) U., 1979; LHD (hon.), Roosevelt U., 1980, Knox Coll., 1980; LLD (hon.), U. Rochester, 1980, U. Notre Dame, 1980, U. So. Calif., 1980, U. Mich., 1981; LHD (hon.), Coe Coll., 1981, Thomas Jefferson U., 1981, Duke U., 1982, New Sch. for Social Research, 1982, Clark U., 1982; LLD (hon.), Princeton U., 1982, Georgetown U., 1983; LHD (hon.), Brandeis U., 1983, Colgate U., 1983, Wayne State U., 1984, Miami U., Oxford, Ohio, 1984, So. Meth. U., Dallas, 1984; LLD (hon.), Marquette U., 1984, W.Va. Wesleyan U., 1985, Hamilton Coll., 1985; LHD (hon.), CUNY, 1985, U. Denver, 1985; LittD, Washington U., St. Louis, 1985; LHD (hon.), Am. Coll. Greece, 1986; LLD, Smith Coll., 1986, U. Miami, 1986; LLD (hon.), Columbia U., 1987; LHD (hon.), Muskingum Coll., 1987, Rush Presbyn. St. Lukes Med. Ctr., Chgo., 1987, N.Y.U., 1988. Instr. Bryn Mawr Coll., 1953-54; teaching fellow Harvard, Pa., 1955-57; instr. Harvard, 1957-59, asst. prof., 1959-60, vis. lectr., 1963-64; asst. prof. U. Chgo., 1961-64, asso. prof., 1964-72; dean, prof. Northwestern U., Evanston, Ill., 1972-74; provost, prof. history Yale U., 1974-78, acting pres., 1977-78; pres., prof. history U. Chgo., 1978—; dir. Cummins Engine Co., J.P. Morgan & Co., Morgan Guaranty Trust Co., Atlantic Richfield Co., Ameritech; fellow Center for Advanced Study in Behavioral Scis., 1966-67, vis. scholar, 1970-71. Editor: (with Charles Gray) Jour. Modern History, 1965-70; contbr. articles to profl. jours. Mem. Nat. Council on Humanities, 1972-78; trustee Yale Corp., 1971-74; bd. dirs. Chgo. Council Fgn. Relations, Andrew W. Mellon Found.; trustee Mus. Sci. and Industry, Ctr. for Advanced Study in the Behavioral Scis, Bryn Mawr Coll., Field Found. Ill., Howard Hughes Med. Inst., Nat. Humanities Ctr. Recipient Medal Liberty award, 1986; Fulbright scholar, 1950-52; U. Chgo. Newberry Library fellow, 1960-61; Phi Beta Kappa vis. scholar, 1971-72; hon. fellow St. Anne's Coll., Oxford U., 1978—. Fellow Am. Acad. Arts and Scis.; mem. Renaissance Soc. Am., Am. Philos. Soc., Nat. Acad. Edn., Phi Beta Kappa. Office: U Chgo 5801 S Ellis Ave Chicago IL 60637

GRAY, HENRY DAVID, minister, congregational center dean; b. Antrim, No. Ireland, Jan. 18, 1908; came to U.S., 1923; s. Nathaniel and Margaret (Lawther) G.; m. Helen Katharine Lorbeer, Aug. 12, 1930; children—Mildred Ellen, David Lawther, Betsey Charisma. B.A. magna cum laude, Pomona Coll., 1930, D.D. (hon.), 1954; M. Div. summa cum laude, Hartford Theol. Sem., 1933; Ph.D., Edinburgh U., Scotland, 1935; cert. in religious edn., Boston U., 1931; Cert. Theology, Tubingen U., Fed. Republic Germany, 1935; D. Litt. (hon.), Piedmont Coll., 1976. Ordained minister Congregational Ch., 1935. Numerous positions Congl. Chs., worldwide, 1935—; missionary Congl. Chs., Western Samoa, 1966; dir. 300th anniversary yr. program Old South Ch., Hartford, Conn., 1969-70; minister emeritus Old South Ch., Hartford, 1970—; dir. summer student study Congl. Ch., Europe, Middle East, worldwide, 1948-70; interim minister Hollywood Congl. Ch., Calif., 1971, North Hollywood Congl. Ch., Calif., 1971-72; dean Am. Congl. Ctr., South Pasadena, Calif., 1972—. Author: A Theology for Christian Youth, 1941, Science and Religion, 1946, Christian Doctrine of Grace, 1948 (best full length theol. book Ind. Press, London, 1948), The Christian Marriage Service, 1950, The Upward Call, 1952, Service Book, 1966, God's Torchbearers, 1970, Congregational Usage, 1976, Congregational Worshipbook, 1978, Pilgrim Fathers Reach the Pacific, 1981, Soundings, 1980, Waymarks, 1983, Plus Ultra, Vol. 1, 1983, Vol. 2, 1985, The Mediators, 1984; editor (monthly mag.) The Congregationalist, 1962-66, (monthly mag.) The Pilgrim Highroad, 1939-42, Congregational Jour., 1975—; contbr. numerous articles to profl. jours., also pamphlets; numerous appearances on TV and radio. Active numerous civic organizations, 1924-70; mem. Hartford City Plan Commn., 1959-70, chmn., 1962-67, 70; organizer Ventura City Environ. Coalition, Calif., 1971; mem. exec. com. Comprehensive Planning Commn., Ventura, Calif., 1973-77; chmn. Cultural Heritage Team, Ventura, 1974-75; pres. South Village, Hartford, 1968-84; mem. Nat. Com. for Scouting, 1939-42; former parliamentarian/vice chmn. Santa Monica Mountains Nat. Commn., Nat. Park Service; founder Congl. World Assembly of Youth, 1949. Recipient numerous awards Boy Scouts Am., Hartford Theol. Sem., Congl. Chs., citation of excellence State of Conn., 1970, Resolution of Profound Appreciation City Council Hartford, 1970, Resolution Commendation award Bd. Suprs. Ventura, 1985, letter of commendation Supt. Nat. Park Service, 1985, citation Conn. Conf. United Ch. Christ, 1985, Spl. Commendation, Internat. Congl. Council, 1987; Gray Hall named in his honor, South Pasadena, Calif., 1955, Hartford, 1960, Alexandroupolis, Greece, 1962, Gray Chapel named for him, Kristocoil, Kerala, India, 1967, Gray Student Union named for him Lady Doak Coll., Madurai, India, 1967. Fellow Royal Anthropol. Inst., Am. Anthropol. Assn.; mem. Calif. West Congl. Assn. Chs. and Ministers (cons. policy 1984—), Nat. Assn. Congl. Christian Chs. (numerous coms., chmn. coms., offices), Clerics Club, Am. Acad. Religion, Soc. Bibl. Lit., Ventura County Hist. Soc., Calif. Hist. Soc., Nat. Hist. Soc., Am. Congl. Assn. (bd. dirs. 1965-70), United Ref. Ch. History Soc., Brit. Congl. Hist. Circle, Inst. Pacific Studies, Congl. World Assembly Youth (founder, bd. dirs. 1962, chmn. 1985), Congl. Christian Hist. Soc., Congl. Fellowship Conn. (life, exec. com.), Hartford Assn. Congl. Christian Chs. and Ministers (exec. com. 1956-60, citation 1985), Nat. Pilgrim Fellowship (founder, life counselor), Nat. Eagle Scout Assn., Phi Beta Kappa, Delta Sigma Rho. Republican. Clubs: Pasadena Athletic, Wranglers (Pasadena); Oneonta Mens Service (San Gabriel); Congl. Ministers (Scotland). Lodge: Order DeMolay (chevilier of hon.). Home: 298 Fairfax Ave Ventura CA 93003 Office: Am Congregational Ctr 1515 Garfield Ave South Pasadena CA 91030

GRAY, JAN CHARLES, lawyer; b. Des Moines, June 15, 1947. s. Charles Donald and Mary C. Gray; m. Anita Marie Ringwald, June 6, 1987. B.A. in

Econs., U. Calif.-Berkeley, 1969; M.B.A., Pepperdine U., 1986, J.D., Harvard U., 1972. Bar: Calif. 1972, D.C. 1974. Law clk. Kindel & Anderson, Los Angeles, 1971-72; assoc. Halstead, Baker & Sterling, Los Angeles, 1972-75; sr. v.p., gen. counsel external affairs, sec. Ralphs Grocery Co., Los Angeles, 1975—; judge pro tem Los Angeles Mcpl. Ct., 1977—; instr. bus. UCLA, 1976—, Pepperdine MBA Program, 1985—; arbitrator Am. Arbitration Assn., 1977—; media spokesman So. Calif. Grocers Assn., Calif. Grocers Assn.; real estate broker, Los Angeles, 1973—. Trustee, South Bay U. Coll. Law, 1978-79; mem. bd. visitors Southwestern U. Sch. Law, 1983—; mem. Los Angeles County Pvt. Industry Council, 1982—, exec. com. 1984-88, chmn. econ. devel. task force, 1986—; mem. Los Angeles County Martin Luther King, Jr. Gen. Hosp. Authority, 1984—; mem. Los Angeles County Aviation Commn, 1986—; Los Angeles Police Crime Prevention Adv. Council, 1986—; Angelus Plaza Adv. Bd., 1983—; bd. dirs. RecyCAL of So. Calif., 1983—; bd. trustees Santa Monica Hosp. Found., 1986—; mem. Los Angeles County Democratic Central Com., 1980-82 ; del. Dem. Nat. Conv., 1980. Recipient So. Calif. Grocers Assn. award for outstanding contbns. to food industry, 1982; Calif./Nev. Soft Drink Assn. appreciation award for No on 11 Campaign, 1983. Mem. ABA, Calif. Bar Assn., Los Angeles County Bar Assn. (exec. com. corp. law depts. sect. 1974-76, 79—, vice-chmn. 1988—, exec. com. barristers sect. 1974-75, 79-81), San Fernando Valley Bar Assn. (chmn. real property sect. 1975-77, Los Angeles Pub. Affairs Officers Assn., Los Angeles World Affairs Council, Calif. Retailers Assn. (supermarket com.), Food Mktg. Inst. (govt. relations com., govt. affairs council), So. Calif. Businessmen's Assn. (bd. dirs. 1981—, mem. exec. com. 1982—, sec. 1986—), Town Hall Los Angeles, U. Calif. Alumni Assn., Ephebian Soc. Los Angeles, Phi Beta Kappa. Club: Harvard of So. Calif. Contbg. author: Life or Death, Who Controls?, 1976; contbr. articles to legal jours. Home: PO Box 407 Beverly Hills CA 90213 Office: PO Box 54143 Los Angeles CA 90054

GRAY, JOHN ARCHIBALD (BROWNE), medical physiologist; b. Mar. 30, 1918; s. Archibald Gray; attended Cheltenham Coll.; Clare Coll., Cambridge (Eng.) U., Univ. Coll. Hosp.; B.A., 1939; M.A., 1942; M.B., B.Chir., 1942; Sc.D., 1962; D.Sc. hon., Exeter, 1985; m. Vera Kathleen Mares, 1946; 2 children. Service research for MRC, 1943-45, mem. sci. staff of MRC at Nat. Inst. for Med. Research, 1946-52, 2d sec. Med. Research Council, 1966-68, sec., 1966-77, dep. chmn., 1975-77, mem. external sci. staff MRC, Marine Biol. Assn. Labs., Plymouth, Eng., 1977-83; in physiology Univ. Coll., London U., 1952-58, prof. physiology, 1959-66. Served as surg. lt. RNVR, 1945-46. Fellow Royal Soc., Royal Coll. Physicians, Inst. Biol. Contbr. articles, mainly on sensory recptors and sensory system, to profl. jours. Office: care Royal Soc, 6 Carlton House Terrace, London SW1 5AG, England

GRAY, JOHN EDMUND, chemical engineer; b. Woonsocket, R.I., Apr. 13, 1922; s. John Joseph and Alice (Naylor) G.; m. Mary Lightbody, Dec. 3, 1944; children: Jane Elizabeth Gray Redmond, John Carlton, Jeffrey Naylor. B.S. in Chem. Engring, U. R.I., 1943. Research engr. Westinghouse Electric Corp., Bloomfield, N.J., 1943-46; sr. design engr. engring. div. Gen. Electric Co., Hanford, Wash., 1946-47; head materials sect. atomic power dept. Gen. Engring. and Cons. Lab., Schenectady, 1948-49; materials adminstr. Naval Reactors br. AEC, U.S. Navy, 1949-50; dir. tech. and prodn. div. U.S. AEC (Savannah River Plant), S.C., 1950-54; project mgr. Shippingport Atomic Power Sta., Duquesne Light Co., Pitts., 1954-60; pres., chmn., chief exec. officer NUS Corp., Rockville, Md., 1960-72; energy cons. Ford Found. Energy Policy Project, 1972-73, Mass. Inst. Tech. Center for Policy Alternatives, 1973, Edison Electric Inst., 1974-77; chmn. Internat. Energy Assocs. Ltd., Washington, 1976—; chmn. IEA of Japan Co., Ltd., Tokyo, 1982—, IEAL Energie Cons., Bonn, 1985—; bd. dirs. ERC Internat., 1978—, pres., 1985—. Author: Energy Policy: Industry Perspectives, 1975; (with others) Energy Research and Development, 1975, Nuclear Fuels Policy, 1976, International Cooperation on Breeder Reactors, 1978, Nuclear Power and Nuclear Weapons Proliferation, 1978, U.S. Energy Policy and U.S. Foreign Policy in the 1980s, 1981, U.S.-Japan Energy Relationships in the 1980's, 1981, Annual Review of Energy, 1985, Energy Supply and Use in Developing Countries, A Fresh Look at Western (OECD) Interests, 1986. Trustee U. R.I. Found., 1983—; bd. dirs. Atlantic Council U.S., 1976—; chmn. energy policy com. North Atlantic Found., 1979-85; vice chmn., 1985—, trustee, 1986—. Served with U.S. Army, 1945-46. Mem. AAAS, Am. Inst. Chem. Engrs., Am. Nuclear Soc., World Econ. Forum, U.S. Energy Assn. (bd. dirs.), Ams. Energy Independence, Am. Soc. Macro-Engring., Inc. Club: Univ. (Washington). Home: 502 Cameron St Alexandria VA 22314 Office: ERC Internat 3211 Jermantown Rd Fairfax VA 22030

GRAY, MARY TAYLOR, bowling center executive; b. Waxahachie, Tex., Jan. 12, 1928; d. Frank Camillus and Christine Elizabeth (Rader) Taylor; BBA, So. Methodist U., 1950; m. John Preston Gray, June 30, 1950 (dec.); children: Sharon Elizabeth, Carol Ann, Mary Jo. Various secretarial positions, 1950-52; corp. sec.-treas., bookkeeper Gray's Lanes, Texas City, Tex., 1955-84, v.p., 1984-85, sec.-treas., 1986-87, pres. 1988—; v.p. C&T Interests, Inc., Texas City, 1970-85, sec.-treas., 1986-87, pres. 1988—; sec.-treas. S.W. Bowling Propers.' Conv., 1971-76. Republican. Baptist. Home: 1921 15th Ave N Texas City TX 77590 Office: 2404 Palmer Hwy PO Box 2007 Texas City TX 77592-2007

GRAY, MIRIAM MARY, educator; b. Nevada, Mo., Nov. 29, 1905; d. Chester H. and Pearl (Welch) Gray; A.A., Cottey Coll., 1925; B.S., U. Mo., 1927; M.A., Columbia U., 1932, Ed.D., 1943. Tchr. phys. edn. high sch. and jr. coll., Moberly, Mo., 1927-30, jr. and sr. high sch., Chickasha, Okla., 1930-31, elem. and jr. high sch., Tulsa, 1934-41; phys. edn. dir. Knox Sch. for Girls, Cooperstown, N.Y., 1932-33; instr. phys. and health edn. U. Tex., 1943-46; asso. prof. health and phys. edn. Ill. State U., 1946-57, prof., 1957-72, emerita, 1972—, dance coordinator, 1946-69; dir. advanced study insts. in dance edn. U.S. Office Edn., summers 1968, 69; dir. Wayside Farm Inc., 1970—, pres., 1980-84. Dir., mem. adv. bd. Vernon County unit Ret. Senior Vol. Program, 1975-78, chmn. bd., 1977-78. Fellow AAHPERD (hon. fellow; life mem.; chmn. midwest dance sect. 1954-55, chmn. nat. sect. on dance 1958-60, editor dance div. 1966-70, program chmn. conf. on dance as a discipline 1965; chmn. dance div. 1970-73, dir. 1971-72, v.p. 1971-72, nat. dance assn. parliamentarian 1974-75, NDA Heritage award 1975, NDA scholar 1978-79, Centennial award 1985, Pres. Recognition award 1987); mem. Nat., Ill. edn. assns., Ill. (hon. life), Mo. (hon. life) assns. health phys. edn. and recreation, Nat. (nat. editorial com. 1955-60, editor biennial publ. 1957-59), Midwest assns. for phys. edn. of coll. women, Internat. Assn. Phys. Edn. and Sports for Girls and Women, Nat. Found. for Health, Phys. Edn. and Recreation, Internat. Council Health, Phys. Edn. and Recreation, Am. Dance Guild, Sacred Dance Guild, Congress on Research in Dance (dir. 1969-73, parliamentarian 1973-74), Nat. Conf. Grad. Edn. (editorial com. 1967), Dance Notation Bur., Am. Dance Therapy Assn., Ill. Square Dance Callers Assn. (roving dir. 1955-57, central dir. 1960-62), Ill. Fedn. Square Dance Clubs (devel. chmn., editor newsletter 1955-57), Vernon County Hist. Soc. (dir. 1973—, corr. sec. 1974-76, pres. 1983, 84), AAUP (chpt. pres. 1953-54, Ill. conf. pres. 1955), Nat., Mo., Vernon County (sec.-treas. 1973-74, pres. 1974-76, dir. 1977-85) ret. tchrs. assns., Am. Assn. Ret. Persons, Ill. State U. Annuitants Assn., Bus. and Profl. Women's Club, AAUW (program topic chmn. 1975-77, dir. 1975-78, 80-84), Am. Cancer Soc. (v.p. Vernon County unit 1977, dir. 1977-85), Delta Kappa Gamma (chpt. 2d v.p. 1964-66, pres. 1978-80, Mo. State Scrapbook-Photog. Com. 1983-85), Phi Theta Kappa (pres. 1924-25), Kappa Delta Pi, Pi Lambda Theta. Clubs: Idlers (pres. 1963-64), Nevada Camera (pres. 1976-78). Author: The Physical Education Demonstration, 1946; A Century of Growth, 1951; editor: Purposeful Action, Workshop Report of NAPECW, 1956; Focus on Dance V, Composition, 1969; co-editor: Designs for Dance, 1968; contbr. to profl., edn. and lay publs. Dance dir. centennial pageants: The Past Is Prologue, Ill. Edn. Assn., 1955; With Faith in the Future, Ill. State U., 1957. Home: The Wayside Rt 1 Nevada MO 64772

GRAY, OSCAR EDWARD, III, electric power research administrator; b. Phila., Dec. 17, 1943; s. Oscar Edward and Josephine Lucille (Hart) G.; B.S., U.S. Naval Acad., 1965; M.S., Ohio State U., 1971; m. Susan Patricia Tate, May 12, 1979; children—Christine Lee, Eric Alan, Scott Thomas. Commd. ensign USN, 1965, advanced through grades to lt., resigned, 1970; nuclear licensing engr. TVA, Chattanooga, 1971-73, mgmt. staff, nuclear engr., 1974-75, supr. environ. planning sect., 1975-77, asst. chief regulatory br., 1977-79, program coordinator gen. mgr.'s office, 1979, chief spl. projects staff, 1979-80, asst. to dir. energy demonstrations, 1980-82; chief nuclear research projects, 1982-83, project mgr., 1983-84; project mgr. Electric Power Research Inst., 1984—; project engr. nuclear reactor licensing AEC, Bethesda, Md., 1973-74. Author papers on advanced reactor safety and design, nuclear plant life extension. AEC spl. fellow, 1970; registered profl. engr., Tenn. Mem. Naval Acad. Alumni Assn., Ohio State U. Alumni Assn. Home: 3452 Cork Oak Way Palo Alto CA 94303 Office: 3412 Hillview Ave Palo Alto CA 94303

GRAY, PAUL EDWARD, university president; b. Newark, Feb. 7, 1932; s. Kenneth Frank and Florence (Gilleo) G.; m. Priscilla Wilson King, June 18, 1955; children: Virginia Wilson, Amy Brewer, Andrew King, Louise Meyer. S.B., Mass. Inst. Tech., 1954, S.M, 1955, Sc.D., 1960. Mem. faculty Mass. Inst. Tech., 1960-71, Class of 1922 prof. elec. engring., 1968-71; dean Sch. Engring. MIT, 1970-71, chancellor, 1971-80, pres., 1980—, mem. corp., 1971—; dir. Shawmut Nat. Corp., Boston, The New England, Boston, A.D. Little Inc., Cambridge, Cabot Corp., Boston. Trustee Wheaton Coll., Mass., chmn. bd. trustees, 1976-87; trustee Kennedy Meml. Trust, WGBH Ednl. Found., Whitaker Health Scis. Fund trustee, mem. corp. Mus. of Sci., Boston; bd. dirs. Nat. Action Council for Minorities in Engring.; corporator Woods Hole Oceanographic Inst. Served to 1st lt. AUS, 1955-57. Fellow Am. Acad. Arts and Scis., IEEE (publs. bd. 1969-70); mem. Nat. Acad. Engring., Mex. Nat. Acad. Engring. (corr.), AAAS, Sigma Xi, Eta Kappa Nu, Tau Beta Pi, Phi Sigma Kappa. Mem. United Ch. Christ. Office: MIT 77 Massachusetts Ave Cambridge MA 02139

GRAY, PHILIP HOWARD, psychologist, educator; b. Cape Rosier, Maine, July 4, 1926; s. Asa and Bernice (Lawrence) G.; m. Iris McKinney, Dec. 31, 1954; children: Cindelyn Gray Eberts, Howard. M.A., U. Chgo., 1958; Ph.D., U. Wash., 1960. Asst. prof. dept. psychology Mont. State U., Bozeman, 1960-65; assoc. prof. Mont. State U., 1965-75, prof., 1975—; vis. prof. U. Man., Winnipeg, Can., 1968-70; pres. Mont. Psychol. Assn., 1968-70; chmn. Mont. Bd. Psychologist Examiners, 1972-74; speaker sci. and geneal. meetings on ancestry of U.S. presidents. Organized exhbns. folk art in Mont. and Maine, 1972-79; author The Comparative Analysis of Behavior, 1966, (with F.L. Ruch and N. Warren) Working with Psychology, 1963, A Directory of Eskimo Artists in Sculpture and Prints, 1974, The Science that Lost its Mind, 1985; contbr. numerous articles on behavior to psychol. jours., poetry to lit. jours. Served with U.S. Army, 1944-46. Recipient Am. and Can. research grants. Fellow Am. Psychol. Assn., AAAS, Internat. Soc. Research on Aggression; mem. History of Sci. Soc., Nat. Geneal. Soc., New Eng. Hist. Geneal. Soc., Gallatin County Geneal. Soc. (charter), Deer Isle-Stonington Hist. Soc., Psychonomic Soc., Internat. Soc. for Human Ethology, Descs. of Illegitimate Sons and Daus. of Kings of Britain, Piscataqua Pioneers, Animal Behavior Soc., Flagon and Trencher, Friends of Freud Museum, Am. Legion, SAR (trustee Mont.), Sigma Xi. Home: 1207 S Black Ave Bozeman MT 59715 Office: Mont State U Dept Psychology Bozeman MT 59717

GRAY, ROBERT LOREN, assn. exec.; b. Sidney, N.Y., Oct. 5, 1929; s. Erlo Charles and Lillian (Berner) B.; B.A., SUNY, 1958; M.B.A., Syracuse U., 1961; D.P.S., Pace U., 1983 children—Carol, James, Laura, Kenneth. Instr. acctg. and fin. Syracuse U., 1960-61; asso. prof. acctg. and fin. SUNY at Binghamton, 1961-70; mgmt. cons., 1961-70; exec. dir. N.Y. State Soc. C.P.A.s, 1970—, also editor C.P.A. Jour., exec. v.p. Found. Acctg. Edn. C.P.A., N.Y. Mem. Am. Acctg. Assn., Am. Inst. C.P.A.s, N.Y. State Soc. C.P.A.s, Nat. Assn. Accts., N.Y. State Assn. Professions. Co-author: Accounting and Data Processing, 1971; Business Systems and Data Processing Procedures, 1972; Cobol and Accounting, 1973, rev. edit., 1976. Home: Rt 1 Upper Station Rd Garrison NY 10524 Office: 600 3d Ave New York NY 10016

GRAY, SHEILA HAFTER, psychiatrist, psychoanalyst; b. N.Y.C., Oct. 19, 1930; m. Oscar Shalom Gray, Apr. 8, 1967. MD, Harvard U., 1958. cert. Washington Psychoanalytic Inst., 1969. Intern St. Elizabeths Hosp., Washington, 1958-59; resident McLean Hosp., Belmont, Mass., 1959-61; clin. and research fellow Mass. Gen. Hosp., Boston, Mass., 1961-62; staff psychiatrist Chestnut Lodge, Inc., Rockville, Md., 1962-64; practice medicine, specializing in psychiatry and psychoanalysis Washington, Rockville, Md., 1964—; clin. asst. prof. psychiatry U. Md. Sch. Medicine, Balt., Md., 1968-75, clin. assoc. prof., 1975-83, clin. prof., 1983—; instr. Washington Psychoanalytic Inst., Balt., Md., 1971-75, teaching analyst, 1975—; mem. staff U. Md. Hosp., Balt.; physician mem. Commn. on Mental Health, Superior Ct. of D.C., 1972—; bd. govs. Nat. Capital Reciprocal Ins. Co., 1981—; cons. Walter Reed Army Med. Ctr., Washington, 1983—. Mem. D.C. Mayor's Adv. Com. on Mental Health Services Reorgn., 1984; exec. com. D.C. Fedn. Civic Assns., 1984—, asst. rec. sec., 1985, rec. sec., 1986—; v.p. programs Women's Equity Action League of Met. D.C., 1986; commr. D.C. Adv. Neighborhood Commn., 1986—. Fellow Am. Psychiat. Assn.; mem. Am. Psychoanalytic Assn. (diplomate Bd. of Profl. Standards), Washington Psychiat. Soc. (councillor 1981-83) Med. Soc. D.C. (exec. bd. 1982), Washington Psychoanalytic Soc. (dir. psychoanalytic clinic and councillor ex officio 1987—), Palisades Citizens Assn. (exec. com. 1980—, treas. 1983-84, pres. 1984-86). Office: PO Box 40612 Palisades Sta Washington DC 20016

GRAY, SIMON JAMES HOLLIDAY, British writer and lecturer; b. Oct. 21, 1936; s. James Davidson and Barbara Cecelia Mary (Holliday) G.; m. Beryl Mary Kevern, 1965; 2 children. Student Westminister Sch., Dalhousie U., Halifax, N.S.; M.A., U. Cambridge. Supr. English, U. B.C., 1960-63, sr. instr., 1963-64; lectr. Queen Mary Coll., U. London, 1965-84. Author novels: Colmain, 1963, Simple People, 1965, Little Portia, 1967, A Comeback for Stark, 1968, An Unnatural Pursuit and Other Pieces, 1985; plays: Wise Child, 1968, Sleeping Dog, 1968, Dutch Uncle, 1969, The Idiot, 1971, Spoiled, 1971, Butley, 1971 (Evening Standard award), Otherwise Engaged, 1975 (Best Play, New York Drama Critics' Circle, Evening Standard award), Plaintiffs and Defendants, 1975, Two Sundays, 1975, Dog Days, 1976, Molly, 1977, The Rear Column, 1978, Close of Play, 1979, Quartermaine's Terms, 1981, Tartuffe, 1982, Chapter 17, 1982, Common Pursuit, 1984, Plays One, 1986, After Pilkington, 1987, Melon, 1987. Address: care Judy Daish Assocs, 83 Eastbourne Mews, London W2 6LQ, England *

GRAY, WILLIAM PATTON, JR., lawyer; b. Tuscaloosa, Ala., Mar. 13, 1943; s. William Patton and Ruth Herndon (Turner) G.; m. Rebecca Story Wright, Apr. 9, 1966; children—Stacy Elaine, Susan Meridith, Ashley Rebecca, John David. B.S. in Acctg., U. Ala.-Tuscaloosa, 1965, J.D., 1968. Bar: Ala. 1968, U.S. Dist. Ct. (no. dist.) Ala. 1972, U.S. Ct. Appeals (5th cir.) 1972, U.S. Ct. Appeals (11th cir.) 1983. Mem. trust dept. staff City Nat. Bank, Tuscaloosa, 1968; judge adv. U.S. Air Force, Columbus, Ohio, 1968-72; assoc. Hubbard & Waldrop, Tuscaloosa, 1972-73; ptnr. Tucker, Gray & Thigpen, Tuscaloosa, 1973-77, Tucker, Gray & Espy, Tuscaloosa, 1977-82, Gray, Espy & Nettles, Tuscaloosa, 1982—; lectr. law U. Ala.-Tuscaloosa, 1982—. Bd. dirs. Mental health Assn., 1983—; co-chmn. Mother's March, March of Dimes, 1973. Mem. Ala. Bar Assn., Ala. Trial Lawyers Assn. (exec. com.), Tuscaloosa C. of C. (subcom. chmn.). Democrat. Presbyterian. Home: 5 Riverdale Rd Tuscaloosa AL 35406 Office: Gray Espy & Nettles 2728 8th St Tuscaloosa AL 35401

GRAYLOW, RICHARD VERNON, lawyer; b. Sept. 4, 1940. BS, U. Wis., Milw., 1965; JD, U. Wis., 1969. Bar: Wis. 1969. Assoc. Lawton & Cates, Madison, Wis., 1969-74, ptnr., 1974—; lectr. ad hoc U. Wis. Sch. for Workers. Served to sgt. USMC, 1958-61. Mem. Wis. Bar Assn., Dane County Bar Assn., Assn. Trial Lawyers Am., Wis. Acad. Trial Lawyers. Office: Lawton & Cates SC 214 W Mifflin St Madison WI 53703

GRAYSON, CECIL, professor; b. Batley, Yorkshire, Eng., Feb. 5, 1920; s. John Micklethwaite and Dora (Hartley) G.; m. Margaret Parry Jordan, Mar. 17, 1947; children: Celia, Catherine, Julia, Robin. MA, Oxford (Eng.) U., 1947. Lecturer in Italian Oxford U., 1948-57, prof. Italian studies, fellow Magdalen Coll., 1958-87, prof., fellow emeritus, 1987—. Author: Cinque Saggi Su Dante, 1972; editor: V. Calmeta, Prose e Lettere, 1959, L.B. Alberti, Opere Volgari (I), 1960, (II), 1966, (III), 1973. Served to major British Army, 1940-45. Recipient Premio Galileo Rotary and U. Pisa, 1974, Serena medal British Acad., 1976; hon. fellow St. Edmund Hall, 1986. Fellow British Acad.; mem. Accademia Nazionale dei Lincei, Accademia della Crusca, Accademia delle Scienze, Bologna, Istituto Veneto. Home: 11 Norham Rd, Oxford OX2 6SF, England Office: U Oxford, Magdalen Coll, Oxford England

GRAYSON, HENRY, psychoanalyst; b. Atmore, Ala., Oct. 25, 1935; s. Henry T. and Ethel (Sageser) G.; m. Elizabeth Cauthen, Apr. 1, 1959; children—Pegine, Douglas. A.B., Asbury Coll., 1957; S.T.M., Boston U., 1963, Ph.D., 1967, postdoctoral cert., psychoanalysis and psychotherapy Postgrad. Ctr. for Mental Health, N.Y.C., 1971. Lic. psychologist, N.Y. Instr. dept. psychology Mt. Ida Jr. Coll., Newton, Mass., 1963-67; from asst. to assoc. prof. CUNY, Bklyn., 1967-78; sole practice psychology, N.Y.C., 1967—; founder, exec. dir. Nat. Inst. Psychotherapies, N.Y.C., 1970-82, chmn. bd., 1970—; dir. Counseling and Family Therapy Assocs., Mahopac and Croton-on-Hudson, N.Y. 1981—; bd. dirs. Ctr. Marital and Family Therapy, N.Y.C., 1981—; pres. F.A.T. Seminars, N.Y.C., 1982—. Author: Three Psychotherapies, 1975; author, editor: Short-term Approaches to the Psychotherapies, 1979, Changing Approaches to the Psychotherapies, 1978. Fellow Am. Group Psychotherapy Assn.; mem. Eastern Group Psychotherapy Soc. (treas. 1978-79), Am. Psychol. Assn., Am. Acad. Psychotherapists, N.Y. State Psychol. Assn. Office: 330 W 58th St New York NY 10019

GRAZIANO, CRAIG FRANK, lawyer; b. Des Moines, Dec. 7, 1950; s. Charles Dominic and Corrine Rose (Comito) G.; m. Diane Weissman, Nov. 17, 1987. BA summa cum laude, Macalester Coll., 1973; JD with honors, Drake U., 1975. Bar: Iowa 1976, U.S. Dist. Ct. (no. and so. dist.) Iowa 1978, U.S. Ct. Appeals (8th cir.) 1977. Law clk. to sr. circuit judge M.D. Van Oosterhout, U.S. Ct. Appeals for 8th Circuit, Sioux City, Iowa, 1976-78; assoc. Dickinson, Throckmorton, Parker, Mannheimer & Raife, P.C., Des Moines, 1978-82, ptnr., 1982—. Mem. ABA, Iowa Bar Assn., Polk County Bar Assn., Nat. Health Lawyers Assn., Order of Coif, Phi Beta Kappa. Office: Dickinson Throckmorton et al 1600 Hub Tower Des Moines IA 50309

GREANEY, VINCENT MARTIN, educational researcher; b. Dunmore, Galway, Ireland, Sept. 21, 1942; s. James J. and Delia (Reynolds) G.; m. Betty Jane Wokanovicz, Jan. 23, 1971; children: Brian, Mark, Kevin, David. BA, U. Coll., Dublin, 1965, Higher Diploma in Edn., 1966; M of Letters, Trinity Coll., 1970; MEd, Boston Coll., 1971, PhD, 1973. Tchr. primary grades Dublin, 1962-68; research asst. Boston Coll. Ctr. for Field Research, 1970-71; research fellow St. Patrick's Coll. Ednl. Research Centre, Dublin, 1972-80, 81—; vis. Fulbright scholar Western Mich. U. Evaluation Ctr., Kalamazoo, 1980-81; pres. Reading Assn. Ireland, 1976, 82; cons. Council of Europe, 1985. Author: Equality of Opportunity, 1985; editor: Children's Needs and Rights, 1985; developer test series, 1975-78; contbr. articles to profl. jours. Mem. Am. Ednl. Research Assn., Internat. Reading Assn. (bd. dirs. 1988—). Office: St Patrick's Coll, Ednl Research Centre, Dublin 9, Ireland

GREASER, CONSTANCE UDEAN, research organization executive; b. San Diego, Jan. 18, 1938; d. Lloyd Edward and Udean Greaser; B.A., San Diego State Coll., 1959; postgrad. U. Copenhagen Grad. Sch. Fgn. Students, 1963, Georgetown U. Sch. Fgn. Service, 1967; M.A., U. So. Calif., 1968; Exec. M.B.A., UCLA, 1981. Advt., publicity mgr. Crofton Co., San Diego, 1959-62; supr. Mercury Publs., Fullerton, Calif., 1962-64; supr. engring. support services div. Arcata Data Mgmt., Hawthorne, Calif., 1964-67; mgr. computerized typesetting dept. Continental Graphics, Los Angeles, 1967-70; v.p., editorial dir. Sage Publs., Inc., Beverly Hills, Calif., 1970-74; head publs. RAND Corp., Santa Monica, Calif., 1974—. Mem. nat. com. Million Minutes of Peace Appeal, 1986, Dept. Commerce Nat. Info. Standards Orgn., 1987—, nat. com. Global Cooperation for Better World, 1988. Mem. Women in Bus. (pres. 1977-78), Soc. for Scholarly Pubs. (nat. bd. dirs.), Women in Communication, Soc. Tech. Communication, World Future Soc., Brahma Kumaris World Spiritual Orgn. Co-author: Quick Writer-Build Your Own Word Processing Users Guide, 1983; Quick Writer-Word Processing Center Operations Manual, 1984; editor: Urban Research News, 1970-74; mng. editor Comparative Polit. Studies, 1971-74; assoc. editor New Realities mag., 1988—; contbr. articles to various jours. Office: The Rand Corp 1700 Main St Santa Monica CA 90406

GREASER, MAYLIN H., retired dredging company executive; b. North Wales, Pa., Jan. 15, 1909; s. John B. and Katie B. Greaser; m. Ruth N. Philipp, Mar. 13, 1943. B.S. in Civil Engring., Pa. State U., 1930. Engaged in constrn. and dredging bus. 1930-79; with Am. Dredging Co., Ft. Washington, Pa., 1949-79; successively gen. supt., dir. Am. Dredging Co., 1951-79, v.p., 1953, pres., 1954-79; ret. 1979; Mem. Delaware River Ports' Council for Emergency Ops. Served as lt. col. C.E., AUS, 1942-45. Fellow Soc. Am. Mil. Engrs. (past pres., dir. Phila. post); mem. Port of Phila. Maritime Soc. (past pres.), ASCE (life), Delaware Valley Council (past pres.), Mil. Order World Wars, Am. Legion, Seamens Church Inst. (bd. mgrs.), Pa. Soc., Permanent Internat. Assn., Nav. Congress. Presbyterian. Clubs: Phila. Cricket (Phila.), Union League (Phila.); Skytop (Pa.). Home: 6003 Cricket Rd Flourtown PA 19031

GREBSTEIN, SHELDON NORMAN, university president; b. Providence, Feb. 1, 1928; s. Sigmund and Sylvia (Skotkin) G.; m. Phyllis Strumar, Sept. 6, 1953; children: Jason Lyle, Gary Wade. B.A. cum laude, U. So. Calif., 1949; M.A., Columbia U., 1950; Ph.D., Mich. State U., 1954. Instr., then asst. prof. English U. Ky., 1953-62; asst. prof. U. South Fla., 1962-63; mem. faculty SUNY, Binghamton, 1963-81; prof. English SUNY, 1968-81, asst. to pres., 1974-75; dean arts and scis. Harpur Coll., 1975-81; pres. SUNY, Purchase, 1981—; Fulbright-Hays lectr. U. Rouen, France, 1968-69; vis. lectr. Caen, Hull and Edinburgh univs., 1969. Author: Sinclair Lewis, 1962, John O'Hara, 1966, Hemingway's Craft, 1973; Editor: Monkey Trial, 1960, Perspectives in Contemporary Criticism, 1968, Studies in For Whom The Bell Tolls, 1971; editorial cons. univ. presses, publishers.; Contbr. articles to profl. jours. Mem. Am. Assn. Higher Edn. Office: SUNY Purchase NY 10577

GRECH, ANTHONY PAUL, law librarian; b. N.Y.C., July 16, 1930; s. Annibale H. and Anna Jane (Cassar) G. B.B.A., Manhattan Coll., 1952; M.L.S., Columbia U., 1961. Asst. reference librarian Assn. Bar City N.Y., 1958-65, reference librarian, 1965-67, librarian, 1967-84, librarian, curator, 1984—; mem. library com. of Eastman Arbitration Library, Am. Arbitration Assn., 1984-85. Mem. Am. Assn. Law Libraries (Joseph L. Andrews Bibliog. award 1967, chmn. micro fascimiles com. 1965-67, chmn. publs. com. 1975-76, exec. bd. 1980-83), Assn. Law Libraries Upstate N.Y. (treas. 1976-77), Bibliog. Soc. Am., Spl. Libraries Assn., Am. Arbitration Assn., Law Library Assn. Greater N.Y. (pres. 1967-68), ALA, Bibliog. Soc. U. Va., Internat. Assn. Law Libraries, Am. Printing History Assn., Nat. Micrographics Assn., Beta Phi Mu. Home: 15 W 72d St New York NY 10023 Office: 42 W 44th St New York NY 10036

GRECIANO DE ALCALÉ, JAVIER EDUARDO, architect; b. Caracas, Venezuela, Apr. 12, 1958; s. Eusebio Greciano Miguel and Luisa (de Alcalé) de Greciano; m. L. Elena Arcia de Greciano, Feb. 5, 1988. Degree in architecture, Cen. U. Venezuela, 1984. Asst. architect Ministry of Justice, Caracas, 1978; architect, bd. dirs. Moulinier-Greciano Architects and Assocs., Caracas, 1984, Grinca S.R.L., Caracas, 1984; architect Constructora Stalca, Caracas, 1985; pvt. practice architecture Caracas, 1985—. Mem. Colegio de Arquitectos de Venezuela, Colegio de Ingenieros de Venezuela. Acción Democrática. Roman Catholic. Home: Calle la Arboleda, Edificio Veneto Piso 8 Apt 83, Urbanización el Bosque, 1050 Caracas Venezuela Office: Calle Villaflor Edicidio Cen, Profl del Este Sóna 1, Oficina S-7 Sabana Grande, 1050 Caracas Venezuela

GRECO, EMILIO, sculptor; b. Catania, Italy, Oct. 11, 1913; m. Anna Greco, 1969; two children. Student, Accad. di Belle Arti, Palermo, Italy. Prof. sculpture Accad. di Belle Arti, Rome. One-man exhbns. in Rome, Milan, London, San Francisco, R.I.; represented in numerous group exhbns. in Italy; works in pub. and pvt. collections in Rome, Milan, London, St. Louis, etc.; permanent collections: Hermitage, Leningrad, USSR, 1980, Emilio Greco Mus., Sabaudia, Italy, 1984; works include Monumento a Pinocchio in Collodi, 1953-56, Grande Bagnante, 1956, Testa di Donna, 1957, Self-portrait, 1982. Mem. Accad. Nazionale di San Luca. Address: Viale Cortina d'Ampezzo 132, Rome Italy *

GREELEY, JOSEPH MAY, advertising consultant; b. Winnetka, Ill., Sept. 13, 1902; s. Morris Larned and Anne (Foote) G.; m. Margery Gerould, Dec. 18, 1928 (div. June 1958); children—Margery (Mrs. Forrest I. Watson),

Samuel Joseph May; m. Elizabeth Knode Conrad, Apr. 8, 1961. Student, Phillips Exeter Acad.; B.S., Harvard, 1925, M.B.A., 1927. Advt. mgr. Quaker Oats, Ltd., London, Eng., 1930-39; asst. gen. mgr. Hecker Products Corp., N.Y.C., 1939-41; account exec. Pedlar & Ryan, N.Y.C., 1941-42; v.p. Dancer, Fitzgerald, Sample, Chgo., 1942-48, Leo Burnett, Chgo., 1948-55; v.p. charge marketing Leo Burnett, 1955-58, exec. v.p. marketing services, 1958-70, cons., 1971—, also former dir., mem. exec. com. Mem. Asso. Harvard Alumni (regional dir. 1972-75). Clubs: University (Chgo.); Harvard of Chicago (pres., dir.), Mid-America, Indian Hill; Port Royal (Naples), Hole-In-The-Wall Golf (Naples). Home: 600 Galleon Dr Naples FL 33940 also: 596 Cedar St Winnetka IL 60093

GREEN, ADELINE MANDEL, psychiatric social worker; b. St. Paul; d. Meyer and Eva Ulanove; B.S., U. Minn., M.S.W.; m. Nathan G. Mandel (div.); children—Meta Susan (Mrs. Richard Katzoff), Myra (Mrs. Jeffrey Halpern); m. Maurice L. Green. Past investigator, Ramsey County Mothers Aid and Aid to Dependent Children, Ramsey County Welfare Bd., St. Paul; then psychiat. social worker Wilder Child Guidance Clinic, St. Paul; then psychiat. social worker, supr. outpatient psychiatry clinic U. Minn. Hosps., Mpls., subsequently supr., clin. instr. psychiatry-social service, outpatient psychiatry clinic; currently in pvt. practice family and marriage counseling South Bay Clinic. Past pres. St. Paul sect. Council Jewish Women; past chmn. Diagnostic Clinic for Rheumatic Fever-Wilder Clinic, St. Paul; assoc. Family and Child Psychiat. Med. Clinic. Lic. social worker. Mem. Nat. Assn. Social Workers, Acad. Certified Social Workers, Minn. Welfare Conf., Am. Assn. Marriage and Family Counselors, Brandeis U. Women. Democrat. Home: 2365 Oakcrest Dr Palm Springs CA 92264 Office: South Bay Psychiatric Clinic 14651 S Bascom Suite 225 Los Gatos CA 95030

GREEN, ALLISON ANNE, educator; b. Flint, Mich., Oct. 5, 1936; d. Edwin Stanley and Ruth Allison (Simmons) James; m. Richard Gerring Green, Dec. 23, 1961 (div. Oct. 1969). B.A., Albion Coll., 1959; M.A., U. Mich., 1978. Cert. tchr., Mich. Tchr. phys. edn. Southwestern High Sch., Flint, 1959-62; tchr. math. Harry Hunt Jr. High Sch., Portsmouth, Va., 1962-63; receptionist Tempcon, Inc., Mpls., 1963-64; tchr. phys. edn. and math. Longfellow Jr. High Sch., Flint, 1964-81, tchr. math., 1981-87, tchr. lang. arts and social studies, 1986-87. Mem. Fair Winds council Girl Scouts U.S.A., 1943—, leader Lone Troop, Albion, Mich., 1957, sr. tchr. aide adviser, 1964-67; mem. Big Sisters Genesee and Lapeer Counties, 1964-68; mem. adminstrv. bd. Court St. United Methodist Ch.; treas. edn. work area, mission commn., sec. council on ministries United Meth. Women Soc. Christian Service, also chmn. meml. com. Mem. NEA, Mich. Edn. Assn., Mich. Assn. Mid. Sch. Educators, United Tchrs. Flint (bldg. rep.), Delta Kappa Gamma (treas. 1982—, profl. affairs chmn. 1978-80, legis. chmn. 1980-82, pres. 1988—), Alpha Xi Delta (pres. Flint, alumnae, v.p., treas., corp. pres. Albion Coll., alumnae dir. province 1972-77, Outstanding Sr. Albion Coll. 1959), Embroiderers Guild Am. (sec. 1977-80, maps rep. 1980-82). Home: 1002 Copeman Blvd Flint MI 48504 Office: 1255 N Chevrolet Ave Flint MI 48504

GREEN, ANNE ELIZABETH, university researcher; b. St. Albans, Hertfordshire, Eng., Nov. 2, 1958; d. Clifford and Jean (Calder) G.; m. David Wynne Owen, June 16, 1987. BA in Geography, U. Coll. of London, 1980; MLitt in Geography, U. Newcastle, 1983. Univ. researcher Centre Urban and Regional Devel Studies U. Newcastle, Newcastle-upon-Tyne, 1983-86, Inst. Employment Research U. Warwick, Conventry, Eng., 1987—. Mem. Regional Studies Assn., Inst. Brit. Geographers, Town & Country Planning Assn. Office: Univ of Warwick, Inst Employment Research, Conventry CV4 7AL, England

GREEN, BARRY, lawyer; b. Bklyn., Oct. 24, 1957; s. Joseph and Anne (Polsky) G. BA, Brandeis U., 1978; JD, Tulane U., 1982. Bar: N.Mex. 1982, U.S. Dist. Ct. N.Mex. 1986. Asst. dist. atty. Dist. Atty.'s Office, Santa Fe, 1983; sole practice Santa Fe, 1983—. Mem. N.Mex. Trial Lawyers Assn., Am. Trial Lawyers Assn., N.Mex. Bar Assn., Greenpeace, The Wilderness Soc., Jacques Cousteau Soc., Amnesty Internat. Democrat. Office: 150 Washington Ave Suite 300 Santa Fe NM 87501

GREEN, BENSON ARTHUR, film and television executive; b. N.Y.C. B.A., Dartmouth Coll., 1956; postgrad. UCLA, 1957. Pres., chief exec. officer N. Lee Lacy Assocs., Los Angeles, N.Y., Chgo., London, Paris, 1971—; pres., chief exec. officer Greenbriar Prodns., Los Angeles, N.Y.C., 1973—; pres., chief exec. officer Greenhouse Properties, Los Angeles, N.Y.C., 1980—; pres., chief exec. officer Photon Pub., Los Angeles, 1981—; pres., chief exec. officer LBA Inc., N.Y.C., 1981—. Mem. Assn. Ind. Comml. Producers (founding pres. 1976-81, bd. dirs.). Office: 8446 Melrose Pl Los Angeles CA 90069

GREEN, CARL JAY, lawyer; b. N.Y.C., Oct. 12, 1939; s. Irving and Ruth (Rispler) G.; m. Judith Lynn Slomoff, May 24, 1964; m. 2d, Pamela Carol Wattenberg, Sept. 21, 1975; children: Adam Mitchell, Brian Jeffrey, Anthony Loeb. A.B. magna cum laude, Harvard U., 1961; postgrad. U. Hong Kong, 1961-62; J.D., Yale U., 1965; postgrad. Japan Research Ctr., Tokyo (Stanford U.), 1973-74. Bar: N.Y. 1965, D.C. 1969, U.S. Supreme Ct. 1981. Assoc. Baker & McKenzie, N.Y.C., 1965-68; atty./advisor U.S. Dept. Transp., Washington, 1968-69; assoc. Caplin & Drysdale, Washington, 1969-72; program officer Ford Found., N.Y.C., 1973-75, rep. for Japan and E. Asia, Tokyo, 1975-80; ptnr. Wender Murase & White, Washington, 1980-86, Milbank, Tweed, Hadley & McCloy, Washington, 1986—; research assoc. East Asian Legal Studies, Harvard Law Sch., 1981-83; Bd. dirs. Korea Econ. Inst. U.S. Nat. Com. Pacific Econ. Cooperation; trustee Asia Study Japan Am. Soc. of Washington, Lingnan U.; advisor U.S.-Japan Econ. Relations (Wise Men) Group, 1980-81. Fulbright fellow, 1961; Harvard U. travelling fellow, 1961-62. Mem. ABA (coms. internat. trade, China, Far Eastern law), Am. Soc. Internat. Law, Assn. Bar City N.Y., D.C. Bar Assn., Council Fgn. Relations, Asia Soc. (trustee 1983—), Trial Lawyers Assn. (internat. trade commn.), Japan Fedn. Bar Assns., Phi Beta Kappa. Democrat. Jewish. Clubs: Cosmos, (Washington); University (N.Y.C.). Contbr. articles to publs. in field. Office: Milbank Tweed Hadley & McCloy, 2-1 Uchisaiwai-Cho 2-Chome, Chiyoda-ku, Tokyo Japan

GREEN, DAVID, manufacturing company executive; b. Chgo., Mar. 22, 1922; s. Harry B. and Carrie (Scheinbaum) G.; m. Mary I. Winton, June 15, 1951; children—Sara Edmond, Howard Benjamin, Jonathan Winton. B.A. in Econs., U. Chgo., 1942, M.A. in Social Scis., 1949. Mgr., Toy Co., Chgo., 1949-54; founder, pres. Quartet Mfg. Co., Skokie, 1954—; pres. Colleague, Inc., Booneville, Miss., 1967-87; chmn. bd. and cons. DG Group, Chgo., 1977—; chmn. Quartet Ovonics, 1986—. Spl. cons. to White House-Trade Expansion Act, Washington, 1962; chmn. Winnetka Caucus (Ill.), 1971; chmn. Ill. state Dan Walker for Gov., 1972, 76; spl. asst. to Gov. for intergovtl. relations, Ill., 1973-76; governing mem. Chgo. Symphony Orchestra. Served with U.S. Army, 1942-45, PTO. Mem. Nat. Office Products Assn., Wholesale Stationers' Assn. Clubs: Metropolitan (Chgo.); Pelican Bay (Naples, Fla.). Home: 969 Tower Manor Dr Winnetka IL 60093 Office: Quartet Mfg Co 5700 Old Orchard Rd Skokie IL 60077

GREEN, FITZHUGH, author, government agency administrator, consultant; b. Jenkintown, Pa., Sept. 12, 1917; s. Fitzhugh and Natalie W. (Elliot) G.; grad. St. Paul's Sch., 1936; student Princeton U., 1940; M.A., Boston U., 1963; 1 dau., Penelope. Fgn. sales and advt. exec. Vick Chem. Co., 1946-49; div. mgr., advt. sales promotion Life mag., 1949-52; asst. to chmn. FTC, 1953-54; with USIA, 1954-66; dir. USIS, Laos, 1955-56, Israel, 1956-58, chief pvt. enterprise div., 1958-60, dir. USIS, Belgian Congo, 1960, Republic of Congo, Leopoldville, 1960-62, grad. Naval War Coll., 1963, USIA rep. U.S. Mission to UN, dir. Fgn. Corrs. Center, N.Y.C., 1964-65; dep. dir. personnel and tng. USIA, 1965-66; oceanography, fgn. affairs expert on staff U.S. Senator Claiborne Pell, 1966-68; dep. dir. Far East ops. USIA, 1968-70; assoc. adminstr. EPA, 1971-77, 83-87; v.p., William D. Ruckelshaus Assocs., 1987—; psychol. warfare cons. Am. U., 1959; rep. UN Conf. on Human Environment, Stockholm, 1972. Dep. vice chmn. Nat. Citizens for Eisenhower, 1954; Republican candidate for Congress from R.I., 1970. Trustee, mem. exec. com. Washington chpt. Nat. Multiple Sclerosis Soc.; bd. dirs. Boys Harbor, Inc., N.Y.C., Nat. Conf. Citizenship, 1982—, Charles A. Lindbergh Fund, 1986—; mem. admissions com. Georgetown U. Grad. Fgn. Service Sch. Served from ensign to lt. USNR, 1942-46; PTO. Clubs: Met., Burning Tree, Federal City (Washington); Spouting Rock Beach Assn. (Newport, R.I.); Explorers (N.Y.C.). Author: Fitz Jr. with the Fleet, 1931; A Change in the Weather, 1977; American Propaganda Abroad, 1988; also numerous articles; editorial bd. Atlantic Council Quar., 1986—. Home: 3630 Prospect St NW Washington DC 20007

GREEN, FRANCIS WILLIAM, investment consultant; b. Locust Grove, Okla., Mar. 17, 1920; s. Noel Francis and Mary (Lincoln) G.; B.S., Phoenix U., 1955; M.S. in Elec. Engring., Minerva U., Milan, Italy, 1959; M.S. in Engring., West Coast U., Los Angeles, 1965; m. Alma J. Ellison, Aug. 26, 1950 (dec. Sept. 1970); children—Sharmon, Rhonda; m. Susan G. Mathis, July 14, 1973 (div. July 1979). With USN Guided Missile Program, 1945-49; design and electronic project engr. Falcon missile program Hughes Aircraft Co., Culver City, Calif., 1949-55; sr. electronic engr. Atlas missile program Convair Astronautics, San Diego, 1955-59; sr. engr. Polaris missile program Nortronics div. Northrop, Anaheim, Calif., 1959-60; chief, supr. electronic engr. data systems br. Tech. Support div. Rocket Propulsion Lab., USAF, Edwards AFB, Calif., 1960-67, dep. chief tech. support div., 1967-69; tech. adviser Air Force Missile Devel. Ctr., Holloman AFB, N.Mex., 1969-70, 6585 Test Group, Air Force Spl. Weapons Ctr., Holloman AFB, from 1970; pvt. investment cons., 1978—. Bd. examiners U.S. CSC; mem. Pres.'s Missile Site Labor Relations Com.; cons. advanced computer and data processing tech. and systems engring.; mem. USAF Civilian Policy Bd. and Range Comdrs. Council. Served as pilot USAAF, 1941-45. Fellow Am. Inst. Aeros. and Astronautics; mem. IEEE, Nat. Assn. Flight Instrs. Contbr. articles to profl. jours. Home and Office: 2345 Apache Ln Alamogordo NM 88310

GREEN, GEORGE FRANCIS, economics educator; b. Brighton, Eng., Nov. 7, 1949; s. Keith and Rosamund (Wickham) G.; m. Alison Culverwell, July 11, 1984. BA, Oxford U., 1970; MSc, London Sch. Econs., 1972; PhD, London U., 1979. Lectr. econs. Kingston Poly. Inst., London, 1972-84, 86-87, U. Mass., Boston, 1985-86, Leicester (Eng.) U., 1987—. Co-editor Economics: An Antitext, 1976; co-author The Profit System, 1987; editor Rev. Radical Polit. Econs., 1985-88. Mem. Labour Party. Office: Leicester U, University Rd, Leicester LE1 7RH, England

GREEN, HAMILTON, prime minister of the Republic of Guyana; v.p. for pub. welfare, until 1982, v.p. for agr. and pub. welfare, 1982-83, v.p. for prodn., 1983, v.p. for social infrastructure, 1983-85, first dep. prime minister, 1984-85, 1st v.p. and prime minister, Republic of Guyana, 1985—. Address: Office of Prime Minister, Georgetown Guyana *

GREEN, HOLCOMBE TUCKER, JR., investment executive; b. Atlanta, Sept. 29, 1939; s. Holcombe Tucker and Mary Katharine (Woltz) G.; A.B., Yale U., 1961; LL.B., U. Va., 1967; m. Nancy Reade Hall, June 18, 1966. Admitted to Ga. bar, 1967; asso. firm Hansell & Post, Atlanta, 1967-70, mem. firm, 1970-87, mgmt. com. 1980-87; gen. ptnr. Green Capital Investors L.P., Atlanta, 1988—; dir. Ga. Gulf Corp., HBO & Co., Rhodes Furniture, Inc., Kusan, Inc., Southeastern Capital Corp. Trustee Atlanta Bot. Garden, 1976—, Atlanta Music Festival Assn., 1983—, exec. com. 1986—; bd. dirs. Child Service and Family Counseling Center, 1972-85, pres. 1982-84; bd. dirs., mem. exec. com. High Mus. of Art, 1982—; bd. dirs., mem. exec. com. Atlanta Ballet, 1987—; active Leadership Atlanta, 1974-75; hon. Swedish consul, State of Ga., 1988—. Served to lt. (j.g.) U.S. Navy, 1961-64. Mem. ABA, State Bar Ga., Raven Soc. of U. Va., Order of Coif. Democrat. Presbyterian. Clubs: Piedmont Driving, Capital City, Commerce, Nine O'Clocks, Buckhead, Wade Hampton, Doubles. Decisions editor Va. Law Rev., 1965-67. Home: 3655 Tuxedo Rd Atlanta GA 30305 Office: Green Capital Investors LP 3333 Peachtree Rd Suite 1420 E Tower Atlanta GA 30326

GREEN, JAMES CRAIG, data systems company executive; b. Gladstone, Mich., Apr. 19, 1933; s. Albert Keene and Margaret Josephine (Craig) G.; student Coll. of Gt. Falls, 1951-53, UCLA, 1962; m. Catherine Maxwell, Nov. 1, 1957; children—Cindi, Shelley, Nancy, James W., Robert. Clk., carrier U.S. Post Office, Gt. Falls, Mont., 1951-57; clk. office and sales Mont. Liquor Control Bd., Gt. Falls, 1957-59; payroll clk. Herald Examiner, Hearst Publs., Los Angeles, 1959-67, data processing mgr., 1967-75, data processing ops. mgr. corp. hdqrs. Hearst Publs., N.Y.C., 1975-78; gen. mgr., v.p. Computer/Data Inc., Billings, Mont., 1978-83; mgr. customer service Big Sky Data Systems, Billings, Mont., 1983-84; pres. FACTS, Inc., 1985—; tax cons., Los Angeles, 1962-75. Cub Scout leader, com. chmn., Los Angeles council Boy Scouts Am., 1973-75; pres. Bus. Office Employees Assn. Los Angeles, 1963-66. Area commr. Black Otter Council Boy Scouts Am., 1982-84, com. chmn., 1982-84. Served with USNR, 1951-59. Recipient degree of Chevalier, Order De Molay, 1951, Legion of Honor degree.; cert. data processing mgr. Mem. Data Processing Mgrs. Assn., Los Angeles Masonic Press Club. Clubs: Masons, Blue Lodge, York Rite, Scottish Rite, Shrine (Grotto charter mem. Gt. Falls), DeMolay (chpt. advisor 1983—, state advisor 1982—). Writer, negotiator contract Bus. Office Employees Assn., Los Angeles, 1965. Office: 2110 Wiligate Ln Billings MT 59102

GREEN, JAMES FRANCIS, lawyer, consultant; b. Pittsfield, Mass., Oct. 1, 1948; s. Earl Levi and Frances Eleanor (Walshe) G.; m. Eileen Mary Kelly, July 31, 1971; children—Michael Walshe, Maura Kelly. B.A., St. Anselm Coll., 1970; J.D., Suffolk U., 1973. Bar: Mass. 1973, U.S. Dist. Ct. Mass. 1974, U.S. Ct. Appeals (D.C. cir.) 1975, U.S. Dist. Ct. D.C. 1975, U.S. Supreme Ct. 1977, U.S. Ct. Appeals (4th cir.) 1978. Research counsel Joint Com. on Jud. Reform of Joint Jud. Com. of Gen. Ct. Commonwealth of Mass., Boston, 1973-74; ptnr. Drucas, Edgerton & Green, Salem, Mass., 1974; gen. ptnr. Ashcraft & Gerel, Washington, 1975—; dir. Ridge Group, Inc., Falls Church, Va. Mem. Mass. Bar Assn., Boston Bar Assn., Fed. Bar Assn. (bd. dirs. Washington chpt., 1985-86, internat. law com.), Bar Assn. D.C., D.C. Bar Assn., ABA (torts and ins. practice law sections, vice chmn. nat. com. on liaison with the judicial adminstrn.), Assn. Trial Lawyers of Am. (section v. chmn. nat. com. on workers compensation), Am. Soc. Law and Medicine. Democrat. Roman Catholic. Home: 6522 Heather Brook Cr McLean VA 22101 Office: Ashcraft & Gerel 2000 L St NW Suite 700 Washington DC 20036

GREEN, JAMES WYCHE, sociologist/anthropologist consultant; b. Alton, Va., Aug. 5, 1915; s. William Ivey and Mary (Crowder) G.; m. Pearl O'Neal Cornett, Mar. 2, 1940 (dec. 1982); 1 child, Margaret Lydia.; m. Arlene Borkenhagen, Mar. 26, 1983. B.S. with honors, Va. Poly. Inst., 1938, M.S., 1939; postgrad., Duke U., 1947-48; Ph.D., U. N.C., 1953; postgrad., Sch. Advanced Internat. Studies, Johns Hopkins U., 1959. Research fellow Va. Poly. Inst., 1938-39; research field supr. Va. Expt. Sta., 1939; asst. specialist program planning N.C. State Coll. Extension Service, 1939-42; v.p. Greever's, Inc., 1946; tchr. high sch., farm operator 1946-47; asst. prof. rural sociology N.C. State Coll., 1949-54; from asso. chief to chief community devel. adv. to Govt. of Pakistan, Karachi, 1954-59; prof. rural sociology dept. Cornell U., Ithaca, N.Y., 1960; community devel. adviser to Govt. of So. Rhodesia, AID, 1960-64; chief community devel., local govt. adviser to Govt. of Peru, 1964-67; chief urban community devel. adviser to Govt. of Panama, 1967-69; prof., chmn. dept. sociology and anthropology U. N.C., Charlotte, 1969-70; chief methodology div. Bur. Tech. Assistance, AID, Washington, 1970-74; sociologist/anthropologist cons. AID, Washington, 1974-75; contractor AID, Yemen Arab Republic, 1975; pvt. practice cons. 1975—. Contbr. book chpts. and articles to profl. jours., also monographs. Served from 1st lt. to capt. AUS, 1942-46; lt. col. Res. ret. 1975. Decorated Croix de Guerre with Silver Star France; Croix de Guerre with Palm Belgium; Bronze Star with cluster; named Outstanding Alumnus Hargrave Mil. Acad., 1979. Fellow Am. Anthrop. Assn., AAAS, Soc. Applied Anthropology; mem. Res. Officers Assn., Public Citizen, ACLU, Common Cause, Amnesty Internat., Alpha Kappa Delta, Omicron Delta Kappa, Alpha Zeta, Phi Kappa Phi. Lutheran. Home and Office: 6430 Lily Dhu Ln Falls Church VA 22044

GREEN, JERRY HOWARD, banker; b. Kansas City, Mo., June 10, 1930; s. Howard Jay and Selma (Stein) G.; B.A., Yale U., 1952; m. Betsy Bozarth, July 18, 1981. Pres., Union Chevrolet, 1955-69, Union Securities, Inc., Kansas City, Mo., 1969—, Union Bancshares, Inc., Kansas City; chmn. Union Bank, Kansas City, 1976—, Budget Rent-A-Car of Mo., Inc., 1961—, Budget Rent-A-Car of Memphis, Inc.; pres. Pembroke Bancshares, Kansas City, Mo., 1983—; chmn., dir. Citizens Bank, Ava, Mo., 1980—; bd. dirs. Century City Artists Corp., Los Angeles, Union Bank, Kansas City. Bd. dirs. Boys' Clubs Kansas City, Jackson County Pension Plan Com.; appointed dir. (by Gov. Ashcroft) Mo. Higher Loan Authority, 1987—. Yale Class of 1952 Reunion Gift. Served to 1st lt. USAF, 1952-55. Mem. Am. Bankers Assn., Yale Alumni Assn. (bd. dirs.). Republican. Clubs: Kansas City, Oakwood Country, Saddle and Sirloin. Home: 5200 Belleview Kansas City MO 64112 Office: Union Bank 12th and Wyandotte Kansas City MO 64105

GREEN, JOHN LAFAYETTE, JR., business executive, investor, educator; b. Trenton, N.J., Apr. 3, 1929; m. Harriet Hardin Hill, Nov. 8, 1962; 1 child, John Lafayette III. B.A., Miss. State U., 1955; M.Ed., Wayne State U., 1971; Ph.D., Rensselaer Poly. Inst., 1974. Asst. to treas. Internat. Paper Co., 1955-57; mem. faculty U. Calif., Berkeley, 1957-65; v.p. U. Ga., Athens, 1965-71, Rensselaer Poly. Inst., Troy, N.Y., 1971-76; exec. v.p. U. Miami, 1976-80; sr. v.p. U. Houston, 1980-81; pres. Washburn U., Topeka, Kans., 1981-88; pres. Strategic Planning/Mgmt. Assocs., Inc., Topeka, 1981—; pres., chmn. bd. dirs. Smoked Brisket Inn, Inc., Topeka, 1987—; bd. dirs. Indsl. Devel. Corp., Topeka, Capital City Bank and Trust, Topeka, KS Properties, Inc., Topeka, SPMA, Inc., Topeka. Author: Budgeting, 1967, (with others) Cost Accounting, 1969, Administrative Data Processing, 1970, Strategic Planning, 1980, Strategic Planning: A System for Businesses, 1986, A Strategic Plannig System for Higher Education, 1987, Strategy Development and Implementation for Banks, 1988. Bd. dirs. Boy Scouts Am., Topeka, 1983-85. Served to lt. U.S. Army 1951-53. Recipient Disting. Kansan of Yr. in Pub. Adminstrn. award Topeka Capital Jour., 1984, Kans. Pub. Adminstr. of Yr. award Am. Soc. Pub. Adminstrn., 1984, Disting. Exec. award Mktg. Exec. Kans., 1984. Mem. Conf. Bd., Am. Mgmt. Assn., Demographics Inst., AAUP, Phi Delta Kappa, Beta Alpha Psi, Phi Kappa Phi, Pi Kappa Alpha, Delta Sigma Pi. Republican. Presbyterian. (elder, deacon). Lodges: Masons, Shriners, Royal Order of Jesters. Home: 3154 Shadow Ln Topeka KS 66604 Office: 3129 Huntoon Topeka KS 66604

GREEN, JOYCE, book publishing company executive; b. Taylorville, Ill., Oct. 22, 1928; d. Lynn and Vivian Coke (Richardson) Reinerd; m. Warren H. Green, Oct. 8, 1960. AA, Christian Coll., 1946; BS, MacMurray Coll., 1948. Assoc. editor Warren H. Green, Inc., St. Louis, 1966-78, dir., 1978—; v.p. Visioneering Advt. Agy., 1972—; exec. dir. Affirmative Action Assn. Am., 1977—; pres. InterContinental Industries, Inc., 1980—; asst. to pres. Southeastern U., New Orleans, 1982-86; mem. bd. regents, v.p. adminstrn. No. Utah U., Salt Lake City, 1986—. Mem. Am. Soc. Profl. and Exec. Women, Direct Mktg. Club St. Louis, C. of C. Democrat. Methodist. Clubs: Jr. League, World Trade, Clayton, Media. Home: 12120 Hibler Dr Creve Coeur MO 63141 Office: 8356 Olive Blvd Saint Louis MO 63132

GREEN, KENNETH NORTON, lawyer, law educator; b. Chgo., Mar. 18, 1938; s. Martin and Sarah (Owens) G.; m. Joan Nemer, Oct. 17, 1968 (div. July 1974); 1 child, Joy. AA, Wright Jr. Coll., 1960; BA, Calif. State U., Los Angeles, 1963; postgrad. Southwestern U., 1965-67; JD, U. San Fernando Valley, 1968; Cert. (hon. teaching) Los Angeles Unified Sch. Dist., 1979. Bar: Calif. 1970, U.S. Dist. Ct. (cen. dist.) Calif. 1970, U.S. Supreme Ct. 1973. Tchr. Los Angeles, Calif., 1964-70; dep. pub. defender Los Angeles County, Calif., 1970-73, 75—; ptnr. Green & Pirosh, Los Angeles, 1973-75; chief pub. defender; instr. Paralegal dept. U. Calif., Los Angeles, 1975—; judge pro tem Los Angeles Mcpl. Ct., 1978. Contbr. articles to legal publs. Ex officio mem. Prison Preventers, Calif. Dept. of Parole; mayor's com. Project Heavy; bd. dirs. City of Hope; Vista Del Mar; legal adv. panel Jewish Family Service; vol. atty. for indigents UCLA Law Sch.; vol. in Parole Program, com. chmn. Research Prejudice-Pvt. Clubs (Disting. Service award 1971). Served with U.S. Army, 1957-58, Korea. Mem. Pub. Defender Assn. (dir. 1971-74, chief wage negotiator 1973-75) ABA, Los Angeles County Bar Assn. (vice chmn. drug abuse 1975, exec. com. criminal justice 1977). Democrat. Jewish. Lodge: Justice (bd. dirs. 1971-72). Office: Pub Defender Los Angeles County 210 W Temple St Los Angeles CA 90012

GREEN, LYNNE, producer, writer, director; b. Krsko, Yugoslavia, Oct. 16, 1944; came to U.S., 1949, naturalized, 1966; d. Robert and Albina (Schmuck) Prusak; m. Sam Robert Bass, Oct., 1974 (div. 1975). BFA with honors in Directing, Webster Coll. Conservatory of Theatre Arts, 1979. Intern Sta. KSDK-TV, 1987-88; producer-dir. videos Kurt Landberg, Architect and Seja Systems, 1987—. Dir. stage shows including Second Verse, N.Y.C., 1980, Button Button, N.Y.C., 1982, Atmosphere of Enforced Discipline, N.Y.C., 1981, Friend of a Friend, N.Y.C., 1982, The Other Woman: A Farce Closing Saturday Night, N.Y.C., 1983, Question Marks and Periods, 1981-83, Mrs. Michaelangelo, N.Y.C., 1983, Crimes of the Heart, Las Cruces, N.Mex., 1984, Antigone, St. Louis, 1985, Vol., Harriett Woods Com., St. Louis, 1986. Recipient Best Dir. award Internat. Dirs. Festival, 1980. Mem. NOW, Ms. Found. for Women, Nat. Abortion Rights Action League. Democrat. Avocation: photography.

GREEN, MARSHALL, consultant, former ambassador; b. Holyoke, Mass., Jan. 27, 1916; s. Addison Loomis and Gertrude (Metcalf) G.; m. Lispenard Seabury Crocker, Feb. 14, 1942; children: Marshall Winthrop, Edward Crocker, Brampton Seabury. A.B., Yale U., 1939; LLD, Hartwick Coll., 1981. Pvt. sec. to Am. ambassador to Japan, 1939-41; vice consul career, sec. Diplomatic Service, 1945; assigned Wellington, N.Z., 1946-47; acting officer in charge Japanese affairs Dept. State, 1947-50; 1st sec. embassy, consul Stockholm, 1950-55; assigned Nat. War Coll., 1955-56; regional planning adviser for Far East Dept. State, 1956-59, acting dep. asst. sec. of state, 1959-60; minister counselor Am. embassy, Korea, 1960-61; Am. consul gen. Hong Kong; personal rank of minister 1961-63; dep. asst. sec. for Far Eastern affairs Dept. State, 1963-65; A.E. and P. Indonesia, 1965-69; to Australia and Nauru 1973-75; asst. sec. state for East Asian-Pacific affairs Washington, 1969-73; coordinator population affairs State Dept., 1975-79; personal rank of career minister 1966-79, cons., 1979—; dir. population crisis com., chmn. adv. com. Asia Soc., Washington.; Mem. U.S. team in Paris for Vietnam negotiations, 1969; chmn. task force on population Nat. Security Council, 1975—; chief U.S. del. to UN Population Commn., 1977, 79; bd. dirs. Nat. Com. U.S.-China Relations. Served to lt. USNR, 1942-45. Recipient Nat. Civil Service award, 1965, Disting. Service award, 1979, Order of Rising Sun, Japan, 1985. Mem. Japan-Am. Soc. Washington (pres.). Episcopalian. Clubs: Metropolitan (Washington); Chevy Chase (Md.); York Golf and Tennis (Maine). Home: 5063 Millwood Ln NW Washington DC 20016

GREEN, MARTIN, manufacturing executive; b. Johannesburg, Republic of South Africa, Apr. 8, 1946; s. Sam and Fanny Green; married; 2 children. Ed. South African schs. Cattle rancher Evergreen Ranch, 1978-88; chmn. African Tube & Pipe Works Pty Ltd., 1982—, also bd. dirs.; bd. dirs. Antonhyl Ranch Pty Ltd., Universal Machine Tool and Grinding Industries Ltd; established spiral pipe mill in Israel. Founder Bruma (Republic South Africa) Ratepayers Assn., 1984—, Cyrildene/Bruma Village Community, 1988—; active numerous Jewish orgns., Johannesburg. Mem. Order of David. Home: 3 Adolf Goerz Pl, Bruma Village, Bedfordview 2008, South Africa

GREEN, SIR OWEN WHITLEY, diversified manufacturing company executive; b. Stockton-on-Tees, Eng., May 14, 1925; m. Doreen Margaret Green; 3 children. With Charles Wakeling & Co., 1947-56; dir. fin. BTR plc, 1956-66, asst. mng. dir., 1966-67, mng. dir., 1967-84, chief exec. officer, from 1984, chmn., 1984—; also chmn., mng. dir. BTR Inc. subs. BTR plc, Stamford, Conn. Served with Brit. Royal Navy, 1942-46. Fellow Inst. Chartered Accts. Avocation: golf. Office: BTR Inc 750 Main Pl Stamford CT 06902 *

GREEN, RAYMOND BERT, lawyer; b. Hartford, Conn., July 12, 1929; s. William Gottlieb and Mayme Pauline (Judatz) G.; m. Barbara Louise Miller, Jan. 31, 1955; children: Elizabeth Hollister, William Goodrich. BA, Yale U., 1951, LLB, 1954. Bar: Conn. 1954, U.S. Dist. Ct. Conn. 1959, U.S. Supreme Ct. 1962, U.S. Ct. Appeals (2d cir.) 1966, U.S. Ct. Mil. Appeals 1974, U.S. Dist. Ct. (so. dist.) N.Y. 1976, U.S. Dist. Ct. (ea. dist.) N.Y. 1976. Assoc., Camp, Williams & Richardson, New Britain, Conn., 1954-55; assoc. Day, Berry & Howard, Hartford, Conn., 1958-65, ptnr., 1966—; dir. New Britain Herald; trustee Collinsville Savs. Soc. (Conn.); judge of probate Dist. of Canton, Conn., 1963—. Pres., bd. dirs. Am. Friends of Coll. Cevenol (France); bd. dirs. YMCA Met. Hartford, 1963-84, 86—; sec., bd. trustees Children's Mus. Hartford, 1977-85, Sci. Mus. of Conn., 1985-86; bd. editors

Conn. Probate Law Jour. Served with USNR, 1955-58; comdr. JAGC, Res., 1958-79. Mem. Hartford County Bar Assn., ABA, Conn. Bar Assn. (chmn. ins. com. 1978-85, ethics com. 1987—), Judge Advs. Assn., Def. Research Inst., Conn. Def. Lawyers Assn. (bd. dirs. 1985-87), Assn. Trial Lawyers Am., Nat. Coll. Probate Judges, Phi Beta Kappa. Republican. Congregationalist. Clubs: Univ. (Hartford), Officers of Conn., Naval Res. Officers Luncheon (N.Y.C.), Assn. Ex-Mems. Squadron A (N.Y.C.). Home: 120 West Rd Collinsville CT 06022 Office: Cityplace 2500 Hartford CT 06103

GREEN, RAYMOND S(ILVERNAIL), radio station executive; b. Torrington, Conn., Jan. 1, 1915; s. Percy Alexander and Amy (Silvernail) G.; m. Rose Basile, June 20, 1942; children: Carol Rae Green Hoffman, Raymond Ferguson. Student, Julius Hartt Sch. Music, 1934-37; student studied violin with, Sarah Newton, 1925-33; voice with, Royal Dadmun, 1934-38, Giuseppe Boghetti, 1938-41, Alfredo Martino, 1942-50; coached with, Frederick Kitzsinger, 1946, Stuart Ross, 1947, Dr. Ernst Knoch, 1947-50; D.H.L. Cabrini Coll., 1982; D.Mus. (hon.), Combs Coll., 1984; D.F.A. (hon.), New Sch. Music, 1984. Producer, dir. musical programs NBC, N.Y.C., 1941-47; prodn. mgr. NBC, 1948; gen. mgr. Sta. WFLN, Phila., 1949-66; pres. Sta. WFLN, 1966—; pres. Franklin Broadcasting Co., Phila., 1966-82, chmn. bd., 1982—; chmn. bd. Magnetik Prodns.; owner, operator conservation tree farm, Washington, Vt. Pres. Phila. Art Alliance, 1966-73, chmn. bd., 1973-77, hon. pres., 1977—; exec. v.p. Schuylkill Valley Nature Center, 1970—; bd. dirs. Presser Found., 1985—, Musical Fund Soc., Union League Phila; v.p. Societa Cavalieri D'Italia, 1987—; chmn. Eugene Ormandy Archive, U. Pa. Served to maj. USAAF, 1942-46. Decorated commendatore Order of merit Italian Republic; recipient William Penn Human Rights award, 1982, George Washington Medal Freedoms Found. at Valley Forge. Fellow Royal Soc. Arts (London); mem. Broadcast Pioneers (pres. 1965-66, life dir.), Musical Fund Soc. Phila. (pres. 1983-86, bd. dirs.), Am. Forestry Assn., Pa. Soc. Clubs: Peale, Franklin Inn, Philobiblon, Union League (bd. dirs. 1984-88), Phila. Cricket (Phila.). Home: 308 Manor Rd Philadelphia PA 19128 Office: 8200 Ridge Ave Philadelphia PA 19128

GREEN, ROBERT EDWARD, neurosurgeon, writer; b. N.Y.C., Mar. 30, 1921; s. Bud and Anna Marie (vonHinken) Green; m. Beverly Jane Horn, Oct., 1945; children—James Kimball, Gwynneth Marie, Thomas Carter, Cathlin Louise. B.A., Columbia U., 1941; M.D., Cornell U., 1944. Diplomate Am. Bd. Neurol. Surgery. Intern U. Chgo. Clinics, 1944-45, resident, 1945-46; resident in neurosurgery Johns Hopkins Hosp., Balt., 1948-51. Instr. neurosurgery John Hopkins U., Balt., 1950-51; attending neurosurgeon St. Barnabas Med. Ctr., Newark, 1951-64, chief div. neurosurgery Med. Ctr. at Livingston, N.J., 1964—, bd. trustees, 1981—; attending neurosurgeon Hosp. Ctr. at Orange, N.J., 1951—, chief div. neurosurgery, 1959—; cons. neurosurgeon St. Mary's Hosp., Orange, 1966—, Montclair Community Hosp. (N.J.), 1964—. Author, mem. editorial bd: A History of Neurological Surgery, 1951; writer, narrator tape recording Forever Green -50 Years of Songs by Buddy Green, 1983; contbr. med. articles to publs. Served to capt. M.C., U.S. Army, 1946-47; ETO. Fellow ACS, Internat. Coll. Surgeons; mem. Am. Assn. Neurol. Surgeons, Congress Neurol. Surgeons, N.J. Neurol. Soc. (pres. 1961-62, peer rev. com. 1983—), Chaine des Rotisseurs (N.Y. Regional Bailli, N.E. 1979-81), Chaine des Rotisseurs (Chambellan 1982-86, hon. 1986—, asst. regional Bailli, N.E., 1988—). Republican. Congregationalist. Office: 22 Old Short Hills Rd Livingston NJ 07039

GREEN, WARREN HAROLD, publisher; b. Auburn, Ill., July 25, 1915; s. John Anderson Logan and Clara Christina (Wortman) G.; m. Joyce Reinerd, Oct. 8, 1960. Student, Presbyn. Theol. Sem., 1933-34, Ill. Wesleyan U., 1934-36; M.B., Southwestern Conservatory, Dallas, 1938; M.M., St. Louis Conservatory, 1940, Ph.D., 1942; H.L.D. (hon.), Southeastern U., New Orleans, 1983; L.L.D. (hon.), Institut de Droit Practique, Limoges, France, 1983; D.D. (hon.), Calif. Theol Sem., 1980; Litt.D. (hon.), Confédération Européenne de L' Ordre Judiciaire, France, 1983. Prof. voice, composition, conducting and aural theory St. Louis Conservatory, 1938-44; program dir. U.S.O., Highland Park, Ill., Brownwood, Tex., Orange, Tex., Waukegan, Ill., 1944-46; community service specialist Rotary Internat., Chgo., 1946-47; editor in chief Charles C. Thomas, Pub., Springfield, Ill., 1947-66; pub., pres. Warren H. Green, Inc., St. Louis, 1966—, Warren H. Green Internat., Inc., 1970—; sec. John R. Davis Assos., Chgo., 1955—; exec. v.p. Visioneering Advt., St. Louis, 1966—; mng. dir. Pubs. Service Center, St. Louis, Chgo. and Longview, Tex., 1967—; mng. dir., v.p. InterContinental Industries, Inc., St. Louis, 1976—; v.p. Epoch Press, St. Louis, 1986—; cons. U.S., European pubs., profl. socs.; lectr. med. publs. Civil War. Contbr. articles to profl. jours., books on Civil War history, writing, editing. Mem. Mayor's Com. on Water Safety, Met. St. Louis Art Mus., Mo. Bot. Gardens; chief exec. officer Affirmative Action, Inc., St. Louis, 1974—; pres. Southeastern U., 1984-85, No. Utah U., 1986—. Recipient Presdl. citation for outstanding contbn. export expansion program U.S., 1973, citation Md. Crime Investating Com., 1962, citation Internat. Preventive Medicine Found., 1977, citation AMA, 1978. Mem. Civil War Round Table (v.p. 1969—), Am. Acad. Criminology, Am. Acad. Polit. and Social Sci., Am. Assn. Med. Book Pubs., Am. Judicature Soc., Great Plains Hist. Soc., Co. Mil. Historians, Am. Soc. Personnel Adminstrs., University City C. of C. (pres. 1978—), Internat. Assn. Chiefs of Police, Mo. Hist. Soc., Ill. Hist. Soc., St. Louis Philharmonic Soc., Mo. Botanical Gardens, St. Louis Art Mus. Clubs: Mo. Athletic, Media, Elks, World Trade, Direct Mktg. (St. Louis); Clayton (Mo.). Home: 12120 Hibler Dr Creve Coeur MO 63141 Office: 8356 Olive Blvd Saint Louis MO 63132

GREEN, WILLIAM PORTER, lawyer; b. Jacksonville, Ill., Mar. 19, 1920; s. Hugh Parker and Clara Belle (Hopper) G.; m. Rose Marie Hall, Oct. 1, 1944; children: Hugh Michael, Robert Alan, Richard William. B.A., Ill. Coll., 1941; J.D., Northwestern U., 1947. Bar: Ill. 1947, Calif. 1948, U.S. Dist. Ct. (so. dist.) Tex. 1986, Ct. Customs and Patent Appeals 1948, U.S. Patent and Trademark Office 1948, U.S. Ct. Appeals (fed. cir.) 1982, U.S. Ct. Appeals (5th and 9th cirs.), U.S. Supreme Ct. 1948, U.S. Dist. Ct. (cen. dist.) Calif., U.S. Dist. Ct. (so. dist.) Tex., 1986. Practice patent, trademark and copyright law Los Angeles, 1947—; mem. firm Wills, Green & Mueth, 1974-83; of counsel Nilsson, Robbins, Dalgarn, Berliner, Carson & Wurst, Los Angeles, 1984—; del. Calif. State Bar Conv., 1982-88, delegation chair 1986. Bd. editors Ill. Law Rev, 1946. Mem. Los Angeles World Affairs Council, 1975—; del., chmn. Calif. State Bar Conv., 1986 Served lt. USNR, 1942-46. Mem. ABA, Calif State Bar, Am. Intellectual Property Law Assn., Los Angeles Patent Law Assn. (past sec.-treas., bd. govs.), Lawyers Club Los Angeles (past treas., past sec., bd. govs., pres.-elect 1983 84, pres. 1985-86), Los Angeles County Bar Assn (trustee 1986-87), Am. Legion (past post comdr.), Phi Beta Kappa, Phi Delta Phi, Phi Alpha. Republican. Presbyn. (deacon 1961-63). Clubs: Big Ten of So. Calif, Northwestern U. Alumni of So. Calif, Phi Beta Kappa Alumni of So. Calif, Town Hall of Calif. Home: 3570 E Lombardy Rd Pasadena CA 91107 Office: Nilsson Robbins Dalgarn Berliner Carson & Wurst 201 N Figueroa St 5th Floor Los Angeles CA 90012

GREENAWALT, MARTHA SLOAN, civic worker; b. Clarksburg, W.Va., Sept. 8, 1906; d. Herbert Elias and Louella (Dye) Sloan; A.B., Wilson Coll., 1928; M.A., Columbia U., 1929; D.H.L. (hon.), Mercy Coll., 1985; m. Kenneth William Greenawalt, Sept. 3, 1929; children—William Sloan, Robert Kent, Ann Cornell (Mrs. William Beaven Abernethy), Kim Chandler. Tchr., Berkeley Inst., Bklyn., 1929-33; pres. Westchester council Women's Coll. Clubs, 1952-53; mem. housing research com., mem. bd. Westchester Council Social Agys.; chmn. Greenburgh Urban Renewal Commn., 1961-75; mem. bd. Westchester citizens com. Nat. Council on Crime and Delinquency, 1975-82; mem. com. for constl. reform, 2d regional plan com., mem. bd. dirs. Regional Plan Assn.; bd. dirs. Westchester Alliance Juvenile and Criminal Justice, 1980—, co-chmn., 1984-85; mem. Nat. Adv. Com. on Comprehensive Health Planning, 1972-74; mem. adv. bd. Greenburgh Neighborhood Health Center, 1974—; bd. dirs. Westchester County Urban League, 1957-62; v.p. United Way of Westchester, 1979-81 (chmn. admissions com., multi-stress com., planning, evaluation and allocations com.), exec. com. Women of Westchester; chmn. Westchester Women's Council, 1981-83; Child Care Council of Westchester (bd. dirs.), Women's Adv. Bd. Westchester County, mem. citizens adv. panel Tri-State Regional Planning Commn.; adv. council Women's Center; mem. Social Services Community Adv. Council, 1979-81; vice chmn. Legal Awareness for Women, 1981-83, chmn., 1983—; vice chair Westchester 2000, 1983-86, bd. dirs. 1986—. Recipient Avon/Westchester Hall of Fame award, 1985; Presdl. Recognition award, 1986. Mem. LWV (pres. Greenburgh 1953-56, pres. Westchester County 1957-59, pres. N.Y. 1963-67, mem. nat. bd. 1968-74, trustee Overseas Edn. Fund, pres. tri-state met. area 1981-85, chair Westchester human needs com.) , Scarsdale-Hartsdale UN Assn., NOW (dir. Central Westchester chpt. 1973-78), Wilson Coll. Alumnae Assn. (dir. 1979-82, Distinguished Alumnae award 1988). Address: 65 Highridge Rd Hartsdale NY 10530

GREENAWALT, WILLIAM SLOAN, lawyer; b. Bklyn., Mar. 4, 1934; s. Kenneth William and Martha Frances (Sloan) G.; m. Jane DeLano Plunkett, Aug. 17, 1957 (div. May 1986); m. Peggy Ellen Freed Tomarkin, Oct. 31, 1987; children: John DeLano, David Sloan, Katherine Downs. A.B., Cornell U., 1956; LL.B., Yale U., 1961. Bar: N.Y. 1962, U.S. Dist. Ct. (so. and ea. dists.) N.Y. 1962, U.S. Ct. Apls. (2d cir.) 1962, U.S. Supreme Ct. 1966. Assoc., Sullivan & Cromwell, N.Y.C., 1961-65; northeast regional legal services dir. U.S. Office Econ. Opportunity, N.Y.C., 1965-68; assoc. Rogers & Wells, N.Y.C., 1968-69, ptnr., 1969-77, sr. ptnr., 1977-81; sr. ptnr. Halperin, Shivitz, Eisenberg, Schneider & Greenawalt, N.Y.C., 1981-86, sr. ptnr. Eisenberg, Honig & Fogler, N.Y.C., 1986—; lectr. in field. Chmn., Applied Resources Inc., N.Y.C., 1968-70; state chmn. Community Aid Employment Ex-Offenders, Westchester, N.Y., 1971; pres. Westchester Legal Services, 1971-74; bd. dirs, 1975—; mem. N.Y. State Gov.'s Task Force Elem. and Secondary Edn., 1974-75; mem. Pres. Carter's Task Force Criminal Justice, 1976; panel comml. arbitrators Am. Arbitration Assn., 1977—, adv. council N.Y. State Senate Dems., 1978—; mem. Greenburgh Recreational Commn., 1976-83, Statewide Spl. Commn. on Polit. Ethics (Dem. Party), 1986-87; pres. Westchester Crime Victims Assistance Agy., 1981-82; commr. Taconic State Parks, Recreation and Historic Preservation Commn., 1984—; moderator Scarsdale Congl. Ch., 1988—. Served to lt. comdr. U.S. Navy, 1956-58, Res., 1961-68. Fellow N.Y. Bar Found.; mem. ABA, N.Y. State Bar Assn. (chmn. com. on availability of legal services 1968-70, chmn. action unit #3 1979-81, chmn. spl. commn. on alternatives to jud. resolution of disputes 1981-85), Assn. Bar City N.Y., Nat. Legal Aid and Defenders Assn., Phi Alpha Delta. Democrat. Congregationalist. Clubs: County Tennis of Westchester (pres. 1979-80) (Scarsdale, N.Y.); Yale. Bd. editors: Yale Law Jour., 1959-61; contbr. articles in field to profl. jours. Address: 24 Lewis Ave Hartsdale NY 10530

GREENAWAY, DONALD, hotel administration educator; b. Frankfort, Mich., Apr. 14, 1911; s. George Henry and Mary Elizabeth (Orr) G.; m. Louise Constance Wadsworth, June 27, 1936; 1 dau., Jeanne Elizabeth Greenaway Des Camp; m. Lorraine Katherine Muellenbach, July 6, 1958 (dec. Feb. 1983); 1 dau., Karen. B.A., Mich. State U., 1934; LL.D., Northwood Inst., 1970. Hotel adminstrn. and mgmt. 1934-41; food service exec. Trans World Airlines, 1946-47; prof. hotel adminstrn. Coll. Bus., Wash. State U., 1947-51; prof. adminstr.-dir. Sch. Hotel, Restaurant and Instl. Mgmt., Coll. Bus., Mich. State U., 1951-58; exec. v.p. Nat. Restaurant Assn., Chgo., 1958-70; asso. dean Sch. Hotel and Restaurant Mgmt., U. Houston, 1970-76; asst. to exec. v.p. Tex. Restaurant Assn., 1976—; Dir. Wilkensburg Hotel Co., Pa., Hotel Elkhart, Ind.; Mem. Gov.'s Com. for Devel. State Wash., 1950-51; pres., founder Nat. Council Hotel and Restaurant Edn., 1946; adviser to bd. dirs. Army and Air Force Exchange Service; adviser USPHS, USAF, World-Wide Food Service; mgmt. cons. Soc. Advancement Food Service Research; mem. 5th Internat. World Food Congress, U.S. Travel Service; also trade assn. adv. com. U.S. C. of C.; trade missions to Europe auspices Dept. Commerce.; Disting. vis. prof. Fla. Internat. U.; First Westin Hotels Disting. prof. Wash. State U. Author: Manual for Resort Operations, 1950, also monographs, papers, articles. Bd. dirs. Govs. Confs. Tourism Pacific N.W., 1947-49, Pacific N.W. Trade Assn., 1947-48. Served to capt. USAAF, 1942-46. Mem. AAUP, Am. Soc. Assn. Execs., Execs. Forum, Mich., Resort Assn., Mich. Pa. hotel assns., Am. Standards Assn. (com. standards for food service industry), Food Execs. Assn., Internat. Ho-Re-Ca, Confrerie de la Chaine des Rotisseurs, Theta Chi, Alpha Kappa Psi. Club: Rotarian. Home: 10610 Morado Circle #1323 Austin TX 78757

GREENBAUM, CHARLES HIRSCH, dermatologist; b. Phila., Feb. 22, 1925; s. Sigmund Samuel and Rae Shirley (Refowich) G.; m. Julia Heimowitz, July 3, 1955; children—Steven Samuel, Lynne Carol, Robert David. A.B., U. Pa., 1948; M.D., Jefferson Med. Coll., 1954. Intern, Phila. Gen. Hosp., 1954-55; resident U. Pa. Grad. Sch. Medicine, 1955-56, Pa. Hosp., 1956-57, Hosp. U. Pa., 1957-58; practice medicine specializing in dermatology, Phila., 1958—; instr. dermatology Jefferson Med. Coll., Phila., 1958-72, clin. asso. prof., 1972-81, clin. prof., 1981—; attending physician, chief dermatology Holy Redeemer Hosp., Meadowbrook, Pa., 1958—; instr. dermatology U. Pa. Grad. Sch. Medicine, 1958-70; med. advisor Pa. Blue Cross, 1973—. Contbr. articles in field to profl. jours. Bd. trustees Dermatology Found.; bd. dirs. Holy Redeemer Hosp. Served with USMC, 1943-46. Diplomate Am. Bd. Dermatology. Fellow Am. Acad. Dermatology, ACP; mem. Am. Dermatol. Assn., Soc. Investigative Dermatology, Am. Acad. Dermatology (chmn. adv. bd. council 1977, chmn. com. eval. 1979-82), AMA (mem. sect. on dermatology 1978), Pa. Acad. Dermatology (pres. 1976-77), Phila. Dermatol. Soc. (pres. 1976-77), Coll. Physicians Phila., Solomon Solis-Cohen Med. Lit. Soc. (pres. 1978), Pa., Phila. County (pres. N. br. 1976, dir. 1977) med. socs. Home: 1420 Lewis Rd Rydal PA 19046 Office: 10125 Verree Rd Philadelphia PA 19116

GREENBERG, IRA ARTHUR, clinical psychologist, mgmt. cons.; b. Bklyn., June 26, 1924; s. Philip and Minnie (S.) G.; BA in Journalism, U. Okla., 1949; MA in English, U. So. Calif., 1962; MS in Counseling, Calif. State U. Los Angeles, 1963; PhD in Psychology, Claremont (Calif.) Grad Sch., 1967. Editor, Ft. Riley (Kans.) Guidon, 1950-51; reporter, copy editor Columbus (Ga.) Enquirer, 1951-55; reporter Louisville Courier-Jour., 1955-56, Los Angeles Times, 1956-62; free-lance writer, Los Angeles, Montclair, Camarillo, Calif., 1960-69, 76—; counselor Claremont Coll. Psychol. Clinic and Counseling Ctr., 1964-65; lectr. psychology Chapman Coll., Orange, Calif., 1965-66; psychologist Camarillo State Hosp., 1967-69, supervising psychologist, 1969-73, part time clin. psychologist, 1973—; part time asst. prof. edn. San Fernando Valley State Coll., Northridge, Calif., 1967-69, lectr. psychodrama, social welfare U. Calif. Extension Div., Santa Barbara, 1968-69; vol. psychologist Free Clinic, Los Angeles, 1968-70; staff dir. Calif. Inst. Psychodrama, 1969-71; tng. cons. Topanga Ctr. for Human Devel., 1970-75, bd. dirs., 1971-74, faculty Calif. Sch. Profl. Psychology, 1970—; founder, exec. dir. Behavioral Studies Inst., mgmt. cons., Los Angeles, 1970—; pvt. practice cons. in psychology, psychodrama, hypnosis, 1970—; founder, exec. dir. Psychodrama Center for Los Angeles, Inc., 1971—, Group Hypnosis Ctr., Los Angeles, 1976—; producer, host TV talk show Crime and Pub. Safety, Century Cable, Channel 3, 1983—. Vol. humane officer State of Calif., 1979—; res. officer Los Angeles Police Dept., 1980-86; capt. Calif. State Mil. Res., 1986—. Served with AUS, 1943-46; ETO; USAR, 1950-51. Fellow Am. Soc. Clin. Hypnosis; mem. Am. Soc. Group Psychotherapy and Psychodrama, Assn. Research and Enlightenment, Los Angeles Soc. Clin. Psychologists (dir. 1975), Am., Western, Calif., Los Angeles psychol. assns., Am. Soc. for Psychical Research, Group Psychotherapy Assn. So. Calif. (dir. 1974-76, 82—, pres. 1987-87), Am. Mgmt. Assn., Am. Soc. Bus. and Mgmt. Cons. (nat. adv. council 1977—), So. Calif. Soc. Clin. Hypnosis (dir., exec. v.p. 1973-76, pres. 1977-78), So. Calif. Psychotherapy Affiliation (dir. 1976-85), Assn. for Humanistic Psychology, Mensa, Am. Zionist Fedn., Nat. Rifle Assn., Calif. Rifle and Pistol Assn., SW Pistol League, Animal Protection Inst. Am., Humane Educators Council (bd. dirs. 1982-86), Airport Psychol. Assocs., Sigma Delta Chi. Clubs: Sierra, Greater Los Angeles Press; B'nai B'rith; Beverly Hills Gun. Author: Psychodrama and Audience Attitude Change, 1968. Editor, author: Psychodrama: Theory and Therapy, 1974; Group Hypnotherapy and Hypnodrama, 1977. Address: Camarillo State Hosp Box A Camarillo CA 93011 also: BSI & Group Hypnosis Ctr 11692 Chenault St Suite 206 Los Angeles CA 90049

GREENBERG, JAMES, lawyer; b. Phila., Feb. 21, 1939; s. Abraham and Tillie (Gold) G.; m. Sarilee Greenberg, Aug. 26, 1961; children—Suellen, Jonathan, Janet. B.S.E., Princeton U., 1961; J.D. cum laude, U. Pa., 1964. Bar: N.J. 1964, Pa. 1977, U.S. Supreme Ct. 1969. Clk., Superior Ct. N.J., 1964-65; assoc., then ptnr. Greenberg, Shmerelson, Weinroth & Etish, P.A., and predecessors, Camden, N.J. and Phila., 1965—; asst. prosecutor Camden County (N.J.), 1969-70; mcpl. prosecutor Cherry Hill Twp. (N.J.), 1971-73, mcpl. judge, 1973-81; mem. N.J. Supreme Ct. Com. on N.J. Dist. Cts. and N.J. Mcpl. Cts. Mem. Camden County Bar Assn. (trustee 1977-80, Peter J. Devine, Jr. award 1981), N.J. Bar Assn., Pa. Bar Assn., ABA, Trial Attys. N.J., Nat. Dist. Attys. Assn., Am. Trial Lawyers Assn., Am. Judicature Soc. Clubs: B'rith Sholom, B'nai B'rith (Cherry Hill, N.J.). Office: 538 Cooper St Camden NJ 08102 Other: Land Title Bldg Broad and Chestnut Sts Suite 2226 Philadelphia PA 19110

GREENBERG, JOHN LEONARD, science historian; b. Kirksville, Mo., Dec. 10, 1945; s. Leonard Stanley and Margaret Shephard (O'Briant) G.; BA, Shimer Coll., 1966; MA, Johns Hopkins U., 1970; PhD, U. Wis.-Madison, 1979; m. Marie-Therese Vercauteren, Dec. 18, 1972; children: Philippe, Sylvie. Instr., Balt. Poly Inst., 1970-71, Am. Coll. Switzerland, Leysin, 1971-72; NSF Nat. Needs postdoctoral fellow Centre de Recherches Alexandre Koyré, Ecole des Hautes Etudes en Sciences Sociales, Paris, 1979-80; instr. Ecole Active Bilingue J.M., Paris, 1980-81; research fellow Robert A. Millikan Meml. Library, Calif. Inst. Tech., Pasadena, 1981-84; Fulbright research scholar, 1984-85 U.S.-France Exchange of Scientists and NSF scholar, Centre de Recherches Alexandre Koyre, Ecole des Hautes Etudes en Sciences Sociales, Paris, 1984-86; vis. research assoc. Centre National de la Recherche Scientifique, 1986; ACLS fellow, 1987-88. Mem. History of Sci. Soc., Am. Soc. for Eighteenth Century Studies, Soc. Française d'Étude du XVIIIe Siècle, Sigma Xi. Contbr. articles to profl. jours. Home: 2 Residence du Val, 91 120 Palaiseau France Office: Centre de Racherches, Alexandre Koyre, 75 002 Paris France

GREENBERG, MARTIN JAY, lawyer, educator, author; b. Milw., Aug. 5, 1945; s. Sol and Phyllis (Schunder) G.; m. Beverly L. Young, Apr. 29, 1969; children—Kari, Steven. B.S., U. Wis., 1967; J.D., Marquette U., 1971. Bar: Wis. 1971. Assoc. Hoyt, Greene & Meissner, Milw., 1971-74, Weiss, Steuer, Berzowski & Kriger, Milw., 1974-76; ptnr. Greenberg & Boxer, Milw., 1976-78; sole practice, Milw., 1978—; asst. prof. law Marquette U., Milw., 1976-79, adj. prof., 1979—; bd. dirs., pres. Law Projects, Inc.; mem. book revisions com. Wis. Real Estate Examining Bd., 1978—. Mem. brotherhood bd. Congregation Emanu-El B'ne Jeshurun, Milw., 1976-78, treas., 1979—; bd. dirs. Community Coordinated Child Care, Milw., 1976-77, Jewish Nat. Fund, Project Re-Unite; dir. Am. Jewish com., 1988—; mem. Shorewood (Wis.) Bd. Rev., 1977-81. Served with Wis. N.G., 1968-74. Morris Guten Vets. scholar, 1965; I.E. Goldberg scholar, 1966; Carnegie grantee, 1966; Wis. Student Assn. scholar, 1967; Thomas More scholar, 1969; Francis X. Swietlik scholar, 1971. Mem. ABA, Wis. Bar Assn., Milw. Bar Assn. (named Lawyer of Yr.-Legal Scholar 1988), Wis. Bar Found. (lectr. Project Inquiry 1980-81, Lawyer's Pro Bono Publico award 1978), Marquette U. Law Alumni Assn. (trustee), Jewish Vocat. Service (corp.), Woolsack Soc., Scribes, Tau Epsilon Rho (chancellor grad. chpt. 1972-73). Lodge: Masons. Author: Real Estate Practice, 1976, rev. edit., 1977; Wisconsin Real Estate, 1982; Mortgages and Real Estate Financing, 1982; Real Estate Tax Guide, 1988; editor Marquette Law Rev., 1969-71. Home: 9429 N Broadmoor Bayside WI 53217 Office: 1139 E Knapp St Milwaukee WI 53202

GREENBERG, MORTON PAUL, lawyer, insurance broker, advanced underwriting consultant; b. Fall River, Mass., June 2, 1946; s. Harry and Sylvia Shirley (Davis) G.; m. Louise Beryl Schindler, Jan. 24, 1970; 1 dau., Alexis Lynn. BSBA, NYU, 1968; JD, Bklyn. Law Sch., 1971; chartered life underwriter Am. Coll., 1975. Bar: N.Y. 1972. Atty., Hanner, Fitzmaurice & Onorato, N.Y.C., 1971-72; dir., counsel, cons. on advanced underwriting The Mfrs. Life Ins. Co., Toronto, Ont., Can., 1972—; mem. sales ideas com. Million Dollar Roundtable, Chgo., 1982-83; speaker on law, tax, and advanced underwriting to various profl. groups, U.S., Can. Author: (tech. jour.) ManuBriefs. Mem. ABA, N.Y. State Bar Assn., Assn. for Advanced Life Underwriting, Internat. Platform Assn., NYU Alumni Assn., Nat. Assn. of Life Underwriters, Denver Assn. Life Underwriters, Am. Soc. CLU. Office: 7617 E Sunrise Trail Parker CO 80134

GREENBERG, MYRON SILVER, lawyer; b. Los Angeles, Oct. 17, 1945; s. Earl W. and Geri (Silver) G.; m. Shlomit Gross; children: David, Amy. BSBA, UCLA, 1967, JD, 1970. Bar: Calif. 1971, U.S. Dist. Ct. (cen. dist.) Calif. 1971, U.S. Tax Ct. 1977; CPA, Calif. Staff acct. Touche Ross & Co., Los Angeles, 1970-71; assoc. Kaplan, Livingston, Goodwin, Berkowitz, & Selvin, Beverly Hills, 1971-74; ptnr. Dinkelspiel, Steefel & Levitt, San Francisco, 1975-80; ptnr. Steefel, Levitt & Weiss, San Francisco, 1981-82; pres. Myron S. Greenberg, a Profl. Corp., Larkspur, Calif., 1982—; professorial lectr. tax. Golden Gate U. Author: California Attorney's Guide to Professional Corporations, 1977, 79; bd. editors UCLA Law Rev., 1969-70. Mem. San Anselmo Planning Commn., 1976-77; bd. dirs. Bay Area Lawyers for Arts, 1979-80, Marin County chpt. Am. Heart Assn. (bd. dirs., pres. 1984—). Mem. ABA, Marin County (Calif.) Bar Assn., Bus. Execs. Assn. of Marin, Am. Inst. CPA's, Calif. Soc. CPA's, Real Estate Tax Inst. of Calif. Continuing Edn. Bar (planning com.), Larkspur C. of C. (bd. dirs. 1985-87). Democrat. Jewish. Office: 80 E Sir Frances Drake Blvd Larkspur CA 94939

GREENBERG, NATHAN, accountant; b. Worcester, Mass., May 17, 1919; s. Samuel and Ida (Katz) G.; m. Mimi Aaron, Mar. 12, 1950 (dec.); children: Henry Aaron, Ruthanne; m. Barbara Rudnick, Feb. 9, 1979. B.S. in Bus. Adminstrn, Boston U., 1942. C.P.A., Mass. With Internal Revenue Service, 1945-47; v.p. finance, dir. Gt. Am. Plactics Co., Worcester, Mass., 1948-68, Gt. Am. Chem. Corp., Fitchburg, Mass., 1968-80; chmn. Greenberg, Rosenblatt, Kull & Bitsoli, P.C., Worcester, 1958—. Trustee Nathan and Barbara Greenberg Charitable Trust, Jewish Home for Aged, Jewish Community Center, Jewish Fedn. Served with AUS, 1942-45, ETO. Decorated Bronze Star. Fellow Am. Inst. C.P.A.'s, Mass. Soc. C.P.A.'s, Controllers Inst. Am.; mem. Mu Sigma. Club: Mt. Pleasant Country (Boylston, Mass.) (v.p. 1962—). Home: 85 Aylesbury Rd Worcester MA 01609 Office: The Day Bldg 306 Main St Worcester MA 01608

GREENBERG, RONALD DAVID, lawyer, educator; b. San Antonio, Sept. 9, 1939. s. Benjamin and Sylvia (Ghetlzer) G. BS, U. Tex., 1957; MBA, Harvard U., 1961, JD, 1964. Bar: N.Y. 1966, U.S. Dist. Ct. (ea. and so. dists.) N.Y. 1970, U.S. Ct. Appeals (2d cir.) 1975, U.S. Supreme Ct. 1975. Engr., bus. analyst Exxon Corp., N.Y.C., 1957-64; atty., engr. Allied Corp., N.Y.C., 1964-67; assoc. Arthur, Dry, Kalish, Taylor & Wood, N.Y.C., 1967-69, Valicenti, Leighton, Reid & Pine, N.Y.C., 1969-70; faculty Columbia U., N.Y.C., 1970—, prof. bus. law and taxation, 1982—; of counsel Delson & Gordon, N.Y.C., 1973-87; lectr., cons. Citibank, Mfrs. Hanover Trust Co., Harcourt, Brace, Jovanovich, Inc., Prudential-Bache, Drexel, Burnham & Lambert, E.F. Hutton; vis. prof. Stanford U., Palo Alto, Calif., 1978, Harvard U., Boston, 1981. Author: Business Income Tax Materials, 1986; editor-in-chief Internat. Law Practicum, 1987—; contbr. chpt. to book, articles to profl. jours. Cons. council City of N.Y., 1971-72, Manhattan Community Coll., 1974-76. Served to lt. USNR, 1957-59. Recipient Outstanding Prof. award Columbia U. Grad. Sch. Bus., 1973. Mem. ABA (chmn. com. on taxation gen. practice sect. 1978-83, chmn. com. on corp. banking and bus. law gen. practice sect. 1985—), NSPE, N.Y. State Bar Assn. (gen. practice sect., chmn. tax law com. 1983—, bus. law com. 1985—), Assn. Bar City of N.Y., N.Y. Acad. Scis., Mensa. Clubs: Harvard (N.Y.C.); Rye Golf (N.Y.). Home: 55 Morton St New York NY 10014 Office: Columbia U 625 Uris Hall New York NY 10027

GREENBERG, STEVEN MOREY, lawyer; b. Jersey City, N.J., Apr. 9, 1949; s. Joseph and Rhoda (Weisenfeld) G. AB cum laude, Syracuse U., 1971; JD, U. Pa., 1974. Bar: N.J. 1974, U.S. Dist. Ct. N.J. 1974, N.Y. 1980. U.S. Dist. Ct. (so. dist.) N.Y., 1986, U.S. Dist. Ct. (ea. dist.) N.Y., 1986. Assoc. firm Carpenter, Bennett & Morrissey, Newark, 1974-77; assoc. firm Cole, Berman & Belsky, Rochelle Park, N.J., 1977-79; sole practice, Hackensack, N.J., 1979—; atty. Bergenfield (N.J.) Rent Leveling Bd., 1985—; trustee, chmn. youth activities com. Jewish Ctr. of Teaneck, 1978—; pres., trustee, past v.p., Group Care Home for Sr. Adults, Bergenfield, 1983—, mem. gov. bd., 1986—; adv. bd. dirs. Jewish Home and Rehab. Ctr. of N.J. and River Vale, 1982—; trustee Jewish Family Service Inc. of Bergen County, 1986—, The Solomon Schechter Day Sch. of Bergen County, 1986-87; mem. Jewish Community Relations Council No. N.J., 1986—. Mem. ABA, N.J. Bar Assn., Bergen County Bar Assn., Assn. Transp. Practitioners, Phi Kappa Phi, Pi Sigma Alpha. Home: 96 Westminster Ave Bergenfield NJ 07621 Office: 2 University Plaza Hackensack NJ 07601

GREENBERGER, I. MICHAEL, lawyer; b. Scranton, Pa., Oct. 30, 1945; s. David and Betty (Kabatchnick) G.; m. Marcia Devins, July 19, 1969; children—Sarah Devins, Anne Devins. A.B., Lafayette Coll., 1967; J.D., U. Pa., 1970. Bar: D.C. 1971, U.S. Dist. Ct. D.C. 1971, U.S. Ct. Appeals (D.C. cir.) 1971, U.S. Supreme Ct. 1975, U.S. Dist. Ct. Md. 1985, U.S. Ct. Appeals (fed. cir.) 1986. Law clk. U.S. Ct. Appeals for D.C. Circuit, Washington,

1970-71; legis. asst. to U.S. Congresswoman Elizabeth Holtzman, 1972-73; atty., advisor Office of Criminal Justice, Office U.S. Atty. Gen., 1973; assoc. Shea & Gardner, Washington, 1973-77, ptnr., 1977—; mem. D.C. Circuit Adv. Com. on Procedures, 1983—; legal cons. Software Engring. Inst., Carnegie-Mellon U., 1986-87. Editor-in-chief U. Pa. Law Rev., 1969-70; contbr. articles to profl. jours. Bd. dirs. MIT ENterprise Forum Washington, 1984-87, Advanced Tech. Assn. Md., 1985-87. Mem. Am. Law Inst., ABA, D.C. Bar Assn. (chmn. adminstrv. law sect. steering com. 1980-82), Phi Beta Kappa. Address: 2757 Brandywine St NW Washington DC 20008

GREENBERGER, MARTIN, scientist, educator; b. Elizabeth, N.J., Nov. 30, 1931; s. David and Sidelle (Jonas) G.; A.B., Harvard, 1955, A.M., 1956, Ph.D., 1958; m. Liz Greenberger; children—Kari, David, Beth Jonit, Jonah Ben. Teaching fellow, resident adviser, staff mem. Computation Lab., Harvard, Cambridge, 1954-58; mgr. applied sci. IBM, Cambridge, 1956-58; asst. prof. mgmt. Mass. Inst. Tech., Cambridge, 1958-61, assoc. prof., 1961-67; prof., chmn. computer sci., dir. info. processing Johns Hopkins U., Balt., 1967-72, prof. math. scis., sr. research asso. Center for Met. Planning and Research, 1972-75, prof. math. scis., 1978-82; IBM chair in computers and info. systems, prof. pub. policy and analysis UCLA Grad. Sch. Mgmt., 1982—; pres. Council for Tech. and the Individual, 1985—; on leave as mgr. systems program Electric Power Research Inst., Palo Alto, Calif., 1976-77; Isaac Taylor vis. prof. Technion-Israel Inst. Tech., Haifa, 1978-79; vis. prof. Internat. Energy Program, Grad. Sch. Bus., Stanford U., 1980, MIT Media Lab. , 1988—. Mem. computer sci. and engring. bd. Nat. Acad. Scis., 1970-72; chmn. COSATI rev. group NSF, 1971-72; mem. evaluation com. Internat. Inst. for Applied Systems Analysis, Laxenburg, Austria, 1980; mem. adv. panels, Office Tech. Assessment, GAO, U.S. Congress; cons. IBM, A.T.&T., CBS, Rand Corp., Morgan Guaranty, Arthur D. Little, TRW, Bolt, Beranek & Newman, Brookings Inst., Resources for Future, Electric Power Research Inst., Atlantic Richfield, Rockwell Internat., Security Pacific Corp.John F. Kennedy Sch. of Govt. Harvard U. Mem. overseers' vis. com. Harvard U., 1975-81; founder and mem. working groups Energy Modeling Forum, Stanford U., 1978-81; mem. adv. com. Nat. Center Analysis of Energy Systems Brookhaven Nat. Lab., 1976-80, chmn., 1977; mem. rev. com. Energy and Environment div. Lawrence Berkeley Lab., 1983, applied sci. div., 1986-88; chmn. forum on electronic pub., Washington program Annenberg, 1983-84; co-founder ICC Forum, 1985; trustee Educom, Princeton, N.J., 1969-73, chmn. council, 1969-70. Served with USAF, 1952-54, with Res., 1954-60. NSF fellow, 1955-56; Guggenheim fellow U. Calif., Berkeley, 1965-66. Fellow AAAS (v.p., chmn. sect. T 1973-75); mem. Phi Beta Kappa, Sigma Xi. Author: (with Orcutt, Korbel and Rivlin) Microanalysis of Socioeconomic Systems: A Simulation Study, 1961; (with Jones, Morris and Ness) On-Line Computation and Simulation: The OPS-3 System, 1965; (with Crenson and Crissey) Models in the Policy Process: Public Decision Making in the Computer Era, 1976; (with Brewer, Hogan and Russell) Caught Unawares: The Energy Decade in Retrospect, 1983. Editor: Management and The Computer of the Future, 1962, republished as Computers and the World of the Future, 1964; Computers, Communications, and the Public Interest, 1971; (with Aronofsky, McKenney and Massy) Networks for Research and Education, 1973; Electronic Publishing Plus: Media for a Technological Future, 1985. Office: Anderson Grad Sch Mgmt UCLA Los Angeles CA 90024

GREENBLATT, EDWARD LANDE, lawyer; b. Augusta, Ga., Mar. 16, 1939; s. Robert B. and Gwendolyn (Lande) G.; m. Sherry Agoos, June 1, 1967; 1 dau., Susan. Student Duke U.; B.A., Birmingham So. Coll., 1961; LL.B., Emory U., 1964; LL.M., NYU, 1965. Bar: Ga. 1963, D.C. 1966, U.S. Supreme Ct. 1971. Atty., U.S. Dept. Treasury, Washington, 1965-66; assoc. Lipshutz, Greenblatt, & King, and predecessors, Atlanta, 1967-71, ptnr., 1971—. Bd. dirs. Atlanta Legal Aid Soc., Atlanta Community Ctr., Paces Battle Assn.; bd. dirs., chmn. Atlanta B'nai B'rith Youth Orgn., 1973-75; pres. The Temple, 1985-87; chmn. Southeastern Med. Research Found., 1987—. Mem. ABA, State Bar Ga., Atlanta Bar Assn., Lawyers Club Atlanta, Am. Judicature Soc. Jewish. Home: 4417 Paces Battle NW Atlanta GA 30327 Office: Lipshutz Greenblatt & King 2300 Harris Tower Peachtree Ctr 233 Peachtree St NE Atlanta GA 30043

GREENBURY, RICHARD, corporate executive; b. July 31, 1936; s. Richard Oswald and Dorothy (Lewis) G.; 4 children from previous marriage; m. Gabrielle Mary McManus, 1985. Student, Ealing County Grammar Sch. Jr. mgmt. trainee Marks and Spencer plc, 1953, alt. dir., 1970, full dir., 1972, joint mng. dir., 1978-86, chief operating officer, 1986—; non-exec. dir. Metal Box, 1985—. Club: Internat. Tennis of Great Britain. Office: 57 Baker St, London W1A 1DN, England *

GREENE, ARTHUR EDWARD, physicist; b. Chgo., Dec. 10, 1945; s. Shirley Edward and Ellen Catherine (Tweedy) G.; m. Nancy Ellen Green, Sept. 12, 1970; 1 child, Ellen Dorothy. Student, Doane Coll., 1963-65; B.S. cum laude, Ohio State U., 1967, Ph.D. in Astronomy, 1971. Staff mem. theoretical chemistry and molecular physics group Los Alamos Nat. Lab., 1975-81, staff mem. thermonuclear application group, 1981-86, staff mem. pulsed energy application group, 1986—. Contbr. articles to profl. jours. Served to capt. USAF, 1971-75. Recipient award of Excellence Dept. Energy, 1986. Mem. Am. Phys. Soc., Phi Beta Kappa. Clubs: Road Runner Cycling, Pajarito Astronomers. Office: Los Alamos Nat Lab X-10 MS B259 Los Alamos NM 87545

GREENE, BEVERLY ANN, clinical psychologist; b. Orange, N.J., Aug. 14, 1950; d. Samuel and Thelma G. B.A., NYU, 1973; postgrad. Marquette U., 1973-74; M.A., Adelphi U., 1977, Ph.D., 1983. Lic. psychologist, N.Y. Fellow in psychology Mental Retardation Inst., N.Y. Med. Coll., Valhalla, N.Y., 1974-76; psychol. cons. Williamsburg Child Devel. Ctr., Bklyn., 1976-78; psychology intern East Orange VA Med. Ctr., 1978-79; research asst. dept. neurosci. N.J. Coll. Medicine and Dentistry, Vet.'s Hosp., 1979-80; psychology trainee, Children's Partial Hospitalization Unit, Brookdale Hosp. and Med. Ctr., 1980; cert. sch. psychologist N.Y.C. Bd. Edn., 1980-82, staff psychologist, 1982-84; sr. psychologist, dir. inpatient child and adolescent psychol. services King's County Psychiat. Hosp., 1984—; clin. instr. in psychiatry Downstate Med. Sch., 1982-85, clin asst. prof., 1985—, acting dir. Children's Inpatient Unit, 1985-86. Contbr. articles to profl. jours. Martin Luther King scholar, 1968-72, NIMH fellow, 1976-77. Mem. Am. Psychol. Assn. (chmn. subcom. ethnic minor women's div.), Internat. Neuropsychol. Soc., Nat. Assn. Black Psychologists, N.Y. Soc. Black Psychologists, Nat. Assn. Women in Psychology, N.Y. Assn. Women in Psychology, N.Y. Coalition of Hosp. and Instnl. Psychologists. Office: 26 St Johns Pl Brooklyn NY 11217

GREENE, CARL WILLIAM, utility company executive; b. N.Y.C., July 29, 1935; B.S., U. Pa., 1957; M.B.A., N.Y.U., 1960; m. Gloria Nissman, June 29, 1958; children—Andrew, Stephen, Suzanne, Nancy. With, Consol. Edison Co., N.Y.C., 1958—, controller, 1976—, v.p., 1982—. Mem. Am. Gas Assn. (chmn. fin. and adminstrv. sect. 1986-87, vice chmn. 1985-86, chmn. fin. div. 1983-84, mng. com., acctg. adv. com.), Am. Acctg. Assn., Am. Inst. Corp. Controllers, Fin. Execs. Inst., Planning Execs. Inst., Am. Fin. Assn., Edison Electric Inst. (acctg. exec. adv. com.), Eastern Fin. Assn., So. Fin. Assn. Home: 3262 Gary Ln Merrick NY 11566 Office: Consol Edison Co NY Inc 4 Irving Pl New York NY 10003

GREENE, CHARLES MICHAEL, lawyer; b. N.Y.C., June 28, 1956; s. Myron J. and Ursula W. (Wertheim) G.; m. Andrea di Bonaventura; 1 son, Michael Andrew. BA in Polit. Sci. cum laude, Union Coll., 1978; JD, Nova U., 1981. Bar: Fla. 1983, U.S. Dist. Ct. (so. dist.) Fla. 1983, U.S. Dist. Ct. (mid. dist.) Fla. 1983, U.S. Ct. Appeals (11th cir.) 1984. Asst. mgr. credit/new accounts Burdines of Fla., Miami, 1978-79; prosecuter State Atty.'s Office 20th Jud. Cir., Ft. Myers, Fla., 1982-83, asst. state atty. 17th Jud. Cir., Ft. Lauderdale, 1983-87; sole practice, Ft. Lauderdale, 1987—. Alumni fundraiser Union Coll. Mem. Fla. Bar Assn., ABA, Nat. Dist. Attys. Assn., Fla. Pros. Attys. Assn., Broward County Bar Assn., Nova U. Law Ctr. Alumni Assn., Phi Alpha Delta, Zeta Beta Tau. Jewish. Lodge: B'nai B'rith. Home: 615 3d Key Dr Fort Lauderdale FL 33304 Office: 200 SE 6th St Suite 400 Fort Lauderdale FL 33304

GREENE, CHARLES NELSON, business educator; b. Springfield, Ohio, Apr. 28, 1937; s. James Edward Pollard and Founta (Davis) Greene Pollard; m. Margaret Ann Pennell, Dec. 18, 1966; 1 child, Charles N. III. BS, Ohio State U., 1959, MBA, 1961, PhD, 1969. Employee relations supr. Owens-Corning Fiberglas, Toledo, 1961-63; manpower and organizational devel. NCR Corp., Dayton, Ohio, 1963-67; prof. Ind. U. Sch. Bus., Bloomington, 1969-86; prof., chair U. So. Maine Sch. Bus., Portland, 1987—; prin. Mgmt. Cons. and Research Services, 1971—. Co-author: Management, 1985; contbr. articles to profl. jours. Mem. Am. Psychol. Assn., Midwest Acad. Mgmt. (pres. 1979-80, Outstanding Service award 1986), Acad. Mgmt. (bd. gov's. 1981-83, Outstanding Service award 1983), Sigma Iota Epsilon, Beta Gamma Sigma.

GREENE, DONALD RICHARD, dermatologist, educator; b. Buffalo, Aug. 20, 1947; s. Norman Sanborn and Helen Jean (Second) Powers; m. JoAnne D'Amico, Mar. 5, 1982; 1 child, Patrick Ryan. B.A., SUNY-Buffalo, 1970, M.D., 1974. Intern, Buffalo Gen. Hosp., 1974-75; resident Hosp. of U. Pa., Phila., 1975-76; resident Yale-New Haven Hosp., 1976-79, chief resident, 1978-79; clin. instr. Yale U. Sch. Medicine, New Haven, 1979-82, clin. asst. prof., 1982—; attending physician Yale-New Haven Hosp., Hosp. St. Raphael, 1979—; med. bd. Branford (Conn.) Health Care Ctr., 1983—. Recipient Physiology award SUNY-Buffalo, 1971; Am. Cancer Soc. grantee, 1972. Fellow Am. Acad. Dermatology (Diplomate Am. Bd. Dermatology); mem. Conn. State Med. Soc. (pres. dermatology sect 1984-85), AMA, New Haven County Med. Assn., New Haven City Med. Assn., New England Dermatologic Soc. Episcopalian. Club: Rotary (Branford). Office: 5 S Main St Branford CT 06405

GREENE, GERALD MICHAEL, clinical psychologist; b. Chgo., May 7, 1940; s. Albert and Ruth (Kaplan) G.; B.A., Carleton Coll., 1961; Candidate I Diplomate Rijksuniversiteit Te Leiden (Netherlands), 1963; MS, U. Okla., 1966, PhD, 1971; PhD, Pacific Western U., 1984, Clayton U., 1988; m. Cynthia Brantner; children: Mark Brantner, Kirk Brantner, Vitoria Swinburne, Erin Kylie, Kegan Ellery, Gavin Gregory. Asst. instr. U. Kans., Lawrence, 1966-68; chief psychologist Head Start Program of East Central Kans., Ottawa, 1967-68; assoc. dir. East Central Kans. Supplementary Tng. Program, adj. instr. Emporia State Tchr's. Coll., 1967-68; instr. Rockhurst Coll., 1968-69; staff psychologist Osawatomie (Kans.) State Hosp., 1968-69; coordinator program, asst. prof. edn. and psychology Central State U., Edmond, Okla., 1969-71; mem. staff Okla. Psychol. and Ednl. Center, Oklahoma City, 1970-71; instr. phys. therapy Northwestern U. Med. Sch., 1971-72, postdoctoral fellow and intern in clin. psychology, 1971-72, project coordinator Rehab. services, 1972-73, assoc. dept. psychiatry, 1972—, dept. community health and preventive medicine, 1973—, Sch. Dentistry depts. pedodontics and orthodontics, 1972—, intervention dir. Multiple Risk Factor Intervention Trial, 1973-80; pvt. practice clin. psychology, Chgo., 1972—; cons. Chgo. Bd. Mental Health, 1972-78; field supr. U. Ill. Jane Adams Sch. Social Work, 1976-78. OEO grantee, 1967-68; Office Edn. tng. grantee, 1969-71; Social and Rehab. Services grantee, 1972-76; City of Chgo. Head Start-Model Cities grantee, 1972-76; Fellow Am. Assn. Profl. Hypnotherapists, Am. Orthopsychiat. Assn.; mem. Am. Assn. for Counseling and Devel., N.Y. Acad. Scis., Am. Mental Health Couselors Assn., Council Exceptional Children, AAUP, NEA, Assn. Tchr. Educators Emotionally Disturbed Children, Council Children with Behavior Disorders, Assn. Children with Learning Disabilities, Assn. Advancement Behavior Therapy, Midwestern Assn. Advancement Behavior Therapy, Chgo. Psychol. Club, Acad. Psychologists in Marital and Family Counseling, Ill. Biofeedback Soc., Council for Nat. Register Health Service Providers in Psychology, Soc. Behavior Medicine, Council for Advancement of Psychologic Professions and Scis., Assn. for Advancement of Psychology, Soc. Police and Criminal Psychology, Am. Soc. Psychologists in Pvt. Practice, Chgo. Soc. Clin. Hypnosis, Am. Soc. Clin. Hypnosis, Am. Group Psychotherapy Assn., Assn. Advance and Promote Hypnosis, Psychol. Soc. (Republic of Panama; hon. diplomate), Sigma Xi, Psi Chi, Phi Delta Kappa, Kappa Delta Pi. Office: 500 N Michigan Ave Suite 542 Chicago IL 60611

GREENE, GRAHAM, author; b. Berkhamsted, Hertfordshire, Eng., Oct. 2, 1904; s. Charles Henry and Marion (Raymond) G.; m. Vivien Dayrell-Browning, 1927; 1 son, 1 dau. Ed., Berkhamsted Sch., Balliol Coll., Oxford, Eng.; Litt.D. (hon.), Cambridge (Eng.) U., 1962, Edinburgh (Scotland) U., 1967; D.Litt. (hon.), Oxford U., 1979. Sub-editor London Times, 1926-30; lit. editor Spectator, 1940-41; with (Fgn. Office), 1941-44; dir. Eyre & Spottiswoode, Ltd., 1944-48, Bodley Head, London, 1958-68. Author: books Babbling April, 1925, The Man Within, 1929, The Name of Action, 1930, Rumour at Nightfall, 1932, Stamboul Train, 1932, It's a Battlefield, 1934, England Made Me, 1935, The Basement Room; short stories The Bear Fell Free, 1935; Journey Without Maps, 1936, A Gun for Sale, 1936, Brighton Rock, 1938, The Lawless Roads, 1939, The Confidential Agent, 1939, The Power and the Glory, 1940 (Hawthornden prize), British Dramatists, 1942, The Ministry of Fear, 1943; short stories Nineteen Stories, 1947; The Heart of the Matter, 1948, The Third Man, 1950, The Lost Childhood and Other Essays, 1951, The End of the Affair, 1951, Essais Catholiques, 1953; short stories Twenty-one Stories, 1954; Loser Takes All, 1955, The Quiet American, 1955, Our Man in Havana, 1958, A Burnt-Out Case, 1961, In Search of a Character, 1961, A Sense of Reality, 1963, The Comedians, 1966; film 1967 May We Borrow Your Husband? and Other Comedies of the Sexual Life; Collected Essays, 1969, Travels with My Aunt, 1969, A Sort of Life, 1971, The Pleasure Dome: The Collected Film Criticism 1935-40; short stories Collected Stories, 1972; The Honorary Consul, 1973, Lord Rochester's Monkey, 1974, An Impossible Woman, 1975, The Human Factor, 1978, Dr. Fischer of Geneva or The Bomb Party, 1980, Ways of Escape, 1980, Monsignor Quixote, 1982, J'Accuse. the Darker Side of Nice, 1982, Getting to Know the General, 1984, The Tenth Man, 1985; plays The Living Room, 1953, The Potting Shed, 1957, The Complaisant Lover, 1959, Carving a Statue, 1964, The Return of A.J. Raffles, 1975, For Whom the Bell Chimes and Yes and No, 1980; children's books The Little Train, 1947, The Little Fire Engine, 1950, The Little Horse Bus, 1952, The Little Steamroller, 1953 (Recipient Black Meml. prize 1949, Shakespeare prize, Hamburg 1968). Decorated Companion of Honour, Companion of Lit., Order of Merit; chevalier Legion of Honor; Grand Cross Order Vasco Nunez de Balboa (Panama); commandeurdes Arts et des Lettres (France); named hon. citizen Anacapri, 1978; hon. fellow Balliol Coll.; recipient Thomas More medal, 1973, John Dos Passos prize, 1980, medal City of Madrid, 1980, Jerusalem prize, 1981. Address: care Bodley Head, 9 Bow St, London WC1B 3RP, England *

GREENE, HARRIS, author, retired foreign service and intelligence officer; b. Waltham, Mass., Oct. 22, 1921; s. Benjamin and Sara (Krongard) G.; B.S., Boston U., 1943; grad. student George Washington U., 1950-51; m. Charlotte Wolk, Oct. 5, 1943; children—Sharon, Deborah. Researcher, reporter Boston Herald Traveler, 1942-43; joined U.S. Fgn. Service, 1949; assigned, Genoa, Italy, 1950, Rome, 1950-51, Athens, 1964-68; 1st sec. embassy, Bern, 1969-73; served with CIA, to 1980. Served with AUS, 1943-46; ETO. Fellow Macdowell Colony, 1966, 71. Mem. Authors Guild, Assn. Former Intelligence Officers. Club: Cosmos (Washington). Author: (novels) The Mozart Leaves at Nine, 1960, The Flags at Doney, 1964, The Thieves of Tumbutu, 1968, Canceled Accounts, 1973; FSO-1, 1977; Inference of Guilt, 1982. Home: 3671 N Harrison St Arlington VA 22207

GREENE, JOHN JOSEPH, lawyer; b. Marshall, Tex., Jan. 19, 1946; William Henry and Camille Anne (Riley) G.; B.A., U. Houston, 1969, M.A., 1974; postgrad. Oxford (Eng.) U., 1976, U. Okla., 1976; J.D., South Tex. Coll., 1978. Bar: Tex. 1978, U.S. Supreme Ct., 1982. Asst. atty. City of Amarillo, Tex., 1978-79; asst. atty. Harris County, Tex., 1979-83; sole practice, 1983—; city atty. City of Conroe (Tex.), 1983-84. Served to capt. USAR, 1969-76. Decorated Bronze Star, Air Medal. Mem. ABA, Houston Bar Assn., Res. Officers Assn., Assn. for Computing Machinery. Democrat. Roman Catholic. Office: 505 W Davis Conroe TX 77301

GREENE, MARGARET CICELY LANGTON, speech therapist; b. London, July 16, 1913; d. Charles and Olivia (Kohler) Smith; m. Herbert Greene, June 27, 1932 (dec. 1964); children: Heather, Sally. Asst. speech therapist Nat. Hosp. Nervous Disorders, London, 1949-54, Royal Nat. Throat, Nose & Ear Hosp., London, 1949-54; sr. speech therapist Chase Farm Hosp., Enfield, 1950-54, Stoke Mandeville Hosp., 1954-64, St. Bartholomew's Hosp., London, 1964-74, Speech and Lang. Unit, Hertfordshire, Eng., 1974-78; cons. S. Ockendan Hosp., 1973-78; dir. speech therapy dept. Cent. Sch. Speech and Drama, London, 1973-80; cons. speech therapist dept. med. electronics, St. Bartholomew's Hosp., London, 1978—; lectr. in field. Author: The Voice and its Disorders, 5th edit. 1989, Learning to Talk, 1960, Kinderen Lernen Praten, 1963, Disorders of Voice-Studies in Communicative Disorders, 1987; contbr. articles to profl. publs. Named officer Order Brit. Empire, 1987. Mem. Assn. Speech Impaired Children (founder, v.p. 1968). Mem. Liberal party. Home: Dean Leys Nup End Ln, Wingrave, Aylesbury HP22, England

GREENE, WILLIAM LEONARD, lawyer; b. Cedros, Trinidad, July 8, 1934; s. Allan Anisette and Doris (Hoating) G.; student Naparaina Coll., 1945-53, Law Soc. Sch. Law, 1954-60; LL.B., Queen's U., Can., 1970; cert. Osgoode Hall Law Sch., 1972; m. Vivian Barrie Walker, Sept. 6, 1966 (div.); children—Lisa Kathryn, Anthony William. Crown law officer Dept. Atty. Gen., Trinidad, 1964-67; Can. law program Queen's U., 1967-70; practicing atty., Toronto, 1972-77; individual practice law, Trinidad and Tobago, 1978—; sr. partner W.L.M. Greene & Co.; mng. dir. Caribbean Fin. Collection Agy., Ltd.; dir. Indsl. Relations & Immigration Cons., Ltd.; dir., gen. mgr. Caribbean Arbitration Services, Ltd. Mem. Am. Bar Assn., Am. Trial Lawyers Assn., Am. Arbitration Assn., Law Soc. Trinidad and Tobago, Trinidad and Tobago Rifle Assn. Club: Forge Health. Home: 10 Hyderabad, Port of Spain Trinidad and Tobago Office: 9 Quamina St, St James, Port of Spain Trinidad and Tobago

GREENEBAUM, LEONARD CHARLES, lawyer; b. Langgoens, Germany, Feb. 6, 1934; came to U.S. 1937, naturalized, 1952; s. Norbert and Henny Lisa (Greenbaum) G.; m. Barbara Rosendorf, Feb. 10, 1957; children—Beth Lynn, Cathy Sue, Steven I. B.S. cum laude in Commerce, Washington and Lee U., 1956, J.D. cum laude, 1959. Bar: D.C. 1959, Va. 1959, Md. 1965 Atty., Sachs, Greenebaum & Tayler and predeccessor firms, Washington, 1959-64, ptnr. 1964-75, mng. ptnr., 1975—; arbitrator Am. Arbitration Assn., Washington, 1975—. Chmn. bd. Davis Meml. Goodwill Industries, Washington, 1979-82; bd. dirs. Council for Ct. Excellence. Served to capt. U.S. Army, 1957. Recipient Service to Handicapped People award Davis Meml. Goodwill Industries 1982. Fellow Am. Bar Found., mem. D.C. Bar Assn., Md. Bar Assn., Assn. Trial Lawyers Am., Internat. Platform Assn., Jud. Conf. D.C. Cir., Order of Coif, Phi Delta Phi. Jewish. Clubs: University (Washington); Bethesda Country (Md.); Wild Dunes (Charleston, S.C.). Home: 6121 Shady Oak Ln Bethesda MD 20817 Office: Sachs Greenebaum & Tayler 1140 Connecticut Ave NW Washington DC 20036

GREENE-MERCIER, MARIE ZOE, sculptor; b. Madison, Wis., Mar. 31, 1911; d. Louis J.A. and Zoé (Lassagne) Mercier; A.B., Radcliffe Coll., 1933; postgrad. New Bauhaus, Chgo., 1937-38; m. Wesley Hammond Greene, June 21, 1937; children: Steven Hardy, Richard Stuart, Roger Hammond. Exhibited solo shows Art Inst. Chgo., 1955, AIA, Chgo., 1957, Paris Galerie Duncan, 1963, Florence Galleria d'arte Arno, 1965, Rome Galleria Numero, 1966, Milan Numero, 1966, Venice Numero, 1966, S.Stefano, 1968, Milan Gian Ferrari, 1969, Trieste Centro Italo Americano, 1968, 70, Venice La Fenice, 1969, Athens, New Forms, 1970, Perpignan, Main de Fer, 1971, Rome, Artivisive, 1972, Chgo. Met. Structures Inc., 1974, Centre Noroit, Arras, France, 1977, Amerika Haus, West Berlin, 1977, Galerie Musée de Poche Paris, 1978, Maison Française, Chgo., 1979, 83, Stadt Bad Homburg v.d. Höhe, 1979, Amerika Haus, Stuttgart, 1979, Alliance Francaise de Washington, 1980, Skulpturenpark Mus., Bad Nauheim Fed. Republic Germany, 1986, Oberhessisches Mus., Giessen, Fed. Republic Germany, 1986; exhibited in group shows Art Inst. Chgo., 1947, 48, 52, 55, Mus. Contemporary Art, Chgo., 1968, Paris Salon d'Automne, 1962, 1971, 72, 73, 74, Salon des Beaux Arts, Salon des Independants, 1952, de la Jeune Sculpture, 1966, Salon de Mai, 1973, 74, 75, 76, 77, 78, 86, London Royal Inst. Galleries, 1954, Trieste II Exhbn. Sacred Art, 1966, Legnano, Pagani Found., 1966, 69, 70, 71, 72, Campo S. Moisé, Commune di Venezia, 1970, 72, Florence Biennale, 1971, 1st Sculpture Triennale, Paris, 1978, UNESCO, Paris, 1979, Bauhaus ArchiV Mus., W. Berlin, 1979, Capitol Children's Mus., Washington, 1980-81, Kurhausgarten, Bad Homburg, 1979, 80, 81 ; represented in permanent collections at Roosevelt U., Radcliffe Coll., S.W. Mo. State Coll., Grinnell Coll., Bauhaus-Archiv Mus., Berlin, Mus. Modern Art, Venice, Stone Container Corp., Internat. Film Bur., 1st Bapt. Ch., Chgo., Bloomington, Ind., Musée des Sables, Barcarès, France, 1971, Govt. Bldg., Homburg-Saar, 1974, C.E.S. Verlaine, Arras, France, 1978, Western Ill. U., 1979, David and Alfred Smart Gallery, U. Chgo., Oberhessisches Mus., Fed. Republic Germany; mem. U.S. del. 9th Congress Internat. Artists Assn., UNESCO, Stuttgart, W. Ger., 1979. Recipient Silver medal and 1st prize Composition, 1968, Gold medal, grand prize modern sculpture, Cannes, Semaines Internat. de la Femme, 1969, Hors Concours, Nice, 1970, Grand prix Humanitaire de France, médaille de vermeil, Ier Prix Internat. de Sculpture, Mérite Belgo-Hispanique Palmes d'Or, Festival de St. Germain-des-Prés, Paris, 1975; USIS West Berlin grantee, 1977; Stadt Bad Hamburg v.d. Höhe grantee, 1979, Mary Mildred Sullivan award Randolph-Macon Coll., 1985. Author: Trieste, 101 Disegni, 1969; Venezia, 101 Disegni, 1970; Salzburg, 101 Zeichnungen, 1970; Editrice Libreria Internazionale Italo Svevo Trieste, 1969; contbr. to mags. Memoir, Leonardo Magazine, 1982; Reminiscences, Harvard Crimson, 1983. Home: 1232 E 57th St Chicago IL 60637 Other: New Forms/9a Valaoritou St, Athens Greece Other: Galleria Artivisive, 60 Sifra Editrice V, Ugo de Carolis Greece Other: Ruth Volid Gallery Inc 225 W Illinois St Chicago IL 60610 Other: Monika Beck Gallery, Schwarzenacker-Homburg, Saarbrucken Federal Republic Germany

GREENFIELD, HELEN MEYERS, real estate executive, publishing company executive, inspection and test service executive; b. Albany, N.Y., Aug. 4, 1908; d. Stephen and Catherine (Bronkov) Meyers; grad. Baker's Bus. Sch., 1924; m. Frank L. Greenfield, Apr. 1, 1929; children—Stuart Franklin, Val Shea. Accounts supr. George G. McCaskey Co., N.Y.C., 1924-29; spl. assignments purchasing dept. McCall's Pub. Co., 1929, Fgn. Affairs Publs., Inc., 1929-31; with purchasing dept. Glidden-Buick Corp., 1931-32; interviewer Civil Works Adminstrn., supr. filing and payroll systems Houston St. Project Center, 1933-36; with dept. accounting Reuben H. Donnelley Co., 1936-37; supr. layouts, makeup prins. of semi-monthly publs. Tide Publs., Inc., 1939-41; asst. to purchasing agt., supr. maintenance perpetual inventory Hopeman Bros., 1941-43; with money order div., corr. dept. U.S. Govt., P.O. Dept., N.Y.C., 1943-44; v.p. Frank L. Greenfield Co., Inc., N.Y.C., 1945-59; v.p. All Purpose Chair Corp., 1950-55; pres. VAL Equipment, Inc., 1950-62; v.p. Am. Testing Labs., Inc., 1950-63; supr. personnel, purchases Irving Lampert Co., 1951-52; account assignment coordinator, advt. contracts dept. Newsweek, N.Y.C., 1970-78; owner, operator Princess Helen Antiques; pres. Helen M. Greenfield Realty Corp., 1968-79; bus. cons., 1979—. Active New York Heart Assn.; founder, coordinator, show producer, dir. and hostess ann. banquet honor of Dr. Manuel Cabral, composer-dir. Mt. Laurel Ctr. Performing Arts, 1960-84. Named Hon. princess Cherokee Tribe by Chief Rising Sun of Richmond, Va. Mem. Internat. Platform Assn. Club: Order Eastern Star (past matron).

GREENFIELD, TAYLOR HATTON, former government official; b. Balt., Dec. 17, 1905; s. Amos Hatton and Lillian Estelle (Taylor) G.; m. Mildred Sophia Albert, Sept. 15, 1928 (dec. June 1984); children: Lillian Greenfield Tilles, Millette Greenfield Barber. LL.B., U. Balt., 1940. Bar: Md. bar 1949. Exec. Glenn L. Martin Co., 1929-43, Gen. Motors, 1944-45; field dir. A.R.C., Germany, 1945-46; property and supply supr. War Assets Adminstrn., 1946-48; practice law Balt., 1949-51; with Hayes Aircraft Co., Birmingham, Ala., 1951-55; adviser to Govt. Vietnam, 1955-62; mem. tech. adv. staff AID, Far East Bur., 1962-67; dir. Far East Logistics Office, 1965-67; chief logistics USOM; supply mgmt. officer USOM, Bangkok, Thailand, 1969-72. Recipient Meritorious Honor award AID, 1966. Mem. Internat. Transactional Analysis Assn. Club: Civitan. Home: 8623 Starcrest Dr San Antonio TX 78217

GREENGRASS, MARK, educator; b. Epsom, Surrey, Eng., July 9, 1949; s. Philip Henry and Joyce (Maddocks) G.; m. Andrea Rosemary Bevan; children: Martha Elisabeth, Daniel Luke. First class hons in Modern History, U. Oxford, 1972, MA, D in Philosophy, 1979. Lectr. U. Sheffield, Sheffield, Eng. Author: (books) John Calvin, 1983, France in the Age of Henri IV, 1984, The French Reformation, 1987; assoc. editor: The Hamlyn/Newnes Atlas of World History, 1982. Pres. Sheffield Hist. Assn.; councillor The Hist. Assn., London; fellow Royal Hist. Soc., London. Fellow Huguenot Soc. of Great Britain, London. Mem. Anglican Ch. Office: Univ Sheffield, Sheffield s10 2TN, England

GREENHOUSE, DENNIS EDWARD, business executive, state official; b. Wilmington, Del., Jan. 17, 1950; s. Bernard and Sylvia (Chesler) G.; B.A., Fairleigh Dickinson U., 1972; m. Adelaide Elizabeth Donovan, Feb. 2, 1979. Asst. v.p. ops. Home Fed. Savs. & Loan Assn., Wilmington, 1973-81; sr. credit rep. Internat. Playtex Inc., Dover, Del., 1981-82, also chmn. supervisory com. Playtex Employees Fed. Credit Union; auditor of accounts State of Del., 1983—. mem. Ednl. Resources, Inc. Mem. Wilmington Mayor's Subcom. for Urban Lending, 1978-79; bd. dirs. Head Start of New Castle County, 1978-80. Mem. Nat. State Auditors Assn. (exec. com. 1984-85), Intergovtl. Audit Forum, Nat. Assn. State Auditors, Comptrollers and Treas., Tau Kappa Epsilon. Democrat. Jewish. Club: Masons (past master). Developer flexiLoan mortgage plan for Del. Home: 9 S Catherine St Middletown DE 19709 Office: Townsend Bldg Dover DE 19901

GREENLAW, ROGER LEE, interior designer; b. New London, Conn., Oct. 12, 1936; s. Kenneth Nelson and Lyndell Lee (Stinson) G.; children—Carol Jennifer, Roger Lee. B.F.A., Syracuse U., 1958. Interior designer Cannell & Chaffin, 1958-59, William C. Wagner, Architect, Los Angeles, 1959-60, Gen. Fireproofing Co., Los Angeles, 1960-62, K-S Wilshire, Inc., Los Angeles, 1963-64; dir. interior design Calif. Desk Co., Los Angeles, 1964-67; sr. interior designer Bechtel Corp., Los Angeles, 1967-70; sr. interior designer, project mgr. Daniel, Mann, Johnson, & Mendehall, Los Angeles, 1970-72, Morganelli-Heumann & Assos., Los Angeles, 1972-73; owner, prin. Greenlaw Design Assos., Glendale, Calif., 1973—; lectr. UCLA; mem. adv. curriculum com. Mt. San Antonio Coll., Walnut, Calif., Fashion Inst. Design, Los Angeles; bd. dirs. Calif. Legis. Conf. Interior Design. Past scoutmaster Verdugo council Boy Scouts Am.; past pres. bd. dirs. Unity Ch., La Crescenta, Calif. Mem. Am. Soc. Interior Designers (treas. Pasadena chpt. 1983-84, pres. 1986-87, 1st v.p. 1985, chmn. So. Calif. regional conf. 1985, nat. com. legis., nat. com. jury for catalog award, speaker ho. dels., nat. bd. dirs., chmn. standards task force), Glendale C. of C. (bd. dirs.), Adm. Farragut Acad. Alumni Assn., Delta Upsilon. Republican. Lodge: Kiwanis. Home: 2100f Valderas Dr Glendale CA 91208 Office: 3901 Ocean View Blvd Montrose CA 91020

GREENLEIGH, ARTHUR DASHEW, business executive, management consultant; b. N.Y.C., May 8, 1903; s. Abraham Morris and Sadie (Dashew) G.; A.B., U. Calif. at Los Angeles, 1929; M.A., U. So. Calif., 1930; postgrad. N.Y. Sch. Social Work, Columbia, 1931-32; m. Frances Nasatir, July 3, 1928; children—Stephen Henry, Esther Ellen. Psychiat. social worker Big Bros. Assn., Los Angeles, 1928-31; dir. state div. adminstrv. surveys N.Y. State Temporary Emergency Relief Adminstrn., 1932-34; dir. field service Calif. Relief Adminstrn., 1934-36; exec. dir. Los Angeles County Bur. Pub. Assistance, 1936-39; lectr. grad. sch. U. So. Calif., 1936-39; asst. exec. dir. Nat. Refugee Service, N.Y.C., 1939-40, exec. dir., 1940-42; asst. to exec. dir. War Manpower Commn., Washington, 1942-44; dir. for Italy Am. Joint Distbn. Com., Rome, 1944, dir. for France, Paris, 1945, dep. European dir. in charge field ops. in Europe and North Africa, Paris, 1946-47; mem. exec. com. Am. Council Vol. Agys. for Fgn. Service, 1948-56; mem. exec. com. U.S. Com. for Care European Children, 1948-53; mem. nat. adv. com. U.S. Displaced Persons Commn., Washington, 1948-50, chmn. com., 1950-52; assoc. exec. dir. United Service New Ams., N.Y.C., 1948-50, exec. dir., 1950-54; exec. dir. United Hias Service (merger Hebrew Immigrant Aid Soc. and United Service for New Ams., 1954-56; pres. Greenleigh Assocs. Inc., 1956—, Mgmt. Scis. Group, Inc., N.Y.C., 1977—; chmn. bd. Greenleigh Internat., Ltd., N.Y.C., 1977-79; partner Western Storage Properties, Los Angeles, 1964—; sec.-treas. Fed. Transfer Co., Los Angeles, 1964—; adviser on refugee programs to Pres. Truman, 1948-52, to Pres. Eisenhower, 1953-56; dir. numerous studies. Mem. exec. com. Am. Immigration Conf., 1954; vice chmn. Internat. Conf. Non-Govtl. Orgns. Interested in Migration (adv. to UN) 1951-52, chmn., 1952-53; cons. to U.S. del. Internat. Migration Conf., Naples, 1951, Intergovtl. Migration Conf., Brussels, 1951. Fellow Am. Sociol. Assn.; mem. Nat. Assn. Social Workers, A.A.A.S., Am. Mgmt. Assn., Am. Pub. Welfare Assn., Am. Acad. Polit. and Social Sci., Am. Soc. for Pub. Adminstrn., Internat., Nat. confs. social welfare, Nat. Conf. Jewish Social Welfare, Nat. Council Family Relations, Fgn. Policy Assn., Zeta Beta Tau, Psi Chi. Author articles on immigration, public welfare, public adminstrn., human relations. Home and Office: 920 Park Ave New York NY 10028

GREENSPAN, ALAN, economist; b. N.Y.C., Mar. 6, 1926; s. Herman Herbert and Rose (Goldsmith) G. BS summa cum laude, NYU, 1948, MA, 1950, PhD, 1977. Pres., chief exec. officer Townsend-Greenspan and Co., Inc., N.Y.C., 1954-74, 77-87; cons. Council Econ. Advisers, 1970-74, chmn., 1974-77; cons. Congressional Budget Office, 1977-87; mem. Pres.'s Econ. Policy Adv. Bd., 1981-87; chmn. Nat. Commn. on Social Security Reform, 1981-83; mem. Task Force on Econ. Growth, 1969, Pres.'s Fgn. Intelligence Adv. Bd., 1982-85; Commn. on an All-Vol. Armed Force, 1969-70; Commn. on Fin. Structure and Regulation, 1970-71; cons. U.S. Treasury, 1971-74, Fed. Res. Bd., 1971-74; mem. econ. adv. bd. Sec. of Commerce, 1971-72; mem. central market system com. SEC, 1972; mem. GNP rev. com. Office Mgmt. and Budget; sr. adviser panel on econ. activity Brookings Instn., 1970-74, 77-87; chmn. bd. govs. Fed. Res. System, 1987—; mem. bd. economists Time mag., 1971-74, 77-87; adj. prof. Grad. Sch. Bus. Adminstrn., NYU, 1977-87. Mem. Nixon for Pres. Com., 1968-69, dir. domestic policy research; personal rep. of Pres.-elect to Bur. Budget for transition period, chmn. task force on fgn. trade policy.; Bd. overseers Hoover Instn. on War, Revolution and Peace, 1973-74, 77-87. Recipient John P. Madden medal, 1975; joint recipient Pub. Service Achievement award, 1976, William Butler Meml. award, 1977. Fellow Nat. Assn. Bus. Economists (past pres.). Clubs: Hillcrest Country (Los Angeles); Metropolitan (Washington); Century Country, University, Harmonie. Office: Fed Res System 20th & Constitution Ave Washington DC 20551

GREENSPAN, LEON JOSEPH, lawyer; b. Phila., Feb. 10, 1932; s. Joseph and Minerva (Podolsky) G.; m. Irene Gordon, Nov. 2, 1958; children: Marjorie, David, Michael, Lisa. AB, Temple U., 1955, JD, 1958. Bar: N.Y. 1959, U.S. Supreme Ct., 1969, N.J. 1985, Fla. 1985, Pa. 1986. Sole practice, White Plains, N.Y., 1959-64; ptnr. Greenspan and Aurnou, White Plains, 1964-77; ptnr. Greenspan and Jaffe, White Plains, 1978-87; ptnr. Greenspan, Jaffe & Rosenbltt, Whiteplains, 1987—; counsel Brown, Boston; atty. Tarrytown (N.Y.) Housing Authority. Pres. Hebrew Inst., White Plains; vice chmn. ann. dinner NCCJ. Recipient Pres.'s award Union Orthodox Synagogues, 1982; Hebrew Inst. honoree, White Plains, 1983. Mem. ABA, Westchester County Bar Assn., White Plains Bar Assn., N.Y. State Trial Lawyers Assn., Criminal Cts. Bar Assn. Westchester County. Home: 14 Pinebrook Dr White Plains NY 10605 Office: 180 E Post Rd White Plains NY 10601

GREENSTONE, JAMES LYNN, psychotherapist, mediator, consultant, author, educator; b. Dallas, Mar. 30, 1943; s. Carl Bunk and Fifi (Horn) G.; children—Cynthia Beth, Pamela Celeste, David Carl. B.A. in Psychology, U. Okla., 1965; M.S. in Clin. Psychology, N. Tex. State U., 1966, Ed.D. in Edn. and Psychology, 1974. Lic. marriage and family therapist, profl. counselor. Psychologist Beverly Hills Hosp., Dallas, 1966-67; therapist Family Guidance Service, Dallas, 1967-68; instr. Dallas County Community Coll. Dist., 1967-72, 78-79, 87—; asst. prof. Tex. Women's U., 1979; assoc. prof. psychology and criminal justice Tarrant County Jr. Coll., 1987—; tng. faculty Am. Acad. Crisis Interveners, Louisville, 1972-78; tng. dir. Southwestern Acad. Crisis Interveners, Dallas, 1977—; police instr. Dallas Sheriff's Acad., 1979-86; hostage negotiator and trainer Lancaster Police Dept., Tex., 1986—; pvt. practice psychotherapy 1966-87; cons. Dallas County Jails, 1979-82, dir. res. tng. Dallas Sheriff's Res., 1983-84; panel arbitrators Am. Arbitration Assn.; adj. prof. psychology Columbia Coll., Northwood Inst., 1987—; adj. faculty dispute mediation North Tex. State U., 1987-88; instr. hostage negotiations North Cen. Tex. Council Govts. Regional Police Acad., 1987—; assoc. prof. psychology, criminal justice. Author: Crisis Intervener's Handbook, Vol. 1, 1980; Crisis Intervener's Handbook, Vol. II, 1982; Hotline: Crisis Intervention Directory, 1981; Crisis Management: Handbook for Interveners, 1983; Winning Through Accommodation: Handbook for Mediators, 1984; cassette tapes: Crisis Management and Intervener Survival, 1981; Stress Reduction: Personal Energy Management, 1982; Training the Trainer, 1983; contbr. chpts. to books, articles to profl. jours.; sr. editor: Crisis Intervener's Newsletter; editor-in-chief Emotional First Aid: A Jour. of Crisis Intervention; and others. Trustee Southeastern U., New Orleans; bd. dirs. Jewish Community Ctr., Jewish Family Service, Temple Shalom, Congregation Shearith Israel, 1975-80; active Dallas Sheriff's Res., 1978-86; v.p. Jewish Nat. Fund Dallas; adv. bd. Parents Without Ptnrs.; founder Carl B. Greenstone Meml. Library; past dir. Carrollton Rotary Club, Nat. Jewish Com., Scouting, Circle 10 Council Boy Scouts Am. Served with USNR, 1961-65; USMCR, 1965-67; USAR, 1967-69. Recipient Disting. Service award Southeastern Acad. Crisis Interveners, 1981; Disting. Service award Res. Law Officers Assn. Am., 1982. Mem. Am. Assn. Marriage and Family Therapy, Soc. Profls. in Dispute Resolution, Acad. Family Mediators, Am. Bd. Examiners in Crisis Intervention (diplomate), Am. Acad. Crisis Intervention, Southwestern Acad. Crisis Interveners, Acad. Criminal Justice Scis., Am. Acad. Psychotherapists, Am. Assn. Profl. Hypnotherapists, Assn. Mil. Surgeons U.S., Dallas Assn. Marriage and Family Therapists. Democrat. Lodges: Masons, Scottish Rite. Office: PO Box 670292 Dallas TX 75367-0292

GREENWELL, ROGER ALLEN, scientist; b. Santa Maria, Calif., Dec. 4, 1941; s. George C. and Bessie Florence (Sutton) G.; m. Jeannine Pendleton, July 25, 1969; 1 child, George Eli. AA, Hancock Jr. Coll., 1961; BS, Calif. Poly. Coll., 1968; MS, U.S. Internat. U., 1974, DBA, 1981. Mathematician Naval Weapons Ctr., China Lake, Calif., 1968, ops. research analyst, Corona, Calif., 1969-70; ops. research analyst Comdr. Naval Forces, Vietnam, 1968-69; mathematician Naval Electronics Lab. Ctr., San Diego, 1970-77; scientist Naval Ocean Systems Ctr., San Diego, 1977-84; sr. scientist Sci. and Engring. Assoc., Inc., 1984—; cons. fiber optics and econ. analysis; mem. NATO Research Study Group, 1983—. Served with U.S. Army, 1964-67. Decorated Bronze Star. Mem. Ops. Research Soc. Am., Inst. Mgmt. Sci., AIAA, Soc. Allied Weight Engrs., Soc. Photo Optical and Instrumentation Engrs., Optical Soc. Am. Home: 3778 Eagle St San Diego CA 92103 Office: 3838 Camino del Rio North Suite 120 San Diego CA 92108

GREENWOOD, IVAN ANDERSON, physicist; b. Cleve., Jan. 31, 1921; s. Ivan A. and Mabel (Harlow) G.; m. Jean Elizabeth Siebrecht, June 18, 1949 (dec. Jan. 1983); children: Kyle Ann, Hilary (dec.). BS, Case Inst. Tech., 1942; postgrad., MIT, NYU, Columbia U. Asst. group leader Radiation Lab., MIT, 1942-46; mgr. research dept., assoc. dir. research and advanced devel. GPL div. Gen. Precision Systems Inc., 1946-69; research mgr. physics research ctr. Kearfott div. Singer Co., 1969-81, mgr. advanced research projects, 1981-85, cons., 1985—; cons. on med. research project Bellevue Med. Ctr. NYU, 1956-60, Albert Einstein Coll. Medicine Yeshiva U., 1960-64; incorporating dir. Bio-Instrumentation Inst., Inc., 1962—; bd. dirs., mem. exec. com. Glen Ellen Corp., 1962-70; ptnr. Bus. Trends Publs., Cleve., 1947-49; past dir., mem. exec. com. Syntha Corp. Patentee in field. Mem. Stamford (Conn.) Rep. Town Com., 1981-84, 88—, treas., mem. exec. com., 1981-84, 88—; past mem. bd. dirs. Conn. Ski Council; v.p., incorporator Vt. Recreation Ctr., Inc., 1971-84; trustee 1st Presbyn. Ch., Stamford, 1984-87; treas. Friends of Stamford Symphony, 1986—. Mem. Am. Chem. Soc. (assoc.), Am. Phys. Soc., Am. Inst. Physics, IEEE, Inst. Nav., Fedn. Am. Scientists, AAAS, Case Alumni Assn., Tau Beta Pi, Theta Tau, Sigma Alpha Epsilon. Presbyterian. Clubs: Landmark; River Hills Ski; Cove Island Yacht (vice comdr. 1979-82). Home: 6 Weed Circle Stamford CT 06902

GREER, DOROTHY LUCILLE LEECH, business executive; b. Fort Morgan, Colo., Nov. 5, 1921; d. Laurance Blakely and Lucille Otis (Gill) Leech; student Mills Coll., 1939-40; B.A., San Diego State Coll., 1943; m. Thomas Keister Greer, Jan. 9, 1943; children—Nancy Tallaferro (Mrs. William Nelson Alexander II), Giles Carter, Celeste Claiborne. Tchr., Franklin County Schs., Rocky Mount, Va., 1944-45, 48-49, Roanoke (Va.) City Schs., 1949-51; dir., sec.-treas. Franklin County Times, Inc., Rocky Mount, 1968—; v.p. Greer Investment Corp., 1977—. Mem. central com. Assistance League So. Calif., Los Angeles, 1952-54; mem. patrons com. Internat. Debutante Ball, 1969-71; nat. patron Met. Opera. Mem. D.A.R., Internat. Platform Assn. Christian Scientist. Clubs: Willow Creek Country (sec.-dir. Rocky Mount 1962-64). Home: The Grove Rocky Mount VA 24151

GREER, MACK VARNEDOE, physician; b. Valdosta, Ga., July 29, 1927; s. Lloyd Barton and Julie Winn (Varnedoe) G.; A.B., Emory U., 1951; postgrad. Valdosta State Coll., 1955-56; M.D., Med. Coll. Ga., 1960; m. Betty Dame English, Dec. 27, 1951; children—Betty June, Mack Varnedoe. Adjuster, Crawford & Co., ins. adjusters, Atlanta, 1951-52; high sch. math. and sci. tchr., football coach Clinch County (Ga.) and Waycross (Ga.) High Sch., 1952-55; rotating intern Bapt. Meml. Hosp., Jacksonville, Fla., 1960-61; gen. practice medicine and surgery, Homerville, Ga., 1961-72; mem. staff South Ga. Med. Center, chief staff, 1980; Coll. athletic physician; coll. physician, also assoc. prof. biology Valdosta State Coll., 1972—. Former bd. dirs. Valdosta (Ga.) Girls Club. Served with USMCR, World War II, Korea; now capt. M.C., USNR. Diplomate Am. Bd. Family Practice. Mem. AMA, So., Ga. med. assns., S.Ga. Med. Soc., Am. Coll. Emergency Physicians, Pi Kappa Alpha, Alpha Kappa Kappa. Presbyterian. Club: Valdosta (Ga.) Touchdown, Exchange, Valdosta Country. Home: PO Box 2196 Valdosta GA 31604 Office: Farber Health Center Valdosta State Coll Valdosta GA 31698

GREER, RAYMOND WHITE, lawyer; b. Port Arthur, Tex., July 20, 1954; s. Mervyn Hardy Greer and Eva Nadine (White) Swain; 1 child, Emily Ann. BA magna cum laude, Sam Houston State, 1977; JD, U. Houston, 1981. Assoc. Hoover, Cox & Shearer, Houston, 1980-83, Hinton & Morris, Houston, 1983-85; sole practice Houston, 1985-86; prin. Morris & Greer, P.C., Houston, 1986—. Mem. ABA, State Bar Tex., Houston Bar Assn., Fort Bend County Bar Assn., Assn. Trial Lawyers Am., Tex. Assn. Bank Counsel. Avocations: golf, water skiing, reading. Office: Morris & Greer PC 952 Echo Ln Suite 110 Houston TX 77024

GREER, SHARI BETH ROTHENSTEIN, software consulting firm executive; b. Reading, Pa., Mar. 1, 1959; d. Martin and Francine Rita (Gross) Rothenstein; m. Martin Brad Greer, Dec. 31, 1979; children: Shannon Leigh, Krista Heather. BA in Biochemistry, Wellesley Coll.-MIT, 1980; postgrad. in bus. adminstrn. Colo. State U., 1982-83. Lead thermal engr. Rockwell Internat. Space div., Downey, Calif., 1980-81; systems engr. Martin Marietta Aerospace, Denver, 1981-82, aerospace new bus. analyst, 1982-84; v.p. Miaco Corp. (Micro Automation Cons.), Englewood, Colo., 1984-87, pres., 1987—. Co-designer life systems monitor for Sudden Infant Death Syndrome, 1980. Recipient Recog. award for satellite work Martin Marietta Aerospace, 1982; VIP at 1st Space Shuttle landing, Rockwell Internat., Vandenberg, Calif., 1981. Mem. Intermountain Humane Soc., MIT Enterprise Forum of Colo. Democrat. Office: Miaco Corp Harlequin Plaza S 7600 E Orchard Suite 230 Englewood CO 80111

GREER, WILLIAM THOMAS, military officer; b. Madrid, Aug. 2, 1960; s. William Thomas and Marian Freda (Buesing) G. BSME, Syracuse U., 1983. Commd. 2d lt. USAF, 1983, advanced through grades to capt., 1987; ordnance project officer USAF, Norton AFB, Calif., 1983-84, stage project officer, 1984-85, chief ordnance br., 1985-87, chief Peacekeeper propulsion br., 1985—, chief propulsion br., 1988—; ptnr., gen. mgr. Greer Bros. Mobile Homes, Sterling, N.Y., 1984—; ptnr., field supr. Penn-Tex Real Estate, San Bernardino, Calif., 1984—. Mem. Rep. Senatorial Inner Circle. Mem. ASME, AAAS, Air Force Assn., Am. Mgmt. Assn., Soc. Automotive Engrs. Methodist. Club: Officer's (Norton AFB). Home: PO Box 385 Lake Arrowhead CA 92352-0385 Office: BMO/ENMP Norton AFB CA 92409-6468

GREESON, GAYLA LEE, accountant; b. Austin, Tex., Dec. 22, 1956; d. Howard Gaylon and Nancy Diane (Thomas) Brown; m. David Thomas Greeson, Aug. 25, 1979; children—Timothy David, Samantha Lea. B.B.A., U. Tex., 1979; grad. Sch. Banking of South, La. State U., 1986. C.P.A., Tex. Accounts examiner Office of State Comptroller, Austin, 1979-80; auditor Tyler, Willingham & Tuffly, C.P.A.s, Houston, 1981-82; advt. dir. Security Bank & Trust Co., Wharton, Tex., 1982-86, comptroller, chief fin. officer, 1982—, treas. Security Capital Leasing Corp., Wharton, 1982—; treas. Wharton Capital Corp. Treas., Wharton Christian Sch., 1984-86. Mem. Am. Inst. C.P.A.s, Tex. Soc. C.P.A.s. Home: 600 Country Club Dr Richmond TX 77469 Office: Security Bank & Trust Co 112 N Fulton St Wharton TX 77488

GREEVEN, RAINER, lawyer; b. Berlin, Dec. 6, 1936; came to U.S., 1947; s. Wolf and Marianne Kolck G.; m. Regina Jouvin, June 13, 1964; children—Andrea, Cristina. B.A., Cornell U., 1959; LL.B., Columbia U., 1962. Bar: N.Y. 1964, U.S. Dist. Ct. (so. dist.) N.Y. 1964. Assoc., Lord, Day & Lord, N.Y.C., 1963-67; assoc. Burke & Burke, N.Y.C., 1967-70, ptnr., 1971-77; ptnr. Morris & McVeigh, N.Y.C., 1977-87, Greeven & Ercklentz, N.Y.C., 1987—; dir. Viatech, Inc., N.Y.C., Triangle Oil, Westport, Conn., Sterling Drilling, N.Y.C.; pres. Stuart (Fla.) Land Co., 1985—. Founder, bd. dirs. South Fork Land Found., 1974. Mem. ABA, N.Y. State Bar Assn., Assn. Bar of City of N.Y., Internat. Bar Assn. Clubs: Knickerbocker (N.Y.C.); Meadow (Southampton, N.Y.). Home: 200 E 71st St New York NY 10021 Office: Greeven & Ercklentz 30 Rockefeller Plaza Suite 3030 New York NY 10112

GREFFET, PHILIPPE JEAN, French cultural organization executive; b. Lyon, France, Mar. 22, 1924; s. Edouard and Claudine (Imbert) G.; m. Nicole Courault, 1952; 3 children. Ed. U. Lyon. Tchr., Lyon, 1947-49, Lyon then Lons-le Saunier, 1960-67; dir. Alliance Francaise, Santa Fe, Argentina, 1949-51, insp. gen. Adjoint of alliances Françaises in Argentina, 1951-53, sec.-gen. Alliance Française, Brazil, 1953-60, sec.-gen., Paris, 1978-88; corr. Le Monde, 1956-60; adviser for cultural affairs, tech. and sci. cooperation French Embassy, Montevideo, 1967-71, Buenos Aires, 1971-76; tech. adviser to High Com. for French Lang., 1976-78; Author: Rio de tous les coeurs, 1957; also author numerous books in Spanish. Decorated officier Legion d'honneur, Ordre nat. du. Merite, Ordre national des Arts et des lettres, officier Ordre des Palmes academiques (France); grand officer Order of May (Argentina), officer Order of So. Cross (Brazil); named hon. prof. in Buenos Aires; recipient Lit. prize of Rio de Janeiro.

GREGG, JOHN NATHAN, fibers corporation executive; b. Charlotte, N.C., Jan. 11, 1934; s. James Murphy and Nancy Olive (Watkins) G.; m. Nancy Carpenter, July 23, 1955; children: Miriam Ashley, Nancy Elizabeth, John Nathan, Mary Kathryn. BS, N.C. State Coll., 1955; AMP, Harvard U., 1975. Sales mgr. So. regional sales Am. Viscose Corp., Charlotte, N.C., 1957-68; mgr. fiber sales ops., fiber div. FMC Corp., Phila., 1968-69, dir. sales, fiber products, 1969-71, div. v.p. mktg., 1971-75; chmn., pres. Avtex Fibers Inc., Valley Forge, Pa., 1976—; pres., chmn. Aston Precision Products, 1981—. Vice-chmn. bd. trustee N.C. State U., Paoli (Pa.) Hosp.; chmn. N.C. State U. textile adv. com.; pres., bd. dirs. N.C. Textile Found., Inc.; past chmn. bd. dirs. Fiber Fabric Coalition for Trade. Served with U.S. Army, 1955-57. Recipient Man of Yr. award N.C. State U. Textile Sch., 1984, Watagua medal N.C. State U., 1985. Mem. Man-Made Fiber Producers Assn. (chmn. bd. dirs. 1984-86), Phi Kappa Phi (hon.). Episcopalian. Clubs: Aronimink Golf (Newtown, Square, Pa.), Harvard (N.Y.C.), Country of N.C., Union League of N.Y.C., Figure 8 Island Yacht. Home: 221 S Aberdeen Ave Saint Davids PA 19087 Office: Avtex Fibers Inc PO Box 880 Valley Forge PA 19482

GREGOIRE, MICHEL R, physician; b. Marseille, Provence, France, Nov. 14, 1946; s. Robert Marcel and Yvonne Claire (Chopard) G.; m. Denise Gabrielle Calvo, July 4, 1970; children: Cecile, Olivier, Sophie. Degree in physics and math., Sci. Faculty Marseille, 1967; MD, Aix U., Marseille, 1974; med. valuation, 1984. Intern Hosp. Complex Gap, France, 1974-75; practitioner Med. Complex, Tallard, France, 1975—; dept. head Rio-Vert Convalescent Home, La Saulce, France, 1975—; cons. Health Services, Upper Alps, 1976—; med. capt. Firemen, Tallard, 1978—. Mem. med. com. Amnesty Internat., Paris, 1981. Fellow Med. Assn. Upper Alps; mem. French Mesotherapy Soc., Hosp. Mesotherapy Soc., Study and Research Circle Mesotherapy of Provence and Mediterranee. Home: La Condamine, Tallard 05130 Hautes-Alpes France Office: Groupe Medical, 31 Ave Jacques Bonfort, 05130 Tallard France

GREGOR-DELLIN, MARTIN, writer; b. Naumburg, Thuringen, Ger., June 3, 1926; m. Annemarie Gregor-Dellin, Nov. 9, 1951; 1 dau., Katja. P.E.N.-Zentrum, Bundesrepublik, 1976-82, pres., Deutschland, 1982—. Author: Catherine, Erzählung, 1954, Judisches Largo, Roman, 1956, Der Mann mit der Stoppuhr, 1957, Der Nullpunkt, 1959, Der Kandelaber, 1962, Jakob Haferglanz, 1963, Moglichkeiten einer Fahrt, 1964, Einer, 1965, Aufbruch ins Ungewisse, 1968, Unsichere Zeiten, Erzahlungen und Essays, 1969, Wagner-Chronik, 1972, Richard Wagner-die Revolution als Oper, 1973, Fohn, 1974, Richard Wagner, 1980, Heinrich Schutz, 1984, Schlabruadorf oder Die Republik, 1985, Italieuisckes Trauembick, 1986, many others; editor: Werkausgabe Klaus Mann und Bruno Frank, Werkauswahl Leonhard Frank, Richard Wagner, Cosima Wagner, Deutsche Schulzeit, others; radio dramas include: Jakob Haferglanz, 1961; Blumen oder keine, 1962; Suche nach einem Zeugen, 1965; Geordnete Verhaltnisse, 1967; Ferdinand wird totgeredet, 1971; Das Gastehaus, 1972. Mem. Verband deutscher Schriftsteller (regional pres. 1972-75). Home: Kochelseestrasse 57, D-8038 Grobenzell bei Munchen Federal Republic of Germany Office: PEN Zentrum Bundesrepublik, Deutschland Sandstr 10, 6100 Darmstadt Federal Republic of Germany

GREGORIO, PETER ANTHONY, retail grocer, artist; b. Chgo., July 29, 1916; s. Frank and Teresa (Marotta) G.; grad. pub. schs., Chgo., 1942; m. Marie Blanton, Mar. 17, 1945; children—Frank Allen, Carole Teresa. Owner, operator Davis Island Supermarket, Tampa, Fla. 1949—; dir. Ellis Nat. Bank of Davis Island, Tampa 1977-78; dir. Consignment Arts Ctr., Tampa; exhibited in one man show Islands Gallery, 1976-77; group shows Am. Bicentennial, Paris, 1976, Rochester (N.Y.) Religious Art Festival, 1972, Tampa Bay Art Center, 1979, Hillsborough Art Festival, 1976, 77, 78, (award of merit) 79, (3d pl. and honorable mention) 81, (3d pl.) 82, Tampa Realistic Art Assn., 1981, Artist Alliance Guild, Tampa, 1981, Tampa Mus., 1982, Tampa Mus. Art, 1987, Le Salon des Nations a Paris, 1984; represented in permanent collection Vatican Library, Rome, also numerous pvt. collections. Vice pres., Nat. Animal Rights, Inc., nat. hdqrs. Tampa, 1983—. Served to capt. USAF, 1941-46. Decorated Air medal with 6 clusters; recipient award of excellence Hillsborough County Art Fair, Tampa, 1984. award of merit Tampa Hispanic Heritage Exhbn., 1987. Mem. Am., Internat. socs. artists, Graphic Soc. Roman Catholic. Home: 149 Bosphorus Ave Tampa FL 33606 Office: 304 E Davis Blvd Tampa FL 33606

GREGORY, CALVIN, insurance service executive; b. Bronx, N.Y., Jan. 11, 1942; s. Jacob and Ruth (Cherchian) G.; m. Rachel Anna Carver, Feb. 14, 1970 (div. Apr. 1977); children—Debby Lynn, Trixy Sue; m. 2d, Carla Deane Deaver, June 30, 1979. A.A., Los Angeles City Coll., 1962; B.A., Calif. State U.-Los Angeles, 1964; M.Div., Fuller Theol. Sem., 1968; M.R.E., Southwestern Sem., Ft. Worth, 1969; Ph.D. in Religion, Universal Life Ch., Modesto, Calif., 1982; D.Div. (hon.), Otay Mesa Coll., 1982. Notary pub., real estate lic., casualty lic., Calif.; ordained to ministry Am. Baptist Conv., 1970. Youth minister First Bapt. Ch., Delano, Calif., 1964-65, 69-70; youth dir. St. Luke's United Meth. Ch., Highland Park, Calif., 1969-70; tchr. polit. sci. Maranatha High Sch., Rosemead, Calif., 1969-70; aux. chaplain U.S. Air Force 750th Radar Squadron, Edwards AFB, Calif., 1970-72; pastor First Bapt. Ch., Boron, Calif., 1971-72; ins. agt. Prudential Ins. Co., Ventura, Calif., 1972-73, sales mgr., 1973-74; casualty ins. agt. Allstate Ins. Co., Thousand Oaks, Calif., 1974-75; pres. Ins. Agy. Placement Service, Thousand Oaks, 1975—; head youth minister Emanuel Presbyn. Ch., Los Angeles, 1973-74; owner, investor real estate, U.S., Wales, Eng., Can., Australia. Counselor YMCA, Hollywood, Calif., 1964, Soul Clinic-Universal Life Ch., Inc., Modesto, Calif., 1982. Mem. Apt. Assn. Los Angeles, Life Underwriter Tng. Council. Republican. Clubs: Forensic (Los Angeles); X32 (Ventura). Lodge: Kiwanis (club speaker 1971). Home: 3307 Big Cloud Circle Thousand Oaks CA 91360 Office: Ins Agy Placement Service PO Box 4407 Thousand Oaks CA 91359

GREGORY, EDWARD MEEKS, clergyman; b. Richmond, Va., Sept. 30, 1922; s. George Craghead and Constance (Heath) G.; A.B., U. Va., 1947; M.Div., Episcopal Theol. Sch., Cambridge, Mass., 1954; postgrad. George Washington U., 1949, Va. Commonwealth U., 1980, Harvard U., 1981; D.Min., U. of South, 1977. Ordained priest Episcopal Ch., 1955; instr. Staunton (Va.) Mil. Acad., 1947-48; master Episc. High Sch., Alexandria, Va., 1948-51; curate St. Mark's Episc. Ch., Richmond, 1954-69; vicar St. Peter's Episc. Ch., Richmond, 1969-79; chaplain Christchurch Sch., 1980—; dean East Richmond, 1974-78; diocesan youth dir., 1956-60; diocesan del. Va. Council Chs., 1967-73; spiritual adviser Dignity-Integrity/Richmond, 1976-79; mem. Diocesan Dept. Social Relations, 1970-72, Diocesan Lit. Commn., 1973-83; pres. Religious Edn. Council, Richmond, 1961-62, Richmond Episc. Clericus, 1972-73. Bd. dirs. Vol. Service Bur., Richmond, 1960-63, Ednl. Therapy Center, 1964-79, Multiple Sclerosis, 1961-66, Va. Community Devel. Orgn., 1968-75, Va. chpt. ACLU, 1970-71, 76-77, Internat. Council; bd. dirs. Va. Council Human Relations, 1965-70, treas., 1972-73; bd. dirs. Richmond Planned Parenthood, 1969-74, Richmond chpt. ARC, 1973-79, Richmond United Neighborhoods, 1977-79, Met. Area Resources Clearing House, 1977-79, Ch. Hill Revitalization Team, 1979; bd. govs. Christchurch Sch., Va., 1978-79; pres. Richmond Council Human Relations, 1960-62; pres. Friends' Assn. for Children, 1967-70, bd. dirs., 1975-79; mem. adv. bd. Richmond Model Neighborhood, 1971-73; bd. dirs. Richmond Community Sr. Center, 1975-78, Daily Planet, 1974-79, Alcohol and Drug Abuse Prevention and Tng. Services, 1978-85, Richmond Health Center, 1981-85; vice chmn. Richmond Health Occupations, 1979. Served with Med. Dept. AUS, 1942-46. Decorated Bronze Star. Mem. Richmond Clergy Assn., Jamestown Soc. (gov. 1951-55), Mayflower Soc. (elder Va. co. 1963-81), Va. Hist. Soc., Braintree (Mass.) Hist. Soc., Episcopal Soc. Cultural and Racial Unity (chmn. Richmond 1964-66), Assn. Preservation Va. Antiquities, Valentine Mus., Va. Mus. Fine Arts, Chi Phi. Silhouettist; works exhibited Va. Hist. Soc. Clubs: James River Catfish, 2300. Home and Office: Christchurch Sch Christchurch VA 23031

GREGORY, LYDIA MAY JENCKS, librarian; b. Cumberland, R.I., Nov. 6, 1903; d. Gerard Dallas and Florence May (Perkins) Jencks; B.S., U. R.I., 1926; A.M., Brown U., 1929; student library sci. SUNY, Geneseo, 1932; m. William Gregory, Dec. 21, 1935. Tchr., librarian Central Sch., Franklin, N.Y., 1929-30; asst. librarian, registrar State Tchrs. Coll., Geneseo, 1930-32; librarian, instr. library sci. State Tchrs. Coll., Geneseo, 1930-32; librarian, instr. library sci. State Tchrs. Coll., Gorham, Maine, 1932-35; trustee Attleboro (Mass.) Pub. Library, 1941—; state librarian Mass. DAR, 1950-53; state librarian Daus. Am. Colonists, 1958—, Mass. regent, 1961-64, nat. chaplain, 1964-67, nat. chmn. nat. awards com., 1979-82; clk., mem. Christian edn. com. Bethany Congl. Ch., chair music com.; mem. Attleboro Republican City Com. Mem. Children Am. Revolution (sr. state pres., 1953-57), Mass. Library Trustees Assn., Attleboro Museum Art and History, Daus. of Founders and Patriots, Woman Descs. Ancient and Honorable Arty. Co., Nat. Trust Hist. Preservation, New Eng. Hist. Geneal. Soc. Author: Course of Study in Use of Library, 1935; co-author: Bethany Congregational Church 1886-1986-A History, 1987; contbr. articles to profl. jours. Home: 39 Angeline St S Attleboro MA 02703

GREGORY, THOMAS BRADFORD, mathematics educator; b. Traverse City, Mich., Dec. 13, 1944; s. Philip Henry and Rhoda Winslow (Hathaway) G. BA, Oberlin (Ohio) Coll., 1967; MA, Yale U., 1969, M of Philosophy, 1975, PhD, 1977. Lectr. Ohio State U., Mansfield, 1977-78, asst. prof. math., 1978-84, assoc. prof. math., 1984—. Reviewer: Math. Revs., 1984—; contbr. articles to profl. jours. Active Mansfield (Ohio) Symphony Chorus, 1977—, Presbytery Youth Ministries Com., New Philadelphia, Ohio, 1980—, Univ. Singers, Mansfield, 1985—. Served to lt. comdr. USNR, 1969—. Fellow NSF, Washington, 1967; hon. fellow U. Wis., Madison, 1987-88. Mem. Am. Math. Soc. (translator 1974-82), Ohio Council Tchrs. Math., Am. Soc. Naval Engrs., Naval Inst., Res. Officers Assn., Naval Res. Assn., Navy League, Phi Beta Kappa, Sigma Xi. Republican. Home: 930 Maumee Ave Mansfield OH 44906 Office: Ohio State U 0-15 1680 University Dr Mansfield OH 44906

GREIDINGER, B. BERNARD, accountant, educator; b. N.Y.C., Mar. 30, 1906; s. Max and Fannie (Oster) G. B.B.A., CCNY, 1928; M.S., Columbia U., 1932, Ph.D., 1939. C.P.A., N.Y. Ptnr. Beame & Greidinger C.P.A., N.Y.C., 1929-42; sr. partner Greidinger and Co. (C.P.A.), 1946-71; partner Hertz, Herson & Co., N.Y.C., 1971—; prof. accounting grad. sch. bus. N.Y. U., 1948-74; prof. emeritus 1974—; prof. accounting U. Calif. at Los Angeles, summer 1947; lectr. accounting Coll. City N.Y., 1930-39, Rutgers U., 1940-42; Disting. vis. prof. acctg. Rider Coll., Lawrenceville, N.J., 1980-81; past dir., mem. exec. com. U.S. Hoffman Machinery Corp.; Rep. dir. gen. UNRRA at inception Internat. Refugee Orgn., 1946; financial adv., chief financial operations UNRRA, 1946-47; cons. budget adv. com. Army-Air Force Post Exchange Serv., 1948; cons. to chief ordnance Dept. of Army, N.Y. dist., 1952—, spl. cons. to comptroller N.Y., 1955; coordinator N.Y.U., U.S. Operation Mission (internat. cooperation adminstrn.), Israel, 1956. Author: Accounting Requirements of the Securities and Exchange Commission, 1941, Preparation and Certification of Financial Statements, 1950, (with others) Big Business Methods for Small Business, 1952, Filings with the Securities and Exchange Commission, 1966, Handbook for Auditors, 1971; Contbr. (with others) chpts. to books; articles to profl. jours. Business, 1952. Mem. Temp. Commn. City Finances, N.Y.C., 1965-66; mem. citizens' commn. on future of City U. N.Y., 1970—; chmn. transition com. Mayor of N.Y.C., 1974; mem. Mayor's Com. on Judiciary, 1974—, Mayor's Council Econ. and Bus. Advisers, 1974—, Commn. Cultural Affairs City of N.Y., 1976—, Indsl. and Comml. Incentive Bd. City of N.Y., 1977—. Served with finance dept. AUS, 1942-44; from maj. to lt. col. USAAF, 1944-46; col. USAFR. Mem. Am. Inst. C.P.A.s, N.Y. State Soc. C.P.A.s, Am. Accountants Assn., Nat. Assn. Accountants, Acad. Polit. Scis., Jewish Acad. Arts and Scis. Clubs: Columbia, New York University. Lodge: Masons. Home: 2 Washington Sq Village New York NY 10012 Office: 2 Park Ave New York NY 10016

GREIG, JAMES CARRUTHERS GORRIE, theologian; b. Moffat, Dumfriesshire, Scotland, Feb. 23, 1927; s. James and Elizabeth (Carruthers) G.; B.A. with honours (Open Maj. scholar 1945-48), Gonville and Caius Coll., Cambridge (Eng.) U., 1948; M.A., 1952; B.D. (Robert James Wyllie fellow 1954), U. Glasgow, 1954; S.T.M. summa cum laude (Scots fellow 1954), Union Theol. Sem., N.Y.C., 1955; m. Elsa Clark Carlile, Sept. 20, 1958; children: Elspeth Carlile, Andrew Carruthers, Jane Clark. Ordained to ministry of Scotland Ch., 1955; minister, Closeburn, Scotland, 1955-59; prof. N.T. lang., lit. and theology Westminster Coll., Cambridge, 1959-63; lectr. religious edn. Jordanhill Coll. Edn., Glasgow, 1963-79; minister St. Matthew's Ch. Scotland, Paisley, 1979-86; English translator World Council of Chs., Geneva, 1986—; temporary lectr. dept. N.T., U. Glasgow, 1981; moderator Presbytery of Paisley, 1981-82; religious editor Oliver & Boyd Ltd., 1962-67; mem. various coms. Ch. of Scotland. Served with Brit. Army, 1948-50. Mem. Studiorum Novi Testamenti Societas, John Buchan Soc. (chmn. 1983-86). Club: Scottish Arts (Edinburgh). Author: The Serpent in the Wilderness, 1961; translator of Bultmann, Wrede, Hengel, and Hübner; editor Scottish Sunday Sch. Tchr., 1965-75; contbr. to John Buchan Jour.; also articles, revs. Office: PO Box 66, Language Service, World Council of Chs, 150 Route de Ferney, 1211 Geneva 20 Switzerland

GREIS, WAYNE RAYMOND, data processing executive; b. Chgo., Sept. 24, 1942; s. Raymond Julius and Lorraine Marie (Rietschel) G.; m. Annette Teresa Plata, May 14, 1965 (div. May 1980); children: Jodie Marie, Michele Antonette; m. Deborah Ann Hardesty, Sept. 25, 1982. Student, U. Ill., Chgo., 1960, Bogan Jr. Coll., Chgo., 1961, Loop Jr. Coll., Chgo., 1962, Northwestern U., 1967-68. Computer programmer Martin Brower Corp., Forest View, Ill., 1962-66; mgr. programming Morton Thiokol, Inc., Chgo., 1966-72, mgr. data processing, 1972-78, mgr. systems quality assurance, 1978-82, mgr. MIS risk mgmt., 1982-85; mgr. MIS Info. security Morton Thiokol, Chgo., 1985—; lectr. various bus. and profl. orgns. Youth coordinator St. Peter's Cath. Ch., Antioch, Ill., 1976-79. Served to staff sgt. U.S. Army, 1963-69. Mem. Computer Security Inst., GUIDE, Chgo. Info. Security Rountable. Republican. Lutheran. Office: Morton Thiokol Inc 110 N Wacker Dr Chicago IL 60606

GREMBOWSKI, EUGENE, insurance company manager; b. Bay City, Mich., July 21, 1938; s. Barney Thomas and Mary (Senkowski) G.; m. Teresa Ann Frasik, June 27, 1959; children: Bruce Allen, Debora Ann. AA, Allan Hancock U., 1963; BA, Mich. State U., 1967; MBA, George Washington U., 1972. Enlisted USAF, 1955, commd. 2d lt., 1968, advanced through grades to capt., 1971; personnel officer USAF, Goldsboro, N.C., 1968-70; chief of procurement USAF, Cheyenne, Wyo., 1971-73; contract analyst USAF, Omaha, 1973-76; chief of contracting USAF, Atwater, Calif., 1976-79; ret. USAF, 1979; office supr. Farmers Ins. Group of Cos., Merced, Calif., 1980-85, office mgr., 1985-86; fleet mgr. Los Angeles, 1986—. Author: Governmental Purchasing: Its Progression Toward Professional Status, 1972. Cubmaster Boy Scouts Am., Goldsboro, 1968; com. chmn. Am. Heart Assn., Merced-Mariposa, Calif., 1985, sec.-treas., 1986. Recipient Meritorious Service medals Office of the Pres., 1973, 76. Mem. Nat. Contract Mgmt. Assn. Home: 14633 Mountain Spring St Hacienda Heights CA 91745 Office: Farmers Ins Group 4750 Wilshire Blvd Los Angeles CA 90010

GREMILLET, NOËL, physics educator; b. Bethune, Pas de Calais, France, Nov. 23, 1943; s. Paul and Zoé (Viard) G.; m. Annie Morel, Aug. 1, 1970; children: Olivier, Guillaume. Lic. in Physics, U. Lille, France, 1966, Diplome d'Etudes Approfoudies, 1967. Asst. faculté scis. U. Lille, 1967-68; asst. IUT, Valenciennes, France, 1968-70, 72-74; asst. faculté scis. U. Alger, Algeria, 1970-72; maître de conférences U. Valenciennes, 1974—; mgr. fin. Intégrated Optics Team, Valenciennes, 1980—; mgr. Opto-Acousto-Electronique Electroncs, VAlenciennes, 1980—. Contbr. articles to profl. jours. Office: Univ, OAE Labs, 59326 Valenciennes France

GREMILLION, CURTIS LIONEL, JR., psychologist, hospital administrator, musician; b. Slaughter, La., Feb. 26, 1924; s. Curtis Lionel and Beatrice (Watson) G.; m. Rosemary Duhon, Dec. 8, 1951; children: Suzanne Lynelle Gremillion (Walden) Curtis Lionel III, Monique Angele. B.A. in Psychology and Music, U. Southwestern La., 1948; postgrad. in psychology, La. State U., 1948-49, 53. Profl. musician 1940-43, 46-52; staff psychologist East La. State Hosp., Jackson, 1949-83; dir. psychology and social service depts. East La. State Hosp., 1953- 57, asst. supt., 1957-62, adminstr., 1961, 62-64, acting supt., 1964-66, asso. adminstr., 1966-81, patient advocate, 1981-83; cons. psychology 1983—; clin. dir. Pace Ctr., Baton Rouge, 1983-88; notary pub., 1954—; dir. regional council Alcoholism and Drug Abuse, 1972-76. Author: History of The East Louisiana State Hospital. Bd. dirs. La. State Credit Union, 1962-68; chmn. East Feliciana Parish United Givers Fund, 1960; regional chmn. Am. Heart Assn., 1968-76, ARC, 1954-55, 62, Boy Scouts Am., 1964-69, Am. Cancer Soc., 1963-64; bd. dirs. So. Behavioral Research Found., 1970-76. Served with USNR, 1943-46. Recipient Outstanding Leadership and Service award La. Dept. Hosps., 1966. Mem. La. Psychol. Assn. (charter), So. Sociol. Assn., La. Music Therapy Assn. (dir. 1966-74), Am. Legion, Internat. Platform Assn., Psi Chi, Sinfonia, Pi Gamma Mu, Kappa Delta Pi. Democrat. Baptist. Clubs: New Orleans Jazz, Lions. Address: PO Box 306 Slaughter LA 70777

GREMMEN, HANS JOHANNES, economics educator, researcher; b. Hulst, Zeeland, The Netherlands, Jan. 24, 1954; s. Johannes Wilhelmus and Johanna (van Schayk) G.; m. Annette Wester, Dec. 27, 1976; 1 child, Gineke. MA, Tilburg (The Netherlands) U., 1979, PhD, 1988. Sci. asst. Tilburg U., 1976-78, prof. econs., 1979—; dir. econs. dept. Hogeschool Interstudie, Arnhem, The Netherlands, 1984—. Creator multi-country macro econ. computer simulation game, 1987; contbr. articles to profl. jours. Home: Waltro 49, 5161 WL Spring-Capelle The Netherlands Office: Tilburg U Dept Econs, Hogeschoolaan 225, 5037 GC Tilburg The Netherlands

GRENET, FRANTZ MAURICE, research historian; b. Gruchet-le-Valasse, Seine-Maritime, France, Nov. 6, 1952; s. Guy Christian and Eliane Geneviève (Héricier) G.; m. Maxine Elizabeth Medcalf, Aug. 21, 1978; children: Julien, Charles. MA, U. Paris Sorbonne, 1973, PhD, 1981; diploma in Persian, Inst. des Langs. Orientales, Paris, 1976. Fellow Ecole Normale Supérieure, Paris, 1972-77; fellow Délégation Archéologique Française en Afghanistan, Kabul, 1977-78, dep. dir., 1978-81; attaché de recherche Ctr. Nat. Recherche Sci., Paris, 1981-85, chargé de recherche, 1985—. Author: (book) Les Pratiques Funéraires dans l'Asie Centrale Sédentaire, 1984 (Académie des Inscriptions prize 1985); mem. editorial com. Jour. Studia Iranica, 1983—; contbr. articles to profl. jours. Mem. Assn. Advancement Iranian Studies (sec. 1985—), Corpus Inscriptionum Iranicarum, Soc. Iranologica Europaea, Soc. Asiatique, Soc. Ernest Renan. Home: 14 rue du Cardinal Lemoine, 75005 Paris France Office: Ctr Nat Recherche Sci, URA DO 67, 45 rue d'Ulm, 75005 Paris France

GRENFELL, RAYMOND FREDERIC, physician, researcher; b. West Bridgewater, Pa., Nov. 23, 1917; s. Elisha Raymond and Pearl (Bolland) G.; m. Maude Byrnes Chisholm, Aug. 19, 1944; children—Raymond Frederic, Milton Wilfred, James Byrnes, Robert Chisholm. B.S., U. Pitts., 1939, M.D., 1941. Intern Western Pa. Hosp., Pitts., 1941-42; practice medicine specializing in internal medicine, Jackson, 1946-79, practice medicine specializing in diagnosis and treatment of hypertension, 1979—; mem. staffs Riverside Hosp., St. Dominic-Jackson Meml. Hosp., Miss. Bapt. Hosp., Humana Hosp.; clin. instr. U. Miss. Med. Sch., Jackson, 1955-59, clin. asst. prof. medicine, 1959—, vis. teaching physician, 1977—, head hypertension clinic, 1956-79. Pres. Jackson Symphony Orch. Assn., 1961, Duling PTA, Jackson, 1963; deacon First Baptist Ch., Jackson, 1960—. Served to maj. U.S. Army, 1942-46. Recipient bronze medal Am. Heart Assn., 1963, silver medal, 1965. gov. Am. Coll. Angiology, 1979-86; Am. Coll. Chest Physicians; mem. Am. Soc. Clin. Pharmacology and Therapeutics (dir. 1968, v.p. 1976), Am. Fedn. Clin. Research, So. Med. Assn. (councilor 1968-73), Miss. Heart Assn. (pres. 1964-65). Republican. Clubs: Country, Univ. (Jackson) (dir. 1974—). Home: 190 Ridge Dr Jackson MS 39216 Office: 514-H E Woodrow Wilson Jackson MS 39216

GRENLEY, PHILIP, physician; b. N.Y.C., Dec. 21, 1912; s. Robert and Sara (Schrader) G.; B.S., N.Y.U., 1932, M.D., 1936; m. Dorothy Sarney, Dec. 11, 1938; children—Laurie (Mrs. John Hallen), Neal, Jane (Mrs. Eldridge C. Hanes), Robert. Intern, Kings County Hosp., Bklyn., 1936-38, resident, 1939; resident in urology L.I. Coll. Hosp., Bklyn., 1939-41; practice medicine specializing in urology, Tacoma, Wash., 1946-—; urologist Tacoma Gen. Hosp., St. Joseph Hosp., Drs. Hosp., Mary Bridge Children's Hosp. (all Tacoma), Good Samaritan Hosp., Puyallup, Wash.; pres. med. staff St. Joseph Hosp., Tacoma, 1968-69, mem. exec. bd., 1950-54, 67-68; cons. urologist to Surgeon Gen., Madigan Army Med. Center, Tacoma, 1954-87, USPHS McNeil Island Penitentiary, 1955-82, Good Samaritan Rehab. Center, Puyallup, 1960-—; lectr. in sociology U. Puget Sound, Tacoma, 1960-—. Trustee Wash. Children's Home Soc., 1951-60, Charles Wright Acad., 1961-69, Wash. State Masonic Home, 1984—; trustee Pierce County Med. Bur., 1949-51, 59-61, 71-73, pres., 1973-74, mem. exec. bd., 1975-77. Served with AUS, 1941-46. Diplomate Am. Bd. Urology. Fellow ACS; mem. Am. Urol. Assn., AMA, Wash., Pan Am. med. assns., Pierce County Med. Soc. Lodges: Masons, Shrine (med. dir. 1965-78, imperial council 1982-85, potentate 1983), Royal Order Jesters (dir. 1986, 87), Lions, Elks, Red Cross of Constantine (knight). Home: 40 Loch Ln SW Tacoma WA 98499 Office: 721 S Fawcett Ave Tacoma WA 98402

GRENNELL, ROBERT LOVELL, psychology educator; b. Irving, N.Y., July 28, 1910; s. John Chapman and Emma (Brehn) G.; student SUNY, 1930; B.S., Pa. State U., 1934; M.A., Cornell U., 1937; Ed.D., NYU,1950; m. Elinor Thorsen, Aug. 16, 1941; children—Donna L., Susanne T., John C. Tchr., Morrisville Pub. Schs., Pa., 1928-32, Silver Creek High Sch., N.Y., 1934-35; tchr., psychologist, research dir. Rockville Centre Pub. Schs., L.I., N.Y., 1935-42; vocat. adviser, psychologist-counselor U.S. VA, Buffalo, 1946-47; prof. edn. and psychology State Univ. Coll., Fredonia, N.Y., 1947-74, prof. emeritus, 1974—. Mem. Bd. Edn., Lake Shore Central Sch. system, Angola, N.Y., 1957-60; mem., chmn. Town of Brant Planning Bd., 1959—. Served from pvt. to capt. AUS, 1942-46; lt. col. USAF Res., ret. Mem. Am. Psychol. Assn., N.Y. State, Psychol. Assn., Western N.Y. Psychol. Assn., Ret. Officers Assn., Air Force Assn., Phi Delta Kappa. Home: 995 Milestrip Rd Irving NY 14081 Office: State U Coll Thompson Hall Fredonia NY 14063

GREPPIN, JOHN AIRD COUTTS, linguist, editor, educator; b. Rochester, N.Y., Apr. 2, 1937; s. Ernest Haquette and Edna Barbara (Kill) G.; m. Mary Elizabeth Cleland Hannan, Sept. 30, 1961; children: Sally Clelland Coutts, Carl Hannan Haquette. AB in Greek, U. Rochester, N.Y., 1961; MA in Classics, U. Wash., 1966; PhD in Indo-European Studies, UCLA, 1972. Tchr. Greek, Latin Stowe (Vt.) Prep. Sch., 1961-62; tchr. Woodstock (Vt.) Country Sch., 1962-65, admissions dir., 1968-69; interim asst. prof. U. Fla., Gainesville, 1971-72; tchr. Isidore Newman Sch., New Orleans, 1972-74; instr. research Yerevan State U., USSR, 1974-75; from asst. to assoc. to prof. linguistics Cleve. State U., 1975—. Author: Initial Vowel and Aspiration in Classical Armenian, 1973, Classical Armenian Nominal Suffixes, 1975, Classical and Middle Armenian Bird Names: A Taxonomic and Mythological Study, 1978, An Etymological Dictionary of the Indo-European Components of Classical Armenian, 1984, Bark Galianosi: The Greek Armenian Dictionary to Galen, 1985, A Handbook of Armenian Dialectology, 1986; editor: (with others) Interrogativity: A Colloquium of the Grammar, Typology and Pragmatics of Questions in Seven Diverse Languages, 1984; editor Proceedings of the First Internat. Conf. on Armenian Linguistics, Phila., July, 11-14, 1979, 80; editor Ann. Armenian Linguistics, 1980—, Anatolian and Caucasian Studies, 1979—; mng. editor Raft, A Jour. of Armenian Poetry and Critism, 1987—; contbr. 130 articles to Am., European and Soviet jours., 120 revs. to Times Lit. Supplement, N.Y. Times Book Rev., others. Fellow Am. Council Learned Socs., 1965, NEH, 1978, NIH, 1984, Internat. Research and Exchanges Bd., 1974, grantee, 1980-82, 84-85, 86-87; grantee AGBU Manoogian Fund, 1977, 79-87, Gulbenkian Found., 1982, 85; recipient Silver medal Congregazione Mekhitarista, Venice, Italy, 1978. Mem. Assn. Internat. des Études Arméniennes, Soc. for Study of the Caucasus, Am. Philological Soc., Soc. for Armenian Studies (mem. exec. bd. 1982-86, sec. 1983-85), Soc. Caucasologia Europaea. Home: 3349 Fairmont Blvd Cleveland Heights OH 44118 Office: Cleve State U Cleveland OH 44115

GRESHAM, ANN ELIZABETH, retailer, horticulturist executive; b. Richmond, Va., Oct. 11, 1933; d. Allwin Stagg and Ruby Scott (Faber) Gresham. Student, Peace Coll., Raleigh, N.C., 1950-52, East Carolina U., 1952-53, Penland Sch., N.C., 1953-54, Va. Commonwealth U., 1960-64. Owner, prin. Ann Gresham's Gift Shop, Richmond, 1953-56; pres., treas. Gresham's Garden Ctr., Inc., Richmond, 1955-79; v.p. Gresham's Nursery, Inc., Richmond, 1959-73, pres., treas., 1973—; pres., treas. Gresham's Country Store, Richmond, 1964—; tchr., 1982—. Bd. dirs. Bainbridge Community Ministry, 1979, Handworkshop, 1984—; class agt. Peace Coll., Raleigh, 1987-88, mem. alumnae council, 1987, bd. visitors, 1987—; focus group mem. Hand Workshop, Richmond, 1983, bd. dirs., 1984-87. Mem. Midlothian Antique Dealers (treas. 1975-79), Richmond Quilt Guild (chpt. v.p. 1983-84), Nat. Needlework Assn., Quilt Inst., Am. Hort. Soc. Episcopalian. Clubs: Chesmond Women's (v.p. 1979-80), James River Woman's (Richmond). Home: 2324 Logan St Bon Air VA 23235 Office: Gresham's Inc 6725 Midlothian Pike Richmond VA 23225

GRESHAM, PERRY EPLER, university official, philosophy educator; b. Covina, Cal., Dec. 19, 1907; s. George Edward and Mary Elizabeth (Epler) G.; m. Elsie Stanbrough, Dec. 9, 1926 (dec. Mar. 1947); 1 son, Glen Edward; m. Alice Fickling Cowan, May 6, 1953; 1 dau., Nancy. A.B. summa cum laude, Tex. Christian U., 1931, B.D., 1933, LL.D., 1949; postgrad., U. Chgo., 1932-33, Columbia, 1931-41; Litt.D., Culver-Stockton Coll., 1954, Findlay Coll., U. Cin., 1966, W. Va. U., 1971; L.H.D., Chapman Coll., 1964, Concord Coll.; Ed.D., Transylvania, 1965, Rio Grande Coll.; LL.D., Alderson-Broaddus Coll.; Pd.D., Youngstown U., 1966; D.B.A., Lawrence Inst. Tech., 1973. Prof. philosophy Tex. Christian U., 1936-42; minister U. Christian Ch., Ft. Worth, 1933-42, Seattle, 1942-45; minster Central Woodward Christian Ch., Detroit, 1945-53; feature writer Detroit Free Press, 1950-52; pres. Bethany (W.Va.) Coll., 1953-72, chmn. bd., 1972-76, distinguished prof. philosophy, 1973—; former adj. prof. U. Wash.; former lectr. U. Mich.; Mem. study com. Commn. on Faith and Order, World Council Chs., 1948-60; pres. W.Va. Found. Colls., 1954-58; mem. clergy industry commn. N.A.M., 1957-65; commn. on liberal edn. Assn. Am. Colls., 1963-78 ; chmn. North Central Assn. Colls. and Univs., 1964-66; pres. Internat. Conv. Christian Chs., 1960-61; dir. emeritus Chesapeake & Potomac Telephone Cos., Cooper Tire and Rubber Co., Findlay, Ohio.; Wesbanco Corp., 1960-83, pres., 1983; Wheeling Dollar Bank.; Bd. dirs. Found. for Econ. Edn., 1960-86, pres., 1983-84, chmn. bd., 1966-68; bd. dirs. Lawrence Inst. Tech., Detroit, John A. Hartford Found., N.Y.C. Author: Incipient Gnosticism in the New Testament, 1933, Disciplines of the High Calling, 1954, The Sage of Bethany, 1960, Answer to Conformity, 1961, Abiding Values, 1972, Campbell and the Colleges, 1973, With Wings As Eagles, 1980, Toasts - Plain, Spicy and Wry, 1986. Mem. Am. Philos. Soc. Internat. Robert Burns Soc., Internat. Platform Assn., Alpha Chi. Mason (Shriner). Clubs: University (N.Y.C.); Duquesne (Pitts.); Williams Country (Weirton); Rotary (Wheeling); Skytop (Pa.); Royal Scottish (Glasgow); Authors (London). Home: Highland Hearth Bethany WV 26032

GRESHAM, THOMAS ANDREW, counselor; b. Tuscaloosa, Ala., Sept. 20, 1953; s. Richard Andrew and Martha (Yow) G. BS, U. Ala., 1983, MA, 1985. Nat. Cert. counselor, 1987. Therapist Cen. Va. Community Services Bd., Lynchburg, 1985-86; substance abuse and Vietnam Vets. readjustment counselor Dist. 19 Alcohol and Drug Services, Petersburg, Va., 1986—. Pres. Handicapped Students Orgn., 1983-85; mem. Mayors Com. on Handicapped and Elderly, Tuscaloosa, 1983; program dir. Nova Clinics, Inc.; developer Juvenile Alcohol Safety Awarness project for Juvenile Cts. Tuscaloosa (Ala.) County. Served with USN, 1972-80, Vietnam. Mem. Am. Assn. Counseling and Devel., Am. Rehab. Counselors Assn., Am. Mental Health Counselors Assn., Va. Assn. Alcoholism and Drug Abuse Counselors, Nat. Assn. Alcoholism and Drug Abuse Counselors. Mem. Baha'i Faith. Avocations: photography, motorcycling, reading. Office: Dist 19 Alcohol and Drug Services 116 S Adams St Petersburg VA 23803

GRESOV, BORIS (VLADIMIR), economist; b. St. Petersburg, Russia, Aug. 7, 1914; s. Paul Vladimir and Maria de Suzor G.; m. Letitia Coxen Graham, June 21, 1945; children: Winston Graham, Christopher Leo. BA with honors, Cambridge U., Eng., 1938, MA with honors, 1932. With Office Econ. Warfare (Unit of War Prodn. Bd.), prodn. mgr. Compania Nacional Minera de Taxco S.A., Mex., 1941-45; v.p. Industrias y Minas S.A., Mex., 1945-49; cons. economist Shields & Co., N.Y.C., 1949-52, G.H. Walker & Co., N.Y.C., 1952-58, E.W. Axe & Co., N.Y.C., 1957-61; dir., mem. exec. com. Western Devel. Co. of Del., Santa Fe, 1954-61; mem. adv. bd. Axe Sci. and Electronics Corp., N.Y.C., 1957-61; dir. The Flying Tiger Line, Inc., Burbank, Calif., 1957-65, Axe-Templeton Growth Fund of Can., Ltd., N.Y.C., 1958-61, Internat. Oil & Gas Corp., Denver, 1961-66; dir., chmn. bd., chief exec. officer Shattuck Denn Mining Corp., N.Y.C., 1958-60, bd. dirs., chmn. exec. com., 1962; founder, pres. Excelsior Fund Inc., 1963—; chmn. Standard Metals Corp., 1963—, pres., chief exec. officer, 1965—; dir. USLIFE Income Fund, Inc., N.Y.C., 1976-86. Mem. Union Soc. (Cambridge, Eng.). Chevalier of Confrerie de la Chaine des Rotisseurs. Mem. Econ. Club N.Y., Nat. Economists Club, N.Y. Soc. Security Analysts Inc., Am. Inst. Mgmt. (pres.'s council), N.Y. Assn. Bus. Economists. Roman Catholic. Clubs: Metropolitan, University, Met. Opera (N.Y.C.); The L.I. Wyandanch Club (Eastport, LI., N.Y.); Westhampton Country (Westhampton Beach, L.I.); Surf (Quoque, L.I.). Home: 45 E 72d St New York NY 10021 Office: 45 Rockefeller Plaza New York NY 10111

GRESS, ESTHER, editor; b. Copenhagen, Aug. 20; d. Gustav Ferdinand and Anna Maria (Ekberg) Hansson; 1 son, Claus Gress. LittD. (hon.), 1984. Editor: Vor Tids Konversations Leksikon Supplement, Aschehoug Dansk Forlag, Copenhagen, 1943-48; mentor Westermann's Forlag, Copenhagen, 1949-50, Dansk Rim-Ordbog, Politikens Forlag, Copenhagen, 1950, newspaper Berlingske Tidende, 1950—, and other publs. of Berlingske Officin A/S, including Radiolytteren, Landet and Berlingske Aftenavis; Danish acad. consul of Accademia d'Europa, Naples, 1982. Recipient awards U.S., Italy, India, Eng., Taiwan; named guest of honor N.Y. Poetry Forum, 1983, Poet Laureate Journalist with Laurel Wreath, N.Y., 1987; decorated grand dame Knights of Malta, 1984. Fellow IBC; mem. World Poetry Soc. Intercontinental, United Poets Laureate Internat., Accademia Internazionale di Lettere, Scienze, Arti Virgiglio-Mantegna, Danish Authors Assn., Danish Press Hist. Assn., Danish Publicistklub, Danish Press Staff Assn., Internat. Acad. Poets, N.Y. Poetry Forum, Inc., Nat. Fedn. State Poetry Socs., Inc. (N.Y.), Internat. Acad. Poets, Accademia Internazionale Leonardo da Vinci. Author: Skal, 1974; Liv, 1977; Ville - Vejen i Vejen, 1979; Det sker-máske, 1982, 85; Det gik, 1983; Raise (with English poems), 1984; Og-se, 1984; Noget, 1985; contbr. poems in 17 langs. to various anthologies, papers and lit. mags. in Denmark and art mags. in Eng., U.S., Italy, Switzerland, Austria, Korea and India; poems set to music in Danish, English, Italian. Home: 27 Ny Strandvej, Humlebaek Denmark 3050 Office: Berlingske Tidende, 34 Pilestraede, 1147 Copenhagen Denmark

GRESSAK, ANTHONY RAYMOND, JR., food distribution executive; b. Honolulu, Jan. 22, 1947; s. Anthony Raymond and Anne Tavares (Ferreira) G.; m. Catherine Streb, Apr. 11, 1981; children: Danielle Kirsten, Anthony Raymond III, Christina Michelle. A.A., Utah State U., 1967; postgrad., U.S. Army Inf. Officers Candidate Sch., 1968. Restaurant mgr. Ala Moana Hotel, Honolulu, 1970-72; gen. mgr. Fred Harvey, Inc., Ontario, Calif., 1972-73; regional mgr. So. Calif., 1972-73, regional mgr. tollway ops., 1973; divisional mgr. Normandy Lanes, 1973; resident mgr. Royal Inns of Am., San Diego, 1974; food and beverage dir. Asso. Inns & Restaurant Co. of Am. (Aircoa), Big Sky, Mont., 1974-75; condonium mgr. Big Sky, 1975; asst. gen. mgr. Naples (Fla.) Bath and Tennis Club, 1975-76; food and beverage dir. Nat. Parks, Grand Canyon, Ariz., 1976-77; gen. mgr. Grand Canyon

Nat. Park Lodges, 1977-79; divisional v.p. food services The Broadway, Carter Hawley Hale, Inc., Los Angeles, 1979-82; exec. v.p. Silco Corp., Los Angeles, 1982-84; interstate restaurant supply mktg. mgr. 1984-85; dir. mktg. and merchandising S.E. Rykoff & Co., Los Angeles, 1986—; maitre de table Chaine des Rotisseurs-Los Angeles; chmn. edn. culinary steering com. Los Angeles Trade Tech. Coll.; bd. dirs. Orange Empire Internat. Food Service Execs.' Assn. Served with U.S. Army, 1967-70. Decorated Silver Star medal, Bronze Star medal, Purple Heart. Mem. Nat. Restaurant Assn., Les Amis d'Escoffier, Internat. Order DeMolay (life mem., chevalier), Smithsonian Assos., Orange Empire Food Service Execs. Assoc., Le Toque Blanche. Roman Catholic. Club: Industry Hills Country. Home: 20301 Minnehaha St Chatsworth CA 91311 Office: SE Rykoff & Co 761 Terminal St Los Angeles CA 90021

GREW, JAMES, spring company executive; b. Portadown, County Armagh, No. Ireland, Oct. 25, 1929; s. James and Mary Kathleen (Darragh) G.; m. Pauline Peta Cunningham, July 20, 1955; children—Jonathan James, Michaela Maria, Philippa Peta, Christopher Nicholas. Mng. dir. Abbicoil Springs, Ltd., Portadown, Northern Ireland, 1957—. Mem. No. Ireland Community Relations Commn., 1971-74; mem. No. Ireland Econ. Council, 1970-74; mem. Craigavon Devel. Commn., 1971-73; mem. Crawford Com. on Broadcasting Coverage, 1973-74; justice of the peace, 1974—; mem. BBC Gen. Adv. Com., London, 1976-81; mem. BBC No. Ireland Adv. Com., 1976-81; chmn. Lisburn and Dist. Group Tng. Scheme, 1977-78; chmn. Lisburn and Dist. Youth Opportunity Workshop, 1980-81; dir. Mgmt. Devel. Services Ltd., 1975—; mem. Standing Commn. on Human Rights, 1980-82; mem. Post Office Users Nat. Council, London, 1976-81; chmn. Post Office Users Council No. Ireland, 1976-81; pres. Brownlow Citizens Advice Bur., 1976-80; dep. lt. County Armagh, 1981; mem. Ind. Broadcasting Authority No. Ireland Adv. Com., 1981-83; dir. Transport Holding Co. No. Ireland, 1983-86 ; dir. No. Ireland Rys., 1986—; chmn. Probation Bd. No. Ireland, 1982—, Independent Commn. Police Complaints, Northern Ireland, 1987; dep. chmn. T.S.B. Found. Bd., Northern Ireland, 1987—. Roman Catholic. Club: Challoner (London). Home: Peacefield Ballinacorr, Portadown Northern Ireland BT63 5RJ Office: Abbicoil Springs Ltd, Obin St, Portadown Northern Ireland BT62 1BX

GREW, ROBERT RALPH, lawyer; b. Metamora, Ohio, Mar. 25, 1931; s. Edward Francis and Coletta Marie G.; m. Anne Gano Bailey, Aug. 2, 1958; 1 son, Christopher Adam. A.B., U. Mich., 1953, J.D., 1955. Bar: Mich. 1955, N.Y. 1958. Assoc., Carter, Ledyard & Milburn, N.Y.C., 1957-68, ptnr., 1968—; lectr. legal problems in banking and in venture capital investments Practising Law Inst. Mem. Pilgrims of U.S., English Speaking Union, Internat. Bar Assn., ABA, N.Y. State Bar Assn. (chmn. health law com. 1986—), Assn. Bar City N.Y. Republican. Clubs: Union, Down Town Assn. Office: Carter Ledyard & Milburn 2 Wall St New York NY 10005

GREY, BERYL ELIZABETH, prima ballerina, ballet director/producer; b. London, June 11, 1927; d. Arthur Ernest and Annie Elizabeth (Marshall) G.; m. Sven Gustav Svenson, July 15, 1950; 1 child, Inguar Neil. Student Dame Alice Owens Girl's Sch., London. Profl. tng. Madeline Sharp Sch., Sadler's Wells Sch. (Scholar) de Vos. Sch. Debut Sadler's Wells Co., 1941, with ballerina roles following same year in Les Sylphides, The Gods Go A'Begging, Le Lac des Cygnes, Act II, Comus. First full-length ballet, Le Lac des Cygnes on 15th birthday, 1942. Prima ballerina Sadler's Wells Ballet, then Royal Ballet, 1942-57; artistic dir. London Festival Ballet, 1968-79. Appeared in leading roles of many ballets including: Sleeping Beauty, Giselle, Sylvia, Checkmate, Ballet Imperial, Donald of the Burthens, Homage, Birthday Offering, The Lady and the Fool. Film: The Black Swan (3 dimensional ballet film), 1952. Left Royal Ballet, Covenent Garden, Spring 1957, to become free-lance ballerina. Regular guest appearances with Royal Ballet at Covenant Garden and on European, African, American and Far Eastern Tours. Guest artist, London's Festival Ballet in London and abroad, 1958-64. First Western ballerina to appear with Bolshoi Ballet, Moscow, Leningrad, Kiev, Tiflis, 1957-58; First Western ballerina to dance with Chinese Ballet Co., in Peking and Shanghai, 1964. Engagements and tours abroad include: Central and S. America, Mexico, Rhodesia, South Africa, Canada, N.Z., Lebanon, Germany, Norway, Sweden, Denmark, Finland, Belgium, Holland, France, Switzerland, Italy, Portugal, Austria, Czechoslovakia, Poland, Rumania. Regular TV and broadcasts in England and abroad. Named Dame Comdr. of the British Empire, 1988. Dir. Gen. Arts Ednl. Trust, 1966-68; trustee London City Ballet, Adeline Genee Theatre. Mem. Council Imperial Soc. of Tchrs. of Dancing (chmn.), Royal Acad. of Dancing (exec. council, v.p.), Dance Council of Wales (pres.), London Coll. of Dance and Drama (vice chmn.), Royal Ballet Benevolent Fund (trustee), Dance Tchrs. Benevolent Fund (vice chmn., trustee), D.Music (hon.), Leicester U., 1971, Brit. Fedn. Music Festivals (v.p.), Keep Fit Soc.; D.Letters (hon.), City of London, C.B.E. Author: Red Curtain Up, 1958; the Bamboo Curtain, 1965; editor: My Favorite Ballet Stories, 1981. Biographical studies (by Gordon Anthony), 1952, (by Pigeon Crowle), 1952; Beryl Grey Dancers of Today (Hugh Fisher), 1955; Beryl Grey; a biography (David Gillard), 1977. Club: Royal Yacht (London). Avocations: swimming; walking; playing piano; painting.

GRIBBLE, CHARLES EDWARD, editor, educator; b. Lansing, Mich., Nov. 10, 1936; s. Charles P. and Elizabeth K. Gribble; B.A., U. Mich., 1957; A.M., Harvard U., 1958, Ph.D., 1967; postgrad. Moscow State U., 1960-61. Instr., asst. prof. Russian, Brandeis U., Waltham, Mass., 1961-68; asst. prof. Slavic langs. Ind. U., Bloomington, 1968-75; asso. prof. Slavic langs. Ohio State U., Columbus, 1975—; pres., editor Slavica Pubs., Inc., Columbus, 1966—; vis. asso. prof. Slavic langs. U. Va., 1977. Woodrow Wilson fellow, 1957-58; Am. Council Learned Socs. fellow, 1972; Internat. Research and Exchanges Bd. grantee, 1960-61, 72, 80. Mem. Am. Assn. Advancement of Slavic Studies, Am. Assn. Tchrs. of Slavic and E. European Langs., Linguistic Soc. Am., MLA, Linguistic Soc. Europe, Am. Assn. S.E. European Studies, Phi Beta Kappa. Author: Russian Root List, 1973; A Short Dictionary of 18th-Century Russian, 1976; editor-in-chief Folia Slavica, 1977—; editor: Studies Presented to Professor Roman Jakobson by His Students, 1968; Medieval Slavic Texts, Vol. 1, 1973; contbr. articles to scholarly jours. Office: PO Box 14388 Columbus OH 43214

GRIBOW, DALE SEWARD, lawyer, business executive; b. Chgo., June 18, 1943; s. Obby and Norma (Howard) G. B.A., U. So. Calif., 1965; J.D., Loyola U., Los Angeles, 1968; advanced legal studies UCLA, U. So. Calif. Bar: Calif. 1970. U.S. Dist. Ct. (cen. dist.) Calif. 1970, U.S. Supreme Ct. 1977. Dep. public defender Los Angeles County, 1970-74; sr. partner Gribow, Benjamin & Sandler, Beverly Hills, Calif., 1974-76; sole practice, Beverly Hills, 1976—; pres., chmn. bd. Nutritional Biol. Corp., Los Angeles, 1981-83; owner Exec. Credit Control, Inc., Los Angeles, 1979-83, DDM Properties, Los Angeles, 1981-86; judge pro tem Los Angeles Mcpl. Ct., 1977—, Van Nuys, West Los Angeles, Beverly Hills mcpl. cts., 1983—; dir. Aspen mktg.; mem. adv. bd. Dist. Atty. Los Angeles, 1976-78; city Atty. Los Angeles, 1980-83; guest lectr. univs. Contbr. articles to profl. jours. Mem. U.S. Congressional Adv. Bd., 1982-83; selected 1982 fund raising chmn. Loyola Law Sch. Alumni; founder Concerned Adults for Dubnoff Sch., a sch. for handicapped children, 1972, pres., 1974-77, 80-81, bd. dirs., 1974-83; bd. dirs. Thalians, 1975—, exec. bd., 1983—, exec. v.p., 1984—, vice chmn., 1988—, program chmn., 1983-84, mem. exec. com. Presidents Club, 1980—, chmn. Thalian Ball, 1987, 88; bd. dirs. Guardians Jewish Home for Aged, 1981—, v.p., 1983-84, chmn. spl. events, 1983; bd. dirs. Westside chpt. Kidney Found., West Side Symphony Assn., 1982-84, Ctr. for Improvement Child Caring, 1983-85, Dubnoff Ctr. for Handicapped Children, 1974-85, Boys and Girls Club Los Angeles, 1982-85, founder, chmn. bd. Beverly Hills Men's Charities, 1981—, Scopus Soc., 1983—; founding mem. Children's Liver Transplant Found., 1983-84; contbg. mem. City of Hope, Nat. Jewish Hosp. and Research Center, St. Jude's Hosp., Simon Weisenthal Center for Holocaust Studies, Patrons Art Soc., Greater Los Angeles Zoo Assn., Los Angeles County Mus., Natural History Mus., Earl Warren Inst., Los Angeles World Affairs Council, Mcpl. League Beverly Hills, Am. Film Inst., Commerce Assocs. of U. So. Calif., West Los Angeles Boosters Assn.; v.p. Am. Friends Hebrew U., 1985—; trustee U. Judaism Continuing Edn., 1984-86. Recipient David Schloss Meml. award, 1974; plaque City of Los Angeles, 1977, 80, 82; named hon. Ky. Col., 1981; commendation from Gov. Jerry Brown, 1982; resolution Calif. State Assembly and Senate, 1982; award for service Ronald McDonald House for Childrens Cancer, 1984; numerous other commendations and proclamations; Dale Seward Gribow Day proclaimed in Beverly Hills, 1982, 88; Dale Seward Gribow Day declared in Los Angeles, 1988. Mem. Los Angeles Jaycees, U. So. Calif. Law Alumni, State Bar Calif., Los Angeles County Bar Assn. (cert. of appreciation 1984), Beverly Hills Bar Assn. (cert. of appreciation 1984), West Hollywood Bar Assn., San Fernando Valley Bar Assn., Calif. Trial Lawyers Assn., Los Angeles Trial Lawyers Assn., Los Angeles Criminal Cts. Bar Assn., Calif. Attys. for Criminal Justice, San Fernando Valley Criminal Cts. Bar Assn., Scopus Soc. (dir. 1983—, chmn. 1986—), Vikings, Blue Key, Phi Alpha Delta. Democrat. Jewish. Clubs: Friars (membership com.), Variety (dir. 1982-85), Magic Castle, Marbles (dir.), PIPS (v.p., dir. 1982—), J. Daniels. Lodge: B'nai B'rith. Office: 9777 Wilshire Blvd Suite 918 Beverly Hills CA 90212

GRIDLEY, DAILA SEFERS, microbiologist, immunologist; b. Riga, Latvia, Jan. 16, 1944; came to U.S., 1949, naturalized, 1954; d. Videvuds and Marta (Snikers) Sefers; B.S., U. Oreg., 1966, M.S., 1971; Ph.D., Loma Linda U., 1978; m. Larry Brown Gridley, Mar. 9, 1968; children—Laila and Laura (twins), Lisa. Med. technologist U. Oreg., 1966-69; sr. med. technologist Loma Linda (Calif.) Med. Center, 1971-74; researcher assoc. Loma Linda U., 1978-81, asst. prof. microbiology, 1981—, asst. prof. radiation sci., 1983—; lectr. in field; lectr. Calif. Poly. U., 1982-84. Recipient Pres.'s award, Loma Linda U., 1978; Clinton Reed Brower scholar, 1978; Oreg. State scholar, 1962; Elsa U. Pardee Found. co-investigator, 1979-81, Nat. Dairy Council co-investigator, 1979-81; Cancer Research Soc. co-prin. investigator, 1987-88. Mem. N.Y. Acad. Scis., Am. Soc. Clin. Pathology, Am. Soc. Microbiology, Nat. Registry Microbiologists, Internat. Interferon Research Soc., AAAS, Sigma Xi (sec. Loma Linda U. chpt. 1984-86, pres. 1986-88), Delta Gamma. Republican. Lutheran. Club: Mothers of Twins, Casa Colina. Contbr. articles to profl. jours. Home: 784 Hillcrest Dr Pomona CA 91768 Office: Loma Linda U Sch Medicine Dept Microbiology Loma Linda CA 92350

GRIEBEL, DIETER, shipping company executive; b. Hamburg, Fed. Republic Germany, Dec. 16, 1933; s. Karl Friedrich Wilhelm and Hertha (Schluchtmann) G.; m. Ingrid Funke, Feb. 20, 1960; children: Andrea, Manuela, Cornelia. Shipbroker apprentice Montan Transpost Gesellschaft, Hamburg, 1951-54, chartering and agy. clk., 1954-55; asst. to ptnrs., mgr. deepsea-chartering dept. D. Oltmann, Bremen, Fed. Republic Germany, 1955-69; head mgr. sea-transport div. chartering, forwarding and agy. Winschermann Transport Gesellschaft, Hamburg, 1969-75; mng. dir. World Trade Chartering (Germany) GmbH, Hamburg, 1975-78; mng. dir., ptnr. Seaway Transport GmbH, Bremen, 1979-81; mng. dir. Schiffahrtskontor Telamar GmbH, Bremen and Hamburg, 1980-86; sole mng. dir. Multi Transport Internat. GmbH, Hamburg and Bremen, 1986—; part-time lectr. German High Sch. for Traffic and Fgn. Trade, Bremen, 1965-66; part-time lectr. in field; vis. prof. World Maritime U., Malmö; approved shipping cons. Internat. Maritime Orgn. Mem. London Maritime Arbitrators Assn. (supporting mem.'s com.), German Maritime Arbitration Assn., Com. Maritime Internat. (German group). Lodge: Zum Silbernen Schlüssel. Home: Koelner Strasse 34, D-2800 Bremen 41 Federal Republic of Germany Office: Multi Transport Internat, Amsinckstrasse 39, D-2000 Hamburg 1 Federal Republic of Germany

GRIER, BARBARA G. (GENE DAMON), editor, lecturer, author; b. Cin., Nov. 4, 1933; d. Phillip Strang and Dorothy Vernon (Black) Grier; grad. high sch. Author: The Lesbian in Literature, 1967, (with others) 2d edit., 1975, 3d edit., 1981; The Least of These (in Sisterhood is Powerful), 1970; The Index, 1974; Lesbiana, 1976; The Lesbian Home Jour., 1976; The Lavender Herring, 1976; Lesbian Lives, 1976; pub. The Ladder mag., 1970-72, fiction and poetry editor, 1966-67, editor, 1968-72; dir. promotion Naiad Press, Reno, Nev., 1973—, treas., 1976—, v.p., gen. mgr., Tallahassee, Fla., 1980—. Democrat. Home: Rt 1 Box 3319 Havana FL 32333 Office: Naiad Press Inc PO Box 10543 Tallahassee FL 32302

GRIES, JOHN PAUL, geologist; b. Washington, June 7, 1911; s. John Matthew and Ethel Martha (Goff) G.; m. Virginia Overbeck, July 5, 1933; children—John Charles, Donald Alan. A.B., Miami U., Ohio, 1932; M.S., U. Chgo., 1933, Ph.D., 1935. Geologist Ill. Geol. Survey, 1935-36; from instr. to asst. prof. geology S.D. Sch. Mines and Tech., Rapid City, 1936-44; from asso. prof. to prof. 1946—, dir. grad. studies, 1951-66, dean grad. div., 1966-76; geologist Magnolia Petroleum Co., Midland, Tex., 1944-46; now geol. cons. in groundwater, engring. geology non-metallics, mineral fuels. Participant Am. Geol. Inst., Internat. Field Inst., Paris Basin, summer 1965. Contbr. articles to profl. jours. Inducted S.D. Hall of Fame, 1986. Mem. Geol. Soc. Am., Am. Inst. Mining, Metall. and Petroleum Engrs., Am. Assn. Petroleum Geologists, Paleontol. Soc., Rapid City Astron. Soc., Sigma Xi, Sigma Tau. Club: Rotary. Home: 238 St Charles St Rapid City SD 57701

GRIESSMAN, BENJAMIN EUGENE, social scientist, author; b. Spartanburg, S.C., Aug. 12, 1934; B.A., Tenn. Temple Coll., 1956; M.A., Baylor U., 1958; M.Div., New Orleans Bapt. Theol. Sem., 1962; Ph.D., La. State U., 1966. Asst. prof. N.C. State U., 1966-68, asso. prof., 1968-70, prof. Auburn U., 1970-82; head dept. sociology and anthropology, 1970-79; dir. nat. media relations, Georgia Inst. Tech., 1982-88,dir. communication and devel., adj. prof. coll. mgmt. ; lectr. Coll. William and Mary, summer 1965; producer TV programs Option, Up Close; prod. spls. WTBS-TV, Ala. Pub. TV, Ga. ETV. Contbr. articles in field. Fellow Am. Anthrop. Assn.; mem. So. Sociol. Soc., Alpha Kappa Delta (pres. chpt. 1957), Phi Kappa Phi. Author: Vocational Education in Rural Areas, 1969; contbg. author: Minorities: A Text With Readings in Intergroup Relations, 1975; co-editor: The Southern Mystique, 1977; Technology, Human Values, and the Southern Future, 1977; Images and Memories: Georgia Tech 1885-1985, The Achievement Factors, 1987; Contbr. articles to newspapers and profl. jours. including USA Today, N.Y. Times. Home: 505-1421 Peachtree St NE Atlanta GA 30309 Office: Georgia Inst Tech Coll Mgmt Atlanta GA 30332

GRIFFIN, BETTY JO ANN, goldsmith, conservator, consultant; b. Dallas, Sept. 22, 1935; d. James Frederick and Mary Audrey (West) G. B.B.A., So. Meth. U., 1957. Prodn. asst. Neiman-Marcus, Dallas, 1957-59; advt. dir. Ramsey Winch Mfg. Co., Tulsa, 1959-60; prodn. mgr. Bloom Advt. Co., Dallas, 1960-61; advt. dir. Swest, Inc., Dallas, 1965; self-employed goldsmith/conservator, Dallas, 1965—; objects conservator Dallas Mus. Art, 1976—; tchr. ptnr. Argent Jewelers Inst., Dallas, 1971—; tech. cons. Museo del Oro, Bogota, Colombia, S.Am., 1977—; presenter 45th Congress Americanists, Bogota, Colombia, 1985. Recipient Gold award Dallas Mus. Art, 1963; 1st award jewelry 18th Nat. Decorative Arts Exhibition, Wichita, Kans., 1964; Diamonds Today awards DeBeers-Diamond Info. Ctr., 1973, 74. Mem. Tex. Designer Craftsman, Am. Inst. Conservators, S.W. Assn. Conservators. Republican. Presbyterian. Home: 6206 Vanderbilt Ave Dallas TX 75214 Office: Dallas Mus Art 1717 N Harwood St Dallas TX 75201

GRIFFIN, DEWITT JAMES, architect; b. Los Angeles, Aug. 26, 1914; s. DeWitt Clinton and Ada Gay (Miller) G.; m. Jeanmarie Donald, Aug. 19, 1940; children: Barbara Jean Griffin Holst, John Donald, Cornelia Caulfield Claudius, James DeWitt. Student, UCLA, 1936-38; B.A., U. Calif., 1942. Designer Kaiser Engrs., Richmond, Calif., 1941; architect CF Braun & Co., Alhambra, Calif., 1946-48; pvt. practice architecture Pasadena, Calif., 1948-50; prin. Goudie & Griffin Architects, San Jose, Calif., 1949-64, Griffin & Murray, 1964-66, DeWitt J. Griffin & Assocs., 1966-69; pres. Griffin/Joyce Assocs., Architects, 1969-80; chmn. Griffin Balzhiser Affiliates (Architects), 1974-80; founder, pres. Griffin Cos., 1980—; founder, dir. San Jose Savs. and Loan Assn., 1965-75, Capitol Services Co., 1964-77, Esandel Corp., 1965-77. Pub. Sea Power mag, 1975-77; archtl. works include U.S. Post Office, San Jose, 1966, VA Hosp, Portland, 1976, Bn. Barracks Complex, Ft. Ord, Calif., 1978. bd. dirs. San Jose Symphony Assn., 1973-84, v.p. 1977-79, pres. 1979-81; active San Jose Symphony Found., 1981—, v.p. 1988—; bd. dirs. Coast Guard Acad. Found., 1974-87, Coast Guard Found., 1987—; founder, bd. dirs. U.S. Navy Meml. Found., 1978-80, trustee, 1980—; trustee Montalvo Ctr. for Arts, 1982-88. Served to comdr. USNR, 1942-46, 50-57. Recipient Navy Meritorious Pub. Service medal, 1971, Disting. Service medal Navy League of U.S., 1973; Coast Guard Meritorious Pub. Service award, 1975; Navy Distinguished Pub. Service award, 1977; Coast Guard Distinguished Pub. Service award, 1977. Fellow Soc. Am. Mil. Engrs.; emeritus mem. AIA; mem. U.S. Naval Inst., Navy League U.S. (pres. Santa Clara Valley council 1963-66, Calif. state pres. 1966-69, nat. dir. 1967—, exec. com. 1968—, pres. 12th region 1969-71, nat. v.p. 1973-75, nat. pres. 1975-77, chmn. 1977-79), U.S. Naval Sailing Assn., San Francisco C. of C., Naval Order of U.S., Phi Gamma Delta. Republican. Congregationalist. Clubs: St. Francis Yacht, Commonwealth of San Francisco. Home and Office: 17653 Tourney Rd Los Gatos CA 95030

GRIFFIN, GARY ARTHUR, technological executive; b. Yonkers, N.Y., Nov. 23, 1937; s. William Edmund and Madeline (Lane) G.; student Manhattan Coll., 1956-57, Westchester Community Coll., 1957-62; diploma LaSalle Extension U., 1968; m. Jacqueline Cahill, June 21, 1958; children: Lynn, Elizabeth, Margaret. Engring. cons. IBM Corp., Yorktown, N.Y., 1960-61; engring. cons. Perkin Elmer Corp., Norwalk, Conn., 1961-63; product devel. mgr. Technicon Corp., Tarrytown, N.Y., 1963-69; chmn., pres. Dynacon Research Corp., Rockland, N.Y., 1969-72; with Nat. Patent Devel. Corp., New Brunswick, N.J., 1973-82, corp. group v.p. new technologies, 1977-82, pres. Hydromed Scis. div., 1978-82, pres. NDP Dental Systems, Inc., 1979-82, pres. NPD Epic Systems, Inc., 1979-82, pres., dir. Amalgamated Fin. Services, Inc., 1979-82, v.p., dir. NPD Productos Mé dicos, S.A., 1979-82, Washburn Ltd., 1979-82; pres., dir. Applied Genetics, Inc., 1981-82; dir. FCS Industries, Inc., Flemington, N.J., 1982—, sr. v.p., 1982-87, treas., 1984-87; chmn. chief operating officer, pres. Circuitech Inc., Eatontown, N.J., 1982-85, now dir.; chmn., pres., treas. Executrex Internat. Inc., Milltown, N.J., 1985—. Served with USNR, 1954-62. Mem. Am. Prodn. and Inventory Control Soc., Am. Mgmt. Assn., IEEE, Am. Assn. Advancement of Med. Instrumentation, Am. Entrepreneurs Assn., Internat. Entrepreneurs Assn., Smithsonian Assos., N.Y. Vet. Police Assn. Republican. Roman Catholic. Patentee in field. Office: Executrex 440 S Main Milltown NJ 08850

GRIFFIN, GRAHAM BARRY, software development and sales company; b. Walkden, Lancashire, Eng., Mar. 7, 1945; s. Alfred and Edna (Berry) G.; m. Anne Marie Vacchiani, Apr. 1971 (div. 1981); 1 child, Nathalie. BSc in Chemistry, U. Salford, Eng., 1967; PhD in Electrochemistry, U. Manchester, Eng., 1971. Supply analyst Brit. Petroleum Co., London, 1970-75; researcher, sr. researcher Battelle Inst., Geneva, 1975-85; dir. Aprotech Appropriate Techs., Geneva, 1985-87; mng. dir. Aptechnologies, Geneva, 1987—; bd. dirs. Aprotec Ltd., Manchester, Eng. Contbr. articles to sci. jours. Office: Aptechnologies SA, 35 Route des Jeunes, 1227 Geneva Switzerland

GRIFFIN, JOHN HENRY, medical researcher; b. Seattle, June 26, 1943; s. John Henry and Lillian Louise (O'Connell) G.; m. Antonia Lastreto, 1965 (div. 1984); children—John, Deanna, Paul; m. Arlene LaPlante, 1985. B.S., U. Santa Clara, 1965; Ph.D., U. Calif.-Davis, 1969. Teaching asst. U. Calif., 1967-69; research fellow Harvard U. Med. Sch., 1969-71; guest worker NIH, 1971-73; on staff Service de Biochimie Centre d'Etudes Nucleaires, Saclay, France, 1973-74; asst. dept immunopathology Scripps Clinic and Research Found., La Jolla, Calif., 1974-75, assoc. depts. immunopathology and molecular immunology, 1975-80, assoc. mem. dept. immunology, 1980—; peer rev. com. NIH, 1979—. Contbr. articles to profl. jours. Treas. San Diego Assn. Gifted Children, 1978-81; active Pub. Sch. Cluster Com., University City, S.D., 1984-85; mem. adv. com. High Sch. Community, University City, 1979-82, 86—. Recipient Research Career Devel. award NIH, 1976-81. RCA physics scholar 1961-64; fellow NIH, 1966-69, 72-73, Helen Hay Whitney Found. 1969-72. Mem. Am. Chem. Soc., Am. Soc. Biol. Chemists, Am. Assn. Pathologists, Am. Assn. Immunologists, Internat. Soc. Thrombosis and Hemostasis, Am. Heart Assn., Sigma Xi, Alpha Sigma Nu, Phi Kappa Phi. Current work: Basic and clinical research on regulation of hemostasis and thrombosis. Subspecialties: Biochemistry (medicine); Hematology.

GRIFFIN, JOSEPH LAWRENCE, transportation executive; b. Utica, Miss., Sept. 5, 1951; s. Shallie, Jr., and Carrie B. (Lyle) G.; student U. Ill., 1969-71; cert. in transp. and traffic mgmt. Coll. Advanced Traffic, 1978; m. Rhonda Evans, July 28, 1970; children: Joel, Jerl, Rael, Marel. Supr. terminal ops. Consol. Rail Corp., Chgo., 1977-78, asst. terminal mgr., 1978-79; asst. terminal mgr. Pa. Truck Lines, Inc., Chgo., 1979-81; multimodal sales rep. Consol. Rail Corp., Chgo., 1981-83, multimodal sales mgr., Detroit, 1983-84, King of Prussia, Pa., 1984-85; pres. Griffin Transp. Services Inc., Chgo., 1985—; pres. Expert Freight, Inc., Chgo., 1985—; transp. cons., 1981—. Mem. Intermodal Operating Com., Am. Mgmt. Assn., Piggyback Assn. Chgo., Detroit Intermodal Assn., Kappa Alpha Psi. Home: 958 Central Park Flossmoor IL 60422 Office: 2000 W 43d St Chicago IL 60609

GRIFFIN, MARY FRANCES, retired library media consultant; b. Cross Hill, Laurens County, S.C., Aug. 24, 1925; d. James and Rosa Lee (Carter) G. AB, Benedict Coll., 1947; postgrad., S.C. State Coll., 1948-51, Atlanta U., 1953, Va. State Coll., 1961; MLS, Ind. U., 1957. Tchr.-librarian Johnston (S.C.) Tng. Sch., Edgefield County Sch. Dist., 1947-51; librarian Lee County Sch. Dist., Dennis High, Bishopville, S.C., 1951-52, Greenville County (S.C.) Sch. Dist., 1952-66; library cons. S.C. Dept. Edn., Columbia, 1966-87; vis. tchr. U. S.C., 1977. Recipient Cert. of Living the Legacy award Nat. Council Negro Women, 1980. Mem. ALA, Assn. Ednl. Communications and Tech. S.C., Assn. Curriculum Devel., AAUW (pres. Columbia br. 1978-80), Southeastern Library Assn. (sec. 1978-80), S.C. Library Assn. (sec. 1979), S.C. Assn. Sch. Librarians, Nat. Assn. State Ednl. and Media Personnel. Baptist. Home: PO Box 1652 Columbia SC 29202 Other: 1100 Skyland Dr Columbia SC 29210

GRIFFIN, WILLIAM JULIAN, II, manufacturing company executive; b. Indpls., Feb. 10, 1925; s. Frank Julian Cox and Mary (Williams) G.; student Butler U., 1942-43, The Citadel, 1943-44; grad. Ind. Bus. Coll., 1948; m. Mary Jane Noel, Apr. 24, 1953; children—William Julian III, Kevin L., Kirk E., Kerry J. Buyer. Griffin Realty Corp., 1946-47; prodn. mgr. Griffin Engring. Co., Worthington, Ind., 1949-51; sec.-treas., gen. mgr. Imperial Machinery & Tool Corp., Worthington, 1952-53; v.p., gen. mgr., dir. So. Ind. Machine Co., Inc., Worthington, 1954-60, pres., gen. mgr., dir. Griffin Engring. div., 1961—; pres., dir. GBF Dodge, Inc., Casa Grande, Ariz., 1964—; owner, mgr. Griffin Audit Service, 1965—. Bd. dirs. Hulen Meml. Youth Center. Served with AUS, 1943-46, 50. Mem. Am. Ordnance Assn., Am. Legion (past local comdr.), V.F.W., DAV. Mem. Disciples of Christ Ch. Mason (Shriner), Elk. Home: 208 Christian St Worthington IN 47471 Office: Southern Ind Machine Co Inc 3d & Williams Sts Worthington IN 47471 also: GBF Motors 841 Gila Bend Hwy Mesa Grande AZ 85222

GRIFFIN, WILLIAM THOMAS, lawyer; b. N.Y.C., Sept. 27, 1905; s. John and Alice (Doonan) G.; m. Joan Mannix, Jan. 10, 1934; children: Christine, William, Gabrielle, Peter. A.B. summa cum laude, Holy Cross Coll., 1927; LL.B. cum laude, Fordham U., 1930. Bar: N.Y. 1931. Practiced in N.Y.C; former v.p. law N.Y., New Haven and Hartford Ry. Co. Corp.; dir. New Eng. Transp. Co., Am. Trust Co.; dir., v.p., gen. counsel Roper Realization Co., Inc., John L. Roper Lumber Co., Norfolk So. Land Co.; dir., v.p., atty. Providence Produce Warehouse Co. Mem. Am., Fed., Richmond County bar assns., Am. Judicature Soc., Nat. Lawyers Club, N.Y. Law Inst., N.Y. County Lawyers Assn., Assn. ICC Practitioners, Internat. Assn. Barristers. Clubs: New York Athletic (N.Y.C.); Quinipiack (New Haven); Richmond County Country (S.I., N.Y.); Princess Anne Country (Virginia Beach, Va.). Home and Office: 37 Howard Ave Grymes Hill NY 10301

GRIFFITH, EMLYN IRVING, lawyer; b. Utica, N.Y., May 13, 1923; s. William A. and Maud A. (Charles) G.; m. Mary L. Kilpatrick, Aug. 13, 1946; children: William L., James R. AB, Colgate U., 1942; JD, Cornell U., 1950; also hon. degrees. Bar: N.Y. 1950, U.S. Supreme Ct. 1954. Gen. practice Lockport, N.Y., 1950-52, Rome, N.Y., 1952—; bd. dirs. various corporations. Contbr. articles on law and edn. to profl. jours. in U.S. and Eng. Mem. N.Y. State Bd. Regents, 1973—, Gov.'s Com. on Libraries, 1976-78, State Conf. on Professions, 1974-77, Forum of Edn. Orgn. Leaders, 1978-80, Intergovtl. Adv. Council on Edn., 1982-86; del. to China U.S. Joint Session on Trade and Law, Beijing, 1987, Soviet-Am. seminar Comparative Edn., Mowcow, 1988; trustee Aerospace Edn. Found., 1979—, Phi Gamma Delta Edn. Found., 1986—; v.p. Hon. Soc. Cymmrodorion, London; pres. Nat. Assn. State Bds. Edn., 1979-80, Nat. Welsh-Am. Found., 1982-84; mem. exec. com. Bd. Pensions United Presbyn. Ch., 1966-72. Served to maj. U.S. Army, 1942-46. Recipient Alumni Disting. Service award Colgate U., 1975, Exceptional Service citation Air Force Assn., 1980. Fellow Am. Bar Found., N.Y. State Bar Found. (recipient Root-Stimson award for pub. service 1986); mem. ABA (com. pub. edn. 1975—), N.Y. State Bar Assn. (ho. of dels. 1974-76, com. lawyer competency 1986—, mem. bd. editors Bar Jour. 1986—), Oneida County Bar Assn. (pres. 1974-75), State Conf. County

Bar Officers (chmn. 1975-76). Clubs: Rome, Fort Orange of Albany, Colgate of N.Y.C. Office: Griffith & Engelbrecht 225 N Washington St Rome NY 13440

GRIFFITH, JERRY DICE, government administrator, nuclear engineer; b. Sturgis, Mich., Sept. 8, 1933; s. Levi Robert and Vivian Marie (LeVeck) G.; m. Gloria Louise Hessie, June 25, 1965; children—Jennifer Lynn, Bradley Jerome. B.S. summa cum laude, Mich. State U., 1955, M.S., 1957; M.E., Calif. Inst. Tech., 1959; P.F.P.A., Princeton U., 1967. Dir. nuclear safety C.E., U.S. Army, Washington, 1967-72; chief research and devel. br. AEC and ERDA, Washington, 1972-76; asst. dir. for reactor safety Dept. Energy, Washington, 1976-79, dir. div. nuclear power devel., 1979-80, dir. office light water reactors, 1980-85, assoc. dept. asst. sec. reactor systems devel. and tech., 1985—. U.S. rep. to com. for safety nuclear installations OECD Nuclear Energy Agy., Paris, 1976-86. Contbr. articles to profl. jours., 1967—. Patentee inherent reactor control concept, small reaction turbine. Served to capt. U.S. Army, 1959-62. Recipient Meritorious Civilian Service award U.S. Army, 1970; Congl. fellow, 1969. Mem. Am. Nuclear soc. Home: 14711 Bauer Dr Rockville MD 20853 Office: Dept Energy NE10 Washington DC 20545

GRIFFITH, MELVIN EUGENE, entomologist, public health official; b. Lawrence, Kans., Mar. 24, 1912; s. George Thomas and Estella (Shaw) G.; m. Pauline Sophia Bogart, June 23, 1941. AB, U. Kans., 1934, AM, 1935, PhD, 1938; postgrad., U. Mich., summers 1937-40. Instr. zoology N.D. Agrl. Coll., Fargo, 1938-39, asst. prof., 1939-41, assoc. prof., 1941-42; commd. officer USPHS, 1943-71, malaria control entomologist dept. health State of Okla., 1943-51, chief, malaria adviser ICA, Bangkok, Thailand, 1951-60, assoc. dir. Malaria Eradication Tng. Ctr., Kingston, Jamaica, 1960, regional malaria advisor SE Asia, AID, New Delhi, 1960-62, Near East and So. Asia, 1962-64, dep. chief malaria eradication br., Washington, 1964-67, chief, 1967-71, ret. as capt., 1971; assoc. prof. zool. scis. U. Okla., Norman, 1946-52, prof., 1952-56; cons. Office of Health, AID, Washington, 1971-75. Contbr. articles and monographs on entomology, malaria control and pub. health. Recipient citation for disting. service U. Kans., 1962. Mem. Am. Pub. Health Assn., Am. Soc. Tropical Medicine and Hygiene, Am. Soc. Limnology and Oceanography, Entomol. Soc. Am., Explorers Club, N.Y. Acad. Scis., Siam Soc., Phi Beta Kappa, Sigma Xi. Address: PO Box DG Williamsburg VA 23187

GRIFFITH, ROBERT CHARLES, allergist; b. Shreveport, La., Jan. 9, 1939; s. Charles Parsons and Madelon (Jenkins) G.; m. Loretta Dean Secrist, July 15, 1969; children—Charles Randall, Cameron Stuart, Ann Marie. B.S., Centenary Coll., 1961; M.D., La. State U., 1965. Intern, Confederate Meml. Med. Ctr., Shreveport, 1965-66, resident in internal medicine, 1966-68; fellow in allergy and chest disease, instr. Va. Med. Sch. Hosp., Charlottesville, 1968-70; practice medicine specializing in allergies, Alexandria, La., 1970-72, The Allergy Clinic, Shreveport, 1972; pres. Griffith Allergy Clinic, Shreveport, 1973—; faculty internal medicine La. State U., 1972—. Bd. dirs. Caddo-Bossier Assn. Retarded Citizens, 1977-84, Access (fomerly Child Devel. Ctr.), Shreveport, 1979-85; mem. med. adv. com., spl. edn. adv. com. Caddo Parish Sch. Bd., 1977—; mem. commission on missions and social concerns First Methodist Ch., 1981-84, mem. adminstrv. bd., 1981-84; mem. med. panel for transfer Caddo Parish Sch. Bd., 1974—. Served to maj. M.C., U.S. Army, 1965-71. Recipient Physician of the Yr. award Shreveport-Bossier Med. Assts., 1984. Fellow Am. Coll. Allergy and Immunology, Am. Thoracic Soc. (assoc.); mem. Am. Acad. Allergy, Am. Coll. Chest Physicians, AMA, So. Med. Assn., La. Med. Soc., Shreveport Med. Soc. (allergy spokesman 1984—), La. Allergy Soc. (charter; past pres.), U. Va. Med. Alumni Assn., La. State U. Med. Alumni Assn., SCV, Mil. Order Stars and Bars, Shreveport C. of C. Methodist. Lodges: Masons, Jesters. Clubs: Shreveport Country, Ambassadors, Cotillion, Royal, Plantation. Home: 7112 E Ridge Dr Shreveport LA 71106 Office: 2751 Virginia Ave Shreveport LA 71103

GRIFFITH, STEVEN FRANKLIN, SR., lawyer, real estate title insurance agent and investor; b. New Orleans, July 14, 1948; s. Hugh Franklin and Rose Marie (Teutone) G.; m. Mary Elizabeth McMillan Frank, Dec. 9, 1972; children—Steven Franklin Jr., Jason Franklin. B.B.A., Loyola U. of the South, 1970, J.D., 1972. Bar: La. 1972, U.S. Dist. Ct. (ea. dist.) La. 1975, U.S. Ct. Appeals (5th cir.) 1975, U.S. Supreme Ct. bar 1976. Law offices Senator George T. Oubre, Norco, La., 1971-75, sole practice, Destrehan, La., 1975—. Served to 1st lt. U.S. Army, 1970-72. Mem. ABA, La. Bar Assn., Assn. Trial Lawyers Am., La. Trial Lawyers Assn., New Orleans Trial Lawyers Assn., Fed. Bar Assn. Democrat. Club: Lions. Office: 9001 River Rd Destrehan LA 70047

GRIFFITH, WINSTON HENRY, Guyana goverment official; b. Guyana, Oct. 10, 1931; s. George and Patricia Griffith; student North Western Poly., 1966-68; diploma in public adminstrn. U. Guyana, 1972; m. Unaleen Munroe, July 30, 1960; children—Beverly, Bernard, June. Supr., S. Davson & Co., Guyana, 1952-53; with Transp. and Harbours Dept., 1953—, gen. mgr., 1970—; dir. Guyana Transp. Services, 1972-78, W.I. Shipping Corp., 1976—, Guyana Nat. Shipping Corp.; adv. Ministry Transp. Recipient Golden Arrow of Achievement award, Govt. of Guyana, 1986. Mem. Chartered Inst. Transport; assoc. mem. Am. Assn. Port Authority. Presbyterian. Clubs: Transp. and Harbours Dept. Sports (pres. 1971), Demerara Cricket, Guyana Cricket. Home: 417 Cane View Ave STH, Ruimveldt Gardens Guyana Office: Transp and Harbours Dept, Battery Rd, Kingston Guyana

GRIFFITHS, DAVID ANTHONY, surgeon, consultant; b. Newport, Gwent, U.K., Aug. 2, 1940; s. David and Lily Doreen (Bateman) G.; m. Denise Rosemary, Dec. 29, 1965; children—James Alexander, Richard David. B.S., Med. U., Bristol, U.K., 1962, B.Medicine and Surgery, 1965, M.D., 1970. Vis. prof. U. Medicine, Iowa City, 1967-69; surg. tutor Oxford U., U.K., 1971-73; sr. house officer Bristol Hosp., U.K., 1969-71, sr. registrar, 1973-76; surgeon, cons. Somerset Authority, Yeovil, 1976—; pres. Ileostomy Assn., Somerset, 1978—; treas. Southwest Surgeons, Eng., 1985—. Contbr. articles to profl. jours. Hon. fellow U. Bologna, 1980. Fellow Brit. Gastroent. Soc., Brit. Assn. Urologists, Royal Coll. Surgeons of Scotland and Eng.; mem. Anatomical Soc. Methodist. Clubs: Sailing (Dorset); Sailing (vice commodore 1980) (Yeovil). Avocations: sailing; sculpture. Office: Yeovil Dist Hosp, Higher Kingston, Yeovil, Somerset BA 21 4AT, England

GRIFFITHS, DEREK JOHN, physics educator; b. London, July 3, 1938; s. Sir Reginald and Jessica Lilian (Broad) G.; m. Mary Buckett, 1967; children: Jane, David. BA, Cambridge U., 1960; PhD, U. St. Andrews, Scotland, 1964. Research assoc. Stanford U., Calif., 1963-65; lectr. Exeter U., Eng., 1965-78; sr. lectr. Erasmus U., Rotterdam, Netherlands, 1978-88; prof. U. Alberta, Edmonton, Canada, 1988—. Author: Urodynamics, 1980; contbr. articles to profl. jours. Royal Soc. fellow, Netherlands, 1977. Mem. Internat. Continence Soc., Internat. Soc. for Dynamics of Upper Urinary Tract, Biol. Engring. Soc. Office: Edmonton Gen Hosp, Div Geriatric Medicine, Edmonton, AB Canada

GRIFFITHS, MICHAEL THOMAS, holding company executive; b. Preston, Eng., July 28, 1947; s. Cedric William Thomas and Joan (Large) G.; m. Karen Cecilia Price, Nov. 14, 1970; children: Tanya, Sam, Max, Lisa. BA in Indsl. Econs., Nottingham (Eng.) U., 1969. Chartered acct., Eng., Wales. Tax supr. Arthur Anderson and Co., Manchester, Eng., 1969-76; chmn. Ace Protective Wear Ltd., Bolton, Eng., 1976-82; group chmn. Mikar Holdings Ltd., Bolton, Eng., 1982—. Dist. commr. Boy Scouts Assn. Greater Manchester 1983-87; gov. Bolton Sch., 1986. Fellow Inst. Chartered Accts. Eng. and Wales; mem. Manchester Soc. Chartered Accts. (Lloyd Piggott Acctg. prize 1973), Old Boltonians Assn. (sec. 1980-87).

GRIFFITHS, WILLIAM PERRY, artist, art educator; b. Traverse City, Mich., Sept. 20, 1937; s. Bonner Perry and Juanita Ellen (Weese) G.; m. Susan M. Boelhower, Sept. 20, 1981; children from previous marriage: William Perry III, Tara Andrea. BS in Art Edn., Western Mich. U., 1961; postgrad., Mich. State U., 1964; MFA, U. Wis., 1968. Tchr. art Flint (Mich.) Pub. Schs., 1961-66; teaching asst. U. Wis., Madison, 1967-68, lectr., 1968; asst. prof. art U. Wis., Fond du Lac, 1968—. Exhibited in group show at Smithsonion Instn., 1968; represented in permanent collection Am. Craft Mus., N.Y.C., 1969, also pvt. collections; included in book Objects USA by Lee Nordness, 1970. Home: 67 N Lincoln Ave Fond du Lac WI 54935 Office: U Wisconsin Ctr Campus Dr Fond du Lac WI 54935

GRIGGS, JILL, data processing executive; b. Mtarfa, Malta, Aug. 19, 1952; arrived to Eng., 1954; d. Arthur William and Barbara (Linter) G. BSc in Computation with honors, U. Manchester (Eng.) Inst. Sci. & Tech., 1973. Coordinator Nat. Computing Centre, Manchester, 1973-77; with Ferranti Computer Systems Ltd., Manchester, 1977-82, market strategist, 1982—. Club: Stockport Harriers (mem. mgmt. com. 1985—). Office: Ferranti Computer Systems Ltd, Simonsway Wythenshawe, Manchester M22 5LA, England

GRIGOROVICH, YURIY NIKOLAYEVICH, choreographer; b. Leningrad, USSR, Jan. 2, 1927; s. Nikolai Eugenievich and Claudia Alfredovna (Rosai) G.; m. Natalia Igorevna Bessmertnova, Aug. 30, 1968. Grad., Kirov Ballet Sch., Leningrad, 1946, Nat. Inst. for Performing Arts, Moscow, 1959. Dancer Kirov Ballet, Leningrad, 1946-64, choreographer, 1962-64; chief choreographer Bolshoi Ballet, Moscow, 1964—; prof. Leningrad Conservatory, Leningrad, 1975—; pres. dance com. Internat. Theatre Inst. UNESCO, Paris, 1973—. choreographer ballets by Bolshoi Company staged in Moscow Stone Flower, 1959, Legend of Love, 1965, Nutcracker Suite, 1966, Spartacus, 1968, Swan Lake, 1969, Sleeping Beauty, 1963, 1973, Ivan the Terrible, 1975, Angara, 1976, Romeo and Juliet, 1979, Golden Age, 1982, Raymonda, 1984; staged ballets in Leningrad, Novosibirsk, Baku, and Tallin in USSR, also Stockholm, Prague, Czechoslovakia, Sofia, Bulgaria, Vienna, Austria, Rome, Paris, Copenhagen, and Ankara, Turkey; editor-in-chief Soviet Ballet Encyclopedia; contbr. articles to profl. jours. Decorated Order of Lenin, 1976, Hero of Socialist Labor, 1987; recipient Lenin prize, 1970, State prize, 1977; named People's Artist of USSR, 1973. Mem. USSR Theatre Union. Home: 6 Sretensky Blvd, Moscow USSR Office: USSR Bolshoi Theatre, 2 Sverdlov Sq, Moscow USSR

GRIM, ALFONS JOSEPH VICTOR, advertising executive, consultant; b. Heerlen, Limburg, The Netherlands, Dec. 3, 1935; s. Jean Henri and Elizabeth (Veugen) G.; divorced; children: Rudolf, Catharina, Adriana. Dir. G. Arnold Teesing BV, Amsterdam, The Netherlands, 1976-77, chief exec. officer, 1977—. Mem. Internat. Advt. Assn., Internat. Pubs. Advt. Reps. Assn. (sec.). Home: Drusushof 4, 6215 EG Maastricht The Netherlands Office: G Arnold Teesing BV, Prof Tulpstraat 17, 1018 GZ Amsterdam The Netherlands

GRIMANIS, APOSTOLOS PAUL, nuclear chemist; b. Mytilene, Lesbos, Greece, Mar. 16, 1926; d. Peter and Maritsika (Goutos) Spanos G.; m. Maria Vassilaki, Sept. 22, 1964; children: Peter, Georgina-Myrsini. BSc with honors, U. Athens, 1952, PhD in Radiochemistry, 1965; cert., Sch. Radioisotopes Greek Atomic Engergy Commn., 1957, Inst. Nuclear Studies, Oak Ridge, Tenn., 1959. Head analytical lab. Greek Industry Powder and Cartridges, Athens, 1952-57; fellow Oak Ridge Inst. Nuclear Studies and Oak Ridge Nat. Lab., 1958-59; research chemist Nuclear Research Ctr. Demokritos, Athens, 1960-61; research fellow Oak Ridge Nat. Lab., 1961-62; head radioanalytical lab. Nuclear Research Ctr. Demokritos, Athens, 1963—; mem. Intergovtl. Oceanographic Commn. UNESCO, Paris, 1977, Office Sci. Dir. Greek Atomic Energy Commn., 1978-81, standing Com. Internat. Symposium for Archaeometry, 1984—. Contbr. articles to profl. jours. Research grantee Internat. Atomic Energy Agy., Vienna, 1969-72, 73-75, 86—, FAO/UN Environ. Program, Rome, 1977-80, European Econ. Community, Brussels, 1983-85; recipient Royal Golden Cross, Phoenix Bn., 1963. Mem. Internat. Com. Modern Trends in Activation Analysis, European Nuclear Soc., Hellenic Nuclear Soc., Hellenic Assn. Chemists, Hellenic Assn. Environ. Polution. Served with Greek Navy, 1947-49. Home: 6 Vournazole Str, Ampelokipi 11521, Athens Greece Office: Greek AEC Nuclear Research Ctr, Demokritos, Aghia Paraskevi Attikis, Athens Greece

GRIMES, HUGH GAVIN, physician; b. Chgo., Aug. 19, 1929; s. Andrew Thomas and Anna (Gavin) G.; m. Rose Anne Leahy, Aug. 21, 1954; children—Hugh Gavin, Paula Anne, Daniel Joseph, Sarah Louise, Nancy Marie, Jennifer Diane. Student, Loyola U., 1947-50; B.S., U. Ill., 1952, M.D., 1954. Diplomate Am. Bd. Ob-Gyn. Intern St. Joseph Hosp., Chgo., 1954-55; resident in ob-gyn St. Joseph Hosp., 1955-58; practice medicine specializing in ob-gyn Chgo., 1960—; lectr., asst. clin. prof. Stritch Sch. Medicine, Loyola U., Chgo.; active staff St. Joseph Hosp., Chgo., also v.p. med. staff, 1977-78, pres. staff, 1979-80; asst. prof. clin. ob-gyn Northwestern U. Med. Sch., 1980—. Contbr. articles to profl. jours. Trustee Regina Dominican High Sch. Served to capt. M.C., AUS, 1958-60. Fellow Am. Coll. Ob-Gyn, Chgo. Gynecol. Soc.; mem. Am. Cancer Soc. (mem. profl. edn. com. Chgo. unit), Am. Fertility Soc., AMA, Ill. Med. Soc., Chgo. Med. Soc., Cath. Physicians Guild, Assn. Am. Physicians and Surgeons, Am. Soc. Colposcopy and Colpomicroscopy, Am. Assn. Gynecologic Laparoscopists, Assn. Art Inst. Chgo., Assn. Field Mus., Assocs. Smithsonian Instn., Pi Kappa Epsilon. Office: 2800 N Sheridan Rd Suite 406 Chicago IL 60657

GRIMES, JOSEPH A., JR., manufacturing company executive, lawyer; b. Providence, 1932. BA in History, Yale U., 1954; JD, Harvard U., 1961. Pvt. practice law Washington D.C.; then with Agy. for Internt. Devel., Washington D.C.; fed.-state coordinator State of Rhode Island; spl. civilian asst., then dep. under-sec. U.S. Navy, Washington; with Honeywell, Inc., Washington, 1973—; v.p. Asia-Pacific Honeywell, Inc., Tokyo, 1979—. Served with U.S. Air Force. Fulbright scholar France, 1954-55. Mem. Am. Chamber of Commerce in Japan (chmn. Asia-Pacific Council 1984, pres. 1986, 87). *

GRIMES, JOSEPH RUDOLPH, tractor company executive; b. Monrovia, Liberia, Oct. 31, 1923; s. Louis Arthur and Victoria Elizabeth (Cheeseman) G.; m. Doris D. Duncan, Oct. 31, 1954; children—Dolly, Doris. B.A., Liberia Coll., 1944; J.D., Harvard U., 1949; M.Internat. Affaris, Columbia U., 1951, LL.D. (hon.), 1971. Bar: Liberia 1952. Cons. Liberia Tractor & Equipment Co., 1972-76, pres., 1976-78, chmn., 1978—, also dir.; chmn. bd. Denco Shipping Lines, Stevfor, Prime Timber Products Ltd.; dir. West African Explosives & Chem. Co., Ins. Co. Africa; counselor Liberian Dept. State, 1951-56, undersec. state, 1956-60, sec. of state, 1960-72. Chancellor Episcopal Diocese of Liberia, 1976—; mem. Nat. Constn. Commn., chmn. drafting com., 1981-83. Decorated grand cordon Order Pioneers Liberia; grand officer Legion of Honor (France); hon. knight comdr. Order Brit. Empire; recipient Disting. Service citation UN Assn. Mem. Bar Assn. Liberia. Episcopalian. Lodge: Masons. Office: PO Box 299, Monrovia Liberia

GRIMES, MARY ANNE, nurse; b. Kansas City, Kans., June 19, 1936; d. John Andy and Bertha Helen (Ball) G. R.N., St. Joseph's Hosp. Staff nurse St. Joseph's Hosp., Phoenix, 1957-61; office nurse Family Med. Clinic, Phoenix, 1961-62; pvt. duty nurse Central Registery, Phoenix, 1962-65; office nurse, mgr. Phoenix Urologic Clinic, 1965-79; sch. nurse Wilson Sch. Dist. 7, Phoenix, 1980-84, Balsz Sch. Dist. #31, 1984—. Primary fund raiser Classical Chorus Bach and Madrigal Soc., also sec., bd. dirs.; campaign worker Republican gubernatorial election, Phoenix, 1968, 70. Mem. Am. Bus. Women's Assn. (pres. 1974-75). Republican. Roman Catholic. Home: 1805 N 21st Pl Phoenix AZ 85006 Office: Balsz Sch Dist 31 4309 E Belleview Phoenix AZ 85008

GRIMM, CLAYFORD THOMAS, architectural engineer, educator; b. Buchannon, W.Va., July 31, 1924; s. Clayford Thomas and Genevieve Fallon G.; B.Arch.E., Cath. U. Am., 1949; m. Elide Lucy Medone, Dec. 27, 1946; 1 dau., Rose Marie. Sr. lectr. archtl. engring. U. Tex., Austin, 1969—; pres. Clayford T. Grimm, P.E., Inc., cons. archtl. engrs., Austin. Pres., Serra Club, Austin, 1970-71. Served with inf. AUS, 1944-46. Fellow ASTM; mem. ASCE (life), Internat. Council for Bldg. Research Studies and Documentation, Internat. Union Testing and Research Labs. for Materials and Structures, Nat. Inst. Bldg. Scis., Constrn. Specifications Inst. (spl. award edn.), Brit. Masonry Soc., Am. Concrete Inst. Republican. Roman Catholic. Contbr. over 90 articles to profl. jours. Home: 1904 Wooten Dr Austin TX 78758 Office: Dept Civil Engring U Tex Austin TX 78712

GRIMMETT, RICHARD FIELDON, government official; b. Akron, Ohio, June 10, 1946; s. Oliver Fieldon and Edna O. (Moore) G.; B.S. cum laude (Eric N. Rackham leadership award), Kent (Ohio) State U., 1968, M.A., 1970, Ph.D. (univ. fellow), 1973. Lectr. history Kent State U., 1973-74; with Congl. Research Service, Library of Congress, 1974—, specialist nat. def., fgn. affairs and nat. def. div. Mem. Soc. Historians Am. Fgn. Relations, Pi Sigma Alpha, Phi Alpha Theta, Pi Gamma Mu, Omicron Delta Kappa. Episcopalian. Contbg. author: U.S. Security Assistance: The Political Process, 1984. Home: 10308 Duvawn Pl Silver Spring MD 20902 Office: Room LM-315 Library of Congress Washington DC 20540

GRIMSHAW, DONALD HARVEY, logistics engineer; b. Turtlecreek Twp., Ohio, June 22, 1923; s. Percy and Louella Rose (Harvey) G.; m. Jean Dolores Mrazek, Nov. 18, 1950; children—Randall, Kimberley, Stuart, Paul, Heather, Matthew. A.B. in Govt., Calif. State U.-Los Angeles, 1959; postgrad. in pub. adminstrn. U. So. Calif., 1960-62. Research asst. Hughes Aircraft, Culver City, Calif., 1951-54, Douglas Aircraft, Santa Monica, Calif., 1954-57; research engr. Northrop Corp., Hawthorne, Calif., 1957-62; research writer Calif. Dept. Water Resources, Los Angeles, 1962-65; mgr. logistics TRW Def. Systems Group, Redondo Beach, Calif., 1965—. Mem. exec. com. Calif., Los Angeles County and 53d Assembly dist. Republican Party, 1978—; Rep. nominee for U.S. Rep. from Calif.'s 31st Dist., 1978, 80. Served with USN, World War II; Korea. Mem. Soc. Logistics Engrs. (mng. editor SPECTRUM 1966-68), AIAA, Soc. Tech. Communications, U.S. Naval Inst., VFW. Office: TRW 1 Space Park Redondo Beach CA 90278

GRIMSLEY, JAMES ALEXANDER, JR., university administrator, retired army officer; b. Florence, S.C., Nov. 14, 1921; s. James Alexander and Anne (Darby) G.; m. Jessie Lawson, Dec. 8, 1945; children: James Alexander III, Anne, William. B.S., The Citadel, 1942; M.A., George Washington U., 1964. Mgr. Peoples Gas Co., Florence, 1946-48; commd. 2d lt. U.S. Army, 1942, advanced through grades to maj. gen., 1974; ret. 1975; v.p. adminstrn. and finance The Citadel, Charleston, S.C., 1975-80; pres. The Citadel, 1980—. Decorated Silver Star medal, D.S.M., Legion of Merit, Bronze Star medal, Purple Heart, Combat Inf. badge. Mem. Assn. U.S. Army. Episcopalian. Address: The Citadel Office of the President Charleston SC 29409

GRIN, S. SPENCER, publisher, lawyer, educator; b. N.Y.C., Jan. 14, 1928; s. Bernard Boris and Clara (Kane) G.; m. Anne Zabol, Oct. 16, 1955; children: Caron, Milton, Robert, Jennifer. B.A., N.Y. U., 1948; J.D., Bklyn. Law Sch., 1952; Ph.D., Union Grad. Sch., Antioch (Ohio) U., 1971. Bar: N.Y. 1952. Partner firm Gorode, Grin & Samuels, N.Y.C., 1953-70; dir. internat. studies Acad. for Ednl. Devel., N.Y.C., 1971-72; cons. Acad. for Ednl. Devel., 1972—; exec. v.p., pub. Saturday Rev., 1972—; vice chmn., dir. Saturday Review Inc., N.Y.C., 1972-77; counsel Delson & Gordon, N.Y.C. and Washington, 1977-82, Hartke and Hartke, N.Y.C. and Washington, 1982—; chmn. bd. dirs. Hartke, Hartke, Grin and Grin Cons., Falls Church, Va., 1983—; cons. Inst. on Man and Sci., Borlan Industries, R.S.V.P. Cinema, Atlanta/Sosnoff Capital; adj. prof. internat. relations and communications Friends World Coll., Westbury, N.Y., 1967-71; adj. prof. communications Adelphi U., 1980, Don Bolles vis. lectr., 1981; adj. prof. Grad. Sch. Bus. Hofstra U., 1982; del. UNESCO Internat. Ednl. Yr. Author: World Education, 1971; co-author: World Education, Emerging Concepts, 1978; editor: (with Richard L. Tobin) The Golden Age Essays, 1974, Jour. World Edn, 1967-70. Trustee Pan Am. Devel. Found., Washington, Am. Mus. Immigration, Liberty Island, N.Y., NCCJ; bd. dirs. Am. Field Service, N.Y.C.; sec. bd. dirs. Statue of Liberty Am. Mus. Immigration., Eye Inst. Found. Served with USCGR, 1951-52. Mem. Am. Bar Assn., Am. Arbitration Assn., Soc. Internat. Law, World Peace Through Law Center, Mag. Pubs. Assn. (chmn. com. on responsibilities and freedom of press 1972), UN Assn., Overseas Press Club. Home: 7 Plant Ct Rowayton CT 06853 Office: Hartke Hartke & Grin 875 Ave of the Americas New York NY 10001

GRINBERG, MEYER STEWART, retail company executive; b. New Brunswick, N.J., Aug. 31, 1944; s. Allen Lewis and Edith (Bart) G.; m. Beryll Susan Chackman, May 28, 1967; children: David, Lee, Benjamin. BA, Franklin and Marshall Coll., 1965; JD, U. Pa., 1968; MBA, George Washington U., 1973. Bar: Pa., U.S. Ct. Claims, U.S. Customs Ct., U.S. Ct. Internat. Trade, U.S. Ct. Mil. Appeals, U.S. Supreme Ct.; CPA, Pa. Tax acct. Arthur Andersen & Co., Pitts., 1973-77; v.p., co-owner Buy-Wise, Inc., Pitts., 1977—. Exec. v.p. Cong. B'nai Israel, Pitts., 1982—; v.p. Western Pa. region United Synagogues Am., Pitts., 1984—, mem. nat. adv. bd., 1986—; v.p. Sch. Advanced Jewish Studies, Pitts. 1983—; pres. Community Day Sch., 1988—, former v.p.; bd. dirs. Solomon Schechter Nat. Day Sch. Assn.; co-founder Solomon Schechter Day Sch., Pitts.; bd. dirs. Forward-Shady Housing Project; chmn. Pitts. delegation to The Maccabai Games of Israel, mem. Israel Bond Cabinet, Jewish Com. Ctr., coach Little League; chmn. health and phys. edn. com. Jewish Community Ctr.; mem. N.Am. Youth Maccabar Games Com.; bd. dirs. Hebrew Inst. of Pitts. Served to lt. USCG, 1968-73. Recipient Latterman Vol. Mitzuah award, 1988. Mem. Am. Inst. CPA's, Pa. Inst. CPA's, Pa. Bar Assn., Commn. on Jewish Edn. Democrat. Lodge: Kiwanis. Home: 213 Anita Ave Pittsburgh PA 15217 Office: Buy-Wise Inc 4516 Browns Hill Rd Pittsburgh PA 15217

GRINDEA, DANIEL, international economist; b. Galatz, Romania, Feb. 23, 1924; came to U.S., 1975; s. Samy and Liza (Kaufman) Grünberg; M.Econs. and M.Law, Inst. Econ. Scis. and Faculty of Law, Bucharest, Romania, 1948; Ph.D. in Econs., Inst. Fin. and Planning, Leningrad, USSR, 1953; m. Lidia Bunaciu; 1 child, Sorin. Asso. prof. Inst. of Econ. Scis., Bucharest, 1953-56, Acad. of Social Scis., Bucharest, 1956-58, U. Bucharest, 1958-62; asso. prof. Inst. of Agronomy, Bucharest, 1962-69, prof., 1969-72; prof. Acad. St. Gheorghiu, Bucharest, 1972-75; cons. State Planning Com., 1953-56, Ministry of Fin., 1956-68; mem. Sci. Council of the Cen. Statis. Office, 1956-68; internat. economist Republic Nat. Bank of N.Y., N.Y.C., 1976-78, sr. internat. economist, dept. head, 1978-79, v.p., sr. internat. economist, 1979-84, sr. v.p., chief economist, 1984—; sr. advisor U.S. Congl. Adv. Bd., 1988; mem. economic adv. bd. of the Inst. of Internat. Fin., Washington; invited vis. prof. l'Institut International de la Planification de l'Education (UNESCO), Paris, 1973; mem. adv. group Com. on Asian Econ. Studies, 1983. Recipient first prize in econ. research Ministry of Edn., Romania, 1969. Mem. Am. Econ. Assn., Nat. Assn. Bus. Economists, Internat. Assn. for Research of Income and Wealth (elected mem.), Internat. Inst. Public Fin. (W.Ger., elected mem.), Acad. Social and Polit. Scis. Bucharest (elected mem. corr.), Soc. Econ. Scis. of Romania (elected, founding mem.). Correct predictions on world economy and individual countries; contbr. articles on forecasts in field U.S. and internat. to publs.; papers presented to profl. confs. U.S., France, Sweden, Ireland. Office: Republic Nat Bank of NY 452 Fifth Ave New York NY 10018

GRIONI, JOHN SERGIO, scenographer, portraitist; b. Rome, May 29, 1938; s. Giovanni and Ruby (Green) G. Degree cert., Acad. of Fine Arts, Rome, 1960. Author: (photo-books) Fascino di Roma, 1968, Via Margutta, 1970, Le Edicole Sacre di Roma, 1974; contbr. articles to art jours. Recipient 1st Prize and Gold medal Nat. Contest for Young Artists, Rome, 1956, 3d Prize, 1957, Silver Cup for Stage Design, City of Rome, 1961.

GRISEUK, GAIL GENTRY, financial consultant; b. Providence, Jan. 24, 1948; d. Marvin Houghton and Gertrude Emma (Feather) Gentry; m. Steven Paul Griseuk, Oct. 20, 1979; 1 child, Christina Deborah. Student (Fla. Power Corp. scholar), Fla. State U., 1966-70. Registry of Fin. Planning Practitioners. Cert. fin. ops. prin.; cert. gen. securities prin.; registered investment advisor. Asst. div. controller Mobile Home Industries, Tallahassee, 1968-70; owner, mgr. BDI Services, Tallahassee and Lake Charles, La., 1970-78; fin. cons. Aylesworth Fin., Inc., Clearwater, Fla., 1978-82; chmn. bd., chief exec. officer Griseuk Assocs. Inc., 1982—; chief exec. officer GAI Internat. Investment Advisors, Inc., 1985—; instr., dir. vet. outreach Angelina Coll., Lufkin, Tex., 1975-76. Contbr. short stories to Redbook, McCall's, Christian Home. Vol., Sunland Tng. Center, 1970-72, George Criswell House, 1969-73. Mem. Inst. Cert. Fin. Planners, Internat. Platform Assn., Internat. Assn. Fin. Planners. Methodist. Home: 1024 Woodcrest Ave Clearwater FL 33516 Office: 5301 Central Ave Saint Petersburg FL 33710

GRISHAM, EDITH PEARL MOLES, librarian; b. Pinch, W.Va., Mar. 27, 1926; d. Edward Lawrence and Effie (Christy) Moles; m. Charles M. Grisham (div.). A.A., San Antonio Coll., 1958; B.B.A. cum laude, St. Mary's U., 1961; postgrad. Our Lady of the Lake, San Antonio, 1964; M.L.S., Tex. Woman's U., 1973. Billing, sales service asst. Uvalde Rock Asphalt Co., San Antonio, Tex., 1953-62; office mgr. Data Processing Ctr., Inc., San Antonio,

1962-64; serials librarian Houston Pub. Library, 1964-65, head lit. biography dept., 1966-68, head bus. and tech. dept., 1968-73; head Tech. Library Brown & Root, Inc., Houston, 1973-83; reference librarian Incarnate Word Coll., 1984—. Editor, compiler: Union List of Engineering Standards, Specifications, and Codes in Selected Texas Libraries, 1978. Served sgt. USAAF and USAF, 1944-53. Mem. Spl. Libraries Assn., Kappa Pi Sigma, Alpha Beta Alpha. Democrat. Lutheran.

GRISWOLD, ERWIN NATHANIEL, lawyer; b. East Cleveland, Ohio, July 14, 1904; s. James Harlen and Hope (Erwin) G.; m. Harriet Allena Ford, Dec. 30, 1931; children: Hope Eleanor Griswold Murrow, William Erwin. A.B., A.M., Oberlin Coll., 1925; LL.B., Harvard U., 1928, S.J.D., 1929; L.H.D. (hon.), Tufts Coll., 1949, Case Inst. Tech., 1950; LL.D. (hon.), U. B.C., 1949, Brown U., 1950, U. Sidney, U. Melbourne, 1951, Dalhousie U., 1952, Harvard, Amherst Coll., 1953, Columbia U., U. Richmond, 1954, Brandeis U., 1956, U. Mich., 1959, Northwestern U., 1960, Notre Dame U., Allegheny Coll., 1961, U. Toronto, 1962, Williams Coll., 1966, Tulane U., Boston Coll., Princeton U., 1968, Ripon Coll., 1972, Suffolk U., 1973, N.Y. Law Sch., 1978, U. Bridgeport, 1982, Oberlin Coll., 1982; D.C.L. (hon.), U. Western Ont., 1961, U. Toronto, 1962, U. Edinburgh, Georgetown U., 1963, Oxford U., 1964; D.Litt. (hon.), Western Res. U., 1967. Bar: Ohio 1929, Mass. 1935, D.C. 1973. With Griswold, Green, Palmer & Hadden, Cleve., 1929; atty. office solicitor gen., spl. asst. to atty. gen. Washington, 1929-34; asst. prof. law Harvard U., 1934-35, prof., 1935-46, dean, Charles Stebbins Fairchild prof. law, 1946-50, dean, Langdell prof. law, 1950-67; solicitor gen. U.S. 1967-73; partner Jones Day Reavis & Pogue, Washington, 1973—; mem. Alien Enemy Hearing Bd. for Mass., 1941-45; cons. expert U.S. Treasury Dept., 1942; mem. U.S. Civil Rights Commn., 1961-67; trustee Oberlin Coll., Bradford Jr. Coll., 1942-49, Tchrs. Ins. and Annuity Assn., 1942-46, Harvard Law Rev. Assn., 1938-67; bd. dirs. Am. Bar Found., pres., 1971-74; pres. Assn. Am. Law Schs., 1957-58; mem. conf. with Soviet lawyers Lawyers Alliance Nuclear ARms Control, 1983—. Author: Spendthrift Trusts, 1936, 2d edit., 1947, Cases on Federal Taxation, 1940, 6th edit., 1966, (with others) Cases on Conflict of Laws, 1941, rev. edit., 1964, The Fifth Amendment Today, Law and Lawyers in the United States. Fellow Am. Acad. Arts and Sci. (v.p. 1946-48), Brit. Acad. (corr.); hon. bencher Inner Temple; mem. ABA (ho. of dels. 1957-85, gold medal 1978), Mass. Bar Assn., Am. Law Inst., Am. Coll. Trial Lawyers, Am. Philos. Soc., Phi Beta Kappa. Clubs: Harvard (N.Y.C.); Burning Tree, Cosmos, Metropolitan (Washington); Century Assn. (N.Y.); Charles River Country. Home: 36 Kenmore Rd Belmont MA 02178 Office: Jones Day Reavis & Pogue 1450 G St NW Suite 600 Washington DC 20005

GRIZI, SAMIR AMINE, finance executive; b. Lagos, Nigeria, Feb. 27, 1942; s. Amine R. and Fedwa (Murad) G.; m. Nermine Galeb, Nov. 14, 1964; children: Inji, Inas, Iman. BA in Adminstrv. Studies, York U., 1974. Asst. ops. mgr. Navco Food Services Ltd., Toronto, Ont., Can., 1970-71; office mgr. Electro Mech. Testing Labs. Ltd., Toronto, 1971; asst. chief acct. Janin Bldg. and Civil Works Ltd., Toronto, 1971-74; mgr. ops. acctg. VS Services Ltd., Toronto, 1974-75; exec. prin. Talal Abughazaleh & Co., Dammam, Saudi Arabia, 1975-84; group v.p. fin. Abdulla Fouad & Sons, Dammam, 1984-85; group v.p. ASAS Internat. Group, Riyadh, Saudi Arabia, 1986—; bd. dirs. ASAS Internat., Nat. Fire Safety Equipment Co. Ltd., Assil Corp., Saudi Beverages Plant, Cedar House Ltd., Jalloul Internat. Ltd., Chafie O. Aburiche Corp., Saudi Techs. Co. Ltd.; fin. cons. ASAS Internat. Served with C.E. U.S. Army, 1966-70. Fellow Inst .Profl. Mgrs., LEB Assn. Certified Accts.; mem. Am. Mgmt. Assn., Nat. Assn. Accts., Am. Acctg. Assn., Arab Soc. Certified Accts. (assoc.), Inst. Internal Auditors (assoc.). Office: ASAS Internat, PO Box 1656, Al-Khobar 31952, Saudi Arabia

GROBE, WILLIAM HOWARD, retired state government official; b. Winnett, Mont., Feb. 19, 1916; s. Wesley H. and Leota H. (Smith) G.; m. Jane Singleton, May 7, 1967 (dec. Nov. 1987); stepchildren: John C. Singleton (dec.), Linda G. Moore; children from previous marriage: William H., Robert. Student, Simpson Coll., Indianaola, Iowa, 1934-37, Mo. State U., 1937-39, Mont. State Tchrs. Coll., 1940-41; BS, Mont. State U., 1948; BS in Health and Phys. Edn., Miss. Coll., 1951; postgrad., U. Nev., summers 1958-62. Clk. N.P. Ry., Livingston, Mont., 1946-47; student and line coach Mont. State U., Bozeman, 1947-48; coach, phys. edn. tchr. Edgar (Mont.) High Sch., 1948-51; athletic dir., coach, phys. edn. tchr., guidance counselor Bridger (Mont.) High Sch., 1951-57, Lassen Union High Sch. Dist., Herlong, Calif., 1957-62; supt. recreaton and phys. edn. Calif. Conservation Ctr., State Dept. Corrections, Susanville, 1962-75, ret., 1975. Served with USAAF, 1941-45. Mem. Calif. Employees Assn., Nat. Recreation Assn., Calif. Correctional Assn. Lodge: Masons. Home: 3485 Lakeside Dr Apt 300 Reno NV 89509

GROCHOWSKI, MACIEJ HENRYK, linguist; b. Warsaw, Poland, July 14, 1948; s. Jerzy Józef Grochowski and Irena Stanislawa (Rejment) Grochowska; m. Alina Jadwiga Budzynska, Oct. 2, 1973; 1 child, Wojciech. MA, U. Warsaw, 1971; PhD, Inst. Lit. Research, Warsaw, 1974; PhD in Habilitation, Mikolaj Kopernik U., Torun, Poland, 1980. Asst. prof. Inst. Polish Lang. Polish Acad. Scis., Warsaw, 1974-80, assoc. prof., 1980—; assoc. prof. Mikolaj Kopernik U., Torun, Poland, 1980—, group leader gen. linguistics, 1980—. Author: The Manner of Action in the Structure of Sentence, 1975, The Notion of Purpose, 1980, An Outline of Lexicology and Lexicography: the Synchronous Questions, 1982, Polish Particles: Syntax, Semantics, Lexicography, 1986, (with Stanislaw Karolak and Zuzanna Topolinska) The Grammar of Modern Polish, 1984; contbr. more than 90 articles to profl. jours. Mem. Polish Linguistic Soc., Polish Semiotic Soc., Soc. Linguistica Europa, Internat. Assn. Semiotic Studies. Office: Inst Polish Lang, Palac Kultury i Nauki, PL-00-901 Warsaw Poland

GROEBEL, JO, editor; b. Juelich, Rheinland, Fed. Republic Germany, Nov. 11, 1950; parents Gerhard and Marie-Louise (Krumbach) G. Degree in Psychology, Tech. U., Aachen, Fed. Republic Germany, 1974, PhD, 1981. Diplomate Psychology. Asst. prof. Tech. U., Aachen, 1974-79; research assoc. U. Hamburg, Fed. Republic Germany, 1980-81, U. Muenster, Fed. Republic Germany, 1981-83; acad. counselor Ed. U. Rheinland Pfalz, Landau, Fed. Republic Germany, 1983—; visiting prof. UCLA, 1987; editor First German TV Research, Fed. Republic Germany, 1986—; cons. Swiss and German TV, 1984—; UN rep. Internat. Soc. Research on Aggression, Geneva, 1984—; bd. dirs. Market and Communication Psychology, Frankfurt, 1985. Author: Fernsehen und Angst, 1988; editor: (with M. Grewe) Mensch und Medien, 1987, (with R. Hinde) Aggression and War, 1988, (with J. Goldstein) Terrorism, 1988; contbr. articles to profl. jours. Symposium chmn. and cons. UN, 1983-88, Harvard, 1988. Grantee The Minister Interior, Bonn, 1980, Thyssen Stiftung, Essen, 1981, Carnegie Corp., 1984, Woodrow Wilson Ctr., 1987, Guggenheim Found., 1988, Kultusminister Rh. Pf., 1988. Mem. Deutsche Gesellschaft f. Psychologie, Deutsche Gesellschaft f. Publizistik, Internat. Council Psychologists (dir. 1987—), Internat. Soc. Research on Aggression (council 1988—). Roman Catholic. Home: An 44 Nr 25, 6740 Landau Rheinpfalz Federal Republic of Germany 6740

GROEN, LAMBERTUS GERARDUS, sales company executive, consultant; b. Vlaardingen, The Netherlands, Mar. 23, 1932; arrived in Eng., 1958.; s. Boudewijn and Cornelia Hendrina Luidina (Kolmeijer) G.; m. Linda Dorothy Blackman, Sept. 9, 1961; children: Mark Gerardus, Emma Louise, Lucy Helen. Degree in commerce, Hanze, Schiedam, The Netherlands, 1952; MBA, Boston U., 1958; postgrad., U. Birmingham, 1958-60. Asst. export mgr. fertilizer factory, Vlaardingen, 1954-55; export mgr. De Heer Chocolate Factory, Rotterdam, The Netherlands, 1955-56; shipping mgr. Lombard's, Boston, 1957-58; export sect. leader T.I. (Export) Ltd., Birmingham, Eng., 1960-65; export mgr., liason officer T.I. Stainless Steel, Birmingham, 1966-74; export mgr., sales exec. Hemo Plastic Molders, Birmingham, 1974-83; dir., owner Fair Internat. Ltd., Codsall, Eng., 1983—; cons. cookware mfrs., U.K. and Africa, 1985—; cons. for export alcohol meters, 1987—. Recipient awards for exports C. of C., Daily Express, 1979, Queen's award, 1981. Home: 13 Queens Gardens, Codsall Nr Wolverhampton, West Midlands WV8 2EP, England

GROENEVELD, HENRY JACK, sales executive; b. Vlaardingen, Zuid-Holland, The Netherlands, Aug. 5, 1955; s. Gerard and Else (Swaving) G.; m. Tineke Sjoukje Visser, Nov. 7, 1955; children: John, Nicky. Degree in bus. adminstrn., U. Nyenrode, 1979. Mgr. merchandising services Procter & Gamble NV, Rotterdam, The Netherlands, 1979-84; sales dir. Gen. Mills, Amsterdam, The Netherlands, 1984-85; v.p. sales Dutch br.of the Bertelsmann AG Book Club div. ECI/Euroboek, Vianen, The Netherlands, 1985—. Served with inf., 1975-76. Home: Noteboom 53, Culemborg 4101 WS, The Netherlands

GROENEWEGEN, PETER DIDERIK, university professor in economics, author; b. Kerkrade, Limburg, The Netherlands, Feb. 13, 1939; s. Jan Barend and Ruth (De Leeuw) G.; m. Eileen Jennifer Allan, Aug. 15, 1962; children: Sarah Joan, Stephen William. B of Econs. with honors, U. Sydney, 1962, M of Econs., 1963; PhD, London Sch. Econs., 1965. Research officer Res. Bank of Australia, Sydney, 1960-61; teaching fellow U. Sydney, 1961-63, lectr., 1965-67, sr. lectr., 1967-73, assoc. prof., 1974-80, prof., 1980—; mem. editorial bd. History Polit. Economy, Durham, N.C., 1987—, Polit. Economy, Rome, Jour. Econ. Surveys, Edinburgh, Rivista Valutaria, Milan. Author: Public Finance in Australia, 1976-84, Economics of Turgot; author 34 articles to prof. jours. Fellow Acad. Social Scis. of Australia (exec. 1986—); mem. Econ. Soc. of Australia (pres. 1978-79), Am. Econ. Assn., History Econs. Soc., Royal Econ. Soc. Office: U Sidney Econs Dept, 2006 Sydney Australia

GROENING, GERT D., landscape architect, educator; b. Stetten, Germany, Sept. 6, 1944. Diploma Engring., Tech. U., Hannover, Fed. Republic Germany, 1970, Dr. rer. hort. habil., 1979. Research asst. Inst. Gruenplanung u. Gartenarch, Hannover, 1970-73, 74-75; postgrad. researcher dept. landscape architecture U. Calif., Berkeley, 1973-74; acad. counselor Lehrg. Landschaftsplanung, U. Hannover, 1975-82; prof. Inst. Freiraumentwicklung, 1982-85, F.B. Architektur/Hochschule D. Kuenste, Berlin, Fed. Republic Germany, 1985—; cons. various state, communal, and pvt. orgns., Fed. Republic Germany, 1973—. Author: Allotment Gardening, 1974, Permanent Caravanning, 1979; co-author: The Love for Landscape, I and III, 1986, 87, 100 Years German Society for Garden Art, 1987; co-editor book series Arbeiten zur sozialwissenschaftlich orientierten Freiraumplanung (8 vols.), 1980—; contbr. numerous articles on garden architecture, history of garden architecture, nature protection and landscape planning to profl. jours. Recipient Beatrix Farrand award U. Calif., Berkeley, 1973; Peter Josef Lenné prize Senat Berlin, Fed. Republic of Germany, 1975. Mem. Internat. Assn. for Study of People and Their Phys. Surroundings, Environ. Design Research Assn., Internat. Soc. Hort. Sci. Office: Hochschule der Kuenste Berlin, FB 2 Architektur Hardenbergstrasse 33, D 1000-12 Berlin Federal Republic of Germany

GROESBECK, ELISE DE BRANGES DE BOURICA, artist; b. Versailles, France, Jan. 31, 1936 (parents Am. citizens); d. Vicount Louis de Branges de Bourcia II and Diane (McDonald) de Branges de Bourcia; student Phila. Coll. Art, 1954-55; m. James Richard Groesbeck, Oct. 3, 1958 (div. June 1969); children: Gretchen Atlee, Genevieve de Branges. One-man shows The Agnes Irwin Sch., Rosemont, Pa., 1973, Phila. Cricket Club, Chestnut Hill, Pa., 1973. Recipient prize Rehoboth Beach Art League, 1944; Agnes Allen Art prize Agnes Irwin Sch., 1954. Repubican. Episcopalian. Home: 3204 Leigh Rd Pompano Beach FL 33062 Office: Box 58 Pompano Beach FL 33061

GROETSCHEL, MARTIN, mathematics educator; b. Schwelm, Fed Republic Germany, Sept. 10, 1948; m. Iris Biesewinkel, July 9, 1976; children: Andrea, Bettina, Claudia. Prof. applied math. U. Augsburg, Fed. Republic Germany, 1982—. Mem. Inst. Mgmt. Sci. (IBM prize 1984), Mathl. Programming Soc. (Fulkerson prize 1982), Am. Mathl. Soc., Ops. Research Soc. Am. (Lanchester prize hon mention 1980). Home: Gotenstrasse 17, D-8901 Stadtbergen Federal Republic of Germany Office: Inst fur Math, U Augsburg, Memminger Strasse 6, 8900 Augsburg Federal Republic of Germany

GROGAN, DENIS JOSEPH, information scientist, educator; b. Bolton, Lancashire, Eng., Oct. 7, 1930; s. Joseph and Mary (Toohey) G.; m. Margaret McGarry, July 24, 1954; children: John, Peter, David, Clare. BA, U. Manchester, Eng., 1951; Fellow Library Assn., Manchester Coll. Tech., 1956. Chartered librarian. Sr. asst. librarian Manchester Reference Library, 1954-57; dep. librarian Manchester Sci. and Tech. Library, 1957-63; sr. tutor librarian Stockport Coll. Tech., Greater Manchester, 1963-64; head dept. bibliog. studies Coll. Librarianship Wales, Aberystwyth, 1964—; cons. sci. info. Govt. Malaysia, 1971, Govt. South Korea, 1973; external examiner U. Sheffield, 1976-81, Queen's U., Belfast, No. Ireland, 1983-86. Author: Practical Reference Work, 1979, Science and Technology: A Guide to the Literature, 1970, 4th rev. edit., 1982, Grogan's Case Studies in Reference Work, 1967, 78, 8 vols. Roman Catholic. Office: Coll Librarianship Wales, Dept Bibliog Studies, Aberystwyth, Dyfed SY23 3AS, Wales

GROGAN, ROBERT HARRIS, lawyer; b. Bklyn., Feb. 25, 1933; s. Robert Michael and Nora Howarth (Johnson) G.; A.B., Harvard U., 1955; LL.B., U. Va., 1961; m. Delia Ann Grossi, Dec. 23, 1967 (div. 1982); m. Lynn D. Habian, June 20, 1987. Admitted to N.Y. State bar, 1962, Va. bar, 1961, Ill. bar, 1977, Fla. bar, 1986; assoc. firm Milbank, Tweed, Hadley & McCloy, N.Y.C., 1961-66; counsel Anaconda Co., N.Y.C., 1966-68; asso. firm Shearman & Sterling, N.Y.C., 1968-75; v.p., gen. counsel staff Citibank, N.Y.C., 1975-76; partner Mayer, Brown & Platt, Chgo., 1976-81; of counsel Olwine, Connelly, Chase, O'Donnell & Weyher, N.Y.C., 1981-87, sr. v.p., dep. sr. counsel, Southeast Bank, N.A., Miami, Fla., 1987—; lectr. in field. Sec., bd. dirs. 3d Equity Owners Corp., coop. housing corp., 1975-77, pres., bd. dirs., 1982-86. Served with U.S. Army, 1956-58. Mem. Am. Bar Assn., N.Y. State Bar Assn. (chmn. retail installment sales-usury subcom. bus. law com. 1975-83, exec. com. banking, corp. and bus. law sect. 1976-83), Va. Bar Assn., Ill. Bar Assn., Fla. Bar, Phi Delta Phi. Club: Harvard N.Y.C. Contbg. author: The Local Economic Development Corporation, 1970.

GROGNARD, CATHERINE-JEANNE, dermatologist; b. Bizerte, Tunisia, July 23, 1952; d. Rene and Colette (Augier) Gourdon; m. Dominique Yves Grognard, July 25, 1970; children: Arnault, Cecile, Anais. MD, U. Tours, France, 1978, CES in Dermatology, 1979. Resident in dermatology and pediatric surgery U. Tours, France, 1977-79; practice medicine specializing in dermatology Tours, France, 1980—; cons. in dermatology and pediatric surgery, Tours. Author: Handbook of Dermatologic Surgery, 1986. Mem. Groupement Etude Techniques Dermato Chirurgicales Centre Ouest (gen. sec.), Assn. Dermatologues Centre Ouest (v.p.). Roman Catholic. Office: Cabinet Dermatologique, 9 Rue Sully, 37000 Tours France

GROH, GABOR GYULA, mathematician; b. Budapest, Hungary, Apr. 26, 1948; came to Switzerland, 1957, naturalized, 1970; s. Julius and Margit (Molnar) G.; m. Keiko Fuse, July 21, 1979; children: Christoph Ken, Miya Valentine. Diploma in physics Eidgenössische Technische Hochschule, Zurich, 1974, Dr. Sci. Math., 1982. Research assoc. Eidgenössische Technische Hochschule, 1975-82, 85—; research fellow, research assoc. Swiss Nat. Sci. Found.-Lawrence Berkeley Lab., Berkeley, Calif., 1982-83; vis. lectr. dept. math. U. Calif.-Berkeley, 1984; assoc., cons. Medichem S.A., Fribourg, Switzerland, 1984-85. Mem. Soc. Indsl. and Applied Math., AIAA, N.Y. Acad. Sci. Office: Inst Energy Tech, Eth-Zentrum, 8092 Zurich Switzerland

GROHS, GERHARD KARL, sociology educator; b. Dresden, Germany, June 24, 1929; m. Elisabeth Beringer; children: Florian and Henrike. DrIUR, U. Heidelberg, 1959; Habilitation, Free U., Berlin, 1966. Sr. lectr. U. Leicester, Eng., 1965-66; research fellow German Inst. for Devel., West Berlin, 1966-67; sr. lectr. U. Dar-Es-Salaam, Tanzania, 1967-69; prof. sociology U. Berlin, 1969-75, U. Mainz, Fed. Republic Germany, 1975—; prof. sociol. research Theodor Heuss New Sch., N.Y., 1985-86. Author: Stufen Afrikan Emanzipation, 1967; co-author: Decolonisation Afrikas, 1973, Kulturelle Identitat, 1980. Chmn. Protestant Research Inst., Heidelberg, 1976—; vice chmn. Commn. for Devel. Protestant Ch. Germany, Bonn, 1975—; del. cen. com. World Council Chs., Geneva, 1975-83, devel. commn., 1983—; mem. Friedrich Naumann Found., Bonn, 1980—; adv. bd. Goethe Inst., Munich, 1988—. Mem. German Sociol. Assn., Assn. Africanists in Germany, Inst. of African Studies. Office: U Mainz, Saarstrasse, 6500 Mainz Federal Republic of Germany

GROMOV, MIKHAEL, mathematician; b. Boksitogorsk, USSR, Dec. 23, 1943. MS, U. Leningrad, USSR, 1965, PhD, 1969, DSc, 1973. Asst. prof. U. Leningrad, 1967-74; prof. SUNY, Stony Brook, 1974-81, U. Paris VI, 1981-82; permanent fellow, chmn. math dept. Inst. Hautes Etudes Scientifiques, Bures-sur-Yvette, France, 1982—; lectr. ICM Nice, France, 1970, Helsinki, Finland, 1978, Warsaw, Poland, 1982, Berkeley, Calif., 1986. Author: Structures Métriques Pour Les Variétés Riemanniennes (Paris), 1981, Partial Differential Relations (Springer), 1986. Recipient prize Moscow Math Soc., 1971, prix Elie Cartan Académie des Sciences Paris, 1984. Mem. Am. Math. Soc. (Oswald Veblen Prize Geometry 1981). Office: Inst Hautes Etudes Sci, 35 Rt Chartres, 91440 Bures-sur-Yvette France

GROMYKO, ANDREY ANDREYEVICH, president of USSR, former minister foreign affairs; b. Starye Gromyky, Byelo-russia, July 6, 1909; ed. Minsk Agrl. Inst., Econ. Inst., Moscow, 1931-36, M.A., 1936; m. Lydia D. Grinevich; children—Anatoli, Emilia. Sr. sci. worker Econ. Inst., Acad. Scis. USSR, 1936-39, also lectr. Moscow univs.; chief div. Am. countries People's Commissariat Fgn. Affairs, 1939; counselor Russian Embassy, Washington, 1939-43; minister to Cuba; ambassador to U.S., 1943-46, to Gt. Brit., 1952-53; USSR rep. on UN Security Council, 1943-46; dep. minister for fgn. affairs, 1946-49, 1st dep. fgn. minister, 1949-57, fgn. minister, 1957-85, pres., 1985—, 1st dep. chair Council of Ministers, 1983-85; mem. Politburo, 1973—. Named Hero Socialist Labor (twice); recipient Order of Lenin (6) Hammer and Sickle gold medal (2), also others. Address: Office of Chmn, Moscow USSR *

GRÖNBÄRJ, KLAUS H., business executive; b. Helsinki, Finland, Feb. 3, 1946; m. Hautala Pirkko, 1970; children: Sari, Marko. BBA, Helsinki Sch. Econs., 1968. Internal auditor Unilever, Helsinki and Stockholm, 1968-72; various fin. mgmt. positions Oy Wartsila Ab, Helsinki, 1972-79, v.p. fin., 1979-85, sr. v.p., chief fin. officer, 1985-86, exec. v.p., 1986—. Home: Ylisrinne 3, 02210 Espoo Finland Office: Oy Wartsila Ab, John Stenbergs Strand 2, 00530 Helsinki Finland

GRONER, BEVERLY ANNE, lawyer; b. Des Moines, Jan. 31, 1922; d. Benjamin L. and Annabelle (Miller) Zavat; m. Jack Davis, Dec. 31, 1940; children—Morrilou Davis Morell, Lewis A. Davis, Andrew G. Davis; remarried Samuel Brian Groner, Dec. 17, 1962. Student Drake U., 1939-40, Cath. U., 1954-56; JD, Washington Coll. Law, Am. U., 1959. Bar: Md. 1959, U.S. Supreme Ct. 1963, D.C. 1965. Sole practice, Bethesda, Md., Washington, D.C., 1963—; chmn. Md. Gov.'s Commn. on Domestic Relations Laws 1977-86; trustee Montgomery-Prince George's Continuing Legal Edn. Inst.; lectr. to lay, profl. groups; speaker to Bar Assns. and numerous seminars; participant continuing legal edn. programs, local and nat.; participant trial demonstration films Am. Law Inst., ABA Legal Consortium; participant numerous TV, radio programs; seminar leader Harvard Law Sch., 1987, Family Law, Georgetown U. Law Ctr., 1988. Cons. editor: Family Law Reporter, 1986—; contbr. numerous articles to profl. jours. Named One of Leading Matrimonial Practitioners in U.S., Nat. Law Jour., 1979, 87, Best Divorce Lawyer in Md., Washingtonian mag., 1981, One of Best Matrimonial Lawyers in U.S., Town and Country mag., 1985, Best Lawyers in Am.; recipient Disting. Service award Va. State Bar Assn., 1982. Fellow Am. Acad. Matrimonial Lawyers; mem. Bar Assn. Montgomery County (exec. com., chmn. family law sect. 1976, chmn. fee arbitration panel 1974-77, legal ethics com.), Md. State Bar Assn. (gov., chmn. family law sect. 1975-77, vice chmn. com. continuing legal edn., ethics com.), ABA (sec. Family Law Sect. 1983-84, vice chmn. 1984-86, chmn. 1986-87, sect. council 1982-83, chmn. sect. marital property com., assn.'s adv. to Nat. Conf. of Commrs. on Uniform State Laws Drafting Com. on Uniform Marital Property Act), Gov.'s Com. Equal Rights Amendment, 1978-80. Phi Alpha Delta. Home: 6710 Western Ave Chevy Chase MD 20815 Office: 4550 Montgomery Ave Air Rights Plaza III 403N Bethesda MD 20814

GRONER, SAMUEL BRIAN, judge; b. Buffalo, Dec. 27, 1916. AB, Cornell U., 1937, JD, 1939; MA in Econs., Am. U., 1950. Bar: N.Y. 1939, D.C. 1952, Md. 1953, U.S. Supreme Ct. 1944. Sole practice Buffalo, 1939-40; atty.-adviser U.S. Dept. Justice, Washington, 1946-53; sole practice Md. and Washington, 1953-63; ptnr. Groner, Stone & Greiger, Washington, 1955-57, Groner & Groner, Silver Spring and Bethesda, Md., 1962—; adminstrv. law judge U.S. Dept. Labor, Washington, 1979—; acting chmn. Dept. Labor of Contract Appeals, 1987; asst. to commr. FCC, Washington, 1953; asst. counsel Naval Ship Systems Command, Washington, 1963-73; trial atty. Office Gen. Counsel, Dept. Navy, Washington, 1973-74, assoc. chief trial atty., 1974-79; instr. Terrell Law Sch., Washington, 1948; mem. faculty USDA Grad. Sch., 1972—; reporter Md. Gov.'s Commn. on Domestic Relations Laws, 1977-87; participant in continuing legal and jud. edn. Author: Modern Business Law, 1983; (with others) The Improvement of the Administration of Justice, 6th edit., 1981; assoc. editor Fed. Bar Jour., 1948-55; contbr. articles to profl. jours. Active PTA, civic assns., Jewish Community Council, Community Chest. Recipient Navy Superior Civilian Service award, 1979. Mem. ABA (vice chmn. pub. contract com. on adminstrv. claims and remedies law sect. 1976-79, chmn. 1979-80, mem. liaison commn. on professionalsim, 1985—, adv. to standing com. on lawyer competence, 1986—, jud. adminstrn. div.), Fed. Bar Assn., Montgomery County Bar Assn. and Bar Fedn., Md. Bar Assn., D.C. Bar Assn., Cornell Law Assn. (pres. D.C. chpt. 1947-54), Govt. Adminstrv. Trial Lawyers Assn., Am. Law Inst., Inst. Jud. Adminstrn., Am. Judicature Soc., Supreme Ct. Hist. Soc., Nat. Lawyers Club, Phi Beta Kappa. Home: 6710 Western Ave Chevy Chase MD 20815 Office: 1111 20th St NW Washington DC 20036

GROOMES, JOHN WOODWARD, manufacturing company executive; b. Brownsville, Pa., Oct. 5, 1920; s. John Clayton and Eliza (Fox) G.; m. Donna D. Swanson, Aug. 23, 1969; children by previous marriage: John Woodward, Charles C., Anita S., Jeffrey W., Michele M. Student, Case Inst. Tech., 1943-44; BA, Alma Coll., 1949; postgrad., U. Mich., 1949, Mich. State U., 1949-50. Prodn. engr. Kaiser Frazer Corp., 1950-51; test engr. Gen. Motors Proving Ground, 1951-52; sr. project engr. Fisher Body div. Gen. Motors Corp., 1952-53, gen. supr. quality control, 1953-54; sr. project engr. Allison div., 1954-55; instr. Math. Traverse City (Mich.) Schs., 1956-57; adminstrv. asst. to dean engring., dir. Jets Program Mich. State U., 1957-59; asst. to exec. sec. Am. Soc. Tool and Mfg. Engrs., Dearborn, Mich., 1959-61, asst. gen. mgr., 1961-65, gen. mgr., 1965-69; mktg. mgr. machine tool group Ex-Cello Corp., Detroit, 1969-72, v.p. tool and abrasive ops., 1972-77; pres. Am. Feldmuehle Corp., Hendersonville, N.C., 1977-78, Universal Engring. div. Houdaille Industries Inc., Frankenmuth, Mich., 1979-86, Comau Productivity Systems Inc., Troy, Mich., 1987—. Office: Comau Systems 466 Stephenson Hwy Troy MI 48083

GROOSMAN, ERNEST FLORIMOND, architect; b. Ovezande, Netherlands, July 21, 1917; s. Leonardus F. Groosman and Emilie Marie Modde; m. Paulina Van Rhenen, July 28, 1941; children—Marcel, Henri, Ernest and Jan Jaap (twins). M., Acad. Architecture, Amsterdam, 1944. Architect with numerous firms, Netherlands, 1938-47; founder Groosman, Rotterdam, 1948, now Groosman Ptnrs. Architects, 1971—; mem. archtl. juries; lectr. U. Delft, U. Eindhoven, U. Milano; archtl. works include: housing projects, factories, shopping ctrs., schools, hotels, univs. Mem. Found. Volkskracht, Rotterdam, 1968-84; sec. Found. Trompenburg Botanic Gardens, Rotterdam, 1970-84. Served to maj. Netherlands Armed Forces, 1939-40, 47-50. Recipient Van Borsselen medal; 1970; Companionship of Order of Orange-Nassau, 1971. Hon. fellow AIA; mem. Netherlands Inst. Architects, Internat. Union Architects, Steel Constrn. Soc., archtl. Research Found. (founder). Clubs: Rotary, Sailing of Rotterdam. Mem. Liberal Party Netherlands. Office: Groosman Ptnrs Architects, Essenburgsingel 28, Rotterdam The Netherlands

GROSCH, HERBERT REUBEN JOHN, computer consultant; b. Saskatoon, Sask., Can., Sept. 13, 1918; s. Reuben John and Bessie Mabel (Adams) G.; B.S., U. Mich., 1938, Ph.D. in astronomy, 1942; postgrad. Harvard U., 1939-40; m. Nancy Mae Hall, Aug. 16, 1975; 1 dau., Diane. Astronomer, U.S. Naval Obs., 1941-42; optical engr. U.S. Navy, Sperry Gyroscope Co., Farrand Optical Co., 1942-45; computer scientist IBM Corp., 1945-51, mgr. space programs, 1958-59; head logical design research Digital Computer Lab. M.I.T., 1951-52; mgr. investigations, aircraft gas turbine div. Gen. Electric Co., Evendale, Ohio, Lynn, Mass., 1952-56, mgr. applications, computer dept., Phoenix, 1956-58; dir. Deacon Project, Center for Advanced Studies, Santa Barbara, Calif., 1965-67; cons. computer mktg.,

N.Y.C., 1959-62, Monte Carlo and Lausanne, 1962-65; dir. Center for Computer Scis. and Tech., Nat. Bur. Standards, Washington, 1967-70, sr. research fellow, 1970-73; editorial dir. Computerworld, Boston, 1973-76; cons. internat. computer mktg. Sunnyvale, Calif., 1976-80, Netherlands, 1980-83, Switzerland, 1983—; assoc. in astronomy Columbia U., 1945-50; adj. prof. Ariz. State Coll., 1956-57, Boston U., 1974-75; Green vis. prof. Tex. Christian U., 1976. Chmn. Intergovtl. Council for ADP, 1968-70; U.S. rep. OECD Computer Experts Group, 1970-72; mem. Mass. Gov.'s Commn. on Privacy and Personal Data, 1973-75. Lawton fellow, 1936-37; Mandelbaum scholar, 1937-38; Rackham fellow, 1938-39, Univ. fellow, 1939-41. Fellow AIAA (pres. 1951), Brit. Computer Soc.; mem. Assn. Computing Machinery (dir. 1968-87 , v.p. 1974-76, pres. 1976-78), Canadian Info. Processing Soc., others. Democrat. Clubs: Mensa; St. Moritz Tobogganing (Cresta). Contbg. editor: Datamation, 1959-63, Internat. Edn., 1972-73, Computing Europe, 1977-85; contbr. articles to profl. jours. Home and Office: 37 rue du Village, 1295 Mies VD Switzerland

GROSCLAUDE, MARTINE, physician; b. Paris, July 30, 1947; d. Philippe and Monique Gros; m. Max Grosclaude, Sept. 4, 1970; children: Sophie, Antoine, Etienne. MD, U. Lyon, Rhône, France, 1977. Pvt. practice medicine specializing in pneumology, allergology 1983—; cons. physician Hosp. Lyons U., 1975; clin. expert for trials, 1985. Fellow French Allergologic Soc.; European Acad. Allergy and Clin. Immunology, Lyon Soc. Allergy and Immunology, Lyon Soc. Allergy, Rhone Moyen Allergology and Immunology Group. Roman Catholic. Home and Office: 41 rue de la Republique, Saint Peray, Ardèche France 07130

GROSENHEIDER, DELNO JOHN, lawyer; b. Litchfield, Ill., Feb. 10, 1935; s. Junas Louis Henry and Esther O'Neil (Knabel) G.; m. Margaret Noel Adams, Aug. 30, 1959; children—John Stephen, Michael Del. Student So. Ill. U., 1953-54; B.A., U. Tex., 1961, LL.B., 1964. Bar: Tex. 1963, U.S. Dist. Ct. (we. dist.) Tex., 1966, U.S. Ct. Appeals (5th cir.) 1985, U.S. Supreme Ct., 1986. Atty. Tex. Securities Bd., Austin, 1964-66, House, Mercer, House & Brock, Austin, 1966-77; ptnr. Wilson, Grosenheider & Burns, Austin, 1977—. Judge, City of Rollingwood, Tex., 1968; city atty. City of Rollingwood, 1969; mem. Bd. of Adjustment, City of Rollingwood, 1975-84. Mem. State Bar of Tex., Travis County Bar Assn., Tex. Assn. Def. Counsel, Def. Research Inst., Internat. Assn. Ins. Counselors. Republican. Episcopalian. Clubs: Austin, University. Home: 311 Pleasant Dr Austin TX 78746 Office: Wilson Grosenheider & Burns 400 W 15th St Suite 1100 Austin TX 78767

GROSJEAN, CARL CLEMENT, retired theoretical physicist, educator; b. Courtrai, Belgium, Sept. 5, 1926; s. Carl Adolphe-Louis and Germaine Marie (Lecompte) G.; BSc, State U. Ghent, Belgium, 1947, Licentiate Sc., 1949, DSc, 1951, Aggrégation Enseign. Sup., 1955; PhD, Columbia U., N.Y.C., 1951; m. Andrea Emma Bernolet, Aug. 7, 1965. Watson Sci. Computing Lab. fellow, 1949-51; research asst. Inst. Interuniversitaire des Scis. Nucléaires, Brussels, 1951, research assoc., 1952-58; lectr. State U. Ghent, 1954-58, prof. applied math., 1958-69, prof. nuclear reactor theory, 1958-70, prof. advanced math. analysis, 1965-70, prof. math. physics, 1969-86, ret., 1988., founder Digital Computing Lab., 1958, dir., 1960-72; vis. fellow Princeton U., 1956-58; vis. prof., hon. research assoc. Univ. Coll. London, 1963; mem. adv. com. Nat. Fund Sci. Research, Brussels, 1969-88. Decorated officer Order of Leopold, 1968, comdr., 1978; laureate, interuniv. contest, 1950; recipient Prix Empain, 1953. Mem. Belgian Math. Soc. (pres. 1970-72), Flemish Astron. Soc., Royal Acad. Scis., Lit. and Fine Arts Belgium (dir. 1978), Sigma Xi. Author: Formal Theory of Scattering Phenomena, 1960; (with W. Bossaert) Table of Absolute Gamma-Ray Detection Efficiencies, 1965; (with J. Meeus, W. Vanderleen) Canon of Solar Eclipses, 1966; (with others) Reinaert Systematic Ency., vol. 14, 15 and 20, 1974-76; contbr numerous articles to profl. jours.; mng. editor Simon Stevin Math. Jour., 1978—; contbg. editor Jour. Computational and Applied Math., 1975—. Home: 29 Recollettenlei, B-9000 Gent Belgium

GROSS, CATHERINE THERESA, underwater research company executive, industrialist; b. Newark, Jan. 20, 1938; d. Dennis James and Kathryn Viola (Dalton) Donahue; m. Ralph L. Liguori, Sept. 7, 1956 (div. 1982); children—Kathryn Rose, Anthony, Lisa, Michael; m. John Charles Gross, Apr. 23, 1983. Student in Bus. Mgmt., Brookdale Community Coll., 1976-78. Exec. v.p. Artifacts Recovery Corp., New Smyrna Beach, Fla., 1982—; exec. v.p., dir. Merchandise Distbrs. Corp., Edgewater, Fla., 1982—; pres., dir. John C. Gross Investment Corp., Edgewater, 1982—; v.p., dir. Yacht Club Island Corp., New Smyrna Beach, 1982—; dir. Ponce de Leon Realty Corp., New Smyrna Beach, 1982—. Pres., Concerned Citizen's Conf., Inc., Edgewater, 1982—. Mem. Treasure Hunting Assn. Republican. Roman Catholic. Clubs: Halifax, Halifax Yacht, Oceans Racquet (Daytona Beach, Fla.); Fairgreen Country (New Smyrna Beach). Avocations: piano, tennis, golf, boating, treasure hunting. Home: 621 N Riverside Dr Edgewater FL 32032 Office: PO Box 596 New Smyrna Beach FL 32069

GROSS, DAVID LEE, geologist; b. Springfield, Ill., Nov. 20, 1943; s. Carl David and Shirley Marie (Northcutt) G.; m. Claudia Cole, June 11, 1966; children—Oliver David, Alexander Lee. A.B., Knox Coll., 1965; M.S., U. Ill., 1967, Ph.D., 1969. Registered profl. geologist, Calif. Asst. geologist Ill. State Geol. Survey, Urbana, 1969-73; assoc. geologist Ill. State Geol. Surbey, Urbana, 1973-80, geologist, 1980—, coordinator environ. geology, 1979-84, head environ. studies, 1984—. Contbr. numerous articles to profl. jours. Bd. govs. Channing-Murray Found., 1973-76, pres., 1976; trustee Unitarian Universlaist Ch., Urbana, 1977-80, chmn., 1977-79; bd. dirs. Vol. Action Ctr., 1981-85 , chmn., 1984-85 ; bd. dirs. United Way Champaign County, 1984—, exec. com. 1984-85, chmn. United Way Campaign, Univ. Ill., 1986. NDEA fellow, 1969. Fellow Geol. Soc. Am., AAAS; mem. Internat. Union Quaternary Research, Am. Quaternary Assn., Internat. Assn. for Gt. Lakes Research, Soc. Econ. Paleontologists and Mineralogists, Am. Inst. Profl. Geologists (pres. Ill.-Ind. sect. 1980), Ill. State Acad. Sci., Sigma Xi. Lodge: Rotary (Urbana, Ill.) (pres. 1986-87). Home: 3 Flora Ct Champaign IL 61821 Office: Ill State Geol Survey Natural Resources Bldg 615 E Peabody Dr Champaign IL 61820

GROSS, DONALD, operations research educator; b. Pitts., Oct. 20, 1934; s. Frank and Marion (Horovitz) G.; m. Alice Gold, Sept. 20, 1959; children—Stephanie Lynne, Joanne Susan. B.S., Carnegie-Mellon U., 1956; M.S., Cornell U., 1959, Ph.D., 1961. Ops. research analyst Atlantic Refining Co., Phila., 1961-65; from asst. prof. to prof. dept. ops. research George Washington U., Washington, 1965—, chmn. dept., 1976—; cons. industry and fed. agys. Co-author: Fundamentals of Queueing Theory, 1974, 2d edit., 1985; contbr. articles to sci. jours. Treas. Williamsburg Civic Assn., Arlington, Va., 1978-79. Served to capt., Signal Corps U.S. Army, 1962-63. Grantee NASA, NSF, Office Naval Research, USAF. Mem. Ops. Research Soc. Am. (council 1982-85, pres. elect 1988), Inst. Mgmt. Scis., Inst. Indsl. Engrs., Washington Ops. Research Mgmt. Council (trustee 1969-73, pres. 1974-75), Sigma Xi, Tau Beta Pi. Research on queuing theory; inventory theory, model devel. and numerical solution techniques. Home: 3530 N Rockingham St Arlington VA 22213 Office: George Washington U Washington DC 20052

GROSS, EARL, artist; b. Pitts., Sept. 11, 1899. Student, Westminster Coll., Carnegie-Mellon U. Sch. Fine Arts. One-man shows include Macbeth Galleries, N.Y.C., 1942, Associated Am. Artists, N.Y.C., 1945, Atlanta Art Mus., Sarasota Art Assn., Wustum Mus., Madison Art Assn., Longboat Key Art Assn., Ill. State Mus., Herron Art Inst., New Orleans Acad. Art, Burpee Art Mus., Butler Art Mus.; exhibited in group shows Manhattan Mus. of Art, 1952, Internat. Water Color Show at Chgo. Art Inst., Illustrators Club of N.Y.C., Bob-O-Link Country Club; represented in permanent collections J. Walter Thompson Collection, U.S. Gypsum Co., Carborundum Co., Internat. Minerals & Chemicals, Brown & Forman, Stizell-Weller of Ky., Northern Trust Co., Am. Hosp. Supply Co., Westclox Co., New Britain Mus. of Am. Art, Atlanta Art Inst., Reading Mus., Ill. State Mus., Chgo. Art Inst., Chgo. Hist. Soc., Frank Oehlschlaeger Galleries, Chgo. and Sarasota, Fla., U.S. Air Force Acad., The Pentagon, Washington, Tavern Club of Chgo., U. Mich., Old Northwest Territory Arts Soc., So. Ill. U., Mitsubishi of Japan, Ford Motor Co., and numerous pvt. collections including Prime Minister Sato of Japan and former N.Y. Yankee baseball player Joe DiMaggio, others. Recipient 1st prize Parkersburg Fine Art Ctr., 2d prize Denver Art Show, Cosmopolitan Mag. Competition, Purchase award Union League Club, 1959-65, Honorable Mention Terry Art Inst.; named Official Combat Artist USAF. Mem. Am. Watercolor Soc., Arts Club of Chgo., Artists' Guild of Chgo. (1st prize in competition, Best Painting of War Subject), Salamagundi Watercolor Club, Phila. Watercolor Club, Washington Watercolor Club, Madison Wis. Arts League, Nat. Soc. Lit. and the Arts. Home: 10501 Lagria de Oro NE Apt 104 Albuquerque NM 87111

GROSS, FELIKS, sociologist, educator, author; b. Cracow, Poland, June 17, 1906; s. Adolf and Augusta (Alexander) G.; came to U.S., 1941; m. Priva Baidaff, July 25, 1937; 1 child, Eva Helena Gross Friedman. LLM Jagiellanian U., 1930, JD, 1931. Bar: Poland 1937. Sec., Gen. Cen. Ea. European Planning Bd., 1941-45; editor New Europe and World Reconstrn. jour., N.Y.C., 1942-45; prof. sociology Bklyn. Coll. and Grad. Center, CUNY, N.Y.C., 1946-77, emeritus, 1977—; resident prof. CUNY Grad. Sch., 1988—; vis. prof. N.Y. U., 1945-68; vis. prof., dir. Inst. Internat. Affairs, U. Wyo., Laramie, summers 1945-52; vis. prof. Woodrow Wilson Sch. Fgn. Affairs, U. Va., Charlottesville, 1951, 54-56, U. Vt., Burlington, 1957; sr. Fulbright prof. U. Rome, 1957-58, 64-65, 74; lectr. other European, Am. univs.; mem. research council Fgn. Policy Research Inst., Phila., 1966—; vis. prof. Columbia U., N.Y.C., 1973; lectr. U. Florence, 1977, Italian Fgn. Office, Rome; cons. Nat. Com. on Causes and Prevention of Violence, 1968. Pres., Taraknath Das Found., N.Y., 1965; hon. pres. CUNY Acad. Humanities and Scis., 1985, Internat. Labor Office of the League of Nations, Geneva, 1930; resident prof. sociology CUNY Grad. Sch., 1988; co-founder, bd. dirs. Non-Profit Coordinating Com. N.Y., 1984-86. Carnegie scholar, Paris, 1931; Public Affairs Found. N.Y.U., 1962-63; Sloane Found. grantee, 1963; Fulbright grantee, 1956-57, 64-65, 74; City U. Research Found. grantee, 1971, 74; NSF grantee, 1972; Rockefeller Found. grantee, 1974; Golden Cross of Phoenix, King of Greece, 1963; Ethnic New Yorker award N.Y.C., 1987. Mem. Polish Inst. Arts and Sci. (pres. 1988), Internat. League Rights of Man (dir. 1960), Am. Sociol. Assn., Acad. Polit. Sci., N.Y. Acad. Sci., Authors League, Sigma Xi. Author: Nomadism, 1936; Polish Worker, 1945; Foreign Policy Analysis, 1954; Seizure of Political Power, 1957; Valori Sociali e Struttura, 1967; World Politics and Tension Areas, 1967; Violence in Politics, 1973; Il Paese, Values and Social Change in an Italian Village, 1974; The Revolutionary Party, 1974; Ethnics in the Borderland, 1979; Ideologies, Goals and Values, 1986; Working Class and Culture (in Polish), 1986, others; contbr. numerous articles to profl. jours. Home: 310 W 85th St New York NY 10024 Office: City U. N.Y. 208 E 30th New York NY 10016

GROSS, JENARD MORRIS, investment executive; b. Nashville, Oct. 7, 1929; s. Edward and Anna Madeline (Rubenstein) G.; m. Gail Marilyn Meyrowitz, July 11, 1973; children: Jay, Stephanie, Amy, Dawn, Shawn. BA magna cum laude, Vanderbilt U., 1950. Investment builder, pres. Gross Builders, Inc., Houston, 1959—, Nationwide Apartment Mgmt. Corp., 1967-76; chmn. bd. Gulf Coast Savs. Assn., 1977-85; bd. dirs. Republic Bank, Spring Branch, 1973-85, mem. loan com., 1974-84, investment com., 1977-85, loan com., 1974-85; pres., chmn., chief exec. officer United Savs. Assn. of Tex., United Fin. Group, Inc.; bds. dirs. Delta Lloyds Ins. Co., WRI Holdings Inc., Equus Transp. Inc. ; mem. Houston br. Fed. Reserve Bd., 1969-80, bd. dirs., 1987—, Lloyd's of London, 1978—, World Bus. Council, 1979; lectr. U. Houston, 1973-75. Speaker profl. assna.; interview Today Show, 1969; testimony U.S. Ho. of reps., U.S. Senate. Treas. com. San Jacinto council Girl Scouts U.S., 1976-85; trustee San Jocinto Girl Scouts Found., 1979-85, bd. dirs., 1978-85, treas. 1979-85; bd. dirs. Houston Symphony Orch., 1979—, March of Dimes, 1979-80, Wortham Theater Ctr., 1981—, Soc. for Performing Arts, 1979-85, Salvation Army, 1982—; gen. chmn. United Jewish Campaign of Houston, 1970; local chmn. Brandeis U., 1970; mem. pres.'s council, 1972—; mem. mayor's citizens adv. com. of Housing, Houston, 1969-71, mayor's urban renewal com., 1967-68, devel. bd. Health Sci. Ctr. U. Tex. at Houston, 1987—; exec. com. Citizens for Decent Housing; vice chmn. pres.'s com. of UN Day of UN Assn., 1972-81; v.p. Jewish Community Council, 1972; co-chmn. bicentennial week Temple Emanu El, 1976; active Rice Assns., 1971—; constrn. industry council, 1969-70; bd. dirs. Salvation Army, 1982—, Wortham Theater Ctr., 1981—; chmn. bd. Houston Grand Opera, 1986, dir. 1977—, pres., 1984-85, v.p., 1982-84; treas. Grand Opera Endowment, Inc., 1982-84, trustee, 1982—; mem. Friend of English Nat. Opera, bd. dirs. 1983-85, pres. 1983-85; trustee Winchendon Sch., trustee, 1985—, Pauline Sterne Wolff Found., 1985—. Served with U.S. Army, 1953-54. Fellow Brandeis U., 1978-79. Mem. Houston Apt. Assn. (pres. 1968, bd. dirs. 1967-76), Nat. Apt. Assn. (pres. 1969-70, bd. dirs. 1968-73, regional v.p., 1968-69, exec. com. 1968-69), Tex. Apt. Assn. (bd. dirs. 1967-69), Vanderbilt Alumni Club of Houston (pres. 1965, class agt. 1972-75, chmn. Living Endowment Drive of Vanderbilt 1966), Tex. Research League (bd. dirs.1987—), Greater Houston Alumni Chpt. Phi Beta Kappa (pres. 1975), cC (pres. 1975), C. of C. (govtl. affairs com. 1975, housing com. 1975-78). Clubs: University, Racquet, Houstonian, Westwood Country (dir. 1969-75, pres. 1971), Ramada. Office: 5718 Westheimer Suite 600 Houston TX 77057

GROSS, JOEL EDWARD, consultant, safety and security executive; b. Paterson, N.J., Mar. 15, 1939; s. Herman and Virginia (Bivens) G.; m. Alma Wilhemi Janner, Aug. 23, 1980. B.A. cum laude, Seton Hall U., 1977; cert. protection profl. Lab. technician Nabisco, Inc., Fairlawn, N.J., 1957-60; detective Lincoln Park (N.J.) Police Dept., 1966-79; tng. specialist Agway, Inc., Syracuse, N.Y., 1980-81; mgr. safety Drake Bakeries-Borden, Inc., Wayne, N.J., 1981-85; dir. risk mgmt. Pinkerton's Inc., N.Y.C., 1986; mgr. safety N.J. Transit, 1986-87; sr. ptnr. Hunter-Rumsen Group, 1987—; lectr. safety, security, risk mgmt., emergency disaster planning. Coordinator, Greater Passaic Area United Way; state del. N.J. State Policemen's Benevolent Assn., Silver Life mem. Recipient commendation Sec. of Navy and Mayor of Lincoln Park, Morris County Prosecutors Office; cert. breathalyzer operator, N.J., instr. and instr. trainer defensive driving Nat. Safety Council. Served as petty officer, USN, 1960-65. Decorated Navy Commendation medal. Mem. Am. Soc. Indsl. Security, Am. Soc. Safety Engrs. Computer Security Inst., Fire Protection Assn., Am. Legion, Nat. Rifle Assn. Contbr. articles on fleet safety programs to periodicals. Research on juvenile delinquents. Home and Office: 45 Hopper Ave Pompton Plains NJ 07444

GROSS, JOHN JACOB, publisher, editor, author; b. London, Mar. 12, 1935; s. Abraham and Muriel Gross; m. Miriam May, 1965; 2 children. M.A., Wadham Coll., Oxford U. Editor Victor Gollancz, 1956-58; lectr. Queen Mary Coll., U. London, 1959-62; fellow King's Coll., Cambridge U., 1962-65; asst. editor Encounter, 1963-65; lit. editor New Statesman, 1972-73; editor Times Lit. Supplement, 1974-82; dir. Times Newspapers Holdings Ltd. (formerly Times Newspapers Ltd.), 1982; dep. chmn., pub. dir. The Weidenfeld Pub. Group, 1982. Author: The Rise and Fall of the Man of Letters, 1969; James Joyce, 1971; editor: The Oxford Book of Aphorisms, 1983. Recipient Duff Cooper Meml. prize, 1969. Address: 24A St Petersburgh Pl, London W2 England *

GROSS, PATRICK WALTER, business executive, management consultant; b. Ithaca, N.Y., May 15, 1944; s. Eric T. B. and Catharine B. (Rohrer) G.; m. Sheila Eve Proby, Apr. 12, 1969; children: Geoffrey Philipp, Stephanie Lovell. Student, Cornell U., 1962-63; B in Engring. Sci., Rensselaer Poly. Inst., 1965; MSE in Applied Math., U. Mich., 1966; MBA, Stanford U., 1968. Cons. info. mgmt. operation Gen. Electric Co., Schnectady, 1965-67; sr. staff mem. Office Sec. Def., Washington, 1968-69, spl. asst., 1969-70; founder, chmn. exec. com., prin. exec. officer Am. Mgmt. Systems, Inc., Arlington, Va., 1970—, also bd. dirs.; chmn. bd. Medlantic Enterprises Inc., 1988—; bd. dirs. Medlantic Healthcare Group, exec. com., 1982—; bd. dirs. Medlantic Mgmt. Corp., Info.-Disc Corp. Trustee Washington Hosp. Ctr., 1977-87, Sidwell Friends Sch., 1980-88; mem. exec. com., treas. Youth for Understanding, 1984—; mem. Econ. Policy Council UNA-USA. Mem. Fgn. Policy Assn. (bd. govs., bd. dirs., mem. exec. com. 1977-86, 87—), World Affairs Council Washington (bd. dirs., founding vice chmn. 1980—), Council Fgn. Relations, Washington Inst. Fgn. Affairs, Internat. Inst. Strategic Studies (London), Council on Competitiveness, Nat. Economists Club, Am. Econ. Assn., Aspen Inst. Soc. Fellows, Pilgrims of U.S., Pres.'s Assn., Smithsonian Luncheon Group, Sigma Xi, Tau Beta Pi. Clubs: Met. (Washington); Chevy Chase (Md.); Univ. (N.Y.C.). Home: 7401 Glenbrook Rd Bethesda MD 20814 Office: Am Mgmt Systems Inc 1777 N Kent St Arlington VA 22209

GROSS, PAUL, physician, educator; b. Berlin, June 8, 1902; s. Martin and Julia (Baumgarten) G.; m. Dorothy J. Mulac, Aug. 4, 1930; children: Julianne Gross Sauvageot, Paul James, Peter Martin, John Edwin. A.B., Western Res. U., 1924, M.D., 1927, M.A. (Crile research fellow pathology 1928-29), 1929. Intern St. Vincent's Charity Hosp., Cleve., 1927-28; resident pathology Cleve. City Hosp., 1929-31; pathologist St. Vincent's Charity Hosp., 1931-35; vol. asst. to Prof. Erdheim, Vienna, Austria, 1931-32; pathologist West Pa. Hosp., Pitts., 1935-44, St. Joseph's Hosp., Pitts., 1944-54; dir. research lab. Indsl. Health Found., Mellon Inst., also sr. fellow Inst., 1948-68, adv. fellow, 1968—; adj. prof. pathology indsl. diseases Grad. Sch. Pub. Health. U. Pitts., 1960-68; research prof. Grad. Sch. Pub. Health, U. Pitts., 1968-71, adj. prof., 1971-76; disting. research prof. pathology Med. U. S.C., 1971-76, adj. prof., 1976—. Author: (with T.F. Hatch) Pulmonary Deposition and Retention of Inhaled Aerosols, 1964, (with D.C. Braun) Toxic and Biomedical Effects of Fibers with Special Reference to Asbestos, Man-Made Vitreous Fibers and Organic Fibers, 1983; also numerous articles. Recipient Adolph G. Kammer merit in authorship award Indsl. Med. Assn., 1967. Fellow ACP; mem. Am. Coll. Chest Physicians, Indsl. Med. Assn., Coll. Am. Pathologists, Am. Thoracic Soc., Am. Indsl. Hygiene Assn. (hon.), Am. Assn. Pathologists and Bacteriologists, Internat. Acad. Pathology, Am. Soc. Clin. Pathologists, AMA, Am. Soc. Exptl. Pathology. Home: 28 Maui Circle Naples FL 33962

GROSS, PETER ALAN, epidemiologist, researcher; b. Newark, Nov. 18, 1938; s. Meyer P. and Nathalie (Bass) Denburg) G.; m. Regina Teri Gittlin, May 30, 1964; children—Deborah Karen, Michael Philip, Daniel Brian. B.A. cum laude, Amherst Coll., 1960; M.D., Yale U., 1964. Diplomate: Am. Bd. Internal Medicine. NIH fellow virology dept. epidemiology Yale U., New Haven, 1969-71; intern Yale-New Haven Hosp., 1964-65, jr. resident, 1965-66; sr. resident Peter Bent Brigham Hosp., Boston, 1968-69; research and edn. assoc. Va Hosp., West Haven, Conn., 1971-73, acting chief infectious disease sect., 1972-73, chief infectious disease sect., 1973-74, Hackensack (N.J.) Med. Center, 1974—, chmn. dept. medicine, 1980—, chmn. med. bd., 1986; prof. medicine N.J. Med. Sch. Newark, 1981—; assoc. clin. prof. medicine Columbia U. Coll. Phys. and Surgs., N.Y.C., 1971-81, asst. clin. prof., 1974-77; asst. prof. medicine Yale U. Sch. Medicine, New Haven, 1971-74; ad hoc reviewer NIH, Nat. Inst. Allergy and Infectious Diseases research grants, 1974—. Author: Gram Strain Recognition, 1975, 2d edit., 1980; editorial bd.; Jour. Clin. Microbiology, 1980—. Infection Control, 1980—. Mem. clin. indicators task force Joint Commn. on Accreditation of Hosps., 1987. Served to lt. comdr. USPHS, CDC, 1966-68. NIH fellow, 1969-71. Fellow Infectious Disease Soc. Am., ACP, Am. Acad. Microbiology (sco. hosp.); mem. Am. Soc. Virology, AAAS, Am. Soc. Microbiology, Soc. Hosp. Epidemiologists Am. (councillor, 1986—). Republican. Jewish. Home: 242 McKinley Pl Ridgewood NJ 07450 Office: Hackensack Med Ctr Hackensack NJ 07601

GROSS, PRIVA BAIDAFF, art historian, retired educator; b. Wieliczka, Poland, June 19, 1911; came to U.S., 1941, naturalized, 1955; d. Israel and Leopolda (Friedman) Baidaff; Ph.M., Jagellonian U., Cracow, Poland, 1937; postgrad. (N.Y. U. scholar 1945-47), N.Y. U. Inst. Fine Arts, 1945-48; m. Feliks Gross, July 25, 1937; 1 dau., Eva Helena Gross Friedman. Mem. faculty Queensborough Community Coll., CUNY, 1961-81, assoc. prof. art history, 1971-81, ret., 1981, co-chmn. art and music dept., 1966-68, chmn. art dept., 1968-74, dir. coll. gallery, 1968-77. SUNY grantee, 1967. Mem. AAUW (dir. 1972-76, 1980-82), Coll. Art Assn. Am., Soc. Archtl. Historians, Gallery Assn. N.Y. State (dir. 1972-73), N.Y. State Assn. Jr. Colls., AAUP, Polish Inst. Arts and Scis. Am., Council Gallery and Exhbn. Dirs. (dir. 1970-72). Contbr. articles, revs. to profl. publs. Home: 310 W 85th St New York NY 10024

GROSS, RAINER, pharmacologist, physiology educator; b. Mosbach, Fed. Republic Germany, Jan. 22, 1943; s. Joseph and Pia Maria Barbara (Zeitler) G.; m. Christiane Koehler, June 16, 1976; children: Michael Andreas, Barbara Christina. Diploma in engring., Tech. U. Karlsruhe, Fed. Republic Germany, 1966; Dr. med., U. Heidelberg, Fed. Republic Germany, 1972, habilitatus, 1979. Research fellow U. Heidelberg, 1967-79, lectr. in physiology, 1979—; head div. cardiovascular pharmacology Inst. Pharmacology, Bayer A.G., Wuppertal, Fed. Republic Germany, 1981—. Bd. editors Archives Internat. Pharmacodynamie et Pharmacotherapie; contbr. articles to research jours. Mem. German Physiol. Soc., Deutsche Gesellschaft für Herz-u. Kreislaufforschung, Medizinisch Naturwissenschaftliche Gesellschaft Wuppertal. Office: Bayer AG, Friedrich Ebert Strasse 217, D5600 Wuppertal 1 Federal Republic of Germany

GROSS, SIDNEY W., neurosurgeon, educator; b. Cleve., Aug. 28, 1904; s. Joseph and Frieda (Weiss) G.; m. Bobbie Bruce, 1983; 1 son by previous marriage, Samuel. A.B., Western Res. U. (now Case Western Res. U.), 1925, M.D., 1928. Diplomate: Am. Bd. Neurol. Surgery. Intern Michael Reese Hosp., Chgo., 1928-29; resident Neurol. Inst., N.Y.C., 1929-31; asst. neurosurgery Washington U., St. Louis, 1931-33; vol. Neuropath. Lab. U. Chgo., 1933; neurosurgeon Mt. Sinai Hosp., Cleve., 1933-34; now emeritus prof. neurosurgery Mt. Sinai Sch. Medicine, N.Y.C.; emeritus dir. dept. neurosurgery City Hosp., Elmhurst, N.Y.; dir. emeritus dept. neurosurgery Mt. Sinai Med. Center, N.Y.C.; prof. neurology U. So. Fla. Coll. Medicine, 1978-79; sr. neurosurg. cons. Tampa (Fla.) VA Hosp., 1978-79; cons. Wadsworth VA Hosp., Los Angeles, 1980—; neurosurgeon Serra Meml. Health Ctr., Sun Valley, Calif.; clin. prof. neurology UCLA Sch. Medicine, 1981—. Author: Diagnosis and Treatment of Head Injuries, 1940; Contbr. numerous articles to profl. jours. Served with AUS, World War II; chief neurosurg. sect. Halloran Gen. Hosp. maj. M.C. U.S. Army, 85th Evacuation Hosp., 180th and 116th gen. hosps., ETO. Fellow A.C.S., N.Y. Acad. Medicine; mem. Am. Neurol. Assn., Am. Assn. Neurol. Surgeons, N.Y. Soc. Neurosurgery (sec.), Phi Beta Kappa, Alpha Omega Alpha. Address: 330 Alta Ave Santa Monica CA 90402

GROSS, THOMAS LESTER, obstetrician/gynecologist, researcher; b. Decatur, Ill., Aug. 17, 1945; s. Gilbert Wayne and Anna (Graham) G.; m. Judy Beth Osborn, Dec. 30, 1967; children—Elizabeth, Matthew, Joshua. B.A. in Chemistry, Bluffton (Ohio) Coll., 1967; M.D., U. Ill., 1971. Diplomate Am. Bd. Ob-Gyn, subsplty. maternal/fetal medicine. Intern and resident Akron (Ohio) Gen. Med. Ctr., 1973-77; fellow in maternal/fetal medicine Case Western Res. U., 1977-79; asst. to dir. perinatal clin. research ctr. Cleve. Met. Gen. Hosp., 1982-85, acting dir. Perinatal Clin. Research Ctr., 1985-86; asst. prof. ob-gyn Case Western Res. U., Cleve., 1977-85, assoc. prof., 1985-86; assoc. prof. ob-gyn U. Ill. Coll. Medicine, Peoria, 1986—, chmn. dept., 1986—; dir. perinatology St. Francis Med. Ctr., Peoria, Ill., 1987—; instr. Internat. Symposium Fetal Eval., Lima, Peru, 1983. Mem. Physicians for Social Responsibility. Mem. Am. Coll. Obstetricians and Gynecologists (1st prize research 1984), Central Assn. Obstetricians and Gynecologists (Community Hosp. Research award 1981, Ann. Prize award for Research, 1982), Soc. Perinatal Obstetricians, Soc. Gynecologic Investigation, Perinatal Research Soc., Peoria Ob-Gyn Soc. Contbr. numerous articles to sci. jours. Office: One Illini Dr Box 1649 Peoria IL 61656

GROSS, WILLIS CHARLES, JR., dentist; b. St. Louis, June 3, 1924; s. Willis Charles and Mary Ida (Kelly) G.; AA, Harris Jr. Coll., 1943; DDS, St. Louis U., 1946; postgrad. U. Detroit, 1952-53; m. Rosemarie Dorothy Horak, Feb. 14, 1948 (dec. 1985); 1 son, Alan Charles; m. Verda N. Politte, Jan. 4, 1986. Commd. 1st lt. Dental Corps, U.S. Army and USAF, 1946, advanced through grades to maj., 1952; ret., 1953; pvt. practice dentistry, Affton, Mo., 1954—; pres. Willis C. Gross Dental Assos.; v.p. C & W Gross Corp. Served with AUS, 1942-44. Fellow Acad. Gen. Dentistry, Royal Soc. Health (Eng.); mem. Am., Mo. Dental Assns., St. Louis Dental Soc., Concord Village Bus. Men's Assn., Oakville Mehlville Concord C. of C. (bd. dirs.), Am. Legion, VFW, Alpha Sigma Nu, Omicron Kappa Upsilon, Delta Sigma Delta (past pres., sec.-treas. St. Louis chpt.), Alpha Phi Omega. Republican. Clubs: Liberty Country (bd. dirs.) (Horine, Mo.); Big Game Hunters (St. Louis), Chaine des Rotisseurs, Ordre Mondial. Lodges: Masons, Shriners (chmn. temple med. staff, 32d degree), Lions (pres. 1965-66). Home: 20 Dorclin Ln Saint Louis MO 63128 Office: 7 Concord Center Dr Saint Louis MO 63123

GROSSER, ALFRED, political science educator; b. Frankfurt, Germany, Feb. 1, 1925; arrived in France, 1933, naturalized, 1937.; s. Paul and Lily (Rosenthal) G.;m. Anne-Marie Jourcin; children: Jean, Pierre, Marc,

Paul. Agrege, nat. competition, 1947; dr Etat lettres et sciences humaines, U. Sorbonne, Paris, 1970. Asst. dir. UNESCO, Germany, 1950-51; asst. prof. German civilization U. Paris, 1951-55; prof. Inst. Polit. Studies, Paris, 1956—; dir. studies and research Nat. Found. Polit. Sci., Paris, %; vis. prof. Sch. Advanced Internat. Studies, Johns Hopkins U., Bologna, Italy, 1955-69; Kratter vis. prof. modern European history Stanford U., 1964-65; prof. politics Ecole Polytechnique, Paris, 1973—, Ecole Hautes Etudes Commerciales, 1986—; pres. Info. and Research Ctr. on Contemporary Germany, Paris, 1982—. Recipient Peace prize Union German Pubs., 1975. Mem. Internat. Polit. Sci. Assn. (exec. com. 1967-73, v.p. 1970-73), French Assn. Polit. Sci. (bd. dirs. 1965—), Inst. Etudes Politiques (pres. sci. council 1986—). Home: 8 rue Dupleix, 75015 Paris France Office: Inst Etudes Politiques, 27 rue St Guillaume, 75007 Paris France

GROSSFELD, BERNHARD THEODOR, lawyer, educator; b. Bentheim, Fed. Republic of Germany, Dec. 30, 1933; s. Hermann Heinrich and Elisabeth (Rotthege) G.; m. Maria Paula Hettlage, May 22, 1964; children: Ursula, Hildegard, Johannes, Adelheid, Angela, Maria. JD, U. Munster, Fed. Republic of Germany, 1960; LLM, Yale U., 1963. Prof. law U. Goettingen, Fed. Republic of Germany, 1966-73; prof. law U. Munster, 1973—, dir. Inst. for Comparative Law, 1973—, dir. inst. Coop. Research, 1974—. Mem. German-Dutch Lawyers Assn. (chair 1974—), Muenster Lawyers Assn. (chair 1974—), Acad. Sci. Roman Catholic. Lodge: Rotary (pres. Munster chpt. 1972-73). Office: U Munster, Universitaetsstrasse 4-6, 44 Munster Federal Republic of Germany

GROSSKREUTZ, JOSEPH CHARLES, physicist, engineering researcher; b. Springfield, Mo., Jan. 5, 1922; s. Joseph Charles and Helen (Mobley) G.; m. Mary Catherine Schubel, Sept. 7, 1949; children—Cynthia Lee, Barbara Helen. B.S. in Math., Drury Coll., 1943; postgrad., U. Calif.-Berkeley, 1946-47; M.S., Washington U., St. Louis, 1948, Ph.D. in Physics, 1950. Research physicist Calif. Research Corp., La Habra, 1950-52; asst. prof. physics U. Tex.-Austin, 1952-56; research scientist Nuclear Physics Lab., Austin, 1952-56; sr. physicist Midwest Research Inst., Kansas City, Mo., 1956-59, prin. physicist, 1959-63, sr. adviser, 1963-67; prin. advisor Midwest Research Inst., Kansas City, 1967-71; chief mech. properties sect. Nat. Bur. Standards, Washington, 1971-72; mgr. solar programs Black & Veatch Cons. Engrs., Kansas City, Mo., 1972-77, mgr. advanced tech. projects, 1979—; dir. research Solar Energy Research Inst., Golden, Colo., 1977-79; spl. cons. NATO, 1967. Contbr. physics and energy articles to profl. jours. Served to lt. USN, 1943-46. Recipient Disting. Service award Drury Coll., 1959; Washington U. fellow, 1948-49. Fellow Am. Phys. Soc., ASTM (dir. 1977-80, Merit award 1972); mem. Sigma Xi, Sigma Pi Sigma. Methodist. Home: 4306 W 111th Terr Leawood KS 66211 Office: Black & Veatch PO Box 8405 Kansas City MO 64114

GROSSMAN, BURTON E., corporate executive; b. Corpus Christi, Tex., Feb. 15, 1918; s. Edward and Bessie G.; m. Miriam Siegel, Apr. 23, 1980; children—Bruce Edward, Cynthia Helene. B.S. in Bus. Adminstrn., U. Tex., 1940; D.B.A. (hon.), John Dewey U., N.Y., 1981; LL.D., U. Far East, 1983; LL.D. (hon.), Mexican Acad. Internat. Law, 1985; D (hon.), U. of the Ams., Mexico City, 1988. Chmn. bd. Grossman y Asociados, Tampico, Mexico, 1964—, Sociedad Indsl., 1972—, chmn. bd., chief exec. officer Grupo Continental S.A., Tampico, 1977—; chmn. bd., chief exec. officer Asesores de Pensiones S.A., Grabados Fernando Fernandes, Mexico, chmn. bd., chief exec. officer Intercontinental Bankshares Corp., San Antonio. Vice chmn. exec. com. Chancellor's Council, U. Tex. System; mem. investment com. Rotary Internat. Served to capt. U.S. Army, 1942-46. Mem. Inst. Advanced Studies (Tamaulipas) (chmn. bd. trustees), U. Tex. Cancer Found. (bd. visitors), Pres.'s Club U. Tex., Pres.'s Club So. Meth. U., Am. Mgmt. Assn., Conf. Bd., Nat. Advt. Assn. Mexico. Avocations: golf; tennis; big game hunting; collection of cigar bands. Office: InterContinental Bankshares Corp 7710 Jones Maltsberger Suite 200 San Antonio TX 78216

GROSSMAN, DAVID, geography educator; b. Turin, Italy, Feb. 13, 1934; s. Eliyau Eliezer and Judith (Lichtenstein) G.; m. Marcia Bialick, Nov. 24, 1959; children: Benjamin D., Hannah E., Ephraim S., Amihai G. BS, NYU, 1961; MA, Columbia U., 1964, PhD, 1968. Lic. tchr., Israel. Instr. geography Hunter Coll., N.Y.C., 1963-67; asst. prof. Ea. Mich. U., Ypsilanti, 1967-69; assoc. prof. Bar-Ilan U., Ramat Gan, Israel, 1969—. Editor: Judea and Samaria, 1977, Between Yarkon and Ayalon, 1983; contbr. numerous articles to profl. jours. Served with Israeli Army, 1955-57. Burgess Hon. fellow Columbia U., 1965-66, traveling fellow, Nigeria 1965-66, Sherman Found. fellow, Gt. Britain, 1983-84; grantee Israeli Acad. Sci., 1973-80; recipient Gezer Meml. award Defenders of Gezer-Israel, 1983. Mem. Assn. Am. Georgraphers, Israel Geographical Assn. (head rural geography sect. 1986-87), Internat. Geographic Union, Regional Sci. Assn. Jewish. Office: Bar-Ilan U Dept Geography, Ramat Gan 52100, Israel

GROSSMAN, JOHN HENRY, obstetrician, gynecologist, educator; b. Rochester, N.Y., Aug. 17, 1914; s. Gustave Adolph and Mabel (Trumeter) G.; A.B., U. Rochester, 1938, M.D., 1941; m. Marya S. Fryczynski, Nov. 30, 1941; children—John Henry III, Marya Mabel. Asst. serologist Rochester (N.Y.) Health Bur., 1940-41; intern surgery New Haven Hosp., 1941-42, asst. resident ob-gyn, 1942-43, asso. resident, 1943-44, resident ob-gyn, 1944-45; asst. obstetrician and gynecologist, mem. faculty Yale U., 1941-43, instr. ob-gyn, 1943-45; asso. attending obstetrician Bridgeport (Conn.) Hosp., 1945-56, sr. attending gynecologist and obstetrician, 1957-70, sr. cons. ob-gyn, 1970—, pres. and chief attending staff, 1960-61; instr. ob-gyn U. Bridgeport and Bridgeport Hosp. Schs. Nursing, 1945-56, asst. prof. Coll. Nursing, U. Bridgeport, 1956—; host talk show Here's To Your Health, Sta. WADS, Ansonia, Conn., 1982—. First v.p. Nichols Village Improvement Assn. Recipient Man of Yr. award Am. Legion, Trumbull, Conn., 1969; Stanley M. Collins Meml. award, 1970; Linking Ring Feature award, 1972; London Magic Circle Silver Wand award, 1981. Diplomate Am. Bd. Ob-Gyn. Fellow Am. Coll. Obstetricians and Gynecologists (founder, hon. life mem.), Am. Soc. Abdominal Surgeons, Royal Soc. Medicine (overseas fellow); mem. Conn. (hon. life), Fairfield County (hon. life), Bridgeport med. socs., Magicians Guild Am., Magic Collectors Assn. (hon. life pres.), Am. Assn. Physicians and Surgeons, Pan Am. Med. Assn. (hon. life), Sigma Chi. Clubs: Univ. (Bridgeport); Magic Circle (London). Feature writer M.U.M. mag., 1958—, also research editor, monthly columnist; feature writer Magicol mag., 1959—; Am. corr. Magic Circular mag., London, 1960—; mem. Am. Magic Hall of Fame, 1977; contbr. to books. Home: 1708 Huntington Turnpike Trumbull CT 06611 Office: 457 Mill Hill Ave Bridgeport CT 06610

GROSSMAN, ROBERT ALLEN, railcar leasing company executive; b. Port Jervis, N.Y., July 24, 1941; s. George and Helen (Garson) G.; student Cornell U., 1959-60, U. Pa., 1960-62; m. Joan Ward, June 15, 1962 (div.); children—Jeffrey, Wendy; m. Gloria Schwartz, Nov. 22, 1987. Mgr. fin. div. North Shore Packing Co., Inc., North Bellmore, N.Y., 1962-64; mgr. refin. and legal dept. Coburn Corp. Am., Rockville Centre, N.Y., 1964-67; stock broker Weis, Voison & Cannon, Inc., N.Y.C., 1967-69, Nadel & Co., N.Y.C., 1969-70; chmn. bd., chief exec. officer, pres. Emons Industries, Inc., York, Pa., 1970—, Emons Holdings, Inc., 1986—. Mem. York Area C. of C. (dir. 1978-83). Office: 1 W Market St York PA 17401

GROSSMAN, SAMUEL, manufacturer, publisher, author; b. Phila., Dec. 6, 1897; s. Mayer and Goldie (Klempner) G.; student Am. Bus. Inst., 1914-15, CCNY, evenings, 1919-20; m. Doris Boxer, Aug. 21, 1932; children—Judith, Lucille, Lawrence. Asso. editorial and acctg. depts. N.Y. Times, 1915-18; founder S. Grossman Co., N.Y.C., 1921; auditor Fox Film Co., 1922-23; pres. Grossman Stamp Co., Inc., N.Y.C., 1927—; founder Longacre Pub. Co., 1957, Hygrade Sports Card Co., 1984. Mem. Am. Philatelic Assn., Am. Stamp Dealer's Assn. (pres. 1966-67, dir.), King County Grand Jurors Assn., Am. Topical Assn., Royal Can. Philatelic Assn., Am. Numis. Assn., Assn. Stamp Exhbns., Grand Street Boys Assn., Internat. Fedn. Stamp Dealers Assns., Judaica Hist. Philatelic Soc. Author: Superior World Stamp Album, 1950; Paramount World Stamp Album, 1951; Monarch World Stamp Album, 1952; Coronet DeLuxe World Stamp Album, 1954; Stamp Collector's Handbook, 17 edits., 1957-81; Regent World Stamp Album, 4 vols., 1957; Academy World Stamp Album, 1958; Capitol United States Stamp Album, 1959; Victory United States Stamp Album, 1959; Columbia U.S. Plate Block Album, 2 vols., 1969, with supplements to 1976; Crown World Stamp Album, 3 vols., 1963; Transworld World Stamp Album, 1963; Philatelic World Atlas, 1965; Flags and Coats of Arms of the World, 1981; Presidents and Famous Americans, 1968; Space Age Stamp Album, 1970; Philatelic Color Guide; Jefferson U.S. Stamp Album, 1981. Home: 10 W 16th St New York NY 10011 Office: 5 E 17th St New York NY 10003

GROSSWEINER, LEONARD IRWIN, physicist, educator; b. Atlantic City, Aug. 16, 1924; s. Jules H. and Rae (Goldberger) G.; m. Bess Tornheim, Sept. 9, 1951; children-Karen Ann, Jane (dec.), James Benjamin, Eric William. B.S., Coll. City N.Y., 1947; M.S., Ill. Inst. Tech., 1950, Ph.D., 1955. Asst. chemist Argonne Nat. Lab., Ill., 1947-50; assoc. physicist Argonne Nat. Lab., 1950-57; assoc. prof. physics Ill. Inst. Tech., Chgo., 1957-62; prof. physics Ill. Inst. Tech., 1962—, chmn. dept. physics, 1970-81, Sang Exchange lectr., 1972-73; vis. prof. radiology Stanford U. Sch. Medicine, 1979; vis. prof. physics U. Ill. Coll. Medicine, 1983—; adj. prof. biomed. engring. Northwestern U. Tech. Inst., Evanston, Ill., 1987—; cons. Donner Lab. U. Calif., Berkeley, Chgo. Med. Sch., North Chicago, Ill., Hines VA Hosp., Ill., Michael Reese Med. Ctr., Chgo., U.S. Com. on Interagy. Radiation Research and Policy Coordination; cons. and research dir. Wenske Laser Ctr. Ravenswood Hosp. Med. Ctr., Chgo.; mem. U.S. Nat. Com. Photobiology, 1977-81, chmn., 1980-81; trustee Midwest Bio-Laser Inst., 1983—, sec., 1986—. Author: Organic Photoconductors in Electrophotography, 1970; contbr. articles to profl. jours. Served with AUS, 1944-46. Fellow Am. Phys. Soc. (sec.-treas. div. biol. physics 1972-76, vice chmn. 1976-77, chmn. 1977-78), N.Y. Acad. Scis.; mem. Am. Chem. Soc., AAAS, Radiation Research Soc., Midwest Bio-Laser Inst. (exec. com. 1985-86, sec. 1986—), Am. Soc. Photobiology (council 1977-80, sec.-treas. 1981-86, pres.-elect 1986-87, pres. 1987-88), Biophys. Soc., Inter-Am. Photochem. Soc. (exec. com. 1976-78), Sigma Xi (disting. faculty lectr. 1970). Home: 231 Wentworth Ave Glencoe IL 60022 Office: Ill Inst Tech IIT Center Chicago IL 60616

GROSZ, KAROLY, government official; b. Miskolc, Hungary, 1930; m. Éva Csontó; children: Iván, Péter. Student, Eötvös Lóránd U., Budapest, Hungry. Ofcl. Cen. Apparatus of the Party, Hungary, 1950; officer Hungarian People's Army; head dept. Borsod-Abauj-Zemplén County Party Com., 1954; mng. editor Észak-Magyarország Daily, 1958; member polit. staff Hungarian Socialist Workers' Party, sec. com. Hungarian radio and TV, 1962-68, dep. head dept. cen. com., 1968-73, 1st sec. Fejér County Com., 1973, head dept. cen. com., 1974-79, 1st sec. Borsod-Abauj-Zemplén County Com., 1979-84, mem. cen. com., 1980—, 1st sec. Budapest Party Com., 1984-87, mem. Polit. Com., 1985—, prime minister, 1987—, gen. sec. cen. com., 1988—. Office: Office of Prime Minister, Hungarian Socialist Workers' Party, Szechenyi rkp 19, 1054 Budapest Hungary

GROTBERG, JAMES BERNARD, biomedical engineer, educator; b. Oak Park, Ill., July 22, 1950; s. John Edward and Edith (Henderson) Burchinal; m. Karen Faith Rubner, June 22, 1980; children: Anna Christine, John Christian. Ph.D., Johns Hopkins U., 1978; M.D., U. Chgo., 1980. Lic. physician, Ill. Assoc. prof. Northwestern U., Evanston, Ill., 1980—. Contbr. articles to profl. jours. Recipient Achievement award Johns Hopkins U., 1973, New Investigator, NIH, 1983, Presl. Young Investigator, NSF, 1984, Research Career Devel. award NIH, 1987. Mem. Am. Phys. Soc., Phi Beta Kappa, Tau Beta Pi. Office: Northwestern Univ Technological Inst Dept Biomed Engineering Evanston IL 60208

GROTE, E. ENID, artist, librarian, editor; b. N.Y.C., Sept. 26, 1909; d. Lewis and Mary Katherine (Engle) Granath; student (Louise Graham Hinsdale scholar) Columbia U., 1928-31, Sch. Library Sci. and Sch. Journalism, 1933-35; m. John H. Grote, Jr., Dec. 28, 1935 (dec.). With Free Public Library, East Orange, N.J., 1932-37; mem. editorial staff fgn. and Washington news AP, N.Y.C., 1937-43; chief librarian, organizer news reference library Pan Am. World Airways, N.Y.C., 1943-44; organizer U.S. Info. Libraries, Office War Info., U.S. State Dept., N.Y.C. and Washington, 1944-45; chief librarian Hort. Soc. N.Y., N.Y.C., 1947-61; free-lance cons. editor to N.Y.C. pubs.; hort. manuscript evaluator, 1950-61; editor, contbr. book revs. and articles The Bulletin; group shows include: Woodstock (N.Y.) Artists Assn., Catskill Art Soc., Hurleyville, N.Y., also other art assn. shows, pvt. galleries; represented in pvt. collections. Mem. Spl. Libraries Assn., Woodstock Artists Assn., Catskill Art Soc., Internat. Soc. Artists, LWV, Internat. Platform Assn., Smithsonian Assocs., Nat. Trust Historic Preservation, Nat. Mus. Women in the Arts. Republican. Presbyterian. Club: Woodstock Country. Home and studio: Box 176 Aspen Rd Shrub Oak NY 10588

GROTH, A. NICHOLAS, psychologist; b. Webster, Mass., Dec. 6, 1937; s. Aloysius Nestor and Sophie Mary (Karabash) G.; BA, Boston U., 1959, MA, 1960, PhD, 1972. Instr. in psychology Wheelock Coll., 1963-68; chief psychologist Mass. Center for Diagnosis and Treatment of Sexually Dangerous Persons, Bridgewater, Mass., 1966-76; clin. dir. Whiting Forensic Inst., Middletown, Conn., 1976-77; dir. forensic mental health program Harrington Meml. Hosp., Southbridge, Mass., 1977-78; co-dir. sex offender program Conn. Correctional Instn., Somers, 1978-86; cons. Wyo. State Honor Farm, Riverton; co-dir. St. Joseph Coll. Inst. for Treatment and Control Child Sexual Abuse, West Hartford, Conn., 1980—; exec. dir. Forensic Mental Health Assocs., 1981—; mem. adv. bd. Nat. Center for Prevention and Control of Rape, Washington, 1981-85. Mem. Am. Psychol. Assn., Conn. Psychol. Assn., Mass. Psychol. Assn., Nat. Orgn. Victim Assistance, Am. Assn. Orthopsychiatry, Am. Psychology-Law Soc. Author: Sexual Assault of Children and Adolescents, 1978; Men Who Rape: The Psychology Of The Offender, 1979; Anatomical Drawings for the Use in the Investigation and Intervention of Child Sexual Abuse, 1984; contbr. numerous articles, chpts., editorials to profl. publs. Home: RR 1 Box 404 Lakeside Beach Webster MA 01570

GROTH, BETTY, conservationist, author, photographer; b. Oak Park, Ill.; d. Herman A. and Bertha L. (Luepke) G.; grad. Vassar Coll., 1932. Sec., Oak Park YMCA, 1935-42; sec. Ill. Commn. for Handicapped Children, 1943-46; pvt. sec. Chgo. Assn. of Commerce and Industry, 1947-53, Chgo. Heart Assn., 1953-75. Mem. Save-The-Dunes Council, North Central Audubon Council; sec., dir. Natural Resources Council of Ill., 1967-71, v.p., 1969-71; v.p., dir. Du Page County Clean Streams, 1967-69; founder, chmn. Northern Conservation Cabinet, 1971-75; landscape gardener Audubon Sanctuary, Wayne, Ill., 1977-79; color film nature lectr. Mem. Nat. Audubon Soc., Ill. Audubon Soc. (v.p. conservation, dir. 1962-73, sec. bd. dirs. 1973-74), Big Bluestem Audubon Soc. (dir., sec.), Du Page Audubon Soc., Nat. Wildlife Fedn., Conservation Explorers Club (pres. 1975-76), Morton Arboretum, Sarasota Jungle Gardens, Am. Bald Eagle Club. Baptist. Club: Wis. Vassar. Author: Open Spaces in Illinois, 1962; Surprise in the North Woods, 1966; Wildlife by John Burroughs Cabin, 1967; King's Ransom to Save a Prairie, 1968; Ivory Bills Found Alive in Texas Big Thicket, 1969; Great Swamp Wildlife Refuge Versus Jetport, 1970; The Fate of Thorn Creek Woods, 1971; Man's Dominion of the Green Earth, 1972; Country Estate, 1973; King of Sky, Land and Water, 1974; North Woods Shoreline, 1975; Vanished Illinois Prairie Returns, 1976; Florida Conservation and Environmental Survey, 3 vols. for Conservation Ctr., Univ. Wyo., 1983, 4 vols. for Vassar Coll. Library, 1984; Wisconsin Wilderness, 3 vols. for Conservation Ctr., Univ. Wyo., 1985; Yellowstone Park 1914; North with Springtime Florida to Maine, 4 vols. for Vassar Coll. Library, 1986; Toward More Beautiful Gardens, 1988, 3 vols.; The Four Seasons, 1988. Contbr. articles to profl. jours. Home: Gull Shores Gills Rock Ellison Bay WI 54210

GROTJAHN, MARTIN, medical writer, retired psychiatrist and analyst; b. Berlin, July 8, 1904; s. Alfred and Charlotte (Hartz) G.; M.D., Kaiser Friedrich U., Berlin, 1929; came to U.S., 1936, naturalized, 1942; m. Etelka Gross, Aug. 18, 1927; 1 son, Michael. Intern, Hosp. Reinikendaf, Berlin; resident Charité Hosp., Berlin, 1933-36, Menninger Clinic, Topeka, 1936-38, Chgo. Psychoanalytic Inst.; head physician Berlin U. dept. psychiatry and neurology, 1933-36; mem. staff Chgo. Inst. Psychoanalysis, 1938-46; mem. faculty U. So. Calif., 1946-86, now prof. emeritus, tng. analyst emeritus; practice psychiatry, Topeka, Chgo., now Los Angeles, Calif. Served with M.C., AUS, 1942-46. Recipient Sigmund Freud award Psychoanalytic Physicians, 1976. Mem. Am. Psychoanalytic Assn. (life), Am. Psychiat. Assn. (life), So. Calif. Psychiat. Assn. (life), So. Calif. Psychoanalytic Soc. (life). Author: Beyond Laughter, 1957; Psychoanalysis and the Family Neurosis, 1960; A Celebration of Laughter, 1970; The Voice of the Symbol, 1972; The Art and the Technique of Analytic Group Therapy, 1977; My Favorite Patient: The Memoirs of an Analyst, 1987; author, co-editor Psychoanalytic Pioneers, 1966. Contbr. 400 articles to profl. jours. Home: 2169 Century Hill Los Angeles CA 90067

GROUES, HUBERT, marketing professional; b. Lyon, Rhône, France, July 2, 1948; s. Pierre and Marie-Therese (Rodet) G.; m. Christine Beguin, m. May 29, 1971; children: Stephanie, Guillaume, Raphaël, Emilie. BAC, Ecole des Hautes Etudes Commerciales, France, 1973. Product mgr. COFNA (Unilever), Tours, France, 1975-80, mktg. dir., 1980-83; mktg. dir. B.N. (General Mills), Nantes, France, 1983-87, mktg., sales dir., 1987—. Home: 5 bis passage Levesque, 44000 Nantes France Office: BN, Ave Lotz Cossē, 44040 Cedex Nantes France

GROUSE, PHILLIP JOHN, computer company executive, consultant, educator; b. Sydney, New South Wales, Australia, May 16, 1933; s. Phillip Edward and Elza Muir (Seawood) G.; m. Margaret Nancy Ford, May 20, 1957 (div. 1988); children—Jennifer, Alison, Margot, John. B.Sc. with 1st class honors, U. Sydney, 1955, M.Sc., 1957; B.D. with honors, London U., 1966. Sr. def. officer Dept. Def., Melbourne, Australia, 1957-60; EDP mgr. AWA Ltd., Sydney, 1961-66; lectr. U. New South Wales, Sydney, 1968-69, sr. lectr., 1969-74, assoc. prof., 1974-84, dean students New Coll., 1968-78; mng. dir. Microshare Systems, Sydney, 1984—, Lamnia Pty Ltd., Sydney, 1981-88, Stylus Software Pty. Ltd., Sydney, 1988—; cons. various govt. bodies, Sydney, 1970—; dep. dir. Inst. of Info. Tech. U. New S. Wales, Sydney, 1988—. Author: Data Processing and Information Systems, 1970; contbg. author: Information Systems Design, 1982, Your Computer Mag., 1983—; author 3 monographs on computer sci. Contbr. numerous articles to profl. jours. Lay preacher Anglican Diocese of Sydney, 1966—. Fellow Australian Computer Soc.; mem. Assn. for Computing Machinery. Avocations: astronomy; bush walking; flute; homoeopathy. Office: Stylus Software Pty Ltd, PO Box 22, 2778 Woodford, New South Wales Australia

GROUSSARD, SERGE HARITON, writer, journalist; b. Niort, Deux-Sevres, France, Jan. 18, 1921; s. Georges Andre and Vera (Bernstein-Woolbrunn) G.; m. Monique Berlioux, Feb. 29, 1956; children by previous marriage: Dominique, Valerie. D.E.S. Lettres, Sorbonne, 1947, Diplome de l'Lettres, 1946, Licence d'Anglais, 1946; Diplome de l'Ecole Libre Des Sciences Politiques, Paris, 1946. With Ecole Nationale D'Administration, 1946-47; grand reporter Le Figaro, 1954-56, 57-62, L'Aurore, 1962-69; conseiller a la direction, Le Figaro, 1969-75; writer, 1947—. Author: Roman La Femmensans Passe, 1950 (Prix Femina); Une Chic Fille, 1957 (Prix de la Nouvelle); Solitude Espanole (Prix du grand Reportage), 1948; Taxi de Nuit, 1971; L'Algerie des adieux, 1972; La médaille de sang, 1973; La guerre oubliée, 1974, others. Served to maj., French Marines. Decorated Officier de la Legion d'Honneur, Medaille de la Resistance, Croix de Guerre, Croix de la Valeur Militaire, others. Clubs: Cercle Interallie, Racing of France. Address: 9 Rue Sebastien Bottin, 75007 Paris France *

GROUX, GUY MARC, sociologist; b. Alger, Algeria, Nov. 6, 1945; s. Marius Louis and Fathma (Rabah) G.; m. Maryvonne Prost, June 7, 1975; 1 child, Sabine. D in Sociology, U. Paris, 1975; LittD, Inst. Study of Politics, Paris, 1986. Asst. prof. Inst. Social Sci. U. d'Oran, Algeria, 1975-77; conservatoire Nat. des Arts et Metiers, Paris, 1977—; sci. researcher Nat. Ctr. Sci. Research, Paris, 1982—; sci. expert European Found., Dublin, Ireland, 1985-86; lectr. Ecole Superieure de Commerce, Paris, 1987—. Author: (with others) Les Cadres, 1983, Cles Pour une Histoire du Syndicalisme-Cadres, 1984, Le Syndicalisme des Cadres en France, 1963-84, 86; co-editor: Syndicats Français et Americains Face aux Mutations Technologiques, 1984, The French Workers' Movement, 1968-82, 84. Mem. Internat. Indsl. Relations Assn. (adminstr. French sect. 1985—), Tocqueville Soc., French Assn. Polit Sci. Roman Catholic. Office: Conserv Nat des, Arts et Metiers, 2 rue Conte 75003 Paris France

GROVE, BRANDON HAMBRIGHT, JR., diplomat; b. Chgo., Apr. 8, 1929; s. Brandon Hambright and Helen Julia (Gasparska) G.; m. Marie Cheremeteff, 1959 (div. 1983); children: John C., Catherine C., Paul C., Mark C. A.B., Bard Coll., 1950; M.P.A., Princeton U., 1952. Joined U.S. Fgn. Service, 1959; vice consul Abidjan, Ivory Coast, also Upper Volta, Niger, and Dahomey, 1959-61; staff asst. to undersec. state 1961-62, spl. asst. to dep. undersec. state for adminstrn., 1962-63; spl. asst. to Am. ambassador New Delhi, India, 1963-65; U.S. liaison officer to city govt. Berlin, 1965-69; dir. Office Panamanian Affairs, State Dept., 1969-71; mem. Sr. Seminar in Fgn. Policy, 1971-72; dep. dir. State Dept. policy planning staff, Washington; also staff dir. Under Secretaries Com. of Nat. Security Council, 1972-74; chargé d' affaires, then dep. chief of mission Am. embassy to German Dem. Republic, Berlin, 1974-76; fgn. service sr. insp. Dept. State, 1976-78; dep. asst. sec. state for Inter-Am. affairs 1978-80; consul gen. Jerusalem, 1980-83; Capstone fellow Nat. Def. U., Fort McNair, Washington, 1984; ambassador to Zaire, Kinshasa, 1984-87; coordinator State Dept. Budget Rev., Washington, 1987-88; dir. Fgn. Service Inst., 1988—; asst. instr. Princeton U., 1953. Served to lt. USNR, 1954-57. Mem. Am. Fgn. Service Assn., Council on Fgn. Relations. Office: Dept of State Washington DC 20520

GROVE, DAVID LAWRENCE, economist; b. Boston, Apr. 25, 1918; s. Lawrence Roger and Emily (Becker) G.; m. Lois Pawlowski, May 13, 1942; 1 child, Carolyn Anne. Grad., Boston Latin Sch., 1935; A.B. magna cum laude, Harvard U., 1940, M.A., 1942, M.P.A., 1942, Ph.D., 1952. Economist Fed. Res. Bd., 1944-52; adviser monetary and banking problems Paraguay, 1944, 51, Ecuador, 1947, 57, 58, Guatemala, 1945, 46, 56, 62, 65, Philippines, 1948, 49, Colombia, Chile, 1950, Israel, 1964; chief economist Bank Am., San Francisco, 1952-58; v.p., head internat. relations Bank Am., 1961-62, v.p., head bond investment dept., 1962-63, v.p., 1959-63; v.p., econ. advisor Fed. Res. Bank San Francisco, 1963-64; v.p., economist Blyth & Co., N.Y., 1965-66; chief economist IBM, 1966-69, v.p., chief economist, 1969-78; pres. David L. Grove Ltd., 1978-85; sr. economic advisor Marine Midland Bank, 1978-83; lectr. Am. U., 1952, Center of Latin Am. Monetary Studies, Mexico, 1954-56, 58, 64, 66; dir. HNG/Internorth Co., 1976-85, Gen. Pub. Utilities Corp., Aetna Variable Fund, Inc., Aetna Encore Fund, Inc., Aetna Income Shares, Inc.; mem. Time Mag. Bd. Economists, 1969-80, N.Y. State Council Econ. Advisers, 1973-74, several U.S. Govt. adv. coms.; bd. dirs. Nat. Bur. Econ. Research; trustee Com. Econ. Devel., N.Y. Med. Coll., 1972-75. Author articles in field.; mem. editorial bd. Fin. Analysts Jour. Served with OSS, 1942-44. Decorated officer Order of Merit, Ecuador). Mem. Am. Econ. Assn., Internat. C. of C. of U.S. (dir. 1967-78), U.S. Council Internat. Bus. (pres. 1978-84), Phi Beta Kappa. Episcopalian. Home and Office: 5 The Knoll Armonk NY 10504

GROVE, HELEN HARRIET, historian, artist; b. South Bend, Ind.; d. Samuel Harold and LaVerne Mae (Drescher) Grove; grad. Bayle Sch. Design, Meinzinger Found., 1937-39, Washington U., 1940-42; spl. studies, Paris, France. Owner studios of historic research and illustration, St. Louis, Chgo., 1943—; dir. archives, bus. history research Sears, Roebuck & Co., 1951-67; commmns. art and research for Northwestern U., Chgo.-Sears Roebuck & Co., art Lawrence U., Appleton, Wis. Home: 6326 N Clark St Chicago IL 60626 Studio: 6328 N Clark St Chicago IL 60626

GROVE, RUSSELL SINCLAIR, JR., lawyer; b. Marietta, Ga., Dec. 25, 1939; s. Russell Sinclair and Miriam (Smith) G.; m. Charlotte Mariam Glascock, Jan. 9, 1965; children—Farion Smith Whitman, Arthur Owen Sinclair. B.S., Ga. Inst. Tech., 1962; LL.B. with distinction, Emory U., 1964; postgrad., U. Melbourne Faculty Law, Australia, 1965. Bar: Ga. 1965, U.S. Supreme Ct. 1971, U.S. Ct. Appeals (11th cir.) 1983. Assoc. Smith, Currie & Hancock, Atlanta, 1966-67; assoc. Hansell & Post, Atlanta, 1968-72, ptnr., 1972—; mem. adv. com. Ctr. for Legal Studies; mem. exec. com. real property law sect. State Bar Ga., joint com. on ptnrship. law. Author: Word Processing and Automatic Data Processing in the Modern Law Office, 1978, Legal Considerations of Joint Ventures, 1981, Structuring Endorsements and Affirmative Insurance, 1981, Management's Perspective on Automation, 1981, Mineral Law: Current Developments and Future Issues, 1983; co-author: The Integrated Data and Word Processing System, 1981, Georgia Partnership Law: Current Issues and Problems, 1982; (with D.E. Glass) Georgia Real Estate Forms-Practice, 1987; editor-in-chief Jour. Pub. Law, 1963-64. Mem. Central Atlanta Progress, Inc.; bd. dirs. Caribbean Mission, Inc. Served with USMCR, 1960-65. Mem. ABA, Ga. Bar Assn., Atlanta Bar Assn., Bryan Soc., U.S. Marine Corps Assn. Ga. Lawyers, Eastern Mineral Law Found., Am. Coll. Mortgage Attys., Ga. State Bar (mem. joint com. partnership law UPA/ULPA), Am. Coll. Real Estate Lawyers, Ga. Oil and Gas Assn., Ga. Cattlemen's Assn., Nat. Cattlemen's Assn., Am. Scotch Highland Breeders Assn., Can. Highland Cattle Soc., Highland Cattle Soc. U.K., Phi Delta Phi, Omicron Delta Kappa. Episcopalian. Clubs: Dunwoody Country, Commerce, Lawyers of Atlanta, Ashford. Office: 56 Perimeter Ctr E NE Suite 500 Atlanta GA 30346

GROVES, CHARLES BARNARD, orchestra conductor; b. London, Mar. 10, 1915; s. Frederick and Annie (Whitehead) G.; m. Hilary Hermione Barchard, June 5, 1948; children—Sally Hilary, Mary Hermione, Jonathan Charles. Student Royal Coll. Music, London, 1932-37; Mus.D. (hon.), Liverpool U., 1970; Dr. (hon.), Open U., Milton Keynes, Eng., 1978; Litt.D. (hon.), Salford U. (Eng.), 1980. Chorus master BBC Opera Unit, London, 1938-44; condr., musical dir. BBC No. Symphony Orch., Manchester, Eng., 1944-51, Bournemouth Symphony Orch. (Eng.), 1951-61, Welsh Nat. Opera Co., Cardiff, 1961-63, English Nat. Opera Co., London, 1977-80; condr., musical dir. Royal Liverpool Philharm. Orch., 1963-77, condr. laureate for life, 1985—; assoc. condr. Royal Philharmonic Orch., London, 1967—; pres. Nat. Fedn. Music Socs., London, 1972-80; chmn. council Royal No. Coll. Music, Manchester, 1974—. Decorated comdr. and knight bachelor Order Brit. Empire; named Freeman, City of London, 1976; fellow Royal Coll. Music, London, 1956, Royal Acad. Music, London, 1963, No. Sch. Music, Manchester, 1972, Trinity Coll. Music, London, 1974, Guildhall Sch. Music and Drama, London, London Coll. Music, 1981, Manchester Poly.; companion Royal No. Coll. Music, Manchester, 1983. Mem. Inc. Soc. Musicians (pres. 1972, 82). Club: Savage (London). Office: Ingpen & Williams, 14 Kensington Ct, London W8 5DN, England

GROVES, DAVID UPDEGRAFF, trade association executive, public relations consultant; b. Lexington, Mo., Nov. 10, 1926; s. William Lester and Adelaide Rebecca (Updegraff) G.; m. Nancy Jane Bustamante, June 23, 1951; children—Nancy Alice, Patricia Rebecca. B.A., U. Md., 1950; M.A., Johns Hopkins U., 1951. Cartoonist, Stars & Stripes, 1946, Washington Post, 1947-48; artist, researcher syndicated newspaper feature Spotlight on Bus., 1949-51; cons. mgmt., pub. relations and indsl. relations, Washington, 1951-54, Guatemala City, 1954-58, Havana, Cuba, 1958-60; gen. mgr. pub. and indsl. relations Relaciones Publicas Interamericanas S.A., Mexico City, 1960-72; Midwest regional dir. Internat. Mgmt. Ctr., Cleve., 1973-78; pres. David U. Groves and Assocs., Cleve., 1977-79, Bethesda, Md., 1979-83, Winter Springs, Fla., 1983—; sr. cons. Silver Inst., Gold Inst., Washington, 1978—; pub. Stamp Research Report, 1980-83; exec. dir. Precious Metals Industry Assn., N.Y.C., Washington, Winter Springs, 1983—. Bd. dirs. Mexican Devel. Found., 1969-72, Fomento Ednl. Found., 1971-72, Precious Metals Industry Assn, 1983—. Served with AUS, 1944-46. Mem. Pub. Relations Soc. Am., Counselors Acad. Pub. Relations Soc. of Am., Internat. Assn. Bus. Communicators, Am. Philatelic Soc., Newsletter Assn. Am., Am. Soc. Assn. Execs., Phi Theta Kappa. Roman Catholic. Clubs: University (Mexico City); Nat. Press (Washington). Home: 649 Tuskawilla Point Ln Winter Springs FL 32708 Office: PO Box 3550 Winter Springs FL 32708

GROVES, RAY JOHN, accountant; b. Cleve., Sept. 7, 1935; m. Anne Keating, Aug. 18, 1962; children: David, Philip, Matthew. BS summa cum laude, Ohio State U., 1957. CPA, Ohio. With Ernst & Whinney, Cleve. and N.Y.C., 1957—; ptnr. Ernst & Whinney, 1966-71, nat. ptnr., 1971-77; chmn., chief exec. officer Ernst & Whinney, N.Y.C., 1977—; pres. adv. council Coll. Bus. Ohio State U., 1979-80; mem. adv. council U. Chgo. Grad. Sch. Bus. Councilman City of Lyndhurst, Ohio, 1969-72; chmn. bd. trustees Leadership Cleve., 1977-79; trustee Hawken Sch., 1976-86; mem. exec. com. Tax Found.; mem. bd. overseers Wharton Sch. U. Pa.; mem. exec. com. U. Calif. Securities Regulation Inst.; vice chmn. bd. trustees Ursuline Coll., Cleve., 1970-86; bd. dirs. Met. Opera Assn. Mem. Am. Inst. CPA's (chmn. bd. dirs. 1984-85), Nat. Assn. Securities Dealers (bd. govs. 1981-84), Nat. Assn. Accts., Am. Stock Exchange (bd. govs.). Republican. Clubs: Union, Cleve. Athletic; Pepper Pike (Ohio); Mayfield Country (South Euclid, Ohio); Board Room, Links (N.Y.C.); Metropolitan (Washington); Blind Brook (Purchase, N.Y.); Laurel Valley Country. Home: 1566 Ponus Ridge New Canaan CT 06840 also: 15 W 53d St Apt 19D New York NY 10019 Office: Ernst & Whinney 787 7th Ave New York NY 10019

GROVES, ROSALIND GANZEL, corporate communications specialist; b. Phila., Aug. 1, 1934; d. John Edward and Flora Edith (Shultz) Ganzel; m. Harold Eber Woodbridge, Dec. 7, 1951 (div. June 1966); children: John Arthur, Martin Alan, June Marie; m. Gary Wayne Groves, Aug. 7, 1975 (div. 1980). AA, Fla. Keys Community Coll., 1972; BA, U. N. Fla., 1975. Cert. profl. Hypnotist, Fla.; registered ins. agt., Fla. Program analyst USN Officer-in-Charge Constrn. Trident, St. Marys, Ga., 1981-83; with acctg. dept. USN Officer-in-Charge Constrn. Trident, St. Marys, 1983-84; telephone communications USN, NAS Jacksonville, Jacksonville, Fla., 1985—; ins. agt. Hill and Co., Jacksonville, 1986—; also freelance writer/editor; dir. Behavior Modification Ctr., Jacksonville, 1983—; cons. hypnosis, Jacksonville, Fla., 1983—. Counselor Vo. Jacksonville, 1975-76; tchr. Duval County Sch. System, 1984; mem. Key West Art & Hist. Soc., 1984—; speaker Naval Air Station Jacksonville Speakers Bur., 1985—; vol. Jacksonville Upbeat Program, 1986—. Named Honorary Fire Reservist #772 Phila. Fire Dept. Mem. Inst. Advanced Hyponology (newsletter editor 1983-85, sec. 1983-85, v.p. 1986-87), Navy League U.S., Fla. Assn. Profl. Hypnosis (newsletter editor 1985-87), The Exec. Female, Assn. to Advance Ethical Hypnosis, Navy League, Jacksonville C. of C., Offshore Power Boat Racing Assn. Republican. Mem. Ch. of Christ. Club: Internat. Toastmistress (sponsored new club). Home: 7212 Cypress Cove Rd Jacksonville FL 32244

GROW, ANN ELIZABETH, chemist; b. Omaha, Apr. 9, 1950; d. John Nolan Baker and Dorothy Alma (Dixon) B.; m. Stephen Warren Grow, June 9, 1971 (div.); m. Phillips G.P. Eliot, Dec. 20, 1986. BA, Grinnell Coll., 1973; postgrad. in embryology, cell physiology, phys. chemistry U. Iowa, 1973-74. Research asst. Grinnell Coll. (Iowa), 1971-73, U. Iowa, Iowa City, 1974-76; chemist Thompson-Hayward Chem. Co., Kansas City, Kans., 1977-79; asst. biochemist Midwest Research Inst., Kansas City, Mo., 1979-80, assoc. chemist, 1980-84, program mgr., 1981-84; staff engr., mgr. analytical systems GA Technologies Inc., San Diego, 1984—. Active Lyric Opera Guild, 1979-80, Friends of the Zoo, 1978—. Mem. Am. Chem. Soc., San Diego Zool. Soc., Phi Beta Kappa. Patentee processes and devices for detection of substances such as enzyme inhibitors, 1983; contbr. articles to profl. jours. Office: PO Box 85608 San Diego CA 92138

GRÜ, RAINER F. W., publisher; b. Freiburg, Fed. Republic of Germany, July 30, 1943; s. Carl and Lydia (Ditter). Diploma Eng., Coll. Fachhochschule, Offenburg, Fed. Republic of Germany, 1967. Publisher Verlag Dr. Grüb Nachf., Freiburg, 1969—. Inventor storage system for wind energy. Mem. Import-Export Promotion Orgn., Publishers Orgn. Home: Richard Wagner Str 55, 7800 Freiburg Federal Republic of Germany Office: Verlag Dr Grüb Nachf, Schwarzwaldstr 26, D-7800 Freiburg Federal Republic of Germany

GRUBB, GERD, mathematics researcher and educator; b. Copenhagen, Feb. 12, 1939; d. Kjeld Tue and Inger (Steffensen) G.; m. Knud Lonsted, Nov. 11, 1969; children—Vilhelm, Lea. Magister Scientiarum, Aarhus U., Denmark, 1963; Ph.D., Stanford U., 1966; Dr. Phil., Copenhagen U., 1975. Research fellow Copenhagen U., 1966-69, assoc. prof., 1969-72, prof. math., 1972—, dir. math. studies com., 1981-85; with Danish Nat. Com. Studies Natural Scis., 1986—. Author: Functional Calculus of Pseudo-differential Boundary Problems, 1986. Contbr. articles to profl. publs. Recipient Marie Longgaards Rejselegat award, 1980; Hermers prize, 1985. Fellow Danmarks Naturvidenskabelige Akademi; mem. Danish Math. Soc., Am. Math. Soc., Assn. Women in Math. Lutheran. Home: Vedbaek Strandvej 452, DK-2950 Vedbaek Denmark Office: Matematisk Institut, Universitetsparken 5, DK-2100 Copenhagen Denmark

GRUBB, ROBERT LYNN, computer system designer; b. Knoxville, Tenn., Nov. 23, 1927; s. William Henry and DoLores Alfisi (Pierucci) Hollinshead; m. Donna Jean Chicado, May 28, 1973; children—Barbara, Robert Lynn, Paul, Werner, Luke, Jubal. B.S., Central State Coll., Edmond, Okla., 1972. Air traffic controller FAA, Fort Worth, 1955-62; engr. Philco-Ford Corp., Oklahoma City, 1962-65; service co. exec. Lear-Siegler Inc., Oklahoma City, 1965-67; computer specialist U.S. Navy, Corpus Christi, Tex., 1967-71, U.S. Army, Petersburg, Va., 1971-77, U.S. CSC, Washington, 1977-79, U.S. Dept. Justice, San Antonio, 1979-80; Defense Mapping Agy., 1980—; pres. Tex. Office Systems Co., Inc., Wetmore 1980—; cons. Durham Bus. Coll., Corpus Christi; cons. Corpus Christi Pub. Sch. Bd. Author: Conversion and Implementation of CS3 Computer System, 1973; Economic Analysis of Automated System-TOPS, 1977. Contbr. articles and stories on Western history to various periodicals. Committeeman, Boy Scouts Am., 1963-64; bd. dirs., athletic coach Southside Youth League, 1970. Served in USNR, 1945-46, PTO. Mem. Western Writers Am., Am. Hist. Soc. (charter). Home and Office: Rt 1 Box 1068 Wetmore TX 78163

GRUBBE, DEBORAH LYNN, chemical company executive; b. Chgo., Apr. 10, 1955; d. Jerome Walter and Domenica Veronica (Salce) G.; B.S. in Chem. Engring. with highest distinction, Purdue U., 1977; cert. (Winston Churchill fellow) U. Cambridge (Eng.), 1978; profl. engr. license, Del. Chem. engr. E.I. duPont de Nemours & Co., Inc., East Chicago, Ind., 1978, services engr., Edge Moor, Del., 1978-80, area engr. constrn. div., Deepwater, N.J., 1980-81, div. engr., Wilmington, Del., 1981-84, project engr., 1985-88, staff engr., 1987—; mem. Mech. Engring. Adv. Bd. Del. Tech. and Community Coll., 1988—. bd. dirs. Del. Devel. Corp.; vis. lectr. Purdue U., U. Del. Bd. dirs. Chesapeake Bay Girl Scout Council, 1986-89; Mem. Nat. Council Engring. Examiners, Del. Assn. Profl. Engrs. (bd. dirs. 1985—), Am. Inst. Chem. Engrs. (chmn. nat. program subcom. 1980-82, nat. career guidance com. 1985-87), Wilmington Women in Bus. (subchmn. program com. 1982-83, bd. dirs. 1983-85, chair community involvement com. 1985-87), Del. Soc. Profl. Engrs. (bd. dirs. 1985-87, v.p., 1987—, Nat. Soc. Profl. Engrs. (project mgr. exec. devel. project 1985-88, mem. student programs com. 1986—), Del. Alliance Profl. Women (Trailblazer award 1986), Am. Mensa, Zeta Tau Alpha (pres. Wilmington alumnae chpt., province pres. Eastern Pa. region 1981-85), Tau Beta Pi, Phi Kappa Phi, Omega Chi Epsilon. Roman Catholic. Home: 103 Falcon Ln Wilmington DE 19808 Office: EI DuPont de Nemours & Co Inc Louviers Bldg PO Box 6090 Newark DE 19714-6090

GRUBBS, DONALD SHAW, JR., actuary; b. Bellvue, Pa., Dec. 15, 1929; s. Donald Shaw and Zora Fay (Craven) G.; m. Margaret Helen Crooke, Dec. 27, 1969; children: David, Deborah, Daniel, Dawson, Dwight, Douglas. AB, Tex. A&M U., 1951; postgrad., Los Angeles State Coll., 1953-54, Fresno State Coll., 1954-55, Boston U., 1955-57, Princeton Theol. Sem., 1959-60, Westminster Theol. Sem., 1960-61; JD, Georgetown U., 1979. Bar: D.C. 1979. Actuarial asst. New Eng. Mut. Life Ins. Co., Boston, 1955-58, Warner Watson, Inc., Boston, 1958-59; cons. actuary John B. St. John, Penllyn, Pa., 1959-65, Grubbs & Co., Phila., 1965-72; v.p. actuary Nat. Health and Welfare Retirement Assn., N.Y.C., 1972-74; dir. actuarial div. IRS, Washington, 1974-76; cons. actuary Buck Cons., Inc., Washington, 1976-86; pres. Grubbs and Co., Inc., Silver Spring, Md., 1986—; chmn. Joint Bd. for Enrollment Actuaries, Washington, 1975-76. Author: (with G.E. Johnson) The Variable Annuity, 1967. V.p. Ambler (Pa.) NAACP, 1961-61; chmn. Warminster (Pa.) Child Day Care Assn., 1962-64. Served to 1st lt. U.S. Army 1951-53, Korea. Decorated Bronze Star with V U.S. Army, 1953; recipient Employee Benefits Outstanding Achievement award Pension World, 1986. Fellow Soc. of Actuaries (sec. 1983-84), Conf. Actuaries in Pub. Practice; mem. Middle Atlantic Actuarial Club. (pres. 1981-82), ABA. Democrat. Unitarian. Home and Office: 10216 Royal Rd Silver Spring MD 20903

GRUBE, JAMES CLARENCE, steel fabricating company executive; b. Milw., Mar. 10, 1936; B.S. in E.E., U. Wis., 1958; m. Carol Jean Pohlhammer, Oct. 6, 1962; children—James Charles, Nancy Anne. With Fabricated Metal Products Co., Brookfield, Wis., exec. v.p., 1971-74, pres., 1974—; also dir. Mem. Brookfield Planning Commn., 1972-74, Waukesha County Pvt. Indsl. Council, 1981-82. Mem. Nat. Fedn. Ind. Bus., Wis. Mfrs. and Commerce Assn., Ind. Bus. Assn. Wis., Mgmt. Resources Assn. Milw., Brookfield C. of C. (dir. 1985—). Lutheran. Club: Highlander Racquet. Office: 12510 W Lisbon Rd Brookfield WI 53005

GRUBER, ROSALIND H., counseling psychologist; b. Bronx, N.Y., Feb. 10, 1943; d. Lazarus L. and Beatrice (England) G.; B.A. cum laude, SUNY, New Paltz, 1974; M.A., Suffolk U., 1978. Nat. Cert. Counselor; lic. clin. social worker. Sch. registrar Assn. Help Retarded Children, N.Y.C., 1970; counselor Neighborhood Youth Corps, Poughkeepsie, N.Y., 1971-73; liason Govt. Subsidized Housing, Cambridge, Mass., 1975-77; dir., counselor Aradia Counseling, Boston, 1978—; ptnr.-owner real estate investment co., 1982—. Mem. Nat. Assn. Social Workers, Am. Personnel and Guidance Assn., Assn. Humanistic Edn. and Devel., Mass. Mental Health Counselors Assn., Assn. Women in Psychology, U.S. Power Squaron. Home: 251 Mill St Newtonville MA 02160 also: 2150 Old Kings Hwy PO Box 272 West Barnstable MA 02668 Office: 520 Comm Ave Boston MA 02215

GRUCHALLA, MICHAEL EMERIC, electronics engineer; b. Houston, Feb. 2, 1946; s. Emeric Edwin and Myrtle (Priebe) G.; m. Elizabeth Tyson, June 14, 1969; children: Kenny, Katie. BSEE, U. Houston, 1968; MSEE, U. N.Mex., 1980. Registered profl. engr., Tex. Project engr. Tex. Instruments Corp., Houston, 1967-68; group leader EG&G Washington Analytical Services Ctr., Albuquerque, 1974-88; engring. specialist EG&G Energy Measurements Inc., Albuquerque, 1988—; cons. engring., Albuquerque; lectr. in field, 1978—. Contbr. articles to tech. jours; patentee in field (2). Judge local sci. fairs, Albuquerque, 1983 —. Served to capt. USAF, 1968-74. Mem. IEEE, Instrumentation Soc. Am., Planetary Soc., N.Mex. Tex. Instruments Computer Group (pres. 1984-85), Sigma Xi, Tau Beta Pi, Eta Kappa Nu. Office: EG&G Energy Measurements Inc Kirtland Ops PO Box 4339 Sta A Albuquerque NM 87196

GRUEN, JOAN WILLARD, accountant; b. Buffalo, June 22, 1933; d. Neil Matthew and Edna Jean (Manson) Willard; m. Mark E. Uncapher, Jr., Sept. 13, 1952 (div. 1968); children—Mark Elson, N. Willard; m. 2d, David Henry Gruen, Jan. 3, 1976; stepchildren—David E., Stephen, Cathryn, Edward, William A. BS summa cum laude, SUNY-Buffalo, 1977; student Wellesley Coll., 1951-52. CPA, N.Y. Corp. sec. Willard Machine Corp., Buffalo, 1968-77; staff accountant Peat, Marwick, Main & Co., Buffalo, 1977-82, mgr., 1983—. Mem. exec. com. N.Y. State Bd. Developmental Disabilities, 1972-77; bd. dirs. People, Inc., 1975-78; bd. dirs. Psychiat. Clinic, Children's Aid Assn., 1969-73; mem. exec. com. of adv. bd. Erie County Dept. Mental Health, 1968-72; trustee United Way of Buffalo and Erie County, 1972—, Buffalo Seminary, 1988—. Mem. Am. Inst. CPA's, N.Y. State Soc. CPA's, Am. Soc. Women Accountants, Beta Sigma Gamma. Republican. Presbyterian (trustee 1980-84). Clubs: Saturn, Country Club of Buffalo, Buffalo. Home: 34 Middlesex Rd Buffalo NY 14216 Office: Peat Marwick Main & Co 700 Main Place Tower Buffalo NY 14202

GRUEN, PETER H., psychiatrist, educator; b. N.Y.C., June 6, 1939; s. Hans and Ilse (Marx) Wertheimer; B.A. in Psychology with honors, U. Calif. at Berkeley, 1961; M.D., U. Calif. at San Francisco, 1965; children—Arthur L., Kim J. Intern, Bronx Municipal Hosp. Center, 1965-66; resident in psychiatry Albert Einstein Coll. Medicine, Bronx, N.Y., 1969-72, chief resident, 1971-72; practice medicine specializing in psychiatry, N.Y.C., 1972—; asst. instr. psychiatry Albert Einstein Coll. Medicine, 1971-72, 1972-74, asst. prof. psychiatry, 1974-76; lectr. psychiat. inst. Columbia U. Coll. Physicians and Surgeons, 1976-77; head clin. research unit dept. of psychiatry Bronx Municipal Hosp. Center, 1973-75, asso. dir. psychobiol. research, 1975-76, dir. div. clin. psychopharmacology, 1977—; asst. prof. neurosci., assoc. prof. psychiatry Albert Einstein Coll. Medicine, 1978-87; clin. prof. psychiatry N.Y. Med. Coll., 1987—; cons. attending psychiatrist Lenox Hill Hosp., N.Y.C., 1976—, Gracie Square Hosp., N.Y.C., 1975—; asst. attending psychiatrist Bronx Municipal Hosp., Center, 1972—, Presbyn. Hosp., N.Y.C., 1976-77; research psychiatrist N.Y. State Psychiat. Inst., 1976-77. Served to maj., M.C., U.S. Army, 1966-69. Recipient Anne Monika Found. prize, 1975; diplomate Am. Bd. Psychiatry and Neurology. Fellow Am. Psychiat. Assn.; mem. Am. Psychosomatic Soc., AAAS, Am. Psychopath. Assn., Alpha Omega Alpha. Contbr. articles on psychopharmacology to profl. jours. Home: 56 Sprain Valley Rd Scarsdale NY 10583 office: 18 E 77th St New York NY 10021

GRUENWALD, GEORGE HENRY, new products management consultant; b. Chgo., Apr. 23, 1922; s. Arthur Frank and Helen (Duke) G.; m. Corrine Rae Linn, Aug. 16, 1947; children: Helen Marie Gruenwald Orlando, Paul Arthur. B.S. in Journalism, Northwestern U., 1947; student, Evanston Acad. Fine Arts, 1937-38, Chgo. Acad. Fine Arts, 1938-39, Grinnell Coll., 1940-41. Asst. to pres. Uarco, Inc., Chgo., 1947-49; creative dir., mgr. mdse. Willy-Overland Motors Inc., Toledo, 1949-51; new products, brand and advt. mgr. Toni Co., Chgo., 1951-53; v.p., creative dir., account supr. E.H. Weiss Agy., Chgo., 1953-55; exec. v.p., supr. mgmt. North Advt., Chgo., 1955-71; pres., treas., dir. Pilot Products, Chgo., 1963-71; pres., dir. Advance Brands, Inc., Chgo., 1963-71; exec. v.p., dir. Campbell Mithun Inc., Mpls. and Chgo., 1971-72; pres., dir. Campbell Mithun Inc., 1972-79, chmn., dir., 1979-81, chief exec. officer, dir., 1981-83, chief creative officer, dir., 1983-84; vice-chmn., dir. Ted Bates Worldwide, N.Y.C., 1979-80; mgmt. cons. new products 1984—. Editor-in-chief Oldsmobile Rocket Circle mag., 1956-64, Hudson Family mag., 1955; author: New Product Development—What Really Works, 1985, New Products - 7 Steps to Success (video), 1988; contbr. articles to profl. jours.; creator numerous packaged consumer products. Trustee Chgo. Pub. TV Assn., 1969-73, Mpls. Soc. Fine Arts, 1975-83, Linus Pauling Inst. Sci. and Medicine, Palo Alto, 1984—; chmn., v.p., chmn. class reps. Northwestern U. Alumni Fund Council, Chgo., 1965-68; trustee, chmn., pres., chief exec. officer, chmn. exec. com. Twin Cities Pub. TV Corp., 1971-84; trustee Minn. Pub. Radio Inc., 1973-77, vice chmn., 1974-75; bd. dirs., exec. com. Pub. Broadcasting Service, Washington, 1978-86, bd. dirs., 1988—; bd. dirs. St. Paul Chamber Orch., 1982-84, San Diego Chamber Orchestra, 1986—; mem. adv. bd. San Diego State U. Pub. Broadcasting Community, 1986—. Served with USAAF, 1943-45, MTO. Recipient Hermes award Chgo. Federated Advt. Clubs, 1963; Ednl. TV awards, 1969, 71. Mem. Am. Assn. Advt. Agys. (mgmt. com. 1976-84), The Am. Inst. Wine and Food (bd. dirs. 1985—). Office: PO Box 1696 Rancho Santa Fe CA 92067

GRUENWALD, ITHAMAR, philosopher, educator; b. Haifa, Israel, May 27, 1937; s. Shimon Heinz and Ruth (Kober) G.; m. Rachel Elstein, May 29, 1960; children: Na'amah, Efrat. PhD, Hebrew U., 1970. Lectr. dept. Jewish philosophy Tel Aviv U., 1967—. Author: Apocalyptic and Merkavah Mysticism, 1980, From Apocalyptism to Gnosticism, 1988. Served with Hebrew mil., 1957-59. Fellow Inst. for Advanced Studies. Home: 3 Divrey Yerucham Bayit Wegan, Jerusalem 96429, Israel Office: Tel Aviv U, Dept Jewish Philosophy, Tel Aviv Israel

GRUENWALD, JAMES HOWARD, association executive, consultant; b. Cin., Aug. 30, 1949; s. Howard Francis and Geraldine Emma (Mueller) G. B.S., Xavier U., 1971. Cert. profl. in recreation and leisure service, Ill. Rep. pub. relations Catholic Youth Orgn., Cin., 1969-72; advtransp. sales rep. Spade Trucking Co., Cin., 1972-73; field rep. Ohio Dept. Transport, Columbus, 1973-76; editorial, sales rep. Cin. Suburban Newspaper, 1976-77; asst. devel. dir. Cin. Art Acad., 1977-79; nat. exec. dir. SAY SOCCER USA, Cin., 1979—; co-founder, exec. dir. U.S. Indoor Soccer Orgn., 1985—; bd. dirs. Buckeye Men's Baseball, Cin., 1982-88, chmn. 1982-86; dir. Amateur Athletic Union, Indpls., 1983-85 ; cert. trainer Am. Coaches Effectiveness Program, Champaign, Ill., 1983—. Author Jour. Nat. Recreation and Parks, 1983; Jour. Ohio Parks and Attractions, 1985, Jour. Mich. Leisure, 1986. Editor jour. Touchline, 1980—, Parents Guide to Soccer, 1985—. Candidate for city council City of St. Bernard, Ohio, 1977; mem. adv. bd. Church Parish, Cin., 1974-76. Recipient Exec. Dir. Service award SAY SOCCER USA, 1979; State of Mich. Community Service award, 1986. Mem. Cin. Assn. Execs., Nat. Council Youth Sports Dirs., Nat. Recreation and Parks Assn., Mich. Recreation and Parks Assn. (Community Service award 1986), Soc. for Non Profits. Avocations: hiking; reading; writing; teaching; conducting workshops. Home: 610 E Mitchell Ave Cincinnati OH 45217 Office: SAY SOCCER USA 5945 Ridge Rd Cincinnati OH 45213

GRUER, WILLIAM E., personnel director, management consultant; b. Oak Park, Ill., Dec. 21, 1937; s. William Earle and Marguerite (Schramm); m. Jewel Susan Gourley Gruer, Nov. 15, 1958; children: Lynn, Mark. BBA, So. Meth. U., 1962; MBA, Calif. Coast U., 1979; PhD, Columbia Pacific U., 1986. Asst. mgr. personnel Mo. Pacific R.R., St. Louis, 1962-67, mgr. personnel planning, 1969-72; labor relations officer Chgo. & Eastern Ill. R.R. (now part of Union Pacific R.R. system), Chicago Heights, Ill., 1967-69; supt. personnel Monsanto Co., Cin., 1972-79, Ligonier, Ind., 1979-82; dir. personnel and risk mgmt., El Paso Products Co., Odessa, Tex., 1982—, pres. commerce and emergency ins., 1988—. Author: Discipline, A Necessity, 1979, Career Counseling in a Changing Economy, 1984. Bd. dirs. Odessa Private Industry Council, 1984—, Odessa United Way, 1987—. Served with USAF, 1955-59. Mem. Am. Soc. Personnel Adminstrs. (dist. dir. 1983-88), Tex. Assn. Bus. (chmn. bd. 1985-87), Permain Basin Internat. Trade Assn. (chmn. bd. 1985—), Permain Basin Personnel Assn. (bd. dirs.; pres. 1984-85), Tex. Alliance for Minority Engrs. (bd. dirs.), Cin. Personnel Assn. (bd dirs., pres. 1978-79). Republican. Baptist. Club: Odessa Country. Office: El Paso Products Co PO Box 3986 Odessa TX 79760

GRUHL, ANDREA MORRIS, librarian; b. Ponca City, Okla., Dec. 9, 1939; d. Luther Oscar and Hazel Evangeline (Anderson) Morris; m. Werner Mann Gruhl, July 10, 1965; children—Sonja Krista, Diana Krista. B.A., Wesleyan Coll., 1961; M.L.S., U. Md., 1968; M. Liberal Arts Program, Johns Hopkins U., 1971; postgrad. U. Md., 1968, 71-73. Tchr., Broward County, Fla., Dept. Def. Montgomery County, Md., 1961-66; librarian Prince Georges County (Md.) Pub. Library, 1966-68, 81-83, U. Md., College Park, 1970-72; art history researcher Joseph Alsop, Washington, 1972-74; librarian Howard County Pub. Library, Columbia, Md., 1969-70, 74-79; European exchange staff Library of Congress, Washington, 1982-86; cataloger fed. documents, GPO, Washington, 1986—; lang. code processing dept. rep. women's program adv. com. Library of Congress, 1983-86, mem. lang. code ofcl. del. Internat. Fedn. Library Assns. ann. conf., Munich, 1983, Chgo., 1985; state del. White House Conf. on Libraries, 1978. Indexer, editor: Learning Vacations, 3d edit., 1980; LCPA Index to Library of Congress Info. Bull., 1984. Trustee, Howard County Pub. Library, Columbia, Md., 1979-87; publ. chmn. LWV of Howard County, Md., 1974; citizen's rep. for Howard County and exec. bd. Balt. Regional Planning Council Library Com., 1976-79; Friends of the Library, Howard County, Md., pres., 1976; vol. Nat. Gallery of Art Library, Washington, 1978-80. Mem. Art Libraries Soc. N.Am. (coordinator, pub. exhbn. 1980-82), ALA (mem. trustee assn. 1982-87, resources and tech. services div., cataloging sect. 1988—, govt. documents roundtable 1988—), Library of Congress Profl. Assn. (coordinator ann. staff art show 1982, 83, chmn. spl. interest group on library sci. 1985-87), Library of Congress Am. Fedn. State County and Mcpl. Employees Union 2477 (program chmn. 1984-86), Md. Library Assn. (pres. trustee div. 1982-83), Kappa Delta Epsilon, Beta Phi Mu. Democrat. Methodist. Lutheran. Home: 5990 Jacob's Ladder Columbia MD 21045 Office: Govt Printing Office Washington DC 20401

GRUHL, JAMES, electrical engineer; b. Milw., Apr. 9, 1945; s. Alfred and Helen (Vanderveer) G.; m. Nancy Lee Huston, July 4, 1974; children—Amanda Natalie, Steven Christopher. S.B., MIT, 1968, S.M., 1968, Ph.D., 1973. Lectr., MIT, 1969-83; research scientist MIT Energy Lab., Cambridge, 1973-83, program mgr., 1978-83, research affiliate, 1984, U.S. Environ. Protection Agy., sci. adv. bd., 1986—; energy cons. U.S. Congress, research insts. energy industries, 1973—. Ednl. counselor MIT, 1978—. Recipient Silver Beaver award Boy Scouts Am., 1986. NSF grantee. Mem. IEEE, AAAS, Math. Programming Soc., MIT Alumni Assn. (officer 1978—), Tau Beta Pi, Eta Kappa Nu. Research on uncertainties and validity of analytic models, validity of govt. and industry energy policy models, econ. and health impacts of energy sources, design of advanced coal combustion techniques. Office: Gruhl Assocs PO Box 36524 Tucson AZ 85740

GRUN, KARL, financial journalist; b. Cologne, Ger., Jan. 15, 1933; s. Karl Julius Philipp and Anna (Kinkartz) G.; m. Helga Johanna Appenrodt, Jan. 6, 1961; children: Tobias, Felix, Henriette. Diploma, Norwich (Conn.) Free Acad., 1951; abitur, Alexander von Humboldt Gymnasium, Schweinfurt, Ger., 1952; diploma Volkswirt, Julius-Maximilians Universität, Wurzburg, Ger., 1956. Trainee, Main-Post, Wurzburg, 1956-58; econs. editor Frankfurter Allgemeine Zeitung, Frankfurt, 1958-68, Publik, Frankfurt, 1968-70, German TV, Wiesbaden, 1970-72; econs. and fin. corr. Die Welt/Borsenzeitung/Neue Zurcher Zeitung/Internat. Reports, London and N.Y.C., 1972—. Author: Finanzplatz London, 1974; contbr. articles to profl. jours. Roman Catholic. Home: 15 Boulderol Rd Stamford CT 06903

GRUNBERG, GERARD RENE, political scientist, researcher; b. Agadir, Morroco, Jan. 23, 1943; s. René and Simone (Nave) G.; m. Anne Marie Saubole; children: Francois, Julien. Diplome superieur de Sci. Polit., Fondation Nat. des Scis. Polits., Paris, 1968; diplome, I.E.P., Paris, 1965.

Research asst. Fondation Nat. des Scis. Polits., 1967-72; research attaché Nat. Ctr. for Sci. Research, Paris, 1972-78, head research, 1978-85, dir. research, 1985—; cons. BULL-TV (AZ), Paris, 1974—. Author-editor: France de Gauche Vote à droite, 1981, L'Univers politique des classes moyennes, 1983, La drole de defaite de la gauche, 1985; author: Electoral Change in Western Democracies, 1985. Cons. opinion polls for staff Michel Rocard, Paris, 1976—; chargé de mission cabinet Prime Minister. Mem. Ctr. Etude de la Vie Polit. Francaise. Socialist. Home: Ave de Chatron 1, 78640 Neauphle le Chateau France Office: CEVIPOF-MSH, 54 Blvd Raspail, 75700 Paris France

GRUNBERG, ROBERT LEON WILLY, nephrologist; b. Bucharest, Romania, July 23, 1940; came to U.S., 1972, naturalized, 1977; s. William A. and Isabelle L. (Rosen) G.; M.D., U. Orleans-Tours (France), 1969; m. Donna M. Fishman, Oct. 19, 1975; children: Wendie I., Andrea B. Intern, then resident in cardiology Vichy (France) Hosp., 1968-72; resident in internal medicine Albert Einstein Med. Center, Phila., 1972-74; fellow in nephrology-hypertension Hahnemann Med. Coll. and Hosp., Phila., 1974-76, sr. clin. instr., then asst. clin. prof. div. nephrology, 1976—; practice medicine specializing in nephrology, Allentown, Pa., 1976—; assoc. attending physician Allentown Hosp., Sacred Heart Hosp. Allentown, St. Luke's Hosp., Bethlehem, Pa., Lehigh Valley Hosp. Center, Allentown; attending charge div. nephrology Easton (Pa.) Hosp.; courtesy staff Hahnemann Med. Coll. and Hosp. Diplomate Am. Bd. Internal Medicine, Am. Bd. Nephrology. Mem. AMA (Physician's Recognition award 1976, 79, 82, 85, 88), Pa. Med. Soc., ACP, Am. Soc. Nephrology, Am. Soc. Artificial Internal Organs, Internat. Soc. Hypertension, Internat. Soc. Nephrology, Assn. for Advancement Med. Instrumentation, Internat. Soc. for Peritoneal Dialysis, Nat. Kidney Found., N.Y. Acad. Scis. Office: 50 S 18th St Easton PA 18042 also: 401 N 17th St Allentown PA 18104

GRUND, CLARENCE B., JR., elec. utility exec.; b. Portland, Oreg., July 31, 1925; s. Clarence B. and Frances (Eckert) G.; BEE, Ala. Poly. Inst., 1951, MEE, 1952; m. Marilyn Grace Hornsby, May 2, 1948. Engr. system planning Ala. Power Co., Birmingham, 1953-58; engr. rate dept. So. Co. Services, Inc., Birmingham, 1958-63, supr. research rate dept., 1964-67, asst. mgr. rate dept., 1967-69, mgr. rate dept., 1969-72, asst. v.p., 1972-85, sr. cons. engr., rates and regulation, 1986, ret., 1986.; pvt. practice, cons. engr., 1986—. instr. Ala. Poly. Inst., 1951-52, extension center U. Ala., 1952. Pres., Rocky Ridge Vol. Fire Dept., 1957-58, bd. dirs., 1956-62. Served with USAAF, World War II. Registered profl. engr., Ala., Miss. Mem. IEEE, Nat. Soc. Profl. Engrs., Birmingham Soc. Engrs., Newcomen Soc. N. Am., Internat. Platform Assn., Am. Legion, Phi Kappa Phi, Tau Beta Pi, Eta Kappa Nu. Contbr. articles to profl. jours. Address: 3421 Cruzan Dr Birmingham AL 35243

GRUNDMANIS, JOHN VISVALDIS, architect, educator; b. Liepaja, Curland, Latvia, Aug. 9, 1926; came to U.S., 1951; s. Christopher and Luise (Dobele) G.; m. Ieva M. Metra, June 21, 1955; children: Lauris J., Markus V., Ava B. BArch., U. Minn., 1955; MEd, U. La Verne, 1979; PhD, Walden U., 1985. Registered architect Minn., Calif., Fla., N.Y., Pa., Ill., Mich., Mass., Tex., Ala., Ind., Iowa, Mo., Nebr., Okla., S.D., Wis. Intern designer Magvolo & Quick, Mpls., 1954-58; architect Hills, Gilbertson & Fisher, Mpls., 1958-66; sr. architect 3M Corp., St. Paul, 1966-71; profl. assoc. Ellerbe Architects Inc., Bloomington, Minn., 1971-76; cons. Grundmanis & Assocs., Fridley, Minn., 1976—; tchr. Anoka (Minn.) Tech. Inst., 1976—. Prin. works include Reflective Products Plant, Tex., 1967, Lab. and Office Bldg., Minn., 1968, Printing Plant, Okla., 1969, Decorative Products Plant, Mo., 1979, Irvin Army Hosp., Riley, Kans., 1972, Med. Products Plant, S.D., 1970, Scott and White Clinic and Meml. Hosp., Tex., 1971, St. Luke's Meth. Hosp., Iowa, 1971, Rochester (Minn.) Meth. Hosp., 1972, St. Paul and Ramsey Med. ctr., 1975. Deacon Latvian Evang. Luth. Ch., Mpls.; pres. Minn. chpt. Latvian Acad. Fraternity Lettonia, 1957-60. Mem. AIA, Minn. Soc. Architects., Minn. Edn. Assn., Am. Inst. Design and Drafting. Home and Office: 185 NE Hartman Circle Fridley MN 55432

GRUNDMANN, EKKEHARD, pathologist; b. Eibenstock/Erzgebirge, Germany, Sept. 28, 1921; s. Fritz and Frieda (Schmidt) G.; student U. Freiburg/Br., U. Vienna; m. Frauke Dosse, Sept. 10, 1949; children: Bernhard, Gesine, Katharina. Asst. then asso. prof. Inst. Pathology, Freiburg U., 1950-63; sci. dir. BAYER AG, Wuppertal Exptl. Pathology, 1963-71; chmn. pathology, dir. Inst. Pathology, U. Munster, Westf., Germany, 1971—. Pres., Gesellschaft zür Bekampfung der Krebskrankheiten Nordrhein-Westfalen e.V. Recipient State award for Public Health, Republic of Italy, 1968. Mem. German Soc. Pathology, European Soc. Pathology, Internat. Acad. Pathology, N.Y. Acad. Sci., Internat. Soc. Hematology, Leopoldina, Halle; hon mem. Am. Assn. of Pathologists, Spanish Soc. Pathology, Hungarian Soc. Pathology, Chilean Soc. Pathology. Club: Rotary. Author: General Cytology, 1964; Special Pathology, I, II; Early Gastric Cancer; Introduction to General Pathology for Students; editor: Handbook General Pathology; Current Topics in Pathology; Pathology in Research and Practice; Jour. Cancer Research and Clin. Oncology; Cancer Campaign; contbr. articles to profl. jours. Home: 20 Roeschweg, D-4400 Munster NRW Federal Republic of Germany Office: 17 Domagkstrasse, D-4400 Munster NRW Federal Republic of Germany

GRUNDMEYER, DOUGLAS LANAUX, lawyer, editor; b. New Orleans, Nov. 6, 1948; s. Raymond Wallace and Eva Myrl (Lanaux) G.; m. Elaine Ann Toscano, Jan. 19, 1977; 1 child, Sarah Elaine. BA, Tulane U., 1970, JD, 1976; MA in English, U. New Orleans, 1974. Bar: La. 1976, Calif. 1980, U.S. Dist. Ct. (no. dist.) Calif. 1980. Sr. law clk. to presiding judge La. State Ct. of Appeal (4th cir.), New Orleans, 1976-78, 1980-88; assoc. legal editor Bancroft-Whitney Co., San Francisco, 1978-80, contract editor, 1981—; assoc. Chaffe, McCall, Phillips, Toler and Sarpy, New Orleans, 1988—. Contbr. editor American Jurisprudence 2d, Criminal Law, 1981; contbg. author La. Appellate Practice Handbook, 1986. Mem. ABA, State Bar Calif., La. Bar Assn. Democrat. Roman Catholic. Home: 5438 Vermillion Blvd New Orleans LA 70122 Office: Chaffe McCall Phillips Toler & Sarpy 2300 Energy Ctr 1100 Poydras St New Orleans LA 70163-2300

GRUNDY, DAVID LATHAM, electronics company executive; b. Oldham, Lancashire, England, Mar. 22, 1939; s. John Hough and Ida May (Jones) G.; m. Sandra Joy Marler, Aug. 17, 1962; children—Heather Jane, John Latham. Higher Nat. Cert. Oldham Mcpl. Tech. Coll. (Eng.), 1956-62; Part III I.E.E. Salford Coll. Advanced Tech. (Eng.), 1962-63. Chartered Engr. With Ferranti Electronics Ltd., Manchester, Eng., 1955—, sr. applications engr., 1965-67, head integrated circuit applications, 1967-68, mgr. integrated circuit engring., 1968-78, chief engr., 1978-80, technical dir. integrated circuits, 1980—. Patentee in field; contbr. numerous articles to profl. jours. Decorated Order Brit. Empire. Fellow Inst. Elec. Engrs. Mem. Ch. of Eng. Home: 30 Lovers Ln, Grasscroft, Oldham, Lancashire OL4 4DT, England

GRUNERT, KLAUS GUNTER, marketing educator; b. Berlin, Jan. 14, 1953; arrived in Denmark, 1987; s. Heinz Ludwig and Ella Waltraute (Freyboth) G.; m. Susanne Charlotte Wächter, July 17, 1987. MBA, U. Köln, Fed. Republic Germany, 1976; PhD, U. Hohenheim, Fed. Republic Germany, 1982. Research asst. Ctl. Archive Empirical Social Research, Cologne, Fed. Republic Germany, 1974-76; research assoc. Inst. Applied Consumer Research, Cologne, Fed. Republic Germany, 1976-77; asst. prof. U. Hohenheim, Stuttgart, Fed. Republic Germany, 1977-86; prof. mktg. Aarhus (Denmark) Sch. Bus. Adminstrn., 1987—; vis. prof. U. Hannover, Fed. Republic Germany, 1986-87, U. Bonn, Fed. Republic Germany, 1987; instr. Vocat. Acad. Stuttgart, 1981-86. Author 4 books, numerous pub. articles and conf. papers; book rev. editor Jour. Consumer Policy, Dordrecht, Netherlands, 1979—. Mem. Am. Mktg. Assn., Am. Psychol. Assn., Assn. Consumer Research, European Mktg. Acad., Internat. Assn. Research in Econ. Psychology, other profl. orgns. Home: Grenavej 844, DK-8541 Skodstrup Denmark Office: Handelshojskolen Aarhus, Ryhavevej 8, DK-8210 Aarhus Denmark

GRUNEWALD, DONALD, educator former college president; b. N.Y.C., Feb. 9, 1934; s. Harry A. and Tina (Gegner) G.; m. Barbara Susan Frees, Feb. 7, 1981; children: 1 child, Donald Frees. A.B., Union Coll., 1954; M.A., Harvard U., 1955, M.B.A., 1959, D.B.A., 1962; LL.D., Emerson Coll., 1973; Litt.D., Suffolk U., 1974; D.Sc., Far East U., 1979, Medaille Coll., 1983; D.Pol.Sci., Kyung Hee U., 1983; L.H.D., Mercy Coll., 1984; Ph.D. honoris causa, U. Mindanao, 1981. Instr. U. Kans. Sch. Bus., 1959-60; lectr. Boston U. Coll. Bus. Adminstrn., 1961-62; research agt. Harvard U. Grad. Sch. Bus., 1962; asst. prof. Rutgers U. Grad. Sch. Bus., 1962-65, assoc. prof., 1965-67; dean, prof. Suffolk U. (Coll. Bus. Adminstrn., Grad. Sch. Adminstrn.), 1967-69; v.p., dean Suffolk U. (Coll. Liberal Arts and Scis. and Coll. Journalism), 1969-72; pres. Mercy Coll., Dobbs Ferry, N.Y., 1972-84; disting. prof. Mercy Coll., Dobbs Ferry, 1984-86; prof. Iona Coll., 1986—; ednl. cons., propr. Boston Athenaeum.; life gov. Manchester Coll., Oxford, Eng.; former trustee Trinity Coll., Washington, chmn. bd., 1984-87. Author: Cases in Business Policy, 1962, (with Moranian and Reidenbach) Business Policy and Its Environment, 1964, (with H. Bass) Public Policy and the Modern Corporation, 1966, Small Business Management, 1966, (with Fenn, Katz) Business Decision Making and Government Policy, 1966, (with Flink) Managerial Finance, 1969, I Am Honored to Be Here Today, 1985. Trustee Dobbs Ferry Hosp., Heidelberg Coll., Lab. Inst. Merchandising. Served as lt. USAF, 1955-57. Decorated knight Sovereign Order St. John of Jerusalem. Fellow Royal Soc. Arts, Inst. Commerce, Coll. Preceptors; mem. Acad. Mgmt., Internat. Assn. Univ. Pres.'s (exec. com.). Clubs: Harvard (N.Y.C. and Boston); Cosmos (Washington); Ardsley Country. Home: 15 Kingsland Rd North Tarrytown NY 10591

GRUNWALD, HENRY ANATOLE, ambassador, editor, writer; b. Vienna, Austria, Dec. 3, 1922; came to U.S., 1940, naturalized, 1948; s. Alfred and Mila (Loewenstein) G.; m. Beverly Suser, Jan. 7, 1953 (dec. 1981); children: Peter, Madeleine, Lisa; m. Louise Melhado, May 1, 1987. AB, N.Y.U., 1944; LHD, NYU, 1975; LLD, Iona Coll., 1981; LHD, Bennett Coll., 1983. Editorial staff Time mag., 1945—, sr. editor, 1951—, fgn. editor, 1961—, asst. mng. editor, 1966-68, mng. editor, 1968-77; corp. editor Time Inc., 1977-79, editor-in-chief, 1979-87; ambassador to Austria Washington, 1987—. Author: Salinger, a Critical and Personal Portrait, 1962, Churchill, The Life Triumphant, 1965, The Age of Elegance, 1966; contbr. to Life and Horizon mags. Trustee NYU, Am. Austrian Found., Scientists' Inst. Pub. Info. Mem. Council on Fgn. Relations, Am. Council on Germany, World Press Freedom Com. (dir.), Met. Opera Guild (dir.), Met. Opera Assn., ASCAP, Phi Beta Kappa. Club: Century Assn. (N.Y.). Office: US Embassy, 16 Boltzmanngasse, A-1090 Vienna Austria

GRUSH, MARY ELLEN, computer company executive; b. Aurora, Ill., Oct. 28, 1947; d. Byron Edward and Olga Marion (Olson) Grush; m. Kenneth Takagi Takara, Oct. 25, 1981; 1 child, Stephanie Suzanne Grush. B.A., Ft. Wright Coll., 1971; M.A., U. Denver, 1975. Mgr. met. info. retrieval network Bibliog. Ctr. for Research, Denver, 1975-77; customer services rep. tng. Lockheed Dialog Info. Systems, Palo Alto, Calif., 1977-78, computer ops. supr., 1978—. Mem. ALA, Spl. Libraries Assn., Beta Phi Mu, Pi Delta Phi. Home: PO Box 1378 Los Altos CA 94023

GRUYS, ROBERT IRVING, physician, surgeon; b. Silver Creek, Minn., Oct. 15, 1917; s. Herman and Dorothy (Vondergon) G.; m. Cornelia Mol, June 30, 1943 (div. 1976); children—Kathy, Robert, William, John. B.S., U. Minn., 1945, B.S. in Medicine, 1946, M.D., 1947. Gen. surgery resident Wayne County Gen. Hosp., Detroit, 1948-49, Mpls. VA Hosp., 1958-62; postgrad. Cook County Gen. Hosp., Chgo., 1957, 63, 64, Mayo Clinic, Rochester, Minn., 1949-58, U. Minn., 1958-68, 70-75; physician, surgeon Watkins Clinic, Wells, Minn., 1950-58, 63-67, 70-75, Ganado Presbyn. Hosp., Ariz., 1953-57, Southwest Clinic, Edina, Minn., part time, 1967-68, Chiayi Christian Hosp., Taiwan, 1968-70, Estes Park Med. Clinic, Colo., 1975-79, St. Cloud Va Med. Ctr., 1979—; mem. staff Wells Community Hosp., 1951-75, Meth. Hosp., Mpls., 1967-68, Mt. Sinai Hosp., Mpls., 1967-68, North Meml. Hosp., Mpls., 1967-76, Fairview Southdale Hosp., Mpls., 1967-68, Met. Med. Ctr., Mpls., 1967-76, Elizabeth Knutson Meml. Hosp., Estes Park, Colo., 1975-79, Weld County Gen. Hosp., Greeley, Colo., 1976-79, St. Cloud VA Med. Ctr., 1979—. Mem. Am. Soc. Abdominal Surgeons, Internat. Coll. Surgeons, Christian Med. Soc., AMA, Physicians Serving Physicians in Minn., Stearns-Benton County Med. Soc., Alpha Omega Alpha. Lutheran. Lodge: Masons. Avocations: flying country-western music. Home: PO Box 1817 Saint Cloud MN 56302 Office: St Cloud VA Hosp 8th St Saint Cloud MN 56301

GRYTE, ROLF EDWARD, internist; b. Mpls., Mar. 8, 1945; s. Ralph Edward and Irene (Lindquist) G.; m. Barbara Lee Deems, June 8, 1971; children—David, Kirsten, Kristofer. B.A., U. Minn., 1967; D.O., Kirksville Coll. Osteopathic Medicine, 1971. Diplomate Am. Osteopathic Bd. Internal Medicine. Intern Kirksville Osteopathic Hosp., Mo., 1971-72, resident in internal medicine, 1972-75, chief resident, 1974-75, assoc. prof. internal medicine, 1975-79, mem. clin. faculty, 1979—, hosp. epidemiologist, 1977-79; practice medicine specializing in internal medicine, Kirksville, 1979-87; med. dir. inhalation therapy dept. Kirksville Osteopathic Hosp., 1975-80, Grim-Smith Hosp., Kirksville, 1979-87, med. dir. pulmonary rehabilitation program, 1983-87; black lung examiner Dept. Labor, Denver, 1983-87; social security disability examiner, Jefferson City, Mo., 1975—; adj. assoc. prof. internal medicine Kirksville Coll., 1987—. Med. dir. Planned Parenthood of Northeast Mo., Kirksville, 1972-82, chmn. med. adv. com., 1972—; mem. Great Lakes Region Med. Adv. Com. Planned Parenthood World Fedn., 1983—, Amnesty Internat., Conservation Fedn. of Mo. Named Outstanding Prof., Kirksville Coll. Osteopathic Medicine sophomore class, 1979; Nat. Osteopathic Coll. scholar. Mem. Am. Coll. Internal Medicine, Am. Heart Assn., Mo. Thoracic Soc., Mo. Assn. Osteopathic Physicians and Surgeons, Northeast Mo. Osteopathic Assn., Sierra Club. Sigma Sigma Phi, Psi Sigma Alpha. Republican. Lutheran. Clubs: Appaloosa Horse (Moscow, Ida.); Central Mo. Appaloosa Horse (Columbia) (pres. 1981-86). Avocations: Appaloosa breeding farm; hunting; fishing. Home: RR 1 Kirksville MO 63501 Office: 1108 E Patterson Ste 2 Kirksville MO 63501

GRZEGORZEK, CARL JOHN, transportation executive; b. Horsham, West Sussex, Eng., Apr. 29, 1948; s. Tadeusz and Katharine (Parker) G.; m. Jacqueline Julia Thomas, Sept. 26, 1970; children: Carl Simon, Paul Andrew. Ops. supt. Thurston Aviation Ltd., Stapleford, Essex, Eng., 1969-71; ops. mgr. Shorelink Aviation, Shoreham Aviation, Spooner Aviation, Shoreham, Sussex, Eng., 1971-74; ground ops. mgr., adminstrv. mgr. British Island Airways, Gatwick Airport, Lowfield Heath Crawley, Eng., 1974—. Roman Catholic. Office: Brit Island Airways Plc, Apollo House Church Rd, Lowfield Heath Crawley RH11 0PQ, England

GRZYBOWSKI, KAZIMIERZ, legal educator; b. Czortków, Poland, June 19, 1911; came to U.S., 1950; s. Ludwik and Maria (Wieckowska) G.; m. Zofia Szczerbowska, Aug. 5, 1936. LL.M., U. Lwow, Poland, 1933, Dr.Jur., 1935; S.J.D., Harvard U., 1934. Bar: Poland 1936. Asst. prof. law Lvov (Poland) U., 1936-39; judge dist. ct. Lvov, 1936-39; dir. Polish Info. Service, Middle East, Jerusalem, 1942-45; exec. officer Govt. Com. Polish Affairs, 1945-48; free-lance journalist London, 1948-50; editor law library Library of Congress, Washington, 1950-60; vis. prof. law U. Mich., Ann Arbor, 1960-61, Yale Law Sch., New Haven, 1961-62, Leiden (Holland) U., 1963-64; sr. research asso. Duke U., Durham, N.C., 1964—; prof. law and polit. sci. Duke U., 1970—; Cons. Rand Corp., Washington, 1961-63, State Dept., 1961, ACDA, Washington, 1964. Author in Polish) Article 18 of the Covenant of the League of Nations, 1934; International Tribunals and Municipal Law, 1937, General Principles of Private International Law Conflicts, 1939; (with V. Gsovski) (in English) Government Law and Courts in the Soviet Union and Eastern Europe, 2 vols, 1959, The Draft of the Civil Code in Poland, 1962, Economic Treaties and Agreements of the Soviet Bloc, 1952, Soviet Legal Institutions, Their Doctrines and Social Functions, 1962, Soviet Private International Law, 1965, The Socialist Commonwealth of Nations: Organization and Institutions, 1964, Soviet Public International Law: Doctrines and Diplomatic Practice, 1970, East West Trade, 1974, Trade with China, 1975, Soviet International Law and World Economic Order, 1987. Served with Polish Army, 1939-42. Decorated Mil. Cross; grantee Gregory and Kosciuszko Found., 1933-34; Recipient grants Fulbright Found., Leiden, 1963-64, grants Fulbright Found., Strasbourg, France, 1967-68, grants Carnegie Endowment, 1964-67. Mem. Am. Soc. Study Comparative Law (bd. govs. 1970—). Home: 2605 University Dr Durham NC 27707

GSTACH, JEAN HUBERT, visceral surgeon; b. Toulouse, France, Feb. 15, 1944; s. Christian and Verdin (Mauricette) G.; m. Alexandre Chantal, June 7, 1967; children: Bruno, Nathalie. Grad., Lycee Augustin Thierry, France. Intern Lille (France) Hosps., 1970, chef de clinique, 1975—. Office: Ctr Hosp, Ave Louis Herbeaux, 593815 Dunkerque, Nord France

GSTEIGER, MANFRED, literature critic; b. Twann, Bern, Switzerland, June 7, 1930; s. Otto and Hanna Lüthi G.; m. Pierrette Favarger, Feb. 4, 1956; children: Fanny, Saïda. PhD, U. Bern, 1956. Lit. redaktor Radio Bern, 1961-66; privat-docent U. Neuchâtel, Switzerland, 1966, chargé de cours, 1967; assoc. prof. Université, Neuchâtel, 1987—; prof. extraordinaire Université, Lausanne, Switzerland, 1972, prof. ordinaire, 1981—; visiting prof. U. Ill., 1971, 72, 76. Author: Franz, Symbolisten in der deutschen Lit., 1972, Wandlungen Werthers, 1980, La nouvelle lit. romande, 1978, Die zeigenössischen Lit. der Schweiz, 1974, 80. Mem. PEN romand, Assn. Internat. de Litt. comparée, Assn. suisse de litt. comp. (pres. 1979-83). Home: Chateau 7, CH 2000 Neuchatel Switzerland Office: U Lausanne Fac lettres, BFSH II, CH 1015 Lausanne Switzerland

GUALTIERI, VINCENT, urologist; b. Reggio Calabria, Italy, Jan. 5, 1934; s. Joseph Anthony and Victoria (Cartizano) G.; A.B., UCLA, 1955; M.D., U. Calif., Irvine, 1962; m. Gina Mirella Coggi, May 19, 1963; children—Lisa, Joseph, Stephen. Resident in urology, Los Angeles County Gen. Hosp., 1962-66; urologist Ross-Loos Med. Group, Los Angeles, 1966-68; practice medicine specializing in urology, Sherman Oaks, Calif., 1968—; chief of staff Sherman Oaks Community Hosp., 1986-88; clin. instr. urology Calif. Coll. Medicine, 1966-68. Diplomate Am. Bd. Urology. Fellow A.C.S.; mem. AMA, Calif. Med. Assn. (ho. dels.), Los Angeles County Med. Assn. (pres. E. San Fernando Valley chpt. 1986-87), Los Angeles Urol. Soc., Am. Urol. Assn. Republican. Office: 4955 Van Nuys Blvd Sherman Oaks CA 91403

GUARINO, JOHN RALPH, physician, scientist; b. N.Y.C., Aug. 17, 1915; s. Joseph J. and Marie (Ferrara) G.; m. Kathleen Paff, Aug. 2, 1947; children: Christopher John, Joseph Charles, Edward James. B.S., L.I. U., 1937; M.D., Coll. Physicians and Surgeons, Boston, 1943. Diplomate: Am. Bd. Internal Medicine. Intern Wyckoff Hosp., Bklyn., 1943-44; resident in internal medicine VA Hosp., Buffalo, N.Y., 1955-57; practice medicine Westford, Mass., 1947-52; research on simplified artificial kidney 1947-52; inaugurated artificial kidney service Harlem Hosp., N.Y.C., 1952-53; chief artificial kidney service Harlem Hosp., 1952-53, L.I. Coll. Medicine Hosp., 1952-53; asst. chief medicine VA Hosp., Livermore, Calif., 1959-69; chief medicine VA Hosp., Poplar Bluff, Mo., 1969-72, Topeka, Kans., 1972-74; internist VA Hosp., Boise, Idaho, 1974—; clin. asst. prof. medicine U. Wash., 1977-79, clin. assoc. prof., 1979-83, clin. prof., 1983—; cons. dialysis and treatment uremia, 1952—, guest lectr. nephrology, 1952—, physical diagnosis, 1983—. Contbr. articles on internal medicine to profl. jours. Served to capt., M.C. USAF, 1953-55. Presdl. Medal of Freedom award nominee, 1982-83. Fellow A.C.P.; mem. Am. Soc. Artificial Internal Organs (charter), Mass. Med. Soc., AMA. Roman Catholic. Address: 2404 Ormond St Boise ID 83705

GUAY, JACQUES, professional society administrator; b. Que., Can., Apr. 19, 1943; s. Albert Guay and Germaine Anderson; m. Diane Grenier; children: Isabelle, Frédéric, Guillaume. BA, Laval U., Sainte Foy, Que, 1969, BAA, 1983, MBA, 1987. Asst. to gen. mgr. Scriptam Industries, Que., Can., 1967-69, gen. mgr., 1969-73; gen. mgr. Alpha Boutique, Que., 1973-74, Beaumont Camping, Que., 1974-77; comptroller Boischatel Structures, Que., 1977-78; pvt. practice cons. Que., 1978-79; adminstrv. dir. Constrn. Assn., Que., 1979-83, asst. to gen. mgr., 1983-88; exec. v.p. Que. Motor Coaches Assn., 1988—. Contbr. articles to profl. jours. Pres. Entraide-Parents, Que., 1986-87. Mem. Can. Soc. Assn. Execs. (cert. 1985), Am. Soc. Assn. Execs., Profl. Corp. Cert. Adminstrs., Soc. Info. Mgmt. Systems, others. Roman Catholic. Lodge: KC. Home: 550 71st St E, Charlesbourg, PQ Canada G1H 1M1

GUBALA, JACK J., editor, publishing company executive, b. Franklin, N.J., Oct. 30, 1938; s. Joseph Leo and Katherine Elizabeth (Weber) G.; B.A., N.Y. U., 1962; student New Sch. Social Research, 1963-64; children—David D., Joan Danette. Directory editor United Bus. Publs., N.Y.C., 1962-64; asst. devel. dir. Columbia Sch. Engring. and Applied Sci., 1965-68; editor Coinamatic Trade Publs., N.Y.C., 1969-72, 74-75; exec. editor Gellert Publs. div. Ziff-Davis Pub. Co., 1964-65, 72-74; editor Reinhardt/Keymer Pub. Co., N.Y.C., 1976; spl. pubs. editor Floor Covering Weekly, Bart Publs., Inc., N.Y.C., 1976-78; dir. communications Nat. Assn. Tobacco Distbrs., 1978-83; editorial dir. Prime Pub., Inc., N.Y.C., 1983—. Mem. N.Y.C. Met. Council Housing, 1973—; Mem. Mcpl. Art Soc. N.Y., Internat. Jazz Fedn., Universal Jazz Coalition, Jazz Research Inst., Music Critics Assn., Friends of Central Park, Greensward Found., ACLU. Democrat., Nat. Trust for Hist. Preservation. Home: 207 E 15th St New York NY 10003

GUCKENHEIMER, DANIEL PAUL, banker; b. Tel Aviv, Oct. 10, 1943; s. Ernest and Eva Guckenheimer; came to U.S., 1947, naturalized, 1957; B.B.A. in Fin., U. Houston, 1970; cert. hosp. adminstrn., Trinity U., San Antonio, 1973; m. Helen Sandra Fox, Dec. 21, 1969; children—Debra Ellen, Julie Susan. Asst. adminstr. Harris County Hosp. Dist., Houston, 1970-76; pres. Mid Am. Investments, Kansas City, Kans., 1976; exec. dir. Allen County Hosp., Iola, Kans., 1977-78; comml. loan officer Traders Bank, Kansas City, Mo., 1979; v.p. and mgr. Traders Ward Pkwy. Bank, 1980, v.p., mgr. installment loans, 1981, v.p., comml. loan officer, 1982; sr. v.p., mgr. comml. loans United Mo. Bank South, 1982—. Bd. dirs. United Way, Iola, Kans., 1977-78, Food Distbn., Inc., 1983—; adv. bd. Country Side Estate Nursing Home, Iola, 1977-78; clinic adminstr. 190th USAF Clinic, 1977-84. Served with USAF, 1962-66, maj. Res., retired 1984. Mem. Am. Coll. Hosp. Adminstrs., N.G. Assn., C. of C. Kansas City (Mo.), Am. Bankers Assn., Mo. Bankers Assn., Olympic Soc., Internat. Platform Assn., Nat. Assn. Credit Mgmt., Robert Morris Assocs. Clubs: Iola Rotary; Kansas City, B'nai Brith (v.p. 1982-83, pres. 1984-85, treas. 1986—). Home: 8439 W 113th St Overland Park KS 66210 Office: 9201 Ward Pkwy Kansas City MO 64114

GUDDEMI, PHILLIP VICKROY, anthropologist; b. Los Angeles, Jan. 25, 1956; s. Leonard Charles and Mary Ruth (Vickroy) G. BA in Anthropology with honors, U. Calif., Santa Cruz, 1977; MA in Anthropology, U. Mich., 1978, postgrad., 1986—; MS in Environ. Mgmt., U. San Francisco, 1982. Librarian Mischa Titieu Library of Anthropology, Ann Arbor, Mich., 1984-85; field researcher Ama Village, Papua New Guinea, 1986—. Contbr. articles to profl. jours. Rackham grantee Papua New Guinea, 1986, Fulbright/Hayes grantee, 1986; fellow U. Mich., 1979. Office: U Mich Dept Anthropology 1054 LS & A Bldg Ann Arbor MI 48109

GUDJOHNSEN, STEFAN, paint manufacturing company executive; b. Reykjavik, Iceland, May 27, 1931; s. Jakob and Elly G.; m. Gudrun Ragnars, Dec. 26, 1954; children—Egill, Sigridur, Jakob, Stefan. Diploma in econs., U. Iceland, 1957. Office mgr. Malning Ltd., Kopavogi, Iceland, 1957-58, mng. dir., 1978—. Avocations: bridge, snooker; billiards. Home: Hafaflot 10, 210 Gardabae Iceland Office: Malning Ltd, Funahofda 7, 112 Reykjavik Iceland

GUDJONSSON, BIRGIR, physician; b. Akureyri, Iceland, Nov. 8, 1938; s. Gudjon and Kristjana (Jakobsdottir) Vigfusson; m. Heidur Anna Vigfusdottir, Oct. 21, 1961; children: Asdis, Gunnar, Sigrun. MD, U. Iceland, 1965; postgrad. fellow Yale U., 1970-72. Diplomate internal medicine and gastro enterology. Intern, Stamford Hosp., Conn., 1966-67, resident, 1967-68; resident in medicine Yale New Haven Hosp., 1968-70; asst. prof. medicine Yale U. Med. Sch., 1972-73, 77-78, 82; practice medicine specializing in internal medicine and gastroenterology, Reykjavik, 1974—; cons. City Hosp., Reykjavik, 1974-77, Med. Clinic, 1974—. Author: (with H.M. Spiro) Controversies in Internal Medicine, 1980; contbr. articles to profl. jours. Mem. council Athletic Union Iceland, 1981—. Fellow ACP, Royal Soc. Medicine; mem. Royal Coll. Physician U.K., Am. Gastroenterol. Assn., Brit. Soc. Gastroenterology, Brit. Assn. Sport and Medicine, Am. Coll. Sports-Medicine, World Assn. Hepato-Pancreato-Biliary Surgery, N.Y. Acad. Sci. Lutheran. Club: Reykjavik Athletic. Home: Alftamyri 51, 108 Reykjavik Iceland Office: Medical Clinic, Alfheimum 74, 104 Reykjavik Iceland

GUDMUNDSSON, FINNBOGI, library administrator; b. Reykjavik, Iceland, Jan. 8, 1924; s. Gudmundur Finnbogason and Laufey Vilhjalmsdottir; m. Kristjana P. Helgadottir, Oct. 1, 1955; 1 child, Helga Laufey. Cand. mag. U. Iceland, 1949, Dr. phil., 1961. Assoc. prof. U. Man., Winnipeg, Can., 1951-56; lectr. Icelandic Univs., Oslo and Bergen, 1957-58; tchr. Icelandic Reykjavik Gymnasium, 1958-64, U. Iceland, Reykjavik, 1962-64; dir. Nat. Library of Iceland, Reykjavik, 1964—. Author: Sveinbjörn Egilsson's Translations of Homer, 1960, Stephan G. Stephansson in Retrospect: Seven Essays, 1982; contbr. articles to profl. jours.; editor: Orkneyinga saga, 1965; Selected Letters Written to Stephan G. Stephansson, 1971-75. Mem. Icelandic Studies Soc. (chmn. 1962-64), Icelandic Research Librarians (chmn. 1966-73), Icelandic Patriotic Soc. (pres. 1967-84), Nordinfo (bd. dirs. 1976-79). Lutheran. Club: Rotary (sec. 1983-84). Office: Landsbokasafn Islands, Hverfisgata 15, 121 Reykjavik Iceland

GUDZENT, DIETRICH EBERHARD, physicist; b. Berlin, June 18, 1926; s. Friedrich Georg and Margarete (Buelow) G. B.S., Humboldt U., 1948, M.S., 1952. Scientist U.S. Army Missile Command, Huntsville, Ala., 1959-66; sci. supr. Melpar, Falls Church, Va., 1966-68; chief engr. Astro Reliability, Alexandria, Va., 1968-70; chief engr. VSE, Alexandria, Va., 1970-78; proposal adminstr. Tracor, Inc., Rockville, Md., 1978—; mgmt. cons. to def. industry. Contbr. articles to profl. jours. Mem. Assn. Old Crows, Am. Def. Preparedness Assn., IEEE (sr.), IEEE Aerospace and Electronic System Soc. (bd. govs.), Electronic Industries Assn. Republican. Lutheran. Avocations: fine arts; classical music. Home: 300 Northwest Dr Silver Spring MD 20901 Office: Tracor Inc 1601 Research Blvd Rockville MD 20850

GUEDES, AMANCIO D'ALPOIM MIRANDA, architect, educator; b. Lisbon, Portugal, May 13, 1925; s. Amilcar Jose de Miranda Guedes and Maria Soledad Francisca d'Alpoim; m. Dorothy Ann Phillips, 1947; 4 children. Ed. U. Witwatersrand, Johannesburg, South Africa, and Escola Superior de Belas Artes, Oporto, Portugal; B.Arch. Self-employed, Lourenco Marques (now Maputo), Mozambique, 1949-75; prof. architecture, head dept. architecture U. Witwatersrand, 1975—; vis. prof. U. Queensland, 1980, U. Calif., 1980, 81. Author: Architects As Magicians, Conjurers, Dealers in magic Goods, Promises, Spells—Myself as Witchdoctor, 1965; Buildings Grow Out Of Each Other Or How My Own Sagrada Familia Came to Be, 1967; Fragments From An Ironic Autiobiography, 1977; Vitruvius Mozambicanus, 1985; author exhbn. catalogue: Amancio Guedes, 1980. Decorated comdr. Order Santiago and Espada. Mem. Inst. South African Architects (Gold medal). Office: Univ of Witwatersrand, Dept Architecture, 1 Jan Smuts Ave, Johannesburg Republic of South Africa *

GUEDES, FERNANDO AIRES, publishing executive; b. Oporto, Portugal, July 1, 1929; s. Augusto Guedes Silva and Celeste A. (Carvalho) Guedes; m. Maria Júlia Magalhães, May 27, 1954; children: João, Nuno, Carlos, Luis. Student, Tech. U., Lisbon, Portugal, 1948-50. Mgr. Harker, Sumner & Co. Ltd., Lisbon, 1950-58; mng. dir. Editorial Verbo, Lisbon, 1959—; chmn. Verbo Publicações Periódicas, Lisbon, 1972—; cons. Empresa de Divulgação Cultural, Lisbon, 1974—; v.p. Groupe Editeurs Livres, EEC, Brussels, 1987, pres. book pub. group, 1988. Author: Poesias Escolhidas, 1968 (Nat. Poetry prize 1969), O Livro e a Leitura em Portugal, 1987. Mem. Soc. Sci. Cath. U. Portugal, Internat. Pub. Union (v.p. 1988). Roman Catholic. Clubs: Grémio Literário, Circle Eça Queiroz. Home: Alameda Linhas de Torres, 144A-20, 1700 Lisbon Portugal Office: Editorial Verbo, Rua Carlos Testa 1, 1000 Lisbon Portugal

GUEHENNO, JEAN MARIE, bank executive; b. Paris, Oct. 30, 1949; s. Jean and Annie (Rospabe) G.; m. Mathilde de la Bardonnie, Mar. 26, 1974 (div.); m. Michele Fahy Moss, Apr. 21, 1981; 1 child, Claire Maia. Student, Ecole Normale Superieure, Paris, 1968-72, Ecole Nationale D'Administration, Paris, 1974-76, Inst. D'Etudes Politiques, Paris, 1972-73. Auditor Cour des Comptes, Paris, 1976-79, referendary counselor, 1978, 1986-87; deputy dir. Policy Planning Staff, Paris, 1979-82; cultural counselor French Embassy, N.Y.C., 1982-86; special advisor to chmn. Banque de l'Union European, Paris, 1987—. Contbr. articles to profl. jours. Home: 63 rue Claude Bernard, Paris France Office: Banque de l'Union Européenne, 4 rue Gaillon, 75107 Paris France

GUENIN, MARCEL ANDRÉ, physics professor; b. Geneva, July 17, 1937; s. Léandre André and Isabella Serafina (Bontempo) G.; m. Ingrid Marina Selbach, Aug. 20, 1962; children: Marc Olivier, Bertrand Frédeéric Andée, Didier Philippe Marcel. Diploma in theoretical physics, Fed. Inst. Tech., Zurich, Switzerland, 1960; PhD, U. Geneva, 1962. Research assoc. Princeton (N.J.) U., 1964-66; lectr. grad. program, Geneva, Lausanne, Neuchatel, Switzerland, 1966-68; asst. prof. U. Geneva, 1968-70, assoc. prof, 1970-73, prof., 1973—, dir. dept. theoretical physics, 1974-77; vice-rector U. Geneva, 1980-83, rector, 1983-87; bd. dirs. Brown Boveri Co., Baden, Switzerland, Societé Financiere de Geveva; chmn. PBG Privatbank, Geneva; mem. sci. adv. com. Asea Brown Boveri, Zurich, 1988—. Author 3 books in field; editor (jour.) Letters in Mathematical Physics, 1975-86; contbr. articles to profl. jours. Served to 1st lt. Swiss Army Res. Fellow European Phys. Soc. (sec. 1973-78; mem. Swiss Phys. Soc. (sec. 1969-73), Am. Phys. Soc., Internat. Assn. Math. Physicists (founding mem.). Lodge: Rotary. Office: U Geneva Dept Theoret Physics, 32 Blvd d'Yvoy, 1211 Geneva 4 Switzerland

GUÉNIOT, YVONNE MARIE, librarian; b. Paris, Dec. 19, 1924; d. Paul Joseph René and Louise Henriette Guéniot. Diploma in gen. documentation, Union Francaise des Organismes de Documentation, Paris, 1949, diploma in library techniques, 1949; cert. analyst in adminstrv. automation, Ministry of Fin., Paris, 1968. Librarian Nat. Library, Paris, 1950-72; librarian-in-chief, dir. univ. library U. Paris, 1972-77; librarian-in-chief, chief div. cooperation and automation Ministry Nat. Edn., Paris, 1977-79; librarian-in-chief, dir. Library Inter-U. Medicine, Paris, 1979—; prof. Diplome Technique puis Superior de Bibliothecaires, Paris, 1950-77, Conservatoire Nat. des Arts et Metiers, Paris, 1967-80. Contbr. articles to profl. jours. Mem. Confedn. Francaise des Travilleurs Chretiens Scenrac (pres. library sect. 1986—, sec. gen. adjointe 1983—), Assn. des Francais Libres. Home: 84 rue Vergniaud, 75073 Paris France Office: Bibiloteque Inter U de Medcine, 12 rue de l'Ecole, 75270 Paris France

GUENTHER, CHARLES JOHN, librarian, writer; b. St. Louis, Apr. 29, 1920; s. Charles Richard and Hulda Clara (Schuessler) G.; m. Esther G. Klund, Apr. 11, 1942; children—Charles John, Cecile Anne, Christine Marie. A.A., Harris Tchrs. Coll., 1940; student, St. Louis U., 1952-54; B.A., Webster Coll., 1973, M.A., 1974; L.H.D. (hon.), So. Ill. U., Edwardsville, 1979. Editorial asst. St. Louis Star-Times, 1938; various positions Social Security Commn. Mo., Dept. Labor, U.S. Employment Service, War Dept., C.E., St. Louis, 1941-43; head archives unit USAAF Aero Chart Service, St. Louis, 1943-45; head research unit USAAF Aero Chart Service, 1945-47; asst. chief, chief of library, translator, historian, geographer, supervisory cartographer, librarian USAF Aero Chart and Info. Center (name changed to DMA Aerospace Center), St. Louis, 1947-57; chief tech. library USAF Aero Chart and Info. Center (name changed to DMA Aerospace Center), 1957-75; Civilian library specialist Project Crossroads, USAF, 1946; instr. creative writing Peoples Art Center, St. Louis, 1953-56; lectr., poetry workshop leader various U.S. writers confs. Author: Modern Italian Poets, 1961, Paul Valery in English, 1970, (poems) Phrase/Paraphrase, 1970, Voices in the Dark, 1974; translator: (with others) Selected Poems of Alain Bosquet, 1963, Selected Translations, 1986; contbr. to Anthology of Spanish Poetry, 1961, Modern European Poetry, 1966, New Directions, 1968-80, Roots and Wings, 1976; Contbr. articles to profl. jours.; Book reviewer: St. Louis Post-Dispatch, 1953—, Globe-Democrat, 1972-82. Decorated commendatore Ordine al Merito della Repubblica Italiana; recipient Shell Co. Found. grant for book Phrase/Paraphrase, 1970; Lit. award Mo. Library Assn., 1974. Mem. Poetry Soc. Am. (Midwest regional v.p., James Joyce award 1974), St. Louis Writers Guild (v.p. 1958, pres. 1959, 76-77), St. Louis Poetry Center (chmn. bd. chancellors 1965-72, pres. 1974-76), Mo. Writers Guild (v.p. 1971-73, pres. 1973-74), Spl. Libraries Assn. (pres. Greater St. Louis chpt. 1969-70), Rose Soc. Greater St. Louis; corr. mem. Academie d'Alsace (diplome d'honneur 1957); hon. mem. Les Violetti Picards et Normands, Paris, Academia de Ciencias Humanisticas y Relaciones, Mexico, Academie Chablaisienne, Thonon-les-Bains, France, Biblioteca Partenopea, Naples; asso. mem. Internat. Am. Inst. Home: 2935 Russell Blvd Saint Louis MO 63104

GUENTHERODT, INGRID, linguistics educator; b. Eschwege, Fed. Republic of Germany, June 6, 1935; s. Kurt Joachim and Gudrun (Doehle) G. Translator Diploma, U.Mainz, 1959; Ph.D. in Germanic Langs., U. Tex., 1963. Teaching asst. U. Tex., Austin, 1960-63; instr. Manhattanville Coll., Purchase, N.Y., 1963-65; lectr. U. Nancy, France, 1965-67; asst. prof. U. Hawaii, Honolulu, 1967-69; asst prof. U. Kans., Lawrence, 1969-72; Akademische Oberraetin U. Trier, Fed. Republic of Germany, 1972—. Coauthor: Women and the European Community, 1980. Author: Phonai: Hessian Dialects, 1982. Contbr. articles to linguistics jours. Fulbright travel grantee, 1959. Mem. MLA, Linguistic Soc. Am., Deutsche Gesellschaft fuer Sprachwissenschaft, Deutscher Akademikerinnenbund.

GUERIN, CHRISTIAN JEAN MARIE, ophthalmologist; b. Grenoble, France, Mar. 14, 1947; s. Andre Gabriel and Colette Marie (Jay) G.; m. Catherine Bernadette Munch, June 2, 1973; children: Sandra, Cedric. MD, U. Lyon, 1976. Intern Vinatier Hosp., Lyon, France, 1971, Jean 23 Hosp., Lyon, 1972; resident specializing in ophthalmology Croix Rousse Hosp., Lyon, 1972-73, 74-76; practice medicine specializing in ophthalmology Venissieux, France, 1977-78, Altkirch, France, 1980—; ophthalmologist Community Clinic, Pierre Benite, France, 1978-80, Community Clinic for Lepers, Meched, Iran, 1973-74. V.p. Walkers of Heimersdorf, 1987; mem. Pupil's Parents of Pub. Teaching, Altkirch, 1987. Mem. Union Ophthalmologists, Functional Practising Group Altkirch. Roman Catholic. Club: Tennis (Altkirch). Office: 5 rue de L'Hotel de Ville, 68130 Altkirch France

GUERIN, DIDIER, magazine publisher; b. Neuilly/Seine, France, Aug. 2, 1950; came to U.S. 1973; s. Jacques Guerin and Janine (Vaesken) Florange; m. Margaret Moray, Dec. 31, 1982. BA in Pub. Law, U. Paris, 1973, BA in Communications, 1973; MA in Journalism, Mich. State U., 1975. Editor Soc. Gen. de Presse, Paris, 1976-79; asst. pub. Look mag., N.Y.C., 1979-81; mng. dir., dir. Hachette Communications Ltd., London, 1982—; exec. v.p., dir. Edi Sept, Inc., N.Y.C., 1983-84, Cogedipresse, Inc., N.Y.C., 1983-86, Union des Edit. Modernes, Inc., N.Y.C., 1983-86; pres., dir. Edi Sept, Inc., N.Y.C., 1984-86; pres., dir. Hachette Publs., Inc., N.Y.C., 1987—; pres., dir. publs. Filipacchi, Inc., N.Y.C., 1987—; chmn. Tokyo Fashion Kaihatsu, 1984—; pub. Elle Mag., N.Y.C., 1984-85; bd. dirs. Intermag. M.b.h., Munich, Elle Pub., N.Y.C., Curtis Circulation Co., West Caldwell, N.J., Premiere Pub. Co., N.Y.C., Diamandis Communications, Inc., N.Y.C.; fgn. trade advisor to French govt., 1988—. Mem. exec. com. Publishing Hall of Fame, 1987. Office: Hachette Publs Inc 1515 Broadway New York NY 10036

GUERIN, JEAN LOUIS, confectionary company executive; b. St. Denis, France, Mar. 17, 1935; s. Marcel and Berthe (Teytaud) G.; m. Marie-France Villain, June 13, 1974; children: Philippe, Pierre, Aurelie, Aude. B.S., Ecole Nationale Superièure de Chimie, Toulouse, France, 1959; postgrad. D'Administration des Entreprises, Paris, 1965; A.M.P., Harvard U., 1978. Chem. engr. Pfizer-France, Paris, 1962-67, Pfizer-Europe, Brussels, Belgium, 1967-68; tech. dir. Ufico, Paris, 1968-71; chief exec. officer Rowntree Mackintosh S.A., Noisiel, France, 1971-84; chmn. Rowntree Mackintosh SpA, Bologna, Italy, 1983—, Rowntree Mackintosh Europe; dir. Rowntree Mackintosh plc. Home: La Renardiere-Allee St Eloi, 77144 Chalifert France Office: Rowntree Mackintosh Europe, 12 rue de la Maison Rouge, Lognes, 77200 Torcy France

GUÉRITÉE, NICOLAS, endocrinologist; b. Bucharest, Romania, Dec. 29, 1920; s. Virgile-Georges and Marie-Antoinette (Gebhardt) G.; m. Gabriela Rizescu, Dec. 6, 1944 (div. 1954); 1 child, Jean-Claude; m. Lucienne Suzanne Taillebois, July 24, 1954; children: Catherine, Virginie. MD, U. Med. Sch., Bucharest, 1944, Faculté de Médecine, Paris, 1952. Practice medicine specializing in endocrinology Paris, 1957-85; cons. in endocrinology Hosp. of Nanterre, Paris, 1958-66, Endocrine Dept. Faculty of Medicine La Pitié-Salpêtrière, Paris, 1960-85; head med. dept. French Sub. of Schering A.G. Berlin, Paris, 1949-58; head research dept. Laboratoire La Théramex SA, Monaco and Paris, 1958-75; bd. dirs. Laboratoire Théramex SA, 1975—; expert WHO, 1958; mem. French Nat. Com. of Qualification of the Endocrinologists, 1976—; founder, exec. ann. Journees Francaises d'Endocrinolgie Clinique, 1980—. founder and chief editor La Revue Francaise d'Endocrinologie Clinique, 1960—; inventor steroid compounds. Mem. French Nat. Union of Endocrinologists (founder, exec. v.p. 1960—), Societe Francaise d'Endocrinolgie, Am. Soc. Bone and Mineral Research, Soc. for Study of Reprodn., Endocrine Soc. (Am.). Christian Orthodox. Club: Racing of France. Office: Laboratoire La théramex, Tour Les Mercuriales, 40 Rue Jean Jaures, 93176 Bagnolet France

GUERRA GONZALEZ, ALFONSO, vice president of Spain; b. Seville, May 21, 1940; married; 1 son. Joined Partido Socialista Obrero Español, 1964; sec. gen. Andalusian Socialist Fedn. until 1970; sec. for info. and the press, 1974-76; elected sec. for orgn. at 27th Congress, Madrid, 1976; dep. to Congress from Seville, from 1977, mem. Standing Com. Congress, from 1979; dep. prime minister of Spain, 1982—; V.P. Socialist Parliamentary Group. Address: Gabinete Tecnico del Vice, Presidente del Gobierno, Palacio de la Moncloa, Madrid 3 Spain *

GUERRA-RULLAN, FRANCISCO JAVIER, federal agency official; b. Mexico City, Sept. 17, 1945; s. Francisco and Francisca (Rullan) G.; m. Elizabeth Millán-Dehesa, Nov. 13, 1982; children: Francisco José, Alejandro. BArch, Univ. Nat. Autónoma de Mexico, Mexico City, 1971; postgrad., Cambridge U., 1971-78. Registered architect. Rural devel. advisor Ministry of Programming and Budget, Mexico City, 1978, tech. coordinator Nat. Plan of Action to Combat Desertification, 1979-81, dir., coordinator Econ. Policy Info. Program, 1983-85; dep. advisor to pres. World Food Council, Mexico City and Rome, 1981-82; dir. info. State-Owned Enterprises of the Agrl. Sector Ministry of Agriculture, Mexico City, 1986—; head grad. and research in architecture dept. Inst. Poly. Nat., Mexico City, 1983-86; cons. in housing, Mexico City, 1983—. Contbr. articles to mags., books. Undersec. nat. confedn. Partido Revolucionario Institucional. Brit. Council scholar at Cambridge U., 1971. Mem. Centro Mexicano de Análisis Regional (founder, chmn. 1987—), Design Research Soc., Colegio de Arquitectos Mexico, Cambridge-Darwin Coll. Alumni Assn. (chmn. 1973-74), Confedn. Nat. Campesina. Home: Michoacán 19-4, Hipódromo de la Condesa, 06170 Mexico City Mexico

GUERRA-VIEIRA, ANTONIO HELIO, electrical engineer, educator; b. Guaratingueta, Sao Paulo, Brazil, June 14, 1930; s. Nilo Vieira and Julia Guerra; m. Syllene Castejon, Oct. 13, 1955; children: Antonio Jr., Eduardo, Silvia, Paulo, Filipe. Diploma in engring., Escola Politecnica, Sao Paulo, 1953, D in Engring., 1964; DSc, U. Paris, 1957. Registered profl. engr., Brazil. Dir. Digital Systems Lab. U. Sao Paulo, 1968—; dir. Escola Politecnica, Sao Paulo, 1980-82; pres. U. Sao Paulo, 1982-86; pres. Found. for Tech. Devel., Sao Paulo, 1972-80, Found. for Sci. Support, Sao Paulo, 1979-85. Mem. Inst. Engring. (Engr. of Yr. 1977). Home: Ave Lopes de Azevedo 284, 05603 Sao Paulo Brazil Office: U Sao Paulo, PO Box 11455, Sao Paulo Brazil

GUERREIRO, ANTÓNIO M.A., investment banker; b. Almada, Portugal, Oct. 26, 1952; s. Antonio C. and Maria C.A. Guerreiro; m. Isabel M.R. Gaspar Paulino; children: David, Sandra. MBA, Harvard U., 1978. Lic. economist, Portugal. Asst. planning Cimianto, Lisbon, Portugal, 1973-74; asst. treas. DCI Trading Co., Lisbon, 1974-75; account officer Banco Lar Chase, Rio de Janeiro, 1975-76; sr. investment officer IFC/World Bank, Washington, 1978-85; credit and market mgr. Chase Manhattan Bank, Lisbon, 1985-87; mng. dir. Finantia Gestao E Consultoria Financeira Internat. SA, Lisbon, 1987—. Contbr. articles to profl. jours. Mem. Assn. Naval de Lisboa. Clubs: Harvard of Portugal (Lisbon) (bd. dirs. 1986—), Negocios. Office: Finantia Gestao E Cons, AV DA Liberdade 40-4, 1200 Lisbon Portugal

GUERREIRO, LUIZ FERNANDO TAVARES, civil engineer; b. São Paulo, Brazil, May 22, 1953; s. Manoel Tavares and Dora Luiza (Tavares) G.; m. Vera Paula Leite Tavares, Dec. 10, 1977; children: Dora Tavares and Luiz Fernando Tavares Guerriero Filho. Degree in civil engring., Mackenzie U., São Paulo, 1977; postgrad. degree in fin. adminstrn., Getúlio Vargas Found., São Paulo, 1984. Registered profl. engr., Brazil. Mgr. sales Confab Indsl. SA, São Paulo, 1983-86; gen. mgr. Confab Montagens Ltd., SãO Paulo, 1986—; bd. dirs. Cia Agricola Usina Jacarezinho, Confab Química Ltd; cons. OCA Mineração Ltd. Home: Al Equador 636, Alphaville II, 06400 Barueri, Sao Paulo Brazil Office: Confab Indsl SA, Al Rio Negro 433, 06400 Barueri, Sao Paulo Brazil

GUERRERO, REUBEN CASTRO, med. oncologist, internist; b. Manila, Aug. 22, 1935; came to U.S., 1962, naturalized, 1978; s. Jacobo Tolentino and Francisca Claravall (Castro) G.; A.A., U. Philippines, Manila, 1952, M.D. (Univ. scholar, 1955-56; United Drug Co. scholar, 1956-57), 1957; m. Celina V. Sison, June 18, 1962; children—Chiarina, Leonora, Anthony Paul. Intern, Philippine Gen. Hosp., Manila, 1956-57; mem. faculty Coll. of Medicine, U. Philippines, 1957-62; resident in medicine, Ch. Home and Hosp., Balt., 1962-64, chief resident, 1965-66; postdoctoral fellow in medicine Johns Hopkins Hosp., Balt., 1964-65, postdoctoral fellow in med. oncology, 1966-68; asst. prof. medicine, chief chemotherapy div. U. Philippines and Cancer Inst., 1968-73; med. oncologist, chmn. cancer com. Straub Clinic and Hosp., Honolulu, 1973—; clin. assoc. prof. John A. Burns Sch. Medicine, U. Hawaii; chmn. research Philippine Cancer Soc., 1969-73; chmn. service and rehab. com., bd. dirs. Hawaii div. Am. Cancer Soc., 1973—. Served with Philippine Army Res., 1957-58. Fellow ACP; mem. Am. Soc. Internal Medicine, Am. Soc. Clin. Oncology, Philippine Soc. Med. Oncology, Honolulu County Med. Soc., Hawaii Med. Assn. (cancer commn.), AMA, Am. Geriatric Soc., Aerospace Med. Assn., Honolulu Marathon Assn. Republican. Roman Catholic. Club: Honolulu. Contbr. articles to profl. jours. Home: 1424 Ohialoke St Honolulu HI 96821 Office: Straub Clinic and Hosp 88 S King St Honolulu HI 96813

GUERRI, SERGIO CARDINAL, titular archbishop of Trevi; b. Tarquinia, Italy, Dec. 25, 1905. Ordained priest Roman Catholic Ch., Mar. 30, 1929; titular archbishop of Trevi, 1969—; elevated to Sacred Coll. Cardinals, 1969; pro-pres. Congregation Pontifical Comm. for State of Vatican City; mem. Congregation Oriental Chs., Congregation Evangelization of Peoples. Address: Vatican City Vatican *

GUERRIERI, TERESA ELLEN, transportation company executive; b. Espanola, N.Mex., Nov. 22, 1934; d. George M. and Irma P. (Muth) Witzke; m. Gasper J. Guerrieri, May. 13, 1950; children: Gasper L., Jimmy George, Robin B. Grad. high sch. Pres., treas. G&G Truck Leasing Inc., Thornton, Colo., 1967—. Recipient Golden Poet award World of Poetry, 1985, 86, 87. Republican. Office: G&G Truck Leasing Inc 5974 Marion Dr Denver CO 80216

GUEST, RITA CARSON, interior designer; b. Atlanta, Aug. 17, 1950; d. Walter Harold and Doris Rebecca (Reeves) Carson; m. John Franklin Guest Jr., Jan. 20, 1979. BVA, Ga. State U., 1973. Designer, Alan L. Ferry Designers, Inc., Atlanta, 1973-80; v.p. Ferry Hayes Designers, Inc., Atlanta, 1980-84; pres., head designer Carson Guest, Inc., Atlanta, 1984—; lectr. in field. Recipient Presdl. citation Am. Soc. Interior Designers, Ga. chpt., 1984, Comml. Design Project award, 1983, First Place Office Design award Ga. chpt. Am. Soc. Interior Designers, 1987, Hon. mention residential design, 1987. Mem. Am. Soc. Interior Designers (dir. 1984, treas. 1985-86, nominating com. 1987, chmn. interprofl. devel. com. Ga. chpt. 1988), Atlanta C. of C. Presbyterian. Clubs: High Mus. of Art, Atlanta Preservation Center, Shallowford Canoe. Avocation: painting. Office: Carson Guest Inc 1720 Peachtree St NW Suite 1001 Atlanta GA 30309

GUEVARA, DOMINADOR BELLEZA, physician, small business owner; b. Manila, Dec. 10, 1911; s. Buenaventura Quiambao and Feliciana (Belleza) G.; m. Ampara Aspe Ordoña, Jan. 14, 1941 (separated 1959); m. Rosita David, June 10, 1972; children: Dominador Soto, Maria Theresa David. G-rad. medicine and surgery, U. Santo Thomas, Manila, 1941. Gen. practice medicine Manila; owner drug store, pawn shop and trucking co.; asst. dir. La Union Provincial Hosp., Phillipines, 1944-45. Author World Peace, 1960, World Peace Salvation of Mankind, 1986; inventor fiberglass battery, 1960. Candidate for mayor of Manila, 1987; founder, pres. Movement for a Peaceful and Prosperous Democracy, 1987; candidate constitutional conv. Phillipines, 1972. Recipient Most Outstanding Physician of Tondo award The Young Achievers Club, 1982, Golden Harvest Achievement award Achievement Research Soc., 1987. Mem. Manila Med. Soc., Tondo Med. Soc. (bd. dirs. 1972-79, 3 awards), Tondo Barangay Council. Club: Franger (Tondo Manila) (Gerona Tondo adviser 1955-72). Home and Office: 502 Francisco, Tondo Manila, Manila Phillipines

GUEVARA MAYORGA, ALEJANDRO JOSE, infosystems specialist; b. Barranquilla, Atlantico, Colombia, Aug. 5, 1957; s. Pedro and Lilia (Mayorga) Guevara Garzon; m. Vilma Orozco, Jan. 13, 1981; children: David, Laura, Alexandra. Grad. high sch., Barranquilla. Technologist computers Cedecomputos, Barranquilla, 1978-80; adminstr. Caribbean Self-Governing Univ., Barranquilla, 1981-87; dir. systems dept. Cementos Del Caribe S.A., 1984-87. Office: Cementos Del Caribe SA, Via 40, Las Flores, 2739 Barranquilla, Atlantico Colombia

GUEX, JEAN-JEROME, phlebologist; b. Aire sur Adour, Landes, France, Sept. 7, 1952; s. Jean Claude and Therese (Plateau) G.; m. Genevieve Meney, July 7; children: Marine, Thibaud. MD, Med. Faculty Nice, France, 1979. Intern Hosp. Pasteur, Nice, 1978-79, Hosp. St. Roch, Nice, 1979; resident Hosp. Notre Dame de Bon Secours, Paris, 1980-81; practice medicine specializing in vascular pathology Nice, 1981—; surgery attache Univ. Hosp., Nice, 1982—. Contbr. articles to profl. jours. Served with French Navy, 1979-80. Mem. Societe Francaise of Phlebologie (sr. mem.), Coll. Francaise de Pathologie Vasculaire. Home: 1389 Route des Sausses, 06510 Gattieres France Office: 32 Dubouchage St, 06000 Nice France

GUGAS, CHRIS, criminologist; b. Omaha, Aug. 12, 1921; s. Nicholas and Vera (Henas) G.; student U. So. Calif., 1946-49, U. Calif. at Northridge, 1955-56; B.A., M.A. in Pub. Adminstrn., U. Beverly Hills, 1977; D.Div., Ch. Living Sci., 1968; Ph.D., U. Beverly Hills, 1983; m. Anne Claudia Setaro, June 27, 1942; children—Chris, Steven Edward, Carol Ann Gugas Hawker. Asst. dir. security Los Angeles Bd. Edn., 1948-49; spl. agt. CIA, Washington, 1950-54; criminol. cons., Los Angeles, 1955-61; pub. safety dir., Omaha, 1962-65; dir. polygraph services Profl. Security Cons., Los Angeles, 1966—; exec. dir. Calif. Acad. Polygraph Scis., Los Angeles, 1974-76, The Truthseekers, 1975—; instr. Los Angeles Inst. Polygraph, 1979—, Gormac Polygraph Sch., Los Angeles, 1972-73; chief instr. Las Vegas Acad. Polygraph Sci., 1982-83; columnist Los Angeles Daily Jour., Security World mag., The Truthseekers. Mem. advisory bd., sec. Calif. Dept. Consumer Affairs, 1971-76; tech. advicor to Pres. MIA/POW Commn., 1986. Served with USMCR, 1940-45, 47-49. Mem. Marine Corps League (comdr. 1946), Marine Corps Combat Corr.'s Assn. (pres. Los Angeles chpt. 1975-77), Nat. Bd. Polygraph Examiners (pres. 1958), Security Officers Assn. (pres. 1968), Am. Polygraph Assn. (pres. 1971, exec. dir. 1972-73), Am. Soc. Indsl. Security. Club: Los Angeles Press. Author: The Silent Witness; co-author: The National Corruptors; Pre-Employment Polygraph; The Polygraphist in Court; Our National Rebellion, 1982; contbr. numerous articles to various jours. Home: 4018 Dixie Canyon Sherman Oaks CA 91403 Office: 1680 Vine St Ste 400 Hollywood CA 90028

GUGERLI, RICHARD, airline sales manager; b. Jonen AG, Switzerland, Sept. 27, 1953; s. Josef and Paula Maria (Carletti) G.; m. Lydia Diem; children: Reto, Sandro, Roman. Fed. comml. diploma, Comml. Sch., 1971; sales mgr. diploma, 1985. Merchant Kuoni Travel, Zurich, Switzerland, 1971-76; sales rep. Icelandair, Zurich, Switzerland, 1977-79, regional mgr., 1982—. Home: Chrumble 5, 5623 Boswil AG Switzerland Office: Icelandair, Stampfenbach Str 117, 8035 Zurich Switzerland

GUGGENHEIM, CHARLES E., motion picture-television producer, political media consultant; b. Cin., Mar. 31, 1924; s. Jack Albert and Ruth Elizabeth (Stix) G.; m. Marion Davis Streett, June 29, 1957; children: Grace Stix, Jonathan Streett, Philip Davis. BA, U. Iowa, 1948; HHD (hon.), Washington U., 1978. Producer Louis G. Cowan, Inc., N.Y.C., 1948-51; producer, dir. Fund for Adult Edn., Ames, Iowa, 1951-52; acting dir. KETC Ednl. TV Commn., St. Louis, 1952-54; pres. Guggenheim Prodns., Inc., Washington, 1955—. Producer TV series Sunday at the Zoo, 1950 (George Foster Peabody award); producer-dir. (films) Nine from Little Rock, 1964 (Acad. award 1964), Robert Kennedy Remembered, 1968 (Acad. award 1969), Monument to the Dream, 1967 (Golden Mercury award Venice Film Festival 1968), Children Without, 1964 (Acad. award nomination 1964), The Klan: A Legacy of Hate in Am., 1982 (Acad. award nomination 1983), High Schools, 1983 (Acad. award nomination 1984). Trustee Danforth Found., St. Louis, 1983—; mem. nat. council World Wildlife Fund, Washington, 1985—; media dir. Stevenson Presdl. Com., 1956, Kennedy Presdl. Com., 1968, McGovern

Presdl. Com., 1972, Kennedy for Pres. Com., 1980, 75 U.S. senator and gov.'s campaigns, 1955-85. Served to sgt. U.S. Army, 1943-46. Recipient Disting. Achievement award U. Iowa, Conservation Service award U.S. Dept. Interior, 1968, Honors, AIA, 1987. Club: Federal City (Washington). Home: 4343 Cathedral Ave NW Washington DC 20016 Office: Guggenheim Prodns Inc 3121 South St NW Washington DC 20007

GUGGENHIME, RICHARD JOHNSON, lawyer; b. San Francisco, Mar. 6, 1940; s Richard E. and Charlotte Guggenhime; m. Emlen Hall, June 5, 1965 (div.); children: Andrew, Lisa, Molly. AB in Polit. Sci. with distinction, Stanford U., 1961; LLB, Harvard U., 1964. Bar: Calif. 1965, U.S. Dist. Ct. (no. dist.) Calif. 1965, U.S. Ct. Appeals (9th cir.) 1965. Assoc. Heller, Ehrman, White & McAuliffe, 1965-71, ptnr., 1972—; spl. asst. to U.S. Senator Hugh Scott, 1964; bds. dir. Comml. Bank of San Francisco, 1980-81, Global Savings Bank, San Francisco, 1984-86. Mem. San Francisco Bd. Permit Appeals, 1978-86; bd. dirs. Marine World Africa USA, 1980-86; mem. San Francisco Fire Commn., 1986—; chmn. bd. trustees San Francisco Univ. High School, St. Ignatius Prep. Sch., San Francisco. Mem. Am. Coll. Probate Counsel, San Francisco Opera Assn. (dir.). Clubs: Bohemian, University, Wine and Food Soc., Olympic, Chevaliers du Tastevin (San Francisco); Silverado Country (Napa, Calif.); Vintage (Palm Springs). Home: 115 Presidio Ave San Francisco CA 94115 Office: Heller Ehrman White & McAuliffe 333 Bush St San Francisco CA 94104

GUGLER, ADOLF EMIL, electricity company executive; b. Laufenburg, Switzerland, Apr. 13, 1929; m. Sylvia Wiederkehr; children—Thomas, Ariane. Diploma in Law, U. Zurich, Switzerland, 1955. Lawyer, Centralschweizerische Kraftwerke, Lucerne, 1958-68, exec. v.p., 1968-79; exec. v.p. Electrowatt Ltd., Zurich, 1979-84, pres., 1984—. Mem. City Council of Lucerne, 1975-79. Lodge: Rotary. Avocations: hiking; skiing; hunting; reading; music. Office: Electrowatt Ltd, Bellerivestrasse 36, CH-8022 Zurich Switzerland

GUGLIELMINO, ROSARIO JOSEPH, lawyer; b. Buenos Aires, Argentina, Apr. 3, 1911; s. Rosario and Giuseppina (Lo Turco) G.; 1 son, Russell John. A.B. with honors, Cornell U., 1934, J.D., 1936. Bar: N.Y. 1936. Sole practice, Rochester, N.Y., 1936—; exec. dir. and counsel Police Adv. Bd., 1963-70; counsel Eye Bank Assn. Am., 1963-70, Assn. Blind of Rochester and Monroe County, Inc., 1975—; pres. Rochester Radio Reading Service, Inc., 1983—. Bd. visitors Albion State Tng. Sch. and Western Reformatory for Women, 1956-66; founder, pres. Rochester Eye and Human Parts Banks, Inc., 1952, pres. emeritus, 1954—; founder, pres. Eye Bank Assn. Am., 1961-63; pres. Children's Meml. Scholarship Fund, 1958-60; mem. Rochester Council State Commn. Against Discrimination, 1956-66; bd. dirs. Assn. Blind of Rochester and Monroe County, Inc., 1973—; bd. visitors Batavia Sch. Blind, 1979—. Named Citizen of Yr., Valguarnera Soc., 1977; recipient Heise award Eye Bank Assn. Am., 1975. Mem. ABA, N.Y. State Bar Assn., Monroe County Bar Assn. (pres. 1969), N.Y. State Trial Lawyers Assn., Am. Judicature Soc., Am. Arbitration Assn., Phi Beta Kappa, Phi Kappa Phi. Home: 68 Fairlane Dr Rochester NY 14626 Office: 134 S Fitzhugh St Rochester NY 14608

GUHA, PHULRENU, Indian government official; b. Calcutta, India, Aug. 13, 1911; d. Surendra Nath and Abala Bala (Bose) Datta; m. Biresh Chandra Guha, July 17, 1943 (dec.). MA, Calcutta U., 1934; DLitt, Sorbonne, 1938. Instr. U. London, 1939-40; lectr. Women's Coll., Calcutta, 1940-45; headmistress Calcutta Girls' High Sch., 1945-58; chmn. West Bengal Social Welfare Bd., 1959-67; mem. Rajiya Sabha (House of Lords) India, 1964-84; Minister of State for Social Welfare 1967-70, mem. Lok Sabha (House of Commons), 1984—; advisor Indian Inst. Social Welfare and Bus. Mgmt., Calcutta. Author 6 books; contbr. numerous articles to profl. jours. Active Congress Party of India; previously active Indian Govt. Com. on Womens' Edn.; pres. Indian Council for Child Welfare, 1970-73; vice-chmn. West Bengal Council for Child Welfare, 1954-65, chmn., 1965-78; v.p., gen. sec. All India Womens' Conf., 1961-67; past chmn. Bharatiya Adim Bati Sangha; founder All India Com. for Eradication of Illiteracy in the Country; past v.p. Indian Com. for Internat. Women's Yr.; sec. U.C.R.W., 1947; working pres. Council Nat. Integration and Democratic Rights; founder, pres. Karma Kutir; chmn. Centre for Womens' Devel. Studies, New Delhi, India. Recipient Padma Bhusan. Mem. Indo-German Friendship Assn. (pres.), Indo-Soviet Cultural Soc., Assn. for Social Health in India (pres. West Bengal Unit). Address: 55/5 Purna Das Rd, Calcutta 700 029, India

GUHA, SATYA PRIYA (NANOD), marketing consultant, educator; b. Serampore, India, Oct. 4, 1925; s. Asutosh and Renuka (Ghosh) G.; m. Sabita Ghosh, July 7, 1950; 2 children; m. Joan Beryl, Oct. 4, 1969; 1 stepchild. B of Commerce, Calcutta (India) U., 1942, MA, 1944. Account exec. Everest Advt. Agy., Ltd., India, 1945-48, research officer, 1954-56, mktg. mgr., 1962-66; asst. account exec. Ogilvy Mathers Ltd., U.K., 1948-54; product mgr. Lever Bros. India Ltd., 1956-62; mktg. exec. Thomson Orgn. Ltd., U.K., 1966-71; sr. lectr. mktg. and advt. Luton Coll., U.K., 1971—; mktg. cons. Rightways, Luton, 1971—. Mem. Inst. Mktg., Brit. Inst. Mgmt., Inst. Export, Communication Advt. and Mktg. Found., Fine Arts Soc. India (sec. 1944-45), Orient Soc. India (sec. 1951-54). Avocations: photography, golf, travel, cooking. Home: 361 Leagrave High St, Luton LU4 0ND England Office: Luton Coll Park Sq, Luton LU1 3JU, England

GUHL, ELDON LOWELL, author, investor, educator, philosopher, raconteur, electrical engineer; b. Denton, Tex., Nov. 17, 1908; s. Columbus Ranthemanthus and Roxie Ella (Johnson) G.; B.S. in E.E., U. N.Mex., 1965, B.B.A., 1973; m. Bertha Catherine Verda, Sept. 27, 1936. Enlisted USN, 1928, advanced through grades to comdr., 1954; served on U.S.S. Melville, U.S.S. Pruitt, U.S.S. McCormick, Pacific, 1929-37; U.S.S. Philadelphia, Atlantic, 1937-38; U.S.S. Cincinnati, Pacific, 1938-39; U.S.S. Portland, Pacific, 1939-45; Stationed Pearl Harbor Naval Shipyard, 1945-48; mem. Mil. Mission to Turkey, 1948-50; assigned Electronics Maintenance Sch., Gt. Lakes, Ill., 1950-51, Armed Forces Spl. Weapons Program, Albuquerque, 1951-58, ret., 1958; investor, 1958—; improved berthing for crew, and improved storage for spare parts, 1948; author: A Guide for Advancement in Electrical Ratings, 1943; How to Make an A or at Least a D in a Subject, 1963; How to have $100,000 in 15 Years, 1969; (essay) How to Gain the Skills to Shape Your Destiny, 1983; How to Have $1,000,000 by the Time you are 78, 1987. Mem. Ret. Officers Assn., Nat. Assn. Uniformed Services, Am. Assn. Ret. Persons, Am. Legion, Boy Scouts of Am. Alumni Family. Home: 1602 Aliso Dr NE Albuquerque NM 87110

GUHL, PETER LINDSAY, optometrist; b. Cleve. May 7, 1951; s. Paul Julius and Elizabeth Ann (Sheesley) G.; m. Susan Sventosky, Aug. 25, 1973; children: Kristin Laura, Matthew Peter. Student Ohio State U., 1969-72; BS, New Eng. Coll. Optometry, 1977; OD, Walter Reed Army Med. Ctr., 1977. Optometrist Robert Wetzel, OD, Wilmington, Del., 1977, Opthalmology Assn., Fairfield, Conn., 1978, Vision Ctr. Assocs., Bridgeport, Conn., 1978-88. Treas. Optometric Polit. Action com. Conn., 1982-85. Chmn. Church Preservation Com., Newtown, Conn., 1985—; mem. Stewardship Com., Newtown, 1985-88, deacon, 1988—, ch. council, 1985—; co-chmn. Outstanding Citizen Award Com., Newtown, 1986; mem. State Reps. Adv. Com. Mem. Am. Optometric Assn. (contact lens sect., low vision sect.), Conn. Optometric Soc. (bd. dirs. 1985, v.p. 1986-88, pres. 1988—), New Eng. Council Optometry, Fairfield Optometric Assn., New Eng. Coll. Optometry Alumni Assn., Newtown Jaycees (pres. 1985-86, chmn. 1986-87, Jaycee of Yr. 1985, Officer of Yr. 1984), Citizen of Yr. Finalist, Newtown, 1985. Am. Acad. Optometry, Beta Sigma Kappa. Republican. Club: Conn. Mother Earth News Chpt. (bd. dirs. 1984-86). Avocations: gardening, skiing, equestrian, music, sailing. Office: Vision Ctr Assocs 161 Boston Ave Bridgeport CT 06610 Office: 3385 Post Rd Southport CT 06490

GUIDANO, VITTORIO FILIPPO, psychiatrist, psycotherapist; b. Rome, Aug. 4, 1944; s. Federico Nicola and Angela (Zambrelli) G. BA in Liberal Arts, G.B. Vico Coll., Rome, 1963; MD, U. Rome, 1969. Residency in psychiatry, research asst. U. Pisa, Italy, 1969-72; research psychiatrist U. Rome, 1970-73, asst. prof. psycotherapy, 1974-85; founder, staff psychiatrist Ctr. for Cognitive Therapy, Rome, 1978—. Author: Cognitive Processes and Emotional Disorders, 1983, Complexity of the Self, 1987. Mem. Assn. for Cognitive-Behavioral Therapies (founder, exec. bd. 1972—). Office: Ctr for Cognitive Therapy, Via Degli Scipioni 245, 00192 Rome Italy

GUIDO, SHAREON CHRISTINE, mechanical contractor; b. Washington, Aug. 5, 1946; d. James Harold and Edna Louise (Mills) McCullough; m. Frank Michael Guido, June 7, 1975; 1 child, Craig Scott. Diploma, George C. Marshall Sch., 1964. Asst. corp. sec. First Charter Land, Falls Church, Va., 1969-70; sec. to v.p. Liberty Loan Corp., Falls Church, 1970-71; gen. mgr. Richards A/C Co. Inc., Falls Church, 1971-83; founder, pres. Precision Air, Inc., Falls Church, 1983—; sponser Va. Apprenticeship Program, Fairfax, 1983—. Contbr. articles to profl. jours. Bd. dirs. Boys Clubs of Am., Falls Church, Va., 1975-76; leader Boy Scouts Am. Falls Church, 1975-78; instr. religious edn. Diocese of Arlington, Va., 1976-77; counselor Telecommunications for the Deaf, 1982; guest lectr. Am. Lung Assn., 1983; notary pub. Va., 1971—; ofcl. Nat. Assn. Stock Car Auto Racing, 1972-74. Recipient Outstanding Service award Am. Lung Assn., 1983. Mem. Air Conditioning Contractors of Am. (mgmt. edn. com. 1987—), Falls Ch. Preservation Soc., Western Eastern Roadracers Assn., Plumbing, Heating, Cooling Contractors Assn., Am. Motorcyclist Assn., Am. Soc. Notaries. Roman Catholic. Lodge: Rotary Internat. Avocations: poetry writing, skiing, camping, reading. Office: Precision Air Inc 6048 Glen Carlyn Dr Falls Church VA 22041

GUIDON, NIEDE, archeologist, educator; b. Jau, São Paulo, Brazil, Mar. 12, 1933; arrived in France, 1965; parents Ernesto Francisco and Candida (Vianna de Oliveira) G. B of Natural History, U. São Paulo, 1958; D of Prehistory, U. Paris, 1974, LHD, 1985. Researcher Inst. Prehistoria, São Paulo, 1962-64, Centre Nat. Recherche Scientifique, Paris, 1966-77; prof. Ecole des Hautes Etudes Sci. Sociales, Paris, 1977—; invited prof. U. Estadual de Campinas, São Paulo, 1986—, U. Fed. de Pernambuco, Recife, Brazil, 1987; bd. dirs. Missão Franco-Brasileira do Piaui, Paris; assessor U. Fed. do Piauí, Brazil and Paris, 1978—; pres. Fundacão Museu do Homem Americano, Piaui, 1987—. Contbr. articles in Brazilian prehistory. Fellow Assn. Brasileira Antropologia, Soc. Arqueologia Brasileira, Union of Americanist, Assn. Brasileira Estudios do Quaternario, Assn. Francaise Anthropologie. Office: Ecole des Hautes Etudes Sci Sociales, 44 Rue de la Tour, 75116 Paris France

GUIDRY, MARY LEE, nursing educator, legal consultant; b. Glenmora, La., Nov. 25, 1928; d. James Thomas and Myrtle Lillian (Young) Walker; m. James Lawrence Guidry, May 29, 1961; children: Michael Wayne, James Stephen Edward. BS, Sacred Heart Dominican Coll., 1962; MS, Tex. Woman's U., 1970. Staff nurse pediatrics St. Joseph's Hosp., Houston, 1950-55; staff nurse, head nurse, supr. VA Hosp., Houston, 1955-61; instr., assoc. dean Prairie View A&M Coll., 1963-70; supr., instr. M.D. Anderson Hosp., Houston, 1971-74; asst. prof. nursing U. St. Thomas, Houston, 1974—; assoc. prof. nursing Prairie View Coll. Nursing, 1985—; coordinator R.N. sect. faculty devel. in nursing project So. Regional Edn. Bd., 1977-82; legal cons. Perdue, Turner, Berry, Law firm, Houston, 1980—. Instr. breast self exam. Am. Cancer Soc., Houston, 1979; mem. Cancer awareness Black Adv. Group, Cancer Info. Service, 1981-84, cert., 1982. Mem. Tex. Nurses Assn. (chmn. council on practice 1979-84, dist. bd. mem. 1983-84), Chi Eta Phi, Sigma Theta Tau, Sigma Gamma Rho. Democrat. Baptist. Home: 2418 Oakdale St Houston TX 77004

GUIGNABODET, LILIANE, writer; b. Paris, Mar. 26, 1939; d. Moise and Luba Olympia (Necheva) Graciani; m. Jean Guignabodet, Aug. 31, 1961; children: Béatrice, Valérie, Jean-Christophe. Cert., Cambridge (Eng.) U., 1961; lic. es lettres, U. Paris Sorbonne, 1965. Tchr. French lang. and lit. San Jose (Calif.) Coll., 1961-62; tchr. art and lit. IBM Sch., Corbeil, France, 1966-69; free-lance writer Paris, 1977—. Author: L'Ecume du Silence, 1977 (George Sand prize 1977), Le Bracelet Indien, 1980, Natalia, 1983 (Acad. Francaise award 1983), Dessislava, 1986. Mem. PEN Club France, Assn. des Ecrivains Croyants. Home: 55 rue Caulaincourt, 75018 Paris France Office: Albin Michel, 22 rue Huyghens, 75014 Paris France

GUIGNARD, JACQUES MARCEL, catering company executive; b. Lausanne, Switzerland, Jan. 16, 1941; s. Jean and Violette Olga (Henry) G.; m. Paulette Jotterand, July 9, 1966; children: Nathalie Genevieve, Berenice Violette. License ès sciences commerciales et economiques, U. Lausanne, 1967, Licence en economie politique, 1969. Sales rep. IBM, Lausanne, 1967-69; dir. Swiss Watch Fedn., Johannesburg, S. Africa, 1970-73; asst. to mng. dir. Stellram, Nyon, Switzerland, 1974-77; mng. dir. D.S.R., Morges, Switzerland, 1978—; chmn. Assn. Vaudoise des Etablissements Sans Alcool, Morges, 1983; vice chmn. Communaute Suisse des Assns. d'Establissements Sans Alcool, 1982, chmn., 1986—. Chmn. Eglise Evangelique Reformee, Morges, 1978-86. Home: Ch de la Plantaz 14, 1110 Morges Switzerland Office: DSR, Rue Centrale 23, 1110 Morges Switzerland

GUIGNARD, JEAN-LOUIS MARIE JOSEPH, botanist, educator; b. Paris, Apr. 21, 1931; s. Raphael and Isabelle (Labonne) G.; m. Denise Guyot, June 29, 1959; children: Françoise, Philippe, Pierre. Ph.D., Sorbonne, 1962. Mem. faculty U. Paris-Sud Faculty Pharmacy, 1972—, prof. botany, 1964—, head dept., 1970—, dean, 1971-74. Recipient Foulon prize Acad. Scis., 1963. Mem. French Bot. Soc. (editor review 1987—), Internat. Soc. Plant Morphologists, Internat. Assn. Plant Tissue Culture, Nat. Acad. Pharmacy. Roman Catholic. Author: Abrege de Botanique, 6th edit., 1986; Abrégé de Biochimie végetale, 2d edit., 1979; Abrégé of Phytochimie, 1984. Home: 38 du Louvre, 75001 Paris France Office: JB Clement, 92297 Chatenay-Malabry France

GUILD, MONTAGUE, JR., financial analyst; b. Los Angeles, June 6, 1942; s. Montague and Dorothy (Duncan) G.; B.A., U. Calif. at Santa Barbara, 1964; M.B.A. in Fin., Calif. State U., 1968; m. Andrea Taylor Cole, Dec. 19, 1973. Fin. analyst Security Pacific Nat. Bank, Los Angeles, 1968-69; securities analyst, portfolio mgr. Taurus Partners, Los Angeles, 1969; gen. partner The Himalaya Fund, Santa Monica, Calif., 1969-82; founder, pres. Guild Investment Mgmt., Inc., Malibu, Calif., 1969-88, Maharishi Heaven on Earth Devel. Corp., 1988—; pres. Calif. Ranch Properties, 1978—; founder, pres. Guild Capital Mgmt., Inc., 1987. Tchr., Transcendental Meditation Program, 1969—; trustee World Plan Exec. Council, 1974—; bd. dirs. Am. Found. for Sci. of Creative Intelligence, 1973-80. Served with Calif. Air N.G., 1966-67. Mem. Internat. Platform Assn., Phi Kappa Phi, Delta Tau Delta. Office: Maharishi Heaven Earth Devel Corp 22761 Pacific Coast Hwy Suite 226 Malibu CA 90265

GUILD, RICHARD SAMUEL, trade associations management company executive; b. Boston, Nov. 5, 1925; s. Walter Rayford and Anna (Hollander) G.; B.S., Boston U., 1949; m. Susan Jane Coughlin, July 3, 1965; children—Laura Ann, Linda Jean. With Guild Assocs., Inc., Boston, 1949—, mng. dir., 1960-65, pres., 1965—; owner Copypro, 1975—; treas. Resource Matching System, Inc., 1982-83; exec. sec. New Eng. Marine Trade Assn., 1963, Liquified Petroleum Gas Assn. New Eng., 1972-1985; mng. dir. Shoe Pattern Mfrs. Assn., 1951—, Mass. Automatic Merchandising Council, 1964—, Telephone Answering Assn. New England, 1983; exec. v.p. Am. Boat Builders and Repairers Assn., 1979; treas. Wet Ground MICA Assn., 1983-87. Served with USNR, 1944-45. Cert. assn. exec. Mem. Multiple Assn. Mgmt. Inst. (past pres.), Am. Soc. Assn. Execs. (past bd. dirs.), N.Am. Paddlesports Assn. (exec. v.p. 1987—), Boston Soc. Assn. Execs. (past pres.), Def. Orientation Conf. Assn., Soc. Mgmt. of Profl. Computing (exec. sec. 1985—, mng. dir. 1986—). Home: 5 Glengarry Rd Winchester MA 01890 Office: 715 Boylston St Boston MA 02116

GUILES, ROBERT EMERSON, artist; b. Addison, N.Y., Oct. 14, 1917; s. Lester E. and Amelia (Kreja) G.; student U. Rochester, 1939, Acad. Art, San Francisco, 1945-46; A.A. cum laude in Art Indian Valley Colls., Novato, Calif., 1981-84; m. Hazel Mae Anderson, June 7, 1947; children—William Alan, Frank Emerson. Asst. art dir. Ruthrauf & Ryan, Advt., 1948; staff artist San Francisco News, 1948-60, News-Call Bull., 1960-65, San Francisco Newspaper Agy., 1965-80; advt. cons., freelance graphic designer, 1980—; polit. cartoonist various labor publs., artist, 1958—; civic art commr., Novato, 1985—. Mem. Black Raven Pipe Band San Francisco, 1966-67. Publicity chmn. Marin Citizens for Responsible Firearms Control. Served to capt. AUS, 1940-45. Mem. Newspaper Guild (pres. local 52 1964, 75-76, treas. 1978-79). Clubs: Sierra. Democrat. Contbr. articles to profl. jours. Home and Office: 1265 Parkwood Dr Novato CA 94947

GUILLEMIN, ROGER, physiologist; b. Dijon, France, Jan. 11, 1924; came to U.S., 1953, naturalized, 1963; s. Raymond and Blanche (Rigollot) G.; m. Lucienne Jeanne Billard, Mar. 22, 1951; children—Chantal, Francois, Claire, Helene, Elizabeth, Cecile. B.A., U. Dijon, 1941, B.Sc., 1942; M.D., Faculty of Medicine, Lyons, France, 1949; Ph.D., U. Montreal, 1953; Ph.D. (hon.), U. Rochester, 1976, U. Chgo., 1977, Baylor Coll. Medicine, 1978, U. Ulm, Germany, 1978, U. Dijon, France, 1978, Free U. Brussels, 1979, U. Montreal, 1979, U. Man., Can, 1984, U. Turin, Italy, 1985. Intern, resident univs. hosps. Dijon, 1949-51; asso. dir., asst. prof. Inst. Exptl. Medicine and Surgery, U. Montreal, 1951-53; asso. dir. dept. exptl. endocrinology Coll. de France, Paris, 1960-63; prof. physiology Baylor Coll. Medicine, 1953—; adj. prof. medicine U. Calif. at San Diego, 1970—; resident fellow Salk Inst., 1970—. Decorated chevalier Legion of Honor (France), 1974, officier, 1984; recipient Gairdner Internat. award, 1974; U.S. Nat. Medal of Sci., 1977; co-recipient Nobel prize for medicine, 1977; recipient Lasker Found. award, 1975; Dickson prize in medicine, 1976; Passano award med. sci., 1976; Schmitt medal neurosci., 1977; Barren gold medal, 1979; Dale medal Soc. for Endocrinology U.K., 1980. Fellow AAAS; Mem. Am. Physiol. Soc., Endocrine Soc. (pres.) 1986), Soc. Exptl. Biology and Medicine, Internat. Brain Research Orgn., Internat. Soc. Research Biology Reprodn., Soc. Neuro-scis., Nat. Acad. Scis., Am. Acad. Arts and Scis., Académie nationale de Médecine (fgn. assoc.), Swedish Soc. Med. Scis. (hon.), Académie des Scis. (fgn. assoc.), Académie Royale de Médecine de Belgique (corr. fgn.), Club of Rome. Office: Salk Inst Box 85800 San Diego CA 92138 *

GUILLERMOND, GABRIEL GEORGES, physician; b. Nice, France, Oct. 22, 1925; s. Georges Fernand and Yvonne Henriette (Chaskin) G.; m. Nelly Cannebotin, Sept. 5, 1953 (Oct. 1971); m. Marguerite Bondin, June 17, 1972; 1 child, Florence. Lic. in Sci., Sci. Inst., 1950; DM, Montpellier Med. Sch., 1952; Diploma of Labour Medicine and Profl. Diseases, Med. U., Marseille, France, 1981. Pvt. practice physician, internal medicine Nice, 1952—; physician Brit. Am. Hosp., Nice, 1952-72; sworn doctor Edn. Ministry, Nice, 1972—; labour medicine, metilliand diseases French Rys., Soc. Social Organisms Edn. Ministry, Nice, 1965—. Club: Babriel L'Annonciateur. Lodge: Lions (hon. mem.). Home and Office: 47 Rue Marechel Joffre, 06000 Nice France

GUINETTI, GIUSEPPINA, business executive; b. Milan, Italy, May 9, 1923; came to Switzerland, 1976; d. Piero and Janina (Szabelska) Araldi; m. Paride Guinetti, Nov. 16, 1972. Diploma Rosa Stampa Coll., Vercelli, Italy, 1944; Ph.D., Cattolica U., Milan, 1946. Tchr., Liceo Scientifico, Milan, 1946-50; founder, mng. dir. Tad Tubi Acciaio E Derivati s.r.l., Milan, 1950-55; pres. Tad S.P.A., Milan, 1981-87, Tad Fin, Milan, 1987—, TQ Tubi Qualificati, Milan, 1972—; chmn. bd. Tad USA, Houston, 1979. mem. bd. Tad Holland, Amsterdam, 1984—, Ct Ceretti Tanfani, Milan, 1987—, IPM, Milan, 1980—. Recipient Internat. Interpetrol Prize, 1978. Roman Catholic. Clubs: Assn. Mondiale Femmes Chefs d' Enterprise: Cercle Foch (Paris); Horticulture Soc., Annabel's, Mark's (London); Donne in Carriera (Milan). Home: Casa Belmonte, 6927 Bigogno d'Agra/TI Switzerland

GUINLE, FRANCIS FERNAND MARCEL, educator, counter-tenor; b. Pau, France, Apr. 18, 1948; s. Guillaume Pierre Fernand and Juliette Marie-Louise (Paupéré) G. Licence d'Anglais, S. Etienne U., 1970, Maitrise d'Anglais, 1971, Agrégation d'Anglais, 1972, Doctorat 3è Cycle (Musicology), 1977, Doctorat d'Etat, 1986. Tchr. Lycée Carnot, Tunis, Tunisia, 1973-75; lectr. ENS, Tunis, 1975-77; Brit. Council scholar London, 1978-79; tchr. French Nat. Edn., Paris, 1980—. Contbr. articles to profl. jours. Mem. French Shakespeare Soc. Avocations: music; reading; writing. Address: 12 Rue de Condé, 69002 Lyon France

GUINN, STANLEY WILLIS, tax professional; b. Detroit, June 9, 1953; s. Willis Hampton and Virginia Mae (Pierson) G.; m. Patricia Shirley Newgord, June 13, 1981. BBA in Acctg. with high distinction, U. Mich., 1979, MBA in Corp. Fin. with distinction, 1981; MS in Taxation with Distinction, Walsh Coll., 1987. CPA, Mich.; cert. mgmt. acct., Mich. Tax mgr. Coopers & Lybrand, Detroit, 1981-87; tax cons. Upjohn Co., Kalamazoo, Mich., 1987—. Served with USN, 1974-77. Mem. Am. Inst. CPA's, Nat. Assn. Accts., Mich. Assn. CPA's, Inst. Mgmt. Acctg., Phi Kappa Phi, Beta Gamma Sigma, Beta Alpha Psi, Delta Mu Delta. Republican. Presbyterian. Home: 8420 Valleywood Ln Portage MI 49081 Office: Upjohn Co Corp Taxes div B111-242-52 7000 Portage Rd Kalamazoo MI 49001

GUINNESS, ALEC, actor; b. London, Apr. 2, 1914; m. Merula Salaman; 1 child, Matthew. Student, Pembroke Lodge, Southbourne, Roborough Sch., Eastbourne, Fay Compton Studio Dramatic Art; DFA (hon.), Boston Coll., 1962; DLitt (hon.), Oxford U., 1978. Copywriter, Arks Publicity, 1933. Debut with walk-on role in Libel!, 1934; Shakespearean debut in Hamlet, 1934; appeared with Old Vic Co., 1936-37; toured Europe and Egypt, 1938-39; with John Gielgud's Co., 1937-38, appeared in Romeo and Juliet, Perth, Scotland, 1939; Great Expectations (also adapted), 1939, Cousin Muriel, The Tempest, Thunder Rock, all 1940, Flare Path, N.Y.C., 1942; appeared in own adaptation of The Brothers Karamazov, 1946; in Vicious Circle, 1946; with Old Vic Co., 1946-48; dir.: Twelfth Night, 1948; appeared in: The Human Touch, 1949, The Cocktail Party, N.Y.C. and Edinburgh, Scotland, 1949-50, Under the Sycamore Tree, 1952; Richard III and All's Well That Ends Well, Stratford Shakespeare Festival, Ont., Can., 1953, The Prisoner, 1954, Hotel Paradiso, 1956, Ross, 1960 (London Evening Standard award), Exit the King, 1963, Dylan, N.Y.C., 1964, Incident at Vichy and Macbeth, 1966, Wise Child, 1967, Time Out of Mind, 1970, A Voyage Round My Father, 1971, Habeas Corpus, 1973, A Family and a Fortune, 1975, Yahoo, 1976, The Old Country, 1977-78, The Merchant of Venice, 1983; actor, dir.: The Cocktail Party, 1968; film appearances include Great Expectations, 1945, Oliver Twist, 1948, Mudlark, 1950, Kind Hearts and Coronets, 1951, The Lavender Hill Mob, 1951 (Acad. award nomination), The Man in the White Suit, 1951, Captain's Paradise, 1953, The Prisoner, 1956, The Bridge on the River Kwai (Acad. award, Golden Globe award, Brit. Film Acad. award 1957), The Horse's Mouth, 1958 (Venice Film Festival award), Our Man in Havana, 1960, Tunes of Glory, 1960, Lawrence of Arabia, 1962, Dr. Zhivago, 1965, The Comedians, 1967, Cromwell, 1970, Scrooge, 1970, Hitler: The Last Ten Days, 1973, Brother Sun, Sister Moon, 1973, Murder by Death, 1976, Star Wars, 1977 (Acad. award nomination), Lovesick, 1982, Passage to India, 1984; Am. TV debut in The Wicked Scheme of Jebal Deeks, 1959; Brit. TV appearances include The Actor, 1968, Twelfth Night, 1969, The Gift of Friendship, 1974, Caesar and Cleopatra, 1975, Tinker Tailor Soldier Spy, 1979 (Brit. Film Acad. TV award), Little Lord Fauntleroy, 1980, Smiley's People, 1981 (Brit. Film Acad. TV award), Edwin, 1983, Monsignor Quixote, 1985, Little Dorritt, 1986, A Handful of Dust, 1987. Served in Vol. Res., Royal Navy, 1941-45; commd. lt. 1942. Created Comdr. Order Brit. Empire, 1955; knight bachelor, 1959; recipient Acad. award for services to cinema, 1980. *

GUIORA, ALEXANDER ZEEV, psychologist; b. Nyiregyhaza, Hungary, June 13, 1925; came to U.S., 1963, naturalized, 1968; s. Solomon and Theresa (Gottlieb) G.; m. Susie N. Neuser, Jan. 20, 1955. Docteur d'Universite, Sorbonne U., Paris, 1951. Prof. psychiatry, psychology and linguistics U. Mich., Ann Arbor, 1964-85; prof. psychology, dir. grad. program in clin. psychology U. Haifa, Israel, 1985-87; head of research authority U. Haifa, 1987—; vis. prof. U. Negev, Israel, 1971; vis. prof., chmn. dept. med. psychology Technion Israel Inst. Tech., 1976-77; vis. prof. Hebrew U., Jerusalem, 1983—. Editor: (with Marrvin Brandwin) Perspectives in Clinical Psychology, 1968, Epistemology for the Language Sciences, 1983; contbr. articles to profl. jours. Mem. Am. Psychol. Assn., Israeli Psychol. Assn. Jewish. Club: Azazels. Home: 38 Harofe St, Haifa Israel 34367 Office: U Haifa, Haifa Israel 31999

GUISE, DAVID EARL, architect, educator; b. N.Y.C., Dec. 29, 1931; s. Jack I. and Frances (Haberman) G.; m. Gretchen Grunenfelder, Nov. 21, 1962; children: Gabrielle Ann, John George, Jacqueline Alexis, Ursula Claire. B. Arch. with honors, U. Pa., 1957. Job capt. Kahn & Jacobs, Architects N.Y.C., 1957-60; designer draftsman E.J. Robin, Architect, N.Y.C., 1961; architect David Guise, Architect, N.Y.C., 1962—; asst. prof. Sch. Architecture, CCNY, 1966-70, assoc. prof., 1970-76, prof., 1976—; adj. prof. Columbia U., 1983-85. Author: Design and Technology in Architecture, 1985; contbr. articles to profl. jours.; architect numerous comml. and residential bldgs. Mem. nat. panel Am. Arbitration Assn., 1967—; sec. Irvington Planning Bd., N.Y. Mem. Constrn. Specifications Inst., Bldg. Research Inst., Assn. Collegiate Schs. Architecture. Home: Fargo Ln Irvington NY 10533 Office: 250 W 57th New York NY 10019

GUITON, PATRICK DE CARTERET, distance language educator; b. Jersey, Channel Islands, Mar. 16, 1935; arrived in Australia, 1974; s. Stanley de Carteret and Bessie Eileen (Wilden) G.; m. Kate Elizabeth Haslam, Sept. 9, 1967; children: Rachel Clare, Sarah Frances. BA with honors, U. York, Eng., 1966; MA in Econs., U. Manchester, Eng., 1968. Trainee Shell Petroleum Co. Ltd., London, 1952-53, 55; adminstrv. officer Her Majesty's Overseas Civil Service, North Rhodesia, 1955-63; lectr. U. Stirling, Scotland, 1967-72; dep. regional dir. Open U., Eng., 1972-74; dir. external studies Murdoch U., Perth, Australia, 1974—; cons. Commonwealth Fund for Tech. Cooperation, Zimbabwe, 1986. Dir. Sta. 6UVS-FM, Perth, 1983—; advisor editorial bd.: Internat. Jour. Distance Edn., 1981—; contbr. articles on distance education, telecommunications and ednl. radio to profl. jours. Recipient Pater award for most outstanding radio innovation Australian Acad. Broadcast Arts and Scis., 1985. Mem. Australian and South Pacific External Studies Assn. (exec. com. 1977-81). Home: 15 Mifflin Pl Leeming, 6155 Perth Australia Office: Murdoch U, South St, 6150 Perth Australia

GUJU, JOHN G., physician, educator; b. Youngstown, Ohio, June 13, 1924; s. George and Frances (Ratz) G.; m. Margaret Ann Poole, May 11, 1952; children—John Howard, Paula Jean, Nancy Elissa. B.A., Youngstown State U., 1944; M.D., Marquette U., 1947. Rotating intern Youngstown Hosp., 1947-48, asst. resident in surgery, 1948-49, chief of ob-gyn, 1972-79; resident in ob-gyn Cleve. City Hosp., 1949-50, U. Hosps., 1950-52; practice medicine specializing in ob-gyn Youngstown, 1955—; med. dir. Planned Parenthood Fedn., Youngstown, 1960-72; clin. prof. ob-gyn Northeastern Ohio Univs. Coll. Medicine, 1975—. Mem. youth com. YMCA, 1965-75; bd. dirs. Ohio div. Am. Assn. for Maternal and Child Health. Served to capt. USAF, 1953-55. Recipient Alan F. Gutmacher award for service and dedication to Planned Parenthood of Mahoning Valley, 1976. Fellow ACS, Am. Coll. Obstetricians and Gynecologists; mem. AMA, Am. Soc. Abdominal Surgeons, Am. Fertility Soc., Youngstown Soc. Obstetricians and Gynecologists, Mahoning County Med. Soc. (council 1979—), Am. Assn. Reproductive Health Profls. Club: Youngstown Country. Lodge: Rotary Internat. Home: 1350 Virginia Trail Youngstown OH 44505 Office: 435 Gypsy Ln Youngstown OH 44504

GULDIMANN, WERNER, civil aviation consultant; b. Olten, Switzerland, Jan. 31, 1916; s. Werner and Berta (Ulrich) G.; m. May Steuer; children: Theo, Till, Tim, Tom, Tobias. LLD, U. Basel, 1940; postgrad., Canton U., Zurich, 1943. Pres. Fed. Com. Aircraft Accident Investigations, Switzerland, 1961-66, Fed. Com. Air Traffic Services, Switzerland, 1966-81; dir. Fed. Office for Civil Aviation, Switzerland, 1967-76; chmn., chief exec. officer Sarna Polymer Ltd., Sarnen, Switzerland, 1981-86; chmn. Internat. Civil Aviation Orgn. legal com., 1967-70; hon. prof. U. Bern, 1973. Author: Die Luftwaffe, 1944, Flieger und Panzer, 1946, Internationales Lufttransportrecht, 1965. Served to col. Swiss Air Force, 1937-71. Recipient Edward Warner award ICAO, 1982. Roman Catholic. Home and Office: Lindenweg 4, CH-8142 Uitikon Switzerland

GULLEKSON, EDWIN HENRY, JR., physician; b. Flint, Mich., May 14, 1935; s. Edwin Henry and Amy Marcella (Graves) G.; student Flint Community Coll., 1953-56; M.D., U. Mich., 1961; m. Rosemary Evelyn Leppien, May 5, 1968; children—Kathryn Dawn, Hans Edwin, Heidi M. Intern McLaren Gen. Hsop., Flint, 1961-62, resident, 1962-63; gen. practice medicine, Flint, 1963—; chief of staff McLaren Gen. Hosp., 1977-81; mem. staffs Hurley, St. Joseph, Genesee Meml. hosps. (all Flint). Served to capt. M.C., AUS, 1966-67. Upjohn Research grantee, 1958, 59, 60. Diplomate Am. Bd. Family Practice. Mem. Mich. Med. Soc., Genesee County Med. Soc. (pres. 1983-84), AMA, Am. Acad. Family Practice, Mich. Acad. Gen. Practice. Patentee surg. instrument. Home: 1721 Laurel Oak Dr Flint MI 48507 Office: 5031 Villa Linde Pkwy Flint MI 48504

GULLER, IRVING BERNARD, psychologist, educator; b. N.Y.C., July 27, 1932; s. Hyman and Mildred (Rothman) G.; B.A., CCNY, 1954, M.S., 1956; Ph.D., N.Y. U., 1962; m. Adele Horowitz, Apr. 5, 1955; children—Robert, Matthew. Dir. psychol. tng. and research Maine Dept. Mental Health and Corrections, Augusta, 1962-63; asst. prof. psychology, also coll. psychologist Franklin and Marshall Coll., 1963-67; asso. prof. psychology John Jay Coll., N.Y.C., 1967-71, prof. psychology, 1971—, doctoral faculty criminal justice City U. N.Y., 1981—; founder, dir. Inst. Forensic Psychology, Inc., 1981—. attending psychologist, cons. St. Joseph's Hosp., Paterson, N.J., 1970—; cons. to police depts. and criminal justice agys. in forensic psychology; family therapist in pvt. practice, Oakland, N.J., 1962—; founding asso. N. Jersey Mental Health Assos., Oakland. Served with AUS, 1954-56. Recipient Founder's Day award N.Y. U., 1963. Diplomate clin. psychology Am. Bd. Profl. Psychology. Mem. Am., Eastern psychol. assns., Am. Assn. Marriage and Family Counselors (clin.), Sex Educators Council. Author: Clinical Psychology Training Guide and Handbook, 1963; The Clinical Psychologist in Institutional Settings, 1976; contbr. articles to profl. jours. Home and Office: 22 Stone Fence Rd Oakland NJ 07436 also: 445 W 59th St New York NY 10019

GULLEY, WARREN L. (BILL), business executive; b. Wetaug, Ill., Nov. 16, 1922; s. J. Walter and Doss M. (Goodman) G.; m. Nancy J. Redmond, May 7, 1947; children: Joseph Michael, William Patrick, John Walter, Timothy James. Student pub. schs., Ill. Adminstrv. asst., then dep. asst. to mil. asst. President U.S., 1966-75; dir. White House Mil. Office, 1976-77; pres. Internat. Six Inc., Washington, RPA Group Internat., Inc. Author: Breaking Cover. Served to sgt. maj. USMC, 1939-68. Decorated Legion of Merit, Purple Heart. Address: 7831 Welch Ct Alexandria VA 22310

GULLO, STEPHEN VITTON, corporate executive, psychologist; b. N.Y.C., Feb. 12, 1950; s. Anthony V. and Rose (Pernice) G.; Ph.D., Columbia U., 1974. Co-dir. Family Bereavement Project, Columbia U. Med. Sch., N.Y.C., 1973-75; asst. prof. Bklyn. Coll., 1974-80; pres., chmn. bd. Inst. Health and Weight Scis., N.Y.C., 1980—; asst. clin. prof. Columbia U. Med. Center, 1980—; com. grants and profl. edn. N.Y.C. region Am. Cancer Soc.; sci. adv. com. Inst. Cancer Research; co-chmn. Internat. Conf. Child and Death, Columbia-Presbyn. Med. Center, 1979; expert witness City Council N.Y. Vice chair ann. dinner Boys' Town of Jerusalem, 1981, assoc. chmn. ann. dinner Girls' Town Jerusalem, 1984; co-chmn. fundraising com. Found. Thanatology, 1982—; life hon. mem. Foss Found. Recipient gran croce al merito Accademia Italiana per lo Sviluppo Economico e Souale, Rome, 1985; Knight Order St. John of Jerusalem, 1986; Paterson Found. fellow, 1972-73; NIH research grantee, 1973-75. Mem. Am. Psychol. Assn., N.Y. Acad. Scis., Found. Thanatology (exec. bd., profl. adv. bd.). Clubs: Columbia U. College Physicians and Surgeons; Rolls Royce Owners. Author: When People Die, 1978; The Child and Death, 1983; Education in Thanatology, 1984, Loveshock: How to Survive a Broken Heart and Love Again, 1988; cons. editor Jour. Thanatology, 1974-80, Archives Found. Thanatology, 1974—; chmn. editorial bd. Thanatology Abstract Series, 1974-76; cons. editor Advances in Thanatology, 1980—; contbr. articles and chpts. med. textbooks. Home: 42 Towd Point Southampton NY 11968 Office: 4 E 64th St New York NY 10022

GUMBEL, HENRY EDWARD, business consultant; b. Bingen, Fed. Republic Germany, Aug. 31, 1913; arrived in Eng., 1936; s. Gustav Ludwig and Elizabeth (Marx) G.; m. Ellen Frank, June 14, 1946; children: Jennifer, Rosemary, John, Peter, Andrew. D of Laws, U. Zurich, Switzerland, 1935. Called to Bar, 1947. Ins. broker Willis Faber & Dumas Ltd., London, 1936-66, chmn. bd. dirs., 1966-83, ins. cons., 1983—; bd. dirs. Heddington Ins., Ltd., London, Allianz Legal Protection, Ltd.; chmn. Willis Faber AG (hon.), Tokio Reinsurance Co. Contbr. papers, articles to profl. jours. Patron London Mozart Soc.; treas., trustee Brit. Trust for the Ecumenical Inst. for Advanced Theol. Studies in Jerusalem; past chmn. exec. com. Ch. Missionary Soc. Recipient Comdr.'s Cross Fed. German Order Merit, 1984. Mem. Brit. Ins. Law Assn. (past chmn.), Chartered Ins. Inst. (v.p.), European Com. U.K. Ins. Brokers. Mem. Church of England. Office: Willis Faber PLC, Ten Trinity Sq, London England EC3P 3AX

GUMPERT, GUSTAV, public relations executive; b. Phila., Nov. 28, 1922; s. Hibbard Gustav and Lillian (Heebner) G.; A.B., Lehigh U., 1944. Reporter, Allentown (Pa.) Morning Call, 1945-46; asso. editor Musical Digest, N.Y.C., 1946-49; health edn. dir. Dept. Public Health, Phila., 1950-52, health info. officer, 1952-60; writing unit head public relations dept. SmithKline Corp., Phila., 1962-63, mgr. writing, editorial services, 1965-66, mgr. planning, editorial services, 1966-73, dir. spl. projects, 1973-78, dir. creative sers., 1978—. Pres. bd. Planned Parenthood Assn. Phila., 1960-62; bd. dirs. Found. for Study Cycles, 1959-60. Mem. AAAS, Am. Med. Writers Assn., Public Relations Soc. Am., Phi Beta Kappa. Contbr. articles to profl. jours. Office: Smith Kline Beckman Corp One Franklin Plaza PO Box 7929 Philadelphia PA 19101

GUMRUKCUOGLU, RAHMI KAMIL, Turkish ambassador to United Kingdom; b. 1927; s. Rasim and Aliye (Kasaci) G.; m. Elcin. Benice, Dec. 15, 1956; 2 children. Student, Faculty of Polit. Sci., Ankara U., 1948; M.Polit. Econ. and Govt., Harvard U., 1965. 2d Sec., Turkish Embassy, London, 1952-55, 1st sec., 1955; head sect. dealing with internat. econ. affairs Turkish Ministry Fgn. Affairs, Ankara, 1958-60; counsellor Turkish Embassy, Cairo, 1960-63; dep. dir. gen. dept. internat. econ. affairs, Ministry Fgn. Affairs, Ankara, 1963-65, head spl. bur. dealing with con. coop. between Turkey and USSR, 1965-67, dir. gen. Dept. Internat. Econ. Affairs, 1967-71; Turkish ambassador to Council of Europe, Strasbourg, 1971-75, to Iran, 1975-78; sr. advisor Ministry Fgn. Affairs and pres. Def. Industry Coordination Bd., Ankara, 1978-79, dep. sec. gen. econ. affairs, 1979-81; Turkish ambassador to U.K., London, 1981—. Decorated knight Grand Cross Order St. Michael and St. George. Address: Turkish Embassy, 43 Belgrave Sq, London SW1X 8PA England

GU MU, government officieal People's Republic of China; b. Roncheng City, Shandong Province, 1914. Joined Chinese Communist Party, 1932; mayor of Tsinan, China, 1950-52; dep. sec. Chinese Communist Party, Shanghai, 1953-54; vice chmn. Constrn. Commn., State Council, 1954-56, Econ. Commn., 1956-65; chmn. State Capital Constrn. Commn., 1965-67, minister, 1973-81; removed from office during Cultural Revolution, 1967; vice premier State Council, 1975-82, state councilor, until 1988; mem. 10th Cen. Com., Chinese Communist Party, 1973, mem. 11th Cen. Com., 1977, mem. Secretariat, 1980-85, mem. Presidium, 12th Cen. Com., 1982—; minister Fgn. Investment Control Commn., 1979-82, minister Adminstrn. Commn. Import-Export Commn., 1980-82; polit. commisar People's Liberation Army, Capital Constrn. Engring. Corps, 1979-81; dep. for Shandong, 5th Nat. People's Congress, 1978; vice chmn. 7th nat. com. Chinese People's Polit. Consultative Conf., 1988—; hon. pres. Soc. Econs. of Capital Constrn., 1980, Soc. Econ. Legis., 1984. Address: care CPPCC, Beijing People's Republic of China *

GUNA-KASEM, PRACHA, diplomat; b. Bangkok, Dec. 29, 1934; s. Jote and Rabieb (Smitasiri) G.-K.; m. Sumanee Chongcharoen, May 11, 1962; 1 child, Pramond. BA with honors, Oxford (Eng.) U., 1956, MA in Internat. Relations, 1959; PhD, Yale U., 1960. Chief press div. dept. info. Ministry Fgn. Affairs, Bangkok, 1968-71, dir. gen. dept. info., 1973-75, dir. gen. dept. Asean affairs, 1982-84, dir. gen. dept. econ. affairs, 1984-85; Thailand consul gen. Hong Kong, 1971-73; Thailand ambassador, permanent rep. to UN N.Y.C., 1975-80, Geneva, 1980-82; Thailand ambassador to Paris, 1985—, Algeria, 1985—; dir. gen. Dept. Internat. Orgns. Ministry of Fgn. Affairs, Bangkok, 1987—; permanent del to UNESCO, Paris, 1985—. Apptd. mem. The Nat. Conv., Bangkok, 1974; dir. gen. dept. internat. orgns. Ministry Fgn. Affairs, Bangkok. Decorated Grand Cordon, Order of White Elephant, Crown of Thailand, Grand Officer, L'Ordre de Merite, France, Grand Companion of the Most Illustrous Order of Chulachomklao. Mem. Thailand World Affairs and Internat. Law Council. Clubs: Bangkok Sports, Nauatanee Golf (Bangkok). Address: Ambassador's Ct, 76/1 Langsuan Rd, Bangkok Thailand also: Royal Thailand Embassy, 8 Rue Greuze, 16 Paris France

GUNDERSON, JUDITH KEEFER, golf association executive; b. Charleroi, Pa., May 25, 1939; d. John R. and Irene G. (Gaskill) Keefer; student public schs., Uniontown, Pa.; m. Jerry L. Gunderson, Mar. 19, 1971; children—Jamie L., Jeff S.; stepchildren—Todd G. (dec.), Marc W., Bookkeeper, Fayette Nat. Bank, 1957-59, gen. ledger bookkeeper, 1960-63; head bookkeeper First Nat. Bank Broward, 1963-64; bookkeeper Ruthenberg Homes, Inc., 1966-69; bookkeeper, asst. sec./treas. Pennisular Properties, Inc. subs. Investors Diversified Services Properties, Mpls., 1969-72; comptroller, stockholder, pres. dir. Am. Golf Fla., Inc., dba Golf and Tennis World, Deerfield Beach, 1972—; sec.-treas., stockholder, dir. Internat. Golf, Inc. County committeewoman, Broward County, Fla., 1965-66. Mem. Nat. Golf Found., C. of C., Beta Sigma Phi.

GUNDERSON, ROBERT VERNON, JR., lawyer; b. Memphis, Dec. 4, 1951; s. Robert V. and Suzanne (McCarthy) G.; m. Anne Durkheimer, May 15, 1982; children: Katherine Paige, Robert Graham. BA with distinction, U. Kans., 1973; MBA, U. Penn., 1974; MA, Stanford U., 1976; JD, U. Chgo., 1979. Bar: Calif. 1979, U.S. Dist. Ct. (no. dist.) Calif. 1979. Assoc. Cooley, Godward, Castro, Huddleson & Tatum, San Francisco and Palo Alto, Calif., 1979-84, ptnr., 1984-88; ptnr. Brobeck, Phleger & Harrison, Palo Alto, 1988—; panelist Venture Capital and Pub. Offering Negotiation, San Francisco and N.Y.C., 1981, 83, 85, Practicing Law Inst., N.Y.C. and San Francisco, 1986; moderator, panelist Third Ann. Securities Law Inst., 1985; sec. Dionex Corp, Sunnyvale, Calif., 1983-88, Southwall Techs., Inc., Palo Alto, 1985—; visiting lectr. U. Santa Clara (Calif.) Law Sch., 1985. Exec. editor U. Chgo. Law Rev., 1978-79; contbr. articles to profl. jours. mem. ABA (corps., banking and business law sects., various coms.), State Bar Calif. (panelist continuing legal edn. 1984), San Francisco Bar Assn., Am. Fin. Assn., Am. Soc. Corporate Secs., Assn. Old Crows. Clubs: Wharton (San Francisco Bay Area). Home: 243 Polhemus Ave Atherton CA 94025 Office: Brobeck Phleger & Harrison 2 Embarcadero Pl 2200 Geng Rd Palo Alto CA 94303

GUNN, JOSEPH RIDGEWAY, III, consulting economist; b. Ross, Calif., Nov. 28, 1928; s. Joseph Ridgeway, Jr. and Melvine Henrietta (Longley) G.; B.S. in Bus. Adminstrn., U. Calif., Berkeley, 1954, M.A. in Econs., 1958; spl. studies Oxford (Eng.) U., 1967; m. Marie Elsie Thurlow, June 16, 1951; children—Dana Carolyn Gunn Winslow, Anita Jayne Gunn Shirley, Janice Marie. Econ. analyst Standard Oil Co., Calif., 1954-61; econ. adv. Ministry Commerce, Govt. Afghanistan, Kabul, 1961-67; cons. economist, 1967—; sr. v.p. Robert R. Nathan Assos., Inc., Washington, 1986—. Chmn. bd. dirs. Terra Linda Community Services Dist., 1954-61. Mem. Am. Econ. Assn., Nat. Assn. Bus. Economists, Washington Internat. Trade Assn., Assn. Transp. Practitioners, Nat. Soc. Rate of Return Analysts, Nat. Economists Club, Asia Soc. Democrat. Episcopalian. Author articles, reports. Home: 10917 Picasso Ln Potomac MD 20854 Office: 1301 Pennsylvania Ave NW Washington DC 20004

GUNN, ROBERT NORMAN, pharmaceutical company executive; b. Edinburgh, Scotland, Dec. 16, 1925; s. Donald Macfie and Margaret (Pallister) G.; m. Joan Parry, Mar. 17, 1956; 1 child, Jane Victoria. M.A. with honors, Oxford U., 1951. Merchandise buyer Boots Co. PLC, London, 1951-70, head warehousing and distbn., Nottingham, 1971-73, dir. property, 1973-78, dir. indsl. div., 1979-83, vice chmn., chief exec., 1983-85, chmn., chief exec., 1985—; dir. Foseco Minsep, Birmingham, 1984—. Served to lt. Army, 1944-47. Mem. Assn. Brit. Pharm. Industry (bd. mgmt. 1981-84, v.p. 1983-84), Confedn. Brit. Industry (council 1985—), Brit. Inst. Mgmt. (bd. Companions 1986—), Inst. Dirs. Mem. Ch. of Scotland. Avocations: gardening; theatre. Office: Boots Co PLC, 1 Thone Rd W, Nottingham NG2 3AA, England *

GUNNARSSON, BIRGIR ISLEIFUR, minister of culture and education; b. Reykjavík, Iceland, July 19, 1936; s. Gunnar E. Benediktsson and Jórunn Isleifsdóttir; m. Sonja Backman, Oct. 6, 1956; children:Björg Jóna, Gunnar Jóhann, Ingunn Mjöll, Lilja Dögg. Grad., U. Iceland, 1961. Avocate to Supreme Ct., 1967. Leader Youth Soc. of Independance Party, Reykjavík, 1959-62; sec. gen. Independence Party Youth Fedn., Reykjavík, 1961-63; sole practice Reykjavík, 1963-72; mayor City of Reykjavík, 1972-78; chmn. exec. com. Independence Party, 1973-87; member Parliment, Can., 1979—; 2nd dep. speaker Althing (Lower House of Parliment), 1983-87; minister Ministry of Culture and Edn., Can., 1987—; bd. dirs. Nat. Power Co., 1965—, Civil Aviation Bd, 1984-87; chmn. Com. Heavy Industry, 1983-87. Mem. City Council of Reykjavík, 1962-82. Club: Rotary (Reykjavík). Home: Fjölnisvegur 15, 101 Reykjavik Iceland Office: Ministry of Edn, Hverfisgata 6, 101 Reykjavik Iceland

GUNNERSEN, UWE, mental health consultant; b. Denmark, Feb. 10, 1935; s. H. Thomas and H. Agneta (Strufe) G.; came to U.S., 1958, naturalized, 1964; B.S., U. Copenhagen, 1956; M.S., U. Hamburg (W. Ger.), 1958; m. Veronica Peper, June 2, 1962; children—Kirsten, Thomas. Psychiat. social worker Div. Psychiatry, Cook County Hosp., Chgo., 1962-68; assoc. adminstr. Martha Washington Hosp., Chgo., 1968-69; program policy adv. Ill. Dept. Mental Health, 1969-71; mental health cons. region V, NIMH, 1971-73; div. dir. Joint Commn. Accrediation of Hosps., 1973-76; pres. Human Services Horizons Inc., San Francisco, 1976-79; exec. dir. Azure Acres Chem. Dependency Treatment Ctr., 1979—; mem. task force Pres.'s Commn. Mental Health, 1978, Contra Costa County (Calif.) Council Aging, 1978-79. Cert. mental health adminstr., social worker. Fellow Royal Soc. Health, Am. Coll. Addiction Treatment Adminstrs.; mem. Nat. Assn. Social Workers, Assn. Mental Health Adminstrs., Assn. Labor Mgmt. Cons. in Alcoholism (bd. dirs. 1980-83), Nat. Assn. Alcoholism Treatment Programs (bd. dirs. 1984-86), Am. Pub. Health Assn., Am. Health Planning Assn. Lutheran. Author manuals. Home: 3153 Lippizaner Ln Walnut Creek CA 94598 Office: Azure Acres Chemical Dependency Treatment Ctr 2264 Green Hill Rd Sebastopol CA 95472

GUNTER, GORDON, zoologist; b. Goldonna, La., Aug. 18, 1909; s. John O. and Joanna (Pennington) G.; B.A., La. State Normal Coll., 1929; M.A., U. Tex., 1931, Ph.D., 1945; m. Frances M. Hudgins, Sept. 7, 1957; children—Edmund Osbon, Harry Allen; children by previous marriage—Charlotte A. Gunter Evans, Miles G., Forrest P. Biologist, U.S. Bur. Fisheries, intermittently, 1931-38; marine biologist Tex. Game, Fish and Oyster Commn., 1939-45; research scientist Inst. Marine Sci., U. Tex., 1945-49, dir., 1949-55; prof. zoology Marine Lab., U. Miami (Fla.), 1946-47; sr. marine biologist Scripps Instn. Oceanography, U. Calif., La Jolla, 1948-49; dir. Gulf Coast Research Lab., Ocean Springs, Miss., 1955-71, dir. emeritus, 1971—; also prof. biology U. So. Miss., prof. zoology Miss. State U., 1956-78; adj. prof. emeritus biology U. Miss., 1979-85; area cons. Tex. Office Coordinator Fisheries, 1942-45; adv. panel comml. seafoods div. La. Commn. Wild Life and Fisheries, 1953-54; vice chmn. biology, com. treatise on marine ecology NRC, 1942-57; sci. adv. panel Gulf State Marine Fisheries Commn., mem. bd. advisors Fla. Bd. Conservation, 1956-68; prin. investigator plankton studies OTEC program, Gulf of Mex., 1978-82; mem. standing com. Gulf of Mexico Fishery Mgmt. Council. Fellow La. Acad. Scis., Internat. Oceanographic Found., Internat. Acad. Fisheries Scientists, Am. Inst. Fisheries Research Biologists, La. Acad. Scis., Explorers Club; mem. Am. Fisheries Soc. (hon.), Am. Ornithologists Union, Am. Soc. Ichthyologists and Herpetologists, Am. Soc. Limnology and Oceanography, Am. Soc. Mammalogists, Am. Soc. Naturalists, Am. Soc. Zoologists, Ecol. Soc. Am., Miss., New Orleans acads. scis., Nat. Shellfisheries Assn. (hon.), Wildlife Soc., World Mariculture Soc. (pres. 1974, hon.), Miss. Acad. Scis. (pres. 1964-65), Sigma Xi, Phi Kappa Phi. Founder editor: Gulf Research Reports, 1961-74. Author: Gunter's Archives No. 1, 1984; Gunter's Archives No. 2, 1985, Gunter's Archives No. 3, 1986, No. 4, 5, 1987. Contbr. over 435 articles on marine biology to profl. and popular publs. in U.S. and fgn. countries. Address: 127 Halstead Rd Ocean Springs MS 39564

GUNTER, PETE ADDISON YANCEY, III, philosophy educator; b. Hammond, Ind., Oct. 20, 1936; s. Addison Yancey and Anna Ruth (Morris) G.; B.A., U. Tex., Austin, 1958; B.A., Cambridge U. (Eng.), 1960; Ph.D., Yale U., 1963; m. Elizabeth W. Ellington, Apr. 12, 1969; 1 dau., Sheila Dewing. Asst. prof. Auburn (Ala.) U., 1963-65; assoc. prof. U. Tenn., Knoxville, 1965-69; chmn., prof. dept. philosophy N. Tex. State U., Denton, 1969-76, prof., 1976—; cons. Oak Ridge Assoc. Univs., 1968-69, Nat. Humanities Faculty, 1972-75. E. Tenn. campaign chmn. Tenn. Vols. for Eugene McCarthy, 1968; bd. dirs. For the People, Inc., 1980-88; pres. Big Thicket Assn., 1971-73; chmn. Big Thicket Coordinating Com., 1973-80; mem. Citizens Com. for Coastal Zone Mgmt. (Tex.), 1977-79, Tex. Inst. Letters, 1973—. NEH Young Scholar grantee, 1968; N. Tex. State U. Honors prof., 1972-73. Mem. Southwestern Philos. Soc. (pres. 1978-79), N. Tex. Philos. Assn. (pres. 1981-82), Found. Philosophy of Creativity (exec. dir. 1981—), Am. Philos. Assn., So. Soc. Philosophy and Psychology. Democrat. Author: Bergson and the Evolution of Physics, 1969; The Big Thicket: A Challenge for Conservation, 1972; Henri Bergson: A Bibliography, 1974, 2d edit rev., 1986; Process Philosophy: Basic Writings, 1978; (novel) River in Dry Grass, 1985; editor: (with Robert Calvert) The Red River Memoirs of W. R. Strong, 1982; Present, Tense. Future, Perfect! 1985; (with Andrew Papanicolaou) Bergson and Modern Thought: Towards a Unified Science, 1987; contbr. articles to philos. jours.; writer Tex. Observer, 1960—; book reviewer Dallas Morning News, 1980—. Home: 225 Jagoe St Denton TX 76201 Office: N Tex State U Denton TX 76203

GUNTER, WILLIAM DAYLE, JR., physicist; b. Mitchell, S.D., Jan. 10, 1932; s. William Dayle and Lamerta Berniece (Hockensmith) G.; m. Shirley Marie Teshera, Oct. 24, 1955; children—Maria Jo, Robert Paul. B.S. in Physics with distinction, Stanford U., 1957, M.S., 1959. Physicist Ames Research Ctr. NASA, Moffett Field, Calif., 1960-81, asst. br. chief electronic optical engring., 1981-85; pvt. practice cons. Photon Applications, San Jose, Calif., 1985—. Patentee in field. Contbr. articles to profl. jours. Served with U.S. Army, 1953-55. Recipient Westinghouse Sci. Talent Search award, 1950; various awards NASA; Stanford U. scholar, 1950. Mem. Am. Assn. Profl. Cons., Optical Soc. Am., IEEE (sr.), Am. Phys. Soc., Soc. Photo-Optical Instrumentation Engrs., Planetary Soc., Nat. Space Soc.

GUNTHEROTH, WARREN GADEN, physician; b. Hominy, Okla., July 27, 1927; s. Harry William and Callie (Cornett) G.; m. Ethel Haglund, July 3, 1954; children: Kurt, Karl. Sten. M.D., Harvard U., 1952. Diplomate: Am. Bd. Pediatrics, Am. Bd. Pediatric Cardiology, Nat. Bd. Med. Examiners. Intern Peter Bent Brigham Hosp., Boston, 1952-53; fellow in cardiology Children's Hosp., Boston, 1953-55; resident in pediatrics Children's Hosp., 1955-56; research fellow physiology and biophysics U. Wash. Med. Sch., Seattle, 1957-58; mem. faculty U. Wash. Med. Sch., 1958—, prof. pediatrics, 1969—, head div. pediatric cardiology, 1964—. Author: Pediatric Electrocardiography, 1965, How to Read Pediatrics ECGs, 1981, 2d edit., 1987, Crib Death (Sudden Infant Death Syndrome), 1982; also numerous articles; mem. editorial bd.: Am. Heart Jour, 1977-80, Circulation, 1980-83, Am. Jour. Noninvasive Cardiology, Jour. Am. Coll. Cardiology, Am. Jour. Cardiology; sect. editor: Practice of Pediatrics, 1979-87. Served with USPHS, 1950-51. Spl. research fellow NIH, 1967. Mem. Am. Physiol. Soc., Soc. Pediatric Research, Biomed. Engring. Soc. (charter), Soc. Exptl. Biology and Medicine, Am. Heart Assn. (chmn. N.W. regional med. research adv. com. 1978-80), Cardiovascular System Dynamics Soc. (charter), Am. Coll. Cardiology. Democrat. Home: 13201 42d Ave NE Seattle WA 98125 Office: Univ Wash Med Sch Dept Pediatrics RD-20 Seattle WA 98195

GUNZEL, WILLEM ANTON, lumber company executive, consultant, arbitrator; b. Amsterdam, The Netherlands, Dec. 25, 1925; s. Frans Anton Wilhelm Paul and Jacoba Geertruida (Sadenkamp) G.; m. Everdina Elisabeth Van Dyk, July 7, 1951; children—Robert W. A., Willem A.F., Everardus Johannes. Grad. Openbare Handelschool (Hogere Economische School, Amsterdam, 1943; grad. Royal Signal Officers Sch., The Hague, The Netherlands, 1947. Mem. staff M. Abas CV, Amsterdam, 1950—, ptnr., Amsterdam and Bussum, The Netherlands, 1964—; mem. bd., pres. Palty BV, Elburg, The Netherlands, 1977—; mem. bd. ZB Industry and Trady Cy, Elburg, 1977—; dir. Transpan BV, Bussum, 1971—. Served to capt. Signal Corps, Dutch Army, 1945-50. Liberal. Roman Catholic. Home: Nieuwe Hilversumseweg 12, 1406 Bussum The Netherlands Office: M Abas CV-Transpan BV, Nieuwe Hilversumseweg, Nieuwe Hilversumseweg 12, 1406 Bussum The Netherlands

GUO, DAJUN, mathematics educator; b. Chengdu, Sichuan, People's Republic of China, Jan. 23, 1934; s. Zhong Yu Guo and Wan Lan Chen; m. Mei Qi; 1 child, Yun Guo. Grad., Sichuan U., 1955. Asst. Taiyuan Inst. Tech., People's Republic of China, 1955-56; asst. Shandong U., Jinan, People's Republic of China, 1956-60, lectr., 1960-78, assoc. prof., 1978-80, prof. math., 1980—; vis. prof. U. Tex., Arlington, 1985-86. Author: Nonlinear Functional Analysis, 1985 (1st place award 1986), Mathematical Analysis, 1982 (2d place award 1986), Nonlinear Integral Equations, 1987 (1st place award 1988); contbr. articles to profl. jours. Office: Shandong U Dept Math, Jinan, Shandong People's Republic of China

GUO, NAI'AN, musicologist, researcher; b. Guiyang, Guizhou, People's Repub. China, Nov. 16, 1920; s. Huaixi Guo and Zhongxuan Zheng; m. Yunzhong Wu, Nov. 25, 1954; children: Xiao'an, You'an, Zhi'an. Grad.,

State Conservatory, Nanjing, China, 1947. Tchr. Zhonghua Coll. Music, Shanghai, People's Repub. China, 1947-49; leader Art Troupe of Trade Union, Shanghai, 1949-50; officer Chinese Ministry Culture, Beijing, 1950-58; assoc. researcher Chinese Research Inst. Music, Beijing, 1959-83; head Research Inst. Music, Beijing, 1978-85, researcher, 1983—; dir. dept. music Grad. Sch., Acad. Arts China, Beijing, 1983—. Co-author, editor: An Introduction to National Music, 1964, 80; editor: Dictionary of Chinese Music, 1984, Musicology in China quar., 1985—. Mem. Assn. Chinese Musicians (council 1979—). Mem. Communist Party. Home: Xiaozhuang Beili Wenhuabu, Sushe 14-5-401, Beijing Peoples Republic China Office: Research Inst Music, Xinyuanli Xi Yi Lou, Beijing Peoples Republic China

GUO, YUANCHUN, mathematics educator; b. Jianping, Hebei, People's Republic of China, Dec. 11, 1944; s. Dianze Guo and Yaqing Wu; m. Enyuan Chui, Jan. 1, 1972; 1 child, Tiankuo. BS, Jilin U., Changchun, People's Republic of China, 1968, MS, 1981; D in Sci., Jilin U., People's Republic of China, 1985. Tchr. Taian Middle Sch., Yushu, People's Republic of China, 1970-81; tchr. Jilin U., 1981-85, assoc. prof., 1985—. Contbr. articles to profl. jours. Mem. Chinese Math. Soc., Am. Math. Soc. Office: Jilin U, Dept Math, Changchun, Jilin People's Republic of China

GUO, ZHI PING, pediatrician, nutrition researcher; b. Shanghai, China, Sept. 3, 1944; d. Zung En and Yun Ching (Chen) G.; m. Zhen Qun Ni, Feb. 4, 1970; 1 child, Li. MS, Shanghai First Med. Coll., 1982. Resident People's Hosp., Fanshi County, People's Republic of China, 1968-79; resident Children's Hosp. of Shanghai First Med. U., People's Republic of China, 1982-86, vis. physician, 1986—; vis. scholar and researcher Ctr. for Disease Control, Atlanta, 1986—. Contbr. articles to profl. jours.. Recipient Red Banner Worker award Shanghai First Med. U., 1985. Mem. Chinese Med. Assn., Shanghai Psychol. Assn., Chinese Nutritional Assn. Office: Children's Hosp of Shanghai, First Med U, Fengling Rd, Shanghai People's Republic of China

GUO, ZHONG-HENG, mathematics and mechanics educator; b. Guangzhou, People's Republic China, Mar. 2, 1933; s. Qi-ping Guo and Shuxian Shao; m. Dieli Zhang, June 18, 1968; children: Hangfeng, Hangfang. MS, Warsaw Tech. U., Poland, 1960; PhD, Polish Acad. Scis., Poland, 1963. Lectr. dept. math. and mechanics Peking U., Beijing, People's Republic China, 1963-78, prof. dept. math., 1979—; research fellow Alexander von Humboldt Found., Bonn, Fed. Republic Germany, 1979-80, 1986-87; vis. prof. Ruhr-U., Bochum, Fed. Republic Germany, 1980-81, Johns Hopkins U., Balt., 1982, U. Waterloo, Ont., Can., 1982, U. Udine, Italy, 1987, U. Md., College Park, 1987. Author: Nonlinear Theory of Elasticity, 1980, Tensors, 1988, Modern Mathematics and Mechanics, 1988; contbr. 86 articles to profl. jours. Chmn. Scientific Com. Intl. Conf. Non-Linear Mechanics, Shanghai, 1985. Mem. Chinese Soc. Applied and Theoretic Mechanics (exec.) Com. Rational Mechanics and Math. Methods (chmn.), Polish Acad. Scis. (fgn. mem. 1988—). Office: Peking U, Dept of Mathematics, Beijing 100871, People's Republic of China

GUPTA, AJAYA KUMAR, civil engineer, educator; b. Allahabad India, Sept. 27, 1944; came to U.S., 1968, naturalized, 1977; s. Chhailbihari Lal and Taravali (Jain) G.; m. Purnima Rani Mital, Feb. 28, 1968; children—Aparna Mini, Suvarna. B.S., U. Roorkee, India, 1966, M.S., 1968; Ph.D., U. Ill., 1971. Supervising engr. Sargent & Lundy, Chgo., 1971-76; sr. research engr. Research Inst., Ill. Inst. Tech., Chgo., 1976-78, assoc. prof., Chgo., 1979-80; assoc. prof. civil engring. N.C. State U., Raleigh, 1980-83, prof. civil engring., 1983—; dir. Southeastern U.S. Seismic Safety Consortium, Charleston, S.C., 1981-85, Tech. Transfer and Devel. Council, 1982-85; cons. industry and research orgns. Editor: Seismic Performance of Low-Rise Buildings, 1981; contbr. articles to profl. jours. NSF grantee, 1979—. Mem. ASCE (Walter L. Huber prize 1982), Am. Concrete Inst. (chmn. shell reinforcement subcom. 1972-85), Earthquake Engring. Research Inst., ASME, Internat. Assoc. Structural Mechanics in Reactor Tech., U. Ill. Alumni Assoc., U. Roorkee Alumni Assoc., Hindu Soc. N.C., Phi Kappa Phi. Hindu. Current work: Reinforced concrete structures, shells, hyperbolic cooling towers; earthquake engineering, multicomponent design, modal combination, secondary systems, low-rise buildings; finite element analysis, nonlinear and dynamic analysis, nuclear power plant structural analysis and design. Subspecialties: Civil engineering; Structural engineering.

GUPTA, ANIL K., management educator; b. Bullandshahar, Uttar Pradesh, India, Apr. 29, 1952; s. Gyan Prakash and Daya G.; m. Sadhna Gupta, Nov. 28, 1977; children: Abhas Abhinav, Prayas Abhinav. BSc in Agr. with honors, Haryana Agrl., Hissar, 1972, MSC in Genetics, 1974; PhD in Mgmt., Kurukshetra (Haryana) U., 1986. Agrl. fin. officer Syndicate Bank, Karnataka, Haryana, AP, UP, 1974-78; mgmt. specialist IIPA, New Delhi, 1978-81; from asst. prof. to assoc. prof. Indian Inst. Mgmt., Ahmedabad, Gujarat, India, 1981—; cons. various nat. and internat. corps. and inst., India, 1981-86; devel. policy lobbyist IIM, Nat. Bank for Agr. and Rural Devel., Planning Commn., Bombay and New Delhi, 1983-84. Mem. Assn. Arid Land Studies, Indian Soc. Pub. Adminstrn., Indian Soc. Agrl. Econs., Internat. Sociol. Assn., Internat. Rural Sociol. Assn. Office: Indian Inst Mgmt, IIM Campus, Ahmedabad Gujarat 380 015, India

GUPTA, GIRDHARILAL SADURAM, economics educator; b. Talchiri, India, May 1, 1941; s. Saduram and Narmada S. (Gupta) G.; m. Lalita Girdharilal, Jan. 30, 1963; children—Indu, Jaya, Manish. B.A., MS Univ., Baroda, India, 1962, M.A., 1964; Ph.D., Johns Hopkins U., 1970. Econs. lectr. MS Univ., 1964-66; prof. econs. Indian Inst. Mgmt., Abmedabad, 1970—; vis. prof. Ill. State U., Normal, 1982, 83, 85-86; vis. scholar Indsl. Credit and Investment Corp. India, Bombay, 1976; cons. Resource Mgmt. Corp., Bethesda, Md., 1968. Co-author: Managerial Economics: Concepts and Cases, 1977; Teaching Manual for Managerial Economics: Concepts and Cases, 1978; co-author: (with Marine) Managerial Economics, 1988, Inland Fish Marketing in India, 1985; Fish Marketing in India, 1984; numerous articles. Mem. bd. studies in econs./mgmt., acad. councils and adv. bds. several Indian univs.; cons. various govt. and pvt. orgns.; mem. sales tax adv. com. Govt. Gujarat, 1977-78. Johns Hopkins Univ. fellow; Indian Govt. scholar; Univ. Merit scholar; gold medalist; others. Mem. Indian Econometric Soc. (exec. com. 1978-79), Indian Econ. Assn., Gujarat Econ. Assn. Avocations: indoor sports; badminton. Office: 314 Indian Inst Mgmt, Ahmedabad, Gujarat 380015, India

GUPTA, HARI PAL, microbiologist, researcher, research institute executive; b. Badaun Islamnagar, U.P., India, Jan. 13, 1939; s. Brij Lal and Ram Kali Gupta; m. Uma Gupta, Nov. 30, 1964; children: Alok, Ashish. BSc, Agra U., 1959, MSc in Botany, 1961; PhD in Botany, Lucknow U., 1967. Lectr. M.I. Coll., Vrindaban, India, 1961; research scholar Birbal Sahni Inst. Paleobotany, Lucknow, India, 1961-64, jr. sci. asst., 1964-67, sr. sci. asst., 1967-71, jr. sci. officer, 1971-75, sr. sci. officer, 1975-83, asst. dir., 1983—, also head dept. Quaternary Biogeography, and Archaeobotany. Author: (with C. Sharma) Pollen Flora of Northwest Himalaya, 1986. Fellow Indian Assn. Palynostratigraphers; mem. Paleobot. Soc. Lucknow, Man and Environment., Palynolog. Soc. India. Home: G1/4 Papermill Colony, Lucknow Uttar Pradesh 226006, India Office: Birbal Sahni Inst Paleobotany, 53 University Rd, Lucknow Uttar Pradesh 226007, India

GUPTA, MUKESH, mathematics educator; b. Agra, Uttar Pradesh, Oct. 26, 1955; s. Jagdish Sharan and Premvati G.; m. Anita Gupta, Nov. 22, 1980; children: Jaya, Jyoti. BS, St. John's Coll., Agra, India, 1975, MS in Math., 1977, PhD, 1980. Lectr. in math. Sri Varshney Coll., Aligarh, Uttar Pradesh, India, 1979-82; postdoctoral fellow Council of Sci. and Indsl. Research, New Delhi at Agra, 1982; lectr. in math. Durga Prasad Baljeet Singh Degree Coll., Anupshahr, Uttar Pradesh, India, 1982—. Contbr. numerous articles to profl. jours. Treas. Tchr. Assn., 1985—. University Grants Commn. research fellow, 1978-79. Mem. Indian Jour. Theoretical Physics (life), Acta Ciencia Indica (life), Indian Soc. Theoretical and Applied Mechanics. Home: Manak Chowk, Anupshahr, Bulandshahr, Uttar Pradesh 202 390, India Office: DPBS Degree College, Anupshahr, Uttar Pradesh 202 390, India

GUPTA, RATAN MALA, immunologist educator; b. Mehrauli, India, Dec. 28, 1930; s. Om Prakash and Krishna Devi Gupta; m. Indu Mohan, May 28, 1954; children: Jyotsna, Rajiv Mohan, Anuradha. MBBChir, Lucknow U., 1953; MD in Bacteriology, Delhi U., 1964; postgrad., Haffkine Inst., Bombay, 1967. Lectr. pathologyInst. Med. Scis. Banaras Hindu U., Varanasi, India, 1964-66, reader, 1966-78, prof. immunopathology, 1979—, coordinator Immunodiagnostic Tng. and Research Ctr., 1986—. Editor: Illustrated Immunopathology Atlas, Vols. 1-3, 1978; contbr. numerous articles to profl. jours., chpts. to books. Fellow Indian Coll. Allergy and Applied Immunology; mem. Am. Acad. Allergy and Immunology, Indian Immunology Soc. (life), Indian Assn. Pathologists and Microbiologists (life), Inst. Med. Scis. (WHO fellow New Delhi 1968, Singapore 1970, Amsterdam, The Netherlands 1979, chmn. Debating and Lit. Soc. 1976). Hindu. Club: Internat. Innerwheel (Varanasi) (pres. 1974). Home: C/3 Banaras Hindu U Campus, Varanasi 221 005, India Office: Banaras Hindu U Inst Med Scis, Varanasi 221 005, India

GUPTA, SURAJ NARAYAN, physicist, educator; b. Haryana, India, Dec. 1, 1924; came to U.S., 1953, naturalized, 1963; s. Lakshmi N. and Devi (Goyal) G.; m. Letty Gupta, July 14, 1948; children—Paul, Ranee. M.S., St. Stephen's Coll., India, 1946; Ph.D., U. Cambridge, Eng., 1951. Imperial Chem. Industries fellow U. Manchester, Eng., 1951-53; vis. prof. physics Purdue U., 1953-56; prof. physics Wayne State U., 1956-61, Distinguished prof. physics, 1961—; vis. physicist Argonne Nat. Lab., Brookhaven Nat. Lab., NRC Can. Author: Quantum Electrodynamics, 1977. Fellow Am. Phys. Soc., Nat. Acad. Scis. India. Home: 1300 E Lafayette Blvd Detroit MI 48207 Office: Dept Physics Wayne State U Detroit MI 48202

GUPTA, USHA, microbiology educator; b. Lucknow, India, Dec. 11, 1934; s. Panna Lal and Jwala Devi (Agarwal) G. MBBS, U. Lucknow, 1958, DCP, 1961, MD, 1962. Pathologist Safdarjang Hosp., New Delhi, 1965-68; asst. prof. microbiology All India Inst. Med. Scis., New Delhi, 1968-80, assoc. prof., 1980-85, 86—; prof. head dept. microbiology All India Inst. Hygiene and Pub. Health, Calcutta, India, 1985-86; registrar Regional Virus Lab., Birmingham, Eng., 1965; guest physician Robert Koch Inst., Free U. Berlin, 1964-65; vis. scientist Inst. Med. Microbiology, Aarhus, Denmark, 1974-75; vis. Pub. Health Lab. Services, Colindale, Eng., 1975-78; pres. 2d All India Conf. on Anaerobic Infections in Man, 1985. Editor: Proceedings Anaerobic Infections in Man, Proceedings Mycoplasma Diseases, 1982. Lucknow U. scholar, 1955. Mem. Internat. Orgn. Mycoplasmology (bd. dirs. 1982-84), Indian Assn. Mycoplasmology. Club: India Internat. Ctr. (New Delhi). Home: DII 37 Ansari Nager, New Delhi 110 029, India Office: All India Inst Med Scis, Microbiology Dept Ansari Nager, New Delhi 110 029, India

GUPTA, VANKAYALA KAMALAKAR, electrical engineering company executive; b. Visakhapatnam, Andhra Pradesh, India, Oct. 16, 1942; s. Vankayala Rajeswar Gupta and Vankayala Sita Devi; m. Vankayala Venkata Ratnam, Aug. 23, 1972; children: Suneeta, Sridhar. BCom with honors, Andhra U., 1961; grad., Inst. Cost and Work Accounts, India, 1964; MBA, Atlanta U., 1967. Cert. cost acct. Cost acct. NPCC Ltd., Bihar, India, 1965-67; fin. analyst E.I. duPont de Nemours and Co., Wilmington, Del., 1967-72; works acct. Union Carbide India Ltd., Calcutta, 1972-81; cost acct. Sandoz India Ltd., Bombay, 1981-85; group fin. controller T.T. Krishnamachari and Co., Madras, India, 1985-86; exec. dir. fin. The English Elec. Co. India Ltd., Madras, 1986—. Mem. British Inst. Mgmt., Bombay Mgmt. Assn., Inst. Cost and Works Accts. India (assoc.). Hindu. Office: The English Elec Co India, Pallavaram, Madras India

GÜRBÜZ, ATABEY, airline executive; b. Erzincan, Turkey, May 10, 1942; s. Fikri and Bahice (Yurdagel) A.; m. Leman Yenigün, Apr. 5, 1968; children: Ayse Gülcin, Mustafa. Grad., Comml. and Econ. Scis. Acad., Istanbul, 1971. With Turkish Airlines, Inc., Istanbul, 1966—; mgr. Turkish Airlines, Inc., Beirut, 1973-74, Milan, 1974-75, Dusseldorf, Fed. Republic Germany, 1975-76; gen. mgr. Turkish Airlines, Inc., Netherlands, Amsterdam, 1980-85; dir. mktg. Turkish Airlines, Inc., Istanbul, 1985. Muslim. Office: Turkish Airlines Inc, Cumhuriyet CAD 201, Istanbul Turkey

GURDON, JOHN BERTRAND, cell biologist; b. Surrey, Eng., Oct. 2, 1933; s. William Nathaniel and Elsie Marjorie (Byass) G.; m. Jean Elizabeth Curtis, June 25, 1965; Elizabeth Aurea, William John. BA, Oxford U., 1956, DPhil, 1960; DSc (hon.), U. Chgo., 1978; D (hon.), Paris U., 1982; DSc (hon.), Oxford U., 1988. Research fellow Oxford U., Eng., 1961-71; mem. staff MRC Molecular Biology Lab, Cambridge, Eng., 1972-78, div. head, 1979-83; prof. Cambridge U., 1984—; lectr. dept. zoology Oxford U., 1962-71; fellow Churchill Coll., Cambridge, 1974—, Eton Coll., Windsor, Eng., 1980—; prof. Royal Instn., London, 1985—. Author: Control of Gene Expression in Animal Development, 1974; contbr. papers to sci. jours. Recipient Paul Ehrlich prize, Fed. Republic Germany, 1977, Charles Leopold Mayer prize, Acad. Scis., France, 1984, Royal medal, London, 1985, Emperor Hirohito Internat. Biology prize, Japan, 1987; Gosney fellow Calif. Inst. Tech., Pasadena, 1961-62; vis. fellow Carnegie Instn., Balt., 1965. Fellow Royal Soc. London. Mem. Ch. of Eng. Club: Goldsmiths Co., London (liveryman 1986). Home: Whittlesford Grove, Cambridge CB2 4NZ, England Office: U Cambridge Dept Zoology, Downing St, Cambridge CB2 3EJ, England

GURLEY, FRANKLIN LOUIS, lawyer, military historian; b. Syracuse, N.Y., Nov. 26, 1925; s. George Bernard and Catherine Veronica (Moran) G.; m. Elizabeth Anne Ryan, June 17, 1950. A.B., Harvard U., 1949, J.D., 1952. Bar: Mass. 1952, N.Y. 1956, Ill. 1956, Mich. 1956, D.C. 1956. Fgn. service staff officer Dept. State, Washington and Germany, 1953-55; atty. N.Y. Central R.R. Co., 1955-56; asst. dist. atty. New York County, 1956-57; atty. firm Dewey, Ballantine, Bushby, Palmer & Wood, N.Y.C., 1957-63; gen. counsel, sec. IBM Europe Corp., Paris; also mng. atty. IBM Corp., Armonk, N.Y., 1963-68; sr. v.p., gen. counsel Nestle S.A., Vevey, Switzerland, 1968-83; spl. legal adv. Nestle S.A., Vevey, 1984-85; internat. legal cons. 1985—; historian 100th Inf. Div. Assn., 1984—. Author: 399th in Action in World War II, 1946, King Philip's War (play), 1952; contbr. articles to profl. jours. Pres. Tappan Landing Assn. Tarrytown N.Y. 1958-60. Served with inf. AUS, 1944-46, ETO. Decorated Bronze Star, Combat Inf. Badge. Mem. ABA, N.Y. County Lawyers Assn., SAR (sec., bd. mgrs. N.Y. chpt. 1957-63), Harvard Law Sch. Assn., Harvard Law Sch. Assn. Europe. Clubs: Harvard (N.Y.C., France, Switzerland); Lausanne Golf, Montreux Golf; Am. Internat. (Geneva). Home and Office: 1626 Romanens, Fribourg Switzerland

GURNEE, ROBERT FRANCIS, retail and financial services company executive; b. Bklyn., Dec. 3, 1927; s. Robert F. and Florence Catherine (O'Brien) G.; B.B.A. in Fin., St. John's U., Jamaica, N.Y., 1955; grad. Consumer Fin. Program, Columbia U., 1963, Aspen Inst. Humanistic Studies, 1969; m. Arline Catherine Degen, May 21, 1950; children—Patricia Gurnee Lloyd, Barbara Gurnee Scarborough, Robert Philip. Credit analyst and comml. paper depts. Goldman, Sachs & Co., N.Y.C., 1951-58; with Sears Roebuck Acceptance Corp., Wilmington, Del., 1958-80, v.p., 1963-67, exec. v.p., 1967-72, pres., chief exec. officer 1972-80, also dir., chmn. exec. com.; v.p., corp. treas. Sears, Roebuck & Co., Chgo., 1981—; chmn. bd., mng. dir. Sears Overseas Fin. N.V.; dir. Sears Securities Sales Inc., Sears Internat. Commodity Corp.; chmn. Bnaco de Credito Internat. S.A.; dir., chmn. exec. com. Discover Credit Corp.; treas. Sears Fin. Corp., Sears Internat. Fin. Co., Sears, Roebuck de P.R.; pres., dir. Sears, Roebuck Internat., Inc.; treas. Sears Buying Services, Inc., Sears Roebuck Overseas, Inc., Sears Buying Service-Japan, Fleet Maintenance, Inc., Terminal Freight Handling Co.; chmn. investment com. Savs. and Profit Sharing Fund Sears Employee; mem. investment com. Sears Pension Plan; dir., chmn. exec. com. Farmers Bank of State of Del., 1976-80. Bd. dirs. Boys Club of Wilmington, 1972-80, United Way, Wilmington, 1972-73, NCCJ, Wilmington, 1973-77; bus. chmn. Del. Heart Assn. Fund Raising, 1976-77; adv. bd. Sch. Bus. and Commerce, St. John's U.; bd. exec. advisers No. Ill. U., DeKalb, Ill. Served with USN, 1945-48, 51-52; Korea. Mem. Nat. Assn. Corporate Treas. (dir. 1981-86), Soc. Internat. Treas., Chgo. Council Fgn. Relations, Japan Am. Soc. Roman Catholic. Clubs: Downtown Assn. (N.Y.C.); Met. (Chgo.). Lodge: K.C. Home: 5975 Stewart Dr Apt 821 Willowbrook IL 60514 Office: Sears Roebuck Acceptance Corp One Customs House Sq Wilmington DE 19899

GURNEY, JAMES THOMAS, lawyer; b. Ripley, Miss., Jan. 24, 1901; s. James Andrew and Mary Jane (Shepherd) G.; m. Blanche Johnson, Mar. 5, 1925 (dec.); 1 son, J. Thomas; m. Lannie W. Jones, Jan. 8, 1985. A.B., Miss. Coll., 1919, LL.D., 1972; student, U. Chgo., 1919-20, Columbia U., 1919; LL.B., Cumberland U., Lebanon, Tenn., 1922, J.D., 1968; LL.D., Stetson U., 1970; D.H.L., U. Fla., 1978. Bar: Fla. 1922. Mem. faculty Miss. Woman's Coll., Hattiesburg, 1919-21; and since practiced in Orlando; original counsel Minute Maid Corp. (div. Coca- Cola Co.); gen. counsel Orlando Utilities Commn., 1925-85; dir. emeritus Beneficial Corp.; mem. Fla. Supreme Court com. for redrafting common law rules of procedure, 1945; mem. examining bd. Fla. Parole Commn., 1945; chmn. bd. control Fla. Insts. of Higher Learning, 1945-49, now bd. regents. Author: Life Insurance Law of Florida, 1934, Disability Claims Resort to Equity, 1940, World War II Construction of War clauses, 1946; contbr. articles to Fla. Bar Jour. Trustee New Orleans Bapt. Theol. Sem., 1960-67; former bd. dirs. Children's Home Soc. of Fla.; mem. Fla. Council of 100; sponsor for establishment J. Thomas Gurney Elem. Sch. of 1st Bapt. Ch. of Orlando, Fla. Recipient Cert. of Merit U. Fla., 1953; Distinguished Service award Stetson U., 1958; Distinguished Service citation New Orleans Bapt. Theol. Sem. and So. Bapt. Found., 1967; award Pres. Ind. Colls. Fla., 1970; Cert. of Appreciation Miss. Coll., 1984. Fellow Am. Bar Found., Am. Coll. Trial Lawyers; mem. ABA (com. on life ins. law, vice chmn. 1944-47, admissions 1944-48, ssn. and adv. spl. com. on pub. relations 1944-46, adminstrv. law 1945, chmn. Fla. membership com. on ins. sect. 1946-48), Fla. State Bar Assn. (pres. 1942-43), Orange County Bar Assn., Internat. Bar Assn., Am. Life Conv. (legal sect.), Assn. of Life Ins. Counsel (exec. com. 1946-48), Orange County Budget Commn. (chmn. 1935-42), Orlando Community Chest (gen. chmn.), Orlando C. of C. (pres. 1930, nat. council 1940-41, J. Thomas Gurney, Sr. ann. leadership award 1984), Internat. Platform Assn., Fla. Blue Key (hon.), Newcomen Soc., Alumni Assn. U. Fla. (hon.). Democrat. Baptist. Clubs: Lions (Orlando) (dist. gov. 35th dist. 1928), University (Orlando), Orlando Country (Orlando), Rotary (Paul Harris fellow) (Orlando). Home: 1701 N Spring Lake Dr Orlando FL 32804 Office: 225 E Robinson St Suite 450 Orlando FL 32801

GURRY, FRANCIS GERARD, international civil servant; b. Melbourne, Victoria, Australia, May 17, 1951; s. Raymond Paul and Eileen (Galbally) G.; m. Sylvie Marie Annick Veit, Aug. 20, 1983; children: Thomas Jerome, Celine Elisabeth. LLB, U. Melbourne, 1973, LLM, 1975; PhD, U. Cambridge, 1980. Solicitor Arthur Robinson & Co., Melbourne, 1974-76; sr. lectr. law U. Melbourne, 1979-83; vis. prof. U. Dijon, France, 1983; solicitor Freehill, Hollingdale & Page, Sydney, Australia, 1984; cons. World Intellectual Property Orgn., Geneva, 1985, sr. program officer, 1986-87, head indsl. property law sect., 1988—. Author: Breach of Confidence, 1984; contbr. articles to profl. jours. Home: 107 Rue de Lausanne, 1202 Geneva Switzerland Office: World Intellectual Property Orgn, 34 Chemin des Colombettes, 1211 Geneva Switzerland

GURSTEL, NORMAN KEITH, lawyer; b. Mpls., Mar. 24, 1939; s. Jules and Etta (Abramowitz) G.; m. Jane Evelyn Golden, Nov. 24, 1984; children: Todd, Dana, Marc. BA, U. Minn., 1960, JD, 1962. Bar: Minn. 1962, U.S. Dist. Ct. Minn. 1963, U.S. Supreme Ct. 1980. Assoc. Robins, Zelle, Larson & Kaplan, Mpls., 1962-67; prin. Norman K. Gurstel and Assocs., Mpls., 1967—; arbitrator Hennepin County Dist. Ct.; lectr. U. Minn. Family Law Seminar. Mem. ABA (corp. banking and bus. law and family law sects.), Minn. Bar Assn. (co-chmn. family ct. com. bankruptcy law sect. 1966-67, family law and bankruptcy law), Hennepin County Bar Assn. (chmn. family law com. 1964-65, vice chmn. 1981-82, fee arbitration bd., creditors remedy com.), Fed. Bar Assn., Assn. Trial Lawyers Am., Minn. Trial Lawyers Assn., Am. Acad. Matrimonial Lawyers, Motor Carrier Lawyers Assn., Nat. Council Juvenile and Family Ct. Judges, Comml. Law League Am. (chmn. midwest region 1979-80, recording sec. 1980-81, sec. fund for pub. edn. 1981-83, bd. govs. 1983-86, pres.-elect 1986, pres. 1987), Phi Delta Phi. Jewish. Club: Oak Ridge Country (Mpls.). Lodges: Shriners, Masons. Office: Norman K Gurstel and Assocs 431 S 7th St Minneapolis MN 55415

GUSSOW, DON, publisher, author; b. Pumpyan, Lithuania, Dec. 7, 1907; came to U.S., 1920, naturalized, 1923; s. Samuel (Simche) and Anna (Chaia) Sonia (Luria) G.; m. Betty Gussow, Oct. 19, 1930; children: Alan, Mel, Paul. Student, CCNY, 1926-27, Maxwell Tng. Sch. Tchrs., Bklyn., 1927-28; tchr. tng. diploma, U. Vt., 1928-29; student, N.Y. U., 1929-31, B.A., 1977. Editor Butcher's Adv., N.Y.C., 1929-30, Confectionery-Ice Cream World, N.Y.C., 1930-34, 39-44, Internat. Confectioner, N.Y.C., 1935-39; founder 1944; since chmn., editor-in-chief, chief exec. officer Magazines for Industry, Inc., N.Y.C.; v.p., editor Harcourt Brace Jovanovich, Inc., N.Y.C., 1982-85; dir. Cowles Communications, Inc., 1966-70, Am. Bus. Press, 1968-71, 76-85; pres., editor-in-chief PG Communications Inc., 1986—; pres. bus. and profl. mags. div. Cowles Communications, Inc., 1966-70. Author: Divorce Corporate Style, 1972, The New Merger Game, 1978, Chaia Sonia, A Family's Odyssey Russian Style, 1980, The New Business Journalism, 1983; contbg. editor: Ency. Brit, 1939-63. Founder Am. Assn. Candy Technologists, 1948, created Kettle award of candy industry, 1946. Recipient Pub. Service award Nat. Confectioners Assn., 1971; Pres.'s award Am. Coll. Legal Medicine, 1974; Honor scroll Am. Bus. Press, 1979; Gallatin fellow N.Y. U., 1980; Disting. Pub. Service award Anti-Defamation League, 1983; Cert. of Distinction NYU, 1983. Clubs: N.Y. U., Overseas Press. Marco Polo (N.Y.C.). Home: 50 Sutton Pl S New York NY 10022 Office: 747 3d Ave New York NY 10017

GUSSOW, JOHN ANDREW, lawyer; b. Bklyn., May 11, 1946; s. Emanuel M. and Jean M. (Gumpert) G.; children—Jerome A., Charles E. A.B., Dickinson Coll., 1967; J.D., Syracuse U., 1970. Bar: N.Y. 1971. Trial atty. civil div. Dept. Justice, N.Y.C., 1970-75; assoc. Melvin D. Kraft P.C., N.Y.C., 1975-76; asst. gen. counsel, asst. sec. M. Lowenstein Corp., N.Y.C., 1976-82, assoc. gen. counsel, asst. sec., 1982—; small claims arbitrator Civil Ct. Richmond County; mem. N.Y. State Cable TV Commn., 1984-86, ptnr. Hart and Gussow, 1986-87; ptnr., Gussow and Emma, 1987—; Law chmn., mem. exec. com. Richmond County (N.Y.) Republican Com.; Rep. candidate for dist. atty. Richmond County, 1983; commr. N.Y. State Cable TV Commn., 1984—; bd. dirs. Camelot Found. ; law chmn. Richmond County Rep. Com. Mem. ABA, Assn. Bar City N.Y., Textile Lawyers Assn., Customs Bar Assn., N.Y. State Bar Assn., Richmond County Bar Assn., Am. Arbitration Assn. (nat. panel). Jewish. Lodge: Richmond County Kiwanis. Home: 50 Yacht Club Cove Staten Island NY 10308 Office: 32 Narrows Rd S Staten Island NY 10305

GUSTAFSON, ALBERT KATSUAKI, lawyer, engineer; b. Tokyo, Dec. 5, 1949; came to U.S., 1951; s. William A. and Akiko (Osada) G.; m. Helen Melissa Laird, July 31, 1971 (div. 1975); m. Karen Jane Ekblad, Dec. 31, 1978 (div. 1987). B.A. with distinction, Stanford U., 1972; J.D., U. Wash., 1980; L.L.M., 1988. Bar: Wash. 1981, U.S. Dist. Ct. (we. dist.) Wash. 1981, U.S. Ct. Appeals (9th cir.) 1984. Acoustics analyst Boeing Co., Seattle, 1973-74, materiel buyer, 1974; legal editor, book pub. co., Seattle, 1975-76; research analyst Batelle Inst., Seattle, 1975-76; legal intern Office of U.S. Atty., Seattle, 1976; engr. U.P.R.R., 1977-85; corp. counsel Ansette Fin. Corp., Inc., Seattle, 1987—; pres. Albert K. Gustafson, P.S., Seattle, 1981—; corp. counsel Dorden, Inc., Centralia, Wash., 1984—, Ansette Fin. Corp., Inc., Seattle, 1987. Sec. local 117-E, United Transp. Union, 1984, local vice-chmn., 1984; Dem. precinct chmn., 1984. Kraft scholar, 1968; Calif. State scholar, 1968-72. Mem. Assn. Trial Lawyers Am., Wash. State Trial Lawyers Assn., ABA, Fed. Bar Assn., Seattle-King County Bar Assn., Seattle C. of C. Democrat. Presbyterian. Club: College. Lodges: Masons, Shriners, Order of DeMolay (master councilor 1968), Rotary. Home: 4322 Wallingford Ave N Seattle WA 98103 Office: 804 First Interstate Ctr 999 3d Ave Seattle WA 98104 also: Fuji Bldg 8F, 3-18-6 Hatchobori Chuo-ku, Tokyo 104, Japan

GUSTAFSON, GEORGE ROBERT, association executive; b. Austin, Tex., May 19, 1928; s. Fred W. and Nell V. (Wheless) G.; student U. Tex., Austin, 1948-51, 59; m. Norma June Windsor, July 22, 1950; children—Cynthia Ann, Deborah Kay, Tami Lynn. With Tex. Dept. Public Safety, 1949-50; pres. Tex. Safety Assn., Austin, from 1950, now pres.; dir. Nat. Safety Council; mem. Citizens Traffic Safety Comm.; adv. com. Tex. Transp. Inst.; adv. com. Tex. Gov.'s Interagy. Council on Job Injuries. Corp. charter mem. Boys Club of Austin. Recipient citation for disting. service to safety Nat. Safety Council, 1980. Mem. Am. Soc. Assn. Execs. (pres.), Assn. Safety Council Execs. (cert.), Tex. Soc. Assn. Execs. (chmn.-elect). Club: Austin Civitan (past pres.). Home: 6510 Auburn Hill Austin TX 78723 Office: PO Box 9345 Austin TX 78766

GUSTAFSSON, KJELL OVE GILBERT, chemical and manufacturing company executive; b. Värnamo, Sweden, July 10, 1941; s. Arvid Sixten Mattias and Elsa Anna Margareta (Johansson) G.; m. Ingrid Johansson, July

29, 1966 (div. Oct. 1985); children: Oscar, Malin; m. Maybrith Ladssott, Oct. 10, 1985; 1 child, Jonah. MS, Chalmers U. Tech., Gothenburg, Sweden, 1968. Research asst. Hoack AB, Hultsfred, Sweden, 1969-73, quality inspection mgr., 1973-75, tech. mktg. mgr., 1975-78, research and devel. mgr., 1979-87, prodn. mgr., 1981-87, tech. dir., 1987—. Home: Frodinge Brantesizd L5, 59800 Vimmerby Sweden Office: Hoack AB, 57700 Holtsfred Sweden

GUSTAFSSON, MADELEINE, literary critic, writer; b. Gothenburg, Sweden, July 2, 1937; d. Joen and Valborg (Holtermann) Lagerberg; m. Lars Gustafsson, Feb. 1962 (div. Jan. 1982); children: Joen, Lotten. MA, M in Social Scis., U. Uppsala, Sweden, 1962. Lit. critic Stockholmstidningen, 1961-65, Göteborgs Handelstidning, Gothenburg, 1965-72; lit. critic Dagens Nyheter, Stockholm, 1972—, asst. cultural editor, 1984-86; editor-in-chief Ord & Bild, Stockholm, 1983-84. Author: (essays) Med andras ögon, 1978, Utopien och dess skugga, 1978; (poetry) Solida byggen, 1979, Vattenväxter, 1983; contbr. articles and transls. to Swedish, German and U.S. profl. jours. Mem. PEN, Council for Humanistic and Social Research, Author's Fund (bd. dirs.). Home: Heleneborgsgatan 6C 1 tr, S-LL7 32 Stockholm Sweden

GUSTAFSSON, STEN, manufacturing company executive; b. Stockholm, July 13, 1923; s. Oskar Wilhelm G.; grad. Stockholm Sch. Econs., 1948; M.B.A., N.Y. U., 1952; Dr. Econs., Stockholm Sch. Econs., 1984; hon. Dr. Tech., Royal Inst. Tech., 1985; m. Harriet Hardberg, 1954; children—Morgan, Jan, Mats. Dir., AB Astra, Södertälje, Sweden, 1955-57, exec. v.p., 1957-63, now chmn.; pres. Incentive AB, Stockholm, 1963-78, now chmn.; pres. Saab-Scania AB, Linköping, Sweden, 1978-83, now chmn.; dir. Skandia, AB Investor, Förvaltnings AB Providentia, Svenska Dagbladet Skandinaviska Enskilda Banken. Chmn. Swedish Natural Sci. Research Council. Mem. Royal Swedish Acad. Engring. Scis. (chmn.). Office: Saab-Scania AB, S-58188 Linköping Sweden

GUSTAVSON, CARL GUSTAV, historian, educator; b. Vinton, Iowa, Aug. 3, 1915; s. Carl Linus and Edla (Gustafson) G.; m. Caryl Jennings, June 30, 1943; children: Carl, Eric, Martha. A.B., Augustana Coll., 1937; M.A., U. Ill., 1938; Ph.D. (Pres. White fellow 1938-40), Cornell U., 1942. Instr. Lake Forest Coll., 1942-43; asst. prof. Miami U., Oxford, Ohio, 1943-45; asst. to assoc. prof. Ohio U., Athens, 1945-56; acting chmn. dept. Ohio U., 1955-56, prof. history, 1956-71, disting. prof. history, 1971-85; disting. prof. history emeritus 1985—, chmn. dept., 1961-65; vis. prof. summer Emory U., 1949, Cornell U., 1950, Wayne State U., 1955, U. Ill., 1961, U. Cin., 1964, Western Res. U., 1965, U. Ga., 1968, U. Pacific, 1969; Fulbright fellow U. Uppsala, Sweden, 1970. Author: A Preface to History, 1955, The Institutional Drive, 1966, Europe in the World Community Since 1939, 1970, The Mansion of History, 1976, The Small Giant: Sweden Enters the Industrial Era, 1986. Del. XI Internat. Congress Hist. Socs., Stockholm, 1960. Ford Found. Fellow, 1953-54; grantee Am. Philos. Soc., 1956, 64; recipient Baker Research award, 1965, Alumni outstanding achievement award Augustana Coll., 1972; Hon. Alumni award Ohio U., 1985. Mem. Am. History Assn., Ohio Acad. History (pres. 1964-65, ann. award 1956, Disting. Service award 1978), French Hist.-Soc., Am.-Scandinavian Found., Societe d'Histoire Moderne (Paris), Phi Beta Kappa, Phi Alpha Theta, Pi Gamma Mu, Lambda Chi Alpha. Episcopalian. Club: Swedish (Chgo.). Home: 14 Utah Pl Athens OH 45701 Address: General Delivery, Kenora, ON Canada

GUT, RAINER EMIL, banker; b. Baar, Switzerland, Sept. 24, 1932; s. Emil Anton and Rosa (Möller) G.; m. Josephine Lorenz, 1957; 4 children. Ed., Cantonal Sch. Zug. N.Am. rep. Union Bank of Switzerland, N.Y.C., 1963-68; gen. ptnr. Lazard Freres & Co., N.Y.C., 1968-71; chair, chief exec. officer Swiss-Am. Corp., N.Y.C., 1971-73; dep. gen. mgr. head office Credit Suisse, Zörich, 1973-75, gen. mgr., 1975-77, spokesman of gen. mgr., 1977-82, mng. dir., 1982-83, chmn., 1983—; bd. dirs. Sulzer Bros.; chmn. Elektrowatt AG, 1981—, Financière Credit Suisse-First Boston, 1979, Centralschweizerische Kraftwerke, 1983. Office: Credit Suisse, Paradeplatz 8, 8021 Zurich Switzerland *

GUT, TAJA EMIL, writer, editor; b. Zurich, Apr. 1, 1949; m. Ursi Aebi. Diploma, Tchr.'s Tng. Coll., Küsnacht, Switzerland, 1969. Tchr. German Pvt. Sch., Zurich, 1976-79; bookseller Antiquariat Im Seefeld, Zurich, 1979—; editor Kaspar Hauser, Zurich, 1982-85, Individualität, Zurich, 1986—; pvt. practice translator. Contbr. articles to profl. jours. Home and Office: Tuggenerstrasse 12, 8008 Zurich Switzerland

GUTCHÉ, GENE, composer; b. Berlin, Germany, July 3, 1907; came to U.S., 1925; s. Maxmillian and Flora (von Zerbst) G.; m. Marion Frances Buchan, Dec. 1, 1935. M.A., U. Minn.; M.A. (creative scholar), 1950; Ph.D. (creative scholar), State U. Iowa, 1953. Guggenheim fellow 1963-65. Contbr. articles to profl. jours.; World premieres include Piano Concerto Opus 24, Mpls. Summer Session, 1956, Third String Quartet Opus 12 No. 3, Arts Quartet, 1958, Holofernes Overture Opus 27 No. 1, Mpls. Symphony, 1959, Rondo Capriccioso Opus 21, N.Y. Chamber Orch., 1960, Concertino for Orch. Opus 28, Mpls. Summer Session, 1961, Fourth String Quartet Opus 29 No. 1, Fine Arts Quartet, 1962, Symphony IV Opus 30, Albuquerque Symphony, 1962, Timpani Concertante Opus 31, Oakland Symphony, 1962, Symphony V for Strings Opus 34, Chautauqua Festival, 1962, Bongo Divertimento Opus 35, St. Paul Chamber Orch., 1962, Raquel Opus 38, Tulsa Philharmonic, 1963, Genghis Khan Opus 37, Mpls. Symphony, 1963, Rites in Tenochtitlàn Opus 39, St. Paul Chamber Orch., 1965, Gemini Opus 41, Mpls. Summer Session, 1966, Hsiang Fei Opus 40, Cin. Symphony, 1966, Rites in Tenochtitlàn Opus 39 No. 1, New Orleans Symphony, 1967, Classic Concerto for Chamber Orch. Opus 44, St. Paul Chamber Orch., 1967, Aesop Fabler Suite Opus 43, Fargo-Moorhead Symphony, 1968, Epimetheus USA Opus 46, Detroit Symphony, 1969, Symphony VI, Opus 45, Detroit Symphony, 1971, Icarus, Opus 48, Nat. Symphony, 1976, Bi-Centurion, Opus 49, Rochester Philharmonic, 1976, Perseus & Andromeda XX, Opus 50, Cin. Symphony, 1977, Helios Kinetic, Opus 52, Fla. Philharmonic, 1978, Akhenaten, Opus 51, Milw. Symphony, 1980, Opus 51, No 2, St. Louis Symphony, 1983; European premieres include Symphony V For Strings, Opus 34, Radio-TV Luxembourg, 1968, Violin Concerto, Opus 36, Orch. Stabile Trieste, 1969, Bongo Divertimento, Opus 35, Munich Philharmoniker, 1967, Hsiang Fei, Opus 40, Oslo Philharm., 1970, Epimetheus U.S.A., Opus 46, Stockholm Philharm., 1969, Genghis Khan, Opus 37; also recs. (Recipient Minn. State Centennial prize 1958, Luria award 1959, prize Albuquerque Nat. Composition 1962, prize Oscar Espla Internat. Composition 1962, XVI Premio Citta di Trieste 1969, Louis Moreau Gottschalk Gold medal 1970, XIX Premio Citta di Trieste 1972), commns. include, St. Paul Philharmonic, 1962, St. Paul Arts and Scis., 1965, regents U. Minn., 1966, Fargo-Moorhead Symphony, 1967, St. Paul Chamber, 1967, Detroit Symphony, 1969, Nat. Symphony Orch., 1975, Rochester Philharmonic, 1976, Cin. Symphony Orch., 1977, Fla. Philharmonic, 1978,, Milw. Symphony, 1980 (nationwide broadcast of Akhenaten, Opus 51 by NPR/N/C radio 1980, by St. Louis Symphony Orch. on Nat. Pub. Radio, 1983). NEA Bicentennial grantee, 1976, 77, 78; Ford Found. rec. grantee, 1976. Mem. Am. Fedn. Musicians, Am. Composers Alliance, Am. Music Center. Address: Regus Pub 10 Birchwood Ln White Bear Lake MN 55110

GUTERMUTH, SCOTT ALAN, accountant; b. South Bend, Ind., Nov. 24, 1953; s. Richard H. and Barbara Ann (Bracey) G. BS in Bus., Ind. U., 1976. CPA, Ind. With Coopers & Lybrand, Indpls., 1976-83, supervising auditor, 1980-83, audit mgr., 1983; v.p., controller Society Nat. Group, Indpls., 1983—; instr., nat. update analyst Becker CPA Rev. Course, 1980—. Adv., Jr. Achievement; mem. Marion County Republican Com., 1978—, Rep. Nat. Com., 1972—. Fellow Life Mgmt. Inst.; mem. Am. Inst. CPA's, Nat. Assn. Accts., Ins. Acctg. and Statis. Assn., Ind. Assn. CPA's (ins. com. 1984—), Life Mgmt. Inst. (assoc.). Methodist. Home: 3132 Sandpiper S Dr Indianapolis IN 46268 Office: 9101 Wesleyan Rd Indianapolis IN 46268

GUTFREUND, JOHN H., investment banker; b. N.Y.C., Sept. 14, 1929. B.A., Oberlin Coll., 1951. With mcpl. desk Salomon Brothers, N.Y.C., 1953-62, mgr. syndicate, 1962-63, ptnr., 1963-66, exec. ptnr., 1966-78; mng. ptnr. Salomon Bros., N.Y.C., 1978-81; chmn. bd., chief exec. officer Salomon Bros. Inc., N.Y.C., 1981—; co-chair Phibro Corp., N.Y.C., 1981-83; co-chief exec. officer Phibro-Salomon Inc. (formerly Phibro Corp.), N.Y.C., 1983-84, chmn., chief exec. officer, pres., 1984-86; vice chmn. N.Y. Stock Exchange, 1985-87; chmn., chief exec. officer, pres. Salomon Inc. (formerly Phibro-Salomon Inc.), N.Y.C., 1986—; past vice chmn. N.Y. Stock Exchange; past bd. dirs. Securities Industry Assn. Trustee Ctr. for Strategic and Internat. Studies, Com. for Econ. Devel., Joint Council on Econ. Edn.; chmn. Downtown-Lower Manhattan Assn., Inc.; hon. trustee Oberlin (Ohio) Coll.; chmn. Wall St. com. Lincoln Ctr.'s Corp. Fund Campaign, 1986-87; treas. bd. trustees, chmn. fin. com. N.Y. Pub. Library; bd. dirs. Montefiore Med. Ctr. Corp.; trustee Ctr. Strategic and Internat. Studies. Served with U.S. Army, 1951-53. Mem. Downtown-Lower Manhatten Assn. (chmn.). Club: Bond of N.Y. (past pres., past bd. govs.). Office: Salomon Inc 1221 Ave of the Americas New York NY 10020

GUTH, WILFRIED, bank executive; b. Fed. Republic of Germany, July 8, 1919. chmn. supervisory bd. Deutsche Bank AG; chmn., dep. chmn., mem. supervisory bds. numerous other maj. cos. Address: Taunusanlage 12, D-6000 Frankfurt am Main Federal Republic of Germany

GUTH, WILLIAM DONALD, educator; b. St. Louis, Jan. 14, 1933; s. John Elias and Helen Agnes (Yonkus) G.; B.S., Washington U., St. Louis, 1953; M.B.A., Ind. U., 1954; D.B.A. (Ford Found. fellow), Harvard U., 1960; m. Janellen M. Stokes, Nov. 19, 1967; children—Suzanne Elizabeth, Kristen Alexandra. Assoc. prof. Harvard U., 1960-67; prof. Columbia U., 1968-72; prof. mgmt. policy NYU, 1972—, chmn. mgmt. and orgn. behavior area, 1977-87, Harold Price prof. entrepreneurship and strategy, 1987; dir. Ctr. for Entrepreneurial Studies NYU, 1987; vis. prof. IMEDE, Lausanne, Switzerland, 1976-77; dir. Pier 1 Imports, Mgmt. Analysis Center; cons. Gen. Electric Co., IBM, Amstar, Olivetti, Nestle. Chmn. div. bus. policy and planning Acad. of Mgmt., 1972-75. Served with AUS, 1954-56. NSF grantee, 1975-76. Mem. Am. Acad. Polit. and Social Scis., Inst. Mgmt. Scis. Clubs: Harvard (N.Y.C.); Knickerbocker Country (Tenafly, N.J.). Author: (with Christensen, Andrews and Learned) Business Policy Text and Cases, 1st and 2d edit., 1969, 73; editor, contbr.: Planning Systems in the Soviet Union and the United States, 1977; Handbook of Business Strategy, 1986; contbr. articles to profl. jours. Home: 253 W Clinton Ave Tenafly NJ 07670 Office: 90 Trinity Pl New York NY 10006

GUTHARDT, HELMUT, banker; b. Breuna, Hesse, Germany, June 8, 1934; s. Wilhelm and Sophie (Schmale) G.; m. Marga Ackermann; children—Florian; children by previous marriage: Martina, Barbara. Grad., Banking Acad., Frankfurt am Main, Fed. Republic Germany 1960. Chmn. bd. of mng. dir. Raiffeisenbank Kurhessen, Kassel, Fed. Republic Germany, 1964-65; mng. dir. Raiffeisen-Zentralbank Kurhessen, Kassel, 1965-69; mng. dir. DG Bank, Frankfurt am Main, 1970-72, vice chmn. bd. of mng. dir., 1973-81, chmn. bd. of mng. dir., 1981—; chmn. bd. dirs. DG Bank Internat. SA, Luxembourg; chmn. supervisory bd. AGAB Aktiengesellschaft fuer Anlagen und Beteiligungen, Frankfurt am Main, Deutsche Genossenschafts-Hypothekenbank AG, Hamburg and Berlin, Deutsche Genossenschafts-Leasing GmbH, Unterfoehring, DG Agropartners Absatzberatungs-und Projekt-GmbH, Frankfurt am Main, DG Fin. Co. BV, Amsterdam, DG Diskontbank AG, Frankfurt am Main, DG Immobilien-Leasing GmbH, Frankfurt am Main, Evangelische Kreditgenossenschaft EG, Kassel Kampffmeyer Muehlen GmbH, Hamburg, Vereinigte Kunstmuehlen AG, Ergolding; vice chmn. supervisory bd. dirs. Froehlich Bauunternehmung AG, Felsberg-Gensungen, Oelmuehle Hamburg AG, Hamburg; mem. supervisory bd. Bausparkasse Schwaebisch Hall AG, Schwaebisch Hall, BHF-Bank Berliner Handel und Frankfurter Bank, Frankfurt am Main, Kreditanstalt fuer Wiederaufbau, Frankfurt am Main, Landwirtschaftliche Rentenbank, Frankfurt am Main, Liquiditaets-Konsortialbank GmbH, Frankfurt am Main, Otto AG fuer Beteiligungen, Hamburg, R&V Allgemeine Versicherung AG, Wiesbaden, SatellitenFernsehen GmbH, Mainz, Sueddeutsche Zuckerruebenverwertungs-Genossenschaft eG, Stuttgart, Thyssen Stahl AG, Duisburg, Veba AG, Duesseldorf, Zuckerfabrik Franken GmbH, Ochsenfurt. Office: DG Bank, Am Platz der Republik, Pf 100651, D-6000 Frankfurt am Main Hesse, Federal Republic of Germany

GUTHKE, KARL SIEGFRIED, foreign language educator; b. Lingen, Germany, Feb. 17, 1933; came to U.S., 1956, naturalized, 1973; s. Karl Hermann and Helene (Beekman) G.; m. Dagmar von Nostitz, Apr. 24, 1965; 1 child, Carl Ricklef. M.A., U. Tex., 1953; Dr.phil., U. Göttingen, Germany, 1956; M.A. (hon.), Harvard U., 1968. Mem. faculty U. Calif., Berkeley, 1956-65; prof. German lit. U. Calif. at Berkeley, 1962-65, U. Toronto, Ont., Can., 1965-68; prof. German lit. Harvard U., 1968-78, Kuno Francke prof. German art and culture, 1978—; vis. prof. U. Colo., 1963, U. Mass., 1967. Author: Englische Vorromantik und deutscher Sturm und Drang, 1958, (with Hans M. Wolff) Das Leid im Werke Gerhart Hauptmanns, 1958, Geschichte und Poetik der deutschen Tragikomödie, 1961, Gerhart Hauptmann: Weltbild im Werk, 1961, rev. edit., 1980, Haller und die Literatur, 1962, Der Stand der Lessing-Forschung: Ein Bericht über die Literatur, 1932-1962, 1965, Modern Tragicomedy: An Investigation into the Nature of the Genre, 1966, Wege zur Literatur: Studien zur deutschen Dichtungs-und Geistesgeschichte, 1967, Hallers Literaturkritik, 1970, Die Mythologie der entgötterten Welt: Ein literarisches Thema von der Aufklärung bis zur Gegenwart, 1971, Das deutsche bürgerliche Trauerspiel, 1972, 23d rev. edit., 1979, G.E. Lessing, 3d edit., 1979, Literarisches Leben im 18. Jahrhundert in Deutschland u. in der Schweiz, 1975, Das Abenteuer der Literatur, 1981, Haller im Halblicht, 1981, Der Mythos der Neuzeit, 1983, Erkundungen, 1983, Das Geheimnis um B. Traven entdeckt, 1984, B. Traven: Biographie eines Rätsels, 1987, also others; transl.: Die moderne Tragikomödie: Theorie und Gestalt, 1968; editor: Haller, Die Alpen, 1987; co-editor: (Hanser) Gotthold Ephraim Lessing, Werke, 1970-72, Joh. H. Füssli, Sämtliche Gedichte, 1973, Lessing Yearbook, Colloquia Germanica, Twentieth Century Literature, German Quarterly. Guggenheim fellow, 1965; fellow Am. Council Learned Socs., 1972-73; Recipient Walter Channing Cabot prize, 1977; Nat. Endowment for Humanities fellow, 1979-80. Fellow Humanities Research Centre, Inst. Advanced Studies; mem. Lessing Soc. (past pres.), Acad. Lit. Studies. Office: German Dept Harvard U Cambridge MA 02138

GUTHRIE, GEORGE RALPH, real estate development corporation executive; b. Phila., Mar. 12, 1928; s. George Ralph and Myrtle (Robertson) G.; m. Shirley B. Remmey; children: Mary Elizabeth, Brenda Ann. B.S. in Econs, U. Pa., 1948. With I-T-E Imperial Corp., Phila., 1948-70; controller, financial planner I-T-E Imperial Corp., 1960-68, treas., 1968-69, v.p. finance, 1969-70; pres. N. K. Winston Corp., N.Y.C., 1970-76; exec. v.p. Urban Investment and Devel. Co., Chgo., 1976-78; pres. Urban Investment and Devel. Co., 1978-82, chmn., 1982—; vice chmn. JMB Institutional Realty Corp., 1987—; dir. Zenith Electronics Corp. Trustee Nat. Coll. Edn.; chmn., bd. trustees Cornerstone Found.; mem. pres.'s council Lutheran Social Services of Ill.; bd. dirs. March of Dimes, Augustana Coll., Jr. Achievement; mem. pres.'s council, assoc. trustee U. Pa.; co-chmn. Chgo. Devel. Council; com. Chgo. Council on Fgn. Realtions; bd. dirs., exec. com. Chgo. Assn. Commerce and Industry. Mem. Financial Execs. Inst., Urban Land Inst. (trustee, asst. chmn., mem. urban devel./mixed use council), Nat. Realty Com., The Civic Fedn. (bd. dirs.), Lambda Alpha Internat. Republican. Clubs: Glen View, Jupiter Hills, Carlton (bd. govs.), Economics, Chicago. Office: 900 N Michigan Ave Suite 1800 Chicago IL 60611

GUTHRIE, JANET, professional race car driver; b. Iowa City, Mar. 7, 1938; d. William Lain and Jean Ruth (Midkiff) G. B.S. in Physics, U. Mich., 1960. Comml. pilot and flight instr. 1958-61; research and devel. engr. Republic Aviation Corp., Farmingdale, N.Y., 1960-67; publs. engr. Sperry Systems, Sperry Corp., Great Neck, N.Y., 1968-73; racing driver Sports Car Club Am. and Internat. Motor Sports Assn., 1963—; profl. racing driver U.S. Auto Club and Nat. Assn. for Stock Car Racing, 1976-80; highway safety cons. Met. Ins. Co., 1980-87. Mem. athlete adv. bd. Women's Sports Found. Recipient Curtis Turner award Nat. Assn. for Stock Car Racing-Charlotte World 600, 1976; First in Class, Sebring 12-hour, 1970; North Atlantic Road Racing champion, 1973; named to Women's Sports Hall of Fame, 1980. Mem. Madison Ave. Sports Car Driving and Chowder Soc., Women's Sports Found. (adv. bd.), Ballet Aspen (bd. trustees).

GUTHRIE, RANDOLPH HOBSON, lawyer; b. Richmond, Va., Nov. 5, 1905; s. Joseph Hobson and Thomasia Harris (Parkinson) G.; m. Mabel Edith Welton, Mar. 24, 1934; children: Randolph Hobson, Jo Carol, George Gordon. B.S. (first honor grad.), The Citadel, 1925, LL.D., 1976; LL.B. magna cum laude, Harvard U., 1931. Bar: N.Y. 1932. Since practiced in N.Y.C.; sr. partner Mudge, Rose, Guthrie, Alexander and Ferdon; chmn. bd. Studebaker Corp., Studebaker-Worthington, Inc., 1963-71, chmn. exec. com., 1971-81; chmn. bd. UMC Industries, Inc., 1969-76, chmn. exec. com., 1976-81. Editor Harvard Law Rev., 1930-31. Mem. ABA, N.Y. Bar Assn., Assn. Bar City N.Y. Episcopalian. Clubs: Knickerbocker (N.Y.C.), Harvard (N.Y.C.). Home: 43 S Beach Lagoon Road Sea Pines Plantation Hilton Head SC 29928 also: 14 E 75th St New York NY Office: 180 Maiden Ln New York NY 10038

GUTHRIE, RANDOLPH HOBSON, JR., plastic surgeon; b. N.Y.C., Dec. 8, 1934; s. Randolph Hobson and Mabel Edith (Welton) G.; A.B., Princeton, 1957; M.D., Harvard, 1961; m. Beatrice Mills Holden, Mar. 20, 1965; children—Randolph Hobson III, Michael Phipps, Philip Holden. Intern N.Y. Hosp., N.Y.C., 1961-62, resident gen. surgery, 1962-63, resident plastic surgery 1969-71, chief resident, 1971, asst. chief plastic surgery, 1971—; resident gen. surgery St. Luke's Hosp., N.Y.C., 1963-66, chief resident, 1966; research fellow Sloan-Kettering Inst., N.Y.C., 1970-71; chief plastic and reconstructive surgery service Meml. Sloan-Kettering Cancer Center, 1971-77, attending surgeon, 1977—; chief dept. plastic and reconstructive surgery N.Y. Infirmary-Beekman Downtown Hosp., 1979—; asst. prof. Cornell U. Med. Coll., 1971-74, asso. prof., 1974—. Pres., East River Med. Found., N.Y.C., 1970—, Acacia Found., N.Y.C., 1980—; alumni dir. St. Paul's Sch., Concord, N.H., 1979-83, form agt., 1983-87, trustee, 1985—. trustee Episcopal Sch., N.Y.C., 1976-84; bd. dirs. Am.-Italian Found. for Cancer Research, N.Y.C., 1985—; bd. dirs., treas. Save Venice, Inc., 1985—; trustee N.Y. Infirmary-Beekman Downtown Hosp., 1985—. Served to maj. M.C., AUS, 1966-69. Mem. ACS, Plastic Surgery Research Council, Am. Geriatrics Soc., Am. Soc. Plastic and Reconstructive Surgeons, Pan Am. Med. Soc., N.Y. Soc. Plastic and Reconstructive Surgery, N.Y. Med. Soc., Med. Soc. County N.Y., Herbert Conway Soc. Clubs: Doubles, Knickerbucker (N.Y.C.). Contbr. articles to books and med. jours. Home: 15 E 74th St New York NY 10021 Office: 15 E 74th St New York NY 10021

GUTIERREZ, AMAURY ROQUE, engineer, oil and gas company executive; b. San Fernando, Pampanga, Philippines, Oct. 1, 1926; m. Mercedes Paez, Aug. 8, 1953; children: Jose, Ramon, Jaime. BSME, Mapua Inst. Tech., Manila, 1949; MSME, U. Wis., 1951. Engr. Batangas Refinery Caltex (Philippines) Inc., Manila, 1952—, dir. mfg., supply, planning, 1952—; regional dir. Caltex Petroleum Corp., N.Y.C., 1979-82; pres., mng. dir. Caltex (Philippines) Inc., Manila, 1982—; bd. dirs. Batangas Land Co., Manila. Trustee Save the Children, Raymond F. Johnson Found., Manila, 1987—. Mem. Philippines Found. Sci. Tech., Philippines Inst. Pure and Applied Chems. (bd. dirs.), Econ. Devel. Found. (trustee). Clubs: Manila Polo, Manila Golf and Country, Baguio Country (Baguio), Puerto Azul Beach and Country (Cavite). Lodge: Rotary. Home: 14 Buchanan St Forbes Park, Green Hills, San Juan, Metro Manila Philippines Office: Caltex Philippines Inc, 540 P Faura, Ermita Manila Philippines

GUTIERREZ, CARLOS JOSÉ, Costa Rican government official, lawyer; b. Costa Rica, Feb. 26, 1927; Licenciado en Derecho, U. Costa Rica, 1948; M.A. in Polit. Sci., U. Pa., 1951; postgrad. Stanford U., 1972; LL.D. (hon.), U. Tex.-San Antonio, 1974. Prof. philosophy of law Universidad de Costa Rica, San Jose, 1952-73; dir. for Costa Rica, Investigative Project on Law and Devel., Stanford U. (Calif.), 1972-74; Costa Rican ambassador to Fed. Republic Germany, Bonn, 1975-76; prof. Escuela Relaciones Internacionales, Universidad Nacional, San Jose, 1976-80; minister of justice Costa Rica, 1982-83, minister fgn. relations, 1983-86; permanent rep. to U.N., 1986; dir. Instituto Nacional de Seguros, 1953-58. Author: Lecciones de filosofia del Derecho, 1964; La Corte de Justicia Centroamericana, 1974; El Funcionamiento del Sistema Juridico, 1980, Derecho Constitucional Costaprecense Ed, 1983, La Social-Democracia, 1986, Neutralidad y Democracia Combativa, 1987. Mem. Colegio de Abogados de Costa Rica, Union Costarricen se de Abagados, Asociacion Costarricen se de Filosofia, Federación Interamericana de Abogados, Am. Polit. Sci. Assn., Asociacion de Autores de Obras Literarias, Artisticas y Cientificas (pres. 1962-63). Address: Costa Rican Mission to UN 211 E 43d St Suite 903 New York NY 10017

GUTIERREZ, GUILLERMO TIRONA, dermatology educator; b. Manila, Mar. 20, 1924; s. Perpetuo D. and Concepcion P. (Tirona) G.; m. Rosario F. Isidro, Dec. 4, 1948; children: Guillermo II, Manuel, Concepcion. AA, U. Philippines, 1943, MD, 1948. Diplomate Philippine Dermatol. Soc. (bd. dirs. 1959-65, 67-69, 84—, pres. 1971-74, chmn. bd. examiners 1973-74, 86—). Resident North Gen. Hosp., Manila, 1948; resident Philippine Gen. Hosp., Manila, 1949-50, resident surgery, 1950-52, cons. dermatologist, 1956—; trainee Skin and Cancer unit NYU, N.Y.C., 1952-53; resident dermatology syphilology NYU-Bellevue Med. Ctr., N.Y.C., 1954-55; instr. dermatology U. Philippines, Manila, 1956-65, asst. prof., 1965-75, chief dept., 1972-85, assoc. prof., 1975-80, prof., 1981—; instr. Far Ea. U., Manila, 1956-57, asst. prof., 1957-58, assoc. prof., chief dept., 1958-65, cons., 1956-65; Yutivo prof. U. Philippines Med. Found., 1981; ofcl. del. XII-XVI Internat. Congresses Dermatology, other confs. Contbr. articles to med. jours. Founding mem. Citizens League for Good Govt. in Quezon City, 1967. Served to 2d lt. Hunters Guerillas of Philippine Army, 1943-45. Mem. Philippine Med. Assn., Am. Acad. Dermatology, Am. Soc. for Dermatologic Surgery (corr.), Internat. Soc. Tropical Dermatology, San Jaun Med. Soc., Nat. Research Council Philippines, Manila Med. Soc., Philippine Motor Assn., Nat. Rifle Assn. of Am., Nat. Rifle and Pistol Assn. Philippines. Roman Catholic. Office: Manila Doctors Hosp, United Nations Ave, Manila Philippines

GUTIERREZ, MAX, JR., lawyer; b. San Salvador, May 26, 1930; came to U.S., 1930, naturalized, 1959; s. Max J. and Elva (Sol) G.; m. Mary Juanita O'Hearn, Jan. 26, 1957; children:Michele M., Michael E., Paul F., William F., Laurelle M., Maxmillian J. AB, U. Calif., Berkeley, 1953; JD cum laude, U. San Francisco, 1959; LLM, Georgetown U., 1960. Bar: Calif. 1960. Assoc. firm Brobeck, Phleger & Harrison, San Francisco, 1960-67; mem. firm Brobeck, Phleger & Harrison, 1967—; lectr. U. San Francisco Sch. Law, 1963-72; dir. Dodge & Cox Stock Fund, Balanced Fund. Bd. dirs. Florence Crittenton Services. Served with AUS, 1953-55. Mem. ABA (council on real property, probate and trust law sect.), State Bar Calif. (family law com. 1967-69, chmn. 1969, chmn. probate and trust law com. 1973), Am. Bar Found., Am. Coll. Probate Counsel (regent 1987—), Internat. Acad. Estate and Trust Law (pres. 1978-80), St. Thomas More Soc., Phi Delta Phi, Sigma Chi. Republican. Office: Brobeck Phleger & Harrison Spear St Tower 1 Market Plaza San Francisco CA 94105

GUTIERREZ, RALPH, engineering educator; b. Los Angeles, Dec. 23, 1931; s. Jose and Antonia (Acosta) G.; m. Lorene Mae Kesler, Aug. 21, 1954; children: Dennie, Denise, Jolie, Ralph. BA in Vocat. Edn., Calif. State U., Los Angeles, 1972; student in community coll. adminstrn., Nova U.; student in human resource mgmt., Redlands U.; student in human resource devel., Chapman Coll. Coll. work study, fin. aids advisor Pasadena (Calif.) City Coll., 1971-73, coordinator coop. edn. and student placement services, 1973-78, coordinator, assoc. prof. coop. work experience edn., 1978-83, assoc. prof. engring. and tech., 1983—; cons. ednl. programs., mktg. and pub. relations; polit. cons. Hispanic candidates. Bd. dirs. Mid-Valley Mental Health, 1979—; mem. Cable TV Selection Adv. Com., El Monte Calif., 1980; mem. adv. com. Nat. Ctr. Vol. Action, 1976-80, Women's Equity Action League, 1976-80; vice pres. Alumni Assn. Roosevelt High Sch., Los Angeles, 1966—; ednl. liaison Am. GI Forum, 1982—; active Tournament of Roses Parade; trustee Rio Hondo Coll., Whittier, Calif., mem. adv. com. Mexican-Am. Cultural Inst.; trustee El Monte Union High Sch. Mem. Am. Legion, San Gabriel Valley Los Angeles Raiders Boosters (dir. mktg. and pub. relations). Lodge: Masons. Home: 10021 Brockway El Monte CA 91733 Office: Pasadena City Coll 1570 E Colo Blvd Pasadena CA 91106

GUTIERREZ-HERAS, JOAQUIN, composer, music educator; b. Oaxaca, Mex., Sept. 28, 1927; s. Joaquin and Eugenia (Heras) Gutierrez. Diploma in Composition, Julliard Sch. Music, 1961. Dir. Radio Universidad, Mexico City, 1966-70; head dept. music Nat. U., Mexico City, 1973; mus. analysis tchr. Conservatory of Music, Mexico City, 1969-70; composition Nat. Inst. Fine Arts, Mexico City, 1974-77. Composer of music for orchestra, chamber and choral ensembles, films and theatre. Grantee French Inst. Latin Am., 1952-53, Rockefeller Found., 1960-61. Mem. Soc. Authors and Composers Mexico. Home: Callejón de Negrete 11, Coyoacán 04330, Mexico

GUTIERREZ-MARULANDA, LUIS FERNANDO, corporate executive; b. Pereira, Risaralda, Colombia, Jan. 20, 1947; s. Gregorio and Lilia (Marulanda de) G.; m. Maria Teresa Sellarés, Aug. 9, 1969; children: Olga Lucia, Maria Fernanda. Ingeniero químico, U. del Valle, Cali, Colombia, 1968; MS, Cornell U., 1971. Asst. prof. U. del Valle, Cali, 1968-73; prodn. and fin. mgr. Cen. Castilla Ltd., Cali, 1971-81; econ. v.p. Fanalca S.A., Cali, 1981—; pres. C.I. Proinco Ltd., Cali, 1983—. Author: Financial Decisions under Inflation, 1985; contbr. articles to profl. jours. Bd. dirs. Columbian Inst. Superior Studies, Cali, 1983—, Inst. Coll. de Adminstrn., Cali, 1982—. Rockefeller Found. scholar, 1968-71. Mem. Cornell U. Alumni Orgn., Sugar Producers Assn. (bd. dirs. 1979-81). Mem. Liberal Party. Roman Catholic. Clubs: Colombia, Campestre (Cali). Home: Ave San Joaquin 08, Cali, Valle Colombia Office: Fanalca SA, Apartado 8066, Cali, Valle Colombia

GUTMAN, I. CYRUS, transportation consultant, business executive; b. Perth Amboy, N.J., Mar. 28, 1912; s. Leon and Jennie (Levine) G.; m. Mildred B. Largman, July 21, 1940; children: Harry L., Peggy Sheren, Richard J.S. BS in Econs., Johns Hopkins U., 1932. Dist. mgr. Motor Freight Express, Inc., Phila., 1933-40; v.p., treas., gen. mgr. Modern Transfer Co., Inc., Allentown, Pa., 1940-67, dir. nat. sales, 1967-70; v.p. Atlantic div. Nat. Resource Recovery Corp., 1982—; mem. labor panel Am. Arbitration Assn., 1980—; bd. dirs. Eastern Industries, Inc., Wescosville, Pa., 1967-76. Pres. Lehigh County Indsl. Devel. Corp., 1959-85, Lehigh's Econ. Advancement Project, Inc., 1960-85; chmn. Lehigh County Indsl. Devel. Authority, 1966-82; mem. adv. com. Central Pa. Teamsters Pension and Health and Welfare Funds, 1969-76; mem. nat. resources com., nat. alumni schs. com. Johns Hopkins; mem. Lehigh-Northampton Counties Joint Planning Commn., 1962-82; chmn. Allentown Sch. Dist. Authority, 1966-86; mem. Lehigh and Northampton Transp. Authority, 1972-74; chmn. Allentown Non-Partisan Com. for Local Govt.; mem. Eastern Conf. Joint Area Com.; assoc. mem. Nat. Jewish Welfare Bd.; hon. bd. mem. Allentown Jewish Community Ctr., 1986—; exec. com. Citizens for Lehigh County Progress, 1965—; chmn. central campaign planning com. Lehigh Valley Hosps., 1966-67; adv. com. Good Shepherd Workshop; adv. bd. Allentown citadel Salvation Army, treas., 1971-80; pres. bd. assocs. Muhlenberg Coll., v.p., 1971-73, pres. 1974-76; bd. assocs. Cedar Crest Coll., 1972—; gen. adv. com. Lehigh County Vocat.-Tech. Sch., Lehigh County Community Coll., 1977; mem. Lehigh County Rep. Exec. Com.; trustee Allentown Hosp., 1970-82, hon. trustee, 1982-87, hon. mem., 1987; hon. Lehigh Valley Hosp. Ctr., 1987—; trustee, Swain Sch., 1977-80; bd. dirs. Lehigh Valley Jr. Achievement, United Fund, Allentown, Jewish Fedn. Allentown, 1953-60, Wiley House, 1969-80; bd. dirs. Lehigh Valley Public TV, Sta. WLVT, 1980—, vice chmn., 1984—; past trustee Rabbi Louis M. Youngerman Found., Internat. Assn. Machinists Local 1099 Dist. Pension Plan, Phi Sigma Delta Found; hon. adv. bd. Lehigh Valley Assn. for Retarded Children, 1969-70; mem. adv. bd. Lehigh Valley Ctr. for Performing Arts, 1975-77. Recipient St. Patrick's Day award Lehigh Valley, 1961, Civic Service commendation Whitehall C. of C.; Golden Deeds award Allentown Exchange Club, 1972, Disting. Citizens Sales award Sales and Mktg. Execs., Allentown and Bethlehem, 1976, Outstanding Service award Lehigh Valley Traffic Club, 1978, citation Pa. Ho. of Reps., 1982, City of Allentown, 1982, Americanism award Anti-Defamation League and B'nai Brith, 1985, citation Assn. for Blind and Visually Impaired, 1985, citation Lehigh County Vocat. Tech. Sch., 1986; Jack Houlihan Community Vol. award Lehigh County United Way, 1985, Presdl. proclamation through Gov. Thornburgh, Pa., 1986; Cyrus Gutman Scholarship established by Lehigh County Bus. and Indsl. Community Johns Hopkins U., 1983; I. Cyrus Gutman Day proclaimed in honor Allentown, Bethlehem, Easton, Pa. Mem. Allentown C. of C. (Disting. Service award 1967, past bd. dirs.), Traffic and Transp. Assn. Pitts., Met. Traffic Assn. N.Y., Central Pa. Motor Carriers Assn. (v.p., exec. com.), Pa. Soc., Am. Trucking Assn. (gov. Regular Common Carrier Conf. 1968), Eastern Labor Adv. Assn. (v.p.), Hon. First Defenders, Johns Hopkins Alumni Assn. (past sec., past pres. Phila. area), Lehigh County Hist. Soc. (exec. com. 1968-71), Nat. Fedn. Temple Brotherhoods, Omicron Delta Kappa, Pi Delta Epsilon, Zeta Beta Tau. Clubs: Berkleigh Country (Kutztown, Pa.) (hon. mem., past pres.); Lehigh Valley (Allentown); Locust Midcity, Traffic and Transp., Traffic (Phila.); Traffic (Balt.); N.Y. Traffic (N.Y.C.), Livingston. Lodges: Masons, B'nai B'rith. Home and Office: 1824 Turner St Allentown PA 18104

GUTMAN, RICHARD EDWARD, lawyer; b. New Haven, Apr. 9, 1944; s. Samuel and Marjorie (Leo) G.; A.B., Harvard U., 1965; J.D., Columbia U., 1968; m. Jill Leslie Senft, June 8, 1969 (dec.); 1 son, Paul Senft; m. Rosann Seasonwein, Dec. 10, 1987. Admitted to N.Y. bar, 1969; asso. firm. Parker Chapin & Flattau, N.Y.C., 1968-72, Marshall Bratter Greene Allison & Tucker, N.Y.C., 1972-76, 78, Bartel Engelman & Fishman, N.Y.C., 1976-78; counsel Exxon Corp., N.Y.C., 1978—; pres., dir. 570 Park Ave Apts., Inc., N.Y.C. Mem. Fed. Regulation Securities Com. ABA, N.Y. State Bar Assn., (exec. com. 1983-86, securities regulation com. 1980—), Assn. Bar of City of N.Y. (securities regulation com. 1980-81, 83-86), N.A.M. (corporate fin. and mgmt. com.). Club: Harvard (admissions com. 1983-86, chmn. 1985-86, nom. com. 1986-87, bd. dirs. 1988—) (N.Y.C.). Home: 570 Park Ave New York NY 10021

GUTMAN, RICHARD MARTIN, lawyer; b. Chgo., Mar. 12, 1946; s. Raymond Tobias and Frieda (Garber) G.; m. Linda Ellen Fisher, June 14, 1987. BA cum laude, Harvard U., 1967; JD, U. Chgo., 1973. Bar: Oreg. 1973, Ill. 1974, U.S. Dist. Ct. (no. dist.) Ill. 1974, U.S. Ct. Appeals (7th cir.) 1977. Vol. Peace Corps, 1967-69; staff atty. ACLU Police Project, Chgo., 1973-74; sole practice, Chgo.; dir. Polit. Surveillance Litigation Project, Chgo., 1975—; investigator, writer Ralph Nader Congress project, Washington, 1972. Author: (with others) The Environment Committees, 1975; contbr. numerous articles to prof. jours. Recipient 5th Anniversary award Alliance to End Repression, Chgo., 1975, Legal Eagle award Ind. Voters Ill.-Ind. Precinct Orgn., Chgo., 1981, Award of Distinction, 1st Unitarian Ch., Chgo., 1982. Office: 407 S Dearborn St Room 455 Chicago IL 60605

GUTSTEIN, SOLOMON, lawyer; b. Newport, R.I., June 18, 1934; s. Morris Aaron and Goldie Leah (Nussbaum) G.; m. Carol Feinhandler, Sept. 3, 1961; children—Jon Eric, David Ethan, Daniel Ari, Joshua Aaron. A.B. with honors, U. Chgo., 1953, J.D., 1956. Bar: Ill. 1956, U.S. Dist. Ct. (no. dist.) Ill. 1957, U.S. Ct. Appeals (7th cir.) 1958, U.S. Ct. Appeals (5th cir.) 1971, U.S. Supreme Ct. 1980; Rabbi, 1955. Assoc., Schradzke, Gould & Ratner, Chgo., 1956-60; ptnr. firm Schwartz & Gutstein, Chgo., 1961-65, Gutstein & Cope, Chgo., 1968-72, Gutstein & Schwartz, Chgo., 1980-83, Gutstein & Sherwin, Chgo., 1983-85; spl. asst. atty. gen. State of Ill., 1968-69; lectr. bus. law U. Chgo. Grad. Sch. Bus., 1973-82; lectr. in field, real estate broker, Author: Illinois Real Estate, 2 vols., 1983, rev. ann. updates, 1984—; co-author: Construction Law in Illinois, annually 1980-84; contbr. chpt. to Commercial Real Estate Transactions, 1962-76. Assoc. editor U. Chgo. Law Rev., 1954-56; editorial adviser Basic Real Estate I, also Advanced Real Estate II, 1960s-70s., Analysis of the Book of Psalms, 1962; contbr. articles to profl. publs. Mem. Cook County Citizens Fee Rev. Com., 1965; alderman from 40th ward Chgo. City Council, 1975-79; mem. govt. affairs adv. com. Jewish Fedn., 1984—. Fuerstenberg scholar U. Chgo., 1950-56; Kosmerl fellow U. Chgo., 1953-56. Mem. Chgo. Bar Assn., Ill. State Bar Assn., Decalogue Soc. Lawyers (25 yr. cert. 1982). Democrat. Jewish. Lodge: B'nai B'rith. Office: 180 N LaSalle St Chicago IL 60601

GUTTENTAG, WERNER, publisher, librarian, bibliographer; b. Breslau, Germany, Feb. 6, 1920; came to Bolivia, 1939; s. Erich and Margarete (Tichauer) G.; m. Eva Mohr, July 28, 1950; children—Esteban, Carola, Ingrid, Petra. Owner, librarian Los Amigos del Libro, Cochabamba, Bolivia, 1945—; pub., pres. Los Amigos del Libro, La Paz, Bolivia, 1950—; bibliographer Biobibliografia Boliviana, Cochabamba, 1962—; pub. Bolivian Bio-Bibliography 25th Vol. Contbr. articles to various newspapers and mags. Decorated Verdienstkreuz (Germany), Condor De Los Andes (Bolivia); recipient meritious citizen award Municipality of Cochabamba, 1974, Orden de las Heroinas de la Coronilla, 1982, Premio de la Cultura, Fundacion Manuel Vocente Ballivian, La Paz, 1984, Torbio Medina award Salalm in the U. Princeton, 1985. Mem. Instituto Panamericano de Geografia e Historia Mex., C. of C. Cochabamba. Office: Los Amigos del Libro, Ave Heroinas 0 311, Casilla 450, Cochamba Bolivia

GUTTERMAN-REINFELD, DEBRA ELLEN, physician, consultant; b. N.Y.C., Nov. 13, 1948; d. George and Nettie (Liss) Gutterman; m. Stuart Glenn Reinfeld, June 20, 1982; children: Alan Jeffrey, Naomi Rebecca. B.S., R.N. magna cum laude, SUNY Downstate Med. Ctr., 1972; postgrad. U. Auton, Guadalajara Sch. Medicine (Mex.), 1973-75; M.D., Coll. Medicine and Dentistry N.J., 1977. Intern, Boston City Hosp., 1977-78; resident in medicine Maimonides Med. Ctr., Bklyn., 1978-79, 79-80, Mt. Sinai Med. Ctr., Miami Beach, Fla., 1982-83; fellow Jackson Meml. Hosp., Miami, Fla., 1980-82; internist, cons. infectious diseases, former chief dept. internal medicine, former assoc. med. dir. Maxicare/Health Am., Ft. Lauderdale, Fla.; med. dir. Humana/Health Am., Plantation, Fla., 1988—.

GUTTMAN, SAMUEL ARNOLD, psychoanalyst; b. N.Y.C., Sept. 13, 1914; s. Morris and Ida (Goldberger) G.; A.B., Cornell U., 1934, M.A., 1935, Ph.D., 1937, M.D., 1940; children—Elizabeth (Mrs. Bradley Sevin), Samuel Adam; m. Irene, 1978. Fellow Woods Hole Marine Biol. Lab., Cornell U., 1935-36; intern, Albert Einstein Med. Center, Phila., 1940-42; asst. resident neurologist Neurol. Inst. N.Y., 1942-43, chief resident neurologist, 1943-44; fellow Pa. Hosp. and Inst. Pa. Hosp., Phila., 1944-45; practice medicine specializing in psychoanalysis, Phila., 1945—, Wilkes-Barre, Pa., 1950-55, Pennington, N.J., 1955—; asst. neurologist Columbia Presbyn. Hosp., N.Y.C., 1942-44, Pa. Hosp., Phila., 1944-46; asst. neuropsychiatrist Jewish Hosp., Phila., 1944-47; psychiat. cons. Southwark Neighborhood Center, Phila., 1946-47; psychiat. cons. Shoemaker Sch., Elkins Park, Pa., 1947-48; dir. Child Guidance Center, Lakawanna County, Pa., 1947-55; psychiat. cons. Family Service, Wilkes-Barre, Pa., 1948-52; chief div. psychiatry and neurology Wilkes-Barre Gen. Hosp., 1948-55; psychiat. cons. Family Service, Scranton, Dunmore, Pa., 1948-55; asst. attending physician Jefferson Hosp., 1963-82; researcher neurophysiology Harvard Med. Sch., 1936; asst. physiology Cornell U. Med. Coll., 1934-37; asst. neurologist Coll. Physicians and Surgeons, Columbia U., 1942-44; sr. clin. assoc. Phila. Inst. Psychoanalysis, 1944-48; assoc. prof. clin. psychiatry Thomas Jefferson Med. Sch., 1962-67, prof. psychiatry and psychoanalysis, 1967-81, hon. prof. emeritus, 1981—; cons. dept. psychology U. Pa. Med. Sch., 1945-47, Wilkes Coll., Wilkes-Barre, Pa., 1948-55, Cleve. Psychoanalytic Inst., Cleve., 1968—; lectr. neurology Phila. Sch. Occupational Therapy, 1944-45, Phila. Assn. Psychoanalysis and Inst. Phila. Assn. Psychoanalysis, 1949-54; sr. clin. assoc., lectr. Phila. Inst. Psychoanalysis, 1948-49; exec. dir., trustee Center for Advanced Psychoanalytic Studies, Princeton, N.J., 1961—, chmn., 1975—; exec. sec., pres. bd. trustees Psychoanalytic Studies at Aspen, Colo., 1968-72, pres., 1972—. Diplomate Am. Psychoanalytic Assn. (mem. bd. profl. standards 1956-82). Mem. Internat. Psycho-Analytical Assn. (co-chmn. program com. internat. psychoanalytic congresses, 1969, 73), AMA, Am. Psychiat. Assn., Assn. Research in Nervous and Mental Disorders, AAAS, N.J. State Med. Soc., Pa., Phila. psychiat. socs., N.Y., N.J. acads. scis., Mercer County Component Med. Soc., Phila. Assn. Psychoanalysis (tng. analyst 1954—). Chief editor Bull. Phila. Assn. Psychoanalysis, 1950-59. Editorial bd. Psychoanalytic Quar., 1958-66; cons. editor Bull. Phila. Assn. Psychoanalysis, 1959-69. Contbr. articles to profl. jours. Home and Office: Hunter's Green Pennington NJ 08534

GUTWIRTH, JACQUES, anthropologist; b. Antwerp, Belgium, 1926. LittD, U. Paris, 1969. Dir. research Cen. Nat. Recherche Scientifique, Paris, 1982—; prof. anthropology Paris V, 1983—. Author: Vie Juive Traditionnelle, 1970, Les Judeo-Chretiens d'Aujourd'Hui, 1987, Chemins de la Ville, 1987. Mem. Assn. Francaise de Sociologie Religieuse (pres. 1981-83), Soc. d'Ethnologie Francaise (v.p. 1983-87). Home: 16 Ave Reille, 75014 Paris France Office: Lab Anthropologie, Urbaine Cen Nat Recherche Sci, Musee l'Homme, 75116 Paris France

GUY, EDWARD LEE, real estate investor; b. Garland, N.C., Oct. 28, 1937; s. Lee Livingston and Mary Susan (Johnson) G.; 1 child, Stacy Lee. BA, Catawba Coll., 1969. Adminstrv. asst. Cons. Services, Inc., Salisbury, N.C., 1969-71; owner, mgr. Inventory Services Co., Tampa, Fla., 1971-72; pres. Multi-Chek Systems, Inc., Tampa, 1972-77, Super Chek Systems, Inc., Tampa, 1977—. Served with U.S. Army, 1960-62. Recipient F. M. Knetsche award, 1967. Mem. Intertel, Mensa. Office: PO Box 262365 Tampa FL 33685

GUY, ERNEST THOMAS, association executive; b. Detroit, May 12, 1921; s. William G. and Anna (Utas) G.; BA, Mich. State U., 1943; postgrad. U. Ga., 1946, U. Mich., 1948; m. Bernice Louise Smith, Mar. 8, 1945 (dec.); children: E. Timothy, Cynthia Louise. State coordinator vets. tng. Ga. Dept. Edn., Atlanta, 1946-47; mgr. sta. WATL, Atlanta, 1947-48; program dir. sta. WKNX, Saginaw, Mich., 1948-50; pub. relations dir. Mich. Heart Assn., Detroit, 1950-53, exec. dir., 1953-58; exec. dir. Tex. Heart Assn., Houston, 1958-68, Chgo. Med. Soc., 1968-69, Calif. Dental Assn., San Francisco, 1969-73, So. Calif. Dental Assn., Los Angeles, 1972-73, Unified Calif. Dental Assn., 1973-74; exec. dir. Am. Soc. Clin. Hypnosis, Des Plaines, Ill., 1974-75; dir. meetings and travel Am. Bar Assn., Chgo., 1975-88, ETG Enterprises, Park Ridge, Ill., 1988—; v.p. sales Cen. U.S.A. Travel Planners, Inc., Park Ridge, 1988—; bd. dirs. Meeting Planners Internat.; mem. industry adv. bd. Meeting World, 1978-80. Mem. adv. com. Tex. Rehab. Assn. Faculty pub. health classes U. Mich., Ann Arbor, 1953-58; del. White House Conf. Edn., 1956; vice chmn. Fed. Service Campaign for Health Agys. in Tex., 1961-62; mem. governing council Soc. Heart Assns. Profl. Staff, 1959-62. Mem. Pres.'s Bicentennial Commn., 1976; Precinct worker Houston Republican Com., 1960-68; mem. fin. com. George Bush for Pres. Campaign, 1978-80. Served to capt. AUS, 1943-46. Co-recipient Blakeslee award, 1953; recipient award of merit Mich. Heart Assn., 1958, Merit award Tex. Heart Assn., 1968, commendation award Calif. Dental Assn., 1974. Certified assn. exec. 1st class, 1968; named one of 5 U.S. Grand Masters of Meeting Planning, Meetings and Conv. Mag., 1986. Mem. Am. Soc. Assn. Execs., Am. Pub. Relations Soc., Nat. Assn. Parliamentarians, Profl. Conv. Mgmt. Assn., Internat. Platform Assn., Am. Assn. Dental Editors, Nat. Pub. Relations Council, Nat. Assn. Exhibit Mgrs., U.S. Parachute Assn. Republican. Episcopalian (lay reader). Contbr. numerous articles to profl. publs. Home: 930 N Northwest Hwy #202 Park Ridge IL 60068 Office: ABA 750 N Lake Shore Dr Chicago IL 60611

GUY, LOUIS LEE, JR., environmental engineer; b. Norfolk, Va., Apr. 26, 1938; s. Louis Lee and Grace (Mayo) G.; m. Suzanne Penn West, Oct. 9, 1965; children: James Thornton, Louis Lee III, Francis West. BSCE, Va. Poly. Inst., 1959. Lic. profl. engr., Va., Md., Del., W.Va., N.C., D.C.; cert. sanitary engr. Design engr. Wiley & Wilson, Lynchburg, Va., 1962-66; civil engr. George, Miles & Buhr, Salisbury, Md., 1966-69; asst. mgr. tech. services Water Pollution Control Fedn., Washington, 1970-73; ptnr., sr. vp. Patton, Harris, Rust & Guy, Fairfax, Va., 1973-81; v.p., dir. engring. SCS Engrs., Inc., Reston, Va., 1981-83; ptnr. Guy & Davis, Burke, Va., 1983—; presdl. apointee bd. dirs. Nat. Inst. Bldg. Scis., treas., 1987—; chmn., vice chmn. Upper Occoquan Sewage Authority, Centreville, Va., 1984-85. Mem. State Water Study Commn., Richmond, 1977-82; chmn. citizens adv. com. Regional Task Force on Water Supply, Washington, 1980-82; mem. Fairfax County Rep. Com., 1986—; chmn. new ch. devel. Nat. Capital Presbytery, 1985-86. Served to 1st lt. U.S. Army, 1959-62. Recipient Citation of Merit award Fairfax Co. Fed. of Citizens Assns, 1981. Fellow ASCE; diplomate Am. Acad. Environ. Engrs. (pres. 1986-87); mem. NSPE (treas. 1975-80, pres. Ednl. Found. 1980-82, chmn. polit. action com. 1983-85, rep. dir. 1987—, named Young Engr. of Yr. 1974), Va. Soc. Profl. Engrs. (nat. dirs. 1984—, accreditation bd. for engring. and tech., pres.-elect 1988—, Engr. of Yr. 1978), Order of the Engr. (nat. chmn. 1987—), Am. Cons. Engrs. Council. Republican. Club: Cosmos (Washington). Home: 8330 Queen Elizabeth Blvd Annandale VA 22003 Office: Guy & Davis Cons Engrs 5200 Rolling Rd Burke VA 22015

GUYARD, MARIUS-FRANCOIS, educator; b. Paris, Mar. 18, 1921; s. Marius and Jeanne (Chabrillat) G.; m. Francoise Bordier, 1947; 4 children. D.èsL., Sorbonne, U. Paris. Prof., U. Athens (Greece), 1955-57; prof. Strasbourg U. (France), 1957-63, vice chancellor, 1970-76; cultural counsellor French embassy, U.K., 1963-65; prof. French lit. Sorbonne, U. Paris, 1965-67, 80—; vice chancellor U. Montpellier (France), 1967-69, U. Amiens, 1969-70, U. Lyon (France), 1976-80; chmn. Conf. des Recteurs Français, 1975-78; mem. Franco-Brit. Council, 1972—. Author: La Grande-Bretagne dans le roman francais, 1954; Recherches Claudéliennes, 1964; editions of Lamartine and Hugo; numerous contbns. to revs., critical anthologies. Decorated officier Lègion d'honneur, comdr. Ordre national du Mèrite, comdr. Ordre des Palmes academiques, chevalier des Arts et Lettres, (France), comdr. Orange-Nassau (Netherlands), officier Merite Italien.

GUYER, JOHN J., internist; b. Portland, Oreg., May 3, 1925; arrived in Thailand, 1952; s. Henry M. and Olive (Clark) G.; m. Betsy Rasmussen, Sept. 15, 1951; children: Janet Ellen, James Robert. BA, Reed Coll., 1946; MD, U. Oreg., 1948. Cert. Am. Bd. Internal Medicine. Intern. St. Luke's Hosp., Chgo., 1948-49, resident in internal medicine, 1949-50; resident in internal medicine Kennedy Vets. Adminstrn. Hosp., Memphis, 1950-51, Cleve. City Hosp., 1951-52; staff physician McCormick Hosp., Chiang Mai, Thailand, 1953-58, chief. med. service, 1958—, med. dir., 1986—; bd. dirs. VanSantvoord Hosp., Lampang, Thailand, Payap U., Chiang Mai, Chang Mai Internat. Sch. Med. missionary Presbyn. Ch., Louisville, Ky., 1952—. Fellow ACP, Royal Coll. Physicians (Thailand); mem. AMA (spl.), Med. Assn. Thailand, Christian Med. Soc. Lodge: Rotary (pres. Chiang Mai club 1980-81). Office: McCormick Hosp, PO Box 56, Chiang Mai 50000, Thailand

GUYER, JOHN PAUL, mechanical engineer; b. Sacramento, Feb. 12, 1941; s. Paul M. and Vivian (Mosher) G.; B.S., Stanford U., 1962; postgrad. McGeorge Law Sch., 1962-66; m. Judith M. Overholser, June 28, 1968; children—John Paul, Christopher Meador. Mech. engr., State of Calif., Sacramento, 1962-66; partner Guyer & Santin, Sacramento, 1967-75; pres. Guyer Santin, Inc., Sacramento, 1975—. Recipient Unit commendation Calif. Dept. Water Resources, 1972; Outstanding Service award, Calif. Soc. Profl. Engrs., 1969; Outstanding Jr. C. of C. award, Sacramento Jr. C. of C., 1967, others. Mem. Calif. Soc. Profl. Engrs. (v.p. 1969), Crocker Art Mus. Assn., Sacramento Symphony Assn., Stanford Alumni Assn., ASME, ASCE (chmn. land use com. 1984). Republican. Clubs: The Tennis, Univ., Stanford, Comstock, El Macero Country, Engrs. (pres. 1968). Home: 3478 Club House Dr El Macero CA 95618 Office: 917 7th St Sacramento CA 95814

GUYOT, JEAN, former archbishop of Toulouse; b. Bordeaux, France, July 7, 1905. Ordained priest Roman Catholic Ch., 1932; various offices in Bordeaux Diocese; titular bishop of Helenopolis, also coadjutor of Coutances, 1949; bishop of Coutances, 1950-66; archbishop of Toulouse, 1966-78; elevated to Sacred Coll. Cardinals, 1973; mem. de la Congrègation de Chargé et des Sèminqires. Decorated oficier Legion d 'Honneur; grande Croix Ordre de Malte. Address: 181 Rue Judaique, 33000 Bordeaux France Office: 26 Rue Perchepeinte, Toulouse France *

GUYTON, SAMUEL PERCY, lawyer; b. Jackson, Miss., Mar. 20, 1937; s. Earl Ellington and Eulalia (Reynolds) G.; m. Jean Preston, Oct. 11, 1959; children—Tamara Reynolds, William Preston, David Sage. B.A., Miss. State U., 1959; LL.B., U. Va., 1965. Bar: Colo. 1965, U.S. Dist. Ct. Colo. 1965, U.S. Tax Ct. 1977, U.S. Ct. Appeals (10th cir.) 1965, U.S. Ct. Appeals (5th cir.) 1981. Ptnr., Holland & Hart, Denver, 1965—; faculty Am. Law Inst. ABA, 1976-88. Sec., trustee Colo. Hist. Found., 1971-88, pres., 1983-87; trustee Music Assn. Aspen and Aspen Music Festival, 1980-88; precinct com. chmn. Democratic party, 1968-70. Served as capt. USAF, 1959-62. Fellow Am. Coll. Tax Counsel (mem. bd. of regents, vice-chmn.); mem. ABA (sect. taxation 1967-87, chmn. sect.'s com. on agr. 1980-82), Colo. Bar Assn. (tax council 1983-86, sec. 1983, chmn. 1985-86), Denver Bar Assn., Rocky Mountain Estate Planning Council, Greater Denver Tax Csls. Assn. (chmn. 1978), Law Club of Denver. Mem. United Ch. of Christ. Clubs: Am. Alpine (life), Colo. Mountain (life). Co-author: Cattle Owners Tax Manual, 1984, Supplement to Federal Taxation of Agriculture, 1983, Colorado Estate Planning Desk Book, 1984; contbr. articles to jours., mags.; bd. advs. Agrl. Law Jour., 1978-82; mem. editorial bd. Jour. Agrl. Tax and Law, 1983-87. Office: Holland & Hart PO Box 8749 Denver CO 80201

GUZMAN, LORETO DE GALINATO, physician, acupuncturist; b. Urdaneta, Pangasinan, The Philippines, June 14, 1918; s. Jose Cruz de Guzman and Fortunata (Galinato) de G. MD, U. St. Tomas, Manila, 1947. Resident physician Urdaneta Emergency Hosp., Pangasinan, 1948-50; mem. Med. Mission Sisters, Phila., 1950-53; resident physician Holy Family Hosp., Rawalpindi, Pakistan, 1953-54; doctor-in-charge St. Michael's Hosp., Mymensingh, Bangladesh, 1955-60; council mem. Philippine Found. for Med. Sisters, Batangas, The Philippines, 1961-65; pioneer Holy Family Hosp., Bongao, Tawi-Tawi, Sulu, 1966-75; coll. physician Mindanao State U., 1971-75; clinic physician East Asian Pastoral Inst., Ateneo de Manila, 1982-87; clinic physician project 4 Ephpheta, Inc. for the Blind, Quezon City, The Philippines, 1985—, in-charge nutrition program, 1986—. Recipient award for humanitarian services Govt. Tawi-Tawi, 1975, Tandang Sora award Bayaning Filipino Found., 1981, award for humanitarian service Bagumbayan Barangay Council, Quezon City, 1985. Mem. Philippine Med. Assn., Philippine Women's Med. Assn., Med. Mission Sisters. Club: PIMS Medic. Home: Med Mission Sisters Dist House, 30-F Collantes St Loyola Heights, Quezon City, Metro Manila Philippines Office: Ephpheta Inc, P Burgos St Project 4, Quezon City, Manila 3008, Philippines

GUZMAN STEIN, ALEJANDRO, computer and software company executive, presidential advisor; b. San Jose, Costa Rica, Aug. 2, 1953; s. Andres Vesalio and Maria Gabriela (Stein) G.; m. Sandra Balladares (div.); 1 child, Maria; m. Dorothy L. Davant; 1 child, Alejandro Edward. Student in agrl. engring., Escuola Agricola Panamericana, Tegucigalpa, Honduras, 1972; BS in Econs., Tex. Tech U., 1974; postgrad. in mktg., Harvard U., 1975; postgrad. in info. systems, Wang Inst., San Jose, 1983. Mgr. Grupo GISA, Liberia, Costa Rica, 1972-74; Latin Am. sales mgr. John Deere L.A., Rio de Janeiro, 1974; gen. consul Fgn. Relations Sec., Costa Rica Govt., Houston, 1972-76; mktg. mgr. Labs. Fide, San Jose, 1976—; pres. Control de Datos S.A., San Jose, 1978—; rep. Wang Labs. Inc., San Jose, 1979—; pres., chief exec. officer Wang de Costa Rica, San Jose, 1981—; pres. Computerland Ltd., 1986—; pres., chief exec. officer AGS Group, Panama and Costa Rica, 1983—; cons. Minister Agriculture, San Jose, 1979—; advisor Pres. of Costa Rica, San Jose, 1982-86, 87—; advisor in econs. Ministry of Planificacion, Costa Rica, 1986—. Logistics coordinator Partido Liberacion, Costa Rica, 1985-86; bd. dirs. Chamber of Reps., San Jose, 1982-83. Recipient Athlete recognition award World Peace U., 1985; named Outstanding Economist, SBA, 1973. Roman Catholic. Clubs: Costa Rica Country, Union. Lodge: Gran Logia Costa Rica. Office: The AGS Group SA, PO Box 4820, 1000 San Jose Costa Rica

GUZY, MARGUERITA LINNES, educator; b. Santa Monica, Calif., Nov. 19, 1938; d. Paul William Robert and Margarete (Rodowski) Linnes; m. Stephen Paul Guzy, Aug. 25, 1962 (div. 1968); 1 child, David Paul. AA, Santa Monica Coll., 1959; student, U. Mex., 1959-60; BA, UCLA, 1966, MA, 1973. Cert. secondary tchr., Calif. Tchr. Inglewood (Calif.) Unified Sch. Dist., 1967—, chmn. dept., 1972-82, mentor, tchr., 1985—; clin. instr. series Clin. Supervision Levels I, II, Ingelwood, 1986-87; tchr. Santa Monica Coll., 1975-76; cons. bilingual edn. Inglewood Unified Sch. Dist., 1975—; mem. ednl. teaching com. Monroe Jr. High Sch., 1985-86, staff devel. com., 1985—, chmn. drug and alcohol awareness com., 1986—. Author: Elementary Education: "Pygmalian in the Classroom", 1975, English Mechanics Workbook, 1986. Named Tchr. of Yr., 1973. Mem. NEA, Calif. Tchrs. Assn., Inglewood Tchrs. Assn. (local rep. 1971-72, tchr edn. and profl. services com. 1972-78), UCLA Alumnae Assn. (life), Prytanean Alumnae Assn. Republican. Club: Westside Alano (Los Angeles)(bd. dirs., treas. 1982-83). Lodge: Masons. Office: Monroe Jr High Sch 10711 10th Ave Inglewood CA 90303

GVOZDIC, GEORGE ANKA, radio, television producer; b. Yugoslavia, 1953; arrived in Switzerland, 1986; AA in Mech. Engring., High Tech. U., Novi Sad, Yugoslavia, 1974; BA in Theology, Bible Theol. Inst., Zagreb, Yugoslavia, 1977; BA in Radio and TV, So. Calif. Coll., 1984. Constructor Mashine Co., Novi Sad-Yu, 1978-86; producer AlphaVision AG, Emmetten, Switzerland, 1986—. Office: Alpha Vision AG, Postfach 98, 6376 Emmetten Switzerland

GWINN, ROBERT P., publishing executive; b. Anderson, Ind., June 30, 1907; s. Marshall and Margaret (Cather) G.; m. Nancy Flanders, Jan. 20, 1942; 1 child, Richard Herbert. PhD, U. Chgo., 1929. With Sunbeam Corp., Chgo., 1936-51, gen. sales mgr. elec. appliance div., 1951-52, v.p., dir., 1952-55, pres., chief exec. officer, 1955-71, chmn. bd., chief exec. officer, 1971-82, also bd. dirs.; chief exec. officer, chmn. bd. Ency. Brittanica, Inc., Chgo., 1973—; chmn. bd., chief exec. officer Ency. Britannica; chmn. bd. dirs. William Benton Found., Exploration, Inc., Riverside, Ill., Titan Oil Co., Riverside; bd. dirs. Continental Assurance Co., Continental Casualty Co., CNA/Fin. Corp., Inst. for Philos. Research, Max McGraw Wildlife Found.

Trustee Chgo. Zool. Soc., U. Chgo., The Orchestral Assn.; active overseers com. med. sch. and sch. dental medicine Harvard U.; Citizens adv. com., Mus. Contemporary Art. Mem. Elec. Mfrs. Club (hon.), Alpha Sigma Phi. Clubs: Comml. of Chgo., Casino (Chgo.), Execs., Soc. of Chgo., Internat. Food & Wine Soc. of Chgo., Mid-Am., U. of Chgo., Whitehall (Chgo.); Bird Key Yacht, U. of Sarasota; Confrerie des Chevaliers du Tastevin; Riverside Golf. Office: Ency Britannica Inc 310 S Michigan Ave Chicago IL 60604

GWYNN, ROBIN DAVID, historian, educator; b. Newtonmore, Scotland, June 5, 1942; arrived in New Zealand, 1969; s. John David and Grace Lawless (Lee) G.; m. Margaret Diana Rodger, Feb. 15, 1971; children: Jennifer Lee, David Morton. BA, Cambridge (Eng.) U., 1964, MA, 1968; PhD, U. London, 1976. Cert. Edn., Cambridge U., 1965. Part-time lectr. Trent Park Coll. Edn., London, 1965-66, U. London, 1966-67; lectr. Massey U., Palmerston North, New Zealand, 1969-76, sr. lectr., 1977-86, reader, 1987—; dir. "Huguenot Heritage", Brit. Nat. Tercentenary Commemoration, 1984-85. Author: Huguenot Heritage, 1985, Collecting New Zealand Stamps, 1988; editor: A Calendar of the Letter Books of the French Church of London 1643-59, 1979; contbr. articles to profl. jours. V.p., pres. Palmerston North Christian Home Trust, 1974-81. Leverhulme research fellow, 1984-85. Fellow Royal Philatelic Soc. New Zealand (v.p.), New Zealand Philatelic Fedn. (v.p.). Anglican. Office: Massey U, Palmerston North New Zealand

GWYNNE, VERNON DAVID, financial planning executive; b. Uniontown Pa., Oct. 24, 1927; s. Edgar Allen and Nell Marie Gwynne; m. Betty Ragan, July 5, 1950; children: Margaret, Janice, Anella. B.A., Wofford Coll., 1950; Cert. Coll. Fin. Planning, Denver, 1974. Pres. subsidiaries Western Union Corp., N.Y.C., 1965-73; sr. v.p. mktg. FSC Atlanta, 1973-77; exec. dir. Internat. Assn. Fin. Planners, Atlanta, 1978-82; pres. Source Internat., Dallas, 1982-87; pres. Fin. Services Exchange, Inc., 1985—; cons. ins. securities firms and banks, 1973. Served to comdr. USNR, 1945-87, ret. Mem. Internat. Assn. Fin. Planners (past exec. dir.), Inst. Cert. Fin. Planners. Republican. Methodist. Avocations: internat. travel, reading, boating. Office: Fin Services Exchange Inc 100 Decker Ct #220 Irving TX 75062

GYLL, JOHN SÖREN, manufacturing executive; b. Skorped, Sweden, Dec. 26, 1940; s. Josef and Gertrud Gyll; m. Lilly Margareta Hellman, 1974; 3 children. Mktg. dir., v.p. Rank-Xerox Corp., 1963-77; head Uddeholm-Sweden, 1977-79, exec. v.p., 1979-81, pres., chief exec. officer, 1981-84; pres., chief exec. officer Procordia AB, Stockholm, 1984—. Office: Procordia AB, PO Box 2278, 10317 Stockholm Sweden *

GYLLENHAMMAR, PEHR GUSTAF, business executive; b. Gothenburg, Sweden, Apr. 28, 1935; s. Pehr and Aina (Kaplan) G.; M.Law, U. Lund, 1959; M.D. honoris causa, U. Gothenburg, 1981; ThD honoris causa, Brunel U., 1987, ED honoris causa, Tech. U. Nova Scotia, 1988; m. Christina Engellau; children—Cecilia, Charlotte, Oscar, Sophie. With Ins. Co. Amphion, 1961-64; asst. adminstrv. mgr. Ins. Co. AB. Skandia, 1965-66, v.p., 1966, dep. mng. dir., 1968-70, mng. dir., chief exec., 1970; mng. dir., chief exec. officer AB Volvo, Gothenburg, 1971-83, chmn., chief exec. officer, 1983—, also dir.; dir. Skandinaviska Enskilda Banken, United Techs. Corp., Kissinger Assocs. Inc., Pearson plc, Reuters Holdings PLC; chmn. bd. Swedish Ships Mortgage Bank, Pharmacia AB; mem. Internat. advisory com. Chase Manhattan Bank. Mem. Fedn. Swedish Industries (dir.). Author 3 books. Office: AB Volvo, S-40508 Gothenburg Sweden

GYRA, FRANCIS JOSEPH, JR., artist, educator; b. Newport, R.I., Feb. 23, 1914; s. Frank Joseph and Ellen Frances (Mahoney) G.; m. Beatrice Anne Vincent, June 25, 1955; children—Maureen Ellen, Mary Frances, Barbara Ann, Michael Francis, Eileen Margaret, Paul Damian, Katherine Mary, Theresa Louise. Grad., R.I. Sch. Design, 1935; student Parsons Sch. Design, Paris, 1935, Italian Research Sch. of Parsons Sch. Design, 1937, Brighton Coll. Art (Eng.), 1945, 48, U. Hawaii, 1951, Froebel Inst. (Roehampton, Eng.), 1953, McNeese State Coll., 1956; B.S., Keene Tchrs. Coll., 1962. Dir., Gyra Sch. Art, Newport, R.I., 1938-39, Gyra Sch. Art, Woodstock (Vt.) Community Recreation Center, 1947, 49; supr. art edn. Woodstock (Vt.) Elem. Sch., Union High and Rural Schs., 1949-69; art tchr. Woodstock Elem. Sch., 1969-84; art tchr. Glyncoed Secondary Modern Sch., Ebbw Vale, Wales, Gt. Brit., 1952-53; exhibited group shows: Chgo. Art Inst., Pa. Acad. Fine Arts, Mpls. Inst. Arts, Toledo Mus. Art, Milw. Art Inst., Meml. Art Gallery, Carnegie Inst., Phila. Art Alliance, Providence Art Mus.; exhibited one-man shows: Art Assn. Newport, Washington Arts Club, Rundell Gallery, Parsons Sch. Design Gallery, N.Y.C., Robert C. Vose Gallery, L.D.M. Sweet Meml., Portland, Maine, Aquinas Jr. Coll., 1963, 64, Beaux Arts Gallery, Scranton, Pa., Dorado Beach Hotel Gallery, P.R., Chaffee Art Mus., Rutland Vt.; represented in collections at Providence Art Mus., Vanderbilt U., Nashville, Checkwood, Nashville Mcpl. Gallery, Nashville; dir. art workshops Vt. State Dept. Edn., 1954-56, 58-62; faculty advisor in art and art edn., Aquinas Jr. Coll., Nashville, 1963; mem. design review bd., Woodstock, 1985—. Served with U.S. Army, 1942-46. Decorated Bronze Star; Fulbright fellow, 1952; named hon. citizen of Nashville Davidson County, 1964; honorary Rotarian, Woodstock Rotary Club, 1972; Outstanding Vt. Tchr. of Yr. for Windsor Central Supervisory Union, 1982; State of Vt. Tchr. of Yr., 1983—; Award of Merit for disting. services to the Arts in State Vt., Vt. Council on the Arts, 1969; New Eng. Art Edn. Conf. award for Vt., 1983; Recognition award, Nat. Endowment for Arts, 1980; Eva Gebhard-Gourgaud grantee, 1963-68, Eva Gebhard Gourgaud grantee, 1973-74. Mem. Vt. Art Tchrs. Assn. (award 1984), So. Vt. Artists Assn. Roman Catholic. Club: Red Carpet (Nashville). Address: 6 Linden Hill Box 540 Woodstock VT 05091

HAACK, RICHARD WILSON, police officer; b. Chgo., July 7, 1935; s. Arthur Frank and Mildred Ann (Meyer) H.; m. Ruth Marie Tietz, May 27, 1972; children—Laura Marie, Karl Richard. Grad., Cook County (Ill.) Sheriff's Police Acad., 1967; A.S., Triton Coll., 1973; cert. Chgo. Police Acad., 1974; B.A., Lewis U., 1975; M.A., Northeastern Ill. U., 1979; B.S. in Bus. Adminstrn., Elmhurst Coll., 1982. Shipping clk. Am. Furniture Mart, Chgo., 1955-60; quality control insp. Nat. Can Co., Chgo., 1961-67; police officer Northlake Police Dept. (Ill.), 1967—, watch comdr. patrol div., 1978-85, dept. chief of police, 1986—; realtor Internat. Realty World-Norton & Assocs., 1984-87. Recipient John Edgar Hoover Meml. Gold medal, 1987. Mem. Bill Bruce fundraising com. Aid Assn. Luths., Christ Evangelical Luth. Ch., Northlake, 1981-82, mem. Gala Variety Show, 1982, chmn. evang. bd., 1981-85, ch. rep. Internat. Luth. Laymen's League, 1984—, pub. relations dir., usher, 1973-85, dir. Project Compassion, 1983-85; ombudsman No. Ill. dist. Luth. Ch.-Mo. Synod, 1984-85; choir Apostles Luth. Ch., 1985-87, Redeemer Luth. Ch. usher, mem. Men's Club, 1987—; dir., emcee German-Am. Police Assn. Oktoberfest, 1980—, chmn. entertainment, 1984—; coach Northlake Little League baseball team, 1985. Served with USMC, 1952-55, Korea, with res. 1955-60. Recipient numerous letters of commendation, competitive shooting awards. Mem. Ill. Police Assn., Fraternal Order Police (sec.-treas. Perri-Nagle Meml. Lodge 18, 1977-85), St. Jude Police League, Nat. Police Officers Assn., Internat. Police Assn. (life), German/Am. Police Assn. (bd. dirs. 1980—), Combined Counties Police Assn., Ill. Juvenile Officers Assn., Emerald Soc. Ill. Irish/Am. Police Assn., Northeastern Ill. U. Alumni Assn. (bd. dirs. 1980-86), Am. Polit. Sci. Assn., Nat. Rifle Assn., Schwaben Verein, N.W. Real Estate Bd., Leyden Real Estate Bd. (inner circle 1984-87), Internat. Platform Assn., Realtors Polit. Action Com. Ill. (inner circle 1984-87), Am. Legion. Republican. Club: Die Hard Cub Fans. Lodge: Moose. Contbr. law enforcement articles to profl. publs.; author Ency. Am. Judiciary. Home: 244 E Palmer Ave Northlake IL 60164 Office: 55 E North Ave Northlake IL 60164

HAAK, ALEX JOHAN HENRI, architect, educator; b. Haarlem, The Netherlands, Feb. 9, 1930; s. Willem Adriaan and Elisabeth Wilhemina Hendrika (Ten Hooven) H. Engr., U. Tech., Delft, 1957; M.A., Harvard U., 1958. Dir. Architektenburo Haak, Delft, 1960—; lectr. interior design U. Tech., Delft, 1960-79, prof. interior design, 1980—; guest lectr. Ball State U., 1965, Birmingham Poly. (Eng.), 1974—; advisor archtl. firms. Author: Mens en Maat, 1980. Served to lt. Netherlands Royal Engrs., 1959-60. Hon. fellow AIA; mem. Alliance of Dutch Architects. Roman Catholic. Lodge: Rotary. Office: Architektenburo Haak bna bv, Oude Delft 159, 2611 HA Delft The Netherlands

HAAKONSSEN, KNUD, philosophical historian; b. Tingsteud, Falster, Denmark, July 9, 1947; arrived in Australia, 1976; s. Helmer Daniel and Laura Eline (Marquardsen) H.; m. Lis Sørensen, June 26, 1968 (div. 1986); children: Eric Christoph; m. Lisbeth Mary Gurholt, Jan. 27, 1987. MA, U. Copenhagen, 1972; PhD, U. Edinburgh, Scotland, 1978. Tutor U. Copenhagen, 1969-70; part-time lectr. Folkeuniv., Copenhagen, 1970-73; sr. tutor, warden Monash U., Melbourne, Australia, 1976-79; lectr. Victoria U. of Wellington, New Zealand, 1979-82; vis. fellow Australian Nat. U., Canberra, 1980-81, research fellow then sr. research fellow, 1982—; vis. prof. U. New Brunswick, Can., 1984; vis. fellow U. Aarhus, Denmark, 1985, U. Edinburgh, 1986. Author: The Science of a Legislator, 1981, Thomas Reid's Practical Ethics, 1988; contbr. articles to profl. jours. Canberra rep. Dansk Samvirke, Copenhagen, 1984—. Office: Australian Nat U, PO Box 4, 2601 Canberra Australia

HAAR, ANA MARIA FERNÁNDEZ, advertising/public relations executive; b. Oriente Province, Cuba, Mar. 25, 1951; came to U.S., 1960, naturalized, 1970; d. Gilberto and Esmeralda Emiliana (Díaz) Fernández. Grad. Miami Dade Community Coll., 1971; student Barry Coll., 1972-78. Adminstrv. asst. thru asst. v.p. nat. accounts Flagship Bank, Miami Beach, Fla., 1971-77; v.p. comml. lending Jefferson Nat. Bank, Miami Beach, 1977-78; pres. IAC Advt. Group, Miami, 1978—; instr. Miami Dade Community Coll. Women in Mgmt. Program, 1980-81; hostess Sta. WPBT Program Viva. Mem. Dade County Commn. on Status of Women, 1979-82; chmn. Econ. Devel. Task Force of Commn. on Status of Women, 1979-82; bd. dirs. Downtown Miami Bus. Assn., 1979-82, Fla. Counseling Services, Miami; Internat. Ctr. of Fla., chmn. healthcare com.; mem. Dist. Export Council; hostess (program) Viva, WPBT-TV; mem. community Services Cedars Med. Ctr. Recipient Gran Orden Martiana of Cuban Lyceum for excellence in community service, 1976, Up and Comers award South Fla. Bus. Jour., 1988. Mem. Advt. Fedn. Greater Miami, Greater Miami Advt. Fedn. (bd. dirs.), Asociación de Publicitarios Latino-Americanos (v.p.), Miami Beach C. of C. (hon. life), Greater Miami C. of C., Hispanic Heritage Festival Com., Home: 2451 Brickell Ave Miami FL 33129 Office: 2725 SW 3d Ave Miami FL 33129

HAAS, DIANE MARGARET, insurance company executive; b. Surrey, Eng., Nov. 26, 1944; arrived in Can., 1946; d. Carl and Mabel (Brine) Roussie; m. Douglas Earl Mann, Sept. 5, 1963 (div. 1970); m. Lawrance James Haas, July 3, 1971; 1 child, Casandra Marie. Matriculation, Beck Collegiate, London, Ont., Can., 1961. Various clerical and supervisory positions London (Ont.) Life Ins. Co., 1961-79, human resource cons., 1979-80, compensation mgr., 1980-82, mgr. product devel., 1982-85, market mgr., 1985-86, dir. ops. improvement, 1986-88; dir. individual bus. 1988—; bd. dirs. Big Sisters, London. Chmn. comml. div. United Way, London, 1987. Fellow Life Mgmt. Inst., Life Office Mgmt. Assn. Club: London Women's Network. Home: RR #4, Denfield, ON Canada N0M 1P0 Office: London Life Ins Co, 255 Dufferin Ave, London, ON Canada N6A 4K1

HAAS, EDWARD LEE, accounting firm executive; b. Camden, N.J., Nov. 9, 1935; s. Edward David and Mildred (Wynne) H.; m. Maryann Lind, Dec. 27, 1958; children: John Eric, Gretchen Lind. B.A., LaSalle U., 1958; postgrad., Temple U., 1960—. Mgr. systems devel. RCA Corp., Cherry Hill, N.J., 1966-71; mgr. computer tech. services Gencorp, Akron, Ohio, 1971-74; sr. mgr. computer applications research and devel. Ernst & Whinney, Cleve., 1974-75; dir. nat. systems group Ernst & Whinney, 1976-77, nat. dir. data processing and software products, 1977, nat. ptnr., 1978—, cons. ptnr., 1983—. Served to 1st lt., arty. U.S. Army, 1958-59. Mem. Data Processing Mgmt. Assn., Assn. Systems Mgmt., Assn. of Inst. for Cert. Computer Profls. Republican. Roman Catholic. Clubs: Phila. Country, Union League of Phila., Hist. Soc. Pa., Phila. Drama Guild, Cotillion Soc. Cleve. Office: Ernst & Whinney 1500 Market St Suite 2900 Philadelphia PA 19102

HAAS, ELEANOR (MRS. PETER RALPH HAAS), business development consultant; b. Jersey City, Mar. 12, 1932; d. Nicholas Mark and Eleanor (Cochran) Alter de Csanytelek; BA, Smith Coll., 1953; cert. N.Y. Sch. Interior Design, 1960; m. Peter Ralph Haas, Oct. 22, 1966. Exec. sec. MCA Artists, Ltd., N.Y.C., 1954-56; exec. sec. Young & Rubicam, Inc., N.Y.C., 1956-58; exec. sec. J. Walter Thompson Co., N.Y.C., 1958-59; exec. sec. Stanford Research Inst., N.Y.C., 1959, Deafness Research Found., N.Y.C., 1960, Earl Newsom & Co., N.Y.C., 1961-65; account exec. Ruder & Finn, Inc., N.Y.C., 1965-68; founder, pres. The Haas Group, Inc., N.Y.C., 1968-87; founder, pres. HTL Ventures, Inc., N.Y.C., 1986—; adj. asso. prof. dept. journalism N.Y. U., 1980-83, lectr. Sch. Continuing Edn., 1981-83. Mem. Info. Industry Assn., Am. Mktg. Assn., Nat. Acad. TV Arts and Scis., Electronic Banking Econs. Soc., Advt. Women N.Y., Hajji Baba Club. Office: HTL Ventures Inc 59 E 54th St New York NY 10022

HAAS, GILBERT ALAIN, physician; b. Paris, Aug. 20, 1937; s. Claude Raymond and Juliette-Rose (Richner) H.; Luna-Olga, Mar. 14, 1946; 1 child, Olivier. Student, Med. U. Paris, 1958-66, MD, 1972. Extern Paris Hosp., intern; with The Am. Hosp., Paris; pvt. practice specializing in internal, forensic medicine Paris. Served as lt. with French Army. Home and Office: 60 Rue Saint-Andre des Arts, 75006 Paris France

HAAS, MARC, industrial executive; b. Cin., Mar. 16, 1908; s. Marc and Alice (White) H.; m. Helen Hotze, Feb. 3, 1951. Grad., Horace Mann Sch., 1925, Princeton U., 1929. Ptnr. Emanuel & Co., mems. N.Y. Stock Exchange, 1933-42; dept. dir. Office Def. Transp., Washington, 1942-45; assoc. Allen & Co., N.Y.C., 1945-55; pres. Am. Diversified Enterprises, Inc. and subs., 1955—; dir. Cave Laurent Perrier. Named Knight Order of St. John. Episcopalian (warden). Club: Princeton (N.Y.C.). Home: 14 E 75th St New York NY 10021 Office: 711 Fifth Ave New York NY 10022

HAAS, MIRIAM LEVIEN, sculptor, civic worker; b. N.Y.C., Sept. 21, 1921; d. Maurice Flexner and Louisa (Davis) Levien; m. Raymond S. Robinson, June 2, 1940 (div. Mar. 1962); children: Donald Alan, Barbara Ellen Schwartz, James Alfred; m. Adrian Lawrence Haas, Apr. 29, 1962 (dec. Nov. 1984). Student, Art Students League, N.Y.C., 1938-39, Elaine Journet Studio, New Rochelle, N.Y., 1945-47, Westchester County Ctr. Art Studios, White Plains, N.Y., 1968-70, 78-79, Art Life Craft Studios, North White Plains, N.Y., 1982—. Exec. sec. to sr. v.p. fin. Flinkote Co., White Plains, 1969-77; profl. fund raiser United Jewish Appeal Fedn. Joint Campaign, Hartsdale, N.Y., 1977-81; mounted NASA exhibit at Sinai Temple, Mt. Vernon, N.Y., 1966. Exhibited at Nelson Rockefeller Collection, N.Y.C., 1984; exhibited in group shows at Va. Mus. Fine Arts, Richmond, 1936, Met. Mus. Art, N.Y.C., 1939, Cork Gallery of Avery Fisher Hall-Lincoln Ctr., 1984, 87, Lever House, N.Y.C., 1984, 88; represented in permanent collections Calif., Fla., Ill., N.Y., N.J. and Va.; pres., producer Theatre Workshop, Mt. Vernon, N.Y., 1956-61; stage mgr. Philharm. Symphony Westchester, Inc., 1979—, v.p., bd. dirs., 1985—. Chmn. Interfaith Inst., Sinai Temple, Mt. Vernon, 1968-69; nat. chmn. cancer service fundraising United Order True Sisters, Inc., N.Y.C., 1957-59. Recipient numerous art awards. Mem. Mamaroneck Artists Guild (v.p., chmn. fund raising 1982-84, bd. dirs. 1982—), Women and Arts Westchester (bd. dirs. 1982—, chmn. nat. open juried show awards 1984-87—, chmn. nominating com. 1986-87, membership sculptor juror 1987—), Art Life Guild (pres. 1986—), N.Y. Artists Equity Assn., Internat. Platform Assn. Republican. Club: Woodlands Golf (tournament chmn. 1985). Avocations: golf, bridge, reading, music. Home: 100B High Point Dr Hartsdale NY 10530

HAAS, PAUL RAYMOND, petroleum company executive; b. Kingston, N.Y., Mar. 10, 1915; s. Frederick J. and Amanda (Lange) H.; m. Mary F. Diedrick, Aug. 30, 1936; children: Rheta Marie, Raymond Paul, Rene Marie. A.B., Rider Coll., 1934, LL.D., 1976. C.P.A., Tex. Acct. Arthur Andersen & Co. (C.P.A.s), N.Y.C. and Houston, 1934-41; with La Gloria Oil & Gas Co., Corpus Christi, Tex., 1941-59; v.p., treas., dir. La Gloria Oil & Gas Co., 1947-59; adminstrv. v.p. Tex. Eastern Transmission Corp., Houston, 1958-59; pres., chmn. bd. Prado Oil & Gas Co., 1959-66, Wiltex Corp., 1950-65, Garland Co., 1956-65, Citronelle Oil & Gas Co., 1967-69, Corpus Christi Oil and Gas Co., 1968—, Corpus Christi Exploration Co., 1976—; ltd. partner Salomon Bros., 1973-81; dir. Corpus Christi Nat. Bank, oil and gas operator, 1959—. Trustee Corpus Christi Ind. Sch. Dist., 1951-58, pres., 1956-58; mem. Tex. Bd. Edn., 1962-72, vice chmn., 1970-72; mem. Gov.'s Com. Edn., 1966-69; Trustee Paul and Mary Haas Found., 1954—, Robert T. Wilson Found., 1954-72, Rider Coll., 1959-67, Moody Found., 1966-73, Found. Center, 1970-75, Council on Founds., 1970-76, Commn. on Philanthropy and Pub. Needs, 1973-75, Univ. Cancer Found. M.D. Anderson Hosp. and Tumor Inst., 1975—. Presbyn. (elder). Home: 4500 Ocean Dr Apt 9A Corpus Christi TX 78412 Office: PO Box 2928 Corpus Christi TX 78403

HAAS, RUTH SHERWOOD, librarian; b. Peoria, Ill., Nov. 28, 1937; d. Abijah Minor and Elizabeth Ida (Krumpe) Sherwood; m. Howard Wendell Dillon, July 27, 1957 (div.); children—Maureen Rachel, Jason Giles; m. 2d, Howard Clyde Haas, May 28, 1971. B.A., Knox Coll., 1959; M.S. in Library Sci., Ind. U., 1961. Adminstrv. asst. Ind. U. div. library sci., Bloomington, 1960-61; cataloguer Harvard Coll. Library, Cambridge, Mass., 1965-68, asst. head, sr. cataloger CONSER office, 1981—; reference librarian Robbins Library, Arlington, Mass., 1976-81. Recipient Lawrence Latin prize Knox Coll., Galesburg, Ill., 1959; Mem. ALA (resources and tech. services div.), Soc. Scribes and Illuminators, Beta Phi Mu. Methodist. Home: 140 Pleasant St Arlington MA 02174 Office: Harvard U Widener Library Cambridge MA 02138

HAAS, VINTON BENJAMIN, JR., electrical engineering educator; b. Terre Haute, Ind., Aug. 30, 1923; s. Vinton Benjamin and Mayme Catherine (Hartzler) H.; m. Jeanne Reak, Mar. 25, 1944; children—Catherine Elizabeth (Mrs. David Francis Bean), Vinton Benjamin III, Douglas Francis, Marjorie Ellen (Mrs. John E. Kalliongis). B.S., Rose Poly. Inst., 1943; M.S., Mass. Inst. Tech., 1949, Sc.D., 1956. Test engr. Gen. Electric Co., 1946-47; instr. Mass. Inst. Tech., 1947-49, 53-56; asst. prof. N.D. State Coll., 1949-50; asst. prof. U. Conn., 1950-53, assoc. prof., 1956, prof., 1957-79, prof. emeritus, sr. lectr., 1979—; head elec. engring. dept., 1968-74; vis. prof. Imperial Coll., U. London, 1963, 78, M.I.T., 1970; dir. research project IBM Corp., 1961-63. Served with C.E. AUS, 1943-46. Mem. I.E.E.E., Am. Soc. Engring. Edn., Sigma Xi, Tau Beta Pi, Eta Kappa Nu. Home: 180 Puddin Ln Mansfield Center CT 06250

HAASE, AXEL, physicist; b. Hof, Bavaria, Fed. Republic Germany, Apr. 6, 1952. Diploma, U. Giessen, Fed. Republic Germany, 1977, PhD, 1980; Hon. degree, U. Frankfurt, Fed. Republic Germany, 1987. Research Max Planck Inst., Goettingen, Fed. Republic Germany, 1977-87, Heisenberg fellow, 1987—. Contbr. numerous articles on magnetic resonance in biol. material to profl. jours. Office: Max Planck Inst Biophys Chem, PO Box 2841, D-3400 Goettingen Federal Republic of Germany

HAASE, WILLIAM EDWARD, professional baseball executive; b. Highland Park, Mich., Dec. 26, 1943; s. Byron C. and Vera Ethel (Techow) H.; m. Sandra Lee Berg, Aug. 24, 1974; 1 child, John William. B.B.A., Western Mich. U. Sr. acct. Copper & Brass Sales, Inc., Detroit, 1971-75; auditor Detroit Baseball Club, 1975-76, bus. mgr., 1976-78, v.p. ops., 1978-83, exec. v.p., chief operating officer, 1983—. Served with USMC, 1963-66. Mem. Western Mich. U. Vets. Assn. (pres. 1970-71), VFW, Western Mich. U. Alumni Assn. Lodges: Masons; Shriners. Office: Detroit Baseball Club 2121 Trumbull St Detroit MI 48216

HAASE, WILLIAM XAVIER, lawyer; b. Cleve., Jan. 1, 1926; s. William Herman and Mary Veronica (McGurren) H.; m. Shirley Rickert, July 7, 1951 (div.); children—William Warren, Nancy Jane, Christian Douglas. A.B., Kent State U., 1949; J.D., Case Western Res. U., 1951. Bar: Ohio, U.S. Dist. Ct., Ohio. Assoc. Griswold and Leeper, Cleve., 1951-59; ptnr. Ford, Whitney & Haase, Cleve., 1960-75, Haase & Dempsey, Cleve., 1975-79, Arter & Hadden, Cleve., 1979—; dir. Reliable Spring and Wire, Cleve. Contbr. articles to profl. jours. Bd. dirs. Cleve. Suburban YMCA, 1968; trustee Cleve. Legal Aid Soc., 1971; law sch. del. Case Western Res. U., Cleve., 1977-78, vis. com. bd. overseers, 1978-80. Served with USN, 1944-46. Mem. ABA, Ohio Bar Assn. (vice-chmn. com. 1986-87, chmn. 1988—), Am. Arbitration Assn., Cleve. Bar Assn. (chmn. com. 1983-84), Newcomen Soc. N.Am., Case Western Res. U. Alumni Assn. (pres. 1972-73). Republican. Unitarian. Clubs: Union, City (Cleve.). Home: 12700 Lake Rd Apt #1103 Lakewood OH 44107 Office: Arter & Hadden 1100 Huntington Bldg Cleveland OH 44115

HAASS, ERWIN HERMAN, lawyer; b. Detroit, Feb. 18, 1904; s. Otto C. and Minnie (Peters) H.; m. Virginia Allmand, Oct. 5, 1937; children: Frederick, Robert, Stephen, Susan, Sandra. A.B., U. Mich., 1925, J.D., 1927. Bar: Mich. bar 1927. Asso. Race, Haass & Allen, Detroit, 1927-30; partner Hitt, Brewer & Haass, Detroit, 1930-41, Haass, Lungershausen, Frohlich & Lawrence, and predecessors, Detroit, 1941-77; of counsel Dickinson, Wright, Moon, VanDusen and Freeman, Detroit, 1977—; cons. dir. First Union Nat. Bank. Fla., North Broward. Served to lt. col. AUS, 1942-46. Clubs: Country, Detroit, Boat, Detroit Athletic (Detroit); Grosse Pointe (Detroit); Royal Palm Yacht and Country (Boca Raton, Fla.). Home: 991 Hillsboro Beach Pompano Beach FL 33062 also: 84 Stephens Rd Grosse Pointe Farms MI 48236 Office: PO Box 2795 Pompano Beach FL 33072 also: 800 First Nat Bldg Detroit MI 48226

HAAVELSRUD, MAGNUS, educator, researcher; b. Fagernes, Norway, Apr. 24, 1940; s. Martin and Marit Ranheim H.; m. Anne Lise Nordbrond, Dec. 2, 1967; 1 child, Hans Ola. Cand. polit., U. Oslo, 1969; PhD, U. Wash., 1970. Lectr. U. Wash., Seattle, 1970-71; assoc. sch. program Inst. for World Order, N.Y.C., 1972-73; assoc. prof. Inst. of Social Sci., U. Tromso, Norway, 1974—; Carl von Ossietzky guest prof. German Council for Peace and Conflict Research, Bonn, W.Ger., 1978-79; program chairperson World Conf. on Edn., U. Keele, U.K., 1974. Author: Foundations of Peace Learning, 1986, Education and Development Towards Peace, 1986. Editor: Education for Peace, 1975; Approaching Disarmament Education, 1981. Contbr. articles to profl. jours. Mem. Internat. Peace Research Assn. (chairperson Peace Edn. Commn. 1975-79). Home: Malselvgt 19, 9000 Tromso Norway Office: Univ Tromso, 9000 Tromso Norway

HABAKKUK, JOHN HROTHGAR, economic historian; b. Barry, S. Wales, U.K., May 13, 1915; s. Evan Guest and Anne (Bowen) H.; M.A., St. John's Coll., Cambridge U., 1940; m. Mary Elizabeth Richards, Aug. 8, 1948; children—David, Alison, Kate, Lucy. Fellow, Pembroke Coll., Cambridge U., 1938-50, univ. lectr. Faculty Econs. and Politics, 1946-50; vis. prof. Harvard U., 1954-55, U. Calif., Berkeley, 1962-63; prof. econ. history, fellow All Souls Coll., Oxford U., 1950-67, prin. Jesus Coll., 1968-84, vice chancellor univ., 1973-77; pres. Univ. Coll., Swansea, 1975-84; trustee Rhodes Scholarships, 1977-86; mem. Adv. Council Public Records, 1958-70, Social Sci. Research Council, 1967-71, Royal Hist. Namuscripts Commn., 1977—. Chmn. Oxfordshire Health Authority, 1982-84. Created knight bachelor, 1976; hon. fellow Pembroke and St. John's colls., Cambridge U. Fellow Brit. Acad.; mem. Royal Hist. Soc. (pres. 1977-80). Author: American and British Technology in the 19th Century, 1962; Population Growth and Economic Development since 1750, 1970; co-editor: Economic History Review, 1950-60, Cambridge Economic History, Vol. VI, 1965. Address: 28 Cunliffe Close, Oxford OX2 7BL, England also: Jesus Coll, Oxford OX1 3DW, England

HABEL, FRITZ PETER, electronics company executive; b. Bruenn, Moravia, Czechoslovakia, Aug. 31, 1931; came to Ger., 1939; s. Josef and Brunhilde (Baschny) H.; m. Charlotte Heimann, Mar. 24, 1956; children—Susanne, Barbara. M.A. in Econs., U. Muenchen, 1955, Ph.D. in History, 1966. With Siemens AG, Muenchen, 1955—, dir. (sr.), 1984—. Author: Key to the Balance Sheet, 1974; Dokumente Zur Sudetenfrage, 1984. Contbr. articles to profl. jours. i.a. delegate, World Assembly of Youth, Gen. Assembly, Brussels, Belgium, 1960-66; exec. com. various German expelle orgns., 1953—. Recipient Bundesverdienstkreuz, Pres. Fed. Republic Germany, 1970; Foerderpreis fuer Wissenschaft, Ministerpresident, State of Bavaria, 1972. Roman Catholic. Office: Siemens AG N GGA, Postfach 700072, D8000 Munich 70 Federal Republic of Germany

HABER, JOYCE, writer, columnist; b. N.Y.C., Dec. 28, 1932; d. John Sanford and Lucille (Buckmaster) H.; m. Douglas S. Cramer, Jr., 1966 (div. 1974); children: Douglas S. III, Courtney Sanford. Student, Bryn Mawr Coll., 1949-50; A.B., Barnard Coll., 1953. Researcher, Time Mag., 1953-63, Los Angeles corr., 1963-66; columnist Los Angeles Times and Los Angeles Times Syndicate, 1966-75; contbg. editor Los Angeles mag., 1977-79; freelance writer. Author: Caroline's Doll Book, 1962, The Users, 1976; contbr.: articles to numerous popular mags. including New West Mag.

HABERER, JEAN-YVES, banker; b. Mazagan, Morocco, Dec. 17, 1932; m. Anne du Crest, June 17, 1959; children: Sylvie, Charles. B.A., Univ. Paris, 1954; grad. Inst. Polit. Sci. (Paris), 1954, Sch. Nat. Adminstrn. (Paris), 1959. Fin. insp., 1959-67; dep. dir. treasury, 1967-78, dir. treasury, 1978-82, insp. gen fin., 1980, chmn. EEC monetary com.; chmn. Compagnie Financière de Paribas and Banque Paribas, Paris, 1982-86, hon. chmn. 1986—; chmn. sup. bd. Compagnie Bancaire, 1982—; chmn. Crédit Lyonnais, 1988—. Author: The Atlantic Fever, 1974, Money and Monetary Policy, 1975, Treasury and Finance Policy, 1976. Decorated knight Legion of Honor, 1978, comdr. Order Isabel the Catholic, 1969, comdr. Order Merit of Fed. Republic Germany, 1982. Home: 10 rue de Remusat, 75016 Paris France Office: Banque Paribas, 3 rue d'Antin, 75002 Paris France

HABERMAN, CHARLES MORRIS, mechanical engineer, educator; b. Bakersfield, Calif., Dec. 10, 1927; s. Carl Morris and Rose Marie (Braun) H. BS, UCLA, 1951; MS in Mech. Engring., U. So. Calif., 1954, ME, 1957. Lead, sr. and group engr. Northrop Aircraft, Hawthorne, Calif., 1951-59, cons., 1959-61; from asst. prof. to prof. mech. engring. Calif. State U., Los Angeles, 1959—; cons. Royal McBee Corp., 1960-61. Author: Engineering Systems Analysis, 1965, Use of Computers for Engineering Applications, 1966, Vibration Analysis, 1968, Basic Aerodynamics, 1971. Served with AUS, 1946-47. Mem. Am. Acad. Mechanics, Am. Soc. Engring. Edn., AIAA, AAUP. Democrat. Roman Catholic.

HABERMEIER, HANNS ULRICH, physicist; b. Crailsheim, Baden-Württenberg, Fed. Republic of Germany, Jan. 27, 1945; s. Julius and Helene (Kett) H.; m. Ingeborg Elisabeth Haake, Nov. 15, 1942. Degree in Physics (Diploma in Physics), U. Stuttgart, Fed. Republic of Germany, 1970; Degree (Dr. rer. nat.), U. Stuttgart, 1974. Scientist metal research Max Planck Inst., Stuttgart, 1974-77; visiting scientist IBM Research Ctr., Yorktown Heights, N.Y., 1978-79; head scientific services technology Max Planck Inst. Solid State Research, Stuttgart, Federal Republic of Germany, 1980—. Mem. German Phys. Soc., European Phys. Soc., Materials Research Soc. Office: Max Planck Inst, Heisenbergstrasse 1, D7000-80 Stuttgart Federal Republic of Germany

HABGOOD, JOHN STAPYLTON, archbishop; b. Stony Stratford, England, June 23, 1927; s. Arthur Henry and Vera (Chetwynd) Stapylton; m. Rosalie Mary Ann Boston, June 7, 1961; children: Laura, Francis, Ruth, Adrian. BA, Cambridge U., 1948, MA, 1952, PhD, 1953; DD (hon.), U. Durham, Eng., 1975, Cambridge U., 1985, Aberdeen U., 1988. Ordained to priesthood Ch. of Eng., 1955. Demonstrator in pharmacology Cambridge U., Eng., 1950-53, fellow King's Coll., 1952-55; vice prin. Westcott House, Cambridge, 1956-62; rector St. John's Episcopal Ch., Jedburgh, Scotland, 1962-67; prin. Queen's Coll., Birmingham, Eng., 1967-73; bishop of Durham, Eng., 1973-83; archbishop Ch. of Eng., York, Eng., 1983—. Author: Religion and Science, 1964, A Working Faith, 1980, Church and Nation in a Secular Age, 1983, Confessions of a Conservative Liberal, 1988. Confessions of conservative liberal, 1988. Hon. fellow King's Coll., Cambridge, 1986. Club: Athenaeum (London). Home and Office: Bishopthorpe, York England YO2 1QE

HABIB, ASADULLAH, university rector; b. Kabul, Afganistan, Oct. 10, 1941; s. Habibullah and Tajwar H.; m. Soraya Habib, Mar. 8, 1953; children: Behram, Mariyam. B, Tchr. Tng. Coll., Kabul, 1960; BA in Lit., Kabul U., 1963; MA and PhD in Lit., State U. Moscow, 1973. Tchr. Faculty of Lit. Kabul U., 1964-68, dir. pubs., 1974, dir. edn., 1974-78, rector, 1982—. Author: (poems) The Red Line, 1965 (award), Collection Short Stories, 1965, (articles) View of Light, 1982 (award), (book) Dari Literature in 20th Century, 1983, (story) Nazar Gul, 1985; contbr. articles to profl. jours. Recipient Soviet-Afghan Friendship award, 1984, Faithful Service award Afghan Govt., 1985, Award of Distinction, Afghan Govt., 1986. Mem. Writer's Assn. Kabul (first pres. 1980-82, bd. dirs.), Acad. Sci. Kabul (candidate 1986—), Afghan Friendship Assn. (bd. dirs.). Muslem. Home: Block 129 Apt 45, Microriyan 2, Kabul Afganistan Office: Pohantoon-E-Kabul, Kabul U, Kabul Afghanistan

HABIB, PHILIP CHARLES, former foreign service officer; b. Bklyn., Feb. 25, 1920; s. Alex and Mary (Spiridon) H.; m. Marjorie W. Slightam, Aug. 27, 1942; children: Phyllis A., Susan W. B.S., U. Idaho, 1942, LL.D., 1974; Ph.D., U. Calif. at Berkeley, 1952. Fgn. service officer 1949-80; 3d sec. Am. embassy Ottawa, Can., 1949-51; 2d sec. Am. embassy Wellington, N.Z., 1952-54; research specialist Dept of State, Washington, 1955-57; Am. consulate gen. Port of Spain, Trinidad, 1958-60; fgn. affairs officer Dept. State 1960-61; counselor for polit. affairs Am. embassy Seoul, Korea, 1962-65, Saigon, Vietnam, 1965-67; personal rank of minister 1966-67; dep. asst. sec. State for East Asian and Pacific affairs, 1967-69; mem. U.S. delegation to meetings on Vietnam, Paris, 1968-71; personal rank of ambassador 1969-71; ambassador to Republic of Korea, Seoul, 1971-74; asst. sec. state for East Asian and Pacific affairs 1974-76, undersec. of state for polit. affairs, 1976-78; diplomat-in-residence Stanford U., 1978-79; sr. advisor to Sec. of State, 1979-80; personal rep. of Pres. to Middle East, 1981-83; sr. research fellow Hoover Instn., 1980—; presdl. envoy to Philippines 1986, pres.' spl. envoy for C.Am., 1986-87; bd. dirs. Pacific Resources Inc., Honolulu. Chmn. Pacific Forum, Honolulu, 1980—; trustee Am. Univ. Beirut, 1983—, Asia Found., 1978—. Served from pvt. to capt. AUS, 1942-46. Decorated comdr. Legion of Honor (France); recipient Rockefeller Pub. Service award, 1969; Nat. Civil Service League award, 1970; Dept. State Disting. Honor award, 1977; Pres.'s award for disting. fed. service, 1979; Presdl. Medal of Freedom, 1982; Lebanon's Order of Cedars, 1982. Roman Catholic. Address: 1606 Courtland Rd Belmont CA 94002

HABLUTZEL, PHILIP NORMAN, law educator; b. Flagstaff, Ariz., Aug. 23, 1935; s. Charles Edward and Electa Margaret (Cain) H.; m. Nancy Zimmerman, July 1, 1980; children—Margo Lynn, Robert Paul. B.A., La. State U., 1958; postgrad. U. Heidelberg, W.Ger., 1959-60, 60-62; M.A., U. Chgo., 1960, J.D., 1967. Bar: Ill. 1967, U.S. Dist. Ct. (no. dist.) Ill. 1967. Research atty. Am. Bar Found., Chgo., 1967-68, sr. research atty., 1968-71; asst. prof. law Chgo.-Kent Coll. Law, Ill. Inst. Tech., 1971-73, assoc. prof., 1973-79, prof., 1979—, dir. grad. program in fin. services law, 1985—; cons. OEO Legal Services Program, 1967-69; reporter Ill. sec. state's com. on revision of not-for-profit corp. act, 1984-87. Pres., trustee, Chgo. Sch. Profl. Psychology, 1979-83; reporter Ill. Sec. of State's corp. laws adv. com., 1986—. Rotary Found. Advanced Study fellow, 1959-60. Fellow Chgo. Bar Found.; mem. ABA (chmn. subcom. on adoption of Uniform Trade Secrets Act 1984-86), Ill. State Bar Assn., Chgo. Bar Assn. (chmn. com. on sci., tech. and law 1971-72, sec. corp. law com. 1986-8, vice chmn. corp. law com. 1987—). Republican. Episcopalian. Author: (with R. Garrett, W. Scott) Model Business Corporation Act Annotated, 2d edit., 3 vols., 1971, (with J. Levi) Model Residential Landlord-Tenant Code, 1969. Avocations: travel, sailing, photography. Office: IIT Chgo-Kent Coll Law 77 S Wacker Dr Chicago IL 60606

HABRAKEN, CLARISSE LIEKE, chemistry educator, researcher; b. Bandung, Indonesia, Oct. 28, 1926; arrived in The Netherlands, 1947; d. Jan Wormerus and Julie Lucie (Heyting) H. MA, U. Leiden, The Netherlands, 1955, PhD, 1961. Sr. lectr.chemistry U. Leiden, 1955-84, reader, 1984—; lectr. land grant centennial U. Del., Newark, 1961-62; asst. prof. U. Mich., An n Arbor, 1973-74; mem. working party chem. educators Fed. European Chem. Socs., 1978083, com. teaching chemistry Internat. Union Pure and Applied Chemistry, 1978-84; planning com. Open U., Heerlen, The Netherlands, 1977-81. Contbr. numerous articles to profl. jours. Bd. dirs. Vrouwen Visie, Rotterdam, The Netherlands, 1980-84, chmn., Zeist, The Netherlands, 1984-87. Guest research fellow Royal Soc. U.K., 1986. Mem. Royal Netherlands Chem. Soc. (chmn. chem. edn. sect. 1979-84), Am. Chem. Soc., Royal Chem. Soc., Internat. Soc. Heterocyclic Chemistry. Club: Vrowwen Netwerk (The Hague, The Netherlands).

HABRÉ, HISSENE, president of Chad. Formerly a leader Front de Libération Nationale du Tchad; head No. Armed Forces Command Council, 1974-77; leader Forces Armées du Nord, 1977—; prime minister Chad, 1978-79, resigning after Kano peace agreement with Front de Libération Nationale led by Goukouni Oueddei; minister of state for def. and war vets. Provisional Govt. Chad, 1979, minister of def., 1979, reported in exile, 1980; became pres. Chad after mil. coup, 1982—. Address: Presidence de la République, N'Djamena Chad *

HABUSH, ROBERT LEE, lawyer; b. Milw., Mar. 22, 1936; s. Jesse James and Beatrice (Liebenberg) H.; m. Miriam Lee Friedman, Aug. 25, 1957; children—Sherri Ellen, William Scott, Jodi Lynn. B.B.A., U. Wis., 1959, J.D., 1961. Bar: Wis. 1961, U.S. Dist. Ct. (ea. and we. dists.) Wis. 1961, U.S. Ct. Appeals (7th cir.) 1965, U.S. Supreme Ct. 1986. Pres. Habush, Habush & Davis, Milw., 1961—; lectr. U. Wis. Law Sch., Marquette U. Law Sch., State Bar Wis., other legal orgns. Author: Cross Examination of Non Medical Experts, 1981. Contbr. articles to legal jours. Served to capt. U.S. Army, 1959-75. Mem. ABA, Wis. Bar Assn., Wis. Acad. Trial Lawyers (pres. 1968-69), Am. Trial Lawyers Assn. (nat. parliamentarian, sec. 1971-73, bd. govs. 1983-86, pres. 1986—), Internat. Acad. Trial Lawyers (bd. dirs. 1983—), Am. Bd. Trial Advocates, Internat. Soc. Barristers, Inner Circle Advocates. Office: Habush Habush & Davis SC 777 E Wisconsin Ave Milwaukee WI 53202

HABYARIMANA, JUVENAL, president Rwanda; b. Rambura, Gisenyi, Rwanda, March 8, 1937; s. Jean-Baptiste Ntibazilikana and Suzanne Nyirazuba; m. Agathe Kanziga, Aug. 17, 1963; 8 children. Student Coll. St. Paul, Bukavu, Zaire, Lovanium U., Kinshana, also Officers Sch., Kigali. Joined Nat. Guard, advanced through grades to comdr.; chief of staff, 1963-65; minister for Nat. Guard, chief staff police, 1965-73; maj. gen., 1973; leader coup to depose Pres. Kayibanda, July 1973; pres. of Rwanda, 1973—; minister nat. def., 1973—; chmn. OCAM Conf. Heads of State and Govt., 1975. Pres., Com. pour la Paix et l'Unité Nat., 1973-75; leader Mouvement Revolutionnaire nat. pour la Devel., 1975—. Decorated Grand Master, Nat. Order of Rwanda, Grand Cross of Leopold II, Grand Cross of The Order of Leopold, Medal of the Order of the Source of the Nile, Grand Cross of the Nat. Order of Mauritania, Grand Ribbon of the Nat. Order of the Republic of Burundi, Golden Heart (Kenya), 1981; others. Address: President of the Republic, Kigali Rwanda *

HACKETT, EARLE, pathologist; b. Cork, Ireland, Apr. 26, 1921; arrived in Australia, 1958; s. James Reginald and Maud Roxana (Belton) H.; m. Eileen Hackett (dec. 1987); children: Jane, Susan, Johnjames. MA, Trinity Coll., Dublin, Ireland, 1945, MD, 1949. Diplomate in pathology. Dep. dir. Inst. Med. and Veterinary Sci., Adelaide, Australia, 1958-78; chmn. BioHealth Internat., Sydney, Australia, 1987—; practice medicine specializing in pathology St. Leonards, Australia, 1958—; vis. fellow Australian Nat. Univ., Canberra, 1983. Author: Blood, 1973, Lady Bones, 1985, Fevers, 1985, All Gustos, 1986. Commr. South Australian Royal Commn. into the Non-Med. Use of Drugs, Adelaide, 1976-78; vice chmn. Australian Broadcasting Commn., Sydney, 1973-75; chmn. bd. Art Gallery South Australia, Adelaide, 1970-78. Fellow Royal Coll. Pathologists of Australasia (pres. 1971-73), Royal Coll. Australasian Physicians.

HACKMAN, HELEN ANNA HENRIETTE, home economist; b. New Melle, Mo., Oct. 8, 1908; d. John Henry and Lydia Eliza (Meier) Hackman; AB, Central Wesleyan Coll., Warrenton, Mo., 1929; BS, U. Mo., 1942, postgrad., 1942; postgrad. U. Wis., 1934, U. Colo., 1953, 75, U. Ariz., 1975, 77. Prin., Wright City High Sch., 1929; home econs. tchr., Cape Girardeau, Mo., 1930-42; sr. extension adviser home econs. U. Ill., Pittsfield, 1942-78; sec. Pike County Health and Social Services Coordinating Com. Dietitian, buyer Oshkosh Wis. Camp Fire Girls Camp, summers 1935, 36, 37; sec.-treas. Western Ill. 4-H Camp Assn., 1952-54; mem. Western Ill. Fair Bd. Com., Griggsville, 1946—; v.p. Tri-county Assn. for Crippled, 1960—; tech. cons. White House Conf., 1960, 70; pres. Pike County Heart Assn., 1969, organizer Family Planning Centers, Diabetic and Blood Pressure Clinics, Pike County Health Dept., 1971; sec. Illini Hosp. Aux., 1978; Bd. dirs. Pike County Mental Health. Recipient Distinguished Service award Nat. Home Demonstration Agts. Assn., 1952; Meritorious Service award Heart Assn., 1960, 61. Mem. Ill. Home Advisers Assn. (sec. 1948), Nat. Assn. Extension Home Economists (3d v.p. 1951-53, pub. relations chmn. 1951-53), Am. Home Econs. Assn. (sec. Ill. nutrition com. 1967-69), Pittsfield Hist. Soc. Epsilon Sigma Phi (chief 1962), Gamma Sigma Delta. Clubs: Pittsfield Woman's (pres. 1979, 80, 81, 82), Pike County Bus. and Profl. (pres. 1970-71). Home: 230 S Illinois St Pittsfield IL 62363 Office: Hwy 36 and 54th St E Po Box 227 Pittsfield IL 62363

HACKNEY, ALLEN LEE, art educator, artist; b. Madison, Ind., Aug. 13, 1938; s. Oakley Lee and Juanita (Leach) H. B.S., Ind. State U., 1962, M.S., 1964. Tchr. art Vigo County Sch. Corp., Terre Haute, Ind., 1962—; with Gibson Enterprises. Recipient Outstanding Painting award Hoosier Salon, 1968, 75, Commemorative medal State of Ind., 1977, 78, other awards, Honors Seminar award R.I. Sch. of Design, 1988; Eli Lilley grantee. Mem., bd. dirs. Brown County Art Gallery Assn, 1984—; pres. Legendmaster Galleries. Nat. Soc. Painters in Casein and Acrylic, Ind. Realists Club (founder, pres.), Internat. Platform Assn. Democrat. Mormon. Lodges: Masons, Shriners. Avocations: golf; swimming, car restoring. Home: RR 21 Box 69 Oak Grove Terre Haute IN 47802

HACKNEY, FRANCIS SHELDON, university president; b. Birmingham, Ala., Dec. 5, 1933; s. Cecil Fain and Elizabeth (Morris) H.; m. Lucy Judkins Durr, June 15, 1957; children: Virginia Foster, Sheldon Fain, Elizabeth Morris. BA, Vanderbilt U., 1955; MA, Yale U., 1963, PhD, 1966. Mem. faculty Princeton U., 1965-75, assoc. prof. history, 1969-72, prof. and provost, 1972-75; pres. Tulane U., New Orleans, 1975-80, U. Pa., Phila., 1981—; prof. history U. Pa., 1981—. Author: Populism to Progressivism in Alabama, 1969; editor: Populism: The Critical Issues, 1971; (with others) Understanding the American Experience, 1973. Bd. dirs. Carnegie Found. for Advancement of Teaching, 1976—, Ednl. Testing Service, Amistad Research Ctr., Dillard U., 1976—. Served with USNR, 1956-61. Recipient Charles S. Sydnor award So. Hist. Assn., 1970; Beveridge prize Am. Hist. Assn., 1970. Mem. Am. Hist. Assn., So. Hist. Assn., Orgn. Am. Historians. Office: U Pa Office of Pres 100 College Hall Philadelphia PA 19104 *

HADDAD, ALAIN NESSIM, psychiatrist; b. Tunis, Tunisia, Mar. 10, 1941; s. Moise and Irene (Tuil) H.; m. Maryline Adhera, Sept. 1, 1968; children: Michael, Laurence, Karinne, Benjamin, Hanna. MD, U. Paris, 1972. Resident Hosp. Maison Blanche, Nevilly sur Marne, France, 1968-72; asst. staff mem. Hosp. Maison Blanche, Neuilly sur Marne, France, 1972-74; sub-chief Hosp. Maison Blanche, Nevilly sur Marne, France, 1974-82, chief div. psychiatry, 1986—; chief div. psychiatry Hosp. Montdidier, Somme, 1982-86; lectr. Coll. Medicine U. Paris, 1975-82, U. Amiens, 1982-86; cons. Tribunal of Bobigny, 1975—, Tribunal of Amiens, 1982-86. Contbr. articles to profl. jours. Pres. Assn. Kisse Rahamim, Paris, 1980—, Assn. Hag Israel, Sarcelles, France, 1987—; v.p. Assn. T.E.C. Sarcelles, Paris, 1968—, Assn. Jewish in Paris, 1978—. Mem. Internat. Soc. Psychoanalysis. Home: 12 Ave du Chateau, 95200 Sarcelles France Office: 3 Place de l'Hotel de Ville, 95140 Garges France

HADDAD, ANEES ADIB, college dean, sociologist, educator, minister; b. Beirut, Lebanon, Apr. 7, 1931; came to U.S., 1966, naturalized, 1976; s. Adib Youssif and Victoria A. (Adbul Messih) H.; m. Nellie Ann Nehme, Feb. 3, 1954; children: Eddie Adib, Hiam Marie, Ella Ilham. BA, Middle East Coll., 1957; MA, Loma Linda U., 1968; PhD, U. So. Calif., 1971. Ordained to ministry 7th-day Adventist Ch., 1957. Exec. dir. Internat. Commn. for Prevention Alcoholism and Drug Addiction, Beirut, 1958-66; lectr. Loma Linda (Calif.) U., 1966-69, asst. prof. sociology, 1969-73, coordinator Middle East studies grad. program, 1970-85, assoc. prof. sociology and family studies, 1973-77, dir. div. behavioral scis., 1976-81, prof., 1977—, dean Coll. Arts and Scis., 1984—; dir. undergrad. advisement, dir. integration research project U. So. Calif., Los Angeles, 1969-71; cons. in field. Author: The Miracle Girl, 1966; assoc. editor Et Al, 1968-70; contbr. over 65 articles to profl. jours. Internat. scholarship fellow Aquinas Fund, 1970-71. Mem. Am. Sociol. Assn., Nat. Council on Family Relations, Am. Assn. Sex Educators and Therapists, Am. Gerontol. Assn., Phi Beta Kappa, Sigma Xi, Alpha Delta Kappa. Home: 11466 Poplar St Loma Linda CA 92354 Office: Loma Linda Univ Coll Arts & Scis Pierce St Riverside CA 92515

HADDAD, FRED, lawyer; b. Waterbury, Conn., Sept. 14, 1946; s. Fred Melad and Nancy Anne (Crean) H.; m. Julia Hester, Aug. 2, 1980; 1 dau., Allison Hester; children by previous marriage—Tonja, Tristan, Matthew. Student U. Conn., 1964; B.A., U. New Haven, 1971; J.D., U. Miami (Fla.), 1974. Bar: Fla. 1974, U.S. Dist. Cts. (so. and mid. dists.) Fla. 1975, U.S. Cts. Appeals (4th, 5th, 6th, 11th cirs.) 1975, U.S. Supreme Ct. 1977, U.S. Dist. Ct. (we. dist.) Tenn. 1982, U.S. Ct. Appeals (10th cir.). Ptnr. Sandstrom & Haddad (changed to Sandstrom & Haddad, Fort Lauderdale, Fla., 1974—. Mem. Fla. Bar (criminal law, reverse sting coms.), Broward County Criminal Def. Attys. Assn., Fed. Bar Assn. (exec. com.), Nat. Fla. Criminal Def. Attys. Assn., Assn. Trial Lawyers Am., Assn. Criminal Def. Lawyers. Democrat. Office: Sandstrom & Haddad 429 S Andrews Ave Fort Lauderdale FL 33301

HADDAD, GEORGE RICHARD, musician, educator; b. East End, Sask., Can., May 11, 1918; s. Richard and Labeeby (Salloum) H.; m. Lilyan Aboud, May 20, 1949; children: Constance Haddad Frecker, Diane, Carolyn Haddad Dougherty. Asso., Toronto Conservatory Music, 1931; asso. licentiate, 1941; Mus.B., U. Toronto, 1940; M.A., Ohio State U., 1954; student, Royal Conservatory Music Toronto, 1936-40, Julliard Grad. Sch., N.Y.C., 1940-43, Paris Conservatoire, 1950-52. Tchr. piano Bay View Summer Coll. Music, summers 1948-51; prof. Sch. Music Ohio State U., Columbus, 1952—. Appeared in various recitals; guest appearances throughout, U.S., Can., Europe, 1944—, guest artist, Detroit Symphony, Toronto Symphony, Luxembourg Symphony, and, others. George Haddad piano scholarship established in his honor Ohio State U., 1986. Mem. Music Tchrs. Nat. Assn., Nat. Music Guild Piano Tchrs., Ohio Music Tchrs. Assn., Musicians Union, Pi Kappa Lambda. Clubs: Faculty, Kinsmen of Can, Torch. Home: 2689 River Park Dr Columbus OH 43220 Office: Ohio State U Sch of Mus Columbus OH 43210

HADDAD, JAMIL RAOUF, physician; b. Mosul, Iraq, Aug. 18, 1923; came to U.S., 1952, naturalized, 1965; s. Raouf Sulaiman and Fadhila (Shaya) H.; m. Mary Lou Scorsone, Aug. 1, 1959; children—Ralph J., John L., James M. M.B., Ch.B., Iraqi Royal Coll. Medicine, Baghdad, Iraq, 1946. Med. officer Khanaqin (Iraq) Hosp., 1946-52; asst. resident pathology Crawford W. Long Meml. Hosp., Atlanta, 1953-54; resident Bellevue Hosp., N.Y.C., 1954-56; practice medicine specializing in pathology N.Y.C., 1963—, Passaic, N.J., 1981—; chmn. dept. anatomic and clin. pathology St. Clare's Hosp. and Health Center, N.Y.C., 1971-81; dir. pathology and clin. lab. Gen. Hosp. Ctr. at Passaic, 1981—; asso. Sloan-Kettering Inst. for Cancer Research, N.Y.C., 1960-66; asst. prof. pathology NYU Coll. Medicine, 1959-65, asst. clin. prof. pathology, 1965-67, asso. clin. prof. pathology, 1967-70, clin. prof. pathology, 1970—; asst. prof. exptl. cell biology Mt. Sinai Grad Sch. Biol. Scis., N.Y.C., 1966-70, lectr., 1971-83, adj. asst. prof., 1983—. Mem. Coll. Am. Pathologists, Am. Soc. Clin. Pathologists, AMA, N.Y. Pathol. Soc., N.Y. State, New York County med. socs. Home: 420 E 23d St Apt MC New York NY 10010 Office: 350 Boulevard Passaic NJ 07055

HADDAD, WADI DAHIR, bank official, medical equipment company executive; b. Aindara, Lebanon, Mar. 14, 1941; came to U.S., 1976; s. Dahir Boutros and Wardy (Khater) H.; m. Houda Nashef, June 27, 1964; children—Sandra, Loubna. B.S., Am. U., Beirut, 1962, M.A., 1964; Ph.D., U. Wis., 1968. Prof., dir. Am. U., Beirut, 1966-72; pres. Ctr. for Ednl. Research and Devel., Beirut, 1972-76; staff mem., div. chief World Bank, Washington, 1976-82, div. chief, 1987—; nat. security adviser to Pres. Lebanon, Beirut, 1982-84; vis. sr. fellow Ctr. for Strategic Studies, Washington, 1984-85; pres. Trans Devel. Corp., Vienna, Va., 1985—; chmn. bd. Digital Medicine, Boston, 1985—; div. chief World Bank, 1987—; cons. Ford Found., Beirut, 1968-71. Author: Physical Science, 1972; Education Sector Policy, 1980; Efficiency of Education Systems, 1982; Lebanon, The Politics of Revolving Doors, 1985. Co-founder Lebanese Assn. for Advancement Sci., Beirut, 1972; pres. Path of Light Philanthropic Soc., Beirut, 1960-66. Ford Found. grantee U. Wis., 1964-66; AID grantee, Beirut, 1959-62; decorated by Pres. Romania. Fellow AAAS; mem. Am. Ednl. Research Assn. Baptist. Avocations: reading; gardening; travel; drawing. Office: World Bank Washington DC 20433

HADDADIN, MUWAFFAK JIRYIS, pharmaceutical company executive; b. Ma'in, Jordan, Mar. 3, 1942; s. Jiryis Khalil and Salma Abdullah (Hamati) H.; m. Lina Yacoub Ayoub, June 26, 1977; children: Farah, Raja. BS in Pharmacy, Am. U. Beirut, 1965; PhD in Pharmaceutics, U. Wash., 1972, U. Kans., 1972. Assoc. prof. medicine, sci. U. Jordan, Amman, 1972-80; prof., dir. sch. pharmacy Yarmouk U., Irbid, Jordan, 1980-83, acting dir. sch. medicine, dentistry, nursing, 1980-83; dir. gen. Arab Co. Drug Industries and Med. Appliances, Amman, 1983—. Contbr. articles to profl. jours. Fellow U. Kans., 1972, in toxicology, 1977; U. Ky. vis. scientist, 1978-79. Mem. Jordan Pharm. Assn. (chmn. sci. com. 1973-77, editorial bd. jour. 1973-77), N.Y. Acad. Scis., Profl. Pharmacists Assn. Office: Arab Co Drug Industries, and Med Appliances, PO Box 925 161, Amman Jordan

HADDOCK, JOHN WOLCOTT, retired industrialist; b. Polo, Ill., Aug. 22, 1904; s. Frank D. and Mabel (Mulford) H.; m. Gladys Baxter, Oct. 2, 1935; m. 2d Patricia Worlton Cosel, May 4, 1974; m. 3d Sibylle Kuhn, May 22, 1987. Mem. Soc. Mining Engrs., Fin. Analysts Soc., Nat. Assn. Bus. Economists, Sons of the Revolution. Clubs: Union League (N.Y.); Tavern (Chgo.); La Jolla (Calif.) Beach & Tennis, Country. Address: 1001 Genter St La Jolla CA 92037

HADFIELD, PAUL JOHN AUGUSTINE, theatre studies educator; b. Manchester, Lancashire, Eng., May 10, 1941; s. John Collingwood and Margretta (Matthews) H.; m. Barbara Elizabeth Johnson, Aug. 3, 1968 (div. Dec. 1981); children: John Paul, Jane Anna. Cert. edn. with distinction, U. Wales, Bangor, 1968; BA with honors, U. Norwich, Eng., 1974. Cert. in edn. Bank officer Nat. Provincial Bank, London, 1960-66; tchr. Norfolk County Edn. Authority, Norwich, 1968-64; lectr. in drama Rolle Coll. Exmouth, Exeter, Devon, U.K., 1974-78; sr. lectr. in theatre Ulster Poly., Jordanstown, U.K., 1978-84; lectr. in theatre U. Ulster, Coleraine, U.K., 1984—; reader in playscripts Irish Nat. Theatre, Dublin, 1983—; bibliographer Theater Research Data Ctr. at CUNY, Bklyn., 1987—; asst. broadcaster BBC, Belfast, 1986—. Mng. editor, dir. Theatre Ireland Ltd., 1982; theater dir. various groups, 1965—. Mem. Irish Theatre Archive. Home: 29 Main St, Castlerock County of Derry BT51 4RA, Ireland Office: Univ Ulster, Coleraine BT52 15A, Northern Ireland

HADFIELD, ROBERT FRANKLIN, patent and trademark executive; b. Manchester, Eng., Aug. 6, 1944; s. Robert and Mary Lilian (Kirkham) H.; m. Valerie Bradbury, July 9, 1966; children: Andrea Theresa, Richard Anthony, Alistair James. BSc, U. Leeds, Eng., 1965. Patent asst. Dunlop Ltd., Birmingham, Eng., 1965-69, patent agt., 1969-71, sect. mgr., 1971-76; patent agt., dep. head patent dept. Turner & Newall, Manchester, 1976-80, head patent and trademark dept., 1980—; bd. dirs. Anti-Counterfeiting Group, London, 1984—. Fellow Chartered Inst. Patent Agts.; mem. European Patent Inst., Comité de Liaison de la Construction d'Equipements et de Pièces d'Automobiles (chmn. counterfeit goods fighting group), Association Europeenne des Industries de Produits de Marque (chmn. anti-counterfeiting com.). Office: T & N plc, Bowdon House, Ashburton Rd W, Manchester England M17 IRA

HADIDA, PAUL JOSEPH, physician, educator; b. Oran, Algeria, Aug. 3, 1931; s. Samuel and Rica (Faradji) H.; m. Michele Seban, Sept. 5, 1945 (div. 1972); children: Eric, Sabrina. PhD in Medicine, U. Aix-Marseille, France, 1961, degree in Geriatrics, 1977. Non-resident Dr. in medicine and surgery U. Civil Hosp., Mustapha, Algiers, 1956-58; non-resident dr. in medicine and surgery Univ. Civil Hosp. Mustapha, Algiers, Algeria, 1959-61; pub. health physician Dellys, Algeria, 1961-64; gen. practice medicine specializing in acupuncture Marseille, France, 1964—; prof. acupuncture French Assn. Acupuncture, Marseille, 1980, U. Sch. Nurses, Santa Cruz y San Pablo Hosps., Barcelona, Spain, 1984-87; assoc. physician Univ. Hosps., Marseille, 1982—; sworn Dr. 2d. Arrondisement, Marseille, 1981—, 1d Arrondisement, 1988—; med. dir. and head master Instituto Mutaner, Scis. and Tech. Applied to Health, Barcelona, 1987; vis. physician U. Hosp. Sch. Medicine, Kunming, People's Republic China, summer, 1982, 84. Contbr. articles to profl. jours. Recipient Commemorative medal, French Navy, 1960. Mem. French Acupuncture Assn., Ofcl. Acupuncture Drs. Assn. Office: 20 rue Colbert, 13001 Marseilles France

HADINATA, JULIUS See GOEI, ING LIAT

HADINATA, RUDY BAMBANG, cigarette company executive; b. Magelang, Central Java, Indonesia, Feb. 24, 1940; s. Paulus Andiko and Paring H.; m. Juliarti Sutanto, Dec. 26, 1964; children—Ariono, Milono, Susilo. Mktg. mgr. Djarum Cigarette Co., Kudus, Central Java, Indonesia, 1964-69, mktg. dir., 1969-82; fin. dir., 1972-84; supervisory dir., 1984—; founder, part owner, dir. P. T. Hadinata Bros. Furniture Co., 1975—. Roman Catholic. Home: IIC/31 AIP KS Tubun, Jakarta Indonesia

HADIPRIONO, FABIAN CHRISTY, engineer, educator, researcher; b. Cirebon, Java, Indonesia, Oct. 6, 1947; came to U.S., 1976; s. Robertus Sudarjo and Wertriani (Yoyoh) H. BCE, MCE, Parahyangan U., 1973; MS, U. Calif., Berkeley, 1978, M of Engring., 1980, DEng, 1982. Registered profl. engr., Ohio. Project engr. various design and constrn. cos., SE Asia, 1965-75; project mgr. Phoenix Inc., Jakarta, Indonesia, 1974-75; engr., asst. bd. dirs. Mahkota Group, Indonesia, 1975-77; instr., teaching assoc. U. Calif., Berkeley, 1981-82; asst. prof. civil and constrn. engring. and mgmt. Ohio State U., Columbus, 1982—; Tech. cons. Carlile Patchen Murphy and Allison, Ohio, 1984; advisor Chandra and Assocs. Inc., Indonesia, 1984—; lectr. in field. Contbr. articles to profl. jours. Recipient Dale Carnegie Human Relation award, 1976; Ohio State U. grantee, 1985, 1986, U.S. Army C.E. grantee, 1986; USAF fellow and grantee 1986; Newhouse Found. fellow U. Calif., Berkeley, 1978, Harry H. Hilp fellow U. Calif., Berkeley, 1981, Robert B. Rothchild Jr. fellow U. Calif., Berkeley, 1982. Mem. ASCE, NSPE, ASME, Internat. Assn. Bridge and Structural Engring., Am. Concrete Inst., Archtl. and Engring. Performance Info. Ctr. (research adv. com. 1984), Associated Sch. Constrn. (research adv. com. 1986). Roman Catholic. Home and Office: Ohio State U 2070 Neil Ave Columbus OH 43210

HADJIDAKI, ELPIDA, marine archaeologist, curator; b. Hania, Crete, Greece, Oct. 12, 1948; d. Nicholas Hadjidakis and Angelika Polychronopoulou; m. Michael Marder, May 19, 1985; 1 child, Nike-Linda. BA in Ancient History and Archaeology, U. Manchester, 1976, MA in Ancient History and Marine Archaeology, 1977; PhD in Marine Archaeology, U. Calif., Santa Barbara, 1987. Cert. marine archaeologist. Marine archaeologist dept underwater antiquities Greek Ministry Culture, Athens, 1978-81; teaching asst. dept. history U. Calif., Santa Barbara, 1982-85; curator antiquities Ministry Culture/Archaeol. Mus. Hania, 1984—. Contbr. articles to profl. jours. Mem. Soc. Hist. Archaeology, Nautical Archaeology Soc. (Eng.), Lit. Soc. West Crete, Inst. Underwater Archaeology (Athens), Archaeol. Soc. Am., Archaeol. Inst. Am. Home: Kydonias 49, 73100 Hania Crete Greece Office: Archaeol Mus, Halidon 21, 73100 Hania Crete Greece

HADJIMANOLIS, JOHN, management consultant; b. Athens, Mar. 28, 1950; s. George and Helen (Balaskas) H. BSc, Newcastle U., 1972; DipEng., Athens Nat. Tech. U., 1974, MBA, 1976; MPhil, Cambridge U., 1978. Internat. bus. mgr. Thrace Paper Mill S.A., Athens, 1978-84; tech. mgr. Paragon (Greece) U.S.A., Athens, 1984-85; dir. econ. analysis div. Agrotiki Techniki S.A., Athens, 1985-87; dir. Analysis and Mgmt. Cons., Athens, 1985—; cons. Thrace Paper Mill S.A., Paragon S.A., Compuform S.A., Ronamita Ltd. Author materials in field. Fellow Hellenic Ops. Research Soc.; mem. Hellenic Chamber Engrs., Hellenic Mech. Engring. Assn. Christian Orthodox. Home: 69 Anagnostopoulou St, Athens GR 106 78, Greece Office: Analysis and Mgmt Cons, 39 Didotou St, Athens GR 106 80, Greece

HADLEY, LEILA ELIOTT-BURTON, author; b. N.Y.C., Sept. 22, 1925; d. Frank Vincent and Beatrice Boswell (Eliott) Burton; m. Arthur T. Hadley, II, Mar. 2, 1944 (div. Aug. 1946); 1 child, Arthur T., III; m. Yvor H. Smitter, Jan. 24, 1953 (div. Oct. 1969); children—Victoria C. Van D. Smitter Barlow, Matthew Smitter Eliott, Caroline Allison F.S. Nicholson; m. William C. Musham, May 1976 (div. July 1979). Student, U. Witwatersrand, Johannesburg, S. Africa, 1954-55. Author: Give Me the World, 1958; How to Travel with Children in Europe, 1963; Manners for Children, 1967; Fielding's Guide to Traveling with Children in Europe, 1972, rev., 1974, 84; Traveling with Children in the U.S.A., 1974; Tibet-20 Years After the Chinese Takeover, 1979; (with Theodore B. Van Itallie) The Best Spas: Where to Go for Weight Loss, Fitness Programs and Pure Pleasure in the U.S. and Around the World, 1988; Assoc. editor: Diplomat mag., N.Y.C., 1964-65, Saturday Evening Post, N.Y.C., 1965-67; editorial cons. TWYCH, N.Y.C., 1985-87; book reviewer Palm Beach Life, Fla., 1967-72. Contbr. articles to various newspapers, mags. Mem. Soc. Woman Geographers (exec. council 1984—), Authors Guild, Nat. Writers Union, Nat. Press Club. Republican. Presbyterian. Home: 300 E 75th St New York NY 10021 Office: care Peter Matson Literistic 264 Fifth Ave New York NY 10001

HADLEY, RUTH BANDY POWELL, educator; b. Honolulu, Mar. 28, 1925; d. Edwin R. and Ruth Bandy (Powell) Millikan; B.A., U. Ariz., 1958; M.A., Calif. State Poly. U., 1967; m. John Calvin Hadley, Oct. 9, 1948; children—John Craige, Ruth Bandy Priest. With Lompoc (Calif.) Unified Sch. Dist., 1959-85; mem. Calif. Math. Framework Com.; math. coordinator publ. Calif. State Bd. Edn.; active Calif. Math. Model Curriculum Guide Com., Curriculum Devel. and Supplemental Materials Commn., 1978-84, Calif. Instrnl. Materials Evaluation Panel for Math., 1986; chairperson Calif. Legal Compliance Com., 1984—, Calif. Math. Initiative Cadre, Calif. assessment program Math. Adv. Com., Calif. Basic Ednl. Skills Test Math. Com. Recipient Presdl. award for Excellence in Sci. and Math. Teaching, 1985, George Polya Meml. award for math., 1987; named Lompoc Unified Sch. Dist. Tchr. of Yr., 1963. Mem. NEA, Nat. Council Tchrs. Math., Calif. Math. Council, Assn. for Supervision and Curriculum Devel., Nat. Council Suprs. Math., Calif. Tchrs. Assn., Delta Delta Delta, Delta Kappa Gamma. Episcopalian. Home: 1414 S Wallis St Santa Maria CA 93454

HADREAS, JAMES DEMETRIOS, motel executive; b. LaCrosse, Wis., Aug. 29, 1910; s. John Demetrios and Anna (Rozakis) H.; student U. Calif., Berkeley, 1947-49; m. Catherine Mountanos, Dec. 6, 1942; children—John J., Peter J. Pres., Md. Hotel Bldg. Corp., San Diego, 1946-51, Los Gables Apt. Hotel, Salt Lake City, 1951-57, Sundial Motor Lodge of Redwood City (Calif.), 1960-67, Sundial Motor Lodge, Inc., Hillsborough, Calif., 1967—, Republican candidate for Congress from 13th Dist. Calif., 1974. Mem. Redwood City C. of C. Club: Commonwealth. Home: 903 Tournament Dr Hillsborough CA 94010

HADŽISELIMOVIC, OMER, philosopher, educator; b. Sarajevo, Bosnia-Herzegovina, Yugoslavia, Jan. 1, 1946; s. Almas and Esrefa (Arnautovic) H.; m. Esma Kaltak, June 2, 1971; children: Belma, Dina. BA, U. Sarajevo, 1970, PhD, 1978; MA, Oberlin (Ohio) Coll., 1972. Instr. faculty U. Sarajevo, 1972-78, asst. prof., 1985-88, assoc. prof., 1981—, vice dean dept. philosophy faculty, 1985—. Author: Messages and Responses: The American Social Novel in Serbo-Croatian Criticism, 1918-1941, 1980. Mem. Communist Party. Home: Mitra Trifunovica Uce 61, 71000, Sarajevo Bosnia-Herzegovina Yugoslavia Office: U Sarajevo, Sch of Philosophy, Rackog 1 Sarajev, Bosnia-Herzegovina Yugoslavia

HAEBERLE, FREDERICK ROLAND, oil company scientist; b. Phila., Oct. 6, 1919; s. Frederick Edward and Faye Vivian (Davis) H.; m. Cynthia Lee Davis, Feb. 22, 1946; children: Cynthia Faye, Frederick Edward. B.S., Yale U., 1947, M.S, 1948; M.B.A., Columbia U., 1962. Geologist Standard Oil Calif., Houston, 1948-52; chief geologist J. J. Lynn Oil Div., Abilene, Tex., 1952-53; div. mgr. Mayfair Minerals, Abilene, 1953-54; cons. geologist, Abilene, 1954-57; chief subsurface geologist Atlantic Refining Co., Caracas, Venezuela, 1957-60; geol. specialist Mobil Oil Corp., Dallas, 1962-83, cons. geologist, 1983—; asst. prof. U. Houston, 1948-50; prof. McMurray Coll., Abilene, Tex., 1954-57. Contbr. articles to profl. jours. Served to 1st lt U.S. Army, 1941-46, PTO. Fellow Geol. Soc. Am.; mem. Am. Assn. Petroleum Geologists, Soc. Profl. Well Log Analysts, Assn. Profl. Geol. Scientists, Tex. Acad. Sci. Republican. Presbyterian. Club: Brook Haven Country (Dallas). Current Work: Statistical studies of exploration drilling activity and reserves recovered, applications of computers to geological work. Subspecialties: Geology; Information systems (Information science).

HAERER, DEANE NORMAN, mktg. and pub. relations exec.; b. N.Y.C., Feb. 14, 1935; s. Frederick Sidney and Florence Agnes (Jackson) H.; A.A., Boston U., 1955, B.S., 1957; postgrad. NYU Grad. Sch. Bus. and Finance, 1958-60. Drake U. Grad. Sch., 1965-67; m. Polly Ann Dunn, Feb. 24, 1961; children—Jennifer A., Heather J. Account exec. pub. relations and advt. Charles Abbott Assos., Inc., N.Y.C., 1957-60; dir. alumni, community and ch. relations Iowa Wesleyan Coll., 1960-61; tech. editor J.I. Case Co., Burlington, Iowa, 1961-64; dir. publs., asst. dir. pub. relations Drake U., 1964-68; pub. relations account supr. Thomas Wolff Assocs., Des Moines, 1968; dir. sch.-community relations Des Moines Pub. Sch. System, 1968-74; dir. mktg. communications and corp. pub. relations Stanley Consultants, Inc., Muscatine, Iowa, 1974-78, dir. corp. public relations and mktg. services, 1978-82; dir. mktg. services Howard Needles Tammen & Bergendoff, Kansas City, Mo., 1982-84; dir. corp. mktg. Robert E. McKee, Inc., 1984-88, pres. Haerer Stoltz and Assocs Inc. Southlake, Tex., 1988; guest lectr. Sch. Journalism, Drake U., 1970-74, U. Iowa, 1974-78. Bd. dirs. Heart of the Hawkeye council Camp Fire Girls, Des Moines, 1969-72. Recipient 1st place publ. award Univ. div. Mid-Am. Conf., Am. Coll. Public Relations Assn., 1965, 66; nat. awards outstanding ednl. publs. Nations Schs. and Sch. Mgmt. mags., 1972, 73. Mem. Pub. Relations Soc. Am. (accredited; charter mem., co-founder, past pres. and dir. Iowa chpt.; charter mem., co-founder, del. assembly, past chpt. dirand v.p. Quad Cities chpt.), Nat. Sch. Pub. Relations Assn., Acad. Am. Educators, Soc. Mktg. Profl. Services, Am. Mktg. Assn., Tex. Indsl. Devel. Council, Soc. Am. Mil. Engrs. Nat. Alumni Council of Boston U. Contbr. articles profl. publs. Home: 17 Cypress Ct Trophy Club TX 76262 Office: 2107-C Greenbriar Southlake TX 76092

HAERTEL, RAINER MARIA, chemical company executive; b. Vienna, June 27, 1947; s. Wilhelm and Gertrude (Pölzl) H.; m. Vera A. Amon, Nov. 15, 1977; children: Daniela, Christoph R. MS, U. for Bus. Econs., Vienna, 1975. Mktg. service control officer Steel div. Sandvik, Vienna, 1976-77; sales and mktg. mgr. for Yugoslavia, Coromant div., Vienna, 1978-81, gen. mgr. saws and tools div., 1981-83; mgr. dir. Loctite Europa, Vienna, 1984—. Home: Paul-Guselstrasse 22, A02105 Langenzersdorf Austria Office: Loctite Europa GmbH, Akazien gasse 34, A1230 Vienna Austria

HAESELER, WILLIAM, III, finance company executive; b. North Tonawanda, N.Y., Aug. 15, 1930; s. William and Mabel (Meyers) H.; B.A., Valparaiso U., 1952; M.S., Boston U., 1954; m. Gloria Ruth Barth, July 15, 1960; children—Susan Beth, Mark William, Karen Ruth, Lisa Ann. With Cert. Fin. Co., Inc., North Tonawanda, 1948—, v.p., 1957-67, treas., 1960-67, pres., 1967—, also dir.; pres. Cert. Travel Tours, North Tonawanda, 1970—, also dir.; dir. Charge Account Service, Inc., North Tonawanda; owner William Haeseler III Assos., North Tonawanda, 1954—. Mem. faculty Millard Fillmore Coll., SUNY, Buffalo, 1955-66, 70-79; travel columnist, 1972—. Corp. mem. DeGraff Meml. Hosp., North Tonawanda, 1967—. Mem. adv. bd. Niagara County Community Colls. Served with AUS, 1956-57. Mem. C. of C., Am. Soc. Travel Agts. (pres. N.Y. chpt. 1984), Luth. Laymens League, Delta Sigma Pi, Tau Mu Epsilon, Lambda Chi Alpha. Republican. Lutheran. Clubs: Skal, Town of the Tonawandas, Travelers Century, Rotary (past pres.). Home: 39 Bentham Pkwy Snyder NY 14226 Office: 1040 Payne Ave North Tonawanda NY 14120

HAFER, PAUL ROBERT, museum executive, tree farm executive; b. Reading, Pa., Nov. 7, 1910; s. Franklin and Elizabeth O. (Goranflo) H.; m. Erminie Florence Shaeffer, Oct. 7, 1933. Student, Lehigh U., 1931-33. Pres., Boyertown Auto Body Works, Pa., 1932-72, chmn. bd., 1972-83; pres. Boyertown Body and Equipment Co., 1945-72, chmn. bd., 1972-83; pres. Battronic Truck corp., Boyertown, 1962-72, chmn. bd., 1972-83; founder Mus. Hist. Vehicles, Boyertown, 1963—; founder, chmn. bd. Hafer Found., Boyertown, 1965—; owner, operator Hafer Tree Farm, Perkiomenville, Pa., 1975—; dir. emeritus Nat. Bank Boyertown, 1984—; dir. Suburban Airlines, Reading, 1975-86. Patentee Electric Vehicle System 1972. Contbr. articles to profl. jours. Bd. dirs. Northeast Region Boy Scouts Am., 1968, nat. adv. bd. 1986—, Hist. Found. Pa., Harrisburg, 1983; dir., chmn. Trust Devel. Commn., Hawk Mountain Council Boy Scouts Am., 1982—; dir., v.p. Berks County Hist. Soc., Reading, 1968; founder, pres. Boyertown Area Community Trust, 1982—; founder Mus. Historic Vehicles, Boyertown, 1963—; chmn. bldg. commn. Berks County Hist. Soc., 1984—, (v.p. 1970—); elder Good Shepherd United Ch. Christ, Boyertown, 1968-84; sec. Nat. United Ch. Christ Scouters Assn., 1985—. Recipient B'nai B'rith Americanism award 1960, 50 Year Masonic Service Emblem award Masonic Grand Lodge 1985, Founders award Am. Truck Hist. Soc. 1983, Shikallemy award Hawk Mountain Council Boy Scouts Am. 1956, Silver Beaver award Hawk Mountain Council Boy Scouts Am. 1958, Silver Antelope award Northeast Region Boy Scouts Am. 1963, God & Service award Nat. Council Boy Scouts Am. 1979, BSA God Scouters award, 1988, Paul Harris Fellow medal Rotary Internat. 1983, Citation Owl Club award Berks County Optometric Soc. 1960; named Man of Year Boyertown Jr. C. of C. 1961. Republican. Lodges: Rotary, Lions (hon. life), Masons. Avocations: golf, travel; music; playing hammond organ; work on antique cars. Home: 28 W Second St Boyertown PA 19512 Office: Mus Historic Vehicles 28 Warwick St Boyertown PA 19512

HAFFNER, ALFRED LOVELAND, JR., lawyer; b. Bklyn., Sept. 11, 1925; s. Alfred Loveland and Mary Ellen (Myers) H.; m. Mary Dolores Hyland, July 10, 1965; children: Mary Elizabeth, Anne Dolores, Jeanne Marie, Catherine Dianne. B.S. in Engring, U. Mich., 1950, J.D., 1956. Bar: N.Y. 1958, U.S. Patent and Trademark Office, 1958, U.S. Dist. Ct. (so. and ea. dists.) N.Y. 1959, U.S. Ct. Claims 1959, U.S. Ct. Appeals (fed. cir.) 1961, U.S. Supreme Ct. 1961, U.S. Ct. Appeals (2d cir.) 1962. Draftsman-engr., indsl. engr., asst. plant engr. Owens-Ill. Glass Co., Bridgeton, N.J., 1950-53, Streator, Ill., 1953-54; since practiced N.Y.C.; asso. firm Kenyon & Kenyon, N.Y.C., 1957-60, Ward, McElhannon, Brooks & Fitzpatrick, N.Y.C., 1960-61; partner Ward, McElhannon, Brooks & Fitzpatrick, 1961-71, Brooks Haidt Haffner & Delahunty, N.Y.C., 1971—; Chmn. Nat. Council Patent Law Assns., 1973-74, councilman, 1971-88 ; bd. dirs. Nat. Inventors Hall of Fame Found., 1972—, pres., 1973-74, sec., 1980—. Served with USNR, 1943-46. Mem. ABA, N.Y. State Bar Assn., Am. Intellectual Property Law Assn., N.Y. Patent Trademark and Copyright Law Assn. (sec. 1964-68, dir. 1968-70, 71-72, pres. 1970-71), Strathmore Assn. Westchester (treas. 1976-79, v.p. 1980-82, pres. 1982-83, exec. com. 1983—), Phi Gamma Delta, Phi Alpha Delta. Club: Westchester Country. Home: 1 Gainsborough Rd Scarsdale NY 10583 Office: 99 Park Ave New York NY 10016

HAFFNER, JOHAN FREDRIK WILHELM, gastroenterologist; b. Oslo, Mar. 2, 1940; s. Johan and Aase H.; m. Kokko Herboldt; children: Wilhelm, Helene, Henriette. MBChB, Glasgow U., 1964; PhD, Oslo U., 1973, degree in Gen. Surgery, 1977, degree in Surg. Gastroenterology, 1981. Research fellow Oslo U. Dept. Pharmacology, 1968-72; from surg. tng. to chief surgeon Ullevaal Hosp., Rikshospitalet, Radium Hospitalet, Oslo, 1967-83; cons. Ullevaal Hosp., 1983—. Author: Kirurgisk Gastroenterologi, 1985; contbr. numerous articles to sci. jours. Mem. Internat. Fed. Surg. Colls. (nat. rep. 1982-86), Scandinavian Assn. Gastrointestinal Motility (founding mem., treas. 1987—), Norwegian Obesity Group (founding mem.), Norwegian Surg. Soc. (pres. 1982-86), Norwegian Med. Assn. (pres. 1988—), mem. other Internat. Surg. and Gastroenterol. Socs. Office: Ullevaal Hosp, Oslo 0407, Norway

HAFNER, KLAUS, researcher; b. Potsdam, Ger., Dec. 10, 1927; s. Alexander and Gertrud (Urban) H.; m. Gisela Schneider, Feb. 14, 1963; children—Ulrike. D.Ph., U. Marburg, 1951, habilitation, 1956. Research asst. MPI fur Kohlenforschung, Mulheim/Ruhr, Fed. Republic Germany, 1951-55; privat-dozent U. Marburg, Fed. Republic Germany, 1956-61; assoc. prof. U. Munich, 1962-64; prof. organic chemistry Technische Hochschule, Darmstadt, 1965—. Contbr. articles to profl. jours. Editor: Liebigs Annalen der Chemie, 1968—. Co-editor Chemische Berichte, 1980—, Topics in Current Chemistry, 1967—, Reactivity and Structure, 1967—. Recipient Adolf von Baeyer Meml. Coin, German Chem. Soc., 1980; Carus medal German Acad. Sci., 1980; Carus prize City of Schweinfurth, 1980. Mem. Am. Chem. Soc., Verein Osterreichischer Chemiker, Gesellschaft Deutscher Chemiker, Chem. Soc. Britain, Deutsche Kunststoff-Institut (bd. trustees) Beilstein-Institut (bd. dirs.), Deutsche Akademie der Naturforscher Leopoldina. Lodge: Rotary. Home: Steinbergweg 32A, 6100 Darmstadt Federal Republic of Germany Office: Institut fur, Organische Chemie der THD, Petersenstr 22, 6100 Darmstadt Federal Republic of Germany

HAFNER, THOMAS MARK, lawyer; b. Evansville, Ind., Aug. 8, 1943; s. Theodore Paul and Josephine Margaret (Herpolsheimer) H.; m. Joy Ruth Roller, June 10, 1967; children—Mark, Sharon, Matthew, Michael, Martin. B.A. with distinction, Valparaiso U., 1965, J.D., 1968. Bar: Ind. 1968, Tenn. 1980. Asso., Nieter, Smith, Blume, Wyneken & Dixon, Ft. Wayne, Ind., 1968-70; atty. Magnavox Co., Ft. Wayne, 1970-73, group counsel, 1973-77; sr. counsel N.Am. Philips Corp., Ft. Wayne, 1977-80, Knoxville, Tenn., 1980—. Author: Legal Guidelines for Regional Managers, 1978, The Bankruptcy Code: An Outline for Creditors, 1980, A Checklist for Distribution Agreements, 1985. Mem. ABA (chmn. subcom. counseling the mktg. function com. corp. counsel 1982—), Electronic Industries Assn. (chmn. govt. and consumer affairs council 1981-86, vice chmn. law com. 1986, chmn. 1987—), Am. Corp. Counsel Assn. (dir. at large Tenn. chpt. 1986—).

HAGEGARD, HAKAN, baritone; b. Karlstad, Sweden, Nov. 25, 1945; ed. Music Acad., Stockholm; student of Tito Gobbi, Rome, Gerald Moore, London, Erik Werba, Vienna; 2 children. Debut as Papageno in The Magic Flute, Royal Opera Sweden, 1968; Met. Opera debut, 1978; mem. Royal Opera, Stockholm; appeared with maj. opera cos. throughout Europe; in film The Magic Flute, 1975; recitalist; created role of Crispin in Tintomara, Royal Opera, Stockholm, 1973. Address: care Thea Dispeker Artist's Rep 59 E 54th St New York NY 10022 *

HAGEMAN, RICHARD PHILIP, JR., educational administrator; b. Derby, Conn., Dec. 21, 1941; s. Richard Philip and Jane Elizabeth (Serafinowicz) H.; B.S., Cen. Conn. State U., 1964; M.S., U. Bridgeport, 1968, profl. diploma, 1972; children—Margaret Anne, Sheila Marie. Cert. counselor Nat. Bd. Cert. Counselors. Tchr., Stony Brook Sch., Stratford (Conn.) Bd. Edn., 1964-69, elem. sch. guidance counselor, 1969-81, secondary sch. guidance counselor, 1981-83; asst. prin. Stratford (Conn.) Acad., 1983—; lectr. edn. Fairfield U. Grad. Sch. Edn., 1971—; head counselor Stratford Continuing Edn. Program, 1981—, chief examiner Gen. Ednl. Devel.; mem. adv. bd. counselor edn. Fairfield (Conn.) U., 1970-74; co-chmn. Stratford Juvenile Deliquency Prevention Team, 1979-81. Mem. Youth Adv. Bd. Stratford, 1981-85, chairperson, 1984-85; radio announcer Sta. WMNR, Monroe, Conn., 1982—. Mem. Am. Assn. Counseling and Devel., Stratford Edn. Assn. (pres. 1978-79), Am. Sch. Counselor Assn., NEA (life), New Eng. Assn. Specialists Group Work (pres. 1982-83), Nat. Assn. Elem. Sch. Prins., Assn. Supervision and Curriculum Devel., Phi Delta Kappa. Roman Catholic. Democrat. Office: Stratford Acad 719 Birdseye St Stratford CT 06497

HAGEN, LARRY WILLIAM, manufacturing and retail executive; b. Pyote, Tex., May 5, 1945; s. Lawrence Herbert and Marjorie Fern (MacFarland) H.; 1 child, Bret William. AA, Highline Coll., 1965; BS cum laude, Seattle U., 1969; MBA, Pacific Luth. U., 1987. Dir. ops. group III The Bon Marche, Seattle, 1967-75; dir. distbn. Brittania Sportswear, Seattle, 1975-77; exec. v.p., chief fin. officer Schoenfeld Neckwear, Seattle, 1977—, also bd. dirs., 1984—; bd. dirs. Mallory & Church Ltd., London, 1985—; cons. Jeans Warehouse, Seattle, 1979-81. Loaned exec. United Way, Seattle, 1966-69; collector YMCA Disadvantaged Youth, Seattle, 1983-86. Served with USNG, 1964-74. Mem. Am. Prodn. Inventory Control Soc., Pacific NW Personnel Mgmt. Assn., Am. Soc. Personnel Adminstrn. (v.p. Seattle chpt. 1970-71, pres. Columbian Basin 1981-82). Democrat. Lutheran. Home: 5021 Ripley Ln N Renton WA 98056 Office: Schoenfeld Neckwear Corp 676 S Industrial Way Seattle WA 98108

HAGEN, PER ROLF, investment banker; b. Kviteseid, Telemark, Norway, Sept. 19, 1927; s. Hans O. and Nora (Simensen) H.; m. Aud F. Furuto, Apr. 15, 1932; children—Bente, Beate. Grad., Oslo Handelsgymnasium, 1947; student Fag., Leeds Coll. Commerce (Eng.), 1955. Ptnr., Gunnar Bohn & Co., Oslo, 1960-72; mng. dir. Shearson Hammill Internat., London, 1972-74; chief exec. officer Norse Securities, Oslo, 1974-80; gen. mgr. Sparebanken Oslo Akershus (name changed to ABC Union Bank of Norway 1986), 1980—. Mem. Soc. Fin. Analysts. Club: Norwegian (London); Golf (Oslo). Home: Bjerkelundsveien 46, 1342 Jar Norway Office: ABC Union Bank of Norway, Kirkegaten 18, 1 Oslo Norway

HAGER, BROR OLOF, engineer; b. Soderhamn, Sweden, Dec. 19, 1907; s. Olof and Britta (Vestberg) H.; grad. Royal Polytechnical U., Stockholm, 1933; m. Irma Maria Ekstrom, July 15, 1939; children—Britt, Eva, Ulla. Chem. research engr. Boliden Co., Stockholm, 1934-46; owner, mgr. Hager Aktiebolag, Taby-Stockholm, 1946—. Recipient Gold medal award Royal Swedish Acad. Engring., 1961; Invention award Nat. Swedish Bd. for Tech. Devel., 1982. Mem. Swedish Inventors Assn. (dir. 1961-65, recipient award 1973), Am. Wood Preservers Assn. Contbr. articles to profl. jours. Patentee in field (300). Home: 5 Forsetevagen, S-182-63 Djursholm Sweden Office: 17 Kryssarvagen, S-183-52 Taby Sweden

HAGER, FRITZ-PETER P., education educator, philosophy researcher; b. Adelboden, Switzerland, Aug. 1, 1939; s. Emil Friedrich and Clara Bertha (Stengele) H. Dr. Phil., U. Bern, 1961, Privatdozent für Philosophie, 1969; Universitätsprofessor für Paedagogik, U. Zürich, 1978; vis. mem. Inst. Advanced Study, Princeton, 1965. Asst., Paedagogisches Seminar der U. Bern (Switzerland), 1968-72, Oberassistent-Dozent, 1972-78; prof. pedagogics, history and theory of edn. U. Zürich, 1978—. Author: Die Vernunft und das Problem des Bösen, 1963, Der Geist und das Eine, 1970; Pestalozzi und Rousseau, 1975, Plato Paedagogus, 1981, Gott und das Böse im antiken Platonismus, 1987; contbr. articles to jours. and publs. Mem. Internat. Soc. Metaphysics, Internat. Soc. Neoplatonic Studies, Internat. Standing Conf. History of Edn. Mem. Freisinnig-demokratische Partei der Schweiz. Mem. Evangelical Reformed Ch. Home: Schwendenhaustrasse 2, 8702 Zollikon Zürich Switzerland Office: Paedagogisches Inst, Rämistrasse 74, CH 8001 Zürich Switzerland

HAGER, NATHANIEL ELLMAKER, JR., physicist; b. Lancaster, Penn., June 3, 1922; s. Nathaniel Ellmaker and Ruth (Mayer) H.; BS, Franklin and Marshall Coll., 1943; MS, Lehigh U., 1948; PhD, 1953; m. Nancy Cleaver, June 26, 1948; children: Nathaniel E., Sarah Wilson. Instr. Lehigh U., Bethlehem, Pa., 1950-51; sect. head physics dept. Vitro Lab., West Orange, N.J., 1952-54; research physicist Armstrong World Industries Inc., Lancaster, Pa., 1954-68, research asso., 1968-76, sr. research asso., 1976—; tchr. creativity sessions for gifted Lancaster County Pub. Schs., 1967—; adv. panel on bldg. energy performance standards Nat. Inst. Bldg. Scis., 1979-81, mem. Consultative Council, 1982—, Radon com., bd. dirs. Am. Lung Assn. Lancaster County, 1987—. Mem. sch. bd. Manheim Twp., Lancaster County (Pa.), Lancaster and Lebanon Counties; dir. radiol. div. Lancaster County Civil Def., 1956—; bd. dirs. Hearing Conservation Center of Lancaster County 1957—. Served with USNR 1943-46. Mem. Internat. Inst. Refrigeration, Optical Soc. Am., Instrument Soc. Am. (sr.), AAAS, ASHRAE, Air Pollution Control Assn., Assn. Energy Engrs., N.Y. Acad. Sci., Internat. Platform Assn., Cliosophic Soc. Lancaster. Clubs: Sphinx, Fortnightly, Hamilton. Contbr. articles in field to profl. jours.; patentee in field; TV interviewee on sci. subjects. Home: 1410 Clayton Rd Lancaster PA 17603 Office: 2500 Columbia Ave Lancaster PA 17604

HAGERMAN, JOHN DAVID, lawyer; b. Houston, Aug. 1, 1941; s. David Angle and Noima L. (Clay) H.; m. Linda J. Lambright, June 25, 1975; children: Clayton Robert, Holly Elizabeth. BBA, So. Meth. U., 1963; JD, U. Tex., Austin, 1966. Bar: Tex. 1966, U.S. Dist. Ct. (so. dist.) Tex. 1967, U.S. Ct. Appeals (5th cir.) 1967, U.S. Supreme Ct. 1969. Pres., ptnr. Hagerman & Seureau, Inc., Spring, Tex., 1966—; condr. bank creditor rights seminars. Contbr. articles to profl. jours. Res. dep. sheriff, Montgomery County, Tex.; bd. dirs. Montgomery County Fair Assn., 1978—. Mem. ABA, Tex. Bar Assn., Houston Bar Assn., Houston Outdoor Advt. Assn., Tex. Assn. Civil Trial Specialists, Tex. Assn. Bank Counsel, Beta Theta Pi. Republican. Club: Petroleum (Houston). Avocations: swimming, tennis, jogging, shooting. Office: Hagerman & Seureau Inc 24800 Interstate 45 #100 Spring TX 77373

HAGERSON, LAWRENCE JOHN, health agency executive, consultant; b. Lakewood, Ohio, Dec. 30, 1931; s. John Lawrence and Ruth Evelyn (Watson) H.; m. Shirley Lorraine Carter, July 2, 1955; children—Nancy Lynn, Tracy Ann, Laura Jane. B.S. in Econs., U. Pa., 1954, postgrad. in Economics, 1957-59. Cons. John Price Jones Co., N.Y.C., 1960-62, U.S Agy. for Internat. Devel. Southeast Asia, 1970-74; asst. to chancellor U. Calif., Santa Barbara, 1962-63, U. Mo., Kansas City, 1967-70; cons. Asia Found., Singapore, Malaysia, 1964-67; exec. v.p. Mid. Am. Health Edn. Consortium, Kansas City, 1970-78; dir. bus. and devel. Inst. Logopedics, Wichita, Kans., 1978—. Mem., officer Kans. City Civic Orchestra Bd., 1976-78; bd. dirs. Greater Kans. City Urban Coalition, 1969-70. Served to lt. USN, 1954-56. Mem. Nat. Soc. Fund Raising Execs. (nat. bd. dirs. 1984—). Republican.

Presbyterian. Lodge: Kiwanis. Avocation: golf. Home: 7115 Chadowes Wichita KS 67206 Office: Inst Logopedics 2400 Jardine Dr Wichita KS 67219

HAGERTY, HARVE JOHN, retired adult corrections consultant, educator; b. New Orleans, Feb. 18, 1934; s. Vaughn Clifton and Wilhelmina (Wettstein) Hagerty Bilbo; m. Elizabeth Anne Garner, Oct. 10, 1959; children—Harve J., Vaughn C., Michael J. B.S., U. Southern Miss., 1959; M.A., U. Okla., 1975. Director classification Okla. State Penitentiary, McAlester, 1976-77; project supr. Ex-Offender Placement Service, San Antonio, 1977-80; program dir. Kerper House Inc., San Antonio, 1980-82; instr. Tex. A&M U., San Antonio, 1982-87. Bd. dirs. Valley Forge Homeowners Assn., San Antonio, 1981-86; adv. bd. Vista, San Antonio, 1985-87. Served to lt. col. U.S. Army, 1954-76. Decorated Bronze Star. Mem. Am. Correctional Assn., Tex. Correctional Assn., Retired Officer's Assn. Republican. Lodges: Lions, Shriners, Masons, Knights Templar. Avocations: writing for profl. jours.; public speaking; community affairs.

HAGEY, WALTER REX, banker; b. Hatfield. Pa., July 24, 1909; s. Justus T. and Martha Mabel Hagey; student U. Pa., 1931-36; LL.B., La Salle Extension U., 1938; S.T.B., Temple U., 1943; grad. Stonier Grad. Sch. Banking Rutgers U., 1951; LL.D., Muhlenberg Coll., 1963; m. Dorothy E. Rosenberger, Oct. 17, 1931; 1 son, Donald C. With Fidelity Bank (formerly Fidelity-Phila. Trust Co.), 1929—, asst. sec., 1948—, asst. v.p., 1957-66, v.p., 1966-74. Supply pastor Eastern Pa. Synod Lutheran Ch. Am., 1950-80, treas., 1950-80, now Luth. Synod S.E. Pa.; treas. Luth. Synod Northeastern Pa., 1969-70; pres., dir. Phila. Luth. Social Union; treas. Luth. Laymens Movement for Stewardship of United Luth. Ch., 1959-63; mem. bd., exec. com. Luth. Council in U.S., 1962-74; mem. bds., treas. home missions, inner missions, Christian edn. Eastern Pa. Synod, Luth. Ch. Am., 1950-69; vice chmn. adminstrn. and fin. Luth. Ch. in Am., 1972-78, mem. bd. pensions, 1978-84, v.p. Bd. Am. Missions, 1972-78; bd. dirs., adv. bd. Muhlenberg Med. Center; bd. dirs., chmn. Prosser Found., 1968—; bd. dirs., treas. Luth. Retirement Homes, 1978-82; mem. com. for investments Luth. Ch. in Am., 1978-82; bd. dirs., sec. Silver Spring-Martin Luther Sch., 1976—; treas. Bethesda House, 1950-69; treas., registrar Luth. Lay Acad., 1981—, ; treas. The Auxiliary-Luth. Theol. Sem. at Phila., 1986—, The Religious Tercentenary Com., 1982—. Mem. Am. Inst. Banking, Phila. Estate Planning Council, Pa. Council Chs. (dir. 1954-70), Pa. Soc., Luth. Hist. Soc. Eastern Pa., Men of Mt. Airy Sem. (pres. 1976-86), Pa. Bible Soc. (treas., sec., now pres., dir. 1971—). Clubs: Rotary. Elm (sec. 1951-63); Midday, Anglers (Phila.). Home: 510 E Lawn Ave Lansdale PA 19446

HAGGARD, FORREST DELOSS, minister; b. Trumbull, Nebr., Apr. 21, 1925; s. Arthur McClellan and Grace (Hadley) H.; m. Eleanor V. Evans, June 13, 1946; children—Warren A., William D., James A., Katherine A. A.B., Phillips U., 1948; M.Div., 1953, D.D. (hon.), 1967; M.A., U. Mo., 1960. Ordained to ministry Christian Ch., 1948; minister Overland Park (Kans.) Christian Ch., 1953—; pres. Kansas City Area Ministers Assn., 1959, Kans. Christian Ministers Assn., 1960; mem. adminstrn. com., gen. bd. Christian Ch., 1968-72; pres. World Conv. Chs. of Christ (Christian/Disciples of Christ), 1975—; chmn. Grad. Sem. Council, Enid, Okla., 1970; pres. Nat. Evangelistic Assn., 1972; pres. bd. dirs. Midwest Counseling Ctr., Kansas City, 1987—. Author: The Clergy and the Craft, 1970, also articles. Pres. Johnson County (Kans.) Mental Health Assn., 1962-63; mem. council Boy Scouts Am., 1964-69; bd. dirs. Kans. Home for Aged, 1960-65, Kans. Children's Service League, 1964-69; pres. bd. dirs. Kans. Masonic Home, 1974-75; mem. bd. dirs. Kans. Masonic Found, 1970—; trustee Nat. Properties Christian Ch., 1987—. Recipient San Houston medal Sesqui-Centential Commn., Tex., 1987. Club: Masons (grand master Kans. Chaplain Genl. Grand Chpt. Royal Arch Internat. 1975—). Home: 6816 W 78th Terr Overland Park KS 66204 Office: 7600 W 75th St Overland Park KS 66204

HAGGERTY, JAMES JOSEPH, writer; b. Orange, N.J., Feb. 1, 1920; s. James Joseph and Anna (Morahan) H.; student pub. schs.; m. Marian Smith Mitten, Nov. 20, 1962; children—Karin, James Joseph, Brian (by previous marriage). Reporter Orange (N.J.) Daily Courier, 1938-40; mil. editor Am. Aviation Publs., 1948-53; aviation editor Collier's, 1953-56; free-lance writer on sci. and aerospace subjects, 1956—; editor Aerospace Year Book, 1957-70; aerospace editorial cons. Aerospace Industries Assn., 1974—, NASA, 1975—, Pres. Commn. on Space Shuttle Challenger Accident, 1986. Served with USAAF, 1942-48. Decorated D.F.C., Air medal with clusters. Mem. Aviation Space Writers Assn. (past pres.), AAAS, Air Force Assn. Clubs: Bethesda Country; Touchdown (Washington). Author: First of the Spacemen, 1960; Spacecraft, 1961; Flight, 1964; The U.S. Air Force: A Pictorial History in Art, 1965; Man's Conquest of Space, 1965; Food and Nutrition, 1966; Apollo Lunar Landing, 1969; Hail To The Redskins, 1973; Aviation's Mr. Sam, 1973. Address: 502 H St SW Washington DC 20024

HAGGLUND, CLARANCE EDWARD, lawyer, computer company executive; b. Omaha, Feb. 17, 1927; s. Clarence Andrew and Esther May (Kelle) H.; m. Dorothy S. Hagglund, Mar. 27, 1953; children—Laura, Bret, Katherine; m. Merle Patricia Hagglund, Oct. 28, 1972. B.A., U. S.D., 1949; J.D., William Mitchell Coll. Law, 1953. Bar: Minn. 1955, U.S. Ct. Appeals (8th cir.) 1974, U.S. Supreme Ct. 1963. Diplomate Am. Bd. Profl. Liability Attys. Ptnr. Hagglund & Johnson and predecessor firms, Mpls., 1973—; sole practice to present; pres. Internat. Control Systems, Inc., Mpls., 1979—, Hill River Corp., Mpls., 1976—; gen. counsel Minn. Assn. Profl. Ins. Agts., Inc., Mpls., 1965-86. Contbr. articles to profl. jours. Served to lt. comdr. USNR, 1945-46, 50-69. Fellow Internat. Soc. Barristers; mem. Minn. Bar Assn., ABA, Lawyer Pilots Bar Assn., U.S. Maritime Law Assn. (proctor), Acad. Cert. Trial Lawyers Minn. (dean 1983-85), Nat. Bd. Trial Advocacy (cert. in civil trial law). Roman Catholic. Clubs: Ill. Athletic (Chgo.); Edina Country (Minn.); Calhoun Beach (Mpls.). Home: 3719 Xerxes Ave S Minneapolis MN 55410 Office: 4000 Olson Memorial Hwy Suite 501 Golden Valley MN 55422

HÄGGSTRÖM, STIG OLOF, regional planning company executive; b. Inkoo, Finland, Jan. 7, 1924; s. Henry Harock and Vivi Emilia (Ginman) H.; widowed; children: Stefan, Ralf, Ann-Helena, Lars. MS in Photogrammetry, Helsinki U. Tech., Finland, 1948, MS in Rural and Urban Planning, 1971. Registered profl. engr., Finland. Geodetic engr. Township of Karis, Finland, 1948-82; dir. West Nyland Regional Assn., Karis, 1968—; dir. tech. dept. Oy Wulff Ab, 1951-58; dep. dir surveying Imatran Voima Oy, 1958-64; dir. Maastro Oy, 1964-68; dir. Kaavakaratta Oy, 1968-86, now bd. dirs. Author articles on aerial photogrammetry and phys. planning. Recipient Suomen Valkoinen Ruusu award Ridderteknet, 1983. Mem. Finnish Photogrammetric Soc. (bd. dirs. 1956-67). Lutheran. Lodges: Rotary, Masons (postmaster). Home: Stabgatan 10, 10300 Karis Finland Office: West Nyland Regional Assn, Kopmansgatan 11, 10300 Karis Finland

HAGL, EWALD WALTER, import-export trade executive, consultant; b. Karlsruhe, Federal Republic of Germany, Dec. 22, 1935; s. Franz and Lydia Christine (Konstantin) H.; m. Margot Anneliese Born, June 14, 1960; children: Dirk Ulf, Andre Daniel, Susann-Kristin, Marc Claude. Degree in Econs., Comml. U., Pforzheim, Federal Republic of Germany, 1970. Co-owner Hagl Export-Import Co., Karlsruhe, 1953-67; mgr. exports IGS Ltd., Karlsruhe, 1970-73, Dibona KG, Ettlingen, Federal Republic of Germany, 1973-85, Ragolds Ltd., Karlsruhe, 1986—; cons. Jamjoom Gen. Agys., Jeddah, Saudi Arabia. Vice-chmn. German Free Dems., Pfinztal, 1983-87. Home: Tiroler Strasse 9, D-7500 Karlsruhe 41 Federal Republic of Germany Office: RAGOLDS Gmbh, Tullastrasse 60, D7500 Karlsruhe Federal Republic of Germany

HAGRUP, KNUT, aviation consultant; b. Bergen, Norway, Nov. 13, 1913; s. Lie-Svendsen and Ebba (Hagrup) H.; math. degree, 1933; grad. Coll. Royal Norwegian Air Force, 1936; Civil Engr., Darmstadt U., 1940; Dr. Laws (hon.), Pacific Luth. U., 1978; Sc.Dr. (hon.), Northrop U., 1978; Dr.econs., Hochschule fur Verkerswesen, Dresden, Germany, 1979; Dr. tech., Stockholm U., 1980; m. Esther Skaugen, Sept. 22, 1944 (dec. 1975); children—Vivi, Bente. Chief engr. Norwegian Civil Aeros. Bd., Oslo, 1945; chief engr. Scandinavian Airlines Systems, Stockholm, 1946, v.p. ops., 1951-56, v.p. engring., 1956-60, v.p. tech. and ops., 1960-62, exec. v.p. tech. and ops., 1962-69, pres., 1969-79; chmn. bd. Saab-Fairchild Airliner program, Stockholm-N.Y.C., 1980-85; cons., dir. various Scandinavian industries; dir. Hennes & Mauritz, Stockholm, SAAB-SCANIA; cons. prof. Pacific Luth. U., Tacoma, 1979; prof., trustee Northrop U., Los Angeles, 1980; chmn. commn. air transport Internat. C. of C., Paris, 1969—; chmn. IATA, 1974-75, Assn. European Airlines, 1975-76 (chmn.); dir. Thai Airways, 1969-76. Served with Royal Norwegian Air Force, 1940-45. Decorated Norwegian War medal; Def. medal; Haakon VII's medal; comdr. Northern Star (Sweden); comdr. Order St. Olav (Norway); grand officer Orange-Nassau (Netherlands); comdr. Legion d'Honneur (France); Brit. Def. medal; comdr. Order White Elephant (Thailand). Fellow Brit. Aero. Soc.; mem. Royal Airforce Club. Author: La Bataille du Transport Aerien, 1978; Die Heutige Weltluftfahrt, 1979; How the Aerospace Industry of Western Europe Will Survive, 1981. Home: 14 rue St-Jean, 1260 Nyon VD Switzerland

HAGSON, CARL ALLAN, utilities executive; b. Haggenas, Jamtland, Sweden, Nov. 4, 1921; s. Olof and Elin (Eriksson) H.; m. Marianne Lallerstedt, Nov. 24, 1967. MS in Elec. Engring., Royal Tech. Inst., Stockholm, 1947. With Swedish State Power Bd., 1947-50; with Swedish Assn. Electricity Supply Undertakings, Stockholm, 1950-86, gen. mgr., 1967-86; pub. electrotech. jour. ERA, 1975-86; mem. govt. coms. on energy consumption forecasting, energy conservation, energy tariffs, 1972-82; mem. tech. council Nat. Bd. Phys. Planning and Bldg., 1970-85; mem. com. action Internat. Electrotech. Commn., 1978-84. Served with Swedish Army, 1942-43, 45. Decorated knight Royal Order of Vasa 1975, knight Finnish Lions Order 1987. Mem. IEEE, Union Internat. Producteurs Distributeurs d'Energie Electrique (dir. com. 1967-86), Swedish Electrotech. Commn. (bd. dirs. 1967-88, pres. 1973-88), Swedish Inst. Testing and Approval Elec. Equipment (bd. dirs. 1967-88), Conv. Nat. Socs. Elec. Engrs. We. Europe (exec. com. 1972-75, pres. 1973-74), Swedish Assn. Elec. Engrs. (bd. dirs. 1952-60, 69-76, pres. 1972-76, hon.), Swedish Union Grad. Engrs., Swedish Taxpayers Assn. (bd. dirs. 1964-87), Assn. Electroheat Promotion (chmn. 1987—), SEF Tariffs Commn. (chmn. 1986—). Home: Torstenssonsgatan 10, 114 56 Stockholm Sweden Office: Box 3192, 103 63 Stockholm Sweden

HAGSTROM, TONY GUNNAR, government official; b. Worthington, Minn., Nov. 15, 1936; s. Gunnar Konrad and Anna Ingeborg (Andersson) H.; B.A., U. Stockholm, 1960; Ph.D. in Econs., U. Lund, 1968; m. Birgitta Christersson, Nov. 8, 1958; children—Thomas, Camilla. Head dept. for indsl. brs. Swedish Ministry of Industry, Stockholm, 1969-72, under sec. of state, 1973-76; gen. dir. Swedish Telecommunications Adminstrn., Farsta, 1977—; chmn. bd. Teleinvest AB, PK Banken, Ellemtel AB; bd. dirs. Astra, Swedish Steel AB. Editor: The Structure and Function of the Swedish Capital Market, 1968; (with others) The Pharmaceutical Industry, 1969, The Swedish Special Steel Industry, 1977. Home: Myrtenstigen 11, 12531 Älvsjö Sweden Office: 11 Marbackagatan Farsta, 12386 Stockholm Sweden

HAGURA, NOBUYA, banker; b. Kyoto, Japan, Jan. 17, 1919; s. Shinichiro H.; married; 2 children. Grad., Keio U., Tokyo. With Nippon Kangyo Bank (now called Dai-Ichi Kangyo Bank), Tokyo, from 1941; dir. Dai-Ichi Kangyo Bank, Tokyo, 1968-71, mng. dir., 1971-75, sr. mng. dir., 1975-76, dep. pres., 1976-82, pres., 1982-88, dir., adviser, 1988—. Mem. Japan Assn. Corp. Execs., Fedn. Econ. Orgn., Japan Fedn. Employers Assn. (dir.). Clubs: Sosei County (Chiba, Japan); Aso Country (Ibaragi, Japan).

HAHN, CARL HORST, auto company executive; b. July 1, 1926; m. Marisa Traina, 1960; 4 children. Chmn. bd. Continental GummiWerk AG, 1973-81; chmn. bd. Volkswagen AG, 1981—; chmn. supervisory bd. Gerling-Konzern Speziale Kreditversicherungs-AG, Cologne; dep. chmn. Supervisory bd. AG fur Industrie und Verkehrswesen, Frankfurt am Main, Gerling-Konzern Zentrale Vertriebs-AG, Cologne; mem. supervisory bd. Gerling-Konzern Allgemeine Versicherungs-AG, Cologne, Wilhelm Karmann GmbH, Norddeutsche Landesbank-Girozentrale, Hanover, Uniroyal Engleberg Reifen GmbH, Aachen. Mem. Fed. Econs. Ministry (adv. com.), Salk Inst. (internat. adv. com. La Jolla, Calif. chpt.), Founders' Assn. German Sci. (bd. mgmt.), Deutsche Bank AG (group cons.). Office: Volkswagen AG, 3180 Wolfsburg Federal Republic of Germany *

HAHN, CHANGGI, publisher; b. Ko-Eup-Ri, Polgyo-Eup, Chollanamdo, Korea, Nov. 11, 1936; s. Kuqsub and Inam (Cho) H.; LL.B., Seoul (Korea) Nat. U., 1961; M.A., Grad. Sch. Mass Communications, 1973. Resident mgr. Washington Meml. Bible Assos., Inc., P.F. Collier, Inc., Ency. Brit., Inc., 1961-68; gen. mgr. Ency. Brit. (Korea) Inc. (name changed to Korea Brit. Corp.), Seoul, 1968-69, exec. v.p., 1969-70, pres., 1970-85; pub., editor Deep-Rooted Tree, A Monthly Cultural Jour., Seoul, 1976-80, pub. Deep-Rooted Tree Pub. House, 1978—; pub., editor Saemikipunmul, monthly cultural jour., Seoul, 1985—; founding chmn., trustee Lang. Teaching Found., Seoul. Vice pres. Hangeul (Korean Alphabet) Cultural Assn., 1974—; bd. dirs. Nat. Museum Assn. Korea. Recipient Nat. Hangeul award, 1974. Mem. Hanguel Soc. Author: A Socio-Linguistic Study of Korean Honorifics, 1974. Home: 330-336 Sungbuk-Dong, Sungbuk-Gu, Seoul 132 Republic of Korea

HAHN, FRANK HORACE, economics educator; b. Berlin, W.Ger., Apr. 26, 1925; s. Arnold and Maria (Katz) H.; m. Dorothy Salter, 1946. B.Sc., 1945; Ph.D., London Sch. Econs., D.Sc. (Econ.), 1985; M.A., Cambridge U., 1950; D.Social Sci. (hon.), Birmingham U. (Eng.); D.Litt. (hon.), U. East Anglia, Norwich, 1984; Doctor honoris causa, U. Strasbourg, 1984. Lectr., reader math. econs. Birmingham U., 1948-60; lectr. econs. U. Cambridge, 1960-66, prof., 1972—; prof. econs. London Sch. Econs., 1967-72. Author: (with K. Arrow) The Share of Wages in the National Income, 1972; Money and Inflation, 1982, Equilibrium and Macroeconomics, 1984, Money, Growth and Stability, 1985; mng. editor: Rev. of Econ. Studies, 1963-66; assoc. editor: Jour. of Econ. Theory, 1971-76. Fellow Brit. Acad.; mem. Econometric Soc. (pres. 1968-69), Am. Acad. Arts and Scis. (hon.), Am. Econ. Assn. (hon.), Royal Econ. Soc. (pres. 1986—). Office: Faculty of Econ and Politics, Sidgwick Ave, Cambridge CB3 9AD, England

HAHN, FRED, emeritus political science and history educator; b. Stankov, Czechoslovakia, May 28, 1906; s. Emil and Helen (Wilhelm) H.; came to U.S., 1939, naturalized, 1947; D.Law and Polit. Sci., U. Prague, 1929; M.A., Columbia U., 1951; m. Edith H. Friedman, Dec. 25, 1949; children: Susan Ann, Jeanette Emily. Atty., Prague, Czechoslovakia, 1929-39; self-employed, N.Y.C., 1941-62; lectr. Fairleigh Dickinson U., Rutherford, Madison, N.J., 1962-64; assoc. prof. Trenton (N.J.) State Coll., 1964-69, prof., 1969-77, emeritus, 1977—; guest prof. U. Frankfurt, Germany, 1968-69, summer 1971, 73, 75; assoc. Inst. on East Central Europe, Columbia U., 1980—. Fulbright grantee, 1968-69, summer 1973. Mem. Am. Hist. Assn., Am. Assn. for Advancement Slavic Studies, Czechoslovakia Acad. Arts and Scis., Soc. for History Czechoslovak Jews (dir.), Internat PEN. Author: Marxist and Utopian Socialists, 1965; History of Russia, 1968; Stürmer, 1978. Contbr. articles to profl. jours. Home: 780 West End Ave New York NY 10025

HAHN, HAROLD THOMAS, physical chemist, chemical engineer; b. N.Y.C., May 31, 1924; s. Gustave Hahn and Lillie Martha (Thomas) H.; m. Bennie Joyce Turney, Sept. 5, 1948; children: Anita Karen, Beverly Sharon, Carol Linda, Harold Thomas Jr. Student, Hofstra U., 1941-43; BSChemE, Columbia U., 1943-44; PhD in Chemistry, U. Tex., 1950-53. Chem. engr. Manhattan Dist. U.S. Army, Los Alamos, N.Mex., 1945-47; chem. engr. U. Calif., Los Alamos, 1947-50; sr. scientist Gen. Electric Co., Hanford, Wash., 1953-58; sect. chief, chem. research dept. Phillips Petroleum Co., Idaho Falls, Idaho, 1958-64; sr. staff scientist Lockheed Missiles & Space Co., Palo Alto, Calif., 1964—. Contbr. articles to profl. jours.; patentee in field. Pres. Edgemont Gardens PTA, Idaho Falls, 1963-64; commr. cub scout div. Stanford area council Boy Scouts Am., Palo Alto, 1973-76, also cubmaster pack 36, 1973-80, chmn. troops 36 and 37, 1975-77; mem. adminstrv. bd. Los Altos Meth. Ch. Served to col. U.S. Army, 1944-46, with res., 1946-84, col. res. ret. Humble Oil Co. fellow, 1952, Naval Bur. Ordnance fellow, 1953. Fellow Am. Inst. Chemists; mem. Calif. Acad. Scis., Internat. Platform Assn., Am. Chem. Soc., AIAA, Sigma Xi, Phi Lambda Upsilon, Kappa Rho. Republican. Home: 661 Teresi Ln Los Altos CA 94022 Office: Lockheed Research Lab Dept 93-50 Bldg 204 3251 Hanover St Palo Alto CA 94304

HAHN, JOAN CHRISTENSEN, drama educator, travel agent; b. Kemmerer, Wyo., May 9, 1933; d. Roy and Bernice (Pringle) Wainwright; m. Milton Angus Christensen, Dec. 29, 1952 (div. Oct. 1, 1971); children—Randall M., Carla J. Christensen Teasdale; m. Charles Henry Hahn, Nov. 15, 1972. B.S., Brigham Young U., 1965. Profl. ballroom dancer, 1951-59; travel dir. E.T. World Travel, Salt Lake City, 1969—; tchr. drama Payson High Sch., Utah, 1965-71, Cottonwood High Sch., Salt Lake City, 1971—; dir. Performing European Tours, Salt Lake City, 1969-76; dir. Broadway theater tours, 1976—. Dir. Salem City Salem Days, Utah, 1965-75; regional dir. dance Latter-day Saints Ch., 1954-72. Named Best Dir. High Sch. Musicals, Green Sheet Newspapers, 1977, 82, 84; recipient 1st place award Utah State Drama Tournament, 1974, 77, 78; Limelight award, 1982; Exemplary Performance in teaching theater arts Granite Sch. Dist., Salt Lake City, 1982. Mem. Internat. Thespian Soc. (sponsor 1968—, internat. dir. 1982-84, trustee 1978-84), Utah Speech Arts Assn. (pres. 1976-78), NEA, Utah Edn. Assn., Granite Edn. Assn., Profl. Travel Agts. Assn., Utah High Sch. Activities Assn. (drama rep. 1972-76), AAUW (pres. 1972-74). Republican. Mormon. Avocations: reading; travel; dancing. Home: 685 S 1st E Box 36 Salem UT 84653 Office: Cottonwood High Sch 5715 S 1300 E Salt Lake City UT 84121

HAHN, LEWIS EDWIN, philosopher, retired educator; b. Swenson, Tex., Sept. 26, 1908; s. Edwin D. and Ione (Brewster) H.; m. Elizabeth Herring, June 30, 1932; children: Helen Elizabeth, Mary, Sharon. B.A., U. Tex., 1929, M.A., 1929; Ph.D., U. Calif., 1939. Teaching fellow U. Calif., 1931-34; instr. philosophy U. Mo., 1936-39, asst. prof., 1939-46, assoc. prof., 1946-49; vis. lectr. Princeton, 1947; prof. philosophy Washington U., 1949-63, chmn. dept., 1949-63, assoc. dean Grad. Sch. Arts and Scis., 1953-54, dean Grad. Sch. Arts. and Scis., 1954-63; research prof. philosophy So. Ill. U., Carbondale, 1963-77; prof. emeritus So. Ill. U., 1977—; vis. prof., editor So. Ill. U. (Library Living Philosophers), 1981—; disting. vis. prof. Baylor U., 1977, 79, 80; Mem. U.S. Nat. Commn. UNESCO, 1965-67. Author: A Contextualistic Theory of Perception, 1942, (with others) Value: A Cooperative Inquiry, 1949; co-author: (with others) Guide to the Works of John Dewey, 1970; editor: Library of Living Philosophers, 1981—; co-editor: The Philosophy of Gabriel Marcel, 1984, The Philosophy of W.V. Quine, 1986; contbr. articles to profl. jours. Fellow AAAS; mem. Am. Philos. Assn. (exec. bd. 1950-54, 70-73, chmn. com. placement, available personnel 1951-54, sec.-treas. West div. 1949-51, sec.-treas. 1960-66, com. on internat. coop. 1967-80), AAUP, Am. Soc. Aesthetics, S.W. Philos. Soc. (pres. 1955), Mo. Philos. Assn. (pres. 1949-50), So. Soc. for Philosophy and Psychology (pres. 1958-59), Ill. Philosophy Conf. (pres. 1969-71), Phi Beta Kappa. Home: Reed Sta Rd Rt 2 Box 621 Carbondale IL 62901

HAHN, THOMAS MARSHALL, JR., forest products corporation executive; b. Lexington, Ky., Dec. 2, 1926; s. Thomas Marshall and Mary Elizabeth (Boston) H.; m. Margaret Louise Lee, Dec. 27, 1948; children: Elizabeth Hahn McKelvy, Anne Hahn Clarke. BS in Physics, U. Ky., 1945; PhD, MIT, 1950; LLD (hon.), Seton Hall U., 1976, Fla. So. Coll., 1986; PhD (hon.), Va. Poly. Inst. and State U., 1987. Physicist U.S. Naval Ordinance Lab., 1946-47; research asst. MIT, Cambridge, 1947-50; assoc. prof. U. Ky., Lexington, 1950-52, prof., 1952-54; prof., head dept. physics Va. Poly. Inst. and State U., Blacksburg, 1954-59, pres., 1962-75; dean arts and scis. Kans. State U., Manhattan, 1959-62; exec. v.p. Ga.-Pacific Corp., 1975-76; pres. Ga.-Pacific Corp., Atlanta, 1976-82, pres., chief operating officer, 1982-83, pres., chief exec. officer, 1983—, also chmn. bd.; mem. Pres.' Export Council; bd. dirs. Norfolk So. Corp., Coca-Cola Enterprises, API, Sun Trust Banks; Trust Co. Bank of Ga., chmn. N.Y. Stock Exchange Listed Co. Adv. Com. Pres. So. Assn. Land Grant Colls. And State Univs., 1965-66; chmn. Va. Met. Area Study Commn., 1966-68, Va. Cancer Crusade, 1972, U.S. Savs. Bond Program, Ga., 1985-87; bd. visitors Air U., 1966-69, Ferrum Jr. Coll.; bd. dirs. Atlanta Arts Alliance, Cen. Atlanta Progress, Keep Am. Beautiful Inc.; mem. adv. bd. Atlanta chpt. Boy Scouts Am.; chmn. capital funds campaign Atlanta Area Services for Blind, 1984, Atlanta C. of C.; bd. visitors Callaway Gardens; mem. Atlanta Action Forum, nat. adv. bd. Salvation Army; campaign chmn. Ga. chpt. Am. Diabetes Assn., 1985-88, United Way of Met. Atlanta Inc., 1987; trustee Emory U., Inst. Paper Chemistry. Served with USN, 1945-46. Named Chief Exec. Officer of Yr. for Lumber Industry, Wall St. Transcript, 1984-86, Papermaker of Yr., Paper Trade Jour., 1984, Chief Exec. Officer of Yr., Forest Products and Paper Industry, 1986; recipient Outstanding Citizen award Toastmasters Internat., 1966, Outstanding Profl. Contbns. award Va. Citizens Planning Assn., 1970, MIT Corp. Leadership award, 1976. Fellow Am. Phys. Soc.; mem. The Conf. Bd., U. Ky. Bd. Trustees (inst. on paper chem.) Phi Beta Kappa, Sigma Xi, Omicron Delta Kappa. Republican. Methodist. Clubs: Piedmont Driving, The Links, Shenandoah, Capital City, Ocean Reef, Commerce. Office: Ga-Pacific Corp 133 Peachtree St NE Atlanta GA 30303

HAHNE, HENRY VICTOR, engineer, consultant; b. Riga, Latvia, Jan. 16, 1924; s. Harold Adolf and Lydia Maria (Aleksejev) H.; m. Iris Helen Suppik, Dec. 31, 1962; 1 dau., Victoria Ann. Dipl., Ingenieur, Technische Hochschule Graz, Austria, 1949; Ph.D., Stanford, 1954. Registered profl. engr., Calif. Engr. Ed. Ast & Co., Graz, 1949-51; engr. Pacific Car & Foundry Co., Seattle, 1951-52; asso. prof. dept. applied mechanics Washington U., St. Louis, 1954-56; research engr. Lockheed Missile & Space Div., Palo Alto, Calif., 1956-59; prof., head dept. civil engring. and applied mechanics U. Santa Clara, Calif., 1959-73; pres. Henry V. Hahne, Inc. (cons. engrs.), Los Altos, Calif., 1973—. Contbg. author: Handbook of Engineering Mechanics, 1961. Mem. Soc. Automotive Engrs., ASTM, ASCE. Home: 422 Cherry Ave PO Box 396 Los Altos CA 94022 Office: 160 Main St Los Altos CA 94022

HAIDT, HAROLD, lawyer; b. Bklyn., Dec. 6, 1926; s. Samuel and Rebecca (Davidson) H.; m. Elaine Meredith Kaplan, July 4, 1954; children: Rebecca, Jonathan, Samantha. B.S. in Chem. Engring, Purdue U., 1947; J.D., George Washington U., 1950. Bar: D.C. 1951, N.Y. State 1965. Examiner U.S. Patent Office, Washington, 1947-51; practiced in N.Y.C., 1964—; trial atty. antitrust div. U.S. Dept. Justice, 1951-53; corp. patent counsel Airco, Murray Hill, N.J., 1953-56; patent counsel Johnson & Johnson, New Brunswick, N.J., 1956-64; dir. Johnson & Johnson (Permacel and Chicoppee divs.), 1961-64; partner firm Brooks Haidt Haffner & Delahunty, N.Y.C., 1971—; cons., lectr. in field. Mem. U.S. del. U.S.-USSR Exchange in Patents and Licensing, 1972-73; cons. working group on intellectual property Joint U.S.-USSR Commn. on Sci. and Tech. Cooperation, 1975-77; chmn. U.S. del. to Poland and E.Ger. on patents and licensing, 1975. Author: U.S. Government Policies Relating to Technology, 1975; contbr. articles to profl. jours. Bd. govs. Old Scarsdale (N.Y.) Assn., 1969-71. Mem. Licensing Execs. Soc. (trustee 1971-74, v.p. 1973-74), Am. Intellectual Property Law Assn., N.Y. Intellectual Property Law Assn., Phi Lambda Upsilon. Home: 35 Church Ln Scarsdale NY 10583 Office: 99 Park Ave New York NY 10016

HAIG, ALEXANDER MEIGS, JR., former secretary state, former army officer, business executive; b. Phila., Dec. 2, 1924; s. Alexander Meigs and Regina Anne (Murphy) H.; m. Patricia Antoinette Fox, May 24, 1950; children: Alexander P., Brian F., Barbara E. Student, U. Notre Dame, 1943; B.S., U.S. Mil. Acad., 1947; M.A., Georgetown U., 1961; grad., Naval War Coll., 1960, Army War Coll., 1966; grad. hon. law degree, Niagara U.; LL.D. (hon.), U. Utah. Commd. 2d lt. U.S. Army, 1947, advanced through grades to gen., 1973; staff officer Office Dept. Chief of Staff for Ops. Dept. of Army, 1962-64; mil. asst. to sec. of army 1964, dep. spl. asst. to sec. and dep. sec. of def., 1964-65; bn. and brigade comdr. 1st Inf. Div., Vietnam, 1966-67; regtl. comdr., dep. comdt. U.S. Mil. Acad., 1967-69; mil. asst. to asst. to the Pres. for Nat. Security Affairs, 1969-70; dep. asst. to the Pres. for Nat. Security Affairs Washington, 1970-73; vice chief of staff U.S. Army, Washington, 1973; asst. to Pres., chief White House staff, 1973-74; comdr.-in-chief U.S. European Command, 1974-79; supreme allied comdr. Europe SHAPE, 1974-79; ret. 1979; pres., chief operating officer, dir. United Technologies Corp., Hartford, Conn., 1979-81; sec. state Washington, 1981-82; bd. dirs. Leisure Tech. Inc.; dir. Commodore Internat., Carteret Savs. Bank; chmn. United Tech. Corp., Atlantic and Pacific Adv. Councils. Decorated D.S.C., Silver Star with oak leaf cluster, Legion of Merit with 2 oak leaf clusters, D.F.C. with 2 oak leaf clusters, Bronze Star with oak leaf cluster, Air medal with 23 oak leaf clusters, Army Commendation medal, Purple Heart U.S.; Nat. Order 5th Class; Gallantry Cross with palm; Civil Actions Honor medal 1st Class; grand officer Nat. Order of Vietnam, Republic of Vietnam; medal of King Abdel-Aziz Saudi Arabia; grand cross Order of Merit W. Ger.; recipient Disting. Service medal Dept. of Def.; Disting. Service medal U.S. Army; Man of Yr. award Air Force Assn.; James Forrestal Meml. award. Mem. Soc. of 1st Div. (v.p.). Office: 1155 15th St NW Suite 800 Washington DC 20005

HAIG, YLVA CHRISTINA, energy information and public relations company executive; b. Stockholm, Feb. 8, 1945; d. Bror Axel and Ingrid (Wijkenstam) Danielsson; m. Ronald Allan Haig, June 12, 1968 (div.); children: Ylva, Emelie. BA in Econs., Uppsala U., Sweden, 1968; Dip., London Sch. Econs., 1969, Europa Inst., Amsterdam, 1979; postgrad., U. Stockholm, 1976-78. Econ. analyst Hambros Bank, London, 1968-70; prof. Meml. U., St. John's, Nfld., Can., 1970-73; econ. advisor Nfld. Ministry Industry, St. John's, Can., 1972-75; coordinator econ. research Wiener Inst. fur Internat. Wirtschaftsvergleiche, Vienna, Austria, 1975-76; research economist Swedish Def. Research Inst., Stockholm, 1980-83; v.p. Swedish Investment Bank, Stockholm, 1983-85; dir. Swedish Nuclear Fuel and Waste Mgmt. Co., Stockholm, 1985-87; pres. Haig Internat. AB, Stockholm, 1987—; pub. SKB News, nuclear periodical, 1986-87. Co-author: Economic Evaluation of the Swedish Energy Saving Program, 1979, Sweden, Europe and the Third World, 1884; author: Large industrial fires in Sweden, a cost-benefit analysis, 1981; editor: Collected Works of East West Economic Research, 1976. Mem. Internat. Pub. Relations Assn., Econs. Assn., Assn. Polit. Econs., Assn. for Soc. and Industry, Traders Club, Svea Order. Lutheran. Office: Haig Internat AB, Box 3192 Kungsgatan 36 7, 10363 Stockholm Sweden

HAIGH, ROBERT WILLIAM, business administration educator; b. Phila., Aug. 22, 1926; s. Harry E. and Mildred (Elliott) H.; m. Jane Stanton Sheble, June 19, 1948; children: Cynthia Jane, Anne Sheble, Robert William, Barbara Lynne. Student, Muhlenberg Coll., 1944-45; AB cum laude, Bucknell U., 1948; MBA with high distinction, Harvard U., 1950, DCS, 1953. Research and teaching faculty Harvard U. Grad Sch. Bus. Adminstrn., 1950-56, asst. prof., 1953-56; asst. to pres. Helmerich & Payne, Inc., Tulsa, 1956, controller and asst. to pres., 1956-57, fin. v.p., dir., 1957-61; fin. v.p., dir. White Eagle Internat. Oil Co., 1957-60; dir. planning Standard Oil Co. (Ohio), Cleve., 1961, v.p. planning, 1961-63, v.p. corp. planning and devel., 1963-64, v.p. chems. and plastics bus., 1964-66; v.p. chems. and plastics bus. Vistron Corp. subs., 1966-67; group v.p., pres. edn. group, dir. Xerox Corp., Stamford, Conn., 1967-72; exec. v.p. Swedlow Corp., 1973-74, pres., chief exec. officer, dir., 1974; pres. Hillsboro Assocs., 1974-75; sr. v.p. Freeport Minerals Co., 1975-76; chmn. bd., chief exec. officer Photo Quest, Inc., Cognitrex, Inc., Seidel-Farris-Clark, Inc., 1977-78; dir. Wharton Applied Research Ctr., lectr. U. Pa., Phila., 1978-79; now Disting. prof. bus. adminstrn. Tayhoe Murphy Internat. Bus. Studies Ctr. Colgate Darden Grad. Sch. Bus. Adminstrn., U. Va.; adv. bd. Atlantic Venture Ptnrs. Author: (with John G. McLean) The Growth of Integrated Oil Companies, 1954, Leading Virginia Industries: Textile and Apparel, A Business Update, 1986, Leading Virginia Industries: Wood and Paper Products, A Business Update, 1987. Served with USNR, 1944-45. Mem. Am. Petroleum Inst., Phi Beta Kappa, Phi Lambda Theta. Home: 404 Ednam Dr Charlottesville VA 22901 Office: Colgate Darden Grad Sch Bus Adminstrn Box 6550 Charlottesville VA 22906

HAIGHT, EDWARD ALLEN, lawyer; b. Rockford, Ill., July 2, 1910; s. John T. and Augusta (Granger) H.; m. Valerie E. Haight, Jan. 1, 1935; children—Edward Allen, George Ives II, Edith Diane, Stephen Holmes. B.A., U. Wis., 1931; LL.B., Harvard U., 1934. Bar: Ill. bar 1934. Since practiced in Chgo.; ptnr. Haight & Hofeldt and predecessor firm Haight, Hofeldt, Davis & Jamor, Chgo., 1956—. Served as lt. USNR, 1943-46. Mem. Am., Ill., Chgo., 7th Circuit bar assns., Am., Chgo. patent law assns., Am. Coll. Trial Lawyers. Clubs: Union League (Chgo.); Skokie Country. Home: 364 Central Ave Highland Park IL 60035 Office: Haight & Hofeldt 224 S Michigan Ave Suite 600 Chicago IL 60604

HAIGHT, GILBERT PIERCE, JR., chemistry educator; b. Seattle, June 8, 1922; s. Gilbert Pierce and Ruth (Gazzam) H.; m. Shirley Myers Grapek, June 30, 1946; children: Jennifer Lea, Loisanne Fox, Charlene Ellen (dec.), Charles Pierce, Stephanie Louise, Christopher Warren (dec.). A.B., Stanford U., 1943; Ph.D., Princeton U., 1946; research fellow, Ohio State U., 1946-47; Rhodes scholar, Oxford (Eng.) U., 1947-48. Asst. prof. U. Hawaii, 1948-49, George Washington U., 1949-52, U. Kans., 1952-54; assoc. prof. Swarthmore Coll., 1954-65; prof. chemistry Tex. A&M U., 1965-66; prof. chemistry U. Ill. at Urbana, 1966-87, prof. emeritus, 1987—; vis. scientist Tech. U. Denmark, 1960-61; vis. fellow Australian Nat. U., 1981-82, 87; cons. in field, 1951—; lectr. UNESCO Conf. Lab. Instrn., Perth, Australia, 1978, Chemistry Found. lectures, S. Africa, 1978, ITM/Mucia Project for Malaysia, 1986; Dodge lectr. Franklin Inst., 1956; others.: Mem. Rhodes scholar selection com. for Kans., 1965-71, 73-79, 83, Rhodes scholar selection com. for Ill., 1972, 82. Author: Introduction to Physical Science, 1964, (with H.B. Gray) Basic Principles of Chemistry, 1967, (with R.E. Dickerson and H.B. Gray) Chemical Principles, 1970, 3d edit., 1979; also articles and lab. manuals; editorial bd.: Jour. Coll. Sci. Teaching, Coordination Chemistry Revs., Inorganic Chemistry, 1984-87. Recipient vis. scientist award in chem. edn. Western Conn. sect. Am. Chem. Soc., 1974; nat. award in chem. edn. Mfg. Chemists Assn., 1976; Chem. Edn. award Am. Chem. Soc., 1979. Mem. Am. Chem. Soc. (vis. scientist, chmn. div. chem. edn. 1976, mem. edn. and sci. commns.), Danish Chem. Soc., AAAS, Ill. Assn. Chemistry Tchrs. (pres. 1980), Am. Inst. Chemists, N.Y. Acad. Scis., Phi Beta Kappa, Sigma Xi (sec. U. Ill. chpt. 1987-88), Phi Lambda Upsilon.

HAIGHT, WARREN GAZZAM, land development and management executive; b. Seattle, Sept. 7, 1929; s. Gilbert Pierce and Ruth (Gazzam) H.; m. Suzanne H., Sept. 1, 1951; children—Paula Lea, Ian Pierce; m. Ottina Mehau, June 25, 1985. A.B. in Econs, Stanford U., 1951. Asst. Treas. Hawaiian Pineapple Co., Honolulu, 1955-64; v.p., treas. Oceanic Properties, Inc., Honolulu, 1964-67; pres., dir. Oceanic Properties, Inc., 1967-85, chmn., 1983-85; v.p. Hawaii, Castle & Cooke Inc., 1983-85; pres. Warren G. Haight & Assocs., 1985—; trustee TransAm. Realty. Bd. dirs. Downtown Improvement Assn., Oahu Devel. Conf., Hawaii Island Econ. Devel. Bd., Econ. Devel. Corp. Honolulu, Pacific Found. for Cancer Research; mem. Transit Coalition, Honolulu; pres., bd. dirs. Land Use Research Found. of Hawaii. Served to lt. USNR, 1951-55. Mem. Housing Coalition, Calif. Coastal Council. Clubs: Outrigger Canoe, Round Hill Country, Plaza, Pacific. Home: 319 Lala Pl Honolulu HI 96734 Office: 220 S King St Honolulu HI 96813

HAIKO, GERALDINE MAE, auto damage appraiser; b. Hartford, Conn., Nov. 5, 1940; d. Frank Joseph and May Lillian (Brandt) Haiko; m. Douglas Allen Gallant, May 27, 1961 (div. Mar. 1965); 1 child, Douglas Allen. A.A., Vt. Coll., 1960. Rating clk. Travelers Ins. Co., Hartford, 1961-65; teller, adminstrv. asst., Soc. for Savs., Wethersfield, 1965-69; teller, asst. head teller, customer service officer Coral Ridge Nat. Bank, Fort Lauderdale, Fla., 1970-74; with customer service dept. Bank Coral Springs, Fla., 1974-76; pres. Frank J. Haiko, Inc., Wethersfield, 1976—. Mem. Ind. Auto Damage Appraisers (sec. treas. NE region 1981—, nat. sec. 1985—), Wethersfield C. of C., U.S. C. of C., Greater Hartford C. of C. Republican. Avocations: cross country skiing; singing; dancing; spectator sports. Office: Frank J Haiko Inc 36 Silas Deane Hwy Wethersfield CT 06109

HAILE, LAWRENCE BARCLAY, lawyer; b. Atlanta, Feb. 19, 1938; m. Ann Springer McCauley, March 28, 1984; children: Gretchen Vanderhoof, Eric McKenzie, Scott McAllister. B.A. in Econs, U. Tex., 1958, LL.B., 1961. Bar: Tex. 1961, Calif. 1962. Law clk. to U.S. Judge Joseph M. Ingraham, Houston, 1961-62; pvt. practice law San Francisco, 1962-67, Los Angeles, 1967—; mem. firm Simon, Buckner & Haile, Marina Del Rey, Calif., 1984—; instr. U. Calif. at Los Angeles Civil Trial Clinics, 1974, 76; lectr. law Calif. Continuing Edn. of Bar, 1973-74, 80-88; mem. nat. panel arbitrators Am. Arbitration Assn., 1965—. Asso. editor: Tex. Law Rev, 1960-61; Contbr. articles profl. publs. Mem. State Bar Calif., Tex., U.S. Supreme Ct. bar assns., Internat. Assn. Property Ins. Counsel (founding mem., pres. 1980), ASTM, London World Trade Centre Assn., Phi Delta Phi, Delta Sigma Rho. Club: Marine (London). Office: 4551 Glencoe Ave #300 Marina del Rey CA 90292

HAILE, LEROY YELLOTT, JR., real estate broker; b. Towson, Md., Feb. 6, 1929; s. LeRoy Yellott and Rachel Lillian (Stabler) H.; B.S., Hampden-Sydney Coll., 1950; m. Felicity Fletcher, June 8, 1957; children—LeRoy Yellott, Rachel Naomi. Pres., LeRoy Y. Haile, Inc., Towson, Md., 1954—. Bd. dirs. Towson Bus. Assn., Gunpowder Youth Camps, 1985-86; chmn. Towson 4th of July Parade, 1978. Served with USN, 1951-54. Mem. Baltimore County Hist. Soc. (pres. 1981-82), Baltimore County Appraisers Soc., Greater Balt. Bd. Realtors. Democrat. Methodist. Club: Kiwanis (past pres.) (Towson). Home: 1503 Providence Rd Towson MD 21204 Office: 5 W Chesapeake Ave Towson MD 21204

HAILE GIORGIS, WORKNEH, civil engineer; b. Gedamgue, Tegulete, Ethiopia, Mar. 16, 1930; parents: Workneh Aschenaki and Atsede Syoum; m. Jember Teferra, Nov. 16, 1969; children: Workneh, Teferra, Memmenasha, Lelo. BCE, Carnegie Inst. Tech., Pittsburgh, Pa., 1952; MCE, Carnegie Inst. Tech., 1954, PhD, 1956. Design engr. Tippetts, Abbett, McCarthy & Stratton, N.Y.C., 1956-58; engr. constrn. supervision War Reparation Commn., Addis Ababa, Ethiopia, 1958; dir. water resource devel. Ministry Pub. Works and Communications, Addis Ababa, 1959-60, vice minister, 1960, vice minister public works, 1960-62, gen mgr. Ethiopian Hwys. Authority, 1962-65, minister pub. works, 1965-69; Lord Mayor Addis Ababa, Addis Ababa, 1969-74; chmn. constrn. housing and urban devel. research council Ethiopian Sci. and Tech. Commn., Addis Ababa, 1982-85; cons. road and road transport UN Econ. Commn. for Africa, Addis Ababa, 1985-86; pvt. cons. civil engring. Addis Ababa, 1987—. Named Man of Year Internat. Road Fedn., 1970. Mem. ASCE. Mem. Ethiopian Orthodox Ch. Home: PO Box 1296, Addis Ababa Ethiopia

HAILEY, ARTHUR, writer; b. Luton, Eng., Apr. 5, 1920; emigrated to Can., naturalized, 1947 (also Brit. citizen); s. George and Elsie (Wright) H.; m. Sheila Dunlop, July 28, 1951; children: Roger, John, Mark (by previous marriage), Jane, Steven, Diane. Student pub. schs., Eng. Author novels: Runway Zero-Eight, 1958 (with John Castle), The Final Diagnosis, 1959, In High Places, 1962, Hotel, 1965, Airport, 1968, Wheels, 1971, The Moneychangers, 1975, Overload, 1979, Strong Medicine, 1984; Author novels pub. in 35 langs.; collected plays Close-up on Writing for Television, 1960; motion pictures include Zero Hour, 1956, Time Lock, 1957, The Young Doctors, 1961, Hotel, 1966, Airport, 1970, The Moneychangers, 1976, Wheels, 1978, Strong Medicine, 1986. Served as pilot/flight lt. RAF, 1939-47. Mem. Writers Guild Am., Authors League Am., Assn. Canadian Television and Radio Artists (hon. life). Home: Lyford Cay, PO Box N-7776, Nassau Bahamas Office: Seaway Authors First Can Place, PO 130 Suite 6000, Toronto, ON Canada M5X 1A4

HAILSHAM OF ST. MARYLEBONE, LORD QUINTIN MCGAREL HOGG, former lord high chancellor of Great Britain; b. Oct. 9, 1907; ed. Eton, Christ Church, Oxford U., also D.C.L. Fellow All Souls Coll., Oxford, 1931-50, 61—; barrister Lincoln's Inn, 1932, Queen's counsel, 1953, bencher, 1956; mem. Parliament, 1938-50, 63-70; mem. Ho. of Lords, 1950-63, 74—, leader, 1960-63; parliamentary undersec. to Air Ministry, 1945; 1st lord of admiralty, 1956-57; minister of edn., 1957; lord pres. of council, 1957-59, 60-64; lord privy seal, 1959-60; minister for sci. and tech., 1959-64; sec. of state for edn. and sci., 1964; minister for unemployment in N.E., 1963-64, Lord Chancellor, 1970-74, 79-87; rector Glasgow U., 1959-62. Chmn. Conservative Party, 1957-59. Created baron, 1970; chancellor U. Buckingham, 1983—; Knight of the Garter, 1988. Fellow Royal Soc. Author: The Law of Arbitration, 1935; One Year's Work, 1944; The Law and Employer's Liability, 1944; The Times We Live In, 1944; Making Peace, 1945; The Left was Never Right, 1945; The Purpose of Parliament, 1946; The Case for Conservatism, 1947; The Law Relating to Monopolies, Restrictive Trade Practices and Resale Price Maintenance, 1956; The Conservative Case, 1959; Interdependence, 1961; Science and Politics, 1963; The Devil's Own Song, 1968; The Door Wherein I Went, 1975; Elective Dictatorship, 1976; The Dilemma of Democracy, 1978; Hamlyn Revisted: The British Legal System, 1983. Office: House of Lords, London SW1A 0PW, England

HAILU, ABAFERDA YILMA, engineering executive; b. Addis Ababa, Shoa, Ethiopia, July 7, 1930; s. Abaferda Bezabh and Elfenesh Derbichaw; divorced; children: Tegest, Fikrte, Ashenafi, Selamawit, Elfenesh, Hailegabriedl, Hiwote. LLB, Haile Selassie U., Addis Ababa, 1965; diploma in internat. relations, 1958. Exec. sec. tech. assistance bd. Ministry Commerce, Industry and Planning, Addis Ababa, 1958-60, dir. gen., 1960-65; asst. minister Prime Minister's Office, Addis Ababa, 1965-68, vice minister, 1968-71; vice minister Ministry of Justice, Addis Ababa, 1971-75; exec. sec. Shipping and Transit Cos. Assn., Addis Ababa, 1975-77; gen. mgr. Savon and Ries Shipping Co., Addis Ababa, 1977-80, Ries Engring. S.C., Addis Ababa, 1980—; participant fgn. ministerial confs. Orgn. African Unity, Addis Ababa, 1965—, also various internat. seminars, Opsala, Sweden, 1970. Exec. sec. Ethiopian Patriotic Assn., Addis Ababa, 1965. Named Star Decoration Officer, Imperial Ethiopian Govt., 1961, Menelik II Decoration Officer, Imperial Ethiopian Govt., 1964, Star Comdr., Imperial Ethiopian Govt., 1970; UN scholar, 1958-59. Mem. Christian Orthodox Ch. Lodge: Rotary (bd. dirs. Addis Ababa chpt. 1982, exec. sec.). Office: Ries Engring SC, Debrezeit Rd PO Box 1116, Addis Ababa Ethiopia

HAIMBAUGH, GEORGE DOW, JR., lawyer, educator; b. Rochester, Ind., Nov. 21, 1916; s. George Dow and Agnes Elizabeth (Sharp) H.; m. Katharine Louise Draper, Aug. 20, 1960. A.B., DePauw U., 1938; postgrad, Georgetown U., 1938-40; J.D., Northwestern U., 1952; J.S.D., Yale U., 1962. Bar: Ill. 1953, S.C. 1973, U.S. Dist. Ct. (no. dist.) Ohio 1962, U.S. Supreme Ct. 1969. Asst. prof. U. Akron Coll. Law, 1960-63; assoc. prof. law U. S.C., Columbia, 1963-70; prof. U. S.C., 1970-79, David W. Robinson prof. law, 1979-87, disting. prof. emeritus, 1987—, assoc. Inst. Internat. Studies, 1967—, mem. Byrnes Internat. Ctr. Adv. Council, 1984—; spl. master U.S. Dist. Ct. (no. dist.) Ohio, 1962-63; mem. adv. bd. Nat. Inst. Justice, 1982-85; assoc. Belle W. Baruch Inst. Marine Biology and Coastal Research, 1978—. Mem. Ga.-S.C. Boundary Commn., 1978—, Columbia's Commn. on Bicentennial of U.S. Constitution, 1987—; deacon 1st Presbyterian Ch., Columbia. Served to maj. USMC, 1940-46. Mem. Am. Law Inst., ABA (chmn. adv. com. to standing com. on law and nat. security 1979-82), S.C. Bar Assn., Richland County Bar Assn., Am. Soc. Internat. Law, Assn. Am. Law Schs. (chmn. sect. constitutional law 1975-77), Phi Gamma Delta, Phi Delta Phi, Delta Phi Epsilon, Sigma Delta Chi, Order of the Coif, Order of Palmetto. Republican. Club: Mil. Order World Wars. Office: Univ SC Law Sch Columbia SC 29208

HAINES, LEWIS FRANCIS, emeritus humanities educator; b. Endicott, N.Y., Oct. 28, 1907; s. William Joseph and Teresa Irene (Lewis) H.; m. Helen Mary Steere, Sept 1, 1930; 1 son, James Lewis. A.B., U. Mich., 1930, A.M., 1932, Ph.D., 1941. Instr. English Boys' Tech. High Sch., Milw., 1930-34; teaching fellow English U. Mich., 1935-41, instr. English, summer 1941; acting instr. English U. Fla., 1941-42, asst. prof., 1942-46, prof. humanities, 1946-67, prof. humanities and comprehensive logic, 1967-73, prof. humanities and behavioral studies, 1973-77, prof. emeritus, 1977—; editor U. Fla. Press, 1945-67, dir., 1949-67; cons. specialist New Century Cyclopedia of Names. Contbr. to: New Century Handbook of English Literature, World Book Ency., Collier's Ency.; Contbr. also to scholastic and lit. jours. Mem. Gov's Hwy. Safety Conf. Recipient Rockefeller research grant, summer 1962. Mem. MLA, South Atlantic MLA, AAUP, Nat. Council Tchrs. English, Fla. Hist. Soc., Newcomen Soc. N.A., Assn. Am. U. Presses, Am. Book Pubs. Council, Acad. Polit. Sci., Assn. for Latin Am. Studies, Phi Kappa Phi, Kappa Phi Sigma. Home: 23 SW 26th St Gainesville FL 32607 Office: Little Hall U Fla Gainesville FL 32611

HAINES, VICTOR YELVERTON, English language and literature educator, poet; b. Toronto, Ont., Can., Mar. 21, 1941; s. Victor Yelverton Haines and Margaret (Saunders) Cameron; m. Lesley Ford, May 18, 1963 (div.); children: Heidi Alice, Victor Yelverton, Martin Edward; m. Beverly Chandler, July 7, 1974; children: Margaret Valary, Cameron Stuart. B.A., Queen's U., Kingston, Ont., 1963, B.A. with honors, 1965; M.A., Carleton U., Ottawa, Ont., 1966; Ph.D. in English, McGill U., Montreal, Que., Can., 1975. Prof. English Acadia U., Wolfville, N.S., Can., 1966-67, Coll. Militaire Royal de Saint Jean, Que., 1967-73; prof. English, Dawson Coll., Montreal, 1974—, chmn. dept. English, 1984-86. Author: The Fortunate Fall of Sir Gawain: The Typology of Sir Gawain and the Green Knight, 1983. Contbr. articles on Mediaeval lit. to profl. jours. and poems to lit. jours. Can. Council fellow, doctoral fellow, 1973-74. Mem. Internat. Arthurian Soc., MLA, Assn. Canadian Univ. Tchrs. of English, Mediaeval Acad. Am. Home: 4729 de Maisonneuve, Westmont, PQ Canada H3Z 1M3

HAINLINE, DOUGLAS RAY, computer science educator; b. Houston, Dec. 21, 1943; arrived in Eng., 1976; s. Ray Vernon and Bernice (Redwine) H.; m. Helene Brosiue, 1967 (div. 1971); m. Judith Clare Shapiro, Sept. 15, 1973. BA, Cornell U., 1967; MSc, North London Poly., 1977; PhD, Thames Poly., Eng., 1986. Lectr. Thames Polytech., London, 1977-86; sr. lectr. computer sci. U. London, 1986—. Editor: New Developments in Computer Aided Language Learning, 1986. Mem. British Computer Soc. (assoc.). Office: U London, Goldsmith's Coll, New Cross, London SE14 6NW, England

HAINLINE, FORREST ARTHUR, JR., retired automotive company executive, lawyer; b. Rock Island, Ill., Oct. 20, 1918; s. Forrest Arthur and Marian (Pearson) H.; m. Nora Marie Schrot, July 7, 1945; children—Forrest III, Jon, Patricia, Judith, Brian, David, Nora. A.B., Augustana Coll., Rock Island, Ill., 1940; J.D., U. Mich., 1947, LL.M., 1948. Bar: Ill. 1942, Mich. 1943, Fla. 1970, U.S. Supreme Ct. 1946. Mem. firm Cross, Wrock, Miller & Vieson and predecessor, Detroit, 1948-71, ptnr., 1957-71; v.p., gen. counsel Am. Motors Corp., Detroit, 1971-84, sec., 1972-84, ret. Chmn., Wayne County Regional Interagy. Coordinating Com. for Developmental Disabilities, Mich., 1972-76; chmn. grievance com. U.S. Tennis Assn., 1970-85, mem. exec. com., 1972-74, 83-85, chmn. constn. and rules, 1983-86, v.p. So. region, 1985-86; arbitrator Men's Internat. Profl. Tennis Council, 1977-85; pres. Cath. Social Services Oakland County, Mich., 1972-75; mem. exec. com. Western Tennis Assn., 1964—, pres., 1972-73, chmn. constn. and rules com., 1976-84; mem. Men's Internat. Profl. Tennis Council, 1985-87; chmn. Internat. Tennis Fedn. rules com., 1987—; pres. Western Improvement Assn., 1969-75; bd. dirs. Augustana Coll., 1974-82, sec., 1975-82; bd. dirs. Providence Hosp., Southfield, Mich., 1975-84, sec. 1980, vice chmn., 1981, chmn., 1982, chmn. exec. com., 1983-84. Served to 1st lt. AUS, 1942-46. Named (with family) Tennis Family of Yr., U.S. Tennis Assn., 1974; recipient Outstanding Service award Augustana Coll., 1977; named to Rock Island High Sch. Sports Hall of Fame, 1977, Mich. Amateur Sports Hall of Fame, 1978, Augustana Coll. Sports Hall of Fame, 1980. Mem. ABA, Fed. Bar Assn., Mich. Bar. Assn., Ill. Bar Assn., Fla. Bar Assn., Am. Judicature Soc., Augustana Coll. Alumni Assn. (pres. bd. dirs. 1973-74), Phi Alpha Delta. Clubs: Suntide Condominiums, Kenmure Golf, Detroit Tennis, Squash. Lodge: KC. Home: 1357 NE Ocean Blvd Stuart FL 34996 also: 148 Overlook Dr Flat Rock NC 28731

HAINSWORTH, DAVID ROGER, historian; b. Bradford, Yorkshire, England, Apr. 21, 1931; s. John Thomas and Lilian (Pickles) H.; m. Margaret Laura Hunter Collis; 1 child, Jonathan Julian. BA, New Coll. Oxford U., Eng., 1954; PhD, Adelaide U., Australia, 1971. Lectr. Townsville U., North Queensland, Australia, 1963-65; lectr. Adelaide U., Australia, 1965-70, sr. lectr., 1971-78, reader, 1979—. Editor: Papers of Sir C. Lowther, 1976, Sir John Lowther Corr., 1983, Builders & Adventurers, 1968, The Sydney Traders 1788-1821, 1972. Fellow Royal Hist. Soc. Home: 6 Tyne St, Gilberton Australia 5081 Office: Adelaide Univ, History Dept, Adelaide Australia 5001

HAINSWORTH, PAUL ANDREW, political science educator; b. Hull, Yorkshire, Eng., Mar. 27, 1950; s. Ullathorne Rhodes and Agatha Philomena (Thornton) H.; m. Elizabeth Jane Phipps, Aug. 4, 1980; children: Jonathan Paul, Kate Elizabeth. BA with honors, Liverpool (Eng.) U., 1971; PhD, Bristol (Eng.) U., 1976; diploma, Abon Sch., Bristol, 1977. Tchr. Inlingua Sch., Lübeck, Fed. Republic Germany, 1978; lectr. in politics Ulster Poly., No. Ireland, 1979-84, U. Ulster, 1984—. Authro: Decentralisation and Change in Contemporary France, 1986; contbr. numerous articles to profl. jours. Chmn. No. Ireland chpt. Amnesty Internat., 1983-85. European fellow Leverhulme, France, 1981; research grantee French Embassy, 1985, Brit. Acad., France, 1987. Office: U Ulster, Jordanstown, Antrim Northern Ireland

HAIRSTON, WILLIAM BURTON, JR., lawyer; b. Birmingham, Ala., Dec. 14, 1924; s. William B. and Kate Lucile (Steele) H.; m. Louise Narden Poe, May 28, 1955; 1 son, William B. III. J.D., U. Ala., 1950. Bar: Ala. 1950, U.S. Ct. Appeals (5th cir.) 1960, U.S. Ct. Appeals (11th cir.) 1980. Ptnr. Engel & Hairston, Birmingham, 1952-77, Engel, Hairston, Moses & Johanson, Birmingham, 1977-87, Engel, Hairston and Johanson, 1987—; instr. Birmingham Sch. Law, 1968-70; judge Recorders Ct., Leeds, Ala., 1970-75; spl. asst. atty. gen. Ala. Personnel Bd., 1981—. Trustee, Birmingham U. Sch. Law, 1969-75, Meth. Ednl. Soc., 1983—, Meth. Leave Soc., 1983—; vice-chair, Jud. Inquiry Commn., 1985-87, chair, 1987—; mem. adv. bd., Cumberland Law Sch., 1986—; mem. adv. com., Assn. Jud. Disciplinary Counsel, 1988—, Civil Rules of Practice and Procedure for Dist. Cts., 1980—. Served with U.S. Army, 1942-46. Recipient Dean's award U. Ala. Sch. Law, 1977, 80; award as outstanding alumni Bench and Bar Legal Honor Soc., U. Ala. Sch. Law, 1981; Thomas Christopher award, 1982; named Lawyer of Yr., Birmingham Legal Secs. Assn., 1982. Mem. ABA (com. on comml. financing 1982—), Am. Bar Found., Am. Judicature Soc., Am. Coll. Trial Lawyers, Ala. Law Inst., Ala. Bar Assn. (award of merit 1977, bar rep. on jud. inquiry commn. 1979—, pres.-elect 1982-83, pres. 1983-84, bd. bar commrs. 1973-79), Birmingham Bar Assn. (pres. 1970), Ala. Jud. Coll. Faculty Assn. (hon.), U. Ala. Alumni Assn. (pres. 1978-80), 11th Cir. Ct. Appeals Hist. Soc. (trustee 1983—, v.p. 1984-86, pres. 1986—), So. Conf. Bar Pres., Nat. Conf. Bar Pres. Methodist. Clubs: Vestavia Country, Downtown, The Club, Birmingham Rose Soc. (Birmingham, Ala.). Author: Detinue, Execution and Mechanic Liens, 1980; contbr. articles to law jours. Home: 2540 Aberdeen Rd Birmingham AL 35223 Office: 109 N 20th St Birmingham AL 35203

HAISER, KARL FRANCIS, JR., accountant; b. Detroit, Dec. 5, 1942; s. Karl Francis Jahutskey and Mae Martha (Schram) H.; m. Linda Kay Clements, Nov. 18, 1967; children—Eric, Bryan, Justin. B.S., Ferris State Coll., 1965; M.B.A., Central Mich. U., 1967; diploma advanced acctg. Internat. Accts. Soc., 1973. C.P.A., Mich. Staff acct. Price Waterhouse & Co., C.P.A.s, 1966-71; asst. to controller Hygrade Food Products, Inc., Southfield, Mich., 1971-73; self-employed C.P.A., Grand Blanc, Mich., 1973—, mng. ptnr., 1987—; instr. Detroit Coll. Bus., 1983—; instr., advisor acctg. Mott Community Coll., 1983—. Twp. chmn. Planning Commn. and Bd. Appeals, 1974-76; cubmaster Boy Scouts Am.; founder Grand Blanc Jr. League Football. Served with USMC, 1967-69. Mem. Am. Inst. C.P.A.s, Mich. Assn. C.P.A.s, Pi Kappa Alpha. Republican. Lutheran. Home: 5186 Greenmeadows St Grand Blanc MI 48439 Office: 610 E Grand Blanc Rd Grand Blanc MI 48439

HAITINK, BERNARD J.H., conductor; b. Amsterdam, Mar. 4, 1929. MusD (hon.), U. of Oxford, 1988, U. of Leeds, 1988. Condr., Netherlands Radio Philharmonic Orch., 1955-61; guest condr. Concertgebouw Orch., Amsterdam, then joint condr., 1956-64, prin. condr., mus. dir., 1964-88; condr. operas by Mozart and Wagner for Netherlands Opera; guest condr. Hallé Orch., London Philharm. Orch., Los Angeles Philharm. Orch., Berlin Philharm. Orch., 1963-64; prin. condr., artistic adviser to London Philharm. Orch., 1967-79, artistic dir., 1970-78; guest condr. Glyndebourne Festival Opera, 1972-77, mus. dir., 1978-88; mus. dir. Royal Opera, Covent Garden, London, 1987—; guest condr. Boston Symphony, Cleve. Philharm., Vienna Philharm., N.Y. Philharm., Chgo. Symphony, Bayerische Rundfunk Symphony, Munich, Berlin Philharm. Decorated Order Oranje Nassau; chevalier Ordre des Arts et des Lettres; hon. knight Brit. Empire; officer Order of Crown (Belgium); recipient Bruckner medal of honor Bruckner Soc., 1970. Fellow Royal Coll. Music; mem. Royal Acad. Music (London) (hon.), Internat. Gustav Mahler Soc. (hon.; gold medal 1970). Address: care Harold Holt Ltd, 31 Sinclair Rd, London W14 ONS England also: care Royal Opera House, Covent Garden, London WC2E 7QA England

HAJEE, MUSA ESMAIL, estate agent; b. Nairobi, Kenya, Jan. 24, 1928; came to Eng., 1970; s. Esmail and Jenabai (Kassam-Lakha) H.; m. Fatima Gulamhusein Kassam, Aug. 24, 1948; children—Mehboob, Shemin, Rozmin, Muneer. Acct., Alibhai & Co. Ltd., Nairobi, 1946-49, dir., Nairobi and Tanzania, 1950-56; exec. dir. Alibhai Group, Kenyz and Tanzania, 1957-65; exec. dir. Wire Products, Kenya, 1965-70, Aco Fin. Ltd., London, 1978—, Hajeeco Ltd., London, 1980—, Musa & Abdullah, London, 1980—. Founder Sch. for Deaf and Dumb-Aga Khan and Kenya Govt., Nairobi, 1966. Conservative. Moslem. Club: Aga Khan (Nairobi, liaison officer 1969-71), Equator 8675. Office: Musa & Abdullah, 18 Garway Rd, London W2, England

HAJEK, FRANCIS PAUL, lawyer; b. Hobart, Tasmania, Australia, Oct. 21, 1958; came to U.S., 1966; s. Frank Joseph and Kathleen Beatrice (Blake) H. BA, Yale U., 1980; JD, U. Richmond, 1984. Bar: Va. 1984, U.S. Dist.

Ct. (ea. dist.) Va. 1984, U.S. Ct. Appeals (4th cir.) 1986. Law clk. to presiding magistrate U.S. Dist Ct., Norfolk, Va., 1984-85; assoc. Seawell, Dalton, Hughes & Timms, Norfolk, 1985-87, Weinberg & Stein, Norfolk, 1987—. Mem. ABA, Assn. Trial Lawyers Am., Va. Bar Assn., Norfolk-Portsmouth Bar Assn. (exec. com. young lawyer's sect.). Roman Catholic. Home: 3901 Beach Ave Norfolk VA 23504 Office: Weinberg & Stein 1825 Dominion Tower 999 Waterside Dr Norfolk VA 23514

HAJEK, ROBERT J., lawyer, real estate broker, commodity broker, nursing home owner; b. Berwyn, Ill., May 17, 1943; s. James J., Sr., and Rita C. (Kalka) H.; m. Maris Ann Enright, June 19, 1965; children—Maris Ann, Robert J., David, Mandie. B.A., Loras Coll., 1965; J.D., U. Ill., 1968. Bar: Ill. 1968, U.S. Tax Ct. 1970, U.S. dist. ct. (no. dist.) Ill. 1971, U.S. Ct. Appeals (7th cir.) 1972, U.S. Supreme Ct. 1972. Lic. real estate broker, Ill., Nat. Assn. Securities Dealers; registered U.S. Commodities Futures Trading Commn. ptnr. Hajek & Hajek, Berwyn, Ill., 1968-76; pres., bd. chmn. Hajek, Hajek, Koykar & Heying, Ltd., Westchester, Ill., 1976-85; pres., chief exec. officer Land of Lincoln Real Estate, Ltd., Glendale Heights, Ill., 1985—, also bd. dirs.; ptnr., owner Camelot Manor Nursing Home, Streator, Ill., 1978—, Ottawa (Ill.) Care Ctr., 1981—, Law Centre Bldg., Westchester, 1976—; owner Garfield Ridge Real Estate, Chgo., 1973-78, Centre Realty, Westchester, 1976-85; ptnr. Westbrook Commodities, Chgo., 1983; v.p., bd. mem., gen. counsel DeHart Gas and Oil Devel., Ltd., 1970-73; prin. Northeastern Okla. Oil and Gas Prodn. Venture, Tulsa, 1982—; exec. v.p., gen. counsel Garrett Plante Corp., 1978—, Ottawa Long Term Care, Inc., 1982—; bd. dirs. Land of Lincoln Savs. and Loan, 1981—, Home Title Services of Am., Inc., 1981—, Land of Lincoln Ins. Agy., Inc., 1982—, Medema Builders, Inc., 1983—, Ptnrs. of Ill., Inc., 1984—, The Ill. Co., 1984—, Ill. Co. Properties, Inc., subs. of Ill. Co., 1984-87 , Ottawa Long Term Care, Inc., 1982—, Garrett Plante Corp., 1978—. Sr. boys' basketball coach Roselle Recreation Assn., Ill., 1981-83. Mem. ABA, Ill. Bar Assn., Nat. Assn. Realtors, Ill. Assn. Realtors, Northwest Suburban Bd. Realtors, Ill. Health Care Assn., Phi Alpha Delta. Republican. Roman Catholic. Clubs: Amateur Radio, No. Ill. DX Assn. Office: Land of Lincoln Real Estate Ltd 2081 Bloomingdale Rd Glendale Heights IL 60139

HAJI HASHIM BIN, KAMARUDIN, constrn. co. exec.; b. Kota Bharu, Kelantan (Malaysia), Aug. 26, 1948; s. Kamarudin Bin Siraj and Fatimah Binti Omar; grad. Cyma Coll., Kuala Lumpur, Malaysia, 1967; banking grad. Mara Inst. Tech., Shah Alam, 1956-71. Exec. sec., mktg. and distbn. mgr. Syarikat Kerjasama Shamelin Bhd., Kuala Lumpur, 1971-72; sales exec. Usharela Sdn Bhd., Kuala Lumpur, 1972-73; sales exec./purchasing exec. Perangsang Trading Sdn. Bhd., Kuala Lumpur, 1973-75; chmn./mng. dir. Panji Alam Sdn. Bhd., Petaling Jaya, Malaysia, 1975—; mng. dir., chief exec. Bumiland Holdings (M) Sdn Bhd, Petaling Jaya, 1980—; exec. chmn. Bumiland Properties Sdn. Bhd., Tijarra (M) Sdn. Bhd.; mng. dir., chief exec. Panji Continental; mng. dir. HKA Cons. & Mgmt. Sdn. Bhd.; chmn. bd. Timber Components Malaysia Sdn. Bhd. Mem. br. com. United Malay Nat. Orgn., 1978—. Mem. Bumiputra Contractors Assn. (br. com.), Bldg. Materials Distbrs. Assn. Malaysia, Bumiputra Exec. and Entrepreneur Assn. Club: Selangor Polo and Riding (Kuala Lumpur). Office: Petaling Jaya AG-10 Blk A, Happy Mansion, Jalan 17-13, Selangor Malaysia

HAKEN, HERMANN PAUL JOSEPH, physicist, educator; b. Leipzig, Germany, July 12, 1927; s. Karl and Magdalena (Vollath) H.; m. Edith Helene Bosch, Mar. 5, 1963 (dec. Aug. 1987); children: Maria, Karl-Ludwig, Karin. Diploma in Math., Friedrich-Alexander U. Erlangen-Nurnberg, Erlangen, Fed. Republic Germany, 1950, PhD, 1951; doctorate (hon.), Essen-Gesamthochschule U., Essen, Fed. Republic Germany, 1983, U. Madrid, 1987. Dozent Friedrich-Alexander U. Erlangen-Nurnberg, 1956-59; vis. assoc. prof. Cornell U., Ithaca, N.Y., 1959-60; prof. physics U. Stuttgart, Stuttgart, Fed. Republic Germany, 1960—; assoc. prof. U. Strasbourg, Strasbourg, France, 1969-74; cons. Bell-Telephone Labs., Murray Hill, N.Y., 1959-60, ITT, Paris, 1960-68. Author: Laser Theory, 1970, Quantenfeld Theorie, 1973, Synergetics, 1977, Advanced Synergetics, 1983, Information and Organization, 1988. Recipient: Maxborn prize and medal Brit. Inst. Physics, London, 1976, Albert A. Michelson medal Franklin Inst., Phila., 1981, Order Pour Le Merite, Fed. Republic Germany, Bonn, 1985. Mem. Chinese Soc. for Systems Engrs. (hon.). Roman Catholic. Home: 1 Sandgrubenstrasze, D-7032 Sindelfingen Federal Republic of Germany Office: U Stuttgart, 57 Pfaffenwaldring, D-7000 Stuttgart Federal Republic of Germany

HAKHVERDYAN, LEVON, philologist; b. Kirovakan, Armenian S.S.R., USSR, Dec. 26, 1924; s. Hovhannes and Margo (Saratikyan) H.; m. Sona Ayunts, Jan. 27, 1949; children: Ruben, Gagik. Student, Inst. Art and Theatre, Erevan, Armenian S.S.R., 1944-49; Dr. Philology, Inst. Lit. Acad. Scis. Armenian S.S.R., Erevan, 1967. Technicist-geologist Geol. Mgmt. Armenian S.S.R., Erevan, 1963-66; mgr. criticism Grakan Tert newspaper, Erevan, 1949-53; editor Editing House Armenian S.S.R., Erevan, 1953-55; responsible sec. Sovetakan Arvest mag., Erevan, 1955-59; sci. asst. Inst. Art Acad. Scis. Armenian S.S.R., Erevan, 1956-65, mgr. theatrical sector, 1965-87, dir., 1987—; prof. Inst. Art and Theatre, Erevan, 1965. Author: The Classics and Our Days, 1962, The World of Toumanyan, 1966, The Life and Work of Isaheakyan, 1976, The History of Armenian Theatre, 1980. Recipient Laureate of State award, 1983; named Meritorious Agt., Art Armenian S.S.R., 1972. Mem. Union of Writers (sec. 1957), Union Theatrical Agts. (sec. 1949). Communist. Home: Charents 70, 91, 375025 Erevan, Armenia USSR Office: Inst Art Acad Scis Armenian SSR, Bagramyan 24-g, 375079 Erevan USSR

HAKIM, ALI HUSSEIN, export company executive, consultant; b. Mushref, Lebanon, Aug. 13, 1943; came to U.S., 1973; s. Hussein A. and Sabah (Wazni) H.; m. Raafat M. Siklawi, July 2, 1972; children—Hussein, Ronny, Sameer, Mazen. B.S.B.A., Beirut U., 1970; postgrad. in acctg. Wayne State U., 1975; M.A. in Econs. and Politics, U. Detroit, 1980. Supr. Al-Mouharer Newspaper, Beirut, 1964-67; prin. Lebanese Soc. for Edn., Beirut, 1967-72; field services adviser Chrysler Corp., Detroit, 1973-75; owner, operator H & R Parking Co., Detroit, 1975-81; comptroller Met. Detroit Youth, 1979-82; pres. Hakim Export Import, Detroit, 1979-82, Hakim Export, Detroit, 1983—; pres. Gen. Bus. for Internat. Trade Corp., N.Y.C.; cons. to trading and investment agys., Africa, Middle East; budget cons. Met. Detroit Youth Found., 1983—. Research on U.S./China trade relations, 1980, U.S. monetary policy, 1981, internat. mktg., 1983. Mem. Republican Presdl. Task Force, 1982—. Mem. Am. Mgmt. Assn., Acctg. Aid Soc. Club: Senatorial (Washington).

HAKIM, LOUISE ZALTA, import company executive; b. Mobile, Ala., July 14, 1922; d. Nouri L. and Zahda M. (Lizmi) Zalta; m. Albert S. Hakim, May 24, 1942; children—Saul, Betty, Theda, Eddie, Jack, Joseph, Shirley. Student Northeast U., Monroe, La., 1956-58. Mgr. York Children Shop, Monroe, La., 1942-60; importer, owner Tidy Ties Corp., Monroe, 1960-70, inventor, 1970—, developer, 1974—, researcher, 1980—, dir., 1960—. Designer, developer infant shoe ties, 1965, medicine container, 1965; inventor, designer, developer blanket holder, 1976, squeeze toys, 1976, pacifier, 1980. Mem. U.S. C. of C. Republican. Jewish. Avocations: tennis; golf; fishing, sculpture. Home: PO Box 4826 Monroe LA 71211 Office: Tidy Corp 2813 DeSiard St Monroe LA 71201

HAKIM, SEYMOUR, educator, writer, artist; b. N.Y.C., Jan. 23, 1933; s. Sol and Renee Hakim; A.B., Eastern N.Mex. U., 1954; M.A., N.Y. U., 1960; postgrad. U. Calif., Brigham Young U., U. Pa.; m. Odetta Roverso, Aug. 18, 1970. Tchr. art and English schs. in N.Mex. and N.Y., 1957-61; tchr. English and art Dept. Def., Vicenza (Italy) Am. Sch., 1962-70, tchr. English and photography, 1972—, chmn. English dept., 1973—; tchr. London Central High Sch., 1971; mem. exec. bd. Italo-Britannica Assos. Served with AUS, 1952-54. Recipient Outstanding Sustained Superior Teaching award Dept. Def., 1976-79, 81-86, 88. Author: (play) The Sacred Family, 1970; (poems) Manhattan Goodbye, 1970; Undermoon, 1970; The Museum of the Mind, 1971; Wine Theorem, 1972; (autobiography) Substituting Memories, 1976; Iris Elegy, 1979; Balancing Act . . . a congruence of symbols, 1981, The Birth of a Poet, 1985, Eleanor Goodbye, 1988; one-man exhbns. of art, 1970, 73, 82-83, 86; group shows, 1971, 76, 78, 84, 85; represented in collections in China, Romania, Japan, Eng., Korea, Germany, U.S.; Internat. Biennial Print Exhibit, 1985, 87, 88; editor Overseas Tchr., 1977. Address: via Chiesanuova 1, 36023 Longare, Vicenza Italy

HAKIM-ELAHI, ENAYAT, obstetrician, gynecologist; b. Teheran, Iran, Nov. 23, 1934; came to U.S., 1959, naturalized, 1973; s. Mohamed-Ali and Masoomeh Rahimi; M.D., Med. Sch., Teheran, 1959; m. Renate Emsters, Nov. 15, 1967; 1 dau., Cristina. Intern, Queens Hosp. Center, N.Y.C., 1960, resident in internal medicine, 1961, resident in ob-gyn, 1961-64, resident in radiotherapy of gynecologic cancer, Am. Cancer Soc. fellow Queens div., 1965; resident in gynecology Cancer Research Inst., Columbia-Presbyn. Med. Center, N.Y.C., 1964-65; practice medicine specializing in ob-gyn, N.Y.C., 1968—; mem. staff Booth Meml. Med. Center, Flushing, N.Y., N.Y. Hosp., N.Y.C., Jamaica Hosp., Jamaica, N.Y., Univ. Hosp., Stonybrook ; med. dir. Margaret Sanger Center, N.Y.C., 1973—, Planned Parenthood of N.Y.C., 1977—; adj. asst. prof. ob-gyn Cornell U. Med. Coll., N.Y.C., 1973—; asst. prof. ob-gyn. SUNY Stonybrook, 1986—, dir. ambulatory care SUNY Stonybrook, 1986—. Served with U.S. Army, 1965-67 as civilian. Lic. physician, Maine, Conn., Vt., N.Y., N.H., Calif. Diplomate Am. Bd. Ob-Gyn. Fellow ACS, Am. Coll. Obstetricians and Gynecologists, Internat. Coll. Surgeons, Am. Fertility Soc.; mem. Am. Soc. Gynecol. Laparoscopists, Am. Soc. Colposcopy and Cervical Neoplasia, Am. Public Health Assn., Am. Assn. Planned Parenthood Physicians, Royal Soc. Medicine (London), World Med. Assn., N.Y. State Med. Soc., Queens Gynecol. Soc. Contbr. articles to profl. jours.

HAKIMOGLU, AYHAN, electronics company executive; b. Erbaa, Turkey, Aug. 19, 1927; came to U.S., 1955; s. Mekki and Mediha H.; m. Geraldine Ann Crilley, Nov. 19, 1982; children by previous marriage: Zeynep B., Incigul R. O'Brien, Deborah A. Cueto, Leyla P. B.S.E.E., Robert Coll., Istanbul, 1949; M.S.E.E., U. Cin., 1950. Founder, pres., chmn. bd. Dynaplex Corp., Princeton, N.J., 1962-67; gen. mgr. Teledyne Telemetry Co., Los Angeles, 1966-67; founder, chmn. bd., pres. Aydin Corp., Horsham, Pa., 1967—; dir. Fischer & Porter Co., 1983. Served to lt. Turkish Army, 1951-52. Named Turkish Am. of Yr., 1985. Moslem. Office: Aydin Corp 700 Dresher Rd PO Box 349 Horsham PA 19044

HAKOMORI, SEN-ITIROH, immunochemist, biochemist, researcher, educator; b. Sendai, Japan, Feb. 13, 1929; came to U.S., 1963, naturalized, 1978; s. Shinichiro and Kiku (Amae) H.; m. Mitsuko Ito, June 16, 1956; children—Yoichiro, Kenjiro, Naoko. M.D., Tohoku U., Sendai, 1952, D. Med. Sci., Inst. Biochemistry, 1957. Intern, Sendai City Hosp., Japan, 1952-53, asst. prof. Tohoku U., 1957-59, prof. Coll. Pharmacy, 1959-63; research assoc. Med. Sch., Harvard U., Boston, 1963-66; vis. prof. Brandeis U., Waltham, Mass., 1966-68; assoc. prof., then prof. U. Wash., Seattle, 1968-75; program head, prof. pathobiology and microbiology F. Hutchinson Cancer Ctr. and U. Wash., Seattle, 1975-86; scientific dir. The Biomembrane Inst., Seattle, 1986—; mem. study sect. NIH, Bethesda, Md., 1975-78, mem. adv. com., 1984. Author: Sphingolipid Biochemistry, 1983; contbr. numerous articles to profl. publs. Recipient Philip Levin award Am. Soc. Clin. Pathology, 1984, Outstanding Investigator Nat. Cancer Inst., 1986. Mem. Am. Soc. Biol. Chemists, Am. Assn. Cancer Research, Am. Soc. Immunology.r Research, Am. Soc. Immunology. Office: The Biomembrane Inst 201 Elliott Ave W Seattle WA 98119

HALABY, RURIK BENDALY, investment banker; b. Jaffa, Palestine, May 20, 1940; s. Bendaly Jacob and Vera (Debbas) H.; S.B., MIT, 1962, S.M., 1964; M.B.A., Stanford U., 1969; m. Cynthia Jean Petre, Mar. 27, 1964; children—Michael Rurik, Nicholas Alexander. Engr., Bechtel Corp., San Francisco, 1964-67; assoc. corp. fin. dept. Paine Webber Jackson Curtis Inc., N.Y.C., 1969-73; v.p. corp. fin. dept. Hornblower Weeks-Hemphill Noyes Inc., N.Y.C., 1973-76; pres. Crescent Diversified Ltd., N.Y.C., 1976-80, R.B. Halaby Co. Inc., N.Y.C., 1981—, Ibec Agri-Finance Co., N.Y.C., 1983-85, AgriCapital Corp., 1985—; dir. Stanchemco Inc., Omaha, Arabian Shield Devel. Corp., Dallas, The Lexington Group, N.Y.C. Mem. ASCE, Arab Bankers Assn. (London), Arab Bankers Assn. N.Am. Republican. Eastern Orthodox. Club: University (N.Y.C.). Home: 374 Evergreen Pl Ridgewood NJ 07450 Office: 420 Lexington Ave Suite 1925 New York NY 10170

HALASZ, GEORGE, psychiatrist, consultant; b. Budapest, Hungary, July 6, 1949; came to Australia, 1957; s. Laszlo and Alice (Klein) H. Intern Prince Henry's Hosp., Melbourne, Victoria, Australia, 1975-76; sr. house officer Brook Gen. Hosp., London, 1976; resident Beilinson Hosp., Petah Tikva, Tel Aviv, 1977; sr. house officer Middlesex Hosp., London, 1977; registrar King's Coll. Hosp., London, 1978-82; sr. registrar Maudsley, Bethlem Royal Hosp., London, 1982-84; cons. Austin Hosp., Melbourne, 1985-87, Monash Med. Ctr., Melbourne, 1987—; tutor Melbourne U., 1985—; hon. sr. lectr. Monash U., 1987-88; sr. lectr. 1988—; chmn. Office Psychiat. Services, Child Psychiatry Computer Group, Melbourne. Fellow Royal Australian and N.Z. Coll. Psychiatrists; mem. Royal Coll. Psychiatrists, Eng., Family Therapy Assn. Victoria, Assn. Psychoanalytic Psychotherapy (assoc.). Club: Lit. of Orlando (Fla.). Home: 1/97 Mathoura Rd, Toorak Victoria 3142, Australia Office: Monash Med Ctr, 246 Clayton Rd, Clayton Victoria 3168, Australia

HALBOUTY, MANAH ROBERT, retired air force officer; physician; b. Beaumont, Tex., Apr. 28, 1914; s. Tom C. and Sodia (Monolley) H.; M.D., Tulane U., 1937; grad. Sch. Aviation Medicine, 1940, Med-Field Service Sch., 1941, Army Air Staff Command and Gen. Staff Sch., 1944; m. Gracye Collinsworth, Mar. 23, 1940; 1 son, Michel Robert William. Intern, St. Paul's Hosp., Dallas, 1937-38, resident internal medicine, 1938-39; house doctor Mo.-Kans.-Tex. R.R. Hosp., Denison, Tex., 1939-40; commd. 1st lt., M.C., USAAF, 1940, advanced through ranks to col., USAF, 1951; aviation med. examiner, flight surgeon, sr. flight surgeon, chief flight surgeon and med. aircraft observer; research aviation medicine Mayo Clinic, 1941-42; asst. chief med. processing center SAACC, Tex., 1942; med. dir. high altitude flying Hdqrs. S.E. Air Tng. Ctr., Maxwell Field, Ala., 1942-43; hosp. comdr., Ohio and Fla., 1943-44; troop carrier wing surgeon, Italy, Germany, 1944-46, comdr. hosps., wing and base surgeon, N.Y. State, Alaska, Ariz., Tex., 1946-57; div. surgeon 43d Air Div., comdr. 8th Tactical Hosp., also 6160th USAF Hosp., Itazuke AFB, Japan, 1957-60; chief flight surgeon, div. surgeon 819th Air Div. USAF Hosp. cmdr., , dir. base med. services hosp. and Group, Comdr. Dyess AFB, Abilene, Tex.; mem. phys. evaluation bd. USAF Hdqrs., 1966-68; USAF surgeon gen.'s staff med. rep. on USAF Phys. Rev. Council, Hdqrs. USAF Mil. Personnel Center, Randolph AFB, Tex., 1968-74; ret., 1974; chief Med. Bd. Rev. Service, Wilford Hall, USAF Med. Center, San Antonio, 1974-80, chmn. dept. med. bds. and exams., 1980-83; ret., 1983; cons. Mil./VA med. disability system cases, 1982—; ltd. practice family medicine; practicing med. clinician Randolph AFB Hosp. and Wilford Hall USAF Med. Center. Decorated Legion of Merit with oak leaf cluster, Purple Heart. 2 Army and 3 Air Force Commendation medals; Gold Flight Surgeon's Wings with citation from Comdg. Gen. Chinese Nationalist Air Force. Mem. Assn. Mil. Surgeon's U.S., Aerospace Med. Assn. U.S., Am. Acad. Family Practice, Japanese-Am. Med. Assn. (founder), Assn. U.S. Flight Surgeons. Contbr. numerous articles to mil. and profl. med. jours. Home and Office: 6002 Wildwind Dr San Antonio TX 78239

HALBOUTY, MICHEL THOMAS, geologist, petroleum engineer, petroleum operator; b. Beaumont, Tex., June 21, 1909; s. Tom Christian and Sodia (Manolley) H.; m. Billye Stevens, Dec. 27, 1981; 1 dau., Linda Fay. B.S., Tex. A&M U., 1930, M.S., 1931, Profl. Degree in Geol. Engring, 1956; D.Eng. (hon.), Mont. Coll. Mineral Sci. and Tech., 1966. Geologist, petroleum engr. Yount-Lee Oil Co., Beaumont, 1931-33; chief geologist, petroleum engr. Yount-Lee Oil Co., 1933-35; v.p., gen. mgr., chief geologist and petroleum engr. Glenn H. McCarthy, Inc., Houston, 1935-37; owner firm cons. geologists and petroleum engrs. Houston, 1937-81; chmn., chief exec. officer Michel T. Halbouty Energy Co., 1981—; discoverer numerous oil and gas fields La. and Tex.; adj. prof. Tex. Tech U.; vis. prof. Tex. A. and M. U. Author several books. Contbr. numerous papers on geology and petroleum engring. to profl. jours. Served as lt. col. AUS, 1942-45. Recipient Tex. Mid-Continent Oil and Gas Assn. disting. service award for an ind., 1965; named engr. of yr. Tex. Soc. Profl. Engrs. and Engrs. Council, 1968; recipient Disting. Alumni award Tex. A&M U., 1968; Michel T. Halbouty Geoscis. Bldg. named for him, 1977; recipient DeGolyer Disting. Service medal Soc. Petroleum Engrs. of Am. Inst. Mining, Metall. and Petroleum Engrs., 1971; hon. mem. Spindletop sect., 1972; hon. mem. inst., 1973; Anthony F. Lucas Gold medal, 1975; Pecora award NASA, 1977; Horatio Alger award Am. Schs. and Colls. Assn., 1978, Spirit of Life award City of Hope, 1978, Breath of Life award Cystic-Fibrosis Found., 1981, merit medal Circum-Pacific Council for Energy and Mineral Resources, 1982, Hoover medal Am. Assn. Engring. Socs., 1982, disting. service award Paul Carrington chpt. SAR, 1983, Tex. Heritage award Angleton C. of C., Tex., 1983. Mem. Am. Assn. Petroleum Geologists (hon., pres. 1966-67, Human Needs award 1975, Sidney Powers Meml. medal 1977), Am. Soc. Oceanography, Internat. Assn. Sedimentology, Inst. Petroleum, London, Am. Petroleum Inst., Am. Inst. Mining and Metall. Engrs., Soc. Econ. Paleontologists and Mineralogists, Soc. Econ. Geologists, Mineral. Soc. Am., Geol. Soc. Am., Soc. Exploration Geophysicists (hon.), Nat. Acad. Engring., Houston Geol. Soc. (hon.), N.Y. Acad. Sci., Tex. Acad. Sci. (Disting. Tex. Scientist of Yr. 1983), A.A.A.S., Am. Inst. Profl. Geologists, Am. Geol. Inst., Tex., Nat. socs. profl. engrs., Gulf Coast Assn. Geol. Socs. (hon.). Episcopalian. Clubs: Ramada, Houston, Petroleum, River Oaks Country (Houston); Dallas Petroleum; Eldorado Country, Vintage (Palm Desert, Calif.); New Orleans Petroleum; Cosmos (Washington); Broadmoor, Kissing Camels (Colorado Springs). Home: 2121 Kirby Dr Houston TX 77019 Office: Halbouty Center 5100 Westheimer Rd Houston TX 77056

HALBREICH, URIEL, psychiatrist; b. Jerusalem, Israel, Nov. 23, 1943; came to U.S., 1978, naturalized, 1982; s. Mordechai and Zipora (Tennenbaum) H.;1 child, Jasmine; m. Judith T. Mrozowski, 1987. M.D., Hebrew U., 1969. Diplomate Tel Aviv U. Psychiatry and Psychotherapy. Vice chief med. officer Israel Navy, 1970-72; 2d, then 1st asst. Hadassah U. Hosp., Jerusalem, 1972-78, temp. chief physician, 1978; chief psychiatrist Israel Navy, 1977-78; asst. prof., research psychiatrist Columbia U., N.Y.C., 1978-80; assoc. prof., dir. div. biol. psychiatry Albert Einstein Coll. Medicine, N.Y.C., 1982-85; prof. psychiatry, dir. biobehavioral research SUNY-Buffalo, 1985—. Contbr. over 130 articles to profl. jours.; editor: Transient Psychosis, 1983; Resistance to Treatment with Antidepressant Drugs, 1986; Hormones and Depression, 1987. Served to comdr. Israeli Navy, 1970-78. Recipient Ben Gurion award Gen. Fedn. Labor, 1976; Yair Gon award Hebrew U. Hadassah Med. Sch., 1978; Nat. Research Service award NIH, 1978; NIMH grantee, 1982. Fellow Am. Coll. Neuropsychopharmacology, Am. Psychopathology Assn.; mem. Coll. Internat. Neuropsychopharmacology, Internat. Soc. Psycho. Neuro. Endocrinol., Am. Coll. Psychiatrists, Soc. Biol. Psychiatry, Endocrine Soc., others. Jewish. Home: 497 Delaware Ave Buffalo NY 14202 Office: SUNY Buffalo 462 Grider St K-Annex Buffalo NY 14215

HALDANE, JOHN JOSEPH, philosopher, educator; b. London, Feb. 19, 1954; s. James and Hilda Ellen (Dunne) H.; m. Hilda Marie Budas, Aug. 9, 1980; children Kirsty Anne. BFA with honors, Wimbledon Sch. Arts, 1975; BA in Philosophy with honors, U. London, 1980, PhD in Philosophy, 1983. Tchr. art St. Joseph's Grammar Sch., London, 1976-79; lectr. dept. Moral Philosophy U. St. Andrews, Scotland, 1983—; vis. lectr. Poly. Cen. London, 1982—, various colls. nursing edn., Scotland, 1986—; research assoc. Ctr. for Philosophy and Pub. Affairs, 1985—, dir. 1988—. Co-editor: Mind, Causation, and Action, 1986; mem. editorial bd. The Philos. Quarterly, 1983—; manuscript cons. Jour. Med. Ethics, 1986—; contbr. articles to profl. jours. Recipient Analysis jour. prize, 1983, Med. Ethics Jour. prize, 1987; vis. fellow U. Pitts. Ctr. for Philosophy of Sci., 1987; vis. scholar U. Del. Ctr. for Study of Values, 1987. Mem. Brit. Soc. for History of Philosophy, Am. Cath. Philos. Assn., Scottish Phenomenology Soc. (founding, sec. 1986—), Aristotelian Soc. Roman Catholic. Clubs: Royal Overseas League (London), Ct. Electors (U. London) (sec. 1982-83). Home: 20 Melbourne Pl, Saint Andrews KY16 9EY, Scotland Office: U St Andrews, Dept Moral Philosophy, Saint Andrews KY16 9AL, Scotland

HALDANE-STEVENSON, JAMES PATRICK, clergy member, minister; b. Llandaff, Wales, Mar. 17, 1910; s. Graham Morton and Jane (Thomson) Stevenson; m. Leila Mary Flack, Nov. 5, 1938 (div. 1967); children: Alan, Keith, Janet; m. Joan Talbot Smith, Aug. 6, 1983. BA, U. Oxford, Eng., 1933, MA, 1941, postgrad., 1934. Ordained to ministry Anglican Ch., 1935. Clk. Westminster Bank, Birmingham, Eng., 1927-30; curate Anglican Ch., Lambeth, Eng., 1935-38; chaplain British Army, Dunkirk & Cassino, 1939-55; rector Anglican Ch., Wongan Hills, Australia, 1956-59; vicar Anglican Ch. of North Balwyn, Melbourne, Australia, 1959-80; free-lance writer 1980—. Author: (as J.P. Stevenson) In Our Tongues, 1944, Religion and Leadership, 1948, Crisanzio and Other Poems, 1948, Beyond the Bridge, 1973, The Backward Look, 1976; represented in anthologies including Soldiers Also Asked, 1943, Padre Presents, 1943, Poems from Italy, 1945, Songs of Australia, 1977; contbr. Australian Encyclopaedia, Australian Dictionary of Biography, Poetry Rev., Poetry Today, Guardian, New Statesman, Spectator; Australian correspondent Le Monde, 1969-73; contbr. articles on Wales under pseudonym Tomos Radyr. Clubs: Freemen of London, Athenaeum (London); Melbourne, Naval and Mil. (Melbourne); Cymdeithas, Llandaff. Home: 3 Argyle Sq, Ainslie Ave, Canberra 2601, Australia

HALDANE-STEVENSON, JOAN TALBOT, interior designer; b. Wellington, N.Z., Dec. 4, 1922; d. Carl William and Hilda Ivy (Talbot) Wilson; m. Ernest Noel Smith, Apr. 19, 1941 (dec.); children—Peter, Bruce, Ian; m. James Patrick Haldane-Stevenson, Aug. 6, 1983. Ed. St. Margaret's Sch., Christchurch, N.Z., Queen Margaret Coll., Wellington. Engaged in community service, Melbourne, Australia, 1950-63; interior designer ch. and domestic decor, 1963-66; founder, prin. Joan Smith & Assocs., Canberra, Australia, 1966—; hon. interior design cons. Royal Canberra Hosp.; mem. 1983 judging com. Housing Industry Assn.; chmn. Blake Prize Com., 1971. Pres. Canberra YWCA, 1969-72. Fellow Royal Soc. Arts (London); mem. Soc. Interior Designers Australia. Anglican. Home: 3 Argyle Sq, Ainslie Ave, 2601 Canberra City Australia Office: 7 Lonsdale St, 2601 Canberra Australia

HALE, ARNOLD WAYNE, army officer, clergyman; b. Colome, S.D., Sept. 2, 1934; s. Archiebald William and Alvena Lucille (Williams) H.; MEd Our Lady of the Lake U., 1971, MEd, 1973; BS Regents Coll. SUNY-Albany, 1976; AA Austin Comm. Coll., 1979; ministerial cert. Gospel Ministry Inst., 1981; DD (hon.), Gospel Ministry Ctr., 1981; diploma ministerial studies, Berean Coll., 1983; ThD Reeves Christian Coll., 1984; m. Mary Alice Mauricio, Nov. 30, 1962; 1 son, Alexander; children by previous marriage—Colleen, Zola; stepchildren—Charles, Marlow. Ordained to ministry Gospel Ministry Ctr. Full Gospel Ch. in Christ, Victory New Testament Fellowship Internat., 1983. Infantryman, U.S. Army, 1953-55, commd. lt., 1959, advanced through ranks to maj., 1973, served in various staff and mgmt. positions with Med. Service Corps, 1959-67, med. adviser Mil. Assistance Command, Vietnam, 1967-68, ednl. tng. officer, U.S. Army Med. Tng. Center, Ft. Sam Houston, Tex., 1968-73, hosp. comdr., Ft. Campbell, Ky., 1973-75, med. adviser Tex. Army N.G., Austin, 1975-77, ret., 1977; librarian Thorndale/Milano Independent Sch. Dists., Milam County, Tex., 1977-78; instr. psychology Austin Community Coll., 1977-79; librarian, dist. test administr. Austwell-Tivoli Ind. Sch. Dist., Tex., 1979-81; adult probation officer Travis County (Tex.), 1981-82; founding Chaplain Biblio Edn. Counseling Ministry, 1983—. Decorated Bronze Star. Recipient Duke of Paducah award, 1975; Experienced Pastoral Counselor award Inst. Experienced Pastoral Counselors, 1981. Fellow Am. Biog. Inst. Research Assn. (life); mem. ALA bibliotherapy discussion group, Am. Personnel and Guidance Assn., Christians United for Israel, PTL Club, NEA, Nat. Chaplains Assn., Internat. Platform Assn. Tex. Jr. Coll. tchrs. assns., CAP (maj., med. advisor, chaplain), Ret. Officers Assn. (life), N.G. Assn. Tex. (life), Mil. Order World Wars, Assn. U.S. Army, U.S. Armor Assn. Clubs: Masons (W. Ger.); Lions. Home: 10412 Firethorn Ln Austin TX 78750

HALE, CHARLES MARTIN, stock broker; b. London, Jan. 19, 1936; s. Charles Sidney and Carmen Rosa (de Mora) H.; m. Kaaren Alexis Garfunkel, Feb. 11, 1967; children: Melissa Lauren, Amanda Suzanne. BS in Geology, Stanford U., 1957; MBA, Harvard U., 1963. Gen. ptnr. Hirsch & Co., N.Y.C., 1963-70; mng. dir. A.G. Becker & Co., London, 1970-83; gen. ptnr. Lehman Bros., Kuhn Loeb & Co., London, 1983-84; mng. dir. Donaldson Lufkin & Jenrette Internat., London, 1984—; bd. dirs. Invitro-Care, Cambridge, Mass. Served to lt. USN, 1958-61. Mem. N.Y. Stock Exchange (allied), Delta Kappa Epsilon. Republican. Episcopalian. Clubs: Harvard (N.Y.C.), Annabel's (London), Hurlingham (London). Home: 33 Lyall Mews, London SW1, England Office: Donaldson Lufkin &. Jenrette Internat, 14 Finsbury Square, London EC2A 1BR, England

HALE, CHARLES RUSSELL, lawyer; b. Talpa, Tex., Oct. 17, 1916; s. Charles L. and Exa (Evans) H.; m. Clementine L. Moore, Jan. 5, 1946; children: Robert R., Norman B. A.B., Stanford U., 1939; J.D., Fordham U., 1950. Bar: N.Y. 1950, Calif. 1953. Supr., United Geophys. Co., Pasadena, Calif., 1940-46; mem. patent staff Bell Telephone Labs., N.Y.C., 1947-48,

Sperry Gyroscope Co., Great Neck, N.Y., 1948-51; practiced in Pasadena 1951-54; mem. firm Christie, Parker & Hale, Pasadena, 1954—. Mem. ABA, Los Angeles Bar Assn., Pasadena Bar Assn. (v.p. 1960-61), Am. Patent Law Assn., AAAS, San Diego County Bar Assn., Am. Soc. Internat. Law, IEEE. Clubs: University (Pasadena); Rancho Santa Fe (Calif.) Golf. Home: PO Box 616 Rancho Santa Fe CA 92067 Office: 350 W Colorado Blvd Pasadena CA 91105

HALE, IRVING, investment executive, writer; b. Denver, Mar. 22, 1932; s. Irving Jr. and Lucile (Beggs) H.; B.A. with distinction, U. Colo., 1964; m. Joan E. Domenico, Dec. 29, 1954; children—Pamela Joan, Beth Ellen. Security analyst Colo. Nat. Bank, Denver, 1955-58; asst. sec. Centennial Fund, Inc., Second Centennial Fund, Inc., Gryphon Fund, Inc., Meridian Fund, Inc., 1959-68; portfolio mgr. Twenty Five Fund, Inc. (formerly Trend Fund, Inc.), Denver, 1969-72; v.p. Alpine Corp., Denver, 1971-72; dir. research Hanifen, Imhoff & Samford, Inc., Denver, 1973-77; v.p. research First Fin. Securities, Inc., 1977-82; arbitrator Nat. Assn. Securities Dealers; contbg. editor Nat. OTC Stock Jour., 1982-83; exec. v.p. research/corp. Fin. R. B. Marich, Inc., 1983—. lectr., Denver Public Schs. Community Talent, 1975—; bd. dirs. Community Resources, Inc., 1981—. Fellow Fin. Analysts Fedn.; mem. Denver Soc. Security Analysts, Radio Hist. Assn. Colo. (pres. 1977-78), Mensa, Beta Sigma Tau. Republican. Episcopalian. Club: Denver Press (assoc. mem.). Columnist, Denver Post; contbr. articles to profl. jours. Home: 1642 Ivanhoe St Denver CO 80220 Office: R B Marich Inc 1512 Larimer St Suite 800 Denver CO 80202

HALE, JOHN ALEXANDER, publishing company executive; b. Harpenden, England, July 10, 1930; s. Herbert Robert and Dorothy Mary (Lendrum) H.; m. Bridget Corboy; children—Helen Rosemary, Robert John, Susan Margaret. Chartered accountant. Articled clk. Farrow, Bersey, Gain, Vencent and Co., London, 1948-53; mng. dir. Robert Hale Ltd., London, 1956—. Mem. Ch. of England. Office: Robert Hale Ltd, 45-47 Clerkenwell Green, London EC1R OHT, England

HALE, JOHN RIGBY, educator; b. Ashford, Kent, Eng., Sept. 17, 1923; s. E. R. S. and Hilda (Birks) H.; m. Rosalind Williams, 1953; 3 children; m. 2d, Sheila Haynes, 1965; 1 son. Ed. Jesus Coll., Oxford U., Johns Hopkins U. and Harvard U.; MA, DLitt Fellow and tutor in modern history Jesus Coll., Oxford U. (Eng.), 1949-64; prof. history U. Warwick (Eng.), 1964-69; prof. Italian lang. and history, Univ. Coll., London U., 1970—; vis. prof. Cornell U., 1959, U. Calif.-Berkeley; chmn. Brit. Soc. for Renaissance Studies, 1973-78; pub. orator U. London, 1980—. Trustee Nat. Gallery, London, 1973-80, chmn. bd. trustees, 1975-81; trustee Victoria and Albert Mus., London, 1983—, The British Mus., London, 1985, chmn. adv. com. Govt. Art Collection, 1983—; mem. Royal Mint Adv. Com., 1979—. Author: England and the Italian Renaissance, 1954; The Italian Journal of Samuel Rogers, 1956; Machiavelli and Renaissance Italy, 1961; The Literary Works of Machiavelli, 1961; The Evolution of British Historiography, 1964; Renaissance Europe 1480-1520, 1971; Italian Renaissance Painting, 1977; Florence and the Medicine: the Pattern of Control, 1977; Renaissance Fortification: Art or Engineering?, 1977; the Italian Journal of Antonio de Beatis, 1979; Renaissance War Studies, 1983; editor: Certain Discourses Military by Sir John Smyth, 1964; Renaissance Venice, 1973; War and Society in Renaissance Europe, 1985. Decorated commendatore Ordine Al Merito della Repubblica Italiana; recipient Socio Straniero, Accademia-Arcadia, Rome, 1972, Knight Bachelor, 1984, Academicus exclasse (bronze award) Academia Medicea, Florence, Italy, 1980, Bolla prize for services to Venice, 1982. Fellow British Acad., Soc. Antiquaries. Home: 13 Montpelier Row, Twickenham TW1 2NQ, England Office: Univ Coll, Dept History, Gower St, London WC1E 6BT, England

HALEFOGLU, VAHIT M., former Turkish minister of foreign affairs; b. Antakya, Nov. 19, 1919; s. Mehmet Mesrur and Samiye (Cabri) H.; m. Fatma Zehra Bereket, July 14, 1951; children: Nilgun Yucaoglu, Melih. Ed. Antakya Coll., U. Ankara; M.A. with Turkish Fgn. Service, from 1943, serving in Vienna, Moscow, London, 1946-59; dir.-gen. 1st polit. dept. Ministry Fgn. Affairs Turkey, 1959-62; Turkish ambassador to Lebanon, 1962-65, Kuwait, 1964-65, USSR, 1965-66, Netherlands, 1966-70; dep. sec. gen. polit. affairs Ministry Fgn. Affairs, Ankara, Turkey, 1970-72; Turkish ambassador to Fed. Republic Germany, 1972-82, USSR, 1982-83; minister of fgn. affairs, Ankara, 1983-87. Decorated by govts. Lebanon, Greece, Italy, W.Ger., Spain, Finland, U.K. Address: Ministry of Fgn Affairs, Ankara Turkey *

HALEMANE, THIRUMALA RAYA, physicist, systems engineer; b. Ednad Village, India, May 27, 1953; s. H. Shama Bhat and Thirumaleshwari; m. Usha Kumari Kailar, Aug. 30, 1976; children—Kaviraj, Shilpi. B.Sc. (hons.), Bangalore U., 1972; M.Sc., Indian Inst. Tech., Madras, 1974; M.A. in Physics, U. Rochester, 1976, M.A. in Math., Ph.D. in Physics, 1980. Research assoc. Rutgers U., Piscataway, N.J., 1979-81; asst. prof. SUNY Fredonia, N.Y., 1981-85; mem. tech. staff AT&T Bell Labs., Holmdel, N.J., 1985—; vis. asst. prof. Pa. State U., University Park, 1984; vis. scientist Phys. Research Lab., Ahmedabad, India, summer 1983. Rush Rhees fellow, 1974; SUNY Found grantee, 1982. Mem. Am. Phys. Soc., IEEE. Contbr. articles to profl. jours. Home: 62 Yellowstone Ln E Howell NJ 07731

HALEVY, ABRAHAM HAYIM, horticulturist, plant physiologist; b. Tel-Aviv, Israel, July 17, 1927; s. Naftali and Henia (Ginzburg) H.; M.S., Hebrew U., Jerusalem, 1955, Ph.D., 1958; m. Zilla Horngrad, Aug. 20, 1952 (dec. 1981); children—Avishag, Noa, Itai. Research asso. Dept. Agr. Plant Ind. Sta., Beltsville, Md., 1958-59; lectr. in horticulture and plant physiology, Hebrew U., Rehovot, Israel, 1960-64, sr. lectr., 1964-67, asso. prof., 1967-71, prof., 1971—; head dept. ornamental horticulture, Hebrew U. of Jerusalem, 1967-83, 86—; vis. prof., Mich. State U., 1964-65, U. Calif., Davis, 1970-71, 75-76, 82-84, 86, 87; sci. adv. to Israeli Ministry of Edn. Served with Israel Def. Forces, 1948-50. Mem. Internat. Soc. Horticulture (council), Am., Scandinavian, Geradi Socs. Plant Physiologists, Am. Soc. Horticultural Sci. (A. Laurie award, 1960-63). Jewish. Editorial bd. Scientia Horticolturae, Plant Growth Regulators; editor-in-chief Israel Jour. Botany, editor Handbook of Flowering, Vols. 1-6, 1985-88, Flowering Newsletter; contbr. over 200 sci. papers in field to publs. Home: 2 Shtrouk, Tel-Aviv 64 042, Israel Office: Hebrew Univ Agricult Faculty, PO Box 12, Rehovot 76 100, Israel

HALEVY, HILDA MARIA, physician, anesthesiologist; b. Havana, Cuba; d. Juan and Raimunda (Valdes) Cheng; B.S., Instituto de Segunda Enseñanza de la Habana, Havana, 1949; M.D., U. Havana, 1957; m. Simon Halevy, 1968; 1 child, Daniel A. Sr. house physician and surgeon Mother Cabrini Meml. Hosp., N.Y.C., 1957-58; resident in anesthesiology Met. Hosp., N.Y.C., 1958-60; fellow in anesthesiology, various hosps., N.Y.C., 1960-67; attending anesthesiologist Astoria (N.Y.) Gen. Hosp., 1967—; vis. scholar to Mexico, Holland, Israel. Recipient Physician's Recognition award. Mem AMA, Am. Soc. Anesthesiologists, Med. Soc. State N.Y., N.Y. State Soc. Anesthesiologists, Med. Soc. County Queens, Am. Soc. Magnesium Research, N.Y. Soc. of Acupuncture for Physicians and Dentists. Democrat. Jewish. Office: Astoria Gen Hosp Dept Anesthesia 25-10 30th Ave Astoria NY 11102

HALEY, JOHN DAVID, petroleum consulting executive; b. Denver, Mar. 16, 1924; s. Peter Daniel and Margaret Dorothy (O'Haire) H.; m. Annie Loretta Breeden, June 20, 1951; children—Laura, Patricia, Brian, Sharon, Norine, Kathleen. Profl. engr. Colo. Sch. Mines, 1948. Registered profl. engr., Colo., Okla. Petroleum engr. Creole Petroleum, Venezuela, 1948-50, Texaco Corp., 1950-52; staff engr. Carter Oil (Exxon), Tulsa, 1954-56; petroleum cons. Earlougher Engring., Tulsa, 1956-61, resident mgr., Denver, 1961-62; v.p. prodn. Anschutz Corp., Denver, 1962-86; dir. Circle A Mud, Denver, 1983-86; pres. Greylock Pipeline, Denver, 1983-86, Anschutz Pipeline, Denver, 1984-86; pres. Haley Engring. Inc., 1987—; bd. dirs. Future Devel., 1985—, Polar III, 1986—. Rep. committeeman, Littleton. Served to lt. comdr. USNR, 1943-46, 52-54. Mem. Soc. Petroleum Engrs. (dir. Denver chpt.), Soc. Petroleum Evaluation Engrs., Ind. Petroleum Assn. Am., Ind. Petroleum Assn. Mountain States, Am. Petroleum Inst. (citation for service), Internat. Assn. Drilling Contractors, Soc. Profl. Well Log Analysts. Petroleum Club (Denver chpt.). Roman Catholic. Home: 561 E Caley Dr Littleton CO 80121

HALEY, JOHNETTA RANDOLPH, musician, educator, university administrator; b. Alton, Ill., Mar. 19; d. John A. and Willye E. (Smith) Randolph; Mus.B. in Edn., Lincoln U., 1945; Mus.M., So. Ill. U., 1972; children—Karen, Michael. Vocal and gen. music tchr. Lincoln High Sch., E. St. Louis, Ill., 1945-48; vocal music tchr., choral dir. Turner Sch., Kirkwood, Mo., 1950-55; vocal and gen. music tchr. Nipher Jr. High Sch., Kirkwood, 1955-71; prof. music Sch. Fine Arts, So. Ill. U., Edwardsville, 1972—, dir. East St. Louis Campus, 1982—; adjudicator music festivals; area music cons. Ill. Office Edn., 1977-78; program specialist St. Louis Human Devel. Corp., 1968; interim exec. dir. St. Louis Council Black People, summer 1970. Bd. dirs. YWCA, 1975-80, Artist Presentation Soc., St. Louis, 1975, United Negro Coll. Fund, 1976-78; bd. curators Lincoln U., Jefferson City, Mo., 1974—, pres., 1978—; mem. Nat. Ministry on Urban Edn., Luth. Ch.-Mo. Synod, 1975-80; bd. dirs. Council Luth. Chs., Assn. of Governing Bds. of Univs. and Colls.; mem. adv. council Danforth Found. St. Louis Leadership Program, nat. chmn. Cleve. Job Corps, 1974-78; trustee Stillman Coll. Recipient Woman of Achievement in Edn. award Elks, 1987, Disting. Citizen award St. Louis Argus Newspaper, 1970; Cotillion de Leon award for Outstanding Community Service, 1977; Disting. Alumnae award Lincoln U., 1977; Disting. Service award United Negro Coll. Fund, 1979, SCLC, 1981; Community Service award St. Louis Drifters, 1979; Disting. Service to Arts award Sigma Gamma Rho, Fred L. McDowell award, 1986, Nat. Negro Musicians award, 1981, Sci. Awareness award, 1984-85, Tri Del Federated award, 1985, Bus. and Profl. Women's Club award, 1985-86, vol. yr. Inroad's Inc., 1986; named Duchess of Paducah, 1973; received Key to City, Gary, Ind., 1973. Mem. Council Luth. Chs., AAUP, Coll. Music Soc., Music Educators Nat. Conf., Ill. Music Educators Assn., Nat. Choral Dirs. Assn., Assn. Tchr. Educators, Midwest Kodaly Music Educators, Nat. Assn. Negro Musicians, Jack and Jill Inc., Women of Achievement in Edn., Friends of St. Louis Art Mus., The Links, Inc., Alpha Kappa Alpha, Mu Phi Epsilon, Pi Kappa Lambda. Lutheran. Club: Las Amigas Social. Lodge: Elks. Home: 30 Plaza Sq Saint Louis MO 63103 Office: So Ill U Box 1200 Edwardsville IL 62026

HALF, ROBERT, personnel recruiting executive, author; b. N.Y.C., Nov. 11, 1918; s. Sidney and Pauline (Kahn) H.; m. Maxine Levison, June 17, 1945; children: Nancy Half Asch, Peggy Half Silbert. B.S., NYU, 1940. C.P.A., N.Y. Staff acct. Ernst & Whinney, 1940-43; mgr. office and personnel Kayser-Roth Corp., 1943-48; founder Robert Half Internat., Inc., N.Y.C., 1948—; founder, pres. Accountemps Inc., U.S., Can., Eng., 1964—; guest speaker Data Processing Mgmt. Assn., Nat. Assn. Accts.; guest on TV and radio shows in, U.S. and Can.; mem. panel of experts Boardroom Reports. Author: The Robert Half Way To Get Hired in Today's Job Market, Robert Half on Hiring, Robert Half's Success Guide for Accountants, Making It Big in Data Processing, How To Hire Smart, How To Keep Your Best People, How to Get Your Employees to Do What They're Supposed To Do, How to Check References When References Are Hard to Check, 52 Good Ideas on Hiring, Firing and More; monthly columnist Nat. Bus. Employment Weekly, Management Accounting, New Accountant, MIS Week, editorial advisor: Jour. Accountancy, Management Accounting, Personnel Jour.; mem. editorial bd.: CPA Personnel Report, Exec. Productivity; contbr. numerous articles to mags. and newspapers. Expert witness subcoms. U.S. Senate; co-author U.S. tax bill Build Am.; mem. Bd. Appeals Village of Saddle Rock, Great Neck, N.Y., 1956-62. Recipient John Madden award NYU, 1985. Mem. Am. Acctg. Assn., Assn. Personnel Consultants N.Y. (pres. 1963-64, dir. 1960-65, Harold Nelson award 1986), Nat. Assn. Personnel Cons., N.Y. State Soc. CPA's, Am. Inst. CPA's, Nat. Assn. Accts., Am. Mgmt. Assn., Adminstrv. Mgmt. Soc., Am. Soc. Personnel Adminstrs., Assn. Human Resources Cons., Accts. Club Am., U.S. C. of C., Employment Mgrs. Assn., Data Processing Mgmt. Assn., Internat. Platform Assn. Lodge: Toastmasters. Office: 522 Fifth Ave New York NY 10036

HALFHIDE, ARNOLD THEODOR, Suriname ambassador to U.S.; b. Paramaribo, Suriname, Dec. 30, 1939; m. Carla Josephine Ooosterlen; 1 child, Diego Rafael. Ed., Comml. Coll., The Netherlands, Century U., Calif., Ashridge Mgmt. Coll., Berkhempstead, U.K., Mgmt. Ctr., Brussels. Regional sales mgr. Bruynzeel Suriname Houtmaatschappij B.V., Paramaribo, 1968-72, first v.p., dir. mktg. and sales, gen. sales mgr., export mgr., 1973-79; pres. Varossieau Suriname Paint Industries (div. Sigma Coatings B.V.), The Netherlands, 1979-81; consul-gen., Suriname, N.Y.C., 1981-83; Minister Plenipotentiary, Paramaribo, Suriname, 1983-84, ambassador-extraordinary and plenipotentiary to Venezuela, 1984-85, Nicaragua, 1985—, to Canada, 1986—; ambassador extraordinary and plenipotentiary to the U.S., 1986—; permanent Suriname rep. to the OAS, 1986—; mem. various delegations rep. govt. of Suriname including mem. Joint Commn. Suriname-Venezuela, 1981; pres. negotiating com. for indsl. nationalization, 1982-85; pres. Joint Commn. Suriname-Brazil, 1982; dir. Nat. Timber Industries, Surinam Timbers, 1980-82. Mem. Suriname Mfrs. Assn. (co-founder 1981). Address: Embassy of Suriname Press Info Office 4301 Connecticut Ave #108 Washington DC 20008

HALFMANN, JOST, sociologist, educator; b. Krefeld, Northrhine-Westfalia, Fed. Republic of Germany, Mar. 19, 1947; s. Hans and Erika (Trapp) H. Diploma in sociology, U. Frankfurt, Fed. Republic of Germany, 1973, PhD, 1976; PhD Habilitation, U. Osnabrück, Fed. Republic of Germany, 1981. Asst. prof. sociology U. Osnabrück, 1975-82, prof., 1982—; vis. prof. U. Nice, France, 1982. Author: Innenansichten der Wissenschaft, 1980, Entstehung der Mikroelektronik, 1984; co-author: Marxismus als Erkenntniskritik, 1976; contbr. articles to profl. jours. Research grantee Deutsche Forschungsgemeinschaft, 1978-79, 83-84, Volkswagenstiftung, 1984. Mem. Am. Polit. Sci. Assn., Internat. Sociol. Assn., Deutsche Gesellschaft Soziologie, Gesellschaft Wissenschafts und Technikforschung. Office: U Osnabruck, Albrechtstrasse 28, D-4500 Osnabruck Federal Republic of Germany

HALFPENNY, JAMES C., scientist, educator; b. Shreveport, La., Jan. 23, 1947; s. Donald Frazier and Dorothy (Carson) H. BS, U. Wyo., 1969, MS, 1970; PhD, U. Colo., 1980. Various positions govt. conservation agys., parks and univ. conservation programs, 1966-80; coordinator long-term ecol. research program U. Colo., Boulder, 1980—; research assoc. Inst. Arctic and Alpine Research, U. Colo., 1980-87, fellow, 1987—; instr. Teton Sci. Sch., Kelly, Wyo., 1980—, Aspen (Colo.) Ctr. for Environ. Studies, 1984—, Yellowstone (Wyo.) Inst., 1984—, Rocky Mountain Nature Assn., 1987; pres. A Naturalist's World, Boulder, 1985—; staff trainer Colo. Div. Wildlife, Sterling, 1979, 83, sci. advisor 1982-85; staff trainer Yellowstone Nat. Park, 1985-86, 88; grant proposal rev. bd. NSF, 1984—, Nat. Geog. Sci., 1984—; trustee Thorne Ecol. Inst., Boulder, 1982-84; mem. Indian Peaks Wilderness Area Adv. Panel, Boulder, 1982-86, others. Author: A Field Guide to Mammal Tracking, 1986; editor (booklets) Mountain Research Sta.; its environment and research, 1982, Long Term Ecol. Research in the U.S.; a network of research sites, 1982, 83, 84; speaker mammal tracking alpine and winter ecology, China's endangered wildlife; contbr. articles to profl. jours. Mem. Sci. Adv. Panel to EOP Program U. Colo., 1982-84; bd. advisors Teton Sci. Sch., Moran, 1985—; bd. dirs. Nat. Outdoor Leadership Sch., Lander, Wyo., 1975-80, chmn. 1978-79. Served with USNR, 1969-71, Vietnam. Decorated Navy Achievement medal with combat "v", Vietnamese Gallantry Cross with palm (Republic Vietnam); recipient Roosevelt Meml. grant Am. Mus. Natural History, 1979, Walker Van Riper grant U.Colo., 1979, Kathy Lichty Fund grant U. Colo., 1979. Mem. Am. Inst. Biol. Scis., AAAS, Am. Soc. Mammalogists, Internat. Soc. Cryptozoology, Southwestern Assn. Naturalists, Northwest Sci. Assn., Colo.-Wyo. Acad. Sci., Orgn. Biol. Field Stas., Sigma Xi. Office: U Colo Inst Arctic/Alpine Research PO Box 450 Boulder CO 80309

HALFWASSEN, HEINZ KARL, paper manufacturing executive; b. Leer, Lower Saxony, Germany, Aug. 11, 1929; s. Beene and Elly Johanne (Stoeltje) H.; m. Helga Margarete Becker; children: Jens, Jnsa, Peer. Abitur, Ubbo-Emmius-Gymnasium, Leer, 1950; diploma, U. Cologne, Fed. Republic Germany, 1956. Fin. asst. Zanders Feinpapiere AG, Bergisch Gladback, Fed. Republic Germany, 1956-63, leader fin. dept., 1963-72, treas., 1972-80, mem. exec. bd., 1980—; chmn. bd. Lother Cos., Belkaw GmbH, Bergisch Gladbach. Mem., chmn. fin. dept. Bergisch Gladbach City Council, 1969—; chmn. bd. Evang. Krankenhaus, Bergisch Gladbach. Recipient hon. ring City of Bergisch Gladbach, 1987. Mem. Employers Assn. North Rhine-Westfalia (exec. bd. 1980—). Mem. Christ Democratic Union. Mem. Evang. Ch. Lodge: Lions. Home: Schreibersheide 42, 5060 Bergisch Gladbach Federal Republic of Germany Office: Zanders Feinpapiere AG, An der Gohrsmuehle, 5060 Bergisch Gladbach Federal Republic of Germany

HALICZER, JAMES SOLOMON, lawyer; b. Ft. Myers, Fla., Oct. 27, 1952; s. Julian and Margaret (Shepard) H. BA in English Lit., U. So. Fla., 1976, MA in Polit. Sci., 1978; JD, Stetson U., 1981. Bar: Fla. 1982. Assoc. Conrad, Scherer & James, Ft. Lauderdale, Fla., 1982-86, ptnr., 1986—; assoc. Bernard & Mauro, Ft. Lauderdale, 1986. Mem. Phi Kappa Phi, Pi Sigma Alpha, Omicron Delta Kappa. Methodist. Home: 2505 Sea Island Dr Fort Lauderdale FL 33301 Office: Conrad Scherer and James 633 S Federal Hwy Fort Lauderdale FL 33301

HALITZKI, ROMAN, architect; b. Szczecin, Poland, July 7, 1952; came to Can., 1959; s. Joseph and Victoria (Borowska) H.; 1 child, Micheal J. Engring. diploma, McGill U., 1971, BS in Architecture, 1974, BArch, 1975. Registered architect, 1977. Architect, owner Roman Halitzki, Architect, Montreal, 1975-82; architect BAE Group, St. John's, Nfld., Can., 1982-87; pres. Integral Cons. and Mgmt. Ltd., St. John's, 1987—; prin. Roman Halitzki Architecture and Design, St. John's, 1987—. Recipient Habitation Space Internat. Award, 1981, 1st prize Nfld. and Labrodor Housing Corp., 1987. Mem. Royal Archtl. Inst. Can., Nfld. Assn. Architects (registration bd. 1986—). Roman Catholic. Avocations: science, history, sports. Home and Office: PO Box 757, Saint John's, NF Canada A1C 5L4

HALKIAS, CHRISTOS CONSTANTINE, electronics educator, consultant; b. Monastiraki, Doridos, Greece, Aug. 23, 1933; s. Constantine C. and Alexandra V. (Papapostolou) H.; m. Demetra Saras, Jan. 2, 1961; children—Alexandra, Helen-Joanna. B.S. in Elec. Engring., CCNY, 1957; M.Sc. in Elec. Engring., Columbia U., 1958, Ph.D., 1962. Prof. elec. engring. Columbia U., N.Y.C., 1962-73; prof. electronics Nat. Tech. U. Athens, Greece, 1973—, Fulbright vis. prof., 1969, dir. infomatics div., 1983-86; dir. Nat. Research Found., Athens, 1983-87; cons. Nat. Bank of Greece, Athens, 1980—, Ergo Bank, Athens, 1975—. Author: Electronic Devices and Circuits, 1967; Integrated Electronics, 1972; Electronic Fundamentals and Applications, 1976, Design of Electronic Filters, 1988; contbr. articles to profl. jours. Recipient D.B. Steinman award CCNY, 1956; Higgins fellow Columbia U., 1958. Mem. IEEE (sr., Centennial medal 1984, chmn. Greek sect. 1982-86), Sigma Xi. Home: 4 Kosti Palama St, Paleo Psyhico, Athens Greece Office: Nat Tech Univ Athens, 42 Patission Ave, Athens Greece

HALL, ALBERT M(ANGOLD), tech. assn. exec.; b. Bklyn., Oct. 8, 1914; s. Edgar A. and Salena A. (Mangold) H.; A.B., Columbia U., 1935, B.S., Engring. Sch., 1936, Metall. Engr., 1937; m. Jean C. Lamb, Dec. 27, 1937 (dec. Oct. 1976); children—Charles H., David A., Peter A.; m. 2d, Lydia W. Pollack, Aug. 15, 1978. Research engr. Huntington Alloy Products (W.Va.), 1937-45; with Battelle Meml. Inst., Columbus, Ohio, 1945-79, sr. tech. adv., 1966-69, asst. mgr. dept. metallurgy, 1969-79; exec. dir. Materials Tech. Inst. of Chem. Process Industries, Inc., Columbus, 1979-86, metall. cons., 1987—; pres. Columbus Tech. Council, 1955-56; sec. com. on effect temperature on properties of metals Joint ASTM-ASME-Metal Properties Council, 1967-73. Organizer and chmn. ARC Bloodmobile for Sharon Twp. (Ohio), 1949-50; treas., Columbus Art League, 1972-73, pres., 1969-71, 78; elder Covenant Presbyn. Ch., Columbus. Recipient various awards for craft and sculpture, 1963-70. Fellow Am. Soc. Metals; mem. AAAS, AIME, ASTM, Ohio Soc. Profl. Engrs., Sigma Xi, Tau Beta Pi. Republican. Author books, including: (with others) Microstructures of Heat-Resistant Alloys, 1970; contbr. numerous articles to profl. jours.; co-patentee iron-base alloys, chromium-base alloy, process to deposit cadmium on metallic surfaces; managed project for adoption of new "sandwich" coinage by U.S. Mint, 1987. Home: 1194 Kenbrook Hills Dr Columbus OH 43220

HALL, ARTHUR RAYMOND, JR., clergyman; b. Danville, Ill., Apr. 16, 1922; s. Arthur Raymond and Hetta Ada (Wheeler) H.; m. Lou Ann Benson, Mar. 16, 1946; children: Janet Marie Hall Graff, Laura Ann Hall Scott, Nancy Marion. A.B., U. Ill., 1946, M.A., 1948; M.Div. cum laude, Union Theol. Sem., N.Y.C., 1951; D.D., Hanover Coll., 1961. Staff asst. McKinley Meml. Ch. and Found., Champaign, Ill., 1946-48; student asst. First Presbyn Ch., N.Y.C., 1948-50; ordained to ministry Presbyn. Ch., 1951; pastor First Presbyn. Ch., Monmouth, Ill., 1951-58, Central Presbyn. Ch., Louisville, 1958-67, Bradley Hills Presbyn. Ch., Bethesda, Md., 1967—; pres. bd. Christian edn. United Presbyn. Ch., 1968-73; sec., bd. dirs. Louisville Presbyn. Sem., 1962-70; chmn. renewal and extension of ministry (United Presbyn. Gen. Assembly), 1965-68; mem. joint com. on Presbyn. Reunion, 1969-83; moderator Synod of Piedmont, 1974-75; trustee U.P. Ch., 1974-83; bd. dirs. U.P. Found., 1974-83; del. Uniting Assembly of World Alliance of Ref. Chs., Nairobi, Kenya, 1970; mem. com. on theol. edn. Presbyn. Ch., U.S.A., 1987, assoc. dir. 1988—. Contbr. articles to periodicals. Pres. Citizens Met. Planning Council, Louisville, 1962; chmn. Mayor's Adv. Com. for Community Devel., 1963-67; v.p. Louisville YMCA Downtown bd., 1963; bd. dirs. Louisville Health and Welfare Council, 1963-67, Greater Washington Council Chs., Johnson C. Smith Theol. Sem., Interdenominational Theol. Center, Atlanta, 1973; trustee Centre Coll. Ky., 1959-73, Union Theol. Sem., N.Y.C., 1975-84; trustee Travelers Aid Soc., Louisville, 1959-67, v.p., 1961-67. Served to lt. (j.g.) USNR, 1943-46. Mem. Am. Guild Organists, Beta Theta Pi, Phi Delta Phi. Democrat. Clubs: Rotary, Interchurch (Washington). Home: 8400 Whitman Dr Bethesda MD 20817 Office: Bradley Hills Presbyn Ch 6601 Bradley Blvd Bethesda MD 20817

HALL, CHRISTINA MARIA, neurobiologist; b. Göteborg, Sweden, Sept. 2, 1958; d. Karl-Gunnar and Gullmai (Lindstedt) Ohlson; m. Per O. Hall, Apr. 27, 1985; 1 child, Hugo. BS, U. Göteborg, 1981, PhD, 1987. Asst. prof. U. Göteborg, 1987—. Mem. Assn. Neurosci. Güteborg, Internat. Soc. Neurochemistry. Office: Inst Neurobiology, U Göteborg, PO Box 33031, S-40033 Göteborg Sweden

HALL, EARL, accountant, educator; b. Bertha, Minn., May 13, 1946; s. Lloyd E. and Esther M. (Fraedrich) H.; m. Lisa Coe Boyce, Aug. 24, 1968; children: Jonathan, Marc. BA, U. Wash., 1971. CPA, Calif. Staff acct. Arthur Andersen & Co., San Francisco, 1971-72; prin. George Hamilton, C.P.A., San Jose, Calif., 1972-73; tax sr. Alexander Grant, San Jose, Calif., 1973-75; tax ptnr. Roberts, McMains, Sellman, Lewiston, Idaho, 1975-80; dir. taxation Boyd, Olofson & Co., Yakima, Wash., 1980-83; pres. Earl Hall, CPA, Inc., Yakima, 1983—; instr. Heritage Coll., Toppenish, Wash., 1984-85. Chmn. radio day Yakima Kiwanis Club, 1984; del. Wash. State Republican Conv., 1982; mem. fin. com. Wesley United Methodist Ch., Yakima, 1982-85, young adult coordinator, 1985, chmn. pastor parish com., 1986—. Served with USAF, 1965-68; PTO. Recipient Haskins & Sells award U. Wash., 1970. Mem. Wash. Soc. CPAs (estate planning com. 1981-83, auditing standards com. 1987—), Am. Inst. CPAs (hon. mention Elijah Watt Sells award 1971), Idaho Soc. CPAs, Greater Yakima C. of C. (tax legis. com. 1981—). Lodge: Apple Valley Kiwanis (v.p. 1985-87, pres. elect 1986-87, pres. 1987-88, chmn. Air Fair 1987). Home: 350 N 24th Ave Yakima WA 98902 Office: PO Box 10883 Yakima WA 98909

HALL, EDWARD DALLAS, pharmacologist, biol. scientist, med. educator; b. Bedford, Ohio, June 16, 1950; s. Edward Ellis and Martha Elaine (Johnston) H.; m. Marilynn Frances Gay, Sept. 12, 1970; children—Edward William, Christian David. B.S., Mt. Union Coll., Alliance, Ohio, 1972; Ph.D. (Nat. Inst. Gen. Med. Sci. fellow), Cornell U., 1976. Postdoctoral fellow dept. pharmacology Cornell U. Med. Coll., N.Y.C., 1976-77; asst. prof. pharmacology Northeastern Ohio Univs. Coll. Medicine, Rootstown, 1978-82, adj. assoc. prof. 1987—, assoc. prof., 1982; asst. prof. Kent State U., 1978-82, adj. assoc. prof., Med. Coll. of Ohio at Toledo, 1985—; research scientist The Upjohn Co. Kalamazoo 1982-84, sr. research scientist, 1984—; adj. clin. assoc. prof. Western Mich. Physicians' Assts. Program, 1983—; cons. on drug-related issues. Contbr. articles and abstracts to sci. and med. jours., chpt. to book. Elder Randolph (Ohio) Christian Ch., 1981-82; deacon Oakland Dr. Ch. of Christ, Kalamazoo, 1983-86, elder 1986—; mem. adv. council Great Lakes Bible Coll.; v.p. Portage County Combined Gen. Health Dist. Bd. Editorial bd. J. Central Nervous System Trauma, 1984-88; assoc. editor Jour. Neurotrauma, 1988—. NIMH grantee, 1978-79, 80-82; Amyotrophic Lateral Sclerosis Soc. Am. grantee, 1978-81, 81-82. Mem. Am. Soc. for Pharmacology and Exptl. Therapeutics, Soc. for Neurosci., Am. Paralysis Assn. (sci. adv. council), N.Y. Acad. Scis., Sigma Xi, Phi Sigma. Lodge: Randolph Lions. Home: 5604 Stoney Brook Rd Kalamazoo MI 49002 Office: The Upjohn Co CNS Research Unit Kalamazoo MI 49001

HALL, EDWIN HUDDLESTON, JR., investment company executive; b. Bklyn., Sept. 5, 1935; s. Edwin H. and Lois W. Hall; B.S. in Bus. Adminstrn., Boston U., 1957; m. Linda Robbins, July 13, 1958; children—Jeffrey, Lisa, Lesley. With Merrill Lynch, Pierce, Fenner & Smith, 1961-77, v.p., 1973-77, v.p. tax investment mktg., 1978-80, dir. sales support group, 1980-81, v.p., dir. mktg., individual investment products div., 1982-84, v.p., dir. corp. human resources, 1984-86; chmn., chief exec. officer Merrill Lynch Bank and Trust, 1986—; chmn., pres. Merril Lynch Trust Co., 1987, pres. Merrill Lynch Trust Services, Inc., 1987, pres. Merrill Lynch Fiduciary Services, Inc. 1987; presdl. interchange exec., Washington, serving as spl. asst. to pres. Govt. Nat. Mortgage Assn., 1977-78. Div. chmn. United Community Chest, Rochester, N.Y., 1975; bd. dirs. Old Colony chpt. ARC, 1966-68; treas. Rochester (N.Y.) Assn. Blind, 1976-77; pres. Opera Theatre Rochester, 1976-77, hon. chmn., 1978. Mem. Nat. Assn. Security Dealers (corp. fin. com. 1978—). Rochester Soc. Analysts, Rochester C. of C. (trustee, chmn. reaccreditation implementation com. 1976), Boston C. of C. (life), Boston U. Alumni Assn. (dir. 1970-72), Washington Valley Community Assn. (pres. 1981-83, chmn. bd. trustees, 1983—); mem. human resource com. SIA, 1984-86; trustee Security Industry Inst. at Wharton, 1986—. Republican. Episcopalian. Clubs: Federal, Fort Hill (Boston); Genesee Valley (Rochester); Club at World Trade Center (N.Y.C.). Lodge: Masons. Address: 173 Washington Valley Rd Morris Township NJ 07960 Office: 800 Scudder Mill Rd Princeton NJ also: World Fin Ctr New York NY also: 5th Ave Naples FL

HALL, ERNEST E., retired government agency administration; b. Dayton, Nov. 17, 1901; s. Ozni and Julia (Schlotterbeck) H.; m. Florence M. Byrnes, Oct. 29, 1948; children: Kendra Elizabeth, Kevin Ernest. With Ozni Hall and Co., 1917-22; jr. acct. George P. Jackson and Co., 1922-25; asst. sec., treas. Hyde Motor Sales Co., 1925-29; asst. to sec. U.S. Dept. Agr., Washington, 1929-33; asst. chief div. control U.S. Bur. Pub. Rds., 1933-42; exec. officer Fed. Works Agy., 1942-47; v.p. C.F. Lytle Co. (heavy constrn.), Sioux City, Iowa, 1947-52; asst. adminstr. for ops. control services FCDA, Battle Creek, Mich., 1952-55; chief industry asst. br. Office Indsl. Devel. AEC, 1956-59; chief reports and statistics br. Div. Reactor Devel., 1959-64; chief reports staff Office Asst. Gen. Mgr. Reactors, Germantown, Md., 1965-70; ret. Chmn. Washington Grove Planning Commn., 1957-60, town treas., 1961-72. Mem. Am. Cheviot Sheep Soc. (dir. emeritus), Eastern Seaboard Sheep Council (pres. 1978-80), Natural Colored Wool Growers Assn. (pres. 1979-83). Home: 13140 Hiney Rd Red Rock Farm Frederick County Keymar MD 21757

HALL, ERNST PAUL, government official; b. Clarksburg, W. Va., Aug. 23, 1925; s. Herbert Paul and Nola (Simmons) H.; m. Mary Louise Hepler, Apr. 2, 1948 (div.); children—Ernst Paul, Barbara Ann, Sandra Lee, Robert P.; m. Suzette Solon, Feb. 14, 1986. B.S. in Chem. Engring., W. Va. U., 1947; M.S., U. Pitts., 1954. Devel. engr. Pennwalt Corp., Natrona, Pa., 1947-48; asst. tech. div. Celina Stearic Acid Co. (Ohio), 1948-51; fellow Mellon Inst., Pitts., 1951-54; sr. engr. Dewey and Almy div. W.R. Grace Co., Lockport, N.Y., 1954-55; product engr. Gen. Electric Co., Coshocton, Ohio, 1955-57; research cons. Consol. Coal Co., Pitts., 1957-66; chief. metals and machinery br. U.S. EPA, Washington, 1966—. Contbr. articles to profl. jours. Recipient Bronze medal for commendable service U.S. EPA, 1973; S.A. Braley award Coal Industry Adv. Com., 1974; Silver medal for superior service U.S. EPA, 1975, 76, 82. Mem. Am. Chem. Soc., Am. Inst. Chem. Engrs., ASME, AIME, Nat. Soc. Profl. Engrs., Pa. Soc. Profl. Engrs. Home: 3800 N Fairfax Dr Arlington VA 22203 Office: US EPA 401 M St SW Washington DC 20460

HALL, GEORGE VINCENT, cardiologist; b. Sydney, New South Wales, Australia, 1915; s. George Francis and Susan Louisa (Pennell) H.; m. Shirley Elizabeth Goldstein, Nov. 29, 1941; children: Anne Knight, Peter, David, Jeremy, Anthony. Grad., St. Aloysius Coll., Sydney, 1932; MB BS, U. Sydney Med. Sch., Australia, 1940. Vis. cardiologist St. Vincent's Hosp., Sydney, 1948—, vice chmn., bd. dirs. Contbr. 21 articles to profl. jours. Mem. senate U. Sydney; mem. council U. New South Wales. Served to maj. Australian mil., 1941-45. Named Knight Comdr. of Gregory the Great, The Vatican, 1970. Fellow Royal Australasian Coll. Physicians, Royal Coll. Physicians, Am. Coll. Cardiologists; mem. Cardiac Soc. Australia and New Zealand, Australian Soc. for Med. Research. Roman Catholic. Clubs: Australian (Sydney), Am. Home: 2/115A Kurraba Rd, Neutral Bay, 2078 Sydney, New South Wales Australia Office: Cons Rooms, 183 Macquarie St, 2000 Sydney, New South Wales Australia

HALL, HÅKAN, research scientist; b. Norrtälje, Sweden, Apr. 26, 1947; s. Harry and Maja (Dahlgren) H.; m. Elisabet Berger, June 3, 1972; children: Sara, Ola. Student, U. Uppsala, Sweden, 1971, PhD, 1976. Lectr. U. Uppsala, Sweden, 1969-75, asst. prof., 1984; group leader dept. pharmacology A.B. Astra, Södertälje, Sweden, 1975-79, dep. head dept. pharmacology, 1979-83, dir. dept. biochem. neuropharmacology, 1983—. Contbr. 70 articles to profl. jours. Office: Astra Alab, Dept Biochem Neuropharm, S-15185 Sodertalje Sweden

HALL, HAL, businessman; b. Colby, Kans., June 7, 1911; s. Robert Ellsworth and Sarah (Myers) H.; m. Liane Hanft, May 23, 1947; children: Robert Eric, Alan Rae, Ronald Frederick. BA U. Ill., 1939. Journeyman welder Shipyards, Oakland and Alameda, Calif., 1941-43; mechanic U.S. Army, 1943-46; journeyman carpenter Kaiser, San Jose, Calif., 1946-49; house designer and builder, Calif., Colo., 1949-53; lodge owner and operator Red Mountain Lodge, Ouray, Colo., 1953-80; farmer, ranch owner, 1980—. Author: The Great Conflict, 1943, Even to the Last Man, 1960, The Wealth of Persons, 1968, Collectivism and Freedom, 1976, The Sleeping Dragon, 1981, 2d rev. edit., 1986; The Road to Freedom, 1988; also polit., econ. and religious critic, various pubs. Served with U.S. Army, 1943-46. Mailing Address: Red Mountain Trading Post Box 129 Ouray CO 81427

HALL, HANSEL CRIMIEL, government official; b. Gary, Ind., Mar. 12, 1929; s. Alfred McKenzie and Grace Elizabeth (Crimiel) H. B.S., Ind. U., 1953; LL.B., Blackstone Sch. Law, 1982. Officer, IRS, 1959-64; gasoline service sta. operator, then realtor, Chgo., 1964-69; program specialist HUD, Chgo., 1969-73, dir. equal opportunity, St. Paul, 1973-75, dir. fair housing and equal opportunity, Indpls., from 1975; human resource officer U.S. Fish and Wildlife Service, Twin Cities, Minn.; cons. in civil rights; pres. bd. dirs. Riverview Towers Cooperative Assn., Inc.; 1984-87. Served with USAF, 1951-53; Korea. Mem. NAACP (Golden Heritage life mem.), Res. Officers Assn., Am. Inst. Parliamentarians, Ind. U. Alumni Assn.; Omega Psi Phi. Club: Toastmasters (past pres. Minnehaha chpt. 2563, past area gov.). Office: Fed Bldg Ft Snelling Saint Paul MN 55111

HALL, HELEN, interior and environmental designer; b. N.Y.C., Jan. 24; d. Maxwell and Bertha Neuhoff; student N.Y. Sch. Interior Design Architecture, 1982—; m. Sidney Manne, Mar., 1937; children—Belinda Elaine Manne Pokorny, Stephen Anthony Manne. Founder Dumont Hall and Helen Hall Studios, N.Y.C., 1955, pres. Dumont Hall, 1955-60, Helen Hall Studios, 1955—; dir. interior design Sherwood Hotels, 1955-65, other hotel chains, 1956—. Pres., founder League for Cardiac Children, 1948-52; founder Sprout Lake Camp for Cardiac Children; mem. Assoc. Nat. Trust for Historic Preservation, 1987—. Served with ARC, Halloran Hosp. with mil. forces, 1942-50. Recipient cert. of merit, 1947. Mem. Am. Soc. Interior Designers, Assn. Antique Dealers. Active restoration and redesign Hotel Lexington, N.Y.C., 1955-65; design works pub. Interior Design mag., 1955-65, N.Y. Times.

HALL, HUGH GASTON, educator, poet; b. Jackson, Miss., Nov. 7, 1931; arrived in U.K., 1960; s. Powell Storrs and Viola (Sly) H.; m. Gillian Gladys Lund, July 16, 1955; children: Cordelia, Emily, Oliver. BA, Millsaps Coll., 1952, Oxford U., 1955; MA, Oxford U., 1959; PhD, Yale U., 1959. Instr. Yale U., New Haven, 1958-60; lectr. Glasgow (Scotland) U., 1960-64; sr. lectr. Monash U., Melbourne, Australia, 1965, French U., Warwick, Coventry, Eng., 1966-74; reader French U., Warwick, 1974—; asst. prof. U. Calif., Berkeley, 1963; prof. CUNY, 1970-72. Author poetry and scholarly books, 1960—; editor various texts and bibliographies, 1963—; contbr numerous articles to profl. jours. Fulbright scholar, Toulouse, France, 1952-53, Rhodes scholar, Oxford U., 1953-55; fellow Humanities Research Ctr., Canberra, Australia, 1984, Camargo Found., Cassis, France, 1987. Home: Richmond House, 18 Abbey End, Kenilworth Warks CV8 1LS, England Office: U Warwick, Coventry England

HALL, JAMES LEO, JR., lawyer; b. St. Paul, Mar. 29, 1936; s. James L. and Mary Z. (Hitch) H.; m. Carol Rae Marshall, May 16, 1959; two children. B.A. with distinction, U. Okla., 1958; J.D., Harvard U., 1963. Bar: Okla. 1963. Mem. Crowe & Dunlevy, Oklahoma City, 1963—, pres., 1981-83; lectr. numerous symposia, convs. and instns. 1964—; instr. Okla. Bar Rev., Inc., 1972-86; dir. Liberty Nat. Bank & Trust Co., Oklahoma City, Community Nat. Bank Okarche, Community State Bank Canton, Okla. Bar Corp., Okla. Bar Profl. Liability Ins. Co., Okla. Health Lawyers Assn.; mem. Okla. Health Care Corp.; adj. prof. banking law Oklahoma City U. Sch. Law, 1985—; health care law U. Okla. Sch. Law, Norman, 1988—. Contbr. articles tp legal jours. Bd. dirs. global ministries Okla. conf. United Methodist Ch., 1978—, chancellor, 1981—; chmn. bd. trustees Crown Heights United Meth. Ch., 1978-86, lay leader, 1978-80, chmn. adminstrv. bd., 1976-77; trustee Oklahoma City U. Served to lt. comdr. USN, 1958-60. Fellow Am. Bar Found., Okla. Bar Found.; mem. ABA, Fed. Bar Assn., Oklahoma County Bar Found. (pres. 1979-82), Oklahoma County Bar Assn. (treas. 1974-77), Okla. Bar Assn. (chmn. labor law sect. 1972), Nat. Assn. Securities Dealers (panel of arbitrators), Am. Acad. Hosp. Attys., Nat. Health Lawyers Assn., U. Okla. Dad's Assn. (pres. 1986-87), Am. Assn. Preferred Provider Organizations, Okla. Zool. Soc., Phi Beta Kappa (pres. Oklahoma City alumni 1979). Republican. Clubs: Oklahoma City Dinner, 75 (pres. 1986-87), Economic of Okla, Oklahoma City Golf and Country, Petroleum (bd. dirs. 1984-87, treas. 1986-87). Lodge: Kiwanis. Home: 1713 Elmhurst Ave Oklahoma City OK 73120 Office: Crowe & Dunlevy 1800 Mid Am Tower Oklahoma City OK 73102

HALL, JOHN ALLEN, international nuclear consultant; b. Benton Harbor, Mich., Sept. 22, 1914; s. Maurice John and Dora (Ferry) H.; m. Alice Greenidge, June 24, 1939; children: John Allen, Sheila Greenidge Hall Swift. B.S., Northwestern U., 1936; A.M., Harvard U., 1940, Ph.D., 1941. Instr. govt. U. Rochester, 1941-43; adviser U.S. del. UN, Washington, 1946, N.Y.C., 1947; chief Office Spl. Projects, AEC, Washington, 1948-52; dir. Office Internat. Affairs, 1952-55, dir. div. internat. affairs, 1955-58, asst. gen. mgr. internat. activities, 1958-61; dep. dir. gen. IAEA, 1961-64; asst. gen. mgr. U.S. AEC, Washington, 1964-67; dep. dir. gen. IAEA, Vienna, Austria, 1967-80; cons. Resources for the Future, Washington; joint sec. Combined Devel. Agy., Washington, 1949-55, U.S. mem., 1955; adviser to U.S. rep. UN Tech. Adv. Com., 1955, 58, 59, 60; chief liaison and protocol First Internat. Conf. on Peaceful Uses Atomic Energy, Geneva, 1955; sr. adviser U.S. rep. Conf. on Statute, IAEA, 1956; alt. U.S. rep. Inter-Am. Nuclear Energy Commn., 1959, 60; sr. adviser to chmn. U.S. del. 1st Gen. Conf., IAEA, Vienna, 1957, 2d Conf., 1958, 4th Conf., 1960, 9th Conf., 1965, 10th Conf., 1966; alt. U.S. rep. Inter-Am. Nuclear Commn., 1966; U.S. rep. Inter-Am. Sci. Symposium, Brazilia, Brazil, 1960. Served to lt. comdr. USNR, 1943-46. Decorated comdr. Papal Order of St. Sylvester. Clubs: Congl. Country (Washington), Harvard (Washington); Confrerie des Chevaliers du Tastevin (comdr.). Home: 8713 Cranbrook Ct Bethesda MD 20817

HALL, JOHN HOPKINS, lawyer; b. Dallas, May 10, 1925; s. Albert Brown and Eleanor Pauline (Hopkins) H.; m. Marion Martin, Nov. 23, 1957; children—Ellen Martin, John Hopkins. Student, U. Tex., 1942, U. of South, Sewanee, Tenn., 1942-43; LL.B., So. Meth. U., 1949. Bar: Tex. bar 1949. Partner firm. Strasburger & Price, Dallas, 1957—. Served with U.S. Army, 1943-45. Fellow Tex. Bar Found., Am. Bar Found., Internat. Acad. Trial Lawyers, Am. Coll. Trial Lawyers; mem. Am. Bar Assn., Tex. Bar Assn., Dallas Bar Assn., Tex. Assn. Def. Counsel, Def. Research Inst. Episcopalian. Clubs: City Club, Royal Oaks Country, Fin and Feather. Office: Strasburger & Price 4300 Interfirst Plaza Dallas TX 75202

HALL, JOHN RICHARD, oil company executive; b. Dallas, Nov. 30, 1932; s. John W. and Agnes (Sanders) H.; m. Donna S. Stauffer, May 10, 1980. B.Chem. Engring., Vanderbilt U., 1955. Chem. engr. Esso Standard Oil Co., Balt., 1956-58, Ashland Oil Co., Ky., 1959-63; coordinator carbon black div. Ashland Oil Co., Houston, 1963-65; exec. asst. v.p. Ashland Oil Co., 1965-66, v.p., 1966-68, sr. v.p., 1970-71; also dir.; pres. Ashland Chem. Co., 1971-74; exec. v.p. Ashland Oil, Inc., 1974—, group operating officer, 1976—, chief exec. officer petroleum and chems., 1978—, vice chmn., chief operating officer, 1979-81, chmn., chief exec. officer, 1981—; bd. dirs. Banc One Corp., Cleve., Reynolds Metals Co., Richmond, Va. Trustee Vanderbilt U., Nashville, mem. com. visitors Engring. Sch.; bd. curators Transylvania U., Lexington, Ky. Served as 2d lt., Chem. Corps AUS, 1955-56. Mem. Chem. Mfrs. Assn., Nat. Petroleum Refiners Assn., Am. Petroleum Inst., Nat. Petroleum Council, Bus. Roundtable, Tau Delta Pi, Sigma Chi, Delta Kappa. Republican. Home: 99 Stoneybrook Dr Ashland KY 41101 Office: Ashland Oil Inc PO Box 391 Ashland KY 41114

HALL, JOHN ROBERT, food company executive; b. Tadcaster, Yorkshire, Eng., Aug. 14, 1952; came to U.S., 1971; s. Robert Rhodes and Elizabeth Greenwell (Smith) H.; m. Elizabeth Marie Rose Sayers, Apr. 7, 1979. B.A. in Natural Sci., Oxford U., Eng., 1974; M.B.A. in Mktg. and Fin., U. Pa., 1976. Lab. technician Procter & Gamble Co., Cin., 1971, mktg. asst., Newcastle, Eng., 1975; product mgr. Nestle Foods, White Plains, N.Y., 1976-80, group product mgr., 1981-83, bus. dir., 1983-85; dir. strategic planning and bus. devel. Kraft Ltd., Montreal, Que., Can., 1985-86, v.p., dir. strategic planning and mktg. cheese div., 1986—. Methodist. Avocations: sports; investing. Home: 296 Pinetree Crescent, Beaconsfield, PQ Canada H9W 5E1 Office: Kraft Ltd, 8600 Devonshire Rd, Mount Royal, PQ Canada H4P 2K9

HALL, JOHN WESLEY, JR., lawyer; b. Watertown, N.Y., Jan. 28, 1948; s. John Wesley and Mary Louise (Hodge) H.; m. Rebecca B. Bane; children: Justin William, Mark Daniel. BA, Hendrix Coll., 1970; JD, U. Ark., 1973. Bar: Ark. 1973, D.C. 1975, U.S. Dist. and Circuit Cts. 1973, U.S. Supreme Ct. 1976; cert. criminal trial adv. Nat. Bd. Trial Advocacy, 1981. Dep. pros. atty., Little Rock, 1973-79, head career criminal div., 1978-79; trial advocacy instr. Ark. Prosecuting Attys. Assn., 1977-79; law clk. Ark. Supreme Ct., 1974; sole practice law, Little Rock, 1979—; adj. prof. law U. Ark., Little Rock, 1985—, criminal law seminars. Mem. Ark. Bar Assn. (ho. of dels. 1976-79), Assn. Trial Lawyers Am., Am. Bd. Criminal Lawyers, Nat. Assn. Criminal Def. Lawyers, Ark. Assn. Criminal Def. Lawyers (pres. 1987-89), First Amendment Lawyer's Assn. Episcopalian. Author: Search and Seizure, 1982, 2d rev. edit 1989, Professional Responsibility of the Criminal Lawyer, 1987; Trial Handbook for Arkansas Lawyers, 1986; editor, author: Arkansas Prosecutor's Trial Manual, 1976-77; Arkansas Extradition Manual, 1978; contbr. articles to profl. jours, speaker to lawyer and police groups. Home: 12920 Southridge Dr Little Rock AR 72212 Office: 523 W 3d St Little Rock AR 72201

HALL, JON EM, oil company executive; b. Columbus, Ohio, July 6, 1956; s. John Milton and Ordena Hill (High) H.; m. Merri Lynn Pugh, May 20, 1978; children—Jessie, Jennifer, Ross, Ashley. B.S. in Petroleum Engring., Marietta Coll., 1978. Registered profl. engr., Ohio. Petroleum engr. Amoco Prodn. Co., Brownfield, Tex., 1979-80, Houston, 1980-81, Atlas Energy Co., Warren, Ohio, 1981-83; asst. v.p., petroleum engr. Huntington Bank, Cleve., 1983-84; v.p. oil and gas ops. Royal Petroleum Properties, Inc., Cleve., 1984-86; chief tech. adv. Hall Energy, Inc., Powell, Ohio, 1982-86, pres., 1986—. Mem. Soc. Petroleum Engr. (bd. dirs. 1984-85), Soc. Profl. Well Log Analysts (v.p. 1984-85), Am. Assn. Petroleum Geologists, Ohio Oil and Gas Assn., Nat. Ohio Soc. Profl. Engrs. (cert. merit 1983). Republican. Methodist. Avocations: bowling; electric organ; sports. Lodge: Kiwanis. Home: 35454 Chesterfield Dr North Ridgeville OH 44039 Office: Hall Energy Inc 4131 Marysville Rd Delaware OH 43015

HALL, KATHRYN EVANGELINE, author, lecturer; b. Biltmore, N.C.; d. Hugh Canada and Evangeline Haddon (Jenkins) Hall; B.A., U. N.C., M.A.; diploma Adams Sch. Music, Montreat, N.C.; postgrad. Yale, U. London, Fla. Atlantic U. Author: The Papal Tiara, History of the Episcopal Church of Bethesda-By-The-Sea, 1964, The Architecture and Times of Robert Adam, 1969, The Pictorial History of the Episcopal Church of Bethesda-By-The-Sea, 1970-71, 86, Joseph Wright of Derby, A Painter of Science, Industry, and Romanticism, 1974, A History of English Architecture, 1976-82; Sir John Vanbrugh's Palaces and the Drama of Baroque Architecture, 1982-84; lectr. history, art and architecture, U.S., Eng. and Scotland, 1961—. Vice pres. The Jr. Patronesses, Palm Beach, Fla., 1964. Mem. Nat. League Am. Pen Women (Owl award 1972, 76, 77, pres. Palm Beach chpt. 1975-80), Palm Beach Quills (historian), Palm Beach County Hist. Soc. (gov.), Internat. Platform Assn., Nat. Soc. Arts and Letters, Soc. Four Arts, Cum Laude Soc., Palm Beach Civic Assn. Episcopalian. Clubs: Everglades (Palm Beach); English Speaking Union (Palm Beach and London). Home: Acadie PO Box 648 Palm Beach FL 33480

HALL, LEE BOAZ, publishing company consultant, author; b. Little Rock, Oct. 8, 1928; s. Graham Roots and Louise (Boaz) H.; m. Mary Louise Reed, Nov. 29, 1951 (div.); children: Gwendolyn, Ann Valerie, Graham; m. Sarah Moore, Dec. 15, 1978. B.A., Yale U., 1950. Reporter Ark. Gazette, Little Rock, 1950-51; officer Dept. Def., Washington, 1951-52; reporter Dept. Def., W.Ger., 1952-53, Washington Post, 1953-55; with Life mag., 1955-70; bur. chief Life mag., Latin Am., 1958-59, Paris, 1963-66; editor Life en Espanol, 1966-69; editor internat. edits. Life, N.Y.C., 1970; pres. Tomorrow Pub. Co., N.Y.C., 1970-72; sr. v.p. internat. pub. Playboy Enterprises, Inc., Chgo., 1972-86; pres. Int.Pub, Inc., 1986—, Donlee, Inc., Little Rock, 1986—; bd. dirs. Online Access Guide, Chgo., 1987—. Author: International Magazine and Book Licensing, 1983. Served with U.S. Army, 1950-51. Mem. Federation Internationale de la Presse Periodique (liasion). Methodist. Clubs: Racquet, Saddle and Cycle (Chgo.); Yale (N.Y.C.). Home and Office: 229 E Lake Shore Dr Chicago IL 60611

HALL, MILES LEWIS, JR., lawyer; b. Fort Lauderdale, Fla., Aug. 14, 1924; s. Miles Lewis and Mary Frances (Dawson) H.; m. Muriel M. Fisher, Nov. 4, 1950; children: Miles Lewis III, Don Thomas. A.B., Princeton U., 1947; J.D., Harvard U., 1950. Bar: Fla. 1951. Since practiced in Miami; ptnr. Hall & Hedrick, 1953—; dir. Gen. Portland, Inc., 1974-81. Author: Election of Remedies, Vol. VIII, Fla. Law and Practice, 1958. Chmn. 3d Appellate Dist. Ct. Nominating Commn., State Fla., 1972-75; pres. Orange Bowl Com., 1964-65, dir., 1950-84, sec., treas. 1984-86, dir. 1986—; vice-chmn., dir. Dade County (Fla.) ARC, 1961-62, chmn., 1963-64, dir., 1967-73; nat. fund cons. ARC, 1963, 66-68, trustee, 1985—; bd. pres. Ransom Sch. Parents Assn., 1966; chmn. South Fla. Gov.'s Scholarship Ball, 1966; mem. exec. bd. South Fla. council Boy Scouts Am., 1966-67; citizens bd. U. Miami, 1961-66; mem. Fla. Council of 100, vice chmn., 1961-62; mem. Coral Gables (Fla.) Biltmore Devel. Com., 1972-73; mem. bd. visitors Coll. Law, Fla. State U., 1974-77; bd. dirs. Coral Gables War Meml. Youth Ctr., 1967—, pres., 1969-72, bd. dirs; bd. dirs. Salvation Army, Miami, 1968-83, Fla. Citizens Against Crime 1984—; sec.-treas., bd. dirs. Am. Found. Inc., 1985-87; sec., treas. Bok Towes Gardens Found. Inc., 1987—. Served to 2d lt. USAAF, 1943-45. Fellow Am. Bar Found.; mem. ABA (Fla. co-chmn. membership com. sect. corp., banking and bus. law 1968-72), Dade County Bar Assn. (dir. 1964-65, pres. 1967-68), Fla. Bar, Am. Judicature Soc., Miami-Dade County C. of C. (v.p. 1962-64, dir. 1966-68), Harvard Law Sch. Assn. Fla. (dir. 1964-66), Alpha Tau Omega. Methodist (bd. stewards). Clubs: Kiwanis, Cottage, Harvard, The Miami, City of Miami (Miami); Princeton of So. Fla. (past pres., dir.). Home: 2907 Alhambra Circle Coral Gables FL 33134 Office: Suite 1400 Republic Nat Bank Bldg 150 SE 2d St Miami FL 33131

HALL, PAMELA S., environmental consulting firm executive; b. Hartford, Conn., Sept. 4, 1944; d. LeRoy Warren and Frances May (Murray) Sheely; m. Stuart R. Hall, July 21, 1967. B.A. in Zoology, U. Conn., 1966; M.S. in Zoology, U. N.H., 1969, B.S. in Bus. Adminstrn. summa cum laude, 1982; student spl. grad. studies program, Tufts U., 1986—. Curatorial asst. U. Conn., Storrs, 1966; research asst. Field Mus. Natural History, Chgo., 1966-67; teaching asst. U. N.H., Durham, 1967-70; program mgr. Normandeau Assocs. Inc., Portsmouth, N.H., 1971-79, marine lab. dir., 1979-81, programs and ops. mgr., Bedford, N.H., 1981-83, v.p., 1983-85, sr. v.p., 1986-87, pres., 1987—. Mem. Conservation Commn., Portsmouth, 1977—, Wells, Estuarine Research Res. Review Commn., 1986—, Great Bay (N.H.) Estuarine Research Res. Tech. Working Group, 1987—. Graham Found. fellow, 1966; NDEA fellow, 1970-71. Mem. Am. Mgmt. Assn., Water Pollution Control Fedn., Am. Fisheries Soc., Estuarine Research Fedn., Nat. Assn. Environ. Profls., ASTM, Sigma Xi. Home: 4 Pleasant Point Dr Portsmouth NH 03801 Office: Normandeau Assocs Inc 25 Nashua Rd Bedford NH 03201

HALL, PETER REGINALD FREDERICK, theatre, opera and film director; b. Bury St. Edmunds, Eng., Nov. 22, 1930; s. Reginald and Grace (Pamment) H.; M.A., St. Catharine's Coll., Cambridge U., 1963; hon. degrees U. York, 1966, U. Reading, 1973, U. Liverpool, 1977, U. Leicester, 1977, Cornell U.; m. Leslie Caron, 1956 (div. 1965); children: Christopher, Jennifer; m. Jacqueline Taylor, 1965 (div. 1981); children: Edward, Lucy; m. Maria Ewing; 1 dau. First profl. prodn., Windsor, 1953; producer Worthing Playhouse, 1954, Oxford Playhouse, 1955; artistic dir. Elizabethan Theatre Co., 1953; asst. dir. London Arts Theatre, 1954, dir., 1955-57; founder Internat. Playwrights Theater, 1957; founder, mng. dir. Royal Shakespeare Co., Stratford, London, 1960-68; mng. dir. Royal Shakespeare Theatre, Stratford-on-Avon, also Aldwych Theatre, London, 1960-68; assoc. prof. drama Warwick U., 1966—; dir. British Nat. Theatre, 1973-88; dir.: Shadow of Heroes, Blood Wedding, Immoralist, The Lesson, South, Mourning Becomes Electra, Waiting for Godot, The Burnt Flowerbed, Waltz of the Toreadors, Camino Real, Gigi, Wrong Side of the Park, Love's Labours Lost, Cymbeline, Twelfth Night, A Midsummer Night's Dream, Coriolanus, Two Gentlemen of Verona, Troilus and Cressida, Ondine, Romeo and Juliet, Becket, The Collection, Cat on a Hot Tin Roof, The Rope Dancers, Henry VI, Richard III, Richard II, Henry IV, Henry V, Eh?, The Homecoming (Tony award 1967), Hamlet, The Government Inspector, Macbeth, A Delicate Balance, Silence, Landscape, The Battle of Shrivings, All Over, Old Times, Tempest, Happy Days, John Gabriel Borkman, No Man's Land, Hamlet, Judgement, Tambourlaine the Great, Bedroom Farce, Volpone, The Country Wife, The Cherry Orchard, Betrayal, Amadeus (Tony award 1981), Othello; (operas) The Moon and Sixpence, Moses and Aaron, The Magic Flute, La Calisto, Eugene Onegin, Tristan and Isolde, Ritorno di Ulysses, Marriage of Figaro, The Knot Garden, Don Giovanni, Cosi Fan Tutte, Fidelio, A Midsummer Night's Dream, Orfeo ed Euridice, Macbeth, The Ring; (films) A Midsummer Night's Dream, Three into Two Won't Go, Perfect Friday, Old Times, All Over, The Homecoming, Akenfield, Landscape, others; dir. plays for BBC-TV: The Wars of the Roses, Alte Zeiten; presenter of Aquarius (arts program for London weekend TV), 1975-77; author: Peter Hall's Diaries, 1983. Decorated comdr. Order Brit. Empire, 1963; knighted, 1977. Fellow St. Catharine's Coll. Mem. Arts Council, 1969-73. Mem. Theatre Dirs. Guild Gt. Britain (founding). Order des Arts et des Lettres. Clubs: Garrick, Athenaeum, RAC. Address: Peter Hall Co Ltd, Waldorf Chambers, 11 Aldwych, London WC2B 4DA, England also: The Wall House, Mongewell Park, Wallingford Oxon, England *

HALL, RALPH CORBIN, forest entomologist, consultant; b. Ellenville, N.Y., May 7, 1899; s. James Harvey and Anna (Newkirk) H.; m. Dorothy Dane Colby, Sept. 7, 1930 (dec. Aug. 1981); children: James Dane, Judith Gilmore Thomson, John Colby, Joanne Newkirk Parrish (dec.). BS, Syracuse U., 1925; MF, Harvard U., 1927; PhD, U. Mich., 1931. Registered profl. entomologist, U.S.; registered profl. forester, Calif. Research forest entomologist Bur. Entomology and Plant Quarantine, Columbus, Ohio, 1931-38, Berkeley, Calif., 1938-53; with U.S. Forest Service, 1953-64; entomologist San Francisco, 1961-64; v.p., dir. Natural Resources Mgmt. Corp., Orinda, Calif., 1970-74; cons. forest entomology Orinda, 1974—; cons. research grants NSF, 1951—. Mem. nat. council Boy Scouts Am., 1955-66, mem. exec. council Mt. Diablo Council, 1947-71; bd. dirs. Wildernees Found., Calif. Forestry Found., Forest Landowners Calif. Named Man of Yr. by City of Orinda, 1949; recipient Silver Beaver award Boy Scouts Am., 1957; award of Merit SUNY, award of Merit Calif. Acad. Scis., award of Merit N.Y. Acad. Scis. Fellow Soc. Am. Foresters (Golden Membership award 1978), AAAS, Internat. Platform Assn., Fedn. Am. Scientists, Explorers Club; mem. Assn. Cons. Foresters, Wildlife Soc., Wilderness Soc., Am. Forestry Assn., Entomol. Soc. Am., Sierra Club, Sigma Xi, Gamma Sigma Delta, Phi Sigma. Address: 72 Davis Rd Orinda CA 94563

HALL, ROBERT ALAN, manager, finance and administration; b. Montgomery, Ala., Oct. 30, 1958; s. Mack Luverne and Miriam (Johnston) H. BS in Commerce and Bus. Adminstrn., U. Ala., 1981. CPA, Ala. Sr. acct. Jackson and Thronton, CPA's, Montgomery, 1981-83; sr. auditor Vulcan Materials Co., Birmingham, Ala., 1983-86, supr. internal audit, 1986-87; mgr., fin. and adminstrn. Saudi Arabian Vulcan Ltd., Jubail, Saudi

Arabia, 1987—. Charter mem. Rep. Presdl. Task Force, Washington, 1984-86. Recipient presdl. achievement award Pres. Ronald Reagan, 1983; named hon. citizen City of Los Angeles, 1984, hon. asst. atty. gen. State of Ala., 1984; named one of Outstanding Young Men of Am., 1986. Mem. Am. Businessman's Assn. of Saudi Arabia, U. Ala. Sr. Execs. Club, Coll. of Commerce, Am. Inst. CPA's, Ala. Soc. CPA's, Honorable Order Ky. Cols. Baptist. Lodge: Civitan. Home: PO Box 10016, Madinat Jubail 31961, Saudi Arabia

HALL, ROBERT ANDERSON, JR., Italian language and literature educator; b. Raleigh, N.C., Apr. 4, 1911; s. Robert Anderson and Lolabel (House) H.; m. Frances L. Adkins, Aug. 31, 1936 (dec. Sept. 1975); children: Philip Adkins, Diana Katherine (Mrs. William C. Goodall), Caroline Amanda (Mrs. C.M. Erickson); m. Alice Mary Colby, May 8, 1976. A.B., Princeton, 1931; A.M., U. Chgo., 1935; Litt.D., U. Rome, 1934. Asst. prof. fgn. langs. U. P.R., 1937-39; instr. modern lang. Princeton, 1939-40; instr. Italian Brown U., Providence, 1940-42; asst. prof. Brown U., 1942-46; lectr. internat. adminstrn. Columbia, 1943-44; vis. asst. prof. internat. adminstrn. Yale, 1943-44; assoc. prof. linguistics Cornell U., Ithaca, N.Y., 1946-50; prof. Cornell U., 1950-76, prof. emeritus, 1976—; dir. Cornell U. (Cornell-Ford English Lang. Program), Rome, 1966-67. Author: Bibliography of Italian Linguistics, 1941, The Italian Questione della Lingua, 1942, Melanesian Pidgin English, 1943, Hungarian Grammar, 1944, Descriptive Italian Grammar, 1948, Leave Your Language Alone, 1950, Short History of Italian Literature, 1951, Haitian Creole, 1953, Hands Off Pidgin English, 1955, Italian for Modern Living, 1958, Bibliografia della Linguistica Italiana, 1958, Italian Stories, 1961, Basic Conversational Italian, 1963, Cultural Symbolism in Literature, 1963, Introductory Linguistics, 1964, New Ways to Learn a Foreign Language, 1965, Pidgin and Creole Languages, 1966, Antonio Fogazzaro e la Crisi dell 'Italia Moderna, 1967, An Essay on Language, 1968, English Phrase and Clause Structure, 1969, La Struttura dell' Italiano, 1971, External History of the Romance Languages, 1974, The Comic Style of P.G. Wodehouse, 1974, Stormy Petrel in Linguistics, 1975, Proto-Romance Phonology, 1976, Antonio Fogazzaro, 1978, Language, Literature, and Life, 1979, Stormy Petrel Flies Again, 1980, The Kensington Rune-Stone is Genuine, 1982, Proto. Romance Morphology, 1983, Papers on Wodehouse, 1985, Linguistics and Pseudo-Linguistics, 1987; contbr. numerous articles and book revs. to learned jours.; Composer: Missa Lanquan li jorn, 1972, Kyrie Praeparatio, 1981. Fulbright lectr. linguistics Rome, 1950-51, 57-58; Guggenheim fellow, 1954, 70; recipient Profl. Achievement award U. Chgo., 1978. Mem. Linguistic Soc. Am. (v.p. 1961), Linguistic Assn. Can. and U.S. (pres. 1984-85), Am. Assn. Tchrs. Italian (v.p. 1945), Modern Lang. Assn. Am., Wodehouse Soc. (pres. 1983-85). Congregationalist. Home: 308 Cayuga Heights Rd Ithaca NY 14850

HALL, ROBERT EMMETT, JR., investment banker, realtor; b. Sioux City, Iowa, Apr. 28, 1936; s. Robert Emmett and Alvina (Faden) H.; m. Marna Thiel, 1969. BA, U. S.D., 1958, MA, 1959; MBA, U. Santa Clara, 1976; grad. Am. Inst. Banking, Realtors Inst. Grad. asst. U. S.D., Vermillion, 1958-59; mgr. ins. dept., asst. mgr. installment loan dept. Northwestern Nat. Bank of Sioux Falls, S.D., 1959-61, asst. cashier, 1961-65; asst. mgr. Crocker Nat. Bank, San Francisco, 1965-67, loan officer, 1967-69, asst. v.p., asst. mgr. San Mateo br., 1969-72; v.p., Western regional mgr. Internat. Investments & Realty, Inc., Washington, 1972—; owner Hall Investment Co., 1976—; pres. Almaden Oaks Realtors, Inc., 1976—; instr. West Valley Coll., Saratoga, Calif., 1972-82, Grad. Sch. Bus., U. Santa Clara (Calif.), 1981—. Treas., Minnehaha Leukemia Soc., 1963, Lake County Heart Fund Assn., 1962, Minnehaha Young Republican Club, 1963. Mem. Am. Inst. Banking, San Mateo C. of C., Calif. Assn. Realtors (vice chmn.), Beta Theta Pi. Republican. Roman Catholic. Clubs: Elks, Rotary (past pres.), K.C., Almaden Country, Mercedes Benz Calif. Home: 6951 Castlerock Dr San Jose CA 95120 Office: 6501 Crown Blvd 100 San Jose CA 95120

HALL, ROBERT JOSEPH, physician, medical educator; b. Buffalo, June 4, 1926; s. Joseph M. and Florence C. (Kirst) H.; m. Dorothy Nowak, Aug. 28, 1948; children: Thomas R., Kathleen A. Hall Noble, Mary J. Hall Stuart, Michael F., Steven E. Student, Canisius Coll., Buffalo, 1943-45; M.D., U. Buffalo, 1948. Diplomate Am. Bd. Internal Medicine, Sub Bd. Cardiovascular Disease (mem. cardiovascular disease sect. 1969-75). Intern Mercy Hosp., Buffalo, 1948-49; commd. 1st lt. M.C. U.S. Army, 1948, advanced through grades to col., 1966; resident in internal medicine Walter Reed Gen. Hosp., Washington, 1949-52; resident in cardiovascular diseases Walter Reed Gen. Hosp., 1956-57, asst. cardiovascular research Walter Reed Army Inst. Research, 1957-58; service in Korea and Japan, 1952-55; chief cardiology service Brooke Gen. Hosp., Ft. Sam Houston, Tex., 1961-66, Walter Reed Gen. Hosp., 1966-69; ret. 1969; clin. assoc. prof. medicine Georgetown U. Med. Sch., 1967-69; clin. prof. medicine Baylor U. Coll. Medicine, Houston, 1969—, U. Tex. Med. Sch., Houston, 1977—; med. dir. Tex. Heart Inst., Houston, 1969—; chmn. exec. com. profl. staff Tex. Heart Inst., 1969—; dir. div. cardiology St. Luke's Episcopal Hosp., Houston, 1969—; assoc. chief med. service St. Luke's Episcopal Hosp., 1970-83; cons. Tex. Children's, VA, Brooke Gen. hosps., M.D. Anderson Hosp. and Tumor Inst.; mem. cardiovascular study sect. NIH, 1958-61; mem. phys. evaluation team Gemini project NASA, 1958-61; mem. nat. adv. heart counseil Dept. Def., 1966-69; adv. council Mended Hearts, 1970-78. Contbr. numerous articles med. jours. Mem. President's Adv. Panel Heart Disease. Decorated Legion of Merit. Fellow A.C.P., Am. Coll. Cardiology (gov. 1968-71-74, chmn. bd. govs. and trustee 1973-74); mem. Am. Heart Assn. (fellow council clin. cardiology; pres. Houston chpt. 1974-75, advisor corp. cabinet 1980—), Assn. Mil. Surgeons U.S., Assn. Advancement Med. Instrumentation, Pan Am. Med. Assn. (chmn. sect. cardiovascular diseases 1978-81), Assn. Univ. Cardiologists, Tex. Med. Assn., Tex. Cardiology Club, Harris County Med. Soc., Houston Cardiology Soc. (chmn. 1976-77), Houston Soc. Internal Medicine. Home: 5504 Sturbridge St Houston TX 77056 Office: 1 Bates St Houston TX 77225

HALL, ROBERT TURNBULL, III, lawyer; b. Norfolk, Va., Aug. 25, 1945; s. Robert Turnbull and Mary Evelyn H.; m. Colleen Coffee, Aug. 17, 1968; children—Meghan, Robert. B.S., Washington and Lee U., 1967; J.D., Georgetown U., 1971. Bar: U.S. Dist. Ct. D.C. 1971, D.C. Ct. Appeals 1971, U.S. Ct. Appeals (D.C. cir.) 1972, U.S. Ct. Appeals (5th cir.) 1972, U.S. Supreme Ct. 1975, U.S. Ct. Appeals (11th cir.) 1981, U.S. Ct. Appeals (9th cir.) 1982, U.S. Ct. Appeals (8th cir.) 1983. Assoc. Reid & Priest, N.Y.C., 1971-77, ptnr., 1978—. Mem. ABA, D.C. Bar Assn., Fed. Energy Bar Assn. Home: 162 Mercer St Princeton NJ 08540 Office: Reid & Priest 40 W 57th St New York NY 10019

HALL, RONALD WILLIAM, agribusiness executive; b. Smethwick, Staffordshire, Eng., Mar. 2, 1929; s. William Herbert and Audrey (Fearn) H.; m. Ann Hatton Delaforce; 1 child, Mark Jocelyn. BA with honors, Oxford (Eng.) U., 1952; MA, Stanford U., 1953. Asst. to pres. W.R. Grace, N.Y.C., 1953-56; personnel dir. London, 1956-58; asst. gen. sales mgr. Boston, 1959-60; territorial mgr. London, 1960-66; mng. dir. Conagra, Madrid, 1966—; chmn. bd. dirs. Frigsa, Spain; bd. dirs., mng. dir. Sapropor, Portugal, Spain, B.D.R., Eng.; exec. v.p. ConAgra Europe. Served to sgt. British Army, 1947-49. Club: Oxford and Cambridge (London). Office: Conagra Spain, Castellana 95, 28046 Madrid Spain

HALL, VANCE MARK DORNFORD, history of science educator; b. Dar es Salaam, Tanga, Tanzania, June 6, 1949; s. Mark Gordon and Olga Christina (Martins) H.; 1 child, Justin Vance. BA with honors, Oxford (Eng.) U., 1973; MSc, London U., 1974, Diploma Imperial Coll. Sci. and Tech., 1974, PhD, 1977. Tutor history of sci. The Open U., Eng., 1975-82, postdoctoral research fellow, 1976-80; sr. lectr. Aarhus U., Denmark, 1981; prof. U. Malaya, Kuala Lumpur, Malaysia, 1982—, vis. prof. Inst. for Higher Studies. Author: A History of the Yorkshire Agricultural Society, 1987; co-author: Recent Developments in History of Chemistry, 1985; co-editor: Darwin to Einstein, 1980; free-lance journalist The Star, The Sunday Star, Kuala Lumput, 1983—; contbr. articles to profl. jours. Fellow Royal Soc. Chemistry (hon. sec. history sci. group 1977-80); mem. British Soc. History Sci., Internat. Soc. History Sci. Mem. Social Dem. Party. Mem. Soc. Friends. Club: Whispers (Kuala Lumpur). Home: #6 Jalan 16/10, Petaling Jaya, 46350 Selangor Malaysia Office: U Malaya, Inst Higher Studies, 59100 Kuala Lumpur Malaysia

HALL, WILLIAM STERLING, psychology educator; b. Lonoke County, Ark., July 6, 1934; s. Joseph William and Mattie (Brock) H. A.B., Roosevelt U., 1957; Ph.D., U. Chgo., 1968. Instr., asst. prof. ednl. psychology NYU, 1966-68; assoc. research psychologist Ednl. Testing Service, Princeton, N.J., 1968-70; asst. prof. psychology Princeton (N.J.) U., 1970-73; assoc. prof. psychology Vassar Coll., Poughkeepsie, N.Y., 1973-74, Rockefeller U., N.Y.C., 1974-78; prof. psychology and ednl. psychology, co-dir. Ctr. for Study Reading, U. Ill., Urbana-Champaign, 1978-81; prof. psychology U. Md., College Park, 1981—; mem. study sect. NIMH, 1977-81; mem. grad. evaluation panel NRC. Bd. dirs. Lazurus Awards Com., NRMA, N.Y.C., 1975-82; bd. dirs. Nat. Coll. Adv. Service, N.Y.C., 1982—. Carnegie Corp. grantee, 1975, 77; Ford Found. grantee, 1975. Fellow Am. Psychol. Assn., N.Y. Acad. Scis.; mem. AAAS (sci. fellows selection com.), Soc. Research Child Devel., Sigma Xi, Alpha Phi Alpha. Republican. Home: 1140 23d St NW Washington DC 20037 Office: Univ Md Dept Psychology College Park MD 20742

HALL, WILLIAM STONE, retired mental health official; b. Wagener, S.C., May 1, 1915; s. Henry F. and Mary (Gantt) H.; m. Oxena Elizabeth Gunter, June 29, 1940; children: William Stone, Carol Lynn, Richard F. M.D., Med. U. S.C., 1937; student, Sch. Mil. Neuropsychiatry, 1944, Columbia U., 1947, U. Chgo., 1959. Diplomate: Am. Bd. Neurology and Psychiatry. Intern Columbia (S.C.) Hosp., 1937-38; mem. staff S.C. State Hosp., Columbia, 1938-52; supt. S.C. State Hosp., 1952-69, Pineland State Tng. Sch. and Hosp., 1953-66, Palmetto State Hosp. (name now Crafts-Farrow State Hosp.), 1952-66; commr. mental health S.C. Dept. Mental Health, 1963-85, ret., 1985; clin. prof. psychiatry Med. U. S.C., 1957—, U. S.C., 1976—; Mem. Presdl. Task Force on Mentally Handicapped, 1970; chmn. planning com. Surg. Gen.'s Conf. State and Ter. Mental Health Authorities, 1971, 72; liaison mem. Nat. Adv. Mental Health Council, Nat. Inst. Mental Health, 1972-73; mem. Gov.'s State Health Planning Council, 1973-74, Gov.'s Social Devel. Policy Council, 1973-74; mem. coordinating council S.C. Commn. on Aging, 1974-85; mem. Adv. Council for Comprehensive Health Planning, 1967-75, 1st vice chmn., 1972, 73; councillor, accreditation council for psychiat. facilities Joint Commn. on Accreditation Hosps., 1973-79; mem. Gov.'s Com. on State Employees and their Employment, 1973-85, S.C. Statewide Health Coordinating Council, 1976-85, S.C. Gov.'s Interagy. Coordinating council on Early Childhood Devel. and Edn., 1980-85, S.C. Pre-trial Intervention Adv. Com., 1980-85. Trustee United Community Fund, 1968-71; bd. dirs. United Way of Midlands, 1976-80; adv. bd. Remotivation Technique Orgn., 1972-75. Served as maj. M.C. AUS, 1942-46. Recipient distinguished service plaque S.C. Mental Health Assn., 1960; recipient Orgnl. award S.C. Vocational Rehab. Assn., 1969; Ann. Distinguished Service award S.C. dept. Am. Legion, 1970; Distinguished Service award S.C. Hosp. Assn., 1972; Distinguished Alumnus award Med. U. S.C., 1974; named to S.C. Hall of Fame, 1975; named in his honor William S. Hall Diagnostic Ctr., Fenwick Hall, Charleston, 1984. Fellow Am. Psychiat. Assn. (life, nominating com. 1968, chmn. program com. 12th Mental Hosp. Inst. 1960, com. certification in adminstrv. psychiatry 1972-80, pres. S.C. dist. br. 1957), Am. Coll. Psychiatrists (charter), Am. Coll. Mental Health Adminstrn.; mem. Am. Hosp. Assn. (chmn. governing council psychiat. hosp. sect. 1971), AMA (com. on nursing 1966-73), S.C. Mental Health Assn., Columbia Med. Soc. (pres. 1958), Assn. Med. Supts. Mental Hosps. (pres. 1964, 65, meritorious service award 1971), Nat. Assn. State Mental Health Program Dirs. (v.p. 1968, 69, pres. 1970, 71), S.C. State Employees Assn. (bd. dirs. 1968-76, v.p. 1971-73, pres. 1973-75, Outstanding State Employee 1967), Am. Assn. Psychiat. Adminstrs. (assoc. editor Jour. 1983—), S.C. Med. Assn. Baptist (deacon). Club: Rotarian. Home: 5314 Lakeshore Drive Columbia SC 29206

HALLAM, CLIFFORD BARRY, professor; b. Teaneck, N.J., Mar. 23, 1939; s. Walter Voorhees and Fancheon Donaldine (Taylor) H.; m. Alyce Spotted-Bear, Aug. 11, 1968 (div. Dec. 1976); 1 child, Travis Dale. BA, Tarkio (Mo.) Coll., 1963; MA, Northeastern U., 1966; PhD, Miami U., Oxford, Ohio, 1979. Instr. English Canaan (N.H.) Coll., 1963-66; asst. prof. English Dickinson (N.D.) State Coll., 1967-70; instr. comparative lit. Ohio State U., Columbus, 1970-80; asst. prof. English King Saud U., Riyad, Saudi Arabia, 1980-83; prof. lit., dir. criticism Thammasat U., Bangkok, 1983—. Contbr. articles to profl. jours. Home: 122 Klong Pra Pa, Bangkok, Samsen Thailand

HALLAM, RICHARD STUART, psychologist; b. London, May 23, 1942; s. Sydney Harvey and Mary Winifred (Sloper) H.; m. Magdalena Halina Szlenkier, Jan. 2, 1982; 1 child, Sophie. BA in Psychology and Philosophy, U. Wales, 1965; diploma in abnormal psychology, U. London, 1966, PhD, 1971, MS in Social Anthropology, 1980. Psychologist Hosp. for Sick Children, Toronto, Ont., Can., 1966-67; research asst. Montreal (Can.) Neurol. Inst., 1967-68, Inst. Psychiatry, U. London, 1968-71; psychologist Maudsley Hosp., London, 1971-75; lectr. N.E. London Poly., 1975-78; psychologist, research fellow Inst. Laryngology and Otology, U. London, 1980—; sr. lectr. Middlesex Hosp. Med. Sch., U. London, 1986—; clin. psychologist Bloomsbury Health Authority, London, 1986—. Author: Nursing in Behavioral Psychotherapy, 1977, Anxiety, 1985; contbr. articles to profl. jours. and chpts. to books. Mem. Brit. Psychol. Soc., Brit. Assn. Behavioral Psychotherapy, Brit. Med. Anthropology Soc. Office: Audiology Ctr, Inst Laryngology and Otology, 330 Gray's Inn Rd, London WCIX 8DA, England

HALLBERG, PAUL THURE, library director; b. Göteborg, Sweden, Dec. 10, 1931; s. Seth Severin and Eva Sofia Armida (Theorell) H.; m. Anna Elisabeth Löfgren, June 21, 1958; 1 child, Olof. Filosofie kandidat, Göteborg U., 1953, filosofie licentiat, 1960; postgrad., Yale U., 1955-56. Teaching fellow Yale U., New Haven, 1955-56; asst. tchr. English dept. Göteborg U., 1958-59, librarian, 1960-68, head dept., 1968-77, dir. library, 1977—; mem. steering com. NORDINFO. Author, editor, contbr. numerous profl. books and articles on bibliography and librarianship. Mem. Royal Soc. Arts and Scis., Nat. Bibliographic Council, Internat. Fedn. Library Assocs. and Instns. (standing com., sec. of U. Libraries sect.), Swedish Library Assn., Scandinavian Fedn. Research Librarians (sec. 1966-69, steering com. 1979-84). Home: Orangerigatan 34, S-412 66 Goteborg Sweden Office: Goteborg U Library, PO Box 5096, S-402 22 Goteborg Sweden

HALLE, ALOYS JEAN, physician; b. Thionville, France, Dec. 23, 1934; s. Louis Jean and Marie (Breyer) H.; m Laura Pratel, Apr. 26, 1971; 1 child, Frederique. MD, U. Strasbourg, France, 1962. Practice medicine Strasbourg, Baerenthal, France, 1963-64, Thionville, France, 1964—; cons., acupuncture practitioner Coll. D'acupunture de L'est de la France, 1973—. Contbr. articles to profl. jours. Correspondant Institute Europeen D'Ecologie. Mem. Acad. Med. D'Acupunture Paris. Roman Catholic. Home and Office: 8 Sq du 11 Novembre, 57100 Thionville France

HALLENBECK, RALPH HENRY, educational administrator; b. Oceanside, N.Y., Jan. 3, 1933; s. Ralph Henry and Marie (Bachman) H.; B.B.A., Hofstra U., 1954, M.S., 1960; cert. in adminstrn. N.Y.U., 1963; Ed.D., Nova U., 1979; m. Dorothy Ann Parker, June 27, 1964; children—Karen Jean, Sherry Leslie. Distributive edn. coordinator Island Trees High Sch., Levittown, N.Y., 1959-60, Seaford (N.Y.) High Sch., 1960-66; vice prin. Dryden (N.Y.) Jr.-Sr. High Sch., 1966-69; prin. Cedarcroft Middle Sch., South Plainfield, N.J., 1969-71, Glassboro (N.J.) Intermediate Sch., 1971-84, J. Harvey Rodgers and Elsmere Schs., Glassboro, 1984—. Bd. dirs. Edn. Improvement Center-South, 1977-84, vice chmn., 1982-84; mem. State Awareness Com., 1975-77. Served to capt. U.S. Army, 1954-56, USAR, 1956-60. Mem. N.J. Prins. and Suprs. Assn. Assn. Supervision and Curriculum Devel., Gloucester County Assn. Elem. and Middle Sch. Adminstrs., Glassboro Assn. Sch. Adminstrs., Holland Soc. N.Y. Home: 61 Country Club Rd Turnersville NJ 08012 Office: J Harvey Rodgers Sch Yale and Dickinson Rds Glassboro NJ 08028

HALLENE, ALAN MONTGOMERY, elevator and escalator company executive; b. Moline, Ill., Mar. 12, 1929; s. Maurice Mitchell and Ruth (Montgomery) H.; m. Phyllis Dorene Welsh, June 16, 1951; children: Alan, Carol Louise, Janet Lee, James Norman. BS, U. Ill., 1951; postgrad., Oak Ridge Sch. Reactor Tech., 1951-52. Reactor engr. U.S. AEC, Oak Ridge and Chgo., 1951-53; sales engr. Montgomery Elevator Co., Moline, 1953-54, mgr. Moline accessories div., 1954-57; br. mgr. Montgomery Elevator Co., Jacksonville, Fla., 1957-58, chief engr., 1958-60, v.p., 1960-64, exec. v.p., 1964-68, pres., dir., 1968—; bd. dirs. 1st Midwest Bank of Moline,1976-88, Butler Mfg. Co., Ill. Bell Telephone., Rolscreen Co., 1st Midwest Bancorp., Inc., The Inst. for Ill., U. Ill. Found., John D. and Catherine T. MacArthur Found; trustee Butterworth Meml. Trust, Lincoln Acad. of Ill. Mem. Moline Dist. 40 Bd. Edn., 1966-70, Ill. Commn. on Atomic Energy, 1968-73, Ill. Gov.'s Adv. Council; mem. adv. com. tchr. corps HEW, 1970-73, nat. adv. bd. Inst. Govt. and Pub. Affairs U. Ill.; bd. dirs. Moline Luth. Hosp., 1967-80, Western Golf Assn., 1972-77, Am. Coll. Testing Program, 1975-81, Augustana Coll., 1977-81. Mem. U. Ill. Alumni Assn. (pres. 1973-75). Lodge: Rotary (pres. Moline chpt. 1961). Home: 1885 24th Ave A Moline IL 61265

HALLER, ARCHIBALD ORBEN, sociologist, educator; b. San Diego, Jan. 15, 1926; s. Archie O. and Eleanor (Brizzee) H.; m. Hazel Laura Zimmermann, Feb. 15, 1947 (dec. Feb. 1985); children: Elizabeth Ann, Stephanie Lynn, William John; m. Maria Camila Omegna Rocha, Apr. 12, 1986 (div. Oct. 1987). B.A., Hamline U., 1950; M.A., U. Minn., 1951; Ph.D. (Univ. fellow), U. Wis., 1954. Project assoc. research U. Wis.-Madison, 1954-56, prof. rural sociology, also sociology, Indsl. Relations Research Inst., 1965—, chmn. dept. rural sociology, 1970-72; from assoc. prof. to prof. sociology Mich. State U., East Lansing, 1956-65; Fulbright prof. Rural U. Brazil, 1962, U. São Paulo, 1987, 88; Fulbright travel grantee Univs. São Paulo, Brasília, Pernambuco, Ceará, 1974, Univs. São Paulo, Pernambuco, Paraíba and Ceará, Brazil, 1979; vis. prof. U. Wis., Madison, 1964, Brigham Young U., Provo, Utah, 1973; disting. vis. prof. rural Sociology Ohio State U., 1982-83; vis. fellow Australian Nat. U., 1981; cons. in field Inter-Am. Inst. Agrl. Sci., 1959, OAS, 1963; Brazilian govt., 1965, AID, 1972, U. São Paulo, 1974-75, 76-77, Justice Dept., 1976-77, U. Ill., 1977, UN Ctr. Sci. and Tech. for Devel., 1984. Author research monographs and tech. articles; contbr. articles to profl. jours. Mem. Mich. Com. Mental Health Policies, 1961-62; sociology fellowship panel Council on Internat. Exchange Scholars, 1977-81. Served with USNR, 1943-46. Decorated Grande Oficial Ordem do Merito do Trabalho, Brazil. Fellow AAAS; mem. Am. Sociol. Assn., Internat. Rural Sociol. Assn., Internat. Sociol. Assn., Latin Am. Sociol. Assn., Midwest Sociol. Assn., Sociol. Research Assn., Latin Am. Studies Assn., N.Y. Acad. Sci., Rural Sociol. Assn. (pres. 1969-70, rep. AAAS 1973-86), Soc. Internat. Devel., Sigma Xi. Home: 529 Edward St Madison WI 53711

HALLER, HANS JOERG, marketing communications consultant; b. Innsbruck, Austria, Nov. 7, 1935; s. Hans and Josephine (Braunias) H.; grad. U. Innsbruck, 1960; m. Dagmar Nemelka, Oct. 25, 1969; children—Astrid, Mirjam. Adv. Cons. Osterreich Landerbank, Innsbruck, 1960-61, desk mgr., 1961-65; advt. and sales promotion mgr. Ford Motor Co. of Austria, Salzburg, 1965-67; mktg. mgr. Anger Plastics Machinery, Vienna, Austria, 1967-70, McGraw-Hill, Frankfurt, W. Ger., 1967-70; mng. dir. Johnston Internat. Pub. Corp., Munich, W. Ger., 1971-80; owner, pres. MCC Internat.-Mktg. Communications & Cons., Hans J. Haller, Munich, 1981—. Home: Stuckstrasse 8, 8000 Munich Federal Republic of Germany Office: Preysing 30, 8000 Munich 80 Federal Republic of Germany

HALLETT, CAROL BOYD, diplomat; b. Oakland, Calif., Oct. 16, 1937; married. Student, U. Oreg.; student, San Francisco State Coll. Field office rep. Calif. State Assemblyman, 1966; staff asst. U.S. Congressman, 1967-76; assemblywoman Calif. State Assembly, Sacramento, 1976-82; cons., dir. Found. for Individual and Econ. Freedom, Sacramento, 1982-83; dir. of parks and recreation Calif. State Assmbly, 1982-83; western regional dir. Citizens For Am., Sacramento, 1984; nat. field dir. Citizens For Am., Washington, 1985-86; U.S. ambassador to the Bahamas 1986—; asst. to U.S. Sec. Interior, 1984-85. Office: Am Embassy Bahamas, Mosmar Bldg Queen St, PO Box N 8197, Nassau The Bahamas *

HALLEUX, ALBERT MARTIN JULIEN, motor vehicle inspection company executive; b. Dison, Belgium, Nov. 18, 1920; s. Albert Julien and Marie (Lemaire) H.; Mech. Engr., U. Liege, 1945, Aero. Engr., 1955; m. Arlette Lehyme, May 20, 1967; 1 son, Emmanuel. Engr., then chief engr. Autosecurite, Verviers, 1949-74, pres., 1974—; dep. WP29 experts group Econ. Commn. for Europe, Geneva, 1962—; gen. sec. Internat. Motor Vehicle Insp. Com., 1969—; adj. gen. sec., founder Union Tech. Assistance for Motor Vehicles and Road Traffic, Geneva, 1978—; v.p. Groupement des Organismes de Contrôle Automobile, Brussels, 1979-82, 86—, pres., 1982-85; v.p. Fonds d'Etudes pour la Sécurité Routière, Brussels, 1982-85, Fonds de pré vision et d'utilité publique de l'Inspection des vehicules automobiles, Brussels, 1983-85. Decorated chevalier Order de la Couronne, Officier de l'Ordre de Leopold. Mem. Soc. Promoting Traffic Safety. Liberal. Roman Catholic. Home: 2 Rue de Louvain, B-4800 Verviers Belgium Office: 4 Rue de la Marne, B-4800 Verviers Belgium

HALLGRIMSSON, JONAS, pathologist, educator; b. Iceland, Sept. 6, 1931; s. Jonsson and Thoranna (Magnusdottir) H.; M.D., U. Iceland, 1958; m. Anna Margret Larusdottir, July 3, 1954; children—Hallgrimur, Petur, Larus, Margret. Resident in pathology U. Iceland Hosp., Reykjavik, 1958-59, U. Minn. Grad. Sch., Mpls., 1959-60; intern Meml. Hosp., Worcester, Mass., 1960-61; resident in pathology Mass. Gen. Hosp., Boston, 1961-65; pathologist U. Iceland Hosp., 1965-69, chief pathologist, 1969-78, dir. dept. pathology, 1978—; assoc. prof. U. Iceland Faculty of Medicine, 1966-78, prof., chmn. dept. pathology, 1978—, dean Faculty of Medicine, 1982-84; dir. Inst. Pathology, U. Iceland, 1978—; chmn. Bd. Public Health, Gardabaer, 1970-78. Fellow Rotary Found., 1959-60, Rockefeller Found., 1961-63, Commonwealth Fund, 1968. Mem. Icelandic Med. Assn., Am. Coll. Pathologists, Am. Soc. Clin. Pathology, European Soc. Clin. Investigation. Club: Gardar Rotary. Contbr. articles to med. jours. Home: 2 Tjarnarflot, 210 Gardabaer Iceland Office: Univ Iceland, PO Box 1465, Reykjavik Iceland

HALLIBURTON, JEAN ELIZABETH, journalist; b. Dallas, Nov. 3; d. Orville G. and Lydie Jeanne (Houghton) H.; B.A. in Journalism, Stanford U.; m. G. Arnold Stevens (dec.); children—Arnold Jr., Carole Stevens Jackson, Harley Stevens Tucker. Women's editor West Los Angeles (Calif.) Ind.; asst. fashion editor Los Angeles Herald Examiner; contbg. editor Los Angeles Mag., mem. founding staff, 1960-63; owner JHPR Public Relations Co., Newport Beach, Calif., 1964-77; lifestyle editor Sutton News Group (Newport Ensign, Irvine Today, Costa Mesa News), Corona del Mar, Calif., 1978-81; v.p. Color Me Beautiful, Inc., McLean Va., 1981—. Mem. Women in Communications, Public Relations Soc. Am., Soc. Profl. Journalists. Clubs: Nat. Press, Capitol Hill. Home: 7640 Tremayne Pl #104 McLean VA 22102 also: 2020 Fullerton Dr Apt #46 Costa Mesa CA 92627 Office: Color Me Beautiful Inc 2721-A Merrilee Dr Fairfax VA 22031

HALLIDAY, JOHN MEECH, investment company executive; b. St. Louis, Oct. 16, 1936; s. William Norman and Vivian Viola (Meech) H.; m. Martha Layne Griggs, June 30, 1962; children: Richard M., Elizabeth. BS, U.S. Naval Acad., 1958; MBA, Harvard U., 1964. Dir. budgeting and planning Automatic Tape Control, Bloomington, Ill., 1964-66; dir. planning Ralston-Purina, St. Louis, 1966-67, v.p. subsidiary, 1967-68, dir. internat. banking, 1967-68; v.p. Servicetime Corp., St. Louis, 1968-70; assoc. R.W. Halliday Assocs., Boise, Idaho, 1970-87; v.p. Sawtooth Communications Corp., Boise, 1970-73, Commdr. Corp., 1979-81; pres., chief exec. officer, bd. dirs. Sonoma Internat., San Francisco, 1971-77, ML Ltd., San Francisco, 1974—, Halliday Labs., Inc., Reno, 1980—, Alta Packaging Corp., San Francisco, 1986—; exec. v.p., bd. dirs. Franchise Fin. Corp. Am., Phoenix, 1980-85. bldg. com. YMCA, 1965; pres. Big Bros. of San Francisco, 1978-81. Served to lt. comdr. USNR, 1958-66. Mem. Nat. Restaurant Assn., Soc. Advancement Food Research, Heart Ill. Restaurant Assn. (v.p. 1969-70), Nat. Assn. Accountants. Republican. Episcopalian. Clubs: Family, Olympic (San Francisco), Scott Valley Tennis (Mill Valley, Calif.). Home: 351 Corte Madera Ave Mill Valley CA 94941 Office: 625 Market St Suite 602 San Francisco CA 94105

HALLIDAY, WILLIAM JAMES, JR., lawyer; b. Detroit, Nov. 16, 1921; s. William James and Katherine Elizabeth (Krantz) H.; A.B. (scholar), U. Mich., 1943, J.D., 1948; m. Lois Jeanne Streelman, Sept. 6, 1947; children—Carol Lynn Halliday Murphy, Richard Andrew, Marcia Katherine, James Anthony. Admitted to Mich. bar, 1948; assoc. Schmidt, Smith & Howlett and successors, Grand Rapids, Mich., 1952-56, ptnr., 1956-66, of counsel Varnum, Riddering, Schmidt & Howlett, 1984—; sec. Amway Corp.

Ada, Mich., 1964-84, gen. counsel, 1966-71, v.p., 1970-79, exec. v.p., 1979-84, also dir.; asst. pros. atty., Kent County, Mich., 1949-51; twp. atty., Wyoming Twp., Mich., 1955-57; city atty., Wyoming, Mich., 1961-66. Bd. dirs. Better Bus. Bur. Western Mich., Met. YMCA of Grand Rapids. Served with M.I., U.S. Army, 1943-46, with JAGC, 1951-52. Decorated Bronze Star; recipient William Jennings Bryan award U. Mich., 1943. Mem. ABA, Mich. Bar Assn., Grand Rapids Bar Assn., Phi Beta Kappa, Phi Kappa Phi, Delta Sigma Rho, Phi Eta Sigma. Republican. Presbyterian. Club: Kiwanis. Home: 3020 Uplands Dr SE Grand Rapids MI 49506 Office: Varnum Riddering Schmidt & Howlett 171 Monroe Ave NW Suite 800 Grand Rapids MI 49503

HALLIDAY, WILLIAM ROSS, retired physician, author, speleologist; b. Atlanta, Ga., May 9, 1926; s. William Ross and Jane (Wakefield) H.; m. Eleanore Hartvedt, July 2, 1951 (dec. 1983); children: Marcia Lynn, Patricia Anne, William Ross III; m. Louise Baird Kinnard, May 7, 1988. BA, Swarthmore Coll., 1946; MD, George Washington U., 1948. Diplomate Am. Bd. Vocat. Experts. Intern Huntington Meml. Hosp., Pasadena, Calif., 1948-49; resident King County Hosp., Seattle, Denver Childrens Hosp., L.D.S. Hosp., Salt Lake City, 1950-57; practice medicine Seattle, 1957-65, 83-84; with Wash. Dept. Labor and Industries, 1965-76; med. dir. Wash. Div. Vocat. Rehab., 1976-82, Comprehensive Med. Rehab. Ctr., Brentwood, Tenn., 1984-87; dep. coroner, King County, Wash., 1964-66. Author: Adventure Is Underground, 1959, Depths of The Earth, 1966, 76, American Caves and Caving, 1974, 82; Editor: Jour. Spelean History, 1968-73; contbr. articles to profl. jours. Mem. Gov.'s North Cascades Study Com., 1967-76; mem. North Cascades Conservation Council, v.p., 1962-63; Dir. Western Speleological Survey, Seattle, 1955-81; pres., 1981-88; Internat. Speleological Found. asst. dir. Internat. Glaciospeleological Survey, 1972-76. Served to lt. comdr. USNR, 1949-50, 55-57. Fellow Am. Coll. Chest Physicians, Am. Acad. Compensation Medicine, Nat. Speleological Soc., Explorers Club, Am. Bd. Vocat. Experts; mem. Soc. Thoracic Surgeons, AMA, Am. Congress Rehab. Medicine, Am. Coll. Legal Medicine, Wash. State Med. Assn., Tenn. State Med. Assn., King County Med. Soc., Am. Fedn. Clin. Research, Am. Spelean History Assn. (pres. 1968), Brit. Cave Research Assn., Nat. Trust (Scotland), Am. Pain Soc., Internat. Soc. for the Study of Pain, Am. Acad. Algology. Clubs: Mountaineers (past trustee), Seattle Tennis. Home: 308 Aaron Ct Sterling VA 22170

HALLISSEY, MICHAEL, accounting company executive; b. Southampton, England, Mar. 6, 1943; s. John Francis and Mary (Kendall) H. Grad., Magdalen Coll., Oxford U., Eng., 1964. Chartered acct., Eng. With Price Waterhouse, 1964—; asst. mgr. Price Waterhouse, Melbourne, Australia, 1968, Milan, Italy, 1969; ptnr. Price Waterhouse, London, 1974—, head practice devel., 1979-81, head strategic planning, 1981-82, head corp. fin. services, 1983—. Contbr. articles to profl. publs. Mem. Inst. Chartered Accts. Eng. and Wales. Mem. Conservative Party. Mem. Ch. of Eng. Home: 49 Whitelands House, London SW3 4QX, England Office: Price Waterhouse, 32 London Bridge St, London SE1 9SY, England

HALLOT, LOUIS HENRI, consulting engineer, educator; b. Villemomble, France, Dec. 8, 1923; s. Jules E. and Eugenie (Hebert) H.; m. Andree M. Lardiere, Sept. 21, 1946; children: Jean-Louis, Marie-Therese. Ingenieur, Ecole Nationale Superieure des Arts and Metiers, Paris, 1945. Cert. engr. With Fonderies de Paris, Seine Noisy-le-Sec, 1952-57; with Foundries of Renault, Billancourt, France, 1957—, asst. mgr. engring. and devel. foundries, 1962-85; prof. Ecole Superieure de Fonderie, 1973—. Author: Electric Furnaces, 1978; also articles. Mem. Association Eng. Arts et Metiers (Silver medal 1972; pres. 1983), Association Technique de Fonderie (v.p. 1953), Société Française de Metallurgie, Ingenieurs et Scientifiques de France. Roman Catholic. Avocations: movies; photography; music. Home and Office: 30 bis Avenue Joffre, 93220 Gagny France

HALLSTRÖM, ARNE PER, education consulting company executive; b. Malmo, Sweden, July 11, 1931; s. Per and Ingeborg (Magnusson) H.; m. Tahka Laakso, Dec. 28, 1980; 1 child, Per. MBA, U. Lund, 1962, D of Philosophy, 1967. Mng. dir. advt. agy. Vaxjo, Sweden, 1965-80, Mammut AB, Norrhult, Sweden, 1980—. Author: Aktiv Kundtjanst, 1982, Att leda och utveckla kundservice, 1984, Medarbetaren i centrum, 1987. Home: Klavrevägen 14, S-36071 Norrhult Sweden Office: Mammut AB, Bokvägen 5, S-36071 Norrhult Sweden

HALLUIN, ALBERT PRICE, biotechnology executive, lawyer; b. Washington, Nov. 8, 1939; s. William Ord and Martha (Blundon) H.; m. Joanne Rita Forbes, Apr. 16, 1966; children—Marcus Anthony, Russell Price. B.A., La. State U., 1964; J.D., U. Balt., 1969. Bar: Md. 1970, U.S. Supreme Ct. 1976, U.S. Ct. Appeals (Fed. cir.) 1982. Examiner U.S. Patent and Trademark Office, Washington, 1965-69; assoc. Jones, Tullar & Cooper, Arlington, Va., 1969-71; sr. patent atty. CPC Internat. Inc., Englewood Cliffs, N.J., 1971-76; counsel Exxon Research and Engring. Co., Florham Park, N.J., 1976-83; v.p., chief intellectual property counsel, mem. mgmt. com. Cetus Corp., Emeryville, Calif., 1983—; lectr. in field. Chmn. troop com., asst. scoutmaster Westfield council Boy Scouts Am. Mem. ABA, Am. Intellectual Property Assn. (past chmn. chem. practice com., dir., sec.), AAAS, N.J. Patent Law Assn. (bd. mgrs., treas., 2d v.p.), Patent Office Soc., License Exec. Soc., Assn. Corporate Patent Counsel. Contbr. articles to profl. jours.; patentee in field. Office: Cetus Corp 1400 53rd St Emeryville CA 94608

HALPERIN, JOSEPH, entomologist; b. Lodz, Poland, July 13, 1922; came to Israel, 1946; s. Haim and Helene (Goldlust) H.; m. Sara Resnik, May 18, 1951 (div. Nov. 1957); 1 child: Efraim. MA, Hebrew U., 1957, PhD, 1971. Tchr., schoolmaster Belorussian Ministry Edn., Dubrovna, Poland, 1940-41; various schs. Israel, 1949-58; head Lab. for Forest Entomology and Protection, Ilanot, Israel, 1958—; cons. extension service Israel Ministry of Agriculture, Tel Aviv, 1987—, Standards Instn. Israel, Tel Aviv, 1987—. Contbr. numerous articles to profl. jours. Founder, mem. anti-Nazi clandestine unit, White Russia, 1941-43; comdr. guerilla group, Poland, 1944; founder, head youth group for Aliya to Israel, Poland, Austria, Italy, 1945. Served with Irael Army, 1947-49. Recipient Efficiency award Israeli Ministry of Agriculture, 1970. Mem. Entomology Soc. Israel. Home: Hapalmah 5, Nes Ziyona 70 400, Israel Office: The Volcanic Ctr, Lab for Forest Ent and Protect, Bet Dagan 50250, Israel

HALPERIN, WARREN LESLIE, management consultant; b. Bklyn., Apr. 12, 1938; s. Abraham and Bertha Gertrude (Aronowitz) H.; m. Sherry Lee Weshner, Mar. 31, 1968; children: Jonathan David, Justin Edward. PhB, Adelphi U., 1959. Dir. mktg. Faust-Day Inc., Los Angeles, 1969-71; product mgr. Hunt-Wesson Foods, Fullerton, Calif., 1972-74; sr. v.p. Searchmasters Inc., Newport Beach, Calif., 1975-79; ptnr. MCS Assocs., Newport Beach, 1979-83; pres. The Halperin Co. Inc., Newport Beach, 1983—; also bd. dirs.; bd. dirs. Capital Savings & Loan Assn., West Helena, Ark. Contbr. articles to profl. jours. Mem. nat. bd. trustees Leukemia Soc. Am., N.Y.C., 1980-85; trustee Amigos De Las Americas, Irvine, Calif., 1975-78; pres. Leukemia Soc. Am. Tri-County chpt., Garden Grove, Calif., 1979. Recipient Exec. of Yr. Exec. Mag., 1986. Mem. U.S. League of Savings Insts., Mortgage Bankers Assn. Am., Bank Adminstrn. Inst. Office: The Halperin Co Inc 23041 Avenida De La Carlotta Suite 360 Laguna Hills CA 92653

HALPERN, GEORGES MAURICE, physician, consultant; b. Warsaw, Poland, Sept. 7, 1935; came to France, 1935, came to U.S., 1981; s. Bernard Neftali and Renee Rachel (Nysenholc) Halpern Gelbard; m. Marie Catherine Guillard, 1958 (div. 1963); m. Genevieve Bourineau, 1965 (div. 1969); m. Emiko Oguiss, May 14, 1971; children: Emmanuelle Miyoko, Emilie Hideko. Baccalaureate summa cum laude, Lycee Henri IV, Paris, 1953; BS in physics, chemistry, biology, Faculty of Scis., Paris, 1954; degree in nuclear medicine, Institut National des Science et Techniques Nucleaires, Saclay, France, 1965; MD silver medal, Faculty of Medicine, Paris, 1964; med. diplomate, U. Paris, 1964. Practicing internist, allergist Allergy and Clinical Immunology Clinic, Paris, 1964-83; dir. program research Inst. ImmunoBiologie, Paris, 1966-78; chief sci. advisor 3M Diagnostic Systems, Santa Clara, Calif., 1983-88; pres. BioDelta, Frame, Medintern, Portola Valley, Calif., 1985—; adj. prof. medicine U. Calif. Sch. Medicine, Davis, 1986—; med. dir. French Pharmacy Hong Kong, Kowloon, 1970-77; cons. Lab. Cassenne, Paris, 1970-78, Pharmacia, Bois d'Arcy, France, 1971-83, Vittel U.S.A., Newport Beach, 1983—; vis. research scholar Stanford U., Palo Alto, Calif., 1981-83. Author: L'Allergie et la Peau, 1976 (gold medal 1977), Allergies, 1985; editor in chief (med. jour.) Allergie et Immunologie, 1969-84; contbr. recipes to cooking mag., 1969-71 (merite agricole 1974); inventor IgG4 FAST. Recipient Prix Auguste Becard, Soc. de Gastronomie Medicale, Paris, 1969, Medal of Honor, Czech. Soc. J.E. Purkynje, Prague, 1977, Medal of Vermeil, City of Paris, 1985. Fellow European Acad. of Allergy, The Royal Soc. Medicine, Am. Acad. Allergy; mem. Colombian Acad. Medicine (corresponding mem.), GAILL (gen. sec.), Internat. Congress Food and Health (co-pres.). Lodge: Pacifica GODF (venerable). Home: 9 Hillbrook Dr Portola Valley CA 94025

HALPERN, JACK, chemist, educator; b. Poland, Jan. 19, 1925; came to U.S., 1962, naturalized; s. Philip and Anna (Sass) H.; m. Helen Peritz, June 30, 1949; children: Janice Henry, Nina Phyllis. BS, McGill U., 1946, PhD, 1949; DSc (hon.), U. B.C., 1986. Postdoctorate overseas fellow NRC, U. Manchester, Eng., 1949-50; instr. chemistry U. B.C., 1950, prof., 1961-62; Nuffield Found. traveling fellow Cambridge (Eng.) U., 1959-60; prof. chemistry U. Chgo., 1962-71, Louis Block prof. chemistry, 1971-83, Louis Block Disting. Service prof., 1983—; vis. prof. U. Minn., 1962, Harvard, 1966-67, Calif. Inst. Tech., 1968-69, Princeton U., 1970-71, Max. Planck Institut, Mulheim, Fed. Republic Germany, 1983—, vis. prof. U. Copenhagen, 1978; Sherman Fairchild Disting. scholar Calif. Inst. Tech., 1979; guest scholar Kyoto U., 1981; Firth vis. prof. U. Sheffield, 1982; numerous guest lectureships; cons. editor Macmillan Co., 1963-65, Oxford U. Press; cons. Am. Oil Co., Monsanto Co., Argonne Nat. Lab., IBM, Air Products Co., EniChem; mem. adv. panel on chemistry NSF, 1967-70; mem. adv. bd. Am. Chem. Soc. Petroleum Research Fund, 1972-74; mem. medicinal chemistry sect. NIH, 1975-78, chmn., 1976-78; mem. chemistry adv. council Princeton U., 1982—; mem. univ. adv. com. Ency. Brit., 1985—. Assoc. editor: Inorganica Chimica Acta, Jour. Am. Chem. Soc; co-editor: Collected Accounts of Transition Metal Chemistry, vol. 1, 1973, vol. 2, 1977; mem. editorial bd. Jour. Organometallic Chemistry, Ency. Britannica, Accounts Chem. Research, Catalysis Revs., Jour. Catalysis, Jour. Molecular Catalysis, Jour. Coordination Chemistry, Gazzetta Chimica Italiana, Organometallics, Catalysis Letters; contbr. articles to research jours. Trustee Gordon Research Confs., 1968-70. Recipient Young Author's prize Electrochem. Soc., 1953, award in inorganic chemistry Am. Chem. Soc., 1968, award in catalysis Noble Metals Chem. Soc., London, 1976, Wilhelm von Hoffman medal German Chem. Soc., 1988, Humboldt award, 1977, Richard Kokes award Johns Hopkins U., 1978; Alfred P. Sloan research fellow, 1959-63. Fellow Royal Soc. London, AAAS, Am. Acad. Arts and Scis., Chem. Inst. Can. (hon.), Royal Soc. Chemistry London, N.Y. Acad. Scis., Japan Soc. for Promotion Sci.; mem. Am. Chem. Soc. (editorial bd. Advances in Chemistry series 1963-65, 78-81, chmn. inorganic chemistry div. 1971, award for disting. service in advancement inorganic chemistry, 1985, Willard Gibbs medal 1986, Bailar medal U. Ill. 1986), Nat. Acad. Scis. (fgn. assoc. 1985—), Max Planck Soc. (sci. mem. 1983—), Art Inst. Chgo., Renaissance Soc. (bd. dirs. 1985—), Sigma Xi. Home: 5630 Dorchester Ave Chicago IL 60637 Office: U Chgo Dept Chemistry Chicago IL 60637

HALPERN, JO-ANNE ORENT, lawyer; b. Balt., Apr. 13, 1944; d. Max Howard and Marjorie (Ginsburg) Orent; m. M. David Halpern, Aug. 22, 1965; children—Hugh Nathanial, Lee Randall (dec.), Lauren Gail. B.A. Dickinson Coll., 1966; J.D., Dickinson Sch. Law, 1968. Bar: Pa. 1968. Law clk. Daupin County and Commonwealth Ct. Pa., 1965-68; assoc. Hurwitz Klein, Benjamin & Angino, Harrisburg, Pa., 1968-70; sole practice, Hollidaysburg, Pa., 1970—; legal asst. to Blair County Cts., Hollidaysburg, 1974—; solicitor Blair County Assn. Citizens with Learning Disabilities, 1979—, Family Violence Intervention, Inc., Altoona, Pa., 1980—; lectr., atty. Hospice Program of Home Nursing Agy. Blair County, 1979—. Adviser, bd. dirs. Agudath Achim Sisterhood, 1970—, pres., 1985-88; mem. Fedn. Jewish Philanthropies Bd, 1985—. Mem. ABA, Pa. Bar Assn. (family law sect., rights of handicapped children sect.), Blair County Bar Assn., Am. Arbitration Assn. (arbitrator), Blair County Assn. Lawyers Wives, Phi Alpha Delta, Phi Mu. Democrat. Jewish. Lodge: Hadassah. Home: 8 Hickory Hill Hollidaysburg PA 16648

HALPERN, LAWRENCE MAYER, pharmacologist, educator; b. N.Y.C., July 3, 1931; s. Jacob and Clara Deborah (Solomon) H.; m. Frances Weingart (div. 1976); children—Gordon Neil, Sharon Lee, Lisa Ann; m. 2d, Gail Arshon, July 12, 1981. B.S. in Biology and Chemistry, Bklyn. Coll., 1953; Ph.D. in Neuropharmacology, Albert Einstein Coll. Medicine, 1961. Neuropharmacologist, Merck Inst. Therapeutic Research, West Point, Pa., 1962-65; prof. U. Wash. Sch. Medicine, Seattle, 1965—, also dir. drug abuse info. service., 1967-75, cons. pain clinic, 1968—; cons. Nat. Inst. Neurol. Disease, Bethesda, Md., 1967-68. Contbr. articles to profl. jours; chpts. to books. Served with USN, 1950-58. Mem. Am. Soc. Pharmacology and Exptl. Therapeutics, Internat. Assn. Study Pain, Intractable Pain Soc. Gt. Britain and Ireland, Soc. Neurosci. Club: Seattle.

HALPERN, NATHAN LOREN, industrialist; b. Sioux City, Iowa, Oct. 22, 1914; s. Aaron and Lena (Robin) H.; m. Edith Kessel, Oct. 7, 1938; 1 son, Michael. B.A., U. So. Calif., 1936; LL.B. cum laude, Harvard, 1939. Bar: Calif., D.C. 1939. Asst. to chmn. SEC, Washington, 1939-41; exec. asst. to dir. WPB, Washington, 1941-42, USIS, France, 1945; asst. to pres. CBS, N.Y.C., 1945-49; pres. TNT Communications, Inc., N.Y.C., 1949—; Former pres. Internat. Center Photography; pres. East Hampton Beach Preservation Soc.; trustee N.Y. Central Park Conservancy. Benefactor, mem. corp. Met. Mus. of Art. Served with USNR, 1942-44. Mem. Soc. Motion Picture and TV Engrs., Phi Beta Kappa. Clubs: Harvard, Players. Home: 993 Fifth Ave New York NY 10028 Office: 575 Madison Ave New York NY 10022

HALPERN, PATRICIA, sales promotion and premiums company executive; b. San Francisco, Jan. 13, 1934; d. William and Alice (Dewey) O'Shaughnessy; student U. Ill., m. Harold Halpern, Apr. 1; children: Rebecca, Jay. Account exec., v.p. sales React Enterprises, N.Y.C., 1974-87; v.p. nat. accounts Logo Promotions, Inc., N.Y.C., 1987—. Mem. Ad Specialty Assn., NOW. Home: 132 E 35th St New York NY 10016 Office: Logo Promotions Inc 230 Fifth Ave Suite 1210 New York NY 10001

HALPERN, RALPH LAWRENCE, lawyer; b. Buffalo, May 12, 1929; s. Julius and Mary C. (Kaminker) H.; m. Harriet Chasin, June 29, 1958; children: Eric B., Steven R., Julie B. LL.B. cum laude, U. Buffalo, 1953. Bar: N.Y. 1953. Teaching assoc. Northwestern U. Law Sch., 1953-54; assoc. firm Jaeckle, Fleischmann, Kelly, Swart & Augspurger, Buffalo, 1957-58; asso. firm Raichle, Banning, Weiss & Halpern (and predecessors), 1958-59, ptnr., 1959-86; ptnr. Jaeckle, Fleischmann & Mugel, Buffalo, 1986—. Pres. Buffalo Council World Affairs, 1972-74, Temple Beth Zion, Buffalo, 1981-83; chmn. Buffalo chpt. Am. Jewish Com., 1975-77; bd. govs. United Jewish Fedn., Buffalo, 1972-78. Served to capt. JAGC U.S. Army, 1954-57. Mem. ABA, N.Y. State Bar Assn. (chmn. com. profl. ethics 1971-76, chmn. com. jud. election monitoring 1983-86, chmn. spl. com. to consider adoption of ABA model rules of profl. conduct 1983-85), Erie County (N.Y.) Bar Assn., Am. Judicature Soc., Am. Law Inst. Home: 88 Middlesex Rd Buffalo NY 14216 Office: Jaeckle Fleischmann & Mugel 800 Norstar Bldg Buffalo NY 14202-2292

HALPERN, SIDNEY, university official; b. Phila., Jan. 18, 1927; s. Bernard M. and Sophie (Swidler) H.; AB, U. Pa., 1947, MA, 1950, PhD, 1964; postgrad. Harvard U., 1947-49; DCL (hon.), U. Vascondurias; m. Phyllis C. Schachter, Dec. 21, 1951; children—Baruch, Nikki. Vice pres. Loyalty Life Ins. Agy., Inc., 1954-67, sec., dir., 1965-67; exec. v.p. Plymouth Mut. Life Ins. Co., 1954-57, pres., dir. 1957-67; pres. editor, pub. Mercury Books, Inc., 1961-67; asst. v.p. George Washington Life Ins. Co., 1965-67; asst. prof. history Temple U., Ambler, Pa., 1967-76, assoc. prof., 1976-83, prof., 1983—, dir. Ambler Campus, 1971—, dean campus, 1975-82, prof., 1982—; pres. Provident Pub. Co., 1969—. Mem. Adath Zion, Zionist Orgn. Am., Jewish Def. League, Phi Beta Kappa, Sigma Rho. Lodge: Order Conrad III. Author: Caesar and the Aurelii Cottae; The Passions of Caesar and Christ; Salvation is from the Jews; On His Father's Business; Cyrus ha'Maschiah; contbr. articles to psychoanalytic jours. Home: 1025 Friendship St Philadelphia PA 19111 Office: Temple U Ambler PA 19002

HALPERN, STANTON DAVID, maintenance supplies company executive; b. Bklyn., July 23, 1949; s. Samuel and Cecelia (Strum) H.; m. Lauri Beth Newman, July 22, 1973; children—Lauren Rachel, Joshua Seth. B.A., Hofstra U., 1971. Notary Pub., N.Y.; lic. pesticide applicator, N.Y. Sales rep. Halbro Control Industries, Farmingdale, N.Y., 1971-79, dir. mktg., 1980-82, chief exec. officer, exec. v.p., 1982—. Contbr. articles to profl. jours. Republican committeeman 145th ea. dist., Huntington, N.Y. Recipient Nat. Honor Soc. award H. Frank Carey High Sch., 1965-67; J.F.K. Meml. Citizenship award Sachs Furniture, 1967; Outstanding Salesmanship award Dale Carnegie Inst., 1973. Mem. Internat. Platform Assn., Internat. Sanitary Supply Assn., Am. Mgmt. Assn., L.I. Assn. environ. com.), 110 L.I. Action Group. Lodge: Masons. Home: 4 Wilmington Dr Melville NY 11747 Office: Halbro Control Industries 2090 Rt 110 Farmingdale NY 11735

HALPERN MONTECINO, PABLO, lawyer, educator; b. Santiago, Chile, Oct. 28, 1947; s. Mauricio Halpern and Marta Montecino de Halpern; m. Alicia Alamos, Apr. 1, 1977; children—Mauricio, Juan Pablo, Maureen, Sebastian. Lawyer, U. Chile, Santiago, 1972; M.Sc. in Econs., London Sch. Econs., 1974. Bar: Chile 1972. Adviser, Fgn. Office Chile, 1974-75; main legal adviser to fgn. investment com. Banco Central, Santiago, 1977-79; ptnr. Errazuriz & Co., Santiago, 1979-86; prof. internat. law Inst. Internat. Studies, U. Chile, 1975—; ptnr. Windsor Plaque Ltda., Santiago, 1968—; adviser, atty. Consorcio Nacional de Seguros, Santiago, 1977-80, Supermercados Unimarc, Santiago, 1982-85. Active Partido Nacional, Chile, 1966-73. Mem. Colegio de Abogados, Soc. Internat. Devel. (sec. 1975-79), Sociedad Chilena de Derecho Internacional, Am. Soc. Internat. Law, ABA. Club: Club de la Union (Santiago). Avocations: classical music; skiing; tennis; jogging. Office: Gardeweg & Halpern Attys, Moneda N 920 of 502, Santiago Chile

HALPIN, PATRICIA, musicologist; b. Sydney, New South Wales, Australia, June 15, 1935; d. Cyril Keith and Phyllis (Parkin) H. Diploma teaching New South Wales Conservatorium Music, 1956, diploma performance, 1957, D.Music, 1986. Solo pianist Australian Broadcasting Commn., also TV, comml. stas., 1951—; concert appearances as soloist with orchs., as accompanist with chamber groups; condr. orchestral and choral groups; mem. faculty New South Wales Conservatorium Music, 1964, State Conservatorium Music, Wollongong, 1975-76; examiner in pianoforte and acad. subjects Australian Music Exams. Bd., 1964-80; owner, founder Orpheus Publs., 1974—. Author textbooks on theoretical and practical aspects of music. Scholar, Federated Music Clubs, 1950, New South Wales Conservatorium Music, 1953-54; recipient Frank Shirley prize, 1957; decorated Order of Australia (with medal), 1980. Fellow Internat. Biog. Assn.; mem. Mus. Assn. New South Wales, Australian Coll. Edn., 1788-1820 Assn., Order of Australia Assn., Australian Soc. Authors, Mensa.

HALSEY, ALBERT HENRY, economics educator; b. London, Apr. 13, 1923; s. William Thomas and Ada (Draper) H.; m. Gertrude Margaret Littler, Apr. 10, 1949; children: Ruth, Robert, Lisa, David, Mark. BSc, London Sch. Econs., U. London, 1950; PhD, U. London, 1954; MA, U. Oxford, Eng., 1962; D in Social Scis. (hon.), U. Birmingham, Eng., 1987. Research assoc. U. Liverpool, Eng., 1952-54; lectr. U. Birmingham, 1954-62; prof. U. Oxford, 1962—. Mem. Am. Acad. Arts and Scis. Mem. Labour Party. Anglican. Home: 28 Upland Park Rd, Oxford OX1 1NF, England Office: Oxford U, Nuffield Coll, Oxford OX2 7RU, England

HALSEY, JAMES ALBERT, international entertainment impressario, theatrical producer, talent manager; b. Independence, Kans., Oct. 7, 1930; s. Harry Edward and Carrie Lee (Messick) H.; m. Minisa Crumbo; children: Sherman Brooks, Gina. Student, Independence Community Coll., 1948-50, U. Kans. Pres. Thunderbird Artists, Inc., Independence, from 1950; pres. Jim Halsey Co., Inc., Tulsa, from 1952, now chmn., chief exec. officer; pres. Norwood Advt. Agy., James Halsey Property Mgmt. Co., Tulsa Proud Country Entertainment, Stas. KTOW/KGOW, Silverline-Goldline Pub., J.H. Radio Mgmt., Cyclone Records, Tulsa Records, J.H. Lighting and Sound Co., Singin' T Prodns.; v.p. Gen. Artists Corp. now Century City Artists Corp., Beverly Hills, Calif., 1956—; chmn., chief exec. officer Century City Artists Corp., Tulsa, Nashville, Pacific Palisades, Calif.; chmn. Churchill Recs. & Video Ltd., from 1981; personal mgr. various entertainment personalities; internat. jurist Golden Orpheus Festival, Bulgaria, 1981-82; pres. Internat. Fedn. Festival Orgns., Pacific Palisades; producer shows for auditoriums, fairs, rodeos, TV, internat. music fests also others in U.S. and internationally including Tulsa Internat. Music Festival, 1977-80, Neewollah Internat. Music Festival, 1981-83; gen. ptnr. Parker Ranch, Tulsa; bd. dirs. Merc. Bank and Trust, Tulsa, Citizens Nat. Bank, Independence, Farmers & Mchts. Bank, Mound City, Kans. Trustee Philbrook Art Ctr., Tulsa; bd. dirs. Thomas Gilcrease Mus. Assn., Tulsa Philharm. Assn., Roy Clark Celebrity Golf Classic. Served with U.S. Army, 1954-56. Recipient Disting. Service award U.S. Jr. C. of C., 1959, Ambassador of Country Music award SESAC Corp., 1978, citation Cashbox Mag., 1980, citation Golden Orpheus Festival, 1982, Hubert Long award Mervyn Conn, Eng., 1982, commendation Los Angeles Mayor Tom Bradley, Gov.'s medal Kans. Commn., 1986, Frederic Chopin medal Polish Artist Bur., 1987; named Disting. Kansan Topeka Capital Jour. Mem. Country Music Assn. (bd. dirs. 1963-64, 70-71, v.p. 1979-80, Founding Pres.'s award 1985), Acad. Country Music (bd. dirs. 1969-70, 73-74, v.p. 1975-76, 78-79, 79-80, , 88—, Jim Reeves Meml. award 1977), UNESCO, Internat. Fedn. Festival Orgns. (pres., Oscar Midem award 1982). Office: 3225 S Norwood Tulsa OK 74135 also: 17351 Sunset Blvd Pacific Palisades CA 90272 also: 24 Music Sq W Nashville TN 37203

HALSTROM, FREDERIC NORMAN, lawyer; b. Boston, Feb. 26, 1944; s. Reginald F. and Margaret M. (Graham) H.; m. Mary Ann Joseph, Aug. 14, 1982; 1 dau., Ingrid Alexandra. Student Northeastern U., 1961-63, U.S. Air Force Acad., 1963-65; A.B., Georgetown U., 1967; J.D., Boston Coll., 1970. Bar: Mass. 1970, U.S. Dist. Ct. Mass. 1971, U.S. Dist. Ct. R.I. 1981, U.S. Tax Ct. 1981, U.S. Ct. Appeals (1st cir.) 1971. Assoc., Schneider and Reilly, P.C., Boston, 1970-73, ptnr. Parker, Coolter, Daley and White, Boston, 1973-78; prin. Frederic N. Halstrom, P.C., Boston, 1978—; spl. prosecutor Dist. Atty., Norfolk County, 1969-70; spl. asst. city solicitor City of Quincy, 1980. Fellow Boston Coll. Law Sch.; mem. Fed. Bar Assn., ABA (chmn. products liability com. gen. practice sect. 1980—, award of achievement young lawyers div. 1978, vice chmn. taxation on ins. cos. sect. 1986—), Assn. Trial Lawyers Am. (gov. 1981-84, 87—, state del. 1976-78, 86-87, chair various coms.), Am. Judicature Soc., Mass. Acad. Trial Attys. (co-chmn. tort law sect. 1980—, bd. of govs. 1976—, sec. 1987—), Mass. Bar Assn. (pres. young lawyers div. 1977-78, bd. of dels. 1978-80), Middlesex County Bar Assn., Trial Lawyers Pub. Justice (sustaining founder). Roman Catholic. Clubs: Algonquin, University (Boston). Editor Mass. Law Quar., 1972; contbr. articles to profl. jours. Home: 483 River Rd Carlisle MA 01741 Office: 132 Boylston St Boston MA 02116

HALTER, EDMUND JOHN, mechanical engineer; b. Bedford, Ohio, May 10, 1928; s. Edmund Herbert and Martha (Demske) H.; student Akron U., 1946-48; B.S. in Mech. Engring., Case Inst. Tech., Cleve., 1952; M.S. in Mech. Engring., So. Meth. U., 1965; m. Carolyn Amelia Luecke, June 29, 1955; children—John Alan, Amelia Katherine, Dianne Louise, Janet Elaine. Flight test engr., analyst Chance Vought Aircraft, Dallas, 1952-59; chief research and devel. engr. Burgess-Manning Co., Dallas, 1959-68; engring. specialist acoustics Vought div. LTV Aerospace Corp., Dallas, 1968-69; mgr. continuing engring. Maxim Silencer div. AMF Beaird, Inc., Shreveport, La., 1969-72; chief research and devel. engr. Burgess-Manning div. Burgess Industries, Dallas, 1972-79; chief engr. Vibration & Noise Engring. Corp., Dallas, 1979—; cons. Organizer Citizen Noise Awareness Seminar, Irving, 1977. Served with USNR, 1946-49. Registered profl. engr., Tex., Ohio; cert. fallout shelter analyst. Mem. Inst. Environ. Scis. (pres. S.W. chpt. 1977-78), Indsl. Silencer Mfrs. Assn. (chmn. 1975-77), Acoustical Soc. Am., Nat., Tex. socs. profl. engrs., ASME. Republican. Lutheran. Contbr. articles to profl. jours. Patentee in field. Home: 200 Hillcrest Ct Irving TX 75062

HALVA, ALLEN KEITH, legal publications consultant; b. Willow River, Minn., Jan. 23, 1913; s. Edward and Frances R. (Allen) H.; m. Julia M. Halva, Oct. 25, 1941; children—Barbara Jo Halva Kachmarzinski, Kurt Edward. Student Pasadena Jr. Coll. and Los Angeles City Coll., 1931-32; LL.B. cum laude, Calif. Assoc. Colls., 1935; LL.M., Los Angeles U. Applied Edn., 1950, S.J.D., 1951. Bar: Calif. 1936, Minn. 1941. With West Pub. Co., 1942-82; law book editor; retired ; legal publs. cons. Mem. State Bar Calif., Minn. State Bar Assn., Ramsey County Bar Assn., Am. Judicature Soc., Am. Security Council, Nat. Taxpayers Union, Am. Assn. Retired Persons.

Presbyterian. Club: Hospitaller Order of St. John of Jerusalem. Home: 253 S Warwick St Saint Paul MN 55105-2452

HALVERSON, THOMAS GEORGE, nuclear facility executive; b. Madison, Wis., Apr. 14, 1948; s. Arthur John and Mary Jane (Hoffman) H.; m. Linda Sue Vandine, Feb. 17, 1977; children—Nuclear Engring., U. Wis., 1971. Tech. engr. Commonwealth Edison Co., Zion, Ill., 1971-74; design engr. Westinghouse Hanford Co., Richland, Wash., 1974-76, engring. sect. mgr., 1976-80; mgr. safety Fast Flux Test Facility, 1980-81, mgr. nuclear facility safety, 1981-85, mgr. Hanford rep. to EPRI-COMO, 1985-86, staff mgr. LMR program coordination, 1986—; Past pres. Lower Columbia Basin Search and Rescue, Kennewick, Wash., 1982; reservist Benton County Sheriff's Office, Kennewick, 1982. Mem. Am. Nuclear Soc. (program chmn. 1980-82). Lutheran. Club: Atomic Ducks Dive (Kennewick) (pres. 1981-82). Research on liquid metal fast reactor application overview of operation of the Fast Flux Test Facility and advanced fuel research labs. Office: Westinghouse Hanford Co PO Box 1970 WB-66 Richland WA 99352

HALVERSTADT, ROBERT DALE, engineer, manufacturing company executive; b. Warren, Ohio, Jan. 25, 1920; s. Roscoe B. and Dorothy (Grubbs) H.; B.S. in Mech. Engring., Case Inst. Tech., 1951; m. Maryella Greene, Dec. 31, 1941; children—Marta Jean (Mrs. Michael Carmen), Linda Anne (Mrs. Gary Orelup), Sally Jo. Journeyman machinist Republic Steel Corp., Cleve., 1939-51; design engr. Gen. Electric Co., Evendale, Ohio, 1951-53; supr. Metalworking Lab., 1953-58, corp. cons., N.Y.C., 1958-59, mgr. Thomson Engring. Lab., Lynn, Mass., 1959-63; gen. mgr. engring. Continental Can Co., N.Y.C., 1963-64; group v.p. Booz, Allen & Hamilton Inc., N.Y.C., 1964-73, chief exec. Foster D. Snell Inc. subs., 1964-72, pres. Design & Devel., Inc. subs., 1966-70; v.p. tech. Singer Co., 1973-74; pres. Spl. Metals Corp. subs. Allegheny Ludlum Industries, Inc., New Hartford, N.Y., 1974-81, pres. Materials Tech. Group, 1981-83, mng. dir. Allegheny Ludlum Industries Ltd.; sr. staff v.p. Allegheny Internat., 1983-85; pres. AIMe Assocs., New Canaan, Conn., 1985-87; chmn. bd. Spl. Metal Corp., 1987—; co-chmn. Titanium Metals Corp. Am.; dir. Oneida Nat. Bank, Carus Corp., Centrex Labs., Inc. Pres., Industry, Labor and Edn. Council Mohawk Valley, Inc. Served with USCGR, 1942-45. Registered profl. engr., N.Y., Ohio. Fellow Am. Soc. Metals (trustee); mem. ASME, Am. Inst. Chem. Engrs., Am. Ordnance Assn., Regional Plan Assn., Am. Water Resources Assn., N.Y. Acad. Scis., Mohawk Valley C. of C. (dir.), Chemists Club, Sigma Xi, Tau Beta Pi, Theta Tau. Mem. United Ch. of Christ. Clubs: Toastmasters; Woodway Country; University (N.Y.C.). Editorial bd. Internat. Jour. Turbo and Jet Engine Tech. Patentee in field. Home: 333 Oenoke Ridge Rd New Canaan CT 06840 Office: PO Box 1649 New Canaan CT 06840

HALVORSON, WILLIAM ARTHUR, economic research consultant; b. Menomonie, Wis., June 26, 1928; s. George Henry and Katherine Eileen (Dietsche) H.; m. Patricia Janet von Trebra, Dec. 27, 1951; children—Robert, James, Janet, Audrey, Katherine. Student Stout Inst., 1945-46, U. Mich., 1948; B.B.A., U. Wis., 1950, M.B.A., 1951. Registered investment advisor. Asst. group actuary N.Y. Life Ins. Co., N.Y.C., 1951-56; cons. actuary Milliman & Robertson, Inc., San Francisco, 1956-61, Milw., 1961-83, exec. v.p., 1972-81; founder Halvorson Research Assocs., econ. and investment research cons., 1983—. Contbg. author: Group Insurance Handbook, 1965. Served with AUS, 1946-47. Recipient Alumni award Menomonie High Sch., 1945. Fellow Soc. Actuaries (v.p. 1973-75, pres. 1977-78); mem. Wis. Actuarial Club (pres. 1964-65), Am. Acad. Actuaries (sec. 1971-73, pres. 1981-82), Beta Gamma Sigma, Phi Kappa Phi, Chi Phi. Roman Catholic. Clubs: Watertown Golf; Cherokee Golf (Madison); Wyndemere Country (Naples, Fla.). Home: 2550 Windward Way Naples FL 33940 Office: 2900 14th St N Naples FL 33940

HAM, GEORGE ELDON, soil microbiologist, educator; b. Ft. Dodge, Iowa, May 22, 1939; s. Eldon Henry and Thelma (Cran) H.; m. Alice Susan Bormann, Jan. 11, 1964; children—Philip, David, Steven. B.S., Iowa State U., 1961, M.S., 1963, Ph.D., 1967. Asst. prof. dept soil sci. U. Minn., St. Paul, 1967-71, assoc. prof., 1971-77, prof., 1977-80; prof., head dept. agronomy Kans. State U., Manhattan, 1980—; dir. Kans. Crop Improvement Assn., Manhattan, 1980—, Kans. Fertilizer and Chem. Inst., Topeka, 1980—, Kans. Crops and Soils Industry Council, Manhattan, 1982—; cons. Internat. Atomic Energy Agy., Vienna, Austria, 1973-79. Assoc. editor Agronomy Jour., 1979-84. Contbr. articles to profl. jours. and biol. nitrogen fixation research. Asst. scoutmaster Indianhead council Boy Scouts Am., St. Paul, 1977-80; pres. North Star Little League, St. Paul, 1979-80. Served to sgt. U.S. Army, 1963-69. Fellow AAAS, Am. Soc. Agronomy, Soil Sci. Soc. Am.; mem. Crop Sci. Soc. Am. Sigma Xi, Gamma Sigma Delta, Phi Kappa Phi. Home: 2957 Nevada St Manhattan KS 66502

HAMADA, ROBERT S(EIJI), economist, educator; b. San Francisco, Aug. 17, 1937; s. Horace T. and Maki G. H.; m. Anne Marcus, June 16, 1962; children: Matthew, Janet. BE, Yale U., 1959; SM, MIT, 1961, PhD, 1969. Economist Sun Oil Co., Phila., 1961-63; instr. U. Chgo., 1966-68, asst. prof. fin., 1968-71, assoc. prof., 1971-77, prof., 1977—, dir. Ctr. for Research in Security Prices, 1980-85, dep. dean Grad. Sch. Bus. U. Chgo., 1985—; vis. prof. univs., including London Grad. Sch. Bus. Studies, 1973, 79-80, UCLA, 1971, U. Wash., Seattle, 1971-72, U. B.C., Vancouver, Can., 1976; bd. dirs. A.M. Castle & Co., Van Straaten Co., Tchrs. Ins. and Annuity Assn., The Northern Trust Co., Manville Corp.; cons. numerous fin. instns., banks, mfg., mgmt. cons., acctg. and law firms. Assoc. editor: Jour. Fin., Jour. Fin. and Quanitative Analysis, Midland Corp. Fin. Jour.; cons. editor: Scott, Foresman & Co. fin. series; contbr. numerous articles to profl. jours. Bd. dirs. numerous neighborhood non-profit orgns., including Hyde Park Neighborhood Club, Chgo., Harper Ct. Found., Chgo., Hyde Park Co-op., U. Chgo. Lab Schs. Recipient First Outstanding Tchr. award Grad. Sch. Bus., U. Chgo., 1970, McKinsey Teaching prize, 1981; named to 8 Outstanding Bus. Sch. Profs., Fortune Mag., 1982; Sloan Found. fellow, 1959-61, Ford Found. fellow, 1963-65, Standard Oil Found. fellow, 1965-66; MIT scholar, 1959-61, Yale scholar, 1955-59. Mem. Am. Fin. Assn. (bd. dirs. 1982-85), Econometric Soc., Nat. Bur. Econ. Research (bd. dirs.), Am. Econ. Assn., Tau Beta Pi. Office: Univ Chicago Grad Sch Bus Chicago IL 60637

HAMADOU, BARKAT GOURAD (BARKAT GOURAD HAMADOU), prime minister of Djibouti. Former mem. French Senate; former minister of health; prime minister Djibouti, 1978—, minister of ports, from 1978; mem. Reassemblement Populaire pour le Progrès. Address: Office of Prime Minister, Djibouti Republic of Djibouti *

HAMADY, THEODORE MICHAEL, marketing company executive; b. Flint, Mich., Aug. 11, 1937; s. Robert Michael and Millie (Salha) H.; B.A., U. Mich., Ann Arbor, 1960; B.B.A., U. Mich., Flint, 1975; M.B.A., George Washington U., 1978; m. Saniya Al-Faqih, July 30, 1960; children—Michael Geoffrey, Peter Winston, Linda Claire. Vice-pres. Hamady Bros., Inc., Flint, 1964-68, chmn., 1969-74; v.p., dir. Boles World Trade Corp., Washington, 1974-79, exec. v.p., dir., 1979-84; pres. T.M. Hamady, Inc., 1984—. 1st v.p. Flint Inst. Music, 1973-74; bd. dirs. Leadership Flint, 1973-75; trustee Valley Sch., 1973-75. Mem. Am. Mgmt. Assn., Am. Mktg. Assn., Clubs: City (Washington). Lodges: Rotary, Masons. Home: 5802 Manchester Pl Washington DC 20010 Office: 655 15th St NW Washington DC 20005

HAMAI, JAMES YUTAKA, business executive; b. Los Angeles, Oct. 14, 1926; s. Seizo and May (Sata) H.; B.S., U. So. Calif., 1952, M.S., 1955; postgrad. bus. mgmt. program industry exec., UCLA, 1963-64; m. Dorothy K. Fukuda, Sept. 10, 1954; 1 child, Wendy A. Lectr. chem. engring. dept. U. So. Calif., Los Angeles, 1963-64; process engr., sr. process engr. Fluor Corp., Los Angeles, 1954-64; sr. project mgr. central research dept. Monsanto Co., St. Louis, 1964-67, mgr. research, devel. and engring. graphic systems dept., 1967-68, mgr. comml. devel. New Enterprise div., 1968-69; exec. v.p., dir. Concrete Cutting Industries, Inc., Los Angeles, 1969-72; pres., dir. Concrete Cutting Internat., Inc., Los Angeles, 1972-78, chmn. bd., 1978—; cons. Fluor Corp., Los Angeles, 1970-72; dir. Nippon Con-Tec Co. Ltd., Tokyo, Intech Systems Co., Ltd., Tokyo, Cutting Industries Co., Ltd., Tokyo, Techno Trading Co., Ltd., Tokyo; internat. bus. cons. Served with AUS, 1946-48. Mem. Am. Inst. Chem. Engrs., Am. Mgmt. Assn., Tau Beta Pi, Phi Lambda Upsilon. Club: Rotary (gov. dist. 1982-83). Home: 6600 Via La Paloma Rancho Palos Verdes CA 90274 Office: 20963 Lamberton Ave Long Beach CA 90810

HAMAJIMA, BIN, English educator; b. Anjo, Aichi, Japan, Mar. 24, 1937; s. Kurazo and Chiyo (Inagaki) H.; B.A., Meiji Gakuin U., 1960, M.A., 1967; m. Chieko Miyazaki, Nov. 3, 1966; children—Shinri, Nozomu, Kaori. Dir. edn. East West Cultural Inst., Chiba, 1961-68; head English dept. Shikoku Christian Jr. Coll., Kagawa, 1976-77; head English lit. dept. Shikoku Christian Coll., 1977-83. Fellow Internat. Biog. Assn.; mem. Soc. English Lang. Teaching in Shikoku (dir. 1975—), Japan Assn. Coll. English Tchrs., English Lit. Soc. Japan, English Linguistic Soc. Japan, Phonetic Soc. Japan, Japan-Brit. Soc., Japan Asian Friendship Assn., The Gideons Internat., Kagawa-Nishi Camp (capt.), Ch. Music Assn. (adv. com. 1986—). Author introduction to Variorum edit. English Bible, 1974. Home: 132-1 Shimoyoshida Zentsuji, 765 Kagawa Japan Office: 2-1 3-chome Bunkyo Zentsuji, 765 Kagawa Japan

HAMALAINEN, RAIMO PERTTI, mathematics educator; b. Helsinki, Finland, July 7, 1948; s. Reino Olavi and Rauha Mirjami (Nieminen) H.; m. Soili Anneli Forsstrom, Aug. 31, 1979; children: Joonas, Sampsa. Diploma in engring., Helsinki U. Tech., 1972, licentiate tech., 1976, D of Tech., 1977. Jr. research fellow Acad. Finland, Helsinki, 1976-79, sr. research fellow, 1979; assoc. prof. applied math. U. Kuopio, 1979; prof. Vaasa Sch. Econs., 1979-81; prof. Helsinki U. Tech., Espoo, 1981—, dir. Systems Analysis Lab., 1984—; vis. Fulbright prof. UCLA, 1985-86; mem. State Research Council for Tech., Helsinki, 1980-82; chmn. Sci. Coop. between Acad. Finland and Internat. Inst. for Mgmt. Sci., 1979—. Contbr. articles to profl. jours. Fulbright research grantee, 1980, Acad. Finland sr. research grantee, 1985-86; CNRS-France fellow, 1984. Fellow Finnish Acad. Tech. Scis.; mem. Internat. Fedn. Automatic Control (math. control com.), Internat. Fedn. Info. Processing. Office: Helsinki U Tech, Systems Analysis Lab, 02150 Espoo Finland

HAMANA, MASAMICHI, mathematician, educator; b. Soma, Fukushima, Japan, Dec. 11, 1950; s. Toshio and Chika (Fukushima) H. MS, Tohoku U., Sendai City, Japan, 1975; DSc, Kyushu U., Fukuoka City, Japan, 1982. Instr. faculty edn. Toyama (Japan) U., 1978-83, asst. prof., 1983—. Mem. Math. Soc. Japan, Am. Math. Soc. Office: Toyama U Faculty Edn, Gofuku 3190, 930 Toyama City Japan

HAMANN, HANS-JÜRGEN, business executive; b. Berlin, Nov. 26, 1914; s. Albrecht and Marie (Hansen) H.; m. Walli Langner. With Schering AG, Berlin, 1933—; domestic and fgn. sales mgr. Schering AG, Buenos Aires and Bogota, Columbia, 1956; bd. dirs. Schering AG, 1958-78, then chmn. supervising bd.; Columbian hon. cons., West Berlin, 1963-78; vice chmn. supervising bd. Zoologischer Garten Berlin Aktiengesellschaft, Berlin; mem. supervising bd. Bergmann Elektrizitäts-Werke AG, Berlin, Deutsche Ges. für wirtschaftl Zusammenarbeit mbH, Cologne. Decorated Grand Fed. Cross of Merit, 1981; named Commdr. Order of San Carlos. Mem. Ibero-Amerika Verein e.V. (bd. dirs.), Stifter Verband für die Dt. Wissenschaft (bd. trustees). Home: Schunemannweg 8, D-1000 Berlin Federal Republic of Germany *

HAMAR, RUDOLF, business executive; b. Tartu, Estonia, Jan. 27, 1925; s. Rudolf and Marta (Ainson) H.; came to U.S., 1955, naturalized, 1960; grad. Am. Inst. of Banking, 1959; m. Ingrid Swars, July 1, 1950; children—Vaike R., Anja K. Bank clk. 1st Nat. City Bank, N.Y.C., 1955-59; loan officer Broad & Wall Corp., N.Y.C., 1960-61; stockbroker Gude, Winmill, Prescott, Merrill, Turben & Co., N.Y.C., 1962-74; pres. Wm. Sander Co., N.Y.C., and R.H.Curt & Co., N.J. 1974—; gen. ptnr. Wm. Sander Realty Assocs., 1982—. Lutheran. Clubs: Sibelius Lodge, various Estonian organizations. Editor, collaborator in philatelic literature. Office: 1432 Queen Anne Rd Teaneck NJ 07666

HAMBLEN, JOHN WESLEY, computer scientist, genealogist; b. Story, Ind., Sept. 25, 1924; s. James William and Mary Etta (Morrison) H.; m. Brenda F. Harrod, Mar. 1, 1947 (div. 1979); 1 son, James; m. Marianne Muhlbauer, Aug. 7, 1987. A.B., Ind. U., 1947; M.S., Purdue U., 1952; Ph.D., 1955. Tchr. math and sci. Kingsbury (Ind.) High Sch., 1946-48, Bluffton (Ind.) High Sch., 1948-51; asst. prof. math. Okla. State U., Stillwater, 1955-57; cons. in statis. methods for research staff Agrl. Expt. Sta., 1955-56, asso. prof. math., 1957-58; dir. Computing Center, 1957-58; asso. prof. stats., dir. Computing Center, U. Ky., Lexington, 1958-61; prof. math and technology Southern Ill. U., Carbondale, 1961-65; dir. Data Processing and Computing Center, 1961-65; project dir. computer scis. So. Regional Edn. Bd., Atlanta, 1965-72; prof. U. Mo., Rolla, 1972-87; prof. emeritus U. Mo., 1987—, chmn. dept. computer sci., 1972-81; mem. tech. adv. com. Creative Application of Tech. to Edn., Tex. A. and M. U., 1966-68; mem. tech. adv. panel Western Interstate Commn. for Higher Edn., 1969-70; vis. scientist Ctr. for Applied Math. Nat. Bur. Standards, 1981-83; program chmn. World Conf. Computers in Edn., 1985, mem. program com., 1990; cons. FTC, 1978-80, NSF, 1975-76; assoc. program dir. NSF, 1985-86, Nat. Bur. of Standards, 1986-88. Editor: Ednl. Data Processing Newsletter, 1964-65; assoc. editor: Jour. Ednl. Data Processing, 1965-67; editor: Jour. Assn. Ednl. Data Systems, 1967-68; assoc. editor, 1968-87; mem. editorial bd. Jour. Computer Sci. Edn., 1987—; computing editor T.H.E. Jour., 1980—; contbr. articles to profl. jours. Purdue Research Found. fellow, 1954-55; NSF grantee, 1966-81; recipient Disting. award Nat. Ednl. Computing Conf., 1988. Fellow AAAS; mem. Assn. Computing Machinery (sec. 1972-76, chmn. curriculum com. computer sci. 1976-80, gen. chmn. 1981 Computer Scis. Conf. 1979-81, co-chmn. 1987, chmn. Disting. Ser. Award com. 1980-81), IEEE Computer Soc., Assn. Ednl. Data Systems (chmn. conv. adv. com. 1977-80, pres. 1968-69, sec. 1976-77, dir. 1965-70, 76-79), Am. Fedn. Info. Processing Socs. (dir. 1981-86, chmn. edn. com. 1971-72, 79-84, edn. award 1985), Soc. Indsl. and Applied Math., Nat. Geneal. Soc., New Eng. Hist. Geneal. Soc., Sigma Xi, Pi Mu Epsilon, Theta Chi, Upsilon Pi Epsilon, Alpha Chi Sigma. Club: Rotary. Lodge: Order Golden Shillelagh. Address: 18305 Amber Meadows Ct Gaithersburg MD 20879

HAMBLING, MAGGI, artist; b. Sudbury, England, Oct. 23, 1945; d. Harry Leonard and Marjorie Rose (Harris) H. Diploma, Camberwell Sch. Art, London, 1967; diploma in fine arts, Slade Sch. Fine Art, London, 1969. artist in residence Nat. Gallery, London, 1980-81. One-woman shows include: London Exhibition, 1973, 77, Nat. Gallery, 1981, Nat. Portrait Gallery, 1983, Serpentine Gallery, 1987, Richard DeMarco Gallery, Edinburgh, 1988, Arnolfini, Bristol, Eng., 1988; pub. collections include: Arts Council, Birmingham City Art Gallery, Brit. Council, Brit. Mus., Clare Coll, Cambridge, Chelmsford and Essex Mus., Contemporary Art Soc., Ea. Arts Collection, European Parliament Collection, Gulbenkian Found., Haddo House, Aberdeen, Imperial War Mus., Minories Corchester, Morley Coll. London, Nat. Gallery, Nat. Portrait Gallery, Petworth House, Preston Art Gallery, Rugby Mus., Royal Army Med. Coll., Southampton Art Gallery, St. Mary's Ch., Hadleigh Suffolk, Tate Gallery, Unilever House, Whitworth Art Gallery, Harris Art Gallery, Preston, Scottish Nat. Gallery of Modern Art, Edinburgh, St. Mary's, Paddington, Strawberry Hill Coll. Address: 1 Broadhinton Rd, London SW4, England

HAMBURG, CHARLES BRUCE, lawyer; b. Bklyn., June 30, 1939; s. Albert Hamburg and Goldie (Blume) H.; m. Stephanie Barbara Steingesser, June 23, 1962; children—Jeanne M., Louise E. B.Ch. Engring., Poly. Inst. Bklyn., 1960; J.D., George Washington U., 1964. Bar: N.Y. 1964. Patent examiner U.S. Patent Office, 1960-63; patent atty. Celanese Corp. Am., N.Y.C., 1963-65; patent atty. Burns, Lobato & Zelnick, N.Y.C., 1965-67; patent atty. Nolte & Nolte, N.Y.C., 1967-75; prin. C. Bruce Hamburg, N.Y.C., 1976-79; ptnr. Jordan & Hamburg, N.Y.C., 1979—. Recipient Superior Service award (2) U.S. Patent Office, 1963, 63. Mem. ABA, Am. Patent Law Assn., N.Y. Patent Law Assn., Internat. Assn. Protection Intellectual Property, Queens Bar Assn., Bklyn. Bar Assn. Club: Masons. Author: Patent Fraud and Inequitable Conduct, 1972, 78; Patent Law Handbook, 1983-84, 84-85, 85-86; monthly columnist Patent and Trademark Rev., 1976-85, Patents and Licensing, Japan, 1986—. Office: 122 E 42d St New York NY 10168

HAMBURGER, CLARA, editor, musicologist; b. Budapest, Sept. 29, 1934; d. Istvan and Georgette (Weiller) H.; m. Ivan Kertesz, July 23, 1957; 1 child, Martha. Diploma in musicology, Ferenc Liszt Music. Acad., Budapest, 1961, dr., 1981; postgrad. in mus. scis., Hungarian Acad. Scis., 1981. Librarian Hungarian Acad. Scis., Budapest, 1959-61; librarian music dept. Nat. Szechenyi Library, Budapest, 1961-66; editor music books Gondolat, Budapest, 1966—. Author: Liszt, 1966, 2d enlarged edit., 1980 (transl. into German and English), Liszt-kalauz, 1986; contbr. articles to profl. jours. Mem. Assn. Hungarian Musicians. Home: Deres u 12, H-1124 Budapest Hungary Office: Gondolat, Brody S u 16, H-1088 Budapest Hungary

HAMBURGER, HENRI, Slavic languages educator; b. Nijkerk, The Netherlands, Feb. 28, 1930. MA, Leiden State U., 1960; PhD, State U. Groningen, The Netherlands, 1981. Lectr. Slavic dept. State U. Groningen, 1965-70, sr. lectr. Slavic dept., 1970-85, assoc. prof. Slavic dept., 1985—. Author: The Function of the Predicate in the Fables of Krylov, 1981. Home: Boteringesingel 9, 9712 XR Groningen The Netherlands Office: State U Groningen, Reitdiepskade 4, 9718 BP Groningen The Netherlands

HAMBURGER, PHILIP (PAUL), writer; b. Wheeling, W. Va., July 2, 1914; s. Harry and Janet (Kraft) H.; m. Edith Iglauer, Dec. 24, 1942 (div. 1966); children: Jay Philip, Richard Shaw; m. Anna Walling Matson, Oct. 27, 1968. B.A., Johns Hopkins U., 1935; M.S., Grad. Sch. Journalism, Columbia, 1938. Mem. staff New Yorker mag., 1939—, writer Profiles, Talk of the Town, Reporter-at-Large articles, Notes for a Gazetteer, Letters from Fgn. Places, Casuals,, music critic, 1948-49, TV critic, 1949-55; on leave from New Yorker as writer, Office of Facts and Figures and O.W.I., 1941-43; Frank R. Kent Meml. lectr., Johns Hopkins U., 1986; past mem. adv. bd. George Foster Peabody Radio and Television Awards; bd. dirs. Authors League Fund.; Cooper Union. non-fiction workshop Ind. U. Writers' Conf., 1969, 75. Author (for govt.): Divide and Conquer, The Unconquered People, Tale of a City; Author: The Oblong Blur and Other Odysseys, 1949, J.P. Marquand, Esquire, 1952, Mayor Watching and Other Pleasures, 1958, Our Man Stanley, 1963, An American Notebook, 1965, Curious World: A New Yorker At Large, 1987. Recipient 50th Anniversary Honors medal Grad. Sch. Journalism, Columbia, 1963. Mem. Authors League Am., Authors Guild (quondam council), P.E.N. Clubs: Nat. Press (Washington); Century Assn. (N.Y.C.), Coffee House (N.Y.C.). Home: 151 E 80th St New York NY 10021 also: Wellfleet MA 02667 Office: care The New Yorker 25 W 43d St New York NY 10036

HAMDOON, NIZAR SAID, Iraqi ambassador; b. Baghdad, Iraq, May 18, 1944; s. Said Hamdoon and Sadia (Jassim) Mohammed; m. Sahar Hamid, July 21, 1972; children: Ula, Sama. B.Sc. in Architecture and Town Planning, Baghdad U., 1967. Politician Ba'Ath Party Offices, Baghdad, 1970-81; under sec. Ministry of Info. and Culture, Baghdad, 1981-83; ambassador to U.S., Washington, 1983-87, under-sec. Ministry Fgn. Affairs, Baghdad, 1987—. Served to lt. Iraqi Army, 1968-70. Avocation: art. Office: Embassy of Iraq 1801 P St NW Washington DC 20036

HAMEED, A. C. S., Sri Lanka government official; b. Apr. 10, 1929. Mem. Sri Lanka Parliment, Harispattuwa, 1960—; minister fgn. affairs Sri Lanka Govt., Colombo, 1977—. Office: Ministry Fgn Affairs, Colombo Sri Lanka *

HAMEEDND DIN, SALEEM, physician; b. Bannu, Pakistan, Feb. 18, 1955; s. Saeed and Jehandara Hameed-Ud Din; m. Nabila Siddiqui, Oct. 6, 1983; children: Umair, Hasaan. B in Medicine, Khyger Med. Coll., Peshawar, Pakistan, 1978; cert., Nat. Inst. Cardiovascular Diseases, Karachi, Pakistan, 1984. Med. officer Bannu (Pakistan) Sugarmills, 1983-84; gen. practice medicine Umair Clinic, Karachi, 1984—. Author numerous poems. V.p. Khyber Med. Coll. Student's Union, Peshawar, 1975-76. Served to capt. Pakistani Army Med. Corps, 1978-83. Recipient Cert. Appreciation, Embassay of Iraq. Islam. Other: 236 D Meelad Park, Bannu Pakistan Office: Umair Clinic, Sultanabad MT Khan Rd, Karachi Pakistan

HAMEISTER, LAVON LOUETTA, farm manager, social worker; b. Blairstown, Iowa, Nov. 27, 1922; d. George Frederick and Bertha (Anderson) Hameister; B.A., U. Iowa, 1944; postgrad. N.Y. Sch. Social Work, Columbia, 1945-46, U. Minn. Sch. Social Work, summer 1952; M.A., U. Chgo., 1959. Child welfare practitioner Fayette County Dept. Social Welfare, West Union, Iowa, 1946-56; dist. cons. services in child welfare and pub. assistance Iowa Dept. Social Welfare, Des Moines, 1956-58, dist. field rep., 1959-64, regional supr., 1964-65, supr., specialist supervision, adminstrn. Bur. Staff Devel., 1965-66, chief Bur. Staff Devel., 1966-68; chief div. staff devel. and tng. Office Dep. Commr., Iowa Dept. Social Services, 1968-72, asst. dir. Office Staff Devel., 1972-79, coordinator continuing edn., 1979-86; now co-mgr. Hameister Farm, Blairstown, Iowa. Active in drive to remodel, enlarge Oelwein (Iowa) Mercy Hosp., 1952. Mem. Bus. and Profl. Women's Club (chpt. sec. 1950-52), Am. Assn. U. Women, Nat. Assn. Social Workers (chpt. sec.-elect 1958-59), Am. Pub. Welfare Assn., Iowa Welfare Assn., Acad. Cert. Social Workers. Lutheran. Home: 1800 Grand Ave West Des Moines IA 50265

HAMER, JEFFREY MICHAEL, consultant and software company executive; b. Los Angeles, Mar. 11, 1949; s. William Chisdes and Barbara Renee (Wager) H.; BArch. with honors, U. So. Calif., 1971; MArch. with honors, UCLA, 1973; m. Deborah Sue Schwartz, Nov. 29, 1975; children: Stephen Andrew, Jonathan Alan. Architect/systems analyst Skidmore, Owings & Merrill, Chgo., 1973-74; dir. R&D Group, Cannell-Heumann & Assocs./ Albert C. Martin & Assocs., Los Angeles, 1974-78; pres., chief exec. officer The Computer-Aided Design Group, Marina del Rey, Calif., 1978—; mem. faculty Grad. Sch. Architecture and Urban Planning, UCLA, 1974—. Bd. dirs. Speech Pathology Found., 1983—, Internat. Facility Mgmt. Assn., 1987—. Mem. Assn. Computing Machinery, AIA, Assn. for Computers in Design (bd. dirs. 1983-86). Author: Facility Management Systems, 1987, Van Nostrand Reinhold; contbr. numerous articles to tech. publs. Office: 4215 Glencoe Ave Marina del Rey CA 90292

HAMFF, LEONARD HARVEY, physician; b. West Blocton, Ala., Nov. 22, 1913; s. Christian F. and Meri (Harvey) H.; A.B., Emory U., 1932, M.D., 1938; m. Elizabeth Anne Babington, Dec. 22, 1936; children—Mary Anne McClemens, Catherine Willis. Intern, Univ. Hosp., Ann Arbor, Mich., 1938-39, asst. resident, 1939-40, resident in internal medicine, 1940-41, instr., 1941-42; practice medicine specializing in internal medicine, Atlanta, from 1942; dir. diabetic service Grady Meml. Hosp., 1945-68; clin. prof. medicine Emory U. Sch. Medicine, 1965. Fellow ACP, Am. Coll. Chest Physicians; mem. Ga. Diabetes Assn., Diabetes Assn. Atlanta, Am. Heart Assn., So. Med. Assn., Fulton County Med. Soc., Atlanta Clin. Soc., Am. Diabetes Assn. Methodist. Clubs: Capital City, Piedmont Driving. Office: 478 Peachtree St NE Atlanta GA 30308

HAMILTON, ANN STANLEY, marketing executive; b. Phila., Mar. 25, 1960; d. Russell and Helen Marcia (Brown) H. B.A. in Psychology, Temple U., 1982. Customer service rep. Continental Bank, Phila., 1977-82; mgr. pub. div. Hay Assocs., Phila., 1983-84; pres. Hamilton Assocs. mktg. cons., Phila., 1985—. Rep. Senatorial Inner Circle, Washington, 1986. Mem. Alliance Française de Philadelphie, Christian Endeavor, Nat. Assn. Female Execs. Republican. Presbyterian. Avocations: travel; reading; foreign cultures and languages.

HAMILTON, BRANDON LESLIE, systems engineer, mathematician; b. Chgo., Nov. 26, 1947; s. Eugene Alexander Hamilton and Gloria Lee (Gladney) Hamilton Atkins; m. Linda Jean Gholson, Dec. 22, 1967 (div. 1971); 1 son, Brandon Hamilton. A.A., Kennedy-King Coll., 1975; B.S., U. Ill.-Chgo., 1979. Engring. cons. Stone & Webster Engring., Boston, 1972-74; tutor/instr. Inroads Inc., Chgo., 1975-78; physics lab. asst. Ill. Inst. Tech., Chgo., 1977; strategic analyst Analytic Services Inc., Arlington, Va., 1979-80; nuclear-computer engr. So. Calif. Edison, San Clemente, 1980-84; project engr. Aerojet ElectroSystems Co., Azusa, Calif., 1984—; bus. cons., 1986-87; ind. mktg. rep. U.S. Sprint, 1986-87. Vol. Los Angeles Youth Network, Project Homeless Youth; active Youth Motivation Task Force, 1987—. Contbr. articles to profl. publs. Bus. cons. Jr. Achievement, 1986-87. Served with USN, 1968-72. Mem. Math. Assn. Am., D.C. Student Math. Soc. (editor newsletter 1979-80), Soc. Indsl. and Applied Mathematicians, Am. Soc. Computer Simulation, Los Angeles Council of Black Profl. Engrs. Home: 410 S Hobart Apt 312 Los Angeles CA 90020 Office: Aerojet ElectroSystems Co 1100 W Hollyvale St Azusa CA 91702

HAMILTON, SIR (CHARLES) DENIS, newspaper editor-in-chief; b. Dec. 6, 1918; s. Charles and Helena Hamilton; m. Olive Wanless, 1939; 4

sons. Grad., Middlesbrough High Sch., Eng.; DLitt (hon.), U. Southampton, 1975, City U., 1977; DCL (hon.), U. Newcastle-upon-Tyne, 1979. With editorial staff Evening Gazette, Middlesbrough, 1937-38; with editorial staff Evening Chronicle, Newcastle, Eng., 1938-39, adirotial asst. to Viscount Kemsley, 1946-50; editorial dir. Kemsley (now Thompson) Newspapers, 1950-67, editor Sunday Times, 1961-67; editor-in-chief Times Newspapers Ltd., 1967-81, chief exec., 1967-70, chmn., 1971-80; chmn. Times Newspapers Holdings, 1980-81; chmn. Reuters Ltd., 1979-85; chmn. Brit. Com. Internat. Press Inst., 1972-78, pres., 1978-83; pres. Commonwealth Press Union, 1981-83; chmn. Brit. Mus. Pubs. Ltd.; past bd. dirs. Std. Chartered Bank, Evening Gazette Ltd., Newcastle Chronicle and Journal Ltd., Internat. Thomson Orgn. plc. Contbr. articles to jours. Bd. dirs. Brit. Library, 1975-87, IBA, 1981-84; trustee Brit. Mus., 1969—, Henry Moore Found., 1980—, Visnews, 1981-85; gov. Brit. Inst. Florence, 1974—; v.p., mem. exec. com. Great Britain-China Ctr., 1986—; joint sponsor exhibitions Tutankhamun, 1972, China, 1973, U.S. Bicentennial, Nat. Maritime Mus., 1976, Gold of Eldorado, 1978, Vikings, 1980. Served with Brit. Army, World War II. Decorated Knight, 1976, Order of Merit Grande Officiale (Italy), 1976. mem. Commonwealth Press Union (pres. 1981-83), Newspaper Publishers' Assn. (mem. council 1950-80, press council 1959-81), Nat. Council for the Tng. of Journalists (chmn. 1957), BOTB. Clubs: Garrick, Royal Automobile, Grillions. Office: 78A Ashley Gardens, Thirleby Rd, London SW1P 1HG, England *

HAMILTON, ELIZABETH VERNER, publisher; b. Charleston, S.C., Nov. 24, 1908; d. Ebenezer Pettigrew and Elizabeth Quale (O'Neill) Verner; A.B., Coll. Charleston, 1930; postgrad. U. N.C. Sch. Library Sci., U. Philippines Sch. Library Sci.; m. John A. Hamilton, Aug. 29, 1931; children—Andrew, David, Ward, Pettigrew. Pres. Tradd St. Press, Charleston, from 1966; now ret. Bd. dirs. Havana Symphony, 1949-50, Home Health Nursing Charleston. Named to Charleston Hall of Fame, Fedn. Women's Clubs, 1979. Mem. Charleston Jr. League, Ladies Benevolent Soc. Democrat. Episcopalian. Author: (poetry) Tall Houses, 1968, Evgard, 1988; (fiction) When Walls Are High, 1972; Storm Center, 1983. Home and Office: 38 Tradd St Charleston SC 29401

HAMILTON, ELWIN LOMAX, lawyer; b. Lubbock, Tex. Mar. 18, 1934; s. Elwin Louis and Mildred (Hunt) H.; children: Lauren, Karen. A.S., Arlington State Coll., 1954; B.A., North Tex. State Coll., 1956; LL.B., U. Tex., Austin, 1959. Bar: Tex. 1959, U.S. Dist. Ct. (no. dist.) Tex. 1961, U.S. Dist. Ct. (we. dist.) Tex. 1972, U.S. Ct. Claims 1972, U.S. Ct. Appeals (5th cir.) 1961. Atty. Humble Oil Co., Corpus Christi, Tex., 1959-60; mem. firm Morton & Brownfield, Tex., 1960-66; mcpl. judge, Morton, Tex., 1960-61; county dist. atty., Terry County, 1963-66; asst. exec. dir. State Bar Tex., 1966-69; asst. atty. gen., State of Tex., 1969-73; atty. Tex. Securities Bd., Austin, 1973-74; asst. gen. counsel to Gov. of Tex., Austin, 1974-82; ptnr. Senterfitt & Childress, Hamilton & Shook, San Saba, Tex., 1982-86, law practice, R. Mayo Davidson, San Saba Legal Services, 1987—; instr. Legal Asst. Studies, Austin Community Coll. Presbyterian. Home: 1206 W Sunset St San Saba TX 76877 Office: Box 547 San Saba TX 76877

HAMILTON, H(ORACE) GEORGE, museum and planetarium administrator; b. Bordentown, N.J., May 15, 1925; s. Alexander and Gladys (Schwoebel) H.; m. Carleen Straus, Oct. 26, 1974; children by previous marriage: Roger John, Marianne Margaret, Alexander George; adopted children: Tia Moneé, Brock Jason, Brandon George, Faun Elyse. B.S., Trenton State Coll., 1948, M.A., 1960; grad. student, Temple U., 1963-65. Tchr. physics, math., chemistry William MacFarland High Sch., Bordentown, 1948-60; physics tchr. Cherry Hill High Sch., N.J., 1960-62; asst. prof. physics Trenton State Coll., 1962-68; asst. dir. edn. and ops. Fels Planetarium of Franklin Inst., Phila., 1968-69; assoc. dir. Fels Planetarium of Franklin Inst., 1969-71, dir., 1972—; assoc. dir. Franklin Inst. Sci. Mus., 1980-82, dep. dir., 1982-85, v.p., 1986—. Served with U.S. Maritime Services, 1945-46. Recipient Shell Merit fellowship, 1962. Mem. Am. Astron. Soc., Astron. Soc. Pacific, Assn. Sci. and Tech. Ctrs., Internat. Soc. Planetarium Educators, Middle Atlantic Planetarium Soc., N.J. Astron. Soc., Sci. Research Soc. Am., AAAS, Am. Assn. Museums. Episcopalian. Club: Mason. Home: 1003 Kingston Dr Cherry Hill NJ 08034 Office: Franklin Inst Sci Mus and Planetarium 20th St and the Parkway Philadelphia PA 19103

HAMILTON, HOWARD LAVERNE, zoology educator; b. Lone Tree, Iowa, July 20, 1916; s. Harry Stephen and Gertrude Ruth (Shibley) H.; m. Alison Phillips, Dec. 22, 1945 (dec. 1972); children: Christina Helen, Phillips Howard, Martha Jayne; m. Elizabeth Burnley Bentley, June 18, 1975; children: Elizabeth Marshall, Catherine Randolph. B.A. with highest distinction, State U. Iowa, 1937, M.S., 1938; postgrad., U. Rochester, 1938-40; Ph.D., Johns Hopkins U., 1941. Asst. prof. to prof. zoology Iowa State U., 1946-62, acting head, 1960-61, chmn. dept. zoology and entomology, 1961-62; prof. biology U. Va., 1962-82, prof. emeritus, 1982—. Author: Lillie's Development of the Chick, 1952; cons. editor, McGraw-Hill Ency. Sci. and Tech., 1962-78; mng. editor: The Am. Zoologist, 1965-70; Author: (with Viktor Hamburger) Citation Classic: A Series of Normal Stages in the Development of the Chick, 1951. Served to capt. MC, AUS, 1941-45, to col. USAR, 1945-69. Mem. Am. Soc. Zoologists, Am. Soc. Naturalists, Soc. Developmental Biology, Internat. Inst. Devel. Biology, Am. Inst. Biol. Sci., Nat. Soc. Ams. of Royal Descent (pres. gen. 1974-80, now hon. life pres. gen.), SAR (nat. exec. com., pres. Va. Soc. 1979-80, registrar gen. 1980-82, pres. gen. 1982-83, Minuteman award and Gold Good Citizenship medal), Order of Three Crusades 1096-1192 (historian gen. 1976-83, 1st v.p. gen. 1983—), Assn. Preservation Va. Antiquities, Va. Hist. Soc., English Speaking Union, Order of Crown of Charlemagne in U.S.A. (pres. gen. 1982-85, hon. life pres. gen. 1985—), Order Ams. of Armorial Ancestry (councillor), Phi Beta Kappa, Sigma Xi, Phi Kappa Phi, Phi Sigma. Club: Farmington Country. Home: Jumping Branch Farm Rt 5 Box 401 Charlottesville VA 22901 Office: U Va Dept Biology Gilmer Hall Charlottesville VA 22901

HAMILTON, JAMES, lawyer, author; b. Chester, S.C., Dec. 4, 1938; s. Herman Prioleau and Edith Muriel (Gilchrist) H.; m. Siri Kristina Hagglund, July 14, 1979; children—William James, Erik Gilchrist, Kathryn Heyward. A.B., Davidson Coll., 1960; LL.B., Yale U., 1963; LL.M., U. London, 1966. Bar: N.C. 1963, D.C. 1967, U.S. Ct. Appeals (9th cir.) 1977, U.S. Supreme Ct. 1978, U.S. Temporary Emergency Ct. Appeals, 1980, U.S. Ct. Claims 1981, U.S. Ct. Appeals (4th cir.) 1983, U.S. Ct. Appeals (11th cir.) 1985, U.S. Ct. Appeals (2d cir.) 1987. Assoc. firm Covington & Burling, Washington, 1966-73; asst. chief counsel Senate Select Com. on Presdl. Campaign Activities (Watergate Commn.), U.S. Senate, Washington, 1973-74; mem. firm Ginsburg, Feldman & Bress, Washington, 1975-87; ptnr. Olwine, Connelly, Chase, O'Donnell and Weyher, Washington, 1987—; chief counsel Spl. Joint Com. on Referendum Rev., Congress of Micronesia, 1978; spl. counsel human resources subcom. for briefing book investigation Ho. of Reps., Washington, 1983-84; dep. chief counsel Alaska Senate impeachment inquiry, 1985; mem. Jud. Conf. of U.S. Ct. Appeals for Fed. Cir., 1986, for D.C. Cir., 1978, 80; mem. GAO investigative task force, 1985. Author: The Power to Probe: A Study of Congressional Investigations, 1975; contbr., editor: Congressional Investigations: Legal Issues and Practical Approaches, 1987; contbr. articles to profl. jours., articles to major newspapers. Issue coordinator, polit. organizer, advance man Presidential Campaign of Edmund S. Muskie, Washington, 1970-72. Served as 1st lt. U.S. Army, 1963-65. Decorated Army Commendation medal; Ford Found. travel and study grantee, 1974-75. Mem. ABA (individual rights subcom., litigation subcom.) D.C. Bar (com. on legal ethics 1983—, vice chmn. 1987-88), Am. Arbitration Assn. (panel of arbiters), Council for Ct. Excellence (dir.). Democrat. Presbyterian. Club: St Albans Tennis (Washington). Home: 3321 Rowland Pl NW Washington DC 20008 Office: Olwine Connelly Chase O'Donnell & Weyher 1850 K St NW Suite 890 Washington DC 20006

HAMILTON, LEONARD DERWENT, physician, molecular biologist; b. Manchester, Eng., May 7, 1921; came to U.S., 1949, naturalized, 1964; s. Jacob and Sara (Sandelson) H.; m. Ann Twynam Blake, July 20, 1945; children—Jane Derwent, Stephen David, Robin Michael. B.A., Balliol Coll., Oxford U., Eng., 1943, B.M., 1945, M.A., 1946, D.M., 1951; M.A., Trinity Coll., Cambridge U., Eng., 1948, Ph.D., 1952. Diplomate Am. Bd. Pathology. USPHS research fellow U. Utah, 1949-50; mem. staff Sloan-Kettering Inst., N.Y.C., 1950-79, head isotope studies sect., 1957-64, assoc. scientist, 1965-79; mem. staff Meml. Hosp., N.Y.C., 1950-65; mem. faculty Sloan-Kettering div. Grad. Sch. Med. Scis. Cornell U., 1956-64; sr. scientist, head div. microbiology Med. Research Ctr. Brookhaven Nat. Lab., Upton, N.Y., 1964-76; head biomed. and environ. assessment div. Office. Environ. Policy Analysis, 1973—; attending physician Hosp. Med. Research Ctr., 1964-85; dir. WHO Collaborating Ctr. for Assessment of Health and Environ. Effects of Energy Systems, 1983—, WHO focal point on health and environ. effects of energy systems and mem. expert adv. panel on environ. hazards, 1983—; prof. medicine Health Sci. Ctr., SUNY, Stony Brook, 1968—; cons. HEW, Ctr. Disease Control, Nat. Inst. Occupational Safety and Health, epidemiology study of Portsmouth Naval Shipyard, 1978—; vis. fellow St. Catherine's Coll., Oxford U., 1972-73; mem. internat. panel experts on fossil fuel UN Environment Programme, 1978, panel on nuclear energy, 1978-79, panel on renewable sources, 1980; mem. various coms. Nat. Acad. Sci.-NRC, Washington, 1975-80; mem. N.Y.C. Mayor's Tech. Adv. Com. on Radiation, 1963-77, N.Y.C. Commr. of Health Tech. Adv. Com. on Radiation, 1978—. Editor: Gerrard Winstanley, Selections from His Works, 1944; Physical Factors and Modification of Radiation Injury, 1964; The Health and Environmental Effects of Electricity Generation—a Preliminary Report, 1974. Am. Cancer Soc. scholar, 1953-58; Commonwealth Fund grantee, 1955-62. Mem. Am. Assn. Cancer Research, Am. Soc. Clin. Investigation, Am. Assn. Pathologists, Soc. for Risk Analysis, Harvey Soc., Internat. Soc. Environ. Epidemiology. Club: Cosmos (Washington). Home: Childs Ln Old Field Setauket NY 11733 Office: Brookhaven Nat Lab Upton NY 11973

HAMILTON, PERRIN C., lawyer, state official; b. Phila., Oct. 15, 1921; m. Bette J. Shadle; children—Deborah, Maribeth, Perrin Jr. Student Dickinson Coll., 1943, LLB, 1948. Bar: D.C., PA. 1949. Spl. counsel U.S. Senate, 1953; ptnr. Hepburn Willcox Hamilton & Putnam, Phila.; commr. Crime Victims Bd., Delaware River Port Authority; dir. Maxim Healthcare Corp. Bd. dirs. Valley Forge Mil. Acad., Freedoms Found.; bd. advisers Dickinson Coll., Salvation Army; State of Pa. Cabinet Official. Served to lt. USNR, World War II. Decorated Order of Merit, Italy; Freedoms Found. award, 1970. Mem. ABA, Pa. Bar Assn., Phila. Lawyers Club (past pres.), Episcopalian. Clubs: Union League (pres.), Merion Cricket. Home: 210 Glenn Rd Ardmore PA 19003 Office: Hepburn Willcox Hamilton & Putnam 1100 One Penn Center Plaza Philadelphia PA 19103

HAMILTON, RICHARD DANIEL, neurosurgeon; b. Itasca, Tex., June 14, 1928; s. Richard McCrary and Maude Geneva (Fowler) H.; m. Edith Nelle Day, Dec. 31, 1948; children: Melanie Hamilton DeAngelis, Daniel, Melissa Hamilton Driscoll, David, John, Anna-Maria Hamilton Daulton, Kristianna Hamilton Plunkett. M.D., Baylor U., 1950. Diplomate: Am. Bd. Neurol. Surgery. Intern Riverside Gen. Hosp., Arlington, Calif., 1950-51; resident in psychiatry and neurology Letterman Army Hosp., San Francisco, 1951-54; resident in gen. surgery Valley Forge Army Hosp., 1955-56; resident in neurosurgery Walter Reed Army Hosp., Washington, 1956-60; asst. chief neurosurgery Walter Reed Army Hosp., 1964-66; cons. neurosurgery U.S. Army, Korea, 1960-61, Europe, 1961-64; chief dept. neuroanatomy Walter Reed Army Inst. of Research, 1964-65; cons. neurosurgery U.S. Army, Vietnam; also comdg. officer U.S. Army (74th Med. bn. and 68th Med. group), Vietnam, 1966-67; asst. chief neurosurgery Letterman Army Hosp., 1967-70, ret., 1970; private practice medicine specializing in neurosurgery San Jose, Calif., 1970-80, Marysville, Calif., 1980—; mem. staff Santa Clara Valley Med. Center, San Jose, 1970—, chief div. neurosurgery, 1971-80, pres. staff, 1978-80; mem. staffs Rideout Hosp., Fremont Hosp.; prof. clin surgery Stanford Sch. Medicine, 1973-80; clin. asso. prof. San Jose State U., 1976-80. Bd. dirs. Calif. Regional Spinal Cord Injury Care System. Commd. 1st lt. M.C. U.S. Army, 1950; advanced through grades to col. 1967. Decorated Legion of Merit with oak leaf cluster. Fellow A.C.S.; mem. AMA, Calif. Med. Assn., Am. Assn. Neurol. Surgeons, Nat. Paraplegia Found., San Francisco Neurol. Soc., Am. Spinal Injury Assn. (dir.), Internat. Paraplegia Soc., Calif-Assn. Neurol. Surgeons (dir.), Yuba-Sutter-Colusa Med. Soc., Beta Beta Beta, Alpha Epsilon Delta. Republican. Presbyterian. Home: 519 Camino Cortez Yuba City CA 95991 Office: 414 G St Marysville CA 95901

HAMILTON, ROBERT APPLEBY, JR., insurance company executive; b. Boston, Feb. 20, 1940; s. Robert A. and Alice Margaret (Dowdall) H.; student Miami U. (Ohio), 1958-62; m. Ellen Kuhlen, Aug. 13, 1966; children—Jennifer, Robert Appleby, III, Elizabeth. With Travelers Ins. Co., Hartford, Conn., Portland, Maine and Phila., 1962-65; with New Eng. Mut. Life Ins. Co., various locations, 1965—, regional pension rep., Boston, 1968-71, regional mgr., Chgo., 1972-83, sr. pension cons., 1983—. Mem. Republican Town Com., Wenham, Mass., 1970-72, Milton Twp., Ill., 1973-75; mem. Wenham Water Commn., 1970-72. C.L.U.; chartered fin. cons. Mem. Midwest Pension Conf., Am. Soc. Pension Actuaries (assoc.), Am. Soc. C.L.U.s, Am. Assn. Fin. Planners, Profit Sharing Council Am., Chgo. Council Fgn. Relations, Alpha Epsilon Rho. Republican. Home: 2 S 110 Hamilton Ct Wheaton IL 60187 Office: 10 S Riverside Plaza Suite 1710 Chicago IL 60606

HAMILTON, TED ALLEN, biostatistician; researcher; b. Niles, Mich., May 13, 1955; s. Harold Keith and Betty Lou (Knapp) H.; m. Jane Ann Long, Aug. 28, 1981. B.S. in Fisheries and Wildlife, Mich. State U., 1977; M.S. in Natural Resources, U. Mich., 1980, M.S. in Biostats., 1982. Fisheries biologist, statistician Ecol. Analysts, Inc., Northbrook, Ill., 1980-81; biostatistician, epidemiologist Ford Motor Co., Dearborn, Mich., 1982-83; coordinator, biostatistician dept. dermatology U. Mich. Hosp., Ann Arbor, 1983—. Mem. Am. Statis. Assn. Avocations: hiking, bird-watching, cooking, horticulture. Home: 7929 Jennings Rd Whitmore Lake MI 48189 Office: Univ Mich Hosp Dermatology Clin Research 1713 Taubman Ctr Ann Arbor MI 48109

HAMILTON, THOMAS EARLE, retired educator, honorary society executive; b. Savannah, Ga., June 10, 1905; s. Homer Francis and Catherine Clitheral (Langford) Hartwell; m. Juanita Vivian Adams, Aug. 2, 1933; children—Earle Hartwell, Charles Lee, Helen Catherine (Mrs. Paul A. Anthony). A.B., So. Methodist U., 1927, A.M., 1929; Ph.D. in Spanish and Classics (advanced fellow), U. Tex., 1940. Tchr. Garland (Tex.) High Sch., 1927-29, Highland Park High Sch., Dallas, 1929-37; instr. classical and Romance langs. Tex. Tech U., Lubbock, 1940-43; asst. prof. Tex. Tech U., 1943-45, asso. prof., 1945-55, prof., 1955-71, prof. emeritus, 1971—; vis. prof. Spanish Tex. Woman's U., Saltillo, Mexico, 1945; vis. prof. Spanish and classics Austin Coll., 1962-63; cons. Houston Pub. Sch. System, 1953, Angelo State U., 1967-68; co-author grad. reading exams. in Spanish Ednl. Testing Service, Princeton, N.J., 1966-67. Editor: South Central Modern Lang. Assn. Bull, 1953-56; asso. editor, 1965-67; editor: El cardenal de Belen (Lope de Vega), 1948; Contbr. articles to profl. jours., various anthologies. Recipient award Sigma Delta Chi, 1965. Mem. MLA (life emeritus), South Central MLA (hon. life), Tex. Fgn. Lang. Assn. (hon. life, co-founder, pres. 1958, founder, editor Bull. 1953-57), Am. Assn. Tchrs. Spanish and Portuguese (emeritus, chmn. nominating com. 1956), Assn. Coll. Honor Socs. (chmn. com. on standards and definitions, spl. award for meritorious service), Nat. Rifle Assn. (endowment), Eta Sigma Phi, Sigma Delta Pi (nat. v.p. 1950-59, nat. pres. 1959-68, 72-78, nat. hon. pres. 1979—), Sigma Delta Mu (founder, nat. pres. 1979—). Methodist. Lodge: Masons. Home: 209 King Dr Columbus TX 78934

HAMILTON-KEMP, THOMAS ROGERS, organic chemist; b. Lebanon, Ky., May 13, 1942; s. Thomas Rogers and Catherine Rose (Hamilton) K.; m. Lois Ann Groce, Sept. 13, 1980. AA, St. Catharine Coll., 1962; BA, U. Ky., 1964, PhD in Chemistry, 1970. Mem. faculty U. Ky., Lexington, 1970—, asst. prof. plant chemistry, 1970-75, assoc. prof., 1975-85, prof., 1985—. Contbr. articles to profl. jours. Mem. Am. Chem. Soc., Am. Soc. Hort. Sci., AAAS, AAUP, SAR, Sigma Xi. Home: 868 Laurel Hill Rd Lexington KY 40504 Office: Univ Ky Agrl Sci Ctr North Dept Horticulture N-318 Lexington KY 40546

HAMLIN, WINBORNE LEIGH, church worker, educator; b. Norfolk, Va., Aug. 12, 1937; d. Southgate and Maud (Winborne) Leigh; m. Jefferson Davis Hamlin, June 27, 1959; children—Jeff, John, Frank. BA magna cum laude, Sweet Briar Coll., 1958; MAT, John Hopkins U., 1959. English tchr. pub. schs., Balt., 1958-59, Lancaster, S.C., 1959-60, 62-63; ch. sch. tchr. Christ Episcopal Ch., Lancaster, 1961-63, St. Michael and All Angels Ch., Dallas, 1974-80; adult Bible study tchr., 1981-84. Leader troop Girl Scouts U.S., Lancaster, 1961-63; tchr., dir. art program High Mus. Art, Atlanta, 1965-67; bd. dirs. St. Michael Sch., 1973-75; pres. University Park Sch. PTA, Dallas, 1978-79; bd. dirs. McCulloch Middle Sch. PTA, 1981-82, Highland Park High Sch. PTA, 1981-83, 85-86; bd. dirs. Jr. League of Dallas, 1972-74, 76-78, exec. com., 1977-78; sec. Citizens' Study Com. to Recommend Best Form of Govt. for City of University Park, Tex., 1976-77; rec. sec. Dallas Mus. of Fine Arts League, 1979-80; pres. Women of St. Michael and All Angels, 1980-81, vestry mem., 1982-85, sec. Ministry with Aging, Inc., 1982-85, pres. parish council, 1983-85; del. Triennial Conv. of Episcopal Ch., 1982, 85, 88; bd. Exec. Council Diocese of Dallas, 1988—; bd. dirs. Province VII, Episc. Ch., 1984-87; leader Camp Fire Girls, Dallas, 1970-73. Mem. Sweet Briar Coll. Alumnae Assn. (exec. bd. 1977-83, 85—), Phi Beta Kappa.

HAMLYN, DAVID WALTER, philosopher, educator; b. Plymouth, Devon, Eng., Oct. 1, 1924; s. Hugh Parker and Gertrude Isabel (Lintern) H.; m. Eileen Carlyle Litt Hamlyn, July 2, 1949; children: Nicholas John, Catherine Jane. Student, Plymouth Coll., 1935-42; BA, U. Oxford, Eng., 1948, 50, MA, 1949. Jr. research fellow Corpus Christi Coll., U. Oxford, 1950-53; lectr. philosophy Jesus Coll., U. Oxford, 1953-54; lectr. Birkbeck Coll., U. London, 1954-63, reader, 1963-64, prof. philosopher, 1964-88, prof. emeritus, 1988—, vice master, 1983-88; also mem. senate U. London, 1981-87; chmn. bd. govs., Heythrop Coll., U. London, 1971-78, mem. bd. govs., 1984—. Author: The Psychology of Perception, 1957, Sensation and Perception, 1961, Aristotle's De Anima II and III, 1968, The Theory of Knowledge, 1970, Experience and the Growth of Understanding, 1978, Schopenhauer, 1980, Perception, Learning and the Self, 1983, Metaphysics, 1984, A History of Western Philosophy, 1987; editor: Mind jour., 1972-84; cons. editor: Jour. Med. Ethics, 1981—; contbr. over 65 articles to profl. jours. Gov. City Lit., London, 1982-86, vice chmn., 1985-86; gov. Cen. London Adult Edn. Inst., 1987—. Served as lt. Brit. Army, 1943-46. Hon. fellow Heythrop Coll., 1978. Mem. Mind Assn., Aristotelian Soc. (pres. 1977-78), Royal Inst. Philosophy (mem. council 1968—, mem. exec. com. 1971—). Home: 7 Burland Rd, Brentwood, Essex CM15 9BH, England Office: U London Birkbeck Coll, Malet St, London WC1 7HX, England

HAMM, VERNON LOUIS, JR., management and financial consultant; b. East St. Louis, Ill., Mar. 14, 1951; s. Vernon Louis and Colleen Ann Hamm; B.S., Murray (Ky.) State U., 1973; M.B.A., St. Louis U., 1975; postgrad. Stanford U., 1975. Jr. exec. corp. accounts Brown Group, Inc., St. Louis, 1973-75; group supr. APC Skills Co., Palm Beach, Fla., 1975-77; account mgr. Inst. Mgmt. Resources, Los Angeles, 1977-78; dir. mgmt. devel. Naus & Newlyn, Inc., Paoli, Pa., 1978-82; pres. Mgmt. Alternatives Ltd., 1982—; mgmt., fin. and energy cons., 1975—; bd. dirs. Ryan's Family Steakhouses, Inc.; dir. Psychosystems Mgmt. Corp., N.Y.C. Mem. Am. Soc. for Tng. and Devel., Am. Prodn. and Inventory Control Soc., Murray State U. Alumni Assn. Contbr. articles to profl. publs.

HAMMAR, HANS BIRGER, international civil servant; b. Stockholm, Aug. 23, 1936; s. Hans B. and Eva (Thorné) H.; m. Elly Lijnse, Jan. 4, 1970; children: Eva, Peter. M. Law, Lund U., Sweden, 1962. Judge, Dist. Ct., Sweden, 1963-64; mng. dir. Brodin A.B., Sweden, 1965-66; internat. lawyer Swedish Employers Confedn., 1966-69; chief employers relations ILO, Geneva, 1969-80, dir. employers activities, 1980—; cons. developing countries to strengthen employer's orgns. Editor various pubs. Home: 1 Chemin A Caillat, 1217 Meyrin Switzerland Office: ILO, CH 1211 Geneva Switzerland

HAMMER, ARMAND, petroleum company executive, art patron; b. N.Y.C., May 21, 1898; s. Julius and Rose (Robinson) H.; m. Olga von Root, Mar. 14, 1927; m. Angela Zevely, Dec. 19, 1943; m. Frances Barrett, Jan. 26, 1956; 1 child. BS, Columbia U., 1919, MD, 1921, LLD, 1978; LLD, Pepperdine U., 1978, Southeastern U., Washington, 1978, U. Aix-en-Provence, 1981; D in Pub. Service, Salem (W.Va.) Coll., 1979; HHD, U. Colo., Boulder, 1979; DSc (hon.), U. S.C., 1983; PhD (hon.), Tel Aviv U., 1986. Pres. Allied Am. Corp., N.Y.C., 1923-25, A. Hammer Pencil Co., N.Y.C., London and Moscow, 1925-30, Hammer Galleries, Inc., N.Y.C., 1930—, J. W. Dant Distilling Co., N.Y.C. and Dant, Ky., 1943-54; pres., chmn. bd. Mut. Broadcasting System, N.Y.C., 1957-58; chmn. bd., chief exec. officer Occidental Petroleum Corp., Los Angeles, 1957—; chmn. M. Knoedler & Co., Inc., N.Y.C., 1972—, Knoedler-Modarco S.A., N.Y.C., 1977—; dir. Nat. State Bank, Perth Amboy, N.J., 1949-56, City Nat. Bank, Beverly Hills, Calif., 1962-71, Can. Occidental Petroleum Ltd., Calgary, Alta.; dir. Raffinerie Belge de Petroles, Antwerp, Belgium, 1968-79, Cities Service Co., Tulsa; hon. dir. Fla. Nat. Bank of Jacksonville, 1966-72; mem. Nat. Petroleum Council, 1968—, Com. on Arctic Oil and Gas Resources, 1980—. Author: The Quest of the Romanoff Treasure, 1936, autobiography (with Neil Lyndon) Hammer, 1987, (with Neil Lyndon) Hammer: Witness to History, 1987; subject of biography: The Remarkable Life of Dr. Armand Hammer (Robert Considine), 1975; Brit. edit. Larger than Life, 1976; The World of Armand Hammer (John Bryson), 1985. Pres. N.J. Aberdeen Angus Assn., 1948-49. Bd. govs. Monmouth County Orgn. Social Service, Red Bank, N.J., 1949-61, Monmouth Meml. Hosp., Long Branch, N.J., 1946-58, Eleanor Roosevelt Cancer Found., N.Y.C., 1960—, Ford's Theatre Soc., 1970—, UN Assn. U.S.A., 1976—; bd. dirs., exec. com. Internat. Council United World Colls., 1983—; mem. Royal Acad. Trust, Eng., 1980—; mem., fellow Met. Mus. Art, 1985; trustee U. North Africa Assn., 1968-71, Los Angeles County Mus. Art, 1968—, UCLA Found., 1973-76, Nat. Symphony, 1977—, United for Calif., 1977—, Capitol Children's Mus., 1978—; chmn. wine and spirits div. Vis. Nurse Service Greater N.Y., 1946, Am. Aid to France, 1947; mem. Citizens Food Com., 1946-47, Cardinal Spellman's Com. of Laity for Catholic Charities, 1946-48, Public Adv. Com. on U.S. Trade Policy, 1968-69, Am. Com. for Nat. Archives, 1974-76, Los Angeles County-U. So. Calif. Cancer Assos., 1975—, George C. Marshall Assos., James Smithson Soc. of Smithsonian Nat. Assos., 1977—, U. Okla. Assos., 1981—, Bus. Adv. Commn. for 1984 Olympics, 1981—, Los Angeles Olympic Citizens Adv. Commn., 1981—; hon. trustee Denver Art Mus., 1980—; mem. adv. bd. Inst. of Peace, 1950-54, Los Angeles Beautiful, Inc., 1969-75, Com. for a Greater Calif., 1969—, Fogg Art Mus. and Fine Arts Library, Cambridge, Mass., 1977—, The Friendship Force, 1977—, Am. Longevity Assn., Inc., 1980—, Center Strategic and Internat. Studies, Georgetown U., 1981—; mem. fine arts com. U.S. Dept. State, 1981—; chmn. Pres.'s Cancer Panel, 1981—; mem. exec. com. Econ. Devel. Bd. City of Los Angeles, 1968-73; trustee, chmn. exec. com. Salk Inst. Biol. Studies, San Diego, 1969—; bd. dirs. Los Angeles World Affairs Council, 1969—, Planned Parenthood World Population/Los Angeles, 1970—, U.S.-USSR Trade and Econ. Council, 1973—, Assos. Harvard Bus. Sch., 1975—, Calif. Roundtable, 1976—, Century City Cultural Commn., 1977—, Corcoran Gallery Art, Washington, 1978—, Keep Am. Beautiful, Inc., 1979—, Bus. Com. for Arts, N.Y.C., 1980—; bd. visitors Grad. Sch. Mgmt., UCLA, 1957—, UCLA Sch. Medicine Center for Health Scis., 1980—; exec. mem. Energy Research and Edn. Found., 1978—; charter mem. Nat. Visiting Council of Health Scis. Faculties, Columbia U., 1978—; mem. univ. bd. Pepperdine U., 1979—; mem. fellows for life New Orleans Mus. Art, 1980—; bd. dirs. Nat. Coordinating Ctr. forat. support council U.S. Com. for UNICEF, 1980—; founder mem. Pepperdine Assos., 1976—; pres. Found. of Internat. Inst. Human Rights, Geneva, 1977—; mem. exec. bd. dirs. UN Assn. Los Angeles; mem. Bd. Mcpl. Arts Commrs. Los Angeles, 1969-73; mem. budget and fin. com. of bd. trustees Los Angeles County Mus. Art, 1972-74; sponsor Internat. Inst. Human Rights Peace Conf., Oslo, 1978, Campobello Peace Park, 1979, Warsaw, 1980, Aix-en-Provence, France, 1981. Served with M.C. U.S. Army, 1918-19. Endowed Armand Hammer Center for Cancer Biology, Salk Inst., 1969; Armand Hammer prof. bus. and public policy UCLA, 1968; Frances and Armand Hammer wing Los Angeles County Mus. Art, 1969; Armand Hammer Animal Facility Salk Inst., 1976; Calif. Inst. Cancer Research UCLA, 1976; Ann. Armand Hammer Cancer Conf. and Fund Salk Inst., 1976; Harvard/Columbia Russian Study Fund, 1977; Julius and Armand Hammer Health Scis. Center Columbia U., 1977; Five-Yr. Funding Program UN Assn., 1978; Five-Yr. Funding Program Corcoran Gallery Art, 1979; Five-Yr. Funding Program Jacquemart-André Mus., Paris, 1979; Ann. Armand Hammer Award Luncheon Los Angeles, 1980; Los Angeles City Dept. Parks and Recreation, 1981, Armand Hammer Cancer Prize, 1982; Hammer-Rostropovich Cello Scholarship award U. So. Calif., 1982; Theatre du Gymnase, Marseille, France, 1983, Armand Hammer chair Leonardo Ctr., UCLA, 1985; Armand Hammer Ctr. for Advanced Studies in Nucelar Energy and Health, Los Angeles, 1986; recipient Humanitarian award Eleanor Roosevelt Cancer Found., 1962; city commendation Mayor of Los Angeles, 1968; decorated comdr. Order of Crown Belgium, 1962; comdr. Order of Andres Bellos Venezuela, 1975; Order of Aztec Eagle Mex., 1977; officer Legion of Honor France, 1978;

Order of Friendship Among Peoples USSR, 1978; Royal Order of Polar Star Sweden, 1979; officer Grand Order of Merit Italy, 1981; Knight Comdr.'s Cross Austria, 1982; comdr. Nat. Order French Legion Honor, 1983; named Hon. Citizen and Seal Bearer of City of Vinci, Italy, 1982; Disting. Honoree of Yr. Nat. Art Assn., 1978; Golden Plate award Am. Acad. Achievement, 1978; Aztec award Mexican-Am. Opportunity Fond., 1978; Appeal of Conscience award N.Y.C., 1978; Spirit of Life award Oil Industry Council of City of Hope, 1979; award Antique Monthly, 1980; Entrepreneur of Yr. award U. So. Calif., 1980; Maimonides award Los Angeles Jewish Community, 1980; Golden Achievement award Andrus Gerontology Center, U. So. Calif., 1981; Ambassador of Arts award State of Fla., 1981; recipient John Jay award Columbia Coll., 1981, Disting. Citizen award Greater N.Y. Councils Boy Scouts Am., 1982, James Ewing Soc. Layman's award, Soc. Surgical Oncology, 1983, Medaille d'Or Mayor of Marseille and French Minister of Interior, 1983, Golda Meir award Israeli Prime Minister, 1984, Hilal-i-Quaid-i-Azam award Pres. Pakistan, 1985, Jubilee Medal Ambassador Zhulev of Bulgaria, 1985, Golden Archigymnaseum Decoration Mayor Renzo Imbeni of Bologna, 1985, Humanitarian award LWV, 1986, Human Achievement award Op. Calif., 1986, Nat. Recognition award Pres. United States Mexico, 1987, 1987 Humanitarian award Internat. Physicians for Prevention of Nuclear War, Inc., 1987, Emma Lazarus Statue Liberty award Nat. Jewish Hist. Soc., 1987, Nat. Arts Medal, 1987, Eleanor Roosevelt Humanitarian award United Nations Assn. San Francisco, 1987, Norman Vincent Peale award Insts. for Religion and Health, 1987, Spl. award Gen. Hosp. Mexico City, Ministry Health, 1987. Mem. Los Angeles Petroleum Club, Royal Acad. Arts (London), hon. corr., Am. Petroleum Inst. (dir. 1975—), Navy League U.S. (Los Angeles council 1980—), Fifty-Yr. Club Am. Medicine, Royal Scottish Acad. (hon.), AMA (life), N.Y. County Med. Assn., Internat. Inst. Human Rights, Alpha Omega Alpha, Mu Sigma, Phi Sigma Delta. Office: Occidental Petroleum Corp 10889 Wilshire Blvd Suite 1500 Los Angeles CA 90024 *

HAMMER, SIGMUND IMMANUEL, retired geology and geophysics educator, consultant; b. Webster, S.D., Aug. 13, 1901; s. Ludvig Erikson and Laura Louise (Anderson) H.; m. Norma Lucille Johnson (dec. 1980); children—Sigmund Lewis, Mary Alice (dec.), John Phillip, Kirsten Norma Hammer Gardner, Paul Ludvig Norman, Laura Blanche Hammer Inglis (dec.), Douglas James, Ludvig Erikson; m. Doris E. Pullman Lomberg, 1985. Student Concordia Coll., 1919-21; B.A., St. Olaf Coll., 1924; Ph.D., U. Minn., 1929. Geophysicist, Gulf Oil Corp., Pitts., 1929-46, sect. head, 1946-67; lectr. U. Pitts., 1946-67, adj. mem. grad. faculty, 1963-67; prof. geology and geophysics, U. Wis., Madison, 1967-72, prof. emeritus, 1972—; cons. in exploration geophysics; exploration advisor United Nations Devel. Projects, Bolivia, 1972-75, Turkey, 1976-78; visiting prof. U. Mex., Mexico City, 1980, U. Minn., Duluth, 1981; mem. Appalachian Ultradeep Corehole Steering Com., 1987—. Contbr. articles to profl. jours. Organizing chmn. French Cultural Ctr. Western Pa., (1965-67; chmn. Norwegian classroom com. U. Pitts., 1962-66; pres. Nationality Council, U. Pitts., 1966-67; organizing pres. Am. Scandinavian Found., Pitts. chpt. 1964-66, Madison chpt. 1970-71. Mem. Am. Physical Soc., Soc. Exploration Geophysicists (hon.), (v.p. 1950-51, pres. 1951-52), Am. Geophysical Union (fellow), Am. Assn. Petroleum Geologists, N.Y. Acad. Scis., Appalachian Ultradeep Core Hole. Republican. Club: Cosmos (Washington). Avocations: Norwegian and American heritage and culture. Home: 110 S Henry St Apt 406 Madison WI 53703 Office: Univ Wisc Geol Sciences 1215 W Dayton St Weeks Hall Madison WI 53706

HAMMOND, DENISE WHITEHEAD, educator; b. Bklyn., Oct. 11, 1951; d. Jackson and Hazel A. (Hoffler) Whitehead. B.S. in Edn. with honors, Northeastern U., Boston, 1974; postgrad. Boston State Coll., 1978. Cert. secondary tchr.; cert. secondary/jr. high prin. Asst. to spl. needs dir. occupational edn. div. Mass. Dept. Edn., Boston, 1972-74; tchr. English, Brookline High Sch., Mass., 1974—, mem. exec. bd., 1976-78, mem. headmaster's adv. council, 1984—, mem. graduation requirements com., 1984—, faculty advisor Asian Culture club, 1987— ; speaker, panelist Boston Shakespeare Co., ednl. services, 1981. Ch. clk. Union Baptist Ch., Cambridge, Mass., 1980-83; mem. conv. reception com. NAACP, Boston, 1982; chmn. personnel com. Individuals Recovering Sound Thinking, Roxbury, 1980-81, 2d v.p., bd. dirs., 1981-83. Mem. Mass. Notary Pub., Kappa Delta Pi. Home: 96 Ruthven St Dorchester MA 02121 Office: Brookline High Sch 115 Greenough St Brookline MA 02146

HAMMOND, GEORGE PETER, historian; b. Hutchinson, Minn., Sept 19, 1896; s. Niels Peter Jensen and Christiane (Svendsen) H.; A.B. U. Calif., 1920; A.M., 1921, Ph.D., 1924, LL.D., 1966; LL.D., U. N.Mex., 1954; m. Carrie Nelson, Aug. 3, 1921; children: Frances Arlene, Helen Elizabeth, Charles Arnold, George Peter. Traveling fellow in Pacific Coast history of Native Sons of Golden West, in Spain, 1922-23; instr. in history, U. of N.D., 1923-25; asst. prof. history, U. Ariz., 1925-26, asso. prof., 1926-27; asst. prof. history, U. So. Calif., 1927-29, asso. prof., 1929-35; prof. history, head dept. and dean Grad. Sch., U. N.Mex., 1935-46; dean Upper Div., Coll. Arts and Scis., 1935-38; dir. Bancroft Library, prof. history, U. Calif. at Berkeley, 1946-65; vis. prof. U. Tex., 1939, U. So. Calif., 1941, U. N.C., 1944; Fulbright lectr. U. Madrid (Spain), 1965-67; U.S. del. 4th Assembly of Pan-Am. Inst. Geography and History, Caracas, 1946; editor The Historian, 1938-46; co-founder Quivira Soc., also editor publs., 1929—; state dir. for N.Mex., Hist. Records Survey, Works Progress Adminstrn., 1936-39. Recipient Serra award of Ams., 1964. Fellow Soc. Am. Archivists, Calif. State Hist. Soc.; mem. nat., state and local hist. assns., Phi Kappa Phi, Sigma Delta Pi, Phi Alpha Theta (nat. pres. 1936-38). Republican. Lutheran. Clubs: Faculty; Roxburghe (president 1951-53) (San Francisco). Author of books about Mexico and West U.S., 1927; latest being: The Larkin Papers-Personal, Business, and Official Correspondence of Thomas Oliver Larkin, Merchant and United States Consul in California Volumes, I-X, 1951-65; the Adventures of Alexander Barclay, Fur Trader, 1976; The Weber Era in Stockton History, 1982; translator and editor alone and with others several books, including: Oñate, Colonizer of New Mexico (with Agapito Rey), 1953. Editor of the Coronado Historical Series, 1940—; editor co. archives of several N.Mex. counties. Office: Bancroft Library U Calif Berkeley CA 94720

HAMMOND, HANNAH, nurse; b. Skibbereen, Ireland, Jan. 26, 1932; came to U.S., 1972, naturalized, 1980; d. Daniel William and Bridget Ellen O'Driscoll; R.N., midwife, Crumpsall Hosp. Sch. Nursing, Manchester, Eng., 1958; B.S. in Health Care Adminstrn., Iona Coll., New Rochelle, N.Y., 1982; m. Joseph Hammond, Apr. 27, 1974; stepchildren—Jodi, Barbara. Served as missionary, Kenya, 1958-71; charge nurse, instr., matron Kaplong Hosp., Kisii, Kenya, 1962-67; charge nurse, midwife Victoria Hosp., Kisumu, 1967-69; charge nurse, emergency nurse, night supr. hosp. Nairobi Hosp., 1969-71; charge nurse, pvt. duty nurse New Rochelle (N.Y.) Hosp., 1972-79; dir. nursing Bapt. Home for Aged, Bronx, N.Y., 1979—. Mem. N.Y. State Nurses Assn., Grad. Nurses of Westchester, Cath. Nurses Assn., Nat. Assn. Female Execs.

HAMMOND, JEROME JERALD, government program administrator, agricultural economist; b. Davenport, Wash., Mar. 16, 1942; s. Gerald Hammond and Mary Avis (Felton) Koch; m. Deanna Lindberg, Aug. 25, 1968 (div. 1980). A.A., Skagit Valley Coll., 1963; B.A. in Econs., Central Wash. U., 1968; Ph.D. in Agrl. Econs., Wash. State U., 1974. Economist, Econ. Research Service U.S. Dept. Agr., Washington, 1974-77, leader Asia programs Office Internat. Cooperation & Devel., 1977-80, dir. div. internat. conservation Soil Conservation Service, 1980—, tech. mem. Sci. and Tech. Exchange Negotiating Team, Sofia, Bulgaria, Bucharest, Romania, Budapest, Hungary, 1985; agy. rep. U.S. Agrl. Attache Conf., Manila, Philippines, 1980, mem. sci. and tech. exchange agrl. working group meetings, Paris and Bonn Germany, 1983; U.S. del. UN-FAO Conf., Arusha, Tanzania, 1978, New Delhi, India, 1980; profl. assoc. East-West Ctr., Honolulu, 1985; cert. candidate Sr. Exec. Service , U.S. Office Personnel Mgmt., 1988. Contbr. numerous articles and reports to profl. jours. Agy. coordinator Combined Fed. Campaign, Washington, 1979; div. rep. ARC, Washington, 1980-81; dep. chmn. Equal Employment Opportunity Com. Soil Conservation Service, Washington, 1985. Served to staff sgt. USAF, 1963-67. Recipient Certificate of Merit, U.S. Dept. Agr., 1975, 82; Combined Fed. Campaign-Honor award Sec. of Agr., 1979; Meritorious Service award Soil Conservation Service, 1984; award patriotism U.S. Savs. Bond program Sec. of Treasury, 1985, Internat. Honor award USDA Office Internat. Coop. and Devel., 1986. Mem. Intermountain Econ. Rev. (assoc. editor 1969-70), Am. Agrl. Econs. Assn., Western Agrl. Econs. Assn., Soil and Water Conservation Soc. (sec. Washington chpt. 1988), World Assn. Soil and Water Conservation (regional v.p. for N.Am. 1988). Presbyterian. Lodge: Am. Legion. Avocation: running; racquetball; stamp collecting. Home: 8413 Ft Hunt Rd Alexandria VA 22308 Office: USDA Soil Conservation Service PO Box 2890 Washington DC 20013

HAMMOND, MICHAEL THOMAS, instrument engineer; b. Letchworth, Hertfordshire, Eng., Oct. 8, 1943; s. Cyril Thomas and Gwen Alice (Burrows) H.; m. Pamela Ann Martin, Oct. 3, 1964; children—Julia Alice, Jacqueline Mary. Higher Nat. Cert. in Engring., Letchworth and Luton Colls. Tech., Eng., 1968. Design engr. Taylor Instrument Co., Rochester, N.Y., 1970-74; engring. mgr. Taylor Servomex, Ltd., Crowborough, Sussex, Eng., 1974-78; sales mgr. GEC Elliott, Ltd., London, 1978-80; mktg. mgr. Fisher Controls Co., Marshalltown, Iowa, 1980-82; gen. mgr. Fisher Controls Ltd., London, 1982-83; mng. dir. Fluid Data (U.K.) Ltd., Crayford, Kent, Eng., 1983—, also dir.; dir. Fluid Data, Inc., Merrick, N.Y., Hallikainen Instruments Ltd., London. Mem. Inst. Measurement and Control. Anglican. Avocations: cricket; golf. Office: Fluid Data (UK) Ltd, 20 Bourne Indsl Park, Crayford Kent DA1 4B2, England

HAMMOND INNES, RALPH, author; b. Horsham, Sussex, Eng., July 5, 1913; s. William Hammond and Dora Beatrice Innes; m. Dorothy Mary Lang, 1937. With Fin. News, 1934-40, R.A., 1940-46. Author: Wreckers Must Breathe, 1940; The Trojan Horse, 1940; Attack Alarm, 1941; Dead and Alive, 1946; The Lonely Skier, 1947; The Killer Mine, 1947; Maddon's Rock, 1948; The Blue Ice, 1948; The White South, 1949; The Angry Mountain, 1950; Air Bridge, 1951; Campbell's Kingdom, 1952; The Strange Land, 1954; The Mary Deare, 1956; The Land God Gave to Cain, 1958; Harvest of Journeys, 1960; The Doomed Oasis, 1960; Atlantic Fury, 1962; Scandinavia, 1963; The Strode Venturer, 1965; Sea and Islands, 1967; The Conquistadors, 1969; Levkas Man, 1971; Hammond Innes Introduces Australia, 1971; Golden Soak, 1973; North Star, 1974; The Big Footprints, 1977; The Last Voyage, 1978; Solomons Seal, 1980; The Black Tide, 1982; High Stand, 1985; Hammond Innes' East Anglia, 1986; Medusa, 1988; works translated into numerous langs.; author films: Snowbound; Hell Below Zero; Campbell's Kingdom; The Wreck of the Mary Deare; TV films: Golden Soak; Levkas Man.

HAMMOND-PARKER, STEPHEN, company executive; b. Wellington, N.Z., Oct. 5, 1944; came to Hong Kong, 1985; s. William Parker and Marion Hammond; m. Kristina Georgieff; children—Andre Stephen, Luisa Kristina. Assoc. dir. J.H. Minet Aviation div., London, 1976-78; mng. dir. Internat. Airline Passengers Assn., London, 1978-82, pres., Dallas, 1981-82; mng. dir. Assn. Bus. Travellers, Sydney, Australia, 1982—; mng. dir.Frequent Bus. Travellers Club, Hong Kong, 1986—; dir. So. Cross, London, 1983. Avocations: music; golf; squash. Home: 16A Terrell Ave, 2076 Sydney, New South Wales Australia

HAMMONDS, OLIVER WENDELL, lawyer; b. De Queen, Ark., Aug. 4, 1911; s. Oliver Overstreet and Mamie Levonia (Scott) H.; m. Ellen Hewes Floweree, May 22, 1941 (div. 1969); children—Oliver Edmund (dec.), Harry Hewes, Patricia, James Wilson, John Scott. B.A., Okla. U., 1932; LL.B., Harvard U., 1936. Bar: Okla. 1936, U.S. Supreme Ct. 1940, Tex. 1946. Atty., office gen. counsel U.S. Treasury Dept., Washington, 1936-37; spl. asst. to atty. gen. tax div. Dept. of Justice, Washington, 1937-42; ptnr. Ray & Hammonds, Dallas, 1946-60; sole practice, Dallas, 1960—; lectr. Oil and Gas Inst., Southwestern Legal Found., 1954-58, Tax Inst. NYU. Contbr. numerous legal articles to profl. jours.; developed financing for endowment Manley O. Hudson chair in Internat. Law, Harvard Law Sch., 1977. Served to maj. USAAF, 1942-45. Decorated Bronze Star; recipient personal letter of commendation Gen. Hap Arnold, comdg. gen. USAAF, 1945. Mem. Tex. Bar Assn., Dallas Bar Assn. (chmn. com. ethics 1959-60), Dallas Council World Affairs (bd. dirs. 1951-87), Phi Delta Phi. Episcopalian. Clubs: Brookhollow Golf (Dallas); Chevy Chase, Metropolitan (Washington). Office: 211 N Ervay Bldg Suite 309 Dallas TX 75201

HAMMONDS, TIMOTHY MERRILL, association executive, economist; b. Cortland, N.Y., June 5, 1944; s. Robert Merrill and Helen Marie (Conrad) H.; m. Karen Stein, June 17, 1966; 1 child, Lynn Vanessa. M.B.A., Cornell U., 1967, Ph.D., 1970. Assoc. prof. agrl. econs. Oreg. State U., Corvallis, 1970-75; sr. v.p. Food Mktg. Inst., Washington, 1975—. Mem. editorial bd. Am. Jour. Agrl. Econs., 1978-80; mem. Nat. Acad. Sci. Bd. on Agrl., 1988—. Editor: Agribus. Jour., 1985—. Author: Producers and Lenders Guide to Futures Trading, 1974. Contbr. articles to profl. jours. Named Outstanding Tchr., Sch. Agr., Oreg. State U., 1972-73. Mem. Am. Agrl. Econs. Assn., Phi Kappa Phi. Republican. Methodist. Home: 1574 Forest Villa Ln McLean VA 22101 Office: Food Mktg Inst 1750 K St NW Washington DC 20006

HAMMOND-STROUD, DEREK, baritone; b. London, Jan. 10, 1929; s. Herbert William and Ethel Louise (Elliott) Stroud; student Trinity Coll. Music, London, 1937-38. Roles include: Alberich in The Ring, Beckmesser in Der Meistersinger, Papageno in The Magic Flute, Tonio in Il Paliacci, Faninal in Der Rosenkavalier, Bartolo in Barber of Seville, also Rigoletto and Falstaff; appearances include: Glyndebourne Festival Opera, 1959-60, Sadlers Wells Opera Co., 1961-71, Royal Opera Covent Garden, 1971—, Met. Opera, N.Y.C., 1977—, Netherlands Opera, 1977-80, Teatro Colón, Buenos Aires, 1981; appeared in concerts Europe, U.S.A.; prof. singing Royal Acad. Music, London, 1974—; recs. for E.M.I., RCA, Phonogram, Célèbre Records. Decorated Order Brit. Empire. Hon. fellow Trinity Coll. Music, 1982. Mem. Inc. Soc. Musicians, Royal Acad. Music (hon.). Home: 18 Sutton Rd, Muswell Hill, London N10 1HE, England

HAMNER, HOMER HOWELL, economist, educator; b. Lamont, Okla., Oct. 22, 1915; s. Homer Hill and Myrtle Susan (Edwards) H.; m. Winnie Elvyn Heafner, May 8, 1943 (dec. Aug. 23, 1946); 1 dau., Jean Lee (Mrs. Richard L. Nicholson); m. Marjorie Lucille Dittus, Nov. 24, 1947; 1 dau., Elaine (Mrs. Alan M. Yard). A.A., Glendale Coll., 1936; A.B., U. So. Calif.; A.B. (Gen. Achievement scholarship 1936-37), 1938, J.D., 1941, A.M., 1947, Ph.D., 1949. Fellow and teaching asst., dept. econs. U. So. Calif., 1945-49; prof. and chmn. dept. econs. Baylor U., 1949-55; editor research com. Baylor Bus. Studies, 1949-55, lectr. summer workshop, 1954; prof., chmn. dept. bus. adminstrn. and cons. U. Puget Sound, Tacoma, Wash., 1955-58; dir. sch. bus. adminstr. and econs. U. Puget Sound, 1959-63, Edward L. Blaine chair econ. history, 1963—; also occasional lectr. Roman Forums, Ltd., Los Angeles, 1936-40; lectr. Am. Inst. Banking, 1949-50; lectr. Southwest Wholesale Credit Assn., 1949, James Connally AFB, 1950; cons. State of Wash. tax adv. council, 1957-58, State of Wash. Expenditures Adv. Council, 1960. Author: Population Change in Metropolitan Waco, 1950; reviewer, contbr. to Jour. of Finance. Served with U.S. Army, 1941-44. Fellow Found. Econ. Edn., Chgo., Inst. on Freedom, Claremont Men's Coll.; mem. AAUP, Am. Econ. Assn., Southwest Social Sci. Assn. (Tex. chmn. membership com.), Nat. Tax Assn., Am. Finance Assn., Am. Acad. Polit. and Soc. Sci., Order of Artus, Waco McLennan County Bar Assn. (hon.), Phi Beta Kappa, Phi Kappa Phi, Omicron Delta Gamma, Delta Theta Phi, Phi Rho Pi (degree highest achievement 1936). Methodist. Home: 4404 N 44th Tacoma WA 98407

HAMON, PHILIPPE, French literature educator; b. Uzel, France, Oct. 5, 1940; s. Albert and Madeleine (Huet) H.; m. Francoise Raymon, June 15, 1967; children: Etienne, Perrine. Licence, Sorbonne, U. Paris, 1963, Maitrise, 1963, Agrégation, 1966, Dr. Etat, 1981. Asst. U. Haute-Bretagne, Rennes, France, 1968-83, prof. French lit., 1983-88; prof. U. Paris, 1988—. Author: Introduction à L'Analyse du Descriptif, 1981, Le Personnel du Roman, 1983, Texte et Idéologie, 1984; editor spl. numbers Poétique; contbr. numerous articles on theory of lit. to French and U.S. jours. Decorated Palmes Academiques (France). Office: U Paris III, 13 rue Santeuil, 75005 Paris France

HAMPE MARTINEZ, TEODORO, historian, educator; b. Lima, Peru, Mar. 20, 1960; s. Teodoro and Clotilde (Martinez) Hampe Bitter. Licenciate in History and Edn., U. Catolica, Lima, 1983; D in History, U. Complutense, Madrid, 1986. Teaching asst. U. Catolica, Lima, 1982-84, prof. history, 1986—; researcher Banco Cen. de Reserva, Lima, 1986—; coordinator Seminario Internacional de Historia Latinoamericana, Lima, 1987. Author: Obra Politica de La Gasca en España y America, 1986, Historia del Peru Colonial en el Siglo XVI, 1987, Cultura, Sociedad y Otros Temas de la Historia Peruana, 1988. Instituto de Coop. Iberoamericana fellow, 1984, Banco de España fellow, 1987. Mem. Soc. Geografica de Lima, Inst. Peruano de Cultura Hispanica, Inst. Peruano de Investigaciones Genealogicas. Home: Sinchi Roca 2638, Lima 14, Peru Office: U Catolica Dept Humanidades, Apartado 1761, Lima 100, Peru

HAMPSHIRE, STUART, ceramic science educator; b. Wakefield, Eng., July 27, 1950; s. Harold and Margaret (Thornberry) H.; m. Alyson Elizabeth Wakeling, Aug. 7, 1971 (div. Feb. 1984); children: Louise Elizabeth, Helene Kathryn; m. Margaret Mary Hurley, July 23, 1984. BScTech. with honors, U. Sheffield, 1972; PhD, U. Newcastle upon Tyne, 1980. Tech. research officer Dyson Group Research and Devel. Labs., Sheffield, 1972-74; jr. research assoc. crystallography lab. U. Newcastle upon Tyne, 1975-77, postdoctoral research assoc., 1978-80; lectr., sr. lectr., asst. dean for research Nat. Inst. Higher Edn., Limerick, Ireland., 1981—; mem. adv. bd. Silicates Indsls. jour., 1985—; mem. sci. bd. Nat. Council for Ednl. awards, Dublin, 1985—; mem. postdoctoral fellowship com. Dublin Dept. Edn., 1986—. Author: The Sintering of Nitrogen Ceramics, 1986; editor: (with J. Bolton) Failure in Engineering Material, 1985, Non-Oxide Technical and Engineering Ceramics, 1986; mem. editorial bd. Materials Chemistry and Physics jour., 1985—; contbr. articles to sci. jours. Recipient award for excellence in research Nat. Inst. Higher Edn., 1987; French Govt. fellow Limoges, 1987; various research grants for engring. ceramics. Mem. Inst. Ceramics, Am. Ceramic Soc., Instn. Engrs. Ireland (companion, regional com. 1986-88), Irish Durability and Fracture Com. (sec. 1986-87), Choral Union (hon. treas. 1984-87). Office: Nat Inst Higher Edn, Plassey Tech Park, Limerick Ireland

HAMPSON, HAROLD ANTHONY, equity holding company executive; b. Montreal, Que., Can., Aug. 18, 1930; s. Harold Ralph and Geraldine Mary (Smith) H. B.A., McGill U., 1950; M.A. in Econs., Cambridge U., 1952. Mem. staff Royal Commn. of Can's Econ. Prospects, Ottawa, Ont., 1955-57; sec. Royal Commn. on Banking and Fin., Toronto, Ont., 1961-64; dir. research and underwriting Burns Bros & Denton, Toronto, 1957-61; v.p. Power Corp. Can. Ltd., Toronto, 1964-68; pres. Capital Mgmt. Ltd., Montreal, 1968-71; chief exec. officer Can. Devel. Corp., Toronto, 1972-87; dir., mgmt. and venture capital investor Connaught Bioscis., Inc.; dir. Trimac Ltd., Telemedia, Inc., C.D. Howe Inst., Domecrete Ltd. Bd. govs. York U.; chmn. exec. com., mem. policy analysis com. C.D. Howe Inst. Office: 8 King St E Suite 300, Toronto, ON Canada M5C 1B5

HAMPSON, NORMAN, historian, educator; b. Leyland, Lancashire, Eng., Apr. 8, 1922; s. Frank and Elizabeth Jane (Fazackerly) H.; m. Jacqueline Gardin, Apr. 22, 1948; children: Francoise Jane, Michele Elizabeth. MA, Oxford (Eng.) U., 1947; PhD, U. Paris, 1955. From lectr. to sr. lectr. U. Manchester, Eng., 1948-67; prof. U. Newcastle Upon Tyne, Eng., 1967-74, U. York, Eng., 1974—. Author books on the Enlightenment and the French Revolution. Served to lt. Brit. Navy, 1941-45. Fellow Brit. Acad.; mem. Royal Hist. Soc. Home: 305 Hull Rd, York YO1 3LB, England Office: U York, Heslington, York Y01 5DD, England

HAMPSON-JONES, HUW WYN, data processing executive; b. Maesteg, Wales, Nov. 30, 1954; s. Victor and Edna Margit (Briffet) H-J.; m. Frances Elsie Jacob, Aug. 30, 1956. BA in Polit. Theory and Govt. with honors, U. Wales, Swansea, 1976. Grad. mgmt trainee human resource dept. Unilever Plc., Port Sunlight, Eng., 1976-78; divisional human resource officer Philips Plc., Colchester, Eng., 1978-81; sr. divisional human resource office Europe div. Harris Corp., Slough, Eng., 1981-82, mgr. sales devel., 1982-85; sr. account mgr. McDonnell Douglas Info Systems Corp., London, 1985-87; with bus. devel. world div. McDonnell Douglas Info Systems Corp., Hemel Hempstead, Eng., 1987—. Mem. Inner Temple (student), Internat. Commn. Jurists (assoc.), Transactions of the Hon. Soc. Cymmrodorion, London Hist. Soc. Roman Catholic. Club: Windsor (Eng.) Hockey (capt. 1982-83). Home: 51 Bolton Rd, Windsor SL4 3JX, England Office: McDonnel Douglas Info Systems, Maylands House Maylands Ave, Hemel Hemstead HP2 4RL, England

HAMPTON, CHRISTOPHER JAMES, writer; b. Horta, Fayal, The Azores, Jan. 26, 1946; s. Bernard Patrick and Dorothy Patience (Herrington) H.; m. Laura Margaret De Holesch, May 15, 1971; children—Alice Jane, Mary Ann. M.A. in Modern Langs., New Coll., Oxford, Eng., 1968. Resident dramatist Royal Ct. Theatre, London, 1968-70; author: (plays) When Did You Last See My Mother?, 1964, Total Eclipse, 1968, rev., 1981; The Philanthropist, 1970 (Evening Standard award, Plays and Players London Critics Best Comedy award 1970), Savages, 1973 (Plays and Players Best Play award 1973, Los Angeles Drama Critics Circle award 1974), Tales from Hollywood, 1982 (Evening Standard award 1983), Les Liaisons Dangereuses, 1985, others, also TV plays and films. Royal Soc. Literature fellow, 1976. Club: Dramatists Garrick (London). *

HAMPTON, EDWARD JOHN, engineering company executive; b. Pitts., July 28, 1952; s. Edward Aloysius and Helen (Litz) H.; B.S.M.E., U. Dayton, 1973; Ph.D. Century U., 1982; m. Rebecca Ann Franklin, Jan. 5, 1974; 1 child, Edward Steven. With Westinghouse Energy Systems, Pa., 1973-82, mgr. product integrity and design assurance, 1981-82; v.p. ops., dir. engring. and tech. O'Donnell & Assocs., Inc., Pitts., 1982—; also bd. dirs.; engring. cons. in structural integrity, fracture mechanics, fatigue and finite element computer analyses of Sci. mgt. Corp. Recipient Engineering Excellence award Westinghouse, 1981; Tech. Excellence award O'Donnell & Assocs., 1983. Mem. ASME, Nat. Soc. Profl. Engrs., Soc. Mech. Engrs., Gamma Beta. Contbr. articles on engring., plant life extension and mechanics to profl. jours. Co-inventor. Institutionalized several programs for design assurance in both foreign and domestic reactors. Office: O'Donnell & Assocs Inc 241 Curry Hollow Rd Pittsburgh PA 15236

HAMPTON, GLEN RICHARD, environmental engineer; b. Detroit, June 11, 1948; s. LaVerne P. and Virginia M. (Hubbard) H.; B.S. in Engring., Mich. Tech. U., 1973; m. Jane E. Fenlon, Jan. 30, 1981; children—Sarah Lynn, Melanie Anne. Project engr. Granger Engring., Inc., Cadillac, Mich., 1973-79; exec. v.p., dir. Chippewa Architects & Engrs., Inc., Kincheloe and St. Ignace, Mich., 1979-82; constrn. mgr. J.H. Granger and Assocs., Sault Ste. Marie, Mich., 1983—; cons. constrn. engring., environ. engring., civil engring., pollution control and solar energy. Registered profl. engr., Mich., Ky., Minn., Wis. Mem. Nat. Soc. Profl. Engrs., Mich. Soc. Profl. Engrs., ASCE (pres. N.W. Mich. chpt. 1980-82), Mich. Water Pollution Control Fedn., Mich. Soc. Civil Engrs., Nature Conservancy (dir. Mich. chpt.), Nat. Audubon Soc. Club: Kiwanis. Home: Rt 2 Box 130 A Saint Ignace MI 49781

HAMPTON, JAMES WILBURN, physician; b. Durant, Okla., Sept. 15, 1931; s. Hollis Eugene and Ouida (Mackey) H.; m. Carol McDonald, Feb. 22, 1958; children—Jaime, Clay, Diana, Neal. B.A., U. Okla., 1952, M.D., 1956. Intern U. Okla. Hosps., 1956-57; also resident; instr. to prof. U. Okla., Oklahoma City, 1959-77, head hematology/oncology, 1972-77; head hematology research Okla. Med. Research Found., Oklahoma City, 1972-77; dir. cancer program and med. oncology Baptist Med. Center, 1977-85, med. dir. Cancer Ctr. S.W., 1985—; cons. NIH, Biomed. and Nat. Cancer Inst.; chmn. med. adv. com. Hospice of Central Okla., 1981; vis. prof. Karolinska Inst., Stockholm; vis. scientist U. N.C., 1966-67. . Contbr. over 100 articles to profl. jours. Bd. dirs. Heritage Hills, Oklahoma City, 1972—, Am. Cancer Soc., 1982—; co-chmn. Save St. Paul's Episcopal Cathedral com., 1983, others. NIH Career Devel. Award., 1966-76. Fellow ACP; mem. Am. Fedn. Clin. Research (pres. 1970-71), Central Soc. Clin. Research (asso. editor jour. 1975-76), Okla. County Med. Soc. (editor bull. 1981—), Internat. Soc. Thrombosis and Hemostasis, Assn. Am. Indian Physicians (pres. 1978-79); Am. Physiol. Soc., Assn. Am. Pathologists, Am. Soc. Hematology, Am. Soc. Clin. Oncology, So. Soc. Clin. Investigation, Am. Psychosomatic Soc., Clubs: Oklahoma City Golf and Country, Blue Cord, Chaine des Rotisseurs. Assoc. editor Jour. Lab. Clin. Medicine, 1975-76, Bulletin, 1981—. Home: 1414 N Hudson St Oklahoma City OK 73103 Office: Ctr of the Southwest at Bapt Med Ctr 3300 NW Expressway Oklahoma City OK 73112

HAMRELL, HARALD IVAR OLOF, film director; b. Uppsala, Sweden, Dec. 13, 1960; s. Sven Bertil Hamrell and Sonja Marie-Louise Lyttkens. Film dir. Hamrell Filmproduktion, Stockholm. Author, dir.: (films) Leak at Reactor #4, 1980, A Sense of Guilt, 1987, Scenes from the Life of a Wash-Basin, 1987; actor (films) Linus, 1979, The Ninth Company,

1987. Mem. Swedish Actors Assn., Swedish Playwriters Union. Home: Raggatan 1, S-116 59 Stockholm Sweden

HAMRICK, JOSEPH THOMAS, mechanical engineer, corporate executive; b. Carrollton, Ga., Mar. 20, 1921; s. James Mayfield and Mattie Almon (Gaston) H.; m. Dorothy Elizabeth Jones, June 19, 1948; children—Jane Elizabeth Hamrick Kneisley, Nancy Ann Hamrick Owen, Thomas Mayfield. B.M.E., Ga. Inst. Tech., 1946, M.S.M.E., 1948. With NACA, Cleve., 1948-55, Thompson Ramo Wooldridge, Euclid, Ohio, 1955-61; pres. Aerospace Research Corp., Roanoke, Va., 1961—; pres. Cogeneration of Tenn., Inc., Red Boiling Springs Contbr. articles to profl. jours. Pres. North Franklin County Pub. Park, Inc. Served to 1st lt. USAAF, 1943-46; PTO. Recipient Tech. Achievement award Dept. Energy, 1984; Dept. of Energy grantee, 1978—; NSF grantee, 1980. Mem. ASME. Republican. Unitarian. Subspecialties: Biomass (energy science and technology); Combustion processes. Current work: Research on fueling gas turbines with wood, operation of 4000 Hp gas turbine with wood fuel. Patentee in field. Home: 6364 JAE Valley Rd SE Roanoke VA 24014 Office: 5454 JAE Valley Rd SE Roanoke VA 24014

HAMRO-DROTZ, FILIP MIKAEL, association professional; b. Helsinki, Finland, Jan. 26, 1948; s. Gösta Mikael Hamro and Karin Irma (Tegström) Drotz; m. Gunilla Margeta Starck, Mar. 17, 1951; children: Markus, Dennis, Robin. MSc in Econs., Swedish Sch. Econs., 1972. Asst. Helsingfors Aktiebank, Helsinki, 1972-73; dep. head Finnish Employers Confedn., Helsinki, 1973-82; permanent del. Representation Finnish Industries, Brussels, 1982-86; councelor Finnish Employers Confedn./Confedn. Finnish Industries, Helsinki, 1986—. Author: Palkkauksen Käsikirja, 1982. Served to dep. lt. Finnish Mil., 1967-68. Club: Handelsgillet (Helsinki). Home: Sigridsgranden 2, 02700 Grankulla Finland Office: Finnish Employers Confedn, Etelaranta 10, 00100 Helsinki Finland

HAMZA, GÜNTER, engineering company executive; b. Vienna, Aug. 14, 1940; s. Ignaz and Herta (Zinnauer) H.; m. Eva Pecinowsky; children: Christine, Andreas. Diploma in engring., U. Tech., Vienna, 1969. Mem. research and devel. staff Siemens AG, Vienna, 1969-70; authorized signatory Bacher Elektronische Geräte, Vienna, 1970-74; mgr. mktg. and sales SAT Schrack, Vienna, 1974-85; mng. dir. SAT Systeme für Automatisierungstechnik, Vienna, 1985—. Contbr. articles to profl. jours. Mem. Internat. Electrotech. Commn. (mem. various coms.). Home: Silbergasse 25, A-1190 Vienna Austria Office: SAT Systeme für, Ruthnergosse, A-1210 Vienna Austria

HAN, ITTAH, political economist, high technology and financial strategist; b. Java, Indonesia, Jan. 29, 1939; came to U.S., 1956, naturalized, 1972; s. Hongtjioe and Tsuiying (Chow) H. BS in Mech. Engring. and Elec. Engring., Walla Walla Coll., 1960; MA in Math., U. Calif., Berkeley, 1962; BA in French, U. Colo., 1965, MS in Elec. Engring., 1961; MSE in Computer Engring., U. Mich., 1970; MS in Computer Sci., U. Wis., 1971; MBA in Mgmt., U. Miami, Fla., 1973; BA in Econs., U. Nev., 1977; MBA in Tax, Golden Gate U., 1979, MBA in Real Estate, 1979, MBA in Fin., 1980, MBA in Banking, 1980, MPA in Adminstrv. Orgn. and Mgmt., 1984. Cert. fin. planner. Salesman, Watkins Products, Walla Walla, Wash., 1956-60; instr. Sch. Engring. U. Colo., Denver, 1964-66; systems engr. IBM Corp., Oakland, Calif., 1967-69, Scidata Inc., Miami, Fla., 1971-72; chief of data processing Golden Gate Bridge, Hwy. and Transp. Dist., San Francisco, 1973-74; mgr. info. systems tech. and advanced systems devel. Summa Corp., Las Vegas, Nev., 1975-78; mgr. systems devel. Fred Harvey Inc., Brisbane, Calif., 1978-80; chmn. corp. systems steering com., mgr. systems planning Amfac Hotel & Resorts, Inc., 1978-80; tax strategy planner, innovative turnaround fin. strategy planner, chief exec. Ittahhan Corp., 1980—; exec. v.p. Developers Unltd. Group, Las Vegas, 1982-84; v.p. Fidelity Fin. Co., Las Vegas, 1984-85; exec. v.p. John H. Midby and Assocs., Las Vegas, 1982-84; sec., treas., dir. River Resorts Inc., Las Vegas, 1983-84; sec., treas. Goldriver Ltd., Las Vegas, 1983-84; pres. Weststar Gen. Ptnr. Co., 1984-85, Developers Group Service Co., 1984-86; chief exec. officer, pres. High Tech. Polit. Economy Turnaround Strategist, Inc., 1986—; chief exec. officer, pres. Innovative Artificial Intelligence Computer Engring., Inc., 1986—; pres. Orion Land Devel. Co., Las Vegas, 1987—; instr. U. Nev. Sch. Elec. Engring., Reno, 1981; systems designer, cons. in field. Mem. IEEE, Assn. Computing Machinery, Am. Assn. Artificial Intelligence, Am. Math. Assn., Inst. Cert. Fin. Planners, Am. Contract Bridge League. Republican. Home and Office: PO Box 27025 Garside Station Las Vegas NV 89126

HAN, JAOK, medical educator, cardiologist, researcher; b. Chinnampo, Korea, July 16, 1930; came to U.S., 1955, naturalized, 1970; s. Choon H. and Chung R. (Kim) H.; m. Yangsook Chun, Jan. 21, 1961; children—Sylvia, Julia, Andrew. M.D., Kyong-Puk Nat. U., Taegu, Korea, 1951; Ph.D., SUNY-Upstate Med. Ctr., 1962. Intern, Jersey City Med. Ctr., 1955-56; resident Mercy Hosp., Pitts., 1956-57; research assoc. Masonic Med. Research Lab., Utica, N.Y., 1961-66; fellow in cardiology U. Rochester Med. Ctr. (N.Y.), 1966-67; assoc. prof. medicine Albany Med. Coll. (N.Y.), 1968-73, attending cardiologist, 1968—, dir. electrocardiography, 1968—; prof. medicine Albany Med. Coll., 1973—; mem. research com. N.Y. State Heart Assn., 1968-73; mem. spl. project rev. coms. Nat. Heart and Lung Inst., 1972—, mem. cardiology adv. com., 1981—. Author: Cardiac Arrhythmias, 1972; mem. editorial bd. Jour. Electrocardiology, 1984—; contbr. numerous articles to med. jours. Fellow: Internat. Soc. Cardiology Found., 1960-61, Masonic Found. for Med. Research, 1961-63; NIH grantee, 1969—. Fellow Am. Heart Assn. (Council on Circulation; pres. northeastern N.Y. chpt. 1980-82; research com. 1976-79), Am. Coll. Cardiology; mem. Am. Physiol. Soc., Am. Fedn. Clin. Research, N.Y. Acad. Scis., Sigma Xi. Home: 29 Cobble Hill Rd Loudonville NY 12211 Office: Dept Medicine Albany Med Coll Albany NY 12208

HAN, QI ZHI, physicist; b. Beijing, Dec. 24, 1932; s. Ming Ju and Yu Ting (Zheng) H.; m. Hong Zhou Sun, July 29, 1956; 1 child, Gang Sun. Grad., Peking U., Beijing, 1955, postgrad., 1961. Author: Group Theory, 1987; reviewer Math. Revs., 1984; contbr. articles to profl. jours. Recipient 1st prize in sci. research achievement Peking U., 1986, 1st prize in sci. and tech. progress Chinese State Ednl. Commn., 1986. Mem. Chinese Physics Soc., Chinese High Energy Physics Soc., Am. Math. Soc. Office: Peking U Dept Physics, Beijing Peoples Republic of China

HAN, SANG YOUL, corporation executive; b. Seoul, Republic of Korea, Dec. 2, 1938; came to U.S., 1957, naturalized, 1975; s. Chong Soo and Doo Chee (Kim) H.; m. Dora Lucia Mesa, Dec. 13, 1969; children: Sang II, Steven, Monica, Michael. BCE, U. So. Calif., 1962, MBA, 1963. V.p. ops. Filtrol Corp., Los Angeles, 1978-80; pres., chief exec. officer Han Indsl. Corp., Pomona, Calif., 1980—. Charter mem. Rep. Presdl. Task Force, Washington, 1983—, Rep. Senatorial Com., 1984—; trustee Rep. Presdl. Task FOrce, Washington; charter founder Ronald Regan Rep. Ctr., Washington, 1988; bd. chmn. Covina Christian Ch., chmn. adv. council Trustee Christian Ch., 1988. Recipient Merit Medal of Honor, Rep. Presdl. Task Force, 1984. Fellow Nat. Assn. Gen. Contractors. Mem. Christian Ch. Lodge: Rotary.

HAN, SHAO GONG, writer; b. Chang Sha, Hunan, People's Republic China, Jan. 1, 1953; m. Liang Yu Li, Feb. 16, 1978; 1 child, Han. B, Hunan Tchr's Coll., 1982. Journalist Master mag., Chang Sha, 1982-83, vice editor-in-chief, 1983-1984; writer Writer's Assn., Chang Sha, 1985—. Author: Yue Nan, 1981, Flying Cross Blue Sky, 1983, Lure, 1986, To Face the Mystical and Wide World, 1986. Vice chmn. Hunan Youth Union, Chong Sha, 1985—; active Hunan Polit. Cons. Standing Com., 1984—. Mem. Chinese Writers Assn. (council 1984—, Best Story prize, 1980, 81). Office: Lit Fedn Hunan, 302 Eight-One Rd, Chang Sha Peoples Republic China

HANAFIAH, ASIKIN, physician; b. Baturaja, S. Sumatra, Indonesia, May 9, 1932; s. Mohamad Ali and Syarifah H.; m. Laksmiati Sulisto, April 8, 1967; children: Ashanti, Alisyarhazad, Andita. MD, U. Indonesia, Jakarta, 1959, degree in pediatrics, 1963, degree in cardiology, 1967. Resident fellow in pediatrics U. Indonesia, 1959-64; Brit. council fellow in pediatric cardiology Royal Liverpool Hosp. for Sick Children, Great Ormons St. Hosp., England, 1961-62; cardiology staff Nat. Heart Inst., Jakarta, 1964-67; head cardiac catheterization lab. Cipto Mangunkusumo Hosp., Jakarta, 1967-72, cons., postgrad. cardiology tng. coordinator, 1972-82; head postgrad. cardiology program U. Indonesia, 1982—; sr. lectr. in cardiology 1986—; head cardiovascular care unit Nat. Cardiac Ctr. Hosp., 1985—; cons., cardiology dir. St. Carolus Hosp., Jakarta, 1959-64; dir. Sarana Medika Med. Services, 1984—; visiting cardiologist Pondok Indah Hosp., 1987—. Cons. editor: Indonesia Journal of Cardiology; contbr. numerous articles to profl. jours. Recipient Satyalancana Karya Staya award Pres. of Indonesia, 1987. Mem. Indonesian Heart Found. (sci. council mem. 1981—), Indonesian Med. Assn., Indonesian Heart Assn. (sec. gen. 1962-78, pres. 1978-81, pres. 1987—), Internat. Soc. Fed. Cardiology. Club: Exec. of Hilton. Office: Sarana Medika, Taman Kimia 1, Jakarta 10320, Indonesia

HANAHAN, JAMES LAKE, insurance company executive; b. Burlington, Iowa, Aug. 27, 1932; s. Thomas J. and Clarice P. (Lorey) H.; B.S., Drake U., 1955; postgrad. George Williams Coll., 1956; m. Marilyn R. Lowe, Dec. 27, 1952; children—Bridget Sue Bahlke, Erin Rose Hoff. Phys. dir. Monmouth (Ill.) YMCA, 1955-56; mem. community relations staff Caterpillar Tractor Co., Peoria, Ill., 1956-57; rep. Conn. Gen. Life Ins. Co., Des Moines, 1957-59, asst. mgr., 1959-63, mgr. group ins. ops., Tampa, Fla., 1963-80; pres., chief exec. officer Wittner Hanahan & Peck, Inc., 1980—, J & H Cons. Group Inc., 1980—; ltd. ptnr. City Ctr. St. Petersburg; ptnr. Crossroads Ltd., Pres.'s Inn; instr. C.P.C.U. courses; seminar leader C.L.U. workshop; cons. ins. seminar Fla. State U. Bd. dirs. Tampa Sports Found., Jr. Achievement; bd. dirs., pres. Pinellas Emergency Mental Health Services, bd. dirs. West Coast Employee Benefit Council; mem. Hillsborough County Health Council. Recipient Double D award Drake U., 1978. Mem. Sales Mktg. Execs. Tampa (pres., Exec. of Yr. 1982), Tampa Commerce Club, Nat. Risk Mgmt. Soc., Greater Tampa C. of C., Minerat Soc. U. Tampa, Tampa Sports and Recreation Council (bd. dirs.), Self Ins. Assn. Am., St. Petersburg Assn. Life Underwriters, Health Ins. Inst. Am., Profl. Benefit Adminstrs. Assn., Com. of 100, Suncoast C. of C. (adv. bd.), Phi Sigma Epsilon. Democrat. Roman Catholic. Clubs: 7th Inning (chmn.), Nat. D (Drake U.) (v.p., dir.), Innisbrook Country Resort. Home: 3301 S Bayshore Blvd #1008 Tampa FL 33629

HANAI, MASAYA, motor vehicle manufacturing company executive; b. Aug. 1, 1912; m. Motoko Hanai. Ed. Kobe U. Commerce, 1938. Former chmn. Toyota Motor Corp., Aichi, Japan, now sr. adviser; dir. Thailand Motor Co., Ltd. Decorated Medal of Honor with Blue Ribbon. Office: Toyota Motor Corp, 1-Toyota Cho, Aichi 471 Japan *

HANAMIRIAN, VARUJAN, mechanical engineer, educator; b. Istanbul, Turkey, June 23, 1952; s. Kurgin and Etil Sona (Azat) H. Dip. in Mech. Engring., U. Stuttgart, Fed. Republic Germany, 1983. Postal mgr. Foto Annemie, Stuttgart, 1977; tchr. Berlitz Sch., Stuttgart, 1980; creative dir. Unver Werbeagentur, Stuttgart, 1986; scientific asst. Fraunhofer-Gesellschaft, Stuttgart, 1987; course leader Volkshochschule, Stuttgart, 1987; educator, cons. Mem. adv. bd. Produktion weekly, 1981-85. Organizer Orgn. Com. EM 1986, Stuttgart; active mem. Freie Demokratische Partei; interviewer various market research assns., 1979—; adminstr. various offices, 1980-87. Mem. Verein Deutscher Ingenieure. Club: Allgemeiner Deutscher Automobil, München.

HANAOKA, MITSUO, insurance company executive; b. Tokyo, Mar. 7, 1950; s. Kimikazu and Yoshiko Hanaoka; m. Akiko Miyake, Dec. 11, 1982; 1 child, Tamaki. B in Engring., Sibaura Inst. Tech., Tokyo, 1973; student, U. Stockholm, 1976-77; M in Engring., Ohara Sch. Ikebana, Tokyo, 1985. With data processing dept. staff The Nikko Securities Co., Ltd., Tokyo, 1973-76; systems analyst Japan System Co., Ltd., Tokyo, 1978; systems planner Am. Family Life Assurance Co. Columbus, Tokyo, 1978-83, VAN service sect. chief, 1983-87, dept. asst. mgr., 1987-88, asst. mgr. dept. sales control, 1988—; research worker Adminstrv. Inst. Info. Processing, Tokyo, 1978, Japan Actuary Assn., Tokyo, 1982-84. Com. chmn. Tokyo jr. mems. club in The Ohara Sch., 1979-81. Mem. Assn. Labor Ins. Cons. Liberal Democrat. The Zen Sect. Clubs: Suntory hall, Bach hall. Home: 3024-3-503 Nogawa Miyamae, Kawasaki Kanagawa 213, Japan Office: Am Family Life Assurance, 2-1-1 Nishishinjuku, Tokyo 163, Japan

HANBACK, HAZEL MARIE SMALLWOOD, management consultant; b. Washington, Sept. 19, 1918; d. Archibald Carlisle and Mary Louise (Mayhugh) Smallwood; m. William B. Hanback, Sept. 26, 1942; 1 child, Christopher Brecht. AB, George Washington U., 1940; MPA, Am. U., 1968. Archivist, U.S. Office Housing Expediter, 1948-50; mgmt. engr. U.S. Archives, 1950-51; spl. asst.-indsl. specialist Sec. Def., 1951-53; dir. documentation div. Naval Facilities Engring., Alexandria, Va., 1953-81; mgmt. cons., 1981—. Author: Military Color Book, 1960—, Status of Women in a Cybernetically Oriented Soc., 1968, (newsletter) Worms Eye View, 1982. Pres., West End Citizens Assn., Washington, 1956-58; trustee George Washington U., 1979—. Nominee Rockefeller Pub. Service award, 1969, Fed. Woman's award, 1969; recipient cert. of merit Dep. Def., 1965. Mem. Mortar Bd., Phi Delta Gamma, Sigma Kappa. Democrat. Episcopalian. Clubs: George Washington U. (chmn. bd. 1971-75), Columbian Women (pres. George Washington U. 1967-69), Order Eastern Star. Home: 2152 F St NW Washington DC 20037 Office: 2154 F St NW Washington DC 20037

HANCOCK, IAN FRANCIS (O YANKO LE REDŽOSKO), educator; b. London, Aug. 29, 1942; came to U.S., 1972; s. John Redzo and Kathleen Elsa (Palmer) H.; married; children: Julian Marko, Adrian Lee Imre, Meilinne Khim. Diploma in Oriental and African Studies, U. London, 1969, Ph.D., 1971. Reporter, photographer Daily Free Press, B.C., 1959-60; various positions Europe, 1961-74; display advt. staff Sears Roebuck Co., B.C., 1964-65; compiler literary index Vancouver Pub. Library, 1971-72; prof. linguistics U. Tex., Austin, 1972—; mem. Jewish Studies Adv. Bd. U. Tex., 1986—; mem. Adv. Council on Jewish Affairs, Haifa, 1983 U.S. del. UN Orgn. for World Romani Union, U.S. rep. UNICEF; spl. advisor U.S. Holocaust Meml. Council, 1985-87. Author: (with David De Camp) Pidgins and Creoles: Current Trends and Prospects, 1974, (with John Reinecke and others) Bibliography of Pidgin and Creole Languages, 1975, Problems in the Creation of Standard Dialect of Romanes, 1975, The Pariah Syndrome, 1987, (with Loreto Todd) International English Usage, 1986; editor: Romani Sociolinguistics, 1979, Readings in Creole Studies, 1979, (with John Reinecke and others) Jour. of Creole Studies, 1972; mem. editorial bd. Jour. of Gypsy Lore Soc., 1975, Roma, 1973, Jour. of Krio Literary Soc, 1970; contbr. (with John Reinecke and others) articles to profl. jours. Mem. Indian Inst. Romani Studies (bd. govs. 1971), Internat. Gypsy Com. (sec. gen. Am. div. 1970), MLA, World Romani Union, Gypsy Soc. Chgo. (academic advisor), Am. Red Dress Gypsies Assn., Caribbean Linguistic Soc., Romano Bashipé Assn., Inst. for Cultural Studies (bd. dirs.), Deutsche Forschungsgemeinschaft (Heidelberg) (adv. bd.), NCCJ (bd. dirs. 1987—). Office: U Tex Dept English Parlin Hall Austin TX 78712 also: World Romani Union (USA) Buda TX 78610-0865

HANCOCK, JOHN STUART, banker; b. Bradford, Eng., Apr. 11, 1936; s. Frederick Rouse and Edith Larner, June 18, 1960; children: Jayne Elizabeth, Sally Louise, Joan Catherine. Clerical officer Bank London and South Africa, Bradford, 1953-61; mgr's. asst. Bank London and South Africa, London, 1961-71; sr. credit officer Lloyds, Bolsa Internat. Bank, Ltd., Bradford, 1971-73; mgr. Lloyds Bank Internat., Ltd., Bradford, 1973-82; mgr. overseas br. Newcastle, Eng., 1982-84; sr. mgr. internat. br. Southampton, Eng., 1984—. Mem. Inst. Export, Inst. Bankers. Home: 14 Forest Glade Close, Brockenhurst SO42 7QY, England Office: Lloyds Bank PLC, Internat Br, 22/23 High St, Southampton SO9 7BT, England

HANCOCK, LANGLEY GEORGE, mining and diversified business executive; b. Perth, Australia, June 10, 1909; s. George and Lilian Hancock; m. Hope Margaret Nicholas, Aug. 4, 1947 (dec.); 1 child, Georgina Hope Rinehart. Ed. Hale Sch., Perth; D.Bus.Adminstrn. (hon.), Hillsdale (Mich.) Coll., 1983. Asst. mgr., then mgr. Mulga Downs Sheep Sta., Western Australia, 1927-34; began prospecting for minerals, 1927, discovered asbestos in Wittenoom Gorge, developed industry, 1936, entered partnership (with E.A. Wright), then sold half of equity to company that became Australian Blue Asbestos Ltd., 1943, asst. mgr. co., 1943-48; became ptnr. (with Wright and Walters) Whim Creek Copper, Mons Cupri Copper, Nunyerry Creek White Asbestos, 1950; made 1st maj. discovery of iron ore in Pibara, Western Australia, 1952, subsequently discovered over 600 major iron ore deposits; entered into joint iron ore devel. agreement with Texasgulf Inc., 1972; founder Nat. Miner Newspaper, also Westralian Secession Movement, 1974; now life governing dir. Hancock Propsecting Pty. Ltd.; dir. Hancock Pilbara Pty. Ltd., Hancock (Nickel) Pty. Ltd., Georgina Hancock (1965) Pty. Ltd., Pilbara Exploration N.L., Ragged Hills Pty. Ltd., Wright Prospecting Pty. Ltd. Author: Wake up Australia, 1979. Contbr. articles on free enterprise to jours. and newspapers. Mem. internat. bd. dirs. Am. U., Washington. Mem. Explorers Club. Office: Hancock Prospecting Pty Ltd, 49 Stirling Hwy, Nedlands, Perth, Western Australia Australia *

HANCOCK, PATRICIA JEAN, body shop owner; b. Norfolk, Nebr., Oct. 18, 1945; d. John Joseph Fagan Jr. and Virginia Ruth (Simpson) Rauert; m. Robert Dale Hancock, Mar. 1, 1965; 1 child, Jennifer Lynn. BS in Math., U. Nebr., 1967, tchrs. cert., 1967, MAT in Math., 1971. Tchr. math., Palmyra, Nebr., 1967-68; grad. asst. U. Nebr., Lincoln, 1968-69; tchr. math. Pound Jr. High, Lincoln, 1969-74; sec.-treas. Bob's Body Shop, Grand Island, Nebr.; developer, organizer Collision Repair Mgmt. Cert. program Ce. Community Coll., Grand Island. Contbr. articles to profl. jours. Coordinator Bible sch. Trinity United Meth. Ch., 1983, 84, 85, leader 4-H Club, 1985—; mem. adminstrv. council ministries, 1984-86; tchr. Soc. Collision Repair Specialists; charter mem. Hall County Leadership Tomorrow Program; co-chmn. Neb. Jr. Girls Golf Assn. Mem. Nebr. Auto Body Assn. (sec., newsletter editor, convention organizer 1981-83). Clubs: Riverside Golf (Grand Island) (treas., v.p., pres. Ladies Golf Assn.). Avocations: golf, tennis, swimming, sewing, organ. Home: Rt 1 PO Box 185 Cairo NE 68824 Office: Bob's Body Shop Inc 1800 W Lincoln Hwy Grand Island NE 68803

HANCOX, RALPH, publisher; b. Hampstead, Eng., Aug. 23, 1929; married; 4 children. Student, Poly. Sch. Modern Langs., London, 1952-53; student Nieman fellow, Harvard U., 1965-66, grad. program mgmt. devel., 1973. Can. corr. Observer Fgn. News Service, London, 1957-66; author radio and TV scripts 1960-64; news editor Weekly Post Newspapers Ltd., Uxbridge, Middlesex, Eng., 1953-55; sr. reporter, daily columnist Kingston Whig-Standard Co. Ltd., Kingston, Ont., Can., 1955-57; asso. editor, then editor-in-chief Peterborough (Ont.) Examiner, 1957-67; editor Reader's Digest Assn. (Can.) Ltd., Montreal, 1967-73; v.p. adminstrn., then v.p. ops. Reader's Digest Assn. (Can.) Ltd., 1973-78, pres., 1978-86, pres., chmn., 1986—; pres., chmn. Reader's Digest Mags. Ltd., 1978—; dir. Mags. Can. Trustee Peterborough Bd. Edn., 1962-66; gov. Conseil du Patronat du Que. Served with RAF, 1947-52. Recipient Nat. Newspaper award for editorial writing, 1966. Mem. Nat. Assn. Maj. Mail Users (pres.). Home: 590 Chelsea Crescent, Beaconsfield, PQ Canada H9W 4N5 Office: Readers Digest Mags Ltd, 215 Redfern Ave, Montreal, PQ Canada H3Z 2V9

HANCOX, ROBERT ERNEST, financial services company executive; b. Newark, Apr. 6, 1943; s. Ernest E. and Laverne (Bruguiere) H.; B.A., Lycoming Coll., 1965; M.B.A., Fairleigh Dickinson U., 1970; Ph.D., Pace U., 1981; m. Judith Hale, Aug. 6, 1966; children—Jennifer Susan, Elizabeth Jane. Coordinator mgmt. devel. State Farm Ins. Cos., Wayne, N.J., 1965-66, asst. personnel mgr., 1968-70, personnel supt., 1970-72, regional personnel mgr., 1972-76, regional personnel dir., 1976-81; v.p. human resources INA Corp., 1981-83; v.p. human resources Penn Mut. Life Ins. Co., 1983-87; exec. v.p., chief operating officer ICMA Retirement Corp., Washington, 1987—; bd. dirs. The Daro Group Inc.; adj. asso. prof. Seton Hall U., 1970—, Fordham U., 1974—; trustee Lycoming Coll. Mem. Am. Soc. Personnel Adminstrn. (accredited personnel exec.), Acad. Mgmt., Phila. Urban Coalition, Indsl. Gerontology Research Inst. (bd. dirs.), Am. Compensation Assn., Assn. Specialists Group Work, Indsl. Relations Research Assn., Am. Soc. Tng. and Devel. Republican. Methodist. Office: ICMA Retirement Corp 1120 G St NW Washington DC 20005

HAND, BRIAN EDWARD, consultant; b. DuBois, Pa., Mar. 16, 1963; s. Homer Edward and Patricia Ann (Delaco) H. BA, Pa. State U., 1985. Asst. to city mgr. City of DuBois, Pa., 1983; coordinator Council Commonwealth Student Govts., University Park, Pa., 1984-85; exec. dir. United Way, DuBois, 1985-87; teaching asst. Cath. U. of Am., 1987—; treas. LTG Assocs., Washington, 1985—; sec. United Way, 1985-87. Dir. DuBois Campus Alumni Soc., 1985—, sec., 1986-87; active in DuBois Area Hist. Soc., 1983-87; pres. Student Govt. Assn. Pa. State U., 1982-83; mem. Profl. Assn. United Way of Pa., 1986-87; pres. DuBois Commmunity Theatre, 1986. Recipient Eric A. and Josephine Walker award Pa. State U. 1983, Outstanding Young Alumni award Pa. State U.-DuBois, 1987. Lodge: Rotary. Avocations: numismatics, photography, genealogy.

HAND, HERBERT HENSLEY, management educator, executive, consultant, inventor; b. Hamilton, Ohio, July 11, 1931; s. Herbert Lawrence and Berta Elizabeth (Hensley) H.; m. Katharine Harris Gucker, July 26, 1952; children—Stephen Harris, Herbert Gucker. B.S., Ind. U., 1953; M.B.A., U. Miami, 1966; Ph.D., Pa. State U., 1969. Vice pres. Hand Oil Co., 1955-65; instr. Pa. State U., 1968-69; asst. prof. Ind. U., Bloomington, 1969-73, assoc. prof., 1973-76; prof. mgmt. U. S.C. Coll. Bus. Adminstrn., Columbia, 1976—; state dir. Small Bus. Devel. Ctr. S.C., 1968-69; exec. v.p. Carter-Miot Engring. Co., Columbia, S.C., 1981; pres. Carolina Consultants, 1973-84; pres. Phronesis, Inc., 1985—, also dir.; cons. to numerous cos., 1973—. Author: (with H.P. Sims, Jr.) Managerial Decision Making in the Business Firm-A Systems Approach, 1972, The Profit Center Simulation, 1975; (with A.T. Hollingsworth) A Guide to Small Business Management, 1979, Practical Readings in Small Business, 1979; contbr. research articles, papers in field to profl. jours.; mem. editorial bd. Bus. Horizons, 1971-73; patentee in field. Served to 1st lt. USAF, 1953-55. Recipient Western Electric award for most innovative bus. course, 1971; Small Bus. Inst. Regional award SBA, 1976, 80, 81, Small Bus. Inst. Nat. award, 1980; Office Naval Research grantee, 1976, 77, 78. Mem. Acad. Mgmt. (editorial bd. Rev. Jour. 1975-79), So. Mgmt. Assn., Am. Inst. Decision Scis., Internat. Council for Small Bus. Episcopalian. Lodge: Rotary. Office: U SC Coll Bus Adminstrn Dept Bus Mgmt Columbia SC 29208 Other: 223 Tram Rd Columbia SC 29210

HANDEL, BERNARD, accountant, actuarial and insurance consultant, lawyer; b. N.Y.C., Sept. 25, 1926; s. Louis and Sarah (Brody) H.; B.B.A., City U. N.Y.; J.D., Pace U.; m. Shirley M. Krom. With Eisner & Lubin, C.P.A.s, N.Y.C., 1946-52; v.p. Davis Assos., N.Y.C., 1952-56; pres. Handel Group div. H.D.L. Assocs., Inc., Poughkeepsie, N.Y., 1956—, Hudson Valley Planning, Poughkeepsie, 1961—; dir. Bankers Assurance Co., 1984—. Bd. dirs. Dutchess County chpt. ARC; bd. dirs. Hudson Valley Health Systems Agy., pres., 1982-84; bd. dirs. Dutchess County Health Planning Council, 1976—; treas. Dutchess County Assn. Sr. Citizens, 1976; past insp. N.Y. State Athletic Commn.; mem. N.Y. State Hosp. Rev. and Planning Council, 1978—; bd. dir. Am. Health Planning Assocs., 1982-85; trustee Vassar Bros. Hosp., 1986—; bd. dirs. Bardavon Opera House, 1985—. Served with U.S. Army, 1945-46. C.P.A., N.Y. Mem. Internat. Found. Employee Benefit Plans (chmn. consultants com., chmn. health care services com. 1980-83, 88—, chmn. health care data base com., 1986-87, dir. 1981-83, 85-87), IS-CEBS (fellow, gov. council 1982-84), N.Y. State Soc. C.P.A.s, Nat. Assn. Securities Dealers, Am. Pension Conf., Soc. Benefit Plan Adminstrs., ABA, N.Y. State Bar Assn. Clubs: Rotary, Amrita. Author books and articles in field. Office: 53 Academy St PO Box 709 Poughkeepsie NY 12602

HANDEL, MORTON EMANUEL, leisure products company executive; b. N.Y.C., Apr. 12, 1935; s. Benjamin and Mollie (Heller) H.; m. Irma Ruby, Aug. 5, 1956; children: Mark, Gary, Karen. B.A., U. Pa., 1956; postgrad., N.Y. U., 1957-59. Vice pres. Dale Plastic Playing Card Corp., N.Y.C., 1955-57; gen. mgr. Handel Nets & Fabrics Corp., N.Y.C., 1957-62; pres. A.M. Industries, Inc., Farmingdale, N.Y., 1962-68, Allan Marine, Inc., Deer Park, N.Y., 1969-71; chmn. bd. Marlow Yacht Corp., Deer Park, 1969-71; v.p. fin., sec.-treas. Aurora Products Corp. (subs. Nabisco Inc.), 1971-73, sr. v.p., chief fin. officer, 1973-74; v.p. Rowe Industries Inc., 1971-74; v.p., dir. Aurora Nederland N.V., 1971-74, Aurora Plastics Can. Ltd., 1971-74; v.p. fin., chief fin. officer Coleco Industries Inc., 1974-78, sr. v.p., chief fin. officer, 1978-82, exec. v.p. fin. and adminstrn., 1982-83, exec. v.p. corporate com., 1983-85, exec. v.p. corp. devel., 1985-88, chmn., dir., chief exec. officer, trustee, 1988—; Coleco Industries, Inc.; trustee Aurora Products Profit Sharing Trust, 1971-74, Coleco Industries Inc. Pension Fund, 1976-85. Pres. Rochdale Vill. Civic Assn., 1964-65; pres., bd. dirs. Symphony Soc. Greater Hartford, 1976—; bd. dirs. Jewish Children's Service Corp., 1976-78; corporator St. Francis Hosp., 1982—; bd. dirs. One Thousand Corp., 1983—. Mem. Am. Mgmt. Assn., Fin. Execs. Inst., Planning Execs. Inst., Alpha Epsilon Pi. Home: 41 Ranger Ln West Hartford CT 06117 Office: Coleco Industries Inc 999 Quaker Ln S West Hartford CT 06110

HANDEL, RICHARD CRAIG, lawyer; b. Hamilton, Ohio, Aug. 11, 1945; s. Alexander F. and Marguerite (Wilks) H.; m. Katharine Jean Carter, Jan. 10, 1970. AB, U. Mich., 1967; MA, Mich. State U., 1968; JD summa cum laude, Ohio State U., 1974; LLM in Taxation, NYU, 1978. Bar: Ohio 1974, S.C. 1983, U.S. Dist. Ct. (so. dist.) Ohio 1975, U.S. Dist. Ct. S.C. 1979, U.S. Tax Ct. 1977, U.S. Ct. Appeals (4th cir.) 1979, U.S. Supreme Ct. 1979; cert. tax specialist. Assoc. Smith & Schnacke, Dayton, Ohio, 1974-77; asst. prof. U. S.C. Sch. Law, Columbia, 1978-83; ptnr. Nexsen, Pruet, Jacobs & Pollard, Columbia, 1983-87; ptnr. Moore & Van Allen, Columbia, 1987-88; ptnr. Nexsen Pruet Jacobs & Pollard, Columbia, 1988—. Contbr. articles to legal jours. Served with U.S. Army, 1969-70, Vietnam. Gerald L. Wallace scholar, 1977-78; recipient Outstanding Law Prof. award, 1980-81. Mem. ABA, S.C. Bar Assn., Richland County Bar Assn., Order of Coif. Office: Nexsen Pruet Jacobs & Pollard 1441 Main St Suite 1500 Columbia SC 29202

HANDEL, WILLIAM KEATING, sales executive; b. N.Y.C., Mar. 23, 1935; s. Irving Nathaniel and Marguerite Mary (Keating) H.; m. Margaret Inez Sitton; children: William Keating II, David Roger. BA in Journalism, U. S.C., 1959, postgrad., 1959-60. With Packaging div. The Mead Corp., Atlanta, 1960-64, Ketchum, MacLeod & Grove, Pitts., 1964-67, Rexall Drug & Chem. Corp., Los Angeles, 1967-68; owner Creative Enterprises/Mktg. Communications, Los Angeles, 1968-71; creative dir., sales promotion mgr. Beneficial Standard Life Ins., Los Angeles, 1971-72; mgr. advt. and public relations ITT Gen. Controls, Glendale, Calif., 1972-80; mgr. corp. recruitment advt. Hughes Aircraft Co., Los Angeles, 1980-81; mgr. corp. communications Fairchild Camera and Instrument Corp., 1981-83; dist. mgr. Cahners Pub. Co., 1984—; pub. relations counsel Calif. Pvt. Edn. Schs., 1978-87; chmn. exhibits Mini/Micro Computer Conf., 1977-78. Bd. dirs. West Valley Athletic League; dir. Los Angeles chpt. USMC Scholarship Found.; public relations cons. Ensenada, Mexico Tourist Commn., 1978; chmn., master of ceremonies U.S. Marine Corps Birthday Ball, Los Angeles, 1979-82. Served with USMC, 1950-53. Decorated Silver Star, Bronze Star, Purple Heart (4), Navy Commendation medal with combat V.; recipient Public Service award Los Angeles Heart Assn., 1971-73. Mem. Bus. and Profl. Advt. Assn. (cert. bus. communicator, past pres.), 1st Marine Div. Assn., Navy League (dir.), Sigma Chi (chpt. adv.). Republican. Roman Catholic. Clubs: AdLinx Golf of So. Calif., Griffith Park Golf, Nueva España Boat, Baiamar Country, Ensenada Country, Ensenada Fish and Game (Baja, Mexico). Home: 4443 Ventura Canyon Ave Sherman Oaks CA 91423

HANDELSMAN, DAVID JOSHUA, endocrinologist, researcher; b. Melbourne, Victoria, Australia, Apr. 16, 1950; s. Salomon and Sulamit (Kagan) H.; m. Penelope Louise Hoskins, Aug. 8, 1986; 1 child, Timothy David. B of Medicine, B of Sci., U. Melbourne, Australia, 1974; PhD, U. Sydney, 1984. Resident med. officer Royal Prince Alfred Hosp., Sydney, 1975-77, endocrinology registrar, 1978-79; research fellow U. Sydney, 1980-83; overseas research fellow Med. Research Council, 1985-86, Wellcome sr. research fellow, 1987—; research fellow UCLA, 1984-85; dir. Andrology unit Royal Prince Alfred Hosp., Sydney, 1985—. Contbr. articles to profl. jours. Mem. Endocrine Soc., Am. Andrology Soc., Am. Fertility Soc., Internat. Soc. Neurendocrinology, Australian Soc. Reproductive Biology, Endocrine Soc. Australia. Home: 82 Goodhope St Paddington, Sydney New South Wales 2021, Australia Office: U Sydney, Dept Medicine, Sydney New South Wales 2008, Australia

HANDLER, EVELYN ERIKA, university president; b. Budapest, Hungary, May 5, 1933; d. Donald D. and Ilona Sass; m. Eugene S. Handler; children: Jeffrey, Bradley. BA, Hunter Coll., 1954; MSc, NYU, 1962, PhD, 1963; LLD (hon.), Rivier Coll., 1981. Research asst. Sloan Kettering Inst., N.Y.C., 1956-58; research asso. Merck Inst. Therapeutic Research, Rahway, N.J., 1958-60; mem. faculty, dept. biol. scis. Hunter Coll., N.Y.C., 1962-77; dean div. scis. and math Hunter Coll., 1977-80; pres. U. N.H., Durham, 1980-83, Brandeis U., Waltham, Mass., 1983—; Mem. nat. adv. gen. med. sci. council NIH, 1981-84; mem. Am. Council Pharm. Edn., 1978-82; mem. exec. com. Nat. Assn. State Univs. and Land Grant Colls., 1981-83, mem. com. on policies and issues, 1981—. Contbr. articles and abstracts to profl. publs. Mem. New Eng. Bd. Higher Edn., 1980—; mem. New Eng. Council Presidents, 1980-83, N.H. Coll. and Univ. Council, 1980-83, Post-Secondary Edn. Commn., 1980—; corp. mem. Woods Hole Oceanographic Instn., 1983—. Mem. Assn. Ind. Colls. and Univs. Mass. (exec. com. 1986—), Assn. Am. Univs. (sci. and research com. 1985), New Eng. Council, Inc. (bd. dirs. 1983 chmn. edn., edn and tech. 1985—), The New Eng. (bd. dirs. 1983—).

HANDLEY, ROBERT EUGENE, photographer; b. Bloomington, Ill., May 23, 1945; s. Bernard A. and Edna Margarete (Manahan) H. Student So. Ill. U., 1966-67, Ill. State U., 1967-68; grad. N.Y. Inst. Photography, 1972, Winona Sch. Profl. Photography, 1974. Formerly publicity photographer Ringling Bros. and Barnum & Bailey Circus; owner Robert E. Handley, Photography, Bloomington, 1969—; lectr. photography for nat., state, regional confs., high schs. Contbr. articles to profl. jours. Pres., Bloomington Down Town Council, 1979-80. Served with AUS, 1962. Recipient Excellence award Profl. Photographers Am., 1973; Ct. of Honor trophy State of Ill.; numerous other awards. Mem. Profl. Photographers Am. (Photog. Craftsman degree 1976; asst. nat. conv. mgr. 1976), Assn. Commerce and Industry Mclean County (dir. 1980), Asso. Profl. Photographers Ill., Profl. Photographers No. Ill. (dir. 1976-80), Profl. Photographers Calif., Profl. Photographers Los Angeles County, Brit Inst. Profl. Photography, Am. Soc. Mag. Photographers, Am. Soc. Photographers, Photog. Soc. Am., Internat. Wedding Photographers Am., Asso. Photographers Internat. (life), Winona Sch. Alumni Assn. Moose. Home: 1920 E Croxton Ave Bloomington IL 61701

HANDOJO, ALIE, trading company executive; b. Ujang Pandang, South Sulawesi, Indonesia; s. Liyanto and Lanny Handojo; m. Lilies Iswani, Jan. 5, 1969; children: Annie Kartini, Anna, Anvi, Anmi, Anwar Handojo. B of Indsl. Mgmt., Nat. U. Singapore, 1967. Adminstrv. mgr. Ho Tot & Co., Singapore, 1967-69; sales mgr. Kedaung Group, Surabaya, Indonesia, 1970-78; mng. dir. Diamond Trading Co., Surabaya, 1978—. Home: Jalan Tokala 10-12, Surabaya Indonesia Office: Diamond Trading Co, Jalan Panggung 3, #7-A, Surabaya Indonesia

HANDS, TERENCE DAVID (TERRY), theater director; b. Jan. 9, 1941; s. Joseph Ronald and Luise Berthe (Kohler) H.; m. Josephine Barstow (div.); m. Ludmila Mikael, 1974 (div. 1980); 1 child. B.A. with honors in English Lang. and Lit., Birmingham U. Founder, artistic dir. Liverpool Everyman Theatre, Eng., 1964-66; artistic dir. RSC Theatregoround, 1966-67; cons. dir. Comedie Francaise, 1975-77; assoc. dir. Royal Shakespeare Co., 1967-77, joint artistic dir., 1978—, artistic dir., chief exec. Dir. theater prodns. including The Importance of Being Ernest, Look Back in Anger, Richard III, The Four Seasons, Fando and Lis; artistic dir. The Proposal, 1966, The Dumb Waiter, 1967, Under Milk Wood, 1967; dir. for Royal Shakespeare Co., The Criminals, 1967, Pleasure and Repentance, 1967, The Merry Wives of Windsor, 1968, Bartholomew Fair, 1969, Women Beware Women, 1969, Murder in the Cathedral, 1972, Romeo and Juliet, 1973, The Bewitched, 1974, The Actor, 1974, Henry VI parts 1, 2 and 3 (Soc. of West End Theatre award, Dir. of Yr., Plays and Players award, Best Prodn. award 1978), The Changeling, 1978, The Children of the Sun, 1979, As You Like It, 1980, Much Ado About Nothing, 1982, Cyrano de Bergerac, 1983, Othello, 1985, Julius Caesar, 1987; dir. for Comedie Franciase, Richard III, 1972 (Meilleur Spectacle de l'Annee award), Twelfth Night, 1976 (Meilleur Spectacle de l'Annee award), Le Cid, 1977, Murder in the Cathedral, 1978; dir. for Paris Oprea, Verdi's Otello, 1976; dir. for Barbican Theatre, Red Noses, 1985 (Laurence Olivier award 1985), Winter's Talk, 1987, Carrir, 1987-88, The Balcony, 1987, numerous others. Contbr. to Theatre 72 and Playback publs. Translator: (with Barbara Wright) Genet, The Balcony, 1971; Pleasure and Repentance, 1976. Address: care Royal Shakespeare Theatre, Stratford-on-Avon, Warwicks CV37 6BB, England

HANDSCHUMACHER, ALBERT GUSTAVE, corporate executive; b. Phila., Oct. 20, 1918; s. Gustave H. and Emma (Streck) H.; children: Albert, David W., Megan, Karin, Melissa. B.S., Drexel Inst. Tech., 1940; diploma, U. Pitts., 1941, Alexander Hamilton Inst., 1948. Prodn. mgr. Jr. Motors Corp., Phila., 1938-40; sales engr. Westinghouse Electric Co., Pitts., 1941; with Lear, Inc., Grand Rapids, Mich., 1945-57; beginning as sales mgr. central dist., successively asst. to pres., asst. gen. mgr., v.p. and gen. mgr., sr. v.p., dir. sales, pres., dir. Lear, Inc., 1959-62; v.p., gen. mgr. Rheem Mfg. Co., 1957-59; pres., dir. Lear Siegler, Inc., 1962-65; chmn. bd. Aeronca, Inc.; dir. First Exec. Corp., Lear Siegler, Inc., Exec. Life Ins. Co., Flight Dynamics Inc.; underwriting mem. Lloyd's of London; chmn. exec. com. First Fin. Group, Inc. Trustee Drexel U.; trustee City of Hope; nat. adv. chmn. Am. Heart Assn.; mem. bus. adv. council UCLA Internat. Student Ctr., Los Angeles World Affairs Council; trustee Nat. Asthma Assn. Served to maj. USAAF, 1942-45. Recipient 60th Anniversary Alumni award for outstanding achievements and services field of indsl. mgmt. Drexel U., 1951, Outstanding Alumni award, 1971; Man of Year award City of Hope, 1970; Man of Year award Nat. Asthma Assn., 1978. Mem. Am. Mgmt. Assn., ASHRE. Clubs: Jonathan, Caiif. Yacht, Bel Air (Calif.) Country; Wings (N.Y.C.), Metropolitan (N.Y.C.); Confrerie de la Chaine des Rotisseurs, Beverly Hills; Le Mirador Country (Switzerland); Astro (Phila.). Home: 1100 Stone Canyon Rd Los Angeles CA 90077 Office: 844 Morago Dr Los Angeles CA 90049

HANDY, JOHN ABNER, JR., business executive; b. Mpls., Apr. 19, 1913; s. John Abner and Winnifred (Hammond) H.; m. Frances P. Slack, July 4, 1936; children: John Abner, Mary Eugenia. A.B., Hamilton Coll., 1935; M.B.A., Harvard U., 1937. Salesman Procter & Gamble Distbg. Co., 1937-40; dept. head, gen. office mgr., asst. controller Carborundum Co., Niagara Falls, N.Y., 1940-47; controller, later controller-asst. sec. Deering Milliken & Co., Inc.; sec. Pendleton Fabrics Corp.; controller numerous corps; sec. corp. Joseph E. Seagram & Sons, Inc., 1952-56, also; sec. subsidiary corps. Seagram Distillers Corp., Calvert Distilling Co., Carstairs Bros. Distilling Co., Inc., Frankfort Distilleries, Inc., Frankfort Distillers Corp., Gallagher & Burton, Inc., Hunter-Wilson Distilling Co., Inc., Julius Kessler Distilling Co., Inc., Lord Calvert Distilleries, Inc., Paul Jones & Co., Inc., Pharma-Craft Corp., Md. Distillery, Inc., Gen. Distillers Corp.; financial v.p., controller, dir. Chem. Constrn. Corp. (subsidiary Electric Bond & Share Co.), 1956-66; v.p., dir. Chem. Constrn. Internat. Del., Chem. Constrn. A.G. Zug, Switzerland; dir. Chem. Constrn. Ltd., Gt. Britain, Can.; dir. Linden Brunswick Corp., 1958-66; exec. v.p., dir. Fabergé, Inc., 1966-72; dir. planning Guideposts Assocs., Inc., 1977—. Contbr. articles to profl. publs. Mem. Fin. Execs. Inst., Am. Mgmt. Assn. (council), Nat. Office Mgmt. Assn. (past pres., dir. Buffalo chpt.), Am. Arbitration Assn. (panel), Tau Kappa Epsilon, Delta Sigma Rho. Clubs: Harvard (N.Y.C.); Gipsy Trail (Carmel, N.Y.). Home: Gipsy Trail Club Carmel NY 10512 Office: Guideposts Assocs Inc Carmel NY 10512

HANDY, ROLLO LEROY, educator, research executive; b. Kenyon, Minn., Feb. 20, 1927; s. John R. and Alice (Kispert) H.; m. Toni Scheiner, Sept. 17, 1950; children—Jonathan, Ellen, Benjamin. B.A., Carleton Coll., Northfield, Minn., 1950; M.A., Sarah Lawrence Coll., 1951; postgrad., U. Minn., 1951-52; Ph.D., U. Buffalo, 1954. Mem. faculty U. S.D., 1954-60, prof. philosophy, head dept., 1959-60; assoc. prof. Union Coll., Schenectady, 1960-61; mem. faculty SUNY-Buffalo, 1961-76, prof. philosophy, 1964-76, chmn. dept., 1961-67, chmn. div. philosophy and social scis., 1965-67, provost faculty ednl. studies, 1967-76; pres. Behavioral Research Council, 1976—, Am. Inst. Econ. Research, 1977—. Author: Methodology of the Behavioral Sciences, 1964, Value Theory and the Behavioral Sciences, 1969, The Measurement of Values, 1970, (with Paul Kurtz) A Current Appraisal of the Behavioral Sciences, 1964; (with E.C. Harwood) rev. edit., 1973, Useful Procedures of Inquiry, 1973; Co-editor: (with E.C. Harwood) Philosophical Perspectives on Punishment, 1968, The Behavioral Sciences, 1968, The Idea of God, 1968. Served with USNR, 1945-46. Mem. AAUP (chpt. pres. 1964-65), Am. Anthrop. Assn., Am. Philos. Assn., Mind Assn., Philosophy Sci. Assn. Office: Am Inst Econ Research Great Barrington MA 01230

HANEMANN, JAMES, JR., lawyer; b. New Orleans, Dec. 31, 1935; s. James and Mary Rollins (Douglass) H.; m. Ann Mahorner, Aug. 7, 1965; children: James Douglass, Katherine Glennon. BS in Civil Engring., Tulane U., 1957, JD, 1963. Bar: La. 1963, U.S. Dist. Ct. (ea. dist.) La. 1963, U.S. Ct. Appeals (5th cir.) 1963, U.S. Supreme Ct. 1967. Assoc. Phelps, Dunbar, Marks, Claverie & Sims, 1963-64, 66-69, ptnr., 1969-74; assoc. Terriberry, Carroll, Yancey & Farrell, 1964-66; ptnr. Poitevent & Hanemann, 1974-81; sole practice 1981-82; ptnr. Hanemann & Little, 1982-83; prin. Hanemann & Assocs., 1983—. Adv. editor The Maritime Lawyer, 1975—, Tulane Law Review. Bd. dirs. Boys Club Greater New Orleans, 1977-81; mem. Marine Fisheries Adv. Com. to Sec. Commerce, 1977—; chmn. U.S. Blind Golfers' Championship, 1980. Served to lt. USN, 1957-63. Mem. ABA, Fed. Bar Assn., La. Bar Assn. (ho. of dels. 1980—), New Orleans Bar Assn., Maritime Law Assn. (mem. exec. com. 1988—), Gulf Steamship Claims Assn. (pres. 1970), Gulf Coast Conservation Assn. (pres. Delta chpt.), Order of Coif, Omicron Delta Kappa, Kappa Delta Phi, Phi Delta Phi. Roman Catholic. Clubs: Bienville (New Orleans) (pres. 1975-76), New Orleans Country (bd. dirs. 1974-75), Pickwick. Lodge: Rotary (pres. New Orleans chpt. 1976-77). Home: 5528 Hurst St New Orleans LA 70115 Office: Hanemann & Assocs 1010 Whitney Bldg New Orleans LA 70130

HANF, JAMES ALPHONSO, poet, government official; b. Chehalis, Wash., Feb. 3, 1923; s. William G. and Willa DeForest (Davis) H.; grad. Centralia Jr. Coll., 1943, DLitt (hon.) World U. Ariz.; m. Ruth G. Eyler, Aug. 16, 1947; 1 child, Maureen Ruth. Naval architect technician P.F. Spaulding, naval architects, Seattle, 1955-56, Puget Sound Bridge & Dredge Co. (Wash.), 1953-55, Puget Sound Naval Shipyard, 1951-53, 56—; cons. Anderson & Assocs., ship bldg.; cons. The Research Bd. Advs., Am. Biographical Inst., Inc.; guest lectr. on poetry and geneal. research methods to various lit. socs., 1969—; contbr. hundreds of poems to lit. jours., anthologies and popular mags.; poetry editor Coffee Break, 1977-82. Recipient Poet Laureate award, 1978, Poet Laureate Wash. State award Internat. Poetry Soc. India and World, 1981, grand prize World Poetry Soc. Conv., 1985, 86, Golden Poet award World of Poetry in Calif., 1985, 86, numerous other awards. Judge poetry contest, Australia and India, 1985. Mem Internat. Poetry Soc., World of Poetry Soc. (Golden Poet award 1985, 86, 87, 88), Kitsap County Writers Club (pres. 1977-78), Internat. Fedn. Tech. Engrs., Nat. Hist. Locomotive Soc., Kitsap County Hist. Soc., Puget Sound Geneal. Soc., Western World Haiku Soc., Olympic Geneal. Soc. (pres. 1974-75), N.Y. Poetry Forum, World Poets Resource Center, Literarische Union, Internat. Platform Assn., Calif. Fedn. Chaparral Poets, Internat. Biog. Assn., Am. Biog. Inst. (Silver Medal of Honor). Baptist. Home: PO Box 374 Bremerton WA 98310

HANGLEY, WILLIAM THOMAS, lawyer; b. Long Beach, N.Y., Mar. 11, 1941; s. Charles Augustus and Faustine Charmillot Hangley; m. Mary Dupree Hangley, July 24, 1965; children—Michele Dupree, William Thomas, Katherine Charmillot. B.S. in Music, SUNY-Coll. at Fredonia, 1963; LLB cum laude, U. Pa., 1966. Bar: Pa. 1966, U.S. Ct. Appeals (3d cir.) 1966, U.S. Dist. Ct. (ea. dist.) Pa. 1966. Assoc. Schnader, Harrison, Segal & Lewis, Phila., 1966-69; mem., pres. Hangley Connolly Epstein Chicco Foxman & Ewing, Phila. 1969—; dir. Pub. Interest Law Ctr. Phila. Mem. ACLU; dir. Ams. for Democratic Action, 1972-81. Fellow Am. Coll. Trial Lawyers; mem. ABA, Pa. Bar Assn. (corp. and litigation coms., securities and antitrust subcoms.), Phila. Bar Assn., Order of Coif. Roman Catholic. Club: Racquet (Phila.). Contbr. articles to profl. publs. Office: Hangley Connolly et al 1515 Market St Philadelphia PA 19102

HANKINSON, RISDON WILLIAM, chemical engineer; b. St. Joseph, Mo., Dec. 11, 1938; s. William Augusta and Rose Mary (Thompson) H.; B.S., U. Mo., Rolla, 1960, M.S., 1962; Ph.D. (Am. Oil fellow), Iowa State U., 1972; Hon. degree, Chem. Engr., U. Mo., Rolla, 1982; m. Lyla Pollard, June 4, 1960; children—Kenneth, Michelle, Michael, Mark, Douglass. Instr. chem. engring. U. Mo., Rolla, 1960-62; instr. chem. engring. Iowa State U., 1964-67; engr. Phillips Petroleum Co., Bartlesville, Okla., 1967-69, group leader, 1969-70, cons., 1970-78, prin., thermodynamics, 1978-80, prin. process engr., 1980-82, sr. staff assoc., 1982-85, mgr. engring. scis. br. tech. systems devel., 1985, mgr. tech. systems br. engring. and services, 1985-87; mgr. comml. systems, Phillips 66 Natural Gas Co., 1985—; adj. prof. math. Okla. State U., 1967-75, Bartlesville Wesleyan Coll., 1969-71. Vice pres. Tech. Careers Adv. Com., 1972-73, pres., 1973-74; v.p. Vol. Okla. Overseas Mission Bd., 1970-71; cub scout leader; tchr. religious edn., minister of Eucharist, lector, Roman Cath. Ch., 1976—; chmn. bd. dirs. Alcohol and Drug Center Inc., 1984-87; bd. dirs., 1987—. Served from 2d lt. to 1st lt. AUS, 1962-63. Recipient Outstanding Alumnus Achievement award Ia. State U., 1971; named Outstanding Young Engr. in Okla., 1970, Outstanding Engr. in Okla., 1984; registered profl. engr. in Okla. Mem. Am. Inst. Chem. Engrs. (dir., past pres. Bartlesville sect.), Okla. Soc. Profl. Engrs. (v.p. membership 1988—), Am. Petroleum Inst. (chmn. phys. properties com. static measurement 1979-82). Clubs: Elks, KC (grand knight, council 1987—), Kiwanis. Contbr. articles to profl., sci. jours. Home: 701 Sooner Park Dr Bartlesville OK 74006 Office: Phillips Petroleum Co 1060 Plaza Office Bldg Bartlesville OK 74004

HANLIN, JAMES PAUL, oil field service executive; b. Douglas, Wyo., Aug. 13, 1939; s. Jack C. and Helen Marie (Shick) H.; m. Sharon Kay Gillespie, Aug. 31, 1962; children—James Todd, Brett, Tracey. Operator Halliburton Co., Warri, Nigeria, 1970-72, Aberdeen, Scotland, 1972-76, supr., Stavanger, Norway, 1978-80, div. test and tools supr., The Hague, The Netherlands, 1980-82, mgr., Ijmuiden, The Netherlands, 1982-88; with Howe Moss Crescent, 1988— . Mem. sch. bd., Stavanger, 1980. Served with U.S. Army, 1954-57. Mem. Soc. Petroleum Engrs. Republican. Methodist. Avocations: skeet and trap shooting, hill walking, photography. Home: 19 Kirkbrae Ave Cults, Aberdeen Scotland Office: Halliburton Co Howe Moss Crescent, Kirkhill Indsl Estate, Dyce Aberdeen 2B2 0ES, Scotland

HANNA, COLIN ARTHUR, management consultant, executive search consultant; b. Abington, Pa., Dec. 3, 1946; s. Arthur and Jean Victoria (McClure) H.; A.B., U. Pa., 1968; m. Anne Price Hemphill, Dec. 28, 1967; children—Jean Price, Colin Alexander. With CBS, Inc., 1969-76; account exec. CBS Radio Spot Sales, N.Y.C., 1969-70; mgr. creative services CBS-Viacom Group, N.Y.C., 1970-71; account exec. CBS Radio Spot Sales, N.Y.C., 1971-72, sales mgr., Phila., 1974-76; account exec. WCAU Radio, Phila., 1972-74; dir. sales devel. WCAU-TV, Phila., 1976; pres. Hanna & Wile Advt., Wayne, Pa., 1976-77, Tri-State Trade Exchange, Inc., West Chester, Pa., 1978-80, Hanna Enterprises Ltd., 1980—; prin. Whittlesey and Assocs., West Chester, 1980-86; pres. The Cheshire Group, West Chester, 1986—, Vestryman Ch. of Good Samaritan, Paoli, Pa.; trustee Upland Country Day Sch., Kennett Square, Pa. Served with USNR, 1968-69. Mem. Am. Mktg. Assn., Am. Mgmt. Assn., Bank Mktg. Assn., Inter-Fin. Assn., Fin. Instns. Mktg. Assn., Nat. Assn. Corp. and Profl. Recruiters, Phila. Direct Advt. Assn., Shakspere Soc. Phila., Newcomen Soc. N.Am., Am. Vets. Assn. (dir.), Alumni Assn. U. Pa. (pres.), Mensa. Republican. Episcopalian. Clubs: Racquet (Phila.); Radley Run Country (West Chester); Tred Avon Yacht (Oxford, Md.). Home: 603 Fairway Dr West Chester PA 19380 Office: 300 S High St West Chester PA 19382

HANNA, KEITH LAWRENCE, photographer; b. Washington, Oct. 19, 1942; s. Keith Lazell and Virginia Victoria (Poston) H.; m. Peggy Lynn Welling, Sept. 25, 1983; children: Brandon Keith, Brittany Lauren. B.S. in Biology and Chemistry, Lynchburg Coll., 1965, postgrad., 1965-66; M.S. in Biochemistry and Nutrition, Va. Poly. Inst. and State U., 1968; postgrad. in physiology Vanderbilt U., 1971; M in Photography, Profl. Photographers Am., 1986. Chemist Nat. Bur. Standards, Washington, summers 1964-66; research biochemist Sch. Medicine, Vanderbilt U., 1969-71; food technologist Pet Food div. Star-Kist Foods, Inc., 1971-76; prin. Larry Hanna Photography, Las Vegas, Nev., 1976—. Mem. Profl. Photographers Am. (cert. profl. photographer, master of photography degree 1986, qualified for comml. studio, Craftsman Photographer award 1983), Profl. Photographers Nev. (Photographer of Yr. award 1981, 83, 84, 87, pres. 1980, 83—, chmn. bd. dirs.). Episcopalian. Home: 4305 Jodi Ave Las Vegas NV 89120 Office: Larry Hanna Photography 3347 S Highland Suite 303 304 Las Vegas NV 89109

HANNA, MARTIN SHAD, lawyer; b. Bowling Green, Ohio, Aug. 4, 1940; s. Martin Lester and Julia Loyal (Moor) H.; m. Sharon Ann Higgins, Feb. 10, 1969; children—Jennifer Lynn, Jonathan Moor, Katharine Anne. Student, Bowling Green State U.; B.S., Purdue U., 1962; J.D., Am. U., 1965. Bar: Ohio 1965, D.C. 1967, U.S. Supreme Ct. 1969. Ptnr. Hanna, Middleton & Roebke, 1965-70; ptnr. Hanna & Hanna, Bowling Green, 1971—; spl. counsel for atty. gen. Ohio, 1969-71, 82-85, Ohio Bd. Regents, 1974; instr. Bowling Green State U., 1970, Ohio Div. Vocat. Edn., 1970—, Ohio Peace Officer Tng. Council, 1968; legal adviser NW Ohio Vol. Firemen's Assn., 1970—. Contbr. articles to profl. publs. Elder, lay minister Presbyterian Ch.; state chmn. Ohio League Young Republican Clubs, 1972-73; nat. vice chmn. Young Rep. Nat. Fedn., 1973-75, counselor to chmn., 1975-77; vice chmn. Wood County Rep. Exec. Com., Ohio, 1972-80, precinct committeeman, 1968-80; trustee Bowling Green State U., 1976-86; mem. Ohio State Fire Commn., 1979-87. Recipient George Washington honor medal award Freedoms Found. at Valley Forge, 1969, award of merit Ohio Legal Ctr. Inst., 1973, Robert A. Taft Disting. Service award, 1974, James A. Rhodes Leadership award, 1975; named one of 10 Outstanding Young Men, Ohio Jaycees, 1968. Mem. ABA, D.C. Bar Assn., Ohio Bar Assn., Northwest Ohio Bar Assn., Wood County Bar Assn., Toledo Bar Assn., Am. Trauma Soc. (trauma and law com.), Phi Delta Phi, Pi Kappa Delta, Omicron Delta Kappa. Home: 506 Knollwood Dr Bowling Green OH 43402 Office: 700 N Main St Bowling Green OH 43402

HANNA, WILLIAM EUGENE, JR., cybernetician, management consultant; b. Chgo., Jan. 25, 1921; s. William Eugene and Elizabeth E. (Calvert) H.; AA in Phys. Sci., Woodrow Wilson Jr. Coll., 1941; AB in Social Studies, Bradley U., 1947; grad. advanced study program Nat. Inst. Public Affairs, 1948; MA in Econs., George Washington U., 1951; m. Annette Antoniow, June 8, 1948; children: Sharon Valli, Karen Michelle, Patrice Marie, Kathleen Louise, Mary Lucille, Teri Sue, Jeanette Gabrielle. Comptroller, Aero. Chart and Info. Center, St. Louis, 1954-61; exec. officer AEC/NASA Space Nuclear Propulsion Office, Germantown, Md., 1961-67; dir. programs and resources Office Advanced Research and Tech., NASA, Washington, 1967; dir. Bur. Data Processing, Office Advanced Systems, Social Security Adminstrn., Balt., 1968-76; v.p. Nat. Inst. Public Mgmt., Washington, 1976-84; dir. Washington studies program San Francisco State U., 1976-80. Councilman, City of Rockville (Md.), 1968-74, mayor, 1974-82; councilman Montgomery County (Md.), 1982—; bd. dirs. Met. Washington Council Govts., 1974-82, U.S. Conf. Mayors, 1977-82. Served to lt. col. USAF. Decorated Air medal with 6 oak leaf clusters; recipient Outstanding Citizen of Yr. award Rockville C. of C., 1978; Good Neighbor award, KC, 1979. Mem. Am. Soc. Cybernetics, AIAA, Am. Soc. Public Adminstrn., Assn. Computing Machinery, Tech. Transfer Soc., Sister Cities Internat. (treas.). Democrat. Roman Catholic. Office: County Office Bldg 100 Maryland Ave Rockville MD 20850

HANNAM, CHARLES, education lecturer; b. Essen, Fed. Republic Germany, July 26, 1925; arrived in Eng., 1939; m. Sue, Aug. 5, 1947; children: David Simon, Toby, Naomi. Sr. lectr., U. Bristol, Eng., 1960-87. Author: Young Teachers and Reluctant Learners, 1971, 2d edit., 1985, First Year of Teaching, 1975, 2d edit., 1986, Parents and Mentally Handicapped Teachers, 1975, A Boy in Your Situation, 1975, 2d edit., 1988, Boy in New Situation, 1977, Almost an Englishman, 1977, Parents of Mentally Handicapped Children, 1980, Becoming a Teacher, 1988, Refugees, Evacuees, 1989. Chmn. Community Health Council, Bristol, 1978-87. Office: U Bristol, Bristol B58 1JA, England

HANNAN, CECIL JAMES, school system administrator, small business owner; b. Sydney, Mont., Oct. 3, 1925; s. Cecil George and Isabelle Mary (Finch) H.; m. Molly M. Roberts, Dec. 16, 1974; children: Matthew G., Kelley J., Marguerite M. BA, Western Wash. State U., 1947, MS, 1948; DEd, Wash. State U., 1961. Exec. sec. Wash. State Edn. Assn., Seattle, 1959-67; assoc. exec. sec. NEA, Washington, 1967-71; pres. NTL Learning Resources Co., Washington, 1971-75; exec. sec. Colo. Edn. Assn., Denver, 1975-77; vice chancellor San Diego Community Coll. Dist., 1977-85; chmn., chief exec. officer Edn. Systems Tech. Co., San Diego, 1985—; ptnr. Tech. Specialists Inc., Phila., 1988—; pres. Tchrs. Services Corp., Washington, 1968-71. Author: Teach Spelling By All Means, 1952, Merit Pay for Teachers, 1953, Cross Value Dialog, 1963, Twenty Exercises for Classroom, 1966. Chmn. Educators Humphrey for Pres., Washington 1964, Educators Jackson for Pres., Washington, 1968. Served to lt. USAF, 1943-46. Recipient Disting. Service award Wash. State Legis., 1967. Mem. NEA (exec. com. 1964-68, bd. dirs. 1960-64), Nat. Tng. Labs. (exec. com. 1964-72), Fla. Edn. Assn. (life), Mass. Tchrs. Assn. (life), Nat. Congress PTA (life). Democrat. Methodist. Home: 2433 7th St Olivenhain CA 92024

Office: Edn Systems Tech Corp 5230 Carroll Canyon Rd San Diego CA 92121

HANNAN, EDWARD LEES, state health services agency administrator, researcher; b. Troy, N.Y., Aug. 21, 1943; s. Edward J. and Marian (Cooper) H.; m. Maryanne Casey, Mar. 25, 1983; children—Elizabeth, Kathleen. B.S., Union Coll., 1964; M.S., 1970; M.S., Syracuse U., 1966; Ph.D., U. Mass., 1973. Instr. math. SUNY-Albany, 1966-68; sr. statistician N.Y. State Dept. Transp., Albany, 1968-70; asst. prof. Inst. Adminstrn. & Mgmt., Union Coll., Schenectady, 1973-78; assoc. prof. Sch. Bus., Fla. Internat. U., Miami, 1978-80; dir. Bur. Health Care Research and Info. Services, N.Y. State Dept. Health, Albany, 1980—; cons. U.S. Coast Guard, 1978-80, N.Y. State Health Dept., 1973-78, Am. Lung Assn., 1972-73. Mem. planning com. Albany area chpt. ARC, 1982-83. Mem. Ops. Research Soc. Am., Am. Pub. Health Assn., Am. Statis. Assn., Inst. Mgmt. Scis., Am. Inst. for Decision Scis., Sigma Xi, Kappa Mu Epsilon, Alpha Pi Mu. Home: 7 Locust Ave Troy NY 12180

HANNAY, SIR DAVID (HUGH ALEXANDER), diplomat; b. London, Sept. 28, 1935; s. J.G. and E.M. (Lazarus) H.; m. Gillian Rosemary Rex, May 9, 1961; children: Richard, Philip, Jonathan, Alexander. BA in Modern History with honors, Oxford (Eng.) U., 1959. With Fgn. and Commonwealth Office, 1959-60, Tehran, 1960-61; oriental sec. Kabul, Afghanistan, 1961-63; with Ea. dept. Fgn. and Commonwealth Office, 1963-65, 1st and 2d sec. UK Del. to EC, 1965-70, 1st sec. UK Negotiating Team with EC, 1970-72; chef de cabinet to Sir Christopher Soames, v.p. of commn. of EC Brussels, 1973-77; head, energy, sci., space dept. Fgn. and Commonwealth Office, 1977-79, head, Middle East dept., 1979, asst., under sec. of state European community, 1979-84; minister Washington, 1984-85; with Brit. Fgn. and Commonwealth Office The European Communities, Brussels, 1985—. Served as 2d lt. 8th Kings Royal Irish Hussars, 1954-56. Anglican. Club: Travellers (London). Office: care The European Commmunities, 6 rond point Robert Schumann, 1040 Brussels Belgium

HANNERZ, ULF, anthropology educator; b. Malmö, Sweden, June 9, 1942; s. Lag. W. and Laila (Hallborg) H.; m. Helena Wulff. BA, U. Stockholm, 1963, PhD, 1969; MA, Indiana U., 1966. Research assoc. Ctr. Applied Linguistics, Washington, 1966-68; asst. to assoc. prof. U. Stockholm, 1970-81, full prof., 1981—; vis. assoc. prof. U. Pitts., 1971-72; Simon Sr. research fellow U. Manchester, Eng., 1976; vis. prof. U. Calif., Berkeley, 1981; fellow Ctr. Advanced Study in Behavioral Scis., Stanford, Calif., 1984-85; vis. prof. U. Adelaide, Australia, 1987; fellow Swedish Collegium for Advanced Study in Social Scis, 1988—; bd. dirs. UNRISD, Geneva, 1983—. Author: Soulside, 1969, Caymanian Politics, 1974, Exploring the City, 1980; editor: Ethnos, Stockholm, 1971—. Grantee Swedish Research Council Humanities and Social Scis., Bank Sweden Tercentenary Found, Swedish Agy. for Research Coop. with Developing Countries. Mem. Royal Swedish Acad. Scis. Home: Kronobergsgatan 9, 112 38 Stockholm Sweden Office: U Stockholm, 106 91 Stockholm Sweden

HANNES, MARTIN ROY, photographic company executive; b. Sydney, NSW, Australia, Mar. 10, 1950; s. Jack Dieter and Morna Jean (Houghton) H. B.Engr., Sydney U., 1973; M.B.A., Harvard U., 1977. Vice pres. ops. Baia Photo Optical, Jackson, Mich., 1977-78; group mgr. photo ops. Hanimex Corp., Sydney, 1978-80, gen. mgr. NSW, Hanimex , Sydney, 1980-84, mng. dir., 1984-86; mng. dir. Palcolor Ltd., Sydney, 1985-86, Graflex Pty Ltd.; pres. Hannex Corp., West Palm Beach, Fla., Seas & Sea, Riviera Beach, Fla. U.S.A., exec. dir. Trans Nat. Investments Ltd., Hong Kong, Hanset Pty. Ltd. Mem. Inst. Engrs. Australia, Australian Inst. Mgmt., Soc. Photofinishing Engrs. Mem. Ch. Eng. Clubs: Harvard (Boston); Royal Prince Alfred (Newport Australia); Yacht. Avocations: Skiing; yachting; tennis. Home: 1754 Pittwater Rd, 2104 Bayview, New South Wales 2104, Australia

HANNIBALSSON, JON BALDVIN, Iceland government official; b. Isafjordur, Iceland, Feb. 21, 1939. MA in Econs., U. Edinburgh, Scotland, 1963; postgrad., Nationalokonomiska Inst., Stockholm, 1963-64, Harvard U. Ctr. for European Studies, 1976-77; diploma in psychology and teaching techniques, U. Iceland, 1985. Tchr. Hagaskoli Elem. Sch., Reykjavik, Iceland, 1964-70; journalist Frigals Thjod, Reykjavik, 1964-68; headmaster Menntaskolinn á Isafirdi, Isafjordur, Iceland, 1970-79; chief editor Althydubladid, Reykjavik, 1979-82; M.P. Iceland, Reykjavik, 1982—, minister fin., 1987—; chmn. Socialist Dem. Party, 1984—. Address: Ministry Finance, Reykjavik Iceland *

HANNIG, KURT BRUNO, biochemist, educator; b. Reichenberg, Czechoslovakia, May 26, 1920; s. Josef and Ida (Peuker) H.; Ph.D., U. Darmstadt, 1963; m. Lauterbach Traudl, June 4, 1949; 1 son, Christian. Research asst. Tech. U., Regensburg, W. Ger., 1948-50, Max-Planck Inst., Regensburg, 1951-57; asst. dir. Max-Planck Inst. of Eiweiss-U. Lederforschung, Munich, 1958-72; prof. biochemistry U. Munich, 1971—; dir. Max-Planck Inst. of biochemistry, Martinsried-Munich, 1973-88. Recipient Dr. Fritz Merck prize, 1968. Mem. Sudetendeutsche Akademie der Kü nste und Wissenschaften, Gesellschaft Deutscher Chemiker, Gesellschaft Biologische Chemie. Tech. and theoretical developer of electrophoretic separation methods; contbr. articles in field to profl. jours. Home: 45 Pentenriederstr, Krailling 8033 Federal Republic Germany Office: MPI Biochemie, 8033 Martinsried Federal Republic of Germany

HANNON, ELIZABETH HALL, information service company executive; b. Washington, Oct. 16, 1941; d. John Richard and Elizabeth Mae (Garber) H.; B.A., U. Md., 1963; m. Kevin Hayes Hannon, Sept. 12, 1964 (div. June 1986); children—Patrick Michael, Kathleen Anne, Megan Theresa. Reporter, Sci. Service, Washington, 1963-64; sci. reporter Syracuse (N.Y.) Post Standard, 1964-72; tech. editor Pacific Gas & Electric Co., San Francisco, 1973-74; mgr. Inforum, Atomic Indsl. Forum, Washington, 1974-80; chmn., chief exec. officer Utility Data Inst., Washington, 1980—. Office: Utility Data Inst 1700 K St NW Suite 400 Washington DC 20006

HANS-ADAM, hereditary Prince of Liechtenstein; b. Feb. 14, 1945; s. Prince Franz Josef II and Princess Gina; m. Countess Marie Aglae Kinsky von Wchinitzund Tettau, 1967; four children. Grad. Sch. Econs. and Social Scis., St. Gallen, Switzerland, 1969. Exec. authority of Liechtenstein, 1984—. Address: Schloss, Vaduz Liechtenstein

HANSCHAR, LAWRENCE JOHN, copper mining executive; b. Medicine Hat, Alta., Can., June 13, 1944; s. John and Sarah (Stahl) H.; m. Kay O'Connor, Oct 19, 1970 (div. 1983); m. Mary Mpundu Mapulanga, Jan. 6, 1984; 1 child, Lawrence Chalwe. BMetE with honors, U. Queensland, Australia, 1970. Chartered engr., Gt. Britain. With Zambia Consol. Copper Mines Ltd., Kitwe, 1970-77, smelter, projects supr., 1977-84, cons. metallurgist, 1984-86, mgr. corp. planning, 1986-88, sr. mgr. tech. services, 1988—. Contbr. articles to profl. jours. Mem. parish council local Roman Cath. ch., Kitwe, 1985—. Mem. AustralAsian Inst. Mining and Metallurgy, AIME (pyrometall. com. 1982-85), Inst. Mining and Metallurgy, Engrs. Inst. Zambia. Office: Zambia Consol Copper Mines Ltd, PO Box 260071, Kalulushi Zambia

HANSELL, EDGAR FRANK, lawyer; b. Leon, Iowa, Oct. 12, 1937; s. Edgar Noble and Celestia Delphine (Skinner) H.; m. Phyllis Wray Silvey, June 24, 1961; children—John Joseph, Jordan Burke. A.A., Graceland Coll., 1957; B.B.A., U. Iowa, 1959, J.D., 1961. Bar: Iowa 1961. Mem. Nyemaster, Goode, McLaughlin, Emery & O'Brien, P.C., Des Moines, 1964—; ptnr. Nyemaster, Goode, McLaughlin, Emery & O'Brien, P.C., 1968—; bd. dirs. Britt Tech. Corp., The Vernon Co. Mem. editorial adv. bd. Jour. Corp. Law, 1985—. Bd. dirs. Des Moines Child Guidance Ctr., 1972-78, 81-87, pres., 1977-78; bd. dirs. Child Guidance Found., 1983—; trustee Iowa Law Sch. Found., 1975—, pres., 1983-87; bd. dirs. Des Moines Community Playhouse, Inc., 1982-87, Iowa Sports Found., 1986—. Served with USAF, 1961-64. Mem. ABA, Iowa Bar Assn. (pres. young lawyers sect. 1971-72, gov. 1971-72, 85-87, mem. grievance commn. 1973-78, Merit award young lawyers sect. 1977, chmn. corp. and bus. law com. 1979-85, pres.-elect 1988—), Polk County Bar Assn. Home: 4001 John Lynde Rd Des Moines IA 50312 Office: Nyemaster Goode McLaughlin et al Hub Tower Des Moines IA 50309

HANSEN, BOBBY JEAN, management consultant, real estate investor and developer; b. Newton, Kans., Jan. 30, 1926; s. Clarence Nielsen and Blanche Eleanore (Andrews) H.; m. Marlene Marie Mendoza, Oct. 18, 1960 (div. May 1986); children: Cherokee E. Ryznar, Jody K. Abbott, Alyson Cottini, Mimi E., Nicole M. BS, U. So. Calif., 1949; MA Pub. Adminstrn., Am. U., 1966. Pres. Trak-Life Inc., Portland, Oreg., 1957-59; staff specialist Lockheed Missile & Space Co., Sunnyvale, Calif., 1959-61; program mgr. Ops. Research Inc., Silver Spring, Md., 1961-62; exec. v.p. Computer Dynamics Corp., Silver Spring, 1961-65; sr. v.p. John I. Thompson & Co., Washington, 1965-68; pres. Decision Research Corp., Washington, 1968-70; county exec. Prince William County, Manassas, Va., 1970-71; county adminstr. Wythe County, Wytheville, Va., 1971-73; city mgr. Marion, Va., 1973-77; mgr. Williams Crane & Rigging Inc., Wytheville, 1977-80; prin. adminstr. and investors coordinator Royal Commn. Jubail (Saudi Arabia)-Yanbu, 1980-83; div. mgr. Al-Rushaid Investment Co., Dammam, Saudi Arabia, 1980-85; investor Hansen Assocs., Wytheville, 1985—; adj. faculty professorial lectr. Wytheville Community Coll., The Am. U. Author: Practical Program Evaluation and Review Technique, 1962; guest editor Government Exec. Mag.; former columnist Southwest Va. Enterprise; patentee in field. Mem., former chmn. small bus. adv. council Metro Washington U.S. SBA ; mem. council Luth. Ch. Served to capt. USNR, 1943-47, WWII, 51-53, Korea, 66-67, Vietnam. Mem. FIABCI-Fedn. Internationale des Professions Immobilieres, Am. Inst. for Mgmt., Am. Mgmt. Assn., Armed Forces Mgmt. Assn. (former v.p.), Def. Orientation Conf. Assn., United Inventors and Scientists, Associated Gen. Contractors, Am. Waterworks Assn., Internat. City Mgrs. Assn., Nat. Assn. County Adminstrs., Nat. Security Indsl. Assn., Am. Arbitration Assn. (nat. panel arbitrators), Naval Res. Oficer's Assn., Beta Gamma Sigma, Kappa Mu Epsilon, Sigma Nu. Lutheran. Clubs: Evergreen Country (Haymarket, Va.); Evansham Swim & Racquet (Wythe County); Va. Masters Swimming Assn. (pres. 1979-80); Chantilly (Va.) Country. Lodges: Rotary, Moose. Home: PO Box 974 Wytheville VA 24382-0974

HANSEN, CARL RICHARD, JR., child psychiatrist, researcher; b. Mankato, Minn., July 21, 1954; s. Carl Richard Sr. and Martha Elisabeth (Sorensen) H.; m. Constance Joann McLeod, June 27, 1981; 1 child, Carl Richard III. BA, BS, Viterbo Coll., 1976; MD, U. Minn., 1979, postgrad., 1979-82. Fellow in psychiatry U. Minn., Mpls., 1979-82; fellow in child psychiatry Yale U. Child Study Fellow, New Haven, 1982-84; pvt. practice child psychiatry North Haven, Conn., 1984-85, Golden Valley, Minn., 1985-87; med. dir. child psychiatry service Golden Valley Health Ctr., Mpls., 1987; chief adolescent psychiatry Riverwood Ctr., Prescott, Wis., 1987-88; clin. dir. Greenshire Sch., Cheshire, Conn., 1984-85; cons. Golden Valley Health Ctr., 1985; chief dept. adolescent psychiatry Riverwood Ctr., Prescott, Wis., 1987-88. Mem. U.S. Congl. Adv. Bd., 1985. Named one of Outstanding Young Men Am., 1981; recipient Eagle award Boy Scouts Am., 1969; fellow John A. Merck Found., Yale U., 1983-84, Leonard Berger, Yale U., 1983-84. Mem. AMA, AAAS, Am. Psychiat. Assn., Minn. Psychiat. Assn., Am. Acad. Child and Adolescent Psychiatry, Minn. Soc. Child and Adolescent Psychiatry, Hastings Ctr., Phi Kappa Phi, Sigma Xi. Republican. Lutheran. Office: 606 24th Ave S Suite 801 Minneapolis MN 55454

HANSEN, CHARLOTTE HELGESON, newspaper editor, publishing company executive; b. Jamestown, N.D., June 1, 1922; d. Louise S. and Ida (Clough) Helgeson; student Jamestown Coll., 1940-41; B.S., U. Minn., 1944; m. Gordon H. Hansen, Oct. 31, 1945; 1 dau., Jo-Ida C. Hematologist, Hanford Engring., Richland, Wash., 1944-45; serologist Tex. Dept. Health, Wichita Falls, 1945-46; instr. microbiology Jamestown Coll., 1951-61; food editor Jamestown Sun, 1949—; v.p., sec.-treas. Hansen Bros., Inc., Jamestown, 1972—; dir. First Bank Jamestown, First Bank System, Mpls., Hansen Bros., Inc. Bd. dirs. Jamestown Indsl. Devel. Corp., James River Sr. Citizens, Inc., Camp Rokiwan; trustee Jamestown Coll.; mem. N.D. Gov's. Human Resources Council, 1982. Recipient Thanks badge Girl Scouts U.S.A., 1969; Outstanding Citizen in Community Service award State of N.D., 1974; Outstanding Citizen award City of Jamestown, 1978. Mem. Jamestown C. of C. (dir., pres. 1981), Nat. Assn. Bank Women, Nat. League Am. Pen Women, N.D. Press Women, AAUW, Nat. Fedn. Press Women, Nat. Food Editors and Writers Assn., PEO, Am. Legion Aux., Delta Kappa Gamma, Sigma Delta Chi. Republican. Clubs: Zonta, Order Eastern Star. Author: Kitchen Magic, 1964; Favorites of My family, 1972; Let's Entertain, 1980. Editors and Writers Assn., PEO, Am. Legion Aux., Delta Kappa Gamma, Sigma Delta Chi. Republican. Clubs: Zonta, Order Eastern Star. Author: Kitchen Magic, 1964; Favorites of My Family, 1972; Let's Entertain, 1980; Then and Now, 1983. Home: 309 11th Ave NE Jamestown ND 58401 Office: 122 2d St NW Jamestown ND 58401

HANSEN, ERIK, political scientist; b. Oslo, Dec. 6, 1956; s. Sverre and Lena (Löchsen) H.; m. Ilse Ramböck, Aug. 22, 1980 (div. June 1987). Grad., U. Oslo, 1981, Candidate in Politics, 1985. Research asst. The Fridtjof Nansen Inst., Oslo, 1985-86, research assoc., 1986-87; research assoc. Resource Policy Group, Oslo, 1987—. Contbr. articles to profl. jours. on natural resources industries, 1984—. Home: Schaeffersgate, N-0558 Oslo 5 Norway Office: Resource Policy Group, Sagveien, N-0458 Oslo 4 Norway

HANSEN, FINN, electrical engineer; b. Copenhagen, May 21, 1945; s. Hans Henning and Nina (Rasmussen) H.; m. Margit Hansen, Aug. 1, 1987; children by previous marriage: Tine, Jakob, Thomas Duus. BEE, Copenhagen Engring coll., 1971. Electrician Danish Cen. Com., 1967; project engr. Det Danske Stallvalsevaerk, Fr. Vaerk, 1973-75; project engr. Nea-Lindberg A/s, Copenhagen, 1975-77, engring. mgr., 1977-80; service mgr. ISS Securities A/S, Copenhagen, 1980-87; regional mgr. Dansk Erhvers Rengoring A/S, Copenhagen, 1987-88; engring. mgr. Kone A/S, Copenhagen, 1988—. Home: Lyngborghave 20, Birkerod, Copenhagen DK 3460, Denmark Office: Kone A/S, Lygten 37, Copenhagen DK 2400, Denmark

HANSEN, FLORENCE MARIE CONGIOLOSI (MRS. JAMES S. HANSEN), social worker; b. Middletown, N.Y., Jan. 7, 1934; d. Joseph James and Florence (Harrigan) Congiolosi; B.A., Coll. New Rochelle, 1955; M.S.W., Fla. State U., 1960; m. James S. Hansen, June 16, 1959; 1 dau., Florence M. Caseworker, Orange County Dept. Pub. Welfare, N.Y., 1955-57, Cath. Welfare Bur., Miami, Fla., 1957-58; supr. Cath. Family Service, Spokane, Wash., 1960, Cuban Children's Program, Spokane, 1962-66; founder, dir. social service dept. Sacred Heart Med. Ctr., 1968-85, dir. Kidney Ctr., 1967—. Asst. in program devel. St. Margaret's Hall, Spokane, 1961-62; trustee Family Counseling Service Spokane County, 1981—, also bd. dirs.; mem. budget allocation panel United Way, 1964-76, mem. planning com., 1968-77, mem. admissions com., 1969-70, chmn. projects com. 1972-73, active work with Cuban refugees; mem. kidney disease adv. com. Wash.-Alaska Regional Med. Program, 1970-73. Mem. Spokane Quality of Life Commn., 1974-75. Mem. Nat. Assn. Social Workers (chpt. pres. 1972-74), Acad. Cert. Social Workers (charter). Roman Catholic. Home: 5609 Northwest Blvd Spokane WA 99205 Office: Sacred Heart Med Ctr W 101 8th St Spokane WA 99204

HANSEN, HANS BERTIL HARALD, motor car body repairs engineering company executive, consultant; b. Strelitz, Germany, Jan. 24, 1921; s. Harald Bonde Oskar and Julia Anna Lovisa (Larsson) H.; m. Maijt Britt Vera Lindbom, Oct. 31, 1943; children: Gunilla, Par, Marten; Maj Britt Ingeborg Nilsson, June 11, 1964. Student, Högre Allmänna Läroverket, Kristianstad, 1940, Royal Naval Coll., Stockholm, 1941-43, Royal Naval Inst. of Advanced Studies and Univ. of Tech., 1949-53. Chief engr., mgr. Skandia Motor Car Ins., Stockholm, 1955-77; mng. dir. Bilskadecenter AB, Stockholm, 1977-81, Bilreko AB, Stockholm, 1981—; chmn. bd. BRK Tech. Com., Stockholm, 1965-73; sec. BRK Scandinavian Countries, 1967-81; mem., sec. RCAR World-Wide, London, 1971-81. Inventor estimating system for auto claims, 1963. Served to maj. Swedish mil., 1940-55. Mem. Swedish Ins. Assn. Club: Royal Automobile. Office: Bilreko AB, Bandhagsvagen 24, S-122 42 Enskede Sweden

HANSEN, JAMES VERNON, computer science, information sytems educator; b. Idaho Falls, May 31, 1936; s. Heber Lorenzo and Myrtle Jane (Simmons) H.; m. Diane Lynne Bradbury, Sept. 18, 1963; children: Tamsin, Jeffrey, Dale, Peter. BS, Brigham Young U., 1963, MS, 1966; PhD, U. Wash., 1973. Systems analyst TRW, Redondo Beach, Calif., 1966-69; sr. research analyst Battelle Meml. Inst., Richland, Wash., 1972-74, also cons.; asst. prof. Ind. U., Bloomington, 1974-77, assoc. prof., 1977-81; prof. Brigham Young U., Provo, Utah, 1982—; prin. EDI Group, Chgo., 1987—. Author: Controls in Microcomputer Systems, 1984—, Data Communications: Concepts and Controls, 1987; research on expert systems in computer auditing, use of inductive methods for knowledge engring., langs. for knowlege-based systems. Mem. Ind. dist. council Boy Scouts Am., 1978. Served with U.S. Army, 1959-62. Grantee Peat, Marwick, Mitchell Found., 1982, 83, Inst. Internal Auditors, 1983, Kellog Found., 1972. Mem. Assn. Computing Machinery, Inst. Mgmt. Sci., Ops. Research Soc. Am., Am. Assn. Artificial Intelligence, Sierra Club. Mormon. Office: Brigham Young U Provo UT 84602

HANSEN, KATHRYN GERTRUDE, former state official, association editor; b. Gardner, Ill., May 24, 1912; d. Harry J. and Marguerite (Gaston) Hansen; BS with honors, U. Ill., 1934, MS, 1936. Personnel asst. U. Ill., Urbana, 1945-46, supr. tng. and activities, 1946-47, personnel officer, instr. psychology, 1947-52, exec. sec. U. Civil Service System Ill., also sec. for merit bd., 1952-61, adminstrv. officer, sec. merit bd., 1961-68, dir. system, 1968-72; lay asst. firm Webber, Balbach, Theis and Follmer, P.C., Urbana, Ill., 1972-74. Bd. dirs. U. YWCA, 1952-55, chmn., 1954-55; bd. dirs. Champaign-Urbana Symphony, 1978-81; sec. Women's Assn. 1st Presbyn. Ch., Champaign, 1986. Mem. Coll. and Univ. Personnel Assn. (hon., life mem., editor jour. 1955-73, newsletter, internat. pres. 1967-68, nat. publs. award named in her honor 1987), Annuitants Assn. State Univs. Retirement System Ill. (state sec.-treas. 1974-75), Pres.'s Council U. Ill. (life), U. Ill. Alumni Assn. (life), Friends of the Library (bd. dirs. 1987—), U. Ill. Found., Campus Round Table U. Ill., Nat. League Am. Pen Women, AAUW (state 1st v.p. 1958-60, 50 yr. mem.), Champaign-Urbana Symphony Guild, Secretariat U. Ill. (life), Grundy County Hist. Soc., Delta Kappa Gamma (state pres. 1961-63), Phi Mu (life), Kappa Delta Pi, Kappa Tau Alpha. Presbyterian. Clubs: Monday Writers, Fortnightly (Champaign-Urbana). Lodge: Order Eastern Star. Author: (with others) A Plan of Position Classification for Colleges and Universities; A Classification Plan for Staff Positions at Colleges and Universities, 1968; Grundy-Corners, 1982; Sarah, A Documentary of Her Life and Times, 1984, Ninety Years with Fortnightly, Vols. I and II, an historical compilation, 1986; editor: The Illini Worker, 1946-52; Campus Pathways, 1952-61; This is Your Civil Service Handbook, 1960-67; author, cons., editor publs. on personnel practices. Home: 1004 E Harding Dr Apt 307 Urbana IL 61801

HANSEN, KENNETH D., lawyer, physician; b. Seattle, Mar. 26, 1947; s. George R. and Elaine D. (Jacobsen) H.; m. Barbara Caleen, Oct. 8, 1976; 1 son, David Scott. B.S. in Psychology, U. Wash., 1969, J.D., 1972, M.D. with honors, 1976. Bar: Wash. 1972, Mich. 1977, Ill. 1984, D.C. 1986, U.S. Supreme Ct. 1981. Diplomate Am. Bd. Ophthalmology. Legal counsel Assn. Wash. Bus., Olympia, 1972-73; asst. atty. gen. State of Wash., Seattle, 1973-74; v.p., gen. counsel Northwest Med. Research Found. Seattle, 1976—; pres. Internat. Health Found., 1986—; intern medicine U. Mich. Hosp., Ann Arbor, 1977, resident in opthalmology, 1978-80; sr. med. staff Henry Ford Hosp., Detroit, 1981-82; dir. ophthalmology Carbondale Clinic, Ill., 1983-86, chmn. dept. surgery, gen. counsel, 1984-86; clin. asst. prof. ophthalmology and med. humanities So. Ill. U., Carbondale 1983-86; clin. asst. prof. ophthalmology U. Md., Balt., 1986—; med.-legal adv. com. U. Mich. Hosp. System; cons. Nat. Def. Med. Coll., China. Recipient U. Wash. Med. Thesis Award, Gold Medal Egyptian Med. Syndicate, 1986; William Wallice Wilshire Meml. scholar; Anna C. Dunlap Meml. scholar; Grad. Research fellow, 1975—. Fellow Am. Coll. Legal Medicine (jud. council, model statutes com.), Internat. Coll. Surgeons; mem. Wash. State Bar Assn. Mich. Bar Assn., Ill. Med. Soc. (med.-legal council), Ill. Bar Assn., Mich. Med. Schs. Council Deans (med.-legal adv. com.), Mich. Ophthalmology Soc. (research award 1981), ABA, AMA, Am. Acad. Ophthalmology, D.C. Bar Assn., Phi Delta Pi, Phi Eta Sigma, Pi Sigma Epsilon. Baptist. Assoc. editor Wash. Law Rev., 1971-72; contbr. articles to legal and med. profl. jours., publs. Home: 1179 Ballantrae Ln McLean VA 22101 Office: Internat Health Found 4601 N Fairfax Dr Suite 100 Arlington VA 22203

HANSEN, LEONARD JOSEPH, writer, editor, publisher, marketing consultant; b. San Francisco, Aug. 4, 1932; s. Einar L. and Margie A. (Wilder) H.; A.B. in Radio-TV Prodn. and Mgmt., San Francisco State Coll., 1956, postgrad. 1956-57; cert. IBM Mgmt. Sch., 1967; m. Marcia Ann Rasmussen, Mar. 18, 1966; children—Barron Richard, Trevor Wilder. Jr. writer (part-time) Sta. KCBS, San Francisco, 1952-54; assoc. producer and dir. Ford Found. TV Research Project, San Francisco State Coll., 1955-57; air promotion dir. and writer Sta. KPIX-TV, San Francisco, 1959-60, crew chief on live and remote broadcasts, 1957-59; pub. relations mgr. Sta. KNTV-TV, San Jose, Calif., 1961; radio and TV promotion mgr. Seattle World's Fair, 1962; pub. relations and promotion mgr. Century 21 Ctr., Inc., Seattle, 1963-64; pub. relations dir. Dan Evans for Gov. Com., Seattle, 1964; propr., mgr. Leonard J. Hansen Pub. Relations, Seattle, 1965-67; campaign mgr. Walter J. Hickel for Gov. Com., Anchorage, 1966; exec. cons. to Gov. of Alaska, Juneau, 1967; gen. mgr. No. TV, Inc., Anchorage, 1967-69; v.p. mktg. Sea World, Inc., San Diego, 1969-71; editor and publisher Sr. World Publs., Inc., San Diego, 1973-84; pres. Sr. Publishers Group, 198487; speaker and mktg. cons. to sr. citizens, 1984—; panelist, pub. affairs radio programs, 1971—; lectr. journalism San Diego State U., 1975-76. Writer weekly syndicated column Mainly for Seniors, 1984—, syndicated column Travel for Adults, 1984—; Editor in chief Mature Life Features, news/feature syndicate, 1987—; chmn. Mature Mkt. Seminars, 1987—. Founding mem. Housing for Elderly and Low Income Persons, San Diego, 1977-78; mem. Mayor's Ad Hoc Adv. Com. on Aging, San Diego, 1976-79; vice chmn. Housing Task Force, San Diego, 1977-78; bd. dirs. Crime Control Commn., San Diego, 1980, San Diego Coalition, 1980-83; del. White House Conf. on Aging, 1981. Served with U.S. Army, 1953-55. Recipient numerous service and citizenship awards from clubs and community orgns. Mem. Public Relations Soc. Am. (accredited), Soc. Profl. Journalists (Best Investigative Reporting award 1979), Internat. Platform Assn., San Diego Press Club (Best Newswriting award 1976-77, Headliner of Yr. award 1980), Am. Assn. Travel Editors (profl. mem.). Home: 704-A Asbury Ct San Diego CA 92109 Office: 1326 Garnet Ave San Diego CA 92109

HANSEN, NIELS BORGE, chemist; b. Fensmark, Denmark, Nov. 10, 1908; M.E., Teknikum, Odense, 1932; certificate in Philosophy, U. Copenhagen, 1940; M.S. in Chem. Engring., Tech. U. Denmark, 1962. Designer, supr. constrn. machinery and waterworks, Denmark, 1932-46, Tanganyika, 1948-49; san. engr. UNRRA, China, 1946-47; procurement of equipment in U.S.A., tchr. Teknikum, Copenhagen, 1950-62; engr. waterworks and sewage plants Municipality of Copenhagen, 1962-65; founder, head microchem. lab. Inst. Mineralogy, U. Copenhagen, 1965-81, lectr., 1972-78. Mem. Danish Chem. Soc., Danish Soc. Chem., Civil, Elec. and Mech. Engrs., Geol. Soc. Denmark, Danish Soc. for Nature Conservation, Norden Assns. Lutheran. Author series of monographs Chemical Analysis of Minerals and Rocks, 1976—. Contbr. profl. papers on analytical chemistry. Office: Inst for Mineralogy, 5 Oster Voldgade, DK-1350 Copenhagen Denmark

HANSEN, PHYLLIS JEAN, librarian; b. Ames, Iowa, Nov. 28, 1934; d. Elmer N. and Florence (Faust) H. A.B. with honors, U. Ill., 1960, M.S., 1961; M.A., Calif. Poly. State U., 1984. Librarian, Queens Borough Pub. Library, N.Y.C., 1961, San Leandro Community Library (Calif.), 1962-63, Calif. Poly. State U., San Luis Obispo, 1963—. Author bibliographies: Vitamin C, 1980, rev., 1984, Sex Role Stereotyping and Career Aspirations of Junior High and High School Students, 1983, Sex Role Stereotyping in Career Literature, 1984. Mem. ALA, Calif. Library Assn., Calif. Soc. Librarians, AAUW, County Hist. Assn. San Luis Obispo, Delta Kappa Gamma, Alpha Lambda Delta. Republican. Presbyterian. Club: Business and Professional Women (v.p. 1984-85) (San Luis Obispo). Home: 1241 Fredericks St San Luis Obispo CA 93401 Office: Calif Poly State Univ Library San Luis Obispo CA 93407

HANSEN, SOREN VIKTOR, management consultant; b. Nykobing, Denmark, July 13, 1943; s. Kaj Viktor and Herdis (Sondergaard) H.; m. Gunvor Eskildsen, Dec. 9, 1967; 1 child, Mikala. MBA, Copenhagen U., 1971. Cons. DLG, Copenhagen, 1967-68; supr. Dansk Esso A/S, Copenhagen, 1968-70; asst. to bd. dirs. J.H. Schultz A/S, Copenhagen, 1970-71; project mgr. Louis Poulsen A/S, Copenhagen, 1971-75; sr. expert ILO, Trinidad, 1975-77; dir. Price Waterhouse, Copenhagen, 1977-83; ptnr. Interpro Mgmt. Cons., Copenhagen, 1983—; chmn. bd. dirs. H.P. Nielsen A/

S, Roskilde; bd. dirs. Proware APS, Copenhagen, Acorn Milling APS, Copenhagen. Contbr. articles to profl. jours. Mem. Inst. Danish Economists, Danish Assn. Mgmt. Cons. Home: Bredengen 23, 4000 Roskilde Denmark Office: Interpro Mgmt Cons, Bomhusvej 13, 2100 Copenhagen O Denmark

HANSEN, STEN STURE, educational administrator, mathematics educator and researcher; b. Middelfart, Denmark, Apr. 10, 1929; s. Carl Gunnar Hansen and Karen Hornelund. M.S., U. Copenhagen, 1953, D.Sc., 1981. Assoc. prof. Sankt Annae Gymnasium, Copenhagen, 1954-56; assoc. prof. Gammel Hellerup Gymnasium, Copenhagen, 1956-71, prof., 1971-84; prin. Ordrup Gymnasium, Copenhagen, 1984—; prof. math. U. Copenhagen, 1982—. Author: Contributions to the Sylvester-Gallai-Theory, 1981; also articles in profl. publs. Mem. Danish Math. Soc., Am. Math. Soc., Assn. Profs. State Colls. (pres. 1959-71), Assn. Higher Civil Servants (bd. dirs. 1960-71). Avocation: oil painting. Home: Aavaenget 3, 2970 Hoersholm, Copenhagen Denmark Office: Ordrup Gymnasium, Kirkevej 5, 2920 Charlottenlund, Copenhagen Denmark

HANSEN, WENDELL JAY, clergyman, gospel broadcaster; b. Waukegan, Ill., May 28, 1910; s. Christian Hans and Anna Sophia (Termansen) H.; m. Bertelle Kathryn Budman, Mar. 9, 1933 (dec. Jan. 6, 1956); 1 child, Sylvia Larson; m. 2d, Eunice Evaline Irvine, Nov. 2, 1957; 1 child, Dean. Grad. Cleve. Bible Coll., 1932; A.B., William Penn Coll., 1938; postgrad. Gletch Berg Skule, Switzerland, 1939; M.A., U. Iowa, 1940, Ph.D., 1947. Ordained to ministry Recorded Friends, 1936, Evang. Reformed Ch., 1944; pastor chs., Grinnell, Iowa, Mpls. and Iowa City, 1934-47; evangelist with talking and performing birds, 1946—, mgr. gospel radio stas. Two Rivers, Wis., Menomonie, Wis., Peru, Ind., Wabash, Ind., East St. Louis, Ill., Indpls., 1952—; pres., chmn. of bd. WESL Inc., East St. Louis, 1962—, cons. radio and TV, 1970—; appointed adv. com. to Indpls. Prosecutor, 1986. Dir. St. Paul Inter-racial Work Camp, 1939; chmn. Minn. Joint Refuge Com., 1940-41. Recipient honor citation Nat. Assn. Broadcasters, 1980; Boss of Yr. award Hamilton County Broadcasters, 1979, award Boys Town, 1983, award Women of Faith, St. Louis, 1984. Mem. Internat. Platform Assn., Internat. Assn. Christian Magicians, Ind. Bird Fanciers, East St. Louis C. of C. (bd. dirs. 1981—), Pi Kappa Delta. Republican. Quaker. Club: Ind. Pigeon (best exotic bird award 1969, 75, 80). Lodge: Kiwanis. Contbr. articles to popular mags.

HANSON, ALDEN WADE, chemist; b. Jennings, Mich., June 19, 1910; s. Yorgan and Goldie (Fairchilds) H.; m. Helen Laurine Bennett, Feb. 22, 1930; children: Peter W., Helen Laurine, Chris Alden, Alden Bennett. BS, Alma Coll., 1934, DSc (hon.), 1980. Chemist Dow Chem. Co., Midland, Mich., 1934-39; project leader Dow Chem. Co., Midland, 1939-41, group leader, 1941-54, dir. nuclear and basic research lab., 1954-73; cons., dir. Hanson Industries Inc., Midland, 1970—, Alden Labs., Midland, 1980—. Contbr. articles on indsl. use of nuclear power, chem. research on plastics and nuclear waste disposal to profl. jours.; patentee plastic processes, mech. apparatus, snow-making processes, knot (dedicated to Boy Scouts Am.). Bd. regents U. Calif., Livermore, 1956-62. Mem. AAAS, ASTM, Am. Chem. Soc., Sigma Xi. Clubs: Midland Country; Otsego Ski; Hidden Valley (Gaylord, Mich.). Home: 3124 Valley Dr Midland MI 48640

HANSON, BRUCE EUGENE, lawyer; b. Lincoln, Nebr., Aug. 25, 1942; s. Lester E. and Gladys (Diessner) H.; m. Peggy Pardun, Dec. 25, 1972. B.A., U. Minn., 1965, J.D., 1966. Bar: Minn. 1966, U.S. Dist. Ct. Minn. 1966, U.S. Tax Ct. 1973, U.S. Ct. Appeals (8th cir.) 1973, U.S. Ct. Appeals (fed. cir.) 1983, U.S. Supreme Ct. 1970. Ptnr., Doherty, Rumble & Butler, St. Paul, 1966—. Mem. Ramsey County Bar Assn., Minn. State Bar Assn., Am. Acad. Hosp. Attys., Minn. Soc. Hosp. Attys. (bd. dirs.), Assn. Trial Lawyers Am. Order of Coif, Phi Delta Phi. Clubs: St. Paul Athletic; North Oaks Golf (Minn.). Home: 23 Evergreen Rd North Oaks MN 55110 Office: Doherty Rumble & Butler 2800 Minn World Trade Ctr Saint Paul MN 55101

HANSON, BRYANT R., health care administrator; b. Price, Utah, Apr. 13, 1946; s. Rex R. and Christine (Passarella) H.; m. Annette Wilson, June 15, 1968; children: Tonya, Stephen. AB cum laude, Regis Coll., 1968; MS in Hosp. Adminstrn., Ohio State U., 1973. Asst. exec. dir. St. Francis Hosp., Blue Island, Ill., 1973-75, assoc. exec. dir., 1975-80, exec. dir., 1980—, healyh ctr., pres., chief exec. officer; preceptor Govs. State U., Park Forest, Ill., 1980—, Ohio State U., Columbus, 1980—; bd. dirs. Family and Mental Health Cook County, Oak Lawn, 1976-85, Met. Chgo. Healthcare Council. Mem. Blue Island Mayor's Adv. Com., 1980-85; hon. chmn. Los Amigos, Blue Island, 1982; bd. dirs. Community Fund South Cook County, 1978-80. Served with U.S. Army, 1968-71, Vietnam. Regis Coll. scholar, 1964-68; decorated Bronze Star. Mem. Blue Island C. of C. (bd. dirs. 1979-83), Am. Coll. Health Care Execs., Am. Acad. Med. Adminstrs., Ill. Hosp. Assn. (region pres. 1982-84), Cath. Hosp. Assn., Chgo. Conf. Cath. Hosps. (v.p. 1984-87), Met. Chgo. Health Care Council (bd. dirs. 1987-90), Cath. Health Alliance (bd. dits.met. Chgo. 1987—). Roman Catholic. Lodges: Rotary (v.p. 1978-80), Deacons, K.C. (Blue Island). Avocations: golf, rose gardening. Home: 15304 Walnut Rd Oak Forest IL 60452 Office: St Francis Hosp & Health Ctr 12935 S Gregory St Blue Island IL 60406

HANSON, JOSEPH J., publishing executive; b. N.Y.C., Sept. 23, 1930; s. Isiah and Mary (Solodow) H.; m. Gloria Hanson; children: Melissa Ann, Leigh Caren, Meri Jenifer, Joshua Joseph, Alexandra Brooke. Student, Rochester Inst. Tech., 1950-52. Eastern sales mgr. Indsl. Pub. Corp., Cleve., 1954-58; v.p. Mgmt. Pub. Corp., Greenwich, Conn., 1958-65; pres. Market Publs., Inc., New Canaan, Conn., 1965-76; chmn. bd. Marketplace Publs., Inc., New Canaan, 1967-69; pub., editor-in-chief Folio, The Mag. for Mag. Mgmt., 1972—; pres. Hanson Pub. Group, Inc. (affiliate Cowles Media Co.), 1988—; chmn. Media Pub. Corp., 1978-80; dir. ann. Mag. Publishing Week, 1979—; producer Face to Face, ann. pub. conf. and expn.; dir. Educat Pubs., Inc., Directories Internat., Inc., 1983-87; v.p., dir. Conf. Mgmt. Corp., 1976-80; U.S. del. Internat. Fedn. Periodical Press, 1982—; dir. Gallatin Div. publishing program NYU, 1986—, publishing program Pace U., 1987, tech./mag. program Rochester Inst. Tech, 1987—; lectr. schs. journalism colls. and univs. Exec. dir. Assn. Supervisory Nurses, New Canaan, 1969-75; trustee Mead Sch., Greenwich, Conn., 1971-74. Recipient Jessie H. Neal award for disting. journalism, 1975; award for disting. journalism Fla. Mag. Assn., 1978; Lee C. Williams award for disting. contbns. to the periodical pub. field, 1979; Marie Archer award for mag. design, 1979. Mem. Am. Bus. Press (dir. 1974-77), Mag. Pubs. Assn. (edn. com.). Clubs: Metropolitan, Overseas Press, Nat. Press. Office: 6 River Bend Box 4949 Stamford CT 06907

HANSON, MONTE KENT, retail and broadcasting executive; b. Mexico, Mo., Jan. 11, 1955; s. Wilmer D. and Velma B. (Montague) H.; m. Glee Anne Brummitt, June 19, 1977; children—Josiah Kent, Lydia Michelle, Micah Franklin. B.S., Northeast Mo. State U., 1977. Salesman, OCCO Feed Co., Oelwein, Iowa, 1973, dist. mgr., 1974-77; asst. mgr. K-Mart Corp., Mo., 1977-80; pres., gen. mgr. Faith Ctr., Kirksville, Mo., 1981—; pres., gen. mgr. No. Mo. Christian Broadcasting, Inc., 1987—. Bd. dirs. Christian Life, Nazarene Ch., Mo., 1981, 82, 83. Named State Farmer, Future Farmers Am., Mo., 1973. Mem. Christian Booksellers Assn., Kirksville C. of C. (chmn. retail com. 1982), Nat. Fedn. Ind. Bus. Republican. Avocations: reading; Bible collecting; softball. Office: Faith Ctr 110 W Harrison St Kirksville MO 63501

HANSON, ROBERT ARTHUR, agricultural equipment executive; b. Moline, Ill., Dec. 13, 1924; s. Nels A. and Margaret I. (Chapman) H.; m. Patricia Ann Klinger, June 25, 1955. B.A., Augustana Coll., Rock Island, Ill., 1948. Various positions Deere & Co., Moline, 1950-62; gen. mgr. Deere & Co., Mexico, 1962-64, Spain, 1964-66; dir. mktg. overseas Deere & Co., 1966-70, v.p. overseas ops., 1972, sr. v.p. overseas div., 1973, dir., 1974—, exec. v.p., 1975-78, pres., 1978-85, chief operating officer, 1979-82, chmn., chief exec. officer, 1982—; bd. dirs. Procter & Gamble Co., Merrill Lynch & Co., Dun & Bradstreet Corp.; mem. Morgan Guaranty Trust Co.'s Internat. Council, N.Y.C. Trustee Com. for Econ. Devel.; trustee Mayo Found.; bd. dirs. Farm and Indsl. Equipment Inst. Served with USMCR, 1943-46. Mem. Bus. Council. Home: 2200 29th Avenue Ct Moline IL 61265 Office: Deere & Co John Deere Rd Moline IL 61265 *

HANSON, ROBERT CARL, sociologist, educator; b. Wichita, Kans., Nov. 5, 1926; s. Otto Albert and Alma Charlotta (Larson) H.; m. Margaret B. Bremner, Jan. 1, 1950; children—Steven, Holly, Juliana. Student, U. Wyo., 1944, Tex. A&M U., 1945; B.A., U. Calif., Berkeley, 1949, M.A., 1951, Ph.D., 1955; postgrad., Harvard U., 1951-52. Instr. Mich. State U., 1955-57, asst. prof., 1957-60; asst. prof. U. Colo., Boulder, 1960-62; asso. prof. U. Colo., 1962-65, dir. Bur. Sociol. Research, 1962-64, acting dir. Inst. Behavioral Sci., 1964-65, prof. sociology, 1965—, research program dir., 1965-75; cons. USPHS (Migrant Health Br.), 1963-65; mem. Com. on Acad. Disciplines for Study Commn. on Undergrad. Edn. U.S. Office Edn., 1972-75. Author: (with Richard Jessor, Theodore D. Graves and Shirley L. Jessor) Society, Personality and Deviant Behavior, 1968; Contbr. articles to profl. jours. Served with AUS, 1944-46. Russell Sage Found. residency grantee, 1960-62; USPHS research grantee, 1960-63; NIMH research grantee, 1960-63, 64-70; Council on Research and Creative Work fellow, 1964-65. Mem. AAAS (mem. com. on desert and arid zones research 1961-62), Peace Research Soc., AAUP, Am. Fedn. Tchrs., ACLU, Am. Sociol. Assn. (com. on social stats. 1964-66), Pacific Sociol. Assn. Office: U Colo Dept Sociology Boulder CO 80309

HANSON, ROBERT DELOLLE, lawyer; b. Harrisburg, Pa., Dec. 13, 1916; s. Henry W. A. and Elizabeth (Painter) H.; B.A., Gettysburg Coll., 1939; LL.B., Dickinson Law Sch., 1942; m. Barbara Esmer, Apr. 22, 1949. Admitted to Pa. bar, 1942; practiced in Harrisburg, 1946—; solicitor, Dauphin County, 1958-76, Dauphin County Redevel. Authority, 1959—. Pres. Family and Children's Service of Harrisburg, 1956-57; mem. Harrisburg Sch. Bd., 1952-57, Dauphin County Housing Authority, 1960; gen. chmn. Tri-County United Fund, 1969, pres., 1971-72; trustee Gettysburg Coll., 1974—, sec., 1980, vice chmn., 1983-866 pres. Keystone area council Boy Scouts Am., 1980-82. Served from 2d lt. to maj. inf. AUS, 1942-46; ETO. Decorated Bronze Star, Purple Heart. Mem. Am., Pa. (sec., treas. taxation sect. 1948-59), Dauphin County (dir. 1958-59) bar assns., Gettysburg Coll. Alumni Assn. (treas. 1958, 59, v.p. 1968-71, pres. 1971-72), Phi Beta Kappa. Lutheran (pres. council of congregation 1953, 54, 55, 57, 58, 59). Clubs: Masons (33 deg., past master, pres. bd. trustees 1982-85), Execs. (pres. 1953), Tuesday, Rotary (pres. 1979). Home: 2500 N 2d St Harrisburg PA 17110 Office: Suite 307 100 Chestnut St Harrisburg PA 17101

HANSON, RONALD WINDELL, cardiologist; b. Jeffersonville, Ind., Apr. 30, 1947; s. Erwin D. and Bernice (Windell) H. B.S. summa cum laude, Ariz. State U., 1968, M.S., 1969, Ph.D. in Physics, 1972; M.D., U. Ala., 1977. Diplomate Am. Bd. Internal Medicine, Am. Bd. Cardiovascular Diseases. Asst. prof. physics U. Ala., 1972-74; resident in internal medicine and cardiology Good Samaritan Hosp., Phoenix, 1977-82; practice medicine specializing in cardiology, Gadsden, Ala., 1982—; entrepreneur in comml. real estate and gas and oil exploration. Served to lt. col. CAP. Fellow Am. Coll. Cardiology; mem. ACP, Phi Kappa Phi. Office: 801 Gaines Ave Suite 400 Gadsden AL 35903

HANSRYD, ROLF, retail executive; b. Karlskrona, Blekinge, Sweden, Oct. 14, 1943; m. Birgitta Ljungstedt, June 14, 1968; children: Jonas, Ulf, Cecilia. BS, Lund U., Sweden, 1968. Mktg. researcher Kooperative Forbundet, Stockholm, 1969-71, controller, mgr. logistics, 1979-85; dep. gen. mgr. Inter Coop, Hamburg, Fed. Republic Germany, 1971-74; gen. mgr. Konsum Skaraborg, Skoude, Sweden, 1985—. Home: Morkullevagen 13, 54156 Skoude Sweden Office: Konsum Skaraborg, PO Box 111, 54122 Skoude Sweden

HANSSON, AKE H., sales executive; b. Stockholm, Sweden, June 2, 1939; s. Anders T. and Ingeborg (Andersson) H.; m. Birgitta K. Wihlborg, May 2, 1947; children: Kristina, Maria. Teletekniker, Tekniker Sch., Sala, Sweden, 1957. Sr. engr. Swedish Air Force, Stockholm, Sweden, 1961-70; gen. mgr. Technitron Sweden AB, Stockholm, 1970-81, sr. sales mgr., 1982—. Club: Odd Fellow (Stockholm). Home: Jakobsdal/Lugn V 16, 13700 V-Haninge Sweden Office: Technitron Sweden AB, PO Box 163 55 Spanga, S-100 28 Stockholm Sweden

HANSSON, INGE LEIF HERBERT, materials scientist, educator, consultant; b. Alvsborg, Sweden, May 31, 1949; came to Denmark, 1973; s. George Herbert and Vivan Margareta (Johanson) H.; m. Carolyn Mary Russell, Mar. 15, 1941; 1 child, Russell Victor. MSc, Chalmers U., Gothenburg, Sweden, 1972; PhD, Chalmers U., 1980, DSc, 1984. Asst. prof. Tech. U. Denmark, Lyngby, 1973-76; assoc. prof. Tech. U. Denmark, 1977-84; materials tech. dept. head F.L. Smidth & Co., Valby, Denmark, 1984-86; assoc. prof. Tech. U. Denmark, 1987—; cons. in field. Author: Ultrasonics, 1978. Mem. ASTM, Danish Soc. Materials Research and Testing (bd. dirs. 1986—). Office: Tech U Denmark, Lab Applied Physics, 2800 Lyngby Denmark

HANSUM, GERARD ARNOLD, accountant; b. Deventer, Overijssel, The Netherlands, Dec. 22, 1939; s. Pieter M. and Krina Visser H.; m. Wilhelmina P. Veenvliet; 3 children. Cert. acctg., 1969. With various auditor's firms, The Netherlands, 1959-75; controller Akzo Zout Chemie, The Netherlands, 1975-82, adjunct dir., adminstrv. affairs, 1982-87; gen. mgr. Akzo Pensioenfonds, The Netherlands, 1987—; tchr., examiner Nederlands Instituut van Register Accts., 1962—. Home: 53 Juniperlaan, 7313 BW Apeldoorn The Netherlands Office: Stricting Akzo-Pensionfonds, PO Box 1002, 6801 Arnhem The Netherlands

HANTON, E. MICHAEL, public and personnel relations cons.; b. Gary, Ind.; s. Zachary and Maria (Suciu) H.; A.B., Ind. U., 1951, M.A., 1955; grad. U.S. Air Force Air War Coll., 1968. Various prodn. positions U.S. Steel Corp., Gary, 1940, 41, 50; prodn. controller Douglas Aircraft Corp., Santa Monica, Calif., 1946-47; classified advt. mgr. Weaver Pub. Co., Santa Monica, 1947-48; reporter Muncie (Ind.) Evening Press, 1952, Gary Post-Tribune, 1952-53; head cashier Office Lake County Treas., Gary, 1955-60; public and personnel relations cons., Gary, 1960—, Plattsburgh, N.Y., 1968—; asst. prof. State U. Coll. Arts and Scis., Plattsburgh, 1966-67; cons. community relations and fund raising. Served with USAAF, 1941-45; mem. Res. Decorated Air medal, Purple Heart. Mem. Am. Med. Writers Assn., Assn. Edn. in Journalism and Mass Communications, Am. Acad. Advt., Gary C. of C., Plattsburgh C. of C., Air Force Assn., Res. Officers Assn. Clubs: Nat. Arts, Steel, Caterpillar, Flying Boot. Author: The New Nurse, 1973. Office: PO Box 803 Plattsburgh NY 12901

HANUSZKIEWICZ, ADAM, director, actor; b. Lvov, USSR, June 16, 1924; s. Wlodzimierz and Stanislawa (Szydlowska) H.; m. Zofia Rys; 3 children; m. 2d, Zofia Kucowna. Ed. State High Sch. of Drama, Lodz, and State Higher Sch. of Drama, Warsaw. Debut as actor, 1945, acted in Cracow, Poznan and Warsaw, Poland; debut as dir., 1953, directed in Poznan and Warsaw; artistic dir. Theatre of Polish TV, 1956-63; dir., producer Teatr Powszechny, Warsaw, 1963-68; gen. mgr., artistic dir. Teatr Narodowy, Warsaw, 1968-82; visited various theatre cos.; actor numerous plays, including: Hamlet, 1951-59, Berenice, 1962, The Tempest, 1963, Crime and Punishment, 1964, Don Juan, 1965, Fantazy, 1967, Un-divine Comedy, 1969, Macbeth, 1972, Antigone, 1973, plays directed include: Wesele, Crime and Punishment, Coriolanus, Don Juan, Platonov, The Columbus Boys, Kordian, St. Joan, 1969, Hamlet, 1970, Norwieg, 1970, Beniowski, 1971, Three Sisters, 1971, Twelfth Night, 1971, Macbeth, 1973, Antigone, 1973, The Inspector General, 1973, Balladyna, 1974, A Month in the Country, 1974, Waclawa dzieje, 1974, Kartoteka, 1974, Don Juan, 1974, Wesele, 1976, Mickiewicz, 1976, Maz i zona, 1977, Phedre, 1977, Peace, 1977, Sen Srebrny Salomei, 1977, Wyszedl z domu, 1978, Dziady, 1978, Biale malzenstwo, 1978, Treny, 1979, The Brothers Karamazov, The Decameron, As You Like It, Platonov, School of Wires. Decorated Order of Banner of Labor 1st class; recipient State prize first class for TV work, award for theatre work City of Warsaw, Theatre Critics' prize, 1964, Ekran Gold Screen TV award, 1968, prize of Minister of Fgn. Affairs, 1979. Office: Teatr Narodowy, Pl Teatralny 3, 00-077 Warsaw Poland *

HANWAY, DONALD GRANT, retired agronomist, educator; b. Broadwater, Nebr., Aug. 6, 1918; s. Frank Pierce and Emma Terrissa (Twist) H.; m. Blanche Elizabeth Larson, Sept. 26, 1942; children—Donald Grant, Wayne Edward, Janice Kay. B.S., U. Nebr., 1942, M.S., 1948; Ph.D., Iowa State Coll., 1954. Tchr. rural schs., Morrill County, Nebr., 1936-40; mem. faculty dept. agronomy U. Nebr., Lincoln, 1947-84, prof. emeritus, 1984—; also extension agronomist, chief of party univ. mission to Ataturk U. U. Nebr., Erzurum, Turkey, 1965-67; agronomic cons., Nigeria, Columbia, Morocco, Tunisia. Contbr. articles to profl. jours. Served with USAAF, 1942-46. Named to Nebr. Hall of Agrl. Achievement. Fellow Am. Soc. Agronomy, AAAS, Crop Sci. Soc. Am.; mem. Crop Sci. Soc. Am., Soil Conservation Soc. Am., Am. Inst. Biol. Scis., Phi Beta Kappa, Sigma Xi, Alpha Zeta, Gamma Sigma Delta. Republican. Episcopalian. Home: 6025 Madison Ave Lincoln NE 68507

HAOUR-KNIPE, MARY LOIS, sociologist; b. Prince Rupert, B.C., Can., Jan. 26, 1945; d. Roger George and Winnifred Lois (Morgan) Knipe; m. Georges Charles Haour, May 29, 1971; children: Anne Claire, Patrick Michael. BS, U. Wash., 1966; MS, Columbia U., 1969; MA, U. Toronto, Ont., Can., 1972. Instr. Columbia U., N.Y.C., 1969-71; research assoc. U. Toronto, 1972-74; lectr. various nursing schs. Geneva, 1978-85; cons. WHO, Geneva, 1985—; researcher Unite D'Investigation Clinique, 1982-85; free-lance researcher, 1982—. Contbr. articles on migration, health, stress, and social equity to sci. jours. Mem. European Soc. Med. Sociology (nat. coordinator 1986), Am. Sociol. Assn., Swiss Sociol. Soc. Home and Office: 5 rue Saint Ours, 1205 Geneva Switzerland

HAPPEL, JOHN, chemical engineer, researcher; b. Bklyn., Apr. 1, 1908; s. John and Emilie (Weinkauf) H.; m. Dorothy Merriam, 1951; children: Jill, George, Ruth. B.S., MIT, 1929, M.S., 1930; D.Ch.E., Poly. Inst. Bklyn., 1948. Registered profl. engr., N.Y. With Socony Vacuum Oil Co., 1930-48; prof. chem. engring., chmn. dept. chem. engring. NYU, N.Y.C., 1949-73, prof. emeritus, 1973—; sr. research assoc. Columbia U., N.Y.C., 1973—, spl. research assoc., 1976—; pres. Catalysis Research Corp.; bd. mgrs. Mohonk Consultations, Inc.; mem. petroleum industry war council, 1942-45; mem. tech. com. charge constrn. and operation world's largest butadiene plant for synthetic rubber, 1942-47; mem. indsl. adv. bd. for chem. engring. U. Conn., Storrs, 1981—; cons. to various cos. on petroleum chems. Author: Chemical Process Economics, 1958, 2d edit. (with Donald Jordan), 1974, (with Howard Brenner) Low Reynolds Number Hydrodynamics, 1965, 2d edit., 1973, paperback edit., 1983; translator: (with M.F. Delleo, Jr., G. Dembinski, A.H. Weiss) Catalysis by Non-Metals (from Russian by O.V. Krylov), 1970, (with Miguel Hnatow and Laimonis Bajars) Base Metal Oxide Catalysts, 1977, Isotopic Assessment of Heterogeneous Catalysis, 1986; assoc. editor: Chem. Engring. Jour.; mem. editorial adv. bd. Ency. Chem. Processing and Design, Oxidation Communications, Chem. Engring. Jour.; contbr. articles to profl. jours., chpts. to tech. books. Recipient Certificate of Distinction Poly. Inst. Bklyn.; Tyler award N.Y. sect. Am. Inst. Chem. Engrs. Fellow N.Y. Acad. Scis. (v.p. 1977), Am. Inst. Chem. Engrs. (Founders award 1987); mem. Am. Chem. Soc. (Honor Scroll), Nat. Acad. Engring., Sigma Xi, Alpha Chi Sigma, Phi Lambda Upsilon, Tau Beta Pi. Episcopalian. Club: Chemists (N.Y.C.). Home: 69 Tompkins Ave Hastings-on-Hudson NY 10706 Office: Columbia U New York NY 10027

HAQUE, MALIKA HAKIM, pediatrician; b. Madras, India; came to U.S., 1967; d. Syed Abdul and Rahimunisa (Hussain) Hakim; M.B.B.S., Madras Med. Coll., 1967; m. C. Azeez ul Haque, Feb. 5, 1967; children—Kifizeba, Masarath Nashr, Asim Zayd. Rotating intern Miriam Hosp., Brown U., Providence, 1967-68; resident in pediatrics Children's Hosp., N.J. Coll. Medicine, 1968-70; fellow in devel. disabilities Ohio State U., 1970-71; acting chief pediatrics Nisonger Center, 1973-74; staff pediatrician Children and Youth Project, Children's Hosp., Columbus, Ohio, also clin. asst. prof. pediatrics Ohio State U., 1974-80; clin. asso. prof. pediatrics Ohio State U., 1981—; pediatrician in charge community pediatrics and adolescent services clinics Columbus Children's Hosp., 1982—; cons. Central Ohio Head Start Program, 1974-79. Contbr. articles to profl. jours. and newspapers. Charter mem. Republican Presdl. Task Force, 1982—, Nat. Rep. Senatorial Com., 1985—, U.S. Senatorial Club; charter founder Ronald Reagan Rep. Ctr. Recipient Physician Recognition award AMA, 1971-86, 88—, Gold medals in surgery, radiology, pediatrics and ob/gyn; Presdl. medal of Merit, 1982; diplomate Am. Bd. Pediatrics. Fellow Am. Acad. Pediatrics (Prep Fellowship award 1986, Ohio chpt.); mem. Ambulatory Pediatric Assn., Acad. Medicine, Ohio State Med. Assn., Cen. Ohio Pediatric Soc. (mktg. and community edn. coms.). Islam. Research on enuresis. Home: 5995 Forestview Dr Columbus OH 43213 Office: 700 Children's Dr Columbus OH 43205

HARA, KENZABURO, government official; b. Hyugo Prefecture, Japan, Feb. 6, 1907; m. Mariko Hara. Student, Waseda U., Japan; grad., Oregon U., Columbia U., Berlin U. Mem. Ho. of Reps. Govt. of Japan, 1946—, parliamentary vice-minister of transport, 1949, vice speaker Ho. of Reps., 1961-62, minister of labour, 1968-71, 71-72, minister of state, 1980-81, now speaker Ho. of Reps.; vice-chmn. exec. council Liberal Dem. Party, 1977-78; past. dir. gen. Nat. Land Agy., Hokkaido Devel. Agy. Home: 131-6 Kitamochida-cho, Matsuyama, Ehime 790 Japan Office: House of Reps, 2-18-1 Nagata-cho, Chujoda-ku, Tokyo 100 Japan *

HARADA, KEIICHI, education educator; b. Nagoya, Japan, Feb. 11, 1929; s. Hiroshi and Yoneko (Ohtani) H.; m. Keiko Kinugasa; children: George, Mari Harada Yuan. BA, Doshisha U., Kyoto, Japan, 1951; MA, Syracuse U., 1954. Tchr. Nagoya (Japan) Gakuin High Sch., 1951-56; instr., assoc. prof. Aoyama Gakuin U., Tokyo, 1956-61; assoc. prof. Chiba (Japan) U., 1961-72, prof., 1972—. Co-editor: American Literature, 1960; author: (with others) The Growth of American Novels, 1976, Self-Formation of American Literature, 1981; contbr. articles to profl. jours. American Council of Learned Socs. fellow Ind. U., 1966-67, Duke U., 1979. Mem. Chiba English Lit. Soc. (pres. 1977—), Japan English Lit. Soc., Japan Am. Lit. Soc., Modern Language Assn. Am., Melville Soc. U.S.A., Hemingway Soc. Home: Shiohama 4-2-15-204, 272-01 Ichikawa-shi Japan Office: Chiba U Faculty of Letters, 1-33 Yayoi-cho, 260 Chiba-sahi Japan

HARADA, TAKASHI, textile executive; b. Kasugai, Aichi, Japan, Apr. 13, 1939. BA, Nagoya U., Japan, 1962, MA, 1964; PhD, Ochanomizu U., Tokyo, 1985. Researcher Toyobo Co. Ltd., Otsu, 1964-73, chief researcher, 1973-75, 78-82; asst. coordinator Toyobo Co. Ltd., Osaka, 1975-78; sr. chief researcher Toyobo Co. Ltd., Otsu, 1982-84; coordinator Toyobo Co. Ltd., Osaka, 1984-86, sr coordinator, 1986—. Contbr. articles to profl. jours. Mem. Soc. Polymer Sci., Soc. Fiber Sci. Tech., Textile Machinery Soc. Japan (meml. award 1984). Home: 18-10 Kinugawa 2-chome, Otsu, Shiga 520-02, Japan Office: Toyobo Co Ltd, 2-8 Dojima-hama 2-chome, Kita-ku, Osaka 530, Japan

HARALAMBOPOULOS, IOANNIS, deputy prime minister Greece; b. Psari, Messinia, Greece, 1919; grad. Greek Mil. Acad., 1939; student Woolwich Inst., London, 1946-50. Commd. Greek Army, 1939; resigned, 1961; mem. faculty Greek Mil. Acad., 1953-54; tech. advisor Greek Ministry of Fin., 1954-58; dep. Greek Parliament, 1963-67; founding mem. Nat. Democratic Resistance Movement, 1967; jailed and deported, 1967, arrested and jailed, 1968, 73-74; leader Panhellenic Liberation Movement, 1972; founding mem. PASOK (Panhellenic Socialist Movement), mem. central com. and exec. office, 1977—; minister of fgn. affairs, 1981-85, dep. prime minister, minister of def., 1986—; PASOK parliamentary rep. European Parliament, 1981, also mem. Socialist Polit. Bur. Office: Office of Deputy Prime Minister, Athens Greece *

HARALDSSON, ERLENDUR, psychology educator, psychical researcher, writer; b. Seltjarnarnes, Iceland, Nov. 3, 1931; s. Haraldur Erlendsson and Anna Elisabet Elimundardottir. Grad., Reykjavik Gymnasium, Reykjavik, 1954; diploma in Psychology, U. Munich, Federal Republic Germany, 1969; Ph.D., U. Freiburg, Federal Republic Germany, 1972. Journalist, Althydubladid, Reykjavik, Iceland, 1960-62; research fellow Inst. for Parapsychology, Durham, N.C., 1969-70; intern in clin. psychology U. Va., Charlottesville, 1970-71; research assoc. Am. Soc. Psychical Research, N.Y.C., 1972-74; asst. prof. psychology U. Iceland, Reykjavik, 1974-77, assoc. prof., 1978—. Author: Land im Aufstand Kurdistan, 1966; At the Hour of Death, 1977; Thessa Heims og Annars, 1978; Modern Miracles, 1988. Contbr. articles to profl. jours. Press agt. Kurdistan Democratic Party, Iraq, 1964-69. Mem. Parapsychol. Assn., Am. Psychol. Assn. (fgn. affiliate), Soc. Sci. Study of Religion, Soc. Psychical Research (corr.), Nordisk Psykologisk Forskerbund. Lutheran. Office: U Iceland Sudurgata, 101 Reykjavik Iceland

HARALDSTED, HANS HENRIK, mechanical engineer, corporate executive; b. Copenhagen, Apr. 14, 1942; s. Mogens and Else (Larsen) H.; m.

Karen Petersen, 1969; children: Henrik, Helle. BSc in Mech. Engring., Tech. High Sch., Copenhagen, 1969; BScCom, Comml. High Sch., Copenhagen, 1979; BScCom in Exports, Comml. High Sch., 1982, BScCom in Mgmt., 1983. Mech. engr. Copenhagen, 1969-74; pres., owner engring. and trading co. Hans H. Haraldsted, Copenhagen/Farum, 1975—. Editor: About Inventions, 1982; patentee in field. Recipient Gold and Silver medals for best invention Eureca, Brussels, 1979. Mem. Daffo-Lyngby (pres. 1980-87). Home and Office: Ellegaardspark 19, PO Box 107, 3520 Farum Denmark

HARALSON, DALE, lawyer; b. Colorado City, Tex., Aug. 7, 1937; m. Betty L. Haralson; children—Wendy, Kristi. B.B.A., Hardin-Simons U., 1959; J.D., U. Ariz., 1963. Bar: Ariz. 1963, U.S. Dist. Ariz., 1976, U.S. Dist. Ct. (we. dist.) Tex. 1976, U.S. Ct. Appeals (5th, 9th and 10th cirs.) 1976, U.S. Surpeme Ct. 1975. Ptnr., Haralson, Kinerk & Morey, P.C., Tucson; lectr. in field. Trustee, Tucson Gen. Hosp., 1968-74, chmn. exec. com., 1969-71, chmn., 1971-72. Fellow Internat. Soc. Barristers, Internat. Acad. Trial Lawyers; mem. Assn. Trial Lawyers Am. (nat. v.p. 1981-82, nat. treas. 1978-81), Ariz. Trial Lawyers Assn. (pres. 1969-70), Western Trial Lawyers Assn. (gov. 1976—, pres. 1987-88), So. Ariz. Trial Lawyers Assn. (pres. 1968-69), Am. Bd. Trial Advs., Ariz. Bar Assn., Tex. Trial Lawyers Assn., Practising Law Inst., Law-Sci. Acad., Am. Arbitration Assn., ABA. Address: 82 S Stone Tucson AZ 85701

HARASAWA, KAZUYUKI, construction company executive; b. Ota, Gunma, Japan, June 18, 1940; m. Taeko Harasawa, Oct. 1, 1967; children: Hiroki, Sumie. Grad. high sch., Ota. Plasterer Harasawa Plasterers, Ota, 1957-63; mng. dir. Harasawa Kogyō Ltd. Co., Ota, 1963-74; pres. Gunma Aurora, Inc., Ota, 1972-73; pres. Sanwa Kogyo, Inc., Ota, 1973-85, also bd. dirs.; pres. Harasawa Kogyō Ltd. Co., Ota, 1974-80, also bd. dirs.; pres. Harasawa Homes Co., Ltd., Ota, 1979—; boading dir. Johnson Group, Inc., Ota, 1988—. Named Hon. Citizen City of Tacoma, Wash., 1987. Mem. Liberal Democratic Party. Mem. The Zen Cult. Clubs: Nōzan Country (Gunma), Futaba Country. Lodge: Rotary. Office: Harasawa Home Co Ltd, 707 Higashi-Kanai, Ota, Gu Japan 376

HARASEVYCH, MARIA S., literary critic; b. Ukraine, Oct. 14, 1918; d. Sava and Iryna (Hannocha) Bilous; came to U.S., 1949, naturalized, 1955; philologist diploma, Kiev State U., 1941; m. Bohdan W. Harasevych, Jan. 24, 1944. Dir. studies, acting high sch. prin. in Russia, 1941-42; mem. bd. edn. Mineralny Vody, Kaukasus, USSR, 1942; dir. dept. ednl. methods and supervising insp. high schs., Mineralny Vody, 1942; wording redactor for novelists, translator and lectr., 1945-49; lit. critic, writer, journalist, tchr., cons. Ukrainian and Russian langs., 1949—. Author: Contemporary Poetry in Ukraine, 1962; Satire and Humor in Soviet Literature, 1963; John Steinbeck, 1966; Works of M. Ponedilok, 1966-70; B. Alexandriv-Poetry, 1973; B. Lepky in Prose and Poetry, 1974; Literary Portrait of O.Veretenchenko, 1976; Literary Portrait of U. Samchuk, 1978; Poet Yar Slarutych, 1980; Unique Writer Marco Vorchok in Perspective of 150 Years, 1985; also articles, revs., essays; staff writer Horizon, Ukrainian quar., 1970—. Mem. Ukrainian Nat. Women's League Am., Ukrainian Writers Assn. in Exile, World Fedn. Ukrainian Women's Orgns. Mem. Ukrainian Orthodox Ch. Club: Ukrainian Community (Detroit). Address: 3061 Firestone St Sterling Heights MI 48077

HARBAY, EDWARD WILLIAM, nuclear engineer; b. Johnstown, Pa., May 16, 1937; s. Edward F. and Helen M. (Virostek) H.; m. Marian M. Belavic, Sept. 4, 1971; children—Katherine Mary, Julie Ann, Marla Jean. B.S., U. Pitts., 1961, postgrad., 1963-64. Rocket devel. engr. Hercules Allegany Ballistics Lab., Cumberland, Md., 1961-66; reactor core engr. Westinghouse Electric Corp. Bettis Atomic Power Lab., West Mifflin, Pa., 1966-74; nuclear engr. Detroit Edison Co., 1974—. Mem. Nat. Soc. Profl. Engrs., Am. Nuclear Soc. Democrat. Roman Catholic. Research on boiling Water Reactor nuclear fuel cycle engineering. Home: 7870 Siding Ct Grosse Ile MI 48138 Office: Detroit Edison Co Fermi 2 Nuclear Power Plant Newport MI 48166

HARBECK, WILLIAM JAMES, real estate executive, lawyer, international consultant; b. Glenview, Ill., Dec. 16, 1921; s. Christian Frederick and Anna (Gaeth) H.; m. Jean Marie Allsopp, Jan. 20, 1945; children: John, Stephen, Timothy, Mark, Christopher. B.A., Wabash (Ind.) Coll., 1947; J.D., Northwestern U., 1950. Bar: Ill. 1950. Land acquisition atty. Chgo. Land Clearance Commn., 1950-51; with Montgomery Ward & Co., Chgo., 1951-81; asst. to pres., dir. corp. facilities Montgomery Ward & Co., 1968-70, v.p., dir. facilities devel., 1970-81; v.p. Montgomery Ward Devel. Corp., 1972-81; pres., chief exec. officer Montgomery Ward Properties Corp., 1974-81; pres. William J. Harbeck Assocs., 1981—; dir. Randhurst Corp., 1972-81, exec. com., 1975-79; bd. dirs. Internat. Council Shopping Centers, 1972-78, exec. com., 1975-78, govt. affairs com., 1977—, awards com., 1980-83, urban com. 1980-83, lectr., 1969—. Author articles in field; mem. editorial bds. profl. jours. Bd. dirs. Chgo. Lawson YMCA, 1973—, chmn. devel. com., 1979—, mem. exec. com., 1985—; bd. dirs. Greater North Michigan Ave. Assn., Chgo., 1979-81; chmn. constrn. com. Chgo. United, 1979-81; co-chmn. Chgo. Bus. Opportunities Fair, 1980-81; mem. real estate com. Chgo. Met. YMCA, 1982—, chmn. Bldg. Task Force, 1985—; mem. pres.'s council Concordia Coll., River Forest, Ill., 1969-87, mem. bd. regents, 1987—, planning com. Inst. for Philanthropic Mgmt., 1985—; youth Bible and Bethel instr. Redeemer Luth. Ch., Highland Park, Ill., 1965, congregation pres., 1968-70, 85-87, chmn. ch. growth com., 1982—; trustee Lutheran Ch. Mo. Synod Found., 1975-76, 81—, mem. Synodical mission study commn., 1974-75, mem. dist. research and planning com., 1981—, mem. task force on synodical constn. by-laws and structure, 1975-79; mem. research and planning com. No. Ill. Dist. Luth. Ch. Mo. Synod, 1984—; sponsor Luth. Chs. for Career Devel., 1979—; corp. chmn. U.S. Bond drive, Chgo., 1976; chief crusader Chgo. Crusade Mercy, 1976-78; div. chmn. Chgo. Cerebral Palsy campaign, 1977-78. Served to lt. (j.g.) USNR, 1942-46. Mem. Ill. Bar Assn., Luth. Layman's League, Alpha Sigma Kappa, Phi Alpha Delta, Pi Alpha Chi. Home and Office: 470 E Linden Ave Lake Forest IL 60045

HARBER, CLIVE ROBERT, social science educator; b. Wau, Papua, New Guinea, June 14, 1951; s. Harold Leslie and Dorothy Margaret (Liley) H.; m. Mary Chrisina Graham, June 30, 1973. BA in Politics, Reading (Eng.) U., 1972; P.G.C.E., Leicester (Eng.) U., 1973, MA in Politics, 1974; PhD in African Studies, Birmingham (Eng.) U., 1982. Tchr. Hampshire County Council, 1974-77; lectr. Kano State (Nigeria) Poly., 1977-79, Birmingham U., 1980—; advisor BBC, London, 1983-85; evaluator, west midlands, West Africa project Devel. Edn. Ctr., Birmingham, 1983-85. Editor Social Education: Principles and Practice, 1986, Social Science Teacher International Journal Education and Development, Political Education in Britain, 1987. Mem. Assn. for Teachers of Social Scis., Politics Assn. Office: U Birminigham, Faculty of Edn, PO Box 363, Birmingham B15 2TT, England

HARBISON, EARLE HARRISON, JR., chemical company executive; b. St. Louis, Aug. 10, 1928; s. Earle Harrison and Rose (Hensberg) H.; m. Suzanne Groves Siegel, Nov. 18, 1952; children—Earle Douglas, Keith Siegel. Student, Harvard U., 1960; AB, Washington U., St. Louis, 1949, LLB, 1957. With CIA, Washington, 1949-67; dir. mgmt. info. systems dept. Monsanto Co., 1967-73, dir. corp. orgn. and mgmt. devel. dept., 1973-75, gen. mgr. specialty chem. div., 1975, gen. mgr. plasticizers div., 1976-77, gen. mgr. detergents and phosphates div. and plasticizers div., 1977; v.p., mng. dir. Monsanto Comml. Products Co., 1977, mem. corp. adminstrv. com., 1977; group v.p., mng. dir. Monsanto Chem. Co. (formerly Monsanto Indsl. Chems. Co.), St. Louis, 1979-84; exec. v.p. parent co. Monsanto Co., St. Louis, 1981-86, pres., chief operating officer, 1986—, also bd. dirs.; chmn. bd. G.S. Searle & Co. (subs. Monsanto Co.), Skokie, Ill., 1985-86; dir. Centerre Trust Co.; former chmn. Fisher Controls Internat., Inc. (subsidiary), St. Louis. Bd. dirs., pres. Mental Health Assn. St. Louis, 1973-78; mem. long-range planning com. United Way of Am., 1976—, chmn. NAV Com., 1980—, mem. program evaluation com., 1977—; bd. dirs. Bethesda Gen. Hosp., 1979—, St. Louis Children's Hosp. Served with U.S. Army, 1950-65. Mem. Fed. Bar. Clubs: Old Warson Country, Ponte Vedra, Log Cabin (Ponte Vedra Beach, Fla.). Office: Monsanto Co 800 N Lindbergh Blvd Saint Louis MO 63167 *

HARBORD, RICHARD LEWIS, local government finance director, accountant; b. London, Apr. 30, 1946; s. Lewis Walter and Dorothy (Mobbs) H.; m. Jenny Berry, May 2, 1970; children: Mark, Adam, Guy. M in Philosophy, Anglican Regional Mgmt. Ctr., Chelmsford, Eng., 1985. chartered acct. Trainee London Borough Southgate, 1963-65; audit asst. London Borough Enfield, 1965-66, City of Westminster, Eng., 1966-67; chief auditor Maidenhead Borough, Berkshire, Eng., 1967-68, Harlow Devel. Corp., Essex, 1968-70; mgmt. acct. London Borough Hounslow, 1970-74; asst. chief officer London Borough Ealing, 1974-76; dep. dir. London Borough Richmond, 1976-81, dir. fin., dep. chief exec., 1981—. Fellow Assn. Chartered Cert. Accts., Brit. Inst. Mgmt., Inst. Data Processing, Rating and Valuation Assn. (mem. council); mem. Chartered Inst. Pub. Fin. (gov. edn. and tng. ctr. Croyden, Surrey). Mem. United Reformed Ch. Lodge: Rotary (pres. Twickenham 1987-88). Office: London Borough Richmond, York House Twickenham, Middlesex TW1 3AA, England

HARCOURT, GEOFFREY COLIN, economist educator; b. Melbourne, Victoria, Australia, June 27, 1931; s. Kenneth Kopal and Marjorie Rahe (Gans) H.; m. Joan Margaret Bartrop, July 30, 1955; children: Wendy Jane, Robert Geoffrey, Timothy William, Rebecca Mary. B of Commerce with honors, U. Melbourne, 1954, M of Commerce, 1956; PhD, U. Cambridge, 1960. Lectr. econs. U. Adelaide, South Australia, Australia, 1958-61; sr. lectr. econs. U. Adelaide, 1962-65; reader econs. U. Adelaide, Australia, 1965-67; prof. econs., personal chair U. Adelaide, 1967-85; univ. lectr. econs. and politics U. Cambridge, 1982—; univ. lectr., econs., politics U. Cambridge, 1964-66, fellow Jesus Coll. and Trinity Hall, 1964-66. Author: Some Cambridge Controversies in the Theory of Capital, 1972, Theoretical Controversy and Social Significance: An Evaluation of the Cambridge Controversies, 1975, The Social Science Imperialists. Selected Essays. G.C. Harcourt, 1982, Controversies in Political Economy, Selected Essays by G.C. Harcourt, 1986; Author: (with others) Economic Activity, 1967; editor (with others): Readings in the Concept and Measurement of Income, 1969, 2d ed., 1986, Capital and Growth, Selected Readings, 1971; editor: The Microeconomic Foundations of Macroeconomics, 1977, Keynes and his Contemporaries. The Sixth Centennial Keynes Seminar held the University of Kent at Canterbury; Editor (with others) International Monetary Problems and Supply Side Economics: Essays in Honour of Lorie Tarshis, 1986; contbr. articles to profl. jours. Pres. Econ. Soc. Australia and New Zealand, 1974-77. Fellow Acad. Soc. Scis. in Australia, Royal Econ. Soc. Mem. Labor Party. Mem. United Ch. Office: U Cambridge, Faculty Econ and Pol, Sedgwick Ave, Cambridge CB1 1EY, England

HARDEN, DOYLE BENJAMIN, import-export company executive; b. Banks, Ala., Oct. 15, 1935; s. J.C. and Gladis C. (Romine) H.; m. Elvira Harden; children: Janet Denice, Misty Lyn, Dusty Lyn, Wesley Doyle, Crystal Elvira. Student pub. schs. Salesman, Gordon Foods, Atlanta, 1955-64; pres. Kwik Shop Markets, Columbus, Ga., 1964-73, Exportaciones Chico, S.A., Juarez, Mex., 1973-76, Chico Arts, El Paso, Tex., 1976—, Transp. Interoceanica, S.A., Honduras, C.Am., 1975—. Office: 1045 Humble Dr El Paso TX 79915

HARDER, HILDA LYBOLT, educator; b. Wurtsboro, N.Y., Oct. 17, 1915; d. Daniel Everett and Nell Evelyn (Bradley) Lybolt; B.S., State U. N.Y. at New Paltz, 1961; M.A., Calif. State U., Northridge, 1968; M.S., Calif. Luth. Coll., 1977; m. Edmund A. Harder, Dec. 25, 1941; children—Linda Anne, Stefanie, Gerald, Daniel, Kristen. Elem. tchr., N.Y. State, 1936-58; reading tchr., 1959-61; asst. dir. Ventura (Calif.) Reading Improvement Center, 1961-63; dir. Calif. Reading Clinics, Thousand Oaks, 1963-68; instr. U. Calif., Santa Barbara, 1966-68; asst. prof. edn. Calif. Luth. U., Thousand Oaks, 1968-77, assoc. prof., 1977-82, prof. emeritus, 1982—; edn. cons. public and pvt. schs. Mem. edn. task force Conejo Future Found. Recipient Woman of Achievement award Bus. and Profl. Women, 1966. Mem. AAUP, Calif. Coll. and Univ. Profs., Calif. Profs. Reading, AAUW, Internat. Reading Assn. (speaker profl. confs. 1980, 82, 83, 85), NEA, Calif. Assn. for Neurologically Handicapped, Bus. and Profl. Women's Assn., Sigma Pi Sigma, Delta Kappa Gamma, Theta Phi Gamma (pres. 1934-36). Contbr. articles to profl. jours. Address: 20191 Village 20 Camarillo CA 93010

HARDIN, TOMMY JOE, electronics professional, photographer; b. Tacoma, Wash., May 13, 1947; s. Zachary Thomas Hardin and Doris Marie (Bezinque) Franchione. BS in Physics, Pittsburg (Kans.) State U., 1970, BS in Edn. Physics, 1974; postgrad., George Washington U., 1983. Technician Gulf Oil Chem. Co., Pittsburg, 1976-79; technician Quality Assurance Material Test Lab. Boeing Mil. Airplane Co., Wichita, Kans., 1979-80, quality assurance coordinator mil. programs, 1980-82, quality assurance corrective action analyst elec., electronics area, 1982-83, quality research and devel. mfg. devel. engr., 1983-86, coordinator product integrity audit group, 1986-87, quality assurance program staff coordinator, 1988—; owner, photographer Free Lance Photography, Wichita, 1986—. Vol. coach, umpire Frontenac (Kans.) Little League Program, 1965-78; rep. materials and mfg. technology Good Neighbor Fund Membership Dr., Wichita, 1985. Mem. Am. Soc. Quality Control, Photographic Soc. Am. (charter mem. Santa Fe Trail and Okla. chpt.), Wichita Internat. Photography Exhibitors Soc. Democrat. Methodist. Clubs: Stereo Camera, Wichita Amateur Camera. Home: 1157 S Webb Rd Apt 1811 Wichita KS 67207

HARDJO PRAKOSO, MASTINI, library director; b. Surakarta, Cen. Java, Indonesia, July 7, 1923; s. Hardjo Prakoso and Mantinah Hardjosumakso. M Library Studies, U. Hawaii, 1972. Cert. library technician. Asst. to circulation sect. library Indonesian Cultural Inst., Jakarta, Indonesia, 1953-56, head serials sect., 1956-59, head processing sect., 1959-62; head library Cen. Mus., Jakarta, 1962-80; dir. Nat. Library, Jakarta, 1980—; compiler bibliography service, 1973; cons. Clearing House on Law, Ministry of Justice, Jakarta, 1976—, Inst. S.E. Asian Studies, Singapore, 1982, Clearing House on Forestry, Jakarta, 1983—. Author: Library and Information Service in Indonesia, 1987. Nat. trainer Indonesian Scouts Movement, Jakarta, 1961-70, nat. commr., 1974—. Recipient Indonesian Award of Merit Govt. of Republic of Indonesia, 1984, Award of Merit Indonesian Scouts Movement, 1985, Award of Dedication Indonesian Scouts Movement, 1987. Mem. Indonesian Library Assn. (pres. 1980-86), Congress S.E. Asian Librarians (exec. bd. 1981—), Conf. Dir. Nat. Libraries. Home: JL. Bank Dagang Negara 11/77, Jakarta 12430, Indonesia Office: Nat Library of Indonesia, Jl Imam Bonjol 1, POB 3624, Jakarta 10002, Indonesia

HARDT, GÜNTHER, philosopher, former educator; b. Gummersbach, Ger., Mar. 22, 1920; s. Otto and Alma (Koch) H.; m. Elisabeth Tonat, Aug. 8, 1958. Cert. tchr. U.Köln, 1952. Tchr. ednl. establishment for tech. vocations, Bonn, W.Ger., 1952-78, sr. asst. master ret., 1978—. Author: (philos. works) Des Menschen Aufbruch in eine Neue Zeit, 1984, Die Bedeutung der Transzendentalphilosophischen Erkenntnistheorie von Kant für den Aufbau einer Modernen Theorie, Teil 1 Kritische Rekonstruktion der empirisch-psychologischen Basis der Kantischen Philosophie, 1985; contbr. numerous articles to profl. jours. Avocations: tennis; skiing. Home: Herresdorfstr 7, D-5463 Unkel am Rhein Rheinland-Pfalz Federal Republic of Germany

HARDY, ANNE DUNLAP, artist, educator; b. Birmingham, Ala., Jan. 15, 1910; d. James Thompson and Georgia Bailey (Dixon) D.; m. Charles Lambdin Hardy Sr., Nov. 18, 1936; children: Albert Sidney II, Charles Lambdin Jr., Georgia Hardy Luck. AB, Brenau Coll., Gainesville, Ga., 1931; postgrad., Mus. Modern Art, L.I., N.Y., 1965, North Ga. Coll., 1966, U. Ga., 1970. Supr. art schs., Dawsonville, Ga., 1963-72; pvt. instr. art, Gainesville, 1960—, Dallas, 1961-63. One women shows include Gainesville, 1960, Piedmont Interstate Fair, Spartanburg, S.C., 1977, Lake Lanier Islands (Ga.) Art Show, 1977; group shows include Telfair Mus., Savannah, Ga., 1952, Columbus Art Mus., 1960, Motorola Art Show, Chgo., 1962, U. Ga. Cortona, Italy, 1970; represented in numerous pvt. collections. Mem. Hall County Library Bd., 1951-61, Atlanta Symphony Orch. Bd., 1953-58; pres. Yonah council Girl Scouts U.S., 1955-57, exec. dir., 1958-61; mem. Gainesville Beautification Com., 1979-81. Mem. Assn. Ga. Artists (v.p. 1952-54), Gainesville Art Assn., Ga. Arts Council, Alpha Delta Pi. Democrat. Episcopalian. Clubs: Garden of Ga. (bd. dirs. 1948-60), Gainesville Garden, Gainesville Book (pres. 1970-71); Chattahoochee Country; Cushman. Avocations: gardening, cooking. Home: 3165 Tan Yard Branch Rd Gainesville GA 30501

HARDY, ASHTON RICHARD, lawyer; b. Gulfport, Miss., Aug. 31, 1935; s. Ashton Maurice and Alice (Baumbach) H.; m. Katherine Ketelsen, Sept. 4, 1959; children: Karin K., Katherine B. BBA, Tulane U., 1958, JD, 1962. Bar: La., 1962, FCC, 1976. Ptnr. Jones, Walker, Waechter, Poitevent, Carrere & Denegre, New Orleans, 1962-74, 76-82; gen. counsel FCC, Washington, 1974-76; ptnr. Fawer, Brian, Hardy, Zatzkis, New Orleans, 1982-86, Hardy & Popham, 1986-88; ptnr. Walker, Bordelon, Hamlin, Theriot & Hardy, New Orleans, 1988—; gen. counsel La. Assn. Broadcasters, 1976-86, Greater New Orleans Assn. Broadcasters, 1976—, La. Assn. Advt. Agys., 1982-86; lectr. advance rep. to Pres. U.S., 1971-74. Served to lt. USN, 1958-60. Mem. Fed. Bar Assn., La. Bar Assn. (del. ho. of dels. 1987—), FCC Bar Assn., Christian Legal Soc. Republican. Evangelical Christian. Clubs: Bienville, Metairie Country. Home: 306 Cedar Dr Metairie LA 70005 Office: 701 S Peters St New Orleans LA 70130

HARDY, BEN (BENSON B.), orchid nursery executive; b. Oakland, Calif., Nov. 22, 1920; s. Lester William and Irene Isabell (Bliss) H.; student pub. schs., Oakland, Calif., Concord, Calif.; grad. photo Intelligence Sch., Denver, 1949. Served as enlisted man U.S. Navy, 1942-48; joined USAF, 1948, advanced through grades to capt., 1957; with 67th Reconnaisance Squadron, Korea, 1951-52, Hdqrs. Squadron, Thule AFB, 1956, resigned, 1957; material requirements analyst-coordinator Teledyne Ryan Aero. Co., San Diego, 1958-73, 83-88; dispatcher-coordinator Cubic Western Data Co., San Diego, 1977-80; owner-partner orchid nursery. Pres. San Diego County Orchid Soc., 1972-73, 75-76, Exotic Plant Soc., 1976-78, 81-84, San Diego Gesneriad Soc., 1978; dir. 23d Western Orchid Congress, 1979. Decorated Bronze Star; recipient Letter of Commendation NASA, also others. Mem. Am. Orchid Soc., N.Z. Orchid Soc., Orchid Soc. SE Asia, Pacific Orchid Soc. Hawaii, Hoya Soc. Internat. (pres. 1981-83), Mexicana de Orquideologia, Sociedad Colombiana de Orquideologia, Cymbidium Soc. Am., Orchid Digest Corp. Contbr. articles to orchid jours.; pub. Western Gesneriad Gazette, 1978-79. Home: 9443 E Heaney Circle Santee CA 92071

HARDY, DUANE HORACE, federal agency administrator, educator; b. Ogden, Utah, June 8, 1931; s. Willis and Julia Mary (Garder) H.; m. Janet Myrnel Slater, Aug. 3, 1951; children: Rochelle Anne Leishman, Leslie Kaye Woolston, Kathy Korinne Davis. AA, Weber State Coll., 1951. Cert. EEO investigator/counselor. Ordained Mormon bishop, 1987. Enlisted U.S. Army, 1951, advanced through grades to lt. col., 1967, ret., 1971; EEO investigator U.S. Postal Service, San Bruno, Calif., 1978—, EEO instr., 1982—. Mem. EEO civic council, Salt Lake City, 1978—. Republican. Mormon. Lodge: Kiwanis. Home: 120 W 5200 S Ogden UT 84405 Office: US Postal Service 3680 Pacific Ave Ogden UT 84401

HARDY, JUNE DORFLINGER, portrait painter and photographer; b. N.Y.C., Feb. 2, 1929; d. William Francis Dorflinger, Jr. and Katheryn (Hait) Dorflinger Manchee; grad. Briarcliff Jr. Coll., 1949; student Parsons Sch. Design, 1949-50, N.Y. Sch. Interior Design, 1953-54, 87-88, Nat. Acad. Art-Art Students League, 1966-85, Columbia U., 1963; m. John Alexander Hardy, Jr., May 26, 1956. Asst. tchr. Peck Sch., Morristown, N.J., 1950-51; with personnel dept. McGraw Hill, Inc., 1951-52; editorial asst., then asst. editor Better Homes and Gardens mag., 1952-57; editorial asst., then asst. editor Successful Farming mag., 1952-57; freelance portrait painter and photographer, 1969—; tchr. drawing and pastel painting Onteora Club, N.Y., summer 1977; mem. Twilight Park Exhbn. Com., 1983-87. Nat. Home Fashions League scholar, 1953; recipient 1st prize portrait in oil Twilight Park Art Show, 1976, 79, 1st prize portrait photography, 1977, 2d prize pastel landscape, 1979, 2d prize for flower photography, 1982, 3d prize oil portrait, 1987; 1st prize for flower photography Onteora Garden Club Show, 1982, 1st and 2d prizes for photography Twilight Park Art Show, 1985. Life mem. Art Students League. Republican. Episcopalian. Clubs: Colony (chmn. entertainment 1979-84), Wednesday (past pres.), Badminton, Onteora. Address: 14 Sutton Pl S New York NY 10022

HARDY, RALPH W. F., biochemist, biotechnology executive; b. Lindsay, Ont., Can., July 27, 1934; s. Wilbur and Elsie H.; m. Jacqueline M. Thayer, Dec. 26, 1954; children: Steven, Chris, Barbara, Ralph, Jon. B.S.A., U. Toronto, 1956; M.S., U. Wis.-Madison, 1958, Ph.D., 1959. Asst. prof. U. Guelph, Ont., Can., 1960-63; research biochemist DuPont deNemours & Co., Wilmington, Del., 1963-67, research supr., 1967-74, assoc. dir., 1974-79, dir. life scis., 1979-84; vis. prof. life scis. Cornell U., 1984-86, now pres. Boyce Thompson Inst.; pres. Bio Technica Internat., Inc., Cambridge, Mass., 1984-86; dep. chmn. Bio Technica Internat., Inc., 1986—; chmn. Bio Technica Diagnostics, 1985-87; mem. exec. com. bd. agr. Nat. Acad. Sci., 1982—, commn. life scis., bd. basic biology Nat. Research Council, 1984—; mem. com. genetic experimentation Internat. Council Sci. Union, 1981—. Author: Nitrogen Fixation, 1975, A Treatise on Dinitrogen Fixation, 3 vols, 1977-79; mem. editorial bd. sci. jours.; contbr. over 100 articles to sci. jours. Recipient Gov. Gen.'s Silver medal, 1956, Sterling Henricks award 1986; WARF fellow, 1956-58; DuPont fellow, 1958-59. Mem. Indsl. Biotech. Assn. (bd. dirs. 1986—), Am. Chem. Soc. (exec. com. biol. chemistry div., Del. award 1969), Am. Soc. Biol. Chemists, Am. Soc. Plant Physiology (exec. com. 1974-77), Am. Soc. Agronomy, Am. Soc. Microbiology. Episcopalian. Home: 330 The Parkway Ithaca NY 14850 Office: Bio Technica Internat Inc 85 Bolton St Cambridge MA 02140 also: Boyce Thompson Inst at Cornell Tower Rd Ithaca NY 14853

HARDY, RICHARD JOHN, loss prevention specialist; b. Chgo., Apr. 18, 1955; s. Arthur John and Elaine Barbara (Piotrowski) H.; m. Rosemary Ann Przybylski, June 11, 1977; 1 child, David. AA in Transp. and Biology, Daley Community Coll., 1979. Dir. safety Fast Motor Service, Brookfield, Ill., 1977-79; div. safety mgr. Gateway Transp., LaCrosse, Wis., 1979-80; regional safety supr. Interstate Motor Freight, Grand Rapids, Mich., 1981; regional loss prevention mgr. ARA/Smith's Transfer, Staunton, Va., 1982-87, Overland Express Inc., Indpls., 1987-88, Area Interstate Trucking, Inc., Gary, Ind., 1988—. Mem. Ill. Trucking Assn., Nat. Com. for Motor Fleet Supr. Tng., Ill. Council Safety Suprs. Office: Area Interstate Trucking Inc 201 Mississippi St Unit 4 Gary IN 46401

HARDY, THOMAS AUSTIN, sculptor; b. Redmond, Oreg., Nov. 30, 1921; s. Orlando Buell and Marie Jane (Austin) H. BS, U. Oreg., 1942, MFA, 1952. Lectr. U. Calif., Berkeley, 1956-58; assoc. prof. sculpture Tulane Univ., New Orleans, 1958-59; artist-in-residence Reed Coll., Portland, Oreg., 1959-61; prof. sculpture Univ. Wyo., Laramie, 1975-76. One man shows, De Young Mus., San Francisco, 1957, Oakland (Calif.) Art Mus., 1958, Pensacola (Fla.) Art Center, 1958, Columbia U., 1959, Seattle Art Mus., 1954, Stanford U. Gallery, 1955, group shows include, Met. Mus., N.Y.C., 1952, Am. Mus. Natural History, 1958, Pa. Acad., Phila., 1958, Mus. Modern Art, N.Y.C., 1959; represented in permanent collections, Whitney Mus. Am. Art, N.Y.C., Seattle Art Mus., Portland (Oreg.) Art Mus., Lloyd Center, Portland, Hilton Hotel, Portland, Chandler Meml. Pavilion, Los Angeles, Fed. Bldg., Juneau, Alaska, Western Forestry Center, Portland, One Civic Center, Salem, U. Calif., Berkeley, Clackamas Town Center, Portland, Seattle Center, High Desert Mus., Bend, Oreg., Santa Barbara (Calif.) Art Mus. Bd. dirs. Art Advocates, 1975—, Friends of Timberline Lodge, 1976—, Portland Center for Visual Arts, 1977-81. Recipient Disting. service award U. Oreg., 1966, Gov.'s award Oreg. Art Commn., 1986, Webfoot award U. Oreg. Alumni Assn., 1986. Mem. Portland Art Assn., Audubon Soc., Am. Mus. Natural History, Kappa Sigma. Democrat. Home: 1422 SW Harrison St Portland OR 97201 Studio: 1023 N Killingsworth Portland OR 97217 Office: Kraushaar Galleries 724 Fifth New York NY 10019

HARDY, WILLIAM ROBINSON, lawyer; b. Cin., June 14, 1934; s. William B. and Chastine M. (Sprague) H.; m. Barbro Anita Medin, Oct. 11, 1964; children: Anita Christina, William Robinson. AB magna cum laude, Princeton U., 1956; JD, Harvard U., 1963. Bar: Ohio 1963, U.S. Supreme Ct. 1975. Life underwriter New Eng. Mut. Life Ins. Co., 1956-63; assoc. Graydon, Head & Ritchey, Cin., 1963-68, ptnr., 1968—; mem. panel comml. and constrn. industry arbitrators Am. Arbitration Assn., 1972—; reporter joint com. for revision of rules of U.S. Dist. Ct. for So. Dist. Ohio, 1975, 80, 83. Bd. dirs. Cin. Union Bethel, 1968—, pres., 1977-82; bd. dirs. Ohio Valley Goodwill Industries Rehab. Ctr., Cin., 1970—, pres., 1981—; mem Cin. Bd. Bldg. Appeals, 1976—, vice chmn., 1983, chmn., 1983—. Served to capt. USAR, 1956-68; lt. col., insp. gen. Ohio Mil. Res. Recipient award of merit Ohio Legal Ctr. Inst., 1975, 76. Mem. ABA, Ohio Bar Assn., Cin. Bar Assn., Am. Judicature Soc., Assn. Trial Lawyers Am., Ohio Acad. Trial Lawyers, 6th Circuit Jud. Conf. (life), AAAS, Ohio Soc. Colonial Wars (gov. 1979), Phi Beta Kappa. Mem. Ch. of Redeemer. Clubs: Princeton (N.Y.C.); Racquet (Cin.). Home: 1339 Michigan Ave Cincinnati OH 45208 Office:

Graydon Head & Ritchey 1900 Fifth Third Ctr 511 Walnut St Cincinnati OH 45202

HARE, A(LEXANDER) PAUL, sociology educator; b. Washington, June 29, 1923; arrived in Israel, 1980; s. Alexander Paul and Lulu Irene (Waters) H.; m. Rachel Diana Thies, 1947 (div. 1972); children: Sharon E., Diana S., Mally M., Christopher P.; m. June Sara Rabson, 1974; children: Simon L., Andrew G. BA, Swarthmore Coll., 1947; BS, Iowa State U., 1948; MA, U. Pa., 1949; PhD, U. Chgo., 1951. Instr. Harvard U., Cambridge, Mass., 1955-60; assoc. prof. Haverford (Pa.) Coll., 1960-66, prof., 1966-73; prof. U. Cape Town, Republic of South Africa, 1973-81, Ben-Gurion U. of the Negev, Beer Sheva, Israel, 1982—. Author: Handbook of Small Group Research, 1962, 2d edt., 1976, Creativity in Small Groups, 1982, Social Interaction as Drama, 1985; co-author: Dramaturgical Analysis of Social Interaction, 1988. Served to 1st lt. U.S. Army, 1943-46, ETO. Univ. Cape Town fellow, 1979. Mem. Am. Sociol. Assn. (cert.), Soc. Exptl. Social Psychology. Mem. Soc. of Friends. Office: Ben-Gurion U, Dept Behavioral Scis, Beer Sheva 84105, Israel

HARE, DAVID, playwright; b. St. Leonards, Sussex, Eng., June 5, 1947; s. Clifford Theodore and Agnes (Gilmour) H.; m. Margaret Matheson, Aug. 1970 (div. 1980); children: Joe, Lewis, Darcy. M.A., Cambridge U., 1968. Author: (plays) Slag, 1970 (Evening Standard Drama award), The Great Exhibition, 1972, Brassneck, 1973, Knuckle, 1974 (John Llewlyn Rhys award), Fanshen, 1975, Teeth 'N Smiles, 1975; author, dir: Plenty, 1978 (N.Y. Critics Circle award for Broadway prodn. 1983), A Map of the World, 1982, Pravda, 1985 (Evening Standard Drama award, Plays and Players Best Play of Yr., City Limits Best Play), The Bay at Nice, 1986, The Secret Rapture, 1988; TV films include Licking Hitler (Best Play of Year award Brit. Acad. Film and TV Arts 1978), Dreams of Leaving, 1980, Saigon: Year of the Cat, 1983; plays performed in, U.S. at Public Theatre, N.Y.C., Goodman Theatre, Chgo., Arena Theatre, Washington,; writer, dir. films: Wetherby, 1985 (Golden Bear award for best film Berlin Fesitval 1985), Paris By Night, 1988; writer screenplay Plenty, 1985, Strapless,

HARE, PAUL J., ambassador; b. Alexandria, Va., Dec. 8, 1937; m. Robbie Anna; two children. B.A., Swarthmore Coll., 1959; postgrad., U. Chgo., 1959-60. Joined Fgn. Service Dept. State, 1960; adminstrv. office Dept. State, Kuwait, 1961-63; consular officer Dept. State, Tunisia, 1963-64; on assignment AID, CORDS and Am. Embassy, Socialist Republic Vietnam, 1964-68; Vietnam desk officer, then Moroccan desk officer Office of Press Relations, Dept. State, 1969-71, dep. dir. for policy planning African Bur., 1971-72, press officer, then dep. dir., 1972-75; consul Am. Consulate, Brisbane, Australia, 1975-77; dir. Peace Corps, Morocco, 1977-79, Office So. African Affairs, Dept. State, 1979-81; counselor Polit. Affairs in Israel, 1981-85; U.S. ambassador to Zambia, Lusaka, 1985—. Office: care US Dept State 2201 C St NW Washington DC 20520 *

HAREL, CLAUDE ALBERT, diplomat; b. Caudebec, Normandy, France, July 25, 1932; s. Jean Harel and Simone Petit; m. Michèle Picot, Mar. 31, 1958; children: Veronique, Valerie, Guillaume. Student, Inst. Polit. Studies, Paris, 1950-53, Johns Hopkins U., Bologna, Italy, 1956, French Nat. Sch. Adminstrn., Paris, 1959-61. Attaché, then 2d sec. French Embassy, London, 1962-65; tech. advisor Minister of State, Paris, 1965-67; advisor to permanent representation for France EEC, Brussels, 1967-73; dep. dir. info. Ministry Fgn. Affairs, Paris, 1973-75, assoc. dir. African and Madagascan affairs, 1976-78; tech. advisor to Pres. of France Paris, 1978-79; ambassador to Jordan Amman, 1979-81; minister, counselor Govt. of France, Washington, 1981-83; ambassador, chief French rep. to Senegal Dakar, 1983-86; ambassador, chief French rep. to The Gambia 1983-86; ambassador to Poland Warsaw, 1986—; sr. lectr. Inst. Polit. Studies, Paris, 1967-73, French Nat. Sch. Adminstrn., Paris. Roman Catholic. Home: 11 rue St Jean, 50400 Granville Normandy, France Office: Ministère des Affaires, Etrangeres, 37 Quai d'Orsay, 75007 Paris France also: Ambassade de France, Piekna 1, Warsaw Poland

HARGIS, BILLY JAMES, clergyman; b. Texarkana, Tex., Aug. 3, 1925; s. Jimmie Earsel and Laura Lucille (Fowler) H.; m. Betty Jane Secrest, Dec. 21, 1951; children—Bonnie Jane, Billy James II, Becky Jean, Brenda Jo. Student, Ozark Bible Coll., 1943-45; B.A., Pikes Peak Bible Sem., 1957; Th.B., Burton Coll., 1958; LL.D., Bob Jones U., 1961. Ordained to ministry Christian Ch., 1943; pastor Christian chs. Sallisaw, Okla., 1944-46, Granby, Mo., 1946-47, Sapulpa, Okla., 1947-50; pastor Christian chs. Ch. of Christian Crusade, Tulsa, 1966-86; founder, pres. Christian Echoes Nat. Ministry, Inc., Tulsa, 1948-86, Am. Christian Coll., Tulsa, 1970-74; Pub. Christian Crusade Newspaper, 1948—; speaker Christian Crusade network radio broadcasts, 1949—, syndicated Daily TV Program, 1970—; founder, chmn. bd. David Livingston Missionary Found., 1970-80, Soc., 1974-80; founder, pres. Billy James Hargis Evang. Assn., 1975 , Ch. of Christian Crusade, 1966 , Christian Ams. For Life, 1971—, Good Samaritan Children's Found., Inc., 1975—; Dir. Rose of Sharon Farm-Log Sch.-Chapel, Neosho, Mo., 1982—. Author: Communist America - Must It Be, 1960, Communism The Total Lie, 1961, Facts About Communism and Churches, 1962, The Real Extremists - The Far Left, 1964, Distortion By Design, 1965, Why I Fight For A Christian America, 1974, Thou Shalt Not Kill—My Babies, 1977, The Depth Principle, 1977, The Disaster File, 1978, Riches and Prosperity Through Christ, 1978, The National News Media, 1980, The Cross and the Sickle-Super Church, 1982, Abortion on Trial, 1982, The Federal Reserve Scandal, 1985; (autobiography) My Great Mistake, 1986, Communist America, Must It Be, vol. 2, 1986, Forewarned, 1987. Home: Rose of Sharon Farm Neosho MO 64850 Office: PO Box 977 Tulsa OK 74102

HARGOUS, DOMINIQUE JEAN MAURICE, trading company executive; b. Paris, Jan. 4, 1945; came to Switzerland, 1984; s. Henri Robert Jean and Claire Alexandrine Suzanne (Bailleux) H.; m. Ursula Gertrud Magda Weingardt, May 15, 1971; children: Yann, Frank, Eric. DECS, ESCP, Paris, 1968; MBA, IESE, Barcelona, Spain, 1970. Asst. dir. fin. Societe Francaise Bunge (Bunge y Born Group), Paris and Buenos Aires, 1971-74; fgn. exchange and money mgr. Finagrain SA, Geneva and N.Y.C., 1974-78; asst. chief exec. officer countertrade sect. Renault Sorimex SA, Boulogne, France, 1979-84; asst. chief exec. officer Sodechanges SA, Geneva, 1979-84, bd. dirs., 1979—; chief exec. officer Sodechanges SA (Renault), Geneva, 1984—; asst. chief exec. officer Sorimex SA, Boulogne, 1979-84, bd. dirs., chief exec. officer, 1984—; chmn. Sodimpek AS, Istanbul, Turkey, 1986—; bd. dirs. Oyak-Renault, Istanbul. Mem. Union Chamber Fgn. Trade Cos. with Offices Abroad (permanant assembly 1987—). Club: St. James (London). Home: 19A route de Malagnou, 1208 Geneva Switzerland Office: Sodechanges SA, 5 rue Pedro-Meylan, 1208 Geneva Switzerland

HARGREAVE, TIMOTHY BRUCE, surgeon, researcher; b. Lytham, Lancashire, Eng., Mar. 24, 1944; s. John Michael and Margaret Isobel (Douglas) H.; m. Molly Dickens, Mar. 27, 1971; children: Alison Lucinda, Sophie Louise. MB, BS, U. Coll. Hosp. Med. Sch., London, 1967, MS, 1984. House surgeon Putney Hosp., London, 1967-68; house physician Addenbrooke's Hosp., Cambridge, England, 1968; med. officer Paray R.C. Missionary Hosp./Lesotho Flying Dr. Service, 1968-70; casualty surgical officer Middlesex Hosp., London, 1970; sr. house officer Victoria Hosp., Blackpool, England, 1971; rotating registrar U. Coll. Hosp., London, 1972-73; urol. registrar Middlesex Hosp., London, 1973-74; sr. surg. registrar U. Coll. Hosp., London, 1974-75; sr. urol. registrar Western Infirmary, Glasgow, Scotland, 1975-78; urol., transplant surgeon Western Gen. Hosp., Edinburgh, Scotland, 1978—; sr. lectr. urology Edinburgh U., 1978—; hon. cons. urological and renal transplant surgery Western Gen. Hosp., Edinburgh; mem. steering com. of the infertility task force WHO, Geneva, 1984—, working party on bladder cancer Med. Research Council, London, 1982—. Author: Diagnosis of Renal and Urinary Diseases, 1982, Male Infertility, 1983, Practical Urological Endoscopy, 1988; assoc. editor Internat. Jour. of Andrology, 1986—; mem. editorial bd. Urol. Research, 1985—; contbr. numerous articles to profl. jours. Fellow Royal Coll. Surgeons Edinburgh (examiner 1984—), Royal Coll. Surgeons; mem. Brit. Assn. Urol. Surgeons, Brit. Andrology Soc. (pres. 1987—), Scottish Urol. Soc. (sec. 1982-87), Brit. Med. Assn., Am. Fertility Soc. Office: Western Gen Hosp, Crewe Rd, Edinburgh EH4 2XU, Scotland

HARGREAVES, ALEC GORDON, language professional; b. Bury, Eng., Mar. 13, 1948; s. Henry Gordon and Margaret (Warburton) H.; m. Patricia Mary Thompson, Sept. 28, 1968; children: Katherine Eleanor, Rosamund Alice. BA in French, Sussex U., 1970, D in Philosophy in French Lit., 1978. Lectr. French Trent Poly., Nottingham, Eng., 1975-87; head dept. French Loughborough (Eng.) U., 1988—. Author: The Colonial Experience in French Fiction, 1981, Immigration in Post-War France, 1987; contbr. articles to profl. jours. Sec. Ruddington Labour Party, Eng., 1981-84. Mem. Soc. French Studies. Home: 57 Brookside Rd, Ruddington NG11 6AW, England Office: Loughborough U, Loughborough LE 11 3TU, England

HARGROVE, BERNARD LEE, marine dealer; b. Devalls Bluff, Ark., Mar. 11, 1928; s. Porter Jackson and Norma Lee (Driskill) H.; m. Virginia Wanda Sullivan, May 24, 1947; children: Brenda Kay, Benny Lee. Student, Batesville Sch., Ark. Dealer, pres. Red River Marine, Inc., Heber Springs, Ark. Republican. Baptist. Home: 1004 Hwy 210 Heber Springs AR 72543 Office: Red River Marine Inc 2001 Hwy 25 N Heber Springs AR 72543 *

HARIANTO, PAUL NOVIAN, physician; b. Kediri, Indonesia, Nov. 1, 1948; s. ing Hie and Gien Nio (Liem) Oei; m. Hadisuwito Wiwik. Kristanti, Jan. 14, 1973. M.D., U. Gadjah Mada, 1973. Intern, Gajah Mada Hosp., Yogyakarta, 1971-73; dir. primary health care Bethesda Hosp., Tomohon/ Minahasa, Indonesia, 1974-77, asst. dir. in charge med. services, 1977-78, med. officer in charge internal medicine, 1976-78, head dept. internal medicine, 1982—. Christian. Home: Kuranga-Talete II, Tomohon, Sulawesi Utara Indonesia Office: Bethesda Hosp, Tomohon, North Sulawesi Indonesia

HARIBHAKTI, SHAILESH VISHNUBHAI, accountant; b. Bombay, India, Mar. 12, 1956; s. Vishnubhai Bhagwandas and Usha (Vishnubhai) H.; m. Amita, Dec. 7, 1977; children—Sejal, Tarun. B. Commerce, Sydenham Coll., 1975. Ptnr. Haribhakti & Co., Bombay, 1977-79, 80; sr. auditor Arthur Young & Co., Chgo., 1979-80; ptnr. Haribhakti & Co., Bombay, 1980—; vis. faculty Indian Inst. Mgmt., Ahmedabad, 1982-83, 83-84 dir. Echbee Mgmt. Services Pvt. Ltd., 1984—. Contbr. articles to profl. jours. and newspapers. Fellow Inst. Chartered Accts. in India; mem. Inst. Cost and Works Accts. in India, Inst. Internal Auditors Fla. Lodge: Rotary. Avocations: reading; swimming. Home: 203 Wallace Apt B, Tukaram Javji Rd (Grant Rd), Bombay 400007, India Office: Haribhakti & Co, 42 Free Press House, 215 Nariman Point, Bombay, Maharashtra 400021, India

HARIBHAKTI, VISHNUBHAI BHAGWANDAS, accountant; b. Baroda, India, Oct. 8, 1929; s. Bhagwandas and Taralaxmi H.; m. Usha; children: Shailesh, Vijay, Sujata. B in Commerce, U. Bombay. Chartered acct., India. Sr. ptnr. Haribhakti & Co. Bombay mem. Moores Rowland Internat., London; dep. leader Indian delegation 9th Internat. Congress of Accts., Paris, 1967; bd. dirs. Kirloskar Leasing and Fin. Ltd., Bifora Watch Co., Ltd., Forward Electronics and Leasing, Rohit Pulp and Paper Mills Ltd., Shri Ram Fibres Fin. Ltd., Futura Packaging (India) Ltd., Shipping Credit and Investment Corp. India Ltd. Mem. Bombay Cricket Assn., Indian Merchants' C. of C. Club: Pransukhlal Mafatalal Hindu Swimming, Bath and Boat; Wilingdon Sports. Lodge: Rotary Internat. Home: 51 Maker Tower B Flat 51, Cuffe Parade, Bombay 400005, India Office: Haribhakti & Co, 42 Free Press House, 215 Nariman Point, Bombay 400021, India

HARING, JOSEPH EMERICK, economist; b. Mansfield, Ohio, July 19, 1931; s. Joseph and Kathryn (Woerner) H.; m. Loreen Carolyn Stuber, June 2, 1956; children—Crystal Janine, Arianne Denise, Elisa Jo, Peter Joseph. B.S., Ohio State U., 1952; Ph.D., Columbia U., 1959. Instr. econs. Columbia U., 1958-59; mem. faculty Occidental Coll., Los Angeles, 1959-77, Richard W. Millar prof. econs. and fin., 1965-77, chmn. dept. econs., 1962-73; econ. planning mgr. Gen. Telephone Co. Calif., Thousand Oaks, 1977-80, planning systems dir., 1980-87; pres., bd. dirs. Calif. Venture Group, 1987—; chief fin. officer Comet Enterprises, Inc., 1987; Brookings Nat. research prof. econs. S.E. Asia, 1961-62; vis. prof. econs. U. So. Calif., 1964-66, UCLA, 1965, U. Vienna (Austria), 1974, U. Munich (W.Ger.), 1974-75; cons. Govt. Thailand, 1963-64; mem. steering com. So. Calif. Research Council, 1959-73; pres. Pasadena Research Inst., 1959—; moderator TV series Inside Business, 1970. mem. Calif. State Adv. Com. on Sch. Dist. Budgeting and Fin., 1967-71; pres. Econ. Literacy Council Calif., 1982-86; bd. dirs. Calif. State Univ. Found., 1984—, vice chmn., 1987—; mem. Calif. Mining and Geology Bd., 1971-74. Author: Utility Regulation During Inflation, 1970; The New Economics of Regulated Industries, 1968; Urban and Regional Economics, 1972. Assoc. editor: Jour. Fin. and Quantitative Analysis, 1965-68; Contbr. articles to profl. jours. Served with U.S. Army, 1953-55. Mem. Planning Execs. Inst., N.Am. Soc. Corp. Planners, Am. Econs. Assn., Western Econ. Assn., So. Calif. Econ. Assn. (past pres.), Western Fin. Assn. Econometric Soc., Regional Sci. Assn., So. Calif. Acad. Scis. (editorial bd.), Lambda Alpha. Office: 607 Laguna Rd Pasadena CA 91105

HARITO, SADAMOTO JACK, financial officer; b. Tokyo, Japan, Oct. 4, 1948, naturalized, 1975; s. Dao-liang and Shu-chin (Dang) Chang; m. Fujiko Koyata, Mar. 24, 1978; children—Li-cka (Irene), Tsugu-se (Alex). B.A., Denison U., Granville, Ohio, 1971; M.B.A., Columbia U., N.Y.C., 1973. Fin. mgr. Merck Sharpe & Dohme, Tokyo, 1973-75; Japan area fin. mgr. Rohm & Haas Asia, Tokyo, 1975-82; fin. consolidation mgr. Far and Middle East Schlumberger Tech. Services Inc., Tokyo, 1982—. Mem. Omicron Delta Kappa. Democrat. Roman Catholic. Home: 16-21 Seta 1-chome Setagaya-ku, 158 Tokyo Japan Office: Schlumberger Tech Services Inc, 7-1 Nishi-Shinjuku 2-chome, 160 Shinjuku, Tokyo Japan

HARIVEL, JEAN HENRI, data processing engineer; b. Valognes, Manche, France, Dec. 12, 1946; s. Marcel Jean Harivel and Cecile Eugenie (Houellebec) Niceron; m. Marie Madeleine Dufrois, Apr. 27, 1974. MS, Inst. Applied Math., Grenoble, France, 1969, degree in engring., 1970. Engr. Cap, Paris, 1971-74; sr. engr. Cap Sogeti Logiciel, Paris, 1975-79, project dir., 1980-85, dir., 1987—; export mgr. Gie Cap Sogeti-Sesa, Paris, 1985-86; expert Cap Gemini Sogeti, Paris, 1986—. Contbr. articles to profl. jours.; designer electronic phone directory. Served with French Army, 1970-71. Mem. Ingenieurs and Scientifiques Club France. Roman Catholic. Office: Cap Sogeti Logiciel, 129 rue de l'Universite, 75007 Paris France

HARJADI, TAN POOTJIANG, machinery manufacturing executive; b. Malang, Jatim, Indonesia, May 15, 1935; s. Kah Kie and Gok Tie (Ong) T.; m. Anggriani, Feb. 15, 1960; children: Harsono, Hartono, Hardjono. ME, Inst. Tech., Bandung, Indonesia, 1959. Trainee Stanvac Oil Co., Sungai, Gerong, Indonesia, 1959-60; supr. Perlona Metal Works, Jakarta, Indonesia, 1960-61; designer Guntur Machinery Factory, Malang, 1961-62; designer Kemajuan Machinery Factory, Malang, 1962-67, pres., bd. dirs., 1967—; cons. Pusat Koperasi Unit Desa, Jakarta, 1983-84, PT Perkebunan XXVI, Jember, Indonesia, 1985-87, San Miguel Corp., Manila, 1987. Inventor coffee drying process, 1978. Recipient Food Tech. award Editorial Office, Spain, 1987. Home: 7 Jln Natuna, Malang Jatim, Indonesia Office: 17 Jln Irian Jaya, Malang Jatim, Indonesia

HARJULA, ARI LASSE JUHANI, cardiovascular surgeon, educator, researcher; b. Tyrvää, Finland, Feb. 17, 1951; s. Pekka Juhani and Aino Tellervo (Väkiparta) H.; m. Päivi Marketta Sten, Jan. 29, 1972; children: Rilla Katariina, Riikka Karoliina, Antti Pekka. Grad. Jr. Coll., Tyrvään Yhteislyseo, Vammala, Finland, 1970; M.D., U. Helsinki, Finland, 1976, D. Med.Sc., 1981. Resident, U. Central Hosp., Helsinki, 1977-83, instr., 1976—, cons. surgeon, 1984, assoc. prof., 1985—. Editorial bd. Annales Chirurgiae et Gynaecologiae, 1985—; contbr. articles to profl. jours. Cons. Finnish Light Athletic Fed. Served to lt. Finnish Armed Forces, 1975-76. Recipient S. Juselius Found. award, 1981—; Matine award, 1985; Evarts A. Graham meml. travelling fellow Am. Assn. for Thoracic Surgery, 1986—. Mem. Nat. Bd. Thoracic and Cardiovascular Surgery (sec. 1984), Nat. Soc. Medicine, Nat. Soc. Surg., Scandinavian Soc. Thoracic and Cardiovascular Surgery, Nat. Soc. Cardiology, Nat. Soc. Angiology. Avocations: sports medicine, tennis, squash. Home: Mitalitie 2A4, 02680 Espoo 68 Finland Office: Helsinki U Cen Hosp, Haartmaninkatu 4, 00290 Helsinki Finland

HARKEY, PAUL, administrative law judge; b. Idabel, Okla., Mar. 4, 1920; s. John Paul and Jessie Ruth (Elliott) H.; m. Lucille Roy, June 1, 1942; children—Cheryl Annette Harkey Nordstrom, Roy Lee, John Paul III. B.A., Southeastern Okla. Coll., 1950; LL.B., U. Okla., 1961, J.D., 1970. Bar: Okla. 1948, U.S. Dist. Ct. (no., ea. and we. dists.) Okla., Tex. 1966, U.S. Dist. Ct. (ea., no. and we. dists.) Tex., U.S. Dist. Ct. (ea. dist.) Pa., Hawaii, also others. Pvt. practice law, Idabel and Norman, Okla., 1948-64; U.S. adminstrv. law judge HEW/HHS, Dallas, 1964—. Mem. Okla. Ho. of Reps., 1946-54; established largest timberland res. in U.S. East of Rocky Mountains. Served to capt. USN, from 1940, ATO, PTO. Mem. ABA. Home: PO Box 22-2122 Dallas TX 75222 Office: Office Hearings & Appeals DHHS Suite 252 10830 N Central Pkwy Dallas TX 75231

HARKEY, VERNA RAE, pianist, educator; b. Ft. Worth, Nov. 20, 1928; d. Verne and Rachel Isabelle (Beam) Morrill; B.A., George Pepperdine Coll., 1950; m. Kenneth L. Harkey, Sept. 21, 1951; children—Karl M., Kevin L. Tchr. piano, Long Beach, Calif., 1950—. Mem. Nat. Guild Piano Tchrs., Nat. Music Tchrs. Assn., Music Tchrs. Assn. Calif., Southwestern Youth Music Festival, Epsilon Eta, Mu Phi Epsilon (founder Long Beach alumae chpt., vice chmn. 1986-87) Republican. Mem. Ch. of Christ. Clubs: Ebell of Long Beach, Musical Arts (Long Beach). Home and Studio: 2243 Canehill Ave Long Beach CA 90815

HARKIN, THOMAS R., U.S. Senator; b. Cumming, Iowa, Nov. 19, 1939; s. Patrick and Frances H.; m. Ruth Raduenz, 1968; children: Amy, Jenny. B.S., Iowa State U., 1962; J.D., Cath. U. Am., 1972. Mem. staff Ho. of Reps. Select Com. U.S. Involvement in S.E. Asia, 1970; mem. 94th-98th Congresses from 5th Iowa Dist., Sci. and Tech. Com., agr., nutrition and forestry coms., U.S. Senate, 1984—, appropriations and small bus. coms., labor and human resources com.; mem. Dem. Steering Com. Served with USN, 1962-67. Named Outstanding Young Alumnus Iowa State U. Alumni Assn., 1974. Democrat. Office: 316 Hart Senate Bldg Washington DC 20510 *

HARKINS, HERBERT PERRIN, otolaryngologist; b. Scranton, Pa., Aug. 13, 1912; s. Percy Stoner and Myra (Perrin) H.; B.S., Lafayette Coll., 1934; M.D., Hahnemann Med. Coll., 1937; M.Sc., U. Pa., 1942; m. Anna Catherine Shepler, July 16, 1938; children—Herbert P., Sally Anne, Nancy Shepler. Lectr. otolaryngology Hahnemann Med. Coll., 1939-44, asso. prof., 1944-51, prof. head dept. otolaryngology, 1951; asst. prof. otolaryngology Grad. Sch. Medicine, U. Pa., 1951—; sr. staff otolaryngology Lankenau Hosp. Bd. Studies in Higher Edn. Trustee, Lafayette Coll. Served as comdr. U.S. Navy, 1945-48; Res. Diplomate Am. Bd. Otolaryngology. Fellow A.C.S., Am. Otorhinol. Soc. Plastic Surgery; mem. Am. Soc. Ophthalmic and Otolaryngologic Allergy (pres.), Am., Pa. acads. ophthalmology and otolaryngology, Coll. Physicians Phila., Phila. Laryngol. Soc., Phila County Med. Soc., AMA, Am. Laryngol., Rhinol. and Otol. Soc. Clubs: Union League, Phila. Country, Bachelors Barge. Contbr. numerous articles on ear, nose and throat to med. jours. Home: 701 Woodleave Rd Bryn Mawr PA 19010 Office: Lankenau Medical Bldg Philadelphia PA 19151

HARLAN, LEONARD MORTON, real estate developer, consultant; b. Newark, June 1, 1936; s. Harold Robinson and Doris Harriet (Siegler) H.; B.M.E., Cornell U., 1959; M.B.A. with distinction, Harvard U., 1961, D.B.A., 1965; m. Elizabeth Nan Kramon, Aug. 27, 1969; children—Joshua, Noah. Security analyst Donaldson, Lufkin & Jenrette, Inc., 1965-69, v.p., 1968-69; founder, chmn. bd. The Harlan Co., Inc. (formerly Harlan, Betke & Myers, Inc.), N.Y.C., 1969—; dir., co-owner San Luis Central R.R., 1970-78; gen. partner Real Estate Partnerships, 1971—; co-owner HBM Properties, Inc., 1976-78; founder, co-owner Mich. Interstate Ry. Co., 1977—; dir. Ryland Group, Inc., 1984-87; pres. Castle Harlan, Inc., 1987—; gen. ptr. Legend Capital Group L.P., 1987—; dir. Del. Group of Mutual Funds, 1988—, Del. Mgmt. Holdings, Inc., 1988—; guest lectr. Harvard U. and Columbia U. grad. schs. bus. adminstrn., 1968—, others; adj. prof. banking and real estate N.Y. U. Real Estate Ist., 1968—, Grad. Sch. Bus. Adminstrn., 1976-80; adj. prof. bus. adminstrn. Columbia U. Grad. Sch. Bus. Adminstrn., 1980—. Mem. Pres.'s Com. on Indsl. Innovation, 1978-80; mem. Urban Devel. Action Grant Task Force, HUD, 1984; mem. exec. com. N.Y. chpt. Am. Jewish Com., 1975-80, Central N.J. chpt., 1980—, nat. budget commn., 1987; mem. Cerberus Soc. (N.Y.C. Citizens Budget Commn.), 1983-88; trustee N.Y.C. Citizens Budget Commn., 1988—. Recipient Charles B. Shatuck Meml. award Am. Inst. Real Estate Appraisers, 1967, 72; Disting. Tchr. award N.Y. U., 1979; Ford Found. fellow, 1964-65; Zurn fellow, 1962-63. Lic. real estate broker, N.Y., N.J. Clubs: Harvard (admissions com. 1973-75), Harvard Bus. Sch. (v.p. 1977-79) (N.Y.C.); Harvard Club N.J. Editorial bd. Real Estate Rev. Jour., 1971-84; contbr. articles to profl. jours. Office: Castle Harlan Inc 150 E 58 St New York NY 10155

HARLAN, NEIL EUGENE, consumer products company executive; b. Cherry Valley, Ark., June 2, 1921; s. William and Mary Nina (Ellis) H.; m. Martha Almlov, Sept. 27, 1952; children: Lindsey Beth, Neil Eugene, Sarah Ellis. Student, U. Edinburgh, Scotland, 1946; B.S., U. Ark., 1947, LL.D., 1969; M.B.A., Harvard U., 1950, D.B.A., 1956. Mem. faculty Harvard U. Grad. Sch. Adminstrn., 1951-62, asst. prof., 1954-58, assoc. prof., 1958-61, prof., 1962; asst. sec. Air Force Washington, 1962-64; v.p., chief fin. officer, dir. Anderson, Clayton & Co., 1964-66, exec. v.p., 1966-67; dir. McKinsey & Co., Inc., 1967-74; with McKesson Corp., San Francisco, 1974—, chmn., 1979—, also dir.; chief exec. officer 1984-86. Author: Management Control in Air Frame Subcontracting, 1956, (with R.H. Hassler) Cases in Controllership, 1958, (with R.F. Vancil) Cases in Accounting Policy, 1961, (with Christenson and Vancil) Managerial Economics, 1962. Trustee San Francisco Ballet, World Affairs Council; bd. dirs. Bay Area Council, Nat. Park Found.; bd. govs. San Francisco Symphony; mem. Calif. Com. on Campaign Fin., Calif. Roundtable, San Francisco Bay Area Council; mem. nat. adv. com. YMCA. Sch. Served with AUS, 1943-46. Mem. Conf. Bd., San Francisco C. of C. (bd. dirs., trustee). Clubs: Congressional Country (Bethesda, Md.); Webhannet Golf, Edgecomb Tennis (Kennebunk Beach, Maine); Bankers, Bohemian, Pacific Union (San Francisco); Menlo Country (Woodside, Calif.); Links (N.Y.C.); Johns Island Golf (Vero Beach, Fla.). Home: 1170 Sacramento St #13D San Francisco CA 94108 also: 400 Ocean Rd Unit 170 Johns Island Vero Beach FL 32973 Office: McKesson Corp Crocker Plaza One Post St San Francisco CA 94104

HARLAN, NORMAN RALPH, construction executive; b. Dayton, Ohio, Dec. 21, 1914; s. Joseph and Anna (Kaplan) H.; Indsl. Engring. degree U. Cin., 1937; m. Thelma Katz, Sept. 4, 1955; children—Leslie, Todd. Pres. Am. Constrn. Corp., Dayton, 1949—, Mainline Investment Corp., 1951—, Harlan, Inc., realtors; treas. Norman Estates, Inc. Mem. Dayton Real Estate Bd., Ohio Real Estate Assn., Nat. Assn. Real Estate Bds., C. of C., Pi Lambda Phi. Home: 303 Glenridge Rd Kettering OH 45429 Office: 2451 S Dixie Hwy Dayton OH 45409

HARLAN, RIDGE LATIMER, corporate executive; b. Pilot Grove, Mo., Feb. 25, 1917; s. George B. and Dale (Latimer) H.; m. Barbara Hawley, Oct. 7, 1939 (div.); children: Brooke, Holly Ann, Robert Ridge; m. Marjory Folinsbee, June 4, 1976. BJ, U. Mo., 1939; postgrad. Harvard, 1943, Colo. U., 1945-46, Stanford U. Grad. Sch. Bus., 1965. Pres. Barnes-Hind Pharms., Inc., 1972-76; prin. Harlan & Clucas, Inc., San Francisco, 1968-82; pres. Charila Found., 1969-73; chmn. bd., pres. Flores de las Americas, 1979-81; chmn. Millenium Systems, Inc., 1978-82; pres. Velo-Bind, Inc., 1983-85, chmn., chief exec. officer 1985-87, chmn. 1987—, also bd. dirs.; bd. dirs. Impulflor de Mexico, Velo-Bind Inc., Bishop, Inc.; chmn. Harlan & Dalton, Inc. Served to lt. (j.g.) USNR, 1943-46. Mem. Nat. Investor Relations Inst. (dir.), Assn. Corp. Growth (dir.), Alpha Delta Sigma, Kappa Tau Alpha. Clubs: Olympic, Family (San Francisco). Home: 839 Seabury Rd Hillsborough CA 94010 Office: 650 Almanor Ave Sunnyvale CA 94086

HARLAN, ROMA CHRISTINE, portrait painter; b. Warsaw, Ind.; d. Charles William and Fern (McCormick) H. Student, Purdue U., Art Inst. Chgo. Art chmn. D.C. Fedn. Women's Clubs. One-man shows, Lake Shore Club, Chgo., Little Gallery of Esquire Theatre, Chgo., Purdue U., W. Lafayette, Ind., Hoosier Salon, Indpls., All.-Ill. Soc. Fine Arts, Chgo., Kaufmann's Galery, Chgo., Lafayette (Ind.) Art Assn., Arts Club, Washington, George Washington U., Washington; exhibited numerous group shows; represented in permanent collections at, U.S. Supreme Ct., D.C. Fed. Ct. House, SEC, U.S. Capitol, Nat. Presbyn. Ch., Va. Theol. Sem., Alexandria, Nat. Guard Bldg., St. Stephen's Sch., Alexandria, Washington Nat. Fedn. Bus. and Profl. Women's Clubs, Washington, Children's Hosp. Nat. Med. Ctr., Alexandria, Lakeshore Club, Chgo., Purdue U. Dau. Ind. scholar. Mem. Nat. Soc. DAR, Ind. State Art Assn. Presbyterian. Club: Arts

(Washington). Lodge: Zonta Internat. Address: 1600 S Joyce St Arlington VA 22202

HARLAND, WILLIAM BRYCE, New Zealand government official; b. Wellington, N.Z., Dec. 11, 1931; s. Edward Dugard and Annie McDonald (Gordon) H.; m. Rosemary Anne Gordon, June 15, 1957 (div. 1976); children—James Edward, David John; m. 2d, Margaret Anne Blackburn, June 29, 1979; 1 son, Thomas Bryce Blackburn. M.A. with honors, Victoria U., Wellington, 1954; A.M., Fletcher Sch. Law and Diplomacy, Medford, Mass., 1955. With New Zealand Ministry of Fgn. Affairs, 1953—, ambassador to China, Peking, 1973-75, asst. sec., 1977-81, dir. external aid, 1981-82, ambassador and permanent rep. to UN, 1982-85; high commr. for N.Z. in London, 1985—. Office: New Zealand House, Haymarket, London England

HARLE, VILHO, peace researcher; b. Nilsiä, Finland, May 21, 1947; s. Konstantin and Anna (Lintu) H.; m. Sirpa Helena Savinainen, May 23, 1971; children: Katja Jelena, Annamaria Helena. D in Social Sci., U. Tampere, Finland, 1975. Lectr. polit. sci U. Tampere, 1973-84; reader U. Jyväskylä, Finland, 1977—; reader internat. relations U. Helsinki, Finland, 1985—; dir. Tampere Peace Research Inst., 1985-88; sr. research fellow Tampere (Finland) Peace Research Inst., 1988—. Author: International Tension, 1975; editor: The Political Economy of Food, 1978, Tampere Peace Research Inst. Yearbook, 1987, Essays in Peace Studies, 1987; contbr. articles to profl. jours. Grantee John D. and Catherine MacArthur Found., 1987. Mem. Center Party. Greek Orthodox. Home: Hauralantie 20, 37500 Lempäälä Finland Office: Tampere Peace Research Inst, PO Box 447, 33101 Tampere Finland

HARLESS, KATHRYN FRANCES, government adminstrator; b. Washington, Feb. 13, 1946; d. Joseph Sr. and Kathryn Winifred (Ashley) Zagami; children—Angela Lynn, Joseph Anthony. Student Wheeling Coll., Montgomery Coll., Prince Georges Community Coll., ITT Bus. Inst. Sec., U.S. Parole Commn., Washington, 1968-74; with adminstrn. office, Burlingame, Calif., 1974-76; staff asst. to dir., Office of Mgmt. and Fin., U.S. Dept. Justice, Washington, 1976-77, mgmt. analyst, 1977-79, staff asst. to dep. asst. atty. gen. Office Personnel and Adminstrn., 1979-86; co-dir. Consol. Adminstrv. Office, 1986—; notary pub. U.S. Parole Commn., 1974-76. Democrat. Roman Catholic. Avocations: boating; traveling; handicrafts; reading; computers. Home: 3820 Mt Olney Ln Olney MD 20832 Office: US Dept Justice Consol Adminstrv Office Room 1229 10th & Constn Ave NW Washington DC 20530

HARLEY, HALVOR LARSON, banker, lawyer; b. Atlantic City, Oct. 7, 1948; s. Robison Dooling and Loyde Hazel (Gauhnauer) H. B.Sc., U. S.C., 1971, M.A., 1973; J.D., Widener U., 1981. Bar: Pa. 1982. Staff psychologist Columbia Area Mental Health Ctr., S.C., 1971-73; dir. Motivational Research Consultants, Columbia, 1973-79; psychologist Family Ct. Del., Wilmington, 1979, sole practice law, Phila., 1982; v.p. investment banking Union Bank, Los Angeles, Calif., 1982-88; v.p., mgr. Tokai Bank, Newport Beach, Calif., 1988—. Bar: Ct. of Appeals (3rd cir.), 1987, US. Dist. Ct. (Eastern Pa.), 1987, U.S. Supreme Ct., 1988. Author: Help for Herpes, 1982; also articles. Fundraiser Orange County Performing Arts Ctr., 1983-84; mem. chair circle Calif. Democratic Party, 1983-84; vol. Hosp. Ship HOPE, Sri Lanka, 1968-69; bd. dirs. Lido Sands Homeowners Assn., Newport Beach, Calif., 1984—. Mem. Orange County Bankers Assn., Assn. Trial Lawyers Am., Am. Judicature Soc., Indsl. League Orange County (membership com. 1983-84), Am. Bankers Assn., World Trade Ctr. Assocs. Orange County (directing com. 1983—), Psi Chi (chpt. pres. 1971-73). Democrat. Capitalist. Home: 5015 Lido Sands Dr Newport Beach CA 92663 Office: Tokai Bank 18831 Von Karman Ave Irvine CA 92714

HARLEY, ROBISON DOOLING, JR., lawyer, educator; b. Ancon, Panama, July 6, 1946; s. Robison Dooling and Loyde Hazel (Gochenauer) H.; m. Suzanne Purviance Bendel, Aug. 9, 1975; children—Arianne Erin, Lauren Loyde. B.A., Brown U., 1968; J.D., Temple U., 1971; LL.M., U. San Diego, 1985. Bar: Pa. 1972, U.S. Ct. Mil. Appeals 1972, Calif. 1976, N.J. 1978, U.S. Supreme Ct. 1980, D.C. 1981, U.S. Dist. Ct. N.J., U.S. Dist. Ct. (cen. and so. dists.) Calif., U.S. Ct. Appeals (9th cir.) 1982, U.S. Dist. Ct. (ea. dist.) Pa. 1987, U.S. Ct. Appeals (3rd cir.) 1987. Cert. criminal law specialist Calif. Bd. Legal Specialization; cert. criminal trial adv. Nat. Bd. Trial Advocacy. Asst. agy. dir. Safeco Title Ins. Co., Los Angeles, 1975-77; ptnr. Cohen, Stokke & Davis, Santa Ana, Calif., 1977-85; sole practice, Santa Ana, Calif., 1985—; instr. Orange County Coll. Trial Advocacy, paralegal program U. Calif.; judge pro-tem Orange County Cts. Bd. dirs. Orange County Legal Aid Soc. Served to lt. col. JAGC, USMCR, 1971—; trial counsel, def. counsel, mil. judge, asst. staff judge adv. USMC, 1971-75, asst. regional def. counsel Western Region, 1986—. Mem. Orange County Bar Assn. (judiciary com., criminal law sect., adminstrn. of justice com.), Orange County Trial Lawyers Assn., Calif. Trial Lawyers Assn., Assn. Trial Lawyers Am., Calif. Attys. for Criminal Justice, Calif. Pub. Defenders Assn., Nat. Assn. for Criminal Def. Attys., Assn. Specialized Criminal Def. Advs., Orange County Criminal Lawyers Assn. (found. com.), Res. Officers Assn., Marine Corps Reserve Officers Assn. Republican. Home: 12 Bayberry Way Irvine CA 92715 Office: 825 N Ross St Santa Ana CA 92701

HARLEY, ROSE MADELINE, training school executive; b. Paris, Ark.; d. Charles V.B. and Ella O. (McVay) H.; B.A. cum laude, Columbia U., M.A. in Adult Edn., 1976. Area mgr. N.Y.-L.I., Dale Carnegie orgn., 1960-63, instr. trainer internat. hdqrs., 1963-67, regional mgr. internat. hdqrs., 1967-76, mgr. Dale Carnegie Inst. of N.Y.C., 1976-79; pres. Harley Inst., Inc., presenting Dale Carnegie courses in No. N.J., Hackensack, 1979— , Accrediting Council for Continuing EDn. and Tng. (former pres. and bd. dirs.).Mem. Mensa, Dale Carnegie Sponsors Assn. (bd. dirs.), Internat. Platform Assn., Commerce and Industry Assn. N.J. (bd. dirs.), Columbia U. Alumni Assn., Sales Execs. Club N.Y.C. Club: Princeton. Home: 280 Prospect Ave Hackensack NJ 07601 Office: 25 E Salem St Hackensack NJ 07601

HARMAN, AVRAHAM, university chancellor; b. London, 1914; B.A., Oxford U., 1936; married; 3 children. With Zionist Fedn. S. Africa, 1939-40, Jewish Info. Dept. Agy., 1940-48; dep. dir. Israel Govt. Press Office, 1948-49; consul gen., Montreal, P.Q., 1949-50; dir. Israel Office Info., counselor Israel Del. UN, 1950-53; consul gen., N.Y.C., 1953-55; asst. dir. gen. Ministry Fgn. Affairs, Jerusalem, 1955-56; ambassador to U.S., 1959-68; pres. Hebrew U., Jerusalem, 1968-83, chancellor, 1983—; mem. exec. Jewish Agy., 1956-59. Address: Hebrew U Jerusalem, Mount Scopus, Jerusalem Israel

HARMAN, CHRISTOPHER JOHN, mathematics educator, researcher; b. Freeling, S.A., Australia, Jan. 10, 1943; s. Walter Martin and Helen Veronica (Watson) H.; m. Carol Ann Ryan, May 13, 1967; children—James Christopher, John Matthew. Diploma in Teaching, Adelaide Tchrs. Coll., Australia, 1964; B.Sc., U. Adelaide, 1964, Ph.D., 1972. Teacher Unley High Sch., South Australia, 1965-66; sci. officer Dept. Defence, Australia, 1968-73, research scientist, 1973-75; lectr. Mitchell Coll. Advanced Edn., N.S.W., Australia, 1975-78, sr. lectr., 1979-84; prin. lectr. Darling Downs Inst. Advanced Edn., Queensland, Australia, 1984—; cons. Coastal Council N.S.W., Sydney, Australia, 1981-85; mem. problems com. Australian Math. Competition, Canberra, 1979—; reviewer Math. Revs., Providence, 1978—. Contbr. articles to profl. jours. Regional chmn. Austcare, Bathurst, N.S.W., 1979-81. Recipient Gov.'s medal Amateur Sports Club South Australia, Adelaide, 1963; research grantee Coastal Council N.S.W., Sydney, Australia, 1981. Mem. Australian Math. Soc., Am. Math. Soc. Roman Catholic. Avocations: baseball; tennis; bushwalking. Office: Darling Downs Inst Advanced Edn, PO Darling Heights, 4350 Toowoomba Queensland Australia

HARMELINK, HERMAN, III, clergyman, author, educator; b. Sheldon, Pa., Dec. 26, 1933; s. Herman II, and Thyrza (Eringa) H.; B.A. cum laude, Central Coll., 1954; M.A., Columbia U., 1955; postgrad. U. London, 1955; M.Div., New Brunswick Theol. Sem., 1958; World Council Chs. scholar U. Heidelberg, 1959; S.T.M. magna cum laude, Union Theol. Sem., N.Y.C., 1964, M.Phil., 1978; m. Barbara Mary Conibear, Aug. 11, 1959; children: Herman IV Alan, Lindsay Alexandra. Ordained to ministry Reformed Ch. Am., 1959; minister Community Ch., Glen Rock, N.J., 1959-64, Woodcliff Community Ch., Woodcliff-on-Hudson, N.J., 1964-71, Ref. Ch., Poughkeepsie, N.Y., 1971—; mem. adj. faculty in philosophy SUNY, 1983—; vice chmn. Faith and Order Commn., Nat. Council Chs., 1976-79, mem. Commn. on Regional and Local Ecumenism, 1981-84; pres. Synod of N.J., 1969; chmn. interch. relations Ref. Ch. Am., 1964-71; pres. Dutchess Interfaith Council, 1977-78; del. gen. council World Alliance Ref. Chs., Frankfurt, 1964, Nairobi, 1970; advisor 4th Gen. Assembly World Council Chs., Uppsala, Sweden, 1968; U.S. del. 50th Anniversary Faith and Order Commn., Lausanne, Switzerland, 1977. Trustee, St. Francis Hosp., 1979—, mem. exec. com. of bd., 1981—, joint conf. com., 1986—, chmn. planning com., 1987—; bd. dirs. Dutchess County Hist. Soc., 1974-78, also life mem.; bd. dirs. Dutchess County Arts Council, 1976-80, Bardavon 1869 Opera House, 1978-79; mem. allocation and planning divs. United Way of Dutchess County; sec. bd. dirs. Rehab. Programs, Inc., 1977-79; bd. dirs. Collingwood Repertory Theatre, 1978-80; Mid-Hudson Meml. Soc., 1981-84; pres. Poughkeepsie Generating Community, 1974—; dir. Literacy Vol. of Dutchess Co., 1985—, pres., 1987—; dir. Poughkeepsie Rural Cemetery, 1986—; pres. Ranfurly Library Service of N.Y. Inc., 1982—. Served to lt. USNR, 1957-61. Fulbright travel grantee to Germany, 1958-59; participant U.S.-S. African Leader Exchange Program, 1971. Mem. N.Am. Acad. Ecumenists, Am. Soc. Ch. History, Presbyn. Hist. Soc., Poughkeepsie C. of C., Dutchess Interfaith Council, Dutchess County Clergy Club. Clubs: Poughkeepsie Rotary (pres. 1977-79, sec. 1979—, sec. Dist. 721, 1980-81, gov. 1982-83, Rotary Internat. Council on Legislation, Monte Carlo, 1983, Rotary Internat. pres.'s rep. to dist. confs. 1984, 88, Paul Harris fellow), Lumanites (sec.-treas.), 251, Poughkeepsie Social Reading (past pres.); Circumnavigators (N.Y.C.), The Club, Travelers Century (life mem.). Author: Ecumenism and the Reformed Church, 1968; The Reformed Church in New Jersey, 1969; Another Look at Frelinghuysen and His Awakening, 1969; contbg. author to Piety and Patriotism, 1976, Vision from the Hill, 1984, The Livingston Legacy, 1987. Office: 70 Hooker Ave Poughkeepsie NY 12601

HARMON, ROBERT LON, lawyer; b. Saginaw, Mich., Jan. 27, 1938; s. Homer W. and Vena M. (Moore) H.; m. Ruth Susan Schaberg, Aug. 25, 1962; children—Matthew Moore, Daniel Palmer. B.S.E. in Elec. Engring., U. Mich., 1960, J.D. with distinction, 1963. Bar: D.C. 1964, Ill. 1965, Wis. 1983. Law clk. to assoc. judge U.S. Ct. Customs and Patent Appeals, Washington, 1963-65; ptnr. Hume, Clement, Brinks, Willian & Olds, Ltd., Chgo., 1965-83, Willian, Brinks, Olds, Hofer, Gilson & Lione, Ltd., Chgo., 1983—. Mem. ABA, Ill. Bar Assn., Chgo. Bar Assn., Am. Patent Law Assn., Chgo. Patent Law Assn. Club: Anglers (Chgo.). Author: Patents and the Federal Circuit, 1988; co-author: Patent Law, 1965; contbr. articles to legal publs. Home: 814 Woodbine Ln Northbrook IL 60062 Office: One IBM Plaza Suite 4100 Chicago IL 60611

HARMS, STEVEN ALAN, lawyer; b. Detroit, Feb. 15, 1949; s. Herbert Rudolph and Elsa Jane (McClelland) H.; m. Nancy Gayle Banta, June 26, 1971; children—Jennifer Elizabeth, Heather Lynn, Robin Ann. B.A., Hope Coll., 1970; J.D., Detroit Coll. Law, 1975. Bar: Mich. 1975, U.S. Dist. Ct. (so. dist.) Mich. 1975, U.S. Ct. Appeals (6th cir.) 1982. Ptnr. Muller, Muller, Richmond, Harms, Myers & Sgroi, P.C., Birmingham, Mich.; sec. gen. practice session State Bar Mich., 1982-83; lectr. in field. Author: Successful Collection of a Judgement, 1981; Rights of Commercial Creditors, 1982, Post Judgement Collection, 1988; editor General Practitioner, State Bar Mich., 1978-82. Mem. adminstrv. bd. St. Paul's United Meth. Ch., Rochester, Mich., 1984—; bd. dirs., fin. com. YMCA, North Oakland County, Calif., 1987—. Mem. ABA, Detroit Bar Assn. Republican. Club: Pearson Yacht Owners Assn. (commodore 1988—), Hunter Sailing Assn. (vice commodore 1985-86, commodore 1987-88). Office: Muller Muller Richmond Harms & Sgroi PC 1880 S Woodward Birmingham MI 48011

HARMS, WOLFGANG, philologist, educator; b. Bellavista, Peru, July 1, 1936; s. Siegfried and Annemarie (Doerwald) H.; m. Ulla-Britta Kuechen, 1981; children: Franka, Felix, Bendix. Dr Phil, U. Kiel, Fed. Republic Germany, 1963; habilitation, U. Munster, Fed. Republic Germany, 1969. Prof. philology U. Hamburg, Fed. Republic Germany, 1969-79; prof. German philology U. Munich, 1979—, dean of faculty, 1985-87; chmn. Commn. Germanic Studies of Deutsche Forschungsgemeinschaft, Bonn, Fed. Republic Germany, 1981-85. Author: Der Kampf mit dem Freund oder Verwandten in der deutschen Literatur bis um 1300, 1963, Homo viator in bivio, 1970; editor books Deutsche illustrierte Flugblaetter, (4 vols.), 1980-87; contbr. articles to profl. jours. Mem. Joachim Jungius Gesellschaft der Wissenschaften (pres. 1975-78), other acad. socs. Evangelical Lutheran. Office: Inst Deutsche Philology, Schellingstrasse 3, D-8000 Munich Federal Republic of Germany

HARNED, DAVID BAILY, educator; b. Allentown, Pa., June 5, 1932; s. William Biechele and Mary (Baily) H.; m. Elaine Paula Heydenreich, July 1, 1961; children: Christopher Baily, Timothy Heydenreich. B.A., Yale U., 1954, B.D., 1957, M.A., 1959, Ph.D., 1963; postgrad., New Coll. Edinburgh U., Scotland, 1954-55. Ordained to ministry Lutheran Ch., 1961; instr. Williams Coll., 1960-61, Yale U., 1962-63; asst. prof. religion Smith Coll., 1963-67, asso. prof., 1967; prof. religious studies U. Va., Charlottesville, 1967-80; chmn. dept. U. Va., 1967-72, 75-80; pres. Allegheny Coll., Meadville, Pa., 1980-86; dean arts & scis., prof. religious studies La. State U., Baton Rouge, 1986—; cons. higher edn. U.K., India, U.S.; vis. research prof. religious studies Punjabi U., Patiala, India, 1970, 78; chmn. bd. selection post-doctoral fellowships for Cross-Disciplinary Study, 1970-73; vis. prof. Christian dogmatics U. Edinburgh, Scotland, 1972-73, 76-77, 79-80, theology Austin Presbyn. Seminary, 1986; Westervelt lectr., 1979, Slover lectr., 1980, and many others. Author: Theology and the Arts, 1966, The Ambiguity of Religion, 1968, 69, Grace and Common Life, 1970 (Indian edit., 1970), rev., 1971, Faith and Virtue, 1973, Brit. edit., 1974, Images for Self-Recognition, 1977, Creed and Personal Identity, 1981, Brit. edit., 1981; Editor: (with J.F. Childress) Secularization and the Protestant Prospect, 1970, 71; mem. editorial bd.: Jour. Religious Studies, India, 1969—; others. Insight. Pres. League Winant Vols., 1951. Recipient Disting. Prof. award U. Va., 1978; Nat. Endowment for Humanities Jr. Humanist, 1970-71; fellow Soc. Religion in Higher Edn.; Kent fellow, 1957-60; Rockefeller doctoral fellow, 1959-60; fellow Princeton Theol. Sem., 1985-86. Lutheran.

HARNER, MICHAEL JAMES, anthropologist, author; b. Washington, Apr. 27, 1929; s. Charles Emory and Virginia (Paxton) H.; m. June Knight Kocher, 1951; children: Teresa J., James E.; m. Sandra Ferial Dickey, 1966. A.B., U. Calif., Berkeley, 1953, Ph.D. (Social Sci. Research Council, Doherty Found., Am. Museum Natural History fellow and grantee), 1963. Asst. prof. Ariz. State U., Tempe, 1958-61; from sr. mus. anthropologist to assoc. research anthropologist and asst. dir. Lowie Mus. Anthropology U. Calif., Berkeley, 1961-67, vis. assoc. prof., 1971-72, vis. prof., 1975; vis. assoc. prof., then assoc. prof. Columbia U., N.Y.C., 1966-70; vis. assoc. prof. Yale U., New Haven, 1970; from assoc. prof. to prof. grad. faculty New Sch. Social Research, N.Y.C., 1970-87, chmn. dept. anthropology, 1973-77; founder, dir. Ctr. for Shamanic Studies, Norwalk, Conn., 1979-87; pres., chmn. bd. dirs. Found. for Shamanic Studies, Norwalk, Conn., 1985—, sr. scholar, dir. research, 1987—; researcher Upper Amazon basin, 1956-57, 60-61, 64, 69, 73, Western N.Am., 1951-53, 59, 65, 76, 78, Lapland, 1983-84, Can. Arctic, 1987. Author: The Jivaro: People of the Sacred Waterfalls, 1972, 2d edit., 1984, Music of the Jivaro of Ecuador, 1972, Cannibal, 1979, The Way of the Shaman, 1980; editor: Hallucinogens and Shamanism, 1973. Fellow Am. Anthrop. Assn., Royal Anthropol. Inst. Gt. Britain and Ireland, AAAS, N.Y. Acad. Scis. (co-chmn. anthropology sect. 1980-81); mem. Soc. Med. Anthropology, Am. Ethnol. Soc., Soc. Am. Archaeology, Soc. Ethnohistory, Assn. Transpersonal Anthropology, Assn. for Humanistic Psychology, Assn. Transpersonal Psychology, Internat. Transpersonal Assn. (bd. dirs. 1982-85), Inst. Ecuatoriano de Anthropologia y Geografia, Assn. for Study of Consciousness. Animist. Club: Explorers (fellow). Office: Found Shamanic Studies Box 670 Belden Sta Norwalk CT 06852

HARNEY, DAVID MORAN, lawyer; b. Marysville, Calif., June 30, 1924; s. George Richard and Eileen M. (Daly) H.; m. Evelyn Brint Turner, Mar. 17, 1945; children: Brian Patrick, David Turner. Student Loyola U., Los Angeles, 1942-43, Ariz. State U., 1943-44, Southwestern La. U., 1944; J.D., U. So. Calif., 1948. Bar: Calif. 1949. Ptnr. Harney Law Offices, Los Angeles, 1950—. Served to 1st lt. USMC, 1942-45. Mem. Internat. Acad. Trial Lawyers (pres.-1983-84). Democrat. Roman Catholic. Club: Jonathan (Los Angeles). Home: 880 W 1st St 705 Los Angeles CA 90012 Office: 201 N Figueroa St #1300 Los Angeles CA 90012

HARNONCOURT, NIKOLAUS, musician, conductor; b. Berlin, Germany, Dec. 6, 1929; s. Eberhard and Ladislaja (Meran) H.; student Matura Gymnasium, Graz, Acad. Music, Vienna; m. Alice Hoffelner, 1953; 4 children. Mem. Vienna Symphony Orch., 1952-69, founder mem. Concentus Musicus, Ensemble for Ancient Music, 1954; pres. Mozarteum and Inst. Musicology U. Salzburg, 1972—; condr. Zurich Opera, Amsterdam Concertgebouw Orkest; numerous concerts in Europe, Australia and U.S.A. Recipient Erasmus prize, 1980, Grand Prix Mondiale; Grand Prix du Disque; Deutscher Schallplattenpreis. Author: Musikals Klangrede; Der Musikalische Dialog. Office: 38 Piaristengasse, A-1080 Vienna Austria Other: Mariedi Anders Artists Mgmt 535 El Camino del Mar San Francisco CA 94121 *

HARNSBERGER, THERESE COSCARELLI, librarian; b. Muskegon, Mich.; d. Charles and Julia (Borrell) Coscarelli; B.A. cum laude, Marymount Coll., 1952; M.L.S., U. So. Calif., 1953; postgrad. Rosary Coll., River Forest, Ill., 1955-56, U. Calif., Los Angeles Extension, 1960-61; m. Frederick Owen Harnsberger, Dec. 24, 1962; 1 son, Lindsey Carleton. Free-lance writer, 1950—; librarian San Marino (Calif.) High Sch., 1953-56; cataloger, cons. San Marino Hall, South Pasadena, Calif., 1956-61; librarian Los Angeles State Coll., 1956-59; librarian dist. library Covina-Valley Unified Sch. Dist., Covina, Calif., 1959-67; librarian Los Angeles Trade Tech. Coll., 1972—; med. librarian, tumor registrar Alhambra (Calif.) Community Hosp., 1975-79; tumor registrar Huntington Meml. Hosp., 1979—; pres., dir. Research Unltd., 1980—; free lance reporter Los Angeles' Best Bargains, 1981—; med. library cons., 1979—. Chmn. spiritual values com. Covina Coordinating Council, 1964-66. Mem. Calif. Assn. Sch. Librarians (chmn. legis. com.), Covina Tchrs. Assn., AAUW (historian 1972-73), U. So. Calif. Grad. Sch. Library Sci. (life), Am. Nutrition Soc. (chpt. Newsletter chmn.), Nat. Tumor Registrars Assn., So. Calif. Tumor Registrars Assn., Med. Library Assn., So. Calif. Librarians Assn., So. Calif. Assn. Law Libraries, Book Publicists So. Calif., Am. Fedn. Tchrs. Coll. Guild, Faculty Assn. Calif. Community Colls., Loyola, Marymount Alumnae Assn. (coordinator), Pi Lambda Theta. Author: (poetry) The Journal, 1982, To Julia: in Memoriam; contbr. articles to profl. jours. Office: 2809 W Hellman Ave Alhambra CA 91803

HAROON, MAHMOUD ABDULLAH, Pakistani minister of defense; b. Karachi, Pakistan, Sept. 19, 1920; s. Haji Sir Abdullah and Lady Nusrat H.; D.J., Sci. Coll.; S.C., Shahani Coll. Law; m. Nov., 1948; children: Nazafreen, Amber Saigol. Pres., Provincial Muslim League, 1944; mem. Sind Legis. Assembly, Pakistan, 1945; mem. W. Pakistan Legis. Assembly, 1954-58; mem. Nat. Assembly, Pakistan, 1965, high commr. in U.K., 1968; minister Central Govt. Pakistan, 1969; former minister for interior Govt. Pakistan, Islamabad, minister of def., 1988—; chmn./dir. various bus., pub. houses. Salar of Muslim League Nat. Guards; Naib salar i-Ala of the Nat. Youth Orgn., 1941; pres. Karachi Harbour Union, 1943; mayor of Karachi, 1953; chmn. Pakistan sect. Commonwealth Press Union, 1965. Mem. Newspaper Soc. Pakistan (pres.). Islam. Clubs: Karachi Gymkhana, Karachi, Sind, Boat, Race. Office: Haroon House, Dr Ziauddin Ahmed Rd, Karachi Pakistan *

HARP, DANA L., sales and marketing executive; b. Dayton, Ohio, Mar. 11, 1950; s. Lorrie Albert and Ruth Agnes (Pohlkotte) H.; m. Barbara Eichner, Aug. 21, 1971; children: Darren Matthew, Christine Elizabeth. Student, Sinclair Community Coll., 1969-71. Printing asst. Reynolds & Reynolds, Dayton, 1969-71, printing estimator, 1971-76, purchasing agt., 1976-78, sales rep., 1978-80; sales rep. John K. Howe Co., Dayton, 1981-83, v.p. sales, 1983—. Dir. projects Midwest chpt. Immune Deficiency Found., 1984—; active Bellbrook Wee Eagles. Mem. Ky. Bus. Advt. Assn., Adminstrv. Mgmt. Soc. Republican. Lodges: Lions. Home: 4100 Locus Bend Dr Dayton OH 45440

HARPER, CARL BROWN, JR., accountant; b. Clover, S.C., Nov. 18, 1934; s. Carl Brown and Nannie Lillian (Dickson) H.; student Presbyn. Coll., 1952-53; B.S. in Acctg., U. S.C., 1957; m. Mary Ann Johnson, Apr. 16, 1954; children—Rhonda Ann Harper Mitchell, Jennifer Lynne Harper Earnhardt, David Scott. Jr. acct. S.D. Leidesdorf and Co. (merger with Ernst & Whinney 1978), Greenville, S.C., 1957-62, audit mgr., 1962-65, Spartanburg, S.C., 1965—, partner in charge Spartanburg office, 1967-81, mng. partner Greenville and Spartanburg offices, 1981—; speaker edni. and civic orgns.; instr. Spartanburg Tech. Coll., 1966, Wofford Coll., 1974, U. S.C., 1969, 75; adj. prof. Clemson U., 1984-85, U. S.C., 1987-88; mem. S.C. Bd. Accountancy, 1979—, sec.-treas., 1983—, chmn., 1985. Deacon, 1st Presbyn. Ch., Spartanburg, 1977-84; elder Westminster Presbyn. Ch., 1984—, chmn. capital needs campaign, 1985; bd. dirs., United Way of Spartanburg, 1973-81, treas., 1976—; chmn. program and budget rev., bd. dirs. United Way Greenville County, 1984—; bd. dirs., treas., Arts Council Spartanburg County, 1975—, 1st v.p., 1986, pres. 1987, chmn. mem. com. 1988; S.C. Legis. Audit Council, 1975—, chmn., 1975-77; mem. adv. council Spartanburg County Commn. Higher Edn., 1976—; bd. dirs. Greenville Art Mus., 1984, treas., 1985—, v.p. 1986—; treas., bd. dirs. Children's Hosp. Family Ctr., Inc., 1987—. Served with U.S. Army, 1953-55. Recipient Presdl. award Spartanburg County United Way, 1981; C.P.A., S.C., N.C. Mem. Nat. Assn. Accts. (pres. Western Carolinas chpt. 1970-71, participant tax panel, speaker), Am. Inst. C.P.A.s (practice rev. com. 1973—, chmn. 1976—, S.C. mem. to council 1976—), S.C. Assn. C.P.A.s (pres. 1972-73, Service to Profession award 1979, Disting. Pub. Service award 1982), Estate Planning Council Spartanburg (pres. 1975), Middle Atlantic States Acctg. Conf. (sec., treas. 1975-81), Nat. Assn. State Bds. Accountancy (dir. 1984—). Clubs: Sertoma Internat. (Centurian award 1972, Honor Club pres. 1972, pres. Spartanburg, 1971-72), Spartanburg County. Lodge: Rotary (program chmn. 1986). Home: 12 Parkins Place Greenville SC 29607 Office: C & S Tower Two Shelter Ctr Greenville SC 29602

HARPER, GLADYS COFFEY, health services adviser; b. Pitts.; d. Clarence William and India Anna (James) Jackson; B.A., U. Pitts., 1970, M.P.A., 1972, M.S.H., 1973; m. Thomas A. Harper, Jan. 21, 1968. With Allegheny County (Pa.) Health Dept., 1958—, chief office tng. and edn. adminstr., 1975-76, adv. curriculum devel. and health adminstrn., 1976—; health technician specialist office health affairs OEO, Washington, 1965; vis. lectr. Grad. Sch. Public and Internat. Affairs, U. Pitts., 1970—; bd. dirs. Heritage Nat. Bank, 1988—; panelist Sta. WQED-TV White House Conf. Food, Nutrition and Health; trustee Mayview State Hosp., 1975—, v.p. bd. trustees, 1978, trustee clin. pastoral edn. program, 1979-80; bd. dirs. United Mental Health, Inc. Program chmn. Law Day, Heritage Nat. Bank, 1988, Allegheny County Assn. Lawyers' Wives, 1975, v.p., 1978, pres., 1980; program chmn. Pa. Bar Assn. Wives Program, 1978; trustee Louis Little Meml. Fund, Allegheny County Bar Assn., 1979; founder Judge Thomas A. Harper Meml. Scholarship, Howard U. Sch. Law, 1984. Active Allegheny County Bicentennial Com., 1987, Afro-Am. Heritage Day Parade Com., 1987, Allegheny County Bicentennial Scholarship Com., 1988; exec. v.p. Afro-Am. Heritage Parade Assn., chmn. judging com., 1988; v.p. Hist. Soc. of Western Pa., 1988. Named Woman of Yr., Greyhound Corp., 1967, 1 of 25 Outstanding Pittsburghers, Wayfarer Mag., Chrysler Corp., 1967, Health Services award Pitts. Club United, 1970, Harold B. Gardner award-Md. Citizen Health award, Allegheny County Med. Soc., 1973, Drug Edn. recognition Pitts. Press, 1971, citation for environ. health curriculum devel. and supervision Chatham Coll., 1976, award African Meth. Episcopal Zion Ch., 1984; crowned Bahamas Princess Christmas Queen, Freeport, 1976. Mem. Am. Pub. Health Assn., Royal Soc. Health, Am. Soc. Pub. Adminstrn., Conf. Minority Pub. Adminstrs., Legis. Council Western Pa. (dir., v.p. elect 1982), Western Pa. Genealogy Soc. (pres. 1983), Legis. Council Western Pa. (pres. 1983), League Community Health Workers, AAUW, NAACP (Isabel Strickland Youth Advisor award 1967, Daisy E. Lampkin Human Rights award 1969), Hist. Soc. Western Pa. (trustee 1984, v.p. bd. trustees 1988), U. Pitts. Alumnae Assn. (Bicentennial scholarship com.), Program to Aid Citizen Enterprises. Co-producer documentary: What's Buggin' The Blacks?, Sta. KDKA-TV, 1968. Home: 5260 Centre Ave Coronada Apts 502 Pittsburgh PA 15232

HARPER, GLENN S., business cons.; b. Phila., Apr. 19, 1940; s. Glenn Samuel and Minnie Marie H. Student U. Dayton (Ohio), 1961-65; B.A., Capital U., 1982. Br. mgr. Household Fin. Corp., Dayton, 1965-69; mgmt. cons. A.B. Cassidy & Assos., Ridgefield, Conn., 1969-70; v.p. sales Lin Conselyea, Inc., Medway, Ohio, 1970-72, exec. v.p., treas., dir., 1972-77; founder Val-Pak Promotions, Inc., Dayton, 1974-77, pres., chief exec. officer, 1977-79; founder Metro Maid, Inc., Dayton, 1978-79, pres., chief exec. officer, 1979—; dir., exec. v.p. San Sal Villas, San Salvador, Bahamas, 1978—;

dir. Carousel Mountain Amusement Park, Owego, N.Y.; co-dir. Group Interaction Inc., Dayton. Dayton Area Bd. Realtors. Mem. Ch. of Brethren. Address: Metro Maid Inc 4336 Gorman Ave Englewood OH 45322

HARPER, HEATHER MARY, soprano; b. Belfast, Ireland, May 8, 1930; d. Hugh Harper; m. Eduardo J. Benarroch, 1973. Student (Coll. fellow), Trinity Coll. Music, London; Mus.D. (hon.), Queen's U., Belfast; student, Frederic Husler, Helene Isepp, Frederic Jackson. prof. and cons. Royal Coll. Music, London, 1985; dir. singing studies Britten-Pears Sch. for Advanced Musical Studies, 1986—; 1st vis. lectr. in residence Royal Scottish Acad. of Music, Glasgow, 1987. Prin. soloist BBC Symphony Orch. tour to U.S., 1965, USSR, 1967, recital tour Australia, 1965, Hong Kong, 1982, Royal Opera House tours to Japan, Korea, 1979, USA, 1984; TV appearances include Ellen Orford, Mrs. Coyle, Ilia, Donna Elvira, La Traviata, La Boheme; created soprano role in world premier Britten's War Requiem, Coventry Cathedral, 1962; soloist opening concerts at Maltings at Snape, 1967, Queen Elizabeth Hall, 1967; ann. concert and opera tours in U.S. 1967—, also concerts in Asia, Middle East, Australia, S.Am., maj. European festivals; performed prin. roles at Covent Garden, Deutsche Oper, Berlin, Netherlands Opera, Bayreuth Festival, Glyndebourne Festival, Sadler's Wells, Teatro Colon, Buenos Aires, Argentina, Frankfort, Japan, Met. Opera N.Y.C., San Francisco, La Scala, Milan, Italy; performs regularly with main symphony orchs. in European capitols; maj. roles include Arabella, Ariadne, Chrysothemis, Kaiserin, Marschallin in Richard Strauss operas; appears with BBC-TV; recs. include Verdi's Requiem, Mahler's Symphony Numbers 2,4 and 8, Beethoven's Missa Solemnis, Britten's Peter Grimes Les Illuminations, R. Strauss' 4 Last Songs, Mozart's Don Giovanni Marriage of Figaro. Decorated Comdr. Brit. Empire; recipient Edison award, 1971, Prix du Disque, 1979, Grammy awards, 1979, 84, Best Solo Recording award. Mem. Royal Acad. Music (hon.). Office: 20 Milverton Rd, London England NW6 7AS

HARPER, JEWEL BENTON, pharmacist; b. Springfield, Tenn., Nov. 14, 1925; s. William Henry and Violet Irene (Benton) H.; m. Josephine Cook, Feb. 12, 1953; children: Pamela Jewel, Karen Jo. BS, Austin Peay State U., 1948, BS, Samford U., 1950. Pharmacist Battlefield Pharmacy, Nashville, 1950-52, VA Hosp., Nashville, 1952-63, Lexington, Ky., 1963-67, Durham, N.C., 1967-76, Manchester, N.H., 1976-82, Vanderbilt U., Nashville, 1982-86, Nashville Meml. Hosp., 1986—. Served to col. Med. Service Corps, USAR, 1944-85. Recipient Hosp. Adminstrn. Diploma, Acad. Health Scis., 1970, Nat. Security Mgmt. Diploma, Indsl. Coll. Armed Forces, 1973, Logistics Exec. Devel. Diploma U.S. Army Logistics Mgmt. Ctr., 1977. Fellow Am. Coll. Apothecaries; mem. Assn. Mil. Surgeons U.S., Am. Pharm. Assn., Am. Soc. Hosp. Pharmacists, Nat. Inst. History Pharmacy, Res. Officers Assn. U.S. (pres. chpt. 1962-63, sec. 1970-73, dept. surgeon 1977-82), Assn. of U.S. Army, The Mil. Order of World Wars, Nat. Assn. Uniformed Services, The Retired Officers Assn., The Gideons Internat., Lambda Chi Alpha, Kappa Psi. Republican. Baptist. Avocations: country music, deep sea fishing. Home: 503 Cuniff Ct Goodlettsville TN 37072 Office: Nashville Meml Hosp 612 West Due West Ave Madison TN 37115

HARPER, WARREN RANDOLPH, land surveyor; b. Glen Ridge, N.J., Sept. 22, 1945; s. Randolph Seward and Marion Elenor (Hilliard) H.; A.A.S., Paul Smith's Coll., 1966; B.S., N.J. Inst. Tech., 1982. m. Sandra Diane Clouse, Sept. 27, 1969; 1 son, David Clouse. Transitman, Miller-McGiffert, Montclair, N.J., 1966-67; party chief Canger Specter Assos., Parsippany, N.J., 1970-76; field dir. Arthur M. DeLuca, Rockaway, N.J., 1976-84; land surveyor Montville Twp., Montville, N.J., 1984-85; v.p. Arthur M. DeLuca, Cons. Engrs., P.A., 1985-87; pres., Arthur M. DeLuca, Constr. Engrs., 1988—; ptnr., DeLuca, Harper, Spillane, Baker Assocs., 1988—. Youth dir. Caldwell United Meth. Ch., 1972-81; trustee Caldwell United Meth. Ch., 1982—, pres. bd. trustees, 1983-85. Scoutmaster Boy Scouts Am., Caldwell; route dir. West Essex area Walk for Hunger, 1977-78. Served with USN, 1967-70; Vietnam. Decorated Vietnam Service medal with bronze star. Mem. N.J. Soc. Profl. Land Surveyors, Am. Congress Surveying and Mapping, N.J. Soc. Profl. Engrs. and Land Surveyors. Home: 161 Brookside Ave West Caldwell NJ 07006 Office: 20 Union St Rockaway NJ 07866

HARPER, WAYNE FRANKLIN, distribution executive; b. Ottawa, Ont., Can., Mar. 31, 1941; s. Francis Patrick and Alice Ruth (Way) H.; m. Sandra Lu, Aug. 17, 1968; children: Todd Jason, Kristen Leigh. Student, U. Western Ont., 1959-60. Distbn. mgr. M. Loeb Ltd., London, Ont., 1965-74; sr. project mgr. M. Loeb Ltd., Ottawa, Ont., 1974-79, mgr. distbn. planning, 1979-82; dir. distbn. Atlantic Wholesalers Ltd., Sackville, N.B., Can., 1982-84, dir. wholesale ops., 1984-86, v.p. wholesale ops., 1986—, also bd. dirs. Bd. dirs. Sackville (N.B., Can.) Meml. Hosp., 1986—. Lodge: Rotary. Office: Atlantic Wholesalers Ltd, 4 Charlotte St, Sackville, NB Canada E0A 3C0

HARPSTER, JAMES ERVING, lawyer; b. Milw., Dec. 24, 1923; s. Philo E. and Pauline (Daanen) H.; Ph.B., Marquette U., 1950, LL.B., 1952. Bar: Wis. 1952, Tenn. 1953; dir. info. services Nat. Cotton Council Am., Memphis, 1952-55; dir. public relations Christian Bros. Coll., 1956; mgr. govt. affairs dept. Memphis C. of C., 1956-62; exec. v.p. Rep. Assn. Memphis and Shelby County, 1962-64; individual practice law, Memphis, 1965; ptnr. Rickey, Shankman, Blanchard, Agee & Harpster, and predecessor firm, Memphis, 1966-80, Harpster & Baird, 1980-83; pvt. practice, 1984—. Mem. Shelby County Tax Assessor's Adv. Com., 1960-61; editor, asst. counsel Memphis and Shelby County Charter Com., 1962; mem. Shelby County Election Commn., 1968-70; mem. Tenn. State Bd. Elections, 1970-72, sec., 1972; mem. Tenn. State Election Commn., 1973-83, chmn., 1974, sec., 1975-83; a founder Lions Inst. for Visually Handicapped Children, 1954, chmn. E. H. Crump Meml. Football Game for Blind, 1956; pres. Siena Student Aid Found., 1960; bd. dirs. Memphis Public Affairs Forum; mem. Civic Research Com., Inc., Citizens Assn. Memphis and Shelby County; Republican candidate Tenn. Gen. Assembly, 1964; v.p. Nat. Council Rep. Workshops, 1967-69; pres. Rep. Workshop Shelby County, 1967, 71, 77, 78, Rep. Assn. Memphis and Shelby County, 1966-67; chmn. St. Michael the Defender chpt. Catholics United for the Faith, 1973, 75. Served as sgt. USAAF, 1942-46. Mem. Am., Tenn., Wis. bar assns., Navy League U.S., Am. Conservative Union, Conservative Caucus, Cardinal Mindszenty Found., Am. Security Council, Am. Cause, Am. Legion, Latin Liturgy Assn. Roman Catholic. Home: 3032 E Glengarry Rd Memphis TN 38128 Office: 100 N Main Bldg Suite 3217 Memphis TN 38103

HARRAK, ALEXANDRE, geriatric physician; b. Ouezzane, Morocco, May 18, 1951; m. Ges Maryse Harrak, May 17, 1986; children: Ronan, William, Kevin. MD, U. Bordeaux, 1978. Intern Clinique Choizy, Guadeloupe, French Antilles, 1975-76; prof. medicine Red Cross Sch., Bordeaux, 1980-84; gen. practice medicine Bordeaux, 1980—; practice medicine specializing in geriatrics Talence, France, 1980—; mem. staff Samu Hosp. Pellegrin, Bordeaux, 1980—; dir. Sarl les Cedres Argentes, Bordeaux, 1986. Served to capt. French armed forces med. service, 1978-79. Mem. Med. Assn. Bordeaux sud France, Union Nat. Medecins Reserve. Home and Office: 61 Cours Pasteur, 33000 Bordeaux France

HARRELL, RUTH FLINN, psychologist; b. Americus, Ga., Apr. 19, 1900; d. Dan and Neva (Poley) Flinn; B.S., Wesleyan Coll., Macon, Ga., 1920; M.A., Columbia U., 1924, Ph.D., 1942; m. William Lee Harrell, Nov. 24, 1928; 1 dau., Ruth Harrell Capp. Psychologist, Norfolk (Va.) Schs., 1926-37; rehab. psychologist neuro-surgery Johns Hopkins Hosp., Balt., 1936-47; prof. psychology Old Dominion U., Norfolk, 1965-70, research prof., 1976—. Found. nutritional Advancement grantee, 1976. Mem. Am. Psychol. Assn., N.Y. Acad. Sci., Va. Psychol. Assn., NEA. Presbyterian. Author: Effect of Mothers Diets on the Intelligence of Offspring; Effect of Added Thiamin on Learning, 1943, Further Effects of Added Thiamin on Learning and Other Processes, 1947; co-author: Can Nutritional Supplements Help Mentally Retarded Children?: An Exploratory Study, 1981. Home: 3100 Shore Dr Virginia Beach VA 23451 Office: 801 W 46 St Norfolk VA 23508

HARRELL, SAMUEL MACY, grain company executive; b. Indpls., Jan. 4, 1931; s. Samuel Runnels and Mary (Evans) H.; m. Sally Bowers, Sept. 2, 1958; children: Samuel D., Holly Evans, Kevin Bowers, Karen Susan, Donald Runnels, Kenneth Macy. B.S. in Econs., Wharton Sch., U. Pa., 1953. Pres., chmn. bd., chief exec. officer, chmn., exec. com. Early & Daniel Industries, Cin., 1971—; chmn. bd., chmn. ecec. com. Early & Daniel Co., Cin., 1971—; chmn. bd., chief exec. officer, chmn. exec. com. Tidewater Grain Co., Phila., 1971—; dir. Wainwright Bank & Trust Co., Wainright Abstract Co., Nat. Grain Trade Council, U.S. Feed Grains Council; mem. Chgo. bd. Trade. Served with AUS, 1953-55. Mem. Young Pres.'s Orgn., U. Pa. Alumni Assn. (past pres.), Terminal Elevator Grain Mchts. Assn. (dir.), Millers Nat. Fedn. (dir.), Assn. Operative Millers, Am. Soc. Bakery Engrs., Am. Fin. Assn., Council on Fgn. Relations, Fin. Exec. Inst., N.Am. Grain Export Assn. (dir.), Mpls. Grain Exchange, St. Louis Mchts. Grain Exchange, Buffalo Corn Exchange, Delta Tau Delta (Past prs. Ind. alumni). Presbyterian. Clubs: Columbia, Indpls. Athletic, Woodstock, Traders Point Hunt, Dramatic, Players, Lambs (Indpls.); Racquet (Phila.); University (Washington and N.Y.C.). Lodges: Masons, Rotary. Home: 5858 Sunset Ln Indianapolis IN 46208 Office: Early & Daniel Industries Inc 733 S Missouri St Indianapolis IN 46225 also: Early & Daniel Industries 733 S Missouri St Indianapolis IN 46225

HARRIES, PATRICK ALLAN LIFFORD, historian, educator; b. Cape Town, Cape, South Africa, May 31, 1950; s. Allan Lifford and Patricia Ruth (Hardy) Harries. BA, U. Cape Town, 1974; PhD, London U., 1983. Lectr. history dept. U. Cape Town, 1980-84; researcher U. Lausanne, Switzerland, 1985-86; sr. lectr. history U. Capetown, 1987—; cons. Internat. Jour. African Hist. Studies, Boston, 1983—, Can. Jour. African Studies, Montreal, 1984—; external examiner Khanya Coll., Cape Town, 1987—. U. Western Cape, 1988—. Contbr. chpts. to books, articles to profl. jours. Fellow Swiss Govt., 1985-86. Home: 21 Milner Rd, Tamboerskloof, 8001 Cape Town Republic of South Africa Office: U Cape Town, Dept History, 7700 Rondebosch Republic of South Africa

HARRIGAN, JOHN FREDERICK, banker; b. Eau Claire, Wis., June 22, 1925; s. Frederick H. and Marion F. (Farr) H.; m. Barbara Heald, July 1, 1950; children—Sarah H. Gruber, Peter Christopher. Student, U. Wis., 1946-49; grad., Rutgers U. Stonier Grad. Sch. Banking, 1965. With First Nat. Bank Oreg., Portland, 1949-71; exec. v.p. First Nat. Bank Oreg., 1971; chmn. bd., chief exec. officer Pacific Nat. Bank Wash., Seattle, 1971-74; dir. Pacific Nat. Bank Wash., 1971-80; vice chmn. bd. dirs. United Calif. Bank, Los Angeles, 1974-75; pres., dir. Western Bancorp., Los Angeles, 1975-80; chmn. bd., chief exec. officer, dir. Union Bank, Los Angeles, 1980—; dir. Nordstrom, Inc. Bd. dirs. Los Angeles Civic Light Opera Assn., So. Calif. chpt. Nat. Multiple Sclerosis Soc.; bd. visitors Grad. Sch. Mgmt., U. Calif., Los Angeles; mem. Peregrine Fund. Served with USMCR, 1943-45. Mem. Assn. Res. City Bankers. Episcopalian. Clubs: Calif, Los Angeles Country, Eldorado Country. Office: Union Bank 445 S Figueroa St Los Angeles CA 90071

HARRIGAN, JOHN THOMAS, JR., physician, educator; b. Perth Amboy, N.J., Apr. 20, 1929; s. John T. and Mary E. (Czapp) H.; m. Marlene Lulka, Apr. 14, 1961 (div.); children: John, Alisa, Edmund. Student, U. Va., 1946-49; M.D., George Washington U., 1953. Diplomate Am. Bd. Ob-Gyn. Intern Doctors Hosp., Washington, 1953-54; resident in ob-gyn Luth. Hosp., Balt., 1954-55, Providence Hosp., Washington, 1957-58, Free Hosp. for Women, Boston, 1958-59; practice medicine specializing in ob-gyn, sub specialist in maternal-fetal medicine Jersey City, 1960-65, Colonia, N.J., 1962-70, Madison Twp., N.J., 1965-70; asst. attending in ob-gyn Margaret Hague Hosp., Jersey City, 1960-65; attending physician in ob-gyn Rahway Hosp., N.J., 1962-70, South Amboy Hosp., N.J., 1965-73; sec. to med. staff South Amboy Hosp., 1970; attending in ob-gyn Martland Hosp. Unit, Newark, 1970-74; dir. dept. ob-gyn Monmouth Med. Ctr., Long Branch, N.J., 1974-76; dir. regional perinatal edn. program Monmouth Med. Ctr., 1975-78; dir. Monmouth Perinatal Center, Long Branch, 1975-78; sr. attending in ob-gyn St. Peters Med. Ctr., 1978—; assoc. prof. ob-gyn Hahnemann Med. Coll., Phila., 1975-78; prof. dir. div. maternal-fetal medicine Rutgers Med. Sch., Piscataway, N.J., 1978—; cons. in maternal-fetal medicine to physicians, Eastern N.J.; mem. maternal and infant care services com. N.J. Dept. Health, 1975—; dir. statewide premature delivery prevention project; med.-legal expert cons.; tech. adv. panel Healthstart program, N.J. Health Dept. Contbr. articles to med. jours.; reviewer med. jours. Mem. task force on biomed. causes and pub. relations Gov.'s Council on Prevention Mental Retardation, N.J. task forces on genetics and fetal defects, 1984—; mem. pub. affairs com., MOD Birth Defects Found. Served to capt. M.C. U.S. Army, 1955-57. Fellow Am. Coll. Obstetricians and Gynecologists (vice chmn. N.J. sect. 1979-82, chmn. N.J. sect. 1982—, nat. adv. council 1982—, legis. rep., treas. dist. III 1986) mem. AMA, N.J. Med. Soc., Am. Fertility Soc., N.J. Perinatal Assn. (v.p. 1980—), Baker Channing Soc., N.J. Ob-Gyn Soc. (council). Democrat. Roman Catholic. Home: 919 Woodland Terr Bridgewater NJ 08805 Office: Dept Ob-Gyn St Peters Med Ctr 254 Easton Ave New Brunswick NJ 08903

HARRIGAN, KENNETH WILLIAM J., automotive products company executive; b. Chatham, Ont., Can., Sept. 27, 1927; s. Charles A. and Olga Jean (Wallace) H.; m. Margaret Jean Macpherson, June 18, 1955; children: Tara Lynne Harrigan Tomlinson, Stephen Charles. BA with honors, U. Western Ont., 1951. With Ford Motor Co. Can. Ltd., Oakville, Ont., 1951—, regional mgr. central region, 1965-68, gen. sales mgr., 1968-71; dir. sales and mktg. Ford Asia Pacific Inc., Australia, 1971-73; group dir. So. Europe Ford Europe, Inc., 1973-76, v.p. truck sales and mktg., 1976-78; v.p., gen. mgr. sales Ford Motor Co. Can. Ltd., Oakville, Ont., 1978-81, pres., 1981—, chief exec. officer, 1982—; mem. policy com. Bus. Council on Nat. Issues, Govt. Sectoral Adv. Group on Internat. Trade, 1986-88; mem. Ont. Bus. Adv. Council; bd. dirs. Ford Motor Co., New Zealand, Ltd., New Holland of Can. Ltd., Dome Corp. Ptnrs., Ford Credit Can. Ltd.; mem. Nat. Adv. Council World Energy Conf.; trustee Brock U., St. Catharines. Bd. govs. Appleby Coll., Oakville; adv. com. U. Western Ont. Sch. Bus. Adminstrn; mem. adv. bd. Provincial Mcpl. Secretariat for 1988 Toronto Summit. Mem. Conf. Bd. Can. (bd. dirs.), Inst. Corp. Dirs. in Can., Toronto Bd. Trade, Can. C. of C., Motor Vehicle Mfrs. Assn. (chmn.). Clubs: Mississauga (Ont.) Golf and Country; Canadian; Empire. Office: Ford Motor Co of Can Ltd, The Canadian Rd Box 2000, Oakville, ON Canada L6J 5E4

HARRINGER, OLAF CARL, architect, museum consultant; b. Hamburg, Germany, Apr. 29, 1919; came to U.S., 1927; s. Henry Theodore and Anke (Berger) H.; m. Helen Ehrat Hedges, Dec. 20, 1975; children—Carla, Brita, Eric. Student, Evanston Acad. Fine Arts, The New Bauhaus, 1937-38, Ill. Inst. Tech., 1942-45. Designer Raymond Loewy Assos., Chgo., 1946-49, H. Allan Majestic Assos., Chgo., 1949-51, Dickens, Inc., Chgo., 1951-52, Olaf Harringer and Assos. (architects/designers), Chgo., 1952-62; account exec. several exhibit firms Chgo., 1962-68; dir. exhibits Mus. Sci. and Industry, Chgo., 1957-60, 68-80; prin. Olaf Harringer Assos., Chgo., 1981—. Mem. AIA, Am. Assn. Museums, ICOM. Home and Office: 3650 N 36th Ave Villa #5 Hollywood FL 33021

HARRINGTON, JOSEPH FRANCIS, historian, educator, educational company executive; b. Boston, Oct. 24, 1938; s. Joseph Francis and Mary Virginia (Lynch) H.; m. Brenda Marie Crowley, Sept. 3, 1966; children: Megan Marie, Christopher Joseph John. BS, Boston Coll., 1960; MA, Georgetown U., 1963, PhD, 1971. Instr. Framingham (Mass.) State Coll., 1966-68, asst. prof., 1968-70, assoc. prof., 1970-72, prof., 1972—, bd. chmn. dept. history, 1972-82; pres. Learning, Inc., Stoughton, 1979—, also bd. dirs.; trustee East European Research Ctr.; pres. MA/AIF, 1987—. Author: Masters of War, Makers of Peace, 1985, Powers, Pawns and Parleys, 1978; contrbr. articles to various jours. Mem. Stoughton, Mass. Sch. Com., 1971-77, 82-87. Served with U.S. Army, 1962-65. Tchg. fellow Georgetown U., Washington, 1960-62, 65-66; hon. fellow Kennedy Presdl. Library, 1986—. Mem. Mass. Assn. for Advancement of Individual Potential (bd. dirs.), Nat. Assn. Creative Children & Adults (bd. dirs. 1985—). Roman Catholic. Home: 119 Holmes Ave Stoughton MA 02072 Office: Framingham State Coll State St Framingham MA 01701

HARRINGTON, MICHAEL DAVID HUGO, marketing professional; b. London, Mar. 8, 1961; s. David George and Lia (Businaro) H.; m. Maria Concetta Mesiti, Sept. 10, 1985; 1 child, Lavinia Maria-Etruria. BS in Aero. and Astronautical Engring. with honors, U. Southampton, 1984. Market analyst British Aerospace, Weybridge, Surrey, Eng., 1984-85, British Aerospace Hdqrs., Kingston, Surrey, Eng., 1985-86; sr. market analyst British Aerospace Mktg. Ops. Centre, Hatfield, Surrey, Eng., 1986—. Pres. British Archeol. Reconnaissance Trust, Surrey, 1976-79; mem. Italian Archeol. Team, 1976-85. Recipient British Aerospace scholarship, 1980-84. Mem. Royal Aero. Soc. (assoc. mem.). Roman Catholic. Office: British Aerospace PLC, PO Box 35 (MOC), Stevenage SG1 2D9, England

HARRINGTON, SANDRA MAY, educator, administrator; b. Geneva, N.Y., Sept. 21, 1948; d. James Jerome and Julia Mary (Deeb) H.; AA, Niagara County Community Coll., 1968; BS in Secondary Edn., SUNY, Buffalo, 1970; M.S., Nova U., 1979. Tchr. trainable mentally handicapped Okeechobee (Fla.) Public Schs., 1971-79, tchr. educable mentally handicapped, 1979-81, dean of students Okeechobee High Sch., 1981-82, Okeechobee Jr. High Sch., 1982-83; tchr. Mt. Dora High Sch. (Fla.), 1983-85, Dabney Elem. Sch., Leesburg, Fla., 1985—. Recipient Entricy Herald Achievement award Niagara County Community Coll., 1968; Cert. of Appreciation, Okeechobee Cub Scouts, 1977; winner Fla. Learning Resources System/Alpha contest, 1979; Fla. Dept. Edn. grantee, 1976. Mem. Assn. Supervision and Curriculum Devel., Council Exceptional Children, Internat. Platform Assn., Bus. and Profl. Women (past pres. Mt. Dora chpt., chmn. com. Eustis chpt.), Lake County Edn. Assn., Nat. Mus. Women in Arts (charter). Democrat. Home: 1224 Palmetto Rd Eustis FL 32726

HARRIOTT, JOHN FRANCIS XAVIER, retired broadcast company executive; b. Darlington, Eng., Jan. 2, 1933; s. Cyril Francis and Elizabeth (McGee) H.; m. Shirley Houssemayne du Boulay, Sept. 15, 1979. Licentiate in Philosophy, Heythrop Coll., 1955, Lic. in Theology, 1966; Cert. Edn., U. London, 1956; MA in English Lang. and Lit., Oxford U., 1959. Ordained priest Roman Catholic Ch., 1965, resigned, 1976. Retreat dir. Loyola Hall, Rainhill, Liverpool, Eng., 1966-70; asst. editor The Month, Jour. Internat. Affairs, London, 1970-76; columnist The Tablet (internat. Cath. weekly), London, 1974—; chief asst. for TV contracts and hearings Ind. Broadcasting Authority, London, 1978-84, chief asst. for TV policy, 1984—; freelance broadcaster and journalist on religion and social issues, 1970—; mem. exec. com. Cath. Inst. for Internat. Relations, London, 1970-75; mem. Justice and Peace Commn., Roman Catholic Hierarchy for Engl. and Wales, 1971-75; mem. exec., com. Social Morality Council, 1972—; mem. edn. com. Cath. Fund for Overseas Devel., 1987—. Author: (essays) A Pride of Periscopes, 1976, (articles and broadcasts) Fields of Praise, 1977; editor Selected Letters of St. Thomas More, 1972, The Future of Broadcasting, 1973. Mem. appeals com. Sue Ryder Found. for Concentration Camp Survivors and Disabled, Cavendish, Eng., 1969-73; mem. Council for Sci. and Soc., London, 1973-74, Found. for Study Christianity and Soc., London, 1986—. Mem. Royal TV Soc. Club: Travellers (London). Home: 180 Woodstock Rd, Oxford OX2 7NG, England

HARRIS, ALLEN, lawyer, educator; b. Bklyn., Feb. 3, 1929; s. Edward and Minnie (Herzog) H.; m. Susanne T. Berger, Sept. 1, 1957. B.A., N.Y.U., 1949; J.D., Columbia U., 1954. Bar: N.Y. 1954, Mo. 1968, U.S. Sup. Ct. 1966, U.S. Ct. Mil. Appeals 1956, U.S. Tax Ct. 1954, U.S. Ct. Appeals (2d cir.) 1955, U.S. Dist. Ct. (so. dist.) N.Y. 1955, (ea. dist.) N.Y. 1957. Assoc. Newman and Newman, N.Y.C., 1954-55, Garey and Garey, N.Y.C., 1955-56; asst. dist. atty. New York County, 1956-59; 1st asst. counsel, trial counsel, coordinating com. on discipline First Jud. Dept., N.Y. State Sup. Ct., 1959-62; law sec. to justice N.Y. State Sup. Ct., 1962-63; gen. counsel, labor negotiator United Board and Carton Corp., N.Y.C., 1963; asst. counsel N.Y. State Commn. on Investigation, 1963-65; assoc. dir. Inst. Jud. Adminstrn., N.Y.U., 1965-67; prof. law, dir. community legal edn., dir. legal research, dir. legal assistance to inmates clinic, dir. public service project in law enforcement U. Mo., Kansas City, 1967-69; prof. law Bklyn. Law Sch., 1969-72; counsel N.Y. State Study Commn. for N.Y.C., 1972; spl. asst. atty. gen. N.Y. State, 1972-76; sole practice, N.Y.C., 1976-79; sr. law asst., appellate div. First Jud. Dept., N.Y. State Sup. Ct., N.Y.C., 1979—; cons. for legal matters N.Y. State Select Com. on Correctional Instns., 1971-72; dir. spl. projects N.Y.C. Patrolmen's Benevolent Assn., 1978; cons. to police in Kansas City, 1968-69; mem. faculty appellate judges seminars N.Y. U., 1965-67; involved in numerous hearings. Served as 1st lt., inf. U.S. Army, 1951-53; col. JAGC. Decorated Combat Infantryman's badge; recipient N.Y. State Conspicuous Service cross. Mem. ABA, N.Y. State Bar Assn., Nat. Dist. Attys. Assn., N.Y. State Dist. Attys. Assn., Assn. Bar City N.Y., N.Y. County Lawyers Assn., Fed. Bar Council, Richmond County Bar Assn., Kansas City Bar Assn., Mil. Order World Wars, Res. Officers Assn. U.S., AAUP, Internat. Assn. Chiefs Police. Jewish. Club: City. Contbr. articles to encys. and legal jours. Home: 700 Victory Blvd 18D Staten Island NY 10301 Office: Appelate Div Court House 25th St & Madison Ave New York NY 10010

HARRIS, BRIAN CRAIG, lawyer; b. Newark, Sept. 8, 1941; s. Louis W. and Lillian (Frankel) H.; m. Ellen M. Davis, Aug. 20, 1978; children: Andrea, Keith. BS, Boston U., 1963; JD, Rutgers U., 1966. Bar: N.J., 1968, D.C. 1968, U.S. Ct. Appeals (3d cir.) 1968, N.Y. 1984, U.S. Ct. Appeals (2d cir.) 1985. Asst. corp. counsel Newark, 1968-70; assoc. Braff, Litvak & Ertag, East Orange, N.J., 1970-72; ptnr. Braff, Litvak, Ertag, Wortmann & Harris, East Orange, 1972-85, Braff, Ertag, Wortmann, Harris & Sukoneck, Livingston, N.J., 1985—. adj. lectr. law and medicine Seton Hall U., South Orange, N.J., 1982-83, trial preparation Rutgers U., Newark, 1983, strategy of def. United Tech. Corp., Chgo., 1986. Chmn. Essex County Heart Assn., East Orange, 1972-73; contbg. mem. Nat. Ileitis Found., N.Y.C., 1983—. Mem. ABA, N.Y. State Bar Assn., N.J. Bar Assn., Essex County Bar Assn., Essex County Trial Lawyers Assn., Middlesex County Trial Lawyers Assn., Assn. Trial Lawyers Am., Def. Research Inst., N.J. Trial Lawyers Assn. Named Master of the Inns of Ct., Arthur J. Vanderbilt Sect., 1988. Jewish. Club: Water Mill Country (N.Y.). Avocations: running, basketball, theater, study of mil. strategy of land forces in World War II. Home: Llewellyn Park West Orange NJ 07052 Office: Braff Ertag Wortman Harris & Sukoneck 570 W Mt Pleasant Ave Livingston NJ 07039 also: 475 Fifth Ave Suite 1614 New York NY 10017

HARRIS, BRUCE ALEXANDER, JR., obstetrics-gynecology educator; b. Ann Arbor, Mich., May 15, 1919; s. Bruce Alexander and Clara Alfreda (Lindquist) H.; m. Joan Leigh Maddy, Feb. 21, 1944; children—William Bruce, Glenn Ferguson, Joan Elizabeth. A.B., Harvard U., 1939, M.D., 1943. Diplomate Am. Bd. Ob-Gyn. Intern, Boston City Hosp., 1943-44, ob-gyn intern Vanderbilt U. Hosp., 1946-47, Johns Hopkins Hosp., Balt., 1947-48, resident, 1948-50, 50, Detroit Receiving Hosp., 1950, Kings County Hosp., Bklyn., 1951; asst. in obstetrics Johns Hopkins U., 1948-50, instr., 1950; clin. instr. ob-gyn SUNY, 1952-53, asst. clin. prof. ob-gyn, 1953-59; assoc. prof. ob-gyn U. Ala., Birmingham, 1974-76, clin. assoc. prof., 1974-76, clin. prof., 1976-78, 78—; prof. ob-gyn U. Ala.-Tuscaloosa, 1986—; prof. and chmn. ob-gyn U. Ala. in Huntsville, 1976-78; various hosp. appts. including cons. in gynecology House of St. Giles The Cripple, Bklyn., 1965-74; mem. ob-gyn staff Druid City Hosp., Tuscaloosa, 1974-76, Hale Meml. Hosp., Tuscaloosa, 1976, Huntsville Hosp., 1976-78, University Hosp., Birmingham, 1978—, Cooper Green Hosp., Birmingham, 1978—; mem. courtesy ob-gyn staff Med. Center Hosp., Huntsville, 1977-78; Charles E. Flowers prof. ob-gyn U. Ala., 1986—; con. in field. Mem. Ala. State Perinatal Adv. Com., 1976—, dist. III com., 1980—; mem. med. adv. bd. HELP Line, Madison County, Ala., 1976-78, v.p., 1977-78; mem. med. adv. com. Well-Child Clinic, Madison County, 1977; mem. MCQ3 Nat. Bd. Med. Examiners, 1983—. Contbr. numerous articles to med. jours.; editor Women's Care Quar., 1979-82, Ala. Perinatal Bulletin, 1981—. Med. dir. N. Suffolk Planned Parenthood, N.Y., 1957-64; Tuscaloosa County Planned Parenthood, 1975-76. Served to capt. AUS, 1944-46. Recipient U. Ala. in Huntsville Student award, 1978; U. Ala. in Birmingham Caduceus Club award, 1979, Chief Residents Dept. Ob-Gyn award, 1979, Superlative award, 1980. Fellow ACS (com. on candidates L.I. eastern dist. 1969-74), Am. Coll. Ob-Gyn; mem. AMA, Am. Fertility Soc., Med. Assn. State of Ala., Ala. Assn. Ob-Gyn (pres. 1978-79), So. Perinatal Assn. (bd. dirs. southeastern regional adv. bd. 1976—, chmn. 1978-79), Jefferson County Med. Soc. (ob-gyn assurance panel 1983—), Charles E. Flowers Jr. Soc., Assn. Profs. Ob-Gyn, Birmingham Ob-Gyn Soc., Soc. Perinatal Obstetricians. Republican. Episcopalian. Clubs: Inverness Country, Relay House (Birmingham). Home: 3527 Conestoga Way Birmingham AL 35243 Office: U Ala Birmingham dept Ob-Gyn div Maternal and Fetal Medicine Birmingham AL 35294

HARRIS, BRUCE EUGENE, finance executive; b. Zanesville, Ohio, Jan. 14, 1950; s. Harold Eugene and Ruth A. (Harbaugh) H.; m. Linda Elaine Vess, Mar. 6, 1971. BS in Acctg., Ohio State U., 1974. Coal miner Peabody Coal Co., New Lexington, Ohio, 1970-72; auditor Boykin Enterprises, 1973-

74; cost acct. Ashland Chem. Co., Dublin, Ohio, 1974-76; acct. Ohio State U., Columbus, 1976-78; systems analyst Gulf Oil Corp., Houston, 1978-81; cons. Deloitte Haskins & Sells, Houston, 1981-82; systems mgr. Info. Service Internat. div. Mars, Inc., Houston and Los Angeles, 1982—. Mem. Smithsonian Assocs., Washington, 1986, Citizens Choice, Washington, 1975—, Air Force Mus. Found. Mem. Data Processing Mgmt. Assn. (cert.), Inst. for Cert. of Computer Profls., Mensa. Republican. Roman Catholic. Lodge: Elks. Home: 2419 Moss Hill Dr Houston TX 77080 Office: Mars Inc Info Services Internat PO Box 1752 Houston TX 77251-1752

HARRIS, CHARLES EDGAR, retired wholesale distribution company executive; b. Englewood, Tenn., Nov. 6, 1915; s. Charles Leonard and Minnie Beatrice (Borin) H.; m. Dorothy Sarah Wilson, Dec. 27, 1916; children: Charles Edgar, William John. Office and credit mgr. H.T. Hackney Co., Knoxville, Greeneville and Athens, Tenn., 1948-66, v.p., 1966-71; treas. H.T. Hacney Co., Knoxville, Greeneville and Athens, Tenn., 1971-72; pres., treas. H.T. Hackney Co., Knoxville, Greeneville and Athens, Tenn., 1972, pres., chmn. bd., chief exec. officer, 1972-82; cons. H. T. Hackney Co., Knoxville, Greeneville and Athens, Tenn., 1982—, hon. dir.; former chmn. bd., chief exec. officer, dir. more than 25 corps. in Tenn., Ky., N.C. and Ga. Bd. dirs., v.p., mem. exec. com. Downtown Knoxville Assn., 1979-83; bd. dirs., mem. exec. bd. Greater Knoxville Smoky Mountain council Boy Scouts Am, 1956-57, 82-83 ; bd. dirs., mem. exec. com. Met. YMCA, Knoxville, 1971-77, treas., 1975-76; mem. budget fin. com. United Way of Knoxville, 1974-80, bd. dirs., treas., chmn. fin. com., 1979-80; mem. budget com. 1982 World's Fair, Knoxville, 1980-82; deacon, trustee Central Baptist Ch., 1961—; active Knox County Assn. Baptists, 1964-77; mem. exec. bd. Tenn. Bapt. Conv., Nashville, 1976-82; asssoc. chmn. Layman's Nat. Bible Week, Washington, 1977-78; trustee Carson Newman Coll., Jefferson City, Tenn., 1983—. Recipient Outstanding Community Leadership award Religious Heritage Am., 1978; recipient Red Triangle award and Silver Triangle award YMCA, 1979. Mem. Greater Knoxville C. of C. (bd. dirs. 1973-76, v.p. 1975-76 Outstanding Corp. Citizenship award), Nat. Assn. Wholesalers-Distrbrs. (trustee 1977-82). Republican. Club: LeConte (Knoxville) (charter mem.). Lodge: Rotary (Knoxville). Home: 7914 Gleason Dr Unit 1071 Knoxville TN 37919 Office: HT Hackney Co 300 Fidelity Bldg Knoxville TN 37901

HARRIS, CHARLES UPCHURCH, clergyman, seminary president; b. Raleigh, N.C., May 2, 1914; s. Charles Upchurch and Saidee (Robbins) H.; m. Janet Jeffrey Carlile, June 17, 1940; children: John C., Diana Jeffrey (Mrs. Melvin). BA, Wake Forest Coll., 1935, DHL (hon.), 1979; BD, Va. Theol. Sem., 1938, DD (hon.), 1958; postgrad., Union Theol. Sem., 1939-40; DCL (hon.), Seabury-Western Sem., 1972. Ordained deacon P.E. Ch., 1938, priest, 1939; rector All Saints Ch., Roanoke Rapids, N.C., 1938-39; asst. rector St. Bartholomew's Ch., N.Y.C., 1939-40; rector Trinity Ch., Roslyn, L.I., 1940-46, Highland Park, Ill., 1946-57; pres., dean Seabury-Western Theol. Sem., Evanston, Ill., 1957-72; pres., dean emeritus Seabury-Western Theol. Sem., 1972—; dean Lake Shore Deanery; vicar St. John's Ch., Harbor Springs, Mich., 1969-85, vicar emeritus, 1985—; founder St. Gregory's Ch., Deerfield, Ill.; hon. canon St. James Cathedral, Chgo., 1975—; pres. Episc. Theol. Sch., Claremont, Calif., 1977-82; trustee Sch. Theology, Claremont, 1979-82; chmn. exam. chaplains 5th and 6th provinces Episcopal Ch.; cons. nat. dept. Christian edn.; pres. Chgo. Theol. Inst., 1966-72; pres. Chgo. Inst. Advanced Theol. Studies, 1968-70; sec. Drafting Com. on Holy Eucharist, 1970-79; pres. Chgo. Inter-Sem. Faculties Union, 1971-72; vice chmn. N.Am. com. St. George's Coll., Jerusalem, 1981-83; pres. Cyprus-Am. Archaeol. Inst., 1984—; mem. exec. com. Nat. Cathedral, Washington, 1978-84; v.p. Chgo. Inst. Advanced Theol. Studies, 1967-72; Dir. Am. Consortium Joint Archaeol. Expdn., 1972-78; mem. Anglican Theol. Rev. Bd., 1959—, pres., 1968-85, v.p., 1985—; mem. Am. Schs. Oriental Research 1959—, trustee, 1969-72, 76—, treas., 1984-87, bd. visitors St. Paul's Coll, Va., Inst. Christianity and Antiquities, Calif. Author: (with A. LeCroy) Harris-LeCroy Report, 1975; Asst. editor: Anglican Theol. Rev, 1958—; contbr.: Sermons on Death and Dying, 1975. Trustee Am. Schs. Oriental Research, 1976—, Little Traverse Conservancy, 1986; mem. bd. visitors Wake Forest U., 1979—, Div. Sch., U. Chgo.; bd. visitors St. Paul's Coll., Richmond, 1986; active Presiding Bishop's Commn. on Evangelism, 1987; mem. adv. com. Inst. for Antiquity and Christianity, 1987. Mem. Am. Theol. Soc., Am. Acad. Religion, Soc. Colonial Warriors, S.A.R., Conf. of Anglican Theologians, Soc. of Biblical Lit. Clubs: University, Wequetonsing Golf (Harbor Springs); Little Sturgeon Trout; Glenview (Golf, Ill.); Desert Forest (Carefree, Ariz.). Home: Flint Hill Delaplane VA 22025

HARRIS, CHAUNCY DENNISON, geographer, educator; b. Logan, Utah, Jan. 31, 1914; s. Franklin Stewart and Estella (Spilsbury) H.; m. Edith Young, Sept. 5, 1940; 1 child, Margaret. A.B., Brigham Young U., 1933; B.A. (Rhodes scholar), Oxford U., 1936, M.A., 1943, D.Litt., 1973; student, London Sch. Econs., 1936-37; Ph.D., U. Chgo., 1940; D.Econ. (honoris causa), Catholic U., Chile, 1956; LL.D. (h.c.), Ind. U., 1979. Instr. in geography Ind. U., 1939-41; asst. prof. geography U. Nebr., 1941-43; asst. prof. geography U. Chgo., 1943-46, asso. prof., 1946-47, prof., 1947-84, prof. emeritus, 1984—, dean social scis., 1955-60, chmn. non western area programs and internat. studies, 1960-66; dir. U. Chgo. Center for Internat. Studies, 1966-84; chmn. dept. geography U. Chgo., 1967-69, Samuel N. Harper Disting. Service prof., 1969-84, spl. asst. to pres., 1973-75, v.p. acad. resources, 1975-78; del. Internat. Geog. Congress, Lisbon, 1949, Washington, 1952, Rio de Janeiro, 1956, Stockholm, 1960, London, 1964, New Delhi, 1968, Montreal, 1972, Moscow, 1976, Tokyo, 1980, Paris, 1984, Sydney, Australia, 1988; v.p. Internat. Geog. Union, 1956-64, sec.-treas., 1968-76; mem. adv. com. for internat. orgns. and programs Nat. Acad. Scis., 1969-73, mem. bd. internat. orgns. and programs, 1973-76; U.S. del. 17th Gen. Conf. UNESCO, Paris, 1972; exec. com. div. behavioral scis. NRC, 1967-70; mem. council of scholars Library of Congress, 1980-83, Conseil de la Bibliographie Géographique Internationale, 1986—. Author: Cities of the Soviet Union, 1970; editor: Economic Geography of the U.S.S.R, 1949, International List of Geographical Serials, 1960, 71, 80, Annotated World List of Selected Current Geographical Serials, 1960, 64, 71, 80, Soviet Geography: Accomplishments and Tasks, 1962, Guide to Geographical Bibliographies and Reference Works in Russian or on the Soviet Union, 1975, Bibliography of Geography, Part I, Introduction to General Aids, 1976, Part 2, Regional, vol. 1, U.S., 1984, A Geographical Bibliography for American Libraries, 1985, Directory of Soviet Geographers 1946-87, 1988; contbr. Sources of Information in the Social Sciences Encyclopaedia Britannica; contbg. editor: The Geog. Rev., 1960-73; contbr. articles to profl. jours. Recipient Alexander Csoma de Körösi Meml. medal Hungarian Geog. Soc., 1971, Lauréat d'Honneur Internat. Geog. Union, 1976; Alexander von Humboldt Gold Medal Gesellschaft für Erkunde zu Berlin, 1978; spl. award Utah Geog. Soc., 1985. Fellow Japan Soc. Promotion of Sci.; mem. Assn. Am. Geographers (sec. 1946-48, v.p. 1956, pres. 1957, Honors award 1976), Am. Geog. Soc. (council 1962-74, v.p. 1969-74; Cullum Geog. medal 1985), Am. Assn. Advancement Slavic Studies (pres. 1962, award for disting. contbns. 1978), Social Sci. Research Council (dir. 1959-70, vice chmn. 1963-65, exec. com. 1967-70), Internat. Council Sci. Unions (exec. com. 1969-72), Internat. Research and Exchanges Bd. (exec. com. 1968-71), Nat. Council Soviet and East European Research (dir. 1977-83), Nat. Council for Geog. Edn. (Master Tchr. award 1986); hon. mem. Royal Geog. Soc. (Victoria medal 1987), geog. socs. Berlin, Frankfurt, Rome, Florence, Paris, Warsaw, Belgrade, Japan, Chgo. (Disting. Service award 1965; dir. 1954-69, 82—). Home: 5649 S Blackstone Ave Chicago IL 60637 Office: Dept Geography U Chgo 5828 University Ave Chicago IL 60637

HARRIS, COLLINGWOOD JAMES, advertising executive; b. Elizabeth, N.J., June 11, 1924; s. Collingwood James and Winifred Caroline (Burgess) H.; student Columbia U., 1947-48, George Washington U., 1972-73, NIH Found. Continuing Edn., 1974-76; m. Joan Rita McGrath, Apr. 21, 1978; children by previous marriage—Shelley, Collingwood, Justine, Mark, Frederick, Patrick. Advt. mgr. Rheem Mfg. Co., 1955-60; mktg. exec. Interpublic, 1960-63; v.p. Tatham-Laird & Kudner, Inc., 1963-70; v.p. Mohawk Airlines, Utica, N.Y., 1970-72; asst. dir. Office Minority Bus. Enterprise, Dept. Commerce, Washington, 1972-74; v.p. Washington office Advt. Council, Inc., 1974-84; now pres Pro Bono Pub. Service Advt. Mem. Monmouth County (N.J.) Republican Exec. Com., 1961-65; Rep. primary candidate for Congress from 3d N.J. Dist., 1966; mem. N.Y. Regional Export Expansion Council, 1966-70. Served with USCGR, 1943-46. Recipient award for disting. contbn. to exec. program for travel and tourism N.Y. U., 1970. Mem. Mensa, Am. Advt. Fedn. Clubs: Wings (N.Y.C.); Internat. (Washington). Contbg. mktg. editor Air Transport World Mag., 1970-73. Home: 10717 Middleboro Dr Damascus MD 20872 Office: Pro Bono Pub Service Advt 1828 L St NW Suite 600 Washington DC 20036

HARRIS, DAVID MICHAEL, financial executive; b. Houston, Mar. 14, 1947; s. Edwin F. and Mary Gayle (McKinney) H.; m. Rachel Anne Williams, June 2, 1970 (div. 1984); 1 child, Matthew Edwin; m. Karol Kaye Kueteman, July 4, 1986. BBA, U. Tex.-Austin, 1970; MS in Accountancy, U. Houston, 1971. CPA, Tex. Staff acct. Arthur Andersen & Co., Houston, 1971-73; with Exxon Co. USA, Houston, 1973-79; v.p., controller Eden Corp./Gen. Homes, Houston, 1979-81; v.p., chief fin. officer, The Johnson Corp., Houston, 1981—; v.p., chief fin. officer Parklane Devel. Co., Houston, 1985—, LDJ Devel. Co. Inc., Houston, 1981—, Instnl. Devel. Corp., Houston, 1986—; cons. in field. Cons., Am. Cancer Soc., Houston, 1982-84; vol. fund raiser U. Houston Acad. Excellence Fund, 1975-82; cons. So. Bible Coll. Named one of Outstanding Young Men Of Am., U.S. Jaycees, 1983. Mem. Am. Inst. CPA's, Tex. Soc. CPA's., Beta Theta Pi, Beta Gamma Sigma. Republican. Methodist. Clubs: Houston City, Dorking Sportsmen (pres.), The Houstonian, Yellow Rose Aquatic. Home: 5220 Weslayan #C309 Houston TX 77005 Office: The Johnson Corp 1300 Post Oak Blvd Suite 1800 Houston TX 77056

HARRIS, DEBRA LYNNE, jewelry sales company executive; b. Columbus, Ohio, Oct. 26, 1956; d. Conrad London and Ruth Evelyn (Bergglas) H. B.S. in Bus., Ind. U., 1978. Founder, owner Gold Connection, Inc., Chgo., 1978—. Mem. Jewelers Bd. of Trade, Jewelers of Am.

HARRIS, DIANA KOFFMAN, sociologist, educator; b. Memphis, Aug. 11, 1929; d. David Nathan and Helen Ethel (Rotter) Koffman; student U. Miami, 1947-48; B.S., U. Wis., 1951; postgrad. Tulane U., New Orleans, 1951-52; M.A., U. Tenn., 1967; postgrad. U. Oxford (Eng.), 1968-69; m. Lawrence A. Harris, June 24, 1951; children—Marla, Jennifer. Advt. and sales promotion mgr. Wallace Johnston Distbg. Co., Memphis, 1952-54; welfare worker Tenn. Dept. Public Welfare, Knoxville, 1954-56; instr. sociology Maryville (Tenn.) Coll., 1972-75; instr. sociology Fort Sanders Sch. Nursing, Knoxville, 1971-78; instr. sociology U. Tenn., Knoxville, 1967—. Chmn. U. Tenn. Council on Aging, 1979—; organizer Knoxville chpt. Gray Panthers, 1978; mem. Gov's. Task Force on Preretirement Programs for State Employers, 1973; mem. White House Conf. on Aging, 1981; bd. mem. Knoxville-Knox County Council on Aging, 1976, Sr. Citizens Info. and Referral, 1979, Sr. Citizens Home-Aide Service, 1977; del. E. Tenn. Council on Aging, 1977. Recipient Meritorious award Nat. U. Continuing Edn. Assn., 1982. Mem. Am. Sociol. Assn., AAAS, Gerontol. Soc. Am., Popular Culture Assn., So. Sociol. Soc., So. Gerontol. Soc. (Pres.'s award 1984), N. Central Sociol. Assn. Clubs: London Competitor's; Nat. Contest Assn.; Knoxville Kontestars. Author: Readings in Social Gerontology, 1975, (with Cole) The Elderly in America, 1977, The Sociology of Aging, 1980; co-author: Sociology, 1984, Annotated Bibliography and Sourcebook: Sociology of Aging, 1985, Dictionary of Gerontology, 1988, Dictionary of Gerontology, 1988; contbr. articles to profl. jours. Home: PO Box 50546 Knoxville TN 37950-0546 Office: U Tenn Dept Sociology PO Box 50546 Knoxville TN 37950

HARRIS, EARL DOUGLAS, lawyer; b. Athens, Ga., Apr. 9, 1947; s. Roland Russell and Martha Sue (Davis) H.; m. Jean Wright, Dec. 26, 1975; children—Jeannette, Stephanie. B.S.A.E., U. Ga., 1970, M.B.A., J.D., 1973. Bar: Ga. 1973, U.S. Dist. Ct. (mid. dist.) Ga. 1973, U.S. Ct. Appeals (5th cir.) 1973, U.S. Ct. Claims 1977, U.S. Tax Ct. 1977, U.S. Patent Office 1977, U.S. Customs Ct. 1977, U.S. Supreme Ct. 1977, U.S. Ct. Customs and Patent Appeals 1980, U.S. Ct. Internat. Trade 1981, U.S. Ct. Appeals (11th cir.) 1981. Sole practice, Watkinsville, Ga., 1973-76, 1986—; city atty. Town of Bogart, 1974-75, 85—; sr. ptnr. Harris & Rice, Watkinsville, 1977-78; mem. Harris, Rice & Alford, P.A., Watkinsville, 1978-80; ptnr., pres. Harris & Alford, P.A., Watkinsville, 1980-85; pres. Fed. Title Corp., 1978—; county atty. Oconee County (Ga.), 1978-80; atty. Town of Bishop, 1980—; corp. sec. Lawlog Corp., 1980—. Bd. dirs. The Oconee Enterprise, Inc., 1987—, Clarke County unit Am. Cancer Soc., 1970-72; mem. Oconee County Dem. Exec. Com., 1976—, treas., 1976-82; pres., trustee N.E. Ga. Presbytery, 1987—; trustee Masonic Children's Home Ga., 1985—. Served with USCMR, 1965-68; with USAF, 1968. Mem. Ga. Trial Lawyers Assn., ABA, Western Cir. Bar Assn., Gridirion Secret Soc., AGHON Soc. (pres.), U. Ga. Agrl. Alumni Assn. (pres. young alumni div. 1975-76), Oconee County C. of C. (dir., sec. 1976-78), Blue Key, Sphinx, Omicron Delta Kappa, Sigma Iota Epsilon, Alpha Zeta. Presbyterian (ruling elder, chmn. Presbyn. trustees). Lodges: Masons (33 degree Scottish Rite, Grand Master of Masons in Ga.) Order of Eastern Star (past patron), Shriners, KT, Tall Cedars of Lebanon, Royal Order of Scotland, Red Cross of Constantine, Knights of York Cross of Honor, York Rite Coll. Home: 8700 Macon Rd Athens GA 30606 Office: PO Box 498 12 Durham St Watkinsville GA 30677

HARRIS, FREDERICK MILO, former securities company executive; b. Ottawa, Kans., Nov. 26, 1915; s. Fred Milo and Helen (Janes) H.; B.A., U. Kans., 1936; m. Josephine Elizabeth Burrow, Nov. 21, 1936; children—Fred Milo III, Nancy (Mrs. Ronald Lee Chandler), Cynthia Ann, David Christopher. With Chanute (Kans.) Tribune, 1936-52, 73-85, assoc. editor, 1942-48, pub., 1948-52, 73-80; promotion-publicity dir. KMBC-TV and Radio, Kansas City, Mo., 1955-59; mgr. S.E. Kans. Westam. Securities, Inc., Chanute, 1959-71; div. mgr. Internat. Securities Corp., Chanute, 1971-75; resident mgr. Weinrich Zitzmann Whitehead Inc., investment securities, 1975-85; pres. Chanute Pub. Co., 1973-80, chmn., 1980-85; pres., Mid-Am., Inc., 1967-68, chmn., 1968-69. Chmn. Kans. Adv. Commn. on Alcoholism; mem. Kans. Adv. Commn. on Drug Abuse; mem. Commn. on Alcoholism and Drug Abuse, Kans. Episcopal Diocese, 1972-84. Mem. Chanute City Commn., 1964-67; mayor Chanute, 1966-67; mem. Kans. Ho. of Reps., 1968-76, chmn. transp. and utilities com., 1973-76; legis. coordinator Kans. Press Assn., 1981-84. Chmn., Neosho Meml. Hosp. Endowment Found., Chanute; bd. advisers Gladys A. Kelce Sch. Bus. and Econ. Devel., Pittsburg (Kans.) State U., 1974-82; trustee William Allen White Found., Sch. Journalism, U. Kans. Served to lt. (j.g.) USNR, 1943-46. Mem. Chanute C. of C. (past dir., pres.), Kans. Assn. Commerce and Industry (past dir.), Am. Legion (past comdr.), V.F.W., Nat. Council Alcoholism, Sigma Delta Chi, Phi Kappa Psi. Republican. Episcopalian. Home: 1208 W 14th St Ct Chanute KS 66720

HARRIS, IRVING, lawyer; b. Cin., May 23, 1927; s. Albert and Sadye H.; m. Selma Schottenstein, June 18, 1950; children: Jeffrey Philip, Jonathan Lindley, Lisa Ann Hollister. Undergrad. degree, U. Cin., 1948, LL.B., 1951. Partner firm Porter, Wright, Morris & Arthur, Cin., mem. exec. com., 1982-88; mem. Ohio Trade Mission to Orient, 1973, to Eng. and Germany, 1974; spl. counsel to Atty. Gen. Ohio, 1963-71 dir. Eagle Chem. Co., Valley Fair Corp.; chmn. exec. com. Hyatt Regency Cin. Mem. Ohio Devel. Financing Commn., 1974-84, vice chmn., 1978-79; trustee Skidmore Coll., 1976—; trustee emeritus Big Bros.; mem. Hamilton County Steering Com. Democratic Party. Served with USN, 1945-46. Mem. Am. Bar Assn. (Sherman Act com., sect. on antitrust), Ohio Bar Assn., Cin. Bar Assn., Am. Judicature Soc., Newcomen Soc., Am. Arbitration Assn. (arbitrator). Democrat. Clubs: Bankers, Camargo Hunt, Cin. Tennis. Home: 18 Grandin Ln Cincinnati OH 45208 Office: Porter Wright Morris & Arthur 250 E 5th St Cincinnati OH 45202

HARRIS, JAMES HERMAN, pathologist, neuropathologist, consultant, educator; b. Fayetteville, Ga., Oct. 19, 1942; s. Frank J. and Gladys N. (White) H.; m. Judy K. Hutchinson, Jan. 30, 1965; children: Jeffrey William, John Michael, James Herman. BS, Carson-Newman Coll., 1964; PhD, U. Tenn.-Memphis, 1969, MD, 1972. Diplomate Am. Bd. Pathology; sub.-cert. in anatomic pathology and neuropathology. Resident and fellow N.Y.U.-Bellevue Med. Ctr., N.Y.C., 1973-75; adj. asst. prof. pathology N.Y. U., N.Y.C., 1975—; asst. prof. pathology and neuroscis. Med. Coll. Ohio, Toledo, 1975-78, assoc. prof., 1978-82, dir. neuropathology and electron microscopy lab., 1975-82; cons. Toledo Hosp., 1979-82, assoc. pathologist/neuropathologist, dir. electron microscopy pathology lab., 1983—, mem. overview com., credentials com., appropriations subcom. medisgroup, interqual task force; chmn. clin. support services com., mem. med. staff quality rev. com.; cons. neuropathologist Mercy Hosp., 1976—, U. Mich. dept. pathology, 1984—; cons. med. malpractice in pathology and neuropathology; mem. AMA Physician Research and Evaluation Panel; mem. ednl. and profl. affairs commn., exec. council Acad. Medicine; mem. children's cancer study group Ohio State U. satellite; bar-acad. liaison com.; mem. adv. com. to Blue Cross, mem. task force on Cost Effectiveness N.E. Ohio, tech. and issues com.; dir. PIE Mut. Ins. Co. Chmn. steering com. Pack 198, Boy Scouts Am.; chmn. fin. com., tech. and issues sub-com., dir. bldg. fund campaign First Baptist Ch., Perrysburg, Ohio; faculty chmn. Med. Coll. Ohio United Way Campaign. Recipient Outstanding Tchr. award Med. Coll. Ohio, 1980; named to Outstanding Young Men Am., U.S. Jaycees, 1973; USPHS trainee, 1964-69, postdoctoral trainee, 1973-75; grantee Am. Cancer Soc., 1977-78, Warner Lambert Pharm. Co., 1978-79, Miniger Found., 1980 Toledo Hosp. Found., 1985, Promedica Health Care Found., 1986. Mem. Am. Profl. Practice Assn., Lucas County Acad. Medicine (bar acad. liaison com.), Ohio State Med. Assn., Am. Assn. Neuropathologists (profl. affairs com., awards com., program com., constitution com. 1987-88), Internat. Acad. Pathologists, Ohio Soc. Pathologists, EM Soc. Am., Sigma Xi. Author med., sci. papers; reviewer Jour. Neuropathology and Exptl. Neurology. Home: 550 Oak Knoll Perrysburg OH 43551 Office: Toledo Mcpl Hosp Dept Pathology 2120 N Cove Blvd Toledo OH 43606

HARRIS, JAMES RIDOUT, retired communications executive; b. Lockhart, Tex., Apr. 14, 1920; s. Walter Karl and Hortense (Ridout) H.; m. Frances Elizabeth Wiley, June 23, 1943; children—Richard Wells, Betty Anne, Beverly Jean. B.S., U. Richmond, 1941; M.E.E., Poly. Inst. N.Y., 1948; postgrad. Williams Coll., summer 1959; Engr. Chesapeake & Potomac Telephone Co., Richmond, Va., 1941-42; with Bell Telephone Labs., N.Y. and N.J., 1942-82, dir. data communications, 1961-65, dir. customer switching and govt. communications, 1965-71, dir. customer equipment studies center, 1971-81, dir. data network spl. studies ctr., 1981-82; dir. spl. studies ctr. AT&T Info. Systems Labs., 1983. Developed pioneer solid state computing equipment, 1950, world's earliest transistor-based computing equipment; supervised devel. world's earliest high speed transistor-based computer, Bell Labs, 1953; patentee computing, communications and solid state circuits; directed preparation of Engineering and Operations in the Bell System, 1977. Mem. IEEE (sr., adminstrv. com. of computer soc. 1962-65), Am. Phys. Soc., Soc. Automotive Engrs., Phi Beta Kappa, Sigma Xi. Presbyterian (elder, trustee, pres. corp.). Home: 8 Dogwood Ln Rumson NJ 07760

HARRIS, JANINE DIANE, lawyer; b. Akron, Jan. 12, 1948; d. Russell Burton and Ethel Harriet (Smith) H.; m. Robert I. Coward, Sept. 14, 1968 (div. 1977); m. John Richard Ferguson, Feb. 1, 1980; children: Brigit Grace, Rachel Anna. AB, Bryn Mawr Coll., 1970; JD, Georgetown U., 1975. Bar: Va. Supreme Ct. 1975, U.S. Dist. Ct. D.C. 1976, U.S. Ct. Appeals (D.C. cir.) 1976, D.C. Ct. Appeals 1976, U.S. Supreme Ct. 1978, U.S. Ct. Appeals (6th cir.) 1981, U.S. Ct. Appeals (8th cir.) 1981. Assoc. Baker & Hostetler, Washington, 1975-78, Pettit & Martin, Washington, 1978-79, Peabody, Lambert & Meyers, Washington, 1979-82, ptnr., 1983-84; sole practice, Washington, 1984—. Contbr. articles to legal jours. Mem. Nat. Conf. Women's Bar Assns. (bd. dirs. 1984-87, pres.-elect 1987-88, v.p. 1986—, pres. 1988-89), Nat. Found. for Womens' Bar Assn. (pres. 1985-88), Women's Bar Assn. D.C. (pres. 1984-85), D.C. Bar (bd. govs. 1984—), ABA (com. on specialization), Va. Women Attys. Assn. Club: Bryn Mawr. Office: 113 W Franklin St Baltimore MD 21201

HARRIS, JESSIE G., retired educational administrator; b. Athens, Ga., May 12, 1909; d. Wiley Jackson and Dora (Hilley) Ginn; BBA, U. Ga., 1956; AB, Ga. State U., 1960; m. Hubert Lamar Harris, Nov. 25, 1930 (dec.); children: Mary Ann (Mrs. William Holley), Hubert Lamar, Dorothy (Mrs. Ronald Zazworksy), Martha Susan (Mrs. R. R. McCue, Jr.). Various secretarial positions ins. and law offices, 1923-30; sec. div. gen. extension U. Ga., 1930-35, asst. dir. div. gen. extension, 1935-47; assisted with compilation survey Univ. System Ga., Atlanta, 1949-50, adminstrv. asst. to regents, 1951-63, asst. exec. sec., 1963-67, assoc. exec. sec., 1967-72, asst. vice chancellor personnel, 1972-74, emeritus, 1974—; cattle farmer, 1972—. Asst. exec. dir. Ga. Scholarship Commn., 1965-66; assoc. exec. sec. Ga. Med. Edn. Bd., 1952-72. Mem. AAUW (chmn. study group 1964-66, treas. 1972, 73), Atlanta Hist. Assn., So. Hist. Soc., Hist. Soc. Walton County (trustee, bd. dirs.), Ga. Trust Hist. Preservation, Crimson Key Honor Soc., Mortar Bd., Phi Chi Theta, Delta Mu Delta, Psi Chi. Club: Atlanta Writers. Home: Rosemont Rt 4 Box 274 Monroe GA 30655

HARRIS, JOE FRANK, governor of Georgia; b. Cartersville, Ga., Feb. 16, 1936; s. Grover Franklin and Frances (Morrow) H.; m. Elizabeth Carlock Harris, June 25, 1961; 1 son, Joe Frank, Jr. BBA, U. Ga., 1958; LLD (hon.), Woodrow Wilson Coll. Law, 1981, Asbury Coll., 1983, Morris Brown Coll., 1983, LaGrange Coll., 1987, Mercer U., 1987. Sec.-treas. Harris Cement Products, Inc., Cartersville, 1958-79; pres. Harris Georgia Corp., Cartersville, 1979-83; mem. Ga. Gen. Assembly, 1965-83; gov. State of Ga., 1983—. Served with U.S. Army, 1958. Democrat. Methodist. Home: 391 W Paces Ferry Rd NW Atlanta GA 30305 Office: State Capitol Room 203 Atlanta GA 30334

HARRIS, JOHN DUNCAN, banker; b. Doncaster, Eng., July 24, 1945; arrived in Hong Kong, 1979; s. Duncan and Mary H.; m. Theresa Weston (Div. 1976); 1 child, Thomas; m. Judi Lerwill, Mar. 18, 1978; children: Timothy, Nicholas. MA in Oriental Studies, Worcester Coll., 1966. Dir. Bankers Trust Asia Ltd., Hong Kong, 1979-81, mng. dir., 1981-83; dir. Lloyds Bank Internat., Hong Kong, 1983-85; sr. v.p. First Interstate Bank Ltd., Hong Kong, 1985—; sr. v.p., div. mgr. Asia-Pacific-Middle East Region; dir. Merchant Banking, Asia. Fellow Inst. chartered Accts. Clubs: Hong Kong, Royal Hong Kong Golf, Aberdeen Boat; Naval (London), Ladies Recreation, Fgn. Corrs. Office: First Interstate Bank Ltd, 29F One Exchange Sq, Hong Kong Hong Kong

HARRIS, KAREN KOSTOCK, manufacturing company executive; b. Chgo., Sept. 11, 1942; d. Kenneth P. and Elsie A. (Raffl) Kostock; student Mundelein Coll., 1979—; m. Roy Lawrence Harris, Feb. 14, 1981. Clerk, loan dept. Evanston (Ill.) Fed. Savs. and Loan, 1960-63, mgr. collection dept., 1963-65; credit adminstr. Packaging Corp. Am., Evanston, 1965-72, adminstrv. asst. to v.p., 1972-74; credit mgr. trainee Am. Hosp. Supply Corp., McGaw Park, Ill., 1974-75; cash mgr. asst. to treas. Pullman Standard, Chgo., 1975-76; nat. credit adminstr. Gen. Binding Corp., Northbrook, Ill., 1976-77; treas. C. H. Hanson Co., Chgo., 1977-79, sec.-treas., 1980—, dir., 1980—, adminstr., trustee C. H. Hanson Co. Pension Plan, 1979—, Employees Savs. and Profit Sharing Trust, 1978—; owner Stock Enterprises, Highland Park, Ill., 1980-81; partner Harris Enterprises, 1981—; pres. Sirrah Enterprises, Inc., 1982—; pres. cottage Keepers Inc., 1986-87; ptnr. Mont. Co., 1984—; cons. in field; lectr. Founder Mundelein Weekend Coll. Scholar Grant. Recipient Cert. of Merit Chgo. Assn. of Commerce and Industry, 1981, 85. Mem. Mundelein Coll. Women's Network, Nat. Fedn. Republican Women. Clubs: Swedish of Chgo. (sec. 1981-82, steering com. 1982), Venice-Nokomis. Office: C H Hanson Co 3630 N Wolf Rd Franklin Park IL 60131

HARRIS, LESLIE GEORGE, manufacturing company executive; b. Birmingham, Eng., June 20, 1905; s. William George and Florence Ann (Deakin) H.; m. Edith Mary Wood, Apr. 11, 1942; children—Andrew, Richard, Geraldine. Founder L. G. Harris & Co. Ltd., Stoke Prior, Worcestershire, Eng., 1928—, chmn., L. G. Harris & Co. (PTY) Ltd., Port Elizabeth S.A., 1951—, E. Africa, Ltd., 1966—, Ireland, Ltd., 1956—, Harris (Ceylon) Ltd., Colombo, 1971—. Chmn. Avoncroft Mus. Bldgs., Worcestershire, 1963-79; pres. Margery Fry Meml. Trust, 1965—; life gov. Birmingham U., 1971—. Mem. Mgmt. Research Groups (chmn. Birmingham group 1965-67). Conservative. Recipient MBE from Queen Elizabeth, 1972. Mem. Soc. of Friends. Club: Blackwell Golf (Barnt Green, Birmingham). Office: L G Harris & Co Lts, Stoke Prior, Worcestershire England

HARRIS, LOUISE, author; b. Warwick, R.I.; d. Samuel P. and Faustine M. (Borden) Harris; A.B., Brown U., 1926; pvt. study organ with T. Tertius Noble, N.Y., 1938-47. Sec., Samuel P. Harris, Inc., 1928-42; tchr. piano and organ, ch. organist, recitalist, Providence, 1928-48; founder, curator C.A. Stephens Collection. Mem. R.I. Hosp. Corp.; 1st founder Brown U. Med. Sch. Mem. Nat. Archives Assocs., Am. Guild Organists, Hymn Soc. Am., Audubon Soc., Brown Alumnae Assn., Nat. Trust Historic Preservation, Am. Bicentennial Research Inst.; Am. Heritage Soc., Am. Mus. Natural History, Smithsonian Instn. Assos., Nat., Western R.I. Author: A Comprehensive Bibliography of C.A. Stephens, 1965; None But the Best, 1966; A

Chuckle and A Laugh, 1967; The Star of the Youth's Companion, 1969; The Flag Over the Schoolhouse, 1971; Our Great American Story-Teller, 1978; Old Glory-Long May She Wave, 1981; compiler: Under the Sea in the Salvador (C.A. Stephens), 1969; C.A. Stephens Looks at Norway, 1970; Charles Adams Tales (C.A. Stephens), 1973; Little Big Heart (C.A. Stephens), 1974; Time For The Truth, 1987. Home: 395 Angell St Apt 111 Providence RI 02906 Office: Box 1926 Brown U Providence RI 02912

HARRIS, MARGARET, pianist, conductor, composer; b. Chgo., 1943; d. William and Clara Harris; B.S., M.S., Juilliard Sch. Music. Debut as pianist at age 3; toured as child prodigy; debut with Chgo. Symphony Orch., 1953; condr., pianist Black New World ballet prodn.; toured Europe twice as mus. dir. Black New World and Negro Ensemble Co. N.Y.; debut Town Hall, 1970; pianist, condr. prodn. Hair; musical dir., condr. Two Gentlemen of Verona; made debut as symphonic condr. with Grant Park and Chgo. Symphonies, 1971; soloist original piano concerto Los Angeles Philharmonic, 1972, 73; condr. St. Louis, Minn., San Diego, Detroit symphonies, Los Angeles Philharmonic, Wolf Trap Park, Opera Ebony, N.Y.C., 1977, Winston-Salem, N.C. Symphony, 1988; mus. dir. One More Time, Israel, Europe, N.Y.; mus. dir./pianist I Love New York, Europe, 1984; mus. dir. Amen Corner, Broadway, 1984; artist-in-residence Hillsborough Coll., Tampa, Fla., 1984; mus. dir., condr. nat. TV spls.; mus. dir., condr. Raisin on Broadway and nat. tour; exec./music dir. Newark Boys Chorus. Panelist Nat. Endowment Arts, Nat. Opera Inst. Affiliate Artists, N.Y.C., Dame Knights of Malta; composer of musical (with Ruby Dee), 1988; artistic dir., cons. N.Y. Boys Choir; pres. Margaret R. Harris Enterprises. Office: 165 West End Ave New York NY 10023

HARRIS, MICALYN SHAFER, lawyer; b. Chgo., Oct. 31, 1941; d. Erwin and Dorothy (Sampson) Shafer. AB, Wellesley Coll., 1963; JD, U. Chgo., 1966. Bar: Ill. 1966, Mo. 1967, U.S. Dist. Ct. (ea. dist.) 1967, U.S. Supreme Ct. 1972, U.S. Ct. Appeals (8th cir.) 1974, N.Y. 1981, N.J. 1988. Law clk. U.S. Dist. Ct., St. Louis, 1967-68; atty. The May Dept. Stores, St. Louis, 1968-70, Ralston-Purina Co., St. Louis, 1970-72; atty., asst. sec. Chromalloy Am. Corp., St. Louis, 1972-76; sole practice, St. Louis, 1976-78, Ridgewood, N.J., 1988—; div. counsel, gen. counsel S.B. Thomas, Inc.; div. counsel CPC N.Am., 1978-84; corp. counsel and asst. sec. CPC Internat., Englewood Cliffs, N.J., 1984-88; counsel Weil, Gotshal and Manges, N.Y., 1988—. Mem. ABA (co-chmn. subcom. counseling the mktg. function, securities law com., tender offers and proxy statements subcom.), Ill. Bar Assn., N.Y. State Bar Assn. (securities regulation com.), Bar Assn. Met. St. Louis (chmn. TV com.), Mo. Bar Assn. (chmn. internat. law com.), Am. Corp. Counsel Assn. N.J. (bd. dirs., chmn. bus. law com.). Address: 625 N Monroe Ridgewood NJ 07450

HARRIS, MICHAEL GENE, optometrist, educator, lawyer; b. San Francisco, Sept. 20, 1942; s. Morry and Gertrude Alice (Epstein) H.; B.S., U. Calif., 1964, M. Optometry, 1965, D. Optometry, 1966, M.S., 1968; J.D., John F. Kennedy U., 1985; m. Andrea Elaine Berman, Nov. 29, 1969; children—Matthew Benjamin, Daniel Evan. Bar: Calif., U.S. Dist. Ct. (no. dist.) Calif. Assoc. practice optometry, Oakland, Calif., 1965-66, San Francisco, 1966-68; instr., coordinator contact lens clinic Ohio State U., 1968-69; asst. clin. prof. optometry U. Calif., Berkeley, 1969-73, dir. contact lens extended care clinic, 1969-83, chief contact lens clinic, 1983—, assoc. clin. prof., 1973-76, asst. chief contact lens service, 1970-76, assoc. chief contact lens service, 1976—, lectr., 1978-80, sr. lectr., 1980—, vice chmn. faculty Sch. Optometry, 1983—, prof. clin. optometry, 1984-86; clin. prof. optometry, 1986—; John de Carle vis. prof. City U., London, 1984; pvt. practice optometry, Oakland, Calif., 1973-76; lectr., cons. in field; mem. regulation rev. com. Calif. State Bd. Optometry; cons. hypnosis Calif. Optometric Assn., Am. Optometric Assn.; cons. Nat. Bd. Examiners in Optometry, Soflens div. Bausch & Lomb, 1973—, Barnes-Hind Hydrocurve Soft Lenses, Inc., 1974—, Contact Lens Research Lab., 1976—, Wesley-Jessen Contact Lens Co., 1977—, Palo Alto VA, 1980—, Primarius Corp., Cooper Vision Optics-Alcon, 1980—; co-founder Morton D. Carver Research Lab., 1986; Planning commr. Town of Moraga, Calif., 1986, vice-chmn., 1987— ; founding mem. Young Adults div. Jewish Welfare Fedn., 1965—, chmn. 1967-68; commr. Sunday Football League, Contra Costa County, Calif., 1974-78. Charter Mem. Jewish Community Ctr. Contra Costa County; founding mem. Jewish Community Mus. San Francisco, 1984; Para-Rabbinic Temple Isaiah, Lafayette, Calif., 1987; life mem. Bay Area Council for Soviet Jews, 1976; bd. dirs. Jewish Community Relations Council of Greater East Bay, 1979—, Campolindo Homeowners Assn., 1981—; pres. student council John F. Kennedy U. Sch. Law, 1984-85. Fellow U. Calif., 1971; Calif. Optometric Assn. Scholar 1965, George Schneider Meml. scholar, 1964. Fellow Am. Acad. Optometry (diplomate cornea and contact lens sect.; chmn. contact lens papers; mem. contact lens com. 1974—, vice chmn. contact lens sect. 1980-82, chmn. 1982-84, 84-86), Assn. Schs. and Colls. Optometry (council on acad. affairs), AAAS; mem. Assn. for Research in Vision and Ophthalmology, Am. Optometric Assn. (proctor 1969—), Calif. Optometric Assn., Assn. Optometric Contact Lens Educators, Am. Optometric Found., Mexican Soc. Contactology (hon.), Nat. Council on Contact Lens Compliance, Internat. Soc. Contact Lens Research, Calif. State Bd. Optometry (regulation rev. com.), Calif. Acad. Scis., U. Calif. Optometry Alumni Assn. (life), ABA, Assn. Trial Lawyers Am., Calif. Trial Lawyers Assn., Calif. Young Lawyers Assn., Contra Costa Bar Assn., Mus. Soc., JFK U. Sch. Law Alumni Assn., Mensa. Democrat. Lodge: B'nai B'rith. Editor current comments sect. Am. Jour. Optometry, 1974-77; editor Eye Contact, 1984—; contbr. chpts. to books; author various syllabuses; contbr. articles to profl. pubs. Home: 43 Corte Royal Moraga CA 94556 Office: U Calif Sch Optometry Berkeley CA 94720

HARRIS, MICHAEL JEFFREY, data processing company executive, consultant; b. Austin, Tex., Feb. 5, 1954; s. Saul George and Isabelle Rose (Soshtain) H.; BA in Psychology, U. Hawaii, 1974-78; grad. with honors U.S. Air Force Sch. Applied Aerospace Sci., 1971-72. Mgr. network services Stanford U., Palo Alto, Calif., 1979-81; sr. cons. G.E. Info. Services, Rockville, Md., 1981-82; assoc. Booz Allen, & Hamilton, Bethesda, Md., 1982-83; mgr. Automated Systems div. Arthur D. Little, Inc., Washington, 1983-86; dir. systems devel. div. Coopers & Lybrand, Washington, 1986—; bd. dirs. Eastern Atlantic Transport, Boston. Served with USAF, 1971-79. Mem. Am. Mgmt. Assn., Armed Forces Communications and Electronics Assn. Republican. Jewish. Avocations: racquetball, squash, golf, skydiving, horseback riding. Office: Coopers & Lybrand 1800 M St NW Washington DC 20036

HARRIS, MORGAN HOVEY, JR., exec. recruiting cons.; b. Cambridge, Mass., Dec. 8, 1932; s. Morgan Hovey and Gladys N. (Nordstrom) H.; B.A., Yale, 1954; m. Elizabeth Colgate Cowles, June 21, 1962; children—Elizabeth Colgate, Jennifer Hovey, Stephanie Morgan. With White Weld & Co. Investment Bankers, N.Y.C., 1957-63; with White Weld & Co., Los Angeles, 1963-71, v.p., 1965-71, gen. partner in charge So. Calif. region, 1968-71; pres. William O'Neil & Co., Securities, Los Angeles, 1971-72; pres. Seidler, Arnett, Spillane & Harris, Los Angeles, 1972-74; sr. v.p., mgr. Los Angeles office Russell Reynolds Assos., 1974-80; sr. partner, mem. exec. com. Korn/Ferry Internat., 1980-84, mng. ptnr., 1984—. Pres., Internat. Student Center, Los Angeles, 1968-72, chmn., 1973-75; mem. St. Matthews Parish Sch. Bd., 1970-71; trustee St. John's Hosp., 1970—, treas., 1977, v.p., sec. 1978; regional chmn. Yale Alumni Fund, 1964-70, bd. dirs., 1969—. Mem. Calif. del. Democratic Nat. Conv., 1968; statewide finance chmn. Jess Unruh for Gov., 1970; div. chmn. United Way, Los Angeles, 1977-78; chmn. bd. trustees Loyola-Marymont U., Los Angeles, 1974-78; trustee John Thomas Dye Sch., Los Angeles, 1975-78, Brooks Sch., North Andover, Mass., 1969-78; trustee Calif. Mus. Found., 1983—, vice-chmn. nominating com. 1985, treas., 1984, pres. 1986—. Served with AUS, 1954-56. Mem. Calif. Exec. Recruiters Assn. (founding pres. 1980), Spring St. Forum of Los Angeles (pres. 1972). Clubs: Los Angeles Country, Calif. (Los Angeles), Regency; Links (N.Y.C.); Beach (Santa Monica, Calif.). Home: 642 Toyopa Dr Pacific Palisades CA 90272 Office: 911 Wilshire Blvd Los Angeles CA 90017

HARRIS, RAYMOND JESSE, retired government official; b. Van Buren, N.Y., Dec. 28, 1916; s. Francis Elbert and Anna Marie (Selinsky) H.; A.B., Harvard U., 1940, postgrad., 1940-42; postgrad. U. Pa., 1952-54, 59-60; m. Rosalba Emilia Prestianni, Jan. 7, 1950. Corr. drafter U.S. State Dept., Washington, 1947, vice consul Am. consulate, Palermo, Italy, 1947-50, Munich, Germany, 1950-51; personnel technician, information officer City of Phila., 1952-59, adminstrv. asst. to water commr., 1959-79; ret., 1979; Republican committeeman 59th ward, City of Phila., 1986—. Served with USAAF, 1942-45; ETO. Named Water Dept. Supr. of Year, 1971, 72, 73, 76; recipient Ted Moses award Pa. Water Pollution Control Assn., 1978. Mem. Am. Water Works Assn., Archeol. Inst. Am., Am. Acad. Polit. and Social Sci., Nat. Trust Historic Preservation, Pa. Hist. Soc., Pa. Trust Historic Preservation, Acad. Polit. Sci., Am. Anti-Vivisection Soc. Club: Harvard of Phila. Home: 275 W Tulpehocken St Philadelphia PA 19144

HARRIS, RICHARD ANTHONY SIDNEY, trust company executive; b. Bklyn., Dec. 22, 1940; s. Stanley Sidney and Rose (Franquelli) H.; m. Sharon Lynne Harvey, Dec. 21, 1975; 1 child, Aaron Nathaniel Graeme. Student St. John's U., Jamaica, N.Y., 1958-61. Adminstr. Harris Trust, N.Y.C., 1972—, trustee, 1972—; adminstr. Beehive Trading Co., Provo, Utah, 1980—, Aaron Reseda Med., Calif., 1976—; pres. Reseda Mgmt., 1976—, also dir. Mem. Am. Assn. Individual Investors, Internat. Platform Assn., Heritage Found. Roman Catholic. Office: PO Box 108 Van Nuys CA 91408

HARRIS, RICHARD FOSTER, JR., insurance company executive; b. Athens, Ga., Feb. 8, 1918; s. Richard Foster and Mai Audli (Chandler) H.; m. Virginia McCurdy, Aug. 21, 1937 (div.); children: Richard Foster, Gaye Karyl Harris Law; m. Kari Melandso, Dec. 29, 1962. BCS, U. Ga., 1939. Bookkeeper, salesman 1st Nat. Bank, Atlanta, 1936-40; agt. Vol. State Life Ins. Co., Atlanta, 1940-41; asst. mgr. N.Y. Life Ins. Co., Atlanta and Charlotte, N.C., 1941-44; mgr., agt. Pilot Life Ins. Co., Charlotte and Houston, 1944-63; mgr., agt. bus. planning div.; city agy. Am. Gen. Life Ins. Co., Houston, 1963—; bd. dirs. Fidelity Bank & Trust Co., Houston, 1965-66. Chmn. fund drive Am. Heart Assn., Charlotte, Mecklenburg County, 1958-59, chmn. bd., 1959-61; gen. chmn. Shrine Bowl Promotion, Charlotte Shriners, 1955; v.p., bd. dirs. Myers Park Meth. Ch. Men's Class, 1956-59, bd. stewards, Charlotte, 1959-61; bd. dirs. Houston Polit. Action Com., 1982—; charter mem. Rep. Presdl. Task Force, pres., 1981-86; co-chmn. Christian Community Service Ctr., 1984-85; mem. Mus. of Fine Arts, Houston, 1986—, First Tuesday Group, Houston, 1985—, Ambassadors Club of Rep. Nat. Com. Recipient Pres.'s Cabinet award Am. Gen. Life Ins. Co., 1964-67, 69, 71, 77-83, Disting. Salesman award Charlotte Sales Exec. Club, 1955, 57-59, Bronze Medallion award Am. Heart Assn., 1959, Nat. Quality award Life Ins. Agy. Mgmt. Assn. and Nat. Assn. Life Underwriters, 1965-87. Mem. Assn. Advanced Life Underwriters, Am. Soc. CLU's, Nat. Assn. Life Underwriters, SAR (v.p., bd. dirs. sec. chpt. 5 Tex. 1974—), Life Underwriters Polit. Action Com. (life), Houston Estate and Fin. Forum, English Speaking Union, Mensa Internat., Houston Assn. Life Underwriters, Lone Star Leaders Club, Tex. Leader's Round Table (life), Million Dollar Round Table, Tex. Assn. Life Underwriters, Am. Security Council (nat. adv. bd. 1979—), Nat. Platform Assn., Tex. Crime Prevention Assn., Pi Kappa Phi. Episcopalian. Clubs: Heritage (charter), Warwick, Napoleon, 100, Kingwood Country (Tex.); Deerwood (Tex.); Forum of Houston, Houston Knife and Fork, U.S. Senatorial Bus. Adv. Bd.; Campaigner; Tex. Circle R, 300. Lodges: Kiwanis (bd. dirs. 1979—), Masons, Shriners, Sertoma (life; v.p. bd. dirs. Charlotte chpt.), Royal Order Jesters. Home: 2701 Westheimer Rd Houston TX 77098 Office: Am Gen Life Ins Co Wortham Tower 2727 Allen Pkwy Suite 500 Houston TX 77019

HARRIS, RICHARD MICHAEL, electronic systems engineer; b. Balt., Nov. 22, 1941; s. Richard Elmer and Alice Alden (Hartline) H.; m. Ann Harris, Dec. 28, 1963; children: Michael, David, Susan, Catherine, Paul. BSEE, MIT, 1963, MSEE in Ops. Research, 1965; PhD in Engring. and Econ. Systems, Stanford U., 1972. Instr., MIT, 1963-65; cons. celestial navigation Jet Propulsion Lab., Calif. Inst. Tech., Pasadena, 1963-65; tech. staff air transp. systems The MITRE Corp., McLean, Va., 1968-71, group leader advanced airport systems, 1972-74, asso. dept. head systems planning, 1975-78, dept. head advanced systems, 1979-81, dept. head advanced air traffic control automation systems engring., 1981-82, assoc. tech. dir. naval systems engring., 1983-84, tech. dir. navy and info. systems div., 1984-88; chief engr. Washington div., 1988—; seminar lectr. Contbr. articles to profl. jours. Served to lt. USNR, 1965-67. Fellow Ford Found., 1967-68, MITRE, 1969-71. Fellow AIAA (assoc.); mem. Naval Inst., Armed Forces Communications Electronics Assn., Navy League, Sigma Xi, Tau Beta Pi, Eta Kappa Nu, Beta Theta Pi. Home: 2038 Freedom Ln Falls Church VA 22043 Office: 7525 Colshire Dr McLean VA 22102

HARRIS, ROBERTA LUCAS, social worker; b. St. Louis, Nov. 13, 1916; d. Robert Joseph and Clara Louise (Mellor) Lucas; A.B., St. Louis U., 1955, M.S.W. (NIMH grantee), 1964; m. William F. Sprengnether, Jr., Aug. 21, 1937 (dec. Aug. 30, 1951); children—Robert Lucas, Madelon Sprengnether Littlejohn, Ronald John; m. 2d, Victor B. Harris, Sept. 13, 1955 (dec. June 14, 1960). Field instr. Sch. Social Work St. Louis U., 1967-70; chief of domestic relations City of St. Louis, 1966—. Dir., Citizens' Housing Council, 1956-60; del. to Community Family Life Clinic, 1957; dir. Landmarks Assn., 1957-63; pres. Compton Heights Improvement Assn., 1973. Mem. Nat., Mo. assns. social workers, Assn. Family Conciliation Cts. (dir. 1968—), Greater St. Louis Probation and Parole Assn. (sec. 1976), St. Louis U. Sch. Social Service Alumni Assn. (sec. 1973), LWV (dir. 1956-61). Methodist. Club: Wednesday. Home: 3137 Longfellow St Saint Louis MO 63104

HARRIS, THOMAS SARAFEN, management consultant; b. Middletown, Ohio, Dec. 17, 1947; s. William Sellers and Ellen Marion (Sarafen) H.; m. Susan Wendy Shuman, Mar. 8, 1968 (div. Apr. 1972); m. Freda Gillian Wooldridge, Dec. 3, 1979; 1 dau., Anna Wooldridge. B.A., Johns Hopkins U., 1969, postgrad., 1969-72. Trainee, Brakeley, John Price Jones, Inc., N.Y.C., 1972-74, account mgr./v.p., 1974-78; directeur service internat. Equip'Contact SARL, Paris, 1978-80; mng. dir. Thos. Harris & Assoc., London, Paris, Essen, Rome, Amsterdam, N.Y.C., 1980—. Contbr. articles to profl. publs. Recipient various awards Boy Scouts Am., 1960-65. Mem. Inst. Fund Raising Mgrs., Nat. Soc. Fund-Raising Execs., Inst. Dirs. (London). Club: Royal Commonwealth.

HARRIS, TIMOTHY CHARLES, farmer, livestock exporting company executive; b. High Wycombe, Surrey, Eng., Dec. 30, 1941; s. Paul Ivor and Kitty (Bennett) H.; m. Rosalind Mary Angier, June 26, 1971; 1 child, Patrick Noel Angier. B.S. in Agr., Edinburgh U. (Scotland), 1961. Self-employed farmer, Nutfield, Surrey, Eng., 1961—; mng. dir. Exporc and Harris Assocs., Nutfield, Surrey, 1973—. Appointed to Farm Animal Welfare Council, 1986. Contbr. articles to profl. jours. Recipient 2d prize farming invention Shell Mex. and BP, London, 1971. Mem. Nat. Farmers Union (Surrey exec. 1968), Royal Agrl. Soc. Eng. (gov. 1970—), Pig Health Control Assn. (com. mem. 1970—), Animal Air Transp. Assn. U.S. (recipient Robert Campbell award, 1988), Rare Breeds Survival Trust. Avocations: conjuring; sailing.

HARRIS, WAYNE MANLEY, lawyer; b. Pittsford, N.Y., Dec. 28, 1925; s. George H. and Constance M. Harris; m. Diane C. Quigley, Sept. 30, 1979; children—Wayne, Constance, Karen, Duncan, Claire. LL.D., Albany Law Sch., U. Rochester, 1951. Bar: N.Y. 1952. Ptnr., Harris, Maloney, Horwitz, Evans & Fox, and predecessors, Rochester, N.Y., 1958—. Pres. Delta Labs., Inc. (non-profit environ. lab.), 1971—, pres. Friends of Bristol Valley Playhouse Found., 1984-87, Monroe County Conservation Council Inc., 1985-87. Served with AUS, 1944-46. Decorated Bronze Star. Recipient Sportsman of Yr. award Genesee Conservation League, Inc., 1960, Conservationist of Yr. award Monroe County Conservation Council, Inc., 1961, Kiwanian of Yr. award, Kiwanis Club, 1965, Livingston County Fedn. of Sportsmen award, 1966, N.Y. State Conservation Council Nat. Wildlife Fedn. Water Conservation award, 1967, Rochester Acad. of Sci. award, 1970, Am. Motors Corp. Conservation award, 1971, Rochester C. of C. award, 1972. Drafter 5 laws passed into law in N.Y. State. Home: 60 Mendon Center Rd Honeoye Falls NY 14472 Office: 700 First Fed Plaza Rochester NY 14614

HARRIS, WHITNEY ROBSON, lawyer; b. Seattle, Aug. 12, 1912; s. Olin Whitney and Lily (Robson) H.; m. Jane Freund Foster, Feb. 14, 1964; 1 child, Eugene Whitney. AB magna cum laude, U. Wash., 1933; JD, U. Calif., 1936. Bar: Calif. 1936, U.S. Supreme Ct. 1945, Tex. 1953, U.S. Ct. Mil. Appeals 1955, Mo. 1964. Gen. law practice Los Angeles, 1936-42; trial counsel U.S. Chief of Counsel, Nuremberg, 1945-46; chief legal advice br. U.S. Mil. Govt. for Germany, 1946-48; prof. law So. Meth. U., 1948-54; staff dir. legal service and proc. Com. Orgn. Exec. Br. Govt., 1954; exec. dir. ABA, 1954-55; solicitor for Tex. Southwestern Bell Telephone Co., Dallas, 1955-63; gen. solicitor Southwestern Bell Telephone Co., St. Louis, 1963-65; practice law St. Louis, 1965—; ptnr. Sumner, Harris and Sumner, Clayton, Mo., 1974—; sr. counsellor Mo. Bar Assn.; lectr. UCLA, Stanford U., Washington U., Wellesley Coll., U. Denver. Author: Family Law, 1953, Tyranny On Trial, 1954, Legal Services and Procedure, 1955; Contbr. numerous articles to legal jours., concentration camps,Ency. Brit., 1954, Justice Jackson at Nuremberg, The Internat. Lawyer, 1986. Pres. St. Louis Civic Ballet, 1970-72; mem. St. Louis Center Holocaust Studies, 1980-85; bd. govs. Winston Churchill Meml. and Library, 1980—; trustee Nat. Jewish Med. Ctr. Immunological and Respiratory Medicine, 1980—; chmn. pres.'s club St. Louis Children's Hosp., 1981-84; bd. dirs. St. Louis Arthritis Found., 1982—, St. Louis Multiple Sclerosis Soc., 1983— ; mem. nat. adv. council Nat. Philanthropy Day, 1986—. Served from ensign to lt. comdr. USN, 1942-46, capt. JAGC, Res. ret. Decorated Legion of Merit, other service medals, officer's cross Order of Merit (Fed. Republic Germany), Churchill fellow Westminster Coll., 1979—; recipient Humanitarian award Nat. Jewish Hosp. and Research Ctr., 1980, Shalom award St. Louis Rabbinical Coll., 1982, Vol. of Yr. award St. Louis chpt. Nat. Soc. Fund Raising Execs., 1983, Nat. Outstanding Fund-Raising Vol. award Nat. Soc. Fund Raising Execs., 1983, Internat. Disting. Communal Service award B'nai B'rith, 1984. Mem. Internat. Bar Assn., ABA (chmn. internat. law sect. 1953-54, chmn. adminstrv. law sect. 1960-61), Japan-Am. Soc. St. Louis (pres. 1978-80), Phi Beta Kappa, Order of Coif, Phi Kappa Psi, Delta Theta Phi. Home: 2 Glen Creek Ln Saint Louis MO 63124

HARRISON, ALINE LANGLOIS, interior designer, color coordinator; b. Montreal, Que., Can., Nov. 17, 1943; d. Henri Noel and Jeanne (Desrochers) L.; m. Arthur A. Harrison, Dec. 21, 1963 (div. 1982); 1 child, Sylvie; m. Michel Lavigne, June 28, 1985. Immatriculation in Classic Sci., Basile Moreau Coll., St. Lauentque, Que., 1960; student Notre Dame Secondary Sch., Montreal, 1961; D.E.C. (Designer), Coll. Old Montreal, 1981; intermediate degree in Spanish, U. Montreal, 1984. Exec. sec. Surveyer, Nenninger & Chenevert, Montreal, 1961-65; adminstr. Nation Wide Bus. Ctr., Montreal, 1967-68; decorator, adminstr. Tapis Horizon, Roxboro, Que., 1973-77; designer, pres. C'est Si Beau Inc., Roxboro, 1978—. Mem. Soc. Decorators Quebec, Design Can., West Island C. of C. Roman Catholic. Avocations: fishing; tennis; skiing; reading. Office: Import Export C'est si Beau Inc, 4557 Des Sources, Roxboro, PQ Canada H8Y 3C5

HARRISON, BRIAN FRASER, military artist, writer; b. Liverpool, Lancashire, Eng., Sept. 6, 1918; s. James Fraser and Bessie Fraser (Broadhurst) H.; m. Constance Kathleen Bennion, Dec. 9, 1939; 1 child, James Fraser. Grad. high sch., Liverpool. Asst. solicitor Mace & Jones Solicitor, Liverpool, 1945-48, ptnr., 1948-83; free-lance writer 1959—; mem. adv. com. Lord Chancellor's Circuit, Liverpool, 1972-81; free-lance mil. artist, 1983—. Author: Advocacy at Petty Sessions, 1956, Work of a Magistrate, 1964, A Business of Your Own, 1973; author, pub. books, articles to profl. publs. Dep. chmn. Liverpool Conservative Assn., 1957-67; chmn. Conservative Constituents, 1959-60. Served to capt. Brit. mil., 1937-44. Home: Mouldsworth House, Mouldsworth, Chester CH3 8AP, England

HARRISON, CHARLES WAGNER, JR., applied physicist; b. Farmville, Va., Sept. 15, 1913; s. Charles Wagner and Etta Earl (Smith) H.; m. Fern F. Perry, Dec. 28, 1940; children—Martha R., Charlotte J. Student, U.S. Coast Guard Acad., 1934-36; B.S. in Engring., U. Va., 1939, E.E., 1940; S.M., Harvard U., 1942, M.E., 1952, Ph.D. in Applied Physics, 1954. Registered profl. engr., N.Mex., Va., Mass. Engr. Sta. WCHV, Charlottesville, Va., 1937-40; commd. ensign U.S. Navy, 1939, advanced through grades to comdr., 1948; research staff Bur. Ships, 1939-41, asst. dir. electronics design and devel. div., 1948-50; research staff U.S. Naval Research Lab., 1944-45, dir.'s staff, 1950-51; liaison officer Evans Signal Lab., 1945-46; electronics officer Phila. Naval Shipyard, 1946-48; mem. USN Operational Devel. Force Staff, 1953-55; staff Comdg. Gen. Armed Forces Spl. Weapons project, 1955-57; ret. U.S. Navy, 1957; cons. electromagnetics Sandia Nat. Labs., Albuquerque, 1957-73; instr. U. Va., 1939-40; lectr. Harvard U., 1942-43, Princeton U., 1943-44; vis. prof. Christian Heritage Coll., El Cajon, Calif., 1976. Author: (with R.W.P. King) Antennas and Waves: A Modern Approach, 1969; contbr. numerous articles to profl. jours. Founder Fellowship Bible Ch., chmn. steering com., 1976-77, deacon, 1978-81, 83-86; mem. Famous Families Va. Fellow IEEE (Electronics Achievement award 1966, best paper award electromagnetic compatibility group 1972); mem. Soc. Harvard Engrs. and Scientists, Internat. Union Radio Sci. (commn. B. and H), Sigma Xi. Home: 2808 Alcazar St NE Albuquerque NM 87110

HARRISON, EARL DAVID, lawyer, real estate executive; b. Bryn Mawr, Pa., Aug. 25, 1932; m. Lisa Philippa Wanderman, Oct. 25, 1981; 1 son, H. Jason. BA, Harvard U., 1954; JD, U. Pa., 1960. Bar: D.C. 1960. Sole practice, Washington; exec. v.p. Washington Real Estate Corp., 1986—. Served to capt. U.S. Army, 1954-57. Decorated Order of Rio Branco (Brazil); Order of Merit (Italy). Mem. ABA, Bar Assn D.C., Washington Assn. Realtors, Montgomery County Md. Assn. Realtors, Nat. Assn. Realtors, Harvard Club of D.C., U. Pa. Club of D.C. Home: 336 Constitution Ave NE Washington DC 20002 Office: 777 14th St NW Suite 305 Washington DC 20005

HARRISON, EMMETT BRUCE, JR., public relations counselor; b. Langdale, Ala., Apr. 3, 1932; s. Emmett Bruce and JeNelle (Williams) H.; A.B., U. Ala., 1954; postgrad. Cath. U. Am., 1966-67; m. Patricia DeStacy, Aug. 26, 1973; children by previous marriage—Susan, Emmett, Joe. Mng. editor Talladega (Ala.) News, 1955; polit. reporter Columbus (Ga.) Ledger, 1956; adminstrv. asst. to U.S. Rep. K.A. Roberts, Washington, 1957-61; public relations dir. Mfg. Chemists' Assn., Washington, 1961-69; v.p. Freeport Minerals Co., N.Y.C., 1969-73; pres. Harrison Assos., Washington, 1973-77; pres., chmn. E. Bruce Harrison Co., Inc., Washington, 1978—; instr. bus. studies George Washington U. Asst. press mgr. J.F. Kennedy campaign Ala., 1960. Named outstanding journalism grad. U. Ala., 1954; recipient AP Radio Award, 1956, Nat. Endowment of Arts Play Award, 1969. Mem. Pub. Relations Soc. Am. (accredited, v.p. N.Y. chpt. 1973, v.p. D.C. chpt. 1982), Counselors Acad. (chair-elect), Nat. Press Club, Senate Press Secs. Club, Chemists Club N.Y., Soc. Profl. Journalists, Sigma Delta Chi, Omicron Delta Kappa, Pi Kappa Phi. Methodist. Clubs: Internat., Capitol Hill, Pisces, City. Producer plays at Dramarena, N.Y.C., and Washington Theatre Club, Arena Stage, 1966-69. Home: 3201 N Vermont St Arlington VA 22207 Office: E Bruce Harrison Co 1440 New York Ave NW Suite 300 Washington DC 20005

HARRISON, SIR ERNEST (THOMAS), electronics company executive; b. May 11, 1926; s. Ernest Horace and Gertrude Rebecca (Gibbons) H.; m. Phyllis Brenda Knight, 1960; 5 children. Student, Trinity Grammar Sch.; DSc (hon.), U. Cranfield, 1981, City U., 1982; DUniv., U. Surrey, 1981, U. Edinburgh, 1983. Chartered acct. With Harker Holloway and Co., 1951; sec., chief acct. Racal Electronics, 1951, bd. dirs., 1958, dep. mng. dir., 1961, chmn., chief exec., 1966—; chmn., chief exec. Decca Ltd., 1980—. Active Nat. Savs. movement, 1964-76; mem. RSA. Decorated Knight, 1981, OBE, 1972; named Businessman of the Yr., 1981. Office: Racal Electronics plc, Western Road, Bracknell, Berkshire RG12 1RG, England *

HARRISON, GEORGE, musician; b. Liverpool, Eng., Feb. 25, 1943; s. Harold and Louise H.; m. Patricia Ann Boyd, 1966 (div. 1977); m. Olivia Arias, 1978; 1 son, Dhani. Mem. The Rebels, 1956-58, The Quarrymen, 1958-60, The Beatles, 1960-70; solo performer 1970—; organizer A Concert for Bangladesh, 1971; co-founder HandMade Films (financing co.). Numerous compositions including Taxman, I Need You, While My Guitar Gently Weeps, Something, Here Comes the Sun, My Sweet Lord, Somewhere in England; films include: A Hard's Day's Night, 1964, Help!, 1965, Magical Mystery Tour, 1967, Let it Be, 1970 (Acad. award for soundtrack), A Concert for Bangladesh, 1972; albums include Wonderwall, Electronic Sounds, All Things Must Pass, Concert for Bangladesh, Living in the Material World, Dark Horse, Extra Texture, 33 & 1/3, Best of George Harrison, George Harrison, Somewhere in England, Gone Troppo, Cloud 9; author, performer video Mind Set On You, 1988; author: I, Me, Mine, 1980; exec. producer films Life of Brian, 1979, Time Bandits, 1981, Monty Python Live at the Hollywood Bowl, 1982, The Missionary, 1982, Privates on Parade, 1984, Scrubbers, 1984, A Private Function, 1985, Water, 1985, Withnail and I, 1987; co-exec. producer film Mona Lisa, 1986. Decorated Order Brit. Empire; recipient numerous Grammy awards with the Beatles; Beatles named to Rock and Roll Hall of Fame, 1988. Home: 4 Halkin Pl, London SW1X 8JG, England Office: care Hand Made Films Ltd, 26 Cadogan Sq, London SW1, England *

HARRISON, HENRY STARIN, author, real estate consultant; b. New Haven, June 19, 1930; s. Julius and Helen (Starin) H.; m. Ruth Lambert, May 30, 1976; children—Julie, Eve, Kate, H. Alex. B.S. in Econs., U. Pa., 1952; M.A., Goddard Coll., 1974. Asst. to pres. Charlton Press, Derby, Conn., 1955-57; assoc., Harris Weissbuck Co., New Haven, 1956-57; pres. Harrison Appraisal Co., New Haven, 1957—, H & R Ins. Agency, 1975—, Health Care Mgmt. Co., 1964-86, The H Co., 1986—; free-lance author, New Haven, 1970—. Author: Houses, Houses, Houses, 1974; Appraising the Single Family Residence, 1978, Home Buying - The Complete Illustrated Guide, 1980, Illustrated Dictionary of Real Estate and Appraisal, 1982; Illustrated FNMA-FHLMC Real Estate Appraisal Series, 1975—; Review Appraisers Handbook, 1988; also articles, book chpts., audio-visual materials. Named Realtor of Yr., Realtors Greater New Haven, 1980; recipient other awards. Mem. Am. Inst. Real Estate Appraisers, Soc. Real Estate Appraisers, Am. Coll. Health Care Adminstrs. Jewish. Home: 224 St Ronan St New Haven CT 06511 Office: Harrison Compound 315 Whitney Ave New Haven CT 06511

HARRISON, KEITH, zoologist; b. North Shields, Northumberland, Eng., Jan. 14, 1954; s. Robert and Cassie Phyllis Marjorie (Avery) H.; m. Mary Patricia Lloyd, Jan. 8, 1988. BSc with honors, Portsmouth (Eng.) Poly., 1977; PhD, Nottingham (Eng.) U., 1982. Officer marine survey Dorset County Council, Dorchester, Eng., 1977-78; research asst. Nottingham U., 1978-82; research fellow Brit. Mus. Natural History, London, 1984-87. Contbr. articles to sci. jours. Fellow Natural Environment Research Council, London, 1984. Fellow Linnean Soc. London; mem. Inst. Biology, Ray Soc. (hon. sec. 1988—). Club: Brit. Sub-Aqua (Nottingham) (diving officer 1979-80). Office: Brit Mus Natural History, Cromwell Rd, London SW7 5BD, England

HARRISON, MARION EDWYN, lawyer; b. Phila., Sept. 17, 1931; s. Marion Edwyn and Jessye Beatrice (Cilles) H.; m. Carmelita Ruth Deimel, Sept. 6, 1952; children: Angelique Marie (Mrs. Kevin B. Bounds), Marion Edwyn III, Henry Deimel. B.A., U. Va., 1951; LL.B., George Washington U., 1954, LL.M., 1959. Bar: Va. 1954, D.C. 1958, Supreme Ct. 1958. Spl. asst. to gen. counsel Post Office Dept., 1958-60, assoc. gen. counsel, 1960-61, mem. bd. contract appeals, 1958-61; ptnr. firm Harrison, Lucey & Sagle (and predecessors), Washington, 1961-78, Barnett & Alagia, 1978-84; ptnr. Scott, Harrison & McLeod, 1984-86, Law Offices Marion Edwyn Harrison, Washington, 1986—; Mem. council Adminstrv. Conf. U.S., 1971-78, sr. conf. fellow, 1984—. mem. D.C. Law Revision Commn., 1975—; lectr. Nat. Jud. Coll., Reno, 1979; adv. dir. Sovran Bank N.A., 1988—. Author articles, manuals.; editor-in-chief: Fed. Bar News, 1960-63; mem. editorial bd. Adminstrv. Law Rev, 1976—. Trustee AEFC Pension Fund, 1986—; pres. Young Rep. Fedn. Va., 1954-55; mem. Va. Rep. Cen. Com., 1954-55; bd. visitors Judge Adv. Gen. Sch., Charlottesville, Va., 1976-78; chmn. Wolf Trap Assn., 1984-87; bd. dirs. Wolf Trap Found., 1984—; pub. mem. USIA Inspection Mission, Argentina, 1971. Served as officer AUS, 1955-58. Decorated Commendation medal. Fellow Am. Bar Found. (life); mem. ABA (chmn. sect. adminstrv. law 1974-75, ho. of dels. 1978-88, bd. govs. 1982-86, chmn. com. on fgn. and internat. orgns. 1986-87, chmn. lawyers in govt. 1980-82), Fed. Bar Assn. (nat. council 1966-82), Inter-Am. Bar Assn., Bar Assn. D.C. (chmn. adminstrv. law sect. 1970-71, bd. dirs. 1971-72), George Washington U. Law Assn. (pres. 1974-77). Episcopalian (vestry). Clubs: Washington Golf and Country, Metropolitan, Nat. Lawyers (Washington); Farmington Country (Charlottesville, Va.). Home: 4111 N Ridgeview Rd Arlington VA 22207 also: 3105 NE 28th St Fort Lauderdale FL 33308 Office: 840 The Watergate 2600 Virginia Ave NW Washington DC 20037 also: Falkenstrasse 14, 8008 Zurich Switzerland

HARRISON, SIR RICHARD, anatomist, marine mammalogist; b. London, Oct. 8, 1920; s. Geoffrey Arthur and Theodora Beatrice (West) H.; m. Barbara Jean Fuller, 1967. BA, Cambridge U., Eng., 1941, MA, 1944; MBBChir, U. London, 1945; DSc, Glasgow U., 1948; MD, U. London, 1953. Demonstrator St. Bartholomew's Hosp. Med. Coll. U. London, 1944-46, lectr. in anatomy Charing Cross Hosp. Med. Coll., 1947-51, prof. anatomy, 1954-68; prof. physiology Royal Instn., London, 1962-68; prof. anatomy U. Cambridge, Eng., 1968-82, prof. emeritus, 1982—; gov. London Hosp., 1963-68. Editor, author and researcher in field. Chmn. Farm Animal Welfare Council Ministry Agriculture, London, 1979-88, bd. trustees Brit. Mus. Natural History, 1984-88; sci. adviser Ministry Environment, Paris, 1986—. Fellow Royal Soc. London, Downing Coll. Cambridge U. (hon.), Am. Assn. Anatomists (hon.). Clubs: Garrick (London); Sheringham Golf (Norfolk, Eng.). Home: 8 Woodlands Rd, Great Shelford Cambridge CB2 5LW, England Office: B2 Downing Coll, Cambridge CB2 1DQ, England

HARRISON, ROBERT WILLIAM, zoologist, educator; b. Napoleon, Ohio, Nov. 3, 1915; s. Charles Foster and Goldie Dell (Fahrer) H.; m. Marion Murlless Billings, May 30, 1943 (div. 1973); children—Suzanne Harrison Marchetti, Elizabeth A. Harrison Greene, Barbara A. Harrison DiOrio; m. Ruth Lightner Hastings, July 31, 1974 (div. Nov. 19, 1980). A.B., Oberlin Coll., 1938; postgrad. Springfield Coll., Mass., 1938-39; M.A., Wesleyan U., Middletown, Conn., 1941; M.S., Yale U., 1942, Ph.D. (Nat. Cancer Inst. research fellow), 1949. Asst. in biology Springfield Coll., 1938-39; asst. Wesleyan U., 1939-41, vis. assoc. prof., 1957; asst. in zoology Yale U., New Haven, 1941-42, 46-48, research asst. pathology Med. Sch., 1942; instr. zoology U. R.I., Kingston, 1949-50, asst. prof., 1950-56, assoc. prof., 1956-65, prof., 1965-77, prof. emeritus, 1977—, assoc. dean div. univ. extension, 1968-69, acting dean, 1969-70, acting chmn. dept. zoology, 1974-75, cons. Crime Lab.; vis. spl. instr. Brown U., 1958; Physiol. Soc. research fellow U. Ill., 1959. Bd. dirs. Animal Rescue League So. R.I.; mem. Republican Town Com. of South Kingstown, R.I., 1962-66, chmn. bipartisan com. on town adminstrn. Town Council, 1966; pres. Friends of U. R.I. Library. Served from ensign to capt. USNR, 1942-46. AEC grantee, 1962. Mem. AAUP, AAAS, Am. Inst. Biol. Scis., R.I. Assn. Health, Phys. Edn. and Recreation (hon. life), N.Y. Acad. Scis., Am. Soc. Zoologists, Am. Coll. Sports Medicine, Ret. Officers Assn., Sigma Xi, Phi Kappa Phi. Congregationalist. Club: Commodore Point Judith Yacht. Home: 40 Dockray St Wakefield RI 02879 Office: Dept Zoology U RI Kingston RI 02881

HARRISON, ROSALIE THORNTON (MRS. PORTER HARMON HARRISON), retired educator; b. Birmingham, Ala., Jan. 24, 1917; d. John William and Zora (Whetstone) Thornton; AB, Samford U., 1937; MA, U. Ala., 1945; postgrad. Tchrs. Coll., Columbia U., Cath. U. Am., George Washington U., Am. U., U. Md., U. D.C.; m. Porter Harmon Harrison, Apr. 12, 1941; 1 child, Porter Harmon. Tchr., Pinson (Ala.). Sch., 1937-41; tchr. Children's Sch., U. Ala., summers 1939-41; tchr., asst. prin. Avondale Estates (Ga.) Elem. Sch., 1941-45; asst. tchr. Horace Mann-Lincoln Sch. of Tchrs. Coll., Columbia U., 1946; instr. English, Samford U., 1948; tchr. Lakeview Sch., Birmingham, 1948-49, Hazelwood and McFerran Sch., Louisville, 1950-53; with pub. schs. of Dist. of Columbia, Washington, D.C., 1956-82; tchr. Congress Heights Elem. Sch., Washington, 1956-63; guidance counselor Barnard Elem. Sch., Washington, 1963-82; adminstr. D.C. Project Head Start, summers 1966-69, coordinator parent program, summers 1968-69; prin. Congress Heights-Savoy Elem. Summer Sch., Washington, 1971, Blow-Bowen Elem. Summer Sch., Washington, 1972. Del. Congress of Baptist World Alliance, Rio de Janeiro, Brazil, 1960, Miami, Fla., 1965; dir. D.C. Bapt. Conv. Summer Mission Camp Girls Aux., 1955, assembly officer Dept. Bapt. Women, 1967-71, 73-77; dir. Bapt. Tng. Union, Riverside Bapt. Ch., Washington, 1954-65, also mem. choir, council, mem. numerous coms., officer, 1953—; past pres. Ministers Wives, D.C. Bapt. Conv. Ky. Col. Mem. NEA (life), Am. Assn. for Counseling and Devel., D.C. Assn. Counseling and Devel., Am. Sch. Counselor Assn., D.C. Sch. Counselor Assn., D.C. Elem. Sch. Counselor Assn. (past v.p.), D.C. Career Devel. Assn. (past pres.), Nat. Career Devel. Assn., Assn. for Multicultural Counseling and Devel., D.C. Assn. for Multicultural Counseling and Devel., Assn. Specialists in Group Work, D.C. Assn. Specialists in Group Work (charter), Am. Mental Health Counselors Assn., D.C. Mental Health Counselors Assn.; also Internat. Platform Assn., Council for Exceptional Children, Nat. Trust Hist. Preservation, D.C. Ret. Tchrs. Assn., The Columbian Women of the George Washington U. (past 1st v.p.), Smithsonian Nat. Assocs., U.S. Capitol Hist. Soc., Concerned Citizens Council Washington (pres.), Washington City Bible Soc. (bd. dirs.), Alpha Delta Kappa (past state pres. Washington, past pres. Gamma chpt.). Home: 3828 17th Pl NE Washington DC 20018

HARRISON, RUPERT KNIGHT, investment banker; b. Oxted, Eng.; s. Roger William and Rose Christine (Noeldechen) H.; m. Tamlyn Jane Nall, 1987. LLB, London U., 1981, M Laws, 1982. Cert. barrister. V.p. Citicorp Investment Bank Ltd., London, 1983—. Mem. Church of England. Club: Reform (London). Office: Citicorp Investment Bank, 335 Strand, London WC2R 1LS, England

HARROD, B(ILLY) J(OE), professional association executive; b. Olney, Tex., Jan. 30, 1933; s. Palmer Francis and Euna Pearl (Dunagan) H. MusB, North Tex. State Coll., 1954; MusM, Ind. U., 1959, Dr. Mus. Edn., 1961. Cert. tchr., Tex. Mgr. trade and edn. div. Alexander Broude Inc., N.Y.C., 1971-79; dir. ednl. div., assoc. editor Summy Birchard Pubs., Princeton, N.J., 1978-80; asst. to exec. dir. ASCE, N.Y.C., 1980-82; mgr. spl. projects Am. Assn. Engring. Socs., N.Y.C., 1982-83, acting exec. dir., 1984; mng. dir. Soc. Women Engrs., N.Y.C., 1984-85, acting exec. dir., 1985—. Bd. dirs. Engring. Socs. Library, N.Y.C., 1986—. Served with U.S. Army, 1954-56. Named Knight Ofcl., Pres. Republic of Liberia, 1966. Mem. Am. Soc. Assn. Execs., N.Y. Soc. Assn. Execs., Council Engring. and Sci. Assn. Execs., Soc. Women Engrs. (affiliate), Sigma Phi Epsilon, Alpha Chi, Phi Theta Kappa. Democrat. Presbyterian. Office: Soc of Women Engrs 345 E 47th St Rm 305 New York NY 10017

HARROLD, GORDON COLESON, environmental consultant; b. Mount Jewett, Pa., July 5, 1906; s. John Joseph and Clarissa H. (Coleson) H.; m. Florence W. Bristow, Oct. 7, 1927 (dec. 1984); children: Dianne Collier, Lynn Batte, Susan Schmidt; m. Lynn Doubleday, Mar. 2, 1986. BS, Antioch Coll., 1930; MA, U. Cin., 1931, PhD, 1934. Indsl. hygiene engr. Indsl. Health Conservacy Lab., Detroit, 1934-35; chief indsl. hygienist Chrysler Corp., Detroit, 1935-45; dir. Indsl. Health Hygiene and Safety Service, Detroit, 1945—; gen. co-chmn. First Midwest Conf. Occupational Diseases, Detroit, 1937, Am. Conf. on Indsl. Diseases, Cleve., 1939; cons. in field. Contbr. articles to profl. jours. Fellow AAAS, Inst. Chemists, Am. Pub. Health Assn. (emeritus); mem. Am. Chem. Soc. (emeritus), Am. Soc. Heating and Ventilating Engrs., Am. Inst. Chemistry (fellow emeritus), Am. Indsl. Hygiene Assn. (co-organizer, 1st sec.-treas. 1939-40, sec. 1940-42, bd. dirs. 1942-45, Donald E. Cummings Meml. award 1960, Gordon C. Harrold Loan fund established in his honor 1982, Borden award 1980, hon. emeritus), Mich. Soc. Ventilating Engrs., Analytical Chemists Soc., Mich. Indsl. Ventilation Soc. (pres. 1951), Am. Soc. Safety Engrs., Am. Air Pollution Control Assn., Engring. Soc. Detroit, Detroit Bd. Commerce (cons. to noise abatement com.), Sigma Xi. Republican. Methodist. Avocations: travel, gardening. Home and Office: PO Box 1116 423 NE 3d St Boca Raton FL 33432

HARROP, WILLIAM CALDWELL, ambassador, foreign service officer; b. Balt., Feb. 19, 1929; s. George A. and Esther (Caldwell) H.; m. Ann G. Delavan, Aug. 22, 1953; children—Mark D., Caldwell, Scott N., George H. A.B., Harvard U., 1950; postgrad., Grad. Sch. Journalism U. Mo., 1953-54; fellow, Woodrow Wilson Sch., Princeton U., 1968-69. Fgn. Service officer 1954—; vice consul Palermo, 1954-55; 2d sec. Rome, 1955-58; internat. relations officer Dept. State, 1958-63; 1st sec. Brussels, 1963-66; consul Lubumbashi, Congo, 1966-68; dir. Office Research for Africa, Dept. State, Washington, 1969; dep. chief mission Am. embassy, Canberra, Australia, 1973-75; U.S. ambassador to Guinea 1975-77, dep. asst. sec. of state for Africa, 1977-80, ambassador to Kenya and Seychelles, 1980-83; insp. gen. Dept. State and Fgn. Service, 1983-86; ambassador to Zaire, 1987—; chmn. Am. Fgn. Service Assn., 1970-73. Served with USMCR, 1951-52. Recipient Dept. State Merit Service award, 1968, Presdl. Disting. Service award, 1985, State Dept. Disting. Service award, 1987. Mem. Am. Fgn. Service Assn. Clubs: Fly (Cambridge Mass.); Metropolitan (Washington). Address: Dept State 2201 C St NW Washington DC 20520 *

HARROP-WILLIAMS, KINGSLEY ORMONDE, civil engineer, educator; b. New Amsterdam, Guyana, Dec. 12, 1947; came to U.S., 1970, naturalized, 1981; s. Edric Christopher and Adelaide (Jardin) H-W.; m. Lynette Gibson, July 1, 1975; children: Kingsley Audwin, Tippi Ann, Cher Anemone. BE magna cum laude, CUNY, 1975, ME, 1976; PhD, Rensselaer Poly. Inst., 1980. Registered profl. engr., Pa. Adj. lectr. CUNY, 1975-76; research asst. Rensselaer Poly. Inst., Troy, N.Y., 1976-80; geotech. engr. D'Appolonia Cons. Engrs., Pitts., 1981-83; asst. prof. Carnegie-Mellon U., Pitts., 1980-85; prin. Innovation Engring. Inc., Pitts., 1984—; engr. The BDM Corp., McLean, Va., 1985—. Contbr. articles to profl. jours. Coach YMCA Soccer, Penn Hills, Pa., 1984. Recipient J. Charles Rathbun award CUNY, 1974, Univ. fellow, 1975; Rensselaer Poly. Inst. grantee, 1980. Mem. ASCE, Am. Acad. Mechanics, Sigma Xi, Chi Epsilon. Democrat. Roman Catholic. Avocations: personal computer software development, soccer.

HARROUN, DOROTHY SUMMER, painter, educator; b. El Paso, Tex., Nov. 29, 1935; d. Daniel Stuart and Eleanor (Flowers) H.; B.F.A., U. N.Mex., 1957; postgrad. (Fulbright scholar) U. Paris, Sorbonne, 1957-58; M.F.A., U. Colo., 1960. One woman shows: The Gondolier Gallery, Boulder, Colo., 1961, 62, Sta. KAFE-FM Gallery, San Francisco, 1963, 64; Lovelace-Bataan Hosp., Albuquerque, 1976, 79; Eastern N.Mex. U., 1981, Rathaus, Kelkheim, W.Ger., N.Mex. State U. group shows include: Whitte Mus., San Antonio, 1960, shows in Hyannis, Mass., Waterbury, Conn., Newport, R.I., 1964-65, Mus. N.Mex., Santa Fe, 1966, Ogunguit (Maine) Art Ctr., 1977, Am. Watercolor Soc. 112th Ann., N.Y.C., 1979, Coos Art Mus., Coos Bay, Oreg., 1980, Western Slope Show, Montrose, Colo., 1981, 82, Ga. Watercolor Soc. Open, 1983, Western Fedn. Watercolor Socs., 1984, Sun Carnival Art Show, El Paso, 1984, Western Fedn. Watercolor Socs., 1984, 85, 86, 87, 88, El Paso Mus. Art, 1987, N.Mex. Watercolors show Gov's Galler, State Capitol, 1988, State Fair Fine Arts Gallery, Albuquerque, 1988; represented in permanent collections U. N.Mex., U. Colo., Fine Arts Mus., Carlsbad, N.Mex., also pvt. collections in U.S., France, Italy, W.Ger.; art dir. Wood-Reich Advt. Agy., Boulder, 1960-61; lectr. U. Colo., Boulder, 1961-62; tchr. art Langley-Porter Neuropsychiat. Inst. U. Calif., 1963; lectr. San Francisco State Coll., 1964-65; tchr. Art Center Sch., Albuquerque, 1975-79; tchr. watercolor, drawing U. N.Mex., 1980-81. Mem. Artist Equity Assn. (pres. Albuquerque chpt. 1977-79), AAUW (state cultural dir.), Nat. League Am. Pen Women (pres. Albuquerque br. 1982-83), N.Mex. Watercolor Soc. (v.p. 1984, pres. 1985). Author and illustrator: Take Time to Play and Listen, 1963, Phun-y Physics, 1975. Address: 3875 Corrales Rd Corrales NM 87048

HARRY, ROLAND JÖRN STEVEN HARRY, nuclear physicist, consultant; b. The Hague, The Netherlands, Nov. 17, 1936; s. Wessel Jan Steven and Sjieuwke Frederika (Fennema) H.; m. Benjamina Maria Stam, Dec. 15, 1962; children: David, Vincent, Ruben. PhD in Exptl. Physics, U. Leyden, 1963. Research scientist Netherlands Energy Research Found. (ECN), Petten, 1963—; mem. adv. groups on nuclear safeguards Internat. Atomic Energy Agy., 1971—; mem. chmn. working groups on nuclear materials mgmt., 1975—; vice chmn. Conv. Phys. Protection Nuclear Materials, 1977-79; chmn. working group ESARDA Non-Destr. An., 1975—. Contbr. articles to profl. jours. Mem. Nederlandse Natuurkundige Vereniging, European Phys. Soc., Inst. Nuclear Materials Mgmt., Netherlands Nuclear Soc. Home: Beemsterlaan 8, NL-1861 LH Bergen The Netherlands Office: Netherlands Energy Research Found, (ECN) PO Box 1, NL-1755 ZG Petten The Netherlands

HARSAGHY, FRED JOSEPH, JR., educator; b. N.Y.C., Sept. 17, 1916; B.A., N.Y. U., 1948, M.P.A., 1953, Ph.D., 1965; M.S. in Library Sci., Columbia U., 1954; m. Helen Krusko, Sept. 13, 1941; children—Andrea Joan, Paula Jean, Beth Hope. Asst. reference dept. N.Y. Public Library, 1930-37; editorial asst. Newsweek mag., 1937-44; supr. reference sect. Dept. State/OWI/Voice Am., 1945-49; dir. Am. info. centers in Nagoya, Kanazawa and Hakodate, Japan, 1949-52; revs. editor Inst. Aero. Scis., N.Y.C., 1952-56; chief field librarian Arabian Am. Oil Co., Dhahran, Saudi Arabia, 1956-60; tchr. social studies Danbury (Conn.) High Sch., 1961-65; prof. polit. sci. and Am. civilization Danbury State Coll., part-time 1962-65, lectr. internat. relations, spring 1974; dir. library services, prof. Coll. Petroleum and Minerals, Dhahran, 1965-69; area dir. libraries, prof. Inter Am. U., P.R., 1969-72; prof., chief librarian York Coll., City U. N.Y., 1972-74; tchr. spl. and adult edn. Danbury Schs., 1975—; lectr. mgmt. and polit. sci. U. New Haven, 1977-79; cons. developing sch. facilities. Served with AUS, 1943. N.Y. State scholar, 1944-48; recipient Founder's Day award N.Y. U., 1966. Mem. AAUP, Am. Soc. Public Adminstrn., AAAS, NEA, Spl. Libraries Assn., ALA, Am. Mgmt. Assn., Am. Acad. Polit. and Social Sci., Assn. Caribbean Univ. and Research Insts., Danbury Community Chorus, Renaissance Singers, Candlewood Chorale Soc. Republican. Roman Catholic. Contbr. to profl. publs. Address: 211A E Gleneagles Rd Ocala FL 32672

HART, CECIL WILLIAM JOSEPH, otolaryngologist, head and neck surgeon; b. Bath, Avon, England, May 27, 1931; came to U.S., 1957.; s. William Theodore Hart and Paulina Olive (Adams) Gilmer; m. Brigid Frances Molloy, June 15, 1957 (dec. Nov. 1984); children: Geoffrey Arthur, Paula Mary, John Adams; m. Doris Crystel Katharina Alm, Mar. 14, 1987; children: Kristen-Linnea Alm, Erik Alm, Britt-Marie Alm. BA, Trinity Coll., Dublin, Ireland, 1952, MB, BCH, BAO, 1955, MA, 1958. Diplomate Am. Bd. Otolaryngology. Intern Dr. Steevens Hosp., Dublin, Ireland, 1956, Little Co. Mary Hosp., Evergreen Park, Ill., 1957; mem. staff Little Co. Mary Hosp., 1958-59; resident in otolaryngology U. Chgo. Hosp. and clinic, 1959-62; instr. U. Chgo. Med. Sch., 1962-64, asst. prof., 1964-65; practice medicine specializing in otolaryngology Chgo., 1958—; mem. staff Northwestern Meml. Hosp., 1972—, Rehab. Inst. Chgo., 1965—, Children's Meml. Hosp., 1972—, Little Co. of Mary Hosp., 1977—, LaGrange Meml. Hosp., 1977—; teaching assoc. Cleft Palate Inst., 1968, dir. otolaryngology, 1969—; asst. prof. dept. otolaryngology and head and neck surgery Northwestern U. Med. Sch., 1965-75, assoc. prof., 1975—; lectr. dept. otorhinolaryngology Loyola U., 1972; med. adv. bd. So. Hearing and Speech Found. Producer videos, movie; contbr. numerous articles to profl. jours. and mags.; also guest appearances various radio and TV talk shows. NIH fellow U. Chgo., 1962-63; NIH grantee, 1985-88. Fellow Am. Neurotology Soc. (pres. 1974-75, chmn. editorial review & publ. com. 1978-79), Am. Acad. Otolaryngology-Head and Neck Surgery (chmn. subcom. on Equilibrium 1980-86, computer com. 1987—), ACS, Inst. Medicine Chgo., Soc. for Ear, Nose and Throat Advances in Children; mem. AMA, Brit. Med. Assn., Ill. State Med. Soc., Chgo. Med. Soc., Nat. Hearing Assn. (sci. adv. com. 1982—, bd. dirs. 1983—), Am. Cleft Palate Assn., Am. Council Otolaryngology, Chgo. Laryngological and Otological Soc. (v.p. 1975-76), Northwestern Clin. Faculty Med. Assn. (vice chmn. 1976-78, pres. 1979-81), Barany Soc., Royal Soc. Medicine, Irish Otolaryngological Soc., So. Hearing and Speech Found (med. adv. bd.), Sigma Xi. Roman Catholic. Clubs: Cliff Dwellers, Carlton, Club Internat. Office: 707 N Fairbanks Ct Chicago IL 60611

HART, EDWARD LEROY, poet, educator; b. Bloomington, Idaho, Dec. 28, 1916; s. Alfred Augustus and Sarah Cecilia (Patterson) H.; m. Eleanor May Coleman, Dec. 15, 1944; children: Edward Richard, Paul LeRoy, Barbara, Patricia. B.S., U. Utah, 1939; M.A., U. Mich., 1941; D.Phil. (Rhodes scholar), Oxford (Eng.) U., 1950. Instr. U. Utah, Salt Lake City, 1946; asst. prof. U. Wash., Seattle, 1949-52, Brigham Young U., Provo, Utah, 1952-55; asso. prof. Brigham Young U., 1955-59, prof., 1959—; vis. prof. U. Calif., Berkeley, 1959-60, Ariz. State U., summer 1968. Author: Minor Lives, 1971, Instruction and Delight, 1976, Mormom in Motion, 1978; (poems) To Utah, 1979, Poems of Praise, 1980; More Than Nature Needs, 1982, God's Spies, 1983; contbr. articles to profl. jours. Served to lt. USNR, 1942-46. Am. Philos. Soc. grantee, 1964; First prize in poetry and biography Utah State Inst. Fine Arts, 1973,75; Fulbright-Hays sr. lectr. Pakistan, 1973-74; recipient Charles Redd award Utah Acad., 1976, Coll. Humanities Disting. Faculty award Brigham Young U., 1977. Fellow Am. Council Learned Socs., Found. Econ. Edn.; mem. MLA, Rocky Mountain MLA, Am. Soc. 18th Century Studies, Utah Acad. Sci., Arts and Letters, Phi Beta Kappa, Phi Kappa Phi. Democrat. Mormon. Home: 1401 Cherry Ln Provo UT 84604 Office: Brigham Young U Dept English Provo UT 84602

HART, GURNEE FELLOWS, investment counselor; b. Chgo., Apr. 26, 1929; s. Percival Gray and Marguerite May (Fellows) H.; B.A. cum laude, Pomona Coll., 1951; M.B.A., Stanford U., 1955; m. Marjorie Walker Leigh, Apr. 23, 1966. With Willis & Christy, Los Angeles, 1955-65; investment counsel Scudder, Stevens & Clark, Inc., Los Angeles, 1965-67; with Scudder, Stevens & Clark, N.Y.C., 1967—, ptnr., 1972-85, mng. dir., 1985—. Vice chmn. bd. dirs., mem. exec. com. N.Y. Philharm.; bd. dirs. Lincoln Center for the Performing Arts, Inc., 1981-86; chmn. Friends of N.Y. Philharm., 1975-82; bd. dirs., v.p. Berkshire Farm Center and Services for Youth, 1972-83; trustee Pomona Coll., 1982—. Served to 1st lt., inf. U.S. Army, 1951-53; Korea. Decorated Bronze Star. Mem. N.Y. Soc. Security Analysts, St. Andrew's Soc. State of N.Y., Soc. Mayflower Desc., Phi Beta Kappa. Republican. Episcopalian. Club: Univ. Home: 133 E 64th St New York NY 10021 Office: Scudder Stevens & Clark 345 Park Ave New York NY 10154

HART, HARVEY, motion picture producer, director; b. Toronto, Can., Mar. 19, 1928; s. Benjamin and Anita (Jessel) Applebaum; m. Helena Esther Postell, Oct. 28, 1951 (div. May 1988); children: Patreena Edana Anne, Bethelene Ellen, Mathew David Harris; m. Katherine Downey, June 26, 1988. Student U. Toronto, 1945-48, Dramatic Workshop, N.Y.C., 1949-50. TV producer, dir. CBC, Toronto, 1952-64; freelance motion picture producer and dir., pres. Rohar Productions Ltd., Toronto, 1964—; co-founder Civic Square Theatre, Toronto, 1962. Theatrical movies include Utilities, The High Country, Shoot, Goldenrod, The Pyx, Fortune and Men's Eyes, The Sweet Ride, Bus Riley's Back in Town. Mini-series for TV include Master of the Game, East of Eden. Pilots for TV films include The Yellow Rose, W.E.B., The Young Lawyers, Judd for the Defense. Specials and movies for TV films include Reckless Disregard, Born Beautiful, Murder or Mercy, The Prince of Central Park, Can Ellen Be Saved, Panic on the 5:22, Like Normal People, Captains Courageous, The Aliens, This is Kate Bennett, Street Killing, Standing Tall, The City, Beverly Hills Madam, Stone Fox, four episodes of Alfred Hitchcock Presents, two episodes of The Name of the Game, four episodes of Columbo. Producer, dir. for the Can. Broadcasting Corp.; The Dybbuk, The Crucible, Enemy of the People, The Lark, The Wild Duck, Ondine, Home of the Brave, The Luck of Ginger Coffey, The Blue Hotel, The Gambler, Queen and the Rebels, A Very Close Family, Mrs. Dally Has a Lover and To-Day is Independence Day, Ward Six, Gallows Humour, Roots, David Chapter II, David Chapter III, The Morning After Mr. Roberts, The Quare Fellow, The Police, Eli the Fanatic, Sun in My Eyes, Flipside, The Double Cure, The Littlest of Kings, Panic at Parth Bay, Mr. Arcularis. New York Videotape Production: He Who Gets Slapped. Recipient of Venice Film Festival Award for Fortune and Men's Eyes, Can. Film award for Goldenrod (named Best Dir. of Feature Film), Golden Globe award for East of Eden, Emmy for Columbo-By Dawn's Early Light. Office: Rohar Prodns Ltd, 344 DuPont St Suite 201, Toronto, ON Canada M5R 1V9

HART, HERBERT MICHAEL, marine officer; b. St. Louis, Oct. 19, 1928; s. Herbert Malcolm and Helen Genevive (Quigley) H.; m. Teresa Keating, Oct. 13, 1958; children: Bridget, Erin, Bret, Tracy, Megan, Michael, Patrick. BS in Journalism, Northwestern U., 1951. Commd. 2d lt. U.S. Marine Corps, 1951, advanced through grades to col., 1972; infantry platoon, co. and bn. comdg. officer Korea, 1952, Vietnam, 1969-70; head profl. edn. Dept. Navy, Washington, 1977-78; head hist. br. Marine Corps. Hqrs., Washington, 1973-77; dir., dep. dir. pub. affairs, 1978-81; ret., 1981; dir. pub. affairs Res. Officers Assn. of U.S., Washington, 1982—; mem. adv. bd. ad hoc com. Nat. Park Service, 1985—, com. on Cemeteries and Memls. VA, 1987—. Author 9 mil. history books; editor ROA Nat. Security Report, 1983—. Decorated 2 Purple Heart medals, Meritorious Service medal, 2 Legion of Merit medals; recipient Award of Merit, Am. Assn. State and Local History, 1976, Cultural Achievement award Sec. of Interior, 1979, Conservation Service award Sec. Interior, 1986. Fellow Co. Mil. Historians; mem. Potomac Westerners (pres. 1974-75, 84-85), Res. Officers Assn. of U.S. (life), Marine Corps Hist. Found. (charter, dir. 1983-87), Assn. U.S. Army, Council Am. Mil. Past. (co-founder 1966, exec. dir. 1971—), Western History Assn. (charter), Apollo Soc. (dir. 1983-87), Am. Mil. Inst. (trustee 1978-83), Sigma Delta Chi, Theta Xi (life). Republican. Roman Catholic. Club: Nat. Press (Washington). Lodge: K.C. Avocation: photography. Home: 3218 Hallran Rd Falls Church VA 22041 Office: Res Officers Assn US 1 Constitution Ave NE Washington DC 20002

HART, JAMES HARLAN, emergency medicine physician; b. Hamilton County, Ill., Dec. 16, 1934; s. Gleason and Elizabeth Jane (Smith) H.; m.

Sharon Lenore Darr, Sept. 20, 1937; m. 2d, Lora Rae Barnett, May 9, 1955; children—Shane, Kyle, Raelene. B.S., Southwestern State U., Weatherford, Okla., 1963; M.D., Okla. U., 1968. Intern, Mercy Hosp., Oklahoma City, 1968-69; resident in ob-gyn St. Anthony Hosp., Oklahoma City, 1969-72; practice medicine specializing in ob-gyn, Woodriver, Ill., 1972-77; emergency medicine physician St. Elizabeth Hosp., Danville, Ill., 1977-80, med. dir. emergency med. service, 1980—; practice medicine specializing in emergency medicine, Lincoln, Ill., 1977-80; emergency medicine physician, Danville, Ill., 1980; med. dir. emergency med. technicians program; clin. assoc. prof. U. Ill. Med. Sch., Urbana. Served with U.S. Army, 1957-59. Mem. Am. Coll. Emergency Physicians, AMA, Ill. State Med. Soc., Vermillion County Med. Soc. Republican. Home: RR 2 Williamsport IN 47993 Office: St Elizabeth Hosp 600 Sager Ave Danville IL 61832

HART, KATHRYN MARY, service company executive; b. Toronto, Ont., Can., July 26, 1947; d. Jack Albert Moore and Marie Hart; children: Janet Linda, Ashley Walter. Mgr. Canadian Studies Engring. Mgmt., Toronto, 1977-79; telemarketing mgr. Southam Communications, Don Mills, Ont., 1979-80; mng. dir. Katimavik Cons., London, 1980-83; pres. The Receptionist, St. Catharines, Ont., 1975-77; pres. The Receptionists, Inc., Toronto, 1983-88, Atlanta, 1988—; internat. dir. Canadian Assn. Message Exchanging, Toronto, 1986—, pres. 1987—. Bd. dirs. Pape Children's House, Toronto, 1983-86. Office: The Receptionists Inc, 1240 Bay St #401, Toronto, ON Canada M5R 2A7

HART, LARRY CALVIN, lawyer; b. Lawton, Okla., Dec. 24, 1942; s. Clifford C. and Evelyn M. (Dupler) H.; m. Leslie K. Bolek, April 1986. A.B.A., Otero Coll., 1963; B.S., Colo. State U., 1967; J.D., Loyola U., Los Angeles, 1974. Bar: Calif. 1974, U.S. Dist. Ct. (cent. dist.) Calif. 1974, U.S. Ct. Appeals (9th cir.) 1979, U.S. Dist. Ct. (ea. and no. dists.) Calif. 1980. Assoc., Ned Good, Los Angeles, 1974-76, Hagenbaugh & Murphy, Los Angeles, 1976-77; ptnr. Hart & Michaelis, Los Angeles, 1977-84; Brill, Hunt & Hart, Los Angeles, 1984-86; Musick, Peeler & Garrett, Los Angeles, 1987—; instr. Inst. Safety and Systems Mgmt., Univ. So. Calif., Los Angeles, 1982—; hearing officer Los Angeles Superior Ct., 1982—. Mem. Assn. So. Calif. Def. Counsel (bd. dirs. 1980-83), Aviation Ins. Assn. Calif. (v.p. 1983-84, pres. 1986-87), Def. Research Inst., Calif. Bar Assn., Lawyer Pilots Bar Assn. Office: Musick Peeler & Garrett One Wilshire Blvd Los Angeles CA 90017

HART, LAWRENCE AUSTIN, chemist, computer engineer; b. Hollywood, Calif., Feb. 16, 1986; s. Robert Ray and Faye Irene (Wohlers) H. BS in Chemistry, U. Calif., Fullerton. Quality control supr. U.S. Polymeric, Santa Ana, Calif., 1979-82; cons. Hart's Labs., Brea, Calif., 1981; research and devel. chemist Xenotech Labs., Irvine, Calif., 1982-85; cons. U.S. Dept. State, Washington, 1980. Mem. AAAS, Am. Chemistry Soc., Soc. of Plastic Engrs. Republican. Episcopalian. Home: PO Box 393 Brea CA 92622

HART, THOMAS, international relations specialist; b. Erie, Pa., Dec. 6, 1936; arrived in Sweden, 1959; s. Merrill Bliss and Norma Grace (Thomas) H.; m. Inger Margareta Lundquist, Aug. 15, 1959; children: Lars Steven, Birgitta Kristina, Karin Maria. AB, Pa. State U., 1959; MA, U. Stockholm, 1962, PhD, 1971. Lectr., assoc. prof. U. Stockholm, 1968—; research assoc. Swedish Inst. Internat. Affairs, Stockholm, 1971—. Author: Cognitive World of Swedish Security Elites, 1976, Sino-Soviet Relations, 1987; contbr. articles to profl. jours. Served to capt. U.S. Army, 1962-65. Office: Swedish Inst Internat Affairs, Box 1253, S-11182 Stockholm Sweden

HART, TIMOTHY RAY, college official, lawyer; b. Portland, Jan. 5, 1942; s. Eldon V. and Wanda J. (Hillyer) H.; m. Mary F. Barlow, Aug. 31, 1964 (div. Dec. 1975); children—Mark, Matthew, Marisa, Martin; m. Annette Bryant, Aug. 8, 1981. A.A., San Jose City Coll., 1968; B.A., San Jose State U., 1970; M.A., Wash. State U., 1973; J.D., San Joaquin Coll. Law, Fresno, Calif., 1983. Bar: Calif. 1983, U.S. Dist. Ct. (ea. dist.) Calif. 1983. Police officer City of Santa Clara, Calif., 1965-71; chief of police U. Idaho, Moscow, 1971-73; crime prevention officer City of Albany, Oreg., 1973-75; instr. criminal justice Coll. of Sequoias, Visalia, Calif., 1975-81, dir. paralegal dept., 1981-83, chmn., dir. adminstrn. justice div., 1983—; sole practice, Visalia, 1983—. Served with USAF, 1960-63. Mem. ABA, Calif. Bar Assn., Assn. Trial Lawyers Am. Mennonite. Home: 3527 McCormick Ave Visalia CA 93277 Office: Coll of Sequoias 310 W Murray Visalia CA 93277

HARTE, ANDREW DENNIS, transportation company executive, travel agent; b. Bronx, N.Y., Jan. 23, 1946; s. Bernard and Gertrude (Romm) H. BA, Hunter Coll., CUNY, 1968; MS in Spanish, SUNY-New Paltz, 1975, MS in English, 1979; MA in French, NYU, 1975; MS in Reading, L.I. U., 1979. Cert. tchr., 48 states. Tchr. Hendrick Hudson Sch., Montrose, N.Y., 1968-69, Mahopac Schs., N.Y., 1969-70, Croton-Harmon Schs., N.Y., 1970-83, travel cons. Travelworks, Fishkill, N.Y., 1983—, mgr. Unltd. Limousine Inc., Briarcliff Manor, N.Y., 1983—; mem. local com. N.E. Conf. on Teaching Fgn. Langs., N.Y.C., 1979-83. Mem. Am. Assn. Tchrs. French (life), Am. Assn. Tchrs. Spanish and Portuguese (life), N.Y. State Assn. Fgn. Lang. Tchrs. (life; bd. dirs. 1983-86), Mensa (life), Phi Delta Kappa (life; editor, historian). Avocations: foreign and domestic travel; language study; philately; reading. Office: Unlimited Limousine Inc 55 Woodside Ave Briarcliff Manor NY 10510-1715

HARTE, NEGLEY BOYD, historian, editor; b. Rochdale, Lancashire, Eng., Aug. 29, 1943; s. Herbert and Dorothy (Stokes) H.; m. Eva Katharina Gottfrieda Maria Hutter; children: Pendle, Piran. Research fellow Inst. Hist. Research, London, 1968-69; lectr. econ. history U. Coll. London, 1969-81, sr. lectr., 1981—; historian Worshipful Co. of Leathersellers, London, 1983—; dir. Pasold Research Fund, London. Author: The World of University College London (1828-1978), 1978, University of London (1836-1986), 1986; editor The Study of Economic History, 1971, Textile History and Economic History, 1973; gen. editor (series of books) Pasold Studies in Textile History, 1983—; asst. editor Econ. History Rev., 1979-84; editor London Jour., 1986—. Fellow Royal Hist. Soc., Soc. of Antiquaries. Home: Flat 8 1 Hornton St, Kensington, London W87NP, England Office: U Coll London Dept History, Gower St, London WCIE 6BT, England

HARTER, DAVID JOHN, oncologist, radiation therapist; b. Milw., Apr. 12, 1942; s. Herbert George and Marion Bertha (Kahl) H.; m. Diane Leigh Kuebler; children: Renée, Andrew, Susannah Lee. BA, U. Wis., Milw., 1964; MD, U. Wis., Madison, 1968. Diplomate Am. Bd. Radiology. Dir. Immanuel Radiation Treatment Ctr., Omaha, 1979—, Norfolk (Nebr.) Regional Radiation Treatment Ctr., 1988—; asst. clin. prof. radiology U. Nebr. Coll. Med., Omaha, 1978—; dir. Great Plains Inst. U. Nebr., Lincoln, pres. Harter Land and Lumber Co., Green County, Va., 1986—; v.p. Aviation Services Nebr. Inc., Omaha, 1986—. Pres. Am. Cancer Soc. Nebr. div., Omaha, 1983-84, bd. dirs. 1980—; vice chmn. Omaha Parks and Recreation Commn., 1983—; bd. dirs. Bemis Found, Omaha, 1988; mem. Omaha Pub. Art Commn., adv. bd. U. Nebr. Sheldon Meml. Art Gallery. Served to lt. comdr. USN, 1968-72. Mem. AMA, Am. Coll. Radiology, Am. Soc. Therapeutic Radiologists, Am. Radium Soc., Am. Soc. Clin. Oncology, Gilbert H. Fletcher Soc. Club: Omaha Country, Omaha; Doctors of Houston. Home: 9927 Essex Rd Omaha NE 68114 Office: Immanuel Med Ctr 6901 N 72d St Omaha NE 68122

HARTER, GEORGES, architect, urban planning consultant; b. Hanoi, Vietnam, Dec. 6, 1942; s. Eugene Louis and Georgette Henriette (Silvestre) H.; m. Jeannine Marie Schilling, July 24, 1971; children: Nicholas, Magali. Diploma in Fine Arts, Nat. Sch., 1969; Diploma in Urban Planning, Paris U., 1970. Registered architect, France. Architect, urban planner B.E.R.U., Paris, 1969, French Mission in Zaire, Kinshasa, 1970; tchr. architecture Housing & Urban Planning Agy., Paris, 1971-73, tchr. architecture head studies sector, 1973-75, cons., 1977-79; new town project mgr. Regional S.W. Devel. Authority, San Pedro, Ivory Coast, 1975-76; chmn.'s cons. Devel. & Cooperation Agy., 1980-85; architect, designer 1986—; tchr. Paris VIII U., 1973-80, Paris VII U., 1979-80; cons. The World Bank, Abidjan, Ivory Coast, 1980, Adma-Opco, 1980. Author: Housing in Developing Countries, 1975, Land Plotting in Developing Countries, 1977, Facilities in Developing Countries, 1984. Recipient award Engrs. and Scientists France Soc., 1981. Mem. Urban Planners French Soc. Office: 20 Rue Saint Romain, F 75006 Paris France

HARTIGAN, IAN GUY STEWART, oil company executive; b. Leicester, England, Aug. 22, 1933; s. Guy Edward Ross Stewart and Evadne Evelyn (Abell) H.; m. Gillian Elizabeth Pryor, Aug. 30, 1958; children: Nicola Crawford, Diana. Student, Wellington Coll., Berks, Eng., 1947-51, Royal Mil. Acad., Sandhurst, Eng., 1951-53; BSc, Royal Mil. Coll. of Sci., Shrivenham, Eng., 1956; student, Staff Coll., Camberley, Eng., 1962-63, U. London, 1976. Commd. Royal Arty., Eng., 1953, advanced through grades to maj., resigned, 1969; with Brit. Petroleum, London, 1969—, mgr. supply unit Gothenburg Refinery, 1971-73, various mgmt. positions supply dept., 1973-76, ops. div. mgr. supply dept., 1976-79; exec. v.p., dep. chmn. Stolt-Nielsen, Inc., Greenwich, Conn., 1979-84; mng. dir. BP Shipping Ltd., London, 1984-86; pres. BP N.Am., Inc., N.Y.C., 1986-87; exec. v.p. BP Am., Inc., N.Y.C., 1987—; bd. dirs. BP America, Inc., Cleve., BP Can., Inc., Calgary, Alta. Trustee U.S. Council for Internat. Bus. Mem. Am. Petroleum Inst. (bd. dirs. 1986), Lloyd's Register of Shipping (mem. com. 1986). Mem. Ch. of England. Clubs: Sky (N.Y.C.), Board Room; Greenwich Golf; Effingham (Eng.) Golf. Lodges: Honourable Arty. Co. (London), Shipwrights. Office: BP Am Inc 620 Fifth Ave New York NY 10020

HARTIGAN, JAMES J., airline executive; b. 1924. With United Air Lines, Inc., Chgo., 1942—; asst. mgr. sales Mt. Prospect, Ill., 1961-63, sales mgr., 1963-67, asst. v.p. sales, 1967, v.p. passenger sales and services planning, 1968-71, v.p. system mktg., 1971-73, sr. v.p., gen. mgr. Western div., 1973-75, group v.p. ops. services, exec. v.p., 1975-81, pres., 1981-87, chief exec. officer, 1985-87, chmn., 1987—, also bd. dirs. Served with USN, 1943-45. Office: United Air Lines Inc PO Box 66100 Chicago IL 60666 *

HARTLEY, BRIAN SELBY, biochemistry educator; b. Apr. 16, 1926; s. Norman and Hilda H.; B.A., U. Cambridge (Eng.), 1947, M.A., 1952; Ph.D., U. Leeds, 1952; m. Kathleen Maude Vaughan, 1949; 4 children. ICI fellow U. Cambridge, 1952; Helen Hay Whitney fellow U. Wash., 1958; fellow, lectr. in biochemistry Trinity Coll., Cambridge U., 1964; sci. staff MRC Lab. Molecular Biology, 1961-74; prof. biochemistry Imperial Coll., U. London, 1974—, also dir. Ctr. for Biotech.; mem. Council European Molecular Biology Orgn., 1978-83; mem. sci. bd. Biogen, N.V., 1978-84. Fellow Royal Soc.; mem. Am. Soc. Biol. Chemists (hon.). Contbr. articles to profl. jours. Address: Imperial Coll Sci and Tech, Centre for Biotech, London SW7 2AZ, England Other: care Royal Soc, 6 Carlton House Terr, London SW1Y 5AG England

HARTLEY, FRED LLOYD, oil company executive; b. Vancouver, B.C., Can., Jan. 16, 1917; came to U.S., 1939, naturalized, 1950; s. John William and Hannah (Mitchell) H.; m. Margaret Alice Murphy, Nov. 2; children: Margaret Ann, Fred Lloyd. BS in Applied Sci., U. B.C., 1939. Engring. supr. Union Oil Co. Calif., 1939-53, mgr. comml. devel., 1953-55, gen. mgr. research dept., 1955-56, v.p. in charge research, 1956-60, sr. v.p., 1960-63, exec. v.p., 1963-64, pres., chief exec. officer, 1964-73, chmn. bd. dirs., pres., 1974-85, chief exec. officer, 1985-88, chmn. bd. dirs., 1985—; bd. dirs. Rockwell Internat. Corp., Union Bank. Bd. dirs. Los Angeles Philharm. Assn.; trustee Calif. Inst. Tech., Tax Found., Com. Econ. Devel.; ambassador and commr. gen. U.S. exhibition EXPO 86. Mem. Nat. Petroleum Council, Am. Petroleum Inst. (bd. dirs., former chmn. bd. dirs.), Council Fgn. Relations, Calif. C. of C. (bd. dirs.). Office: Unocal Corp PO Box 7600 Los Angeles CA 90051

HARTLEY, JAMES, psychologist, researcher; b. Alnwick, Northumberland, Eng., Feb. 19, 1940; s. George William and Joan Routlidge. BA with honors, U. Sheffield, Eng., 1961; PhD, U. Sheffield, 1964. Lectr. U. Keele, Staffordshire, Eng., 1964-72, reader, head of dept. psychology, 1982—; vis. scholar Meml. U., Newfoundland, Can., 1970-71; sr. lectr. U. Keele, 1972-82; vis. mem. tech. staff Bell Labs., 1977-78. Author: Psychology of Written Communication, 1980, Designing Instructional Text, 2d edit., 1985; co-author Teaching and Learning in Higher Education, 1984, also over 200 papers. Fellow Brit. Psychol. Soc., Am. Psychol. Assn.

HARTLEY, JAMES MICHAELIS, manufacturing and printing co. exec.; b. Indpls., Nov. 25, 1916; s. James Worth and Bertha S. (Beuke) H.; student Jordan Conservatory of Music, 1934-35, Ind. U., Purdue U., Franklin Coll.; m. E. Lea Cosby, July 30, 1944; children—Michael D., Brent S. With Arvin Industries, Inc., 1934-36; founder, pres. J. Hartley Co., Inc., Columbus, Ind., 1937—. Pres., Columbus Little Theatre, 1947-48; founding dir. Columbus Arts Guild, 1960-64, v.p., 1965-66, dir., 1971-74; musical dir., cellist Guild String Quartet, 1963-73; active Indpls. Mus. of Art; founding dir. Columbus Pro Musica, 1969-74; dir. Regional Arts Study Commn., 1971-74; v.p. Ind. Council Republican Workshops, 1965-69, pres., 1975-77; pres. Bartholomew County Republican Workshop, 1966-67. Served with USAAF, 1942-46. Mem. NAM, Nat. Fedn. Ind. Bus., U.S. C.of C. Office: 101 N National Rd Columbus IN 47201

HARTLEY, ROBERT FRANK, educator, author; b. Beaver Falls, Pa., Dec. 15, 1927; s. Frank Howell and Marie Eleanor (Thies) H.; m. Dorothy Mayou, June 30, 1962; children: Constance Ann, Matthew. B.B.A., Drake U., 1949; M.B.A., U. Minn., 1962, Ph.D., 1967. Store mgmt. staff S.S. Kresge Co., 1949-54; J.C. Penney Co., 1954-59; mdse. staff Dayton's, Mpls., 1959-61; central buyer subs. Dayton Target, 1961-63; asst. prof. George Washington U., Washington, 1965-69; asso. prof. George Washington U., 1969-72; prof. mktg. Cleve. State U., 1972—. Author: Marketing: Management and Social Change, 1972, Retailing—Challenge and Opportunity, 1975, 2d edit., 1980, 3d edit., 1984, Marketing Fundamentals for Responsive Management, 1976, Marketing Mistakes, 1976, 3d edit., 1986, Japanese translation, Sales Management, 1979, Spanish translation, Management Mistakes, 1983, 2d edit., 1986, Marketing Fundamentals, 1983, Marketing Successes, 1985, Bullseyes and Blunders, 1987, Export Channel Management, 1987 Pricing for Export, 1987; co-author: Essentials of Marketing Research, 1983. Mem. Am. Mktg. Assn., So. Mktg. Assn., Case Research Assn. Home: 17405 S Woodland Rd Shaker Heights OH 44120 Office: Dept Mktg Cleveland State U Cleveland OH 44115

HARTLEY, STUART LESLIE, diversified company executive, accountant; b. Luton, Eng., Apr. 3, 1938; emigrated to Can., 1960; s. Leslie and Isobel (Buchan) H.; m. Patricia Holmes, Dec. 27, 1960; children: Stephen, Caroline, Susan. Gen. cert. edn., Royal Liberty Sch., London, 1955. chartered acct. Ont., Eng., Wales, 1960. Controller IBM Can. Ltd., Toronto, Ont., 1971-73; dir. fin. for Latin Am. area IBM Am.'s Far East Corp., Rio de Janeiro, Brazil, 1973-74; v.p. fin. and planning Gen. Bus. Group, IBM Can. Ltd., Toronto, Ont., 1975-79; exec. v.p., chief fin. officer Molson Cos. Ltd., Toronto, Ont., Can., 1979—; mem. Fin. Execs. Council, Conf. Bd. Can., Ottawa, Ont., 1981—. Fellow Inst. Chartered Accts. (Eng. and Wales); mem. Inst. Chartered Accts. (Ont.), Fin. Execs. Inst. (pres. Toronto chpt. 1983-85, dir. for Can. 1985—). Office: Molson Cos Ltd, 2 International Blvd, Toronto, ON Canada M9W 1A2

HARTLEY-LINSE, BONNIE JEAN, health nurse clinician, administrator, consultant; b. Chgo., July 26, 1923; d. Frank and Anna Kathleen (Koutecky) Kadlec; m. Robert William Hartley, June 23, 1949 (div. Feb. 1961); children: Robert Greig, Franklin James; m. Howard Albert Linse, June 10, 1978 (dec. Nov. 1985); stepchildren: Michael Howard, Janet Stokes. BS in Nursing, St. Xavier Coll., Chgo., 1945; cert. edn. Portland State Coll., 1965; MS in Nursing Edn., U. Oreg., 1972; cert. coll. health nurse practitioner program Brigham Young U., 1976. R.N., Oreg. Mem. faculty nursing St. Xavier Coll., 1945-47; head nurse U. Chgo. Clinics, 1947-48; nurse research newborn neurology U. Oreg. Med. Sch., Portland, summer 1961; coordinator dental assistant program, instr. biology Portland Pub. Schs., Oreg., 1965-67; health service clinician, adminstr. Clackamas Community Coll., Oregon City, Oreg., 1970-84; cons. Health Services Community Colls. of Oreg., 1972-84; pres. Coll. Health Nurses, State of Oreg., 1976-78. Mem. N.W. Oreg. Health Systems, Clackamas County Sub-Area Council, Oregon City, 1980-86. Recipient Recognition for Outstanding Service award Clackamas Community Coll., 1984; USPHS grantee, 1968. Mem. Am. Nurses Assn., Oreg. Nurses Assn. (Clackamas County unit 26), Pacific Coast Coll. Health Assn. (ann. conf. program coordinator 1980), Oreg. Coll. Health Dirs. Assn., Oreg. Health Decisions. Avocations: travel, piano, choral singing, swimming. Home: 18633 Roundtree Dr Oregon City OR 97045

HARTLING, PETER, writer, journalist; b. Chemnitz, Germany, Nov. 13, 1933; s. Rudolf and Erika (Hantzschel) H.; m. Mechthild Maier, 1959; 4 children. Student Gymnasium Nurtingen/Neckar. Journalist, 1953—; lit. editor Deutsche Zeitung und Wirtschaftszeitung, Stuttgart and Cologne, 1955-62; editor of mag. Der Monat, 1962-70, also co-pub.; editor, mng. dir. S. Fischer Verlag, Frankfurt, 1968-74; editor Die Vater, 1968—. Author: Yamins Stationem, 1955, In Zeilen zuhaus, 1957, Palmstrom grusst Anna Blume, 1961, Spielgeist-Spiegelgeist, 1962, Niembsch oder Der Stillstand, 1964, Janet, 1966, Das Familienfest, 1969, Gilles, 1970, Ein Abend, Eine Nacht, Ein Morgen, 1971, Zwetti-Nachprufung einer Errinerung, 1973, Eine Frau, 1974, Holderlin, 1976, Anreden, 1977, Hubert oder Die Ruckkehr nach Casablanca, 1978, Nachgetragene Liebe, 1980, Die dreifache Maria, 1982, Das Windrad, 1983, Felix Guttmann, 1985, Waiblingers Augen, 1987, Der Wanderer, 1988. Recipient Literaturpreis des Deutschen Kritikerverbandes, 1964, Literaturpreis des Kulturkreises der Deutschen Industrie, 1965, Literarischer Forderungspreis des Landes Niedersachsen, 1965, Prix du Meilleur livre estranger, Paris, 1966, Gerhart Hauptmann Preis, 1971, Deutscher Jugendbuchpreis, 1976, Stadtschreiber von Bergen-Enkheim, 1978-79, Hoelderlin-Preis, 1987. Mem. PEN, Akademie der Wissenschaften und der Literatur Mainz, Akademie der Kunste Berlin, Deutsche Akademie fur Sprache und Dichtung Darmstadt. Address: Finkenweg 1, 6082 Morfelden-Walldorf Federal Republic of Germany

HARTLING, POUL, former United Nations official; b. Copenhagen, Aug. 14, 1914; s. M. and Mathilde Hartling; M.Div.; m. Elsebeth Kirkemann, 1940; 4 children. Sec. to Student Christian Movement, 1934-35; sec. to Denmark's Christian Movement of Sr. Secondary Students, 1939-43; curate of Frederiksberg Ch., 1941-45; chaplain St. Luke Found., 1945-50; prin. Zahle's Tchrs. Tng. Coll., 1950-68; mem. Folketing, 1957-60, 64-77; chmn. Liberal Party Parliamentary Group, 1965-68; mem. Nordic Council, 1964-68, pres., 1966-73, v.p., 1977; minister of Fgn. Affairs, 1968-71; prime minister, 1973-75; chmn. Liberal Party, 1973-77; UN high commr. for refugees, Geneva, 1978-85. Author: Sursum corda (History of Student Christian Movement); The Danish Church, 1964; From 17 Years in Danish Politics, 1974; I dine haender, 1977.

HARTMAN, HEDY ANN, fund raising company executive, consultant; b. Sept. 24, 1954; d. Alan Stuart Hartman and Joan Marcia (Lederman) Hartman Goldsmith; m. Jon Abbott Mersereau, Nov. 27, 1976 (div. June 1981); m. William Bainbridge Everett, June 2, 1984. B.A. with distinction, U. Pa., 1975; M.A., U. Wash., 1982, Ph.C., 1983. Researcher Am. Mus. Natural History, N.Y.C., 1974; curatorial asst. Univ. Mus., U. Pa., Phila., 1974-75; instr. Children's Mus., Indpls., 1976; curatorial asst. Indpls. Mus. Art, 1975-76; program adminstr. statewide services S.C. State Mus., Columbia, 1977-80; pres. Hartman Planning & Devel. Group Ltd., Bellevue, Wash., 1980—; S.C. state rep. Southeastern Mus. Conf., 1979-80. Author: Funding Sources and Technical Assistance for Museums and Historical Organizations, 1979; Fund Raising for Museums, 1985. Editor: Official Museum Guide to Products and Services, 1980. Mem. Am. Assn. Museums, Am. Assn. State and Local History (bd. dirs. 1983—), Western Museums Conf. (bd. dirs. 1980-83), Wash. Mus. Assn. (bd. dirs. 1985—; sec. 1986—). Office: Hartman Planning and Devel Group Ltd PO Box 818 Redmond WA 98073

HARTMAN, NANCY LEE, physician; b. Philipsburg, Pa., July 29, 1951; d. Richard Lee and Ann Hartman; grad. Barbizon Sch. Modeling, 1970; A.A., Harcum Jr. Coll., 1969-71; B.A., Lycoming Coll., 1974; M.S., L.I. U., 1977; M.D., Am. U. of Caribbean in Plymouth, Montserrat, W.I., 1981. Med. technologist Lock Haven (Pa.) Hosp., 1971-72, Williamsport (Pa.) Hosp., 1972-73, Renovo (Pa.) Hosp., 1974; microbiologist and med. technologist Jersey Shore (Pa.) Hosp., 1974; microbiologist N.Y. Hosp. and Cornell Med. Center, N.Y.C., 1974-75, Drekter and Heisler Labs., N.Y.C., 1975, North Shore Labs., Inc., Syosset, N.Y., 1976-78. Lab. technician North Shore Hosp., Manhasset, N.Y., 1981-82, Nat. Health Labs. Inc., Bethpage, N.Y., 1982; resident internal medicine program Interfaith Med. Ctr., Bklyn., 1983-84; med. cons. Shapiro, Baines, Saasto & Shainwald, Mineola, N.Y., 1985-88; resident pathology program Lenox Hill Hosp., N.Y.C., 1986-88; resident clin. pathology Beth Israel Med. Ctr., N.Y.C., 1988. Author: The Pocket Handbook of Infectious Agents and their Treatments. Recipient Allied Health Professions Traineeship grant, 1975-77. Mem. AMA, Am. Women's Med. Assn., Am. Soc. Clin. Pathologists (registered med. technologist), Internat. Platform Assn., Am. Soc. Microbiology. Home: PO Box 847 Glenwood Landing NY 11547

HARTMAN, PATRICK JAMES, mechanical engineer, researcher; b. Ann Arbor, Mich., Dec. 5, 1944; s. Norman James and Mary Jane (Cottrill) H.; m. Lee Ann Walraff, Oct. 5, 1968; children—Elizabeth Marie, Suzanne Caroline. B.M.E., Marquette U., 1968; M.S., U. R.I., 1974, Ph.D., 1976. Researcher U. R.I., Kingston, 1972-76; research engr. E. I. duPont de Nemours Co., Wilmington, Del., 1976-79; sr. ocean engr. Gould, Inc., Glen Burnie, Md., 1979-80; sr. mech. engr. USN, Washington, 1980—. Organizer, Community Assn. Tasks, Columbia, Md., 1982. Served to lt. (j.g.) USCG, 1969-72. Recipient Sci. award Bausch and Lomb, 1963, Vigil Honor award Boy Scouts Am., 1963; M. Kollinski Found. scholar, 1967; U. R.I. fellow, 1972-74. Mem. ASME (chmn. ocean engring. div. 1982-84, Bd. Govs. award 1985, ocean engring. div. Gold cert. 1985), Soc. Reliability Engrs., Tau Beta Pi, Pi Tau Sigma. Subspecialties: mechanical and ocean engineering; current work: supervisory mechanical, ocean and reliability engineering to improve shipboard equipment design; application of expert systems and artificial intelligence to design and reliability assessment. Office: Naval Sea Systems Command Code 05MR Washington DC 20362

HARTMAN, WILLIAM ELLIS, sociologist, emeritus educator; b. Meadville, Pa., Feb. 17, 1919; s. Hartley J. and Janet A. (Ellis) H.; student N.Y. U., 1937-41, Centenary Coll., 1943; A.B., U. So. Calif., 1947, M.A., 1948, Ph.D., 1950; m. Iva R. Decker, June 30, 1944 (div. 1980); children—Carol, William Ellis, Taylor, Paul, Beverly, Stephen, Lawrence. Instr. sociology and psychology El Camino (Calif.) Coll., 1950-51; faculty Calif. State U. at Long Beach, 1951-80, prof. sociology, 1961-80, prof. emeritus, 1980—, chmn. dept. sociology and social welfare, 1960-63; dir. Center for Marital and Sexual Studies, Long Beach, Calif. Fellow Soc. Sci. Study of Sex (pres.); mem. Am. Assn. Sex Educators, Counselors and Therapists. Home: 5251 Los Altos Plaza Long Beach CA 90815

HARTMANN, DONALD OTTO, SR., beverage corporation executive; b. St. Louis, Jan. 24, 1934; s. Otto Frederic and Mabel Lena (Schuessler) H.; B.S., U. Mo., 1963, M.Ed., 1964, Assoc. EED, 1966; m. Linda Lou Sparks, Sept. 8, 1962; children—Kimberly Lynn, Donald Otto, Jacqueline Marie, Michele Lee. Profl. scout exec. Boy Scouts Am., 1959-60; asst. prof. U. Mo., 1960-63; coordinator co-op. edn. Mo., 1963-67; dir. personnel, rehab. Goodwill Industries of Am., 1967-69; dir. forms mgmt., graphics communications, supply services Anheuser-Busch Cos., Inc., St. Louis, 1969—; tchr., counselor, cons. in graphic arts, forms design and mgmt., 1969—. Chmn. bd. Christian edn. United Ch. of Christ, St. Louis, 1974-77; bd. dirs. local bd. edn., 1972—, pres., 1973-76; active Boy Scouts Am., 1942—, Eagle Scout reviewer/presenter, 1960—; mem. community wide youth services panel United Way of St. Louis, 1970—; mem. White House Panel on Childhood Edn., Mo. Gov.'s Panel on Edn., 1977; active Lindbergh PTA, 1968—. Served with USN, 1953-59. Recipient Eagle Scout award Boy Scouts Am., 1952, Silver Explorer award, 1956, Gt. Grant award, 1962, Regional Service award, 1973, Silver Beaver award; Outstanding Loaned Exec. award United Way, 1970, Community Service award Girl Scouts U.S.A. Mem. Am. Sch. Bds. Assn., Nat. Sch. Bds. Assn., Mo. Sch. Bds. Assn., St. Louis Suburban Sch. Bds. Assn., In-Plant Mgrs. Assn., Council of Reprographics Execs., Am. Mgmt. Assn., Nat. Eagle Scout Assn. (St. Louis area council 1982), Phi Delta Kappa, Sigma Phi Epsilon (alumni bd. pres. 1963-70). Home: 4824 Gatesbury Dr Saint Louis MO 63128 Office: Anheuser-Busch Companies Inc One Busch Pl Saint Louis MO 63118

HARTMANN, LUIS FELIPE, health science association administrator, endocrinologist; b. La Paz, Bolivia, Nov. 25, 1923; s. José A. and Victoria (Lavadenz) H.; m. Beatriz de Grandchant Luzio; children: Beatriz, Felipe, Carlos, Isabel. MD, U. San Simon, Cochabamba, Bolivia, 1949; Degree in Endocrinology, Inst. Exptl. Biology and Medicine, Buenos Aires, Argentina, 1954; MS in Endocrinology, London, 1961. Medico cirujano H. Researcher Inst. Exptl. Biology and Medicine, 1951-54; prof. Biology Sch. Pharmacy U. San Simon, 1954-55; prof. med. diagnosis Sch. Medicine, La Paz, Bolivia, 1956-71; rector U. San Andrés, La Paz, 1972-74; prof. medicine UMSA Endocrinology, La Paz, 1975-84; pres. Bolivian Univs. Bur., La Paz, 1982-83;

chief med. dept. Univ. Hosp., La Paz, 1984-86; pres. Nat. Acad. Scis., La Paz, 1986—; bd. dirs. Inst. Human Genetics, La Paz, Univ. Hosp., La Paz, med. chief women's ward, 1965-85; hon. prof. U. Gral Ballivian, Trinidad, Beni, 1972, U. Autonoma Guadalajara, Mex., 1973; med. adv. Polyclinic Nat. Social Security, La Paz, 1963-64. Author: Fisiologia Médica, 1965, Citogenética Médica, 1970 (award). Pres. Com. Mal. Coordi. Desarro. C. Biol., Bolivia, 1975-85; v.p. Fund. Bol. Capacit. Dem., Bolivia, 1985. Named Huesped Illustre, Ciudad de Sucre, 1973, Ciudad de Tarija, 1974; Eisenhower Exchange fellow, Phila., 1962. Fellow ACP, Third World Acad. Scis., N.Y. Acad. Scis.; mem. Acad. Mex. Cirujia, Acad. Nat. Scis. (pres. 1966), Univ. Council Edn. (v.p. 1971-72). Roman Catholic. Clubs: Golf, La Paz, Tennis, La Paz. Home: Av Julio C Patino 755, La Paz Murillo Bolivia Office: Bolivian Nat Acad of Scis, PO Box 5829 Avda 16 de Julio 1732, 5829 La Paz Murillo, Bolivia

HARTMANN, PETER CLAUS, historian, educator; b. Munich, Mar. 28, 1940; s. Alfred and Manfreda (Knote) H.; m. Beate Just, Sept. 29, 1972; children: Pia, Emanuel, Aurelia, Patrick. D in Philosophy, U. Munich, 1976, D in Philos. Habil., 1976; Doctorat d'U., Sorbonne U., Paris, 1969. Research asst. German Hist. Inst., Paris, 1970-81; privatdozent U. Munich, 1978-81; prof. modern history U. Regensburg, Fed. Republic Germany, 1981; prof. modern and Bavarian history U. Passau, Fed. Republic Germany, 1982-88; prof. modern history U. Mainz, Fed. Republic Germany, 1988—. Author: Pariser Archive, Bibl. u. Dokumentationszentren, 1976, Geldals Instrument europ. Machtpolitik im Zeitalter d. Merkantilismus, 1978, Steuersystem d. europ. Staaten a. Ende d. Ancien Régime, 1979, Karl Albrecht - Karl VII, 1985, Französ. Gesch. 1914-45, 1985, Franzö s. Verfassung d. Neuzeit, 1985. Office: U Mainz, Hist Seminar, D-6500 Mainz Federal Republic of Germany

HARTMANN, WALTER LORENZ, safety engineer; b. Chur, Switzerland, Sept. 15, 1923; s. Lorenz and Liny (Mandle) H.; m. Elisabeth Filli, Sept. 19, 1950; children: Andrea Lorenz, Robert Lorenz, Ursina Elisabeth. M.Sc., Fed. Inst. Tech., Zurich, Switzerland, 1947, Dr. Sc., 1957, Privatdozent, 1967. Cert. mech. engr. Project engr. Sulzer Bros. Ltd., Winterthur, Switzerland, 1948-49; asst. mgr. Hartmann Unfallverhütung, Winterthur, 1949-56, sr. mgr., 1956-68, pres., 1968—; chmn. Schweiz Tagung fur Unfallverhütung, 1962-84. Author: Wissenschaftl Methoden fur Unfallverhütung, 1967; (with Locher) Risiken erkennen u meistern, 1980; editor newsletter Salvo, 1950—; contbr. to profl. publs. Elder, Zwinglian Protestant Ch., Winterthur, 1964-72. Served to 1st lt. arty. Swiss Army, 1945. Mem. Swiss Actuarial Soc., Konferenz Schweiz Sicherheitsfachleute (co-founder). Office: L Hartmann Unfallverhutung, Technikumstr 82, 8401 Winterthur Switzerland

HARTMANN-JOHNSEN, OLAF JOHAN, physician; b. Aalesund, Norway, Aug. 22, 1924; s. Odd and Helga Elisabeth (Hartmann) Johnsen; M.B., B.S., U. Queensland (Australia), 1956; M.D., Oslo U., 1974; m. Mary Essil Archibald, 1956 (dissolved 1968); children: Sally, Helga Elizabeth; m. Mary Eldbjørg Hestad, May 23, 1969; children: Olaf Johan, Else Margrete. Physician, Royal Brisbane (Australia) Hosp., 1956-63, Oslo Univ. Hosp., 1964-65, Bundaberg Gen. Hosp., 1966, Hornsby Dist. Hosp., 1967-70, Upton Hosp., Slough, Eng., 1970, Blacktown Dist. Hosp., 1971-73, Ullevål Hosp., 1974-77, Vefsn Hosp., 1977-78, Kragerø Hosp., 1978-79; physician-in-chief St. Joseph's Hosp., Porsgrunn, 1979-82; cons. physician, chief med. officer Nesset County, 1982—; cons., govt. med. officer, 1982—; tutor in medicine U. Oslo Med. Sch., 1975-77. Served with Royal Norwegian Air Force, 1942-47. Decorated King Haakon VII medal. Mem. Norwegian Med. Assn., Coll. Norwegian Internists, N.Y. Acad. Scis. Conservative. Lutheran. Contbr. articles to med. jours. Office: 2 Helsesenteret, 6460 Eidsuaag 1 R Norway

HARTNESS, SANDRA JEAN, venture capitalist; b. Jacksonville Fla., Aug. 19, 1944; d. Harold H. and Viola M. (House) H. A.B., Ga. So. Coll., 1969; post-grad., San Francisco State Coll., 1970-71. Researcher Savannah (Ga.) Planning Commn., 1969, Environ. Analysis Group, San Francisco, 1970-71; dir. Mission Inn, Riverside, Calif., 1971-75; developer, venture capitalist Hartness Assocs., Laguna Beach, Calif., 1976—; ptnr. Western Neuro-Care Ctr., Tustin Calif.; former edu. dir. Laguna Bd. Realtors, 1982. V.p., mem. bd. dirs. Evergreen Homes, Inc.; recipient numerous awards for community service. Democrat. Club: Soroptimists (Riverside, Calif.). Home: 32612 Adriatic Dr Laguna Niguel CA 92677 Office: Hartness Assocs 301 Forest Ave Laguna Beach CA 92651

HARTNETT, THOMAS ROBERT, III, lawyer; b. Sioux City, Iowa, July 19, 1920; s. Thomas R. and Florence Mary (Graves) H.; m. Betty Jeanne Dobbins, Mar. 3, 1943; children—Thomas Robert Joseph, Jeanine Elizabeth, Dennis Edward, Glenn Michael. Student Trinity Coll., 1937-39; LL.B., U. So. Calif., 1948. Bar: Tex. 1948, U.S. Dist. Ct. (no. dist.) Tex. 1949, U.S. Ct. Appeals (5th cir.) 1954, U.S. Ct. Appeals (10th cir.) 1955, U.S. Supreme Ct. 1957, U.S. Ct. Appeals (11th cir.) 1983. Sole practice law, Dallas, 1948—. Served with USAAF, 1939-45. Mem. State Bar Tex., Dallas Bar Assn. Republican. Roman Catholic. Home: 5074 Matilda St #224 Dallas TX 75206 Office: 2800 M Bank Bldg Dallas TX 75201

HARTOG, JOOST, economics educator; b. Sliedrecht, The Netherlands, June 29, 1946; s. Arie and Lena (Wijngaarden) H.; m. Anthonia Kuil, June 19, 1970; children: Marleen, Johan Willem. Diploma in econs., Netherlands Sch. Econs., Rotterdam, 1970; MA, Queen's U., Kingston, Ont., Can., 1971; PhD in Econs., Erasmus U., Rotterdam, 1978. Asst. prof. econs. Erasmus U., 1978-81; prof. econs. U. Amsterdam, The Netherlands, 1981—; vis. assoc. U. Wis.-Madison, 1978, Sch. Edn., Stanford (Calif.) U., 1984, Queen's U., Kingston, 1986. Author: Personal Income Distribution, 1981; contbr. articles to econs. publs. Can. Council scholar, 1970-71, Fulbright scholar, 1986. Mem. Am. Econs. Assn., Vereniging voor de Staathuishoudkunde. Office: U Amsterdam, Jodenbreestraat 23, 1011 NH Amsterdam Holland The Netherlands

HARTOKO, DICK, clergyman, writer, lecturer; b. Jatiroto, Lumajang, East Java, Indonesia, May 9, 1922; s. Mathijs Jan Willem Geldorp and Theresia Elisabeth (van't Wout Hoflad) Geldorp. Grad., Canisius Coll., Batavia, N.E. Indies, 1941; BA in Philosophy, Ignatius Coll., Yogyakarta, Indonesia. Lic. theology, Canisianum, Maastricht, Hollland, MO in history, 1952. Joined Soc. of Jesus, Roman Cath. Ch., Yogyakarta, Indonesia, 1942; chief editor cultural mag. Basis, Yogyakarta, Indonesia, 1957—; lectr. Weda Bhakti Theology Faculty, Yogyakarta, Indonesia, 1957—, Sanata Dharma Tchr. Tng. Coll., Yogyakarta, Indonesia, 1957—, Gadjah Mada U. Faculty of Letters, Yogyakarta, Indonesia, 1970—; chmn. Karta Pustaka Cultural Ctr., Yogyakarta. 1968—; trustee Gadjah Mada U., 1982—, Indonesian Inst. Arts, 1985—. Author: Man and Art, 1987; translator of 17 books from Engl. and Dutch into Indonesian. Home: Jl ID Nyoman, Oka 18, 55224 Yogyakarta Indonesia Office: Basis Mag, Jl Abu Bakar, Ali 14, 55224 Yogyakarta Indonesia

HARTONO, MICHAEL BAMBANG, tobacco company executive; b. Semarang, Central Java, Indonesia, Oct. 2, 1939; s. Wie Gwan Oei and Tjoe Nio Goei; m. Ikawati Budiarto, Oct. 22, 1964; 1 child, Stefanus Wijava. Student, Diponegoro U., Semarang, 1960-63. Purchasing dir. PT Djarum Cigarette Factory, Kudus, Central Java, Indonesia, 1964-70, dir. research and devel., 1971-79, pres., dir., 1980—; chmn. bd. dirs. Hartono Istana Electronics, 1979—; commr. Busana Rama, Jakarta, Indonesia, 1981—. Mem. Golkar Party. Roman Catholic. Office: PT Djarum Cigarette Factory, 28 Jl Jen A Yani, Kudus Indonesia

HARTSAW, WILLIAM O., mechanical engineering educator; b. Tell City, Ind., Oct. 17, 1921; s. William A. and Hazel (Barr) H.; m. Delma Stuckey, June 30, 1946; 1 son, Mark Alan. BS in Mech. Engring., Purdue U., 1946, MS in Engring., 1953; PhD, U. Ill., 1966. Instr. engring. U. Evansville (Ind.), 1946-52; asst. prof. U. Evansville, 1952-54, assoc. prof., 1954-63, prof. engring., 1963-85, disting. prof. mech. engring., 1985—, dir. engring., 1958-68, dean engring., 1968-76, chmn. dept. mech. engring., 1977-85; vice chmn. Evansville Environ. Protection Agy., 1980—. Author: The Peltier Effect, 1958, Low Cycle Fatigue Strength Investigation of a High Strength Steel, 1966. Mem. exec. bd. Buffalo Trace council Boy Scouts Am., 1969—, chmn. service com., 1975-76; mem. Evansville Urban Transp. Advisory, 1975—. Served with USAAF, 1942-43. Recipient Alumnus Certificate of Excellence U. Evansville, 1972, Tech. Achievement award Tri-State Council for Sci. and Engring., 1979; Lilly Found. fellow, 1960; NSF fellow, 1961-62. Mem. ASME (faculty adviser student chpt. 1968—, nat. com. div. solar energy com. on components 1975—, vice chmn. faculty advisers region VI 1975-76, chmn. faculty advisors region VI 1976-78, vice chmn. Evansville sect. 1980-81, chmn. Evansville sect. 1981-82, v.p. elect Region VI 1982-83, v.p. Region VI 1983-85, advisor to regional v.p. 1985-87, Centennial Service award 1980, Centennial medal 1980), Am. Soc. Engring. Edn., ASHRAE (pres. Evansville chpt. 1966-67), ASME, ASTM, AAUP, AAAS, Am. Soc. Metals, Phi Kappa Phi, Phi Beta Chi, Phi Tau Sigma. Methodist. Home: 1407 Green Meadow Rd Evansville IN 47715

HARTSHORNE, CHARLES, philosopher, retired educator; b. Kittanning, Pa., June 5, 1897; s. Francis Cope and Marguerite (Haughton) H.; m. Dorothy Eleanore Cooper, Dec. 22, 1928; 1 dau., Emily Lawrence (Mrs. Nicolas D. Goodman). Student, Haverford Coll., 1915-17; A.B., Harvard U., 1921, A.M., 1922, Ph.D., 1923; postgrad., U. Freiburg, Germany, 1923-25, U. Marburg, 1925; L.H.D. (hon.), Haverford Coll., 1967, Episcopal Theol. Sem. of Southwest, 1977; Litt. D. (hon.), Emory U., 1969; Ph.D. (hon.), U. Louvain, Belgium, 1978. Sheldon travelling fellow Harvard U., 1923-25, instr., research fellow, 1925-28; mem. faculty U. Chgo., 1928-55, mem. federated theol. faculty, 1943-55, prof. philosophy, 1949-55; prof. philosophy Emory U., Atlanta, 1955-62, U. Tex., Austin, 1962-63; Ashbel Smith prof. philosophy U. Tex., 1963-76, prof. emeritus, 1976—; Vis. prof. Stanford U., 1937, New Sch. Social Research, 1941-42, Johann Wolfgang Goethe U., Frankfurt, Germany, 1948-49, U. Wash., 1958, Banaras Hindu U., Varanasi, India, 1966, Colo. Coll., 1977, 79, U. Louvain, 1978; Terry lectr. Yale, 1947; Fulbright lectr., Melbourne, 1952; Fulbright prof., Kyoto, Japan, 1958, 66; Dudleian lectr. Harvard U., 1963; Morse lectr. Union Theol. Sem., 1964; Lowell lectr. Harvard U., 1979, 86; others. Author: The Philosophy and Psychology of Sensation, 1934, Beyond Humanism, 1937, Man's Vision of God, 1941, The Divine Relativity, 1948, Reality as Social Process, 1953, (with Wm. Reese) Philosophers Speak of God, 1953, The Logic of Perfection, 1962 (Lecomte du Noüy award 1963), Anselm's Discovery, 1965, A Natural Theology for Our Time, 1967, Creative Synthesis and Philosophic Method, 1970, Whitehead's Philosophy, 1972, Born to Sing: An Interpretation and World Survey of Bird Song, 1973, Aquinas to Whitehead: Seven Centuries of Metaphysics of Religion, 1976, (with Creighton Peden) Whitehead's View of Reality, 1981, Insights and Oversights of Great Thinkers, 1983, Omnipotence and Other Theological Mistakes, 1983, Creativity in American Philosophy, 1984, Wisdom as Moderation: a Philosophy of the Middle Way, 1987; also numerous articles in profl. jours. Editor: (with Paul Weiss) The Collected Papers of Charles S. Peirce, 1931-35. Served with U.S. Army, 1917-19. Fellow Am. Acad. Arts and Scis.; mem. Am. Philos. Assn. (pres. 1948-49), Metaphys. Soc. Am. (pres. 1954-55), Charles Peirce Soc. (pres. 1950-51), Soc. for Philosophy of Religion (pres. 1963-64), So. Soc. for Philosophy and Psychology (pres. 1964-65). Home: 724 Sparks Ave Austin TX 78705 Office: U Tex Waggener Hall Austin TX 78712

HARTSOOK, ROBERT FRANCIS, educational administrator; b. Eureka, Kans., July 12, 1948; s. Herbert Edwin and Beverly Mercia (James) H.; m. Karin Oliver Hartsook. B.A., Kans. State Tchrs. Coll., 1970, M.S., 1972; J.D., Washburn U., 1979. V.p. Colby Community Coll., Kans., 1972-76; exec. v.p., chief exec. officer Kans. Engring. Soc., Inc., Topeka, 1978-82; v.p. Washburn U., Topeka, 1982-85, Wichita State U., Kans. 1985—. Bd. editors Washburn Law Jour. 1977-79, exec. editor, 1977-78. Commn. Kansas State Educ. Commn., Topeka, 1975-78; mem. adv. panel Gov.'s Commn. Criminal Admin., Topeka, 1975-78. Danforth Found. fellow, summer 1973. Mem. Council for Advancement and Support of Educ. (most improved univ. 1984, 86, exceptional achievement in fin. support 1985). Club: Wichita. Home: 9433 Bent Tree Circle Wichita KS 67226 Office: Wichita State U Wichita KS 67208

HARTWELL, ERIC, company executive; b. East Sheen, Surrey, Eng., Aug. 10, 1915; s. Alfred and Edith Maud (Brunning) H.; m. Gladys Rose Bennett (div. 1954); children: Anthony Charles, Susan; m. Dorothy Maud Mowbray, June 14, 1954; children: Janine Erica, Keith Alan. With Elec. Industry, Worthing, Sussex, Eng., 1932-38; dir. Fortes Milk Bars, London, 1938—; mng. dir. Fortes Holdings Ltd., London, 1969—; chief exec. Trusthouse Forte PLC, London, 1972—, joint chief exec., 1980—, non-exec. vice chmn., 1983—. Dir. LV Catering Edn. Trust Ltd., 1960—; council mem. Confedn. Brit. Industry, 1972—, chmn. fin. subcom., 1982—; chmn. Trusthouse Forte Group Subscription Com. and Charity, 1980—; vice chmn. Thames Heritage Trust, 1983—; mem. Nuffield Nursing Home Trust, Enfield Hosp. Adv. Bd., 1983-86; gov., life mem. Royal Nat. Lifeboat Instn., 1983—; chmn. Brit. Hotels and Catering Assn. Nat. Council, 1982—; freeman Worshipful Co. Upholders, London, 1953. Served with Royal Engrs., 1940-46. Appt. ordinary comdr. of Most Excellent Order of British Empire, 1983. Fellow Hotel and Catering Inst., Royal Soc. Encouragement Art, Mfr., and Commerce; mem. Inner Magic Circle with Gold Star, Compainion Brit. Inst. Mgmt. Clubs: Thames Motor-Yacht (commodore 1969—, v.p., trustee), Terenure Country (hon. mem.), South Herts Golf. Avocations: navigation; golf; painting; music; photography. Home: Tall Trees, 129 Totteridge Lane, London N20 8NS, England Office: Trusthouse Forte PLC, 86 Park Ln, London W1A 3AA, England

HARTWIG, GERT KARL, technical physics engineer, consultant; b. Hamburg, Fed. Republic Germany, Jan. 23, 1936; s. Friedrich Robert and Gertrud (Juerss) H. Degree, U. Hamburg, 1958, Wedel, Fed. Republic of Germany, 1964. Registered profl. engr. Well-logging engr. IBM Deutschland, Bonn, Fed. Republic Germany, 1964—, systems engr., project leader, 1974—; data processing cons. in acad. sci., 1987—. Club: Blau-Gelb (Bonn). Home: Kantstrasse 7, D-5300 Bonn 2 Federal Republic of Germany Office: IBM Deutschland, Godesberger Allee 115, 5300 Bonn 2 Federal Republic of Germany

HARTWIG, THOMAS LEO, civil engineer; b. Pitts., June 16, 1952; s. Leo William and Bertha Barbara (Lukas) H.; m. Cynthia L. Grupp, 1987. B.S.C.E., U. Notre Dame, 1974. Registered profl. engr., Pa. Mgr. infiltration, inflow Duncan, Lagnese & Assoc., Pitts., 1974-76, ops. engr., 1976-80, mgr. ops. div., 1980-81, mgr. ops., assoc., 1981, v.p., 1981-83, v.p., mgr. mcpl. environ. engring., 1983-86, sr. v.p., mgr. mcpl. environ. engring., 1986—, also dir. Mem. Water Pollution Control Fedn., Nat. Soc. Profl. Engrs., ASCE, Water Pollution Control Assn. Pa. (program co-chmn. 1983), Profl. Engrs. in Pvt. Practice, Western Pa. Pollution Control Assn. (1st v.p.), Chi Epsilon. Democrat. Roman Catholic. Home: 9131 Ridgefel Ave Pittsburgh PA 15237 Office: Duncan Lagnese and Assoc Inc 3185 Babcock Blvd Pittsburgh PA 15237

HARTWIGSEN, NELSON LEROY, rubber company executive; b. Nanticoke, Pa., Mar. 4, 1941; s. Norman L. and Anna (Rowland) H.; B.S., Wilkes Coll., 1963; m. Lucille Bartish, June 11, 1963; children—Dawn Marie, Deborah Ann, Eric Norman. Trade service asst., mech. rubber goods div. UniRoyal, Inc., Buffalo, 1963, salesman, 1964, inside salesman, Pitts., 1964-65, salesman, Balt., 1965-68, asst. mgr. hose sales, Passaic, N.J., 1968-69, dist. sales mgr., Detroit, 1969-70; v.p., gen. mgr. Md. Rubber Corp., Balt., 1970-71, pres., 1971—; pres. Keystone Rubber Corp., York, Pa., 1974—; mng. gen. ptnr. OMR Ltd., gen. ptnr. Key Mar Gen. Ptnrs. Bd. dirs. Bel Air Amateur Sports Assn.; mgr., coach Bel Air Travel League, Little League. Served with Md. Army N.G., 1965-71. Home: 1506 Donegal Rd Bel Air MD 21014 Office: 8661 Towne Courte Ct White Marsh MD 21236

HARTZLER, CHERYL ELAINE, financial planner; b. Kokomo, Ind., Feb. 16, 1945; d. Lowell Jay and Juanita Monell (Gasaway) Somsel; m. Edward W. Hartzler, June 11, 1967 (div. June 1981); children: Bryan Joseph, Andrea Lisabeth. BA, Ind. U., 1968; MBA, So. Ill. U., 1985; postgrad., Pacific Luth. U., 1982-83, Seattle Cen. Community Coll., 1979, S.Seattle Community Coll., 1980, Highline Community Coll., 1980-82, U. Washington, 1978, 83, Coll. for Fin. Planning, 1987—. Boutique mgr., jr. asst. buyer trainee Block's, Indpls., 1967-68; tchr. Indpls. Pub. Schs., 1968-71; with sales and inventory dept. Frederick & Nelson's Dept. Store, Seattle, 1971-72; co-owner video store Video World, Inc., Seattle, 1978-81; fin. planner and account exec. Investors Fin. Planning/Southmark Fin. Services, Bellevue, Wash., 1983—; pres. C.E. Hartzler and Assocs., 1986—; instr. continuing edn. N. Seattle Community Coll., 1985—; coordinated reorgn. of pvt. med. practice, Seattle, 1976; registered rep. Southmark Fin. Services. Mem. Seattle Repertory Orgn., 1973—; bd. dirs. Seattle Opera Guild, 1978-80; cultural chmn. Highline Sch. Dist. Parent Teachers Students Assn., Seattle, 1978-83. Mem. Internat. Assn. Fin. Planners, Wash. Women United, Women's Bus. Exchange, Assn. MBA Execs., Nat. Assn. for Female Execs., Am. Soc. Women Accts., Internat. Platform Assn., Alpha Chi Omega Alumni. Clubs: Olympic View Swim (Seattle); Leads (mgmt. team South Seattle chpt.). Home: 718 SW 199th Pl Seattle WA 98166 Office: Investors Fin Planning/Southmark 1300 114th Ave SE Suite 232 Bellevue WA 98004

HARUHARA, AKIHIKO, communications educator; b. Tokyo, Aug. 24, 1927; s. Masaki and Seiko (Yoshitaka) H. BA, Sophia U., 1953; MA, Keio U., 1955. Chief research sect. Japan Newspaper Pubs. and Editors Assn., Tokyo, 1954-69, chief researcher, 1975-76, cons. research inst., 1976—; acting sec.-gen. Japan Nat. Press Club, Tokyo, 1969-75; prof. journalism and communications Sophia U., Tokyo, 1976—. Author: The History of Newspapers in Japan, 1987. Fellow Internat. Assn. for Mass Communication Research; mem. Japan Soc. for Studies in Journalism and Mass Communication (bd. dirs. 1951—). Club: Japan Nat. Press., Tokyo. Home: Suginamiku Asagaya-kita, 6-47-14, Tokyo 166, Japan Office: Sophia U Chiyodaku, kioicho 7-1, Tokyo 102, Japan

HARUNA, KAZUO, corporate executive; b. Mar. 15, 1920; m. Mikiko Haruna. Grad., Toa Dobun Shoin, 1940. Mng. dir. Marubeni Corp., 1975-83, pres., 1983—; bd. dirs. Hoko Fishing, Ltd., Tokyo Sugar Refineries. Home: Motoyoyogi Heights 305, 50-2 Motoyoyogi-cho, Shibuya-ku, Tokyo Japan *

HARUO, SUZUKI, electronics company executive; b. Omiya, Ibaragi, Japan, Jan. 4, 1935; s. Kikuji and Toyo Suzuki; m. Takako Nasuhara, Jan. 22, 1963; children: Chiharu, Rie, Miho. Mgr. acctg. and cost control Katsuta Works Hitachi Ltd., Ibaragi, 1970-78, Sawa Works Hitachi Ltd., Katsuta, Ibaragi, 1978-85; mgr. mgmt. improvement ctr. Head Office Hitachi Ltd., Tokyo, 1985-87; dir. Hitachi Car Electronics Ltd., Katsuta, 1987—. Chmn. Ibaragi Indirect Tax Orgn., 1983-85; com. mem. Japan Industry Efficiency Orgn., 1985-87. Home: 3428-14 Higashi-Ishikawa 312, Katsuta City Ibaragi, Japan Office: Hitachi Car Electronics Ltd, 3085-5 Saikouchi Higashi-Ishikawa, 312 Katsuta Ibaragi, Japan

HARVEY, CYNTHIA, ballet dancer; b. San Rafael, Calif.. Studied with, Christine Waltone, The Novato Sch. Ballet; student, San Francisco Ballet Sch., Marin Ballet Sch., Sch. Am. Ballet Theatre, N.Y.C., Am. Ballet Theatre Sch., N.Y.C., Nat. Ballet Sch. Can., Toronto. With Am. Ballet Theatre, N.Y.C., from 1974, soloist, from 1978, prin. dancer, from 1982; now with Royal Ballet, London, 1986-88. Creator: role of Gamzatti in La Bayadere; appeared in: Apollo, Billy the Kid, Fancy Free, Giselle, Raymonda. Recipient John Anthony Bitson award, 1973. Office: care of Am Ballet Theatre 890 Broadway New York NY 10003

HARVEY, DOROTHY MCDONALD, retired home economist; b. Junction City, Ark., May 5, 1917; d. Robert John and Annie (Nolley) McDonald; B.S., La. Tech. Coll., 1939; postgrad. La. State U., 1953, 69; M.S., Iowa State U., 1951; Ph.D., Tex. Women's U., 1957; m. J.P. Harvey, June 6, 1946. Tchr., Junction City High Sch., 1937-38; tchr. home econs. Rocky Mount (La.) High Sch., 1939-43; asst. home demonstration agt. Rapids Parish, Alexandria, La., 1943; assoc. home demonstration agt. Caddo Parish, Shreveport, La., 1944-46; home demonstration agt. Jackson Parish, Jonesboro, La., 1946-55; asst. prof. clothing and textiles Tex. Woman's U., Denton, Tex., 1957-60; sci. tchr. Jonesboro Schs., 1960-67; assoc. prof. Wis. State U., Stevens Point, 1968-69, Ga. So. Coll., Statesboro, 1969-70; prof. Miss. U. for Women, Columbus, 1970-80. Tex. Woman's U. fellow, 1955-57. Mem. AAUW, La. Home Demonstration Agts. Assn. (sec. 1954), AAUP, Am. Home Econs. Assn., ASTM, Miss. Home Econs. Assn., Central Region Coll. Profs. Clothing and Textiles, Delta Phi Delta, Phi Upsilon Omicron, Epsilon Sigma Phi. Methodist. Democrat. Club: Jonesboro Hodge Garden. Home: 820 Polk Ave S Jonesboro LA 71251

HARVEY, FREDERICK WILFRED, JR., quality control engineer; b. Everett, Mass., May 12, 1929; s. Frederick Wilfred and Ethel Blanche (Strong) H.; cert. in quality control Northeastern U., 1970; m. Jean Gwendolyn Long, May 9, 1952 (div.); children—Debra Jean, Frederick Wilfred, Amy Louise; m. 2d, Carol Ann Clark, July 2, 1983. Sr. technician GTE Sylvania, Bedford, Mass., 1965-67, supr. quality control GTE Info. Systems, 1967-72; mgr. quality control Jerrel-Ash div. Scientific, Waltham, Mass., 1972-73; mgr. quality control Hendrix Corp., Manchester, N.H., 1973-76; quality control engr. Centronics Data Computer, Hudson, N.H., 1976-80, Sanders Assocs., 1980-85; quality control specialist U.S. Dept. Def., 1980—; quality assurance rep. Def. Logistics Agy., U.S. Dept. Def., 1985—. Chmn. bldg. com. local Episcopal Ch., 1968, mem. vestry, 1969; mem. N.H. Gov.'s Council for Employment and Tng., 1980-81. Served with U.S. Army, 1947-48, 52-54. Mem. Am. Soc. Quality Control, Engring. Soc. New Eng., Centronics Mgmt. Club, VFW (state chief of staff 1974-75, nat. dep. chief of staff 1975-76, state judge adv. 1976-77, state jr. vice comdr. 1977-78, state sr. vice comdr. 1978-79, state comdr. 1979-80, named All-Am. State Comdr. 1980, mem. nat. legis. com. 1981-84, nat. community activities com. 1985-88; jr. vice chmn. Eastern States Conf. 1981-82, sr. vice chmn. 1982-83, chmn. 1983-84), Am. Legion (1st vice comdr. 1980-81, comdr. 1981-82), N.H. Vets. Assn. (sec.-treas. 1981-83). Home: 78 Village Glen Falls Goffstown NH 03045

HARVEY, HERSCHEL AMBROSE, JR., glass and marketing company executive; b. Steubenville, Ohio, Sept. 16, 1929; s. Herschel Ambrose and Josephine (Bernert) H.; B.S. in Bus. Adminstrn., U. Notre Dame, 1951; postgrad. Mich. State U., 1958; m. Thelma F. Freeman, July 4, 1974; children—Debera, H.R., Herschel Ambrose III. Indsl. engr. Uniroyal, N.Y.C., 1951-53; indsl. relations mgr. Brunswick Co., Chgo., 1956-64; pres. Harvey Industries, Inc., Clarksburg, W.Va., 1964—, Hersh Harvey Assocs., Inc., Georgetown, S.C., 1974—, Harvey Glass, Inc., Georgetown, S.C., 1986—. Bd. dirs. Am. Cancer Soc. Served to lt. USNR, 1953-56. Mem. Am. Ceramic Soc., Alumna Club U. Notre Dame. Republican. Roman Catholic. Home: 3 Prospect Ct West DeBordieu Colony Georgetown SC 29440 Office: PO Box 1099 Georgetown SC 29442-1099

HARVEY, JAMES ROSS, diversified service company executive; b. Los Angeles, Aug. 20, 1934; s. James Ernest and Loretta Berniece (Ross) H.; m. Charlene Coakley, July 22, 1971; children: Kjersten Ann, Kristina Ross. B.S. in Engring., Princeton U., 1956; M.B.A., U. Calif.-Berkeley, 1963. Engr. Standard Oil Co. (Calif.), San Francisco, 1956-61; acct. Touche, Ross, San Francisco, 1963-64; chmn. bd., chief exec. officer, dir. Transamerica Corp., San Francisco, 1965—; bd. dirs. Transam. Occidental Life Ins. Co., Transam. Fin. Corp., Transam. Ins. Co., Transam. Interway Inc., Transam. Title Ins. Co., Sedgwick Group, Pacific Telesis Group, McKesson Corp. Bd. regents St. Mary's Coll.; bd. dirs. U. Calif. Bus. Sch., Calif. State Parks Found., Bay Area Council. Served with AUS, 1958-59. Mem. San Francisco C. of C. (dir., pres.). Clubs: Bohemian, Pacific-Union (San Francisco); Union League (N.Y.C.). Office: Transam Corp 600 Montgomery St San Francisco CA 94111

HARVEY, KATHERINE ABLER, civic worker; b. Chgo., May 17, 1946; d. Julius and Elizabeth (Engelman) Abler; student La Sorbonne, Paris, 1965-66; A.A.S., Bennett Coll., 1968; m. Julian Whitcomb Harvey, Sept. 7, 1974. Asst. librarian McDermott, Will & Emery, Chgo., 1969-70; librarian Chapman & Cutler, Chgo., 1970-73, Coudert Freres, Paris, 1973-74; adviser, organizer library Lincoln Park Zool. Soc. and Zoo, Chgo., 1977-79, mem. soc.'s women's bd., 1976—, chmn. library com., 1977-79, sec., 1979-81, mem. exec. com., 1977-81 ; mem. jr. bd. Alliance Francaise de Chgo., 1970-76, treas., mem. exec. com., 1971-73, 75-76, mem. women's bd., 1977-80; mem. Fred Harvey Fine Arts Found., 1976-78; hon. life mem. Chgo. Symphony Soc., 1975—; mem. Phillips Acad. Alumni Council, Andover, Mass., 1977-81, mem. acad.'s bicentennial celebration com. class celebration leader, 1978, co-chmn. for Chgo. acad.'s bicentennial campaign, 1977-79, mem. student affairs and admissions com., 1980-81; mem. aux. bd. Art Inst. Chgo., 1978-88; mem. Know Your Chgo. com. U. Chgo. Extension, 1981-84; mem. guild Chgo. Hist. Soc., 1978—; mem. women's bd. Lyric Opera Chgo., 1979—, chmn. edn. com., 1980, mem. exec. com., 1980-84, 88—, treas. women's bd., 1983-84, 1st v.p. 1988—; mem. women's bd. Northwestern Meml. Hosp.,

1979—, treas., chmn. fin. com., 1981-84, mem. exec. com., 1981—; bd. dirs. Found. Art Scholarships, 1982-83; bd. dirs. Glen Ellyn (Ill.) Children's Chorus, 1983—, founding chmn. pres.'s com., 1983; mem. women's bd. Chgo. City Ballet, 1983-84; trustee Chgo. Acad. Scis., 1986-88; bd. dirs. Grant Park Concert Soc., 1986—; adv. council med. program for performing artists Northwestern Meml. Hosp., 1986—; pres., bd. dirs. William Ferris Chorale, 1988—. Mem. Antiquarian Soc. of Art Inst. Chgo. (life); bd. dirs. Grant Park Concerts Soc., 1986—. Clubs: Arts of Chgo., Friday (corr. sec. 1981-83), Casino (gov. 1982-88, sec. 1984-85, 1987-88, 1st v.p. 1985-86, 2d v.p. 1986-87), Cliff Dwellers. Home: 1209 N Astor St Chicago IL 60610

HARWOOD, DOUGLAS AMEND, retired government official; b. N.Y.C., June 17, 1912; s. Brunn and Elsie Amelia (Amend) H.; B.A., Yale U., 1932; postgrad. Columbia, 1934; m. Laura Lucille Turner, Apr. 16, 1952 (div. Nov. 1980); 1 son, Douglas Turner. Exec. asst., liaison officer to Maritime Commn., WPB, 1941-42; regional mgr., asst. dir. devel. N.A.M., 1946-51; cons. Office Civilian Requirements, dir. program planning staff NPA, 1951-52; dir. sales promotion, fleet div. Chrysler Corp., 1952-54; with Mut. Security Program and Fgn. Aid Program, 1955-64, dir. in East Pakistan, 1958-60, head team Fgn. Service personnel to Oxford U. African Studies Program, Eng., 1960-61, regional dir. U.S. Mut. Security Program for Equatorial Africa, Congo, 1961-64; sr. market devel. officer, dir. mktg. activities Bur. Internat. Commerce, Dept. Commerce, 1964-68, nat. export sales mgr., dir. global mktg. campaigns, dir. program coordination staff, export devel. activities program, 1968-72, dir. U.S. exhbns., 1972-79; internat. trade cons. govt. and pvt. industry. Served to 1st lt. AUS, 1942-46; PTO. Clubs: Yale (N.Y.C., Washington, Ft. Lauderdale, Fla.). Home: 1000 S Ocean Blvd Apt 12-K Pompano Beach FL 33062

HARWOOD, ELEANOR CASH, librarian; b. Buckfield, Me., May 29, 1921; d. Leon Eugene and Ruth (Chick) Cash; B.A., Am. Internat. Coll., 1943; B.S., New Haven State Tchrs. Coll., 1955; m. Burton H. Harwood, Jr., June 21, 1944 (div. 1953); children—Ruth (Mrs. William R. Cline), Eleanor, James Burton. Librarian, Rathbun Meml. Library, East Haddam, Conn., 1955-56; asst. librarian Kent (Conn.) Sch., 1956-63; cons. to Chester (Conn.) Pub. Library, 1965-71. Served from ensign to lt. (j.g.) USNR, 1944-46. Mem. Am., Conn. library assns., Chester Hist. Soc. (trustee 1970-72), D.A.V., Am. Legion Aux., Soc. Mayflower Descs. Mem. United Ch. Author: (with John G. Park) The Independent School Library and the Gifted Child, 1956; The Age of Samuel Johnson, LL.D., 1959. sec.,(essay) Remember When, 1987. Recipient The Commemorative medal of Honor Am. Biog. Inst., 1987; biog. tribute Dr. Katie Wilcox, 1975. Home: Maple St Chester CT 06412

HARWOOD, WENDY ANN, science researcher; b. Braintree, Eng., Apr. 16, 1961; d. David Arthur and Pamela Marjorie (French) Lawrence; m. Martin Barry Harwood, May 24, 1986. BSc, U. London, 1982; PhD, U. East Anglia, Norwich, Eng., 1985. Higher scientific officer John Innes Inst. Norwich, 1985—. Office: John Innes Inst, Colney Ln, Norwich NR4 7UH, England

HARWOOD-BEE, JOHN, international business consultant; b. Nottingham, Eng., Feb. 11, 1945; s. Kenneth Metcalf and Margaret (Harwood) Bee; m. Anne Robinson (div. 1979); children: Sharon, Mellony; m. Joy Carol Trinder, Sept.26, 1981. Dir. Douglas Group, Eng., 1966-68, Field Mktg. Ltd., Eng., 1968-70; mktg. dir. Beryl Richards Orgn., Eng., 1970-74; mng. dir. mktg. div. Freeman, Mathes, Milne, Eng., 1974-76, Harwood-Bee Ltd., 1976—; chmn. Acts Internat., Buntingford, Hertfordshire, Eng., 1985—; mng. dir. Home Gallery Ltd., 1986—; cons. Brunning Ltd., Eng., 1986-69, Internat. Mktg. and Fin. Services, 1987—, Internat. Sounds Ltd., 1987—. Author papers on internat. mktg. Conservative. Mem. Ch. of Eng. Office: Acts Internat Ltd, 94 Fairfield, Buntingford S99 9NX, England

HARWOOD-NUSS, ANN LATIMER, physician; b. Sigourny, Iowa, July 22, 1948; d. Arthur Manning and Nyta Pauline (Latimer) Harwood; m. Gary Larsen, June 22, 1974 (div. 1976); m. Robert C. Nuss, Sept. 21, 1984. B.S., U. Iowa, Iowa City, 1969, M.D., 1973. Diplomate Am. Bd. Emergency Medicine. Resident in gen. surgery and urology Mich State U.-Grand Rapids, 1973-76, residency dir. in emergency medicine Mich. State U., Grand Rapids, 1976-80; resident dir. U. Chgo., 1980-81; chmn. emergency medicine University Hosp., Jacksonville, Fla., 1981-85; div. chief U. Fla., 1981-85, assoc. prof., 1984 ; mem. Nat. Adv. Council Grad. Med. Edn.; Cons. Am. Heart Assn., Dallas, 1981, Smith-Kline-French, Los Angeles, 1982, cost containment Am. Coll. Emergency Physicians, 1983. Author: Cardiopulmonary Resucitation, 1982; Textbook of Emergency Medicine: Urologic Emergencies, 1983; editor: Clin. Practice of Emergency Medcine, 1988; series editor Churchill Livingstone Pubs., 1986—; mem. editorial bd. Jour. Emergency Medicine, 1983, sect. editor, 1984—. Mem. affiliate faculty Am. Heart Assn., Dallas, 1979—. Mem. Am. Coll. Emergency Physicians (chmn. comprehensive rev. emergency medicine 1980-82, pres. future workshop Chgo. 1979, bd. dirs. Fla. chpt. 1981-84), Soc. Tchrs. Emergency Medicine (bd. dirs. 1979-81, orators award Atlanta 1979), Fla. Med. Found. Emergency Med. Service, Duval County Med. Soc. (emergency medicine service), Univ. Assn. Emergency Medicine (moderator 1982) ACS (trauma com. 1982-84, symposium speaker 1986), So. Med. Assn. (chmn. sect. on emergency medicine 1985-86). Office: University Hosp 655 W 8th St Jacksonville FL 32209

HASANFATTA, UMAR SALEHMOHMED, oil company executive; b. Dhoraji, Gujarat, India, Apr. 5, 1950; s. Salehmohmed Latif Hasanfatta and Jenambai (Alimohmed) Godil; m. Sunhera Hasanfatta, Dec. 13, 1981; children: Sofia, Ahmed. BS in Computers, Navgujarat Coll., 1974. Cashier Dist. Panchayat Office, Gondal, Gujarat, India, 1974-75; asst. acct. Hamosons Exports Pvt. Ltd., Madras, Tamilnadu, India, 1975-76, chief acct., 1976-79; adminstrv. aide Arabian-Am. Oil Co., Dhahran, Saudi Arabia, 1979-81, cable traffic operator, 1981-85, billing systems analyst, 1985-86, message switch operator, 1986-88; adminstrv. asst. Arabian-Am. Oil Co., Dhahran, 1988—. Office: Arabian-American Oil Co, PO Box 7284 Al-Munirah, 31311 Dhahran Saudi Arabia

HASANI, SINAN, government official of Yugoslavia; b. Pozaranju, SAP Kosovo, 1922. Active Nat. Liberation Struggle, from 1941, participant in formation of partisan unit, 1942; mem. League Communists Yugoslavia, 1942—, mem. central com. at XI Congress; former sec. regional bd. National Liberation Front for Kosovo and Metohija; past sec. dist. com. League of Communists in Cnjilane; former mem. regional com. League Communists; past pres. provincial com. Socialist Alliance of Working People of Kosovo; former mem. provincial exec. council and dir. Rilindija pub. house; elected various times mem. Republican and Fed. Assembly; pres. Serbian Assembly; former Yugoslavian ambassador to Denmark; past v.p. Yugoslavian Assembly; elected mem. presidency of provincial com. League of Communists of Kosovo, elected pres. provincial com., 1982; elected various times mem. Fed. Conf. of Socialist Alliance of Working People of Serbia and mem. central com. League of Communists of Serbia; mem. Presidency of Socialist Fed. Republic of Yugoslavia from Kosovo, Novi Beograd, 1984—, pres. of Presidency, 1986-87. Author various publs. Decorated Yugoslavian and fgn. decorations; recipient Anti-Fascist Council of Nat. Liberation of Yugoslavia award. Office: Mem Presidency, Bulevar Lenjina 2, Novi Beograd Yugoslavia *

HASCHKA, HELMUT, business educator; b. Graz, Austria, Sept. 22, 1925; s. Max and Hermine (Roschger) H.; m. Beverly Bleakley, Sept. 9, 1960; children: Martin Walter, Paul Helmut. Diploma in Econs. and Polit. Sci., U. Oxford, 1951; PhD in Philology, U. Graz, 1952; MBA in Econs. and Bus., Vienna U., Austria, 1954. Habilitation Englischer Sprachwissenschaft. Acct. various firms in Austria and Fed. Republic Germany, 1954-55; asst. prof. econs. U. Vienna, 1955-60; research scholar U. Mich., Ann Arbor, 1960-61; assoc. prof. bus. U. Vienna, 1962-66, prof. bus., 1966—, head dept. bus. English, 1962—; guest prof. econs. Wilmington (Ohio) Coll., 1970-71; seminar leader various orgns. Author: Die fremdsprachlich beeinflussten Bezeichnungsweisen, 1960, Die englische Wirtschaftssprache, 1964, American Business English, 1986. Office: U Wien, Augasse 2-6, A-1090 Vienna Austria

HASEGAWA, KENKO, industrial executive; b. Fukushima, Japan, June 8, 1916; s. Kenjuro and Sumino (Hasegawa) H.; B.A. in Naval Architecture, Tokyo Imperial U., 1941; m. Eiko Matsui, Apr. 16, 1944; children—Hiromichi, Atsuko. With Kawasaki Heavy Industries Ltd., Tokyo, 1942—, sr. mng. dir., 1978, exec. v.p., 1980-81, pres., 1981-87, chmn., 1987—; also dir. Recipient award Ministry of Transport, 1982; Blue Ribbon award, 1983.

HASEGAWA, MASARU, electronics executive; b. Aichi, Japan, Jan. 20, 1937; s. Shima and Fumi Hasegawa; m. Keiko Takemoto, Nov. 11, 1969; 1 child, Emiko. B in Econs., U. Nagoya, Japan, 1959. Rep. Mitsubishi Electric Corp., Chgo., 1966-67; gen. mgr. Mitsubishi Electric Corp., N.Y.C., 1967-69, Manila, 1980-82; mgr. automotive equipment div. Mitsubishi Electric Corp., Tokyo, 1987—; sr. v.p. Internat. Elevator and Equipment Inc., Muntinlupa, Philippines, 1980-82. Democrat. Clubs: Nanzan Country, Tsurugashima Country. Office: Mitsubishi Electric Corp, 2-2-3 Marunouchi Chiyoda-ku, Tokyo 100, Japan

HASEGAWA, MINORU, computer science educator; b. Tokyo, Dec. 15, 1937; s. Shoichi and Kuniko (Takatsu) H.; m. Fumi Masuda, Apr. 15, 1962; children—Wanda, Richard, David. M.Sc., Tokyo Met. U., 1962, D.Sc., 1967. Lectr., Waseda U., Tokyo, 1965-67; asst. prof. Tokyo Met. U., 1967-71; asst. to pres. ILSCO of Can. Ltd., Mississauga, Ont., 1974-78; database coordinator Ont. Govt., Toronto, 1978-81; assoc. prof. computer sci. Lakehead U., Thunder Bay, Ont., 1981—. Contbr. articles to profl. jours. Mem. Am. Math. Soc., Can. Math. Soc., IEEE, Computer Soc. of IEEE. Home: 131 Pine St, Thunder Bay, ON Canada Office: Lakehead U, Dept Math Scis, Thunder Bay, ON Canada P7B 5E1

HASEGAWA, YOZO, industrial company executive; b. Yokosuka, Kanagawa, Japan, Dec. 3, 1932; s. Sakujiro and Sugi Hasegawa; m. Keiko Kimura, May 28, 1961; children: Miho, Naho, Hiroko. LLB, Chuo U., Tokyo, 1956. Dir. managerial planning Teisan Industries Corp., Tokyo, 1977-78, exec. dir., 1978-80, sr. v.p., 1980—; pres. Temco Corp.; bd. dirs. Mizusawa Industry Co., Ltd., Amtic Corp., Madison Precision Products, Inc., Metalfino da Amazonia, Ltd. Office: Teisan Industries Corp, 10350-1 Shimoyama, Minobu-cho, Minami-Komagun, Yamanashi Japan 409-25

HASELMANN, JOHN PHILIP, advertising agency executive; b. Summit, N.J., Feb. 25, 1940; s. John and Elizabeth Haselmann; divorced; children—Terri Lee, Karen Lynn, Guy Philip. BSEE, N.J. Inst. Tech., 1961; MBA in Indsl. Mgmt., Ops. Research and Mgmt. Sci., U. Pa., 1963. Asst. dir. Behavior Systems, Phila., 1961-63; mgr. mgmt. sci. div. Western Electric Co., Princeton, N.J., 1970-73; mgt. mktg. sci. div. AT&T Long Lines, Bedminster, N.J., 1974-78; pres. Info. Mgmt. Group, Morristown, N.J., 1978-83, Trinet Inc., Morristown, N.J., 1984-85, Entity Advt. and Graphics, Inc., Florham Park, N.J., 1986—. Mem. Am. Mgmt. Assn., Am. Soc. Profl. Cons. Republican. Lutheran. Office: Entity Advt & Graphics Inc 325 Columbia Turnpike Florham Park NJ 07932

HASHIGUCHI, YASUO, language professional; b. Sasebo, Nagasaki, Japan, July 31, 1924; s. Keikichi and Shitsu (Fukumoto) H.; m. Eiko Uchida, Jan. 8, 1957; children: Aoi, Keimei. BA, U. Tokyo, 1948; MEd, Ohio U., Athens, 1951. Assoc. prof. English Kagoshima U., Japan, 1951-64; assoc. prof. English Kyushu U., Fukuoka, Japan, 1964-68, prof. English, 1968-82; prof. English Fukuoka U., Fukuoka, Japan, 1982-88; pres. Fukuoka Jo Gakuin Jr. Coll., 1988—. Editor: The Complete Works of John Steinbeck, 1985. Recipient Dick A. Renner prize and named Best Steinbeck Tchr. of Yr. Steinbeck Soc. of Am., 1977. Mem. Kyushu Am. Lit. Soc. (pres. 1977—), Steinbeck Soc. Japan (pres. 1977—), Internat. John Steinbeck Soc. (sr. cons. 1983—). Club: Japan-Am. Soc. of Fukuoka. Home: 7-29-31-105 Iikura, Sawara-ku, Fukuoka 814-01, Japan Office: Fukuoka Jo Gakuin Jr Coll, 3-42-1 Osa, Minami-ku, Fukuoka 816, Japan

HASHIMOTO, ISAO, dermatologist, educator; b. Aomori City, Japan, May 3, 1935; m. Atsuko Murai, Apr. 30, 1967. MD, Hirosaki U., 1960, Doctor of Med. Sci, 1965. Intern Aomori Prefectural Cen. Hosp., 1961; resident Hirosaki (Japan) U. Hosp., Japan, 1961-65; asst. prof. dept. dermatology Hirosaki (Japan) U. Hosp., 1966-83; assoc. prof. Hirosaki (Japan) U. Hosp., 1983-86, prof., 1986—, chmn. dept., 1986—. Contbr. articles to profl. jours. Japan Ministry Health and Welfare research grantee, 1984. Mem. Japanese Soc. for Investigative Dermatology (councilor 1984—), Japanese Soc. for Connective Tissue Research (councilor 1984—), Japanese Dermatol. Assn. (councilor 1988—). Home: 3 6 2 Matsubara Nishi, Hirosaki 036, Japan Office: Hirosaki U, Dept Dermatology, 5 Zaifu-chu, Hirosaki 036, Japan

HASHIMOTO, KUNIO, architect, educator; b. Tokyo, Jan. 6, 1929; s. Shinichi and Tomiko (Fuse) H.; m. Masako Takahashi, Dec. 24, 1969; 1 child, Mami. BArch, Tokyo Nat. U. Fine Art and Music, 1948. Registered architect, Japan. Participate assoc. Yokokawa Komusho Architects & Engrs., Tokyo, 1948-50; assoc. Takashi Matsumoto Architect & Assocs., Tokyo, 1950-54, Baker, Butler & Tripllet Architects & Engrs., Tokyo, 1954-56; chief architect R. Kitadai Architect & Assocs., Tokyo, 1956-62; pres. K. Hashimoto Architect & Assocs., Tokyo, 1962—; lectr. Shibaura Inst. Tech., Tokyo, 1958-67, assoc. prof. architecture, 1967-79, prof. architecture, 1979—. Former mem. Nomination Com. of Annon-Grand Prix, Tokyo, 1960-65, Com. on Constrn. of City Mus., 1980-81; judge Jury Competition for Refreshing Ctr. of Health Orgn., Atami, Japan, 1986-87. Recipient Honorable Mention award Jury Competition for City Hall, 1951, 2d prize for Model House Chiba Prefectural Gov., 1956, 1st prize for Model House Asahi Newspaper Office, 1957. Mem. Japan Architect Assn. (chmn. coms. 1963-66, 68-71, 74-78, bd. dirs. 1970-74, 81-85), Kawaski Architects Club (bd. dirs. 1980—), Archtl. Inst. Japan, Japan Inst. Architect. Clubs: Tokyo Shinagawa. Lodge: Rotary. Home: 4-3-1 Saginuma, Miyamae-ku, 213 Kawasaki-shi Japan Office: K Hashimoto Architect & Assocs, 3-15-18 Meguro, Meguro-ku, Tokyo 153, Japan

HASHIMOTO, TAKUJI, restaurant executive; b. Tokyo, Nov. 28, 1934; s. Yoshio and Fumi Hashimoto; m. Chie Hashimoto, Jan. 17, 1959; children: Chizuru (Nakano), Takuma. BA in Commerce, Hitotsubashi U., Kunitachi, Tokyo, 1958. Acct. Asahi Breweries Ltd., Hakata Brewery, Fukuoka Kyushu, 1958-60; fin. officer Asahi Breweries Ltd., Kyobashi Tokyo, 1960-66, adv. to pres., 1966-69, mgr planning div., 1969-71, mgr. mktg. div., 1971-73; also bd. dirs. Asahi Breweries, Ltd., Kyobashi Tokyo; sr. mng. dir. Pizza Hut Japan, Ltd., Kanda Tokyo, 1973-75; pres. Pizza Hut Japan, Ltd., Ohta-ku Tokyo, 1975—. Club: Jyosuikai. Home: 1-5-5 Nishinogawa, Tokyo Komae-shi 201, Japan Office: Pizza Hut Japan Ltd, 1-6-1 Kitasenzoku, Tokyo Ohta-ku 145, Japan

HASHIMOTO, YOSHIO, architect; b. Tokyo, Aug. 29, 1928; s. Saburo and Teruko (Ichimura) H.; m. Emiko Kobori, May 25, 1964 (div. 1975); 1 child, Kayoko. BArch, Tokyo U. Arts, 1949. Designer Seichi Washizuka Architects & Engrs., Tokyo, 1949-55; architect, pres. Sanshin Associated Architects, Tokyo, 1955-61; draftsman Neptune & Thomas Architects, Pasadena, Calif., 1961-63; architect, pres. Yoshio Hashimoto J.I.A. Architects & Engrs., Tokyo, 1963—. Mem. Japan Inst. Architects. Office: 5-2-5 Roppongi Minatoku, 106 Tokyo Japan

HASKELL, HELEN BEAUMONT PARK (MRS. WILLIAM PECKHAM HASKELL), real estate executive; b. N.Y.C., Feb. 3, 1916; d. Halford Woodward and Helen Irene (Curtis) Park; B.A., Wellesley Coll., 1939; M.S., Mass. Inst. Tech., 1941; m. William Peckham Haskell, May 12, 1945; children—William Beaumont, Halford Whittier, Helen Hilton. With research and devel. Inst. Optics, U. Rochester, 1941-45, tchr. math. Rosemary Hall, Greenwich, Conn., 1947-61; owner Helen Park Haskell, Realtor, West Chop, Mass., 1968—. Trustee, Rosemary Hall Found., Inc., 1956-62. Mem. U.S. Field Hockey Assn., U.S. Women's LaCrosse Assn., Sigma Xi (asso.). Home: 54 Butternut Hollow Rd Greenwich CT 06830

HASKINS, CARYL PARKER, chemical company executive, educator; b. Schenectady, Aug. 12, 1908; s. Caryl Davis and Frances Julia (Parker) H.; m. Edna Ferrell, July 12, 1940. Ph.B., Yale U., 1930; Ph.D., Harvard U., 1935; D.Sc., Tufts Coll., 1951, Union Coll., 1955, Northeastern U., 1955, Yale U., 1958, Hamilton Coll., 1959, George Washington U., 1963; LL.D., Carnegie Inst. Tech., 1960, U. Cin., 1960, Boston Coll., 1960, Washington and Jefferson Coll., 1961, U. Del., 1965, Pace U., 1974. Staff mem. research lab. Gen. Electric Co., Schenectady, 1931-35; research asso. Mass. Inst. Tech., 1935-45; pres., research dir. Haskins Labs., Inc., 1935-55, dir., 1935—, chmn. bd., 1969-87; dir. E.I. du Pont de Nemours, 1971-81; research prof. Union Coll., 1937-55; pres. Carnegie Instn. of Washington, 1956-71, also trustee, 1949—; Asst. liaison officer OSRD, 1941-42, sr. liaison officer, 1942-43; exec. asst. to chmn. NDRC, 1943-44, dep. exec. officer, 1944-45; sci. adv. bd. Policy Council, Research and Devel. Bd. of Army and Navy, 1947-48; cons. Research and Develop. Bd., 1947-51, to sec. def., 1950-60, to sec. state, 1950-60; mem. Pres.'s Sci. Adv. Com., 1955-58, cons., 1959-70; mem. Pres.'s Nat. Adv. Commn. on Libraries, 1966-67, Joint U.S.-Japan Com. on Sci. Coop., 1961-67, Internat. Conf. Insect Physiology and Ecology, 1971-73; panel advisers Bur. East Asian and Pacific Affairs, Dept. State, 1966-68; mem. Sec. Navy Adv. Com. on Naval History, 1971-83, vice chmn., 1975-83. Author: Of Ants and Men, 1939, The Amazon, 1943, Of Societies and Men, 1950, The Scientific Revolution and World Politics, 1964; contbr. to anthologies and tech. papers.; Editor: The Search for Understanding, 1967; Chmn. bd. editors: Am. Scientist, 1971-83 ; chmn. publs. com., 1971-83 . Trustee Carnegie Corp. N.Y., 1955-80, hon. trustee, 1980—, chmn. bd., 1975-80; trustee Rand Corp., 1955-65, 66-75, adv. trustee 1988—; fellow Yale Corp., 1962-77; regent Smithsonian Instn., 1956-80, regent emeritus, 1980—, mem. exec. com., 1958-80; bd. dirs. Council Fgn. Relations, 1961-75, Population Council, 1955-80; bd. dirs. Ednl. Testing Service, 1958-61, 67-71, chmn. bd., 1969-71; trustee Center for Advanced Study in Behavioral Scis., 1960-75, Thomas Jefferson Meml. Found., 1972-78, Council on Library Resources, 1965—, Pacific Sci. Center Found., 1962-72, Asia Found., 1960—, Marlboro Coll., 1962-77, Wildlife Preservation Trust Internat., Inc., 1976—, Nat. Humanities Center, 1977—; trustee Woods Hole Oceanographic Instn., 1964-73, mem. council, 1973—; bd. dirs. Franklin Book Programs, 1953-58; mem. Save-The-Redwoods League, 1943—, mem. council, 1955—; Mem. vis. coms. Harvard, Johns Hopkins; bd. visitors Tulane U. Recipient Presdl. Certificate of Merit U.S., 1948, King's medal for Service in Cause of Freedom Gt. Britain, 1948, Joseph Henry medal Smithsonian Inst., 1980. Fellow Am. Phys. Soc., A.A.A.S. (dir. 1971-75), Am. Acad. Arts and Scis., Royal Entomol. Soc., Entomol. Soc. Am., Pierpont Morgan Library; mem. N.Y. Zool. Soc., Washington Acad. Scis., Nat. Geog. Soc. (trustee 1964-84 , honorary trustee, 1984—, fin. com. 1972-85, com. on research and exploration 1972—, exec. com. 1972-84), Royal Soc. Arts (Benjamin Franklin fellow), Faraday Soc., Met. Mus. Art, Am. Mus. Natural History (trustee 1973—, bd. mgmt. 1973—), Am. Philos. Soc. (councillor 1976-78, 81-83), Brit. Assn. Advancement Sci., Linnean Soc. London, Internat. Inst. Strategic Studies, Asia Soc., Japan Soc., Biophys. Soc., Nat. Acad. Sci., N.Y. Acad. Scis., Audubon Soc., N.Y. Bot. Garden, P.E.N., Pilgrims, Phi Beta Kappa, Sigma Xi (nat. pres. 1966-68, dir. 1966-83), Delta Sigma Rho, Omicron Delta Kappa. Episcopalian. Clubs: Somerset (Boston), St. Botolph (Boston); Century (N.Y.C.), Yale (N.Y.C.); Mohawk (Schenectady); Metropolitan (Washington), Cosmos (Washington) (bd. mgmt. 1973-76); Lawn (New Haven). Home: 22 Greenacre Ln Westport CT 06880 Office: 1545 18th St NW Washington DC 20036

HASKINS, REGINALD JAMES, management consultant; b. Saskatoon, Sask., Can., Sept. 27, 1950; s. Reginald Hinton and Shirley Elieta (Koester) H.; m. Nancy Jean Keehr, July 7, 1984. BA, U. Sask., 1973, MA, 1975. Research asst. U. Sask., Saskatoon, 1973-75; research officer Human Resource Devel. Agy., Regina, Sask., 1975-77; mgmt. analyst Sask. Supply and Services, Regina, 1977-81; cons. Sask. Fin., Regina, 1981-85; dir. Sask. Urban Affairs, Regina, 1985-87; mng. ptnr. Haskins and Assocs., Regina, 1987—. Pres. Sask. Scouts Can., 1984—; bd. dirs. Boy Scouts Can., Ottawa, 1984—. Mem. Can. INfo. Processing Soc. (bd. dirs. 1979-81), Inst. Pub. Adminstrn. Can., Am. Mgmt. Assn. Mem. United Ch. Home: 3270 Rae St, Regina, SK Canada S4S 1S2 Office: Haskins and Assocs, 2241 Smith St, Regina, SK Canada S4P 2P5

HASKINS, THOMAS MARSTON, lawyer; b. Bryn Mawr, Pa., July 20, 1950; s. Jefferson Porterfield and Alice Marston (Sloan) H.; m. Margo L. Witt, Feb. 3, 1971 (div. Feb. 1986); children: William E., David M., Nicole L. BA in Philosophy, Dickinson Coll., 1972, JD cum laude, 1975. Bar: Va. 1975, U.S. Dist. Ct. (ea. dist.) Va. 1975, U.S. Ct. Appeals (4th cir.) 1975. Assoc. Kellam, Pickrell & Lawler, Norfolk, Va., 1975-79, Breeden, Mac Millan & Green, Norfolk, 1983-87; sole practice Virginia Beach, Va., 1979-83; sr. v.p., gen. counsel 1st Fed. Savs. and Loan Assn. of Colorado Springs, Colo., 1987—; sr. v.p. First Colo. Fin. Corp., 1987—. Mem. ABA, Virginia Beach Bar Assn., Norfolk-Portsmouth Bar Assn., Aircraft Owners and Pilots Assn. (legis. counsel), Virginia Beach Jaycees (v.p. 1979-81). Republican. Methodist. Clubs: Toastmasters, Colorado Country, Colorado Springs Plaza (gov.). Office: 1st Fed Savs and Loan Assn 5225 N Academy Blvd Colorado Springs CO 80918

HASPESLAGH, PHILIPPE C., business educator; b. Roeslaere, Belgium, May 11, 1950; arrived in France, 1973; s. Richard and Rachel (DeBruyne) H.; m. Martine Y. van den Poel, Sept. 28, 1973; children: Frederik, Sophie. B in Comml. Engr., U. Louvain, Belgium, 1972; MBA, Ghent (Belgium) U., 1973, Harvard U., 1977; DBA, Harvard U., 1983. Advisor Prime Minister Belgium, Brussels, 1973-75; cons. P.A. Mgmt. Co., London, 1975-77; research assoc. Harvard U., Cambridge, Mass., 1977-79; asst. prof. European Inst. Bus. Adminstrn., Fontainebleau, France, 1979-84, assoc. prof., 1985—, dir. advanced mgmt. program, 1987—. Nat. Bur. mem. Belgian Christian-Dem. Party, Brussels, 1973-74. Mem. Assn. Internat. des Etudiants en Scis., Econs., et Commls. (pres. Belgian chpt. 1971-73), Acad. Mgmt. (Kearney award 1984), Strategic Mgmt. Soc. (founding mem., editorial bd. 1984—). Roman Catholic. Home: 11 Bis Rue de Neuville, 77300 Fontainebleau France Office: INSEAD, Blvd de Constance, 77300 Fontainebleau France

HASSAN, HIS MAJESTY II, King of Morocco; b. Rabat, Morocco, July 9, 1929; s. King Mohammed V; ed. Imperial Coll. at Rabat; Baccalaureat, U. Bordeaux, 1947, Law degree, 1951, diploma higher studies in Civil Law, 1952; m. Lalla Litifa, 1961; children: Lalla Mariam, Sidi Mohammed, Lalla Asmaa, Lalla Hassnaa, Moulay Rachid. Tng. course French Navy, served aboard battleship Jeanne d'Arc; with royal family exiled by French govt. to Island of Corsica, then Madagascar, 1953-55; participated negotiations on treaty granting independence, 1953-55; in Morocco, 1955-56; became chief dep. to father; comdr. in chief Royal Moroccan Army, 1957, 72—; vice premier, 1960, became King Hassan II of Morocco, 1961; prime minister, 1961-63, 65-67; minister of def., 1960-61, 72-73; chmn. Orgn. African Unity Assn. of Heads of State, 1972; wrote democratic constn. providing for elected parliament, 1962; participant Non-Aligned Conf., Belgrade, 1961. Developer irrigation of previously uncultivated land. Address: Royal Palace, Rabat Morocco *

HASSAN, JOSHUA (ABRAHAM), lawyer, government official; b. Gibraltar, Aug. 21, 1915; s. Abraham M. and Lola (Serruya) H.; m. Daniela Salazar (div. 1969); children: Loli Netto, Rosette Yonatan; m. Marcelle Bensimon, July 30, 1969; children: Fleur, Marlene. Student, Line Wall Coll., Gibraltar; LLD (hon.), Hull U., Eng., 1985. Called to bar Mid. Temple, London, 1939; sr. ptnr. J.A. Hassan & Ptnr., Gibraltar, 1939; dep. coroner Gibraltar, 1941-64; chief mem. leg. co. Gibraltar, 1950-63; leader of opposition Gibraltar, 1969-72, chief minister, 1964-69, 72-87; chmn. Cen. Planning Commn., 1947-70, chmn. Lottery Com., 1955-70. Mayor Gibraltar, 1945-50, 53-69; chmn. Gibraltar Mus., 1952-65; pres. Gibraltar Labour Party, Assn. Advancement Civil Rights. Named Mem. Royal Victoria Order, Comdr. Order Brit. Empire, 1957, Knight Comdr. St. Michael and St. George, Knight Grand Cross Order of Brit. Empire, 1987, Justice of the Peace, 1949. Jewish. Clubs: Oxford and Cambridge U.; Royal Gibraltar Yacht. Address: 11/18 Europa Rd, Gibraltar British Dependent Territory Office: 57/63 Line Wall Rd, Gibraltar British Dependent Territory

HASSAN, KAMAL YOUSIF, oil company executive, personnel manager, consultant; b. Sharjah, United Arab Emirates, Mar. 31, 1958; s. Yousif Hassan and Hajar (Ali) Mohammed; m. Yohanna T. Al Hassen, Aug. 7, 1981. AA, Miami-Dade Community Coll., 1979; BA, U. Miami, 1981. Summer trainee Brit. Bank Middle East, Sharjah, 1974-75, City Bank, Dubai, United Arab Emirates, 1981; head pub. and employee relations Abu Dhabi Gas Industries Ltd., United Arab Emirates, 1981-83; mgr. human resources and adminstrn. Total Abu Al Bukhoosh, Abu Dhabi, 1983—; cons. in human resources, 1986—. Editor Center mag., 1979. Mem. Islamic Cultural Ctr. (pres. 1979-81), Am. Mgmt. Assn., Nat. Geog. Soc., Gulf Inst. (gen. sec.

1984-85). Club: U. Miami Alumni. Office: Total Abu Al Bukhoosh, Hamdan St, PO Box 4058, Abu Dhabi United Arab Emirates

HASSAN, NAJMA NAJMUL, physician; b. Simla, India, Jan. 16, 1943; d. Ghulam Mustafa and Mahmooda Rizvi; m. Syed Najmul Hassan, Aug. 23, 1970; children: Rubab, Farwa, Saima. MBBS, Fatima Jinnah Med. Coll., Lahore, Pakistan, 1965. House surgeon Liaquat Med. Coll., Hyderabad, Pakistan, 1966; med. officer ob-gyn dept. Nishtar Hosp., Multan, Pakistan, 1967; demonstrator pharamcology dept. King Edward Med. Coll., Lahore, 1967-72; gen. practice medicine Kutchery Bazar, Sargodha, Pakistan, 1973—. Muslim. Home: 28-A Satellite Town, Sargodha, Punjab Pakistan Office: Al Hassan Clinic, Kutchery Bazar, Sargodha Pakistan

HASSAN, RIAZ UL, sociologist; b. Gurdaspur, Punjab, Aug. 14, 1937; s. Atta Mohammad and Muhmuda Begum; m. Selva Devi Arulampalam, Apr. 20, 1970; children: Haroon, Tirana. BA, Punjab U., 1959; MA, Dacca U., Bangladesh, 1961; PhD, Ohio State U., 1968. Social welfare officer Mcpl. Corp., Lyallpur, Pakistan, 1961-63; asst. prof. Wright State U., Dayton, Ohio, 1966-68; lectr., sr. lectr. U. Singapore, 1968-77; reader Sch. Social Scis. Flinders U., S. Australia, 1977—; vis. prof. Griffith U., Brisbane, Australia, 1984-85, Gadja Mada U., Yogyakarta, Indonesia, 1984-85; cons. Internat. Survey Research Corp., Chgo., 1974—. Author: Singapore: Society in Transit, 1976, Families in Flats, 1977, Ethnicity, Culture and Fertility, 1980, A Way of Dying, 1983, Islam, 1986. Advisor Singapore Juvenile Ct., 1972-76. Scholar, Asia Found., 1959-61, Fulbright Commn., 1963-65; vis. fellow Japan Ctr. Area Studies, Tokyo, 1970. Mem. Am. Sociol. Assn., N.Y. Acad. Scis., Internat. Union Sci. Study of Population, Internat. Sociol. Assn., Sociol. Assn. Australia and New Zealand, Am. Assn. Suicidology. Home: 585 Fullarton Rd, Mitcham, 5062 Adelaide Australia Office: Flinders U Bedford Park, 5042 Adelaide Australia

HASSAN, SYED AZMAT, diplomat; b. Sialkot, Pakistan, Aug. 7, 1944; s. Syed Fida and Zeenat Hassan; m. Shagufta Hassan, Oct. 12, 1967; 1 child, Rabia. BA, Govt. Coll., Lahore, Pakistan, 1963; MA, King's Coll., Eng., 1969; MS in Strategic Studies, Quald-e-Azam U., Islamabad, Pakistan, 1984. 3d, then 2d sec. Embassy of Pakistan, Rome, 1968-71; sect. officer Ministry Fgn. Affairs, Islamabad, 1971-74, dir., 1974-76; 1st sec. Pakistan Mission to UN, N.Y.C., 1976-78, dep. permanent rep., 1979-80; dep. chief of mission Pakistan Embassy, Abu Dhabi, United Arab Emirates, 1980-82; dir. gen. Ministry Fgn. Affairs, Islamabad, 1983-85; Pakistan ambassador to Malaysia Kuala Lumpur, 1985—. Club: Royal Selangor Golf (Kuala Lumpur). Office: Embassy of Pakistan, 132 Jalan Ampang, Kuala Lumpur 50450, Malaysia

HASSANAL BOLKIAH, HIS MAJESTY MUI'ZZADDIN WADDAULAH, Sultan of Brunei; b. July 15, 1946; s. Sultan Omar Ali Saifuddin; m. Rajah Isteri Anak Saleha, 1965; 6 children; m. Pengiran Isteri Hajjah Mariam, 1981, 1 child. ed. Victoria Inst., Kuala Lumpur, Malaysia, Royal Mil. Acad., Sandhurst, Eng. Apptd. crown prince and heir apparent State of Brunei, 1961, ruler of state, Sultan, 1967—, prime minister, 1984—, minister fin. and home affairs, 1984-86, minister of def., 1986—. Hon. capt. Coldstream Guards, 1968. Address: Istana, Darul, Bandar Seri Begawan Brunei *

HASSANALI, NOOR MOHAMED, president of Republic of Trinidad and Tobago; b. San Fernando, Trinidad and Tobago, Aug. 13, 1918; s. Ashraph and Rasulan (Ramjohn) H.; m. Zalayhar Mohammed, May 17, 1953; children: Khalid, Amena. BA in Law (hon.), U. Toronto, Can., 1947; barrister-at-law, Gray's Inn, Eng., 1948. Pvt. practice law Republic of Trinidad and Tobago, 1948-53; magistrate Magistracy of Republic of Trinidad and Tobafo, 1953-59, sr. magistrate, 1960; sr. crown counsel Office of Attorney General, Republic of Trinidad and Tobago, 1961-64, sr. law officer; solicitor general Ministry of Legal Affairs, Republic of Trinidad and Tobago, 1965; judge of the High Court Supreme Court of Judicature, Republic of Trinidad and Tobago, 1966-77, judge of Court of Appeal, 1978-84; president of the Republic of Trinidad and Tobago 1987—; master of the Moots Hugh Wooding Law Sch., 1985-86; mem. judicial and legal service commn., 1985-86, Trinidad and Tobago Defense Force Commns. Bd., 1985-86. Exec. mem. Scout Assn. Tidad and Tigo, Trinidad and Tobago, 1965-86; mem. bd. control Naparima Coll., San Fernando, 1948-60. Home and Office: President's House, Saint Ann's Port of Spain Trinidad and Tobago

HASSAN BIN TALAL, crown prince of Jordan; b. Amman, Jordan, Mar. 20, 1947; brother of King Hussein of Jordan. BA, Christ Ch., Oxford U. Heir to throne of Jordan, acting regent in absence of King Hussei, ombudsman for nat. devel., 1971—; hon. gen. Jordanian Army. Author: A Study on Jerusalem, 1979, Palestinian Self-Determination, 1981. Mem. Royal Sci. Soc. Jordan (founder 1970). Address: Office of Crown Prince, Royal Palace, Amman Jordan *

HASSELL, MORRIS WILLIAM, judge; b. Jacksonville, Tex., Aug. 9, 1916; s. Alonzo Seldon and Cora Lee (Rainey) H.; m. Mauriete Watson, Sept. 3, 1944; children—Morris William, Charles Robert. A.A., Lon Morris Coll., 1936; J.D., U. Tex., Austin, 1942. Bar: Tex. 1941, U.S. Dist. Ct. 1948, U.S. Supreme Ct. 1973. County atty. Cherokee County, Tex., 1943-47; mem. Norman Hassell Spiers & Thrall of Rusk and Jacksonville, Tex., 1948-78; judge 2d Jud. Dist. Tex., 1978—; chmn. bd. Swift Oil Co., 1964-77, H & I Oil Co., 1968-77; dir. First State Bank, Rusk, Tex., 1959-78. Mayor, City of Rusk, Tex., 1959-63, 73-78; trustee Rusk Ind. Sch. Dist., 1967-73; chmn. bd. trustees, chmn. exec. com. Lon Morris Coll., Jacksonville; chmn. bd. trustees Tex. conf. United Methodist Ch.; vice-chmn. bd. trustees Lakeview Meth. Assembly; trustee Tex. ann. conf. United Meth. Found. Mem. State Bar Tex., ABA; fellow Tex. Bar Found., Am. Bar Found. Democrat. Lodges: Kiwanis (lt. gov. 1964), Masons, Odd Fellow. Home: 1300 Copeland St Rusk TX 75785 Office: 2d Jud Dist Ct PO Box 196 Rusk TX 75785

HASSELQUIST, MAYNARD BURTON, lawyer; b. Amador, Minn., July 1, 1919; s. Harry and Anna F. (Froberg) H.; m. Lorraine Swenson, Nov. 20, 1948; children—Mark D., Peter L. B.S.L., U. Minn., 1941; J.D.L., U. Minn., 1947. Bar: Minn. 1948. Asst. mgr. taxation Gen. Mills Inc., Mpls., 1947-53; chmn. internat. dept. Dorsey & Whitney, Mpls., 1953-81, sr. ptnr.; dir. Graco Inc., Mpls., McLaughlin Gormley King Co., Mpls., ADC Telecommunications, Inc., Mpls., Wesco Resources, Billings, Mont., Gustavus Adolphus Coll., St. Peter, Minn., Soprea S.A., Paris. Gen. counsel, bd. dirs. Swedish Council Am.; past chmn. Japan-Am. Soc. Minn.; bd. dirs., counsel James Ford Bell Library; past. chmn. Fairview Hosps. Internat., Ltd., Cayman Islands. Served with USN, 1941-46. Mem. ABA, Minn. Bar Assn., Internat. Bar Assn., Am. Soc. Internat. Law. Republican. Lutheran. Club: Mpls. Office: Dorsey & Whitney 2200 First Bank Pl East Minneapolis MN 55402

HASSELQVIST, SVEN ARNE, architect; b. Karlshamn, Sweden, Feb. 5, 1937; arrived in St. Vincent, 1964; s. Sven Gustav and Edla (Johansson) H.; m. Anita Stenholm; children: Petronella, Karolina, Lukas. Degree in Engring. and House Constrn., Hogre Tekniska Laroverket, Stockholm, 1955. Prin. Arne Architect Services, St. Vincent, W.I., 1969—. Prin. works include Petit St. Vincent Resort, 1969, Mustique Island, 1969—; contbr. articles to profl. jours. Home: Mustique Island Saint Vincent and Grenadines

HASSETT, CAROL ALICE, psychologist; b. Bklyn., Apr. 19, 1947; d. Joseph and Anna (Portanova) Lusardi; B.S., St. John's U., 1968; M.Ed., Hofstra U., 1974, Ph.D. in Psychology (teaching asst.), 1981; m. John J. Hassett, June 29, 1968; 1 son, John J. Tchr. Day Elem. Sch., Bklyn., 1968-69; psychologist Nassau County Dept. Drug and Alcohol also Mental Health Assn. Nassau County, East Meadow, N.Y., 1981-84; chief supervising psychologist Queens Outreach Project, 1985—; pvt. practice clin. psychology, 1984—; adj. asst. prof. Hofstra U., 1980—. Trustee Malverne (N.Y.) Pub. Libray, 1986—; bd. dirs. Malverne Vol. Ambulance Corps, 1976—; bd. govs. Kings County Cadet Corps, 1966-72; bd. trustees Malverne Pub. Lib., 1986—. Cert. advanced emergency med. technician, prehosp. critical care technician; permanently cert. tchr., N.Y. Mem. Am. Psychol. Assn. Republican. Roman Catholic. Contbr. articles profl. jours. Home: 105 Franklin Ave Malverne NY 11565 Office: 230 Hilton Ave Hempstead NY 11550

HASSINGER, MARK ALAN, optometrist; b. Cleve., Jan. 4, 1956; s. Elwood Charles and June Bernice (Swaffield) H.; m. Angela Marie Federico, Aug. 18, 1984; children: Jennifer Lynn, Mark Alan Jr. BS, Ohio State U., 1978; BS in Visual Sci., OD, Ill. Coll. Optometry, 1982. Lic. optometrist, Ohio, Wis., Ill. Assoc. optometrist Dr. Daniel Geiger, Parma, Ohio, 1983—; staff optometrist Ohio Permanente Med. Group, Willoughby, 1983-86; assoc. optometrist Dr. Ronald Mesnick, Lyndhurst, Ohio, 1983. Named one of Outstanding Young Mem of Am., 1984; Recipient Faculty Meml. award Ill. Coll. Optometry, Chgo., 1982. Mem. Am. Optometric Assn., Ohio Optometric Assn., Phi Theta Upsilon (v.p. 1981-82).

HASSLER, SANDRA LEE, controller; b. Allentown, Pa., Jan. 3, 1949; d. Harold Elmer and Ruth Eleanor (Dahlof) H.; A.A. in Bus. Adminstrn., Northampton County Community Coll., 1969; B.S. in Bus. Mgmt., Indiana (Pa.) U., 1971. Engaged in retail fin., 1971-77; corp. controller, asst. to chmn. bd. Apparel Affiliates, Inc., Quakertown, Pa., 1977-81; ind. fin. and retail cons. computer programming and internal auditing, Phila., 1981-82; div. controller Honeybee, women's retail apparel chain, Huntington Valley Pa., 1982-84; asst. controller Wall to Wall Sound & Video, Inc., Cinnaminson, N.J., 1984—. Mem. Am. Mgmt. Assn., Nat. Assn. Female Execs. Mem. Moravian Ch. Author ops. and retail manuals/booklets for design of data collection devices. Home: 800 Trenton Rd #275 Langhorne PA 19047 Office: 200 S Rt 130 Cinnaminson NJ 08077

HASSLOCHER, MARCEL DEZON COSTA, ambassador. Sec. state Govt. Rio de Janeiro's Industry-Commerce and Tourism Offices, Brazil, 1975-79; head of pres's cabinet Nuclebras, Brasilia, Brazil, 1979; pres. Radiobras, Brasilia, 1980-81; ambassador Brazilian Govt., Maputo, Mozambique, 1982-85, Rabat, Morocco, 1986—.

HASSON, HASKIA, mathematician, computer scientist, consultant, educator; b. Los Angeles, May 28, 1951; s. Sam and Victoria (Coen) H.; B.A. (scholar), U. Calif., Los Angeles, 1972, postgrad., 1973-75; M.A., U. Calif., Berkeley, 1973. Asst. prof. Pepperdine U., 1975-78; lectr. Calif. State U., Long Beach, 1977-78; mathematician Hughes Aircraft Co., 1978-82, TRW, Inc., 1982-85; liaison officer Atenisi Inst., Nuku'alofa, Tonga, 1975—, guest lectr., 1975, adj. lectr., 1978—; adj. prof. Pepperdine U., 1978-80; cons. Microexpert Systems, Inc, 1986—. Mem. AAAS, Am. Math. Soc., Math. Assn. Am., Assn. Computing Machinery, N.Y. Acad. Scis., Vols. in Tech. Assistance (vol.). Author: The Equivalence of Real Numbers Under Unimodular Transformations, 1973. Home: 304 3d St Manhattan Beach CA 90266

HASSON, JAMES KEITH, JR., lawyer, law educator; b. Knoxville, Tenn., Mar. 3, 1946; s. James Keith and Elaine (Biggers) H.; m. Jayne Young, July 27, 1968; 1 son, Keith Samuel. B.A., Duke U., 1967, J.D., 1970. Bar: Ga. 1971, D.C. 1971. Assoc. Sutherland, Asbill & Brennan, Atlanta, 1970-76, ptnr., 1976—; prof. law Emory U., Atlanta, 1976—; dir. House-Hasson Hardware Co., Knoxville, 1971—. Contbr. articles to profl. jours. Chmn. Met. Atlanta Crime Commn., 1986-87, also trustee; mem. Atlanta Civilian Review Bd.; mem. Leadership Atlanta, 1981-82; mem. IRS Commr. exempt orgn. adv. group; bd. dirs. Foxfire Fund, 1988—. Served to 1st lt. U.S. Army, 1970-71. Mem. ABA (com. chmn. 1983-85), Atlanta Bar Assn. (counsel 1977-80, Pres's. Disting. Service award 1980). Presbyterian. Club: Lawyers. Home: 3185 Chatham Rd NW Atlanta GA 30305 Office: Sutherland Asbill & Brennan 3100 First Atlanta Tower Atlanta GA 30383

HASSOUNA, FRED, architect, educator; b. Cairo, Mar. 26, 1918; s. Amin Sami and Dawlat (Mansour) H.; came to U.S., 1948, naturalized, 1953; diploma in architecture with honors Higher Sch. Fine Arts, Cairo, 1940; diploma in Egyptology with 1st class honors U. Cairo, 1944; diploma in civic design U. Liverpool (Eng.), 1946; M.Arch., M.S. in Pub. Adminstrn., U. So. Calif., 1950; m. Verna Arlene Dotter, Mar. 9, 1950. Architect, curator Cairo Mus., Egypt, 1940-44; lectr. archaeology and architecture Alexandria U., Egypt, 1944-45, 47-48; dir. planning Huyton-with-Roby Urban Dist. Council, Huyton, Eng., 1946-47; lectr. city planning U. So. Calif., 1950-55; architect Kistner, Wright and Wright, architects and engrs., Los Angeles, 1952-53; project architect Welton Becket and Assocs., architects and engrs., Los Angeles, 1954-56, Albert C. Martin and Assocs., architects and engrs., 1956-58; faculty architecture East Los Angeles Coll., 1958-75, prof. architecture, head dept. architecture; prof., head dept. architecture Saddleback Coll., 1975-83; pvt. planning cons., architect, Los Angeles, 1950-75, Laguna Niguel, 1975—. Mem. indsl. tech. adv. bd. Calif. State U. at Long Beach, 1963-83; mem. adv. bd. on environ. and interior design U. Calif., Irvine, 1976-83; pres. Calif. Council Archtl. Edn., 1977; mem. liaison com. architecture, landscape architecture, urban and regional planning in Calif. higher edn., 1976-83. Registered architect, Calif.; recipient hon. cultural doctorate World U. Roundtable, Tucson, 1983. Fellow Internat. Inst. Arts and Letters (life); mem. emeritus AIA, Am. Planning Assn. Home and Office: 31242 Flying Cloud Dr Laguna Niguel CA 92677

HAST, MALCOLM HOWARD, medical educator; b. N.Y.C., May 28, 1931; s. Irving William and Rose Lillian (Berlin) H.; m. Adele Krongelb, Feb. 1, 1953; children: David Jay, Howard Arthur. B.A., Bklyn. Coll., 1953; postgrad., U. So. Calif., 1955-57; M.A., Ohio State U., 1958, Ph.D. (NIH fellow), 1961. Instr. U. Iowa, 1961-63; NIH spl. fellow U. Iowa (Coll. Medicine), 1963-65, asst. prof., 1965-69; assoc. prof. otolaryngology Med. Sch., Northwestern U., 1969-74, prof., 1974—, dir. research otolaryngology, 1969—; prof. anatomy med. and dental schs. Northwestern U., 1977—; assoc. staff Northwestern Meml. Hosp., 1969—; guest scientist Max Planck Inst. für Psychiatrie, 1976; vis. prof. Royal Coll. Surgeons Eng., 1980-86, U. Edinburgh, 1987; mem. task force on new materials Am. Bd. Otolaryngology, 1969-72; dir. Ill. Soc. Med. Research, 1973-77; mem. Internat. Anat. Nomenclature Com., 1983—; guest scientist Zoologisches Forchungsinstitut und Museum A. Koenig, 1988. Contbr. articles to profl. jours., chpts. to books. Mem. adv. bd. Center on Deafness, 1977-80; bd. dirs. Cliff Dwellers Arts Found., 1979-82; trustee Wilmette Library Bd., 1982-83. Served with AUS, 1953-55. Recipient Gould Internat. award, 1971, Alumnus award of honor Bklyn. Coll., 1977, Alumnus of Yr. award Bklyn. Coll., 1984; NIH research grantee, 1964-84; NSF research grantee, 1975-77; NATO sr. fellow in Sci. Oxford U., Eng., 1978; Arnott demonstrator Royal Coll. Surgeons Eng., 1985. Fellow Linnean Soc. (London), Am. Speech and Hearing Assn., Royal Soc. Medicine, AAAS; mem. Am. Acad. Otolaryngology Head and Neck Surgery, Am. Physiol. Soc. (animal care and experimentation com. 1976-82), Am. Assn. Clin. Anatomists, Chgo. Laryngol. and Otol. Soc. (Council of Seven 1988—), Am. Soc. Mammalogists, AAUP (chpt. pres. 1977-82), Anat. Soc. Gt. Britain and Ireland, Am. Assn. Anatomists, Am. Assn. History of Medicine, Amnesty Internat. (coordinator Chgo. health profls. group 1986-87), Sigma Xi (pres. chpt. 1971-72), Sigma Alpha Eta. Office: 303 E Chicago Ave Chicago IL 60611

HASTINGS, DAVID ALAN, research geoscientist, consultant, educator; b. Newton, Mass., Dec. 26, 1946; s. Carlton Herbert and Frances J. (McMahon) H.; m. Vasanta Devi Suppiah, June 6, 1979. Cert. in Italian, U. degli Studi, Bologna, Italy, 1968; B.A. in Physics, Tufts U., 1969; postgrad. in geophysics, Brown U., 1969-70; M.S. in Geol. Engring., U. Ariz., 1972; postgrad. in geophysics/geology U. Alaska, 1976-85; supervisory research geophysicist Nat. Geophys. Data Ctr., NOAA, Boulder, Colo., 1986—; geophysicist World Data Ctr. A for Solid Earth Geophysics, Boulder, 1986—; lectr., U. Sci. and Tech., U.S. Peace Corps, Kumasi, Ghana, 1972-74; cons., researcher EnerDesign Assocs., Weston, Mass., 1974-75; sr. geophysicist, asst. dir. Ghana Geol. Survey, Takoradi, 1976-78; vis. instr. Mich. Tech. U., Houghton, 1978-80; sr. applications scientist geophysics/geology Technicolor Govt. Services Inc., EROS Data Ctr., Sioux Falls, S.D., 1980-86; mem. non renewable resources program adv. panel NASA, Washington, 1979-81; adj. prin. geophysicist Ghana Geol. Survey, Accra, 1983—; co-founder, editor N.Am. NOAA Polar Orbiter Users Group, 1986—; cons./advisor various orgns., U.S. and overseas. Co-author: Geology and Mineral Resources of West Africa, 1985. Editor: Geophysics, Tectonics and Mineral Deposits in Africa, 1980-82; co-editor N.Am. NOAA, 1987, monthly AVHRR (NOAA Satellite System); 1988—; mem. editorial com. Geodynamique Jour., 1984—. Contbr. articles to profl. jours. Recipient Magsat research award NASA, 1983, hon. mention paper award U.S. Geol. Survey, 1984. Mem. Geol. Soc. Am., Am. Geophys. Union, Am. Inst. Profl. Geologists (cert. profl. geol. scientist), Assn. Geoscientists for Internat. Devel., Am. Soc. Photogrammetry and Remote Sensing. Home: PO Box 958 Boulder CO 80306 Office: NOAA Nat Geophys Data Ctr 325 Broadway Boulder CO 80303

HASTINGS, EDMUND STUART, petroleum geologist, retired naval officer; b. New Orleans, Jan. 2, 1924; s. James Stuart and Winnie Dorothy (Miller) H.; student U.S. Naval R.O.T.C., U. Tex., 1943, Command Staff Course Naval War Coll., 1959, Gen. Staff Coll., 1969; B.S., U. So. Calif. 1950; m. Elizabeth Theresa Dean, June 21, 1947; children—Theresa Christine (Mrs. Aaron R. Folse), Margaret Elizabeth, James Stuart. Commd. ensign USN, 1943, advanced through grades to comdr., 1971; with weapons tng. unit NAS, Dallas; with Naval Ammunition Depot, Pusan, Korea; ret.; spl. projects geologist Phillips Petroleum Co., Lafayette, La., 1956-59, dist. div. geologist, 1959-62, regional staff geologist, Bartlesville, Okla., 1962-64, petroleum geologist, Houston, 1964-70, 1973-85, Lafayette, 1970-73; chmn., chief exec. officer Pet Cons & Assocs., Houston, 1985—; expert witness petroleum exploration, devel., drilling prodn. opns., onshore offshore pipeline and acquisitions worldwide; v.p., then chief exec. officer Hastings Properties, Gautier, Miss., 1967-75; ship's master Oceans Unltd.; dir. First Nat. Bank. Recipient commendations U.S. Dept. Def., 1962, 68, 69. Mem. Explorers Club, Am. Inst. Profl. Geologists (state v.p. 1973), Soc. Profl. Well Log Analysts (state v.p. 1972-73), Am. Assn. Petroleum Geologists (del., foreman, silver cert. for 25 yrs., exec. com.), Naval Res. Assn., Soc. Exploration Geophysicists (silver cert. for 25 yrs.), SAR, Soc. Ind. Profl. Earth Scis., Phi Kappa Tau. Club: Phillips (bd. dirs.). Lodges: Elks, Optimists. Home: 8414 Braes Meadow Dr Houston TX 77071 Office: PO Box 710607 Houston TX 77271

HASTINGS, HAROLD, mathematics educator, researcher, author; b. Dayton, Ohio, Nov. 21, 1946; s. Julius M. and Celia A. (Morse) H.; m. Gretchen E. Saalbach, June 2, 1968; children: Curtis, Matthew. BS, Yale U., 1967; MA, Princeton U., 1969, PhD, 1972. From instr. to assoc. prof. math. Hempstead U., N.Y., 1968-81, prof., 1981—, dept. chmn., 1985—; vis. assoc. prof. SUNY-Binghamton, 1974-75, U. Ga., Athens, 1978-79; founder, prin. Hastings, Saalbach Assocs., Inc., Garden City, N.Y., 1983—; mem. working group on supercomputers NASA, Greenbelt, Md., 1985—; founder, prin. Advanced Med. Computing, Inc., Great Neck, N.Y., 1988—. Author: (with D. Edwards) Cech and Steenrod Homotopy Theory, 1974; editor: (with M. Kochen) Advances in Cognitive Science, 1988; contbr. articles to profl. jours. Patentee in field. Pres., v.p. Garden City Lay Ecumenical Com., N.Y., 1983—. NSF grantee, 1977, 80. Mem. Am. Math. Soc., Assn. Computing Machinery, Soc. Math. Biology. Avocations: running, photography, music. Home: 23 Lindbergh St Garden City NY 11530 Office: Hofstra U Hempstead NY 11550

HASTINGS, LAWRENCE VAETH, physician, lawyer; b. Flushing, N.Y., Nov. 23, 1919; s. Henry Luftman and Lillian (Vaeth) H.; m. Doris Lorraine Erickson, Dec. 11, 1971; children: Lance Clifford Hastings Shepard, Wilhelmina Streeton and Laura Thynne (twins),. Student, Columbia U., 1939-40, student Law Sch., 1949-50; student, U. Mich. Engring. Sch., 1942-43, Washington U., 1943-44, U. Vt., 1943; M.D., Johns Hopkins U., 1948; J.D., U. Miami, 1953. Bar: Fla. 1954, U.S. Supreme Ct. 1960, D.C. 1976; cert. Am. Bd. Legal Medicine. Intern, U.S. Marine Hosp., S.I., N.Y., 1948-49; asst. surgeon, sr. asst. surgeon USPHS, 1949-52; asst. resident surgery Bellevue Hosp. Med. Ctr., 1951; med. legal cons., trial atty. Miami, Fla., 1953—; assoc. Sams, Donato, Purdy and Hastings, P.A.; asst. prof. medicine U. Miami, 1964—, lectr. law, 1966; adj. prof. St. Thomas of Villanova Law Sch., Biscayne Coll., Miami, Fla. Contbr. articles to profl. publs. Bd. dirs. Miami Heart Inst.; trustee Barry Coll., Miami, 1976—, Fla. Internat. U., 1979—. Served with AUS, 1943-46. Fellow Acad. Fla. Trial Lawyers, Am. Coll. Legal Medicine, Law-Sci. Acad. Found. Am.; mem. Am. Acad. Forensic Scis., Assn. Trial Lawyers Am., Fla. Bar (vice chmn. med. legal com. 1957, vice chmn. trial tactics com. 1963-65, chmn. steering com. trial tactics and basic anatomy seminars), Pitts. Inst. Legal Medicine, AMA, Fla., Dade County med. assns., Johns Hopkins Med. and Surg. Assn., Pithotomy Club, Assn. Mil. Surgeons, U. Miami Law Alumni Assn. (pres. 1967), ABA, Fla., Dade County bar assns., Acad. Psychosomatic Medicine, Com. of 100 Miami Beach, Alpha Delta Phi, Phi Eta Sigma, Phi Alpha Delta. Roman Catholic. Clubs: Two Hundred, Bankers; Bal Harbour (Fla.); LaGorce Country, Bath, Surf (bd. govs. 1976—, chmn. bd. 1978-82, pres. 1978-80), Com. 100, Indian Creek Country, Miami Beach, River of Jacksonville; N.Y. Athletic, Metropolitan, Princeton (N.Y.C.). Home: 256 Bal Bay Dr Bal Harbour FL 33154 Office: 530 City National Bank Bldg 300 71st St Miami Beach FL 33141 Office: Concord Bldg 66 W Flagler St Suite 700 Miami FL 33130

HASTINGS, ROBERT EUGENE, city-county official; b. Council Bluffs, Iowa, June 17, 1932; s. Elmer Wayne and Lillian Irene (Potts) H.; student appraisal courses Omaha U., Iowa State U., Iowa Western Community Coll., 1967-78; m. Marcia Ann Martin, Aug. 2, 1969. Meter reader Council Bluffs Gas Co., 1950; clk. Milw. R.R., Council Bluffs, 1951-52; with Harding Cream Co., Omaha, 1952-54; clk. Safeway Stores, Council Bluffs, 1954-56; circulation mgr. World Herald Newspaper, Eastern Nebr., 1956-58; agt. Met. Life Ins., Omaha, 1958-59; asst. county assessor Pottawattamie County, Iowa, Council Bluffs, 1959-72; city assessor Council Bluffs, 1972-74; city-county assessor Pottawattamie County, 1974—; instr. real estate appraisal Iowa Community Coll., Nebr., Kans. Taxation and fin. steering com. Nat. Assn. Counties, Washington, 1974-79; pres. C of C Cee Bees (Goodwill Ambassadors), 1978; county govt. lobbyist, 1974-75; mem. Iowa State Assessors Edn. Commn., 1983-85. Recipient ICA degree, Iowa Inst. Certified Assessors, Outstanding AAO Profl. Designer, 1988. Mem. Internat. Assn. Assessing Officers (CAE degree; contbr. report 1974; profl. admissions com. 1981-85, profl. standards com. 1987—, mem. exec. bd. 1985-87, sr. nat. edn. instr.), Nat. Assn. Review Appraisers (C.R.A. degree), Am. Soc. Appraisers (charter pres. Nebr. chpt. 1985-88, Northeast chpt. pres., state dir. 1986-88, sr. mgr., R.E. appraiser instr.), Iowa State Assn. Assessors, C. of C. (dir. 1975-77). Lutheran. Clubs: Kiwanis (pres. Downtown Council Bluffs 1976-77, On-To dist. Nebr.-Iowa Dist. conv. chmn. 1979, internat. conv. dist. chmn. 1983, 1987, club sec. 1983, lt. gov. div. 13, trustee Nebr.-Iowa Dist. 1981-82, dist. youth chmn. 1983-84, dist. community services chmn. 1985-86, dist. retention chmn. 1987-88, dist. major emphasis chmn. 1988—). Home: 72 Bellevue Ave Council Bluffs IA 51503 Office: Court House PO Box 1076 Council Bluffs IA 51502

HASUMI, MORISUKE, mathematics educator; b. Mito, Ibaraki, Japan, Oct. 14, 1932; s. Moribumi and Ume (Kuriyama) H.; m. Shizuka Kamei, Nov. 6, 1965; children—Moriyoshi, Satoko, Masako. B.Sc., Ibaraki U., 1955; Ph.D., U. Calif.-Berkeley, 1966; D.Sc., U. Tokyo, 1966. Asst. math. Ibaraki U., Mito, 1955-62, lectr. math., 1962-66, asst. prof., 1966-68, prof., 1968—; instr. math. U. Calif.-Berkeley, 1962-63, lectr. math., 1963-64; vis. mem. Mittag-Leffler Inst., Djursholm, Sweden, 1976-77. Author: Hardy Classes on Infinitely Connected Riemann Surfaces, 1983. Contbr. research articles to math. jours. Mem. Math. Soc. Japan, Am. Math. Soc. Home: 2-7-9 Joto, 310 Mito Ibaraki Japan Office: Ibaraki U, Dept Math, 2-1-1 Bunkyo, Mito, 310 Ibaraki Japan

HATA, SACHIO, leasing company executive; b. Kakogawa, Hyogo, Japan, Feb. 20, 1932; s. Koichi and Kino H.; m. Kiyoko Hashiguchi. BA in Econs., Keio U., 1956. With Sanwa Bank Ltd., Tokyo, 1956-67; with Orient Leasing Co. Ltd., Tokyo, 1967—, gen. mgr. internat. dept., 1974, bd. dirs., 1979, mng. dir., 1987—. Home: Hatandodai Shinagawa-ku, 6-21-18, Tokyo Japan Office: Orient Leasing Co Ltd, 2-4-1 Hamamatsucho, Minato-ku, Tokyo Japan

HATADA, KAZUYUKI, mathematician, educator; b. Maebashi, Gunma, Japan, Dec. 23, 1951; s. Kiyoshi and Tokiko H.; m. Kumiko Yoshikawa, Dec. 15, 1985; 1 child, Hidehiko. BS, U. Tokyo, 1974, MS, 1976, DSc, 1979. Research fellow faculty sci. U. Tokyo, 1979-80; assoc. prof. math. faculty edn. Gifu U., Gifu City, Japan, 1981—. Contbr. articles to profl. jours. Fellow Internat. Biog. Assn.; mem. Am. Biog. Inst. Research Assn. (Life), (recipient Commemorative Medal of Honor (Gold) 1988, Internat. Cultural Diploma of Honor 1988), World Inst. Achievement (Life), Math. Soc. Japan, Am. Math. Soc. Avocation: music. Home: 6-2 Chiyoda 2 chome, 371 Maebashi Gunma, Japan Office: Faculty Edn, Gifu U, Dept Math, 1-1 Yanagido, 501-11 Gifu Japan

HATANAKA, HIROSHI, neurosurgeon; b. Toyama Prefecture, Japan, Apr. 20, 1932; s. Taichi and Hana (Takahashi) H.; m. Anita Louisa Beck, Oct. 15, 1973; children: Elsa, Clara. MD, U. Tokyo, 1957, D of Med. Scis., 1963. Resident in surgery and neurosurgery U. Tokyo Hosp., 1958-62, asst. in surgery, 1963-64; Fulbright scholar, surg. research fellow Harvard U., 1964-67; clin. and research fellow Mass. Gen. Hosp., Boston, 1964-67, vis. fellow neurosurgery, 1971-72; asst. in neurosurgery U. Tokyo Hosp., 1967-73; prof. neurosurgery Teikyo U., Tokyo, 1971—; vis. resident in neurosurgery Montreal Neurol. Inst. and Hosp. at McGill U., summer 1966. Mem. Japanese Cancer Assn., Japanese Surg. Soc., Japanese Congress Neurosurgeons, World Fedn. Neurol. Surgeons, Japan Neurosurg. Soc., Japan Soc. Practicing Surgeons, Internat. Coll. Surgeons, Japan Assn. Cancer Research, Asian and Australasian Soc. Neurol. Surgeons, Japan Soc. Cen. Nervous System Computed Tomography, Japan Radiol. Soc., Internat. Soc. Radiology, Japan EEG Soc., Japan Neuropathol. Soc., Japan Neurochemistry Soc., Internat. Soc. for Neutron Capture Therapy (founder, 1st pres. and sec.), Japan Soc. Clin. Imaging (exec. bd.), J.E. Purkyne Czech. Med. Assn. (hon.), Czech Neurosurg. Soc. (hon.). Mem. Society of Friends. Home: 4-15-29 Mita, Minato-ku, Tokyo Japan Office: Teikyo U Hosp, 2-11-1 Kaga, Itabashi-ku, Tokyo Japan

HATCH, GERALD GORDON, engineer; b. Brockville, Ont., Can., July 30, 1922; s. Earle Clifton and Ethel Helen (Goodfellow) H.; m. Sheila Pamela Baillie, Sept. 4, 1946; children—Linda, Douglas, Christopher, Joan. B.Engring., McGill U., Montreal, Que., Can., 1944; Sc.D., MIT, 1948. Registered profl. engr. Research engr. Armour Research Found., Chgo., 1948-52; dir. research and devel. Que. Iron and Titanium Co., Sorel, Can., 1952-54, works mgr., 1954-58; pres. W.S. Atkins & Assocs., Ltd., Toronto, Ont., 1958-65, Hatch Assocs., Ltd., Toronto, 1965—. Author tech. papers. Mem. Assn. Profl. Engrs. Ont. (council), Can. Inst. Mining and Metallurgy (Past Pres.'s Gold medal 1961, Airey award 1986), Ordre des Ingenieurs de Que., Am. Iron and Steel Inst., AIME (metall. soc.). Clubs: National, St. George's Golf and Country (Toronto). Avocations: golf, tennis. Office: Hatch Assocs Ltd, 21 St Clair Ave E, Toronto, ON Canada M4T 1L9

HATCH, MARY WENDELL VANDER POEL, nonprofit organization executive, interior decorator; b. N.Y.C., Feb. 6, 1919; d. William Halsted and Blanche Pauline (Billings) Vander Poel; m. George Montagu Miller, Apr. 5, 1940 (div. 1974); children—Wendell Miller Steavenson, Gretchen Miller Elkus; m. Sinclair Hatch, May 14, 1977. Pres. Miller Richard, Inc., interior decorators, Glen Head, N.Y., 1972—, bd. dirs. Eye Bank Sight Restoration, N.Y.C., 1975—, pres., 1980-88, hon. chair, 1988—; bd. dirs. Manhattan Eye Ear and Throat Hosp., N.Y.C., 1966—, v.p., 1978—; sec. 1985—, bd. dirs. Cold Spring Harbor Lab., N.Y., 1985—; v.p. North Country Garden Club, Nassau County, N.Y., 1979-81, 1983-85; dir. Planned Parenthood Nassau County, Mineola, N.Y., 1982-84, Hutton House C.W. Post Coll., Greenvale, N.Y., 1982—. Republican. Episcopalian. Clubs: Colony (N.Y.C.), Church (N.Y.C.), Order St. John Jerusalem (N.Y.C.). Home: Mill River Rd Box 330 Oyster Bay NY 11771

HATCH, ORRIN GRANT, U.S. senator; b. Homestead Park, Pa., Mar. 22, 1934; s. Jesse and Helen (Kamm) H.; m. Elaine Hansen, Aug. 28, 1957; children: Brent, Marcia, Scott, Kimberly, Alysa, Jesse. B.S., Brigham Young U., 1959; J.D., U. Pitts., 1962. Bar: Pa. 1962, Utah 1962. Ptnr. firm Thomson, Rhodes & Grigsby, Pitts., 1962-69, Hatch & Plumb, Salt Lake City, 1976; mem. U.S. Senate from Utah, 1977—; past chmn. labor and human resources com.; ranking minority mem. Senate Labor and Human Resources Com, mem. Senate Judiciary Com., Select Com. on Intelligence, Spl. Senate Com. Investigating Iran Arms Deal. Contbr. articles to newspapers and profl. jours. Mem. Am., Nat., Utah, Pa. bar assns., Am. Judicature Soc. Republican. Mormon. Office: 135 Russell Senate Bldg Washington DC 20510

HATCHER, JOHN CHRISTOPHER, psychologist; b. Atlanta, Sept. 18, 1946; s. John William and Kay (Carney) H.; B.A., U. Ga., 1968, M.S., 1970, Ph.D., 1972. Psychologist, Clayton Mental Health Center, Atlanta, 1971-72; dir. intern training psychology service Beaumont Med. Center, El Paso, Tex., 1972-74; dir. family therapy program Langley Porter Inst., U. Calif., San Francisco, 1974—; adj. prof. dept. psychology U. Tex., 1972-74, dept. ednl. psychology and guidance, 1972-74; asst. clin. prof. psychology U. Calif., San Francisco, 1974-80, assoc. clin. prof., 1980-86, clin. prof., 1986—; cons. city and state govts. in U.S., Europe, Mexico, Asia, Far East; internat. cons. in hostage negotiation and terrorism chmn., Mayors Commn. on Family Violence, San Francisco; advisor arson task force San Francisco Fire Dept.; adv. bd. Nat. Firehawk Found., Kevin Collins Found. for Missing Children; advisor CBS-TV; spl. asst. to Mayor of San Francisco in charge of People's Temple Jonestown Case; mem. Calif. State Legis. Task Force on Missing Children; prin. investigator U.S. Dept. Justice Families of Missing Children Project. Mem. Am. Psychol. Assn. (chmn. com. hostage families), Calif. State Psychol. Assn. (chmn. task force on terrorism), Soc. Police and Criminal Psychology, Assn. Advancement Psychology, Am. Family Therapy Assn., Internat. Council Psychologists, Phi Kappa Phi. Author: (with Himelstein) Handbook of Gestalt Therapy, 1976; (with Brooks) Innovations in Counseling Psychology, 1977, (with Gaynor) Psychology of Child Firesetting, 1987; assoc. editor Am. Jour. Family Therapy; sr. editor Family Therapy Jour., mem. editorial bd. Family Psychology Jour. Office: U Calif Psychiatry Dept 401 Parnassus San Francisco CA 94143

HATCHER, MARTHA OLIVIA TAYLOR (MRS. FRANK PRIDGEN HATCHER, SR.), biologist, educator; b. Birmingham, Ala., Feb. 17, 1920; d. Sanford Allia and Mary (McCullough) Taylor; B.S., Howard Coll., 1936-40; M.Ed. in Sci. Edn., U. Ga., 1966, Ed.D., 1973; tchrs. cert. Brenau Coll., 1964; m. Frank Pridgen Hatcher, Sr., Nov. 7, 1941; children—Frank Pridgen, Martha Elizabeth, Nancy Louise. Chief bacteriologist veterinary div. Ga. Dept. Agr., Atlanta, 1943-45; supr. surg. pathology lab. Jefferson Hillman Hosp., Med. Coll. Ala., Birmingham, 1945-46, research asst. in pathology, 1945-46; mgr. offices Fran Mar Farms, Inc., Gainesville, Ga., 1957-66; instr. biology Gainesville Jr. Coll., 1966-67, asst. prof. biology, 1967-74, assoc. prof., 1974-77, prof., 1977-82, acting chmn. div. natural scis. and maths., 1968-74, chmn., 1974-82; prof. biology, adminstrv. asst. Brenau Coll., 1982-87, dean student devel., 1986-87; accompanist music dept. Brenau Coll., Gainesville, 1959-61. Chmn. Gray Ladies Vol. Services, Gainesville chpt. ARC, 1957-62; sec. Yohah council Girl Scouts U.S.A., 1959-61; bd. dirs. Community Concert Assn. Gainesville, 1968-70; active Ed Dodd Mark Trail Found., 1986—, Lanier Orchestra League, 1984—, Pro Musica, 1984—, City of Gainesville. NSF sci. faculty fellow in microbiology, 1970-71. Mem. AAUP, AAAS, Am. Guild Organists, Am. Inst. Biol. Scis., Nat. Assn. Biology Tchrs., Assn. S.E. Biologists, Nat. Assn. Research Sci. Teaching, Ga. Acad. Sci., Nat. Sci. Tchrs. Assn., Am. Legion Aux. (pres. 1948-50), Am. Soc. Zoologists, Southeastern Assn. Educators of Tchrs. Sci. (pres. 1983-84; editor Newsletter), UDC (chpt. pres. 1949-51), Am. Soc. Microbiology, AAUW, Kappa Delta Pi, Alpha Epsilon Delta, Delta Kappa Gamma, Phi Delta Kappa, Phi Theta Kappa, Delta Zeta. Clubs: Music (pres. 1950-52), Federated Music (sec. 1957-58), Phoenix Soc., Pilot Internat. (pres. 1983-84) (Gainesville). Home: 840 Memorial Dr NE Gainesville GA 30501 Office: Brenau Coll PO Box 4668 Gainesville GA 30501

HATCHER, THOMAS FOUNTAIN, management consultant; b. Monroe, Mich., Dec. 26, 1931; s. Fountain H. and Cecilia E. (Boylan) H.; B.S., N.Y. U., 1968; m. Rosemary K. Downs, June 23, 1956; children—Mary Kathleen, Roberta Joan, Margaret Ann. With Equitable Life Assurance Soc., N.Y.C., 1955-71, mgr. learning systems, 1968-71; owner Thomas Hatcher Assos., Mpls., 1971-79; pres., owner Futures Unlimited, Inc., Mpls., 1979—. Mem. Nat. Speakers Assn., Am. Soc. Profl. Cons., Am. Soc. Tng. and Devel. Roman Catholic. Author: The Definitive Guide to Long Range Planning, 1981, Facilitator's Handbook for Planning, 1985. Home: 18525 Texas Ave Prior Lake MN 55372 Office: Futures Unlimited Inc 5200 W 73d St Minneapolis MN 55435

HATELEY, ENID ELLEN, real estate broker; b. Guayaquil, Ecuador, Mar. 22, 1925; came to U.S., 1944, naturalized, 1948; d. Harry Hawkes and Silia (Blanco) Shephard; B.S., Colegio Guayaquil, 1942; B.A., U. So. Calif., 1946; m. James Charles Hateley, II, Aug. 24, 1946; children—James Charles, Robert, Donald. Asst. credit mgr. Bank of Calif., 1946-49; with IBEC, 1950-51, E.H. Imports, 1952-60; trust adminstr. Bank of Am., 1973-75; broker Coldwell Banker, Los Altos, Calif., 1976-84; pres. City Resources, 1984—. Mem. Orange County Philharmonic Soc. Mem. Women in Commercial Real Estate, Beverly Hills Bd. of Realtors MLS, Trojan League. Republican. Roman Catholic. Clubs: Los Angeles Athletic, University. Home: 2 La Quinta Turtle Rock Pointe Irvine CA 92715 Office: City Resources PO Box 9935 Newport Beach CA 92658-9935

HATFIELD, MARK, U.S. senator; b. Dallas, Oreg., July 12, 1922; s. Charles Dolen and Dovie (Odom) H.; m. Antoinette Kuzmanich, July 8, 1958; children: Mark, Elizabeth, Theresa, Charles. A.B., Willamette U., 1943; A.M., Stanford U., 1948. Instr. Willamette U., 1949, dean students, asso. prof. polit. sci., 1950-56; mem. Oreg. Ho. of Reps., 1951-55, Oreg. Senate, 1955-57; sec. State of Oreg., 1957-59, gov., 1959-67; U.S. senator from Oreg. 1967—, ranking minority mem. appropriations com.; mem. energy and natural resources com., rules and adminstrn. com. Author: Not Quite So Simple, 1967, Conflict and Conscience, 1971, Between A Rock and A Hard Place, 1976; co-author: Amnesty: The Unsettled Question of Vietnam, 1973, Freeze! How You Can Help Prevent Nuclear War, 1982, The Causes of World Hunger, 1982. Served to lt. j.g. USN, 1943-45. Recipient numerous hon. degrees. Republican. Baptist. Office: Room SH-711 US Senate Washington DC 20510

HATHAWAY, AMOS TOWNSEND, retired naval officer, educator; b. Pueblo, Colo., Dec. 5, 1913; s. James Amos and Nina (North) H.; B.S., U.S. Naval Acad., 1935; postgrad. U.S. Naval War Coll., 1947-48; M.A. in Teaching, Duke U., 1965-66; m. Marianne Langdon Train, June 10, 1937 (dec. Dec. 1972); children—Joan Langdon, Marianne Train, Melinda North (dec.), Barbara Spencer, Sarah Townsend; m. Gay Johnson Blair, Jan. 2, 1979. Commd. ensign U.S. Navy, 1935, advanced through grades to capt., 1954; exec. officer, navigator destroyer minesweeper Zane, Guadalcanal, 1942; command destroyer Heermann, Battle off Samar, 1944; mem. faculty U.S. Naval Acad., 1945-47, U.S. Naval War Coll., 1951-53; mem. war staff Gen. MacArthur, Korea, 1948-50, writer theater logistic plan Inchon Landing, 1950; exec. officer cruiser St. Paul, 1950-51; command Destroyer Div. 92, 1953-54, command attack transport Okanogan, 1958-59; command cruiser Rochester, 1959-60; mem. joint staff Joint Chiefs of Staff, 1961-63, dir. logistic plans Office Chief of Naval Operations, 1963-65, ret., 1965; asst. prof. math. and computer sci. The Citadel, Charleston, S.C., 1966-79. Decorated Navy Cross, Legion of Merit (2), Bronze Star (2). Mem. Math. Assn. Am., U.S. Naval Acad. Alumni Assn., U.S. Naval Acad. Athletic Assn. (dir. 1945-47), U.S. Naval Inst., Kappa Delta Pi. Club: Army Navy (Washington). Home: 11 Sayle Rd Charleston SC 29407 also: PO Box 5463 Charlottesville VA 22905-0463

HATHAWAY, RICHARD DEAN, language professional, educator; b. Chillicothe, Ohio, Aug. 8, 1927; s. Dale and Edith (Hart) H.; m. Viola Hale, Apr. 16, 1978; children by previous marriage: Linda Hathaway Ellis, Bruce. A.B. summa cum laude, Oberlin Coll., 1949; A.M., Harvard U., 1952; Ph.D., Western Res. U., 1964. Exec. sec. New Eng. Fellowship of Reconciliation, Boston, 1953-55; instr. in English, Rensselaer Poly. Inst., Troy, N.Y., 1957-62; asst. prof. SUNY, New Paltz, 1962-65; asso. prof. SUNY, 1966-69, prof., 1970—; asso. prof. Millsaps Coll., Jackson, Miss., 1965-66. Author: Sylvester Judd's New England, 1981; contbr. poems to mags. and revs. Chair legis. com. SCLC Poor People's Campaign, 1968. Served with USNR, 1945-46. Mem. MLA, Phi Beta Kappa. Mem. Religious Soc. of Friends. Home: 11 Crescent Ln New Paltz NY 12561 Office: SUNY New Paltz NY 12561

HATKANAGALEKAR, MADHUKAR DATTATRAYA, English language educator; b. Sangli, Bombay, Maharashtra, India, Feb. 1, 1927; s. Dattatraya Khemrao and Mathubai Hatkanagalekar; m. Sudha M. Arwade; children: Pradeep, Revati, Vishrabdha. BA, Bombay U., 1948; MA, Poona U., 1950. Lectr. in English Willingdon Coll., Sangli, 1950-62, prof., head dept. English, 1962—; chmn. Maharashtra Sanitya Parishad, Sangli City, 1982—. Author: Sahityatil Adherekhite Katha: Rup Ani Parisar, 1981 (State and U. award 1983); editor Sahitya: Prerana Ani Pravarti Wangmayin Tantra Ani Shaili. Chmn. Young Men Edn. Soc. G.A. Arwade High Sch., Sangli City, 1980—. Recipient Best Coll. Tchr. award Maharashtra State, 1976. Mem. Bhartiya Dnyanpith. Hindu. Home: Kupwad Rd, Nirved, Vishrambaug, Sangli, Maharashtra 416 415, India Office: Balak Mandir, Vishrambag, Sangli City 416 415, India

HATOGAI, YASUO, engineering company executive; b. Osaka, Japan, Oct. 3, 1924; s. Kinzo and Fumiko (Sohda) H.; B.S., Osaka Tech. Coll., 1945; m. Toshiko Fujimoto, Dec. 18, 1956; children—Koichi, Sachiko. Chief engr. composite research Rolling Stock div. Kawasaki Heavy Industries, Ltd., Kobe Hyogoken, Japan, 1957-68; vice supt. Yashiro Kako KK., Hyogoken, Japan, 1968-72, dir., chief engr., 1972-88; cons. engr., 1988—; lectr. Kobe Tech. Coll., 1966-68. Mem. Japanese Soc. Material Sci., Japanese Soc. Reinforced Plastics, Soc. for Advancement of Material and Processing Engring. Editor various books and jours.; inventor of more than 10 items. Home: 3-15 5-chome Nishiokamoto Higashinadaku, Kobe 658 Japan also: 435 Yashiro Yaskirocho, Katogun, Hyogo 673-14, Japan Office: 506 Kita Yashirocho Katogun, Hyogoken 673-14 Japan

HATSCHEK, RUDOLF ALEXANDER, electronics company executive; b. Grafenberg, Austria, May 10, 1918; s. Rudolf Bernhard and Maria (Zischka) H.; m. Erika Lucia Satory, Jan. 10, 1946. Student, U. Prague, Czechoslovakia, 1936-40, U. Graz, Austria, 1945-46; Doctorate, U. Graz, 1946. Biochemist Interpharma AG, Prague, 1940-45; head of lab. Fux, Vienna, Austria, 1946-54; v.p. engring. BCF, Vienna, 1954-59; gen. mgr. instrumentation dept. AVL Engine Inst., Graz, 1959-65; v.p. research and devel. Vibro-Meter S.A., Fribourg, Switzerland, 1965-77; v.p. engring. div. ASULAB S.A., Neuchatel, Switzerland, 1978-83; cons. advanced piezo-electric applications in medicine, chronometry, automation and telecommunication; introduced piezo-electric aircraft-engine vibration monitoring. Mem. ASME, IEEE, Swiss Phys. Soc. Home: 3 Rue Vogt, CH1700 Fribourg Switzerland

HATTIS, ALBERT D., business executive, educator; b. Chgo., Oct. 12, 1929; s. Robert E. and Victoria C. (Kaufman) H.; m. Fern Hollobow; children: Kim Allyson Hattis Mercer, Kay Arlene Hattis Draper, John Elmore, Michael Allen, Sharon Beth. BS with highest distinction, Northwestern U., 1948, postgrad. in bus. adminstrn., 1950, DD (hon.), 1968. Vice-pres., sec.-treas. Robert E. Hattis Engrs., Inc., Hattis Service Co., Inc., Deerfield, Ill., 1950-73; v.p., sec.-treas. Servbest Foods, Inc., Highland Park, Ill., 1973-78; A.C. Equipment Co., 1978-80, Prime Packing Co., Inc., Haitian Am. Meat & Provision Co. SA, Spanish-Am. Foods, Inc.; pres., chief exec. officer Frigidmeats, Inc., Chgo., 1978-80; pres. Gits Enterprises, Inc., 1978-80, Double K Bar J Ranch, Inc., 1968—; prof. bus., holder Schwan Endowed Chair for Free Enterprise, S.W. State U., Marshall, Minn., 1981—; dir. S.W. Minn. Small Bus. Devel. Ctr., 1984-87, S.W. Minn. Homegrown Economy Local Cooperation Office, 1984—; chmn. Minn. Small Bus. Procurement Adv. Council, 1986-87. Exec. dir. The Lambs, Inc., Libertyville, Ill., 1980-81; trustee Orphans of the Storm Found., 1972-74, Cobblers Found., 1972-74; mem. adv. bd. Northwestern Psychiat. Inst., 1972-74; bd. dirs. Marshall Industries Found.; chmn. Marshall Planning Commn., 1982-85. Served to capt. USAF, 1946-48, 50-52. Mem. Assn. Pvt. Enterprise Edn., Internat. Council Small Bus., U.S. Assn. Small Bus. and Entrepreneurship, Minn. C. of C. (small bus. council 1984-87), Marshall Area C. of C. (bd. dirs.), Beta Gamma Sigma. Lodges: Lions, Rotary. Syndicated columnist, broadcaster Straight Talk, 900 newspapers, 500 radio stas. Home: 100 E Marshall St Marshall MN 56258 Office: AS-321 SW State U Marshall MN 56258

HATTON, JOHN ERNEST, brokerage house executive; b. Melbourne, Australia, Dec. 30, 1938; came to U.S., 1983; s. Ernest Roy and Jean Beryl Christina (Edney) H.; m. Elizabeth Anne Wilkinson, Nov. 19, 1960; children: Jacqueline Anne, Allison Jean, Fiona Jane. Grad., Adminstrv. Staff Coll., Henley, U.K., 1977. Mng. dir. Baillieu Bowring, Hobart, Tasmania, 1968-74; mng. dir. Baillieu Bowring, Melbourne, 1974-78, dep. chief exec. officer, 1978-80, chief exec. officer, 1980-83; chief, exec. officer Group IV Marsh & McLennan, Inc., N.Y.C., 1983-85, mng. dir. Pacific Basin ops., 1986—; Mem. Law Reform Rev. Council, Melbourne, 1976-77; assoc., bd. dirs. Australian Ins. Inst., 1972-73. Chmn. bd., trustee The Cheshire (Conn.) Acad., 1985—; commr. declarations and affidavits State Law Dept., Victoria, Australia, 1979—. Episcopalian. Clubs: Kew Golf (Victoria, Australia); Australian Club (Melbourne); Pine Orchard Yacht and Country (Branford, Conn.). Home: 15 Hart Ave Pine Orchard Branford CT 06405 Office: Marsh and McLennan Inc 1221 Avenue Americas New York NY 10020

HATTON, KAY SMITH, geologist; b. Henryetta, Okla., Dec. 22, 1937; d. Hayward Bennett and Mary Kathryn (Ford) Smith; m. Donal Clay Hatton, Mar. 21, 1964; 1 child, Karen Markley. B.S., U. Tulsa, 1960; postgrad., U. Colo., U. San Carlos, Lab. technician Scripps Inst. Oceanography, La Jolla, Calif., summer 1959; geol. librarian Exxon, Tulsa, 1960-62; lab. technician Amoco, Tulsa and Oklahoma City, 1962-66; field environmentalist N.Mex. Environ. Improvement Agy., Santa Fe, 1974-76; staff geologist IV, N.Mex. Energy and Minerals Dept., Santa Fe., 1976-87; dir. County Energy Resource Inventory. Author: (with others) New Mexico's Energy Resources, 1976-87; Oil and Gas Fields of the Four Corners Area, 1978; Geothermal Exploration and Research in New Mexico, 1980; Keystone Coal Industry Manual, 1983-87; Geothermal Resources Council Trans., Vol. 8, 1984; Interstate Oil Compact Commn., Vol. XXIII, No. 2, 1981; editor Ann. Resources Report. U. Tulsa scholar, 1955-60; U. San Carlos scholar 1960. Mem. Geol. Soc. Am., Am. Assn. Petroleum Geologists (cert.), Am. Inst. Profl. Geologists (cert.), AIME, N.Mex. Geol. Soc. (pres., mem. exec. com. 1983-87). Home: Rt 4 Box 58 A Santa Fe NM 87501 Office: New Mex Dept Energy Minerals and Natural Resources 525 Camino de los Marquez Santa Fe NM 87501

HATTORI, MASARU, manufacturing executive; b. May 5, 1919; married. Grad., Kyoto U., 1941. With Hitachi Shipbuilding and Engring. Co. Ltd., Japan, 1943—, exec. dir., from 1973; currently v.p. Hitachi Shipbuilding and Engring. Co. Ltd.; chmn. Hitachi Zosen Corp., Osaka, Japan. Home: 1-10 Horikiri-cho, Nishinomiya Japan Office: Hitachi Zosen Corp, 6-14 Edobori, 1-chome Nishi-ku, Osaka Japan *

HAU, MICHEL, historian, educator; b. Reims, France, July 16, 1943; s. Jean and Germaine (Appert) H.; m. Nicole Delcleve, Dec. 21, 1973; children: Stephane, Sophie. Maitrise, U. Paris, 1966; Diplome, Inst. Etudes Polit., Paris, 1966; Doctorat, U. Paris, 1985. Asst. U. Strasbourg, France, 1970-74, asst. prof. contemporary history, 1974—. Author: La Croissance de la Champagne, 1976, L'industrialisation de l'Alsace, 1987. Served with French Army, 1969-70. Mem. Soc. des Amis des Univs. Acad. Strasbourg (sec. gen. 1986—), Soc. Histoire Moderne etr Contemporaine. Roman Catholic. Home: 50 rue d'Altkirch, 67100 Strasbourg France Office: U Strasbourg 2, Palais Univ, 67000 Strasbourg France

HAU, THEODOR FRIEDRICH, psychoanalyst; b. Essen, Germany, Jan. 29, 1924; s. Maximilian and Frieda (Pruemm) H.; Diploma in Psychology, U. Goettingen (W. Ger.), 1953, Diploma of Physician, 1954, M.D., 1957; Diploma in Psychoanalysis, Inst. Psychoanalysis, Goettingen, 1960; Habilitation in Psychosomatic Medicine, U. Freiburg (W. Ger.), 1971; m. Elisabeth Maria Oelkers, Mar. 22, 1952; 1 dau., Cornelia. Intern, resident in psychiatry and internal medicine Univ. Clinic, Goettingen, 1953-55; asst. dept. Niedersaechsisches Landeskrankenhaus Tiefenbrunn, Goettingen, 1955-63, head dept., 1963-64; physician psychosomatic dept. U. Freiburg Internal Hosp., 1964-73, head dept., 1968-73; head Inst. for Psychoanalysis, Freiburg, 1965—; docent U. Freiburg, 1965-75, prof. psychosomatic medicine, 1975—; med. dir. Werner-Schwidder-Klinik für Psychosomatische Medizin, Bad Krozingen/Freiburg, 1979—. Served to lt. German Army, World War II. Mem. Deutsche Psychoanalytische Gesellschaft, Deutsche Gesellschaft fü r Psychotherapie, Psychosomatic und Tiefenpsychologie, Deutsche Gesellschaft fü r Psychologie, Allgemeine Aerztliche Gesellschaft für Psychotherapie, Am. Acad. Psychoanalysis. Clubs: Deutscher Jagdschutz-Verband, Freiburger Reit. Author: Frühkindliches Schicksal und Neurose, 1968; Psychoanalytische Perspektiven der Persoenlichkeit, 1979; contbr. numerous articles to profl. jours.; editor: Psychosomatische Medizin, 1973; Klinische Psychotherapie, 1975; (with H.G. Arnds) Psychoanalyse heute, 1977; (with S. Schindler) Praenatale u. Perinatale Psychosomatik, 1982; (with F. Wyatt) Therapeutische Anwendungen der Psychoanalyse, 1985; Psychosomatische Medizin, Krankheitsbilder, 1986, (with K.L. Messner) Psychoanalyse urd Klirische Psychotherapie, 1988. Home: 25 Becherwaldstrasse, 7802 Merzhausen/Freiburg Federal Republic of Germany Office: Inst of Psychoanalysis, 239 Kaiser-Joseph-Strasse, 7800 Freiburg Federal Republic of Germany

HAUCK, RICHARD HENRY, science educator; b. Harrisburg, Pa., Apr. 19, 1930; s. George Washington and Kathryn Irene (Daniels) H.; m. Gilda Tan, Jan. 19, 1977; children—Richard Daniels, Richelle Kathryn. B.S., Shippensburg State Coll., 1957; M.Sc., U. Bridgeport, 1983. Tchr. pub. schs., Los Angeles, 1957-59, Harrisburg, 1959-61, Conn., 1961-74, Morgan City, La., 1979-82, Dillsburg, Pa., 1984-85; instr. Prin. Tech. DCTS, Harrisburg, 1986-87; chemist research and devel. staff Gen. Dynamics Corp., 1964-65; cons. fed. edn. project LEARN; audio-visual and ednl. closed circuit TV dir. Montville-Groton Pub. Sch. (Conn.), 1965-69; pres. Ednl. Research Assocs., Old Saybrook, Conn., 1969-79, Morgan City, La., 1979-82, Mechanicsburg, Pa., 1982-85; instr. chemistry and physics U.S. Nat. Def. Cadet Corps, New Bloomfield, Pa., 1982-84; v.p. Hauck Bros. Ltd., Mechanicsburg, Pa., 1979—. Editor: Raintree Illustrated Sci. Ency., 1978—. Bd. dirs. World Monies Mus. Served with USAF, 1952-53, U.S. Army, 1982-84. Mem. AAAS, NEA, Nat. Sci. Tchrs. Assn., Pa. State Ednl. Assn., Gt. Eastern Numis. Assn., New Eng. Numis. Assn., N.Y. Acad. Scis., Conn. Ednl. Media Assn. (founding mem.), Am. Legion, Mensa. Republican. Episcopalian. Lodges: Lions, Masons.

HAUER, ANN, educator; b. Braddock, N.D., Sept. 19, 1942; d. Ray Joseph and Mildred Elizabeth (Kippes) Splonskowski; m. Jim Hauer, June 26, 1965; children: Todd, Missy. BA, Mary Coll., 1969; MA in Ednl. Adminstrn., U. N.D., 1981. Cert. elem. prin. Elem. tchr. Richholt Sch., Bismarck, N.D., 1970-74, tchr., asst. prin., 1974-76; tchr. Roosevelt Sch., Bismarck, 1976—; elem. rep. Bismarck Pub. Schs. Curriculum Steering Com., developer curriculum metrics, nutrition, career edn., chmn. dist. social studies standing com., chmn. social studies curriculum com. Tchr. rep. N.D. adv. bd. Project Wild. Recipient Tchr. Yr award C. of C., 1987. Mem. NEA, N.D. Edn. Assn., Bismarck Edn. Assn. (govt. relations com., elem. negotiator, profl. rights and responsibilities chmn., pres. 1983-84, 1987—, health curriculum evaluation and standing com.), Bismarck C. of C. (Tchr. of Yr. award 1987, edn. com.), Phi Delta Kappa (v.p. 1985-86), Delta Kappa Gamma. Roman Catholic. Lodge: Elks. Home: 2600 Mercury Ln Bismarck ND 58501 Office: 613 Ave B West Bismarck ND 58501

HAUGHEY, CHARLES JAMES, Irish political leader; b. Castlebar, County Mayo, Ireland, Sept. 16, 1925; s. John and Sarah Ann (McWilliams) H.; B.Commerce, Univ. Coll., Dublin; B.L., Kings Inns, Dublin; m. Maureen Lemass, Sept. 18, 1951; children: Eimear, Conor, Ciaran, Sean. Ptnr., Haughey Boland & Co., chartered accts., 1950-60; called to bar, 1948; bloodstock breeder, 1950—; mem. Dublin Corp., 1953-55; mem. Irish Parliament for Dublin (Artane) Constituency, 1957—; parliamentary sec. to minister justice, 1960-61; minister for justice, 1961-64, minister for agr., 1964-66, minister for fin., 1966-70; chmn. Irish Parliamentary com. on EEC, 1973-77; minister for health and social welfare, 1977-79; prime minister Ireland, 1979-81, 82, 87—; leader opposition party, 1981-82, 82-87; pres. Fianna Fail Party, 1979—. Fellow Inst. Chartered Accts. Ireland; Mem. Royal Hibernian Acad. Arts (hon.). Clubs: St. Stephens Green, Ward Union Hunt. Address: Office of Prime Minister, Upper Merion St, Dublin 2 Ireland *

HAUMONT, DANIEL VICTOR, air transport industry executive; b. Clichy, France, Mar. 8, 1942; s. Adrienne-Andree H.; m. Monique Marie-France Hapchette, Oct. 25, 1969; children: Christophe, Pascal, Nicolas. License en scis., U. Paris, 1965. CPA, France. Tchr. math. Pontoise, France, 1963-67, 69-72; systems analyst Burroughs France, Paris, 1969-72; engr. EDP, project mgr., cons. mgr., services promotion mgr. SITA, Neuilly, France, 1975-85; cons. Telematique Cons., Montgé, France, 1985; mgr. air transport McDonnell Douglas, St. Cloud, France, 1986—. Mcpl. councillor Town of Montgé-en-Goële, 1977-83; officer Republican Party, 1978—. Served to lt. French Air Force, 1967-68. Mem. Centre Perfectionnement aux Affaires. Roman Catholic. Club: French Res. Officers (Meaux) (pres.). Home: 3 Rue Simonard, 77230 Montgé-en-Goële France Office: McDonnell Douglas, Bureaux de la Collins, Saint Cloud, 92213 Hauts de Seine France

HAUPTMAN, HERBERT AARON, mathematician, educator, researcher; b. N.Y.C., Feb. 14, 1917; s. Israel and Leah (Rosenfeld) H.; m. Edith Citrynell; children—Barbara, Carol Fullerton. B.S. in Math., CCNY, N.Y.C., 1937; M.A., Columbia U., N.Y.C., 1939; Ph.D., U. Md., College Park, 1955. Statistician U.S. Census Bur., 1940-42; civilian instr. electronics and radar U.S. Army Air Force, 1942-43, 46-47; physicist, mathematician Naval Research Lab., 1947-70, head math. physics br., 1965-67, acting supt. math. and info. scis. div., 1967-68, head applied math. br., 1968-69, head math. staff, 1969-70; research prof. biophys. scis. SUNY, Buffalo, 1970—; prof. math. U. Md., 1956-70; head math. biophysics lab. Med. Found. of Buffalo Inc., 1970-72, dep. research dir., 1972, exec. v.p., research dir., 1972-85, pres., research dir., 1986-88, pres., 1988—; cons. and lectr. in field. Contbr. chpts. to books, articles to profl. jours. Bd. dirs. Med. Found., Buffalo. Served with USNR, 1943-46. Recipient numerous prizes for excellence in math. including co-recipient Nobel Prize in Chemistry, 1985. Fellow Washington Acad. Scis.; mem. U.S. Acad. Scis., Nat. Acad. Scis., Endocrine Soc., Am. Math. Soc., Am. Phys. Soc., Am. Crystallographic Assn., Math. Assn. Am., AAAS, Sigma Xi. Clubs: Cosmos (Washington); Saturn (Buffalo). Office: Med Found of Buffalo 73 High St Buffalo NY 14203

HAUSAFUS, JOHN EARL, architect; b. Marshalltown, Iowa, Dec. 8, 1946; s. William Wayne and Margaret A. (Hastie) H.; m. Cheryl Ann Olmstead, May 26, 1973; children: Michael Todd, Tara Ann. AS, Marshalltown Community Coll., 1970; BArch, Iowa State U., 1973. Archtl. draftsman Englebrecht/Rice Architects, Des Moines, 1973-75; asst. prof. architecture Smith-Voorhees-Jensen, Des Moines, Iowa, 1975-80; project architects J.E.H. Architects, Des Moines, 1980-84, FEH Assocs. Inc., Des Moines, 1985-87; assoc. project architect KGRA Architects, Engrs, Planners, Inc., Des Moines, 1987—. Chmn. archtl. adv. com. City of Des Moines, 1986—. Mem. Constrn. Specifications Inst. (reg. award chmn. 1983-85, regional editor chmn. 1986-87 editor cen. Iowa chpt. 1978-82, pres. 1984-86, regional award 1983, 84, 85, Nat. award 1984, 85). Clubs: Bohemian, Cosmopolitan Internat. Des Moines (pres. 1982-83). Home: 3700 Rollins Ave Des Moines IA 50312 Office: KGRA Architects Engrs Planners Inc 3030 Ruan Ctr Des Moines IA 50309

HAUSER-DANN, JOYCE ROBERTA, marketing professional; b. N.Y.C.; d. Abraham and Helen (Lesser) Frankel; B.A., SUNY, 1976; Ph.D., Union Grad. Sch., 1987; m. Asher Dann, Sept. 7, 1987. children—Mitchell, Mark, Ellen; stepchildren: Laurence, Michael. Editor, Art in Flowers, 1955-58; pres. Joyce Advt., 1958-65; partner Hauser & Assocs., Pub. Relations, 1966-75; dir. broadcasting Bildersee Pub. Relations, 1973-75; pres. Hauser & Assocs., Inc., Pub. Relations, 1975-78, Hauser-Roberts, Inc., Pub. Relations/Mktg., N.Y.C., 1978-85, Mktg. Concepts & Communications Inc., N.Y.C., 1985—; moderator show Perceptions, Sta. WEVD, 1975-77, Speaking of Health, WNBC, 1977—, 97 Health Line, Sta. WYNY, 1980-83, Conversations with Joyce Hauser, Sta. WNBC, 1975-86, What's on Your Mind, Sta. WYNY, 1983-84, Talk-Net, 1983—; entertainment critic Sta. WNBC, 1986—; instr. Baruch Coll., CCNY, 1980-85; asst. prof. NYU, 1987— . Mem. Citywide Health Adv. Council on Sch. Health, 1970—, treas., 1980—; mem. adv. bd. degree programs NYU Sch. Continuing Edn.; mediator/artitrator Victim Services Agy., 1986-87, Inst. Mediation & Conflict Resolution, 1985-86. Named one of 10 Top Successful Women, Cancer Soc., 1976; recipient Professionalism award Sta. WNBC, 1980. Mem. AFTRA, Am. Women in Radio and TV (corr. sec. 1973, chmn. coll. women in broadcasting 1974), Acad. Family Mediators, Soc. Profl. Dispute Resolutions. Contbg. editor Alive, 1976-77. Home: 115 E 82d St New York NY 10028 Office: 20 E 53d St New York NY 10022

HAUSMAN, HOWARD, electronics executive; b. N.Y.C., July 4, 1945; s. Edward A. and Bella (Bloom) H.; m. Marsha Stone, Aug. 24, 1968; children: Lawrence Stuart, Bradley Russel. BSEE, Poly. Inst. N.Y., 1967, MSEE, 1971. Computer programmer Harry Kahn Assocs., Great Neck, N.Y., 1965-67; engr. Airborne Instruments Lab., Deer Park, N.Y., 1967-72; dept. head Miteq Inc., Hauppauge, N.Y., 1972-81; pres. Labred Electronics Corp., Bohemia, N.Y., 1981—; mem. tech. cons. com. 2d supervisory dist. Bd. Coop. Ednl. Services, Suffolk County, N.Y., 1986—; cons. Arista Devices, Inc., Ronkonkoma, N.Y., 1974-81; instr. Hofstra U., Hempstead, N.Y., 1971-78; lectr. Poly. U., Farmingdale, N.Y., 1978—. Contbr. articles to profl. jours. Mem. IEEE, Nat. Contracts Mgmt. Assn., AAAS, N.Y. Acad. Scis. Home: 4 Mark Ln Farmingville NY 11738 Office: Labred Electronics Corp 170 Wilbur Pl Bohemia NY 11716

HAUSMAN, ROBERT, dermatopathologist; b. Takengon, Acin, Indonesia, June 19, 1914; s. Pawel Rudolph and Geertruida Roosje (Stap) H.; m. Helen B. Rasch, Aug. 19, 1944; children: David P., Benson A. Doctorandus, U. Leiden, The Netherlands; MD, U. Amsterdam, The Netherlands; MS in Pathology, Baylor U.; PhD in Medicine, Free U., Amsterdam. Med. examiner Bexar County, San Antonio, 1956-67; prof. forensic medicine U. Calif., San Francisco, 1963-65; dep. chief med. examiner Med. Examiner's Office City of N.Y., N.Y.C., 1968-70; practice medicine specializing in pathology Ft. Worth, 1970-71, Utrecht, The Netherlands, 1972-74; pathologist Acad. Hosp. U. of Amsterdam, 1974-81; pathologist Acad. Hosp. Free Univ., Amsterdam, 1981-83, cons., 1983—. Contbr. articles to profl. jours. Served to 1st lt. Indonesian M.C., 1945-47. Mem. Am. Soc. Clin. Pathologist. Home: Wilhelminapark 16, 3581 NC Utrecht The Netherlands

HAUSMANN, WERNER KARL, pharmaceutical executive; b. Edigheim, Germany, Mar. 9, 1921; came to U.S., 1948, naturalized, 1954; s. Carl and Johanna (Sprenger) H.; m. Helen Margaret Vas, Sept. 29, 1949; 1 child, Gregory. M.S. in Chem. Engring., Swiss Fed. Inst. Tech., 1945, D.Sc., 1947. Cert. quality engr. Research fellow U. London, 1947-48; research assoc. Rockefeller Inst. Med. Research, N.Y.C., 1949-57; research group leader Lederle Labs., Pearl River, N.Y., 1957-66; assoc. dir. quality control Ayerst Labs., Rouses Point, N.Y., 1966-71; dir. quality control Stuart Pharms., Pasadena, Calif., 1971-74; dir. quality assurance, analytical research and devel. Adria Labs., Inc., Columbus, Ohio, 1974-84; cons. Columbus, Ohio, 1985-86, San Diego, 1986—. Contbr. articles to profl. jours. Pres. Ednl. TV Assn., 1970-71; radiation officer CD, 1962-66; scoutmaster, 1942-45. Served to 1st lt. Swiss Army, 1939-46. Fellow Royal Soc. Chemistry, Chem. Soc. London, Am. Inst. Chemists, N.Y. Acad. Scis., AAAS, Am. Soc. Quality Control (chmn. Columbus sect.); mem. Acad. Pharm. Scis., Am. Soc. Biol. Chemists, Am. Chem. Soc., Am. Soc. Microbiology, Parenteral Drug Assn. Presbyterian. Office: 4332 Post Rd San Diego CA 92117

HAUSPURG, ARTHUR, utilities company executive; b. N.Y.C., Aug. 27, 1925; s. Otto and Charlotte (Braul) H.; m. Catherine Dunning Mackay, July 26, 1947; children: Peter R., David A., Daniel L. B.S.E.E., Columbia U., 1945, M.S.E.E., 1947. Asst. v.p. Am. Electric Power Corp., 1968; v.p. Consol. Edison Co. N.Y., Inc., N.Y.C., 1969-73, sr. v.p., 1973-75, exec. v.p., chief operating officer, 1975, chief operating officer, 1975-81, pres., 1975—, chief exec. officer, 1981—, chmn., 1982—, also dir.; dir. Prudential-Bache High Yield Fund, Inc., Prudential-Bache High Yield Mcpls., Inc., Prudential-Bache Tax-Free Money Fund, Inc., Prudential-Bache Growth Opportunity Fund, Inc., Prudential-Bache Govt. Securities Trust; Bd. dirs. Com. for Econ. Devel., Regional Plan Assn., N.Y.C. Partnership, Econ. Devel. Council N.Y.C., Electric Power Research Inst., Cen. Park Conservancy. Contbr. articles to profl. jours. Bd. dirs. N.Y. Zool. Soc. Served with USNR, 1943-46. Fellow IEEE; mem. Nat. Acad. Engring., Council Fgn. Relations (dir.), Chamber Commerce and Industry (bd. dirs.). Office: Consol Edison Co of NY Inc 4 Irving Pl New York NY 10003 •

HAUT, GUILLERMO ENRIQUE, biology educator; b. Buenos Aires, July 17, 1951; s. Federico Guillermo Carlos and Emma Maria (Frahm) H.; m. Elsa Meinazdi, Apr. 11, 1979 (div. Apr. 1981); m. Florencia Sofia del Pino, Aug. 8, 1982. B, Colegio Nat. NG Manuel Belgrano, Buenos Aires, 1978; M in Biol. Scis., Buenos Aires U., 1984. Chmn. biol. chemistry dept. U. Buenos Aires, 1984-86, chmn. animal physiology dept., 1985—, auxiliar docente de ira, 1988—. Contbr. articles to profl. jours. Pres. Argentine's Youth Hostel Assn., Buenos Aires, 1984-86. Mem. Assn. Argentina Ciencias Naturales. Partido Justicialista. Roman Catholic. Home: Argerich 4035, 3d Dept, Capital Federal, 1419 Buenos Aires Argentina Office: Ciudad U, Dept Ciencias Biologicas, 1428 Nunez Argentina

HAUZINGER, HEINZ-HELLMUTH, personnel executive; b. Jestetten, Federal Republic Germany, Jan. 21, 1944; s. Willibald and Gertrud Julie (Fink) H.; m. Carmen Michelle Castro, July 17, 1969; children: Katja Maria, Philipp Edouardo Willibald. Grad. high sch., 1963. With various banking instns. Federal Republic Germany, 1963-68; treas. Schoeller Textil, Switzerland, 1968-69; trainer personnel Union Bank Switzerland, St. Gallen, 1969-71; head of tng. Credit Swiss, St. Gallen, 1971-79; dir., mgr. Inst. für Handelskunde, St. Gallen, 1979-85; cons. banking Suter & Suter AG, Zurich, Switzerland, 1983-85; head personnel tng. and devel. Shell Switzerland, Zurich, 1985—; cons., dir. IKU Inst. d'Etudes Comml., St. Gallen, 1985—. Author, editor various banking tng. books. Mem. Swiss Mgmt. Assn., Zentralstelle für betriebliche Ausbildung. Mem. Liberal Party. Roman Catholic Club: Alpin. Home: Dorfstrasse 131, CH-8802 Kilchberg-Zurich Switzerland Office: Shell Switzerland, Bederstrasse 66, CH-8802 Zurich Switzerland

HAVELKA, THOMAS EDWARD, choral director; b. Wheeling, W.Va., July 10, 1947; s. Alfred and Marilyn Eleanor (Hays) H.; m. Susan Kay Wilson, June 16, 1973; children: Trevor Hays, Havaleh Ann. BFA, Ohio U., 1969, MusM, 1975. Cert. tchr., Ohio. Music instr., chmn. fine arts dept. Bellaire (Ohio) Bd. Edn., 1969-74; choir dir., chmn. music dept. Coshocton (Ohio) City Bd. Edn., 1975—; founder Coshocton City Schs. Arts Festival, 1985—; state rep. All Am. Youth Honor Musicians, Miami, Fla., 1970—; asst. condr. All Am. Youth Honor Choir, 1970, 77-78, condr., 1980—; adjudicator Internat. Choir Fest., Mexico City, 1978, Dulcimer Festival, Roscoe Village, Ohio, 1986—, Show Choir Competition, Lancaster, Ohio, 1986, Show Choir Festival, Portsmouth, Ohio, 1986. Composer: Piece for String Quartet, 1974, (choral) Offertorium from Missae Requiem Brevis, 1974, Bless Ye the God of All, 1975. Mem. Big Bros./Big Sisters Assn., Columbus, 1970—; dist. exec., chmn. bd. Boy Scouts Am., Coshocton, 1979-80; sect. leader, asst. accompanist Coshocton Community Choir, 1984—; active various theater groups, Coshocton and Wheeling, 1974—; singer St. Matthew's Episcopal Ch., Wheeling, W. Va., 1973-75; asst. organist Grace United Meth. Ch., Coshocton, 1986—. Recipient awards from Mayors of Malaga, Spain, 1981, Agnani and Fuiggi, Italy, 1984 and Paris, 1985, award of Merit Coshocton City Schs., 1984. Mem. Ohio Edn. Assn., Ohio Music Edn. Assn. (asst. contest chmn., chmn. county membership com. 1977-78), Internat. Soc. for Music Edn., Internat. Fedn. for Choral Music, Am. Guild Organists, Am. Choral Dirs. Assn., Ohio Choral Dirs. Assn. (chmn. county membership 1978-79), Coshocton City Edn. Assn. (sec. 1984-85), Am. Film Inst., Met. Opera Guild, NEA, Music Educators Nat. Conf., Soc. Research in Music Edn., Soc. Music Tchr. Edn., Nat. Fedn. Interscholastic Music Assn., Kappa Kappa Psi, Phi Mu Alpha, Pi Kappa Lambda. Republican. Methodist. Home: 1628 Woodland Dr Coshocton OH 43812 Office: Coshocton High Sch 1205 Cambridge Rd Coshocton OH 43812

HAVEN, THOMAS KENNETH, financial consultant; b. Muskegon, Mich., June 27, 1906; s. Ole B. and Minnie B. (Larson) H.; m. Marion L. Reading, Dec. 11, 1935; children: Carl, Donna, Madge, Daniel. A.B., U. Mich., 1928, M.B.A., 1929, Ph.D., 1940. Research assoc. Bus. Adminstrn. Sch., U. Mich., Ann Arbor, 1929-36, grad. teaching staff, summer 1940; prof. fin. Sch. Bus. Adminstrn. U. Mich., Ann Arbor, 1970-74, prof. fin. for exec. devel. program, 1973; with Watling, Lerchen & Co., Detroit, 1936-42; v.p. fin. Reichhold Chems., Inc., Detroit, 1942-47, exec. v.p., 1947-54; v.p. Detrex Corp., 1954, Beaver Precision Products, Inc., 1957-65; pres. Pioneer Fin. Co., Mobile Homes Life Ins. Co., 1958-66; founding dir., v.p. Detroit Med. Ctr. Devel. Corp., 1961-65; cons. fin. Malaya, 1966-67, Banco de Desarrollo (formerly Financiera Dominicana S.A.), Dominican Republic, 1968—; rep. bd. dirs. Wabash Portland Cement Co., Dayton, Ohio, 1940-44; officer, bd. dirs. various cos. Can., Japan, Australia, Eng., Fed. Republic of Germany and France, 1943-76; founding bd. dirs. Ferndale Nat. Bank, 1948-58; adv. dir. Comerica (formerly Detroit Bank and Trust Co.), 1958-66; cons. fin. and econs. DuPont Corp., 1974-79, Levi Strauss, 1981; lectr. on fin. Govt. Australia, 1965; bd. dirs. Detrex Chem. Industries, Inc. Author: Investment Banking Under the Securities and Exchange Commission, 1940. Past pres., trustee Grace Hosp.; trustee Harper-Grace Detroit; treas., vice chmn., chmn. Cranbrook Ednl. Community, 1963-76. Mem. Delta Sigma Pi. Clubs: Circumnavigators, Bloomfield Hills Country, Detroit, Pres.'s U. Mich, Century (Oakland U.). Home: 3675 Ward Point Dr Orchard Lake MI 48033

HAVENS, TIMOTHY MARKLE, investment advisory firm executive; b. New Haven, Oct. 20, 1945; s. Walter Paul and Ida Markle (Hessenbruch) H.; m. Margaret Jean Stockdale, Nov. 1, 1969; children—Paul Markle, David Stockdale. B.A., U. Pitts., 1969. V.p. Drexel Burnham Lambert, Phila., 1970-79; pres. Newbold's Asset Mgmt., Phila., 1979—; bd. dirs. Federal Union, Washington, 1982—, Game Conservation Internat., San Antonio; mem. adv. bd., Phila. Coll. Physicians; trustee Independence Hall Assn., Phila. Served with USAR, 1968-74. Republican. Episcopalian. Clubs: Racquet (Phila.); Merion Cricket (Haverford, Pa.). Avocation: hunting. Home: 418 Fishers Rd Bryn Mawr PA 19010 Office: Newbold's Asset Mgmt 1500 Walnut St Philadelphia PA 19102

HAVERS, LORD MICHAEL (LORD (ROBERT) MICHAEL (OLDFIELD) HAVERS), government chancellor; b. London, Mar. 10, 1923; s. Cecil Robert Havers; m. Carol Elizabeth Snelling, Sept. 3, 1949; children: Philip, Nigel. MA, Cambridge U., 1948. Atty. 1948-87; Queen's counsel Brit. Govt., 1964-87, solicitor gen., 1972-74, atty. gen., 1979-87, lord chancellor, 1987—; Mem. Parliament from Wimbledon, Eng., 1970-87. Served as lt. Royal Navy Vol. Res., 1941-46, ETO, NATOUSA, CBI, MTO, U.S.A. Conservative. Mem. Ch. of England. Office: Admiralty House, Whitehall, London SW1, England also: Lord Chancellor, House of Lords, London England

HAVILAND, CAMILLA KLEIN, lawyer; b. Dodge City, Kans., Sept. 13, 1926; d. Robert Godfrey and Lelah (Luther) Klein; m. John Bodman Haviland, Sept. 7, 1957. A.A., Monticello Coll., 1946; B.A., Radcliffe Coll., 1948; J.D., Kans. U., 1955. Bar: Kans. 1955. Assoc. Calver & White, Wichita, Kans., 1955-56; sole practice, Dodge City, 1956—; probate, county and juvenile judge Ford County (Kans.), 1955-77; mem. Jud. Council Com. on Probate and Juvenile Law. Mem. adv. bd. Salvation Army, U. Kans. Sch. Religion. Recipient Nathan Burkan award ASCAP, 1955. Mem. Ford County Bar Assn. (pres. 1980), S.W. Kans. Bar Assn. (pres. 1968), Kans. Bar Assn., ABA, C. of C., Order of Coif, PEO, Phi Delta Delta. Democrat. Episcopalian. Clubs: Prairie Dunes Country (Hutchinson, Kans.); Soroptimists. Contbr. articles to profl. jours. Home: 2006 E Lane Dodge City KS 67801 Office: 203 W Spruce Box 17 Dodge City KS 67801

HAVILAND, LEONA, librarian; b. Stamford, Conn., Nov. 10, 1916; d. Howard Brush and Ada Grace (Jewell) Haviland; B.S., U. Ala., 1940; M.S., U. Ill., 1951; postgrad. Columbia, 1943, 56-60; m. Warren John Burke, Sept. 10, 1973. Jr. asst. Ferguson Library, Stamford, 1936-37, summers 1938-39, sr. asst., 1940-44; student asst. U. Ala., 1937-40; asst. to cataloguer U.S. Nat. Mus. Library, Washington, 1944-48; librarian Arts and Industries Mus., Smithsonian Instn., Washington, 1948-50; reference librarian U.S. Mcht. Marine Acad., Kings Point, N.Y., 1952-77. Mem. council YWCA, Washington, 1945-47. Mem. A.L.A., Spl. Libraries Assn. (past group membership chmn.), L.I. Hist. Soc., N.Y. Geneal. and Biog. Soc., Smithsonian Assos., South Street Seaport Mus., Alpha Beta Alpha, Alpha Lambda Delta. Home: 809 Pennsylvania Ave Saint Cloud FL 32769

HAVILLAND, BEN, lawyer, policy specialist; b. Charleston, W.Va., Mar. 11, 1924; s. Benjamin Charles and Elizabeth (Battreall) Grosscup; A.B., Wittenberg U., 1948; J.D., U. Wash., 1953; m. Michele Drapeau, Sept. 16, 1950; children—Stephen John, Lance. Admitted to Wash. State bar, 1954, D.C. bar, 1973, U.S. Supreme Ct. bar; practice law, 1954—; prof. bus. law Palomar Coll., San Diego County, Calif., 1956-59; adj. prof. Internat. Sch. Law, Washington, 1975; specialist policy and procedures, program mgr. fgn. mil. sales U.S. Air Force, Washington, 1967—. Active, Boy Scouts Am. Served with USNR, 1942-45, USMCR, 1945-59, maj. ret. Decorated Peruvian Cross Aero. Merit; recipient Outstanding Service to Conservation award Hartford Ins. Co., 1973; Silver Beaver award Boy Scouts Am.; hon. pilot, Guatemala. Mem. Alpha Phi Omega, Phi Sigma Alpha, Beta Theta Pi. Episcopalian. Author: Earthquakes and Cities, 1950. Home: 4214 River Rd NW Washington DC 20016 Office: Hdqrs USAF (PRI) Washington DC 20330

HAW, DAVID WILLIAM MARTIN, orthopedic surgeon; b. Batticoloa, Ceylon, Mar. 17, 1926; s. Albert and Kathleen Ellen (Turk)H.; m. Marjorie Elise Hetherington, Mar. 27, 1948; children: Judith Mary, Catherine Elise, Roger John David, Sally Jane, Marcus Peter. B.Sc., Leeds U., 1948, M.B.Ch.B., 1951, E.R.C.S., Eng. 1960. House surgeon Leeds Gen. Infiramry, 1956-57; sr. house surgeon Manchester Royal Infirmary, 1957-58; registrar surgeon, Ashton Under Lyne, 1958-59; sr. house officer Royal Nat. Orthopedic Hosp., Stanmoor, 1959-60; regisrar orthopedic surgeon Lord Mayor Trelaors Orthopedic Hosp., 1960-61; registrar orthopedics Guys Hosp., 1961-63; sr. registrar orthopedics Leeds Regional Bd., Hull, Bradford, Leeds, 1963-65; cons. orthopedic surgeon York Dist. Hosp., 1965—. Demonstrator in anatomy Leeds U., 1955-56. Served to lt. RAF, 1952-55. Fellow Royal Coll. Surgeons Eng., Brit. Orthopedic Assn.; mem. Ridings Orthopedic Club (pres. 1966), Holdsworth Orthopedic Club (sec. 1978-85). Conservative. Methodist. Clubs: Lord Mayor Treloars and Gauvain Dining; Thirk and Malton Conservative Dining (chmn. 1978-81); No. Counties Vets. Athletic (pres. 1975-77). Rep. Eng. in English Univs. Cross-country race (champion 3 mi. 1947). Avocations: Skiing; oil painting; gardening. Home: East Court, Shipton By Beningbrough, York YO6 1AR, England Office: York Dist Hosp, Wigginton Rd, York England

HAW, JOHN RICHARD, quality assurance manager; b. Springs, Transvaal, S Africa, June 21, 1941; s. William and Magdalena (Hewson) H.; m. Johanna Freda du Preez, Aug. 3, 1963; children: Daryl Bruce, Wayne Ronald. Student, Tech. Coll. of South Africa, 1960-63. Cert. Auditing Quality, Engring. Mgmt. Services, Joahhanesburg, 1976, Quality Programs, Stat-A-Matrix USA, Johannesburg, 1974, Mech./ Structural Draughtman, Watt and Wilkenson, Springs, 1965. Cost and estimating prodn. mgr. Watt and Wilkinson, Ltd., Springs, 1965-67; works mgr. Watt and Wilkinson, Ltd., 1969-73; asst. to works dir. D.C. Vortex Ltd., Springs, 1967-69; estimating and planning dept. mgr. Bresco Engring., Brakpan, S. Africa, 1973-74; quality control mgr. Cementation Engring. & Forging, Boksburg, S. Africa, 1974-79; materials mgr. Catronics Cables Ltd., Springs, 1980-81; quality assurance mgr. Catronics Cables Ltd., 1981-82; divisional quality assurance mgr. Aberdare Calbes Ltd., Johannesburg, 1982—. Group Chmn., Boy Scouts of S. Africa, Nigel, 1982—. Served with the S. African Army, 1987—. Mem. S. African Inst. Draughtsman, S. African Soc. Quality Control, Prodn. Mgmt. Inst., Associated Sci. and Tech. Socs. of S. Africa, Am. Soc. for Quality Control. Anglican. Club: E. Rand Hiking. Lodge: Golden Reef Alomner. Home: 3 Craib Ave, PO Box 175, Dunnottar Transvaal 1590, Republic of South Africa Office: Aberdare Cables Ltd, PO Box 1679, Edenvale Transvaal 1610, Republic of South Africa

HAWAWINI, GABRIEL ALFRED, finance educator; b. Alexandria, Egypt, Aug. 29, 1947; arrived in France, 1965; s. Alfred Goubrane and Renee (Eddi) H.; m. Marci Serene Garber, July 16, 1977; children: Alfred, Alana. MS in Chem. Engring., Ecole Nat. Superieure de Chimie de Toulouse, France, 1972; MBA, NYU, 1974, PhD, 1977. Asst. prof. fin. NYU, N.Y.C., 1977-79; assoc. prof. CUNY, 1979-81; prof., head dept. fin. European Inst. Bus. Adminstrn., Fontainebleau, France, 1981-87, Yamaichi prof. fin., assoc. dean, dir. Euro-Asia Ctr., 1988—; vis. prof. fin. Wharton Sch., U. Pa., Phila., 1987-88. Author: European Equity Markets, 1984, Mandatory Financial Disclosure and Capital Market Equilibrium, 1987; editor: Finance, 1985—; contbr. over 50 articles to profl. jours. Recipient Money Marketeers Internat. award NYU, 1975, Presdl. award Baruch Coll., CUNY, 1982, Helen Kardon Moss Anvil Wharton Sch., 1988. Mem. Am. Fin. Assn., Am. Econ. Asns., French Fin. Assn. (v.p. 1985—). Home: 7 Bernard de Clairvaux, 75003 Paris France Office: European Inst Bus Adminstrn, Boulevard de Constance, 77305 Fontainebleau France

HAWE, DAVID LEE, consultant; b. Columbus, Ohio, Feb. 19, 1938; s. William Doyle and Carolyn Mary (Hassig) H.; m. Margret J. Hoover, Apr. 15, 1962; children—Darrin Lee, Kelly Lynn. Project mgr. ground antenna systems W.D.L. Labs., Philco Corp., 1960-65; credit mgr. for Western U.S., Am. Hosp. Supply Corp., Burbank, Calif., 1965-74; owner, mgr. Hoover Profl. Equipment Co., contract health equipment co., Guasti, Calif., 1974-75; pres. Baslor Care Services, owners convalescent homes, Santa Ana, Calif., 1975-80; pres. Application Assocs., 1980—; bd. dirs., chmn. of bd. Xiron, Inc., 1984—; dir. Medisco Co., Casa Pacifica, Broadway Assocs. Bd. dirs. Santa Ana Community Convalescent Hosp., 1974-79, pres., 1975-79. Served with USN, 1954-56. Lic. real estate broker, Calif. Mem. Am. Vacuum Soc. Republican. Roman Catholic. Home: 18082 Hallsworth Circle Villa Park CA 92667

HAWK, ROBERT STEVEN, library administrator; b. Athens, Ohio, June 6, 1949; s. John Paul and Mary Lois (Briggs) H.; m. Constance Lynne Jodoin, June 16, 1979. B.S., Wright State U., 1971; M.S. in L.S., U. Ky., 1974. Library asst. Dayton and Montgomery County Pub. Library, Dayton, Ohio, 1972-73; project dir. Miami Valley Library Orgn., Dayton, 1974-76; library devel. cons. State Library of Ohio, Columbus, 1976-77; librarian, asst. dir. main library Akron Summit County Pub. Library, 1977-79, librarian, asst. dir. brs., 1979-80, librarian, dir., 1980—. Host, writer: cable TV program INFOCUS, 1982. Mem. Gov's Pub. Library Fin and Support Com., Columbus, Ohio, 1983-86; mem. Ohio Multiple Interlibrary Coop. Com., 1980-81, Library and Info. Services to Citizens of Ohio Implementation Adv. Com., Columbus, 1983—; mem. adv. com. Kent State U. Sch. Library Sci., 1980—, U. Akron Continuing Edn. and Pub. Services, 1981—; bd. dirs. Project Learn, Akron, 1988—. Mem. ALA, Ohio Library Assn. (bd. dirs. 1982-85, v.p. 1985-86, pres. 1986-87), Beta Phi Mu. Methodist. Lodge: Kiwanis. Home: 311 Merriman Rd Akron OH 44303 Office: 55 S Main St Akron OH 44326

HAWKE, ROBERT JAMES LEE, prime minister of Australia, union official; b. Bordertown, South Australia, Australia, Dec. 9, 1929; s. Clement Arthur and Edith Emily (Lee) H.; m. Hazel Masterson, Mar. 3, 1956; children—Susan, Stephen, Rosslyn. B.A., LL.B., U. Western Australia; B.Litt., Oxfrod U., 1955. Research scholar Australian Nat. U., Canberra, 1956; research officer, adv. Australian Council Trade Unions, 1958-70, pres., 1970-80 , leader, from 1983; M.P. for Wills, 1980—; prime minister Australia, Canberra, 1983—; mem. bd. Res. Bank Australia, 1973-83; mem. Australian Mfg. Council, 1977; rep. trade union movement Nat. Labour Cons. Council, 1977—; mem. governing body ILO. Author: Hawke on Israel; also articles. Decorated Companion of Australia; recipient UN Media Peace prize, 1980; Rhodes scholar Oxford U., Eng., 1953; fellow Univ. Coll., Oxford U., 1984. Mem. Federated Misc. Workers Union Australia, Federated Clks. Union Australia, Amalgamated Metal Workers Union. Office: Parliament House, Canberra Australia •

HAWKES, GLORIA DAWN, consulting company executive; b. Batavia, N.Y., Mar. 7, 1934; d. Arthur Keating and Hazel A. (Laufer) Gore; m. Norman Harry Hawkes, May 7, 1955; children—Brett Allen, Guy Norman. Adminstrv. asst. Erdman Anthony & Hosley, Rochester, N.Y., 1958-59; office mgr. Tex. Instruments, Rochester, 1960-62; acting office mgr. P K Mgmt., Henrietta, N.Y., 1972-73; exec. dir. March of Dimes, Rochester, 1974-78; cons. G. Hawkes/Cons., McLean, Va., 1982-84; pres. H & H Cons. Co., Oakton, Va., 1984—. Mem. Rochester Women's Polit. Caucus, 1974-78, McLean Citizens Assn., 1980; mem., coordinating com. Genesee region Internat. Women's Yr., 1975-78. Mem. Fairfax County Bus. and Profl. Women's Club, Community Assns. Inst. (bd. contbg. editors 1986-88, officer/dir. Washington Met. chpt. 1982—), Epsilon Sigma Alpha (life). Republican. Lutheran. Office: H & H Cons Co 10124 Oakwood Chase Ct Oakton VA 22124

HAWKING, STEPHEN, astrophysicist, mathematician; b. Oxford, England, Jan. 8, 1942; s. F. and E.I. Hawking; m. Jane Wilde, 1965; two sons, one daughter. BA, Oxford U., DSc (hon.), 1978; PhD, Cambridge U.; DSc (hon.), U. Chgo., 1981, Notre Dame U., 1982, NYU, 1982, Leicester U., 1982. Research asst. Inst. Astronomy, Cambridge, Eng., 1972-73; research asst. dept. applied maths. and theoretical physics Inst. Astronomy, Cambridge, 1973-75, reader in gravitational physics, 1975-77, prof., 1977-79, Lucasian prof. math., 1979—. Author: (with G.F.R. Ellis) The Large Scale Structure of Space-Time, 1973; A Brief History of Time: From the Big Bang to Black Holes, 1988; co-editor: 300 Years of Gravitation, 1987. Decorated comdr. Brit. Empire, 1981; recipient Eddington medal Royal Acad. Sci., 1975, Pius XI Gold medal Pontifical Acad. Sci., 1975, Danne Heinemann prize for math. and physics Am. Phys. Soc.-Am. Inst. Physics, 1976, William

Hopkins prize Cambridge Philos. Soc., 1976, Maxwell medal Inst. Physics, 1976, Einstein award Strauss Found., 1978, Albert Einstein medal Albert Einstein Soc. of Berne, 1979. Fgn. mem. Am. Philos. Soc., AAAS; fellow Royal Soc. (Hughes medal 1976). Address: 5 West Rd, Cambridge England 351905 *

HAWKINS, ALBERT EDWARD, manufacturing company executive; b. El Paso, Nov. 18, 1930; s. Albert Edward and Vida Jane (Lewis) H.; B.S. in Civil Engring., U. Colo., 1952; postgrad. nuclear engring. UCLA, 1956-58; Advanced Mgmt. Program, Harvard U. Grad. Sch. Bus., 1980-81; m. Shirley Jean Henley, Dec. 16, 1951; children—Richard Albert, Sherri Kathleen. Sr. specification engr. Radioplane Co., Van Nuys, Calif., 1954-58; contract engr. Titan I & II, Martin Marietta Corp., Denver, 1958-64, bus. mgr., 1964-70, dir. adminstrn., 1970-73, corp. dir. strategic planning, Washington, 1973-75, dep. dir. bus. mgmt., New Orleans, 1975-77, v.p. solar energy systems, Denver, 1977-84; v.p. bus. ops., Denver, 1984-85; v.p. Denver Info. and Communications Systems, 1985-88; prin. Arrowhead QH Ranch, 1988—. Bd. dirs. Roxbrough Found., Porter Meml. Hosp.; trustee Mile High United Way, 1979—. Served with USMC, 1952-54. Mem. Nat. Contract Mgmt. Assn. (cert.). Club: Ridge Rider's Saddle. Office: Martin Marietta Info & Communications Systems PO Box 1260 Denver CO 80201-1260

HAWKINS, BRIAN, sales executive; b. Staffordshire, Eng., July 10, 1944; s. Cyril and Irene (Bull) H.; m. Barbara Hilary Bedson, Mar. 15, 1969; children: Richard, Marie. Chartered engr. Stress engr. Dorman Diesels, Stafford, Staffordshire, 1968-71, sr. stress engr., 1971-73, chief stress engr., 1973-74; sales engr. Holset Engring., Huddersfield, Yorkshire, Eng., 1974-77, sr. sales engr., 1977; sr. sales engr. Laycock Engring., Sheffield, Eng., 1977-79, indsl. sales mgr., 1979-84; sales mgr. couplings Twiflex Couplings Ltd., London, 1984-86; regional sales mgr. Twiflex Ltd., London, 1986—. Mem. Instn. Mech. Engrs. Anglican. Home: 22 Fenwick Close, Woking Surrey GU21 3BY, England Office: Twiflex Ltd, 104 The Green, Twickenham TW25AQ, England

HAWKINS, DAVID ROLLO, psychiatrist, educator; b. Springfield, Mass., Sept. 22, 1923; s. James Alexander and Janet (Rollo) H.; m. Elizabeth G. Wilson, June 8, 1946; children: David Rollo, Robert Wilson, John Bruce, William Alexander. B.A., Amherst Coll., 1945; M.D., U. Rochester, N.Y., 1946. Intern Strong Meml. Hosp., Rochester, 1946-48; Commonwealth Fund fellow in psychiatry and medicine U. Rochester, 1950-52; instr. psychiatry U. N.C. Sch. Medicine, 1952-53, asst. prof., 1953-57, asso. prof. psychiatry, 1957-62, prof., 1962-67, dir. curriculum rev. and revision, 1965-67; prof., chmn. dept. psychiatry U. Va. Sch. Medicine, 1967-77, Alumni prof. psychiatry, 1977-79, asso. dean, 1969-70; psychiatrist-in-chief U. Va. Hosp., 1967-77; prof. psychiatry Pritzker Sch. Medicine, U. Chgo., 1979—; dir. liaison and consultation services dept. psychiatry Michael Reese Hosp., Chgo., 1979-87, chmn., 1987—; assoc. attending physician N.C. Meml. Hosp., Chapel Hill, 1952-63, attending physician, 1962-67; cons. Watts Hosp., Durham, 1952-67, VA Hosp., Fayetteville, N.C., 1956-67, Eastern State Hosp., Williamsburg, Va., 1971—; spl. research fellow Inst. Psychiatry, U. London, 1963-64, Fogarty internat. research fellow, 1976-77; U.S.-USSR and Romania health exchange fellow, 1978; cons. VA Hosp., Salem, Va., 1969—, mem. deans com., 1971-77. Review editor: Psychosomatic Medicine, 1958-70; asso. editor, 1970—, Psychiatry. Mem. small grants com. NIMH, 1958-62; mem. nursing research study sect. NIH, 1965-67; mem. Gov.'s Commn. Mental, Indigent and Geriatric Patients, 1968-72; mem. research evaluation com. Va. Dept. Mental Hygiene and Hosps., 1971-73, chmn., 1972-73; mem. behavioral sci. test com. Nat. Bd. Med. Examiners, 1970-74. Served as capt. MC Aus, 1948-50. Fellow Am. Coll. Psychoanalysts (charter, bd. regents 1979-81), Am. Psychiat. Assn.; mem. Am. Psychosomatic Soc. (mem. council 1959), AMA, Group for Advancement Psychiatry (bd. dirs. 1987), Assn. Am. Med. Colls. (council assoc. socs. 1973-78), Am. Psychoanalytic Assn., Am. Coll. Psychiatrists, AAAS, Va. Psychoanalytic Soc., Washington Psychoanalytic Soc., Chgo. Psychoanalytic Soc., Ill. Psychiat. Soc. (council 1981-82, pres.-elect 1987), AAUP, Soc. Neurosci., Am. Assn. Chmn. Depts. Psychiatry (sec.-treas. 1971-73, pres. 1974-75), Sleep Research Soc., Nat. Bd. Med. Examiners (exam. com. 1983-87), Phi Beta Kappa, Sigma Xi, Alpha Omega Alpha. Office: Michael Reese Hosp Dept Psychiatry Lake Shore Dr at 31st St Chicago IL 60616

HAWKINS, ELLIS DELANO, manufacturing executive; b. Princeton, Ark., Feb. 13, 1941; s. Eddie and Anne Beadie (Smith) H.; m. Vera Mae Smith, Aug. 19, 1969 (div. Sept. 1979); children: Angela, Stacey, Rhonald. AA, Shorter Jr. Coll., 1958; BBA, Calif. Coast U., 1981, MBA, 1983. Cert. in statistical process control; lic. ins. agt., Ill. Operator drill press Choctaw Inc., Poyen, Ark., 1962-65; supr. Chrysler Corp., Detroit, 1965-76; Alcan Aluminum, Terre Haute, Ind., 1976—; pres., chief exec. officer Jes-El-Ed Inc., Chgo., 1980—; also bd. dirs. Jes-El-Ed Inc.; bd. dirs., sec. Idlewild Civic Investment, Inc. Scoutmaster troop 48 Boy Scouts Am., Malvern, Ark., 1962; solicitor United Found., Detroit, 1971. Served with USN, 1958-62. Recipient Commendation Letter Tribune Star, 1986, Appreciation Letter, M.L. King Convocation com., 1986. Mem. NAACP (life), Am. Legion (chmn. Spl. Olympics 1982—, plaque 1985), Idlefellows Social Club. Democrat. Club: Chgo. Idlewilders (parlimentarian 1982-85). Lodge: Masons (sr. warden So. Dist. 1984—). Home: 3216 W 166th St Markham IL 60426-5504 Office: Jes-El-Ed Inc 3216 W 166th St Markham IL 60426

HAWKINS, FREDERICK CAMPBELL, JR., osteopathic physician; b. Phila. Dec. 16, 1937; s. Frederick Campbell and Margaret Josephine (Rosell) H.; m. Monique Pressoir, July 13, 1963; children—Frederick 3d, Dominique, Daniel, Linda. B.A., Lincoln U., 1959; D.O., Phila. Coll. Osteo. Medicine, 1965. Night physician in charge Eageville Hosp., Pa., 1966; physician Sch. Bd. of Phila., 1966-67; physician in charge U.S. Customs House, Phila., 1966-69; practice osteo. medicine specializing in family medicine, Phila., 1967—; instr. dept. internal medicine Phila. Coll. Osteo. Medicine, 1966-72; med. dir. Medicosurg. Diagnostica, Inc., Phila., 1974—; cons. Mansion Mgmt. Corp., Phila., 1974—; asst. prof. medicine Temple U., Phila., 1988—. Del. Chinese Med. Assn., Beijing, Nanjing, Shanghei, Hong Kong, 1988. Recipient Legion of Honor Chapel of Four Chaplains. Mem. AAAS, World Med. Assn., Am. Osteo. Assn., Pa. Osteo. Med. Assn., Am. Coll. Gen. Practitioners, N.Y. Acad. Sci. Episcopalian. Home: PO Box 425 Villanova PA 19085 Office: Medicosurg Diagnostica Inc 3035 W Diamond St Philadelphia PA 19121

HAWKINS, IDA FAYE, educator; b. Ft. Worth, Dec. 28, 1928; d. Christopher Columbus and Nannie Idella (Hughes) Hall; student Midwestern U., 1946-48; B.S., N. Tex. State U., 1951; student Lamar U., 1968-70; M.S., McNeese State U., 1973; m. Gene Hamilton Hawkins, Dec. 22, 1952; children—Gene Agner, Jane Hall. Tchr., DeQueen Elem. Sch., Port Arthur, Tex., 1950-54; tchr. Tyrrell Elem. Sch., Port Arthur, 1955-56; tchr. Roy Hatton Elem. Sch., Bridge City, Tex., 1967-68; tchr. Oak Forest Elem. Sch., Vidor, Tex., 1968—. Second vice pres. Travis Elem. PTA, 1965-66, 1st v.p., 1966-67; corr. sec. Port Arthur City council PTA, 1966-67. Named Tchr. of Yr., Oak Forest Elem. 1984-85. Mem. NEA, Tex. State Tchrs. Assn., Classroom Tchrs. Assn., McNeese State U. Alumni Assn. Presbyterian (Sunday sch. tchr. 1951-53, 60-66). Home: 4075 Laurel Apt 73 Beaumont TX 77707 Office: Oak Forest Elem Sch 2400 Hwy 12 Vidor TX 77662

HAWKINS, PETER JOSEPH, salesperson; b. Four Marks, Alton, Eng., Apr. 19, 1944; s. Patrick Peter and Josephline (Coonan) H.; m. Gillian Frances Mott, June 28, 1969; children: Johanna Mary, Benjamin Charles. Diploma, Tech. Coll., Eng., 1963. Salesman NCR (UK) Ltd., Birmingham, Eng., 1978-79, Wilcex Computers Ltd., Chester, Eng., 1979-84, JBA (UK) Ltd., Birmingham, 1984-86, Kalamazoo PLC, Birmingham, 1986—. Roman Catholic. Home: Castle House, Castle Pulverbatch, Shrewsbury England SY5 8DS Office: Kalamazoo PLC, Northfield, Birmingham England B31 2RW

HAWKINS, RICHARD SPENCER DADDOW, personnel director; b. Boston, Apr. 29, 1943; s. Joseph Elmer Jr. and Jane Elizabeth (Daddow) H.; m. Roberta Rosenthal, Dec. 24, 1974 (div. Oct. 1984); 1 child, Jessica Clayton. Baccalaureate, Goteborgs Hogre Samskola, Sweden, 1963; BA, Harvard U., 1967; MA, Yale U., 1970. Exec. v.p. Media Engring. Cambridge, Mass., 1970-73; sales trainer John Hancock Life Ins. Co., Westwood, Mass., 1974-77; dir. employee tng. asst. Commonwealth of

---

Mass., Boston, 1977-78; mgmt. devel. specialist Wang Labs., Lowell, Mass., 1978-80, mgr. mfg. tng., 1980-81; mgr. tng. and devel. electro-optics div. Honeywell Inc., Lexington, 1981-86, mgr. staffing, 1986-87; mgr. mgmt. devel. Otis Elevator Co., Farmington, Conn., 1987—; adj. faculty Northeastern U., Boston, 1983-85, Bryant Coll., 1987—. Contbr. articles to bus. and econs. jours. Harvard U. Scholar, 1961; Nat. Merit scholar, 1961; Fulbright Found. fellow, Singapore, 1967. Mem. Am. Soc. for Tng. and Devel. (bd. dirs. Mass. chpt. 1982-84, chmn. community devel. com. 1982-84, regional conf. program, 1984), Human Resource Planning Soc. Episcopalian. Club: Appalachian Mountain (Boston). Home: PO Box 931 Farmington CT 06034 Office: Otis Elevator Co 10 Farm Springs Farmington CT 06032

HAWKINS, ROBERT LEE, social work administrator; b. Denver, Feb. 18, 1938; s. Isom and Bessie M. (Hugley) H.; A.A., Pueblo Jr. Coll., 1958; B.S., So. Colo. State Coll., 1965; M.S.W., U. Denver, 1967; m. Ann Sharon Hoy, Apr. 28, 1973; children—Robert, Jeanne, Julia, Rose. Psychiat. technician Colo. State Hosp., Pueblo, 1956-58, 1962-63, occupational therapist asst., 1964-65, clin. adminstr. psychiat. team, 1969-75, dir. community services, 1975—, supr. vol. services, 1975—, mem. budget com., 1975—; counselor (part-time) Family Service Agy., Pueblo, 1968-69, exec. dir., 1969-70; mem. faculty U. So. Colo., 1968-75; partner Human Resource Devel., Inc., 1970-75. Mem. Pueblo Positive Action Com., 1970; chmn. adv. bd. Pueblo Sangre de Cristo Day Care Center, 1969-72; chmn. Gov.'s So. Area Adv. Council of Employment Service, 1975-76, chmn. Pueblo's City CSC, 1976-77, Pueblo Community Corrections, 1985-87, Pueblo Civil Service Commn., 1988—; commr. Pueblo Housing Authority, 1986—, Colo. Commn. Higher Edn., 1987—; mem. gov's. adv. com. Mental Health Standards, 1981—; mem. Colo. Juvenile Parole Bd., 1977; bd. dirs. Pueblo United Fund, 1969-74, pres.. 1973; bd. dirs. Pueblo Community Orgn., 1974-76, Spanish Peaks Mental Health Center, 1976—, Neighborhood Health Center, 1977-79, Pueblo Community Corrections, 1983—, Pueblo Legal Services, 1983—. Served with U.S. Army 1958-62. Mem. Nat. Assn. Social Workers (nominating com. 1973-76), ACLU (dir. Pueblo chpt. 1980—), NAACP, Broadway Theatre Guild. Democrat. Methodist. Club: Kiwanis. Home: 520 Gaylord St Pueblo CO 81004 Office: 1600 W 24 St Pueblo CO 81003

HAWKLAND, WILLIAM DENNIS, educator; b. Willmar, Minn., Nov. 25, 1920; s. Douglas F. and Lola (Johnston) H.; B.S., U. Minn., 1942, J.D., 1947; LL.M., Columbia U., 1949; m. Rosemary Neal, Aug. 27, 1949; children—William Dennis, Stephen D. Admitted to Minn. bar, 1947, Ill. bar, 1961, N.Y. bar, 1970; asst. prof. U. Tenn. Law Sch., 1949-50; from asst. prof. to prof. Temple U. Law Sch., 1950-56; vis. prof. UCLA Law Sch., 1956; prof. Rutgers U. Law Sch., 1956-60; vis. summer lectr. N.Y.U., 1957, Tex. Law Sch., 1961; prof. Faculté Internat. Pour L'Enseignment Du Droit Comparé, Strasburg, France, 1970; prof. U. Ill. Law Sch., 1960-64, 70-79, dean, prof. SUNY, Buffalo Law Sch., 1964-67, prof., provost, 1968-70; adv. Dept. State; vis. prof. U. Minn., 1974-75; chancellor, prof. La. State U. Law Center, 1979—. Bd. dirs. Am. Arbitration Assn. Vice chmn. Republican Com. to Elect Senator Kenneth Keating, 1964. Served to lt. USNR, 1942-46. Mem. Am., N.Y. State, Minn., Ill., Erie County bar assns., Am. Law Inst., Order of Coif. Author: (with George Bogert and William Britton) Sales and Security, 1962; A Transactional Guide to the Commercial Code, 1964; Commercial Paper and Bank Deposits and Collections, 1966; Bills and Notes, 1956; Sales and Bulk Sales Under The Uniform Commercial Code, 2d edit., 1959; (with Marion Benfield) Sales, 1979; (with Pierre Loiseaux) Debtor-Creditor Relations, 1979; Uniform Commercial Code Series, 9 vols., 1986; also articles; editorial bd. Uniform Commercial Code. Home: 3651 S Lakeshore Rd Baton Rouge LA 70808

HAWLEY, PHILLIP EUGENE, investment banker; b. Tecumseh, Mich., Dec. 9, 1940; s. Paul P and Vadah Arlene (Lawhead) H.; m. Linda Darlene Miller, Feb. 14, 1957; children—Pierre Lee, Paul Marvin, Danny Parke, David Eugene, Martin Edward. Student in mgmt. Yale U., 1959-63; B.S. in Bus. Adminstrn., Northwestern Coll., Tulsa, 1980. With Credit Bur. Fort Myers, Inc., Fla., 1956—, chmn. bd.; pvt. investigator Transworld Investigators, Inc., 1964; now v.p.; founder real estate co. (now Gold Coast Develop. Corp.), 1965, pres.; pres. Phillip Hawley Investment Banking Co.; bd. dirs. Caribbean Industries Internat. Corp., Future Investment Corp. Co-founder, bd. dirs. Collier-Lee Wrestling Assn., 1974—. Named Outstanding Speaker, Fla. Collectors Assn., 1967; Outstanding Individual, Fla. Fedn. Young Republicans, 1971; recipient Presdl. Sports award, 1979. Author: Law And It's Alternative to Chaos, 1958; The Happiest Man in the World, 1970; The Best Buys In Fort Myers, 1982. Mem. Fla. Collectors Assn., Am. Collectors Assn., Assn. Credit Burs. Am., Med.-Dental Hosp. Burs. Am., Fla. Assn. Mortgage Brokers, Fla. Assn. Pvt. Investigators. Republican. Mem. Nazarene Ch. Clubs: Gideons Internat., Collier Lee Wrestling Assn.; Am. Numismatic Assn. Home: 6435 Winkler Rd Fort Myers FL 33907 Office: 2083 Cleveland Ave Fort Myers FL 33901

HAWRYLYSHYN, BOHDAN W., business educator; b. Koropec, Ukraine, Oct. 19, 1926; s. Dmytro and Teodosia (Sadowska) H.; m. Leonida Hayowsky, June 10, 1950; children—Leslie, Patricia, Christine. Officer UNRRA in Germany, 1946-47; positions in research, engring. and mgmt. in Can., 1954-60; mem. faculty Internat. Mgmt. Inst., Geneva, 1960—, dir., 1968-86, scholar in residence, 1986—; lectr. in more than 40 countries; cons. to govts., internat .orgns. and bds. of transnat. corps.; mem adv. council McGraw-Hill. Trustee Resources for Future. Recipient Gold medal Pres. of Italian Republic, various scholarships and awards. Fellow World Acad. Art and Sci., Internat. Acad. Mgmt., Club of Rome. Ukrainian Catholic. Author: Road Maps to the Future, in six lang. edits., other books and more than 40 articles; editorial bd. several jours. Home: 5 chemin du Reposoir, CH 1255 Geneva-Veyrier Switzerland Office: 4 Chemin de Conches, CH 1231 Geneva-Conches Switzerland

HAWRYLYSHYN, LESLIE MICHAEL, investment firm executive; b. Toronto, Ont. Can., Sept. 9, 1954; arrived in Switzerland, 1960; s. Bohdan and Leonida (Hayes) H.; m. Fabienne Valentine Morin, July 3, 1982. BA in Econs., U. Alta., Can., 1979; MBA, Inst. European d'Adminstrn. Affaires, Fontainebleau, France, 1982. Adminstrn. mgr. Bank of Montreal, Edmonton, Alta., 1979-81; corp. credit officer Citibank NA, Geneva, 1982-85; ptnr., mng. dir. Genevest Cons. Group, Geneva, 1985-87; founding ptnr., mng. dir. Euroventures - Genevest Mgmt., Geneva, 1987—. Mem. Swiss-Am. C. of C., Swiss Venture Capital Assn., European Venture Capital Assn., Office Promotion Industrielle Geneva (affilate), Assn. Petite-Moyenne Enterprise. Clubs: Assn. Dialogue (co-founder) (Brussels and Geneva); Richelieu Internat. (Ottawa, Can. and Geneva). Office: Euroventures-Genevest Mgmt, 16 Rue Grand Bureau, 1227 Geneva Switzerland

HAWTHORNE, MARION FREDERICK, chemistry educator; b. Ft. Scott, Kans., Aug. 24, 1928; s. Fred Elmer and Colleen (Webb) H.; m. Beverly Dawn Rempe, Oct. 30, 1951 (div. 1976); children: Cynthia Lee, Candace Lee; m. Diana Baker Razzaia, Aug. 14, 1977. B.A., Pomona Coll., 1949; Ph.D. (AEC fellow), U. Calif. at Los Angeles, 1953; D.Sc. (hon.), Pomona Coll., 1974. Research asso. Iowa State Coll., 1953-54; research chemist Rohm & Haas Co., Huntsville, Ala., 1954-56; group leader Rohm & Haas Co., 1956-60; lab. head Rohm & Haas Co., Phila., 1961; vis. lectr. Harvard, 1960, Queen Mary Coll., U. London, 1963; vis. prof. Harvard U., 1968; prof. chemistry U. Calif. at Riverside, 1962-68, U. Calif. at Los Angeles, 1968—; vis. prof. U. Tex., Austin, 1974; Mem. sci. adv. bd., USAF, 1980-86, NRC Bd. Army Sci. and Tech., 1986—. Editor: Inorganic Chemistry, 1969—; Editorial bd.: Progress in Solid State Chemistry, 1971—, Inorganic Syntheses, 1966—; Organometallics in Chemical Synthesis, 1969—, Synthesis in Inorganic and Metalorganic Chemistry, 1970—. Recipient Chancelors Research award, 1968, Herbert Newby McCoy award, 1972, Am. Chem. Soc. award in Inorganic Chemistry, 1973, Tolman Medal award, 1986, Nebr. sect.Am. Chem. Soc. award, 1979, Disting. Service in the Advancement of Inorganic Chemistry award Am. Chem. Soc., 1988, Boron U.S.A. award, 1988; Sloan Found. fellow, 1963-65, Japan Soc. Promotion Sci. fellow, 1986; named Col. Confederate Air Force, 1984. Fellow AAAS; mem. U.S. Nat. Acad. Scis., Am. Acad. Arts and Scis., Aircraft Owners and Pilots Assn., Sigma Xi, Alpha Chi Sigma, Sigma Nu. Club: Cosmos. Home: 3415 Green Vista Dr Encino CA 91436

HAY, ALEXANDRE, retired humanitarian organization executive; b. Berne, Switzerland, Oct. 29, 1919; s. Frederic and Lydia (Trachsler) H.; m. Helene Morin Pons, 1945 (dec. 1973); children—Isabelle, Frank-Olivier, Cedric, Beatrice; m. Verena Vogler, 1980. Student Mat. class, Geneva Coll.: 1931-38; LL.B., U. Geneva, 1942, Lawyer's Cert., 1944, LL.D. (hon.), 1986; Ph.D. (hon.), U. St.-Gall. Sole practice, Geneva, 1942-45; with Fed. Polit. Dept., Berne, 1945-48, Swiss Legation, Paris, 1948-53; dir. Swiss Nat. Bank, Zurich, 1953-55, dir., acting chief dept. II, Berne, 1955-61, gen. mgr., v.p., Berne, 1961-76; pres. bd. mgmt. European Monetary Agreement, Paris, 1961-66; pres. Internat. Cm. Red Cross (ICRC), Geneva, 1976-87. Active Internat. Cm. Red Cross (ICRC). Office: ICRC, 17 ave de la Paix, CH 1202 Geneva Switzerland

HAY, GEORGE AUSTIN, motion picture producer, director, artist, actor; b. Johnstown, Pa., Dec. 25, 1915; s. George and Mary Louise (Austin) H. B.S., U. Pitts., 1938; postgrad., U. Rochester, 1939; M.Litt., U. Pitts. 1948; M.A., Columbia U., 1948. dir. Jr. League hosp. shows, N.Y.C., 1948-53. Producer, dir. off-Broadway prodns., 1953-55; motion picture casting dir. for Dept. Def. films, Astoria Studios, N.Y., 1955-70, motion picture producer-dir., U.S. Dept. Transp., Washington, 1973—; group exhbns. of paintings and sculpture include, Lincoln Ctr., N.Y.C., 1965, Parrish Art Mus., Southampton, N.Y., 1969, Carnegie Inst., 1972, Duncan Galleries, N.Y.C., 1973, Bicentennial Exhbn. Am. Painters, Paris, 1976, Chevy Chase Gallery, 1979, Watergate Gallery, 1981, Le Salon des Nations a Paris, 1983; rep. permanent collections, Met. Mus. Art, N.Y.C., Library Congress, also, pvt. collections; bibliog. reference to works pub. in History of Internat. Art, 1982. Author, illustrator: Seven Hops to Australia, 1945; Dir.: Bicentennial documentary Highways of History, 1976; dir.: film World Painting in Museum of Modern Art, 1972; Composer: Rhapsody in E Flat for piano and strings, 1950; writer: TV program Nat. Council Chs., 1965; Broadway appearances include: What Every Woman Knows, 1954; original Broadway run of Inherit the Wind, 1955-57; created role of Prof. Fiveash in premiere of The Acrobats, White Barn Theater, Westport, Conn., 1961; feature films include: Pretty Boy Floyd, 1960, The Landlord, 1970, Child's Play, 1971, Chekhov's The Bet, 1978, Being There, 1980, No Way Out, 1986, Her Alibi, 1988; TV appearances include Am. Heritage, 1961, Americans-A Portrait in Verses, 1962, Naked City, 1962, U.S. Steel Hour, 1963, Another World, 1965, Edge of Night, 1968, As the World Turns, 1969, Love Is a Many-Splendored Thing, 1972, The Adams Chronicles, 1976; piano soloist in concerts and recitals, 1937; editor: Cultural Chronicles; performer Cruise Ship, Europe, 1938; author, illustrator: The Arts Scene; entrepreneur in mgmt. of property, portfolio of stocks and bonds; contbr. articles to periodicals. Apptd. to pres.'s council Coll. William and Mary; mem. World Affairs Council; bd. govs., trustee Hist. Home of Pres. James Monroe; mus. donor Am. doctor's office turn-of-century period preservation; bd. dirs. Washington Film Council. Served with AUS, 1942-46, PTO. Recipient Loyal Service award Jr. League, 1953, St. Bartholomew's Silver Leadership award, 1966, Gold medal Accademia Italia, 1980, Smithsonian Instn. Pictorial award, 1982; Fed. Govt. Honor award in recognition 30 yrs. dedicated service, 1985; subject of biog. work: Austin Hay Careers of a Christmas Child. Mem. Nat. Acad. TV Arts and Scis., Am. Fedn. TV and Radio Artists, Screen Actors Guild, Am. Artists Profl. League, Allied Artists Am. Internat. Bach Soc., Beethoven Soc., Music Library Assn., AFTRA, Actors Equity, Washington Film Council (bd. dirs.), Nat. Assn. Investors, Nat. Trust Hist. Preservation, SAR, Nat. Parks and Conservation Assn., Shakespeare Oxford Soc., St. Andrew's Soc., Cambria County Hist. Soc., Am. Philatelic Soc., Am. Mus. of the Moving Image, Washington Film Council (bd. dirs.), Fed. Design Council, Sigma Chi, Phi Mu Alpha. Clubs: Nat. Arts, Players (N.Y.C.); Nat. Travel, Nat. Press, Arts (Washington); English Speaking Union, Classic Car Club of Am. Home: 2022 Columbia Rd NW Washington DC 20009 also: Hay Ave Johnstown PA 15902 Office: US Dept Transp 400 7th St SW Washington DC 20590

HAY, JOHN LEONARD, lawyer; b. Lawrence, Mass., Oct. 6, 1940; s. Charles Cable and Henrietta Dudley (Wise) H.; m. Millicent Victoria, Dec. 16, 1967; 1 child, Ian. AB with distinction, Stanford U., 1961; JD, U. Colo., 1964. Bar: Colo. 1964, Ariz. 1965, D.C. 1971. Assoc. Lewis and Roca, Phoenix, 1964-69, ptnr., 1969-82; ptnr. Fannin, Terry & Hay, Phoenix, 1982-87, Allen, Kimerer & LaVelle, Phoenix, 1987—; dir. Ariz. Life and Disability Ins. Guaranty Fund, 1983—, Ariz. Licensors and Franchisors Assn., 1985—. Mem. Democratic Precinct Com., 1966-78, Ariz. State Dem. Com., 1968-78; chmn. Dem. Legis. Dist., 1971-74; mem. Maricopa County Dem. Cen. Com., 1971-74; bd. dirs. ACLU, 1973-78; bd. dirs. Community Legal Services, 1983—, pres. 1987-88. Mem. ABA, Maricopa County Bar Assn. (bd. dirs. 1985—), State Bar of Ariz., Ariz. Licensors and Franchisors Assn. (bd. dirs. 1985—, pres. 1988—), Ariz. Civil Liberties Union (bd. dirs. 1973-77, 1984-87; chmn. 1973-77, Disting. Citizen award 1979). Home: 201 E Hayward Ave Phoenix AZ 85020 Office: Allen Kimerer LaVelle 2715 N 3d St Phoenix AZ 85004

HAY, RAYMOND A., steel and diversified manufacturing company executive; b. L.I., N.Y., July 13, 1928; m. Grace Mattson; children: John Alexander, Susan Elizabeth. BS in Econs., L.I. U., 1949; MBA, St. John's U., 1960. Mgr. Northeastern div. Monroe Calculating Machine Co. (now Monroe-Swede), 1958-61; with Xerox Corp., Rochester, N.Y., 1961-75; br. mgr. Xerox Corp., N.Y.C., 1961-62, zone mgr. Western Region, also asst. dir. sales ops. and dir. mktg., 1962-68, group v.p. and gen. mgr. info. systems, 1968, exec. v.p. to 1975; pres., chief operating officer LTV Corp., Dallas, from 1975, chief exec. officer, 1982—; also chmn., dir. Bd. dirs. First City Bancorp., Tex., Diamond Shamrock Corp. Bd. govs. Kennedy Ctr. for Performing Arts; trustee Dallas Mus. Fine Arts, Dallas Symphony Orch.; bd. dirs. Dallas Civic Opera Assn. Mem. Am. Mgmt. Assn., Nat. Business Club: Dallas C. of C. (council steering com.). Office: LTV Corp 2001 Ross Ave P O Box 655003 Dallas TX 75265 *

HAY, ROBERT PETTUS, history educator; b. Eagleville, Tenn., Oct. 23, 1941; s. Ira James and Alice Elizabeth (Pettus) H.; m. Carla Jean Humphrey, Dec. 31, 1966. B.S. with highest honors, Middle Tenn. State U., Murfreesboro, 1962; Ph.D., U. Ky., 1967. Instr. history Middle Tenn. State U., summer 1964; lectr. history U. Ky., 1966-67; instr. history sch. edn. NDEA Inst., U. Ky., summer 1967; asst. prof. history Marquette U., Milw., 1967-71, assoc. prof., 1975, chmn. dept., 1975, chmn. dept., dir. grad. study, 1975-79. Assoc. history editor USA Today, 1980—; contbr. numerous articles and commentaries to hist., popular and profl. jours.; book reviewer numerous jours.; author poetry and chpts. in books. Mem. Milw. County Zool. Soc., Milw. Art Mus., Friends of Milw. County Pub. Mus., Tenn. State Mus. Assn. Colonial Williamsburg Found. Univ. research grantee Marquette U., 1968; summer faculty fellow Marquette U., 1969, 73, life mem. Pres.'s Council Marquette U., U. Ky. Fellows. Commd. Ky. col., 1980; Woodrow Wilson fellow, 1962-63, 65-66; NDEA fellow, 1962-65; Nat. Endowment Humanities fellow, 1969-70. Mem. Orgn. Am. Historians (life), So. Hist. Assn. (life), Soc. Historians Early Am. Rep. (life), Tenn. Hist. Soc. (life), Am. Cath. Hist. Assn. (life), Milw. County Hist. Soc. (life), Ky. Hist. Soc. (life), Filson Club (life), Am. Hist. Assn. (life), Milw. Met. Historians Assn. East. Tenn. Hist. Soc. (life), West Tenn. Hist. Soc. (life), Inst. Early Am. History and Culture, Ctr. for Study of Presidency, Wis. Assn. Promotion History, AAUP, Phi Alpha Theta, Pi Gamma Mu. Democrat. Roman Catholic. Clubs: Wisconsin. Helfaer Recreation Center, Atlanta Track Avocations: running, gardening, poetry, weight-lifting, basketball. Home: 2146 Laura Ln Waukesha WI 53186 Office: Marquette U Dept History Milwaukee WI 53233

HAYAKAWA, KAN-ICHI, food science educator; b. Shibukawa, Gumma, Japan, Aug. 12, 1931; came to U.S., 1961, naturalized, 1974. s. Chyogoro and Kin (Hayakawa) H.; m. Setsuko Maekawa, Feb. 18, 1967. B.S., Tokyo U. Fisheries, 1955; Ph.D., Rutgers U., 1964. Research fellow Canners' Assn. Japan, 1955-60; asst. prof. food sci. Rutgers U., New Brunswick, N.J., 1964-70; assoc. prof. food sci. Rutgers U., 1970-77, prof. food engring. and physics, 1977-82, Disting. prof. food engring. and physics 1982—; OAS visit. prof. U. Campinas, Brazil, summers 1972, 73; cons. to food processing cos. prof. U. Campinas, Brazil, summers 1972, 73; cons. to food processing cos. Organizer, chmn.; participant NSF sponsored U.S.-Japan Coop. Conf., Tokyo, 1979; lectr. Industry Research and Devel. Inst. and Nat. Taiwan U., both Taiwan, June 1982, Wuxi Inst. of Light Industry, China, 1985. Co-editor: Heat Sterilization of Food, 1983. Contbr. articles to books; chpts. jours. and encys. research grantee USPHS, 1966-73, Nabisco Found., 1975-76, NSF, 1981-82, travel grantee NSF; 1972, Rutgers Research Found. 1977, grantee Advanced Food Tech. Ctr. grantee, 1985—. Fellow Inst. Food Technologists; mem. AAAS, Am. Inst. Chem. Engrs., ASHRAE (chmn tech. com. on thermophys. property values of food 1981-85, mem. com. 1981—), Am. Soc. Agrl. Engrs., Can. Inst. Food Sci. and Tech., Sigma Xi. Home: 631 Lake Dr Princeton NJ 08540 Office: Rutgers U Food Sci Dept PO Box 231 New Brunswick NJ 08903

HAYASAKA, TAIJIRO, social psychology educator; b. Sendai, Miyagi-ken, Japan, Feb. 20, 1923; s. Ichiro and Teru (Ito) H.; m. Misako Suruga, Feb. 28, 1955; children: Makiko, Shigeki, Mikiko. MA, Tohoku U., 1948. Asst. Tohoku U., Sendai, 1948-52, lectr., 1952-53; lectr. Rikkyo U., Tokyo, 1953-54, asst. prof., 1954-62, prof. social psychology, 1962-88, prof. emeritus, 1988—; prof. social psychology Tokyo Internat. U., 1988; cons. TDK Co., Ltd., Tokyo, 1984—. Author: Interpersonal Psychology, 1978, Learning Phenomenology, 1985, Science of Interpersonal Relationships, 1986. Mem. Japanese Theoretical Psychology Assn. (pres. 1984—), Interpersonal Relationship Tng. Programme (pres. 1971—), Assn. of Japanese Humanistic Psychology (bd. dirs. 1976—). Home: 2228 Ohkura-Machi, Machida Tokyo 19401, Japan Office: Rikkyo U, Nishi-Ikeoukuro, Toshimo-ku Tokyo 171, Japan

HAYASHI, HAJIME, trading company executive; b. San Mateo, Calif., Apr. 13, 1925; s. Kiyoichi and Masue H.; m. Emiko, Feb. 4, 1953; 1 child, Mami. BA, Doshisha U., 1947; student, Stanford U., 1949; BA, San Francisco State U., 1952. Sr. corp. advisor Matsushita Electric Indsl. Co. Ltd., Osaka, Japan, 1953—; chmn. bd. dirs. numerous subs. including Matsubo Equipment and Instrument Corp., Matsubo Electronic Compnonents Co., Matsubo Credit Sales Co., Osaka, 1975—; chmn. AMAC Corp., Los Angeles and N.Y.C., 1981—, Jetro Import Promotion Council, Osaka. Mem. Japan Machinery Import Assn. Lodge: Lions (decorated insignia of Commdr., Finland, 1983). Home: 700 Okadaura Sennan-City, Osaka 590-05, Japan Office: 3-2 Minamisemba 4-chrome, Minami-Ku, Osaka 542, Japan also: 300 S Grand Ave Suite 3140 Los Angeles CA 90017 also: 375 Park Ave Suite 3708 New York NY 10152 also: 400 18th Ave NE Suite 302 Bellevue WA 38004

HAYASHI, MASAKI, pharmaceutical company executive; b. Wakayama, Japan, Jan. 3, 1927; s. Minenoshin and Teruko (Yumikura) H.; m. Yoshiko Tohtani, May 21, 1959; 1 child, Yukako. B.S., Osaka Sci. and Engring. U., 1951; Ph.D., Osaka U., 1979. Researcher Ono Pharm. Co., Osaka, Japan, 1951-65, dir. chemistry dept., 1965-81, dir. research inst., 1981-82, cons., 1982—. Author: Prostaglandins, 1982. Contbr. articles to profl. jours. Patentee in field. Mem. Chem. Soc. Japan, Pharm. Soc. Japan (chmn. 1982), Soc. Synthetic Organic Chemistry (Creative prize 1979), Am. Chem. Soc. Home: 4-5-10 Nanpeidai, Takatsuki, 569 Osaka Japan Office: Ono Pharm Co Ltd, 3-1-1 Sakurai Shimamoto-cho, Mishima-gun, 618 Osaka Japan

HAYASHI, SHIGEO, medical research institute director, parasitology researcher; b. Tokyo, June 26, 1922; m. Teruyo Hayashi, Oct. 25, 1952; children: Maya Nagumo, Sae Hayashi. MD, U. Tokyo, 1947, PhD, 1954. Intern, then resident Hosp. of Faculty of Medicine, U. Tokyo, 1947-48; assoc. prof. Inst. Infectious Diseases U. Tokyo, 1960-66; prof. parasitology Sch. Medicine Yokohama (Japan) City U., 1966-75, dean, 1971-74; dir. dept. parasitology NIH, Tokyo, 1975-81, dep. dir.-gen., 1981-83, dir.-gen., 1983-88; epidemiologist WHO, Rangoon, Burma, 1964-65; chmn. Japanese Panel on Parasitic Disease, U.S.-Japan Coop. Med. Sci. Program, Tokyo, 1979-88. Author, editor: Control of Soil, 1980, Helminthiases I, II, III, 1980, 83, 86. Mem. Japanese Soc. Parasitology (pres. 1982, Katsurada Meml. Prize 1980), Japan Soc. Sanitary Zoology (23d Sanitary Zoology Prize 1977), Japanese Soc. Tropical Medcine. Office: Nat Inst of Health, 10-35, Kamiosaki 2 chome, Shinagawa-ku, Tokyo 141, Japan

HAYASHI, YOSHIHIRO, architect; b. Hikone, Japan, Sept. 29, 1940; s. Genzo and Koshie (Yoshida) H. B of Engring., Kogakuin U., Tokyo, 1965; MA, U. Mich., 1975. Supt. Sato Hide Komuten Co. Ltd., Tokyo, 1965-72; dir. Yoshihiro Hayashi Architecs and Assoc., Tokyo, 1975—. Author: Zosaku, 1981. Recipient Nika-Ten award Nika Orgn., Japan, 1981, 83. Fellow Archtl. Inst. Japan, Japan Inst. Architects, Tokyo Soc. Architects and Bldg. Engrs. Roman Catholic. Home: 3-35 2-Chome Shibaura Minato, Tokyo 108, Japan Office: 1-2-19 Hamamastu-Cho Minato, Tokyo 105, Japan

HAYASHI, YUKIKO, biochemist, educator; b. Manchuria, China, 1943; arrived in Japan, 1946; DSc, Hokkaido U., Sapparo, Japan, 1979. Asst. dept. of clin. lab. Asahikawa Med. Coll., Japan, 1979—.

HAYDEE, MARCIA (PEREIRA DA SILVA), ballerina; b. Niteroi, Brazil, Apr. 18, 1939. Student, Royal Ballet Sch., London; studied in Paris with Olga Preobrajenska and Lubov Egorova. Mem., Grand Ballet du Marquis de Cuevas, 1957-61; prin. dancer, Stuttgart Ballet, 1961—, artistic dir., 1976—; created roles in John Cranko's Romeo and Juliet, Eugene Onegin, The Taming of the Shrew, Carmen, Variation, Homage au Bolshoi, Four Images, Initials R.B.M.E., Legend; Kenneth Macmillan's Las Hermanas, Song of the Earth, Miss Julie, Requiem; Glen Tetley's Voluntaries, Daphnis and Chloe, Algerias; John Neumeier's Steeetcar Named Desire, Hamlet Connotations, Night, Lady of the Camellias; Maurice Bejart's Divine, Gaite Parisienne, and Wien, Wien nur du allein, Isadora and Chairs; choreographer: Sleepint Beauty, 1987, Enas. Office: Stuttgart Ballet, Oberer Schlossgarten 6, 7000 1 Stuttgart Federal Republic of Germany

HAYDEN, WILLIAM (BILL) GEORGE, Australian minister for foreign affairs and trade; b. Brisbane, Queensland, Australia, Jan. 23, 1933; m. Dallas Broadfoot, May 7, 1960; 3 children. B in Econs., U. Queensland. Mem. Queensland police force, 1953-61; mem. Australian Ho. of Reps., Canberra, 1961—, opposition spokesman on health and social welfare Australian Labor Party, 1967-72, minister for social security, 1972-75, treas., 1975, opposition spokesman on def., 1975, opposition spokesman for econ. affairs and econ. devel., 1977, leader of the opposition, 1977-83, opposition spokesman on fgn. affairs, 1983, minister for fgn. affairs, 1983—. Mem. exec. com. Parliamentary Labor Party of Australia, 1967-72. Office: Ministry Fgn Affairs, Canberra Australia *

HAYDEN-WING, LARRY DEAN, wildlife consulting company executive; b. Webster City, Iowa, Aug. 13, 1935; s. Orlie C. Wing and Ruth Vivian (Erickson) Wing Stafford; m. Sandra Marlene Bullington, June 30, 1958 (div. Dec. 1977); 1 child, Chris E. Wing; m. Susan L. Hayden, Dec. 20, 1977 (div. Sept. 1980); m. Mary Marina Hawkins, Feb. 13, 1982; stepchildren—Mark G. Hawkins, John M. Hawkins. B.S. in Forestry and Wildlife, U. Idaho, 1958, M.S. in Wildlife, 1962, Ph.D. in Wildlife Ecology, 1969. Research assoc. U. Idaho, Moscow, 1965-69; asst. prof. animal ecology Iowa State U., Ames, 1969-72, assoc. prof., 1972-77; assoc. prof. zoology U. Wyo., Laramie, 1977-78; dir. wildlife div. Mine Reclamation Cons., Laramie, 1978-80; chief exec. officer Hayden-Wing Assocs., Sheridan, Wyo., 1980—, also dir. Coauthor monograph: Elephants and Forests, 1970; author: Wildlife Conservation Manual, 1972. Co-editor symposium procs.: North American Elk, 1979. Mem. U.S. Delegation Forestry and Wildlife Mgmt. to People's Rep. China for U.S. People to People Internat. Citizen Ambassador Program. Served to lt. (j.g.) USN, 1958-60. Mem. Wildlife Soc., Sigma Xi, Xi Sigma Pi, Phi Sigma (Nat. award of Merit 1968), Phi Kappa Phi. Lodge: Elks. Home: 1695 Hillcrest Sheridan WY 82801 Office: PO Box 6083 1695 Hillcrest Sheridan WY 82801

HAYEK, FRIEDRICH AUGUST (VON), economist, educator; b. Vienna, Austria, May 8, 1899; s. August and Felicitas (von Juraschek) von H.; Dr.jur., U. Vienna, 1921, Dr.re.pol., 1923; D.Sc. in Econs., U. London, 1941; Dr. (hon.), U. Rikkyo, Tokyo, Japan, 1964, U. Salzburg, 1974, U. Dallas, 1975, Marroquin U., Guatemala, 1977, U. Santa Maria, Valparaiso, 1977, U. Buenos Aires, 1977, U. Giessen, 1982; children—Christine M. F., Lorenz J. H.; m. 2d, Helen Bitterlich, 1950. With Austrian Civil Service, 1921-26; dir. Austrian Inst. for Bus. Cycle Research, 1927-31; lectr. econs. and stats. U. Vienna, 1929-31; Tooke prof. econ. sci. and stats. U. London, London Sch. Econs., 1931-50; prof. social and moral sci. U. Chgo., 1950-62; prof. econs. U. Freiburg (Germany), 1962—; vis. prof. U. Salzburg (Austria), 1970-74. Decorated Companion of Honor (Great Britain), Order Pour le Merite (Germany); Austrian Distinction for Arts and Sci.; recipient Nobel Prize for Econs., 1974. Fellow Brit. Acad.; hon. fellow Austrian Acad. Sci. Author: Prices and Production, 1931; Monetary Theory and the Trade Cycle, 1933; Monetary Nationalism and International Stability, 1937; Profits, Interest and Investment, 1939; The Pure Theory of Capital, 1941; The Road to Serfdom, 1944; Individualism and Economic Order, 1949; John Stuart Mill and Harriet Taylor, 1951; The Sensory Order, 1952; The Counter-Revolution of Science, 1952; The Constitution of Liberty, 1960; Studies in Philosophy, Politics and Economics, 1967; Freiburger Studien, 1969; Law, Legislation and Liberty, Vol. I, 1973, Vol. II, 1975, Vol. III, 1979; Denationalization of Money, 1976; Further Studies in Politics, 1978; also numerous articles. Acting editor Economica, 1940-50. Research on evolution of civilization. Home: Urachstrasse 27, D7800 Freiburg, Breisgau Federal Republic of Germany

HAYES, ANN CARSON, art director; b. Hamlin, Tex. Apr. 25, 1941; d. Fred Elbert and Nona Faye (Riddle) Carson; m. Robert Lee Hayes, Nov. 15, 1975; m. James Russell Brown, May 7, 1959 (div. July 1973); children: James Allen, Daniel Russell, Robert Anthony, Debra Faye Mead. AAS, Howard Coll., Tex., 1972; student Regents Coll., N.Y.C., 1986. Freelance artist, Big Spring, Tex., 1956-76; real estate agt. Century 21, Littleton, Colo., 1976-78, Huntsville, Ala., 1978-79; art dir. Hayes and Co., Splendora, Tex. 1979—; income tax cons. H&R Block, Porter, Tex. Mem. Nat. Assn. Female Execs., Am. Bus. Womans Assn., LWV. Democrat. Episcopalian. Club: Toastmasters. Avocations: sculpting, glass etching, bowling, tennis. Home: 176 Split Oak Dr New Caney TX 77357 Office: PO Box 1209 Splendora TX 77372

HAYES, ARTHUR CHESTER, state legislator; b. Ft. Wayne, Ind., Aug. 24, 1918; s. Walter F. and Marie P. (Hardesty) H.; B.S., Ind. U., 1948; m. Miriam E. Peck, Feb. 1, 1946 (dec. Nov. 1968); children—Arthur C., Bethany M., Gayle W. Crosby. Sales corr. Magnavox Corporation, 1948-54; supr. Budget State Hwy. Dept., 1954-58; owner Vernors Bottling Co., Ft. Wayne, 1959-63; became dist. mgr. Colonial Life & Accident Ins. Co., 1963; mem. Ind. Ho. of Reps., 1963-72, 77—, ho. mem. Ind. Statutory com. on Commn. on Protection and Advocacy for Developmentally Disabled, 1977-78; safety cons. Chmn. Interstate Cooperation Com., Recodification of Cities and Towns Commn.; mem. Sesquicentennial Commn.; chmn. speakers bur. Ind. Am. Revolution Bicentennial Commn.; mem. Ind. Am. Negro Emancipation Centennial Commn. Served with AUS, 1941-45. Mem. Ft. Wayne C. of C., Am. Legion. Clubs: Ft. Wayne Civitan (pres. 1963-68; lt. gov. Midwest 1967). Home: 2001 Oakland St Fort Wayne IN 46808 Office: State House Bldg Indianapolis IN 46204

HAYES, BETTINE J., investment executive; b. Boston, Sept. 6, 1928; d. Reginald W. P. and Ethel (Thomas) Brown; B.A., Wellesley Coll., 1950; m. M. Vinson Hayes, June 10, 1961; children—M. Vinson III, Juliet Dorothy. Security analyst Merrill Lynch, Pierce, Fenner & Smith, Inc., N.Y.C., 1950-60, 76—, portfolio analyst, 1960-73, Canadian research coordinator, 1967-69; mgr. N.Y. Wellesley Club, 1973-74; researcher Nat. Information Bur., Inc., N.Y.C., 1974-76. Mem. D.A.R. (chpt. treas. 1958-59, historian 1961-62, rec. sec. Colonielles 1961-71, 73-77, treas., 1971-73), N.Y. Soc. Security Analysts. Club: New York Wellesley. Home: 39 Gramercy Park New York City NY 10010 also: 11 Spring Close Ln East Hampton NY 11937 Office: Merrill Lynch World Hdqrs North Tower World Fin Ctr New York NY 10281-1215

HAYES, BYRON JACKSON, JR., lawyer; b. Los Angeles, July 9, 1934; s. Byron Jackson and Caroline Violet (Scott) H.; m. DeAnne Saliba, June 30, 1962; children—Kenneth Byron, Patricia DeAnne. Student, Pomona Coll., 1952-56; B.A. magna cum laude, Harvard U., LL.B. cum laude, 1959. Bar: Calif. 1960, U.S. Supreme Ct. 1963. Assoc., McCutchen, Black, Verleger & Shea, Los Angeles, 1960-68, ptnr., 1968—. Trustee, Los Angeles Ch. Extension Soc. United Methodist Ch., 1967-77, pres., 1974-77; Dir., pres. Pacific and S.W. United Methodist Found., 1978-83, chancellor annual conf., 1979-86. Served to capt. U.S. Army, 1959-65. Named layperson of yr. Pacific and S.W. Annual Conf., United Methodist Ch., 1981. Mem. Am. Coll. Mortgage Attys. (regent 1984—), Calif. Bar Assn., ABA, Assn. Real Estate Attys., Los Angeles County Bar Assn. (chmn. real property sect. 1982-83), Pomona Coll. Alumni Assn. (pres. 1984-85). Club: Lakeside Golf (Toluca Lake, Calif.). Office: 600 Wilshire Blvd 9th Floor Los Angeles CA 90017

HAYES, CHARLES, religious organization executive, clergyman; b. Chgo., Aug. 4, 1950; s. Charles and Doris Yvonne (Davis) H.; children: Tammy, Beverly. Degree in Theology, Emmaus Bible Sch., 1977; AA in Data Processing, Kennedy King Coll., 1982, AS in Acctg., 1985; BA, Chgo. State U., 1986; AA in Bus. Mgmt., Ctr. Degree Studies, Scranton, Pa., 1988. Lic. minister. Assoc. pastor St. Mary's Ch., Chgo., 1978—; instr. Kennedy King Coll., Chgo., 1980-82; pres. Christians Taking Action, Inc., Chgo., 1983—; bd. dirs. Organized Urban Resource, Inc., Chgo. Contbr. articles to profl. jours. Recipient Recognition award Ch. Christ, 1977, Appreciation award U.S. Com. for UNICEF, 1985, Disting. Leadership award Am. Biog. Inst., 1988, Men of Achievement award Internat. Biog. Centre, Cambridge, Eng., Internat. World Leaders award. Democrat. Baptist. Home: 6619 S Maryland Chicago IL 60637

HAYES, CLAUDE QUINTEN CHRISTOPHER, research scientist; b. N.Y.C., Nov. 15, 1945; s. Claude and Celestine (Stanley) H. BA in Chemistry and Geol. Sci., Columbia U., 1971, postgrad., 1972-73; postgrad., N.Y. Law Sch., 1973-75; JD, Western State Law Sch., 1976. Cert. community coll. tchr. earth scis., phys. sci., law, Calif. Tech. writer Burroughs Corp., San Diego, 1978-79; instr. phys. scis. Nat. U., San Diego, 1980-81; instr. bus. law, earth scis. Miramar Coll., 1978-82; sr. systems analyst Gen. Dynamics Convair, 1979-80, advanced mfg. technologist, sr. engr., 1980-81; pvt. practice sci. and tech. cons. Calif., 1982-86; instr. phys. sci., phys. geography, bus. law San Diego Community Coll. Dist., 1976-82, 85-87; U.S. Dept. Def. contractor Def. Nuclear Agy., Strategic Def. Initiative Agy., USAF, Def. Advance Projects Agy., 1986-87; adj. prof. phys. chemistry San Diego State U., 1986-87; adj. prof. internat. bus. and computer sci. U. Redlands (Calif.) Grad. Sch., 1986-88; def. research contractor to Maxwell Labs., Naval Oceans Systems Ctr. Contbr. articles to profl. jours.; patentee in field. Mem. Am. Chem. Soc., N.Y. Acad. Sci. Home: 7980 Linda Vista Rd #49 San Diego CA 92111

HAYES, DOUGLAS MARTIN, investment banker; b. Cleve., Nov. 27, 1943; s. Douglas Anderson and Anna Carolyn (Martin) H.; m. Constance Anne Maezes, July 22, 1967; 1 child, Stephanie Janet. AB, Dartmouth Coll., 1965; MBA, Harvard U., 1969. Assoc. A.G. Becker Co., Chgo., 1969-72, asst. v.p., 1972-73, v.p., Los Angeles, 1973-77; mng. dir. Warburg, Paribas, Becker, Los Angeles, 1977-82, A.G. Becker Paribas, Los Angeles, 1982-84, Merrill Lynch Capital Markets, Los Angeles, 1984-86; prin., sr. v.p. Donaldson, Lufkin & Jenrette, Los Angeles, 1986—; guest speaker U. Chgo. Bus. Sch., 1972, Harvard U. Bus. Sch., Boston, 1974, UCLA Grad. Sch. Adminstrn., 1982-84. Treas. Calif. Chamber Symphony, Los Angeles, 1981-85, chmn. bd., 1985—; bd. dirs. UCLA Internat. Students Assn., 1982-83, Children's Bur. Los Angeles, 1985—. Clubs: Calif., Regency (Los Angeles). Home: 2545 Roscomare Rd Los Angeles CA 90077 Office: Donaldson Lufin & Jenrette 2121 Ave of Stars Suite 3000 Los Angeles CA 90067

HAYES, GEORGE NICHOLAS, lawyer; b. Alliance, Ohio, Sept. 30, 1928; s. Nicholas John and Mary Irene (Fanady) H. B.A., U. Akron, 1950; M.A., Western Res. U., 1953, LL.B., 1955. Bar: Ohio 1955, U.S. Dist. Ct. Alaska 1957, Alaska 1959, U.S. Ct. Appeals (9th cir.) 1958, U.S. Supreme Ct. 1964, Wash. 1972. Mcpl. ct. prosecutor, asst. county prosecutor Portage County, Ravenna, Ohio, 1955-57; asst. U.S. atty. Fairbanks and Anchorage (Alaska), 1957-59; dep. atty. gen. State of Alaksa, 1959-62; dist. atty. 3d Jud. Dist., Anchorage, 1960-62; atty. gen., Juneau, Alaska, 1962-64; spl. counsel to Gov., State of Alaska on earthquake recovery program at Washington, 1964; ptnr. Delaney, Wiles, Hayes, Reitman & Brubaker, Inc., Anchorage, 1964—. Mem. ABA, Washington State Bar Assn., Alaska Bar Assn., Ohio Bar Assn., Anchorage Bar Assn., Am. Coll. Trial Lawyers. Democrat. Office: 1007 W 3d Ave Anchorage AK 99501

HAYES, JAMES WILLIAM, municipal administrator; b. Fife, Scotland, Nov. 8, 1930; s. Eric Henry John and Anne Munro (Pegrum) H.; divorced 1972; children: Philippa, Susanna, Jacquetta; m. Mabel Chiu Woon Wong, Sept. 7, 1974. BA in History with honors, U. London, 1952, MA in History, 1956, PhD in History, 1975. Adminstr. Her Majesty's Oversea Civil Service Govt. Hong Kong, 1956-87; companion Imperial Service Order, 1986; ret. Govt. Hong Kong, 1987. Author: Hong Kong Region 1850-1911, 1977, Rural Communities of Hong Kong, 1983; contbr. articles to profl. jours. Served to capt. inf. Brit. army Hong Kong vols., 1953-66. Mem. Royal Asiatic Soc. (councillor 1966-70, v.p. 1970-83, pres. 1983—). Conservative. Mem. Ch. England. Club: Army and Navy (London). Home: 14B MacDonnell House, 6-8 MacDonnell Rd, Hong Kong Hong Kong

HAYES, JOHN TREVOR, museum administrator; b. Jan. 21, 1929; s. Leslie Thomas and Gwendoline (Griffiths) H.; attended (hon. fellow) Keble Coll., Oxford (Eng.) U., Courtauld Inst. Art, London, Inst. Fine Arts, N.Y.; MA, Oxford U.; PhD, London U.; Asst. keeper London Mus., 1954-70, dir., 1970-74; dir. Nat. Portrait Gallery, London, 1974—; Commonwealth Fund fellow N.Y. U., 1958-59; vis. prof. history of art Yale U., 1969. Decorated Comdr. Order of Brit. Empire. Fellow Royal Soc. Antiquaries. Clubs: Beefsteak, Arts. Author: London: a pictorial history, 1969; The Drawings of Thomas Gainsborough, 1970; Catalogue of Oil Paintings in the London Museum, 1970; Gainsborough as Printmaker, 1971; Rowlandson: Watercolours and Drawings, 1972; Gainsborough: Paintings and Drawings, 1975; The Art of Graham Sutherland, 1980; (catalogue) Gainsborough Exhbns., 1980-81; The Landscape Paintings of Thomas Gainsborough, 1982; various London Mus. and Nat. Portrait Gallery publs.; contbr. numerous articles to Burlington Mag., Apollo and other jours. Office: Nat Portrait Gallery, St Martin's Pl, London WC2H 0HE, England

HAYES, MARY PHYLLIS, savings and loan association executive; b. New Castle, Ind., Apr. 30, 1921; d. Clarence Edward and Edna Gertrude (Burgess) Scott; m. John Clifford Hayes, Jan. 1, 1942 (div. Oct. 1952); 1 child, R. Scott. Student, Ball State U., 1957-64, Ind. U. East, Richmond, 1963; diploma, Inst. Fin. Edn., 1956, 72, 76. Teller Henry County Savs. and Loan, New Castle, 1939-41, loan officer, teller, 1950-62, asst. sec., treas., 1962-69, sec., treas., 1969-73, corp. sec., 1973-84; v.p., sec. Ameriana Savs. Bank (formerly Henry County Savs. and Loan), New Castle, 1984—; exec. sec. Am. Nat. Bank, Nashville, 1943-44; corp. sec. HCSS Corp., New Castle, 1984—; bd. dirs. Ameriana Ins. Co. Treas. Henry County Chpt. Am. Heart Assn., New Castle, 1965-67, 76-87, vol. Indpls. chpt. 1980—; membership sec. Henry County Hist. Soc., New Castle, 1975—; sec. Henry County Chpt. ARC, New Castle, 1976—. Recipient Gold medallian Am. Heart Assn., 1973, diploma of merit Inst. Fin. Edn., 1984, 20-Yr. award, 1983, 25-Yr. award Ind. affiliate Am. Heart Assn., 1987. Mem. Inst. Fin. Edn. (sec., treas. E. Cen. Ind. chpt. 1973—), Ind. League Savs. Insts. (25-Yr. award 1975), Psi Iota Xi (past sec., treas.). Mem. Christian Ch. Lodges: Altrusa (past officer, bd. dirs. New Castle chpt.), PEO (past chaplain, sec.). Office: Ameriana Savs Bank 2118 Bundy Ave New Castle IN 47362

HAYES, MONSON HENRY, III, electrical engineering educator; b. Washington, Oct. 27, 1949; s. Monson Henry Jr. and Anna Lois (Tufts) H.; m. Sandra Gayle Song, Dec. 18, 1971; children—Michael Young, Kimberly Song. B.A., U. Calif., Berkeley, 1971; S.M. in Elec. Engring., MIT, 1978, Sc.D., 1981. Systems engr. Aerojet Electrosystems, Azusa, Calif., 1971-74; tchr., research asst. MIT, Cambridge, Mass., 1974-81; assoc. prof. Ga. Inst. tech., Atlanta, 1981—; cons. Hayes Micrcomputers, Norcross, Ga., 1983-84, Lockheed-Ga., Marietta, 1985—. Contbr. articles to profl. jours. Recipient NSF Presdl. Young Investigator award, 1984. Mem. IEEE (chmn. digital signal processing tech. com. 1985—, assoc. editor 1984—, sr. award 1983).

HAYES, RICHARD JOHNSON, association executive, lawyer; b. Chgo., May 25, 1933; s. David John Arthur and Lucille Margaret (Johnson) H.; m. Mary R. Lynch, Dec. 2, 1961; children: Susan, Richard, John, Edward. B.A., Colo. Coll., 1955; J.D., Georgetown U., 1961. Bar: Ill. 1961. Assoc. firm Barnabas F. Sears, Chgo., 1961-63, Peterson, Lowry, Rall, Barber and Ross, Chgo., 1963-65; staff dir. Am. Bar Assn., Chgo., 1965-70; exec. dir. Internat. Assn. Ins. Counsel, Chgo., 1970—; instr. various legal programs 1966—, Ins. Counsel Trial Acad., 1973—. Editor: Antitrust Law Jour, 1969—. Served to 1st lt. AUS, 1955-57. Mem. Am., Chgo. socs. assn. execs., ABA (chmn. prepaid legal services 1977-78), Ill. Bar Assn., Chgo. Bar Assn., Jr. Bar (chmn. 1965), Nat. Conf. Lawyers and Ins. Cos. (bd. dirs. 1983—), Phi Alpha Delta, Beta Theta Pi. Clubs: Rotary/One (Chgo.), Tower (Chgo.); Mich. Shores (Wilmette, Ill.). Home: 1920 Thornwood St Wilmette IL 60091 Office: 20 N Wacker Dr Chicago IL 60606

HAYES, WAYLAND JACKSON, JR., toxicologist, educator; b. Charlottesville, Va., Apr. 29, 1917; s. Wayland Jackson and Mary Lula (Turner) H.; m. Barnita Donkle, Feb. 1, 1942; children: Marie Hayes Sarneski, Maryetta Hayes Hacskaylo, Lula Hayes McCoy, Wayland, Roche del Hayes Moser. B.S., U. Va., 1938, M.D., 1946; M.A., U. Wis., 1940, Ph.D., 1942. Chief vector-transmission investigations USPHS, Savannah, Ga., 1947-48; chief toxicology sect. USPHS, 1949-60, Atlanta, 1960-67; chief toxicologist USPHS, 1967-68; prof. biochemistry Vanderbilt U. Sch. Medicine, Nashville, 1968—; Vol. asso. prof. pharmacology Emory U., Atlanta, 1962-68; cons. WHO, 1950—, Nat. Acad. Scis.-NRC, 1964-86. Author: Clinical Handbook on Economic Poisons, 1963, Toxicology of Pesticides, 1975, Pesticides Studied in Man, 1982; Mem. editorial bds.: Jour. Pharmacology and Exptl. Therapeutics, 1962-64, Archives Environmental Health, 1965-72, 76-85, Food and Cosmetics Toxicology, 1967-78, Essays in Toxicology, 1972-76; Contbr. sci. papers to profl. lit. Served with AUS, 1943-46. Recipient Meritorious Service medal USPHS, 1964. Mem. Soc. Toxicology (charter, pres. 1971-72, ambassador of toxicology award 1985), Am. Soc. Pharmacology and Exptl. Therapeutics, Am. Soc. Tropical Medicine and Hygiene, Am. Conf. Govtl. Indsl. Hygienists. Home: 2317 Golf Club Ln Nashville TN 37215

HAYLOCK, JOHN MERVYN, English literature educator; b. Bournemouth, Hampshire, Eng., Sept. 22, 1918; s. Sydney John and Winifred Margaret (Baker) H. Diplôme Français, Institut de Touraine, Tours, France, 1937; Cert. d'Immatriculation, U. Grenoble, France, 1938; BA with honors, Cambridge (Eng.) U., 1942, MA with honors, 1946, Dip. Edn., 1948. Tchr. English Primary Tchrs. Tng. Coll., Baghdad, Iraq, 1948-52, Coll. of Commerce and Econs., Baghdad, Iraq, 1952-56, Waseda U., Tokyo, 1958-60, 62-65; vis. prof. English lit. Rikkyo U., Tokyo, 1975-82, Japan Women's U., Tokyo, 1982-84. Author: (novels) See You Again, 1963, It's All Your Fault, 1964, One Hot Summer in Kyoto, 1980; (with Desmond Stewart) New Babylon, Portrait of Iraq, 1956; contbr. articles and fiction to jours. and mags. Served to capt. Brit. Army, 1940-46. Decorated Ordre de Leopold II (Belgium), Croix de Guerre avec palme (Belgium). Mem. Ch. of England. Club: Oriental (London). Home: 5 Powis Grove, Brighton BN1 3HF, England

HAYNAL, ANDRE EMERIC, psychiatrist educator, psychoanalyst; b. Budapest, Hungary, Aug. 13, 1930; arrived in Switzerland, 1956; s. Imre G. and Margit L. (Nagy) H.; m. Litza R. Guttieres, Feb. 2, 1971 (div. 1984); m. Veronique Reymond, Jan. 6, 1985; children: Cleo E., David S. BA, Cistercian Coll., Budapest, 1948; MA in Philosophy and Psychology, U. Budapest, 1951; MD, U. Zurich, 1959; FMH, U. Berne, 1966. Diplomate Fedn. of Swiss Doctors in neurology, psychiatry and psychotherapy. Intern, resident Zurich (Switzerland) U. Gen. Hosp., 1960-64; from asst. prof. psychiatry to prof. Med. Sch. U. Geneva, 1973—; practice medicine specializing in psychiatry and psychoanalysis Geneva; med. dir. psychiat. service U. Clinic for Psychiatry II, 1971—; vis. prof. psychiatry Stanford (Calif.) U., 1980-81. Author: Le Fanatisme, 1980 (pub. in English as Fanatacism 1983), Le Sens du Desespoir, 1976 (transl. into Italian, pub. in English as Depression and Creativity 1985), Abrege de medecine psychosomatique, 1978 (transl. into Italian, Spanish and Portuguese), Les Orphelins menent-ils le monde?, 1978, Technique en question - Controverses en psychanalyse, 1987. Recipient Dubois prize Swiss Med. Soc. Psychotherapy, 1977, Merit award Am. Mental Health Found., 1982. Mem. Swiss Psychoanalytic Soc. (pres. 1976-79), European Psychoanalytical Fedn. (v.p. 1979-85), Internat. Psychoanalytical Assn., Internat. Coll. Psychosomatic Medicine, Internat. Inst. for Mental Health Research, Sigmund Freud Gesellschaft. Home: 20 bis Ch de la Gradelle, 1224 Geneva Switzerland Office: U Geneva Dept Psychiatry, 16-18 Blvd St Georges CP 79, 1211 Geneva 8 Switzerland

HAYNES, ARDEN R., oil company executive; b. Sask., Can., B.Commerce, U. Man., Winnipeg, 1951. With Imperial Oil Ltd., throughout Can., 1951-68, 1972—, Standard Oil Co. (N.J.) (now Exxon Corp.), N.Y.C., 1968-72; v.p., gen. mgr. mktg. dept. Imperial Oil Ltd., Toronto, 1973-74, dir., sr. v.p., 1974-78, pres., chief exec. officer Esso Resources Can. Ltd., 1978-81; chmn. bd. Esso Resources Can. Ltd. subs. Imperial Oil Ltd., 1981-85; exec. v.p. Imperial Oil Ltd., Toronto, 1982, pres., chief operating officer, 1982, chmn., pres., chief exec. officer, 1985, chmn., chief exec. officer, 1988—;

assoc. faculty adminstrv. studies, co-chmn. devel. fund., U. Man.; mem. fed. govt.'s adv. group on energy products and services, fed. govt.'s adv. com. on bus./govt. exec. exchange program; bd. dirs. Royal Bank Can., Power Corp. Can., Moore Corp. Ltd. Chmn. fund-raising campaign Diabetes Can., 1982-87; bd. dirs. Jr. Achievement of Can., Alzheimer Soc. of Can., Centre for Research in Neurodegenerative Diseases at U. Toronto; gov. Olympic Trust Can.; founding mem., bd. dirs. Ont. Trillium Found.; patron Bob Rumball Centre for the Deaf, Toronto; chmn. Nat. Adv. Council for World Energy Congress in Montreal. Office: Imperial Oil Ltd, 111 St Clair Ave W, Toronto, ON Canada M5W 1K3

HAYNES, FREDERICK LESLIE, industrial engineer, government official; b. Portsmouth, N.H., Oct. 27, 1934; s. James Edwin and Elizabeth (Crankshaw) H.; m. Patricia Marie Griffith, July 29, 1960. BS, Northeastern U., 1960; MBA, Am. U., 1968. Registered profl. engr., Mass. Indsl. engr. Alcoa, Edgewater, N.J., 1962-64; sr. indsl. engr. USAF Mgmt. Engring Program, Pentagon, 1964-72; asst. dir. U.S. Gen. Acctg. Office, Washington, 1972-79; dir. office coop. generic tech. U.S. Dept. Commerce, Washington, 1979-81; assoc. dir. product and market devel. Nat. Tech. Info. Service, Washington, 1981-85, assoc. dir., mktg. and customer services, 1985—; assoc. for research and devel. ltd. partnerships, office of asst. sec. PTI; lectr. in field. Contbr. articles to profl. jours. Served with USN, 1955-57; U.S. Army, 1960-62. Decorated U.S. Army Commendation medal. Fellow Am. Inst. Indsl. Engrs.; mem. Soc. Mfg. Engrs., World Future Soc., Order of the Engr. Home: 3806 Fort Hill Dr Alexandria VA 22310 Office: Nat Tech Info Service Springfield VA 22161

HAYNES, JEAN REED, lawyer; b. Miami, Fla., Apr. 6, 1949; d. Oswald Birnam and Arleen (Weidman) Dow; m. William Rutherford Reed, Apr. 15, 1974 (div. Sept. 1981); m. Thomas Beranek Haynes, Aug. 7, 1982. AB with honors, Pembroke Coll., 1971; MA, Brown U., 1971; JD, U. Chgo., 1981. Bar: Ill. 1981, U.S. Dist. Ct. (no. dist.) Ill. 1983, U.S. Ct. Appeals (7th cir.) 1982. Tchr. grades 1-4 Abbie Tuller Sch., Providence, 1971-72; tchr./facilitator St. Mary's Acad., Riverside, R.I., 1972-74; tchr./head lower sch. St. Francis Sch., Goshen, Ky., 1974-78; law clk. U.S. Ct. Appeals (7th cir.), Chgo., 1981-83; assoc. Kirkland & Ellis, Chgo., 1983-87, ptnr., 1987—. Sustaining fellow Art Inst. Chgo., 1982—, mem. aux. bd. 1986—, membership com. aux. bd., 1987—, v.p. for devel., 1988—. Mem. ABA (litigation sect., com. on affordable justice 1988—), Chgo. Bar Assn., Ill. Bar Assn. (life), Am. Judicature Soc. (life). Club: Internationale, East Bank. Home: 179 East Lake Shore Dr Chicago IL 60611 Office: Kirkland & Ellis 200 E Randolph Dr Chicago IL 60611

HAYNES, LILITH MARGARET VON MUTIUS, linguist, translator, educator, researcher; b. Kitty, Greater Georgetown, Guyana, Sept. 9, 1944; d. Oscar Elgin and Lucille Maude (Sobryan) Haynes; m. Ludwig Alexander von Mutius, July 11, 1980; children—Lindi Dorothée, Alexander Lael. B.A. in French and Spanish with gen. honors, Univ. West Indies, Barbados, 1966, M.A. in Linguistics and Ethnobotany, Jamaica, 1969; Ph.D. in Linguistics, Stanford U., 1973. Asst. prof. N. Mex. State U., Las Cruces, 1973-76; project specialist Ford Found., Middle East, Africa, 1976-79; Benedict Disting. vis. prof. Carleton Coll., Northfield, Minn., 1979-80, vis. assoc. prof., 1980-81; Brückenkursleiterin U. Essen (W.Ger.), 1981—; cons. Ford Found., N.Y.C., Middle East, 1982-83. Editor 2 books, including: (with Werner Enninger) Studies in Language Ecology, 1984; contbr. articles to profl. jours. Soprano Meml. Ch. Choir, Stanford U. (Calif.), 1971-73, sr. house assoc. Manzanita Park, 1971-73. Mem. Linguistic Soc. Am. (Summer stipend 1971), Soc. Caribbean Linguistics, Stanford Alumni Assn. (life), Delta Sigma Theta (student adviser 1975-76). Home: Goldfinkstrasse 52, 4300 Essen 1 Federal Republic of Germany Office: Fachbereich 3, Literatur-und, Sprachwissenschaften, U Essen, Universitätstrasse 12, 4300 Essen 1 Federal Republic of Germany

HAYNES, RICHARD CHRISTOPHER, government official; b. June 10, 1936; married; 2 sons. Student, Harrison's Coll., Barbados, Edinburgh (Scotland) U. Lectr. Edinburgh U., 1963, research fellow, 1967; assoc. lectr. U. West Indies, head dept. medicine, 1969; chief of staff Queen Elizabeth Hosp., 1974-76, head intensive care, 1970-76; M.P. Barbados, 1978—, shadow minister, 1978-86, minister of fin., 1986-87. Office: Govt Hdqrs, Bay St, St Michael, Bridgetown Barbados *

HAYNIE, HUGH, editorial cartoonist; b. Reedville, Va., Feb. 6, 1927; s. Raymond Lee and Margaret Virginia (Smith) H.; m. Oleta Joanne Stevens; children: Hugh Smith, Tiffany Dawn. A.B., Coll. William and Mary, 1950; L.H.D., U. Louisville, 1968. Cartoonist Richmond (Va.) Times-Dispatch, 1950-53; Cartoonist, Greensboro (N.C.) Daily News, 1953-55, 56-58, Atlanta Jour., 1955-56; with Louisville Courier Jour., 1958—, now editorial cartoonist. Author: Hugh Haynie: Perspective, 1974. Served to lt. USCGR, 1944-46, 51-52, PTO, ATO. Recipient Headliner award, 1966; Freedoms Found. award, 1966-70; Disting. Service award and bronze medallion Sigma Delta Chi, 1971; Alumni medal for service and loyalty Coll. William and Mary, 1977; Civil Libertarian of Yr. award Ky. Civil Liberties Union, 1978; named to Ky. Journalism Hall of Fame, 1987 and Best of Gannett, 1987. Mem. Soc. Alumni Coll. William and Mary (past dir.), Phi Beta Kappa, Omicron Delta Kappa, Pi Kappa Alpha. Democrat. Episcopalian. Clubs: Windmill Point, Yacht (Windmill Point, Va.); Filson (life mem.). Home: 6609 Upper River Rd Harrods Creek KY Office: Courier-Jour 525 W Broadway Louisville KY 40202

HAYOUN, MAURICE-RUBEN, educator; b. Paris, Sept. 22, 1950; s. Isaac and Gracia (Benarroch) H. Doctorat d'Etat es Lettres, U. Paris Sorbonne, 1985. Prof. U. Strasbourg, France, 1979—; assoc. prof. U. Heidelberg, Fed. Republic Germany, 1984, U. W. Berlin, 1985. Author: Gershom Scholem/Le Nom et Les Symboles de Dieu Dans la Mystique Juive, 1983, Gershom Scholem/La Kabbale/Les Themes fondamentaux, 1985, Solomon Maimon/Histoire de Ma Vie, 1984, Samson Raphael Hirsch/Les Dix-Neuf Epitres Sur le Judaisme, 1987, Moise Maimonide Que Sais Je?, 1987, Moshe Narboni, 1986. Fellow Meml. Found. for Jewish Culture, N.Y., 1979085, Alexander Von Von Humboldt Stiftung, Bonn, Fed. Republic Germany, 1984-85. Mem. Soc. des Etudes Juives, Soc. Asiatique. Home: 16 Rue Paul Bert, 75011 Paris France Office: Inst Etudes Hebraiques, Strasbourg France

HAYRY, PEKKA JUHA, transplant surgeon, immunologist; b. Vihti, Finland, Dec. 13, 1939; s. Olavi K. and Aili (Harjula) H.; m. Annamari Ranki, July 17, 1976 (div. 1982); 1 child, Valtteri. M.D., Univ. Helsinki (Finland), 1965, Ph.D., 1966. Postdoctoral fellow Wistar Inst., Phila., 1967-70; resident in surgery U. Helsinki Hosp., 1971-73, assoc. chief surgery, 1973-79; asst. prof. immunology U. Helsinki, 1970-79; asst. prof. surgery U. Oulu, Finland, 1973-79; prof. transplantation surgery and immunology U. Helsinki and Helsinki U. Central Hosp., 1979—; vis. prof. U. Rene Descartes, Paris, 1974, Duke U., 1977, U. N.C., 1977, U. Adelaide, Australia, 1981. Contbr. chpts. to books, articles to profl. jours. Served to lt. Finnish Med. Corps, 1960-61. Mem. Transplantation Soc., Scandinavian Soc. Immunology (bd. dirs. 1980-85), Am. Assn. Immunologists, Am. Soc. Transplant Surgeons, Internat. Soc. Heart Transplantation (v.p. 1988—), Internat. Soc. Nephrology. Avocations: sheep breeding. Office: U Helsinki Transplant Lab, Haartmaninkatu 3, SF 00290 Helsinki Finland

HAYS, HERSCHEL MARTIN, electrical engineer; b. Neillsville, Wis., Mar. 2, 1920; s. Myron E. and Esther (Marquardt) H.; E.E., U. Minn., 1942; grad. student U. So. Calif., 1947; children—Howard Martin, Holly Mary, Diane Esther, Willet Martin Hays II. Elec. engr. City of Los Angeles, 1947-60; pres. Li-Bonn Corp. Served as radio officer, 810th Signal Service Bn., U.S. Army, 1942-43; asst. signal constrn. officer, E.T.O., 1943-45, tech. supr. Japanese radio systems, U.S. Army of Occupation, 1945-46; mem. tech. staff, Signal Corps Engring. Labs., U.S. Army, 1946; col. U.S. Army, ret. Signal Officer Calif. N.G. 1947-50. Registered profl. engr. Calif. Mem. Eta Kappa Nu, Pi Tau Pi Sigma, Kappa Eta Kappa. Republican. Episcopalian. Home: 603 Alhambra Venice FL 34285

HAYS, MARILYN PATRICIA, lawyer, rancher, real estate executive; b. Yarrow, Mo., Sept. 19, 1935; d. John Dewey and Ruth (McKim) H.; m. Harold Clifton Ledbetter, Dec. 13, 1953 (div. 1972); children—Latricia Lyn, Lisa Ledbetter Cerio, David Clifton, Laura Lizanne; Harold Clifton, Jr.; m. Dean Leon Fortney, July 21, 1978. BS, Northeast Mo. State U., 1958; broker cert. U. Fla., 1976; MA, U. Mo., 1983; JD, Washburn U., 1987. Lic. real estate broker, Mo., Kans., Fla., Grad. Realtors Inst. Fashion coordinator Ashells, Regina's Co., Kirksville, Mo., 1951-54; instr. pub. schs., Crocker, Novinger, Kirksville and University City, Mo., 1954-61; real estate salestaff Goldman's Assocs., Daytona Beach, Fla., 1975-76; real estate broker Kellogg Century 21, Daytona Beach, 1976-78; pres. M.P. Hays Co., Olathe, Kans., 1978-82, Bucyrus, Kans., 1982—; cons. Goldman, Kellogg, Daytona Beach, 1975-78. Contbr. articles on real estate edn. to profl. jours. Pres. Fla. Osteopathic Med. Assn. Aux., Dist. IV, 1964-65, 73-74, pres.-elect, 1967-68; major chmn. Assn. of Jr. League, Daytona Beach, 1968-69, 72-73; Pan Hellenic del., 1972-78; adviser Ormond Beach Hosp. Guild, Fla., 1972-74; tchr. CCD Holy Rosary Cath. Ch., Bucyrus, 1987—. Scholar, Mo. Council PTAs, 1953, K.C., 1954; recipient Outstanding Sales Achievement award Kellogg Century 21, 1977. Mem. Kans. Bar Assn., ABA, Miami County Bd. Realtors, Johnson County Bd. Realtors, Nat. Assn. Realtors, Kans. Assn. Realtors, Kans. Farm Bur., Women's Legal Forum, AAUW, Am. Quarterhorse Assn., Holy Rosary Alter Soc., Alpha Sigma Alpha, Phi Delta Phi. Republican. Roman Catholic. Clubs: Ormond Beach Woman's, Oceanside Country. Avocations: photography; cooking; horseback riding. Home: Rt 1 Box 161 Bucyrus KS 66013 Office: M P Hays Co 223d St and State Line Rd Bucyrus KS 66013

HAYS, MARY KATHERINE JACKSON (MRS. DONALD OSBORNE HAYS), civic worker; b. Flora, Miss.; d. Rufus Lafayette and Ada (Collum) Jackson; student U. Miss., 1925-26, Millsaps Coll., 1926-27, 43-44; grad. Clark Bus. Sch., 1934; student Columbia U., 1935, Strayer Bus. Coll., 1951; m. Halbert Puffer Oliver, Aug. 9, 1927 (dec. 1934); m. 2d, Donald Osborne Hays, Aug. 30, 1937. Sec. to pres. McCullough Box and Crate Co., Pharr, Tex., 1934-36; sec. to field supr. Miss. Unemployment Compensatio Commn., 1936-37; rep. Homes of Tomorrow, 1940 N.Y. World's Fair; sec. to head interior design Lord & Taylor, N.Y.C., 1940; sales dept. Knabe Piano Co., N.Y.C., 1941-43. Active, Little Theatre, Wilkes Barre, Pa., 1937-39; charter mem. and incorporator Conf. State Socs., Washington, 1952; vol. worker Am. Cancer Soc., Washington, 1957; mem. Center City Residents Assn., Phila., 1956; mem. women's com. Nat. Symphony Assn., vol. worker USO, 1945-48, symphony sustaining com. drives, 1957-66; mem. women's com. Corcoran Gallery Art, Washington, 1957-62; mem. Pierce-Warwick Adoption Assn. of Washington Home for Foundlings; vol. Washington Heart Assn., 1959-66; mem. Nat. Capital Area chpt. United Ch. Women, 1957-72; mem. D.C. Episcopal Home for Children, 1961-86, D.C. Salvation Army Aux., 1962—. Mem. Miss. State Soc. D.C. (sec. 1950-53), Miss. Women's Club D.C., DAR (vice regent chpt. 1970-72, regent chpt. 1972-74, vice chmn. D.C. com. celebration Washington's birthday 1972-76, state librarian 1974-76), chpt. chmn. DAR Service for Vet. Patients Com., 1986-88, UDC (chpt. historian 1982-84, 86—, chaplain 1984-86), Johnstone Clan Am. (exec. council 1976-81), First Families of Miss. Episcopalian. Club: The Washington. Home: 4000 Massachusetts Ave NW Washington DC 20016

HAYS, ROBERT ALEXANDER, lawyer; b. Westerly, R.I., June 20, 1944; s. William Henry and Margaret Elizabeth (Tefft) H.; m. Norma Marie Camerlin, Aug. 23, 1969; children—Stephanie Rebecca, Gregory Alexander. Assoc. Sci., Mitchell Coll., 1967; B.S., NYU, 1969, M.S., 1970; J.D., Del. Law Sch., 1976. Bar: N.J. 1976, U.S. Dist. Ct. N.J. 1976, U.S. Patent Office 1974, U.S. Ct. Appeals (fed. cir.) 1982. Mem. tech. staff RCA, Moorestown, N.J., 1970-73, patent atty., Princeton, N.J., 1973-78, resident patent counsel, Cherry Hill, N.J., 1978-80; group patent counsel Perkin-Elmer, Norwalk, Conn., 1980-84; patent counsel ITT, Shelton, Conn., 1984-86, patent atty. Pitney Bowes, Stamford, Conn., 1986-88; sr. patent atty. Hughes Aircraft Co., Los Angeles, 1988—. Mem. Conn. Patent Law Assn., Tau Beta Pi, Eta Kappa Nu.

HAYS, SAMUEL SPARTAN, lawyer, consultant; b. Fairfield, Ala., Apr. 15, 1920; s. Samuel Spartan and Mabel (Vines) H.; m. Edwina Mallette Pringle, Jan. 26, 1942; children—Mary Mallette, Sally Ellen. B.S., U. Ala., 1942, J.D., 1952; M.S. in Govt. Mgmt., U. Denver, 1944. Bar: Ala. 1952, U.S. Supreme Ct. 1965. Tax research assoc. Tax Found., N.Y.C., 1944; rep. Tax Assn. Md., 1944-45; research dir. Tax Assn. Mo., 1945-46; exec. dir. Tax Assn. Ark., 1946-50; cons. Tax Assn. Pa., summer 1952; ptnr. law firm, Birmingham, Ala., 1952-59; tax and fiscal adv. Dept. State to Govt. of Iran, 1959-65, Govt. of Jordan, 1965, also intermittent cons. to other nations; sole practice, Mountain Brook, Ala., 1965—; cons. internat. bus. and taxes. Served with USN, 1943. Alfred P. Sloan Found. grantee, 1942-44. Episcopalian. Club: Masons. Editor Ala. Law Rev., 1952.

HAYWARD, ROGER PHILIP, cardiologist; b. London, July 8, 1947; s. Sidney Thomas and Irene (Ackerley) H.; m. Mary Rothwell Bromley; children: Rosemary Claire, Michael Thomas George. BS in Medicine and Surgery, U. London, 1970, MD, 1985. Med. house physician St. Bartholomew's Hosp., London, 1970-71, house officer, 1972-73, research registrar, 1974-77; registrar Nat. Heart Hosp., London, 1977-79; sr. registrar Middlesex Hosp., London, 1980—. Contbr. numerous articles on cardiology to profl. jours. Mem. Brit. Cardiac Soc., Brit. Pharmacological Soc., European Soc. Cardiology. Office: Middlesex Hosp, Cardiac Dept, London W1N 8AA, England

HAYWARD, TERESA CALCAGNO, educator; b. N.Y.C., Jan. 28, 1907; d. Vito and Rosalie (Amato) Calcagno; m. Peter Hayward, Feb. 6, 1932; children—Nancy, Peter. B.A., Hunter Coll., 1929; M.A., Columbia U., 1931. Tchr. romance langs. Jr. High Sch. 164, N.Y.C., 1936-57, Jr. High Sch. 141, Riverdale, N.Y., 1957-71; tchr. English to Japanese women Nichibei Fujinkai, Riverdale, 1972—. Chmn. Riverdale chpt. Nichibei Fujinkai, Riverdale, 1976-88; bd. dirs. Riverdale chpt. UN Assn., 1976-88. Mem. Hunger and Social Outreach com. Christ Ch., Riverdale. Democrat. Episcopalian. Avocations: concerts; piano; art lectures; travel.

HAZAMA, YOSHIKAZU, environmental engineer; b. Tokushima, Japan, Jan. 1, 1948; s. Tamotsu and Toshiko (Iwata) H.; m. Toshi Omori, July 24, 1974; children: Yusuke, Youko. B in Engring., Nagoya (Japan) Inst. Tech., 1972. Engr. Toyo Netsu Kogyo Kaisha, Ltd., Tokyo, 1972-85, chief planning engr., 1986—; cons. in field. Author: Solar System Design Guide, 1981, Knowledge of Solar System, 1982. Mem. Soc. Heating, Air-Conditioning and Sanitary Engrs., Japan Cons. Engrs. Assn. Home: 1-15 Kaijin 3-Chome, Funabashi, Chiba 273, Japan Office: Toyo Netsu Kogyo Kaisha Ltd, 5-12 Kyobashi 2-Chome, Tokyo 104, Japan

HAZARD, JOHN NEWBOLD, retired public law educator; b. Syracuse, N.Y., Jan. 5, 1909; s. John Gibson and Ada Bosarte (DeKalb) H.; m. Susan Lawrence, March 8, 1941; children: John Gibson, William Lawrence, Nancy, Barbara Peace. Ed., The Hill Sch., 1926; A.B., Yale U., 1930; LL.B., Harvard U., 1934; certificate, Moscow Juridical Inst., 1937; J.S.D., U. Chgo., 1939; LL.D., U. Freiburg, 1969, Lehigh U., 1970, Leiden U., 1975, U. Paris, 1977, U. Louvain, 1979, U. Sydney, 1986. Bar: N.Y., U.S. Supreme Ct. Fellow Inst. of Current World Affairs (student of Soviet law), 1934-39; asso. with law firm Baldwin, Todd & Young, N.Y.C., 1939-41; dep. dir. U.S.S.R. br. Fgn. Econ. Adminstrn. (and predecessor agys.), 1941-45; adv. on state trading Dept. State, 1945-46; prof. public law Columbia, 1946-77, Nash prof. law, 1976-77, Nash prof. law emeritus, 1977—; adviser on Soviet law to U.S. chief of counsel for prosecution of Axis criminality, 1945; lectr. Soviet law U. Chgo., 1938-39; lectr. Soviet polit. instns. Columbia U., 1940-41; lectr. internat. politics Fgn. Service Ednl. Found., 1944-46; vis. prof. law Yale U., spring 1949, 50, 52, 54, 56; vis. Fulbright prof. U. Cambridge, London Sch. Econs., 1952-53, U. Louvain, Belgium, 1979; vis. prof. U. Tokyo, summer 1956, Grad. Sch. Internat. Studies, Geneva, 1959-60; prof. Luxembourg Comparative Law Faculty, summers 1958-60, Strasbourg Comparative Law Faculty, summers 1962—; vis. prof. U. Teheran, fall 1966, U. Sydney, 1978, summer 1986; Goodhart prof. Cambridge U., 1981-82; prof. European U. Inst., 1984-85; sr. specialist East-West Center Hawaii, spring 1967; fellow Center for Advanced Study in the Behavioral Scis., 1961-62. Author: Soviet Housing Law, 1939, Law and Social Change in the USSR, 1953, The Soviet System of Government, 1957, Settling Disputes in Soviet Society, 1960, (with I. Shapiro) The Soviet Legal System, 1962, Communists and Their Law, 1969, Managing Change in the USSR, 1983 (enlarged edition 1987); Recollections of a Pioneer Sovietologist, 1983; Editor: Soviet Legal Philosophy, 1951; Bd. editors: Am. Slavic and East European Rev; mng. editor, 1951-59; bd. editors: Am. Polit. Sci. Rev, 1950, Am. Jour. Internat. Law, 1956-72, hon. editor, 1974—; bd. editors: Am. Jour. Comparative Law, 1952—. Dir. and sec. Am. Assn. for the Advancement of Slavic Studies, 1948-60, treas., 1961-65. Recipient Pres.'s Certificate of Merit, 1947. Mem. ABA (vice chmn. internat. and comparative law 1951-58), Assn. of Bar of City of N.Y. (chmn. com. fgn. law 1947-50), Am. Polit. Sci. Assn., Am. Soc. Internat. Law (exec. council 1946-49, 51-54, v.p. 1971-73, hon. v.p. 1973-84, hon. pres. 1984-86), Am. br. of Internat. Law Assn. (chmn. exec. com. 1958-59, v.p. 1957-73, pres. 1973-79), Internat. Acad. Comparative Law (pres. 1984—), Internat. Assn. Legal Sci. (pres. 1968-70), Am. Philos. Soc., Am. Acad. Arts and Scis., World Assn. Law Profs. (co-chmn. 1975-84), Consular Law Soc. (pres. 1986-87), Am. Fgn. Law Assn. (pres. 1973-76), Brit. Acad. (corr.), Phi Alpha Delta, Alpha Delta Phi. Democrat. Episcopalian. Clubs: Century (N.Y.); University (Washington); Wolf's Head. Home: 20 E 94th St New York NY 10128 Office: 435 W 116th St New York NY 10027

HAZARD, THOMAS WILLIAM, JR., business management consultant; b. San Jose, Calif., Nov. 13, 1925; s. Thomas William and Bernice Vernice (Butts) H.; m. Audrey Marie Knecht, July 29, 1957 (div. 1977); children—Scott Thomas, Jeanmarie Ann, Gregory Michael; m. Gloria Joan Lee, July 26, 1977. B.S., U.S. Mil. Acad., 1948; M.A., Stanford U., 1968; LL.B., LaSalle U., 1969; Ph.D., Calif. Coast U., 1977. Commd. 2d lt. U.S. Army, 1948, advanced through grades to capt. 1957; tech. engr. Gen. Electric Co., Cin., 1957-59; chief spl. publs. AEC, Washington, 1959-63; regional sci. officer AID, 1963-74; mgmt. cons., 1975-81; asst. prof. Embry-Riddle Aero. U., Prescott, Ariz., 1981-83; mem. faculty U. Phoenix, 1983—; pres. T&L Assocs., mgmt. cons., 1984—. Contbr. articles to profl. jours. Decorated Purple Heart. Mem. Inst. Indsl. Engrs., Indsl. Mgmt. Soc., Assn. for Advancement of Policy, Research and Devel., West Point Alumni Assn., Stanford U. Alumni Assn. Republican. Home: 8001 E Broadway 968 Mesa AZ 85208

HAZELRIGG, MEREDITH KENT, education consultant; b. Allegan, Mich., Feb. 28, 1942; s. Burke Browning and Genevieve (Sakal) H.; m. Niimi Junko, Dec. 23, 1980; children: Niimi Ken. BA, Mich. State U., 1965, MA, 1967. With Mich. Dept. Social Services, Lansing, 1964-68; tchr. Lansing Pub. Schs., 1965-67; faculty dept. English Lansing Community Coll., 1966-69; lang. skills program dir. Malcolm X Communication Skills Acad., Lansing, 1970-71; owner Red Carpet Bus. Service, Lansing, 1972-77; dir., owner KLS, Sayama-shi, Japan, 1979—; prof. English Dept. Kanagawa U., Yokohama, Japan, 1987—; writer, advt. dir. West Side News, Lansing, 1970-71; adj. prof. U. Md., Tokyo, 1979-83. Author: (with Antico) Insight through Fiction, 1970; (with Snowden and Atkin) NihONSENSE, 1987; Sound and Sense for International Communication, 1987, Uncle Ebeneezer's Book for Creative Children, 1988; columnist Allegan County Photo Jour., Allegan News-Gazette, 1972-76. Bd. dirs. Lansing Community Art Gallery, 1966-68, Capital Art Gallery, 1970-72, Boar's Head Players, 1967-70; research dir. Allegan Potato Producers Assn., 1972; commr., sec., chmn. Allegan City Planning Commn., 1972-78. Mem. The Phonetic Soc. Japan, Japan Assn. of Practical English., Soc. Writers, Editors and Translators, Japan Assn. Translators, Tokyo English Lit. Soc. Lodge: Kiwanis. Home: PO Box 155 Hooker Rd Allegan MI 49010 Office: KLS, 468-1 Mizuno, Sayama-shi, Saitama-Ken 350-13, Japan

HAZEWINDUS, NICOLAAS, corporate executive; b. Dordrecht, The Netherlands, Aug. 2, 1937; s. Pieter and Krijntje E. (Waling) H.; m. Martine Gelijns, Dec. 22, 1960; children: Pieter J., Geertrui E. Ir in Physics, Tech. U., Delft, Netherlands, 1959, Dr, 1964. Researcher Philips Research Labs, Amsterdam, Netherlands, 1964-67; researcher Philips Research Labs, Eindhoven, Netherlands, 1967-77, internat. coordinator, 1977-80; internat. coordinator corp. product devel. coordination Philips Internat. BV, Eindhoven, Netherlands, 1980-82, dir. corp. product devel. coordination, 1982—; research fellow Ctr. Sci. and Tech. Policy, NYU, 1981. Author: The U.S. Microelectronics Industry, 1982; contbr. articles on nuclear physics, accelerators and ednl. tech. to profl. jours. Mem. IEEE, Nederlandse Natuurkundige Vereniging. Office: Philips Internat BV, PO Box 218, 5600 MD Eindhoven The Netherlands

HAZI, VENCEL, ambassador; b. Okany, Hungary, Sept. 3, 1925; came to U.S., 1983.; m. Judit Zell; 1 child: Judit. D. in Econ., U. Econ. Sci, Budapest, Hungary, 1965. Entered Fgn. Service, Ministry Fgn. Affairs, Budapest, Hungary, 1950—; diplomate London, 1951-53; minister for fgn. affairs Budapest, 1953-57; diplomate Stockholm, Sweden, 1957-58; ambassador Hungarian Embassy, Baghdad, Iraq, 1958-61, Athens, Greece, 1961-64; dep. minister for fgn. affairs Ministry Fgn. Affairs, Budapest, Hungary, 1968-70; ambassador Hungarian Embassy, London, Eng., 1970-76; ambassador to U.S. Hungarian Embassy, Washington, 1976—. Decorated Order of Labor, Golden Merit, Order of People's Republic, Liberation Meml. award, Petofi Centennial award, Govt. of Hungary.

H'DOUBLER, FRANCIS TODD, JR., surgeon; b. Springfield, Mo., June 18, 1925; s. Francis Todd and Alice Louise (Bemis) H'D; m. Joan Louise Huber, Dec. 20, 1951 (dec. Dec. 1983); children—Julie H'Doubler Thomas and Sarah H'Doubler Muegge (twins), Kurt, Scott; m. Marie Ruth Duckworth, Jan. 18, 1986. Student, Washington U., St. Louis, 1943, Miami U., Oxford, Ohio, 1943-44; B.S., U. Wis., 1946, M.D., 1948. Intern Milw. Hosp., 1948-49; resident in surgery U.S. Naval Hosp., Oakland, Calif., 1950-51; practice medicine specializing in thyroid surgery Springfield, Mo., 1952—; mem. staff St. John's Hosp., Springfield; mem. courtesy staff L.E. Cox Hosp., Springfield; dir. Landmark Nat Bank. Active YMCA; mem. Commn. to Reapportion Mo. Senate, 1971; chmn. Sch. Bond and Tax Levy Com., 1958; chmn. Greene County Republican Com., 1974-75; mem. Rep. State Fin. Com., 1972-75; bd. dirs. Shrine Galveston Burns Inst., St. Louis Shrine Hosp. for Crippled Children; trustee Shriners Hosps.; mem. steering com. Wilson's Creek Battlefield Nat. Park, 1951-61; mem. pres.'s adv. council Sch. Ozarks, Point Lookout, Mo., 1975—. Served with USNR, 1943-46, 49-51, Fleet Marines, 1950. Decorated Bronze Star with V, Purple Heart with oak leaf cluster; recipient Disting. Service award Mo. Jaycees, 1959; Humanitarian award S.W. Mo. Drug Travelers Assn., 1971; named Young Man of Yr., City of Springfield, 1959. Fellow Am. Coll. Nuclear Medicine (founder's group); mem. AMA, Greene County Med. Assn., Mo. Med. Soc., Southwestern Surg. Congress, Mo. Surg. Assn., Soc. Nuclear Medicine, Royal Order of Scotland, Am. Thyroid Assn., Springfield Jr. C. of C. (past pres.), Springfield C. of C., Sigma Nu (Outstanding Alumnus nat. award 1980), Green Gang, Nu Sigma Nu. Presbyterian. Club: Hickory Hills Country. Lodges: Mason (33 deg.), Shriners (imperial potentate 1980-81), Red Cross of Constantine, Order DeMolay Legion Honor (hon.), Royal Order Scotland. Home: 2445 Melbourne Rd Springfield MO 65804 Offfice: 1900 S National Suite 2950 Springfield MO 65804

HE, SHAOZENG, research institute executive; b. Ninpo, Chekiang, China, Feb. 27, 1929; s. Qinyuan and Yueqing (Yu) H.; m. Zhuying Yu, Nov. 26, 1956; children—Ping, Cheng, Ting. Grad. Shanghai Inst. Tech., 1950; postgrad. Jiao Tong U., 1950-52. Engr., China Chem. Works, Shanghai, 1952-57; engr. to sr. engr. Shanghai Watch Factory, 1957—, chief engr., 1978—; tech. dir., 1979—; tech. dir., chief engr. Shanghai Research Inst. of Timepiece, 1984—. Mem. China Mech. Engring. Soc., China Instrument Soc., (chmn. mem. Shanghai br. 1980-87), Shanghai Sci. and Technique Cons. Assn.

HEAD, PATRICK JAMES, lawyer; b. Randolph, Nebr., July 13, 1932; s. Clarence Martin and Ellen Cecelia (Magirl) H.; m. Eleanor Hickey, Nov. 24, 1960; children: Adrienne, Ellen, Damian, Maria, Brendan, Martin, Sarah, Daniel, Brian. A.B. summa cum laude, Georgetown U., 1953, LL.B., 1956, LL.M. in Internat. Law, 1957. Bar: D.C. 1956, Ill. 1966. Assoc. firm John L. Ingolsby (and predecessor firm), Washington, 1956-64; gen. counsel internat. ops. Sears, Roebuck & Co., Oakbrook, Ill., 1964-70; counsel midwest ter. Sears, Roebuck & Co., Skokie, Ill., 1970-72; v.p. Montgomery Ward & Co., Inc., Washington, 1972-76; v.p., gen. counsel, sec. Montgomery Ward & Co., Inc., Chgo., 1976-81; v.p., gen. counsel FMC Corp., Chgo., 1981—. Mem. Chgo. Crime Commn.; bd. regents Georgetown U., Washington; mem. bd. visitors Norwestern U. Law Sch., 1988. Mem. ABA, D.C. Bar Assn., Chgo. Bar Assn., Am. Law Inst. Democrat. Roman Catholic. Clubs: Met. (Washington); Chgo, Internat. Office: FMC Corp 200 E Randolph St Chicago IL 60601

HEAD, WILLIAM CARL, lawyer, real estate developer; b. Columbus, Ga., Mar. 4, 1951; s. Louis Bernice and Betty June (Vickery) H.; m. Sandra Earle, Sept. 3, 1972 (div. 1979); m. Kathleen Crenshaw, Aug. 8, 1981 (div. 1988); 1 stepchild, Stephanie A. Hansen. BA cum laude, U. Ga., 1973, JD, 1976.

Bar: Ga. 1976, U.S. Dist. Ct. (mid. dist.) Ga. 1976, U.S. Ct. Appeals (5th and 11th cirs.) 1979. Ptnr. Galis, Timmons, Andrews & Head, Athens, Ga., 1977-79, Andrews & Head P.C., Athens, 1979-82; sole practice Athens, 1982-85; ptnr. McDonald, Head, Carney & Haggard, Athens, 1985—; real estate developer, Athens, 1979—. Pres. Joseph Henry Lumpkin Found., Inc., Athens, 1979; chmn. Bridge the Gap seminar, Atlanta, 1980. Awardee Athens-Clarke Heritage Found. Inc., Athens, 1983. Mem. ABA, Assn. Trial Lawyers Am., Ga. Trial Lawyers Assn., Am. Bankruptcy Inst., Order of Barristers. Democrat. Baptist. Club: Pres's. (U. Ga.). Home: PO Box 1428 Athens GA 30603 Office: McDonald Head Carney & Haggard 345 W Hancock Ave Athens GA 30603

HEAD, WILLIAM IVERSON, SR., retired chemical company executive; b. Tallapposa, Ga., Apr. 4, 1925; s. Iverson and Ruth Britain (Hubbard) H.; m. Mary Helen Ware, June 12, 1947; children: William Iverson, Connie Suzanne, Alan David. BS in Textile Engring. with honors, Ga. Inst. Tech., 1949; D of Textile Engring. (hon.), World U., 1983; PhD in Indsl. Mgmt., Columbia Pacific U., 1988. Research and devel. engr. Tenn. Eastman Co., Kingsport, 1949-56, quality control-mfg. sr. engr., 1957-67, dept. supt., 1968-74; supt. acetate yarn dept. Chems. div. Eastman Kodak Co., Kingsport, 1975-85; info. officer U.S. Naval Acad., 1983—; mem. adv. bd., Trinity Resources Inc., 1988—, POINT ONE Adv. Group, Inc., 1988—. Patentee textured yarns tech. in U.S., Great Britain, Fed. Republic of Germany, Japan and France. Served with USN, 1943-46, capt. Res., 1946-83. Decorated Meritorious Service medal, 1980. Mem. Internat. Soc. Philos. Enquiry (personnel cons. 1978-79, sr. research fellow and internat. pres. 1980-85, diplomate and chmn. bd. trustees 1987—), Am. Chem. Soc., Prometheus Soc., Internat. Platform Assn., Naval Res. Assn., Mil. Order World Wars, Res. Officers Assn. (pres. Tenn. dept. 1981-82), Retired Officers Assn., VFW, Mensa (pres. Upper East Tenn. 1976-79), Cincinnatus Soc., Internat. Legion of Intelligence. Unitarian. Home: 4035 Lakewood Dr Kingsport TN 37663

HEADLEE, WILLIAM HUGH, emeritus educator; b. Morristown, Ind., June 15, 1907; s. Walter C. and Nellie Ann (Adams) H.; A.B., Earlham Coll., 1929; M.S. (Rockefeller Found. fellow), U. Ill., 1933; Ph.D. (Rockefeller Found. fellow), Tulane U., 1935; cert. of proficiency in tropical and mil. medicine Army Med. Sch., 1943; m. Gabrielle Mills, Aug. 4, 1937; children—Joan Headlee Bowden, Anne. Instr. biology Am. U., Cairo, Egypt, 1929-31; research asst. internat. health div. Rockefeller Found., Cairo, 1930-32; asst. prin. Friendsville Acad., Tenn., 1933-34; instr. biology Purdue U., 1935-42, asst. prof. zoology, 1942-43; asst. prof. parasitic diseases Ind. U. Sch. Medicine, Indpls., 1943-46, assoc. prof., 1946-53, prof., 1953-77, prof. emeritus Grad. Sch., 1977—, parliamentarian of faculty, 1973-75, sec., 1973-74, exec. sec., 1974-75; dir. Parasitology Diagnostic Lab., Ind. U. Med. Ctr., 1943-57; cons. parasitologist dept. dermatology Indpls. Gen. Hosp., 1946-57; prof. parasitic diseases Ind. U. Sch. Med., 1953-77; prof. emeritus, 1977—; mem. faculty council Ind. U.-Purdue U.-Indpls., 1973-75, chmn. faculty bd. rev., 1974-75; chmn. dept. biology Nat. Pedagogic Inst., Caracas, Venezuela, 1937-38; sr. scientist USPHS Res., 1953-71; attache, med. parasitologist U.S. ops. mission Fgn. Ops. Adminstrn., Am. embassy, Bangkok, 1953-55; vis. prof. med. parasitology Sch. of Medicine, Chulalongkorn U. and Thailand Sch. Public Health, Bangkok, 1953-55; U.S. del. to 9th Pacific Sci. Congress, Bangkok, 1957; coordinator, dir. Ind. U.-AID, Pakistan Project to develop Jinnah Postgrad. Med. Center, 1957-66; asso. dir. Div. Allied Health Scis., Ind. U. Sch. Medicine, 1968; cons. epidemiologist Ind. Regional Med. Program, 1969-77. Bd. dirs. Central Ind. Council on Aging, 1979-82, mem. nominating com., 1979, long range planning com., 1979-82, program services com., 1978-81 ; del. Older Hoosiers Assembly of Commn. on Aging of State of Ind., 1977—, mem. at large, floor leader, 1982—, mem. aging network legis. com., steering com., 1978—; mem. Mayor's Adv. Com. on Aging and the Aged, Indpls., 1978-81; bd. dirs. Marion County Council on Aging, 1978-81; adv. council Ind. U. Center on Aging and Aged. Recipient Arts and Humanities award Shelbyville (Ind.) Rotary Club, 1980; John and Mary Markle Found. fellow, 1943, 44. Emeritus fellow AAAS (life, council 1957-62), Ind. Acad. Sci. (exec. com. 1944, chmn. zoology sect. 1944, mem. membership com. 1950-60, fellows com. 1972-77), Royal Soc. Tropical Medicine and Hygiene; emeritus mem. AAUP (sec.-treas. Ind. Conf. 1972-73, pres. 1974-75, Disting. Mem. award 1976), Am. Soc. Parasitologists (sr.; com. on hon. and emeritus mems. 1967), Am. Soc. Tropical Medicine and Hygiene (emeritus; program com. 1959, 60, nominating com. 1971), Sigma Xi (emeritus); mem. Soc. Internat. Devel., Internat. Coll. Tropical Medicine, Nat. Council on Aging, Nat. Ret. Tchrs. Assn., Ret. Profs. Ind., Soc. Ret. Execs., Am. Assn. Ret. Persons, Ind. Partners of Ams. (dir. 1978—, treas. 1986), Tulane U. Med. Alumni Assn. (life mem.), U. Ill. Alumni Assn. (life), Phi Sigma. Unitarian (bd. trustees 1953, 70-73, chmn. nominating com. 1948-49, 70-71). Clubs: Ind. U. Emeritus, Earlham Coll. Emeritus; Pan Am Clipper. Contbr. numerous articles on epidemiology of parasite infections, med. edn., higher edn. to profl. jours., also poems and miscellaneous articles, manuals. Home: 6413 Peace Pl Indianapolis IN 46268

HEAKAL, M. SABRY, accountant; b. Shebin El-Koum, Egypt, Mar. 20, 1940; came to U.S., 1961; s. Mohamed E. and Ghadiga H.; B.Com. with honors, U. Cairo, 1960; M.S., U. Ill., 1965, Ph.D., 1968; m. Tity I. Kamel, Aug. 2, 1964; children—Hanan, Reem, Delilah. Asst. prof. acctg. St. Cloud State U., 1968-70, asso. prof. acctg., 1970-71, prof., chmn. acctg., 1971-78; vis. prof. acctg. U. Minn., 1975-78, lectr., 1978—; vis. prof. U. Fla., 1977-78; partner McGladrey Hendrickson & Pullen, Mpls., 1978—, nat. coordinator audit and acctg., 1985—. C.P.A., Minn. Mem. Am. Acctg. Assn., Am. Inst. C.P.A.'s, Minn. Soc. C.P.A.'s. Club: Wayzata Country. Home: 2710 Everest Ln Plymouth MN 55447 Office: 1300 Midwest Plaza E 800 Marquette Ave Minneapolis MN 55402

HEALD, BRUCE DAY, educator; b. Boston, June 5, 1935; s. Henry M. and Muriel D. (Day) H.; A.A., Boston U., 1956; B.S. in Music Edn., Lowell State U., 1959; M.A., Columbia Pacific U., 1984, Ph.D., 1985; m. Helen Peaslee, May 21, 1960; children—William Forristall III, Craig, Eric Bentley, Allyson Kaye. Supr. music Ashland-Meredith Union 2, Meredith, N.H., 1959-64; dir. music, lectr. fine arts Belknap Coll., Center Harbor, N.H., 1963-65; dir. bands Plattsburgh (N.Y.) City Schs., 1969-70; supr. music Inter-Lakes Sch. Dist., Meredith, 1965-69, dir. music edn., 1970-77; dir. instrumental music Kennebunk (Maine) High Sch., 1977-79; prodn. mgr. Annalee Mobilitee Dolls, Meredith, 1979-81; lectr. English and journalism Moultonborough Acad., 1981-86; dir. music Congl. Ch., Laconia, N.H., 1985—; chair English dept. Holy Trinity Sch., Laconia, 1987—; mentor Columbia Pacific U., 1986—; instr. music N.H. Coll., Manchester, 1988—. Commr. Parks and Playgrounds, Meredith, 1966-69; selectman Town of Meredith, 1971-76. Served with USMC, 1954-62. Mem. NEA, N.H. Tchrs. Assn., Moultonborough Tchrs. Assn., Nat. Music Educators Assn. Republican. Clubs: Masons, Order Eastern Star. Author: Follow the Mount, 1968, 2d edit., 1970; Postmaster of the Lake, 1971; Mail Service on the Lake, 1980; Steamboats in Motion, 1984; composer Kennebunk Concert March, The Hills of Old N.H., Moultonboro Concert March, Cascades, Trilogy, New Hampshire Learnin' Days. Home: RFD 2 Meredith NH 03253 Office: Holy Trinity Sch Laconia NH 03254

HEALY, GEORGE WILLIAM, III, lawyer; b. New Orleans, Mar. 8, 1930; s. George William and Margaret Alford H.; m. Sharon Saunders, Oct. 26, 1974; children: George W. IV, John Carmichael, Floyd Alford, Hyde Dunbar, Mary Margaret. B.A., Tulane U., 1950, J.D., 1955. Bar: La. bar 1955, U.S. Supreme Ct. bar 1969. Asso. firm Phelps, Dunbar, Marks, Claverie & Sims, New Orleans, 1955-58; partner Phelps, Dunbar, Marks, Claverie & Sims, 1958—; mem. U.S. del. Comite Maritime Internat., Tokyo, 1969, Lisbon, 1985; lectr. in field. Served with USN, 1951-53. Fellow Am. Coll. Trial Lawyers, Maritime Law Assn. U.S. (exec. com. 1984-87), Am. Bar Assn.; mem. La. State Bar Assn., New Orleans Bar Assn. (1st v.p. 1987), La. Assn. Def. Counsel, New Orleans Assn. Def. Counsel, Internat. Assn. Def. Counsel. Republican. Episcopalian. Clubs: Boston, La, Stratford, Plimsoll, Whitehall, Yale, India House, Recess (pres. 1978), Pinfeathers Hunting, New Orleans Lawn Tennis, Propeller, Mariners. Home: 6020 Camp St New Orleans LA 70118 Office: 30th Floor Texaco Bldg 400 Poydras St New Orleans LA 70130

HEALY, JAMES BRUCE, cooking school administrator, writer; b. Paterson, N.J., Apr. 15, 1947; s. James Burn and Margaret Mercy (Patterson) H.; m. Alice Fenvessy, May 9, 1970; 1 child, Charlotte Alexandra. BA, Williams Coll., 1968; PhD, The Rockefeller U., 1973. Mem. faculty Inst. Advanced Study, Princeton, N.J., 1973-75; J.W. Gibbs instr. physics Yale U., New Haven, Conn., 1975-77, research affiliate, 1977-80; dir. Healy-Lucullus Sch. French Cooking, New Haven, 1978-80, Boulder, Colo., 1980—; cons. Claudine's, Denver, 1985-86; vis. instr. Salem (Mass.) State Coll., 1984, and various culinary schs. Author: Mastering the Art of French Pastry, 1984; contbr. articles and revs. on restaurants and cooking to mags. and profl. jours. Mem. Internat. Assn. Cooking Profls. (cert.), Confederation Nationale des Patissiers, Glaciers, et Confiseurs de France. Presbyterian. Home and Office: Healy-Lucullus Sch French Cooking 840 Cypress Dr Boulder CO 80303

HEALY, JOHN RUSSELL, education administrator; b. Brookline, Mass., June 6, 1951; s. John James and Dorothy (Johnston) H.; m. Irene Foster, Feb. 20, 1972; 1 child, Melissa Ann. BS, Empire State Coll., New Paltz, 1984; MBA, Manhattan Coll., 1987; Dr. of Philosophy, Coll. of New Rochelle, 1988. Asst. mgr. Trefz Mgmt. Corp., Bridgeport, Conn., 1971-73; gen. mgr. Spain Oil Corp., Mahopac, N.Y., 1973-77; pres. DTA Mid-Hudson, Poughquag, N.Y., 1977—; coordinator bus. dept. Beacon (N.Y.) High Sch., 1985—; adj. prof. Dutchess Community Coll., 1984-87, Poughkeepsie, SUNY New Paltz, 1984—; guest speaker on half-hour safety talk show, Cablevision Channel 10, Poughkeepsie, 1984; asst. prin. Circleville Mid. Sch., 1987—. Dir. Teen Ctr., Beekman Recreation Assn., Poughquag, 1977. Empire State Challenger fellow, 1986. Mem. Driver Tng. Assocs., So. Dutchess C. of C., Nat. Assn. Secondary Sch. Prins., N.Y. State Middle Sch. Assn., Assn. Sch. Curriculum Devel. Home: Rural Rt 2 Box 264 Poughquag NY 12570 Office: DTA Mid-Hudson Pleasant Ridge Rd Poughquag NY 12570

HEALY, JOSEPH FRANCIS, JR., lawyer, airline executive; b. N.Y.C., Aug. 11, 1930; s. Joseph Francis and Agnes (Kett) H.; m. Patricia A. Casey, Apr. 23, 1955; children: James C., Timothy, Kevin, Cathleen M., Mary, Terence. B.S., Fordham U., 1952; J.D., Georgetown U., 1959. Bar: D.C. 1959. With gen. traffic dept. Eastman-Kodak Co., Rochester, N.Y., 1954-55; air transp. examiner CAB, Washington, 1955-59; practiced in Washington, 1959-70, 80-81; asst. gen. counsel Air Transport Assn. Am., 1966-70; v.p. legal Eastern Air Lines, Inc., N.Y.C. and Miami, Fla., 1970-80; ptnr. Ford, Farquhar, Kornblut & O'Neill, Washington, 1980-81; v.p. legal affairs Piedmont Aviation, Inc., Winston Salem, N.C., 1981-84, sr. v.p., gen counsel, 1984—. Served to 1st lt. USAF, 1952-54. Mem. ABA, Fed. Bar Assn., Internat. Bar Assn., Am. Soc. Corp. Secs., Am. Irish Hist. Soc., Nat. Aero. Assn., Beta Gamma Sigma, Phi Delta Phi. Clubs: Univ., Internat. Aviation (Washington); Wings (N.Y.C.); Piedmont (Winston-Salem). Home: 236 Heatherton Way Winston-Salem NC 27104 Office: Piedmont Aviation Inc One Piedmont Plaza Winston-Salem NC 27156

HEALY, NICHOLAS JOSEPH, lawyer, educator; b. N.Y.C., Jan. 4, 1910; s. Nicholas Joseph and Frances Cecilia (McCarthy) H.; m. Margaret Marie Ferry, Mar. 29, 1937; children: Nicholas, Margaret Healy Parker, Rosemary Healy Bell, Mary Louise Healy White, Donall, Kathleen Healy Hamon. A.B., Holy Cross Coll., 1931; J.D., Harvard U., 1934. Bar: N.Y. 1935, U.S. Supreme Ct. 1949. Pvt. practice N.Y.C., 1935-42, 48—; mem. Healy & Baillie (and predecessor law firms), 1948—; chmn. bd. dirs. Victory Carriers, Inc. (and affiliated cos.); spl. asst. to atty. gen. U.S., 1945-48; tchr. admiralty law NYU Sch. Law, 1947-86, adj. prof., 1960—; Niels F. Johnsen vis. prof. maritime law Tulane Maritime Law Ctr., 1986. Contbr.: chpts. on admiralty to Annual Survey Am. Law, 1949—; author: (with Sprague) Cases on Admiralty, 1950, (with Currie) Cases and Materials on Admiralty, 1965, (with Sharpe), Cases and Materials on Admiralty, 1974, 2d edit., 1986; editor: Jour. Maritime Law and Commerce; assoc. editor: American Maritime Cases; mem. bd. editors: Il Dirittimo Marittimo; contbr. to Ency. Brit. Chmn. USCG adv. panel on Rules of the Road, 1966-72; mem. permanent adv. bd. Tulane Admiralty Inst. Served to lt. (s.g.) USNR, 1942-45. Mem. Maritime Law Assn. U.S. (pres. 1964-66), Assn. Average Adjusters U.S. (chmn. 1959-60), ABA (ho. dels. 1964-66), N.Y. State Bar Assn., Comité Maritime Internat. (exec. council 1972-79, v.p. 1985—), Assn. Bar City N.Y., Soc. Friendly Sons St. Patrick. Democrat. Roman Catholic. Clubs: Harvard (N.Y.C.), India House (N.Y.C.), Downtown Athletic (N.Y.C.). Home: 132 Tullamore Rd Garden City NY 11530 Office: Healy & Baillie 29 Broadway New York NY 10006

HEALY, STEVEN MICHAEL, accountant; b. Chgo., July 20, 1949; s. Daniel Francis and Angelina (Massino) H. BA, U. Ill., Chgo., 1971; MBA, Rosary Coll., 1984. Br. mgr. Assocs. Capital Co., Chgo., 1971-74; credit analyst Motorola, Inc., Schaumburg, Ill., 1974-76; office mgr. Triple "S" Steel Corp., Franklin Pk., Ill., 1976-79; accounts payable supr. Zenith Electronics, Chgo., 1979-84; supr. acctg. Village of Oak Park, Ill., 1984-86; bus. analyst Cablevision of Chgo., Oak Park, 1986-87; dir. fin. Village of Maywood, Ill., 1988—. Mem. Oak Park Village Players Group; bd. dirs. Oak Park Employees Credit Union. Mem. Nat. Soc. Pub. Accts., Nat. Govt. Fin. Officers Assn., Ill. Govt. Fin. Officers Assn., U. Ill. Alumni Assn., Rosary Coll. MBA Alumni Assn. (founder, mem. soc. com. 1984—), Friends of the Oak Park Library, Friends of the Conservatory, Cath. Alumni Club. Club: Village Oak Park Chess (pres. 1984-86). Home: 728 S Ridgeland Ave Oak Park IL 60304 Office: Village of Maywood 115 S 5th Ave Maywood IL 60153

HEALY, THOMAS MARTIN, manufacturing company executive; b. Milw., May 9, 1921; s. Thomas and Helen (Galewski) H.; m. Ruth Marcella Johnson, Jan. 30, 1943; children: Kathleen Healy Brey, Maureen Ann Warzon, Timothy James, Eileen Marie, Daniel Michael. Student Milw. Area Tech. Sch., 1945-48; student U. Wisc., 1948-49. Engring. rep. Oilgear Co., Milw., 1952-59; mgr. Houston office, 1959-63, mgr. speciality sales, 1963-73, mgr. corp. devel., 1973-83, v.p. corp. devel., 1984-87; pres. Healy Assocs., Austin, Tex., 1987—. Campaigner Rep. Nat. Com. Served as non-commissioned officer USN, 1943-45, PTO. Mem. Am. Mgmt. Assn., World Future Soc., Am. Def. Preparedness Assn. Roman Catholic. Club: Onion Creek. Avocations: travel, philosophy, business and professional ethics.

HEALY, TIMOTHY STAFFORD, university president; b. N.Y.C., Apr. 25, 1923; s. Reginald Stafford and Margaret Dean (Vaeth) H. B.A., Woodstock Coll., Md., 1946, Ph.L., 1947, M.A., 1948; S.T.L., Facultes St. Albert, Louvain, Belgium, 1954; M.A., Fordham U., N.Y.C., 1957; D.Phil., Oxford U., 1965; M.A., 1979. Joined S.J., 1940; ordained priest Roman Cath. Ch., 1953; instr. Latin and English Fordham Prep. Sch., N.Y.C., 1947-50; instr. English, asst. prof., assoc. prof., prof. Fordham U., 1955-69, exec. v.p., 1965-69; prof. English, vice chancellor for academic affairs City U. N.Y., 1969-76; prof. English, pres. Georgetown U., Washington, 1976—; mem. Pres.'s Commn. on Fgn. Lang. and Internat. Studies, 1978-79, mem. conf. bd., 1987—; mem. Middle States Assn. Commn. on Higher Edn., 1976-79; mem. Nat. Adv. Com. on Accreditation and Instl. Eligibility U.S. Dept. Edn., 1981-83; mem. Council for Fin. Aid to Higher Edn., 1979-85; mem. Nat. Assn. Ind. Colls. and Univs., 1977-80, 84-87, chmn., 1980; mem. Commn. for Study of Migration and Cooperative Econ. Devel., 1986—; bd. dirs. Am. Council on Edn., 1979-85, chmn., 1983-84; mem. exec. com. Consortium of Univ. of Washington, 1976—, chmn., 1978-79, 84-85; dir. Washington Urban League, 1984—; mem. U.S. sec. of state's adv. com. on South Africa, 1985-87; trustee LeMoyne Coll., 1985—, Xavier U., 1986—. Author: John Donne: Ignatius His Conclave, 1969; editor: (with Dame Helen Gardner) John Donne: Selected Prose, 1967; articles to profl. publs. Mem. Folger Com., Folger Shakespeare Library, 1980-86, Fed. City Council, Washington, 1976—; bd. dirs. Folger Theatre, 1986—; trustee Shakespeare Theatre at Folger, 1986—, Regis High Sch., N.Y.C., 1987—. Kent fellow, 1963-65, Supernumerary fellow St. Cross Coll., Oxford, 1979—; Am. Council Learned Socs. grantee, 1971. Fellow Soc. for Religion in Higher Edn., 1969; mem. Phi Beta Kappa, Alpha Sigma Nu. Democrat. Office: Georgetown U Office of Pres Washington DC 20057

HEALY, WALTER FRANCIS XAVIER, lawyer; b. N.Y.C., Sept. 15, 1941; s. Walter Patrick and Helen Theresa (Fischer) H.; B.A., St. Joseph's Coll., Yonkers, N.Y., 1963; LL.B., Fordham U., 1966; m. Margaret O'Hanlon, Nov. 26, 1966; 1 child, Katherine Siobhan. Admitted to N.Y. State bar, 1967, Pa. bar, 1980; asso. firm Dewey, Ballantine, Bushby, Palmer & Wood, N.Y.C., 1966-76; corp. counsel Singer Co., N.Y.C., 1976; corp. sec., asst. gen. counsel Studebaker-Worthington, Inc., N.Y.C., 1976-79; v.p., gen. counsel UGI Corp., Valley Forge, Pa., 1979-84; ptnr. Windels, Marx, Davies & Ives, N.Y.C., 1984—. Mem. Assn. Bar City N.Y., Am. Bar Assn., N.Y. State Bar Assn. Pa. Bar Assn. Clubs: N.Y. Athletic, N.Y. Skating, Philadelphia Skating. Office: Windels Marx et al 156 W 56th St New York NY 10019

HEANEY, SEAMUS JUSTIN, poet, educator; b. County Derry, No. Ireland, Apr. 13, 1939; s. Patrick and Margaret H.; B.A., Queen's U., Belfast, 1961; m. Marie Devlin, 1965; 3 children. Tchr., St. Thomas's Secondary Sch., Belfast, No. Ireland, 1962-63; lectr. St. Joseph's Coll. Edn., Belfast, 1963-66; lectr. Queen's U., Belfast, 1966-72; free-lance writer, 1972-75; lectr. Carysfort Coll., 1975-80; now Bolyston prof. rhetoric and oratory Harvard U. Author: Eleven Poems, 1965; Death of a Naturalist, 1966 (Somerset Maugham award 1967, Cholmondeley award 1968); Room to Rhyme (with Dairo Hammond and Michael Longley), 1968; A Lough Neagh Sequence, 1969; Door into the Dark, 1969; Night Drive: Poems, 1970; Boy Driving His Father to Confession, 1970; Land, 1971; Wintering Out, 1972; North, 1975 (W.H. Smith award, Duff Cooper prize); Stations, 1975; Bog Poems, 1975; Field Work, 1979; Poems: Nineteen Sixty-Five to Nineteen Seventy-Five, 1980; Preoccupations: Selected Prose 1968-1978, 1980; Sweeney Astray: A Version from the Irish, 1984; Station Island 1984; The Haw Lantern, 1987; also ed. poetry anthologies. Recipient Eric Gregory award, 1966, Faber Meml. prize, 1968, Irish Acad. Letters award, 1971, Denis Devlin Meml. award, 1973, Am.-Irish Found. award, 1975, Nat. Inst. Arts and Letters E.M. Forster award, 1975. Mem. Irish Acad. Letters. Office: care Faber & Faber, 3 Queen Sq, London WC1N 3RU England also: Havard U Dept English Cambridge MA 02138 *

HEAP, JAMES CLARENCE, retired mechanical engineer; b. Trinidad, Colo.; s. James and Elsie Mae (Brobst) H.; m. Alma Mae Swartzendruber. Registered profl. engr., Wis. Sr. mech. engr. Cook Electric Research Lab, Morton Grove, Ill., 1955-56; assoc. mech. engr. Argonne (Ill.) Nat. Lab., 1956-66; sr. project engr. Union Tank Car Co., East Chicago, Ind., 1966-71; sr. engr. Thrall Car Mfg. Co., Chicago Heights, 1971-77; research design engr. Graver Energy Systems, Inc., Chicago Heights, 1977-79; mech. cons. design engr. Pollak & Skan, Inc., Chgo., 1979-83, ret., 1983; cons. mech. design and stress analysis, 1965-83. Author: Formulas for Circular Plates Subjected to Symmetrical Loads and Temperatures, 1966; contbr. tech. papers to profl. jour.; patentee in field. Served with USAF, 1946-47. Mem. ASME, Christian Businessmen's Com. US. Lodge: Masons. Home: 1913 Lambert Ln Munster IN 46321

HEAP, SYLVIA STUBER, civic worker; b. Clifton Springs, N.Y., Sept. 25, 1929; d. Stanley Irving and Helen (Hill) Stuber; B.A. cum laude, Bates Coll., 1950; postgrad. U. Conn. Sch. Social Work, 1952-54, Boston U. Sch. Social Work, 1953-54, SUNY, Brockport, 1979, SUNY-Potsdam, 1980, Syracuse U., 1980-83, 85—; m. Walker Ratcliffe Heap, June 9, 1951; children—Heidi Anne, Cynthia Joan, Walker Ratcliffe III. Dir. Y-Teens, YWCA, Holyoke, Mass., 1950-51; social group worker West Haven (Conn.) Community House, 1951-54; program dir. YWCA, Ann Arbor, 1954-55, part-time, 1955-59; mem. adv. bd. div. continuing edn. Jefferson Community Coll., 1965—, chmn. adv. bd., 1968—; pres. Jefferson County Med. Soc. Aux., 1971-72; bd. dirs. St. Lawrence Valley Ednl. TV, 1973-83, sec., 1976-80, treas., 1980-82; v.p., 1982-83, dir. Chem. People Project, 1983; bd. dirs. Watertown Lyric Theatre, 1973-83; bd. dirs. N.Y. State Med. Soc. Aux., 1974-85, 2d v.p. bd., 1979-80; fitness instr. Jefferson Community Coll., Watertown, 1977-86; chmn. health projects N.Y. State Med. Soc. Aux., 1981-85. Named Citizen of Yr. Greater Watertown C. of C., 1975. Mem. Friends of Public TV, AAUW, Coll. Women's Club Jefferson County, Phi Beta Kappa. Unitarian Universalist. (UN office envoy 1978—).

HEAPS, MARVIN DALE, food services company executive; b. Boone, Iowa, June 26, 1932; s. Donald and Mary Isabel (Robson) H.; m. Martha Coleman Davis, July 4, 1957; children—Mitchell, Matthew, Martha. B.A. in Econs, Whitworth Coll., 1953; postgrad., George Washington U., 1957; M.B.A. (Achievement scholar), U. Pa., 1959. Asso. McKinsey & Co. (mgmt. cons.), Washington, Geneva and N.Y.C., 1960-66; dir. service systems engring. Automatic Retailers of Am., Phila., 1967; v.p. Automatic Retailers of Am., 1968; sr. v.p. ARA Services, Inc., Phila., 1969-71; exec. v.p. ops. ARA Services, Inc., 1975-77, pres., chief operational officer, 1977-81; also dir.; pres. Marvin D. Heaps Assos., Inc., 1981—; pres. ARA Food Services Co., 1971-75; dir. Morse/Diesel, Inc., Jerricho, Inc., Primus Devel. Grou, Ltd., Provident Am. Co.; cons. to Office Edn., HEW; mem. food service industry adv. com. Exec. Office of Pres., 1969—. Bd. dirs., chmn. Young Life; bd. dirs. Whitworth Coll., U. of Arts, Greater Phila. YMCA, Salvation Army, Evang. Ministries, Inc.; chmn. Acad. Nat. Sci. Served to lt. USNR, 1955-59. Mem. Conf. Bd., Am. Mgmt. Assn., Soc. Personnel Adminstrn., Assn. Internat. Devel., Nat. Automatic Mdse. Assn. (dir.), Wharton MBA Alumni Club. Republican. Presbyterian (elder). Clubs: Metropolitan (Washington); Union League (Phila.). Home: 301 Elm Ave Swarthmore PA 19081 Office: 301 Elm Ave Swarthmore PA 19106

HEARD, WILLIAM ROBERT, insurance company executive; b. Indpls., Apr. 25, 1925; s. French and Estelle (Austin) H.; attended Ind. U.; m. Virginia Ann Patrick, Feb. 6, 1951; children—Cynthia Ann, William Robert, II. With Grain Dealers Mut. Ins. Co., 1948, exec. v.p., Indpls., 1978-79, pres., chief exec. officer, dir., 1979—; pres., chief exec. officer, dir. Companion Ins. Co., 1979—; chmn., dir., exec. and fin. com. Alliance Am. Insurers; chmn., exec. com. IRM; pres., dir. Grain Dealers Mut. Agy., Inc.; chmn. bd. 15 N. Broadway Corp. Served with USNR, 1942-46. Mem. Assn. Mill and Elevator Ins. Cos. (chmn., dir.), Ins. Inst. Ind. (dir., exec. com.), Mut. Reins. Bur. (dir., exec. com.), Indiana Better Bus. Bur. (dir., exec. com., vice chmn.), Excess of Loss Assn. (vice chmn., dir.), Sales and Mktg. Execs. Indpls. (past pres.), Sales and Mktg. Execs. Internat. (past dir.), Fla. 1752 Club (past pres.), Property and Casualty Ins. Council, Ind. Insurors Assn. (dir.), Hoosierland Rating Bur. (dir.), Ind. Mill and Elevator Rating Bur. (dir.), Ins. Claims Service (dir.), Property Loss Research Bur. (dir., chmn.), Mill and Elevator Rating Bur. (dir.), Mill and Elevator Fire Prevention Bur. (dir.), Econ. Club of Indpls., Am. Legion, Hon. Order Ky. Cols., Pi Sigma Epsilon. Club: Indpls. Skyline. Office: Grain Dealers Mut Ins 1752 N Meridian Indianapolis IN 46202

HEARST, BELLA RACHAEL, physician, researcher, artist; b. Pitts.; d. Aba and Bertha (Alpern) H. B.M., Chgo. Med. Sch., 1949, M.D., 1950; postgrad., Johns Hopkins U., 1952-53, Art Inst. Chgo., 1958-68. Rotating intern Norwegian Am. Hosp., Chgo., 1949-50; jr. asst. pathologist Cook County Hosp, Chgo., 1950-52; fellow med. legal pathology U. Md., 1953-54; sr. pathology resident Charity Hosp., New Orleans, 1955-56; spl. cardiac researcher Armed Forces Inst. Pathology, Washington, 1956-57; dir., coordinator pathology dept Hosp. O'Horan Menda Yucatan, Mexico, 1957-58; founder Bertha Hearts Found., Inc., 1958, exec. dir., 1958-63; founder Diabetic Inst. Am., Inc., Chgo., 1959, exec. dir., 1959-63; founder Internat. Diabetic Inst., Inc., Chgo., 1963, exec. dir, 1963—; dist. med. dir. compensation U.S. Dept. Labor, Chgo., 1968—; with Chgo. Dept. Health, 1977—, Uptown Neighborhood Health Ctr., 1977-78, Copernicus Multipurpose Ctr., 1978-79, Lakeview Neighborhood Health Ctr., Chgo., 1979—; research dir. Fed. Safety and Fire Council, Chgo.; research assoc. microbiology Stritch Sch. Medicine, Loyola U., Chgo.; staff physician Western Ill. U., 1971-72, assoc. prof., 1971-72. Author: Diabetes and Juvenile Delinquency, 1964, Diabetes and Fitness, 1964, Diabetic Statistical Research Survey, 1961-65, Diabetes and Blood Groups, 1965, Diabetes and Aging, 1965, Diabetes and Newborns; contbr. articles to various publs., art exhibit, Shuster Art Gallery, N.Y., 1966, Internat. Dermatology Congress, Munich, 1967. Recipient 3d prize AMA Conv., Chgo., 1962; recipient testimonial plaque for work sr. citizens Chelsea House, Chgo. Fellow Am. Coll. Angiology, Internat. Coll. Angiology, Am. Geriatric Soc., Royal Soc. Pub. Health; mem. Internat. Acad. Pathology, Am. Women's Med. Assn., Am. Soc. Microbiology, Am. Assn. for Study Neoplastic Diseases, Reticuloendothelial Soc. Office: 8 S Michigan Blvd Chicago IL 60603 also: PO Box A3579 Chicago IL 60690

HEARST, STEPHEN, writer, television producer; b. Vienna, Austria, Oct. 9, 1919; arrived in Eng., 1938; m. Lisbeth Edith Neumann, July 17, 1948; children: Daniela Carol, David Andrew. Student, U. Vienna, 1937; diploma in horticulture, Reading U., Eng., 1940; grad. with honors in Modern History, Oxford U., Eng., 1948. Newsreel writer BBC, London, 1952, TV documentary writer, 1952-55, TV writer/producer, 1955-64, TV exec. producer arts, 1965-67, head TV arts features, 1967-71, radio controller, 1971-78, controller future policy, 1978-82, spl. advisor to dir. gen., 1982-86; free-lance writer, producer, broadcasting policy cons. London, 1986—; cons. Bavarian TV, Munich, 1970's, European Broadcasting Union, 1981, Italia Prize, 1982. Author: 2000 Million Poor, 1965; co-author: The Third Age of Broadcasting, 1984. Served to capt. Brit. Army, 1940-46, ETO, NATO-U.S. Decorated comdr. Order Brit. Empire; recipient 1st prize Vancouver Festival, 1958, award State of Ohio, 1963. Fellow Royal Soc. Arts; mem. Brit. Acad.

Film and TV Arts. Home and Office: Orsino Prodns Ltd, 78 Elm Park, Stanmore, Middlesex HA7 4BQ, England

HEARST, WILLIAM RANDOLPH, JR., editor; b. N.Y.C., Jan. 27, 1908; s. William Randolph and Millicent Veronica (Willson) H.; m. Austine McDonnell, July 29, 1948; children—W.R. Hearst III, John Augustine Chilton. Student, U. Calif., 1925-27; LL.D., U. Alaska. Began career with N.Y. Am., N.Y.C., 1928; as reporter, asst. to city editor, pub. N.Y. Am., 1936-37; pub. N.Y. Jour.-Am., N.Y.C., 1937-56; served as war corr. 1943-45; now chmn. exec. com., dir. Hearst Corp. Bd. dirs. Hearst Found., William Randolph Hearst Found., USO of Met. N.Y., Research to Prevent Blindness, Ear Research Inst. Recipient Pulitzer prize, 1956; Overseas Press Club award, 1958. Mem. UPI Inter-Am. Press Assn. (dir.), Sigma Delta Chi, Phi Delta Theta. Clubs: Madison Square Garden (N.Y.C.); Nat. Press (Washington), F St. (Washington); Pacific Union (San Francisco). Office: The Hearst Corp 959 8th Ave New York NY 10019

HEATH, ADRIAN LEWIS ROSS, artist, educator; b. Maymyo, Burma, June 23, 1920; s. Percy Charles Petgrave and Adria Fredrica (Porter) H.; m. Corinne Elizabeth Lloyd; children: Damon, Clio. Student, Sch. Fine Arts U. Coll., London, 1939-40, 45-47. Mem. art panel Arts Council of Gr. Britain, London, 1964-71; mem. com. of art and design Council Nat. Acad. Awards, London, 1975-82; vis. lectr. Bath (Eng.) Acad. Art, 1956-76, U. Reading (Eng.), 1980-85. One-man exhibitions include London, Sweden, Norway, Holland, Germany, France, Italy; represented in permanent collections British Mus., Victoria and Albert Mus., Tate Gallery, Gulbenkian Found., Bklyn. Mus., Boston Mus., Hirschorn Mus., Washington. Chmn. Artists Internat. Assn., London, 1954-64. Served with RAF, 1940-45, prisoner of war Germany. Address: 28 Charlotte St, London W1P 1HJ, England

HEATH, CHARLES DICKINSON, lawyer, telephone company executive; b. Waterloo, Iowa, June 28, 1941; s. George Clinton and Dorothy (Dickinson) H.; m. Carilyn Frances Cain, June 3, 1972. B.B.A., U. Iowa, 1962, J.D., 1966; M.B.A., U. Ariz., 1963. Bar: Iowa 1966, Pa. 1969, Ind. 1970, U.S. Supreme Ct. 1971, Wis. 1973, Ariz. 1975, Mich. 1979, Fla. 1979. Asst. gen. counsel Kohler Co. (Wis.), 1973-79; securities and tax counsel Kellogg Co., Battle Creek, Mich., 1979-81; assoc. gen. counsel Universal Telephone Inc., Milw., 1981—, also sec., 1987—.

HEATH, EDWARD RICHARD GEORGE, British statesman; b. Broadstairs, Kent, Eng., July 9, 1916; s. William and Edith Heath; grad. (Organ scholar) Balliol Coll. Oxford, 1939, DCL (hon.) Oxford, DCL (hon.), Kent, D Tech. (hon.), Bradford Tech. Inst., Westminster Coll., Salt Lake City, Sorbonne. With Civil Service, 1946-47; mem. Parliament, from 1950; lord commr. of Treasury, 1951-53; dep. chief whip, 1953-55; parliamentary sec. to Treasury, and govt. chief whip, 1955-59; Minister of Labor, 1959-60; Lord Privy Seal, 1960-63; sec. state for industry, trade and devel., and pres. Bd. of Trade, 1963-64; leader Conservative party, 1965-75; Prime Minister, 1970-74; mem. Ind. Commn. Internat. Devel. Issues, 1977-79; lectr. Harvard U., Yale U., Princeton U., Cornell U., Dartmouth Coll., Calif. Pomona U., U. Ga., Gothenburg (Sweden) U., also others. Chmn., London Symphony Orch. Trust, 1963-70, also guest condr.; guest condr. nat. and internat. symphonies including Berlin Philarm., Chgo. Symphony, Zurich Chamber Orch.; founding com. European Community Youth Orch., also pres., 1977-80; rec. artist EMI, RCA, albums include Elgar's 'Cockaigne Overture, European Brass by The Black Dyke Mills Band. Served to lt. col. Brit. Army, 1939-46. Decorated mem. Brit. Empire privy councillor, 1955; Godkin lectr., Harvard U., 1967; recipient various awards for efforts in EEC, including Charlemagne prize City Aachen, 1963, Freiherr Von Stein Found., award, 1971, Estes J. Kefauver prize, 1971; gold medal City of Paris, 1978, World Humanity Award, 1980, Gold Medal, European Parliament, 1981; winner Classic Sydney Hobart yacht race, 1969; capt. Brit. Admiral Cup Team, 1971, 79, Brit.-Sardinia Cup Team, 1980; vis. Chubb fellow, Yale U., 1975; Montgomery fellow, Dartmouth Coll., 1980. Hon. fellow Royal Coll. Organists, Royal Can. Coll., Bailliol Coll. and Nuffield Coll., Oxford, Organists. Clubs: Carlton, Royal Yacht Squadron, N.Y. Yacht, Brit. Sportsman (chmn.). Author: One Nation: A Tory Approach to Social Problems, 1950; Old World, New Horizons, 1970; Sailing—A Course of My Life, 1975; Music—A Joy for Life, 1976; Travels—Peoples and Places in My Life, 1977; Carols—The Joy of Christmas, 1977, also others. Address: House of Commons, London SW1A 0AA, England

HEATHCOCK, JOHN HERMAN, manufacturing company executive; b. Jacksonville, Ala., June 20, 1943; s. John Herman and Fallie Mae (Ford) W.; m. Yvonne Larue Sisk, July 31, 1965 (div. Feb. 1974); 1 child, Deven Scott; m. Janice Carol McCrary, Dec. 31, 1974; 1 child, Johnathan Adam. BBA, Jacksonville State U., 1961-65. CPA, Tenn., Ga. Acct.-in-charge Ernst & Whinney, Chattanooga, 1970-72; acctg. mgr., controller Sykland Internat., Chattanooga, 1973-81; controller Riverside Mfg. Co., Moultrie, Ga., 1981-83, Sunkist Soft Drinks, Inc., Atlanta, 1983-85; v.p., controller Del Monte Franchise Beverages (formerly Sunkist Soft Drinks), Atlanta, 1985-86; v.p. ops., chief fin. officer Digital Transmissions Systems Inc., Duluth, Ga., 1986—; fin. cons. Seabrook Blanching, Inc., Albany, Ga., 1983. Served as capt. U.S. Army, 1965-70, Vietnam. Decorated Bronze Star, Air medal; recipient Outstanding Service plaque Riverside Mfg. Co., 1982. Mem. Tenn. State Soc. CPA's, Ga. State Soc. CPA's, Am. Inst. CPA's, Assn. Corp. Growth, The Planning Forum, Fin. Execs. Inst. Republican. Presbyterian. Home: 3932 Millwood Ln Lilburn GA 30247 Office: Digital Transmissions Systems Inc 4830 Rivergreen Pkwy Duluth GA 30136

HEBALD, CECILLE ANNETTE, painter; b. N.Y.C.; d. Samuel and Anna (Bauman) Rosner; m. Milton Elting Hebald, June 10, 1938; 1 child, Margo Hebald Heyman. BA, CUNY, 1938; MFA, NYU, 1945; postgrad., Bklyn. Mus. Art Sch., 1936, 48; pvt. studies with, Moses Soyer, Daniel Green, Jack Levy, Richard Piccolo. Represented in numerous pvt. and pub. collections, N.Y.C., Los Angeles, Washington, Geneva, Oslo, Bangkok, London, Rome. Recipient Premio Citta de Bracciano, 1976. Club: Am. Women's (Rome). Home: Traversa Quarto del Lago 13, 00062 Bracciano, Lazio Italy

HEBERT, A. HERVE, utilities company executive; b. Montreal, Que., Can., Apr. 3, 1929; s. Calixte and Yvonne H.; children: Gilles, Jean-Charles, Johanne, Jocelyne, Nathalie. BSc, U. Montreal, Que., Can. Actuarial asst. Sun Life Assurance, Montreal, Que., Can., 1951-55; actuary Desjardins Mut., Levis, Que., Can., 1955-65; cons. actuary Hebert, Le Houillier & Assocs., Inc., Quebec, Montreal, Que., Can., 1965-77; pres. Fiducie du Que., Can., 1977—; chancellor U. Montreal, Que., Can.; chmn. bd. Hydro-Que., 1985—; dir. various cos. Fellow Soc. Actuaries, Can. Inst. Actuaries; mem. Montreal Bd. Trade, Chambre de Commerce de Montreal. Office: Hydro Quebec, 505 De Maisonneuve Blvd W, Montreal, PQ Canada H3A 3E4 *

HEBRON, STEPHEN FRANCIS, surgeon; b. Quezon City, Philippines, Jan. 22, 1950; s. Godofredo and Rosario Hebron; m. Wevina Tuico, June 16, 1984; 1 child, Camille. BS, U. Philippines, 1972; MD, U. of East, 1976. Med. intern Vets. Meml. Med. Ctr., Quezon City, 1976-77, resident in surgery, 1978-82, cons. in surgery, 1985—; gen. practice medicine rural health unit Candelaria, Zambales, Philippines, 1977; vis. cons. in surgery Delgado Hosp., Quezon City, 1982—, Santa Teresta Gen. Hosp., Quezon City, 1982—; cons. in surgery Olongapo Gen. Hosp., Zambales, 1984. Mem. Philippine Med. Assn. Roman Catholic. Home: 40 Visayas Ave Diliman, Quezon City 3008, Philippines

HECHT, CHIC, U.S. senator; b. Cape Giradeau, Mo., Nov. 30, 1928; m. Gail Hecht; children: Lori, Leslie. B.S., Washington U., St. Louis, 1949; postgrad., Mil. Intelligence Sch., Ft. Holibird, Mo., 1951. Mem. Nev. State Senate, 1966-74, Rep. minority leader, 1968-72; mem. U.S. Senate from Nev., 1982—, mem. Banking, Housing and Urban Affairs Com., chmn. housing and urban affairs subcom., mem. Energy and Natural Resources Com., mem. Senate Select Com. on Intelligence. Served with U.S. Army, 1951-53. Mem. Nat. Counter Intelligence Corps. (past pres.), Nat. Mil. Intelligence Assn. Office: 302 Hart Senate Office Bldg Washington DC 20510

HECK, JAMES BAKER, university administrator; b. Columbus, Ohio, Aug. 26, 1930; s. Arch O. and Frances (Agnew) H.; m. Jo Ann Gatton, Nov. 18, 1950; children—Janice M., Judith L., J. Jeffrey. B.S., Ohio State U., 1953, M.A. (Nat. Def. Edn. Act fellow), 1961, Ph.D., 1967. Comml. sales engr. Ohio Bell Telephone Co., Dayton, 1955-57; tchr. Ohio Pub. Schs., Dayton, 1957-59; sch. counselor Ohio Pub. Schs., 1959-60; instr. Ohio State U., 1960-63; asst. to dean Ohio State U. (Coll. Edn.), 1963-66, asst. dean faculties, research asso., 1966-67, asso. dean faculties, asst. prof. edn., 1967-68; prof., dean, dir. Ohio State U. (Mansfield campus), 1971-78; dean regional campus affairs U. South Fla., 1978-81, assoc. v.p. acad. affairs, dean regional campus affairs, 1981-84, assoc. v.p. acad. affairs, dir. office of technology, 1984-86, dean Sch. Extended Studies and learning techs., gen. mgr. pub. broadcasting, spl. asst. to provost, dir. office tech., 1986—; asst. state supr. for guidance service Ohio Dept. Edn., 1962-63; Am. Council on Edn. fellow in academic adminstrn. U. Ill., 1965-66; prof., dean Coll. Edn., U. Del., Newark, 1968-71; evaluator Nat. Council for Accreditation Tchr. Edn., 1972-78; mem. planning com. Nat. Conf. Br. and Regional Campus Adminstrs., 1973-82, chmn., 1972, 80; chmn. planning com. Am. Council Edn. Acad. Fellows Working Reunion, 1972, 79, 85; vice chmn. Am. Council Edn. Council Fellows, 1980-81, chmn., 1981-82, exec. com., 1980-83; cons., lectr. in field. Co-author: Counseling; Selected Readings, 1962, Educational Administration: Selected Readings, 1965, 2d edit., 1971, Analysis of Educational Change in Ohio Public Schools, 1968; also numerous articles, monographs, papers, book revs., abstracts in field. Gen. chmn. Mansfield Area United Way campaign, 1975, bd. dirs., 1976-78, v.p., 1977, 78; bd. dirs. Mansfield Symphony Orch., 1972-78, pres., 1978; bd. dirs. Research for Better Schs., Inc., 1968-71, pres., 1970-71; mem. citizens adv. com. Richland County Regional Planning Commn., 1973-74, bd. dirs., 1975-78, v.p., 1977, 78; mem. Manpower Adv. Council Richland and Morrow Counties; trustee Hillsbrough County Hosp. Authority, Tampa, Fla., 1980-84; mem. Leadership Tampa, 1982-83; mem. Tampa Leadership Conf., 1983—; instl. rep. PBS and Nat. Pub. Radio. Served with USAF, 1953-55; Res., ret. 1973. Mem. Am. Assn. Higher Edn. (life), Mansfield-Richland Area C. of C. (dir. 1972-78, v.p. 1974, 75, 76, 77, 78), Ohio State U. Assn. (life), Nat. U. Continuing Edn. Assn. (instl. rep., bd. dirs. region III), So. Ednl. Communications Assn. (bd. dirs.), Greater Tampa C. of C., Phi Delta Kappa (life), Kappa Delta Pi, Phi Kappa Phi. Club: Univ. Area Civitan (founding pres. 1980-81). Office: U South Fla Tampa FL 33620

HECKADON, ROBERT GORDON, plastic surgeon; b. Brantford, Ont., Can., Jan. 30, 1933; s. Frederick Gordon and Laura (Penrose) H.; B.A., U. Western Ont., 1954, M.D., 1960; postgrad. U. Toronto, 1960-66, U. Vienna, 1966; m. Camilla Joyce Russell, July 11, 1959; children—David, Louise, Peter, William, Barbara. Intern, Toronto Gen. Hosp., 1960-61; asst. resident Toronto Western Hosp., 1961, Toronto Wellesley Hosp., 1962, Toronto Gen. Hosp., 1962-63; resident in plastic surgery St. Michael's Hosp., Toronto, 1963, Toronto Western Hosp., 1964, Toronto Gen. Hosp., 1964, Toronto Hosp. for Sick Children, 1965; asst. resident orthopedics Toronto East Gen. Hosp., 1965-66; practice medicine specializing in plastic surgery, Windsor, Ont., Can., 1966—; chief med. staff Hotel Dieu; mem. staff Grace Hosp., Met. Hosp. (all Windsor). Served with RCAF, 1951-56. Fellow A.C.S.; mem. Canadian Med. Assn., Ont. Med. Assn., Essex County Med. Assn., Windsor Acad. Surgery, Royal Coll. Physicians and Surgeons, Can. Soc. Plastic Surgeons.

HECKER, JOSIE RIEGER, ophthalmologist; b. Metz, France, Sept. 23, 1946; d. Marc and Rachel (Weinberg) Rieger; m. Jean-Louis Hecker, July 29, 1969; children: Emmanuelle, Pascale, Marc. MD, Faculté Rédecéne, 1979. Hosp. extern Strasbourg, France, 1969-74; hosp. attaché Strasbourg, 1974—. Mem. Soc. French Ophthalmologists. Office: 18 Ave des Vosges, 67000 Strasbourg France

HECKER, RICHARD, utility executive; b. N.Y.C., Nov. 25, 1930; s. Harry and Gertrude (Hertzberg) H.; m. Sheila Davis, Sept. 6, 1953; children: Philip Davis, Mark Robert. Student, U. Fla., 1948-49; BBA, U. Miami, 1958; MBA, Nova U., 1976; spl. course, Ga. Inst. Tech., 1976. Chmn. exec. bd. Local 359 Internat. Brotherhood Elec. Workers, 1959-65, pres., 1966, sec., 1967-69; supr. labor relations Fla. Power & Light Co., Miami, 1971-76, mgr. workers' compensation, 1976-78, mgr. safety, 1979; mgr. workers' compensation Fla. Power & Light Co., West Palm Beach, Fla., 1980—; mem. Rules adv. com. of self-insurers Fla. Dept. Labor, 1979—, workers compensation council, 1988—. Pres. U.S.O. Council of Dade County, 1980, bd. dirs. 1965. Mem. Am. Soc. Safety Engrs., Am. Soc. Law Medicine, Acad. Trial Lawyers (safety awards com.), Internat. Assn. Indsl. Accidents Bds. and Commns., Southern Assn. Workers Compensation Adminstrs., Assoc. Self Insurers Fla. (pres. 1983-85, bd. dirs. 1986—). Lodges: Masons, Shriners, K.P. Home: 1012 Green Pine Blvd West Palm Beach FL 33409 Office: Fla Power & Light Co 400 N Congress Ave West Palm Beach FL 33402

HECKERT, RICHARD EDWIN, chemical company executive, chemist; b. Oxford, Ohio, Jan. 13, 1924; s. John W. and Winifred E. (Yahn) H.; m. Barbara Kennedy, 1945; children: Alex Y., Andra Heckert Rudershausen. B.A., Miami U., Ohio, 1944; M.S. in Organic Chemistry, U. Ill., 1947, Ph.D. in Organic Chemistry, 1949. With E.I. DuPont de Nemours & Co., 1949—; research chemist E.I. DuPont de Nemours & Co., Wilmington, Del., 1949-54; from supr. cellophane research and devel. lab. film dept. to asst. mgr. lab. E.I. DuPont de Nemours & Co., Richmond, Va., 1954-57, tech. supt. cellophane plant, 1957-58; tech. supt. cellophane plant E.I. DuPont de Nemours & Co., Clinton, Iowa, 1958-59; plant mgr. E.I. DuPont de Nemours & Co., Circleville, Ohio, 1959-63; dir. supporting research and devel. E.I. DuPont de Nemours & Co., Wilmington, 1963-65, asst. gen. mgr. film dept., 1965-67, asst. gen. mgr. plastics dept., 1967-69, gen. mgr. fabrics and finishes dept., 1969-72, v.p., 1972-73, sr. v.p., dir., 1973-81, pres., 1981-85; vice chmn., chief operating officer DuPont Co., Wilmington, 1981-85, dep. chmn., 1985-86, chmn., chief exec. officer, 1986—; bd. dirs. Provident Mut. Life Ins. Co. Phila. Contbr. articles on cyanocarbon chemistry to sci. jours.; patentee in field. Pres. Longwood Gardens, Inc.; dean's assoc. bus. adv. council Miami U. Sch. Bus. Adminstrn.; chmn. bd. trustees Carnegie Instn. of Washington; trustee Del. Council on Econ. Edn., Med. Ctr. Del., Tuskegee U.; bd. dirs. U. Ill. Found. Nat. Action Council for Minorities in Eng.; mem. Bretton Woods Com., bus. adv. com. to Edn. Com. of States, Conf. Bd., Environ. Assessment Council, Gov.'s High Tech. Task Force, fin. com. of Joint Council on Econ. Edn. Served with U.S. Army, 1944-46. Mem. AAAS, NAM (bd. dirs.), Am. Chem. Soc., Bus. Roundtable. Clubs: Pine Valley Golf, Rodney Sq., Wilmington, Vicmead Hunt. Office: E I du Pont de Nemours & Co 1007 Market St Wilmington DE 19898 *

HECKETSWEILER, CLAUDE PIERRE, sales manager; b. Metz, Switzerland, Dec. 9, 1951; s. Paul Ernest Hecketsweiler and Carole (Raymonde) Sieffer; m. Carole Villa (div. 1983).; m. 2d, Marie-France Kohli, Jan. 28, 1957; 1 child, Pierre Daniel. MBA, Cath. U., 1971; cert., Internat. Inst. Mgmt., Montreux, Switzerland, 1975. Asst. sales mgr. GMM, London, 1975-76; sales rep. overseas-French territories Anfa SA, Paris, 1976-79; country mgr. Exxon Offices Systems, Geneva, 1980-82; sales mgr. Geneva-Dayton USA, Dayton, Ohio, 1985-86; sales mgr. South Europe, Middle East, Africa, Digital Communications Assocs. Inc., Atlanta, 1987—. Mem. Internat. Council Aircraft Owners and Pilots Assn., Internat. Airline Passengers Assn. Home: 24 Rt de Lausanne, 1180 Rolle Switzerland Office: DCA SA, Air Ctr Blandonnet, 1214 Geneva Switzerland

HECKHAUSEN, HEINZ, psychologist; b. Wuppertal, Fed. Republic Germany, Mar. 24, 1926; s. Max and Hedwig (Steinhoff) H.; m. Christa Kraneburg, Oct. 24, 1954; children: Jutta, Dorothee, Cordula, Felix. Diploma, U. Münster, Fed. Republic Germany, 1952, PhD, 1956; PhD, U. Münster, Fed. Republic Germany, 1962; hon. degree, U. Oslo, 1981. Docent U. Münster, 1962-64; prof. Ruhr-U. Bochum, Westfalia, Fed. Republic Germany, 1964-83; research dir. Max-Planck-Inst. for Psychol. Research, Munich, 1983—. Author books and articles. Fellow The Netherlands Inst. for Advanced Study, 1971-72. Mem. German Soc. Psychology (pres. 1980-82), Am. Psychol. Assn., Bavar. Acad. Scil., Sci. Council Fed. Republic Germany (chmn. 1985-87). Roman Catholic. Office: Max-Planck-Inst for Psychol Research, Leopoldst 24, 8000 Munich 40 Federal Republic of Germany

HECKHAUSEN, JUTTA, research psychologist; b. Münster, Fed. Republic Germany, Mar. 28, 1957; d. Heinz and Christa (Kraneburg) H. MA in Psychology, Ruhr U., 1980; PhD in Psychology, Strathclyde, Glasgow, Scotland, 1984. Post-doctoral fellow Max Planck Inst., Berlin, 1984-86, research scientist, 1987—; lectr. Tech. U., Berlin, 1984—. Research fellow U. Strathclyde; recipient scholarships German Acad. Exchange Service, 1981, Volkswagen, 1983, Max Planck Inst. 1984. Mem. Deutsche Gesellschaft Für Psychologie, Internat. Soc. Study Behavioral Devel., Soc. Research Child Devel. Office: Max Planck Inst, Lentzeallee 94, 1000-33 Berlin Federal Republic of Germany

HECKLER, MARGARET MARY, ambassador; b. Flushing, N.Y., June 21, 1931; d. John and Bridget (McKeon) O'Shaughnessy; children—Belinda West, Alison Anne, John M. B.A., Albertus Magnus Coll., 1953; LL.B., Boston Coll., 1956; student, U. Leiden, Holland, 1952; numerous hon. degrees. Bar: Mass. bar 1956, also U.S. Supreme Ct 1956. Mem. 90th to 97th Congresses, 10th Dist. Mass.; founder co-chmn. Congl. Women's Caucus; sec. HHS, 1983-85; ambassador to Ireland 1985—; mem. Mass. Gov.'s Council, 1963-66; Alternate del. Republican Nat. Conv., 1964, del., 1968, 72, 80, 84. Named Outstanding Mother of Year in Politics, 1984; Prince Henry the Navigator award (Portugal). Office: Am Embassy care US Dept State Washington DC 20520 *

HECKMAN, HENRY TREVENNEN SHICK, steel company executive; b. Reading, Pa., Mar. 27, 1918; s. H. Raymond and Charlotte E. Shick H.; A.B., Lehigh U., 1939; m. Helen Clausen Wright, Nov. 28, 1946; children—Sharon Anita, Charlotte Marie. Advt. prodn. mgr. Republic Steel Corp., Cleve., 1940-42, editor Enduro Era, 1946-51, account exec., 1953-54, asst. dir. advt., 1957-65, dir. advt., 1965-82; partner Applegate & Heckman, Washington, 1955-56; advt. mgr. Harris Corp., 1956-57. Permanent chmn. Joint Com. for Audit Comparability, 1968—; chmn. Media Comparability Council, 1969-83; chmn. indsl. advertisers com. Greater Cleve. Growth Assn., 1973-76; chmn. publs. com. Lehigh U., 1971-76; pres.'s adv. council Ashland Coll., 1966-76; advt. adv. council Kent State U., 1976-81; exec. com. Cleve. chpt. ARC, 1968-74; mem. Republican Fin. Exec. Com., 1966-87 . Served to comdr. USNR, 1942-46, 51-53; Korea. Named to Advt. Effectiveness Hall of Fame, 1967; named Advt. Man of Yr., 1969; recipient G.D. Crain, Jr. award, 1973; Disting. Alumnus award Lehigh U., 1979; elected to Cleve. Graphic Arts Council Hall of Distinction, 1981. Mem. Indsl. Marketers Cleve. (past pres., Golden Mousetrap award 1968), Bus./Profl. Advt. Assn. (pres. 1968-69, Best Seller award 1966), Assn. Nat. Advertisers (chmn. shows and exhibits com. 1966-74, dir. 1969-72), Am. Iron and Steel Inst. (com. chmn. 1961-69), Steel Service Center Inst. (advt. adv. com. 1965-77), Employee Support for the Guard and Res. (coordinator pub. service campaign council 1973-83), SAR (pres. 1979), Mil. Order World Wars (comdr. 1980), Early Settlers, Cleve. Advt. Club (pres. 1961-62, Hall of Fame 1980), Center for Mktg. Communications (chmn. bd. 1965), Internat. Platform Assn. Clubs: Cheshire Cheese (pres. 1982), Cleve. Grays (trustee 1980-82), Mid-Day, Cleve. Skating. Home: 375 Bentleyville Rd Chagrin Falls OH 44022

HECKMAN, JOANN, small business owner; b. Newton, N.J., Feb. 23, 1950; d. James Richard and Frances Margaret (Bertram) H. A.S. in Communications, Centenary Coll., 1982, B.A. cum laude in Communications and Journalism, 1984. Freelance reporter, editorial asst. Daily Advance, Roxbury Twp., N.J., 1979-81; asst. mgr., pressperson Jag-Ton Print World, Hackettstown, N.J., 1985; owner, operator Words-Worth Word Processing Services, Budd Lake, N.J., 1984—; word processor MetLife Security Ins. Co., East Hanover, N.J., 1985-87; co-owner, pres. The Crystal Works, Hackettstown, N.J., 1987—. Mem. Nat. Assn. Female Execs., AAUW, Phi Theta Kappa (Merit cert. 1982), Alpha Chi. Republican. Baha'i. Avocations: photography, graphic art and design, freelance writing, crafting. Home: 313 Shore Rd PO Box 114 Budd Lake NJ 07828 Office: The Crystal Works PO Box 7101 Hackettstown NJ 07840

HECKMAN, RICHARD AINSWORTH, chemical engineer; b. Phoenix, July 15, 1929; s. Hiram and Anne (Sells) H.; BS, U. Calif. at Berkeley, 1950, cert. hazardous mgmt. U. Calif., Davis, 1985; m. Olive Ann Biddle, Dec. 17, 1950; children—Mark, Bruce. With radiation lab. U. Calif. at Berkeley, 1950-51; chem. engr. Calif. Research & Devel. Co., Livermore, 1951-53; assoc. div. leader Lawrence Livermore Nat. Lab., Livermore, 1953-77, project leader, 1977-78, program leader, 1978-79, energy policy analyst, 1979-83, toxic waste group staff engr., 1984-86, waste minimization project leader, 1986—; mem. Calif. Radioactive Materials Forum. Bd. dirs. Calif. Industries for Blind, 1977-80, Here and Now Disabled Services for Tri-Valley, Inc., 1980. Registered profl. engr., Calif. Fellow Am. Inst. Chemists, Acad. Hazardous Materials Mgmt.; mem. AAAS, Am. Acad. Environ. Engrs. (diplomate), Am. Chemistry Soc., Am. Inst. Chem. Engrs., Soc. Profl. Engrs., Water Pollution Control Assn., Air Pollution Control Assn., Internat. Union Pure and Applied Chemistry (assoc.), Nat. Hist. Soc., N.Y. Acad. Scis., Am. Nuclear Soc., Internat. Oceanographic Soc. Clubs: Commonwealth (San Francisco); Island Yacht (commodore 1971) (Alameda, Calif.), Midget Ocean Racing Club (sta. 3 commodore 1982-83), U.S. Yacht Racing Union, Midget Ocean Racing Assn. No. Calif. (commodore 1972). Co-author: Nuclear Waste Management Abstracts, 1983. Patentee in field. Home: 5683 Greenridge Rd Castro Valley CA 94552 Office: PO Box 808 Livermore CA 94550

HEDGES, ROBERT ERNEST MORTIMER, university research scientist; b. London, June 9, 1944; s. Ernest Sydney and Elizabeth Dorothy (Lamb) H.; m. Laureen Susan, May 6, 1946; children: Donna Claire, Cara Jessamy. BA, MA, Cambridge U., 1965, PhD, 1968. Research assoc. U. Colo., 1969-70; research fellow U. Cambridge, 1968-72; research officer U. Oxford, Eng., 1971—, dir. radiocarbon accelerator lab., 1978—; Contbr. articles to profl. jours. Home: Lautrec Kiln Ln, Wheatley, Oxford England Office: Research Lab Archaeology, 6 Keble Rd, Oxford England

HEDIEN, COLETTE JOHNSTON, lawyer; b. Chgo.; d. George A. and Catherine (Bugan) Johnston; m. Wayne E. Hedien; children—Mark, Jason, Georgiana. B.S. with honors, U. Wis., 1960; J.D., DePaul U., 1981. Bar: Ill. 1981. Tchr., Sch. Dist. 39, Wilmette, Ill., 1960-63, Tustin Pub. Schs. (Calif.), 1964-66; extern law clk. to judge, Chgo., 1980, U.S. Atty.'s Office, Chgo., 1980; sole practice, Northbrook, Ill., 1981—; atty. Chgo. Vol. Legal Services; mem. Chgo. Appellate Law Com., 1982-83. Chmn. Northbrook Planning Commn; founder Am. Women of Surrey (Eng.), 1975-77; founding dir. U. Irvine Friends of Library, 1965-66; guidance vol. Glenbrook High Sch., 1984—. NSF scholar, 1962. Mem. Chgo. Bar Assn., Ill. Bar Assn., ABA (com. on real property), Phi Kappa Phi, Kappa Alpha Theta.

HEDIN, ROBERT ARNOLD, corporation executive; b. Burbank, Calif., Dec. 28, 1937; s. Ragnar Sigfred and Florence Coreene (Perry) H.; m. Ann Christine Carlsson, Nov. 3, 1968 (div. 1987); children—Eric, Thor. B.E.E., U. So. Calif., 1960, M.E.E., 1962; Bus. Cert., UCLA, 1968. Mem. tech. staff Electronic Specialty Co., Glendale, Calif., 1962-65; mgr. systems engring. Xerox Data Systems, El Segundo, Calif., 1965-70; mgr. engring. Eaton Electronic Security, Anaheim, Calif., 1970-73; research engr. Eaton Research Ctr., Southfield, Mich., 1973-76; range ops. mgr. Dynalectron, Waimea, Kauai, Hawaii, 1977-87; electronics engr. Pacific Missile Range, Barking Sands, Kauai, 1987—; pres., founder Light On Industries Inc., Anaheim, 1970-73, Tropical Shirts, Kalaheo, Hawaii, 1982—; founder, mgr. Digital ID Systems, Anaheim, 1968-73; pres., dir. Electronic Message Corp., Novi, Mich., 1973-76. Patentee in field. Contbr. articles to profl. jours. Served with USNR, 1955-63. Litton Industries fellow, 1962. Mem. IEEE, UCLA Bus. Alumni Assn., Kauai Soc. Artists, Eta Kappa Nu, Sigma Nu, Tau Beta Phi. Republican. Home: PO Box 1027 Kalaheo HI 96741

HEDLEY, RONALD HENDERSON, mus. dir.; b. Durham, Eng., Nov. 2, 1928; s. Henry Armstrong and Margaret (Hopper) H.; B.Sc. in Zoology, King's Coll., U. Durham, 1950, Ph.D., 1953, D.Sc., 1968; m. Valmai Mary Griffith, 1957; 1 son, Iain. Sr. sci. officer Brit. Mus. Natural History, 1955-61, prin. sci. officer, 1961-64, dep. keeper, zoology, 1964-71, dep. dir. mus., 1971-76, dir., 1976-88; vis. lectr. microbiology U. Surrey, 1968-75; trustee Percy Sladen Meml. Fund, 1972-77. N.Z. natural research fellow, 1960-61. Mem. council Royal Albert Hall, 1982-88. Fellow Inst. Biology, Zool. Soc. London (hon. sec. 1977-80, v.p. 1980-85); mem. Freshwater Biol. Assn. (council 1972-76), Soc. Protozoology (pres. Brit. sect. 1975-78), Marine Biol. Assn. (council 1976-79, 81—, council nat. trust 1985-88). Co-author: Atlas of Testate Amoebae, 1980; co-editor: Foraminifera, vols. 1-3, 1974-78; contbr. articles to profl. jours. Office: Brit Mus, Cromwell Rd, South Kensington, London SW7 5BD, England

HEDLEY, WILLIAM JOSEPH, engineer; b. St. Louis County, Mo., Nov. 6, 1902; s. Charles Henry and Elizabeth Frances (Smith) H.; B.S., Washington U., 1925; m. Katherine Henby (dec. Jan. 1988), May 14, 1927; children—William Henby, Mary Anne Hedley Speer (dec. 1978). Draftsman, Miss. Valley Structural Steel Co., Maplewood, Mo., 1925; with Wabash R.R., St. Louis, 1925-57, chief engr., 1957-63, asst. v.p. exec. dept., 1963-64; asst. v.p. Norfolk & Western Ry., St. Louis, 1964-67; cons. U.S. Dept. Transp., Washington, 1968-85, Sverdrup & Parcel & Assoc., St. Louis, 1968—. Chmn., Clayton (Mo.) City Plan Commn., 1957-62; mem. St. Louis County Planning Commn., 1958-62; mayor City of Clayton, 1963-67; pres. St. Louis County Municipal League, 1966-67; trustee Washington U., St. Louis, 1959-62. Named Engr. of Year, Mo. Soc. Profl. Engrs., 1964; recipient Alumni citation Washington U., 1966; Achievement award medal Engrs. Club St. Louis, 1967; Civil Govt. award ASCE, 1969; Hoover medal Joint Bd. Engrs. Found. Soc., 1973; Alumni Achievement award Washington U., 1976. Mem. Joint Council Asso. Engring. Soc. St. Louis (pres. 1951-52), Am. Ry. Engring. Assn. (pres. 1956-57), ASCE (pres. 1965-66), Interprofl. Council on Environ. Design (chmn. 1967), Mo. Soc. Profl. Engrs., Transp. Research Bd. (exec. com. 1968-71), Am. Ry. Bridge and Bldg. Assn., Roadmasters and Maintenance of Way Assn., Am. Rd. Builders Assn., Am. Soc. Planning Ofcls., AAAS, Nat. Def. Transp. Assn., Smithsonian Assos., St. Louis Acad. Sci. (dir. 1963-81, v.p. 1973-81), Mo. Hist. Soc., Nat. Council State Garden Clubs (dir. 1954-65), World Affairs Council of St. Louis, Internat. Platform Assn., St. Louis Sci. Ctr., Nat. Space Soc., Theta Xi (nat. pres. 1961-64), Tau Beta Pi, Sigma Xi, Chi Epsilon. Republican. Presbyterian. Clubs: St. Louis, Engrs. of St. Louis (pres. 1950-51), Rotary, Circle (St. Louis); University (Washington). Author: The Achievement of Grade Crossing Protection, 1949; The Effectiveness of Highway-Railway Grade Crossing Protection, 1954; State of the Art Report on Railroad-Highway Grade Crossing Surfaces, 1973; Railroad-Highway Grade Crossing Surfaces, 1979. Home: 824 N Biltmore Dr Clayton MO 63105 Office: 801 N 11th St Saint Louis MO 63101

HEDRICK, LOIS JEAN, investment company executive, state official; b. Topeka, Kans., Jan. 25, 1927; d. Arthur Lenard and Nellie Cecelia (Johnson) Lungstrum; m. Clayton Newton Hedrick, Apr. 26, 1949; 1 dau., Carol Beth. Cert., Strickler's Bus. Coll., 1947; student Washburn U., Topeka, 1980-83. Staff sec. Kans. State Senate, Topeka, 1946-65; co-owner Hedrick's Market, Topeka, 1953-67; exec. sec. to sr. legal counsel Security Benefit Life Ins. Co., Topeka, 1963-73; asst. corp. sec. Security Mgmt. Co., Topeka, 1973—, Security Distbrs. Inc., SBL Planning Inc., SBL Fund, Security Action Fund, Security Equity Fund, Security Investment Fund, Security Ultra Fund, Security Bond Fund, Security Cash Fund, Security OmniFund, Security Tax-Exempt Fund, Security Benefit Group, Ins., Security Mgmt. Co.; mgmt. cons. United Way of Greater Topeka, 1981—, mem. pub. relations staff, 1982—, rep. precinct woman. Organizer, chmn. Topeka Crime Blockers, 1976—; vol. fundraiser Am. Heart Assn., Stermont-Vail Hosp. Expansion, 1976-77; chmn. Plant a Tree for Century III, 1976; mem. Greater Topeka Career Edn. Com., 1981—; staff sec., fundraiser Christian Rural Overseas Program, 1951, staff sec. USAF Supply Depot, 1951-53. Named Woman of Year, Am. Bus. Women's Assn., 1970; Sec. of Yr., Profl. Secs. Inc., 1975. Mem. Greater Topeka C. of C. (chmn. edn. com. 1981—, ambassador chmn. high sch. honors banquet, 1982—), Adminstrv. Mgmt. Soc. (dir., pres. 1976—). Republican. Home: 1556 SW 24th St Topeka KS 66611

HEEB, CAMILLE STOREY, physician, educator; b. Brookfield, Mo., May 26, 1944; d. Kenneth Paul and Virginia May (Bailey) Storey; children: Marsha, Sarah. BA with honors in Sociology, U. Kans., 1966, MS in Spl. Edn., 1967, MD with honors 1979. Diplomate Am. Acad. Pediatrics. Corrective reading tchr., Chandler, Ariz., 1968-69; ednl. diagnostician Dept. Spl. Edn., Abilene, Tex., 1970-72; staff mem. dept. spl. edn. U. Kans., Lawrence, 1974-76, sponsor student chpt. Council for Exceptional Children; intern and pediatric resident U. Kans. Med. Ctr., 1979-81; pediatric resident Children's Mercy Hosp., Kansas City, Mo., 1981-82; staff physician Kans. Neurol. Inst., Topeka, 1982-84; pvt. practice, Topeka, Kans., 1984—; staff physician Stormont Vail Hosp., Topeka, St. Francis Hosp.; chmn. dept. pediatrics Meml. Hosp. Author: An Oral Language Development Program for the Educable Mentally Retarded, 1969. U.S. Office Edn./Bur. Handicapped fellow in spl. edn., 1966-67; U. Buffalo research grantee, 1968; recipient Daniel C. Darrow award, Paul Gyorgy award La Leche League. Mem. Council for Exceptional Children, Am. Assn. for Edn. Severely and Profoundly Handicapped, PEO, AMA, Am. Acad. Pediatrics, Phi Beta Phi. Home: 3120 W 15th St Topeka KS 66604 Office: Pediatric Assocs 1125 Gage Blvd Topeka KS 66604

HEER, EWALD, engineer; b. Friedensfeld, Germany, July 28, 1930; s. Johannes and Lilli Friedericke (Jauch) H.; Engr., Engring. Sch. Hamburg, 1953; B.S., CUNY, 1959; M.S., Columbia U., 1960, C.E., 1962; Dr. Eng. Sc. magna cum laude, Tech. U., Hannover, W. Ger., 1964; m. Hannelore M. Oehlers, Jan. 26, 1952; children—Thomas Ewald, Eric Martin. Engr., Hinz Architects, Hamburg, W. Ger., 1952-55; design engr. Hewitt Robins Co., N.Y.C., 1956-59; research engr. Weidlinger Cons., N.Y.C., 1959-62, McDonnell Douglas, St. Louis, 1964-65; research mgr. Gen. Electric Co., Phila., 1965-66; research mgr. Jet Propulsion Lab., Pasadena, Calif., 1966-70, program mgr. advanced studies, 1971-76, dir. research program autonomous systems and space mechanics, 1976-84, pres. Heer Assocs., Inc., 1984—; program mgr. Lunar exploration office NASA, Washington, 1970-71; adj. prof. U. So. Calif., 1973-84, dir. Inst. Technoecon. Studies, 1978-84. Fellow ASME; asso. fellow AIAA; mem. ASCE, IEEE, Am. Mgmt. Assn., Internat. Fedn. Theory Machines and Mechanisms, Sigma Xi. Republican. Lutheran. Editor: Remotely Manned Systems, 1973; Robots and Manipulator Systems I & II, 1977; Machine Intelligence and Autonomy for Aerospace Systems, 1988; contbr. articles to profl. jours. Home: 5329 Crown Ave La Canada CA 91011 Office: 4800 Oak Grove Dr Pasadena CA 91103

HEESELER, EDGAR CARLTON, investment banker; b. Bklyn., Oct. 28, 1921; s. Edgar Bernard and Florence Esther (Williams) H.; B.S. in Fin., Hofstra U., 1955, M.B.A. in Fin., 1958; m. Prudence Elizabeth La Plac, Feb. 17, 1945; 1 child, Richard Carlton. Wind tunnel facilities designer NASA, 1945; trainee C.J. Devine & Co. (now merged with Merrill Lynch Capital Mkts.), 1945, founder, mgr. dept. mcpl. research, 1946-49; research analyst mcpl. dept. Moody's Investors Service 1949-54; mgr. dept. mcpl. buying White, Weld & Co. (now merged with Merrill Lynch Capital Mkts.), 1954-64; mgr. new bus. dept., underwriter, fin. cons. Kidder Peabody & Co., 1964-71; v.p. in charge mcpl. fin. dept., underwriter, fin. cons. Shearson, Hammill & Co., Inc., 1971-74; v.p. in charge mcpl. fin. dept., underwriter, fin. cons. Shearson Hayden Stone, Inc. (merger Shearson, Hammill & Co. and Hayden, Stone & Co.), 1974-76; v.p. in charge mcpl. fin., underwriter, fin. cons. Thomson McKinnon Securities, Inc., N.Y.C., 1977-79; v.p. public fin. dept., underwriter, fin. cons. Loeb Rhoades, Hornblower & Co., N.Y.C., 1979; v.p. pub. fin. dept., underwriter, fin. cons. Shearson Loeb Rhoades Inc. (merger Loeb Rhoades, Hornblower & Co. and Shearson Hayden Stone, Inc.), N.Y.C., 1979-81, Shearson/Am. Express, Inc., N.Y.C., 1981-84, Shearson Lehman Bros., Inc., 1984—; dir. Walker Parking Cons., Inc., Kalamazoo; instr. mcpl. fin. N.Y. Inst. Fin., 1959-64; speaker on mcpl. parking fin. and downtown devel. Active local council Boy Scouts Am., 1933-51, Little League, Wantagh, N.Y., 1954-64. Served as navigator USAAF, 1941-44. Mem. Mcpl. Forum, Mcpl. Bond Club N.Y., L.I. Hist. Soc., Govtl. Fin. Officers Assn., Conn. Assn. Mcpl. Parking Authorities, Nat. Parking Assn. (dir., chmn. Parking Cons. Council 1983-84), Assn. Parking Authorities N.J., Am. Hist. Soc., Instnl. and Mcpl. Parking Congress, Internat. Downtown Execs. Assn., Mich. Parking Assn., Fla. Parking Assn., Internat. Platform Speakers Assn., Internat. Bridge, Tunnel and Turnpike Assn., Mensa., Lambda Chi Alpha. Republican. Episcopalian. Clubs: Down Town Assn., Analysts Lunch. Contbr. articles to profl. jours. Home: 2225 Jones Ave Wantagh NY 11793 Office: World Fin Ctr Am Express Tower 16 New York NY 10285

HEESTERBEEK, YVAN JOSEPH, management consultant; b. Antwerp, Belgium, Dec. 13, 1934; s. Henry Edmond and Charlotte Marie (de Weert) H.; m. Catherine Renee Bert, Sept. 4, 1964; children—Nathalie, Sontja. LL.D., U. Gent, 1958, M.Sc., U. Basel, 1962. Mgmt. trainee Ford Motor Co., Cologne, Germany, 1963-65; dir. fin. ITT Industries, Brussels, 1965-71; v.p. Gould Europe, Brussels, 1971-74; pres. Hunter Douglas Europe, Rotterdam, Holland, 1974-80; vice-chmn. Holec N.V., Utrecht, Holland, 1980-84; chmn. Heesterbeek Co., De Bilt-Utrecht, Barcelona, Brussels, Paris, N.Y.C., Rio de Janeiro, Brisbane, 1984—. Served to 2d lt. Commando, 1959-61. Mem. Am. Mgmt. Assn., Fin. Execs. Inst., Nederlands Centrum van Direkteuren. Club: Cercle Gaulois (Brussels). Avocations: tennis, golf, epistemology studies, art collecting. Home: Kortrykesteenweg 1009, 9000 Gent Belgium

HEFFER, JEAN, historian, educator; b. Paris, Oct. 1, 1933; s. Ernest and Marguerite (Labarre) H.; m. Yvette Marty, July 27, 1961; children: Patrick, Gabriel. Agregation, Sorbonne, 1957; D 3d cycle, U. Toulouse, 1967; D. U. Paris I, 1984. Asst. prof. history Sorbonne, Paris, 1969-70, U. Paris, 1970-84; prof. history Ecole Hautes Etudes en Sciences Sociales, Paris, 1985—. Author: The Port of New York and the American Foreign Trade, 1860-1900, 1986. Mem. French Assn. Econ. Historians (pres. 1987), French Assn. Am. Studies (v.p. 1987—). Home: 42 bis ave Carnot, 94500 Champigny sur Marne France Office: Ecole Hautes Etudes en Scis, Sociales Ctr Etudes NAm, 11 rue Pierre et Marie Curie, 75005 Paris France

HEFFNER, RICHARD EUGENE, petroleum geologist; b. Altoona, Pa., July 24, 1928; s. Eugene Vance and Florence Gertrude (Hamilton) H.; student La. Tech., 1946-49; B.S. in Geology, Centenary Coll., 1954; postgrad. U. Wyo., 1954; m. Imogene McEntire, Apr. 21, 1950; children—Cheryl Ann, Gail Elizabeth, Brian Eugene. Staff geologist Union Producing Co., Shreveport, La., 1954-67, Columbia Gas, Houston, 1967-69; pres. Atwater Cons., Ltd., New Orleans, 1979—; exec. v.p. Lamark Energy, Inc., New Orleans, 1973—. Profl. geol. scientist Am. Inst. Profl. Geologists. Mem. Am. Assn. Petroleum Geologists (cert. profl. geologist), Soc. Petroleum Engrs., AIME, Soc. Exploration Geophysicists, Geol. Soc. Am., AAAS. Republican. Methodist. Clubs: Lakewood Country, Internat. House, New Orleans Petroleum. Home: 1 Tennyson Pl New Orleans LA 70131 Office: 318 Camp St New Orleans LA 70130

HEFLIN, HOWELL THOMAS, U.S. senator, lawyer, former chief justice; b. Poulan, Ga., June 19, 1921; s. Marvin Rutledge and Louise D. (Strudwick) H.; m. Elizabeth Ann Carmichael, Feb. 23, 1952; 1 son, Howell Thomas. AB, Birmingham So. Coll., 1942; JD, U. Ala., 1948, LLD (hon.); LLD (hon.), U. No. Ala., Samford U., Tuskegee Community, Del. Law Sch., Widener Coll., Widener Coll., Troy State U., Ala. Christian Coll., Livingston U., Stillman Coll.; DHH (hon.), Birmingham So. Coll., 1980; DHL (hon.), Talledega Coll. Bar: Ala. 1948. Practiced in Tuscumbia; sr. partner firm Heflin, Rosser and Munsey; chief justice Supreme Ct. Ala., 1971-77; chmn. Nat. Conf. Chief Justices, 1976-77; U.S. senator 1979—; chmn. Ethics Com.; mem. Judiciary Com., Agr. Com. Bd. dirs. Meth. Pub. House, 1952-64; lectr. U. Ala., 1946-48, U. North Ala., 1948-52; Tazewell Taylor vis. prof. law Coll. William and Mary, 1977. Mem. Ala. Edn. Commn., 1957-58; chmn. Colbert County A.R.C., 1950; Ala. field dir. Crusade for Children, 1948; pres. Ala. Com. Better Schs., 1958-59; chmn. Tuscumbia Bd. Edn., 1954-64, Ala. Tenure Commn., 1959-64; pres. U. Ala. Law Sch. Found., 1964-66; co-chmn. NCCJ, Tri-Cities area, 1949-70; chmn. Brotherhood Week; bd. dirs., v.p. Nat. Center for State Cts., 1975-77; trustee Birmingham So. Coll.; hon. pres. Troy State U. Served to maj. USMC, 1942-46. Decorated Silver Star, Purple Heart; recipient Ala. Citizen of Yr. award Ala. Cable TV Assn., 1973, 82; Outstanding Alumnus award U. Ala. and Birmingham So. Coll., 1973; Herbert Lincoln Harley award Am. Judicature Soc., 1973; Justice award, 1981; Ala. Citizen of Year award Ala. Broadcasters Assn., 1975; mem. Ala. Acad. Honor; named Outstanding Appellate Judge in U.S. Assn. Trial Lawyers Am., 1976; recipient Highest award Am. Judges Assn., 1975, Thomas Jefferson award Ala. Press Assn., 1979; Inst. Human Relations award, 1980; Silver Chalice award Am. Council on Alcoholism, 1980; Disting. Am. award Nat. Football Found. and Hall of Fame; Warren E. Burger award Inst. Ct. Mgmt.; Leadership award Am. Security Council, 1985-87; Leadership award Southeastern Soc. Am. Forresters, 1986, Taxpayers Hall of Fame, 1987, Patriotic Civilian award U.S. Army, 1987, Henry Jackson Senatorial Leadership award, 1987, others. Fellow Internat. Acad. of Law and Scis., Internat. Acad. Trial Lawyers, Internat. Soc. Barristers, Am. Coll. Trial Lawyers; mem. Ala. Law Inst. (v.p.), ABA, Ala. Bar Assn. (pres. 1965-66), Colbert County Bar Assn. (past pres.), Ala. Bar Found. (past pres.), Am. Judicature Soc. (v.p. 1977-79), Ala. Law Sch. Alumni Assn. (past pres.), Ala. Trial Lawyers Assn. (pres.), VFW, Am. Legion, 40 and 8, DAV, Third Marine Div. Assn., Order of Coif, Omicron Delta Kappa, Phi Delta Phi, Tau Kappa Alpha, Lambda Chi Alpha. Methodist. Office: Office of the Senate 728 Hart Senate Bdlg Washington DC 20510

HEFTER, LAURENCE ROY, lawyer; b. N.Y.C., Oct. 13, 1935; s. Charles S. and Rose (Postal) H.; m. Jacqulyn Maureen Miller, June 13, 1957; children—Jeffrey Scott, Sue-Anne. B.M.E., Rensselaer Poly. Inst., 1957, M.S. in Mech. Engring., 1960; J.D. with honors, George Washington U., 1964. Bar: Va. 1964, N.Y. 1967, D.C. 1973. Instr. Rensselaer Poly. Inst., Troy, N.Y., 1957-59; patent engr. Gen. Electric Co., Washington, 1959-63; sr. patent atty. Atlantic Research Corp., Alexandria, Va., 1963-66; assoc. firm Davis, Hoxie, Faithfull & Hapgood, N.Y.C., 1966-69; mem. firm Ryder, McAulay & Hefter, N.Y.C., 1970-73, Finnegan, Henderson, Farabow, Garrett & Dunner, Washington, 1973—; prof. lectr. trademark law George Washington U., 1981—; mem. adv. com. U.S. Patent and Trademark Office, 1988—, Trademark Rev. Commn., 1986—. Mem. ABA (chmn. patent office affairs com. patent, trademark and copyright sect. 1976-80, unfair competition com. 1980-81), N.Y. State Bar Assn., D.C. Bar Assn., Va. Bar Assn. (dir. patent, trademark and copyright sect. 1976-78), Internat. Bar Assn. (chmn. trademark com. 1986—), Am. Patent Law Assn. (chmn. trademark com. 1979-81, dir. 1981-84), U.S. Trademark Assn. (dir. 1982-84), Internat. Assn. Advancement of Teaching and Research in Intellectual Property, Order of Coif, Alpha Epsilon Pi. Home: 7405 Pinehurst Pkwy Chevy Chase MD 20815 Office: 1775 K St NW Washington DC 20006

HEGARTY, MARY FRANCES, lawyer; b. Chgo., Dec. 19, 1950; d. James E. and Frances M. (King) H. B.A., DePaul U., 1972, J.D., 1975. Bar: Ill. 1975, U.S. Dist. Ct. (no. dist.) Ill. 1976, U.S. Supreme Ct. 1980. Ptnr. Lannon & Hegarty, Park Ridge, Ill., 1975-80; sole practice, Park Ridge, 1980—; dir. Legal Assistance Found. Chgo., 1983—. Mem. revenue study com. Chgo. City Council Fin. Com., 1983; mem. Sole Source Rev. Panel, City of Chgo., 1984; pres. Hist. Pullman Found., Inc., 1984-85. Mem. Ill. State Bar Assn. (real estate council 1980-84), Chgo. Bar Assn., Women's Bar Assn. Ill. (pres. 1983-84), NW Suburban Bar Assn., Park Ridge Women Entrepreneurs. Democrat. Roman Catholic. Club: Chgo. Athletic Assn. Office: 301 W Touhy Park Ridge IL 60068

HEGARTY, WILLIAM EDWARD, lawyer; b. N.Y.C., Nov. 18, 1926; s. William Alfred and Mary Johanna (Condon) H.; m. Barbara Meade Fischer, Oct. 26, 1950; children: Katharine Hegarty Bouman, Mary Hegarty Colombo, William, Amanda. AB, Princeton U., 1947; LLB, Yale U., 1950. Bar: N.Y. 1951, D.C. 1973, U.S. Supreme Ct. 1962. With Cahill, Gordon & Reindel (and predecessors), N.Y.C., 1950—, ptnr., 1962-69, sr. ptnr., 1969-87, sr. counsel, 1988—; counsel Mcpl. Art Soc. N.Y., 1988—. Bd. dirs. Florence J. Gould Found., French Inst./Alliance Française, Mcpl. Art Soc.; mem. Greenwich Inland Wetlands and Watercourses Agy. Served with USNR, 1944-46. Mem. ABA, Am. Bar Found., Assn. Bar City N.Y., Am. Law Inst., Am. Coll. Trial Lawyers., N.Y.C. Legal Aid Soc. (bd. dirs.). Clubs: Indian Harbor Yacht (bd. dirs.), India House, Coffee House, Cercle de l'Union Interallie. Home: Meads Point Greenwich CT 06830 Office: Cahill Gordon & Reindel 80 Pine St New York NY 10005

HEGAZY, ISMAIL SEDKI ABDEL-HAMID, trading company executive; b. Cairo, Oct. 1, 1932; s. Abdel Hamid Hegazy Mohamed and Zeinab Moustafa Helmy; B.S.C., Alexandria U., 1958; diploma bus. adminstrn. Cairo U., 1965, PhD in mktg., 1965; m. Soheir, Feb. 8, 1968; children—Amr, Abdel Hamid, Afaf, Cherine, Khaled. Mgr., Oils and Soap Co., Cairo, 1962-68; dir. Sudan Internat. Trade Office, 1960-62; dir. Pharaonic Internat. Trade Office, Cairo, 1968-88 , cons. 1968, pres. 1988—. Served with Egyptian Commandos, 1951-52. Moslem. Clubs: Lions, Gezira, National, Swissair. Address: 37 Talaat Harb Fl 5, Cairo Egypt

HEGEMAN, JAMES ALAN, corporate executive; b. Indpls., Jan. 8, 1943; s. Frank Anderson and Helene Anna (Sudbrock) H.; B.S. in Acctg. cum laude, U. Tenn., 1973; M.B.A., Harvard U., 1975; m. Catherine Louise Mallers, May 1, 1966 (div. 1973); 1 son, Christopher Scott; m. Janet Lee Scherf Nystrom, May 24, 1986. Pres., chmn. Nat. Rent-A-Cycle, Inc., Indpls., 1964-68, Fairfield Electronics Corp., Indpls., 1965-68; gen. mgr. H & R Block, Inc., Knoxville, Tenn., 1967-73; asst. controller Rohm & Haas, Inc., Knoxville, 1973-75; v.p. Gerson Co., Middleboro, Mass., 1975-76; controller Acton Corp. (Mass.), 1976-79; chief exec. officer Acton Films, Inc., N.Y.C., Telaction Phone Corp., Palisades Park, N.J., 1976—; corp. controller Golden Eye Seafoods, Inc., New Bedford, Mass., 1977-78; chief fin. officer Simon Konover & Assocs., K&P Mgmt., Inc., Anthony Assocs. (all West Hartford, Conn.), 1978-79; v.p. fin. Audio Specialists, Inc. and Sound Playground, Newington, Conn., 1979—; fin./mgmt. cons. Standex Internat. Corp., Salem, N.H., 1979-84; chief cons. APC Skills Co., Palm Beach, Fla., Alexander Proudfoot Co., Chgo., 1984; chief fin. officer State St. Technologies, Hartford, Conn., 1984—; pres. LWC Industries, Inc., Miami, Fla., also dir.; treas., dir. Kenmore Rd. Assn., 1987—; dir. Window Corp. Am. Mem. Ind. Republican Central Com., 1967-68; bd. govs. U. Tenn., 1975-79. Named to Tenn. Gov.'s staff, Tenn. Col. Continental Grain Co. fellow, 1973; Cabot fellow, 1974. C.P.A., Tenn. Mem. Am. Film Inst., Am. Inst. C.P.A.s, Tenn. Soc. C.P.A.s, U. Tenn. Alumni Assn. (pres.), Wally Byam Caravan Club Internat., Inc. (dir. 1982—), Beta Alpha Psi. Lutheran. Club: Harvard (Boston). Home: 58 Kenmore Rd Bloomfield CT 06002

HEGGE, PER EGIL, magazine editor; b. Skatval, Norway, June 3, 1940; s. Ole and Mary (Braa) H.; m. Birgit Wedege, June 22, 1963; children: Tanja Kristine, Trond Ivar, Thomas. Degree in journalism, Oslo U., 1966. Reporter Aftenposten, Oslo, 1962-69; fgn. corr. Aftenposten, Moscow, 1969-71; commentator Aftenposten, Oslo, 1971-77; fgn. corr. Aftenposten, Washington, 1977-81; editorial writer Aftenposten, Oslo, 1981-84; editor A-Magasinet of Aftenposten, Oslo, 1984—. Author: Go-Between in Moscow, 1971, The News From Moscow, 1972, USA-Right Turn?, 1981, US Foreign Policy, 1983. Recipient Narvesen Prize Norwegian Editors Assn., 1985. Mem. PEN (Norwegian pres. 1985—). Lutheran. Home: Taasenveien 135, 0880 Oslo 8, Norway Office: Aftenposten, Akersgatt 51, 0180 Oslo 1, Norway

HEGGLAND, RADOY WITT, energy company executive, consultant; b. Chgo., July 15, 1928; s. Thurlow Martin and Alice Marie (Witt) H.; m. Nancy Elizabeth Redd, June 12, 1949 (dec. Aug. 1983); children: Sherry, Sally; m. Shirley M. Agnew, Apr. 12, 1985. B.S., Calif. Inst. Tech., 1949; M.S. (Sloan fellow), Mass. Inst. Tech., 1965. Mem. geol. dept. staff Conoco (formerly Continental Oil Co.), Wichita Falls, Tex., Roswell, N.Mex., New Orleans, Houston, 1949-62; divs. exploration mgr. Conoco (formerly Continental Oil Co.), Lafayette, La., 1962-64; chief geologist internat. Conoco (formerly Continental Oil Co.), N.Y.C., 1965-67; mgr. exploration for N. Am. Conoco (formerly Continental Oil Co.), Houston, 1967-69; v.p. Conoco (Western Hemisphere exploration), 1970-76; exec. v.p. minerals Conoco (formerly Continental Oil co.), Denver, 1976-83, energy cons., 1983—. Mem. Am. Assn. Petroleum Geologists, Am. Mining Congress., Soc. Mining Engrs. Clubs: Hiwan Golf. Home and Office: 31428 Tamarisk Ln Evergreen CO 80439

HEGRENES, JACK RICHARD, educator; b. Fargo, N.D., Feb. 27, 1929; s. John and Ivy Anna (Jacobson) H.; B.S., U. Oreg., 1952, M.S., 1955; M.A., U. Chgo., 1960, Ph.D., 1970. Caseworker, Clackamas County Public Welfare Commn., Oregon City, Oreg., 1956-59, casework supr., 1960-62; instr. dept. psychiatry U. Oreg. Med. Sch., Portland, 1962-64, instr. Crippled Children's div., 1966-68, asst. prof., 1969-73, asso. prof. dept. public health and preventive medicine, and Crippled Children's div. Oreg. Health Scis. U., 1973—; adj. asso. prof. social work Sch. Social Work, Portland State U., 1973—. La Verne Noyes scholar, U. Chgo., 1958-60; NIMH fellow, U. Chgo., 1964-66. Fellow Am. Orthopsychiat. Assn.; mem. Nat. Assn. Social Workers, Am. Public Health Assn., Soc. for Gen. Systems Research, Am. Assn. for Advancement of Behavior Therapy, Am. Assn. Marriage and Family Therapists. Lutheran. Contbr. articles to profl. jours. Home: 3101 McNary Pkwy 12 Lake Oswego OR 97035 Office: Oreg Health Scis U PO Box 574 Portland OR 97207

HEGSTROM, WILLIAM JEAN, educator; b. Macomb, Ill., Oct. 21, 1923; s. Carl William and Thelma (Canavit) H.; student Western Ill. U., 1941-42; B.Sc., Rutgers U., 1949, Ed.M. 1952; M.A. in Teaching, Purdue U., 1964; postgrad. U. Fla., 1961, Fla. Atlantic U., 1965-68; Ed.D., U. Miami, 1971; m. Grace Ann Paladino, May 3, 1944; children—Elizabeth Louise (Mrs. Edward Cook), William Jean II, Jean. Tchr. jr. high sch., South Plainfield, N.J., 1949-52, high sch., Bernardsville, N.J. 1952-54, Oak St. Sch., Bernard's Twp., N.J., 1954-55, high sch., Summit, N.J., 1955-58, jr. high sch., Delray Beach, Fla., 1958-65; chmn. math. dept. John I. Leonard High Sch., Lake Worth, Fla., 1965-68, dir. Palm Beach County research project, 1966-68; adj. prof. Fla. Atlantic U., 1965-69, assoc. prof., 1969-70; counselor coordinator John Leonard Adult Center, Lake Worth, 1965-68; supr. research and evaluation Palm Beach County Sch. Bd., West Palm Beach, Fla., 1970-74; adj. prof. Palm Beach Jr. Coll., 1981-88, asst. prof., 1986-87; Palm Beach Atlantic Coll., 1984-87; cons. math. prof. Palm Beach County Sch. Bd., 1985—. Served with USAAF, 1942-46. Mem. NEA, Nat. Council Tchrs. Math., Nat. Assn. Investors Corp., Am. Assn. Individual Investors, Phi Delta Kappa. Contbr. articles to profl. jours. Home: 225 NE 22d St Delray Beach FL 33444

HEGYELI, RUTH INGEBORG ELISABETH JOHNSSON, physician, government official; b. Stockholm, Aug. 14, 1931; came to U.S., 1963; d. John Alfred and Elsa Ingeborg (Sjogren) Johnsson; m. Andrew Francis Hegyeli, July 2, 1966 (dec. June 1982). B.A. in Scis., U. Toronto, 1958, M.D., 1962. Sr. research pathologist Battelle Meml. Inst., Columbus, Ohio, 1967-69; intern Toronto Gen. Hosp., 1962-63; med. officer Nat. Heart and Lung Inst., 1969-73; chief program devel. and evaluation Nat. Heart, Lung and Blood Inst., Bethesda, Md., 1973-76, acting dir. office program planning, 1975-76, asst. dir. internat. relations, 1976-86, assoc. dir. internat. relations, 1986—; mem. sci. adv. bd. Giovanni Lorenzini Found., Inc., N.Y.C., Milan, 1982—. Coordinating editor Jour. Soviet Research in Cardiovascular Diseases, 1979-86. Editor 10 sci. books. Contbr. poetry to nat. anthologies. Named Hon. Mem., Eagle Tribe of Haida Indians, Queen Charlotte Islands, B.C., Can., 1961; recipient Outstanding Scientist award Battelle Meml. Inst., Columbus, Ohio, 1966; Cert. for Superior Service, HEW, 1975. Fellow Acad. Medicine, Toronto; mem. Am. Soc. Cell Biology, Am. Soc. Artificial Internal Organs, World Affairs Council, Nat. Council Internat. Health, N.Y. Acad. Scis. Republican. Avocations: poetry; fiction writing; non-fiction writing; art; music; travel; hiking; singing; swimming; ecology. Home: 24301 Hanson Rd Gaithersburg MD 20879

HEIBERG, JENS GERHARD, manufacturing executive; b. Oslo, Apr. 20, 1939; s. Gerhard and Ba Heiberg; m. Else Cathrine Matheson, July 3, 1970; children: Christian, Line, Halvor. Student, Coll. Commerce, Oslo, 1960; MBA, Copenhagen Grad. Sch. Econs. and Bus. Adminstrn., 1963; student in human relations in bus. and industry, Calif. State U., San Jose, 1964. Asst. controller Guardian Packaging Corp., Newark, Calif., 1963-64; market analyst Norsk Hydro A/S, Oslo, 1964-66; v.p. sales pulp and paper products Borregaard A/S, Paris, 1966, Salzburg, 1966-72; v.p. A/S Norcem, Oslo, 1972-73, pres., chief exec. officer, 1973-87; pres., chief exec. officer Aker Norcem A/S now Aker A/S, Oslo, 1987—; bd. dirs. Norske Fina A/S, Cia Valenciana de Cementos Portland S.A., Valencia, Spain, Industri AB Euroc, Sweden, Norval Inc. USA; mem. corp. assembly Saga Petroleum A/S & Co., 1980—. Chmn. Found. for Promotion Norwegian Athletics, Oslo, 1982-88, The Norwegian Found., Oslo, 1985-88. Recipient The Farmand award, Oslo, 1986. Mem. Fedn. Norwegian Industries (bd. dirs. 1984—), Norwegian Employers Confedn. (vice chmn. bd. dirs. 1984—). Office: Aker A/S, Bryggegaten 3, 0250 Oslo 2 Norway

HEICHBERGER, ROBERT LEE, educator; b. Boston, N.Y., Jan. 19, 1930; s. Norman Allen and Louise (Gross) H.; B.S., State Univ. Coll., Buffalo, 1951; Ed.M., SUNY, Buffalo, 1962, Ed.D., 1970; m. Elaine Boldt, Apr. 14, 1956; children—Lisa Elaine, Mark Robert. Prin. schs. in E. Aurora, N.Y., 1953-64; asst. dean, then dean State Univ. Coll., Fredonia, N.Y., 1964-72, exec. asst. to pres., 1972-77, prof. ednl. adminstrn., 1977—; lectr., cons. in field. Vice pres. Tri-County Hosp., Gowanda, N.Y., 1976-79. Mem. Am. Assn. Sch. Adminstrs., Elementary Sch. Prins. Assn., Nat. Assn. Higher Edn., Fredonia C. of C. (v.p. 1972-80), Phi Delta Kappa (pres. 1973-76; Educator of Year award 1979, Disting. Service award 1975). Lutheran. Author: Leadership Development: Theory and Practice, 1975, A Strategy for Humanizing the Change Process in Schools, 1976. Home: 110 Memorial Dr Gowanda NY 14070 Office: State Univ Coll Fredonia NY 14063

HEID, HANS, education educator; b. Velbert, W.Ger., Mar. 3, 1932; s. Hans and Ilse (Engelbert) H.; m. Karla Kolk, Apr. 8, 1958; children—Dagmar, Jutta. Magister Artium, U. Köln, 1964; Dr.paed., U. Essen, 1974. Tchr., Realschule Heiligenhaus, 1958-68; wiss. asst. U. Duisburg, W.Ger., 1968-71; prof. sci. of edn. U. Essen, W.Ger., 1972—. Author numerous books and essays. Mem. sci. orgn. com. World Congress of Sexology, New Delhi, India, 1985. Mem. Deutsche Gesellschaft für Geschlechtserziehung. Home: Dürerstr 42, 5628 Heiligenhaus Federal Republic Germany Office: Univ Essen, Universitestrasse 2, 4300 Essen Federal Republic of Germany

HEIDEKING, JÜRGEN, historian, educator; b. Hameln, Fed. Republic Germany, Apr. 17, 1947; s. Karl and Anna (Mann) H.; m. Anna-Maria Ellinger; children: Claudia, Martin. Grad., U. Tübingen, Fed. Republic Germany, 1974, PhD, 1978, habilitation, 1987. Asst. prof. history U. Tübingen, 1977-87, pvt. dozent history, 1987—. Author: Areopag der Diplomaten, 1979, Die Verfassung vor dem Richterstuhl, 1988; editor: Holocaust, 1982; contbr. articles to mags. Mem. Assn. Documentary Editing, German Hist. Soc. Evangelical Lutheran. Office: Univ Tubingen, Wilhelmstr 36, 7400 Tubingen Federal Republic of Germany also: German Hist Inst 1759 R St NW Washington DC 20009

HEILER, SIEGFRIED, statistics educator; b. Wangen, Allgaeu, Fed. Republic Germany, Oct. 20, 1938; s. August and Lotte (Fleischer) H.; m. Ilse Hoptner, Mar. 21, 1963 (div. Mar. 1976); 1 child, Eva; m. Hildegard Rausch-Heiler, June 16, 1977; children—Mark, Patrick. Verwaltungs-inspektor, Staatl Verwaltungs Schule, Stuttgart, Bad-Wuertt, 1959; Diplom Volkswirt, U. Tubingen/Hamburg/Munchen, 1963; Dr.rer.pol., U. Tubingen, 1966. Asst. prof. Tech. U. Berlin, 1969-71, prof., 1971-72; prof. stats. U. Dortmund, Fed. Republic Germany, 1972-87, dean dept. stats. 1974-75, 79-80; prof. statistics U. Konstanz, Fed. Republic Germany, 1987—. Author: Einfuhrung in die Statistik, 1971, Wirtschaftprognosen, 1973; editor: Recent Trends in Statistics, 1983; contbr. articles to sci. jours. Mem. Internat. Statis. Inst., Deutsche Statistische Gesellschaft. Home: Mozartstrasse 8, Konstanz, 7750 Baden-Wurttemberg Federal Republic of Germany Office: Fak Wirtschafftswiss u, Statistik U Konslanz, Postfach 5560, 7750 Konstanz Federal Republic of Germany

HEILIG, MARGARET CRAMER, nurse; b. Lancaster, Pa., Jan. 17, 1914; d. William Stuart and Margaret White (Snader) Cramer; m. David Heilig, June 1, 1942; children—Judith, Bonnie, Barbara. B.A. in Psychology, Wilson Coll., 1935; M.S.W., U. Pa., 1940; AASci. in Nursing Delaware County Community Coll., 1970. Registered nurse. Caseworker Children's Bur., Lancaster, Pa., 1935-37, 39-42; group worker Ho. of Industry Settlement Ho., Phila., 1937-39; curriculum chmn. Upper Darby Adult Sch. (Pa.), 1958-68; health asst., camp mother Paradise Farm Camp, Downington, Pa., 1960-70, camp nurse, 1970-78, infirmary dir., 1978-86; med. surg. nurse Crozer-Chester Med. Ctr., Chester, Pa., 1970; out-patient nurse Maternal Infant Care, Chester, 1971; coll. nurse Delaware County Community Coll., Media, Pa., 1971-76, dir. health services, 1976-84, health cons., 1984—, writer coll. health newsletter, 1973—, health fair dir., 1979—. Author: First Aid Booklet, 1976; also articles and columns in health field. Nurse for health screening children's program Tyler Arboretum, Media, 1982—, Update on Personal Health, Broadmeadows Women's Prison, 1973, 82; former leader Delaware County Council Girl Scouts U.S.; clk. Lansowne Friends Meeting, 1986—; mem. Upper Darby Recreation Bd., 1956-58, Upper Darby Adult Sch. Bd., 1956-68, curriculum chmn., 1958-68; provider host home for fgn. exchange students, 1965-75; participant Audubon Ann. Bird Count, 1970—; coordinator, dir. Ann. Soc. of Friends Ch. Retreat, 1970—; ARC Speakers' Bur.-AIDS; tchr. Beginning Birding course Del. County Community Coll. Recipient Ollie B. Moten award Am. Coll. Health Assn., 1987. Mem. Am. Coll. Personnel Assn., Am. Nurses Assn., Pa. Nurses Assn., Delaware County Nurses Assn. (membership chmn. 1977-78), Southeastern Pa. Coll. Health Nurses Assn. (co-founder, pres. 1983-85), Middle Atlantic Coll. Health Assn., Delaware Valley Soc. for Adolescent Health, LWV, Women's Internat. League for Peace and Freedom, Brandywine Conservance. Quaker. Avocations: piano and choral music, nature walking, handicrafts. Home: 605 Mason Ave Drexel Hill PA 19026 Office: Del County Community Coll Media PA 19063

HEILIGENSTEIN, CHRISTIAN E., lawyer; b. St. Louis, Dec. 7, 1929; s. Christian A. and Louisa M. (Dixon) H.; children: Christie, Julie; m. Liselotte Warbanoff, Feb. 6, 1981. BS in Law, U. Ill., 1953, JD, 1955. Bar: Ill. 1955, U.S. Dist. Ct. (ea. dist.) Ill. 1955, U.S. Ct. Appeals (7th cir.) 1956, U.S. Dist. Ct. (so. dist.) Ill. 1960, U.S. Supreme Ct. 1982. Assoc. Listeman & Bandy, East St. Louis, Ill., 1955-61; sole practice, Belleville, Ill., 1962-84; ptnr. Heiligenstein & Badgley, Belleville, 1984—; dir., exec. com. 1st Nat. Bank of Belleville, dir. Magna Group, Inc. Recipient Alumni of Month award U. Ill. Law Sch., 1982. Mem. Ill. State Bar Assn., Internat. Acad. Trial Lawyers, St. Clair County Bar Assn., St. Louis Bar Assn., Inner Circle Advs., Am. Bd. Trial Advs., Am. Acad. Profl. Liability Attys., Assn. Trial Lawyers Am. (bd. govs. 1985-87), Ill. Trial Lawyers Assn. (bd. dirs. 1975—, v.p. 1987). Democrat. Clubs: Mo. Athletic (St. Louis); Union League (Chgo.); Beach (Palm Beach, Fla.). Home: RR 5 PO Box 231 Belleville IL 62222 Office: 30 Public Sq Belleville IL 62220

HEILMAN, CARL EDWIN, lawyer; b. Elizabethville, Pa., Feb. 3, 1911; s. Edgar James and Mary Alice (Bechtold) H.; m. Grace Emily Greene, Nov. 29, 1934 (div. 1952); children—John Greene, Elizabeth Greene; m. 2d, Claire Virginia Phelps, Oct. 10, 1952. B.A., Lafayette Coll., Easton, Pa., 1932, M.A., 1933; J.D. magna cum laude, U. Pa., 1939. Bar: N.Y. 1940, Pa. 1940, Mass. 1973, U.S. Supreme Ct. 1960. Tchr. English, Easton High Sch., 1934-36; assoc. Dwight, Harris, Koegel & Caskey, N.Y.C., 1939-42; atty. OPA, Washington, 1942-43; atty. N.Y. Gov.'s Commn. to Investigate Workmen's Compensation Law, N.Y.C., 1943-44; assoc. Dewey, Ballantine, Bushby, Palmer & Wood, N.Y.C., 1944-59, ptnr., 1959-73; counsel to firm Csaplar & Bok, Boston and San Francisco, 1973—. Trustee Upsala Coll., East Orange, N.J., 1970-73. Fellow Am. Bar Found.; mem. ABA, Boston Bar Assn., Order of Coif. Republican. Episcopalian. Club: Down Town (Boston). Home: One Devonshire Pl Apt 2605 Boston MA 02109

HEILMANN, WOLF-RÜDIGER, mathematics and insurance sciences educator; b. Rendsburg, Fed. Republic of Germany, Sept. 27, 1948; s. Wilhelm Heilmann and Ursula (Schröder) Hansen; m. Ingrid Benn, Mar. 20, 1970; children: Larissa-Valeska, Lisa-Maria, Lydia Sara. Diploma in Math., U. Hamburg, Fed. Republic Germany, 1974, Doctoral Promotion, 1977, Habilitation, 1979. Asst. math. U. Hamburg, 1974-80, asst. prof., 1980-82, assoc. prof., 1982-85; prof. ins. scis. U. Karlsruhe, Fed. Republic Germany, 1985—. Author: Grundbegriffe der Risikotheorie, 1987; editor: Versicherungsmärkte im Wandel, 1987; contbg. editor Insurance Abstracts and Reviews Jour., 1987—. Mem. Deutsche Gesellschaft Versicherungsmathematik, Deutsche Mathematiker-Vereinigung, Deutscher Verein für Versicherungswissenschaft, Bernoulli Soc., ASTIN Internat. Home: Parkstrasse 21, D-7500 Karlsruhe 1, Federal Republic of Germany Office: Univ Karlsruhe Versicherungswissenschaft, Kronenstrasse 34, D-7500 Karlsruhe 1, Federal Republic of Germany

HEIM, BRUNO BERNARD, archbishop; b. Olten, Switzerland, Mar. 5, 1911; s. Bernhard and Elizabeth (Studer) Heim-Studer. Student Benedictine Coll., Engelberg, Switzerland, 1926-31; Dr. phil., Thomas Aquinas U., Rome, 1934; BD, Fribourg U., Switzerland, 1937; DCL, Gregorian U. (Rome), 1946; grad. Pontifical Diplomatic Acad., Rome, 1947. Ordained priest Roman Cath. Ch., 1938, consecrated bishop, 1961. Curate in parishes Arbon and Basel, Switzerland, 1938-42; chief chaplain for Italian and Polish mil. internees in Switzerland, 1943-45; sec. Nuncio Roncalli, Pope John XXII in Paris, 1947-51; auditor Nunciature, Vienna, Austria, 1951-54; councillor Nunciature, Bonn, Fed. Republic of Germany, 1954-61; apostolic del., Scandinavia 1961-69; pro nuncio, Finland, 1966-69, Egypt; pres. of Caritas, Egypt, 1969-73; apostolic del. Gt. Britain, 1973-82, pro nuncio, Gt. Britain, 1982-85. Author: Coutumes et droit héraldiques de l'Eglise, 1950; Heraldry in the Catholic Church, 1978; 82 Liber amicorum, 1982. Decorated officer Legion d'honneur France, 1951, knight of honour Teutonic Order, 1961; Cross of Merit with star (Germany), 1961; gt. cross Order of Malta, 1962; Golden Cross with star (Austria), 1962; gt. officer of Merit, Italy, 1965; gt. cross of Finnish Lion, 1969; gt. cross Order of St. Maurice and Lazarus, Savoy, 1973; Gt. Cordon first class Order of Republique, Egypt, 1974; gt. cross Order of St. John, Britain, 1979; Order of Isabel la Catolica, Spain, 1982; bailiff gt. cross Constantinian Order of St. George, 1982; gt. officer Order of Polonia Restituta, 1985. Mem. Internat. Heraldic Acad., Soc. Suisse d'Heraldique, Accademia del Collegio Araldico, Real Acad. de la Historia, Accad. Atcheologica Italiana, Societa' Italiana di studi Araldici, French Heraldic and Geneal. Soc., Adler Vienna, Herold Berlin, Socs. Heraldica Scandinavica, Cambridge U. Heraldic and Geneal. Soc. (patron). Club: Atheneum (London). Avocations: heraldic painting; gardening; cooking. Address: Zehnderweg 31, CH 4600 Olten Switzerland

HEIM, KAARE, banker; b. Oslo, June 9, 1945; s. Fredrik and Inger (Arnesen) H.; m. Irene Rasmussen, Jan 9, 1971 (div. Oct. 1979); 1 child, Siv; m. Ragnhild Herland, Oct. 25, 1981; 1 child, Cecilie. MBA, Norwegian Sch. Bus. Adminstrn. and Econs., 1973. Fgn. exchange dealer Bergen (Norway) Bank, 1971-83; head fgn. dept. A/S Bergens Skillingsbank, Bergen, 1983—. Home: Herland, N-5234 Garnes Norway Office: A/S Bergens Skillingsbank, Raadstuplass 4, N-5017 Bergen Norway

HEIMAN, GROVER GEORGE, JR., editor, writer; b. Galveston, Tex., July 26, 1920; s. Grover George and Rose Mary (Ulch) H.; m. Virginia Deene Williamson, Feb. 14, 1942 (dec.); children: Virginia, Grover, Deborah, Richard. Student, Lee Coll., 1937-40, U. Tex., 1940-41; B.S. in Commerce cum laude, U. So. Calif., 1959. News reporter Corsicana (Tex.) Daily Sun, 1945-47; commd. 2d lt. USAAC, 1942; advanced through grades to col. U.S. Air Force, 1963; spl. asst. to USAF Chief of Staff, Pentagon, Washington, 1959-63; chief of info. Allied Air Forces So. Europe, Naples, Italy, 1963-66; chief mags. and books Dept. Def., Pentagon, 1966-68; ret. 1968; mng. editor Armed Forces Mgmt. mag., Washington, 1968-70; assoc. editor Nation's Business mag., Washington, 1970-76; industry editor Nation's Business mag., 1976-78, mng. editor, 1978-80, editor, 1980-82, editor emeritus, 1982—; chmn. Naples Dependent Schs. bd., 1964-65. Author: (with Rutherford Montgomery) Jet Navigator, 1959, Jet Tanker, 1961, Jet Pioneers, 1963, (with Virginia Myers) Careers For Women In Uniform, 1971, Aerial Photography, 1973. Served with USAAF, 1941-45, USAF, 1945-68. Decorated Legion of Merit. Mem. Authors League, Authors Guild, Jet Pioneers Am., Beta Gamma Sigma. Roman Catholic. Clubs: Cedar Crest Country, National Press. Home: 2881 Glenvale Dr Fairfax VA 22031

HEINDL, DENNIS DUANE, mfg. co. exec.; b. St. Mary's, Pa., June 30, 1942; s. Harold H. and Marion M. Heindl; student public schs., Ridgway area; m. Rose E. DeGroat, Oct. 13, 1962; 1 dau., Paula. Press operator Keystone Carbon Co., St. Mary's, 1959-61; sales mgr. Nat. Molded Products, St. Mary's, 1963-70; founder, owner, pres. Compacted Powdered Metals, Ridgway, Pa., 1970—, Atlas Pressed Metals, DuBois, Pa., 1975—, Laurel Mfg. Inc., Dubois, 1980—; dir. Keystone Nat. Bank; owner, operator radio Sta. WLMI; pres. Laurel Media Inc. Served with USN, 1960-62. Roman Catholic. Club: Elks (past exalted ruler). Home: 613 Dewey St Ridgway PA 15853 Office: PO Box J DuBois PA 15801

HEINDORFF, MICHAEL, artist, educator; b. Braunschweig, Niedersachsen, Germany, June 26, 1949; arrived in Eng., 1975; s. Hans Heindorff and Sigrid (Hampe) Bootz; m. Monica Buferd, July 8, 1983; children, Roman, Paloma. MA, Royal Coll. Art, London, 1977. Sr. lectr. St. Martins Sch. Art, London, 1980-81; tutor Royal Coll. Art, London, 1981-88, fellow, 1988—; represented by Bernard Jacobson Gallery, London and N.Y.C. Recipient German Acad. Exchange Council award, London, 1976-77, Karl Schmidt-Rottluff prize, Bonn, Fed. Republic Germany, 1980-83, Villa Massimo prize, Rome, 1983-84. Club: Freds, Chelsea Arts (London). Studio: 33 Charlotte Rd, London EC2 3PB, England

HEINE, ELIZABETH, editor; b. N.Y.C., Feb. 3, 1939; d. T.C. and Anne Meade H. BA in English and Math., Cornell U., 1960; MA in English, Radcliffe Coll., 1961; PhD in English Lit., Harvard U., 1965. Resident fellow Radcliffe Coll., 1961-62; teaching fellow in English and gen. edn. Harvard U., 1962-65; instr. English, Bklyn. Coll., 1965-66; asst. prof. English, U. Hawaii, Manoa, 1966-71; lectr. humanities U. of Sci., Penang, Malaysia, 1972-73; assoc. prof. English, U. Tex., San Antonio, 1974-78; assoc. editor Abinger Edition, E.M. Forster, King's Coll., Cambridge, Eng., 1978-79, editor, 1980—. Editor: The Hill of Devi and Other Indian Writings, 1983; The Longest Journey, 1984; co-editor: (with Oliver Stallybrass) Arctic Summer and Other Fiction, 1980. Contbr. articles and reviews to profl. jours. Woodrow Wilson fellow, Nat. Merit scholar. Mem. Modern Lang. Assn., Phi Beta Kappa, Phi Kappa Phi.

HEINEMAN, NATALIE (MRS. BEN W. HEINEMAN), civic worker. Formerly med. social worker Chgo.; pres. Child Welfare League Am., 1971-74, now hon. life mem.; chmn. citizens com. Ill. Adoption Service, 1959-71; pres. Chgo. Child Care Soc., 1967-71, now bd. dirs.; mem. citizens' com. Juvenile Ct. of Cook County; bd. dirs. United Way Am., 1973-79, Erickson Inst. for Advanced Study in Child Devel., Chapin Hall Ctr. for Children, U. Chgo., Chgo. Fedn. Settlements, 1957-68; mem. women's bd. Field Mus. Natural History, U. Chgo., Northwestern U.; vis. com. U. Chgo. Sch. Social Service Service. Bd. dirs. United Way Met. Chgo., 1975-86. Address: 180 E Pearson St Chicago IL 60611

HEINEMANN, KATHERINE (KAKI), author; b. St. Louis; d. Herbert N. and Elsa S. (Straus) Arnstein; B.S., Washington U., St. Louis, 1950, M.A. (Arts and Scis. Faculty award 1950), 1956; m. Morton D. May, 1937; children—David A., Philip F.; m. Sol Heinemann, July 8, 1950; 1 dau., Kate Heinemann Taucher. Freelance writer, poet, 1960—; prof. English, U. Tex., El Paso, 1968-74; condr. poetry readings, workshops, 1968—; mem. El Paso Art Resources Dept. Bd., 1980-81; author: Brandings, 1968; Some Inhuman Familiars, 1983; taping for Poetry Collection of Library of Congress, 1982. Mem. PEN, Nat. Soc. Arts and Letters. Clubs: Coronado Country, El Paso Tennis, Sunset Heights Garden. Home: 4252 Ridge Crest Dr El Paso TX 79902

HEINIG, NORMAN THOMAS, cons. co. exec.; b. Chgo., Feb. 20, 1928; s. Oscar William and Agnes Kerchville (Lamar) H.; B.S., Northwestern U., 1955; children—Norman, William, Mary, Barbara, Tanya, Randy. Apprentice, Sanger Plumbing, 1945-50; engr., project mgr. Commonwealth Plumbing Co., Chgo., 1957-65; cons. engr. Architects Mech. Design Service Corp., Chgo., 1965-73; owner Heinig Cons. Plumbing Engring. Co., Mission Viejo, Calif., 1974—. Bd. dirs. Chgo. Boys Club, 1961; pres. PTA, 1967; leader Boy Scouts Am., 1955-65. Mem. Am. Soc. Plumbing Engrs. Republican. Roman Catholic. Clubs: Chgo. Athletic, Royal League, Elks. Home and office: PO Box 2777 Mission Viejo CA 92690

HEINLE, ROBERT ALAN, physician; b. Tarentum, Pa., Oct. 26, 1933; s. Edward William and Mary Alice (Purvis) H.; B.S., U. Pitts., 1955, M.D., 1959; m. Barbara Klimeck, Aug. 23, 1958; children—Richard, Jeffrey, Ronald, Robert, Thomas, Timothy. Intern, U. Pitts. Health Center, 1959-60, resident, 1962-65; research fellow in medicine Peter Bent Brigham Hosp., 1965-67; research asso. in medicine Harvard Med. Sch., 1967-68; asst. prof. medicine U. Rochester (N.Y.) Med. Sch., 1968-71, asso. prof., 1971-75, clin. asso. prof., 1975—; dir. cardiovascular lab. Genesee Hosp., Rochester, 1975—; sr. asso. physician Strong Meml. Hosp., Rochester, 1975—; cons. Am. Heart Jour., 1973—; NIH research fellow, 1965-68. Bd. dirs. Blue Cross in Rochester, Blue Shield in Rochester. Served with U.S. Army, 1960-62. Fellow ACP, Am. Coll. Cardiology; mem. Am. Heart Assn., AMA, Am. Fedn. Clin. Research, Rochester Individual Practice Assn. (dir.), Phi Beta Kappa, Omicron Delta Kappa, Alpha Omega Alpha. Republican. Roman Catholic. Home: 415 Warren Ave Rochester NY 14618 Office: 224 Alexander St Rochester NY 14607

HEINRICH, RUDOLF WOLFGANG, archivist; b. Mering, Fed. Republic Germany, Jan. 4, 1940; s. Rudolf and Emma (Faaber) H.; m. Ingeborg Waldmann (dec. July 1988). Degree in Electronic Engring., Tech. U., Munich, 1965; Degree in Higher Librarianship, Bayerische Bibliotheksschule, Munich, 1976; D of Chemistry, Tech. U., Munich, 1984. Devel. engr. Studio for Electronic Music, Munich, 1963-66; head lab. Max Planck Inst. for Physics, Munich, 1966-74; head archives Deutsches Mus., Munich, 1976—. Author: Vom Atom zum Weltgefüge, 1984, (with others) Wittelsbacher Hausverträge des späten Mittelalters, 1987; contbr. articles to profl. jours. Home: Ludwigstrasse 87, 8210 Prien-Bachham Federal Republic of Germany Office: Deutsches Mus, Museumsinsel 1, 8000 Munich 22, Federal Republic of Germany

HEINZ, HENRY JOHN, III, U.S. senator; b. Pitts., Oct. 23, 1938; s. Henry John II and Joan (Diehl) H.; m. Teresa Simoes-Ferreira, 1966; children: Henry John IV, Andre, Christopher Drake. Grad., Phillips Exeter Acad., 1956; B.A., Yale U., 1960; M.B.A., Harvard U., 1963; Litt.D.(hon.), Wilkes Coll., 1979; LL.D.(hon.), Temple U., 1978. Gen. product mgr. marketing H.J. Heinz Co., Pitts., 1965-70; lectr. Carnegie-Mellon U. Grad. Sch. Indsl. Adminstrn., 1970-71; mem. 92d-94th congresses from 18th Dist. Pa., 1971-77; U.S. senator from Pa., 1977—; chmn. Senate spl. com. on aging; Del. Republican Nat. Conv., 1968, 72, 76, 80; chmn. Pa. Rep. Platform Com., 1970. Trustee Howard Heinz Endowment, Childrens Hosp., Pitts., U. Pitts.; bd. overseers Grad. Sch. Bus., Harvard U.; chmn. H.J. Heinz II Charitable and Family Trust. Served with USAF, 1963. Recipient Nat. Americanism award Anti-Defamation League of B'nai B'rith, 1977. Mem. Am. Inst. Pub. Service. Office: 277 Russell Senate Office Bldg Washington DC 20510 *

HEINZ, WERNER, physicist; b. Dusseldorf, Fed. Republic Germany, Jan. 9, 1927; s. Kurt and Marie Luise (Schmitz) H.; m. Margrit Heskamp (dec. 1962); m. Helga Joerger; children: Gerd-Ulrich, Corinna. Diploma in physics, U. Wurzburg, Fed. Republic Germany, 1950. Physicist Gebruder Haake, Berlin, 1953-62; mng. dir., ptnr. Brabender MessTechnik K.G., Duisburg, Fed. Republic Germany, 1962—. Contbr. articles to profl. jours.; patentee in field. Mem. Deutsche Rheologische Gesellschaft, Verein Deutscher Ingenieure. Home: Dabringhauser Str 72, Cologne 80 Federal Republic of Germany Office: Brabender Messtechnik KG, Kulturstr 51-55, Duisburg Federal Republic of Germany

HEINZE, LINDA HOLLI, promotion agency executive, lecturer; b. N.Y.C., Dec. 31, 1939; d. Rudolf Ley and Jessica Mary (Babcock) H. A.A., N.Y.C. Community Coll., 1959; student in bus. adminstrn. Pace Coll., 1964-68, New Sch. Social Research, 1969, Baruch Coll. CCNY, 1970. Asst. mgr. advt. makeup Look mag., N.Y.C., 1959-64; prodn. mgr. McCall mag., N.Y.C., 1964-70; asst. promotion mgr. treasury div. J.C. Penney Co., N.Y.C., 1970-72; sr. v.p. Robert Brian Assocs., N.Y.C., 1972—. Mem. bus. games com. L.I. U.; bd. dirs. N.Y. chpt. Medic Alert, 1984-89. Mem. Am. Advt. Fedn. (Silver medal 1971), Advt. Women N.Y. (ELA award 1972). Office: Robert Brian Assocs 149 Fifth Ave New York NY 10010

HEINZLE, JOACHIM, philologist, educator; b. Konstanz, Fed. Republic Germany, Aug. 2, 1945. PhD, U. Berlin, 1969. Habilitation, U. Cologne, 1975. Asst. prof. German philology U. Cologne, Fed. Republic Germany, 1976-78; prof. U. Kassel, Fed. Republic Germany, 1978-84; prof. German philologpy U. Marburg, Fed. Republic Germany, 1984—. Author: Stellenkommentar zu Wolframs Titurel, 1972, Mittelhochdeutsche Dietrichepik, 1978, Das Nibelungenlied, 1987, Geschichte der Deutschen Literatur im 113 Jahre, 1984. Office: U Marburg, Wilhelm-Röpke-Str 6A, D-3550 Marburg Federal Republic of Germany

HEIRES, JOHN HOPKINS, international banker, lawyer; b. Sioux City, Iowa, Sept. 19, 1918; s. Arthur Francis and Frances (Hopkins) H.; m. Alice Rea Chamberlin, May 14, 1955; children: John Hopkins, David Chamberlin, Gregory Norris. B.A. magna cum laude, Yankton Coll., 1939; J.D., Yale, 1946; M.Litt (Rhodes scholar), Oxford (Eng.) U., 1948. Bar: D.C. 1950, also U.S. Supreme Ct. 1950. With Dept. Justice, 1941; legal asst. Pillsbury, Madison & Sutro, San Francisco, 1949-50; asso. Covington & Burling, Washington, 1950-53; asst. to chief estimates staff and estimates officer Bd. Nat. Estimates, 1953-57; sec. intelligence adv. com. Nat. Security Council, 1957-58; exec. sec. U.S. Intelligence Bd., 1958-62; dep. legis. programs coordinator AID, 1962, officer charge Pakistan affairs, 1962-64; moderator Naval Acad. Fgn. Affairs Conf., 1964; regional legal counsel, attache for embassy and U.S. AID missions to India, Nepal and Ceylon, New Delhi 1964-69; v.p., sec. Pvt. Investment Co. for Asia (PICA), S.A., Tokyo, 1969-72, Singapore, 1972-73; v.p., internat. sec. Marine Midland Bank, N.Y.C.; corporate sec. Marine Midland Internat. Corp., Marine Midland Overseas Corp., Marine Midland, Inc., 1973-76; adviser Fed. Res. Bank N.Y., 1976-86; mem. Nat. Com. on U.S.-China Relations; mem. U.S. ofcl. del. to ann. Asian devel. bank meetings, 1977-85. Note editor: Yale Law Jour, 1942; case editor, 1946. Served to lt. USNR, 1942-46. Mem. ABA, Internat., D.C. Bar Assns., Am. Soc. Internat. Law, Assn. Am. Rhodes Scholars, Fgn. Policy Assn., Asia Soc., Japan Soc., Yale Law Assn., English Speaking Union, Pi Kappa Delta, Phi Delta Phi. Clubs: Chevy Chase (Washington), Internat. (Washington); Yale (N.Y.C.), Nat. Press. (Washington); Delhi Gymkhana (New Delhi); Fgn. Corrs. (Tokyo), American (Tokyo); Tokyo Lawn and Tennis; American (Singapore). Home: 3535 Hamlet Pl Chevy Chase MD 20815 Office: 3535 Hamlet Pl Chevy Chase MD 20815 *Died July 2, 1988.*

HEISER, ROLLAND VALENTINE, former army officer, foundation executive; b. Columbus, Ohio, Apr. 25, 1925; s. Rudolph and Helen Cecile H.; BS, U.S. Mil. Acad., 1947; MS in Internat. Affairs, George Washington U., 1965; m. Gwenne Kathleen Duquemin, Feb. 26, 1949; children—Helen Heiser Sanford, Charlene Heiser Geiger. Commd. 2d lt. U.S. Army, 1947, advanced through grades to lt. gen., 1978; served in Europe, Korea, Vietnam; army planner, Washington, 1973-74; comdr. 1st Armored div., Ger., 1974-75; chief of staff U.S. Army Europe, 1975-76; chief staff U.S. European Command, 1976-78; pres. New Coll. Found., Sarasota, Fla., 1979—; dir. Coast Fed. Savs. & Loan Assn., Sarasota. Mem. Sarasota Com. 100; bd. dirs. Suncoast Offshore Grand Prix, Inc., gen. chmn., 1986—. Decorated D.S.M. (2), Def. Disting. Service medal, Legion of Merit (3), Bronze Star, others. Mem. Ret. Officers Assn., Sarasota County C. of C. Republican. Episcopalian. Clubs: Bird Key Yacht, Univ., Ret. Officers of Sarasota (past pres., dir.), Sarasota City (founding chmn.). Lodge: Masons. Home: 4104 Las Palmas Way Sarasota FL 34238 Office: 5700 N Tamiami Trail Sarasota FL 34243

HEISKANEN, TUULA AULIKKI, social science researcher, educator; b. Tampere, Finland, Sept. 1, 1949; d. Kalevi Armas and Helga Helena (Laurunen) Lahovuori; m. Hannu Juhani Heiskanen, 1972; children: Iikka Antero, Aki Santeri. Doctor of Social Scis., U. Tampere, 1984. Researcher Finnish Acad., 1973-77; researcher, lectr. U. Tampere, 1977—, acting assoc. prof., 1984-87, acting prof., 1987—. Author: Automation, Work Content and Work Requirements, 1984; contbr. articles to profl. jours. Mem. The Westermarck Soc., Soc. Psychology, Soc. Social Medicine. Home: Kolvukuja 25, 33900 Tampere Finland Office: U Tampere, PO Box 607, 33101 Tampere Finland

HEISLER, ELWOOD DOUGLAS, hotel executive; b. Wilmington, Del., June 29, 1935; s. Elwood Dean and Laura Matilda (Hutchison) H.; B.A., Mich. State U., 1957; postgrad. Johns Hopkins U., 1979—. Asst. mgr. Kents Restaurants, Atlantic City, 1957; mgr. Korean Mil. Adv. Group Officers' Club and Housing Office, Tague, 1958-59; innkeeper Treadway Inns Corp., N.Y., Mass., Colo., Ohio, Va., Del., 1960-68, Holiday Inns, Inc., Lansing and Troy, Mich., 1969-77; gen. mgr. Quality Inns, Inc., Towson, Md., 1977—. Mem. St. George's Soc. of Baltimore, German Soc. of Md., L'Amicale-Soc. Francaise de Baltimore, Hist. Soc. of Delaware, Md. Hist. Soc., Nantucket Hist. Assn., Md. Retired Officers Assn., sec. Md. state adv. council Future Bus. Leaders of Am./Phi Beta Lambda; bd. dirs. Gunpowder Youth Camps, Inc.; mem. greater Balt. Com.; chmn. Balt. Country Travel Council; mem. Balt. Council on Fgn. Affairs, Md. Travel Council. Served to 1st lt. U.S. Army, 1957-59. Named Top Ten Innkeeper Holiday Inns Internat., 1975; Md. Bus. Person of the Year, Future Bus. Leaders of Am., 1981, Bus. Person of Year nat. chpt., 1981, award of Merit Baltimore County C. of C., 1982, Paul Harris fellow Rotary Found., 1983, Outstanding Service award Md. Future Bus. Leaders of Am., 1984, Baltimore Mayor's Citation, 1984. Mem. Balt. Econ. Soc., Balt. Public Relations Council, Am. Hotel and Motel Assn., Hotel Sales Mgmt. Assn., Md. Hotel and Motor Inn Assn., Balt. Country Lic. Beverage A Assn., Md. Internat. Trade Assn., Travel and Tourism Research Assn., Balt. County C. of C. (v.p.). Republican. Congregationalist. Clubs: Univ., Towson Rotary (pres.), Advt. of Balt. (bd. govs.). Clubs: Baltimore Yacht. Author manual for resort ops., 1965; author: The Rising Sun of the Japanese Hotel Industry, 1980. Home: 516 Charles Street Ave Towson MD 21204 Office: Quality Inn 1015 York Rd Towson MD 21204

HEISLER, STANLEY DEAN, lawyer; b. The Dalles, Oreg., Jan. 11, 1946; s. Donald Eugene and Roberta (Van Valkenburgh) H. BA, Willamette U., Salem, Oreg., 1968, JD, 1972. Bar: Oreg. 1972, D.C. 1973, U.S. Ct. Claims 1972, U.S. Tax Ct. 1972, U.S. Ct. Appeals (9th cir.) 1972, U.S. Ct. Mil. Appeals 1973, U.S. Ct. Customs and Patent Appeals 1973, N.Y. 1985, U.S. Supreme Ct. 1985. Assoc. Heisler & Van Valkenburgh, The Dalles, 1973-74; ptnr. Heisler, Van Valkenburgh & Coats, The Dalles, 1975-81, Heisler & Heisler, The Dalles, 1982-84, Cohen & Shalleck, N.Y.C., 1985-88, Phillips, Nizer, Benjamin, Krim and Ballon, N.Y.C., 1988—. Speechwriter Sec. of State Tom McCall, Salem, 1965, Gov. Tom McCall, Salem, 1966-68; speechwriter, legis. asst. U.S. Senator Bob Packwood, Washington, 1969-73; vice chmn. Pres.'s Air Quality Adv. Bd., Washington, 1973-76. Mem. ABA, N.Y. State Bar Assn., Assn. Bar City of N.Y. Republican. Clubs: Arlington, Univ. (Portland). Home: 201 East 69th St Apt 12K New York NY 10021 Office: Phillips Nizer Benjamin Krim and Ballon 40 W 57th St New York NY 10019

HEISTEIN, JOSEF, literature educator; b. Jaworow, Poland, Jan. 3, 1925; s. Simche and Hena (Nadel H.; 1 child, Anna; m. Stefania Brzozowska, Apr. 29, 1974. MA, U. Krakow (Poland), 1963, Doctor of Human Scis., 1966, Habilitation, 1971. Officer Polish Army, 1944-64; asst. U. Wroclaw (Poland), 1964-66, adj./asst. prof. French, Italian, comparative lit., 1967-68, lectr. prof., docent, 1969-78, extraordinary prof., 1979-86, ordinary prof., 1986—; dir. Romance Philology chair, U. Wroclaw, 1969-71, dir. Romance Philology Inst., U. Wroclaw, 1972—; editor Romanica Wratislaviensia, 1974—; assoc. prof. U. Paris III, 1985-86. Author: History of Italian Literature, 1979, 2d edit., 1986, French 20th Century Literature, 1982, Decandentism, Symbolism, Avantguard, 1987; author, editor: Futurism in European Literature, 1977; mem. editorial bd. Beitraege zur Romanischen Philologie, 1979—, Francofonia, 1982—. Decorated cavalier Polonia Restituta (Poland), officer Order of Merit (Italy), officer Acad. Palms (France). Mem. European French Dept. Assn. (com. 1979—), Polish Acad. Scis. (modern lang. com. 1969—). Home: Wejherowska 67/6, 54 239 Wroclaw Poland Office: Wroclaw Univ, Plac Nankera 4, 50 140 Wroclaw Poland

HEISTEIN, ROBERT KENNETH, obstetrician and gynecologist; b. Newark, Oct. 14, 1940; s. Samuel M. and Elizabeth M. (Jellinek) H.; B.A., U. Vt., 1962, M.D., 1966; m. Vallery Gubner, Aug. 26, 1967; children—Jonathan, Erica, Michael. Intern, Newark Beth Israel Med. Center, 1966-67, resident in ob-gyn 1967-70, attending staff, 1972—; asst. chief, dept. ob-gyn Patuxent River Naval Hosp., Md., 1970-72; pvt. practice medicine, specializing in ob-gyn Millburn, N.J., 1972—; mem. staffs St. Barnabas Med. Ctr., Livingston, N.J., Newark Beth Israel Med. Center, Overlook Hosp., Summit, N.J.; clin. instr. N.J. Med. Sch., 1974—. Served with USNR, 1970-72. Diplomate Am. Bd. Ob-Gyn. Fellow Am. Coll. Obstetricians and Gynecologists, ACS, Internat. Coll. Surgeons, Am. Fertility Soc., N.J. Acad. Medicine, Am. Soc. Abdominal Surgeons; mem. AMA, Pan Am. Med. Assn., N.J. Med. Soc., Essex County Med. Soc., Am. Assn. Gynecol. Laparoscopists, Royal Soc. Medicine. Office: 68 Essex St Millburn NJ 07041 also: 23 Green Village Rd Madison NJ 07940

HEITUN, ODD GUNNAR, psychiatrist; b. Fredrikstad, Norway, Mar. 6, 1947. MD, U. Oslo, 1972, M in Social Sci., 1979. Asst. physician Diakonhjemmet Hosp., Oslo, 1972-74; physicain Dikemark Hosp. and Youth Clinic, Oslo, 1974-76; cons. Gaustad Mental Hosp., Oslo, 1976-79, asst. chief psychiatrist, 1980-86; cons. Louisenberg Hosp., Oslo, 1979-80; med. dir. Reitgjerdet Mental Hsop., Trondheim, Norway, 1981, Dikemar Mental Hosp., Oslo, 1986-87; chief psychiatrist Nat. Directorate Health, Oslo, 1987—; prof. U. Oslo, 1982-84. Author: The Psychiatric Youth Teams, 1987; contbr. articles to profl. publs. Served to capt. mil. psychiatry, Norwegian armed forces, 1977-78. Office: Nat Directorate Health, Calmeyersgaten 1, Oslo 1 Norway

HEIZER, EDGAR FRANCIS, JR., venture capitalist; b. Detroit, Sept. 23, 1929; s. Edgar Francis and Grace Adelia (Smith) H.; m. Molly Bradley Hunt, June 17, 1952; children: Linda Heizer Seaman, Molly Hunt, Edgar Francis III. BS, Northwestern U., 1951; JD, Yale U., 1954. Bar: Ill. 1954; CPA, Ill. Mem. audit and tax staff Arthur Andersen & Co., Chgo., 1954-56; fin. analyst Kidder, Peabody & Co., Chgo., 1956-58; mgmt. cons. Booz, Allen & Hamilton, Chgo., 1958-62; asst. treas. Allstate Ins. Co., Northbrook, Ill., 1962-69; chmn., founder, chief exec. officer Heizer Corp., Chgo., 1969-85; venture capitalist Tucker's Town, Bermuda, 1985—; bd. dirs. Amdahl Corp., Sunnyvale, Calif., Computer Consoles, Inc., Rochester, N.Y., Material Sci. Corp., Elk Grove Village, Ill.; adv. bd. Kellogg Sch. Mgmt.; bd. dirs. John Evans Soc. of Northwestern U. Mem. Delta Upsilon (chmn. bd. dirs. 1985-88). Republican. Presbyterian. Clubs: Chgo. Curling, Shoreacres, Econ. of Chgo., Coral Beach and Tennis, Mid-Ocean; Riddells Bay Golf and Country (Bermuda). Home and Office: Dover House, Tuckers Town Bermuda also: 261 Bluffs Edge Dr Lake Forest IL 60045

HEJNA, WILLIAM FRANK, surgeon, executive administrator; b. Chgo., May 13, 1932; s. William H.; m. Eva Lee Goodale, June 11, 1955; children: William, David, Michael, Susan. B.A., Grinnell Coll., 1954, D.Sc., 1974; M.D., Washington U., St. Louis, 1958. Diplomate: Am. Bd. Orthopedic Surgery (examiner 1969-74). Intern Presbyn.-St. Luke's Hosp., Chgo., 1958-59; coordinator orthopedic clinics and med. sch. tng. Presbyn.-St. Luke's Hosp., 1963-70, dir. electromyography lab., 1963-70, asst. chmn. dept. orthopedic surgery, 1965-70, assoc. attending surgeon, 1967-70, sr. attending surgeon, 1971—; resident in orthopedic surgery U. Ill. Research and Ednl. Hosps., Chgo., 1959-63; assoc. dean Office Surg. Scis. and Services, Rush-Presbyn.-St. Luke's Med. Center, 1970-73; v.p. med. affairs, dean Rush Med. Coll., 1973-76; sr. v.p. Rush U., 1976-84, also prof. orthopedic surgery; pres. BioService Corp., 1977-80, Bus. Cons., Inc., 1970—, Biotech. Maintenance and Repair Corp., 1978-82, Affiliated Med. Arts, Inc., 1984—, Met. Orthopedic Surgeons, 1985—, Combined Orthopedic Resources, Inc., 1984—; mng. ptnr. Orthopedic Assocs., 1983—, U. Orthopaedics, 1986—; chmn. bd. trustees Anchor HMO, 1980-85; cons. Whittaker Corp., 1978-84; chmn. physician adv. bd. Smith Labs., 1980-83; pres. Council Med. Deans, Ill., 1974-76; chmn. Rush Faculty Council, 1973-76; trustee Orthopaedic Research and Edn. Found., Park Ridge. Contbr. articles to profl. jours.; editorial bd. Health Care Mgmt. Rev., 1982—. Trustee MacNeal Meml. Hosp., 1982—; trustee Ripon Coll., 1982—, exec. com., 1985—. Fellow ACS, Am. Acad. Orthopedic Surgeons; mem. AMA, Ill. Med. Soc., Chgo. Med. Soc., Chgo. Surg. Soc., Inst. Medicine, Orthopedic Research Soc., Clin. Orthopedic Soc. Club: Econs. (Chgo.). Home: 321 N Delaplaine Rd Riverside IL 60546 Office: 1725 W Harrison St Chicago IL 60612

HEJTMANCIK, MILTON RUDOLPH, medical educator, physician; b. Caldwell, Tex., Sept. 27, 1919; s. Rudolph Joseph and Millie (Jurcak) H.; B.A., U. Tex., 1939, M.D., 1943; m. Myrtle Lou Erwin, Aug. 21, 1943; children—Kelly Erwin, Milton Rudolph, Peggy Lou; m. 2d, Myrtle M. Granberry, Nov. 27, 1976. Resident in internal medicine U. Tex., 1946-49, instr. internal medicine, 1949-51, asst. prof., 1951-54, assoc. prof., 1954-65, prof. internal medicine, 1965-80, dir. heart clinic, 1949-80, dir. heart sta., 1965-80; chief of staff John Sealy Hosp., 1957-58; chief staff U. Tex. Hosps., 1977-79; prof. medicine Tex. A&M Coll. Medicine, 1981-82; cardiologist Olin E. Teague VA Hosp., Temple, Tex., 1981-82, VA Clinic, Beaumont, Tex., 1982-86. Served from 1st lt. to capt., M.C., AUS, 1944-46; ETO. Diplomate in cardiovascular diseases Am. Bd. Internal Medicine. Fellow ACP, Am. Coll. Chest Physicians, Am. Coll. Cardiology; mem. Am. (fellow council clin. cardiology), Tex. (pres. 1979-80), Galveston Dist. (pres. 1956) heart assns., AMA (Billing's Gold medal 1973), Am. Fedn. Clin. Research, AAAS, Tex. Acad. Internal Medicine (gov. 1971-73, v.p. 1973-74, pres. 1976-77), N.Y. Acad. Scis., Tex. Club Cardiology (pres. 1972), Galveston County (pres. 1971), Tex. (del. 1972-80) med. assns., Am. Heart Assn. (pres. Tex. affiliate 1979-80), Phi Beta Kappa, Sigma Xi, Alpha Omega Alpha, Phi Eta Sigma, Mu Delta, Phi Rho Sigma. Contbr. articles to profl. jours. Home: 500 N Spruce St Hammond LA 70401

HEJTMANEK, DANTON CHARLES, lawyer; b. Topeka, July 22, 1951; s. Robert Kieth and Bernice Louise (Krause) H.; m. Jenny Jordan, May 26, 1973; 1 child, Brian J. BBA in Acctg., Washburn U., 1973, JD, 1975. Bar: Kans. 1976, U.S. Dist. Ct. Kans. 1976, U.S. Tax Ct. 1976. Ptnr. Schroer, Rice, Bryan & Lykins, P.A., Topeka, 1975-86, Bryan, Lykins, Hejtmanek & Wulz, P.A., Topeka, 1986—. Mem. ABA (rep. young lawyers Kans. and Nebr.), Kans. Bar Assn. (pres. young lawyers 1985), Am. Trial Lawyers Assn., Kans. Trial Lawyers Assn. Republican. Presbyterian. Lodge: Sertoma (pres. 1983). Home: 2800 Burlingame Rd Topeka KS 66611 Office: 115 E Seventh St Topeka KS 66603

HELDENSTEIN, CARLO, insurance company executive; b. Luxembourg, Dec. 5, 1944; s. Edmond and Claire (Mich) H.; m. Liliane Lacave, Apr. 8, 1969; children—Bettina, Max. Cand Law, Athenee Grand-Ducal, Luxembourg, 1967, Docteur en Droit, U. Strasbourg, France, 1972. Lawyer, Luxembourg, 1972-76; attaché de direction Assurlux S.A., Luxembourg, 1976-80, counseillor de direction, 1980-81, sous-dir., 1981-86, dir. adj. 1987— ; corp. gen. mgr. Sosuelux S.A., 1985-87, dir. adj. TENE Reins., 1986— ; adminstr. FCGA, 1985-87, dir. adj. RHEA S.A. 1987— . Mem. Assn. des Cies d' Assurance. Clubs: Round Table, Rotary. Avocations: photography; travelling; nautical sports. Home: 29 Allee L Goebel, 1635 Adolphe Luxembourg Office: Assurlux 4 rue, 1116 Adolphe Luxembourg

HELFERT, ERICH ANTON, management consultant, author, educator; b. Aussig/Elbe, Sudetenland, May 29, 1931; came to U.S., 1950; s. Julius and Anna Maria (Wilde) H.; m. Anne Langley, Jan. 1, 1983; children: Claire L., Amanda L. BS, U. Nev., 1954; MBA with high distinction, Harvard U., 1956, DBA, 1958. Newspaper reporter, corr., Neuburg, Fed. Republic of Germany, 1948-52; research asst. Harvard U., 1956-57; asst. prof. bus. policy San Francisco State U., 1958-59; asst. prof. fin. and control Grad. Sch. Bus. Adminstrn., Harvard U., 1959-65; internal cons., then asst. to pres., dir. corp. planning Crown Zellerbach Corp., San Francisco, 1965-78, asst. to chmn., dir. corp. planning, 1978-82, v.p. corp. planning, 1982-85; cons. mgmt., San Francisco, 1985—. Author: Techniques of Financial Analysis, 1963 , 6th edit., 1987, Valuation, 1966, (with others) Case Book, 1963, Controllership, 1965; contbr. articles to profl. jours. Exchange student fellow U.S. Inst. Internat. Edn., 1950; Ford Found. fellow, 1956. Mem. Assn. Corp. Growth (past pres., bd. dirs. San Francisco chpt.), Corp. Planners Assn. (past pres., bd. dirs.), Phi Kappa Phi. Roman Catholic. Clubs: Commonwealth, Comml., Harvard U. Bus. Sch. of No. Calif. (chmn. bd. dirs., past pres.). Home: 111 W Third Ave #401 San Mateo CA 94402 Office: 1777 Borel Pl 508 San Mateo CA 94402

HELGADOTTIR, RAGNHILDUR, Icelandic government official; b. Reykjavik, Iceland, May 26, 1930; m. Por Vilhjalmsson; 4 children. Grad. Reykjavik Coll., 1949; degree in law, U. Iceland, 1958. Mem. Parliament of Iceland, Reykjavik, 1956-63, 71-79, 83—, speaker of Lower House of the Althing, 1961-62, 74-78, mem. various parliamentary coms. on edn., social security and old age pensioners, minister of edn., from 1983, former minister of health and social security legal counsellor Soc. for Assistance to Mothers, 1959-60; Icelandic del. Nordic Council, 1974-78, council pres., 1975. Mem. central com. Independence Party of Iceland, 1963-71, 79-81, chmn. Women's Assn., 1965-69. Office: Parliament, Reykjavik Iceland *

HELGASON, JON, minister of agriculture Iceland; b. Seglbudir, Vestur-Skaftafellssysla, Iceland, Oct. 4, 1931; m. Gudrun Porkelsdottir; 2 children. Grad. Reykjavik Coll., 1950. Farmer, Seglbudir, 1951—; mem. Althing, Reykjavik, Iceland, 1974—, mem. steering com. parliamentary group, 1978—, 1st v.p. Upper House, 1978-79, pres. Althing, 1979-83; minister of agr., 1983—, minister of justice and ecclesiastical affairs, 1983-87; mem. bd. State Elec. Network, 1978—; chmn. bd. Jardefnaidnadur, 1980—. Chmn. Youth Assn. of Progressive Party, Vestur-Skaftafellssysla; chmn. Progressive Party, Vestur-Skaftafellssysla. Mem. Dist. Agrl. Soc. (council 1966—, chmn. council 1967-76), Vestur-Skaftafellssysla Coop. Soc. (chmn. 1972—), Mjolkursamsalan (steering com. 1964—), Farmers Union (dir. and mem. Agrl. Bd. 1972-79). Office: Ministry of Agriculture, 101 Reykjavik Iceland

HELGASON, SIGURDUR, airline executive; b. Rekjavik, Iceland, July 20, 1921; s. Helgi and Olof (Sigurjonsdottir) Hallgrimsson; m. Unnur Einarsdottir, Dec. 20, 1952; children: Olof, Edda, Helgi, Sigurdur. BBA, Columbia U., 1947. Vice chmn. Icelandic Airlines/Loftleidir, Reykjavik, 1953-74; pres. Icelandic Airlines Inc., N.Y.C., 1961-74; chief exec. officer Internat. Air Bahama, 1969-74; mng. dir. Flugleidir hf (Icelandair), Reykjavik, 1974-79, pres., chief exec. officer, 1979-84, chmn. bd., 1984—; bd. dirs. Alafoss H.F., Reykjavik. Trustee St. Joseph Hosp., Reykjavik, 1979, Am. Scandinavian Found., 1982—. Decorated knight Order Falcon, comdr. Cross of Order of Falcon, (Iceland), grand officer Order Oak Crown, Luxembourg, 1986; named Hon. Citizen, Winnipeg, Man., Can., 1965; recipient Order of Merit award Iceland Sports Fedn., 1983, Gold medal Icelandic Aero. Soc., 1986. Mem. Icelandic-Am. Soc. (chmn. 1975-87), Internat. C. of C. (bd. dirs. Iceland chpt. 1982). Lutheran. Clubs: Wings (bd. dirs. 1972-75), Internat. House (trustee 1968—) (N.Y.C.). Lodge: Rotary. Home: 52 Skildinganes, 101 Reykjavik Iceland Office: Icelandair, Reykjavik Airport, 101 Reykjavik Iceland

HELGASON, SIGURDUR, mathematician, educator; b. Akureyri, Iceland, Sept. 30, 1927; came to U.S., 1952; d. Helgi and Kara (Briem) Skulason; m. Artie Gianopulos, June 9, 1957; children:Thor Helgi, Anna Loa. Student, U. Iceland, 1946, Dr. Honoris Causa, 1988; MS, U. Copenhagen, 1952; PhD, Princeton U., 1954. C.L.E. Moore instr. MIT, Cambridge, 1954-56, asst. prof. math., 1960-61, assoc. prof. math., 1961-65, prof. math., 1965—; lectr. Princeton (N.J.) U., 1956-57; Louis Block asst. prof. math. U. Chgo., 1957-59; vis. mem. Inst. Advanced Study, Princeton, 1964-66, 74-75, 83-84. Author: (books) Differential Geometry, Lie Groups and Symmetric Spaces, 1978, Groups and Geometric Analysis, 1984, others; editor Progress in Math., 1980-86, Perspectives in Math. Academic Press, Cambridge, 1985—; contbr. articles to profl. jours. Recipient Gold medal U. Copenhagen, 1951, Jessen diploma, Danish Math. Soc., 1982, Steele Prize in Math., 1988; Guggenheim fellow, 1964-65. Mem. Am. Acad. Arts and Scis., Royal Danish Acad. Scis. and Letters, Icelandic Acad. Scis., Am. Math. Soc. Office: MIT Dept Math 77 Massachusetts Ave Cambridge MA 02139

HELIOFF, ANNE GRAILE, painter; b. Liverpool, Eng.; d. Max and Frances Elizabeth (Beilenson) H.; student Columbia U., Art Students League, N.Y.C.; m. Benjamin Michael Hirschberg. One-woman exhbns. include: Capricorn Gallery, N.Y.C., 1966-69, Phoenix Gallery, N.Y.C., 1972, 74, 76, 82, 85, Woodstock (N.Y.) Artists Assn., 1988; group exhbns. include Milch Gallery, N.Y.C., 1940, Pepsi-Cola Nat., travelling show, maj. museums, U.S., 1947, Nat. Gallery Art, Washington, Pa. Acad. Ann., Art U.S.A., also bicentennial exhbn., 6 Americans in France, traveling show, 1976, museums in Florence and Naples, Italy; mem. U.S. del. 5th Congress Internat. Assn. Art, Tokyo, 1966; dir. exhbns. including 50 Yrs. of Woodstock Art (N.Y.), N.Y. State Tri-Centennial, 1959. Recipient Silver medal Albany (N.Y.) Mus. Art and Sci., 1957; Homer Boss scholar, 1939; Y. Kuniyoshi scholar, 1940-45. Mem. Woodstock Artists Assn. (life, past dir.), Art Students League (past dir.), Am. Soc. Contemporary Artists (past dir.; awards in oil, watercolor and acrylic), Nat. Assn. Women Artists, N.Y. Soc. Women Artists (past dir.), Archives of Am. Art, Smithsonian Mus. Home: 14 Neher St Woodstock NY 12498 Office: 340 W 28th St New York NY 10001

HELLAN, LARS, linguist; b. Trondheim, Norway, Jan. 12, 1945; s. Kaare and Ragnhild (Stav) H.; m. Guri Hjelde, July 3, 1970; 1 child, Yngve. Magister Artium, U. Oslo, Norway, 1971; PhD (hon.), U. Trondheim, 1981. Amanuensis U. Trondheim, Norway, 1971-81, første amanuensis, 1981-87, prof., 1987—; head linguistics dept. U. Trondheim, 1980-82, 84-86, dir. summer sch. syntax, 1984, project leader Scandinavian Syntax, 1983—, Lang. Tech., 1987—. Author: An Integrated Analysis of Comparatives, 1981, Anaphora in Norwegian and the Theory of Grammar, 1987; co-editor: Topics in Scandinavian Systems, 1986. Research grantee U. Trondheim, 1973-75, 84-85; grantee Norwegian Council of Arts and Scis., 1979-80; recipient numerous travel grants at various univs. including, U. Trondheim, MIT, Stanford U., Tilburg U., and others, 1981-87. Mem. Generative Linguistics in the Old Word (assoc. editorial bd., linguistic inquiry, 1981—), Linguistics Soc. Am. Home: Tingveien 15A, 7046 Trondheim Norway Office: U Trondheim, Linguistics Dept, 7055 Trondheim Norway

HELLEMAA, PERTTI ARTTURI, tannery company executive; b. Ulvila, Finland, Dec. 1, 1930. BS in Econs., Helsinki (Finland) Sch. Econs., 1952; postgrad., U. Chgo., 1954-55. Pres. Friitala Oy, Ulvila, 1963-77; chmn. bd. Frihansa Oy, Lauttakyla, Finland, 1970—, Friitala-Lauter, Fed. Republic Germany, 1970—, Friitala-London, 1970—, Friitala Group, Ulvila, 1978—; v.p. Modeurop, 1979—; chmn. bd. Friitala GesmbH, Austria, 1984—, Friitala USA, 1985—; bd. dirs. Finnish Employers' Cen. Fedn., 1983-84, 87—; adv. bd. Ins. Co. Pohjola, 1970—. Served to capt. Finnish Army. Mem. Internat. Council Tanners (pres. 1982-87, honorary pres. 1987—), Finnish Leather Industries Assn. (chmn. 1968—), Leather Industries Employers Assn. (chmn. 1968—). Lodge: Rotary. Office: Friitala Group, PO Box 5, 28401 Ulvila Finland

HELLEN, MARIE EVOLINE, safety engineer; b. Burbank, Calif., July 31, 1950; d. Robert Owen and Ruth Naomi (Clark) Griffin; m. Jeffrey Hearn Hellen, July 11, 1971 (div. Oct. 1984); 1 child, Scott Alexander. BS in Health and Safety, San Diego State U., 1978. Safety dir. Sharp Meml. Hosp., San Diego, 1979-83, cons., 1985; safety engr. IVAC Corp., San Diego, 1983—. Bd. dirs. Am. Lung Assn. San Diego, 1984—, San Diego Safety Council, 1985—. Mem. Am. Soc. Safety Engrs. (pres. San Diego chpt. 1984-85), Nat. Fire Protection Assn., Am. Indsl. Hygiene Assn., Am. Lung Assn. (bd. dirs. San Diego chpt. 1984-87, com. on occupational and environ. health 1982—, chmn. 1986—), Internat. Health Care Safety Assn. (cert. health care safety profl.). Democrat. Office: IVAC Corp 10300 Campus Point Dr San Diego CA 92121

HELLENTHAL, LINDA BROUGHTON, psychologist; b. Seattle, May 22, 1947; d. Ray Munroe and Margret (Ryno) Broughton; m. Marc Edwin Hellenthal, June 10, 1967; children—Kristine Tara, Megan LaRue. B.A. with honors, Whitman Coll., 1969; M.A., Boston U., 1973, Ph.D., 1977. Lic. psychologist, Alaska. Lectr., Boston U., 1973-77; clin. psychologist Bear River Community Mental Health Ctr., Logan, Utah, 1978; asst. prof. U. Alaska, Anchorage, 1978-79; clin. psychologist, Anchorage, 1980—; cons. Standing Together Against Rape, Anchorage, 1980-81; treas., co-owner Hellenthal & Assocs., Anchorage, 1978—. Recipient Boston U. Grad. Scholarship award, 1971-77. Mem. Am. Psychol. Assn., Alaska Psychol. Assn. Presbyterian. Club: P.E.O. Home: 2200 Vanderbilt Cr Anchorage AK 99508 Office: 608 W 4th Suite 21 Anchorage AK 99501

HELLER, ADAM, chemist, researcher; b. Cluj, Romania, June 25, 1933; s. Ephraim and Blanche (Nissel) H.; m. Ilana Grossbard, July 26, 1956; children—Ephraim, Jonathan. M.Sc., Hebrew U., 1957, Ph.D., 1961. Postdoctoral research assoc. U. Calif.-Berkeley, 1962-63; mem. tech. staff Bell Labs., Murray Hill, N.J., 1963-64, 1975-77; mem. tech. staff GTE Labs., Bayside, N.Y., 1964-70, mgr. exploratory research, Waltham, Mass., 1970-75; head electronic materials research dept., AT&T Bell Labs., Murray Hill, 1977-88; Ernest Cockrell Sr. Chair of Chem. Engring., prof. Chemistry and Materials Sci., U. Tex., Austin, 1988—; mem. vis. com. Chem. and Materials Research div. Lawrence Berkeley Lab. U. Calif., 1984—, chmn., 1987—; mem. adv. bd. Solar Energy Research Inst., Golden, Colo., 1987—; research prof. Brandeis U., Waltham, 1972-75; adj. prof. chemistry CUNY, 1968—; vis. prof. Coll. de France, Paris, 1982; regents lectr. UCLA, 1984; disting. prof. U. Guelph, Ont., Can., 1984; Beverly and Raymond Sackler disting. lectr. Tel-Aviv U., 1987. Editor: Semiconductor Liquid Junction Solar Cells, 1977, Inorganic Resists, 1982; contbr. articles to profl. jours.; patentee in field. Mem. Nat. Acad. Engring., Electrochem. Soc. (Battery Div. award 1978, Grahame award Phys. electrochemistry div. 1987, Vittorio DovNora-Diamond Shamrock award 1988), Am. Chem. Soc., Am. Phys. Soc., Internat. Soc. Electrochemistry, Internat. Union Pure and Applied Chemistry (assoc., com. photochemistry). Jewish. Current work: electron transfer in chemically-modified redox-enzymes; hydrogen-evolving solar cells; photoelectrochemistry; chemistry and materials science of microelectronic devices; batteries (lithium-thionyl chloride). Subspecialties: physical chemistry; electronic materials; biosensors. Home: 5317 Valburn Circle Austin TX 78731

HELLER, MAX M., state agency administrator; b. Austria, 1919; m. Trude Schonthal; three children. LLD (hon.), Furman U., 1975. Founder Maxon Shirt Co., Greenville, S.C., 1948-69; elected mem. Greenville City Council, 1969-71; mayor City of Greenville, 1971-79; chmn. State Devel Bd., 1979-83; bd. dirs. Asten Group Inc., Greenville; selected mem. of fact-finding mission German Marshall Fund and Kettering Found. Bd. dirs. St. Francis Community Hosp., Greenville, Greenville chpt. United Fund, Nat. Conf. of Christians and Jews, Greenville, Phillis Wheatley Ctr., Greenville, Greenville Community Council, Greenville chpt. Cerebral Palsy Assn., Greenville Symphony Assn., Nat. League of Cities, Carolina Exec. Service; pres. Mcpl. Assn. S.C., Beth Israel Synagogue, Greenville; mem. adv. bd. Robert Wood Johnson Found., Greenville, Greenville chpt. Jr. League, Greenville Higher Edn. Consortium; mem. bd. of Alliance of Quality Edn. of Furman U. Adv. Council; past mem. Greenville Community Found., Winthrop Coll. Adv. Bd., med. sch. com. of U. S.C. Adv. Bd., Greenville Housing Found., Family and Children's Service Adv. Council on Drug Abuse, Gov.'s Commn. on Childcare, Gov.'s Adv. Council on Housing, Greenville Health Planning Council. Named Man of Yr. Nat. Council Jewish Women, 1970, NAA, 1978, Vol. of Yr. S.C. Econ. Devel. Assn., 1983; recipient Freedom award DAR, 1973, Disting. Service award Greater Greenville Ministerial Alliance, 1976, Service to Mankind award Sertoma, 1976, Life Speaks honor Greenville County Found. to Library, 1976, Human Relations award Greenville Human Relations Commn., 1976, Share Community Service award S.C. Econ. Devel. Assn., 1984; Disting. Service award Greenville Jaycees, 1987, Whitney Young Humanitarian award Urban League, 1988; Greenville Housing Found. Max. M. Heller Neighborhood Improvement award and Greenville Community Found. Max Heller Internship Program in City Govt. named in his honor. Lodge: B'Nai Brith (Man of Yr. North and South Carolina clubs 1972). Office: 220 N Main St Greenville SC 29601

HELLIE, RICHARD, Russian history educator, researcher; b. Waterloo, Iowa, May 8, 1937; s. Ole Ingeman and Mary Elizabeth (Larsen) H.; m. Jean Laves, Dec. 23, 1961; 1 son, Benjamin. B.A., U. Chgo., 1958, M.A., 1960, Ph.D., 1965; postgrad., U. Moscow, 1963-64. Vis. asst. prof. Rutgers U., 1965-66; asst. prof. Russian history U. Chgo., 1966-71, assoc. prof., 1971-80, prof., 1980—. Author: Muscovite Society, 1967, Enserfment and Military Change in Muscovy, 1971 (Am. Hist. Assn. Adams prize 1972), Slavery in Russia 1450-1725, (Laing prize U. Chgo. Press 1985), 1982, The Russian Law Code (Ulozhenie) of 1649, 1987; editor: The Plow, the Hammer and the Knout: An Economic History of Eighteenth Century Russia, 1985, Ivan the Terrible: A Quarcentenary Celebration of His Death, 1987; editor quar. jour. Russian History. Ford Found. Fgn. Area Tng. fellow, 1962-65; Guggenheim Found. fellow, 1973-74; NEH fellow, 1978-79; NEH grantee, 1982-83, 1988, NSF grantee, 1988—, grantee Bradley Found., 1988—. Mem. Am. Hist. Assn., Am. Soc. Legal History, Am. Assn. Advancement Slavic Studies, PEN, Economic History Assn. Home: 4917 S Greenwood Ave Chicago IL 60615 Office: Dept History U Chgo 1126 E 59th St Box 78 Chicago IL 60637

HELLMAN, F(REDERICK) WARREN, banking executive; b. N.Y.C., July 25, 1934; s. Marco F. and Ruth (Koshl) H.; m. Patricia Christina Sander, Oct. 5, 1955; children: Frances, Patricia H., Marco Warren, Judith. B.A., U. Calif.-Berkeley, 1955; M.B.A., Harvard U., 1959. With Lehman Brothers, N.Y.C., 1959-84; ptnr. Lehman Brothers, 1963-84; exec. mng. dir. Lehman Bros., Inc., 1970-73, pres., 1973-75; ptnr. Hellman Ferri Investment Assocs., 1981—, Matrix Ptnrs., 1981—; gen. ptnr. Hellman & Friedman, San Francisco; dir. DN & E Walter, Alamitos Land Co., Shaughnessy Holdings Inc., Levi Strauss & Co., Mut. N.Y., Idetek, Inc., Consilium Inc., Williams-Somona, Inc., Il Fornaio Inc., ITEL Corp. Chmn. bd. trustees Mills Coll. Served to 1st lt. AUS, 1955-57. Mem. Explorers Club. Clubs: Bond, Piping Rock, Century Country, Family, Pacific Union. Office: Hellman & Friedman One Embarcadero Ctr #4000 San Francisco CA 94111

HELLMUTH, GEORGE FRANCIS, architect; b. St. Louis, Oct. 5, 1907; s. George W. and Harriet M. (Fowler) H.; m. Mildred Lee Henning, May 24, 1941; children: George William, Nicholas Matthew, Mary Cleveland, Theodore Henning, Daniel Fox. B.Arch., Washington U., 1928, M.Arch., 1930; Steedman traveling fellow, 1931; diploma, Ecole des Beaux Arts, Fontainebleau, France. Founder Hellmuth, Yamasaki & Leinweber, 1949-55, Hellmuth, Obata & Kassabaum, 1955-78, HOK Internat., Inc., 1977-86; numerous offices including St. Louis, N.Y.C., San Francisco, Dallas, Washington, Houston, Kansas City, Mo., Tampa, Fla., Los Angeles, Riyadh, Saudi Arabia, Cairo, Egypt, Stuttgart, Germany, Hong Kong; pres. Bald Eagle Co., Gladden, Mo.; Chmn. St. Louis Landmarks and Urban Design

Commn., 1950-70. Prin. archtl. works include: King Saud U., Riyadh, Saudi Arabia; King Khaled Internat. Airport, Riyadh; (outside U.S.) Nile Tower, Cairo, Egypt, U. West Indies, Trinidad, Spanish Honduras secondary sch. system, Am. Embassy, El Salvador, Am. embassy housing, Cairo, Canadian medium and maximum prisons, Taipei World Trade Ctr., Taiwan, Housing for Royal Saudi Naval Forces, Saudi Arabia, Military Secondary Schools, Saudi Arabia, Air Def. Command Hdqtrs. Complex, Saudi Arabia, Burgan Bank Hdtrs., Kuwait, Asoka Dev., Kuala Lumpur, Chesterton Retail Mall, U.K.; prin. archtl. works include: (U.S.) Nat. Air and Space Mus., Washington, Marion Fed. Maximum Security Prison, (Ill.), IBM Advanced systems Lab, Los Gatos, Calif., Dallas/Ft. Worth Regional Airport, U. Wis. Med. Center, Madison; Internat. Rivercenter, New Orleans; SUNY Health Scis. Complex, Buffalo, The Galleria/Post Oak Center, Houston, E.R. Squibb Co, Lawrenceville, N.J., McDonnell Planetarium, St. Louis, Dow Research and Devel. Facility, Indpls.; Commonwealth P.R. Penal System; Duke U. Med. Center, Durham, N.C.; Lubbock Regional Airport, (Tex.), Lambert-St. Louis Internat. Airport, St. Louis, D.C. Courthouse, St. Louis U. Sch. Nursing, No. Ill. U. Library, Mobil Oil Hdqtrs., Fairfax, Va., Cities Service Research Ctr., Tulsa, Marriott Corp. Hdqtrs., Bethesda, Md., McDonnell Douglas Automation Ctr., St. Louis, Moscone Conv. Ctr., San Francisco, Piers 1. 2. 3., Boston, Clark County Dentention Ctr., Las Vegas, Nev., Pillsbury Research and Devel. Facility, Mpls., Saturn Automotive Facility, Tenn., Burger King World Hdqrs., Miami, Exxon Research and Egrning. Ctr., Clinton, N.J., Incarnate Word Hosp., St. Louis, Kellogg Co. Hdqrs., Battle Creek, Mich., Fleet Ctr., Providence, Phillips Point, West Palm Beach, Fla., Sohio Corp. Hdqrs., Cleve., Lincoln Tower, Miami, 2000 Pennsylvania Ave., Washington, Providence Park, Fairfax, Va., Tower One, Houston, Griffin Tower, Dallas, ARCO Tower, Denver, Levi's Plaza, San Francisco, Southwestern Bell Telephone Hdqrs., St. Louis, Met. Life Bldg., St. Louis, Burger King Hdqrs., Miami, Fla., Saturn Automotive Facility, Tenn., many other indsl. and bus. corporate hdqrs., research centers. Recipient First Honor award AIA, 1956; knight Sovereign Mil. Order Malta in U.S.A. Fellow AIA. Clubs: Racquet (St. Louis); Sky (N.Y.C.). Home: 5 Conway Lane Saint Louis MO 63124 Office: 100 N Broadway Saint Louis MO 63102

HELLSTROM, GUNNAR STEN, chemical executive; b. Stockholm, May 3, 1947; s. Sten Oskar and Greta (Nylinder) H.; m. Birgitta Naemi, May 15, 1971; 1 child, Maria. MSc in Chem. Engring., Royal Inst. Tech., Stockholm, 1972. Lab. engr. AB Astra, Sodertalje, Sweden, 1972-73; lab. engr. Kema Nobel AB, Stockholm, 1973-75, sales mgr., 1976-79; mktg. mgr. Kenobel AB, Stockholm, 1980-84, gen. mgr., 1985—; bd. dirs. Amphoterics Internat., Leamington Spa, Eng., Kenochem C.C., Johannesburg, Republic of South Africa. Mem. Am. Oil Chemists Soc., Comité Européen des Agts. de Surface et leurs Intermédiaires Organiques. Office: Kenobel AB, Box 11536, S-10061 Stockholm Sweden

HELM, DEWITT FREDERICK, JR., association executive; b. Charlotte, N.C., Apr. 24, 1933; s. DeWitt Frederick Sr. and Blanche Buchanan (DeBusk) H.; m. Mary McNair Jones, Oct. 5, 1957; children: DeWitt Frederick III, Mary McNair Helm Bishop. BS in History, Davidson (N.C.) Coll., 1956. Mgr. advt. Vick Chem. Co., N.Y.C., 1956-63; mgr. consumer products Pfizer, Inc., N.Y.C., 1963-66; mgr. consumer product acquisition and devel. A.H. Robins Co., Richmond, Va., 1966-69; exec. v.p. Miller Morton Co., Richmond, 1969-72, pres., 1972-81; v.p. Miller Morton of Can. Ltd., 1969-81; sr. v.p. Jack Morton Prodns. Inc., Washington, 1981-84; exec. v.p. Assn. Nat. Advertisers, Inc., N.Y.C., 1984, pres., 1984—, also bd. dirs. Deacon, elder Presbyn. Ch.; bd. dirs. Nat. Tobacco Festival, Richmond, 1977-81, Traffic Audit Bur., N.Y.C., 1984—. Served with U.S. Army, 1956-58. Mem. Proprietary Assn. (bd. dirs., exec. com. 1972-80, chmn. 1973-75), Cosmetic, Toiletry and Fragrance Assn. (bd. dirs. 1977-80), Advt. Council (bd. dirs., treas. 1984—), Advt. Research Found. (bd. dirs. 1984—), World Fedn. Advertisers (bd. dirs., mgmt. com. 1984—), Davidson Coll. Nat. Alumni Assn. (v.p. 1974-75), N.C. Soc. of N.Y., Advt. Media Partnership for a Drug Free Am. (mgmt. bd. 1986—), Omicron Delta Kappa. Clubs: Bull and Bear (Richmond, Va.); Wintergreen (Va.); Sky, Metropolitan (N.Y.C.). Office: Assn Nat Advertisers 155 E 44th St New York NY 10017

HELM, HUGH BARNETT, retired judge; b. Bowling Green, Ky., Dec. 27, 1914; s. Hugh Barnett and Ermine (Cox) H.; B.A., Vanderbilt U., 1935, postgrad. law sch., 1936-37, 52-53, Stanford U., 1953-56, Nat. Coll. Judiciary, 1976, m. Vivian Loreen Downing, June 5, 1943; children: Beverly, Hugh B. III, Nathaniel Henry. Admitted to Ky. bar, 1938, Tenn. bar, 1938, U.S. Supreme Ct. bar, 1942; atty. Trade Practice Conf., FTC, Washington, 1938-42; asso. counsel U.S. Internat. Prosecution Sect. Gen. Hdqrs., SCAP, Tokyo, 1946; practiced in Nashville, 1946-53; bond specialist Swett & Crawford, San Francisco, 1956-57; resident mgr. Totten & Co., San Francisco, 1958, v.p. gen. mgr., 1959-60; sr. trial atty. Bur. Restraint of Trade, FTC, Washington, 1961-66, chief div. of adv. opinions, 1966-70, acting dir. Bur. Industry Guidance, 1969-70, atty. adviser FTC Bur. Consumer Claims, until 1971; adminstrv. law judge Bur. Hearing and Appeals, Social Security Adminstrn., HEW, Chattanooga, 1971-73, adminstrv. law judge charge Western Ky. and So. Ill., Paducah, Ky., 1973-76, Louisville, 1976-78; adminstrv. law judge in charge Miami (Fla.) Office Hearings and Appeals, 1979-81, adminstrv. law judge, Louisville, 1981-82; mem. regional jud. council Social Security Adminstrn. Pres. Surety Claims Assn. No. Calif., 1957-58. Mem. Tenn. Ho. of Reps., 1949-50. Served with inf. USAAF, 1941-45; served to capt. U.S. Army, 1950-52. Decorated Bronze Star, Combat Infantry Badge; recipient Founders medal for oratory Vanderbilt U., 1935, Disting. Service Commendation FTC, 1969. Mem. Am. (com. on civil service law), Ky., Tenn. bar assns., Nat. Lawyers Club, Pi Sigma Alpha, Tau Kappa Alpha. Presbyterian (deacon). Home: 23301 Lago Mar Circle Boca Raton FL 33433

HELMER, DAVID ALAN, lawyer; b. Colorado Springs, May 19, 1946; s. Horton James and Alice Ruth (Cooley) H.; m. Jean Marie Lamping, May 23, 1987. BA, U. Colo., 1968, JD, 1973. Bar: Colo. 1973, U.S. Dist. Ct. Colo. 1973. Assoc., Neil C. King, Boulder, Colo., 1973-76; mgr. labor relations, mining regulations Climax Molybdenum Co., Inc. div. AMAX, Inc., Climax, Colo., 1976-83; prin. Law Offices David A. Helmer, Frisco, Colo., 1983—; sec., bd. dirs. Z Comm. Corp., Frisco, 1983—. Editor U. Colo. Law Rev., 1972-73; contbr. articles to legal jours. Bd. dirs. Summit County Council Arts and Humanities, Dillon, Colo., 1980-85, Advs. for Victims Assault, Frisco, 1984—; legal counsel, v.p. Summit County United Way, 1983—, bd. dirs., 1983-88; bd. dirs., legal counsel Summit County Alcohol and Drug Task Force, Inc., 1984—. chmn. Summit County Reps., 1982—; chmn. 5th Jud. Dist. (Colo.) Rep. Com., 1982—; chmn. resolutions com. Colo. Rep. Conv., 1984, del. Rep. Nat. Com., 1984; chmn. chmn. reaccreditation com. Colo. Mountain Coll., Breckenridge, 1983; founder, bd. dirs. Dillon Bus. Assn., 1983—; atty. N.W. Colo. Legal Services Project, Summit County, 1983—. Served to master sgt. USAR, 1969. Mem. Continental Divide Bar Assn., Colo. Bar Assn., ABA, Phi Gamma Delta. Presbyterian. Club: Dillon Corinthian Yacht (commodore 1987-88). Home: 121 Three Rivers Box 300 Dillon CO 80435 Office: 619 Main St Drawer E Frisco CO 80443

HELMERICKS, HARMON, author, explorer; b. Gibson City, Ill., Jan. 18, 1917; s. Clarence James and Abbie (Cornelius) H.; m. Constance Chittenden, Apr. 27, 1941; children—Constance Jean, Carol Ann; m. Martha M. Paxton; children—James Woodrow, Mark Harmon, Jeffrey Todd. Student, U. Ariz., 1940-41. Sheet metal worker Army Engrs., Seaward, Alaska, 1941- 44; assoc. with Constance Helmericks in study of Arctic, 1944-46; writer, lectr. on Arctic Am. 1946—; organizer expdn. by air north of Arctic Circle Alaska and Can., 1947; co-founder, with Martha M. Helmericks Arctic Tern Fish-Freight Co., 1952; chmn. bd. Colville Inc.; asst. curator Kansas City Mus.; cons. Arctic oil operation Gulf Oil Co., Sohio Oil Co., Union Oil Co.; founder (with Martha M. Helmericks) Arctic Sch. for Boys, 1974; Arctic cons. to Eastman Kodak Co.; chmn. bd. Colville Environ. Services; dir. Alaska Interior Resources; master guide Alaskan Game Commn.; active in conservation in Africa, India, Europe Arctic Inst. N. Am., Airplane Owners and Pilots Assn. Author: Oolak's Brother, 1952, Arctic Hunters, 1955, (with Constance Helmericks) We Live in the Arctic, 1947, Our Summer With the Eskimos, 1948, Our Alaskan Winter, 1949, Flight of the Arctic Tern, 1952, Arctic Bush Pilot, 1968, The Last of the Bush Pilots, 1968; also mag. articles.; films for, Am. Motors Corp., TV shows on Arctic research. Mem. Daedalians. Clubs: Circumnavigators, Explorers. Address: 930 9th Ave Fairbanks AK 99701-9998

HELMFRID, STAFFAN, human geography educator, university president; b. Stockholm, Dec. 13, 1927; s. Hartwig E. W. and Greta (Kristiansson) H.; m. Antje Teichmann, June 19, 1954; children—Sigrun, Gudrun, Hillevi. Fil.mag., Stockholm U., 1951, fil.lic. in Geography, 1958, fil.dr., 1962. Teaching asst. dept. geography Stockholm U., 1951-61, docent, 1962-67, forskar docent, 1967-69, prof. human geography, 1969—, rektor, 1978—; sec. gen. 19th Internat. Geog. Congress, 1960; chmn. bd. Bank of Sweden Tercentenary Found., Stockholm, 1980-86, Swedish-Am. Fulbright Commn., 1984-85; mem. Swedish del. Council of Europe Com. on Univ. Problems, 1983-88. Author books, including: Östergötland Västanstång. Studien über die ältere Agrarlandschaft und ihre Genese, 1962; Europeiska agrarlandskap, 1963; Geografi for realskolan gymnasiet 1-3, 1960-63; also numerous articles, conf. papers in hist. and agrarian geography. Editor: Morphogenesis of the Agrarian Cultural Landscape, 1961; editor Ymer, 1959-64, Geografiska Annaler, Series B, Human Geography, 1965-78. Served to capt. Swedish Inf. Res., 1952-77. Decorated knight Royal Order North Star, Mem. Royal Swedish Acad. Letters, History and Antiquities, Royal Swedish Acad. Scis., Doctor h.c. Helsinki, 1986, Lord in Waiting, 1987. Office: Stockholm U, 10691 Stockholm Sweden

HELMS, DAVID ALONZO, lawyer; b. Evanston, Ill., July 5, 1934; s. Hugh Judson and Edna (Peterson-Holmes) H.; div.; children—Donald Anthony, Cybil Estelle. B.B.A., Northwestern U., 1956; J.D., U. Calif.-Berkeley, 1969. Bar: N.Y. 1972, Calif. 1973, Ill. 1974. With Matson Navigation Co., San Francisco, 1958-66, mgr. mktg. research, passenger ops., 1963-66; assoc. law firm Paul, Weiss, Rifkind, Wharton & Garrison, Esqs., N.Y.C., 1969-72; spl. asst. to mayor of Berkeley, Calif., 1972-73; dep. sec. state, spl. asst. to gov. Calif., 1973-75; exec. sec. Civil Rights Bar Assn., San Francisco, 1975-80; asst. dean, mem. faculty Chgo.-Kent Coll. Law, Ill. Inst. Tech., Chgo., 1979-81; atty., regional counsel FAA, Des Plaines, Ill., 1982-84; vol. atty. Howard Area and Cabrini-Green Law Clinics, Chgo. Vol. Legal Services Found., 1981—; sole practice law, David A. Helms & Assocs., Evanston and Chgo., 1981—; legal advisor to nat. pres. op. Push, 1986; real estate broker. Editor: Civil Rights Law Jour., Vol. I & II, 1974-78. Bd. dirs. Pub. Advocates, San Francisco, 1977-79. Mem. ABA, Chgo. Council Lawyers, Cook County Bar Assn., Chgo. Bar Assn. Baptist (mem. legal com., law clinic 1984—).

HELMS, FRED BRYAN, lawyer; b. Union County, N.C., Apr. 12, 1896; s. Emanuel M. and Frances P. (Austin) H.; m. Margaret V. Harrelson, July 14, 1927 (dec.); children: Margaret Harrelson (Mrs. Joseph B. Tyson), Frances (Mrs. Frances H. Abernethy); m. Susan Erwin Williamson, Mar. 3, 1978. Student, U. Ga., 1919-20; J.D., Wake Forest Coll., 1922; postgrad., Columbia U., 1922. Bar: N.C. 1922. Tchr. pub. schs. Union County, 1914-15; mgr. chain clothing stores Athens, Ga., East Moline, Ill., Muscatine, Iowa, 1919-22; since practiced in Charlotte; pros. atty. City of Charlotte, 1925-27; county judge Mecklenburg County, N.C., 1927-31; pvt. practice, specializing in civil law 1931—; ptnr. firm Helms Mulliss & Johnston and predecessors. Organizer, 1st pres. Charlotte Community Chest (now United Way), 1932-33; chmn. Citizens Com., 1941-45; mem. Commn. to Study and Revise Ins. Laws N.C., 1945-47, Commn. for Improvement Adminstrn. of Justice in N.C., 1947-49, N.C. Jud. Council, N.C. Gov.'s adv. commn. on segregation, Nat. Commn. Reform Fed. Criminal Laws.; Past trustee Wingate Coll. Presdl. elector N.C., 1956; Organizer, atty., commr. Charlotte Meml. Hosp. Authority. Served as 2d lt., F.A. U.S. Army, 1918-19. Recipient Silver medallion NCCJ, 1958; Distinguished Service Citation in law Wake Forest U., 1971. Fellow Am. Coll. Trial Lawyers; mem. Am. Soc. Internat. Law, Am. Legion, Am., Mecklenburg County bar assns., N.C. State Bar, Inc. (v.p. 1944-46, pres. 1946-47), Am. Judicature Soc., Am. Law Inst. Democrat. Clubs: Kiwanis (Charlotte), City (Charlotte), Charlotte Country (Charlotte). Home: 1571 Queens Rd W Charlotte NC 28207 Office: 227 N Tryon St Charlotte NC 28202

HELMS, JESSE, U.S. senator; b. Monroe, N.C., Oct. 18, 1921; s. Jesse Alexander and Ethel Mae (Helms) H.; m. Dorothy Jane Coble, Oct. 31, 1942; children: Jane (Mrs. Charles R. Knox), Nancy (Mrs. John C. Stuart), Charles. Student, Wingate (N.C.) Jr. Coll., Wake Forest Coll. City editor Raleigh (N.C.) Times, 1941-42; news and program dir. Sta. WRAL, Raleigh, 1948-51; adminstrv. asst. to U.S. senators Willis Smith and Alton Lennon, 1951-53; exec. dir. N.C. Bankers Assn., 1953-60; exec. v.p., vice chmn. Capitol Broadcasting Co., Raleigh, 1960-72; U.S. senator from N.C., 1973—; mem. Nutrition and Forestry; ranking mem. Com. on Fgn. Relations; mem. Select Com. on Ethics; chmn. Rules Com., also asst. minority whip.; chmn. bd. Specialized Agrl. Publs., Inc., Raleigh, 1964-72; mem. Raleigh City Council, 1957-61, chmn. law and finance com. Bd. dirs. N.C. Cerebral Palsy Hosp., Durham, United Cerebral Palsy N.C., Wake County Cerebral Palsy and Rehab. Center, Raleigh, Camp Willow Run, Littleton, N.C.; former trustee Campbell Coll., Wingate Coll., Meredith Coll., John F. Kennedy Coll. Served with USNR, 1942-45. Recipient Freedoms Found. award for best TV editorial, 1962, for newspaper article, 1973, So. Bapt. Nat. award for Service to mankind, 1972; Gold medal VFW; Conservative Congressional award, 1976; Liberty award Am. Econ. Council, 1978; Disting. Public Service award Public Service Research Council, 1978; Watchdog of Treasury award; Guardian of Small Bus. award; named Man of Yr. Women for Constl. Govt., 1978; Legislator of Yr. award Nat. Rifle Assn., 1978; other awards. Republican. Baptist (deacon). Clubs: Rotary (past pres. Raleigh), Raleigh Executives (past pres.), Masons (32 deg.). Office: Office of the Senate 403 Dirksen Senate Bldg Washington DC 20510

HELMS, MARY ANN, nurse; b. Compton, Calif., Jan. 7, 1935; d. Raymond Whitfield and Amanda Zelpha (Hancock) Spencer; AA in Nursing, El Camino Coll., 1971; BS in Nursing, Calif. State U., Los Angeles, 1976; MA in Mgmt., St. Mary's Coll., 1978; MS in Nursing, Ariz. State U., 1985; postgrad., Columbia Pacific U., 1988—; cert. clin. specialist; m. Willard Ford Helms, Mar. 15, 1958; children: Michael Steven, Steven Allen. Med. sec., bookkeeper Palm Springs (Calif.) Med. Clinic, 1956-61; office mgr. William R. Stevens Ins. Agy., Santa Ana, Calif., 1961-63, I.J. Weinrot & Son Ins. Agy., Los Angeles, 1963-67; staff nurse Kaiser Found. Hosp., Harbor City, Calif., 1971-76; supr., coordinator pediatrics Maricopa County Gen. Hosp., Phoenix, 1976-80; critical care nurse Phoenix Baptist Hosp., 1980-81, critical care mgr., 1981—, critical care cons., 1986—. Mem. Am. Nurses Assn., Am. Soc. Women Accts., Natural History Mus., Met. Mus. Art, Smithsonian Instn., Phoenix Zoo, Phoenix Art Mus., Cousteau Soc., Calif. State U. Alumni Assn., KAET Public Broadcasting System, Am. Assn. Critical Care Nurses, Ariz. Nurses Assn. Nat. League Nursing, Ariz. State U. Alumni Assn., Phi Kappa Phi, Alpha Gamma Sigma, Sigma Theta Tau. Republican. Mormon. Research on noise pollution on phys. and mental health of citizenry, phenylketonuria testing in Los Angeles, measurement of attitudes toward children in pediatric nurses, nursing practice, physiological changes with back massage, incidence of prolonged Q-T internal in critically ill patients. Home: 1007 E Michelle Dr Phoenix AZ 85022 Office: 6025 N 20th Ave Phoenix AZ 85015

HELPMAN, ELHANAN, economics educator; b. Dzalabad, USSR, Mar. 30, 1946; arrived in Israel, 1957; s. Matis and Feige (Edelstein) H.; m. Ruth Sticlar, Dec. 23, 1969; children: Limor, Liat. BA cum laude, Tel Aviv U., 1969, MA summa cum laude, 1971; PhD, Harvard U., 1974. Lectr. Tel Aviv. U., 1974-76, sr. lectr., 1976-78, assoc. prof., 1978-81, prof., 1981-88; Archie Sherman Prof. Internat. Econ. Relations 1988—; vis. prof. Harvard Univ., Cambridge, Mass., 1982-83, MIT, 1983-84, 87-88. Author: International Trade Under Uncertainty, 1978, Market Structure and Foreign Trade, 1985; editor: Social Policy Evaluation, 1983; co-editor Jour. Internat. Econs., 1982—; contbr. articles to profl. jours. NSF grantee, 1977-78, Ford Found. grantee, 1975-77, 80-82. Fellow Econometric Soc., Israel Econ. Soc., Am. Econ. Assn., Royal Econ. Soc., European Econ. Soc.

HELTON, DANNY ORVILLE, chemist; b. Booneville, Miss., Oct. 5, 1944; s. Orville and Thelma Yvlette (Green) H.; B.S., U. Louisville, 1966, Ph.D., 1972; m. Sarah Frances Cole, Aug. 21, 1966; children—Raymond Orville. Asso. chemist Midwest Research Inst., Kansas City, Mo., 1973-75; sr. chemist, 1975-81; with Alcon Labs., Ft. Worth, 1981—; lectr. U. Mo., Kansas City. Mem. Republican Nat. Com., 1980—. NDEA fellow, 1968-69. Mem. Am. Chem. Soc. (chmn. Ft. Worth Dallas), Mid-Am. Cancer Center Program, Phi Lambda Upsilon. Baptist. Pioneer in rapid assay method for N 5 rocket propellant. Home: 1024 CR 1017 Joshua TX 76058 Office: Alcon Labs 6201 S Freeway Fort Worth TX 76058

HEMANN, RAYMOND GLENN, aerospace company executive; b. Cleve., Jan 24, 1933; s. Walter Harold Marsha Mae (Colbert) H.; B.S., Fla. State U., 1957; postgrad. U.S. Naval Postgrad. Sch., 1963-64, U. Calif. at Los Angeles, 1960-62; M.S. in Systems Engring., Calif. State U., Fullerton, 1970, M.A. in Econs., 1972; m. Lucile Tinnin Turnage, Feb. 1, 1958; children—James Edward, Carolyn Frances; m. Pamela Lehr, Dec. 18, 1987.Aero. engring. aide U.S. Navy, David Taylor Model Basin, Carderock, Md., 1956; analyst Fairchild Aerial Surveys, Tallahassee, 1957; research analyst Fla. Rd. Dept., Tallahassee, 1957-59; chief Autonetics div. N.Am. Rockwell Corp., Anaheim, Calif., 1959-69; v.p., dir. R. E. Manns Co., Wilmington, Calif., 1969-70; mgr. avionics design and analysis dept. Lockheed-Calif. Co., Burbank, 1970-72, mgr. advanced concepts div., 1976-82; gen. mgr. Western div. Arinc Research Corp., Santa Ana, 1972-76; dir. future requirements Rockwell Internat., 1982-85; dir. Threat Analysis, Corp. Offices, Rockwell Internat., 1985—; cons. various U.S. govt. agys.; mem. naval studies bd. Nat. Acad. Scis., 1985—; asst. prof. ops. analysis dept. U.S. Naval Postgrad. Sch., Monterey, Calif., 1963-64, Monterey Peninsula Coll., 1963; instr. ops. analysis Calif. State U., Fullerton, 1963, instr. quantitative methods, 1969-72; adj. fellow Ctr. Strategic and Internat. Studies, Washington, 1987—; pres. Asso. Aviation, Inc., Fullerton, 1965-74; lectr. Brazilian Navy, 1980, U. Calif., Santa Barbara, 1980, Yale U., 1985, Princeton U., 1986, U.S. Naval Postgrad. Sch., 1986; cons. to various corps. and govt. agys. Troop chmn. Boy Scouts Am. Bd. dirs. Placentia-Yorba Jr. Athletic Assn. Served with AUS, 1950-53. Syde P. Deeb scholar, 1956; recipient certificate appreciation U.S. Naval Postgrad. Sch., 1963; Honor awards Nat. Assn. Remotely Piloted Vehicles, 1975, 76. Comml., glider and pvt. pilot. Fellow AAAS; mem. Ops. Research Soc. Am., IEEE, AIAA, Air Force Assn., N.Y. Acad. Scis., Soaring Soc. Am., Nat. Acad. Scis. (Naval Studies Bd. 1985—), Assn. Old Crows, Phi Kappa Tau (past pres.). Episcopalian. Contbr. articles to profl. jours. and news media. Home: 1215 Hartwood Point Dr Pasadena CA 91107 Office: 2230 E Imperial Hwy El Segundo CA 90245

HEMBERG, BENGT SVEN ESKIL, composer, conductor; b. Stockholm, Jan. 19, 1938; s. Bengt Emil Esse and Rut Ingeborg (Thelander) H.; diploma Stockholm Music Tchrs. Degree, 1961; diploma organ and orch. conducting Royal Coll. Music, Stockholm, 1964; m. Birgit Sofia Ohlsson, July 8, 1962; children—Anna Maria, Johan Eskil Olof, Fredrik Eskil Love. Exec. producer Swedish Radio, 1963-70; planning mgr. Nat. Inst. Concerts, 1970-83; condr. Stockholm U. Chorus, 1958-83; mng. dir. Göteborgs Teateroch Konsert AB and artistic dir. Stora Teatern, Göteborg, 1984-87; gen. dir. Stockholm Royal Opera, 1987—; guest prof. choral conducting, U.S., 1974—; mem. Konstnärsnämnden Artists Council Sweden, 1976-80; pres. Swedish NOMUS, 1979-83, Swedish nat. com. IMC, 1975—; composer: (operas) Love, Love, Love, 1973, The Pirates of the Deep Green Sea, 1977, Saint Erik's Crown, 1979, Canticles, 1981; other vocal works; rec. artist EMI, Fabo records. Grantee Swedish Govt., 1972, 73, 75, 81, City of Stockholm, 1970, City of Nacka, 1977; recipient Gustaf Aulén prize, Ture Rangström prize, Stim grant, Stockholm Music Assn. prize. Mem. Swedish Composers Soc. (pres. 1971-83), Stim Performing Rights Soc. (v.p. 1971-83), Royal Acad. Music, Internat. Fedn. Choral Music (exec. com.), Internat. Music Council UNESCO (v.p. 1987—). Club: Rotary. Home: Floravägen 3, 131 41 Nacka Sweden Office: Royal Opera Stockholm, Box 16094, 103 22 Stockholm Sweden

HEMBRE, JOHN IVER, advertising executive; b. Baker, Mont.; s. Julius O. and Cora (Lanning) H.; m. Florence M. Wilson, July 19, 1953; children—Jane Cora, Julie Florence, Ellen Ruth. BBA, U. Minn., 1951. With Nat. Outdoor Advt. Bur., various locations, 1952-62; supr. outdoor and transit media Young & Rubicam, Inc., N.Y.C., 1962-64; sr. v.p., dir. mktg. and sales, mem. exec. com. of bd. dir. Transp. Displays, Inc. subs. internat. Tel. & Tel. Co., N.Y.C., 1964-72; pres., chmn. bd. The Hembre Co., Inc., Huntington, N.Y., 1972—; founder, chmn. bd. D-Cube Inc., Huntington, N.Y., 1976—.

HEMBREE, JAMES D., retired chemical company executive; b. Morris, Okla., Feb. 27, 1929; s. James D. and Mary Eleanor (Hacker) H.; m. Joyce Pickrell, Aug. 25, 1951; Victoria Lee Stilwell, Alex James, Kent Douglas. B.S.Ch.E., Okla. State U., 1951; M.S.Ch.E., U. Mich., 1952. Dir. mktg. inorganic chems. Dow Chem U.S.A., Midland, Mich., 1968-78, gen. mgr. designed products dept., 1976-78, v.p., 1978-80, group v.p., 1980-83; pres., chief exec. officer Dow Chem. Can., Sarnia, Ont., 1983-86; ret. 1986. Home and Office: 4620 Jupiter Dr Salt Lake City UT 84124

HEMINGWAY, RICHARD WILLIAM, lawyer, educator; b. Detroit, Nov. 24, 1927; s. William Oswald and Iva Catherine (Wildfang) H.; m. Vera Cecilia Eck, Sept. 12, 1947; children: Margaret Catherine, Carol Elizabeth, Richard Albert. B.S. in Bus, U. Colo., 1950; J.D. magna cum laude (J. Woodall Rogers Sr. Gold medal 1955), So. Meth. U., 1955; LL.M. (William S. Cook fellow 1968), U. Mich., 1969. Bar: Tex. 1955, Okla. 1981. Assoc. Fulbright, Crooker, Freeman, Bates & Jaworski, Houston, 1955-60; lectr. Bates Sch. Law, U. Houston, 1960; assoc. prof. law Baylor U. Law Sch., Waco, Tex., 1960-65; vis. assoc. prof. So. Meth. U. Law Sch., 1965-68; prof. law Tex. Tech U. Law Sch., Lubbock, 1968-71, Paul W. Horn prof., 1972-81, acting dean, 1974-75, dean ad interim, 1980-81; prof. law U. Okla., Norman, 1981-83, Eugene Kuntz prof. oil, gas and natural resources law, 1983—; of counsel McAfee & Taft, attys., Oklahoma City; mem. legal com. Interstate Oil Compact Com., Oklahoma City, 1982—. Author: The Law of Oil and Gas, 1971, 2d edit., 1983, lawyer's edit., 1983, West's Texas Forms (Mines and Minerals), 1977, West's Forms (Mines and Minerals), 1985; contbg. editor various law reports, cases and materials. Served with USAAF, 1945-47. Mem. ABA, Okla. Bar Assn., Tex. Bar Assn., Cleveland County Bar Assn., Lubbock Bar Assn., Scribes, Order of Coif (faculty), Beta Gamma Sigma. Lutheran. Home: 1411 Greenbriar Dr Norman OK 73072 Office: U Okla Law Sch Norman OK 73019

HEMLEY, EUGENE ADAMS, trade association executive, former navy officer; b. Bklyn., Feb. 20, 1918; s. Benjamin and Fannie (Gottlieb) H.; B.E.E., U.S. Naval Acad., 1940; M.S. in Internat. Affairs, George Washington U., 1968; m. Charlotte McClure, Dec. 22, 1948; children—Philip, Paul, Anne, Margaret. Served as midshipman U.S. Navy, 1936-40, commd. ensign U.S. Navy, 1940, advanced through grades to capt., 1959; comdg. officer USS Bang, 1951, USS Volador, 1952, USS Bristol, 1956-57, USS Taconic, 1961-62, USS Northampton, 1965-66; dir. fleet communications div. Office Chief of Naval Ops., 1958-61, dep. dir. info. systems div., 1968-70; comdg. officer U.S. Naval Communications Sta., Japan, 1962-65; ret., 1970; dir. mgmt. info. systems Nat. Girl Scout Orgn., N.Y.C., 1970-74; computerization mgr. Nat. Council on Internat. Trade Documentation, N.Y.C., 1974-84 (name changed to The Internat. Trade Facilitation Council), assoc. dir., 1984-85, exec. dir., 1985—; U.S. bus. adviser meetings UN Econ. Commn. for Europe, 1982—. Mem. Citizens nominating commn. Town of Scarsdale, 1982-83. Decorated Silver Star. Mem. U.S. Naval Inst., Naval Acad. Alumni Assn. (v.p. N.Y. chpt. 1982-83, pres. 1984-85, trustee 1985—). Clubs: N.Y. Yacht, Army-Navy Country, Scarsdale Town, County Tennis (v.p. 1983-84, pres. 1985-87). Editor: Cardis Standards Manual, 1981, Nat. Council on Internat. Trade Documentation Computerization News, 1982-84. Home: 20 Cohawney Rd Scarsdale NY 10583 Office: 350 Broadway New York NY 10013

HEMMER, JAMES P., lawyer; b. Oshkosh, Wis., Mar. 28, 1942; s. Joseph John and Margaret Louise (Nuernberg) H.; m. Francine M. Chamallas, June 4, 1967; children—James, Christopher, Sarah. A.B. summa cum laude, Marquette U., 1964; LL.B., Harvard U., 1967. Bar: Ill. 1967. Assoc. Bell, Boyd & Lloyd, Chgo., 1967-74, ptnr., 1975—; adj. prof. law Marquette U., 1985-86; lectr. Ill. Inst. Continuing Legal Edn.; bd. dirs. Sanford Corp., Constrn. Projects Mgmt. Inc., Holco Corp. Mem. Kenilworth (Ill.) Sch. Dist. 38 Bd. Edn., v.p. 1985-87, pres. 1987—, Kenilworth Citizens Adv. Caucus; bd. dirs. Jos. Sears Sch. Devel. Fund. Wickersham fellow. Mem. ABA, Ill. Bar Assn. (editor banking and comml. law newsletter), Alpha Sigma Nu, Phi Theta Psi, Phi Sigma Tau, Sigma Tau Delta. Clubs: University, Law, Legal (Chgo.); Kenilworth. Contbr. articles to legal jours.

HEMMERLIN, ALBERT JOSEPH, publishing company executive; b. Angleur-Liege, Belgium, Feb. 2, 1938; s. Albert Jules Hemmerlin and Yvonne Vandenberght; m. Danielle Previnaire; children—Laetrtra, Lionel, Michael, Fabien, Gilles. Doctor in Law, U. Leuven, Belgium, 1963. Direction asst. Hemma, Chevron, Belgium, 1964-76, gen. mgr., 1976—. Home: rue de Chevron 118, 4081 Chevron Belgium Office: Hemma Publisher, rue de Chevron 106, 4081 Chevron Belgium

HEMMING, HEATHER JOAN, psychology educator; b. Lincoln, Lincolnshire, Eng., Aug. 9, 1942; d. William Wycliffe and Helen Graham Finch (Dawson) H. BS in Psychology with honors, Cardiff U., South Wales, U.K., 1969; M in Psychology, Southhampton (Eng.) U., 1977. Sci. asst. Inst. Aviation Medicine, Farnborough, Eng., 1961-64; research asst. U. Southampton, 1969-73, U. Coll. Swansea, South Wales, Eng., 1975-78; lectr. in psychology Paisley (Scotland) Coll. Tech., 1978—. Contbr. articles to profl. jours. Mem. Brit. Psychol. Assn. Office: Paisley Coll Tech, High St, Paisley PA1 2BE, Scotland

HEMPHILL, ALAN POLK, management consultant; b. Montgomery, Ala., Aug. 22, 1933; s. Alan Polk and Elizabeth Evans (Orr) H.; m. Jean Tilden Baker, June 8, 1957; children—Elizabeth, Alan, Laurie. BSEE., U.S. Naval Acad., 1957; MA in Mgmt., Nat. U., 1987. Commd. ensign U.S. Navy, 1957, advanced through grades to lt. comdr., 1977; various assignments, San Diego, 1957-77; mgr. Prestige Properties, Poway Calif., 1977-80; founder Orion Bus. Systems, San Diego, 1980-82; pres., chief exec. officer Sta. KBSC-TV, Glendale, Calif., 1982-83; chmn., bd. dirs. Oak Broadcasting Systems, Glendale, 1983-84; pres. Community Bus. Cons., San Diego, 1984-85; prof. computer sci. Nat. U., Vista, Calif., 1984—; trustee Sta. KBSC-TV Stock of Oak Industries, San Diego, 1982-84; panelist TV series On Edge, 1986-87; cons. Oak Industries, San Diego, 1984; bd. dirs. Community Bus. Cons., San Diego, 1984. Contbr. articles and columns to profl. jours., chpts. to books. Gen. mgr. Remember the Pueblo, San Diego, 1968; pres., chmn. bd. Green Valley Civic Assn., Poway, 1974-75; pres., bd. dirs. N. County Bd. of Jr. Achievement, 1979. Lodge: Kiwanis (pres. Rancho Bernardo chpt. 1980-81). Pres., chief exec. officer, chmn. while Sta. KBSC-TV received 12 Emmys, 1982-84.

HEMPHILL, BERNICE MONAHAN (MRS. CHARLES D. HEMPHILL), association executive, civic leader; b. San Francisco; d. Thomas E. and Anne J. (McGinerty) Monahan; m. Charles D. Hemphill, June 30, 1939. Bioanalyst, U. Calif. Supervising technologist Honolulu Blood Plasma Bank, 1941- 43; exec. dir., sec. Irwin Meml. Blood Bank, San Francisco Med. Soc., 1944-82, dir. emeritus, 1983—; sec. Calif. Blood Bank System, 1951-57; charter mem., treas. Am. Assn. Blood Banks, 1949-74, pres. elect, 1975, pres., 1976-77, emeritus dir., 1978—, originator bloodbank clearinghouse concept, 1951, chmn. nat. clearing house program, 1953-84, mem. com. on external affairs, com. on internat. relations, 1978; mem. Pres.'s exec., fin., personnel coms. Am. Blood Commn., 1978-80, bd. dirs., 1981-83; cons. blood bank projects AMA, Am. Hosp. Assn., other nat. health orgns., other countries; Mem. adv. com. blood and blood derivatives Calif. Dept. Pub. Health, 1964—; mem. Nat. Adv. Council for Disease Control, 1969-72; exec. sec. Zone 1 Federacion Pan Americana Pro Donacion Voluntaria de Sangre, 1980—; bd. dirs. Health Care Found. of San Francisco, 1983, Nat. Center for Voluntary Action, 1976-77; bd. dirs. San Francisco unit Am. Cancer Soc., 1978-83, sec. San Francisco unit, 1981-83; mem. steering com. Learn Through Internat. Vol. Effort Conf., 1975-76; mem. adv. bd. U. Santa Clara Bus. Sch., 1980-83; pres. (vol.) Blood Research and Devel. Found., 1984—; mem. (appointee) Sickle Cell Disease Adv. com. Nat. Heart, Lung and Blood Inst., 1984-87, chmn., 1987-88; active San Francisco United Way Bay Area, mem. health council, mem. joint budget study com. program for hosps. and health agys., 1966-75, mem. casework services com. program for aging, 1961-62, Hispanic affairs com., 1981-82; mem. Cath. Social Service San Francisco, Mayor San Francisco Citizens Com. Centennial Golden Gate Park, 1969-70; also mem. hosp. aux. U. Calif.; aux. St. Francis Hosp., Calif., Laguna (Calif.) Honda Home; women's aux. San Francisco Dental Soc.; aux. Little Children's Aid, St. Francis Yacht Club, St. Anthony's Dining Room, Guide Dogs for Blind., S.F. Opera Guild, S.F. Symphony Assn.; bd. dirs. Marshal Hale Meml. Hosp., 1984—, San Francisco Heart Inst., 1987—; mem. San Francisco-Shanghai Friednship com., 1986—; bd. devel. Sisters of Notre Dame de Namur, 1987—. Mem. Women for Nixon-Agnew Com., 1968; co-chmn. Women's Adv. Com. for Re-election Pres., 1972; mem. nat. adv. com. Women for Pres. Ford, 1976; mem. adv. com. on fiscal affairs Republican Nat. Com., 1977-80; mem. Manila-San Francisco Sister City Com., 1981-82; bd. dirs. San Francisco Convention and Visitors Bureau, 1982—; bd. dirs., chmn. vol. com. Hearing Soc. for Bay Area, Inc., 1983; bd. dirs. Green Hills Towers, 1983; mem. San Francisco-Osaka Sister City Com., 1983; San Francisco City and County Planning Commn., 1985—. Named Distinguished Woman San Francisco Examiner, 1960, U.S. Lady of Month U.S. Lady mag., 1963; recipient John Elliot award contbns. blood banking Am. Assn. Blood Banks, 1960, Award of Merit for Cath. charities services Archdiocese San Francisco, 1962, commendation exceptional services to patients Ft. Miley VA Hosp., San Francisco, 1961, 80, citation for vol. community services Lane Bryant, 1965, 66, 67, 68, Cert. of Honor City and County of San Francisco Bd. of Supervisors, 1971, 82, diploma 2000 Women of Achievement, 1972, Award of Honor Pan Am. Fedn. for Voluntary Blood Donations, 1972, Award of Merit Nat. Orgn. of Voluntary Blood Donors of Venezuela, 1973, Key of Guild award Medico Dental Study Guild, Calif., 1973; 1st. Ann. Lecture award S. Central Assn. of Blood Banks, 1975; KABL Citizen of the Day award, 1975, 82; cert. of appreciation Kiwanis Club of Benicia, 1977; Owen Thomas Meml. award Calif. Blood Bank System, 1978; Woman of Achievement award Bus. and Profl. Women's Club of San Francisco, 1981; commendation Calif. State Senate, 1982; commendation VA, 1982; Resolution of Recognition Calif. Med. Assn., 1983; Hon. Life Mem. Calif. Blood Bank System, 1983, recipient Internat. Woman Year award, 1986. Mem. Women's Forum West (v.p. 1980-81), San Francisco Assn. Mental Health, Med. Dental Study Club San Francisco (life mem.), Internat. Soc. Blood Transfusion, Ambassador League of San Francisco, Am. Women for Internat. Understanding (pres. 1973—, chmn. bd. 1987—), World Affairs Council No. Calif., Host Com. San Francisco, Nat. Conf. Social Welfare (chmn. sponsoring com. 1975), San Francisco C. of C. (dir., exec. com. 1980-82, chmn. health care com. 1983); (award for Lifetime Dedication to People and to a City 1981); Mem. UN Assn. San Francisco (steering com. for internat. women's com. 1975, coordinating com. Calif. Internat. Women's Year 1977), UN Assn. of U.S., Nat. Com. on U.S.-China Relations; hon. mem. Pan Am. Fedn. Voluntary Blood Donations. Republican. Clubs: Doctors' Wives, Francisca; Commonwealth (San Francisco) (membership com. 1983); Capitol Hill (Washington). Home: 1070 Green St San Francisco CA 94133 Office: 270 Masonic Ave San Francisco CA 94118

HEMPHILL-HAMMOND, BETTY, retired teacher, civic worker; b. Guthrie, Okla., Mar. 22, 1911; d. Rolla Kellogg and Bertha Louise Ferrier; m. Frederic Hemphill, May 23, 1936 (dec. 1978); 1 child, Patricia Steinke; m. Russell I. Hammond, Sept. 1, 1984. Student Kans. U., 1930-31, Coll. William and Mary, 1935, Midland Coll., 1942. Cert. elem. tchr., Kans., Okla. Tchr. Clay Ctr., Kans., 1928-30, 34-36, Merrimac, Okla., 1932-33; dir. Youth Art Contest, Tekamah, Nebr., 1942-65; milk technologist Fed. Milk Market, Chgo., 1943-45; prodn. asst. weekly newspaper Tekamah, 1936-65; sec. Wyo. Vets. Affairs Commn., 1975-88; chmn. for securing govt. and state grants for State Vets. Cemetery, VFW Aux., 1946-58. Vol. local library and mus.; chaplain Wyo. Silver-Haired Legis., 1985-86. Mem. Am. Legion Aux. (regional v.p., nat. historian 1947—), VFW Aux. (past pres.), Daus. of Nile, Eastern Star, Alpha Gamma Delta. Democrat. Methodist. Club: Laramie Woman's (pres. 1977). Avocations: art; fishing; bridge, handcrafts; china painting. Home: 816 S 17th Laramie WY 82070

HENBEST, WILLIAM HARRISON, insurance agent; b. Elmira, N.Y., Nov. 14, 1955; s. Robert Leroy and Grace Edith (Rowley) H.; m. Cynthia Jean Rohde, Apr. 26, 1980; 1 child, Danielle Christine. BBA, Rochester Inst. Tech., 1978. Fin. analyst A&P, Horseheads, N.Y., 1979-80; multi-line underwriter Gen. Accident Ins., Syracuse, N.Y., 1980-82; v.p. Henbest & Morrisey Inc., Elmira, 1982—; sec., treas. Chemung County Agts. Assn., Elmira, 1982—. Com. mem. United Way, Elmira, 1986. Mem. Profl. Ins. Agts. Assn., Ind. Ins. Agts. Assn., Chemung County C. of C. (bd. dirs.), Sigma Pi. Republican. Lodge: Kiwanis. Home: 82 Demarest Pkwy Elmira NY 14905 Office: Henbest & Morrisey Inc 305 E Water St Elmira NY 14901

HENDARTO, HENDARMIN, otolaryngologist, educator; b. Jakarta, Indonesia, Aug. 16, 1937; s. Sastrosoepono Hendarmin and Juariah Soetawidjaja; m. Sri Koemarjati, Apr. 7, 1963; children: Heru, Hari, Hendi, Hani. MD, U. Indonesia, Jakarta, 1963, postgrad. otolaryngology, 1966; postgrad. otolaryngology, Royal Victorian Eye and Ear Hosp., Melbourne, Australia, 1969. Diplomate otolaryngology. Head audiology dept. U. Indonesia Med. Sch., 1969-75, head otology dept., 1975-78, head postgrad. ear, nose and throat tng., 1978—. Pres. Indonesian Fedn. for the Welfare of the Deaf, Jakarta, 1975—; bd. dirs. Indonesian Nat. Council on Social Welfare, 1975—; dep. chmn. Found. for Med. Rehab., Jakarta, 1983—. Hon. award for social work Gov. Jakarta, 1977, 84. Fellow Internat. Coll. Surgeons; mem. Indonesia Med. Assn., Asian Oceanian Otorhinolaringology Assn. (exec. bd.). Golongan Karya. Moslem. Lodge: Rotary. Home: Jl T Cik di Tiro II/4, Jakarta 10350, Indonesia

HENDEL, MARK SCOTT, data processing executive; b. Miami Beach, Fla., Oct. 28, 1955; s. David Hendel and Gwendolyn Evette (London) Tanner; m. Isabelle Lucette Germaine Wild, Apr. 10, 1982; children: Samantha, Caroline. Cert. in internat. bus., Netherlands Sch. Bus., Breukelen, Holland, 1975; BS in Bus. Adminstrn., U. Fla., 1976; MS, Am. Grad. Sch. Internat. Mgmt., Glendale, Ariz., 1979. Lic. ins. agt., real estate agt., mortgage broker. Tech. advisor U.S. Peace Corps, Cameroon, Africa, 1976-78; adminstr., sales engr. Garrett Corp., Los Angeles, 1980-81; asst. gen. mgr. D.H. Assocs., Inc., Palm Beach Gardens, Fla., 1981-82; mgr. info. systems Garrett Corp., Strasbourg, France, 1983-86; mgr. European telecom and bus. system Skelmersdale, Eng., 1986—. Mem. Brit. Computer Soc., Internat. Telecommunications Users Group, Soc. Automotive Engrs., World Trade Council Palm Beach. Clubs: Hesketh Golf, Argyle Tennis (Southport, Eng.). Office: Garrett Automotive Ltd, Potter Place West Pimbo, Skelmersdale, Lancs WN8 9PH, England

HENDERSON, ALAN, physician; b. Newcastle-Upon-Tyne, Eng., Dec. 11, 1951; s. Adam Halla and Gertrude (Bulman) H.; m. Arlene Bette Holley, July 10, 1976; children: Lindsay Jane, Duncal Alan, Hope Catriona Elizabeth. BMSci with 1st class honors, Nottingham U., 1973, BM and BS with honors, 1975; Diploma of Tropical Medicine and Hygiene, 1988. House physician Derbyshire Royal Infirmary, Derby, Eng., 1975; house surgeon Nottingham City Hosp., Eng., 1976; registrar in pathology Hammersmith Hosp., Eng., 1976-77; sr. house physician Gen. Hosp., Newcastle, 1977-78; registrar in cardiology Freeman Hosp., Newcastle, 1978-79; registrar in medicine Edinburgh Hosp., Scotland, 1980-81; sr. registrar in medicine Brit. Army, 1981-84; cons. physician Brit. Mil. Hosp., Hong Kong, 1984-86, Trent Reg. Health Authority, Eng., 1987—; sr. physician Brit. Mil. Hosp., Hong Kong, 1984-86; clin. mem. Hong Kong Govt. Malaria Control Com., 1984-86; cons. physician Argyle Vietnamese Refugee Camp, Hong Kong, 1984-86; advisor AIDS Brit. Army, 1986—. Contbr. articles to profl. jours. Served to maj. Royal Army Med. Corps, 1981-83. Recipient Leishman prize Brit. Army, 1984, Bupa Doctor of the Yr. award Brit. Army, 1986. Mem. Royal Coll. Physicians. Office: Grantham and Kesteven Gen Hosp, Manthorpe Rd, Lincolnshire England

HENDERSON, DAVID ANDREW, biochemist; b. Alyth, Scotland, Apr. 9, 1948; s. Frank Patterson and Moira Scott (Stewart) H.; m. Lorraine Anne Erickson, Mar. 23, 1975; children: Kirsten, Daniel, Peter. BSc, U. Edinburgh, 1970; PhD, Vanderbilt U., 1974. Research fellow Calif. Inst. Tech., Pasadena, 1975-76; staff scientist Max Planck Inst. Biophys. Chemistry, Gottingen, Fed. Republic Germany, 1976-82, Schering Aktiengesellschaft, Berlin, 1982—. Patentee pharm. compounds; contbr. over 40 sci. articles to profl. publs. Mem. Am. Soc. Cell Biology, N.Y. Acad. Scis., Sigma Xi. Office: Schering AG, Muellerstrasse 170-178, D1000 Berlin 65 Federal Republic of Germany

HENDERSON, DENYS HARTLEY, chemical company executive; b. Colombo, Sri Lanka, Oct. 11, 1932; s. John Hartley and Nellie (Gordon) H.; m. Doreen Mathewson Glashan, Mar. 16, 1957; children: Nicola Mary, Fiona Elizabeth. MA, U. Aberdeen, LLB, LLD (hon.), 1987; Dr. Univ., U. Brunel, 1987. Legal apprentice Messrs. Esslemont & Cameron, Aberdeen, 1952-55; comml. asst. Imperial Chem. Industries plc, London, 1957-58; various positions Imperial Chem. Industries plc, various locations, 1958-74; gen. mgr. Imperial Chem. Industries plc, London, 1974-77; chmn. paints div. Imperial Chem. Industries plc, Slough, 1977-80; main bd. dir. Imperial Chem. Industries plc, London, 1980—, dep. chmn., 1986-87, chmn., 1987—; chmn. adv. com. Stock Exchange Listed Cos., London, 1988—; non-exec. Barclays Bank plc, London, Barclays plc, London. Mem. ct. govs. Henley-The Mgmt. Coll., 1986—; adv. council Prince's Youth Bus. Trust, 1986—; mem. pres.'s com. Confedn. Brit. Industry, London, 1987—; mem. The Opportunity Japan Campaign com., 1988—; mem. Adv. Com. Stock Exchange Listed Co., N.Y., 1988—. Served as capt. Brit. Army, 1955-57. Fellow Royal Soc. Arts, Inst. of Mktg.; mem. Law Soc. Scotland, Brit. Inst. Mgmt. (companion). Presbyterian. Club: Royal Automobile (London). Office: Imperial Chem Industries plc, Imperial Chem House, Millbank, London SW1P 3JF, England

HENDERSON, DONALD AINSLIE, university dean; b. Cleve., Sept. 7, 1928; s. David Alexander and Grace Eleanor (McMillan) H.; m. Nana Irene Bragg, Sept. 1, 1951; children: Leigh Ainslie, David Alexander, Douglas Bruce. B.A., Oberlin (Ohio) Coll., 1950, D.Sc. (hon.), 1979; M.D., U. Rochester (N.Y.), 1954, D.Sc. (hon.), 1977; M.P.H., Johns Hopkins U., 1960; LL.D. (hon.), Marietta (Ohio) Coll., 1978; D.Sc. (hon.), U. Ill., 1979, U. Md., 1980; M.D. (hon.), U. Geneva, 1980; L.H.D. (hon.), SUNY, 1981; D.Sc. (hon.), Yale U., 1986. Diplomate: Am. Bd. Preventive Medicine. Intern, then resident Mary Imogene Bassett Hosp., Cooperstown, N.Y., 1954-55, 57-59; chief epidemic intelligence service Center Disease Control, USPHS, Atlanta, 1955-57; chief surveillance sect. Center Disease Control, USPHS, 1960-66; chief med. officer smallpox eradication WHO, Geneva, 1966-77; dean Johns Hopkins U. Sch. Hygiene and Pub. Health, 1977—. Contbr. articles to med. jours. Recipient Commendation medal USPHS, 1962, Disting. Service medal, 1976; Ernst Jung prize, 1976; award Govt. India-Indian Soc. Malaria and Other Communicable Diseases, 1975; Rosenhaus internat. award for excellence, 1975; George MacDonald medal London Sch. Hygiene and Tropical Medicine, Royal Soc. Tropical Medicine and Hygiene, 1976; Health medal Govt. Afghanistan, 1976; Spl. Albert Lasker Pub. Health Service award for WHO, 1976; Public Welfare medal Nat. Acad. Scis., 1978; Joseph C. Wilson award in internat. affairs, 1978; James D. Bruce Meml. award, 1978; 50th Anniversary Disting. Service award Blue Cross-Blue Shield, 1979; medal for contbns. to health Govt. of Ethiopia, 1979; Outstanding Alumnus award Delta Omega, 1980; Disting. Alumnus award Johns Hopkins U., 1982; Internat. Merit award Gairdner Found., 1983; Albert Schweitzer Internat. prize for medicine, 1985; Nat. Medal Sci., 1986; Richard T. Hewitt award Royal Soc. Medicine, 1986, Charles Dana Found.award for Pioneering Achievement in Health, 1986; Japan prize in Preventative Medicine, 1988. Fellow Nat. Acad. Arts and Scis., Am. Acad. Pediatrics (hon.), Royal Coll. Physicians U.K. (hon.); mem. Nat. Acad. Arts & Scis., Inst. Medicine Nat. Acad. Scis., Am. Public Health Assn., Internat. Epidemiol. Assn., Royal Coll. Physicians (Edinburgh), Royal Soc. Tropical Medicine and Hygiene, Indian Soc. Malaria and Other Communicable Diseases. Home: 3802 Greenway Baltimore MD 21218 Office: John Hopkins U Sch Hygiene Pub Health 615 N Wolfe St Baltimore MD 21205

HENDERSON, ERNEST, III, business executive; b. Boston, Oct. 25, 1924; s. Ernest and Mary G. (Stephens) H.; m. Mary Louise Campbell, Dec. 31, 1953; children—Ernest Flagg IV, Roberta Campbell. S.B., Harvard, 1944, M.B.A., 1949; L.H.D. (hon.), Bard Coll., 1976. With Sheraton Corp. Am., 1946-69, dir., 1953-69, treas., 1956-63, pres., 1963-69, chief exec. officer, 1967-69; pres. Henderson Houses Am., Inc. (and affiliates), 1969—; pres. Fidelity Products Corp. 1985—. Mem. permanent com. Harvard Class, 1946; permanent sec. Harvard U. Bus. Sch. Class, 1949; Mass. Republican jr. nat. committeeman, 1956-57; mem. Wellesley Town Meeting, 1970—; grand marshal Wellesley Vets. Day Parade, 1978; trustee, mem. exec. com. Northeastern U.; trustee Henderson Estate, Henderson Found., George B. Henderson Found., Boston Biomed. Research Inst.; trustee, treas. Boston Biomedical Research Inst.; bd. dirs. Wellesley Community Center, Inc, Robin Moore Entertainment, Inc. Served as lt. (j.g.) USNR, World War II. Named hon. Big Chief Many Tepees and blood brother Creek Indian Nation. Mem. Chief Exec.'s Orgn. Marlowe-Shakespeare Soc. (dir.), Mensa. Clubs: Wellesley Country; Harvard Business School Assn. (Boston) (past pres.); Circumnavigators. Home: 171 Edmunds Rd Wellesley Hills MA 02181 Office: Fidelity Products Corp 105 Bodwell St Avon Indsl Park Avon MA 02322

HENDERSON, EUGENE LEROY, lawyer; b. Columbus, Ind., July 21, 1925; s. Harry E. and Verna (Guffey) H.; m. Mary Louise Beatty, Sept. 6, 1948; children—Andrew, Joseph, Carrie Henderson Walkup. B.A., Franklin Coll., 1950; J.D., Harvard U., 1953. Bar: Ind. 1953. Assoc. Baker & Daniels, Indpls., 1953-59, ptnr., 1959-65; sr. ptnr. Henderson, Daily, Withrow & DeVoe and predecessor firms, Indpls., 1965—; bd. dirs. Maplehurst Group, Inc., Maplehurst Farms, Maplehurst Deli-Bake, Inc., PHD Venture Capital Corp.; sec. Ind. Fin. Investors, Inc. Mem. Ind. State Bd. Edn., 1984—; past pres. Hoosier Art Salon, bd. dirs.; trustee Franklin Coll., Lacy Found.; bd. dirs. Indpls. Boys' Club. Served with U.S. Maritime Service, 1943-44, AUS, 1944-46. Mem. Indpls. Bar Assn., Ind. Bar Assn., ABA, Internat. Law Assn., Indpls. Mus. Art. Democrat. Clubs: Indpls. Athletic, Meridian Hills Country, Skyline, Venture, Lawyers, Econ. Lodge: Rotary. Home: 6225 Sunset Ln Indianapolis IN 46260 Office: Henderson Daily Withrow & DeVoe 2450 One Indiana Sq Indianapolis IN 46204

HENDERSON, HENRY LORENZO, retired food products executive; b. Greenville, S.C., Dec. 10, 1915; s. John Clyde and Lydia (Ross) H.; m. Eugenia McMahan, Sept. 21, 1940; children: Michael L., Richard R. Certificate, Carolina Sch. Commerce, 1936; student, N.Y.U., 1951-53; advanced mgmt. program, Harvard Grad. Sch. Bus., 1964. Mgr. Nabisco Inc., N.Y.C., 1940-43, auditor, 1946-50; mgr. plant Nabisco Inc., Atlanta, 1954-59; gen. mgr. Chgo. bakeries Nabisco Inc., 1959-69, dir. mfg., 1969-72, corporate v.p. new products div., 1972, pres. spl. products div., 1973-77; chmn. bd. Nabisco-Astra Corp., 1973-77; dir. Cereal Inst., Pet Foods Inst., 1973-77; S.C.O.R.E. counselor and cons. SBA. Served to capt. AUS, 1943-46. Mem. Ill. State C. of C. (dir. 1965-69, chmn. exec. com. 1966-69), Am. Mgmt. Assn. Republican. Methodist (steward 1955—, trustee 1967-69, chmn. fin. com., mem. adminstrv. bd.). Clubs: Harvard of Chgo., Harvard of S.C., Lakeview Golf (Piedmont, S.C.). Home and Office: 407 Golf Course Rd Piedmont SC 29673

HENDERSON, ISAAC CRAIG, medical oncologist, researcher; b. Paullina, Iowa, Aug. 10, 1941; s. Isaac C. and Ora E. (Tjossem) H.; m. Mary Turner Henderson, June 11, 1966; children—Isaac Craig, Amy Hudson. A.B., Grinnell (Iowa) Coll., 1963; M.D., Columbia U., 1970. Cert. internal medicine, 1977, med. oncology, 1979. Intern Presbyterian Hosp., N.Y.C., 1970-71, resident, 1971-72; research assoc. NIH, 1972-74; instr. medicine Harvard U. Med. Sch., Boston, 1975-76, asst. prof., 1976-84, assoc. prof., 1984—; dir. Breast Evaluation Center, Dana Farber Cancer Inst., 1980—. Contbr. articles to profl. jours. Served with USPHS, 1972-74. Fulbright Research scholar, 1964-65; Merck, Sharpe and Dohme Internat. fellow, 1966; recipient Columbia Presbyterian Med. Soc. Research prize, 1970. Mem. Am. Soc. Clin. Oncology, Am. Assn. Cancer Research. Fellow ACP; mem. Soc. of Friends. Research on clin. protocols evaluating new treatment modalities for the treatment of breast cancer. Home: 8 Glengarry Rd Winchester MA 01890 Office: 44 Binney St Dana 1720 Boston MA 02115

HENDERSON, JOHN ROBERT, lawyer; b. Ft. Worth, Apr. 21, 1950; s. Julius Adrian and Jane Marie (Fitts) H.; m. Cynthia Lynn Wendland, May 27, 1972; 1 child, Michael Robert. B.B.A., U. Tex., 1972; J.D. with honors, Tex. Tech. U., 1975. Bar: Tex. 1975, U.S. Dist. Ct. (no. dist.) Tex. 1976, U.S. Dist. Ct. (ea. dist.) Tex. 1981, U.S. Ct. Appeals (5th and 11th cirs.) 1981, U.S. Dist. Ct. (we. dist.) Tex. 1983. Briefing atty. 12th Dist. Tex. Ct. Appeals, Tyler, 1975-76; assoc. Stalcup, Johnson, Meyers & Miller, Dallas, 1976-78, Meyers, Miller & Middleton, Dallas, 1978-80; assoc. Jones, Day, Reavis & Pogue, Dallas, 1981-83, ptnr., 1984—. Bd. dirs. The 500 Inc., Dallas, 1982-83, sponser, 1984, 85; bd. dirs. Dallas Opera, 1982-84, Dallas Repertory Theater, 1983-84, Dallas Civic Music Assn., 1987—. Fellow Tex. Bar Found.; mem. ABA (litigation sect., forum com. on constrn. industry), Dallas Assn. Def. Counsel, Tex. Assn. Def. Counsel, Tex. Bd. Legal Specialization (cert.), Dallas Bar Assn. (council constrn. law sect. 1983-85), Order of Coif. Episcopalian. Club: Argyle. Office: Jones Day Reavis & Pogue 2300 LTV Ctr PO Box 660623 2001 Ross Ave Dallas TX 75201

HENDERSON, KENNETH ATWOOD, investment counseling executive; b. Watertown, Mass., Oct. 18, 1905; s. Charles William and Anna Lyons (Atwood) H.; B.S., Harvard U., 1926; m. Elizabeth Berry Marshall, June 10, 1944; 1 dau., Caroline Marshall. With fgn. dept. Brown Bros. & Co., Boston, 1926-30; analyst Weil McKey & Co., Boston, 1931; salesman, engr. home and comml. heating dept. Standard Oil Co. N.J., Boston, 1932-36; investigator Raymond E. Bell, Inc., N.Y.C., 1936; analyst, editor Poor's, Babson Park, Wellesley, Mass., 1937; investment counsellor Cromwell & Cabot, Inc., Boston, 1937-42, 46-50; sr. v.p. John P. Chase, Inc., Boston, 1950-74; pvt. practice investment counselling, Waban, Mass., 1975—; dir., treas. Henniker Crutch Co. Active investment, fin. coms. 2d Ch., Newton, Mass. Served to comdr. USNR, 1942-46. Fellow Harvard Travellers Club (hon.); mem. Boston Security Analysts Soc., Bond Analysts Soc. of Boston, Public Utility Analysts Boston, Am. (asst. treas., Angelo Heilprin award 1982), Can., London alpine clubs, Harvard Mountaineering Club, Explorers Club, Appalachian Mountain Club (hon.). Author: Handbook of American Mountaineering, 1942; New England Canoeing Guide, 1965; editor: Appalachia, 1947-55; contbr. articles Am. Alpine Jour., Appalachia, Alpine Jour., others. Home: 29 Agawam Rd Waban MA 02168

HENDERSON, KENNETH REED, physician; b. Wheatland, Wyo., Jan. 19, 1935; s. Ralph Elliott and Mansella (Davis) H.; B.S. in Pharmacy, U. Wyo., 1957; postgrad. U. Tulsa, 1959-61; D.O., U. Health Sci., Kansas City, Mo., 1965; m. Nancy Alene Davis, July 31, 1962; children—Trenton Reed, Kira Leigh. Intern, Phoenix Gen. Hosp., 1965-66; gen. practice medicine, Denver, 1966—; mem. staff Valley View Hosp. and Med. Center, Gen. Rose Meml., St. Anthony's North and Mercy hosps.; chief staff Valley View Hosp. and Med. Center, 1975-77, vice chief, 1979; pres. Columbine Med. Group, 1980; bd. dirs. Comprecare, 1978—; mem. Sloans Lake Med. Group, 1980—; founder, dir., chmn. bd. Community First Nat. Bank, Thornton, Colo. Chmn., N. Denver physicians com. United Way, 1980; pres. N. Denver chpt. Colo. Assn. Children with Learning Disabilities, 1977; mem. adv. bd. Ramses II exhibit Denver Mus. Nat. Hist.; elder Broomfield Presbyn. Ch. Diplomate Am. Bd. Family Practice, Am. Osteo. Bd. Gen. Practice. Fellow Am. Acad. Family Physicians; mem. AMA (Physicians Recognition award 1977, 80), Colo. Acad. Family Physicians (chpt. pres. 1980-81, dir. 1981-82), Colo. Med. Soc. (ho. dels.), Colo. Osteo. Med. Soc. (trustee), Clear Creek Valley Med. Soc. (chmn. continuing med. edn. com. 1978, chmn. bd. censors and bd. trustees 1980-81, sec.-treas. 1981-82, v.p. 1984, pres. 1985), Tri-County Osteo. Soc. Clubs: Northglenn-Thornton Rotary, Shriners. Office: 8989 Huron St Denver CO 80221

HENDERSON, LENNEAL JOSEPH, JR., political science educator; b. New Orleans, Oct. 27, 1946; s. Lenneal Joseph and Marcelle (Heno) H. A.B., U. Calif. at Berkeley, 1968, M.A., 1969, Ph.D., 1976; postgrad. in Sci., tech. and pub. policy, George Washington U. Asst. dean students, asst. prof. govt. St. Mary's Coll., Calif., 1969-71; vis. prof. polit. sci. Xavier U., New Orleans, 1970, Howard U., Washington, 1971; dir. ethnic studies, asst. prof. govt. U. San Francisco, 1971—; prof. Morgan State U., Balt., 1975—; asst. dean Sch. of Mgmt. John F. Kennedy U., Martinez, 1974-75; vis. faculty city and regional planning dept. U. Calif. at Berkeley, 1974-75; vis. prof. Howard U., Washington, 1975-76; also lectr. polit. sci. Morgan State U., Balt.; asso. dir. research Joint Center Polit. Studies, Washington, 1977-78; pub. adminstrn. fellow U.S. Dept. Energy, 1979—; lectr. urban studies Inst. Urban Studies U. Md., College Park; for U.S. State Dept. in, Somalia, Tanzania and Nigeria, South Africa, Swaziland, India; prof. Sch. Bus. and Public Adminstrn., Howard U., 1979—; v.p. sci. and tech. Ronson Mgmt. Corp., Alexandria, Va., 1986—; prof., head dept. polit. sci., dir. Bur. Pub. Adminstrn. U. Tenn., Knoxville, 1988—; cons. Booz-Allen Pub. Adminstrn. Services, Inc., 1973-74, Shepard Assos., 1973-74, Morrison & Rowe, Inc., 1974, Dukes, Dukes & Assos., 1974-75; mem. U.S. del. Energy and Human Habitat Conf., EEC, Ottawa, Can., 1977. Editor: Black Political Life in the U.S, 1972; mem. editorial bd. Bureaucrat; contbr. articles to profl. jours. Pres., bd. dirs. Children and Youth Service Agy. of San Francisco, 1974-75; chmn. local reviewing com. San Francisco County Campaign for Human Devel., 1973-74; pres. San Francisco Youth Assn., 1964-65; mem. regional task force on open space Assn. of Bay Area Govt., 1973-75; pres., bd. dirs. African Am. Hist. and Cultural Soc., Inc., 1975-76; chmn. Mayor's Citizen Adv. Com. for Washington, 1981, Mayor's Budget Adv. Com., Washington, 1983. Recipient Disting. Faculty award Howard U., 1984, Outstanding Faculty award, 1986; Calif. State fellow, 1969-71; Urban Affairs fellow, 1969-

70; fellow Moton Center Ind. Studies, summer 1978; Nat. Assn. Schs. Public Affairs and Public Adminstrn. fellow U.S. Dept. Energy, 1978-79; research fellow Rockefeller Found.; research asso. Harvard U.; NRC postdoctoral fellow Johns Hopkins U. Sch. Advanced Internat. Studies, 1983-84; Kellogg nat. fellow, 1986. Mem. Am. Polit. Sci. Assn., Am. Soc. Pub. Adminstrn., AAAS, Western Govtl. Research Assn., Internat. Personnel Mgmt. Assn., Am. Social and Behavioral Sci. Assn. Democrat. Roman Catholic. Home: 1208 Sundew Rd Knoxville TN 37914 Office: U Tenn Dept Polit Sci 1001 McClung Tower Knoxville TN 37914

HENDERSON, LESLIE, psychology educator; b. Dalbeattie, Scotland, Apr. 13, 1942; s. George Alan and Rosina Alice Murray (Macnab) H.; m. Sheila Elizabeth Headridge. MA with 1st class honors, Glasgow (Scotland) U., 1965, DSc in Psychology, 1987; PhD in Psychology, Waterloo U., 1971. From lectr. to asst. prof. to assoc. prof. U. Guelph, Ont., Can., 1967-74; prin. lectr., reader in exptl. psychology Hatfield (Eng.) Poly., 1974—. Author: Orthography and Word Recognition in Reading, 1982; editor: Orthographies and Reading, 1984; editor Quar. Jour. of Exptl. Psychology, 1980-85; contbr. over 50 articles on cognitive psychology to profl. jours. Grantee Nat. Research Council, 1971-74, Can. Council, 1973-74, Econ. and Social Research Council, 1975-77, 78-79, 86-88, Med. Research Council, 1985-88. Mem. Exptl. Psychology Soc., British Psychol. Soc., European Soc. for Cognitive Psychology. Clubs: Zinfadel, Coonawarra (London). Office: Hatfield Poly Psychology Div, Sch Natural Scis PO Box 109, Hatfield AL10 9AB, England

HENDERSON, ROSS, business administration educator; b. Winnipeg, Man., Can., Aug. 5, 1928; s. Douglas Dudgeon and Annie Colville (Douglas) H.; m. Jeanette Kirk, Oct. 10, 1953; children—Scott Douglas, Craig Alexander, Eric Grant. B.Sc.M.E., U. Manitoba, 1955; M.B.A., Harvard U., 1957; Ph.D. in Bus., U. Western Ont., Can., 1975. Registered profl. engr., Man. Prin. Ross Henderson Ins. Co., Winnipeg, 1950-66; analyst U.S. Steel Co., Cleve., 1958-60; pres. Damascus Steel Products Ltd., Winnipeg, 1960-65; asst. gen. mgr. Dosco Steel Ltd., Montreal Works, Montreal, Que., Can., 1965-68; prof. bus. adminstrn. U. Man., Winnipeg, 1968—. Author: Plant Startup Productivity, 1975. Contbr. articles to profl. jours. Recipient Gov. Gen.'s medal, 1945; George F. Baker scholar, 1956; recipient Stanton award for Teaching Excellence, U. Man., 1977, Grad. Students' award for Teaching Excellence, U. Man., 1986, Saunderson award for Teaching Excellence at convocation 1988, U. Man. Fellow Fin. Analysts Fedn.; mem. Assn. Profl. Engrs. Man., Am. Soc. Quality Control. Avocations: running, swimming. Office: U Man, Dept Bus Adminstrn, Winnipeg, MB Canada R3T 2N2

HENDERSON, VICTOR WARREN, neurologist, educator; b. Little Rock, Aug. 20, 1951; s. Philip S. and N. Jean (Edsel) H.; m. Barbara Ann Curtiss, May 24, 1975; children—Gregory Philip, Geoffrey Victor, Stephanie Ann, Nicole Curtiss. B.S., U. Ga., 1972; M.D., Johns Hopkins U., 1976; Diplomate Am. Bd. Psychiatry and Neurology. Intern in internal medicine Duke U., Durham, N.C., 1976-77; resident in neurology Washington U., St. Louis, 1977-80; fellow in behavioral neurology Boston U., 1980-81; asst. prof. neurology U. So. Calif., Los Angeles, 1981-86, assoc. prof. neurology and gerontology, 1986—, dir. Alzheimer's Disease Research Ctr. Consortium So. Calif. Clin. Core, 1985—, co-dir. Neurobehavior Clinic/Bowles Ctr. for Alzheimer's and Related Diseases, 1981—; vis. scientist MIT, 1988—. Author: (with others) Principles of Neurologic Diagnosis, 1985. Contbr. articles to profl. jours. Nat. Merit scholar, 1968; grantee Hurd Found., Mather Found., Doheny Found., NIH, French Found., 1984—. Fellow Am. Acad. Neurology; mem. Soc. for Neurosci., Acad. of Aphasia, Gerontol. Soc. Am., Behavioral Neurology Soc., Internat. Neuropsycol. Soc., Am. Soc. for Neurol. Investigation.

HENDERSON, WILLIAM DONALD, antiquarian, consultant; b. Bluefield, W.Va., June 20, 1914; s. Thomas Ewell and Cordie Ethel (Nelson) H.; B.S.E.E., Va. Poly. Inst., 1936, postgrad. in Mech. Engring., 1938-39; postgrad. in Bus. Adminstrn., U. Pa., 1937, in Edn., U. Md., 1939-40; m. Edythe May Edwards, 1957. Docent, Am. Automobile Assn., Washington; jr. engr. Washington Inst. Tech., College Park, Md., 1940-41; civilian electronics engr. Airborne Communications and Nav., Design Br., Bur. Ships, Navy Dept., Washington, 1941-46; pvt. practice real estate mgmt., Cleveland, Ga., 1946-52, 54—; owner Henderson Lumber Co., 1945—; field service rep. nav. electronic guidance and control of Matador, Glenn L. Martin Co., Essex, Md., 1953; surveyor White County, Ga., 1960-64, 76-80. Mem. AAAS, Am. Def. Preparedness Assn. (life), U.S. Naval Inst. (life), History of Sci. Soc. (life), Tailhook Assn. (life). Developer surveying techniques; inventor entrance lock and deadbolt, doorknocker; author: Minerals of White County, Georgia, 1987. Avocation: genealogy. Office: PO Box 164 Cleveland GA 30528

HENDERSON, WILLIAM JOHN, educator; b. Germiston, S. Africa, Aug. 3, 1937; s. William John and Evelyn May (Smith) H.; m. Dorothy Ann Forster, Jan. 1, 1963; children: Frances, John, Graham, Catherine, Andrew. BA, U. Stellenbosch, 1958, BA with honors, 1960, MA, 1964, D.Litt., 1971. Lectr. U. Orange Free State, Bloemfontein, 1960-66; sr. lectr. U. Natal, Pietermaritzburg, 1967-69; sr. lectr. Rand Afrikaans U., Johannesburg, 1970-74, prof., 1974—. Co-author: Kalliope I, 1986, Kalliope II, 1988, Bibliographia Classica Austro-Africana, 1986; contbr. articles to profl. jours. Brit. Council scholar, 1965-66; Human Scis. Research Council Pretoria scholar, 1976, sr. scholar, 1983. Mem. Classical Assn. S. Africa (chmn. 1979-81). Methodist. Office: Rand Afrikaans U, Empire Rd, Johannesburg Republic of South Africa

HENDRAWAN, FRANS, oil company executive; b. Mataram, Indonesia, Nov. 12, 1936; s. Kusuma Widjaja and Bie Nio Kam; m. Yokki Ratnawati Hendrawan, Sept. 4, 1972; children—Albert Mulyadi, Andrew Darmadi, Henry Setiadi. M. Degree in Econs., Parahyangan U., 1971. Lectr. Parahyangan U., Bandung, 1969-71; adminstrn. mgr. PT Astra Internat. Inc., Jakarta, Indonesia, 1972-73, adminstrn., fin. mgr., 1973, gen. mgr., 1973-75; fin., adminstrn. dir. PT Djaya Pirusa, Jakarta, 1976-78; mng. dir. PT Midas Oil, Jakarta, 1978—. Mem. Ikatan Sarjana Ekonomi Indonesia (dep. chmn.), Indonesia Fin. Execs. Assn. (sec. II). Home: Jln Surya Utama 111/7, Kedoya, Jakarta 11520, Indonesia Office: PT Midas Oil, Jln Gaya Motor Raya #6, Sunter II, PO Box 41, Jakarta Utara JKT 14001, Indonesia

HENDREN, ROBERT LEE, JR., furniture company executive, academic administrator; b. Reno, Oct. 10, 1925; s. Robert Lee and Aleen (Hill) H.; student U. Idaho, 1943-44, 46-47; BA magna cum laude Coll. Idaho; m. Merlyn Churchill, June 14, 1947; children: Robert Lee IV, Anne Aleen. Pres., Hendren's Furniture Co., Boise, Idaho; pres. Coll. Idaho, Caldwell; dir. Shore Club Lodge, Inc., 1st Interstate Bank Idaho., Blue Cross of Idaho. Trustee Boise Ind. Sch. Dist.; charter dir. Boise Valley Indsl. Found.; chmn. bd. trustees Coll. of Idaho; trustee Boise Ind. Sch. Dist.; mem. Boise Redevel. Agy. Mem. Boise Retail Mchts. (chmn.), C. of C. (pres., dir.), Am. Inst. Interior Designers, Idaho Sch. Trustees Assn., Sigma Chi. Clubs: Arid, Hillcrest, Masons, K.T., Shriner, Rotary. Home: 3504 Hillcrest Dr Boise ID 83705 Office: College of Idaho Caldwell ID 83605-9990

HENDRICK, NANCY CROWELL, educator; b. Nashua, N.H., Feb. 4, 1914; d. Walter Andrew and Bertha Jane (Griffin) Crowell; m. Paul Hendrick, Nov. 29, 1941; children—Constance Jane Hendrick Post, Sandra Margaret Hendrick Adler, Peter Crowell Hendrick. A.B., Barnard Coll., 1935; postgrad. U. N.H., U. Maine, Boston U., Harvard U. Tchr. Alvirne High Sch., Hudson, N.H., 1953-57, West High Sch., Manchester, N.H., 1957-60, Nashua High Sch., N.H., 1960-68, Pinkerton Acad., Derry, N.H., 1969-71. Founding dir. N.H. Council World Affairs, Durham, 1979—; mission council rep. and vice chmn. Women's concerns team Presbyn. Synod of the Northeast, Syracuse, N.Y., 1980-87; dir., past pres. N.H. Assn. Conservation Commns., Concord, 1974-87; mem., past. chmn. Litchfield Conservation Commn., N.H., 1970-87; state rep. N.H. Gen. Ct., Concord, 1978-86; bd. dirs. Merrimack River Watershed Council, West Newbury, Mass., 1984-87, Matthew Thornton Health Plan, Nashua, 1978-82; vice moderator No. New Eng. Presbytery, 1978-87; founder, bd. dirs. Litchfield LWV. Mem. Orgn. Women Legislators. Democrat. Avocations: skiing; canoeing; theatre drama coach; choir director. Home: 6177 W Pebble Beach Dr Banning CA 92220

HENDRICKS, NATHAN VANMETER, III, lawyer; b. Decatur, Ga., Dec. 16, 1943; s. Nathan VanMeter and Ella L. (Ward) H.; B.A., Washington and Lee U., 1966, LL.B., 1969; m. Kathryn A. Barnes, Aug. 19, 1972; children—Nathan VanMeter, Seaton Grantland. Bar: Ga. 1970. Practiced in Atlanta, 1969—; assoc. firm Swift, Currie, McGhee and Hiers, 1969-70, Henning, Chambers and Mabry, 1970-71; asso. firm Redfern, Butler and Morgan, 1971-73, partner, 1973-77; partner firm Cobb, Hyre, Hendricks & Ferguson, Atlanta, 1978—. Chmn. Younger Lawyers Com. Campaign for mayor, Atlanta, 1972, re-election campaign for chmn. of Fulton County Bd. Commnrs., 1986; active host com. 1988 Dem. Nat. Conv. Mem. High Mus. of Art, group leader ann. fund-raising campaign, 1973-75, chmn. young careers group, 1972-73, sec. young men's round table, 1974-75; active ann. fund raising campaign Atlanta Symphony Orch. Assn., 1977-78, Atlanta Arts Alliance, 1977-79, Atlanta Botanical Garden, 1986-88; bd. dirs. Atlanta Hunter-Jumper Classic, 1978-79, pres., 1979; bd. dirs. Save America's Vital Environment, sec., 1971-74; bd. dirs. Merrie-Woode Found., v.p., 1978-79, chmn., pres., 1981—, exec. com. Give Wildlife a Chance fund Ga. Dept. Natural Resources, 1988. Mem. Am., Atlanta (mem. real estate sect. 1972—, com. 1978) bar assns., State Bar of Ga. (mem. real estate sect. 1972—), Lawyers Club Atlanta, Washington and Lee U. Alumni Assn. (dir. 1972—, pres. Atlanta chpt. 1973-75), Beta Theta Pi, Phi Delta Phi. Episcopalian. Clubs: Ansley Golf, Piedmont Driving, Wildcat Cliffs Country, The Nine O'Clocks, Pan Tex. Assembly, N.C. Soc. of the Cincinnati. Home: 230 The Prado Atlanta GA 30309 Office: 6085 Lake Forrest Dr Suite 200 Atlanta GA 30328

HENDRICKSON, JEROME ORLAND, trade association executive, lawyer; b. Eau Claire, Wis., July 25, 1918; s. Harold and Clara (Halverson) H.; student Wis. State Coll., 1936-39; J.D., U. Wis., 1942; m. Helen Phoebe Harty, Dec. 27, 1948; children—Jaime Ann, Jerome Orland. Bar: Wis., 1942, U.S. Supreme Ct., 1955; sole practice, Eau Claire, 1946; sales and advt. mgr. Eau Claire Coca-Cola Bottling Co., Inc., 1947-48; exec. sec. Eau Claire Community Chest, 1948-49; in charge dist. office Am. Petroleum Inst., Kansas City, Mo., 1950-53, Chgo., 1953-55; exec. dir. Nat. Assn. Plumbing-Heating-Cooling Contractors, 1955-64; sec. Joint Apprentice Text, Inc., 1955-64; exec. v.p. Cast Iron Soil Pipe Inst., Washington, 1964-74; pres. Valve Mfrs. Assn., McLean, Va., 1975-80; exec. v.p. Plumbing and Piping Industry Council, Inc., 1981—. Treas., Wis. Community Chest, 1948-49. Treas., All-Industry Plumbing & Heating Modernization Com., 1956-57; co-sec. Joint Industry Program Com., 1958-64. Served to lt. USNR, 1943-46. Mem. ABA, Wis. Bar Assn., Am. Soc. Assn. Execs., Washington Soc. Assn. Execs., Wis. State Soc. Washington (pres. 1966-68), Nat. Conf. Plumbing-Heating-Cooling Industry (chmn. 1967-69), NAM, U. Wis. Alumni Assn., U. Wis. Law Sch. Alumni Assn. Washington (pres. 1970-74), C. of C. of U.S., Gamma Eta Gamma (pres. Upsilon chpt. 1941-42). Episcopalian. Mason (32 deg., Shriner). Clubs: Washington Golf and Country, Internat. (Washington). Home: 4621 N 33d St Arlington VA 22207 Office: Plumbing & Piping Industry Council 501 Shatto Pl Suite 405 Los Angeles CA 90020

HENDRICKSON, ROBERT AUGUSTUS, lawyer; b. Indpls., Aug. 9, 1923; s. Robert Augustus and Eleanor Riggs (Atherton) H.; m. Virginia Reiland Cobb, Feb. 3, 1951 (div. 1980); m. Zita Davisson, May 12, 1981; children—Alexandra Kirk, Robert Augustus III. Cert., Yale U., 1943, U. Besancon, France, 1945, U. Sorbonne, France, 1946; J.D., Harvard U., 1948. Bar: N.Y. 1949, Ind. 1948, Fla. 1971, U.S. Supreme Ct. 1959, U.S. Ct. Internat. Trade 1978. Assoc. Lord, Day & Lord, N.Y.C., 1948-52; law asst. to Surrogates of N.Y. County, 1952-54; assoc. Breed, Abbott & Morgan, 1954-67; ptnr. Lovejoy, Wasson, Lundgren & Ashton, 1967-76; counsel Coudert Bros., N.Y.C., 1977-78, ptnr., 1979-86; counsel Citibank N.A., 1986-87; ptnr. Eaton & Van Winkle, N.Y.C., 1987—; bd. dirs. Sebring Lakes Inc., St. Martin's Press, Inc., Grove's Dictionaries of Music Inc.; chmn., bd. dirs. Hendrickson Asset Mgmt. Assistance Cons.; vis. prof. U. Miami, Coral Gables, Fla., 1976; mem. sec. of State's Adv. Group on Trusts, 1983—; trade rep. U.S. Sec. of Commerce Industry Sector Adv. Com. on Services in Trade, 1985—. Author: The Future of Money, 1970; The Cashless Soc., 1972; Hamilton I 1757-1789; Hamilton II 1789-1804; The Rise and Fall of Alexander Hamilton, 1981; others; producer The Ramayana, 1975; contbr. articles to profl. jours. Bd. dirs., sec. Mental Health Assn. of N.Y.C. and Bronx Counties, 1964-74; trustee, v.p. Friendly Homes Inc., 1960-80; trustee Hosp. Chaplaincy, 1960-85, Internat. Ctr. Disabled, 1968—, St. Hilda's and St. Hugh's Sch., 1968-81, Clinton Hall Assn., 1987—, Carl Duisberg Soc., 1976—, chmn., chief exec. officer, 1983-87. Served to 1st lt. U.S. Army, 1951. Decorated Bronze Star, Purple Heart with oak cluster; Yale U. regional scholar, 1941-42; Phelps Assn. scholar, 1942; Officer's Cross of Order of Merit, 1st Class (Bundesverdienst-Kreuz ersteklasse), Fed. Republic Germany, 1987. Mem. ABA, N.Y. State Bar Assn. (editor-in-chief N.Y. Internat. Law Rev., sect. of internat. law and practice), Am. Coll. Probate Counsel, SAR, Ind. Bar Assn., Assn. of Bar of City of N.Y., Fla. Bar, Consular Law Soc. (pres. 1982-83, chmn. 1983-85), Am. Fgn. Law Assn. (v.p. 1982, pres. 1983-87), Internat. Acad. Estate and Trust Law (exec. council), Am. Soc. Internat. Law, Am. br. Internat. Law Assn., Maritime Law Assn. of U.S., Bankruptcy Lawyers Bar Assn., N.Y. Commerce and Industry Assn. (chmn. com. on trusts 1964-68), Union Internat. des Avocats, Inst. Mgmt. Cons. Inc., Assn. Mgmt. Cons. Inc. Republican. Episcopal. Clubs: Century Assn., Union, Racquet and Tennis, Sky, Colonial Wars, Sons of the Revolution, Pilgrims of U.S., The Church (pres. 1977-79). Office: Eaton & Van Winkle 600 Third Ave 39th Floor New York NY 10016

HENDRICKSON, ROBERT MELAND, insurance company executive; b. Fargo, N.D., Aug. 23, 1929; s. Reinhard Oscar and Beatrice Harriet (Meland) H.; m. Kathleen McCauley, 1950 (div. 1979); children: David, Nancy; m. Patricia Kruk, 1981. BS, N.D. State U., 1950; DCL (hon.), St. Augustine Coll., 1986; LLD (hon.), N.D. State U., 1987. With Equitable Life Assurance Soc., N.Y.C., 1950—, exec. v.p., chief investment officer, 1975-80, exec. v.p., chief ins. officer, 1980-81, exec. v.p., asst. to chief exec. officer, 1981-86, vice chmn., 1986—, also bd. dirs. Chmn. investment com. U.S. Olympic Com., 1980—; former dir. United Student Aid Funds, Burlington No., Inc.; past mem. N.Y. State Employees Retirement System Adv. Bd., Mfrs. Hanover Trust Co. Adv. Bd. Mem. Am. Econs. Assn., Am. Fin. Assn. Clubs: Econ. N.Y., Huntington Country, Waccabuc Country, Univ. Office: Equitable Fin Cos 787 7th Ave Suite 4804 New York NY 10019

HENDRIE, ELAINE, public relations executive; b. Bklyn., d. David and Pearl (Saltzhauer) Kostell; m. Joseph Mallam Hendrie, July 9, 1949; children: Susan, Barbara. Asst. account exec. Benjamin Sonnenberg Public Relations firm, N.Y.C., 1953-57; pub. relations cons., writer, editor, 1957-72; dir. pub. relations and media Religious Heritage of Am., Washington, 1973-75; producer, interviewer Woman to Woman radio program, sta. WRIV and stas. WALK-AM and -FM, L.I., N.J., Westchester County, N.Y., Conn., 1974-77; exec. dir. Women in New Directions, Inc., Suffolk County, N.Y., 1974-77, cons. 1978—; nat. media coordinator NOW, Washington, 1978; media dir. Am. Speech-Lang.-Hearing Assn., Washington, 1979-80; pub. info. officer, head media and mktg. Dept. Navy, Washington, 1980-81; pres. Triangle Enterprises, 1982, Hendrie & Pendzick, 1982—; resource person for media Nat. Commn. on Observance of Internat. Women's Yr., 1977—; cons. Multi-Media Prodns. Inc., N.Y.C., 1978—, Women in New Directions, Inc., 1981—. Mem. adv. bd. Women's Ctr., SUNY-Farmingdale; mem. exec. bd. Energy Edn. Exponents, 1983—; chmn. Bellport (N.Y.) Bd. Archtl. Review, 1986—; mem. exec. bd. L.I. chpt. Am. Nuclear Soc. Club: Bellport Bay Yacht. Home: 50 Bellport Ln Bellport NY 11713

HENDRIX, DENNIS RALPH, energy industry, engineering and construction executive; b. Selmer, Tenn., Jan. 8, 1940; s. Forrest Ralph and Mary Lee (Tull) H.; m. Jennie L. Moore, Dec. 28, 1960; children—Alisa Lee, Natalie Moore, Amy Louise. B.S., U. Tenn., 1962; M.B.A., Ga. State U., 1967. C.P.A., Ga. Staff accountant, cons. Arthur Andersen & Co., Atlanta, 1962-65; faculty Ga. Inst. Tech., 1965-67; sr. cons. Touche, Ross & Co., Memphis, 1967-68; pres. United Foods, Inc., Memphis, 1968-73; asst. to pres. Tex. Gas Transmission Corp., Owensboro, Ky., 1973-75, pres., 1976-83, chief exec. officer, 1978-83; vice chmn. CSX Corp., 1983-84; exec. v.p., dir. Halliburton Co., Dallas, 1984-85; pres., chief exec. officer, dir. Tex. Eastern Corp., Houston, 1985-87, chief exec. officer, 1987—; dir. First City Bancorp. of Tex., Inc.; mem. U. Tex. Coll. Engring. Adv. Council, Ga. State Adv. Council. Bd. dirs. Nat. Jr. Achievement, Tex. South Coast United Way, Cen. Houston, Inc., U. Tenn. Devel. Council, Tex. Dept. Corrections; mem. Ga. State U. Bus. Sch. Adv. Bd., U. Tex. Coll. Engring. Adv. Council. Mem. Am Petroleum Inst. (bd. dirs.), Conf. Bd. Presbyterian. Clubs: Burning Tree (Washington); Ramada, Houston Ctr., River Oaks Country, Forum (Houston) (bd. dirs.); Castle Pines (Castle Rock, Colo.). Office: Tex Eastern Corp PO Box 2521 Houston TX 77001

HENDRY, ROBERT RYON, lawyer; b. Jacksonville, Fla., Apr. 23, 1936; s. Warren Candler and Evalyn Marguerite (Ryon) H.; m. Lee Comstock, June 21, 1956; children: Lorraine Evalyn, Lynette Comstock, Krista Ryon. BA, in Polit. Sci., U. Fla., 1958, JD, 1963. Bar: Fla. 1963. Assoc. Harrell, Caro, Middlebrooks & Wiltshire, Pensacola, Fla., 1963-66; assoc. Helliwell, Melrose & DeWolf, Orlando, Fla., 1966-67, ptnr., 1967-69; ptnr., pres. Hoffman, Hendry, Parker & Smith and predecessor Hoffman, Hendry & Parker, Orlando, 1969-77, Hoffman, Hendry & Stoner and predecessor, Orlando, 1977-82, Hendry, Stoner, Sims & Sawicki, Orland, 1982-88, Hendry, Stoner, Townsend & Sawicki, 1988—. Author: U.S. Real Estate and the Foreign Investor, 1983; contbr. articles to profl. jours. Mem. Dist. Export Council, 1977—, vice chmn., 1981; bd. dirs. World Trade Ctr. and predecessor, Orlando, 1979—, pres., 1980-82, 84; chmn. Fla. Gov.'s Conf. on World Trade, 1983; mem. internat. fin. and mktg. adv. bd. U. Miami Sch. Bus., Fla. Commn. on Internat. Edn., 1986-88. Served to 1st lt. U.S. Army, 1958-60, to capt. Army N.G., 1960-70. Mem. Fla. Council Internat. Devel. (bd. dirs. 1972-85, chmn. 1977-79, adv. bd. 1985—), Fla. Bar (vice chmn. internat. law com. 1974-75, chmn. com. 1976-77, mem. exec. council internat. law sect. 1982—, v.p. Fla. Assn. Voluntary Agys. for Caribbean Action 1987—), Orange County Bar Assn. (treas. 1971-74), Brit.-Am. C. of C. (bd. dirs., sec. 1984-85). Club: University (Orlando). Office: Hendry Stoner Townsend & Sawicki 205 E Central Blvd Orlando FL 32801

HENDRY, ROSEMARY JOY, social anthropology educator; b. Birmingham, Eng., Oct. 23, 1945; d. Duncan William and Edna Beatrice (Woodley) H.; m. Dennis Charles Kay; children: James Dennis Burke, William John Hendry. BSc with honors, Kings Coll., London, 1966; diploma in Social Anthropology, Oxford U., 1972; BLitt in Social Anthropology, 1974, DPhil in Social Anthropology, 1979. Tchr. Casablanca, Morocco, 1966-67, Montreal, Que., Can., 1967-68, Tokyo, 1970-71; journalist Mexico City, 1968-70; sr. lectr. social anthropology Oxford Poly., 1979—; cons. BBC, U.K. and Japan, 1979, Brit. Airways, U.K. and Japan, 1985. Author: Marriage in Changing Japan, 1981, Becoming Japanese, 1986, Understanding Japanese Society, 1987; co-editor Interpreting Japanese Society, 1986. Japan Found. fellow, 1981. Fellow Royal Anthrop. Inst.; mem. Assn. Social Anthropologists, Brit. Assn. Japanese Studies, European Assn. Japanese Studies, Japan Anthropology Workshop (sec.). Office: Oxford Poly, Dept Social Studies, Headington Oxford OX3 0BP, England

HENEIN, RAFICK GARAS, pharmaceutical company executive; b. Cairo, Apr. 18, 1940; s. Garas and Daisy (Badir) H.; m. Nelly Bishara, July 27, 1963; children: Tarik, Natalie. BS in Pharmacy, Cairo U., 1960, diploma in Indsl. Pharmacy, 1961; MS in Pharm. Scis., Budapest U., 1970; PhD in Pharm. Tech., Acad. Scis., Hungary, 1971; diploma in Mgmt., McGill U., Montreal, 1977, MBA, 1982. Chief pharmacist Egyptian Air Force, 1961-62; head extraction dept., liquids and ointments dept., packaging dept., Chem. Industries Devel., Cairo, 1962-65; dir. pharm. research and devel. Chinoin Labs., Budapest, Hungary, 1970-71; adminstrv. asst. to plant mgr. Ayerst Labs., Inc., Montreal, Que., 1971, prodn. control mgr., 1972-73, asst. dir. prodn., 1973-76, dir. prodn., 1977-79, dir. prodn. ops., 1980, v.p. materials mgmt., 1980-82, v.p. plant, distbn. ops., 1983-86, sr. v.p. plant, distbn. ops., 1987-88; exec. v.p. NovoPharm Ltd., Scarborough, Ont., Can., 1988—; bd. dirs. Ayerst Organics, Ltd. div. of API Lab. Products, Ltd.; lectr. U. Montreal Dept. Pharmacy, 1980—, John Abbott Coll., St. Anne de Bellevue, Que., 1982—. Mem. Order Pharmacists of Que., Pharm. Mfrs. Assn. (vice chmn. 1980-81, chmn. plant ops. sect. 1981-82, past chmn. 1982-83). Mem. Coptic Ch. Office: NovoPharm Ltd, 1290 Ellesmere Rd, Scarborough, ON Canada M1P 2Y1

HENG SAMRIN, head of state of the People's Republic Kampuchea; b. 1934. Polit. commissar and comdr. of Khmer Rouge 4th Inf. Div., 1976-78; led abortive coup against Pol Pot and fled to Vietnam, 1978; pres. Nat. Front for Nat. Salvation of Kampuchea, 1978—; pres. People's Revolutionary Council, 1979—; sec.-gen. People's Revolutionary Party of Kampuchea, 1981—. Address: Office of the Pres, Phnom-Penh People's Republic of Kampuchea *

HENGSTMENGEL, MARINUS, manufacturing executive; b. Rotterdam, Netherlands, Feb. 24, 1927; s. Pieter Jan and Jacoba Rookje (Van Noort) H.; grad. Naval Coll. (Royal), 1946; m. Wilhelmina Wildschut, May 29, 1952; children—Wilma M., Lidewey J., Richard W. Sales tech. adv. Royal Dutch Shell Group, London and The Hague, Netherlands, 1952-74, sr. exec. mktg., 1974-76, oil trader, 1976-80; founder, owner, mng. dir. ICC Ind. Coal Co. and R.S.V. Mining Equipment B.V., The Hague, 1974—; dir. Hy-Test Europe B.V., The Hague, Hy-Test Holding N.V., Holland Coal Co. N.V. (both Curacao, Netherlands Antilles), Minetech Holdings Ltd., Guernsey, Int. Mining Techn. Inc., Lexington, Ky., Foremco Corp., Lexington, ICC Inc., Houston, Tradimex Precisie Prod. B.V., Vianen, Netherlands, Tradimex Real Estate, Voorburg, Netherlands, Multifoam B.V., Varsseveld, Netherlands, N.Am. Mining Services, Inc., Lexington, Holland Am. Energy Systems Corp., Corona del Mar, Calif. Mem. Dutch industry adv. council on energy matters, 1980—. Served with Royal Dutch Navy, 1946-48. Chartered engr., Gt. Britain. Fellow Inst. Marine Engrs. Inst. Energy. Liberal. Club: Lions. Home: 2 Dr A Diepenbrockstr, 2631 BJ Nootdorp The Netherlands Office: 265 Kon Julianaln, 2273 JG Voorburg The Netherlands

HENICAN, CASWELL ELLIS, lawyer; b. New Orleans, Feb. 10, 1905; s. Joseph Patrick and Alice (Boning) H.; m. Elizabeth Cleveland, June 18, 1930 (dec. Nov. 1987); children: Alice (Mrs. Claude V. Perrier, Jr.), Caswell Ellis Jr., Margaret (Mrs. F. Gordon Wilson, Jr.), Dorothy (Mrs. Charles E. Heidingsfelder), Joseph Patrick III. LLB, Tulane U., 1926. Bar: La. 1926. Sole practice law New Orleans; assoc. Lemle, Moreno & Lemle, 1926-33; sr. ptnr. Henican, Carriere & Cleveland, 1933-40, Henican, James & Cleveland, 1940—. Chmn. La. State Bd. Pub. Welfare, 1940-47; pres. New Orleans Community Chest, 1940, Council Social Agencies, 1939, Assoc. Cath. Charities New Orleans, 1938; chmn. bd. Mercy Hosp.; mem. exec. com., pres. Magnolia Sch. Bd. Decorated Knight St. Gregory, Knight St. Louis; named Most Outstanding Young Man New Orleans Jr. C. of C., 1940; named to Tulane U. Hall of Fame, 1978, Greater New Orleans Hall of Fame, 1980. Mem. New Orleans Bar Assn., La. Bar Assn., ABA (charter mem.), Am. Acad. of Hosp. Attorneys. Home: 1401 Nashville Ave New Orleans LA 70115-4349 Office: Henican James & Cleveland 111 Veterans Blvd Suite 1200 Metairie LA 70005

HENKEL, JOHN HARMON, physics educator; b. Kentwood, La., Aug. 14, 1924; s. William Hatton and Margaret Gwendolyn (Watson) H.; student Southeastern La. Coll., 1941-43; B.S., Tulane U., 1947, M.S., 1948; Ph.D., Brown U., 1954; m. Sara Ernestine Saucier, Apr. 23, 1948; children—Wendolyn Elizabeth (dec.), Sally Lee Henkel Bone (dec.), Jenny Saucier, Margaret Loraine, Pamela Ann (dec.). Jr. research technologist Magnolia Petroleum Co., Dallas, 1948-51, sr. research technologist, 1954-55; research asst. Brown U., Providence, 1951-54; asst. prof. physics U. Ga., Athens, 1955-58, assoc. prof., 1958-64, prof., 1964—. Served with USNR, 1943-46. NSF fellow, 1959-60, grantee, 1962-69. Fellow AAAS; mem. Am. Phys. Soc., Ga. Acad. Sci., Sigma Xi, Sigma Chi. Methodist. Clubs: Kiwanis, Green Hills Country. Office: U Ga Dept Physics Athens GA 30602

HENLEY, JOSEPH OLIVER, manufacturing company executive; b. Sikeston, Mo., June 25, 1949; s. Fred Louis and Bernice (Chilton) H.; B.S.B.A., U. Mo., 1972; M.B.A., Mich. State U., 1973; m. Jane Ann Rhodes, Aug. 21, 1971. Ops. analyst Midland-Ross, Inc., Cleve., 1974, prodn. control mgr., 1974-75, engring. systems mgr. Cameron-Waldron div. Somerset, N.J., 1976; prodn. control mgr., 1976-77; prodn. planning and mfg. systems mgr. ICM div. Massey Ferguson, Inc., Akron, Ohio, 1977-78; sr. audit specialist (mfg.) United Techs. Corp., Hartford, Conn., 1978-82, mfg. control systems mgr. UT Diesel Systems div., 1983-84, materials mgr., 1983-84, internal cons., 1984-86; inventory mgr. Pratt & Whitney Aircraft div., 1986—. Served with Army N.G., 1970-72. Mem. Nat. Assn. Purchasing Mgmt., Am. Prodn. and Inventory Control Soc., Beta Gamma Sigma, Sigma Iota Epsilon, Omicron Delta Epsilon. Presbyterian. Home: 25 Duncaster Ln Vernon CT 06066 Office: 400 Main St East Hartford CT 06108

HENLEY, PRESTON VANFLEET, former banker, financial consultant; b. Fort Madison, Iowa, July 7, 1913; s. Jesse vanFleet and Ruth (Roberts) H.; m. Elizabeth Artis Watts, Mar. 31, 1940 (div. June 1956); children: Preston Edward VanFleet, Stephen Watts, John vanFleet; m. 2d, Helena Margaret Greenslade, Nov. 29, 1964; 1 adopted son, Lawrence D. Student Tulane U., 1931-34, Loyola U., New Orleans, 1935-36; A.B., Calif. State Coll. at Santa Barbara, 1939; postgrad. U. Wash., 1939-40, N.Y. U., 1943, 46. Teaching fellow U. Wash., 1939-40; sr. credit analyst, head credit dept. Chase Nat. Bank, 45th St. br. N.Y.C., 1942-49; Western sales rep. Devoe & Raynolds, Inc., N.Y.C., 1949-51; v.p., comml. loan officer, mgr. credit dept. U.S. Nat. Bank, Portland, Oreg., 1951-72; loan agtminstr. Voyageur Bank Group, Eau Claire, Wis.; v.p. Kanabec State Bank, Mora, Minn., Montgomery State Bank (Minn.), Park Falls State Bank (Wis.), Montello State Bank (Wis.), 1972; v.p., mgr. main office, sr. credit officer So. Nev. region Nev. Nat. Bank, Las Vegas, 1973-75; bus. and fin. cons., 1975—; loan cons. Continental Nat. Bank, Las Vegas, 1983—; instr. Am. Inst. Banking, Portland, 1952-65, Multomah Coll., Portland, 1956-62, Portland State U., 1961-72, Mt. Hood Community Coll., 1971-72, Clark County Community Coll., 1979-83; adv. dir. Vita Plus, Inc., 1979-83; exec. dir. Nev. Minority Purchasing Council, 1979-80; dir., treas. Consumer Credit Counselling Service of Oreg. 1965-72. Treas., Ore. chpt. Leukemia Soc., 1965-66; mem. Menninger Found. 1965-67; trustee, exec. com. St. Rose delima Hosp. Found., 1982-87;dir. So. Nev. chtp. Assn. Part-Time Profls., 1985-87. Served with USNR, 1943-45. Mem. Oreg. Bankers Assn., Robert Morris Assos. (pres. Oreg. chpt. 1959-60, nat. dir. 1961-64), Nat., Oreg. assns. credit mgmt., Credit Research Found., Inst. Internal Auditors, S.A.R., Am. Legion, Navy League, Beta Mu, Leaf and Scarab, Alpha Phi Omega, Portland C. of C., Oreg. Retail Council. Republican. Episcopalian. Mason (32 deg., Shriner), Elk. Club: International. Contbr. articles to profl. jours. Home and Office: 4235 Gibraltar St Las Vegas NV 89121

HENLEY, WILLIAM BALLENTINE, lawyer, rancher; b. Cin., Sept. 19, 1905; s. William Herbert and May G. (Richards) Ballentine (later assumed name of stepfather, Charles E. Henley); m. Helen McTaggart, 1942. A.B., U. So. Calif., 1928; postgrad., Sch. Religion, 1928-29, Yale, 1929-30; M.A., U. So. Calif., 1930, J.D., 1933, M.S. in P.A, 1935; LL.D., Willamette U., 1937; Sc.D., Kansas City Coll. Osteopathy and Surgery, 1949; R.Sc.D., Inst. Religious Sci. and Philosophy, 1949; L.H.D. Los Angeles Coll. Optometry, 1958; Sc.D., Pepperdine Coll., 1966. Lectr. pub. adminstrn., asst. to coordination officer U. So. Calif., 1928-29; dir. religious edn. First Meth. Ch., New Haven, 1929-30; lectr. in pub. adminstrn. U. So. Calif., 1930-33; exec. sec. U. So. Calif. (Women's Civic Conf.), 1930-40; acting dean U. So. Calif. (Sch. of Govt.), 1937-38; dir. U. So. Calif. (8th and 9th Inst. Govt.), 1937-38; asst. to dean U. So. Calif. (Sch. Govt., in charge in-service tng., Civic Center), 1934-36, asst. prof. pub. adminstrn., 1935-39, asso. prof., 1939-40, dir. co-ordination, 1938-40; pub. speaking instr. and debate coach Am. Inst. Banking, 1928-40; pres. Calif. Coll. Medicine, Los Angeles, 1940-66, Coll. Osteopathic Surgeons, 1940-66; provost U. Calif. at Irvine-Calif. Coll. Medicine, 1966-69; pres., chmn. bd. trustees United Ch. Religious Sci., 1969—; prof. United Ch. Religious Sci. (Sch. Ministry), 1972—; exec., speakers' panel Gen. Motors Corp., 1956-75. Author: The History of the University of Southern California, 1940, Man's Great Awakening, or Beautiful Mud, 1974, also mag. articles. Bd. dirs. Glendale Community Hosp., Glendale Adventist Med. Center, 1978-85; mem. Bd. Water and Power Commrs., Los Angeles, 1944-62, pres., 1946, v.p., 57-58; mem. Employees' Pension and Retirement Bd. Mgmt, 1946; mem. adv. bd. Los Angeles County Gen. Hosp., 1940-65; v.p. Los Angeles County Safety Council, 1971—; mem. Los Angeles Def. Council, 1941-44, War Council, 1944-45, Calif. Civil Def. Com.; guest observer UN Conf., San Francisco, 1945, A.T. Still Meml. lectr., Washington, 1958. Mem. Am., Calif., Los Angeles bar assns., NEA, Am. Pub. Health Assn., AAAS, Am. Saddle Horse Breeding Futurity Assn. (dir.), Am. Aberdeen Angus Breeders Assn., Sigma Alpha Epsilon, Phi Delta Phi, Phi Kappa Phi, Phi Sigma Gamma, Sigma Sigma Phi, Delta Sigma Rho, Phi Delta Kappa, Pi Sigma Alpha, Alpha Delta Sigma, Phi Eta Sigma, Sigma Sigma, Skull and Dagger. Republican. Clubs: Mason (32 deg.), Los Angeles Rotary (pres. 1955-56, chmn. conf. dist. 160-A, gov. dist. 528 1959-60, mem. internat. community service consultative group, chmn. host club exec. com. for 1962 internat. conv., mem. world community service com.). Home and Office: Creston Circle Ranch Paso Robles CA 93446

HENNAGE, JOSEPH HOWARD, publisher, printing company executive; b. Washington, Jan. 2, 1921; s. Joseph Howard and Helen (Cook) H.; m. June Elizabeth Stedman, Sept. 29, 1947. Founder, pres. Hennage Creative Printers, Washington, 1945—; pres. Jonage Investment Corp., Washington, 1958—, Highland House Pubs. Inc., Washington, 1969—; mem. adv. bd. 1st Nat. Bank Washington, 1963-69, Am. Security and Trust Co., Washington, 1969—; chmn. joint govt.-industry adv. bd. Govt. Printing Office, 1972-78; bd. dirs. Graphic Arts Mut. Ins. Co., N.Y.C.; bd. dirs. emeritus United Ins. Co. Ltd., Hamilton, Bermuda, 1975-85; mem. fine arts com. U.S. Dept. State. Bd. dirs. Washington Bd. Trade, 1970-76, Potomacland ambassador, 1970. Mem. bus. adv. bd. George Washington U., 1967-75; chmn. Americana com. Nat. Archives, 1972-77, Printing Mgmt. Edn. Trust Fund, 1972—; mem. adv. bd. Am. Freedom Train, 1975-77; trustee Am. Cancer Soc., D.C. Cancer Soc., Balt. Mus. Art; mem. pres.'s house restoration com. Coll. of William and Mary; chmn. bd., trustee Carlyle House Found., 1978—, past pres.; bd. dirs. Boys' Club Washington, 1949-79, Gadsby's Tavern, local Meth. Ch., 1966-70. Served with USNR, 1942-45. Recipient Disting. Service award Boys' Club Washington, 1951, Alumni award Boys' Club Washington, 1959, Freedom Found. award, 1969, Brit. Fedn. Master Printers citation, 1971, Bronze medal Boys' Clubs Am., 1976; named Graphic Arts Man of Yr., 1971. Mem. Master Printers Am. (pres. 1967-69, Man of Yr. 1969), Printing Industries Am. (bd. dirs. 1964-76, exec. com. 1966-76, chmn. bd. 1969-70, v.p. pub. relations 1970-77, Disting. Service award 1972), Printing Industry Washington (pres. 1964-65, bd. dirs. 1960-74, Disting. Service award 1969), Creative Printers Am. (pres. 1963-64), Master Printers Washington (pres. 1960-61), Met. Washington Bd. Trade (bd. dirs.-at-large 1972, 78), Supreme Ct. Hist. Soc. (trustee, chmn. acquisitions com. 1975-79), Fellows of Va. Mus. Fine Arts, Raleigh Tavern Soc. of Colonial Williamsburg Found., Ash Khan Soc. (King Khan). Clubs: City Tavern of Georgetown (Washington); Columbia Country (Chevy Chase, Md.); Farmington Country (Charlottesville, Va.); Met. (N.Y.C.); La Coquille (Palm Beach, Fla.); Chatmoss (Martinsville, Va.); Med Ocean (Bermuda); Golden Horseshoe (Williamsburg, Va.); Confrerie des Chevaliers du Tastevin. Lodge: Optimist (gov. 1957-58, dir. bd. dirs. Leonard Cheshire Found., Disting. Gov. award 1958). Metropolitan (N.Y.C.); La Coquille (Palm Beach, Fla.); Chatmoss (Martinsville, Va.); Mid Ocean (Bermuda); Golden Horseshoe (Williamsburg, Va.); Confrerie des Chevaliers du Tastevin. Home: 405 S England St Williamsburg VA 23185 Office: 500 N Henry St Alexandria VA 22314

HENNBY, BO ALBERT, business consultant; b. Malmo, Scania, Sweden, Dec. 18, 1930; s. Albert B. and Annie H. (Nilsson) H.; m. Kerstin M. Sjolin; 1 child, Torbjorn. AB, Malmo (Sweden) Handels, 1951. Cert. real estate broker, Hollviken. Acct. Ewert Gussler AB, Malmo, 1959-63; sales rep. Burroughs AB, Stockholm, 1963-68; pres. Plastmo AB, Malmo, 1968-74, JW Hus AB, Malmo, 1978-82, Phildar AB, Wellinge, Sweden, 1975-78, Bo Hennby AB, Hollviken, 1968—; real estate broker Aktiv Fastighetsbyra AB, Hollviken, 1983—; tchr. Malmo Handels, 1964-66, Lunds U., 1976-77. Treas. Malmo Jr. C. of C., 1961-65; chmn. Bldg.-Planning Bd., Vellinge, 1974-79, Social Welfare Bd., 1980-85; mem. Vellinge City Bd., 1967-85. Paul Harris fellow, Rotary Youth Exchange USA, 1976-86. Mem. C. of C. (sec. 1983-85, chmn. 1986—). Lodge: Rotary (world chmn. youth exchange 1983-84). Office: Bo Hennby AB, Falsterbovagen 26, S-236 00 Hollviken Sweden

HENNECY, BOBBIE BOBO, English language educator; b. Tignall, Ga., Aug. 11, 1922; d. John Ebb and Lois Helen (Gulledge) Bobo; AB summa cum laude, Mercer U., Macon, Ga., 1950; postgrad. Oxford (Eng.) U., 1961 English-Speaking Union Scholar; MA (NDEA fellow), Emory U., 1962; postgrad. Cambridge U., Eng., 1987; m. James Howell Hennecy, Dec. 28, 1963; 1 dau., Erin. Adminstrv. asst. to pres., instr. Mercer U., 1950-61, instr. English, 1961-76, asst. prof., 1976—; a founder Tattnall Sq. Acad., Macon, 1968, sec. acad. corp., 1968-73, dir., 1968-78; Bobbie Bobo Hennecy scholarship named in her hon. Tattnall Sq. Acad., Mercer U. . Mem. AAUW (chpt. pres. 1964), MLA, S. Atlantic MLA, So. Comparative Lit. Assn., Am. Comparative Lit. Assn., Internat. Comparative Lit. Assn., Nat. Assn. Tchrs. English, Ga. Assn. Tchrs. English, English Speaking Union, LWV, Pres. Club of Mercer U., YWCA (life), Nat. Soc. So. Dames, Nat. Soc. Magna Charta, DAR (registrar 1980-82), Daus. of 1812, Descendants, Colonial Clergy, Daus. of Am. Colonists, Jamestowne Soc., UDC, Colonial Dames XVII Century (chpt. 1st v.p. 1988-90), Colonial Order of the Crown (descendents of Charlemagne), Mid. Ga. Hist. Soc., Cardinal Key, Sigma Tau Delta, Sigma Mu (past pres.), Phi Kappa Phi, Alpha Psi Omega, Chi Omega (alumnae adviser). Baptist. Home: 1347-B Adams St Macon GA 31201 Office: Mercer U Macon GA 31207

HENNEKEUSER, HANS HEINRICH, internist; b. Bonn, Fed Republic Germany, Mar. 20, 1937; s. Hans and Julia Hennekeuser; married, 1964; children: Johannes, Matthias, Christian, Delmira. MD, U. Bonn, 1962; Prof. Medicine, U. Freiburg, Fed. Republic Germany, 1971. Chief dept. medicine Krankenhaus Barmherzige Breuder, Trier, Fed. Republic Germany, 1976—. Mem. Deutsche Gesellschaft Innere Medizin, N.Y. Acad. Sci., Deutsche Gesellschaft Haematologie Onkologie, Deutsche Gesellschaft Pneumologie. Club: Bavaria (Bonn). Office: Krankenhaus Barmherzige Brueder, Nord Allee 1, D 5500 Trier Federal Republic of Germany

HENNELLY, EDMUND PAUL, lawyer, oil company executive; b. N.Y.C., Apr. 2, 1923; s. Edmund Patrick and Alice (Laccorn) H.; m. Josephine Kline; children: Patricia A. Anglin, Pamela J. Farley. BCE, Manhattan Coll., 1944; postgrad. Columbia U.; JD, Fordham U., 1950. Bar: N.Y. 1950. Instr., Manhattan Coll., 1947-50; litigation assoc. law firm Cravath, Swaine and Moore, 1950-51, sr. litigation assoc. 1953-54; asst. gen. counsel CIA, Washington, 1951-52; assoc. counsel Time, Inc., N.Y.C., 1954-56; asst. legis. cons. Mobil Oil Corp., N.Y.C., 1956-60, legis. cons., 1960-61, mgr. domestic govt. relations dept., N.Y.C., 1961-67, mgr. govt. relations dept., 1967-73, gen. mgr. govt. relations dept., 1974-78, gen. mgr. pub. affairs dept., 1978-86, pres., chief exec. officer Citroil Enterprises, 1986—; dir. South Cay Trust; dir., mem. exec. com. Home Savs. Bank, N.Y.C. Trustee, vice chmn. Daytop Village Found.; mem. adv. com. N.Y. State Legis. Com. on Higher Edn., Nassau County (N.Y.) Energy Commn., L.I. Citizens' Com. for Mass Transit, N.Y. State Def. Council; mem. White House Conf. on Natural Beauty, 1963; bd. dirs. Nat. Council on Aging; exec. com. Pub. Affairs Research Council of Conf. Bd.; mem. Nassau County Econ. Devel. Planning Council; commr. nat. com. Commn. for UNESCO, 1982-85, head U.S. del. with personal rank of ambassador 22d Gen. Conf., 1983; mem. Pres.' Intelligence Transition Team, 1980-81; cons. Pres.'s Intelligence Oversight Bd.; trustee Austen Riggs Ctr., Pub. Affairs Found. Served from ensign to lt., USNR, 1943-46, PTO, ETO. Decorated Knight of Malta, Knight of Holy Sepulchre. Mem. ABA, Fed. Bar Assn., Assn. Bar City of N.Y., Acad. Polit. and Social Scis., Am. Good Govt. Soc. (trustee), Tax Council (dir.), Pub. Affairs Council (dir.), Freedom House (trustee), Am. Mgmt. Assn., Pi Sigma Epsilon, Delta Theta Phi. Clubs: Army-Navy, Southward Ho Country, Babylon Yacht, Explorers, Metropolitan, International, George Town; Capitol Hill. Lodges: K.M., Knights Holy Sepulcher. Contbr. articles on engring. and law to profl. jours. Home: 84 Seqüams Ln E West Islip NY 11795 Office: 275 Madison Ave New York NY 10016

HENNEN, THOMAS WALDO, lawyer; b. Tacoma, Nov. 28, 1945; s. Waldo Gerhart and Ruth Elzora (George) H. A.A., Highline Coll., 1966; B.S.M.E., Wash. State U., 1969; J.D., U. Maine, 1973. Bar: Wash. 1973, U.S. Ct. Claims 1975, U.S. Patent Office, 1975, U.S. Ct. Customs and Patent Appeals 1975. Design engr. Boeing Aircraft Co., Seattle, 1969-70; patent atty. Office Naval Research, Arlington, Va., 1975, patent staff asst. for tech. and adminstrv. ops., 1979-82; patent atty. Naval Weapons Ctr., China Lake, Calif., 1975-78, dep. patent counsel, Ridgecrest, Calif., 1982-86; sr. patent atty. Boeing Aerospace Co., Kent, Washington, 1986—; patent atty. Naval Sea Systems Command, Washington, 1978-79; instr. basic patent prosecution Naval Weapons Ctr. Coach, Civitan Soccer Club, Arlington, Va., 1981-82. Mem. ASME, Wash. State Bar Assn., Govt. Patent Lawyers Assn., Nat. Rifle Assn. (life), Indian Wells Valley Bar Assn. (pres. 1977). Clubs: Sierra Desert Gun, China Lake Trap and Skeet (Ridgecrest). Author: Navy Patent Administrative Guide, 1981, 2d edit., 1982. Office: Boeing Aerospace PO Box 3999 Mailstop 84-74 Seattle WA 98124-2499

HENNEQUET, JEAN-PIERRE, business executive; b. Paris, May 3, 1947; s. Andre and Jacqueline (Morelle) H.; m. Agnes Le Roux, Nov. 27, 1969 (div. 1976); m. Nicole Torck, July 7, 1977; children—Maxime, Martin, Claire. Diploma, Inst. Polit. Studies, Paris, 1969. Attache Ministry of Planification, Abidjan, Ivory Coast, 1970-71; buyer Societe Ah! Internationale, Chaignolles, France, 1972-77, pres., 1977—; co-founder, mgr. Societe l'Entrepot, Paris, 1977—; pres. Salon Table & Cuisine, Paris, 1984-86, Euro-Devel. S.A., 1986—; gen. mgr. Z.E.U.S., Paris, 1986—; expert EEC Dept for Devel. Utilitarian Handicrafts in Third World Countries, Brussels and Paris, 1975-80. Co-editor Intra-Muros, 1985—. Gen. sec. French Nat. Ctr. for Culinary Arts, 1985-86; dir. Nat. Housewares Trade Show, 1986—. Mem. Association pour la Promotion des Arts et Ustensiles culinaires (founder), Centre Etudes Prive-Public. Avocations: travel; skiing. Home: 8 rue Edouard Fournier, 75116 Paris France Office: ZEUS, 2 rue de la Paix, 75002 Paris France also: L'Entrepot, 50 rue de Passy, 75016 Paris France

HENNESSEY, WILLIAM JOSEPH, physician; b. Troy, N.Y., Mar. 8, 1947; s. Joseph William and Loretta (Brooks) H.; m. Patricia McMahon, Jan. 23, 1983; children—Bridget Marie, Jason William, Matthew Brian. B.S., Rensselaer Poly. Inst., 1969; M.D., Albany Med. Coll., 1973. Resident in ob-gyn Albany (N.Y.) Med. Center Hosp., 1973-76; pvt. practice specializing in ob-gyn. Troy, N.Y., 1976—; attending physician St. Peter's Hosp., Leonard Hosp., Meml. Hosp., Albany Med. Ctr. Hosp., Samaritan Hosp., treas. med. staff Samaritan Hosp., 1988; clin. asst. dept. ob-gyn Albany Med. Center and Albany Med. Coll., 1976—; bd. dirs. PSRO, 1981-85, PRO, 1985-86. Fellow Am. Coll. Ob-Gyn; mem. Am. Chem. Honor Soc., AMA, N.Y. State Med. Soc., Rensselaer County Med. Soc., Northeast Ob-Gyn Soc., Northeastern N.Y. Health Care Consortium, Am. Assn. Gynecol. Laparoscopists. Republican. Roman Catholic.

HENNESSY, EDWARD LAWRENCE, JR., diversified aerospace/automotive products and engineered materials executive; b. Boston, Mar. 22, 1928; s. Edward Lawrence and Celina Mary (Doucette) H.; m. Ruth Frances Schilling, Aug. 18, 1951; children: Michael E., Elizabeth R. BS, Fairleigh Dickinson U., 1955; student, NYU. With Heublein, Inc., Hartford, Conn., 1965-72; v.p. fin. Heublein, Inc., 1965-68, sr. v.p. adminstrn., fin., 1969-72; sr. v.p. fin. and adminstrn. United Techs. Corp., Hartford, 1972-77; chief fin. officer, group v.p. United Techs. Corp. (Systems and Equipment Group), 1977, exec. v.p., 1978-79; chmn., pres., chief exec. officer Allied Corp., Morris Township, N.J., from 1979; chmn., chief exec. officer Allied-Signal Inc., 1985—; bd. dirs. Nova Pharm. Corp., Martin Marietta Corp., DNA Plant Tech., Bank of N.Y. Trustee Cath. U. Am.; trustee Fairleigh Dickinson U., USCG Found. Served with USNR, 1949-55. Mem. Fin. Execs. Inst., Econ. Club N.Y. Roman Catholic. Clubs: Cat Cay (Bahamas); N.Y. Yacht; Ocean Reef, Anglers (Key Largo, Fla.).

HENNESSY, JOHN FRANCIS, consulting engineer; b. N.Y.C., July 18, 1928; s. John F. and Dorothy (O'Grady) H.; m. Barbara McDonnell, Oct. 24, 1953; children—John, Kathleen, James, Kevin, Peter, David; m. Bruce Rial, Dec. 30, 1971. B.S. in Physics, Georgetown U., 1949; B.S. in Engring, Mass. Inst. Tech., 1951. Registered profl. engr., N.Y., Calif., Colo., Conn., Va., D.C., Ga., N.J., Ill., Ind., others. With Syska & Hennessy, Inc., N.Y.C., 1951—; exec. v.p. Syska & Hennessy, Inc., 1955-66, pres., 1967—, chmn., chief exec. officer, 1973—; former dir. Franklin Soc. Fed. Savs. & Loan; chmn. pres. In The Pink, Inc., N.Y.C., WTB, Inc., N.Y.C. Mem. exec. bd. Greater N.Y. council Boy Scouts Am., 1958—; former chmn. bd. trustees Whitby Sch.; past trustee Clark Coll., Atlanta; former mem. bd. dirs. Catholic Interracial Council; bd. dirs. N.Y. Heart Assn., Battery Park City Authority; former mem. MIT Ednl. Council; mem. vis. com. Sloan Sch. Mgmt., MIT. Served with USAF, 1951-52. Fellow Am. Cons. Engrs. Council; mem. Nat., N.Y. State, Conn. socs. profl. engrs., N.Y. Assn. Cons. Engrs. (past pres.), N.Y. Bldg. Congress, Soc. Am. Mil. Engrs., ASME. Clubs: River (N.Y.C.), Links (N.Y.C.), Univ. (N.Y.C.); Capitol Hill (Washington), Fed. City (Washington), Met. (Washington); Annabels, Marks (London); Castells, Travellers (Paris). Office: 11 W 42 St New York NY 10036

HENNESSY, PETER JOHN, journalist, writer; b. London, Mar. 28, 1947; s. William Gerald and Edith (Wood-Johnson) H.; m. Enid Mary Candler, June 14, 1969; children: Cecily Frances, Polly Louise. BA, Cambridge U., 1969; postgrad., London Sch. Econs., 1969-71, Harvard U., 1971-72. Reporter Times Higher Edn. Supplement, London, 1972-74; reporter The Times, London, 1974-76, Whitehall corr., 1976-82, Whitehall leader writer, 1982-84; polit. corr. Fin. Times, London, 1976; Britain specialist The Economist, London, 1982; sr. fellow Policy Studies Inst., London, 1984-85, vis. fellow, 1984—; co-dir. Inst. Contemporary Brit. History, London, 1986—; columnist New Statesman, London, 1987-88, The Independent, London, 1987—; presenter Analysis, BBC, London, 1987-88; vis. lectr. politics Strathclyde U., Glasgow, Scotland, 1983-84, hon. research fellow, 1984—. Co-author: States of Emergency, 1983, Sources Close to the Prime Minister, 1984; author: What The Papers Never Said, 1985, Cabinet, 1986, Whitehall, 1988. Trustee Attlee Found., London, 1986—. Mem. Politics Assn. (v.p. 1986—). Office: Inst Comtemporary Brit History, 34 Tavistock Sq, London WC1H 9EZ, England

HENNESY, GERALD CRAFT, artist; b. Washington, June 11, 1921; s. Gerald Craft and Frances Lee (Moore) H.; m. Elizabeth Ann Lovering, Mar. 4, 1950; children—Kathleen, Paul, Brian, Shawn, Hugh, Craig. Student Corcoran Sch. of Art, 1939; George Washington U., 1940; B.S., U. Md., 1948. Artist advt. dept. Times Herald Newspaper, Washington, 1941-42; enlisted U.S. Navy, 1942; advanced through grades to comdr., 1956; mgmt. analyst U.S. Air Force Hdqtrs., Pentagon, Washington, 1948-52, 54-56; asst. dir. for orgn. and mgmt. AEC., 1956-72; artist, dir. Studio of Hennesy, Clifton, Va., 1972—; exhbns. include: Corcoran Gallery Art, Washington, 1957, 59, 67, Smithsonian Inst., Washington, 1962, 64, Allied Artists of Am., N.Y.C., 1975, 76; one man shows include: PLA Gallery, McLean, Va., 1967, Gallery Kormendy, Alexandria, Va., 1979, Tolley Galleries, Washington, 1983; represented in permanent collections: U.S. House of Reps., Washington, Md. State Exec. Mansion, Annapolis, Md., Nat. Hdqtrs. Am. Legion, Washington; Nat. Hdqrs. DAR, Washington; Hdqrs. Fed. Deposit Ins. Corp., Washington, and others. Decorated Air Medal with one star. Mem. Artists Equity Assn., Fairfax County Council of Arts, Washington Soc. Landscape Painters. Republican.

HENNEY, MAC LEE, lawyer; b. Columbus, Ohio, May 25, 1915; s. John Langford Wolbach and Ruth Oleta (Wilson) H.; m. Judith Ann Kauffman, May 29, 1947; children—Scott K., Cynthia Lee Henney Ayers, Deborah Lou Henney Krall, Christina Ann. J.D., Ohio State U., 1937. Bar: Ohio 1937. Sole practice, Columbus, Ohio, 1937-42; 1st officer Pan Am. Airways, Miami, Fla., 1942-46; mem. firm Henney & Walcutt, Columbus, 1946-60, Henney & Shaefer, 1960-70, White, Rankin, Henry, Morse & Mann, Columbus, 1970-85, White & Rankin, L.P.A., Columbus, 1985-87; counsel to Robins Preston & Beckett Co., Columbus, 1987—; corp. sec. Ohio Bar Title Ins. Co., 1955-87. Contbr. articles to profl. jours. Fellow Ohio State Bar Found.; mem. ABA, Ohio Bar Assn., Columbus Bar Assn. Republican. Episcopalian. Avocations: sailing; flying. Home: 2840 Canterbury Rd Columbus OH 43221 Office: Robins Preston & Beckett Co LPA 1328 Dublin Rd Columbus OH 43215

HENNING, EDWARD BURK, museum curator; b. Cleve., Oct. 23, 1922; s. Harold and Marguerite (Burk) Wagner; m. Margaret Revacko, Dec. 31, 1942; children: Eric M., Lisa A. Henning Puzder, Geoffrey A. B.S. magna cum laude, Western Res. U., 1949; cert., Cleve. Inst. Art, 1949; postgrad., Acad. Julian, Paris, 1949-50; M.A., Western Res. U., 1952. Instr. Cleve. Mus. Art, 1951-53, asst. curator edn., 1953-56, asso. curator edn., 1956-58, asst. to dir., 1958-70, curator contemporary art, 1970-72, curator modern art, 1972-78, chief curator modern art, 1978-85, research curator, 1985—; adj. prof. art history Case Western Res. U., Cleve., 1967—; cons. in field. Author: Paths of Abstract Art, 1960, Fifty Years of Modern Art, 1966, The Spirit of Surrealism, 1979, Creativity in Art and Science, 1987; contbr. articles to profl. jours. Served with U.S. Army, 1942-46. Mem. Coll. Art Assn., Am. Assn. Museums, New Orgn. Visual Arts. Office: 11150 E Boulevard Cleveland OH 44106

HENNING, HANS HELMUT FRITZ, German literature educator, library director; b. Altenburg, Thuringia, German Democratic Republic, Dec. 16, 1927; s. Otto and Martha (Taatz) H.; m. Renate Quenzer, Mar. 5, 1950; children: Ulrike, Thomas. Diploma in library sci., U. Jena, Democratic Republic Germany, 1949, PhD, 1964. Chief librarian Pub. Library, Erfurt, German Democratic Republic, 1950-55; dir. Cen. Library German Classic Lit., Weimar, German Democratic Republic, 1955—; prof. German lit. U. Jena, 1987—; vis. prof. U. Ill., Urbana, 1973, U. Beijing, Republic of China, 1986. Author: Faust Bibliography, 5 vols., 1966-76, Druckgeschichte der Faustt--Bücher, 1963, Kupferstiche zu Goethes Werken, 1982, 2d edit., 1987; editor: Goethe Almanac, 5 vols., 1967-71, Faust Historia 1587, 1963, 3d edit. 1984. Recipient Nat. prize Govt. German Dem. Republic, 1969, Kunst prize City of Weimar, 1975. Mem. Goethe Gesellschaft, German Shakespeare Soc. (v.p. 1973—), Winckelmann Gesellschaft, Internat. Assn. Comparative Lit., Internat. Shakespeare Assn., German Library Assn. Home: Helmholtzstrasse 23, 5300 Weimar German Democratic Republic Office: Deutsche Shakespeare Gesellschaft, Markt 15, 5300 Weimar German Democratic Republic

HENRICH, DIETER, philosopher, educator; b. Marburg, Hessen, Fed. Republic of Germany, Jan. 5, 1927; s. Hans Harry and Frieda (Blum) H.; m. Johanna U. Friederike. PhD, U. Heidelberg, Fed. Republic of Germany, 1950, habilitation, 1956. Prof. philosophy Free U. Berlin, 1960-65; prof. U. Heidelberg, 1965-81, U. Munich, 1981—; pres. Internat. Hegel-Vereinigung, Heidelberg, 1970-86; vis. prof. philosophy Columbia U., N.Y.C., 1968-72, U. Mich., Ann Arbor, 1969, Harvard U., Cambridge, Mass., 1973-86, Tokyo U., 1979, Yale U., New Haven, 1987. Author: Der Ontologische Gottesbeweis, 1960, Identität u Objektivität, 1976, Fluchtlinien, 1982, Der Gang des Andenkens, 1986. Mem. Heidelberg Acad. Wissenschaften, Bayerische Acad. Wissenschaften. Home: Gerlichstrasse 7 A, 8000 Munich 60 Federal Republic of Germany Office: Univ Munich, Inst Philosophy Ludwig, Maximilians, 8000 Munich 22 Federal Republic of Germany

HENRICHSEN, MELVIN BURT, univ. bookstore dir.; b. Altamont, S.D., Dec. 14, 1913; s. Claus John and Alice Marie (Bauer) H.; B.S., S.D. State U., 1938; m. Alvina Kay Preuss, Apr. 7, 1939; children—Melvin John, Dean Douglas. Tchr., Elkton (S.D.) Public Sch., 1938-41; with supts. office Swift & Co., Watertown, S.D., 1941-45; dir. Pugsly Union, S.D. State U., Brookings, 1945-46, dir. housing and bookstore, 1946-65, dir. Student Assn. Bookstore, 1946—; tchr., cons. bookstore mgmt. Oberlin Coll., Calif. State U., U. Utah, Stanford U.; speaker profl. meetings. Dist. camping chmn. Boy Scouts Am.; state chmn. This is the Life, Luth. Laymen Men's Club. Recipient cert. of merit for cons. and teaching bookstore classes, 1970, student appreciation award for outstanding service, S.D. State U., 1978, award for service to Tri-State area, 1979. Mem. Nat. Assn. Coll. Stores (Mgr. of Yr. 1970), Am. Booksellers Assn., Christian Bookstore Assn., Tri-State Bookstore Assn. Republican. Club: Elephant. Home: 1625 Calumet Dr Brookings SD 57006 Office: Bookstore Univ Student Union S D State U Brookings SD 57007

HENRIKSON, LENNART KARL NILS, construction company executive; b. Courbevoire, France, Apr. 13, 1935; s. Arne Nils Erik and Ingrid Maria (Toll) H.; married; children: Maria, Louise, Tomas, Magnus. MBA, Stockholm U., 1962; PMD, Harvard U., 1970. Auditor Seth Svensson Rev. Byra, Stockholm, 1962-64; bank clk. Götabanken, Stockholm, 1965-68; fin. mgr. Sand o grus AB Jehander, Stockholm, 1969-70, v.p., 1971-73, mgn. dir., 1974-79; chmn. AB Betongindustri, Stockholm, 1979—. Home: Thaliavagem 47, 16142 Stockholm Sweden Office: AB Betongindustri, 132 Lindhagensg, Stockholm Sweden

HENRIKSSON, JAN HUGO LENNART, architect, educator; b. Halmstad, Sweden, Feb. 28, 1933; s. John Hugo and Anna Kristina (Göransson) H.; m. Eva Anita Olson, Nov. 28, 1959 (div. June 1981); children: Lars Jonas, Mattias, Jan Andreas. Diploma in Bldg. Engring., Tekniska Gymnasiet, Gothenburg, Sweden, 1954; MArch, Royal Inst. Tech., Stockholm, 1960, PhD in Architecture, 1982. Cert. architect. Architect Peter Celsing Arkitektkontor AB, Stockholm, 1962-74; ptnr. AFHJ Arkitektkontor AB, Stockholm, 1974-78; owner Jan Henriksson Arkitektkontor AB, Stockholm, 1978—; prof. architecture U. Lund, Sweden, 1984-87, Royal Inst. Tech., Stockholm, 1987—. Author: Lägenheter på verkstadsgolvet; prin. works include Sveriges Riksbank, Stockholm, Malmö, Örebro. Served as sgt. Swedish Armed Forces, 1954. Recipient Stadsbyggnadspris, Malmö kommun, 1986. Mem. Svenska Arkitekters Riksförbund, Sveriges Praktiserande Arkitekter, Arkitektförbundet, Stockholms Byggnadsförening. Mem. Social Dem. Party. Home: Riksrådsvägen 45, 121 60 Johanneshov Stockholm Sweden Office: Kocksgatan 50, 116 29 Stockholm Sweden

HENRIQUES, NELSON DA SILVA SIMÕES, pharmaceutical company executive; b. Pedrogão Grande, Portugal, Feb. 16, 1946; s. Antônio Simões Henriques and Ilda Jesus Silva; m. Maria Fernanda Henriques; children: Christina Isabel, Nuno João. Student in mktg., Columbia U., Paris, 1982, Insead, Fontainbleu, France, 1984. Sales rep. Eli Lilly Co., Lisbon, Portugal, 1973-78; sales rep. Merck Sharp & Dohme, Lisbon, 1978-79, product mgr., 1979-82, mktg. bus. mgr., 1982-84, mktg. dir., 1986—. Home: Rua 4 Lote 60 80B, Urb Pimenta and Rendeiro, 2745 Massama-Queluz Portugal Office: Merck Sharp & Dohme, Rua Consiglieri Pedroso 123, 2745 Queluz Baixo Portugal

HENRY, CARL FERDINAND HOWARD, theologian; b. N.Y.C., Jan. 22, 1913; s. Karl F. and Johanna (Vaethroeder) H.; m. Helga Bender, Aug. 17, 1940; children: Paul Brentwood, Carol Jennifer. B.A., Wheaton (Ill.) Coll., 1938, M.A., 1940; B.D., No. Baptist Theol. Sem., Chgo., 1941, Th.D., 1942; Ph.D., Boston U., 1949; Litt.D. (hon.), Seattle-Pacific Coll., 1963, Wheaton Coll., 1968; L.H.D. (hon.), Houghton Coll., 1973; D.D. (hon.), Northwestern Coll., 1979, Gordon-Conwell Theol. Sem., 1984. Ordained to ministry Bapt. Ch., 1941; asst. prof., then prof. theology No. Bapt. Theol. Sem., 1942-47; acting dean Fuller Theol. Sem., Pasadena, Calif., 1947; prof. Fuller Theol. Sem., 1947-56, Peyton lectr., 1963, vis. prof., 1980; vis. prof. theology Wheaton Coll., Gordon Div. Sch., Columbia Bible Coll., 1977, 80, Japan Sch. Theology, 1974, Trinity Evang. Div. Sch., 1974, 87, 88, Bethel Theol. Sem., W. San Diego, 1988, Denver Conservative Bapt. Sem., 1981, 83, So. Bapt. Theol. Sem., 1988; vis. prof. Eastern Bapt. Theol. Sem., 1969-70, prof.-at-large, 1970-74; lectr.-at-large World Vision, 1974-87; Disting. vis. prof. Christian studies Hillsdale Coll., 1983-84; Disting. vis. prof. systematic theology Calvin Theol. Sem., 1986; faculty mem. flying seminar to Europe and Nr. East, Winona Lake (Ind.) Sch. Theology, 1952; daily radio commentator Let the Chips Fall, Los Angeles, 1952-53; chmn. World Congress Evangelism, Berlin, 1966, Consultation Scholars, Washington, 1967; program chmn. Jerusalem Conf. Bibl. Prophecy, Israel, 1971; Latin Am. Theol. Frat. lectr., 1973; lectr. Evangelism Internat., Singapore, 1976, 78, 86, All-India Evang. Conf. on Social Action, Madras, 1979, Liberia Bapt. Theol. Sem., Monrovia, 1982, Cameroun Bapt. Theol. Coll., Ndu, 1982; vis. lectr. Asian Center Theol. Studies and Mission, Seoul, Korea, 1974, 74, 76, 78, 80, Teoloski Facultet, Matija Vlacic Illrik, Zagreb, Yugoslavia, 1977, Asian Theol. Sem., Manila, 1980, Soong Sil Univ. Inst. Christian Culture Research, Seoul, 1987, C.S. Lewis Summer Inst., Oxford, 1988; bd. dirs. Inst. Advanced Christian Studies, 1976-79, 81-85, pres., 1971-74; bd. dirs. Ethics and Public Policy Center, 1979—, Inst. Religion and Democracy, 1981—, v.p., 1985—, Prison Fellowship, 1981—; trustee Gordon Conwell Theol. Sem., 1965-68, Elmer Bisbee Found., 1986—; bd. dirs. Ministers Life and Casualty Union, 1968-77; co-chmn. Rose Bowl Easter Sunrise Service, 1950-56. Author: A Doorway to Heaven, 1941, Successful Church Publicity, 1942, Remaking the Modern Mind, 1948, The Uneasy Conscience of Modern Fundamentalism, 1948, Giving a Reason for Our Hope, 1949, The Protestant Dilemma, 1949, Notes on the Doctrine of God, 1949, Fifty Years of Protestant Theology, 1950, The Drift of Western Thought, 1951, Personal Idealism and Strong's Theology, 1951, Glimpses of a Sacred Land, 1953, Christian Personal Ethics, 1957, Evangelical Responsibility in Contemporary Theology, 1957, Aspects of Christian Social Ethics, 1964, Frontiers in Modern Theology, 1966, The God Who Shows Himself, 1966, Evangelicals at the Brink of Crisis, 1967, Faith at the Frontiers, 1969, A Plea for Evangelical Demonstration, 1971, New Strides of Faith, 1972, Evangelicals in Search of Identity, 1976, God, Revelation and Authority, vols. 1 and 2, 1976, vols. 3 and 4, 1979, vol. 5, 1982, vol. 6,, 1983,, The Christian Mindset in a Secular Society, 1984, Christian Countermoves in a Decadent Culture, 1986, Confessions of a Theologian, 1986, Conversations with Carl Henry: Christianity for Today, 1986; editor: Contemporary Evangelical Thought, 1957; Editor: Revelation and the Bible, 1959, The Biblical Expositor, 1960, Basic Christian Doctrines, 1962, Christian Faith and Modern Theology, 1964, Jesus of Nazareth: Saviour and Lord, 1966, Fundamentals of the Faith, 1969, Horizons of Science, 1978 ; editor-in-chief: Baker's Dictionary of Christian Ethics, 1973; cons. editor: Baker's Dictionary of Theology, 1964; editor: Christianity Today, 1956-68, editor at large, 1968-77; contbg. editor: World Vision Mag., 1976-87. Recipient Freedoms Found. award, 1954, 66, Religious Heritage Am. award, 1975; honored with Carl F.H. Henry manuscript collection, Syracuse U., 1975—, The Carl F.H. Henry Study and Resource Ctr., Trinity Evangelical Divinity Sch., Deerfield, Ill., 1987. Mem. Soc. Sci. Study Religion, AAAS, Am. Soc. Christian Ethics, Am. Acad. Religion, Am. Theol. Soc. (v.p. 1974-75, pres. 1979-80), Evang. Theol. Soc. (pres. 1969-70), Conf. Faith and History, Nat. Assn. Evangelicals (bd. administrn. 1956-70), Am. Philos. Assn., Am. Soc. Ch. History, Soc. Oriental Research, Soc. Christian Philosophers, Nat. Assn. Bapt. Profs. of Religion, Evang. Press Assn. (hon. life), Soc. Bibl. Lit. Address: 3824 N 37th St Arlington VA 22207

HENRY, DAVID HOWE, II, former diplomat and international organization official; b. Geneva, N.Y., May 19, 1918; s. David Max and Dorothy (Buley) H.; m. Margaret Beard, Nov. 16, 1946; children: David Beard, Peter York, Michael Max, Susan. Student, Hobart Coll., 1935-37, Sorbonne, 1937-38; A.B., Columbia U., 1939; student, Russian Inst., 1948-49, Harvard U., 1944-45, Nat. War Coll., 1957-58. Ins. agt. 1939-41; mem. fgn. service Dept. State, 1941-71; assigned Dept. State, Montreal, 1941-42, Beirut, 1942-44, Washington, 1944-45, 48-52, 57-66, 70, Moscow, 1945-48, 52-54, Vladivostok, 1945-46, Berlin, 1955-57; acting dir. Office Research and Intelligence Sino-Soviet bloc, 1958-59; dir. dept. polit. affairs Nat. War Coll., 1959-61; dep. dir. Office Soviet Affairs, 1961-64, dir., 1964-65; mem. Policy Planning Council, 1965-66; dep. chief of mission Am. embassy, Reykjavik, Iceland, 1966-69; information systems specialist 1970; polit. and security council affairs UN, N.Y.C., 1971-78. Mem. Kappa Alpha. Presbyterian. Club: Rotarian. Home: Seaside Apt 20 3541 NE Ocean Blvd Jensen Beach FL 34957

HENRY, EDWARD FRANK, computer accounting service company executive; b. East Cleveland, Ohio, Mar. 18, 1923; s. Edward Emerson and Mildred Adella (Kulow) H.; B.B.A., Dyke Coll., 1948; student Cleve. Inst. Music, 1972; m. Nicole Annette Peth, June 18, 1977. Internal auditor E.F. Hauserman Co., 1948-51; office mgr. Frank C. Grismer Co., 1951-52; Broadway Buick Co., 1952-55; treas. Commerce Ford Sales Co., 1955-65; nat. mgr. Auto Acctg. div. United Data Processing Co., Cin., 1966-68; v.p. Auto Data Systems Co., Cleve., 1968-70; pres. Profl. Mgmt. Computer Systems, Inc., Cleve., 1970—, ComputerEase, Small Bus. Computer Ctrs. div. Profl. Mgmt. Computer Systems, Inc., 1985—, VideoEase Computerized Video Rental Systems div. Profl. Mgmt. Computer Systems, Inc., 1987—. Charter pres. No. Ohio Council Little Theatres, 1954-56; founder, artistic and mng. dir. Exptl. Theatre, Cleve., 1959-63; dramatic dir., actor various community theatres, 1955-65; actor Cleve. Playhouse, 1961-63; bd. dirs. Cleve. Philharmonic Orch., 1972-73. Served with USAAF, 1943-46; CBI. Notary public. Mem. Am. Mgmt. Assn., Nat. Assn. Accountants, Mil. Order World Wars, Air Force Assn. (life), Ky. Cols., Mayfield Area C. of C., Phi Kappa Gamma (charter pres., past nat. pres.). Republican. Presbyterian. Clubs: Rotary, Acacia Country, Hermit, Univ., Cleve. Grays, Deep Springs Trout, Nat. Sojourners (Nat. Pres.'s cert. 1977-78, pres. Cleve. chpt. #23 1978), Heroes of '76 (comdr. Cleve. 1977). Lodges: Masons (33d degree), DeMolay (past master Cleve. chpt., Legion of Honor 1970), Ancient Accepted Scottish Rite (dramatic dir. 1967—, TPM 1982-84), K.T., Grotto, Shriners (dramatic dir. 1968—), Cleve. Ct. #14, Jesters (dir. 1981, impresario 1984—, dramatic dir./producer 1971—), Kachina, SOBIB. Home: 666 Echo Dr Gates Mills OH 44040 Office: Profl Mgmt Computer Systems Inc 19701 S Miles Ave Cleveland OH 44128

HENRY, HUNTER WOODS, chemical company executive; b. McComb, Miss., 1928. B.S., Miss. State U., 1950. With Dow Chem. Co., Midland, Mich., 1951—; dir. mfg. Dow Internat., 1964-66; dir. ops. Dow Chem. Latin Am., 1966-73, bus. devel. mgr., 1966-73; v.p. Dow Badische, 1973-76; mgr. organic chemicals dept. Dow Chem. U.S.A., 1976-77; mgr. Dow Mich. div., Midland, 1976-77; pres. Dow Quimica S.A., Brazil, 1977-82; corp. v.p. Dow Chem. U.S.A., Midland, 1982-83, pres., 1982-87; exec. v.p. Dow Chem. Co., Midland, 1983—; in charge all non-U.S. geographic locations and global mfg. Dow Chem. Co., 1987—; also bd. dirs. Dow Chem. U.S.A., Midland; dir. Dow Corning Corp., Comerica Bank-Midland, Am. Indsl. Health Council. Office: The Dow Chem Co 2030 Willard H Dow Ctr Midland MI 48674 *

HENRY, JOHN ALFRED, lawyer; b. Westbrook, Maine, Feb. 11, 1931; s. Donald M. and Josephine M. (Perry) H.; children—James Richard, Jeffrey Alan. B.A. cum laude, Bowdoin Coll., 1952, J.D. with honors, George Washington U., 1960. Bar: Va. 1960, Mass. 1961, Ariz. 1968. Tax law specialist Rulings div. Nat. Office IRS Washington 1959-61; assoc. Ropes & Gray, Boston, 1960-68, Lewis & Roca Phoenix, 1968-70; founding ptnr. Henry, Kimerer & La Velle, 1970-84; of counsel Allen, Kimerer & LaVelle, Phoenix, 1985—. Chmn. bd. Legal Profls. Credit Union; mem. exec. com. Am. Cancer Soc. Ariz. Div., Inc., 1969—, pres., 1976-77, chmn. bd., 1977-79, chmn. legacy com., 1979-83; vice chmn. ann. dinner NCCJ, 1983, 84. Served with USAF, 1952-56. Recipient Am. Cancer Soc. Annual Nat. Divisional award, 1978, 83. Mem. ABA, State Bar Va., State Bar Mass., State Bar Ariz. Republican. Clubs: Univ., Mansion, Plaza (Phoenix). Contbr. to legal jours. Home: 4936 E Arroyo Verde Dr Paradise Valley AZ 85253 Office: Allen Kimerer & LaVelle 2715 N 3d St Phoenix AZ 85004

HENRY, JOHN JAMES, physicist; b. White Pine, Tenn., Feb. 12, 1929; s. Herbert Holloway and Clara (Spurgeon) H.; student U. Fla., 1946-48; B.S., Lincoln Meml. U., 1954; m. Audrey Duffield, Sept. 14, 1954; children—Mark Stephen, Claudia Alexandra, John James. Instrument technician Carbide & Carbon Chem. Co., Oak Ridge, 1954-56; asso. physicist Union Carbide Corp., Oak Ridge, 1956-61, physicist nuclear div., 1961-74, devel. specialist, 1974-76, devel. staff I, 1976-84; devel. staff I, Martin Marietta Energy Systems, Oak Ridge, 1984—. Instr. transistor circuit theory Oak Ridge Adult Edn. Program, 1962-65. Scoutmaster, Boy Scouts Am., Oak Ridge, 1960-62; tympanist Oak Ridge Symphony Orch., 1965-73, publicity chmn., 1966-67, v.p., 1966-68. Served with USMC, 1949-52. Recipient IR-100 award Industrial Research Mag., 1979. Mem. Instrument Soc. Am. (sr.), AAAS, IEEE. Episcopalian (vestryman 1974-76, 84-86, chmn. music and worship com. 1974-75, chmn. outreach com. 1976, Evangelism com. 1985, pastoral care com., 1986). Clubs: Atomic City Stamp (editor 1978, v.p. 1981-88); Commodore Users (pres. 1984) (Oak Ridge). Patentee in field. Home: 639 Pennsylvania Ave Oak Ridge TN 37830 Office: Y-12 Plant Oak Ridge TN 37830

HENRY, NANCY LOUISE, conference center-hotel executive, mayor; b. Somerville, N.J., July 18, 1940; d. Robert Lewis and Mary Louise (Skinner) Twyman; student Rutgers U., 1973-75, Trenton State Coll., 1976-77; children—Lionel N., Robert Lewis. With Johnson & Johnson, New Brunswick, N.J., 1959-77, v.p., 1965-77; conv. coordinator Nat. Conf. Center, East Windsor, N.J., 1977-78; sales mgr. Scanticon-Princeton (N.J.) Conf. Center-Hotel, 1982—; dep. mayor City of Somerset (N.J.), 1982—; mayor Franklin Twp. (N.J.), 1982—; pres. Henry's Constrn. Clean Up Service; spl. asst. to gov. State of N.J., Trenton, 1978-79, dir. resources and community participation Office of Ombudsman for Instnl. Elderly, Trenton, 1979—. Councilwoman Franklin Twp. (N.J.), 1977—; committeewoman 4th Ward, Franklin Twp., 1977-79, ward chmn., 1978-79; mem. adv. council Somerset County Employment and Tng. Agy., 1977-81, chmn. youth adv. council, 1978-80; del. Democratic Nat. Conv., 1980; v.p. N.J. Fedn. Dem. Women. Methodist. Home: 15 DeWald Ave Somerset NJ 08873 Office: Scanticon-Princeton 100 College Rd E Princeton NJ 08540

HENRY, PETER YORK, lawyer; b. Washington, Apr. 28, 1951; s. David Howe II and Margaret (Beard) H.; m. Rebecca Jo Csajka, Aug. 1976; children—Ryan York, Zachary Price. B.B.A., Ohio U., 1973; J.D. St. Mary's U., San Antonio, 1976. Bar: Tex. 1976. Sole practice, San Antonio, 1976—. Mem. Tex. Bar Assn., Am. Trial Lawyers Assn., Tex Trial Lawyers Assn., San Antonio Trial Lawyers Assn., San Antonio Bar Assn., Phi Delta Phi. Home: 6806 Forest Haven San Antonio TX 78240 Office: 224 Casa Blanca San Antonio TX 78215

HENRY, SANDRA KEDNOCKER, civic worker, small business investment corporation executive; m. Charles J. Henry; children: Brendan Allan, Garratt Hill. BA, U. N.C., 1959; postgrad., U. Cin., 1966-67; grad. fin. forum, The Harris Bank, Chgo. Pres. Intervest Group, 1984-85. Bd. dirs. North Shore Country Day Sch., Illinois Club, House of the Good Shepherd; mem. Consular Ball benefit com. of Library of Internat. Relations; chmn. Sept. Ball of the Children's Home and Aid Soc. Ill., 1984; bd. mgmt., v.p. sustaining membership, benefit chmn. Jr. League Chgo., 1984-85; mem. woman's bd., mem. ball com. Chgo. Heart Assn., 1985; mem. benefit coms. Brookfield Zoo, 1985-88, Women's Bd. Goodman Theatre, Women's Bd. USO of Ill., 5 hosp. homebound programs for elderly; women's bd., history of active leadership in geneal. socs., pub. TV, archtl. preservation, community and ednl. orgns., symphony orchs., convalescent hosp. for children; benefit chmn. Am. Cancer Soc., 1987, 88, mem. woman's bd.; bd. dirs. Midwest region Shakespeare Globe Ctr. N.Am., Inc. Mem. Nat. Soc. Fund Raising Execs., Harris Bank Fin. Network, U. N.C. Alumni Assn., Nat. Soc. Daus. Am. Colonists, Nat. Soc. Daus. Founders and Patriots Am., Nat. Soc. Daus. Colonial Wars (state officer), Nat. Soc. Sons and Daus. Pilgrims, U.S. Daus. 1812, Hotchkiss Family Assn., Descs. Colonial Clergy, numerous others. Clubs: Fortnightly of Chgo., Woodley Road Garden (bd. dirs), Woman's Athletic, The Glenview.

HENSEL, GEORG, editor, critic; b. Darmstadt, Germany, July 13, 1923. Grad., Gymnasium, Darmstadt. Editor, theatre critic Darmstädter Echo, Darmstadt, 1945-74, Frankfurter Allgemeine Zeitung, Frankfurt, 1975—. Author: Spielplan, 2 vols., 1966; contbr. to Stuttgarter Zeitung, Die Welt, Süddeutsche Zeitung, also radio and TV programs; author essays, criticisms. Recipient Julius Bab award Deutsche Volksbühnen-Vereine, Essen, 1982, Carl Zuckmayer medal Rheinland-Pfalz Country-A, Mainz, 1982, Egon Erwin Kisch award Stern mag., Hamburg, 1983. Mem. Deutsche Akademie für Sprache und Dichtung, PEN. Lodge: Rotary. Home: Park Rosenhohe 1, D-6100 Darmstadt Federal Republic of Germany Office: Frankfurter Allgemeine Zeitung, Hellerhofstrasse 2-4, D-6000 Frankfurt Federal Republic of Germany

HENSEL, WITOLD, archaeologist; b. Poznan, Poland, Mar. 29, 1917; s. Maksymilian and Maria (Formanowicz) H.; m. Maria Chmielewska, June 5, 1941; children: Wojciech, Zdzislaw, Leszek, Barbara. M in Philosophy, U. Poznan, 1938, Docent, 1948; PhD, U. Lublin, Poland, 1945; Dhc, U. Poznan, 1987. Lectr. U. Lublin, 1944-45; prof. extraordinary, head chair archaeology U. Poznan, 1951-55, dean history and philosophy dept.,, 1951-53; vice dir. to dir. Inst. History Material Culture Polish Acad. Scis., Warsaw, 1954—; prof. extraordinary U. Warsaw, 1954-56, prof. ordinary, 1956—, head chair Slavonic dept., 1956-65, head chair prehistoric and early medieval archaeology, 1965-70; leader expdns. Poland, Yugoslavia, France, Italy, Algeria. Author: Slowianszczyna wczesnosredniowieczna, 1952, 56, 65, 80, Polska przed tysiacem lat, 1960, La naissance de la Pologne, 1966, The Beginnings of the Polish State, 1960, Najdawniejsze stolice Polski, 1960, Archeologia o poczatkach miast sowianskich, 1963, Anfänge der Städte bei der Ost and Westslawen, 1967, Ziemie polske w pradziejach, 1969, Archeologia i prahistoria, 1971, Polska starozytna, 1973, 80, Ur-und Frühgeschichte Polens, 1974, others; contbr. to profl. lit. Decorated comdrs. cross with star Polonia Restituta; comdr. Cross al Merito della Republica Italiana; recipient Polonia State prize, 1955, 66, Copernicus medal Polish Acad. Scis., 1977, Gold medal Czechoslavak Acad. Scis., 1975. Mem. Polish Acad. Scis. (mem. presidency 1984—), Acad. Scis. DDR, Mak. Acad. Scis., Sächsische Acad. Scis., Union Pre and Protohist. Scis. (internat. council 1956—), Union Studies Origin Towns (chmn. internat. com. 1962-77), Internat. Congress Slavists (v.p. 1971—), Internat. Union Anthropol. and Ethnographic Studies (chmn. nat. com. 1986—), Polish (chmn. 1969-70), Jugoslavian (hon.) archaeol. socs. and polit. archeol. soc., and Soc. of Scis. of Ptock. Home: Marszalkowska 84/92, m 109, 00-514 Warsaw Poland Office: Al Swierczewskiego 105, 00-140 Warsaw Poland

HENSON, PAUL HARRY, communications company executive; b. Bennet, Nebr., July 22, 1925; s. Harry H. and Mae (Schoenthal) H.; m. Betty L. Roeder, Aug. 2, 1946; children: Susan Irene Flury, Lizbeth Henson Barelli. B.S. in Elec. Engring. U. Nebr., 1948, M.S., 1950; hon. doctorates, U. Nebr., Ottawa U., Bethany Coll. Registered profl. engr., Nebr. Engr. Lincoln (Nebr.) Tel. & Tel. Co., 1941-42, 45-48, div. mgr., 1948-54, chief engr., 1954-59; v.p. United Telecommunications, Inc., Kansas City, Mo., 1959-60; exec. v.p. United Telecommunications, Inc., 1960-64, pres., 1964-73, chmn., 1966—, also dir.; dir. Armco, Duke Power; vice chmn. Pres.'s Nat. Security Telecommunications Adv. Com.. Trustee Midwest Research Inst., Tax Found., U. Nebr. Found., U. Mo. at Kansas City. Served with USAAF, 1942-45. Mem. Nat. Soc. Profl. Engrs., IEEE, Armed Forces Communications Electronics Assn., U.S. Telephone Assn. (dir. 1960-76, pres. 1964-65), Sigma Xi, Eta Kappa Nu, Sigma Tau, Kappa Sigma (Man of Yr. 1987). Clubs: Mason (Shriner), Kansas City, Kansas City Country, Mission Hills Country, Castle Pines, El Dorado Country, River. Office: United Telecommunications Inc Box 11315 Kansas City MO 64112

HENSTOCK, RALPH, mathematician, educator; b. Newstead, Nottingham, Eng., June 2, 1923; s. William and Mary Ellen (Bancroft) H.; m. Marjorie Jardine, July 16, 1949; 1 child, John Patrick. MA, Cambridge (Eng.) U., 1948; PhD, U. London, 1948. Exptl. officer Ministry of Supply, London, 1943-46; asst. Bedford Coll. U. London, 1947-48, lectr. Birkbeck Coll., 1948-51; lectr. Queen's U., Belfast, Northern Ireland, 1951-56, sr. lectr., reader, external examiner, 1960-64; lectr. Bristol (Eng.) U., 1956-60; reader Lancaster (Eng.) U., 1964-70; prof. math. U. Ulster (formerly New U. Ulster), Coleraine, Northern Ireland, 1970—, chmn. dept. math., 1971-84. Author: Theory of Integration, 1963, Linear Analysis, 1968, Lectures on the Theory of Integration, 1988; contbr. articles to profl. publs. Fellow Royal Stats. Soc., Inst. Math. and Applications; mem. London Math. Soc., Am. Math. Soc., Irish Math. Soc. Mem. Ulster Democratic Unionist Party. Methodist. Lodge: Loyal Orange. Home: 11 Regent Park, Portstewart BT55 7NP, Northern Ireland Office: U Ulster Dept Math, Coleraine BT52 1SA, Northern Ireland

HENTSCHEL, DAVID A., oil company executive; b. 1934; married. B.S. in Phys. edn., La. State U.; B.S. in Meteorology, Okla. State U. Reservoir engr. Ark. Fuel Corp., 1957-61; with Cities Service Co., Tulsa, 1961—, prodn. engr., 1961-64, gas. ops. engr., 1964-65, buyer purchasing div., 1965-68, auto services mgr., 1968-70, gen. mgr. purchasing, 1970-74, gen. mgr. so. region, 1974-77, v.p. Western area energy resources group, 1977-79, v.p. Western internat. area energy resources group, 1979-80, exec. v.p. planning, tech. and services, 1980-82, corp. exec. v.p., 1982-85, chmn., chief exec. officer, 1985—, pres., from 1985, pres. PPG group, from 1982, also dir.; also exec. v.p. Occidental Petroleum Corp., Los Angeles. Served with USAF, 1957-59. Office: Cities Service Co Cities Service Bldg Tulsa OK 74102 *

HENTSCHEL, UWE, psychology educator; b. Greifswald, Pommern, Fed. Republic Germany, Jan. 23, 1940; arrived in The Netherlands, 1987; s. Wilhelm Rudolf and Elsa (Anderson) H.; m. Henriette Streffer, Oct. 19, 1962 (div. June 1987); children: Caterin, Ludger; m. Maria Helena van der Voort, Sept. 16, 1987; 1 child, Mayke. Diploma in pyschology, U. Giessen, Fed. Republic Germany, 1964; Dr. Philosophy, U. Freiburg, Fed. Republic Germany, 1969; postdoctoral, U. Mainz, Fed. Republic Germany, 1977. Researcher Marplan, Frankfurt, Fed. Republic Germany, 1964-67; research dir. McCann, Hamburg, Fed. Republic Germany, 1971; research asst. Max Planck Inst. for Psychiatry, Munich, 1974-75; asst. prof. U. Mainz, 1975-81, prof., 1981-87; prof., head dept. psychology of personality Rijksuniversiteit te Leiden, The Netherlands, 1987—. Editor: Experimentelle Persönlichkeitspsychologie, 1980, Persönlichkeitsmerkmale und Familienstruktur, 1984, The Roots of Perception, 1986; contbr. articles to profl. jours. Research grantee Deutsche Forschungsgemeinschaft, Lund, Sweden, 1972-73. Mem. Deutsche Gesellschaft für Psychologie, Soc. for Psychotherapy Research, Gesellschaft zur Förderung persönlichkeits-und sozialpsychologischer Forschung (chmn. 1984). Office: Rijksuniversiteit te Leiden, Hooigracht 15, 2312 KM Leiden The Netherlands

HENYCH, IVO, metal processing company executive; b. Skvorec, Prague, Switzerland, Jan. 12, 1935; s. Rudolf and Vera (Stadelmann) H.; m. Alexandra Spada; 1 child, Blanka. MS in Engring., State U. Mining and Metallurgy, Ostrava, Czechoslavakia, 1962. Metallurgist, mgr. Kralodv Zelezarny, Kraluvdvur, Czechoslovakia, 1961-68; metall. researcher Georg Fischer, Ltd., Schaffhausen, Switzerland, 1968-80, br. mgr., 1980—; mgr. Foundry Tech. Transfer. Contbr. articles to profl. jours.; patentee in field. Mem. Verein Deutsche Giessereifachleute, Lic. Exec. Soc. Home: IM Buel 201, 8211 Stetten Switzerland

HENZE, HANS WERNER, composer, conductor; b. Gutersloh, Ger., July 1, 1926; s. Franz and Margarete (Geldmacher) H.; Dr. Mus., Edinburgh U., 1971. Mus. dir. Heinz Hilpert's Deutsches Theater, Constance, 1948-50; artistic dir. Ballet of the Hessian State Theatre, Wiesbaden, from 1950; prof. composition Mozarteum, Salzburg, from 1961; dir. Accademia Filarmonica Romana, Rome, 1981—; compositions include: operas: Das Wundertheater, Blvd. Solitude, Konig Hirsch, Der Prinz von Homburg, Elegy for Young Lovers, 1961, Der Junde Lord, 1964, Die Bassariden, 1965; radio operas: Ein Landarzt, Das Ende einer Welt; ballets: Jack Pudding, Tancred under Cantylene, Variationen, Labyrinth, The Idiot, Apoll und Hyazirth, Ondine; oratorio: Novae de Infinito Laudes, 1962; cantatas: Being Beauteous, 1963, Ariosl, 1963, Cantata della Fiaba Estrema, 1963; choral works: Chorfantasie, 1964, Musen Siziliens, 1966; oratorio: Medusa, 1968, 6 symphonies, violin, piano and violoncello concertos, double concerto for oboe, harp and strings, 2 string quartets, wind quintet, Kammermusik, 1958, El Cimarron, 1969, The Tedious Way to the Place of Natasha Ungeheuer, 1970, Heliogabalus Imperator, 1971, La Cubana, 1972, Voices, 1973, Tristan, 1974, Ragtime and Habarera, 1975; music for films including Muriel. Recipient Robert Schumann prize, 1952; Prix d'Italia, 1954; North Rhine Westphalia Art prize, 1956; Sibelius Gold medal; Music Critics prize Buenos Aires, 1958; Ludwig Spohr Preis, 1976. Author: Undine, Dairy of a Ballet, 1958; Essays, 1964; (with H. Enzenberger) El Cimmarron-A Work Report, 1971; Musik und Politik, 1976. Address: care ICM Artists Ltd 40 W 57th St New York NY 10019 *

HENZE, PAUL BERNARD, author, former government official; b. Redwood Falls, Minn., Aug. 29, 1924; s. Paul Henry and Elizabeth Ann (Rush) H.; m. Martha Elaine Heck, Sept. 15, 1951; children: John, Elizabeth, Martin, Mary, Alexander, Samuel. A.B., St. Olaf Coll., 1948; A.M., Harvard U., 1950; postgrad., U. Nebr., 1943-44, U. Maine, 1947, U. Minn., 1948. Fgn. affairs officer Dept. Def., 1950-51; policy adviser Radio Free Europe, Munich, West Germany, 1952-58; communications adviser Turkey, 1958-59; mem. sr. research staff Ops. Research Office, Johns Hopkins, 1960-61; exec. Dept. Def., 1961-68; 1st sec. Am. embassy, Addis Ababa, Ethiopia, 1969-72; assigned Dept. State, Washington, 1973; 1st sec. Am. embassy, Ankara, Turkey, 1974-77; mem. staff NSC, Washington, 1977-80; Wilson fellow Smithsonian Inst., 1981-82; resident cons. RAND Corp., 1982—; v.p. Fgn. Area Research, Inc. Author: Ethiopian Journeys, 1977, The Plot To Kill the Pope, 1983; contbg. author: The USSR and the Muslim World, 1984, Soviet Nationalities in Strategic Perspective, 1985, Hydra of Carnage, 1986; contbr. articles to profl. jours. Trustee Am. Friends of Turkey Found. Served with AUS, World War II, ETO. Mem. Brit. Inst. Archaeology at Ankara, Archeol. Inst. Am., French Soc. for Ethiopian Studies (Paris), Am. Assn. for Advancement of Slavic Studies, Nat. Parks Assn., Royal Soc. for Asian Affairs (London), AAAS, Appalachian Trail Conf., Textile Mus. (Washington), Piedmont Environ. Council, Rappahannock League Environ. Protection, Am.-Turkish Soc., East African Wildlife Soc., Soc. for Central Asian Studies, Brit. Inst. in Eastern Africa (Nairobi), Hakluyt Soc. Club: Federal City (Washington). Home: 6014 Namakagan Rd Bethesda MD 20816

HEONG, TOH, TV producer; b. Singapore, Aug. 8, 1953. B in Commerce, Nanyang U., Singapore, 1976. Def. exec. officer Ministry Def., Singapore, 1978-80; TV producer Singapore Broadcasting Corp., 1980-85, producer, 1985—. Producer numerous TV dramas including Children Playhouse, 1981, The Flying Fish, 1983, CID '83, 1983, Blossoms In The Sun, 1984, Growing Up, 1984, Son of Pulau Tekong, 1985, Take Over, 1985, The Happy Trio, 1986, Crossroads, 1986, Five-Foot-Way, 1987, The Airforce, 1988. Home: 7 Bright Hill Dr #19-03, Thomson View Condominium, Singapore Singapore 2057 Office: Singapore Broadcasting Corp, Caldecott Hill Thomson Rd, Singapore Singapore 1129

HEPBURN, KATHARINE HOUGHTON, actress; b. Hartford, Conn., Nov. 8, 1909; d. Thomas N. and Katharine (Houghton) H.; m. Ludlow Ogden Smith (div.). Student, Bryn Mawr Coll, 1928. Appeared in films A Bill of Divorcement, 1932, Christopher Strong, 1933, Morning Glory, 1933

(Acad. award for best performance by actress 1934), Little Women, 1933, Spitfire, 1934, The Little Minister, 1934, Alice Adams, 1935, Break of Hearts, 1935, Sylvia Scarlett, 1936, Mary of Scotland, 1936, A Woman Rebels, 1936, Quality Street, 1937, Stage Door, 1937, Bringing up Baby, 1938, Holiday, 1938, The Philadelphia Story, 1940 (N.Y. Critic's award 1940), Woman of the Year, 1941, Keeper of the Flame, 1942, Stage Door Canteen, 1943, Dragon Seed, 1944, Undercurrent, 1946, Sea of Grass, 1946, Song of Love, 1947, State of the Union, 1948, Adam's Rib, 1949, The African Queen, 1951, Pat and Mike, 1952, Summertime, 1955, The Rainmaker, 1956, The Iron Petticoat, 1956, The Desk Set, 1957, Suddenly Last Summer, 1959, Long Day's Journey into Night, 1962, Guess Who's Coming to Dinner, 1967, (Acad. award for best actress 1968),The Lion in Winter, 1968 (Acad. award for best actress 1969), Madwoman of Chaillot, 1969, Trojan Women, 1971, A Delicate Balance, 1973, Rooster Cogburn, 1975, Olly, Olly, Oxen Free, 1978, On Golden Pond, 1981 (Acad. award for best actress 1981), The Ultimate Solution of Grace Quigley, 1985; appeared in plays The Czarina, 1928, The Big Pond, 1928, Night Hostess, 1928, These Days, 1928, Death Takes a Holiday, 1929, A Month in the Country, 1930, Art and Mrs. Bottle, 1930, The Warrior's Husband, 1932, Lysistrata, 1932, The Lake, 1933, Jane Eyre, 1937, The Philadelphia Story, 1939, Without Love, 1942, As You Like It, 1950, The Millionairess, Eng. and U.S.A., 1952, The Taming of the Shrew, The Merchant of Venice, Measure for Measure, Old Vic Co., Eng. and Australia, 1955, Merchant of Venice, Much Ado about Nothing, Am. Shakespeare Festival, 1957, toured later, 1958, Twelfth Night, Antony and Cleopatra, Am. Shakespeare Festival, 1960, Coco, 1969-70, toured, 1971, The Taming of the Shrew, Old Vic, 1970, A Matter of Gravity, 1976-78, West Side Waltz, 1981; appeared in TV movies The Glass Menagerie, 1973, Love among the Ruins, 1975, The Corn Is Green, 1979, Mrs. Delafield Wants to Marry, 1986; Laura Lansing Slept Here, 1988; author: The Making of the African Queen, 1987. Recipient gold medal as world's best motion picture actress Internat. Motion Picture Expn., Venice, Italy, 1934; ann. award Shakespeare Club, N.Y.C., 1950; award Whistler Soc., 1957; Woman of Yr. award Hasty Pudding Club, 1958; outstanding achievement award for fostering finest ideals of acting profession, 1980; lifetime achievement award Council Fashion Designers Am., 1986. Office: William Morris Agy 151 El Camino Beverly Hills CA 90212 *

HEPFNER, LYNNE BERNARD, school system administrator; b. Richmound, Sask., Can., June 10, 1940; s. Bernard S. Hepfner and Annie Lannan; m. Linda J. Franks; children: Kara, Joy, Jayme. Student, U. Sask., Regina, 1960; P.G. diploma in ednl. psychology, U. Sask., Alta., 1970; EdB, U. Calgary, Alta., 1967. Cert. in edn., Sask. Tchr. Regina Separate Schs., 1960-62; tchr. Maple Creek (Sask.) Sch. Div., 1962-70, guidance counsellor, 1970-75, supr. asst., 1975-80, asst. supt., 1981-86, dir. edn., 1986—. Mem. League of Ednl. Adminstrs., Dirs., Suprs. (leader Sask. sect.), Sas. Assn. Cons. and Suprs. (pres. 1984), South-West Adminstrs. (conf. chairperson local chpt. 1987), Maple Creek Tchrs. Assn. (pres. 1975). Liberal. Roman Catholic. Lodge: KC. Office: Box 400, Maple Creek, SK Canada S0N 1N0

HEPLER, KENNETH MAX, manufacturing company executive; b. Streator, Ill., Feb. 7, 1922; s. Max C. and Florence Roberta Hepler; B.S. in Mech. Engring., Ill. Inst. Tech., 1949; cert. mktg., UCLA, 1971; m. Wanda Ettamae Sines, Jan. 22, 1944; children—Kenneth F., Keith L., Kevin S., Vidabeth O. With U.S. Gypsum Co., 1949—, pres. subs., Yeso Panamericano SA de CV, Yeso Mexicana SA, Cia Terminal de Yeso SA, 1971-74, pres. U.C. Industries Co., 1977-79, corp. gen. mgr. mineral fiber div., Chgo., 1979-82, corp. gen. mgr. wood fiber products div., Chgo., 1982—; group v.p. wood fiber div. Masonite Corp., Chgo., 1986—. Served with USNR, 1941-46. Mem. Chgo. C. of C. Republican. Clubs: Union League (Chgo.); Jonathan (Los Angeles); Masons. Office: 101 S Wacker Dr Chicago IL 60606

HEPLER, MARTIN EUGENE, management analyst; b. Lancaster, Pa., Oct. 4, 1949; s. James Painter Hepler and Janet Marie (Hess) Bucher; m. Phyllis Ann Seymour, Apr. 23, 1977 (div. June 1983). AS, Miramar Coll., San Diego, 1977; BS, San Diego State U., 1980, M in Pub. Adminstrn., 1983. Registered indsl. engr., technician, Calif.; cert. post secondary edn. Prodn. mgr. Cerebronic, Inc., San Diego, 1973-74; aircraft engine mechanic Naval Aviations Depot, San Diego, 1974-80; indsl. engring. technician Naval Aviations Depot, 1980-83, program coordinator, 1983-86, internal cons., 1985—; pres. Bremman & Assocs., San Diego, 1984—; cons. Richman Mgmt., San Diego, 1983-86. Mem. Zoological Soc., San Diego, 1979—; instr. Heart Assn., San Diego, 1976—; bd. dirs. Clairemont Friendship Ctr., San Diego, 1978-80. Served with USN 1968-72, with Res. 1974—. Mem. Nat. Rifleman's Assn., Deming User's Group (pres. 1986—), Western Criminology Soc., Internat. Assn. Quality Circles (bd. dirs. San Diego chpt. 1984—), VFW. Democrat. Roman Catholic. Home and Office: 14560 Vintage Dr San Diego CA 92129

HEPWORTH, JAMES MICHAEL (MIKE), sociology educator; b. Wakefield, Yorkshire, U.K., Dec. 21, 1938; s. James and Mary (Stockdale) H.; m. Mary Ellworthy, Dec. 21, 1963 (div. 1973); children—Rachel, Virginia; m. Marian Bywell, Apr. 20, 1974; 1 son, Guy. B.A. in Social Studies, U. Hull, 1961. Asst. careers adv. officer Warwickshire (U.K.) Youth Employment Service, 1961-65; asst. lectr. social studies Monkwearmouth Coll., Sunderland, County Durham, U.K., 1965-66; lectr. sociology Teesside Poly. Inst., Middlesbrough, Cleveland, Eng., 1967-71; sr. lectr. Lanchester Poly. Inst., Coventry, Warwickshire, 1971; lectr. sociology Aberdeen (Scotland) U., 1972-81, sr. lectr., 1981—; chmn. Mid Life Centre Devel. Group, Birmingham, 1983—; dir. MidLife Style Ltd. Author: Blackmail, 1975; (with others) Surviving Middle Age, 1982, Confession: Studies in Deviance and Society, 1982; joint rev. editor Theory, Culture and Soc. Jour., 1983—. Mem. Age Concern Scotland, Brit. Soc. Gerontology, Crime Writers' Assn., Scottish Assn. for Study of Delinquency. Home: Rose Cottage, Whiterashes, Aberdeen AB5 0QP, Scotland Office: U Aberdeen, King's College, Aberdeen AB9 2TY, Scotland

HERALD, GEORGE WILLIAM, foreign correspondent; b. Berlin, Jan. 3, 1911; came to U.S., 1941; s. Bruno H. and Paula J. (Levy) H.; m. Martha A. Dubois, Mar. 24, 1948; children—Steve Andrew, Patricia Claudia. LL.D. cum laude, Basle U. (Switzerland), 1934; postgrad. Columbia U., 1950-52. Staff corr. INS, N.Y., London and Paris, 1945-46, bur. chief, Berlin and Vienna, 1946-49; spl. writer United Features, N.Y.C., 1949-52; assoc. editor UN World mag., N.Y.C. and Europe, 1952-55; head bur. Vision, Inc., Paris, 1955—. Author: My Favorite Assassin, 1943; (with others) Off the Record, 1952; (with Soraya Esfandiary) My Life as an Empress, 1962; The Big Wheel, 1963, Art and Money, 1977; contbr. numerous articles to mags. including Reader's Digest, Harper's, McCall's. Served to capt. U.S. Army, 1942-45. Mem. Authors League Am., Internat. Press Inst., Overseas Press Club Am., Anglo-Am. Press Club, Internat. Arts Council. Unitarian. Office: Vision Inc, Vision Bldg 13 E 75th St New York NY 10021

HERBERT, GILBERT, architectural educator; b. Johannesburg, Republic of South Africa, June 22, 1924; arrived in Israel, 1968; s. Benjamin and Sophia (Miller) H.; m. Valerie Ryan, June 18, 1953; children: Barry (dec.), Margalit. BArch, U. of the Witwatersrand, Johannesburg, 1947, MArch, 1955, DArch (hon.), 1986; D Litt et Phil., U. South Africa, Pretoria, 1969. Lectr. architecture U. Witwatersrand, Johannesburg, 1947-61; reader U. Adelaide, Australia, 1961-68; assoc. prof. Technion, Haifa, Israel, 1968-72, dean faculty of architecture, 1973-74, Mary Hill Swope prof. architecture, 1974—; pvt. practice architecture Johannesburg and Adelaide, 1947-68; vis. prof. U. Witwatersrand, 1975, 85, 88, Fed. Univ. Paraná, Curitiba, Brazil, 1980; disting. vis. scholar U. Adelaide, 1979, Harvard U., Cambridge, Mass., 1981. Author: Synthetic Vision of Walter Gropius, 1959, Martienssen and the International Style, 1975, Pioneers of Prefabrication, 1978, The Dream of the Factory-Made House, 1984; assoc. editor South African Archtl. Record, 1949-60; contbr. chpts. to various books, articles to profl. jours. Pres. Jewish Nat. Fund of South Australia, 1965-67. Recipient Myer Found. award Australian Humanities Research Council, 1967, Advanced Studies award Graham Found., Chgo., 1981, Joseph H. Hazen award Israel Mus., 1982; Sir Herbert Baker scholar, 1957. Fellow Royal Inst. Brit. Architects, Royal Australian Inst. Architects; mem. Inst. South African Architects (Archtl. Writers and Critics' award 1979), Am. Soc. Archtl. Historians, Assn. Engrs. and Architects Israel. Jewish. Home: 8 Eder St, Haifa 34752, Israel Office: Technion Sch Architecture, Technion City, Haifa 32000, Israel

HERBIG, GUNTHER, conductor; b. Aussig, Germany, Nov. 30, 1931; s. Emil and Gisela (Hieke) H.; diploma Franz-Liszt-Hochschule, Weimar, Germany, 1956; m. Jutta Czapski, Oct. 30, 1958; children: Beate, Thomas. Mus. asst. Erfurt Theatre, 1956-57; condr. Deutsches Nat. Theatre, Weimar, 1957-62; prin. condr. Potsdam (Ger.) Theatre, 1962-66; condr. Berliner Sinfonie-Orchester, Berlin, 1966-72, chief condr., artistic dir., 1977-83; music dir. Detroit Symphony Orch., 1984-88; chief condr., artistic dir. Dresden (Ger.) Philharmonic Orchester, 1972-77; prin. guest condr. Dallas Symphony Orch., 1978-80; artistic advisor Toronto Symphony Orch., 1988, music dir., 1988—. Recipient Theodor Fontane Arts prize, 1964; German Democratic Republic Arts prize, 1970; Nat. prize German Democratic Republic, 1977. Mem. Composers League German Democratic Republic. Roman Catholic. Office: Toronto Symphony Orch, 60 Simcoe St Suite C116, Toronto, ON Canada M5J 2H5 *

HERBST, TODD LESLIE, lawyer; b. N.Y.C., July 15, 1952; s. Seymour and Charlotte (Wolper) H.; m. Robyn Beth Kellman, June 3, 1979; children: Scott Marshall, Carly Nicole. BA, CUNY, 1974; JD, John Marshall Law Sch., 1977. Bar: N.Y. 1978. Assoc. Max E. Greenberg, Cantor & Reiss, N.Y.C., 1977-83, mng. ptnr., 1984-87; ptnr. Max E. Greenberg, Cantor, Trager & Toplitz, N.Y.C., 1988—; bus. cons. Shimizu Am. Corp., N.Y.C., 1983—, Dillingham Constrn. Holdings, Inc., San Francisco, 1987—. Pres. Congregation Eitz Chaim Anshei Wolozon, N.Y.C., 1986. Mem. ABA, N.Y. State Bar Assn., N.Y. County Lawyers Assn. Jewish. Home: 2 Settlers Ct New City NY 10956 Office: Max E Greenberg Cantor et al 100 Church St New York NY 10057

HERDEG, HOWARD BRIAN, physician; b. Buffalo, Oct. 14, 1929; s. Howard Bryan and Martha Jean (Williams) H.; student Paul Smith's Coll., 1947-48, U. Buffalo, 1948-50, Canisius Coll., 1949; DO, Phila. Coll. Osteopathic Medicine, 1954; MD, U. Calif.-Irvine Coll. Medicine, 1962; m. Beryl Ann Fredricks, July 21, 1955; children: Howard Brian III, Erin Ann Kociela. Intern, Burbank (Calif.) Hosp., 1954-55; practice medicine specializing in family practice, Woodland Hills, Calif., 1956—; chief med. staff West Park Hosp., Canoga Park, Calif., 1971-72, trustee, 1971-73; chief family practice dept. Humana Hosp. West Hills, Canoga Park, 1982-83, mem. exec. com., 1984-85. Mem. Hidden Hills (Calif.) Pub. Safety Commn., 1978-82, 1988—, chmn., 1982, exec. com. 1982—; bd. dirs. Hidden Hills Community Assn., 1971-73, pres., 1972; bd. dirs. Hidden Hills Homeowners Assn., 1973-75, pres., 1976-77; bd. dirs. Woodland Hills Freedom Season, 1961-67, pres., 1962; mem. Hidden Hills City Council, 1984—, mayor pro tem, 1987—. Recipient disting. service award Woodland Hills Jr C. of C., 1966. Mem. Woodland Hills C. of C. (dir. 1959-68, pres. 1967), San Fernando Valley Bus. and Profl. Assn., Theta Chi, Gamma Pi. Republican. Home: 24530 Deep Well Rd Hidden Hills CA 91302 Office: 22600 Ventura Blvd Woodland Hills CA 91364

HERENSTEIN, ARNOLD FREDERICK, insurance company executive; b. N.Y.C., Dec. 21, 1948; s. Henry and Jessie (Cohen) H.; m. Deborah Hope Shay, June 6, 1971; children—Beth Nicole, Monica Leigh. B.A. in Econs., CCNY; 1971; M.B.A., St. John's U., 1978. Cons. Standard Research Cons., N.Y.C., 1971-73; mgr. Royal Ins., N.Y.C., 1973-81, asst. to gen. mgr., London, 1981-83, asst. sec., N.Y.C., 1983-85; Dir. CIGNA Property Casualty Cos., Phila., 1985—, Ins. Cons. Services, N.Y.C., 1984—, dir. P&H Display Corp., Bklyn. Mem. Ins. Inst. Am., Am. Ins. Assn. (manpower cost com. 1977-80), Geneva Assn. (corr.). Democrat. Jewish. Office: CIGNA 1600 Arch St Philadelphia PA 19103

HERGE, HENRY CURTIS, SR., retired educator; b. Bklyn., June 29, 1905; s. Henry John and Theresa (Maaz) H.; m. Josephine E. Breen, July 2, 1931 (dec. Oct. 8, 1975); children: Joel Curtis, Henry Curtis; m. Alice V. Wolfram, Apr. 21, 1976. B.S., NYU, 1929, M.A., 1931, Ed.D., 1942; M.A. (hon.), Wesleyan U., 1946; Ph.D., Yale U., 1956. Instr. English Sr. High Sch., Port Washington, N.Y., 1928-38; dist. prin. Bayville, N.Y., 1938-41, Bellmore, N.Y., 1941-45; asst. dir. study on Armed Services edn. programs Am. Council Edn., Washington., 1945-46; dir. higher edn., tchr. edn. cert. Conn. Dept. Edn., 1946-53; dean, prof. edn. Rutgers U., 1953-64, prof. edn., 1964-75, assoc. dir. Ctr. for Internat. Programs, 1968-75; vis. prof. Hartford U., 1950-52, Fairfield U., 1950-53, U. So. Calif., summer 1964, NYU, 1964-65; del. White House Conf. Edn., 1957; edn. cons. USOM Asuncion and ICA dir. ednl. priorities study for ministry of edn., Paraguay, 1961; team leader Rutgers-U.S. AID field survey, Zambia and Malawi, 1961-62; chief human resource devel. officer U.S. AID, Jamaica, 1966-68; Fulbright rapporteur Seminar in Univ. Adminstrn., U.S. and Italy, 1970; OAS sr. research fellow, Paraguay and Jamaica, 1972-73. Author: Wartime College Training Programs of Armed Services, 1948; The College Teacher, 1966; editor: Disarmament in the Western World, 1968; Common Concerns in Higher Education: An Italian-American Universities Project, Phase I, 1970; contbr. numerous articles to profl. publs. Pres. Shadow Lake Assn., Vt., 1976-78; sec. Fed. Lake Assns., No. Vt., 1980-84; project dir. Hilton Head Plantation Public Forum for Humanities, 1980-81; chmn. bd. trustees Coll. Hilton Head (S.C.), 1984-86, Town Council Com. for Higher Edn., 1986-88. Served as comdg. officer Wesleyan U. Navy V-12 unit 1943-45; lt. comdr. USNR (Ret.). Recipient certificate of recognition NCCJ, 1958. Mem. Nat. Assn. State Dirs. Tchr. Edn. and Certification (past pres.. Hono Citation 1986), Nat. Soc. for Study Edn., N.J. Congress Parents and Tchrs. (hon. life), N.J. Secondary Sch. Tchrs. Assn. (trustee 1954-66, merit award 1966), Am. Assn. Higher Edn., N.J. Council on Edn., N.J. Schoolmasters Club, AAUP, Fulbright Alumni Assn. (v.p. S.C. chpt. 1983—), Naval Res. Assn. (life), The Retired Officers Assn., Phi Delta Kappa (emeritus), Epsilon Pi Tau (laureate trustee), Kappa Delta Pi (Compatriot in Edn. award 1976). Republican. Presbyterian. Home: 39 Pineland Rd Hilton Head Island SC 29928

HERING, GUNTHER ERWIN, investment banking executive; b. Munich, Germany, Sept. 22, 1936; came to U.S., 1959; s. Erwin and Wera (Binder) H.; m. Jan T. Turner, Dec. 2, 1978; children: John Gunther, Bren Elizabeth. M.B.A., U. Hamburg, Germany, 1959. Mgmt. cons. McKinsey & Co., N.Y.C., 1971-75; v.p. corp. devel. Fluor Corp., Irvine, Calif., 1975-86; sr. v.p. Shearson Lehmann, N.Y.C., 1986-87; pres., chief exec. officer Harpener AG, Dortmund, Fed. Republic Germany, 1988—; chmn. Wanderer AG, Munich, Bowe GMBH, Augsburg, Fed. Republic Germany; dir. Phenol Chemie, Gladbeck, Fed. Republic Germany; prin., mng. dir. Hering & Co., Greenwich, Conn., 1988—. Mem. 552 Club Hoag Meml. Hosp., Newport Beach, Calif., 1976. Recipient Johanniter Orden, Bonn, Germany, Ven. Order St. John, London. Clubs: N.Y. Yacht, Indian Harbor Yacht, Norddertscher Regatta Verein, Big Canyon Country. Home: 62 Royal St George Rd Newport Beach CA 92660 also: 45 Greenwich Hills Dr Greenwich CT 06831 Other: Hering and Co 100 Putnam Green Greenwich CT 06831

HERINGER, HANS JÜRGEN, professor of German philology; b. Apr. 26, 1939; married Doris Fröhlich, 1971; children: Georg, Anja. Student, U. Mainz, 1961, U. Heidelberg, Fed. Republic Germany, 1959-61, 62-64; PhD Dissertation, U. Heidelberg, Fed. Republic Germany, 1965, Habilitation for German Philology and Linguistics, 1969. Asst. prof. U. Heidelberg, 1969-70; prof. German philology U. Copenhagen, 1970, U. Tübingen, Fed. Republic of Germany, 1971-81, U. Augsburg, Fed. Republic of Germany, 1981—. Author: Practical Semantics, 1974, Wort für Wort, 1978, Wege zum Verstehenden Lesen, 1987; editor linguistic jour. Sprache und Literatur. Home: Seestrasse 30, Schondorf, 8913 Ammersee, Bayern Federal Republic of Germany Office: Uinv Augsburg, Universitatsstrasse 10, Augsburg 8900, Federal Republic of Germany

HERLITZIUS, ERWIN GEORG, political science educator; b. Erfurt, German Democratic Republic, Mar. 15, 1921; s. Ferdinand Joachim and Marie (Keck) H.; m. Rosemarie Jobst, Jan. 1950; children: Jobst Ulrich, Thomas. Diploma in Social Scis., Friedrich-Schiller U., Jena, German Democratic Republic, 1950; PhD, Humboldt U., Berlin, German Democratic Republic, 1959, Habilitation, 1965. Asst. U. Jena, German Dem. Republic, 1949-50; docent Deutsches Theater-Inst., Weimar, German Dem. Republic, 1950-51; docent, prof. Bergakademie Freiberg Mining Acad., Freiberg, German Dem. Republic, 1951-63; prof., dean Technische U., Dresden, German Dem. Republic, 1964—, prof. emeritus, 1986—; leader nat. com. Internat. Union of History and Philosophy Sci., 1967-71; vis. scholar to U.S., 1970, 72, 74, 77. Author: G. Agricola-Philosophy of Renaissance, 1960; Entstehung und Entwicklung der Technikwissenschaften, 1982; contbr. articles to profl. jours. Recipient Humboldt medal Verdienter Hochschullehrer Ministerium für das Hoch- und Fachschulwesen der German Dem. Republic, 1981-82. Home: Leonhard-Frank-Strasse, 43 (69-44), 8027 Dresden German Democratic Republic

HERMAN, FRED L., lawyer; b. New Orleans, Mar. 25, 1950; s. Harry and Reba (Hoffman) H.; m. Amanda Luria, Mar. 4, 1975. BA, Tulane U., 1972; JD, Loyola U.-New Orleans, 1975. Bar: La. 1975, U.S. Dist. Ct. (ea. dist.) La. 1975, U.S. Ct. Appeals (5th cir.) 1978, U.S. Dist. Ct. (we. and mid. dists.) La. 1981, U.S. Ct. Appeals (11th cir.) 1981. Assoc. Herman & Herman, New Orleans, 1975-80; ptnr. Herman, Herman, Katz & Cotlar, New Orleans, 1980-87; sole practice, New Orleans, 1987—; ltd. ptnr. New Orleans Saints, 1985, legis. counsel, chief negotiator for mng. ptnr., 1987; adj. faculty Tulane U.; lecturer Loyola Sch. Law, New Orleans, La. Trial Lawyers Assn. Commr. New Orleans Pub. Belt R.R. Commn., 1983—; mem. Jefferson Parish Child Abuse Advocacy Program, 1980-81; spl. counsel litigation council, State of La.; spl. counsel City of New Orleans; bd. dirs. Odyssey House Substance Abuse Treatment Ctr. Mem. Fed. Bar Assn. (bank counsel sect.), La. Bankers' Assn., La. State Bar Assn., Assn. of Trial Lawyers of Am. Office: One Shell Square New Orleans LA 70139

HERMAN, HERBERT, materials science educator; b. N.Y.C., June 15, 1934; s. Samuel and Frances (Friedman) H.; m. Barbara R. Budin, July 1, 1963; 1 child, Daniel. B.S., DePaul U., 1956; M.S., Northwestern U., 1958, Ph.D., 1961. Fulbright scholar U. Paris, 1961-62, Argonne Nat. Lab., 1962-63; asst. prof. U. Pa., 1963-68, Ford Found. prof. in industry, 1967-68; prof., chmn. dept. materials sci. SUNY, Stony Brook, 1968—; liaison scientist U.S. Office Naval Research, London, 1975-76; mem. and chmn. NRC panels, 1978-81; indsl. cons. Editor-in-chief: Treatise on Materials Science and Technology, 1972—, Materials Sci. and Engring., internat. jour.; co-editor: series Ocean Technology, 1976—; contbr. articles to profl. jours. NSF grantee, 1964-69, 78—; AEC grantee, 1968-74; Office Naval Research grantee, 1974—; NASA grantee, 1980—; also others. Mem. AIME, Am. Soc. Metals, Am. Phys. Soc., Am. Ceramic Soc., Am. Crystallogrphic Soc., Marine Tech. Soc. (chmn. marine materials com.), Am. Soc. Engring. Edn., AAAS, Am. Soc. Metals (tech. divs. bd., chmn. thermal spray div. 1986—), Sigma Xi. Office: SUNY Dept Materials Sci Stony Brook NY 11794

HERMAN, KENNETH, psychologist; b. Englewood, N.J., Mar. 4, 1927; s. Joseph and Rose (Sattenstein) H.; m. Benita Saievetz, June 7, 1959; children: Michael Robert, Deborah Lynn, Joseph Todd, Rebecca Jane. A.B., Fla. So. Coll., 1950; M.Ed., Boston U., 1952; Ed.D., Columbia U., 1955, N.Y. U., 1956. Diplomate: Am. Bd. Clin. Psychology; cert. sex therapist. Research Bergen County Dept. Probation, Hackensack, N.J., 1948; investigator Child Welfare Home, Hackensack, 1948; psychometrist Student Clinic, Fla. So. Coll., Lakeland, 1948-50; clin. psychologist Mass. Gen. Hosp., Boston, 1951-54; research psychologist Med. Sch., Harvard, 1952-53; psychologist Speech Clinic, Boston U., 1952-53; research asst. State U. Iowa, 1954; founder Psychol. Service Center, Teaneck, N.J., 1955; dir. Psychol. Service Center, 1955—; dir. Reading Clinic, Child Study Center, 1965-66; chmn. bd., pres. Child Growth and Devel. Corp., 1969. Contbr. articles to profl. jours. Dir. Antipoverty Program, Garfield, N.J., 1965-66; bd. examiners Internat. Assn. Counseling Services, 1973-80; dir. Center Sexual and Relationship Enrichment, 1978—, Psycom Corp., 1980, 2d Self Discovery Program, 1980; cons. Hackensack Juvenile Counseling Program, 1974-76, N.Y. and N.J. Council of Chs., 1979—, participant radio and TV programs. Served with AUS, 1945-46. Mem. Am. Soc. Clin. Hypnosis, Soc. Clin. Exptl. Hypnosis, N.J. Personnel and Guidance Assn., Eastern Psychol. Assn., N.J. Clin. Psychologists, Nat. Council on Family Relations, Bergen County Sch. Psychologists Assn., Psychologists Interested in Advancement Psychotherapy, Am. Group Psychotherapy Assn., Psychologists Interested in Pvt. Practice, Am. Assn. Sex Educators, Counselors and Therapists, Nat. Vocat. Guidance Assn., Acad. Psychologist Marital Counseling, Am. Personnel and Guidance Assn., Am. Speech and Hearing Assn., N.J. Speech Assn., Tau Epsilon Phi, Kappa Delta Pi, Pi Gamma Mu, Omicron Delta Kappa. Home: 342 Orchard Rd Wyckoff NJ 07481 Office: 175 Cedar Lane Teaneck NJ 07666

HERMAN, ROBERT LEWIS, cork co. exec.; b. N.Y.C. July 16, 1927; s. Nat W. and Ruth (Stockton) H.; A.B., Columbia, 1948, B.S., 1949; m. Susan Marie Volper, Dec. 10, 1966; children—Candia Ruth, William Neal. Vice pres. Joseph Samuels & Sons, Inc., Whippany, N.J., 1953-62; pres. Dependable Cork Co., Inc., Morristown, N.J., 1962—; chmn. bd. Global Technology Systems. Co., Trevor, Wis., 1980—. Served to comdr. C.E. Corps, USNR, 1949-53. Mem. N.J. Mfrs. Assn., Naval Res. Assn., U.S. C. of C. Clubs: Navy League; Columbia University, Princeton (N.Y.C.). Inventor Corticiera natural cork wallcovering. Home: PO Box 1023 Morristown NJ 07960-1023 Office: POB 1102 Morristown NJ 07960-1102

HERMAN, STEPHEN GERALD, ophthalmologist; b. Boston, Sept. 23, 1939; s. Louis M. and Ruth F. H.;m. Bettina Gershinzon, Mar., 1965. BS, Rensselaer Poly. Inst., 1961; MD, Chgo. Med. Sch., 1965. Diplomate Am. Bd. Ophthalmology, Am. Acad. Ophthalmology. Intern USPHS, Boston, 1965-66; resident Bronx Eye Infirmary, N.Y.C., resident, 1968-71; practice medicine specializing in ophthalmology, St. Petersburg and Seminole, Fla., 1971—; mem. staff. Lake Seminole Hosp., All Children's Hosp., Palms of Pasedena Hosp., Humana Sun Bay Hosp.; clin. asst. prof. U. South Fla. Coll. Medicine, Tampa, 1974-77, 84—. Served with USPHS, 1966-68, Fellow Am. Acad. Ophthalmology; mem. Fla. Med. Assn., Pinellas County Med. Soc. Republican. Clubs: Treasure Island Tennis and Yacht (Fla.); Tiger Bay. Avocations: gardening, boating, travel, archeology, collecting antiques. Office: 9375 Seminole Blvd Seminole FL 34642

HERMAN, WITOLD WALENTY, cellist, educator; b. Torun, Poland, Feb. 14, 1932; s. Alojzy and Margaret (Grosser) H.; Diploma, Copernic Lyceum, Torun, 1950, Szymanowski Conservatory, Torun, 1950; M.A., Acad. Music Cracow, 1956; Diploma, Ecole Normale de Musique, Paris, 1960; D.Philosophy of Music, World U., Tucson, 1984; Dr. Phil. in Music (hon.), U. Ariz., 1984; m. Catharine Bromboszcz, June 13, 1970; children—Margaret-Monika, Adam Raphael. Soloist France, Luxemburg, Belgium, Germany, Hungary, Rumania, Poland, 1954—; prof. Acad. Music Cracow, 1960—, chief of cello and doublebass/contrebass faculty; mem. jury Pablo Casals Competition, Budapest, 1968—; senator State Acad. Music, Cracow; prof. summer acad. Franz Liszt Music Acad., Weimar, 1972, Acad. for Strings, Lancut, 1981; prof. Summer Music Acad. for String Instruments, Lancut, 1981; rec. artist Radio Luxemburg, Polish radio and TV. 1972, 81, spl. prize Polish Ministry Culture and Arts, 1972, 82, Golden Cross Merit, Polish Govt., 1977; Honor medal 40th Anniversary of Polish Republic, 1984 Chevalier Cross, Polonia Restituta, 1986. Mem. Polish Musicians Union, Internat. Jeunesse Musicale. Roman Catholic. Club: Tennis (Torun, Cracow). Home: 49/m5 ul Friedleina, 30 009 Cracow Poland Office: Academy Music, ul Bohat Stalingradu 3, Cracow Poland

HERMANIES, JOHN HANS, lawyer; b. Aug. 19, 1922; s. John and Lucia (Eckstein) H.; m. Dorothy Jean Steinbrecher, Jan. 3, 1953. A.B., Pa. State U., 1944; J.D., U. Cin., 1948. Bar: Ohio 1948. Atty. Indsl. Commn. Ohio, 1948-50; asst. atty. gen. State of Ohio, 1951-57, asst. to gov., 1957-59; ptnr. Hermanies & Major (formerly Beall, Hermanies, Bortz & Major), Cin., 1958-82; mem. bd. grievances and discipline Supreme Ct. Ohio, 1976-82; mem. Ohio Bd. Bar Examiners, 1963-68. Mem. Southwest Ohio Regional Transit Authority, 1973-76, trustee U. Cin., 1977—; bd. election Hamilton County, Ohio, 1984—; chmn. exec. com. Hamilton County Rep. Party, 1974—. Served with USMC, World War II. Mem. ABA, Ohio Acad. Trial Lawyers Assn., Am. Judicature Soc. Clubs: Bankers, Queen City, Highland Country. Home: 2110 Columbia Pkwy Cincinnati OH 45202 Office: Hermanies & Major 30 Garfield Pl Suite 740 Cincinnati OH 45202

HERMANN, HORST, philosopher, educator; b. Frankfurt, Hesse, Fed. Republic Germany, July 19, 1930; s. Paul and Else (Nies) H.; m. Gudrun Anna Theresia Kempe, 1960; 1 child, Maili. Student, Johann Wolfgang Goethe U. Frankfurt, Fed. Republic Germany, 1953-54, Johannes Gutenberg U. Mainz, Fed. Republic Germany, 1951-53, 54-57; PhD, Johannes Gutenberg U. Mainz, Fed. Republic Germany, 1959. Asst. prof. Johannes Gutenberg U., 1958-63; tchr. College, Langen, Hesse, Fed. Republic Germany, 1964-69; trainer student tchrs. Tchrs Coll., Offenbach, Hesse, Fed. Republic Germany, 1969-73; cons. Ministry Edn., Wiesbaden, Hesse, Fed.

Republic Germany, 1973-75; prin. College, Bruchköbel, Hesse, Fed. Republic Germany, 1975-77; trainer student tchrs. Tchrs. Coll., Darmstadt, Bensheim, Hesse, Fed. Republic Germany, 1977—; lectr. philosophy Univ., Kassel, Hesse, Fed. Rep. Germany, 1975—. Author: (with F. Delekat) Immanuel Kant, 1963; contbr. articles, essays to periodicals. Friends of the Hebrew U. Jerusalem. Home: Friedrich Ebert St 5, D 6070 Langen Federal Republic of Germany

HERMANN, THOMAS GEORGE, lawyer; b. Cleve., June 15, 1935; s. George James and Elizabeth Virginia (Kreckel) H.; m. Maria Veres, Aug. 31, 1968 A.B., John Carroll U., Cleve., 1963; J.D., Cleve. State U., 1969. Bar: Ohio 1969, U.S. Dist. Ct. (no. dist.) Ohio, 1970, U.S. Ct. Appeals (6th cir.) 1971, N.Y. 1986, U.S. Dist. Ct. (so. dist.) N.Y. 1986. Atty., Legal Aid Soc. Cleve., 1969-70; assoc. Squire, Sanders & Dempsey, Cleve., 1970-79, ptnr., 1979—; lectr. seminars, Cleve. Advocacy Inst., life mem. 8th Jud. Conf., 1987—; mem. com. ct. tech. Ohio Supreme Ct., 1988—. Served with U.S. Army, 1954-57. Recipient Prize Project award ABA-AMA, 1982; Exceptional Performance citation Def. Research Inst., 1982; Merit Service award Bar Assn. Greater Cleve., 1981-82. Mem. ABA (chmn. tech. in legal practive and jud. systems div.1988—, chmn. law office tech. com. 1982-88, sect. sci. and tech.), Bar Assn. Greater Cleve. (chmn. med.-legal com., chmn. group travel com.), Cuyahoga County Bar Assn., Cleve. Assn. Civil Trial Attys. (pres. 1981-82). Republican. Club: Cleve. Athletic. Office: Squire Sanders & Dempsey 1800 Huntington Bldg Cleveland OH 44115

HERMANNSSON, STEINGRIMUR, minister foreign affairs Iceland; b. Iceland, June 22, 1928; s. Hermann Jonasson and Vigdis Steingrímsdottir; Grad. Reykjavik Coll., 1948; BSEE, Ill. Inst. Tech., Chgo., 1951; MS, Calif. Inst. Tech., Pasadena, 1952; m. Gudlaug Edda Gudmundsdottir, Oct. 19, 1962; children: Hermann, Hlif, Gudmundur; children by previous marriage: John, Ellen, Neil. Elec. engr. City of Reykjavik Elec. Power Works, 1952-53, Fertilizer Plant Inc., Iceland, 1952-54, So. Calif. Edison Co., Los Angeles, 1955-56; ptnr. Bldg. Contractors Ltd., Reykjavik, 1957; dir. Nat. Research Council Iceland, 1957-78; minister of justice, ecclesiastical affairs and agr., 1978-79, minister of fisheries and communications, 1980-83; prime minister of Iceland, 1983-87, minister of fgn. affairs, 1987—; M.P., 1971—; mem. council of Europe com. on higher edn. and research 1959-75; sec. Progressive Party, 1971-79, chmn., 1979—; del. UN, 1956. Mem. Elec. Engring. Soc., Engring. Soc. Iceland. Lutheran. Club: Rotary. Author papers on sci. and politics. Home: 19 Mavanes, 210 Gardabaer Iceland Office: Ministry for Fgn Affairs, Hverfisgata 115, 150 Reykjavik Iceland

HERMES, HEINZ OTTEN, engineer; b. Rheine, Westfalia, Fed. Republic Germany, Dec. 9, 1931; s. Josef and Sophia (Schmiemann) H. Student, Tech. U. Brunswick, Fed. Republic Germany, 1958; D in Engring., Tech. U. Berlin, 1976. Tech. asst. Tech. U. Brunswick, 1957-58; developer navy electronics Allgemeine Elektricitats-Gesellschaft Shipbuilding, Hamburg, Fed. Republic Germany, 1958-62; dept. mgr. avionics devel. Allgemeine Elektricitats-Gesellschaft Shipbuilding, Wedel, Fed. Republic Germany, 1962-67; mng. dir. Allgemeine Elektricitats-Gesellschaft Shipbuilding, Wedel, 1967—; trustee Flugzeug-Elektronik-Gesellschaft, Munich, 1970-71; cons. Adv. Group Aerospace, Bonn, Fed. Republic Germany, 1971—. Contbr. articles to profl. jours; inventor avionics and automatic check-out systems. Mem. German Meteorol. Soc., Soc. Detection and Navigation. Mem. Christian Dem. Party. Roman Catholic. Clubs: Tennis, Rowing. Office: AEG, Industriestr, 2000 Wedel Federal Republic of Germany

HERMODSSON, LARS FRITIOF, philologist, educator; b. Orsa, Sweden, Oct. 5, 1916; s. Carl Harald and Amalie Lydia (Fausel) H.; m. Gunborg Ingegärd Barck, May 15, 1948; children: Gunlög, Örjan, Erland, Hedvig. PhD, Uppsala U., Sweden, 1952. Tchr. Lappish Volumtary Sch., Jokkmokk, Sweden, 1947; lectr. U. Zürich, Switzerland, 1948-49; lectr. Uppsala U., 1952-60, prof., 1960-82. Author: Reflexive u intransitive Verba, 1952, Semantische Strukturen der Satzgefüge, 1978, Spätlese, 1986; editor: Dat Boec van den Houte, 1959; co-editor Studia Neophilologica, 1965-75, chief editor 1975—. Named Knight of Order Northern Star Royal Com. Stockholm, 1964; recipient Goethe medal Goethe Inst., Munich, 1974.

HERNANDEZ, KATHLEEN NYMAN, nurse; b. Chester, Pa., June 21, 1945; d. Ralph Henry and Beatrice Frances (Arico) Nyman; m. Alfred Joe Hernandez, Jr., July 18, 1970; children—Katelena Laura, Marc Andrew, Elizabeth Ann. B.S. in Nursing, U. Mich., 1967. R.N., Tex., Mich. Staff nurse Citizens Hosp., Houston, 1975; office mgr., gastrointestinal asst. nurse A.J. Hernandez, Jr., M.D., P.A., Houston, 1976—. Served to lt. USNR, 1966-70. Mem. Soc. Gastrointestinal Assts., Tex. Med. Soc. Aux., Sigma Kappa. Presbyterian. Home: 12206 Clearfork Dr Houston TX 77077 Office: 1200 Binz Suite 650 Houston TX 77004

HERNANDEZ, WILBERT EDUARDO, physician; b. Progreso, Mex., Mar. 17, 1916; s. Alonso C. and Adolfina (Camara) H.; came to U.S., 1947, naturalized, 1949; B.S., U. Yucatan, 1937; M.D., Hahnemann Med. Coll. Phila., 1941; m. Jayne Rhodes, Oct. 4, 1941; children—Mary Jayne (Mrs. Charles S. Horgan III), Patricia (Mrs. James Wheeler). Intern, Wyoming Valley Hosp., Wilkes-Barre, Pa., 1941-42; gen. practice medicine, Merida, Mex., 1942-46, Allentown (Pa.) State Hosp., 1947-48, Wilkes-Barre, 1948-51; specialized in anesthesiology St. Catherine's Hosp., Bklyn., 1955-57; chief dept. anesthesia Wyoming Valley Hosp., 1957-82; asso. in anesthesiology Geisinger Med. Group, NPW Med. Center, 1982-83; med. dir. Blue Cross of Northeastern Pa., 1970-87. Served as capt. M.C., AUS, 1951-53. Fellow Am. Coll. Anesthesiologists; mem. AMA, Pa. Med. Soc., Luzerne County Med. Soc., Am. Soc. Anesthesiologists, Pa. Soc. Anesthesiologists. Author: The Blood of the Conquistador, 1967. Contbr. articles to profl. jours. Home: 1172 Scott St Wilkes-Barre PA 18705 Office: 70 N Main St Wilkes-Barre PA 18711

HERNÁNDEZ ÁLVAREZ, JOSÉ, entrepreneur; b. Mexico City, Mar. 26, 1948; s. Ignacio Hernández-Pons and Mari a Elena Álvarez; m. Cynthia Elisa Smith, Oct. 15, 1971; children—José Daniel, Andrés, Marisa. Student U. Anahuac, 1970. Prodn. supr. Con-Papel, mfrs. carbon paper, 1967-68; with Herdez, S.A., food processors and distbrs., 1969-76, purchasing mgr., 1972-76; pres. Tipólito, S.A., graphic arts, 1976-82; treas. Herdez, S.A., 1977-82; vice chmn. Stafford de Méx. S.A., 1978-80; chmn. bd. Multi-Pak, S.A., 1980-81; founder, pres. Tianex, Inc., computer cons., info. gateway, 1982—; founder Printoptions, 1986—. Author: Love Sign, 1970; Tetrahedral Calendar, 1977; The Market Expander, 1983. Mem. Property Owners Assn. la Herradura. Roman Catholic. Home: 848 Farm Quarter Rd Mount Pleasant SC 29464 Office: 701 E Bay St S-200 Charleston SC 29403

HERNÁNDEZ CERVANTES, HÉCTOR, secretary of commerce and industrial development of Mexico; b. Mexico City, Dec., 1923. Student Nat. U. Mex. Colegio de Mexico, U. Melbourne. Past tchr. econ. theory U. Mex., Centre of Latin Am. Monetary Studies; then economist Banco de Mexico; asst. dir. fin. studies Ministry of Fin.; dir.-gen. industry and commerce, Ministry of Commerce, dir.-gen. fin. and internat. studies, Ministry of Fin.; under-sec. fgn. trade Ministry of Commerce and Indsl. Devel., 1982-83; sec. commerce and indsl. devel., 1983—. Office: Dept Industria y Comercio, Ave Cuauhtemoc 80, Mexico City DF, Mexico *

HERNÁNDEZ-COLÓN, RAFAEL, governor of Puerto Rico; b. Ponce, P.R., Oct. 24, 1936; s. Rafael Hernández Matos and Dorinda Colón; m. Lila Mayoral, 1959; children: Rafael, José Alfredo, Dora Mercedes, Juan Eugenio. A.B., Johns Hopkins U., 1956; LL.B., U. P.R. Assoc. commr. P.R. Pub. Service Commn., 1960-62; atty. gen. Commonwealth of P.R. San Juan, 1965-67; mem., pres. P.R. Senate, San Juan, 1969-73; gov. Commonwealth of P.R., San Juan, 1973-77, 85—. Author: The Commonwealth of Puerto Rico, Territory or State. Mem. pres.'s com. Popular Democratic Party P.R., 1968—; Dem. nat. committeeman, P.R., 1968-78; del. Dem. Nat. Conv., 1972, 76, 80; trustee Johns Hopkins U. Office: La Fortaleza PO Box 82 San Juan PR 00901 *

HERNANDEZ MURILLO, JOSE, agronomic engineer; b. Cali, Valle, Cauca, Colombia, Dec. 12, 1955; s. Alvaro Hernandez L. and Maria (Violet) De Hernandez. B in Agronomic Engring., Nat. U., Palmira, Valle, Colombia, 1984. Registered profl. engr., Colombia. Asst. investigator Cen. Inst. Agrl. Tropical, Cali, 1982—; cultivator individual property, Cali, 1975—. Contbr. articles to profl. jours. Mem. Assn. Colombiana Fitopatologia (Gozalo Ochoa prize 1984), Assn. Vallecaucana Orquideologia. Roman Catholic. Home: Calle 50 N #8N61 El Bosque, Cali, Valle Colombia Office: Cen Inst Agrl Tropical, AA 6713 FPY, Cali, Valle Colombia

HERNSTADT, JUDITH FILENBAUM, city planner, real estate executive, broadcasting executive; b. N.Y.C., Nov. 18, 1942; d. Alex and Ruth Selena (Silberman) Filenbaum. B.A., NYU, 1964, M.Urban and Regional Planning and Housing, 1966; certificate, Harvard Bus. Sch., 1977. With Office Planning Coordination, State of N.Y., 1966-68; partner Devel. Planning Assos., N.Y.C., 1967-68; with engring. scis. dept. Service Bur. Corp., N.Y.C., 1968-69; planning cons. Llewelyn-Davies Assos., N.Y.C., 1969-71, Arlen Realty & Devel. Corp., N.Y.C., 1971-73; partner Planning & Devel. Team, N.Y.C. and Las Vegas, 1974—; v.p. Nev. Ind. Broadcasting Corp. (KVVU/TV), Las Vegas, 1974-75; pres. Nev. Ind. Broadcasting Corp. (KVVU/TV), 1976-77, Hernstadt Broadcasting Corp., 1978-81. Condr. TV interview programs. Del. Fine Arts Fedn. N.Y., 1970—; bd. dirs. Hudson Inst., 1980—; mem. fine arts com. U.S. Dept. State; bd. dirs. Hebrew Immigrant Aid Soc.; bd. dirs. Am. Assocs. of Royal Acad. Art, London; mem. exec. com. Nat. Com. on Am. Fgn. Policy; bd. dirs. Afghan Relief Com., dirs. Decorative Arts Trust; vis. com., bd. dirs. Allen Meml. Art Mus. Oberlin Coll.; bd. dirs. Eastside Internat. Community Ctr., Prodemca, Coalition for Democratic Majority. Mem. Am. Soc. Planning Ofcls. Clubs: Harvard (N.Y.C.), Lotos (N.Y.C.); Sleepy Hollow Country (Scarborough, N.Y.). Home: 927 Fifth Ave New York NY 10021

HERNU, CHARLES, French political leader; b. Quimper, France, July 3, 1923; s. Eugene and Laurence (Prost) H.; m. Dominique Tetreau, July 4, 1975. Dir. Le Jacobin, newspaper, 1954; dep. from Rhone dept. French Nat. Assembly, 1956-58, 78-81, dep. from Lyons, 1986—; mayor, Villeurbanne, from 1977; minister of def. French Govt., 1981-86; mem. steering com. French Socialist Party, from 1971. Author: la Colère Usurpée, 1959; Priorité à Gauche, 1969; Soldat Citoyen, 1975; Chroniques d'Attente, 1976; Nous, les Grands, 1980; Defendre la Paix, 1985. Office: care Parti Socialiste, 10 rue de Solferino, 75333 Paris France *

HERON, PATRICK, painter; b. Leeds, Yorks, Eng., Jan. 30, 1920; s. T. M. and Eulalie (Davies) H.; m. Delia Reiss, 1945 (dec. 1979); 2 children. Ed. Slade Sch., London. D.Litt. (hon.), Exeter, 1982. Art critic New English Weekly, 1945-47, New Statesman and Nation, 1947-50; London corr. Arts, N.Y.C., 1955-58; tchr. painting Central Sch. Arts and Crafts, London, 1953-55; John Power lectr. Sydney U. (Australia), 1973; Doty prof. U. Tex., Austin, 1978; trustee Tate Gallery, 1980—. Numerous one-man shows, including: (retrospectives) Wakefield City Art Gallery, 1952, Demarco Gallery, Edinburgh, 1967, Mus. Modern Art, Oxford, Eng., 1968, U. Tex. at Austin Art Mus., 1978; Sao Paulo Bienal, 1954, 65; Whitechapel Art Gallery, London, 1972; numerous group shows, Europe, Am.; represented in permanent collections, including: Tate Gallery, Brit. Mus., Victoria and Albert Mus., Arts Council; Brit. Council, Nat. Portrait Gallery, Stuyvesant Found., C. Gulbenkian Found., London, Nat. Mus. of Wales, Cardiff, Montreal Mus. Fine Art (Que., Can.), Musé e d'Art Contemporain, Montreal, Toronto Art Gallery (Ont., Can.), Vancouver Art Gallery (B.C., Can.), Nat. Gallery of W. Australia, Perth, Power Collection, Sydney, Bkly. Mus., Boymans Mus., Rotterdam, Netherlands, Smith Coll. Mus. Art, Toledo Mus. Art (Ohio), Albright-Knox Art Gallery, Buffalo, U. Mich. Mus. Art, Ann Arbor, U. Tex. at Austin Art Mus.; author: Vlaminck, 1947; The Changing Forms of Art, 1955; Ivon Hitchens, 1955; Braque, 1958; The Shapes of Colour, 1943, 78; Paintings by Patrick Heron 1965-77, 1978; The Colour of Colour, 1978; numerous articles on art. Decorated Comdr. Order Brit. Empire; recipient Main prize John Moores Liverpool Exhbn. II, 1959, Silver medal Sao Paulo Bienal, 1965. Address: Eagle's Nest, Zennor near St Ives Cornwall, England *

HERPST, ROBERT DIX, lawyer, optical company executive; b. Teaneck, N.J., Jan. 23, 1947; s. Harold Dix and Anita Augusta (Adams) H.; children: Katherine Elizabeth, Lauren Gabriel; m. Theresa M. Jacobini, Oct. 24, 1987. BS, NYU, 1969; JD, Rutgers U., 1972. Bar: N.J., U.S. Supreme Ct. Assoc. Pitney, Hardin & Kipp, Morristown, N.J., 1972-77; assoc. BOC Group, Inc., Montvale, N.J., 1977-87, div. counsel, 1978-80, assoc. corp. counsel, 1980-82, corp. counsel, asst. sec., 1982—; pres. Internat. Crystal Labs., Inc., Garfield, N.J., 1982-88, chmn. bd. dirs., 1988—. Mem. ABA (internat. bus. law com., overseas equity and joint venture investment subcom. of corp., banking and bus. law sect.). Home: 1 Lincoln St Suffern NY 10901 Office: The BOC Group Inc 85 Chestnut Ridge Rd Montvale NJ 07645

HERR, DAN, association executive; b. Huron, Ohio, Feb. 11, 1917; s. William Patrick and Wilhelmina Margaret (Slyker) H. B.A., Fordham U., 1938; postgrad., McGill U., 1938, Columbia U., 1939; LL.D. (hon.), Rosary Coll., 1967. Asst. to editor Inf. Jour., Washington, 1945-46; free lance writer 1946-48; pres. Thomas More Assn., Chgo., 1948-85, chmn. bd., 1985—; pub. The Critic, 1948-81, 85—; editor Overview, 1967-73. Author: Stop Pushing, 1961, Start Digging, 1987; co-editor six anthologies. Pres. Nat. Catholic Reporter, 1968-71; trustee Rosary Coll., 1969-73, chmn. bd. trustees, 1970-72. Served to maj. inf. AUS, 1941-45. Decorated Purple Heart, Silver Star; recipient Pere Marquette award Marquette U., 1957; Assn. Chgo. Priests award, 1978. Office: 223 W Erie St Chicago IL 60610

HERRERA, AMILCAR OSCAR, science policy educator; b. San Martin, Argentina, Oct. 23, 1920; arrived in Brazil, 1979; s. Sebastian and Elena (Masotti) H.; m. Lia Guarnieri, July 2, 1949; children: Alejandra Estela, Cristina Maria, Isabel Monica, Federico Alberto. BS, U. Buenos Aires, 1947, PhD, 1952; MS, Colo. Sch. Mines, 1951. Dir. tech. research Indsl. Bank Mining Dept., Buenos Aires, 1951-53; geol. cons. Buenos Aires, 1953-55; prof. faculty exact scis. U. Buenos Aires, 1953-55; v.p. Nat. Inst. Geology and Mining, Buenos Aires, 1964-66; prof., dir. geoch sect. dept. geology U. Chile, 1966-69; asst. dir. dept. natural resources Found. Bariloche, Argentina, 1969-76; sr. vis. fellow U. Sussex, 1976-78; dir. Inst. Geosci. and Ctr. Sci. Policy, U. Campinas, Brazil, 1979—; cons. internat. orgns.; mem. com. geol. data Internat. Union Geol. Scis., 1966-72; project coordinator UN U., Tokyo, 1978—. Team dir., main author: Latin American World Model Catastrophe or New Society? (translated into French, German, Dutch, Japanese, Spanish), 1976; author 5 books, 50 articles on natural resources, science policy. Grantee Internat. Devel. Research Ctr., Ottawa, Can., 1970-72, 79—, UN U., 1978—. Mem. Internat. Found. Devel. Alternatives (mem. internat. council 1981-84), Internat. Inst. Ednl. Planning (mem. adv. bd. 1984—), World Assn. Internat. Relations, Third World Forum (founding mem.), Interamerican Council Research on Sci. Policy (mem. adv. bd. 1985—). Home: Rua: Antonio Augusto de Almeida, 131 CEP 13083 Campinas, Sao Paulo Brazil Office: U Estadual de Campinas, Insto de Geociencias Unicamp, 6152 Sao Paulo Brazil

HERRERA, CHRISTIAN YANEZ, flight surgeon, pediatrician; b. Santiago, Chile, Mar. 9, 1938; came to U.S., 1968, naturalized, 1973; s. Arturo Segundo and Ernestina Carmen (Yanez) H.; M.D. with scholastic honors, magna cum laude, Univ. Chile, 1962; m. Shirley Mae Lagasse, Apr. 29, 1975; children—Karen Anne, Gary John, Ivan Edward, Iwonne Ester. Intern, U. Chile Med. Sch., Santiago, 1960-62; resident in pediatrics Children's Hosp., Boston, 1968-69; fellow in pediatrics Harvard Univ. Med. Sch., Boston, 1962-64, 69-70, instr. in pediatrics, 1971-73; asst. clin. prof. pediatrics Wright State U., Fairborn, Ohio, 1975-77, assoc. clin. prof., 1977-79; assoc. clin. prof. pediatrics U. Utah Sch. Medicine, 1980—; chief pediatric services USAF Hosp., Hill AFB, Utah, 1979-82; chief clin. services Andersen AFB, Guam, 1982-83; practice medicine specializing in pediatrics, Boston and Stoneham, Mass., 1971-74, Dayton, 1975-79, Provo, Utah, 1979-82; practice medicine specializing in pediatrics, flight medicine and emergency medicine, Guam, 1982-83; chief med. services USAF Hosp., Hill AFB, Utah, 1983-85, flight surgeon, 1985-86; chief aeromed. services USAF Clinic, Randolph AFB, Tex., 1986-88; dir. Base Med. Services & Clinic Comdr., USAF Clinic, Pope AFB, N.C., 1988—; regional mil. cons. pediatrics, 1974-79. Served to col., USAF, 1974-82. Recipient Pioneer award Ohio Occupational Therapy Assn., 1978; Physician's Recognition award in Continuing Med. Edn. AMA, 1973—. Diplomate Am. Bd. Pediatrics. Fellow Am. Acad. Pediatrics, A.C.P.; assoc. fellow Aerospace Med. Assn., mem. AMA, Soc. Air Force Physicians, Soc. USAF Flight Surgeons, Air War Coll. Alumni Assn. (founder and 1st v.p. Alamo chpt.), Internat. Platform Assn., Assn. Mil. Surgeons, Population Action Council. Course dir. Am. Heart Assn. Advanced Cardiac Life Support; instr. Am. College Surgeons' Advanced Trauma Life Support. Republican. Contbr. articles to med. jours. Home: 3637 Creek Path Pl Fayetteville NC 28301-4736 Office: USAF Clinic Pope Pope AFB NC 28308-5300

HERRHAUSEN, ALFRED, banker; b. Jan. 30, 1930. Mem. bd. mng. dirs. Deutsche Bank AG, Frankfurt, Fed. Republic Germany, main chmn., dep. chmn. and mem. supervisory bd. of numerous cos. Address: Taunusanlage 12 Postfach 100601, D-6000 Frankfurt am Main Federal Republic of Germany

HERRICK, PHILIP FIELD, lawyer; b. Washington, Apr. 18, 1909; s. Samuel and Fanny (Field) H.; m. Eleanor Collbran, Apr. 22, 1939; children—Philip F., Christine H., Sue H. B.A., Williams Coll., 1929; LL.B., George Washington U., 1933, LL.M., 1936. Bar: D.C., 1932, Va., 1937, P.R., 1940. Lectr. law George Washington U., Washington, 1948-73; U.S. atty. for P.R., 1942-48; mem. Appeal Bd. Office Contract Settlement, 1948-52; mem. U.S. Dist. Cts. Com. on Admissions and Grievances, 1970-77; sr. ptnr. Herrick, Allen & Glassman, Washington, 1952—; adj. prof. law George Washington U., 1986. Pres., Belle Haven Citizens Assn., Alexandria, Va., 1960-61. Mem. Am. Coll. Trial Lawyers, ABA, Bar Assn. D.C., Interam. Bar Assn. (mem. council) The Barristers, Phi Delta Phi, Phi Beta Kappa, Order of the Coif. Republican. Baptist. Clubs: Univ., Good-let Racquet, Belle Haven Country (pres. 1967-68). Home: 126 Moorings Park Dr Naples FL 33942 Office: 1000 Connecticut Ave NW Washington DC 20036

HERRING, CHARLES DAVID, lawyer, educator; b. Muncie, Ind., Mar. 18, 1943; s. Morris and Margaret Helen (Scherbaum) H.; children—David, Margaret, Christopher. B.A., Ind. U., 1965, J.D. cum laude, 1968. Bar: Ind. 1968, Calif. 1971, U.S. Dist. Ct. (so. dist.) Ind., U.S. Dist. Ct. (so. dist.) Calif. Research assoc. Ind. U., 1965-68; intern Office of Pros. Atty., Monroe County, Inc., 1967-68; ptnr. Herring, Stubel & Lehr, and predecessor Herring and Stubel, San Diego, 1972—; prof. law Western State U., 1972—. Vice chmn. Valle de Oro Planning Com., Spring Valley, Calif., 1972-75; chmn. Valle de Oro Citizens Exec. Com. for Community Planning, Spring Valley, 1975-78. Served with JAGC, U.S. Army, 1968-72. Mem. ABA (nat. best brief award 1968), Ind. Bar Assn., Calif. Bar Assn., San Diego County Bar Assn., Conf. Spl. Ct. Judges, Calif. Trial Lawyers Assn., Order of Coif. Author: (with Jim Wade) California Cases on Professional Responsibility, 1976. Home: 1968 Treseder Circle El Cajon CA 92021 Office: Herring Stubel & Lehr 101 W Broadway Suite 1670 San Diego CA 92101

HERRING, MONVILLE (LEE), county official; b. Brookhaven, Miss., May 14, 1935; s. Lonnie E. and Mildred Ada (Lea) H.; student U. New Orleans, 1945-52, U. Kans., 1963-64; 1 child, Suzie Ray. With Woodward White Co., New Orleans, 1952; standards coordinator Water Dist. #1 of Johnson County, Mission, Kans., 1962—. Served with USN, 1952-61. Mem. Nat. Wildlife Fedn., C. of C., Am. Water Works Assn., Kansas Rural Water Assn., Purchasing Mgrs. Assn. (dir. 1964-65), Kansas City Purchasing Agts., Am. Fedn. Police, Nat. Aubudon Soc., Am. Legion. Baptist. Home: 5702 Earnshaw St Shawnee KS 66216 Office: 5930 Beverly St Mission KS 66202

HERRINGER, FRANK CASPER, diversified service company executive; b. N.Y.C., Nov. 12, 1942; s. Casper Frank and Alice Virginia (McMullen) H.; m. Nancy Lynn Blair, Dec. 21, 1968; 1 son, William Laurence. A.B. magna cum laude, Dartmouth, 1964, M.B.A. with highest distinction, 1965. Prin. Cresap, McCormick & Paget, Inc. (mgmt. cons.), N.Y.C., 1965-71; staff asst. to Pres., Washington, 1971-73; adminstr. U.S. Urban Mass Transp. Adminstrn., Washington, 1973-75; gen. mgr., chief exec. officer San Francisco Bay Area Rapid Transit Dist., 1975-78; exec. v.p., dir. Transamerica Corp., San Francisco, 1979-86, pres., 1986—; dir. Sedgwick Group plc (London), Occidental Life Ins. Co., Transam. Ins. Co., Fred S. James Corp., Transam. Fin. Corp., Transam. Interway. Trustee Pacific Presbyn. Med. Ctr., Amos Tuck Sch. Bus. Adminstrn. Dartmouth Coll., Mills Coll. Mem. Phi Beta Kappa. Republican. Clubs: Olympic, Bankers, Commonwealth. Home: 4175 Canyon Rd Lafayette CA 94549 Office: Transam Corp 600 Montgomery St San Francisco CA 94111 *

HERRINGTON, JOHN STEWART, government official; b. Los Angeles, May 31, 1939; s. Alan D. and Jean (Stewart) H.; m. Lois Haight, Apr. 10, 1965; children—Lisa Marie, Victoria Jean. A.B. in Econs., Stanford U., 1961; J.D., U. Calif., San Francisco, 1964. Bar: Calif. 1964. Dep. dist. atty. Ventura County Dist. Atty.'s Office, Calif., 1965-66; ptnr. Herrington & Herrington, Walnut Creek, Calif., 1966-81; dep. asst. to Pres. White House, Washington, 1981, asst. to Pres., 1983-85; asst. sec. Dept. Navy, Washington, 1981-83; sec. Dept. Energy, Washington, 1985—; mem. Res. Forces Policy Bd., Washington, 1981-83; chmn. Def. Dept. Per Diem Com., Washington, 1982-83; chmn. U.S. Del. IEA Ministerial Conf.; U.S. Rep. annual gen. conf. IAEA, spl. session on Chernobyl. Trustee Ronald Reagan Presdl. Found., 1985—. Served to 1st lt. USMC, 1962. Recipient Disting. Service medal U.S. Dept. Def., 1983. Mem. U.S. Naval Inst., Calif. Bar Assn., Hastings Alumni Assn., Stanford U. Alumni Assn. Republican. Office: Dept of Energy 1000 Independence Ave SW Washington DC 20585

HERRIOT, JAMES (JAMES ALFRED WIGHT), veterinary surgeon, author; b. Oct.3, 1916; s. James Henry and Hannah Wight; m. Joan Catherine Danbury, 1941; 2 children. Ed. Glasgow Vet. Coll.; D.Litt. (hon.), U. Heriot-Watt, 1979; DVSc (hon.), Liverpool, 1983. Practice veterinary medicine, Thirsk, Yorks, Eng., 1940—. Author: If Only They Could Talk, 1970; It Shouldn't Happen to a Vet, 1972; All Creatures Great and Small, 1972; Let Sleeping Vets Lie, 1973; All Things Bright and Beautiful, 1973; Vet in Harness, 1974; Vets Might Fly, 1976; Vet in a Spin, 1977; James Herriot's Yorkshire, 1979; The Lord God Made Them All, 1981; The Best of James Herriot, 1982; James Herriot's Dog Stories, 1985; (also juvenile books) Moses the Kitten, 1984; Only One Woof, 1985; The Christmas Day Kitten, 1986; Bonny's Big Day, 1987; numerous translations. Served with RAF, World War II. Decorated Order Brit. Empire. Mem. Royal Coll. Vet. Surgeons, Brit. Vet. Assn. *

HERRMANN, BERND GOTTLIEB, biology educator; b. Berlin, Feb. 3, 1946; m. Susanne Lindner, Sept. 18, 1970; children: Daniel, David. Diploma in Biology, Free U. Berlin, 1970, PhD, 1973. Asst. prof. biology Free U. Berlin, 1975-78; prof. U. Göttingen, Fed. Republic Germany, 1978—, dean Biology faculty, 1983-84. Author: (with others) Methods of Preparation for Electromicroscopy, 1985; editor: Mensch und Umwelt im Mittelalter, 1986, (with R. Sprandel) Determinanten der Bovölkerungsentwicklung in Mittelalter, 1987, Innovative Trends in Prehistoric Anthropology, 1981, (with G. Grupe) Trace Elements in Environmental History, 1988. Office: U Göttingen, Bürgerstrasse 50, 3400 Göttingen Federal Republic of Germany

HERRMANN, CHARLENE ALICE, transportation executive; b. Chgo., Nov. 19, 1937; d. Floyd Alvin and Alice Elise (Stach) Schraufnagel; m. George Edward Herrmann, Aug. 5, 1961; children: Kyle Ann, Jeffrey Edward. BS in Edn., No. Ill. U., 1959. Cert. elem. tchr., Ill. Tchr. Sch. Dist. 163, Park Forest, Ill., 1959-61, Sch. Dist. 33, West Chgo., Ill., 1961-65; tax rep. IRS, Chgo., 1979-81; rt. supr. Crosstown Services, Inc., subs. Willett, Inc., Glen Ellyn, Ill., 1981-86, br. mgr., 1986—; mem. transp. task force Special Assn. for Special Edn. in Du Page County (North Region), Roselle, Ill., 1986—. 4-H leader-dir. DuPage County Coop. Extension Service, 1976—. Democrat. Roman Catholic. Club: Winfield Jr. Women's (Ill.) (com. chmn. 1970-75).

HERRMANN, CLAUDINE FANCHETTE, writer, lawyer, educator; b. Brussels, Nov. 19, 1926; came to France, 1967; d. Léon Isaie and Hélène Marie (Manon) H. Licence de Droit, U. Paris, 1948, Doctorat de Droit, 1954. Lawyer Avocat à la Cour de Paris, 1949-61; prof. Kabul U., 1961; editor Les Femmes Pub. Co., Paris, 1962—, Gallimard Pub. Co., Paris, 1962—; assoc. prof. Boston U., 1971-77; vis. prof. U. Colo., 1967-68, U. Mass., 1970-71, Tufts U., fall 1978, Paris VII, spring 1983, Boston Coll., fall 1987; lectr. in field. Author: Le Rôle Judiciaire et Politique des Femmes sous la République Romaine, 1964; (novels) L'Etoile de David, 1958, Maître Talmon, 1961, Le Cavalier des Steppes, 1963, Le Diplôme, 1965; (criticism) Les Voleuses de Langue, 1976, German edit., Italian edit., New French Feminisms, 1980; translator: Les Italiens, 1966; contbr. articles to profl.

jours. Recipient Union de Jeunes Avocats, 1949; grantee Caisse des Lettres Ministère de la Culture, 1963. Fellow Bar of Paris (Coupe d'Eloquence Prix d'improvisation 1953), Société Staelienne, Société Chateaubriand. Address: 69 Revere St Boston MA 02114 also: 8 rue Tournefort, 75005 Paris France

HERRMANN, JOACHIM, archaeologist, educator; b. Lübnitz, Potsdam, German Democratic Republic, Dec. 19, 1932; s. Albert and Martha (Paul) H.; m. Ursula Becher, 1954; children: Albrecht, Mathias, Ulrike. BS in History and Archaeology, Humboldt U., 1955, PhD in Philosophy, 1958, PhD in Philosophy (habilitation), 1965. Research asst. Humboldt U., Berlin, 1955-56; research asst. Acad. of Scis., Berlin, 1956-64, head dept., 1964-69, dir. cen. inst., 1969—; prof. history and archaeology Acad. of Scis. and Humboldt U., Berlin, 1972—; chmn. Dept. Social Scis. II Acad. Scis., Berlin, 1980—; pres. Nat. Com. of Historians of German Democratic Republic, 1981—. Author and editor of 25 books and 300 articles on history, archaeology, world history, early history of slave peoples, German and European ancient history. Recipient Nat. Prize of German Democratic Republic, 1971, Frantisek Palecky Medal, Acad. Scis. of Czechoslovakia, 1975, M. Drinov Metal, Acad. Scis. of Bulgaria, 1977, Metal d'Hommage U. Libre de Bruxelles, 1980. Mem. Acad. Scis., Polish Acad. Scis. (corresponding mem. 1985), Comitee Internat. de Scis. Historiques (mem. bur. 1985—), Union Internat. des Scis. Préhistoriques et Protohistoriques (mem. permanent council 1971—, exec. com. 1987—), Urania, Soc. for Dissemination Sci. Knowledge (pres. 1986—). Office: Acad Scis, Leipziger St 3-4, 1086 Berlin German Democratic Republic

HERRMANN, KENNETH JOHN, JR., social work educator; b. Lackawanna, N.Y., Apr. 13, 1943; s. Kenneth John and Alice Jane (Gray) H.; B.A., Canisius Coll., 1972; M.S.W., SUNY, Buffalo, 1975; m. Kathleen Wolf, Oct. 1969 (div. 1986); children—Aaron Kim-Eui, Gabe Sang-Koo, Mark Hoi-Duk, Rachele Hoi-Im, Ruth Myung-Hee. Tchr., St. Monica's Sch., Buffalo, 1963-67; sr. caseworker Erie County Child Welfare, 1969-73; family therapist Wyndham Lawn Home for Children, Lockport, N.Y., 1975-77; dir. children's services Dept. Social Service, County of Genesee (N.Y.), 1977-78; assoc. prof. social work SUNY, Brockport, 1978—; pvt. practice psychotherapy, East Pembroke, N.Y., 1975—; adoption social worker Dillon Children's Services Intercountry Adoption Program, 1982-84; mem. state bd. for social work N.Y. State Edn. Dept., 1984—; cons. UN Children's Fund, U.S. Senate, U.S. Congress; radio and TV appearances, lectr., cons. on children's rights, child abuse and neglect, family violence. Served with U.S. Army, 1967-69. Mem. Nat. Assn. Social Workers, Am. Group Psychotherapy Assn., N.Y. State Soc. Clin. Social Work Psychotherapists, Def. for Children, Internat. Soc. for Prevention and Treatment Child Abuse and Neglect, Children's Alliance of Monroe County, Am. Humane Assn., Vietnam Vets. Am., OURS, Inc. Author: I Hope My Daddy Dies, Mister, 1975; I'm Nobody's Child, 1982; author studies on internat. children's issues; contbr. articles to profl. jours. Home: 2614 E Main Rd East Pembroke NY 14056 Office: SUNY U Faculty Office Bldg Brockport NY 14420

HERRMANN, KLAUS PETER, mechanical engineering educator; b. Koenigszelt, Silesia, Ger., May 20, 1937; s. Erich Fritz and Margarete Emma (Berger) H.; m. Rosemarie Schauer, July 17, 1965; 1 son, Thomas. Diploma physics, U. Halle, 1961, Ph.D., 1964, D.Sc., 1969. Asst. dept. physics, U. Halle, 1961-69, sr. asst., 1970-71; lectr. Inst. Mechanics, U. Karlsruhe, 1973-74; assoc. prof. U. Karlsruhe, 1975-77; prof. mechanics U. Paderborn, 1977—; research scholar U. Warsaw, Poland, 1970-71; vis. prof. Stanford U., 1979, Va. Poly. Inst. and State U., Blacksburg, 1983. Editor (with L. H. Larsson) Fracture of Non-metallic Materials, 1987; contbr. articles to profl. jours. Fellow N.Y. Acad. Sci.; mem. Hochschulverband, Assn. Applied Math. and Mechanics, German Assn. for Materials Testing. Office: Univ Paderborn, Pohlweg 47-59, Paderborn, D 4790 Nordrhein-Westfalen Federal Republic of Germany

HERRMANN, LACY BUNNELL, investment company executive, financial entrepreneur, venture capitalist; b. New Haven, May 12, 1929; s. James Joseph and Helen Georgia (Bunnell) H.; A.B., Brown U., 1950; postgrad. London Sch. Econs., 1953-54; M.B.A., Harvard U., 1956; m. Elizabeth Ocumpaugh Beadle, May 23, 1953; children—Diana Parsons, Conrad Beadle. Asst. to purchasing mgr. and buyer Westinghouse Elec. Corp., Metuchen, N.J., 1956-60; asst. v.p. Douglas T. Johnston & Co., Inc., N.Y.C., 1960-66; v.p. Johnston Mut. Fund, Inc., N.Y.C., 1964-66; gen. partner Tamarack Assos., N.Y.C., 1966-84; chmn. bd., pres. Family Home Products, Inc., N.Y.C., 1972-84, Buxton's Country Shops, Jamesburg, N.J., 1973-86; pres., dir. STCM Mgmt. Co., Inc., N.Y.C., 1974—; founder, pres. STCM Corp., money market fund, N.Y.C., 1974-76; vice chmn. bd. trustees, v.p. Centennial Capital Cash Mgmt. Trust, N.Y.C. successor to STCM Corp., 1976-81; chmn. bd. trustees, pres. successor fund Capital Cash Mgmt. Trust, 1981—; pres., dir. Incap Mgmt. Corp., 1982—; founder, chmn. bd. trustees, pres. Trinity Liquid Assets Trust, 1982-85, Oxford Cash Mgmt. Fund, 1982—, Prime Cash Fund, 1982—, Cash Assets Trust, 1984—, Short Term Asset Reserves, 1984—, Hawaiian Tax-Free Trust, 1985—, Churchill Cash Res. Trust, 1985—, Tax Free Trust Ariz., 1986—, Tax Free Trust Oreg., 1986—, 88—, Tax Free Fund Colo., 1987—, Churchill Tax-Free Fund Ky., 1987—, Churchill Tax-Free Cash Fund, 1988—, Tax-Free Cash Asset Trust, 1988—, U.S. Treasuries Cash Assets Trust, 1988—; chmn., pres. Aquila Mgmt. Corp., 1983—; v.p. Aquila Distbrs. Inc., 1981—, bd. dirs.; bd. dirs. Quest for Value Fund Inc., Quest for Value Cash Mgmt. Fund; founder, chmn. bd. trustees, pres. N.Y. Localities Legal Obligations Cash Access Trust, 1983—; chmn. Fiduciary Mgmt. Inc.; adviser Access, 1982—; organizer, dir. and/or cons. to numerous small to medium sized corps. and orgns.; founding dir. mgmt. cons. firm merged with Towers, Perrin, Forster & Crosby; instr. Rutgers U., 1958-59. Organizer, trustee endowed award Internat. div. Grad. Sch. Journalism, Columbia U., 1962—; trustee Meml. and Endowment Trust of St. Paul's Ch., Westfield, N.J., 1968—; mem. capital devel. com. St. Luke's Ch., Darien, Conn., 1978-85; mem. coll. scholarship fund com. St. Luke's Ch., Darien, Conn., 1976-85. Served to lt. (j.g.) USN, 1951-54; Korea; lt. USNR ret. Mem. N.Y. Soc. Security Analysts, Harvard Bus. Sch. Alumni Assn. N.Y. (dir. and officer 1958-71), Assn. Alumni Brown U. (dir. 1978—, exec. com. 1980-85, pres. 1983-85). Republican. Episcopalian. Clubs: Harvard, N.Y. Athletic (N.Y.C.); Brown U. (bd. dirs. 1981-84); Brown U. of Fairfield County (pres. 1977-82); University (R.I.); Faculty of Brown U. (Providence); Stratton Mountain Country (Vt.). Contbr. articles to profl. jours. Home: 6 Whaling Rd Darien CT 06820 Office: 200 Park Ave New York NY 10017

HERSANT, ROBERT JOSEPH EMILE, publications company executive, journalist, editor; b. Vertou, France, Jan. 31, 1920; s. Victor and Juliette (Hugot) H.; married, 8 children. Student Lycées of Rouen and Le Havre, France. Editor, 1945—; founder, pres.-dir. gen. Groupe de Presse Robert Hersant, Paris, 1950—; editor/owner of dailies including: Le Figaro, 1975, Paris-Normandie, Nord-Eclair, Nord-Matin, Centre-Presse, Le Berry Républicain, L'Eclair de l'Quest, France-Antilles, La Liberté du Morbihan, L'Action Républicain, Le Havre Presse, La République des Pyrenées, France-Soir, 1976—; editor/owner other publs. including: L'Auto-Jour., Yachting, Sport-Auto, Bateaux, Revue de la Chasse, La Pêche et les Poissons, Pointe de Vente, Votre tricot, La Bonne Cuisine, Layettes, Market, L'ami des Jardins, France-Amérique; owner Le Dauphine Libé ré, 1982—; pres. Nat. Assn. Gen. or Specialized Periodic Press and French Periodic Press Fedn., 1971—; v.p. French Nat. Press Fedn. Assn. of Provincial Dailies, 1972—; pres., dir. gen. Socpresse, La 5 television channel; mayor of Ravenel, France, 1953-59; mayor of Liancourt, France, 1967-74; counsel gen. Saint-Just-en-Chaussée, 1954-72. Active Nat. Assembly for l'Oise, 1956-78. Address: Groupe de Presse Robert Hersant, 12 rue de Presbourg, 75116 Paris France *

HERSCHBACH, DUDLEY ROBERT, chemistry educator; b. San Jose, Calif., June 18, 1932; s. Robert Dudley and Dorothy Edith (Beer) H.; m. Georgene Lee Botyos, Dec. 26, 1964; children: Lisa Marie, Brenda Michele. BS in Math., Stanford U., 1954, MS in Chemistry, 1955; AM in Physics, Harvard U., 1956, PhD in Chem. Physics, 1958; DSc (hon.), U. Toronto, 1977. Jr. fellow Harvard U., Cambridge, Mass., 1957-59, prof. chemistry, 1963-76, Frank B. Baird prof. sci., 1976—, mem. faculty council, 1980-83, master Currier House, 1981-86; asst. prof. U. Calif., Berkeley, 1959-61, assoc. prof., 1961-63; cons. editor W.H. Freeman lectr. Haverford Coll., 1962; Falk-Plaut lectr. Columbia, 1963; vis. prof. Göttingen (Germany) U., summer 1963, U. Calif. at Santa Cruz, 1972; Harvard lectr. Yale U., 1964; Debye lectr. Cornell U., 1966; Rollefson lectr. U. Calif. at Berkeley, 1969; Reilly lectr. U. Notre Dame, 1969; Phillips lectr. U. Pitts., 1971; Disting. vis. prof. U. Ariz, 1971, U. Tex., 1977, U. Utah, 1978, Gordon Lectr. U. Toronto, 1971, Clark lectr. San Jose State U., 1979, Hill lectr. Duke U., 1988, Flory lectr. Stanford U., 1988, Flugare lectr. U. Ill., 1988. Assoc. editor: Jour Phys. Chemistry. Guggenheim fellow U. Freiburg, Germany, 1968; vis. fellow Joint Inst. for Lab. Astrophysics U. Colo., 1969; Fairchild Disting. scholar Calif. Inst. Tech., 1976; Sloan fellow, 1959-63, Exxon Faculty fellow, 1980—; recipient pure chemistry award Am. Chem. Soc., 1965, Centenary medal, 1977, Pauling medal, 1978; Spiers medal Faraday Soc., 1976, Polanyi medal, 1981, Langmuir prize, 1983, Nobel Prize in Chemistry, 1986; named to Calif. Pub. Edn. Hall of Fame, 1987. Fellow Am. Phys. Soc. (chmn. chem. physics div. 1971-72), Am. Acad. Arts and Scis.; mem. Am. Chem Soc., AAAS, Nat. Acad. Scis., Royal Soc. Chemistry (fgn. hon. mem.), Phi Beta Kappa, Sigma Xi. Office: Harvard U Dept Chemistry 12 Oxford St Cambridge MA 02138

HERSCHORN, MICHAEL JULIUS, mathematics educator; b. Montreal, Que., Can., Apr. 21, 1933; s. Sheea and Molly (Surkes) H.; m. Shirley Sand, June 20, 1954 (dec. 1985); children—Sally Deborah, Madelyn Grace. B.A., McGill U., 1953, M.A., 1956, Ph.D., 1958. Asst. prof. math. McGill U., Montreal, 1959-67, assoc. prof., 1967-79, prof., 1979—, chmn. math. and stats. dept., 1982—. Chmn. bd. edn. Solomon Schechter Acad., Montreal, 1969-78; pres. Jewish Edn. Council Greater Montreal, 1977-79; v.p. Assn. Jewish Day Schs., Montreal, 1979—; v.p. Allied Jewish Community Services, 1980-85, chmn. exec. com., 1985—. Recipient Anne Molson Gold medal in math. and natural philosophy McGill U., 1953. Mem. Am. Math. Soc., Can. Math. Soc., Am. Schs. Oriental Research, AAAS, Sigma Xi. Home: 5235 Saranac Ave, Montreal, PQ Canada H3W 2G5 Office: McGill U, Dept Math and Stats, 805 Sherbrooke St W, Montreal, PQ Canada H3A 2K6

HERSHATTER, RICHARD LAWRENCE, lawyer, novelist; b. New Haven, Sept. 20, 1923; s. Alexander Charles and Belle (Blenner) H.; B.A., Yale U., 1948; J.D., U. Mich., 1951; m. Mary Jane McNulty, Aug. 16, 1980; children by previous marriage—Gail Brook, Nancy Jill, Bruce Warren; 1 stepdau., Kimberly Ann Matlock. Bar: Conn. 1951, Mich. 1951, U.S. Supreme Ct. 1959. Sole practice law, New Haven, 1951-85, Clinton, Conn., 1985—; state trial referee, 1984—. Chmn., Clinton Rep. Town Com. (Conn.), 1984-88, Rep. town Com., Conn., 1984-88. Author: The Spy Who Hated Licorice, 1966; Fallout For a Spy, 1968; The Spy Who Hated Fudge, 1970. Mem. Branford (Conn.) Bd. Edn., 1963-71. Served with U.S. Army Air Corps, 1942-44, AUS, 1944-46. Mem. Conn. Sch. Attys. Council (pres. 1977), New Haven County Bar Assn., Conn. Bar Assn., Middlesex County Bar Assn., Mystery Writers Am., West Haven C. of C. (pres. 1956). Lodge: Masons. Office: 2 Rt 81 Suite 1 Clinton CT 06413

HERSHEY, ALFRED DAY, geneticist; b. Owosso, Mich., Dec. 4, 1908; s. Robert Day and Alma (Wilbur) H.; m. Harriet Davidson, Nov. 15, 1945; 1 son, Peter. B.S., Mich. State U., 1930, Ph.D. in Chemistry, 1934, D.M.S., 1970; D.Sc. (hon.), U. Chgo., 1967. Asst. bacteriologist Washington U. Sch. Medicine, St. Louis, 1934-36; instr. Washington U. Sch. Medicine, 1936-38, asst. prof., 1938-42, asso. prof., 1942-50; mem. staff, genetics research unit Carnegie Inst. of Washington, Cold Spring Harbor, N.Y., 1950-62; dir. Carnegie Inst. of Washington, 1962-74; ret. 1974. Contbr. articles to profl. jours. Recipient Nobel prize in Medicine (joint), 1969; Albert Lasker award Am. Pub. Health Assn., 1958; Kimber Genetics award Nat. Acad. Scis., 1965. Mem. Nat. Acad. Scis. Address: RD 1640 Moores Hill Rd Syosset NY 11791

HERSHHORN, BERNARD SEYMOUR, veterinarian; b. Bklyn., June 17, 1928; s. Max and Ida (Bersson) H.; student Bklyn. Coll., 1945-46, 49-50; D.V.M., Cornell U., 1955. Asst. veterinarian Nickerson Animal Hosp., Stamford, Conn., 1955-58; assoc. veterinarian Meisel's Dog and Cat Hosp., N.Y.C., 1958-65; owner, dir. West End Vet. Clinic, with spl. interest in geriatrics, cardiology and exotic pets, N.Y.C., 1965—; research partner James A. Baker Inst. for Animal Health, Cornell U., 1970—; guest lectr. Chulalongkorn U., Bangkok, Thailand, 1983, Udorn Tchrs. Coll., Thailand, 1985; dep. examiner N.Y. State Bd. Vet. Medicine Dept. Edn., mem. campaign com. N.Y.C. div. Am. Cancer Soc., 1978, 79, 80, 81; asst. scoutmaster Boy Scouts Am., 1946-49, asst. explorer adv., 1949-55, merit badge counselor, 1955—; trustee Sunnyside Jewish Center, 1980, treas., 1981—, chmn. Israel Bond Drive, 1982-87. Recipient Reinald C. Werrenrath music medal, 1945. Mem. AVMA, N.Y. State Vet. Med. Soc. (ethics com. 1984—, Merit award 1979), Vet. Med. Assn. N.Y.C. (dir. 1968-77, sec. 1972, treas. 1973-77, historian 1979, Recognition award 1978, Merit award 1984, Veterinarian of Yr. 1985), Am. Animal Hosp. Assn., Am. Heartworm Soc. (charter), Am. Assn. Feline Practitioners, Assn. Avian Veterinarians (charter mem.), Am. Assn. Zoo Veterinarians, Am. Vet. Radiology Soc., Acad. Vet. Cardiology, Vet. Cancer Soc., Soc. Vet. Anesthesiology, Am. Vets. for Israel. Am. Assn. Avian Pathologists, N.Y. State Assn. of Professions, N.Y. Turtle and Tortoise Soc., N.Y. Choral Soc. (dir., pres. 1962-63), Williamsburg Community Soc. (trustee, rec. sec.), Smithsonian Instn. Author: Active Years for Your Aging Dog, 1978; editor A Word from the Veterinarian, Am. Kennel Gazette monthly, 1960-63; contbr. articles to profl. jours. Home and Office: 711 West End Ave New York NY 10025

HERSLEVEN, GUY PATRICK, impresario, publisher; b. Antwerp, Belgium, Oct. 20, 1947; s. Jacques Robert Pierre and Marianne (van Cutsem) H.; m. Francine Vercammen, Nov. 25, 1969; 1 child by previous marriage, Pascal. Second degree cert., Antheneum Kapellen, Antwerp, 1965. Sales promotor numerous firms Antwerp, Brussels, 1970-74; dir. G.P. Prodns. Cy. internat. concert and tour orgn., Antwerp, 1974—, Publi G.P., Antwerp, 1985—. Club: Derby Hockey (Antwerp). Home and Office: Ruytenburgstraat 46, 2600 Antwerp Belgium

HERSOV, BASIL EDWARD, mining executive; b. Johannesburg, Republic South Africa, Aug. 18, 1926; s. Abraham Sundell (Bob) and Gertrude Aronson H.; m. Antoinette Herbert, Sept. 28, 1957; children: Rowena Mary, Robert Basil, James Ronald, Alexandra Diana. BA with honors, U. Cambridge, Eng., 1949, MA, 1952; LLD (hon.), Rhodes U., Republic South Africa. Learner offcl. Anglovaal Group Ltd., Johannesburg, 1949-52, asst. mgr., 1952-58, mgr., 1958-62, asst. mng. dir., 1962-67, mng. dir., 1967-73, chmn., chief exec. officer, 1973—; chmn. bd. 1st Nat. Bank, Republic South Africa, Hartesbeestfontein Gold Mine, Republic South Africa, Assoc. Manganese Mines, Republic South Africa, Good Year Tyre, Republic South Africa. Gov. Rhodes U., 1980—, Urban Found., 1985—; hon. pres. South Africa Found., 1979—; patron Avril Elizabeth Children's Homes, Republic South Africa, 1978—, Johannesburg Child Welfare, Alexandra Progress Thru Prosperity. Served to capt. South African Air Force, 1943-45. Recipient Decoration for Meritorious Service Pres. South Africa, 1981; named hon. col. South African Air Force, 1985. Fellow Inst. Dirs. (pres. 1986—), South African Inst. Mining and Metalurgy, South African Inst. Mgmt.; mem. South Africa Chamber of Mines (council). Jewish. Clubs: Rand, Inanda (South Africa); Hawks, Pitt (Eng.). Office: Anglovaal Ltd, 56 Main St, Johannesburg 2000, Republic of South Africa

HERTER, FREDERIC PRATT, university administrator; b. Bklyn., Nov. 12, 1920; s. Christian Archibald and Mary Caroline (Pratt) H.; m. Annabel Toland, May 27, 1942 (dec. Dec. 1946); m. Harriet Ames Conel, Nov. 22, 1947 (div.); m. Solange Batsell, May 31, 1978; children: Frederic Pratt Jr., Caroline Ames, Brooke. BS, Harvard U., 1941, MD, 1944. Diplomate Am. Bd. Gen. Surgery. Intern Presbyn. Hosp., N.Y.C., 1944-45, resident, 1947-53, attending surgeon, 1954—; from asst. prof. to prof. Columbia U., N.Y.C., 1954—, Auchincloss Prof. of Surgery, 1970—; pres. Am. U., Beirut, 1987—; chmn. bd. trustees Am. U., Beirut, 1985-87; trustee Mary Imogene Bassett Hosp., Cooperstown, N.Y., 1970—, Jackson Labs., Bar Harbor, Maine, 1975-85. Contbr. more than 75 articles to profl. jours. Served to capt. M.C. AUS, 1945-47, PTO. Mem. Council on Fgn. Relations. Republican. Episcopalian. Clubs: Century, River (N.Y.C.). Home: 345 E 57th St New York NY 10022 Office: Am U of Beirut Office of President 850 3d Ave New York NY 10022

HERTWECK, E. ROMAYNE, educator; b. Springfield, Mo., July 24, 1928; s. Garnett Perry and Nova Gladys (Chowning) H.; m. Alma Louise Street, Dec. 16, 1955; 1 child, William Scott. B.A., Augustana Coll., 1962; M.A., Pepperdine U., 1963; Ed.D., Ariz. State U., 1966; Ph.D., U.S. Internat. U., 1978. Cert. sch. psychologist, Calif. Night editor Rock Island (Ill.) Argus Newspaper, 1961; grad. asst. psychology dept. Pepperdine Coll., Los Angeles, 1962; counselor VA, Ariz. State U., Tempe, 1963; assoc. dir. Conciliation Ct., Phoenix, 1964; instr. Phoenix Coll., Phoenix, 1965; prof. Mira Costa Coll., Oceanside, Calif., 1966—, mem. senate council, 1968-70, 85-87, chmn. psychology-counseling dept., 1973-75, chmn. dept. behavioral sci., 1976-82, 87-88; part-time lectr. dept. bus. adminstrn. San Diego State U., 1980-84, Sch. Human Behavior U.S. Internat. U., 1984—; prof. psychology Chapman Coll. World Campus Afloat, 1970; pres. El Camino Preschs., Inc., Oceanside, Calif., 1985—. Bd. dirs. Lifeline, 1969, Christian Counseling Center, Oceanside. Mem. Am., Western, North San Diego County (v.p. 1974-75) psychol. assns., Am. Personnel and Guidance Assn., Nat. Educators Fellowship (v.p. El Camino chpt. 1976-77), Am. Coll. Personnel Assn., Phi Delta Kappa, Kappa Delta Pi, Psi Chi. Club: Kiwanis (charter mem. Carlsbad club, dir. 1975-77). Home: 2024 Oceanview Rd Oceanside CA 92056 Office: Mira Costa Coll 1 Barnard Dr Oceanside CA 92056 Office: El Camino Preschs Inc 2002 California St Oceanside CA 92054

HERTZBERGER, HERMAN, architect, educator; b. Amsterdam, Netherlands, July 6, 1932; s. Herman and Margaretha Johanna (Prins) H.; m. Johanna C. van Seters, 1957; children—Akelei, Veroon, Titus. Grad. Tech. U. Delft (Netherlands), 1958. Practice architecture, Amsterdam, 1958—; prof. archtl. design Tech. U. Delft., 1970—, U. Geneva, 1986—. Archtl. designs include: Centraal Beheer, Apeldoorn, Netherlands, 1972; De Drie Hoven, Amsterdam, 1974; Music Ctr. Vredenburg (A.J. v. Eck award 1980), Utrecht, Netherlands, 1979; 2 schs., Amsterdam, 1983; Lima housing complex, West Berlin, 1986; co-editor (Dutch) Forum, 1959-63. Recipient Archtl. award Town of Amsterdam, 1968, Eternit award, 1974, Fritz Schumacher award, 1974, A.J. van Eck award, 1980, award Town of Amsterdam, 1985. Office: Architectenburo Hertzberger, Vossiusstraat 3, 1071 AB Amsterdam The Netherlands

HERVÉ-BAZIN, JEAN-PIERRE MARIE, author; b. Angers, France, Apr. 17, 1911; s. Jacques and Paule (Guilloteaux) Herve-B.; licenice es lettres, Faculté des Lettres, Paris; m. Odile L'Hermitte, Aug. 1967; children—Jacques, Jean-Paul, Maryvonne, Catherine, Dominique, Claude, Nicolas. Critic newspaper Journal du Dimanche; mem. staff Edits. Grasset, Edits. Seuil; pres. Commn. d'Aide a la Creation; author: (poetry) Jours, 1947, A la poursuite d'Iris, 1948, Humeurs, 1953; Traits, 1976; (novels) Vipere au Point, 1948, La Tete contre les Murs, 1949, La Mort du Petit Cheval, 1950, Le Bureau des Mariages, 1951, Leve-toi et Marche, 1952, L'Huile sur le Feu, 1954, Qui j'ose aimer, 1956, La Fin des Asiles, 1959, Au Nom du Fils, 1960, Chapeau bas, 1963, Plumons l'Oiseau, 1966, Le Matrimonie, 1967, Les Bienheureaux de la Desolation, 1970, Tristan, 1972, Cri de la Chouette, 1972, Madame Ex, 1975; Ce que je croix, 1977; Un Feu devore un autre Feu, 1978; L'Eglise verte, 1981; L'abecedaire, 1984. Decorated officier Legion of Honor; commandeur des Arts et des Lettres, des Palmes Academiques. Mem. Assn. Writers (v.p.), Acad. Goncourt, (pres. 1973—), PEN, Soc. des Gens et Lettres, Nat. des Lettres (council). Address: La Gasnaudiere, Barneville, 27310 Bourg-Achard France

HERZ, JOACHIM, operatic stage director, educator; b. Dresden, Germany, June 15, 1924. Staatsexamen, Musikhochschule, Dresden, German Dem. Republic, 1949; student Humboldt-Universität, Berlin, 1949-51. Mng. stage dir. Landesoper Dresden, 1951-53; stage dir. Komische Oper Berlin, 1953-56, dir., chief regisseur, 1976-81; stage dir. Operhaus Köln, 1956-57; chief regisseur Opernhaus Leipzig, 1957-59, opera dir., 1959-76; chief regisseur, leader stage div. Staatsoper Dresden, 1981—; lectr. Opernschule Dresden, Humboldt-Universitat, Musikhochschule, Cologne, Germany; dir. Abt. Musiktheaterregie Musikhochschule, Dresden, 1981—; lectr. Theaterhochschule, Leipzig, Germany, U. Salzburg, Austria, U. Munich; vis. lectr. U. Calif., U. B.C., NYU, Eichstaff U., U. Paris VIII, U. London.; hon. prof. U. Leipzig, 1976—; hon. bd. mem. Musiktheaterkomitee, Internationales Theaterinstitut; hon. mem. Bolschoi Theater, Moscow; mem. Direktorium East German Internationales Theaterinstitut. Guest prodns. include Buenos Aires, London, Vancouver, Zurich, Moscow, Cardiff, Stockholm, Belgrade, Bern, Munich, Hamburg, Frankfurt, Vienna. Recipient Nationalpreis 1/2/3 klasse German Democratic Republic, Kritikerpreise, Berliner Zeitung, Kunstpreis, Stadt Leipzig, Vaterlandischer Verdienstorden in gold, Grand prix du Disque, Goldener und Silberner Lorbeer des Fernsehens German Dem. Republic, Best Staging of Yr. award Zauberflote, Belgrad; named Best Dir. of Yr., London. Mem. Akademie der Kunste. Office: Staatsoper Dresden, Semper Opera Theaterplatz Pf 75, 8010 Dresden German Democratic Republic

HERZBERG, GERHARD, physicist; b. Hamburg, Ger., Dec. 25, 1904; emigrated to Can., 1935, naturalized, 1945; s. Albin and Ella (Biber) H.; m. Luise H. Oettinger, Dec. 29, 1929 (dec.); children: Paul Albin, Agnes Margaret; m. Monika Tenthoff, Mar. 21, 1972. Dr. Ing., Darmstadt Inst. Tech., 1928; postgrad., U. Goettingen, U. Bristol, 1928-30; D.Sc. hon causa, Oxford U., 1960; D.Sc., U. Chgo., 1967, Drexel U., 1972, U. Montreal, 1972, U. Sherbrooke, 1972, McGill U., 1972, Cambridge U., 1972, U. Man., 1973, Andhra U., 1975, Osmania U., 1976, U. Delhi, 1976, U. Bristol, 1975, U. Western Ont., 1976; Fil. Hed. Dr., U. Stockholm, 1966; Ph.D. (hon.), Weizmann Inst. Sci., 1976, U. Toledo, 1984; LL.D., St. Francis Xavier U., 1972, Simon Fraser U., 1972; Dr. phil. nat., U. Frankfurt, 1983, others. Lectr., chief asst. physics Darmstadt Inst. Tech., 1930-35; research prof. physics U. Sask., Saskatoon, 1935-45; prof. spectroscopy Yerkes Obs., U. Chgo., 1945-48; prin. research officer NRC Can., Ottawa, 1948; dir. div. pure physics NRC Can., 1949-69, disting. research scientist, 1969—; Bakerian lectr. Royal Soc. London, 1960; holder Francqui chair U. Liege, 1960. Author books including: Spectra of Diatomic Molecules, 1950; Electronic Spectra and Electronic Structure of Polyatomic Molecules, 1966, The Spectra and Structures of Simple Free Radicals, 1971, (with K.P. Huber) Constants of Diatomic Molecules, 1979. Recipient Faraday medal Chem. Soc. London, 1970, Nobel prize in Chemistry, 1971; named companion Order of Can., 1968, academician Pontifical Acad. Scis., 1964. Fellow Royal Soc. London (Royal medal 1971), Royal Soc. Can. (pres. 1966, Henry Marshall Tory medal 1953), Hungarian Acad. Sci. (hon.), Indian Acad. Scis. (hon.), Am. Phys. Soc. (Earle K. Plyler prize 1985), Chem. Inst. Can.; mem. Internat. Union Pure and Applied Physics (past v.p.), Am. Acad. Arts and Scis. (hon. fgn. mem.), Am. Chem. Soc. (Willard Gibbs medal 1969, Centennial fgn. fellow 1976), Nat. Acad. Sci. India, Indian Phys. Soc. (hon.), Japan Acad. (hon.), Chem. Soc. Japan (hon.), Royal Swedish Acad. Scis. (fgn., physics sect.), Nat. Acad. Sci. (fgn. assoc.), Faraday Soc., Am. Astron. Soc., Can. Assn. Physicists (past pres., Achievement award 1957), Optical Soc. Am. (hon., Frederic Ives medal 1964). Home: 190 Lakeway Dr, Rockcliffe Park, Ottawa, ON Canada K1L 5B3 Office: Nat Research Council, Ottawa, ON Canada K1A 0R6

HERZBERG, RICHARD ARNOLD, financial executive; b. Newark, Sept. 11, 1915; s. Max John and Edna (Newman) H.; A.B., Harvard U., 1937; M.S., Columbia U., 1938; m. M. Olga Roston, May 1, 1946; children—Deborah Robboy, Elizabeth Hoffman. Free lance journalist, 1937-41; mgr. publs. Prudential Ins. Co., Newark, 1942-65; founder, investor, pres. Morris Cablevision, Morristown, N.J., 1970-82. Mem. sch. bd., Hanover Twp., N.J., 1957-59; bd. trustees Trenton Psychiat. Hosp., 1968-82, chmn., 1981-82; v.p. bd. trustees N.J. Shakespeare Festival, Madison, N.J., 1980-82; bd. mgrs. Vis. Health Service, Morris County, 1987—, 1st v.p. 1988—. Served to capt., AUS, 1942-46. Democrat. Unitarian. Home: PO Box 273 Peapack NJ 07977

HERZBERGER, JUERGEN PAUL, mathematician, educator; b. Berlin, Dec. 17, 1940; s. Paul Ernst and Elisabeth (Ueckert) H. Degree, Munich Tech. U., 1966; Doctorate, Karlsruhe Tech. U., Fed. Republic of Germany, 1969, Karlsruhe Tech. U., 1972. Asst. Munich Tech. U., 1966-67, Karlsruhe Tech. U., 1967-72; research assoc. U. Calif., Berkeley, 1974-75; lectr. Karlsruhe Tech. U., 1972-75, assoc. prof., 1975-76; prof. math. Oldenburg U., Lower Saxony, Fed. Republic of Germany, 1976—. Co-author: Introduction to Interval Computations, 1983. Mem. Soc. for Indsl. and Applied Math., German Math. Soc., Soc. for Applied Math. and Mechanics. Home: Dahlienweg 1, 2906 Wardenburg Lower Saxony, Federal Republic of Germany Office: U Oldenburg, PO Box 2503, 2900 Oldenburg Federal Republic of Germany

HERZER, RICHARD KIMBALL, franchising company executive; b. Ogden, Utah, June 2, 1931; s. Arthur Vernon and Dorothy (Cortez) H.; B.S., UCLA, 1958; m. Phyllis Ann McCullough, Mar. 29, 1958; children—Diane E., Mark V., Craig K. Vice pres., controller United Rent All, Inc., Los Angeles, 1967-71; dir. fin. planning Internat. Industries Inc., North Hollywood, Calif., 1971-73, v.p., controller, 1973-75, v.p. fin., 1975-79, pres., 1979—, chmn. bd., chief exec. officer, 1983—; pres. IHOP Corp., 1979—, also dir. Trustee So. Calif. chpt. Multiple Sclerosis, 1984—. Served to 1st lt. U.S. Army, 1953-56. Mem. Calif. Restaurant Assn. (bd. dirs. 1985—), Phi Delta Theta. Republican. Home: 1550 Sunshine Dr Glendale CA 91208 Office: IHOP Corp 6837 Lankershim Blvd North Hollywood CA 91605

HERZFELD, CHARLES MARIA, physicist; b. Vienna, Austria, June 29, 1925; came to U.S., 1942, naturalized, 1949; s. August Alfred and Frieda Auguste (Poehlman) H.; m. Norma Ann Krause, May 15, 1954 (div. 1979); children: Charles Christopher, Thomas Augustine, Paul Vincent; m. Zofia E. Dziewanowska, Aug. 1, 1981. BS in Chem. Engring. cum laude, Cath. U. Am., 1945; PhD (Carnegie Found. fellow), U. Chgo., 1951. Lectr. chemistry Cath. U. Am., 1946; lectr. gen. sci. Coll. U. Chgo., 1946-47; lectr. physics DePaul U., Chgo., 1948-50; physicist Ballistic Research Lab., Aberdeen, Md., 1951-53, Naval Research Lab., Washington, 1953-55; lectr. physics U. Md., 1953-57, prof. physics, 1957-61; cons. chief heat and power div. Nat. Bur. Standards, 1955-56, acting asst. chief, 1956-57, chief heat div., 1957-61, asso. dir. bur., 1961; asst. dir. Advanced Research Project Agy., Dept. Def., 1961-63, dir. ballistic missile def., 1963; dep. dir. Advanced Research Projects Agy., 1963-65, dir., 1965-67; tech. dir. def. space group ITT, Nutley, N.J., 1967-74; tech. dir. aerospace-electronics-components-energy group ITT, 1974-76, tech. dir. telecommunications and electronics group N.Am., 1978-79; v.p., dir. research ITT Corp., 1979-83, v.p., dir. research and tech., 1983-85; vice chmn. Aetna, Jacobs and Ramo, N.Y.C., 1985—; chmn. bd. Westronix Co., Midvale, Utah; bd. dirs. T Cell Scis. Inc., Cambridge, Mass., Coordination Tech. Inc., Stamford, Conn., Memorex N.V., Internat. Sch. for Synthesis of Expert Knowledge, Glasgow; mem. Def. Sci. bd., 1968-83, Def. Policy Adv. Bd., 1985—, Nat. Commn. on Space, 1985-86; cons. USN, Nat. Security Council, Contel Corp., Atlanta, SAIC, San Diego, RDA Inc., Marina del Rey, Calif.; fellow mem. Hudson Inst.; mem. Brookings Inst. Fifth Conf. for Career Execs. in Fed. Govt., 1958; mem. engring. council Columbia U. Editor: Temperature, Its Control in Science and Industry, vol. III, 1962; contbr. articles to profl. jours. Recipient Flemming award, 1963; Meritorious Civilian Service medal Dept. Def., 1967. Fellow Phys. Soc., Council Fgn. Relations, AAAS, Conf. on Sci., Philosophy and Religion; mem. N.Y. Acad. Scis., Inst. for Strategic Studies (London), Cath. Assn. Internat. Peace (pres. 1959-61), Sigma Xi. Clubs: Cosmos (Washington); Explorers (N.Y.C.); Raritan Yacht (Perth Amboy, N.J.). Home: 86 Harbor Key Secaucus NJ 07094 Office: Aetna Jacobs and Ramo 375 Park Ave New York NY 10152

HERZIG, JULIE ESTHER, architect; b. N.Y.C., Jan. 23, 1951; d. Philip R. and Helene J. (Phillips) H. B.A., Mt. Holyoke Coll., 1973; B.Arch. with honors, Pratt Inst., 1983. Draftsman Red Roof Design, N.Y.C., 1977-80; designer Phillips Janson Group, N.Y.C., 1983-84; pres. Herzig, Knechtel Assocs., N.Y.C., 1984-85, Herzig Design, N.Y.C., 1985—. Mt. Holyoke Coll. grantee, 1972. Mem. Alliance Women in Architecture, AIA, N.Y. Soc. Architects. Clubs: Mt. Holyoke (N.Y.C.); North Shore Country (Glen Head, N.Y.).

HERZOG, BERNARD MAURICE JEAN, radiology educator; b. Nancy, Meurthe et Moselle, France, Dec. 28, 1935; s. Eugène and Elisabeth (Dufour) H.; m. Anne-Marie Vlasak (div. 1974); children: Xavier, Bertrand, Hedwige; m. Christine Renaud, 1984; 1 child, Irvin. Licencié-ès sciences, Facultè des sciences, Nancy, 1961; Doctorat en Médecine, Facultè de Médecine, Nancy, 1961; nat. degree in electroradiology, Paris, 1963. Biophysics research chief Facultè de Médecine, Nancy, 1961-63; asst. electroradiologist Facultè de Médecine, Grenoble, France, 1964-66; prof. electroradiology Facultè de Médecine, Nantes, France, 1966—; head radiology depts. Nantes Hosp. System, 1966—; consistent research in med. pathology and immunology, Nancy, 1959-64, musicotherapy and psychoanalysis, Nantes, 1975—. Author: Death, Love and Dreams, 1987, The Cancerous Imaginary, 1987; exhibited artist (oil paintings, stained glass, lithography, charcoal) throughout Europe.

HERZOG, CHAIM, president of Israel; b. Belfast, No. Ireland, Sept. 17, 1918; emigrated to Israel, 1935; ed. Wesley Coll., London U., Cambridge U.; LLB Hebron Yeshiva; m. Aura Ambache; 4 children. Admitted as barrister-at-law, advocate, 1947; head security dept. Jewish Agy., 1947-48; mil. naval and air attaché Israeli embassy, Washington, 1950-54; comdg. officer Jerusalem Dist., 1954-57; chief of staff So. Command, 1957-59; dir. Mil. Intelligence, 1948-50, 59-62; appointed comdr. Israel Def. Forces, 1st mil. gov. for West Bank, 1967; polit. and mil. broadcaster during Six Day War, 1967, Yom Kippur War, 1973; polit. and mil. publicist for Israeli, Brit. and U.S. periodicals; regular radio and TV commentator in Israel and abroad; A.E. and P. from Israel to UN, 1975-78; former dir. Israel Discount Bank, Tel Aviv, N.Y.C.; former leadership bur. Israel Labour Party; mem. Knesset, 1981-83; pres. Israel, 1983—. Served as maj. Brit. Army, World War II; maj. gen. Res. Israeli Army. Decorated knight comdr. Brit. Empire. Mem. World ORT Union (past pres.). Author: Israel's Finest Hour, 1967, Days of Awe, 1973, The War of Atonement, 1975, Who Stands Accused?, 1978, The Arab-Israeli Wars, 1982; co-author: Battles of the Bible, 1978. Office: Office of President, Beit Hanassi, Jerusalem Israel *

HERZOG, WERNER, film director; b. Munich, Ger., Sept. 5, 1942; m. Marthe Grohmann. Dir. films: Signs of Life, 1967, Even Dwarfs Started Small, 1970, Fata Morgana, 1971, The Land of Silence and Darkness, 1971, Aguirre, Wrath of God, 1973, The Enigma of Kaspar Hauser, 1974, The Great Ecstasy of Woodcutter Steiner, 1974, How Much Wood Would Woodchuck Chuck?, 1976, Heart of Glass, 1976, Stroszek, 1976-77, Nosferatu, 1979, Woyzeck, 1979, Le pays du silence et de l'obscurité, 1980, Huie's Sermon, 1980, God's Angry Man, 1980, Fitzcarraldo, 1982, Where the Green Ants Dream, (also author screenplay), 1984; appeared in films Man of Flowers, 1984, Tokyo-Ga, 1985. Address: care New Yorker Films 16 W 61st St New York NY 10023 *

HESDORF, HANS, aeronautical and industrial consultant, international government and defense liaison; b. Copenhagen, Denmark, May 30, 1921; s. Hans and Christine (Hald) H.; m. Gertrud Fielers (dec. 1978). Cert. airline capt., Air Trg. Ctr., Cranwell, Eng., 1958; high security clearence for negotiations, sales, and presentation of defence and security equipment, for British, Danish, German govs. and NATO. Airline capt., second officer Zone Salvage Ambulance Flying Corps, Copenhagen, 1948-49, capt., 1949-57; trainer, tester for first pilots Lufthansa Airlines, 1954-55; head of flight ops. Mestersvig, E. Greenland, 1957-58; chief pilot Continental Airlines, Germany, 1958-60; head flight ops. UN Exec. Flying div., Leopoldville, Congo, 1960-63; pres. British Electronic Agys. GmbH., Bonn, Federal Republic of Germany, 1963-81; owner, pres. Hesdorf Consultancy Ltd., Copenhagen, 1981—; internat. liason, rep. numerous bus., govts. Author: Greenland from the Air, 1964, Congo Tragedy, 1968; contbr. numeruos articles to newspapers, 1936—. Served with the Royal Danish Lifeguard, 1941-42; prisoner of war, Germany, 1942-43; resistance fighter, Holger Danske, 1943-44. Escaped to Sweden. Camp chief of various refugee camps under Royal Danish Embassy, Refugee office, Stockholm, 1944-45; mem. staff UN Relief and Rehab. Adminstrn., Denmark, Paris, 1945-47. Recipient Resistance medal Danish govt., 1962, Salvation medal Danish govt., 1971. Fellow Armed Forces Com. and Electronics Assn.; mem. Danish Officers Club, Danish Aviator Club (recipient flying medal 1979), Royal Danish Guards Soc.(com. mem. 1981), Danish Flyers (com. mem. 1982), Deutsche Gesellsch. für Wehrtechnik. Lutheran. Home and Office: Jagtvej 107D, DK 2200 Copenhagen N Denmark

HESS, BARTLETT LEONARD, clergyman; b. Spokane, Wash., Dec. 27, 1910; s. John Leonard and Jessie (Bartlett) H.; B.A., Park Coll., 1931, M.A. (fellow in history 1931-34), U. Kan., 1932, Ph.D., 1934; B.D., McCormick Theol. Sem., 1936; m. Margaret Young Johnston, July 31, 1937; children—Daniel Bartlett, Deborah Margaret, John Howard and Janet Elizabeth (twins). Ordained to ministry Presbyn. Ch., 1936; pastor Effingham, Kan., 1932-34, Chgo., 1935-42, Cicero, Ill., 1942-56, Ward Meml. Presbyn. Ch., Detroit, 1956-68, Ward Presbyn. Ch., Livonia, Mich., 1968-80, Presbyn. Ch., 1980—. Tchr. ch. history, bible Detroit Bible Coll., 1956-60, bd. dirs., 1956—; minister radio sta. WHFC, Chgo., 1942-50, WMUZ-FM, Detroit, 1958-68, 78—, WOMC-FM, 1971-72, WBFG-FM, 1972—; missioner to Philippines, United Presbyn. Ch. U.S.A., 1961; mem. Joint Com. on Presbyn. Union, 1980; adviser Mich. Synod council United Presbyn. Ch.; mem. com. Billy Graham Crusade for S.E. Mich., 1976; mem. adminstrv. com. Evang. Presbyn. Ch., 1980-85; mem. joint com. missions Evang. Presbyn. Ch. and the Presbyn. Ch. of Brazil. Mem., organizer Friendship and Service Com. for Refugees, Chgo., 1940. Bd. dirs. Beacon Neighborhood House, Chgo., 1945-52, Presbyns. United for Bibl. Concerns, 1975-80; pres. bd. dirs. Peniel Community Center, Chicago, 1945-52. Named Pastor of Year, Mid-Am. Sunday Sch. Assn., 1974; recipient Service to Youth award Detroit Met. Youth for Christ, 1979. Mem. Cicero Ministers Council (pres. 1951), Phi Beta Kappa, Phi Delta Kappa. Author: (with Margaret Johnston Hess) How To Have a Giving Church, 1974; (with M.J. Hess) The Power of a Loving Church, 1977, How Does Your Marriage Grow, 1982, Never Say Old, 1984; contbr. articles in field to profl. jours. Traveled in Europe, 1939, 52, 55, 68; also in Greece, Turkey, Lebanon, Syria, Egypt, Israel, Iraq; condr. tour of Middle East and Mediterranean countries, 1965, 67, 73, 74, 76, 78, 80, China and Far East, 1982; missioner, India, 1981, Brazil, 85, 86, 87, Argentina, 87. Home: 16845 Riverside Dr Livonia MI 48154 Office: 17000 Farmington Rd Livonia MI 48154

HESS, DAVID FREDRIC, foundation executive; b. Long Beach, Calif., Oct. 11, 1946; s. William Nelson and Maryellen (Nickson) H.; B.S., Calif. State U., Long Beach, 1969; postgrad. U. So. Calif., 1980—; m. Donna Darleen Kaspereit, Jan. 31, 1968; children—Jennifer Darleen, Joshua David. Fiduciary tax specialist Security Pacific Nat. Bank, Los Angeles, 1969-75; analyst CCH/Computax, El Segundo, Calif., 1975-76; asst. v.p. Security Pacific Nat. Bank, 1976-80; asso. dir., sec.-treas. and chief fin. officer Calif. Community Found./CCF, Inc., Los Angeles, 1977-83; exec. dir. Pasadena City Coll. Found., 1983; exec. dir. Sacramento Regional Found., 1983—; cons. Japan Assn. for Charitable Trusts, 1974-75; lectr. in field. Treas., Los Angeles Council on Careers for Older Ams., 1981-85; pres. Planned Giving Forum of Sacramento; charter mem. Nat. Council on Careers for Older Ams., 1981—; bd. dirs. SCAPA Praetors, U. So. Calif. Sch. Public Adminstrn., 1980-83. Mem. So. Calif. Assn. for Philanthropy (dir. 1979-81), Council on Founds. Ind. Sector, Soc. for Advancement of Mgmt. Republican. Office: 1900 Point West Way Suite 128 Sacramento CA 95815

HESS, GEOFFREY LAVERNE, accountant; b. Gettysburg, Pa., Dec. 20, 1949; s. Richard LaVerne and Beatrice Geraldine (Brown) H.; B.S. in Acctg., Mt. St. Mary's Coll., 1976. Acct., United Bldg. Corp., Germantown, Md., 1976-77; NAD resident auditor U.S. Army Corps Engrs., Balt., 1977-78; sr. acct., Councilor Buchanan and Mitchell, Bethesda, Md., 1979-80; internal auditor George Washington U., 1981; sr. acct. Buchanan and Co., Frederick, Md., 1981-82; acctg. mgr. PATS, Inc., Flight Refueling, Inc., Patrick Aircraft Tank Systems, Inc., 1983-85; controller Annapolis Fed. Savs. Bank , 1985—. Served with USAF, 1968-72. C.P.A., Md. Mem. Am. Inst. C.P.A.s, Md. Assn. C.P.A.s, Am. Legion. Republican. Roman Catholic. Home: 1223 Cherrytown Rd Westminster MD 21157 Office: 140 Main St Annapolis MD 21404

HESS, GEORGE FRANKLIN, II, lawyer; b. Oak Park, Ill., May 13, 1939; s. Franklin Edward and Carol (Hackman) H.; m. Diane Ricci, Aug. 9, 1974; 1 son, Franklin Edward. B.S. in Bus., Colo. State U., 1962; J.D., Suffolk U., 1970; LL.M., Boston U., 1973. Bar: Pa. 1971, Fla. 1973, U.S. Tax Ct. 1974, U.S. Dist. Ct. (so. dist.) Fla. 1975. Assoc. Hart, Childs, Hepburn, Ross & Putnam, Phila., 1970-72; instr. Suffolk U. Law Sch., Boston, 1973-74; ptnr. Henry, Hess & Hoines, Ft. Lauderdale, Fla., 1974-79; sole practice George F. Hess, II, P.A., (merged with Mousaw, Vigdor, Reeves, Heilbronner & Kroll., Rochester, N.Y., 1981, name now Mousaw, Vigdor, Reeves & Hess), Ft. Lauderdale, 1979—, now ptnr. Bd. dirs. Children's Home Soc., Ft. Lauderdale, 1985—, Nadeau Charitable Found.; Served to lt. USNR, 1963-66. Mem. ABA, Fla. Bar Assn., Broward County Bar Assn., SAR, Phi Alpha Delta. Episcopalian. Clubs: Lago Mar, Lauderdale Yacht (Ft. Lauderdale); U.S. Navy League. Home: 2524 Castilla Isle Fort Lauderdale FL 33301 Office: Mousaw Vigdor Reeves & Hess 333 N New River Dr E Fort Lauderdale FL 33301

HESS, HANS OBER, lawyer; b. Royersford, Pa., Nov. 8, 1912; s. Samuel Harley and Annamae (Wenger) H.; m. Dolores Groke, May 18, 1940; children: Antonine (Mrs. Joseph J. Gal), Roberta (Mrs. Edward S. Trippe), Liese (Mrs. Arleigh P. Helfer, Jr.), Kristina (Mrs. Charles H. Bonner). A.B., Ursinus Coll., 1933, LL.D., 1979; LL.B., Harvard U., 1936; LL.D., Muhlenberg Coll., 1964; D.F.A. (hon.), Phila. Coll. Art, 1981. Sr. partner Ballard, Spahr, Andrews & Ingersoll, Phila.; dir. Ferag Corp. Editor: Fiduciary Rev, monthly, The Nature of a Humane Society, 1976. Former mem. exec. council Lutheran Ch. in Am.; trustee Lankenau Hosp., Phila. Coll. Art; former Mary J. Drexel Home; chmn. Lankenau Med. Research Ctr.; trustee Marie M. Barclay Endowment; former bd. dirs., sec. Phila. Orch. Assn., Acad. Music Phila.; former mem. Harvard Overseers Com. to Visit Law Sch.; former nat. chmn. Harvard Law Sch. Fund. Mem. ABA, Pa., Phila., Montgomery County bar assns., Harvard Law Sch. Assn. Clubs: Philadelphia, Union League, Philadelphia Country (Phila.). Home: 143 Woodside Rd Ardmore PA 19003 Office: 30 S 17th St Philadelphia PA 19103

HESS, LAWRENCE EUGENE, JR., lawyer; b. Phila., Aug. 18, 1923; s. Lawrence Eugene and Charlotte (Engel) H.; m. Jane Strayer, June 11, 1949; children—Lawrence Edward, Charlotte Jane. Student Princeton U., 1942-43; B.S., U.S. Naval Acad., 1947; J.D. with honors, George Washington U., 1954. Bar: Pa. 1954, D.C. 1954, U.S. Supreme Ct. 1963. Commd. ensign U.S. Navy, 1946, advanced through grades to lt. comdr.; assigned to various ships and stas.; ret., 1966; house counsel Nat. Liberty Life Ins. Co., Valley Forge, Pa., 1966-67, Standard Computers, Inc., 1967-68; atty. Def. Personnel Support Center, Phila., 1968-69; counsel Am. Acceptance Corp., Phila., 1969-74; sole practice, Fort Washington, Pa., 1974—. Mem. Sch. Bd. Upper Dublin Sch. Dist. Montgomery County, Pa., 1981-85; pres. bd. trustees Glenside (Pa.) United Meth. Ch., 1973-76, trustee, 1987—. Mem. ABA, Fed. Bar Assn., Pa. Bar Assn., Phila. Bar Assn., Montgomery Bar Assn., Comml. Law League Am., Judge Advocates Assn., Pa. Trial Lawyers Assn., Montgomery Trial Lawyers Assn., Navy League U.S., U.S. Naval Acad. Alumni Assn. Phila. (past pres., dir.), Ret. Officers Assn. (life mem.; bd. dirs. Willow Grove chpt.), Am. Legion, Mil. Order World Wars. Republican. Clubs: Army-Navy (Arlington, Va.); Mfrs. Golf and Country (Oreland, Pa.); Princeton (N.Y.C.) Lodge: Masons. Mem. editorial bd. George Washington U. Law Rev., 1952-53. Home: 515 Dreshertown Rd Fort Washington PA 19034

HESS, LEON, oil company executive; b. Asbury Park, N.J., Mar. 13, 1914; (married). With Hess Oil & Chem. Corp. (and predecessor), 1946-69, pres., 1962-65, chmn. bd., chief exec. officer, 1965-69; also dir. Hess Oil & Chem. Corp.; chmn. bd. Amerada Hess Corp. (merger Hess Oil & Chem. Corp. and Amerada Petroleum Corp.), N.Y.C., 1971—, chief exec. officer, 1971-82, 86—, also dir.; co-owner, now sole owner, chmn. bd. N.Y. Jets Football Team, N.Y.C., 1963—; dir. ABC, Mut. Benefit Life Ins. Co., Monmouth Park Jockey Club. Served with AUS, 1942-45. Office: Amerada Hess Corp 1185 Ave of Americas New York NY 10036 *

HESS, MARGARET JOHNSTON, religious writer, educator; b. Ames, Iowa, Feb. 22, 1915; d. Howard Wright and Jane Edith (Stevenson) Johnston; B.A., Coe Coll., 1937; m. Bartlett Leonard Hess, July 31, 1937; children—Daniel, Deborah, John, Janet. Bible tchr. Community Bible Classes Ward Presbyn. Ch., Livonia, Mich., 1959—, Christ Ch. Cranbrook (Episcopalian), Bloomfield Hills, Mich., 1980—. Co-author: (with B.L. Hess) How to Have a Giving Church, 1974, The Power of a Loving Church, 1977, How Does Your Marriage Grow?, 1983, Never Say Old, 1984; author: Love Knows No Barriers, 1979; Esther: Courage in Crisis, 1980; Unconventional Women, 1981, The Triumph of Love, 1987; contbr. articles to religious jours. Home: 16845 Riverside Dr Livonia MI 48154

HESS, ORVAN W., medical educator, obstetrician-gynecologist. m. Carol Woodruff Maurer; children—Katherine Hess Halloran, Carolyn Hess Westerfield. B.S., Lafayette Coll., 1927; M.D., SUNY-Buffalo, 1931. Diplomate Am. Bd. Ob-Gyn (fellow). Intern Children's Hosp., Buffalo, 1931-32; intern New Haven Hosp., 1932-33, asst. resident, 1934-36, resident in ob-gyn, 1936-37; research fellow in gynecol. surgery Yale U. Sch. Medicine, New Haven, 1933-35; instr. ob-gyn Yale U. Sch. Medicine, 1936-37, clin. instr., 1937-43, asst. clin. prof., 1949-69, sr. assoc. ob-gyn, 1969-71, assoc. clin. prof., 1971-75, clin. prof., dir. perinatal monitoring program, 1975—, sr. research scientist, 1986—; co-dir. Fetal Heart Inst. Yale-New Haven Hosp., 1982—, co-dir. Fetal Cardio-Vascular Ctr., 1985—; attending Yale-New Haven Med. Ctr.; staff Hosp. St. Raphael, New Haven, Middlesex Hosp., Middletown, Conn.; mem. Gov.'s Ad Hoc Planning Com. on Heart Disease, Cancer and Stroke; mem. Conn. Comprehensive Health Planning Council, New Eng. Title XIX Adv. Council, Tri-State Council; mem. adv. com. pub. health nursing Conn. Dept. Health; med. dir. Conn. Welfare Dept., 1967-70, adminstr. Medicaid, 1967; mem. Conn. Drug. Adv. Council, Conn. Com. Perinatal Mortality; dir. Corometrics Electronics, Inc., New Haven Health Care, Inc. Contbr. articles to profl. jours. Bd. dirs. Compac, Conn. Med. Inst. Served to col. M.C., U.S. Army, 1942-45; ETO. Fellow Morse Coll., Yale U. Fellow ACS, Am. Coll. Ob-Gyn., Am. Bd. OB-Gyn.; mem. AMA (del. 1969-84), Conn. Med. Soc. (sec. 1960-64, v.p. 1964-65, pres.-elect 1965-66, pres. 1966-67, councillor-at-large 1967-68, chmn. coms.), Conn. Health Assn. (pres.), New Haven Med. Soc., New Haven Obstetrical Soc., New Haven County Med. Assn., Assn. Mil. Surgeons U.S., World Med. Assn., N.Y. Acad. Scis., AAAS, IEEE, Internat. Assn. Bio-telemetry, Am. Assn. Pub. Welfare Med. Dirs., Sigma Xi, Nu Sigma Nu, Knife and Stork Club. Clubs: Lawn, Yale (New Haven). Home: 29 Old Orchard Rd North Haven CT 06473

HESS, ROBERT, JR., ambulance service executive; b. East Cleveland, Ohio, Oct. 22, 1957; s. Robert and Patricia Lou Hess; m. Susan Hole, Jan. 28, 1983; children: Christine Renee, Robert III, Jessica Marie. Student John Carroll U., 1976-81, Cuyahoga Community Coll., 1977-78. With Physician's Ambulance Service, South Euclid, 1972—, v.p. in charge fin., data processing, med. assurance, 1978-86, sr. v.p., chief operating officer, 1986—; pres., chief exec. officer Medflight, Inc., South Euclid, Ohio, 1986—; dir. Hess Enterprises, Inc.; adj. faculty Cuyahoga Community Coll., vice chmn. Emergency Med. Technician Tng. Dept., 1986—, v.p. Allan R. Sussberg Builders, Inc., Beachwood, Ohio. mem. paramedic admissions com. Cuyahogo Community Coll.; dir. research U.S. Emergency Med. Technician Assn., 1981. Instr. advanced cardiac life support Am. Heart Assn., 1981—; mem. Ohio Bd. Regents Paramedic Adv. Com., 1980-86; alternate mem. emergency med. service adv. com. Ohio Bd. Edn., 1986—; mem. paramedic adv. council Hillcrest Hosp.; mem. local legis. com. Cleve. Growth Assn. Mem. Ohio Ambulance Assn. (pres. 1981-82, trustee 1980-81, chmn. govtl. affairs com. 1985—), Am. Ambulance Assn. (dir. 1980-83, fin. com., govtl. affairs com., accreditation com.), Nat. Assn. Emergency Med. Technicians, Ohio Assn. Emergency Med. Services. Republican. Roman Catholic. Club: Rotary (community service com.). Office: 4349 Monticello Blvd South Euclid OH 44121

HESSAYON, DAVID GERALD, corporate executive author; b. Manchester, Eng., Feb. 13, 1928; s. Jack and Lena H.; B.Sc., Leeds U., 1950; Ph.D., Manchester U., 1954; m. Joan Parker, Apr. 2, 1951; children—Angelina, Jacqueline. Asst. lectr. biology Manchester U., 1951-53; research fellow Univ. Coll. of Gold Coast, 1953-54; with Pan Britannica Industries, Ltd., Waltham Cross, 1955—, mng. dir., 1964—, chmn. bd., 1972—; dir. Tennants Consol. Ltd., 1982—. Fellow Brit. Inst. Mgmt.; mem. Guild of Freemen of City of London, Inst. Dirs. Club: London Press. Author: Be Your Own Gardening Expert, 1959; Be Your Own House Plant Expert, 1960; Potato Growers Handbook, 1961; Silage Makers Handbook, 1961; Be Your Own Lawn Expert, 1962; Be Your Own Rose Expert, 1964; Garden Book of Europe, 1973; Vegetable Plotter, 1975; Be Your Own Garden Doctor, 1978; Be Your Own Vegetable Doctor, 1978; The House Plant Expert, 1980; The Rose Expert, 1981; The Lawn Expert, 1982; The Cereal Disease Expert, 1982; The Tree and Shrub Expert, 1983; The Armchair Book of the Garden, 1983; The Flower Expert, 1984; The Vegetable Expert, 1985; The Indoor Plant Spotter, 1985; The Garden Expert, 1986, The Gold Plated House Plant Expert, 1987, The Home Expert, 1987. Home: Hilgay, 12 Mill Ln, Broxbourne, Hertfordshire EN10 7AX England Office: Britannica House, High St Waltham Cross, Hertfordshire EN8 7DY, England

HESSE, CHRISTIAN AUGUST, mining company executive; b. Chemnitz, Germany, June 20, 1925; s. William Albert and Anna Gunhilda (Baumann) H.; B.Applied Sci. with honors, U. Toronto (Ont., Can.), 1948; m. Brenda Nora Rigby, Nov. 4, 1964; children: Robin Christian, Bruce William. In various mining and constrn. positions, Can., 1944-61; jr. shift boss N.J. Zinc Co., Gilman, Colo., 1949; asst. layout engr. Internat. Nickel Co., Sudbury, Ont., 1949-52; shaft engr. Perini-Walsh Joint Venture, Niagara Falls, Ont., 1952-54; project engr. B. Perini & Sons (Can.) Ltd., Toronto, Ottawa, and New Brunswick, 1954-55; field engr. Aries Copper Mines Ltd., No. Ont., 1955-56; instr. in mining engring. U. Toronto, 1956-57; planning engr. Stanleigh Uranium Mining Corp. Ltd., Elliot Lake, Ont., 1957-58, chief engr., 1959-60; field engr. Johnson-Perini-Kiewit Joint Venture, Toronto, 1960-61; del. Commonwealth Mining Congress, Africa, 1961; with U.S. Borax & Chem. Corp., 1961—, gen. mgr. Allan Potash Mines Ltd., Allan, Sask., Can., 1974, chief engr. U.S. Borax & Chem. Corp., Los Angeles, 1974-77, v.p. engring., 1977-81, v.p. and project mgr. Quartz Hill project, 1981—; v.p. Pacific Coast Molybdenum Co., 1981—, v.p. mining devel., 1984—, v.p. engring., 1987—. Sault Daily Star scholar, Sault Sainte Marie, Ont., Can., 1944. Mem. AIME, Can. Inst. Mining and Metallurgy (life), Assn. Profl. Engrs. Ont. Lutheran. Clubs: Los Angeles, Los Angeles Tennis. Office: US Borax & Chem Corp 3075 Wilshire Blvd Los Angeles CA 90010

HESSELFELD, HEINRICH JOSEF, missionary, physics educator, researcher; b. Lohne, Vechta, Germany, Dec. 28, 1930; emigrated to Taiwan, 1966; s. Heinrich and Josefa (Westerhoff) H. Abitur, St. Xaver's Coll., Bad Driburg, W.Ger., 1952; M.A. in Physics Catholic U., Washington, 1963, Ph.D., 1966. Ordained priest Soc. of the Divine Word, Roman Catholic Ch., 1958. Assoc. prof. physics Fu Jen U., Taipei, Taiwan, 1966-72, prof., 1972—, chmn. dept. physics, 1968-75, dir. Grad. Sch. Physics, 1972-77, dean Coll. Scis., 1973-84; sci. advisor in Tacloban, Philippines, 1984-86. Editor-in-chief: Fu Jen Studies, 1971—. Mem. Optical Soc. Am., Acoustical Soc. Am., Phys. Soc. Am., Phys. Soc. Republic of China, Sigma Xi. Home and Office: Steyler Mission, Arnold Janssen Str 26, 5205 Sankt Augustin 1 Federal Republic of Germany

HESSELINK, WIM H., computer information scientist, researcher; b. Deventer, The Netherlands, Feb. 21, 1946; s. Albert A. and Coletta E.M. (Holsboer) H.; m. Maria C.L. Baljon, Feb. 24, 1971; children: Katink, Kryn Peter, Sieger Odmar. Grad., Rijksuniversiteit, Utrecht, The Netherlands, 1966, D in Math., 1970, 75. With math. dept. Rijksuniversiteit U., Utrecht, 1970-75; with math. dept. Rijksuniversiteit U., Groningen, 1976-85, with dept. computer sci., 1985—; researcher, lectr. C.S. U. Tex., Austin, 1986-87. Office: U Groningen Vakgroep Info, PO Box 800, 9700 AV Groningen The Netherlands

HESSELS, JOSEPH MAXIMILIAAN ELISABETH, chemical company executive, educator; b. The Hague, The Netherlands, Jan. 27, 1956; s. Aloysius F.J.M. and A.M.M. (Oliesiagers) Kampschöer. MBA, Mich. State U., 1979; Dr. Erasmus U., 1981. Asst. project coordinator Billiton Internat. Metals, Leidschendam, The Netherlands, 1982-83; project coordinator Billiton Internat. Metals, Brazil, 1983-84; mktg. mgr. Billiton Aluminium, Leidschendam, 1985-86; bus. developer Billiton Mktg. & Trading Co., Leidschendam, 1987; unit mgr. Shell Nederland Chemie BV, Rotterdam, The Netherlands, 1987—; lectr. Webster U. Mem. Nederlands Inst. Mktg. Roman Catholic. Home: PO Box 1031, 2240 BA Wassenaar The Netherlands Office: Shell Nederland Chemie BV, Hofplein #19, 3032 AC Rotterdam The Netherlands

HESSLUND, BRADLEY HARRY, manufacturing engineer; b. Mpls., June 27, 1958; s. Harry A. and Dorothy (Tishi) H. AA, Normandale Community Coll., 1978; BS, U. Wis., Menomonie, 1981; MBA, U. Pitts., 1984. Indsl. engr. Thermo King Corp. sub. Westinghouse Electric Corp., Bloomington, Minn., 1981-82; quality engr. Westinghouse Electric Corp., Beaver, Pa., 1983; cost engr. IBM Corp., East Fishkill, N.Y., 1984-85; mfg. engring. supr. Fed.-Hoffman Inc., Anoka, Minn., 1985—; sr. cost analyst Naval Systems div. FMC Corp., Fridley, Minn., 1988—. Mem. Soc. Mfg. Engrs. Republican. Lutheran. Home: 3200 Zane Ave N Crystal MN 55422 Office: FMC

Corp Naval Systems Div PO Box 59043 4800 E River Rd Fridley MN 55459-0043

HESTAD, BJORN MARK, metal distributing company executive; b. Evanston, Ill., May 31, 1926; s. Hilmar and Anna (Aagaard) H.; student Ill. Inst. Tech., 1947; m. Florence Anne Ragusi, May 1, 1948; children—Marsha Anne, Patricia Lynn Krueger, Peter Mark. Sales corr., Shakeproof, Inc., Chgo., 1947-50; indsl. buyer Crescent Industries, Inc., Chgo., 1950-51; purchasing agt. Switchcraft, Inc., Chgo., 1951-73, materials mgr., 1973-74, dir. purchasing, 1974-77; pres. Tool King, Inc., Wheeling, Ill., 1977—; pres. H & H Enterprises of Northfield. Mgr. youth orgns. Northfield Jr. Hockey Club, 1968-71, Winnfield Hockey Club, 1972-73; bus. mgr. West Hockey Club, 1973-74. Served as cpl. USAAF, 1944-46. Mem. Tooling and Mfg. Assn., Sons of Norway. Republican. Mem. United Ch. Christ. Clubs: Waukegan Yacht, Lions. Home: 850 Happ Rd Northfield IL 60093 Office: Tool King Inc 275 Larkin Dr Wheeling IL 60090

HESTER, JAMES FRANCIS, JR., fastener mfg. co. exec.; b. Chgo., May 6, 1928; s. James Francis and Marion A. (Meservey) H.; student Marquette U., 1948; B.S. in Commerce, De Paul U., 1951; m. Doris Bauer, Nov. 17, 1951; children—James III, Timothy, Maureen, Stacie, Deidre. Credit mgr. St. Joseph Hosp., Chgo., 1950-53; with Am. Rivet Co., Inc., Franklin Park, Ill., 1953—, v.p., dir., 1960—, sec., 1981—. Served with U.S. Army, 1946-47. Mem. Franklin Park C. of C. (dir. 1967-70), Ill. Mfg. Assn., Chgo. Assn. Commerce and Industry, Purchasing Mgmt. Assn. Chgo., Nat. Assn. Purchasing Mgmt., Chgo. Midwest Credit Mgmtm. Assn., NAM, N.W. Suburban Mfrs. Assn. (dir. 1967-70, pres. 1976-77). Roman Catholic. Club: River Forest Golf (Elmhurst, Ill.) (dir. 1984-86, sec. 1985, 86). Office: 11330 W Melrose St Franklin Park IL 60131

HESTON, CHARLTON, actor; b. Evanston, Ill., Oct. 4, 1924; s. Russell Whitford and Lilla (Charlton) Carter; m. Lydia Marie Clarke, Mar. 17, 1944; children—Fraser Clarke, Holly Ann. Student, Northwestern U., 1941-43. Mem. Nat. Council on the Arts, 1967-72. Stage appearances in Antony and Cleopatra, 1947, Leaf and Bough, 1948, Design for a Stained Glass Window, 1949, The Tumbler, 1960; TV appearances in Wuthering Heights, Macbeth, Taming of the Shrew, Of Human Bondage, Jane Eyre; motion picture star appearing in: Gray Lady Down, Dark City, Greatest Show on Earth, Ruby Gentry, Naked Jungle, The Ten Commandments, The Big Country, Ben Hur, El Cid, 55 Days of Peking, The Greatest Story Ever Told, The Agony and the Ecstasy, Khartoun, Will Penny, Planet of the Apes, Julius Caesar, The Hawaiians, The Omega Man, Antony and Cleopatra, Soylent Green, The Three Musketeers, Airport, Earthquake, Midway, Two-Minute Warning, The Prince and the Pauper. Trustee Los Angeles Center Theatre Group, Am. Film Inst., 1971—, chmn., 1973; head President's Task Force on Arts and Humanities, 1981—. Served in USAAF, World War II. Recipient Acad. award for best actor in Ben-Hur, 1959; Jean Hersholt award as humanitarian of yr. Am. Acad. Motion Picture Arts and Scis., 1978. Mem. Screen Actors Guild (pres. 1966-71). Office: Michael Levine Pub Relations 8730 Sunset Blvd 6th Floor Los Angeles CA 90069 *

HETHERWICK, GILBERT LEWIS, lawyer; b. Winnsboro, La., Oct. 30, 1920; s. Septimus and Addie Louise (Gilbert) H.; m. Joan Friend Gibbons, May 31, 1946 (dec. Aug. 1964); children—Janet Hetherick Pumphrey, Ann Hetherwick Lyons Winegeart, Gilbert, Carol Hetherwick Sutton, Katherine Hetherwick Hummel; remarried Mertis Elizabeth Cook, June 7, 1967. BA summa cum laude, Centenary Coll., 1942; JD, Tulane U., 1949. Bar: La. 1949. With legal dept. Arkla, Inc., Shreveport, La., 1949-53; ptnr. Blanchard, Walker, O'Quin & Roberts, Shreveport, 1953—. Mem. Shreveport City Charter Revision Com., 1955; Shreveport Mcpl. Fire and Police Civil Service Bd., 1956, vice chmn., 1957-78, chmn., 1978—. Served with AUS, 1942-46. Recipient Tulane U. Law Faculty medal, 1949. Mem. La. Bar Assn., Shreveport Bar Assn. (pres. 1987), Fed. Energy Bar Assn., Order of Coif, Phi Delta Phi, Omicron Delta Kappa. Episcopalian. Club: Petroleum of Shreveport. Home: 4604 Fairfield Ave Shreveport LA 71106 Office: First Nat Bank Tower Shreveport LA 71101

HETLAND, JAMES LYMAN, JR., banker, lawyer, educator; b. Mpls., June 9, 1925; s. James L. and Evelyn E. (Lundgren) H.; m. Barbara Anne Taylor, Sept. 10, 1949; children: Janice E., James E., Nancy L., Steven T. B.S.L., U. Minn., 1948, J.D., 1950. Bar: Minn. 1950. Law clk. Minn. Supreme Ct., 1949-50; asso. firm Mackall, Crounse, Moore, Helmey & Palmer, Mpls., 1950-56; prof. U. Minn. Coll. Law, 1956-71; v.p. urban devel. First Nat. Bank Mpls., 1971-75, sr. v.p. law and urban devel., 1975-82, sr. v.p., gen. counsel, sec., 1982—; sr. v.p. First Bank System, 1987—; adj. prof. Hubert Humphrey Inst., U. Minn., 1976—, Bus. Coll. extension, 1975-81, Coll. Law, 1980—; labor arbitrator, 1967—; chmn. Minn. Citizens Council Crime and Delinquency, 1978-83; chmn. adv. coms. Minn. Supreme Ct.; regents adv. com. Hubert Humphrey Inst., U. Minn., 1982—. Co-author: Minnesota Practice, 3 vols., 1970, Minnesota Jury Instruction Guides, 2d edit., 1974. Chmn. Met. Council Twin Cities, St. Paul, 1967-71, Mpls. Charter Commn., 1963-70; chmn. Mpls. Citizens League, 1963-64, bd. dirs., 1953-67; bd. dirs. Mpls. Downtown Council, 1971—, vice chmn., 1978-82, chmn., 1982-83; chmn. bd. Minn. Zool. Garden, 1978-83; nat. v.p., mem. exec. com. Nat. Mcpl. League, 1979-82, pres., 1982-85, chmn. bd., 1985-87; vice chmn. Minn. Press Council, 1973-81; vice chmn. bd. Minn. Health Care Cost Coalition, 1980; bd. dirs. Interstudy, 1972-79, chmn., 1974; mem. Bus. Urban Issues Council, Conf. Bd., 1980—; bd. dirs. Freshwater Biol. Research Found., 1971-85, adv. bd., 1985—; bd. dirs. Mpls. Community Coll. Found., 1978-83, Minn. Exptl. City, 1972-75, Minn. Campfire Girls, 1974-79, Mpls. YMCA, 1957-76; bd. dirs. Health Central, Inc., 1973-87, exec. com., 1977—; mem. exec. com. Partnership Dataline U.S.A., 1983; bd. dirs., exec. com. Health One, 1987. Served with AUS, 1943-46. Mem. ABA, Am. Bankers Assn., Minn. Bar Assn., Hennepin County Bar Assn. Republican. Lutheran. Clubs: Mpls. Athletic, St. Anthony Athletic, N.W. Tennis Assn. Lodge: Rotary. Office: First Bank Pl Minneapolis MN 55480

HETLAND, JOHN ROBERT, lawyer, educator; b. Mpls., Mar. 12, 1930; s. James L. and Evelyn (Lundgren) H.; m. Mildred Woodruff, Dec. 1951 (div.); children: Lynda Lee, Robert John, Debra Ann.; m. Anne Kneeland, Dec. 1972; children: Robin T. Kneeland, Elizabeth J. Kneeland. B.S.L., U. Minn., 1952, J.D., 1956. Bar: Minn. bar 1956, Calif. bar 1962. Practice law Mpls., 1956-59; asso. prof. law U. Calif., Berkeley, 1959-60; prof. law U. Calif., 1960—; practice law Berkeley, 1959—; vis. prof. law Stanford U., 1971, 80, U. Singapore, 1972, U. Cologne, Fed. Republic Germany, 1988. Author: California Real Property Secured Transactions, 1970, Commercial Real Estate Transactions, 1972, Secured Real Estate Transactions, 1974, 1977, (with Maxwell, Riesenfeld, and Warren) California Cases on Security Transactions in Land, 2d edit., 1975, 3d edit., 1984; contbr. articles to legal, real estate and fin. jours. Served to lt. comdr. USNR, 1953-55. Mem. state bars Calif. and Minn., Am. Bar Assn., Order of Coif, Phi Delta Phi. Republican. Home: 20 Redcoach Ln Orinda CA 94563 Office: 2600 Warring St Berkeley CA 94704

HETSKO, CYRIL FRANCIS, retired lawyer, corporation executive; b. Scranton, Pa., Oct. 4, 1911; s. John Andrew and Anna (Lesco) H.; m. Josephine G. Stein, Nov. 12, 1932; children—Jacqueline V. (Mrs. Charles F. Kaufer), Cyril M., Cynthia F. (Mrs. William J. Rainey). Jeffery F. A.B., Dickinson Coll., 1933; J.D., U. Mich., 1936. Bar: Pa. 1937, N.Y. 1938, U.S. Supreme Ct. 1965. Assoc. Chadbourne, Parke, Whiteside & Wolff (name now Chadbourne & Parke), 1936-55, partner, 1955-64; gen. counsel Am. Brands, Inc., 1964-77, v.p., 1965-69, sr. v.p., 1969-77, also former dir.; former dir. Acme Visible Records, Inc., Acushnet Co., Am. Brands Export Corp., Am. Tobacco Internat. Corp., James B. Beam Distilling Co., James B. Beam Distilling Internat. Co., Duffy-Mott Co., Inc., Gallaher Ltd. (Gt. Britain), Master Lock Co., Master Lock Export, Inc., Swingline, Inc., Andrew Jergens Co., Sunshine Biscuits, Inc., Swingline Export Corp., Wilson Jones Co. Mem. ABA, Fed., N.Y. State bar assns., U.S. Trademark Assn. (dir. 1959-67, 68-72, 73-77, pres. 1965-66, hon. bd. chmn. 1966-67, mem. council past presidents 1977—), Order of Coif, Phi Beta Kappa, Phi Delta Theta, Delta Theta Phi. Republican. Presbyterian. Clubs: Intrepids, Explorers, Williams (N.Y.C.); Nat. Lawyers (Washington); Ridgewood (N.J.) Country. Home: 714 Waverly Rd Ridgewood NJ 07450

HETSKO, CYRIL MICHAEL, physician; b. Montclair, N.J., May 25, 1942; s. Cyril Francis and Josephine (Stein) H.; m. Theresa Hottenroth, Jan. 2, 1988; B.A., Amherst Coll., 1964; M.D., U. Rochester, 1968. Intern, U. Wis. Hosps., Madison, 1968-69, resident in internal medicine, 1969-72, clin. assoc. prof. medicine U. Wis., 1975—; practice internal medicine Dean Med. Ctr., Madison, 1975—, dir. Dean Care HMO, Inc., 1983—; chmn. dept. medicine St. Mary's Hosp. Med. Ctr., Madison, 1985-87. Served to maj. M.C., AUS, 1972-75. Diplomate Nat. Bd. Med. Examiners, Am. Bd. Internal Medicine. Mem. AMA (alt. del. 1983—), Am. Soc. Internal Medicine, Am. Soc. Microbiology, Am. Thoracic Soc., Assn. Mil. Surgeons U.S., State Med. Soc. Wis. (Councillor 1979-81, dir. 1981—, chmn. task force on AIDS 1987—), Dane County Med. Soc. (chmn. com. on prepaid health plans 1977-82; Pres.'s award 1981), Wis. Soc. Internal Medicine (councillor 1981-87, pres. 1987-88), N.Y. Acad. Scis., New Eng. Soc. in City N.Y., Nat. Found. for Infectious Disease, Madison Acad. Medicine. Club: Madison. Home: 1114 Sherman Ave Madison WI 53703 Office: Dean Med Ctr 1313 Fish Hatchery Rd Madison WI 53715

HETZEL, FREDERICK ARMSTRONG, publisher, editor; b. Pitts., Sept. 6, 1930; s. Louis and Jean Bowman (Armstrong) H.; m. Nancy Miller, Dec. 14, 1957; children: Jean Armstrong, Jennifer Elizabeth, Frederick Armstrong, Emily Miller. B.A., Washington and Jefferson Coll., 1952; M.A., U. Va., 1957. Assoc. editor Inst. Early Am. History and Culture, Williamsburg, Va., 1957-61; asso. editor U. Pitts. Press, 1961-64, dir., 1964—; sec., dir. United Pocahontas Coal Co., 1960-68; dir. Second Nat. Bank, Connellsville, Pa., 1972-75; commentator WQED-FM, 1976-79. Mem. editorial bd.: Western Pa. Hist. Mag., 1981—. Bd. dirs., sec. U. Pitts. Book Center, 1969-72, chmn., 1970-72; bd. dirs. Loaves and Fishes Coffee House, 1969-70; trustee Winchester-Thurston Sch., 1969-77, 79-83, mem. exec. com., 1970-77, 79-83, chmn., 1971-74; bd. dirs. Mendelssohn Choir Pitts., 1977-79; bd. dirs. Pitts. Dance Council, 1977-83, vice pres., 1978-79. Served to 1st lt. AUS, 1952-54, Korea. Decorated Bronze Star. Mem. Assn. Am. Univ. Presses (dir. 1972-74), Am. Hist. Assn., Pitts. History and Landmarks Found., Hist. Soc. Western Pa., Pitts. Bibliophiles (vice chmn. 1970-72, chmn. 1972-73), Phi Beta Kappa, Phi Kappa Sigma, Pi Delta Epsilon. Presbyn. Club: University (Pitts.). Home: 1221 Wightman St Pittsburgh PA 15217 Office: 127 N Bellefield Ave Pittsburgh PA 15213

HEURLEN, BENT BORGE, airline executive; b. Holbaek, Denmark, Mar. 28, 1934; s. Herluf and Doris (Hansen) Pedersen; children: Jesper, Kamilla. B Com, Copenhagen Sch. Economics, 1977. Fighter pilot Royal Danish Air Force, 1952-60; flight ops. officer Scandanavian Airlines, Copenhagen, 1960-63, EDP programmer, 1963-66, EDP analyst, 1966-68, EDP project mgr., 1968-73, EDP integration mgr., 1973-77, adminstrv. mgr. stas., 1977-81, dir. SAS mgmt. cons., 1981-83, dir. airport projects, govtl. changes, 1983—; tchr. orgns. theory Comml. Sch., Copenhagen, 1987—. Author: Systems Integration and Data Base Adminstration, 1977. Mem. Orgn. Danish Civil Economists. Home: Vadum Alle 21, DK-2770 Kastrup Copenhagen Denmark Office: SAS Copenhagen Airport, PO Box 150, DK-2770 Copenhagen Denmark

HEUTGER, NICOLAUS CARL, canon; b. Rinteln, Hanover, Fed. Republic Germany, July 1, 1932; s. Fritz Heutger and Laura (Spanuth) Klein; m. Ursula Reinhard, Feb. 8, 1964; children: Nicolaus, Viola. ThD, U. Münster, Fed. Republic Germany, 1959, Theol. Faculty Montpellier, France, 1968. Pastor St. Martin Ch., Nienburg, Fed. Republic Germany, 1961-82; hon. canon Monastery of Bassum, Fed. Republic Germany, 1973—; lectr. U. Hildesheim, 1973—; pastor St. Lamberti Ch., Hildesheim, Fed. Republic Germany, 1982—. Author: Evangelische Konvente in den Welfischen Landen, 1961, Das Kloster Amelungsborn, 1968, Die Evangelisch-Theologische Arbeit der Westfalen, 1969, Bursfelde und Seine Reformklöster, 1975. Mem. Nienburg Town Parliament, 1968-71. Lutheran. Lodge: Lions. Home: Kaiser-Friedrich Strasse, D 32 Hildesheim Federal Republic of Germany

HEWETT, ARTHUR EDWARD, real estate developer; b. Dallas, Oct. 16, 1935; s. Arthur Elton and Clara Mae (Wagoner) H.; m. Helen Yvonne Barry, May 20, 1959; children: Julie, Matthew, Clara. B.B.A., So. Methodist U., 1957, LL.B., 1965. Bar: Tex. bar 1965. Asst. to exec. v.p. Diversa, Inc., Dallas, 1960-61; asst. to pres. RichPlan Corp., Dallas, 1961-62; mng. ptnr. firm Hewett Johnson Swanson & Barbee, 1970-80; pres. Thompson Realty Corp., Dallas, 1980-83; pres., chief exec. officer Republic Property Group, Inc., 1983—; dir. Inter First Bank Park Cities. Served to lt. USNR, 1957-60. Mem. Tex. Bar Assn. Presbyterian. Clubs: Park City, Stonebridge Country. Home: 3705 Euclid Ave Dallas TX 75205 Office: Republic Property Group 5956 Sherry Ln Suite 930 Dallas TX 75225

HEWISH, ANTONY, radioastronomer; b. May 11, 1924; s. Ernest William and Frances Grace Lanyon (Pinch) H.; B.A., Cambridge U., 1948, M.A., 1950, Ph.D., 1952; D.Sc. (hon.), Leicester, 1976, Exeter, 1977; m. Marjorie Elizabeth Catherine Richards, 1950; 1 son, 1 dau. Research fellow Gonville and Caius Coll., 1952-54, asst. dir. research, 1954-62, fellow, 1955-62, hon. fellow, 1976—; lectr. physics U. Cambridge, 1962-69, prof. radioastronomy, 1971—, reader, 1969-71, fellow Churchill Coll., 1962—; vis. prof. astronomy Yale U., 1963; prof. astronomy Royal Instn. Gt. Britain, 1977—; dir. Mullard Radio Astronomy Obs., Cambridge, 1982—. Recipient Eddington medal Royal Astron. Soc., 1969; Charles Vernon Boys prize Inst. Physics and Phys. Soc., 1970; Dellinger Gold medal Internat. Union Radio Sci., 1972; Michelson medal Franklin Inst., 1973; Hopkins prize Cambridge Philos. Soc., 1973; Holweck medal and prize Soc. Française de Physique, 1974; Nobel prize for Physics (with other), 1974; Hughes medal Royal Soc. London, 1977. Fellow Royal Soc. London, Indian Acad. Scis. (fgn.); mem. Am. Acad. Arts and Scis. Address: Pryor's Cottage, Kingston, Cambridge England Office: Univ of Cambridge, Cavendish Lab, Cambridge CB3 OHE England *

HEWITT, DESMOND JAMES, barrister-at-law; b. Opotiki, N.Z., Oct. 26, 1908; s. Leonard and Frances Orme (Webb) H.; student Christ's Coll., 1923-26; LL.M., U. Canterbury, N.Z., 1937; m. Reita Edith Nicholls, Apr. 3, 1972. Admitted to N.Z. bar, 1937; practice as barrister, Christchurch, N.Z., 1937—; lectr. constl. law U. Canterbury, N.Z., 1952-60. N.Z. rep. Asso. Bd. Royal Schs. Music, 1950-79; bd. dirs. Christchurch Civic Trust, 1970—, chmn., 1974-76; vice-chmn. N.Z. sect. Internat. Commn. Jurists, 1977; diocesan lay reader Anglican Ch. Christchurch, 1945—; mem. exec. council South Island Promotion Assn., Inc., 1978-80. Decorated officer Order Brit. Empire. Mem. Royal Coll. Music (hon.). Clubs: Elmwood, Masons. Author books: Practical Guide to the Land Sales Act, 1943; The Control of Delegated Legislation, 1953; Natural Justice, 1972. Home: 38 B Mansfield Ave, Christchurch New Zealand

HEWKIN, JOHN, electronics executive, consultant; b. Bristol, Eng., Aug. 13, 1943. Degree in elec. engring., Bath (Eng.) U. Tech., 1966. Design engr. various firms, Eng., 1966-69; engr. dist. mktg. Tex. Instruments Ltd., Bedford, Eng., 1969-71; product mktg. engr. Tex. Instruments Inc., Houston, 1971-78; mgr. European product mktg. Mostek Internat., Brussels, 1978-85; mng. dir. Mostek U.K. Ltd., London, 1985-86; dir. European mktg. Honeywell Control Systems Ltd., Bracknell, Eng., 1986-87; cons. semiconductor industry Reading, Eng., 1987—. Conservative.

HEWLETT, C(ECIL) JAMES, interior designer; b. Russell, N.Y., Apr. 24, 1923; s. Orin Stanley and Grace Josephine (Heffernan) H. Student, U. Md., 1949-51, Syracuse U., 1953-60. Mem. design staff Colony Shop, Syracuse, N.Y., 1952-55, Sagenkahn Co., Syracuse, 1955-61; design dir. Halle Bros. Co., Cleve., 1961-72, Nahan Co., New Orleans, 1973-75; pvt. practice interior design New Orleans, 1975-76; owner Hewlett Mack Design Assocs., New Orleans; design dir. Hemenway Co., Inc., New Orleans, 1976-77; lectr. various profl. groups, nat. convs. Contbr. articles to profl. publs. Trustee, chmn. Found. for Interior Design Edn. Research, 1970-74, trustee emeritus, 1983—, chmn. futures conf., coll. curricula planning, 1981—; del. Coalition for Nat. Growth Policy, 1971-74; mem. adv. panel Washington Center for Met. Studies, HUD, 1970-74; founder, mem. Nat. Council for Interior Design Qualification, 1969-73. Served with USAAF, 1942-51. Decorated Air medal with 8 oak leaf clusters. Fellow Am. Soc. Interior Designers (position papers com.); mem. Nat. Soc. Interior Designers (pres. 1967-69, chmn. bd. dirs. 1969-71), Interior Design Educators Council (hon.), Internat. Soc. Arts, Scis. and Tech., World Future Soc. Office: P O Box 70166 New Orleans LA 70172

HEXNER, LILA M., entrepreneur, educator, consultant; b. Kimberly, Wis., May 14; d. Harold George and Florence Esther (McCabe) Fird; BS in Edn., U. Wis.; M.Phil.Ed., Boston Coll., 1973; m. Peter E. Hexner (div. 1986); children: Michael T., Holly A., Thomas S. Women's adv., mem. adminstrn. Middlesex Community Coll., 1971-78, founder, dir. women's center, 1971-75, founder dir. Widening Opportunity Research Center, 1975-78, founder, dir. div. community services, 1978; founder, Edn. for Commercialization div. No. Energy Corp., N.E. Regional Solar Energy Center Edn. Dept., Boston, 1978-82; founder, pres. Cons. Exchange, Inc., 1982—; mem. adv. com. Internat. Solar Renewable Energy Conf., 1981; chmn. Bus. Resource Ctr., Small Bus. Assn.; cons. in field. Mem. Mass. Adv. Council on Vocat. Tech. Edn., 1972-79; mem. Mass. Gov.'s Spl. Commn. on Youth Unemployment, 1978—; mem. exec. com. Mass. coordinating com. Internat. Women's Yr., 1978. Recipient Disting. Service award Middlesex Community Coll., 1973; grants include Fund for Improvement Postsecondary Edn., 1976-78. Mem. Women in Solar Energy (nat. adv. bd. 1980-82), Boston Computer Soc., Smaller Bus. Assn. New Eng. (chmn. first bus. conf., bd. dirs. 1987—), Research Mgmt. Assn. (bd. govs.). Home: 105-1 Trowbridge Cambridge MA 02138

HEYCK, GERTRUDE PAINE DALY, social club administrator; b. Houston, Nov. 30, 1910; d. David and Gertrude (Paine) Daly; m. Theodore R. Heyck, May 1, 1935; children: Jane Peel (Mrs. Donald H. Gaucher), Theodore Daly. Student, Wellesley Coll., 1929; BA, Brown U., 1934. Bd. dirs. Union Stock Yards, San Antonio, 1961-64. Mem. Jr. League. Clubs: Wellesley, Brown-Pembroke (v.p. 1950-60), Brown (Houston); Brown Faculty (Providence). Home: 1907 Bolsover Rd Houston TX 77005

HEYCK, THEODORE DALY, lawyer; b. Houston, Apr. 17, 1941; s. Theodore Richard and Gertrude Paine (Daly) H. B.A., Brown U., 1963; J.D., N.Y. Law Sch., 1979. Bar: N.Y. 1980, Calif. 1984, U.S. Ct. Appeals (2nd cir.) 1984, U.S. Supreme Ct. 1984, U.S. Dist. Ct. (so. and ea. dists.) N.Y. 1980, U.S. Dist. Ct. (we. and no. dists.) N.Y. 1984, U.S. Dist. Ct. (cen. and so. dists.) Calif. 1984, U.S. Ct. Appeals (9th cir.) 1986. Paralegal dist. atty. Bklyn., 1975-79; asst. dist. atty. Bklyn. dist., Kings County, N.Y., 1979-85; dep. city atty., Los Angeles, 1985—; bd. dirs. Screen Actors Guild, N.Y.C., 1977-78. Mem. ABA, AFTRA, Bklyn. Bar Assn., Assn. Trial Lawyers Am., N.Y. Trial Lawyers Assn., N.Y. State Bar Assn., Calif. Bar Assn., Fed. Bar Council, Los Angeles County Bar Assn., Screen Actors Guild, Am. Fedn. TV and Radio Artists, Actors Equity Assn., Nat. Acad. TV Arts and Scis., Screen Actors Guild, Home: 2106 Live Oak Dr E Los Angeles CA 90068 Office: Office of City Atty City Hall East 200 N Main St Los Angeles CA 90012

HEYDEGGER, H(ELMUT) ROLAND, physical chemist, educator, researcher, cons.; b. Phila., Dec. 3, 1935; s. Helmut and Allyse (Paulich) H. B.S., Queens Coll., CUNY, 1956; M.S., U. Ark., Fayetteville, 1958; Ph.D. (Gen. Electric Found. fellow), U. Chgo., 1968. Phys. chemist U.S. Bur. Mines, Bartlesville, Okla., 1958; instr. Prairie State Coll., 1961-62; asst. prof. chemistry Purdue U. Calumet, Hammond, Ind., 1970-75, assoc. prof., 1975-81, prof. 1981—, head dept. chemistry and physics, 1979—, dir. Inst. Environ. Edn., 1982-84, acting dean Sch. Sci. and Nursing, 1983-84; research assoc. Enrico Fermi Inst., U. Chgo., 1968-78, sr. research asso., 1978—; cons. Argonne Nat. Lab., 1973-74; vis. fellow Australian Nat. U., 1976-77, 84; vis. staff mem. Los Alamos Nat. Lab., 1978-84; NRC assoc. NASA Johnson Space Ctr., 1985-86. Contbr. articles to profl. jours. Mem. Am. Chem. Soc., Am. Phys. Soc., Am. Geophys. Union, Geochem. Soc., Internat. Assn. Geochemistry and Cosmochemistry, Meteoritical Soc. Office: Purdue U Dept Chemistry and Physics Calumet Hammond IN 46323

HEYDEN, FRANCIS JOSEPH, astronomer; b. Buffalo, May 3, 1907; s. Frederick John and Clara Elizabeth (Drescher) H.; B.S., Woodstock Coll., 1930, M.A. in Philosophy, 1931, licenciate theol., 1938; M.A. in Astronomy, Harvard U., 1942, Ph.D. in Astronomy, 1944; D.Sc. (hon.), Georgetown U., 1963. Joined Soc. of Jesus, Roman Catholic Ch., ordained priest; chief astronomer Manila (Philippines) Obs., 1931-34, dir. Solar Div., 1972—; teaching fellow Harvard U., 1942-44; prof. math. St. Peter's Coll., 1944-45; dir. Georgetown Coll. Obs., 1945-72, dir. radio/TV activities, 1946-72. Mem. Internat. Astron. Union, Internat. Union Geodesy and Geophysics, Am. Astron. Soc., Royal Astron. Soc., Nat. Research Council Philippines, AAAS, IEEE, Harvard Grad. Soc., Religious Heritage Am., Phi Beta Kappa Sigma Xi. Roman Catholic. Author texts and articles in profl. jours. Home and Office: 1101 PO Box 122, UP Post Office, Diliman, QC Philippines

HEYDT, HELMUT, dental association executive; b. Cologne, Germany, Aug. 16, 1928; came to South Africa, 1936; s. Emil and Kaethe (Katzenstein) H.; m. Ruth Abrahamsohn, Oct. 4, 1953 (dec. July, 1983); children—Arlene, Beverley, Dana, Kevin; m. Ellen, June 10, 1986. D.D.S., U. Witwatersrand, 1951. Pvt. practice dentistry, Benoni, South Africa, 1951-69; specialist, sr. lectr. U. Witwatersrand, 1970-72; exec. dir., mng. editor Dental Assn. South Africa, Johannesburg, 1972—, pres. South Transvaal br., 1961-62, fed. councillor, 1959-72, hon. sec., 1968-72; mem. Dental Technicians Council, 1964—, past vice-chmn., treas., chmn. edn. com. 1974. Mem. Dental Assn. South Africa (J. C. Middleton-Shaw fellow 1970, R.V. Bird gold medal 1973), Zimbabwean Dental Assn., Internat. Coll. Dentists, South African Dental Technicians Council, Prosthodontic Soc. South Africa, Acad. Prosthodontics, ADA, South African Soc. Periodontology, Federation Dentaire Internationale. Jewish. Office: Dental Assn South Africa, Private Bag One, Houghton 2041 Republic of South Africa

HEYER, JOHN WHITEFOORD, film company executive; b. Devonport, Australia, Sept. 14, 1916; s. Frederick George and Marcia (Elliston) H.; m. Dorothy Agnes Janet Greenhalgh, Nov. 18, 1942; children: Elizabeth Lewis, Frederick, Anna. Student, Scotch Coll., Melbourne, Australia, 1929-31, Prahran Coll., Melbourne, 1932-33. Mem. film com. Australian Edn. Council, Sydney, 1940-45; dir. Ealing Studios, Sydney, 1945-46; producer Australian Nat. Film Bd., Sydney, 1946-48, Shell Film Unit, Sydney, 1948-56, Shell Internat., London, 1956-67; mng. dir. John Heyer Film Co. Ltd., London, 1958—. Mem. Govt. Film Council New South Wales, Australia, 1947-56, Film and TV Com. Australian Council Arts, 1970—. Decorated Order Brit. Empire; recipient Venice Internat. Festival Grand Prize Absoloto, 1954, Gran Premio Montevideo-UNESCO, 1956, 1st prize Melbourne Film Festival, 1957, 1st prize Venice Film Festival, 1958, 60, Film of Yr. prize London Film Festival, 1962, Coupe de Venice, 1964. Mem. Fedn. Film Socs. (pres. 1944-56), Brit. Film Inst., Assn. Cinema and TV Technicians, Sci. Film Assn. (v.p. 1950-56), Sydney Film Soc. (pres. 1944-54), Producers and Dirs. Assn., Soc. Film and TV Arts, European Acad. Arts and Scis. Home: 3 Ulva Rd, London SW15 6AP, England also: PO Box 89, 2021 Paddington NSW Australia

HEYL, ALLEN VAN, JR., geologist; b. Allentown, Pa., Apr. 10, 1918; s. Allen Van and Emma (Kleppinger) H.; student Muhlenberg Coll., 1936-37; B.S. in Geology, Pa. State U., 1941; Ph.D. in Geology, Princeton U., 1950; m. Maxine LaVon Hawke, July 12, 1945; children—Nancy Caroline, Allen David Van. Field asst., govt. geologist Nfld. Geol. Survey, summers 1937-40, 42; jr. geologist U.S. Geol. Survey, Wis., 1943-45, asst. geologist, 1945-47, asso. geologist, 1947-50, geologist, Washington and Beltsville, Md., 1950-67; staff geologist, Denver, 1968—; disting. lectr. grad. coll. Beijing, China and Nat. Acad. Sci., 1988; chmn. Internat. Commn. Tectonics of Ore Deposits. Fellow Instn. Mining and Metallurgy (Gt. Brit.), Geol. Soc. Am., Am. Mineral. Soc.; mem. Inst. Genesis of Ore Deposits, Soc. Econ. Geologists, Geol. Soc. Wash., Colo. Sci. Soc., Rocky Mountain Geol. Soc., Friends of Mineralogy (hon. life), Evergreen Naturalist Audubon Soc., Sigma Xi, Alpha Chi Sigma. Lutheran. Contbr. numerous articles to profl. jours., chpts. to books. Home: PO Box 1052 Evergreen CO 80439 Office: US Geol Survey Cen Mineral Resources Br MS 905 Denver Fed Br Denver CO 80225

HEYMAN, IRA MICHAEL, university chancellor; b. N.Y.C., May 30, 1930; s. Harold Albert and Judith (Sobel) H.; m. Therese Helene Thau, Dec. 17, 1950; children—Stephen Thomas, James Nathaniel. AB in Govt., Dartmouth Coll., 1951; JD, Yale U., 1956; LLD (hon.), U. Pacific, 1981; LHD (hon.), Hebrew Union Coll., 1984; LLD (hon.), U. Md., 1986. Bar: N.Y. 1956, Calif. 1961. Legis. asst. to U.S. Senator Ives, 1950-51; assoc. Carter, Ledyard & Milburn, N.Y.C., 1956-57; law clk. to presiding justice U.S. Ct. Appeals (2d cir.), New Haven, 1957-58; chief law clk. to Supreme Ct. Justice Earl Warren, 1958-59; acting assoc. prof. law U. Calif. at Berkeley, 1959-61, prof. law, 1961—, prof. city and regional planning,

1966—, vice chancellor, 1974-80, chancellor, 1980—; vis. prof. Yale Law Sch., 1963-64, Stanford Law Sch., 1971-72; bd. dirs. Pacific Gas & Electric Co., 1985—; counsel task force on demonstrations and protest Pres.'s Commn. on Violence, 1968-69; mem. Pub. Land Law Rev. Commn., 1968-70, Commn. on Isla Vista, U. Calif.-Santa Barbara, 1970; cons. various orgns. Editor Yale Law Jour.; contbr. articles to profl. jours. Sec. Calif. adv. com. U.S. Commn. Civil Rights, 1962-67; trustee Dartmouth Coll., 1982—, Lawyers' Commn. for Civil Rights Under Law, 1977—; chmn. exec. com. Nat. Assn. State Univs. and Land Grant Colls., 1986; chmn. Div. I subcom. Nat. Collegiate Athletic Assn. Pres.'s Commn., 1986-88; chmn. Human Rights and Welfare Commn. City of Berkeley, 1966-68; chmn. acad. senate policy com. U. Calif., Berkeley, 1965-67, state-wide acad. assembly, 1964-66, 72-73; pres. Pres. and Chancellor group Pacific 10 Conf., 1984-85; mem. research adv. com. Oakland Inter-Agy. Project, 1964-65; bd. dirs. Am. Council on Edn., 1984-85. Served to 1st lt. USMC, 1951-53, to capt. USMCR, 1953-58. Named Chevalier de la Legion D'Honneur Govt. France, 1985. Mem. Am. Law Inst. (asst. reporter). Democrat. Office: Univ Calif Office of the Chancellor Berkeley CA 94720

HEYNINCK, JEAN-MARIE, personnel manager; b. Familleureux, Hainaut, Belgium, Dec. 18, 1944; parents: Isidore Heyninck and Anna-Marie Hennau; m. Patricia De Cooman; children: Stephane, Xavier, Alexis. Grad. in Psychology, U. Louvain, Belgium, 1969, grad. in Safety and Health, 1982. Scientific researcher U. Louvain, 1969-70; personnel supr. Don Internat., Manage, Belgium, 1970-71; personnel mgr. Stewart Warner Corp., Ghlin, Belgium, 1971-77; psychologist Cen. PMS, Bersilles L'Abbaye, Belgium, 1977-78; human relations mgr. S.A. Signode N.V., Carnieres, Belgium, 1978-87; personnel mgr. S.A. Match, Fleurus, Belgium, 1987—. Social judge Work Ct., Charleroi, Belgium, 1979. Served as 1st sgt. para-commando unit Belgian mil., 1964-66. Mem. Compagnie des Dirigeants de Service du Personnel. Home: Rue Saint Pierre 61, Besonrieux (La Louviere), Hainaut B7100, Belgium

HIAI, FUMIO, mathematician; b. Toyama, Japan, Mar. 1, 1948; s. Fujio and Kimi (Sanga) H.; m. Rieko Tabata, Nov. 11, 1950; 1 child, Shinji. BS, Tokyo Inst. Tech., 1970, MS, 1975, D.Sc., 1979. Mem. staff Kawasaki Steel Co., Ltd., Kobe, Japan, 1970-72; research asst. Tokyo Inst. Tech., 1975-76; lectr. Sci. U. Tokyo, Chiba, Japan, 1976-84; assoc. prof. U. Tokyo, Chiba, 1984-85, Research Inst. Applied Electricity, Hokkaido U., Sapporo, Japan, 1985—. Office: Research Inst Applied Electricity, Hokkaido U, Sapporo 060, Japan

HIBBARD, RICHARD PAUL, industrial ventilation consultant, lecturer; lectr.; b. Defiance, Ohio, Nov. 1, 1923; s. Richard T. and Doris E. (Walkup) H.; B.S. in Mech. Indsl. Engring., U. Toledo, 1949; m. Phyllis Ann Kirchoffer, Sept. 7, 1948; children—Barbara Rae, Marcia Kae, Rebecca Ann, Patricia Jan, John Ross. Mech. engr. Oldsmobile div. Gen. Motors Corp., Lansing, Mich., 1950-56; design and sales engr. McConnell Sheet Metal, Inc., Lansing, 1956-60; chief heat and ventilation engr. Fansteel Metall. Corp., North Chicago, Ill., 1960-62; sr. facilities and ventilation engr. The Boeing Co., Seattle, 1962-63; ventilation engr. environ. health div. dept. preventive medicine U. Wash., 1964-70, lectr. dept. environ. health, 1970-82, lectr. emeritus, 1983—; prin. Indsl. Ventilation Cons.Services, 1983—; chmn. Western Indsl. Ventilation Conf., 1962; mem. com. indsl. ventilation Am. Conf. Govtl. Indsl. Hygienists, 1966—; mem. staff Indsl. Ventilation Conf., Mich. State U., 1955—. Served with USAAF, 1943-45, USAR, 1946-72. Recipient Disting. Service award Indsl. Ventilation Conf., Mich. State U., 1975. Mem. Am. Soc. Safety Engrs. (R.M. Gillmore Meml. award Puget Sound chpt.), ASHRAE, Am. Inst. Plant Engrs., Am. Indsl. Hygiene Assn. (J.M. Dallevalle award 1977), Am. Foundryman's Soc. Lodges: Elks, Masons. Contbr. articles on indsl. hygiene and ventilation to profl. jours. Home: 41 165th Ave SE Bellevue WA 98008

HIBBERT, ELEANOR, (JEAN PLAIDY, VICTORIA HOLT, PHILIPPA CARR, KATHLEEN KELLOW, ELLALICE TATE, ELBUR FORD, ELEANOR BURFORD), author; b. London, 1906; d. Joseph and Alice (Tate) B.; m. G. P. Hibbert. Ed. privately. Author: (as Jean Plaisy) Together They Ride, 1945, Beyond The Blue Mountains, 1947, Murder Most Royal (and as The King's Pleasure, U.S.), 1949, The Goldsmith's Wife, 1950, Madame Serpent, 1951, Daughter of Satan, 1952, The Italian Woman, 1952, Sixth Wife, 1953, new edit, 1969, Queen Jezebel, 1953, St. Thomas's Eve, 1954, The Spanish Bridegroom, 1954, Gay Lord Robert, 1955, The Royal Road to Fotheringay, 1955, new edit., 1968, The Wandering Prince, 1956, A Health Unto His Majesty, 1956, Here Lies Our Sovereign Lord, 1956, Flaunting Extravagant Queen, 1956, new edit., 1960, Triptych of Poisoners, 1958, new edit., 1970, Madonna of the Seven Hills, 1958, Light on Lucrezia, 1958, Louis the Wellbeloved, 1959, The Road to Compiegne, 1959, The Rise of the Spanish Inquisition, 1959, The Growth of the Spanish Inquisition, 1960, Castile for Isabelle, 1960, Spain for the Sovereigns, 1960, The End of the Spanish Inquisition, 1961, Daughters of Spain, 1961, Katherine, The Virgin Widow, 1961, Meg Roper, Daughter of Sir Thomas More (for children), 1961, The Young Elizabeth (for children), 1961, The Shadow of the Pomegranate, 1962, The King's Secret Matter, 1962, The Young Mary, Queen of Scots, 1962, The Captive Queen of Scots, 1963, Mary, Queen of France, 1964, The Murder in the Tower, 1964, The Thistle and the Rose, 1965, The Three Crowns, 1965, Evergreen Gallant, 1965, The Haunted Sisters, 1966, The Queen's Favourites, 1966, The Princess of Celle, 1967, Queen in Waiting, 1967, The Spanish Inquisition, its Rise, Growth and End (3 vols. in one), 1967, Caroline The Queen, 1968, Katharine of Aragon (3 vols. in one), 1968, The Prince and the Quakeress, 1968, The Third George, 1969, Catherine de Medici (3 vols. in one), 1969, Perdita's Prince, 1969, Sweet Lass of Richmond Hill, 1970, The Regent's Daughter, 1971, Goddess of the Green Room, 1971, Victoria in the Wings, 1972, Charles II (3 vols. in one), 1972, The Captive of Kensington Palace, 1972, The Queen and Lord M, 1973, The Queen's Husband, 1973, The Widow of Windsor, 1974, The Bastard King, 1974, The Lion of Justice, 1975, The Passionate Enemies, 1976, The Plantagenet Prelude, 1976, The Revolt of the Eaglets, 1977, The Heart of the Lion, 1977, The Prince of Darkness, 1978, The Battle of the Queens, 1978, The Queen from Provence, 1979, Edward Longshanks, 1979, The Follies of the King, 1980, The Vow on the Heron, 1980, Passage to Pontefract, 1981, Star of Lancaster, 1981, Epitaph for Three Women, 1981, Red Rose of Anjou, 1982, The Sun in Splendour, 1982, Uneasy Lies the Head, 1982, Myself My Enemy, 1983, Queen of this Realm, 1984, Victoria Victorious, 1985, The Lady in The Tower, 1986, The Courts of Love, 1987, In the Shadow of the Crown, 1988; (as Eleanor Burford) Daughter of Anna, 1941, Passionate Witness, 1941, Married Love, 1942, When All The World Was Young, 1943, So the Dreams Depart, 1944, Not In Our Stars, 1945, Dear Chance, 1947, Alexa, 1948, The House At Cupid's Cross, 1949, Believe The Heart, 1950, Love Child, 1950, Saint Or Sinner?, 1951, Dear Delusion, 1952, Bright Tomorrow, 1952, When We Are Married, 1953, Leave Me My Love, 1953, Castles in Spain, 1954, Hearts Afire, 1954, When Other Hearts, 1955, Two Loves In Her Life, 1955, Married in Haste, 1956, Begin To Live, 1956, To Meet A Stranger, 1957, Pride of the Morning, 1958, Blaze of Noon, 1958, Dawn Chorus, 1959, Red Sky At Night, 1959, Night of Stars, 1960, Now That April's Gone, 1961, Who's Calling?, 1962, (as Ellalice Tate) Defenders of the Faith, 1956 (under name of Jean Plaidy, 1970), Scarlet Cloak, 1957 (2d edn. under name of Jean Plaidy, 1969), Queen of Diamonds, 1958, Madame Du Barry, 1959, This Was A Man, 1961, (as Elbur Ford) The Flesh and The Devil, 1950, Poison in Pimlico, 1950, Bed Disturbed, 1952, Such Bitter Business, 1953 (as Evil in the House, U.S., 1954), (as Kathleen Kellow) Danse Macabre, 1952, Rooms At Mrs Oliver's, 1953, Lilith, 1954 (2d edit. under name of Jean Plaidy, 1967), It Began in Vauxhall Gardens, 1955 (2d edit. under name of Jean Plaidy, 1968), Call of the Blood, 1956, Rochester-The Mad Earl, 1957, Milady Charlotte, 1959, The World's A Stage, 1960, (as Victoria Holt) Mistress of Mellyn, 1961, Kirkland Revels, 1962, The Bride of Pendorric, 1963, The Legend of the Seventh Virgin, 1965, Menfreya, 1966, The King of the Castle, 1967, The Queen's Confession, 1968, The Shivering Sands, 1969, The Secret Woman, 1971, The Shadow of the Lynx, 1972, On the Night of the Seventh Moon, 1973, The Curse of the Kings, 1973, The House of a Thousand Lanterns, 1974, Lord of the Far Island, 1975, The Pride of the Peacock, 1976, My Enemy the Queen, 1978, The Spring of the Tiger, 1979, The Mask of the Enchantress, 1980, The Judas Kiss, 1981, The Demon Lover, 1982, The Time of the Hunter's Moon, 1983, The Landower Legacy, 1984, The Road to Paradise Island, 1985, Secret for a Nightingale, 1986, The Silk Vendetta, 1987, The India Fan, 1988; (as Philippa Carr) The Miracle at St Bruno's, 1972, Lion Triumphant, 1974, The Witch from the Sea, 1975, Saraband for Two Sisters, 1976, Lament for a Lost Lover, 1977, The Love Child, 1978, The Song of the Siren, 1979, The Drop of the Dice, 1980, The Adulteress, 1981, Zipporah's Daughter, 1983, Voices in a Haunted Room, 1984, The Return of Gypsy, 1985, Midsummers Eve, 1986, The Pool of St. Branok, 1987. Office: care Robert Hale Ltd, 45-47 Clerkenwell Green, London EC1, England also: co AM Heath Ltd, 40 William IV St, London WC2N 4DD, England

HIBBERT, WILLIAM ANDREW, JR., surgeon; b. Pensacola, Fla., June 15, 1932; s. William Andrew and Blanche Marie (Blair) H.; BS, U. of South, 1953; MD, Emory U., 1957; children: Andy III, Blair, Reb Stuart. Diplomate Am. Bd. Surgery, also recert., Am. Bd. Colon and Rectal Surgery. Intern, Duval Med. Center, U. Fla., Jacksonville, 1957-58; resident in gen. surgery Grady Meml. Hosp., Emory U., Atlanta, 1958-62; fellow in colon-rectal surgery Ochsner Found. Hosp., New Orleans, 1962-63, Baylor U. Med. Center, Dallas, 1964-65; practice medicine specializing in colon-rectal surgery, Austin, Tex., 1965—; mem. staff St. David, Seton, Brackenridge, Holy Cross hosps.; instr. Tulane U. Med. Sch., New Orleans, 1962-64; cons. U. Tex. Student Health Center. Bd. govs. Shrine Burn Hosp., Galveston, Tex.; bd. dirs. St. David Hosp. Found., Austin. Served with USPHS, 1963-64. Fellow ACS, Am. Soc. Colon and Rectal Surgeons, Am. Soc. Gastrointestinal Endoscopists, Am. Soc. Laser Surgery, Soc. of Am. Gastrointestinal Surgeons, Internat. Soc. Univ. Colon and Rectal Surgeons; mem. Pan Am. (past chmn. colon-rectal sect.), So. Med. Assn. (past sect. chmn.), Tex. Med. Assn. Tex. Colon-Rectal Soc. (past pres.), Pan Pacific Surg. Soc., Royal Soc. Medicine (hon.). Club: Austin Downtown. Lodges: Masons, Shriners (potentate 1985; past bd. govs. Shrine Hosp., rep. Imperial Council Shrine North Am.), Royal Order of Jesters (officer), Order of DeMolay (Legion of Honor, chmn. bd. trustees Ben Hur Shrine Temple). Contbr. articles to med. jours. Office: 4210 Medical Pkwy Austin TX 78756

HIBBS, WILLIAM ERNEST, III, clergyman; b. Norfolk, Va., Sept. 28, 1950; s. William Edward and Ruby Adelle Holley Hibbs Peed; BBA, George Washington U., 1970; ThM, U. St. Thomas, Houston, 1976. Ordained priest Roman Catholic Ch., 1975; sec., treas. Parker Supply Co., Inc., Houston, 1974-75, Interfaith Council on Human Rights, Washington, 1978—, Mandinka Village Projects, Inc., Balt., 1978; chmn., co-exec. dir. Washington based Nat. Ecumenical Coalition, Inc., 1976-88; pres. The Dr. James F. Holloran III Meml. Nat. AIDS Bereavement Ctr., Georgetown Station, Washington, 1988—. Active Boy Scouts Am.; bd. dirs. Balt. Theatre Festival; bd. dirs. Balt. Performing Arts Workshop Assn. Mem. Am. Soc. Assn. Execs., Internat. Platform Assn. Contbr. articles to profl. publs. Office: The Dr James F Holloran III Meml Georgetown Station PO Box 25696 Washington DC 20007

HIBDON, JAMES EDWARD, economist, educator; b. McAlester, Okla., Sept. 1, 1924; s. William Wesley and Minnie Irene (McBride) H.; m. Mina Mae Gilreath, Aug. 20, 1944; children—Mary Ann, Jennifer Lee. Student, Okla. Bapt. U., 1942-43, Syracuse U., 1943; B.A., U. Okla., 1948, M.A., 1949; Ph.D., U. N.C., 1957. Asst. prof. econs. Ga. State U., 1954-57, asso. prof., 1957-59; asso. prof. Tex. A&M U., 1959-61, U. Okla., Norman, 1961-67; prof. U. Okla., 1967—, chmn. dept. econs., 1971—; vis. scholar U.S. Dept. Commerce, 1977-78. Author: Price and Welfare Theory, 1969; editor: Rev. of Regional Econs. and Bus, 1975—, Okla. Bus. Bull, 1970-71; contbr. articles to profl. jours. Trustee annuity bd. So. Bapt. Conv. Served with AUS, 1943-46, 50-51. Mem. Am. Econs. Assn., So. Econs. Assn., S.W. Econs. Assn. (pres. 1977-78), Midwest Econs. Assn., Southwestern Social Sci. Assn., Western Social Sci. Assn., Beta Gamma Sigma, Omicron Delta Epsilon.

HICK, KENNETH WILLIAM, business executive; b. New Westminster, B.C., Can., Oct. 17, 1946; s. Les Walter and Mary Isabelle (Warner) H. BA in Bus., Eastern Wash. State Coll., 1971; MBA (fellow), U. Wash., 1973, PhD, 1975. Regional sales mgr., San Leandro, Calif., 1976-79; gen. sales mgr. Moore Internat., Inc., Portland, 1979-80; v.p. sales and mktg. Phillips Corp., Anaheim, Calif., 1980-81; owner, pres., chief exec. officer K.C. Metals, San Jose, Calif., 1981-87; owner, pres., chief exec. officer Losli Internat. Inc., Portland, Oreg., 1987—; communications cons. Asso. Public Safety Communication Officers, Inc., State of Oreg., 1975-77; numerous cons. assignments, also seminars, 1976-81. Contbr. to numerous publs., 1976—. Mem. Oreg. Gov.'s Tax Bd., 1975-76; pres. Portland chpt. Oreg. Jaycees, 1976; bd. fellows U. Santa Clara, 1983—. Served with USAF, 1966-69. Decorated Commendation medal. Mem. Am. Mgmt. Assn., Am. Mktg. Assn., Assn. M.B.A. Execs., Asso. Gen. Contractors, Soc. Advancement Mgmt. Roman Catholic. Home: 3101 McNary Pkwy #6 Lake Oswego OR 97034 Office: Losli Internat 8015 SW Hunziker Rd Tigard OR 97223

HICKEY, LADY BARBARA STANDISH, company executive; b. Washington, June 7, 1946; d. Robert Adams and Nell (Green) Thayer; m. Sir Justin Hickey, May 9, 1964; children: Justine, Simon, Portia. Dir. Mrs. World Pagent, Surfers Paradise, Queensland, Australia, 1986, Accident Ins. Mutual, 1986—, Bartinon Securities, 1985—. Patron Lifeline Support Com., Surfers Paradise, Keystone Rehab. Ctr., Brisbane, Australia; found. council mem. Goldcoast Coll. Advanced Edn.; found. mem. Bond U., Queensland. Office: Mrs World Pagent-Australia, PO Box 306, 4217 Surfers Paradise Queensland, Australia

HICKEY, HOWARD WESLEY, educator; b. Bozeman, Mont., Oct. 20, 1930; s. Wesley Grandon and Frances Mildred (Howard) H.; m. Gwen Callahan, Feb. 14, 1987; children—Darcianne, Benjamin, Morris, Stuart, Bryan; 1 dau. by previous marriage, Brooks. B.A., Western Wash. U., 1953, M.Ed., 1958; M.A., Bowdoin Coll., 1962; Ph.D., Mich. State U., 1968. Dir. fed. programs Puyallup (Wash.) Schs., 1962-66; asst. prof. elem. edn. Mich. State U., East Lansing, 1968-71; assoc. prof., dir. Mott Inst. for Community Improvement, Mich. State U., 1971-77, prof. higher edn., 1978—; cons. in field. Author: (with Curt Van Voorhees) Role of the School in Community Education, 1969; assoc. editor: (with Curt Van Voorhees) Community Edn. Jour, 1971-74; contbr. (with Curt Van Voorhees) articles to profl. jours. NSF fellow, 1958, 61-62; Mott fellow, 1966-67. Mem. Nat. Community Edn. Assn., Nat. Soc. Study Edn., Phi Delta Kappa. Episcopalian. Club: Rotary (pres. 1965-66). Home: 2609 Woodhill Dr Okemos MI 48864 Office: Mich State U 420 Erickson Hall East Lansing MI 48824

HICKEY, LEO DENIS, Spanish educator; b. Cappawhite, Tipperary, Ireland, Nov. 2, 1934; arrived in Eng., 1962; s. Daniel and Lillie (O'Byrne) H.; m. Sioned Kenrick, May 24, 1969; children: Laura, Daniel, Yvonne. BA, Univ. Coll. Dublin, 1956, MA, 1958, LLB, 1958; L in F and L, U. Madrid, 1965, PhD, 1966. Lectr. in Spanish Univ. Salford, Eng., 1966-74, sr. lectr., 1974-78, reader in Spanish, 1978-84, prof. Spanish, 1984—. Author: Cinco Horas Con Miguel Delibes, 1968, Usos y Estilos del Español Moderno, 1972, Realidad y Experiencia de la Novela, 1974, Curso de Pragmaestilística, 1987. Mem. Assn. Hispanists, Internat. Pragmatics Assn. Office: U Salford, Salford England M5 4WT

HICKEY, TIMOTHY DANIEL, banker; b. Tacoma, Wash., Jan. 6, 1949; s. Maurice Burke and Geraldine Marie (Smith) H.; B.A. in Bus. Adminstrn., Seattle U., 1976. Revenue agt. IRS, Seattle, 1975-76; sr. acct. Ernst & Whinney, Seattle, 1976-80; v.p., controller First Interstate Bank of Wash., Seattle, 1980-83, sr. v.p., chief fin. officer, 1983-86, exec. v.p., chief fin. officer, 1987—; regional dir. Bank Adminstrn. Inst., Rolling Meadows, Ill., 1983-84; dir. First Interstate Bank, Seattle, 1988; bd. dirs., sec., treas. Bank Adminstrn., Inst. Mem. Am. Inst. C.P.A.s, Wash. State Soc. C.P.A.s, Fin. Execs. Inst., Nat. Assn. Accts. Office: 1st Interstate Bank of Texas, NA PO Box 3326 Houston TX 77253-3326

HICKIE, JOHN BERNARD, cardiology educator; b. Sydney, New South Wales, Australia, Mar. 6, 1926; s. Thomas Staniclaus and Sarah Ann (Hopkinson) H.; m. Noelene Rosemary Walden, Dec. 1, 1951; children: David, Christopher, Thomas, Ian, Robyn, Marea, Kathleen. Student, Waverley Coll., Sydney, 1940-42; MBBS with honors, U. Sydney, 1948. Intern St. Vincents Hosp., Sydney, 1948-49, resident, 1950, registrar, 1951-53, physician, cardiologist, 1960—; house officer registrar St. Thomas Hosp., London, 1954-56; sr. lectr. medicine U. Sydney, 1960-63, assoc. prof. medicine, 1963-68; prof. medicine U. New South Wales, Sydney, 1968—; chmn. sch. medicine, U. New South Wales, Sydney, 1970-73, 77-79; cons. physician Australian Army, 1980—; dir. Bankstown Hosp., Sydney, 1971-76, 82-85. Patentee in field. Served to col. Australian Army Res., 1980-87. Fellow Royal coll. Physicians (Saltwell scholar 1955—56), Royal Australian Coll. Physicians (pres. 1984-86), ACP (hon.), Council Atherosclermis (corr.), Am. Heart Assn. (corr. council cardiology); mem. Cardiac Soc. Australian and New Zealand (pres. 1982-86), Brit. Cardiac Soc. (corr.). Roman Catholic. Club: Royal Sydney Golf. Home: 2A Coolong Rd, Vaucluse Sydney 2030, Australia Office: St Vincent Hosp, Victoria St, Darlinghurst, Sydney 2010, Australia

HICKMAN, HOYT LEON, clergyman; b. Pitts., May 22, 1927; s. Leon Edward and Mayme (Hoyt) H.; B.A. magna cum laude, Haverford Coll., 1950; M.Div. cum laude, Yale U., 1953; S.T.M., Union Theol. Sem., 1954; D.D. (hon.), Morningside Coll., 1978; m. Martha Jean Whitmore, Dec. 16, 1950; children—Peter, John, Stephen, Mary. Ordained to ministry Meth. Ch., 1953; pastor 1st Meth. Ch., Windber, Pa., 1954-57, Claysville and Stony Point Meth. Chs., Claysville, Pa., 1957-59, Coll. Hill Meth. Ch., Beaver Falls, Pa., 1959-64, Cascade United Meth. Ch., Erie, Pa., 1964-72; dir. office local ch. worship, bd. discipleship United Meth. Ch., Nashville, 1972-78, asst. gen. sec. bd. discipleship, 1978-85, dir. resource devel. bd. discipleship, 1985—; exec. sec. Commn. on Worship, United Meth. Ch., 1968-72; mem. Commn. on Worship, World Meth. Council, 1971-81; mem. nat. program com. Christian Family Movement, 1969-73; pres. Erie County Council Chs., 1970-71. Bd. dirs. Liturgical Conf., 1973-80. Served with USN, 1945-46. Mem. Phi Beta Kappa. Democrat. Author: At the Lord's Table, 1981, Strengthening Our Congregation's Worship, 1981, United Methodist Altars, 1984, A Primer for Church Worship, 1984, The Acolyte's Book, 1985; co-author: Handbook of the Christian Year, 1986; author: Holy Communion, 1987, Planning Worship Each Week, 1988. Contbr. numerous articles to mags. Home: 2034 Castleman Dr Nashville TN 37215 Office: PO Box 840 Nashville TN 37202

HICKMAN, JOHN HAMPTON, III, entrepreneurial industrialist, investment banker, educator; b. Wilmington, Del., May 19, 1937; s. John Hampton Jr. and Martha (Barnett) H.; m. Barbara Spurlin, 1953; children: Erica Delius Hickman-Downs, Gretchen Leigh Hickman-Jewett, Rochanya Charlotte Hickman-Generous, John Hampton IV. Attended Randolph-Macon Coll., 1954-56; AB, Brown U., 1959; certificate in Chinese, Yale U., 1960, JD, 1962. Dir. internat. dept. McDonnell & Co., N.Y.C., 1964-68; partner investment banking firm The Hickman Corp., 1969—; chmn., chief exec. officer First Bancorp., Reno, 1968—; chmn. bd., chief exec. officer Seilon, Inc., 1968-69, Lockwood Corp., Gering, Nebr., 1968-69; chmn. bd. Thomson Internat. Co., Thibodaux, La., 1968-69; chmn. bd., pres. Nev. Nat. Bancorp, Las Vegas, 1968-69; pres. Delanair, Inc. (name now Nexus Industries), N.Y.C., 1969-70; chmn. bd. C.R. Burr & Co. (name now United Nurseries Corp.), Middlefield, Conn., 1972-75, Buffalo Capital Corp., 1984—, Palm Beach County Utilities Corp., 1986—; founder, chmn. bd. Peninsula Corp.; prof. bus., chmn. dept. mgmt. Tenn. Wesleyan Coll.; prof., chmn. dept. mgmt. studies Rochester Inst. Tech., 1977-83; mem. faculty U. Conn.; vis. exec. U. N.C., Boone, vis. prof. bus. La. State U., Fordham U. Grad. Sch. Bus., N.Y.C., 1986—; vis. disting. prof. Barry U., Miami, Fla., 1984-85; bd. dirs., mem. fin. com. Aberdeen Petroleum (name now Adobe Oil and Gas Co.), Tulsa, 1970-73; bd. dirs. Dissen & Juhn Corp., Macedon, N.Y., 1980, Nat. Health Care Affiliates, Inc., Buffalo, 1982—, HTE, Inc., Orlando, Fla., 1986— ; founding mng. dir. Acad. for Advancement Corp. Governance, N.Y.C., 1986—. Author: Financing in the Entrepot Capital Market, 1968, East-West Investments, 1969, Spin-Offs As A Management Tool, Corporate Reorganization, 1972; Contbr.: Business Handbook for Photographers, 1980; articles to profl. jours. Trustee, treas. Oceanic Soc., Washington, 1972—; trustee N.Y. State Assn. for Human Services, 1977-80; bd. dirs. Genesee Valley Arts Found., Rochester, 1978-84; mem. Yale U. Alumni Assembly, 1976-79; chmn. The Rochester Fund, 1978-81. Mem. Am. Mgmt. Assn. (world council pres.'s assn., lectr., editor publs.), Internat. Law Assn. (Am. br.), Fin. Execs. Inst., Acad. Mgmt. Clubs: Rochester Yacht, Univ., Yale (N.Y.C.), Metropolitan, Canadian (N.Y.), Arts and Letter (Toronto, Can.), The Beach (Palm Beach). Office: Mount Morris Rd Geneseo NY 14454

HICKOX, WILLIAM HORACE, III, real estate corporation executive; b. Borger, Tex., May 29, 1941; s. William Horace and Mildred Elizabeth (Barnett) H.; m. Suzanne Lillian Permenter, Nov. 29, 1969; children: William Horace IV, Amy Elizabeth. Student, U. Tex., 1959-64. Lic. real estate broker, Tex. Regional mgr. Avis Rent A Car, Dallas and Houston, 1968-74; owner William H. Hickox Investments, Houston, 1971—; pres., chief exec. officer Hickox Devel. Corp., Houston, 1982—; owner Hickox Electronic Group, Houston, 1987—. Pres. Ed White PTO, Houston, 1984-85; mem. fin. com. Gethsemane United Meth Ch., 1977, adminstrv. bd., 1985-87. Named Adm. in the Tex. Navy, Gov. Tex., 1973, Col. and A.D.C., Gov. Miss., 1973, Col. Gov.'s staff, Gov. La., 1973; named hon. mem. KHIVA Temple, Amarillo, Tex., 1984. Mem. Houston Bd. Realtors, U. Tex. Longhorn Singers Alumni Assn. (co-founder, organizer, dir.), Quarter Century Wireless Club, Houston Amateur Radio Club. United Methodist. Office: Hickox Devel Corp 9896 Bissonnet Suite 100 Houston TX 77036

HICKROD, GEORGE ALAN KARNES WALLIS, educational adminstration educator; b. Fort Branch, Ind., May 16, 1930; s. Hershell Roy and Bernice Ethel (Karnes) H.; m. Ramona Dell Poole, 1952 (div.); m. Lucy Jen Huang, June 17, 1964 (dec. Apr. 26, 1987); 1 stepson, Goren Wallis Liu. A.B., Wabash Coll., 1954; M.A., Harvard U., 1955; Ph.D., Harvard U., 1966. Asst. prof. ednl. and social scis. Lake Erie Coll., 1962-67; assoc. prof. ednl. adminstrn. Ill. State U., Normal, 1967-71, prof., 1971-83, disting. prof., 1983—, dir. Ctr. for Study Ednl. Fin., 1974—; dir. McArthur/Spencer Ill. Sch. Fin., 1987—, Ctr. for Ednl. study on ednl. fin. to profl. jours., chpts. to books. Served with USMC, 1950-52, Korea. State of Ill. and U.S. Govt. grantee. Mem. Am. Edn. Fin. Assn. (v.p. 1983-84, pres. 1984-85). Democrat. Unitarian. Clubs: Scottish-Am. Soc. Central Ill. (past chief), Clan Wallace Internat. Royal Order of Scotland. Lodges: Masons, Elks. Avocations: history; genealogy; travel; cooking. Home: 2 Turner Rd Normal IL 61761

HICKS, BETHANY GRIBBEN, lawyer; b. N.Y., Sept. 8, 1951; d. Robert and DeSales Gribben; m. William A. Hicks III, May 21, 1982; children: Alexandra Elizabeth, Samantha Katherine. AB, Vassar Coll., 1973; MEd, Boston U., 1975; JD, Ariz. State U., 1984. Bar: Ariz. 1984. Sole practice Scottsdale, Ariz., 1984—. Mem. Jr. League of Phoenix, 1984—; parliamentarian Girls Club of Scottsdale, Ariz., 1985-87, bd. dirs. 1988—. Mem. ABA (family law sect.), State Bar Ariz. (family law sect.), Maricopa County Bar Assn. Democrat. Episcopalian. Club: Paradise Valley Country. Office: 4824 E Sparkling Ln Paradise Valley AZ 85253

HICKS, JAMES THOMAS, physician, lawyer; b. Brownsville, Pa., June 5, 1924; s. Thomas and Florence Julia (O'Donnell) H.; B.S., U. Pitts., 1945, A.B., 1946, M.S., 1946; Ph.D., George Washington U., 1950; M.D., U. Ark., 1956; J.D., DePaul U., 1975; m. Ellen Elliott, Aug. 25, 1950; children—Ellen, Mary Jo. Intern USPHS, Balt., 1958-60; resident VA Hosp., Pitts., 1958-60. Bar: Ill. 1977, D.C. 1987, N.Y. 1987, Pa. 1977, U.S. Ct. of Appeals, 1977, U.S. Supreme Ct., 1980, U.S. Ct. Appeals D.C. 1988; practice medicine specializing in forensic and legal medicine, River Forest, Ill., 1964—; dir. labs. Oak Park (Ill.) Hosp., 1964-87 ; pres. Oakton Service Corp., 1968—; Oakton Service Corp. of Pa. Served with USPHS, 1956-57. Fellow Nat. Cancer Inst., 1949-50. Fellow ACP, Internat. Coll. Surgeons; mem. AMA, ABA, Ill. Bar Assn., Pa. Bar Assn., Assn. Am. Trial Lawyers, Am. Assn. Hosp. Lawyers, Sigma Xi. Clubs: Univ., Whitehall, Oak Park Country, Carlton. Contbg. editor Hosp. Formulary Mgmt., 1966-70. Office: 7980 W Chicago Ave River Forest IL 60305

HICKS, JOHN RICHARD, economist; b. Warwick, U.K., Apr. 8, 1904; s. Edward H.; ed. Clifton Coll., also Balliol Coll., Oxford; m. Ursula Kathleen Webb, 1935 (dec. 1985). Prof. polit. economy U. Manchester, 1938-46; fellow Nuffield Coll., Oxford, 1946-52, univ. prof. polit. economy, 1952-65, research fellow All Souls Coll., 1965—. Created knight; recipient Nobel prize in econs., 1972. Author: Theory of Wages, 1932; Value and Capital, 1939; The Social Framework, 1942; Contribution to the Theory of the Trade Cycle, 1950; A Revision of Demand Theory, 1956; Essays in World Economics, 1959; Capital and Growth, 1965; Critical Essays in Monetary Theory, 1967; A Theory of Economic History, 1969; Capital and Time, 1973; The Crisis in Keynesian Economics, 1974; Economic Perspectives, 1977; Causality in Economics, 1979; Collected Essays on Economic Theory, 3 vols., 1981-83.

Address: All Souls Coll, Oxford England Office: British Acad, 20-21 Cornwall Terrace, London NW1 4QP England *

HICKS, JOHN TRIMMER, rheumatologist, consultant; b. Bethesda, Md., Mar. 11, 1946; s. Samuel Pendleton and Mary Louise (Trimmer) H.; m. Deborah Rehberg, July 30, 1977; children—Julie Pendleton, Melissa Anne. B.S., U. Mich., 1968; M.D., Columbia U., 1972; hon. F.A.C.P., Am. Coll. Physicians, 1982. Diplomate Am. Bd. Med. Examiners, Am. Bd. Internal Medicine. Intern St. Luke's Hosp. Ctr., Columbia U. Coll. Physicians and Surgeons, N.Y.C., 1972-73; research assoc. div. virology Bur. Biologics-FDA, Bethesda, 1973-75; resident in internal medicine Georgetown U. Hosp., Washington, 1975-76; sr. investigator div. virology Bur. Biologics, 1976-78, instr. medicine Georgetown U., 1976-78, fellow rheumatology, 1976-78; from instr. to asst. prof. medicine, fellow rheumatology W.Va. U., Morgantown, 1978-79; pvt. cóns. practice rheumatology, Phila., 1979-82; clin. asst. prof. medicine and rheumatology Temple U., Phila., 1979-82; group dir. med. affairs div. rheumatology/immunology Smith Kline Beckman Corp., Phila., 1982-84; pvt. cons. rheumatology, Phila., 1982-84; med. dir. Arthritis Inst. Nat. Hosp., Arlington, Va., 1984-87; dir. rheumatological research Anderson Orthopaedic Research Inst., Arlington, 1987—; pvt. cons. rheumatology, Arlington, 1984—; staff Chestnut Hill Hosp., Phila., 1979—, Roxborough Hosp., Phila., 1979-84, Nat. Hosp. Orthopaedics and Rehab., Arlington, 1984—, Fairfax (Va.) Hosp., 1987—. Contbr. articles to profl. jours. Active Arthritis Found. (chmn. patient clubs and pub. edn. subcoms. Eastern Pa. chpt.); adv. com. Pa. Lupus Found., Inc. Served with USPHS, 1976-78. Recipient Disting. Service award Arthritis Found., 1979; Active Tchr. in Family Practice award Am. Acad. Family Practice, 1981, 82. Fellow Am. Rheumatology Assn. (co-founder); mem. AAAS, Am. Soc. Microbiology, ACP, Am. Fedn. Clin. Research, Am. Assn. Immunologists, N.Y. Acad. Scis., Phila. Rheumatism Soc., Phila. Med. Club, AMA (Physician's Recog. award 1982-87), Am. Soc. Clin. Pharmacology and Therapeutics. Current work: Clinical trials of various pharmaceutical agents in rheumatic diseases; microbial etiology of rheumatic diseases. Subspecialties: Rheumatology; Virology (medicine).

HICKS, RONALD EDWARD, archaeologist, educator; b. Kingman, Ind., Aug. 26, 1940; s. Winfield Spencer and E. Genevia (Clements) H.; m. Adrienne Martinez, 1964 (div. 1968); 1 son, Geoffrey; m. Robin Michelle Hines, Apr. 23, 1982; children: Cameron, Gwendolyn. BA, Purdue U., 1963; PhD, U. Pa., 1975. Asst. prodn. editor Prentice-Hall, 1965-66; asst. editing supr. World Publ., 1966-67; mng. editor American Anthropologist, 1968-70; teaching fellow U. Pa., Phila., 1970-71, 72-73, staff dir. univ. devel. commn., 1972, instr./lectr., 1974-76; instr. Community Coll. of Phila., 1974-76; asst. prof. Ball State U., Muncie, Ind., 1976-80, assoc. prof. dept. anthropology, 1980-84, prof., 1984—, dir. Archaeol. Resources Mgmt. Service, 1978-83; dir. Ctr. Internat. Programs, 1985—; active field research, N.J., 1970, 72, 75-76, Ireland, 1971, 73-74, 77, 83-84, 87, Scotland, 1976, Ind., 1978-81; Fulbright-Hays fellow, Ireland, 1973-74; bd. dirs. Council for Conservation of Ind. Archaeology, 1977—, pres., 1979-81. Served to lt. j.g. USN, 1963-65, lt. comdr. Res. ret. Grantee Am. Council Learned Socs., 1977, fellow, 1983-84; grantee U.S. Dept. Interior Heritage Conservation and Recreation Service/Ind. Div. Hist. Preservation, 1979, 80, 81, 82, 85, 87. Fellow Am. Anthrop. Assn., Royal Soc. Antiquaries of Ireland, Soc. Antiquaries of Scotland; mem. Archaeol. Inst. Am. (com. of European Archaeology, 1977—), Soc. for Am. Archaeology (pub. relations com. 1985—), Ind. Acad. Scis. (chmn. anthropology sect. 1986), AAAS, Folklore Soc. Co-editor: Old World Archaeology Newsletter, 1977-81; cons. editor Archaeoastronomy, 1979—; contbr. articles to publs. including Bull. Phila. Anthrop. Soc., Expedition, Jour. Royal Soc. Antiquaries Ireland, Irish Archaeo. Research Forum, Archaeology, Mondo Archeologico, Archaeoastronomy. Office: Ball State Univ Dept Anthropology Muncie IN 47306

HICKS, STEPHEN DALE, consumer electronics executive; b. Greensboro, N.C., 1956; s. Earlie Ray and Celia Mae (Wright) H.; m. Angela Rhyne Connor, July 30, 1983; 1 child, Michael Allen. BBA, Cen. Wesleyan U., 1978. Salesperson Telma Electronics GMBH, Pfungstadt, West Germany, 1978-79, mgr. sales, 1979-81, pres., chief exec. officer, 1982—; pres., chief exec. officer Delco Enterprises, Inc., Greensboro and Europe, 1984—; founder Reach UP Internat., Greensboro and Europe, 1984—; bd. dirs. ARCH Prodns., Inc., Greensboro and Europe, 1985—. Mem. Reps. Abroad, Frankfurt, West Germany, 1980—. Mem. Assn. U.S. Army, Am. Logistics Assn. (bd. dirs. exchange com. 1982—). Club: Protestant Men of the Chapel (West Germany). Home: Hildebrand Str 7, 6084 Gernsheim Federal Republic of Germany Office: Telma Electronics GMBH, Hauptstrasse 27, 6102 Hessen Federal Republic of Germany

HICKS-GOMEZ, EDGARDO, chemical oceanographer, consultant; b. Mexico City, Oct. 24, 1951; s. Edgardo and Amalia (Gomez) H. BSc, Nat. Aut. U. Mex., Unam, 1976; PhD in Oceanography, U. Liverpool (Eng.), 1981. Research Politech. Mex., Merida, Yucatan, Cinvestav, 1980-81; cons. Environ. Impact, Mexico City, 1980-81; mining co. exec. Rofomex, S.A. de C.V., La Paz, Mex., 1981-83; cons. Analysts, Inc., Mexico City, 1983—; research Inter-Disciplinary Marine Scis. Inst., Cicimar, La Paz, 1983—; sci. affairs specialist state dept. U.S. Embassy, Mexico, 1986. cons; analyst urban ecosystems, U. Utah Research Inst., 1986. Mex. Marine Mil. Forces, 1983—, Ministry of Fisheries, 1983, Nat. Council Sci. and Tech., Conacyt, 1984, Ecoingenieria, S.A., 1985, Tecma, S.A., 1986, ERT, 1986, remote sensng urban ecosystems U. Utah Research Inst., seafood quality assurance U. Tex. A&M, 1987. Contbr. articles to profl. jours. Mem. Ocean Research Intersecretarial Commn. Office: Sci Office, US Embassy Reforma 305, 06500 Mexico City DF Mexico

HIDA, TAKEYUKI, mathematics researcher, educator; b. Okazaki, Japan, Nov. 12, 1927; s. Koichi and Fumi (Mitsui) Ota; m. Minami Hida, Mar. 30, 1953; children—Misachi Isogawa, Fumikazu Hida. B.S., Nagoya U., 1952; Ph.D., Kyoto U., 1961. Instr. Aichi-Gakugei U., Okazaki, Japan, 1952-59; asst. prof. Kyoto U., Japan, 1959-64; prof. math. Nagoya U., Japan, 1964—, dean sch. sci., 1976-77 . Author: Stationary Stochastic Processes, 1970; Brownian Motion, 1980. Recipient Chunichi Culture prize, The Chunichi (newspaper company), 1980. Mem. Math. Soc. Japan, Am. Math. Soc., Internat. Statis. Inst. Avocation: painting. Home: 6-2 Hirabari-danchi, Tenpaku-cho, Tenpaku-ku, Nagoya 468 Japan Office: Nagoya U, Faculty of Sci, Furo-cho, Chikusa-ku, Nagoya 464 Japan

HIDALGO, DIEGO, publisher, development economist; b. Madrid, Nov. 5, 1942; s. Diego and Gerda (Schnur) H.; children—Marta, Silvia, Diego, Daniel. LL.B., Madrid Law Sch., 1964; M.B.A., Harvard U. (Mass.), 1968. Trainee Chase Manhattan Bank, N.Y.C., 1966; young profl. World Bank, Washington, 1968-69, ops. officer, 1969-74, chief African div., 1974-77; chmn. bd. FRIDA, London and Paris, 1977—; managing dir. Alianza Editorial, Madrid, 1983—; dir. El Pais, Madrid, 1981—; chmn. Devel. Fin. Cons., London, 1977—. Founder Fund for Research and Investment for Devel. of Africa Ltd., 1976; v.p. CEAR, 1985; chmn. bd. U. Extremadura, 1986. Served to 2d lt. Spanish Army, 1964-65. Office: Alianza Editorial, Milan 38, Apdo 9107, Madrid 33 28043, Spain

HIDALGO, EDWARD, lawyer, former secretary U.S. Navy; b. Mexico City, Oct. 12, 1912; came to U.S., 1918, naturalized, 1936; s. Egon and Domitila (Hidalgo) Kunhardt; m. Belinda Bonham; children: Joanne, Edward, Richard, Tila. B.A. magna cum laude, Holy Cross Coll., 1933; J.D., Columbia U., 1936; civil law degree, U. Mexico Law Sch., 1959. Bar: N.Y. 1936, Mexico 1959, D.C. 1976. Law clk. 2d Circuit Ct. Appeals, N.Y., 1936-37; assoc. Wright, Gordon Zachry & Parlin, N.Y.C., 1937-42; mem. Eberstadt Com. on Unification of Mil. Services, Washington, 1945; spl. asst. to Sec. of Navy James Forrestal, Washington, 1945-46; partner Curtis, Mallet-Prevost, Colt & Mosle, 1946-48; founder, sr. partner Barrera, Siqueiros & Torres Landa, Mexico City, 1948-65; spl. asst. to Sec. of Navy Paul H. Nitze, Washington, 1965-66; partner Cahill, Gordon & Reindel, Paris, 1966-72; spl. asst. econ. affairs to dir. USIA, Washington, 1972; gen. counsel Congl. liaison USIA, 1973-76; asst. sec. for manpower, res. affairs and logistics U.S. Navy Dept., Washington, 1977-79; sec. U.S. Navy Dept., 1979-81. Served with USNR, 1942-46. Decorated Bronze Star, Royal Order of Vasa (Sweden); Order of Aztec Eagle (Mex.). Roman Catholic. Clubs: Chevy Chase, Met. Office: 1828 L St NW Suite 1111 Washington DC 20036

HIDDEN, GREGORY RICHARD, investment company executive; b. Fresno, Calif., Mar. 25, 1947; s. Morton Earl and Jannette Marshall (Bridger) H.; m. Sharon Lee Krejcu, Dec. 16, 1973; 1 child, Jennifer Michelle. B.S., Tex. Christian U., 1976. Cert. Fin. Planner. Account exec. Prudential Ins. Co., Fort Worth, 1973-76; mgr. Great So. Ins. Co., Dallas, 1976; account exec. E.F. Hutton & Co., Inc., N.Y.C., 1976-80; regional v.p. Anchor Nat. Fin. Services, Phoenix, 1980-81, Putnam Funds Distbn. Co., Boston, 1981-82; sr. v.p. Equitec Securities Co., Oakland, Calif., 1982-86; owner, Wholesale Investment Network, Dallas, 1986—, v.p. G.T. Global Fin. Services, 1987—, Fort Worth, 1966—, Colleyville, 1984.Mem. Inst. Cert. Fin. Planners, Internat. Assn. Fin. Planners, Pvt. Idustry Council. Republican. Methódist. Club: Sertoma. Lodge: Kiwanis.

HIDDLESTON, JAMES ANDREW, French literature educator; b. Edinburgh, Scotland, Oct. 20, 1935; s. James Andrew Sr. and Helen Cochrane (Hall) H.; m. Janet Suzanne Taylor, Oct. 8, 1971; children: Anna, Jane Barbara. MA, Edinburgh U., Scotland, 1957, PhD, 1961. Lectr. Leeds U., Yorkshire, Eng., 1960-66; fellow Exeter Coll. Oxford U., Eng., 1966—. Author: L'Univers de Jules Supervielle, 1965, Malraux: La condition humaine, 1973, Poems: Jules Laforgue, 1975, Essai sur Laforgue et les Derniers Vers, 1980, Baudelaire and Le Spleen de Paris, 1987. Office: Exeter College, Oxford Ox1 3DP, England

HIEBERT, ELIZABETH BLAKE, civic worker; b. Mpls., July 18, 1910; d. Henry Seavey and Grace (Riebeth) Blake; student Washburn U., 1926-30; B.S., U. Tex. 1933; m. Homer L. Hiebert, Aug. 29, 1935; children—Grace Elizabeth (Mrs. John E. Beam), Mary Sue (Mrs. Donald Wester), John Blake, Henry Leonard, David Mark. Sec. Topeka Regional Sci. Fair, 1958-60, bd. dirs., 1964-—; bd. dirs. YMCA 1968-74, Topeka (Kans.) Friends of the 300; water safety instr. and swimming tchr. of handicapped; freelance writer; mem. adv. com. Kans. Ctr.; former mem. Shawnee County Advocacy Council on Aging; Shawnee County chmn. Arthritis Found. Hon. fellow Harry S. Truman Library; recipient Paul Harris award Rotary, 1985. Mem. D.A.R., Daus. Am. Colonists, AAUW (dir. 1944-62, 65-—), N.E. Hist. and Geneal. Soc., Tex. U. Alumni, Am. Home Econs. Assn., Shawnee County Med. Aux. (past pres.), Nat. Audubon, Met. Mus. Art, P.E.O. (past local pres. coop. bd.), Topeka Art Guild, Nat. Soc. Ancient and Hon. Arty., Nat. Trust Historic Preservation, Internat. Oceanographic Found., Nat. League Am. Pen Women (pres. Topeka 1970-72), Washburn Alumnae Assn., Am. Assn. State and Local History, Colo. Hist. Assn., Shawnee County Hist. Soc., Mont., Minn., Kans. hist. socs., Smithsonian Assos., Oceanic Soc., Internat. Platform Assn., Topeka Friends of the Library, Cousteau Soc., Am. Assn. Zookeepers, Nat. Assn. for Mature People, Am. Assn. Ret. Persons, K.U. Spencer Mus. Art, Conn. Soc. Genealogists, Nat., New Eng. geneal. socs., Topeka Beautification Assn. (sec.), People to People, Archives Assos., Am. Space Found., Mus. Fine Arts Boston, Kans. Reading Assn., Am. Assn. Museums, San Diego Zool. Soc., Nat. Space Inst., Oriental Inst., Delta Kappa Gamma (hon.), Delta Gamma, others. Club: Topeka Knife and Fork. Editor children's page Household mag., 1934-39. Home: 1517 Randolph Topeka KS 66604

HIELSCHER, UDO ARTUR, educator; b. Ger., Oct. 23, 1939; s. Arthur Paul and Bertha Irmgard (Koehler) H.; Diplom Wirtschaftsingenieur, U. Darmstadt, 1964; Dr. rer. pol., 1968; m. Ursula Hartmann, Jan. 20, 1965. Prof. bus. adminstrn. and fin. Tech. Hochschule Darmstadt, 1971—, exec. dir. Inst. Bus. Adminstrn., 1982-84, dean Faculty of Law and Econs., 1985-86. Mem. European Fin. Assn., German Soc. Fin. Analysts, Soc. U. Profs. Mgmt. Sci., German Soc. Advt. Scis., Soc. German Engrs., Assn. U. Profs. in Germany. Author: Das optimale Aktienportefeuille, 3d edit., 1970, Finanzierungskosten, 1976; Innovationsfinanzierung Mittelstaendischer Unternehmungen, 1982; Historische Amerikanische Aktein, 1987; contbr. articles to sci. jours.; editor: Industrielle Kommunikation, 1978; also various newsletters. Office: 1 Hochschulstrasse, D 6100 Darmstadt Federal Republic of Germany

HIEMSTRA, VICTOR GUSTAV, retired supreme court judge, university chancellor; b. Lydenburg, Transvaal, Republic of South Africa, June 9, 1914; s. Sybren Wybren and Johanna (Oppermann) H.; m. Hazel Moolman, Apr. 14, 1945; children: Jan, Grietje, Christina, Victor, Recht. BA, Stellenbosch U., Republic of South Africa, 1932; LLB, U. Cape Town, Republic of South Africa, 1936; LLD (hon.), U. Potchefstroom, Republic of South Africa, 1984, U. Bophuthatswana, Republic of South Africa, U. S. Africa, 1987. Journalist Nat. Press, Cape Town, 1933-42; advocate Pretoria, Republic of South Africa, 1943-56; judge Supreme Ct. of Province, Pretoria, 1956-84; chief justice Republic of Bophuthatswana, Mmabatho, 1977-84; mem. exec. council U. South Africa, 1965-77, chancellor, 1977-87. Author: (textbook) Criminal Procedure, 1967, 4th rev. edit., 1987; Trilingual Legal Dictionary, 1981, 2d rev. edit., 1987. Chmn. Constitutional Council for Southwest Africa/Namibia, 1985-87. Mem. South African Acad. for Sci. and Art (mem. council 1959-73). Home: 371 Delphinus St, Waterloof Ridge, Pretoria 0181, Republic of South Africa

HIEU, NGUYEN-TRUNG, social science educator, voluntary agency executive; b. Nghe-An, Viet Nam, Dec. 15, 1946; came to U.S., 1974, naturalized, 1980; s. Ngoc-Duc and Thu-Ba Nguyen; B.A., U. Saigon, 1970; M.A., Govs. State U., 1975, 76, 77, 78; M.Ed., Loyola U., Chgo., 1979, Ed.D., 1985; C.A.S., U. Chgo., 1980; Ph.D., Heed U., 1981. Tchr., Viet Nam Ministry Edn., Saigon, 1966-67; tng. officer U.S. AID, Viet Nam, 1968-69; instr. Nat. Sch. Social Work, Viet Nam, 1970-74; tchr. counselor Jones Community Ctr., Inc., Ill., 1974-75; counselor Catholic Charities, Lombard, Ill., 1975-76; tchr. Chgo. Bd. Edn., 1977—; instr. Nat. Coll. Edn., Chgo., 1979—; founder, pres. NghiaSinh Internat., Saigon, Chgo., 1963—; exec. dir. Social Service Ctr., Saigon, 1968-70; prin. NghiaViet High Sch., Saigon, 1971-74; exec. dir. Vietnamese Community for Human Devel. Inc., Chgo., 1976-80. Author: English-Vietnamese Idioms, 1977, 2d edit., 1981; Nineteen Songs for Love and Peace, 1974; English-Vietnamese Social Science Concepts, 1972. Editor: Lien-Nghia News, 1963—. Recipient Goldern Apple award PBS-TV Chgo., 1987. Mem. Ill. Bilingual Adv. Council, Chgo., 1978-82, Asian Am. Adv. Council to Gov. Ill., 1983—; dir. Access, Inc., Chgo., 1979-84; sponsor more than 1,000 refugees, Chgo., 1975-84. Recipient Nat. Medal of Youth, 1969, Nat. Medal of Edn., 1970, Nat. Medal of Social Service, 1971, Nat. Medal of Labor, 1972; Edn. award Ill. Bd. Edn., 1979; Citizen of Yr. award Chgo. Citizenship Council, 1981; Pres.'s Vol. award White House, 1983-84. Mem. Nat. Assn. Vietnam-Am. Edn., Asian Am. Educators, Ill. Bilingual Edn. Assn., Chgo. Bilingual Educators Assn., Chgo. Citizenship Council. Office: Clemente Community Acad 1147 N Western Ave Chicago IL 60622

HIGASHINO, KAZUYA, medicine educator, internist; b. Higashiosaka, Osaka, Japan, Sept. 20, 1930; s. Toshimasa Oue and Aiko H.; m. Tamiko Okuda, Feb. 27, 1962; children—Koji, Mayuko. M.D., Osaka U., 1954; postgrad., 1960, Ph.D., 1960. Diplomate Japanese Bd. Internal Medicine. Intern, Osaka U. Hosp., 1954-55; mem. staff dept. medicine, 1960-72, lectr., 1972-74, asst. prof., 1974-78, assoc. prof., 1978-81; research assoc. U. Pitts, 1964-65; v.p. Kinki Cen. Hosp., Itami, Hyogo, 1981-82; prof. Medicine Hyogo Coll. Medicine, Nishinomiya, Hyogo, 1983—; dir. Research Found. for Gout, Shinjuku, Tokyo, 1983—. Author: Purine Metabolism, 1982; Alkaline Phosphatase in Cancer, 1983; editor: Metabolism, 1974—. Winner Kurokawa prize Kanae Found. for New Remedies, Tokyo, 1977. Mem. Japanese Soc. Internal Medicine (councilor 1979—), Japanese Soc. Gastroenterology (councilor 1987—), Japanese Soc. Hepatology (councilor 1980—), Japan Soc. Clin. Biochemistry and Metabolism (councilor 1984—), Japanese Cancer Assn. (councilor 1984—), Japanese Soc. Uric Acid, Purine and Pyrimidine Disorders (councilor 1976—), N.Y. Acad. Scis. Buddhist. Home: 1-3 Inaba 3-Chome Higashiosaka-shi, Osaka 578, Japan Office: Third Dept Internal Medicine 1-1 Mukogawa-Cho, Dishinomiya-Shi, Hyogo 663, Japan

HIGASHITANI, IWAHITO FRANCISCO, anthropologist-linguist, educator; b. Osaka, Japan, Mar. 9, 1938; s. Ichiro and Kimi (Hosoda) H.; m. Sabine Anne Marie-Therese Roesch, Sept. 7, 1979. B.Spanish Studies, Osaka U. Fgn. Studies, 1961. Lectr. linguistics and anthropology Kansai U. of Fgn. Studies, Hirakata, Japan, 1965-68; asst. prof. Kyoto U. Fgn. Studies (Japan), 1968-71; lectr. Hosei U., Tokyo, 1971—; researcher in field. Author: Bontoc Rituals, 1979; Collectives in Andalucia, 1979; Spain—Life and Death of a Revolution, 1983, others; contbr. articles to profl. jours. Mem. Phonetic Soc. Japan, Inst. Study of Human Issues, Universala Esperanto-Asocio, Sennacieca Asocio Tutmonda. Roman Catholic. Office: Hosei U, 2-7-1- Fujimi, Chiyodaku, 102 Tokyo Japan

HIGBY, EDWARD JULIAN, safety engineer; b. Milw., June 9, 1939; s. Richard L. Higby and Julie Ann (Bruins) O'Kelly: m. Frances Ann Knoodle, 1959 (div. 1962); 1 child, Melinda Ann Mozader. BS in Criminal Justice, Southwestern U., Tucson, 1984. Tactical officer Miami Police Dept., Fla., 1967-68; intelligence officer Fla. Div. Beverages, 1968-72; licensing coordinator Lums Restaurant Corp., Miami, 1972-73; legal asst. Walt Disney World, Lake Buena Vista, Fla., 1973-78; loss control cons. R.P. Hewitt & Assocs., Orlando, Fla., 1978-79; safety coordinator City of Lakeland, Fla., 1979—. Author: Safety Guide for Health Care, 1979. Bd. dirs. Tampa Area Safety Council, 1983—, Imperial Traffic Safety Council, Lakeland, 1983—; mem. Bay Lake City Council, 1974-76, mayor, 1975-76; bd. dirs. Greater Lakeland chpt. ARC, 1980-86, chmn. bd. dirs., 1983-84. 85-86, chmn. health services, 1980-86; mem. budget com. United Way Central Fla., 1983-85; mem. Fla. League Cities, 1974-76, Tri-County League Cities, 1974-76, Orange County Criminal Justice Council, 1974-78, Central Fla. Safety Council, 1978-79, Fla. Pub. Health Assn., World Safety Orgn.; mem. Polk County Disaster Coordination Com.; bd. dirs. Employers Health Care Group Polk County, 1987—. Served with U.S. Army, 1963-64. Named Vol. of Yr., Greater Lakeland chpt. ARC, 1983-84. Fellow Am. Biog. Inst. Research Assn., Internat. Biog. Assn.; mem. Fla. Sheriffs Assn. (hon. life), Internat. Assn. Identification, Internat. Assn. Identification (life, Fla. div.), Pub. Risk and Ins. Mgmt. Assn., Nat. Rifle Assn., Imperial Polk Mgmt. Assn., Fla. Fedn. Safety, Risk and Ins. Mgmt. Soc., Am. Soc. Safety Engrs. (chpt. pres. 1984-85, Safety Profl. of Yr. 1984-85), Heartland Safety Soc. (pres. 1983), Fla. Citrus Safety Assn. (pres. 1981-83), Nat. Fire Protection Assn., Am. Indsl. Hygiene Assn., Aircraft Owners and Pilots Assn. Republican. Club: Lakeland Rifle and Pistol. Avocations: hunting, fishing. Office: 1108 E Parker St Lakeland FL 33801

HIGGINBOTHAM, JOHN TAYLOR, lawyer; b. St. Louis, Feb. 10, 1947; s. Richard Cann and Jocelyn (Taylor) H.; m. Lauren Flint Totty, Aug. 9, 1975 (div. 1979). B.A., UCLA, 1969; J.D., Columbia U., 1972. Bar: N.Y. 1975, Calif. 1976. Assoc., Kirlin, Campbell & Keating, N.Y.C., 1972-74; atty. Nat. Bank of N.Am., N.Y.C., 1974-76; atty., dir. real estate Korvettes Inc., N.Y.C., 1979-82; assoc. Leon Katz, Bklyn., 1983-84; assoc. Finley, Kumble, Wagner, Heine, Underberg, Manley & Casey, N.Y.C., 1984-86; assoc. regional counsel HUD, N.Y.C., 1986-88; assoc. Fink, Weinberger, Fredman, Berman, Lowell & Fensterheim, N.Y.C., 1988—. Editor: Safe Deposit Decisions and Practice, 1977—. Mem. ABA, Assn. Bar City N.Y.

HIGGINS, CHRISTOPHER IAN, state agency administrator; b. Murwillumbah, New South Wales, Australia, Apr. 3, 1943; s. George Patrick and Muriel Adelaide (McEwan) H. m. Paula Abigail Gomberg, Dec. 22, 1966; children: David Wallace, Timothy Sean. B in Econs., Australian Nat. U., Canberra, 1964; PhD, U. Pa., 1968. Research officer Australian Bur. Statistics, Canberra, 1968-69; head of section Australian Treasury, Canberra, 1970-73, asst. sec., 1975-79, dep. sec. econ., 1984—; vis. prof. U. Pa., Phila., 1973-74, U. B.C., Vancouver, 1974; econ. minister Australian Del. OECD, Paris, 1980-81, dir. gen. econ. br., 1982-84; cons. UN Devel. Program, Bratislava, Czechoslavakia, 1972. Wharton Econometric Forecasting Assocs., U. Pa., 1973-74; adj. lectr. Australian Nat. U., 1972; mem. Australian Statistics Adv. Council, Canberra, 1984—. Co-author: SOMVOD I: A Macroeconometric Model of the Soviet Union; contbr. articles to profl. jours. Treas. Internat. Sch., Paris, 1980-84, Canberra Symphony Orch., 1984—. Sr. Fullbright Hayes fellow, 1973-74. Fellow Acad. Social Scis; mem. Econ. Soc. Australia (pres. 1975), Statistics Soc. Australia,, Am. Econ. Assn. Home: 12 Savery St, 2605 Garran, Australian Capital Terr Australia Office: The Treasury, Parkes Pl, 2600 Parkes, Australian Capital Terr Australia

HIGGINS, FRANCIS EDWARD, educator; b. Chgo., Nov. 29, 1935; s. Frank Edward and and Mary Alyce (Fahey) H.; B.S., Loyola U., Chgo., 1959, M.A., 1964; postgrad. Exeter Coll., Oxford (Eng.) U., 1962, Am. U. Beirut, 1966, McGill U., Montreal, Que., Can., 1967; adminstrn. cert. St. Xavier Coll., 1971; Ed.D., U. Sarasota, 1977. Tchr., Washington Jr. High Sch., Chicago Heights, Ill., 1959; tchr. Chgo. Vocat. High Sch., 1960-68, dept. chmn., 1964; asst. prof. social sci. Moraine Valley Community Coll., 1968-69; tchr. history Hillcrest High Sch., Country Club Hills, Ill., 1969—; instr. nursing continuing edn. St. Francis Coll., 1978—. Mem. pres.'s council St. Xavier Coll., 1978—; mem. St. Germaine Sch. Bd., 1972-73, St. Alexander Sch. Bd., 1978-84; active Chgo. council Boy Scouts Am., 1969-77, asst. dist. commr., 1971-75, mem. dist. scout com., 1976-77; co-historian Palos Heights Silver Jubilee Com., 1984. Recipient Disting. Service award Chgo. council Boy Scouts Am., 1974; Brit. Univ. scholar, 1962; Fulbright fellow, summer 1966; English Speaking Union fellow, 1967. Mem. Ill. Hist. Soc., Del. Hist. Soc., Am. Cath. Hist. Soc., Nat. Council Social Studies, Ill. Council Social Studies, Nat. Curriculum and Supervisory Assn., Ill. Supervisory Assn., Ill. Assn. Supervision and Curriculum Devel. (editorial rev. bd. Jour. 1984-86), Chgo. Hist. Soc., Nat. Hist. Soc., Brit. Hist. Assn., Brit. Hist. Assn., Nat. Soc. Study Edn., Phi Delta Kappa, Phi Gamma Mu. Republican. Roman Catholic. Contbr. revs. to Am. Cath. Hist. Jour., History Tchr. Jour. Home: 7660 W 131st St Palos Heights IL 60463 Office: Hillcrest High Sch 175th and Pulaski Rd Country Club Hills IL 60477

HIGGINS, KENNETH RAYMOND, landscape architect; b. Holyoke, Mass., Nov. 2, 1915; s. Alfred and Lillie (Ritter) H.; student R.I. State Coll., 1934; BS Mass. State Coll., 1937, B in Landscape Architecture, 1939; m. Mary Douthat Smith, Sept. 5, 1942; children: Kenneth Hewlett, Ralph Barton, Janie Lyle. Landscape architect, site planner Richmond (Va.) Field Office Pub. Housing Adminstrn., 1948-51; pvt. practice landscape architecture, Richmond, 1951-76; prin. Higgins Assos., 1976—. Instr., Richmond Profl. Inst., evenings 1956; cons. in field. Chmn., Richmond Beautification Com., 1954-64; treas. River Rd Citizens Assn., 1956, bd. dirs., 1983—, pres. 1988—; bd. dirs. Lewis Ginter Bot. Garden; chmn. Monument Av. Commn., 1969-85. Bd. dirs. Berkeley Thanksgiving Fest. Served to capt. USAAF, 1942-46. Recipient Landscape award Am. Assn. Nurserymen, 1969; Richmond Urban Design award, 1970; Masonry Contractors Assn. Va. award, 1977. Mem. Am. Soc. Landscape Architects (past Va. chmn., Pres.'s award Potomac chpt. 1968), Landscape Architects Va., U. Mass. Landscape Archtl. Assn., Va. Hist. Soc., Soc. Archtl. Historians, Nat. Trust for Historic Preservation, Eastern Nat. Park and Monument Assn., Assn. for Preservation Va. Antiquities (life), Am. Arbitration Assn. Lambda Chi Alpha. Episcopalian (former vestryman). Club: Country of Virginia. Address: 908 S Gaskins Rd Richmond VA 23233 also: 8501 Patterson Ave Richmond VA 23229

HIGGINSON, THEODORE N., electrical manufacturing company; b. N.Y.C., Dec. 6, 1935; s. Edward and Mary (Cochrane) H.; B.E.E., Villanova U., 1962; M.B.A., N.Y. U., 1966; m. Barbara T. Lesnik, July 29, 1967; children—Jonathan Edward, Laura Maria, Karen Ann, Michelle Teresa. Asst. mgr. div. staff Western Electric Co., Newark, 1970-71, sales service cons. mgr., 1971-76, revenue systems mgr., 1976-77, mgr. corp. account mgmt., 1977-78, mgr. sales (nat. accounts), 1978-86, dir. sales affiliated accounts and network cons. AT&T Network Systems, 1986, dir. sales, new markets, 1987—, v.p. mktg. ops. and devel., 1988—. Served with USNR, 1954-58. Mem. IEEE (sr.). Democrat. Roman Catholic. Home: 69 Delwick Ln New Providence NJ 07974 Office: 111 Madison Ave Morristown NJ 07960

HIGHBERGER, WILLIAM FOSTER, lawyer; b. Suffern, N.Y., May 15, 1950; s. John Kistler and Helen Stewart (Foster) H.; m. Carolyn Barbara Kuhl, July 12, 1980; 1 child, Helen Barbara. AB, Princeton U.; JD, Columbia U. Bar: Calif. 1976, U.S. Dist. Ct. (cen. dist.) Calif. 1976, U.S. Ct. Appeals (2d cir.) 1976, U.S. Ct. Appeals (9th cir.) 1977, U.S. Dist. Ct. (so. and ea. dists.) Calif. 1979, U.S. Supreme Ct. 1980, D.C. 1981, U.S. Dist. Ct. (no. dist.) Calif. 1981, U.S. Dist. Ct. D.C. 1982, U.S. Ct. Appeals (D.C. cir.) 1982, U.S. Ct. Appeals (3d cir.) 1983, N.Y. 1984, U.S. Dist. Ct. (so. dist.) N.Y. 1984, U.S. Dist. Ct. (ea. dist.) N.Y. 1985. Law clk. to judge U.S. Ct. Appeals (2d cir.), Bridgeport, Conn., 1975-76; assoc. Gibson, Dunn & Crutcher, Washington and Los Angeles, 1976-82, ptnr., 1983—. Notes and comments editor Columbia U. Law Rev., 1974. Mem. Nat. Trust for Hist. Preservation, Washington, 1980—, Nature Conservatory, Calif., 1981—, Pacific Palisades (Calif.) Presbyn. Ch., 1987—. James Kent scholar

Columbia U., 1973. Mem. ABA (com. on individual rights and repsonibilities in workplace, labor sect., litigation sect.), Indsl. Relations Research Assn., Am. Judicature Soc., Internat. Soc. for Social Security and Labor Relations Law. Republican. Clubs: Princeton (N.Y.C.); Univ. Cottage (Princeton, N.J.). Home: 11688 Picturesque Dr Studio City CA 91604 Office: Gibson Dunn & Crutcher 333 S Grand Ave Los Angeles CA 90071

HIGHSMITH, PATRICIA, writer; b. Ft. Worth, Jan. 19, 1921; d. Jay Bernard Plangman and Mary Coates. Attended Barnard Coll.; BA, Columbia U., 1942. Author: (novels) Strangers on a Train, 1950, The Blunderer, 1955, The Talented Mr. Ripley, 1956, Deep Water, 1957, A Game for the Living, 1958, This Sweet Sickness, 1960, The Cry of the Owl, 1962, The Two Faces of January, 1964, The Glass Cell, 1965, A Suspension of Mercy, 1965, Those Who Walk Away, 1967, The Tremor of Forgery, 1969, Ripley Under Ground, 1971, A Dog's Ransom, 1972, Ripley's Game, 1974, Edith's Diary, 1977, The Boy Who Followed Ripley, 1980, People Who Knock on the Door, 1983, Found in the Street, 1986; (short story collections) The Animal Lover's Book of Beastly Murder, 1975, Little Tales of Misogyny, 1977, Slowly, Slowly in the Wind, 1979, The Black House, 1981, Mermaids on the Golf Course, 1985, Tales of Natural and Unnatural Catastrophes, 1987; (non-fiction) Plotting and Writing Suspense Fiction, 1966, 2d edit., 1983. Club: Detection. Office: care Marianne Liggenstorfer, Diogenes Verlag Sprecherstrasse 8, 8032 Zurich Switzerland

HIJIKATA, TAKESHI, chemical company executive; b. Ena, Japan, Mar. 18, 1915; s. Kikusaburo and Sue Hijikata; m. Michiko Kumakura; children—Sonoko, Ryo, Atsushi. B.Agr., Tokyo Imperial U., 1937, B.Econs., 1941. Dir. Sumitomo Chem. Co., Ltd., Osaka, Japan, 1971-73, mng. dir., 1973-77, exec. v.p., 1977, pres., 1977-85, chmn. bd., 1985—; pres. Japan-Singapore Petrochems. Co., Ltd., Sumitomo Pharms. Co., Ltd.; dir. Fuji Oil Co., Ltd., Seitetsu Kagaku Co., Ltd.; ad hoc com. mem. AEC; mem. indsl. structure council Ministry Internat. Trade and Industry, trade conf. Office of Prime Minister. Recipient Blue Ribbon medal Govt. of Japan, 1980. Mem. Fedn. Econ. Orgns. (exec. dir.), Japan Com. for Econ. Devel. (bd. dirs.), Kansai Econ. Fedn., Japan Fedn. Employers' Assns. (standing bd. dirs.). Buddhist. Lodge: Rotary. Avocations: golf; reading. Office: Sumitomo Chem Co Ltd, 15 5-chome, Kitahama Higashi-ki, Osaka 541 Japan *

HILBRECHT, NORMAN TY, lawyer, state legislator; b. San Diego, Feb. 11, 1933; s. Norman Titus and Elizabeth (Lair) H.; m. Mercedes L. Sharratt, Oct. 24, 1980. B.A., Northwestern U., 1956; J.D., Yale U., 1959. Bar: Nev. 1959, U.S. Supreme Ct. 1963. Atty., assoc. firm Jones, Wiener & Jones, Las Vegas, 1959-62; assoc. counsel Union Pacific R.R., Las Vegas, 1962; partner firm Hilbrecht & Jones, Las Vegas, 1962-69; pres. Hilbrecht, Jones, Schreck & Bernhard, 1969-83, Hilbrecht & Assocs, 1983—, Mobil Transport Corp., 1970-72; gen. counsel Bell United Ins. Co., 1986—; assemblyman Nev. Legislature, 1966-72, minority leader, 1971-72; mem. Nev. Senate, 1974-78; asst. lectr. bus. law U. Nev., Las Vegas. Mem. labor mgmt. com. NCCJ, 1963; mem. Clark County (Nev.) Democratic Central Com., 1959-80, 1st vice chmn., 1965-66; del. Western Regional Assembly on Ombudsman; chmn. Clark County Dem. Conv., 1966, Nev. Dem. Conv., 1966; pres. Clark County Legal Aid Soc., 1964, Nev. Legal Aid and Defender Assn., 1965-83. Served to capt. AUS, 1952-67. Named Outstanding State Legislator Eagleton Inst. Politics, Rutgers U., 1969. Mem. Am. Judicature Soc., Am. Bar Assn., Clark County Bar Assn., Am. Assn. Rev. Appraisers, Am. Acad. Polit. and Social Sci., Am. Trial Lawyers Assn., State Bar Nev., Nev. Trial Lawyers (state v.p. 1966), Nat. Assn. Real Estate Appraisers, Fraternal Order Police Assos. (v.p.), Phi Beta Kappa, Delta Phi Epsilon, Theta Chi, Phi Delta Phi. Lutheran. Lodge: Elks. Office: 723 S Casino Center Blvd Las Vegas NV 89101

HILDEBRAND, KLAUS, historian; b. Bielefeld, Fed. Republic Germany, Nov. 18, 1941; s. Ewald and Maria (Taüsch) H.; m. Erika Hildebrand; 1 child, Daniel. PhD, U. Mannheim, 1967, habilitation, 1972. Research asst. U. Mannheim, 1967-72; prof. modern history U. Bielefeld, Fed. Republic Germany, 1972-74; prof. U. Frankfurt, 1974-77, U. Münster, Fed. Republic Germany, 1977-82, U. Bonn, 1982—; mem. Commn. for History Parliamentarism and Polit. Parties, 1982, Hist. Commn. with the Bavarian Acad. Scis., 1983. Author: Bundesrepublik Deuhcchlarest, 1963-67, Vom Reich zum Weltreich, 1967, Bethmann Hollweg, 2d edit. 1970, Deutsche Aubenpolitik, 4th edit. 1980, Das Dritte Reich, 3d edit., 1987; co-editor: Deutschland und Frankscich, (1936-39), 1981, Internationale Beziehungen (1929-1933), 1981, Deutsche Frage und europäisches Gleichgewicht, 1985. Office: 11 Konviktstrasse, 5300 Bonn Federal Republic of Germany

HILDEBRANDT, FREDERICK DEAN, JR., insurance company executive; b. Upper Darby, Pa., Apr. 17, 1933; s. Frederick Dean and Ruth Taylor (Barry) H.; A.B. magna cum laude, Dartmouth, 1954, M.S., Tuck Sch. of Bus. Adminstrn. and Thayer Sch. Engring., 1955; m. Marjorie Louise Smith, July 27, 1968; children—Frederick Dean III, Elizabeth Florence. Engr., Eastman Kodak Co., Rochester, N.Y., 1957-60; systems mgr. J.T. Baker Chem. Co., Phillipsburg, N.J., 1960-63; asso. Booz, Allen & Hamilton Inc., N.Y.C., 1963-72, v.p., 1972-78; sr. v.p. Am. Ins. Assn., N.Y.C., 1978-81; v.p. Travelers Ins. Cos., Hartford, Conn., 1981—; adminstr. All-Industry Research Adv. Council, 1979, dir., 1982—, vice chmn. bd. dirs. Workers Compensation Research Inst. 1987—. Served with U.S. Army, 1955-57. Mem. Phi Beta Kappa. Home: 38 Lincoln Lane Simsbury CT 06070 Office: One Tower Square Hartford CT 06183

HILFSTEIN, ERNA, science historian, educator; b. Kraków, Poland; came to U.S., 1949, naturalized, 1954; d. Leon and Anna (Schornstein) Kluger; B.A., CCNY, 1967, M.A., 1971, Ph.D., City U. N.Y., 1978; m. Max Hilfstein; children—Leon, Simone Juliana. Tchr. secondary schs., N.Y.C., 1968-84, 86—; vis. prof. Queens Coll., 1973; affiliate Grad. Sch./Univ. Center, City U. N.Y. NEH grantee, 1984-85. Mem. History Sci. Soc., Polish Inst. Arts and Scis. in Am., N.Y. Acad. Scis., United Fedn. of Tchrs. (chpt. chmn. 1978-84, 86—, del. 1980—). Democrat. Jewish. Author: Starowolski's Biographies of Copernicus, 1980; collaborator English version of Nicholas Copernicus Complete Works, vol. 1, 1972, vol. 2, 1978, vol. 3, 1985; contbr. articles and revs. to profl. jours. Editor: Science and History, 1978. Home: 1523 Dwight Pl Bronx NY 10465

HILGER, FREDERICK LEE, JR., real estate executive, banker, lawyer; b. Dallas, Feb. 17, 1946; s. Frederick Lee Sr. and Maryann Taylor (Ayers) H.; m. Terri Lynn Wilson, May 13, 1984; children: Matthew Charles, Kristen Leigh. BA, U. Pacific, Stockton, Calif., 1967; JD, U. Calif., Berkeley, 1970. Bar: Calif. 1971. Sr. tax acct. Touche Ross and Co., San Francisco, 1971-73; atty. F. L. Hilger Prof. Corp., Eureka, Calif., 1973-75; mng. ptnr. Moses Lake (Wash.) Farms, 1975-78; sr. cons. Sites and Co. Inc., Seattle, 1978-79; v.p. ops. mgmt. U.S. Cruises, Inc., Seattle, 1980-83; pres., chief fin. officer First Nat. Bank, Chico, Calif., 1984-86; pres., chief exec. officer FreeHill Corp., Sacramento, 1986—. Recipient Outstanding Banker award Am. Bankers Assn. First Nat. Bank, 1984, 85. Mem. ABA, Calif. Bar Assn., Sacramento Bar Assn. Republican. Presbyterian. Club: Olympic (San Francisco). Office: FreeHill Corp Box 40 Roseville CA 95661

HILGER, WOLFGANG, manufacturing executive; b. Leverkusen, Fed. Republic Germany, Nov. 16, 1929. Ed., U. Bonn, Fed. Republic Germany. Joined Hoechst AG, 1958; chmn. Hoechst AG, Frankfurt, 1985—, also bd. dirs.; pres. adv. bd. Hoechst Holland, Hoechst CeramTec, Riedel de Haen, Wacker Chemie. Named an Hon. Prof. U. Frankfurt. Office: Hoechst AG, 6230 Frankfurt/Main 80, Federal Republic of Germany *

HILKER, WALTER ROBERT, JR., lawyer; b. Los Angeles, Apr. 18, 1921; s. Walter Robert and Alice (Cox) H.; m. Ruth Margaret Hibbard, Sept. 7, 1943; children: Anne Katherine, Walter Robert III. B.S., U. So. Calif., 1942, LL.B., 1948. Bar: Calif. 1949. Sole practice Los Angeles, 1949-55; ptnr. Parker, Milliken, Kohlmeier, Clark & O'Hara, 1955-75; of counsel Pacht, Ross, Warne, Bernhard & Sears, Newport Beach, Calif., 1980-84. Trustee Bella Mabury Trust; bd. dirs. Houchin Found. Served to lt. USNR, 1942-45. Decorated Bronze Star. Mem. ABA, Calif. Bar Assn., Orange County Bar Assn. Republican. Clubs: Spring Valley Lake Country (Apple Valley, Calif.); Balboa Bay (Newport Beach, Calif.). Home and Office: 34 Georgetown Irvine CA 92715

HILL, ALAN EUGENE, physicist, inventor; b. Durango, Colo., Sept. 4, 1939; s. Glenn Worland and Minnie (Hermsmeier) H.; m. Carol Ann Havens, Mar. 26, 1960; children—Larry Glenn, Roy Leon. B.S.E., U. Mich., 1964, M.S., 1965. Leader laser research br. Lear Siegler Corp., Ann Arbor, Mich., 1965-67; sr. scientist, tech. dir. Laser div. USAF Weapons Lab., Kirtland AFB, Albuquerque, 1967-77; pres., chief scientist Plasmatronics, Inc., Albuquerque, 1977—; adj. prof. U. Ariz., Tucson, 1975—; founder, past dir. Photon Sources Corp., 1969-82; founder, dir. Indsl. Lasers Inc. Contbr. articles to profl. jours. Patentee in field. Mem. Cave Research Found., 1963—. Recipient Sci. Achievement award Air Force Systems Command, 1971; Air Force Assn. Citation of Honor, 1972; Air Force Outstanding Performance award, 1968-72. Mem. Nat. Speleological Soc. (bd. dirs.). Address: Plasmatronics Inc 2460 Alamo SE #101 Albuquerque NM 87106

HILL, SIR AUSTIN BRADFORD, retired physician; b. July 8, 1897; s. Sir Leonard Erskine Hill; ed. Univ. Coll. London; Ph.D., 1926; D.Sc., 1929; m. Florence Maud (dec. 1980); 3 children. Staff Med. Research Council and Indsl. Health Research Bd., 1923-33; reader in epidemiology and vital stats. London Sch. Hygiene and Tropical Medicine, 1933-45, prof., prof. emeritus, dean, 1955-57; honr. dir. statis. research unit Med. Research Council, 1955-57; lectr. in field. Served with Royal Naval Air Service, 1916-18; seconded to Dept. Ministry of Home Security, 1940-42, to med. directorate RAF, 1943-45, civilian cons., 1943-78. Fellow Royal Soc.; knighted, 1961; decorated comdr. Brit. Empire, 1951. Fellow Royal Coll. Physicians (hon.), FFCM, FRSM, FAPHA. Recipient Galen medal Soc. Apothecaries, 1959, Harben Gold medal, 1961, Herbenden Soc., 1965, numerous others. Author: Internal Migration and Its Effects upon the Death Rates, 1925; The Inheritance of Resistance to Bacterial Infection in Animal Species, 1934; Principles of Medicial Statistics, 1937, 11th edit., 1985. Office: care Royal Soc, 6 Carlton House Terr, London SW1Y 5AG England *

HILL, BRUCE MARVIN, Bayesian statistician, scientist educator; b. Chgo., Mar. 13, 1935; s. Samuel and Leah (Berman) H.; m. Linda Ladd, June 18, 1958; children—Alec Michael, Russell Andrew, Gregory Bruce; m. Anne Edith Gardiner Bruce, Aug. 5, 1972. B.S. in Math., U. Chgo., 1956; M.S. in Stats., Stanford U., 1958, Ph.D. in Stats., 1961. Mem. faculty U. Mich., Ann Arbor, 1960—, assoc. prof. stats. and probability theory, 1964-70, prof., 1970—; vis. prof. bus. Harvard U., 1964-65; vis. prof. systems engring. U. Lancaster, U.K., 1968-69; vis. prof. stats. U. London, 1976; vis. prof. econs. U. Utah, 1979. Editor Jour. Am. Statis. Assn., 1977-83, Jour. Bus. and Econ. Stats, 1982—; contbr. articles to profl. jours., chpts. to books on stats. NSF grantee, 1962-69, 81—; USAF grantee, 1971-73, 87—. Fellow Am. Statis. Assn., Inst. Math. Stats.; mem. AAUP, Research Club U. Mich., N.Y. Acad. Sci., Psi Upsilon, Sigma Chi. Home: 1657 Glenwood Ann Arbor MI 48104 Office: U Mich Dept Statistics Ann Arbor MI 48104

HILL, BRYCE DALE, school administrator; b. Seminole, Okla., Mar. 5, 1930; s. Charles Daniel and Ollie (Nichols) H.; B.S., East Central State Coll., 1952, M.Teaching, 1957; postgrad. U. Okla., 1959-70; profl. adminstrs. certificate, 1969; m. Wilma Dean Carter, Aug. 16, 1956; children—Bryce Anthony, Brent Dale. Tchr. pub. schs., New Lima, Okla., 1952-56, supt. pub. schs., 1956—; owner New Lima Gas Co., 1958-82. Chmn. bd. dirs. Seminole County chpt. ARC, 1969—; v.p. bd. dirs. Redland Community Action Program, 1968-71, Okla. Assn. Sch. Adminstrs., 1979-81, Org. Okla. Rural Schs., 1986—; mem. Seminole County Bd. Health, 1985—, v.p., 1986—; mem. Seminole County Rural Devel. Council. Chmn. Seminole County Democratic Central Com., 1962-64, 70—. Mem. NEA, Okla. Edn. Assn., Am. Assn. Sch. Adminstrs., Okla. Assn. Sch. Adminstrs. (exec. com. 1976-78, 79-81, bd. dirs. 1979-81, Adminstr. of Yr. 1983), Org. Okla. Rural Schs. (bd. dirs. 1986—), Seminole County Tchrs. Assn. (pres. 1964-65, 71-72, 79-80), Seminole County Sch. Adminstrs. Assn. (chmn. 1969-70), Seminole County Schoolmasters Club (pres. 1963-64, 69-70, 77-78), Seminole Hist. Soc. (v.p. 1971-73, 74-76). Baptist. Home: Rt 1 Box 96 Wewoka OK 74884

HILL, CHARLES MICHAEL, oral and maxillofacial surgeon, consultant; b. Bolton, Lancashire, Eng., June 23, 1950; s. George Bernard and Lilian (Morris) H.; m. Jennifer Margaret James; children: Kathryn Louise, Joanna Ruth, Peter James. B in Dental Surgery, Bristol U., Avon, Eng., 1972; MDSc, Leeds (Eng.) U., 1986. House officer Bristol (Eng.) Dental Hosp., 1973-74; dental officer Manorom Hosp., Thailand, 1974-75; registrar Frenchway/Bristol Hosps., 1976-79; sr. registrar Leeds/Bradford Hosps., Yorkshire, 1979-86; oral and maxillo-facial surgeon, cons. Univ. Hosp. Wales, Cardiff, 1986—. Author: General Anaesthesia and Sedation in Dentristry, 1983; contbr. articles to profl. jours., 1983-87. Grantee Boots PLC, Nottingham, Eng., 1986. Fellow Brit. Assn. Oral and Maxillo-Facial Surgeons, Brit. Dental Assn. (sect. com. 1986—). Baptist. Office: Cardiff Dental Hosp Dept, Oral and Maxillo-Facial, Surgery, Cardiff CF4 4XY, Wales

HILL, (JOHN EDWARD) CHRISTOPHER, history educator, author; b. Feb. 6, 1912; B.A., Oxford U., 1934, D.Litt., 1965; D.Litt. (hon.), U. Hull, 1966, U. East Anglia, 1968, U. Exeter, 1979, U. Wales, 1979; Litt.D. (hon.), U. Sheffield, 1967; LL.D. (hon.), U. Bristol, 1976; D.Univ. (Hon.), York U., 1978; hon. doctorate Sorbonne, Paris, 1979; m. Inez Waugh, 1944; 1 dau.; m. 2d, Bridget Irene Sutton, 1956; 1 son, 2 daus. (1 dec.). Asst. lectr. Univ. Coll., Cardiff, Wales, 1936; fellow and tutor in modern history Balliol Coll., Oxford U., 1938; pvt. field Security Police, commd. Oxford and Buckinghamshire Light Inf., 1940; seconded to Fgn. Office, 1943; lectr. history oxford U., 1959, Ford's lectr., 1962, master of Balliol Coll., 1965-78; vis. prof. Open U., 1978-80, Preston Poly., 1982—. Recipient Hanford award Milton Soc. Am., 1978. Fellow Brit. Acad.; fgn. hon. mem. Am. Acad. Scis. Author: The English Revolution 1640, 1940; (under name K. E. Holme) Two Commonwealths, 1945; Lenin and the Russian Revolution, 1947; Economic Problems of the Church, 1956; Puritanism and Revolution, 1958; Oliver Cromwell, 1958; The Century of Revolution, 1961; Society and Puritanism in Pre-Revolutionary England, 1964; Intellectual Origins of the English Revolution, 965; Reformation to Industrial Revolution, 1967; God's Englishman, 1970; Antichrist in 17th Century England, 1971; The World Turned Upside Down, 1972; Change and Continuity in 17th Century England, 1975; Milton and the English Revolution (Heinemann award), 1978; Some Intellectual Consequences of the English Revolution, 1980; (The Experience of Defeat: Milton and Some Contemporaries, 1984; Writing and Revolution in 17th Century England, 1985; Religion and Politics in 17th Century England, 1986; People and Ideas in 17th Century England, 1986); also articles. Editor: (with E. Dell) The Good Old Cause, 1949; (with B. Reay and W. Lamont) The World of the Muggletonians, 1983. Home: Woodway House, Sibford Ferris, Banbury England

HILL, DAVID LAWRENCE, research corporation executive; b. Boonville, Miss., Nov. 11, 1919; s. David Alexander and Mabel Clair (Brown) H.; B.S., Calif. Inst. Tech., 1942; Ph.D. (Socony Vacuum Co. fellow), Princeton U., 1951; m. Mary M. Shadow, Dec. 31, 1950; children—David A., Mary C., Robert L., John Frederick, Cynthia A., Sandra E., James A. With U. Chgo. Metall. Lab. and Argonne Nat. Lab., 1942-46, assoc. physicist, group leader, 1944-46; asst. prof. physics Vanderbilt U., Nashville, 1949-52, assoc. prof., 1952-54; guest scholar Inst. Theoretical Physics, Copenhagen, summer 1950; cons. theoretical physics U. Calif., Los Alamos (N.Mex.) Sci. Lab., 1952-54, staff mem., 1954-58, group leader theoretical nuclear physics, 1955-58; mgmt. cons., 1958-60; pres. Phys. Sci. Corp., Fairfield, Conn., 1960-62, Nanosecond Systems, Inc., Fairfield, 1963-72, Particle Measurements, Inc., Southport, Conn., 1965-81, Harbor Research Corp., 1978—; chmn. bd. Integrated Total Systems, Inc., Hingham, Mass., 1968-81; pres. Southport Computers, Inc., Conn., 1973-81, Valutron N.V., Netherlands Antilles, 1980—; lectr. in field; sci. advisor to Vice Presdl. nominee, Senator Estes Kefauver, 1956; incorporator, exec. v.p. dir. Los Alamos Investment Corp., 1956-58; cons. physicist in field. Adv. com. on sci. and tech. of Adv. Council of Dem. Nat. Com., 1959-61. Fellow Am. Phys. Soc., AAAS; mem. IEEE, Fedn. Am. Scientists (nat. chmn. 1953-54), Sigma Xi. Contbr. articles to profl. jours. Address: 1074 Harbor Rd Southport CT 06490

HILL, DENNIS PATRICK, electrical engineer, educator; b. Wilmington, Del., Jan. 28, 1960; s. James A. and Irene P (Kelly) H. BS in Engring., Marquette U., 1982, MSEE and Computer Sci., 1983, postgrad., 1986—. Research engr. Gen. Electric Co., Milw., 1981-82; computer scientist VA Med. Ctr., Wood, Wis., 1982-83, Med. Coll. Wis., Milw., 1982—; dir. computing services Milw. Sch. Engring., 1983-87, exec. dir. Sch. Industry and Govt. Relations, 1987—, prof. electrical engring. and computer scis., 1984—, exec. dir. industry and govt. relations, 1987—; pres. Athletic Info. Systems, Milw., 1986—; tech. advisor High Tech. Specialists, Milw., 1984—, Bradford Computer Group, Skokie, Ill., 1983—; TV commentator on computer security for Milw. affiliates NBC, CBS, ABC., 1986—; cons. computer security Honeywell Fed. Systems, HBL-Can., HBL-U.K., 1986—. Author numerous articles. Advisor Milw. Sch. Engring. Explorers Post, 1985; pres. Parc Renaissance Assn., Inc., Milw., 1987—. Recipient Engring. Educator award, Falk Corp., Milw., 1985, Minority Affairs award Milw. Sch. Engring., 1987. Mem. Am. Soc. Engring. Edn. (exec. bd. north midwest sect., 1985—, IEEE (exec. bd. Milw. 1982—), Soc. Mfg. Engring., Computer and Automated Systems Assn. (program chmn. Milw. sect. 1985-87), Computer Security Inst., Milw. Urban League, Alpha Eta Mu Beta, Eta Kappa Nu, Triangle Frat. (advisor 1984). Republican. Roman Catholic. Lodge: Masons. Home: 4123 W Meinecke St Milwaukee WI 53210 Office: Milw Sch Engring PO Box 644 Milwaukee WI 53201

HILL, EARL MCCOLL, lawyer; b. Bisbee, Ariz., June 12, 1926; s. Earl George and Jeanette (McColl) H.; m. Bea Dolan, Nov. 22, 1968; children: Arthur Charles, John Earl, Darlene Blain, Tamara Gentry. BA, U. Wash., 1960, JD, 1961. Bar: Nev. 1962, U.S. Ct. Clms. 1978, U.S. Ct. Apls. (9th cir.) 1971, U.S. Sup. Ct. 1978. Law clk. Nev. sup. ct., Carson City, 1962; assoc. Gray, Horton & Hill, Reno, 1962-65, ptnr. 1965-73; ptnr. Hill Cassas de Lipkau and Erwin, Reno, 1974—, Sherman & Howard, Denver, 1982—; judge pro tem Reno mcpl. ct., 1964-70; lectr. continuing legal edn. Mem. Nev. Commn. on Jud. Selection 1977-84; trustee Rocky Mountain Mineral Law Found. 1976—, sec. 1987—. Mem. ABA, State Bar Nev. (chmn. Com. on Jud. Adminstrn. 1971-77), Washoe County Bar Assn., Am. Judicature Soc., Soc. Mining Law Antiquarians. Club: Prospectors. Contbr. articles to profl. publs. Office: Holcomb Profl Ctr Suite 300 333 Holcomb Ave PO Box 2790 Reno NV 89505

HILL, GEORGE JAMES, surgeon, educator; b. Cedar Rapids, Iowa, Oct. 7, 1932; s. Gerald Leslie and Essie Mae (Thompson) H.; m. Helene Zimmermann, July 16, 1960; children: James Warren, David Hedgcock, Sarah, Helena Rundall. A.B., Yale U., 1953; M.D., Harvard U., 1957. Intern N.Y. Hosp., 1957-58; fellow and resident in surgery Peter Bent Brigham hosp. and Harvard Med. Sch., 1958-61, 63-66; instr. surgery U. Colo., 1966-67, asst. prof., 1967-72, asso. prof., 1972-73; prof. Washington U., 1973-76; prof., chmn. Marshall U., 1976-81; prof., dir. surg. oncology U. of Medicine & Dentistry of N.J.-N.J. Med. Sch., Newark, 1981—; chmn. clin. cancer edn. com. Nat. Cancer Inst., 1978-80; vis. fellow in molecular biology Princton U., 1988. Author: Leprosy in Five Young Men, 1970, Outpatient Surgery, 1973, 2d edit., 1980, 3d edit., 1988, Clinical Oncology, 1977; contbr. articles in field to profl. jours. Pres. Tri-State Area council Boy Scouts Am., Huntington, W.Va., 1980-81, v.p. Essex Council, 1983—, chmn. nat. med. exploring com., 1987—; pres. W.Va. div. Am. Cancer Soc., 1980-81, pres. N.J. div., 1987—; pres. Am. Assn. Cancer Edn., 1985-86; mem. N.J. State Commn. on Cancer Research, 1983-84; trustee Frost Valley YMCA, 1986-89. Served with USPHSR, 1961-63, with USNR, 1976—. Recipient Civic Actions medal Republic S. Vietnam, 1972, Lederle Med. Faculty award 1970, Silver Beaver award Boy Scouts Am., 1981; Damon Runyon fellow, 1958; Am. Cancer Soc. jr. faculty fellow, 1973-76; named Physician of Yr., N.J. div. Am. Cancer Soc., 1985, Jerseyan of Week Newark Star Ledger, 1987. Mem. Acad. Medicine N.J. (trustee 1986—), ACS (mem. commn. on cancer 1987-90), Soc. Univ. Surgeons, Soc. Surg. Oncology (exec. council 1985-88), Central Surg. Assn., Am. Assn. Cancer Edn. (pres. 1985-86), Am. Assn. Cancer Research, Essex County Med. Soc. (trustee 1987-89), Med. Soc. N.J. (chmn. com. cancer control 1986—), N.J. Med. and Dental Sch. Chpt. AAUP (pres. 1988—, 1st v.p. 1986-87), Sigma Xi (pres. Newark chpr. 1986-87), Alpha Omega Alpha. Republican. Episcopalian. Clubs: Harvard (Boston); Univ. (Denver); Army and Navy (Washington); Explorers (N.Y.C.), Harvard (N.Y.C.); Yale of Cen. N.J. (trustee 1985—). Office: 100 Bergen St Newark NJ 07103

HILL, HAMNETT PINHEY, accountant; b. Ottawa, Ont., Can., Oct. 11, 1943; s. Hamnett Pinhey and Cynthia Benson (Jaffray) Hill Eberts; m. Terry Delany, Aug. 23, 1969; children: Catherine, Hamnett, Austin, Jeremy, Darcy, Ashley, Jaffray, Morgan. BA, Carleton U., 1971. Chartered acct., 1974. Chief acct. Locweld & Forge Products Ltd., Montreal, Que., Can., 1966-69; acct. Peat Marwick Mitchell & Co., Ottawa, 1971-75, ptnr. Hudson & Co., Calgary, Alta., Can., 1975-88; pres., dir. Nine Hills Resources Inc., Calgary, 1981—. Bd. dirs. Calgary French Sch., 1977-82, U. Calgary Swim Club, 1984-87. Mem. Inst. Chartered Accts. Alta., Inst. Chartered Accts. Ont., Can. Tax Found. Progressive Conservative. Mem. Ch. Jesus Christ Latter-day Saints. Office: Hamnett P Hill Profl Corp, 420 Superior Ave SW, Calgary, AB Canada T2R 1J4

HILL, HEYWARD GIBBES, diplomat, retired foreign service officer; b. Hammond, La., Jan. 16, 1900; s. Samuel Lindsay and Kate Turpin (McKnight) H. Ed., La. State U., 1916-20; also private tutors in, France and Switzerland. Apptd. fgn. service officer, vice consul and sec. in the diplomatic service 1930; fgn. service Sch. Dept. State, 1930; vice consul Kobe, Japan, 1930; temporary vice consul Taihoku, 1931; vice consul Kobe, 1931; vice counsul Yokahama, 1931; vice consul Buenos Aires, 1933; asst. sec. Am. del. 7th Internat. Conf. of Am. States, Montevideo, 1933; sec. Am. del. Pan Am. Comml. Conf., Buenos Aires, 1935, Chaco Peace Conf., Buenos Aires, 1935-36; vice consul Geneva, Switzerland, 1936; consul 1937; sec. Am. del. Intergovernmental Com. on Polit. Refugees meeting, Evian, France and London, 1938, Eighth Internat. Conf. Am. States, Lima, Peru, 1938; consul Basel, Switzerland, 1939; second sec. embassy Panama, 1939; 2d sec. embassy for duty with U.S. rep. to Politico-Mil. Commn., Algiers, 1943; temporarily detailed European div. Dept. of State, 5 mos. in 1944; 1st sec. embassy Ankara, Turkey, June, 1945; counselor of embassy, charge d' affaires Jidda, Saudi Arabia, 1949-50; consul gen. Marseilles, France, 1951-54; counselor of embassy, consul gen. Manila, P.I., 1954-56; consul gen. Alexandria, Egypt, U.A.R., 1957-61. Decorated comdr. Order St. Mark, 1961. Clubs: University (Washington); Athens Lawn Tennis. Address: Hilton Hotel, Athens Greece

HILL, JOHN MCGREGOR, physicist, corporate executive; b. Feb. 21, 1921; s. John Campbell and Margaret Elizabeth (Park) H.; m. Nora Eileen Hellett, 1947; 3 children. BS, King's Coll., London; PhD, St. John's Coll., Cambridge U. Research physicist Cavendish Lab., Cambridge, Eng., 1946-48; lectr. London U., 1948-50; formerly with U.K. Atomic Energy Authority, London, from 1950, mem. for prodn., 1964-67, chmn., 1967-81; chmn. Brit. Nuclear Fuels, Ltd., 1971-83, Amersham Internat., 1975-88; chmn. Aurora PLC, 1984—. Mem. Adv. Council on Tech., 1968-81. Served to flight lt. RAF, World War II. Decorated knight Queen Elizabeth II. Fellow Royal Soc., Inst. Physics, Fellowship Engring.; mem. U.S. Nat. Acad. Engring. (fgn. assoc.). Club: East India. Home: Dominic House, Sudbrook Ln, RichmondSurrey TW10 7AT, England Office: Aurora House, 61 Manchester Rd, S10 5DY Sheffield England

HILL, JOHNSON DAVIS, JR., life insurance executive; b. El Dorado Springs, Mo., Nov. 20, 1916; s. Johnson Davis and Lura (Phillips) H.; m. Elizabeth Dodge Jones, Dec. 20, 1940; children—Stephen Davis, Lucinda Marie, Susan Elizabeth. A.A., Wentworth Coll., Lexington, Mo., 1935; B.J., Stanford U., 1937. Reporter, Longview Daily News, Wash., 1937-39, Sacramento Bee, 1939-48; v.p., Atlas Life Ins. Co., Tulsa, Okla., 1948-52, exec. v.p., 1952-67, pres., 1967-77, chmn., chief exec. officer, 1977-86, chmn., 1986—. Chmn. Tulsa County chpt. ARC, 1952-53. Served to 1st lt. U.S. Army, 1942-46. Mem. Assn. Okla. Life Cos. (pres.), Am. Life Conf. (state v.p.). Democrat. Episcopalian. Club: Tulsa (pres. 1963), Southern Hills (Tulsa). Home: 2140 E 32d St Tulsa OK 74105 Office: Atlas Life Ins Co 415 S Boston St PO Box 1919 Tulsa OK 74102

HILL, JONEL C., gas company executive; b. Mankato, Minn., 1925. Attended, Mankato State Coll.; LLB, St. Paul Coll. of Law, 1950. Formerly editor West Publishing Co.; past public utilities commr. State of Oreg.; former atty. Am. Telephone & Telegraph Co.; exec. asst. So. Calif. Gas Co., 1968-70, asst. v.p., 1970-74, v.p. regulatory affairs, 1974-80, sr. v.p., 1980-83, exec. v.p., 1983-85; pres. So. Calif. Gas Co., Los Angeles, 1985—, also dir. Office: So Calif Gas Co 810 S Flower St Los Angeles CA 90017 *

HILL, JUDITH DEEGAN, lawyer; b. Chgo., Dec. 13, 1940; d. William James and Ida May (Scott) Deegan; m. Dennis M. Havens, June 28, 1986; children by previous marriage: Colette M., Cristina M. BA, Western Mich. U., 1960; cert. U. Paris, Sorbonne, 1962; JD, Marquette U., 1971. Bar: Wis. 1971, Ill. 1973, Nev. 1976, D.C. 1979. Tchr., Kalamazoo (Mich.) Bd. Edn., 1960-62, Maple Heights (Ohio), 1963-64, Shorewood (Wis.) Bd. Edn., 1964-68; corp. atty. Fort Howard Paper Co., Green Bay, Wis., 1971-72; sr. trust adminstr. Continental Ill. Nat. Bank & Trust, Chgo., 1972-76; atty. Morse, Foley & Wadsworth Law Firm, Las Vegas, 1976-77; dep. dist. atty., criminal prosecutor Clark County Atty., Las Vegas, 1977-83; atty. civil and criminal law Edward S. Coleman Profl. Law Corp., Las Vegas, 1983-84; sole practice, 1984-85; atty. criminal div. Office of City Atty., City of Las Vegas, 1985—. Bd. dirs. Nev. Legal Services, Carson City, 1980-87, state chmn., 1984-87; bd. dirs. Clark County Legal Services, Las Vegas, 1980-87; mem. Star Aux. for Handicapped Children, Las Vegas, 1986—; Greater Las Vegas Women's League; jud. candidate Las Vegas Mcpl. Ct, 1987. Recipient Scholarship, Auto Specialties, St. Joseph, Mich., 1957-60; St. Thomas More Scholarship, Marquette U. Law Sch., Milw., 1968-69; juvenile law internship grantee Marquette U. Law Sch., 1970. Mem. ABA, Nev. Bar Assn., Woman's Bar Assn. of Ill., So. Nev. Assn. Women Attys., Ill. Bar Assn., Washington Bar Assn. Democrat. Club: Children's Village (pres. 1980) (Las Vegas, Nev.). Home: 1110 S 5th Pl Las Vegas NV 89104 Office: City Atty's Office 400 E Stewart 6th Floor Las Vegas NV 89101

HILL, LESLIE CLYDE, construction company executive; b. Bell, Calif., Aug. 9, 1934; s. Noble Clyde and Leona Pearl (Franks) H.; m. Gilda Ann Kay, Nov. 27, 1977. Grad. high sch., Whittier, Calif., 1952. Pres., chmn. bd. Schmid Insulation Contractors, Inc., San Diego, 1965—, The Hill Cos. Inc., San Diego, 1979-86, Sacramento Insulation Contractors Inc., 1984—; bd. dirs. The Bank Rancho Bernardo, San Diego, co-chmn. San Diego County Energy Conservation Orgn., 1978-80. Served to cpl. U.S. Army, 1952-55, Korea. Mem. Insulation Contractors Assn. Am. (v.p. 1978-80, bd. dirs.), Sports Car Club Am. Clubs: De Anza Desert Country, San Diego. Lodge: Golden Eagles. Home: 230 W Laurel St #604 San Diego CA 92101 Office: The Hill Cos Inc 5151 Murphy Canyon Rd Suite 200 San Diego CA 92123

HILL, PATRICIA ARNOLD, management consultant, realtor, former government official; b. Balt., Oct. 29, 1936; d. George Henry and Mildred Mae (Kress) Arnold; student No. Va. Community Coll., part time 1966-76; m. Richard Denzil Hill, Oct. 24, 1970; children—Terry Marlene Fomby, Debra Michelle Hill. Sec. firm McEwan & Walker, Chattanooga, 1955; clk.-typist Bur. Aeros., Washington, 1956-58, security clk., 1958, security asst., 1959-62, security specialist Bur. Aeros. and Naval Weapons Washington, 1962-66; security specialist Bur. Naval Weapons, 1962-66, Naval Ordnance Systems Command, 1966-74; security specialist Naval Sea Systems Command, Washington, 1974-75, head classification mgmt. br., asst. dir. security div., 1975-80, dep. dir., head info. security br. security div., 1980-83, security mgr. and dir. security div., 1983-86; realtor, Town and Country Properties; cons. in mgmt., adminstrn. and security, Alexandria, Va., 1986—. Mem. Nat. Assn. Female Execs., Nat. Classification Mgmt. Soc., Ind. Sec. Assn., Va. State Soc., Profl. Bus. Women. Baptist. Home: 1003 Collingwood Rd Alexandria VA 22308

HILL, PETER WAVERLY, lawyer; b. White River Junction, Vt., June 24, 1953; s. Richard Bert and Elaine Etta (Kimball) H.; m. Suzanne Miller, Nov. 21, 1983; 1 stepchild, Marshall Jackson Miller. BA in Philosophy and Govt., U. Ariz., 1975, JD, 1978. Bar: Ariz. 1978, U.S. Dist. Ct. (no. dist.) N.Y. 1979, N.Y. 1980, U.S. Ct. Appeals (2d cir.) 1982. Staff atty. Legal Aid Soc. Mid N.Y., Utica, 1978-79, Oneonta, 1979-83; assoc. Law Offices of Paternoster & O'Leary, Walton, N.Y., 1983-84; sole practice Oneonta, 1985—; bd. dirs. OURS-Delaco Assn., Inc., Delhi, N.Y. Contbr. articles to profl. jours. Mem. N.Y. State com. Socialist Party, Syracuse. Mem. ABA, N.Y. State Bar Assn., Otsego County Bar Assn., Delaware County Bar Assn., Assn. Trial Lawyers Am., N.Y. State Trial Lawyers Assn., Nat. Lawyers Guild, Nat. Orgn. Social Security Claimants Reps. Unitarian Universalist. Home: 103 Elm St Oneonta NY 13820 Office: 37 Dietz St PO Box 823 Oneonta NY 13820

HILL, ROBERT EVERAGE, lawyer; b. Mobile, Ala., Feb. 20, 1946; s. Robert and Lauretta (Ladner) H.; m. Glenda Robinson, Jan. 21, 1967 (div. 1975); 1 child, Erica Yvette Hill. BA, Grambling U., 1968; M in Pub. Adminstrn., San Jose State U., 1977; JD, So. U., Baton Rouge, 1982; grad. in law, Loyola U., New Orleans, 1986; grad. Nat. Jud. Coll., U. Nev., 1986. Bar: La. 1984; notary pub., La. Buyer Western Electric Co., Inc., N.Y.C., 1973-74; mgr. procurement Western Progress, Inc., Mountain View, Calif., 1974-77; asst. mgr. purchasing Peterbilt Motor Co., Newark, Calif., 1977-79; analyst Legis. Fiscal Office State of La., 1985; ptnr. Robert E. Hill, Atty. at Law, Baton Rouge, 1984; asst. sec. worker compensation Dept. Labor State of La., Baton Rouge, 1986-88, mem. 2d inquiry bd., %. Mem. So. U. found., Baton Rouge, 1986; bd. dirs., legal counselor Benefit Soc. Nat. Bapt. Conv., U.S.A., Inc., 1986; advisor Boy Scouts Am., Baton Rouge, 1985-86. Served with U.S. Army, 1969-71. Recipient Community Service in Govt. award Baton Rouge Examiner Newspaper, 1984; named one of Outstanding Young Men Am., 1980. Mem. ABA, La. State Bar Assn., Assn. Trial Lawyers Am., Nat. Inst. for Trial Advocacy, Nat. Jud. Coll., Nat. Assn. Securities Dealers (cert.), NAACP, Kettering Found., Nat. Issues Forum. Democrat. Baptist. Lodge: Kiwanis. Home: 2421 Guilford Dr Baton Rouge LA 70808

HILL, ROBYN LESLEY, artist, designer; b. Sydney, Australia, Apr. 28, 1942; d. Frank Bragg and Florence Margorie (Turnham) H. Grad., Nat. Art Sch., Sydney, 1962; studies with Edward Betts, Claude Croney, Fred Leach, Maxine Masterfield, 1969-85. Art mistress S.C.E.G.G.S., Sydney, 1963-66; art dir. Am. Greetings, Cleve., 1967-78; sr. program dir. Those Characters From Cleve., 1978-88. Creative, designer (TV program) The Special Magic of Herself the Elf (Can. Emmy award 1982). Mem. Nat. Watercolor Soc. (signature), Nat. Watercolor USA Hon. Soc. (award Springfield Art Mus. 1984, signature), Ohio Watercolor Soc. (So. Ohio Bank award 1983, signature), North Coast Collage Soc., Ky. Watercolor Soc. Episcopalian. Home: 2812 Wooster Rd Rocky Road OH 44116 Office: Those Characters from Cleve 8800 E Pleasant Valley Rd Cleveland OH 44131

HILL, SARA LYNN, architectural company executive, artist, architectural delineator; b. Montclair, N.J., May 25, 1951; d. Lawrence and Mary (Allanson) H.; m. William James Van Cleve., Jr. B.Arch. cum laude, Tulane U., 1974; B.F.A. magna cum laude, Newcomb Coll., 1974. Lic. architect, contractor, La. Archtl. designer J. Buchanan Blitch & Assocs., Architects, New Orleans, La., 1975-76; archtl. cons. F. Monroe Labouisse, Jr., Architect, New Orleans, 1976-79; staff architect, plans examiner Vieux Carre Commn., New Orleans, 1979; ptnr. V.C. Builders, Gen. Contractors, New Orleans, 1980—; sole propr. Hill Co., Architects, New Orleans, 1979—; v.p. Robin Riley & Assocs., Architects, New Orleans, 1981-84; designer, project architect S. Stewart Farnet, AIA, Architect & Assoc., Inc., 1984—; founding mem., sec. Art-Op Coop., New Orleans, 1975; agt. Tulane U. Alumni Assn., New Orleans, 1975—. Illustrator: New Orleans Home Care Handbook, 1978; Great Louisiana Recipes, 1977; Razing the Roofs, 1978. Co-editor, founder Marsharch Jour., 1973-74. Mem. Preservation Resource Ctr., New Orleans, Friends of the Cabildo, New Orleans, 1978—, Contemporary Arts Ctr., New Orleans, 1977—. John W. Lawrence fellow Tulane U., 1973, Dorothy Lubbe Dunkerley fellow Tulane U., 1972; recipient 2d place award Reynolds Aluminum Corp., 1973, 1914 prize in Art Newcomb Coll., 1974. Mem. AIA (medal, cert. 1974), Nat. Trust for Historic Preservation, Constrn. Specifications Inst., Urban Land Inst., Internat. Platform Assn., Tulane U. Alumni Assn. (bd. dirs. 1977-82). Methodist. Clubs: So. Yacht, Corinthian Sail (New Orleans). Office: S Stewart Farnet AIA and Assocs Architects 2331 St Claude Ave New Orleans LA 70117

HILL, SUSAN SLOAN, safety engineer; b. Quincy, Mass., June 1, 1952; d. Ralph Arnold and Grace Elenore (Sloan) Crosby; m. William Loyd Hill, Dec. 16, 1973 (div. July 1982); m. William Joseph Graham, Sept. 10, 1983 (div. Feb. 1985). Assoc. Sci. in Gen. Engring., Motlow State Community Coll., Tullahoma, Tenn., 1976; BS in Indsl. Engring., Tenn. Technol. U., 1978. Intern, safety engr. Intern Tng. Ctr., U.S. Army, Red River Army Depot, Tex., 1978-79, Field Safety Activity, Charlestown, Ind., 1979, system safety engr. Communications-Electronics Command, Ft. Monmouth, N.J., 1979-84, gen. engr., 1984-85; chief system safety Arnold Air Force Sta., USAF, Tullahoma, 1984; system safety engr. U.S. Army Safety Ctr., Ft. Rucker, Ala., 1985—. Recipient 5 letters of appreciation U.S. Army, 1982. Mem. Assn. Fed. Safety and Health Profls. (regional v.p. 1980-84), Soc. Women Engrs., Nat. Safety Mgmt. Soc., Am. Soc. Safety Engrs., System Safety Soc., Nat. Assn. Female Execs., Order Engr. Republican. Episcopalian. Avocations: bowling, needlework, sewing, cooking, golf. Home: 115 Liveoak Dr Enterprise AL 36330 Office: US Army Safety Ctr Attn CSSC-SE Fort Rucker AL 36362

HILL, THOMAS WILLIAM, JR., lawyer; b. N.Y.C., Dec. 25, 1924; s. Thomas William Sr. and Marion (Bond) H.; m. Elizabeth Rowe, June 18, 1949; children: Gretchen P., Catharine B., Thomas William III. BS, U. Pa., 1948; MBA, NYU, 1950; JD, Columbia U., 1953. Bar: N.Y. 1953; CPA, N.Y. Sr. tax acct. Hurdman & Cranstoun, 1949-50; asst. U.S. atty. So. Dist. N.Y., 1953-54; assoc. Cahill, Gordon, Reindel & Ohl, 1954-58; sr. ptnr. Spear & Hill, 1958-75; ptnr. Sidley & Austin, 1981-86; pres. Belco Petroleum Co., N.Y.C., 1962-63; legal adviser Sultanate of Oman, 1972-76; adj. prof. law U. Miami, 1986—. Contbr. articles to profl. jours. Pres., trustee Internat. Coll., Beirut, Lebanon, 1978—. Served as 1st lt. AUS, 1943-46. Decorated Bronze Star, Purple Heart, Medal of Oman (Sultanate of Oman), Order of Homayun (Iran). Mem. ABA, Assn. Bar City of N.Y., Am. Inst. CPA's, N.Y. State Soc. CPA's, Phi Delta Phi, Kappa Sigma. Clubs: Racquet and Tennis (N.Y.C.); Winged Foot Golf; Woburn Golf (Eng.); Dubai Golf (United Arab Emirates); Palm Beach Polo and Country. Home: 2627 Muirfield Ct West Palm Beach FL 33414 Office: Sidley & Austin 520 Madison Ave New York NY

HILL, WILLIAM FRANK, university dean; b. Weston-super-Mare, Eng., Aug. 10, 1942; s. William Charles and Irene Brenda (Channing) H. B.Arch., U. Bristol, Eng., 1965. Asst. lectr. Ahmadu Bello U., Zaria, Nigeria, 1965-68; asst. architect R.J. Cole Friba, Camberley, Eng., 1968-70; lectr. U. Sci. & Tech., Kumasi, Ghana, 1970-77, sr. lectr., 1977-84, head dept. architecture, 1983-84; sr. lectr. Sch. Environ. Studies Copperbelt U., Kitwe, Zambia, 1984, head dept. architecture and bldg. sci., 1985-87, dean Sch. Environ. Studies, 1987—. Mem. Royal Inst. Brit. Architects. Mem. Ch. of Eng. Home: 4873 Kariba Rd, Kitwe Zambia Office: The Copperbelt U, Jambo Dr, Kitwe Zambia

HILLABRANDT, LARRY LEE, service industry executive; b. Amsterdam, N.Y., Apr. 5, 1947; s. Ronald Edward and Marion Alice (Smith) H.; B.S., Purdue U., 1969, M.S., 1971; m. Beverly Ann Johnson, Jan. 25, 1969; 1 son, Larry Lee. With Mobil Chem. Co., various locations, 1971-84, fin. analyst, Jacksonville, Ill., 1973, sr. systems analyst Macedon, N.Y., 1973-74, fin. analyst, 1974, plant controller, Frankfort, Ill., 1974-77, distbn. supt. NE region, Macedon, 1979-80, div. gen. mgr., Belleville, Ont., Can., 1980-84; bus./fin. mgr. George Heisel Corp., Rochester, N.Y., 1984-85; pres. ZIP Computer Systems, 1985—; owner, mgr. Datemate, 1985—. Mem. Purdue Alumni Assn., Krannert Grad. Sch. Alumni Assn., Mendon Community Orgn. (treas.), Scot-Grove Conservation Club, Zeta Psi Alumni Assn. Club: Lima Gun (bd. dirs.). Home: 53 Stoney Lonesome Rd Honeoye Falls NY 14472

HILLARY, EDMUND PERCIVAL, diplomat, explorer, bee farmer; b. Auckland, N.Z., July 20, 1919; s. Percy and Gertrude H.; ed. U. Auckland; LL.D. (hon.), Victoria U., B.C., Can., U. Victoria, (New Zealand); m. Louise Mary Rose, 1953 (dec. 1975); 1 son, 2 daus. (1 dec.). Bee farmer; dir. Field Ednl. Enterprises of Australasia Pty. Ltd.; went to Himalayas on N.Z. Garwhal expdn., 1951, with Brit. expdn. to Cho Oyu, 1952, Brit. Mt. Everest Expdn. under Sir John Hunst, 1953; leader N.S. Alpine Club Expdn. to Barun Valley, 1954, N.Z. Antarctic Expdn., 1956-58; reached South Pole, 1957; leader Himalayan Expdns., 1961, 63, 64; leader climbing expdn. on Mt. Herschel, Antarctica, 1967, River Ganges Expdn., 1977; built hosp. for Sherpa tribesmen, Nepal, 1966; high commr. to India, also accredited to Bangladesh, Bhutan and Nepal, 1985—. Served with Royal N.Z. Air Force, 1944-45; PTO. Decorated Gurkha Right Hand 1st Class; Star of Nepal 1st Class; recipient Cullum Geog. medal, 1954; Hubbard medal, 1954; Polar medal, 1958; Founders Gold medal Royal Geog. Soc., 1958; James Wattle Book of Yr. award N.Z., 1975. Author: High Adventure, 1955; (with Sir Vivian Fuchs) The Crossing of Antarctica, 1958, No Latitude for Error, 1961; (with Desmond Doig) High in the Thin Cold Air, 1963, Schoolhouse in the Clouds, 1965, Nothing Venture, Nothing Win, 1975, From the Ocean to the Sky, 1978. Office: High Commn of New Zealand, 25 Golf Links, New Delhi 110003, India *

HILLBRUNER, ANTHONY, educator, scholar, critic; b. Chgo., Feb. 10, 1914; s. Walter and Hedwig (Senk) H.; m. Laura Zino, Nov. 26, 1942; children—Anthony James, Tina Laurie. B.S., Northwestern U., 1949, M.A., 1950, Ph.D., 1953. Inst. U. Denver, 1950-51, U. Oreg., 1951-52, Stanford U., 1952-54; mem. faculty Calif. State U., Los Angeles, 1954—; now prof. rhetoric emeritus and Am. studies, dir. Am. studies program Calif. State U., 1954-69; vis. prof. Whittier Coll., 1962, Pa. State U., 1963; cons. Los Angeles County Execs., 1965-70, univ. presses, 1979—; vis. scholar U. Cambridge, Eng., 1972, U. Oxford, Eng., 1979. Author: Critical Dimensions, 1966; Contbr. articles to profl. jours., chpts. to books. Grantee Calif. State U. Found., 1965. Mem. Am. Studies Assn., Speech Communication Assn., Western Speech Communication Assn. (Disting. Service award 1981), Center Study Democratic Instns. Home: 407 N Mission Dr San Gabriel CA 91775 Office: 5151 State College Dr Calif State U Los Angeles CA 90032

HILLEMAND, BERNARD JEAN PIERRE HIPPOLYTE, medical educator; b. Paris, Aug. 22, 1923; s. Pierre and Françoise (Durand) H.; m. Monique Antoinette Janine Philbert, Jan. 31, 1959. Grad., Faculté des Scis., Paris, 1941-42; postgrad. in medicine, Faculté de Medicine, Paris, 1942-48. Externe des Hôpitaux de Paris Assistance Publique de Paris, 1946-51, interne des Hôpitaux de Paris, 1951-55, medicin asst. des Hçpitaux de Paris, 1959-66; dr. en médecine Faculté de Médecine de Paris, 1955, chef med. clinique, 1956-59; maître de Conf. Agrégé Médecin des Hôpitaux, U. de Médecine et de Pharmacie, Rouen, France, 1966—; chef de service hospitalier U. Rouen de Médecine et de Pharmacie, 1969—, prof. sans chaire, 1971—, prof. titulaire à titre personnel en thérapeutique, 1974—; médecin chef de service de Médecine Interne et Pathologie Digestive Hotel-Dieu, Rouen; expert permanent, mem. du haut com. d'Etude et d'Info. sur l'Alcoolisme, 1975—; conseiller Départemental du Conseil de l'Ordre des Médecins de Seine Maritime; rédacteur, chef de la Revue de l'Alcoolisme, 1983—; participant various coms. Contbr. articles to profl. jours. Served with med. aux. French Army, 1945, ETO. Named Officier des Palmes Académiques. Mem. Soc. Nat. Française de Gastroentérologie, Soc. Nat. Française de Proctologie, Soc. Nat. Française d'Allergologie, Soc. Med. des Hôpitaux de Paris (corr.), Soc. Royale Belge de Gastro-entérologie (corr.), Soc. de Gastro-entérologie de l'Ouest, Soc. Italiana di Gastroenterologia (corr.), Soc. Espanòle de Pathologia Digestiva, Assn. Française d'Hépatologie, Soc. Française d'Alcoologie (co-fondateur), Acad. Nat. Médecine (corr.), European Soc. For Biomed. Research on Alcoholism. Roman Catholic. Lodge: Rotary (past pres. Rouen-Bruyeres). Office: Hotel Dieu de Rouen, rue Lecat, 76000 Rouen France

HILLENMEYER, JACQUES HENRI, business executive; b. Nimes, France, July 19, 1946; s. Henri and Henriette (Le Normand) H.; m. Agnes Ferrin, July 23, 1977; 1 child, Alexandra. Superior degree, Ecole Francaise Commerce de Detail, Nantes, 1968, Inst. Adminstn. Enterprises, Nantes, 1976; Engr., Bur. des. Temp Elémentaires, Paris, 1977. Chief regional sales SA Fregecreme, Herblain, France, 1969-74; dir. SA DISPA, Nantes, 1977; mem. engring. council Bur. des Temp El'46mentaires, Nantes, 1977-78; dirs. cons. CADES Mgmt., Bouaye, France, 1978—; dir. gen. Group del Govt Safi Guyomarc'h, Vannes, France, 1985-86; ins. broker Mutuelles du Mans, 1988—; prof. mktg. Ecole Techniciens du Commerce, St. Nazaire, France, 1980-82; in charge assignment U. Nantes, 1982-85. Author: La Pratique en Management, 1981; contbr. econ. articles to mag. Mem. Institut Econ. Paris. Home: Allee de le Roseraie, Domaine de la Noe, 44830 Bouaye Pays de Loire France Office: 20 Rue Carnot, PO Box 9, 9290 Chalonnes SIL France 40 326466

HILLER, WILLIAM ARLINGTON, agricultural executive; b. East Stroudsburg, Pa., Jan. 15, 1928; s. John Jacob and Marguerite Laura H.; m. Joan Drake, June 2, 1947; children: William A., Joel, Jay S. BS cum laude, Upper Iowa U., 1950; MS, Pa. State U., 1952. Mgmt. trainee Agway Inc., Lakewood, N.J., 1951-53, retail store mgr., 1953-71; v.p. corp. mktg. Agway Inc., Syracuse, N.Y., 1971-73, group v.p., 1973-79, asst. gen. mgr., 1979-81, pres., chief exec. officer, 1981—; chmn. Texas City (Tex.) Refining Inc., also bd. dirs.; chmn. bd. Agway Ins. Co.; vice chmn., bd. dirs. Nat. Council Farmer Coops; bd. dirs. Syracuse Research Corp., Chase-Lincoln First Bank, Rochester; corp. adv. council Syracuse U. Sch. Mgmt. Trustee Crouse-Irving Meml. Hosp., Syracuse; trustee Upper Iowa U., Fayette; pres. Hiawatha Council Boy Scouts Am., Syracuse; mem. adv. council Cornell Coll. Agrl. and Life Scis; mem. FFA Sponsors' Adv. Bd.; nat. v.p. admnstrn. Boy Scouts Am. Recipient Silver Beaver award Boy Scouts Am., 1981, Silver Antelope award, Distinguished Citizen award. Mem. Alpha Zeta. *

HILLERY, MARY JANE LARATO, editor, columnist, reserve army officer; b. Boston, Sept. 15, 1931; d. Donato and Porzia (Avellis) Larato; Asso. Sci. (scholar), Northeastern U., 1950; BS, U. Mass. Harvard Extension, 1962; m. Thomas H. Hillery, Feb. 25, 1961; 1 son, Thomas H. Sales agt., linguist Pan Am. Airways, Boston, 1955-61; interpreter Internat. Conf. Fire Chiefs, Boston, 1966; tchr. Spanish, YWCA, Natick, Mass., 1966-67; community relations cons., adv. bd. dirs., lectr. for migrant edn. project div. Mass. Dept. Community Affairs, Boston, 1967-69; editor-in-chief Sudbury (Mass.) Citizen, 1967-76; assoc. editor The Beacon, 1976-79, contbg. editor, 1979-83 ; area editorial adviser Beacon Pub. Co., Acton, Mass., 1970-80, editor, 1976-80; columnist Town Crier, 1987—; contbg. editor Towne Talk, 1975-79, Citizens' Forum, 1975-81; dir. public affairs Mass. Dept. Environ. Quality Engring., 1981-83. Mem. Bus. Adv. Com., 1972-77, Sudbury Sch. Com., 1976-77; mem. Meml. Day Celebration Com., 1972—, master of ceremonies, 1973-88, paradè marshal, 1973-75, 82, 84, chmn., 1973-74. Bd. dirs., incorporator Sudbury Nonprofit Housing Corp., 1973-74; mem. Sudbury Town Report, 1967-72, 85-88, chmn., 1969-72; panelist Internat. Women's Year Symposium, 1975, Women in Politics, 1987, Women In Mil., 1987; columnist Town Crier, 1987—. Served with USN, 1950-54; lt. col. USAR; liaison officer U.S. Mil. Acad., 1976—; pub. affairs officer 94th USAR Command, 1982-83(meritorious service medal 1985); mem. Congl. Nominating bd. USMA, 1985—; editor Hansconian, 1983-85. Decorated Meritorious Service medal. Named Editor of Year, Beacon Pub. Co., 1970; recipient medal of appreciation Internat. Order DeMolay, 1969, certificates of appreciation U.S. Def. Civil Preparedness Agency, 1975, Mass. Bicentennial Commn., 1976, Res. Officers Assn., 1986; citations Mass. State Senate, 1979, 82; Newswriting award Media Contest, Air Force Systems Command, 1984. Mem. Nat. Editorial Assn., Nat. Newspaper Assn., New Eng. Press Assn., Bus. and Profl. Women's Club (1st v.p. 1973-74, pres. 1974-76, parliamentarian 1978-88, state bylaws com. 1977-78, 79-81, 1986-88, state legis. chmn. 1979-81, 86-88, State Polit. Action Com. Chmn., 1988-89, Woman of Yr. 1979, Woman of Achievement 1982), LWV (dir. 1964-68), Nat. League Am. Pen Women (exec. bd. Boston 1974-76, 78-88, pres. 1976-78, publicity chmn. 1979-80, chmn. bylaws com. 1979-80, 86-88, parliamentarian 1978-80, 82-88, auditor 1980-82, 84-88), Res. Officers Assn. (life; state sec. 1978-79, pres. Boston chpt. 1986-88, army council rep. 1989—; Outstanding Service award 1978-79), Omega Sigma. Home: 66 Willow Rd Sudbury MA 01776

HILLERY, PATRICK JOHN, president of Ireland; b. Miltown-Malbay, Ireland, May 2, 1923; s. Michael Joseph and Ellen (McMahon) H.; ed. Rockwell Coll., Cashel and Univ. Coll., Dublin; BSc, 1943; MB, BCh, BAO, 1947; DPH with honors, 1952; LLD (hon.), Nat. U. Ireland, 1962, U. Dublin, 1977, U. Melbourne, 1985, Pontifical U. Maynooth, 1988; m. Mary Beatrice Finnegan, Oct. 27, 1955; 1 child, John. Mem. Health Council, Ireland, 1955-57; med. officer Miltown-Malbay, Ireland, 1957-59; coroner, West Clare, Ireland, 1958-59; minister for edn. Govt. of Ireland, 1959-65, minister for industry and commerce, 1965-66, minister for labour, 1966-69, minister fgn. affairs, 1969-72; v.p. Commn. European Communities, Brussels, 1973-76; pres. Ireland, 1976—. Fellow Royal Coll. Surgeons Ireland (hon.), All-India Inst. Med. Scis. (hon.), Royal Coll. Gen. Practitioners (hon.), Royal Coll. Physicians Ireland (hon.), Pharm. Soc. Ireland; mem. Royal Irish Acad., Irish Med. Assn. (hon. life). Office: Áras an Uachtaráin, Phoenix Park, Dublin 8, Ireland

HILLION, PIERRE THÉODORE MARIE, mathematical physicist; b. Saint-Brieuc, France, Jan. 31, 1926; s. Pierre Auguste Alexandre and Olive Jane (Marion) H.; Licencié es Sciences, Engineer Ecole Supérieure d'Electricité, 1950, Docteur es Sciences, 1957; m. Jane Garde, July 9, 1955; children—Catherine, Pierre, Joëlle, Hervé . Engr., Le Matériel Electrique Schneider-Westinghouse, 1950-55; math. physicist Section Technique de L'Armée, 1955-64; head math. phys. dept. Laboratoire Central de L'Armement, 1964-83; sci. cons. Centre D'Analyse de De'fense, 1983—; maitre de conferences Ecole Nationale Supérieure des Techniques Avancées, 1976—. Mem. du bureau Assocation de Parents d'É lèves, 1965-76. Served with French Army, 1950. Recipient Mérite pour la Recherche et l'Invention, 1965; Palmes Académiques, 1970; Ordre National pour le Mérite, 1978, Legion d'Honneur, 1988. Mem. Societé Mathématique de France, Societé Française de Radioprotection, Syndicat de la Presse Scientifique, Internat. Assn. Math. Physics. Roman Catholic. Contbr. articles on high energy physics, math. physics and numerical analysis to profl. jours. Home: 86 bis Route de Croissy, 78110 Le Vesinet Yvelines France Office: 16 bis Prieur de la Cote d'or Arcueil, 94114 Val de Marne France

HILLIS, RANDOLPH DALES, mfrs. agent; b. Hobart, N.Y., Jan. 31, 1907; s. Frederick Wager and Lydia (Dales) H.; ed. U. Ill., 1930; m. Virginia Pearl Rankin, Nov. 25, 1932 (dec. Feb. 1981). With load bldg. sales Asso. Gas & Electric, 1928-32; sta. mgr. Mobile Oil, 1932-35; div. sales Am. Seating Co., 1935-39; final assembly mechanic Brewster Aircraft-Bell Aircraft, 1939-41; civil exptl. flight test technician U.S. Army Air Force, Wright-Patterson Field, Ohio, 1941-42; exptl. technician Curtiss Wright, Columbus, Ohio, 1942-45; record systems Diebold Inc., 1945-47; vending sales NEHI Corp., Columbus, Ga., 1949-55; prodn. engr. div. Sperry Rand, Cobleskill, N.Y., 1957-61; pres. Tinkertown, Inc., Hobart, N.Y., 1966—; chmn. engring. adv. com. N.Y. State U., Delhi, 1968-78. Mem. Bldg. Industries Employees, Gen. Bldg. Contractors, Constrn. Specifications Inst. (emeritus), Am. Def. Preparedness Assn., N.Y. State Bus. Council. Episcopalian. Lodges: Elks, Masons, Shriners. Home: W Main St Hobart NY 13788

HILLMAN, ARYE LEO, economics educator; b. Bad Verishofen, Fed. Republic Germany, Jan. 13, 1947; s. Sol and Rosa (Borenstein) H.; m. Jeannette Mann, Mar. 12, 1967; children: Tamara, Ilana, Nachman Eliyahu, Benjamin. BA with honors, U. Newcastle, Australia, 1967; M in Econs. with honors, Macquarie U., Sydney, Australia, 1970; PhD, U. Pa., 1973. Lectr. econs. Tel Aviv U., 1974-79; prof. econs. Bar-Ilan U., Ramat Gan, Israel, 1980—; vis. fellow Australian Nat. U., Canberra, 1979; vis. prof. dept. econs. UCLA, 1985-87; cons. Ctr. for Policy Studies, Melbourne, Australia, 1982-85, World Bank, Washington, 1987. Author: The Political Economy of Protection, 1988; contbr. articles to numerous profl. jours. Mem. Am. Econ. Assn., Western Econ. Assn., Econometric Soc., Pub. Choice Soc. Jewish. Home: Ha'Arava 5, Ra'anana 43575, Israel Office: Bar-Ilan U, Ramat Gan 52100, Israel

HILLMAN, GORDON CHARLES, archaeology educator; b. Hailsham, Eng., July 29, 1943; s. Albert William and Annie Joyce (Connett) H.; m. Wendy Ursula MacIness, May 1974 (div. 1977); children: Thilaka, Emma, Wendy. ScB in Agrl. Botany, U. Reading (Eng.), 1969; postgrad., U. Mainz (Fed. Republic Germany), 1969-70. Asst. sci. officer Nature Conservancy Council Alston Moor Nature Reserve, Cumbria, Eng., 1961; asst. sci. officer dept. botany Brit. Mus. Natural History, London, 1961-65; research fellow Brit. Inst. Archeology, Ankara, Turkey, 1970-75; lectr. botany dept. plant sci. U. Coll. Cardiff (Wales), 1975-81; lectr. archeobotany Inst. Archeology U. Coll. London, 1981—; cons. archeobotanist Welsh Archeol. Trusts, Wales, 1975-81. Author: (with others) Abu Hureyra..., 1988; editor: Foraging and Farming..., 1988; contbr. articles to profl. jours. Sci. Engring Research Council grantee, 1983-85. Mem. Assn. Environ. Archeology. Liberal. Home: 5A Ersham Rd, Hailsham East Sussex BN27 3LG, England Office: U Coll Inst Archaeology, 31-34 Gordon Sq, London WC1H OPX, England

HILLMAN, MELVILLE ERNEST DOUGLAS, chemist; b. Winnipeg, Man., Can., Aug. 3, 1926; came to U.S., 1954, naturalized, 1976; s. Frank Ernest and Elizabeth (Grindlay) H.; m. Linda Lou Brown, Dec. 21, 1985. B.A. with honors, U. B.C., 1952, M.Sc., 1954; Ph.D., Ohio State U.,

1958. Research chemist E.I. DuPont de Nemours & Co., Wilmington, Del., 1958-61, Chevron Research, Richmond, Calif., 1961-64; research supr. W.R. Grace Co., Columbia, Md., 1964-68; group leader Celanese Research Co., Summit, N.J., 1968-71; program leader Ethicon, Inc., Somerville, N.J., 1971-73; prin. research scientist Battelle Columbus Labs., Ohio, 1973-75, sr. research scientist, 1975-79, research leader, 1979—; cons. in field. Contbr. articles to profl. jours.; patentee in field. Fellow Socony-Mobil, 1955-56; fellow Lubrizol, 1956-57, DuPont, 1957-58. Mem. Am. Chem. Soc., N.Y. Acad. Scis., N.Y. Catalyst Soc., Sigma Xi, Phi Lambda Upsilon. Home: 3317 Darbyshire Dr Columbus OH 43026 Office: Battelle Columbus Labs 505 King Ave Columbus OH 43026

HILLMAN, STANLEY ERIC GORDON, former corporate executive; b. London, Eng., Oct. 13, 1911; came to U.S., 1951, naturalized, 1957; s. Percy Thomas and Margaret Eleanor Fanny (Lee) H.; m. May Irene Noon, May 2, 1947; children: Susan, Deborah, Katherine. Educated pub. schs., Eng. With Brit.-Am. Tobacco Co., Ltd., London, Shanghai, 1933-47; dir. Hillman & Co., Ltd., Cosmos Trading Co., FED Inc., U.S.A., Airmotive Supplies Co. Ltd., Hong Kong, 1947-52; v.p. Gen. Dynamics Corp., 1953-61; v.p., group exec. Am. Machine & Foundry Co., N.Y.C., 1962-65; v.p., dir. Gen. Am. Transp. Corp., 1965-67; pres., vice chmn., dir. IC Industries, 1968-78; bankruptcy trustee Chgo., Milw., St. Paul & Pacific R.R., 1978-79; dir. Bandag Corp., Conrail Corp., Axla Corp. Clubs: Chgo., Mid Am.; Onwentsia (Lake Forest, Ill.); Royal Poinciana. Home: 414 Thorne Ln Lake Forest IL 60045

HILTON, GREGORY STEVEN, credit manager; b. Haleyville, Ala., Oct. 20, 1956; s. Lester E. and Luvena (Pickard) H.; m. Tracy Wells, Sept. 4, 1982. A in Sci., Walker Coll., 1976; BS in Bus. Adminstrn., Samford U., 1980. Sales rep. Life of Va., Birmingham, Ala., 1980-81; regional credit mgr. Baker Bros., Inc., Birmingham, Ala., 1981-86, corp. credit mgr., 1986—. Named one of Outstanding Young Men Am., 1985. Mem. Nat. Inst. Credit (assoc.), Nat. Assn. Credit Mgmt., Internat. Platform Assn., Fla. Credit Council. Republican. Baptist. Home: 11640 Cape Horn Ave Jacksonville FL 32216 Office: Baker Bros Inc 7892 Baymeadows Way Jacksonville FL 32216

HILTON, ROBERT LEROY, insurance company executive; b. Chgo., July 30, 1928; s. Harold and Myrtle E. (Osgood) H.; m. Patricia Ann Robertson, Apr. 22, 1950; children—Michael, Lee Ann Carrol, Sandra R. Brown. Student S.E. Mo. State U., 1946-49, Washington U., St. Louis, 1949-50. Insp. Nat. Council on Compensation Ins., St. Louis, 1949-53, mgr., Salt Lake City, 1953-56, Des Moines, 1956-62; v.p., Birmingham, Ala., 1962-83, sr. v.p., N.Y.C., 1983—; chmn. employees stock ownership plan Statesman Group, Des Moines, 1976—. Pres. Ladies Profl. Golf Assn. Sponsors Assn., 1977, Birmingham Golf Assn., 1976, Dixie Golf Course Rating and Handicap Assn., 1979, Mt. Brook High Sch. Athletic Assn., 1975. Served with USAF, 1951-53. Named to Hall of Fame, Birmingham Golf Assn., 1976. Clubs: Green Valley Country (pres. 1971), Apple Ridge Country, Boca Woods Country, N.Y. Athletic.

HILTON, ROBERT PARKER, SR., national security affairs consultant, retired naval officer; b. Atlanta, Mar. 17, 1927; s. William Linwood and Elizabeth Shumate (Parker) H.; m. Joan Maxine Mader, Sept. 3, 1955; children: Robert Parker, Wendy Hilton-Jones. B.A., U. Miss., 1948; M.A. in Russian Affairs, Georgetown U., 1964; postgrad., Sino-Soviet Inst. George Washington U., 1964-68. Commd. ensign U.S. Navy, 1948, advanced through grades to rear adm., 1972; service in all operational fleets in cruisers/destroyers, and in Korea, Japan, Vietnam, Italy, Belgium; asst. chief staff logistics CINCSOUTH, Naples, Italy, 1972-74; dep. dir. force devel. and strategic plans Office Joint Chiefs Staff, 1974-76; dir. East Asia and Pacific region Office Sec. Def., Washington, 1976-77; dir. Strategy plans and policy div. OPNAV (OP60), 1977-78; asst. dep. CNO, Plans and Policy, 1979; dep. asst. chief staff Plans and Policy SHAPE, 1979-81; vice dir. ops. Office Joint Chiefs Staff, 1981-83; retired USN, 1983; cons. nat. security affairs 1983—; cons. nat. security and def. matters IDA, 1984—. Decorated Legion of Merit, Bronze Star, Joint Service Commendation medal. Mem. U.S. Naval Inst., Nat. Trust Historic Preservation, Assn. Polit. Risk Analysts, Pi Sigma Alpha, Pi Kappa Phi, Phi Delta Theta. Episcopalian. Clubs: Masons, Army Navy Country. Home: 3628 Orlando Pl Alexandria VA 22305

HIMEL, CHESTER MORA, entomologist, educator; b. Des Plaines, Ill., Mar. 10, 1916; s. Charles Maurice and Mary Eleanor (Mora) H.; m. Ann Walter, June 21, 1943; children: Barbara Holly Himel Pietrowski, Shelley Jeanne Himel Scharnberg. B.S. in Chemistry, U. Chgo., 1938; Ph.D. in Organic Chemistry, U. Ill., 1942. Research chemist E.I. duPont de Nemours & Co., Wilmington, Del., 1942-43, Allied Chem. Co., N.Y.C., 1943-44; research group leader Phillips Petroleum Co., Bartlesville, Okla., 1944-49; sr. organic chemist, dir. organic research div. Stanford Research Inst., 1949-65; research prof. entomology U. Ga., Athens, 1965-85; prof. emeritus U. Ga., 1985—; chmn. bd. Environ. Chem. Co., 1979—, Spray Control Systems, 1984—; indsl. cons. Intra-Sci. Contbr. articles to sci. jours., chpt. in book. Research Found. fellow, 1968—; grantee NIH, Office Naval Research, Dept. Agr., EPA, Army Med. Research and Devel. Command. Mem. Entomol. Soc. Am., Am. Chem. Soc., AAAS, Ga. Entomol. Soc., Sigma Xi, Gamma Sigma Delta. Episcopalian. Home: 2005 East View Dr Sun City Center FL 33570 Office: Spray Control Systems 1020 Industrial Dr Watkinsville GA 30677

HIMELSTEIN, MANDEL EDWIN, lawyer; b. Ft. Wayne, Ind., Jan. 4, 1933; s. Max Alexander and Rose (Kaufman) H.; m. Judith Carol Benjamin, Nov. 6, 1955; children—Scott B., Lisa K., Linda B. B.S., Northwestern U., 1954, J.D., 1959. Bar: Ill. 1959, Ariz. 1964, U.S. Dist. Ct. (no. dist.) Ill. 1960, U.S. Dist. Ct. Ariz. 1964, U.S. Supreme Ct. 1972. Assoc. Zlatnick, Gaines & Boyer, Chgo., 1959-63; assoc. Dushoff & Sacks, Phoenix, 1963-64; sole practice, Phoenix, 1964-70; ptnr. Himelstein & Timbanard and predecessor Johnson, Himelstein & Timbanard, Phoenix, 1970-74; sole practice, Phoenix, 1974-80; ptnr. Himelstein & Aquilar, Phoenix, 1980-82; prin. Mandel E. Himelstein, P.C., 1983—. Pres. Nat. Council on Alcoholism, 1970-72; mem. Phoenix Mayor's Com. on Cable TV, 1974; chmn. sch. bd. Temple Beth Israel, Phoenix; bd. dirs. Phoenix Jewish Community Ctr., Ariz. Sr. Olympics; mem. Ariz. Acad. Town Hall. Served to sgt. U.S. Army, 1954-56. Mem. ABA, Ill. Bar Assn., Chgo. Bar Assn., Lawyer-Pilots Bar Assn., Ariz. Bar Found., Ariz. Bar Assn., Maricopa County Bar Assn., Am. Judicature Soc., Internat. Assn. Jewish Lawyers and Jurists, Phi Delta Phi. Democrat. Legal columnist Ariz. Apt. News, 1968-75. Office: 5125 N 16th Std St B 223 Phoenix AZ 85016 also: 1001 B St #317 Coronado CA 92118

HIMMELHEBER, GEORG, art historian; b. Karlsruhe, Baden, Fed. Republic of Germany, Aug. 4, 1929; s. Bernhard and Kathinka (Herrmann) H.; m. Irmtraud Schmidt, June 30, 1955; children: Liat, Wendelin, Judith. PhD, U. Freiburg, 1954. Conservator Staatliches Amt für Denkmalpflege, Stuttgart, 1956-61, Badisches Landesmuseum, Karlsruhe, Fed. Republic of Germany, 1961-65; chief conservator Bavarian Nat. Mus., Munich, 1966-73, vice dir., 1974-84, landeskonservator, 1985—. Author: Die Kunstdenkmäler des Oberamts Künzelsau, 1962, Der Ostchor des Augsburger Doms, 1963, Karlsruhe, Pforzheim, Baden-Baden, 1965, Spiele, Gesellschaftsspiele aus einem Jahrtausend, 1972, Die Kunst des deutschen Mobels, 1973, Biedermeier Furniture, 1974, Kleine Möbel, Modell-, Andachts-, und Kassettenmöbel, 1979; contbr. articles on furniture to jours. in field. Mem. Furniture History Soc. of London. Office: Bavaria Nat Mus, Prinzregentenstrasse 3, 8000 Munich Federal Republic of Germany

HIMSWORTH, HAROLD PERCIVAL, physician, researcher; b. May 19, 1905; M.D., U. London, also LL.D.; Dr. honoris causa, Toulouse; LL.D. (hon.), U. Glasgow, U. Wales; D.Sc. (hon.) U. Manchester, 1956, Leeds, 1968, U. W.I., 1968; Sc.D. (hon.), Cambridge U., 1964. Former prof. medicine U. London; former dir. med. unit Univ. Coll. Hosp. Med. Sch., London, 1939-49. Sec., Med. Research Council, 1949-68; chmn. bd. mgmt. London Sch. Hygiene and Tropical Medicine, 1969-76. Fellow Univ. Coll., London; decorated knight comdr. Bath. Fellow Royal Soc., Royal Coll. Physicians, Royal Coll. Radiologists (hon.), Royal Coll. Physicians Edinburgh (hon.), Royal Soc. Medicine (hon.), Royal Coll. Surgeons (hon.), Royal Coll. Pathologists; mem. Belgian Royal Acad. Medicine (hon.), Swedish (hon.), Norwegian med. socs., Am. Acad. Arts and Scis. (fgn. hon.), Royal Soc. Arts and Scis. Gothenburg, Am. Philos. Soc. (fgn. hon.), Assn. Am. Physicians (hon.). Author: The Development and Organisation of Scientific Knowledge and Philosophic Thought, 1970; also sci. and med. papers. Address: 13 Hamilton Terr, London NW8 9RE, England also: care Royal Soc, 6 Carlton House Terr, London SW1Y 5AG, England

HINCKLEY, ELMER DUMOND, psychologist; b. Margaretville, N.Y., Jan. 11, 1903; s. Elmer Lewis and Mary Louise (Sears) H.; A.B., U. Fla., 1924; Ph.D., U. Chgo., 1929; m. Martha Brown, Jan. 1, 1927. Diplomate clin. psychology Am. Bd. Examiners in Profl. Psychology. Statistician Merrill-Palmer Sch., Detroit, 1925-26; asst. prof., U. Fla., 1926-29, assoc. prof., 1929-30, prof., head psychology dept., 1930-57, prof. psychology, 1957-63, now emeritus; dir. Bur. Vocat. Guidance and Mental Hygiene, 1931-50, asso., 1950—; dir. (part-time) Fla. Merit Systems, 1936-44, cons., 1944-46, cons. Fla. Parole Commn., VA. Honored for founding 1st dept. psychology and 1st psychol. clinic in Fla. Fellow AAAS, Am. Psychol. Assn. (helped establish clin. div.); mem. Psychometric Soc., Psychol. Corp., Fla. Acad. Scis., Nat. Vocational Guidance Assn. (profl. mem.), AAUP, So. Soc. Philosophy and Psychology, Fla. Edn. Assn., Southeastern, Fla. (pres. 1948-49) psychol. assns., SAR, Blue Key, Phi Beta Kappa, Sigma Xi, Phi Kappa Phi, Pi Gamma Mu, Delta Tau Delta. Democrat. Methodist. Clubs: Masons, Rotary. Contbr. Jour. Soc. Psychology, Jour. Gen. Psychology, U. Fla. Press, U. Chgo. Press, Am. Jour. Psychology, others. Home: Box 12007 University Sta Gainesville FL 32604

HINDO, WALID AFRAM, radiology educator, oncologist; b. Baghdad, Iraq, Oct. 4, 1940; came to U.S. 1966, naturalized 1976; s. Afram Paul and Laila Farid (Meshaka) H.; m. Fawzia Hanna Batti, Apr. 20, 1965; children—Happy, Rana, Patricia, Heather, Brian. M.B., Baghdad U., 1964, Ch.B., 1964. Diplomate Am. Bd. Radiology. Instr. radiology Rush Med. Coll. Chgo., 1971-72; asst. prof. Northwestern U., Chgo., 1972-75; assoc. prof. medicine and radiology Chgo. Med. Sch., 1975-80, prof., chmn. dept. radiology, 1980—; cons. Ill. Cancer Council. Contbr. articles on cancer treatment to profl. jours. Bd. dirs. Lake County div. Am. Cancer Soc., Ill., 1975-80. Served to lt. M.C., Iraq; Army, 1965-66. Named Prof. of Yr., Chgo. Med. Sch., 1981, 82, 83, 85. Mem. Am. Coll. Radiology, Am. Soc. Acad. Radiologists, Am. Soc. Therapeutic Radiologists. Republican. Roman Catholic. Home: 2789 Greenwood Rd Northbrook IL 60062 Office: Univ of Health Scis Chgo Med Sch 3333 Greenbay Rd North Chicago IL 60064

HINDSØ, OLE, consulting company executive; b. Copenhagen, May 26, 1935; arrived in Sweden, 1946; s. Svend Martin and Tove (Christiansen) H.; m. Margareth Clary Ann Anderson, July 11, 1959; 1 child, Helena. Degree in chem. engring., High Tech. Coll., Malmö, Sweden, 1959; M in Bus., U. Lund, Sweden, 1974. Devel. mgr. Skanska, Bromöolla and Simrishamn, 1959-62; devel. mgr. Tetra Pak, Lund, 1963-64; prodn. mgr. Ericsson, Kristianstad, Sweden, 1965-68, Vouge/Nivella, Malmö, 1969-74; mng. dir. Hunt Sport AB, Örebro, Sweden, 1975-77, Interprint AB, Falun, Sweden, 1978-79, Wigéns AB, Tranås, Sweden, 1980-84, L.R. Konsult AB, Stockholm, 1984—. Lodges: Rotary (pres. 1983-84), Odd Fellows. Home: Åkergatan 3, Tranås S-57300, Sweden Office: L R Konsult AB, Klarabergsgatan 33, Stockholm S-10533, Sweden

HINE, HARRY MORRISON, Latin educator; b. Portsmouth, Eng., June 19, 1948; s. Frank and Cynthia Kathleen (Morrison) H.; m. Rosalind Mary Ford, Dec. 31, 1977; children: Catriona Joy, Jonathan Richard. MA, U. Oxford, Eng., 1973, PhD, 1976. Lectr. humanity U. Edinburgh, Scotland, 1975-85; Scotstarvit prof. U. St. Andrews, Scotland, 1985—. Author: An Edition with Commentary of Seneca Natural Questions Book Two, 1981; co-editor: Classical Rev. jour., 1987—. contbr. articles to profl. jours. Home: 33 Drumcarrow Rd, St Andrews, Fife KY16 8ER, Scotland Office: St Salvator's Coll Humanity Dept, St Andrews, Fife K16 9AL, Scotland

HINGSON, ROBERT ANDREW, physician, educator, inventor, farmer; b. Anniston, Ala., Apr. 13, 1913; s. Robert A. and Elloree Elizabeth (Haynes) H.; m. Gussie Dickson, Mar. 2, 1940; children: Dickson James, Andrew T., Roberta Ann, Ralph W., Luke L. AB, U. Ala., 1935, postgrad., 1933-35; MD, Emory U., 1938; LHD, Monrovia (Liberia) Coll., 1962; LLD, William Jewell Coll., 1963, Eastern Bapt. Coll., 1963; LittD (hon.), Hardin-Simmons U., 1965; DSc (hon.), Thomas Jefferson U. Medicine, 1970; LHD (hon.), U. Ala., 1970. Commd. med. officer USPHS, 1938, advanced through grades to surgeon, med. officer various ships USCG and USN, 1939-40; fellow anesthesiology Mayo Clinic USPHS, Rochester, Minn., 1940-41; chief of dept. anesthesia, U.S. Marine Hosp. USPHS, Staten Island, N.Y., 1941-42; dir. Lying-in Hosp., Jefferson Med. Coll., Phila. USPHS, 1943-45, dir., first prof. anesthesiology, U. Tenn., 1945-48; assoc. prof. obstetrics, anesthesiologist dept. obstetrics Johns Hopkins U., 1948-51; prof. anesthesia, founder dept. Case Western Res. U., 1951-68; prof. pub. health and anesthesiology, dir. anesthesiology Magee Women's Hosp. U. Pitts. Sch. Medicine, 1968-73; cons. U.S. VA Hosp., Sunny Acres Hosp., Highland View Hosp., Met. Hosp., St. Anne's Hosp.; sr. cons. Amigos de Honduras Med. Service Mission; vis. prof. at univs. in New Guinea, New Zealand, Australia, S. Am., Asia, Africa, Europe, 1958-80. Author: Control of Pain in Childbirth; co-author: Anesthesia for Obstetrics; co-editor: Pitkin's Conduction Anesthesia; contbr. articles to profl. jours., chpts. to books; developer clin. methods including hypospray, dermojet, Med-e-jet, continuous caudal and peridural analgesia; inventor. Trustee Religious Heritage Found., 1968; chmn. Polio Plus Program Rotary dist. 692, Ga.; deacon local Bapt. ch.; dir. Bapt. World Alliance Interdenominational, Inter-Racial Med. Mission Survey of Asia-Africa, 1958, Operation Bro.'s Bro. in Liberia vaccination program, 1962, med. survey in Cen. Am. nations, 1967; pres., med. dir. Bro.'s Bro. Found.; pres. Edn. and Relief Found., World Fedn. Soc. Anesthesiologists, 1960-70. Served as med. dir. USPHS Res., 1951-78. Named Man of Yr. in Medicine Pitts. Acad. Medicine, 1974, 75, one of Ten Outstanding Young Men Am. U.S. Jaycees, 1947, Knight Grand Comdr. Humane Order African Redemption, 1962, Man of Distinction Pitts. Bapt. Assn., 1980, Man of Yr. Rotary of Ocilla, 1985; named to Gen. Francisco Morizan, 1968, Order Ruben Dario, 1968, Order Rodolfo Robles, 1974; recipient Service citation Costa Rica, 1967, service citation govts. of Nicaragua, Guatemala, Republic of Panama, El Salvador, Peru, Honduras, Dominican Republic, Haiti, Venezuela, Colombia, Cuba, Jamaica, Hadassah Service award Israel, 1968, Dahlberg Peace award Am. Bapt. Chs., 1977, Human Rights award UN Assn. Pitts., 1978, William O McQuiston Lectureship award Ill. Soc. Anesthesiologists, 1978, Paul Harris Fellowship award Rotary, 1978, Gaston Labat award Am. Soc. Regional Anesthesia, 1981, U.S. Pres.' award Internat. Volunteerism, 1987, Gov.'s Humanitarianism award, 1987; Hingson Day named in his honor, Oxford, Ala., 1985. Fellow Internat. Coll. Anesthesia, William Crawford Gorgas Med. Soc., Am. Soc. Anesthetists, Internat. Coll. Surgeons, Royal Coll. Surgeons (faculty aenesthesiology), Am. Coll. Anesthesiology; mem. Coll. Physicians and Surgeons, Republic of Costa Rica (hon.), Internat. Research Soc. (v.p.), Am. Soc. Anesthesiologists (bd. dirs.), Sigma Xi, Pi Kappa Alpha. Rotary. Home: 801 S Irwin Ave Ocilla GA 31774 Office: Bros Bro Found 824 Grandview Ave Pittsburgh PA 15211

HINKELMAN, LOREN G., engineering company executive; b. 1931. BSCE, Stanford U., 1953; MBA, Golden Gate U., 1975. With Bechtel Power Corp., 1960—, v.p., mgr. Los Angeles Power, 1983; now pres., dir. Bechtel Western Power Corp., Norwalk, Calif.; also bd. dirs. Bechtel Group Inc., San Francisco. Office: Bechtel Western Power Corp Box 60860 12440 E Imperial Hwy Norwalk CA 90060 *

HINMAN, EDWARD JOHN, health care administrator; b. New Orleans, Nov. 10, 1931; s. E. Harold and Katharine (Fradenburgh) H.; m. Emma Jean Richmond, June 15, 1954; children—Cynthia, Alan, David. B.A., U. Okla., 1951; M.D., Tulane U., 1955; M.P.H., Johns Hopkins U., 1971. Diplomate: Am. Bd. Preventive Medicine. Intern USPHS Hosp., New Orleans, 1955-56, resident, Balt., 1958-61; dir. spl. research and devel. project Nat. Center Health Service Research, Rockville, Md., 1973-74; asst. surgeon gen., dir. div. hosps. and clinics USPHS, 1974-78; exec. dir. Group Health Assn., Washington, 1978-83; pres. Risk Control Services, Washington, 1984-86; med. dir. PruCare of Washington, 1986—; bd. dirs. Am. Assn. Med. Systems and Informatics, 1980—, pres., 1985-86; bd. dirs. Coop. League U.S.A., Washington, 1982-85. Contbr. articles in field to profl. jours. Bd. dirs. Greater Southeast Community Hosp. Found., 1983—. Served with USPHS, 1955-78. Recipient Bronze Letzeiser medal U. Okla., 1951; Meritorious Service award USPHS, 1976; Outstanding Achievement award Md. chpt. Federally Employed Women, 1976. Fellow ACP, Am. Coll. Med. Informatics, Am. Coll. Preventive Medicine (v.p. 1976-77), Am. Pub. Health Assn., Soc. Advanced Med. Systems (dir. 1968-82, pres. 1976-77), Am. Fedn. Clin. Research, Phi Beta Kappa. Home: Box 48D Cape Leonard Dr Saint Leonard MD 20685 Office: PruCare of Washington 2001 L St NW Suite 500 Washington DC 20036

HINMAN, MYRA MAHLOW, educator; b. Saginaw County, Mich., Jan. 11, 1926; d. Henry and Cynthia (Mims) Mahlow; B.S., Columbia U., 1946; M.A., U. Fla., 1954, Ph.D., 1959; m. George E. Olstead, 1948 (div. 1967); 1 son, Christopher Eric; m. Charlton Hinman, 1968 (dec. 1977); 1 stepdau., Barbara. Asst. prof. Memphis State U., 1959-61; instr. U. Kans., Lawrence, 1961-63, asst. prof., 1963-68, asso. prof. English lit., 1968—. Travel grantee Am. Council Learned Socs., 1966. Mem. MLA, Internat. Arthurian Soc. (conf. speaker), Shakespeare Assn. Am. (conf. presenter), U. Va. Bibliog. Soc., AAUP, Kans. Folklore Soc., Midwest MLA, S. Atlantic MLA, United Burmese Cat Fanciers, Am. Shorthair Cat Assn., Phi Kappa Phi. Asst. editor: Hinman Text, Complete Works of Shakespeare; mem. editorial bd. Computer-Assisted Composition jour.; contbr. articles to profl. jours. Home: 1932 Maine St Lawrence KS 66046 Office: U Kans Wescoe Hall Lawrence KS 66045

HINSHAW, HORTON CORWIN, physician; b. Iowa Falls, Iowa, 1902; s. Milas Clark and Ida (Bushong) H.; m. Dorothy Youmans, Aug. 6, 1924; children—Horton Corwin, Barbara (Mrs. Barbara Baird), Dorothy (Mrs. Gregory Patent). A.B., Coll. Idaho, 1923, D.Sc., 1947; A.M., U. Calif., 1926, Ph.D., 1927; M.D., U. Pa., 1933. Diplomate Am. Bd. Internal Medicine, Nat. Bd. Med. Examiners. Asst. prof. zoology U. Calif., 1927-28; adj. prof. parasitology and bacteriology Am. U., Beirut, Lebanon, 1928-31; instr. bacteriology U. Pa. Sch. Medicine, 1931-33; fellow, 1st asst. medicine. Mayo Found., U. Minn., 1933-35, asst. prof., 1937-46, asso. prof., 1946-49; cons. medicine Mayo clinic, 1935- 49, head sec. medicine, 1947-49; clin. prof. medicine, head div. chest diseases Stanford Med. Sch., 1949-59; clin. prof. medicine U. Calif. Med. Sch., 1959-79, emeritus prof., 1979—; chief thoracic disease service So. Pacific Meml. Hosp., 1958-69; dir. med. services and chief staff Harkness Community Hosp. and Med. Center, San Francisco, 1968-75; Dir. med. operations Health Maintenance No. Calif., Inc.; Mem. Calif. Com. Regional Med. Programs, 1969-75. Author: Diseases of the Chest, rev. edit., 1980; co-author: Streptomycin in Tuberculosis, 1949; contbr. over 215 articles to med. publs. Del. various internat. confs., 1928-59. Fellow A.C.P., Am. Coll. Chest Physicians; hon. mem. Miss. Valley Med. Assn.; mem. Nat. Tb Assn. (bd. dirs., chmn. com. therapy, v.p. 1946- 47, 67-68, research com.), Am. Thoracic Soc. (pres. 1948-49, hon. life 1979), Am. Clin. and Climatol. Soc., Minn. Med. Assn., Am. Bronchoesophalogical Assn., A.M.A., Am. Soc. Clin. Investigation, Central Soc. Clin. Research, Soc. Exptl. Biology and Medicine, Aero-Med. Assn., Am. Lung Assn. (hon., Hall of Fame 1980), Minn. Soc. Internal Medicine, Sigma Xi, Phi Sigma, Gamma Alpha.; Mem. Soc. of Friends. Home: Box 546 512 San Rafael Ave Belvedere CA 94920 Office: 450 Sutter St San Francisco CA 94108

HINSON, HOWARD HOUSTON, petroleum company executive; b. Fletcher, Okla., Mar. 3, 1913; s. Jasper Lafayette and Dana (Wunsch) H.; m. Louise Lawson, May 31, 1934 (dec.); children: Barbara Ann Hinson Brightwell, Larry Howard; m. Doris Lloyd Findley, 1976. B.S., Tex. Tech Coll., Lubbock, 1934, M.S., 1945; postgrad., Advanced Mgmt. Program, Harvard U. Registered profl. engr., Tex. Jr. petroleum engr. helium plants U.S. Bur. Mines, Tex., 1936-40; asst. petroleum engr. U.S. Bur. Mines, 1940-42, asso. petroleum engr., 1942-43, petroleum engr., 1943-44, sr. petroleum engr., 1944-47, asst. supervising engr., 1947-48; chief prodn. research engr. Continental Oil Co., 1948-50, asst. mgr. prodn., 1950-52, southwestern regional gen. mgr., 1952, v.p. fgn. dept., 1953-57, dir., 1958-66, v.p. fgn. exploration and prodn., 1957-61, v.p., gen. mgr. internat. exploration, prodn., 1961-66, cons., 1966-68; pres., dir. Imperial-Am. Mgmt. Co., Houston, 1968-69; partner Hinson & Hall, 1969-72, Hinson, Hall & Smith, 1971-72; pres. Tex. Pacific Oil Co., Inc., Dallas, 1972-82. Contbr. articles to profl. jours. Recipient Distinguished Engr. award Tex. Tech U., 1975, Distinguished Alumnus award, 1976. Mem. Soc. Petroleum Engrs., Am. Assn. Petroleum Geologists, Tau Beta Pi. Clubs: Petroleum, Plaza (Dallas); Willowbrook, Holytree (Tyler, Tex.).

HINSON, PEGGY MILDRED, educator; b. Thomaston, Ga., July 19, 1936; d. Robert LeGrand, Sr. and Mildred Sara (Keever) H.; B.S. in Edn., Auburn U., 1958; B.S. in Med. Adminstrn. and Supervision, Ga. State U., 1978. Head English dept. Faith Sch., Ft. Benning, Ga., 1958-61, Daniel Jr. High Sch., Columbus, Ga., 1961-63; tchr. Rothschild Jr. High Sch., Columbus, 1965-75, head English dept., 1976—; secondary English cons., Columbus, 1975-76; curriculum steering com. Columbus Coll. Speaker Ga. Writing Conf., Atlanta, 1986-87. Recipient commendation Pres. of U.S., 1976, commendation U.S. Congress, 1976; named Star Tchr., 1975, Tchr. of Yr., Ga. Council Tchrs. of English, 1988. Mem. Nat. Council Tchrs. of English, NEA, Ga. Assn. Educators, Muscogee Assn. Edn., Columbus Exec. Club, AAUW, Ga. Walking Horse Assn., Phi Delta Kappa, Alpha Delta Kappa, Delta Delta Delta. Home: 3312 Gail Dr Columbus GA 31907 Office: 1136 Hunt Ave Columbus GA 31907

HINTERSCHEID, MATHIAS, labor union administrator; b. Düdelingen, Luxembourg, Jan. 26, 1931; married, Apr. 2, 1953. Grad. high sch., Düdelingen; apprentice, Esch-sur-Alzette tech. sch.; student, Ecole supérieure du Travail. Exec. bd. Düdelingen br. Luxembourg Workers Union, 1955-59, mem. mng. com. ARBED, mng. com. old age pension and disablement ins. fund, 1956-58, sec. youth issues, edn. and info., 1958-63, pres., 1970-76; gen. sec. Luxembourg Confed. Generale du Travail, 1963-70, pres., 1970-76; gen. sec. European Trade Union Confederation, Luxembourg, 1976; mem. exec. com. European Confederation Free Trade Unions and many coms. on the Confederation Generale du Travail, 1965—, Luxembourg Econ. and Social Com., 1966-76; gen. sec. Luxembourg Consumers Union; mem. various state commns. including Labour Exchange, Price Commn. and Index Commn.; mng. dir. Luxembourg Consumers Union Bank. Luxembourg Socialist Labour (v.p. 1963-68). Address: European Trade Union Confedn, 37-41 rue Mongagne aux Herbes Potageres, 1000 Brussels Belgium

HINTIKKA, HARRI JUHANI, construction company executive; b. Helsinki, Mar. 27, 1937; s. Vaino Johannes and Maija (Kyrohanka) H.; m. Rita Anja Helena Oila, Aug. 28, 1965; children: Kari Juhani, Anja Kaarina. Grad., Helsingin Suomalainen Yhteiskoulu Coll., Helsinki, 1955; MSc in Civil Engring., Helsinki U. Tech., 1961. Design engr. Henauer Lee, Zurich, Switzerland, 1961-62, STUP, Paris, 1962-63, Erkki Paloheimo & Co., Helsinki, 1963; tech. mgr. Elementtituote Oy, Helsinki, 1964-67; mgr., pres. Lemminkäien Oy, Helsinki, 1967-83; chmn., chief exec. officer Lemminkäien Oy, 1986—; pres. Polarrakennusosakeyhtio, Helsinki, 1983-86, chief exec. officer, 1986—; bd. dirs. KOP Bank, Pohjola Ins., Uusi Suomi Oy Pub., Karl Fazer Oy. Mem. Confedn. Finnish Industries, Assn. Gen. Contractors Finland, Assn. Finnish Fgn. Trade. Home: Liinasaarentie 3, 02160 Espoo 16 Finland Office: Polarrakennusosakeyhtio, Pasilanraitio 9, 00240 Helsinki Finland

HINTON, DEANE ROESCH, ambassador; b. Fort Missoula, Mont., Mar. 12, 1923; s. Joe A. and Doris (Roesch) H.; m. Angela E. Peyraud, May 10, 1946 (div. 1971); children: Deborah, Christopher, Jeffrey, Joanna, Veronica; m. Miren de Aretxabala, Dec. 6, 1971 (dec. Nov. 1979); stepchildren: Pedro, Guillermo, Miren, Maria, Juan, Sebastian; m. Patricia Lopez, Feb. 14, 1983; 1 child, Deane Patrick. Grad., Elgin (Ill.) Acad., 1940; B.A., U. Chgo., 1943, postgrad., 1946; postgrad., Fletcher Sch. Law and Diplomacy also Harvard U., 1951-52; grad., Nat. War Coll., 1962. Apptd. fgn. service officer 1946; with Dept. State, Washington, 1946, 51-52, 55-58; 3d sec., vice consul Damascus, Syrian Arab Republic, 1947-48, 2d sec., vice consul, 1948-49; vice consul Mombasa, Kenya, 1949, consul, 1949-51; 2d sec., consul Paris, 1952-55; attache U.S. Mission to European Communities, Brussels, 1958-59, 1st sec., 1959-61; chief commodity programming div. Dept. State, Washington, 1962-63; dir. Office Atlantic Polit. Econ. Affairs, 1963-67; dir. AID mission to, Guatemala, 1967-69, Chile; econ. counselor AID mission to, Santiago, Chile, 1969-71; asst. dir. Council Internat. Econ. Policy, Washington, 1971-73, dep. dir., 1973-74; ambassador Kinshasa, Zaire, 1974-75; U.S. rep. U.S. mission to European Communities, Brussels, 1976-79, asst. sec. state for econs. and bus., 1980-81; ambassador San Salvador, El Salvador, 1981-83; ambassador Islamabad, Pakistan, 1983-87, career ambassador; ambassador to Costa Rica, 1987—; professorial lectr. Am. U., Washington. Served to 2d lt. AUS, 1943-45. Recipient Dept. State Superior Service award, 1967; recipient Presdl. award for disting. diplomatic service, 1983. Mem. Council Fgn. Relations, Fgn. Service Assn., Royal Central Asian Soc., Soc. Internat. Devel. Office: US Embassy San Jose, Costa Rica APO Miami FL 34020 Other: Am Embassy, Avenida 3 and Calle I, San Jose Costa Rica *

HIRABAYASHI, SHINICHI, computer company executive, consultant; b. Tokyo, Japan, Apr. 30, 1949; s. Ichiro and Tamee Hirabayashi; m. Kaoru Imai, May 13, 1978; 1 child, Makoto. BOS, Hokkaido U. Math. diplomate. Software developer Toshiba Computer Div., Tokyo, 1971-78, market, planning mgr., 1983-85; pres. Japan Communication Corp., Tokyo, 1985—; tech., mktg. mgr. Computer Div. in Toshiba Europe, Frankfurt, W.Ger., 1979-83. Patentee in field. Avocation: golf, auther. Office: Japan Communication Corp, Kobayashi Blvd 2-3-2, Hacchou-Bori, Chouou-Ku, Tokyo 104, Japan

HIRAGA, MASAHARU, automotive products company executive; b. Maebashi, Gunma-ken, Japan, Apr. 13, 1939; s. Minoru and Fusa (Kanai) H.; m. Keiko Sunaga, Oct. 29, 1975; children: Tomoko, Fumiko. BS, Tohoku U., Sendai, Japan, 1963; MS, Tohoku U., 1969, D of Engring., 1972. Electronic engr. OKI Electric Co., Takasaki, Japan, 1963-65; asst. to prof. Tohoku U., 1965-67; mgr. sales engring. Sanden Internat. Inc., Dallas, 1975-77; mech. engr. Sanden Corp., Isesaki, Japan, 1972-74; mgr. research and devel. Sanden Corp., Isesaki, 1977-78, gen. mgr. research and devel., chief engr., 1979-87, sr. gen. mgr. product devel., 1988—. Patentee in field. Recipient Nat. Invention award Japan Inst. Invention and Innovation, Tokyo, 1986. Mem. Soc. Automotive Engrs. Home: 4-8-34 Honjo Honjoshi, Saitamaken 367, Japan Office: Sande Corp, Yattajima Plant, 350 Yattajima-cho, Isesaki-shi, Gunma-ken 372, Japan

HIRAHARA, MASAKATU, architect; b. Kure, Hiroshima, Japan, July 2, 1945; s. Masaaki and Saeko (Ishino) H. B in Engring., Kogakuin U., Tokyo, 1974; B in Lit., Waseda U., Tokyo, 1978. Registered architect. Architect Nikken Sekkei, Ltd., Tokyo, 1964—. Author: Hotel Architecture, 1986; prin. works include A.I.J. Hall (Excellence award 1981), Indira Gandhi Nat. Ctr. for Arts. mem. Archtl. Inst. Japan. Club: Half Moon Beach (Kamakura City). Home: Obirin-Haitu C-504 Minesawacho, Yokohama, Kanagawa 240, Japan Office: Nikken Seikkei Ltd, Koraku 1-4-27, 112 Tokyo Japan

HIRAHARA, PATTI, public relations agency executive; b. Lynwood, Calif., May 10, 1955; d. Frank C. and Mary K. Hirahara. A.A., Cypress Coll., 1975; B.A., Calif. State U.-Fullerton, 1977. Pub. affairs dir. United Television, Los Angeles, 1977-80; v.p. Asian Internat. Broadcasting Co., Los Angeles, 1980-81; mktg. cons. Disneyland, Anaheim, Calif., 1982; pub. relations agt. Japan External Trade Orgn., Los Angeles, 1982-86, 87—; owner, pres. Prodns. By Hirahara, Anaheim, 1982—; comml. photographer Hirahara Photography, Anaheim, 1977-83; publicist Tokyo Met. Govt., 1981; advisor State Colo. Trade Mission to Japan, 1986, State Ariz. Trade/Investment Mission to Japan, 1987, County Riverside, Calif. for Japanese trade, investment, tourism, 1986-88; coordinator JETRO's Bus. Study Series, Los Angeles, 1988; advisor Japan External Trade Ordgn., 1987-88. Bd. dirs. Nisei Week Japanese Festival, Los Angeles, 1980-81. Nat. scholar Seventeen Mag. Youth Adv. Council, 1973; named Orange County Nisei Queen, Suburban Optimist Club, Buena Park, Calif., 1975, nat. semi-finalist Outstanding Young Working Women Competititon Glamour mag., 1983-84; recipient service award Suburban Optimist Club of Buena Park, 1975. Mem. Soc. Profl. Journalists (bd. dirs. 1980-81), Nat. Assn. Female Execs., World Trade Ctr. Assn. Orange County, Japanese Am. Citizens League, Am. Women in Radio and TV (bd. dirs. So. Calif. chpt. 1980-82, vice-chair western area conf. 1981), Alpha Gamma Sigma.

HIRAIZUMI, WATARU, government official; b. Tokyo, Nov. 26, 1929; s. Kiyoshi and Hayako (Morishita) H.; m. Mieko Kajima, Mar. 5, 1957; children: Nobuyuki, Tomiko. LLD, Tokyo U., 1952; student, Ecole Nat. d'Adminstrn., Aix-en-Provence, France, 1952-54. Mem. Japanese Fgn. Service, 1951-64, Japanese Ho. Councillors, 1965-76; vice minister Sci. and Tech. Agy. Govt. of Japan, 1971; mem. Japanese Ho. of Reps., 1976—; dir. gen. Econ. Planning Agy., 1985—; exec. v.p. Kajima Corp., 1969-71; mem. exec. council Liberal Dem. Party, 1976-79, 81-82, dir. gen. internat. bur., 1983-85; vice-chmn. research commn. on fgn. affairs, 1976—; v.p. Japan Inst. Internat. Affairs, 1975—; pres. Kajima Inst. Internat. Peace, 1979—. Mem. Anglo-Japanese Parliamentary Group, Franco-Japanese Parliamentary Group, Japan-E C Parliamentary Group. Shindo. Office: Kajima Inst Internat Peace, 6-5-33 Akasaka, Minato-ku, Tokyo 107 Japan *

HIRAKAWA, KIMIYOSHI, neurosurgeon, educator; b. Fukuyama, Hiroshima, Japan, Aug. 18, 1934; s. Takesaburo and Fuji (Date) H.; m. Atsuko Nakatsuka, May 30, 1968; children—Yukako, Minako. M.D., U. Tokyo, 1959, D.M.Sc., 1970. Med. diplomate. Intern U. Tokyo, 1959-60, resident, 1960-63, asst. U. Tokyo, 1963-69, chief asst., 1966-69, asst. prof. neurosurgery, 1969-72, assoc. prof, 1972-88; prof., head neurosurgery Tokyo Med. and Dental U., 1988—; prof., head neurosurgery Kyoto Prefectural U. of Medicine, Japan, 1978—. Recipient 20th Med. awards Igaku-Shoin Pub. Co., Tokyo, 1971. Mem. Japan Neurosurg. Soc. (editorial staff 1972-81, editorial bd. 1981—), Japanese Soc. Neurotraumatology (pres. 1979-80), Japanese Congress Neurol. Surgeons (pres. 1985-86), Academia Eurasiåna Neurochirugica. Buddhist. Home: Kohinata 1-22-11, Bunkyo-ku, Tokyo 112 Japan Office: Tokyo Med and Dental U, Dept Neurosurgery Yushima 1-5-45, Bunkyo-ku, Tokyo 113, Japan

HIRANO, ATSUO, banker; b. Tokyo, May 12, 1931; s. Hiroshi and Teru (Ohta) H.; m. Yoko Hoshino, Jan. 22, 1958; children: Hirofumi, Atsuhiko. BA in Economics, Keio U., Tokyo, 1954. Exec. v.p. Mitsubishi Bank of Calif., Los Angeles, 1973-79; gen. mgr. Mitsubishi Bank Ltd. of N.Y., N.Y.C., 1981-85; dir. Mitsubishi Bank Ltd. Tokyo, 1984-86, mng. dir., 1986—. Mem. com. Internat. Council Edn., Tokyo, 1986—. Clubs: Kasumigaseki C.C. (Saitama, Japan), Shonan C.C. (Kanagawa, Japan). Office: Mitsubishi Bank Ltd, Marunouchi 2 7 1, Tokyo 100, Japan

HIRANO, KEN-ICHI, metallurgist, educator; b. Hamamatsu-City, Japan, May 18, 1927; s. Etsuhei and Toki (Takabayashi) H.; B.Eng., Tokyo Inst. Tech., 1952; Sc.D., Hokkaido U., 1959; m. Tetsuko Kondo, Dec. 21, 1963; children—Mitsuko, Hiromi. Research asso. M.I.T., Cambridge, Mass., 1957-62; asso. prof. Tohoku U., Sendai, Japan, 1962-69, prof., 1969—, head dept. metallurgy and materials sci., 1971—; vis. prof. univs. including U. Tokyo, Tokyo Inst. Tech., Nat. Cheng-Kung U., Taiwan; also cons. Recipient Achievement award Japan Inst. Metals, 1970. Fellow Am. Soc. Metals; mem. Phys. Soc. Japan, Metal Soc. of AIME, Japan Inst. Metals (trustee), Sigma Xi. Club: Japan Polar Philatelist (pres.). Author: Metal Physics, 1975; editor Jour. Japan Inst Metals, 1971-72, 79-80, 82-83, 87—. Home: 7-5-13 Nakayama, Sendai 981 Japan Office: Dept Material Scis, Tohoku Univ, 980 Aoba Sendai Japan

HIRATA, HIRONORI, educator; b. Hiroshima, Japan, June 2, 1948; s. Shigeki and Toshie (Yamaguchi) H.; m. Yoko Horii Hirata, Mar. 14, 1976; children: Maki, Mari, Toshiki. BEng., Waseda U., Tokyo, 1971; MEng., Tokyo Inst. Tech., 1973, Dr. Eng., 1976. Assoc. research Chiba U., Chiba-shi, Japan, 1976-81; vis. assoc. prof. U. Md., Solomons, 1982-84; assoc. prof. elect. engr. Chiba U., Chiba-shi, 1981—. Mem. IEEE, Internat. Soc. Ecol. Modeling, Internat. Neural Network Soc., Inst. Elec. Engring. of Japan, Soc. Instrument and Control Engrs., Inst. Electronics, Info. and Communication Engrs. of Japan, Info. Processing Soc. of Japan. Office: Chiba U Dept Electronics, 1-33 Yayoi-cho, Chiba-shi, Chiba 281, Japan

HIRATA, KUSUO, photographic equipment company executive; b. Sept. 7, 1909. Grad., Kanseigagui U., 1933. Chmn. Fuji Photo Film Co., Ltd.; exec. trustee Japan Fedn. Econ. Orgns. Decorated Medal of Honor with Blue Ribbon, 2d Class Order Sacred Treasure. Home: 48-12 Utsukushigaoka, 2-chome Midori-ku, 227 Yokohama Japan Office: Fuji Photo Film Co Ltd, 26-30 Nishiozabu, 2-chome Minato-ku, Tokyo Japan *

HIRAYAMA, CHISATO, medical educator, physician; b. Kajiki, Kagoshima, Japan, Nov. 6, 1923; s. Shigeki and Hide (Kokusho) H.; m. Kimiko Ueno, May 4, 1954; children—Toko, Tomoo. M.D., Kyushu U., Fukuoka, Japan, 1947, Ph.D., 1956. Intern Kyushu U. Hosp.; asst. Kyushu U., 1953-62, asst. prof., 1962-66, assoc. prof., 1966-76; prof. medicine Tottori U., Yonago, Tottori, Japan, 1976—, dean Sch. Medicine, 1986—; dir. Tottori U. Hosp., 1984-86. Author: Diseases of the Liver, 1977; editor: Plasma Proteins, 1979; Treatment of Hepatobiliary Diseases, 1980; Pathobiology of Hepatic Fibrosis, 1985. Recipient prize Japan Soc. Electrophoresis, 1968. Fellow Japan Soc. Internal Medicine (bd. dirs. 1985—), Japan Soc. Gastroenterology; mem. Japan Soc. Hepatology (dir. 1980—), Internat. Assn. Study Liver, N.Y. Acad. Scis. Lodge: Rotary (Yonago). Office: Tottori U Sch Medicine, 86 Nishimachi, 683 Tottori Japan

HIROHITO, HIS MAJESTY, Emperor of Japan; b. Tokyo, Apr. 29, 1901; s. Emperor Yoshihito and Empress Sadako; ed. special tutors and The Peers' Sch.; m. Princess Nagako Kuni, Jan. 26, 1924; children: Shigeko (dec.), Kazuko, Atsuko, Akihito (Crown Prince), Masahito, Takako. Regent because of father's illness, 1921-26, became emperor, 1926; formally enthroned, 1928. Fellow Royal Soc. (U.K.). Author 9 books on marine biology. Address: Imperial Palace, Tokyo Japan *

HIROTA, JITSUYA, reactor physicist; b. Hyogo-ken, Japan, Oct. 31, 1924; s. Jitsuki and Isoko (Adachi) H.; m. Hiroko Terasaka, Apr. 17, 1954; 2 children. Grad. Kyoto U., 1948, Sc.D., 1961. Research scientist Japan Atomic Energy Research Inst., Tokai Research Establishment, 1956-64, prin. scientist, 1965-83, chmn. com. reactor physics, 1967-81; cons. Mitsubishi Atomic Power Industries, Inc., 1984—; mem. com. on exam. reactor safety Nuclear Safety Commn., 1964-83 (award 1987); Japanese rep. nuclear energy agy. com. reactor physics OECD, 1966-81. Author papers in field. Mem. Atomic Energy Soc. Japan (spl. prize 1973), Am. Nuclear Soc. Home: 11-5 Okusawa 4-chome, Setagaya-Ku, 158 Tokyo Japan Office: Mitsubishi Atomic Power Ind Inc, 4-1 Shibakouen 2-chome Minato-Ku, 105 Tokyo Japan

HIROTA, TAKASHI, pharmacologist; b. Suita, Osaka, Japan, Feb. 1, 1943; s. Minoru and Kisae Hirota; m. Tizuru Hirota, Feb. 3, 1973; 1 child, Takayuki. Degree in pharmacology, Kyoto (Japan) U. Registered pharmacist. Rep. sales Inabata Co. Ltd., Osaka, 1968-73, acting mgr. market devel., 1973-78; various positions Sawai Pharm. Industry Co. Ltd., Osaka, 1978-82; clin. research mgr. Squibb Japan Inc., Tokyo, 1982-85, mktg. planning mgr., 1985—. Mem. Japanese Pharmacist Assn., Japanese Classical Hematological Congress, Japanese Chemotherapy Assn., Natural Resource Developing Assn. (mng. dir., 1976-87). Mem. Liberal-Democratic party. Club: Japanese I Go Found. (Tokyo). Home: 19-32 Sakura 2 chome, Setagaya-ku Tokyo Japan Office: Squibb Japan Inc, 12-19 Shibuya 2-chome, Shibuya-ku Tokyo Japan

HIROTANI, ATSUSHI, pharmaceutical company executive; b. Fukuyama, Hiroshima, Oct. 3, 1934; s. Masashi and Hiroko Hirotani; m. Noriko Goto, May 27, 1962; children: Takashi, Satoko. BChemE, U. Tokyo, 1958. Dep. mgr. planning dept. Mitusbishi Chem. Industries Ltd., Tokyo, 1971-78, gen. mgr. research and devel. dept., 1973-82; gen. mgr. research and devel. dept. SS Pharm. Co. Ltd., Tokyo, 1982-84, gen. mgr. prodn., 1984—, also bd. dirs. Mem. Soc. Chem. Engrs. Japan. Home: 765-99 5-chome Numama, 249 Zushi, Kanagawa Japan Office: SS Pharm Co Ltd, 12-4 2-chome Hihonbashi Hamacho, Chuo-ku, Tokyo 103, Japan

HIRSCH, ROBERT HENRY, retail company executive; b. Kansas City, Mo., May 29, 1925; s. Clarence A. and Ruth (Auerbach) H.; student U. Kans., 1943-44; B.S. in Mech. Engring., U. Calif.-Berkeley, 1946; postgrad. Harvard U., 1946-47, NYU, 1948; m. Pamela; children—Sydney Suzanne, Leslie Joan, Robert Henry Jr. Trainee, Abraham & Straus, Bklyn., 1948, buyer accessories, coats, suits, 1951-57; founder, owner Brooks Hirsch, Inc., Westport, Trumbull, Fairfield, Stamford and Hamden, Conn., 1957, pres., 1962— ; dir. Shawmut Bank, Westport. Pres., Comml. Bd., Westport, 1963—, Westport Devel. Commn., 1964-66; trustee Mid-Fairfield County Youth Mus., 1964-76, v.p., 1972-76; chmn. bur. bus. adminstrn. and public relations Fairfield U., 1971—, bd. dirs., 1971—, v.p., 1972, chmn., 1973. Served to lt. (j.g.) USN, 1943-47. Mem. Nat. Retail Mchts. Assn., Westport C. of C. (pres. 1964-65). Republican. Jewish. Clubs: Birchwood Country (gov.), Saints and Sinners Jumbo Tent, Racquet, Sportsman (v.p.) (Westport). Office: 403 E State St Westport CT 06880

HIRSCHBERG, GARY EDWARD, computer company executive; b. Mt. Vernon, N.Y., Oct. 2, 1939; s. Sanford Leon and Helen (Felton) H.; m. Peggy Gropper Rosenberg, Nov. 16, 1968; children: Stacy Lynn, Amanda Ruth. BS in Naval Architecture, MIT, 1961. Head computer-aided design Hull Design br. USN Dept. Bur. Ships, Washington, 1961-66, M. Rosenblatt & Son, N.Y.C., 1966-68; pres. Marine Computer Applications Corp., N.Y.C., 1968-70; cons. systems analysis, N.Y.C., 1970-72; v.p. computer ops. Felton Internat. Inc., N.Y.C., 1972-76, v.p. prodn., 1976-82, sr. v.p. fragrance div., 1982-85, sr. v.p. ops., mem. exec. com., dir., 1985-88; chmn. ops. and controls steering group Felton Worldwide, 1986-88; pres. MacinTosh Bus. Systems, Inc., Mamaroneck, N.Y., 1988—. Author, contbr. MacUser mag. Mem. Coastal Zone Mgmt. Commn., Mamaroneck, N.Y. Recipient Superior Performance award USN Dept. Bur. Ships, 1964. Mem. U.S. Naval Inst. Clubs: Beach Point (Mamaroneck, N.Y.) (chmn. entertainment com., bd. govs.), Beach Point Yacht (bd. dirs., purchasing com., protest com., co-chmn.). Home: 3 Country Ln Mamaroneck NY 10543 Office: 599 Johnson Ave Brooklyn NY 11237

HIRSCHFELD, MICHAEL AVIGDOR, distribution executive; b. Oct. 27, 1944; m. Vivien Elizabeth Flack; 3 children. BA with honors in Polit. Sci., Victoria U., Wellington, New Zealand, 1965, MA in Polit. Sci., 1958. Chmn. Mico/Wakefield Ltd., Wellington, Auckland, New Zealand, mng. dir.; chmn. Acorn Pacific Corp., Edenlite Garden Products Ltd., Acorn Plastics Ltd., 1984, The Shipping Corp. New Zealand Ltd., 1984; dep. chmn. Pacific Forum Line; mem. adv. com. dept. bus. studies, extension Victoria U.; participant Ford Found. research Pacific Basin Devel., Japan, Hong Kong, Indonesia, Malaysia, Singapore, Eng., 1980, Pacific Marine Commons meeting, Tokyo, 1980, Changing Indsl. Structure Pacific Basin, Seoul, Korea, 1981, Food and Devel., Mexico City, 1982, Info. Revolution Pacific, Singapore, 1984; mem. organizing com. New Zealand's Prospects Pacific Basin, 1983; bd. dirs. New Zealand Blueberries Ltd., Endeavor Prodns. Ltd., Metal Import Group Holding Ltd., Container Terminals Ltd., Wellington Steel Ltd., Wellington Fasteners Ltd. Corr. radio sta. NZBC, Israel, 1967, broadcaster numerous stas.; contbr. articles to profl. jours. Sec. trust appeal com. Wellington Sculpture, 1983-84; chmn. Circa Theatre Trust, 1987, m. ministerial responsibility Inst. Policy Studies, 1985-86, bd. dirs.; mem. univ. council Wellington, New Zealand;. Mem. Labour Party. Office: Mico-Wakefield, PO Box 38471, Petone New Zealand

HIRSCHMANN, FRANZ GOTTFRIED, aerospace executive; b. Kempten, Fed. Republic Germany, Oct. 4, 1945; came to U.S., 1973; s. Kurt Rudolf G. and Linda (Krieger) H.; m. Martha L. Ossa, Dec. 27, 1978 (div. May 1982). BS, FWG Coll., Cologne, Fed. Republic Germany, 1965; MA, U. Bonn, Fed. Republic Germany, 1973; MBA, Pepperdine U., 1981. Mktg. mgr. Western U.S. and S. Am. regions United Techs./Ambac, Los Angeles, 1978-80; mktg. mgr. Western U.S. and Pacific regions Buehler Inc., Los Angeles and N.C., 1981-83; mgr. internat. ops. Gen. Dynamics, Pomona, Calif., 1983-84, mgr. info. services, 1984—. Author: Mandaic Inscription, 1970; inventor deciphering language computer. Vol. Lincoln Club, Los Angeles, 1981. Mem. Nat. Mgmt. Assn., Pepperdine Alumni Assn., Sierra Club, Retinitis Pigmentosa Found. (co-founder). Republican. Lutheran. Home: PO Box 7000-391 Palos Verdes CA 90274 Office: Gen Dynamics #303-5 PO Box 2507 Pomona CA 91769

HIRSCHSOHN, CLIVE LOUIS, retail company executive; b. Cape Town, Cape, South Africa, July 28, 1932; s. Phillip Hirschsohn and Nita Esther (Myers) Steinberg; m. Helen Pamela Brahms, Apr. 29, 1956; children—Philip, Lindy, Martine. B. Commerce, U. Witwatersrand, 1951; LL.B., U. South Africa-Pretoria, 1955. Exec. dir. Am. Swiss Jewelers, Cape Town, 1958-67; mng. dir., 1967-80; dep. mgr. dir. Foschini Ltd., Cape Town, 1980—; mng. dir. subs. Foshini Stores Pty Ltd., 1982-85. Fellow Gemmological Assn. Gt. Britain. Club: Milnerton Golf (pres. 1969-71) (Cape Town). Home: Rathfelder Ave Constantia, Cape Town 7800, Republic of South Africa Office: Foschini Ltd, 342 Voortrekkor Rd, Parow, Cape 7501, Republic of South Africa

HIRSCHSON, NIEL, writer; b. Victoria West, Cape Province, Republic of South Africa, Jan. 21, 1934; s. Zvi Gedalia and Rachel (Zamunoff) H.; m. Rona Merle Kiel, Sept. 17, 1967; children: Lydia, Gideon; stepchildren: Julia, Paul. Author: The Naming of Johannesburg, 1974; contbr. articles to periodicals, jours.; speaker in field. Mem. Inst. Contemporary Life and Thought (chmn. 1978-85). Jewish. Office: PO Box 11381, Johannesburg 2000, Republic of South Africa

HIRSH, NORMAN BARRY, helicopter company executive; b. N.Y.C., Apr. 20, 1935; s. Samuel Albert and Lillian Rose (Minkow) H.; m. Christina M. Poole, Sept. 21, 1957 (div. 1967); children: Richard Scott, Lisa Robin; m. Sharon Kay Girot, Dec. 29, 1973. BSME, Purdue U., 1956; cert. in mgmt., UCLA, 1980. Mech. engr. Ford Motor Co., Dearborn, Mich., 1956-58; design engr. Gen. Dynamics, San Diego, 1958-62; mech. engr. aircraft div. Hughes Tool Co., Culver City, Calif., 1962-65, project engr. aircraft div., 1965-69, engr. mgr. aircraft div., 1969-72; dep. program dir. Hughes Helicopters, Culver City, 1972-79, v.p., 1979-84; v.p., gen. mgr. Hughes Helicopters, Mesa, Ariz., 1984-85; exec. v.p. McDonnell Douglas Helicopter Co., Mesa, 1986—. Served with U.S. Army. Mem. Am. Helicopter Soc. (chmn. 1986—), Assn. U.S. Army, Army Aviation Assn. Am., Am. Def. Preparedness Assn., Nat. Aeronautic Assn. Office: McDonnell Douglas Helicopter Co 5000 E McDowell Rd Mesa AZ 85205

HIRST, WILMA ELIZABETH, consulting educational psychologist; b. Shenandoah, Iowa; d. James H. and Lena (Donahue) Ellis; m. Clyde Henry Hirst (dec. Nov. 1969); 1 dau., Donna Jean (Mrs. Alan Robert Goss). A.B. in Elementary Edn., Colo. State Coll., 1948, Ed.D. in Ednl. Psychology, 1954; M.A. in Psychology, U. Wyo., 1951. Elem. tchr., Cheyenne, Wyo., 1945-49, remedial reading instr., 1949-54; assoc. prof. edn., dir. campus sch. Nebr. State Tchrs. Coll., Kearney, 1954-56; sch. psychologist, head dept. spl. edn. Cheyenne (Wyo.) pub. schs., 1956-57, sch. psychologist, guidance coordinator, 1957-66, dir. research and spl. projects, 1966-76, also pupil personnel, 1973-84; pvt. cons., 1984—; vis. asst. prof. U. So. Calif., summer 1957, Omaha U., summer 1958, U. Okla., summers 1959, 60; vis. assoc. prof. U. Nebr., 1961, U. Wyo., summer 1962, 64, extension div., Kabul, Afghanistan, 1970, Catholic U., Goias, Brazil, 1974; investigator HEW, 1965-69; prin. investigator effectiveness of spl. edn., 1983—; participant seminar Russian Press Women and Am. Fedn. Press Women, Moscow and Leningrad, 1973. Sec.-treas. Laramie County Council Community Services, 1962; mem. speakers bur., mental health orgn.; active Little Theatre, 1936-60, Girl Scout Leaders Assn., 1943-50; mem. Adv. Council on Retardation to Gov.'s Commn.; mem., past sec. Wyo. Bd. Psychologist Examiners, vice chmn., 1965-74; chmn. Mayor's v.p. Model Cities Program, 1969; mem. Gov.'s Com. Jud. Reform, 1972; adv. council Div. Exceptional Children, Wyo. Dept. Edn., 1974; mem. transit adv. group City of Cheyenne, 1974; bd. dirs. Wyo. Children's Home Soc., treas., 1978-84, sec. 1984—; del. Internat. Conv. Ptnrs. of Ams., Jamaica, 1987 ; bd. dirs. Goodwill Industries Wyo., chmn., 1981-83; mem. Wyo. exec. com. Partners of Americas, 1970-86; ambassador to Honduras, summer 1979; del., voice moderator bd. deacons Friendship Force ambassador to Honduras, 1988; chmn. bd. SE Wyo. Mental Health Center; elder 1st Presbyn. Ch., Cheyenne, 1978—; chmn. adv. assessment com. Wyo. State Office Handicapped Children, 1980, 81; mem. allocations com. United Way of Laramie County. Named Woman of Year, Cheyenne Bus. and Profl. Women, 1974. Diplomate Am. Bd. Profl. Psychology. Fellow Internat. Council Psychologists (chmn. Wyo. div. 1980-85); mem. AAUP, Am. Assn. State Psychology Bds. (sec.-treas. 1970-73), Am., Wyo. (pres. 1962-63) psychol. assns., Laramie County (bd. mem., corr. sec. 1963-69, pres.), Wyo. mental health assns. (bd. mem.), Internat. Platform Assn., Am. Ednl. Research Assn., Assn. Supervision and Curriculum Devel., Assn. for Gifted (Wyo. pres. 1964-65), Am. Personnel and Guidance Assn., Am. Assn. Sch. Adminstrs., NEA (life, participant seminar to China 1978), AAUW, Cheyenne Assn. Spl. Personnel and Prins. (pres. 1964-65, mem. exec. bd. 1972-76), Nat. Fedn. Press Women (dir. 1979—), DAR (vice regent Cheyenne chpt. 1975-77), AARP (state coordinator 1988—, preretirement planning specialist 1986—), Psi Chi, Kappa Delta Pi, Pi Lambda Theta, Alpha Delta Kappa (pres. Wyo. Alpha 1965-66). Presbyn. Lodge Soc. Colonial Dames XVII Century, Order Eastern Star, Daus. of Nile. Clubs: Wyo. Press Women, Zonta (pres. Cheyenne 1965-66, treas. dist. 12 1974). Author: Know Your School Psychologist, 1963; Effective School Psychology for School Administrators, 1980. Home and Office: 3458 Green Valley Rd Cheyenne WY 82001

HIRVENOJA, MAURI KALEVI, zoology educator; b. Riihimaki, Finland, Sept. 3, 1928; s. Otto Kustaa and Aino Gustava (Viren) H.; m. Elina Sofia Kostama, Aug. 16, 1964; children—Markku Antero, Jukka Pekka, Antti Juha Kustaa. Dr. phil., U. Helsinki, 1973. Tchr. biology and geography secondary sch. Riihimaki, Finland, 1954-58; asst. U. Helsinki, 1962-75, assoc. prof. zoology, 1975—; bd. dirs. Kalataloussaatio, Helsinki, 1977-83. Contbr. articles to profl. jours. Served to lt. Finnish Armed Forces. Lutheran. Home: Sotilaskorventie 13, SF 01730 Vantaa Finland Office: Zoological Inst U Helsinki, P Rautatiekatu, 13 Helsinki Finland

HISAM, HORST GUENTHER, business advisor and investment company executive; b. Berlin, May 2, 1921; came to U.S., 1976, naturalized, 1977; s. Theodor Friedrich Wilhelm and Helene Amalie Rosalie (Meyer) H.; J.D., U. Tuebingen, 1945; m. Ursula M. Domdey, May 25, 1965; children—Thorsten G., Nicole. Bus. cons., Germany, 1946-76; prof. mgmt. U. Bad Harzburg, 1957-73; pres. various investment cos., Germany, 1958-76; bus. cons., U.S.A., 1976—; pres. Swiss and German Investments, Inc., Ft. Lauderdale, Fla., 1976—, Investment and Holding Co. of Fla., Inc., Ft. Lauderdale, 1976—. Mayor, City of List auf Sylt (Germany), 1969-73. Club: Lions (pres. 1982-83) (Lauderdale by the Sea.). Author: Die Satzungsgewalt der Gemeinde, 1945; Der Handel in der industriellen Gesellschaft, 1963. Home and Office: 2218 NE 17th Ct Fort Lauderdale FL 33305

HITAM, DATO YUSOF M., ambassador; b. Mentakab, Pahang, Malaysia, Jan. 1, 1936. BA, U. Malaya, Singapore, 1959; BA with honors, U. Malaya, Kuala Lumpur, 1960. Asst. dist. officer Malaysian Civil Service, Pahang, 1961-63, magistrate first class, 1963; asst. sec. prime ministers office Malaysian Civil Service, Kuala Lumpur, 1963; elections returning officer Malaysian Civil Service, 1964; from asst. sec. to prin. asst. sec. Minstry of Home Affairs, Kuala Lumpur, 1967; Malaysian consul to Indonesia Ministry of Home Affairs, Sumatra, Medan, 1968-69; counsellor Embassy of Malaysia, Manila, 1969-72; Malaysian minister to Indonesia Jakarta, 1972-74; undersec. for S.E. Asia Ministry of Fgn. Affairs, Kuala Lumpur, 1974-76; ambassador to Hanoi Vietnam, 1976-78; high commr. to N. Zealand Ministry of Fgn. Affairs, Wellington, 1978-80; dir. gen. Nat. Secretariat of Malaysia Ministry of Fgn. Affairs, Kuala Lumpur, 1980-86; permanent rep. of Malaysia UN, N.Y.C., 1986—; also accredited as ambassador of Malaysia to Cuba; liaison officer Paris Conf. on Indochina, Paris, 1973; del. to 34th session UN Gen. Assembly, N.Y.C., 1980. Contbr. articles to profl. jours. Council mem. IAPA, Hong Kong and Pacific, 1976; mem. Malaysian Red Cross Soc., Malaysia, 1961. Decorated P.P.M.G. His Majesty King of Malaysia, 1968, J.S.M., 1976, D.I.M.P. Sultan of Pahang, 1986. Club: Nat. Writers (Malaysia). Office: Permanent Mission of Malaysia to the U N 140 East 45th St 43rd Floor New York NY 10017

HITCH, CHARLES JOHNSTON, economist, institution executive; b. Boonville, Mo., Jan. 9, 1910; s. Arthur Martin and Bertha (Johnston) H.; m. Nancy Winslow Squire, Mar. 20, 1942; 1 dau., Caroline Reto. A.A., Kemper Mil. Sch., 1929; B.A. with highest distinction, U. Ariz., 1931, LL.D., 1962; postgrad., Harvard, 1931-32; B.A. with first class honors (Rhodes scholar), Oxford U., 1934, M.A., 1938; D.Sc. in Commerce, Drexel U., 1963; LL.D., U. Pitts., 1968, U. Mo., 1968, George Washington U., 1976; D.Engring., Colo. Sch. Mines, 1979; L.H.D. honoris causa, U. Judaism, 1973; D. Pub. Policy, Rand Grad. Inst., 1985. Began as fellow, praelector, tutor Queen's Coll., Oxford U., 1935-48; gen. editor Oxford Econ. Papers, 1941-48; vis. prof. U. São Paolo, Brazil, 1947; chief econs. div. Rand Corp., Washington, 1948-61, dir. research program; asst. sec. def. (comptroller), 1961-65; v.p. bus. and finance U. Calif., 1965-66, v.p. of adminstrn., 1966-67, pres. univ., 1968-75; prof. econs. U. Calif. at Berkeley, 1965-75; now emeritus; pres. Resources for the Future, 1975-79, also dir.; vis. prof. UCLA, 1949-50; Irving Fisher research prof. Yale, 1957; Staff economist Mission for Econ. Affairs, U.S. Embassy, London, 1941-42; staff economist planning com. WPB, 1942-43; chief stblzn. controls div. Office War Moblzn. and Reconversion, 1945-46; chmn. gen. adv. com. ERDA, 1975-77; mem. Energy

Research Advisory Bd. Dept. Energy, 1978-85, Assembly Engring., NRC, 1975-78, Nat. Petroleum Council, 1975-78; mem. advisory council Gas Research Inst., 1976-84, Electric Power Research Inst., 1978-85; mem. Research Coordination Council, Gas Research Inst., 1984-87 ; dir. Aerospace Corp., 1975-82. Author: The Economics of Defense in the Nuclear Age, 1960, Decision Making for Defense, 1965; Editor: Introduction to Economic Analysis and Policy, 1938, Energy Conservation and Economic Growth, 1978. Trustee Asia Found., Center Biotech. Research; bd. dirs. Am. Council on Edn., 1971-74. Served as 1st lt., OSS U.S. Army, 1943-45. Recipient Pub. Service award U.S. Navy, 1965; Phi Beta Kappa vis. scholar, 1977-78; Hon. fellow Queen's Coll., Oxford; Hon. fellow Worcester Coll., Oxford. Fellow AAAS, Am. Acad. Arts and Scis., Econometric Soc.; mem. Am. Econ. Assn. (v.p. 1965), Royal Econ. Soc., Ops. Research Soc. Am. (council 1955-58, pres. 1959-60), Council Fgn. Relations, Nat. Acad. Pub. Adminstrn., Phi Beta Kappa. Democrat. Presbyn. Clubs: Bohemian (San Francisco); Cosmos (Washington). Home: 1515 Oxford St Berkeley CA 94709 Office: Lawrence Berkeley Lab U Calif Berkeley CA 94720

HITCH, HORACE, lawyer; b. Princeton, Ind., July 3, 1921; s. Horace and Edith Mae (Ervin) H.; m. Helen Tuttle, Oct. 7, 1943; children: Peter H., Thomas E. B.Sc., U. Minn., 1942, LL.B., 1947. Bar: Minn. 1947. Ptnr. Dorsey & Whitney, Mpls., 1947—. Chancellor Episcopal Diocese Minn., 1974—. Served with USNR, 1942-46, 51-52. Mem. ABA, Minn. Bar Assn., Am. Judicature Soc., Order of Coif. Clubs: Minikada, Mpls.; Beach and Tennis, Pebble Beach, Calif. Office: Dorsey & Whitney 2200 First Bank Pl E Minneapolis MN 55402

HITCH, THOMAS KEMPER, economist; b. Boonville, Mo., Sept. 16, 1912; s. Arthur Martin and Bertha (Johnston) H.; m. Margaret Barnhart, June 27, 1940 (dec. Nov. 1974); children: Hilary, Leslie, Caroline, Thomas; m. Mae Okudaira. Student, Nat. U. Mexico, 1932; A.B., Stanford U., 1934; M.A., Columbia U., 1946; Ph.D., U. London, 1937. Mem. faculty Stephens Coll., Columbia, Mo., 1937-42; spl. study commodity markets Commodity Exchange Adminstrn., Dept. Agr., 1940; acting head current bus. research sect. Dept. Commerce, 1942-43; labor adviser Vets. Emergency Housing Program, 1946-47; economist labor econs. Pres.'s Council Econ. Advisers, 1947-50; dir. research Hawaii Employers Council, Honolulu, 1950-59; sr. v.p., mgr. research div. First Hawaiian Bank, 1959-82; chmn. Hawaii Gov.'s Adv. Com. on Financing, 1959-62; chmn. research com. Hawaii Vistors Bur., 1962-69; chmn. Mayor's Fin. Adv. Com., 1960-68; chmn. taxation and fin. com. Constl. Conv. Hawaii, 1968. Contbr. articles to profl. jours. Trustee Tax Found. of Hawaii, 1955-80, pres., 1968; trustee McInerny Found.; chmn. Hawaii Joint Council Econ. Edn., 1964-68. Served as lt. O.R.C., 1933-38; as lt. USNR, 1943-46. Mem. C. of C. Hawaii (chmn. bd. 1971), Nat. Assn. Bus. Economists, Am., Hawaii econs. assns., Indsl. Relations Research Assn., Am. Statis. Assn., Phi Beta Kappa, Pi Sigma Alpha, Alpha Sigma Phi. Clubs: Waialae Country (pres. 1979), Pacific. Home: 5329 Olapa St Honolulu HI 96821 Office: First Hawaiian Bank Honolulu HI 96847

HITCHCOCK, J. GARETH, retired judge; b. Putnam County, Ohio June 10, 1914; s. Roy C. and Laura (Adam) H.; m. Helen M. Eck, June 10, 1941 (dec. Oct. 1972); children—James Edward, David Louis; m. 2d, Ruth E. Fessel, Aug. 18, 1973. LL.B., Ohio State U., 1939, J.D., 1969. Bar: Ohio 1939, U.S. Dist. Ct. (no. dist.) Ohio 1945, U.S. Dist. Ct. (no. dist.) Ind. 1960, U.S. Supreme Ct. 1960, U.S. Ct. Appeals (7th cir.) 1960. Sole practice, Paulding, Ohio, 1939-40; spl. agt. FBI, 1940-42; sole practice, Port Clinton, Ohio, 1946-51; protection chief Joseph Home Co., Pitts., 1951-57; investment sales Federated Investors Inc., Pitts., 1957-59; practice, Paulding, Ohio, 1959-60; judge Common Pleas Ct. Paulding County (Ohio), 1960-86. Served with AUS, 1942-46. Mem. Ohio State Bar Assn. (bar activities com. 1963-80, com. jud. adminstrn. and legal reform 1981—), Paulding County Bar Assn., N.W. Ohio Bar Assn., Am. Judicature Soc., Judge Advocates Assn., Ohio Common Pleas Judges Assn., Soc. Former Spl. Agts. of FBI. Republican. Episcopalian. Club: Kiwanis (lt. gov. 1970-71). Contbr. articles to profl. jours. Home: 733 N Cherry St Paulding OH 45879

HITTLE, DAVID WILLIAM, lawyer; b. Medford, Oreg., Apr. 28, 1947; s. Merritt Lyle and Mary Jane (Williams) H.; m. Sharon Lea Crowley, Sept. 27, 1969 (div. June 1975). BS, Oreg. State U., 1969; JD, Lewis & Clark Coll., 1974. Bar: Oregon 1974, U.S. Dist. Ct. Oreg. 1974, U.S. Ct. Appeals (9th cir.) 1976, U.S. Supreme Ct. 1977. Assoc. William Claussen PC, Salem, Oreg., 1974-75, Dye & Olson, Salem, 1975-79; ptnr. Olson, Hittle & Gardner, Salem, 1979-82, Callahan, Hittle & Gardner, Salem, 1982—; instr. Linfield Coll., McMinnville, Oreg., 1982—, Coll. of Law Willamette U., Salem, 1988—; mcpl. judge pro tem City of Salem, 1978-85; dist. judge pro tem Oreg., 1982-85. Mem. Oreg. Trial Lawyers Assn. (legis. chmn. workers compensation 1985), Oreg. Bar Assn. (worker's compensation sect., sec. 1982, chmn. 1984, bd. govs. 1985—, v.p. 1987-88, contbr. author Bar book on Worker's Compensation 1980, 84, Real Property 1985, Legislation, 1985), Marion County Bar (bd. dirs. 1984-86, v.p. 1987, pres. 1988), Oreg. Workers' Compensation Attys. (exec. com. 1978—), Oreg. Supreme Ct. Disciplinary Bd. 1984-85. Home: 1570 Fairmount Ave S Salem OR 97302 Office: Callahan Hittle & Gardner 2659 Commercial St SE Suite 200 Salem OR 97302

HITTLE, JAMES D., government and business consultant; b. Bear Lake, Mich., June 10, 1915; s. Harry F. and Margaret Jane (McArthur) H.; m. Edna Jane Smith, Dec. 9, 1939 (dec. 1969); children: Harry McArthur, James Richard; m. Patricia Ann Herring, Sept. 5, 1970. B.A., Mich. State U., 1937; M.S. in Oriental History and Geography, U. Utah, 1952. Commd. 2d lt. USMC, 1937, advanced through grades to brig. gen., 1958, legis. asst. to comdt., 1952-58; asst. to sec. def. legis. affairs 1958-60, retired, 1960; dir. nat. security and fgn. affairs VFW, 1960-67; syndicated columnist Copley News Service, 1964-69; mil. commentator MBS, 1964-69; dir. DISC, Inc., 1960-67; spl. counsel Senate Armed Services Com., 1968-69; cons. House Armed Services Com., 1968-69; founder, dir. D.C. Nat. Bank, 1965-69; asst. sec. navy for manpower and res. affairs 1969-71; sr. v.p. govt. affairs Pan Am. World Airways, Washington, 1971-73; cons. to adminstr. VA, 1973-77; cons. to pres. Overseas Pvt. Investment Corp., 1974-75; participant comml. air mgmt. survey S.E. Asian Transp. and Communications Commn., 1975; cons. Gleason Assos. Inc., 1974—, LTV Aerospace and Def. Corp., 1975—, Marriott Corp., 1978—, KMS Industries, Inc., 1985—; comdt. U.S. Marine Corps, 1979-81; sec. U.S. Navy, 1981-82; counselor to Sec. of Navy, 1982-87; mem. adv. com. USN Postgrad. Sch., 1983-86. Author: History of the Military Staff, 1949; also articles.; Editor: Jomini's Art of War, 1945; columnist: Navy Times, 1974—. Bd. dirs. Stafford County (Va.) Indsl. Devel. Authority, 1974—; vice chmn. Belleau Woods U.S. Mil. Cemetary Meml. Day Services, 1978—. Decorated Legion of Merit with combat V, Purple Heart; Medal of Combat Merit France; Cross of Chevalier, Mil. Order European Vets.; recipient Alfred Thayer Mahan award Navy League U.S., 1960, Scroll of Honor, 1967; silver medal City of Paris, 1961; gold medal, 1972; George Washington award Freedom Found., 1967, 69; Selective Service System Distinguished Service award, 1971; U.S. Navy Civilian Distinguished Service award, 1971, 87; Meritorious Pub. Service citation U.S. Marine Corps, 1981; Outstanding Alumnus award Mich. State U., 1987. Mem. VFW, Am. Legion, Brit. Legion (hon.), La. State Hist. Soc. (hon. life), Mil. Order World Wars, Clan MacArthur Soc. Am., Navy League, U.S. Marine Corps League (legis. com. 1980-82), Battleship Assn. U.S., 1st Marine Div. Assn. (life), 3d Marine Div. Assn. (life), Co. Mil. Historians, Mil. Order of Carabao, China-Burma-India Vets. Assn., Phi Kappa Phi, Phi Kappa Delta. Club: Army-Navy Washington (pres. 1983-87, pres. emeritus 1988—). Mailing Address: 3137 S 14th St Arlington VA 22204

HITTMAIR, OTTO HEINRICH, physics educator; b. Innsbruck, Austria, Mar. 16, 1924; s. Rudolf and Margarete (Schumacher) H.; m. Anni Rauch, Dec. 3, 1956; children—Christine, Elisabeth, Georg, Margarete. Ph.D., U. Innsbruck, 1949, dozent, 1953; D.Tech. (hon.), Tech. U. Budapest, 1982. Vis. scientist Inst. Advanced Studies, Dublin, 1951, MIT, Cambridge, Mass., 1951-52; attache CNRS, Paris, 1952-54; sr. fellow U. Sydney (Australia), 1954-56; vis. scientist Comision Nacional de Energia Atomica, Buenos Aires, 1957; scientist Atomic Inst. Austrian U., 1958-60; prof. physics Tech. U. Vienna, 1960—, dean Faculty Scis., 1968-69, rector, 1977-79; Author: (With S.T. Butler) Nuclear Stripping Reactions, 1957; Quantum Theory, 1972; (with G. Adam) Theory of Heat, 1971, 77; (with H. Weber) Superconductivity, 1979. Recipient Jubilee medal U. Innsbruck, 1970; prize for sci. and tech. City of Vienna, 1982; Wilhelm Exner medal Austrian Trade Assn., 1982. Mem. Austrian Acad. Scis. (sec. 1983-87, pres. 1987—, Erwin Schrodinger prize 1974); Internat. Soc. Engring. Edn. (v.p. 1973—), Royal Soc. Sci. Uppsala, Austrian Phys. Soc., European Phys. Soc. Roman Catholic. Office: Tech Univ, Karlsplatz 13, A-1040 Vienna Austria

HITZIG, BERNARD MICHAEL, physiology and biophysics scientist educator; b. N.Y.C., Apr. 17, 1935; s. Joseph B. and Martha (Steiger) H.; m. Jacqueline Freeman, Feb. 8, 1960 (div. 1967); 1 child, Jennifer Beth; m. Harlyn Anne Behrmann, Aug. 5, 1972; 1 child, Kathryn Anne. B.S., Wagner Coll., 1958; postgrad. Columbia U., 1958-61; Ph.D., Brown U., 1977. Parker Francis Found. fellow Dartmouth Med. Sch., Hanover, N.H., 1978-79; asst. prof. Howard U., Washington, 1979-81; asst. prof. physiology and biophysics Harvard U. Med. Sch., Boston, 1981-86, assoc. prof. physiology and biophysics, 1987—; asst. biologist Mass. Gen. Hosp., Boston, 1981-86, assoc. biologist, 1987—; vis. scientist MIT, Cambridge, 1983—. Contbr. articles to profl. jours. Hinds Found. fellow, 1977-78; NIH grantee, 1978, 80, 84, 85; Am. Heart Assn. grantee, 1986. Mem. Am. Soc. Zoologists, Biophys. Soc., Nuclear Magnetic Resonance Soc., Sigma Xi.

HIYAMA, TAMEJIRO, research chemist, chemistry educator; b. Ibaraki, Osaka, Japan, Aug. 24, 1946; s. Hachiro and Sumie Hiyama; m. Hisako Tsujimoto, Feb. 15, 1975; children—Kazuko, Taichi, Hitoshi. B., Kyoto U., 1969, M.Eng., 1971; D. Eng., Kyoto U., 1975. Lectr. Kyoto U., Japan, 1972-81; jr. research fellow Sagami Chem. Research Ctr., Sagamihara, Kanagawa, Japan, 1981-83, sr. research fellow, 1983-88, exec. research fellow, 1988— . Author: (in Japanese) Highly Selective Synthesis in Organic Chemistry, 1982. Contbr. articles to profl. jours. Harvard U. fellow 1975-76. Mem. Chem. Soc. Japan (Progress award 1980), Kinki Chem. Soc., Assn. Synthetic Organic Chemistry Japan, Am. Chem. Soc. Home: 4-29-3-101 Kamitsuruma, Sagamihara, Kanagawa 229, Japan Office: Sagami Chem Research Ctr, 4-4-1 Nishiohnuma, 229 Sagamihara, Kanagawa Japan

HIYOSHI, JUNICHI, ceramics company executive; b. Jakarta, Indonesia, May 5, 1923; s. Kingo and Enko (Asami) H.; B., Tokyo U. Tech. Coll., 1946; m. Noriko Takahashi, Oct. 24, 1953; children—Koichi, Kenji. Dir., Toshiba Corp., Tokyo, 1978-80, dir. home appliance sect., 1980, mng. dir. in research and devel., 1980-82, sr. mng. dir., 1982-84; exec. v.p. Toshiba Ceramics Co., Tokyo, 1984-85, pres., 1985-88, exec. advisor 1988—. Mem. Japan Soc. Mech. Engrs., Inst. TV Engrs. Japan. Home: 2-16-1 Senzoku Meguroku, T 152 Tokyo Japan Office: Shinjuku Nomura Bldg 1-26-2, Nishi-Shinjuku Shunjukuk, T 163 Tokyo Japan

HJALMAR, LARS-OLOF, electrical company executive; b. Karlsham, Sweden, May 21, 1939; m. Marie-Louise Mortenson, Mar. 24, 1962; children: Viktoria, Lukas. MSc, Chalmers U., Gothenburg, 1964; MBA, Stockholm U., 1976. V.p. tech. PLM Packaging, Malmo, Sweden, 1964-68, v.p. plastics group, 1968-78; pres., chief exec. officer Noack Batteries, Stockholm, 1974-78, Bahco, Stockholm, 1978-83, Siemens, Stockholm, 1983—; pres. bd. dirs. Hellectron, Siemens Data; bd. dirs. PK-Banken, Comparex Indo. Systems, Gunnebo, Siemens-Elema, others. Bd. dirs. Cancer Union, Stockholm, 1978, S.W. Fedn. Employers, Stockholm, 1976, S.W. Indsl. Fedn., 1978. Home: Vaarvaegen 18, S-182 74 Stocksund Sweden Office: Siemens AB, Helsingeg 40, S-104 35 Stockholm Sweden

HJARTARSON, RAGNAR, food products company executive; b. Reykjavik, Iceland, May 21, 1965; parents: Hjortur and Rosa Bjorg (Karlsdottir) H. Student, Comml. Coll. Iceland, Reykjavik, 1985; postgrad., U. Iceland, Reykjavik, 1986. Mgr. purchasing Smjorlik Sol..Ltd., Reykjavik, 1985—. Mem. Motel Choir Iceland, Reykjavik, 1985—. Mem. Liberal Party Iceland. Lutheran. Home: Granaskjol 64, 107 Reykjavik Iceland Office: Smjorlik Sol Ltd, Thverholt 17 21, 105 Reykjavik Iceland

HJERTAGER, BJORN HELGE, research scientist; b. Bergen, Norway, Feb. 26, 1947; s. Harald A. and Annie E. (Hovdenes) H.; m. Inger-Lill Storhaug, Dec. 31, 1969; children—Hilde B., Lene K., Nina. Ing., Bergen Engring. Coll., 1968; M.Sc., U. Trondheim, Norway, 1972, Ph.D., 1979. Sci. asst. U. Trondheim, 1973, asst. prof., 1976-78; head dept. Norwegian Underwater Inst., Bergen, 1979; sr. scientist Christian Michelsen Inst., Bergen, 1980-83, head research program, 1984—. Author: Flow Heat Transfer and Combustion in Three-Dimensional Enclosures, 1979; contbg. author Handbook for Heat and Mass Transfer Operations, 1986; contbr. articles to profl. jours. Served with Norwegian Navy, 1968-69. Mem. Combustion inst., AIAA, Internat. Assn. Math. and Computers in Simulation, Internat. Centre Heat and Mass Transfer, Polyteknisk Forening. Home: Vakleiva 101, N 5062 Bergen Norway Office: Chr Michelsen Inst, Fantoftvegen 38, N 5036 Bergen Norway

HLEBEC, BORIS, linguist, translator; b. Belgrade, Yugoslavia, Aug. 4, 1945; s. Franjo and Bosiljka (Stoisavljevic) H.; m. Mila Trifunovic, Aug. 24, 1980; 1 child, Darko. BA in Philology, U. Belgrade, 1968, MA, 1973, D.Linguistics, 1979. Bookshop asst. Foyles, London, 1968; grad. asst. Faculty Philology, U. Belgrade, 1970-73, asst., 1973-80, asst. prof., 1980—, dep. head dept. English, 1983-85; mem. orgn. com. 12th World Congress Internat. Fedn. Translators. Translator: A. Tennyson: Ulysses, 1977, The Canterbury Tales (Chaucer) 1983; co-translator A Dictionary of Linguistics, 1987. Mem. Soc. Linguistics Europe. Home: XI Krajiske Divizije 67, 11090 Belgrade Yugoslavia Office: Faculty Philology, U Belgrade, Knez-Mihajlova 40, 11000 Belgrade Yugoslavia

HO, CHESTER SHOU-TIE, biochemical engineering executive; b. Chia-Yi, Taiwan, Dec. 25, 1950; came to U.S., 1974; s. Kuan-Wen and Su-Wen (Fu) H.; m. Angela Fong-Chu Chang, June 21, 1975; children: Joey C., Arkady C. BSChem E, Chung-Yuan U., 1972; MSChemE, Kans. State U., 1977; PhDChemE, MIT, 1987. Prof. dept. chem. engring. SUNY, Buffalo, 1983-87, dir. Cell Culture Lab., 1983-87; dir. Biochem. Engring. dept. Invitron Corp., St. Louis, 1987—; affiliate prof. chem. engring., Wash. U., St. Louis, 1988—; panelist small bus. innovative research com. NSF; mem. organizing com. U.S./Japan Collaborative Research in Biotech. Author: Biotechnology Processes: Scale-Up and Mixing, 1987; contbr. articles to profl. jours.; patentee in field. Mem. Am. Inst. Chem. Engrs., Am. Chem. Soc., AAAS, N.Y. Acad. Scis., Tissue Culture Assn., Sigma Xi. Home: 753 Westbrooke Terrace Dr Ballwin MO 63021 Office: Invitron Corp 4649 LeBourget Dr Saint Louis MO 63134

HO, CHUNG FAI, tooling company executive; b. Hong Kong, July 19, 1949; s. Kon and Lai (Lee) H.; m. Magy Poon Ho, Mar. 26, 1976; children—Frankie, Dickie. B.Sc., U. Hong Kong, 1971, Ph.D., 1977. Cons., Chen Hsong Co., Hong Kong, 1973-75; lectr. Hong Kong Polytechnic, 1975-77; mgr. factory Yan Hing Engring. Co., Hong Kong, 1977-81; cons. Hong Kong Productivity Council, 1981-84; sr. elec. and mech. engr. Hong Kong Govt., 1984; gen. mgr. Hong Kong CAD/CAM Services Co., 1985—. Editor: Hong Kong Plastics Technology, 1985. Mem. Instn. Mech. Engrs., Hong Kong Instn. Engrs. Avocation: Ball games. Home: 7/F Block B, Oriental Height, 33 Shatin Hong Kong Office: HK CAD/CAM Services Ltd, 9-11 Dai Wang St, Tai Po Industrial Estate, Tai Po Hong Kong

HO, IWAN, research plant pathologist; b. Souzhou, Jiangsu, China, Apr. 15, 1925; came to U.S., 1956; m. Mei-Chun Chang, Nov. 29, 1975; 1 child, Tomur M. BS, Nat. Shanghai U., 1946; MS, La. State U., 1958; PhD, Oreg. State U., 1984. Microbiologist Seattle Pub. Health Dept., 1962-66; research plant physiologist Forestry Scis. Lab., Corvallis, Oreg., 1970—; courtesy asst. prof. Coll. Forestry, Oreg. State U. Mem. Mycol. Soc. Am., Am. Soc. Plant Physiologists, Internat. Soc. Plant Molecular Biology, Sigma Xi. Democrat. Episcopalian. Home: 1686 Bullevard Philomath OR 97370 Office: Forestry Sci Lab Pacific Northwest Research Sta 3200 Jefferson Corvallis OR 97333

HO, KAM-FAI, university administrator; b. Hong Kong, June 10, 1933; s. Shu-Fong Ho and Sai-Ying Pang; m. Christine Yuk-Chin Tse; children: Joy, Edmond, Eugene. BA in Econs., Nat. Taiwan U., 1959; Diploma in Social Scis., Hong Kong U., 1960; MSW, Columbia U., 1964, DSW, 1974. Sr. social worker Internat. Social SErvices, Hong Kong, 1959-62; reader in social work Chinese U. of Hong Kong, 1964-83, dir. dept. extramural studies, 1983—; external cons., Pupua-New Guinea U., 1968; external examiner, Hong Kong Poly., 1983-86. Contbr. articles to profl. jours. Mem. Hong Kong Legis. Council, 1978—. Recipient Justice of the Peace award His Excellency the Gov., Hong Kong, 1980; named Order Brit. Empire, Her Majesty the Queen, Hong Kong, 1981. Clubs: Beas River Country (Hong Kong), Urban Services Recreation.

HO, LEO CHI CHIEN, education administrator; b. Tai Hu, An-Wei, Republic of China, Sept. 2, 1940; came to U.S., 1964, naturalized, 1971; s. Yu Yuan and Hung (King) H.; m. Julie Yu-Ling Hou, May 11, 1967; children: Albert, Alexander. BA, Nat. Cheng Chi U., Taipei, Republic of China, 1964; MLS, Atlanta U., 1967; PhD, Wayne State U., 1975. Librarian Tex. Tech U., Lubbock, 1966-69; dir. China Sci. Pub., Taylor, Mich., 1969-77; bus. librarian Detroit Pub. Library, 1970-75; librarian Washtenaw Community Coll., Ann Arbor, Mich., 1977—; pres. Fin. Brokers' Exchange, Farmington Hills, Mich., 1978-87; edn. adminstr. Sylvan Learning Ctr.Mich., West Bloomfield, 1987—; bd. dirs. Sylvan Learning Ctr. of Mich. Mem. adv. council Guide to Ethnic Museums, Libraries, and Archives in the U.S., 1984. Bd. govs. Internat. Inst. of Greater Met. Detroit, 1985—; commr. Mich. Gov.'s Adv. Com. on Asian Affairs, Lansing, 1986—. Mem. Detroit Chinese Cultural Ctr. (pres. 1984-86, Outstanding Service award 1984), Assn. Chinese-Ams. (v.p. 1985—, dedicated service award 1988). Lodge: Rotary. Home: 3810 Manchester Ct Bloomfield Hills MI 48013 Office: Sylvan Learning Ctr 5755 W Maple Suite 115 West Bloomfield MI 48033

HO, ROBERT EN MING, physician; b. Honolulu, Nov. 13, 1942; s. Donald Tet En Ho and Violette (Weeks) Gould; m. Edie Olsen, June 27, 1964; children: Lisa, Amy. BS cum laude, Mich. State U., 1964; MD, Wayne State U., 1968. Diplomate Am. Bd. Neurol. Surgery. Surg. intern Detroit Gen. Hosp., 1968-69, surg. resident, 1969-70, neurosurg. resident, 1972-76; microsurg. fellow Neurochirurgische Universtatskilinik, Zurich, Switzerland, 1976; instr. dept. neurosurgery Wayne State U., Detroit, 1977-79, dir. dept. neurosurgery Gertrude Levin Pain Clinic, 1977-80, asst. prof., 1979-84, chief neurosurg. services Health Care Inst., 1979-84, founder, dir. Microneurosurg. Lab., 1977—, clin. asst. prof., 1984—; dir. neuroscis. intensive care unit Harper Hosp., Detroit, 1980-84; mem. audit com. Detroit Gen. Hosp., 1977-80, mem. med. device com., 1977-80, mem. credentials com., 1978-84; sec., treas. Detroit Neurosurg. Acad. Program Com., 1978-84; mem. emergency room com. Harper Hosp., 1980-84, neuroscis. intensive care unit com., 1980-84; dir. Oakland-Macomb PPO; chief neurol. sect. William Beaumont Hosp., Troy, Mich., trustee, 1986—; presenter of numerous exhibits, profl. papers; organizer numerous med. meetings.; lectr. in field. Contbr. articles to profl. jours. Served with U.S. Army, 1970-72, Vietnam. Recipient Intern of Yr. award Detroit Gen. Hosp., 1969. Mem. AMA, ACS, Congress Neurol. Surgeons, Detroit Neurosurg. Acad., Mich. Assn. Neurol. Surgeons (sec.-treas. 1979-82, v.p. 1982-84, pres. 1984-86, bd. dirs. 1986—), Mich. State Med. Soc., Oakland County Med. Soc., Wayne County Med. Soc., Internat. Coll. Surgeons (U.S. sect.), Am. Assn. Neurol. Surgeons (spinal disorders sect. 1981, cerebrovascular surgery sect.). Office: 44199 Dequindre Rd Suite 402 Troy MI 48098

HO, TAO, architect, designer, lecturer, art critic; b. Shanghai, China, July 17, 1936; s. Ping Yin Ho and Chin Haw Chiu; m. Chi Ping Lu, June 6, 1960 (div. 1978); children—Suenn, Shu, Dien; m. 2d Irene Yue Chi Lo, Aug. 23, 1978; 1 daughter, Noelle. B.A., Williams Coll., 1960, L.H.D. (hon.), 1979; M.Arch., Harvard U., 1964. Research asst. Albright Art Gallery, Buffalo, 1959; asst. architect Architects Collaborative, Cambridge, Mass., 1960-64; architect Hsin Yieh Architects, Hong Kong, 1964-65; lectr. design Chinese U., Hong Kong, 1965-67; prin. Taoho Design Architects, Hong Kong, 1968—; core mem. Asian Planning & Archtl. Collaborative, Hong Kong, 1975—; founder, dir. Vision Press Ltd., Hong Kong, 1982—; hon. lectr. art and architecture U. Hong Kong, 1982—; adviser Hong Kong Mus. Art, 1981, design dept. Hong Kong Poly., 1982. Archtl. designs include: Hong Kong Internat. Elem. Sch.; Hong Kong Arts Centre (Hong Kong Inst. Architects Silver medal for design 1978), 1977; Hong Kong St. Stephen's Coll. (Hong Kong Inst. Architects Design Excellence award 1982), 1981; designer 8 sets of commemorative stamps for Hong Kong Govt., 1975—. Cofounder Hong Kong Arts Centre; mem. tech. edn. bd. Hong Kong Govt., 1983—. Arthur Lehman fellow Harvard U., 1960; vis. fellow Hong Kong and Macau Study Centre, Zhongshan U., Guangzhou, China, 1984—. Mem. Hong Kong Inst. Architects, World Soc. for Ekistics, Chartered Inst. Arbitrators, (assoc.), Hong Kong Designers Assn. (chmn.), Hong Kong Arts Centre. Lodge: Rotary. Office: Taoho Design Architects, 33-35 Leighton Rd, 22d Floor, Causeway Bay Hong Kong *

HO, TIEH-CHI, architect; b. Canton, China, Oct. 20, 1937; came to U.S., 1966; s. Huy-Dinh and Thoai-Anh (Ha) H.; m. Betty Ju-Wuan, July 9, 1966; children—Winnie, Anne. B.S., Cheng Chung U., 1962; M.S. in Tropical Architecture, Pratt Inst., 1967. Designer, Lee-Tai Architects/Engrs., Taipei, Taiwan, 1962-65, Brodsky, Hopf & Adler, N.Y.C., 1967-68; architect I.M. Pei & Ptnrs., Architects & Planners, N.Y.C., 1968-74; ptnr., architect Babusis & Ho Architects, Hackensack, N.J., 1974-76; prin. Ho Assocs., Architects, N.Y.C., 1976—; cons. Viet-Am. Consl. Benevolent Assn., N.Y.C., 1983—; designer Statue of Confucius, N.Y.C., 1983, Chinese Gate in Chinatown, N.Y.C., 1984. Mem. Beautifying of Chinatown Com., 1984. Mem. AIA. Lodge: Viet-Am. Lions (pres. N.Y.C.). Office: Ho Assocs Architects 33 Bowery New York NY 10002

HOADLEY, WALTER EVANS, economist, financial executive; b. San Francisco, Aug. 16, 1916; s. Walter Evans and Marie Howland (Preece) H.; m. Virginia Alm, May 20, 1939; children: Richard Alm, Jean Elizabeth (Mrs. Donald A. Peterson). A.B., U. Calif., 1938, M.A., 1940, Ph.D., 1946; Dr.C.S., Franklin and Marshall Coll., 1963; LL.D. (hon.), Golden Gate U., 1968, U. Pacific, 1979; hon. degree, El Instituto Technologico Autonomo de Mexico, 1974. Collaborator U.S. Bur. Agrl. Econs., 1938-39; research economist Calif. Gov.'s Reemployment Commn., 1939, Calif. Gov.'s Reemployment Commn. (Planning Bd.), 1941; research economist, teaching fellow U. Calif., 1938-41, supr. indsl. mgmt. war tng. office, 1941-42; econ. adviser U. Chgo. Civil Affairs Tng. Sch., 1945; sr. economist Fed. Res. Bank Chgo., 1942-49; economist Armstrong Cork Co., Lancaster, Pa., 1949-54; treas. Armstrong World Industries, 1954-60; v.p., treas. Armstrong Cork Co., 1960-66, dir., 1962-87; sr. v.p., chief economist, mem. mng. com. Bank of Am. NT & SA, San Francisco, 1966-68; exec. v.p., chief economist, mem. mng. com., mem. mgmt. adv. council, chmn. subs. Bank of Am. NT & SA, 1968-81; ret. 1981; sr. research fellow Hoover Inst., Stanford U., 1981—; dir. Transcisco Industries, Inc., Pacific Gas Transmission, Selected Funds, PLM Inc.; dep. chmn. Fed. Res. Bank, Phila., 1960-61, chmn., 1962-66; chmn. Conf. Fed. Res. Chairmen, 1966; faculty Sch. Banking U. Wis., 1945-49, 55, 58-66; adviser various U.S. Govt. agys.; Wright Internat. Bd. Econ. and Investment Advisors, 1987—; spl. adviser U.S. Congl. Budget Office, 1975-87; mem. pub. adv. bd. U.S. Dept. Commerce, 1970-74; mem. White House Rev. Com. for Balance Payments Statistics, 1963-65, Presdl. Task Force on Growth, 1969-70, Presdl. Task Force on Land Utilization, Presdl. Conf. on Inflation, 1974; gov. Com. on Developing Am. Capitalism, 1977—, chmn. 1987—. Mem. Meth. Ch. Commn. on World Service and Fin. Phila. Conf., 1957-64, chmn. investment com., 1964-66; bd. dirs., exec. com. Internat. Mgmt. and Devel. Inst., 1976—; trustee Pacific Sch. Religion, 1968—; adviser Nat. Commn. to Study Nursing and Nursing Edn., 1968-73; trustee Duke U., 1968-73, pres.'s assoc., 1973-80; trustee Golden Gate U., 1974—, chmn. investment com., 1977—; trustee World Wildlife U.S.-Conservation Found., 1974-87; mem. periodic chmn. adminstrv. bd. Trinity United Meth. Ch., Berkeley, Calif., 1966-84; mem. bd. advisors Lafayette (Calif.) United Meth. Ch., 1984—; mem. bd. overseers vis. com. Harvard Coll. Econs., 1969-74; chmn. investment com. Calif.-Nev. Meth. Found., 1968-75, mem., 1976—; mem. Calif. Gov.'s Council Econ. and Bus. Devel., 1978-82, chmn., 1980-82; trustee Hudson Inst., 1979-84; co-chmn. San Francisco Mayor's Fiscal Adv. Com., 1978-81, mem. 1981—; spl. adviser Presdl. Cabinet Com. Innovation, 1978-79; mem. Calif. State Internat. Adv. Com., 1986—. Fellow Am. Statis. Assn. (v.p. dir. 1952-54, pres. 1958), Nat. Assn. of Bus. Economists (vice-chmn. 1975-86, chmn. 1987—), Com. Devel. Am. Capitalism, Internat. Acad. Mgmt.; mem. Am. Fin. Assn. (dir. 1955-56, pres. 1969), Conf. Bus. Economists (chmn. 1962), Atlantic Council of U.S. (dir. 1985—), Internat. C. of C. (vice chmn. commn. on econ. and fin. policy, trustee, chmn. com. on internat. monetary affairs U.S. council), Commonwealth Club of Calif. (pres. 1987), Internat. Conf. Comml. Bank Economists (chmn. 1978-81), Am., Western Econ. Assns., Am. Marketing Assn., Fin. Analysts San Francisco, Conf. Bd. (econ. forum), Am. Bankers Assn. (chmn. urban and community affairs com. 1972-73, mem. econ. adv. council 1976-78), Nat. Bur. Econ. Research (dir.), Western Fin. Assn., dir., mem. steering com., U. Calif. Alumni Council (chmn. investment com. 1983—, v.p. 1985—), U.S. Nat. Com. on Pacific Econ. Cooperation (vice chmn. 1984—, pres.-elect 1988), Phi Beta Kappa (v.p. Western region, dir. 1986—), Kappa Alpha. Clubs: St. Francis Yacht (San Francisco), Commonwealth (San Francisco), Pacific Union (San Francisco), Bankers (San Francisco); Silverado Country. Office: 555 California St Suite 500 San Francisco CA 94104

HOAG, W(ILLIAM) GIFFORD, management consultant; b. N.Y.C., Aug. 22, 1909; s. William J. and Anna L. (Puckhafer) H.; m. Diane Fisler, Feb. 24, 1939; children—Peter Marshall, John Gifford. B.S., Cornell U., 1931, M.S., 1934. Info. specialist Farm Credit Assn., Washington, 1934-51, dir. info., 1951-69, exec. asst. to gov., 1969-74; sr. assoc. E.A. Jaenke & Assocs., Washington, 1975-85; prin. W. Gifford Hoag Assocs., Washington, 1985—; treas. Fairfax Cable Assn., Va., 1982—, also dir.; pres. Potomac Coop. Fedn., Washington, 1958-62; bd. dirs. Group Health Assn., 1963-69, pres., 1965-68; vice chmn., treas. Greenbelt Coop., Savage, Md., 1960-71, 81-84. Author: (with others) Banks for Cooperatives-Quarter Century of Progress, 1959; The Farm Credit System: A History of Financial Self Help, 1976. Editor News for Farmer Cooperatives Mag., 1944-53. Contbr. articles on coops. and credit to profl. jours. Pres. Coop. Inst. Assn., Ithaca, N.Y., 1964-66. Recipient Career award Am. Inst. Cooperation, 1972; Travel award Coop. Found., 1980, 50 Yr. medal Fed. Land Banks, 1967; named to Coop. Hall of Fame, Coop. League of U.S.A., 1983. Mem. Advt. Council Coops. Internat. (treas. 1964-66), Coop. Editorial Assn. (bd. dirs. 1966-68, Klinefelter award 1965), Nat. Coop. Bus. Assn., Am. Agrl. Econ. Assn., Agrl. Relations Council, Am. Agrl. Editors Assn., Am. Mktg. Assn., Nat. Agrl. Mktg. Assn., Internat. Platform Assn., Alpha Zeta. Club: Nat. Press (Washington). Home: 1695 Beulah Rd Vienna VA 22180 Office: 1401 New York Ave NW Washington DC 20005

HOAGLAND, ALBERT JOSEPH, JR., psychotherapist, minister; b. Clayton, N.J., July 2, 1939. Cert. psychiat. tech., Ancora State Hosp., 1958; RN, Monmouth Med. Ctr., 1961; BS, Monmouth Coll., 1964; MSW, Rutgers U., 1966; M.Div., Fuller Theol. Sem., 1978; D in Ministry, Boston U., 1981; postgrad., Am. Inst. Hypnotherapy. Ordained to ministry Disciples of Christ, 1978; lic. clinical social worker, Calif., marriage, family and child counselor, Calif.; cert. sch. psychologist, anger therapist. Pvt. practice counseling 1959—; psychiat. technician N.J. State Hosp., 1958-66; instr., cons. Los Angeles County Dept. Probation, 1972-75; instr. psychology Calif. Grad. Inst., 1973; instr. Chapman Coll., 1972-74; instr. psychology Calif. State U., Dominguez Hills, 1974; instr. Torrance (Calif.) Adult Sch., 1977-79, 81-85; pastor Ariz., 1984-85, Calif., 1978-79, 81-84, Mass., 1977-81; subs. tchr. Marana (Ariz.) Sch. Dist., 1985; instr. Beverly Hills Adult Sch., 1984—; exec. clin. dir. Personal Counseling Services, San Pedro, 1986—; religious educator various retreats, programs, summer camps, etc., 1975—. Author: Anger to Intimacy, 1987; editor Jonestown Collection, 1978, Professional Papers from the Desert, 1970; producer (film) Gestalt Therapy, 1974. Mem. Congress of Disciples Clergy, Disciples of Christ Hist. Soc., Disciples Peace Fellowship; trainer, cons. Los Angeles Council Exploring div. Boy Scouts Am., 1971-74; coach Palos Verdes (Calif.) Soccer Program, basketball Torrance City Sports Program; dir. YWCA Delinquency Prevention Program, San Pedro, 1986—; chair community adv. council San Pedro High Sch.; campaigning for mayor. Mem. Nat. Tchrs. Assn., Nat. Assn. Social Workers, Am. Assn. Marriage and Family Therapists, Am. Osteo. Assn., Nat. Assn. Christians in Soc. Work, Harbor Area Police Clergy Council (pres.), Am. Guild Hypotherapists, Clowns of Am., Phi Delta Kappa. Democrat. Lodge: San Pedro Rotary (sec.). Home: 3318 W Torrance Blvd Torrance CA 90503 Office: Personal Counseling Services 1044 S Gaffey St #2 San Pedro CA 90731

HOAGLAND, HENRY WILLIAMSON, JR., investment consultant; b. Colorado Springs, Colo., Sept. 5, 1912; s. Henry W. and Harriet (Seldomridge) H.; B.A., Stanford U., 1934, LL.B., 1937; M.B.A., Harvard U., 1939; m. Ray Watkin, June 24, 1961. Exec. asst. to dir. mil. planning div. Office of Q.M. Gen., Washington, 1942-46; dep. dir. Joint Com. on Atomic Energy, U.S. Congress, 1946-48; sr. v.p. Am. Research and Devel. Co., Boston, 1949-69; with Fidelity Mgmt. and Research Co., Boston, 1969—, Fidelity Venture Assos., sr. gen. partner Fidelity Ventures, Ltd., Boston, 1969-79, ltd. ptnr., 1979-87; bd. overseers Hoover Instn., Stanford, Calif. Mem. Stanford Assos., Soc. Colonial Wars Mass., Holland Soc. N.Y., Order Founders and Patriots Am. in Mass., Delta Theta Phi. Republican. Clubs: Harvard (Boston and N.Y.C.); Boston (New Orleans); Houston Country; Tucson Country. Home: PO Box 728 30 S Main St Kennebunkport ME 04046 Office: 82 Devonshire St Boston MA 02109

HOAGLAND, PAMELA REDINGTON, educational consultant, administrator; b. Phoenix, June 2, 1937; d. George Appleton and Margaret Tweed (Rae) H. B.A., U. Ariz., 1959; MEd in Reading Edn., 1965, EdD in Reading and Psychology, 1973. Tchr. Tucson Unified Sch. Dist., 1959-73, asst. dir. instruction, reading, lang. arts, library services, 1980—; co-founder, co-dir. Learning Devel. Ctr., Tucson, 1970-74; curriculum specialist and supr. Pima County Spl. Edn. Coop., Tucson, 1973-76; ednl. cons. Redington Cons. Corp., Tucson, 1970—; founder, pres. Redinton Cons. Corp.; lectr. in field; bd. dirs. Behavior Assocs. Chmn. Ariz. Right to Read Council, 1978-80; bd. dirs. Tucson Westside Coalition, 1979-80, bd. dirs. Friends of Tucson Pub. Library, v.p., 1984—, pres. 1986-88; edn. supr. Grace Episcopal Ch., 1965-67; pres. Tucson Area Reading Council, 1968; mem. alumni bd. U. Ariz. Coll. Edn., 1984—, pres. 1986-88. Mem. Nat. Council Tchrs. English, Internat. Reading Assn. (field cons.), Ariz. State Reading Council (pres. 1969), Assn. Supervision and Curriculum Devel., Tucson Adminstrs., Inc. (v.p. 1987-88, pres. 1988-89), Alpha Delta Kappa, Pi Delta Kappa (Disting. lecture series award 1978), Pi Beta Phi. Democrat. Contbr. articles to profl. publs. Office: 2025 E Winsett St Tucson AZ 85719

HOAGLUND, JOHN ARTHUR, philosophy educator, editorial consultant; b. Houston, June 15, 1936; s. Rudolph Arthur and Doris Antoinette (Barker) H.; m. Lilian Nilsson, June 18, 1966; children—Glen Arthur, Larissa Ann. Student Ludwig Maximilians U., Munich, W.Ger., 1957-58, U. Vienna (Austria), 1958-59; Ph.D., Free U., Berlin, 1967. Lectr. Padagogische Hochschule, Berlin, 1966-67, Free U., Berlin, 1967-72; prof. Christopher Newport Coll., Newport News, Va., 1972-80, 81—; editorial cons. Vale Press, Newport News, 1982—; lectr., Eng., Scotland, Norway, W.Ger., Poland, Yugoslavia, Can., U.S., 1972—. Author: Kants Kritik der reinen Vernunft in England, 1971; Critical Thinking, 1984; contbr. articles on logic, ethics, and aesthetics to profl. lit. Served with USMC, 1953-55. Am. Council Learned Socs. grantee, 1975; NEH summer seminar grantee, 1977; Fulbright fellow, 1980-81. Mem. AAUP (chpt. v.p. 1977-79, 83-87, pres. 1979-80), Assn. for Informal Logic and Critical Thinking (founding mem., exec. com., 1983—, pres. 1985-87), Brit. Soc. for Aesthetics. Democrat. Home: 13 Cherbourg Dr Newport News VA 23606 Office: Christopher Mewport Coll 50 Shoe Ln Newport News VA 23606

HOAK, JOHN CHARLES, physician, educator; b. Harrisburg, Pa., Dec. 12, 1928; s. John Andrew and Anna Bell (Holley) H.; m. Dorothy Elizabeth Witmer, Dec. 21, 1952; children: Greta Elizabeth, Laurinda Elaine, Thomas Emory. B.S., Lebanon Valley Coll., 1951; M.D., Hahnemann Med. Coll., 1955. Diplomate: Am. Bd. Internal Medicine. Intern Harrisburg Polyclinic Hosp., 1955-56; resident internal medicine VA Hosp., Iowa City, 1958; resident internal medicine U. Iowa Hosps., 1958-61, research fellow blood coagulation, 1958-59; mem. faculty U. Iowa Med. Sch., 1961-62, 63-84, assoc. prof. internal medicine, 1967-70, prof., 1970-84, dir. div. hematology, 1970-72, dir. div. hematology-oncology, 1973-84; prof. medicine, chmn. dept. U. Vt., Burlington, 1984-87, assoc. dir. Specialized Ctr. Research in Thrombosis, 1986-87; prof. dept. medicine U. Iowa, Iowa City, 1987—; vis. research staff Sir William Dunn Sch. Pathology, Oxford (Eng.) U., 1962-63; prin. research and tng. grants Nat. Heart and Lung Inst., assoc. dir. Specialized Center for Research in Atherosclerosis U. Iowa, 1970-84; Research fellow, then advanced research fellow Am. Heart Assn., 1961-63. Editorial bd.: Jour. Lab. and Clin. Medicine, 1972-78, Jour. Arteriosclerosis, 1986—; Contbr. articles to profl. jours. Fellow ACP; mem. Am. Soc. Hematology, Internat. Soc. Thrombosis and Haemostasis, Am. Heart Assn., Am. Fedn. Clin. Research, Central Soc. Clin. Research, Phi Alpha Epsilon, Alpha Omega Alpha., Assn. Am. Physicians. Office: U Iowa Hosps Dept Medicine Iowa City IA 52242

HOANG, NGUYEN-TRONG, physician, consultant; b. Huê, Repulbic of Vietnam, Sept. 4, 1936; parents: Nguyen-Trong Hiep and Nguyen-Phuoc Ton-Nu-Thi Sung. B in Math., Lycée d'Etat Michel Montaigne, Bordeaux, 1956; state diploma of medicine, Sch. Medicine, Paris, 1966, also cert. aeronautical medicine and health and sanitation. Resident surgeon Compiegne State Hosp., 1963-64, Meaux State Hosp., 1964-66, Lagny State Hosp., 1966; specialist in health and sanitation Paris Sch. Medicine, 1965—; specialist in family planning action French Action of Family Planning, Paris, 1968—; practice medicine, Nanterre, France, 1969—; cons. physician various pharm. labs., Paris, 1987. Contbr. articles to profl. jours. Mem. French Soc. Aviation and Space Physiology and Medicine (titulary, specialist in aviation medicine), Assn. Nanterre Physicians, Assn. Vietnamese Practitioners in France. Club: Ex du XIVe Shooting (Paris). Home: Quartier Villon, Tour Eve 3602, 92800 Puteaux la Defense France Office: Cabinet Med Privé, 38 Rue des Fontenelles, 92000 Nanterre France

HOARE, JOSEPH ANDREW CHRISTOPHER, farmer, currency specialist, investment consultant; b. London, Mar. 23, 1925; s. Sir Reginald Hervey and Lady Lucy Joan (Cavendish-Bentinck) H.; m. Lady Christina Alice McDonnell, Jan. 23, 1963; children: Jane Alice Patience, Charles William Reginald, Lucy Mary Christina. Student, Eton Coll., 1938-39, 41-43, higher sch. cert., 1943; student LeRosey, Rolle, Switzerland, 1939-40; MA with 2d class honors, Balliol Coll., Oxford U. (Eng.), 1950. Agt. Charles Hoare & Co., London, 1950-55; govt. securities specialist Ford Motor Co., London, 1955-56; ptnr. Akroyd & Smithers, London, 1957-59, Blackwell & Co., London, 1960-73; founder, dir. Can. Overseas Packaging Industries, St. John, N.B., 1962—; mktg. cons. Encase Holdings Ltd., London, 1980-85; econ. advisor to Can. overseas packaging industries, 1986—; chmn. Assn. Chart and Tech. Analysts, 1969-73. Mem. Manorial Soc. Gt. Britain, London, 1981—. Served with RAF, 1946-47, 52-57. Recipient His Majest the King's Prize for French, 1942; Andre Maurois Shield, 1943; Silver Badge, Internat. Aero. Fedn. for Gliding and Soaring of Gt. Britain, 1947. Mem. Nat. Farmers Union, Lloyd's of London (underwriting). Club: Brooks (London). Home: Hartridge Manor Farm, Cranbrook, Kent England Office: Internat Packaging Services, 24 Blvd Princesse Charlotte, IPS SAM, Monte Carlo 98000, Monaco

HOBANA, ION ION, writer; b. Sînnicolaul Mare, Timis, Romania, Jan. 25, 1931; s. Ion and Antonia Hobana; m. Sofia Hobana, Dec. 23, 1950; 1 child, Ion Sorin. BA, U. Bucharest, Romania, 1954. Newspaper reporter Scînteia Tineretului, Bucharest, 1950-52; chief literary dept. Luminita mag., Bucharest, 1953-55; chief dept. sci. fiction pub. house Editura Tineretului, Bucharest, 1955-68; chief sci. dept. newspaper Scînteia, Bucharest, 1968-72; sec. Writers Union of S.R. Romania, Bucharest, 1972—. Author: The Golden Age of Romanian Science Fiction, 1969, 20,000 Pages in Search of Jules Verne, 1979, Science Fiction, 1983, A Kind of Space, 1988. Recipient Polish Ministry Art and Culture award, 1974, Short Story award European Science Fiction Conf., 1985. Mem. World Sci. Fiction Com. (Harrison award 1984), European Sci. Fiction Soc. (coordinator, awards 1972, 80), H.G. Wells Soc. Home: Nicolae Balcescu #24, 70122 Bucharest Romania Office: Writers Union SR Romania, Calea Victoriei #115, 71102 Bucharest Romania

HOBART, PETER CAHILL, welding company executive; b. Troy, Ohio, Dec. 4, 1934; s. William Harrison and Rachel (Cahill) H.; m. Anna Serena Zawbon, July 16, 1960; children: Michelle, Peter John. V.p. Hobart Bros. Co., Troy, 1959—; pres. Hobart Bros. Internat. A.G., Switzerland, 1962—; also holds other mgmt. positions Hobart Bros. Internat. A.G., throughout the world; cons. in field. Contbr. articles to profl. jours. and mags. Served with U.S. Army, 1957-59. Fellow British Welding Inst.; mem. Internat. Inst. Welding, Am. WElding Soc., Am. C. of C. (Italy), Internat. Sculpture Ctr., (bd. dirs. 1985—). Republican. Episcopalian. Office: Hobart Bros Internat Ltd, Via Di Porta Pinciana 34, I-00185 Rome Italy

HOBBS, JOHN RAYMOND, immunology educator; b. Aldershot, Eng., Apr. 17, 1929; s. Frederick Walter Haydn and Anna Helena (Froseler) H.; m. Patricia Lilian Arnott, Aug. 7, 1954; children—Wendy, Lucy, Trudy. B.Sc. with spl. honors, Middlesex Hosp. Med. Sch., 1953, M.B.B.S., 1956, M.D., 1963. Tutor in chem. pathology Westminster Med. Sch. (Eng.), 1959-62, Chmn. bone marrow team, 1971—; lectr. in chem. pathology Royal Free Hosp. Med. Sch., London, 1962-63, sr. lectr. in chem. pathology Postgrad. Med. Sch., 1963-70; prof. chem. pathology U. London, 1970-84, prof. chem. immunology, 1984—; chmn. numerous sci. coms., 1959—; mem. council Royal Coll. Pathologists, 1971-74; pres. sect. pathology Royal Soc. Medicine, London, 1972-73; vis. prof. numerous univs., 1969—; rep. Overseas Devel. Ministry, India, 1968-70. Contbr. numerous articles to profl. jours. Served with Royal Army Med. Corps, 1947-49. Recipient Vicker's award Assn. Clin. Biochemists, G.B., 1981; Silver medal City of Bruges (Belgium), 1972; named Disting. Clin. Chemist Can. Soc. Clin. Chemists, 1977; winner Paul Martini prize, 1973. Mem. Internat. Coop. Group for Bone Marrow Transplant, Bd. of European Bone Marrow Transplantation, Internat. Fedn. Clin. Chemists (chmn. expert panel on proteins 1970-79). Mem. Ch. of Eng. Club: Athenaeum (London). Home: 5 Dormywood, Ruislip, Middlesex England Office: Westminster Hosp, London SW1P 2AR, England

HOBBS, MARVIN, engineering executive; b. Jasper, Ind., Nov. 30, 1912; s. Charles and Madge (Ott) H.; B.S. in Elec. Engring., Tri-State Coll., Angola, Ind., 1930; postgrad. U. Chgo., 1932; PhD in Mgmt., Calif. U. Advanced Studies, 1985; m. Bernadine E. Weeks, July 4, 1936. Chief engr. Scott Radio Labs., Chgo., 1939-46; cons. engr. RCA, Camden, N.J., 1946-49; v.p. Harvey-Wells Electronics, Southbridge, Mass., 1952-54; asst. to exec. v.p. Gen. Instrument Corp., Newark, N.J., 1958-62; mgr., cons. engr. Design Service Co., N.Y.C., 1963-68; v.p. Gladding Corp., Syracuse, N.Y., 1968-71, cons. corporate devel., 1971-79; mem. adminstrv. group Bell Telephone Labs., Naperville, Ill., 1979-82; prof. Calif. U. Advanced Studies, 1985—. Mem. Electronics Prodn. Bd., ODM, Washington, 1951-52; operations analyst Far East Air Force, 1945. Recipient Certificate of Appreciation War Dept., 1945, Certificate of Commendation, Navy Dept., 1947. Registered profl. engr., Ill. Mem. IEEE (life). Author: Basics of Missile Guidance and Space Techniques, 1959, Fundamentals of Rockets, Missiles and Spacecraft, 1962; Modern Communications Switching Systems, 1974, 2d edit., 1981; Modern CB Radio Servicing, 1979; Servicing Home Video Cassette Recorders, 1982; Techniche Moderne Di Riparazione Delle Radio CB, 1982; E.H. Scott—The Dean of DX-A History of Classic Radios, 1985. Inventor low radiation radio receiver. Home and Office: 655 W Irving Park Rd Chicago IL 60613

HOBSBAUM, PHILIP DENNIS, English educator; b. London, June 29, 1932; s. Joseph and Rachel (Shapira) H.; m. Hannah Kelly, Aug. 7, 1957 (div. 1968); m. Rosemary Phillips, July 20, 1976. MA, Cambridge U., PhD; lic., Royal Acad. Music, Guildhall Sch. Music. Cert. Licentiate Royal Acad. Music, Guildhall Sch. Lectr. in English Queen's U. Belfast, Ireland, 1962-66; lectr. in English lit. U. Glasgow, Scotland, 1979-84, sr. lectr. English lit., 1972-79, reader English lit., 1979-84, prof. Eng. Lit., 1984—. Author: A Theory of Communication, 1970, A Reader's Guide to Charles Dickens, 1972, Tradition and Experiment, 1979, A Reader's Guide to D.H. Lawrence, 1981, Essentials of Literary Criticism, 1985, A Reader's Guide to Robert Lowell, 1988. Labour. Clubs: College, BBC (Glasgow). Home: 156 Wilton St, Glasgow G20 6BS, Scotland Office: U Glasgow, Glasgow G12 8QQ, Scotland

HOBSON, ANNE GLEN, pharmacist; b. Lawrence, Mass., Apr. 11, 1925; d. William Harvey and Alexanderina (Brown) Sparks; student Radcliffe Coll., 1942-43; B.A., Stanford U., 1946, M.A., 1947; postgrad. U. Houston, 1969-70; Ph.D., U. Tex., 1972, B.S. in Pharmacy, 1974; m. William C. Hobson, Jan. 9, 1960; children—Floyd, Bruce, Scott, William. Research asst. in preventive medicine U. Calif., San Francisco, 1947; research asso. in pharmacology Stanford Med. Sch., San Francisco, 1948; tchr. U.S. Army Dependents Sch., Manila, Philippines, 1949-51, Miss Harker's Sch., Palo Alto, Calif., 1951-53; med. lab. technician Palo Alto Clinic, 1953-54; tchr. Anglo-Am. Sch., Kifissia, Athens, Greece, 1954-56; chief lab. technician Dale County Hosp., Ozark, Ala., 1956-57; tchr. Bloomfield (N.J.) High Sch., 1957-58, Clark (N.J.) High Sch., 1958-59; asst. prof. Hellenika Anglaise Collegion, Athens, Greece, 1959-60; tchr. Molesworth AFB, Eng., 1960-61; asst. prof. Ashton Community Coll., Ashton-under-Lyne, Eng., 1961-62; tchr. Hartshead Sec. Sch., Ashton-under-Lyne, 1962-63, Droylsden (Eng.) Secondary Sch. for Girls, 1963-64; asst. coordinator Trenton Jr. 5 Exptl. Sch. program, for Disadvantaged, 1964-65; tchr. Trenton High Sch., 1965-66; research asso. Princeton (N.J.) U., 1966-67; tchr. Sam Rayburn High Sch., Pasadena, Tex., 1967-70; chief adult councilor Juvenile Drug Addiction, Pasadena, 1970-72; NSF grantee U. Tex., Austin, 1970-74; pharmacist, asst. mgr., mgr. Sommers Drug Stores, Austin, 1974-76; owner, pharmacist Hobson Pharmacy, Pflugerville, Tex., 1976-87. Recipient Outstanding Alumna award U. Tex., 1977; registered pharmacist, Tex. Fellow Am. Coll. Apothecaries; mem. Am. Soc. Hosp. Pharmacists, Am. Pharm. Assn., Tex. Pharm. Assn., Capital Area Pharm. Assn., Am. Inst. History of Pharmacy (cert. of recognition 1973), Am. Tchrs. Assn., Tex. Tchrs. Assn., AAUW, Bus. and Profl. Women, Better Bus. Bur., Greater Pflugerville C. of C. (treas. 1985-86), Kappa Epsilon. Republican. Episcopalian. Clubs: Rainbow Girls, Am. Luth. Ch. Women's Assn. Contbr. articles to profl. jours; researcher in RH blood factor and leukemia, possible relationship with epilepsy, and mongolism, possible causal relationship between jaundice and hepatitis, others. Home: 20 Storth Meadow Rd, Simmondly Glossop, Derbyshire SK139UZ, England

HOBSON, PATRICIA JADE, magazine executive; b. N.Y.C., Mar. 12, 1945; d. John Louis Campo and Elizabeth (Anne) Stanton; m. David Alan Hobson, Dec. 30 (div. 1972); m. Martin Charnin, Dec. 18, 1984. BA, NYU, 1967. Asst. editor Glamour mag., N.Y.C., 1970; accessory editor Vogue mag., N.Y.C., 1970-78, fashion editor, 1978-81, fashion dir., 1981-86, creative dir. fashion, 1987—; cons. editor Self mag., N.Y.C., 1979-81. Mem. Nat. Assn. Female Execs. Democrat. Avocations: gardening, opera, ballet, theater, skiing. Office: Conde Nast Publs 350 Madison Ave New York NY 10017

HOBSON, ROBERT WAYNE, II, surgeon; b. DeKalb, Ill., Dec. 21, 1939; s. Robert Wayne and Jean Helen (Sampson) H.; m. Joan Patricia Souza, Dec. 5, 1985; children: Lisa, Wayne, Laura, Matthew. BS in Chemistry, George Washington U., 1959, MD, 1963. Cert. Am. Bd. Surgery; cert. of spl. qualification in gen.-vascular surgery. Intern Tripler Gen. Hosp., Honolulu, 1963-64; resident gen. surgery Walter Reed Gen. Hosp., Washington, 1967-71, fellow peripheral vascular surgery, 1972-73; group surgeon 3rd Spl. Forces Group, Ft. Bragg, N.C., 1964-65; surgeon Detachment C-3, 5th Spl. Forces Group, Republic of Vietnam, 1965-66; chief exptl. surgery, dep. dir. Div. Surgery, Walter Reed Inst. Research, Washington, 1971-75; asst. chief peripheral vascular surgery service Walter Reed Army Med. Ctr., Washington, 1973-75; chief surg. service East Orange VA Med. Ctr., N.J., 1975-83; chief sect. vascular surgery Univ. Medicine and Dentistry of N.J., Newark, 1978-86, assoc. prof. surgery, 1975-79, prof. surgery, 1980-86, vice chmn. dept. surgery, 1980-86; James Utley prof. surgery, chmn. dept. surgery Boston U. Sch. Medicine. 1986-88; surgeon-in-chief Univ. Hosp., Boston U. Med. Ctr., 1986-88; prof. surgery, chief sect. vascular surgery U. Medicine and Dentistry of N.J., Newark, 1988—; editorial cons. Jour. AMA, 1982—; mem. editorial bd. Jour. Surg. Research, 1983—; contbr. articles to profl. jours. Served to col. M.C., U.S. Army, 1963-75. Recipient Franklin Metcalfe award for surg. research U.S. Army Med. Dept., 1969-70; decorated Bronze Star, Air Medal, Medal of Honor, Cross of Gallantry, Airborne (all Republic of Vietnam); NIH grantee, 1979-82, other research project grants. Fellow ACS, Am. Surg. Assn., Stroke Council Am. Heart Assn.; mem. Internat. Cardiovascular Soc., Soc. Vascular Surgery, Soc. Univ. Surgeons, Assn. VA Surgeons (v.p. 1983), Southeastern Surg. Congress, Am. Fedn. Clin. Research, Chesapeake Vascular Soc., Assn. Mil. Surgeons, Assn. Acad. Surgery (pres.-elect 1980, pres. 1981), Assn. Surg. Edn., Soc. Med. Cons. to Armed Forces, Assn. Internat. Vascular Surgeons, Soc. Surgeons of N.J., Boston Surg. Soc., Vascular Soc. N.J. (pres.-elect 1980, pres. 1981). Republican. Office: U Medicine & Dentistry NJ Sect Vascular Surgery Dept Surgery G-532 185 S Orange Ave Newark NJ 07103

HOCH, ORION LINDEL, corporate executive; b. Canonsburg, Pa., Dec. 21, 1928; s. Orion L.F. and Ann Marie (McNulty) H.; m. Jane Lee Ogan, June 12, 1952 (dec. 1978); children: Andrea, Brenda, John; m. Catherine Nan Richardson, Sept. 12, 1980; 1 child, Joe. B.S., Carnegie Mellon U., 1952; M.S., UCLA, 1954; Ph.D., Stanford U., 1957. With Hughes Aircraft Co., Culver City, Calif., 1952-54; with Stanford Electronics Labs., 1954-57; sr. engr., dept. mgr., div. v.p., div. pres. Litton Electron Devices div., San Carlos, Calif., 1957-68; group exec. Litton Components div., 1968-70; v.p. Litton Industries, Inc., Beverly Hills, Calif., 1970, sr. v.p., 1971-74, pres., 1982-88, chief exec. officer, 1986—, chmn., 1988—, also dir.; pres. Intersil, Inc., Cupertino, Calif., 1974-82; bd. dirs. Measurex Corp., Maxim Integrated Products. Trustee Carnegie-Mellon U. Served with AUS, 1946-48. Mem. IEEE, Am. Electronics Assn. (bd. dirs.), Sigma Xi, Tau Beta Pi, Phi Kappa Phi. Office: Litton Industries Inc 360 N Crescent Dr Beverly Hills CA 90210

HOCHBERG, FREDERICK GEORGE, accountant; b. Los Angeles, July 4, 1913; s. Frederick Joseph and Lottie (LeGendre) H.; Ann C. Hochberg May. BA, UCLA, 1937. Chief acct., auditor Swinerton, McClure & Vinnell, Managua, Nicaragua, 1942-44; pvt. acctg. practice, Avalon, Calif., 1946-66; designer, operator Descanso Beach Club, Avalon, 1966; v.p. Air Catalina, 1967; treas. Catalina Airlines, 1967; pres. Aero Commuter, 1967; v.p., treas., dir. bus. affairs William L. Pereira & Assocs., Planners, Architects, Engrs., Los Angeles, 1967-72; v.p., gen. mgr. Mo. Hickory Corp., 1972-74; prin. Fred G. Hochberg Assocs., Mgmt. Cons., 1974—; v.p. Vicalton S.A. Mexico, 1976—; v.p., gen. mgr. Solar Engring. Co., Inc., 1977-79; pres. Solar Assocs. Internat., 1979-83. Chmn. Avalon Transp. Com., 1952, Avalon Harbor Commn., 1960, Avalon Airport Com., 1964-66, Harbor Devel. Commn., 1965-66; sec. Santa Catalina Festival of Arts, 1960, Avalon City Planning Commn., 1956-58; pres. Avalon Music Bowl Assn., 1961, Catalina Mariachi Assn., 1961-66; treas. City of Avalon, 1954-62, councilman, 1962-66, mayor, 1964-66; bd. dirs. Los Angeles Child Guidance Clinic, 1975-86, treas., 1978-79, pres., 1979-81; bd. dirs. Los Aficionados de Los Angeles, 1980-86, pres., 1980-83, 87-88; pres. Nat Assn. Taurine Clubs, 1982-85. Served as ensign USNR, 1944-45. Named Catalina Island Man of Yr., 1956. Mem. Avalon Catalina Island C. of C. (past pres.), Soc. Calif. Accountants, Mensa, Am. Arbitration Assn. (panel), Catalina Island Mus. Soc. (treas. 1964), El Monte chambers commerce, Town Hall-West (vice chmn.). Lodge: Rotary (Avalon pres. 1956). Home and Office: 936 Trout St Staunton VA 24401

HOCHBERG, HOWARD MARTIN, medical device company executive, physician; b. N.Y.C., Mar. 4, 1935; s. Philip and Jean (Lieber) H.; m. Gaye Marcia Berlfein, Dec. 24, 1957; children—Sharon, Philip, Michael, Jane. B.E., B.A., NYU, 1957; M.D., U. Buffalo, 1961. Intern, resident Montefiore Hosp., N.Y.C., 1961-64; chief med. devel. Heart Disease Control Program USPHS, Washington, 1964-69; fellow in cardiology George Washington U. Hosp., Washington, 1967; v.p. med. services Roche Med., Cranbury, N.J., 1969-81; mng. dir. Cranbury Med., 1981-82; v.p. product devel. Squibb Med., Bellevue, Wash., 1982-83; exec. v.p. med. sci. Internat. Biomedics, Bothell, Wash., 1983—; cardiologist Helene Fuld Med. Ctr., Trenton, N.J., 1972-82; asst. prof. Hahnemann Med. Coll., Phila., 1972-82; cons. Spacelabs, Bellevue, 1984—, Nuclear Pharmacy, Albuquerque, 1984—. Author and editor: Clinical Perinatal Biochemistry, 1981. Contbr. articles to profl. jours. Served to LCDR USPHS, 1964-69. Mem. Soc. Critical Care Medicine, Tau Beta Pi. Jewish. Home: 14474 156th Ave NE Woodinville WA 98072 Office: Internat Biomedics Inc 1631 220th SE Bothell WA 98021

HOCHBERGER, SIMON, educator; b. York, Pa., Aug. 29, 1912; s. Charles Michael and Lena (Freireich) H.; m. Bella Hirschfield, Dec. 26, 1937; 1 son, Charles Michael. B.Jour. (Eugene Field scholar), U. Mo., 1933, M.A., 1935. Engaged in publicity and pub. relations 1933-34, 35-37; mem. faculty U. Miami, Fla., 1937—; prof. journalism, chmn. dept. U. Miami, 1947-66, prof. mass communications, chmn. dept., 1966-72, prof. communications, 1972-78, emeritus, 1978—; vis. prof. U. Nev., Reno, 1962, 69, 71-72, 73, 74; asso. editor Fla. Tchr. mag., 1937-42; book reviewer Miami News, 1939-40, 48-51; editorial adviser, manuscript editor Glade House Book Pubs., Miami, 1942-45; copy editor, Sunday mag. writer, editorial writer Nashville Tennessean, 1946-47, 53; asso. editor, drama reviewer Playtime mag., Miami, 1957, Beachcomber mag., 1957-59; v.p. Beachcomber Pub. Co., Inc., Miami, 1957-59; mem. editorial bd. Journalism Educator, 1958-65; editorial cons., 1940—. Editor: (with Lambert Greenawalt) The Student's Macbeth, 1954, 2d edit., 1959; Author articles and revs.; editor and or editorial cons. Mem. pub. information com. Heart Assn. Greater Miami, 1967-71; editorial cons. Dade

County (Fla.) Bd. Pub. Instrn., 1970-71. Recipient Gold Key award Columbia Scholastic Press Assn., 1949. Mem. Am. Soc. Journalism Sch. Adminstrs. (sec.-treas. 1962-65, chmn. internat. relations com.), Assn. Edn. Journalism (nat. dep. sec.-treas. 1962-65), Mo. Hist. Soc. (life), AAUP, Inter-Am. Press Assn. (asso.), Am. Acad. Polit. and Social Sci., Phi Kappa Phi (pres. U. Miami chpt. 1961-62), Iron Arrow, Omicron Delta Kappa, Kappa Tau Alpha (mem. nat. council 1958-78, nat. sec. 1968-70), Soc. Profl. Journalists, Sigma Delta Chi (life). Club: Univ. Miami Faculty (v.p. 1959-61, bd. dirs. 1959-63). Home: 5329 Granada Blvd Coral Gables FL 33146

HOCHSCHILD, CARROLL SHEPHERD, company administrator, educator; b. Whittier, Calif., Mar. 31, 1935; d. Vernon Vero and Effie Corinne (Hollingsworth) Shepherd; m. Richard Hochschild, July 25, 1959; children—Christopher Paul, Stephen Shepherd. B.A. in Internat. Relations, Pomona Coll., 1956; Teaching credential U. Calif.-Berkeley, 1957; M.B.A., Pepperdine U., 1985. Cert. elem. tchr., Calif. Elem. tchr. Oakland Pub. Schs. (Calif.), 1957-58, San Lorenzo Pub. Schs. (Calif.), 1958-59, Pasadena Pub. Schs. (Calif.), 1959-60, Huntington Beach Pub. Schs. (Calif.), 1961-63, 67-68; adminstrv. asst. Microwave Instruments, Corona del Mar, Calif., 1968-74; co-owner Hoch Co., Corona del Mar, 1978—. Rep. Calif. Tchrs. Assn., Huntington Beach, 1962-63. Mem. AAUW, Bus. Women's Inst., Internat. Dance-Exercise Found., Nat. Assn. Female Execs. Republican. Presbyterian. Clubs: Toastmistress (corr. sec. 1983), Jr. Ebell (fine arts chmn. Newport Beach 1966-67).

HOCHSCHWENDER, HERMAN KARL, science and management consultant; b. Heidelberg, Federal Republic Germany, Mar. 1, 1920; came to U.S., 1930, naturalized, 1935; s. Karl G. and Maria (Recken) H.; B.S., Yale U., 1941; postgrad. Harvard U. Bus. Sch.; m. Jane Elliott (div. 1961); children—Lynn Anne Hochschwender McGowin, Herman Karl, Irene Hochschwender Pate, James E.; m. 2d, Mary Koger, July 3, 1965; 1 son, J. Michael. Asst. indsl. relations mgr. Sargent & Co., New Haven, 1943-45; mgr. corp. planning Firestone Tire & Rubber Co., Akron, Ohio, 1945-56; pres. Mohawk Rubber Co., N.Y.C., 1959; founder, pres. Hochschwender & Assocs., Akron, 1959-72, Smithers Sci. Services, Inc., Akron, 1972—; lectr. in field. Contbr. articles to profl. jours. Vice-chmn. Bd. Trustees Akron Gen. Med. Ctr. Mem. Am. Council Ind. Labs., Union Internat. des Laboratoires Independents (pres., bd. govs.), ASTM, Soc. Automotive Engrs., Am. Assn. Lab. Accreditation, Yale U. Alumni Assn. Clubs: Akron City (trustee), Portage Country (Akron); Yale (N.Y.C.); Naples Yacht; Royal Poinciana Golf. Lodge: Rotary. Home: 2400 Gulfshore Blvd N Apt #603 Naples FL 33490 Office: 425 W Market St Akron OH 44303

HOCHSCHWENDER, KARL ALBERT, government relations consultant; b. Mannheim, Ger., Feb. 1, 1927; came to U.S., 1931, naturalized, 1938; s. Karl Georg and Maria Irma (Recken) H.; m. Lilli Gettinger, July 4, 1964. BA, Yale U., 1947, MA, 1949, PhD, 1962. Instr. polit. sci. Fla. State U., Tallahassee, 1949-51; assoc. Mott of Washington & Assocs., Washington, 1954-58; research analyst U.S. govt., 1959-60; asst. to mgmt. Am. Hoechst Corp., Bridgewater, N.J., 1961-63, mgr. govt. relations, 1963-68, dir. public relations, 1968-72, dir. public affairs, 1972-83; prin. Palatine Assocs., Princeton, N.J., 1983—; mem. Roster of Tech. Specialists, Office of Spl. Rep. for Trade Negotiations, Exec. Office of Pres., 1964-67. Trustee United Fund of Somerset Valley (N.J.), 1969-75. Yale U. fellow, 1952-54; recipient Am. Polit. Sci. Assn. Leonard D. White Meml. award, 1963. Mem. Am. Assn. Exporters and Importers (bd. dirs. 1963—, v.p. 1967-83, pres. 1983, chmn. 1983-85), Am. Polit. Sci. Assn., Chem. Communications Assn. (bd. dirs. 1976-80), Soc. Plastics Industry, Inc. (chmn. food, drug & cosmetics packaging material com. 1972-76). Club: Yale of N.Y.C. Office: PO Box 1466 Princeton NJ 08542

HOCKEIMER, HENRY ERIC, government official; b. Winzig, Germany, Apr. 3, 1920; came to U.S., 1946, naturalized, 1951; s. Erich and Gertrude (Masur) H.; m. Margaret Feeny, May 26, 1956; children: Ellen Patricia, Henry Eric. Student, RCA Insts., 1946-47; electronics and bus. mgmt., N.Y.U., 1948-51. With Philco-Ford Corp., Phila., 1947—, gen. mgr. communications and tech. services div., 1962-63, corp. v.p., 1963-72; v.p., gen. mgr. refrigeration products div. Connorsville, Ind., 1972-75; pres. Ford Aerospace & Communications Corp., Dearborn, Mich., 1975-85; v.p. Ford Motor Co., 1981-85; cons. USIA, Washington, 1985-86, dep. dir. TV and film service, 1985-87, acct. dir., 1987—, asst. dir. for mgmt., 1988—. Bd. regents Cath. U. Am., Hampton U. Mem. Engring. Soc. Detroit, Electronic Industries Assn., Smithsonian. Clubs: Capitol Hill (Washington); Renaissance, Detroit Econ., Nat. Space.

HOCKNEY, DAVID, artist; b. Bradford, Yorkshire, Eng., July 9, 1937; s. Kenneth and Laura H. Attended, Bradford Coll. Art, 1953-57, Royal Coll. Art, 1959-62. Lectr. U. Iowa, 1964, U. Colo., 1965, U. Calif. Berkeley, 1967; lectr. UCLA, 1966, hon. chair of drawing, 1980. Exhibited in one-man shows, Kasmin Gallery, 1963, Mus. Modern Art, N.Y.C., 1964, 68, Stedelijk Mus., Amsterdam, Netherlands, 1966, Andre Emmerich Gallery, N.Y.C., 1972, 83, 84, Musee des Arts Decoratifs, Paris, 1974, Mus. Gerona, Spain, 1976, Goteborg (Sweden) Mus., 1976, Gulbenkian Found., Lisbon, Spain, 1977, Susan Gersh Gallery, Los Angeles, 1982, Flanders Mus. Contemporary Arts, Mpls., 1982, Met. Mus. Art, 1988, others; designer: Rake's Progress, Glyndebourne, Eng., 1975; sets for Magic Flute, Glyndebourne, 1978, Met. Opera House, 1979, Tristan und Isolde, Los Angeles Music Ctr. Opera, 1987; Author: David Hockney by David Hockney, 1976, David Hockney: Travels with Pen, Pencil and Ink, 1978, Paper Pools, 1980, David Hockney Photographs, 1982; illustrator: Six Fairy Tales of the Brothers Grimm, 1969. Recipient Guinness award and 1st prize for etching, 1961, Gold medal Royal Coll. Art, 1962, Graphic prize Paris Biennale, 1963, 1st prize 8th Internat. Exhbn. Drawings Lugano, Italy, 1964, 1st prize John Moores Exhbn. Liverpool, Eng., 1967. Office: 7506 Santa Monica Blvd Los Angeles CA 90041 Other: The Old Bath House, Manor Lane, Shipley, West Yorkshire BD18 3EA, England *

HOCQUET, JEAN-CLAUDE, historian, educator; b. Aulnoye, Nord, France, Feb. 3, 1936. Licence d' histoire, U. Lille, France, 1958; agrégation d' histoire, U. Paris, 1961; doctorate, U. Paris-Sorbonne, 1975. Prof. agregé Lycée Faidherbe, Lille, 1961-66; asst. U. Paris-Sorbonne, 1966-69; prof. Facoltà di Lettere, Venice, Italy, 1969-71; researcher Ctr. Nat. Recherche Sci., Paris, 1971-74; prof. U., Lille, 1974-85; dir. recherche premiée classe U. Paris, 1985—; dir. d'études associé EHESS, Paris, 1987—; v.p. Univ. Lille, 1980-83; dir. Unité Ctr. Nat. Recherche Sci., Paris, 1985—. Author: Le Sel et la fortune de Venise, 2 vol., 1979, Le Sel et le Pouvoir, 1985, Le Roi, le Marchand et le sel, 1987. Mem. Comité Internat. pour la Métrologie Hist. (sec. gen. 1986), Commission Internationale D'Histoire du Sel (pres. 1988—). Home: 34 Alle e La Comedie, 59650 Villeneuve D Ascq France Office: Universite de Lille 3, BP 149, 59653 Villeneuve d'Ascq Cedex France

HODARA, RALPH LEON, consulting company executive; b. Buenos Aires, Aug. 30, 1921; s. Isaac and Fortunée (Levy) H.; m. Dolly D. Azicri, Oct. 1, 1948; children: Christian Yves, Alain Didier, Carole Anne. Student, Facultad de Ingenieria, Buenos Aires, 1941; BS, Columbia U., 1944; MS, MIT, 1945. Asst. researcher MIT, Cambridge, Mass., 1945-46; field engr. Barnes Textiles Assocs., Boston, 1946-47; mng. dir. BTCI, Paris, 1948—; also bd. dirs. BTCI, London. Contbr. articles to profl. jours. Mem. Textile Inst. Home: 34 rue du Docteur Blanche, 75016 Paris France Office: BTCI, 178 rue Montmartre, 75002 Paris France

HODEL, CHRISTIAN M., pathologist, toxicologist; b. Basel, Switzerland, June 24, 1936; s. Peter and Elly H.; student U. Geneva, 1955-56, U. Basel, 1956-62; M.D., U. Hamburg, 1960; m. Deike Von Westernhagen, July 5, 1962; children—Jan, Arne. Postdoctoral fellow U. Basel, 1962-67; research asso. Yale U., New Haven, Conn., 1967-69; head electronmicroscopy unit Sandoz Ltd., Basel, 1969-72, head pathology in toxicology, 1972-80; dir. drug safety monitoring Hoffmann-La-Roche & Co. Ltd, 1980-84; med. dir. Sterling-Europa, Basel, 1984—. Tech. dir. Swiss Military First Aid Soc., 1974-78. Served to maj., Swiss Army, 1956-74. Mem. European Soc. Toxicology (sec. 1975-86, pres. 1986—), Swiss Soc. History Medicine, Swiss Soc. Pharm. and Toxicology, Internat. Union Toxicology (treas. 1980-83). Contbr. articles to profl. jours. Home: 83 Neubadstrasse, CH 4054 Basel Switzerland Office: Sterling-Europa, PO Box 4658, CH 4002 Basel Switzerland

HODEL, DONALD PAUL, government official; b. Portland, Oreg., May 23, 1935; s. Philip E. and Theresia Rose (Brodt) H.; m. Barbara Beecher Stockman, Dec. 10, 1956; children: Philip Stockman (dec.), David Beecher. B.A., Harvard Coll., 1957; J.D., U. Oreg., 1960. Bar: Oreg. 1960. Treas., Harvard Young Republican Club, 1955-56, pres., 1956-57; precinct organizer Clackamas County Rep. Central Com., Oreg., 1964; sec. Clackamas County Rep. Central Com., 1964-65, chmn., 1965-66; chmn. Oreg. Rep. State Central Com., 1966-67; alt. del. Rep. Nat. Conv., 1968; dep. adminstr. Bonneville Power Adminstrn., 1969-72, adminstr., 1972-77; pres. Nat. Elec. Reliability Council, Princeton, N.J., 1978-80, Hodel Assos. Inc., 1978-81; undersec. Dept. Interior, Washington, 1981-82; sec. Dept. Energy, Washington, 1982-85, Dept. Interior, Washington, 1985—; atty. Davies, Biggs, Strayer, Stoel & Boley, 1960-63, Ga. Pacific Corp., 1963-69. Mem. Oreg. Bar Assn. Presbyterian. Office: Sec Dept Interior 18th & C Streets NW Washington DC 20240

HODGE, GAMEEL BYRON, surgeon; b. Spartanburg, S.C., Sept. 16, 1917; s. Charles B. and Mary (Bargot) H.; m. Katie Adams, Sept. 22, 1943; children: Susan, Byron, John Adams. BS, Wofford Coll., 1938; MD, Vanderbilt U., 1942, D Pub. Service (hon.), U. S.C., 1982. Diplomate Am. Bd. Surgery. Intern Duke U. Med. Sch. and Hosp., Durham, N.C., 1942-43, asst. resident, 1943-47, chief resident surgeon, 1947-48; practice medicine specializing in gen., thoracic and cardiovascular surgery, Spartanburg, 1948—; attending surgeon Spartanburg Gen. Hosp.; cons. surgeon St. Luke's Hosp., Tryon, N.C., 1948-58, Cherokee County (S.C.) Meml. Hosp., 1948-74; thoracic surgeon Spartanburg County Tb Hosp., 1948-69; chief of surgery Mary Black Meml. Hosp., 1969-72; assoc. clin. prof. surgery Med. U. S.C., Spartanburg, 1970—. Contbr. articles on surgery and gen. medicine to profl. jours. Chmn. Spartanburg County Commn. for Higher Edn., 1967—; trustee Spartanburg Day Sch., 1958—. Served with M.C., USAR, 1942-53. Fellow Am. Coll. Chest Physicians, Internat. Acad. Proctology, N.Y. Acad. Sci., Am. Fedn. Clin. Research, Indsl. Medicine Assn.; mem. Am. Heart Assn., S.C. Med. Assn., S.C. Surg. Soc., S.C. Vascular Surg. Soc., AMA, Spartanburg Med. Soc., Am. Geriatrics Soc., Deryl Hart Surg. Soc., Duke U. Med. Alumni Assn. (past pres.), Spartanburg Area C. of C. (past pres., Neville Holcombe Disting. Service award 1988), Omicron Delta Kappa, Order of Palmetto, Phi Beta Kappa, Phi Beta Pi. Episcopalian. Clubs: Spartanburg Country, Piedmont, Carolina Country. Lodge: Kiwanis (Citizenship of Yr. award 1969). Home: 2500 Old Knox Rd Spartanburg SC 29302 Office: 3 Catawba St Spartanburg SC 29303

HODGE, JAMES ROBERT, psychiatrist; b. Martins Ferry, Ohio, Jan. 28, 1927; s. Robert Gabriel and Ethel Melissa (Ashton) H.; m. Marilyn Jane Dinklocker, June 10, 1950; children: Sharon, Scott. B.S., Franklin and Marshall Coll., 1946; M.D., Jefferson Med. Coll., 1950; M.A., U. Akron, 1981. Intern U.S. Naval Hosp., St. Albans, N.Y., 1950-51; resident Menninger Sch. Psychiatry, Topeka, 1951-52, U.S. Naval Hosp., Oceanside, Calif., 1952-53, Univ. Hosps., Cleve., 1954-55; USPHS fellow in adult psychiatry Sch. Medicine Case-Western Res. U., 1955-56; practice medicine specializing in psychiatry Akron, Ohio, 1956—; head psychiatry Akron City Hosp., 1962-75, cons. staff, 1975-79, chmn. dept. psychiatry, 1979-85; assoc. program dir., clinic dir. St. Thomas Med. Ctr., 1986—; adj. prof. psychology U. Akron, 1963-85; prof. psychiatry Northeastern Ohio Univs. Coll. Medicine, 1980—; mem. council chiefs psychiatry Northeastern Ohio U. Coll. Medicine, Akron, 1974-76, 79—, dir. psychiat. residency tng. program, 1981-83, chmn. dept. of psychiatry, 1982—; grad. faculty in psychology Fla. Inst. Tech., 1976-83. Author: Practical Psychiatry for the Primary Physician, 1975, also articles in med. and psychiat. jours.; feature writer: Med. Times mag; producer: movie The Use of Hypnosis in Psychotherapy, 1975. Served to lt. USNR, 1944-45, 50-51, 52-54. Recipient spl. recognition award Ohio Psychiat. Assn., 1976, Meritorious Service award Ohio Psychiat. Assn., 1981. Fellow Am. Psychiat. Assn., Am. Bd. of Med. Psychotherapist, Am. Soc. Clin. Hypnosis, Internat. Soc. Clin. and Exptl. Hypnosis, Acad. Psychosomatic Medicine, Am. Coll. Psychiatrists; mem. Am. Psychol. Assn., Ohio Psychiat. Assn. (pres. 1980-81), Cen. Neuropsychiat. Assn. (v.p. 1986-87, pres. 1988—). Home: 295 Pembroke Rd Akron OH 44313 Office: Dept Psychiatry St Thomas Med Ctr 444 N Main St Akron OH 44310

HODGE, STANLEY BERTRAND JOHN, corporate professional, accountant; b. Greenock, Scotland, Sept. 14, 1936; s. James Henry Campbell and Elizabeth Struthers (Bertrand) H.; m. Nan Carse, Aug. 25, 1961; children: Russell James, Gordon Stanley, Nicola Elizabeth Ann. Chartered acct. degree, Inst. Chartered Accts. Scotland, 1960. Sec. Blacks of Greenock Ltd., 1960-67; group co. sec. Black and Edgington PLC, London, 1967-84; sr. acct. IBM (U.K.) Ltd., Greenock, 1984-88; group co. sec. Shanks & McEwan Group PLC, Glasgow, Scotland, 1988—. Mem. Inst. Chartered Accts. (mem. regional com. 1984—), Inst. Personnel Mgmt. Club: Royal Gourock Y.C. Lodge: Rotary (Gourock). Home: 140 Newton St, Greenock PA16 8SJ, Scotland

HODGES, JOT HOLIVER, JR., lawyer, business executive; b. Archer City, Tex. Nov. 16, 1932; s. Jot Holiver and Lola Mae (Hurd) H.; m. Virginia Cordray Pardue, June 11, 1955; children—Deborah, Jot, Darlene. BS, BBA, Sam Houston State U., 1954; JD, U. Tex.-Austin, 1957. Bar: Tex., U.S. dist. ct. (so. dist.) Tex., U.S. Ct. Appeals (5th cir.). Asst. atty. gen. State of Tex., 1958-60; gen. counsel Tex. Pharm., 1960-61; assoc. gen. counsel Tex. Med. Assn. and Tex. Hosp. Assn., 1960-61; founder, sr. ptnr. Hodges & Grant; chmn. bd. Presidio Devel. Corp.; bd. dirs., gen. counsel First Nat. Bank of Missouri City; gen. ptrs. Double Eagle Ranch, Ltd., Pinto Creek Ranch, Ltd. Served to capt. U.S. Army. Methodist. Club: Houston Contbr. articles to legal, med., pharm. and hosp. jours. Home: 3527 Thunderbird Missouri City TX 77459 Office: Hodges & Grant 3660 Hampton Dr Suite 200 Missouri City TX 77459-3016

HODGES, THOMPSON GENE, librarian; b. Clinton, Okla., Jan. 30, 1913; s. Kiah and Allie Lee (Thompson) H.; m. Claire Surbeck, June 19, 1935 (dec. 1979); 1 son, Thompson Gene; m. Dorothea Arnold Ray, 1980. B.S., U. Okla., 1934, M.L.S., 1955; B.D., McCormick Theol. Sem., Chgo., 1939. Ordained to ministry Presbyn. Ch., 1939; minister supply Ch. of Scotland, 1939; pastor Pawhuska and Lawton, Okla., 1939-47; aquisitions librarian U. Okla., 1955-58; dean library services Central State U., Edmond, Okla., 1958-76; dean emeritus Central State U., 1976—; library cons. Univ. Microfilms, 1977; vis. prof. bibliography U. Okla., 1980-81; library cons. Mem. ALA, Southwestern Library Assn., Okla. Library Assn. (pres. 1965-66), Okla. Ednl. Assn., Kappa Sigma, Beta Phi Mu, Kappa Kappa Psi. Home and Office: 415 Macy St Norman OK 73071

HODGKIN, ALAN LLOYD, biophysicist; b. Feb. 5, 1914; s. G.L. and M.F. (Wilson) H.; student Trinity Coll., (fellow) Cambridge, 1936; M.A., Sc.D., Cambridge; M.D. (hon.), univs. Berne, Louvain; D.Sc. (hon.), univs. Sheffield, Newcastle-upon-Tyne, East Anglia, Manchester, Leicester, London, Nfld., Wales, Rockefeller U., Bristol, Oxford; LL.D., U. Aberdeen; m. Marion de Kay Rous, 1944; 1 son, 3 daus. Sci. officer radar Air Ministry, also Ministry Aircraft Prodn., 1939-45; lectr., then asst. dir. research Cambridge, 1945-52; Foulerton research prof. Royal Soc., 1952-69; John Humphrey Plummer prof. biophysics U. Cambridge, 1970-81; master Trinity Coll., Cambridge, 1978-84; mem. Med. Research Council, 1959-63; chancellor U. Leicester, 1971—. Decorated knight Order Brit. Empire, 1972, Order of Merit, 1973; recipient Baly medal, 1955, Nobel prize for medicine or physiology (with A.F. Huxley, J.C. Eccles), 1963, Lord Crook Medal, 1983. Fellow Royal Soc. (Royal medal 1958, Copley medal 1965, pres. 1970-75), Imperial Coll. Sci., Indian Nat. Sci. Acad. (hon.) Girton Coll., Cambridge (hon.); mem. Physiol. Soc. (fgn. sec. 1960-67), Nat. Acad. Scis., Am. Acad. Arts and Scis. (fgn. hon.), Royal Danish Acad. Scis. (fgn.), Leopoldina Acad., Royal Swedish Acad. Scis. (fgn.), Pontifical Acad. Scis., Am. Philos. Soc. (fgn.), Royal Irish Acad. (hon.), USSR Acad. Scis. (fgn.), Marine Biol. Assn. U.K. (pres. 1966-76). Author: Conduction of the Nervous Impulse, 1963; also sci. papers on nature of nervous conduction, muscle, and vision. Devised (with Andrew Huxley) system of math. equations describing nerve impulse; worked with giant nerve fibers of squid, proving that electricity was direct causal agt. of impulse propagation. Office: Cambridge U, Physiol Lab/Downing St, Cambridge CB2 3EG, England

HODGKIN, DOROTHY CROWFOOT, chemist; b. Cairo, 1910; student Somerville Coll., Oxford, Eng., 1928-32, Cambridge U., 1932-34; Sc.D. (hon.) U. Leeds, U. Manchester, Cambridge U. and others; m. Thomas L. Hodgkin, 1937 (dec. 1982). Mem. faculty Oxford U., from 1934, now prof. emeritus; chancellor Bristol U., 1970—. Decorated Order of Merit; First Freedom of Beccles; recipient Nobel Prize in chemistry, 1964; Mikhail Lomonosov gold medal, 1982. Fellow Royal Soc. (Royal medal 1956, Copley medal 1976), Australian Acad. Sci., Akad. Leopoldina; mem. Nat. Acad. Scis., Brit. Assn. Advancement of Sci. (pres. 1977-78); fgn. mem. Royal Netherlands Acad. of Sci. and Letters, Am. Acad. Arts and Scis.; hon. fgn. mem. USSR Acad. Scis. Determined structure of vitamin B12, cholesterol iodide, and penicillin using X-ray crystallographic analysis. Home: Crab Mill, Ilmington, Shipston-on-Stour Warwickshire, England Office: U Oxford, Chem Crystallography Lab, 9 Parks Rd, Oxford OX1 3PS, England

HODGKINSON, MICHAEL FRANCIS, oil company executive; b. Derby, Derbyshire, Eng., Nov. 4, 1945; arrived in New Zealand, 1961; s. Authur Whawell and Marjorie Ella (Pritchard) H.; m. Gillian Peggy Fraser; children: Jane Margot, Sally Anne, Claire Sue. Degree in bus. mgmt., Otago U., Dunedin, New Zealand, 1978. With sales and adminstrn. depts. No. Steel Supplies Ltd., Auckland, New Zealand, 1965-68; supt. purchasing New Zealand Steel Ltd., Auckland, 1969-76, supt. projects adminstrn., 1979-80, mgr. adminstrn. and purchasing projects, 1976-79; mng. dir., v.p. fin. Seatec Internat. Ltd., Singapore, 1980-81; mgr. purchasing Petralgas Chems. NZ Ltd., Auckland, 1981-82; group supply mgr. Petroleum Corporation Ltd., Auckland, 1983-84; gen. mgr. comml. projects, corp. sec. Wellington, New Zealand, 1987—, Petroleum Corp. of New Zealand, New Plymouth, 1984-85. Councillor Waiuku Borough Council, New Zealand, 1975-78. Mem. New Zealand Inst. Purchase and Supply, New Zealand Inst. Mgmt. Presbyterian. Club: Taranaki (New Plymouth). Lodge: Lions. Office: Petroleum Corp New Zealand, 86 Lambton Quay, Wellington New Zealand

HODGKINSON, WILLIAM JAMES, marketing company executive; b. Bklyn., July 31, 1939; s. William James and Augusta Anne (Botka) H.; A.B., Bucknell U., 1961; M.B.A., Columbia U., 1963; m. Virginia Evelyn Humphreys, Sept. 7, 1963; 1 dau., Elizabeth Anne. Mktg. research analyst Singer Co., N.Y.C., 1963-66; asst. adminstrn. Writing Paper div. Am. Paper Inst., N.Y.C., 1966-67; market research mgr. Diners Club, N.Y.C., 1967-68; with Dun & Bradstreet Cos., Inc., 1968—, mgmt. cons. William E. Hill Co. div., N.Y.C., 1971-73, mgr. fin. services group Donnelley Mktg. div., Stamford, Conn., 1973-86, v.p., 1987—. Bd. dirs. Bklyn. Pub. Library br., 1974-79, Enlightenment Together, Inc., 1971-76; research coordinator Presdl. Task Force on Improving Small Bus., 1969-70; v.p., trustee Montessori Sch. Bklyn., 1975-79; trustee Greens Farms Congl. Ch., 1983-85; co-chmn. Save Fairfield Com., 1984—. Served with U.S. Army, 1963. Grantee Columbia U., 1962-63; recipient Brotherhood award Bucknell U., 1960. Mem. Bank Mktg. Assn., Am. Mktg. Assn., Direct Mail Mktg. Assn., Phi Lambda Theta. Congregationalist. (bd. deacons 1971-78, pres. 1977-78). Club: Princeton of N.Y. Contbr. articles to profl. jours. Home: 4454 Black Rock Turnpike Fairfield CT 06430 Office: Donnelley Mktg div Dun & Bradstreet 1515 Summer St Stamford CT 06905

HODGKISS, WAYNE, mechanical engineer; b. Birmingham, Eng., Mar. 5, 1958; s. Frank and Doris Jean (Smith) H.; m. Janet Ward, Aug. 15, 1981. Higher nat. cert. in applied electronics, Birmingham Polytech., 1976, higher nat. cert. in mech. engring., 1984. Devel. technician T.I. Sunhouse, Walsall, Eng., 1981; devel. engr. T.I. Creda, Stoke-on-Trent, Eng., 1981-86; design engr. Servis Group Ltd., Darlaston, Eng., 1982, project engr., 1982-84, lab. mgr., 1984-85, head. design sect., 1985—. Mem. Safety and Reliability Soc., Brit. Inst. Mgmt., Inst. Purchasing and Supplies. Conservative. Anglican. Home: 11 Stone Pine Close, Staffordshire WS12 4St, England Office: Servis Group, Darlaston Rd, Wednesbury England WS10 7TE

HODGMAN, VICKI JEAN, school system administrator; b. Joliet, Ill., May 22, 1933; d. Joseph and Mary (Desman) Mikolic; divorced; children: Michael James, Tudy Magnuson, Kathy Lynn. BEd, Ill. State U., 1954, MEd, 1970; postgrad., U. Bridgeport, 1972, U. Hawaii, 1982, No. Ill. U., 1978, 79, 80, Nat. Coll., 1983, 86, U. Utah, 1984, U. Ill., 1988. Cert. tchr., Ill., Md. Tchr. Will County (Ill.) Pub. Schs., Joliet, Rockdale and Lockport, 1954-55, 58-68, Balt. County (Md.) Pub. Schs., Sparrow's Point, 1955-56, McLean County (Ill.) Pub. Schs., Heyworth, 1957; tchr. spl. edn. So. Will County Coop. for Spl. Edn., 1969-79, supr., coordinator, 1979—; sec. Pulse-Chicagoland Spl. Edn. Suprs., 1983-85. Vol. Youth with a Mission, Gospel Outreach, 1985; treas. Women's Ch. Council, Rockdale, Ill., 1966-67, Band Parents Assn., Rockdale, 1966-67. Mem. Council Exceptional Children, Ill. Council Exceptional Children, Ill. Council Children with Behavior Disorders (pres.-elect 1988, bd. dirs. 1986-87), Will County Reading Assn. (bd. dirs. 1986-88), Will County Council for Exceptional Children, Ill. Alliance for Exceptional Children and Adults, Assn. for Children with Learning Disabilities, Assn. for Supervision and Curriculum Devel., Secondary Reading League, Heritage Quilters Guild (sec. 1987, treas. 1988). Republican. Mem. Assembly of God Ch. Home: 310 Reedwood Dr Joliet IL 60436 Office: So Will County Co-op Spl Edn 106 Tryon Channahon IL 60436

HODGSON, ARTHUR CLAY, lawyer; b. Little River, Kans., Aug. 22, 1907; s. Edward Howard and Flora Cleveland (Perry) H.; m. Annie Letitia Green, Jan. 5, 1939; children: Richard, David, Edward, Alice Anne, James. A.B., U. Kans., 1929; J.D., George Washington U., 1937. Bar: Kans. 1936, D.C. 1936, U.S. Supreme Ct. 1950. Sole practice, Washington, 1936-38; practice, Lyons, Kans., 1938—, ptnr. Hodgson & Kahler, 1969—. Pres. Lyons Jaycees; bd. dirs. Lyons C. of C. Served with USN, 1943-45. Mem. Kans. Trial Lawyers Assn. (bd. govs. 1957—, pres. 1972-73), Assn. Trial Lawyers Am. (bd. govs. 1973-76), Rice County Bar, S.W. Kans. Bar, Kans. Bar Assn. (del., disting. service award 1985), ABA (ho. of dels. 1976-82), City Attys. Assn. Kans. (pres. 1960-61). Democrat. Congregationalist. Clubs: Rotary (Lyons). Lodge: Masons. Home: Rural Rt Little River KS 67457 Office: 119 1/2 W Main Lyons KS 67554

HODGSON, ERNEST, toxicology educator; b. Durham, Eng, July 26, 1932; came to U.S., 1955; s. Ernest Victor and Emily (Moses) H.; m. Mary Kathleen Devlin, Dec. 21, 1957; children—Mary Elizabeth, Audrey Catherine, Patricia Emily Devlin, Ernest Victor Felix. B.Sc. with honors, Kings Coll. U. Durham, Eng., 1955; Ph.D., Oreg. State U., 1959. Research fellow Oreg. State U., Corvallis, 1955-59; research fellow U. Wis., Madison, 1959-61; asst. to assoc. prof. N.C. State U., Raleigh, 1961—, prof. toxicology, William Neal Reynolds prof., 1977—, chmn. toxicology dept., 1982—; mem. adv. panel U.S. EPA, Washington, 1982-85; mem. toxicology study sect. NIH, Washington, 1985—; pres. Toxicology Communications, Raleigh, 1982—; vis. scientist U. Wash., Seattle, 1975. Author, editor: Introduction to Biochemical Toxicology, 1980, Modern Toxicology, 1987, Dictionary of Toxicology; editor: Reviews in Biochemical Toxicology, 1979—, Reviews in Environmental Toxicology, 1984—; contbr. articles to profl. jours.; mem. editorial bd. Chemico-Biol. Interactions, Jour. Toxicology and Applied Pharmacology, Drug Metabolism and Distbn. Jour. Toxicology and Environ. Health. Chmn. policy rev. com. Gov.'s Waste Mgmt. Bd., Raleigh, 1984. NIH grantee, 1964—. Mem. Soc. Toxicology (edn. com. 1984—, Edn. award 1984, N.C. chpt. pres. 1984-85), Am. Soc. Pharmacology (drug metabolism com. 1981-84), Am. Chem. Soc., AAAS, Internat. Soc. Study Xenobiotics (council mem. 1986-98), Sigma Xi (chpt. pres. 1974). Democrat. Office: N C State U Toxicology Program Box 7633 Raleigh NC 27695

HODGSON, MAURICE ARTHUR, manufacturing and retailing executive; b. Bradford, Yorkshire, Eng., Oct. 21, 1919; s. Walter and Amy (Walker) H.; C.Eng., C.Chem., Merton Coll., Oxford (Eng.) U., 1938, B.Sc., M.A., 1942; D.Sc. (hon.), Loughborough U. Tech., 1981, Heriot-Watt, 1979; Hon. D. Tech., U. Bradford, 1979; m. Norma Fawcett, Mar. 20, 1945; children—Vivien, Tom Howard. With Imperial Chem. Industries Ltd. and subsidiaries, various locations, 1942-82, research dir. petrochem. div., 1960-66, gen. mgr. corp. planning, 1966-70, dir., 1970, dep. chmn., 1972, chmn., 1978-82; chmn. Brit. Home Stores PLC, 1982-87, chief exec. officer, 1982-85; chmn. Dunlop Holdings plc, 1984; non-exec. dir. Storehouse PLC, 1985—; vis. fellow Sch. Bus. and Organisational Studies, U. Lancaster; gov. London Grad. Sch. Bus. Studies, 1978-87; mem. ct. Brit. Shippers Council, 1978-82; mem. council Confedn. Brit. Industry, 1978-82; mem. internat. adv. com. Chase Manhattan Bank, 1980-83; mem. internat. adv. bd. AMAX Inc., 1982-85. Trustee The Civic Trust, 1978-82; mem. internat. council Salk Inst., 1978—; mem. ct. U. Bradford, 1979—; MEM. Council of Lloyd's, 1987—. Recipient Messel medal Soc. Chem. Industry, 1980, George F.

Davis medal Instn. Chem. Engrs., 1983. fellow Merton Coll., Oxford, 1979; hon. fellow U. Manchester Inst. Sci. and Tech., 1979. Office: Brit Home Stores PLC, Marylebone Rd House 129-137, London NW1 5QD, England

HODJAT, YAHYA, metallurgist; b. Tehran, Iran, Aug. 8, 1950; came to U.S., 1977; s. Javad and Robabeh (Fayaz) H.; m. Patricia Anne Gray, Dec. 17, 1980. BS, Arya-Mehr U., Tehran, Iran, 1972; MS, Ohio State U., 1978, PhD, 1981. Engr. trainee August Thyssen Corp., Oberhausen, W. Ger., 1974-75; project mgr. Pahlavi Steel Corp., Ahwaz, Iran, 1975-77; grad. research assoc. Ohio State U., Columbus, 1977-81; dir. ops. Intercontinental Metals, Miami, 1981-82; research scientist The Standard Oil Co., Cleve., 1982-83; mgr. pulley devel. Dyneer Corp., Bloomfield Hills, Mich., 1983—; cons. Intercontinental Metals Corp., Miami, 1978-80. Asst. inventor Pyro-Technique Silver Refining, 1980. Served to lt. Iranian Imperial Army, 1972-74. Mem. AIME, Am. Soc. Metals, Am. Foundrymen's Soc., Alpha Sigma Mu. Home: 45200 Keding St Apt 304 Utica MI 48087 Office: Dyneer Corp 1133 W Long Lake Rd Bloomfield Hills MI 48013

HODNETT, EARNESTINE, labor relations specialist; b. Virginia Beach, Va., Feb. 1, 1949; d. David and Mary Elizabeth (Scott) H. B.S. in Bus. Adminstrn., Norfolk State U., 1978; MBA in Pub. Adminstrn. Valdosta State Coll., 1988. Acctg. technician, Navy Pub. Works Ctr., Norfolk, 1967-78; personnel mgmt. specialist Naval Air Rework Facility, Norfolk, 1978-80, personnel staffing specialist, 1980-83, employee relations specialist, 1982-84; employee relations specialist Naval Submarine Base, Kings Bay, Ga., 1984-85, personnel mgmt. specialist, 1985-86, supervisory labor relations specialist, 1986-88, Eighth Army CPO, Seoul, Republic of Korea, 1988—. Bd. dirs. United Way, Camden County, Ga., 1985. Mem. Black Profl. Women Club Inc. (chairperson scholarship com. 1983-84), Soc. Labor Relations Profls., Federally Employed Women, Personnel Mgmt. Soc., Phi Delta Kappa, NAACP. Democrat. Avocations: reading; golf; aerobics; camping. Office: Seoul CPO Attn: East-CP-Mer APO San Francisco CA 96204

HOEFELMEYER, ALBERT BERNARD, cosmetic company executive; b. San Antonio, Mar. 27, 1928; s. Albert H. and Anna Theresa (McMonigal) H. BS in Chemistry, St. Mary's U., San Antonio, 1949; MA in Chemistry, U. Tex., 1950; PhD in Chemistry, Tex. Agrl. and Mech. U., 1954. Research chemist Celanese Corp. Am., Clarkwood, Tex., 1953-55; asst. prof. chemistry Tex. Coll. Arts and Industries, Kingsville, 1955-57; sr. nuclear engr., sr. research scientist Gen. Dynamics, Ft. Worth, 1957-71; v.p. Burkhart Trailer Mfg. Co., Ft. Worth, 1971-74; pres., owner Eagle Beauty Labs., Inc., Dallas, 1974—; sci. cons. Bac Stat Systems, Inc., Dallas, HS&N Corp., Dallas, 1976—; adj. prof. chemistry evening coll. Tex. Christian U., Ft. Worth, 1958-68. Mem. Soc. Cosmetic Chemists, Am. Chem. Soc., Radiation Research Soc., S.W. Sci. Forum, N.Y. Acad. Scis., Ft. Worth Bowling Assn. (former pres., life mem., Hall of Fame), Sigma Xi, Phi Lambda Upsilon. Roman Catholic. Home: 7355 Greenacres Dr Fort Worth TX 76112 Office: 3778 W Northwesr Hwy Dallas TX 75220

HOEFFLIN, RICHARD MICHAEL, lawyer, judicial administrator, contractor; b. Los Angeles, Oct. 20, 1949; s. David Greenfield and Gloria (Harrison) H.; m. Susan J. Amoroso, Mar. 29, 1969; children: Alyssa, Jennifer, Richard, II. BS in Acctg. cum laude, Calif. State U.-Northridge, 1971; JD, Loyola U., Los Angeles, 1974. Bar: Calif. 1974, U.S. Dist. Ct. (cen. dist.) Calif. 1974, U.S. Tax Ct. 1976, U.S. Dist. Ct. (no. and so. dists.) Calif. 1976, U.S. Supreme Ct. 1982. With Lewitt, Hackman, Hoefflin, Shapiro & Marshall, 1974—, ptnr., 1977—; judge pro tem Los Angeles Mcpl. Ct., 1982—; family law mediator Los Angeles Superior Ct., 1982-86. Co-founder Ventura County Homeowners For Equal Taxation, Westlake Village, Calif., 1978-79; pres., counsel Westlake Hills Homeowners Assn., 1975-77. Mem. Los Angeles Bar Assn., Ventura County Bar Assn., ABA, San Fernanado Valley Bar Assn. Republican. Roman Catholic. Club: North Ranch County (pres. tennis assn. 1984-85). Office: Lewitt Hackman Hoefflin et al 16633 Ventura Blvd Suite 1100 Encino CA 91436

HOEFLING, JOHN ALAN, former army officer, corporation executive; b. Milw., Sept. 3, 1925; s. Frederick Adolph and Lorraine (Braun) H.; m. Patricia Eileen Flynn, Apr. 12, 1947; children: Peggy Ann, Mary Kathleen, John Patrick. B.S., U.S. Mil. Acad., 1946; M.B.A., U. Ala., 1957; M.S. in Indsl. Relations, George Washington U., 1965; grad., Advanced Mgmt. Program, Harvard U., 1970. Commd. 2d lt. U.S. Army, 1946, advanced through grades to maj. gen., 1974; service in Japan, Korea, Germany, Vietnam, India; U.S. def. rep. to India New Delhi, 1970-72; asst. div. comdr. (3d Armored Div.), 1972-74; coordinator Army Security Assistance Washington, 1974-76; program gen. mgr. Vinnell Corp., 1976-79; v.p. Litton Data Command Systems and v.p., gen. mgr. Litton Saudi Arabia Ltd., 1979-84; v.p. Litton Data Command, Washington, 1980—; pres. HHS Inc., 1986—. Pres. Republicans Abroad, 1980-82. Decorated D.S.M., Silver Star, Legion of Merit, D.F.C., Soldier's medal, Bronze Star. Mem. Assn. U.S. Army 3d Armored Div. (pres. 1972-74), Assn. U.S. Army, Army Athletic Assn., Harvard Bus. Sch. Assn. Roman Catholic. Address: 1457 Cockleys Meadow Dr Boiling Springs PA 17007

HOEGES, DIRK, educator; b. July 27, 1943; s. Heinz and Helene (Lersch) H. Studied history, sociology, philosophy and Romance philology, U. Cologne, U. Paris and U. Siena, Italy, 1964-72; Diploma, Staatsexamen, U. Cologne, 1972. Habilitation, 1977. Prof. U. Bielefeld, Siegen, Fed. Republic Germany, 1977-87; prof. Romance philology and cultural scis. U. Hanover, Fed. Republic Germany, 1987—. Author: F. Guizot und die Französische Revolution, 1973 (Stiftung F.V.S.1974), Aufklärung und die List der Form, 1979, Literatur und Evolution, 1980, Alles Veloziferisch, 1985, Kontroverse vor dem Abgrund, E.R. Curtius, Karl Mannheim, 1929-33, 88; editor: Emile Hennequin, La Critique Scientifique, 1982, André Gide, Aufzeichnungen über Chopin, 1987; contbr. historiography, theory of literature and literature articles to profl. jours. Recipient Viutor-von-Scheffel-Preis, 1964, Prix Strassbourg, 1974. Mem. Deutscher Romanistenverband, Marcel-Proust-Gesellschaft, Freiherr-vom-Stein-gesellschaft, Gesellschaft für Interkulturelle Germanistik. Home: Classen-Kappelmannstr 26, Cologne 41, 5000 Nordrhein-Westfalen Federal Republic of Germany Office: Univ Hanover, Im Moore 21, 12 3000 Hanover Federal Republic of Germany

HOEK, HANS WYBRAND, psychiatrist; b. Amsterdam, The Netherlands, Apr. 6, 1955; s. Willem Andreas and Martha Maria (Keuls) H. BA in Psychology, State Univ. Groningen, The Netherlands, 1977, MD, 1982, PhD, 1987. Hosp. intern Surinam, 1979, Netherlands Antilles, 1981-82; researcher Groningen State U., 1982-87; fellow Columbia U., N.Y.C., 1986; advisor Nat. Health Council, The Hague, The Netherlands, 1985—. Author: Psychiatric Examination, 1987; contbr. sci. articles to profl. jours., 1983-87. Office: State U Groningen, Psychiatric Clinic, PO Box 30001, 9700 RB Groningen The Netherlands

HOEKEMA, DAVID ANDREW, philosophy educator, association administrator; b. Paterson, N.J., June 10, 1950; s. Anthony Andrew and Ruth Alberta (Brink) H.; m. Susan Alice Bosma, Jan. 2, 1972; children—Janna Elizabeth, Nicolas John. AB, Calvin Coll., 1972; PhD, Princeton U., 1981. Asst. prof. philosophy St. Olaf Coll., Northfield, Minn., 1977-84; prof. U. Del., Newark, 1984—; exec. dir. Am. Philos. Assn., Newark, 1984—; bd. dirs. Philosophy Documentation Ctr., Nat. Humanities Alliance; vis. fellow Calvin Ctr. for Christian Scholarship, Grand Rapids, Mich., 1982-83; cons. Del. Humanities Forum; project dir. Nat. Endowment Humanities Translation Grant. Author: (books) Rights and Wrongs: Coercion, Punishment and the State, 1986; guest editor Teaching Philosophy; contg. editor The Reformed Jour.; contbr. articles to profl. publs. Fellow Soc. for Values in Higher Edn. (bd. dirs.); mem. Am. Philos. Assn. (exec. dir.), Soc. Christian Philosophers, Am. Soc. for Aesthetics, Internat. Soc. Polit. and Legal Philosophy, Concerned Philosophers for Peace, Brandywine Friends of Old-Time Music. Home: 335 Park Ave Swarthmore PA 19081 Office: Am Philos Assn U Del Newark DE 19716

HOENACK, PEG COURSE, music educator; b. Moses Lake, Wash., Mar. 6, 1916; d. Herbert Moore and Mary (Hart) Course; BA in Music and Edn., magna cum laude, Wash. State U., 1937; MusM, Catholic U. Am., 1972; m. August Hoenack, June 14, 1939; children—Stephen A., Judith Hoenack Schultz, Francis A., August Jeremy. Tchr., cons. music edn. in Washington, Va. and Md., 1940-53; music specialist, Bethesda, Md., 1954-65; group piano instr. Montgomery County Pub. Schs., Md., 1960-70; lectr. elementary music edn. Am. U., 1972-74, George Mason U., Fairfax, Va., 1976, Trinity Coll., Washington, 1977, Chautauqua Inst. N.Y., 1977, Cath. U., Washington, 1979, Capitol Children's Mus., Washington, 1980-82, Washington State U., 1984; music cons. and workshop clinician Montessori, parochial and pub. schs., 1967—; founder, 1967, since dir. Music for Young People, studios and pub., Bethesda; founder Com. for Music in Pub. Schs., Montgomery County, 1953; steering com. Cultural Arts in Schs., 1970-75; bd. dirs. Concerned Citizens for Arts in Pub. Schs., 1972-80. Grantee Rockefeller Found., 1967, Ednl. Profl. Devel. Act, 1968, Philip Stern Family Fund, 1967-68. Mem. Internat. Soc. Music Edn., Music Educators Nat. Conf., Md. Music Educators, Am. Montessori Soc., Assn. Childhood Edn. Internat., Nat. Assn. Edn. Young Children, Washington Folklore Soc., Am. Orff Schulwerk Assn., Am. Recorder Soc., N.Y. Koto Club, Washington Koto Club (performing mem.), Washington Friday Morning Music Club (performing mem., violist), Phi Kappa Phi, Pi Lambda Theta, Psi Chi, Mu Phi Epsilon. Presbyterian. Author music textbooks, charts, teaching aids, programmed learning materials; contbr. profl. jours. Home: 8409 Seven Locks Rd Bethesda MD 20817

HOENIGSWALD, HENRY MAX, linguist, educator; b. Breslau, Germany, Apr. 17, 1915; s. Richard and Gertrud (Grunwald) H.; m. Gabriele Schoepflich, Dec. 26, 1944; children: Frances Gertrude, Susan Ann. Student, U. Munich, 1932-33, U. Zurich, 1933-34, U. Padua, 1934-36; D.Litt., U. Florence, 1936, Perfezionamento, 1937; L.H.D. (hon.), Swarthmore Coll., 1981, U. Pa., 1988; M.A. (hon.), U. Pa., 1971. Staff mem. Istituto Studi Etruschi, Florence, 1936-38; lectr., research asst., instr. Yale U., 1939-42, 44-45; lectr., instr. Hartford Sem. Found., 1942-43, 45-46; lectr. Hunter Coll., 1942-43, 46; lectr. charge Army specialized tng. U. Pa., Phila., 1943-44, assoc. prof., 1948-59, prof. linguistics, 1959-85, prof. emeritus, 1985—, chmn. dept. linguistics, 1963-70, co-chmn., 1978-79, mem. Ctr. for Cultural Studies, 1987—; P-4 Fgn. Service Inst., Dept. State, 1946-47; asso. prof. U. Tex., 1947-48; sr. linguist Deccan Coll., India, 1955; Fulbright lectr., Kiel, summer 1968, Oxford U., 1976-77; corp. vis. com. fgn. lits. and linguistics MIT, 1968-74; chmn. overseers com. to visit dept. linguistics Harvard U., 1978-84; vis. assoc. prof. U. Mich., 1946, 52, 68, Princeton U., 1959-60; vis. assoc. prof. Georgetown U., 1952-53, 54, Collitz prof., 1955; vis. prof. Yale U., 1961-62; mem. Seminar, Columbia U., 1965—; vis. staff mem., Leuven, 1986; fellow St. John's Coll., Oxford U., 1976-77; del. Comparative Linguistics Irex., 1986—; cons. Etymological Dictionary of Old High German, 1980—. Author: Spoken Hindustani, 1946-47, Language Change and Linguistic Reconstruction, 1960, Studies in Formal Historical Linguistics, 1973; Editor: Am. Oriental Series, 1954-58, The European Background of American Linguistics, 1979, (with L. Wiener) Biological Metaphor and Cladistic Classification, 1987; assoc. editor: Folia Linguistica Historica, 1979—, Indian Jour. Linguistics, 1977—; cons. editor: Jour. History of Ideas, 1978—; adv. bd. Lang. and Style, 1968—; editorial bd. Oxford Internat. Ency. Linguistics, 1986—. Am. Council Learned Socs. fellow, 1942-43, 44; Guggenheim fellow, 1950-51; Newberry Library fellow, 1956; NSF and Center Advanced Study Behavioral Scis. fellow, 1962-63; Festschrift in his honor, 1987. Corr. fellow British Acad.; mem. Nat. Acad. Scis., Am. Philos. Soc. (research com. 1972-84, research cons. 1984—, library com. 1984-87, chmn. 1988—, membership com. class IV 1984-87, chmn. 1987—, exec. com. 1988—), Am. Acad. Arts and Sci., AAAS, N.Y. Acad. Scis., Linguistic Soc. Am. (pres. 1958, archives com. 1983—), Am. Oriental Soc. (editor 1954-58, pres. 1966-67), Philol. Soc. (London), Linguistic Soc. India, Societas Linguistica Europaea, Linguistics Assn. Gt. Britain, Internat. Soc. Hist. Linguistics, Indogermanische Gesellschaft, Am. Philol. Assn., Archaeol. Inst. Am., Società di linguistica Italiana, Henry Sweet Soc. Home: 908 Westdale Ave Swarthmore PA 19081 Office: U Pa 618 Williams Hall Philadelphia PA 19104-6305

HOEPKER, WILHELM-WOLFGANG, pathologist, educator; b. Frankfurt, Fed. Republic of Germany, July 15, 1942; s. Wilhelm and Ruth (Gaetjens) H.; m. Doris Herfel, July 18, 1970; children: Tilo Martin, Katja Anne. MD, U. Hamburg, Fed. Republic of Germany, 1966; degree, U. Heidelberg, Fed. Republic of Germany, 1969, privatdozent, 1976. Physician Inst. Pathology U. Heidelberg, 1971-74, prof., 1979-87; prof. Inst. Pathology, U. Munster, Fed. Republic of Germany, 1977-79; chief Inst. Pathology, Hosp. Barmbek, Hamburg, 1987—; exchange pathologist Peoples Republic China, 1983-87. Author: Starvation Diseases, 1974, Autopsy, 1976, Diagnosis, 1976, General Pathology, 1976, Malformations, 1983, Lung Carcinoma, 1987. Mem. several sci. assns. Home: Ruebenkamp 148, 2000 Hamburg 60 Federal Republic of Germany Office: Allgem Krankenhaus Barmbek, Inst Pathology, 2000 Hamburg 60 Federal Republic of Germany

HOERNER, ROBERT JACK, lawyer; b. Fairfield, Iowa, Oct. 12, 1931; s. John A. and Margaret (Simmons) H.; m. Judith Chandler, Apr. 11, 1954; children: John Andrew, Timothy Chandler, Blayne Marie, Michelle Margaret; m. Susan Priscilla Warren, Aug. 27, 1980. BA, Cornell Coll., 1953; JD, U. Mich., 1958. Bar: Ohio 1960, U.S. Supreme Ct. 1964. Law clk. to Chief Justice Earl Warren, U.S. Supreme Ct., Washington, 1958-59; chief evaluation sect. antitrust div. Dept. Justice, Washington, 1963-65; ptnr. Jones, Day, Reavis & Pogue, Cleve., 1967—. Contbr. articles to legal jours. Mem. ABA, Ohio Bar Assn., Cleve. Bar Assn. Office: Jones Day Reavis & Pogue 901 Lakeside Ave North Point Cleveland OH 44114

HOERNI, JEAN AMÉDÉE, electronics consultant; b. Geneva, Sept. 26, 1924; came to U.S., 1953, naturalized, 1959; s. Robert and Jeanne (Berthoud) H.; children—Michael, Anne, Susan. B.S., U. Geneva, 1947, Ph.D., 1950; Ph.D., Cambridge U., 1952. Founder, research physicist Fairchild Semiconductor Corp., 1957-61; v.p. Teledyne, Inc., Mountain View, Calif., 1961-63; cons. Los Altos, Calif., 1963-67; founder, pres. Intersil, Inc., Cupertino, Calif., 1967-75; electronics cons. Hailey, Idaho, 1975—. Patentee in semiconductor planar process field. Recipient John Scott medal City of Phila., 1966; Longstreth medal Franklin Inst., 1969; Semmy award, 1985. Fellow IEEE. Address: PO Box 1400 Hailey ID 83333

HOETINK, HENDRIK RICHARD, museum director; b. Utrecht, Netherlands, Feb. 12, 1929; s. Hendrik Richard and Johanna Cornelia (Gertges) H.; D. History of Art, U. Amsterdam, 1959; m. Jacomina Louis Gilberte Ter Meulen, Dec. 19, 1959; children—Linda, Hendrik Richard. Chief curator drawings dept. Mus. Boymans van Beuningen, Rotterdam, 1959-71; dir. Royal Cabinet of Paintings Mauritshuis, The Hague, 1972—; dir. Erasmus Found., Amsterdam, 1975—. Served with Dutch Armed Forces, 1950-52. Author mus. and exhbn. catalogues; contbr. articles to profl. jours. Home: 8 Korte Vijverberg, 2513 AB Hague The Netherlands

HOFER, CHARLES WARREN, strategic management educator, consultant; b. Phoenixville, Pa., Nov. 11, 1940; s. Charles Emil and Alice May (Howard) H.; m. Judith Racella Millner, Oct. 22, 1980. BS in Engring. Physics summa cum laude, Lehigh U., 1962; MBA in Mktg. with distinction, Harvard U., 1965, MS in Applied Math., 1966, D in Bus. Policy, 1969. Research asst. Harvard Bus. Sch., Boston, 1965-66; asst. prof. Northeastern U., Boston, 1968-69; vis. lectr. Singapore Inst. Mgmt., 1969-70; asst. prof. Northwestern U., Evanston, Ill., 1970-75; assoc. prof. Northwestern U., 1975-76; vis. assoc. prof. Stanford (Calif.) U., 1976-77, Columbia U., N.Y.C., 1978, NYU, 1978-80; vis. prof. U. Calif., Riverside, 1980; prof. U. Ga., Athens, 1981—; lectr. Chgo. C. of C., 1976-78; campaign cons. Congressman (now Senator) Donald W. Riegle, Jr., Flint, Mich., 1968-72. Author: Toward a Contingency Theory of Business Strategy, 1975 (ranked 16th in world Acad. Mgmt. survey 1985), Strategy Formulation: Analytical Concepts, 1978 (ranked 30th in world Acad. Mgmt. survey 1985); co-author: Strategic Management: A Casebook in Policy and Planning, 1980, 84; co-editor: Strategic Management: A New View of Business Policy and Planning, 1979 (ranked 6th in world Acad. Mgmt. survey 1985); editor: Strategic Planning Mgmt., 1987—; assoc. editor: Jour. of Bus. Strategy, 1980-85; contbg. editor Am. Jour. Small Bus., 1987—. Pa. Scholar, 1958-62, Baker Scholar Harvard U., 1965; NSF fellow, 1962-63, Ford Found. Fellow, 1966-67. Mem. Acad. Mgmt. (chmn. policy div. 1977-78), Strategic Mgmt. Soc. (charter), Decision Scis. Inst. (policy track chmn. 1985-86), Inst. Mgmt. Scis., Am. Econ. Assn., Phi Beta Kappa, Phi Eta Sigma, Pi Mu Epsilon, Tau Beta Pi, Sigma Iota Epsilon, Beta Gamma Sigma. Republican. Lutheran. Clubs: Harvard Bus. Sch. of Atlanta, Harvard of Ga.; Lehigh Chess (pres. 1961-62). Home: 4445 Stonington Circle Dunwoody GA 30338 Office: U Ga Mgmt Dept Athens GA 30602

HOFER, TAMÁS, anthropologist educator; b. Budapest, Hungary, Dec. 29, 1929; S. Miklós J. and Irén Pantó H.; m. Mária Florián, Apr. 2, 1974, 1 child, Tamás Jr. MA, L Eötvös U., Budapest, Hungary, 1952, PhD, 1958. Research asst. Ethnographical Mus., Budapest, 1952-63, dept. head, 1963-80; vis. prof. U. N.C., Chapel Hill, 1971; dept. head Hungarian Acad. Sci. Ethnographical Inst., Budapest, 1980-86, dep. dir., 1986—. Author: Hungarian Folk Art, 1979; co-author Proper Peasants, 1969; editor Ethnographia (jour.); contbr. articles to profl. jours. Recipient Erixon award Nordiska Museet, Stockholm, 1973; Ford fellow, 1966-67. Mem. Hungarian Ethnographical Soc. (sec. gen. 1973-75, bd. dirs.), Hungarian Nat. Com. (pres.), Internat. Congress Anthrop. and Ethnol. Scis., Ethnologia Europaea (editorial bd.). Office: Ethnographical Inst, Orszaghaz u 30, H-1014 Budapest Hungary

HOFF, HELLMUT ECKART WALTER, West German ambassador to Ecuador; b. Rellingen, Germany, May 14, 1924; s. Walter and Frida (Hoff) H.; m. Waltraut Hawer, Dec. 30, 1956; children—Sabine, Andrea. Ph.D., U. Hamburg, Germany, 1955; Diploma Diplomatic and Consular Service, 1958. Attache Minstry Fgn. Relations, Bonn, Germany, 1956-58; 2d sec. Embassy Santiago de Chile, Chile, 1954-62; 1st sec. Embassy Kabul, Afghanistan, 1962-66; dep. consul gen., Montreal, Can., 1969-75; West German ambassador to Paraquay, Asuncion, 1975-78, to Bolivia, La Paz, 1982-86, to Ecuador, Quito, 1986—. Decorated Grand Gross (Paraquay), Grand Cross (Bolivia); comdr. Order of Merit (Chile); comdr. Order of Merit (Brazil). Lutheran. Office: Embassy of Fed Repub Germany, Casilla 537, Quito Ecuador

HOFFBERG, ALAN MARSHALL, accountant; b. Chgo., Apr. 15, 1940; s. Nathan and Evelyn Ruth (Zelensky) H.; m. Janet C. Glunts, Aug. 7, 1966; children—Amy, Donna, Wendy. B.Sc. in Acctg., DePaul U., 1962; postgrad. DePaul Law Sch., 1961-63; M.B.A. with honors, Roosevelt U., 1966. C.P.A., Ill., N.Y.; cert. systems profl. Adminstrv. v.p. Williams & Co., N.Y.C., 1969-80, Williams Real Estate Co., Inc., N.Y.C., 1969-80; pres. Info. Resource Mgmt. Inc., N.Y.C., 1980—; acct., cons. Ernst & Whinney, N.Y.C., 1966-69. Author: Fortran IV, 1975, 2d edit., 1980, Apple Supplement, 1980, (chpt.) Handbook of Management for the Growing Business, 1986. Contbr. articles to profl. publs. Treas. Broadview Police Pension Fund (Ill.), 1961, trustee, 1961-65; pres. Wantagh Scholarship Fund Inc. (N.Y.), 1978, treas., 1977. Mem. Am. Inst. C.P.A.s, N.Y. State Soc. C.P.A.s (chmn. coms.), Assn. for Systems Mgmt. (pres., v.p., treas., merit and achievement awards 1976, disting. service award 1979). Jewish. Home: 1644 Jane St Wantagh NY 11793 Office: Info Resource Mgmt Inc 1644 Jane St Wantagh NY 11793

HOFFER, DIANE LYNN, psychologist; b. Coral Gables, Fla., Dec. 29, 1953; d. Harold Herman and Charlotte May (Bernstein) H.; B.A. in Sociology, U. Miami, 1974; M.Ed. in Psychology, Counseling and Psychol. Services, Ga. State U., 1975; Dr. Psychology, Nova U., 1981. Practicum student Community Mental Health S. Dade, Dade County, Fla., 1978-79; clin. psychology intern Univ. Health Services U. Mass., Amherst, 1980-81; psychologist in pvt. practice, Coral Gables, 1981—; co-owner Jazz Workout, dance and exercise studio, 1982-84; dance instr.; instr. Parent Effectiveness Tng. Lic. marriage and family therapist, mental health counselor, clin. psychologist. Mem. Am. Psychol. Assn., Counselors and Therapists, Fla. Psychol. Assn, Friends of Fla. Psychoanalytic Soc., Soc. for Personal Assessment. Democrat. Jewish. Contbr. articles to profl. jours. Office: 6851 Yumuri St Suite 17 Coral Gables FL 33146

HOFFERT, PAUL WASHINGTON, surgeon; b. N.Y.C., Feb. 22, 1923; s. Charles and Rose (Isaacs) H.; m. Rosolyn Sheiman, Apr. 20, 1947; children—Marvin Jay, Renée Beth, Deborah Susan. A.B., with honors, Columbia U., 1942; M.D., cum laude, Yale U., 1945. Diplomate Am. Bd. Surgery, Am. Bd. Abdominal Surgery. Intern New Haven (Ct.) Hosp., 1945-46; fellow radiology Hosp. U. Pa., 1948-49; resident surgery VA Hosp., Bronx, N.Y., 1949-53; practice medicine specializing in gen. and vascular surgery, Yonkers, N.Y., 1953—; attending surgeon Yonkers Gen. Hosp., 1953—, chief of surgery, 1987—; sr. gen. and vascular surgeon St. Joseph's Hosp., 1953—; assoc. vascular surgeon Montefiore Hosp., 1965—; asst. prof. surgery Albert Einstein Coll., 1955—. Contbr. articles to profl. jours. Served to capt. U.S. Army Med. Corps, 1946-48. Recepient citation Am. Cancer Soc., 1960. Fellow Am. Coll. Surgeons (pres. Westchester, N.Y. chpt.), Am. Coll. Angiology N.Y. Acad. Medicine, Westchester Acad. Medicine (charter), Clin. Soc. N.Y. Diabetes Assn.; mem. N.Y. Surgical Soc., N.Y. Soc. Cardiovascular Surgery, Am. Zionist Orgn. (life) (past pres. Lincoln Park, Yonkers region), Phi Beta Kappa, Alpha Omega Alpha, Phi Delta Epsilon. Lodge: Masons. Home: 1450 Flagler Dr Mamaroneck NY 10543 Office: 45 Ludlow St Yonkers NY 10705

HOFF-JESSEN, ALLAN, financial consulting company executive; b. Copenhagen, May 31, 1942; s. Volmer Buris and Else (Pedersen) H.; m. Anne-Grete Ballieu Petersen, June 7, 1969; children—Alexander Ballieu, Kristina Anastasia. Asst. acct. Boesberg, Copenhagen, 1961; asst. Copenhagen Telephone Co., 1962-63, 64-66; chief acct. Forlaget-Sabroe, Copenhagen, 1967-69; Thomas Bergsoe Advt., Copenhagen, 1969-73; mng. dir. Allan Hoff-Jessen Co., Copenhagen, 1973—, Ty/pho/grafen, Copenhagen, 1975-78, Revisionsselskabet, Copenhagen, 1982—; chmn. bd. Forenede Danske Revisorer A/S., Odense, 1986—, Halding & Co., Advt., 1987—; bd. dirs. Copenhagen Communication Ctr. A/S . Served with Danish Army, 1963-64. Theatrechief grantee, 1976. Mem. Guild Freemasons, Lodge Dannevirke, Lodge Cubus Frederici Septimi, Dansk Revisor Union. Conservative. Home: 6 Holck Winterfeldts Alle, DK 2900 Hellerup Denmark Office: 12 Vestergrade, PO Box 1039, K 1007 Copenhagen Denmark

HOFFMAN, ALFRED JOHN, mutual fund executive; b. Amarillo, Tex., Apr. 16, 1917; s. Kurt John and Mabel (Beven) H.; m. Falice Mae Pittinger, Jan. 5, 1946; children: Susan Terry, John. J.D., U. Mo., 1942. Atty. Prudential Ins. Co. Am., 1946-50, Kansas City Fire & Marine Ins. Co., 1950-59; vice chmn. dir., past pres., chief exec. officer Jones & Babson, Inc., Kansas City, Babson Enterprise Fund; v.p. Babson Value Fund; v.p., dir. Babson Tax Free Income Fund, Babson Money Market Fund; trustee Babson Bond Trust; vice chmn., dir. Am. Cablevision of Kansas City; v.p., bd. dirs. UMB Bond Fund, UMB Stock Fund, UMB Money Market Fund, UMB Tax-Free Money Market Fund, UMB Qualified Dividend Fund; bd. dirs. Frankona Am. Life Reins. Co. Bd. dirs. Crittenton Ctr. Served with USN, 1942-46. Mem. ABA, Mo. Bar Assn., Western Golf Assn. (bd. dirs.), Kansas City Golf Assn. (pres., bd. dirs.), Kansas City Srs. Golf Assn. (past pres.), U.S. Golf Assn. (com.). Home: 6701 High Dr Mission Hills KS 66208 Office: 2440 Pershing Rd Kansas City MO 64108

HOFFMAN, CLYDE HARRIS, dean emeritus technical institute; b. Jamestown, N.D., Mar. 24, 1925; s. Clarence William and Ada Catherine (Gensrich) H.; B.S.E.E., U. N.D., 1950; M.S.E.E., U. Notre Dame, 1952, Ph.D. in Applied Mechanics, 1962; m. Betty Myra Ledingham, May 29, 1950. Instr. elec. engring. U. Notre Dame, 1951-52, asst. prof., 1953-62; project engr. Jack & Heintz, Inc., Cleve., 1952-53; asso. prof. elec. engring. Ill. Inst. Tech., Chgo., 1962-70, also head elec. engring. dept. Kabul (Afghanistan) U., 1966-68; mgr. IIT/TV Instructional Television Network, 1968-70; tng. mgr. Page Communications Engrs. INTS Program, Tehran, 1970-72; dir. tech. and vocat. tng. Harza Engring. Co., Chgo., 1972-73; 1st officer, program specialist UNESCO, Paris, 1973-78; mgr. transit communications systems IIT Research Inst., Chgo., 1978-80; dean acad. affairs DeVry Inst. Tech., Chgo., 1980-85; prin. Edutech Assocs. Cons., 1986—; evaluation panels undergrad. sci. instructional equipment program NSF, 1963-65; mem. Nat. Acad. Scis. adv. com. to electronics instrumentation div. Nat. Bur. Standards, 1965-68; mem. Nat. Def. Exec. Res., U.S. Dept. Transp. trustee Nat. Electronics Conf., Inc. Sustaining mem. Republican Nat. Com.; mem. nat. adv. bd. Am. Security Council. Served with inf. AUS, 1943-46; ETO, PTO. Decorated Bronze Star; registered profl. engr., Ill., Ind., Calif. Mem. Instrument Soc. Am. (sr. mem., governing bd. 1964-65, v.p. Chgo. sect. 1980-81, v.p. dist. 6 1986—), IEEE (sr.), Am. Def. Preparedness Assn. (life), DAV, (life), Nat. Rifle Assn. (life), Nat. Assn. Watch and Clock Collectors, Am. Soc. Tng. and Devel., Am. Legion, Inst. Radio Engrs. (chmn. South Bend sect. 1960-61), IEEE (exec. com. Chgo. 1964-65), Am. Ordnance Assn., AAAS, ASME, Assn. Computing Machinery, Am. Soc. Engring. Edn., Nat. Electronics Conf. (dir. 1957-64), Art Inst. Chgo. Republican. Club: Elks. Contbr. numerous articles to profl. jours. Home: 184 Cascade Dr Indian Head Park IL 60525 Office: PO Box 275 Western Springs IL 60558

HOFFMAN, DARNAY ROBERT, management consultant; b. N.Y.C., Nov. 25, 1947; s. Bill and Toni (Darnay) H.; B.A., SUNY, 1977; M.B.A., Baruch Coll., City U. N.Y., 1980; J.D., Yeshiva U., 1982; m. Jennifer Lea Sheppard, Aug. 20, 1984; children by previous marriage—Brandon, Brett. Pres., Darnay Hoffman Assos., Inc., mgmt. cons., N.Y.C., 1969—, Hoffman Research Group, Inc., mgmt. cons., N.Y.C., 1977—; research asso. Baruch Coll., 1977-79; bd. dirs. Hobton Realty Corp.; dir. Nat. Conf. Law Historians Am., 1987—. Mem. ABA, Am. Mgmt. Assn., Am. Mktg. Assn., Acad. Mgmt. Scis., Beta Gamma Sigma, Alpha Delta Sigma. Club: Player's. Author: Murder in the Wilderness, Alien Contact, 1980; (pamphlet) Products in Decline, 1980.

HOFFMAN, DONALD BROOKS, former county ofcl., bus. exec.; b. Franklin, Pa., Nov. 20, 1911; s. Camilla C. and Hazel (Brooks) H.; m. Margaret Jane Gruber, July 27, 1935; children—Margaret J. (Mrs. Harry Adams), Donald Brooks, Edwin P., William G. Ph.B., Muhlenberg Coll., 1932; M.A., Lehigh U., 1963; LL.D., Otterbein Coll., 1964. Claims mgr. Liberty Mut. Ins. Co., 1934-45; bus. mgr. Phoebe Floral Co., Allentown, Pa., 1945-52; county treas. Lehigh County, Pa., 1952-55, 64-67; with firm Yarnall, Biddle & Co., Allentown, 1955-75; v.p. investments Janney Montgomery Scott, Allentown, 1975—. Chmn. bd. commrs. Lehigh County, 1968-75. Trustee Muhlenberg Coll., 1963—. Mem. Orgn. Am. Historians, Am. Hist. Assn., So. Hist. Assn., Western Hist. Assn., County Treas. Assn. Pa. (sec., treas. 1954-71), Pa. Assn. Elected County Ofcls. (sec., treas. 1954-71), Assn. Coll. Honor Socs. (sec.-treas. 1965-75, pres. 1977-79), Pa. Dist. Exchange Clubs (pres. 1977-78, nat. dir. 1979-80), Phi Alpha Theta (exec. sec.-treas. 1937—). Republican. Mem. United Ch. of Christ. Clubs: Masons, Odd Fellows, Exchange. Home: 2812 Livingston St Allentown PA 18104

HOFFMAN, ERIC ALFRED, cardiopulmonary physiologist, educator; b. Rochester, Minn., Sept. 5, 1951; s. Murray Stanley Hoffman and Doris (Creamer) Kal. B.A., Antioch Coll. Yellow Springs, Ohio, 1974; Ph.D., U. Minn.-Mayo Grad. Sch. Medicine, 1981. Research cons. Royal Berkshire Hosp., Reading, Eng., 1972; research asst. Fels Research Inst., Yellow Springs, Ohio, 1973-74, U. Colo. Med. Ctr., Denver, 1974-75; pre-doctoral fellow Mayo Clinic Found., 1975-81, postdoctoral fellow, 1981-83, instr. physiology, 1982-83, assoc. cons., 1983-87, asst. prof., 1984-87; asst. prof. radiologic sci. and physiology U. Pa., Phila., 1987—; chief, sect. of cardiac imaging research, Dept. Radiol., Hosp. of U. Pa., Phila., 1988—; mem. research com. Colo. Heart Assn., 1974-75; new investigator Nat. Heart, Lung and Blood Inst., Washington, 1983-86, Searle/Mayo fellow, 1983-86. Established investigator grantee Am. Heart Assn., 1986; recipient Research Career Devel. Award NIH, 1987, Outstanding Film award Am. Coll. Chest Physicians, 1987. Mem. Am. Physiol. Soc. (fellow cardiovascular sect. 1986—), Am. Thoracic Soc., Am. Heart Assn. Council Cardiopulmonary Disease (exec. com., newsletter editor), Am. Heart Assn. Council Cardiovascular Radiology, Am. Heart Assn. Council Circulation, N.Am. Soc. for Cardiac Radiology, AAAS, Internat. Union Concerned Scientists, Sigma Xi. Office: Dept Radiol 3400 Spruce St Philadelphia PA 19104

HOFFMAN, JAMES PAUL, lawyer, hypnotist; b. Waterloo, Iowa, Sept. 7, 1943; s. James A. and Luella M. (Prokosch) H.; m. Debra L. Malone, May 29, 1982; 1 dau., Tiffany K. B.A., U. No. Iowa, 1965, J.D. U. Iowa, 1967. Bar: Iowa 1967, U.S. Dist. Ct. (no. dist.) Iowa 1981, U.S. Dist. Ct. (so. dist.) Iowa 1968, U.S. Dist. Ct. (so. dist.) Ill, U.S. Tax Ct. 1971, U.S. Ct. Appeals (8th cir.) 1970, U.S. Supreme Ct. 1974. Sr. mem. James P. Hoffman, Law Offices, Keokuk, Iowa, 1967—; chmn. bd. Iowa Inst. Hypnosis. Fellow Am. Inst. Hypnosis; mem. ABA, Iowa Bar Assn., Lee County Bar Assn., Assn. Trial Lawyers Am., Ill. Trial Lawyers Assn., Iowa Trial Lawyers Assn. Democrat. Roman Catholic. Author: The Iowa Trial Lawyers and the Use of Hypnosis, 1980. Home and Office: Middle Rd PO Box 1066 Keokuk IA 52632

HOFFMAN, JEROME, publishing data processing executive; b. N.Y.C., Feb. 5, 1924; s. Adolph Louis and Lillian H.; B.S., Fordham U., 1943; m. Judith Sterling Banks, Aug. 14, 1948; children—John, Matthew, Daniel, Gabriel. Mgmt. cons., 1953-61; systems mgr. Simon and Schuster, N.Y.C., 1961-65; dir. electronic data processing Forbes Mag., N.Y.C., 1965—. Served with U.S. Army, 1943-46. Mem. Assn. Computing Machinery, Assn. Systems Mgmt., Data Processing Mgmt. Assn., Fulfillment Mgmt. Assn., Mag. Pubs. Assn. Home: 53 Harbor Hills Dr Port Washington NY 11050 Office: 60 Fifth Ave New York NY 10011

HOFFMAN, JOHN RAYMOND, lawyer; b. Rochester, N.Y., July 24, 1945; s. Raymond Edward and Ruth Emily (Karnes) H.; m. Linda Lee Moore, Aug. 22, 1970; 1 child, Heather Anne. B.A., Washburn U., 1967; J.D., U. Mo.-Kansas City, 1971. Bar: Mo. 1972, Tenn. 1976, Kans. 1980, U.S. Supreme Ct. 1975. Law clk. United Telecom, Kansas City, Mo., 1967-70, gen. atty., 1970-75; gen. counsel, sec. United Telephone System-Southeast Group, Bristol, Tenn., 1975-80; v.p., gen. counsel United Telephone System Inc., Kansas City, Mo., 1980-84; sr. v.p. legal, dir. US Telecom, Inc., Kansas City, Mo., 1984-86 ; sr. v.p. external affairs, US Sprint Communications Co., Kansas City, 1986—. Bd. dirs. Trinity Luth. Hosp., Kansas City, 1984—, Health Initiatives, Inc., Kansas City, 1985, pres. 1986—, Kansas City Young Audiences, 1981-85, Johnson County Fire Dist., Prairie Village, Kans., 1982-86, Kansas City/Coro Found., 1983-84. Mem. ABA, Mo. Bar Assn., Tenn. Bar Assn., Kans. Bar Assn., Kansas City Bar Assn., Competitive Telecommunications Assn. (chmn. 1986-88), Kappa Sigma, Phi Delta Phi. Club: Optimist. Home: 6607 Willow Ln Mission Hills KS 66208 Office: US Sprint PO Box 8417 Kansas City MO 64114

HOFFMAN, MARK, finance executive; b. Greensboro, N.C., Dec. 14, 1938; s. Mark and Elaine (Faulkner) H.; m. Mary Jo Pyles, Nov. 30, 1968; children—Nicholas, John, James. A.B. in Applied Physics, Harvard U., 1959, MA, 1961, M.B.A., 1963; B.A., Cambridge U., Eng., 1961. Undersec. fin. East African Common Services Orgn., Nairobi, Kenya, 1963-65; investment officer World Bank, Washington, 1966-68; dir. Hambros Bank, London, 1969-74; fin. dir., resource group pres. George Weston Ltd., Toronto, Ont., Can., 1975-82; mng. dir. Guinness Peat Group Plc, London, 1982-83; chmn. Internat. Fin. Mkts. Tng. Ltd., London, 1984—; dir. Millipore Corp., Bedford, Mass., 1975—, George Weston Ltd., Toronto, 1975—, B.C. Packers Ltd., Vancouver, 1975—. prin. Hamilton Lunn Ltd., London, 1988—; overseer com. Harvard U. Ctr. for Internat. affairs; chmn. Harvard Cambridge Scholarship com.; trustee Oxford and Cambridge Rowing Found.; fin. chmn. Toronto Zoo Bd., 1975-78. Mem. Fin. Exec. Inst. Home: 21 Campden Hill Square, London W8, England also: Estabrook Woods Concord MA 01742 Office: 1 Finsbury Ave, London EC2 M2PA, England

HOFFMAN, MARVIN, computer company executive; b. Wauwatosa, Wis., July 27, 1933; s. Sam and Anna (Cohen) H.; m. F. Evelyn Lazar, Sept. 28, 1955; children: Loren William, Darryl Scott. BA in Math., Calif. State U., Northridge, 1962. Systems supr. N.Am. Rockwell, 1961-66; dir. software devel. Control Date Corp., 1966-69, Ampex Corp., 1969-72; mgr. software devel. F&M Systems Co., 1972-73; dir. research and devel. div. Computer Machinery Corp., 1973-76; founder, pres., chmn. bd. dirs. XXCAL, Inc., Los Angeles, 1976—; instr., mem. adv. com. Los Angeles City Coll.; bd. dirs. Rimtec. Bd. dirs. Los Angeles City Coll. Found. Served with USN, 1952-56. Mem. AMA, Data Processing Mgrs. Assn., So./Cal/Ten, West Los Angeles C. of C., Alpha Gamma Sigma. Republican. Jewish. Home: 2423 S Beverly Dr Los Angeles CA 90034 Office: XXCAL Inc 11500 Olympic Blvd Los Angeles CA 90025

HOFFMAN, MARY CATHERINE, nurse anesthetist; b. Winamac, Ind., July 14, 1923; d. Harmon William Whitney and Dessie Maude (Neely) H.; R.N., Methodist Hosp., Indpls., 1945; cert. obstet. analgesia and anesthesia, Johns Hopkins Hosp., 1949, grad. U. Hosp. of Cleve. Sch. Anesthesia, 1952; Staff nurse Meth. Hosp., 1945-49; research asst., then staff anesthetist Johns Hopkins Hosp., 1949-62; staff anesthetist Meth. Hosp., 1962-64, U. Chgo. Hosps., 1964-66; chief nurse anesthetist Paris (Ill.) Community Hosp., 1966-80; staff anesthetist Hendricks County Hosp., Danville, Ind., Ball Meml. Hosp., Muncie, Ind., 1981-86; instr.-trainer CPR, 1975-81; mem. Terr. 08 CPR Coordinating Com., 1975-80. Mem. Am. Assn. Nurse Anesthetists, Am. Heart Assn., Ind. Fedn. Bus. and Profl. Women's Clubs (Ill. dist. chmn. 1977-78, state found. chmn. 1978-79; found. award 1979). Republican. Presbyterian. Home: 1700 N Maddox Dr Muncie IN 47304

HOFFMAN, MERLE HOLLY, social psychologist, political activist, author; b. Phila., Mar. 6, 1946; d. Jack Rheins and Ruth (Dubow) H.; B.A. magna cum laude in Psychology, Queens Coll., 1972; postgrad. CUNY, 1972-75; m. Martin Gold, June 30, 1979. Founder, pres. Choices Women's Med. Ctr., Forest Hills, N.Y., 1971—; family planning cons. Health Ins. Plan, N.Y.C., 1973—; founder, pres. Ctr. for Comprehensive Breast Services, N.Y.C., 1979—; founder, pres. Merle Hoffman Enterprises, 1986—; speaker, debator on women's rights and polit. issues. Bd. dirs. Found. for the Creative Community, 1979—; founder, pres. Nat. Liberty Com., 1981. Mem. Am. Health Assn., Nat. Assn. Abortion Facilities (co-founder, pres. 1976-77), Nat. Abortion Fedn. (co-founder, sec. 1977-78), Phi Beta Kappa. Cons. editor Female Health Topics and Diagnostic Reporter, 1979-81; editor, pub. ednl. jour. On The Issues; contbr. articles in field to various publs.; producer documentary film Abortion A Different Light; founder N.Y. Pro-Choice Coalition; host cable TV series MH: On the Issues, 1986. Office: Choices 97-77 Queens Blvd Forest Hills NY 11374

HOFFMAN, MIMI SARA, educator; b. Pitts., June 23, 1931; d. Joseph and Mary (Kaufman) Edelstein; B.S. cum laude, U. Pitts., 1973, M.Ed., 1976, Ph.D., 1983; m. Marvin A. Hoffman, Apr. 19, 1970; children—Larry, Sharon. Tech. advisor Fermodyl Labs., Pitts., 1967-69; tng. supr. Am. Totalisator Co., Pitts., 1969-70; supr., curriculum coordinator, tchr. No. Area Spl. Purpose Schs., Pitts., 1974—; resident resource person, inservice presenter; ednl. cons. Active, Pitts. PBS Sta. WQED, Pitts. Symphony Soc. Coordinator Wellness program, Mem. Western Pa. Conservency, Pa. Edn. Assn., Assn. Supervision and Curriculum Devel., Pitts. Zoo, Carnegie Instn., U. Pitts. Doctoral Assn., U. Pitts. Consortium Profl. Ednl. Orgns., Adminstrv. Women in Edn., Buhl Sci. Ctr., Pi Lambda Theta (pres. delta chpt.). Jewish. Home: 3737 Beechwood Blvd Pittsburgh PA 15217

HOFFMAN, PHILIP EISINGER, lawyer, real estate company executive; b. N.Y.C., Oct. 2, 1908; s. David S. and Hildegarde (Eisinger) H.; m. Florence L. Lehman, Sept. 9, 1933 (dec.); children: David L., Lynn B. (Mrs. Roger L. Manshel); m. Bee Beham, June 18, 1972. A.B. cum laude, Dartmouth Coll., 1929; LL.B., Yale U., 1932. Bar: N.Y. 1933. Since practiced in N.Y.C.; corp. law practice 1933-42, 45—; partner Goodell, Hoffman & Spark, 1937-42, Hoffman & Tuck, 1962—; chmn. exec. com. U.S. Realty & Investment Co., Newark, 1962—; also dir.; former dir. Comml. Mortgage Co., Ray Miller, Inc., Realty Capital Corp., Ltd., Toronto, Ont., Can.; Mem. N.J. Commn. on Civil Rights, 1969-75, Bipartisan Conf. on Civil Rights, 1960—, mem. N.J. adv. com., 1964-69; N.J. adv. com. U.S. Commn. on Civil Rights, 1969-75; U.S. rep. Human Rights Commn. UN, 1972-75; chmn. Community Relations Council Essex County, N.J., 1960-63; co-chmn. housing com. Com. of Concern Newark, 1967-69; asst. gen. counsel WPB, Washington, 1942-45; hearing commr. Nat. Prodn. Authority, 1950-53; chmn. coodinating com. Retail Jewelry Industry, 1954-60; chmn. bd. govs. Am. Jewish Com., 1963-67, pres., 1969-73, hon. pres., 1973—, chmn. nat. exec. bd., 1967-68; hon. chmn. Appeal for Human Relations, 1962—; mem. exec. com. Nat. Community Relations Adv. Council, 1966-73, Am. Israel Pub. Affairs Com., 1969-73; chmn. adminstrv. council Jacob Blaustein Inst. for Advancement Human Rights, 1975—; trustee Leonard M. Sperry Research Center, East Orange Gen. Hosp., Jewish Community Council Essex County; chmn. bd. dirs. Nat. Assn. for Visually Handicapped, 1978-79; bd. dirs. Am. Friends of Jerusalem Mental Health Center, 1973-76; bd. govs. Hebrew U. Jerusalem, 1973—, Internat. League for Human Rights, 1975—, Com. for Econ. Growth in Israel, 1975; v.p. acad. affairs Am. Friends of Hebrew U., 1978—. Recipient numerous awards in human relations field. Mem. ABA, Assn. Bar City N.Y., N.Y. County Lawyers Assn., Phi Beta Kappa. Jewish. Clubs: 744 (Newark); Mountain Ridge Country (Caldwell, N.J.). Home: Claridge 1 Verona NJ 07044 Office: Aetna Realty Co 909 Broad St 5th Floor Newark NJ 07102

HOFFMAN, WILLIAM KENNETH, obstetrician, gynecologist; b. Milw., Jan. 18, 1924; s. William Richard and Marian (Riegler) H.; student U. Wis., 1942-43; student U. Pa., 1943-44, postgrad, 1954-55; M.D., Marquette U., 1947; m. Peggy Folsom, July 28, 1952; children—Janet Susan, Ann Elizabeth. Intern, Columbia Hosp., 1947-48, resident in obstetrics and gynecology, 1948-49, mem. staff, 1949—; preceptor R.E. McDonald, M.D., Milw., 1949-50; resident in ob-gyn U. Chgo., 1950-51; practice medicine specializing in ob-gyn, Milw., 1955-74; mem. staff, Columbia Hosp.; dir. health service U. Wis.-Milw., 1974—, cons. Sch. Nursing, 1976-77, clin. assoc. prof., 1979—, vice chmn. mem. Instl. rev. bd. 1976—, mem. instl. safety and health com., 1981—, chmn., 1984—. Mem. Am. Coll. Ob-Gyn, Am. Coll. Health Assn., Am. Coll. Sports Medicine, Milw. Acad. Medicine, N.Y. Acad. Scis., Royal Soc. Medicine, Am. Cancer Soc. (public edn. com. Milw. div., bd. dirs. 1983—). Home: 4629 N Murray Ave Milwaukee WI 53211

HOFFMAN, WILLIAM WALTER, surgeon; b. Evanston, Ill., July 20, 1928; s. William and Stella (Krygiel) H.; m. Doris Rosemary McNamara, Aug. 4, 1956; children: Jo Ann, Virginia, William Walter III. Student, Loyola U., Chgo., 1945-47; BS, Northwestern U., Evanston, 1949, MD, 1951. Diplomate Am. Bd. Urology, Am. Bd. Med. Examiners. Intern Cook County Hosp., Chgo., 1951-52; resident Northwestern U., Wesley Meml. Hosp., Chgo., 1954-57; staff urologist Chgo. VA Research Hosp., 1957-58; staff urologist Dallas Med. and Surg. Clinic, 1958—, mem. exec. com., 1969-87, chmn. bd. dirs., 1969—; dir. Dallas Med. and Surg. Clinic Investment Co., 1969-87, chmn. bd. dirs., 1977-87; clin. asst. prof. urology U. Tex. Southwestern Med. Sch., Dallas, 1958-79, assoc. clin. prof. urology, 1979—; vice chief urology Baylor U. Med. Ctr., Dallas, 1975-76, chief urology, 1976-86, chmn. med. bd., mem. exec. com., 1980-81; mem. staffs Children's Med. Ctr., Dallas, Parkland Meml. Hosp., Dallas, Presbyn. Hosp., Bristol Hosp., Gaston Episcopal Hosp.; cons. ambulatory health care accreditation program Joint Commn. on Accreditation of Hosps., 1972—. Contbr. articles to profl. jours. and chpts. to books. Served to capt. USAF, 1952-54. Fellow ACS, Internat. Coll. Surgeons, Am. Acad. Pediatrics; mem. AMA (Physicians Recognition award 1971), Tex. Med. Assn., Dallas County Med. Soc. (treas. 1976-78, del. 1981—), Soc. Pediatric Urology, Am. Urol. Assn., Intercity Urol. Soc. (pres. 1970-71), Am. Group Practice Assn. (trustee 1976-79, 84-88, pres. South Cen. sect. 1974-76), Am. Assn. Med. Clinics (commr. accreditation 1970-73, 76-78, chmn. editorial adv. com. 1979-84, trustee liaison editorial adv. com. 1984-87). Home: 6727 Meadow Lake Ave Dallas TX 75214 Office: 4105 Live Oak St Dallas TX 75221

HOFFMANN, MANFRED WALTER, oil company executive; b. Bklyn., Apr. 21, 1938; s. Hermann Karl and Emilie (Talmon) H.; B.S., Cornell U., 1960; M.Ed., Temple U., 1972, Ph.D., 1977; m. Barbara Ann Kenvin, Aug. 5, 1961; children—Lisa Joy, Lauren Kimberly, Kurt William. Mktg. rep. H. T. Heinz Co., N.Y.C., 1960-61; regional mgr. Swift & Co., Curtis Bay, Md. and Reading, Pa., 1961-63; salesman Sun Oil Co., Syracuse, N.Y., 1963-67, personnel mgr., 1967-71, mgr. mktg. devel., Rosemont, Pa., 1971-72, mgr. tng., 1973-77, dir. orgn. and mgmt. devel., 1977-79; dir. human resources and adminstrn. Sun Prodn. Co., Dallas, 1979-83; dir. human resources Sun Exploration & Prodn. Co., 1983-86; gen. dir. World Wide Human Resources Services, Dallas, Tex., 1986—; lectr. Grad. Sch., U. Tex., Dallas, 1979—. Pres., PTA, bd. mem. Beechwood Sch., 1975-77; cons. exec. com. Orgns. Industrialization Congress Am., 1975-79; bd. dirs. Job Opportunity for Youth, 1980-81; bd. dirs. Dallas SER, 1986—. Served with USMCR, 1956-62. Mem. Am. Soc. Tng. and Devel. (mgr. petroleum industry spl. interest group 1977-78, cert. of Appreciation 1977), Am. Soc. Personnel Adminstrn. (cert. of Appreciation 1977, 78), Am. Psychol. Assn. Republican, Am. Mgmt. Assn. Am. Petroleum Inst. Episcopalian. Home: 2210 Forest Creek McKinney TX 75069

HOFFMANN, MICHAEL RICHARD, lawyer; b. Des Moines, Apr. 26, 1947; s. Robert Wyman and Margaret Inez Wagner (stepmother) H.; m. Carol Elaine Tomb, July 29, 1973; children—Kurt Michael, Kristen Elaine, Kevin Richard. B.S. in Chemistry and Zoology, U. Iowa, 1969; J.D., Drake U., 1972; LL.M. in Patent and Trade Regulation, George Washington U., 1973. Bar: Iowa 1972, U.S. Ct. Customs and Patent Appeals 1972, U.S. Patent and Trademark Office 1973, U.S. Dist. Ct. (so. and no. dists.) Iowa 1974, U.S. Ct. Appeals (8th cir.) 1976, U.S. Supreme Ct. 1977. Clerk Jones, Hoffmann & Davison, Des Moines, 1970-73; assoc. Bacon and Thomas, Arlington, Va., 1973-74; assoc. Jones, Hoffmann & Davison, Des Moines, 1974-79, ptnr., 1979-83; pres. Michael R. Hoffmann, P.C., Des Moines, 1983—; mem. Iowa Def. Counsel, Def. Research Inst., Inc. Recipient Am. Jurisprudence award Bancroft-Whitney Co. and Lawyers Coop. Pub. Co., 1970-72. Mem. Iowa State Bar Assn., ABA (sci. and tech. sect.), Iowa Patent Bar Assn. (charter mem.), Am. Patent Law Assn., Am. Judicature Soc., Polk County Bar Assn., Iowa Assn. Workers' Compensation Lawyers. Phi Alpha Delta (dist. marshall 1970). Lutheran. Clubs: Prairie (Des Moines); Nat. Rifleines); Nat. Rifle (Washington). Office: Jones Hoffmann & Davison 1000 Des Moines Bldg Des Moines IA 50309

HOFFMANN, ROALD, chemist, educator; b. Zloczow, Poland, July 18, 1937; came to U.S., 1949, naturalized, 1955; s. Hillel and Clara (Rosen) Safran (stepson Paul Hoffmann); m. Eva Börjesson, Apr. 30, 1960; children: Hillel Jan, Ingrid Helena. B.A., Columbia U., 1958; M.A., Harvard U., 1960, Ph.D., 1962; D.Tech. (hon.), Royal Inst. Tech., Stockholm, 1977; D.Sc. (hon.), Yale U., 1980, Columbia U., 1982, Hartford U., 1982, CUNY, 1983, U. P.R., 1983, U. Uruguay, 1984, U. La Plata, SUNY, Binghampton, 1985, Colgate U., Rennes U., 1987. Jr. fellow Soc. Fellows Harvard, 1962-65; asso. prof. Cornell U., Ithaca, N.Y., 1965-68; prof. Cornell U., 1968-74, John A. Newman prof. phys. sci., 1974—. Author (with R.B. Woodward) Conservation of Orbital Symmetry, 1970, (poetry) The Metamict State, 1987. Recipient award in pure chemistry Am. Chem. Soc., 1969, Arthur C. Cope award, 1973; Fresenius award Phi Lambda Upsilon, 1969; Harrison Howe award Rochester sect. Am. Chem. Soc., 1970; ann. award Internat. Acad. Quantum Molecular Scis., 1970; Pauling award, 1974; Nobel prize in chemistry, 1981; inorganic chemistry award; Am. Chem. Soc., 1982; Nat. Medal of Sci., 1983; Award in Chem. Scis., Nat. Acad. Sci., 1986. Mem. Nat. Acad. Scis., Am. Acad. Arts and Scis., Internat. Acad. Quantum Molecular Scis.; fgn. mem. Royal Soc., Indian Nat. Sci. Acad., Royal Swedish Acad. Scis.

HOFFMANN, ROBERT S., museum administrator, educator; b. Evanston, Ill., Mar. 2, 1929; s. Robert C. and Dorothy E. (Shaw) H.; m. Sally A. Monson, June 17, 1951; children—Karl R., John F., David R., Brenna E. B.S., Utah State U., 1950; M.A., U. Calif.-Berkeley, 1954, Ph.D., 1955; PhD (hon.), Utah State U., 1988. From instr. to prof. U. Mont., Missoula, 1955-68; prof. U. Kans., Lawrence, 1968-86; dir. Nat. Mus. Natural History, Washington, 1986-87; asst. sec. for research Smithsonian Inst., Washington, 1988—; cons. Faisalabad U., Pakistan, 1971—; adviser Inst. Arctic and Alpine Research, Boulder, Colo., 1980—, Quaternary Research Ctr., Seattle, 1981—. Co-author: Mammals in Kansas, 1981, Mammals of the Northern Great Plains, 1983; coordinator Mammal Species of the World, 1982; contbr. articles to profl. jours. Recipient Summerfield Disting. Prof. award U. Kans., 1982; NSF grantee, 1957-87. Fellow Am. Assn. Adv. Sci.; mem. Am. Soc. Mammalogists (bd. dirs. 1965—, pres. 1981-82). Office: Smithsonian Inst Washington DC 20560

HOFFMANN, TAMÁS, anthropology educator, museum director; b. Budapest, Hungary, May 29, 1931; s. Béla and Erzsébet (Kniesz) H.; m. Gabriella Kladek, Sept. 5, 1957; children: Judit, Tamás. MA in Philosophy, U. Budapest, 1954. Asst. prof. anthropology U. Budapest, 1957-63, prof., 1963—; dir. gen. Ethnographic Mus., Budapest, 1969—; dir. open air mus. Hungary, 1969-75. Author A gabonanemuek nyomtatása, 1963, Ethnography and Feudalism, 1975. Pres. Mus. Council Hungary, 1986—. Mem. Hungarian Acad. Scis. (dep. pres. com. agrl. history 1985—). Home: Berend 11, H-1035 Budapest Hungary Office: Ethnographic Mus, Kossuth Plaza 12, H-1035 Budapest Hungary

HOFFMANN-OSTENHOF, OTTO, retired biochemistry educator, researcher; b. Vienna, Austria, Oct. 18, 1914; s. Otto and Margit (Kolarik) Hoffmann-O.; m. Christel Gloege, Apr. 20, 1950; children—Thomas, Georg, Margit, Peter. Ph.D., U. Zurich (Switzerland), 1940. Research asst. U. Vienna, 1944-50, lectr., 1950-59, assoc. prof., 1959-71, prof. biochemistry, 1971-84, head dept. gen. biochemistry, 1971-84; sec. Enzyme Commn., 1955-61; chmn. Commn. Biochem. Nomenclature, 1965-77; pres. Fedn. European Biochem. Socs., 1965-66. Author: Enzymologie, 1954, Intermediary Metabolism, 1987; research, numerous publs. in field, 1946—; contbr. rev. articles to profl. jours.; editor: Affinity Chromatography, 1978. Served with mountaineering troops German Army, World War II; Russia. Decorated Cross of Honor for Sci. 1st class, Sign of Honor for Liberation Austria, Gt. Sign Honor Diet of Burgenland; recipient medal U. Liege (Belgium), 1964. Fellow N.Y. Acad. Scis.; mem. Biochem. Soc. (London), Societe de Chimie Biologique (Paris) (Jubilee medal 1965), Austrian Biochem. Soc. (hon.), Suomalaisten Kemistien Seura (Helsinki, Finland) corr.), Biochem. Soc. of German Dem. Republic (hon.), Union Socialist Acads. Austria (hon.), Austrian Pugwash Group (pres.). Socialist. Home: Leopold-Steiner-Gasse 26, A-1190 Vienna Austria

HOFFMANN-OSTENHOF, PETER, lawyer; b. Vienna, Austria, Oct. 28, 1955; s. Otto and Christel Hoffmann-Ostenhof. JD, U. Vienna, 1978; MBA, European Inst. Bus. Adminstrn., Fontainebleau, France, 1979. Mgmt. trainee Ford Motor Co., Colone, Fed Republic of Germany, 1979-80; asst. to gen. mgr. Mühlendorfer Kreidefabrik, Vienna, 1981-85, gen. mgr., 1985—; atty. Law Office of Braunegg, Hoffmann and Preslmayer, Vienna, 1981-82, Law Office of Dr. Schilhan, Vienna, 1982-85; sole practice Vienna, 1986—. Mem. European Inst. Bus. Adminstrn. Alumni Assn. (pres. Austrian nat. group 1980—). Home: Hackhofergasse 22, A 1190 Vienna Austria Office: Plankengasse 4, A 1010 Vienna Austria

HOFFMEYER, ERIK, banker; b. Raarup, Denmark, Dec. 25, 1924; s. Skat and Aase (Thejll) H.; m. Eva Kemp, Jan. 6, 1949. D.Sc., U. Copenhagen, 1958. With Danmarks Nationalbank, 1951-59; Rockfeller fellow, 1954-55; prof. U. Copenhagen, 1959-64; econ. counsellor Danmarks Nationalbank, Copenhagen, 1959-62; gen. mgr. Bikuben Savs. Bank, 1962-64; chmn. bd. govs. Danmarks Nationalbank, 1965—; gov. for Denmark to IMF, 1965—. Bd. dirs. Assn. Polit. Economy, pres. 1951-53; bd. dirs. Danish Econ. Assn., 1960-66, Precidency of Econ. Council, 1962-65, Danish Acad. Tech. Scis., 1963, Econ. Council, 1965—, Danish Sci. Adv. Council, 1965-72; chmn. C.L. David Collection, 1977—; chmn. Danmarks Nationalbank Anniversary Found., 1977—; Housing Mortgage Fund, 1969-72, European Investment Bank, 1973-77; com. govs. Central Banks EEC-Countries, chmn. 1975-76, 79-81; dep. chmn. Danish Export Fin. Corp., 1975—. Chmn., Found. for Trees and Environment Protection, 1979—. Laurits Andersen Found., 1982—; Group of Thirty 1984—; King Frederik V11 Found., 1985—, chmn. 1987—. Author: Price Stability and Full Employment, 1960; Structural Changes in the Money and Capital Markets, 1960; The Theory of Economic Welfare and the Welfare State, 1962; Industrial Growth, 1963; Monetary History of Denmark, 1968. Contbr. to Nationaløkonomisk Tidsskrift and internat. econ. jours. Office: Denmark Nationalbank, Havnegade 5, K 1093 Copenhagen Denmark

HOFFMEYER, WILLIAM FREDERICK, lawyer; b. York, Pa., Dec. 20, 1936; s. Frederick W. and Mary B. (Stremmel) H.; m. Betty J. Hoffmeyer, Feb. 6, 1960 (divorced); 1 child, Louise C.; m. Karen L. Semmelman, 1985. AB, Franklin and Marshall Coll., 1958; JD, Dickinson Sch. Law, 1961. Bar: Pa. 1962, U.S. Dist. Ct. (mid. dist.) Pa. 1981, U.S. Supreme Ct. 1983. Sole practice, 1962-81; sr. ptnr. Hoffmeyer & Semmelman, 1982—; instr. real estate law York Coll. Pa. Author: The Abstractor's Bible, 1981, Pennsylvania Real Estate Installment Sales Contract Manual, 1981, Real Estate Settlement Procedures, 1982, Contracts of Sale, 1985, How to Plot a Deed Description, 1986; author and lectr. of Pa. Bar Inst.'s audio-cassette program: Recent and Recently Remembered Developments in Real Estate Financing, 1981, and numerous other programs. Mem. ABA, Pa. Bar Assn., York County Bar Assn., York County Bd. Realtors, Am. Coll. Real Estate Lawyers. Lodges: Lions (past pres. East York club); Masons (past pres. York county club). Address: 30 N George St York PA 17401

HOFSTADTER, ROBERT, physicist, educator; b. N.Y.C., Feb. 5, 1915; s. Louis and Henrietta (Koenigsberg) H.; m. Nancy Givan, May 9, 1942; children: Douglas Richard, Laura James, Mary Hinda. B.S. magna cum laude (Kenyon prize), Coll. City N.Y., 1935; M.A. (Procter fellow), Princeton U., 1938, Ph.D., 1938; LL.D., City U. N.Y., 1961; D.Sc., Gustavus Adolphus Coll., 1963; Laureate Honoris Causa, U. Padua, 1965; D.Sc. (hon.), Carleton U., Ottawa, Can., 1967, Seoul Nat. U., 1967; Honoris Causa, U. Clermont-Ferrand, 1967; D. Rerum Naturalium honoris causa, Julius Maximilians U., Würzburg, W. Ger., 1982, Johannes Gutenberg U. Mainz (W. Ger.), 1983; D.Sc. (hon.), Israel Inst. Tech., 1985. Coffin fellow

Gen. Electric Co., 1935-36; Harrison fellow U. Pa., 1939; instr. physics Princeton U., 1940-41, CCNY, 1941-42; physicist Norden Lab. Corp., 1943-46; asst. prof. physics Princeton U., 1946-50; assoc. prof. physics Stanford U., 1950-54, prof., 1954-85, Max H. Stein prof. physics, 1971-85, prof. emeritus, 1985—, dir. high energy physics lab., 1967-74; dir. John Fluke Mfg. Co. Author: (with Robert Herman) High-Energy Electron Scattering Tables, 1960; editor: Investigations in Physics, 1958-65, Electron Scattering and Nucleon Structure, 1963; co-editor: Nucleon Structure, 1964; assoc. editor: Phys. Review, 1951-53; mem. editorial bd.: Review Sci. Instruments, 1953-55, Reviews of Modern Physics, 1958-61. Bd. govs. Technion, Israel Inst. Tech., Weizmann Inst. Sci. Calif. Scientist of Year, 1959; co-recipient of Nobel prize in physics, 1961; Townsend Harris medal Coll. City N.Y., 1961; Guggenheim fellow Geneva, Switzerland, 1958-59; Ford Found. fellow; recipient Röntgen medal, Wurzburg, Germany, 1985, U.S. Nat. Sci. medal, 1986, Prize of Cultural Found. of Fiuggi, Italy, 1986. Fellow Am. Phys. Soc., Phys. Soc. London; mem. Nat. Acad. Scis., Am. Acad. Arts and Scis., AAUP, Phi Beta Kappa, Sigma Xi. Home: 639 Mirada Ave Stanford CA 94305 Office: Stanford Univ Dept of Physics Stanford CA 94305 *

HOFSTEAD, JAMES WARNER, laundry machinery company executive; b. Jackson, Tenn., Feb. 3, 1913; s. Harry Oliver and Agnes Lucile (Blackard) H.; m. Ellen Frances Bowers, Dec. 27, 1940; 1 dau., Eda Lucile. A.B., Vanderbilt U., 1935, LL.B., 1938. Bar: Tenn. Sole practice law; v.p., dir. United Telephone Co., 1969—; pres., dir. Wishy Washy, Inc., Nashville, 1946—; pres., dir. Wishy Sales Inc., 1959—. Served to capt. USMC, 1942-45. Mem. SAR (nat. committeeman, state pres. elect), So. Srs. Golf Assn., Soc. of the Cincinnati, English Speaking Union (chmn.), Soc. Colonial Wars, C. of C., Sigma Chi. Methodist. Clubs: Belle Meade, Cumberland, 200, Exchange (Nashville); Eccentric (London). Home: 215 Deer Park Circle Nashville TN 37205 Office: 3729 Charlotte Ave Nashville TN 37209

HOFSTEDE, GERARD HENDRIK, management educator; b. Haarlem, The Netherlands, Oct. 2, 1928; s. Gerrit and Evertine G. (Veenhoven) H.; m. Maaike A. Van den Hoek, June 4, 1955; children: Gert-Jan, Rokus, Bart P., P. Gideon. Diploma in mech. engring., Delft (The Netherlands) Tech. U., 1953; PhD in Social Sci., U. Groningen, The Netherlands, 1967. Engr. Stork Engring., Hengelo O, The Netherlands, 1955-59; plant mgr. Jovanda Hosiery, Hengelo O, 1959-60; various mgmt. positions Menko Textiles, Enschede, The Netherlands, 1960-65; mgr. personnel research IBM Europe, Blaricum, The Netherlands, 1965-71; vis. lectr. IMEDE Mgmt. Devel. Inst., Lausanne, Switzerland, 1971-73; prof. organizational behavior European Inst. Advanced Studies Mgmt., Brussels, 1973-79, INSEAD Bus. Sch., Fontainebleau, France, 1973-79; dir. human resources Fasson Europe, Leiden, The Netherlands, 1980-83; dean Semafor Sr. Mgmt. Coll., Arnhem, The Netherlands, 1983-86; prof. organizational anthropology and internat. mgmt. U. Limburg at Maastricht, The Netherlands, 1985—; vis. scholar Internat. Inst. Applied Systems Analysis, Laxenburg, Austria, 1979. Author: The Game of Budget Control, 1967 (NIVE award 1968), Culture's Consequences, 1980. Served to 1st lt. The Netherlands Army, 1953-55. Recipient Royal Dutch Shell Study award, 1949, Berenschot Meml. award European Fedn. Mgmt. Development, 1973, Internat. Research award Am. Soc. Tng. and Devel., 1988. Mem. Internat. Assn. Cross Cultural Psychology, European Group Organization Studies. Home: den Bruyl 15, 6881 AN Velp The Netherlands Office: U Limburg, PO Box 616, 6200 MD Maastricht The Netherlands

HOGAN, CLARENCE LESTER, retired electronics executive; b. Great Falls, Mont., Feb. 8, 1920; s. Clarence Lester and Bessie (Young) H.; m. Audrey Biery Peters, Oct. 13, 1946; 1 child, Cheryl Lea. BSChemE, Mont. State U., 1942, Dr. Engring. (hon.), 1967; MS in Physics, Lehigh U., 1947, PhD in Physics, 1950, D in Engring. (hon.), 1971; AM (hon.), Harvard U., 1954; D in Sci. (hon.), Worcester Poly. U., 1969. Research chem. engr. Anaconda Copper Mining Co., 1942-43; instr. physics Lehigh U., 1946-50; mem. tech. staff Bell Labs., Murray Hill, N.J., 1950-51, sub dept. head, 1951-53; assoc. prof. Harvard U., Cambridge, Mass., 1953-57, Gordon McKay prof., 1957-58; gen. mgr. semi-conductor products div. Motorola, Inc., Phoenix, 1958-60, v.p., 1960-66, exec. v.p., dir., 1966-68; pres., chief exec. officer Fairchild Inst., Mt. View, Calif., 1968-74, vice chmn. of bd. dirs., 1974-85; bd. dirs. Timeplex, Inc., Woodcliff Lake, N.J., Varian Assocs., Palo Alto, Calif., TAB Products, Palo Alto; gen. chmn. Internat. Conf. on Magnetism and Magnetic Materials, 1959, 60; mem. materials adv. bd. Dept. Def., 1957-59; mem. adv. council dept. electrical engring. Princeton U.; mem. adv. bd. sch. engring. U. Calif., Berkeley, 1974—; mem. nat. adv. bd. Desert Research Inst., 1976-80; mem. vis. com. dept. electric engring. and computer sci. MIT, 1975-85; mem. adv. council div. electrical engring. Stanford U., 1976-86; mem. scientific and ednl. adv. com. Lawrence Berkeley Lab., 1978-84; mem. Pres.'s Export Council, 1976-80; mem. adv. panel to tech. adv. bd. U.S. Congress, 1976-80. Patentee in field. Chmn. Commn. Found. Santa Clara County, Calif., 1983-85; mem. vis. com. Lehigh U., 1966-71, trustee, 1971-80; trustee Western Electronic Edn. Fund; mem. governing bd. Maricopa County Jr. Coll.; bd. regents U. Santa Clara. Served to lt. (j.g.) USNR, 1942-46. Recipient Community Service award NCCJ, 1978, Medal of Merit Am. Electronics Assn., 1978, Berkeley Citation U. Calif., 1980; named Bay Area Bus. Man of Yr. San Jose State U., 1978, One of 10 Greatest Innovators in Past 50 Yrs. Electronics Mag., 1980. Fellow IEEE (Frederick Philips Gold medal 1976, Edison Silver medal Cleve. Soc., 1978), AAAS, Inst. Electrical Engrs. (hon.); mem. Am. Phys. Soc., Nat. Acad. Engring., Sigma Xi, Tau Beta Pi, Phi Kappa Phi, Kappa Sigma. Democrat. Baptist. Club: Menlo Country (Redwood City, Calif.). Lodge: Masons. Home: 36 Barry Ln Atherton CA 94025

HOGAN, CURTIS JULE, union executive, industrial relation consultant; b. Greeley, Kans., July 25, 1926; s. Charles Leo and Anna Malene (Roussello) H.; m. Lois Jean Ecord, Apr. 23, 1955; children—Christopher James, Michael Sean, Patrick Marshall, Kathleen Marie, Kerry Joseph. B.S. in Indsl. Relations, Rockhurst Coll., 1950; postgrad., Georgetown U., 1955, U. Tehran, 1955-57. With Gt. Lakes Pipeline Co., Kansas City, 1950-55; with Internat. Fedn. Petroleum and Chem. Workers, Denver, 1955-85; gen. sec. Internat. Fedn. Petroleum and Chem. Workers, 1973-85; pres. Internat. Labor Relations Services, Inc., 1976—; cons. in field; lectr. Rockhurst Coll., 1951-52. Contbr. in field. Served with U.S. Army, 1945-46. Mem. Internat. Indsl. Relations Assn., Indsl. Relations Research Assn., Oil Chem. and Atomic Workers Internat. Union. Office: PO Box 6565 Denver CO 80206

HOGAN, PAUL, actor; b. Sydney, Australia; m. Noelene Hogan; 5 children. Actor films Crocodile Dundee, 1986, Crocodile Dundee II, 1988; former host TV shows A Current Affair, The Paul Hogan Show. Office: care ABC, 145-153 Elizabeth St, PO Box 9994, Sydney Australia *

HOGARTH, BURNE, cartoonist, illustrator; b. Chgo., Dec. 25, 1911; s. Max and Pauline H.; m. Constance Holubar, June 27, 1953; children—Michael, Richard, Ross. Student Art Inst. Chgo., 1925-27, Chgo. Acad. Fine Arts, 1926-29, Crane Coll., 1928-30, U. Chgo., 1930-32, Northwestern U., 1931-32, Columbia U., 1956-57. Asst. cartoonist to Lyman Young, Tim Tyler's Luck, N.Y.C., 1934; cartoonist Pieces of Eight, McNaught Syndication, N.Y.C., 1935; free lance artist King Features, N.Y.C., 1935-36; staff artist Johnstone Agy., N.Y.C., 1936-37; cartoonist Sunday Color Page, Tarzan, United Feature Syndication, N.Y.C., 1937-50, Sunday page Drago, Post-Hall Syndication, N.Y.C., 1946, Miracle Jones, United Features, N.Y.C., 1948; founder Sch. Visual Arts, N.Y.C., 1947-70, v.p., coordinator curriculum, instr., 1947-70; author Watson-Guptill, N.Y.C., 1958-85; instr. Parsons Sch., N.Y.C., 1976-79; pres. Pendragon Press Ltd., N.Y.C., 1975-79; with Art Ctr. Coll. Design, Pasadena, Calif., 1982—, Otis Art Inst., Parsons Sch. Design, Los Angeles, 1981—; numerous exhbns. worldwide including Musee des arts decoratives, Louvre, Paris, 1968, 69; one man show Paris, 1967, Bibliotheque Municipale, 1985, Palais de Longchamps, Marseille, France, 1985; represented in permanent collections: Smithsonian Instn., Mus. Cartoon Art, U. Colo., U. Wyo., Mus. Art, Gijon, Spain, others. Author: Dynamic Anatomy, 1958, Drawing the Human Head, 1965, Dynamic Figure Drawing, 1970, Drawing Dynamic Hands, 1977; Dynamic Light and Shade, 1981; creator graphic novels Tarzan of the Apes, 1972, Jungle Tales of Tarzan, 1976, Golden Age of Tarzan, 1979; Life of King Arthur, 1984. Trustee NCS Milt Gross Fund., 1980. Named Best Illustration Cartoonist, Nat. Cartoonists Soc., 1974, 75, 76, Artist of Yr., Pavilion of Humour, 1975, Premio Emilio Freixas Silver plaque V-Muestra Internat. Conv., 1978, Pulcinella award V-Mostra Internat. del Fumetto, 1983, Caran D'Ache Silver plaque Internat. Comics Conv., 1984, Adamson Silent Sam award Comics '85 Internat. Conv., 1985, Golden Palms award Cesar Illustration Group, Paris, 1988. Mem. Nat. Cartoonists Soc. (pres. 1977-79), Mus. of Cartoon Art, Am. Soc. Aesthetics, Nat. Art Edn. Assn., WHO, Graphic Arts Soc., Internat. Assn. Authors of Comics and Cartoons. Address: 6026 W Lindenhurst Ave Los Angeles CA 90036

HOGBEN, MONICA MARGARET, physician; b. Kaifeng, Honan, China, Sept. 22, 1919; d. Rowland and Alexina (Beckett) H. MBBS, Royal Free Hosp., London, 1944; Diploma in Obstetrics, Royal Coll. Obstetricians and Gynaecologists, Royal Free Hosp., London, 1946; D in Tropical Medicine and Hygiene, London Sch. Hygiene and Tropical Medicine, 1952. House surgeon Royal Free Hosp., 1943-44, asst. med. registrar, 1944-45; gen. practice medicine Newbury, Eng., 1946; resident doctor China Inland Mission, Langchung, China, 1948-50; clinic doctor China Inland Mission, Nanchung, China, 1950-51; family doctor Overseas Missionary Fellowship, Karuizawa, Japan, 1952-55, Aomori, Japan, 1957-62; internat. med. officer Overseas Missionary Fellowship, Singapore, 1963—. Mem. Royal Coll. Surgeons, Royal Coll. Physicians (licentiate). Office: Overseas Missionary Fellowship, 2 Cluny Rd, 1025 Singapore Singapore

HOGBERG, CARL GUSTAV, retired steel company executive; b. Escanaba, Mich., July 19, 1913; s. Claus Emil and Anna C. (Franson) H.; BS in Metall. Engring., Mich. Coll. Mining and Tech., 1935, DEng (hon.) Mich. Tech. U., 1968; m. June Loraine Evans, June 10, 1935; children—David K., Janet H. (Mrs. Nicholas A. Matwiyoff). Blast-furnace apprentice South Chicago works, Carnegie-Ill. Steel Corp., 1935, various operating positions blast-furnace dept., 1935-39, sec. blast-furnace and coke-oven com., Pitts., 1939-41; asst. chmn. blast-furnace com. U.S. Steel Corp., Pitts., 1942-54, asst. to v.p. Mich. Limestone div., Detroit, 1955, asst. v.p., 1956, v.p., 1957-60, pres., 1960-63, v.p. raw materials service, parent co., 1964, pres. Orinoco Mining Co. subs., Caracas, Venezuela, 1965-70, v.p. internat. U.S. Steel Corp., 1970-73. Mem. AIME (J.E. Johnson, Jr. award 1945), Assn. Iron and Steel Engrs. (Kelly award 1950), Am. Iron and Steel Inst., Eastern Western States Blast Furnace and Coke Assns. Contbr. tech. articles trade publs. Home: Sherwood Oaks 100 Norman Dr Mars PA 16046

HOGFORS, MARIE, journalist; b. Danderyd, Sweden, Oct. 10, 1938; d. Knut G. and Cecilia (Nordenfelt) Winroth; m. Sven Hogfors, Sept. 7, 1940; children: Carl, Hanna, Hedvig. BA, U. Stockholm, 1968; Degree in (acad. journalism), Journalist Sch. Stockholm, 1973. Freelance guide Europe and Am., 1963-68; asst. Am. Cultural Attache, Stockholm, 1969-70; journalist Svenska Dagbladet, Stockholm, 1974—. Office: Svenska Dagbladet, 10517 Stockholm Sweden

HOGG, CHRISTOPHER ANTHONY, manufacturing company executive; b. London, Aug. 2, 1936; s. Anthony Wentworth and Monica (Gladwell) H.; B.A., Marlborough, Trinity Coll., Oxford U., 1960; (fellow hon., 1982) M.B.A., Harvard U., 1962; m. Anne Cathie, 1961; 2 daus. Tchr., Institut pour l'Etude des Mé thodes de Direction de l'Entreprise, Lausanne, Switzerland, 1962-63; with Philip Hill, Higginson, Erlangers Ltd., 1963-66; staff mem. Indsl. Reorganisation Corp., London, 1966-68; with Courtaulds Group, London, 1968—, dir. The Internat. Paint Co. Ltd., 1968, Overseas dir., 1969, mng. dir., 1971, dep. chmn., 1972-73, chmn., 1973-78, dir. Courtaulds Ltd., 1973—, a dep. chmn., 1978-80, chief exec., 1979—, chmn., 1980—; non-exec. dir. Brit. Celanese Ltd., 1971-72, exec. dept. chmn. 1972; dir. Brit. Cellophane Ltd., 1978—, chmn., 1979—; mem. Dept. Industry Indsl. Devel. Adv. Bd., 1976-81. Mem. Com. of Award for Harkness Fellowships, 1980-86. Served with Nat. Service, parachute regt., 1955-57. Harkness fellow, 1960-62. Author: Masers and Lasers, 1962. Office: Courtaulds PLC, 18 Hanover Sq, London W1A 2BB, England

HOGG, RUSSELL E., credit card company executive; b. Cranston, R.I., Apr. 28, 1928; s. Walter and Julia H.; m. Dorothy Hogg; 1 child, Jason. BS, U. R.I., 1951, LLD (hon.), 1986; postgrad. in bus. adminstrn., Harvard U., 1965. With Joseph E. Seagram's & Sons, 1951-54; agt. FBI, Washington, 1954-61; sr. fin. officer Am. Airlines, 1961-69; with Am. Express Co., 1970-78; sr. v.p., internat. gen. mgr. card div. Am. Express Co., London; sr. v.p., operating group exec. Macmillan, Inc., N.Y.C., 1978-80; pres., chief exec. officer MasterCard Internat., Inc., N.Y.C., 1980—, also bd. dirs. Trustee, mem. bus. adv. council U. R.I.; mem. Muscular Dystrophy Assn.; chmn. bd. dirs. Inst. Internat. Sport. Clubs: Union League (N.Y.C.); Sleepy Hollow Country (Scarborough, N.Y.); Quidnessett Country (North Kingstown, R.I.). Office: MasterCard Internat Inc 888 7th Ave New York NY 10106

HOGUE, TERRY GLYNN, lawyer; b. Merced, Calif., Sept. 23, 1944; s. Glynn Dale and Lillian LaVonne (Carter) H.; m. Joanne Laura Sharples, Oct. 3, 1969; children: Morgan Taylor, Whitney Shannon. BA, U. Calif., Fresno, 1966, postgrad., 1967; JD, U. Calif., San Francisco, 1972. Bar: Calif. 1972, U.S. Dist. Ct. (cen. dist.) Calif. 1973, Idaho 1975, U.S. Dist. Ct. Idaho 1975, U.S. Supreme Ct. 1976. Assoc. Reed, Babbage & Coyle, Riverside, Calif., 1972-75; sole practice Hailey, Idaho, 1975-77; ptnr. Campion & Hogue, Hailey, 1977-80, Hogue & Speck, Hailey and Ketchum, Idaho, 1980-82, Hogue, Speck & Aanestad, Hailey and Ketchum, Idaho, 1982—. Bd. dirs. Blaine County Med. Ctr., Hailey, 1975—. Served to sgt. U.S. Army, 1969-71. Mem. ABA, Calif. Bar Assn., Idaho Bar Assn., Idaho Trial Lawyers Assn. (bd. govs. 1982—, treas. 1985-86, sec. 1986-87), Hailey C. of C. (bd. dirs. 1975-83, v.p. 1988—). Lodge: Rotary (bd. dirs. Hailey club 1975-80). Home: PO Box 1259 Ketchum ID 83340 Office: Hogue Speck & Aanestad 120 East Ave Box 987 Ketchum ID 83340

HÖHER, MARTIN, cardiologist; b. Cologne, Fed. Republic of Germany, Oct. 6, 1957; s. Karl-Heinz and Annemarie (Mauel) H. Student, U. Cologne, 1976-83, MD, 1987. Fellow dept. physiology U. Cologne, 1984-87, fellow dept. cardiology, 1987-88; fellow dept. cardiology Univ. of Ulm, Fed. Republic of Germany, 1988—. Contbr. articles to profl. jours. Fellow German Soc. Heart and Circulation Research. Roman Catholic. Home: Tokajerweg 19, 7900 Ulm Federal Republic Germany Office: U Ulm, Oberer Eselberg, 7900 Ulm Federal Republic Germany

HOHLER, G. ROBERT, fundraising consultant; b. Boston, Sept. 24, 1932; s. Robert Anthony and Eileen (Dutcher) H.; children: Robert Tillman, Cynthia Ann, Julie Barbara. B.A. magna cum laude, Northeastern U., 1960. Asst. to dep. comptroller Harvard, 1956-60; dir. office information Unitarian Universalist Assn., Boston, 1960-63; exec. dir. Laymen's League, 1963-69; dir. devel. Putney (Vt.) Sch., 1970-76; dir., partner Resource Devel. Assos., Brattleboro, Vt., 1976-77; dir. devel. and communication Oxfam-Am., 1978-82; Pres. Liberty Tree Assoc., cons. vol. orgns., 1966—; pres. Robert Hohler Assocs., Orgn. Devel., Communications and Fund Raising, 1981; editor Respond mag., 1966-70, Challenge mag., 1964-65, Putney Post, 1970-76. Author: You Can't Jail Us All, 1964, My Father Played for Me, 1977, Cambodia: Does It Have a Future, 1980. Founding mem. Citizens Boston Schs., 1961; founder Bostonian of Year award, 1960; founder, mem. bd. Boston Center for Arts, 1970—; del., vice-chmn. Vt. del. Nat. Democratic Conv., 1976. Hon. distinguished minister congregation Arlington St. Ch., 1967. Mem. Nat. Soc. Fund Raising Execs., N.E. Direct Mktg. Assn. Office: Robert Hohler Assocs 16 Shawmut St Boston MA 02116

HOHNER, KENNETH DWAYNE, fodder company executive; b. St. John, Kans., June 24, 1934; s. Courtney Clinton and Mildred Lucile (Forrester) H.; m. Sherry Eloi Anice Edens, Feb. 14, 1961; children: Katrina, Melissa, Steven, Michael. BS in Geol. Engring., U. Kans., 1957. Geophysicist Mobil Oil Corp., New Orleans, Anchorage, Denver, 1957-72; sr. geophysicist Amerada Hess Corp., Houston, 1972-75, ARAMCO, London, 1975-79; far east area geophysicist Hamilton Bros., Denver, 1979-83; owner Hohner Poultry Farm, Erie, Colo., 1979—; pres. Hohner Custom Feed, Inc., Erie, Colo., 1982—. Mem. Soc. Exploration Geophysicists. Home and Office: 3398 Weld County Rd 4 Erie CO 80516

HO-JIN, MYUNG, neurologist; b. Seoul, Republic of Korea, Mar. 11, 1931; s. Joo-wan and Woo-sik (Lim) M.; m. Chong-min Chang, Nov. 15, 1961; children: Jay, Jung-eun, Jea-sung, Jea-yoon. BS in Medicine, Seoul Nat. U., 1958, MS in Medicine, 1962; D of Med. Scis., Korea U., Seoul, 1972. Lic. med. practitioner, neuropsychiat. specialist. Asst. prof. neuropsychiatry Coll. Medicine, Seoul Nat. U., 1968-70, assoc. prof., 1970-77, prof., chmn. dept. neurology, 1977—; cons. Capital Armed Forces Gen. Hosp., Seoul, 1976—; dir. EEG lab. Seoul Nat. U. Hosp., 1978—; advisor Republic of Korea Office VA, 1981—; chief Korean Dels. to Asia Pacific Conv. of Neurology, 1984; founding mem. Phronesis World Confederation Neuroscis. Mem. Korean Neuropsychiat. Assn. (pres., chmn. 1976-77), Korean Neurol. Assn. (pres. 1982-83). Roman Catholic. Home: Soojong Apt A-103, Yoido-dong, 150 Seoul Republic of Korea Office: Seoul Nat U Hosp, 28 Yunkeun-dong, 110 Seoul Republic of Korea

HOKENSTAD, MERL CLIFFORD, JR., social work educator; b. Norfolk, Nebr., July 21, 1936; s. Merl Clifford and Flora Diane (Christian) H.; m. Dorothy Jean Tarrell, June 24, 1962; children: Alene Ann, Laura Rae, Marta Lynn. B.A. summa cum laude, Augustana Coll., 1958; Rotary Found. fellow, Durham (Eng.) U., 1958-59; M.S.W., Columbia U., 1962; Ph.D., Brandeis U., 1969, Inst. Ednl. Mgmt., Harvard U., 1977. With Lower East Side Neighborhood Assn., N.Y.C., 1962-64; community planning assoc. United Community Services, Sioux Falls, S.D., 1964-66; instr. Augustana Coll., Sioux Falls, 1964-66; research assoc. Ford Found. Project on Community Planning for Elderly, Brandeis U., Waltham, Mass., 1966-67; prof., dir. Sch. Social Work, Western Mich. U., Kalamazoo, 1968-74; prof., dean Sch. Applied Social Scis., Case Western Res. U., Cleve., 1974-83; Ralph and Dorothy Schmitt prof. Sch. Applied Social Scis., Case Western Res. U., 1983—; vis. prof. Inst. Sociology, Stockholm U., 1978, Fulbright lectr., 1980; vis. prof. Nat. Inst. Social Work, London, 1981; vis. prof. Sch. Social Work, Stockholm U., 1986; vis. scholar Inst. Applied Social Research, Oslo, 1989—. Author: Participation in Teaching and Learning: An Idea Book for Social Work Educators. Editor: Meeting Human Needs: An International Annual, Vol. V. Editor-in-chief Internat. Social Work Jour., 1985-87, Linking Health Care and Social Services: Internat. Perspectives; co-editor Internat. Issue Jour. Gerontol. Social Work, 1988. Contbr. articles to profl. jours. Mem. alcohol tng. rev. com. Nat. Inst. Alcoholism and Alcohol Abuse, 1974-78; workshop leader Am. Assn. State Colls. and Univs., 1974; chmn. U.S. com. XVIII Internat. Congress Schs. Social Work, 1976; chmn. Kalamazoo County Community Mental Health Services Bd., 1971, vice chmn., 1972; mem. edn. and tng. task force Mich. Office Drug Abuse and Alcoholism, 1972-73; mem. Mich. Assn. Mental Health Bds., 1972; bd. dirs. Cleve. United Way Services, 1982-84, del. assembly, 1974-82, mem. periodic rev. oversight com., 1982—, mem. leadership devel. com., 1978—; bd. dirs. Kalamazoo United Way, 1968-72; trustee Cleve. Internat. Program for Youth Workers and Social Workers, chmn. program com., 1985-87; mem. program devel. com. Cleve. Center on Alcoholism, 1976; trustee Alcoholism Services Cleve., Inc., 1977-86, v.p., 1982-85; trustee Community Info./Vol. Action Ctr., 1982—, chmn. leadership devel. com., 1984-86, chmn. unmet needs com., 1986-88, exec. com., 1985-88, v.p., 1986-88. Named Outstanding Alumnus, Augustana Coll., 1980; Fulbright Research fellow; NIMH trainee, 1960-62; Vocat. Rehab. trainee, 1966; Gerontology trainee, 1967; Rotary Found. fellow, 1958-59. Mem. Acad. Cert. Social Workers, Internat. Assn. Schs. Social Work (exec. bd., treas. 1978—, treas. 1978-86), Internat. Council on Social Welfare (dir. U.S. com. 1982—), Council on Social Work Edn. (del. 1972-75, 77-83, chmn. ann. program meeting 1973, chmn. com. on nat. legis. and adminstrv. policy 1975-79, mem. nominating com. 1978-81, internat. com. 1980-86, chmn. com. 1982-84, dir. 1979-82, exec. com. 1986—, pres. 1986—), Nat. Assn. Social Workers, Nat. Conf. on Social Welfare (bd. dirs. 1978-80, chmn. sect. V program com. 1977-78), World Future Soc. (area coordinator 1972-74), Fulbright Alumni Assn. Democrat. Episcopalian. Home: 2917 Weymouth Rd Shaker Heights OH 44120 Office: 2035 Abington Rd Cleveland OH 44106

HOLBROOK, DAVID KENNETH, language professional, writer; b. Norwich, Norfolk, Eng., Jan. 9, 1923; s. Kenneth Redvers and Elsie Eleanor (Grimmer) H.; m. Frances Margaret Davies-Jones, Apr. 23, 1949; children: Suki, Kate, Jonathan, Thomas. MA with honors, Cambridge U., 1947. Asst. editor Bur. Current Affairs, London, 1947-51; tutor Worker's Ednl. Assn., Leicestershire, Eng., 1951-53, Village Coll., Bassingbourn, Cambridge, 1954-61; fellow King's Coll., Cambridge, 1961-65; lectr. Jesus Coll., Cambridge, 1968-70; writer in residence Dartington Hall, Eng., 1971-73; fellow, dir. English studies Downing Coll., 1980-88, Leverhulme Emeritus Research Fellow, 1988690; Emeritus Fellow Downing Coll. 1988—; disting. vis. prof. MacMaster Univ., Hamilton, Ont., Can., 1985. Author: English for Maturity, 1961, English for the Rejected,1964, Human Hope and the Death Instinct, 1971, The Pseudo-Revolution, 1972, English for Meaning, 1980, Evolution and the Humanities, 1986, numerous others; (novels) Flesh Wounds, 1966, A Play of Passion, 1978, Nothing Larger than Life, 1987, Worlds Apart, 1988; (poetry) Against the Cruel Frost, 1963, Old World, New World, 1969, Selected Poems, 1980, numerous others. Served to lt. British Mil., 1942-45. Recipient Arts Council grants, numerous lit. awards; King's Coll. Sr. Leverhulme research fellow, 1965. Mem. Soc. Authors. Home: Denmore Lodge, Brunswick Gardens, Cambridge CB58DQ, England Office: Downing Coll, Cambridge England

HOLBROOK, DONALD BENSON, lawyer; b. Salt Lake City, Jan. 4, 1925; s. Robert Benson H.; m. Betty J. Gilchrist, Apr. 24, 1947; children—Mark, Thomas, Gregory, Mary. JD, U. Utah, 1952, Phd (hon.) Weber State Coll. Bar: Utah 1953. Pres. Jones Waldo, Holbrook and Mc Donough, Salt Lake City, 1973—; dir. Kearns-Tribune Corp.; bd. adv. Mountain Bell, 1974-84. Bd. dirs. Utah Assn. UN, 1963-64; bd. dirs. and exec. com. Utah Coop. Assn., 1962-82; vice chmn., chmn fin. com. bd. regents U. Utah, 1965-67, chmn. bd. 1965-67, 67-69, vice chmn., 1970-73, chmn., 1974-82, 83—; commr. Western Interstate Commn. Higher Edn., 1978-83, chmn. 1982; chmn. Edn. Task Force for Econ. Devel. in Utah, 1987—; pres. and chmn. bd. Ballet West, 1982-84; bd. dirs. Utah Democratic Party, exec. sec. 1955-65, exec. com. 1956-65; chmn. resolutions com. State Dem. Conv., 1958, antitrust and monopoly subcom. Western States Dem. Conf., 1962-66; campaign mgr. Gov. Calvin L. Rampton, 1964, 68; Dem. Conv., 1968; del. Dem. Nat. Conv., 1968; candidate for U.S. Senate, 1974. Recipient Disting. Alumni award U. Utah, 1985. Fellow Internat. Acad. Trial Lawyers, Am. Bar Found., mem. U. Utah Coll. Law Alumni Assn. (pres. 1957), ABA (gen. chmn. Rocky Mountain Region 1962, Utah chmn., mem. com. sect. corp., banking and bus. law 1962—), Utah State Bar Assn. (bd. commrs., 1982—), Salt Lake County Bar Assn. (chmn. com. continuing legal edn. 1961, chmn. com. World Peace Through Law, 1964, pres. 1964-65, chmn. com. jud. retirement 1968), Beta Theta Phi, Phi Kappa Phi, Delta Theta Phi (disting. alumni award 1967), Order of Coif (award for contbns. to law, scholarship and community service 1968). Clubs: Alta, Jeremy Ranch Country. Editor-in-chief Utah Law Rev., 1951-52. Office: First Interstate Bank Plaza Suite 1500 Salt Lake City UT 84111

HOLCOMB, DOROTHY TURNER, publicist; b. Roanoke, Va., June 15, 1924; d. Wiley Bryant and Lena Mae (Gray) Turner; m. Joseph E. Baxter, Aug. 1, 1944 (dec. Nov. 1944); m. 2d, G. William Holcomb, May 8, 1948 (div. 1962). Student Coronet Bus. Sch., Roanoke, 1943; interior decorator certificate N.Y. Sch. Interior Design, 1953; student U. Miami, 1962-63. Exec. sec. Am.'s Jr. Miss Pageant, Mobile, Ala., 1962; exec. asst. to pres. Gilbert Mktg. Group, Inc., N.Y.C., 1963-65; br. dirs. Heart Assn., Miami, Fla., 1965-66; publicist in charge on-air promotion Screen Gems, Hollywood, Calif., 1966-68; publicity dir. Mus. of Sci./Planetarium, Miami, 1968-71, Bryna Cosmetics, Inc., Miami, 1973-74; freelance publicist, 1971-73, 76—; pub. relations/communications ECKANKAR, Menlo Park, Calif., 1974-75. Mem. Publicists Guild, Internat. Alliance Theatrical Stage Employees, Moving Picture Machine Operators, Women in Communications. Home: Ridgewood Farm 2400 Gate House Ln Salem VA 24153

HOLCOMBE, CRESSIE EARL, JR., ceramic engineer; b. Anderson, S.C., Dec. 18, 1945; s. Cressie Earl Sr. and Blanche Elizabeth (Keaton) H.; m. Catherine Joselyn Brockman, Dec. 27, 1966; children—Justin Kent, Eric Benjamin. B.S., Clemson U., 1966, M.S., 1967; postgrad. U. Mo.-Rolla, 1973. Assoc. devel. engr. Union Carbide Corp., Oak Ridge, 1967-72, devel. engr., 1972-76, mem. devel. staff, 1977-80, mem. advanced devel. staff, 1980-84; advanced devel. staff Martin Marietta Energy Systems, Inc., Oak Ridge, 1984-88, sr. devel. staff, 1988—; founder ZYP Coatings Inc., Oak Ridge, 1982—. Author: (with others) Metallurgical Coatings, Vol. 1, 1976. Contbr. articles to profl. jours., unclassified spl. tech. reports for AEC/Dept. Energy. Patentee on refractory materials, metals and ceramics. Recipient Top Twenty award Materials Engring. mag., 1984, Excellence-Inventor award Martin Marietta Energy Systems, 1985; Weapons Complex award Excellence, Dept. Energy, 1986; IR-100 award for innovation Research and Devel. mag., 1987;

scholar Vol. Cement Co., 1964, 3-M Co., 1965; indsl. fellow Cabot Corp., 1966. Mem. Am. Ceramic Soc., Nat. Inst. Ceramic Engrs. (cert.), Keramos, Inventors Forum (v.p. 1985-86), Sigma Xi, Tau Beta Pi. Republican. Methodist. Office: Martin Marietta Energy Systems Inc PO Box Y Bldg 920 Oak Ridge TN 37830

HOLDEN, ANTHONY JAMES, physicist; b. Walsall, West Midlands, Eng., Oct. 8, 1953; s. Stanley and Marjorie (Scoffham) H.; m. Michele Abell, July 17, 1976; 1 child, Sophie Michele. BSc in Physics with honors, Victoria U. of Manchester, Eng., 1975; PhD in Physics, Gonville & Caius Coll., Cambridge, Eng., 1978. Chartered physicist. Postdoctoral research asst. Cavendish Lab. U. Cambridge, 1978-80; prin. scientist Allen Clark Research Ctr., Plessey Research Caswell Ltd., Towcester, Eng., 1980-86, sr. prin. scientist, 1986-88; chief physicist theory Allen Clark Research Ctr., Plessey Research Caswell Ltd., Towcester, 1988—. Contbr. numerous articles to profl. jours.; inventor: Linear Gate Transistor, Automatic Gain for ANR, Coplanar Balun Circuit. Ch. warden St. Peter and St. James Parish, Brackley, Eng., 1984—; leader 1st Helmdon (Eng.) Scout Group, 1981—. Mem. Inst. Physics in U.K. Mem. Ch. of Eng. Office: Plessey Research Caswell Ltd, Caswell, Towcester, Northants NN12 8EQ, England

HOLDEN, DONALD, writer, artist; b. Los Angeles, Apr. 22, 1931; s. Mack and Miriam (Epstein) H.; m. Wilma Shaffer, Jan. 10, 1954; children: Wendy, Blake. B.A., Columbia U., 1951; M.A., Ohio State U., 1952; LLD (hon.), Portland (Maine) Sch. Art, 1986. Teaching asst. English Ohio State U., Columbus, 1951-52; dir. pub. relations Phila. Coll. Art, 1953-55; dir. pub. relations and personnel Henry Dreyfuss (indsl. designer), N.Y.C., 1956-60; assoc. mgr. pub. relations Met. Mus. Art, N.Y.C., 1960-61; art cons. Fortune mag., N.Y.C., 1962; editorial dir. Watson-Guptill Publs. (art books), 1963-79, Am. Artist mag., N.Y.C., 1971-75; lectr. in field; mem. faculty, mem. artist adv. bd. Scottsdale Artists Sch., Ariz. Author: Art Career Guide, 1961, rev. edits., 1967, 73, 83, Whistler Landscapes and Seascapes, 1969; under pseudonym Wendon Blake: Acrylic Watercolor Painting, 1970, Complete Guide to Acrylic Painting, 1971, Creative Color: A Practical Guide for Oil Painters, 1972, Landscape Painting in Oil, 1976, The Watercolor Painting Book, 1978, The Acrylic Painting Book, 1978, The Oil Painting Book, 1979, The Portrait and Figure Painting Book, 1979, The Drawing Book, 1980, The Color Book, 1981, Complete Guide to Landscape Painting in Oil, 1981, Painting in Alkyd, 1982, Creative Color for the Oil Painter, 1983, The Complete Painting Course, 1984. Contbr. articles to profl. publs.; editorial cons., Watson-Guptill Publs., 1979—, drawings exhibited in one-man exhbns., sculpture, watercolors, and drawings in numerous group shows. Mem. Authors Guild, N.Y. Artists Equity Assn., Am. Inst. Graphic Arts, Nat. Art Edn. Assn., Phi Beta Kappa. Club: Century Assn. Home and Studio: 128 Deertrack Ln Irvington-on-Hudson NY 10533

HOLDEN, GEORGE FREDRIC, brewing company executive, consultant; b. Lander, Wyo., Aug. 29, 1937; s. George Thiel Holden and Rita (Meyer) Zulpo; B.S. in Chem. Engring., U. Colo., 1959, M.B.A. in Mktg., 1974; m. Dorothy Carol Capper, July 5, 1959; children—Lorilyn, Sherilyn, Tamilyn. Adminstr., plastics lab. EDP, indsl chems. plant, prodn. process engring., tool control supervision, aerospace (Minuteman, Polaris, Sparrow), Parlin, N.J., Salt Lake City, Cumberland, Md., 1959-70; by-product sales, new market and new product devel., resource planning and devel. and pub. relations Adolph Coors Co., Golden, Colo., 1971-76; dir. econ. affairs corp. pub. affairs dept., 1979-84, dir. pub. affairs research, 1984-86; owner Phoenix Enterprises, Arvada, 1986—; mgr. facilities engring. Coors Container Co., 1976-79; instr. brewing, by-products utilization and waste mgmt. U. Wis.; cons., speaker in field. Del. Colo. Rep. Conv., 1976—; bd. dirs. Colo. Pub. Expenditures Council, 1983-86, Nat. Speakers Assn., Colo. Speakers Assn., Nat. Assn. Bus. Economists, Colo. Assn. Commerce and Industry Ednl. Found. Mem. U.S. Brewers Assn. (chmn. by-products com., Hon. Gavel, 1975), Am. Inst. Indsl. Engrs. (dir. 1974-78). Co-author: Secrets of Job Hunting, 1972; The Phoenix Phenomenon, 1984; contbr. articles to Chem. Engring. Mag., 1968-76, over 150 published articles. Regular guest columnist La Voz, Colo. Statesman. Spkr. Heritage Found. Guide to Pub. Policy Experts, Spkrs. Bur., Commn. on the Bicentennial, U.S. Constn. Home: 6463 Owens St Arvada CO 80004 Office: Phoenix Enterprises PO Box 1900 Arvada CO 80001

HOLDEN-BROWN, SIR DERRICK, business executive; b. Surrey, Feb. 14, 1923; s. Harold Walter and Beatrice Florence (Walker) H.; m. Patricia Mary Ross Mackenzie, 1950; 2 children. Ed Westcliff. Chartered acct., Scotland. Joined Hiram Walker & Sons, 1949-54;mgr. dir. Ind Cooper, 1954-57, ; dir. Ind Coope Ltd., 1962; chmn. Victoria Wine Co., 1964; dir. Allied Breweries Ltd., 1967; chief exec. SVPW, 1969; fin. dir. Allied Breweries, 1972; chmn. and chief exec. Allied-Lyons, 1982—. Chmn. FDF, 1984-85, pres. 1985-86; dir. Sun Alliance and London Ins., 1977, Midland, 1984; chmn. 87; dep. chmn. Food From Britain Council, 1986; mem. CBI/Industry Task Force, 1986. Mem. Brewers' Soc. (chmn. 1978-80, pres. 1980). Address: Copse House, Milford-on-Sea Hampshire, England Office: Allied Lyons PLC, 156 Saint John St, London EC1P 1AR, England

HOLDER, BARRY KEITH, state safety administrator; b. Owensboro, Ky., Jan. 3, 1933; s. William O. and Mary E. (Hart) H.; m. Pamela M. Leake, Apr.1, 1956 (dec.); children: Kim E., Barry Keith. Student, U. Md., 1953-54. Quality control insp. W.R. Grace Chem. co., Owensboro, 1961-67; occupational safety compliance officer Ky. Dept. Labor, Owensboro, 1968-71, asst. dir. occupational safety and health div., 1972, asst. dir. div. edn. and tng., 1973-76, asst. dir. safety compliance, 1976-79; asst. dir. safety and health Ky. Dept. Labor, Frankfort, 1979, asst. dir. edn. and tng., 1984—; lectr., instr. labor edn. classes various state coll. and univs. Contbr. articles to profl. jours. Bd. dirs. various groups including PTA, 1962-70, United Way, 1966-71, Assn. Mental Retardation, 1967-72, Big Bros., 1974-79, Frankfort Arts Found., 1983-87; moderator, chmn. bd. deacons Crestwood Bapt. Ch., 197386; mem. Frankfort Civil Service BD., 1980-87. Served to master sgt. U.S. Air Force, 1952-60. Paul Harris fellow 1983. Mem. AFL-CIO (various offices), Boilermakers (pres. 1964-68), Am. Conf. Indsl. Hygienists, Am. Soc. Safety Engrs. (pres. Louisville chpt. 1973-74), Nat. Fire Protection Assn. (adv. council). Democrat. Lodges: Frankfort Rotary (pres. 1980-81, Rotarian Yr. 1982, dist. gen. 1987-88, v.p. UN 1988—), Masons. Home: 516 Menominee Trail Frankfort KY 40601 Office: US 127 S Frankfort KY 40601

HOLDER, HAROLD DOUGLAS, investor, industrialist; b. Anniston, Ala., June 25, 1931; s. William Chester and Lucile (Kadle) H.; children—Debra Holder Greene, Harold Douglas, Robert Douglas. Student, Anniston Bus. Coll., 1949, Jacksonville State U., 1954-57, Druitt Sch. Speech, 1962. Dept. mgr. Sears, Roebuck & Co., Anniston, 1954-57; merchandising mgr. Sears, Roebuck & Co., Atlanta, 1957-59; dir. coll. recruiting Sears, Roebuck & Co., 1959-61, dir. exec. devel. program, 1961, asst. personnel dir., 1962-63; store mgr. Sears, Roebuck & Co., Cocoa, Fla., 1965-67, Ocala, Fla., 1963-65; asst. zone mgr. Sears, Roebuck & Co., Atlanta, 1967-68; asst. gen. mgr. mdse. Sears, Roebuck & Co., 1968-69; sales promotion mgr. Sears in South, 1968; pres., bd. dirs. Cunningham Drug Stores, Inc., Detroit, 1969-70; v.p. Interstate Stores, 1971; pres., bd. dirs. Rahall Communications Corp., 1971-73; chmn. bd., chief exec. officer, dir. Am. Agronomics Corp., 1973-86; chmn. exec. com. Holder Internat. Industries, Inc., 1979-86; pres. Harold Holder Leasing; exec. com., bd. dirs. Coastland Corp., Fla., 1979-84; pres., dir. Golden Harvest, Inc., 1976-88; bd. dirs. Westbank Enterprises Inc.; bd. dirs., treas. Bay Capital Corp. of Tampa. Author: Don't Shoot, I'm Only a Trainee, 1975. Chmn., bd. dirs. Miracle, Inc., Brevard County; chmn. United Appeal, Ocala, Fla., 1964, Cocoa, Fla., 1966; bd. dirs. United Way Hillsborough County (Fla.); Chmn. Heart Fund Drive, Ocala, 1964, Marion (Fla.) Com. of 100.; bd. dirs. So. Coll. Placement Assn., Am. Acad. Achievement; exec. com., bd. dirs. Marion chpt. ARC, Opera Arts Assn.; exec. com. SHARE, U. Fla.; chmn. bd. trustees Eckerd Coll.; trustee U. Tampa, Eckerd Coll.; trustee U. Tampa. Endowed Harold D. Holder chair of mgmt. Eckerd Coll. Recipient Disting. Service award Marion County 4-H Club, 1965, Golden Plate award, 1983, Champion of Higher Edn. award, 1982, Fla. NAACP Humanitarian award, 1984. Mem. Chief Execs. Forum, C. of C. (chmn. beautification com., retail bus. com.), Young Pres. Orgn. (past chmn. Fla. chpt.). Episcopalian. Clubs: Univ., Tampa, Tampa Yacht and Country, Palma Ceia Golf and Country , (Tampa, Fla.). Office: The Holder Group 4600 W Cypress St Suite 300 Tampa FL 33607

HOLDER, HOWARD RANDOLPH, broadcasting corporation executive; b. Moline, Ill., Nov. 14, 1916; s. James William and Charlotte (Brega) H.; m. Clementi Lacey-Baker, Feb. 21, 1942; children: Janice Clementi Holder Collins, Susan Charlotte Holder Mason, Marjory Estelle Holder Turnbow, Howard Randolph. BA, Augustana Coll., 1939. With radio stas. WHBF, Rock Island, Ill., 1939-41, WOC, Davenport, Iowa, 1945-47, WINN, Louisville, 1947, WRFC, Athens, Ga., 1948-1956, WGAU & WNGC, Athens, 1956—; pres. Clarke Broadcasting Corp., Athens, 1956—; v.p. and treas. H. Group, Inc., 1986—; pres. Mid-West Ga. Broadcasting, Inc., 1983-86; bd. dirs. AP Broadcasters Inc. Chmn. adv. bd. Salvation Army, 1962-63, mem., 1952—; chmn. Athens Parks and Recreation Bd., 1952-62; chmn. Cherokee dist. Boy Scouts Am., 1966-67, bd. N.E. Ga. council, 1950—; mem. adv. bd. Clarke County Juvenile Ct., 1960-72; chmn. region IV Ga. div. Am. Cancer Soc., 1968; bd. dirs. Athens Crime Prevention Com., 1960-70; mem. Georgians for Safer Hwys., 1970; mem. adv. bd. Athens-Clarke County ARC, 1950-70; trustee Ga. Rotary Student Fund, Inc., 1969—; mem. Model Cities Policy Bd., 1970-71, Ga. Criminal Justice Coordinating Com.; mem. Ga. Productivity Bd., 1984-85; mem. bicentennial alumni activities com. U. Ga., 1982; co-pres. Friends U. Ga. Mus. Art, 1973-75; state bd. advisors Ga. Mus. Art, 1984—; sec. adv. bd. Henry W. Grady Sch. Journalism, U. Ga., 1973-74, mem., 1972-76; mem. adv. com. Ga. Commn. for Nat. Bicentennial, 1976; bd. dirs. Rec. for the Blind, 1977-83, Athens Symphony, 1981-85; mem. Ga. Gov.'s Jail/Prison Overcrowding Com., 1982. Served with AUS, 1941-46, ETO, maj. USAR ret. Named Boss of Yr., Athens Jr. C. of C., 1959, Broadcaster-Citizen of Yr., Ga. Assn. Broadcasters, 1962, Employer of Yr., Bus. and Profl. Women's Club, 1969, Athens Citizen of Yr., Rotary Club, 1971, Athens Citizen of Yr., Athens Woman's Club, 1971; recipient Silver Beaver award Boy Scouts Am., 1973, Liberty Bell award Athens Bar Assn., 1977, Robert Stolz medaille, 1973, Nat. DAR medal of Honor, 1983, cert. of Merit United Daus. of the Confederacy, 1983; Paul Harris fellow, 1978, Will Watt fellow, 1984. Mem. Res. Officers Assn. (pres. Athens chpt. 1962), Am. Ex-prisoners War, Ga. Assn. Broadcasters (pres. 1961), Athens Area C. of C. (pres. 1970), Ga. AP Broadcasters (pres. 1963), Augustana Coll. Alumni Assn. (bd. dirs. 1973-76; Outstanding Achievement award 1973), Golden Quill, Gridiron, Sigma Delta Chi, Alpha Psi Omega, Alpha Delta Sigma, Di Gamma Kappa (Ga. Pioneer Broadcaster of Yr. award 1971), Phi Omega Phi. Club: Touchdown (Athens) (pres. 1963-64). Lodge: Rotary (pres. Athens club 1957-58, gov. dist. 692, 1969-70, internat. pub. relations com. 1987—). Home: 383 Westview Dr Athens GA 30606 Office: 850 Bobbin Mill Rd Athens GA 30610

HOLDSWORTH, JANET NOTT, nurse, educator; b. Evanston, Ill., Dec. 25, 1941; d. William Alfred and Elizabeth Inez (Kelly) Nott; children—James William, Kelly Elizabeth, John David. B.S. in Nursing with high distinction, U. Iowa, 1963; M.Nursing, U. Wash., 1966; postgrad. U. Colo., 1981, U. No. Colo., 1982. Registered nurse, Colo. Staff nurse U. Colo. Hosp., Denver, 1963-64, Presbyn. Hosp., Denver, 1964-65, Grand Canyon Hosp., Ariz., 1965; asst. prof. U. Colo. Sch. Nursing, Denver, 1966-71; counseling nurse Boulder PolyDrug Treatment Ctr., Boulder, 1971-77; pvt. duty nurse Nurses' Official Registry, Denver, 1973-82; cons. nurse, tchr. parenting and child devel. Teenage Parent Program, Boulder Valley Schs., Boulder, 1980—; bd. dirs., treas. Nott's Travel, Aurora, Colo., 1980—; instr., nursing coordinator ARC, Boulder, 1979—, instr., nursing tng. specialist, 1980-82. Mem. adv. bd. Boulder County LaMaz Inc., 1980—; mem. adv. com. Child Find and Parent-Family, Boulder, 1981—; del. Republican County State Congl. Convs., 1972-86, sec. 17th Dist. Senatorial Com., Boulder, 1982—; vol. chmn. Mesa Sch. Parent Tchr. Orgn., Boulder, 1982—, bd. dirs., 1982—, v.p., 1983—. Mem. Am. Nurses Assn., Colo. Nurses Assn. (bd. dirs. 1975-76, human rights com. 1981-83, dist. pres. 1974-76), Soc. Adolescent Medicine, Council High Risk Prenatal Nurses, Council Intracultural Nurses, Sigma Theta Tau. Republican. Presbyterian (elder). Home: 1550 Findlay Way Boulder CO 80303 Office: Teenage Parent Program 3740 Martin Dr Boulder CO 80303

HOLDSWORTH, SIR (GEORGE) TREVOR, business executive; accountant; b. Bradford, Eng., May 29, 1927; m. Patricia June Ridler, 1951; 3 children. Ed. Keighley Grammar Sch. and Hanson Grammar Sch., Bradford; D. Tech. (hon.), U. Loughborough, 1981; D.Sc. (hon.), U. Aston, 1982. With Rawlinson, Greaves and Mitchell, Bradford, 1944-51; with Bowater Corp., 1952-63, becoming dir. and controller of U.K. paper-making subs.; dep. chief acct. Guest Keen and Nettlefolds Ltd., 1963-64, group chief acct., 1965-67; gen. mng. dir. GKN Screws and Fasteners Ltd., 1968-70, dir. and group controller, 1970-72, group exec. vice chmn., corp. controls and services, 1973-74, dep. chmn., 1974, mng. dir. and dep. chmn., 1977, chmn., 1980; dir. Thorn EMI PLC, 1977, Equity Capital for Industry Ltd., 1976-83, Midland Bank PLC, 1979; mem. council C.B.I., 1974—, mem. econ. and fin. policy com., 1976-80; mem. council Inst. Dirs., 1978-80, mem. steering group on unemployment, 1982, mem. programmes unit, 1982; bd. govs. Ashridge Mgmt. Coll., 1978—; v.p. Eng. Employers' Fedn., 1980; mem. exec. com. Soc. Motor Mfrs. and Trades, 1980; mem. Eng. Industries Council, 1980; trustee Anglo-German Found. for Study Indsl. Soc., 1980; mem. Brit. N. Am. Com., 1981-85; mem. European Adv. Council AMF Inc., 1982-85, Council Royal Inst. Internat. Affairs, 1983—, Lord Mayor's Appeal Com., 1981. Vice pres. Ironbridge Gorge Mus. Devel. Trust, 1981; trustee Royal Opera House Trust, 1981. Recipient Duke of Edinburgh's award Bus. and Comml. Enterprises Group, 1980; freeman City of London; liveryman Worshipful Co. Chartered Accts. in Eng. and Wales. Mem. Brit. Inst. Mgmt. (council 1974—, vice chmn. 1978-80, chmn. 1980, v.p. 1982). Office: Guest Keen & Nettlefolds PLC, 7 Cleveland Row, London SW1A 1DB, England *

HOLGATE, GEORGE JACKSON, university president; b. Lakewood, Ohio, Feb. 19, 1933; s. George Curtis and Melba Marguerite (Klein) H.; m. Sharon Joy, Dec. 20, 1954 (div. 1961); 1 child, Leigh Meredith. Mus.B., Baldwin-Wallace Coll., 1953; Mus.M., U. So. Calif., 1954, Ed.D., 1962; Ph.D., Riverside U., 1970, LL.D., 1971. Tchr. Oxnard High Sch., Calif., 1954-56; tchr. Ventura Coll., Calif., 1956-60; exec. v.p. Sierre Found., Santa Barbara, Calif., 1960-62; campus coordinator Congo Poly. Inst., Leopoldville, 1962-64; exec. dir. Automation Inst., Sacramento, 1964; pres. Riverside Bus. Coll., Calif., 1965-67, Riverside U., Calif., 1967—. Minister music St. Paul's Methodist Ch., Oxnard, Calif., 1954-55; condr. So. Calif. Council Protestant Chs. Messiah Chorus, 1954; dir. Ventura Coll. concert Chorale, 1956-60; condr. Ojai Festivals, Calif., 1958, Ventura Bach Festival, 1960; pres. Oxnard Community Concert Assn., 1958; pres. Vineyard Estates Property Owners Assn., 1958; me. Calif. State Democratic Central Com., 1962-63; chmn. 13th Congl. Dist. Dem. Council, 1963; bd. dirs. Riverside U., 1967—, Riverside Opera Assn., 1966-71, Riverside Symphony Orch. Soc., 1966—, So. Calif. Vocal Assn., 1955-56, USCG Found. Flotilla comdr. USCG Aux., 1983—, div. capt., 1986-87. Recipient Disting. Service U.S. Jaycees, 1962. Mem. NEA, Calif. Council Bus. Schs. (pres. 1970), Calif. Assn. Pvt. Edn. (treas. 1969), Music Educators Nat. Conf., Calif. Choral Condrs. Guild, Internat. Platform Assn., Phi Delta Kappa, Phi Mu Alpha Sinfonia, Sigma Phi Epsilon, Delta Epsilon. Office: Riverside U 890 N Indian Hill Blvd Pomona CA 91767

HOLIEN, KIM BERNARD, historian; b. Bad Cannstadt-Stuttgart, Fed. Republic of Germany, Mar. 10, 1948; s. Maurice Joel and Margaret Alice (Wild) H. BS, Bethel Coll., 1970; MA, George Mason U., 1984. With Dept. State, Washington, 1971-73; adjudicator GAO, Washington, 1975-76; with Nat. Archives, Washington, 1977-79; mil. historian Dept. Army, Washington, 1979—; historian Nat. Guard Bur., 1984; officer First North-South Brigade, Inc., 1974-84. Recipient Letter of Commendation, Dept. State, 1971, Disting. Service award Va. div. Sons of Confederate Vets., 1980; Outstanding Service award, 1980, Sustained Outstanding Service award and Spl. Service award, 1981 (all Dept. Army); Comdr.-in-Chief's award Sons Confederate Vets., 1982, Comdr.'s award Sons Union Vets., 1982; cert. of achievement U.S. Army Ctr. Mil. History, 1984. also letters of commendation/appreciation Dept. Army, Sec. Def., 1983, spl. service award Chief of Mil. History, 1986, official commendation, 1988. Author: Battle at Ball's Bluff, 1985, Battle at 1st Manassas, 1988; asst. editor The Sharpshooter, 1976-79; editor Clarion's Call, 1980-83, Ann. Rev. N.G. Bur., 1984. Mem. Am. Hist. Assn., Co. of Mil. Historians, D.C. Civil War Round Table (past pres.), Am. Mil. Inst., No. Va. Assn. of Historians, Alexandria Civil War Round Table (past pres.), Sons of Norway, Bethel Coll. Alumni Assn. (dir.), Heritage of Honor (pres.). Lutheran.

HOLKERI, HARRI HERMANNI, prime minister of Finland; b. Oripää, Finland, Jan. 6, 1937; m. Marja-Liisa Lepisto. MA in Polit. Sci. Sec. Nat. Coalition Party Youth League, 1959-60, info. sec., 1960-62; info. sec. Nat. Coalition Party, 1962-64, research sec., 1964-65, party sec., 1965-71, chmn., 1971-78; M.P. Finland, Helsinki, 1970-78, prime minister, 1987—; mem. bd. mgmt. Bank Finland, 1978—. Mem. Helsinki City Council, 1969—, chmn., 1981—. Address: Office Prime Minister, Aleksanterinkatu 3D, 00170 Helsinki Finland *

HOLLADAY, WILHELMINA COLE, real estate, interior design and museum executive; b. Elmira, N.Y., Oct. 10, 1922; d. Chauncy E. and Claire Elizabeth (Strong) Cole; m. Wallace Fitzhugh Holladay, Sept. 27, 1946; children: Wallace Fitzhugh, Scott Cole. BA, Elmira Coll., 1944; postgrad. art history U. Paris, 1953-54, U. Va., 1960-61, HHD (hon.), Moore Coll. Art, 1988, Mt. Vernon Coll., 1988. Exec. sec. Howard Ludington, Rochester, N.Y., 1944-45, Chinese Embassy, Washington, 1945-48; staff Nat. Gallery of Art, Washington, 1957-59; dir. interior design div. Holladay Corp., Washington, 1970—; dir. Holladay-Tyler Printing Corp., 1982-86; dir. Adams Nat. Bank, 1978-86, chmn. 1978-86; pres., chmn. bd. Nat. Mus. Women in the Arts; pres. First Corp.-WNB, 1980-86. Founder archival library of periodicals, books, exhbn. catalogs on women's art for research purposes; bd. dirs. Am. Field Service, 1964-80, Internat. Student House, 1973—, Leeds Castle Found.; mem. council Friends of Folger Shakespeare Library, 1978-82; mem. world service council YMCA; trustee Corcoran Gallery of Art, 1980—; pres. Holladay Found., 1980—; mem. profl. adv. com. interior design Mt. Vernon Coll.; mem. Mayor's Blue Ribbon Com., Met. Mus. Art. Recipient Horizon's Theatre award, 1986, Anti-Defamation award, 1987, Thomas Jefferson award Am. Soc. Interior Designers; named Woman of Achievement Washington Ednl. TV Assn., 1984, Woman of Distinction Council Ind. Colls., 1987. Mem. Am. Assn. Mus., Am. Fedn. Art, Women's Caucus for Arts, Met. Mus. Art, Mus. Modern Art, Art Libraries of N.Am., Archives Am. Art, Golden Circle of Kennedy Center, Arttable, Smithson Soc., Internat. Women's Forum, Women's Econ. Alliance (dir. 1984—), Phillips Gallery Art (patron). Episcopalian. Home: 3215 R St NW Washington DC 20007 Office: Nat Mus Women in the Arts 1250 New York Ave Washington DC 20005

HOLLÁN, SUSAN R., hematologist, educator; b. Budapest, Hungary, Oct. 26, 1920; d. Henrik and Maria (Hornik) Hollan; m. Gyorgy Révész, 1944; children—Thomas, Mary Christine. M.D., Univ Budapest, 1947, candidate of medicine, 1956; D.Sc., Univ Budapest Med. Sch. and Hungarian Acad. Sci., 1971. Research fellow I dept. medicine U. Budapest, 1950-54; sci. adviser Inst. for Exptl. Medicine, Budapest, 1954—; dir. Nat. Inst. Hematology and Blood Transfusion, Budapest, 1959-85, dir. gen., 1985—; prof. hematology Postgrad. Med. Sch., 1970—. Author: Basic Problems of Transfusion, 1965; Haemoglobins and Haemoglobinopathies, 1972; author numerous profl. papers; editor: Hungarian Medical Encyclopedia, 1967-72; Advances in Physiological Science, vol. 6 of Genetics, Structure, Function of Blood Cells, 1981; editor-in-chief Haemotologia, 1967—. Recipient Hungarian Acad. award, 1970, Hungarian Nat. prize, 1974. Mem. Hungarian Acad. Sci. (presidium 1976-85), Soc. Biologie (corr.), College de France (corr.); hon. mem. Purkinje Soc., Turkish Soc. Haematology, German Soc. Haematology, Soviet Soc. Haematology, Polish Soc. Haematology, Romanian Soc. Haematology, Hungarin Soc. Genetics (hon. pres.). Office: Nat Inst Hematology & Blood, Transfusion, Daroczi ut 24, 1113 Budapest Hungary

HOLLAND, CHARLES HEPWORTH, geology educator; b. Southport, Eng., June 30, 1923; s. William James and Elizabeth (Hepworth) H.; m. Eileen Storey, Aug. 9, 1952; 1 child, Celia Victoria. BSc in Geology with honors, U. Manchester, Eng., 1950; PhD in Geology, U. London, 1956; MA (hon.), Trinity Coll., Dublin, Ireland, 1968. Asst. lectr. geology U. Manchester, 1951-52; lectr. paleontology and stratigraphy Bedford Coll., U. London, 1953-64, sr. lectr. geology, 1965-66; prof. geology and mineralogy, head dept. geology Trinity Coll., 1966—. Author, editor: A Geology of Ireland, 1981, A Global Standard for the Silurian System, 1988; contbr. numerous articles to profl. jours. Recipient T.N. George medal Glasgow Geol. Soc., 1982. Fellow Geol. Soc. London (pres. 1984-86); mem. Palaeontol. Assn. (pres. 1974-76), Internat. Union Geol. Scis. (chmn. subcommn. on Silurian stratigraphy 1976-84), Geologists Assn., Paleontol. Soc., Royal Irish Acad. Office: Trinity Coll, Dept Geology, Dublin 2 Ireland

HOLLAND, CHARLES MALCOLM, JR., banker; b. Dallas, Dec. 5, 1932; s. Charles Malcolm and Kathryn (Hargon) H.; B.B.A., So. Meth. U., 1955, LL.B., 1957; m. Allison Allen, June 28, 1958; children—Malcolm, Hargon, Edith, Taryn. Admitted to Tex. bar, 1957; asso. law firm Lyne, Blanchette, Smith & Shelton, Dallas, 1960; with Hawaiian Trust Co., Honolulu, 1961-65; with First Hawaiian Bank, Honolulu, 1965—, sr. v.p., mgr. corp. banking div., 1980-87, sr. v.p., bus. devel. div. mgr., 1987—. Bd. dirs., mem. exec. com., chmn. strategic planning com., audit com., budget and fin. com. Queen's Med. Ctr.; trustee Queen Emma Found., Queen's Health Care; bd. dirs. Hawaii Heart Assn., Hawaiian Humane Soc; sr. warden vestryman, treas. St. Clement Epis. Ch.; mem. profl.-amateur com. Hawaiian Open Golf Tournament, also co-chmn. Satellite Tournament. Served to maj. USAF, 1959-65. Mem. Tex. Bar Assn., Hawaii Bar Assn., Am. Inst. Banking. Episcopalian. Clubs: Oahu Country (bd. dirs., treas.), Maui Country, Waialae Country, Beretania Tennis. Home: 168 Poloke Pl Honolulu HI 96822 Office: First Hawaiian Bank 161 S King St Honolulu HI 96847

HOLLAND, DAVID SCOTT, oil company executive; b. Havana, Ark., Mar. 26, 1931; s. William Lafayette and Mae Elizabeth (Scott) H.; m. Jacque Nell Hunter, July 11, 1952; children: David Scott, Terrence Hunter. Student, Hardin-Simmons U., 1949-51; B.S. in Geology, U. Tex., Austin, 1957. Geologist Marathon Oil Co., Midland, Tex., 1957-66; with Pennzoil Co., 1966—; v.p. Pennzoil Offshore Gas Operators, Inc., Houston, 1974-77; v.p., dir. Pennzoil La. and Tex. Offshore, Inc., Houston, 1974—, Pennzoil Producing Co., Pennzoil Oil & Gas, Inc., 1977—; sr. v.p. exploration Pennzoil Exploration & Prodn. Co., Houston, 1979-84, pres., chief exec. officer, 1984—. Contbr. papers to profl. lit. Active PTA, Boy Scouts Am., YMCA, Midland, 1957-68; bd. dirs. Christian Child Help Found., Sharpstown Sch. Served with USAF, 1951-54. Mem. Ind. Petroleum Assn. Am., Am. Assn. Petroleum Geologists (continuing edn. com., chmn. com. indsl. liason), Am. Petroleum Inst. (chmn. gen. com. experimental affairs), West Tex. Geol. Soc., Houston Geophys. Soc., Houston Geol. Soc., Permian Basin Soc. Exploration Geophysicists, Western Gas and Oil Assn., Assn. Citizens Polit. Action Com., Atlantic Council (China policy com.), Nat. Ocean Industries Assn. Clubs: Univ. of Houston, Petroleum of Houston and Lafayette (bd. dirs.), Forum. Home: 2914 Ann Arbor St Houston TX 77063 Office: Pennzoil Co PO Box 2967 Houston TX 77252

HOLLAND, GENE GRIGSBY (SCOTTY), artist; b. Hazard, Ky., June 30, 1928; d. Edward and Virginia Lee (Watson) Grigsby; B.A., U. S. Fla., 1968; pupil of Ruth Allison, Talequah, Okla., 1947-48, Ralph Smith, Washington, 1977, Clint Carter, Atlanta, 1977, R. Jordan, Winter Park, Fla., 1979, Cedric Baldwin Egeli Workshop, Charleston, S.C., 1984; m. George William Holland, Sept. 22, 1950; 3 children. Various clerical and secretarial positions, 1948-52; news reporter, photographer Bryan (Tex.) Daily News, 1952; clk. Fogarty Bros. Moving and Transfer, Tampa and Miami, Fla., 1954-57; tchr. elem. Schs., Hillsborough County, Fla., 1968-72; salesperson, assoc. real estate, 1984—; owner, operator antique store, 1982-87. One-woman/group shows include: Tampa Woman's Clubhouse, 1973, Cor Jesu, Tampa, 1973, bank, Monks Corner, S.C., 1977, Summerville Artists Guild, 1977-78, Apopka (Fla.) Art and Foliage Festival, 1980, 81, 82, Fla. Fedn. Women's Clubs, 1980, 81, 82; numerous group shows, latest being: Island Gifts, Tampa, 1980-82, Brandon (Fla.) Station, 1980-81, Holland Originals, Orlando, Fla.; represented in permanent collections including Combank, Apopka, also pvt. collections. Vol., ARC, Tampa, 1965-69, United Fund Campaign, 1975-76; pres. Mango (Fla.) Elem. Sch. PTA, 1966-67; pres. Tampa Civic Assn., 1974-75; vol. Easter Seal Fund Campaign, 1962-63. Recipient numerous art awards, 1978-82. Mem. Internat. Soc. of Artists, Council of Arts and Scis. for Central Fla., Fedn. of Women's Clubs (pres. Hillsborough County 1974-75, v.p. Tampa 1974-75), Meth. Women's Soc. (sec. 1976-77), Nat. Trust for Historic Preservation, Nat. Hist. Soc., Central Fla. Geneal. and Hist. Soc., Am. Guild Flower Arrangers, Methodist Soc. Clubs: Internat. Inner Wheel (past chmn. dist. 696, pres. Tampa 1972-73), Musicale (1st v.p. bd. incorporators Tampa 1974-75), Apopka Woman's (pres. 1981-82, dir. 1983-85). Home: 1080 Errol Pkwy Apopka FL 32712 Office: PO Box 700 Plymouth FL 32768

HOLLAND, GEORGE MCINTOSH, electronic company executive; b. Orange, Australia, Aug. 13, 1921; s. George Robert and Ann (McIntosh) H.; Eng.Diploma, Sydney Tech. Coll., 1950; m. Margaret Ruth Thomson, Aug. 31, 1950; children—Rebecca, Steven, Amanda, Timothy, Belinda, Jane, Matthew. Cadet engr. Cocatoo Docks, 1940-42; prodn. mgr. T.S. Skillman & Co., Sydney, Australia, 1946-50, London, 1950-53; works mgr. United Capacitor Co., Sydney, 1954-57; mgr. Esbray Pumps, Sydney, 1957-59; dir. Ferris Industries Ltd., Sydney, 1959-68; chmn. bd. dirs. New Metal Mines Ltd., Sydney, 1968-82, also Holland & Thomson Pty. Ltd., Holland Thomson Drilling Pty. Ltd., Joma Engring. Pty. Ltd., Orange, Australia, Lawrence Throwgrip Clutches Pty. Ltd., Sydney, Australian Drilling Inst. Tng. Com. Ltd. Served with Royal Australian Navy, 1942-46. Mem. Instn. Radio and Electronic Engrs. Australia. (sr.). Liberal. Methodist. Home: 15 Woodside Grove, 2087 Forestville Australia Office: 137 Boundary Rd, 2210 Peakhurst Australia

HOLLAND, JOHN BEN, clothing manufacturing company executive; b. Scottsville, Ky., Mar. 26, 1932; s. Elbridge Winfred and Lou May (Whitney) H.; m. Margaret Irene Pecor, Jan. 31, 1954; children: John Sandra, Robert. B.S. in Acctg., Bowling Green Bus. U., 1959. With Union Underwear Co., Inc., Bowling Green, Ky., 1961—, v.p.-adminstrn., 1972-74, vice chmn., 1975, chmn., chief exec. officer, 1976—; dir. 1st Ky. Nat. Corp., Louisville, Dollar Gen. Corp.; mem. N.Y. Cotton Exchange, 1985—. Bd. dirs. Ky. Council Econ. Edn., Louisville, 1981—, Ky. Advocates for Higher Edn. Inc., 1985—, Camping World Inc., 1985-88; chmn. corp. council Western Ky. U., also mem. devel. Steering com.; bd. dirs. Ky. C. of C., 1987—. Mem. Bowling Green-Warren County C. of C. (bd. dirs. 1981-85), Am. Arbitration Assn. (panel 1985—). Office: Fruit of the Loom Inc 1 Fruit of the Loom Dr Bowling Green KY 42101

HOLLAND, LEWIS ELBERT, investment banking executive; b. Denver, Dec. 6, 1942; s. Lewis E. Sr. and Josephine (Nash) H.; m. Judith Douglas Hamner, Jan. 14, 1965 (div. Oct. 1982); children: William Lewis, Melanie Lisa; m. Lunida Bell Jackson, May 21, 1985; 1 child, Sarah Elizabeth Trosper. BS, Miss. State U., 1965. CPA, Tenn. Ptnr. Ernst and Whinney, Memphis, 1970-83; pres. UMIC, Inc., Memphis, 1983—. Div. chmn. United Way, Memphis, 1986; bd. dirs. Memphis Orchl. Soc., Memphis, 1987. Mem. Tenn. Soc. CPA's (pres. 1984, bd. dirs. 1987—), Fin. Mgrs. Soc. (investment com.), Securities Industry Assn. (regional dealers com.). Republican. Clubs: Economic, University, Exchange (Memphis). Home: 4099 Gwynne Rd Memphis TN 38117 Office: UMIC Inc 850 Ridge Lake Blvd Memphis TN 38119

HOLLAND, MARTIN JEFFREY, educator; b. London, Dec. 8, 1954; s. Jeffrey Henry and Marie Josephine (Martin) H.; m. Susanne Haberstock, Dec. 30, 1960. BA with hons., Exeter U., Eng., 1982, PhD, 1982; MA, U. Kent, Eng., 1978. Lectr. U. Cape Town, Republic of South Africa, 1982-84; lectr. U. Canterbury, Christchurch, New Zealand, 1984-86, sr. lectr., 1988—. Author: The EEC in the 1980s, 1983, Candidates for Europe, 1986, The 4th Labour Government, 1987, The EEC and South Africa, 1988. Jean Monnet fellow, EEC, European U. Inst., Florence, Italy, 1987. Mem. Polit. Studies Assn., New Zealand Polit. Studies Assn. (treas. 1985-86), New Zealand Inst. Internat. Affairs. Mem. Labour Party. Office: U Canterbury, Dept Polit Sci, Christchurch 1 New Zealand

HOLLAND, RANDY JAMES, judge; b. Elizabeth, N.J., Jan. 27, 1947; s. James Charles and Virginia (Wilson) H.; m. Ilona E. Holland, June 24, 1972; B.A. in Econs., Swarthmore Coll., 1969; J.D. cum laude, U. Pa., 1972. Bar: Del. 1972. Ptnr., Dunlap, Holland & Rich and predecessors, Georgetown, Del., 1972-80; ptnr. Morris, Nichols, Arsht & Tunnell, Georgetown, 1980-86; justice Supreme Ct. Del., 1986—. mem. Del. Bd. Bar Examiners, 1978-86; mem. Gov.'s Jud. Nominating Commn., 1978-86, sec., 1982-85, chmn., 1985-86; mem. Del. Supreme Ct. Consol. Com., 1985-86. Pres. adminstrv. bd. Ave. United Methodist Ch., Milford, Del., trustee Peninsula Ann. Conf. Recipient Henry C. Loughlin prize for legal ethics U. Pa. 1972. Trustee Del. Bar Found.; mem. ABA, Assn. Trial Lawyers Am., Del. Trial Lawyers Assn. (bd. govs.), Del. State Bar Assn. (exec. com. 1988—), Am. Soc. Hosp. Attys., Am. Judicature Soc. Republican. Mem. editorial bd. Del. Lawyer Mag., 1981-85; contbr. chpt. Del. Appellate Handbook, 1985—.

HOLLAND, RAY LAURIMORE, accountant; b. Rich Hill, Mo., Sept. 10, 1916; s. Ralph Lee and Florence Grace (Horton) H.; AB, U. Mo., 1937; certificate advanced mgmt. U. Chgo., 1960; m. Thasia G. Tidd; children: Dennis L., Laurel M., Ray C. Accountant, Arthur Andersen & Co., Chgo. and Seattle, 1940-57, sr. mgr., 1947-57; controller Transunion Corp., Chgo., 1957-65; pvt. practice accounting, Arlington Heights, Ill., 1966-78; pres. Holland & Asso., Inc., Aurora, Ohio, 1972—; mng. ptnr. Laurimore Investors, Ltd., Aurora, 1983—; v.p. fin. Speed Selector Inc., 1988—. CPA, Kans., Ill., Wash., Wis., Ohio. Mem. Am. Inst. CPA's (hon. life). Home: 166 N Park Dr Aurora OH 44202 Office: 8589 Darrow Rd Twinsburg OH 44087

HOLLAND, SANDRA GUNTER, businesswoman, journalist; b. Mount Airy, N.C., Jan. 12, 1952; d. Joseph Bernard and Rondalene Geralda (Stanley) Gunter; m. Gasper O. Holland, Feb. 14, 1981; children: Abraham Justus, Noah Jonah. BS in Journalism, Va. Commonwealth U., Richmond, 1973; postgrad. U. Tex., Austin, 1974, North Tex. State U., Denton, 1975-78. Report writer Va. Dept. Hwys., 1973; newsletter editor Tex. Employment Commn., Austin, 1977-80; former tchr. English, journalism and ESL; part-time reporter Sta. KBOP, 1985-87; columnist, bus. newspaper, 1987-88; owner Holland Secretarial Services (also doing bus. as Holland Editorial Services and Holland Keepsake Clipping Services), 1982—. Pub. (mags.) Austin, Go, Income Opportunities, Lady's Circle, Women's Circle, Woman's World, Income Opportunities; (newspapers) Grit, San Antonio Light, Pleasanton Express, Brush Country Advertiser, Wilson County News, Medina Valley Times, Devine News, Horesville Chronicle-Jour. Mem. Pleasanton Friends of Library, San Antonio Zoological Soc., Friends of the San Antonio Zoo, Friends of Sta. KLRN-TV, Longhorn Mus. Assn., Nat. Arbor Day Found.; mgr. fundraiser bike-a-thon, Cystic Fibrosis; chmn. Atascosa County chpt. ARC, 1987—; media contact congl. candidate, office mgr., election coordinator Rep. Party of Atascosa County, 1986, 88, cofounder and charter pres. Atascosa County Rep. Women's Club, 1986-87, publicity chmn. 1986—, sec. 1988. Served with USAR; mem. Tex. Army N.G. Recipient letter of Appreciation USAR, 1982, cert. of Commendation Tex. Com. for Employer Support of Guard and Res., 1982, U.S. 5th Army Minaret award, 1982, Danforth award, 1973, Freedom Found. awards, 1980, 82. Mem. Mensa, UDC, Pleasanton C. of C., Nat. Soc. Notaries. So. Baptist. Home and Office: 529 Oakhaven Dr Pleasanton TX 78064

HOLLANDER, ELLEN COLLINS, hospital personnel executive; b. Cambridge, Mass., Mar. 6, 1946; d. John Ambrose and Marjorie Emma (Merrifield) Collins; BA, Boston Coll., 1967; MA, Incarnate Word Coll., 1976; 1 child, Christopher Antony Botto. Teaching supr. dept. clin. adminstrn. Mass. Gen. Hosp., Boston, 1963-67; supr. radiology dept. Genesee Hosp., Rochester, N.Y., 1969-70; coordinator edn. S.W. Tex. Meth. Hosp., San Antonio, 1970-77, asst. dir. personnel, 1977—; adj. faculty Sch. Health Professions, S.W. Tex. State U., San Marcos, 1976—; bd. dirs. South Tex. Healthcare Fed. Credit Union, 1986—, vice chair, 1988—. Mem. Am. Hosp. Assn., Am. Soc. Healthcare Edn. and Tng. (dir. 1977-80, Disting. Service award 1982), San Antonio Area Soc. Healthcare Edn. and Tng. (pres. 1972, 74-75), Tex. Soc. Hosp. Educators (Outstanding Service award 1981), Tex. Hosp. Assn. Author: Identifying Healthcare Training Needs, 1984; contbr. articles to profl. jours.; bd. dirs. Inservice Tng. and Edn. Mag., 1972-76. Home: 6123 Walking Gait Dr San Antonio TX 78240 Office: 7700 Floyd Curl Dr San Antonio TX 78229

HOLLAND-MARTIN, BERNARD, company executive, systems analyst, programmer; b. Leigh, Eng., Jan. 15, 1939; s. Bernard Eric and Kathleen Winifred (Holland) M.; m. Edwina Janeczka, Feb. 23, 1963 (div.); children—Anthony David, Amanda Jane; m. 2d, Susan Wilson, Apr. 24, 1976; 1 son, Matthew John. Diploma Chorley Coll. Edn. (Eng.), 1964. Jr. cashier Westminster Bank, Salford, Lancashire, Eng., 1956-61; asst. tchr. Lancashire County Council, Bolton, 1964-68; chief librarian Harper Green Sch., Farnworth, Lancashire, 1968-72; head resources Millfield Sch., Thornton Cleveleys, Lancashire, 1972-74; dir. learning resources Forest Sch., Walsall, West Midlands, Eng., 1975-82; exec. dir. Actrason Internat. Ltd., Walsall, West Midlands, 1982—; studio mgr. HRS Broadcasting, Stafford, Eng., 1980-82; owner Travel Tapes, Cannock, Staffordshire, 1982—, Tocota Bus. Systems, 1985-87; gen. mgr. Tiger Travel, Walsau. West Midlands, 1985—. Author, dir. film: Christmas Party, 1966; The Other Half, 1967; librettist, coproducer stage rev.: Knock, Knock, Who's Fair?, 1970. Found. scholar Manchester Grammar Sch., 1949-56. Home: 2A Essex Dr, Hednesford, Staffordshire WS12 5LG, England

HOLLANDSWORTH, KENNETH PETER, management consultant; b. York, Pa., Jan. 18, 1934; s. Dover Daniel and Sarah Kathryn (Meyers) H.; B.A. in Econs., Gettysburg Coll., 1956; m. Edith D. Butera, Oct. 15, 1960; children—Stephanie, Tracy. Purchasing clk. Certain-Teed Products Corp., York, 1958-59; territorial salesman Todd div. Burroughs Corp., Allentown, Pa., 1959-61; dir. presentation and incentive sales, then nat. dir. retail sales Hamilton Watch Co., Lancaster, Pa., 1962-69; gen. mgr. Vendome Watch div. Coro Inc., N.Y.C., 1969-71; pres., chief exec. officer Jules Jurgensen Corp. subs. Downe Communications, Inc., N.Y.C., 1972-75; exec. v.p., sec. to corp. Optel Corp. Princeton, N.J., 1975-76, also dir.; pvt. fin. and gen. mgmt. cons., 1976-80, 82—; pres., dir. Thomas-Pond Bus. Devel. Group, Inc., 1978-80; v.p. consumer products Commodore Internat. Ltd., 1980-82; gen. cons. to v.p. ops. Timex Computer Corp., also cons. to exec. v.p. Timex Corp., 1983—; bus. devel. cons. AT&T Consumer Products Group, 1984. Mem. Conn. Task Force on Computers and Instrn., 1983. Served with U.S. Army, 1956-58. Author: The Emerging Watch Industry, 1978. Home: PO Box 296 Yardley PA 19067

HOLLAWAY, RAYMOND LAWSON, JR., manufacturing executive; b. Olmstead, Ky., July 4, 1924; s. Raymond Lawson and Katie Agnes (Kemp) H.; student Western State Tchrs. Coll., Mt. Union Coll., U. Hawaii, Internat. Corr. Schs.; m. Mary Beth Schroeder, Jan. 1, 1944; children—Judi Rae, Jeffrey Jay. Layout draftsman Doug Turner Engring., Salem, Ohio, 1946-47; asst. chief engr. Strong Mfg. Co., Sebring, Ohio, 1947-51; factory mgr. and chief engr. Belmont Co., New Philadelphia, Ohio, 1951-55; asst. to plant mgr. Anchor Hocking Corp., Lancaster, Ohio, 1955-60, mgr. customer engring. services, 1960-67, mgr. adminstrv. services, 1967-68, plant mgr., 1968-73, factories mgr., 1973-74, v.p. factories mgr. container div., 1974-75, v.p. mfg. and engring., 1975-78, v.p. and gen. mgr. closure div., 1978-83, v.p. closure products group, 1983-86, v.p. hardware and packaging group, 1986-87, mgmt. cons., 1987—. Active YMCA; pres. Methodist Youth Council, Connellsville, Pa., 1957-58, mem. ofcl. bd., 1958, 59, 60, vice chmn. Commn. Stewardship and Fin., 1958-59, gen. chmn. every mem. canvass, 1959, chmn. stewardship and fin., 1958-59, mem. choir, Lancaster, Ohio, 1961-62. Served with AUS, 1943-47. Mem. Closure Mfg. Assn. (pres. 1980-82, dir. 1978-85), Glass Packaging Inst. (dir. 1983-85), ASME (numerous offices, sec. region V, 1957-60, chmn. v.p. adv. and planning com. for region V 1957-62, nat. nominating com. 1960-61, chmn. subcom. to rewrite nominating com. manual 1961, 70, chmn. profl. divs. interest com. Columbus, Ohio 1961, sects. group chmn. region V 1960-62, exec. com. Columbus 1960-63, chmn. adv. com. on nominations 1962, chmn. orgn. group, 1960-62, vice chmn. membership devel. group 1964-66, nat. bd. on membership 1964-68, nat. constn. and by-laws com. 1969-72). Republican. Clubs: Pleasant Valley Country (Connellsville), Lancaster Country, Lakeview County (Morgantown, W.Va.), P.G.A. Nat. Golf (Palm Beach Garden, Fla.), P.G.A. Hole-In-One. Lodge: Masons. Home and Office: Harbor Point Apt 403 5000 Ocean Dr Singer Island FL 33404

HOLLERAN, CONSTANCE ANN, nursing association executive; b. Manchester, N.H., June 19, 1934; d. Martin Peter and Veronica (Trinity) H. Diploma in nursing, Mass. Gen. Hosp., 1956; BS, Columbia U., 1958; MS in Nursing Edn. Adminstrn., Cath. U. Am., 1965. Nurse cons. div. nursing USPHS, Washington, 1965-70, chief sect. project grants, 1968-70; dep. exec. dir. Am. Nurses Assn., Washington, 1971-81; exec. dir. Internat. Council Nurses, Geneva, 1981—. Fellow Am. Acad. Nursing; mem. Am. Nurses Assn., Nat. League Nursing, Am. Pub. Health Assn. Office: Internat Council Nurses, 3 place Jean Marteau, 1201 Geneva Switzerland

HOLLEY, LAWRENCE ALVIN, retired labor union official; b. Elkhart, Ind., Nov. 7, 1924; s. Olin Coet and Carrie (Erwin) H.; m. Joyce Reed, Mar. 5, 1946; 1 child, Claudia Joyce. Student public schs., Elkhart. Bus. rep. Vancouver (Wash.) Aluminum Trades Council, 1951-57; pres. Wash. State Card and Label Council, 1952-57; internat. rep. Aluminum Workers Internat. Union, St. Louis, 1957-65, wage engr., 1965, research and ednl. dir., 1967-75; dir. Region 5 Aluminum Workers Internat. Union, Vancouver, Wash., 1975-77; pres. Aluminum Workers Internat. Union now Aluminum, Brick and Glass Workers Internat. Union, St. Louis, 1977-85; farmer La Center, Washington, 1985—; v.p. Union Label and Service Trades Dept., AFL-CIO, 1980-85, exec. bd. Maritime Trades Dept., 1981-85. Served with U.S. Army, 1943-46, PTO. Decorated Bronze Star with oak leaf cluster. Mem. Am. Legion. Democrat. Club: Voyageur 40/8. Lodge: Eagles. Office: Aluminum Brick & Glass Workers Internat Union 3362 Hollenberg Dr Bridgeton MO 63044

HOLLEY, ROBERT WILLIAM, biologist; b. Urbana, Ill., Jan. 28, 1922; s. Charles E. and Viola (Wolfe) H.; m. Ann Dworkin, Mar. 3, 1945; 1 son, Frederick. A.B., U. Ill., 1942; Ph.D., Cornell U., 1947. Fellow Am. Chem. Soc. State Coll. Wash., 1947-48; asst. prof., then assoc. prof. organic chemistry N.Y. State Agr. Expt. Sta. Cornell U., Ithaca, 1948-57, research chemist plant, soil and nutrition lab. USDA, 1957-64, prof. biochemistry, 1964-69, chmn. dept. biochemistry, 1965-66; resident fellow Salk Inst. Biol. Studies, La Jolla, Calif., 1968—; mem. biochemistry study sect. NIH, 1962-66; vis. fellow Salk Inst. Biol. Studies; vis. prof. Scripps Clinic and Research Found., La Jolla, 1966-67. Recipient Distinguished Service award U.S. Dept. Agr., 1965, Albert Lasker award basic med. research, 1965; U.S. Steel Found. award in molecular biology Nat. Acad. Scis., 1967; Nobel prize for medicine and physiology, 1968; Guggenheim fellow Calif. Inst. Tech., 1955-56. Fellow AAAS; mem. Am. Acad. Arts and Scis., Am. Soc. Biol. Chemists, Am. Chem. Soc., Nat. Acad. Scis., Phi Beta Kappa, Sigma Xi. Home: 7381 Rue Michael La Jolla CA 92037 Office: Salk Inst for Biolog Studies PO Box 85800 San Diego CA 92138

HOLLIER, YVES, lawyer; b. Chaumont, France, Mar. 7, 1949; s. Raymond and Yvette (Moretti) H.; m. Ramain Hollier, Sept. 3, 1983; children: Clemence, Julie. Baccalaureat Philosophie Langues, Lycee Bouchardon, 1969; lic. en Droit, Faculte de Droit, Dijon, France, 1973. Stagiaire Chez Maitre Xavier Vincent, Paris, 1974-76; collaborator Chez Gide, Loyrette et Nouel, Paris, 1977-79; sole practice Paris, 1980—. Roman Catholic. Home and Office: 33 Rue des Ardennes, 75019 Paris France

HOLLINGS, ERNEST FREDERICK, senator; b. Charleston, S.C., Jan. 1, 1922; s. Adolph G. and Wilhlemine D. (Meyer) H.; m. Rita Louise Liddy, Aug. 21, 1971; children by previous marriage—Michael Milhous, Helen Hayne, Patricia Salley, Ernest Frederick III. B.A., The Citadel, 1942, LL.D. (hon.), 1960; LL.B., U. S.C., 1947, LLD (hon.), 1980. Bar: S.C. 1947, U.S. Supreme Ct. Mem. S.C. Ho. of Reps., 1949-54, speaker pro tem, 1951-54; lt. gov. of S.C., 1955-59, gov., 1959-63; practiced in Charleston, 1963-66; U.S. senator State of S.C., 1966—, chmn. commerce sci. and transp. com., chmn. communications subcom., chmn. commerce justice state judiciary and related agys. subcom., mem. various coms. and caucuses; mem. Hoover Comm. on Intelligence Activities, 1954-55; mem. President's Adv. Comm. on Intergovernmental Relations, 1959-63, on Federalism, 1981—; mem. Jud. Council, 1957-59, State Planning and Urban Regional Devel. Conv.; chmn. Legis. Council, 1955-59, Regional Adv. Council on Nuclear Energy; mem. adv. com. Nat. River and Harbors Congress; del. Law of Sea Conf. Author: The Case Against Hunger: A Demand for a National Policy, 1970. Served to capt. U.S. Army, 1942-45, ETO, NATOUSA. Recipient Founders award S.C. Com. for Tech. Edn., 1963, Nat. Vet. award, 1968, Friend of Edn. award S.C. Edn. Assn., 1974, Neptune award Am. Oceanic Orgn., 1978, James Woodruff award Assn. U.S. Army, 1980, Nat. Future award Am. Space Found., 1984, Disting. Pub. Service award, 1985, Consumer Fedn. award, 1985, Govt. Social Responsibility award Martin Luther King Jr. Ctr., 1986; named one of Ten Outstanding Young Men U.S. Junior C. of C., 1954, S.C. Vet. of Yr., 1957, Guardian of Small Bus., 1973, 76, 85, 86, Legislator of Yr., Nat. Wildlife Fedn., 1975, S.C. Man of Yr., WIS-TV, 1975, Textile Man of Yr., N.Y. Bd. Trade, 1979. Mem. ABA, Charleston County Bar Assn., S.C. Bar Assn., Assn. Citadel Men, Hibernian Soc., Am. Legion, Univ. S.C. Law Fedn., St. Andrews Soc. Democrat. Lutheran. Lodges: Elks, Masons. Office: 125 Russell Office Bldg Washington DC 20510 *

HOLLINGSWORTH, VERNON C., banker, insurance executive; b. Lebanon, S.D., Apr. 29, 1905; s. William Sylvester and Bertha May (Patterson) H.; m. Lois A. Miller, Sept. 11, 1930; children—Diane Hollingsworth Barry, Jean Hollingsworth Peterson, Alene Hollingsworth Beck. B.A., U. Mont., 1927. Asst. cashier Ronan State Bank (Mont.), 1927-30; liquidating agt. Close Bank div. Mont. State Banking Dept., Helena, 1930-38; pres., chmn. bd., chief exec. officer Citizens State Bank, Hamilton, Mont., 1938—; pres. V.C. Hollingsworth Ins. Co., 1939—; state dir. Mont. Blue Shield Corp., 1976-82. State senator from Ravalli County, Mont., 1943-46; bd. dirs. Daly Meml. Hosp., Hamilton, 1941—, vice chmn., 1944—. Mem. Am. Bankers Assn. (exec. council 1961-63), Mont. Bankers Assn. (pres. 1959-61, pres. 25 Yr. Club 1961), N.Am. Hwy. Assn. (pres. 1956-60), Mont. Automobile Assn. (state dir. 1972—), State Bank Suprs. Assn. (adv. com. conf. 1964-70), Alpha Kappa Psi (Mont. Outstanding Businessman of Yr. 1958), Theta Chi. Republican. Presbyterian. Lodges: Masons, Elks, Eagles, Lions (pres. Hamilton 1944, dep. dist. gov. 1945-47). Home: 416 S 5th St Hamilton MT 59840 Office: Citizens State Bank PO Box 393 Hamilton MT 59840

HOLLINSHEAD, EARL DARNELL, JR., lawyer; b. Pitts., Aug. 1, 1927; s. Earl Darnell and Gertrude (Cahill) H.; m. Sylvia Antion, June 29, 1957; children: Barbara, Kim, Earl III, Susan. AB, Ohio U., 1948; LLB, U. Pitts., 1951. Bar: Pa. 1952, U.S. Ct. Mil. Appeals 1954, U.S. Dist. Ct. (we. dist.) Pa. 1955, U.S. Supreme Ct. 1956, U.S. Ct. Appeals (3d cir.) 1959, U.S. Dist. Ct. (ea. dist.) Ohio 1978. Sole practice Pitts., 1955-70; ptnr. Hollinshead & Mendelson, Pitts., 1970—; mem. Pitts. Estate Planning Council. Contbr. articles to profl. jours. Served to lt. USNR, 1951-55. Fellow Pa. Bar Found. (life); mem. Pa. Bar Assn. (chmn. real property div. 1983-85, real property, probate and trust sects. 1985-86), Allegheny County Bar Assn. (chmn. real property sect. 1975-76), Pa. Bar Inst. (lectr., planner), Am. Coll. Real Estate Lawyers. Home: 2535 Windgate Rd Bethel Park PA 15102 Office: Hollinshead & Mendelson 230 Grant Bldg Pittsburgh PA 15219

HOLLIS, SHEILA SLOCUM, lawyer; b. Denver, July 15, 1948; d. Theodore Doremus and Emily M. (Caplis) Slocum; m. John Hollis, 1 child, Windsong Emily. B.S. in Journalism cum laude with honors, U. Colo., 1971; J.D. (Law Sch. scholar), U. Denver, 1973. Bar: Colo. 1974, D.C. 1975, U.S. Supreme Ct. 1980. Trial atty. Fed. Power Commn., Washington, 1974-75; asso. firm Wilner & Scheiner, Washington, 1975-77; dir. office enforcement Fed. Energy Regulatory Commn., Washington; 1977-80; ptnr. Butler & Binion, 1981-84, Broadhurst, Brook, Mangham & Hardy, 1984-87, Vinson & Elkins, Washington, 1987—; profl. lectr. in law Nat. Law Center, George Washington U., 1980-88. Co-author: Energy Decision Making, 1983, Energy Law and Policy, 1988; contbr. articles to profl. publs. Established and developed Enforcement Program of Fed. Energy Regulatory Commn. Mem. ABA (mem. council Natural Resources sect. 1985-88, coordinating group on energy law, liaison with Southwestern Legal Found.), Oil and Gas Ednl. Inst. (adv. bd.), Southwestern Legal Found. (adv. com.), Nat. Gas Inst. (chmn. 1983-88), Fed. Energy Bar Assn. (sec. 1975-77, exec. bd. 1981-84) Internat. Bar Assn., Colo. Bar Assn., D.C. Bar. Roman Catholic. Club: National Press. Office: Vinson & Elkins 1455 Pennsylvania Ave NW Washington DC 20004

HOLLOWAY, DONALD PHILLIP, librarian; b. Akron, Ohio, Feb. 18, 1928; s. Harold Shane and Dorothy Gayle (Ryder) H.; B.S. in Commerce, Ohio U., Athens, 1950; J.D., U. Akron, 1955; M.A., Kent State U., 1962. Title examiner Bankers Guarantee Title & Trust Co., Akron, 1950-54; acct. Robinson Clay Product Co., Akron, 1955-60; librarian Akron-Summit Pub. Library, 1962-69, head fine arts and music div., 1969-71, sr. librarian, 1972-82. Payroll treas. Akron Symphony Orch., 1957-61; treas. Friends Library Akron and Summit County, 1970-72. Mem. Music Library Assn., Am., Ohio, Akron bar assns., Ohio Library Assn., ALA, Nat. Trust for Hist. Preservation, Internat. Platform Assn., Soc. Archtl. Historians, Coll. Art Assn., Art Libraries North Am. Republican. Episcopalian. Club: Nat. Lawyers (Washington). Home: 601 Nome Ave Akron OH 44320

HOLLOWAY, JAMES LEMUEL, III, merchant marine association executive, retired naval officer; b. Charleston, S.C., Feb. 23, 1922; s. James Lemuel and Jean Gordon (Hagood) H.; m. Dabney Hix Rawlings, Dec. 14, 1942; children—Lucy Dabney Lyon, Jane Meredith. B.S.E.E., Naval Acad., Annapolis, 1942. Cert. naval aviator, naval nuclear reactor operator. Commd. ensign U.S. Navy, 1942, advanced through grades to adm.; comdr. U.S. 7th Fleet, 1971-73, vice chief naval ops., 1973-74, mem. Joint Chiefs of Staff, Dept. Def., 1974-78, chief naval ops., 1974-78, ret., 1978; pres. Council Am.-Flag Ship Operators, Washington, 1981-88; cons. Paine Webber, Washington, 1980—; dir. U.S. Life Ins. Co., Washington, 1984—, UNC Inc., Annapolis, 1987—; chmn. spl. rev. group investigating Iranian hostage rescue, 1981; exec. dir. V.p.'s Task Force on Terrorism, 1985; spl envoy of v.p. to Mid. East, 1986; commr. Presdl. Blue Ribbon Commn. on Def. Mgmt., 1985, Congl. Commn. on Mcht. Marine and Def., 1987—, Presdl. Commn. on Longterm Integrated Strategy, 1987—. Contbr. articles to mags. Expert witness Congl. Coms., 1978—; trustee St. James Sch., Md., 1968—; dir. Olmsted Found., Washington, 1978—; mem. bd. advisors The Citadel, 1981-86; chmn. adv. bd. U.S. Naval Acad., 1983—. Decorated Bronze Star, Air Medals, Legion of Merit, D.F.C., Def. D.S.M. with two bronze oak leaf clusters, Navy D.S.M. with four bronze oak leaf clusters, Order of Rising Sun (Japan), Grand Cross (Germany), Legion of Honor (France), others. Mem. Assn. Naval Aviation (chmn. 1985—), Naval Hist. Found. (pres. 1980—). Republican. Episcopalian. Clubs: Metropolitan (Washington); Brook, N.Y. Yacht (N.Y.C.); Maryland (Balt.); Annapolis Yacht; Soc. of Cincinnati. Avocation: sailing. Home: 1694 Epping Farms Ln Annapolis MD 21401 Office: United Shipowners Am 1627 K St NW Suite 1200 Washington DC 20006

HOLLOWAY, JOHN CHRISTOPHER, tourism educator; b. London, Feb. 11, 1934; s. John Henry and Christina Henrietta (Brown) H.; m. Irmgard Mathilde Peters, Oct. 4, 1958; children: Lynn Irmgard, Britt Tryfan. BEd, London U., 1974; MS, U. Surrey, Eng., 1979; diploma in mgmt. studies, Cunard. Asst. mgr. Cunard, N.Y.C., 1956-66; sales promotion officer Cunard, Southampton, Eng., 1966-67; tours mgr. Assoc. Tours, Reigate, Eng., 1967-69; mgr. group travel Barry Aikman Travel, London, 1969-70; lectr. Bournemouth (Eng.) Coll., 1974-76; sr. lectr. Dorset Inst. of H.E., Bournemouth, 1976-80; prin. lectr. Bristol (Eng.) Poly., 1981—; resource editor annals of tourism research U. Wis., Madison, 1983-85. Author: THe Business of Tourism, 1983 (2d edit. 1985), Marketing for Tourism, 1988; contbr. articles to profl. jours. Fellow The Tourism Soc., The Inst. Travel and Tourism; mem. The Inst. Mktg., Assn. Tchrs. of Tourism (chmn. 1985-88). Home: 21 Rownham Mead, Hotwells, Bristol BS8 4YA, England Office: Bristol Poly Bus Sch, Bristol BS16 1QY, England

HOLLOWAY, LAWRENCE MILTON, osteopathic physician, plastic surgeon; b. Kirksville, Mo., Sept. 8, 1913; s. Edward Lee and Vetta (Elmore) H.; student Kirksville Bus. Coll., 1933, NE Mo. U., 1933-36; D.O., Kirksville Coll. Osteopathy and Surgery, 1940; M.D., U. Santo Tomas, 1951; m. Roena Jane Williams, Dec. 24, 1935; children—Lawrence Milton, Lynette Jane. Intern, A.S.O. Hosp., Kirksville, 1939-40, Detroit Osteo. Hosp., 1940-42; gen. practice osteo. medicine, Byron, Mich., 1942-56, plastic surgeon, Flint, Mich., 1956—; examining physician Am. Pres. Life Ins. Co.; fellow in surgery Am. Coll. Osteo. Physicians and Surgeons, Byron, 1940-56; instr. Physiol. Chemistry Lab., Kirksville Coll. Osteopathy and Surgery, 1938-40; founder, chief surgeon, chief staff Lawrence Osteo. Hosp., Byron, 1942-56; dir., bus. mgr. L. M. Holloway Clinic; plastic and cosmetic surgeon Flint Gen. Hosp. Pres., L.M. Holloway Mfg. Co., Byron, 1944-47; v.p. Owosso Finance Co. (Mich.), 1952-56, pres., 1956—; adv. bd. Hamilton Internat. Life Ins. Co. Physician, Byron High Sch., 1940-54. Adviser Swartz Creek chpt. Boy Scouts Am.; sec. Orgn. for World Wide Postgrad. Study. Fellow Am. Soc. Clin. Hypnosis (life); mem. Am. (life mem.), Genesee County (life mem.) osteo. assns., Mich. Assn. Osteo. Physicians and Surgeons, Am. Osteo. Physicians and Surgeons, Am. Coll. Osteo. Surgeons (life mem.), Am. Soc. Endocrinology and Nutrition, Am. Soc. Clin. Arthritis, Kirksville Osteo. Alumni Assn., Future Farmers Am. (life), Psi Sigma Alpha. Lodges: Masons (32 deg., life mem.), Shriners, Elks, 750 (pres. Mich. chpt. 1958-59, 61, 64-66). Home: 10283 Corunna Rd Swartz Creek MI 48473 Office: G 5200 Corunna Rd Flint MI 48504

HOLLOWAY, LAWRENCE MILTON, JR., wholesale executive, physician, surgeon; b. Detroit, Jan. 14, 1946; s. Lawrence Milton and Roena Jane (Williams) H.; B.S., Mich. State U., 1968; M.A., Drake U., 1977; D.O., U. Osteo. Medicine and Health Scis., 1983; m. Charlotte Jane Spiter, June 19, 1970; children—Tiffany Jane, Marque Spiter, Tiara Lynn, Topaz Jerilyn, Lawrence Milton III. Collection supr. Owosso (Mich.) Fin. Co., 1963-66; supr. med. lab. L.M. Holloway Clinic, Flint, Mich., 1966-68, mem. staff, 1983—, vice chmn. dept. surgery, 1985-87, chmn. dept. surgery, 1987—; lab. supr. Ferris State U., Big Rapids, Mich., 1968-69; tchr. St. Matthew Sch., Flint, 1969-70; fin. cons. Hamilton Internat. Corp., Farmington, Mich., 1970-71; v.p. Nat. Potential Devel. Co., St. Louis, 1971—; pres. Holloway House, Des Moines, 1971—; instr. Des Moines Area Community Coll., 1978-79. Active Iowans for L.I.F.E., Inc., 1975-83, state conv. chmn., 1982, past mem. exec. com. of bd.; bd. dirs. Des Moines Right to Life, 1978-83, polit. chmn., 1979-83; Republican princinct chmn. Iowa, 1976-83, precinct del. Mich., 1986—; bd. dirs. Pro-Life Action Council, 1980-83, treas., 1981-83; chmn. Am. Com. for Life, 1978—. Mem. Nat. Assn. Federally Lic. Firearms Dealers, Am. Chem. Soc., Am. Inst. Hypnosis, Iowa Acad. Sci., Iowa Soc. Osteo. Physicians and Surgeons, Christian Med. Soc. (disting. mem. presdl. task force), Am. Osteo. Assn., Am. Soc. Nondestructive Testing. Republican. Mem. Evangelical Ch. Lodges: Masons Shriners. Author: Dry Cell Therapy, Its Future, 1964; Biochemical Basis of Learning, 1977. Home: 1099 N Dye Rd Flint MI 48532 Office: L M Holloway Clinic G-5200 Corunna Rd Flint MI 48532

HOLLWEG, ARND, clergyman; b. Moenchengladbach, Germany, Mar. 23, 1927; s. Ernst and Henriette (Voswinckel) H.; m. Astrid Blomerius, Aug. 30, 1961; children—Heike, Uta, Karen. Student U. Bonn, 1946-48, U. Goettingen, 1948-50, U. Tuebingen, 1952-53, U. So. Calif., 1953-54, U. Muenster, 1955-56; Dr. theol., U. Bonn, 1967. Ordained to ministry United Chs. Rhineland, 1958. Tchr. religion Gymnasium and Berufsschule, Lobberich, Germany, and asst. minister ch., Essen, Germany, 1955-57; lectr. Inst. Theology and Edn. of Rhineland Protestant Ch. (W.Ger.) and regional pastor Rhineland for Christian Edn., 1958-63; researcher Ecumenical Inst., U. Bonn (W.Ger.), 1964-65; pastor, ch., Bad Honnef, W.Ger., 1966-72; dept. head, hdqrs. diaconical relief ctr. German Protestant Ch., Stuttgart, 1973-76; pastor Ch. of Bethlehemsgemeinde, Berlin, and chmn. German Reformed Ch. of West Berlin, 1976—; lectr. Free U., Berlin, 1978-79, Kirchliche Hochschule, Berlin, 1979-84. Author: Theologie und Empirie, 3d edit., 1974; Gruppe-Gesellschaft-Diakonie, 1976; (with others) Obdachlosenhilfe, 1981; contbr. numerous essays to profl. publs.; editor Innere Mission and Diakonie, 1973-76. Served with Germany Army, 1943-44, German Inf., 1945. Mem. Deutsche Gesellschaft fü r Pastoralpsychologie, Gemeinschaft Evangelischer Erzieher, Christliche Presseakademie. Home: Holbeinstrasse 15, D1000 Berlin 45 Federal Republic of Germany Office: Richardstrasse 97, D1000 Berlin 44 Federal Republic of Germany

HOLLYWOOD, GERARD, language educator; b. Glasgow, Scotland, June 2, 1934; s. Edward and Bridget (Gormley) H.; m. Petra Fritsche, Feb. 9, 1967 (div. 1972); children: Stuart, Gerhard. Sr. cert. with hons., Royal Coll. Preceptors, London, 1955. Tchr. English Sprachwissenschaftliches Inst., Berlin, 1958-61; personal tutor to governing mayor and Senators Berlin, 1959-65; sr. lectr., dept. head Zentrale Sparchenstelle Fur Die Verwaltung, Berlin, 1965-84; prin. Internat. Translators' Sch., Berlin, 1965—; accredited interpreter Dept. Justice, Berlin, 1967—; dir. ITS English Sch., Hastings, Eng., 1977-87; sec. Assoc. Examining Bd. GCE Examinations, Eng., 1972—. Author: Law of Establishment, 1973, Motor Insurance, 1978, Conference, 1984, Office Terminology, 1987. Mem. German Fed. Assn. Interpreters and Translators, German Soc. Modern Langs., Internat. Inst. for Legal and Adminstrv. Terminology (v.p. 1981—). Clubs: British Officers' (Berlin); English Speaking Union (Mayfair, London). Office: Internat Translators Sch. Uhlandstr 175, Berlin 15 Federal Republic of Germany

HOLMAN, B. LEONARD, radiologist, nuclear medicine physician, educator; b. Sheboygan, Wis., June 26, 1941; s. Max and Sophia (Penn) H.; m. Dale Elyse Barkin, Jan. 22, 1971; children: Amy Lynn, Allison Stacy. BS, U. Wis., 1963; MD, Washington U., St. Louis, 1966, AM (hon.), Harvard U., 1988. Diplomate Am. Bd. Nuclear Medicine, Am. Bd. Radiology. Intern Mt. Zion Hosp., San Francisco, 1966-67; resident Mallinckrodt Inst. Radiology, St. Louis, 1967-70; nuclear radiologist Peter Bent Brigham Hosp., Boston, 1970-75; from instr. to assoc. prof. Harvard U. Med. Sch., Boston, 1970-82, prof. radiology, 1982-88, Philip H. Cook prof., 1988 ; nuclear radiologist Children's Hosp., Boston, 1970—, Dana-Farber Cancer Ctr., 1976—; attending nuclear radiologist West Roxbury (Mass.) VA Hosp., 1973—; cons. radiology New Eng. Deaconess Hosp., Boston, 1981—, Beth Israel Hosp., 1982—; dir. clin. nuclear medicine Brigham and Women's Hosp., Boston, 1975-86, acting chmn. dept. radiology, 1986-88, chmn., 1988—; mem. med. adv. com. U.S. NRC, Bethesda, Md., 1980—; bd. dirs. Am. Bd. Nuclear Medicine, Los Angeles, 1980-86, vice chmn., 1986; chmn. residency rev. com. in nuclear medicine Accreditation Council for Grad. Med. Edn., 1980-86; George V. Tapla lectr. Western region Soc. Nuclear Medicine, 1985; Jamieson lectr. Royal Can. Soc. Physicians and Surgeons, 1986; Marc Tetalman lectr., 1988. Author: (with J.A. Parker) Computer Assisted Cardiac Nuclear Medicine, 1981; editor: (with P.J. Ell) Emission Computed Tomography, 1982, Radionuclide Imaging in the Brain, others; contbr. articles to profl. jours., chpts. to books. Recipient Hermann Blumgart Pioneer award New Eng. chpt. Soc. Nuclear Medicine, 1986, Disting. Lectr. award Southwestern chpt. Soc. Nuclear Medicine, 1988; Nat. Inst. Gen. Med. Sci. fellow, 1968-70. Fellow Am. Coll. Chest Physicians, Am. Coll. Radiology, Am. Coll. Nuclear Physicians, Am. Heart Assn. (council cardiovascular radiology, council circulation, established investigator 1977-79), Am. Coll. Cardiology (trustee 1980-83), Chgo. Radiol. Soc. (hon.); mem. Tex. Radiol. Soc. Nuclear Medicine (trustee 1976, 80-83, sec. 1983-86, pres. 1987-88), N.Y. Acad. Sci., Radiol. Soc. N.Am., Assn. Univ. Radiologists, AMA, N.Am. Soc. Cardiovascular Radiology, Soc. Thoracic Radiology, Sigma Xi. Home: 25 Nancy Rd Chestnut Hill MA 02167 Office: Brigham and Women's Hosp 75 Francis St Boston MA 02115

HOLMAN, JAMES LEWIS, financial and management consultant; b. Chgo., Oct. 27, 1926; s. James Louis and Lillian Marie (Walton) H.; m. Elizabeth Ann Owens, June 18, 1948 (div. 1982); children: Craig Stewart, Tracy Lynn, Mark Andrew; m. Geraldine Ann Wilson, Dec. 26, 1982. BS in Econs. and Mgmt., U. Ill., Urbana, 1950, postgrad., 1950; postgrad. Northwestern U., 1954-55. Traveling auditor, then statistician, asst. controller parent buying dept. Sears, Roebuck & Co., Chgo., 1951-54; asst. to sec.-treas. Hanover Securities Co., Chgo., 1954-65; asst. to controller chem. ops. div. Montgomery Ward & Co. Inc., Chgo., 1966-68; controller Henrotin Hosp., Chgo., 1968; bus. mgr. Julian, Dye, Javid, Hunter & Najafi, Associated, Chgo., 1969-81, cons. 1981-84; vol. cons., adminstrv. asst. Fiji Sch. Medicine, Suva, U.S. Peace Corps, 1984-86, cons., 1987—; cons., dir., sec.-treas. Comprehensive Resources Ltd., Glenview (Ill.), Wheaton (Ill.) and Walnut Creek, Calif., 1982; bd. dirs., sec.-treas. Medtran, Inc., 1980-83; sec. James C. Valenta, P.C., 1979-82; sponsored project adminstr. Northwestern U., Evanston, Ill., 1984. Sec., B.R. Ryall YMCA, Glen Ellyn, Ill., 1974-76, bd. dirs., 1968-78; trustee Gary Meml. United Meth. Ch., Wheaton, 1961-69, 74-77; bd. dirs. Goodwill Industries Chgo., 1978-79, DuPage (Ill.) Symphony, 1954-58, treas., 1955-58. Served with USN, 1944-46. Baha'i. Lodge: Kiwanis (bd. dirs. Chgo. 1956-60, bd. dirs. youth found. 1957-60, pres. 1958-60). Home and Office: 3 Wheaton Ctr Suite 302 Wheaton IL 60187

HOLMAN, REGINALD ALBERT, consultant medical microbiologist, educator; b. Castleford, Yorkshire, U.K., Aug. 12, 1923; s. Albert Edward and Elsie Pauline (Hilborne) H.; m. Dorothy Elizabeth McNeill, Sept. 18, 1948; children—Rury, Jacqueline, Brandon, Charlotte. M.B., Ch.B., Med. Sch., Leeds, U.K., 1947, M.D., 1955. Intern Leeds, 1946-47; resident Gen. Infirmary, Leeds, house surgeon, 1947; demonstrator Med. Sch., Leeds, 1947-49; specialist in pathology M.C., Royal Army, 1949-51; lectr. Med. Sch., Leeds, 1951-55; clin. bacteriologist Med. Sch., Cardiff, U.K., 1955—; cons. advisor Lystun, London, 1965—, Yad Products, Cardiff, 1978—, Searle, London, 1965-75. Mem. South Glamorgan Health Authority, Cardiff, 1980-84; chmn. Control of Infection, Med. Equipment Panel, 1965-87; chmn. South Glamorgan Div. Pathology, 1976-86; chmn. Sterile Services Mgmt. Coms., 1974-87. Served to capt. M.C., Royal Army, 1949-57. Cancer grantee Tenovus Cardiff, 1966. Fellow Royal Coll. Pathologists, Royal Coll. Surgeons; mem. Pathology Soc. Gt. Britain, Central Soc. Sterilization, Cardiff Med. Soc. Mem. Ch. of England. Avocations: genealogy; numismatica; chess. Home: Laylocks Broadclyst Exeter, Devon EX5 3EJ, England Office: Dept Med Microbiology, Royal Infirmary, Cardiff England

HOLMAN, STEELE, management consultant, property developer; b. Ottawa, Ill., Dec. 31, 1909; s. Harland D. and Esther Lady Jane Lowe Holman Sutherland; B.S., U. Calif.-Berkeley, 1936, postgrad., 1937-41; m. Elizabeth K. Kniveton, Aug. 30, 1941; children—Rodwin William Steele IV, Tamara Holman Baren, Soñ a H. Holman Lawrence. Spl. agt. Sears, Roebuck & Co., 1935; probation officer Alameda County (Calif.), 1937; chief supr. So. Calif. Prison, 1941; master shipfitter United Engring. Co., San Francisco, 1941; chief San Francisco Bay Area Tng. Staff, Oakland Vocat. Schs., 1942; head bus. conf. moderator State of Calif., 1945; pres. Steele Holman & Assocs., 1943—; govt. cons. Mexican-Am. Aftosa Commn., Mex., 1948-50; auditor Atlas Constructors, Africa, 1951; bus. cons. Trust Ter. Pacific Islands, 1952, 70-72; cons. Govt. Philippines, 1955; moderator So. Pacific Co., Pacific G & E, Merco Nordstrum Valve Mfg. Co., Pacific Motor Transport, 1946; pres. Golden Desert Acres, Nev., 1973—; developer homesites Lahonton Lake, Golden Desert Acres, Lake Lahonton, Nev. Candidate for gov. U.S. Samoa, 1961. Pres., Steele Holman Found.; bd. dirs. Spanish Speaking Citizens Assn., Samoan Civic Assn., Sino-Asian Inst.; mem. Washoe County Grand Jury, Reno, 1985-86. Mem. World Trade Club, Inst. Indsl. Engrs., Nat. Soc. Programmed Instrn., Western Govtl. Research Assn., Am. Geophys. Union, Urban Renewal Assn., U. Calif. Alumni Assn. (life), Am. Arbitration Assn. (panel), Mechanics Inst., Nat. Geog. Soc. (life), Smithsonian Instn., Public Personnel Assn., World Affairs Council San Francisco, Philippine Assn. Mgmt. and Indsl. Engrs. (hon. life), Engrs. and Scientists of Calif., Marin County Property Owners Assn. (budget analyst), Mgmt. Assistance Council San Francisco (co-founder 1968). Home: 910 Harold Box 5498 Incline Village NY 89450 Office: PO Box 1209 Dayton NV 89403

HOLME, THOMAS TIMINGS, industrial engineering educator; b. Frankford, Pa., Mar. 12, 1913; s. Justus Rockwell and Margaret (Mitchell) H.; m. Marjory Evans Walton, July 7, 1936; children: Judith Walton Holme Harrell, Thomas Timings, Penelope Walton. B.S., Lehigh U., 1935, M.S., 1940, I.E. (profl.), 1948; M.A. (hon.), Yale U., 1950; Dr. Engring., Lehigh U., 1970. Registered profl. engr., Pa., Conn. Indsl. engr. E. I. duPont de Nemours & Co., Wilmington, Del. and Fairfield, Conn., 1935-37; asst. prof. mech. engring. Lehigh U., Bethlehem, Pa., 1937-41; assoc. prof. indsl. engring. Lehigh U., 1946-49, prof. indsl. engring., head dept. and dir. curriculum, 1949-50; prof. of indsl. engring., dept. adminstrv. sci. Yale U., 1950-73, emeritus prof., 1973—, chmn. dept., dir. grad. studies, 1954-63; fellow Trumbull Coll.; cons. U.S. Army Ordnance Corps, 1952-53, 56-57, Hughes Aircraft, 1959, 61-62, Hamilton Standard div. United Aircraft, 1963; nat. exec. sec. Sigma Xi, 1953-69, nat. exec. dir., 1969-81, exec. dir. emeritus, 1981—. Chmn. Commn. Pub. Service, Dist. of Fripp Island, S.C., 1983—; bd. dirs. Yale Coop., New Haven, exec. com., 1951-72; mem. Yale-Industry Com. of New Haven. With Ordnance Dept. U.S. Army, 1941-46; asst. works mgr. 1941-42, Springfield Armory; asst. works mgr. July 1942-Mar. 1944, E.T.O.; officer in charge engring. 1944-46, Springfield Armory; disch. rank of lt. col. lt. col. Ordnance Res. 1946-53. Recipient U.S. Army Citation medal, Ordnance Certificate of Commendation, Legion of Merit. Mem. Am. Inst. Indsl. Engrs., Am. Soc. Engring. Edn., Newcomen Soc., Sigma Xi, Tau Beta Pi, Pi Tau Sigma, Pi Gamma Mu. Club: Fripp Island (S.C.) Beach and Golf. Home: 773 Marlin Dr Fripp Island SC 29920 Office: 345 Whitney Ave New Haven CT 06511

HOLMES, CARL DEAN, landowner, state legislator; b. Dodge City, Kans., Oct. 19, 1940; s. Haskell Amos and Gertrude May (Swander) H.; m. Wilynda Coley, Nov. 29, 1986. Student, Kans. U., 1958-60; BBA, Colo. State U., Ft. Collins, 1962. Mgr. Holmes Motor Co., Plains, Kans., 1962-65; v.p. Holmes Chevrolet, Inc., Meade, Kans., 1962-78; owner Holmes Sales Co., Plains, 1965-80; land mgr. Holmes Farms, Plains, 1962—. Chmn. Greater Southwest Regional Planning Commn., Garden City, Kans., 1980-82; del. Rep. Dist. Conv., Great Bend, Kans., 1984, Rep. State Conv., Topeka, 1984, Rep. Dist. Conv., Russell, Kans., 1988, Rep. State Conv., Topeka, Kans., 1988; City of Plains Councilman 1977-82, Council Pres. 1979-82, Mayor, 1982—; mem. 125 dist. Kans. Ho. Reps., Topeka, Kans., 1985—; precinct committeeman, Meade County Reps., 1986—, pres. Kans. Mayors Assn., 1984-85; v.p. League Kans. Municipalities, 1986-87, pres., 1987-88; vice chmn. Kans. Ho. of Reps. Energy & Natural Resources com., chmn. Energy sub-com., 1987—. Mem. Liberal C. of C. Methodist. Lodge: Masons. Home and Office: Box 578 Plains KS 67869

HOLMES, DAVID LARSON, psychologist, educational administrator; b. Stamford, Conn., Feb. 25, 1948; s. Erwin Wiedlich and Teckla Hildegaard (Larson) H.; B.S., Western Conn. State U., 1970; M.Ed., Rutgers U., 1971, Ed.D., 1976; m. Karen Louise Parnak, July 26, 1969; children—Paige Annette, Corinne Ashley. Teaching fellow Children's Psychiat. Center, Rutgers U., New Brunswick, N.J., 1970-71, adj. prof. Rutgers U., 1974-77, 81; dir. Princeton (N.J.) Child Devel. Inst., 1971-75; adj. prof. Princeton U., 1977-87; dir. Eden Inst. Children and Adults with Autism, Princeton, 1975—; chmn. Nat. Council Affiliated State Assns. Pvt. Schs. for Handicapped; vice chmn. N.J. Adv. Council on Handicapped. Mem. Bd. Edn. Stockton (N.J.), 1980—. Cert. supr., prin., elem. tchr., tchr. of handicapped, N.J. Mem. Assn. Advancement of Behavior Therapy, Am. Psychol. Assn., Am. Assn. Spl. Educators, Nat. Assn. Children and Adults with Autism (cert. of commendation 1974), Council Orgns. and Schs. for Autistic Citizens (trustee), Kappa Delta Pi. Contbr. articles to profl. publs. Office: Eden Inst One Logan Dr Princeton NJ 08540

HOLMES, GEORGE ARTHUR, university professor, historian; b. Aberystwyth, Wales, Apr. 22, 1927; s. John and Margaret (Thomas) H.; m. Evelyn Anne Klein, Dec. 19, 1953; children: Susan, Catherine, Nicholas. BA, Cambridge U., Eng., 1948; PhD, Cambridge U., 1952. Fellow St. John's Coll. Cambridge U., 1951-54; tutor St. Catherine's Coll., Oxford, Eng., 1954-62, fellow, 1962—, vice master, 1969-71; joint editor English Hist. Rev., 1974-81; chmn. Victoria County History Com., London, 1981—; del. Oxford U. Press, 1982—. Author: The Estates of the Higher Nobility in Fourteenth Century England, 1957, The Later Middle Ages, 1962, The Florentine Enlightenment 1400-1450, 1969, Europe: Hierarchy and Revolt 1320-1450, 1975, The Good Parliament, 1975, Dante, 1980, Florence, Rome and the Origins of the Renaissance, 1986. Fellow British Acad.; Inst. Advanced Study. Home: Highmoor House, Bampton, Oxon OX8 2HY, England Office: St Catherine's Coll, Oxford OX1 3UJ, England

HOLMES, HENRY ALLEN, government official; b. Bucharest, Rumania, Jan. 31, 1933 (parents Am. citizens); s. Julius Cecil and Henrietta (Allen) H.; A.B., Princeton U., 1954; certificat d'etudes politiques (Woodrow Wilson fellow) U. Paris, 1958; m. Marilyn Janet Strauss, July 25, 1959; children—Katherine Anne, Gerald Allen. Intelligence research analyst Dept. State, 1958-59; commd. fgn. service officer Dept. State, 1959; assigned to Am. embassy, Yaounde, Cameroun, 1959-61, Dept. State, Washington, 1961-63, 67-70, Am. embassy, Rome, 1963-67, counselor polit. affairs Am. Embassy, Paris, 1970-74; sr. exec. Seminar in Fgn. Policy, Washington, 1974-75; assigned as dir. Office NATO and Atlantic polit. mil. affairs Bur. European Affairs, Washington, 1975-77; dep. chief of mission U.S. embassy, Rome, 1977-79; prin. dep. asst. sec. state for European affairs, Washington, 1979-82; ambassador to Portugal, 1982-85; asst. sec. Bur. Politico Military Affairs, U.S. Dept. State, Washington, 1986—. Served as capt. USMCR, 1954-57. Mem. Am. Fgn. Service Assn., Council Fgn. Relations. Episcopalian. Club: Met. (Washington). Office: US Dept of State Bur Politico Mil Affairs 2201 C St NW Washington DC 20520

HOLMES, JACK DAVID LAZARUS, historian; b. Long Branch, N.J., July 4, 1930; s. John Daniel Lazarus and Waltrude Helen (Hendrickson) H.; m. Anne Elizabeth Anthony, Sept. 6, 1952 (div. 1965); children—David H., Jack Forrest, Ann M.; m. Martha Rachel Austin, Feb. 11, 1966 (div. 1967); m. Gayle Jeanette Pannell, July 1967 (div. 1970); 1 child, Daniel; m. Stephanie Pasneker, Apr. 10, 1971; 1 child, Sean Burkett. B.A. cum laude, Fla. State U., 1952; M.A., U. Fla., 1953; postgrad., Universidad Nacional Autonoma de Mexico, 1954; Ph.D., U. Tex.-Austin, 1959. Instr. history Memphis State U., 1956-58; asst. prof. McNeese State U., Lake Charles, La., 1959-61; lectr. U. Md., Constantina, Spain, 1962; assoc. prof. U. Ala., Birmingham, 1963-68, prof., 1968-79; hist. cons. 1962—; cons. U.S. Parks Service, 1962, Pensacola Hist. Commn., Fla., 1969-70, New Orleans Cabildo Mus., 1968-73, NEH, 1972-83, Miss. Dept. Archives-History, 1978—, scholar-in-residence, 1986-87, State of Ala., 1980-85, Granadero de Galvez Hidalgo of San Antonio, 1981, State of La., 1983—, Mowa Indians, 1983—, P.K. Yonge Library, U. Fla., 1985-86; substitute tchr. Jefferson County schs., Ala., 1985—. Author: Documentos ineditos para la historia de la Luisiana, 1963; Gayoso, 1965; Honor and Fidelity, 1965; Jose de Evia, 1968 Francis Baily's Journal, 1969; New Orleans: Facts and Legends, 1970; Luis de Onis Memoria, 1969; Guide to Spanish Louisiana, 1970; New Orleans Drinks and How to Mix Them, 1973; History of the University of Alabama Hospitals and Clinics, 1974; The 1779 Marcha de Galvez: Louisiana's Giant Step Forward in the American Revolution, 1974; Galvez, 1981; Stephen Minor, 1983; contbg. author World Book Ency., Acad. Am. Ency., others; editor, dir. La. Collection Series, 1965—; contbr. to numerous hist. books, also articles to U.S. and fgn. hist. jours. Served with inf. AUS, 1951. Created knight cruz de caballero Royal Order Isabel La Catolica, Spain, 1979; Charles W. Hackett fellow, 1959; Am. Philos. Soc. fellow, 1961, 66; Fulbright fellow, 1961-62; Assn. State and Local History grantee, 1966, Nat. Endowment Humanities grantee, 1986-87, numerous others; recipient award of merit, 1978. Mem. Tenn. Squires, So. Hist. Assn. (life), La. Hist. Assn. (dir. 1977-78), Laffite Study Group (pres. 1980-88), Soc. History of Discoveries, Phi Beta Kappa, Phi Kappa Phi, Sigma Delta Pi, Phi Alpha Theta, Pi Kappa Phi. Home: 520 S 22d Ave Birmingham AL 35205

HOLMES, JAMES PARKER, investment executive; b. Chgo., Nov. 6, 1940; s. Parker M. and Dorothy (Thomas) H.; m. Barbara A. Marshall; 1 child, Elizabeth K. B.S., Marquette U., 1962; M.B.A., Northwestern U., 1963. Investment analyst Equitable Life Assurance Co., N.Y.C., 1963-66; mgr. investments CBS Inc., N.Y.C., 1966-69; sr. investment analyst Dean Witter, N.Y.C., 1969-72, portfolio strategist Ford Found., 1972-82; ptnr. Value Quest, N.Y.C., 1982-86; mng. dir. Dreman Value Mgmt., N.Y.C., 1986—. Contbr. chpts. to books. Treas. Ridgewood Republican Club, 1982-84. Mem. N.Y. Soc. Security Analysts (Vol. of Yr. award 1985), Am. Rhododendron Soc. (v.p. Tappan Zee chpt.), Inst. Chartered Fin. Analysts, Am. Iris Soc., Garden State Iris Soc. (sec.). Republican. Roman Catholic. Avocations: gardening; reading; jogging. Home: 210 Greenway Rd Ridgewood NJ 07450 Office: Dreman Value Mgmt 70 Pine St New York NY 10005

HOLMES, JAMES STEVENS, JR., utility company executive; b. Jackson, Miss., May 21, 1926; s. James Stevens and Frances Glynn (Tyler) H.; m. Dorothy Miriam Singletary, June 11, 1951; children—James Stevens III, Benjamin Ford III. B.S., Millsaps Coll., 1948; B.S., Ga. Inst. Tech., 1950, M.S., 1950. With So. Bell Tel. & Tel. Co., 1957—, gen. mgr., Atlanta, 1966-71, dir. labor relations, 1971-82, sec., 1982—. Bd. dirs. United Way, Atlanta, 1968, Jr. Achievement, Atlanta, 1979; scoutmaster Atlanta Area council Boy Scouts Am., 1970-76; trustee Gerontology Ctr., Ga. State U., 1983—; mem. Internat. Exec. Service Corps. Served to comdr. USN, 1944-47, ETO. Decorated comdr. Mil. Order Stars and Bars. Fellow Alpha Epsilon Delta; mem. SAR, SCV. Republican. Mem. Christian and Missionary Alliance Ch. Lodge: Lions (pres. Louisville 1951-54). Home: 2216 Springwood Dr Decatur GA 30033 Office: So Bell Tel & Tel Co 675 W Peachtree NE Room 42P75 Atlanta GA 30375

HOLMES, LUCILLE MARTIN, florist; b. Tylertown, Miss., Jan. 9, 1921; d. Lawrence M. and Ella (Smith) Martin; m. Donald E. Holmes, Apr. 15, 1940; 1 child, Donette Holmes Titus. Student floral designing Am. Florist Assn., V. I., 1975, U. Miami 1976, Florist Trans World, London, 1980. Owner, operator Tylertown Florist, 1960—; tchr. floral designing, 1985-88. Mem. Southeastern Florist Assn., La. Florist Assn., Ala. Florist Assn., Miss. Florist Assn. Democrat. Baptist. Clubs: Garden, Country. Avocations: tennis; camping; reading; traveling. Home and Office: Tylertown Florist 425 Beulah Ave Tylertown MS 39667

HOLMES, MARIA LEE, communication consultant, lecturer, writer; b. San Francisco, Mar. 2, 1944; d. Tracy Sherlock Holmes and Alda Maria (Baranzelli) Holmes-Lyddy. B.A., Calif. State U.-Long Beach, 1967; postgrad, Columbia Pacific U. Cert. secondary tchr., Calif. Tchr., Los Angeles City Schs., 1967-80; cons. Maria Holmes Co., Harbor City, Calif., 1971—; owner Maria Holmes Communication Services, Harbor City, 1980—; dir. bus. and program devel. TranSyn, Ltd. Cons., Venice, Calif., 1982; tchr. bus. and psychology Harbor Coll., Wilmington, Calif., 1982, Torrance Adult Sch., Calif., 1980-81; lectr. various community organizations, Greater Los Angeles, 1978—; faculty chair Chapman Sch.; tchr. Long Beach State U. Free Coll., 1967, Orange Coast Coll., 1987—, U. San Diego, 1987—, Pierce Coll., 1987—; cons. Los Angeles County, Carson, Calif., 1980; guest radio and TV talk shows, Los Angeles. Author: Dealing with Difficult People, 1985; Getting Your Message Across: How to Let Others Know You Mean Business, 1985. Mem. AAUW, Nat. Speakers Assn. (corr. sec. greater Los Angeles chpt.), Women in Mgmt., Los Angeles United Tchrs. Office: Maria Holmes & Assocs 760 W Lomita Blvd #144 Harbor City CA 90710

HOLMES, OPAL LAUREL, publisher; b. Laurens, Iowa, Oct. 14, 1913; d. Ila Laurel and Jessie Merle (Hesselgrave) Holmes; ed. pub. and pvt. schs.; m. Vardis Fisher, Apr. 16, 1940. Publisher, Opal Laurel Holmes, Pub. Coauthor: Gold Rushes and Mining Camps of the Early American West. Recipient Golden Spur award, 1969. Mem. Authors Guild, Authors League Am., Nat. Soc. Lit. and Arts, Internat. Platform Assn. Office: PO Box 2535 Boise ID 83701

HOLMES, PETER F., petroleum company executive; b. Athens, Greece, Aug. 27, 1932; s. Gerald Holmes and Caroline Morris Holmes; m. Judith M. Walker, 1955; 3 children. Ed. Malvern Coll., Trinity Coll., Cambridge, Eng. With Shell Group of Cos., 1965—, chief exec. officer Shell Markets, Middle East, Ltd., 1965-68, Shell Cos. in Libya, 1970-73, mng. dir. and chief exec. officer Shell Petroleum Devel. Co. of Nigeria, Ltd., 1977-81, pres. Shell Internat. Trading Co., 1981-83, mng. dir. Shell Transport and Trading, 1982—, chmn. bd., 1985—; mng. dir. Royal Dutch/Shell Group, 1982—, vice chmn. com. Author: Mountains and a Monastery, 1958, Nigeria, Giant of Africa, 1985. Avocations: mountaineering; travel; 19th century travel literature. Address: Shell Transp & Trading Co PLC, Shell Centre, London SE1 7NA England *

HOLMES, ROBERT ALLEN, lawyer, educator, consultant, lecturer; b. Sewickley, Pa., Dec. 12, 1947; s. Lee Roy John and Nellie Ann (Kupits) H.; m. Linda Lee Freeman Aug. 16, 1969; children—Wesley Paige, Ashley Reagan. BA in Bus. Adminstrn., Coll. William and Mary, 1969, JD, 1972. Bar: Md. 1972, U.S. Dist. Ct. Md. 1972, Va. 1973, U.S. Dist. Ct. (ea. dist.) Va. 1973. Assoc. Ober, Grimes & Shriver, Balt., 1972-73, Kellam, Pickrell & Lawler, Norfolk, Va., 1973-75; ptnr. Holliday, Holmes & Inman, Norfolk, 1975-77; asst. prof. law Bowling Green State U., Ohio, 1977-82, assoc. prof., 1982—; dir. Purchasing Law Inst., 1979—, EEO-Affirmative Action Research Group, 1978—; lectr. profl. seminars and workshops throughout country onpurchasing, discrimination and affirmative action law. Author: (books) (with others) Computers, Data Processing and the Law, 1984; numerous manuals on discrimination and affirmative action law. Contbg. editor, monthly columnist Midwest Purchasing, 1983-84. Recipient Outstanding Young Man award William and Mary Soc. Alumni, 1973. Mem. Md. Bar Assn., Va. Bar Assn., Am. Bus. Law Assn., Am. Soc. Personnel Adminstrs., Nat. Assn. Purchasing Mgmt., Mensa. Republican. Home: 1034 Conneaut Ave Bowling Green OH 43402 Office: Ohio Supreme Ct 30 E Broad St 2nd floor Columbus OH 43266-0419

HOLMES À COURT, (MICHAEL) ROBERT (HAMILTON), oil company executive; b. July 27, 1937; s. Peter Worsley and Ethnée Celia Holmes à Court; m. Janet Lee Ranford, 1965; 3 children. Grad., U. West Australia. Barrister, solicitor Supreme Ct. Western Australia, 1965-82; chmn. Associated Communications Corp., Australia, 1982—, Weeks Petroleum Co., Australia, 1984—, Bell Group Ltd., 1970-88, The Bell Group Internat. Ltd., 1982—. Office: The Bell Group Internat Ltd, 22 The Esplanade, Peppermint Grove, 6011 Perth Australia *

HOLMGREN, LATON EARLE, clergyman; b. Mpls., Feb. 20, 1915; s. Frank Albert and Freda Ida (Lindahl) H. Student, U. Minn., 1934-35; A.B. cum laude, Asbury Coll., 1936; M. Div. summa cum laude, Drew U., 1941; postgrad., Edinburgh (Scotland) U., 1947; D.D., Ill. Wesleyan U., 1956, Asbury Theol. Sem., 1972. Ordained to ministry United Methodist Ch., 1942; assoc. minister Calvary Meth. Ch., East Orange, N.J., 1940-42, Christ

Ch. Meth., N.Y.C., 1943-48; minister Tokyo (Japan) Union Ch., 1949-52; lectr. internat. dept. Tokyo U. Commerce, 1950-52; adviser Japanese Fgn. Office, Tokyo, 1951; sec. for Asia Am. Bible Soc., N.Y.C., 1952-54; exec. sec. Am. Bible Soc., 1954-62, gen. sec., rec. sec., 1963-78, cons., 1978—; mem. exec. com. United Bible Socs., Stuttgart, Germany, 1957-78, chmn., 1963-72, spl. cons., 1978—. Recipient Gutenberg award, 1975; Disting. Alumni award Asbury Coll., 1981; Baron von Canstein award, 1982. Mem. Japan Soc. Clubs: Union League, Metropolitan, Monday. Home: 322 W 57 St New York NY 10019 Office: 1865 Broadway New York NY 10023

HOLMGREN, THEODORE J., food company executive; b. N.Y.C., May 2, 1927; s. Oscar F. and Madeline (Thompson) H.; m. Miriam Brady, June 3, 1950; children: Miriam Jane (Mrs. James C. McCrea III), Barbara Lynn (Mrs. Benjamin Fowler), Theodore Douglas. A.B., Brown U., 1949; M.B.A., Harvard U., 1955. Asst. to Donald Deskey, Indsl. Designer, 1955-60; dir. design services Gen. Foods Corp., White Plains, N.Y., 1960-62; corp. new products mgr. Gen. Foods Corp., 1962-65, sr. product mgr., 1965-68; sr. cons. mktg. Peat, Marwick, Mitchell & Co., N.Y.C., 1968; v.p. mktg. Curtice-Burns, Inc., Rochester, N.Y., 1968—; sec. Curtice-Burns, Inc., 1974—, sr. v.p., 1985—; co. rep. to Grocery Mfrs. Am., Washington. Pres. Community Council Chs. Irvington, Ardsley, Dobbs Ferry, Hastings, and Hartsdale, N.Y., 1961-63; trustee Orphan Asylum Soc. City N.Y., 1962-68, Curtice-Burns Charitable Found., 1970—; mem. corp. bd. United Way of Greater Rochester; life assoc. Pres.'s Soc. U. Rochester. Served to lt. (j.g.) USNR, 1951-53. Mem. Nat. Food Processors Assn. (alt. dir.), Rochester Acad. Sci., Alpha Delta Pi. Clubs: Harvard Bus. Sch. (Rochester); U. Rochester Faculty. Home: 16 Esternay Ln Pittsford NY 14534 Office: Curtice-Burns Foods Inc 1 Lincoln First Sq Rochester NY 14603

HOLMSTROM, VALERIE LOUISE, clinical psychologist, educator; b. Seattle, June 13, 1948; d. Frank Gottfried and Laura (Lofthus) H. AB, Boston U., 1968; PhD, U. Wash., 1972. Diplomate Am. Bd. Profl. Pschology. Lic. clin. psychologist, S.C. Staff psychologist VA Med. Ctr., Brockton, Mass., 1972-75, asst. chief psychology service, Charleston, S.C., 1975-81, chief psychology service, 1981—; asst. prof. dept. psychiatry and behavioral scis. Med. U. S.C., Charleston, 1975—; cons. Mass. Rehab. Commn., Boston, 1974-75, S.C. Div. Vocat. Rehab., Charleston, 1979—; lectr. Boston U., 1974, Grad. Sch. Edn., The Citadel, Charleston, 1979-80. USPHS fellow, 1968-69; recipient Outstanding Performance award VA Med. Ctr., Brockton, 1975, VA Med. Ctr., Charleston, 1982. Mem. Am. Psychol. Assn., S.C. Assn. Profl. Psychology, Am. Epilepsy Soc., VA Chiefs Assn. Democrat. Home: 1775 Dunbarton Dr Charleston SC 29407 Office: VA Med Ctr 109 Bee St Charleston SC 29403

HOLOUBEK, GUSTAW, actor, director; b. Cracow, Poland, Apr. 21, 1923; s. Gustaw and Eugenia H.; m. Danuta Kwiatkowska; m. 2d Maria Wachowiak; m. 3d Magdalena Zawadzka; 2 children. Ed. State Higher Dramatic Sch., Cracow. Actor, Cracow theatres, 1947-49; actor Wyspianski Theatre, Katowice, artistic mgr., 1954-56; actor Polish Theatre, Warsaw, 1958-59; actor Dramatic Theatre, Warsaw, Poland, 1959-82, dir., artistic mgr., 1972-82; assoc. prof. State Higher Theatrical Sch.; vice chmn. SPATIF (Assn. Polish Theatre and Film Actors), 1963-70, chmn., 1970-81; dep. to Seym, 1976-82; now actor in various Warsaw theatres. Stage appearances include: Leprosy at the Palace of Justice; Le diable et le bon Dieu; Dziady; Rzeznia; Electra; The Iceman Cometh; King Lear; Oedipus; Hamlet; Richard II and Hadrian VII; November Night; Operetka; also film and TV play appearances; dir. film: Mazepa, 1976. Decorations include State prize 1st class, Order of Banner of Labor 2d class, Knight's Cross of Polonia Restituta; recipient award Meritorious Activist of Culture, 1972, Warsaw City prize, 1975, Com. for Polish Radio and TV award, 1980. *

HOLOWAY, THEODORE RODNEY, electrical engineer; b. Springfield, Mass., Oct. 11, 1949; s. Clayton Frank and Irene (Siemaszko) H.; B.S. in E.E. with honors, U. Tenn., 1972, postgrad., 1979-81; postgrad. Middle Tenn. State U., 1981—. Elec. maintenance engr. Scottish Inns of Am., Knoxville, 1973-77; with Sverdrup Tech./ARO, Inc., Tullahoma, Tenn., 1977—, project lead elec. engr.-indsl. computer automation, distbd. process control systems, machinery vibration analysis, computer-aided design, mfg. engring, expert systems and artificial intelligence, 1980—. Mem. IEEE, Middle Tenn. Soc. Profl. Engrs. (Young Engr. of Yr. award 1981). Methodist. Lodges: Kiwanis, Toastmasters, Masons, Shriners. Home: PO Box 4441 Fort Walton Beach FL 32549 Office: Sverdrup Tech Inc Tech Evaluation and Analysis Support Group Eglin AFB FL 32542

HOLSINGER, JAMES WILSON, JR., physician; b. Kansas City, Kans., May 11, 1939; s. James Wilson and Ruth Leona (Reitz) H.; student Duke U., 1957-60, M.D., 1964, Ph.D., 1968; M.S., U. S.C., 1981; m. Barbara Jenn Craig, Dec. 28, 1963; children—Anna Elizabeth, Martha Ruth, Sarah Frances, Rachel Catherine. Intern, Duke Hosp., Durham, N.C., 1964, resident in surgery, 1965, fellow in thoracic surgery, 1966; fellow in anatomy Duke U., Durham, 1966-68; resident in surgery U. Fla., Gainesville, 1968-70, fellow in cardiology, 1970-72; with VA, 1969—, chief of staff VA Med. Ctr., Augusta, Ga., 1978-81, dir. VA Med. Ctr., Richmond, Va., 1981—; prof. medicine and anatomy Med. Coll. Ga., Augusta, 1978-81; prof. medicine and allied health edn. Med. Coll. Va., Richmond, 1981—; asst. v.p. health scis. Va. Commonwealth U., Richmond, 1985—. Mem. com. evangelism N. Ga. conf. United Meth. Ch., 1980-81; mem. com. 80, World Meth. Council, 1981—, mem. bd. discipleship Va. Conf., 1982-86, lay mem., 1984—, assoc. dist. day leader, 1983-86, dist. lay leader, 1984-86, conf. lay leader, 1986—; mem. World Meth. Council, 1986— (exec. com.), del. gen. conf., 1988, del. SE Jurisdictional Conf., 1988. Served to brig. gen. M.C., USAR, 1986—. Fellow Am. Coll. Cardiology, ACP; mem. Am. Coll. Hosp. Adminstrs., Am. Assn. Anatomists, Am. Heart Assn. (fellow clin. council), Am. Soc. Pub. Adminstrn. Internat. Brotherhood Magicians. Republican. Author/editor med. books; contbr. articles to med. and religious publs. Home: 8915 Tresco Rd Richmond VA 23229 Office: Hunter Holmes McGuire Vet Adminstrn Med Ctr 1201 Broad Rock Blvd Richmond VA 23249

HOLST, HERMANN GEORG, manufacturing company executive; b. Neumunster, Germany, June 5, 1940; s. Georg Wilhelm and Agnes (Kreutz) H.; Engr., State Coll. Engring., Mannheim, W. Ger., 1965; m. Heidrun Monika Busch, Dec. 1, 1967; children—Torsten Holger, Katrin Anke Susanne. Design engr. Standard Elektrik Lorenz AG, Mannheim, 1965-68, group leader, 1968-78, project mgr. navigation system, 1978-79, program mgr., 1979—. Served with German Air Force, 1961-62. Mem. Verein Deutscher Elektrotechniker, Nachrichtentechnische Gesellschaft. Home: 47 Ludwig-Beck Strasse, D6800 Mannheim Federal Republic of Germany Office: 62 Weinheimer Strasse, D6800 Mannheim Federal Republic of Germany

HOLST, JOHAN JORGEN, minister of defense of Norway; b. Oslo, Nov. 29, 1937; s. Nils Oluf and Ester (Salvesen) H. Grad. in Polit. Sci., Columbia U. and U. Oslo, 1965; postgrad. Harvard U. Research assoc. Norwegian Def. Research Establishment, 1963-67; head of research Norwegian Inst. of Internat. Affairs, 1969-76, dir., 1981-86; state sec. Norwegian Ministry of Def., 1976-79, state sec. Ministry of Fgn. Affairs, 1979-81, Minister of Def., 1986—. Mem. Norwegian Labor Party. Office: Ministry of Defense, Oslo Norway

HOLSTEIN, JENS CHRISTIAN, pharmaceutical company executive; b. Hamburg, Federal Republic of Germany, June 16, 1930; s. Christian A. and Helene E. (Esser) H.; m. Margarete O. born Weth, Aug. 28, 1956; children: Cecil, Claudine, Peter, Gabriele. BA in Econs., Heidelberg U., 1954. Bd. dirs. Holstein Co. Group, Hamburg, Federal Republic of Germany, 1955; chief exec. officer C. Holstein Co., Osaka, Japan, 1956, chief operating officer, chief exec. officer, 1957—; v.p., bd. dirs. German C. of C. in Japan, 1970-83. Contbr. articles to profl. jours. Mem. Japan Pharm. Assn., Japan C. of C. Clubs: Rotay (Osaka) (bd. dirs. 1980-81); Kobe (Japan) (pres. 1976-80). Home: 24-31 Rokurokuso-cho, Ashiya City 659, Japan Office: C Holstein Co, Doshomachi, 541 Osaka Japan

HOLSTI, KEIJO KALEVI, educator; b. Koski Tl, Finland, Oct. 23, 1932; s. Kustaa Verner and Helvi Helena (Saharanta) H.; M.A., U. Turku (Finland), 1964, Lic. Ph., 1966; Ph.D., U. Tampere (Finland), 1971; m. Hanna-Maija Vä limaa, July 31, 1960; children—Aino Kristiina, Martti Tapani. Tchr. Swedish and English, Finnish secondary schs., Evijä rvi, Kolari, Mikkeli, Oripä ä , 1952-55, 60-66; asst. in gen. lit. U. Tampere, 1966-73, docent, 1971—, prof. gen. lit., 1973—, dean Faculty Humanities, 1976, 81-82, dir. dept. art studies, 1979-81, mem. univ. council, 1979-80; grantee Salzburg Seminar, 1977, U. Turku grantee, 1965-66; Niilo Helander Found. grantee, 1966; U. Tampere grantee, 1967; Sci. Fund Tampere grantee, 1969; Emil Aaltonen Found. grantee, 1971; Acad. Finland grantee, 1984. Mem. Finnish Lit. Soc., Lit. Scholars Assn., Nordic Assn. Am. Studies, Nordic Assn. for Can. Studies, Am. Assn. Aesthetics, Internat. Comparative Lit. Assn., Deutsche Bibliothek. Lutheran. Club: Rotary. Author books, including: Motiivin kä site kirjallisuudentutkimuksessa (The Concept of Motif in Literary Study) (in Finnish with an English summary), 1970; editor: Kanadan kirjallisuuden vaiheita (Introduction to Canadian Literature), 1988. contbr. articles in lit. and lit. theory to profl. jours. Home: Soinilankatu 30 H 33, 33730 Tampere 73 Finland Office: PO Box 607, 33101 Tampere 10 Finland

HOLT, ALAN CRAIG, government space agency administrator; b. Camp Lejeune, N.C., Mar. 16, 1945; s. Floyd Marshall and Bernice Ann (Schmidt) H.; m. Susan Carol Darnall, Aug. 8, 1970; 1 son, Christopher Scott. B.S., Iowa State U.-Ames, 1967; M.S., U. Houston, Clear Lake, 1979. Expt. procedures specialist NASA, Manned Spacecraft Ctr., Houston, 1967-70, Skylab crew proceedings and tng. specialist, 1970-74; Spacelab crew ops. specialist Johnson Space Ctr., 1974-78, Spacelab systems tng. supr., 1978-80, payload group leader, 1980-84, space sta. tech. mgr., 1985-87, chief user requirements and accommodations br. NASA Space Sta. Program, 1987—; pres., dir. Holt Research & Devel. Co., 1983-86; bd. dirs. Vehicle Internal Systems Investigative Team, Inc., Friendswood, Tex., 1978-86. Recipient Sustained Superior and Outstanding Performance award NASA, Johnson Space Center Hdqrs., 1973, 82, Super Achievement award NASA Hdqrs., 1988. Mem. Am. Astron. Soc. (assoc.), AIAA (sr.), Armed Forces Communications and Electronics Assn., Nat. Def. Preparedness Assn., Nat. Classification Mgmt. Soc. Lutheran. Club: AMORC (regional monitor 1979-81, 85—). Home: PO Box 787 Herndon VA 22070 Office: NASA Code SSU Space Sta Program Office 10701 Parkridge Blvd Reston VA 22094

HOLT, BARBARA BERTANY, management consultant; b. Bridgeport, Conn., Nov. 4, 1940; d. Stephen Edward and Mary G. Bertany; student Regis Coll., 1958-59; B.A. in English, U. Bridgeport, 1962; m. Robert Holt, Dec. 5, 1971; children—Pamela Maren, Laura Kimbel, Mary Brooke. Instr. speech and theatre, U. Bridgeport (Conn.), 1962-69; gen. mgr. BFL Assos., Exec. Recruitment, N.Y.C., 1969-72; founder, pres. Barbara Holt Assos., mgmt. cons., N.Y.C., 1972—; mem. faculty New Sch. for Social Research. Chmn. bd. advisers Fine Arts Acad. Fairfield. Mem. N.Y. Fashion Group, Women in Mgmt. Club: Atrium (N.Y.C.). Developer, producer video career mgmt. series for public TV, 1976. Office: Barbara Holt Assocs Box 713 Southport CT 06490

HOLT, BERTHA MERRILL, state legislator; b. Eufaula, Ala., Aug. 16, 1916; d. William Hoadley and Bertha Harden (Moore) Merrill; AB, Agnes Scott Coll., 1938; LLB, U. Ala., 1941; m. Winfield Clary Holt, Mar. 14, 1941; children: Harriet Wharton Holt Whitley, William Merrill, Winfield Jefferson. Admitted to Ala. bar, 1941; with Treasury Dept., Washington, 1941-42, Dept. Interior, Washington, 1942-43; mem. N.C. Ho. of Reps. from 22d Dist., 1975-80, 25th Dist., 1980—, chmn. select com. govtl. ethics, 1979-80, chmn. constl. amendments com., 1981, 83, mem. joint commn. govtl. ops., 1982—, chmn. appropriation com. justice and pub. safety, 1985-88 . Pres., Democratic Women of Alamance, 1962, chmn. hdqrs., 1964, 68; mem. N.C. Dem. Exec. Com., 1964-75; pres. Episcopal Ch. Women, 1968; mem. council N.C. Episcopal Diocese, 1972-74, 84-87 , chmn. budget com. 1987—; chmn. fin. dept., 1973-75, parish grant com., 1973-80, mem. standing com., 1975-78; chmn. Alamance County Social Services Bd., 1970; mem. N.C. Bd. Sci. and Tech., 1979-83; bd. dirs. Hospice N.C., State Council Social Legis., U. N.C. Sch. Pub. Health Adv. Bd., Salvation Army Alamance County, N.C., Alternatives for Status Offenders and Burlington (N.C.) Health Adv. Bd. Recipient Outstanding Alumna award Agnes Scott Coll., 1978, Legis. award for service to elderly Non-Profit Rest Home Assn., 1985, health, 1986, ARC, 1987, Faith Active in Pub. Affairs award N.C. Council of Churches, 1987. Mem. Women's Forum N.C., Law Alumni Assn. U. N.C. Chapel Hill (dir. 1978-81), N.C. Bar Assn., NOW, English Speaking Union, N.C. Hist. Soc., Les Amis du Vin, Pi Beta Phi, Phi Kappa Gamma (hon. mem.). Club: Century Book. also: PO Box 1111 Burlington NC 27215

HOLT, GORDON ARTHUR, broadcast executive, media broker; b. Austin, Tex., Oct. 27, 1951; s. Arthur Henry and Phyllis Imogen (Jones) H. BFA, North Tex. U., 1971. With pub. relations dept. Universal Studios, Los Angeles, 1971-72; print salesman Sta. WTMI-FM, Miami, 1972-73; dir. gen. Holt Corp. Internat., Bogota, Colombia, 1977-78; v.p. Holt Corp., Bethlehem, Pa., 1974-86; exec. v.p., chief operating officer, Holt Media Group, Holt Tech. Service, Stas. WZZO-FM, Bethlehem, Pa., WUSQ-AM/FM, Winchester, Va., 1986—; exec. v.p. Holt Communications Corp., Del. including Stas. WJMI, WOKJ, Jackson, Miss., WGCM-AM/FM, Biloxi, Miss., WTKX, WBOP, Pensacola, Fla., 1986—; pres. Holt Communications Corp., Pa., 1986—; dir. Pa. Assn. Broadcaster, 1985-86; v.p. KMXQ, Socorro, N.Mex.; v.p. WBNE-FM, Benton, Pa. Contbr. articles to profl. jours. Mem. Inter-Am. Assn. Broadcasters, Internat. Inst. Communications, Nat. Assn. Broadcasters, Fla. Broadcasters Assn., Pensacola Broadcasters Assn.. Republican. Office: Holt Corp Pa Inc Suite 205 Westgate Bethlehem PA 18017 also: 111 N Baylen St Pensacola FL 32501

HOLT, HERBERT, psychiatrist; b. Vienna, Austria, Apr. 27, 1912; s. Leon and Cecilia (von Lempel) H.; Absolvent der Medizin, U. Vienna, 1937; Docteur en Medicine, U. Lausanne (Switzerland), 1938; m. Dolores Bolla di Osasco, July 14, 1961; children—Renata, Gerhard. Came to U.S., 1936, naturalized, 1941. Intern, Bellevue Hosp., N.Y.C., 1938-39, resident, 1939-41; practice medicine specializing in psychiatry and psychoanalysis, N.Y.C., 1951—; dean Westchester Inst., Rye, N.Y., 1970—; dir. N.Y. Inst. Existential Analysis, 1965—. Med. dir. Cathedral Counseling Service Cathedral Ch. St. John the Divine, N.Y.C., Actors Counseling Service, N.Y.C. Fellow Assn. for Applied Psychoanalysis (founding pres.), Am. Assn. for Social Psychiatry, Am. Soc. Psychoanalytic Physicians, Am. Ontoanalytic Assn., Am. Soc. Existential Psychiatry (pres. 1972—), Am. Acad. Psychoanalysis. Author: Free to Be Good or Bad, 1976; contbg. author Comprehensive Textbook of Psychiatry II, 1975. Editor: Jour. Modern Psychotherapy. Contbr. chpts. to textbooks, articles to profl. jours. Office: 185 E 85th St New York NY 10028

HOLT, JOSEPH WILLIAM, reinsurance company executive; b. Apr. 16, 1930; s. Joseph W. and Helen G. Holt; m. Irina von der Launitz, July 19, 1952; children: Lise Margaret Bradley, Helen Alexandra Lizotte. BA, Maryville Coll., 1950; MA, U. Pa., 1954. Mgr. Parker & Co. Internat., Phila., 1952-54, with Price Forbes, London, 1955, Interocean Agy., N.Y.C., 1956-67; co-founder, exec. v.p., dir. Duncanson & Holt, Inc., 1967—; pres. RA Fulton & Co., Inc., 1968—; v.p. Reed & Brown, 1974—; v.p. Aerospace Mgrs., 1974—, D & H Tech. Services, Inc., 1974—; exec. v.p. ERG Mgmt. Corp., 1975—; exec. v.p., dir. Rochdale Ins. Co., 1976—; pres., dir. United Ams. Ins. Co., 1978—, Holt Corp., 1981—; bd. dirs. First Manhattan Intermediaries Inc., 1979—; chmn., pres., chief exec. officer Federated Reins. Corp., 1982—; mgr. Pinehurst Accident Reins. Group, 1982—; bd. dirs. RMS, Inc., CIU, Inc.; chmn. bd. dirs. Nat. Marine Underwriters, 1983—; chmn. John Hewitt and Assocs. 1986—, Nat. Marine Ins. Co., 1987—, Mgmt. and Facilities Corp., 1987—. Clubs: Union, World Trade. Home: 1100 Rahway Rd Plainfield NJ 07060 also: Amen Farm Brooklin ME 04616 Office: 206 E 61st St New York NY 10021

HOLTE, CLARENCE LE ROY, retired marketing executive and publisher; b. Norfolk, Va., Feb. 19, 1909; s. Samuel and Dora (Whitted) H.; student Lincoln U., 1930-32, LL.D. (hon.), 1982; student Am. Inst. Banking, 1932-34, New Sch. Social Research, 1940-42; m. Audrey M. Proctor, Dec. 22, 1945; 1 dau., Helen Ruth Holte-Fields. Teller, Dunbar Nat. Bank, N.Y.C., 1932-35; race relations specialist Works Progress Adminstrn., N.Y.C., 1935-40; traffic mgr. Conlan Electric Corp., Bklyn., 1940-44; sales rep. Lever Bros. Co., 1944-52; with Batten, Barton, Durstine & Osborn, N.Y.C., 1952-72; founder, pub., Nubian Press, Inc., N.Y.C., 1971-86; editorial cons. Nat. Scene, newspaper supplement, 1974-78. Mem. Nat. Assn. Mktg. Developers, Alpha Phi Alpha. Club: Masons. Contbr. articles to profl. jours.; editor: Nubian Baby Book, 1971. Donor collection Africana housed in Clarence L. Holte Africana Room, Ahmadu Bello U., Zaria, Nigeria, biennial Clarence L. Holte lit. prize, 1979; established Clarence L. Holte Lectureship, Lincoln U., 1982. Home: 555 Edgecombe Ave New York NY 10032

HOLTE, JOHAN BERTHIN, industrialist; b. Notodden, Norway, Feb. 19, 1915; m. Eva Bull; Degree in Chem. Engring., Tech. U. Norway, 1938. With Norsk Hydro, Norway, 1958-85, dir. research div., 1957-66, v.p., 1964-66, pres., 1967-77, chmn., 1977-85; chmn. Banque Paribas Norge A.S., Oslo, Amerada Hess Norway Ltd., Oslo; dir. Amerada Hess (U.K.) Ltd., London, Qatar Fertiliser Co. S.A.Q., Umm Said, Qatar. Decorated comdr.'s cross Royal Order St. Olav; officier Legion of Honor; recipient Dr. Ing. Sam Eyde's prize of honor. Avocations: fishing; walking. Office: Bygdøyallè 2, 0257 Oslo 2 Norway

HOLT-HARRIS, JOHN EVAN, JR., lawyer; b. Stapleton, N.Y., Feb. 10, 1917; s. John E. and Edith Ellen (Screen) H.-H.; m. Susan E. Schenck, Aug. 10, 1941; children—John Evan III, Susan E. A.B., Cornell U., 1937, LL.B., J.D., 1939. Bar: N.Y. State 1939, U.S. Dist. Ct. (no. dist.) N.Y. 1940. Assoc. Milbank, Tweed, Hope & Webb, N.Y.C., 1939-40, Brown & Gallagher, Albany, N.Y., 1940-41; assoc. DeGraff, Foy, Conway, Holt-Harris & Mealey and predecessor firms, Albany, 1945-51, ptnr., 1951—; lectr. Albany Law Sch., 1951-70; judge Recorders Ct., Albany, 1952-77; mem. N.Y. State Bd. Law Examiners, 1969—; mem. Chief Justices Coordinating Council on Lawyer Competency, 1982—. Trustee Albany Med. Ctr. Hosp., 1952-79, Albany Acad. for Boys, 1952-79; bd. dirs. Mid-Hudson Library Assn., 1956—; bd. dirs. Albany Pub. Library, 1952-85, pres., 1985—; mem. Albany Bd. Edn., 1952-70; mem. adv. council Cornell U. Law Sch., 1979-81; mem. test drafting com. Multi-State Profl. Responsibility Examination, 1980—; chmn. com. on ethical stds. and conduct of officers and employees, City of Albany, 1987—, strategic planning com., 1984—; chmn. adminstrv. bd. com. to relarize bar admission procedures, State of N.Y., 1985—; pres. Fedn. of the Bar, 3d Jud. Dist., 1962-65; chmn. Jud. Conv. 3d Jud. Dist. N.Y., 1982, 83; chmn. N.Y. State Bd. Law Examiners, 1985—; qualifier staff course, Royal naval Coll., Greenwich, Eng., 1944-45. Served to lt. comdr. USN, 1941-46. Mem. ABA (N.Y. State del. 1980, mem. Law Sch. Site Evaluation com.), N.Y. State Bar Assn., Albany County Bar Assn. (pres. 1955), Assn. Trial Lawyers Am., The Am. Judicature Soc., Nat. Conf. Bar Examiners (chmn. elect 1982-83, chmn. 1983-84), Nat. Conf. State Trial Judges. Democrat. Episcopalian. Clubs: Ft. Orange, Schuyler Meadows, Albany Country, Oriskany, YMCA (Albany) (bd. dirs. 1953-61). Office: 11th Floor 90 State St Albany NY 12207

HOLT-JENSEN, ARILD, geographer, educator; b. Horten, Norway, Dec. 5, 1937; s. Rolf and Ingrid (Holt) J.; m. Elisabeth Offersen, Oct 24, 1964; children: Roald, Ingvild. MA in Geography, U. Oslo, 1963; PhD, U. Bergen, Norway, 1986. Amanuensis U. Aarhus, Denmark, 1963-65; lectr. Sch. Econs., Bergen, 1965; lectr. U. Bergen, 1966-69, sr. lectr., 1970—, mem. acad. collegium, 1986-87, chmn. dept. geography, 1977-78. Author: The Norwegian Wilderness, 1978, Geography, Its History and Concepts, 1981, revised edit., 1988; mem. editorial bd. GeoJournal, 1985—; editor newsletter, 1987-88; contbr. articles to profl. jours. Chmn. environ. com. Liberal Party of Norway, 1969-75, mem. Bergen city council, 1971-79. Norwegian Authors Orgn. travel grantee, 1982, 87. Mem. Norwegian Assn. Human Geographers (chmn. 1981-82, mem. editorial bd. GeoJournal. 1985—, editor newsletter 1987-88). Lutheran. Office: Dept Geography, Helleveien 30, 5035 Bergen Norway

HOLTKAMP, DORSEY EMIL, medical research scientist; b. New Knoxville, Ohio, May 28, 1919; s. Emil H. and Caroline E. (Meckstroth) H.; m. Marianne Church Johnson, Mar. 20, 1942 (dec. 1956); 1 son, Kurt Lee, 1 stepchild; m. Marie P. Bahm Roberts, Dec. 20, 1957 (dec. 1982); 2 stepchildren; m. Phyllis Laurence Bradfield, Sept. 1, 1984; 3 stepchildren. Student, Ohio State U., 1937-39; AB, U. Colo., 1945, MS, 1949, PhD, 1951. Sr. research scientist biochemistry sect. Smith, Kline & French Labs., Phila., 1951-57, endocrine-metabolic group leader, 1957-58; head endocrinology dept. Merrell-Nat. Labs. div. Richardson-Merrell, Inc., Cin., 1958-70, group dir. endocrine clin. research, med. research dept., 1970-81; group dir. med. research dept. Merrell Dow Pharms. subs. Dow Chem. Co., Cin., 1981-87; ind. cons. in med. research Lebanon, Ohio, 1987—. Research and publs. on various phases endocrinology, pharmacology, tumor metabolism, fertility-sterility control, biochemistry, teratology, inflammation, nutrition; research and devel. on new drugs. U. Colo. Med. Sch. fellow, 1946, biochemistry research fellow, 1948-51. Fellow AAAS; mem. AMA (affiliate), Am. Soc. Clin. Pharm. and Therapeutics, Endocrine Soc., Am. Fertility Soc., Am. Chem. Soc., Am. Soc. Pharmacology and Exptl. Therapeutics, N.Y. Acad. Sci., Soc. Exptl. Biology and Medicine, Sigma Xi, Nu Sigma Nu. Republican. Presbyterian. Home and Office: 130 S Liberty-Keuter Rd Lebanon OH 45036

HOLTON, WILLIAM CHESTER, engineer, consultant; b. Caldwell, Idaho, May 2, 1939; s. Chester Clayton and Margaret Ann (MacLaren) H.; m. Rhoberta Phaigh Romo, June 1, 1958 (div. Sept. 1976); children: William Lee, Robert Charles, Ronald Clayton. AS, Regents Coll., 1986. lic. FCC. Electronic technician Litton Industries, Los Angeles, 1963-66; applications engr. 3M Co., Camarillo, Calif., 1966-74; program analyst USN, Port Magu, Calif., 1974-75; video supr. U. Calif., Santa Barbara, 1975-77; cons. Great Am. Tech. Services, Los Angeles, 1977-87; founder, pres. G&B Electronics Inc., Hollywood, Calif., 1987—; project engr. Amblin Entertainment, Universal City, Calif., 1983-84, Beijing (People's Republic of China) Film Studios, 1982. Creator first digitally controlled screening theater for sound/film/video at Universal Studios, first high speed sound-on-film editing suite in People's Republic of China. Mem. Soc. Motion Picture TV Engrs. (voting). Office: G&B Electronics Inc 747 N Seward Hollywood CA 90038

HOLTSMARK, ERIC BIRGER, architect; b. Malmköping, Sweden, July 25, 1937; came to U.S., 1945; s. Bent Erling and Birgit M. (Egerström) H.; m. Aase Kristoffersen, Sept. 5, 1976; children: Devon, Eric II, Mindi, Jenni, Nicole. BArch, U. Calif., Berkeley, 1963. Registered profl. architect, Calif.; cert. architect Nat. Council Archtl. Registration Bds. Journeyman carpenter La Jolla and Berkeley, Calif., 1954-63; owner Modell Design, Berkeley, 1960-63; field engr. Masonic Home Project, Union City, Calif., 1963-64; project coordinator Bechtel Internat., San Francisco, 1964-66; field engr. Bechtel Pacific Ltd., Tasmania, Australia, 1966-68; sr. engr. Bechtel, Inc., N.Y.C., 1968-69; architect, project mgr. Hotel Inter-Continental, Helsinki, Finland, 1969-71, London, 1971-76; mgr. Saudi Arabian projects Bechtel Corp., San Francisco, 1976-78; owner, prin. Comml. and Hotel Devels. (name changed to Holtsmark Architects 1985), San Francisco, 1978—; chmn. Mark-Bentland Properties, San Francisco, 1976—; ptnr., bd. dirs. Eurocal Hotel Devel. Co., London, 1986—; mem. commn. State of Calif. Archtl. Lic. Bd. Author: "Putyshestvinik" - Russian Travels Alone, 1960. Office: Holtsmark Architects 1 Market Plaza San Francisco CA 94105 Summer: Ytterbyvik Resarö, Vaxholm Sweden

HOLTUS, GUNTER, linguistics educator; b. Bremen, Fed. Republic Germany, Oct. 14, 1946; s. Wilhelm and Dora (Bosking) H.; m. Elisabeth Dahmen, May 22, 1948; children: Verena, Marisa, Pamela. PhD, U. Marburg, Fed. Republic Germany, 1971. Prof. U. Saarbrucken, Fed. Republic Germany, 1977, U. Mainz, Fed. Republic Germany, 1980-86, U. Bonn., Fed. Republic Germany, 1986, U. Trier, Fed. Republic Germany, 1987—. Author: Celine, 1972, Lexikalische Interferenzen, 1979; editor: Italienische Varietatenlinguistik, 1983, Linguistica e dialettologia veneta, 1983, Umgangssprache in der Iberoromania, 1985, La Bataille d'Aliscans, 1985, Gesprochenes Italienisch, 1985, Rumanistik, 1986, Sprachlicher Substandard, 1986, Raetia Antiqua et moderna, 1986, Latein und Romanisch, 1987, Theaterwesen, 1987, Romania et Slavia Adriatica, 1987, Rätovomanisch hente, 1987, Lesikon der Romanistishen Linguistik (LRL), 1988. Societe de Linguistique Romane, Societa Linguistica Italiana, Deutscher Romanistenverband. Office: U Trier FB2, D-5500 Trier Federal Republic of Germany

HOLTZ, GILBERT JOSEPH, steel co. exec.; b. N.Y.C., Jan. 23, 1924; s. Al S. and Carrie (Schindler) H.; student N.Y.U., 1940-42; m. Carla Kahn, July 18, 1948; children—Steven J., Robert A. Vice pres. Hanger Service Co., Yonkers, N.Y., 1946-48; owner Economy Sales Co., Yonkers, 1948-50; v.p. Belvedere Space Saving Products, Inc., 1951-72; pres. Walnut Metal Industries, Inc., Yonkers, 1955-72, Belvedere Home Products Inc. (formerly 411 Walnut St. Corp.), 1962—, Holtz Realty Corp., 1962—, Walnut Assn. Inc.,

1961—, Belvedere Internat. Ltd., 1970—. Ward leader 2d Ward Republican County Com., Yonkers. Served with AUS, 1943-46. Mem. Yonkers C. of C. Club: Kiwanis. Patentee in field. Home: 182 Tibbetts Rd Yonkers NY 10705 Office: 937 Saw Mill River Rd Yonkers NY 10710

HOLTZAPFEL, PATRICIA KELLY, health facility executive; b. Madison, Wis., Jan. 29, 1948; d. Raymond Michael and Laura Margaret (Stegner) Kelly; m. Robert Adrian Bunker, Oct. 4, 1975 (div. June 1979); children: Donald, Theresa, Nicole, Douglas; m. Raymond Paul Holtzapfel, Mar. 12, 1983; children: David, Richard. RN; cert. pub. health nurse. Staff nurse Madison Gen. Hosp., 1970-72; bloodmobile staff nurse ARC, Madison, 1972-73; pub. health nurse Dane County Pub. Health Dept., Madison, 1973-75; field health nurse CIGNA Health Plan, Phoenix, 1975-84; dir. nursing Olsten Health Care, Phoenix, 1984-85; mgr. bus. Holtzapfel Phys. Therapy and Pain Control Clinic, Phoenix, 1985—; bd. dirs. Deer Valley Vocat. Arts Adv. Council, Phoenix. Bd. dirs. Deer Valley Vocat. Arts Adv. Council, Phoenix, 1986—. Mem. The Exec. Female Assn., Ariz. Networking Council. Office: Holtzapfel Phys Therapy Pain Control 4025 W Bell Rd Suite #2 Phoenix AZ 85023

HOLTZINGER, ALBERT HARRISON, retired chemistry educator; b. Wrightsville, Pa., Aug. 2, 1901; s. Albert Joseph and Cordelia Campbell (Slep) H.; m. Almira Van Brunt Smith (dec.), Nov. 4, 1922; children—Harrison (dec.), Joseph, James (dec.), Edward. B.S., Pa. State U., 1927, Ph.D., 1939. Analyst, Warner Lab., Creson, Pa., 1921-26; instr. to assoc. prof., dir. chem. labs. Pa. State U., University Park, 1936-61. Fellow Am. Inst. Chemists, AAAS; mem. Am. Chem. Soc., Pa. Acad. Sci., Pa. Inst. Chemists, Internat. Union of Pure and Applied Chemistry, N.Y. Acad. Scis., Sigma Xi, Alpha Chi Sigma, Phi Lambda Upsilon. Republican. Presbyterian. Lodge: Lions. Avocations electronic equipment. Home: 13239 Buena Vista Rd Waynesboro PA 17268

HOLTZMAN, ARNOLD HAROLD, chemical company executive; b. Phila., May 11, 1932; s. William and Rae (Shapiro) H.; B.S., Drexel Inst., 1954; M.S., Lehigh U., 1956, Ph.D., 1957; m. Phyllis Raskow, June 26, 1955; children—Rosalind Ann, Linda Susan, William Lewis. Asst. metallurgist J. Bishop & Co., Malvern, Pa., 1954; with duPont Co., various locations, 1957—, research mgr., dist. sales mgr. Polymer Intermediates dept., Wilmington, Del., 1973-76, mgr. new bus. programs, central research and devel. dept., Wilmington, 1976-78, mgr. health products, 1980-81, dir. devel. div. central research and devel. dept., 1982—; dir. Perceptive Systems, Inc. Recipient John Price Wetherill medal Franklin Inst., 1969. Fellow Am. Soc. Metals; mem. Sigma Xi. Patentee in processing of metals and non metals. Home: 208 Stone Crop Rd Wilmington DE 19810 Office: 1007 Market St Wilmington DE 19898

HOLUB, MIROSLAV, author, scientist; b. Pilsen, Czechoslovakia, Sept. 13, 1923; s. Josef and Frantiska (Dvorakova) H.; M.D., C.Sc., Charles U., Prague, Czechoslovakia; m. 3d, Jitka Langrová , 1969; 3 children. Sci. worker, Microbiol. Inst., Czechoslovak Acad. Scis., Prague 1953-71, Pub. Health Research Inst., N.Y.C., 1965-67, Max-Planck Inst. Immunobiology, Freiburg, 1968-69, Inst. Clin. and Exptl. Medicine, 1972—. Mem. Union Czechoslovak Writers (central com. 1963-69), Union Czech Sci. Workers (cen. com. 1969-71, Bavarian Acad. Arts, Internat. PEN. Author: (poetry) Day Shift 1958, Archilles and the Tortoise, 1960, 63. The Primer, 1961, 65, Go and Open the Door, 1961, Entirely Unsystematic Zoology, 1963, Where Blood Flows, 1963, So-called Heart, 1963, Anamnesis (Selected Poems, 1958-63), 1964, Selected Poems, 1967, Obwohl, 1969, Although, 1969, Concrete, 1970, Model of a Man, 1969, Events, 1971, Aktschlüsse, 1974, Een Machine Van Woorden, 1975; Vantunum Mool, 1976; Notes of a Clay Pigeon, 1977; Sagittal Section, 1980; On the Contrary, 1982; Interferon or On Theater, 1982, The Fly, 1987; (prose) Angel on Wheels, 1963, Three Steps on the Ground, 1965, Die explodierende Metropole, 1967; To Live in New York, 1969; Poe or The Valley of Unrest, 1971; The Principle of a Jingle Bell, 1987; (sci. works) Experimental Morphology of Antibody Formation, 1958, Mechanisms of Antibody Formation, 1960 (editor); The Lymphocyte and The Immune Response, 1967; Zellulä re Grundlagen der Antikö rperbildung, 1978; Structure of the Immune System, 1979; Immunology of Nude Mice, 1988. Home: Hrncire 107, 14900 Prague 4 Czechoslovakia Office: Inst Clinical & Exptl Medicine, 14622 Prague 4 Czechoslovakia

HOLUB, ROBERT FRANTISEK, nuclear chemist, physicist; b. Prague, Czechoslovakia, Sept. 19, 1937; came to U.S., 1966; s. Stanislav and Marie (Prochazkova) H.; m. Johnna S. Thames, Dec. 27, 1977; children—Robert M., John F., Elisabeth J. B.S., Charles U., Prague, 1958, M.S., 1960; Ph.D., McGill U., 1970. Research assoc. Fla. State U., Tallahassee, 1970-73; teaching intern U. Ky., Lexington, 1973-74; research physicist Bur. Mines, U.S. Dept. Interior, Denver, 1974—; cons. Internat. Atomic Energy Agy., Vienna, 1984—; faculty affiliate Colo. State U., Ft. Collins, 1982—; key participant radon intercalibration OECD, Paris, 1983—. Patentee continuous working level exposure apparatus. Contbr. articles to sci. jours. NRC Can. scholar, 1967-70. Mem. Am. Phys. Soc., Health Physics Soc.

HOLWAY, JAMES COLIN, steel co. exec.; b. Youngstown, Ohio, Nov. 14, 1927; s. Robert G. and Marie W. (Kane) H.; B.S., Ohio State U., 1950; M.B.A., Pa. State U., 1952; m. Patricia Ann Touscany, Aug. 31, 1957; children—Moira Ann, Colin A., Brent Patrick, Jamesin McAndrew, Jonathan Lynch. Sales trainee U.S. Steel Corp., 1951-55; salesman Republic Steel Corp., Cleve. and Detroit, 1955-58; dist. sales mgr. Tenn. Products & Chem. Corp., Detroit, 1958-60; dist. sales mgr. Nat. Steel Corp., Charlotte, N.C., 1960-72; founder, pres. Southeastern Steel Rolling Mills, Charlotte, 1972-73; co-founder, pres. Decker-Holway Steel Co., 1973-77; chmn. bd. Mid-Atlantic Industries, Inc., 1979—; adj. prof. corp. fin., bus. policy, econs. Queens Coll., Charlotte, 1987—. Served with USNR, 1945-46. Mem. AIME (asso.). Clubs: Country of Detroit (Grosse Pointe, Mich.); Charlotte City, Charlotte Country; Pike Run Country (Jones Mills, Pa.). Home: 2312 Pembroke Ave Charlotte NC 28207 Office: PO Box 15057 Charlotte NC 28211

HOLYER, ERNA MARIA, author, educator, artist; b. Weilheim, Bavaria, Germany, Mar. 15, 1925; d. Mathias and Anna Maria (Goldhofer) Schretter; A.A., San Jose Evening Coll., 1964; student San Mateo Coll., 1965-67, San Jose State U., 1968-69, San Jose City Coll., 1980-81; DLitt World U., 1984; m. Gene Wallace Holyer, Aug. 24, 1957. Free lance writer under pseudonym Ernie Holyer, 1960—; tchr. creative writing San Jose (Calif.) Met. Adult Edn., 1968—; artist, 1958—. mem. research bd. advisors Am. Biographical Inst., 1986; exhibited in group shows Crown Zellerbach Gallery, San Francisco, 1973, 74, 76, 77; I.B.C. Gallery, San Francisco, 1978, Los Angeles 1981. Recipient Woman of Achievement Honor cert. San Jose Mercury-News, 1973, 74, 75. Recipient Lefoli award for excellence in adult edn. instrn. Adult Edn. Senate, 1972; various art awards. Mem. Calif. Writers Club. Author: Rescue at Sunrise, 1965; Steve's Night of Silence, 1966; A Cow for Hansel, 1967; At the Forest's Edge, 1969; Song of Courage, 1970; Lone Brown Gull, 1971; Shoes for Daniel, 1974; The Southern Sea Otter, 1975; Sigi's Fire Helmet, 1975; Reservoir Road Adventure, 1982; Wilderness Journey, 1985. Contbr. articles to various mags. and newspapers. Home and Office: 1314 Rimrock Dr San Jose CA 95120

HOLZACH, ROBERT, banker; b. Zurich, Switzerland, Sept. 28, 1922; s. Ernst and Hertha (Schrenk) H. Dr.iur., U. Zurich, 1949. Trainee in atty.'s office, Arbon, Switzerland, 1950-51; trainee Union Bank of Switzerland, Geneva and London, 1951-52, mem. secretariat, Zurich, 1952-56, asst. mgr., 1956-66, mem. gen. mgmt., 1966-80, chmn. bd., 1980-88, hon. chmn., 1988—. Office: Union Bank of Switzerland, Bahnhofstrasse 45, 8021 Zurich Switzerland

HOLZER, MARC, educator; b. Bronx, N.Y., Feb. 28, 1945; s. Philip and Ann Lee (Blinder) H.; B.A. in Polit. Sci., U. Rochester, 1966; M.P.A., U. Mich., 1967, Ph.D. in Polit. Sci., 1971; m. Madeleine Fuchs, Aug. 31, 1969; children—Matthew, Benjamin. Asst. prof. govt. and public adminstrn. John Jay Coll. Criminal Justice, CUNY, 1971-74, asso. prof., 1975-79, prof., 1980—, founder, exec. dir. Nat. Center for Public Productivity, 1975—; founder, chmn. Internat. Productivity Network, 1986—; cons. internat. and fed. depts. agys., city, state and county agys.; dir. numerous funded projects in field; mem. Croton-Harmon Bd. Edn., 1984-87, pres. 1986-87. Mem. Am. Soc. Public Adminstrn. (chmn. nat. tng. com. 1981-82, 83-84, nat. council 1982-85; chairperson mgmt. sci. sect. 1981-82; pres. N.Y Met. chpt. 1978-79; 79-80; N.Y. Met. Outstanding Acad. award 1985); founder, co-chairperson Pub. Adminstrn. Teaching Roundtable, 1980—. Author: (with Arie Halachmi) Public Sector Productivity, editor: Productivity in Public Organizations, 1976; (with K. Morris and W. Ludwin) Literature in Bureaucracy; Readings in Administrative Fiction, 1979; (with Ellen D. Rosen) Current Cases in Public Administration, 1981; (with Stuart Nagel) Productivity and Public Policy, 1984; (with Arie Halachmi) Strategic Issues in Public Sector Productivity, 1986, The Bureaucrat, Pub. Adminstrn. Quar.; New Directions in Public Administration Research; founder, editor-in-chief Public Productivity Rev., 1975—; contbr. numerous chpts. to books, articles to profl. jours. Sr. Fellow Rockefeller Inst. Gov., 1986-87. Home: 4 Giglio Ct Croton-on-Hudson NY 10520 Office: 445 W 59th St New York NY 10019

HOLZER, WERNER, editor; b. Zweibruecken, Palatinate, Germany, Oct. 21, 1926; s. Robert and Barbara H.; m. Monika Aschke, 1962; children—Katharina, Philip. Editor, Frankfurter Rundschau, (Germany), 1973—. Decorated commendatore Italian Order Merit, Order of Merit 1st class Fed. Republic Germany; recipient European prize Cortina Ulisse, 1962, Theodor-Wolff prize, 1964, Nat. Journalism award, 1968. Mem. PEN. Author: Das nackte Antlitz Afrikas, 1961; 26mal Afrika, 1967; Vietnam oder die Freiheit zu sterben, 1968; Bei den Erben Ho Tschi Minhs, 1971; 20mal Europa, 1972. Home: 20 Am Zollstock, 638 Bad Homburg, Hesse Federal Republic Germany Office: 16-18 Gr Eschenheimer, D-6000 Frankfurt/Main Federal Republic of Germany

HOLZHEIMER, HERMANN, West German diplomat; b. Aschaffenburg, Ger., Oct. 23, 1928; s. Franz and Christine (Nahm) H.; m. Flora Kevorkian, Feb. 1, 1952. Student univ. Bamberg and Wü rzburg, Ger., 1947-51, U. Mich., 1952, U. Dijon, France, 1952. Joined West German Diplomatic Service, 1954; served in Brazil, India, Can., Iraq; ambassador to Chile, Santiago, 1983-86; dep. sec., gen. Western European Union, 1986— . Decorated Order of Merit (W.Ger.). Mem. Brazilian Acad. Fine Arts (hon.). Office: Western European Union, 9 Grosvenor Pl, London SW1X 7HL, England

HOLZMAN, ROBERT STUART, tax consultant; b. Paterson, N.J., Nov. 18, 1907; s. Samuel and Lillian (Hamburger) H.; m. Eleanore Grushlaw, May 27, 1938. B.S., U. Pa., 1929; A.M., N.Y. U., 1947, Ph.D., 1953. Tax cons., lectr. fin. NYU Grad. Sch. Bus. Adminstrn., 1946-53; prof. taxation NYU Sch. Adminstrn., 1953-73, dir. univ. budget, 1958-61; prof. acctg. U. Conn., 1973-74, 76-80; dir. Standard Security Life Ins. Co., N.Y. Author: Corporate Reorganizations: Their Federal Tax Status, 1948, Guide to Pension and Profit-sharing Plans, 1953, rev., 1969, Stormy Ben Butler, 1954, General Baseball Doubleday, 1955, The Romance of Fire Fighting, 1956, The Tax on Accumulated Earnings, 1956, Arm's Length Transactions, 1958, Sound Business Purpose, 1958, Federal Income Taxation, 1960, The Taxpayer's Problem of Proof, 1962, Tax Basis for Managerial Decisions, 1965, Tax-Free Reorganizations, 1967, Holzman on Estate Planning, 1967, Federal Taxation of Capital Assets, 1969, Tax Free Reorganizations After the Tax Reform Act of 1969, 1970, Dun & Bradstreet's Handbook of Executive Tax Management, 1974, Accountant's and Treasurer's Complete Guide to the Accumulated Earnings Tax, 1974, Take It Off!, 1984, Tax-Free Organizations After the Pension Reform Act of 1974, 1976, Adapt or Perish, 1976, New Tax Traps and New Opportunities, 1975, The Complete Book of Estate Planning, 1978, Landmark Tax Cases, 1979, Business Tax Traps, 1979, A Survival Kit for Taxpayers, 1979, Encyclopedia of Estate Planning, 1987, Estate Planning—The New Golden Opportunities, 1983, Complete Book of Tax Deductions, 1988; editor: Tax Practitioners Library, 15 vols, 1956-62; co-editor: Big Business Methods for the Small Business, 1952; contbg. editor: Boardroom Reports; editorial bd.: Taxation for Accountants; estate planning editor: Bottom Line Personal; contbr. articles to profl. publs. Past pres. Fed. Tax Forum, Civil War Round Table, N.Y.C. Mem. Am. Hist. Assn., Fin. Execs. Inst., Estate Planners Council N.Y.C., Beta Alpha Psi, Beta Gamma Sigma. Club: N.Y. Univ. Home: Carlyle Rd Candlewood Vista Danbury CT 06811 Office: PO Box 1013 Danbury CT 06813

HOLZWORTH, MONTA LAVERN, retired nuclear manufacturing executive; b. Barberton, Ohio, June 21, 1923; s. Monta Dean and Ruth Elizabeth (Wardell) H.; m. Frances Marie Fager, June 18, 1949; children—Donald Alan, Marie-Laverne, Peter Dale, Monta Raymond, Clara Frances. B.S., U. Notre Dame, 1947, M.S., 1949; Ph.D., Ohio State U., 1952. Metallurgist, Battelle Meml. Inst., 1948-50; research assoc. Ohio State U., 1950-52; research supr. Du Pont Corp., Aiken, S.C., 1952-62, staff metallurgist, 1962-78, sr. editor Savannah River plant, Aiken, S.C., 1978-86; instr. metallurgy U. S.C.-Aiken. Active Boy Scouts Am., 1955-85, unit commr., 1983-85. Served with USMC, 1943-45. Mem. Sigma Xi. Presbyterian. Lodge: Masons. Contbr. articles to profl. jours. Home: 816 Woodlawn Ave North Augusta SC 29841

HOM, STEPHEN, communications executive; b. San Francisco, Feb. 13, 1932; s. Joseph Heng and Anna (Wong Shee) Hom; m. Nellie Dolores Chew, Apr. 21, 1956; children: Christopher Shannon, Valeria Saint Elizabeth (Mrs. L. McDonald), Randolph Stevenson, Lawrence Sterling. B.S., U. San Francisco, 1980; B.A., U. Calif.-Berkeley, 1983; M.B.A., Calif. Coast U., 1984. Field engr. heavy mil. electronics div. Gen. Electric Co., Syracuse, N.Y., 1956-60; tech. dir. KRON-TV, NBC affiliate, Chronicle Broadcasting Co., San Francisco, 1960-80; del. 31st internat. conv. Internat. Brotherhood Elec. Workers Union, Atlantic City, 1978, mem. exec. bd., 1975-80, pres. Local 202, San Francisco, 1978-80; del. San Francisco Labor Council, 1978-80, Alameda Central Labor Council, Calif., 1978-80; ops. mgr. TV Broadcast Sta. KTSF, San Francisco, 1980; corp. dir. Lincoln TV, Inc., San Francisco, 1980-82; pres. Marshall Telecommunications, Inc., Oakland, Calif., 1982-83; mgmt. cons. KTSF, San Francisco, 1982-83; spl. cons. corporate pres. Radar Devices, Inc., San Leandro, Calif., 1982-83; tech., mgmt. cons. Maharlika Broadcasting System, Philippines, 1983-85; bus. cons. Shelter Metropolis, Inc., Philippines, 1983-85, Ministry Human Settlements, Devel. Communications Service Bur., Philippines, 1983-84; pres. Stevens Assocs., Cons., Oakland, Calif., 1983-85; Charlex Corp., USA, 1984-85; agt. Roblett Indsl. Constrn. Corp., Philippines, 1984-86; v.p. bus. devel. Roblett Constr. (USA) Ltd., Los Angeles, 1984-86; v.p. bus. devel. Engring. Traders Corp., Tokyo, 1986—; pres. The Pinnacle Group Contractors, Traders, Cons., Oakland, Calif., 1984—. Author: Managerial Supervision: A Systems Approach to Planning, Organizing and Coordinating, 1983; RF Pulse Analysis, 1983. Chmn. Oakland Civil Service Commn., Calif., 1984—. Mem. adv. com. Calif. State Welfare Dept. Social Services, Sacramento, 1986—. Served with Signal Corps, U.S. Army, 1953-55. Recipient Nat. Acad. TV Arts and Scis. award for engring. achievement, 1977-78; Dist. Leadership award, Subscription TV of Am., 1980-81; Maharlika Broadcasting System Meritorious award Philippine Ministry Pub. Info., 1983-84. Mem. Inst. Radio Engrs., Soc. Motion Picture and TV Engrs., Am. Rocket Soc., Nat. Acad. TV Arts and Scis., Assn. Cons. Mgmt. Engrs., Inst. Mgmt. Cons., Soc. Broadcast and Communications Engrs. Republican. Roman Catholic. Office: ENT Internat Inc 15800 Piazza Ave PO Box 949 Clackamas OR 97015

HOMAN, RALPH WILLIAM, finance company executive; b. Wilkes-Barre, Pa., June 7, 1951; s. Norman Ryan and Adelaide Bernice (Sandy) H.; m. Donna Marie Webb, Jan. 25, 1975. BS in Acctg., Wheeling Coll., 1977; MBA in Mktg., Nat. U., 1986. Paymaster-Dravo Corp., Pitts., 1974-75; tax preparer H&R Block, Wheeling, W.Va., 1977; fin. services exec. NCR Credit Corp., Sacramento, 1977-84; leasing exec. CSB Leasing, Sacramento, 1984-85; pres. Convergent Fin. Services, Sedona, Ariz., 1985—. Co-winner Name the Plane Contest Pacific Southwest Airlines, 1984. Republican. Episcopalian. Club: Toastmasters (treas. Oak Creek chpt. 1988—). Lodge: Kiwanis. Home and Office: Convergent Fin Services 210 Canyon Diablo Rd Sedona AZ 86336

HOMAN VAN DER HEIDE, JAN NICO, cardiac surgeon; b. Soebang, Indonesia, Dec. 25, 1926; s. Jacob and Lydia (Meihuizen) H.; m. Henriette Dinger, Feb. 2, 1952; children—Jaap, Jetske, Carey. M.D., U. Utrecht, 1953; Ph.D., State U. Groningen, 1961. Lectr. thoracic surgery State U. Groningen, 1963, prof. cardiac surgery, 1965—. Mem. Dutch Soc. Thoracic Surgery, Soc. Thoracic Surgeons of Gt. Britain, European Soc. Cardio Vascular Surgeons. Home: Goeman Borgesius Laan 17, Groningen 9722 RB, The Netherlands Office: Academic Hosp Faculty Medicine, State U Groningen, Dept Thoracic Surgery, Groningen The Netherlands

HOMBURGER, FREDDY, physician, scientist, artist; b. St. Gall, Switzerland, Feb. 8, 1916; came to U.S., 1941, naturalized, 1952; s. Ludwig and Cécile (Gaille) H.; m. Regina Thürlimann, Nov. 8, 1939. Student, U. Vienna, Austria, 1936-37; M.D., U. Geneva, Switzerland, 1941. Diplomate Nat. Bd. Med. Examiners., Am. Bd. Toxicology. Research fellow, intern pathology Yale Med. Sch. and New Haven Hosps., 1941-43; intern, research fellow in medicine Harvard Med. Sch., Thorndike Meml. Lab., Boston City Hosp., 1943-45; fellow in medicine Meml. Hosp., N.Y.C., 1946-48; chief clin. investigation Sloan-Kettering Inst. Cancer Research, N.Y.C., 1945-48; instr. medicine Cornell U. Med. Coll., 1946-48, research prof. medicine, 1948-57; dir. cancer research and control unit Tufts U. Sch. Medicine, Boston, 1948-57; mem. courtesy staff Mt. Desert Island Hosp., Bar Harbor, Maine, 1955-73, Eastern Meml. Hosp., Ellsworth, Maine, 1957-60; sci. assoc. Jackson Lab., Bar Harbor, 1951-60; research prof. oncology, div. basic scis. Sch. Grad. Dentistry, Boston U., 1973—; research prof. pathology Sch. Medicine, 1974—; mem. sci. staff Mallory Inst. Pathology, Boston City Hosp., 1979—; mem. Grad. Sch. Faculty Boston U., 1981—; Mem. corp. Gesell Inst. Child Devel., 1960-78; chmn. adv. com. Am. Students U. Geneva; pres., dir. Bio-Research Inst., Inc., 1957—, Bio-Research Cons., Inc., 1957—; pres. Trenton Exptl. Lab. Animal Co., Bar Harbor, 1969-81; treas., dir. Cambridge Coordinating Com. Drugs, 1972-74; hon. consul of Switzerland in Boston, 1964-86; neutral mem. mixed med. commn. War Dept., 1944-46. Author: The Medical Care of the Aged and Chronically Ill, 3d edit, 1973, The Biological Basis of Cancer Management, 1957; also numerous sci. papers.; Editor: The Physiopathology of Cancer, 3d edit, 1974-76, Progress in Experimental Tumor Research, vols. I-XXVII, 1960—; sr. editor: Symposia on Research Advances Applied to Medical Practice, Current Concepts in Toxicology; Exhibited paintings one-man shows, N.Y.C., Paris, Zurich, Geneva, Boston. Mem. overseers com. to visit Harvard U., 1965-71, 76—; bd. dirs. Cambridge Soc. Early Music, 1970—; trustee Opera Co., Boston, 1967-84; chmn. Friends Busch-Reisinger Mus., 1974-85; visitor paintings Boston Mus. Fine Arts, 1974—; mem. adv. bd. Lachaise Found.; bd. overseers Mt. Desert Island Biol. Lab., 1985—; bd. dirs. Copley Soc. Boston, 1986—, Longy Sch. Music, Cambridge; exec. sec. Friends of Switzerland, Boston, 1986—. Fellow AAAS, N.Y. Acad. Scis. (ednl. adv. com. 1967); mem. Nat. Hypertension Assn. (nat. adv. council 1978—), AMA, Endocrine Soc., Am. Assn. Cancer Research, Am. Fedn. Clin. Research, N.Y. Acad. Medicine, Soc. Exptl. Biology and Medicine, Am. Assn. Pathologists, Soc. Toxicology, Am. Soc. Pharmacology and Exptl. Therapeutics, Royal Soc. Health, Brit. Soc. Toxicology, Soc. Pharmacol. and Environ. Pathologists, Endocrine Soc., New Eng. Soc. Pathologists, Acad. Toxicological Scis., Cambridge C. of C. (dir. 1969-73), Sigma Xi. Clubs: Harvard (Boston); Yale (N.Y.C.); Cosmos (Washington). Home: 759 High St Dedham MA 02026 also: Trenton ME 04605 Office: 380 Green St Cambridge MA 02139

HOMEN, CARL-OLAF, insurance company executive; b. Helsinki, Finland, Mar. 24, 1936; s. Lars Herman and Arna (Thyra) (Strahlmann) H.; LL.B., U. Helsinki, 1959; postgrad. U. Del., 1959-60; m. Beat-Marie Wangel, Feb. 22, 1964; children—Carina, Bettina, Susanne, Christian. Legal sec., asst. chief internat. dept. Finnish Employers Confedn., 1960-64; legal adviser Employers Fedn. Woodworking Industries, 1964-66; lawyer, sec. bd. Oy Wilh. Schauman Ab, 1966-70, adminstrv. dir., 1970-74; sec. of state for def. Finland, 1974-75; mng. dir. Indsl. Mut. Ins. Co., Helsinki, 1975—; dir. Ins. Co. Fennia, Ins. Co. Otso, Ins. Co. Finnish Marine. Pres., Swedish People's Party, Esbo, 1974-77; pres. Nat. Union Finnish Students, 1965; sec. gen. Finnish Olympic Com., 1969-73, v.p., 1981-84, pres., 1985—; v.p. State Sports Council, 1975-76; pres. Finnish Amateur Athletic Assn., 1977-80; mem. council European Athletic Assn., 1980-87, pres. 1987—, council Internat. Amateur Athletic Fedn., 1987—. Author: Finnish-Swedish Labour Market Dictionary, 1966. Home: Forsbacka 02780, Esbo 78 Finland Office: Vattuniemenkuja 8A, 00210 Helsinki 21 Finland

HOMER, CHARLES ROSS, consumer products company executive; b. Toronto, Ont., Can., Apr. 23, 1945; s. William James and Enid Jean (Kirby) H.; m. Eva Linnea Norberg, Dec. 31, 1971; children: Per Charles, Sara Kristina, Nils William. B of Commerce, U. Toronto, 1967; MBA, Harvard U., 1969. Mktg. mgr. Lever Detergents, Ltd., Toronto, 1969-71; sr. brand mgr. Lever Bros., Ltd., London, 1972-74; mktg. mgr. Shopsy's Foods, Ltd., Toronto, 1974-81; gen. mgr. Shopsy's Food, Ltd., Toronto, 1982-84; v.p. mktg. and sales Unox, Inc., Toronto, 1984-86; v.p., gen. mgr. LePages, Ltd., Brampton, Can., 1987, pres., 1988—; bd. dirs. Can. Hardware Housewares Mfrs. Assn., Toronto, 1987—. Bd. dirs. Alfred Adler Inst. Ont., Toronto, 1981-85, Peel Family Edn. Council, Brampton, 1987. Clubs. Brampton Golf; Harvard Bus. Sch. (Toronto).

HOMER, TAMARA KUKRYCKA, advertising executive; b. Warsaw, Poland, Feb. 23, 1932; came to U.S., 1949, naturalized, 1953; d. Basil and Alexandra (Masiuk) Kukrycka; m. Edward John Homer, Sept. 6, 1954. B.A., Hunter Coll., 1954; postgrad. New Sch. for Social Sci., 1956-58. Pres. Sunwear, Inc., N.Y.C., 1964-66; exec. v.p. Allerton, Berman & Dean, N.Y.C., 1966-73; founder, pres. Homer & Durham Advt., Ltd., N.Y.C., 1973—. Author travel guides for European countries. Trustee New Eyes for the Needy, Short Hills, N.J., 1982—; bd. dirs. Nat. Assn. to Prevent Blindness, March of Dimes, N.Y.C., 1983—. Recipient Matrix award Women Execs. in Communication, 1983, Extraordinary Service to Nation's Tourism, Republic of Ireland, 1976, Leadership award March of Dimes, 1987; named to Hall of Fame, Hunter Coll., 1983. Mem. Advt. Women of N.Y. (bd. dirs.; pres. 1983-85), Women Execs. in Pub. Relations, Fashion Group, Am. Advt. Fedn. (com. chmn. 1985—). Republican. Ukrainian Orthodox. Avocations: painting; tennis; fresh water fishing. Home: 2 Joanna Way Short Hills NJ 07078 Office: Homer & Durham Advt Ltd 115 Fifth Ave New York NY 10003

HOMET, RAQUEL AMALIA, medieval history researcher, educator; b. Firmat, Argentina, Oct. 21, 1940; d. Esteban and Pilar (Florensa) H. PhD, U. Buenos Aires, 1982. Prof. ancient history Inst. Nat. del Profesorado, Azul, Argentina, 1966-76; prof. modern history U. Nat. de Rosario, Buenos Aires, 1976-82; prof. medieval history U. Catolica Argentina, Rosario, 1979-82; adj. researcher Consejo Nat. de Investigaciones Cientificas y Technicas, Buenos Aires, 1982—; asst. prof. Spanish history U. Buenos Aires, 1971-74, adj. prof. medieval history, 1976—. Author: Un Senorio Bajomedieval, 1985; selector sources La Educacion Medieval, 1979; contbr. articles to profl. jours. Mem. Assn. of Univ. Profs. of European History (treas. 1985—), Ctr. European de Recherches sur les Congregations et Ordres Religieux, Coll. Grads. of Philosophy and Letters. Home: Alsina 2520, 2DO A Buenos Aires 1090, Argentina

HOMEYER, FRED CARL, banker; b. Austin, Tex., Apr. 7, 1920; s. Fred C. and Mamie (Wilke) H.; B.S., A. and M. Coll. Tex., 1942; postgrad. Savs. and Loan Grad Sch., 1963; m. Betty Sue Tumey, Apr. 3, 1942; children—Fred Charles, William Polk, Janice Sue. Adjuster, asst. office mgr. Comml. Credit Corp., 1946-48; sec. asst. Austin Savs. & Loan Assn., 1948-55; pres. Home Savs. Assn., Odessa, Tex., 1955-66, Northport Fed. Savs. & Loan Assn. L.I., N.Y., 1966-69; sr. v.p. First City Nat. Bank, Houston, 1969-82; pres. First City Nat. Bank of Northline, Houston, 1982-84, chmn. bd., 1984-86; pres., chmn. bd. Petroplex Savings Assn., Midland, 1986—. Pres. Odessa Day Nursery Bd., 1959; dir. Odessa Community Chest and United Fund, campaign chmn., 3d v.p., 1959; pres. Go-Dessa orgn., 1959-60; chmn. Black Gold dist. Boy Scouts Am., 1959, mem. exec. com. Buffalo Trail council, 1959-60, recipient Silver Beaver award. Served to maj. AUS, 1942-46; lt. col. Res. Mem. Odessa C. of C. (past dir.), Am. Savs. and Loan Inst. (instr.), Odessa Real Estate Bd., Home Builders Assn., Permian Hist. Soc. (dir.), Soc. Residential Appraisers, U.S. (com. supervision and exams., legis. com.), Nat. (Tex. gov. 1963-65, mem. legis. com.), Tex. (past dir., chmn. edn. com., chmn. by-laws com., mem. league services com., exec. com.) savs. and loan leagues, Chuck Wagon Gang. Presbyterian (deacon). Club: Rotary (pres. Odessa 1962-63). Home: PO Box 61373 Houston TX 77208 Office: PO Box 16340 Houston TX 77022

HOMOLA, DUSAN, cardiologist, researcher; b. Brno, Czechoslovakia, Oct. 16, 1925; s. Antonin and Stanislava (Nowak) H. MD, J.E. Purkynje U., Brno, 1950, DSc, 1956. Intern, asst. J.E. Purkynje U., 1950-55, physician faculty hosp., 1950-55, cardiologist researcher 3d Internal Clinic, asst. prof. cardiology, 1955—. Author: The Mechanism of the WPW Syndrome, 1967; contbr. over 100 articles to med. jours. Mem. Czechoslovakian Cardiol. Soc., Czechoslovakian Biol. Soc., J.E. Purkynje Soc. Home: Botanicka 5,

602 00 Brno Czechoslovakia Office: IIId Internal Clinic, Faculty Hosp, Pekarska 53, 65691 Brno Czechoslovakia

HOMS QUIROGA, JORGE, manufacturing executive; b. Veracruz, Mexico, Aug. 21, 1957; s. Ricardo Homs Mir and Elizabeth Quiroga Molloy; m. Delfina Lopez Vives De Homs, Sept. 5, 1987. Degree in mech. engring., Instituto Tecnologico y de Estudios Superiores de Monterrey, Monterrey, Mex., 1979; postgrad., U. Colo., 1980; M in Indsl. Engring., Cranfield Inst. Tech., Bedford, Eng., 1982. Cons. HMC Brauer LTD, Bedford, 1981-82; mgr. prodn. Tubos de Acero de Mex. S.A., Veracruz, 1983-84; exec. HOMSA, Veracruz, 1984—; cons. Broker Agy. R.H., Veracruz, 1983-87. Mex. Council Sci. and Tech. scholar, 1980. Mem. Regional Ctr. Mex. Employers (bd. dirs. 1986), Orgn. Ex-students of Technol. Inst. Hight Studies Monterrey. Club: Spanish. Home: Pizarro 78, 91910 Veracruz Mexico

HONDA, KIN-YA, mathematics educator; b. Nagasaki, Kyushu, Japan, Mar. 31, 1924; s. Eisaku and Hanako (Sakai) H.; m. Masami Funo, Apr. 10, 1955; 1 child, Michiya. BS, Tokyo U., 1947, DSc, 1958. Lectr. math. St. Paul's U., Tokyo, 1949-52, asst. prof., 1952-61, prof., 1961—; chmn. math. dept. St. Paul's U., Tokyo, 1968-75; chief grad. sch. St. Paul's U., Tokyo, 1976-79. Author: Abelian Groups, 1969, Centennial History of Japanese Mathematics, 1984. Mem. Math. Soc. Japan, Am. Math. Soc. Buddhist. Home: Sakuradai 2-22-19, Nerima-ku, Tokyo 176, Japan Office: St Paul's U, Nishi-Ikebukuro 3-34-1, Tokyo 171, Japan

HONE, JOSEPH, broadcasting professional; b. London, Feb. 25, 1937; s. Nathaniel and Bridget (Anthony) H.; m. Jacqueline Yeend, Mar. 5, 1964; children: Lucy, William. Grad. high sch., London, 1954. Radio producer BBC, 1963-66; staff office pub. info., radio and TV producer UN Secratariat, N.Y.C., 1967-68; novelist, broadcasting official BBC, 1968—. Author: Flowers of Forest, 1978, Africa of the Heart, 1985. Club: Upton House Cricket (Banbury, Eng.). Address: c/o Deborah Rogers, 49 Blenheim Crescent, London W11, England

HONECKER, ERICH, government official; b. Neunkirchen, Saarland, Aug. 25, 1912; s. Wilhelm H.; m. Edith Baumann, 1947 (div.); 1 dau.; m. Margot Feist, 1953; 1 dau. Mem. Communist Party of Germany, 1929-46, youth sec. central com., 1945, mem. central com., 1946; imprisoned for anti-fascist activity, 1935-45; mem. mng. com. Socialist Unity Party, 1946—; mem. Volkskammer, 1949—; kandidat politburo, central com. Socialist Unity Party, 1950-58, Mitglied, 1958—, 1st sec. central com., 1971-76, gen. sec., 1976—; mem. State Council, 1971—, chmn., 1976—; sec. Nat. Def. Council, 1960-71, chmn., 1971—. Author: From My Life, 1981. Decorated Karl Marx Order, German Democratic Republic, Order of Merit Fatherland in Gold, medal Antifascist Resistance, Held der Sowjet-Union Order of Lenin (USSR). Office: Sozialistische Einheitspartei, Am Marx-Engles Platz 2, 102 Berlin German Democratic Republic

HONEYMAN, LOUISE MARY, orchestra administrator; b. Shrewsbury, Salop, Eng., Feb. 23, 1933; d. George Edward and Mary Eleanor (Crowe) Huffa; student Brit. schs.; divorced; children—Karen Philippa, Andrea Louise, Iain Peter. Orch. mgr. London Mozart Players, 1966-73, now gen. adminstr. Elected mem. exec. com. Greater London Arts; mgr. English Bach Festival Orch., English Symphony Orch. and Ensemble; rep. Assn. of Brit. Orchs. on Nat. Campaign for the Arts. Address: 12 Tiverton Rd, London NW10 3HL England

HONG, GEON HEE, hotel executive; b. Kangwon-Do, Korea, Nov. 3, 1946; s. Chung-Sik Hong and Chung-Hwa Lee; m. Yeon-Soon Bang; children: KeyJo, OakJo. BA, Kyung Gi U., Seoul, 1979; MS, Kyung Hee U., Seoul, 1982. Cert. hotel mgr. Sales mgr. Hotel Lotte, Seoul, 1975-82; mktg. mgr. Seoul Plaza Hotel, 1982-87, tng. dir., 1987—. Contbr. articles to jours. in field. Mem. Korea Tourist Hotel Mgmt. Club. Office: Seoul Plaza Hotel, 23 S-KA Taipyung-Ro Chung-Ku, Seoul Korea

HONG, JOHN JOONPYO, physician; b. Seoul, Republic of Korea, Aug. 27, 1938; Came to U.S., 1968; s. Myung Kil and Kil Sang (Song) H.; m. Judith Kyuwon Lee, May 12, 1965; children: Richard, Rosamond, Raymond. Grad. premedical sch., Seoul Nat. U., 1960, MD, 1964, M in Med. Sci., 1966, postgrad., 1967. Diplomate Am. Bd. Abdominal Surgery. Intern The Victoria Gen. Hosp., Halifax, N.S., Can., 1967-68; resident in surgery Aultman Hosp., Canton, Ohio, 1968-69, Fairview Gen. Hosp., Cleve., 1969-72; mem. med. staff Deaconess Hosp. of Cleve., 1974-86; owner, operator Brook Park (Ohio) Med. Clinic, 1980—; mem. med. staff S.W. Gen. Hosp., Middleburg Heights, Ohio, 1976-86. Fellow Am. Soc. Abdominal Surgeons, Internat. Coll. Surgeons; mem. Acad. Medicine of Cleve., Ohio State Med. Assn., Korean Assn. Greater Cleve. (pres. 1979), Brook Park C. of C. Home: 2684 Goldwood Dr Rocky River OH 44116 Office: Brook Park Med Clinic 15400 Snow Rd Brook Park OH 44142

HONG, YUN-LIN, cardiologist, educator; b. Shanghai, China, Apr. 24, 1931; s. Chun-Zhi and Yun-Xian (Cheng) H.; m. Tu Gui-Yi, Apr. 24, 1955; 1 child, Tu Jun. MD, Med. Coll. Shanghai, 1955. Resident physician 1st Teaching Hosp., Beijing Med. Coll., 1955-60, vis. physician, lectr., 1960-79, assoc. prof., 1980-83; assoc. prof., dep. head dept. fgn. patients Peking Union Med. Coll., Acad. Med. Scis., Beijing, 1983-84, head dept., 1985—; cons. physician Cancer Hosp., Cancer Inst., 1986—. Author numerous publications on heart diseases; translator: UICC Classification of Tumor, 1983. Vis. scholar Australia-China Council, Sydney, 1981. Mem. Chinese Heart Assn., Chinese Physician Assn., Chinese Assn. Scis. and Tech., St. Johns' Alumni Assn., European-Am. Alumni Assn. Home: PO Box 2258, Beijing Peoples Republic of China Office: PUMC Hosp, Beijing 100730, Peoples Republic of China

HONIG, MERVIN, artist, art conservator; b. N.Y.C., Dec. 25, 1920; s. Joseph and Frances (Flaum) H.; m. Rhoda Sherbell, Apr. 28, 1956; 1 dau., Susan. Student with, Francis Criss, Amadee Ozenfant, Hans Hofmann; B.A., Bklyn. Coll., 1973; postgrad., Hofstra U., 1974—. Apprentice Bklyn. Mus., 1956-58, Keck Studio, 1956-58; asst. Mus. Modern Art, 1958; lectr. conservation of paintings Hofstra U., 1972—, Channel 21, L.I., N.Y., 1976-77; mem. faculty New Sch., 1975—. Exhibited one-man shows at: Kingsworthy Art Gallery, N.Y.C., 1961, County Art Gallery, Westbury, N.Y., 1963-65, Grace Gallery, N.Y.C., Community Coll., 1968, Westbury Meml. Pub. Library, 1969, Frank Rehn Gallery, N.Y.C., 1970, Nassau Community Coll., 1971, New Sch. Assocs., N.Y.C., 1978, Bergen Mus. Art and Sci., Paramus, N.J., 1984, Bronx Mus. Arts, 1986, retrospective exhbn., Nat. Art Mus. of Sport, N.Y.C., 1977-78, William Benton Mus. Art, Storrs, Conn., 1985; exhibited in group shows at: Met. Mus. Art, 1944, Carnegie Inst., 1945, Los Angeles County Mus., 1945, Wm. Rockhil Nelson Gallery, Kansas City, 1945, Whitney Mus. Artists Ann., 1949, Bklyn. Mus., 1960, Nat. Acad. Galleries, 1963, 77, 78, 79, 80, 81, 82, 83, Wadsworth Atheneum, Conn. Acad. Fine Arts, 1965-66, Soc. 4 Arts, 1965, Jersey City Mus. Ann. Exhbn., 1966, Locust Valley Art Show, 1966 (1st prize), Am. Vets. Soc., 1966 (Meml. Gold medal), Purdue U., 1966, Butler Inst. Am. Art, Youngstown, Ohio, 1967, 69, Nat. Art Mus. Sport, N.Y.C., 1968, 69, Audubon Artists Ann., 1968-85, Spectrum Gallery, N.Y.C., 1977, Queens Mus., 1978, Port Washington Library, 1978, L.I. Artists, 1978, Allied Artists Am., 1978-85, C.W. Post Art Gallery, 1981, The Eye on Sport, CUNY, N.Y.C., 1983, Islip Art Mus., 1983, Pensacola (Fla.) Mus. Art, 1982, Owenboro (Ky.) Mus. Fine Art, 1982, Phila. Coll. Art, 1984, Guild Hall Mus., East Hampton, N.Y., 1986, Castle Gallery Coll. New Rochelle, N.Y., 1987, Nat. Acad. Ann. Exhibition, N.Y.C., 1987; represented in permanent collections: Okla. Mus. Art, Oklahoma City, Colby Coll. Art Mus., Met. Mus. Art, N.Y.C., Okla. Mus. Art, Emily Lowe Gallery/Hofstra Mus.-Hofstra U., Colby Coll. Art Mus., Met. Mus. Art, Nassau County Mus., Siena Hts. Coll., William Benton Mus. Art, NAD, N.Y.C., also pvt. collections: Author papers on art conservation. Bd. advisors Nassau County Mus., 1978; trustee Nat. Art Mus. Sport, 1978. Recipient Bronze medal, hon. mention Am. Vets. Soc. Artists, 1968, also Gold medal; award of excellence Mainstream '70; award of excellence Grover M. Hermann Arts Center, 1970; prize Knickerbocker Artists, 1978; Samuel Morton Meml. award Audubon Artists, 1983; others. Mem. Internat. Inst. Conservation Historic and Artistic Works, Coll. Art Assn. Am., Audubon Artists N.Y. (corr. sec. N.Y.C. 1977), Nat. Acad. (assoc.), L.I. Hist. Soc., Allied Artists Am. (dir. oil), (v.p. 1980-83), Nassau Council Contemporary Art (sec. 1973-74), Nassau County Mus. Fine Art (adv. bd. 1979—). Address: 64 Jane Ct Westbury NY 11590

HOO, JOE JIE, geneticist, pediatrician; b. Malang, Java, Indonesia, July 7, 1944; s. Heng-Seng and Roe-Ing (Oei) H.; M.D., Philipps U., Marburg, W. Ger., 1972; m. Lanlan Koo, Jan. 12, 1973. Sci. asst. U. Inst. Human Genetics, Marburg, Hamburg, W. Ger., 1973-75; pediatric resident Mercy Hosp., Buffalo, 1975-78; Med. Research Council fellow, Auckland, N.Z., 1978-79; sr. research assoc. U. Inst. Human Genetics, Hamburg, 1979-81; med. geneticist U. Inst. Human Genetics, Giessen, W.Ger., 1981-82; asst., then assoc. prof. U. Calgary, Alta., Can., 1982-85; assoc. prof. U. Ill.-Chgo., 1985—. Volkswagenswerk Found. grantee, 1979-81; Alta. Heritage Found. for Med. Research grantee, 1983-85. Mem. Am. Soc. Human Genetics, Am. Acad. Pediatrics, Internat. Soc. Twin Studies, European Soc. Human Genetics, Internat. Soc. Twin Studies. Office: U Ill Dept Pediatrics 840 S Wood St Chicago IL 60612

HOOD, DOROTHY, artist; b. Bryan, Tex., Aug. 22, 1919; d. Frank and Earl and Georgianna B. (Simpkins) H.; B.A., R.I. Sch. Design, 1940; student Art Students League N.Y., 1940. Tchr., Houston Mus. Sch. Mus. Fine Art, 1961-79, part-time, 1979—; artist-in-residence across U.S., 1974—; one-man exhibits: McNay Art Inst., San Antonio, 1978, Phila. Art Alliance, 1961, Witte Meml. Mus., San Antonio, 1965, Contemporary Arts Mus., Houston, 1970, Rice U., Houston, 1971, Everson Mus., Syracuse, N.Y., 1972, 74, 76, Mus. Fine Arts, Houston, 1961, 74, N.Y. State U., Art Mus. South Tex., Tibor de Nagy Gallery, N.Y.C., 1974, Internat. Kunstmesse, Basel, Switzerland, 1974, Michener Galleries, U. Tex., Austin, 1975, Meredith Long Contemporaries, N.Y.C., 1978, 80, 82; group shows include: Am. Acad. Arts and Letters, N.Y.C., 1975, Kunsthalle, Dusseldorf, W. Ger., McNay Art Inst., 1976, Meredith Long Contemporaries, N.Y.C., Everson Mus., 1976, Vice Presdl. Mansion, Washington, 1978-79, Tamarind Inst., Albuquerque, 1979, "The Comet Show" Light Gallery, N.Y., 1985, "Am. Women in Art: Works on Paper" U.N. Conf. on Women, Nairobi, Kenya, 1985, Mus. Fine Arts, Houston, 1985, Wallace Wentworth Gallery, Washington, 1986-88, Images on Stone: Two Centuries of Artists Lithographs U. Houston Blaffer Gallery, 1987; setting for ballet Allen's Landing, Bicentennial Celebration Houston Ballet, 1975, settings for Toronto Truck Theater's Gold for the Golds celebration, Royal Ont. Mus., 1976; retrospective U. Houston, 1979, Stavanger and Oslo (Norway) Mus., 1982; New Work from a New City, 1983-84; represented in permanent collections: Mus. Modern Art, N.Y.C., Phila. Mus. Art, San Francisco Mus. Modern Art, Santa Barbara (Calif.) Mus. Art, Whitney Mus. Am. Art, N.Y.C., Worcester (Mass.) Art Mus., LaJolla (Calif.) Mus., Salzburg Kuntsverein, Galerie an der Stadmauer, Villach, Austria, Palazzio Lichenstein, Vienna, State Galerie, Lintz, Austria, Am. House, Berlin, Frankfurt Mus. other instnl. collections in Switzerland, Mexico City, U.S. Recipient Childe Hassam award Am. Acad. Arts and Letters, 1973, Outstanding Achievement in the Visual Arts Nat. award Women's Caucus for Art, 1988; subject of documentary films, 1981, 85; Mayor's award for contbn. to visual arts, Houston, 1983.

HOOD, LESLIE LYNN, publishing executive; b. Indpls., June 24, 1948; s. John Marquis and Gloria (Bennett) H.; m. Jean Marie Rawlings, Dec. 12, 1969; children—Derek, Heath, Brecka, Shamene. B.S., Mo. Valley Coll., 1970. Student personnel adminstr. Mo. Valley Coll., Marshall, 1969-71; ministerial degree Berear Coll., 1985. Ordained to ministry, 1985. Dist. dir. Crossroads of Am. council Boy Scouts Am., Indpls., 1971-74, fin. dir. Dan Beard council, Cin., 1974-83; v.p. Lay Leadership Internat., Christian lit. pub. co., Fairfield, Ohio, 1983—; pres. C.C.S. Cons., Cin., 1980—; bd. dirs. Santa Marie Neighborhood, Cin., 1976-80, H.I.P. Inc., Cin., 1977-79. Author: Financing Local Institutions, 1981; Baptist Church in Scouting, 1983. Named Eagle Scout, 1965. Kansas City Council Higher Edn., 1969. Mem. Nat. Assn. Ch. Adminstrs. (pres. 1987—), Nat. Soc. Fund Raising Execs. (cert.; Honors scholar 1983; mem. exec. bd. 1980—), Cin. Soc. Fund Raisers, Advt. Council. Republican. Mem. Assemblies of God. Clubs: Hamilton (Ohio); Kiwanis (Cin.). Lodge: Elks. Avocations: hiking; camping; canoeing. Home: 5841 Gilmore Dr Fairfield OH 45014 Office: Lay Leadership Internat 1267 Hicks Blvd Fairfield OH 45014

HOOD, THOMAS RICHARD, artist, graphic designer, educator; b. Phila., July 13, 1910; s. Thomas Richard and Anne Lovering (Grubb) H. Student, U. Pa., 1929-30; B.F.A. in Advt. Design, Phila. Mus. Coll. Art, 1953. Prof., design coordinator, exhbn. dir. Phila. Coll. Art; dir. Pa. Art Program, 1940-42, Pa. War Services Program, 1943. Exhibited nationally, 1936—; represented in permanent collections, Phila. Mus., Carnegie Library, Phila. Public Library, N.Y. Public Library, Library of Congress, Phila. Mus. Natural History, Mus. Modern Art, N.Y.C., Bryn Mawr Coll., Yale U., Nat. Portrait Gallery, Smithsonian Instn., also pvt. collections. Served with AUS, 1943-45. Recipient over 60 awards, including Phila. Print Club, 1937, 48, over 60 awards, including Western Pa. Prints, 1940, Soldier Art, 1945, 1st prize Times Herald Exhbn., Washington, 1945, Franklin medal, 1959 (2), 69, 70, award Del. Valley Graphic Arts, 1971, Silver and Bronze medals Art Dirs. Gold medal, 1966, 69, 73, Silver medal, 1971, 73, Neographics Gold, Silver and Bronze medals, 1973, Nat. Graphic Arts Design award U.S. and Can., 1968, (2) 70, Disting. Design award Phila. Coll. Art, 1971, Andy award of Merit, 1973, Neographics Gold Medal, 1976; named to Wisdom Hall of Fame in Edn., 1975. Fellow Internat. Inst. Arts and Letters (life); mem. Am. Color Print Soc. (pres. 1956), Artist Decoys, The Authors, Phila. Art Alliance (chmn. print com. 1977-81), Mus. Modern Art, Phila. Print Club. Club: Peale. Home: 1452 E Cheltenham Ave Philadelphia PA 19124 Office: Phila Coll Art Broad and Spruce Sts Philadelphia PA 19102

HOODENPYLE, RICHARD LEE, peridontist; b. Gainesville, Ga., Aug. 16, 1946; s. Hugh Charles and Colleen (Hughes) H.; m. Miriam Dianne Pinnell, June 7, 1970; children—Leigh Anne, Lauren Emily. B.A., Emory U., 1969; D.M.D., Med. Coll. Ga., 1973; cert. in periodontics, Columbia U., 1975. Staff Luth. Med. Ctr. Dental Clinic, Bklyn., 1973-75, staff periodontist, 1975-76; pvt. practice, Nyack and White Plains, N.Y., 1975-76, High Point, N.C., 1976—; med. staff dental sect. High Point Meml. Hosp., 1977-83, chief dental sect., 1979-82, med. staff exec. com., 1979-82, mem. profl. quality assurance com., 1982-83; clin. instr. periodontics Columbia U., 1975-76; clin. asst. prof. Sch. Dentistry, U. N.C., Chapel Hill, 1980-81, 81-82, 82-83; guest lectr. periodontics Guilford Tech. Inst., Jamestown, N.C., 1977-81. Contbr. articles to profl. jours. Mem. adminstrv. bd. Wesley Meml. United Methodist Ch., High Point, 1979-82 and various coms.; mem. N.C. Urban Transp. Policy Task Force; bd. dirs. High Point Rescue Squad, 1979-81, chmn. bd. dirs., 1980-81; mem. nominating com. High Point Mental Health Assn., 1985; chmn. dental adv. com. Guilford Tech. Inst., 1980-81, member com. 1979-83; chmn. Area Health Edn. Com., 1980-83; mem. Council on Missions, 1980-83, Early Childhood Com., 1979-82, Wesley Meml United Meth. Ch. Mem. ADA, N.C. Dental Soc. (legis. com. 3d dist. 1981-83), High Point Dental Soc. (pres. 1979-80, exec. com. 1980-81, children's dental health com. 1977-81), Guilford County Dental Soc., Assn. Piedmont Periodontists, Am. Acad. Periodontology, N.C. Soc. Periodontists (pub. relations com. 1979-83), So. Acad. Periodontology (Pub. relations com. 1981-84), Northeastern Soc. Periodontists, Am. Acad. Implant Dentistry (supporting), Internat. Coll. Implantologists, Am. Coll. Implantology, Am. Acad. Implant Prosthodontics, High Point Dental Soc. (children's dental health com. 1977-81), Alpha Oral Implant Study Group (pres. 1987-88), High Point C. of C. (bd. dirs. 1983-86, chmn. transp. com. 1983-85 and numerous other coms.). Democrat. Methodist. Avocations: travel; tennis; family, basketball. Home: 802 Kingston Ct High Point NC 27260 Office: 100 Westwood Ave High Point NC 27262

HOOG, MARJORIE, architect; b. Paris, Feb. 28, 1947; came to U.S., 1951; d. Armand and Marie Jacques (Debrix) H.; m. John L. Young, Nov. 2, 1974 (div. 1984); stepchildren—Marcolm, Lila, Anina, Dara; 1 child, Madeleine Hoog-Crellin. B.A., NYU, 1969; student Cooper Union, N.Y.C., 1966-68; M.Arch., Harvard Grad. Sch. Design, 1972. Registered architect, N.Y. Designer, Ulrich Franzen & Assoc., N.Y.C., 1971-73; architect Urban Deadline Architects, N.Y.C., 1974-76; prin. Marjorie Hoog Architect, N.Y.C., 1976-81; assoc. Prentice & Chan, Ohlhausen, N.Y.C., 1981-86; propr. Marjorie Hoog Architect, 1986-87; assoc. Herbert Beckhard-Frank Richlan & Assocs., N.Y.C., 1987—. co-founder Archive Women in Architecture, N.Y.C., 1974; coordinator Women's Sch. Planning and Architecture, Bristol, R.I., summer 1978; vis. asst. prof. Pratt Inst., N.Y.C., fall 1983; guest lectr., panelist in field. Appeared in show Firing the Imagination, Urban Ctr., N.Y.C. and Bennington (Vt.) Coll., 1988. Named co-leader del. Archtl. Soc. China, 1977, 80. Mem. Alliance Women in Architecture (co-founder), China Study Group on Environ. Issues (co-founder), Archtl. League, AIA, NOW. Home: 172 E 4th St New York NY 10009 Office: Herbert Beckhard-Frank Richlan and Assocs 333 Seventh Ave New York NY 10001

HOOGERHUIS, RUDOLF PIETER, manufacturing equipment import executive; b. Amsterdam, The Netherlands, Jan. 11, 1943; s. Pieter and Anna (Gabriël) H.; m. Ina Veldman, Nov. 2, 1967; 1 child, Bastiaan Rudolf Pieter. Grad., Hendrick de Keyser coll. Middelbaar Tech. Sch., Amsterdam, 1963; diploma, Inst. Social Studies Coll. for Mktg. Mgmt., Amsterdam, 1974. Tech. translator Lindeteves Jacoberg, Amsterdam, 1965-66; claim specialist Koopman and Co., Amsterdam, 1966-68; rayon mgr. Zwaans b.v., Sittand, 1968-73; dir. sales Vorklift b.v., Amsterdam, 1973-75; mgr. Louis Reyners b.v., Amsterdam and Purmerend, The Netherlands, 1975—. Served as sgt. The Netherlands Air Force, 1963-65. Club: Law and Tennis de Rijp (chmn. 1977-84). Home: Julianalaan 60, 1483 VM De Rijp The Netherlands Office: Louis Reyners BV, Neckerstraat 79-91, 1441 KV Purmerend The Netherlands

HOOGLANDT, JAN DANIEL, steel company executive; b. Tangiers, Morocco, Feb. 15, 1926; Dr.Econs., U. Amsterdam, 1953; 4 children. With Hoogovens, 1954—, sec. to mng. dir., asst. mgr., 1963, adminstrv. mgr., 1968, mng. dir., 1970; chmn. bd. mng. dirs. Hoogovens Groep BV, Beverwijk, Netherlands, 1972—; vice-chmn. Internat. Iron and Steel Inst.; v.p. Eurofer; dir. Algemene Bank Nederland and Westland/Utrecht HypotheekbankNV, Heineken NV, Nederlandse Participatie Maatschappij NV. Decorated Knight of the Order of the Dutch Lion. Office: Hoogovens Groep BV, PO Box 10.000, 1970 CA Ijmuiden The Netherlands

HOOGSTEDEN, ALOYSIUS FRANCISCUS, manufacturing company executive; b. Rotterdam, The Netherlands, May 12, 1936; s. Fredericus Josephus and Cornelia Maria Christi (Baereveldt) H.; m. Johanna Cornelia Henrica Floris; children: Aloysius Franciscus Jr., Maurice Danielle Frederique. BA, Rotterdam High Sch. Jr. clk. Shipping & Forwarding Co., Rotterdam, 1952-62; mgr. various shipping lines, trading houses, Rotterdam, 1962-74; dir. Freight Forwarding Group, Rotterdam, 1974-80; pres. Intern. Freight Specialists B.V., Gravenzande, Netherlands, 1980-87, A.F. Hoogsteden Holding B.V., Gravenzande, 1980-87, Globe Trading B.V., Gravenzande, 1982-87; pres. Globe Oilfield Services, Gravenzande, 1985-87, dir., 1985-87; dir. Anembo Trading and Forwarding Inc., Latham, N.Y., 1980-87, Hoco Mfg. Co., Ltd., Sunninghill, Eng., 1984-87, Hoco Shipping Co. Ltd., Sunninghill, 1984-87. Home: Frejo Parallelweg 27, 's-Gravenzande 2691 JM, The Netherlands Office: AF Hoogsteden Holding BV, PO Box 58, 's-Gravanzande 2690 AB, The Netherlands

HOOKSTRATTEN, EDWARD GREGORY, lawyer; b. Whittier, Calif., June 12, 1932; s. E.G. and Winona (Hewitt) H.; children: Jon Crowley, Ann. B.S., U. So. Calif., 1953; J.D., Southwestern U., Los Angeles, 1957; LL.D., Southwestern U., 1984. Bar: Calif. 1958, U.S. Supreme Ct. 1974. Individual practice law Beverly Hills, Calif., 1960—; pres. Broadcast Artists, Ltd.; dir. Nat. Athletic Health Inst., Los Angeles Rams Football Co., 1973-79; mem. Dist. Attys. Adv. Council. Commr. bd. adminstrn. Los Angeles Retirement System, 1970-71; commr. Los Angeles Dept. Pub. Utilities and Transp., 1971-73, v.p., 1973; commr. Los Angeles Dept. Recreation and Parks, 1973-75, v.p., 1974; commr. State of Calif. Motion Picture Council, 1979—; bd. dirs., life mem. U. So. Calif. Assocs.; bd. dirs. Los Angeles Police Meml. Found.; trustee Southwestern U., 1984—. Mem. Los Angeles County Bar Assn., Beverly Hills Bar Assn. Clubs: Bel Air Country, Bohemian (San Francisco), Beverly Hills Tennis (pres. 1988—). Office: 9489 Dayton Way Beverly Hills CA 90210

HOOPER, EDITH FERRY, museum trustee; b. Detroit, Nov. 30, 1909; d. Dexter Mason and Jeannette (Hawkins) Ferry; m. Arthur Upshur Hooper, June 22, 1945; children—Jeannette Williams, Kate Gorman, Queene Ferry. B.A., Vassar U. Indsl. design dept. asst. Mus. Modern Art, N.Y.C., 1939-40; clk. U.S. Procurement Office, Detroit, 1941-43; asst. Roeper City and Country Schs., Detroit, 1944; trustee Balt. Mus. Art., 1957—, pres. bd., 1973-75, accessions com., 1977—. Bd. dirs. Friends Art Gallery, Vassar Coll., Poughkeepsie, N.Y., 1974-76; pres. bd. trustees Bryn Mawr Sch., Balt., 1965-71, chmn. bldg. com., 1971-73; pres. DM Ferry Jr. Trustee Corp. (found.), Balt., 1973. Presbyterian. Clubs: Cosmopolitan (N.Y.C.), Hamilton St. (Balt.). Home: 1100 Copper Hill Rd Baltimore MD 21209

HOOPER, JAMES MURRAY, service association executive; b. Waco, Tex., Jan. 4, 1928; s. Murray Robertson and Ersey (Cawthon) H.; m. Lorraine Marian Voehl, Mar. 9, 1967; children—William David, John Charles, Walter Brooks, Paul Ryan. B.Arch., Tex. Tech U., 1953. Vol., staff positions Peace Corps, Bolivia, Guatemala, Colombia, 1962-69; dir. Brazil, Rio de Janeiro, 1969-71; owner N.Mex. Office Supply Co., Santa Fe, 1971-72; adminstrv. officer Ohio Dept. Fin., Columbus, 1972-76; exec. dir. Sertoma Internat., exec. v.p. Sertoma Found., Kansas City, Mo., 1976—. Served with USN, 1946-48. Mem. Am. Soc. Assn. Execs., Mid Am. Soc. Assn. Execs. Club: Sertoma (Kansas City, Mo.). Office: Sertoma Internat 1912 E Meyer Blvd Kansas City MO 64132

HOOPER, JERE MANN, hotel executive; b. Brownsville, Tenn., July 6, 1933; s. Carmon Thomas and Annie (Mann) H.; B.A., Vanderbilt U., 1955; m. Alice Anne Caldwell, Feb. 5, 1966; 1 dau., Emily. Exec. trainee Irving Trust Co., N.Y.C., 1958-61; asst. v.p. franchise Holiday Inns, Inc., Memphis, 1961-66; v.p. Chatmar, Inc., San Francisco, 1967-72; sr. v.p. franchise Forte Hotels Internat., Inc., El Cajon, Calif., 1972—, also mem. exec. mgmt. group and coordinating council. Served with AUS, 1955-57. Mem. Am. Hotel and Motel Assn., Calif. Hotel and Motel Assn. (dir.), Internat. Franchise Assn., Sigma Alpha Epsilon. Republican. Episcopalian. Club: Cuyamaca. Home: 5141 Marlborough Dr San Diego CA 92116 Office: 1973 Friendship Dr El Cajon CA 92090

HOOTMAN, HARRY EDWARD, nuclear engineer, consultant; b. Oak Park, Ill., June 5, 1933; s. Merle Albert and Rachel Edith (Atkinson) H.; m. Linda P. Smith, Nov. 23, 1963; children—David, Holly, John. B.S. in Chemistry, Mich. Technol. U., 1959, M.S. in Nuclear Engring., 1962. Registered profl. engr., S.C. Research assoc. Argonne (Ill.) Nat. Lab., 1959-62; process engr. Savannah River Plant, Aiken, S.C., 1962-65; research assoc. reactor physics group, nuclear engring. div. Savannah River Lab., Aiken, 1965—; cons. transuranic waste disposal and incineration, radioisotope prodn., separation and shielding. Inventor alpha waste incinerator. Bd. dirs. Central Savannah River Area Sci. and Engring. Fair, Inc., Augusta, Ga., 1972—. Served to sgt. USAF, 1953-57. Mem. Am. Acad. Environ. Engrs., Nat. Soc. Profl. Engrs. (local chmn. 1978-79), Am. Nuclear Soc. (local chmn. 1979-80), Am. Phys. Soc., Sigma Xi. Baptist. Home: 820 Brandy Rd Aiken SC 29801 Office: Savannah River Lab Aiken SC 29808

HOOTON, BRUCE DUFF, editor, publisher; b. Waukegan, Ill., Dec. 11, 1928; s. Bruce Duff and Romine (Garrison) H.; 1 son, Harold Hart. Student Memphis Acad. Arts, 1946-47, Southwestern Coll., 1948-50, Harvard U., 1951-52. Editor, pub. Drawing mag., 1957-61; art critic, editor, reviewer N.Y. Herald Tribune, 1962-65; head N.Y. office Archives Am. Art, 1965-66; editor ARTnews, 1968-69; exec. dir. Save Venice, N.Y.C., 1973-75; assoc. Lee Ault & Co., 1971—; editor, pub. Art/World, N.Y.C., 1976—. Founder, v.p. Stravinsky-Diaghilev Found., N.Y.C., 1970-72; acting chmn. Venice Com., N.Y.C., 1969-70. Editor: Mother and Child in Modern Art, 1964. Republican. Episcopalian. Mem. Drawing Soc. N.Y.C. (founder, v.p. 1960—). Clubs: Coffeehouse (N.Y.C.), Century Assn., Piping Rock. Home: 40 E 94th St New York NY 10128 Office: 1295 Madison Ave New York NY 10128

HOOVER, DAVID CARLSON, lawyer; b. Waterville, Maine, Apr. 22, 1950; s. Jack Cauldwell and Mary Elizabeth (Donavan) H.; m. Kathleen Delia Powell, June 28, 1981; children: Maegan Elizabeth, Peter Daniel. BA, U. N.H., 1972; JD cum laude, Suffolk U., 1976. Bar: Mass. 1977, U.S. Dist. Ct. Mass. 1982, U.S. Supreme Ct. 1982, U.S. Ct. Appeals (1st cir.) 1983. Atty. advisor NOAA, Washington, 1976-79; gen. counsel Mass. Div. Marine Fisheries, Boston, 1979-83; spl. asst. atty. gen. Mass. Dept. Atty. Gen., Boston, 1980—; gen. counsel Mass. Dept. of Fisheries, Wildlife and Environ.

Law Enforcement, Boston, 1983—; adminstrv. law magistrate Commonwealth of Mass., 1979—; lectr. Franklin Pierce Law Ctr., Concord, N.H., 1984. Contbr. articles to profl. jours. Mem. Cen. Congl. Ch. Recipient Am. Jurisprudence award Lawyers Cooperative Pub. Co. Mem. Mass. Bar Assn., Com. on Chemical Dependency, Lawyers Concerned for Lawyers. Home: 808 Watertown St West Newton MA 02165 Office: Dept Fisheries Wildlife and Environ Law Enforcement 100 Cambridge St Boston MA 02202

HÖPCKE, KLAUS, government official; b. Cuxhaven, Germany, Nov. 27, 1933; s. Erich and Hertha (Böttcher) H.; m. Monika Vosz, 1983; children: Heike, Ute, Kerstin, Steffen, Franziska. Student, Karl-Marx U., 1955. Asst. Karl-Marx U., Leipzig, German Democratic Republic, 1955-60; dep. sec. Socialist Unity Party at Karl-Marx U., Leipzig, 1961-62; 1st sec. Dist. Com. FDJ Leipzig, 1962-63; mem. collegium Neues Deutschland, 1964-73; vice minister of culture German Democratic Republic, 1973—. Author: Probe für das Leben, 1982, Chancen der Literatur, 1986. Mem. presdl. council Kulturbund, Berlin, 1967—. Mem. PEN. Socialist Unity Party of Germany. Office: Ministry of Culture, Clara-Zetkin-Str 90, Berlin German Democratic Republic

HOPE, ALEC DERWENT, poet; b. Cooma, New South Wales, Australia, July 21, 1907; s. Percival Hope and Florence Ellen Scotford; m. Penelope Robinson, May 21, 1938; children: Emily (dec.) Andrew, Geoffrey. BA, U. Sydney, 1928, U. Oxford, 1931; LittD (hon.), Australian Nat. U., Canberra, Australialian Capital Ter., 1972, Monish U., Melbourne, Australia, 1976, U. Melbourne, 1976. Tchr. New South Wales Dept. Edn., Sydney, 1932; vocat. psychologist New South Wales Dept. Labour and Industry, Sydney, 1933-36; lectr. English Sydney Tchrs. Coll., 1937, 38-44; sr. lectr. U. Melbourne, 1945-46; prof. U. Canberra, Australian Nat. U., 1951-67; library fellow Australian Nat. U., Melbourne, 1967-72, vis. fellow, 1973—. Author: (book) The Wandering Island, 1956; (poems) Collected Poems: 1930-65, 1966, New Poems: 1965-69, 1969, Dunciad Minor, 1970, Collected Poems: 1930-70, 1972, A Late Picking, 1975, A Book of Answers, 1978, The Drfting Continent, 1979, Antechinus, 1981, The Age of Reason, 1985; (drama) Ladies From The Sea, 1987; (prose) The Cave and the Spring, 1968, A Midsummer Eves Dream, 1970, Native Companions, The Pack of Autolyeus, 1979, The New Cratylus, 1979; contbr. articles to profl. jours. Decorated Order Brit. Empire; Order Australia. Recipient Grace Lenin prize, 1956, Award for Poetry Arts Council Great Britain, 1965, Award for Lit. Britannic Australia Com., 1965, Award for Lit. Volkswagen Com., 1966. Award for Australian Lit. Myer Com., 1967. Levinson prize, 1969, Ingram Merril award, 1969. Mem. Australian Acad. Humanities. Home: 66 Arthur Circle, Canberra, ACT 2603, Australia Office: Australian Nat U, GPO Box 4, Canberra 2601, Australia

HOPE, BOB, actor, comedian; b. Eltham, Eng., May 29, 1903; m. Dolores Reade, Feb. 19, 1934; children: Linda, Anthony, Kelly, Nora. Ed. pub. schs., Cleve.; DFA (hon.), Brown U., Jacksonville (Fla.) U.; LHD (hon.), Quincy (Ill.) Coll., Georgetown U., So. Meth. U., Dallas, Ohio State U., Ind. U., John Carroll U., U. Nev., Monmouth Coll., Whittier Coll., Pa. Mil. Coll., Miami U., Oxford, Ohio, U. Cin., Calif. State Colls., Mercy Coll., N.J., Coll. of Desert, Baldwin-Wallace Coll.; LLD (hon.), U. Wyo., Northwestern U., Evanston, Ill., St. Bonaventure U., Pace Coll., Pepperdine U., U. Scranton, Western State U., Calif.; HHD (hon.), Ohio Dominican Coll., Bowling Green U., Santa Clara U., Fla. So. Coll., Wilberforce U., Northwood Inst., Mich., Norwich U., Bethel Coll., Tenn., Utah State U., St. Anselm's Coll., N.H.; D of Internat. Relations (hon.), Salem Coll.; D of Pub. Service (hon.), St. Ambrose Coll.; D of Humane Service (hon.), Drury Coll.; D of Humane Humor (hon.), Benedictine Coll., Kans.; D of Performing Arts (hon.), Dakota Wesleyan U.; LittD (hon.), Gonzaga U. Began in vaudeville and also appeared on stage; now in motion pictures, TV, radio; actor: (stage) Ballyhoo, 1932, Roberta, 1933, Ziegfeld Follies, 1935, Red Hot and Blue, 1936, (films) College Swing, 1938, Give Me a Sailor, 1938, Thanks for the Memory, 1938, Never Say Die, 1939, Some Like It Hot, The Cat and the Canary, 1939, The Road to Singapore, 1940, The Ghostbreakers, 1940, Caught in the Draft, 1941, Nothing But the Truth, 1941, Road to Zanzibar, 1941, Louisiana Purchase, 1941, Road to Morocco, 1942, My Favorite Blonde, 1942, Star Spangled Rhythm, 1942, They Got Me Covered, 1943, Let's Face It, 1943, The Princess and the Pirate, 1944, The Road to Utopia, 1945, Monsieur Beaucaire, 1946, My Favorite Brunette, 1947, Where There's Life, 1947, Road to Rio, 1948, Palefacc, 1948, Sorrowful Jones, 1949, The Great Lover, 1949, Fancy Pants, 1950, Lemon Drop Kid, 1951, My Favorite Spy, 1951, Son of Paleface, 1952, Road to Bali, 1953, Off Limits, 1953, Here Come the Girls, 1953, Casanova's Big Night, 1954, 7 Little Foys, 1955, That Certain Feeling, 1956, Iron Petticoat, 1956, Beau James, 1957, Paris Holiday, 1958, Alias Jesse James, 1959, The Facts of Life, 1960, Bachelor in Paradise, 1961, Road to Hong Kong, 1962, Critic's Choice, 1963, Call Me Bwana, 1963, A Global Affair, 1964, I'll Take Sweden, 1965, Boy, Did I Get the Wrong Number, 1966, Eight on the Lam, 1967, The Private Navy of Sargeant O'Farrell, 1968, How to Commit Marriage, 1969, Cancel My Reservation, 1972; also TV variety shows including The Bob Hope Christmas Special, 1987, The Bob Hope Birthday Special, 1988; author: They Got Me Covered, 1941, I Never Left Home, 1944, So This is Peace, 1946, Have Tux, Will Travel, 1954, I Owe Russia, 1963, Five Women I Love, 1966, The Last Christmas Show, 1974, Road to Hollywood, 1977. Decorated Hon. Comdr., Order of Brit. Empire; recipient 4 Spl. Acad. awards, Emmy award, 3 People's Choice awards for best male entertainer, 1975-76, Congrl. Gold medal Pres. Kennedy, medal of freedom Pres. Johnson, People to People award Pres. Eisenhower, Peabody award, Jean Hersholdt Humanitarian award, Criss award, Disting. Service medals from all branches of Armed Forces, Poor Richard award, Kennedy Ctr. honors, 1985, numerous others; fellow Westminster Choir Coll., N.J.). Office: 3808 Riverside Dr Burbank CA 91505 *

HOPE, NICHOLAS MARTIN, historian, educator; b. Oxford, Eng., Feb. 13, 1944; s. Constantine Ludwig and Hilde (Linde) H.; m. Susanne Kock Danielsen; 1 child, Agnes Louise. MA, Oxford U., 1967, PhD, 1971. Lectr. in history U. Glasgow, Scotland, 1971—; examiner in history U. Edinburgh, Scotland, 1987—. Author: The Alternative to German Unification, 1973; contbr. articles and revs. to profl. jours. Mem. Great Britain Hist. Assn., German History Soc., St. Antony's Soc. (com. mem. 1985—). Anglican. Club: Glasgow U. Angling (sec. 1980—). Home: 40 Highburgh Rd, Glasgow G12 9EF, Scotland Office: U Glasgow, Dept Modern History, Glasgow G12 8QQ, Scotland

HOPE, THEODORE SHERWOOD, JR., lawyer; b. N.Y.C., Oct. 7, 1903; s. Theodore Sherwood and Winifred (Ayres) H.; m. Emily Louise Blanchard, June 28, 1934; 1 son, Peter Blanchard. AB, Harvard U., 1925; LLB, Columbia U., 1928. Bar: N.Y. 1931, U.S. Supreme Ct. 1936. Instr., Columbia U. Law Sch., N.Y.C., 1928-29; assoc. instr. Johns Hopkins U. Inst. Law, Balt., 1929-32; sole practice, N.Y.C., 1932-33; with Paramount Bankruptcy Trustees, N.Y.C., 1933-34; assoc. Donovan Leisure Newton & Lumbard, name changed to Donovan Leisure Newton & Irvine, N.Y.C., 1934-40, 1941-49, ptnr., 1949-86, counsel, 1986—; assoc. prof. law Cornell U. Law Sch., 1940-41. Life mem. Browning Inst., Inc.; fellow Pierpont Morgan Library, 1974—, mem. Fellows Council, 1983-87. Mem. Assn. Bar City N.Y., N.Y. State Bar Assn., N.Y. County Bar Assn., Am. Soc. Internat. Law. Clubs: Lotos, Harvard of N.Y.C. Contbr. articles to legal jours. Home: 11 Fifth Ave New York NY 10003 Office: 30 Rockefeller Plaza New York NY 10012

HOPKINS, ANTHONY PHILIP, actor; b. Port Talbot, South Wales, U.K., Dec. 31, 1937; s. Richard Arthur and Muriel Annie (Yeates) H.; m. Petronella Barker, 1967 (div. 1972); 1 child, Abigail; m. Jennifer Ann Lynton, Jan. 13, 1973. Student, Welsh Coll. Music and Drama, Cardiff, Wales, 1954-56, Royal Acad. Dramatic Art, London, 1961-63. Ind. stage, screen, TV actor 1963—. Made London stage debut in Julius Caesar, 1964; mem. Nat. Theatre Co., 1966-73; appeared in Juno and the Paycock, 1966, A Flea in Her Ear, 1966, The Dance of Death, 1967, Three Sisters, 1967, As You Like It, 1967, The Architect and the Emperor of Assyria, 1971, A Woman Killed with Kindness, 1971, Coriolanus, 1971, Macbeth, 1972, The Taming of the Shrew, 1972, Equus, N.Y.C., 1974-75, Los Angeles, 1977, The Tempest, Los Angeles, 1979, Old Times, N.Y.C., 1983, The Lonely Road, London, 1985, Pravda, Nat. Theatre, London, 1985-86 (Olivier award 1985, Stage Actor award Variety Club), King Lear, Nat. Theatre, London, 1986-87, Anthony & Cleopatra, Nat. Theatre, London, 1987; films include (debut) The Lion in Winter, 1968, The Looking Glass War, 1970, When Eight Bells Toll, 1971, Young Winston, 1972, A Doll's House, 1973, The Girl from Petrovka, 1974, Juggernaut, 1974, A Bridge Too Far, 1977, Audrey Rose, 1977, International Velvet, 1977, Magic, 1978, The Elephant Man, 1979, A Change of Seasons, 1980, The Bounty, 1984 (Film Actor award Variety Club), The Good Father, 1985, 84 Charing Cross Road, 1986 (Best Actor award Moscow Film Festival 1987), The Old Jest, 1987, The Dawning, 1987, A Chorus of Disapproval, 1988; BBC-TV series War and Peace, 1972; TV shows include All Creatures Great and Small, 1975, The Lindbergh Kidnapping Case, 1976 (Emmy award), Victory at Entebbe, 1976, Dark Victory, Mayflower: The Pilgrim's Adventure, 1979, The Bunker, 1980 (Emmy award), Peter and Paul, 1980, Othello, BBC, 1981, Little Eyolf, BBC, 1981, The Hunchback of Notre Dame, 1982, A Married Man, 1984, The Arch of Triumph, CBS, 1984, Hollywood Wives, ABC, 1984, Guilty Conscience, CBS, 1984, Blunt, BBC, 1985. Decorated Comdr. of the Order of the Brit. Empire; recipient Best TV Actor award Soc. Film and TV Arts 1973, Best Actor award N.Y. Drama Desk 1975, Outer Critics Circles award 1975, Am. Authors and Celebrities Forum award 1975, Los Angeles Drama Critics award 1977; included on Queen's Birthday Honours List, 1987. Office: care Jeremy Conway Ltd, 109 Jermyn St, London SW1, England also: care The Lantz Office 9255 Sunset Blvd Los Angeles CA 90069

HOPKINS, BARBARA PETERS, writer, editor; b. Santa Monica, Calif., Sept. 26, 1948; d. Philip Rising and Caroline Jean (Dickason) Peters; m. Philip Joseph Hopkins, May 23, 1981. AA, Santa Monica Coll., 1971; BS, San Diego State U., 1976; postgrad. UCLA, 1981-82, 84. Gen. ptnr. Signet Properties, Los Angeles, 1971-85; tech. editor C. Brewer & Co., Hilo, Hawaii, 1975-76; editor The Aztec Engineer mag., San Diego, 1976-77; regional publicist YWCA, San Diego, 1977-78; campaign cons. Rep. Congl. and Assembly Candidates San Diego Pollster, Los Angeles Times, 1983; pres. Humbird Hopkins Inc., Los Angeles, 1978—; pub. relations cons. ASCE, San Diego, 1975-76, Am. Soc. Mag. Photographers, San Diego, 1980. Author: The Layman's Guide to Raising Cane: A Guide to the Hawaiian Sugar Industry, 1975, The Student's Survival Guide, 1976, 2d edit. 1977. Council mem. Mayor's Council on Libraries, Los Angeles, 1969; mem. Wilshire Blvd. Property Owners Assn., Santa Monica, 1972-78; docent Mus. Sci. and Industry, Los Angeles, 1970; founding mem. Comml. and Indsl. Properties Assn., Santa Monica, 1982—. Recipient Acting award Santa Monica Coll., 1970. Mem. Internat. Assn. Bus. Communicators, Sales and Mktg. Execs. Assn. Avocations: writing, travel, opera. Office: Humbird Hopkins Inc PO Box 39 San Clemente CA 92672

HOPKINS, CHARLES PETER, II, lawyer; b. Elizabeth, N.J., June 16, 1953; s. Charles Peter Sr. and Josephine Ann (Battaglia) H.; m. Elizabeth Anna Altinger, Jan. 21, 1984; 1 child, Courtney Alexandra. AB summa cum laude, Boston Coll., 1975, JD, 1979; MBA, Rutgers U., 1987. Bar: N.J. 1979, U.S. Dist. Ct. N.J. 1979, U.S. Ct. Appeals (3d cir.) 1982, U.S. Supreme Ct. 1985. Assoc. Gagliano, Tucci & Kennedy, West Long Branch, N.J., 1980; sole practice West Long Branch, 1980-81; staff atty. Sparks & Sauerwein, Shrewsbury, N.J., 1981-83, trial atty., 1983-87, sr. trial atty., 1987—; arbitrator U.S. Dist. Ct. N.J., 1985—. Mem. West Long Branch Sch. Bd., 1980-82. Mem. ABA, N.J. Bar Assn., Monmouth Bar Assn., N.J. Def. Assn., Phi Beta Kappa. Republican. Roman Catholic. Office: Sparks & Sauerwein 655 Shrewsbury Ave Shrewsbury NJ 07701

HOPKINS, EDUARDO FRANCISCO, literature educator; b. Lima, Peru, Dec. 5, 1947; s. Edward Forsyth and Zoila Rosa (Rodriguez) H.; m. Martha Irene Barriga, Sept. 19, 1975; children: Aranzazu, Simon, Sofia. Licenciate in Hispanic Lit., U. Nacional Mayor de San Marcos, Lima, 1975. Prof. lit. U. Nacional Mayor de San Marcos, Lima, 1974—, prof. sec., 1974-79, chief edits. and libraries, 1985-86, mem. dir. com. Escuela Profl. Lit., 1985—; prof. lit. Pontificia U. Catolica, Lima, 1984-86; dir. teatro U. Lima, 1985—; prof. drama Escuela Nacional de Arte Dramatico, Lima, 1984-85; dir. Teatro U. de San Marcos, Lima, 1988—; mem. dir. com. Asociacion Cultural Peruano-Brasilera, Lima, 1985-87. dir. theatre universal plays, 1969—; contbr. articles and poetry to profl. jours. Mem. Instituto Investigaciones Humanisticas. Roman Catholic. Home: Mariscal Ureta, 185 Miraflores, Lima Peru Office: U Nacional Mayor de San Marcos, Ciudad U Callao, Lima Peru

HOPKINS, GARY WAYNE, retail sales executive; b. New Rochelle, N.Y., Oct. 22, 1942; s. George and Veronica Violet (Tymon) H.; m. Jean Elizabeth Bassett, Jan. 20, 1937; children—Darcy, Meredith. B.S., Rider Coll., 1965; postgrad. Stetson Coll. Law, 1968; M.Mgmt., Aquinas Coll., 1981. Sales coordinator, prodn. coordinator Luxo Lamp Corp., Port Chester, N.Y., 1965-67; prodn. control supr. Clover Mfg., Norwalk, Conn., 1968-69; self-employed distbr. Conn. Sunday Herald, 1969-70; distbr. specialist, direct retail salesman The Nestle Co., Inc., White Plains, N.Y., 1970-86, unit mgr., 1986—. Sustaining mem. Republican Nat. Com. Recipient NATD Nat. Sales award, 1973, Nat. Sales Idea award, 1978, Honor award, 1975, 79; Nestle awardee, 1971, 75, Highest Cycle award, 1980, 83, Cycle I award, 1983; named to Million Dollar Club, 1977, 79, 80, 81, Centurion Club, 1984, 85. Roman Catholic. Address: Nestle Co Inc 719 Plymouth Blvd SE Grand Rapids MI 49506

HOPKINS, GEORGE MATHEWS MARKS, lawyer, business executive; b. Houston, June 9, 1923; s. C. Allen and Agnes Cary (Marks) H.; m. Betty Miller McLean, Aug. 21, 1954; children: Laura Corrigan, Edith Cary. Student, Ga. Sch. Tech., 1943-44; B.S. in Chem. Engring, Ala. Poly. Inst., 1944; LL.B., J.D., U. Ala., 1949; postgrad., George Washington U., 1949-50. Bar: Ala. 1949, Ga. 1954; Registered profl. engr., Ga. registered patent lawyer, U.S., Can. qualified deep-sea diver. Instr. math. U. Ala., 1947-49; assoc. firm A. Yates Dowell, Washington, 1949-50, Edward T. Newton, Atlanta, 1950-62; asst. dir. research, legal counsel Auburn (Ala.) Research Found., 1954-55; ptnr. firm Newton, Hopkins and Ormsby (and predecessor), Atlanta, 1962-87; sr. ptnr. Hunt, Richardson, Garner, Todd & Cadenhead, Atlanta, 1987—; spl. asst. atty. gen. State of Ga., 1978; chmn. bd. Southeastern Carpet Mills, Inc., Chatsworth, Ga., 1962-77, Thomas-Daniel & Assocs., Inc., 1981-85, Eastern Carpet Mills, Inc., 1983-87; dir. Xepol Inc. Served as lt., navigator, Submarine Service USNR, 1944-46, 50-51. Mem. ABA, Ga. Bar Assn. (chmn. sect. patents 1970-71), Atlanta Bar Assn., Am. Intellectual Property Law Assn., Am. Soc. Profl. Engrs., Submarine Vets. World War II (pres. Ga. chpt. 1977-78), Phi Delta Phi, Sigma Alpha Epsilon. Episcopalian. Clubs: Nat. Lawyers (Washington); Atlanta Lawyers, Phoenix Soc, Cherokee Town and Country, Atlanta City. Home: 795 Old Post Rd NW Atlanta GA 30328 Office: Hunt Richardson Garner Todd & Cadenhead SW 1400 999 Peachtree St Atlanta GA 30303

HOPKINS, JEANNE SULICK, accountant; b. Fair Lawn, N.J., Oct. 14, 1952; d. Peter and Margaret (McLaughlin) Sulick; m. Ronald T. Hopkins, Aug. 23, 1975. B.S., Syracuse U., 1974, M.B.A., 1975. With Price Waterhouse, Syracuse, 1975-83, staff acct., 1975-78, sr. acct., 1978-80, audit mgr., 1980-83; mgr. cost acctg. United Technologies/Carrier Corp., Syracuse, 1983-85; owner J.S. Hopkins & Co., CPA's, 1985-87, ptnr. Dannible & McKee, CPAs, 1987—; instr. in field. Mem. fund raising com. Syracuse Symphony Orch.; mem. Nat. Assn. Panhellenics. Mem. Am. Inst. C.P.A.s, Planning Execs. Inst., Hosp. Fin. Mgmt. Assn., N.Y. State Soc. C.P.A.s, Syracuse U. Alumni Assn., Delta Delta Delta. Club: Zonta. Office: Dannible & McKee 499 S Warren St Syracuse NY 13202

HOPKINS, JOHN LIVINGSTON, novelist; b. Orange, N.J., Aug. 5, 1938; s. John Livingston Hopkins and Anita (Bradshaw) Hopkins Wattles; m. Ellen Ann Ragsdale, June 24, 1977; children—Jonathan, Beauregard, Cabell. B.A., Princeton U., 1960. Author: The Attempt, 1967; Tangier Buzzless Flies, 1972; The Filght of the Pelican, 1983. Clubs: Princeton of N.Y. (N.Y.C.); Queen's (London). Home and Office: The Old Parsonage, Buscot, Oxfordshire SN7 8DQ, England

HOPLIN, HERMAN PETER, educator, consultant; b. Brandon, Minn., June 23, 1920; s. Peter Nelson and Edna Viola (Larson) H.; B.S., St. Cloud State U., 1942; M.B.A., Syracuse U., 1955; M.A. in Internat. Affairs, George Washington U., 1963, D.B.A., 1975; m. Eleanor Irene Johnson, Dec. 20, 1943; 1 child, Barbara Lee. Commd. 2d lt. U.S. Army, 1942, advanced through grades to col., 1965; longrange logistic planner Joint Chiefs Staff, Washington, 1968-69; dir. material acquisition U.S. Army, Washington, 1970-72; ret., 1972; sr. cons. Howard Finley Corp., Houston, 1974-75; ind. cons. McLean, Va. and Manlius, N.Y., 1976—; listed Strategic Innovations Internat. Experts Registry; mem. faculty Am. U., Washington, 1976-79; assoc. prof. Sch. Mgmt., Syracuse (N.Y.) U., 1979—; dir. NYSET Services, Inc., Boyertown, Pa., 1978-80, mem. exec. com. Syracuse Systems. Mem. exec. bd. Am. Nat. Red Cross, Umatilla County, Oreg., 1966, 67. Decorated Legion of Merit with two oak leaf clusters, Bronze Star medal; recipient Disting. Service award Rotary Internat., 1967. Mem. Am. Mgmt. Assn., Data Processing Mgmt. Assn., Assn. Computing Machinery (chmn. Syracuse chpt. 1982-83), IEEE Computer Soc., Internat. Cons. Found. (exec. bd., regional v.p. for Ams.), Soc. Gen. Systems Research, Soc. Info. Mgmt. (editorial bd.), Computer Measurement Group, Assn. Human Resources Mgmt. and Organizational Behavior (pres. N.Y. chpt.), Am. Soc. Tng. and Devel., Inst. Mgmt. Sci., Am. Def. Preparedness Assn., Pi Omega Pi, Beta Gamma Sigma. Club: Rotary. Mem. reviewing staff Computing Reviews, 1976—; referee Systems Research mag.; contbr. articles to profl. jours. Home: 8188 Pembroke Dr Manlius NY 13104 Office: Sch Mgmt Syracuse U Syracuse NY 13244

HOPPE, RUDOLF REINHOLD OTTO, chemist, educator; b. Wittenberge, Germany, Oct. 29, 1922; s. Rudolf and Meta Hoppe; Dipl.Chem., U. Kiel, later Dr. rer. nat. h.c.; Dr. rer. nat., U. Muenster; m. Karin Saborowski, 1951; children—Klaus-Dieter, Jens Reimar. Mem. faculty U. Giessen, 1965—, prof. and dir. Inst. Inorganic and Analytical Chemistry, 1965—. Bd. dirs. Max Planck Inst.; mem. Kuratorium-Gmelin Inst., 1967-86. Recipient Akademie-Preis U. Goettingen, 1962, Henry Moissan Medal Chem. Soc. France, 1986, Josef-Stefan Medal U. Ljubljana, 1986. Mem. German Chem. Soc. (Alfred Stock prize 1974), Austrian Chem. Soc., Royal Netherlands Chem. Soc., Chem. Soc. London, Am. Chem. Soc., Union Internat. Amies di cirque, German Soc. Ornithology, German Soc. Herpetology, German Soc. Natural Scientists and Physicians, German Mineral. Soc., Acad. Deutscher Naturforscher und Ärzte Leopoldina (senator, adj.), Mitglied der Osterreichischen Akademie der Wissenschaften. Author: The Chemistry of Noble Gases, 1961; over 500 articles; adv. bd. several chem. jours.; bd. dirs. Gmelins Handbuch Anorganischen Chemie, 1967-86. Address: Heinrich Buff Ring 58, D-63 Giessen Federal Republic of Germany

HOPPER, WALTER EVERETT, lawyer; b. Houghton, Mich., Oct. 29, 1915; s. Walter E. and Maude (Crum) H.; m. Jeannette Ross, Aug. 23, 1941 (dec. 1947); 1 dau., Nancy Cameron Hopper Marcouci; m. Diana Kerensky, Sept. 24, 1958; 1 stepdau., Nicole Sudrow Hopper Neilan. A.B., Cornell U., 1937, J.D., 1939. Bar: N.Y. 1939, U.S. Supreme Ct. 1946, D.C. 1959. Practice in Ithaca, 1939-42, N.Y.C., 1946—; chmn., chief exec. officer Fort Amsterdam Corp., 1973-81; dir. Davis Brake Beam Co. Chmn. trustees Loyal Legion Found.; trustee Inst. on Man and Science, 1969-71, Signal Hill Ednl. Center; bd. dirs. U.S. Flag Found. Served from 1st lt. to lt. col. inf. AUS, World War II, ETO; col. U.S. Army Res. ret. Decorated Army Commendation medal with oak leaf cluster; N.Y. State Conspicious Service Cross with Maltese Cross; Order Ruben Dario Nicaragua; comdr. Order Orange-Nassau, Netherlands; Order St. John of Jerusalem. Mem. Internat. Assn. Protection Indsl. Property (exec. com. Am. group 1958-71), Internat. Fiscal Assn., Nat. Fgn. Trade Council (mem. coms.), Internat. C. of C. (U.S. council 1949-71, mem. coms.), Am. Arbitration Assn. (panelist), U.S. Trademark Assn. (past v.p., dir., chmn. internat. com.), UN Assn. (dir. N.Y. chpt. 1964-66), Holland Soc. (pres. 1966-71), Loyal Legion (comdr.-in-chief 1964-67), Assn. Bar City N.Y., N.Y. State Criminal Bar Assn., Res. Officers Assn. (pres. N.Y. State 1949), Confrerie des Chevaliers du Tastevin, Pilgrims, Soc. War 1812, Founders and Patriots of Am., Mayflower Descs., Soc. Colonial Wars, St. Nicholas Soc. (pres. 1982-84), S.R., Huguenot Soc. Am. (pres. 1972-75), Mil. Order Fgn. Wars, Soc. of Cincinnati. Clubs: Explorers (N.Y.C.), University (N.Y.C.), Leash (N.Y.C.); Metropolitan (Washington), Army-Navy (Washington). Home: 715 Park Ave New York NY 10021

HORA, HEINRICH, physicist; b. Bodenbach-Elbe, Bohemia, July 1, 1931; s. Otto and Elisabeth (Schneider) H.; m. Rosemarie Weiler, July 1, 1956; children—Michael, Ulrike McCluskey, Maria Carmody, Beate, Dorle Minilin, Regina. Dipl. Phys., U. Halle-Wittenberg (Democratic Republic Germany), 1956; Dr. rer. nat., U. Jena, 1960; D.Sc., U. New South Wales, 1981. Research asst. to dir. R & D, Zeiss Jena, 1956-60, Oberkochen, 1960-61; research scientist IBM Lab., Boblingen, Fed. Republic Germany, 1961-62; research scientist Max-Planck-Institut fur Plasmaphysik, Garching, Fed. Rep. Germany, 1962-67, prin. research scientist, 1969-75; sr. research scientist Westinghouse Research Ctr., Pitts., 1967-68; assoc. prof. Rensselaer Poly. Inst.-Hartford Grad. Ctr., 1969-75; prof. theoretical physics, head dept. theoretical physics U. New South Wales, Sydney, Australia, 1975—; vis. prof. U. Rochester, 1973-74, U. Bern, 1978-79, U. Tokyo, Weizmann Inst., 1984, U. Giessen, U. Iowa, 1985-86; mem. convenor Dirac Funds for Theoretical Physics, U. New South Wales, 1979—; hon. lectr. Nuclear Club of Wall St., 1978; cons. in field. Author: Laser Plasmas and Nuclear Energy, 1975; Nonlinear Plasma Dynamics at Laser Irridation, 1979; Physics of Laser Driven Plasmas, 1981; Equation of State (with others), 1986. Editor-in-Chief: Laser and Particle Beams; Physics of High Energy Density, 1982—; co-editor: Laser Interaction and Related Plasma Phenomena 10 vols., 1971—; contbr. research and articles to profl. jours. Patentee: Radiation, energy, laser and basic physics. Mem. bd. City Council Ottobrunn, Bavaria, 1972-75. Recipient medal Lebedev Inst. Acad. Sci., U.S.S.R,m,' 1978; USAF grantee, 1972; Ritter-von-Gerstner medal, 1985; German Sports Gold medal, 1982. Fellow Inst. Physics (London), Australian Inst. Physics (dir. New South Wales 1979-85); mem. Am. Phys. Soc., European Phys. Soc., German Phys. Soc., Soc. to Advance Fusion Energy (N.Y., dir. 1979—) . Roman Catholic. Lodge: Rotary. Home: 12 Duggan Crescent, Connels Point 2221, Australia Office: U New South Wales, Dept Theoretical Physics, Sydney 2033, Australia

HORAN, CLARK JAMES, III, priest, corporate executive; b. Syracuse, N.Y., Feb. 3, 1950; s. Clark James Horan Jr. and Joan Roumage (Kelsey) Bergin. BA, U. Waterloo, Ont., Can., 1972, LLD (hon.), 1982; STB, BTh, St. Peter's Sem., London, Ont., Can., 1975; MDiv, U. Western Ont., London, 1975. Ordained priest Roman Cath. Ch., 1976. Priest Diocese of Honolulu; chief exec. officer Abercrombie & Waterhouse, Del., Can. Air Travellers; v.p. The Checkley Found., Can.; chmn. bd. dirs. Horan, Macmillan, Bache & Chapman, Ottawa, Ont., Can.; cons. Wardair Internat., Calgary, Alta., Can., 1978-82; bd. dirs. Horan-in-Trust, N.Y.C. Decorated Order of Can.; named Knight Bachelor, Queen Elizabeth II, 1978, Knight of the Holy Sepulchre, Pope John Paul II, 1982, officer Order Brit. Empire, Queen Elizabeth II, 1977; ascendency 5th Earl Dunsmere and Baron Horan Antwerp, 1988. Fellow Royal Commonwealth Soc., Can. Commonwealth Council (chancellor, editor Can. Commonwealth newsletter 1978-84), Monarchist League Can. (editor Monarchy Today mag. 1979-81). Clubs: Plaza, Honolulu; Ottawa Hunt and Golf, Albany (Toronto, Can.), Empire, Confederation. Lodges: Elks, KC. Address: PO Box 38016 Honolulu HI 96837-1016

HORAN, HUME ALEXANDER, ambassador; b. Washington, Aug. 13, 1934; s. Harold and Margaret Robinson (Hume) H.; m. Nancy Jane Reinert, Apr. 2, 1960; children: Alexander Hume, Margaret Robinson, Jonathan Theodore. AB cum laude, Harvard U., 1958, AM, 1963. Joined Fgn. Service, Dept. State, 1960; 3d sec. Am. embassy, Baghdad, Iraq, 1960-62; attaché Beirut, Lebanon, 1963-64; polit. officer, 2d sec. Baida, Libya, 1964-66; personnel officer Dept. State, 1966-67; desk officer Libya, 1967-69; 1st sec., chief polit. sec. Am. embassy, Amman, Jordan, 1970-72; minister, counselor Jidda, Saudi Arabia, 1972-77; mem. sr. seminar Dept. State, Washington, 1977-78; sr. dep. asst. sec. State Bur. Consular Affairs, 1978-80; ambassador to Cameroon, 1980-83; non-resident ambassador to Republic of Equatorial Guinea, 1980-82; ambassador to Sudan, 1983-86, Saudi Arabia, 1987-88; prof. diplomacy Georgetown U., Washington, 1988—. Served with U.S. Army, 1954-56. Presbyterian.

HORE, JOHN EDWARD, commodity futures educator; b. Kingston-on-Thames, Surrey, Eng., Dec. 13, 1929; came to Can., 1954; s. Ernest and Doris Kathleen (Horton) H.; m. Diana King, May 3, 1958; children: Edward John Bruce, Celia Kathleen Hore Milne, Timothy Frank. B.A. with honors, King's Coll., Cambridge, Eng., 1952, M.A., 1957. Chartered fin. analyst. Asst. sales mgr. Borthwicks, London, 1952-54; security analyst Dominion Securities, Toronto, Ont., Can., 1955-57; asst. mktg. mgr. Rio Algom, Toronto, 1957-61; dir. Bell, Gouinlock & Co., Toronto, 1961-75; v.p., dir.

futures Can. Securities Inst., Toronto, 1979—, seminar leader, 1980—; founding sec. Can. Nuclear Assn.; past v.p. Brit. Can. Trade Assn.; chmn. 1st Can. Internat. Futures Research Seminar, 1985, also editor Proc., 2 vols., 1986; chmn. Can. Futures Conf., 1986; chmn. Third Can. Internat. Futures Conf. and Research Seminar, 1987 (mng. editor Selected Papers, 1988), chmn. proposed 4th Conf., 1988. Author: Trading on Canadian Futures Markets, 1984, 3rd edit., 1987; co-editor Canadian Securities Course, 1980—; co-author Fin. Analysts Fedn. Standards of Practice Handbook, 1982 (Pres. Reagan citation 1984); mng. editor Selected papers Third Can. Internat. Futures Conf. and Research Seminar, 1988—. Gov. Montcrest Sch., 1970-73; mem. internat. com. Futures Industry Assn., Washington (appointed), rowing com. Upper Can. Coll., Toronto, 1982-86; pres. St. George's Soc. Toronto, 1978-80, chmn. edn. com., 1987. Served with Royal Army Ednl. Corps., 1948-49; Singapore. Mem. Toronto Soc. Fin. Analysts (bd. dirs. 1968-71), Fin. Analysts Fedn. (bd. dirs. investment analysis standards 1974-85, emeritus 1985). Progressive Conservative. Anglican. Clubs: University (bd. dirs. 1980-83) (Toronto); Leander (assoc.) (Henley-on-Thames), United Oxford, Cambridge U., Hurlingham, Royal Overseas League (hon. corr. sec. for Toronto) (London). Avocations: historical research, squash, choral music. Office: Can Securities Inst, 33 Yonge St, Toronto, ON Canada

HOŘENÍ, ZDENĚK, editor; b. Frydštejn, Czechoslovakia, Feb. 9, 1930; s. Karel and Anna (Kovářová) H.; m. Irena Fuxová, 1955; children: Igor, Monika. Student, Acad. Commerce, Liberec, Czechoslovakia, 1945-49; D of Research, High Party Sch., Moscow, 1960. Redacteur Liberec Jour., 1950-51, Vítězná křídla, Prague, Czechoslovakia, 1951-54, Rudé právo, Prague, 1954; corr. Moscow, 1962-68; dep. editor in chief Prague, 1968, 69-83, editor in chief, 1983—; redacteur Prague Tribuna, 1969; chmn. Union Journalists Czechoslovakia, Prague, 1972-83. Author: Jaroslav Hašek, 1983. Mem. Czechoslovakia Nat. Assembly, Prague, 1976-86, Fedn. Essembly, Czechoslovakia, 1986—; candidate mem. CC of CPC, 1976-83, mem., 1983, sec., 1984—; chmn. Union Czechoslovakia-Soviet Friendships, 1987—. Recipient Czechoslovakia Nat. prize of journalism, 1970. Home: Kjezeru 475, 149 00 Prague 4 Haje Czechoslovakia Office: Rude pravo, Na porici 30, 112 86 Prague 1 Czechoslovakia

HORGAN, PAUL, writer, educator; b. Buffalo, Aug. 1, 1903; s. Edward Daniel and Rose Marie (Rohr) H. Student, N.Mex. Mil. Inst., 1919-23; Litt.D., Wesleyan U., 1956, So. Meth. U., 1957, Notre Dame U., 1958, Boston Coll., 1958, N.Mex. State U., 1962, Coll. Holy Cross, 1963, U. N.Mex., 1963, Fairfield U., 1964, St. Mary's Coll., 1976, Yale U., 1977; D.H.L., Canisius Coll., 1960, Georgetown U., 1962; Litt.D., D'Youville Coll., 1965, Pace U., 1968, Loyola Coll., Balt., 1968, Lincoln Coll., 1968, St. Bonaventure U., 1970, Cath. U., 1973; L.H.D., LaSalle Coll., 1971, U. Hartford, 1987. Prodn. staff Eastman Theatre, Rochester, N.Y., 1923-26; librarian N.Mex. Mil. Inst., Roswell, 1926-42; asst. to pres. N.Mex. Mil. Inst., 1947; sr. fellow Center Advanced Studies, Wesleyan U., Middletown, Conn., 1959-61; dir. Center Advanced Studies, Wesleyan U., 1962-67, sr. fellow in letters, 1967-68, adj. prof. English, 1967-71, prof. emeritus, 1971—, author in residence, 1971—; lectr. Grad. Sch. Letters, U. Iowa, Feb.-June 1946; lectr. English, Yale U., 1969; hon. trustee Aspen Inst. Humanistic Studies, scholar in residence, 1968, 70, 71, 73; past mem. Nat. Council Humanities; mem. nat. adv. bd. Center for the Book, Library of Congress, 1978—. Author: Men of Arms, 1931, The Fault of Angels, 1933 (Harper prize), No Quarter Given, 1935, Main Line West, 1936, From the Royal City, 1936, The Return of the Weed, 1936, A Lamp on the Plains, 1937, New Mexico's Own Chronicle, (with Maurice Garland Fulton), 1937, Far from Cibola, 1938, Figures in a Landscape, 1940, The Habit of Empire, 1941, A Tree on the Plains, An American Opera (music by Ernst Bacon 1942), (play) Yours, A. Lincoln; (novel) The Common Heart, 1942; (novella) The Devil in the Desert, 1952, One Red Rose for Christmas, 1952; (history) Great River: The Rio Grande in North American History (Pulitzer prize, Bancroft prize, Tex. Inst. Letters award, 1954); (fiction) Humble Powers, 1954; (novella) The Saintmaker's Christmas Eve, 1955; (history) The Centuries of Santa Fe, 1956; (novel) Give Me Possession, 1957; (film narration) Rome Eternal, 1959; (novel) A Distant Trumpet, 1960; (biography) Citizen of New Salem, 1961; (collected novels) Mountain Standard Time, 1962; (history) Conquistadors in North American History, 1963; (juvenile) Toby and the Nighttime, 1962; (novel) Things as They Are, 1964; (poetry) Songs after Lincoln, 1965; (biography) Peter Hurd: A Portrait Sketch from Life, 1965; (novel) Memories of the Future, 1966; (short stories) The Peach Stone, 1967; (novel) Everything To Live For, 1968; (history) The Heroic Triad, 1970; (novel) Whitewater, 1970; (criticism) Maurice Baring Restored, 1970; (biography) Encounters with Stravinsky, 1972; (criticism) Approaches to Writing, 1973; (biography) Lamy of Santa Fe, His Life and Times (Pulitzer prize, Tex. Inst. Letters award, 1975); (novel) The Thin Mountain Air, 1977; (biography) Josiah Gregg and His Vision of the Early West, 1979; (novel) Mexico Bay, 1982; (selected writings) Of America East and West, 1984, Under the Sangre de Cristo, 1985, The Clerihews of Paul Horgan, 1985, A Writer's Eye: Field Notes and Water Colors, 1988, A Certain Climate: Essays in History, Arts and Letters, 1988; articles, fiction to mags.; exhbns. field drawings for research. Chmn. bd. Santa Fe Opera, 1958-69, mem., 1969—; mem. adv. bd. John Simon Guggenheim Found., 1963-69; pres. bd. dirs. Roswell Mus., 1948-55; mem. bd. Roswell Pub. Library, 1958-62, hon. mem., 1962—; hon. life fellow Sch. Am. Research; fellow Pierpont Morgan Library, 1974—, mem. council, 1975-79, 82-83, life fellow, 1977—; trustee Assocs. Yale U. Library, 1976-79; bd. dirs. Witter Bynner Found., 1972-79; founding trustee Lincoln County (N.Mex.) Heritage Trust, 1976—. Served from capt. to lt. col. AUS, 1942-46; recalled temp. active duty gen. staff Dept. Army, 1952, Washington. Created knight of St. Gregory, 1957; Guggenheim fellow, 1947-48, 58; Hoyt fellow Saybrook Coll., Yale U., 1965; asso. fellow Saybrook Coll., 1966—; Decorated Legion of Merit; recipient Tex. Inst. Letters awards, 1955, 71, 76; Campion award of Catholic Book Club, 1957; Cath. Book award Cath. Press Assn., 1965, 68; Laetare medal U. Notre Dame, 1976; Bronze medal Smithsonian Instn., 1980; medal Nat. Portrait Gallery, 1981; Baldwin medal Wesleyan U., 1982; medal Washington Coll., 1985; Robert Kirsch award Los Angeles Times, 1987; Roswell Mus. addition named after him; N.Mex. Mil. Inst. library named after him. Fellow Am. Acad. Arts & Scis., Conn. Acad. Arts & Scis.; mem. Am. Cath. Hist. Assn. (pres. 1960), Am. Antiquarian Soc., Wesleyan Writers Conf. (adv. bd.), Nat. Inst. Arts and Letters, Phi Beta Kappa (orator 1973, hon. Alpha of Conn. chpt.), Soc. Am. Historians. Roman Catholic. Clubs: Yale (N.Y.C.); Athenaeum (London, Eng.). Address: Wesleyan U Middletown CT 06457

HORIGAN, JAMES EUGENE, lawyer, author; b. Oklahoma City, Sept. 4, 1924; s. Joseph D. Horigan and Mary (Swirczynski) Horigan McRill; stepson Albert L. McRill; student Okla. U., 1942-44, Northwestern U., 1944; J.D., Okla. U., 1949; postgrad. So. Meth. U., 1958, Colo. U., 1966; m. Joan Murry, Mar. 8, 1945; children—Susan, Daniel James, Nancy Jean Horigan Datz. Bar: Okla. 1949, Tex. 1957, N.Y. 1959, Colo. 1961, Law Soc. Eng. (hon.), 1973. Asst. county atty. Oklahoma County, 1949-51; atty. Mobil Oil Corp., Oklahoma City, 1951-57, Beaumont, Tex., 1957, Dallas, 1958; U.S. and Can. counsel, office gen. counsel, N.Y.C., 1959-61, regional gen. atty. Denver regional office, 1961-63; gen. counsel Hamilton Bros. Oil Co. and affiliates, Denver, 1963-69; ptnr. Foliart, Shepherd, McPherson & Horigan, Oklahoma City, 1963, Horigan Thompson & Miller, Denver, 1965-69; individual practice internat. law, London, 1969-70; ptnr. Horigan & Boss, 1971; sr. resident ptnr. London office law firm Vinson, Elkins, Searls, Connally & Smith, 1971-75; of counsel Burns & Wall, 1978; ptnr. Horigan, Jumonville, Broadhurst, Brook & Miller, 1978, Holland & Hart, Denver, 1979-81; sole practice law, 1981—; bd. dirs., gen. counsel Charterhall N.Am. P.L.C., 1985-87; gen. agt. Charterhall Australia Ltd. 1983-87. Trustee Town of Bow Mar (Colo.), 1976-78; mem. U.S. Congl. Adv. Bd., 1982-87; mem. adv. bd. Internat. Comparative Law Ctr., Southwestern Legal Found., 1983—. Served to lt. USNR, 1943-46. Mem. ABA, Colo. Bar Assn., Okla. Bar Assn., Denver Bar Assn., Internat. Bar Assn., Am. Soc. Internat. Law, Rocky Mountain Mineral Law Found. (gen. chmn. spl. legal inst. 1975), Internat. Platform Assn., Internat. Trade Assn. Colo. (v.p. 1979-81. bd. dirs.), Phi Delta Phi, Phi Gamma Delta, Delta Sigma Rho. Roman Catholic. Clubs: American (London); Rotary; Denver Petroleum (bd. dirs. 1987—). Author: Chance or Design?, 1979; The Key to Reconcile Modern Science and Religious Thought, 1983; Petroleum Laws of the North Sea, 1975; contbg. author: The Law of Transnational Business Transactions, 1980; Foreign Participation in Domestic Oil and Gas Ventures, 1982; contbr. articles to legal jours.; charter mem. bd. editors Okla. Law Rev., 1947-49. Home: 5230 Lakeshore Dr Littleton CO 80123

HORLING, ROBERT, photographer, art director; b. Budapest, Hungary, Apr. 19, 1931; s. Lajos and Maria (Szély) H.; m. Helen Gonda, Sept. 24, 1955; 1 child, Catherine Dianna. Student, Sch. Photography, Budapest, 1952-55; diploma, Acad. Journalism, Budapest, 1957. With Hungarian News Agy., Budapest, 1949—, apprentice photographer, 1949-52, now art dir. illustrating and advt. office, 1978-88, dep. gen. editor-in-chief photo editorial office, 1988—; tchr. functional photography and photo aesthetics U. Art, Budapest, 1986—. Author, photographer 1 book. Recipient over 300 prizes at various exhbns. and competitions, including Artiste Fiap Fedn. Internat. Fedn. Fotogrphic Art,,1959, Excellence Fiap., Internat. Fedn. Fotographic Art, 1967, Gold Medal Interpress-Photo World Competitions, 1962, 66, 72; Balázs Béla Artistic award Ministry of Culture, 1980, Ministry award for 35 yrs. in field of photography, 1983; named to Order Labour, Presidium Hungarian People's Republic, 1976, 85. Mem. Hungarian Journalist Assn., Hungarian Photographic Artist's Assn. (found. and active staff), Hungarian Advt. Assn. (found. and active staff photo sect., Pécsi József award 1978), Fèdèration Internationale De L'Art Photographique. Home: XIII Katona J-25-III, 1137 Budapest Hungary Office: Magyar Távirati Iroda, T Fém Utca 8, 1016 Budapest Hungary

HORMUTH, STEFAN EDMUND, university educator; b. Heidelberg, Fed. Republic Germany, Nov. 29, 1949; s. Kurt and Priska (Schlienz) H. Diploma in Psychology, U. Heidelberg, 1975; PhD, U. Tex., 1979. Asst. prof. U. Heidelberg, 1981-87, assoc. prof., 1987—. Author: The Self-Concept and Change: An Ecological Approach in Press; editor: Social Psychology of Attitude Change, 1979. Mem. Soc. Exptl. Social Psychology, European Assn. Exptl. Social Psychology, Am. Psychol. Assn., Deutsche Gesellschaft für Psychologie, Fachgruppe Sozialpsychologie (treas. 1987, bd. dirs. 1985-87). Club: Seglervereinigung (Heidelberg) (pres. 1984—). Home: Albert Ueberle-Str 8, D-6900 Heidelberg 1 Federal Republic of Germany Office: Dept Psychology, U Heidelberg, Haupstr 47-51, D-6900 Heidelberg Federal Republic of Germany

HORN, ANDREW WARREN, lawyer; b. Cin., Apr. 19, 1946; s. George H. and Belle (Collin) H.; m. Melinda Fink; children—Lee Shawn, Ruth Belle. B.B.A. in Acctg., U. Miami, 1968, J.D., 1971. Bar: Fla. 1971, U.S. Dist. Ct. (so. dist.) Fla. 1972, U.S. Tax Ct. 1974. Ptnr. Gillman & Horn P.A., Miami, Fla., 1973-74; sole practice Miami, 1974—. Bd. dirs. Young Democrats of Dade County. Recipient Am. Jurisprudence award Lawyers Coop. Pub. Co., 1970. Mem. ABA, Fla. Bar. Club: Tiger Bay. Office: Children's Hosp Civic Council Miami FL 33130

HORN, FRIEDEMANN HANS CHRISTIAN, minister; b. Oppeln/Upper Silesia, Poland, Apr. 30, 1921; came to Switzerland, 1950, naturalized, 1972; s. Johannes Rudolf and Gertrud (Muller) H.; ed. U. Jena; Dr. Religious Sci., U. Marburg, 1952; m. Hella Merseburger, Dec. 29, 1948; children—Christiane, Beate, Johannes. Ordained to ministry Swedenborgian Ch., 1952; asst. minister Swedenborgian Ch., Zurich, 1952-56, minister, 1956-77, gen. pastor European field, 1977—, pres. Theol. Sem., Newton, Mass., 1977-79. Served with German Air Force, 1940-45. Mem. Swedenborg Gesellschaft, German Swedenborg Gesellschaft, Swedenborg Found., Swedenborg Soc. London, Schweizer Akademie fur Grundlagenstudien. Author: Schelling und Swedenborg, 1954; Der innere Sinn des Alten Testaments, 1972; Der innere Sinn der Bergpredigt, 1965; Wie dachte Jesus uber Tod und Auferstehung, 1970; Reinkarnation-Ja oder Nein, 1988; editor: Offene Tore, Beitrage zu linem neuen christl Zeitalter, 1957—, Neukirchenblatt, 1963—; translator from Latin and English. Home: 2 Apollostr, CH 8032 Zurich Switzerland

HORN, JOHN CHISOLM, management consultant; b. N.Y.C., Jan. 16, 1915; s. William M. and Marguerite E. (Jacobs) H.; A.B., Cornell U., 1936, postgrad., 1937; LL.D., Susquehanna U., 1965; m. Solveig E. Wald, June 22, 1938; children—Phyllis Downing, John Chisolm, Stephen Lunde, Eric Laurens, Robert Gregg, Thomas Wald, Dorothy Traill, James Melchior. With John R. Wald Co., 1937-39; sec. Prismo Safety Corp., 1939-45, sec., treas., 1945-49, v.p., 1949-57, exec. v.p., 1957-62, pres., 1962-69; pres. John C. Horn Assos., 1970—; pres. Prismo Universal Corp., 1969-70, vice chmn. bd., 1970—; asst. sec. Wald Industries, Inc., 1950-51, pres., 1951-69; exec. dir. Church Mgmt. Service, Inc., 1971—; dir. Long Siding Corp., Prismo France, Paris, Prismo Universal Ltd., Eng. cooperating cons. Tech. Diversification Services, 1972—; dir. Springfield Corp. Dir. Huntingdon Bus. and Industry, Inc., 1958—; chmn. Indsl. Devel. Commn., 1959-60, area devel. chmn., 1960-62. Bd. dirs., vice chmn. Wald Found., 1954-63; mem. nat. council Boy Scouts Am., 1950—, nat. com. on cubbing, 1961-68, nat. com. exec. profl. tng., 1971—, exec. com Region III, 1961—, v.p. Juniata Valley council 1951-57, pres., 1957—; pres., bd. dirs. Huntingdon County United Fund, 1959-68; mem. indsl. and profl. council Pa. State U. Bd. dirs. Juniata Valley Schs., St. James Huntington Choir; pres. bd. dirs. Susquehanna U.; mem. bd. publ. Luth. Ch. Am., 1968-74. Recipient Silver Beaver, Lamb and Silver Antelope awards Boy Scouts Am., also Outstanding Civic Leader award, 1967. Mem. Army Ordnance Assn., NAM, AIM, Am. Mgmt. Assn., Am. Road Builders Assn., Internat. Bridge Tunnel and Toll Rd. Assn., Inst. Traffic Engrs., C. of C. (dir. 1955), Juniata Mountains Devel. Assn. (pres. 1956). Lutheran (home mission bd. Central Pa. Synod 1948—, com. on music and worship; synodical proposal com. 1957—, exec. bd. 1962-67, higher edn. com. 1967—). Clubs: Huntingdon Music, Huntingdon Country. Home: Killmarnock Hall Alexandria PA 16611 Office: 301 Penn St Huntingdon PA 16652

HORN, RUSSELL EUGENE, engineering executive, consultant; b. Yoe, Pa., May 4, 1912; s. Eugene M. and Charlotte (Snyder) H.; m. Eleanor B. Baird, Jan. 12, 1934; children: Russell Eugene, Ralph Elliot, Rosalind Emily (Mrs. Lee Kunkel), Robert Errol. BS, Pa. State U., 1933. Foreman Pa. Dept. Hwys. dist. office, York, Pa., 1933-35; draftsman, supr., designer C.S. Buchart, architect, 1935-41; exec. v.p., chief engr. Buchart Engring., 1945-59, pres., chief engr., 1959-61; pres., chief engr. Buchart-Horn, Inc., cons. engrs., 1961-72, chmn. bd. dirs., 1972—; pres., chmn. bd. dirs. Pace Resources, Inc., 1970-87, chief exec. officer, chmn. bd. dirs., 1987—; dir. emeritus Dauphin Deposit Bank and Trust Co.; dir. emeritus adv. bd. So div. Dauphin Deposit Bank & Trust Co.; bd. dirs. AAA White Rose Motor Club, chmn., 1975-78; bd. dirs. Auto Club So. Pa., bd. dirs. York County chpt. ARC; bd. dirs. emeritus Retirement Homes of Meth. Ch., 1978—. Served to col. AUS, 1940-45. Mem. Soc. Am. Mil. Engrs., NSPE, Pa. Soc. Profl. Engrs. (pres. Lincoln chpt. 1961), Pa. Assn. Cons. Engrs. (pres. 1965, bd. dirs. 1966), Pa. Hwy. Information Assn. (bd. dirs.), Am. Soc. Hwy. Engrs. (nat. pres. 1962), Tech. Socs. Council Southeastern Pa. (chmn. 1963), Engring. Soc. York, Profl. Engrs. Pvt. Practice, Am. Concrete Inst., Assn. Pa. Constructors, Assn. Hwy. Ofcls. N. Atlantic States, Assn. U.S. Army, Res. Officers Assn., ASCE, VFW, Cons. Engrs. Council, Am. Rd. Builders Assn., Am. Legion, Pa. State U. Alumni Club York County. Clubs: Univ., Lake, Dutch, Exchange ((Golden Deeds award 1979), Mt. Nittany Soc. Pa. State U. Lodges: Masons (32 deg.; Order of the Double Eagle award, 1983, Legion of Freedom award 1986), Moose. Home: 1270 Brockie Dr York PA 17403 Office: 40 S Richland Ave York PA 17405

HORNBRUCH, FREDERICK WILLIAM, JR., corporate consultant; b. Roselle, N.J., July 14, 1913; s. Frederick William and Elsa M. (Becker) H.; M.E., Stevens Inst. Tech., 1934; m. Helen Novak, Apr. 10, 1936; children—Frederick William III, Harlan Richard. Engr., Weston Elec. Instrument Corp., Newark, 1934-40, Falstrom Co., Passaic, N.J., 1940-41; indsl. engr. Bendix Aviation Corp., Phila., 1941-43; prodn. mgr. Columbia Machine Works, Bklyn., 1943-44; chief engr., dir. Rath & Strong, Inc., Boston, 1944-57; v.p. Landers, Frary & Clark, Inc., New Britain, Conn., 1957-59; v.p. Atlas Corp., N.Y.C., 1959-64, dir., 1962-64; pres., dir. Titeflex, Inc., Springfield, Mass., 1960-64; chmn. bd. Mertronics Corp., Santa Monica, Calif., 1960-64; pres., dir. Internat. Air, Inc., N.Y.C., 1962; v.p. Calumet & Hecla, Inc., Chgo., also gen. mgr. Flexonics div., 1964-68; v.p. Aero-Chatillon Corp., Inc., N.Y.C., 1968-69; v.p. adminstrn. Macrodyne-Chatillon Corp., N.Y.C., 1969; dir. Macrodyne Industries, Inc., 1974-78; pvt. practice corp. cons., Barrington Hills, Ill., 1969-83, Laguna Hills, Calif., 1984—. Mem. ASME (chmn. mgmt. div. 1957, chmn. orgn. com. 1966, chmn. confs. 1955, 56), Soc. Advancement Mgmt. (pres. Phila. chpt. 1948-49, chmn. 1949-50, co-chmn. conf. 1953), Newcomen Soc., Tau Beta Pi, Pi Delta Epsilon, Phi Sigma Kappa. Presbyterian. Author: (with Bruce and Chadruc) Practical Planning and Scheduling, 1950; Raising Productivity, 1977. Contbr. to Handbook of Bus. Administrn., 1967; mem. adv. bd., contbr. Handbook of Modern Mfg. Mgmt., 1967-68, Handbook of Product Design for Mfg., 1986. Patentee instrument for synchronizing aircraft engines. Address: 26532 Wildview Terr Laguna Hills CA 92653

HORNE, JAMES ANTHONY, psychology educator; b. Bromley, Eng., Apr. 16, 1946; s. Frank Edward and Joyce Georgina (Freeman) H.; m. Helen Monica Dallosso, Mar. 14, 1985; 1 child, Rosie Louise. BSc in Zoology, Psychology, U. London, 1968; MSc in Applied Psychology, U. Aston, Birmingham, Eng., 1969, PhD in Psychophysiology, 1972. Post doctoral lectr. U. Aston, Birmingham, 1972-73; lectr. U. Loughborough, Leicestershire, Eng., 1973-80, sr. lectr., 1980-84, reader, dir. sleep research lab., 1984—. Author: Function of Sleep, 1987; contbr. articles to profl. publs. Mem. Loughborough Parish Council, 1983—. Fellow Brit. Psychol. Soc., Inst. Biology; mem. Electroencephalography Soc., Sleep Research Soc. (exec. com. 1981-85), European Sleep Research Soc. (exec. com. 1986—), Amnesty Internat. (sec. Loughborough sect. 1980—). Office: Loughborough Univ, Human Scis Dept, Leicestershire LE11 3TU, England

HORNE, MARILYN, mezzo-soprano, soprano; b. Bradford, Pa.; m. Henry Lewis (div.); 1 child. Ed., U. So. Calif.; MusD (hon.), Rutgers U., 1970, Jersey City State Coll.; DLitt (hon.), St. Peter's Coll. Operatic debut as Hata in The Bartered Bride, Los Angeles Guild Opera; La Scala debut in Oepidus Rex, 1969; Met. Opera debut as Adalgisa in Norma, 1970; other roles include Rosina in Barber of Seville, Cleonte in The Siege of Corinth, Isabella in L'Italiana in Algieri, Carmen at Met. Opera, 1972-73, Laura in Harvest, Chgo. Lyric Opera, Marie in Wozzeck, San Francisco Opera; also appeared in Phigenie en Tauride, Semiramide, Samson et Dalila at Met. Opera, 1987; other appearances include Venice Festival by invitation of Igor Stravinsky, Am. Opera Soc., N.Y.C., for several seasons, Vancouver Opera, Philharm. Hall, N.Y.C., Paris, Dallas, Houston, Covent Garden, London, roles at La Scala, Italy, Rossini Opera Festival, Pesaro, Italy, Met. Opera, 1987; recital debuts in Madrid, Dresden, East Berlin, 1987; ann. recital at Carnegie Hall, European tour with husband for Dept. State, 1963; rec. artist for London, Columbia and RCA records. Address: care Columbia Artists Mgmt Inc 165 W 57th St New York NY 10019 *

HORNELL, AKE GUNNAR, optical company executive; b. Falun, Sweden, Aug. 15, 1948; s. Gunnar C. and Ester K. (Eld) H.; m. Lisbeth M. Jalnas, Apr. 13, 1974; children: Dan A., Mats G. MS, Chalmers U. Tech., Gothenburg, Sweden, 1972. Engr. Gotaverken AB, 1972-73; researcher Chalmers U. Tech., 1974-77; pres. Hornell Elektrooptik AB, Gagnef, Sweden, 1978—. Patentee in field. Bd. dirs. Local Cos. Assn., Gagnef, 1985—. Recipient Inventor's Prize Regional Devel. Found., 1986. Mem. Internat. Soc. Optical Engring., Soc. Info. Display. Office: Tjarnhedsvagen 2, S-78041 Gagnef Sweden

HORNER, CHARLES DALLAS, lawyer; b. Kansas City, Mo., Mar. 21, 1939; s. Bryan Ridgway and Alma Louise (Dallas) H.; m. Mary Katherine Hall, Aug. 18, 1962; children: Charles Walton, Katherine Hall, Stephen Bryan. BA cum laude, Princeton U., 1961; JD, U. Mich., 1964. Bar: Mo. 1964, Kans. 1985. Assoc. atty. Watson, Ess, Marshall & Enggass, Kansas City, 1964-69; ptnr. Hillix, Brewer, Hoffhaus, Whittaker & Horner, Kansas City, 1969—, mng. ptnr., 1985—; bd. dirs., exec. com. St. Luke's Hosp., Kansas City, 1979—, chmn. Mid-Am. Heart Inst., 1985—; sec. Wyandotte Garage Corp., Kansas City, 1983—; bd. dirs. Mid-Am. Healthnet, Inc., Kansas City. Author: Real Estate Tax Shelters, 1982. Legal advisor Downtown Council, Kansas City, 1982—; treas. Audrey Langworthy Kans. Senate campaign, 1984; chmn. tax policy com. Johnson County (Kans.) Rep. Party, 1984—; vestry, chancellor St. Andrews Episcopal Ch., Kansas City, 1968-84. Mem. ABA (real property and trusts sect.), Mo. Bar Assn., Lawyers Assn. Kansas City, Kansas City Bar Assn. Club: Kansas City Country (Johnson County); Univ., Mercury (bd. dirs., v.p., pres.) (Kansas City). Lodge: Rotary (pres. Kansas City chpt.). Home: 6143 Reinhardt Dr Shawnee Mission KS 66205 Office: Hillix Brewer Hoffhaus Wittaker & Horner 911 Main Suite 2700 PO Box 13367 Kansas City MO 64199

HORNER, LEE, foundation executive, speaker, consultant, computer specialist; b. Sault Ste. Marie, Ont., Can., Mar. 18, 1944; came to U.S., 1976; d. William E. and Gladys (Boomhower) H.; m. Claude Lavallee, Jan. 21, 1960 (div. Sept. 1969); children—Kevin Lauren Lavallee/Petalos, Cynthia Lee Lavallee; m. James G. Petalos, Jan. 9, 1970 (dec. Jan. 1977). Student Concordia U., Montreal, Que., Can., 1975-76, U. Nev.-Las Vegas, 1977, 88. Pres., LHP Investments, Inc., Las Vegas, 1978—; v.p. Casa Mobile Corp., real estate, San Francisco, 1979—; founder, chmn. bd. PMS Research Found., Las Vegas, 1982—; pub. speaker premenstrual syndrome, health, wellness, cycles. Author: How to Chart Your Course to Freedom, 1983; Mini-Nutrition and Exercise Manual, 1983; PMS Minder, 1983; PMS Wellness Workbook, 1985, PMS Support Group Manual, 1985. Mem. Am. Soc. Fund Raising Execs., Am. Bus. Women's Assn., Nat. Speakers Assn. (founding pres. Las Vegas chpt. 1984-85, 88). Club: Windjammer, Toastmasters (ednl. v.p. 1980, adminstrv. v.p. 1983, 88). Home: 2754 El Toreador Las Vegas NV 89109 Office: LHP Investments Inc/ PMS Research Found PO Box 14574 Las Vegas NV 89114

HORNER, MATINA SOURETIS, college president; b. Boston, July 28, 1939; d. Demetre John and Christine (Antonopoulos) Souretis; m. Joseph L. Horner, June 25, 1961; children: Tia Andrea, John, Christopher. A.B. cum laude, Bryn Mawr Coll., 1961; M.S., U. Mich., 1963, Ph.D., 1968; LL.D., Dickinson Coll., 1973, Mt. Holyoke Coll., 1973, U. Pa., 1975, Smith Coll., 1979, Wheaton Coll., 1979; L.H.D. (hon.), U. Mass., 1973, Tufts U., 1976, U. Hartford, 1980, U. New Eng., 1987. Teaching fellow U. Mich., Ann Arbor, 1962-66; lectr. motivation personality U. Mich., 1968-69; lectr. social relations Harvard U., 1969-70, asst. prof. clin. psychology dept. social relations, 1970-72; also cons. univ. health services; pres. Radcliffe Coll., 1972—; dir. Time, Inc., Fed. Res. Bank Boston, Liberty Mut. Life Ins. Co., Boston Edison Co. Contbr. psychol. articles on motivation to profl. jours. Mem. adv. council NSF, 1977—, chmn., 1980-86; trustee Twentieth Century Fund, 1973—, Mass. Eye and Ear Infirmary, 1986—; bd. dirs. Revson Found., 1986—, Council for Fin. Aid to Edn., 1985—; bd. dirs. Women's Research and Edn. Inst., 1979—, chmn. research com., 1982—; mem. President's Commn. for Nat. Agenda for 1980s, 1979-80; chmn. Task Force on Quality Am. Life in '80s, 1979-80; mem. adv. com. Women's Leadership Conf. on Nat. Security, 1982—. Recipient Roger Baldwin award Mass. Civil Liberties Union Found., 1982, citation of merit Northeast Region NCCJ, 1982, Career Contbn. award Mass. Psychol. Assn., 1987. Mem. Council Fgn. Relations, Nat. Inst. Social Scis. (award 1973), Phi Beta Kappa, Phi Delta Kappa, Phi Kappa Phi. Office: Radcliffe Coll Office of Pres 10 Garden St Cambridge MA 02138

HORNING, ROSS CHARLES, JR., historian, educator; b. Watertown, S.D., Oct. 10, 1920; s. Ross Charles and Harriett (Meaghan) H. B.A., Augustana Coll., 1948; M.A., George Washington U., 1952; Ph.D. (Sanders fellow), 1958; postgrad. Russian, Inst. Langs. and Linguistics, Georgetown U., 1952-53. Instr. Wis. State U., Eau Claire, 1958-59; asst. prof. St. John's U., Collegeville, Minn., 1959-64; assoc. prof. Russian history and internat. affairs Creighton U., Omaha, 1964-68, prof., 1968—, pres. faculty, 1984-86, chmn. athletic bd., Athletic Hall of Fame com., 1987-88. Mem. council Nebr. com. for humanities NEH. Served with USAF, 1943-46. Recipient Disting. Faculty Service award Creighton U., 1982; Fulbright scholar India, summer 1967. Mem. AAAS, Am. Assn. Advancement Slavic Studies, Am. Hist. Assn., Am. Soc. Internat. Law, AAUP, Orgn. Am. Historians, Conf. Slavic and European Studies, Am. Com. for Irish Studies, Assn. Profl. Baseball Players, Omaha Urban League, Joslyn Liberal Arts Soc., S.W. Am. Assn. Advancement Slavic Studies, Western Social Sci. Assn., Am. Fgn. Service Assn., Canadian History Assn., Assn. Canadian Studies in U.S. (exec. council), Assn. Asian Studies, Omaha Symphony Assn., Assn. Canadienne de Sci. Politique, Internat. Law Assn. (Am. br.), World Peace Through Law Center, Ctr. for Study of Presidency, Fgn. Service Club (Washington), Nebr. Arts Council, Asia Soc., Opera/Omaha, Fulbright Alumni Assn., Omaha Press Club (bd. dirs.), Alpha Sigma Nu. Home: 4955 Cuming St Omaha NE 68132

HORNTHAL, PHILIPP RICHARD, management consultant; b. Chgo., Feb. 25, 1950; s. William J. and Sally (Schultz) H.; B.S. in Indsl. Engring., Purdue U., 1972, M.S. in Indsl. Engring., 1972; m. Sheila Maureen, Apr. 21, 1974; children—Jennifer Lynn, David Adam. Mgmt. cons., Arthur Andersen & Co., Chgo., 1973—, mgr. mgmt. info. cons. div., 1978—, dir. mktg. Chgo.

Cons. Group, 1988—. Mem. fund drive com. Jr. Achievement; mem. Northbrook Civic Found. (Northbook Days Com. 1980—); bd. dirs. Better Boys Found.-Arthur S. Arkush Scholarship Found., Coffee Break Service Ala., USA Sports Inc. Mem. Am. Prodn. and Inventory Control Soc. (flight chmn. 1974, 75, cert. in inventory mgmt., speaker internat. conf. 1980, internat. conf. com. 1981, 1982, 83, 84, 85), Inst. Indsl. Engrs. (sr. mem.), Am. Materials Mgmt. Soc. (flight chmn. 1979-80, treas. 1982, dir. 1979—), Purdue U. Engring. Alumni Assn. (bd. dirs. 1983-89, v.p. 1986-89). Home: 4135 Yorkshire Ln Northbrook IL 60062 Office: 33 W Monroe St Chicago IL 60602

HORNUNG, GERTRUDE SEYMOUR, art educator; b. Boston; d. Samuel Parker and Rose Anne Seymour; A.B., Wellesley Coll., 1929; M.A., Western Res. U., 1939, Ph.D., 1949; m. Robert M. Hornung, Oct. 31, 1932; 1 dau., Elizabeth Zimri Luce Smith. Lectr., instr., supr. adult programs Cleve. Mus. Art, 1937-60; lectr. Am. U., Rome, 1974-75; lectr. Tehran, Iran, 1975, Bangkok, Thailand, 1978, Dublin, Ireland, 1970; free lance lectr., Cleve., 1960—; lectr. Honolulu Acad. Arts, 1973-85. Pres. Decorative Arts Trust Cleve Circle, 1987; trustee Kent (Ohio) U. Mus., 1987—. Mem. Nat. Art Educators Assn., Internat. Council Mus., Internat. Com. Mus. Edn., Am. Assn. Mus. Republican. Episcopalian. Home: 2240 Elandon Dr Cleveland OH 44106

HORNUNG, ULRICH, educator; b. Dortmund, Fed. Rep. Germany, Nov. 21, 1941; s. Walter and Luise (Stadtler) H. Dr. rer. nat., U. Münster, 1970, Habilitation, 1979. Prof. U. Münster, Fed. Rep. Germany, 1982-83, U. of the Fed. Armed Forces, Munich, 1983—; vis. prof. Ariz. State U., Tempe, 1987-88; dir. SCHI, Ottobrunn, Fed. Rep. Germany, 1986—. Contbr. articles to profl. jours. Office: SCHI, PO Box 1222, D-8014 Neubiberg Federal Republic of Germany

HORNYCH, ANTONIN FRANÇOIS, physician, researcher; b. Prague, Czechoslovakia, Sept. 8, 1930; arrived in France, 1970.; s. Antonin and Anna (Faltusova) H.; m. Helena Jarosova, June 1959 (dec. March 1981); 1 child, Pierre; m. Yvetta Zlatovsky, April 4, 1986. MD, Charles U. Med. Sch., Prague, 1956, Marie Curie Med. Sch., Paris, 1974. cert. internal med. 1st, 2nd degrees; cardiology, nephrology Inst. for postgrad. Edn., Czechoslovakia. Intern in internal medicine Prague, 1955-56; intern dept. internal medicine Most Regional Hosp., Czechoslovakia, 1956-57; resident Inst. for Cardiovascular Research, Prague, 1958-59, staff mem. cardiology dept., 1958-65; staff mem., lectr. 1969-70; assoc. dir. hemodial and transplant programs Inst. for Cardiovascular Research, 1965-67; research fellow U. Paris Coll. of Med., 1967-68; asst. prof. experimental med. dept. U. Paris Med. Sch., 1970-74; staff mem., researcher Inst. Nat. Santé Recherche Med., Paris, 1970—; visiting prof. Munich Med. Sch. TUM, 1986, dir. hypertension lab. U-28 INSERM, Paris, 1980-87. contbr. over 98 articles to numerous profl. jours. Active Czechoslovakian Sportive Orgn., Prague; mem. Czechoslovakian Soc. for Arts and Scis., Internat. Acad. Human Rights, Paris, 1986-87. Served with the French Med. Reserves. Mem. Order of Med., Internat. Soc. of Nephrology, French Soc. of Nephrology, Internat. Soc. of Hypertension, French Soc. of Cardiology, Hypertension Br. Roman Catholic. Office: Hosp Broussais, 96 Rue Didot, 75674 Paris 14, France

HOROVITZ, ISAAC LUCAS, surgeon; b. Berlin, Feb. 19, 1927; arrived in Israel, 1934.; s. Moisi and Eva (Binder) H.; m. Miriam Swisha, Sept. 26, 1954; children: Ronen, Shirly, Roy. MD, Hebrew U., 1954. Intern, then resident Rambam Govt. Hosp., Haifa, 1960-73; resident, then chief resident surgery Rothschild Mcpl. Hosp., Haifa, 1960-73; head dept. surgery Rambam Govt. Hosp., 1973—. Served to capt. Israeli armed forces, 1977-82. Mem. Israel Med. Assn. (mem. cent. com. 1976-85). Home: 6 En Gedi, Haifa 3452P, Israel

HOROWITZ, BARNEY LOUIS, banker; b. Johannesburg, South Africa, Oct. 20, 1938; s. Robert and Rachel Horowitz; m. Andrea Benice Kimmel, Jan. 7, 1962; children: Sharon Anne, Robert Vernon, Daniel Alexander, Steven Michael. BA, U. Witwatersrand, 1958, LLB, 1961. Dir., Pioneer Holdings & Finance Corp., Johannesburg, 1961-73, mng. dir., vice chmn., 1973-78; pres. Barbenco USA, Inc. Investment Bankers, Stamford, Conn., 1978—. Address: Barbenco USA Inc 9 W Broad St Stamford CT 06902

HOROWITZ, BEN, medical center executive; b. Bklyn., Mar. 19, 1914; s. Saul and Sonia (Meringoff) H.; B.A., Bklyn. Coll., 1940; LL.B., St. Lawrence U., 1935; postgrad. New Sch. Social Research, 1942; m. Beverly Lichtman, Feb. 14, 1952; children—Zachary, Jody. Admitted to N.Y. bar, 1941, dir. N.Y. Fedn. Jewish Philanthropies, 1940-45; Eastern regional dir. City of Hope, 1945-50, nat. exec. sec., City of Hope Los Angeles, 1950-53, exec. dir., 1953-85, gen. v.p. City of Hope, 1986—; chmn. bd. dirs. com. City of Hope Nat. Med. Ctr., 1980—, pres., bd. dirs. 1986-87; bd. dirs. Beckman Research Inst. City of Hope, 1980—. Mem. Gov.'s Task Force on Flood Relief, 1969-74. Bd. dirs., v.p. Hope for Hearing Found., UCLA, 1972—. Recipient Spirit of Life award, 1970, Gallery of Achievement award, 1974, Profl. of Yr. award So. Calif. chpt. Nat. Soc. Fundraisers, 1977; Ben Horowitz chair in research established at City of Hope, 1981. Los Angeles City street named in his honor, 1986. Jewish (dir. temple 1964-67, 1986—). Home: 221 Conway Ave Los Angeles CA 90024 Office: City of Hope 208 W 8th St Los Angeles CA 90014

HOROWITZ, FRED L., dentist, educator, consultant; b. Chgo., June 10, 1954; s. Jacob and Celia (Morgenstern) H. BA, Washington U., St. Louis, 1976, DMD, 1979; cert. of residency, Sinai Hosp. Detroit, 1980. Gen. practice dentistry Chgo., 1981—; chief dental cons. Charter Barclay Hosp., Chgo., 1985—; mem. med. teaching staff Ravenswood Hosp., Chgo., 1983—, Michael Reese Hosp., Chgo., 1984—; mem. med. staff St. Francis Hosp., Evanston, 1987—; chmn. bd. Plan Adminstrs. Ill., Inc.; cons. Michael Reese Health Maintenance Orgn. Contbr. articles to Ravenswood Hosp. publs. Mem. Am. Assn. Hosp. Dentists, Acad. Gen. Dentistry, Alpha Omega (leadership award 1979). Office: Ravenswood Health Care Ctr 4211 N Cicero Chicago IL 60641 also: Plan Adminstrs of Ill 2545 S King Dr Chicago IL 60616

HOROWITZ, HERBERT EUGENE, foreign service officer; b. Bklyn., July 10, 1930; s. Max and Jean (Pomerantz) H.; m. Lenore Joan Glasser, Jan. 6, 1963; children: Jason, Richard. B.A., Bklyn. Coll., 1952; M.A., Columbia U., 1964, Fletcher Sch. Law, 1965; diploma, Nat. War Coll., 1972. Econ. officer Am. Embassy, Taipei, Taiwan, 1957-62; chief China econ. unit U.S. Consulate, Hong Kong, 1965-69; chief comml. and econ. sect. U.S. Liaison Office, Beijing, 1973-75; dir. Office for Research of East Asia, Dept. State, Washington, 1975-78; dir. Office East-West Econ. Policy Dept. Treasury, Washington, 1979-80; consul gen. U.S. Consulate Gen., Sydney, Australia, 1981-84; deputy chief of mission U.S. Embassy, Beijing, Peoples Republic of China, 1984-86; ambassador to Republic of Gambia 1986—. Mem. Assn. Asian Studies, Am. Fgn. Service Assn. Club: Fajara (Banjul, The Gambia). Office: Am Embassy Banjul The Gambia care Dept State Washington DC 20520

HOROWITZ, IRVING LOUIS, educator, publisher; b. N.Y.C., Sept. 25, 1929; s. Louis and Esther (Tepper) H.; m. Ruth Lenore Horowitz, 1950 (div. 1964); children: Carl Frederick, David Dennis; m. Mary Curtis Horowitz, 1979. B.S.S., CCNY, 1951; M.A., Columbia U., 1952; Ph.D., Buenos Aires (Argentina) U., 1957; postgrad. fellow, Brandeis U., 1958-59. Asst. prof. sociology Bard Coll., 1960; assoc. prof. social theory Buenos Aires U., 1955-58; chmn. dept. sociology Hobart and William Smith Colls., 1960-63; assoc. prof., then prof. sociology Washington U., St. Louis, 1963-69; chmn. dept. sociology Livingston Coll., Rutgers U., 1969-73; prof. sociology grad. faculty Rutgers U., 1969—, Hannah Arendt prof. social and polit. theory, 1979—; vis. prof. sociology U. Caracas, Venezuela, 1957, Buenos Aires U., 1959, 61, 63, SUNY, Buffalo, 1960, Syracuse U., 1961, U. Rochester, fall 1962, U. Calif., Davis, 1966, U. Wis., Madison, 1967, Stanford U., 1968-69, Am. U., 1972, Queen's U., Can., 1973, Princeton U., 1976; vis. lectr. London Sch. Econs. and Polit. Sci., 1962; Prin. investigator for numerous sci. and research projects. Author: Idea of War and Peace in Contemporary Philosophy, 1957, Philosophy, Science and the Sociology of Knowledge, 1960, Radicalism and the Revolt Against Reason: The Social Theories of Georges Sorel, 2d edit, 1968, The War Game; Studies of the New Civilian Militarists, 1963, Historia y Elementos de la Sociologia del Connocimento, 1963, Professing Sociology: The Life Cycle of a Social Science, 1963, The New Sociology: Essays in Social Science and Social Values in Honor of C. Wright Mills, 1964, Revolution in Brazil: Politics and Society in a Developing Nation, 1964, The Rise and Fall of Project Camelot, 1967, rev. edit., 1976, Three Worlds of Development: The Theory and Practice of International Stratification, 1966, rev. edit., 1972, Latin American Radicalism: A Documentary Report on Nationalist and Left Movements, 1969, Sociological Self-Images, 1969, The Knowledge Factory: Masses in Latin America, 1970, Cuban Communism, 1970, 6th edit., 1986, Foundations of Political Sociology, 1972, Social Science and Public Policy in the United States, 1975, Ideology and Utopia in the United States, 1977, Dialogues on American Politics, 1979, Taking Lives: Genocide and State Power, 1979, Beyond Empire and Revolution, 1982, C. Wright Mills: An American Utopian, 1983, Winners and Losers, 1985, Communicating Ideas, 1987; pres., editor-in-chief: Transaction/SOCIETY; pres. transaction books and periodicals. Fellow AAAS; mem. AAUP, Am. Polit. Sci. Assn., Am. Sociol. Assn., Authors Guild, Center for Study The Presidency, Council Fgn. Relations, Internat. Studies Assn., Latin Am. Studies Assn., Internat. Soc. Polit. Psychology (founder), Council on Fgn. Relations, Soc. Internat. Devel., Soc. Study Social Problems (chmn. awards com. 1964-66), Assn. Am. Pubs. (exec. dir.). Home: Rt 206 1247 State Rd Blawenburg Rd/Rocky Hill Intersection Princeton NJ 08540 Office: Rutgers Univ Dept Sociology Livingston Campus New Brunswick NJ 08903

HOROWITZ, STEPHEN PAUL, lawyer; b. Los Angeles, May 23, 1943; s. Julius J. and Maxine (Rubenstein) H.; m. Nancy J. Shapiro, Apr. 4, 1971; children: Lindsey Nicole, Keri Lyn, Deborah Arielle. B.S., UCLA, 1966; J.D., 1970; M. Acctg., U. So. Calif., 1967. CPA, Calif. Bookkeeper, various law and acctg. firms, 1963-70; staff acct. Touche, Ross & Co., C.P.A.s, Los Angeles, 1968, 69; admitted to Calif. bar, 1971, U.S. Dist. Ct. bar, 1971, U.S. Ct. Appeals bar, 1972; individual practice law, Los Angeles, 1971-77; partner firm Horowitz & Horowitz, Los Angeles, 1978-79, prin. firm, 1979—; judge pro tem Los Angeles Mcpl. Ct.; classroom speaker Los Angeles County Bar Assn.; arbitrator Better Bus. Bur., Los Angeles County Bar Assn., Am. Arbitration Assn.; ombudsman VA, 1970. Bd. dirs. Vols. Am. Detoxification and Rehab. Center, Los Angeles, 1975-81, treas., 1979, vice chmn., 1980-81; legal adv. chmn., parliamentarian Temple Ramat Zion, Northridge, Calif., 1983-88, v.p., 1988. Served with U.S. Army, 1961-62. Mem. Calif. State Bar, Calif. Trial Lawyers Assn., Los Angeles Trial Lawyers. Jewish. Lodge: Masons. Editorial bd. UCLA-Alaska Law Rev., 1968-70, co-editor-in-chief, 1969-70. Office: 8383 Wilshire Blvd Suite 528 Beverly Hills CA 90211

HOROWITZ, TAMAR RUTH, behavioral science researcher, educator; b. Jerusalem, June 29, 1935; d. Natan Aharon and Malka (Many) Zuta; m. Dan Horowitz, Nov. 9, 1955; children: Yael, Avner. BA, Hebrew U., Jerusalem, 1959, MA, 1962; PhD, Leicester (Eng.) U., 1970. Lectr. sociology Leicester U., 1963-67; sr. researcher Szold Inst. for Behavioral Sci., Jerusalem, 1967—; vis. scholar dept. higher edn. U. Mich., Ann Arbor, 1975, Gallaudet Coll., Washington, 1983; vis. lectr. Ben Gurion U., Beer Sheva, Israel, 1980—; mem. coms. on ednl. planning and sch. violence Ministry of Edn., 1976—. Author: The Teaching Profession in Israel, 1985, Between Two Worlds - Soviet Children in Israel, 1987. Trustee Chan Theatre, Jerusalem, 1979—; mem. Com. to Preserve Hist. Bldgs. in Jerusalem, 1985—. Internat. Soc. for Research on Aggression fellow, 1987—. Mem. Internat. Assn. Cross Cultural Psychology. Office: Szold Inst for Behavioral Sci, 9 Columbia St, Jerusalem 96538, Israel

HOROWITZ, VLADIMIR, pianist; b. Kiev, Russia, Oct. 1, 1904; s. Samuel and Sophia (Bodik) H.; m. Wanda Toscanini, Dec. 21, 1933; 1 dau., Sonia (dec.). Ed., Kiev Conservatory; study under, Felix Blumenfeld, Sergei Tarnowsky. Made first appearance at age 17, Kiev, Russia; made debut Europe, 1925, made debut in U.S. with N.Y. Philharm., Jan. 1928; concert tours of U.S., 1928—; most recent performances White House, 1978, 1986, Royal Festival Hall, London, 1982, Japan tour, 1983, USSR tour, 1986. Recipient 23 Grammy awards for best classical performance, instrumental soloist or soloists, 1966-81, 87, for best classical recording, 1987; recipient Best Classical Performance/Instrumental Soloist for Kreisleriana Ministry Edn. Japanese Govt., 1971, Acad. Award/Classic Best Instrumental Soloist, Rec. Geijutsu, 1971, Best Performance Award-Classic Instrumental Soloist CBS/SONY, 1970, Prix Mondial du Disque for Kreisleriana, 1971, Gold Medal Royal Philharm. Soc., 1972, Grand Prix des Discophiles, 1966; decorated Medal of Freedom; Comdr. Legion of Honor (France); Knight grand cross Order of Merit (Italy); recipient President's Merit award, Nat. Acad. of Recording Artists & Scis., 1987. Address: care Columbia Artists Mgmt 165 W 57 St New York NY 10019 *

HORRIGAN, EDWARD A., JR., food and consumer products company executive; b. N.Y.C., Sept. 23, 1929; s. Edward A. and Margaret V. (Kenny) H.; m. Elizabeth R. Herperger, June 27, 1953; children: Ellen, Christopher, Gordon, Brian. B.S. in Bus. Adminstrn, U. Conn., 1950; grad., Advanced Mgmt. Program, Harvard U., 1965. Mgr. sales Procter & Gamble Co., N.Y.C., 1954-58; gen. mgr. Ebonite Co., Boston, 1958-61; div. v.p. T.J. Lipton Inc., 1961-73; chmn. bd., pres. Buckingham Corp., N.Y.C., 1973-78; chmn. bd., chief exec. officer R.J. Reynolds Tobacco Internat., Inc., Winston-Salem, N.C., 1978-80; chmn. bd., pres., chief exec. officer R.J. Reynolds Tobacco Co., Winston-Salem, 1980-81, chmn., chief exec. officer, 1987—; exec. v.p. RJR Nabisco, Inc., 1981-84, pres., chief operating officer, 1984-85, vice chmn. bd., 1985—; chmn., chief exec. officer R.J. Reynolds Tabacco Co., 1987—. Served as officer, inf. U.S. Army, 1950-54. Decorated Silver Star, Purple Heart, Combat Inf. badge, Parachute badge. Mem. Knights of Malta. Clubs: Old Town Country, Vintage. Home: 2815 Bartram Rd Winston-Salem NC 27106 Office: RJ Reynolds Tobacco Co 401 N Main St Winston-Salem NC 27102

HORROCKS, FREDERICK JOHN, electrical engineer; b. Birmingham, West Midlands, Eng., Nov. 8, 1941; s. Hubert and Muriel Arch (Tustin) H.; m. Mary Dungey, July 25, 1963; children: Diana Mary, Judith Anne. AA, City and Guilds Inst., U. London, 1963, BSc in Engring., 1963, diploma, Imperial Coll., 1965; MSc in Indsl. Adminstrn., U. Aston, Birmingham, Eng., 1969. Design engr. B.K.B. (Electric Motors) Ltd., Birmingham, 1964-66, mgr. prodn., 1966-69, gen. mgr., 1969-73; mgr. quality control Otis Elevator (UK) Ltd., Liverpool, Eng., 1973-75, mgr. contracts, 1975-80; mgr. tech. Bull Elec. Ltd., Ipswich, Eng., 1980-82, mgr. mktg., 1982-84; mgr. tech. mktg. Ling Dynamic Systems Ltd., Royston, Eng., 1984-87, mgr. applications engring., 1987—; cons. in field. Mem. Inst. Elec. Engrs. (chair Ipswich area chpt. 1986-87), The Combined European Environ. Engring. Socs. (sec. 1986-88), Soc. Environ. Engrs. Anglican. Office: Ling Dynamic Systems Ltd, Baldock Rd, Royston SG8 5BQ, England

HORSLEY, JACK EVERETT, lawyer, author; b. Sioux City, Iowa, Dec. 12, 1915; s. Charles E. and Edith V. (Timms) H.; m. Sallie Kelley, June 12, 1939 (dec.); children: Pamela, Charles Edward; m. Bertha J. Newland, Feb. 24, 1950 (dec.); m. Mary Jane Moran, Jan. 20, 1973; 1 child, Sharon. AB, U. Ill., 1937, JD, 1939. Bar: Ill. 1939. With Craig & Craig, Mattoon, Ill., 1939—, sr. counsel; vice chmn., bd. dirs. Cen. Nat. Bank, 1976—, Harlan Moore Heart Research Found., 1968—; mem. lawyers adv. council U. Ill. Law Forum, 1960-63; lectr. Practising Law Inst., N.Y.C., 1967-73, Ct. Practice Inst., Chgo., 1974—, U. Mich. Coll. Law Inst. Continuing Legal Edn., 1968; vis. lectr. Orange County (Fla.) Med. Soc., 1975, San Diego Med. Soc., 1970, U. S.C., 1976, Duquesne Coll., 1970; chmn. rev. com. Ill. Supreme Ct. Disciplinary Commn., 1973-76. Narrator: Poetry Interludes, Sta. WLBH-FM; author: Trial Lawyer's Manual, 1967, Voir Dire Examinations and Opening Statements, 1968, Current Development in Products Liability Law, 1969, Illinois Civil Practice and Procedure, 1970, The Medical Expert Witness, 1973, The Doctor and the Law, 1975, The Doctor and Family Law, 1975, The Doctor and Business Law, 1976, The Doctor and Medical Law, 1977, Testifying in Court, 1973, 2d edit., 1983, 3d edit., 1987, Anatomy of a Medical Malpractice Case, 1984; contbr. articles to profl. jours. including RN Mag. and Forensic Scis.; cons., contbr. Med. Econs., 1969—; legal cons. Mast-Head, 1972—. Pres. bd. edn. Sch. Dist. 100, 1946-48; bd. dirs. Harlan Moore Heart Research Found., 1968—; vol. reader in recording texts Am. Assn. for Blind, 1970-72. Served to lt. col. U.S. Army, 1942-46. Fellow Am. Coll. Trial Lawyers; mem. ABA, Ill. Bar Assn. (exec. council ins. law 1961-63, lectr. law course for attys. 1962, 64-65, Disting. Service award 1982-83), Coles-Cumberland Bar Assn. (v.p. 1968-69, pres. 1969-70, chmn. com. jud. inquiry 1976-80, chmn. meml. com. 1981—), Am. Arbitration Assn. (nat. panel arbitrators), U. Ill. Law Alumni Assn. (pres. 1966-67, Alumni of Month Sept. 1974), Ill. Def. Counsel Assn. (pres. 1967-68), Soc. Trial Lawyers (chmn. profl. activities 1960-61, bd. dirs. 1966-67), Adelphic Debating Soc., Assn. Ins. Attys., Internat. Assn. Ins. Counsel, Am. Judicature Soc., Appellate Lawyers Assn., Scribes, Delta Phi (exec. com. alumni assn. 1960-61, 67-68), Sigma Delta Kappa. Republican. Lodge: Masons (32 degree). Home: 50 Elm Ridge Mattoon IL 61938 Office: Craig & Craig 1807 Broadway PO Box 689 Mattoon IL 61938

HORSLEY, PAULA ROSALIE, accountant; b. Smithfield, Nebr., Sept. 7, 1924; d. Karl and Clara Margaret (Busse) Fenske; m. Phillip Carreon (div.); children—Phillip, James, Robert, David, Richard; m. Norby Lumon, Apr. 5, 1980. Student AIB Bus. Coll., Des Moines, 1942-44, YMCA Coll., Chgo., 1944-47, UCLA Extension, 1974. Acctg. mgr. Montgomery Ward & Co., Denver, 1959-62; acct. Harman & Co., C.P.A.s, Arcadia, Calif., 1962-67; controller, officer G & H Transp., Montebello, Calif., 1967-78; comptroller Frederick Weisman Co., Century City, Calif., 1978-80; chief fin. officer Lutheran Shipping, Madang, Papua, New Guinea, 1980-82; prin. Village Bookkeeper, acctg. cons., Monreno Valley, Calif., 1982—; chief fin. officer Insight Computer Products and Tech., Inc., San Diego, 1988—. Vol. crises counselor, supr. and instr. Melodyland Hotline, Anaheim, Calif., 1976-79. Mem. Riverside Tax Cons., Nat. Assn. for Female Execs., Internat. Platform Assn. Republican. Lutheran. Avocations: church activities, reading, cooking, phys. fitness. Home: 4660 N River Rd SP 129 Oceanside CA 92054 Office: Insight Computer Products and Techs Inc 4883 Ronson Ct Suite T San Diego CA 92111

HORSMAN, DAVID A. ELLIOTT, author, educator, financial services executive; b. Calvert County, Md., June 28, 1932; s. Alvin W. and Bessie L. (Elliott) H.; student U. Chgo.; B.A., San Francisco State U., 1964; M.A., N.Y. U., 1967, Ph.D., 1970, M.Div., Episcopal Div. Sch., 1984. Floor dir., stage mgr. WTOP-TV, Washington, 1959-61; TV writer/producer Insight, Nat. Council Chs., Washington, 1961-62; English master, dir. studies Searing Sch., N.Y.C., 1965-67; asst. prof. humanities Acad. Aeros., Flushing, N.Y., 1967-68; instr. humanities Rensselaer Poly. Inst., Troy, N.Y., 1969-70; asso. prof., founder and coordinator film sequence U. South Fla., Tampa, 1970-80; adj. prof. Union Grad. Sch., Yellow Springs, Ohio, 1976—; headmaster All Hallows Acad., Alexandria, Va., 1985-87; asst. mgr., sr. account exec. Blinder, Robinson and Co., Columbia, Md., 1987-88; pres. Elliott Horsman & Assocs., 1988—. Served with U.S. Army, 1957-59. Recipient Founders Day award N.Y. U., 1971. Fellow Intercontinental Biog. Assn. (Cert. of Merit 1974); mem. MLA, Nat. Soc. Hist. Preservation, Univ. Film Assn., Am. Film Inst., Internat. Platform Assn., Soc. Edn. in Film and TV, Alcuin Club. Episcopalian. Author: The Liturgy as Communication, 1970; (novel and screenplay) Pilgrims on Strange Strands, 1979; Introduction to Structural Description of Liturgical Dromena, 1979. Home: 212 East Main St Salisbury MD 21801 Office: Blinder Robinson & Co 10480 Little Patuxent Pkwy Columbia MD 21044

HORSNELL, WALTER CECIL, artist; b. Ware, Hertfordshire, Eng., Dec. 18, 1911; s. John William and Emily Agatha (Baker) H.; studied at Bolt Ct. Sch. Art, London and St. Martin's Sch. Art, London; m. Kathleen Leslie, Oct. 2, 1963; children by previous marriage: Lionel, Thelma, Elva, Adrian. Painter in oil, pastel, watercolor, mixed media of landscapes, figures and portraits, 1928—; graphic artist various art studios, London, 1929-39; art designer for motion picture presentations, 1936-39; ofcl. illustrator Brit. Ministry Aircraft Prodn., London, 1942-47; one-man shows Harrogate Festival Arts, 1970, various pvt. galleries London and provinces, 1928—; numerous group shows including Nat. Portrait Gallery, London, 1944, Royal Soc. Brit. Artists, 1946, Royal Acad. Arts, London, 1949, mcpl. galleries Leeds, Blackpool, Bradford, Brighton, Harrogate, Keighley (U.K.), 1945-70, Yorkshire Arts Assn., 1974, Rural Preservation Assn., Edinburgh and Liverpool, 1977; represented in permanent collections Grundy Gallery, Blackpool, Lambeth Palace, London, Canterbury (Kent) Palace, also pvt. collections; mural paintings at Barclays Bank, Carlton Lodge Hosp., Midland Bank, Harrogate (Eng.) Coll., Harrogate Gen. Hosp., Nat. Westminster Bank, 1960—; demonstrator painting art socs., 1947-77. Served with Nat. Fire Service, 1939-40, RAF, 1941-42. Recipient 1st prize nat. poster design RAF, Brit. Ministry Def., 1975; diploma and Gold medal Accademia delle Arte, Italy, 1981; Premio d'Italia award, Cremona, Italy, 1985; Majestic Trusthouse Forte Design award, 1987; Targa d'Oro Italia award Town of Harrogate, 1987. Home: Studio 89, Knox Ave, Harrogate North Yorkshire HG1 3JF, England

HORTON, PAUL BRADFIELD, lawyer; b. Dallas, Oct. 19, 1920; s. Frank Barrett and Hazel Lillian (Bradfield) H.; m. Susan Jeanne Diggle, May 19, 1949; children: Bradfield Ragland, Bruce Ragsdale. B.A., U. Tex., Austin, 1943, student Law Sch., 1941-43; LL.B., So. Methodist U., 1947. Bar: Tex. 1946. Ptnr. McCall, Parkhurst & Horton, Dallas, 1951—; lectr. mcpl. bond law and pub. finance S.W. Legal Found.; drafter Tex. mcpl. bonds legislation, 1963—. Mem. Gov.'s Com. Tex. Edn. Code, 1967-69. Served to lt. USNR, 1943-46. Mem. Am., Dallas bar assns., Nat. Water Resources Assn., Tex. Water Conservation Assn., Govt. Finance Officers Assn., The Barristers, Delta Theta Phi, Beta Theta Pi. Clubs: Dallas Country, Crescent, Tower, 2001 (Dallas). Home: 5039 Seneca Dr Dallas TX 75209 Office: McCall Parkhurst & Horton 717 N Harwood St Suite 900 Dallas TX 75201

HORTON, ROBERT ANDREW, chemical engineer; b. Oradell, N.J., Feb. 22, 1929; George Francis and May (Acker) H.; m. Lillian Marie Brandow, Sept. 23, 1950; children: Robert A., William T., Thomas J., Nancy K. BChemE, Cooper Union Sch. Engring., 1955. Chemist Austenal, Inc., Dover, N.J., 1955-59; pilot plant mgr. Precision Metal Smiths, Inc., Cleve., 1959-72, dir. research and devel., 1972-80; sect. mgr., project leader TRW, Inc., Cleve., 1980-86; mgr. casting tech. PCC Airfoils, Inc., Cleve., 1986—. Contbr. papers to tech. jour.; holder of 33 U.S. Patents. Fellow Am. Inst. Chemists; mem. AAAS, Am. Ceramic Soc., Am. Soc. for Metals, Ductile Iron Soc. (mem. research com. 1976-80), Investment Casting Inst. (pattern materials com. 1986). Home: 12781 Caves Rd Chesterland OH 44026 Office: PCC Airfoils Inc 23555 Euclid Ave Cleveland OH 44117

HORTON, ROBERT BAYNES, petroleum company executive; b. Bushey, Eng., Aug. 18, 1939; s. William H. Horton and Dorothy Joan (Baynes) Dunn; m. Sally Doreen Wells, July 28, 1962; children: Simon, Ruth. BSME, U. St. Andrews, Scotland, 1960; MS, MIT, 1971. With Brit. Petroleum Ltd. (now BP plc), London, 1957—; gen. mgr. BP Tankers, London, 1975-76, gen. mgr. corp. planning, 1976-79; mng. dir. BP Co. plc, 1983-86, 1988—; vice chmn., chief exec. officer BP Am. Inc., 1987-88; chmn., chief exec. officer Standard Oil Co., Cleve., 1986-88, also bd. dirs.; bd. dirs. API, Nat. City Corp., Emerson Electric Co. Trustee Case Western Res. U., Cleve.; mem. Com. for Econ. Devel., MIT Corp. Fellow Royal Soc. Arts; mem. Nat. Petroleum Council, Chem. Industries Assn. (pres. 1982-84), Bus. Roundtable, British Inst. Mgmt. (companion, vice chmn. 1984—), Musical Arts Assn. (trustee), Univ. Circle Inc. (trustee). Anglican. Clubs: Carlton (London); Leander (Henley, Eng.); Union, Pepper Pike (Cleve.). Office: BP Co PLC, Britannic House, Moor Ln, London EC24 9BU, England *

HORTON, THOMAS CLIFFORD, SR., farmer, rancher, water cooperative executive; b. Venus, N.Mex., Jan. 23, 1916; s. Claude C. and Ethel M. (Madole) H.; m. Rita Shook, Dec. 27, 1937; children—Rita-Loy Horton Thomas, Sharron Horton Geilenfeldt, Thomas Clifford. Grad. Menaul Sch. of United Presbyn. Ch., 1936. Farmer, rancher Santa Fe and Bernalillo Counties (N.Mex.), 1936—; farm instr. Edgewood Dist. (N.Mex.) State Coll., 1947-49; sub-contractor road constrn. Allison-Haney Co., Albuquerque, 1953-54, Northwestern Engrs., Denver, 1953-54, Floyd Hake, Santa Fe, 1953-54; gen. contractor, Albuquerque, 1954—; bldg. supr. Bd. Nat. Missions United Presbyn. Ch. U.S.A., N.Mex., Ariz., Utah, Tex., Alaska, 1954-71, asst. dir. Bd. Properties div., 1961-69; founder Entranosa Water Corp. (name changed to Entranosa Water Cooperative 1981), Santa Fe and Bernalillo Counties, 1974—, comptroller, 1982—; founder El Monte Sol Water Cooperative Assn., 1987—. Sec. Edgewood Soil Conservation Dist., 1942-43; mem. adv. com. Santa Fe County Long Range Planning Program, 1948-49; organizer no. half Estancia Valley for REA com., 1949-50; pub. relations officer Cen. N.Mex. Elec. Coop., 1950-52. Mem. Menual Sch. Alumni Assn. Democrat. Clubs: Mason, Moriarty Rotary. Address: PO Box 150 Edgewood NM 87015

HORTON, WARREN, national library administrator; b. Sydney, Australia, June 23, 1938; m. Patsy Hardy, Nov. 1983. BA, U. Sydney, 1973. Various positions State Library of New South Wales, Sydney, 1957-75, dep. state librarian, 1975-81; state librarian Library Council of Victoria, Melbourne, 1981-85; dir. gen. Nat. Library Australia, Canberra, 1985—; chmn. Australian Libraries and Info. Council, 1985-86. Fellow Library Assn. Australia (pres. 1984). Office: Nat Library of Australia, Parkes Place, Canberra 2600, Australia

HORTTOR, DONALD J., lawyer; b. Fort Scott, Kans., May 3, 1932; s. Elmer J. and Cleda C. (Cox) H.; m. Jane Ann Ausherman, Mar. 22, 1959; children—Daun Ann, Bretton J. A.B. in Econs., U. Kans., 1953, J.D., 1959; LL.M. in Taxation, NYU, 1961. Bar: Kans. 1959, U.S. Dist. Ct. Kans. 1959, U.S. Ct. Appeals (10th cir.) 1963, U.S. Supreme Ct. 1965, U.S. Tax Ct. 1965. Adj. prof. Washburn U. Law Sch., Topeka, 1965-76; Assoc. Cosgrove, Webb and Oman, Topeka, 1959-63, ptnr., 1963—. Served to capt. USAF, 1953-56. Mem. ABA, Topeka Bar Assn., Kans. Bar Assn. Republican. Congregationalist. Clubs: Topeka Country, Masons, Elks, Moose. Author: Estate Planning, Why a Will; Kansas Estate Administration. Office: Bank IV Tower Suite 1100 Topeka KS 66603

HORVATH, WILLIAM JOHN, health systems educator, research scientist; b. N.Y.C., Sept. 13, 1917; s. John and Anna (Horvath) H.; m. Rebecca Sue Badger, Feb. 23, 1963; children—Susan, John. B.S., CCNY, 1936; M.S., NYU, 1938, Ph.D., 1940. Physicist U.S. Navy-Bur. Ordnance, Washington, 1940-43; ops. analyst Chief of Naval Ops., Washington, 1943-49; sci. advisor Weapons Systems Evaluation Group, Sec. of Def., Washington, 1949-52; staff cons. Sylvania Electric Co., Bayside, N.Y., 1952-55; sect. head. Airborne Instrument Lab., Mineola, N.Y., 1955-58; prof. health systems, research scientist U. Mich., Ann Arbor, 1958—; cons. Nat. Acad. Sci., 1952-55, NIH, 1962-70, NIMH, 1967-72. Author numerous chpts. and articles in nuclear physics, ops. research, math. sociology, med. physics, health care delivery, health behavior. Bd. dirs. Washtenaw Community Services, Ann Arbor, 1978-80, Community Systems Found., Ann Arbor, 1978-81. Recipient Naval Ordnance Devel. award U.S. Dept. Navy, 1945; Presdl. Cert. of Merit, 1947. Fellow AAAS, Am. Pub. Health Assn.; mem. Am. Phys. Soc., Ops. Research Soc. Am. (Kimball medal 1977), Royal Soc. Health. Club: Cosmos (Washington). Home: 2451 Trenton Ct Ann Arbor MI 48106 Office: Mental Health Research Inst U Mich Ann Arbor MI 48109

HORWIN, LEONARD, lawyer; b. Chgo., Jan. 2, 1913; s. Joseph and Jennie (Fuhrmann) H.; m. Ursula Helene Donig, Oct. 15, 1939; children—Noel Samuel, Leonora Marie. LLB cum laude, Yale U., 1936. Bar: Calif. 1936, U.S. Dist. Ct. (cen. dist.) Calif. 1937, U.S. Ct. Appeals (9th cir.) 1939, U.S. Supreme Ct. 1940. Assoc., Lawler, Felix & Hall, 1936-39; ptnr. Hardy & Horwin, Los Angeles, 1939-42; counsel Bd. Econ. Warfare, Washington, 1942-43; attache, legal advisor U.S. Embassy, Madrid, Spain, 1943-47; sole practice, Beverly Hills, Calif., 1948—; dir., lectr. Witkin-Horwin Rev. Course on Calif. Law, 1939-42; judge pro tempore Los Angeles Superior Ct., 1940-42; instr. labor law U. So. Calif., 1939-42. U.S. rep. Allied Control Council for Ger., 1945-47; councilman City of Beverly Hills, 1962-66, mayor, 1964-65; chmn. transp. Los Angeles Goals Council, 1968; bd. dirs. So. Calif. Rapid Transit Dist., 1964-66; chmn. Rent Stabilization Com., Beverly Hills, 1980. Fellow Am. Acad. Matrimonial Lawyers; mem. ABA, State Bar Calif., Order Coif. Clubs: Balboa Bay, Aspen Inst. Contbr. articles to profl. jours. Office: 121 S Beverly Dr Beverly Hills CA 90212

HORWITT, MAX KENNETH, biochemist, educator; b. N.Y.C., Mar. 21, 1908; s. Harry and Bessie (Kenitz) H.; m. Frances Levine, 1933 (dec.); children: Ruth Ann Horwitt Singer, Mary Louise Horwitt Goldman; m. Mildred Gad Weitzman, Jan. 1, 1974. B.A., Dartmouth Coll., 1930; Ph.D., Yale U., 1935. Diplomate: Am. Bd. Nutrition, Am. Bd. Clin. Chemistry. Research fellow physiol. chemistry Yale U., 1935-37, lab. asst., 1932-34, asst., 1934-35; dir. biochem. research lab. Elgin (Ill.) State Hosp., 1937-59; dir. biochem. research lab. L.B. Mendel Research Lab., 1960-68, dir. research, 1966-68; asso. dept. biol. chemistry U. Ill. Coll. Medicine, Chgo., 1940-43; asst. prof. U. Ill. Coll. Medicine, 1943-51, asso. prof., 1951-62, prof., from 1962; prof. dept. biochemistry St. Louis U. Sch. Medicine, 1968-76, prof. emeritus, 1976—, cons. in nutrition div. endocrinology dept. internal medicine, 1976—, chmn. univ. instl. rev. bd., 1981-82; acting dir. div. research services Ill. Dept. Mental Health, Chgo., 1967-68; cons. human nutrition Rush Med. Sch., Chgo., 1967-83, vis. prof. dept. internal medicine, 1979-82; mem. expert group on Vitamin E WHO, 1981-82; field dir. Anemia and Malnutrition Research Center, Chiang Mai Med. Sch., Thailand, 1968-69; cons., 1976—. Contbr. numerous articles on clin. nutrition, biochemistry and psychopharmacology to profl. publs.; editorial bd.: Jour. Nutrition, 1967-71; co-editor: Am. Jour. Clin. Nutrition, 1974. Pres. Kneseth Israel Congregation, Elgin, 1965. Recipient Osborne and Mendal award Am. Inst. Nutrition, 1961. Fellow AAAS, N.Y. Acad. Scis., Am. Inst. Nutrition, Am. Inst. Chemists, Gerontol. Soc.; mem. Am. Soc. Biol. Chemists, Am. Soc. Clin. Nutrition, NRC (food and nutrition bd. 1980-86, com. dietary allowances), Soc. Exptl. Biology and Medicine, Soc. Biol. Psychiatry, Assn. Vitamin Chemists, Am. Chem. Soc. Office: St Louis Univ Sch Medicine 1402 S Grand Blvd Saint Louis MO 63104

HORWITZ, DAVID LARRY, health care executive, researcher, educator; b. Chgo., July 13, 1942; s. Milton Woodrow and Dorothy (Glass) H.; m. Gloria Jean Madian, June 20, 1965; children—Karen, Laura. A.B., Harvard U., 1963; M.D., U. Chgo., 1967, Ph.D., 1968. Diplomate Am. Bd. Internal Medicine. Resident in internal medicine U. Chgo. Hosp., 1971-72; fellow in endocrinology U. Chgo., 1972-74, asst. prof., 1974-79; assoc. prof. U. Ill.-Chgo., 1979—; med. dir. Baxter Healthcare Corp., Deerfield, Ill., 1982—. Contbr. articles to profl. jours. Bd. dirs. No. Ill. affiliate Am. Diabetes Assn., 1976—, pres. 1987—. Served to comdr. USNR, 1969-71. Recipient Research and Devel. award Am. Diabetes Assn., 1974-76; Outstanding Young Citizen of Chgo. award Chgo. Jr. C. of C., 1976; Outstanding Young Citizen Ill. award Ill. Jaycees, 1977. Fellow ACP; mem. Endocrine Soc., Am. Diabetes Assn. (chmn. com. on planning and orgn. 1986-88), Am. Assn. Clin. Nutrition. Office: Baxter Healthcare Corp One Baxter Pkwy Deerfield IL 60015

HORWOOD, ELLIS GEORGE, publisher; b. Bromley, Eng., Oct. 13, 1911; s. William and Emma (Binley) H.; m. Felicity Mary Hodges, Aug. 18, 1972; children—Susan, Michael, Clive, Margaret, Mark. Asst. pub. Macmillan & Co. Ltd., London and Madras, 1927-48; pub., bus. mgr. Elsevier Pub. Co., London, 1949-57; mng. dir. Cleaver-Hume Press/D. Van Nostrand Co., London, 1957-72; founder, chmn., pub. Ellis Horwood Ltd., Chichester, Eng., 1973—. Author: Publishing with Ellis Horwood, 1983. Served to maj. Gurkha Brigade, 1941-46. Decorated mem. Order Brit. Empire. Fellow Royal Soc. Chemistry; mem. Soc. Chem. Industry, Liverymen, Worshipful Co. of Blacksmiths City of London. Club: Hurlingham. Avocations: gardening; music; spectator sports. Office: Ellis Horwood Ltd, Market Cross House, Cooper St, Chichester, West Sussex PO19 1EB, England

HOSBACH, HOWARD DANIEL, publishing company executive; b. North Bergen, N.J., Mar. 9, 1931; s. Howard D. and Marjorie V. (Hoffer) H.; m. Eugenia Elizabeth Paracka, Apr. 10, 1954; children: Susan Hosbach Murray, Cynthia Hosbach Miezeiewski, Beth Ann, Alyssa. B.S., Fairleigh Dickinson U., 1953, M.B.A., 1967. Advt. mgr. McGraw-Hill Book Co., N.Y.C., 1958-62; dir. mktg. McGraw-Hill Book Co., 1962-66, gen. mgr. dealer and library sales, 1966-69; group v.p. Standard & Poor's Corp., N.Y.C., 1970-73; exec. v.p., chief operating officer Standard & Poor's Corp., 1973-80, pres., chief exec. officer, 1981-84, chmn., chief exec. officer, 1985-88; exec. v.p. ops. McGraw-Hill, Inc., 1985-88; bd. dirs. Interlake Corp., Chgo. Trustee Fairleigh Dickinson U., Peirce Jr. Coll.; chmn. Assn. for Help Retarded Children, 1983—; mem. Governing Bds. of Univs. and Colls., 1983—. Served with AUS, 1953-55. Recipeint Alumni medal for disting. service Fairleigh Dickinson U. Trustees. Roman Catholic. Home: 104 Green Way Allendale NJ 07401 Office: McGraw-Hill Inc 1221 Ave of the Americas New York NY 10020 also: Standard & Poor's Corp 25 Broadway New York NY 10004

HOŠEK, ANKICA, sociology educator; b. Banja Luka, Yugoslavia, Jan. 11, 1949; d. Venceslav and Miroslava (Savaric) H.; m. Konstantin Momizovic, Oct. 4, 1975. BS, U. Zagreb, Yugoslavia, 1972, MS, 1976, PhD, 1978. Lab. technician Inst. for Kinesiology, Zagreb, 1971; asst. U. Zagreb, 1972-78, asst. prof., 1978-82, assoc. prof., 1982-87, prof., 1987—, dean, 1987—; visiting prof. Fac. of Phys. Culture, U. Ljubljana, Yugoslavia, Faculty of Sci. and Math. U., Zagreb, Faculty of Physical Edn. U., Novi Sad, Yugoslavia. Author: Social Stratification, 1975, Sociology of Sport, 1987; contbr. over 85 articles to various profl. jours. Recipient state award for Scientific Achievement, Republic of Croatia, 1987. Me. Internat. Sociol. Assn., European Anthrop. Assoc., Internat. Assn. for Genetics and Somatology, Croatian Anthro. Assn. (v.p. 1975). Home: Brace Domany 4, 41000 Zagreb Yugoslavia Office: Fac of Physical Culture, Horvacanski Zavoj 15, 41000 Zagreb Yugoslavia

HOSEMAN, DANIEL, lawyer; b. Chgo., Aug. 18, 1935; s. Irving and Anne (Pruzansky) H.; m. Susan H. Myles, Aug. 7, 1960; children—Lawrence N., Joan E., Jonathan W. B.A., U. Ill., 1956, J.D., 1959. Bar: Ill. 1959, U.S. Dist. Ct. (no. dist.) Ill. 1960, U.S. Ct. Appeals (7th cir.) 1967, U.S. Supreme Ct. 1976. Sole practice, Chgo., 1959—; mem. panel pvt. atty. trustees U.S. Bankruptcy Ct. No. Dist. Ill., 1979—. Trustee Ill. Legal Services Fund, 1978—; v.p. Allied Jewish Sch. Bd. Met. Chgo., 1977—; v.p. United Synagogue Am., 1978—. Served with USAFR, 1959-65. Mem. Decalogue Soc. Lawyers (pres. 1981-82, award of merit 1979-80), Ill. Bar Assn. (gen. assembly, long-range planning com.), Lake County Bar Assn. (com. on bankruptcy 1980—), Chgo. Council Lawyers, Am. Bankruptcy Inst., Advocates Soc., Comml. Law League Am. Home: 2151 Tanglewood Ct Highland Park IL 60035 Office: 105 W Madison St Suite 704 Chicago IL 60602

HOSIE, PETER JOHN, educator; b. Perth, Australia, Jan. 8, 1957; s. John Stuart and Yvonne Mary (Hathway) H.; m. Sari Maree Smith, Dec. 31, 1978; children: Simone, Camille. Diploma of Teaching, Western Australian Secondary Tchrs. Coll., 1977; B Ed, Western Australia Inst. Tech., 1981; BA with honors, Murdoch U., 1986. Secondary tchr. Edn. Dept. Western Australia, Bunbury, 1978-81, master spl. duties, 1982-86, edn. officer, 1986-87; tng. program designer State Energy Commn. of Western Australia, 1988—. Contbr. articles to profl. jours.; coordinator ednl. videotapes, profl. confs. Recipient Jiout award, Mobie award Internat. TV Assn., 1986, Adesic award Nat. Tng. Film Awards, 1986. Mem. Australian Coll. Edn., Australian Soc. Ednl. Tech., Ednl. Computing Assn. Western Australia. Home: 15 Adare Way Kingsley, 6026 Perth Australia

HOSKINS, ROBERT WILLIAM, actor; b. Oct. 26, 1942; s. Robert and Elsie Lilian Hoskins; m. Jane Levesey, 1970 (div.); 2 children; m. Linda Banwell, 1984; 2 children. Grad., Stroud Green Sch. With Intimate Theatre, Palmers Green, Eng., 1966, Victoria theatre, Stoke on Trent, Eng., 1967, Century Travelling Theatre, 1969, Royal Court, 1972. Performances include (plays) Pygmalion, 1974, Aldwych, 1976, The World Turned Upside Down, 1978, Has Washington Legs, 1978, True West, 1981, Guys and Dolls, 1981; (TV) On the Move, 1976, Pennies from Heaven, 1978, Flickers, 1980, The Dunera Boys, 1985; (films) Zulu Dawn, 1980, The Long Good Friday, 1981, The Honorary Consul, 1982, Lassiter, 1984, Cotton Club, 1984, Sweet Liberty, 1986, Mona Lisa, 1986 (Best Actor award Cannes festival). Office: care Anne Hutton, Hutton Mgmt, 200 Fulham Rd, London SW10, England *

HOSOE, EIKOH, photographer, educator; b. Yonezawa, Japan, Mar. 18, 1933; s. Yonejiro and Mitsuko (Nakagawa) H.; m. Misako Imai, Apr. 2, 1962; children—Kenji, Kanako, Kumiko. B.A., Tokyo Coll. Photography, 1954. Prof. Tokyo Inst. Poly., 1975—; individual exhibitions: Konishiroku Gallery, Ginza Tokyo, 1956, 60, Nikon Salon, Ginza, 1969, Smithsonian Instn., Washington, 1969, Light Gallery, N.Y.C., 1973, 75, 83, Nikon Salon, 1977, Photographers' Gallery, Melbourne, Australia, 1979, Silver Image Gallery, Ohio State Univ., Columbus, 1979; FNAC Forum, Paris, 1980, Galerij Paule Pia, Antwerp, Belgium, 1981, Internat. Mus. Photography, Rochester, N.Y., 1982; public exhibitions: Shadai Gallery, Tokyo, Nihin Univ., Tokyo, Mus. Modern Art, N.Y.C., Internat. Mus. Photography, George Eastman House, Rochester, N.Y., Smithsonian Instn., Washington, Nat. Gallery of Can., Ottawa, Victoria and Albert Mus., London, Bibliotheque Nationale, Paris, Musee d'Art de Ville de Paris, Nat. Gallery of Australia, Canberra. Recipient Photographer of Yr. award Japan Photo Critics Assn., 1963; Art award Ministry of Edn., 1970. Mem. Japan Profl. Photographers Soc. Other: care Light Gallery 724 Fifth Ave New York NY 10019

HOSOKAWA, MORIHIRO, governor; b. Kumamoto, Japan, Jan. 14, 1938; s. Morisada and Yoshiko (Konoe) H.; m. Kayoko Ueda, Oct. 23, 1971; children: Morimitsu, Satoko, Yuko. BA, Sophia U., Tokyo, 1963. Journalist Asahi Shimbun Pub. Co., Tokyo, 1963-68; member House of Councillors, Tokyo, 1971-83; vice-minister Parliament Ministry of Fin., Tokyo, 1975-76; vice-chmn. Nat. Diet Steering Commn. Liberal Dem. Party, Tokyo, 1977-79; vice-sec. gen. Liberal Dem. Party, Tokyo, 1979-80; pres. Info. Industry Research Commn. Liberal Dem. Party, Tokyo, 1980-81; chmn. Energy Problem Commn. House of Councillors, Tokyo, 1981; head dir. Steering Com. House of Councillors, Tokyo, 1981-83; gov. Kumamoto Prefecture, 1983—. Pres. Japanese Red Cross, Kumamoto Br., 1983—, Kumamoto UNESCO Assn., 1983—; chmn. Kumamoto Council Social Welfare, 1984—, Kumamoto Technopolis Found., Kamimashiki, 1985—. Office: Kumamoto Prefectural Govt, 18-1 Suizenji 6-chome, Kumamoto Japan 862

HOSSAIN, A. K. M. MOSHARRAF, chemical company executive; b. Mymensing, Bangladesh, Jan. 10, 1939; s. Mohammed Kashem and Hamida (Begum) Ali; m. Zeenat Hossain, Nov. 24, 1966; children: Zonaid, Zubair. Degree in commerce, U. Dhaka, Bangladesh, 1957; diploma in bus. adminstrn., City of Birmingham (Eng.) Coll. of Commerce, 1959. Chartered acct. Sr. dep. chief acct. East Pakistan Indsl. Devel. Corp., Dhaka, 1965-67; chief acct. Titas Gas Transmission and Distribution Co., Ltd., Dhaka, 1967, Jute Trading Corp., Dhaka, 1967-71; accounts exec. Bangladesh Tobacco Co., Dhaka, 1972; dir. fin. Bangladesh Food and Allied Industries Corp., Dhaka, 1973-76; dir. fin. Bangladesh Chem. Industries Corp., Dhaka, 1976-79, chmn., 1979—; chmn. Consultative Com. Pub. Enterprise, 1983—; bd. dirs. Bangladesh Biman Air Lines, Sonali Bank, Titas Gas Transmission and Distribution Co., Ltd., Karnaphuli Fertilizer Co., Ltd.; chmn. bd. dirs. Dhaka Match Industries Co., Ltd., Wavin Ltd.; convenor cost and price consultative com. of price adv. com. Ministry of Commerce, 1974-78. Contbr. articles to profl. jours. Mem. fin. com. Bangladesh U. Engring. and Tech., 1978-86, Commerce Faculty Dhaka U., 1980—, Bangladesh Olympic Com., 1980—, Council Indsl. Devel., 1985—, Nat. Council Bangladesh Inst. Tech., 1986—, re-organization com. Nat. Council for Energy and Mineral Resources, 1986—, promotion and recruitment com. Agrl. U., Mymensingh and Chittagong U., 1986—, com. tech. and engring. edn. Nat. Edn. Commn., 1986—; dir. promotions Bangladesh Chamber of Industry, 1984—; dep. sec. gen. 3d South Asian Fedn. Games, 1986, pres. souvenir and publ. com., 1980; bd. dirs. Nat. Sports Control Bd., 1980—, Inst. Bus. Adminstrn., 1986—. Recipient Sharathi award Bangladesh Agrl. Coll., 1984, Asafaddowla Spastabadi award Asfaddowla Meml. Parishad, 1984, Wrishiz Shilpi Goshthi award, 1984, Sergeant Zahirul Huq Parisad award, 1985, Sher-e-Bangla award Bangladesh Youth Front, 1986, 87, Sreegan Atish Deepankar Gold medal, 1986, Pres.'s Commendation award Hon. Pres. People's Republic of Bangladesh, 1987. Fellow Inst. Chartered Accts. Bangladesh (mem. council 1972-73, pres. 1982), Inst. Chartered Accts. Eng. and Wales, Brit. Inst. Mgmt.; mem. Bangladesh Judo and Karate Fedn. (pres. 1980—), Grindlays Assn. (chmn. 1984—). Islamic. Clubs: Dhaka, Gulshan, Officers. Lodge: Lions (cabinet sec. 1975-76, dist. gov. 1984-85, chmn. Lions Found., 1985-86). Home: 37 DOHS, Banani, Dhaka Cantt Bangladesh Office: Bangladesh Chem Industries Corp, 30-31 Dilkusha Commercial Area, Dhaka 2 Bangladesh

HOSSAIN, ANWAR, government official; b. Dhaka, Bangladesh, Jan. 1, 1931; s. Velayet Hossain and Jobeda Khatun; m. Regina Hossain, July 16, 1955; children: Muntasir, Nargis, Bulbuli; m. Sabiha Begum, Mar. 23, 1980. BSc in Physics with honors, Dhaka U., 1950, MSc in Physics, 1951; PhD in Nuclear Physics, Bristol U., U.K., 1955. Prof. physics Sir Ashutosh Coll., Kanungopara, Bangladesh, 1952; postdoctoral research asst. Bristol U., 1955-57; successively sr. sci. officer, prin. sci. officer, chief sci. officer Pakistan AEC, 1960-66; dir. Pakistan AEC, Karachi, 1960, 69, Lahore, 1963; dir. Pakistan AEC, Dhaka, 1964-67, dir., chief sci. officer, 1966-67; chief sci. officer, dir. gen. PINSTECH, Rawalpindi, Pakistan, 1967-69; mem. staff Bangladesh AEC, 1973-77, chmn., 1977—; Ford Found. vis. scientist CERN, Geneva, 1960-61; guest scientist Atomic Energy Research Establishment, Studsvik, Sweden, 1967-68; mem. planning bd. Govts. East Pakistan, Bangladesh, 1969-72; dir. gen., chmn. Space Research and Remote Sensing Orgn., 1974-82. Author: Introduction to Nuclear Physics, 1962, Nuclear Structure, 1967, Nuclear Science and Modern Physics in Bangladesh, 1987; contbr. over 100 articles and 50 papers in field; mem. internat. adv. bd. Fusion Asia jour. Mem. acad. council, senate Dhaka U. Fellow Bangladesh Acad. Sci.; mem. UNESCO, Nat. Com. Sci. and Tech., Nat. Com. on Man in Biosphere, World Energy Conf. (nat. com.), Commonwealth Human Ecology Council, Nuclear Soc. Bangladesh (vice chmn.), Bangladesh Assn. Advancement Sci., Bangla Acad. (life). Home: 155 Gulshan Ave, Dhaka Bangladesh Office: Bangladesh AEC, PO Box 158, Dhaka 2 Bangladesh

HOSSEIN, ROBERT, actor, director. s. Amin Hossein and Anna Mincovschi; m. Marina de Poliakoff, 1955 (div.), 2 children; m. Caroline Eliacheff, 1962 (div.), 1 child; m. Candice Patou. Plays include Haute surveillance, Les Voyous; films include Quai des blondes, Toi le Venin, Le vice et la virtu; author: As A Last Resort. Address: Sinfonia Films, 17 rue de la Tremolle, 75008 Paris France *

HOSTETTER, AMOS BARR, JR., cable television executive; b. N.Y.C., Jan. 12, 1937; s. Amos Barr and Leola (Conroy) H. BA cum laude, Amherst Coll., 1958; MBA, Harvard U., 1961. Asst. to v.p. fin. Am. & Fgn. Power Co., N.Y.C., 1958-59; investment analyst Cambridge (Mass.) Capital Corp., 1961-63; co-founder, exec. v.p. Continental Cablevision, Inc., Boston, 1963-80, pres., chief exec. officer, 1980-85, chmn., chief exec. officer, 1985—; founder, bd. dirs. Cable Satellite Pub. Affairs Network, 1979—; bd. dirs. Commodities Corp., Princeton, N.J. ; trustee various mut. funds Mass. Fin. Services, 1985—; bd. dirs. Corp. Pub. Broadcasting, Washington, 1975-79, The Walter Kaitz Found., 1981—; trustee Children's TV Workshop, N.Y.C., 1980—, New Eng. Med. Ctr. Hosp., Boston, 1981—, Nantucket Conservation Found., 1986—; corporator Perkins Sch. for Blind, Watertown, Mass, 1982—; bd. overseers Mus. Fine Arts, Boston, 1987—. Named Man of Yr., Cablevision Mag., 1972. Mem. Nat. Cable TV Assn. (nat. chmn. 1973-74, dir. 1968-75, 82—, Larry Boggs award 1975), Amherst Coll. Soc. Alumni (pres. 1982-84, exec. comm. 1982—, chmn. 1987—), Internat. Radio and TV Soc. Office: Continental Cablevision Inc Pilot House Lewis Wharf Boston MA 02110

HOSTIE, RAYMOND GEORGES, psychologist; b. Antwerp, Belgium, Mar. 9, 1920; s. Georges and Mathilde (DeVroey) H.; degree in philosophy U. Louvain (Belgium), 1944, degree in theology, 1951; Th.D., U. Nijmegen (Netherlands), 1954. Prof. social and pastoral psychology U. Louvain, 1966-85, Internat. Inst. of Lumen Vitae, Brussels, 1965-74; vis. prof. U. Pontificia Gregoriana, Rome, 1966-74; dir. Center for Psychosociol. Tng., Brussels, 1970-84; cons. human relations various orgns. and industries, 1960—. Mem. Assn. Flemish Group Psychotherapists (pres. 1975-77), Internat., European (treas. 1976-78, pres. 1978-80) assns. transactional analysis, Internat. Assn. Study of Med. Psychology and Religion. Roman Catholic. Editor monthly rev. Streven, 1954-55, quar. rev. Actualites en Analyse Transactionnelle, Brussels, 1977-86 ; dir. weekly rev. De Linie, 1956; author 6 books, translated into 5 langs. Home: 220 Waverse baan, 3030 Louvain Belgium Office: 153 Ave Gribaumont, 1200 Brussels Belgium

HOTCHKISS, HENRY, petroleum geologist; b. New Haven, June 6, 1909; s. Henry Stuart and Elizabeth (Washington) H.; B.S., Yale U., 1933, postgrad., 1933-35; m. Mary Bell Clark, May 19, 1936 (dec. Dec. 1979); children—Henry Washington, Anne Perrine Clark (Mrs. Robert Norton Ganz, Jr.), Frederick Hatfield Clark; m. 2d, Prudence Wagoner Robinson, July 26, 1980. Miner, Idaho, 1935-36; asst. seismic observer Phillips Petroleum Co., La., Tex., Okla., 1936-37; asst. dist. geologist Phillips Petroleum Co., Ardmore, Okla., 1937; field geologist Amiranian Oil Co., Iran, 1937-38; field geologist Iraq Petroleum Co. and asso. cos., Oman, Dhofar and Iraq, 1938-41; divisional geologist Persian Gulf, 1946-48, N. Iraq, 1948-50, asst. fields mgr. Qatar and Trucial Coast, 1950-53, fields mgr., 1953-55; regional geologist Middle East and Far East, Standard Oil Co. (N.J.), N.Y.C., 1955-64, exploration adviser Middle East and Far East, N.Y.C., 1964-69, exploration adviser Esso Middle East, 1969-70. Asso., Woods Hole (Mass.) Oceanographic Inst. Served to capt. USNR, 1941-46. Decorated Commendation medal. Fellow Geol. Soc. London, Explorers Club, AAAS, Am. Geog. Soc., Inst. Petroleum, London; mem. Am. Assn. Petroleum Geologists (asso. editor bull. 1956-65, East sect. pres. 1960-61), Am. Inst. Profl. Geologists, N.Y. Acad. Scis., Mass. Archaeol. Soc., Mass. Soc. Mayflower Desc., Soc. Colonial Wars, Order Founders and Patriots Am., Soc. Cincinnati, SAR. Republican. Methodist. Clubs: Little Ship (London); East Chop Beach, East Chop Yacht, Barnacle of Vineyard Haven (Mass.). Home: Fuller Rd Box 231 Vineyard Haven MA 02568 also: 80 Fort St Fairhaven MA 02719

HOTTOIS, GILBERT PIERRE, philosopher, educator, writer; b. Brussels, Mar. 29, 1946; s. Leon Pierre and Malvina Regina (Janssens) H.; m. Anny Monique Van Holsbeek, Dec. 23, 1967; 1 child, Roland. PhD in Philosophy, U. Brussels, 1977. Prof. philosophy U. Brussels, 1977—; researcher FNRS, Brussels, 1973-79; dir. Inst. Philosophy, Brussels, 1984—. Author: La Philosophie du Langage de Wittgenstein, 1976, L'Inflation du Langage dan la Philosophie Contemporaine, 1979, Metaphilosophie du Langage, 1981, Le Signe et La Technique, 1984, Pour Une Ethique dans un Univers Technicien, 1984; editor: Ethique et Technique, 1973, La Philosophie du Langage, 1982, Science Fiction et Fiction Speculative, 1985. Mem. Soc. Philosophique du Bruxelles, Soc. de Logique et de Philosophie des Scis., Soc. Belge du Philosphie. Home: Mettewie 79 BP 19, 1080 Brussels Belgium Office: U Brussels, 143 Ave Buyl, 1050 Brussels Belgium

HOU, LIANHAI, paleontologist; b. Shandong, Republic of China, Sept. 16, 1935; s. Yunde Hou and Zheng Cao; m. Ge Minghua; 1 child, Hou Xianzhong. BS, Lanchow (Republic of China) U., 1961. Asst. prof. Inst. Vertebrate Paleontology and Paleoanthropology, Acad. Sinica, Beijing, Republic of China, 1961—. Contbr. articles to profl. jours. Mem. Paleontol. Soc. China, Ornithol. Soc. China. Office: Inst Vertebrate Paleontology and Paleoanthropology, 142 Xi Wai St, Beijing Peoples Republic of China

HOUCK, LEWIS DANIEL, JR., management consultant; b. Cleve., July 9, 1932; s. Lewis Daniel and Mary Clark (Dowds) H.; A.B., Princeton U., 1955; M.B.A. with distinction, N.Y. U., 1964, Ph.D., 1971; m. Ellen Dorothy Thayer, Sept. 8, 1962 (div. 1975); children—Marianne Jennifer, Leland Daniel. Mgr. spl. research Young & Rubicam, Inc., N.Y.C., 1957-59; mktg. mgr. Selling Research, Inc., N.Y.C., 1959-62; ednl. projects mgr. Nat. Assn. Accts., N.Y.C., 1969-71; spl. cons. U.S. Dept. Agr., Washington, 1971-73; project leader nat. econ. analysis div. Econ. Research Service, 1973-79; pres. Houck Mktg. and Mgmt. Cons., Inc., 1979-85; pres. Houck & Assocs. Inc., Kensington, Md., 1986—; instr. N.Y.U. Grad. Sch. Bus. Adminstrn., 1966-69; trustee World U., 1982—, v.p., 1983—. Served as 1st lt., AUS, 1955-56. Recipient Founders Day award N.Y.U. Grad. Sch. Bus. Adminstrn., 1971. Ford Found. fellow, 1964-66. Fellow Am. Biog. Inst. (Medal of Honor 1986), Internat. Biog. Assn. (hon. editorial adv. bd. 1981—); mem. Am. Acctg. Assn., Am. Econ. Assn., AIM, Am. Mktg. Assn., Am. Statis. Assn., AAAS, Acad. Polit. Sci., Am. Acad. Polit. and Social Sci., Internat. Platform Assn., Ind. Cons. Am., Internat. Council Small Bus. Episcopalian. Club: Princeton (Washington). Author: A Practical Guide to Budgetary and Management Control Systems, 1979. Home: 11111 Woodson Ave Kensington MD 20895 Office: PO Box 2485 Kensington MD 20895

HOUDEK, ROBERT G., U.S. ambassador; b. Chgo., Feb. 26, 1940; m. Mary Elizabeth Wood; 2 children. B.A., Beloit Coll., 1961; M.A., Fletcher Sch. Law and Diplomacy-Tufts U., 1962. With U.S. Fgn. Service, 1962—; jr. officer trainee U.S. Fgn. Service, Brussels, Belgium, 1963-65; polit. officer U.S. Fgn. Service, Conakry, Guinea, 1965-67; staff officer Exec. Secretariat U.S. Dept. State, 1967-69; spl. asst. to Nat. Security Adviser Nat. Security Council, 1969-71; dep. chief mission U.S. Dept. State, Freetown, Sierra Leone, 1972-76; polit. counselor U.S. Dept. State, Jamaica, 1976; dep. dir. Office West African Affairs U.S. Dept. State, 1976-78, dir. Office Intra-African Affairs, 1978-80; dep. chief mission U.S. Dept. State, Nairobi, Kenya, 1980-84; mem. exec. seminar in internat. and nat. affairs U.S. Dept. State, 1984-85; U.S. ambassador U.S. Dept. State, Uganda, 1985-88; U.S. charge d'affaires U.S. Dept. State, Ethiopia, 1988—. Office: Dept of State Embassy to Ethiopia Washington DC 20520-2030

HOUDRET, JEAN-CLAUDE ANDRE, physician; b. Bourges, France, June 21, 1942; s. Jean and Augustine (Lagier) H.; m. Pascale Roger, July 23, 1961; children: Marie Louise Vinel Houdret Antoine, Monique Djellouli Houdret Aurelien. BA, Coll. Orleans, 1959; MD, U. Tours, 1967. Resident Hosp. Tours (France), 1963-67, asst., 1970-74; chief service Hosp. Orleans (France), 1970-74; gen. practice medicine Orleans, 1969-78; practice medicine specializing in homeopathic medicine and iridology Paris, 1978—; cons. to pharm. labs., Paris, 1982—. Author: Traité d'Iridologies, 1983, Medicines differentes, 1984, Fatigues-Etes-Vous Spasmophiles, 1985, L'Iridologie, 1988 - Dictionnarire Familial des Medecines Douces, 1988; contbr. numerous articles to med. jours. European cons. on parliamentary info., Paris, 1987&. Recipient Gold medal Lutetia Acad., 1983, Great Gold medal Ministry Social Edn., 1984. Mem. Med. Inst. Iridology (pres. 1981), Esthetical Med. Soc. Mem. Republican Party. Roman Catholic. Home: Chateau de l'Air, 45560 Saint Denis en Val France Office: Medical Cabinet, Rue Vavin 26, 75006 Paris France

HOUGH, JAMES RICHARD, economics educator; b. Hornchurch, England, Aug. 2, 1837; s. George and Eileen (Donovan H.; m. Jane Louise Vincent, Aug. 31, 1968; children: Steven, Richard, Catherine. BA with honors, U. Keele, 1969; MSc, London Sch. Econs., 1974; PhD, U. Leicester, 1980. Exec. Lloyd's Underwriters, London, 1953-65; lectr. Luton (Eng.) Coll. Tech., 1969-71; sr. lectr. Huddersfield (Eng.) Poly., 1971-72; mem. faculty dept. edn. Loughborough (Eng.) U., 1972—, reader, 1984—; dean Ech. Edn. and Humanities, 1985—; cons. UNESCO, Paris, 1976—, Brit. Council, London, 1982—, World Bank, Washington, 1987—. Author: A Study of School Costs, 1981, The French Economy, 1982, Educational Policy, 1984, Education and the National Economy, 1987. Fellow Chartered Ins. Inst; mem. Econs. Assn., Brit. Edn. Mgmt. Adminstrn. Soc. Office: Loughborough U, Loughborough LE11 3TU, England

HOUGHTON, JAMES RICHARDSON, glass manufacturing company executive; b. Corning, N.Y., Apr. 6, 1936; s. Amory and Laura (Richardson) H.; m. May Tuckerman Kinnicutt, June 30, 1962; children: James DeKay, Nina Bayard. AB, Harvard U., 1958, MBA, 1962. With Goldman, Sachs & Co., N.Y.C., 1959-61; with Corning Glass Works, 1962—, v.p., gen. mgr. consumer products div., 1968-71, vice chmn. bd., dir., chmn. exec. com., 1971-83, chmn. bd., chief exec. officer, 1983—; v.p., European area mgr. Corning Glass Internat., Zurich, Switzerland, Brussels, Belgium, 1964-68; bd. dirs. Met. Life Ins. Co., J. P. Morgan Co. Inc., Dow Corning Corp., CBS, Inc. Trustee Corning Glass Works Found., Corning Mus. Glass, Pierpont Morgan Library, N.Y.C., The Bus. Council of N.Y. State, Met. Mus. Art; mem. Bus. Com. for Arts, N.Y.C., Council on Fgn. Relations.; bd. dirs. US-USSR Trade and Econ. Council. Served with AUS, 1959-60. Mem. Bus. Council, Bus. Roundtable. Episcopalian. Clubs: Corning Country; River, Harvard, Univ., Links (N.Y.C.); Brookline (Mass.) Country; Tarratine (Dark Harbor, Maine); Augusta (Ga.) Nat. Golf; Rolling Rock, Laurel Valley Golf (Ligonier, Pa.). Home: The Field Spencer Hill Rd RD 2 Corning NY 14830 Office: Corning Glass Works Houghton Park Corning NY 14831

HOUGHTON, WILLIAM HENRY, publishing company executive; b. Hartford, Conn., Apr. 13, 1925; s. Henry Ernest and Frances Mary (Plaunt) H.; m. Marion Jensen, Jan. 28, 1959; children: Robert G., Bradley J. BS magna cum laude, Babson Coll., 1949. Comml. mgr. Associated Program Service, Inc., N.Y.C., 1949-52; v.p. mktg. Ency. Brit., Inc., Chgo., 1952-62; exec. v.p. Marketways, Inc., Chgo., 1962-63; pres. Collier Services, Inc., Riverside, N.J., 1963-67; pres., chief exec. officer Macmillan Book Clubs, Inc., N.Y.C., 1967—; group v.p. Macmillan, Inc., N.Y.C., 1985—; bd. dirs. Berlitz Pubs., Inc., Gryphon Edition, Inc. Mem. Assn. Am. Pubs., Direct Mktg. Assn., Pres. Assn. Club: Chappaqua (N.Y.) Country. Office: Macmillan Inc 866 Third Ave New York NY 10022

HOUGHTON, WOODSON PLYER, lawyer; b. Washington, Apr. 19, 1893; s. Harry Sherman and Alice Virginia (Ballentine) H.; m. Geta Triester, July 21, 1933. B.A., Washington and Lee U., 1915; LL.B., Georgetown U., 1918. Bar: D.C. bar 1918. Asst. sec. 2d Pan Am. Sci. Congress, 1916-17; since practiced in Washington; mem. firm Ellis, Houghton and Ellis, 1919-68, sr. partner, 1948-68; prof. law Nat. U. Law Sch., 1923-26; formerly mem. bd. Mut. Protection Fire Ins. Co., Norfolk and Washington Steamboat Co. Pres. Family Service Assn. (Asso. Charities); mem. bd. Family Welfare Assn. Am., Council Social Agys., Community Chest, D.C.; bd. govs. Nantucket Boys Club. Served as 1st lt. judge adv. gen. corps. U.S. Army, 1918-19; asst. port judge adv. Port Embarkation, Newport News. Va. Mem. Am., D.C. bar assns., DuPont Circle Citizens Assn., Sheridan-Kalorama Neighborhood Council, S.A.R., Barristers, Sigma Chi, Phi Delta Phi, Omicron Delta Kappa. Clubs: Nantucket Yacht, Sankaty Head Golf, Metropolitan, Chevy Chase, 1925 F Street (gov.), Pacific, Wharf Rat. Home: 2337 California St NW Washington DC 20008 Office: 815 Connecticut Ave NW Washington DC 20006

HOUNSFIELD, GODFREY NEWBOLD, scientist; b. Aug. 28, 1919; s. Thomas H.; ed. City and Guilds Coll., London; diploma Faraday House Elec. Engring. Coll., London; M.D. (hon.), U. Basel, 1975; D.Sc. (hon.), City U., 1976, U. London, 1976; D.Tech. (hon.), U. Loughborough, 1976. Joined EMI Ltd., Hayes, Middlesex, Eng., 1951, head med. systems sect., central research labs., 1972-76, sr. staff scientist, 1977—; professorial fellow in imaging scis. Manchester U., 1978—. Recipient Nobel prize in Physiology or Medicine, 1979; MacRobert award, 1972; Wilhelm-Exner medal Austrian Indsl. Assn., 1974; Ziedses des Plantes medal Physikalishe Medizinische Gesellschaft, Wü rzburg, 1974; Prince Philip Medal award CGLI, 1975; ANS Radiation Industry award Ga. Inst. Tech., 1975; Lasker award Lasker Found., 1975; Duddell Bronze medal Inst. Physics, 1976; Golden Plate award Am. Acad. Achievement, 1976; Reginald Mitchell Gold medal Stoke-on-Trent Assn. Engrs., 1976; Churchill Gold medal, 1976; Gairdner Found. award, 1976; decorated comdr. Order Brit. Empire, 1976, knight, 1981. Fellow Royal Soc. Contbr. articles to sci. jours. Led design team for 1st large all-transistor computer to be built in Gt. Britain; invented EMI-scanner computerized transverse axial tomography system for X-ray exam.; developed new X-ray technique (EMI-scanner system). Office: Thorn EMI Research Labs, Dawley Rd, Hayes, Middlesex UB3 1HH, England

HOUPHOUET-BOIGNY, FELIX, president Republic of Ivory Coast; b. Yamoussoukvo, Ivory Coast, Oct. 18, 1905; student William Ponty Coll. of Gore (Senegal); grad. Fed. Med. Sch. Dakar, 1925; m. Marie-Therese Brou; 3 sons, 1 dau. Doctor for Asst. Medicale, 1925-40; pres. Syndicat Agricole Africain, 1944; mem. French Constituent Assembly, 1945-46, mem. French Nat. Assembly, 1946, 51, 56; minister to French prime minister, 1956-57, minister state, 1957-59, minister pub. health and population, 1957-58, cabinet mem., 1958-59; pres. assembly Ivory Coast Republic, 1958-59, prime minister, councilor French Govt., 1959-60; pres. Council, 1959-60, pres. Republic of Ivory Coast, 1960—, minister fgn. affairs, 1961, minister interior, edn. and agr., 1963, minister def., 1963-74; pres. Council of Ministers; pres. Reassemblement Democratique Africain, Parti Democratique de la Cote d'Ivoire. Decorated grand cross French Legion of Honor, grand master Nat. Order of Ivory Coast, also others. Address: Presidence de la Republique, Abidjan Ivory Coast *

HOUSE, CARLEEN FAYE, director management information systems; b. Sparta, Wis., Dec. 14, 1950; d. Clarence Frederick and Ida Mae (Murdock) Anderson; m. Gregory Allen House, Aug. 25, 1984. BS, U. Wis., 1978, MS, 1982. Cert. engr., Wis. Prin. Customized Research and Design, 1979-81; sci. tchr. Wis. Ednl. System, 1981-82; systems analyst Hewlett Packard, 1982-83, software systems engr., 1983-86, MIS dir., 1986-88; chief exec. officer House Research, 1986—; pres. HPII Lt. Partnership, 1987—, Chisago County Office Supply, Chisago City, Minn., 1988—; area project dir. Hewlett Packard, 1988—; dir. devel. House Properties One, 1985—; pres. HPII Ltd. Partnership, 1986—. Mem. Women in Engring., Aircraft Owners and Pilots Assn., Omicron Nu, League of Women Voters. Republican. Lutheran. Home and Office: 10579 Point Pleasant Rd Chisago City MN 55013

HOUSEN-COURIEL, DEBORAH ANDREA, jurist, educator; b. Erving, Mass., Apr. 9, 1960; arrived in Israel, 1982; d. Charles Bernard and Margorie Mildred (Grodner) Housen; m. Lior Amir Couriel, Apr. 13, 1986. Certificat d'Etudes Politiques, Inst. D'Etudes Politiques, Paris, 1981; BA in Anthropology, History, Wellesley Coll., 1982; LLB, Hebrew U., Jerusalem, 1987. Tchr. Hadassah Youth Ctr., Jerusalem, 1984-85, Hebrew U., 1986—; legal intern Bur. Legal Adv. Ministry Fgn. Affairs, Jerusalem, 1985-87, Yehuda Raveh and Co., Jerusalem, 1987—. Recipient Oberlander Pub. Internat. Law prize Hebrew Univ., 1987. Mem. Am. Soc. Internat. Law, Israel Oriental Soc., Wellesley Coll. Alumnae Assn., Northfield-Mt. Hermon Alumni Assn., Phi Beta Kappa. Jewish. Office: Yehuda Raveh and Co, 3 Metudela St, Jerusalem 92305, Israel

HOUSER, JOHN EDWARD, lawyer; b. Richmond, Va., Dec. 24, 1928; s. Aubrey Alphin and Winnifred (Savage) H.; m. Elizabeth Rives Pollard, Apr. 1, 1967; children—Allen Rives Cabell Lybrook, Andrew Murray Lybrook. B.S., U. Va., 1959, LL.B., 1959. Bar: Fla. 1959, U.S. dist. ct. (so. and mid. dists.) Fla. 1959, U.S. Ct. Appeals (5th cir.) 1963, U.S. Supreme Ct. 1970, U.S. Ct. Appeals (11th cir.) 1981. Assoc., Jennings, Watts, Clarke & Hamilton, Jacksonville, Fla., 1959-61, Howell, Kirby, Montgomery & Sands, Jacksonville, 1961-63; ptnr. Howell & Houser, Jacksonville, 1963-65; sole practice, Jacksonville, 1965—; lectr. on Long shore and Harbor works Comp. Act Loyola U., 1979, 88; dir. William P. Polythress & Co., Richmond, Neal F. Tyler & Sons, Jacksonville. Active Jacksonville U. Council, Jacksonville Symphony Assn., Fla. Hist. Soc., Jacksonville Hist. Soc., Cummer Gallery of Art, Jacksonville Art Mus.; mem. English-Speaking Union, dir., 1970-79, pres., 1974-78, nat. regional chmn., 1973-76, nat. dir., 1976-81; hon. sec. Live Oak Hounds; active Thomasville Landmarks, Thomasville Arts Guild, Thomas County Hist. Soc. Served with AUS, 1953-57. Mem. Internat. Assn. Indsl. Accident Bds. and Commns., Maritime Law Assn., Southeastern Admiralty Law Inst., Jacksonville Claimsmen Assn., Atlanta Claimsmen Assn., ABA, Jacksonville Bar Assn., Fla. Bar, Fla. Def. Scl. Assn., Am. Judicature Soc., Am. Arbitration Assn., Nat. Trust Hist. Preservation, Fla. Inst. Pub. Affairs, Navy League, Jacksonville Assn. Def. Counsel, Def. Reearch Inst., Theta Delta Chi, Sigma Nu Phi. Clubs: River, Fla. Yacht, Deerwood, Ponte Vedra River, Exchange, German, Ye Mystic Revellers, Univ., Princeton of N.Y., Glen Arven, Commonwealth (Richmond, Va.); 2300. Office: 403 St James Bldg Jacksonville FL 32202

HOUSTON, ELIZABETH REECE MANASCO, education educator, consultant; b. Birmingham, Ala., June 19, 1935; d. Reuben Cleveland and Beulah Elizabeth (Reece) Manasco; m. Joseph Brantley Houston; 1 child, Joseph Brantley Houston III. BS, U. Tex., 1956; MEd, Boston Coll., 1969. Cert. elem. tchr., Calif., cert. spl. edn. tchr., Calif., cert. community coll. instr., Calif. Tchr., elem. Ridgefield (Conn.) Schs., 1962-63; staff, spl. edn. Sudbury (Mass.) Schs., 1965-68; staff intern Wayland (Mass.) High Sch., 1972; tchr., home bound Northampton (Mass.) Schs., 1972-73; program dir. Jack Douglas Ctr., San Jose, Calif., 1974-76; tchr., specialist spl. edn., coordinator classroom services, dir. Juvenile Ct. Schs. Santa Clara County Office of Edn., San Jose, Calif., 1976—; instr. San Jose State U., 1980-87, U. Calif., Santa Cruz, 1982-85; cons. Houston Research Assocs., Saratoga, Calif., 1981—. Author: (manual) Behavior Management for School Bus Drivers, 1980, Classroom Management, 1984, Synergistic Learning, 1986. Bd. dirs. Ming Quong Children's Ctr., Los Gatos, Calif. Grantee Santa Clara County Office Edn. Tchr. Advisor Program U.S. Sec. Edn., 1983-84; Recipient President's award Soc. Photo-Optical Instrumentation Engrs., 1979, Classroom Mgmt. Program award School Bds. Assn., 1984. Mem. Assn. for Supervision and Curriculum Devel., Assn. Calif. Sch. Adminstrs., Council Exceptional Children. Home: 12150 Country Squire Ln Saratoga CA 95070 Office: Santa Clara County Office Edn 100 Skyport Dr San Jose CA 95115

HOUSTON, SHIRLEY MAE (MRS. THOMAS H. HOUSTON), court reporter; b. Jasper, Tex., Oct. 4, 1938; d. Walter Louis and Effie Marie (Hulett) Gordon; student U. Houston, 1957, South Tex. Jr. Coll., Houston, 1958; grad. Robert Krippner Sch. Reporting, 1965; m. Thomas Harold Houston, Aug. 3, 1957. Various secretarial positions, 1956-65; ct. reporter, owner Houston Reporting Service, 1965—; owner H-R-S, 1975—; v.p. Tradewinds Indsl. Park, Inc., 1974-83, dir., 1984—; partner Houston Video Service, 1977-86; dir. Skate City USA, 1980-86; owner Bear Creek Skating Rink, 1985—, Houston Litigation Support Service, 1986—. Vol. juvenile counselor; advisor Houston Community Coll., 1976-78, Alvin Community Coll., 1980-84. Registered profl. reporter, cert. shorthand reporter, cert. legal video specialist, Tex. Mem. Greater Houston Ct. Reporters Assn. (pres. 1975, chmn. tech. com. 1986-87, disting. service award 1983), Nat. Shorthand Reporters Assn. (state chmn. membership com. 1977-78, dir. 1979-80, placement com. 1980-82, ins. com. 1982-84, co-chmn. word processing com. 1981-83, chmn. videotape com. 1985, mem. 1986, seminar instr. nat. conv. 1978, 79, 81, 82, 83, 84, fund-raising task force 1986-88, chmn. videotape com. 1987-88, nat. membership award 1980), Tex. Shorthand Reporters Assn. (advt. chmn. conv. 1967, dir. 1978-80, spl. advisor to bd. dirs. 1988, state liaison to state bar of Tex. 1986-88, chmn. mktg. & pub. relations 1987-88, disting. service award 1987, seminar instr. 1985, 86, 87, reporters coop. sec. 1986-87, v.p. 1987-88), Nat. Assn. Legal Secs., Tex. Assn. Legal Secs., Greater Houston Legal Secs. Assn. (dir. 1969), Legal Assts. Assn., DAR, UDC, Harris County Heritage Soc., Theatre Under the Stars, Baron Users Group (bd. dirs. 1984-87, treas. 1987-88, seminar instr. 1986, 87, chmn. conv. 1988). Baptist. Club: Cotillion (Houston). Address: 1001 Texas Suite 1100 Houston TX 77002

HOUSTON, WILLIAM ROBERT MONTGOMERY, ophthalmic surgeon; b. Mansfield, Ohio, Nov. 13, 1922; s. William T. and Frances (Hursh) H.; B.A., Oberlin Coll., 1944; M.D., Western Res. U., 1948; m. Marguerite LaBau Browne, Apr. 25, 1968; children—William Erling Tenney, Marguerite Elisabeth LaBau, Selby Cabot Truitt Vanderbilt. Intern, Meth. Hosp. Bklyn., 1948-49, Ill. Eye and Ear Infirmary, Chgo., 1949-50; resident N.Y. Eye and Ear Infirmary, 1950-52; practice medicine specializing in ophthalmic surgery, Mansfield, 1952—; mem. staffs Mansfield Gen. Hosp., Peoples Hosp., Mansfield, N.Y. U. Bellevue Med. Center, N.Y.C.; assoc. prof. clin. ophthalmology N.Y. U. Sch. Medicine. Pres. Mansfield Symphony Soc., 1965-68, Mansfield Civic Music Assn., 1965; mem. Mansfield City Sch. Bd., 1962-65, v.p., 1965. Served to capt. M.C. USAF, 1952-55. Diplomate Am. Bd. Ophthalmology. Recipient Honor award Acad. Ophthalmology. Fellow Internat. Coll. Surgeons; mem. SAR (color guard 1961-71), Ohio Hist. Soc. (life), Western Res. Hist. Soc. (life fellow), N.Y. Geneal. and Biog. Soc. (life), Ohio Geneal. Soc. (trustee 1955—). Editor, Ohio Records and Pioneers Families, 1970—. Address: 456 Park Ave W Mansfield OH 44906

HOUTS, MARSHALL WILSON, author, editor, lawyer; b. Chattanooga, June 28, 1919; s. Thomas Jefferson and Mary (Alexander) H.; m. Mary O. Dealy, Apr. 27, 1946; children: Virginia, Kathy, Marsha, Patty, Tom, Cindy, Tim. AA, Brevard Jr. Coll., 1937; BS in Law, U. Minn., 1941, JD, 1941. Bar: Tenn. 1940, Minn. 1946, U.S. Supreme Ct. 1967. Spl. agt. FBI, Washington, Brazil, Havana, Boston, 1941-44; ptnr. Palmer & Houts, Pipestone, Minn., 1946-51; mcpl. judge Pipestone, 1947-51; gen. counsel Erle Stanley Gardner's Ct. of Last Resort, Los Angeles, 1951-60; prof. law UCLA, 1954, Mich. State U., East Lansing, 1955-57; adj. prof. Pepperdine U. Law Sch., 1972-80; clin. prof. forensic pathology Calif. Coll. Medicine, U. Calif., Irvine, 1972—; cons. police depts. Creator, editor: TRAUMA, 1959-88; author: Houts: Lawyer's Guide to Medical Proof, 4 vols., 1967, From Gun to Gavel, 1954, From Evidence to Proof, 1956, The Rules of Evidence, 1956, From Arrest to Release, 1958, Courtroom Medicine, 1958, Courtroom Medicine: Death, 3 vols., 1964, Photographic Misrepresentation, 1965, Where Death Delights, 1967, They Asked for Death, 1970, Proving Medical Diagnosis and Prognosis, 14 vols., 1970, Cyclopedia of Sudden, Violent and Unexplained Death, 1970, King's X: Common Law and the Death of Sir Harry Oakes, 1972, Art of Advocacy: Appeals; Art of Advocacy: Cross Examination of Medical Experts, 1980; Courtroom Toxicology, 7 vols., 1981, Who Killed Sir Harry Oakes?, 1988. Served with OSS, 1944-46, CBI. Decorated Bronze Arrowhead. Address: 33631 Magellan Isle Laguna Niguel CA 92677

HOVE, ARNE, power co. exec.; b. Time, Rogaland, Norway, Mar. 29, 1928; s. Staale and Astri Loice (Hognestad) H.; B.Sc., Norwegian U. Tech., 1955; M.Sc., Carnegie Inst. Tech., 1960; m. Johanne Meland, July 14, 1956; children—Stein Arne, Ina Kristine. Jr. engr. Asea, Norway, 1955-57; load dispatcher Samkjoringen, Norway, 1957-59, cons. engr., 1961-66; sr. engr. Ringerike Kraftverk, Honefoss, Norway, 1966-72, mng. dir., 1972-82; elec. engr. Bechtel Corp., San Francisco, 1960-61; mng. dir. Sandnes Elverk (Norway), 1982—; dir. Samkjoringen, Norway. Mem. Norwegian Engrs. Assn., Sigma Xi. Author: Cooperation of Power Stations, 1966. Home: Jadar vn 17, 4300 Sandnes Norway Office: Sandnes Elverk, Hoveveien 9, 4300 Sandnes Norway

HOVEY, JUSTUS ALLAN, JR., political scientist; b. Cambridge, Mass., May 13, 1922; s. Justus Allan and Lois Eugenia (Clark) H.; m. Peggy Streit, 1983; 1 dau., Anne Elisabeth (Mrs. Alan R. Brandolini). A.B. magna cum laude, Swarthmore Coll., 1948; cert., Institut Universitaire de Hautes Etudes Internationales, 1948; M.A., Columbia U., 1950, Ph.D., 1965. Intern, Office Sec. Gen. UN, 1949; study dir. Council Fgn. Relations, N.Y.C., 1952; exec. dir. Am. Com. United Europe, N.Y.C., Paris, 1952-60; Washington rep. Olin Corp., 1960-68; Washington dir. Allen & Murden, Inc., 1965-68; v.p., sec. Radio Free Europe (Free Europe, Inc.), N.Y.C., 1968-76; internat. relations specialist GAO, Washington, 1976—; on assignment Ho. of Reps. subcom. on legislation and nat. security, Washington, 1985-88; adj. assoc. prof. Manhattan Community Coll., CUNY, 1969-72, Queens Coll., 1973-75; Bd. dirs. Atlantic Council of U.S., Washington, Citizens Network for Fgn. Affairs, Washington, Ontario Owners, Inc., Washington, English in Action, N.Y.C., 1973-76. Author: The Superparliaments, 1966, U.S. International Leadership for the 21st Century: Building a National Foreign Affairs Constituency, 1987; author various GAO reports, Atlantic Council policy papers; editor: Toward a Consensus on Military Service, 1982; contbr. articles to profl. jours. Served to 1st lt., inf. AUS, 1943-46. Mem. N. Y. Council Fgn. Relations, Am. Acad. Polit. and Social Sci., Internat. Studies Assn., Phi Beta Kappa. Club: Nat. Press (Washington). Home: 2853 Ontario Rd NW Washington DC 20009 Office: U S Gen Acctg Office #4132 Washington DC 20548

HOVING, JOHN HANNES FORESTER, consulting firm executive; b. N.Y.C., July 18, 1923; s. Hannes and Mary Alma (Gilbert) H.; m. Anne Fisher Spiers, Feb. 1, 1958; children: Christopher, Karen Anne, Katherine Jean. BA in History, U. Chgo., 1947. Radio news editor, reporter Milw. Jour., also Capital Times, Madison, Wis., 1947-51; asst. to chmn. Democratic Nat. Com., 1952-54; exec. positions Kefauver, Stevenson, Johnson, Humphrey, Sanford presdl. campaigns; asst. to presdl. asst. for trade policy 1962; v.p. exec. action Air Transp. Assn. Am., Washington, 1956-64; propr. cons. firm Washington, 1964-72; sr. v.p. Federated Dept. Stores, Inc., Cin., 1972-82; pres. The Hoving Group (cons. firm), Washington, 1982—. Mem. vestry Christ Episcopal Ch., Cin.; bd. dirs. Am. Council Young Polit. Leaders., Fashion Inst. of Design Merchandising; former dep. chmn. for planning Democratic Nat. Com. Served with AUS, 1943-46. Decorated Purple Heart, Bronze Star. Mem. Am. Assn. Polit. Cons. Democrat. Clubs: Met. (Washington), Nat. Press (Washington), Nat. Capital Dem. (Washington); Queen City (Cin.); Lotos (N.Y.C.). Home: 4831 Albemarle St NW Washington DC 20016 Office: The Hoving Group 910 17th St NW Washington DC 20006

HOVNANIAN, H. PHILIP, biomedical engineer; b. Aleppo, Syria, Dec. 17, 1920; s. Philip and Rosa (Jebejian) H.; m. Siran Norian, June 10, 1948; children: Rosemary Janice, Joan Anita, John Philip. B.S., Am. U., Beirut, 1942, postgrad., 1945-47; postgrad., Brown U., 1947-49; M.S., State Coll., Boston, 1951; Ph.D., U. Beverly Hills, Calif. Registered profl. engr., N.Y., Mass.; chartered physicist (U.K.). Prin. investigator, research grant Nat. Heart Inst., NIH; faculty dept. physics Am. U., Beirut, 1942-47, Brown U., 1947-49; sr. engr. Western Electric Co., Haverhill, Mass., 1951-52; asst. chief engr. Calidyne Co., Winchester, Mass., 1952-53; sr. physicist, project head, asst. research dir. Boston Electronics div. Norden-Ketay Corp., 1953-56; partner, research and devel. dir. physics Neutronics Research Co., Waltham, Mass., 1956-58; sr. staff scientist Avco Corp., 1958, mgr. med. sci. dept., 1959-66; mgr. lunar biosci. NASA, Washington, 1966-67; mgr. biomed. engring. and biophysics Kollsman Instrument Corp., Syosset, N.Y., 1967-68; v.p., dir. biomed. products Cavitron Corp. and Cooper Med. Corp., 1969—; dir. Donti Instruments Inc., Milab, Inc.; guest lectr. biomed. engring. Northeastern U., MIT-Harvard Study Group on Biomed. Engring.; research asso. in surg. research Lahey Clin. Found.; mem. workshop interaction between industry and biomed. engring. Nat. Acad. Engring.; mem. ob-gyn. devices panel, former mem. panel on ear, nose and throat devices and dental devices FDA. Contbr. tech. papers to profl. jours. Trustee Haigazian Coll. of Beirut, Lebanon. Fellow Inst. Physics (chartered, Brit.), Phys. Soc. (Brit.), Am. Soc. Laser Med. and Surgery; mem. Optical Soc. Am., Am. Inst. Physics, IEEE (sr. mem., profl. group biomed. electronics), Internat. Fedn. Med. Electronics, Biomed. Engring. Soc., Research Soc. Am., Internat. Microscopy Assn., Am. Inst. Ultrasound in Medicine, Am. Soc. Microbiology, N.Y. Acad. Scis., AAAS, Assn. for Advancement Med. Instrumentation, Am. Dental Trade Assn. (com. on dental materials and devices), Am. Inst. Biol. Scis., Armenian Missionary Assn. of Am. (bd. dirs.), Sigma Xi. Congregationalist (United Ch. of Christ) (chmn. bd. trustees, moderator). Lodge: Masons. Home: 3902 Manhattan College Pkwy Unit 1B Bronx NY 10471

HOWARD, ALAN MACKENZIE, actor; b. London, Aug. 5, 1937; s. Arthur John and Jean (Compton Mackenzie) H.; student Ardingley Coll.; m. Stephanie Hinchcliffe Davies, 1965; m. 2d Sally Beauman, 1976, 1 son. Stage hand, asst. stage mgr., actor Belgrade Theatre Coventry, 1958-60; debut London West End, Duke of York's Theatre In Roots, 1959, N.Y. debut, 1971; with Royal Shakespeare Co., 1966—, assoc. artist, from 1967, plays include: Twelfth Night, As You Like It, The Relapse, King Lear, Much Ado About Nothing, Dr. Faustus, Camlet, Midsummer Night's Dream, Mand od Mode, The Balcony, The Bewitched, Henry Iv parts 1 and 2, Henry V, Henry VI parts 1, 2 and 3, Anthony and Cleopatra, Children of the Sun, Richard II, Richard III; films include: The Heroes of Telemark, Work is a Four Letter Word; TV appearance include: The Way of the World, Comet Among the Stars, Coriolanus, The Holy Experiment. Served with RAF, 1956-58. Recipient Plays and Players London Theatre Critics most promising actor award, 1969, Best Actor award, 1977, Soc. West End Theatre Mgrs. Best Actor in a Revival award, 1976, 78; Evening Standard Drama award for best actor, 1978, Variety Club of Britain Best Actor award, 1980. Address: care Julian Beflrage Assocs, 60 St James's St, London SW1, England *

HOWARD, ALLEN RICHMOND, JR., corporate executive; b. San Francisco, Dec. 15, 1920; s. Allen Richmond and Elizabeth Mead (Coates) H.; student Brown U., 1940-41; B.S., U.S. Naval Acad., 1944; m. Carlotta Greenfield, Mar. 7, 1953; children—Charles F., Allen Richmond III, Derek G. Commd. ensign USN, 1944, advanced through grades to lt. comdr., 1954; assigned to USS Lake Champlain, USS San Diego, various aircraft squadrons and air stas.; ret., 1954; with Singer Mfg. Co., Bridgeport, Conn., 1954-55. Thalheimer & Wertz, Architects & Engrs., 1955-58; pres. McCullough Howard & Co., Phila., 1959-69; pres. Williard Inc., Jenkintown, Pa., 1969-79; chmn. Greenfield Co., Phila., 1980-82; mgmt. cons., 1982-87; pres. Quaker City Internat. Inc., 1987—. Registered profl. engr., Pa. Episcopalian. Clubs: Sunnybrook Golf (Plymouth Meeting, Pa.); Pine Valley (N.J.) Golf; Mid Ocean (Bermuda); Overbrook Golf (Bryn Mawr, Pa.); Union League (Phila.).

HOWARD, BERNARD EUFINGER, mathematics and computer science educator; b. Ludlow, Vt., Sept. 22, 1920; s. Charles Rawson and Ethel (Kearney) H.; m. Ruth Belknap, Mar. 29, 1942. Student Middlebury Coll., 1938-40; B.S., MIT, 1944; M.S., U. Ill., 1947, Ph.D., 1951. Staff mem. Radiation Lab, MIT, Cambridge, 1942-45; asst. math. U. Ill., Champaign-Urbana, 1945-49; sr. mathematician Inst. Air Weapons Research, U. Chgo., 1951, asst. to dir. Inst. for Systems Research, 1951-54, assoc. dir., 1956-60, assoc. dir. Labs. for Applied Sci., 1958-60; dir. Sci. Computing Ctr. U. Miami, Coral Gables, Fla., 1960-64, prof. math. and computer sci., 1960—; exec. sec. Air Force Adv. Bd. Simulation, 1951-54; cons. Systems Research Labs, Inc., Dayton, Ohio, 1963-67, acting dir. math. scis. div., 1965; cons. Variety Children's Research Found., Miami, 1964-66, Fla. Power & Light Co., Miami, 1968, Shaw & Assocs., 1964-75; vis. fellow Dartmouth Coll., Hanover, N.H., 1976; co-investigator Positron Emission Tomography Ctr., U. Miami Dept. Neurology/Mt. Sinai Med. Ctr., 1981-84. Co-creator: (with Henry W. Kunce) Sociocybernetics, 1971, Optimum Curvature, 1964, Torsion, 1974, (with J.F.B. Shaw) Principles in Highway Routing. Chmn. bd. dirs. Blue Lake Assn., Inc., Miami, 1969—. Am. Soc. Engring. Edn.-Office of Naval Research fellow Naval Underwater Systems Ctr., 1981, 82. Mem. Am. Math. Soc., Soc. Indsl. and Applied Math. (treas. S.E. sect. 1964), Am. Phys. Soc., Assn. Computing Machinery (chpt. chmn. 1969-70), IEEE, AAUP (chpt. sec. 1974—), Sigma Xi, Phi Kappa Phi, Pi Mu Epsilon, Alpha Sigma Phi. Home: 7320 Miller Dr Miami FL 33155 Office: U Miami Coral Gables FL 33124

HOWARD, DAGGETT HORTON, lawyer; b. N.Y.C., Mar. 20, 1917; s. Chester Augustus and Olive Ree (Daggett) H.; m. Patricia McClellan Exton, Sept. 1950; children: Daggett Horton Jr., Jeffrey, David, Patricia. B.A. magna cum laude, Yale U., 1938, J.D., 1941. Bar: N.Y. 1942, D.C. 1961. Legal staff Root, Clark, Buckner & Ballantine, N.Y.C., 1941-43, Lend Lease Adminstrn., Fgn. Econ. Adminstrn., 1943-44; exec. asst. to spl. counsel to Pres. White House, 1945; legal adviser on WWII Allied war settlements, developing Marshall Plan Dept. State, 1945-47; internat. atty. on world-wide civil aviation bilateral agreements, asst. chief internat. and rules div. CAB, 1947-52; assoc. gen. counsel Dept. Air Force, 1952-56, dep. gen. counsel, Dept. Def. rep., 1956-58; gen. counsel FAA, 1958-62; partner Cox, Langford & Brown, Washington, 1962-66, Howard, Poe & Bastian, Washington, 1966-83, Howard & Law, Washington, 1983—. Bd. editors: Yale Law Jour. Past mem. policy com. Daniel and Florence Guggenheim Aviation Safety Center; corp. mem. Children's Hosp. D.C. Recipient Exceptional Civilian Service award Dept. Air Force, 1958; Disting. Service award FAA, 1962. Mem. Yale Law Sch. Assn. Washington, Corbey Ct., Fed., Am. bar assns., Phi Beta Kappa, Alpha Sigma Phi. Clubs: Yale (Washington), Metropolitan (Washington), Nat. Capital Democratic (Washington); Chevy Chase. Home: 4319 Cathedral Ave NW Washington DC 20016 Office: 1900 M St NW Suite 620 Washington DC 20036

HOWARD, EDWARD IAN, plastics company executive, accountant; b. Oakmere, Cheshire, Eng., June 20, 1921; s. Edward William Vincent and Kathleen Louise (Emerson) H.; m. Marian Gertrude Moore, Apr. 3, 1944; children—Gregory Carmen, Brenton Ian. B.Commerce, U. B.C., 1947. Chartered acct., B.C. With Peat-Marwick-Mitchell, Chartered Accts., Vancouver, B.C., Can., 1947-52; founding ptnr. Dyke & Howard, Chartered Accts., Vancouver, 1952-62; pres. Columbia Plastics Ltd., Vancouver, 1962—; mem. adv. bd. Med. Device Devel. Ctr., Vancouver, 1979-86; mem. mfrs. reference group B.C. Innovation Office, Vancouver. Served to lt. comdr. Royal Can. Navy, 1941-45. Mem. Inst. Chartered Accts. of B.C., Soc. Plastics Engrs., Naval Officers Assn., Phi Kappa Sigma. Club: Royal Vancouver Yacht. Home: 1930 Queens Ave, West Vancouver, BC Canada V7V 2X7 Office: Columbia Plastics Ltd, 19320 60th Ave, Surrey, BC Canada V3S 4N9

HOWARD, GEORGE SALLADÉ, conductor, music consultant, educator; b. Reamstown, Pa., Feb. 24, 1903; s. Hayden H. and Florence (Salladé) H.; m. Sadako Takenouchi, Apr. 5, 1957. Mus.B. with honors, Ithaca Conservatory, 1925; A.B., Ohio Wesleyan U., 1929; Mus.B., Chgo. Conservatory Music, 1934, Mus.M., 1935, Mus.D., 1939; M.A., N.Y. U., 1936; Mus. D. (hon.), Ithaca Coll., 1984. Dean Ernest Williams Sch. Music, Bklyn., 1935-36; dir. music, condr. bands Pa. State Tchrs. Coll., 1936-39; dir. bands, orch. and chorus sch., dir. music in extension Pa. State Coll., 1939-42; commd. capt. U.S. Army, 1942; advanced through grades to col. USAF, 1951; organizer, condr. music programs Greenland, Iceland, Newfoundland, 1942-43; comdg. officer, condr. Ofcl. Army Air Forces Band, Washington, 1944; chief music and radio br. AAF Hdqrs., 1946; established, organized AAF Band Sch., 1946; chief bands and music USAF; condr. USAF (USAF Band and Symphony Orch.), 1947; condr. USAF Band on tour, U.S., Can., Eng., Scotland, Wales, Ireland, Germany, Austria, Norway, Denmark, Libya, Iceland, Azores, Japan, Korea, P.I., Cambodia, others; condr. command performances Buckingham Palace, Royal Palace of Cambodia, The White House; ret. USAF, 1963; distinguished prof. music Troy (Ala.) State U., 1974—; vis. prof., dir. wind ensemble U. Houston, 1977; music cons. (rank of insp.) Met. Police Dept., Washington, 1973—; condr. Met. Police Band, Washington, 1963-73, Air Force Village Voices, San Antonio, 1977—; guest condr. Goldman Band, 1961-75, hon. life mem., 1973; hon. comdr. Tokyo (Japan) Youth Symphony Orch., Tex. Longhorn Band U. Tex., 1975. Clarinetist, Patrick Conway Band, 1922-27, soloist, 1927-29, condr., Ohio Wesleyan U. Band, 1925-29, dir. music, condr., Moosehart Band, 1929-35; Author: Ten Minute Self-Instructor for Pocket Instruments, 1943, The Big Serenade, 1961; Composer: Niece of Uncle Sam, 1944, American Doughboy, 1945, My Missouri, 1945, General Spaatz March, 1947, The Red Feather; theme song, Community Chest, Official March of the Washington Evening Star, Official March of the Central Canada Exhibition, Official March Pacific Nat. Exhbn, Vancouver, B.C., Alfalfa Club March, Cougar's Victory, Bachelors of the Sky, others. Chmn. John Philip Sousa Meml., Kennedy Center for the Performing Arts, Washington. Decorated Legion of Merit with cluster U.S.; Guarde Republique medal; comdr. Order of Nonsaraphon Cambodia, Star of the Order, gold medal Sudler Found.; recipient Gold record for furthering Japanese-Am. relations thru music Nippon-Columbia Co., 1962; named to Hall of Fame for Disting. Band Condrs. Mem. ASCAP, Nat. Assn. Composers and Condrs. (citation for contbn. Am. music), Am. Bandmasters Assn. (pres. 1956-57, elected hon. life pres. 1986), Tex. Bandmasters Assn. (hon. life), Nat. Band Assn. (pres. 1970-74), Phi Mu Alpha, Pi Kappa Lambda, Phi Kappa Tau, Kappa Kappa Psi, Phi Beta Mu. Club: Alfalfa (Washington). Address: Air Force Village 4917 Ravenswood Dr Apt 1615 San Antonio TX 78227

HOWARD, GROVER LATHAM, III, data processing and management consultant; b. New Brunswick, N.J., Apr. 29, 1945; s. Grover Latham and Joy Elizebeth (Gibson) H.; m. Mary Catherine Jones, Oct. 14, 1966 (div. July 1973); children—Grover Latham IV, Peter W.; m. Ana Cristina Eichman, Feb. 24, 1974; children—Mathew M., M. Tazewell. Student La. State U., New Orleans, 1963-65. Enlisted U.S. Air Force, 1965, advanced through grades to sgt., 1969; planning research corp. project mgr. World Wide Mil. Command and Control System, Heidelberg, W.Ger., 1972-74; project mgr. USAF Europe Tactical Air Intelligence system architecture design, Ramstein, W.Ger., 1980-81; pres. GCM, Inc., Alexandria, Va., 1981—. Mem. Alexandria Republican City Com. Mem. Am. Security Council, Center for Entrepreneurial Mgmt., Alexandria Crime Solvers (pres.), Aircraft Owners and Pilots Assn., Nat. Trust for Historic Preservation, Alexandria C. of C. Republican. Methodist. Lodge: Kiwanis. Office: 4601 H Pinecrest Office Park Dr Alexandria VA 22312

HOWARD, JAMES WEBB, investment banker, lawyer; b. Evansville, Ind., Sept. 17, 1925; s. Joseph R. and Velma (Cobb) H.; m. Phyllis Jean Brandt, Dec. 27, 1948; children: Sheila Rae, Sharon Kae. B.S. in Mech. Engring, Purdue U., 1949; postgrad., Akron (Ohio) Law Sch., 1950-51, Cleve. Marshall Law Sch., 1951-52; M.B.A., Western Res. U., 1962; J.D., Western State Coll. Law, 1976. Registered profl. engr., Ind., Ohio. Jr. project engr. Firestone Tire & Rubber Co., Akron, 1949-50; gen. foreman Cadillac Motor Car div. Gen. Motors Corp., 1950-53; mgmt. cons. M.K. Sheppard & Co., Cleve., 1953-56; plant mgr. Lewis Welding & Engring. Corp., Ohio, 1956-58; underwriter The Ohio Co., Columbus, 1959; chmn. Growth Capital, Inc., Chgo., 1960—; pres. Meister Brau, Inc., Chgo., 1965-73; others. Co-chmn. Chgo. com. Ill. Sesquicentennial Com., 1968. Served with AUS, 1943-46. Decorated Bronze Star, Parachutist badge, Combat Inf. badge. Mem. ASME, Nat. Assn. Small Bus. Investment Companies (past pres.), Am. Mgmt. Assn., ABA, State Bar Calif., Grad. Bus. Alumni Assn. Western Res. U. (past gov.), Tau Kappa Epsilon, Pi Tau Sigma, Beta Gamma Sigma. Methodist. Club: Masons.

HOWARD, JOHN WILFRED, artist; b. Corinth, Ky., Aug. 20, 1924; s. John David and Veral (Kemper) H.; m. Leona Belle Thompson, June 22, 1979; children—Bonnie, Connie, Sharon, Terresa, Sandra. Farmer, 1940-45, 1947-72; life and health ins. agt., 1972-79; comml. artist, Corinth, Ky.; works displayed in Artists U.S.A. (internationally distributed art book), 1981-82. Served with AUS, 1945-47. Mem. Nat. Mus. Women in Arts, Creative World, Nat. Trust Hist. Preservation Am. Democrat. Baptist. Home and Office: Rural Rt 2 Corinth KY 41010

HOWARD, MARGUERITE EVANGELINE BARKER (MRS. JOSEPH D. HOWARD), business executive, civic worker; b. Victoria, B.C., Can., July 30, 1921; d. Reuel Harold and Frances Penelope (Garnham) Barker; brought to U.S., 1924, naturalized, 1945; B.A., U. Wash., 1943; m. Joseph D. Howard, June 16, 1952; children—Wendy Doreen Frances, Bradford Reuel. Vice pres., dir. Howard Tours, Inc., Oakland, Calif., 1953—; co-owner, gen. mgr. Howard Travel Service, Oakland, 1956—, mng. dir. Howard Hall, Berkeley, Calif., 1964-75; co-owner, asst. mgr. Howard Investments, Oakland, 1960—; sec., treas. Energy Dynamics Inc. Bd. dirs. Piedmont council Campfire Girls, 1969-79, pres., 1974-79, mem. nat. council, 1972-76, zone chmn., 1974-76, 77-83, zone coordinator, 1976, nat. v.p., 1975, nat. bd. dirs., 1976-83, bd. dirs. Alameda Contra Costa council, 1984—; bd. dirs. Oakland Symphony Guild, 1969—, pres., 1972-74; mem. exec. bd. Oakland Symphony Orch. Assn., 1972-74, bd. dirs., 1972-86; 1st pres. Inner Wheel Club of East Oakland, 1983-84; bd. dirs. Piedmont Jr. High Sch. Mothers Club, 1968-69. Recipient Wohelo Order award Campfire, Inc. 1985. Mem. Oakland Mus. Assn., U. Wash. Alumni Assn., East Bay Bot. and Zool. Soc., Young Audiences, Am. Symphony Orch. League, Assn. Calif. Symphony Orchs., Chi Omega Alumni Seattle, Chi Omega East Bay Alumni Berkeley. Republican. Clubs: Womens Univ. (Seattle); Womens Athletic (Oakland) (bd. dirs. 1986—). Home: 146 Bell Ave Piedmont CA 94611 Office: 526 Grand Ave Oakland CA 94610

HOWARD, MARTHA WALLING, educator, writer; b. Shreveport, La., Jan. 28, 1916; d. Joseph Macon and Moss (Turner) Walling; B.A., Randolph-Macon Woman's Coll., 1937; M.A., George Washington U., 1942; Ph.D., U. Md., 1967; m. George Wilberforce Howard, June 5, 1938; children—George Wilberforce III, James Ewing. Instr. Latin, All Saints Coll., Vicksburg, Miss., 1937-39, Gunstan Hall Jr. Coll., Washington, 1940-42, public schs. Stafford and Fairfax Counties, Va., 1950-66; lectr. Greek and Latin, Am. U., Washington, 1965-66; lectr. humanities U. Ariz., Tucson, 1966-74, asso. prof. humanities, 1974-76; freelance writer, 1976—; books include: All Things to Sea (lyric poetry), 1942; Plutarch in the Major European Literatures of the Eighteenth Century, 1970; Comparative Literature Study (Choice List of outstanding acad. books), 1972; The Roland Woman: A Biography, 1983. Named to Hall of Fame, U. Ariz., 1975. Mem. Humane Soc. Tucson, Ariz. Hist. Soc., Phi Beta Kappa (Alpha chpt. Ariz.), Mortar Bd. Republican. Episcopalian. Club: U. Ariz. President's. Home: 177-C S Paseo Sarta Green Valley AZ 85614

HOWARD, MELVIN, office equipment and financial services company executive; b. Boston, Jan. 5, 1935; s. John M. and Molly (Sagar) H.; m. Beverly Ruth Kahan, June 9, 1957; children: Brian David, Marjorie Lyn. BA, U. Mass., 1957; MS, Columbia U., 1959. Fin. exec. Ford Motor Co., Dearborn, Mich., 1959-67; v.p. adminstrn. Shoe Corps. of Am., Columbus, Ohio, 1967-70; asst. controller Bus. Products group Xerox Corp., Rochester, N.Y., 1970-72; v.p. fin. Bus. Devel. group Xerox Corp., 1972-74, sr. v.p., sr. staff officer, 1974-75, corp. v.p., controller, 1975-77, corp. v.p. fin., 1977-78, sr. corp. v.p. fin., 1978-81, sr. v.p., chief fin. officer, 1981-84, exec. v.p., pres. fin. services, 1984-86, vice chmn., 1986; chmn. Xerox Fin. Services, Inc.; also bd. dirs. Xerox Corp.; bd. dirs. LMH Fund Ltd., Crum and Forster, Inc., Van Kampen Merritt, Inc., Gould Pumps, Inc., Xerox Credit Corp., Bond Investors Group, VMS Realty Ptnrs. Trustee Norwalk Hosp. Served to 1st lt. AUS, 1957. Mem. AIA (conf. bd.), Fin. Execs. Inst., Am. Mgmt. Assn., Beta Gamma Sigma. Club: Birchwood Country. Home: 42 Red Coat Rd Westport CT 06880 Office: Xerox Corp 800 Long Ridge Rd Stamford CT 06904

HOWARD, MICHAEL ELIOT, university professor, historian; b. London, Nov. 29, 1922; s. Geoffrey Eliot and Edith Julia Emma (Edinger) H. MA, U. Oxford, 1948, LittD, 1976; LittD, Leeds (Eng.) U.; DLitt, U. London, 1988. Asst. lectr. history Kings Coll. U. London, 1947-53, lectr. war studies, 1953-62; prof. war studies U. London, 1963-68; fellow higher defence studies All Souls Coll., Oxford, 1968-77; prof. history of war U. Oxford, 1977-80, regius prof. modern history, 1980—; pres. Internat. Inst. Strategic Studies, London, 1987. Author: The Franco Prussian War, 1961 (Duff Cooper Prize, 1962), Grand Strategy,, vol. IV, 1971 (Wofson award for history); many others. Served to capt. English Army, 1942-45. Decorated Mil. Cross His Majesty King George VI, 1943; named Knight Bachelor Her Majesty Queen Elizabeth II, 1986, Commdr. of the British Empire, 1987. Fellow British Acad., U.S. Acad. Arts and Scis. Mem. Ch. of Eng. Clubs: Athenaeum, Garrick (London). Office: Oriel Coll, Oxford OX1 4EW, England

HOWARD, PHILIP MARTIN, insurance agent; b. Chgo., Dec. 16, 1939; s. Anthony Gerald and Mary Elizabeth (Smith) H.; m. Diane R. Miller, Sept. 12, 1964; children: Anne Marie, Philip Martin II, Kevin Vincent. Student Chgo. parochial schs. Laborer, tree trimmer Chgo. Bur. Forestry, 1963-66; sales rep. O.H. div. Bell & Howell, Chgo., 1966; sr. account agt. Allstate Ins. Co., Chgo., 1967—; ins. officer Mt. Greenwood Youth Baseball, Chgo., 1981-86. Served with USMCR, 1962-67. Mem. Nat. Assn. Life Underwriters, Ill. Life Underwriters Assn., Chgo. Assn. Life Underwriters, Worth C. of C. Republican. Roman Catholic. Home: 11324 S Lawndale Ave Chicago IL 60655 Office: 7000 W 111th St Worth IL 60482

HOWARD, RICHARD CHARLES EDWARD, Canadian government official; b. Bath, Eng., May 13, 1944; s. Geoffrey John Eliot and Patricia Doreen (Chesney) H.; m. Judith Faye Shakespeare, Jan 20, 1968 (div. 1974); children: Geoffrey John Eliot, Catherine Anne; m. Patricia Kathleen Leach, Sept. 28, 1985. Grad. pvt. sch., Eastbourne, Eng. Apprentice Cadbury Bros. Ltd., Bournville, Eng., 1962-65; mktg. mgr. East Asiatic Co. (Can.), Vancouver, B.C., 1965-73; mktg. cons. Govt. of Ont. (Can.), Toronto, 1973-82; rep. Govt. of Ont. (Can.), Brussels, 1982-85; sr. rep. Govt. of Ont. (Can.), Frankfurt, Fed. Republic Germany, 1985—. Anglican. Home: Mailaenderstrasse 9 70, Frankfurt/Main Federal Republic of Germany Office: Govt of Ont, Bockenheimer Landstrasse 51/53, D 6000 Frankfurt/Main Federal Republic of Germany

HOWARD, TREVOR WALLACE, actor; b. Sept. 29, 1916; student Clifton Coll., Bristol, Eng.; m. Helen Cherry, 1944. Plays include: French Without Tears, The Recruiting Officer, 1944, Anna Christie, 1944, The Devil's General, 1953, The Cherry Orchard, 1954, Two Stars for Comfort, 1962, The Father, 1964, Table Number Seven, The Waltz of the Toreadors, 1974, Scenario, Toronto, 1977; films include: Brief Encounter, 1945, The Third Man, 1949, An Outcast of the Islands, 1951, The Heart of the Matter, 1953, Les amants du Tage, 1955, Cockleshell Heroes, 1955, The Key, 1958, Roots of Heaven, 1958, Sons and Lovers, 1960, Mutiny on the Bounty, 1962, Von Ryan's Express, 1966, The Charge of the Light Brigade, 1968, Ryan's Daughter, 1970, Mary Queen of Scots, 1972, The Offense, 1973, A Doll's House, 1973, II Harrowhouse, 1974, The Visitor, Hennessy, 1975, Conduct Unbecoming, 1976, Count of Monte Cristo, 1976, Eliza Fraser, 1977, The Last Remake of Beau Geste, 1977, Slavers, 1978, Meteor, 1978, Ludwig, Stevie, Hurricane, 1979, The Sea Wolves, 1980, Sir Henry at Rawlinson End, 1980, Windwalker, 1981, Light Years Away, 1982, The Missionary, 1983, Gandhi, 1983, Dust, 1986, White Mischief, 1987; TV plays include: Hedda Gabler, 1962, The Invincible Mr. Disraeli (Acad. award), 1963, Napoleon at St. Helena, 1966, Catholics, Night Flight, Staying On, 1980, And the Band Played On, 1981, No Country for Old Men, 1982, The Long Exile of Jonathan Swift, 1983, The Deadly Game, 1983, George Washington, 1984, Time After Time, 1985, This Lightning Always Strikes Twice, 1985, Shaka Zulu, 1986, Sir Isaac Newton in Peter the Great, 1986; TV miniseries Peter the Great, 1986. Served with Royal Army, 1940-43. *

HOWARD, WILLIAM FRANCIS, writer, educator; b. Albany, N.Y., Sept. 18, 1960; s. William Guilford and Laura May (Bailey) H. B.A. cum laude Manhattanville Coll., 1983; Hon. Diploma, St. Louis Occidental U., 1977; M.A., SUNY-Albany, 1984. Policy analyst N.Y. State Senate, 1984—. Author: Neighbors Not Victims, 1988; book reviewer: Jour. Civil War, 1981—; editor: (book) Dear Eliza: The Civil War Letters of Sgt. Darwin R. Field, 1983, The Battle of Gettysburg, 1988, The Peninsula, 1988; contbr. articles to periodicals. Block capt. Republican Party, Delmar, 1982—; town committeeman Rep. Party, 1984—; hist. lectr. to civic groups. Recipient Howard R. Bloomquist award Manhattanville Coll., 1983; Herbert H. Lehman fellow, 1984. Fellow Co. Mil. Historians; mem. Orgn. Am. Historians, So. Hist. Assn., Mus. of the Confederacy, Hist. Gettysburg Assn., Civil War Roundtable. Lutheran. Home: 155 Cherry Ave Delmar NY 12054 Office: Senate Chamber Albany NY 12247

HOWAT, GRAHAM, aviation executive; b. Eng., Nov. 17, 1944; arrived in Hong Kong, 1972; s. Robert Alexander and Sarah Ada Howat; m. Denise Elliott, Aug. 10, 1968; children: Emma, Matthew. MS, Cranfield Inst. Tech., 1968. Chartered engr., Eng. Apprentice Hawker Siddeley Aviation Ltd., Eng., 1962-68; sr. work study officer Brit. Airways, Eng., 1968-72; mgmt. devel. engr. Hong Kong Aircraft Engring. Co. Ltd., 1972-75, maintenance supt., 1975-76, overhaul mgr., 1976-78, gen. mgr. mktg., 1978-84, dir., chief exec., 1984-87, mng. dir., 1987—; chmn. bd. South China Aero. Tech. Ltd., Hong Kong, 1984—, Thompson Aircraft Tire Co. Ltd., Hong Kong, 1985—, Kai Tak Refuellers Ltd., Hong Kong, 1987—; chmn. transport services council Fedn. Hong Kong Industries, 1987—. Chmn. commn. on apprenticeship and trade testing Vocat. Tng. Council, Hong Kong, 1984—; mem. Outward Bound Trust, Hong Kong, 1987—. Fellow Royal Aero. Soc., Hong Kong Inst. Engrs.; mem. Brit. Inst. Mgmt. Clubs: Tower, Aviation (Hong Kong). Home: 29 Kadoorie Ave, Kowloon Hong Kong Office: Hong Kong Aircraft Engring Co, 60 Concorde Rd, Hong Kong Hong Kong

HOWATT, HELEN CLARE, library director; b. San Francisco, Apr. 5, 1927; d. Edward Bell and Helen Margaret (Kenney) H. B.A., Holy Name Coll., 1949; M.S. in Library Sci., U. So. Calif., 1972. Joined Order Sisters of the Holy Names, Roman Catholic Ch., 1945; cert. advanced studies Inst. Sch. Librarians, Our Lady of Lake U., San Antonio, 1966. Life teaching credential, life spl. services credential, Calif. Prin., St. Monica Sch., Santa Monica, Calif., 1957-60, St. Mary Sch., Los Angeles, 1960-63; tchr. jr. high sch. St. Augustine Sch., Oakland, Calif., 1964-69; tchr. jr. high math St. Monica Sch., San Francisco, 1969-71, St. Cecilia Sch., San Francisco, 1971-77; library dir. Holy Names Coll., Oakland, Calif., 1977—. Contbr. math. curriculum San Francisco Unified Sch. Dist., Cum Notis Variorum, publ. Music Library, U. Calif., Berkeley. Contbr. articles Cath. Library World, 1987, 87. NSF grantee, 1966; NDEA grantee, 1966. Mem. Cath. Library Assn. (chmn. No. Calif. elem. schs. 1971-72), Calif. Library Assn., ALA, Assn. Coll. and research Libraries. Home and Office: 3500 Mountain Blvd Oakland CA 94619

HOWE, BRIAN LESLIE, minister social security of Australia; b. Melbourne, Australia, Jan. 1, 1936; m. Renate Morris, May 8, 1962; children: John, Abbey, Sarah. B.A., Melbourne U., Diploma in Criminology; postgrad. McCormick Theol. Sem., Chgo. Mem. faculty Swinburne Inst. Tech., Melbourne, sr. lectr. in sociology, until 1977, also chmn. dept. social and polit. studies; mem. Australian Labor Party, 1961—, Australian Ho. of Reps., Canberra, 1977—, mem. standing com. on environment, 1978—, mem. joint com. on publs., 1978—, minister for def. support, 1983-84, minister social security, 1984—; founder, first dir. Centre for Urban Research and Action, Melbourne. Mem. various nat. policy coms. Australian Labour Party, chmn. caucus econs. com., mem. caucus resources com., mem. urban and regional affairs com. Office: Ministry of Social Security, Canberra Australia

HOWE, DAVID GLEN, ceramic engineer; b. Wellsville, N.Y., Nov. 21, 1933; s. Glen Henry and Frances Annvernette (Hills) H.; m. Beatriz Aldunate Lewis, July 25, 1987; B.S. in Ceramic Engring., Alfred (N.Y.) U., 1955. Ceramic engr. U.S. Gypsum Co., Oakfield, N.Y., 1955-56, U.S. Naval Research Lab., Washington, 1958-86, Mar, Inc., Severna Park, Md., 1987—. Served with U.S. Army, 1956-58. Recipient Applied Research Pub. award Naval Research Lab. Material Scis. Div., 1977. Mem. Am. Ceramic Soc., Am. Soc. Metals, Md. Inst. Metals, U.S. Naval Inst. Republican. Mem. Disciples of Christ Ch. Holder six patents on alloy formulation and metall. processing of superconducting materials, world record for highest critical current density obtained in a superconducting wire. Home: 46 Ridge Rd Greenbelt MD 20770 Office: Mar Inc 838 Ritchie Hwy Suite 4 Severna Park MD 21246

HOWE, EDITH L. MILLER, real estate investment firm executive; b. Bowling Green, Ohio, Apr. 29, 1913; d. Christie and Alta (Clark) Miller; B.S., Bowling Green State U., 1945; M.A., U. Toledo, 1948; student Ohio State U., 1949, Temple U., 1965-66; m. W. Asquith Howe, Feb. 2, 1936. Tchr. public schs., Wood County, Ohio, 1941-47; tchr. dept. psychology U. Toledo, 1947-48; pres., mgr. Howe Real Estate Investments, Ohio, Fla., N.J., 1948—. Home: 4409 Crews Ct Port Charlotte FL 33952

HOWE, FISHER, management consultant, former government official; b. Winnetka, Ill., May 17, 1914; s. Lawrence and Hester (Davis) H.; m. Deborah Froelicher, June 4, 1945; children: Elizabeth, Shippen. A.B., Harvard, 1935; student, Nat. War Coll., 1948. Salesman Coats & Clarks Thread Co., N.Y.C., 1935-40, Patons & Baldwins, Ltd., Yorkshire, Eng., 1936-37; mem. staff Office of Dir., OSS, Washington, London, Mediterranean, Far East, 1941-45; spl. asst. under sec. of state, econ. affairs 1945-46; exec. sec. Bd. Fgn. Service, Dept. State, 1947, dep. spl. asst. to sec. state, 1948-56; exec. sec. Dept. State, 1956-58; counselor of embassy Dept. State, Oslo, Norway, 1958-62, The Hague, Netherlands, 1962-65; mem. policy planning council Dept. State, 1965-68; exec. dir., asst. dean Johns Hopkins U. Sch. Advanced Internat. Studies, 1968-72; dep. exec. dir. Commn. on Orgn. of Govt. for Conduct of Fgn. Policy, Washington, 1973-75; sec., gen. adv. com. Energy Research and Devel. Adminstrn., 1975-77; asst. to pres., dir. instl. relations Resources for the Future, Inc., 1978-82; v.p. Lavender/Rice & Assocs., 1982—. Author: Computer and Foreign Affairs, 1968. Trustee Fountain Valley Sch., Colorado Springs, Colo., Hospice Care of D.C., Pilgrim Soc., Plymouth, Mass., Washington Area Council on Alcoholism and Drug Abuse. Served as lt. USNR, 1943-44, overseas service. Club: Metropolitan, Mill Reef (Washington). Home: 2015 48th St NW Washington DC 20007 Office: 1730 Rhode Island Ave NW Suite 912 Washington DC 20036

HOWE, (RICHARD EDWARD) GEOFFREY, British secretary of state foreign and commonwealth affairs; b. Dec. 20, 1926; s. B.E. Howe and E.F. (Thomson) H.; m. Elspeth Rosamund Morton Shand; 1 son, 2 daus. M.A., 1950, LL.B. (scholar), 1951, Trinity Hall, Cambridge. Chmn., Cambridge U. Conservative Assn., 1951, Bow Group, 1955; mng. dir. Crossbow, 1957-60; editor, 1960-62; called to bar Middle Temple, 1952, created Queen's counsel, 1965, bencher, 1969; mem. Parliament from Bebington, 1964-66, Reigate, 1970-74, East Surrey, 1974—; solicitor-gen., 1970-72; minister for trade and consumer affairs, 1972-74; M.P., mem. Conservative shadow cabinet, 1974-79, chief front bench spokesman on treasury and econ. affairs, 1975-79; chancellor of Exchequer, 1979-83; chmn. interim com. IMF, 1982-83; sec. state for fgn. and Commonwealth affairs, 1983—; dep. chmn. Glamorgan Quarter Sessions, 1966-70. Mem. Gen. Council of the Bar, 1957-61, Council of Justice, from 1963; sec. Conservative Parliamentary Health and Social Com., 1964-65. Mem. Interdepartmental Com. on Age of Majority, 1965-67; chmn. bd. Ely Hosp. Inquiry, Cardiff, 1969; mem. council mgmt. Pvt. Patients' Plan, 1969-70. Created Knight, 1970, privy councillor, 1972. Office: Fgn and Commonwealth Office, King Charles, London SW1, England

HOWE, JAMES EVERETT, investment company executive; b. N.Y.C., Mar. 30, 1930; s. Ernest Joseph and Gladys Montgomery (Sills) H.; m. Judith DePuy Keating, May 9, 1959; children—James E., Jr., David K. B.A., Williams Coll., 1952; M.B.A., Columbia U., 1954. Chartered fin. analyst. Statistician J.P. Morgan & Co., N.Y.C., 1956-59; investment research officer Morgan Guaranty Trust Co., N.Y.C., 1959-65; sr. analyst Tri-Continental Corp., N.Y.C., 1965-80; asst. v.p., shareholder J&W Seligman & Co., N.Y.C., 1980-81; chmn. investment com. Charles Edison Fund, East Orange, N.J., 1981—; trustee Brook Found., N.Y.C., 1966-72, Charles Edison Fund, 1972—; bd. deacons Brick Presbyn. Ch., N.Y.C., 1963-66. Served to 1st lt. USAF, 1954-56, ETO. Recipient Fin. award Wall St. Jour., 1954, award of Appreciation Thomas A. Edison Found., 1977. Mem. N.Y. Soc. Security Analysts, Inst. Chartered Fin. Analysts, Machinery Analyst of N.Y. (pres. 1967-68, charter mem.), Environ. Control Analysts of N.Y. (pres. 1975, charter mem.), Steel Analysts Group, Jamestown Soc. (charter), Alpha Kappa Psi (pres. 1953-54). Republican. Presbyterian. Clubs: Genesee Valley (Rochester, N.Y.); Short Hills (N.J.). Avocation: photography. Home: 33 Keats Rd Short Hills NJ 07078 Office: Charles Edison Fund 101 S Harrison St East Orange NJ 07018

HOWE, JOHN KINGMAN, sales and marketing executive; b. Everett, Wash., Nov. 7, 1945; s. John Cutler and Nancy Carpenter (Kingman) H.; m. Loretta Kerr, Aug. 27, 1966; children—Steven Cutler, Nancy Kingman. Student Ohio State U., 1963-65. Field technician Data Corp., Dayton, Ohio, 1965-66; letter carrier U.S. Post Office, Dayton, 1966; sales rep. E.S. Klosterman Co., Dayton, 1966-71, v.p. 1971-72; v.p. sales, dir. Springfield Binder Corp., Ohio, 1981-84, pres., chief exec. officer, 1984—; pres. The John K. Howe Co., Inc., Dayton, Ohio, 1972-87, chmn., chief exec. officer, dir. 1987—; pres. Cutler-Kingman, Inc. div. Thump Properties, Dayton, 1979-86, owner, 1986—; gen. ptnr. H&B Enterprises, Dayton, 1977-86, Design Investment Properties, Dayton, 1979-86, BMR Properties, Ltd., Dayton, 1979-82; adminstr. John K. Howe Co./Profit Sharing, Dayton, 1973—, John K. Howe Co./Pension Plan, 1976—; owner Androscoggin Designs, Dayton, 1979-86. Pres. South Dixie Bus. Assn., Kettering, Ohio, 1978-82. Mem.

Adminstrv. Mgmt. Soc. Internat., Dayton C. of C. Republican. Presbyterian. Home: 889 Lincoln Woods Ct Dayton OH 45429-3480 Office: John K Howe Co Inc 400 Pike St 9th Floor Cincinnati OH 45202-4216 Also: Dayton Distbn Ctr 2711 Lance Dr Dayton OH 45409-1574

HOWE, ROBERT WILSON, education educator; b. Klamath Falls, Oreg., July 9, 1932; s. Fred Phillip and Adelaide Alice H.; m. Alma Ann Felton, Mar. 1955; children—Jeanine Adele, Jeffrey Philip. B.A., Willamette U., 1954; M.S., Oreg. State U., 1960, Ed.D., 1964. Tchr., counselor Arlington (Wash.) public schs., 1955-60; inst. Oreg. State U., 1961-63; asst. prof. Ohio State U., 1963-66, asso. prof., 1967-70, prof., 1970—, chmn. dept. sci. and math edn., 1969-77; dir. ERIC Clearinghouse, EQ/IRC; cons. fed. agys., schs., state govts. Author, co-author books; mem. editorial bd.: Jour. Sci. Edn, 1970—; contbr. articles to profl. jours. Trustees Center Sci. and Industry, Columbus, Ohio. NSF fellow, 1959, 60, 61; EPA grantee, 1977-84, 87. Fellow Ohio Acad. Sci.; mem. Nat. Sci. Tchrs. Assn., Am. Ednl. Research Assn., Assn. Educators Tchg. of Sci., Phi Delta Kappa, Sigma Alpha Epsilon. Methodist. Home: 283 Weydon Rd Worthington OH 43085 Office: Ohio State U 1200 Chambers Rd Columbus OH 43212

HOWE, WILLIAM HUGH, artist; b. Stockton, Calif., June 18, 1928; s. Edwin Walter and Eugenia (Mercanti) H. AB, Ottawa (Kans.) U., 1951. Exhibited paintings of butterflies at Philbrook Art Center, Tulsa, Ft. Worth Children's Mus., Witte Meml. Art Mus., San Antonio, Anthropology Mus., Chapultepec Park, Mexico City; represented in permanent collections: Smithsonian Instn., Washington, Franklin Mint (Pa.), Cranbrook Inst., Bloomfield Hills, Mich., U. Mich. Exhibits Mus., Ann Arbor, Oak Knoll Mus., Clayton, Mo., Hax Art Center, St. Joseph, Mo., Am. Mus. Natural History, N.Y.C., Central Mo. State Coll., Warrensburg, Mich. State U., East Lansing, U. Wyo. Art Mus., Laramie, San Diego Mus. Nat. History, Balboa Park, U. Ariz., Tucson, Ill. State Mus. Art, Springfield, Mont. Hist. Soc., Helena, Wyo. State Art Mus., Cheyenne, Ariz. State U., Tempe, Milw. Pub. Mus., State Capitol Bldg., Denver, Denver Pub. Library, Kansas City (Mo.) Mus. History Sci., Presdl. Palace, Tamazunchale, San Luis Potosi, Mexico, Ottawa (Kans.) Jr. High Sch., others; Am. Heritage Wildlife cards Am. Butterflies, 1983. Author-artist: Our Butterflies and Moths, 1964, The Butterflies of North America, 1975, Butterfly Chart of North America, 1979, Butterfly sect. Readers Digest North American Wildlife, 1980; co-author (with Carlos R. Beutelspacher Baights), U.N.A.M., Mexico City, 1984; one man show Caroline Kingcade Gallery, North Kansas City, Mo., 1988; TV show Hoy Mismo, Mexico City, 1986. Mem. Jour. Lepidopterists Soc., Burroughs Nature Club, Audubon Soc. Mo., Central States Entomo. Soc., Los Angeles County Mus. Democrat. Episcopalian. Home: 822 E 11th St Ottawa KS 66067

HOWELL, ARTHUR, lawyer; b. Atlanta, Aug. 24, 1918; s. Arthur and Katharine (Mitchell) H.; m. Caroline Sherman, June 14, 1941; children: Arthur, Caroline, Eleanor, Richard, Peter, James; m. Janet Kerr Franchot, Dec. 16, 1972. A.B., Princeton U., 1939; J.D., Harvard U., 1942; LL.D. (hon.), Oglethorpe U., 1972. Bar: Ga. 1942. Assoc. F.M., 1942-45; ptnr. Alston & Bird (and predecessor firms), 1945—; dir., gen. counsel Atlantic Steel Co.; pres., dir. Creomulsion Co.; dir. Enterprise Funds, J.S. Tech., Inc.; past pres. Atlanta Legal Aid Soc. Pres. Met. Atlanta Community Services, 1956, dir., 1953—; pres. Community Planning Council, 1961-63; gen. chmn. United Appeal, 1955; spl. atty. gen. State Ga., 1948-55; spl. counsel Univ. System Ga., State Sch. Bldg. Authorities, 1951-70; adv. com. Ga. Corp. Code, 1967—; chmn. Atlanta Adv. Com. Parks; Trustee Princeton, 1964-68, Atlanta Speech Sch.; trustee, past chmn. Oglethorpe U.; trustee Morehouse Coll., Westminister Schs., Atlanta, Episcopal High Sch., Alexandria, Va., Inst. Internat. Edn. (exec. com. 1969-72). Named hon. alumnus Ga. Inst. Tech. Fellow Am. Coll. Probate Counsel (chmn. com. on profl. standards 1982-85, regent 1984—); mem. Am. Law Inst., Am., Ga., Atlanta bar assns., Internat. Acad. of Estate and Trust Law (academician), Lawyers Club of Atlanta (past pres.), Am. Judicature Soc., Soc. Colonial Wars, Phi Beta Kappa. Presbyn. (elder, trustee, chmn. bd. trustees 1985—). Clubs: Mill Reef, Capital City, Piedmont Driving, Commerce, Homosassa Fishing; Nassau (Princeton, N.J.); Princeton (N.Y.C.). Home: 33 Ivy Ridge Atlanta GA 30342 also: Petit Ridge Dr Big Canoe GA 30143 Office: 1200 C & S Bank Bldg Atlanta GA 30335

HOWELL, CHARLES MAITLAND, dermatologist; b. Thomasville, N.C., Apr. 14, 1914; s. Cyrus Maitl and Lilly Mae (Ammons) H.; m. Betty Jane Myers, Feb. 12, 1949; children—Elizabeth Myers, Pamela Jane. B.S., Wake Forest U., Winston-Salem, N.C., 1935; M.D., U. Pa., 1937. Intern Charity Hosp., New Orleans, 1937-38; resident in medicine Burlington County Hosp., Mt. Holley, N.J., 1938-39; sch. physician Lawrenceville (N.J.) Sch., 1939-42; resident in pathology N.C. Baptist Hosp., Winston-Salem, 1947-48; resident in dermatology Columbia-Presbyn. Med. Center, N.Y.C., 1948-50; resident in allergy Roosevelt Hosp., N.Y.C., 1950-51; practice medicine specializing in dermatology Winston-Salem, 1951—; mem. staff N.C. Bapt., Forsyth Meml. hosps.; mem. faculty Bowman Gray Sch. Medicine, Wake Forest U., 1951-86, head sect., 1984-86, prof. dermatology, 1967-84, prof. emeritus, 1984, head sect., 1961-86, acting head sect., 1984-86. Served as officer M.C. AUS, 1942-46. Fellow Am. Acad. Dermatology, Am. Acad. Allergy; mem. N. Am. Clin. Dermatol. Soc., N.Y. Acad. Scis. Democrat. Baptist. Clubs: Old Town (Winston-Salem); Bermuda Run Country (Clemmons, N.C.). Home: 1100 Kent Rd E Winston-Salem NC 27104 Office: 340 Pershing Ave Winston-Salem NC 27103

HOWELL, DAVID ARTHUR RUSSELL, British legislator, economist, journalist; b. London, Jan. 18, 1936; s. Arthur and Beryl (Bowater) H.; M.A. with 1st class honours, King's Coll., Cambridge U., 1959; m. Davina Wallace, Aug. 10, 1967; children—Fanny, Kate, Toby. With econ. sect. Treasury, 1959-60; econ. corr., editorial writer Daily Telegraphy, 1960-64; dir. Conservative Polit. Centre, 1964-66; M.P. for Guildford, 1966—; parliamentary sec. Civil Service Dept., 1970-72, Dept. Employment, 1972-74; minister of state No. Ireland Office, 1972-74; sec. state Dept. Energy, 1979-81; sec. state Dept. Transport, 1981-83; privy councillor, 1979; dir. Savory Milln Ltd. Author: Freedom and Capital, 1980; Blind Victory, 1986. Chmn. Bow Group, 1962-63. Served with Brit. Army, 1954-56. Clubs: Carlton, Bucks (London). Address: House of Commons, Westminster, London SW1 England *

HOWELL, DONALD LEE, lawyer; b. Waco, Tex., Jan. 31, 1935; s. Hilton Emory and Louise (Hatchett) H.; m. Gwendolyn Avera, June 13, 1957; children—Daniel Liege, Alison Avera, Anne Turner. BA cum laude, Baylor U., 1956; JD with highest honors, U. Tex., 1963. Bar: Tex. 1963. Assoc. Vinson & Elkins, Houston, 1963-70, ptnr., 1970—, mem. mgmt. com., 1980—. Served to capt. USAFR, 1956-59. Woodrow Wilson fellow U. Tex., 1959-60. Fellow Am. Bar Found., Tex. Bar Found., Houston Bar Found.; mem. ABA, Houston Bar Assn., Am. Law Inst., Nat. Assn. Bond Lawyers (pres. 1981-82, bd. dirs. 1979-83), Tex. Research League (bd. dirs. 1987—), Order of Coif, Phi Delta Phi. Democrat. Baptist. Clubs: Houston Ctr., Ramada (Houston).

HOWELL, FRANK MOBLEY, sociology educator; b. Duluth, Ga., Dec. 23, 1952; s. William Thomas and Sara Ruth (Mobley) H.; m. Mary Elizabeth Robbins, Aug. 3, 1974 (div. Aug. 1983); 1 child, Jonathan Clark. BA, Ga. Coll., 1975; MA, Miss. State U., 1977, PhD, 1979. Dir. news Sta. WXLX, Milledgeville, Ga., 1974-75; asst. prof. Tex. Christian U., Ft. Worth, 1981-83; asst. prof., assoc. dir. social sci. research and instructional computing lab. N.C. State U., Raleigh, 1983-85; assoc. prof., dir., monitor Miss. Lab., Miss. State U., 1985—; cons. Nat. Inst. Edn., Washington, 1977, Assn. Univ. Programs in Health Adminstrn., Washington, 1982-83; vis. research scientist O'Hara Ctr. for Youth Devel., Dallas, 1985—. Author: Making Life Plans, 1982; contbr. articles to profl. jours.; creator SocNet: internat. computer network for sociologists. Hon. chmn. Ga. Mental Health Assn., Milledgeville, 1975. Grantee Miss. Dept. Edn., 1980, 86-88, Wadsworth, Inc., 1985, USDA Human Nutrition Info. Service, 1987, Southeastern Ednl. Improvement Lab., 1987; postdoctoral fellow Miss. State U., 1979-80. Mem. Am. Sociol. Assn., Am. Ednl. Research Assn., Rural Sociol. Soc., Sigma Xi. Democrat. Baptist. Avocations: chess, fishing, shortwave listening, running. Home: 411 Critz St Starkville MS 39757 Office: Miss State U Dept Sociology Drawer C Mississippi State MS 39762

HOWELL, HARLEY THOMAS, lawyer; b. Chgo., June 5, 1937; s. Harley W. and Geneva (Engelmann) H.; m. Aliceann A. McLaughlin, Apr. 23, 1983; children by previous marriage: Shelley A., Rebecca L., Emily S. A.B., Princeton U., 1959; J.D., Yale U., 1962. Bar: Md. 1962, U.S. Supreme Ct. 1966, D.C. 1972. Law clk. to chief judge U.S. Ct. Appeals (4th cir.) 1962-63; assoc. Semmes, Bowen & Semmes, Balt., 1966-72, ptnr., 1972—; mem. Gov.'s Commn. to Revise Annotated Code Md., 1975-85; mem. standing com. on rules of practice and procedure Ct. Appeals of Md., 1985—. Bd. dirs. Balt. Symphony Orch., 1975—, sec., 1986—; trustee Edn. Ctr. of Sheppard Pratt, 1986—. Served to capt. JAG Corps, U.S. Army, 1963-66. Decorated Army Commendation medal. Mem. ABA, Md. State Bar Assn., Balt. City Bar Assn., D.C. Bar Assn., Fed. Bar Assn. Democrat. Clubs: Center, Wine and Food Soc., Wranglers Law (Balt.). Home: 1012 Chestnut Ridge Dr Lutherville MD 21093 Office: 250 W Pratt St Baltimore MD 21201

HOWELL, JAMES BURT, III, technical sales consultant; b. Bridgeton, N.J., Dec. 11, 1933; s. James Burt and Catharine Stanger (Sparks) H. BS with high honors, Rutgers U., 1956; MBA, U. Del., 1980. Agrl. sales rep. Allied Chem. Corp., Phila., 1957-59; sales cons. Asgrow Seed Co. subs. Upjohn Co., Vineland, N.J., 1960—; bd. dirs. Advance Weight Systems, Inc., LaGrange, Ohio. Mem. ofcl. bd. (session) 1st Presbyn. Ch. of Cedarville (N.J.), 1960—; admissions liaison officer U.S. Mil. Acad., West Point, N.Y., 1973—. Served with U.S. Army, 1957, served to col. U.S. Army Res. Recipient Burpee Hort. award Rutgers U., 1955. Mem. Am. Def. Preparedness Assn., Vegetable Growers Assn. N.J., Pesticide Assn. N.J. (bd. dirs.), Res. Officers Assn. U.S., Phi Beta Kappa, Alpha Gamma Rho, Alpha Zeta. Home: Sayres Neck Cedarville NJ 08311 Office: 1740 E Oak Rd Vineland NJ 08360

HOWELL, RICHARD PAUL, SR., transportation engineer; b. Sarasota, Fla., Nov. 20, 1927; s. Paul Augustus and Mary Amanda (Snead) H.; m. Judith Kay Eshelman, Sept. 6, 1958; children—Richard Paul, Thomas Bradford, Robert Greggson, Mary Amanda. BSCE, Mich. State U., 1949. Registered profl. engr., Ohio, Mass., R.I., Conn., N.Y., N.J., Pa., Del., D.C., Md. Track supr. to div. engr. Pa. R.R. and successor co. Penn Central R.R., 1949-71; from chief r.r. engr. to v.p. Deleuw, Cather & Co., Washington, 1971—; mem. Mich. State U. Alumni Engring. Council, East Lansing, 1968-72. Contbr. articles on transp. to profl. publs. Dist. chmn. Md. gubernatorial campaign, 1967. Served to lt. j.g. USN, 1945-46, Civil Engr. Corp. USNR. Recipient Toulmin medal Am. Soc. Mil. Engrs., 1979; named Railroader of Mo., Progressive Railroads, 1979. Mem. Am. Ry. Engring. Assn., Transp. Research Bd., Camp Hill Jr. C. of C. (pres. 1961-62), Phi Delta Theta. Republican. Presbyterian. Lodge: Masons. Avocations: golf; racquetball; sailing; skiing; travel. Home: 15205 Hannans Way Rockville MD 20853 also: 27 South Terr Chautauqua NY 14722 Office: De Leuw Cather & Co 1133 15th St NW Washington DC 20036

HOWELL, WILLIAM ROBERT, retail company executive; b. Claremore, Okla., Jan. 3, 1936; s. William Roosevelt and Opal Theo (Swan) H.; m. Donna Lee Hatch, June 7, 1956; children: Ann Elizabeth, Teresa Lynn. BBA, U. Okla., 1958. With J.C. Penney Co., Inc., 1958—, store mgr. J.C. Penney Co., Inc., Tulsa, 1968-69, dist. mgr., dir. Treasury Stores subs., Dallas, 1969-71, div. v.p., dir. domestic devel., N.Y.C., 1973-76, regional v.p., western regional mgr., 1976-79, sr. v.p., dir. merchandising, mktg. and catalog, 1979-81, exec. v.p., 1981-82, vice chmn. bd. dirs., 1982-83, chmn., chief exec. officer, 1983—, also bd. dirs.; bd. dirs. Exxon Corp., Warner-Lambert Corp., NYNEX Corp., Bankers Trust Co. Trustee Nat. Urban League. Mem. Am. Mgmt. Assn., Bus. Council, Bus. Roundtable, Am. Retail Fedn., Retail Tax Com. of Common Interest, Am. Soc. of Corp. Execs., Nat. Retail Mchts. Assn. (bd. dirs.), Dirs.' Table, Delta Sigma Pi, Beta Gamma Sigma. Baptist. Clubs: Morris County Country, Econ. (N.Y.), Pres.'s. *

HOWELL, WILSON NATHANIEL, ambassador; b. Portsmouth, Va., Sept. 14, 1939; s. Wilson Nathaniel Sr. and Josephine Wilkens (Edwards) H.; m. Margie Anne Saunders, June 25, 1961; children: Wilson Nathaniel III, Edward Vaughan. BA with honors, U. Va., 1961, PhD, 1965; diploma, Nat. War Coll., 1983. Instr. in govt. and fgn. affairs U. Va., Charlottesville, 1964-65; exec. asst. Am. Embassy, Cairo, 1966-67; polit. officer U.S. Mission to NATO, Paris and Brussels, 1967-68; polit. analyst Dept. State, Washington, 1968-70; Arabic student Am. Embassy, Beirut, Lebanon, 1970-72; dep. prin. officer Am. Embassy, Abu Dhabi, United Arab Emirates, 1972-74; polit. officer Am. Embassy, Beirut, 1974-76; Lebanon country officer Dept. State, Washington, 1976-77, dep. dir. NEA/ARN, 1977-79, spl. asst. Near East,, 1979, dir. NEA/ARN, 1980-82; dep. chief of mission Am. Embassy, Algiers, Algeria, 1983-85; polit. advisor CinC, U.S. Cen. Command, MacDill AFB, Tampa, Fla., 1985-87; A. E. and P. Am. Embassy, Kuwait, 1987—. Contbg. editor: Soviet Foreign Relations and World Communism, 1965. Recipient Nat. Def. fellowship U. Va., 1961-64, Superior Honor award Dept. State, Washington, 1967, National Notable award City of Portsmouth, Va., 1987, Meritorious Civilian Service medal Sec. of Def., 1988. Mem. Nat. War Coll Alumni Assn., U. Va. Alumni Assn., Middle East Inst., Phi Beta Kappa. Club: Army & Navy (Washington). Home and Office: US Ambassador of Kuwait Dept of State Washington DC 20520

HOWELL-PRICE, OWEN, retail and food manufacturing executive; b. Sumatra, Indonesia, 1926; m. Louisa Chin-Kim Giam; 2 children. Student, Newington Coll., Sydney. Trainee exec. Woolworths Ltd., Australia, 1947-58, supermkt. controller, 1958-61, distbn. controller, 1961-65, dir. trading, 1965-69, chief exec., 1969-74; gen. mgr. Dairy Farm Ltd., South East Asia, 1974-81; mgr. dir. Dairy Farm Ltd., Hong Kong, 1981—; bd. dirs. Dairy Farm Internat. Holdings Ltd., HK Land Co. Ltd., Maxims Caterers Ltd., Kwik Save P.L.C. Served with Royal Australian Navy. Home: Domum, 6 Sassoon Rd, Pokfulam Hong Kong Office: Dairy Farm Internat Ltd, Windsor House 33d Floor, Causeway Bay Hong Kong

HOWELLS, CHRISTINA MARY, French language educator; b. Frimley, Surrey, Eng., Apr. 13, 1950; d. John Frederick and Elizabeth Mary (Johnston) Mitchell; m. Bernard Patrick Howells, July 21, 1973; children: Marie-Elise, Dominic. BA, King's Coll., U. London, 1972, PhD, 1975. Fellow, tutor in French Wadham Coll. U. Oxford, Eng., 1979—. Author: Sartre's Theory of Literature, 1979, Sartre: The Necessity of Freedom, 1988; contbr. articles to profl. jours. Office: U Oxford Wadham Coll, Oxford OX1 3PN, England

HOWELLS, MURIEL GURDON SEABURY (MRS. WILLIAM WHITE HOWELLS), civic worker; b. White Plains, N.Y., May 3, 1910; d. William Marston and Katharine Emerson (Hovey) Seabury; student Chapin Sch., 1928; m. William White Howells, June 15, 1929; children—Muriel Gurdon Howells Metz, William Dean. Founder Brit. War Relief Soc., Madison, Wis., 1941, pres., 1941-43; apptd. visitor, dept. decorative arts and sculpture Boston Mus. Fine Arts, 1955-72, dept. Am. decorative arts, 1972—; ladies com. Inst. Contemporary Art, Boston, 1955-65, 67-68, asso., 1965-67; bd. dirs. Boston br. English-Speaking Union, 1955-80, v.p., 1973-74; a founder, trustee Strawbery Banke, Inc., Portsmouth, N.H., 1958-75, overseer, 1975-81, hon. overseer, 1981—; a founder, mem. steering com. Guild, 1959—; bd. dirs. Garden Club Am., 1959-62, nat. chmn. medal award com., 1962-65, judge flower arrangements; pres. Piscataqua Garden Club, 1952-54; mem. Harvard Solomon Islands Expdn., Malaita, 1968; chmn. Boston chpt. Venice Com., Internat. Fund for Monuments, 1970-71; vice chmn. Boston chpt. Save Venice Inc., 1971-77, mem. exec. com., 1971—. Recipient King's medal for Service in the Cause of Freedom (Britain), 1946; Historic Preservation award, zone 1 Garden Club Am., 1976. Mem. Nat. Soc. Colonial Dames N.H., Soc. Preservation New Eng. Antiquities (mem. Maine council 1976-78). Clubs: Women's Travel (pres. 1967-69), Chilton (Boston); Colony (N.Y.C.). Home: 274 Beacon St Boston MA 02116 Other: Kittery Point ME 03905

HOWELLS, WILLIAM WHITE, anthropology educator; b. N.Y.C., Nov. 27, 1908; s. John Mead and Abby MacDougall (White) H.; m. Muriel Gurdon Seabury, June 15, 1929; children—Gurdon Howells Metz, William Dean. S.B., Harvard U., 1930, Ph.D., 1934; D.Sc. (hon.), Beloit Coll., 1975, U. Witwatersrand, 1985. From asst. prof. to prof. anthropology U. Wis., 1939-54, prof. integrated liberal studies, 1948-54; prof. anthropology Harvard U., 1954-74, prof. emeritus, 1974—; hon. fellow Sch. Am. Research, 1975. Author: Mankind So Far, 1944, The Heathens, 1948, Back of History, 1954, Mankind in the Making, 1959, rev. edit., 1967, The Pacific Islanders, 1973, Cranial Variation in Man, 1973, Evolution of the Genus Homo, 1973; editor: Early Man in the Far East, 1949, Ideas on Human Evolution, 1962, Paleoanthropology in the People's Republic of China, 1977, Am. Jour. Phys. Anthropology, 1949-54; assoc. editor Human Biology, 1955-74. Served as lt. USNR, 1943-46. Recipient Viking Fund medal in phys. anthropology, 1954. Fellow Indian Anthrop. Assn. (fgn.), Am. Acad. Arts and Scis., Am. Anthrop. Assn. (pres. 1951, Disting. Service award 1978), AAAS, Soc. Antiquaries London; mem. Nat. Acad. Sci., Austrian Acad. Scis., Mass. Hist. Soc.; corr. mem. Geog. Soc. Lisbon, Anthrop. Soc. Paris (Broca prix du Centenaire 1980), Anthrop. Soc. Vienna (hon.), Royal Soc. South Africa (fgn.), Soc. for Biol. Anthropology Spain (corr.). Clubs: Somerset, Tavern (Boston); Harvard Faculty. Home: Lawrence Ln Kittery Point ME 03905 Office: Peabody Mus Harvard U Cambridge MA 02138

HOWITT, FRANCIS, educational administrator; b. Oxford, Eng., Dec. 8, 1929; s. Reginald and Doris Elizabeth (Quinn) H.; m. Patricia Chatten, Dec. 29, 1956. Diploma, Royal Naval Engring. Coll., 1953; M in Engring., McGill U., Montreal, Can., 1961. Chartered engr., Eng. Sci. master Crown Hills Sch., Leicester, Eng., 1954-55; researcher Nat. Coal Bd., Cheltenham, Eng., 1956; lectr. Tech. Coll., Coventry, Eng., 1957; lectr., asst. prof. McGill U., Montreal, 1957-61; sr. lectr. Tech. Coll., Gateshead, Eng., 1961-63; prin. lectr. Robert Gordon's & Aberdeen (Scotland) U., 1963-66; head dept. engring. Marine and Tech. Coll., South Shields, Eng., 1967-71; coll. prin. Canterbury (Eng.) Coll. Tech., 1971—; mem. council Southern Examining Group, Guildford, Eng., 1987—. Designer hand prosthesis, counter-pulsation blood pump. Served to lt. Royal Navy, 1947-53. Fellow Inst. Marine Engrs.; mem. Instn. Mech. Engrs., Assn. Coll. Mgmt., Assn. Prins. of Colls., Nat. Assn. Tchrs. Further and Higher Edn. Marine and Allied Industries Tng. Assn. City and Guilds of London Inst. Anglican. Club: Army & Navy (London). Office: Canterbury Coll, New Dover Rd, Canterbury Kent CT1 3AJ, England

HOWLAND, WILLARD J., radiologist; b. Neosho, Mo., Aug. 28, 1927; s. Willard Jay and Grace Darlene (Myrphy) H.; m. Kathleen V. Jones, July 28, 1945; children—Wyck, Candice, Charles, Thomas, Heather. A.B., U. Kans., 1948, M.D., 1950; M.A., U. Minn., 1958. Intern U.S. Naval Hosp., Newport, R.I., 1950-51; gen. practice medicine Kans., 1951-55; resident Mayo Clinic, Rochester, Minn., 1955-58; radiologist Ohio Valley Gen. Hosp., Wheeling, W.Va., 1959-67; prof., dir. diagnostic radiology U. Tenn. Med. Units, Memphis, 1967-68; dir., chmn. dept. radiology Aultman Hosp., Canton, Ohio, 1968-87, pres. med. staff, 1978; prof., chmn. radiology council Northeast Ohio U. Coll. Medicine, Rootstown, 1976-87, program dir. integrated radiology residency, 1976-87. Author, co-author two books and research papers in field. Served with U.S. Army, 1945-46, USN, 1950-51. Fellow Am. Coll. Radiology; mem. AMA, Radiol. Soc. N.Am., Am. Roentgen Ray Soc., Ohio State Radiol. Soc. (pres. 1980-81). Republican. Presbyterian. Lodge: Masons. Office: Aultman Hosp 2600 6th St SW Canton OH 44710

HOWLAND, WILLIAM STAPLETON, educator, anesthesiologist; b. Savannah, Ga., July 21, 1919; s. William and May (Stapleton) H.; m. Miriam Adams, Feb. 14, 1974; children by previous marriage: Karen, William Stapleton. BS, Notre Dame U., 1941; MD, Columbia, 1944. Surg. intern Grady Hosp., Atlanta, 1944-45; asst. resident urology Grady Hosp., 1945-46; asst. resident anesthesiology Presbyn. Hosp., N.Y.C., 1948-50; asst. anesthesiologist Presbyn. Hosp., 1950-52, asso. staff anesthesiologist, 1952-53; staff anesthesiologist, chmn. dept. anesthesiology Meml. Hosp., N.Y.C., 1953-79; dep. chief med. officer Meml. Hosp., 1967-81, dep. gen. dir., 1974-81; asst. prof. anesthesiology Columbia, 1953; asso. prof. surgery Sloan Kettering div. Cornell U. Med. Coll., N.Y.C., 1954-55; head exptl. surgery Sloan Kettering div. Cornell U. Med. Coll., 1967-69, asso. prof. surgery, 1955-68, prof. anesthesiology, 1968-87, prof. emeritus, 1988—, chmn. dept. anesthesiology, 1953-79, chmn. dept. critical care, 1979-86, v.p. for clin. affairs, 1977-81, emeritus staff, 1987—; mem. Sloan-Kettering Inst., 1976-87 ; mem. panel on blood and blood products Bur. Biologics, FDA, 1975-78. Contbr. articles profl. jours. Served to capt. M.C. AUS, 1946-48; chief urology sect. 121st Gen. Hosp. 1946-48, Bremerhaven, Germany. Mem. Nat. bd. Med. Examiners, Meml. Hosp. Med. Bd. (pres. 1966, 67, 68-69), Am. Soc. Anesthesiologists, N.Y. State Soc. Anesthesiologists (v.p. 1958, pres. 1966), N.Y. Acad. Medicine, N.Y. Acad. Sci. Home: Box 97 Wilmington VA 05363

HOWLETT, ROBERT GLASGOW, lawyer; b. Bay City, Mich., Nov. 10, 1906; s. Lewis Glasgow and Anne Lucile (Hurst) H.; m. Barbara Withey, Sept. 19, 1936; children: Eleanor Howlett Burton, Craig G., Douglas W. BS, Northwestern U., 1929, JD, 1932. Bar: Ill. 1932, N.Y. 1940, D.C. 1945, Mich. 1947, Tenn. 1947. Ptnr. Varnum Riddering Schmidt & Howlett, Grand Rapids, Mich., 1949-83; of counsel Varnum Riddering, Schmidt & Howlett, Grand Rapids, Mich., 1983—; mem. Mich. Employment Relations Commn., 1963-76, chmn., 1964-76; chmn. Fed. Service Impasses Panel, 1976-78, 82-84, mem., 1984—; sec., bd. dirs. Light Metals Corp., Elston Richards Inc.; mem. Fgn. Service Impasse Disputes Panel, 1976-78, 81—; industry mem. shipbldg. commn. Nat. War Labor Bd., 1943-45; spl. asst. atty. gen., dept. aero. State of Mich., 1957-61; vis. prof. Mich. State U., East Lansing, 1972, 75. Contbr. articles to profl. jours. Chmn. Kent County Republican Com., 1956-61; del. Rep. Nat. Conv., 1960. Mem. ABA, Grand Rapids Bar Assn. (pres. 1962-63), State Bar Mich., Nat. Acad. Arbitrators, Indsl. Relations Research Assn. (pres. Detroit chpt. 1978-79), Soc. Profls. in Dispute Resolution (pres. 1974-75), Assn. Labor Relations Agys. (pres. 1977-78), Am. Arbitration Assn. (bd. dirs. 1975—, Disting. Service award 1982, Whitney North Seymour Sr. award 1984), Soc. Labor Relations Profls. (Disting. Service award 1988). Clubs: Kent Country, Peninsular (Grand Rapids). Home: 2910 Oak Hollow Dr SE Grand Rapids MI 49506 Office: Varnum Riddering Schmidt & Howlett Suite 800 171 Monroe St NW Grand Rapids MI 49503

HOWORTH, LUCY SOMERVILLE, lawyer; b. Greenville, Miss., July 1, 1895; d. Robert and Nellie (Nugent) Somerville; m. Joseph Marion Howorth, Feb. 16, 1928. A.B., Randolph-Macon Woman's Coll., 1916; postgrad., Columbia U., 1918; J.D. summa cum laude, U. Miss., 1922. Bar: Miss. 1922, U.S. Supreme Ct. 1934. Asst. in psychology Randolph-Macon Woman's Coll., 1916-17; gauge insp. Allied Bur. Air Prodn., N.Y.C., 1918; indsl. research nat. bd. YWCA, 1919-20; gen. practice law Howorth & Howorth, Cleveland, Greenville and Jackson, Miss., 1922-34; U.S. commr. So. Jud. Dist. Miss., 1927-31; assoc. mem. Bd. Vet. Appeals, Washington, 1934-43; legis. atty. VA, 1943-49; v.p., dir. VA Employees Credit Union, 1937-49; assoc. gen. counsel War Claims Commn., 1949-52, dep. gen. counsel, 1952-53, gen. counsel, 1953-54; ptnr. James Somerville & Assocs. (overseas trade and devel.), 1954—; atty. Commn. on Govt. Security, 1956-57; pvt. law practice Cleveland, Miss., 1958—; mem. nat. bd. cons. Women's Archives, Radcliffe Coll.; mem. lay adv. com. study profl. nursing Carnegie Corp. N.Y., 1947-48; chmn. Miss. State Bd. Law Examiners, 1924-28; mem. Miss. State Legislature, 1932-36, chmn. com. pub. lands, 1932-36; treas. Com. for Econ. Survey Miss., 1928-30; mem. Research Commn. Miss., 1930-34. Editor: Fed. Bar Assn. News, 1944; assoc. editor: Fed. Bar Assn. Jour., 1943-44; editor: (with William M. Cash) My Dear Nellie-Civil War Letters (William L. Nugent), 1977; contbr. articles profl. jours. Keynote speaker White House Conf. on Women in Postwar Policy Making, 1944, at conf. on opening 81st Congress. Recipient Alumnae Achievement award Randolph-Macon Woman's Coll., 1981, Lifetime Achievement award Schlesinger Library of Radcliffe Coll., 1983. Mem. AAUW (nat. dir., 2d v.p. 1951-55, mem. found. 1960-63), Nat. Fedn. Bus. and Profl. Women's Clubs (nat. dir.; rep. to internat. 1939, chmn. internat. conf. 1946), Nat. Assn. Women Lawyers, Miss. Library Assn. (life), Miss. Hist. Soc. (dir. 1982—, Merit award 1983), DAR, Daus. Am. Colonists, Am. Legion Aux. (past sec. Miss. dept.), Assembly Women's Orgns. for Nat. Security (chmn. 1951-52), Phi Beta Kappa, Pi Gamma Mu, Phi Alpha Delta, Alpha Omicron Pi (Wyman award 1985), Delta Kappa Gamma, Omicron Delta Kappa, Phi Kappa Phi (hon.). Democrat (del. nat. conv., 1932). Methodist. Club: Soroptimist (Washington). Address: 515 S Victoria Ave Cleveland MS 38732

HOXIE, RALPH GORDON, author, educational administrator; b. Waterloo, Iowa, Mar. 18, 1919; s. Charles Ray and Ada May (Little) H.; m. Louise Lobitz, Dec. 23, 1953. B.A., U. No. Iowa, 1940; M.A., U. Wis., 1941; Ph.D., Columbia, 1950; LL.D., Chung-ang U., 1965; Litt.D.,

D'Youville Coll., 1966; grad., Air War Coll., 1971; L.H.D., Gannon U., 1988. Roberts fellow Columbia, 1946-47, Roberts travelling fellow, 1947-48, asst. to provost, 1948-49; asst. prof. history, gen. editor Social Sci. Found.; asst. to chancellor U. Denver, 1950-53; project asso. Columbia Bicentennial History, 1953-54; dean Coll. Liberal Arts and Scis., L.I. U., 1954-55; acting dean C. W. Post Coll., 1954-55, dean, 1955-60, provost, 1960-62, pres., 1962-68; chancellor L.I. U., 1964-68, cons., 1968-69; pres. Center for Study of Presidency, 1969—; Pub. mem. Fgn. Service Officer Selection Bd., U.S. Dept. State; vis. lectr. U. Ala., U. Calif., Irvine, Columbia U., U. Colo., Colo. State U., U. Wyo., Chapman Coll., U. No. Colo., Colo. Coll., Gannon U., Naval War Coll., Nat. Archives, Nat. War Coll., Oglethorpe U., U. Pitts., U. Tex. at El Paso, U. Wis., Northwestern U.; Bd. govs. La Banque Continentale br. Franklin Nat. Bank. Author: John W. Burgess, American Scholar, 1950, Command Decision and the Presidency, 1977, (with others) A History of The Faculty of Political Science, Columbia University, 1955, Organizing and Staffing the Presidency, 1980; Editor: Frontiers for Freedom, 1952, The White House: Organization and Operations, 1971, Presdl. Studies Quar, 1971—, The Presidency of the 1970's, 1973, The Presidency and Information Policy, 1981, The Presidency and National Security Policy, 1984; Contbg. author: (with others) Freedom and Authority in Our Time, 1953, The Coattailless Landslide, 1974, Power and the Presidency, 1976, Classics of the American Presidency, 1980, The Blessing of Liberty, 1987, Popular Images of American Presidents, 1988, Rating Game in American Politics, 1988, The Presidency in Transition, 1988, Science and Technology Advice to the President, Congress, and Judiciary, 1988, The American Presidency: Historical and Contemporary Perspectives, 1988, Points of View, 1988; Contbr. articles to profl. jours. and encys. Bd. dirs. United Fund L.I., Bklyn. Inst. Arts and Scis., Tibetan Found., L.I. Council Alcoholism, Bklyn. chpt. A.R.C. Greater N.Y.; chmn., pres. bd. dirs. Am. Friends Chung-ang U.; pres. Pub. Mems. Assn. Fgn. Service; trustee Air Force Hist. Found., Kosciuszko Found. N.Y., Mackinac Coll., North Shore chpt. Am. Assn. UN, Downtown Bklyn. Assn., Council Higher Ednl. Instns. N.Y.C.; mem. adv. bd. L. I. Air Res. Center; mem. adv. council Robert A. Taft Inst. Govt.; sec. Nassau County Commn. on Govt. Revision; co-chmn. Nassau-Suffolk Conf. Christians and Jews; dir., pres. Great-N.Y. Council Fgn. Students; bd. govs. Human Resources Ctr., N.Y. Korean Vets. Meml. Commn. Served from pvt. to capt. USAAF, 1942-46; brig. gen. USAF ret. Decorated Meritorious Service medal, Legion of Merit, numerous other medals; recipient Distinguished Service medal City N.Y., 1965; Paderewski Found. Man of Yr. award, 1966; Eloy Alfaro Internat. Found. Republic Panama Man of Year award, 1966; Alumni Achievement award U. No. Iowa; decorated Korean Cultural medal. Fellow Am. Studies Assn. Met. N.Y.; mem. Am. Hist. Assn., Internat. Assn. Univ. Pres., Am. Polit. Sci. Assn., Acad. of Polit. Sci., Navy League, Air Force Assn., Res. Officers Assn. (pres. Mitchel chpt.), V.F.W., Am. Legion, L.I. Assn. (dir.), Am. Polar Soc., Kappa Delta Pi, Pi Gamma Mu, Alpha Sigma Lambda, Delta Sigma Pi, Gamma Theta Upsilon. Republican. Episcopalian. Clubs: Century Assn., Met., Columbia Univ. Faculty House (N.Y.C.); Met. (Washington); Bklyn., Montauk (Bklyn.); Old Westbury Golf and Country and Mill River (hon.). Home: 10 Laurel Cove Rd Oyster Bay Cove NY 11771 Office: 208 E 75th St New York NY 10021

HOXTER, CURTIS JOSEPH, international economic adviser, public relations counselor; b. Marburg, Germany, July 20, 1922; s. Jacob and Hannah (Katzenstein) H.; A.B., N.Y.U., 1948, M.A., 1950; m. Grace Lewis, Feb. 4, 1945 (dec.); children—Ronald Alan, Victoria Ann Finder, Audrey Therese Strecker; m. 2d, Allegra Branson. Staff contbr. AUFBAU-Reconstn., N.Y.C., 1939-40; feature writer, reporter L.I. Daily Press, 1940-42; editor, writer OWI, 1943-45; public info. officer Dept. State, 1945-47; info. cons. ECA, 1950-55; public relations cons. various cos.; dir. public relations Internat. C. of C., U.S. Council Internat. C. of C., 1948-53; freelance columnist Scripps-Howard Newspapers; exec. v.p. George Peabody and Assos., Inc., 1953-56; pres. Curtis J. Hoxter, Inc., internat. public relations counsels and econ. and fin. advs., 1956—; dir. Internat. Capital and Tech. Corp. Adviser, U.S. Com. for UN Day; adv. on internat. econ. and fin. problems to govt. agys.; adv. U.S. Del. Disarmament Conf., London. Served with AUS, World War II. Mem. Public Relations Soc. Am. Clubs: Metropolitan, Overseas Press (N.Y.C.); Nat. Press, University; Royal Auto (London); Bankers (San Juan, P.R.); Bonnie Briar Country. Author weekly column Scripps-Howard papers, The Foreign Economic Scene. Contbr. nat. mags. Office: 350 Lexington Ave New York NY 10016

HOY, JORGEN ANCHER, oil and natural gas company executive; b. Copenhagen, Jan. 4, 1934; s. Peter Ancher and Agnes (Schultz) H.; m. Helen Raben, June 23, 1957; children—Christian, Soren, Henriette. With SAS, Copenhagen, 1958-60, Royal Greenland Trade Dept., Copenhagen and Godthaab, Greenland, 1960-65; pres. Greenlandair, Godthaab, 1965-79; purchase mgr. Dansk Ollie & Naturgas A/S, Copenhagen, 1979-80, pres., 1981—. Home: Christiansholmsvej 21, 2930 Klampenborg Denmark Office: Dansk Olie & Naturgas A/S, Agern Alle 24-26, 2970 Horsholm Denmark

HOY, WILLIAM IVAN, clergyman educator; b. Grottoes, Va., Aug. 21, 1915; s. William I. and Ileta (Root) H.; student Lees-McRae Coll., 1933-34; B.A., Hampden-Sydney Coll., 1936; B.D., Union Theol. Sem., 1942; S.T.M., Bibl. Sem. N.Y., 1949; Ph.D., U. Edinburgh, 1952; m. Wilma J. Lambert, Apr. 29, 1945; children—Doris Lambert Hoy Bezanilla, Martha Virginia. Tchr. high sch., Va., 1936-39; interim pastor Asheboro (N.C.) Presbyn. Ch., 1948, 52-53; asst. prof. Bible, Guilford Coll., 1947-48; asst. prof. religion U. Miami, from 1953, prof., 1963—, chmn. dept. religion, 1958-79; cons. World Council Christian Edn., Lima, Peru, 1971. Moderator, Presbytery of Everglades, 1960-61, stated clk., 1968-73, 78-79; moderator Synod of Fla., 1985-86; pres. Greater Miami Ministerial Assn., 1964, 80-82; mem. bd. Christian edn. Presbyn. Ch. U.S., 1969-73, mem. Gen. Assembly Mission Bd., 1978-88; bd. dirs. Met. Fellowship Chs., 1970—, v.p., 1972-73, exec. sec., 1974-76, mem. Task Force on World Hunger, 1978-81; trustee Davidson Coll., 1975-87; participant profl. internat. confs., Barcelona, Lausanne, Rome, Melbourne, Goettingen, others, and three White House confs. for religious leaders. Served to comdr. USNR. Decorated Purple Heart; given key to Cities of Miami Beach (twice) and Coral Gables, 1987; named Ky. Col. Mem. Soc. Bibl. Lit., Am. Acad. Religion, Am. Soc. Ch. History, Studiorum Novi Testamenti Societas, Scottish Ch. History Soc., Soc. for Sci. Study Religion, Religious Research Assn., Internat. Assn. Historians of Religion, Internat. Conf. Sociology of Religion, Am. Oriental Soc., Internat. Sociol. Assn., Res. Officers Assn. (past nat. chaplain, nat. councilman 1965-66, pres. Fla. dept. 1965-66, v.p. for navy dept. Fla.), Seabee Vets. Am., Iron Arrow, Phi Kappa Phi, Omicron Delta Kappa (province dep., mem. gen. council 1971-76, Disting. Service Key 1976), Lambda Chi Alpha, Alpha Psi Omega, Theta Delta, Omega. Club: Tiger Bay. Co-author: History of the Chaplains Corps, USN, Volume 6; also articles and book revs. in various publs. Home: 5881 SW 52d Terr Miami FL 33155 Office: PO Box 248348 Coral Gables FL 33124

HOYE, WALTER BRISCO, college administrator; b. Lena, Miss., May 19, 1930; s. William H. and LouBertha (Stewart) H.; m. Vida M. Pickens, Aug. 28, 1954; children—Walter B. II, JoAnn M. B.A., Wayne State U., 1953. Sports/auto editor Detroit Tribune, 1958-65; sports editor Mich. Chronicle, 1965-68; assoc. dir. pub. relations San Diego Chargers Football Co., 1968-76; media liason NFL, 1972-75; community services officer San Diego Coll. Dist., 1976-78; placement officer Ednl. Cultural Complex, San Diego, 1978-80, info. officer, 1980-82, placement officer, adminstrv. asst., 1982-83, placement/program support supr., 1983—; cons. in field. Bd. dirs. San Diego County ARC; active San Diego Conv. and Tourist Bur., Joint Ctr. Polit. Studies, Am. Cancer Soc., San Diego Urban League, Neighborhood Housing Assn., Public Access TV. Named San Diego County Citizen of Month, May, 1979; recipient United Way Award of Merit, 1974. Mem. Am. Personnel and Guidance Assn., San Diego Career Guidance Assn., Nat. Mgmt. Assn., Assn. Calif. Community Coll. Adminstrs., Calif. Community Coll. Placement Assn. Home: 6959 Ridge Manor Ave San Diego CA 92120 Office: Ednl Cultural Complex 4343 Ocean View Blvd Suite 177 San Diego CA 92113

HOYE, WILLIAM JOSEPH, educator; b. Waterbury, Conn., May 20, 1940; came to W. Ger., 1966; s. Joseph William and Margaret (Brignole) H.; m. Holle Frank, May 27, 1972; children—Niclas J., Lukas T. B.A., Boston Coll., 1965; postgrad. U. Strasbourg, France, 1966, U. Munich, 1966-68; Dr.Theol., U. Muenster, 1971. Research asst. Cusanus Institut, Mainz, Ger., 1971-76; teaching asst. Ednl. Coll., Landau, Ger., 1976-78; prof. Ednl. Coll., Muenster, 1978-80; prof. theology U. Muenster, 1980—. Author: Actualitas Omnium Actuum: Man's Beatific Vision of God as Apprehended by Thomas Aquinas, 1975, The Eclipse of the Absolute Mystery: A Critique of Karl Rahner's Teaching on God, 1979. Contbr. articles to profl. jours. Andrew W. Mellon fellow, Cath. U. Am., 1983-84; vis. prof. Marquette U., Milw., 1979-80; German Acad. Exchange Service grantee, 1967-69, Interior Ministry of Bavaria grantee, 1966-67, others. Mem. Internat. Soc. Medieval Philosophy, Cusanus Soc., Internat. Soc. Neo-Platonic Studies. Home: Hittorfstrasse 23, 4400 Muenster Federal Republic of Germany Office: U Muenster Kath Theologie, Scharnhorststrasse 103 FB 2, 4400 Muenster Federal Republic of Germany

HOYNE, THOMAS TEMPLE, dentist; b. Salina, Kans., May 13, 1935; s. John Thomas and Opal Louise (Fisher) H.; m. Naomi Jeanette Nelson, June 21, 1961. BS in Chemistry, U. Kans., 1957; DDS, U. Kansas City, Mo., 1963. Gen. practice dentistry Stover, Mo., 1963—; cons. Handicapped Dental Patients of Mo., 1980-83. Contbr. articles on archeology to profl. jours. Scoutmaster to council exec. bd. Boy Scouts Am., Stover, 1963—. Served to 1st lt. U.S Army, 1957-59. Recipient Silver Beaver award Boy Scouts Am., 1972, Silver Lamb award Boy Scouts Am. and Luth. Ch., 1976. Mem. ADA, Mo. dental Assn., Royal Soc. Health, U. Kans. Chemistry Dept. Alumni Assn., State Mo. Archeol. Soc. (trustee 1987—), W. Cen. Mo. Archeol. Soc. (pres. 1986, 87), Morgan county Archeol. Soc. (pres. 1963-68). Republican. Lutheran. Lodge: Lions. Home: Woodland Dr and Hughes Ave Stover MO 65078 Office: Mimosa Dr and Hwy 52 Stover MO 65078

HOYT, COLEMAN WILLIAMS, postal consultant; b. N.Y.C., Nov. 11, 1925; s. Colgate and Muriel (Williams) H.; m. Cecilia Lucia Guarana, Oct. 21, 1972; children: Coleman Williams, Andrew Erskine, Stephen Tecumseh. B of Naval Sci., Tufts U., 1945; BS, Yale U., 1948. With Reader's Digest Assn., Pleasantville, N.Y., 1948-87, mgr. book prodn., 1950-61, mgr. book subscription service, 1961-63, mgr. subscription service RCA Victor Record Club, 1963-65, mgr. corp. distbn., 1965-76, v.p., dir. distbn., 1976-87; pvt. practice cons., Woodstock, Vt., 1987—; mem. Postmaster General's Mailers Tech. Adv. Com., 1968—, chmn., 1971-73; bd. dirs. Carbon Tech. Inc. Pub. mem. USIA inspection team, Lebanon, 1971; nat. trustee Outward Bound, Inc., 1972—; trustee Vermont Land Trust, 1988—. Served as ensign USNR, 1943-46. Recipient Disting. Service award U.S. Postal Service, 1973, Donald Mumma award Graphics Communications Assn., 1987, Miles Kimball award Mail Advt. Service Assn., 1987. Mem. Mag. Pubs. Assn. (chmn. postal com. 1974-80), Direct Mktg. Assn. (bd. dirs. 1973-79, chmn. govt. affairs com. 1983-86), Assn. Am. Pubs., Pub. Mems. Assn. of Fgn. Service, Third Class Mail Assn. (bd. dirs. 1982—). Republican. Episcopalian. Clubs: Yale U. of N.Y., Squadron A (N.Y.C.); Lakota (Woodstock). Home and Office: Saddlebow Farm RFD 2 Box 764 Woodstock VT 05091

HOYT, JACK WALLACE, engineering educator; b. Chgo., Oct. 19, 1922; s. Claire A. and Fleta M. (Wheeler) H.; B.S., Ill. Inst. Tech., 1944; M.S., UCLA, 1952, Ph.D., 1962; m. Helen Rita Erickson, Dec. 27, 1945; children—John A., Katheryn M. (Mrs. Richard Everett), Annette M. (Mrs. Walter Butler), Denise M. (Mrs. Paul Kruesi). Research engr. gas turbines Cleve. Lab., NACA, 1944-47; mem. staff Naval Ocean Systems Center, Navy Dept., DOD, San Diego, 1948-79, asso. for sci. fleet engring. dept., 1967-79, now cons.; vis. prof. mech. engring. Rutgers U., New Brunswick, N.J., 1979-81; Benjamin Meaker vis. prof. U. Bristol (Eng.), 1987; prof. mech. engring. San Diego State U., 1981—. Mem. ASME (Freeman scholar 1971), N.Y. Acad. Scis., Soc. Naval Architects and Marine Engrs. Author, patentee in field. Editorial bd. Internat. Shipbldg. Progress, 1965—. Spl. research propulsion and hydrodynamics. Home: 4694 Lisann St San Diego CA 92117

HOYTE, HUGH DESMOND, president Republic of Guyana; b. Georgetown, Guyana, Mar. 9, 1929; s. George Alphonso and Gladys Marietta Hoyte; married. B.A., U. London, 1950, LL.B., 1959. Bar: Hon. Soc. Middle Temple 1959, Queen's counsel, 1970, sr. counsel, 1970. Practice law, Guyana, from 1960. Mem. gen. council People's Nat. Congress, 1962—, mem. cen. exec. com., 1972—, legal adviser to gen. sec., from 1973—, chmn. prodn. sub-com. of cen. exec. com. from 1984; chmn. Customs Tariff Tribunal, 1966-68; elected to Parliament, People's Nat. Congress, 1968; minister of home affairs Republic of Guyana, 1969-70, minister of fin., 1970-72, minister works and communication, 1972-74, minister econ. devel., 1974-80, v.p. econ. planning and fin., 1980, v.p. prodn., 1983, prime minister and 1st v.p., 1984-85, pres. Guyana, leader People's Nat. Congress, 1985—; mem. Nat. Elections Commn., from 1966; chmn. Timber Grants Wages Council, 1967; legal adviser Guyana Trades Union Congress, several other trade unions. Mem. Guyana Bar Assn. (chmn. legal practitioners com. 1964). Office: Office of President, Georgetown Guyana *

HRACHOVEC, HERBERT WOLFGANG, philosopher, educator; b. Vienna, Austria, Mar. 30, 1947. PhD, U. Vienna, 1971. Habilitation, U. Vienna, 1980. Asst. prof. philosophy U. Vienna, 1972—. Author: Vorbei. Frege, Wihgenstein Heidegger, 1981, Ausgefallene Figuren, 1988. Home: Windmuhlgasse 16/5, A1060 Vienna Austria Office: U Vienna, Universitätsstrasse 7, A1010 Vienna Austria

HRACHOVINA, FREDERICK VINCENT, osteopathic physician and surgeon; b. St. Paul, Sept. 2, 1926; s. Vincent Frank and Beatrice (Funda) H.; m. Joan Halverson, July 2, 1955. B.A. in Chemistry, Macalester Coll., 1948; D.O., Kirksville Coll. Osteo. Medicine, Mo., 1956. Chemist Twin City area, 1948-51; intern Clare Gen. Osteo. Hosp., Mich., 1956-57; pvt. practice Mpls., 1957-84; asst. prof. osteo. principles and practices Southeastern Coll. Osteo. Medicine, 1985—; lectr. Internat. Acad. Osteo. Medicine, 1984; founder, pres. Physician Placement Service, 1973—; asst. prof osteo. principles and practice Southeastern Coll. Osteo. Medicine, 1985-88; mem. Northlands Regional Med. Program, Inc. 1971-73; mem. Health Services Devel. Com., Regional Adv. Group.; founder, faculty advisor Fla. Acad. Osteopathy Student Assn. Southeastern Coll. Osteo. Medicine, 1987. Author: Microscopic Anatomy, 1952; Methods of Development of New Osteopathic Medical Colleges in the Next Millennium, 1977. Contbr. articles to profl. jours. Grantee Smith Kline & French Labs., 1973, Hill Labs, Gusman Med. Equipment, 1987. Mem. Am. Osteo. Assn. (council fed. health programs, drug enforcement adminstrn. prescribers working com. 1974-75), Minn. State Osteo. Assn. (pres. 1965-66, exec. dir. 1966-74, pub. relations dir. 1974-75), Assn. Osteo. State Exec. Dirs. (pres. 1970-71, dir. 1971-74, founder nat. legis. sem. 1974), Am., Fla. Soc. Coll. Gen. Practitioners Osteo. Medicine and Surgery (lectr. Mo. soc.), Am. Acad. Osteopathy, Fla. Acad. Osteopathy (bd. trustees, chmn. audit and membership com.), Fla. Osteo. Found. (v.p.), Am. Assn. Sr. Physicians, Fla. Osteo. Med. Assn. (chmn. osteo. lit. com.), Internat. Acad. Osteo. Medicine (bd. trustees), Am. Osteo. Acad. Sports Medicine, Am. Blood Resources Assn., Minn. Gymnastic Assn. (founder 1962-72), Fla. Acad. Osteopathy Student Assn. at Southeastern Coll. Osteopathic Medicine (originator, advisor), Phi Sigma Gamma (life mem., grand council adv. and chmn. bd. trustees to fraternity Southeastern Coll. Osteo. Medicine, Phi Sigma Gamma Found. (nat. pres. grand council 1986-87), Am. Assn. Blood Banks, Twin City Model A Ford Club, Pierce-Arrow Soc. (sec. Fla. region). Clubs: Breakfast, Optimist (dir. Mpls. 1959-62, 69-72, pres. 1970-71, gen. chmn. floor exercise gymnastic program 1959-65), Antique Auto Club Am. (life), Classical Club Am. (life mem., membership chmn. Minn. Region 1977, sec. upper midwest region 1978, gold coast region-Fla.), Cadillac LaSalle (founder, treas. North Star Region 1978-83), Pierce Arrow Soc. (news reporter Arrow Driver, life, founder midwest region 1983, dir. and treas. 1983-84, nat. dir. 1983-84, sec. 1987—). Lodges: Masons, Shriner. Home: 1799 Northeast 171st St North Miami Beach FL 33162

HRITZ, GEORGE F., lawyer; b. Hyde Park, N.Y., Aug. 28, 1948; s. George F. and Margaret M. (Callahan) H.; m. Suzan Courtney Hritz, July 6, 1982; 1 child, Amelia Courtney Hritz. A.B., Princeton U., 1969; J.D., Columbia U., 1973. Bar: N.Y. 1974, D.C. 1978, U.S. Supreme Ct. 1979. Law clk. U.S. Dist. Ct. (ea. dist.) N.Y., N.Y.C., 1973; assoc. Cravath, Swaine & Moore, N.Y.C., 1974-77; counsel U.S. Senate Select Com. Ethics Korean Inquiry, Washington, 1977-78; ptnr. Moore & Foster, Washington, 1978-80, Davis, Markel & Edwards, N.Y.C., 1980—; assoc. ind. counsel, Washington, 1986—. Bd. dirs. Internat. Rescue Com. Mem. ABA (internat. law sect.), D.C. Bar Assn., Bar Assn. City of N.Y. Club: Princeton. Office: Davis Markel & Edwards 100 Park Ave Suite 3200 New York NY 10017

HRIVNAK, PAVOL, government official; b. 1931. Student, Slovak Tech. U., Bratislava, Czechoslovakia. Mem. Communist Party, Czechoslovakia, 1956—; Slovak dep. minister of industry 1974-82, minister of industry, 1982-84; Slovak dep. premier, chmn. Slovak Planning Com., 1984-86; mem. Presidium, Communist Party of Slovakia, 1986—; fed. dep. premier Czechoslovakia, 1986-88; minister-chmn. Fed. Price Office, 1988—. Office: Fed Price Office, Prague Czechoslovakia *

HRNA, DANIEL JOSEPH, educator, lawyer, pharmacist; b. Taylor, Tex., March 19, 1940; s. Stephan Peter and Anna Ludmilla (Baran) H.; B.S., U. Houston, 1963, J.D., 1970; m. Velma Isobel Lesson, Sept. 3, 1963; children—Anna Marie, Daniel Steven, Brian Keith. Bar: Tex. 1972. In mgmt., Gunning-Casteel Co., El Paso, Tex., 1963-65; dir. pharmacy services Tex. Inst. Rehab. and Research, Houston, 1966-79; dir. pharmacy Alief Gen. Hosp., Belhaven Hosp., Houston, 1979-85, West Houston Med. Ctr., 1985—; mem. faculty Baylor U. Coll. Medicine, 1977-79; with Houston Continental Enterprises, Tex. Rampage, Inc. Mem. ABA, Am. Pharm. Assn., Tex. Pharmacy Assn., State Bar Tex., Tex. Soc. Hosp. Pharmacists, Am. Soc. Pharmacy Law, Am. Hosp. Assn., Harris County Pharm. Assn., Houston Bar Assn., Galveston-Houston Pharm. Hosp. Assn., Profl. Photographers Guild Houston (hon.), Delta Theta Phi, Kappa Psi, Phi Delta Chi. Roman Catholic. Address: 11920 Beechnut Houston TX 77072

HRUSKA, FRANCIS JOHN, marine surveyor and consultant; b. Trnovec N/V, Czechoslovakia, Jan. 19, 1935, came to U.S., 1977; s. Ferdinand and Julia (Klepanec) H.; m. Ludmila Liptak, Apr. 19, 1958; children—Zuzana, Daniela, Martin. Grad. with honors, Nautical Sch. for Inland Waterways, Czechoslovakia, 1952, State Nautical Sch., Poland, 1955; student Walsey Hall Corr. Coll., Oxford, Eng., 1973-74. Cert. master mariner, 1961, marine pilot, 1969. Ships nautical officer Czechoslovak Ocean Shipping, Prague, 1955-62; exec. nautical engr. State Nautical Authority, Czechoslovakia, 1962-66; master C.S.P.D. Sea Branch, Czechoslovakia, 1966-68; marine pilot Ghana Rys. and Ports, 1968-72, Nat. Port Authority, Liberia, 1972-75; harbour master, chief marine officer, 1975-77; marine surveyor Nautech, Inc., Latham & Assocs., Master Marine Cons., Inc., New Orleans, 1978-82; pres. Plimsoll Marine Surveyors, Inc., Covington, La., 1983—; chmn. exam. bd. for pilots Nat. Port Authority, Monrovia, Liberia, 1975-77; nautical advisor Govt. of Liberia, 1975-77; cons. Comprehensive Study for Devel. of Port of Monrovia, 1975-77, Elbe-Oder-Danube Waterways System, Czechoslovakia, 1963-66. Contbr. articles to profl. jours. Office: Plimsoll Marine Surveyors Inc PO Box 8528 Mandeville LA 70448

HRYCAK, PETER, mechanical engineer, educator; b. Przemysl, Poland, July 8, 1923; came to U.S., 1949, naturalized, 1956; s. Eugene and Ludmyla (Dobrzanska) H.; m. Rea Meta Limberg, June 13, 1949; children: Maria (dec.), Michael Paul, Orest W.T., Alexandra Martha. Student, U. Tubingen, Germany, 1946-48; B.S. with high distinction, U. Minn., 1954, M.S., 1955, Ph.D., 1960. Registered profl. engr., N.J. Adminstrv. asst. French Mil. Govt. in Germany, 1947-49; instr. engring. U. Minn., Mpls., 1955-60; mem. tech. staff Bell Telephone Labs., Murray Hill, N.J., 1960-65; sr. project engr. Curtiss-Wright Corp., Woodridge, N.J., 1965; assoc. prof. mech. engring. N.J. Inst. Tech., 1965-68, prof., 1968—; Participant in Internat. Conf. on Engring. and Applied Sci. Contbr. articles to profl. jours.; one of original Telstar designers. Bd. dirs. Ukrainian Congress Com. Am., Mpls., 1956-60, Plast Camp, East Chatham, N.Y., 1963-68; v.p. Ukrainian Music Found., 1977-86. NASA grantee, 1967-68; NSF grantee, 1982-84. Sr. mem. Inst. Environ. Scis.; mem. ASME, AIAA, Am. Soc. Engring. Edn., Ukrainian Engrs. Soc. Am. (pres. 1966-67), Am. Geophys. Union, AAUP, Shevchenko Sci. Soc., Ukrainian Acad. Arts and Scis. in U.S.A., Am. Chem. Soc., Pi Tau Sigma, Tau Beta Pi, Sigma Xi. Home: 19 Roselle Ave Cranford NJ 07016 Office: 323 Martin Luther King Blvd Newark NJ 07102

HSI, DAVID CHING HENG, plant pathologist and geneticist, educator; b. Shanghai, China, May 17, 1928; came to U.S., 1948, naturalized, 1961; s. Yulin and Sue Jean (King) H.; m. Kathy S.W. Chiang, 1952; children: Andrew C., Steven D. B.S. in Agr, St. John's U., Shanghai, 1948; M.S., U. Ga., Athens, 1949; Ph.D. (grad. teaching asst. 1950), U. Minn., St. Paul, 1951. Postdoctoral fellow U.S. Cotton Field Sta., Sacaton, Ariz., 1951-52; mem. faculty N.Mex. State U., Las Cruces, 1952—; prof. plant pathology and genetics N.Mex. State U., 1968—; adj. prof. biology U. N.Mex., 1986—; cons. AID, Pakistan, 1970; acad. exchange, People's Republic China, 1978, 84, 85, Taiwan, Republic China, 1979, 81, 82, Brazil and Argentina, 1980, Australia, 1983, S. Africa, 1981; judge sr. botany N.Mex. Sci. and Engring. Fair, 1979, 80, 81, 83, 85. Author research papers in field. Past bd. dirs., treas. Carver Pub. Library, Clovis, N.Mex.; elder, worship com. chmn., adult edn. com. chmn. First United Presbyn. Ch., Albuquerque, 1981, 82; mem. nat. adv. council discipleship and worship Gen. Assembly United Presbyn. Ch. U.S.A., 1978-81, mem. nat. theol. reflections working group, 1980-81; mem. bd. edn. Albuquerque Pub. Schs., 1982, sec. bd. edn., 1983, v.p., 1984; bd. dir. Middle Rio Grande Council Govts., 1983, 84; chmn. Albuquerque Sister Cities Bd., 1986-88. Recipient Disting. Research award Coll. Agr. and Home Econs., N.Mex. State U., 1971, Disting. Service award, 1985. Fellow AAAS (hon.); mem. Internat. Soc. Plant Pathology, Am. Phytopath. Soc. (judge Internat. Sci. and Engring. Fair 1983), Nat. Sweet Potato Collaborators Group (chmn. sprout prodn. and root piece propagation com. 1982-84), Nat. Geog. Soc., Am. Peanut Research and Edn. Soc. (chmn. site selection com. 1981, award com., pres.-elect 1981, pres. 1982), N.Mex. Acad. Sci. (chmn. membership com. 1980, pres. 1981, 82, treas. 1984—, Dist. Scientist award 1984), N.Y. Acad. Sci., N.Mex. Chinese Assn. (pres. 1983-84, treas. 1985-86), Sigma Xi (life mem., N.Mex. coordinator Centennial celebration). Club: Kiwanis Internat. (past pres. Clovis, past chmn. spl. program com., bd. dirs. Albuquerque). Office: NMex State U-Agrl Sci Ctr 1036 Miller St SW Los Lunas NM 87031

HSIAO, LING, mathematician; b. Beijing, People's Republic of China, Feb. 20, 1940; s. Ching-Lin Hsiao and Li Zhau; m. Zhi-yau Li, Oct. 30, 1966; 1 child, Mong Li. Grad., Chinese U. of Sci. and Tech., 1963. Asst. prof. Inst. Math., Academia Sinica, Beijing, 1963-79, lectr., 1979-82, assoc. prof., 1982-86, prof., 1986—; vis. prof. Brown U., Providence, 1981-82, Rutgers U., New Brunswick, N.J., 1984-85, U. Heidelberg, Fed. Republic of Germany, 1985, U. Wash., Seattle, 1987-88, Ind. U., Bloomington, 1988—. Contbr. articles to profl. jours. Mem. Am. Math. Soc., Chinese Math. Soc. Home: Baofusi Zhong Guan Cun, Bldg 940 Room 306, Beijing Peoples Republic of China Office: Academia Sinica, Inst Math, Zhong Guan Cun St, Beijing Peoples Republic of China

HSIEH, AN-TIEN, educator, management consultant; b. Kaohsiung, Taiwan, China, Oct. 28, 1939; s. Pai and Chung H.; B.S., Nat. Taiwan U., 1966; M.S., U. Philippines, 1971; Ph.D., Harvard U., 1977; m. Chein-hui Hsu, July 25, 1967; children—Hong-Ping, Er-Jou. Prof. bus. adminstrn., dean Grad. Sch. Mgmt., Tatung Inst. Tech., Taipei, Taiwan, China, 1978—; prof. Nat. Taiwan Inst. Tech., 1980—, Inst. Bus. Adminstrn., Nat. Cheng Chi U., 1979—; mgmt. cons. Tatung Co., Taipei, 1978-82; chmn. Ta Yeh Securities Investment Consulting Co., Ltd., 1984—; pres. Kaiser Plastic Corp., 1986—. Chmn. Bus. Negotiation Assn. of Republic of China. Mem. Acad. Internat. Bus. Author: Business Research Methods, 1979; Business Policy and Strategy, 1980. Home: No 56 Lane 170 Sec 5, Roosevelt Rd, Taipei Republic of China Office: F8 No 71 Min Chuan E Rd, Taipei Republic of China

HSIEH, SAM-CHUNG, bank executive; b. Kwantung, People's Republic of China, Nov. 13, 1919; s. Kung-Hsuen and Hao-Mei (Wen) H.; m. Alice Hsieh, Sept. 28, 1946; children: Wen-Ning, Wen Hsieh Lin, Wendy Chiou, Wen-An. BS, Nat. En. U., Nanking, People's Republic of China, 1943; MS, Nat. En. U., 1945; PhD, U. Minn., 1957. Prof. econs. Nat. Taiwan U., Taipei, Republic of China, 1950-60; dir. projects dept. Asian Devel. Bank, Manila, 1967-81; vice chmn. Council for Econ. Planning and Devel., Taipei, 1981-83; chmn. Bank of Communications, Taipei, 1983—; Bd. dirs. Cen. Bank China, Taipei. Home: 7F 244 Kuang-Fu S Rd, Taipei, Taiwan Republic of China Office: Bank Communications, 91 Heng Yang Rd, Taipei, Taiwan Republic of China

HSIEH, YING-HEN, mathematician, educator; b. Taipei, Taiwan, Sept. 1, 1954; s. Yao-Chu and Kuo-Chen (Pei) H.; m. Woan-Shu Chen, Mar. 29, 1986. PhD, Carnegie-Mellon U., 1982. Prof. math. Nat. Chung-Hsing U., Tai Chung, Taiwan, 1982—. Contbr. 11 articles to profl. jours. Internat.

Rotary scholar Baldwin-Wallace Coll., 1975; recipient Loomis Math. Prize, Baldwin-Loomis Coll., 1975. Mem. Am. Math. Soc., Math. Soc. of Republic of China. Office: Nat Chung-Hsing U, Dept of Applied Math, Tai Chung Republic of China

HSU, CHEN-CHIN, child psychiatrist, educator; b. Taipei, Republic of China, Aug. 11, 1927; parents: Ming-hsiun and Lu-mei (Tseng) H.; m. Mien-mien Tzao, Jan. 22, 1953; children: Tseng-chieh, Tseng-jan, Tseng-yang. MD, Nat. Taiwan U., Taipei, 1950; PhD, Nat. Kobe Med. Sch., Kobe, Japan, 1966. Diplomate Taiwan Bd. Psychiatry. Teaching fellow Harvard U. Med. Sch., Boston, 1958-60; lectr. psychiatry Nat. Taiwan U., 1961-66, assoc. prof., 1966-72, prof., 1972—, chmn. dept. psychiatry, 1984—. Contbr. articles to profl. jours. Fellow Am. Orthopsychiatric Assn. (life), Internat. Acad. for Research in Learning Disabilities, Internat. Soc. for Study in Behavioral Devel.; mem. World Psychiatric Assn. (child and adolescent psychiatry sect.)(mem. exec. com. 1982—), Soc. for Neurology and Psychiatry (pres. 1987—). Office: Nat Taiwan U Hosp, Dept Psychiatry, No 1 Chang-te St, Taipei 10016, Republic of China

HSU, CHIH YUN, retired biologist, educator, researcher; b. Jui An, Chekiang, Republic of China, Sept. 12, 1915; s. Hsin Yu Hsu and Yueh Yeh; m. Hsu Mu Liang, July 26, 1942; children—Wei Min, Ai Min, Yi Min. B.S., Yenching U., 1939; M.S., 1942; Ph.D., Washington U., St. Louis, 1948. Asst. Yenching U. (China), 1940-43; lectr. Nat. Defense Med. Ctr., Taipei, Taiwan, Republic of China, 1943-49, assoc. prof., 1949-55, prof., 1955-85, prof. emeritus, 1985—; mem. Biol. Sci. Ctr., Nat. Sci. Council, Republic of China, Taipei, Taiwan, 1983-85; mem. Com. Biol. Textbooks in Middle Schs., Nat. Inst. Compilation and Translation, Taipei, 1983—. Recipient medal for eminent service in teaching Chinese Army, 1955; honor for disting. work in devel. endocrinology Chung's Fund Adminstrn. Com., 1981; Eminent Research award Ministry of Edn. and Nat. Sci. Council, 1985-87. Mem. Am. Assn. Anatomists, Chinese Soc. Biology (exec. com. 1978-79, award for excellence in research 1981), N.Y. Acad. Scis., Chinese Soc. Electron Microscopy (control com. 1982—), Sigma Xi. Buddhist. Home: No 27 Alley 25 Ln 24, Sec 4 Roosevelt Rd, Taipei, Taiwan 10764, Republic of China Office: Nat Defense Med Ctr, PO Box 8244, Taipei, Taiwan Republic of China

HSU, CHING-YU, philosopher, educator, writer; b. Liuyang, Hunan, China, Dec. 25, 1898; s. Shih-kang and Shu-yi (Li) H.; m. Anna Yuen-Chi Ting, June 1, 1935; children: Stephen, Margaret (Mrs. Bob Mirsky), Victor, Yin-po (Mrs. H. N. Ma), Yin-sho (Mrs. William Cheng), Yu-Kuan. Ed., Hunan Coll. Law, Changsha, 1917-21; postgrad., Oxford (Eng.) U., 1922-25. Prof. philosophy Kwan Hwa U., Shanghai, 1926-28; dep. dir. transl. bur. exam. Juan, Nanking, 1928-30; acting chmn. nat. com. planning Nationalist Gov. China, 1932-34; spl. adminstr. Hunan, 1938-44; research fellow Hongkong U., 1953-58; spl. lectr. philosophy Chunchi Coll., Hongkong, 1952-53, Chee-loo U. (Shantung Christian U.), Tsinan, China, 1946-48. Author: Philosophy of Love, 1921, Philosophy of Confucious, 1925, Philosophy of the Beautiful, 1925, Co-wealthism and the New Age, 1975, Problem of China, 1966. Mem. adv. bd. Am. Nat. Security Council, 1974—; Mem. Presdl. Task Force; state advisor U.S. Congl. Adv. Bd., Commr. interior central polit. council, Kuomintang, Nanking, 1936-39. Mem. Internat. Sci. Soc. Shanghai (dir. 1937-39), Chinese Co-wealthist Soc. Hongkong (founder 1956), China Rebuilding Fedn. (cochmn. 1964—). Address: 21-20 21st St Long Island City NY 11105

HSU, DER-ANN, statistician, financial researcher; b. Canton, Peoples Republic of China, Dec. 9, 1943; s. Jen-Lin and Su-Yun (Lee) Hsu; m. Jane C. Hsu, July 27, 1974; children—Patricia, Andrew. B.A. in Econs., Nat. Taiwan U., Tapei, 1965; Ph.D. in Bus. Statistics, U. Wis., Madison, 1973. Research asst. prof. Princeton U., N.J., 1974-77; asst. prof. U. Wis., Milw., 1977-79, assocs. prof., 1979-83, prof. statistics and finance, 1983-87, disting. research prof. fin., 1987—; cons. FAA, Atlantic City, 1977—, various investment cos., 1986—. Contbr. articles to profl. jours. Recipient Outstanding Research award Sch. Bus. Adminstrn., U. Wis., 1984; Research Com. award Grad. Sch., U. Wis., 1985. Fellow Royal Inst. Nav., Royal Statis. Soc.; mem. Am. Statis. Assn., Inst. Mgmt. Scis., Am. Finance Assn. Avocation: violin. Home: 9485 N Range Line Rd River Hills WI 53217 Office: U Wis Sch of Bus Adminstrn PO Box 742 Milwaukee WI 53201

HOU, JOHN J., psychiatrist; b. China, Oct. 11, 1919; s. Ku Chin and Juan Mei (Shih) H.; m. Elizabeth Chang, Oct. 14, 1946; children—James, Nancy, Timothy, Hwayling, John R. M.D., Nat. Central U., Nanking, China, 1944. Asst. dept. physiology Coll. Medicine Nat. Central U., 1945-49; gen. practice medicine Taipei, Taiwan, 1950-54; resident physician Camden County Hosp., N.J., 1954-56; resident Pontiac State Hosp., Mich., 1957-60; dir. male in-patient dept. Pontiac State Hosp., 1960-62, dir. research, 1962-65; practice medicine specializing in psychiatry 1965-74, Bloomfield Hills, Mich., 1974-86, Birmingham, Mich., 1986—; mem. staff dept. psychiatry Pontiac Gen. Hosp., 1963—, chmn. dept. psychiatry, 1973-75; mem. staff St. Joseph Mercy Hosp., 1965—; pres. Bio Electronics Lab., Inc., 1976—. Author Hsu's method of counting blood-platelets used in People's Republic of China since 1950; contbr. articles to med. jours; patentee med. devices. Pres. Com. on Alcoholism, Pontiac, 1965-66, Oakland County Com. on Alcoholism, Mich., 1966-67; bd. dirs. Alcoholics Anonymous, Pontiac, 1965-74; mem. med. bd. City Drug Abuse Treatment Program, 1970-74. Fellow Am. Assn. Social Psychiatry; mem. AAAS, Am. Psychiat. Assn., Mich. Psychiat. Soc., AMA, Am. Soc. Clin. Hypnosis. Home: 7224 Old Mill Rd Birmingham MI 48010

HSU, SHIH-ANG, meteorologist, educator; b. Hangchou, China, Sept. 15, 1936; came to U.S., 1965, naturalized, 1976; s. Jan-Jin and Joan-Ing (Hwa) H.; Ph.D., U. Tex., Austin, 1969; m. Hwei Chou, Sept. 28, 1963; children—Helen, Julie, Jerry. Meteorol. officer Taiwan Sugar Corp., 1961-63, Taiwan Ministry of Communication, 1963-65; research asso. Atmospheric Sci. group U. Tex., Austin, 1965-69; asst. prof. dept. marine scis. and Coastal Studies Inst., La. State U., 1969-72, assoc. prof., 1972-77, prof., 1977—. Cert. cons. meteorologist. Mem. Am. Meteorol. Soc., Am. Geophysical Union, Sigma Xi, Chi Epsilon Pi. Contbr. articles in field. to profl. jours. Home: 5256 Chenango Dr Baton Rouge LA 70808 Office: Louisiana State U Coastal Studies Inst Baton Rouge LA 70803

HSU, YAU QUE, physician; b. Hong Kong, Feb. 28, 1953; s. Tak and Pui Chu (Yeung) H.; m. Brenda Kwok, June 22, 1986. BSc, U. Wis., 1975; AM, Harvard U., 1976; MBBS, Hong Kong U., 1981. Registrar U. Med. Unit Hong Kong U. Queen Mary Hosp., 1983-86; physician St. Teresa's Hosp., Hong Kong, 1986—; hon. clin. lectr. Hong Kong U., 1987—. Mem. Royal Coll. Physicians, Hong Kong Med. Assn., Phi Kappa Phi. Club: Harvard (Hong Kong). Office: St Teresa's Hosp, 327 Prince Edward Rd, Hong Kong Hong Kong

HSU, ZUEY-SHIN, physiology educator; b. Shinin, Taiwan, Republic of China, Dec. 13, 1930; s. Kua and Mun Mei (Kuo) H.; m. Pan Tsu Wu, Feb. 1, 1964; 1 child, Sheng Chin. M.D., Nat. Taiwan U., 1956. Intern in internal medicine Nat. Taiwan U., 1956-57; asst. Kaohsiung Med. Coll., Kaohsiung City, Republic of China, 1957-59, instr., 1959-62, assoc. prof. legal medicine, 1962-68, assoc. prof. physiology, 1968-72, prof. physiology, 1972—, acting dir. dept. pharmacology, 1972-73, dir. dept. pharmacology, 1973-74, dir. dept. physiology, 1972-85. Inventor method of detoxicating heterologous blood for transfusion, 1978; Immunological method for desensitizing allergic individuals, 1981, preparation of tumor vaccine 1987. Nat. Sci. Council of Taipei grantee, 1967. Fellow Inst. Med. Sci., Tokyo U., Internat. Biographical Assn. (life); mem. Formosan Med. Assn., Chinese Physiol. Soc., Chinese Soc. Immunology, Endocrine Soc. of Republic of China, Chinese Pharmacological Soc. Home: 24 157 Ln Fu-Herng 1st Rd, Kaohsiung Taiwan Office: Kaohsiung Med Coll, 100 Shih-Chuan 1st Rd, Kaohsiung 80708, Taiwan

HU, CAN BEVEN, chemist; b. Taipei, Taiwan, Oct. 31, 1949; came to U.S., 1975, naturalized, 1987; s. Der-Chang and Shen-Chi Hu; m. Li-Wen Yu, Nov. 24, 1982; children: Alexander, Irene. B.S., Nat. Taiwan U., 1972; M.S. U. Ky., 1976, Ph.D., MIT, 1980. Polymer scientist Thoratec Labs. Corp., Berkeley, Calif., 1980-83; staff scientist Procter & Gamble Co., Cin., 1983-84; sr. scientist Becton Dickinson Polymer Research, Dayton, Ohio, 1984—. Whitaker Health Scis. fellow, 1978-80. Mem. Am. Chem. Soc., Soc. Plastics Engrs., Sigma Xi. Mem. Christian Ch. Contbr. articles on polymer science to jours. Home: 9410 Meadow Woods Ln Spring Valley OH 45370 Office: Becton Dickinson Polymer Research 11125 Yankee St PO Box 1285 Dayton OH 45401

HU, DONG-SHENG, opera historian; b. Beijing, Dec. 6, 1925; s. Lin Hu and Shiu-yin Wen; m. Jianchu Nei, Mar. 24, 1951; 1 child, Yuan-jie. BA in History, Yenchin U., Beijing, 1950; student grad sch., Beijing Inst. Chinese Opera, 1959-62. Asst. prof. polit. econs. Med. Coll. Dalian, Republic of China, 1951-59; researcher Beijing Inst. Chinese Opera, 1962—, dir. history dept., 1980—. Mng. editor, edit. bd.: Beijing Opera History of China, 1983-87; editor: Beijing Opera History Research, 1986; contbg. editor Asian Theatre Jour., Honolulu, 1983-87. Mem. Soc. Beijing Opera History (sec. gen. 1982-87), Assn. Chinese Dramatists. Home: Bldg 19, 4-35, Beijing Normal U, Beijing People's Republic of China Office: Beijing Inst Chinese Opera, Min Zoo Gong Nan Jai, Beijing People's Republic of China

HU, JOHN CHIH-AN, chemist, research engineer; b. Nanchang, Hubei, China, July 12, 1922; came to U.S., 1954, naturalized, 1965; s. Chi-Ching and Chao-Xien (Tsen) H.; B.S. in Chemistry, Nat. Central U., Nanjing, China, 1946; M.S. in Organic Chemistry, U. So. Calif., 1957, postgrad., 1957-61; PhD (hon.) Marquis Giuseppe Scicluna Internat. Univ. Foundation, 1985; m. Betty Siao-Yung Ho, Oct. 26, 1957; children—Arthur, Benjamin, Carl, David, Eileen, Franklin, George. Dir. research dept. Plant 1, Taiwan Fertilizer Mfg. Co., Chilung, 1947-54; research assoc. chemistry dept. U. So. Calif., Los Angeles, 1957-61; research chemist Chem Seal Corp. Am., Los Angeles, 1961-62; research chemist Products Research & Chem. Corp., Glendale, Calif., 1962-66; sr. research engr., materials and tech. unit, Boeing Co., Seattle, 1966-71, specialist engr. Quality Assurance Labs., 1971—; cons. UN; lectr., China, profl. confs. Fellow Am. Inst. Chemists; mem. Am. Chem. Soc. (chmn. exec. com. Puget Sound sect. 1988), Royal Soc. Chemistry (London), N.Y. Acad. Sci., Phi Lambda Upsilon. Patentee Chromatopyrography; contbg. author: Analytical Approach, 1983, Advances in Chromotography, vol. 23, 1984; contbr. articles on analytical pyrolysis, gas chromatography, mass spectrometry, polymer characterization, chemistry and tech. of sealants and adhesives profl. publs. in Chinese and English; editor Puget Sound Chemist; referee profl. jours. Analytical Chemistry, Analytica Chimica Acta, Am. Chem. Soc. short courses. Home: 16212 122 SE Renton WA 98058 Office: Boeing Co M/S 8J-55 PO Box 3999 Seattle WA 98124

HU, SHAU-CHUNG, international trade company executive; b. China, Nov. 1, 1941; s. Po-han and Ti-fei (Wu) Hu; BS, Tamkang U., 1967; postgrad. Iowa State U., 1972-76; m. Margaret M. Liu, Feb. 14, 1984; 1 son, Zongguang. Instr. math. Iowa State U., Ames, 1972-76; exec. v.p. Chinese Native Products, Ltd., N.Y.C., 1976-85, Pearl River Chinese Products Emporium, N.Y.C., 1978-85; chmn. Lowbet Realty Corp., N.Y.C., 1979—, Salpang Co., Hong Kong, 1983-85, Pearl River Chinese Food Mfg., Inc., Clive, Iowa, 1983-85, China Natural Fabric Corp., Bklyn., 1985—, China Constructional Material Corp., Bklyn., 1987—. Mem. steering com. Ames chpt. U.S.-China Friendship Assn., 1972-74. Named hon. friend Taipei City Council. Mem. Sino Am. C. of C. (vice chmn. 1981—). Office: 973 44th St Suite 1A Brooklyn NY 11219

HU, STEVE SENG-CHIU, scientific research company director; b. Yangchou City, Kiangsu Province, Republic of China, Mar. 16, 1922; s. Yubin and Shuchang (Lee) H.; m. Lily Li-Wan Liu, Oct. 2, 1977; children: April, Yendo, Victor. MS, Rensselaer Poly. Inst., 1940; PhD, MIT, 1942; postgrad., UCLA, 1964-66. Mng. tech. dir. China Aircraft/China Motor Programs, Douglas Aircraft Co., Calif. and N.J., 1945-48, Kelly Engring Co., N.Y. and Ariz., 1949-54; systems engr., meteorol. sci. dir. R.C.A., Ariz., 1955-58; research specialist Aerojet Gen., Calif., 1958-60; research scientist Jet Propulsion Lab., Calif., 1960-61; dir. research analysis Northrop Corp., Calif. and Ala., 1961-72; dir. Century Research, Inc., Am. Tech. Coll., and U. Am. United Research Inst., Gardena, San Bernardino, Calif., 1973—; pres. U. Am. Found. and U. Am. Research Found., Calif. and Taiwan, Republic of China, 1981—; dir., exec. v.p. Am. Astronautical Soc., Wash., 1963-70; cons. Hsin-Hwa Nuclear Reactor Program, Taiwan, 1954-58; prof. Auburn (Ala.) U., U. Ala., U. Ariz., U. So. Calif., Los Angeles, 1957-73. Fellow Calif. Inst. Tech., 1943-44. Recipient MIT Salisbury prize and Sloane prize, 1941-42, Commission Aeronautical Affairs, Republic of China cert. of merit and cash award, 1945, Northrop Corp. cert. of merit, 1965. Mem. Am. Astronautical Soc., AIAA, Nat. Assn. Tech. Schs. Office: Century Research Bldg Office Sect 16935 S Vermont Ave Gardena CA 90247

HU, WEIBAI, mineral engineer, metallurgist, educator; b. Jiangxi, Peoples Republic of China, Nov. 26, 1922; came to U.S., 1981; BS, Chaotung U., Peoples Rep. of China, 1945; MS, U. Utah, 1949. Prof. and chmn. Cen.-South U. of Tech., Changsha, Peoples Republic of China, 1952-82; vis. prof. Colo. Sch. Mines, Golden, 1982, U. Calif., Berkeley, 1983; research prof. U. Utah, Salt Lake City, 1983—; vice-chmn. mineral processing, Chinese Soc. Metals, 1978-83; sr. adv. China Nonferrous Metal Industry Corp., 1983—; cons. ministry of Metallurgy, Peoples Republic of China, 1979—, ministry of Geology, 1976—. Author Chinese lang. univ. textbooks; editor: Ency. Sinica, Eng.-Chinese Dictionary of Mineral Technology; contbr. articles to profl. jours.; inventor and patentee in field. Recipient Nat. Prize of Invention Chinese Govt., 1987, awards for Research U.S. Dept. Energy, 1987-88, 1988-91. Mem. AIME, Am. Chem. Soc., Math. Assn. Am., Soc. Plastic Engrs., Fine Particle Soc., Chinese Soc. Metals, Chinese Soc. Non-ferrous Metals, Chinese Soc. Mineral Processing, Internat. Assn. Colloid and Surface Chemistry. Office: U Utah Dept Metallurgy 412 Mineral Sci Bldg Salt Lake City UT 84112

HU, YAO-SU, economist, educator, author; b. Tashkent, USSR, Aug. 7, 1946; s. Hung-Lick and Chi-Yung (Chung) H.; m. Magdalene Hü benthal, Dec. 17, 1968; children—Michele, Claire, Victor. BA with honors, Oxford U., 1968, MA, 1972, PhD, 1973. Research fellow Polit. and Econ. Planning, London, 1974-76; indsl. economist World Bank, Washington, 1976-78; sr. research fellow Chatham House, London, 1978-80; sr. tutor Adminstrv. Staff Coll., Henley, U.K., 1980-83, reader in mgmt. studies Hong Kong U., 1983-88; gov. Shue Yan Coll., Hong Kong, 1984—; dir. internat. studies Henley-The Mgmt. Coll., Eng., 1988—. Author: Impact of U.S. Investment in Europe, 1973; National Attitudes and Financing of Industry, 1976; Europe Under Stress, 1981; Industrial Banking and Special Credit Institutions, 1984; (with Nicolas Jé quier) Banking and the Promotion of Technological Development, 1988. Avocations: music, travel, zen. Office: Henley-The Mgmt Coll, Greenlands, Henley-on-Thames RG9 3AU, England

HUA, HSICHUN MIKE, aeronautical industry executive; b. China, Dec. 6, 1925; m. Margaret Hua, Jan. 1, 1954. M.S., Purdue U., 1965, Ph.D., 1968; postgrad. Harvard U. Grad. Sch. Bus., 1979. Aerodynamicist Cessna A/C Co., Wichita, Kans., 1968-69; aerodynamics engr. Lockheed A/C Co., Burbank, Calif., 1969-70; chief A/C design Aero Industry Devel. Center, Taichung, Taiwan, Republic of China, 1970-74, dep. dir. engring. and research, 1974-82, dir., 1982—; assoc. prof. Cheng-Kung U., Taiwan, 1970-72; prof. Tunghai U., Taiwan, 1972-74; v.p.,dir. Internat. Turbine Engine Corp., Phoenix, 1982—. Served with Chinese Air Force, 1949-64. Decorated D.F.C. Fellow AIAA (assoc.); mem. Aero. and Astron. Soc. Republic of China (dir. 1972—), Soc. Theoretical and Applied Mechanics, Republic of China (dir. 1978—), Sigma Xi. Clubs: Am. U. (Taipei, Taiwan); Harvard.

HUA GUOFENG, former vice chairman Chinese Communist Party; b. Jiaocheng County, Shanxi Province, China, 1920; m. Han Zhijun; children: Xiaoli, 3 others. Vice gov., Hunan Province, 1958-67; alt. mem. Secretariat, Communist Party, Hunan Province, 1958; vice chmn. Revolutionary Com., Hunan Province, 1968-70, acting chmn., 1970-74; mem. 9th Cen. Com., Chinese Communist Party, 1969; 1st sec., Hunan Province, 1970; polit. commr. Canton Mil. Region, People's Liberation Army, 1972; 1st polit. commissar Hunan Mil. Dist., 1973-74; mem. Politburo, 10th Cen. Com., Chinese Communist Party, 1973; dep. premier, 1975, minister pub. security, 1975-77, acting premier, 1976, premier, 1976-80; 1st vice chmn. Cen. Com., Chinese Communist Party, 1976, chmn., 1976-81, chmn. mil. affairs com., 1976-81, chmn. 11th Cen. Com., mem. Standing Com., 1977, vice chmn. Cen. Com., 1981-82, mem. 12th Cen. Com., from 1982; mem. Presidium, Nat. People's Congress, 1981. Office: Office of Vice Chmn, Chinese Communist Party, Beijing People's Republic of China *

HUANG, ANNETTE MARGARET MARY, librarian; b. Devonport, New Zealand, June 5, 1947; d. Bernard Noel and Kathleen Margaret (Watts) Marsh; m. Edward Tien Heng Huang, May 6, 1972. MA, U. Auckland, New Zealand, 1971; diploma, New Zealand Library Sch., 1971. Sr. cataloguer Auckland Pub. Library, 1972-78; librarian Manukau Polytech., Auckland, 1978—. Mem. New Zealand Library Assn. Office: Manukau Poly, Otara Rd, Manukau 6, New Zealand

HUANG, DANNY HUAK KWANG, marketing executive; b. Kuching, Malaysia, Sept. 23, 1961; s. Tiong Huang and Hie Chai Ting. Salesman Mitsubishi Corp., Kuching, Malaysia, 1981-83; sales mgr. Ngee Hong Heavy Machinery SDN BHD, Kuching, 1984—. Founder Rotaract Club, Kuching, 1983, v.p., 1983-84, pres. 1984-85, zonal rep., 1985-86. Office: Ngee Hong Heavy Machinery, 7 Lot 358 Pending Rd, 93450 Kuching Malaysia

HUANG, FRANCIS FU-TSE, engineering educator; b. Hong Kong, Aug. 27, 1922; came to U.S., 1945, naturalized, 1960; s. Kwong Set and Chen-Ho (Yee) H.; m. Fung-Yuen Fung, Apr. 10, 1954; children: Raymond, Stanley. B.S., San Jose State Coll., 1951; M.S., Stanford U., 1952; profl. mech. engr., Columbia U., 1964. Design engr. M.W. Kellogg Co., N.Y.C., 1952-58; faculty San Jose (Calif.) State U., 1958—, assoc. prof. mech. engring., 1962-67, prof., 1967—, chmn. dept., 1973-81; hon. prof. heat power engring. Taiyuan (People's Republic of China) U. Tech., 1981—. Author: Engineering Thermodynamics—Fundamentals and Applications, 1976, 2d edit., 1988. Served to capt. Chinese Army, 1943-45. NSF faculty fellow, 1962-64; Named Tau Beta Pi Outstanding Engring. Prof. of Year, 1967, 76, Pi Tau Sigma Prof. of Yr., 1985; recipient Calif. State Coll. System Disting. Teaching award, 1968-69. Mem. ASME, AIAA, Am. Soc. Engring. Edn., AAAS, AAUP, N.Y. Acad. Scis. Home: 1259 Sierra Mar Dr San Jose CA 95118 Office: Dept Mech Engring San Jose State U San Jose CA 95192

HUANG, HOU WEN, naval architect; b. Nanking, China, Mar. 25, 1931; came to U.S., 1962, naturalized, 1974; D.Eng. in Naval Architecture, U. Calif., Berkeley, 1968; m. Anna Wen; children—Merle, Patricia. Naval instr. Chinese Naval Acad., Taiwan, 1956-57; chief engring. officer First Floating Drydock, Taiwan, 1957-58; assoc. naval architect Ingalls-Taiwan Shipbldg. and Drydocks, Taiwan, 1959-61; naval architect, mgr. hull structural analysis dept. John J. McMullen Assocs., N.Y.C., 1968—; cons. oil tanker structural improvement for maj. oil cos., 1968—. Mem. Soc. Naval Architects and Marine Engrs., Sigma Xi. Home: 7 Stradford Rd Parlin NJ 08859 Office: John J McMullen Assos Inc 1 World Trade Ctr New York NY 10048

HUANG, JACOB CHEN-YA, physician, city official; b. Chia-Yi, Taiwan, Dec. 25, 1937; came to U.S., 1966, naturalized, 1974; s. Chang-Chiang and Agenes Cheng-Jen H.; m. Vivian Lin, Oct. 3, 1970; children—Phyllis, Albert, Edward. Intern, Taipei City Hosp., 1964-65, house officer in pediatrics, 1965-66; fellow in clin. pathology Albert Einstein Coll. Medicine-Lincoln Hosp., 1968-70; resident in family medicine Lutheran Med. Center, N.Y.C., 1970-71; clin. asso. prof. NYU, 1972-76; dist. health dir. N.Y.C., Dept. Health, 1971-76; med. dir. Paterson City (N.J.) Health Dept., 1977—; chmn. dept. family practice Dover (N.J.) Gen. Hosp. and Med. Center, 1980—; trustee N.J. Passaic PRO, 1987—; bd. dirs. ambulatory care adv. bd. Beth Israel Hosp., N.Y.C., 1972-76, community adv. bd. ambulatory services St. Vincent Med. Center, N.Y.C., 1972-76, COMED-IPA Inc., N.J., 1980—. Recipient Physician's Recogniation award AMA, 1966, 69, 72—; diplomate Am. Bd. Family Practice. Fellow Am. Coll. Preventive Medicine, Am. Acad. Family Physicians; mem. Am. Public Health Assn., Am. Chinese Med. Assn. N.J. (pres., founder), Chinese Am. Med. Soc. (bd. dirs.). Home: 3 Walnut Hill Dr Chester NJ 07930 Office: Bartley Sq Route 206 Flanders NJ 07836

HUANG, JOSEPH CHEN-HUAN, civil engineer; b. Nanking, China, Oct. 18, 1933; came to U.S., 1962, naturalized, 1972; M.S. in Structural Engring., Va. Poly. Inst. and State U., 1964; m. Elizabeth C. Huang, Sept. 3, 1966; children—Edith, Eleanor, Evelyn, Edna. Project engr. Green Assos., Inc., Balt., 1964-68; pres. Gen. Engring. Consultants, Inc., Balt., 1968-76; chmn., chief exec. officer HSC Engring. Corp., Towson, Md., 1976—. Mem. ASCE, Am. Concrete Inst., Nat. Soc. Profl. Engrs. Author; Prestressed Steel Structures; also tech. papers. Home: 3506 Templar Rd Randallstown MD 21133 Office: 1248 E Joppa Rd Towson MD 21204 Office: 1045 Taylor Ave Towson MD 21204

HUANG, KAO-KANG, pediatrician; b. Taichung, Republic of China, Sept. 3, 1941; s. Ta-lu Huang and Shih-Mei (Chan) Chang; m. Hsiu-Jung Tseng, May 1, 1942; children: Yi-yang, Yi-yueh. MD, Nat. Def. Med. Ctr., 1967. Lic. physician, Republic of China. Commd. Taiwan Air Force, 1967, advanced through grades to lt. col., retired, 1981; flight surgeon Air Force Col. of China, Kangsan, 1967-70; resident in pediatrics Triservice Gen. Hosp., Taipei, 1969-71, chief resident, 1972-73, pediatric attendant, 1973-74, chief pediatric sect., 1974-81; practice medicine specializing in pediatrics Taipei, 1981—. Recipient Standard Mil. Doctor award Ministry Nat. Def., Taipei, 1973. Fellow Formosan Med. Assn., Rep. China Soc. Cardiology, Pediatric Assn. Rep. China, Internat. Coll. Pediatrics. Home and Office: 227 Wen-Chang St, Taipei 10664, Republic of China

HUANG, PATRICK FUH-SHYONG, insurance company executive; b. Taipei, Taiwan, Republic of China, Mar. 20, 1943; s. Shu and Gan (Wong) H.; m. Teng-Mei Chou, Dec. 14, 1970; children: Grace, Ted, Kenneth. BS in Internat. Trade, Tam Kang U., 1973. Asst. to gen. mgr. Tung Tao Indsl. Co., Taipei, 1960-64, Wang Shen Trading Co., Taipei, 1965-67; sr. acct. Motorola Electronics Co., Taipei, 1968-70; chief acct. Deluew Cather Engring. Consulting Co., Taipei, 1971-72; v.p. controller Nan Shan Life Ins. Co., Taipei, 1973—. Fellow Life Ins. Mgmt. Inst. (chmn. 1986-87, analyst). Buddhist. Club: Yuan Shan. Home: 3-2 Alley 16 Lane 81, Roosevelt Rd Sect 2, Taipei Republic of China Office: Nan Shan Life Ins Co Ltd, 11F 302 Ming Chuan East Rd, Taipei 10461, Republic of China

HUANG, POR JAU, cardiologist, educator; b. Tainan, Taiwan, Oct. 30, 1939; d. King Tau and Wu Mee (Tsai) H.; M.D., Nat. Taiwan U., 1966; m. Su-Fen Jung, Jan. 15, 1968; children—Irene Y., James C., Brian C. Intern, then resident in cardiology Nat. Taiwan U. Hosp., 1966-71; fellow cardiology Osaka City (Japan) U. Med. Coll. and Hosp., 1972; mem. faculty Nat. Taiwan U. Coll. Medicine and Hosp., 1973—, assoc. prof. medicine, 1980-85, prof., 1985—; nuclear cardiology sect., 1980—; fellow nuclear cardiology Columbia U.-St. Luke's Hosp. Center, N.Y.C., 1978-79. Fellow Am. Bur. Med. Advancement China, 1978-79. Mem. Formosan Med. Assn., Republic China Soc. Cardiology. Author articles in field. Home: 20 Lane 127, Sect 2, Sien-Sun N Rd, Taipei 104, Republic of China Office: 1 Chang-Te St, Taipei 100, Republic of China

HUANG, QICHANG CHI-CHIANG, mathematics educator; b. Chongqing, Sichuan, People's Republic of China, June 11, 1931; s. Fang-gu Huang and Lenhe Xui; m. Suzen Zhou, Dec. 31, 1958; children: Xiaogang, Kui. Student, Yale-in-China Sch., 1947-50, Dalian (People's Republic of China) Inst. Tech., 1950-52, Northeast Normal U., Changchun, People's Republic of China, 1952-53. Lectr. Jilin Normal U., Changchun, 1961-78; asst. Northeast Normal U., 1953-61, assoc. prof., 1978-83, chairperson dept. math., 1980-83, v.p., 1983-86, prof., 1983—, pres., 1986—. Author: Math. Physics Equations, 1956, Ordinary Differential Equations, 1983, Nonlinear Differential Equations, 1983. Named Preeminent Scientist, Jilin Province Govt., 1983, State Preeminent Specialist, State Sci. Commn., Beijing, 1987; State Edn. Commn. grantee, 1984, NSF grantee, Beijing, 1983, 85, 88. Fellow State Textbook Com.; mem. Chinese Math. Soc. (bd. dirs. 1983—), Chinese Ednl. Soc. (standing mem. bd. 1987—), Am. Math Soc. (reviewer 1983—). Office: Northeast Normal U, Office of Pres, Changchun, Jilin Peoples Republic of China

HUANG, SUN-YI, polymer chemist, researcher; b. Su-Ao, Ilan, Taiwan, Sept. 14, 1940; came to U.S., 1966; s. Su Sen and Shaw Lin H.; m. Misa Lin, June 9, 1968; 1 son, Herman Lin. B.S., Nat. Cheng Keng U.; M.S., N.Mex. Highlands U., 1968; Ph.D., U. Mo.-Kansas City, 1973. Research assoc. U. Mo.-Kansas City, 1973-74; postdoctoral U. Akron, 1974-76; research chemist Am. Cyanamid Co., Stamford, Conn., 1976-78, sr. research chemist, 1978—. Contbr. articles to profl. jours. Served to 2d lt. Chinese Army, 1963-64. Recipient Sci. Achievement award Am. Cyanamid Co., 1981; research grantee. Mem. Am. Chem. Soc., Am. Phys. Soc., Chinese-Am. Chem. Soc.,

Chinese-Am. Polymer Soc. Research on elastomers, engineering plastics, block and Graft copolymers, water soluble polymers, novel polyelectrolytes for enhanced oil recovery, paper additives and water treating; patentee in field U.S. and fgn. countries; co-inventor long-last electrochromic device watch. Home: 106 New England Dr Stamford CT 06903 Office: American Cyanamid Co 1937 W Main St Stamford CT 06904

HUANG, TAYUAN, mathematician; b. Chung-Li, Taiwan, Aug. 26, 1950; s. Chin-Chuan and Tien-Mei (Wu); m. Mei-Chiao Chen, Mar. 27, 1977; children: Kuo-Lung, Kuo-Hua. BS in Math., Chung-Yuan U., Taiwan, 1972; MS in Math., Tsing-Hua U., Taiwan, 1976; PhD in Math., Ohio State U., 1985. Instr. Chung-Yuan U., 1976-78, Fu-Jen U., Taipei, Taiwan, 1978-79; assoc. prof. Nat. Chiao-Tung U., Hsin-Chu, Taiwan, 1985—. Contbr. articles to profl. jours. Grantee Nat. Sci. Council, Republic of China, 1986—. Mem. Math. Soc. of Republic of China, Am. Math. Soc. Home: 49 Sec 2, Chung-Yang West Rd, Chung-Li 32013, Taiwan Office: Nat Chiao-Tung Univ, Dept of Applied Math, Hsin-Chu 30050, Taiwan

HUANG, THERESA C., librarian; b. Nanking, China; m. Theodore S. Huang, Dec. 25, 1959. B.A., Nat. Taiwan U., 1955; M.S. in L.S., Syracuse U., 1958. Cataloger, Harvard U., Cambridge, Mass., 1958-60; with Bklyn. Pub. Library, 1960-78, regional librarian, 1978—. Joint compiler bibliography: Asia: A Guide to Books for Children, 1966; Nuclear Awareness, 1983; The U.S.A. through Children's Books, 1986, 88. Mem. ALA, Assn. Library Service to Children, Pub. Library Assn., Chinese Am. Librarians Assn., Asia Pacific Am. Librarians Assn. Office: Bklyn Pub Library 240 Division Ave Brooklyn NY 11211

HUANG, THOMAS WEISHING, lawyer; b. Taipei, Taiwan, Feb. 1, 1941; arrived U.S., 1967; s. Lienden and Helen (Yen) H. B.A., Taiwan U., 1964; J.D. magna cum laude, Ind. U., Indpls., 1970; LL.M., Harvard U., 1971, S.J.D., 1975. Bar: D.C. 1975, Mass. 1976, U.S. Dist. Ct. Mass. 1976, U.S. Ct. Appeals (1st cir.) 1978, N.Y. 1980. Judge advocate Chinese Army, Taiwan, 1964-65; legal officer Treaty and Legal Dept., Ministry of Fgn. Affairs, Taiwan, 1966-67; assoc. Chemung County Legal Services, Elmira, N.Y., 1975-76; assoc. law firm Taylor Johnson & Wieschhoff, Marblehead, Mass., 1980; prin. Reiser & Rosenberg, Boston, 1982-86, Huang & Assocs., Boston, 1987-88; ptnr. Hale, Sanderson, Byrnes & Morton, Boston, 1988—; exec. v.p. Excel Tech. Internat. Co., Brunswick, N.J., 1982—; legal counsel Nat. Assn. Chinese Ams., Washington, 1979-80. Mem. editorial bd. Ind. Law Rev., 1969-70; contbr. articles to legal jours. Bd. dirs. Chinese Econ. Devel. Council, Boston, 1978-80; mem. Gov.'s Adv. Council on Guangdong, 1984—. Mem. Boston Bar Assn. (mem. internat. law sect. steering com. 1979—, mem. ad hoc com. on code of profl. conducts), ABA, Nat. Assn. Chinese Ams. (v.p. Boston chpt. 1984-86, pres. 1986—). Democrat. Home: 30 Farrwood Dr Andover MA 01810 Office: Hale Sanderson Byrnes & Morton One Center Plaza Suite M-100 Boston MA 02108

HUANG, XIANG-PENG, musicologist, educator; b. Nanjing, Jiangsu, People's Republic of China, Dec. 26, 1927; s. Qi-miao and Hui-li (Dong) H.; m. Zhou Chen, Aug. 8, 1954; children: Tian-lai, Tian-jian. BA, Cen. Conservatory of Music, Tianjin, People's Republic of China, 1951. Asst. Cen. Conservatory for Music, Tianjin, People's Republic of China, 1951; vice dir. study class early youth Cen. Conservatory for Music, Tianjin, 1952-56, lectr. dept. musicology, 1956-58; research fellow, lectr. Research Inst. Music, Beijing, 1958, dir. research sect. Chinese music history, 1980-85, research fellow, prof., 1983—, dir., 1985—; mem. com. Council Acad. degree conferring of Chinese Acad. Arts, 1984—; dir. Bd. Chinese Tradition Music, 1985—. Chief author (collected works) Zeng Hou Yi's Bells, 1981; chief author, editor: (music dictionary) Theories of Tonal Systems, 1984; chief editor, author: (ency.) Chinese Ancient Music, 1985. Grantee 31st Internat. Congress Human Sci. in Asia and North Africa, Tokyo, 1983, Symposium on Traditional Music in Asia and the Pacific, UNESCO, Beijing, 1987. Mem. Soc. Historiography in Chinese Music (vice chmn. 1985—), Soc. Chinese Traditional Music (chmn. 1986—), Internat. Council Traditional Music (study group music archaeology 1982—).

HUBBARD, CHARLES RONALD, engineering executive; b. Weaver, Ala., Feb. 4, 1933; s. John Duncan Hubbard and Athy Pauline (Lusk) Thorpe; m. Betty Lou McKleroy, Dec. 29, 1951; 1 son, Charles Ronald Hubbard II. BSEE, U. Ala., 1960. Mktg. mgr. Sperry Corp., Huntsville, Ala., 1969-71, head engring. sect., 1971-74; sr. staff engr. Honeywell Inc., Clearwater, Fla., 1974-76, mgr., 1976-79, chief engr., West Covina, Calif., 1979-83, assoc. dir. engring., 1983-84, assoc. dir. advanced systems, 1984-87, assoc. dir. programs, 1987-88; v.p. govt. systems div. Integrated Inference Machines, Anaheim, Calif., 1988—. Served as staff sgt. USAF, 1953-57. Mem. IEEE (sect. chmn. 1972-73). Methodist. Home: 5460 Willowick Circle Anaheim CA 92807 Office: Honeywell Inc 1200 E San Bernardino Rd West Covina CA 91790

HUBBARD, THOMAS EDWIN (TIM), lawyer; b. Roseboro, N.C., July 10, 1944; s. Charles Spence and Mary Mercer (Reeves) H.; m. Leslie Howard, July 20, 1985; 1 child, Marvin Gannon. BS in Biomed. Engring., Duke U., 1970, postgrad., 1970-71; JD, U. N.C., 1973. Bar: N.C. 1973. Regulation writer, med. devices FDA, Washington, 1974-75; asst. dir. clin. affairs Zimmer USA, Warsaw, Ind., 1975, dir. regulatory affairs, 1975-76; house counsel Gen. Med. Corp., Richmond, Va., 1976-79; sole practice, Pittsboro, N.C., 1979—; pres. Chathamborough Research Group, Inc., Pittsboro, 1979—, Chathamborough Farms Inc., 1982—; sec., treas. Hubbard-Corry, Inc., Pittsboro, 1981—; chmn. Hubbard Bros., Inc., Chapel Hill, N.C., 1982-87; bd. dirs. No. State Legal Service, Hillsborough, N.C., 1980—, pres., 1986—; adj. instr. U. N.C. Law Sch., 1983. V.p. N.C. Young Dems. 4th Congl. Dist., 1970-71; mem. State Dem. Exec. Com., 1972-73; mem. paralegal adv. com. Cen. Carolina Community Coll., Sanford, N.C., 1987—. Served to sgt. USMC, 1963-67. Named Top N.C. Young Dem., 1971. Mem. ABA, N.C. Bar Assn., Chatham County Bar Assn., Assn. for Advancement Med. Instrumentation (govt. affairs com. 1976). Democrat. Methodist. Office: PO Drawer 929 Pittsboro NC 27312 also: Chathamborough Research Group Inc 105 West St Pittsboro NC 27312

HUBBELL, ERNEST, lawyer; b. Trenton, Mo., Aug. 28, 1914; s. Platt and Maud Irene (Ray) H.; m. Nevah Smith, Apr. 25, 1943; 1 child, Platt Thorpe. AA, Trenton Jr. Coll., 1934; JD, Georgetown U., 1938. Bar: D.C. 1937, Mo. 1938, U.S. Supreme Ct. 1946. Practice Trenton, 1938-39, Jefferson City, Mo., 1939-42; sole practice Kansas City, Mo., 1947-52; ptnr. Hubbell, Sawyer, Peak & O'Neal (formerly Hubbell, Lane & Sawyer), Kansas City, Mo., 1952—; asst. atty. gen. Mo., 1939-42; first chmn. bench, bar com. 16th Jud. Cir. Ct., Kansas City, 1964-69, mem 16th Cir. Jud. Nominating Commn., 1970-75; mem. U.S. Cir. Judge Nominating Commn., 1977-80. Trustee Legal Aid and Defender Soc. Greater Kansas City, 1964-73; mem. Law Found. U. Mo. Kansas City, 1966-71; chmn. Nat. Council on Crime and Delinquency, 1966-76; pres. Hubbell Family Hist. Soc., 1981-85; mem. Soc. Fellows Nelson Art Gallery. Served with USAAF, 1942-44; to capt. AUS, 1944-46. Mem. ABA, Kansas City Met. Bar Assn. (pres. 1963-64, ann. Achievement award 1974, 1st ann. Litigator Emeritus award), Mo. Bar Assn., Assn. Trial Lawyers Am. (assoc. editor R.R. law sect. of jour. 1951—), Mo. Assn. Trial Attys. (pres. 1954, editor bull. 1955), Lawyers Assn. Kansas City, Lawyers Assn. St. Louis, Archeol. Inst. Am., SAR. Episcopalian. Democrat. Club: Kansas City. Home: 1210 W 63d St Kansas City MO 64113 Office: Hubbell Sawyer Peak O'Neal Power & Light Bldg 106 W 14th St 25th floor Kansas City MO 64105

HUBBERT, MARION KING, geologist, geophysicist; b. San Saba, Tex., Oct. 5, 1903; s. William Bee and Cora Virginia (Lee) H.; m. Miriam Graddy Berry, Nov. 11, 1938. Student, Weatherford Coll., 1921-23; B.S., U. Chgo., 1926, M.S., 1928, Ph.D., 1937; D.Sc. (hon.), Syracuse U., 1972, Ind. State U., 1980. Asst. geologist Amerada Petroleum Corp., Tulsa, summer 1926, 27-28; teaching asst. geology U. Chgo., 1928-30; instr. geophysics Columbia, 1930-40; geophysicist Ill. Geol. Survey, summers 1931-32, 35-37; assoc. geologist U.S. Geol. Survey, summer 1934; pvt. research, writing 1940-41; sr. analyst Bd. Econ. Warfare, Washington, 1942-43; research geophysicist Shell Oil Co., Houston, 1943-45; assoc. dir. research Shell Oil Co., 1945-51, chief cons. gen. geology, 1951-55; cons. gen. geology Shell Devel. Co., 1956-64; vis. prof. geology and geophysics Stanford U., 1962-63, prof., 1963-68, prof. emeritus, 1968—; vis. prof. geography Johns Hopkins U., spring 1968; regents prof. U. Calif. at Berkeley, spring 1973; mem. adv. bd. U. Calif. at Berkeley (Coll. Engring.), 1974-77; research geophysicist U.S. Geol. Survey, 1964-76; cons. 1976—; mem. U.S. delegation UN Sci. Conf. Conservation and Utilization Resources, Lake Success, N.Y., 1949; mem. com. geophysics Nat. Research Council; adviser Office Naval Research, 1949-51; mem. com. Disposal Radioactive Waste Products, 1955-63; mem. Adv. Selection Com. for Allowing Grants under Fulbright Act, 1950-51; vis. lectr. Calif. Inst. Tech., 1953; mem. vis. com. earth scis. Mass. Inst. Tech., 1958-60; mem. earth scis. adv. panel NSF, 1953-57, chmn., 1954-57; vis. lectr. Stanford U., 1955, M.I.T., 1959; regents lectr. UCLA, 1960; mem. vis. com. inst. geophysics and planetary scis. U. Calif., 1961; mem. com. natural resources Nat. Acad. Scis., 1961-62; chmn. div. earth scis. Nat. Acad. Scis.-NRC, 1963-65; nat. adv. bd. U. Nev. Desert Research Inst., 1967-73; mem. com. resources and man NRC, 1966-70. Author: Energy Resources, The Theory of Groundwater Motion and Related Papers, U.S. Energy Resources, A Review as of 1972; co-author: Energy for Ourselves and Our Posterity, Resources and Man, Structural Geology; Editor: Geophysics, 1947-49; assoc. editor: Jour. Geology, 1958-82, Bull. Am. Assn. Petroleum Geologists, 1955-74; Contbr. articles to profl. jours. Trustee, sec. Population Reference Bur., 1966-72; lectr. exec. seminars U.S. Civil Service, Office of Personnel Mgmt., 1971-84, USIA lectr., Europe, 1975, 77. Recipient Lucas medal AIME, 1971, hon. mem. 1978; Rockefeller Pub. Service award, 1977; William Smith medal Geol. Soc. London, 1978; Elliott Cresson medal for outstanding work in field of geology Franklin Inst., Phila., 1981; Vetlesen prize gold medal and cash award Columbia U., 1981. Mem. Am. Acad. Arts and Scis. (life), AAAS (life), Nat. Acad. Scis., Geol. Soc. Am. (Day medal 1954, Penrose medal 1973, council 1947-49, pres. 1962), Internat. Union Geol. Scis. (U.S. nat. com. 1961-64, com. on geosci. and man 1972-76); mem. Am. Assn. Petroleum Geologists (hon., Distinguished lectr. U.S. and Can. 1945, 52, 73-74), Am. Geophys. Union (life), Soc. Petroleum Engrs. (hon., Distinguished lectr. 1963-64), Soc. Exploration Geophysicists (hon.), Canadian Soc. Petroleum Geologists (hon.), 28th Interat. Geol. Congress (hon.), Sigma Xi, Gamma Alpha. Club: Cosmos (Washington). Home: 5208 Westwood Dr Bethesda MD 20816 *

HUBBS, RONALD M., retired insurance company executive; b. Silverton, Oreg., Apr. 27, 1908; s. George W. and Ethel (Burch) H.; B.A., U. Oreg.; LL.D. (hon.), William Mitchell Coll. Law, Macalester Coll. H.L.D., (hon.), Carleton Coll.; m. Margaret S. Jamie, Sept. 9, 1935; 1 son, George J. With St. Paul Fire & Marine Ins. Co., 1936-77, asst. to pres., 1948-52, v.p., 1952-59, exec. v.p., 1959-63; pres., chief exec., 1963-68, chmn., 1968-73; pres., chief exec. officer St. Paul Cos., Inc., 1968-73, chmn., 1973-77; past dir. Western Life Ins. Co., chmn. Toro Credit Co.; past chmn. AFIA Worldwide Ins. Past bd. dirs. Minn. Council on Econ. Edn.; bd. dirs., founding trustee Twin Cities Pub. TV Corp.; trustee James H. Hill Reference Library; adv. bd. U. Minn. Sch. Mgmt.; task force U. Minn. Writing Standards, Lt. Gov. Minn. on Womens' History Ctr.; Gov.'s Adv. Com. on Literacy; bd. dirs. emeritus William Mitchell Coll. Law; trustee Coll. St. Thomas, Carleton Coll.; retired chmn. bd. trustees F.R. Bigelow Found.; past trustee, past chmn. Ins. Inst. Am.; mem., past chmn. pres.'s council St. Catherine's Coll.; gov. Internat. Inst. Seminars, Inc.; bd. dirs. Charles Lindbergh Fund, Cath. Digest; bd. overseers emeritus U. Minn. Sch. Mgmt.; bd. dirs. Inst. Philos. Research; trustee St. Paul Found., North Star Found.; bd. overseers Hill Monastic Manuscript Library and Univ. Without Walls; trustee Sci. Mus. Minn. elector Ins. Hall Fame. Served from 1st lt. to col. AUS, World War II. Decorated Legion of Merit; recipient St. Thomas Aquinas medal Coll. St. Thomas; creative leadership in adult edn. award MACAE; Life-long learning award Met. State U.; Disting. Community Builder award Indianhead council Boy Scouts Am.; Great Living St. Paulite award St. Paul C. of C.; Pres. Council award Minn. Pvt. Colls.; King's medal Carl XVI Gustaf of Sweden; Disting. Service award Minn. Humanities Commn.; Humanitarian award St. Paul YWCA; Headman award Minn. Council on Edn.; John Myers award for community service. Mem. Am. Inst. Property and Liability Underwriters (past chmn., trustee), Orgn. Am. Historians, Minn. Hist. Soc. (past pres.), Co. Mil. Historians, Sherlock Holmes Soc. of London, Orchid Soc., Alpha Tau Omega, Phi Delta Phi, Scabbard and Blade, Friars, Beta Gamma Sigma. Episcopalian (past trustee diocese Minn.). Club: Minn. (past pres.). Home: 689 W Wentworth Ave #102 Saint Paul MN 55118 Office: 385 Washington St Saint Paul MN 55102

HUBEL, DAVID HUNTER, physiologist, educator; b. Windsor, Ont., Can., Feb. 27, 1926; s. Jesse Hervey and Elsie (Hunter) H.; m. Shirley Ruth Izzard, June 20, 1953; children: Carl Andrew, Eric David, Paul Matthew. B.Sc., McGill U., 1947, M.D., 1951, D.Sc. (hon.), 1978; A.M. (hon.), Harvard U., 1962; D.Sc. (hon.), U. Man., 1983. Intern Montreal Gen. Hosp., 1951-52; asst. resident neurology Montreal Neurol. Inst., 1952-53, fellow clin. neurophysiology, 1953-54; asst. resident neurology Johns Hopkins Hosp., 1954-55; sr. fellow neurol. scis. group Johns Hopkins U., 1958-59; faculty Harvard U. Med. Sch., 1959—, George Packer Berry prof. physiology, chmn. dept., 1967-68, George Packer Berry prof. neurobiology, 1968-82, John Franklin Enders univ. prof., 1982—; George H. Bishop lectr. exptl. neurology Washington U., St. Louis, 1964; Jessup lectr. biol. scis. Columbia, 1970; James Arthur lectr. Am. Mus. Natural History, 1972; Ferrier lectr. Royal Soc. London, 1972; Harvey lectr. Rockefeller U., 1976; Weizmann meml. lectr. Weizmann Inst. Sci., Rehovot, Israel, 1979; Fenn lectr. 30th internat. congress Internat. Union Psychol. Sci., Vancouver, B.C., Can., 1986. Served with AUS, 1955-58. Recipient Trustees Research to Prevent Blindness award, 1971; Lewis S. Rosenstiel award for disting. work in basic med. research, 1972; Karl Spencer Lashley prize Am. Philos. Soc., 1977; Louisa Gross Horwitz prize Columbia U., 1978; Dickson prize in Medicine U. Pitts., 1979; Ledlie prize Harvard U., 1980; Nobel prize, 1981; Sr. fellow Harvard Soc. Fellows, 1971—. Fellow Am. Acad. Arts and Scis.; mem. Nat. Acad. Sci., Am. Physiol. Soc. (Bowditch lectr. 1966), Deutsche Akademie der Naturforscher Leopoldina, Soc. for Neurosci. (Grass lecture 1976), Assn. for Research in Vision and Ophthalmology (Friedenwald award 1975), Johns Hopkins U. Soc. Scholars, Am. Philos. Soc. (Karl Spencer Lashley prize 1977), Royal Soc. London (fgn.). Home: 98 Collins Rd Waban MA 02168 Office: Harvard Med Sch Dept Neurobiology 220 Longwood Ave Boston MA 02115

HUBENY, PHILLIP CHARLES, oil company executive, inventor; b. Chgo., Aug. 18, 1952; s. Charles Raymond and Arlene Francis (Dresden) H. B.A. in Lit., U. Md.-Balt., 1974; postgrad. Nicholls State U., 1980, U. Tex.-Austin, 1983, La. State U., 1983; B.S. in Mech. Engring., Kennedy Western U., 1986. Security cons., Atlanta, 1975-77; operator Texhoma Contractors, Grand Island, La., 1977-79; head maintenance operator Conoco Inc., New Orleans, 1979—; sole propr. Sunset Enterprises, Cottonport, La., 1982—. vice chmn. Gulf South Compression Conf., 1987. Inventor pressure sensor, pressure relief valve. Mem. Cottonport Vol. Fire Dept., 1981; adv. bd. Am. Security Council, 1983. Served with U.S. Army, 1971-75. Mem. U.S. Jaycees. Roman Catholic. Home: 823 Coco Ave Cottonport LA 71327 Office: Sunset Enterprises PO Box 247 Cottonport LA 71327

HUBER, BRUNO, corporate executive; b. Zurich, Switzerland, Oct. 8, 1934; s. Hermann and Ida (Manz) H.; m. Barbara Freitag, Feb. 20, 1970; children—Pascale, Michael. Grad. Zurich (Switzerland) Comml. High Sch. Mng. dir. Sankyo Seiki Mfg. Co. of Japan, Bern, Switzerland, 1976—, European exec., 1982—. Home: Pourtalesstr 93, Muri bei, CH-3074 Bern Switzerland Office: Sankyo (Schweiz) AG, Morgenstrasse 70, 3018 Bern Switzerland

HUBER, DAVID, oil company executive; b. Toronto, Ont., Can., Apr. 19, 1950; s. David Grant and Mary (Shelley) H.; m. Cynthia Kirk, Apr. 24, 1976. B.S.M.E., U. Alta., Edmonton, Can., 1972; M.S. in Ocean Engring., Oreg. State U., 1974. Sr. drilling engr. Exxon Corp., Houston, 1974-78, drilling engring. supr., Rio De Janeiro, Brazil, 1978-79; cons. drilling supt. Danish Oil & Natural Gas, Copenhagen, 1979-81; chief drilling engr. Hamilton Bros. Oil Co., Aberdeen, Scotland, 1981-82, engring. mgr., 1982-86, planning and econs. mgr., 1986—. Inventor subsea prodn. trees, diving vessel well system. Recipient Best Paper award and Gold medal Engring. Inst. Can., 1972. Mem. Soc. Petroleum Engrs. Avocations: sailing; tennis; climbing. Office: Hamilton Bros Oil & Gas Ltd, Devonshire House, Piccadilly, London W1X 6AQ, England

HUBER, GERHARD, philosopher; b. Basel, Switzerland, Sept. 4, 1923; s. Adolf and Emma (Gertsch) H.; Dr.iur., U. Basel, 1947, Dr.phil., 1950; m. Elfriede Abrahamowicz, Sept. 7, 1948; 2 children. Lectr., then reader Basel U., 1954-62; prof. philosophy and edn. Swiss Fed. Inst. Tech., Zurich, 1956—; pres. Swiss Sci. Council, 1978-82. Mem. Internat. Inst. Philosophy, Swiss Philos. Soc. Author: Das Prinzip der Effektivität im Völkerrecht, 1947, Platons dialektische Ideenlehre nach dem zweiten Teil des Parmenides, 1951, Das Sein und das Absolute, 1955, Gegenwärtigkeit der Philosophie, 1975. Home: Berghaldenstrasse 36c, CH-8053 Zürich Switzerland Office: ETH Zentrum, CH-8092 Zürich Switzerland

HUBER, HELMUTH PAUL, psychology educator; b. Vienna, Austria, Apr. 26, 1937; s. Franz and Helene (Ostermeyer) H.; m. Helga Fremuth, June 15, 1961; children: Christian, Helmut. PhD, U. Vienna, 1961. Head of exptl. clin. psychology unit U. München (Fed. Republic Germany), 1972-74; prof. clin. psychology U. Hamburg (Fed. Republic Germany), 1974-80, U. Graz (Austria), 1980—; dir. Inst. Psychology U. Graz, 1983—; faculty dean natural scis. U. Graz, 1987—. Author: Psychometric Single-Case Assessment, 1973. Mem. Deutsche Gesellschaft Für Psychologie, Deutsche Gesellschaft Für Psychophysiologie U. Ihre Anwendung, Deutsche Gesellschaft Für Neuropsychopharmakologie, Internat. Biometric Soc. Office: U Graz, Schubertstrasse 6a, A-8010 Graz Austria

HUBER, JÜRG, microbiologist, researcher; b. Zurich, Switzerland, Sept. 14, 1944; came to Fed. Republic of Germany, 1973; s. Gustav and Verena (Holzmann) H.; m. Monika Rösselet, Sept. 21, 1973. MS, Swiss Fed. Inst. Tech., 1967, PhD, 1973. Asst. prof. Swiss Fed. Inst. Tech., Zurich, 1968-73; research biologist Fed. Biol. Research Ctr., Darmstadt, Fed. Republic of Germany, 1973—; section organizer Internat. Entomology Congress, Hamburg, Fed. Republic of Germany, 1984, Vancouver, B.C., Can., 1988; nominated mem. study group Internat. Orgn. for Biol. Control, 1985—. Contbr. 50 articles on insect pathology to profl. jours. and books; research dir. for programs on microbiological pest control. Mem. Soc. Invertebrate Pathology, Swiss Entomol. Soc. Office: Biologische Bundesanstalt, Heinrichstr 243, 6100 Darmstadt Federal Republic of Germany

HUBERMAN, ALAN MICHAEL, psychology and education educator; b. Cambridge, Mass., Dec. 25, 1940; s. Joel Milton and Dorothy (Frankel) H.; m. Laurie Lamartine, Sept. 9, 1974; children—Yvan, Anthony, Benjamin, David. B.A. magna cum laude, Princeton U., 1962; M.A., Harvard U., 1965, Ph.D., 1970. Program specialist UNESCO, Paris, 1967-70; vis. assoc. prof. U. Geneva, 1970-72, prof., 1972—, co-dir. faculty of psychology and edn., 1972-76; vis. prof. U. Bristol, Eng., 1972, Stanford U., Calif., 1977-78, U. Montreal, Que., Can., 1983, Am. U., Washington, 1979-81; cons. UNESCO, OECD, World Bank, univs., founds., govt. Author 8 books including Qualitative Data Analysis, 1984; Innovation Up Close, 1984; contbr. numerous articles to profl. jours. Recipient numerous research grants, 1972—. Mem. Am. Edni. Research Assn., Swiss Ednl. Research Assn. (mem. editorial bds. Edn. et Recherche 1981—, Knowledge 1985—). Avocations: skiing; tennis. Office: U Geneva, Pl de l'Universite, 1211 Geneva 4 Switzerland

HUBERT, JEAN-CLAUDE, information services executive; b. Nevilly, France, Sept. 22, 1941; s. Jacques and Jeanne-Marie H.; m. Michele Rousseau, July 19, 1965; children—Martin, Nicolas. License es Sciences, Institut du Genie Chimique-Toulouse, 1966, Engr., 1967; grad. in chem. engring., U. London, 1968. Sales mgr. Honeywell Bull., Paris, 1971-76; mktg. mgr. HBNIS, Paris, 1976-78; v.p. GSI, Paris, 1978-82; chmn., chief exec. officer GSI-ECO, Paris, 1982—; dir. Carnegie Group Inc., Pitts. Office: GSI-ECO, 25 Bd Amiral Bruix, 75782 Paris France

HUBERT, JEAN-LUC, chemical executive; b. Metz, Moselle, France, Mar. 13, 1960; s. Andre and Franziska (Schmidt) H. Diplome Ingenieur, Ecole Centrale Paris, 1982, advanced engring., 1982; MS in Mech. and Nuclear Engring., Northwestern U., 1985. Simulation engr. Didier Werke, Wiesbaden, Fed. Republic Germany, 1981; engr. Iron and Steel Research inst., Metz, France, 1983; applications engr. L'Air Liquide, Paris, 1985-86; R&D mgr. cryogenic refrigeration processes Liquid Air Corp., Countryside, Ill., 1986—; new process devel. cons. Liquid Air Corp./Energy Systems, Lake Charles, La. Served to 2d lt. French Navy, 1982-83. Tuition fellow Georges Lurcy Found., 1984, Henri Blanchenay fellow French Inst., 1984, Bieneck/Didier fellow, Fed. Republic of Germany, 1984. Mem. Am. Soc. Mech. Engrs. (assoc.), Internat. Inst. Refrigeration (assoc.), Inst. Food Technologists. Home: 6103 Knollwood Rd Willowbrook IL 60514 Office: Liquid Air Corp Applied Tech Ctr 5230 S East Ave Countryside IL 60525

HÜBLER, ANDRÁS, phycist; b. Székesfehérvár, Hungary, Nov. 6, 1951; s. József and Julianna (Geszler) H.; m. Éva Hajba, Feb. 26, 1977; children: Gábor, Márton, Veronika. MS, Eötvös U. Scis., Budapest, Hungary, 1976; Doctor Tech., Tech. U., Budapest, Hungary, 1984. External researcher Tech. U., Budapest, 1974-83; researcher Research Inst. for Electronics, Budapest, 1976-78; asst. prof. Kandó Coll. for Electronics, Székesfehérvár, 1978-87; phycist Medata Datenverarbeitung, Sinsheim, Fed. Republic Germany, 1987—; cons. Ikarus Wehicle Works, Székesfehérvár, 1983-87. Contbr. articles to profl. and sci. jours. Roman Catholic. Office: Medata Datenverarbeitung, Am Breiten Bäumchen, 6920 Sinsheim Federal Republic of Germany

HUBLER, JULIUS, artist; b. Granite City, Ill., Dec. 11, 1919; s. Voyle and Marie (Lewedag) H.; m. Loretta Lanter, Apr. 26, 1943; children: Stuart Alden, Ann Marlowe McClure. B.S., S.E. Mo. U., 1943; M.A., Ed.D., Columbia U., 1951. Sci. tchr. Wibaux High Sch., Mont., 1942-43, Ashton High Sch., Idaho, 1943-45; art instr. CCNY, 1946-48; prof. art SUNY-Buffalo, 1948-82; freelance artist Buffalo, 1982—; painter, graphic designer, sculptor, photographer. Exhibited in internat. show Taipei Mus. Fine Arts, 1983-88. Mem. Western N.Y. Peace Ctr. Deans scholar State U. Iowa grad. scholar, 1944; Arthur W. Dow scholar Columbia U., 1947; disting. service awardee U. Buffalo, 1958. Mem. AAUP (dir., pres. N.Y. state chpt. 1956-60), Soc. Am. Graphic Artists (Warren Mack Meml. purchase award 1962), NAD (assoc.; Samuel F.B. Morse medal 1977, Anonymous prize 1980), Amnesty Internat., Brit.-N.Am. Philatelic Assn. Clubs: Buffalo Stamp, Helvetia Am. Address: 94 Danbury Ln Buffalo NY 14217

HUBLEY, DOROTHY GRAYBILL, musician, educator; b. Lititz, Pa., Sept. 9, 1921; d. Rufus Royce and Mary Elizabeth (Fink) Graybill; student Washington U., St. Louis, 1939, St. Louis Inst. Music, 1964, Ithaca Coll., 1959; m. John A. Hubley, Jr., Aug. 6, 1943; 1 son, John A. III. Music tchr., Lititz, 1940-43, 59—. Bd. dirs. Lancaster County Youth Symphony, 1966-73. Mem. Lancaster (pres. 1971-73, 86—), Pa. (treas 1971-86, Disting. Service award 1976) Music Tchrs. Assns., Nat. Guild Piano Tchrs. (chmn. Lancaster center), Music Tchrs. Nat. Assn., Nat. Fedn. Music Clubs., Am. Coll. Musicians (cert. tchr.). Address: 413 S Cherry St Lititz PA 17543

HUBLEY, REGINALD ALLEN, publisher; b. New Rochelle, N.Y., Aug. 21, 1928; s. Reginald McDonald and Eleanor Francis (Stock) H.; m. Karleen J. Smith, Apr. 7, 1979; children: Brandon, Caroline, Matthew. B.S. in Commerce and Fin., Bucknell U., 1952. Salesman McGraw Hill Pub. Co., N.Y.C., N.J., 1952-54; dist. mgr. Elec. Constrn. and Maintenance, and Elec. Wholesaling publs., Cleve., 1954-59; sales mgr. Elec. Constrn. and Maintenance, and Elec. Wholesaling publs., N.Y.C., 1959-63; pub. Elec. Constrn. and Maintenance, and Elec. Wholesaling publs., 1963-69, Nucleonics Week, Nucleonics & Sci. Research, N.Y.C., 1966-69, Aviation Week and Space Tech., N.Y.C., 1969—, Am. Machinist, N.Y.C., 1976—; v.p. European ops. McGraw-Hill Pub. Co., London, 1979-87, v.p. internat., 1987—. Served with USN, 1946-48, PTO. Fellow Inst. of Dirs., London; mem. Internat. Fedn. Periodical Pubs. (exec. com.), Aviation Hall of Fame (bd. nominations 1971—). Republican. Baptist.

HUC, PIERRE VINCENT FRANCOIS, neurologist; b. Antibes, France, Jan. 29, 1935; s. André and Yvonne (Marcerou) DeDainville; m. Maryse Comes, July 26, 1956; children: Henri, Catherine. Student, Ecole Santé Nevale, Bordeaux, 1955-60; MD, Med. U., Bordeaux, 1960. Externe des hopitaux Bordeaux's Hosp., 1956-60, attaché de neurologie, 1961-65; neurologist Med. U., Bordeaux, 1961-65; epileptologist Med. U., Marseille, 1969—; cons. in neurology and epileptology, 1966—; expert près les Tribunaux. Served to capt. French Mil., 1961-62. Mem. Ligue Française Contre Epilepsie, Internat. Bur. for Epilepsy. Home: 8 Pl Gambetta, 66000 Perpignan France Office: 2 Rue Elie Delcros, 66000 Perpignan France

HUCK, LEWIS FRANCIS, lawyer, real estate consultant and developer; b. Bklyn., Mar. 19, 1912; s. Frank and Jessie (Green) H.; LL.B., St. John's U., 1938, LL.M., 1939; m. Frances M. Love, Jan. 7, 1950 (dec. 1985); children—Janet Ahearn, L. Frank, William G., Robert L., James J.; m. Virginia I. Reid, Apr. 18, 1987. Admitted to N.Y. bar, 1939, also Tex., Mass. bars; practice law, 1939—; with trust dept. Guaranty Trust Co. N.Y., 1929-41; atty. Gen. Electric Co., Schenectady, 1945-47, chem. counsel, 1947-48, atomic energy counsel, 1948-51, gen. mgr., Richland, Wash., 1951-55; asst. to exec. v.p. Gen. Dynamics Corp., 1955-57; lawyer, real estate cons. and developer, 1957-68; v.p., dir., cons. real estate devel. Eastern Airlines, Inc., 1968-88; pres. Huck Enterprises Co. Inc., 1980—. Served maj. AUS, 1941-45. Mem. Tex., N.Y., Mass. Bar Assns. Democrat. Home: 15084 Kimberley Ln Houston TX 77079 Office: Huck Enterprises Co Inc 14518 Hempstead Way Houston TX 77040

HUDDLESTON, LAUREN B(EULAH), futurist researcher, oil company executive, human resource developer; b. Nashville, Nov. 19, 1933; d. John and Chattie (Rich) H.; m. Gilbert Taylor, Aug. 25, 1950 (div. July 1972); children: Jeffrey, Charles, Marianne; m. Robert W. Fisher, Apr. 5, 1976. BA, Stephens Coll., 1980; MSW, U. Denver, 1984, PhD, 1988. Clinician, psychotherapy tchr. Halcyon, Inc., Lafayette, Ind., 1972-76; biofeedback specialist New Orleans Ctr. for Psychotherapy, 1976-78; cons. organizational design and human resource devel., orgnl. design The Anchoring System, Denver, 1972—; adminstrv. dir., v.p. Bradden Exploration, Denver, 1981-86; pres., chief exec. officer Fisher Energy Group, Denver, 1986—; developer wellness and peer counseling program Srs. Resource Ctr. Jefferson County, Denver, 1982-84. Co-organizer Citizens for Responsible Devel. of Bergen Park, Evergreen, Colo., 1983; dean search com. Grad. Sch. Social Work, Denver U., 1982—. Mem. Nat. Assn. Social Workers, World Future Soc., Internat. Transactional Analysis Assn. (clin. cert.), Nat. Assn. Female Execs., Ind. Petroleum Assn. Mountain States, Am. Mgmt. Assn., Internat. Platform Assn. Office: Fisher Energy Group 1020 15th St 4 L Denver CO 80202

HUDDLESTON, ROBERT LESLIE, metallurgist; b. Covington, Va., Nov. 15, 1928; s. George Leslie and Leslie Blanche (McCaleb) H.; B.S. Metall. Engring., Va. Poly. Inst., 1950; M. Liberal Arts, Johns Hopkins U., 1971; m. Shirley Jean Reynolds, May 29, 1953; children—Rebecca, Robert Leslie, Emily. Metallurgist, Detroit Induction Heating Co., 1950-51; ordnance engr. Aberdeen Proving Ground (Md.), 1951-53, supervisory metallurgist, 1956-74, chief, phys. test br., material testing directorate, 1974-81; head internat. test standardization group Army Test and Evaluation Command, 1981-85; cons., 1985—; sr. metallurgist Koppers Co., Balt., 1953-54; project leader Quadripartite Standardization Project, 1974-81; mem. NATO Working Party on Standardization, 1975-81. State div. dir. Izaak Walton League Am., 1974-75. Registered profl. engr., Calif. Served with Ordnance Corps. U.S. Army, 1954-56. Fellow Am. Soc. Nondestructive Testing; mem. Am. Soc. Metals, ASTM, Nat. Soc. Profl. Engrs., Am. Def. Preparedness Assn., Nat. Rifle Assn., Washington Soc. Engrs., Alpha Phi Omega, Tau Beta Pi. Republican. Mem. Christian Ch. Contbr. articles to profl. jours. Home: 301 Glenville Rd Churchville MD 21028

HUDELSON, GEORGE DAVID, retired manufacturing company executive; b. Bedford, Ind., Nov. 16, 1920; s. William E. and Mabel C. (Bair) H.; m. Patricia L. Night; children: David, Peter, Patricia. B.M.E., Purdue U., 1943; M.Sc., Ohio State U., 1951. Registered profl. engr., Ohio. Research engr. Wright Aero. Corp., 1943-44, NACA, 1944-47; asst. prof. mech. engring. Ohio State U., 1947-57; with Carrier Corp., 1957-86; asso. dir. research Carrier Corp., Syracuse, N.Y., 1970-72; v.p. engring. and dir. research Carrier Corp., 1972-86, retired; mem. indsl. adv. com. Herrick Labs., Purdue U.; mem. audit and rev. com. Accreditation Bd. Engring. and Tech., 1980—; cons. air conditioning design. Charter mem. industry adv. com. to Coll. Engring., Syracuse U., 1981. Contbg. editor: Production Handbook, 2d edit, 1958—. Recipient Disting. Alumnus award Purdue U., 1977, Disting. Alumnus award Ohio State U., 1979. Fellow ASHRAE. Presbyterian. Club: Willowbank Yacht. Home: 1946 Chard Rd Cazenovia NY 13035

HUDGINS, CATHERINE HARDING, business executive; b. Raleigh, N.C., June 25, 1913; d. William Thomas and Mary Alice (Timberlake) Harding; m. Robert Scott Hudgins IV, Aug. 20, 1938; children: Catherine Harding, Deborah Ghiselin, Robert Scott V. BS, N.C. State U., 1929-33; grad. tchr. N.C. Sch. for Deaf, 1933-34. Tchr. N.C. Sch. for Deaf, Morganton, 1934-36; sec. Dr. A.S. Oliver, Raleigh, 1937; tchr. N.J. Sch. for Deaf, Trenton, 1937-39; sec. Robert S. Hudgins Co., Charlotte, N.C., 1949—, v.p., treas., 1960—, also bd. dirs. Mem. Jr. Service League, Easton, Pa., 1939; project chmn. ladies aux. Profl. Engrs. N.C., 1954-55, pres., 1956-57; pres. Christian High Sch. PTA, 1963; program chmn. Charlotte Opera Assn., 1959-61, sec., 1961-63; sec. bd. Hezekiah Alexander House Restoration, 1949-52, Hezekiah Alexander House Aux., 1975—, treas., 1983-84, v.p., 1984-85, pres., 1985—; sec. Hezediah Alexander Found., 1986—; past chmn. home missions, annuities and relief Women of Presbyn. Ch., past pres. Sunday Sch. class. Mem. N.C. Hist. Assn., English Speaking Union, Internat. Platform Assn., Mint Mus. Drama Guild (pres. 1967-69), Daus. Am. Colonists (state chmn. nat. def. 1973-74, corr. sec. Virginia Dare chpt. 1978-79, 84-85, state insignia chmn. 1979-80), DAR (mem. nat. chmn.'s assn., nat. officers club; chpt. regent 1957-59, chpt. chaplain 1955-57 N.C. program chmn. 1961-63, state chmn. nat. def. 1973-76, state rec. sec. 1977-79, state regent 1979-82, hon. state regent 1982—), Children Am. Revolution (N.C. sr. pres. 1963-66, sr. nat. corr. sec., 1966-68, sr. nat. 1st v.p. 1968-70, sr. nat. pres. 1970-72, hon. sr. nat. pres. life 1972—; 2d v.p. Nat. Officers Club, 1st v.p. 1977-79, pres. 1979-81), Huguenot Soc. N.C. Club: Carmel Country (Charlotte), Viewpoint 24 (v.p. 1986, pres. 1987). Home: 1514 Wendover Rd Charlotte NC 28211 Office: PO Box 17217 Charlotte NC 28211

HUDGINS, DUDLEY RODGER, pharmaceutical company official; b. Chgo., Nov. 4, 1937; s. Dudley Wallace and Helen (Sterling) H.; B.A. in Psychology, Kans. U., 1959; m. Pegge Resch, Aug. 8, 1975; children—Brian, Randy; stepchildren—Todd Woods, Mianne Woods. With Marion Labs., Inc., 1961—, tng. mgr., also bids and contracts mgr., 1970-72, dir. pharm. div., 1972-82, dir. sales tng. and devel. for entire co., Kansas City, Mo., 1982—; cons. in field. Pres. Zion Luth. Ch., 1980; condr. chapel service City Union Mission, Kansas City. Served with AUS, 1960. Recipient Nat. Builder's award Marion Labs., 1979, 85, Marion Presdl. award, 1985. Mem. Nat. Soc. Pharm. Sales Trainers (chpt. pres. 1978-79, nat. pres. 1979-80, hon. life). Home: 511 W 123d Terr Kansas City MO 64145 Office: 10236 Bunker Ridge Rd Kansas City MO 64137

HUDIK, MARTIN FRANCIS, hospital administrator, educator, consultant; b. Chgo., Mar. 27, 1949; s. Joseph and Rose (Ricker) H; 1 child, Theresa Abraham. BS in Mech. and Aerospace Engring., Ill. Inst. Tech., 1971; BPA, Jackson State U., 1974; MBA, Loyola U., Chgo., 1975; postgrad. U. Sarasota, 1975-76. Cert. health care safety mgr., hazard control mgr., hazardous materials mgr.; cert. police and security firearms instr., Ill. and Nat. Rifle Assn. With Ill. Masonic Med. Ctr., Chgo., 1969—, dir. risk mgmt., 1974-79, asst. adminstr., 1979—; lt. tng. div. Cicero (Ill.) Police Dept., part-time 1971—; instr. Nat. Safety Council Safety Tng. Inst., Chgo., 1977-85; cons. mem. Council Tech. Users Consumer Products, Underwriters Labs., Chgo., 1977—; instr., lt. U.S. Def. Civil Preparedness Agy. Staff Coll., Battle Creek, Mich., 1977-85. Pres. sch. bd. Mary Queen of Heaven Sch., Cicero, 1977-79, 84-86; pres. Mary Queen of Heaven Ch. Council, 1979-81, 83-86; pres. I.M.M.C. Employee Club, 1983-86. Ill. State scholar, 1969-71. Mem. Am. Coll. Healthcare Execs., Am. Soc. Hosp. Risk Mgmt., Nat. Fire Protection Assn., Am. Soc. Safety Engrs., Am. Soc. Law and Medicine, Ill. Hosp. Security and Safety Assn. (co-founder 1976, founding pres. 1976-77, hon. dir. 1977-82), Cath. Alumni Club Chgo. (bd. dirs. 1983-84, 86, exec. bd 1984, 86), Mensa, Pi Tau Sigma, Tau Beta Pi, Alpha Sigma Nu. Republican. Roman Catholic. Lodges: KC (Cardinal council), Masons. Office: 836 W Wellington Ave Chicago IL 60657

HUDSON, CELESTE NUTTING, educator, reading clinic administrator, consultant; b. Nashville, Sept. 18; d. John Winthrop Chandler and Hilda Bass (Alexander) Nutting; m. Frank Alden Hudson III, Dec. 30, 1948 (dec.); children—Frank Alden IV (dec.), Jo Ann Hudson Algermissen, Celeste Jane Hudson Hayes, John Winthrop Nutting. B.S., Oreg. Coll. Edn., 1952; M.S., So. Ill. U., 1963, Ph.D., 1973. Cert. tchr., Tenn., Oreg., Mo., Iowa. Tchr. pub. schs., Crossville, Tenn., 1949-51, Salem, Oreg., 1952-53, West Walnut Manor and Jennings, Mo., 1953-54, Normandy Sch. Dist., St. Louis County, Mo., 1954-66; reading coordinator Sikeston (Mo.) Pub. Schs., 1966-71; traveling cons. Ednl. Devel. Labs., Huntington, N.Y., 1970-71; mem. clin. staff So. Ill. U. Reading Ctr., 1972; asst. prof. edn. St. Ambrose Coll., 1972-75, U. Tenn.-Chattanooga, 1975-76; project dir. Learning Skills Ctr., St. Ambrose Coll., 1976-80, asst. prof. edn., 1976-78, assoc. prof., 1979-86 , dir. elem. edn., 1972-75, 76—, chmn. dept. edn., 1980-84, div. chmn., 1984-87, prof. edn., 1986—, dir. Reading Clinic, 76—; cons. reading. Mem. Kimberly Village Bd., Davenport, Iowa, 1979-83; chmn. worship comm. Asbury Meth. Ch. Mem. Assn. Tchrs. Educators, Assn. Supervision and Curriculum Devel., Internat. Reading Assn. (Scott County council), Am. Assn. Colls. Tchr. Edn., Assn. Tchr. Educators, New Eng. Women (past pres.), Orgn. Tchr. Educators Reading, Internat. Platform Assn., Women in Ednl. Adminstrn., DAR, United Daus. Confederacy, Alpha Delta Kappa (past pres.), Kappa Delta Pi, Phi Delta Kappa. Methodist. Master gardner. Author: Handbook for Remedial Reading, 1967; Cognitive Listening and the Reading of Second Grade Children, 1973. Office: Saint Ambrose U Davenport IA 52806

HUDSON, DENNIS LEE, lawyer, government official; b. St. Louis, Jan. 5, 1936; s. Lewis Jefferson and Helen Mabel (Buchanan) H.; m. Linda Kay Adamson; children—Karen Marie, Karla Sue, Mary Ashley. B.A., U. Ill., 1958; J.D., John Marshall Law Sch., 1972. Bar: Ill. 1972, U.S Dist. Ct. (so. dist.) Ill. 1972, U.S. Dist. Ct. (no. dist.) Ill. 1972. Insp., IRS, Chgo., 1962-72; spl. agt. GSA, Chgo., 1972-78, spl. agt.-in-charge, 1978-83, regional insp. gen., 1983—; supervisory spl. agt., Dept Justice-GSA Task Force, Washington, 1978. Bd. govs. Theatre Western Springs, Ill., 1978-81; deacon Grace Lutheran Ch., LaGrange, Ill., 1977-81. Served with U.S. Army, 1959-61. John N. Jewett scholar, 1972. Mem. ABA, Ill. Bar Assn., Assn. Fed. Investigators. Home: PO Box 113 Western Springs IL 60558 Office: Office Insp Gen GSA Suite 408 230 S Dearborn St Chicago IL 60604

HUDSON, EDWARD VOYLE, linen supply company executive; b. Seymour, Mo., Apr. 3, 1915; s. Marion A. and Alma (Von Gonten) H.; student Bellingham (Wash.) Normal Coll., 1933-36, also U. Wash.; m. Margaret Carolyn Greely, Dec. 24, 1939; children—Edward G., Carolyn K. Asst. to mgr. Natural Hard Metal Co., Bellingham, 1935-37; partner Met. Laundry Co., Tacoma, 1938-39; propr., mgr. Peerless Laundry & Linen Supply Co., Tacoma, 1939—; propr. Independent Laundry & Everett Linen Supply Co., 1946-74, 99 Cleaners and Launderers Co., Tacoma, 1957-79; chmn. Tacoma Public Utilities, 1959-60; trustee United Mut. Savs. Bank; bd. dirs. Tacoma Better Bus. Bur., 1977—. Pres., Wash. Conf. on Unemployment Compensation, 1975-76; pres. Tacoma Boys' Club, 1970; v.p. Puget Sound USO, 1972—; elder Emmanuel Presbyn. Ch., 1974—; past campaign mgr., pres. Tacoma-Pierce County United Good Neighbors. Recipient Disting. Citizen's cert. U.S. Air Force Mil. Airlift Com., 1977; U.S. Dept. Def. medal for outstanding public service, 1978. Mem. Tacoma Sales and Mktg. Execs. (pres. 1957-58), Pacific NW Laundry, Dry Cleaning and Linen Supply Assn. (pres. 1959, treas. 1965—), Internat. Fabricare Inst. (dir. dist. 7 treas. 1979, pres. 1982), Am. Security Council Bd., Tacoma C. of C. (pres. 1965), Air Force Assn. (pres. Tacoma chpt. 1976-77, v.p. Wash. state 1983-84, pres. 1985-86), Navy League, Puget Sound Indsl. Devel. Council (chmn. 1967), Tacoma-Ft. Lewis-Olympia Army Assn. (past pres.) Republican. Clubs: Elks (vice chmn. bd. trustees 1984, chmn. 1985-86), Shriners (potentate 1979), Masons, Scottish Rite, Tacoma, Tacoma Country and Golf, Jesters, Rotary (pres. Tacoma chpt. 1967-68), Tacoma Knife and Fork (pres. 1964). Home: 3901 N 37th St Tacoma WA 98407 Office: Peerless Laundry & Linen Supply Co 2902 S 12th St Tacoma WA 98405

HUDSON, HAROLD DON, veterinarian; b. Audrain County, Mo., Nov. 22, 1943; s. Harold F. and Greta Arlene (Boyd) H.; A.A., Hannibal (Mo.) La Grange Coll., 1963; B.S., U. Mo., 1967, D.V.M., 1970; m. Carole Jacqueline Spence, Aug. 30, 1964; children—Dale Brent, Kim Marie. Asso. Clarinda (Iowa) Vet. Clinic, 1970-71, Bethany (Mo.) Vet. Clinic, 1971-72, Vet. Clinic, Mexico, Mo., 1972—. Mem. AVMA, Mo. Vet. Med. Assn., Am. Assn. Bovine Practitioners, Am. Assn. Swine Practitioners. Baptist. Home: 933 Emmons St Mexico MO 65265 Office: 1624 Hwy 54 E Mexico MO 65265

HUDSON, LEONARD LESTER, former school administrator; b. Decatur, Tex., July 23, 1910; s. Harve Hubert and Laura Hilda (Watson) H.; A.S., Decatur Bapt. Coll., NEA, B.S., N. Tex. State U., 1957, M.Ed., 1960; D.D., Kansas City Bible Coll., 1958; Ph.D., Central Christian Coll., 1963; D. Arts-Religion, Internat. U., 1977, Ph.D. 1978; H.D., World U., 1983; m. Reba Fae Porter, Oct. 16, 1928; children—Robert Lester, Frank L. Clk., asst. mgr. Griffin Grocery, Chickasha, Okla., 1928-43; aircraft foreman Douglas Aircraft Mfg., Oklahoma City, 1943-45; owner Hudson Grocery, Chickasha, 1945-53; instr. Decatur (Tex.) Bapt. Coll., 1953-55, North Tex. State U., Denton, 1955-57; prin. Era (Tex.) Consol. Schs., 1957-61; supt. schs., Beeler, Kans., 1961-66, Ingalls-Alta Vista, Kans., 1966-70, Ford, Kans., 1970-73; adminstr. Bill's Mobile Home Park, Oklahoma City, 1973—. Mem. NEA, Assn. Higher Edn., Am. Assn. Higher Edn., Pi Sigma Alpha. Author: Faith, 1948. Inventor in aircraft field. Home: 5945 S Terry Joe Ave Oklahoma City OK 73129 Office: 2145 SE 59th St Oklahoma City OK 73129

HUDSON, MAURICE GEORGE, transportation engineering and planning executive; b. Hastings, Sussex, Eng., Feb. 22, 1929; s. George Henry and Dorothy Edith (Tildesley) H.; m. Pamela Marjorie Wilkins, Aug. 28, 1954; children: Carolyn Wendy Susan, Timothy Martin George. Diploma in transport studies with merit, U. London, 1969, diploma in urban land studies with merit, 1970. Adminstr., chief engr. London County Council, 1949-59, town and highway planner, chief engr., 1959-65; town and highway planner Dept. Planning and Transp., Greater London Council, 1965-67, project asst. to chief adviser on transport policy, 1967-71, aviation and marine planner, 1971-86; exec. dir. The Avmar Consultancy, London, 1984—; expert adviser, econ., and social com. European Community, Brussels, 1980-81; cons. Parkman Buck Ltd., London, 1987—; vis. lectr. U. Tech., Loughborough, Eng., 1980—. Editor: Airport Technology International, 1988; contbr. articles to profl. jours. Spl. adviser Parliamentary Aviation Com., London, 1981-84; mem. tourism com. London Borough Greenwich, London, 1984-86. Served as sgt. Brit. Army, 1947-49, with Territorial Army, 1949-80. Fellow Royal Soc. Arts, Instn. Highways and Transp.; mem. Royal Aero. Soc. (chmn. air transport com. 1977-80), Chartered Inst. Transport (met. com. 1980—). Mem. Ch. of Eng. Lodges: Guild Freemen City of London, Freemen Co. of Watermen and Lightermen of River Thames. Home: 136 Jerningham Rd, London SE14 5NL, England Office: Avmar Consultancy, 19 Queen Anne's Gate, London SW1H 9BU, England

HUDSON, RICHARD LLOYD, retired educator, clergyman; b. Watertown, N.Y., Dec. 1, 1920; s. Milo Alfred and Marion (Davidson) H.; AB, Syracuse U., 1944; BD, Yale U., 1947, STM, 1950; PhD, Syracuse U., 1970; m. Beatrice Evalin Olson, Apr. 23, 1955; children: Margery Elise, Pamela Kristine. Ordained to ministry United Methodist Ch., 1947; asst. minister Rome (N.Y.) Meth. Ch., 1946-48, Meth. Ch., Parish, N.Y., 1950-54; dir. pub. relations Syracuse Area United Meth. Ch., 1954-56; minister Meth. Ch., Carthage, N.Y., 1956-58; Cokesbury fellow, grad. asst. Syracuse U., 1958-61; mem. faculty Wyoming Sem., Kingston, Pa., 1961-64; mem. faculty New Eng. Coll., Henniker, N.H., 1964-83, prof., 1971-83, prof. emeritus, 1983—, acting dean div. humanities, 1970-71, chmn., Am. studies, 1972-79, coordinator liberal studies, 1981-83, prof. emeritus, 1983—; adj. prof. history Post Coll., Waterbury, Conn., 1985—, Quinnipiac Coll., Haden, Conn., 1987—; resident mgr. The Old Homestead, North Haven, Conn., 1983—. Chmn., Henniker Historic Dist. Commn., 1976-83; docent Canterbury Shaker Village, 1975-83, New Haven Colony Hist. Soc., 1984—. Mem. AAUP, Orgn. Am. Historians, Henniker Hist. Soc. (pres. 1975-81). Author: A Burden for Souls, 1950; A Student's Guide to the New Testament, 1963; The Challenge of Dissent, 1970; editor: The Only Henniker on Earth, 1980. Home and Office: 44 Cloudland Rd North Haven CT 06473

HÜE, JOSEPH ALPHONSE, conservator; b. Foulognes, Calvados, France, Mar. 19, 1932; s. Emile and Marie (Cairon) H.; m. Nicole Lhottelain, Mar. 2, 1957; children: Pascal, Jérôme, François. Lic. ès lettres, U. Sorbonne, Paris, 1964. Diplôme Supérieur des Bibliothèques, Concours de Conservateur. Directeur, fondateur Bibliothèque de l'Univ. Paris X, Nanterre, France, 1964-84; chargé de cours Univ. Paris X, Nanterre, 1967-72; dir. Bibliothèque de Documentation Internat. Contemporaine, Nanterre, 1984—, Musée d'Histoire Contemporaine, Paris, 1984—; cons. AUPELF, Paris, 1964-87, Communautés Européennes, Brussels, 1974-75, Univ. d'Annaba d'Alger de Batna (Algeria), 1977-82, Univ. de Cotonou, Benin, 1984. Co-author: Soldat et Société 1850-1950, 1986, Images de 1917, 1987, Mois de la Photo à Paris, 1986; editor: La France et les Français de la Libération 1944-45, 1984, Soldat et Société 1850-1950, 1986, Législatives, 1986, Les Affiches de la Campagne, 1986, Images de 1917, 1987; contbr. articles to profl. jours. Mem. Conseil Sci. Univ. Paris X, Commn. de sauvegarde des Archives Privées Contemporaines, Conseil de Coordination Sci. de l'Inst. d'Histoire du Temps Présent, Commn. Interministérielle des Musées des Deux Guerres Mondiales, Commn. pour Publ. Documents Diplomatiques, Com. Sci. de la Revue Matériaux pour l'histoire de Notre Temps. Home: 48 rue Monsieur le Prince, 75006 Paris France Office: BDIC, 6 rue de l'Université, 92001 Nanterre France also: Musée d'histoire contemporaine, Hotel National des Invalides, 75007 Paris France

HUENIKEN, HORST ECKHARD, investment banker; b. Ostenholzer Moor, Fed. Republic Germany, June 20, 1958; arrived in Can., 1967; s. Horst Hans and Gerda Ilse (Guenther) H. BASc in Mech. Engring., U. Waterloo, 1982; MBA, U. Western Ont., 1987. Registered profl. engr., Ont.; registered securities broker, Ont. Machine operator Sarco Can. Ltd., Toronto, 1978; programmer IBM Can. Ltd., Toronto, 1978-79; prodn. engr. Hein Lehmann AG, Dusseldorf, Fed. Republic Germany, 1980; nuclear researcher Atomic Energy Can. Ltd., Toronto, 1980; oil and gas engr. Dome Petroleum Ltd., Calgary, Alta., Can., 1981; cons. engr. Giffels Assocs. Ltd., Toronto, 1982-85; mgmt. cons. U. Western Ont., London, 1986; investment banker Burns Fry Ltd., Toronto, 1987—. Editor Mgmt. Cons. Industry Profile, 1987. Organizer Guildwood Community Assn., 1985. Can. Dept. External Affairs internat. bus. scholar, 1986, U. Western Ont. Dean's Honour List scholar, 1987. Mem. Assn. Profl. Engrs. Ont., Ont. Securities Commn. Progressive Conservative party. Lutheran. Home: 133 Euclid Ave, West Hill, Toronto, ON Canada M1C 1K2 Office: Burns Fry Ltd, 1 First Canadian Pl, Suite 5000, PO Box 150, Toronto, ON Canada M5X 1H3

HUESTIS, CHARLES BENJAMIN, educational administrator; b. Seattle, Jan. 27, 1920; s. Claude Erwin and Eloise Marie (Pettit) H.; m. Kathryn Alice Porter, Mar. 1, 1942; children: Stephen Porter, Jeffrey Charles, Robin Rebecca. Student, Griffin Murphy Coll., Seattle, 1938-39, U. Calif. Berkeley, 1946. With Seattle First Nat. Bank, 1941; acct. Rheem Mfg. Co., Richmond, Calif., 1946-51; chief acct. aircraft div. Rheem Mfg. Co., Downey, Calif., 1951-54; corp. comptroller Rheem Mfg. Co., 1954-56; v.p., treas. Hall-Scott Inc., Berkeley, Calif., 1956; exec. v.p., dir., treas. 1956-57; adminstrv. cons. Overseas Nat. Airways, Oakland, Calif., 1957-58; controller El Segundo div. Hughes Aircraft Co., 1958-59, controller Tucson div., 1959, treas., chmn. finance com., 1960-66, v.p., 1962-66; v.p., treas., dir. Am. Mt. Everest Expdn., 1963; v.p. bus. and finance Duke U., Durham, N.C., 1966-83, sr. v.p., 1983-85, sr. v.p. emeritus, 1985—; dir. Technomics, Inc., Falls Church, Va., 1966-76; chmn. bd. Sta. WDBS, 1970-76. Bd. dirs. Santa Barbara (Calif.) Research Ctr., 1959-66; bd. dirs., mem. exec. com. Research Triangle Found., Research Triangle Park, N.C., 1969-85; trustee Research Triangle Inst., Research Triangle Park, 1967-79, Sierra Club Found., 1969-79; commr. N.C. Marine Fisheries, 1985-87; trustee N.C. Nature Conservancy., 1977-86, 87—, chmn., 1979-83; bd. dirs. Univ. Tech. Corp., 1987—, N.C. Ednl. Facilities Fin. Agy., 1987—; climbing leader Duke-Gettysburg Expdn. to Kurdistan, 1982. Mem. Explorers Club (v.p. research and edn. 1987-88), Am. Alpine Club. Home: 1803 Woodburn Rd Durham NC 27705 Office: Duke U Durham NC 27706

HUET, DENISE, mathematics educator; b. Nancy, France, Feb. 2, 1931; d. Maximilien Eugène and Suzanne Henriette (Dubas) H. Agrégation, U. Nancy, 1954; Doctorat d'ét, U. Paris, 1959. Researcher Centre Nat. de la Recherche Sci., Paris, 1955-59; prof. U. Dijon, Dijon, France, 1959-66; vis. prof. Georgetown U., Washington, 1966-67; prof. U. Maryland, College Park, 1967-72, U. Nancy, 1972—. Author: Spectral Analysis, 1976; contbr. articles to profl. jours. Mem. Am. Math. Soc., Soc. Math. de France. Home: 86 Rue FéLix Faure, 54000 Nancy France Office: U Nancy I, Dept de Math BP239, 54506 Vandoeuvre 54506, France

HUETING, JUERGEN, internist; b. Bad Oeynhausen, Fed. Republic Germany, May 21, 1956; s. Karl and Lotte H. Grad. magna cum laude, Groton Sch., Mass., 1974; grad. summa cum laude, Immanuel Kant Gymnasium, Bad Oeynhausen, 1975, MD, U. Giessen, Fed. Republic Germany, 1985. Intern, then resident in internal medicine U. Giessen, 1983-87; mem. staff clin. cardiology Max Planck Soc., Bad Nauheim, Fed. Republic Germany, 1987—. Contbr. articles to prof. jours. Home: Schillerstrasse 39, 6307 Grossen Linden Federal Republic of Germany Office: Kerckhoff-Klinik, Max Plank Soc, Beuehestr 4-6, 6350 Bad Nauheim Federal Republic of Germany

HUETTIG, GERHARD ERNST, purchasing administrator; b. Nuremberg, Fed. Republic of Germany, Dec. 4, 1950; s. Ernst Rolf and Lotte (Lindbuchl) H.; m. Heidrun D. Hoyns, Sept. 2, 1976 (div. 1984). MS, Tech. U., Berlin, 1976, PhD, 1981. Asst. prof. Tech. U., Berlin, 1977-83; sr. scientist Nato-Shape Tech. Ctr., The Hague, The Netherlands, 1983-84; mgr. tech. support Airbus Industries, Toulouse, France, 1984-86; mgr. purchasing Deutsche Lufthansa, Hamburg, Fed. Republic of Germany, 1987—. Office: Deutsche Lufthansa AG, Flughafen, Hamburg Federal Republic of Germany

HUETTNER, RICHARD ALFRED, lawyer; b. N.Y.C., Mar. 25, 1927; s. Alfred F. and Mary (Reilly) H.; children—Jennifer Mary, Barbara Bryan; m. 2d, Eunice Bizzell Dowd, Aug. 22, 1971. Marine Engrs. License, N.Y. State Maritime Acad., 1947; B.S., Yale U. Sch. Engring., 1949; J.D., U. Pa., 1952. Bar: D.C. 1952, N.Y. 1954, U.S. Ct. Mil. Appeals 1953, U.S. Ct. Claims 1961, U.S. Supreme Ct. 1969, U.S. Ct. Appeals (fed. cir.) 1982, also other fed. cts, registered to practice U.S. Patent and Trademark Office 1957, Canadian Patent Office 1968. Engr. Jones & Laughlin Steel Corp., 1954-55; assoc. atty. firm Kenyon & Kenyon, N.Y.C, 1955-61; mem. firm Kenyon & Kenyon, 1961—; specialist patent, trademark and copyright law. Trustee N.J. Shakespeare Festival, 1972-79, sec., 1977-79; trustee Overlook Hosp., Summit, N.J., 1978-84, 86—, vice chmn. bd. trustees, 1980-82, chmn. bd. trustees, 1982-84; trustee Overlook Found., 1981—, chmn. bd. trustees, 1986—; trustee Colonial Symphony Orch., Madison, N.J., 1972-82, v.p. bd. trustees 1974-76. pres. 1976-79; chmn. bd. overseers N.J. Consortium for Performing Arts, 1972-74; mem. Yale U. Council, 1978-81; bd. dirs. Yale Communications Bd., 1978-80; chmn. bd. trustees Center for Addictive Illnesses, Morristown, N.J., 1979-82; rep. Assn. Yale Alumni, 1975-80, chmn. com. undergrad. admissions, 1976-78, bd. govs., 1976-80, chmn. bd. govs., 1978-80; chmn. Yale Alumni Schs. Com. N.Y., 1972-78; assoc. fellow Silliman Coll., Yale U., 1976—; bd. dirs., exec. com. Yale U. Alumni Fund, 1978-81; mem. Yale Class of 1949 Council, 1980—; bd. dirs. Overlook Health Systems, 1984—. Served from midshipman to lt. USNR, 1945-47, 52-54; cert. JAGC 1953; Res. ret. Recipient Yale medal, 1983. Fellow N.Y. Bar Found.; mem. Am., N.Y. State bar assns., Assn. Bar City N.Y., N.Y. Patent-Trademark-Copyright Law Assn. (chmn. com. meetings 1961-64, chmn. com. econ. matters 1966-69, 72-74), AAAS, N.Y. Acad. Scis., N.Y. County Lawyers Assn., Am. Intellectual Property Law Assn., Internat. Patent and Trademark Assn., Am. Judicature Soc., Yale Sci. and Engring. Assn. (v.p. 1973-75, pres. 1975-78, exec. bd. 1972—), Fed. Bar Council. Clubs: Yale (N.Y.C.); Yale of Central N.J. (Summit) (trustee 1973—, pres. 1975-77), Morris County Golf (Convent, N.J.); The Graduates (New Haven). Home: 150 Green Ave Madison NJ 07940 Office: Kenyon & Kenyon One Broadway New York NY 10004

HUEY, WILLIAM EDWARD, food products broker, career consultant, writer; b. Lakewood, Ohio, Apr. 14, 1930; s. William Edward and Virginia (Higgins) H. B.A., Dartmouth, 1952. Sales rep. Mobil Oil Corp., Los Angeles, Tacoma, 1954-56; ptnr. Elmer Langguth Brokerage Co., San Francisco, 1957-75, Forrest Randolph Co., San Francisco, 1957-75; cons. Dalgety Ltd., San Francisco and London, 1976-79; internat. sales/mktg. exec. William Sherman Co., San Rafael, Calif., 1980-85; with Hay Career Cons., San Francisco, 1986—. Adviser Black Boys' Clubs, San Francisco, 1959—; mem. Job Therapy Calif., Spl. Com. on Parolee Employment, San Quentin; pres. bd. dirs. Booker T. Washington Community Service Ctr.; house organ U.S. Jr. C. of C. Contbr. articles to Future mag.; editor: (internat. newsletter) Greenline, Export Fedn., (with others) San Franciscan, 1960-61. Served with USNR, 1952-54, Korea, 1961-62, Vietnam. Mem.

U.S. Navy League, World Affairs Council No. Calif., Kappa Sigma. Clubs: Dartmouth of Calif., Commonwealth of Calif. (San Francisco); W. Atwood Yacht (Los Angeles). Lodges: Masons (32 deg.), Shriners, Elks. Home and Office: 258 Chester Ave San Francisco CA 94132-3215

HUFBAUER, GARY CLYDE, economist, lawyer, educator; b. San Diego, Apr. 3, 1939; s. Clarence Clyde and Arabelle Maxwell (McKee) H.; m. Carolyn Revelle, June 25, 1961; children: Randall Clyde Revelle, Ellen Arabelle Scripps. A.B., Harvard U., 1960; Ph.D., King's Coll., Cambridge U., Eng., 1963; J.D., Georgetown U., 1980. Bar: D.C. 1980, Md. 1980. Mem. faculty dept. econs. U. N.Mex., 1963-74, prof., 1970-74; dir. internat. tax staff Dept. Treasury, Washington, 1974-77; dep. asst. Sec. Treasury, Internat. Trade and Investment Policy, 1977-80; mem. firm Rose, Schmidt, Chapman, Duff & Hasley, Washington, 1980-85; dep. dir. Internat. Law Inst., Georgetown Law Center, 1980-82; sr. fellow Inst. Internat. Econs., 1982-85; Wallenberg prof. fin. Georgetown U., 1985—; mem. Harvard Devel. Adv. Service, Pakistan, 1967-69; vis. prof. Stockholm Sch. Econs., 1974, Cambridge U., 1973, Georgetown U., 1975. Author: Synthetic Materials and the Theory of International Trade, 1966, Economic Sanctions Reconsidered, 1985. Ford Found. fellow, 1966-67; Fulbright research scholar, 1973. Mem. Am. Econ. Assn., Nat. Economists Club. Episcopalian. Home: 3213 Farmington Dr Chevy Chase MD 20815 Office: Georgetown U Sch Fgn Service Washington DC 20057

HUFF, NORMAN NELSON, data processing executive ; b. San Diego, Apr. 22, 1933; s. George Kleineberg Peabody and Norma Rose (Nelson) H.; B.S., San Diego State U., 1957; cert. UCLA, 1972; M.B.A., Golden Gate U., 1972; A.A., bus. cert., Victor Valley Coll., 1972; Cultural D, World U., 1987; m. Sharon Kay Lockwood, Sept. 30, 1979. Chemist, Convair, San Diego, 1954-55, astrophysicist, 1955-56; mgmt. trainee, chem. engr. U.S. Gypsum Co., Plaster City, Calif., 1957-58; instr. data processing Victor Valley Coll., Victorville, Calif., 1967-70, chmn. data processing, 1970-81; owner High Desert Data Systems, 1972-82, chmn. Computer Sci., 1984—; dir. Deputy Gen. Internat. Biog. Ctr., 1987, Congress Proclamation, 1987; mgmt. info. systems cons. Pfizer Inc., 1970-72, Mojave Water Agy. Calif., 1972-74. Served with USNR, 1950-54, to capt. USAF, 1954-67; Vietnam. Recipient Presdl. Achievement award, 1982, Presdl. Medal of Merit, 1983. Mem. Calif. Ednl. Computing Consortium, Am. Mgmt. Assn., Calif. Bus. Edn. Assn. (treas. 1967-73), Inst. Aero. Sci. (pres. 1956-57), Soaring Soc. Am. (life). Author 4 computer sci. texts. Office: 16173 Rimrock Rd Apple Valley CA 92307

HUFF, RUSSELL JOSEPH, public relations and publishing executive; b. Chgo., Feb. 24, 1936; s. Russell Winfield and Virgilist Marie (McMahon) H.; B.A. in Philosophy cum laude, U. Notre Dame, 1958; BS in Theology, Cath. U. Santiago (Chile), 1960; M.A. in Communication Arts, U. Notre Dame, 1968; ordained priest Roman Cath. Ch., 1962; m. Beverly Diane Staschke, 1968, 1 dau., Michelle Lynn. Exec. editor Cath. Boy, and Miss, Notre Dame, Ind., 1963-68; mng. editor Nation's Schs., McGraw Hill, Chgo., 1968-70; v.p. pub. affairs Homart Devel. Co., Chgo., 1971-76; dir. public relations Sears, Roebuck Co. Internat. Ops., Chgo., 1976-82, dir. public affairs Sears Roebuck Found. Internat. Projects, 1981-82; sr. v.p., sales and mktg. dir. Mineca Internat., Inc., Chgo., 1982-84; v.p. pub. relations Lofino Poppa Devel. Corp., Sarasota, Fla., 1984-85; pres., co-owner R.J. Huff & Assocs., Inc., 1985—; real estate broker, 1985—. Recipient Outstanding Mag. award Cath. Press. Assn., 1965, 67; named for Best Cover, Nation's Schs., 1968; cert. Gemological Inst. Am. cert. jr. coll. tchr., Calif. Mem. Pub. Relations Soc. Am. (accredited, past chmn., mem. accreditation com. Chgo. chpt.), Chicagoland Mil. Collectors Soc. (dir. quar. expositions 1981-82), Am. Soc. Mil. Insignia Collectors, Orders and Medals Soc. Am., Nat. Fgn. Trade Council, Public Affairs Council, Conf. Bd., Internat. Bus. Council, Internat. Visitors Center Chgo., Partners of the Ams. (cert. for advancement Latin Am. relations 1980), São Paulo Partners (cert. for advancement Brazil-U.S. relations 1979, dir. Ill.), Chgo. Assn. of Commerce and Industry, U.S.-Spanish C. of C. of Middle West (dir.), War Memorabilia Collectors Soc. (exec. dir.). Roman Catholic. Author: Come Build My Church, 1966; On Wings of Adventure, 1967; Wings of WW II, 1985, Companion to Wings of World War II, 1987; editor, publisher (quarterly jour.) Wings and Things of the World. Home: 4062 Kingston Terr Sarasota FL 34238 Office: PO Box 40023 Sarasota FL 34242-0023

HUFF, WILLIAM JENNINGS, lawyer, educator; b. Summerland, Miss., Mar. 3, 1919; s. William Yancey and Hattie Lenora (Robinson) H.; BS with honors, Miss. State U., 1956; MA (asst. fellow 1956-59), Rice U., 1957, PhD (Tex. Gulf Producing Co. fellow 1960), 1960; LLB, U. Miss., 1947, JD, 1968; m. Frances Ellen Rossman, Feb. 26, 1944; 1 son, John Rossman. Bar: Miss. 1947, Tenn. 1948. Closing atty. Commerce Title Guaranty Co., Memphis, 1947-49; atty., adviser FCC, Washington, 1953-54; asso. prof. geology U. So. Miss., Hattiesburg, 1960-65; asst. prof. natural scis. Mich. State U., East Lansing, 1966-68; assoc. prof. geology U. S. Ala., Mobile, 1968-82; ret., 1982; practice law, Pascagoula, Miss., 1982—. Served with USAF, 1941-45, judge adv., 1949-52; lt. col. USAF ret. Decorated Air medal with ten oak leaf clusters. Mem. ABA, Miss. Bar, Tenn. Bar, Miss. Trial Lawyers Assn., Am.. Trial Lawyers Assn., Am. Assn. Petroleum Geologists, Soc. Econ. Mineralogists and Paleontologists, Paleontol. Research Soc., N.Y. Acad. Sci., Sigma Xi, Phi Delta Phi, Sigma Gamma Epsilon. Lodges: Masons, Shriners. Contbr. articles to various publs. Home: 5917 Montfort Rd S Mobile AL 36608

HUFFMAN, ROBERT ALLEN, JR., lawyer; b. Tucson, Dec. 30, 1950; s. Robert Allen and Ruth Jane (Hicks) H.; m. Marjorie Kavanagh Rooney, Dec. 30, 1976; children—Katharine Kavanagh, Elizabeth Rooney, Robert Allen III. B.B.A., U. Okla., 1973, J.D., 1976. Bar: Okla. 1977, U.S. Dist. Ct. (no. dist.) Okla. 1977, U.S. Ct. Appeals (10th cir.) 1978, U.S. Supreme Ct. 1982. Assoc. Huffman, Arrington, Kihle, Gaberino & Dunn, Tulsa, 1977-81, ptnr. 1981—. Mem. ABA, Tulsa County Bar Assn., Fed. Energy Bar Assn. Republican. Roman Catholic. Clubs: Southern Hills Country (Tulsa), Tulsa Club. Home: 5808 S Delaware Tulsa OK 74105 Office: Huffman Arrington Kihle Gaberino & Dunn 1000 ONEOK Plaza Tulsa OK 74103

HUGDAHL, KENNETH JAN, psychology educator; b. Ostersund, Sweden, Jan. 15, 1948; s. Werner Johan and Selma Kristina (Persson) H.; m. Marit Irene Eriksson, Sept. 14, 1974; children—Anna, Emilia. B.A., Uppsala U., Sweden, 1973, Ph.D. in Psychology, 1977. Research asst. Uppsala U., 1974-78, lectr., 1980-84; prof. psychology U. Bergen, Norway, 1984—; mem. research council Hjellestad Clinic, Bergen, 1985—. Author: Design of Experiments in Psychology, 1988; editor: Handbook of Dichotic Listening, 1988. Editor-in-chief Scandinavian Jour. Behavior Therapy, 1983-84, Uppsala Psychol. Reports, 1980-84, Scandinavian Jour. of Psychology, 1988—; assoc. editor, Jour. of Psychophysiology, 1987—; cons. editor various internat. sci. jours. Contbr. articles to profl. jours., chpts. to books. Am.-Scandinavian Found. research scholar, 1978; Fulbright scholar, Phila., 1979; Recipient NAVF award, Norway, 1988. Mem. Soc. Psychophysiol. Research, Swedish Assn. Behavior Therapy (v.p. 1982-83), Internat. Neuropsychol. Soc., European Neurosci. Assn., Internat. Orgn. Psychophysiology, Pavlovian Soc. Biol. Scis. Home: Birkelundsbakken 36A, N-5040 Paradis Norway Office: U Bergen Dept Somatic Psychology, Arstadveien 21, N-5000 Bergen Norway

HUGE, HARRY, lawyer; b. Deshler, Nebr., Sept. 16, 1937; s. Arthur and Dorothy (Vor de Strasse) H.; m. Reba Kinne, July 2, 1960; 1 child, Theodore. A.B., Nebr. Wesleyan U., 1959; J.D., Georgetown U., 1963. Bar: Ill. 1963, D.C. 1965, S.C. 1985. Assoc. Chapman & Cutler, Chgo., 1963-65; assoc. Arnold & Porter, Washington, 1965-71, ptnr., 1971-76; sr. ptnr. Rogovin, Huge & Schiller, Washington, 1976—; bd. dirs. DBA Systems, Inc., Melbourne, Fla., Huge Sales, Inc., Gatlinburg, Tenn., Washington Bancorp., Washington, The Washington Bank, Fairfax, Va., United Coasts Corp., Hartford, Conn., ACMAT Corp., Hartford; chmn. Am. Equity Investors, Inc., Washington, 1986—; chmn., trustee United Mine Workers Health and Retirement Funds, 1973-78. Contbr. articles to legal jours. Pres. Voter Edn. Project, Atlanta, 1974-78; mem. Pres.'s Gen. Adv. Com. Arms. Control, 1977-81; bd. trustees Nebr. Wesleyan U., 1978—; mem. task force local govt. Greater Washington Research Ctr., 1981-82. Served with U.S. Army, 1960; with USNG, 1960-65. Mem. ABA (co-chmn. legis. com. litigation sect. 1981), D.C. Bar Assn. (bd. profl. responsibility 1976-81). Home: 628 Boyle Ln McLean VA 22102 Office: Rogovin Huge & Schiller 1250 24th St NW Washington DC 20036 also: Suite 311 Marriott Ctr Hilton Head Island SC 29938

HUGGINS, CHARLES BRENTON, surgical educator; b. Halifax, N.S., Can., Sept. 22, 1901; s. Charles Edward and Bessie (Spencer) H.; m. Margaret Wellman, July 29, 1927; children: Charles Edward, Emily Wellman Huggins Fine. BA, Acadia U., 1920, DSc (hon.), 1946; MD, Harvard U., 1924; MSc, Yale, 1947; DSc (hon.), Washington U., St. Louis, 1950, Leeds U., 1953, Turin U., 1957, Trinity Coll., 1965, U. Wales, 1967, U. Mich., 1968, Med. Coll. Ohio, 1973, Gustavus Adolphus Coll., 1975, Wilmington (Ohio) Coll., 1980, U. Louisville, 1980; LLD (hon.), U. Aberdeen, 1966, York U., Toronto, 1968, U. Calif., Berkeley, 1968; D of Pub. Service (hon.), George Washington U., 1967; D of Pub. Service (hon.) sigillum magnum, Bologna U., 1964. Intern in surgery U. Mich., 1924-26, instr. surgery, 1926-27; with U. Chgo., 1927—, instr. surgery, 1927-29, asst. prof., 1929-33, assoc. prof., 1933-36, prof. surgery, 1936—, dir. Ben May Lab. for Cancer Research, 1951-69, William B. Ogden Disting. Service prof., 1962—; chancellor Acadia U., Wolfville, N.S., 1972-79; Macewen lectr. U. Glasgow, 1958, Ravdin lectr., 1974, Powell lectr., Lucy Wortham James lectr., 1975, Robert V. Day lectr., 1975, Cartwright lectr., 1975. Trustee Worcester Found. Exptl. Biology; bd. govs. Weizmann Inst. Sci., Rehovot, Israel, 1973—. Decorated Order Pour le Mérite Germany; Order of The Sun Peru; recipient Nobel prize for medicine, 1966, Am. Urol. Assn. award, 1948, Francis Amory award, 1948, AMA Gold medals, 1936, 40, Société Internationale d'Urologie award, 1948, Am. Cancer Soc. award, 1953, Bertner award M.D. Anderson Hosp., 1953, Am. Pharm. Mfrs. Assn. award, 1953, Gold medal Am. Assn. Genito-Urinary Surgeons, 1955, Borden award Assn. Am. Med. Colls., 1955, Comfort Crookshank award Middlesex Hosp., London, 1957, Cameron prize Edinburg U., 1958, Valentine prize N.Y. Acad. Medicine, 1962, Hunter award Am. Therapeutic Soc., 1962, Lasker award for med. research, 1963, Gold medal Virchow Soc., 1964, Laurea award Am. Urol. Assn., 1966, Gold medal Worshipful Soc. Apothecaries of London, 1966, Gairdner award Toronto, 1966, Chgo. Med. Soc. award, 1967, Centennial medal Acadia U., 1967, Hamilton award Ill. Med. Soc., 1967, Bigelow medal Boston Surg. Soc., 1967, Disting. Service award Am. Soc. Abdominal Surgeons, 1972, Sheen award AMA, 1970, Sesquicentennial Commemorative award Nat. Library of Medicine, 1986; Charles Mickle fellow, 1958. Fellow ACS (hon.), Royal Coll. Surgeons Can. (hon.), Royal Coll. Surgeons Scotland (hon.), Royal Coll. Surgeons England (hon.), Royal Soc. Edinburgh (hon.); mem. Am. Philos. Soc., Nat. Acad. Scis. (Charles L. Meyer award for cancer research 1943), Am. Assn. Cancer Research, Canadian Med. Assn. (hon.), Alpha Omega Alpha. Home: 5807 Dorchester Ave Chicago IL 60637 Office: Univ of Chgo Ben May Lab for Cancer Research 950 E 59th St Chicago IL 60637

HUGGINS, CHARLES EDWARD, surgeon, cryobiologist; b. Chgo., May 7, 1929; s. Charles Brenton and Margaret (Wellman) H.; m. Gareth Whittier; children: Elizabeth Ann, Margaret Ruth, Nancy Wellman, Charles Edward, Gordon Spencer. Ph.B., U. Chgo., 1947; M.D. cum laude, Harvard U., 1952. Diplomate: Am. Bd. Surgery, Am. Bd. Pathology (in immunohematology and blood banking). Surg. intern Mass. Gen. Hosp., 1952-53, surg. resident, 1953-60, asst. surgery, 1960-64, asst. surgeon, also asst. dir. blood bank and transfusion service, 1964-67, clin. dir. blood bank and transfusion service, 1968-73, chief surg. low temperture unit, 1969—, asso. vis. surgeon, 1968—, dir. blood transfusion service, 1973—; instr., then clin. asso. surgery Harvard Med. Sch., 1960-63, 64-68, asst. prof. surgery, 1968-69, asso. prof. surgery, 1969—. Bd. dirs. N.E. region ARC Blood Services, 1980—. Served to lt., USN, 1954-56, comdr. Res. ret. Moseley Traveling fellow, 1958-59; clin. fellow Am. Cancer Soc., 1959-60. Fellow ACS; mem. Soc. Cryobiology (gov. 1965-66, 77-78, pres. 1968), Internat. Soc. Blood Transfusion, Soc. Univ. Surgeons, AMA, Soc. Internat. de Chirurgie, Mass. Med. Soc., Am. Assn. Blood Banks (dir. 1976-78), Alpha Omega Alpha. Office: Mass Gen Hosp Boston MA 02114-2690

HUGGINS, PETER, engineer; b. Newport, Gwent, Wales, Apr. 17, 1918; s. Henry Audibert and Vashti (Allen) H.; m. Joan Cynthia Wormell, Apr. 25, 1942; children—Carol, Eve. Chartered engr., U.K. Chief electronics engr. Sargrove Electronics Co., 1952-55; sect. head Tube Investments, 1955-63; chief engr. Girling Indsl. Products div., 1963-73; tech. dir. Mangood Ltd., 1973-75; proprietor Sensemaster Ltd., Newport Gwent, South Wales, U.K., 1985—; cons. Huntleigh Group, Cardiff, Wales, 1978-84. Author: Proximity Switch Practice, 1984. Contbr. articles to profl. publs. Patentee in field. Served with Brit. Mcht. Navy, 1940-45. Fellow Inst. Radio and Electronic Engrs. Mem. Ch. of England. Avocation: fellwalking. Home: 23 Caestory Ave, Raglan, Gwent, South Wales NP5 2EH, United Kingdom Office: Sensemaster Ltd, 218 Stow Hill, Newport, Gwent, South Wales NP9 4HA, United Kingdom

HUGHES, BRADLEY RICHARD, marketing executive; b. Detroit, Oct. 8, 1954; s. John Arthur and Nancy Irene (Middleton) H.; AA, Oakland Coll., 1974; BS in Bus., U. Colo., 1978, BJ, 1979; MBA in Fin. and Mktg., 1981; MS in Telecommunications U. Colo., 1988; m. Linda McCants, Feb. 14, 1977; children: Bradley Richard Jr., Brian Jeffrey. Cert. Office Automation Profl. Buyer, Joslins Co., Denver, 1979; mktg. adminstr. Mountain Bell, Denver, 1980-82, tech. cons. AT&T Info. Systems, mktg. exec. AT&T, 1983-86, acct. exec., 1986-87; mktg. mgr. U.S. West, 1987—. Bd. dirs. Brandychase Assn.; state del., committeeman Republican Party Colo. Mem. Assn. MBA Execs., U.S. Chess Fedn., Internat. Platform Assn., Mensa, Intertel, Assn. Telecommunications Profls., Am. Mgmt. Assn., Am. Mktg. Assn., Info. Industry Assn., Office Automation Soc. Internat., World Future Soc., Internat. Soc. Philos. Inquiry. Republican. Methodist. Home: 5759 S Jericho Way Aurora CO 80015 Office: AT&T 6200 S Syracuse Englewood CO 80111

HUGHES, CARL DOUGLAS, lawyer; b. Sapulpa, Okla., Aug. 29, 1946; s. Kenneth Gordon and Louise (Coffield) H.; m. Alice M. Hughes, May 12, 1978; children—Sarah Elizabeth, Kenneth James. B.B.A., U. Okla., 1968, J.D., 1971. Bar: Okla. 1971, U.S. Sup. Ct. 1974. Assoc. Stipe, Gossett, Stipe & Harper, Oklahoma City, 1971-76; ptnr. Hughes & Nelson, and predecessors, Oklahoma City, 1976—. Legal counsel Okla. Democratic Party, 1978-83; gen. counsel Spl. Olympics, 1976—, chmn., 1981, 84, 85, 86, 87. Served to capt. U.S. Army Res., 1968-73. Mem. Okla. Trial Lawyers Assn. (dir. 1971-78, chmn. judiciary com. 1977-78, chmn. criminal law com. 1981), Okla. Bar Assn., Oklahoma County Bar Assn. Episcopalian. Mem. editorial bd., torts editor Advocate mag., 1975-78. Home: 5909 Oak Tree Rd Edmond OK 73034 Office: 5801 N Broadway Ext Suite 302 Oklahoma City OK 73118

HUGHES, EDWIN LAWSON, management consultant; b. Pittsburg, Kans., Aug. 11, 1924; s. Edwin Byron and Vera (Lawson) H.; m. Ann Turner Nolen, Oct. 21, 1961; 1 child, Andrew George; children from previous marriage: John Lawson, James Prescott. BSEE, Mo. Sch. Mines, 1949; MSEE, U. Ill., 1950. Registered profl. engr. Fla. Group leader Systems Devel. Corp., Santa Monica, Calif., 1957-60; tech. dir. Gen. Motors, Oak Creek, Wis., 1960-71; v.p. engring. Xerox Corp., Webster, N.Y., 1971-81, Santec Corp., Amherst, N.H., 1981-82; chmn., pres., chief exec. officer Fla. Data Corp., Melbourne, 1982-83; pvt. practice cons. Melbourne, 1984—. Contbr. articles and papers to profl jours.; inventor computers, copiers; patentee in field. Com. mem. Boy Scouts Am., Pittsford, N.Y., 1974-76. Served with U.S. Army, 1943-46, ETO. Mem. IEEE, AAAS, Fla. Engring. Soc., Nat. Soc. Profl. Engrs. Republican. Club: Coast, Space Coast Ski, Suntree Country (Melbourne). Home and Office: 447 Pauma Valley Way Melbourne FL 32940

HUGHES, GEORGE, technological executive; b. Liverpool, Eng., May 4, 1937; s. Peter and Anne (Pickersgill) H.; m. Janet Nichols, June 29, 1963; children—David Robert, Edward William. B.A. with 1st class honors, Caius Coll., Cambridge U., 1959, M.A. with honors, 1963; M.B.A., Harvard U., 1968. Switerland ski instr., 1960; head strategy unit IBM, London, 1960-69; vice chmn., group mng. dir. Duple Group Ltd., 1970-71; chmn., chief exec. Willowbrook Worldwide, London, 1971—, Willowbrook Internat., 1971-83; chmn. Hughes Internat. Ltd., Leominster, Eng., 1970—, chmn. Hughes Technology, 1983— ; chmn. Castle Hughes Group Ltd., Hampton Ct. Castle, 1975—, Castle Hughes Farms Internat., Leominster, 1975—, Hampton Ct. Farms, Leominster, 1975—. Author: The Effective Use of Computers, 1968; Military and Business Strategy, 1968; How to Get Things Done, 1979; Strategy for Survival and Road to Recovery, 1983, Superthinking, 1988. Recipient Queen's award for export achievement, 1979. Mem. Mensa. Clubs: Carlton, MCC, Annabels, Derbyshire County Cricket (chmn. 1976-77). Home: Hampton Court Castle, Leominster HR6 0PN, England Office: Xanadu, Matthews Green, Wokingham RG11 1JN, England

HUGHES, GEORGE EDWARD HARCOURT, English literature educator; b. London, Oct. 21, 1944; s. William Hughes and Mary (Hillersdon) Vincent; m. Clair Fauerby Bock, Mar. 3, 1973; 1 stepchild, Pernille Rudlin. BA, U. Sussex, 1969; PhD, U. Cambridge, 1973. Lectr. in English Tohoku U., Sendai, Japan, 1972-75, Osaka (Japan) U., 1975-77; English lit. dept. head U. Buckingham, Eng., 1978-83, dean vis. students; lectr. in English lit. Hiroshima (Japan) U., 1983-87, Tokyo U., 1988—; vis. prof. Bucknell U., Pa., 1981. Author: Ice on a Summer Sea, 1983; (radio play) Harriet's Weekend, 1983; contbr. articles to profl. jours. Fgn. advisor Hiroshima Internat. Relations Orgn., 1985-87; mem. leading project planning com. Japan Ministry Home Affairs, 1987, founding com. Internat. U., Hiroshima, 1987. Mem. Japan-Brit. Soc. (trustee, founder, various coms. 1986-87). Mem. Anglican Ch. Home: Musashino-shi, Nakamachi 3-16-13, Tokyo 180, Japan Home: Musashino-Shi, Nakamach 3-16-13, Tokyo 180, Japan Office: Tokyo U, Faculty Letters, Tokyo Japan

HUGHES, JOHN, chemical company executive; b. London, Jan. 6, 1942; s. Joseph Henry and Edith Annie (Hope) H.; m. Madeleine Jennings, 1967 (div. 1981); 1 child, Katherine Bryony; m. Julie Pinnington; children: Georgina Anne, Joseph Francis. BS, Chelsea Coll., London, 1964; PhD, U. London, 1967; postgrad., Yale U., 1967-69; Dh Causa (hon.), Liege (Belgium) U., 1978. Lectr. Pharmacology U. Aberdeen, Eng., 1969-73; dep. dir. Addiction Research Unit, Aberdeen, 1973-77; reader Biochemistry Imperial Coll., London, 1977-79, prof., 1979-82; dir. Parke-Davis Reseach Unit, Cambridge, Eng., 1983—; cons. Reckitt & Colman Ltd., Hull, Eng., 1975-77, Imperial Chem. Industries, Macclesfield, 1977-82, Squibb, Inc., Princeton, N.J., 1978-82, NRDC, London, 1980-82. Contbr. articles to profl. jours. Recipient Pacesetter award, U.S. Nat. Inst. Drug Abuse, Washington, 1977, Albert Lasker Found. award, 1978, Felberg Found. Prize Anglo-German Sci. Exchange Com., 1981, Gaddum award British Pharmacology Soc., 1982, Lucien Dautrebande Prize, Belgium, 1983. Mem. Academie Royale de Medicine de Belgique, British Pharmacology Soc. Office: Parke-Davis Research Unit, Addenbrooke's Hosp Site, Hills Rd, Cambridge CB2 2QB, England

HUGHES, KENNETH ROBERT, mathematics educator; b. Cape Town, Republic of South Africa, Dec. 10, 1945; s. Donald Richie and Mary Jean (Wale) H. PhD, U. Cape Town, 1970, U. Warwick, Eng., 1976. Lectr. U. Cape Town, 1973-80, sr. lectr., 1981—. Contbr.: Democratic Liberalism in South Africa, 1987. Chmn. Civil Rights League, Cape Town, 1975-80, Friends of Dist. 6, Cape Town, 1981-82. Royal Commn. for Exhbn. of 1851 scholar, 1970-72. Office: U Cape Town, Dept Math/Econs, Rondebosch 7700, Republic of South Africa

HUGHES, MICHAEL ANTHONY, chemistry educator; b. Leeds, Yorkshire, Eng., Dec. 20, 1933; s. Stanley Albert and Florence Mildred (Hambleton) H.; m. Iris Atkinson, Aug. 18, 1956; children: Elizabeth Wendy, Barbara Elaine. BSc with honors, London U., 1956; MSc with distinction, Leeds U., 1958; PhD, Bradford (Eng.) U., 1971. Sci. officer U.K. Atomic Energy Authority, Preston, Eng., 1958-61; lectr., sr. lectr. Bradford Inst. Advanced Tech., 1961-69; lectr., sr. lectr. Bradford U., 1969-82, reader solvent extraction chemistry, 1982—. Contbr. articles, books chpts. to profl. publs. Recipient numerous research grants; Royal Soc. scholar, 1984. Fellow Inst. Energy, Royal Soc. Chemistry, Chartered Chemist, Chartered Engr. Anglican. Home: 38 Woodhall Ln, Pudsey, West Yorkshire LS28 7TT, England Office: Bradford U, Sch Chem Engring, Bradford BD7 1DB, England

HUGHES, PERRYN JOANNA, sculptor; b. Valletta, Malta, July 24, 1953; d. Terence Brinsley John Danvers Butler and Beryl Mary (Trotter) Giardelli; m. Robert Gay Hughes, Dec. 15, 1984. Sculptor. Prin. works included in private collections. Mem. Soc. Indsl. Artists Designers, Soc. Designer Craftsmen (lic.). Conservative. Mem. Ch. Eng. Home: 16 Goat St, Haverford West, Dyfed, SW Wales England

HUGHES, ROBERT MERRILL, engineer; b. Glendale, Calif., Sept. 11, 1936; s. Fred P. and Gertrude G. (Merrill) H.; A.A., Pasadena City Coll., 1957; 1 dau., Tammie Lynn Cobble. Engr. Aerojet Gen. Corp., Azusa, Calif., 1957-64, 66-74; pres. Automatic Electronics Corp., Sacramento, 1964-66; specialist Perkin Elmer Corp., Pomona, Calif., 1974-75; gen. mgr. Hughes Mining Inc., Covina, Calif., 1975-76; project mgr. L&A Water Treatment, City of Industry, Calif., 1976-79; dir. Hughes Industries Inc., Alta Loma, Calif., 1979—; pres. Hughes Devel. Corp., Carson City, Nev.; chmn. bd. Hughes Mining Inc., Hughes Video Corp. Registered profl. engr., Calif. Mem. AIME, Nat. Soc. Profl. Engrs., Instrument Soc. Am., Am. Inst. Plant Engrs. Republican. Patentee in field. Home: 10039 Bristol Dr Alta Loma CA 91701 Office: Box 723 Alta Loma CA 91701

HUGHES, STEVEN JAY, lawyer; b. Fayetteville, Ark., Nov. 7, 1948; s. Howard and Jimmie Louise (Williams) H.; m. Leora Donna Halfhill, July 22, 1972; children: Christopher Blake, Clayton Brent. BS in Edn., U. Ark., Fayetteville, 1970; JD, U. Ark., Little Rock, 1978. Bar: Ark. 1978, U.S. Dist. Ct. (ea. dist.) Ark. 1978, U.S. Ct. Appeals (8th cir.) 1978, U.S. Supreme Ct. 1981. Sole practice Jacksonville, Ark., 1978—. Alderman Jacksonville City Council, 1979-81; commr. Jacksonville Planning Commn., 1982-85; mem. U. Ark. Razorback Letterman's Club, Little Rock, 1985, Ark. Sports Hall of Fame, 1985; bd. dirs. Jacksonville Boys Club, 1979—, pres. 1982-83. Mem. Assn. Trial Lawyers Am., Ark. Bar Assn., Delta Theta Phi (lifetime, dist. chancellor 1983—). Baptist. Lodge: Kiwanis (pres. Jacksonville club 1983-84, Kiwanian of Yr. award 1979-80, Disting. Club Pres. award 1984). Home: 5 Silver Fox Cove Jacksonville AR 72076 Office: 3000 N 1st St PO Box 5266 Jacksonville AR 72076

HUGHES, SUE MARGARET, librarian; b. Cleburne, Tex.; d. Chastain Wesley and Sue Willis (Payne) H. BBA, U. Tex., Austin, 1949; MLS, Tex. Woman's U., 1960, PhD, 1987. Sec.-treas. pvt. corps. Waco, Tex., 1949-59; asst. in public services Baylor U. Library, Waco, 1960-64; acquisitions librarian Baylor U. Library, 1964-79, acting univ. librarian, summer 1979; librarian Moody Library, 1980—. Mem. AAUP, ALA, Southwestern Library Assn., Tex. Library Assn., AAUW, Delta Kappa Gamma, Beta Phi Mu, Beta Gamma Sigma. Methodist. Club: Altrusa. Office: Box 6307 Waco TX 76706

HUGHES, TED, poet, author; b. 1930; s. William Henry and Edith (Farrar) H.; m. Sylvia Plath, 1956 (dec. 1963); 2 children; m. Carol Orchard, 1970. Student, Pembroke Coll., Cambridge (Eng.) U. Author: The Hawk in the Rain, 1957, Lupercal, 1960; (children's poems) Meet My Folks, 1961, The Earth-Owl and Other Moon People, 1963; (children's stories) How the Whale Became, 1963; Wodwo, 1967, Poetry in the Making, 1967, The Iron Man, 1968, Crow Wakes, 1970, A Few Crows, 1970, Crow, 1971, Eat Crow, 1971, Shakespeare's Poems, 1971, Prometheus on His Crag, 1973, Spring, Summer, Autumn, Winter, 1974, Season Songs, 1975, Cave Birds, 1976, Moon-Whales & Other Poems, 1976, Gaudete, 1977, Remains of Elmet, 1979, Moortown, 1980, Under the North Star, 1981, New Selected Poems, 1982, River, 1984, Colors, 1986, The Trouble With Jack, 1986, Two Shoes, New Shoes, 1986, Flowers and Insects, 1987, Out and About, 1988; editor: A Choice of Emily Dickinson's Verse, 1968, A Choice of Shakespeare's Verse, 1971; joint editor Five American Poets, 1963, Selected Poems of Keith Douglas, 1964; contbr. poems to leading mags. Recipient 1st prize Guinness Poetry awards, 1958; Somerset Maugham award, 1960; Hawthornden prize, 1961; Premio Internazionale Taormina, 1973; Queen's medal for Poetry, 1974; Guggenheim fellow, 1959-60. Office: care Faber & Faber, 3 Queen Sq, London WC1 England *

HUGHES, VESTER THOMAS, JR., lawyer; b. San Angelo, Tex., May 24, 1928; s. Vester Thomas and Mary Ellen (Tisdale) H. Student, Baylor U., 1945-46; B.A. with distinction, Rice U., 1949; LL.B. cum laude, Harvard U., 1952. Bar: Tex. 1952. Law clk. U.S. Supreme Ct., 1952; asso. firm Jackson, Walker, Winstead, Cantwell & Miller (and predecessors), Dallas, 1955-58; partner Jackson, Walker, Winstead, Cantwell & Miller (and predecessors),

1958-76; partner firm Hughes & Luce (and predecessor), 1976—; dir. Exell Cattle Co., LX Cattle Co., Murphy Oil Corp., Austin Industries, Inc.; adv. dir. First Nat. Bank Mertzon; tax counsel Communities Found. of Tex., Inc.; mem. adv. com. Tex. Supreme Ct., 1985—. Bd. dirs. Larry and Jane Harlan Found.; trustee Dallas Bapt. Coll., 1967-77; v.p., trustee, exec. com. Tex. Scottish Rite Hosp. for Crippled Children; bd. overseers vis. com. Harvard Law Sch., 1969-75. Served to lt. AUS, 1952-55. Mem. Am. Bar Assn. (council sect. taxation 1969-72), Am. Law Inst. (council 1966—), Harvard Law Sch. Assn. (sec. 1984-86), Phi Beta Kappa, Sigma Xi. Baptist. Clubs: Masons (33 deg.), Order Eastern Star. Home: 3310 Fairmount PlD Dallas TX 75201 Office: 2800 Momentum Pl 1717 Main St Dallas TX 75201

HUGHSTON, LANE PALMER, mathematician, merchant banker; b. Corpus Christi, Tex., Dec. 24, 1951; s. Edward Wallace and Joan Lorraine (Palmer) H. Student, MIT, 1969-71, Princeton U., 1971-72; MA, D Philosphy, Oxford U., Eng., 1976. Vis. assoc. prof. physics U. Tex., Austin, 1974; research fellow Wolfson Coll. Oxford U., Eng., 1977-80; fellow, tutor in applied math. Lincoln Coll., 1980-87; far east trading research analyst Robert Fleming & Co., London, 1988—. Author: Twistors and Particles, 1979; editor: Advances in Twistor Theory, 1979; contbr. articles to sci. publs. Mem. Am. Math. Soc., Am. Phys. Soc., London Math. Soc. Home: PO Box 2764 Taos NM 87571 Office: Robert Fleming & Co, 25 Copthall Ave, London EC2R 7DR, England

HUGIN, ADOLPH CHARLES EUGENE, lawyer, inventor; b. Washington, Mar. 28, 1907; s. Charles and Eugenie Francoise (Vigny) H. BS in Elec. Engring., George Washington U., 1928; MS in Elec. Engring., MIT, 1930; cert. in patent law and practice, JD, Georgetown U., 1934; cert. radio communication (electronics) Union Coll., 1944; cert. better bus. mgmt. Gen. Electric Co., continuing edn. program, 1946; LLM, Harvard U., 1947; SJD, Cath. U. Am., 1949; cert. in Christian Doctrine and Teaching Methods, Conf. of Christian Doctrine, 1960; cert. in social services and charity Ozanam Sch. Charity, 1972. Bar: D.C. 1933, U.S. Ct. Customs and Patent Appeals 1934, U.S. Supreme Ct. 1945, Mass. 1947, U.S. Ct. Claims, 1953, U.S. Ct. Appeals (fed. cir.) 1982; registered U.S. Patent and Trademark Office Atty. Bar, 1933; registered profl. elec. and mech. engr., D.C. Examiner U.S. Patent and Trademark Office, 1928; with Gen. Electric Co., 1928-46, engr. Instruments Research and Devel. Lab., West Lynn Works, Mass., 1928, engr.-in-charge Insulation Lab. River Works, Lynn, 1929, Engine-Electric Drive Devel. Lab., River Works, 1929-30, patent legal asst., Schenectady, 1930, patent investigator, Washington, 1930-33, patent lawyer, Washington, 1933-34, Schenectady, 1934-46; engr.-in-charge section aeros. and marine engring. div., Schenectady, 1942-45; organizer, instr. Gen. Electric patent practice course, 1945-46; sole practice law and cons. engring., Cambridge and Arlington, Mass., 1946-47; vis. prof. law Cath. U. Am., Washington, 1949-55; assoc. Holland, Armstrong, Bower & Carlson, N.Y.C., 1957; sole practice law and cons. engr. Washington and Springfield, Va., 1947—. Author: International Trade Regulatory Arrangements and the Antitrust Laws, 1949; editor-in-chief Bull. Am. Patent Law Assn., 1949-54; editor notes and decisions Georgetown U. Law Jour., 1933-34, staff, 1930-34; contbr. articles on patents, copyrights, antitrust, radio and air law to profl. jours.; inventor dynamoelectric machines, insulation micrometer calipers, ecology and pollution controls, musical instrument dynamometers, viscosimeters, heavy-duty inherent constant voltage characteristic generators, water-cooled eddy-current clutches, brakes, and 12 U.S. and several foreign patents. Mem. Schenectady N.Y. Com. Boy Scouts Am., 1940-42, North Springfield Civic Assn.; charter mem., 1st bd. mgrs. Schenectady Cath. Youth League, 1935-38, hon. life mem., 1945; mem. adv. bd. St. Michael's Parish, Va., 1974-77, lector, commentator, 1969-80; bd. dirs. St. Margaret's Fed. Credit Union, 1963-67, 1st v.p., 1965-67; chmn. St. Margaret's Bldg. Fund, 1954; lector St. Margaret's Parish, 1966-69, retreat group capt., 1965-68, Parish Council, 1969-71; mem. legis. com. Schenectady C. of C., 1940-46. Recipient Dietzen Drawing prize, George Washington U., 1926, Georgetown U. Law Jour. Key award, 1934, Aviation Law prize Cath. U. Am., 1948, Radio Law prize Cath. U. Am., 1949, Charities Work award St. Margaret's Ch., 1982; elected to Gen. Electric Co. Elfun Soc. for Disting. Exec. Service, 1942. Mem. Am. Intellectual Property Law Assn. (life; cert. of Honor for 50 Yrs. Service), ABA (life), John Carroll Soc., D.C. Socs. Profl. Engrs., St. Vincent de Paul Soc. (parish conf. v.p. 1949-65, pres. 1965—, pres. Prince Georges County, Md. council 1958-61, founding pres. Arlington, Va. Diocesan council 1975-77, nat. trustee 1975-77), Nocturnal Adoration Soc., St. Margaret's Parish Confraternity Christian Doctrine (pres., instr. 1960-61), Archdiocesan Council Cath. Men (pres. So. Prince George's County deanery 1936-38, 63-68), Holy Name Soc. (pres. parish 1950-52, Prince George's County section 1953, Washington Archdiocesan Union 1953-55), Retired Tchrs. Assn., Men's Retreat League (Wash. exec. bd. 1954-58), Delta Theta Phi(Georgetown U. Law Sch. Scholarship Key award 1934). Avocations: travel, photography, sketching, horticulture. Address: 7602 Boulder St North Springfield VA 22151

HUGO, GRAEME JOHN, geography educator; b. Adelaide, South Australia, Australia, Dec. 5, 1946; s. John Argent Ronald and Phyllis Odette Marjorebanks Hugo; m. Meredith Ann Le Leu, Dec. 27, 1969; 1 child, Justine Ann. BA with hons., U. Adelaide, 1967; MA, Flinders U., Adelaide, 1971; PhD, Australia Nat. U., Canberra, Australia, 1975. Geography tutor Flinders U., Adelaide, 1968-71, lectr., 1975-80, sr. lectr., 1980-83, reader, 1983—; research scholar Australian Nat. U., Canberra, 1972-75; vis. fellow Hasanuddin U., Ujung Pandang, Indonesia, 1977-78; vis. prof. U. Hawaii, Honolulu, 1981; prof. U. Iowa, Iowa City, 1985; cons. Indonesian Ministry Population and Environment, Jakarta, 1987, Dept. Immigration and Ethnic Affairs, Canberra, 1987-88. Author: Population Mobility in West Java, 1978, Australia's Changing Population, 1986; co-author: (with others) The Demographic Dimension in Indonesian Development, 1987; editor: Famine as a Geographical Phenomenon, 1984. Recipient John Lewis medal South Australian Matriculation Bd., 1963. Fellow Acad. Social Scis. Australia; mem. Internat. Union Sci. Study Population, Population Assn. Am., Australian Population Assn., Inst. Australian Geographers, Royal Geog. Soc. South Australia. Home: 1 Grove St, Eden Hills, 5051 Adelaide Australia Office: Flinders U Sch Social Scis, Sturt Rd, Bedford Park, Adelaide 5042, Australia

HUGO, NORMAN ELIOT, plastic surgeon, medical educator; b. Beverly, Mass., Sept. 23, 1933; s. Victor Joseph and Helen Bernadette (Box) H.; m. Geraldine P. Tonry, Oct. 10, 1959; children—Helen, William, Geraldine, Norman, Catherine. Intern, resident Cornell U. Surg. Service, Bellevue Hosp., N.Y.C., 1959-63, resident N.Y. Hosp.-Cornell Med. Ctr., 1963-65, univ. instr. surgery, 1965-66; asst. prof. Ind. U., asst. chief plastic surgery, 1966-67; assoc. prof. U. Chgo., 1967-69; chief plastic and reconstructive surgery Michael Reese Hosp., Chgo., 1969-71, Passavant Hosp., Chgo., 1971-79; assoc. prof. Northwestern U., Chgo., 1971-82; dir. plastic surgery Lakeside VA Hosp., 1971-77; chief plastic and reconstructive surgery Columbia U.-Presbyn. Med. Ctr., N.Y.C., 1982—; prof. Columbia U. Coll. Physicians and Surgeons, 1982—. Served to maj. M.C., AUS, 1967-69. Diplomate Am. Bd. Plastic and Reconstructive Surgeons, dir., 1982—, vice chmn., 1987-88. Mem. Am. Soc. Plastic and Reconstructive Surgeons (trustee 1981-84, historian 1982-84, v.p. 1985-86, pres. elect 1986-87, pres. 1987-88, bd. dirs. Ednl. Found.), ACS, Am. Assn. Plastic and Reconstructive Surgery (trustee 1982-84), Am. Soc. Aesthetic Plastic Surgery (sec. 1979-82), Chgo. Soc. Plastic Surgery (sec. 1979-81, v.p. 1981-82), Plastic Surgery Research Council, Am. Cleft Palate Soc., Assn. Acad. Surgery, Soc. Head and Neck Surgeons, N.Y. Acad. Sci., AMA (del. 1983-88), Am. Burn Soc. Clubs: Williams, Union (N.Y.C.); University (Chgo.). Home: 37 Carriage Ln New Canaan CT 06840 Office: Columbia Univ Coll Physicians & Surgeons 161 Fort Washington Ave New York NY 10032

HUGUENIN, BERNARD ANDRÉ, scientific research government officer; b. Algiers, Algeria, Sept. 22, 1934; s. André Edouard and Suzanne Marguerite (Revel) H.; m. Jacqueline Baldou, Sept. 10, 1956; children—Stephane, Isabelle, Laurence, Christine. Engr., Nat. Agronomy Inst., Paris, 1957; PhD, U. Rouen, 1968. plant pathologist ORSTOM, Nouméa, New Caledonia, 1961-68, head of div., Brazzaville, Congo, 1969-76, Abidjan, Ivory Coast, 1976-80, with sci. programming, Paris, 1976-80, rep. Lome, Togo, 1982-87, chmn. plant sci. scientific. com., Paris, 1987—. Contbr. articles to profl. jours. Served to lt. arty. French army, 1959-61. Mem. Plant Pathology French Soc., British Soc. Plant Pathology. Roman Catholic. Club: Trieux Yacht. Avocation: sailing. Home: 28 Blvd Albert Thomas, 44000 Nantes France Office: ORSTOM, 213 rue Lafayette, 75010 Paris France

HUHTALA, CHRISTOPHER, marketing executive; b. Cardiff, Wales, July 12, 1946; s. William Joseph and Vera H.; children—Simon, Alexander. Dip CAM, 1978. Advt. controller Revlon Internat. Corp., London, 1974-78; publicity mgr. Richard Ellis, London, 1978-80; gen. mgr. Key Pass (UK) Ltd., London, 1980-83; mktg. dir. Middle East Econ. Digest, London, 1983-86; now with Metals & Minerals Publs. Ltd., London; cons. in field. Fellow Inst. Sales and Mktg., Brit. Inst. Mgmt.; mem. Brit. Inst. Mktg., Brit. Mktg. Soc., Internat. Advt. Assn. Roman Catholic. Clubs: Publicity, Wig & Pen. National Liberal. Avocations: astronomy; theatre; travel. Home: 37 The Towers, Lower Mortlake Rd, Richmond, Surrey TW9 1JR, England Office: Metals & Minerals Publs Ltd, 60 Worship St, London EC2, England

HUI, PETER WING-TAK, hand surgeon; b. Canton, China, May 23, 1946; s. Kam-Chun and Wen-Yu (Siu) H.; came to U.S., 1971, naturalized, 1978; M.D., Nat. Def. Med. Center, Taipei, 1970; married. Intern Mt. Sinai Hosp., Chgo., 1971-72, resident in surgery, 1972-76; fellow in hand surgery Cook County Hosp., Chgo., 1976—; practice medicine specializing in hand surgery, Hinsdale, Ill., 1977-86, Elmhurst, Ill., 1986—; attending hand surgeon Cook County Hosp., 1977—; clin. instr. surgery Rush Med. Coll., Chgo., 1978—. Fellow A.C.S.; mem. Am. Assn. for Hand Surgery, AMA, Chgo. Soc. Surgery of the Hand, Ill. Med. Soc., DuPage Med. Soc., Chgo. Soc. Indsl. Medicine and Surgery. Roman Catholic. Address: 493 S York Rd Elmhurst IL 60126

HUI, STEPHEN S.F., geologist, mining engineer; b. Tsamkong, China, June 13, 1912; s. Oi Chow and Tsang Sze; came to Hong Kong, 1925; naturalized, 1963; Geol. Engr., Colo. Sch. Mines, 1940, D.Engring. (hon.), 1986; Engr. of Mines, 1940; LL.D. (hon.), U. Hong Kong, 1980; m. Anna K.C. Kong, Aug. 23, 1946; children—Sylvia S.L., Richard C.Y., William C.L. Asst. mgr. Shun Cheong Shipping Co., Ltd., Hong Kong, 1941-42; exploration geologist and mining engr. Yan Liu Tung and Tai Hang Ling Coal Fields, Kwangsi Province, China, 1942-46; chief mining engr. Sam Toi Ling Talc Mine, Luck Chuen Dist., Kwangsi Province, China, 1947-50; processing engr. Yan Hing Non-metallic Indsl. Minerals Processing Factory, Yan Hing Mining Co., Ltd., Hong Kong, 1951-56; chief mining engr. and mine mgr. Needle Hill Wolfram Mine, Yang Hing Mining Co., Ltd., Hong Kong, 1956-70, mng. dir., gen. mgr., 1970-72, chmn. and mng. dir., 1973—; chmn. and mng. dir. Chow Hing Investment Co., Ltd., 1973—; geol. cons., 1950—. Mem. Ct. of U. Hong Kong, 1977—. Recipient Distinguished Achievement award Colo. Sch. of Mines, 1974; registered profl. geol. engr. Council Engring. Instns., Eng. Fellow Instn. Mining and Metallurgy (U.K.) (hon.), Hong Kong Instn. Engrs., Chinese gen. C. of C. ; hon. assoc. Royal Sch. Mines; mem. Soc. Mining Engrs., Soc. Petroleum Engrs., Metallurgical Soc., Minerals Engring. Soc., Am. Inst. Mining, Metall. and Petroleum Engrs., Mineral. Soc. Am., Am. Assn. Petroleum Geologists, Am. Inst. Profl. Geologists, Geol. Soc. Hong Kong (hon.), Chinese Gen. C. of C., St. John's U. Alumni Assn., Chinese Mfrs. Assn. (chmn. subcom. mining div. 1972—), Huis Clan Assn. (chmn. 1973—), Central Dist. K-F Welfare Assn. Ltd. (hon., permanent chmn. 1977—). Anglican. Clubs: Hong Kong Country, Royal Hong Kong Golf, Royal Hong Kong Jockey. Hong Kong Racehorse Owners Assn., Chinese Recreation, Sports, South China Athletic Assn., American, Hong Kong, Pacific, Culture. Contbr. reports on mineral resources and mining problems to profl. publs. Home: A-7 Woodland Heights, 2A Wongneichong Gap Rd, Hong Kong Hong Kong Office: Central Bldg, Top Floor, Hong Kong Hong Kong

HUIJING (ALLEN), RICHARD PATRICK JAN, pianist, composer; b. Voorschoten, Holland, The Netherlands, May 29, 1956; arrived in Eng., 1978; s. Jan and Maureen Margaret (Irwin) H. Student, Royal Conservatory of Music, The Hague, The Netherlands, 1972-78. Lectr. Leiden (The Netherlands) Sch. of Music, 1977-78; head of studies Exeter Sch. Music, Eng., 1981-82; free-lance performer, composer 1978; cons. dept. psychology Univ. Exeter, 1985-86; freelance cons. Composer mono drama, clarinet quartet, clarinet concerto, song cycles, cantata, diverse works for piano, lit. translator Dutch-English and vice versa; contbr. articles to profl. jours. Mem. European Piano Tchrs. Assn. Office: Alma Music Ltd, 8 Swift St, London SW6 5AG, England

HUISMAN, STEVEN, economist; b. Amsterdam, Netherlands, Mar. 20, 1939; s. Tiemen and Wilhelmina Suzanna (Eswilder) H.; B.A. in Econs., Free U. Amsterdam, 1963, M.A., 1966, Ph.D., 1969; m. Catharina Juliana van der Harst, Apr. 14, 1967; children—Sylvia Alicia, Timotheus Maarten. Research asso. dept. econs. Free U. Amsterdam, 1967-71, lectr., 1971-80, prof. gen. econs., 1980—, dean dept. econs. and econometrics, 1987—. Mem. Am. Econ. Assn. Mem. Reformed Church. Author: Economic Growth and International Trade, 1969; Economic Growth and Economics, 1972; Employment and Effective Demand, 1981; Potential output, 1983; Disequilibrium analysis, 1984. Home: 28 Handelstraat, 1901 VA Castricum The Netherlands also: 1105 De Boelelaan, 1081 HV Amsterdam The Netherlands

HUITT, JIMMIE L., oil, gas, real estate investor; b. Gurdon, Ark., Aug. 21, 1923; s. John Wesley and Almedia (Hatten) H.; m. Janis C. Mann, Oct. 30, 1945; children—Jimmie L., Jr., Allan Jerome. B.S. in Chem. Engring., La. Tech. U., 1944; M.S. in Chem. Engring., U. Okla., 1948, Ph.D., 1951. Registered profl. engr., La. Research engr. Mobil Oil Corp., Dallas, 1951-56, Gulf Research Co., Pitts., 1956-67; ops. coordinator Kuwait Oil Co., London, 1967-71; gen. mgr. Gulf Oil-Zaire, Kinshasa, 1971-74; mng. dir. Gulf Oil-Nigeria, Lagos, 1974-76; sr. v.p., exec. v.p. Gulf Oil Exploration and Prodn. Co., Houston, 1976-81, pres., 1981-85; rancher Four Jays Ranch, Industry, Tex., 1986—. Contbr. articles to profl. jours.; patentee in field. Served to 1st lt. U.S. Army, 1944-47. Mem. Soc. Petroleum Engrs. (chmn. various coms. 1956—). Republican. Lodges: Masons, Shriners. Office: Four Jays Ranch PO Box 236 Industry TX 78944

HUKKINEN, LARS JOHAN, research and development executive; b. Kuopio, Finland, May 30, 1928; s. Hugo Johannes and Laila Regina (Stålhane) H.; m. Maija Kaisa Turja, Oct. 27, 1931; children: Kalle, Janne, Ville, Sanna. MSc. in Engring/Chemistry, Inst. Tech., Helsinki, Finland, 1955. Tchr. Inst. of Tech., Helsinki, 1955-61; lab. mgr. Oy Fiskars Ab, Åminnefors, Finland, 1962-69, Ovako Oy, Åminnefors, 1969-80; research and devel. mgr. Ovako Oy Ab, Helsinki, 1980-86, Ovako Steel Oy Ab, Åminnefors, 1986-87, Dalsbruk Oy Ab, Åminnefors, 1987—; chmn. Finnish Nat. Com. Standardization Reinforcing Steels, Helsinki, 1977—; del. ISO Spl. Com. Standardization Reinforcing Steels, 1978—. Served with Finnish mil., 1944. Decorated Finnish Lion Pres. of Republic, 1986. Mem. Finnish Tech. Soc., Finnish Chem. Soc., Finnish Mining Soc., Internat. Com. Conservation Indsl. Heritage. Conservative. Lutheran. Lodge: Rotary (pres. 1977-78). Home: Vaunukatu 14, SF-10300 Karjaa Finland Office: Dalsbruk Oy Ab, SF 10410 Åminnefors Finland

HULBERT, WILLIAM ROWSELL, JR., lawyer; b. N.Y.C., Apr. 8, 1916; s. William Rowsell and Olga Craven H.; m. Aline Davis, Mar. 13, 1948; children—David, William Truxton, Lucy. A.B., Brown U., 1937; J.D., Harvard U., 1940. Bar: Mass. 1940, U.S. Dist. Ct. Mass. 1946, U.S. Ct. Appeals (1st cir.) 1953, U.S. Ct. Appeals (Fed. cir.) 1982, Maine 1973, U.S. Dist. Ct. Maine 1974, U.S. Supreme Ct. 1956. Assoc. Fish, Richardson & Neave, Boston, 1940-53, ptnr., 1953-68; ptnr. Fish & Richardson, Boston, 1968—, Lincolnville, Maine, 1976—; spl. agt. FBI, 1941-45; legal attaché Am. embassy, Quito, Ecuador, 1943, Asunción, Paraguay, 1944. Dir. Camden, Maine, Area YMCA, 1984—. Mem. Boston Patent Law Assn. (past pres.), Am. Patent Law Assn. (past. dir.), ABA, Maine Bar Assn., Waldo County Bar Assn., Am. Coll. Trial Lawyers, Inter-Am. Bar Assn. Clubs: Cumberland, Union (Boston); Harvard Faculty. Office: Fish & Richardson PO Box 90 Lincolnville ME 04849 also: One Financial Ctr Boston MA 02111

HULEN, MARJORIE JANE, med. center exec.; b. Denver, Sept. 23, 1921; d. Perry E. and Garnet W. (Doty) Kellogg; student pub. schs., Redondo Beach, Calif.; m. Ray Romaine Hulen, June 10, 1950; 1 child, Lynn Robert. With A. O. Smith Corp., Los Angeles, 1948-60, exec. sec., 1956-60; exec. sec. Sterling Electric Motors, Los Angeles, 1960-61; research sec. Pasadena (Calif.) Found. for Med. Research, 1961-65; exec. sec. Profl. Staff Assn., Los Angeles County/U. So. Calif. Med. Center, Los Angeles, 1965-70, office mgr., 1970-74, bus. mgr., 1974-79, exec. dir., 1979—. Instl. rep. Los Angeles Regional Family Planning, 1977-79. Nat. Pub. Relations award Nat. Assn. Accts., 1979. Mem. Am. Soc. Assn. Execs., Nat. Secs. Assn., Soc. Research Adminstrs., Nat. Assn. Accts., Nat. Council Univ. Research Adminstrs., Assn. Ind. Research Insts., Nat. Assn. Female Execs. Democrat. Home: 2311 El Paseo St Alhambra CA 91803 Office: 1739 Griffin Ave Los Angeles CA 90031

HULESCH, WILLIAM STANLEY, physician; b. Cleve., Apr. 28, 1946; s. Stanley and Beatrice R. (Suchma) H.; B.S., U. Dayton, 1968; M.D., Loyola U., Chgo., 1972; m. Jane S. Liebel, Aug. 9, 1969. Resident in family practice MacNeal Hosp., Berwyn, Ill., 1972-75; practice medicine specializing in family practice, Downers Grove, Ill., 1975—; past chmn. family practice dept. Good Samaritan Hosp.; past chmn. family practice dept. Hinsdale Hosp.; mem. faculty George Williams Coll., Hinsdale Hosp., Ill. Benedectine Coll. Family Practice Residency; pres. D.G. Family Practice, H.S.M. Inc. Advisor, Downers Grove Sch. System, Hinsdale Sch. System. Diplomate Am. Bd. Family Practice, Nat. Bd. Med. Examiners. Bd. dirs. Hinsdale Community Nursery Sch., mem. com. health edn. Fellow Am. Acad. Family Physicians (chmn. com. by-laws com. 1987—, acting exec. direct, 1988—); mem. AMA (Physicians Recognition award), Ill. Acad. Family Physicians (dir., chpt. pres., chmn. bd., pres. 1986), Family Health Found. Ill. (pres. 1987-88), Alpha Epsilon Delta. Republican. Office: 6800 Main St Downers Grove IL 60515

HULL, MARGARET RUTH, artist, educator, consultant; b. Dallas, Mar. 27, 1921; d. William Haynes and Ora Carroll (Adams) Leatherwood; m. LeRos Ennis Hull, Mar. 29, 1941; children: LeRos Ennis, Jr., James Daniel. BA, So. Meth. U., Dallas, 1952, postgrad., 1960-61; MA, North Tex. State U., 1957. Art instr. W.W. Bushman Sch., Dallas Ind. Sch. Dist., 1952-57, Benjamin Franklin Jr. High Sch., Dallas, 1957-58; art instr. Hillcrest High Sch., Dallas, 1958-61, dean, pupil personnel counselor, 1961-70; tchr. children's painting Dallas Mus. Fine Art, 1956-70; designer, coordinator visual art careers cluster Skyline High Sch., Dallas, 1970-71, Skyline Career Devel. Ctr., Dallas, 1971-76, Booker T. Washington Arts Magnet High Sch., Dallas, 1976-82; developer curriculum devel./writing art, 1971-82; artist, ednl. cons., 1982—; mus. reprodns. asst. Dallas Mus. Art, 1984—. Group shows include Dallas Mus. Fine Arts, 1958, Arts Magnet Faculty Shows, 1978-82, Arts Magnet High Sch., Dallas Art Edn. Assn. Show, 1981, D'Art Membership Show, Dallas, 1982-83; represented in pvt. collections. Trustee Dallas Mus. Art, 1978-84. Mem. Tex. Designer/Craftsmen, Craft Guild Dallas, Fiber Artists Dallas, Dallas Art Edn. Assn., Tex. Art Edn. Assn., Nat. Art Edn. Assn., Dallas Counselors Assn. (pres. 1968), Delta Delta Delta.

HULL, ROBERT BETTS, landscape architect; b. Oklahoma City, May 1, 1944; s. Robert Cowles and Edna Louise (Betts) H.; m. Eileen Brown, Dec. 14, 1985; children—Jory Anson, Jeremy Snedecor, Lisa, Gregory, Christine. B.S.L.A., U. Mass., 1968. Registered landscape architect, S.C. With Richard Strong Assocs., Toronto, Ont., Can., 1967-68, Bur. State Parks, Commonwealth of Pa., Harrisburg, 1968-70, Emil Hanslin Assocs., Grantham, N.H., 1970-72, Charles Delk & Assocs., Walnut Creek, Calif., 1972-73, Sea Pines Co. and Kiawah Island Co., Charleston, S.C., 1973-79, EDAW, Inc., Atlanta, 1979-80; pres. Hull-Mozley Assocs., Inc., Atlanta, 1981-85; pres. Robert B. Hull & Assocs., 1985—. Vice pres. Arts Festival Atlanta, 1979-81. Recipient Aurora award Nat. Assn. Home Builders. Speaker Smithsonian Inst. Mem. Am. Soc. Landscape Architects (Merit award 1978), Am. Planning Assn., Urban Land Inst. (mem. exec. council of recreation devel. council), Aircraft Owners and Pilots Assn., Mooney Aircraft Pilots Assn. Congregationalist. Developed master plans for Kiawah Island, S.C., Foxfire, N.C., Stratton Mountain, Vt., others. Home: 635 Old Dorris Rd Alpharetta GA 30201 Office: Robert B Hull & Assocs 227 Dekalb-Peachtree Airport Atlanta GA 30341

HULLAR, THEODORE LEE, university chancellor; b. Mar. 19, 1935; m. Joan J. Miller, Aug. 2, 1958; children: Theodore W., Timothy E. BS with high distinction, U. Minn., 1957, PhD in Biochemistry, 1963. Asst. prof. medicinal chemistry SUNY, Buffalo, 1964-69, assoc. prof., 1969-75, assoc. dean grad. sch., 1969-71; dep. commr. programs and research N.Y. State Dept. Environ. Conservation, 1975-79; assoc. dir. Cornell U. Agrl. Experiment Sta., 1979-81, dir., 1981-84; assoc. dir. research N.Y. State Coll. Agriculture and Life Scis., Cornell U., 1979-81; adj. prof. natural resources Cornell U. Agrl. Experiment Sta., 1979-81; prof. natural resources, dir. research N.Y. State Coll. Agriculture and Life Scis., Cornell U., 1981-84; exec. vice chancellor U. Calif., Riverside, 1984-85, chancellor, prof. biochem., 1985-87; chancellor, prof. environ. toxicology U. Calif., Davis, 1987—; chmn. hazardous waste mgmt. com. So. Calif. Assn. Govs., 1986-87, chmn. air quality task force, 1985-87, mem. regional adv. council, 1985-87; chmn. com. on environment Nat. Assn. State Univs. and Land Grant Colls., 1985—, com. on biotech., 1985—, chmn. program devel. subcom., 1982—; chmn. Gov. Deukmejian's Task Force on Toxics, Waste and Tech., 1985-86; lectr. various orgns. Contbr. articles to profl. jours. Commr. Environ. Quality Erie County, N.Y., 1974-75; alternate to Gov. N.Y. on Delaware and Susquehanna River Basin Commns., 1975-79; mem. N.Y. State Agrl. Resources Commn., 1974-75; mem. Arlington Heights Greenbelt Study Com., 1986-87; mem. Monday Morning Group, 1985-87; active various community orgns. NSF postdoctoral fellow SUNY Buffalo, 1963-64. Mem. Am. Chem. Soc., AAAS, Chem. Soc. London, Regional Inst. So. Calif., Greater Riverside C. of C., (bd. dirs. 1985-87), Sigma Xi. Home: 16 College Park Davis CA 95616 Office: U Calif Davis Office of the Chancellor Davis CA 95616

HULLINGER, CRAIG HARLAN, city planning consultant; b. Brookings, S.D., Dec. 1, 1947; s. Clifford Harlan and Louise Edna (Liffengren) H.; m. Elizabeth S. Ruyle, Oct. 24, 1985; children: Clint, Bret, Leigh Ann. B.A., Govs. State U., 1975, M.A., 1976; postgrad. U. Ill., 1980. Exec. dir. Will County Planning Dept., Joliet, Ill., 1973-77; planner, acting mgr. City of Park Forest South, Ill., 1977-78; chief devel. Prairie Devel. Ltd., Crete, Ill., 1978-80; pres. Planning Devel. Services, Chgo., 1980—; cons. to cities in Ind., Ill. and Mich., 1978—. Author: Dreams and Schemes-Proposals to Improve the Chicago Region, 1987. Candidate, Will County Bd., Frankfort, Ill., 1979, precinct committeeman, 1980. Served to lt. col. USMC, 1966-71, Vietnam. Recipient Navy Commendation medal. Mem. Am. Inst. Cert. Planners, Am. Planning Assn., Misericordia Parents Assn. (chmn. ways and means com. 1981-83), Marine Corps Res. Officers Assn. (sec. 1983-84), Plank Rd. Trail Assn. (bd. dirs. 1984—), Friends of Park. Lutheran.

HULME, GEORGE, humane society administrator; b. Hulme, Manchester, Eng., July 1, 1913; s. George and Emily (Cavanagh) H.; m. Ruth M. McRory, Oct. 14, 1944; children—Sheila Miriam, George David. Chartered sec., U. Toronto. Sec., treas., Art Gallery Toronto, Ont., Can., 1946-54; sec. to bd. trustees, bus. adminstr. Nat. Gallery Can., Ottawa, 1954-57; engaged in advt., 1958; sec., gen. mgr. Toronto Humane Soc., 1959-72; sec., exec. dir. Animal Rescue League of Palm Beaches, Inc., West Palm Beach, Fla., 1972—. Sec., treas. Can. Mus. Assn., 1952-57, Art Inst. Ont., 1948-64, Can. Group Painters, 1965-72, Sculptors Soc. Can., 1966-72. Served to lt. comdr. Royal Can. Navy, 1939-46. Recipient cert. of merit Ont. Humane Soc., 1963, plaque honoring vision, energy and perseverance in monolithic dome shelter-clinic, West Palm Beach, 1985; named to $100,000 Club, Animal Rescue League of the Palm Beaches, 1982; plaque built in his honor Dome Shelter-Clinic, West Palm Beach, 1985. Fellow Inst. Chartered Secs. and Adminstrs. (profl.); mem. Soc. Animal Welfare Adminstrs. (charter 1970—), Naval Officers Assn. Can., English Speaking Union. Anglican. Club: Arts and Letters (Toronto), English Speaking Union (Palm Beach). Lodges: St. George's Soc. (life); Masons (Ottawa); Shriners (Ottawa Valley). Office: Animal Rescue League Palm Beach 3200 N Military Trail West Palm Beach FL 33409

HULTIN, BJORN ANDERS, company executive; b. Uddevalla, Sweden, Nov. 19, 1945; s. Johan Arne Berglin and Inga (Hultin). M.A., Stockholm U., 1970; M.B.A., Stockholm Sch. Econs., 1970. Researcher, Swedish Inst. Polit. Research, Stockholm, 1968-71; fin. analyst Atlas Copco, Stockholm, 1973-76; mng. dir. Polytron, Stockholm, 1976-84; chmn. A kerberg & Fogelströ m, 1984—. Home: Elfviksv 64, 18147 Lidingo Sweden

HULTZSCH, HAGEN EUGEN, computer information company executive; b. Birkenfeld, Fed. Republic Germany, Nov. 26, 1940; s. Hans. E. and Stefanie (Rose) H.; m. Barbel E. Ebhardt, June 3, 1967; children: Stefanie, Philip, Anne. Diploma in physics, U. Gutenberg, Mainz, Fed. Republic Germany, 1965, D in Nat. Laws, 1970. Mem. staff Inst. Nuclear Physics,

Mainz, 1968-72, asst. prof. physics, 1972-76; postdoctoral fellow T.J. Watson Research Ctr., Yorktown Heights, U.S.A., 1973-74; dir. computing data Gesellschaft fuer Schwerionenforschung, Darmstadt, Fed. Republic Germany, 1977-85; dir. Tech. Services Group Electronic Data Systems, Russelsheim, Fed. Republic Germany, 1985-88; corp. exec. dir. Orgn. & Info. Systems, Wolfsburg, Fed. Republic Germany, 1988—. Author: Prozessdaten Verarbeitung, 1981. Mem. Computer Soc. IEEE, Assn. Computer Machinery, European Phys. Soc., Gesellschaff für Info., Deutsche Physikalische Gesellschaft, Europmicro, Share European Assn. (pres. 1983-84), Deutsche Forshungsgemeinschaft (computer com. 1983-85), European Acad. Research Network (chmn. 1983-86), German Research Network (co-chmn. 1984-87). Home: Kruseweg 39, D 3300 Darmstadt 23 Federal Republic of Germany Office: Volkswagen AG, Postfach 1, D 3180 Wolfsburg Federal Republic of Germany

HUMBLE, JIMMY LOGAN, transportation company road engineer; b. Columbia, Ky., Dec. 6, 1944; s. William Rymon and Maxine (Brockman) H. B.S. in Elem. Edn., Western Ky. U., 1972. Field reporter Adair County, Columbia, 1963-66; surveyor Agr. Stabilization Com., Muskingum County Edn. Dept., Zanesville, Ohio, 1966-73; road engr. ARA/Smith's, Columbus, Ohio, 1974—; trustee Teamster's Local 413, Columbus, 1983-85. Mem. Fraternal Order Police, Smithsonian Instn., Regenerative Agr. Assn., Pub. Library Columbus and Franklin County (fellow). Democrat. Methodist. Clubs: Ohio Auto, Centurian (Columbus); 4-H (Columbia); Future Farmers Am. Sentinel. Avocations: reading; travel; writing. Home: 351 Garden Heights Ave PO Box 28098 Columbus OH 43228-0098

HUME, BASIL (GEORGE HALIBURTON) CARDINAL, archbishop; b. Newcastle-upon-Tyne, Eng., Mar. 2, 1923; s. William Errington and Marie Elisabeth (Tisseyre) H.; M.A. in History, Oxford U., 1947, S.T.L., Fribourg (Switzerland) U., 1951; D.Div. (hon.), U. Newcastle-upon-Tyne, 1979, Cambridge U., 1979; D.D. (hon.), Manhattan Coll., 1980, Cath. U., 1980, U. London, 1980, Oxford U., 1981, U. York, 1982, U. Kent, 1983, U. Durham, 1987, Benedictine Internat. Athenaeum St. Anslem, 1988. Professed Benedictine monk, 1942, ordained priest Roman Cath. Ch., 1950; abbot of Ampleforth, 1963-76; consecrated archbishop of Westminster, 1976; created cardinal priest San Silvestro in Capite, 1976; chmn. Benedictine Ecumenical Commn., 1972-76; v.p. Episcopal Conf. Eng. and Wales, 1976-79, pres., 1979—; mem. Sacred Congregation for Religious and Secular Insts.; mem. Pontifical Secretariat Ch. Unity; mem. council for secretariat for Synod of Bishops, 1978-87; pres. European com. of Bishops Confs., 1979-87; mem. Pontifical Commn. Revision of Code of Canon Law; mem. Synod Council for Internat. Synod. Author: Searching for God, 1977; In Praise of Benedict, 1981; To Be a Pilgrim, 1984. Address: Archbishop's House, Ambrosden Ave, Westminster, London SW1P 1QJ, England

HUME, HORACE DELBERT, manufacturing company executive; b. Endeavor, Wis., Aug. 15, 1898; s. James Samuel and Lydia Alberta (Sawyer) H.; student pub. schs.; m. Minnie L. Harlan, June 2, 1926 (dec. May 1972); 1 son, James; m. 2d, Sarah D. Lyles Rood, Apr. 6, 1973. Stockman and farmer, 1917-19; with automobile retail business, Garfield, Wash., 1920-21, partner and asst. mgr., 1921-27; automobile and farm machine retailer, Garfield, partner, mgr., 1928-35, gen. mgr. Hume-Love Co., Garfield, 1931-35, pres., 1935-57; partner, gen. mgr. H.D. Hume Co., Mendota, Ill., 1944-52; pres. H.D. Hume Co., Inc., 1952—; partner Hume and Hume, 1952-72; pres. Hume Products Corp., 1953—; pres., dir. Hume-Fry Co., Garden City, Kans., 1955-73; dir. Granberry Products, Inc., Eagle River, Wis. Mayor, Garfield, Wash., 1938-40. Bd. dirs. Mendota Hosp. Found., 1949-73, pres., 1949-54; bd. dirs. Mendota Swimming Pool Assn.; mem. City Planning Commn., 1953-72, chmn., 1953-69; mem. Regional Planning Commn., LaSalle County, Ill., 1965-73, chmn., 1965-71; mem. Schs. Central Com., 1953—, LaSalle County Zoning Commn., 1966—, LaSalle County Care and Treatment Bd., 1970-73; chmn. Mendota Watershed Com., 1967-73. Mem. Am. Soc. Agrl. Engrs., Eagle River (Wis.) C. of C. (pres., dir. 1962-63), Mendota C. of C. (pres. 1948-49, dir. 1946-49, Community Service award 1972). Republican. Presbyterian (elder). Clubs: Kiwanis (pres. 1953, dir. 1954), Masons, Shriners, Order Eastern Star, Elks; Lakes (Sun City, Ariz.). Patentee in various fields. Home: 709 Carolyn St PO Box 279 Mendota IL 61342 Office: 1701 1st Ave Mendota IL 61342

HUME, LEONARD JOHN, political science educator; b. Sydney, New South Wales, Australia, Apr. 2, 1926; s. Frederick Roy and Alice Clare (Stapleton) H.; m. Angela Marguerite Burden, Nov. 19, 1955; children: Fiona, Rowena, Alexander, Richard. B. of Econs., U. Sydney, 1947, M. of Econs., 1950; PhD in Govt., London U., 1954. Research officer Prime Minister's dept. Gov.t of Australia, Canberra, 1950-58; sr. economist Bur. Agrl. Econs., Canberra, 1958-61; sr. lectr. econs. Australian Nat. U., Canberra, 1961-65, reader polit. sci., 1965—. Author: Bentham and Bureaucracy, 1981, chpts. of various books. Mem. Australasian Polit. Studies Assn. (treas. 1963-65), Royal Australian Inst. Pub. Adminstrn., Internat. Bentham Soc. (v.p. 1985—). Clubs: Nat. Press, Rugby (Canberra). Home: 36 Jansz Crescent, Manuka Canberra 2603, Australia Office: Australian Nat U, PO Box 4, Canberra 2601, Australia

HUMES, CHARLES WARREN, counselor educator; b. Cambridge, Mass.; s. Charles W. and Alice E. Humes; m. Marilyn A. Harper, Aug. 7, 1965; children—Rebecca Ellyn, Malinda Maye. M.A., NYU, 1952; Ed.M., Springfield Coll., 1956; Ed.D., U. Mass., 1968. Lic. profl. counselor, Va. Sch. psychologist Westfield Pub. Schs. (Mass.), 1955-62; dir. guidance Westfield Pub. Schs. (Mass.), 1962-70; assoc. prof. Springfield Coll. (Mass.), 1968-70; dir. pupil service and spl. edn. Greenwich Pub. Schs. (Conn.), 1970-80; assoc. prof. No. Va. Grad. Ctr., Va. Tech. U., Falls Church, 1980-88, prof. 1988—; cons. Am. Assn. Counseling and Devel. Vice pres. Westfield Area Child Guidance Clinic, 1963-65, pres., 1965-66; mem. Greenwich Hosp. Nursing Council, 1970-75. Mem. Am. Psychol. Assn., Conn. Assn. Counselor Edn. and Supervision (pres. 1979-80), Am. Assn. Counseling and Devel., Am. Sch. Counselors Assn., InterAm. Soc. Psychology, Phi Delta Kappa (v.p. Va. Tech. 1982-83), Phi Kappa Phi. Author: Pupil Services: Development, Coordination, Administration, 1984; Contemporary Counseling: Services, Applications, Issues, 1987. Book rev. editor Sch. Counselor, 1984—. Contbr. over 50 articles on counseling to profl. jours.

HUMES, SAMUEL, IV, academic administrator, business educator; b. Williamsport, Pa., Aug. 2, 1930; came to Belgium, 1984; s. Samuel Hamilton and Elenor (Graham) H.; m. Maryke Oudegeest, Sept. 9, 1959 (div. 1975); children: Samuel Hamilton, Willem Johannes; m. Lynne De Lay, May 14, 1976. BA in Polit. Sci. with honors, Williams Coll., 1952; MGA, U. Pa., 1954; PhD, DrPhil, U. Leiden, The Netherlands, 1959. Research assoc. Internat. Union Local Authorities, The Hague, The Netherlands, 1956-59; exec. dir. Met. Washington Council Govts., 1960-65; adminstr. County of Balt., 1965-67; sr. cons., prof. U. Ife, Ibadan, Nigeria, 1967-70, Ctr. for African Research, Tangier, Morocco, 1970-72; dir., prof. Nova U., Ft. Lauderdale, Fla., 1973-79, Rider Coll., Lawrenceville, N.J., 1979-83, Boston U., Brussels, 1984—; chmn. bd. Mgmt. Devel. Internat., Brussels, 1988—; adj. prof. U. Pitts., 1962-63, Grad. Sch. Pub. and Bus. Adminstrn., George Washington U., Washington, 1964-65; sr. cons. Inst. Pub. Adminstrn., N.Y., 1967; lectr. Fels Ctr., U. Pa., 1966-67, 1983-84. Author: The Structure of Local Governments Throughout the World, 1961, The Structure of Local Governments, 1969; co-author Managing Administration, 1984. Mem. council Am. Protestant Ch., Brussels, 1984—. Served with U.S. Army, 1955-56. Graham Roberts scholar, The Hill, Pottstown, Pa., 1946; Fels Ctr. fellow, 1952, Netherlands-Am. fellow The Netherlands Found., N.Y., 1956. Mem. Internat. Inst. Adminstrv. Scis. (U.S. del. 1976-80), European Found. for Mgmt. Devel., World Alliance Reformed Chs. (U.S. del. 1968-74). Home: 351 Ave Louise, 1050 Brussels Belgium Office: Boston U Brussels, Laarbeeklaan 121, 1090 Brussels Belgium

HUMICK, THOMAS CHARLES CAMPBELL, lawyer; b. N.Y.C., Aug. 7, 1947; s. Anthony and Elizabeth Campbell (Meredith) H.; m. Nancy June Young, June 7, 1969; 1 dau., Nicole Elizabeth. B.A., Rutgers U., 1969; J.D., Suffolk U., 1972; postgrad. London Sch. Econs. and Polit. Sci., 1977-78. Bar: N.J. 1972, U.S. Ct. Appeals (3d cir.) 1976, U.S. Supreme Ct. 1977, N.Y. 1981. Law clk. Superior Ct. N.J., 1972-73; assoc. Riker, Danzig, Scherer & Debevoise, Newark and Morristown, N.J., 1973-77; ptnr. Francis & Berry, Morristown, 1978-84, Dillon, Bitar & Luther, Morristown, 1985—; arbitrator U.S. Dist. Ct. N.J., 1985—; del. to Jud. Conf. for Third Jud. Cir. U.S., 1975-79; counsel to Bd. Edn. of Borough of Middlesex (N.J.), 1977—; mem. dist. x ethics com. N.J. Supreme Ct., 1983-87. Trustee, Richmond Fellowship of N.J., 1982—, pres., 1984. Mem. ABA, N.J. Bar Assn., Fed. Bar Assn., Morris County Bar Assn. Republican. Presbyterian. Clubs: Bay Head Yacht (N.J.), Roxiticus Golf. Editorial bd. Suffolk U. Law Rev., 1970-71; contbg. author: Valuation for Eminent Domain, 1973. Home: Hardscrabble Rd Bernardsville NJ 07924 Office: Dillon Bitar & Luther 53 Maple Ave Morristown NJ 07960

HUMMEL, MARTIN HENRY, III, advertising agency executive; b. Glen Ridge, N.J., Feb. 2, 1955; s. Martin Henry, Jr. and Evelyn Kathryn (Mayer) H.; m. Leslie Hulsbus, June 29, 1985. AB, Cornell U., 1978. Account exec. Ted Bates & Co., N.Y.C., 1978-80; advt. dir. Atari, Inc., Sunnyvale, Calif., 1983-84; v.p. Doyle Dane Bernbach, N.Y.C., 1980-83, Saatchi & Saatchi Compton, Inc., N.Y.C., 1984-85; v.p. Batten, Barton, Durstine & Osborn Inc., N.Y.C., 1985-87, account dir., 1987—. Mem. Cornell U. Alumni Assn. Republican. Presbyterian. Club: N.Y. Athletic. Home: 55 E 65th St Apt 5A New York NY 10021 Office: Batten Barton Durstine & Osborn Inc 1285 Ave of the Americas New York NY 10019

HUMPHERY-SMITH, CECIL RAYMOND JULIAN, genealogist, educational administrator; b. Clayton, Eng., Oct. 29, 1928; s. Frederick and Violet Agnes (Boxall) H.-S.; m. Alice Elizabeth Gwendoline Cogle, Sept. 22, 1951; 6 children. Academician, Acad. Internat. d' Heraldique, 1976. Research asst. London Sch. Hygene and Tropical Medicine, 1951-54; consumer service mgr. H.J. Heinz, London, 1954-60; U.K. cons. DeRica S.P.A., 1960-74; prin. Sch. Family History, London, 1957—; prin., trustee Inst. Heraldic and Geneal. Studies, Canterbury; dir. Achievements Inc., Tabard Press; lectr. London U., 1952—, Kent U., 1970—; Atlas of Parish Maps and Registers, 1984. Author: Heraldry of Canterbury Cathedral, 1961,; A Genealogist's Bibliography, 1980; Anglo-Norman Armory, Vol. I, 1976, Vol. II, 1985. Editor: Family History, 1962—. Contbr. articles to profl. jours. Decorated knight of obedience Order of St. John of Jerusalem (Malta). Fellow Am. Soc. Heraldry, Utah Geneal. Soc., Heraldry Soc., Soc. Genealogists, Soc. Antiquaries, Inst. Heraldic and Geneal. Studies; mem. Confedn. Internat. de Généalogie et Héraldique (pres. 1986—), Cambridge U. Heraldic and Geneal. Soc. (v.p. 1958—). Roman Catholic. Clubs: Royal British (Lisbon); Challoner (London). Home: Alcroft Grange Hackington, Canterbury CT2 9NN, England Office: Heraldry Centre, Northgate, Canterbury CT1 1BA, England

HUMPHREY, BINGHAM JOHNSON, chemical company executive; b. Proctor, Vt., Feb. 9, 1906; s. Albert Parmlee and Angie T. (Tenney) H.; B.S., U. Vt., 1927, hon. LL.D., 1978; Ph.D., Yale U., 1930; m. Esther R. Stanley, Oct. 25, 1930; children—Eugene B., James R., Sarah. Sr. research chemist Firestone Corp., 1930-42; tech. dir. Conn. Hard Rubber Co., 1942-49; pres. Humphrey-Wilkinson, Inc., 1949-64; pres. The Humphrey Chem. Co., Hamden, Conn., 1964-72, chmn. bd., 1972—; dir. Milfoam Corp. Chmn., Hamden Bd. Edn., 1958-66; trustee U. Vt., 1968-74, chmn. trustees, 1973-74. Mem. Am. Chem. Soc., U. Vt. Nat. Alumni Assn. (pres. 1969-70), Sigma Xi. Clubs: N.Y. Chemists, Rotary. Office: Humphrey Chem Co PO Box 325 North Haven CT 06473

HUMPHREY, GORDON JOHN, U.S. senator; b. Bristol, Conn., Oct. 9, 1940; s. Gordon H. and Regina H.; m. Patricia Green, July 14, 1978; 1 child, Daniel. Ed., George Washington U., U. Md. Ferry pilot 1964-65; with Universal Air Transport Co., Detroit, 1966-67; pilot Allegheny Airlines, 1967-78; mem. U.S. Senate from N.H., 1979—. Coordinator, dir. N.H. Conservative Caucus, 1977-78. Served with USAF, 1958-62. Mem. Airline Pilots Assn. Republican. Baptist. Home: Chichester NH 03301 Office: US Senate 531 Hart Senate Bldg Washington DC 20510 *

HUMPHREY, JOHN WILLIAM, management and sales training executive; b. Des Moines, June 20, 1937; s. James Arthur and Emeline Louise (Atkinson) H.; m. Pamela Dennison Petri, Oct. 20, 1980; 3 children. B.S. in Indsl. Engring., Iowa State U., 1959; M.B.A., Harvard Bus. Sch., 1964. Asst. to pres. Formulast, 1963-64; sales rep. IBM, 1964-66; v.p., dir. Sterling Inst., Boston, 1966-71; pres., chief exec., founder Sterling Edn. Network, Boston, 1969-71; pres., founder Instructional Systems Assocs., Boston, 1978-80; chmn., chief exec. officer, founder Forum Corp., Boston, 1971—; chmn., cofounder Humphrey Mgmt. Corp., 1984—; lectr. in field. Co-author: Legacy of Neglect: History of Mental Health in Industry, 1964. Mem. editorial adv. bd. Training Mag., 1978. Contbr. articles to profl. jours. Trustee exec. com. Boston Zool. Soc., v.p., 1982—; chmn. bd. trustees, exec. com. Boston Ballet Soc., 1984-88 ; adv. bd. Jr. League of Boston, 1979-80; orgnl. devel. policy bd. Columbia Tchrs. Coll., 1979. Served to lt. (j.g.) USN, 1959-62. Mem. Am. Soc. for Tng. and Devel. (chmn. bd. govs.). Clubs: Harvard (N.Y.C. and Boston). Office: The Forum Corp One Exchange Pl Boston MA 02109

HUMPHREY, LOUISE IRELAND, civic worker, horsewoman; b. Morehead City, N.C., Nov. 1, 1918; d. R. Livingston and Margaret (Allen) Ireland; m. Gilbert W. Humphrey, Dec. 27, 1939; children—Margaret (Mrs. K. Bindhart), George M. II, Gilbert Watts; ed. pvt. schs. Mem. corp., adv. bd. Tall Timbers Research Inc. Nurse's aide ARC, 1944—; past. dir. Nat. City Bank, Cleve., Nat. City Corp., Cleve., 1981-86; trustee Mus. Arts Assn.; hon. trustee, past pres. Vis. Nurse Assn.; hon. trustee Lake Erie Coll., life trustee United Way Cleve., trustee Archbold Hosp., Thomasville, Ga.; hon. trustee Case Western Res. U.; bd. dirs. Monticello (Fla.) Opera House; mem., past trustee, 2d v.p. Jr. League; pres. bd. dirs. Met. Opera Assn.; bd. dirs. Thomas County Entertainment Found.; past pres. No. Ohio Opera Assn.; mem. adv. bd. Coll. of Veterinary Medicine Bd. U. Fla., gainseville; past mem. Ohio Arts Council; treas., trustee Wildlife Conservation Fund Am.; former master foxhounds Chagrin Valley Hunt, Gates Mills, Ohio; past dir., zone v.p. U.S. Equestrian Team, Inc., now hon. life dir.; mem. Garden Club Cleve.; bd. dirs., past pres. Nat. Homecaring Council; treas., bd. mem. Wildlife Legis. Fund Am.; bd. dir. Thomasville Cultural Ctr.; mem., vice chmn. Fla. Game and Fresh Water Fish Commn. Home: Woodfield Springs Plantation Miccosukee FL 32309

HUMPHREY, WILLIAM ROLAND, aerospace co. exec.; b. Wilcoe, W.Va., Dec. 2, 1917; s. Church Gordon and Clarice (Booth) H.; student Harvard, 1937, Am. Mgmt. Assn., 1962-63; B.S. cum laude, U. Hartford, 1968, M.B.A. magna cum laude, 1978; postgrad. Indsl. Coll. of Armed Forces, 1968-69; m. Alice E. Waters, June 30, 1956; children by previous marriage—Clarice Hilda, Margaret Helena, Stephen William. With N.Y., N.H. & H. R.R., 1937-50, traffic rep., Hartford, Conn., 1944-50; asst. traffic mgr. Billings & Spencer Co., Hartford, 1950-52; traffic mgr. Mattatuck Mfg. Co., Waterbury, Conn., 1952-56; traffic rep. Clipper Carloading Co., Chgo., 1957; traffic mgr. Kaman Aerospace Corp., Bloomfield, Conn., 1957—. Asst. dir. carrier agy. coordination and liaison Office Emergency Transp., 1964—; mem. Nat. Def. Exec. Res., 1954—; asst. dir. for resource mgmt. U.S. Dept. Transp., 1971—; adj. prof. dept. marketing Austin Dunham Barney Sch. Bus. and Pub. Adminstrn., U. Hartford, 1974—. Trustee East Hartford Inter-Ch. Housing Adminstrn., v.p., 1971—. Served with USCGR, 1940-44. Mem. Aerospace Industries Assn. (nat. vice chmn. traffic com. 1962-63), New Eng. Shipper-Carrier Council, New Eng. Shippers Adv. Bd., Am. Soc. Traffic and Transp., Conn. Internat. Trade Assn., U.S. Naval Inst., Nat. Def. Transp. Assn., Am. Soc. Internat. Execs., Greater Hartford C. of C., Capitol Region Transp. Assn., Nat. Wildlife Fedn., Am. Mktg. Assn., Nat. Assn. Purchasing Mgmt. (life cert. purchasing mgr.), Charter Oak Shippers Assn., Am. Security Council (com. strikes in transp.), Internat. Platform Assn., Delta Nu Alpha. Methodist (pres. ofcl. bd. 1965—, pres. bd. trustees). Kiwanian. Clubs: Transportation, Conn. Quarter-Century Traffic, City (Hartford). Home: 40 Mountain View Dr East Hartford CT 06108 Office: Old Windsor Rd Bloomfield CT 06002

HUMPHREYS, GARRY PAUL, librarian, musician; b. Hucknall, Nottingham, Eng., Feb. 22, 1946; s. Howard and Ivy (Genders) H.; m. Janet Louise Zimmermann, July 30, 1977 (div. 1987). Student, North Western Poly. Sch. of Librarianship, London, 1967-68; pvt. musical studies with, Norman Platt, Nigel Rogers, John Carol Case. Dep. bus. librarian City of London Libraries, 1971—; profl. chorister, soloist; lectr., writer on bus. info. and mus. topics; council mem. Aslib, London, 1983—; mem. Standing Com. Ofcl. Publs., 1984—; chmn. The English Song Award, 1986—. Contbr. articles to profl. jours. Fellow Royal Soc. Arts, 1978. Mem. Library Assn. (assoc., com. Info Services Group 1980—), Inc. Soc. Musicians, Assn. English Singers and Speakers (sec. 1988—), Elgar Soc. (com. mem. 1984-87). Home: 25 Tamar House, Kennington Ln, London SE11 4XA, England Office: City Bus Library, Gillett House, 55 Basinghall St, London EC2V 5BX, England

HUMPHREYS, ROBERT HAROLD, medical association executive; b. Los Angeles, Feb. 18, 1936; s. John Harold and Dollie (McCutcheon) H.; m. Beverly Williams Bailey, June 10, 1972; 1 stepchild, Michael Jay. Student George Washington U., 1954-58, 62-63. Congl. aide U.S. Ho. of Reps., Washington, 1954-58; planning officer Asian Cultural Exchange Found., Washington, 1960-65; exec. asst. Life Underwriter Tng. Council, Washington, 1966-69; adminstrv. asst. Gen. Agts. and Mgrs. Conf., Washington, 1969-70, exec. adminstr., 1970-73, exec. dir., 1974-76, exec. v.p., 1976-82; chief exec. officer Am. Acad. Med. Preventics, Los Angeles, 1982-86, Am. Inst. Med. Preventics, 1982-86; mng. dir. Bio-Med Health Svcs., North Hollywood, Calif., 1986—; exec. dir. Am. Acad. Esthetic Medicine, 1987—; bd. govs. Nat. Health Fedn., 1984—; cons. Oriental art Towson Coll., Balt., 1969—; chief exhibit curator Audubon Naturalistic Soc., 1968—; curator Turner Collection, Washington, 1960—. Bd. dirs. Asian Cultural Exchange Found., Lilliputian Found., Gatchell Sch., Atlanta. Served with USNR, 1958-60. Hold-Fannie B. Scheffries scholar, 1962-64. Mem. Smithsonian Assocs. Clubs: Nat. Press, Capital Yacht. Home: 32448 Saddle Mountain Dr Westlake Village CA 91361 Office: Bio-Med Health Svcs 11311 Camarillo St Suite 103 North Hollywood CA 91602

HUMPHRIES, ELLEN THOM, banker; b. Oskaloosa, Iowa, Aug. 4, 1947; d. Theodore A. Thom and Catherine A. (Wilkes) Betts; m. Quinn F. Humphries, Jr., Dec. 4, 1965 (div. Feb. 1979); 1 child, Laura Amanda Kelly Humphries. Diploma, Killeen Comml. Coll., Tex., 1966. Banking officer, asst. mgr. First Nat. Bank, Metairie, La., 1967-78; banking officer Jefferson Bank & Trust, Metairie, 1978-80; banking officer, mgr. First Nat. Bank, Metairie, 1980-84; v.p. Gulf Fed. Savs. Bank, Metairie, 1984-85; account exec. First Fin. Bank, New Orleans, 1985-87; mgr. Sussex Trust Co., 1987—. Bd. dirs. New Orleans YWCA, 1982-85. Lutheran. Clubs: Metairie Central Bus. Dist. Assn. (sec. 1982-83, pres. 1983-84). Avocations: drama, dance, swimming, reading, youth counseling.

HUMPHRIES, JOAN ROPES, psychologist, educator; b. Bklyn., Oct. 17, 1928; d. Lawrence Gardner and Adele Lydia (Zimmermann) Ropes; B.A., U. Miami, 1950; M.S., Fla. State U., 1955; Ph.D., La. State U., 1963; m. Charles C. Humphries, Apr. 4, 1957; children—Peggy Ann, Charlene Adele. Part-time instr. U. Miami, Coral Gables, Fla., 1964-66; prof. dept. psychology Miami-Dade Community Coll., 1966—. Pres. Inst. Evaluation, Diagnosis and Treatment, Miami, 1987—, bd. dirs. 1975—, v.p. 1975-87. Recipient Cert. of Achievement Phi Lambda, 1987. Mem. AAUP (chpt. pres.1987-88, v.p., sec., mem. exec. bd., v.p. Fla. conf. 1986—), Internat. Platform Assn. (gov.), Am. Psychol. Assn., AAUW (v.p. Tamiami chpt. 1983-88), Dade County Psychol. Assn. (Fla. chpt.), Colonial Dames 17th Century, N.Y. Acad. Scis., Regines in Miami, Soc. Mayflower Descs. (elder William Brewster colony). Democrat. Clubs: Country of Coral Gables, Jockey. Editorial staff, maj. author: The Application of Scientific Behaviorism to Humanistic Phenomena, 1975; researcher in biofeedback and human consciousness. Home: 1311 Alhambra Circle Coral Gables FL 33134 Office: Miami Dade Community Coll North Campus Miami FL 33167

HUMPHRIES, KENNETH B., accountant; b. Rahway, N.J., Jan. 16, 1928; s. John Phillip and Mary Amy (Miller) H.; m. Juanita Jean Hemsel, May 27, 1950; children—Donald Scott, Amy Jane, Fred Henry. B.S. in Commerce, Rider Coll., 1951. C.P.A., Pa., N.J. Indsl. accountant Vikon Tile Corp., Washington, N.J., 1951-58; pub. accountant Washington, 1958-66; C.P.A. 1966—; sec.-treas., dir. Ferguson Containers, E.L. Baxter Co. Inc.; sec. Alpha Press Co. Mem. Washington Borough Bd. Edn., 1966-68; treas. Nature Unltd. Served with AUS, 1945-47. Fellow Am. Inst. C.P.A.'s, N.J. Soc. C.P.A.'s, Pa. Inst. C.P.A.'s. Roman Catholic. Home and Office: 317 March St Easton PA 18042

HUMPHRY, DEREK JOHN, society executive, writer; b. Bath, Somerset, U.K., Apr. 29, 1930; came to U.S., 1978; s. Royston Martin and Bettine (Duggan) H.; m. Jean Edna Crane, May 5, 1953 (dec. Mar. 1975); children—Edgar, Clive, Stephen; m. Ann Wickett Kooman, Feb. 16, 1976. Student pub. schs. Reporter, Evening News, Manchester, Eng., 1951-55, Daily Mail, London, 1955-63; editor Havering Recorder, Essex, Eng., 1963-67; sr. reporter Sunday Times, London, 1967-78; spl. writer Los Angeles Times, 1978-79; founder, exec. dir. Hemlock Soc. N.Am., Los Angeles, 1980—. Author: Because They're Black, 1971 (M.L. King award 1972), Police Power and Black People, 1972; Jean's Way, 1978, Let Me Die Before I Wake, 1982, The Right to Die, 1986. Served with Brit. Army, 1948-50. Mem. World Fedn. Right-to-Die Socs. (newsletter editor 1979-84, sec.-treas. 1983-84, pres. 1988-90). Office: Hemlock Soc PO Box 11830 Eugene OR 97440

HUNDERTWASSER, FRIEDENSREICH (FRIEDRICH STOWASSER), painter, ecologist; b. Vienna, Austria, Dec. 15, 1928; s. Ernst and Elsa (Scheuer) Stowasser; m. 1st, 1958 (dissolved 1960); m. 2d U Yuko Ikewada, 1962 (dissolved 1966). Student Acad. Fine Arts, Vienna, 1948. Exhibited 1st painting at the Secession, Vienna, 1949, 1st one-man show Art Club, Vienna, 1952; later exhbns. include: Studio Paul Facchetti, Paris, 1954, 56, Galerie H. Kamer, Paris, 1957-60, Galerie Raymond Cordier, Paris, 1960, Austrian pavilion Biennale di Venezia, 1962, Triennale di Milano, 1973, Aberbach Fine Art, N.Y.C., 1973; work shown worldwide in travelling exhbns., first arranged by Kestner-Gesellschaft, starting in Paris, 1964; 2d travelling exhbn. 'Stowasser 1943-Hundertwasser 1974' assembled by State Collection Graphic Art Albertina, Vienna, 1974, 3d travelling show 'Austria Presents Hundertwasser to the Continents', starting in Paris, 1975; 4th exhbn. tour 'Hundertwasser Is Painting', starting at Aberbach Fine Art, N.Y.C., 1979; his 1st Japanese woodcut portfolio, Nana Hiaku Mizu, produced after 11 years collaboration with woodcutters, 1973; other work includes postage stamp designs for Austria, Senegal, Cape Verde Islands, UN, relief medallions for Austrian mint, environmental posters (many donated to environ. protection groups), archtl. models. Conceived theory of transautomatism, 1954, developed into a 'Grammer of Vision', 1957; issued manifesto against rationalism in architecture, 1958, (with others) attack on lack of creativity in edn1. system, 1959, archtl. boycott manifesto, 1968, manifesto on recycling, 1979; cooperated with Peter Schamoni on film Hundertwasser's Rainy Day, also prepared portfolio 'Look at It on a Rainy Day', 1970-72; developed plans for The Hundert-Wasser Haus, City of Vienna, 1983-85 Recipient Sanbra prize 5th São Paolo Biennale, 1959; Mainichi prize 6th Internat. Art Exhbn., Tokyo, 1961; Austrian State award for Arts, 1980; Austrian Protection of Nature award, 1981. Address: care Joram Harel Mgmt, PO Box 28, A-1182 Vienna Austria Other: POB 145, A-1013 Vienna Austria

HUNDRIESER, KENNETH ERICH, nutritional science researcher; b. Chgo., Sept. 24, 1955; s. Richard Allen and Erika (Lemke) H. BS in Engring., Northwestern U., 1977; MS in Nutritional Scis. and Biochemistry, U. Conn., 1981, PhD in Nutritional Scis., 1987. Quality control technician Owens-Ill., Milford, Conn., 1977-79; research technician dept. nutritional scis. U. Conn., Storrs, 1979-87; pvt. tutor Tolland Regional Ctr., Manchester, Conn., 1981-87; research fellow Biochemistry dept. E.K. Shriver Ctr., Waltham, Mass., 1987—. Contbr. articles to profl. jours. U. Conn. Research Found. fellow, 1982; Lloyd Matterson scholar dept. nutritional scis. U. Conn., 1983-84; recipient Am. Oil Chemist's Soc. award, 1986. Mem. R.I. Recorder Soc., Am. Recorder Soc., Conn. Herpetological Soc., Sigma Xi, Phi Kappa Phi, Gamma Sigma Delta. Episcopalian. Avocations: recorder, antique instruments, snake breeding, stamp collecting, jogging. Home: 181 Pleasant St Apt 1 Providence RI 02906 Office: EK Shriver Ctr Dept Biochem 200 Trapelo Rd Waltham MA 02254

HUNEEUS, FRANCISCO C(OX), psychiatrist; b. Santiago, Chile, Apr. 28, 1936; s. Agustin S. Huneeus and Virginia B. Cox; m. Barbara S. Cooper, Sept. 23, 1961 (div. Feb. 1972); children: Barbara Francesca, Catalina Andrea; m. Loreto V. Valenzuela, Oct. 12, 1983; 1 child, Luis Sebastian. MD, U. Chile, Santiago, 1961. Research assoc. MIT, Cambridge, 1961-68; spl. postdoctoral fellow Brandeis U., Waltham, Mass., 1969-70; asst. prof. psychiatry U. Chile, Valparaiso, 1970-74; pvt. practice psychiatry Santiago, 1974—; founder, gen. mgr. Editorial Cuatro Vientos, Santiago, 1974—; cons. human relations various cos. Author: Language, Thought and Disease, 1986, also papers in field of neurobiology. Bd. dirs. Camerata Santiago Chamber Music, 1981—. Mem. Soc. Psiquiatria, Soc. Biologia Valparaiso (pres. 1972-

73), Gestalt Inst. Santiago (pres. 1985—). Home: Ave Simon Bolivar 3781, Santiago Chile Office: Editorial Cuatro Vientos, PO Box 131, Santiago 29, Chile

HUNG, BENJAMIN MING FU, physician; b. Fongliao, Pingtung, Taiwan, Nov. 8, 1941; s. Jen Shang and Shu Chi (Chen) H.; m. Mei Yuan Hsu; children: Chai Jen, Tsai Yuan. Bachelor'd degree, Nat. Defense Med. Ctr., Taipei, 1967. Intern Vet. Gen. Hosp., Taipei, 1966-77; resident in surgery China Air Force Gen. Hosp., Taipei, 1971-74; chief resident C.A.F. Gen. Hosp., 1974-75, attending physician, 1975-76; practice med. Fangyean Chungshin Clinic, Fangliao, Taiwan, 1976—. Served to maj. Taiwanese Air Force, 1975-77. Mem. Surg. Assn. Republic of China, Urol. Assn. Republic of China. Lodge: Lions (pres.). Home and Office: Fangyean Chungshin Clinic, 11 Chung Whao Rd, 94004 Fangliao Pingtung, Taiwan

HUNG, KAW-YUNG EDWARD, banker, accountant; b. Amoy, Peoples Republic of China, Aug. 17, 1955; s. Ying-Hsiang Hung and Suk Chong Cheng. Diploma in acctg. Acct. Price Waterhouse, Hong Kong, 1979-83; mgr., co. sec. Hong Kong Indsl. & Comml. Bank Ltd., 1983—; owner Hung Kaw Yung CPA, Hong Kong, 1983—. Fellow Chartered Assn. Cert. Accts.; mem. Chartered Secs. and Adminstrs. (assoc.), Hong Kong Soc. Accts. (assocs.). Home: Block 26A Baguio Villa, Victoria Rd, Pokfulam Hong Kong Office: Hong Kong Indsl & Comml Bank Ltd, 99-105 Des Voeux Rd Central, Hong Kong Hong Kong

HUNG, MIMI WONG, electronics company executive; b. Shanghai, China, July 22, 1948; d. James and Diana (Chu) Wong; m. Raymond K. Hung, Apr. 22, 1971; children: Renee, Nina, Marcus. ScB in Econs., Purdue U., 1971. Exec. dir. Applied Electronics Ltd., Hong Kong, 1966—, Applied Toys, Hong Kong, 1984; bd. dirs. Applied Internat. Ltd., Hong Kong, Applied E&T Inc., N.J. Clubs: Royal Hong Kong, Jockey, Marina, Clear Water Bay Country (Hong Kong). Office: Applied Electronics Inc, Good Prospect Indsl Bldg, 33-35 Wong Chuk Hang Rd, Hong Kong Hong Kong

HUNG, NGUYEN MANH, political science educator, consultant; b. Hanoi, Vietnam, Mar. 8, 1937; s. Nguyen Quan Chinh and Pham Thi Tho; m. Do Kim Ninh, May 6, 1968; children—Nguyen Hung Phi, Nguyen Hung Phong. LL.B., U. Saigon, 1960; M.A. in Internat. Relations, U. Va., 1963, Ph.D., 1965. Prof. internat. politics Nat. Sch. Adminstrn., Saigon, Vietnam, 1965-74; professorial lectr. Sch. Law, U. Saigon and Nat. Def. Coll., 1965-74; vice dean Sch. Econs. and Bus., Minh Duc U., Vietnam, 1970-72; advisor for planning Nat. Econ. Devel. Fund, Vietnam, 1973-74; dep. minister Nat. Planning and Devel., Republic of Vietnam, 1974-75; vice chmn. Nat. Bd. Investment, 1974-75; dir. Nat. Econ. Devel. Fund, 1974-75; assoc. prof. govt. and politics George Mason U., Fairfax, Va., 1976—, dir. Indochina Inst.; lectr. Catholic U. Am., 1976-77; grant reviewer div. pub. programs NEH, 1979—. Author: Introduction to International Politics (Vietnamese), 1971. Co-author: Peace and Development in the Republic of Vietnam (Vietnamese), 1973. Contbr. articles to Vietnamese and Am. jours. Chmn. subcom. on Reorgn. of Supreme Council of Civil Service and Central Office of Personnel Mgmt., Vietnam, 1967; chmn. Interagy. to Draft New Civil Service Statute for Vietnam, 1968; mem. Postwar Planning Bd., 1968-69; mem. Nat. Sci. Research Council, 1970-75, Vietnam Council on Fgn. Relations, 1971-75; v.p. Vietnam Econ. Assn., 1974-75, Vietnam Found., 1975-81, League of Vietnamese Assns. in the Washington Met. area, 1984-86; mem. adv. group on Indochinese Refugees to Dep. Dir. ACTION, 1979; bd. dirs. Nat. Congress of Vietnamese in Am., 1987—; pres. Nat. Assn. for Vietnamese Am. Edn., 1982-84; governing bd. Woodburn Ctr. for Community Mental Health, 1980-82; bd. advisors Vietnamese Lawyers Assn., 1978-80. Smith-Mundt-Fulbright scholar, 1960-62; grad. scholar U.S. AID, 1962-64; Woodrow Wilson Dept. Fgn. Affairs fellow, U. Va., 1965, Social Sci. Research Council fellow, 1985. Mem. Internat. Studies Assn., Am. Polit. Sci. Assn., Assn. for Asian Studies. Buddhist. Home: 3206 Wynford Dr Fairfax VA 22031 Office: George Mason U Dept Pub Affairs Fairfax VA 22030

HUNG, WILLIAM PING-CHEUNG, shipyard director; b. Hong Kong, Oct. 4, 1935; s. Kai and Siu Chun (Au Young) H.; m. Mei-Chun Hui, Jan. 1971; children: Carmen Hoi-Man, William Wing-Lim. Cert., Hong Kong Tech. Coll. Mechanic U.K. Whampoa Docks, Hong Kong, 1955-61; jr. engr. Swire Shipping Co., Hong Kong, 1961-65; marine engr. A.P. Moller Co., Denmark, 1965-70, prodn. mgr. Am. Marine Ltd., Hong Kong, 1970-75, Kong & Halvorsen Co., Hong Kong, Australia, 1975-82; dir. Mesco Club Ltd., Hong Kong, 1982—, Starcraft Ltd., Hong Kong, 1988—; cons. Aberdeen Marina, Hong Kong, 1982-86. Mem. Inst. Marine Engrs., Soc. Naval Architects and Marine Engrs. Club: Royal Hong Kong Yacht. Home: 11B, Mt Sterling Mall, 5/F, Mei T-00 Sun Chuen, Kowloon Hong Kong Office: Mesco Club Ltd, AML 21, PO Chong Wan, Aberdeen Hong Kong

HUNGER, GUNTHER KARL, research advisor; b. Dresden, Saxony, Germany, Sept. 14, 1922; d. Karl Ernst and Ida Hedwig (Von Katte) H.; m. Ria Elisabeth Pfaff, Sept. 30, 1956; children—Thilo, Claudia. B.S., U. Tubingen, 1950; M.S., Tech. U. Darmstadt, 1954, Dr.Sci.Nat., 1959. Research assoc. Inst. Cellulose Chemistry Tech. U. Darmstadt, 1959-61; research scientist Wastvaco Corp., Luke, Md., 1961, dir. research, Luke, Laurel, Md., 1962-76; corp. dir. research Fedlmuehle AG, Duesseldorf, W.Ger., 1976-85, research advisor, 1986-87; cons. for paper industry, 1988—. Author books; contbr. articles to profl. jours., encys. Patentee in field. Recipient Alexander Mitscherlich medal Verein Zellcheming, 1983. Fellow TAPPI (coating div. award 1983); mem. Am. Chem. Soc., Zellcheming (com. chmn. 1977-85). Lutheran. Avocations: watersports; poetry; political and religious discussion groups. Home: An der Kreukapelle 4, Korschenbroich, D-4052 North Rhine Federal Republic of Germany

HUNGER, J(OHN) DAVID, business educator; b. New Kensington, Pa., May 17, 1941; s. Jackson Steele and Elizabeth (Carey) H.; m. Betty Johnson, Aug. 2, 1969; children: Karen, Susan, Laura, Merry. BA, Bowling Green (Ohio) State U., 1963; MBA, Ohio State U., 1966, PhD, 1973. Selling supr. Lazarus Dept. Store, Columbus, Ohio, 1965-66; brand asst. Procter and Gamble Co., Cin., 1968-69; asst. dir. grad. bus. programs Ohio State U., Columbus, 1970-72; instr. Baldwin-Wallace Coll., Berea, Ohio, 1972-73; prof. U. Va., Charlottesville, 1973-82; strategic mgmt. prof. Iowa State U. Coll. Bus., Ames, 1982—; prof. bus. George Mason U., Fairfax, Va., 1986-87; cons. to bus., fed. and state agys. Served to capt. Mil. Intelligence, U.S. Army, 1966-68. Decorated Bronze Star. Mem. Acad. Mgmt., N.Am. Case Research Assn., Midwest Case Research Soc. (v.p.), Strategic Mgmt. Soc. Author: (with T.L. Wheelen) Strategic Management and Business Policy, 1983, rev. edit., 1989, An Assessment of Undergraduate Business Education in the U.S., 1980, Strategic Management, 1983, rev. edit., 1987, Cases in Strategic Management and Business Policy, 1987; contbr. articles to publs. Office: Iowa State U Coll Bus 300 Carver Hall Ames IA 50011

HUNGERFORD, HERBERT EUGENE, nuclear engineering educator; b. Hartford, Conn., Oct. 3, 1918; s. Herbert Eugene and Doris (Emmons) H.; m. Edythe Lugene Green, Nov. 4, 1949. B.S. in Physics, Trinity Coll., Hartford, 1941; M.S. in Physics, U. Ala., 1949; Ph.D. in Nuclear Engring., Purdue U., 1964; part-time grad. student, U. Tenn., 1951-55, Wayne State U., 1956-61. Tchr. sci. Brent Sch., Baguio, Philippines, 1941; tchr. math. Choate Sch., 1945-46; head physics dept. Marion Mil. Inst., 1946-48; grad. instr. U. Ala., 1948-49; physicist Oak Ridge Nat. Lab., 1950-55; shielding specialist, head shielding and health physics sect. Atomic Power Devel. Assocs., 1955-62; research assoc. Purdue U., 1963-64, assoc. prof., 1964-68, prof. nuclear engring., 1968-83; prof. emeritus 1983—; on leave Argonne Nat. Lab., 1977-78; adj. prof.mech. engring. Fla. Inst. Tech., 1984—; cons. in field. Author chpts. in books, articles. Prisoner of War, 1941-45. Recipient Presdl. citation Kiwanis Internat., 1970. Mem. Am. Nuclear Soc. (sec. shielding and dosimetry div. 1960-62, div. vice chmn. 1969-70, div. chmn. 1970-71, mem. standards com. 1959-82), Am. Phys. Soc., Lafayette Organ Soc. (pres. 1971-72), Amateur Organists Assn. Internat., Health Physics Soc., Am. Assn. Physics Tchrs., Sigma Xi, Sigma Pi Sigma. Episcopalian (vestryman 1965-68). Club: Kiwanis (dir.) (1966-68). Home: 2104 4th Ct SE Vero Beach FL 32962

HUNGSBERG, GOTTFRIED HEINRICH, composer, microelectronics consultant; b. Tutzing, Bavaria, Germany, Nov. 22, 1944; s. Leopold Christian and Eva Maria (Koristca) H.; B.S. in Engring., U. Aachen, 1968; m. Elfriede Jelinek, June 12, 1974. Leader, Arbeitsgruppe Elektronische Musik, Munich, 1967—; owner microelectronics cons. firm a-e-m GmbH, Vienna and Munich, 1975—; composer screen music Welt am Draht, Rainer Werner Fassbinder, 1973; numerous compositions for radio, theatre and films; founder working group Electronic Films, 1980. Mem. German Composers Assn., Internat. Computer Software Users Assn. Home: 42 Sendlingerstrasse, D-8000 Munich 2 Federal Republic of Germany Office: 8 Bauerstr, D-8000 Munich 40 Federal Republic of Germany

HUNNICUTT, M(ARY) SHARON, speech engineer, researcher; b. Oklahoma City, Dec. 28, 1942; arrived in Sweden, 1981; d. William Vernon and Mary Ellen (Cabbage) H.; m. Rolf Tore Carlson, July 25, 1981. AB, Gettysburg Coll., 1964; MA in Math., U. N.Mex., 1967; postgrad., MIT, 1971-73; PhD in Speech Communication, Royal Inst. Tech., Stockholm, 1988. Tchr. Calvert Acad., Albuquerque, 1964-65; teaching asst. math. U. N.Mex., Albuquerque, 1965-66, lectr., 1966-67; mathematician Civil Engring. Research Facility, Albuquerque, 1968, Quantum Systems, Inc., Albuquerque, 1968-70; mem. research tech. staff MIT, Cambridge, 1971-81; research engr. Royal Inst. Tech., Stockholm, 1981-88, research assoc., 1988—. Co-author: From Text to Speech, 1987; contbr. articles to profl. publs. Swedish Humanities and Social Sci. Research scholar, 1984-87. Mem. Acoustical Soc. Am., Internat. Soc. Augmentative and Alt. Communication. Christian Scientist. Home: Tojnavagen 16C, S19144 Sollentuna Sweden Office: Royal Inst Tech, Box 70014 Dept Speech, Communication & Music Acoustics, S10044 Stockholm Sweden

HUNNICUTT, RICHARD PEARCE, metallurgical engineer; b. Asheville, N.C., June 15, 1926; s. James Ballard and Ida (Black) H.; B.S. in Metall. Engring., Stanford, 1951, M.S., 1952; m. Susan Haight, Apr. 9, 1954; children—Barbara, Beverly, Geoffrey, Anne. Research metallurgist Gen. Motors Research Labs., 1952-55; sr. metallurgist Aerojet-Gen. Corp., 1955-57; head materials and processes Firestone Engring. Lab., 1957-58; head phys. scis. group Dalmo Victor Co., Monterey, 1958-61, head materials lab., 1961-62; v.p. Anamet Labs., Inc., 1962—; partner Pyrco Co. Served with AUS, 1943-46. Mem. Electrochem. Soc., AIME, Am. Soc. Metals, ASTM, Am. Welding Soc., Am. Soc. Lubrication Engrs. Research on frictional behavior of materials, devel. armored fighting vehicles; author: Pershing, A History of the Medium Tank T20 Series, 1971; Sherman, A History of the American Medium Tank, 1978; Patton, A History of the American Main Battle Tank, Vol. 1, 1984, Firepower, A History of the American Heavy Tank, 1988. Home: 2805 Benson Way Belmont CA 94002 Office: 3400 Investment Blvd Hayward CA 94545

HUN SEN, minister of foreign affairs People's Republic Kampuchea; b. Kompang-Cham Province, People's Republic Kampuchea, 1950. Ed. in Phnom Penh, People's Republic of Kampuchea. Joined Khmers Rouges, 1970, rising to comdt.; in Vietnam with pro-Vietnamese Kampucheans, 1978; returned to People's Republic Kampuchea after Vietnamese-backed takeover; minister for fgn. affairs People's Republic Kampuchea, 1979—, former prime minister; chmn. Council of Ministers, 1985—. Office: Council of Ministers, Phnom Penh People's Republic of Kampuchea *

HUNSPERGER, ELIZABETH JANE, art and design consultant, educator; b. Phila., Aug. 30, 1938; d. Francis Charles and Elizabeth Julia (Rudolph) Thorpe; m. Robert George Hunsperger, Sept. 13, 1958; 1 child, Lisa Marie. A.A. in Design, Santa Monica Coll., 1974; student UCLA, 1975-76; B.A. in Art History, U. Del., 1978; student Rutgers U., 1978-81. Designer, Huntingdon Mills, Phila., 1960-63, Rothschild's, Ithaca, N.Y., 1963-65, Cornell U., Ithaca, 1965-67; freelance designer, Malibu, Calif., 1967-76; art and design cons., lectr. Art & Sci. Assocs., Newark, Del., 1980—; bd. dirs. Gallery 20, Newark, Del., 1982—. Exhibitions include: Malibu Art Assn. Show, 1973, 74, Newark Art Show, 1987, 88. Founding mem. bd. dirs., v.p. Newark Housing Ministry, Inc., 1983—; mem. social concerns com. and drug and alcohol task force Del. Episcopal. Recipient Outstanding Service award YWCA, Santa Monica, Calif., 1972, Award of Recognition, Missionhurst, 1982. Mem. Nat. Art Edn. Assn., Am. Craft Council. Club: Debutante Assembly (N.Y.C.). Home: 1014 New London Rd Newark DE 19711

HUNT, EARL GLADSTONE, JR., bishop, college president; b. Johnson City, Tenn., Sept. 14, 1918; s. Earl Gladstone and Tommie Mae (DeVault) H.; m. Mary Ann Kyker, June 15, 1943; 1 son, Earl Stephen. BS, East Tenn. State U., 1941; MDiv, Emory U., 1946, DD, 1983; DD, Tusculum Coll., 1956, Lambuth Coll., 1978; LLD, U. Chattanooga, 1957; DCL, Emory and Henry Coll., 1965; DD, Duke U., 1969; LHD, Belmont Abbey Coll., 1976, Fla. So. Coll., 1981, Drew U., 1986; DD, Cookman Coll., 1988. Ordained to ministry Methodist Ch., 1944; pastor Sardis Meth. Ch., Atlanta, 1942-44; asso. pastor Broad Street Meth. Ch., Kingsport, Tenn., 1944-45, Wesley Meml. Meth. Ch., Chattanooga, 1945-50, First Meth. Ch., Morristown, Tenn., 1950- 56; pres. Emory and Henry Coll., 1956-64; resident bishop Charlotte Area, United Meth. Ch., 1964-76, Nashville area, 1976-80, Fla. area, 1980-88; vis. prof. Evangelical Christianity, Emory U., 1988—; participant Meth. series Protestant Hour, nationwide broadcast, 1956; mem. Meth. Gen. Bd. Edn., 1956-68; bd. fellows Interpreters' House, Inc., 1967-78; del. Meth. Gen. Conf., 1956, 60, 64, S.E. Jurisdictional Conf., 1952, 56, 60, 64; chmn. gen. commn. family life United Meth. Ch., 1968-72, mem. gen. council ministries, 1972-80, chmn. bicentennial planning com., 1978-80; chmn. Gen. Conf. Study Commn. on Our Theol. Task, 1984-88; pres. Southeastern Jurisdictional Coll. Bishops, 1973, Southeastern Jurisdictional Conf. Council on Ministries, 1978-80; pres. United Meth. Ch. Council of Bishops, 1987-88; Gen. Bd. Higher Edn. and Ministry, 1980-84; lectr. numerous religious and ednl. founds. Author: I Have Believed, 1980, A Bishop Speaks His Mind, 1987; Editor: Storms and Starlight, 1974; Contbr. numerous articles to scholarly jours., mags. Trustee Emory U., Fla. So. Coll., Bethune-Cookman Coll., Lake Junaluska United Meth. Assembly; keynote speaker World Meth. Conf., Dublin, 1976; exec. com. World Meth. Council, 1976-88, chmn. N.Am. div., 1981-86; mem. governing bd. Nat. Council Chs., 1968-84; mem. Com. One Hundred, Emory U. Named young man of year Morristown Jr. C. of C., 1952. Mem. Newcomen Soc., Blue Key, Pi Kappa Delta. Address: care Emory U Candler Sch Theology Atlanta GA 30322 also: 1120 Hunt Ave Lakeland FL 33801

HUNT, ERIC, chemist; b. Kendal, Cumbria, England, Dec. 23, 1946; s. William Henry and Florence Mary (Dixon) H.; m. Sheila Nicholson, July 24, 1971 (Oct. 1972); m. Jill Dorothy Grinstead, Apr. 2, 1977; 1 child, Nigel. BS in Chemistry with honors, U. Leeds, Eng., 1968, PhD in organic chemistry, 1971. Research chemist Beecham Pharm. Research Div., Betchworth, Surrey, Eng., 1973—. Mem. Royal Soc. Chemistry. Office: Beecham Pharm Research Div, Brockham Park, Betchworth, Surrey RH3 7AJ, England

HUNT, H. GUY, governor of Alabama; b. Holly Pond, Ala., June 17, 1933; S. William Otto and Frances (Orene) Holcombe; m. Helen Chambers, Feb. 25, 1951; children: Pam, Sherrie Hunt Williams, Keith, Lynn Gaddis Brock. LLD (hon.), U. North Ala., 1987, Troy State U., 1987, Ala. A&M U., 1987. Probate judge Cullman (Ala.) County, 1964-76; state chmn. for Ronald Reagan, Cullman, 1975-80; state exec. dir. agrl. stabilization and conservation service USDA, Montgomery, Ala., 1981-85; Gov. State of Ala., 1987—. V.p. Ala. Reps., 1974-75, state senatorial candidate, 1962, chmn. delegation Nat. Conv., Kansas City, 1976, candidate for governor, Ala., 1978; mem., chmn. Cullman County Lurleen Wallace Cancer Dr. to Raise Funds for Birmingham Cancer Hosp.; chmn. United Fund Dr.; treas. ARC; officer, mem. Bd. Mental Health Assn. and Retarded Children. Served with inf. U.S. Army, Korea. Decorated D.S.M. Mem. Probate Judges Assn., Juvenile Ct. Judges Assn. Baptist. Lodge: Lions (charter mem. Holly Pond). Office: Office of the Gov 11 S Union St 2nd Floor Montgomery AL 36130

HUNT, JOHN WESLEY, English language educator; b. Tulsa, Jan. 19, 1927; s. John Wesley and Alta (Johnson) H.; m. Marjorie Louise Bowen, Aug. 8, 1951; children: Stuart Griggs, Susan Scott, Emily Johnson. B.A., U. Okla., 1949; student, U. Minn., 1947; Ph.D., U. Chgo., 1961. Asst. prof. English Earlham Coll., Richmond, Ind., 1956-62, assoc. prof., 1962-66, prof., 1966-72, chmn. English dept., Bain-Swiggett prof. English lang. and lit., 1968-71, assoc. acad. dean, 1971-72; dean Coll. Arts and Sci. Lehigh U., Bethlehem, Pa., 1972-87, prof., 1972-87, univ. service prof., 1987—. Author: William Faulkner: Art in Theological Tension, 1965; Asst. editor, Bull. Ill. Soc. Med. Research, 1954-56; mem. editorial bd.: Quest, 1952-56, Earlham Rev, 1966-72; co-editor: Perspectives on a Cuckoo's Nest, 1977; Contbr. chpts. to books, articles to profl. jours. Served with USNR, 1944-46. Recipient Danforth Tchr. Study grant, 1960-61, E. Harris Harbison award for distinguished teaching Danforth Found., 1965, Carnegie Humanities Program grant, 1967-68; Ira Doan Distinguished Tchr. Travel award Earlham Coll., 1970; Ford Found. Humanities Devel. Fund grant, summers 1970, 71; U. Chgo. fellow, 1952-54; Kent fellow, 1952—; Lilly postdoctoral fellow Lilly Endowment, Inc., 1964-65. Fellow Soc. for Values in Higher Edn. (chmn. postdoctoral selection com. 1968-70); mem. Nat. Council Tchrs. English, Modern Lang. Assn., Ann. Conf. Modern Lit., Soc. for Study So. Lit., Gt. Lakes Colls. Assn. (acad. council 1967-72, exec. com. 1968-72, sec. 1968-71, dir. 1971-72), Lawrence Henry Gipson Inst. for 18th Century Studies (council 1972—), Phi Beta Kappa. Home: Box 432 Springtown PA 18081 Office: Lehigh U Dept English Maginnes Hall 9 Bethlehem PA 18015

HUNT, PIERRE, ambassador; b. Paris, Mar. 9, 1925. Diploma, Ecole Nat. des Langs. Orientales, Paris; cert., Ecole Nat. de la France d'Outre Mer, Paris. Serving in Far East 1946-56; sec. Embassy of France, Rabat, Morocco, 1958-63; dir. Ministry of Fgn. Affairs, Paris, 1965-69; ambassador French Embassy, Brazzaville, People's Republic of Congo, 1972-76, Tananarive, Democratic Madagascar, 1976-78, Tunis, Tunisia, 1980-83, Cairo, Arab Republic of Egypt, 1985—. Office: Embassy of France, 29 Sharia Giza, Cairo Arab Republic of Egypt

HUNT, ROBERT WAYNE, manufacturing company executive; b. Tipton County, Ind., May 28, 1940; s. Wayne G. Hunt and Janet Marie (Harris) Messick; children—Rhonda Jean, Jeffrey Robert. B.S. in Bus. Adminstrn., U. Evansville, 1963. Sr. mktg. exec. Ford Motor Co., Phila., 1965-71; dir. adminstrn., personnel W.E. Walker Co., Jackson, Miss., 1971-73; plant mgr. Northwest Industries, Jackson, 1973-80; asst. v.p. mfg., UNR-Leavitt Co., Chgo., 1980-81, v.p. mfg., 1981-82, sr. v.p. ops., 1982-84, sr. v.p. ops., 1984— ; chmn. energy Miss. Mfrs. Assn., Jackson, 1979-80. Dist. commr., Boy Scouts Am., Canton, Ohio, 1969. Recipient Outstanding Leadership award Internat. Brotherhood Elec. Workers, Jackson, 1980. Mem. Am. Mgmt. Assn. Republican. Methodist. Home: 8956 SE Harbor Island Way Hobe Sound FL 33455 Office: UNR Leavitt Co 1717 W 115th St Chicago IL 60643

HUNT, RUTH CECELIA, association and communications executive; b. Chgo., Apr. 5, 1923; d. Leslie Edward and Gladys Esther (Pratt) Hunt; B.S., Loyola U. Chgo., 1943, M.A., 1969, Ph.D., 1975. Asst. editor Am. Osteopathic Assn., Chgo., 1946-48, acting editor, 1948-51; advt. coordinator J.B. Roerig Co., Chgo., 1951-52; copy editor Jordan-Sieber & Assos., Chgo., 1952-53; sci. editor Am. Peoples Ency., Chgo., 1953-57, mng. editor, 1957-59, editor-in-chief, 1959-63; editorial dir. La Salle Extension U., Chgo., 1963-65; freelance writer, editor, Chgo., 1965-75; adminstr., research and evaluation Am. Coll. Obstetricians and Gynecologists, Chgo., 1974-76; med. evaluator Planned Parenthood-World Population, N.Y.C., 1976-79; mng. editor Riverside Pub. Co., Iowa City, Ia., 1979-83; sr. project dir. Psychol. Corp., 1983-85; exec. dir. Am. Assn. Sex Educators, Counselors, and Therapists, 1986—; lectr. edn. Loyola U. Chgo., 1969-80; cons. in psychometrics. Mem.-at-large Nat. Accreditation Bd. for Continuing Edn., Am. Nurses Assn., 1975-79. HEW fellow, 1967-69. Mem. AAAS, Am. Statis. Assn., Am. Ednl. Research Assn., Nat. Council for Measurement in Edn., MLA, N.Y. Acad. Sci., Nat. Soc. for Study of Edn., Am. Assn. Sex Edn. Counselors and Therapists, Phi Delta Kappa. Republican. Episcopalian. Author: Job Tests for Women, 1980; editor Jour. Am. Assn. Sex Educators, Counselors and Therapists, 1979-82. Office: 11 DuPont Circle NW Washington DC 20036

HUNT, WAYNE PHILIP, psychologist; b. Balt., Feb. 4, 1947; s. Henry Adus and Nancy Hanna H.; m. Janice Lee Staples; 1 child, Scott Waldo. B.S., Mars Hill Coll., 1969; M.S., Johns Hopkins U., 1974; Ed.D., George Washington U., 1982. Lic. psychologist, Md. Cons. psychologist Community Residential Facility for Youth, Balt., 1974; investigator Pre-Trial Release-Supreme Bench Baltimore City, 1973-76; intern psychologist Psychol. Services, Bd. Edn. Baltimore County, 1976; counseling psychologist Glass Mental Health Clinic, Balt., 1977-78; mental health counselor Health and Welfare Council Central Md., Balt., 1975-78; coordinator counseling services Counseling and Consultation Services, Balt., 1978-80; psychologist St. Francis Sch. Spl. Edn., Balt., 1978-83, cons. psychologist Chestnut Hill Devel. Center, Inc., 1982-84, bd. dirs., 1983-84; clin. psychologist Youth Diagnostic Ctr., State of Del., Wilmington, 1983-84; chief psychologist Md. Reception-Diagnostic and Classification Ctr., State of Md., Balt., 1984—. Served to 1st lt. U.S. Army, 1969-72. Mem. Am. Psychol. Assn., Md. Psychol. Assn., Md. Sch. Psychologists Assn., Am. Correctional Psychologists Assn., Am. Psychol. Practitioners Assn., Assn. Hostage Negotiators. Club: Johns Hopkins. Home: 708 Dunkirk Rd Baltimore MD 21212 Office: Psychology Dept 550 E Madison St Baltimore MD 21202

HUNT, WILLIAM EDWARD, neurosurgeon, educator; b. Columbus, Ohio, Nov. 26, 1921; s. William Willard and Marian Almina (Lerch) H.; m. Charlotte M. Curtis, June 15, 1972 (dec. Apr. 1987); children: William W., C. David, Virginia R. B.A. cum laude, Ohio State U., 1943, M.D. with honors, 1945. Diplomate Am. Bd. Neurol. Surgery. Rotating intern Phila. Gen. Hosp., 1945-46; asst. resident in gen. surgery White Cross Hosp., Columbus, 1948-49; asst. resident in neurosurgery Barnes Hosp., St. Louis, 1949-50; resident Barnes Hosp., 1951-52; fellow neurosurgery Washington U. Med. Sch., St. Louis, 1950-51; instr. neurosurgery Washington U. Med. Sch., 1952-53; asst. anatomy Ohio State U. Med. Sch., 1945, mem. faculty, 1953—, prof. neurosurgery, dir. div. neurol. surgery, 1964—; mem. attending staff Ohio State U. Hosps.; cons. staff Children's, St. Anthony's hosps., both Columbus, affiliated teaching staff Riverside Methodist Hosp., Columbus; courtesy staff Mt. Carmel Hosp., Columbus; hon. staff Grant Hosp., Columbus. Author numerous papers in field. Served to capt. M.C., AUS, 1946-48. Grantee USPHS, Spinal Cord Injury Research Center, Bremer Fund, others. Mem. Pan Am. Med. Assn., Royal Soc. Medicine, Soc. Internat. Chirurgie, Am. Surg. Assn., World Fedn. Neurosurg. Soc., Internat. Assn. Study of Pain, Congress Neurol. Surgeons (v.p. 1967), Neurosurg. Soc. Am. (pres. 1979), Am. Assn. Neurol. Surgeons (chmn. coms., v.p. 1983), Soc. Neurol. Surgeons (pres. 1979-80), Assn. Brain Tumor Research (med. adv. com.), Am. Acad. Neurol. Surgeons, ACS, AMA, Soc. Neurosci., Interurban Neurosurg. Soc., Ohio State Neurosurg. Soc. (pres. 1961, 78), Ohio State Med. Assn. (del. 1968-69), Acad. Medicine Columbus and Franklin County (chmn. public relations com. 1975), Central Ohio Neuropsychiat. Assn., Phi Beta Kappa, Alpha Omega Alpha, Sigma Xi. Episcopalian. Office: 410 W 10th Ave Room N-935 Columbus OH 43210

HUNT, WILLIAM LUTHER, III, sales and marketing executive; b. Washington, Jan. 21, 1939; s. William L. and Lois (Trimmer) H.; m. Judith Fellows Ingraham, Sept. 3, 1960; children: Caroline, Jenifer, Alison. BA in Econs. with honors, U. Va., 1962; postgrad., MIT, 1967; postgrad. in mktg. mgmt. program, Harvard U., 1977. Dist. sales mgr. Sunbeam Corp., Chgo., 1962-66; nat. field sales mgr. Cornwall Corp., Boston, 1966-75; v.p. sales and mktg. Patton Electric Co., Inc., New Haven, Ind., 1975-88; v.p., sec. Leisure Design Inc., Elkhart, Ind., 1986—; lectr. Ind. Entrepreneurial Workshop, Ft. Wayne, 1985. Contbr. articles to trade mag. Served with USN, 1957-59. Recipient S.P.O.K.E. award, U.S. Jaycees, 1967. Mem. Nat. Housewares Mfrs. Assn., Assn. Home Appliance Mfrs. (heater exec. com. 1984-88, bd. dirs. portable appliance div. 1984-88; chmn. fan exec. com. 1985-87), Am. Fan Assn. (pres. 1984-88), Am. Mgmt. Assn., Home Ventilating Inst. (bd. dirs. 1983), U.S. C. of C., Arlington (Va.) Jaycees, U. Va. Alumni Assn. (life), Alpha Tau Omega (pledge chmn.). Methodist. Home: 10808 Morning Mist Trail Fort Wayne IN 46804 Office: Leisure Design Inc 52640 Thorne Dr Elkhart IN 46514

HUNTER, CHARLES ORVIS, psychologist; b. Warren, Ohio, Aug. 6, 1943; s. George H. and Gayle (Bandy) H.; m. Susan Wynn Clough, Aug. 1, 1972; children: Christopher B., Matthew Charles. BS in Edn. and Sociology, Findlay Coll., 1969; MS in Psychology, St. Francis Coll., 1971. Asst. dir. Irene Byron Drug Rehab. Ctr., Ft. Wayne, Ind., 1971; clin. psychologist Mental Health Ctr. of Western Stark County, Inc., Massillon, Ohio, 1972-77; dir. psychol. services Child and Adolescent Service Ctr., Canton, Ohio, 1977-79; exec. dir. Child and Adolescent Service Ctr., Canton, 1979-81; pvt. practice in psychology Canton, 1976—; guest lectr. Massillon City Hosp.

Sch. Nursing, 1975-76; cons. in field. Contbr. articles to newspaper. Served to capt. Ohio Army N.G., 1966-72. Named one of Outstanding Young Men Am., 1974, Outstanding Alumnus Findlay Coll., 1978; recipient Cert. Commendation Mental Health Assn. of Stark County, 1975, Cert. Commendation North Lawrence Police Dept., 1976. Mem. Acad. for Edn. and Research in Profl. Psychology (trustee, treas.), Ohio Psychol. Assn. (membership com.), State Assn. Psychology and Psychology Assts. (cert. commendation 1978), N.E. Ohio Psychol. Assn., Am. Psychotherapists Guild. Home: 228 21st NW Canton OH 44709 Office: 4450 Belden Village Ave Suite 205B Canton OH 44718

HUNTER, DONALD FORREST, lawyer; b. Mpls., Jan. 30, 1934; s. Earl Harvey and Ruby Cecilia (Lagerson) H.; m. Marlys Ann Zilge; Jeffrey, Cheri, Kathryn. BA, U. Minn., 1962, JD, 1963. Bar: Minn. 1963, U.S. Dist. C. Minn. 1965, U.S. Ct. Appeals (8th cir.) 1965, Ill. 1977, U.S. Supreme Ct. 1986. Assoc., then ptnr. Gislason, Dosland, Hunter & Malecki, New Ulm, Minn., 1963-76; exec. v.p., sec., gen. counsel Wirtz Prodn. Ltd. Ice Follies/Holiday on Ice, Chgo., 1976-79; ptnr. Gislason, Dosland, Hunter & Malecki, Mpls., 1979—; chmn. bd. dirs. Chgo. Milw. Corp., 1977-81. Fellow Am. Coll. Trial Lawyers; mem. ABA, Minn. Bar Assn. (bd. of govs. 1973-76), 5th Dist. Bar Assn. (pres. 1971-72), Hennepin County Bar Assn., Minn. Def. Lawyers Assn. (bd. dirs. 1976), Internat. Assn. Ins. Counsel. Club: Decathlon Athletic (Bloomington, Minn.). Office: Gislason Dosland Hunter & Malecki 10201 Wayzata Blvd Minnetonka MN 55343

HUNTER, EMMETT MARSHALL, lawyer, oil investments co. exec.; b. Denver, Aug. 18, 1913; s. Emmett Marshall and Pearl Joe (Hubby) H.; m. Marjorie Louise Roth, Nov. 21, 1941; children—Marsha Louise, Marjorie Maddin, Margaret Anne. LL.B., So. Meth. U., 1936, grad. U.S. Naval Mine Warfare Sch. Bar: Tex. 1936. Assoc. Vaughan & Work, Dallas, 1936, Thornton & Montgomery, 1937; sole practice, Dallas, Longview, Houston, 1937-42; with Humble Oil & Refining Co., and successor firm Exxon Co. USA, 1945-78; pres., gen. counsel Internat. Oil Investments, Tyler, Tex., 1978—. Bd. dirs. Tex. Rose Festival, Tyler; bd. mgrs. SAR Tex., state registrar, 1973-85, registrar emeritus, pres. Tyler chpt., 1973. Served with USN, 1942-45; PTO. Recipient Gold Good Citizenship medal SAR, 1979, Patriot's medal, Meritorious medal, 1984. Mem. Am. Petroleum Inst., State Bar Tex., U.S. Naval Inst., Pi Upsilon Nu, Lambda Chi Alpha. Author: Adventuring Abroad on a Bicycle, 1938; Marinas, A Boon to Yachting, 1948. Office: PO Box 7402 Tyler TX 75711

HUNTER, EVA SHIREEN, eucator; b. Cape Town, Republic South Africa, Oct. 3, 1944; m. Cedric Hunter; 1 child, Catherine. BA, U. South Africa, 1978; BA with honors, U. Cape Town, 1980, MA with distinction, 1985. Sec., personal asst. various corp. orgns., 1962-73; lectr. English U. Western Cape, Bellville South, Republic South Africa, 1973—. Contbr. articles on feminism and women writers to profl. jours. Office: U Western Cape, English Dept, Bellville South Republic of South Africa

HUNTER, (JAMES) GRAHAM, cartoonist, caricaturist, watercolorist, writer, advertising producer; b. LaGrange, Ill.; s. William Clarence and Rebecca (Faul) H.; m. Cornelia Isabel Seward. Student, Landon Sch. Cartooning, Cleve., Art Inst., Chgo., Art Instrn. Schs., Mpls. Formerly with Assoc. Editors' Syndicate, Chgo., Pub. Ledger Syndicate, Phila., McClure Syndicate, N.Y.C. Creator Jolly Jingles strip, Chgo. Sunday Tribune and McClure Newspaper Syndicate, Bob Hope Golf Classic souvenir cartoon series, 1980—, Christmas Corners full-page watercolor feature for ann. Christmas book Augsburg. Pub. House, Mpls., 1982—, Hometown America cartoon series in Good Old Days mag., Motor Laffs, Biceps Brothers, Getting the Business, Motor mag., full page color illustrations Charisma mag.; cartoon series for Custom Comic Services; Sycamore Center cartoon feature, So. Agriculturalist and Farmer Stockman; Rhubarb Ridge cartoon feature, Curtis Pub. Co.; full-page bus. cartoons, full color covers Am. Bankers Assn.; Hometown Am., Only Yesterday, The Office Cat, Indsl. Press Service, hometown Am. cartoon series for good old days mag.; cartoon strip Am. Farm Bur. Fedn.; watercolor covers Our Sunday Visitor; religious book illustrations David C. Cook Pub. Co., Elgin, Ill., sch. bag art Acme Brief Case Co.; full color Christmas covers, Christian Life mag.; editorial cartoons NAM newspaper service; cartoon strip Bessie's Barnyard Banter, Milk Marketer, Strongsville, Ohio; ann. calendar art for Winthrop-Atkins, Middleboro, Mass.; safety cartoons N.J. Bell Co., Newark; editorial cartoons for Tobacco Inst., 1977—; indsl. cartoons for BASF Wyandotte Corp.; children's monthly cartoon feature in Marvel Comics, Electric Co. mag.; illustrations for Hoard's Dairyman mag., sales cartoons Chock Full O'Nuts Corp., also advt. cartoons and copy, mag. cover drawings, light verse, prose humor,; specialist detailed busyscene drawings, automotive cartoons, humorous animal art caricatures; Work has appeared in numerous nat. mags., newspapers, and advt.; represented in permanent FBI Cartoon Collection, Washington, Freedoms Found. Cartoon Collection, Valley Forge, Pa., Wayne State U. Cartoon Exhbn., Detroit, Peter Mayo Editorial Cartoon Collection, State Hist. Soc., Columbia, Mo.; author: Cartoon Humor in Advertising, Doin's in Sycamore Center, Art Instr. Schs. Lesson: Creating the Busy Scene Cartoon. Recipient Distinguished Service citation U.S. Treasury Dept., George Washington Honor medal Freedoms Found., 1959, 62, Honor cert. Editorial Cartoon award, 1960, 61, 75, 76. Presbyterian. Home and Studio: Lindenshade 42 Clonavor Rd Silver Spring Park West Orange NJ 07052

HUNTER, HARLEN CHARLES, orthopedic surgeon; b. Estherville, Iowa, Sept. 23, 1940; s. Roy Harold and Helen Iola (King) H.; m. JoAnn Wilson, June 30, 1962; children—Harlen Todd, Juliann Kristin. B.A., Drake U., 1962; D.O., Coll. Osteo. Medicine and Surgery, Des Moines, 1967. Diplomate Am. Osteo. Bd. Orthopedic Surgery. Intern Normandy Osteo. Hosp., St. Louis, 1967-68, resident in orthopedics, 1968-72, chmn. dept. orthopedics, 1976-77; founder, orthopedic surgeon Mid-States Orthopedic Sports Medicine Clinics of Am., Ltd. (St. Louis Orthopedic Sports Medicine Clinic, Union, Md., St. Peters, and Chesterfield), 1977—; mem. staff Normandy Osteo. Hosp., St. Louis, St. Peters Community Hosp. (Mo.), Faith Hosp.; clin. instr. Kirksville Coll. Osteo. Medicne; orthopedic cons., team physician to high schs.; pres. Health Specialists, Inc. mem. med. adv. bd. Mo. Athletic Activities Assn.; cons. sports medicine Sports St. Louis newspaper; founder Ann. Sports Medicine Clinic for Trainers and Coaches, 1 yr. fellowship in sports medicine; nat. lectr. various social, profl. orgns.; adj. clin. assoc. prof. Coll. Osteo. Surgery, Des Moines; orthopedic surgeon Iowa State Boys Basketball Tournament, 1966-85. Contbr. articles to profl. publs. Recipient Clinic Speaker award Iowa High Sch. Baseball Coaches Assn., 1982, 83, Hall of Fame award Mo. Athletic Trainers Assn., 1987. Fellow Am. Coll. Osteo. Surgeons, Am. Osteo. Acad. Orthopedics (past chmn. com. on athletic injuries); mem. Am. Osteo. Assn., Mo. Assn. Osteo. Physicians and Surgeons, Am. Coll. Sports Medicine, Am. Orthopedic Soc. Sports Medicine (del. sports medicine exchange program to China 1985), AMA, St. Louis Met. Med. Assn. Republican. Methodist. Lodges: Masons (Des Moines); Shriners. Home: 1230 Walnut Hill Farm Chesterfield MO 63017 Office: St Louis Orthopedic Sports Medicine Clinic 14377 Woodlake Chesterfield MO 63017

HUNTER, HARRY LAYMOND, physician, pharmaceutical company executive; b. Girard, Kans., Mar. 7, 1923; s. Adolphus Osborne and Mary Elizabeth (White) H.; m. Louise R. Leone, Aug. 19, 1949 (dec. July 1982); children—John Patrick, Mary Anne; m. Emily F. Esau, Oct. 19, 1985. A.B., U. Ill., Urbana, 1944; B.S., U. Ill.-Chgo., 1944, M.D., 1946. Diplomate: Am. Bd. Internal Medicine. Intern Gorgas Hosp., C.Z., 1946-47, resident in internal medicine, 1947-48; resident Ill. Central Hosp., Chgo., 1949-50, U. Mich., Ann Arbor, 1950-51; assoc. chief medicine Blanchard Valley Hosp., Findlay, Ohio, 1951-52; dir. exec. health Ill. Central Hosp., Chgo., 1953-57, assoc. chief medicine, 1957-64, chief med. officer, 1968-74; clin. assoc. prof. medicine U. Ill. Coll. Medicine, Chgo., 1953-76; assoc. dir. clin. pharmacology Abbott Labs., North Chicago, Ill., 1965-67, med. dir., 1975-76; dir. clin. studies Mead Johnson & Co., Evansville, Ind., 1976-83, dir. med. services, 1984-88. Contbr. numerous articles to profl. jours.; patentee med. devices. Bd. dirs. Ill. Council on Alcoholism, Chgo., 1970-74, Am. Cancer Soc., Evansville, 1978-80. Served to capt. U.S. Army, 1943-49; Panama. Fellow ACP, Am. Soc. Clin. Oncology, Chgo. Soc. Internal Medicine, Chgo. Inst. Medicine; mem. AMA. Home: 4141 Orchard Rd Evansville IN 47721 Office: Mead Johnson & Co 2404 Pennsylvania Evansville IN 47721

HUNTER, JAMES GALBRAITH, JR., lawyer; b. Phila., Jan. 6, 1942; s. James Galbraith and Emma Margaret (Jehl) H.; m. Pamela Ann Trott, July 18, 1969 (div.); children—James Nicholas, Catherine Selene. B.S. in Engring. Sci., Case Inst. Tech., 1965; J.D., U. Chgo., 1967. Bar: Ill. 1967, U.S. Dist. Ct. (no. dist.) Ill. 1967, U.S. Ct. Appeals (7th cir.) 1967, U.S. Ct. Claims, 1976, U.S. Ct. Appeals (4th and 9th cirs.) 1978, U.S. Supreme Ct. 1979, U.S. Dist. Ct. (cen. dist.) Ill. 1980, Calif. 1980, U.S. Dist. Ct. (cen. and so. dists.) Calif. 1980, U.S. Ct. Appeals (5th cir.) 1982, U.S. Ct. Appeals (fed. cir.) 1982. Assoc. Kirkland & Ellis, Chgo., 1967-68, 70-73, ptnr., 1973-76; ptnr. Hedlund, Hunter & Lynch, Chgo., 1976-82, Los Angeles, 1979-82; ptnr. Latham & Watkins, Hedlund, Hunter & Lynch, Chgo. and Los Angeles, 1982—. Served to lt. JAGC, USN, 1968-70. Mem. ABA, State Bar Calif., Los Angeles County Bar Assn., Chgo. Bar Assn. Clubs: Metropolitan (Chgo.), Chgo. Athletic Assn., Los Angeles Athletic. Exec. editor U. Chgo. Law Rev., 1966-67. Office: Latham & Watkins Sears Tower Suite 5800 Chicago IL 60606 also: 555 S Flower St Los Angeles CA 90071

HUNTER, JOHN HARNDEN, artist; b. Westmiddlesex, Pa., Sept. 26, 1934; s. John A. and Dorothea H.; children—Gregory Andrew, Christopher John. B.A., Pomona Coll., 1956; M.F.A., Claremont Grad. Sch., 1958. prof. studio art San Jose (Calif.) State U., 1965—; adviser, critic textbooks Holt, Rinehart & Winston, N.Y.C., 1972-80; Bd. dirs. San Jose Mus. Art.; guest artist Tamarind Lithography Workshop, 1969, Lakeside Studios, Mich., 1978, 79. One-person show, Cannes Film Festival, 1966; exhibited in group shows, Basel Art Fair, Documenta VI, Kassel, Germany, Cologne Art Fair, Galerie Wolfgang Ketterer, Munich; represented in permanent collections, Nat. Gallery Art, Washington, Mus. Modern Art, N.Y.C., Norton Simon Mus. Art, Pasadena, U. Minn., Mpls., Scripps Coll., Morrison Library, U. Calif., Berkeley, Los Angeles County Mus. Art, Amon Carter Mus. Western Art, Fort Worth, Grunwald Graphic Arts Found, UCLA, others. Served with AUS, 1958-62. Fulbright fellow Florence, Italy, 1963-64, 64-65. Office: San Jose State U Dept Art San Jose CA 95192

HUNTER, LELAND CLAIR, JR., management consultant; b. Phila., Feb. 22, 1925; s. Leland Clair and Lillian Mae (Failor) H.; m. Elva Joy Charlton, July 5, 1946; children: Charlton Lee, Steven Kent, Brian Scott, Donna Joy. B.S., Villanova U., 1948; postgrad., Columbia U., 1944-45; M.B.A., Fla. Research Inst., 1971; grad., Advanced Mgmt. Program, Harvard U., 1973. Test engr. Gen. Electric Co., Phila., 1949-50; with Fla. Power & Light Co., 1950-88; v.p. indsl. relations Fla. Power & Light Co., Miami, 1966-72; v.p. transmission and distbn. Fla. Power & Light Co., 1972-73, group v.p., 1973-78, sr. v.p., 1978-88; pres. Leland Hunter Mgmt. Cons., Miami, 1988—; mem. spl. labor com. Sec. of Labor U.S., 1975-76; mem. Labor and Mgmt. Polit. Action Com. for Utility Industry, 1977, Gov.'s Adv. Council Productivity, 1981—; pres. Leland & Hunter Mgmt. Cons. Vice chmn. adv. com. Dade County (Fla.) Sch. Bd., 1966; bd. govs. Gold Coast AAU, 1967-68; bd. dirs. Crime Commn. of Greater Miami, 1974—; chmn. bd. Victoria Hosp., 1984-88; dir. Pro-Fish of Fla.; Fla. Lawyers Prepaid Legal Services Inc. Crime Commn. of Greater Miami, 1980—; bd. advisors Stetson U.; mem. bus. adv. com. Brookings Instn., Washington; exec. v.p. Atlantic Gamefish Found. Served with USN, 1943-46. Recipient Key to City Toledo and Coral Gables Fla. Mem. Am. Soc. Tng. Dirs. (pres. local chpt. 1955-56). Clubs: Fla. Athletic (pres. 1962), Coral Gables (Fla.) Country; Univ. (Miami); Univ. (Jacksonville, Fla.). Home: 5577 SW 100 St Miami FL 33156 Office: FPL Bldg Suite 3305 PO Box 029100 Miami FL 33102-9100

HUNTER, MATTHEW CHARLES, pharmaceutical chemist, consultant; b. Greenville, Ohio, May 8, 1922; s. Matthew Charles and Catherine (Foody) H.; m. Barbara Bell, June 13, 1948; children—Katherine, Elizabeth, Matthew. B.S. La. Coll., Pineville, 1943; M.S., La. State U., 1945; Ph.D. in Microbiology and Biochemistry, Ohio State U., 1949. Sr. research microbiologist Smith, Kline & French Labs., Inc., Phila., 1949-51; research microbiologist, devel. engr. Monsanto Chem. Co., St. Louis, 1951-53; pres. Hunter Labs., Inc., New Orleans, 1953-61; assoc. prof. med. tech., prof. Dental Coll., Grad. Sch., Loyola U. South, New Orleans, 1954-55; head quality control labs., research labs., prodn. dept. Carrtone Labs., Inc., Metairie, La., 1958-61; research assoc., product mgr. pharms., dir. small animal mktg. Diamond Labs., Inc., Des Moines, 1961-66; v.p. corp., pres. labs. Hart-Delta, Inc., Delta Labs., Inc., Baton Rouge, La., 1966-69; owner Chemage Co., Bay St. Louis, Miss., 1969-72; v.p. sci. Medico Industries, Inc., Elwood, Kans., 1972-75; pres. Technel, Inc., Waveland, Miss., 1975—; cons. new product devel. Vice pres. Jefferson Democratic Assn., 1956; pres. Council Civic Orgns. Greater New Orleans, 1955, Bridgedale Civic Assn., 1954-55. La. State U. teaching fellow, 1944-45. Mem. Am. Soc. Microbiology, Am. Pharm. Assn., AAAS, Am. Mgmt. Assn., Am. Pub. Health Assn., Tissue Culture Soc., Sigma Xi, Beta Beta Beta, others. Club: Bay-Waveland Yacht. Lodge: Rotary. Contbr. articles to profl. publs.

HUNTER, PAUL WILSON, management consultant; b. London, Dec. 16, 1954; arrived in Australia, 1966; s. Noel Julian Wilson and Christine Murial (Knight) H.; m. Lynelle Cynthia Palser, June 23, 1978; children: Simon Wilson, Elissa Sarah, Rhys Wilson. BBA, New South Wales Inst. Tech., Sydney, 1982; MBA, Royal Melbourne Inst. Tech., 1986. Mgmt. cadet Arnotts Ltd., Sydney, 1973—, head office acct., 1978=80; asst. state acct. Humes Ltd., Sydney, 1980-81; mgmt. acct. Oakbridge Ltd., Sydney, 1981-82; plant acct. Pilkington ACI Ltd., Sydney, 1982-83; sr. mgmt. acct. Pilkington ACI Ltd., Melbourne, 1983-85; product mgr. mktg. Pilkington Aci Ltd., Melbourne, 1985-86; project mgr., mgmt. cons. Price Waterhouse, Jakarta, Indonesia, 1986—. Mem. Australian Soc. Accts., Australian Inst. Mgmt. Mem. Ch. of Eng. Club: Krakatau Country (Indonesia). Office: Price Waterhouse, 215 Spring St, 3000 Melbourne Australia

HUNTER, RICHARD EDMUND, plant pathologist; b. Jersey City, Jan. 26, 1923; s. Frederick William and Margaret (Dahlgren) H.; m. Edith Earline Clark, June 2, 1946; children—Catherine Hunter Hays, Margaret Ann Hunter Adamson, Richard Clark. B.S., Rutgers U., 1949; M.S., Okla. State U., 1951, Ph.D., 1968. Asst. in biology N. Mex. State U., State College, 1951-55; instr., research plant pathologist Okla. State U., Stillwater, 1958-68, asst. prof., 1968-71, asso. prof., 1971-72; research plant pathologist Nat. Cotton Pathology Research Lab., College Station, Tex., 1972-75; research plant pathologist Southeast Fruit and Tree Nut Lab., Byron, Ga., 1975-79, research leader Nut Prodn. unit, 1976-79, supervisory research plant pathologist, research leader, location leader W.R. Poage Pecan Field Sta., Brownwood, Tex., 1979-87. Contbr. articles to various jours. Southeastern regional editor Pecan Quar., 1977-79. Served to capt. USAAF, 1943-46. Mem. Tex. Horticultural Soc., Alpha Zeta, Phi Sigma, Sigma Xi. Methodist. Home: 3903 Glenwood Dr Brownwood TX 76801

HUNTER, RICHARD MORROW, architect; b. Phoenix, Nov. 4, 1930; immigrated to Can., 1968; s. Benjamin Franklin and Dorothy (Lewis) H.; married; children: Ivan, Shon, Silla. B.Arch., U. Okla., 1958; studied Zen Buddhism, Daitokuji Temple, Kyoto, Japan, 1958-59. Engaged in research, photographic recording in village, Buddhist architecture, Japan, 1962-63; archtl. study tour of Korea, Cambodia, Thailand, India, Iran, Turkey, Greece, Italy, 1964; chemigrapher, Victoria, B.C., 1970-78; design architect for hosps., nursing homes, heritage bldgs., cons., B.C. Govt., Victoria, 1974-81; self-employed architect, 1981—; study tour Japan, Korea, China, Sri Lanka, India, Nepal, Egypt, 1983-84. Chemigraphic exhbns. include: B.C. Crafts, 1972; Victoria Art Gallery, 1972; Can. Nat. Exhbn., Toronto, 1973; World Craft Exhbn., In Praise of Hands, Toronto, 1974; Habitat: UN Conf. on Human Settlements, Vancouver, 1976; Fiberworks Internat. Exhbn., Cleve. Mus. Art, 1977; designed and produced (with others) Eric Mendelsohn Portfolio; photographs pub.: A Concise History of East Asia, 1966; master plan for Rinzai Zen monastery, N.Mex., 1987. Served with U.S. Army, 1953-55. Recipient Nat. Council Archtl. registration Bds. cert., 1987. Mem. Archtl. Inst. B.C. Zen Buddhist. Home and Office: 203 Goward Rd, Victoria, BC Canada V8X 3X3

HUNTINGTON, ROBERT WATKINSON, pathologist, retired; b. Hartford, Conn., July 2, 1907; s. Robert W. and Constance (Alton) H.; m. Katherine Bond UpChurch, Mar. 21, 1936; children—Robert W., Ann Heldman (dec.), Edith Huntington, Deborah Ward. B.A., Yale U., 1928, M.D., 1933. Lic. physician, Conn., Calif. Instr. pediatrics Washington U., St. Louis, 1935-38, pathology Cornell Med. Ctr., N.Y.C., 1938-41; assoc. prof. pathology U. So. Calif., Los Angeles, 1946-50; pathologist, Kern Med. Ctr., Bakersfield, Calif., 1950-75, pathologist emeritus, 1975—; assoc. clin. prof. U. So. Calif., 1950-70, clin. prof. pathology, 1970, clin. prof. emeritus, 1975—. Contbr. articles to profl. jours. Served to comdr., M.C. USNR, 1941-46. Recipient citation for Outstanding Contbrns. to Study of Coccidioidomycosis, Am. Coll. Chest Physicians, 1984; for contbrn. in Neoplastic and Non-neoplastic Disease, Calif. Tumor Tissue Registry, 1986. Fellow Am. Soc. Clin. Pathologists, Coll. Am. Pathologists.; mem. Am. Soc. Microbiology, Acad. Forensic Sci. Republican. Episcopalian. Address: 470 Wellington Cambria CA 93428

HUNTLEY, ALICE MAE, mfg. exec.; b. Atoka, Okla., May 9, 1917, d. Joseph LaHay and Lula May (Stapp) Howe; B.A. U. Okla., 1939; m. Loren Clifford Huntley, Nov. 7, 1942; children—Loren Lee, Marcia Lynn. Reporter, McAlester (Okla.) News Capital, 1939-41; sec., asst. to pres. and chmn. bd. N.Am. Aviation, Los Angeles, 1941-63; v.p., co-owner Tubular Specialties Mfg., Inc., Los Angeles, 1966—. Former sec. 1st Baptist Ch. of Westchester; sec. Westchester-Del Rey Republican Women, 1959-60; asso. mem. Rep. State Central Com., 1973. Cert. profl. sec.; named Outstanding Sec. in So. Calif., So. Calif. chpt., 1954, Internat. Sec. of Year, 1955 (both Nat. Secs. Assn.). Home: 8238 Calabar Ave Playa del Rey CA 90293 Office: 13011 S Spring St Los Angeles CA 90061

HUNTLEY, ROBERT JOSEPH, management consultant; b. Rochester, N.Y., May 28, 1924; s. Carroll Thomas and Margaret (Mosier) H.; student U. Redlands, 1943-44; B.S., U. So. Calif., 1947, M.S., 1952, D. Pub. Adminstrn., 1974; m. Patricia Ann Poss, Aug. 25, 1945; children: Timothy Robert, Debra Ann, Jon Joseph. Mem. Budget Bur. City of Los Angeles, 1947-52; asst. adminstrv. officer City of Beverly Hills, Calif., 1952-56; city adminstr. City of Santa Paula, Calif., 1957-58, City of La Habra, Calif., 1959-64; exec. Alpha Beta Acme Markets, La Habra, 1964-67; city adminstr. City of Westminster, Calif., 1967-77; exec. asst. County of Orange (Calif.), 1977-80, chief, labor relations, 1980-82, chief personnel ops., 1982-84; exec. dir. Hughes Enterprises, Laguna Hills, Calif., 1984-85; lectr., U. So. Calif., 1953-58, 70-74, Ventura Coll., 1958; asst. prof. Calif. State U., Fullerton, 1964-65; lectr. Golden West Coll., Orange Coast Coll., Calif. State U. at Davis, prof. Calif. State U. at Long Beach, 1971-79. Mem. Gov.'s Policy Com. of Local Govt. Reform Task Force, 1973; active United Crusade. Served with USN, 1941-45; PTO. Mem. Am. Acad. Polit. and Social Sci., Am. Soc. Pub. Adminstrn., Western Govtl. Research Assn., Internat. City Mgmt. Assn., League Calif. Cities (exec. com. 1964-72), Blue Key, Pi Sigma Alpha, Phi Kappa Tau. Republican. Roman Catholic. Author: History of Administrative Research, 1952; Public Relations Training, 1954; The American City Manager, 1974. Home: 15172 Vermont St Westminster CA 92683 Office: Box 430 Westminster CA 92684-0430

HUNTOON, ROBERT BRIAN, chemist, food company official; b. Braintree, Mass., Mar. 1, 1927; s. Benjamin Harrison and Helen Edna (Worden) H.; BS in Chemistry, Northeastern U., 1949, M.S., 1961; m. Joan Fairman Graham, Mar. 1, 1952; children: Brian Graham, Benjamin Robert, Elisabeth Ellen, Janet Lynne, Joelle. Analytical chemist Mass. Dept. Public Health, microbiologist Met. Dist. Commn., Boston, 1950-53; research and devel. chemist Heveatex Corp., Melrose, Mass., 1953-56; with Gen. Foods Corp., 1956-70, acting quality control mgr., Woburn, Mass., 1965-67, head group research and devel., Tarrytown, N.Y., 1967-70; dir. quality control U.S. Flavor div. Internat. Flavors & Fragrances, Teterboro, N.J., 1970-83, mgr. tech. services, 1983-87, mgr. product devel., 1987—. Served with USCG, 1945-46. Com. mem. Essential Oils Assn., Flavor and Extracts Mfg. Assn.; mem. Am. Chem. Soc., Inst. Food Technologists, Internat. Platform Assn. Republican. Lutheran. Clubs: Indsl. Mgmt. (v.p. 1967) (Woburn); Croton Yacht, Saugus River Yacht (treas. 1967-68). Contbr. articles on flavor and food quality control to profl. and co. publs.; patentee gelatin compositions and mfg. processes. Office: 150 Dock's Corner Rd South Brunswick NJ 08810

HUNTSMAN, LAWRENCE DARROW, lawyer; b. Salt Lake City, Jan. 21, 1934; s. Orson Lawrence and Vera Maude (Day) H.; B.S., Pa. State U., 1956; LL.B., George Washington U., 1959; m. Lynn Maroe; children by previous marriage—Laura, Kathleen, Marguerite, Holbrook. Admitted to Va. bar, 1959, D.C. bar, 1961; clk. D.C. Superior Ct., 1959-60; asst. corp. counsel, D.C., 1960-61; assoc. Welch, Mott & Morgan, 1961-64, Miller, Brown, Gildenhorn, 1964-69; ptnr. Brown, Gildenhorn & Statland, Washington, 1969-75; pres. Pan Mediterranean Shipping Corp., 1975-82, Designed Chem. Systems Inc.; dir. Ashley Corp. Mem. Am., D.C., Va. bar assns. Club: Fairfax (Va.) Country. Home: 11645 Chapel Rd Clifton VA 22024 Office: 1101 17th St NW Washington DC 20036 also: 10374 Democracy Ln Fairfax VA 22030

HUON, HUBERT JOHN, psychiatrist, neurologist; b. Douarnenez, France, June 6, 1936; s. Frank Allen and Mary Ann (Simon) H.; m. Mikaelle Huon, Mar. 31, 1964; children: Nathalie, Renaud, John-Christopher, Valerie. BS, Coll. St. Francois Xavier, Vannes, France, 1953; MD, Faculty Medicine, Paris, 1971; Cert. in Psychiatry, Pediatrics, Faculty Medicine Paris, 1971-72; Cert. in Neurophysiology, Faculty Medicine, 1973. Intern, resident, asst. prof. biochemistry Hosps. of Paris, 1966-70, prof. asst. neurophysiology, psychiatry, 1968-72; prof. asst. psychiatry Hosp. Brest, France, 1972-74; chief psychiat. service Ctr. Hosp. Specialise de St. Ave, Vannes, France, 1977—; dir. sleep lab. Ctr. Hosp. Specialise de St. Ave, 1980—; dir. clin. teaching Hosp. Rennes, France, 1977—; cons. neurologist, Paris; expert ct. of justice, Rennes, 1973; clin. expert Ministry of Health, 1973; French del. World Council for Gifted and Talented Children, 1981-83; mgr. house constrn. firm. Author: The Children's Sleep, 1974; contbr. med. research articles to profl. publs. Served as sgt. French armed forces, 1957-60, lt. col. res. Mem. Sleep Research Soc., European Sleep Research Soc., French Soc. EEG and Neurophysiology, Mensa, Nat. Fedn. Promotion and Constrn. Roman Catholic. Lodge: Rotary. Home: Kerjaffre, 56610 Arrandon France Office: Hospital, 56896 Saint Ave Britany France

HUPPERT, ERWIN, director of photography, educator; b. Baden/Wien, Austria, Oct. 23, 1923; arrived at France,; s. Eduard and Charwat (Ludmilla) H.; m. Anna Frantz, May 15, 1952; 1 child, Matthias. Diploma, Ecole Photo, Locarno, SWitzerland, 1945, Beaux-Art, Lausanne, Switzerland, 1946. Dir. photography various prodn. cos.; prof. Ecole Nationale Louis Lumiere, Paris, 1983—. Author: (with others) Manuel du Technicien du Film, 1973. Mem. Commission Superieur Technique of France, Groupe de Recherche Et D'Essais Cinematographiques. Home: 20 Rue du Commandant Repe, Mouchotte, 75014 Paris France

HU QILI, Chinese political official; b. Yulin County, Shaanxi Province, People's Republic of China, 1929. Grad. dept. mechanics Beijing U., People's Republic of China. Joined Chinese Communist Party, 1948; sec. Communist Youth League Com., Beijing U., 1954, alt. sec., 1964, sec. 1978-80; vice chmn. Students' Fedn., 1954; mem. standing com. Youth Fedn., 1958, vice-chmn., 1965, chmn., 1979-80; purged, 1967; v.p. Qinghua U., Beijing, 1978-80; mem. standing com. 5th CPPCC, 1979-83; mayor Tianjin, 1979-82; sec. com. Chinese Communist Party, Tianjin, 1981-82, dir. gen. office Central Com., 1982-84, mem. 12th Central Com., permanent sec. Secretariat, 1982—, mem. Politburo, 1985—, mem. Standing Com., 1987—. Office: Chinese Communist Party, Standing Com, Tianjin People's Republic of China

HUQUE, AHMED SHAFIQUL, political science educator, researcher; b. Dhaka, Bangladesh, Aug. 1, 1952; s. Mohammad Manirul and Tabinda Akhtar (Khatun) H.; m. Khaleda Yasmin, Oct. 02, 1979; children: Shineen, Sakeen. BA with honors, U. Dhaka, 1974, MA, 1975; MA, U. Man., Winnipeg, Can., 1979; PhD, U. B.C., Vancouver, Can., 1984. Lectr. U. Chittagong, Bangladesh, 1976-78; teaching asst. U. Man., 1978-79, U. B.C., 1979-84; asst. prof. U. Chittagong, 1984-85, assoc. prof., 1985-88; assoc. prof. U. Dhaka, 1988—; mem. publ. com. U. Chittagong, 1985-86. Author: Problems of Participation, 1988; contbr. articles to profl. jours.; editor Bangladesh Polit. Studies, 1987; mem. editorial bd. several acad. jours. Sec. World U. Service Local Com., U. Chittagong, 1986-87. Mem. Bangladesh Assn. for Am. Studies, Bangladesh Polit. Sci. Assn. Moslem. Office: U Dhaka, Dept Pub Adminstrn, Dhaka 1000, Bangladesh

HURD, DOUGLAS RICHARD, British member Parliament, secretary state for the home office; b. Marlborough, Wilts, Eng., Mar. 8, 1930; s. Anthony Richard and Stephanie (Corner) H.; m. Tatiana Elizabeth Michelle Eyre, Nov. 10, 1960 (div. 1982); children: Nicholas, Thomas, Alexander; m. Judy

Smart, May 7, 1982; 2 children. King's scholar, Newcastle scholar Eton, Trinity Coll., Cambridge. With Her Majesty's Diplomatic Service, Peking, UN, Rome, 1952-56; mem. staff research dept. Conservative Party, 1966-68; pvt. sec. to leader of opposition, 1968-70; M.P. for Witney, Oxfordshire; polit. sec. to prime minister, 1970-74, opposition spokesman on European affairs, 1976-79, minister of state Fgn. and Commonwealth Office, 1979-83, minister of state Home Office, 1983-84, sec. of state Home Office, 1985—, sec. of state for No. Ireland, 1984-85. Author 2 hist. works, 7 polit. thrillers. Decorated comdr. Order Brit. Empire. Conservative. Mem. Ch. of Eng. Club: Beefsteak (London). Avocation: writing thrillers. Office: Secretary of State Home Dept, London SW1A 2AZ England *

HURD, RICHARD NELSON, pharmaceutical company executive; b. Evanston, Ill., Feb. 25, 1926; s. Charles DeWitt and Mary Ormsby (Nelson) H.; m. Jocelyn Fillmore Martin, Dec. 22, 1950; children: Melanie Gray, Suzanne DeWitt. BS, U. Mich., 1946; PhD, U. Minn., 1956. Chemist, Gen. Electric Co., Schenectady, 1948-49; research and devel. group leader Koppers Co., Pitts., 1956-57; research chemist Mallinckrodt Chem. Works, St. Louis, 1956-63, group leader, 1963-66; group leader Comml. Solvents Corp., Terre Haute, Ind., 1966-68, sect. head, 1968-71; mgr. sci. affairs G. D. Searle Internat. Co., Skokie, Ill., 1972-73, dir. mfg. and tech. affairs, 1973-77, rep. to internat. tech. com. Pharm. Mfrs. Assn., 1973-77; v.p. tech. affairs Elder Pharms., Bryan, Ohio, 1977-81; v.p. research and devel. U.S. Proprietary Drugs & Toiletries div. Schering-Plough Corp., Memphis, 1981-83; v.p. sci. affairs Moleculon Inc., Cambridge, Mass., 1984—. Patentee in field; contbr. articles to profl. jours. Mem. Ferguson-Florissant (Mo.) Sch. Bd., 1964-66; bd. dirs. United Fund of Wabash Valley (Ind.), 1969-71. Served with USN, 1943-46, 53-55. E. I. DuPont de Nemours & Co., Inc. fellow, 1956. Mem. Am. Acad. Dermatology, Soc. Investigative Dermatology, Am. Soc. Photobiology, Am. Chem. Soc., N.Y. Acad. Sci., Am. Pharm. Assn., Am. Assn. Pharm. Scientists, AAAS, Sigma Xi. Presbyterian. Club: Mich. Shores (Wilmette, Ill.). Home: 49 Austin Rd Sudbury MA 01776 Office: 230 Albany St Cambridge MA 02139

HURET, BARRY S., mktg. exec.; b. N.Y.C., May, 1938; s. Benjamin and Anna (Berko) H.; B.A. with honors, Cornell U., 1961; M.B.A. with distinction, N.Y. U., 1970; m. Marilynn Moskowitz, Feb., 1961; children—Abbey, Eric. Asst. sales engr. Westinghouse Corp., Pitts., 1962-64; sales engr. MultiAmp Corp., Cranford, N.J., 1964-65; sales engr., regional mgr., nat. sales mgr. Gould, Inc., St. Paul, 1965-77; successively mktg. mgr., dir. mktg., dir. new bus. ventures, v.p. new bus. and govt. sales, dir. splty. product mktg. Exide Corp., Horsham, Pa., 1977-82; nat. sales mgr. battery sales div. Panasonic Indsl. Co., Secaucus, N.J., 1982-86; asst. gen. mgr. battery sales div., 1986—. Served to lt. U.S. Army, 1961-62. Recipient Hector Lazo Meml. Mktg. award N.Y. U., 1970, Alumni Key, 1970. Mem. Cornell U. Alumni (v.p. class of '59), Phi Beta Kappa. Author: A User Friendly Guide to Selcting Rechargeable Batteries. Home: 484 Kings Rd Yardley PA 19067

HUREWITZ, J(ACOB) C(OLEMAN), educator, author, consultant; b. Hartford, Conn., Nov. 11, 1914; s. Isaac S. and Ida (Aronson) H.; m. Miriam Freund, Mar. 29, 1946; children—Barbara Jean, Ruth Anne. B.A., Trinity Coll., Hartford, 1936; M.A., Columbia U., 1937, Ph.D., 1950. Sr. polit. analyst OSS, 1943-45, Dept. State, 1945-46; polit. adv. U.S. Cabinet Com. on Palestine, 1946; polit. affairs officer UN Secretariat, 1949-50; prof. Middle East polit. history Dropsie Coll., Phila., 1949-56; mem. faculty Grad. Sch. of Arts and Scis., Sch. Internat. Affairs, Columbia U., N.Y.C., 1950—; prof. govt. Grad. Sch. of Arts and Scis., Sch. Internat. Affairs, Columbia U., 1958-84, prof. emeritus, 1985—; dir. Middle East Inst., 1971-84; vis. prof. polit. sci. Johns Hopkins Sch. Advanced Internat. Studies, 1956, Cornell U., 1970; cons. Carnegie Endowment for Internat. Peace, 1954, Rand Corp., 1962-71, Am. Council Learned Socs., 1963-64, Dept. State, 1966-71, Dept. Def., 1970-74, Stanford Research Inst., 1973-76, ABC News, 1979; founder, chmn. Univ. Seminar on the Middle East, Columbia U., 1971—; bd. research cons. Fgn. Policy Research Inst., Phila., 1972—, Inst. Fgn. Policy Analysis, Cambridge, Mass., 1976—; resident fellow Center for Advanced Studies in the Behavioral Scis., Stanford, Calif., 1962-63, Council on Fgn. Relations, N.Y.C., 1965-66; organizer, dir. internat. confs. on Middle East; participant Dartmouth Am.-Soviet Conf. XII, 1979. Author: The Struggle for Palestine, 1950, Middle East Dilemmas, 1953, Diplomacy in the Near and Middle East, 1956, Undergraduate Instruction on the Middle East in American Colleges and Universities, 1962, Middle East Politics: The Military Dimension, 1969, The Middle East and North Africa in World Politics: I, European Expansion 1535-1914, 1975, II, British-French Supremacy, 1914-1955, 1979; Editor and contbr.: Soviet-American Rivalry in the Middle East, 1969, Oil, the Arab-Israel Dispute and the Industrial World, 1976; Bd. editors: Middle East Jour, 1947-81, Orbis, 1974—, Terrorism, 1977-81. Mem. adv. panel on tech. transfer to Middle East, Cong. Office of Tech. Assessment, 1982-84. Served with U.S. Army, 1942-43. Social Sci. Research Council grantee, 1946-48; Ford Found. fellow, 1954, 86-88; Guggenheim fellow, 1958-59; Am. Philos. Soc. grantee, 1960; Rockefeller Found. fellow, 1960-62; Ford Found. grantee, 1970; Exxon Edn. Found. grantee, 1981. Fellow Middle East Studies Assn. (founding fellow); mem. Am. Hist. Assn., Middle East Inst. Washington (gov. 1964—), Am. Polit. Sci. Assn., Acad. Polit. Sci., Council Fgn. Relations, Am. Inst. Iranian Studies (founding mem., 1st v.p. 1968-69), Internat. Inst. Strategic Studies, Inter-Univ. Seminar on Armed Forces and Soc. (founding mem.), Am. Research Center in Egypt (gov.), Phi Beta Kappa. Office: Columbia U Middle East Inst New York NY 10027

HURFORD, JOHN BOYCE, investment counselor; b. Bryn Mawr, Pa., Feb. 28, 1938; s. James Rayner and Helen Alice (Simon) H.; m. Hildegard Martha Drueke, Jan. 25, 1982; 1 child, Jennifer Elizabeth. B.A., Haverford Coll., 1960; M.B.A., Harvard U., 1965. With investment mgmt. dept. Lazard Freres & Co., N.Y.C., 1967-69; mng. dir. BEA Assocs. Inc., N.Y.C., 1969—. Bd. mgrs. Haverford Coll., 1984—, chmn. investment com., 1987—, mem. corp., 1984—; founder, dir., pres. The Hurford Found., 1986—; mem. Republican Presdl. Task Force, 1981—. John Hancock fellow, 1963; Fulbright scholar, 1966-67. Mem. N.Y. Soc. Security Analysts, U.S. Naval War Coll., Fulbright Alumni Assn. (life). Clubs: University, Harvard (N.Y.C.). Avocations: sailing, swimming, skiing, travel, reading. Home: 220 E 63d St New York NY 10021 also: 347 Meadow Ln Southampton NY 11968 Office: BEA Assocs Inc 153 E 53d St New York NY 10022

HURLBURT, GRAHAM CHARLES, university counselor; b. Winnipeg, Man., Can., May 7, 1936; s. William Erastus and Mildred Irene (Jackson) H.; m. Patricia Helen Mueller, June 30, 1964. B.A., U. Man., Winnipeg, 1957; A.M., Ind. U., 1960; M.Ed., U. Man., 1962; Ph.D., U. N.D., 1980. Cert. tchr., counselor, Man. Geography tchr. St. Vital Sch. Div., Winnipeg, 1963-68, English tchr., 1968-76; instr. New Careers, Provincial Govt., Winnipeg, 1976-78; prof. Brandon U., Winnipeg, 1979-80, 86—; counselor U. Man., 1980—, cons., 1982—, U. Winnipeg, 1985—; researcher Man. Indian Edn. Assn., Winnipeg, 1982—; asst. prof. BUNTEP; bd. dirs. Can. Internat. Coll., Nelson, B.C., Can. Contbr. articles to profl. jours. Mem. Can. Guidance Counseling Assn., Man. Tchrs. Soc., Can. Assn. Colls. and Univs. Mem. United Ch. Clubs: Winnipeg Press, Fort Garry Legion. Avocations: reading; cycling; sailing; camping; cartooning. Home: 645 Viscount Pl, Winnipeg, MB Canada R3T 1J1 Office: U Winnipeg, 515 Portage Ave, Winnipeg, R3B 2E9,, Canada

HURLBURT, HARLEY ERNEST, oceanographer; b. Bennington, Vt., Apr. 12, 1943; s. Paul Rhodes and Evelyn Arlene (Lockhart) H.; B.S. in Physics (scholar), Union Coll., Schenectady, 1965; M.S., Fla. State U., 1971, Ph.D. in Meteorology, 1974. NASA trainee Fla. State U., 1970-72; postdoctoral fellow advanced studies program Nat. Center Atmospheric Research, Boulder, Colo., 1974-75; staff scientist JAYCOR, Alexandria, Va., 1975-77; oceanographer Naval Ocean Research and Devel. Activity, Bay St. Louis, Miss., 1977—, br. head, 1983-85; mem. nat. adv. panels NASA satellite surface stress working group, 1981-84, minerals mgmt. service interagy. adv. group, 1982—, world ocean circulation experiment working group on numerical modeling, 1984—, USN space oceanography working group, 1986—, co-chmn. working group on global prediction systems, ocean prediction workshop, 1986. Contbr. numerous articles to profl. jours. V.p. Burgundy Citizens Assn., 1976-77. Recipient Disting. Scientist medal 13th Internat. Colloquium, Liege, Belgium, 1981, publ. award for best basic research paper Naval Ocean Research and Devel. Activity, 1980; Office Naval Research grantee, 1975-77, 84—; Dept. Energy grantee, 1975-78; Tex. A&M U. grantee, 1976; Office of Naval Technology grantee, 1987—. Mem. Am. Meteorol. Soc., Am. Geophysical Union, Phi Sigma Kappa, Sigma Xi, Sigma Tau, Chi Epsilon Pi. Methodist. Home: 274 Hermitage Ct Pearl River LA 70452 Office: Naval Ocean Research and Devel Activity Code 323 Bldg 1103 Nat Space Tech Lab Bay Saint Louis MS 39529

HURLBUT, ELVIN MILLARD, JR., petroleum geologist, former technical editor; b. El Campo, Tex., Dec. 4, 1921; s. Elvin Millard and Iva Sarepta Marie (Leech) H.; m. Virginia Lee Andrews, Nov. 21, 1950. B.S. in Geology, U. Tex., 1943; M.A. in Geology, U. Calif.-Berkeley, 1948. Tech. writer, data retrieval specialist Fed. Electric Corp., Houston, 1969-71; tech. writer, data retrieval specialist, tech. editor Service Tech. Corp., Houston, 1971-72; engr., publs. engr. Lockheed Electronics Co., Inc., Houston, 1972-74; tech. editor Kentron Internat., Inc., Houston, 1974-83, Omniplan Corp., Houston, 1983-85. Charter mem. Republican Presdl. Task Force, 1984-85; contbr. Nat. Rep. Senatorial Com., 1984-85, Nat. Rep. Congl. Com., 1984-85. Recipient Merit medal Rep. Presdl. Task Force, 1984. Mem. Am. Assn. Petroleum Geologists, Soc. Tech. Communication (sr. mem.), Assn. Earth Sci. Editors, N.Y. Acad. Scis. Mem. Disciples of Christ Ch. Avocations: music; movies; reading; economics.

HURLBUT, ROBERT HAROLD, health care services executive; b. Rochester, N.Y., Mar. 9, 1935; s. Harold Leroy and Martha Irene (Fincher) H.; student Coll. Hotel Adminstrn. Cornell U., 1953-56; m. Barbara Cox, June 14, 1958; children—Robert W., Christine A. Adminstr., dir. Pillars Nursing Home, Rochester, 1956—, Elmcrest Nursing Home, Churchville, N.Y., 1960—, Elm Manor Nursing Home, Canandaigua, N.Y., 1960—, Penfield Nursing Home, Rochester, 1963—, Avon (N.Y.) Nursing Home, 1964—, Newark (N.Y.) Nursing Home, 1965—, Lakeshore Nursing Home, Rochester, 1972—, others; organizer, adminstrv. dir. Rohm Services Corp., hdqrs. Rochester, 1964—organizer, pres. Vari-Care, Inc., hdqrs. Rochester, 1969—; mem. long-term healthcare planning program fund Monroe Community Coll.; mem. nat. adv. bd. Rochester Inst. Tech. Sch. Hotel and Tourism Mgmt. Trustee St. John Fisher Coll., Eastman Dental Ctr.; mem., bd. dirs. Rochester Area Found.; bd. dirs. Rochester Philharm. Orch., Monroe County Long-Term Care Program, Marine Midland Bank; mem. exec. adv. bd. Roberts Wesleyan Coll.; mem. N.Y. State Sen. Lombardi's Task Force on Hosp. Alternate Care. Fellow Am. Coll. Health Adminstrs.; mem. N.Y. State Health Facilities Assn. (multi-facility com.); bd. trustees Rochester Area C. of C., Lambda Chi Alpha. Clubs: Genesee Valley, Oak Hill, Cornell (Rochester). Home: 200 Sheldon Rd Honeoye Falls NY 14472 Office: 277 Alexander St Rochester NY 14607

HURLEY, FRANK EDWARD, cardiologist; b. Springfield, Mass., Feb. 14, 1917; s. John F. and Mary V. H.; B.S., Am. Internat. U., 1940; M.D., Tufts U., 1943; m. Mary Ann Barbara Leddy, Dec. 27, 1945. Intern, Mercy Hosp., Springfield, 1943-44; resident St. Vincent's Hosp., Worcester, Mass., 1946-47; sr. attending physician Mercy Hosp., Springfield, from 1950, chief dept. medicine, 1964-70, dir. medicine, med. edn., from 1950, adv. bd. sch. nursing, 1954-70, med. dir., 1973-75; practice medicine specializing in internal medicine and cardiology, Springfield, from 1948; cons. cardiologist Springfield Mcpl. Hosp. Served with M.C., U.S. Army, 1944-46. Decorated medal of Valor, Legion of Merit; recipient Pynchon award, 1973; AMA Physicians Recognition award, 1969, 72, 75, 78, 82. Mem. ACP, AMA, Am. Coll. Cardiology, Mass. Med. Soc., Mass., Am. socs. internal medicine, Springfield Acad. Medicine (pres. 1962-63). Roman Catholic. Home and Office: 1090 Worthington St Springfield MA 01109

HURLEY, SUSAN LYNN, philosopher, educator; b. N.Y.C., Sept. 16, 1954; d. Roy Thomas and Esther (Sarchian) H. AB summa cum laude, Princeton U., 1976; B Philosophy with distinction, Oxford U., Eng., 1979, MA, 1981, D Philosophy with distinction, 1983; JD cum laude, Harvard U., 1988. Jr. research fellow All Souls Coll., Oxford, Eng., 1981-84; Brockhues fellow, lectr. philosophy St. Edmund Hall Oxford U., 1985—; vis. prof. law U. Calif., Berkeley, 1984; Meyer vis. profl. program law, philosophy, social theory NYU, 1987; vis. lectr. Harvard U. Law Sch., Cambridge, Mass., 1987; vis. fellow in Council of the Humanities, Princeton, 1988. Contbr. articles on philosophy and law to profl. jours. Grad. scholar St. Catherine's Coll., Oxford, 1977-80. Mem. Philos. Soc. (sec. 1986-87), Am. Philos. Assn., Aristotelian Soc., Anmesty Internat., Oxford Acads. Against Apartheid. Home and Office: St Edmund Hall, Queens Ln, Oxford OXI 4AR, England

HURLOCK, JAMES BICKFORD, lawyer; b. Chgo., Aug. 7, 1933; s. James Bickford and Elizabeth (Charls) H.; m. Margaret Lyn Holding, July 1, 1961; children: James Bickford, Burton Charls, Matthew Hunter. A.B., Princeton U., 1955; B.A., Oxford U., 1957, M.A., 1960; J.D., Harvard U., 1959. Bar: N.Y. 1960, U.S. Supreme Ct. 1967. Assoc. firm White & Case, N.Y.C., 1959-66, ptnr., 1967—; bd. dirs. Altex Resources Ltd., Calgary, Alta., Can., Bekaert N.Am., N.Y.C. Trustee Columbia Presbyn. Hosp., Parker Sch. Internat. and Comparitive Law, Hofstra U., Western Rev. Acad. Rhodes scholar, 1955. Mem. ABA, Assn. Bar City N.Y., N.Y. Bar Assn., Am. Law Inst., Am. Assn. Internat. Law. Republican. Episcopalian. Clubs: Links, River, N.Y. Yacht. Home: 46 Byram Dr Greenwich CT 06830 Office: White & Case 1155 Ave of Americas New York NY 10036

HURN, DAVID, photographer, lecturer; b. Redhill, Surrey, Eng., July 21, 1934; s. Stanley and Joan (Maynard) H.; m. Alita Naughton, 1964 (div. 1971); 1 child, Sian. Student Royal Mil. Acad., Sandhurst, U.K., 1952-54. Asst. photographer Reflex Agy., London, 1955-57; free-lance photographer, London, 1957-70, Tintern, Gwent, Wales, 1971—; mem. Magnum Photos coop. agy., N.Y.C. and Paris, 1967—; editorial adviser Album Photog. Mag., London, 1971; mem. photography com. Art Council Gt. Britain, 1972-77, mem. art panel, 1975-77; head Sch. Documentary Photography, Gwent Coll. Higher Edn., 1973—; com. mem. Council for Nat. Acad. Awards, 1978—; disting. vis. artist and adj. prof. Ariz. State U., Tempe, 1979-80. One-man shows, the most recent being: Imperial War Mus. Arts, 1987, Fifth Ave. Gallery, Scottsdale, Ariz., 1980; Sterling Coll. Art, Kans., 1980; Contrasts Gallery, London, 1982; Olympus Gallery, London, 1982; Malmö Mus. (Sweden), 1982; Palais des Congres, Lorient, France, 1982; Olympus Gallery, Tokyo, 1983; Palais des Beaux Arts, Charlerois, Belgium, 1983; Photogallery, Cardiff, 1984; Nat. Mus. Photography, Bradford, 1985; Axiom Gallery, Cheltenham, 1986, Stills Gallery, Edinburgh, 1986; group shows include: Personal Views 1850-1970, on tour U.K. and Europe, 1972; Images des Hommes, on tour Europe, 1978; Phoenix Art Mus., 1980; Photographers Gallery, London, 1983; Centre Nat. de La Photographie, Paris, 1985, Stills Gallery, Edinburgh; represented in permanent collections, including: Welsh Arts Council, Cardiff; Contemporary Arts Soc. for Wales, Cardiff; Arts Council Gt. Britain, London; Brit. Council, London; Bibliotheque Nationale, Paris; FNAC, Paris; Musé e du Chateau d'Eau, Tolouse, France; Internat. Ctr. Photography, N.Y.C.; George Eastman House, Rochester, N.Y.; Ctr. for Creative Photography, U. Ariz., Tucson; U. N.Mex. Art Mus., Albuquerque; San Francisco Mus. Modern Art; Calif. Mus. Photography, U. Calif.; Internat. Mus. Photography, George Eastman House, Rochester; Mus. Modern Art, N.Y.C., also pvt. collections; author: David Hurn: Photographs 1956-1976, 1979; author, subject profl. publs. Recipient award for outstanding merit in living artist Welsh Arts Council, 1971, award for social photography Kodak Photog. Bursary, 1975; U.K./U.S.A. Bicentennial fellow, 1979-80.

HURRELMANN, KLAUS, sociology educator; b. Gdynia, Germany, Jan. 10, 1944; s. Kurt and Elisabeth (Albrecht) H.; m. Bettina Ahrendts, Mar. 25, 1971; children: Achim, Annette. MA, U. Munster, Fed. Republic Germany, 1968; PhD, U. Bielefeld, Fed. Republic Germany, 1971. Asst. prof. sociology U. Bielefeld, Fed. Republic Germany, 1972-75, prof., 1980—; assoc. prof. U. Essen, Fed. Republic Germany, 1975-79; bd. dirs. Research Ctr. Social Prevention, Bielefeld. Author books; editor: German Jour. Socialization, 1980—; series editor: Social Prevention and Intervention; journalist in field. Recipient Sr. Scientist award German Research Assn., 1976, 80, 86; grantee Office Minister Edn., Dusseldorf, 1982, Office Minister Health, Bonn, 1984; research fellow Office Edn., Dusseldorf, 1968. Mem. German Sociol. Assn. (chmn. com. edn. 1978-82). Home: Wertherstr 122, D-4800 Bielefeld Federal Republic of Germany Office: U Bielefeld, Univ Str 25, D-4800 Bielefeld Federal Republic of Germany

HURSON, BRIAN JOHN, orthopedic surgeon; b. Dublin, Ireland, July 29, 1945; s. John Alphonsus and Marie (McCarthy) H.; m. Ruth Claire Bradley, July 29, 1971; children—Conor, Niall, Cliona. M.B., B.Ch., Univ. Coll. Dublin, 1970, M.Ch., 1980. Intern St. Vincent's Hosp., Dublin, 1970-71, resident in medicine, 1971-72, resident in surgery, 1973-76, resident in orthopedic surgery, Cappagh Ortho. Hosp., Jervis St. Hosp., St. Vincent's Hosp. and Hosp. for Sick Children, Dublin, 1976-80; fellow in orthopedic surgery Harvard Med. Sch.-Brigham and Women's Hosp., Boston, 1981; fellow in knee and arthroscopic surgery Toronto Western Hosp.-U. Toronto, Ont., Can., 1982; fellow in orthopedic oncology Sloan-Kettering Meml. Cancer Ctr. and Hosp. for Spl. Surgery, Cornell U. and Hosp. Spl. Surgery, N.Y.C., 1982-83; fellow in orthopedic trauma, Switzerland, 1983; practice medicine specializing in orthopedic surgery, Dublin, 1983—; cons. James Connolly Meml. Hosp., Cappagh Orth. Hosp., Dublin, The Blackrock Clinic, Dublin; gen. practice Australia and Papua, New Guinea, 1972-73. Author: Tumours about the Knee, 1984; Limb preservation in Bone Tumours, 1983; Pathological fractures, 1984; Bone Tumors of the Upper Limb, 1986. Contbr. articles to profl. jours. Fellow Brit. Orthopaedic Assn., Royal Coll. Surgeons in Ireland; mem. Herodicus Soc. Roman Catholic. Club: Fitzwilliam Lawn Tennis. Avocations: tennis, golf, squash. Home: 38 Nutley Ave, Dublin 4 Ireland Office: Blackrock Clinic, Rock Rd, Blackrock, Dublin Ireland

HURST, CHARLES ANGAS, physicist, educator; b. Adelaide, South Australia, Australia, Sept. 22, 1923; s. Walter William and Audrey Carrie (Morris) H.; m. Barbara Leigh Stevens, Dec. 15, 1945; children: Angas John, Elinor Mary, Rachel Louise. Student, Scotch Coll., Melbourne, Australia, 1930-40; BA with honors, Melbourne U., 1947, BSc, 1948; PhD, Cambridge (Eng.) U., 1952. Sr. lectr. Melbourne U., 1952-56; sr. lectr. Adelaide U., 1957-60, reader, 1960-64, prof. physics, 1964—, pro-vice chancellor, 1986—. Author: Order Disorder Phenomena, 1964; editor: Symmetry Principles At High Energy, 1968; contbr. papers to sci. jours. Served with Royal Australian Air Force, 1942-45. Fellow Australian Acad. Sci., Australian Inst. Physics. Home: 99 5th Ave, 5070 Joslin, South Australia Australia Office: U Adelaide, 5001 Adelaide, South Australia Australia

HURST, ERNEST CONNOR, lawyer; b. Lexington, Tex., Sept. 27, 1926; s. Ernest V. and Grace E. (King) H.; m. Barbara Ann Glaze, Oct. 19, 1951; 1 dau., Susan D. Hurst Hensley. Student Sam Houston State U., 1946-48; J.D. with honors, U. Tex.-Austin, 1950. Bar: Tex. 1950, U.S. Dist. Ct. (so. dist.) Tex. 1956, U.S. Ct. Appeals (5th cir.) 1969. Assoc. Liddell, Austin, Dawson & Huggins, Houston, 1951-57; mng. sr. ptnr. Caldwell & Hurst, Houston, 1958—; corp. sec. Adams Resources & Energy, Inc., Houston, 1979-84, KSA Industries, Inc., Houston, 1979—; exec. v.p., bd. dirs. Derrick Oil & Gas, Inc., Houston, 1977—; pres., bd. dirs. Bayou Helicopters, Inc., Houston, 1985—. Served with USN, 1944-46. Mem. Houston Bar Assn., Tex. Bar Assn., Am. Judicature Soc., Internat. Platform Assn., Nat. Trust for Hist. Preservation, Phi Delta Phi. Republican. Methodist. Avocations: spectator sports, traveling, camping. Student editor Tex. Law Rev., 1950-51.

HURT, FRANK BENJAMIN, emeritus educator, banker; b. Ferrum, Va., Oct. 22, 1899; s. John Kempleton and Lelia (Angle) H.; A.B., Washington and Lee U., 1923; M.A., U. Va., 1925; A.M., Princeton U., 1926; postgrad. Johns Hopkins, 1929-30, Harvard, summers 1938-40; H.H.D. (hon.), Ferrum Coll., 1982; m. Mary Ann Wescott, June 3, 1943. Teaching fellow U. N.C., 1926-27; instr. Ferrum Coll., 1927-29; asso. prof. polit. sci. Western Md. Coll., 1930-65, prof. emeritus, 1965—, head div. polit. sci., 1949; head div. social sci. Ferrum Jr. Coll., 1965—, prof. emeritus, 1970—, trustee 1983—; lectr. sch. spl. and continuation studies U. Md., 1950-65; instr. summers Hun Sch., Princeton, 1927-32; dir. First Nat. Bank, Ferrum, v.p., 1977—, pres., 1908-87 . Trustee, Longwood Coll. Found., 1976-82 . Mem. Am. Polit. Sci. Assn., Am. Hist. Assn., Am. Acad. Polit. and Social Sci., Nat. Collegiate Fgn. Lang. Soc., Franklin County Hist. Soc. (pres. 1969-70), AAUP, Pi Gamma Mu, Phi Theta Kappa. Democrat. Methodist. Lion (pres. Ferrum 1968). Author: History of Ferrum College, 1975; The Heritage of the German Element in Franklin County, Virginia in the Eighteenth Century. Address: Ferrum Coll Ferrum VA 24088

HURT, VALINA KAY, science educator, researcher; b. Bowling Green, Ky., Jan. 3, 1953; d. Ottis C. and Geraldine (Andrew) H. B.S. (Regents' scholar), Western Ky. U., 1975, M.S., 1979; postgrad., U. Okla., 1979—. Dental asst., Bowling Green, 1974, 75; grad. teaching asst. Western Ky. U., Bowling Green, 1978, 79, U. Okla., Norman, 1979-83; assoc. prof. sci. Hazard Community Coll., Ky., 1983—. Contbr. articles on botany to profl. jours. Okla. Mining and Mineral Resources Research Inst. scholar, 1980-83. Mem. AAUP, Ecology Soc. Am., Ky. Acad. Sci., Am. Genetic Assn., AAAS, Assn. for Women in Sci., Bot. Soc. Am., Southeastern Assn. Biologists, Okla. Acad. Sci., Southwestern Assn. Naturalists, Sigma Xi, Alpha Epsilon Delta, Beta Beta Beta, Beta Sigma Phi. Republican. Home: PO Box 250 Combs KY 41729 Office: Hazard Community Coll Hazard KY 41701

HURTIG, SERGE, political scientist, educator, administrator; b. Bucharest, Rumania, Apr. 16, 1927; s. Alexander and Anna (Stern) H.; student Sch. Fgn. Service, Georgetown U., 1946-48, Inst. Polit. Studies, U. Paris, 1948-50; m. Christiane Tirimagni, July 8, 1965; 1 dau., Marie-Odile. Mem. Documentation Services, Fondation Nationale des Sciences Politiques, Paris, 1951, asso. dir., 1957-69, tech. adviser, 1969-71, sec. gen., 1971-—, dir. studies and research grad. program polit. sci.; lectr. Paris Inst. Polit. Studies, 1952. Bd. dirs. Fondation Franco-Amé ricaine, 1976—, v.p., 1982—; exec. com. European Consortium for Polit. Sci. Research, 1970-76. Mem. Internat. (sec. gen. 1961-67, v.p. 1979-85), French (mem. council), Am. polit. sci. assns. Editor: Internat. Polit. Sci. Abstracts, 1963—. Contbr. articles on U.S., French and European politics to profl. jours. Home: 86 rue de la Fédération, 75015 Paris France Office: 27 rue Saint-Guillaume, 75007 Paris France

HURTUBISE, JACQUES, editor; b. Ottawa, Ont., Can., Nov. 5, 1950; s. Jean-Claude Hurtubise and Gisele Marchand; m. Hélène Fleury, Apr. 7, 1977; 1 child, Simon Etienne d'Azerbaïdjan. Degree in engring., Poly. U., Montreal, Que., Can., 1971; degree in cultural communication, U. Quebec, Can., 1973. Dir. L'Hydrocephale Entêté Inc., Montreal, 1970-73, Les Petits Dessins Coop., Montreal, 1971-75, Quadriga Publicité, Montreal, 1972-73; animateur Radio Can. TV, Montreal, 1973; cartoonist Jour. Le Jour, Montreal, 1973-77; chroniqueur L'Actualité, Montreal, 1977-79; publiciste Les Entreprises du Maître du Monde, Montreal, 1978-79; pub., editor Mag. Croc, Montreal, 1979—; cartoonist Le Sombre Vilain, 1973; photographer Les Incompressibles. Writer: live album Mort Ou Vif, 1984. V.p. Le Parti Rhinoceros, 1977, Le Parti sans Laisser D'Adresse, 1980; pres. hon. Le Parti d'en Rire, Montreal, 1987. Named Chevalier de L'Ordre de Drummondville, 1981. Mem. Salon de L'humour (officer 1987—), Assn. des Createurs et Intervenants de la Bande Dessinee (officer, founder 1986). Office: Ludcom Inc Croc, 5800 Monkland, Montreal, PQ Canada H4A 1O1

HURVELL, BENGT OLOF, microbiologist; b. Lund, Sweden, Aug. 31, 1935; s. Thure George Hurvell and Helga Elvira (Olsson) Johansson; m. Mariann Wijkstrom, Apr. 19, 1962. B of Veterinary Medicine, Royal Veterinary Coll., Stockholm, 1958; DVM, Royal Veterinary Coll., 1964, PhD, 1973. Diplomate Sweden Bd. Veterinary Medicine. Asst. prof. Royal Veterinary Coll., Stockholm, 1961-64; from asst. prof. to prof. microbiology Nat. Vet. Inst., Uppsala, Sweden, 1964—, head cen. lab., 1982—. Author books and papers in immunology and bacteriology. Fulbright-Hay scholar, 1977. Mem. Swedish Soc. Microbiology (bd. dirs. 1978-82), Swedish Soc. Med. Microbiology, Swedish Assn. Veterinary Research (bd. dirs. 1978—), Soc. Gen. Microbiology, Am. Soc. Microbiology, N.Y. Acad. Scis. Home: Kasbylund, 74100 Knivsta Sweden Office: Nat Veterinary Inst, PO Box 7073, 75007 Uppsala Sweden

HUSA, KAREL JAROSLAV, composer, conductor, educator; b. Prague, Czechoslovakia, Aug. 7, 1921; came to U.S., 1954, naturalized, 1959; s. Karel and Bozena (Dongresova) H.; m. Simone Perault, Feb. 2, 1952; children: Catherine, Anne-Marie, Elizabeth, Caroline. M summa cum laude, Conservatory and Acad. Music, Prague, 1945, 47; grad., Conservatoire de Paris, France, 1948; license for conducting, Ecole Normale de Paris, 1947; MusD (hon.), Coe Coll., 1976, Cleve. Inst., 1985, Ithaca Coll., 1986. Guest condr. Czechoslovak Radio, Prague, 1945-46; guest condr. orchs. in Hamburg, Brussels, Paris, Zurich, Suisse Romande, London, Manchester, Prague, Stockholm, Hong Kong; guest condr. orchs. in Singapore, Japan; guest condr. orchs. in Cin., Buffalo, N.Y.C., Boston, Rochester, N.Y., Balt., San Diego, Syracuse, N.Y.; faculty Cornell U., Ithaca, N.Y., 1954—; prof. music Cornell U., 1954—, dir. univ. symphony and chamber orchs., 1972—,

Kappa Alpha prof. in music. Composer: Symphony, 1953, Fantasies for Orchestra, 1957, Divertimento for Brass, 1959, Poem for Viola and Orchestra, 1959, Elegy and Rondeau for Saxophone and Orchestra, 1961, Divertimento for String Orchestra, 1948, String Quartet No. 2, 1952, Portrait for String Orch., 1953, Mosaiques for Orchestra, 1961, Fresque for Orchestra, rev, 1964, Sonatina for Piano, 1943, Sonatina Violin and Piano, 1945, Sonata for Piano, 1949, Evocations of Slovakia for Clarinet, Viola and Cello, 1951, Eight Duets for Piano, 1955, Twelve Moravian Songs, 1956, Poem for Viola and Piano, 1962, Serenade for Woodwind Quintet and Orchestra, 1963, Concerto for Brass Quintet and Orch, 1965, Two Preludes; flute, clarinet, bassoon, 1966, Music for Percussion, 1966, Concerto for alto saxophone, concert band, 1967, String Quartet No. 3, 1968 (Pulitzer prize 1969), Music for Prague; for Band, 1968, for Orch., 1969, Apotheosis of this Earth for Winds, 1970, Concerto for Percussion and Winds, 1971, Two Sonnets from Michelangelo for Orch, 1971, Concerto for Trumpet and Wind Orch, 1973, Apotheosis of this Earth for Chorus and Orch, 1973, Sonata for Violin and Piano, 1972-73, The Steadfast Tin Soldier; for narrator and orch., 1974, Sonata for Piano, No. 2, 1975, Monodrama, ballet for orch, 1975, An American Te Deum; for mixed chorus, baritone solo, band and organ, 1976, for orch., 1978, Landscapes for Brass Quintet, 1977, Fanfare for Brass Ensemble, 1980, Pastoral for Strings, 1980, Three Moravian Songs, 1981, The Trojan Women, ballet for orch., 1981, Sonata a Tre, 1982, Concerto for Wind Ensemble, 1982, Cantata, 1983, Smetana Fanfare for Wind Ensemble, 1984, Variations for Violin, Viola, Cello and Piano, 1984, Symphonic Suite for Orch., 1984, Intrada for Brass Quintet, 1984, Concerto for Orchestra, 1986, Concerto for Organ and Orch., 1987, Frammenti for Organ solo, 1987, Concerto for Trumpet and Orch., 1987, also others, commns. from, UNESCO, Koussevitsky Found., Nat. Endowment for Arts, Friends of Music at Cornell, Fine Arts Found. Chgo., Chgo. Symphony Orchestra, Butler U., Washington Music Soc., Coe Coll., N.Y. Philharmonic, also others.; Editor: French Barok Music: Reconstructions of old French Barok works by Lully and Delalande, 1961-68. Recipient prize Prague Acad. Arts, 1948, French Govt. award, 1946, 47, L. Boulanger award, 1952, Pulitzer prize in music, 1969; Guggenheim fellow, 1964-65. Fellow Internat. Inst. Arts and Letters (life), Royal Acad. Arts and Scis.; mem. Am. Music Ctr., Internat. Soc. Contemporary Music, French Soc. Composers, Am. Fedn. Musicians, Kappa Gamma Psi (hon.), Kappa Kappa Psi (hon.), Delta Omicron (hon.). Home: 1032 Hanshaw Rd Ithaca NY 14850 Office: Cornell U Music Dept Lincoln Hall Ithaca NY 14853

HUSAIN, JAVED, physicist, educator; b. Aligarh, India, Jan. 2, 1950; s. Masud and Najma (Khan) H.; BSc with honors, Aligarh Muslim U., 1970, MSc, 1972; MPhil, Columbia U., 1977, PhD, 1979. Guest jr. research assoc. Brookhaven Nat. Lab., 1974-76; grad. teaching and research asst. Columbia U., 1974-79; research asst. prof. U. Mo., Rolla, 1979-80; asst. prof. physics U. Petroleum and Minerals, Dhahran, Saudi Arabia, 1980-84; reader Rani Durgavati Univ., Jabalpur, 1984-85; prof. physics Aligarh Univ., India, 1985—. Mem. editorial adv. bd. World Peace News, 1982—; cons. editor for sci. Manorama Yr. Book, 1983—. Fellow Optical Soc. India, World Acad. Arts and Sci.; mem. World Fedn. Sci. Workers, (corr.), Nat. Acad. of Sci., India, Internat. Soc. Philos. Enquiry, Internat. Assn. Univ. Profs. and Lectrs., Mensa, Sigma Xi, Sigma Pi Sigma. Contbr. articles to profl. jours.; author: What Must Humanity Do?, 1980; coined name Laser Isotope Dating in sci. lit. Javed Husain Prize Young Scientists named in his honor UNESCO. Office: AM Univ, Dept Applied Physics, Faculty Engring, Aligarh 202002, India

HUSAIN, MAZHAR, cement company executive; b. Karachi, Pakistan, Aug. 18, 1949; s. Irshad and Subhun (Nisa) H.; m. Rukhsana Karimuddin, May 20, 1982; children: Salman, Maria . BS, Middle East Tech. U., Ankara, Turkey, 1972, MBA, 1974; MS, Union U., Schenectady, N.Y., 1976. Mgmt. counselor Pakistan Inst. of Mgmt., Karachi, 1977-79; mgr. purchasing-mktg. dept. So. Province Cement Co., Abha, Saudi Arabia, 1979—. Contbr. articles to profl. jours. Merit scholar Cen. Treaty Orgn., 1968-74; research fellow Union U., 1974-76. Mem. Pakistan Inst. Engrs. Home: PO Box 826, Abha Saudi Arabia

HUSAIN, SAFDAR ABIDALLY, international trading company executive; b. Bombay, India, Mar. 31, 1947; s. Abidally Abdul and Sugra Hassan (Bhai) H.; came to Singapore, 1951; m. Amina Abdul Kader Tyebally, May 11, 1979; children: Ashraf, Soraya, Farah. Diploma in bus. studies So. West London Coll., 1967. Dir., A. Abdulhusain & Co., Singapore, 1967-80; mng. dir. A. Shiraz Pte Ltd., Singapore, 1980—; dir. Stradcom Pte Ltd., Singapore, 1980—, Transemirates Pte Ltd., Singapore, 1980—. Pres., Dale Carnegie Rock Chpt., Singapore, 1974; appeals chmn. Singapore Children's Soc., 1978— (recipient Pub. Service medal, Pres. Singapore, 1987); trustee Quaide Azam Meml. Fund, 1979—; dir. Children Charities Assn., 1978—, chmn. 1986-88; v.p. Singapore Children's Soc., 1985-86. Named Outstanding Carnegian of Yr., Dale Carnegie Alumni Assn., 1973; award for outstanding contbn. to Allama Mohd Iqbal Centenary Symposium, Govt. Pakistan, 1979; recipient Gopal Haridas award Singapore Children's Soc., 1983. Mem. Singapore Jaycees (Flag Day chmn. 1979, 80). Moslem Lodge: Singapore Rotary (dir., vocat. service chmn. 1983, 84, v.p. 1985-86). Home: 33 Sennett Ln, Singapore 1646 Singapore Office: A Shiraz Pte Ltd, 9 Malacca St, 18 Nunes Bldg, 1646 Singapore Singapore

HUSAK, GUSTAV, president of Czechoslovakia; b. Bratislava, Czechoslovakia, Jan. 10, 1913; m. Viera H. (dec. 1977). LL.D., Law Faculty Comenius U., 1937, C.Sc., 1965. Jr. lawyer, Bratislava, 1938-42; office worker, 1943-44; commr. Interior, 1944-45; commr. Transport and Tech., 1945-46; chmn. bd. commrs., 1946-50; commr. Agr., 1948; head cen. com. Communist Party of Slovakia, 1st sec., 1968-69, 1st chmn., from 1969; sci. worker Inst. State and Law, Slovak Acad. Scis., 1963-68; dep. premier Czechoslovakia, 1968; mem. cen. com. Communist Party Czechoslovakia, 1945, 49-51, 68—, mem. presidium, 1945-50, 68—, exec. com. presidium, 1968-69, mem. secretariat, from 1969, 1st sec., 1969-71, gen. sec., 1971-87; dep. to Ho. of Nations, Fed. Assembly, 1968-71, mem. presidium, 1969-75; mem. presidium, gen. com. Nat. Front, 1971—, chmn. cen. com., 1971—; comdr.-in-chief People's Militia, 1969, Armed Forces, 1975—; pres. Czechoslovak Socialist Republic, 1975—. Decorated Disting. Order Slovak Rising, Mil. Cross, Mil. medal for Services, Order of Lenin, (3), Hero of Czechoslovak Socialist Republic (3); recipient Karl Marx Gold medal USSR Acad. Scis., 1981, other awards. Author: On the ther awards. Author: On the Agricultural Problem in Slovakia, 1948; The Struggle for Tomorrow, 1948; Testimony on the Slovak National Rising, 1964; contbr. articles to mags., newspapers. Office: Office of President, Prague Czechoslovakia *

HUSAR, JOHN PAUL, newspaper columnist; b. Chgo., Jan. 29, 1937; s. John Z. and Kathryn (Kanupke) H.; AA, Dodge City Coll., 1958; BS in Journalism, U. Kans., 1962; m. Louise Kay Lewis, Dec. 28, 1963; children: Kathryn, Laura. Reporter, Clovis (N.Mex.) News-Jour., 1960; night wire editor Okinawa Morning Star, 1961; city editor Pasadena (Tex.) Daily Citizen, 1962; bus. editor Topeka Capital-Jour., 1963; regional news editor Wichita (Kans.) Beacon, 1963-65; sports columnist and writer Chgo. Tribune, 1966—. Chmn., Village of Willow Springs (Ill.) Zoning Commn., 1975-77; mem. Ill. Forestry Adv. Com., 1981-82; mem. adv. com. Ill.-Mich. Canal Nat. Heritage Corridor, 1982; profl.-in-residence U. Kans. Sch. Journalism, 1985. Served with U.S. Army, 1960-62. Recipient 1st pl. award in sportswriting Ill. UPI, 1977, Ill. AP, 1984, 1st pl. award in feature writing Bowling mag., 1979, environ. reporting award Chgo. Audubon Soc., 1979, Disting. Alumnus award Dodge City Coll., 1983, 2d pl. award for public service reporting Ill. AP, 1980, 2d pl. award for sports column writing, 1981, spl. writing award Chgo. Tribune, 1980, Jacob A. Riis award Friends of Parks, 1981, Peter Lisagor award Chgo. chpt. Sigma Delta Chi, 1985, Du-Pont Stren Edit. Excellence award, 1986, Founders award Ill.-Mich. Canal Nat. Heritage Corridor Civic Ctr. Authority, 1987. Mem. Assn. of Great Lakes Outdoor Writers (bd. dirs.), Golf Writers Assn. Am. (past dir.), Baseball Writers Assn. Am., Outdoor Writers Assn. Am., Phi Kappa Theta. Office: 435 N Michigan Ave Chicago IL 60611

HUSBAND, RICHARD LORIN, SR., business executive; b. Spencer, Iowa, July 28, 1931; s. Ross Twetten and Frances Estelle (Hall) H.; A.A., Rochester State Community Coll., 1953; A.B., U. Minn., 1954; m. Darlene Joyce Granberg, 1954; children—Richard Lorin, Thomas Ross and Mark Thurston (twins), Julia Lynn, Susan Elizabeth. Pres., Orlen Ross Inc., Rochester, Minn., 1962-87; partner The Gallery, European antiques, china, gifts, Rochester, 1968—, Millenium III, home furnishings, Rochester, 1975-81; pres., founder R.L. Husband & Assocs., Cons., Minn., St. Paul and Roschester; corp. cons. Coll. St. Thomas. Nat. Editor: The Mayflower Quaterly. Active Episcopal Diocese of Minn., 1951-52, 58—, nat. dept., 1969-73, alt. dept., 1973-75; trustee Seabury Western Theol. Sem., 1975-87, exec. com., 1983-84, 2d v.p., 1986-87; founder Rochester Arts Council, Rochester PTA Community Coll. Scholarship Program, H.D. Mayo Meml. Lecture in Theology, others; pres. Olmsted County (Minn.) Hist. Soc., 1976-77; bd. dirs. Rochester Symphony Orch., Choral, Opera, 1970-78, pres., 1974-75; del. Olmsted County Republican Com., 1974-82; mem. exec. council Minn. Hist. Soc., 1984—, chmn. Minn. Air & Space Mus. & Aviation Hall of Fame, founding trustee Minn. Transp. Mus., St. Paul. Recipient Disting. Service award Rochester Jaycees, 1965, Fifty Mem. award YMCA, 1968, award for Minn. Bicentennial, Gov. Minn., 1976; named 1 of Minn's, 10 Outstanding Young Men, Minn. Jaycees, 1966, Disting. Christian Service award Seabury Western Sem. Mem. Minn. Home Furnishings Assn. (pres. 1976-79, trustee 1968—), First Dist. Hist. Assembly Minn. (pres. 1969-71), Minn. Retail Fedn. (trustee 1972—), Olmsted County Archeology Soc. (founder), Rochester Civil War Roundtable (founder), Rochester Revolutionary War Roundtable (founder), Rochester Arts Council (founder), Am., Nat. (charter), Minn., Norwegian/Am. hist. socs., Minn. Archeology Soc., Am. Assn. State and Local History, U. Minn. Alumni Assn. (life), U. Minn. Alumni Club (charter) Rochester C. of C., Alpha Delta Phi Alumni Assn., Soc. Mayflower Descs. (trustee Minn., gov. 1987—), SAR (Minn. pres. 1980-82), Descs. Colonial Clergy, Sons Union Vets of Civil War, Minn. Territorial Pioneers (trustee 1978—, pres. 1981-84), Soc. Archtl. Historians. Clubs: Rotary (historian 1980-82) (Rochester); Sertoma (Austin) (founder). Public speaker. Home: 1820 26th St NW Rochester MN 55901 Office: Orlen Ross Inc 105 N Broadway Rochester MN 55904

HUSBY, VONNA KAY, brokerage house executive; b. Colfax, Wash., Feb. 8, 1944; d. George W. and Patti (Chase) Von Arb; m. Fredric M. Husby, Sept. 2, 1971; children: Kimberly C., Martin F. AA, Stephens Coll., 1964. Asst. br. mgr. Foster & Marshall, Fairbanks, Alaska, 1982-83, Shearson Lehman Bros., Fairbanks, 1983-85; account exec. Dean Witter Reynolds, Inc., Fairbanks, 1985—. Past pres. Univ. Womens Assn., Fairbanks. Recipient Buz Lukens award for Outstanding D.C. Young Rep. of Yr., Nat. Sales Dirs. Achievement award Dean Witter Reynolds, Inc., IRA Achievement award Dean Witter Reynolds, Inc., Nat. Sales Tng. award Dean Witter Reynolds, Inc., Pacesetters award Dean Witter Reynolds, Inc., 1986. Mem. Univ. Womens Assn., DAR (state chairwoman). Clubs: Kiwanis (bd. dirs.), Soroptimists. Home: 1354 Chena Ridge Fairbanks AK 99701 Office: Dean Witter 305 Lacey St Fairbanks AK 99701

HUSEBYE, EYSTEIN SVERRE, seismologist; b. Fauske, Norway, Feb. 9, 1937; s. Sverre Daniel and Ragnhild (Bruun) H.; m. Hildur Wigdahl Monsen, Aug. 27, 1960; children—Eystein Sverre, Signe Stine, Barbro Indiane, Tomas Hauk. Cand.real., Bergen U., 1962; fil.lic., Uppsala U., 1966, fil.dr., 1972; Dr.philos., Oslo U., 1976. Research fellow Bergen U., Norway, 1964-68; postdoctoral fellow MIT, Cambridge, Mass., 1966-68; chief seismologist NTNF/NORSAR, Kjeller, Norway, 1968—; adj. prof. Oslo U., 1979—; sci. dir. NATO ASI, Norway, 1974, 80; assoc. editor various sci. jours.; nat. del. UN Expert Group, Geneva, 1977—. Contbr. articles to profl. jours.; editor: Identification of Seismic Sources, 1981; Polar Regions Geophysics, 1984. Invited scientist MIT, 1975, USSR Acad. Sci., 1976. Mem. Seismology Soc. Am., Am. Geophys. Union, Royal Astron. Soc. London, Internat. Union Geodesy & Geophysics, European Union Geoscis., Norwegian Acad. Scis. Lutheran. Home: Solvangen 20, Skjetten N-2013, Norway Office: NTNF/NORSAR, Post Box 51, Kjeller N-2007, Norway

HUSS, CHARLES MAURICE, municipal building official; b. Chgo., Nov. 11, 1946; s. Charles Maurice and June Pierce (Bailey) H.; m. Winifred Louise Traughber, Dec. 24, 1973; children—Amber Elaine, Ra Ja Lorraine, Micah Alexander, Gabriel Joe, Cameron M., Jordan Charles. A.A., Kendall Coll., 1984; student Oregon State U., Western Oreg. State Coll., U. Cinn., U. Alaska, Western Ill. U., City U., Nat. Fire Acad. Traffic mgr. The Harwald Co., Evanston, Ill., 1966-67, asst. v.p., 1968-69; traffic mgr. Northwestern U. Press, Evanston, 1969-71; fire chief City of Kotzebue (Alaska), 1971-76, asst. city mgr., 1973-76; dir. maintenance USPHS Hosp., Kotzebue, 1976-79; pres., gen. mgr. Action Builders, Inc., Kotzebue, 1979-82; gen. mgr. Husky Maintenance Services, 1982—; chief bldg. insp. City of Kotzebue, 1985—; adj. faculty Nat. Fire Acad., Emmitsburg, Md. Chmn., Kotzebue Planning Commn., 1978-82, Kotzebue Sch. Bd., 1974-79, 83—; founding vice chmn. Kotzebue chpt. ARC; mem. Alaska Criminal Code Revision Commn., 1976-78; mem. Alaska Fire Fighter Tng. Commn.; vol. Kotzebue Vol. Fire Dept., 1972-76, 82-86; bd. dirs. instr. Alaska Craftsman Home Program 1986—; instr. Kotzebue Regional Fire Tng. Ctr., 1982—. Pullman Found. scholar, 1964-65; Blackburn Coll. scholar, 1964-65; Ill. State scholar, 1964-66. Mem. Constrn. Specifications Inst., Soc. Fire Service Instrs., Bldg. Officials and Code Adminstrs. Internat., Alaska Firefighters Assn., Internat. Assn. Fire and Arson Investigators, ASHRAE, Western Fire Chiefs Assn., Internat. Conf. Bldg. Ofcls. (cert. bldg. ofl., fire inspector), Am. Soc. Safety Engrs., Internat. Assn. Plumbing and Mech. Ofcls., Internat. Assn. Elec. Insps., Internat. Assn. Fire Chiefs, Home Builders Assn. Alaska, Nat. Fire Protection Assn., Coalition for Home Fire Safety, Am. Soc. Safety Engrs., Kotzebue C. of C. Guest essayist: Seven Days and Sunday (Kirkpatrick), 1973; contbr. Alaska Craftsman Home Building Manual. Home and Office: PO Box 277 Kotzebue AK 99752

HUSS, SALIM AL-, politian, economics educator. Chair Banking Control Com., Lebanon, 1967-73, Nat. Bank for Indsl. and Tourist Devel., Lebanon, 1973-76; prime minister Govt. of Lebanon, 1976-80, caretaker prime minister, 1980, 87—, minister of econ. and trade and info., 1976-79, minister of industry and petroleum, 1976-77, minister of labour, fine arts and edn., 1984-85, 85—, now acting minister of fgn. affairs; chair Compagnie Arabe et Internat. d'Investissement, 1981—; dir. Banque Arabe et Internat. d'Investissement, 1983—. Author: The Development of Lebanon's Financial Markets, 1974, Nafiza Ala Al Mustakbal (Window on the Future), 1981. Office: BAII Centre Gefinor Bloc B, Apt 1401 14th Floor, PO Box 11-9692, Beirut and Doha, Na'meh, Beirut Lebanon *

HUSSAIN, AKMAL, manufacturing executive, consultant; b. Lahore, Pakistan; s. Syed Alamdar H.; m. Tazeen Hussain Sayed; children: Syed Savail, Syed Jalal. BA in Econs., Philosophy, Punjab U., 1969; BA in Econs. with honors, U. Cambridge, 1972; PhD in Econs., Sussex U., Eng., 1980. Lectr., asst. prof. Punjab U., Lahore, Pakistan, 1973-76, 80-83; vis. prof. Pakistan Adminstrv. Staff Coll., Lahore, 1974—, Nat. Inst. Pub. Adminstrn., Lahore, 1974—, U. Calif., Riverside, 1983-84; cons. ILO/ARTEP, Lahore, 1983-85; dir. Econ. Policy Research Unit, Lahore, 1983-85; chief exec. Sayyed Engrs. Ltd., Pakistan; country coordinator, assoc. project dir. UN U. Asian Perspectives Project, South Asia, 1984-87; dir. Econ. Policy Research Unit, Lahore, 1985—; cons. Swiss Devel. Corp.; mem. small farmers com. Nat. Commn. on Agri., Pakistan. Author: Strategic Issues in Pakistan's Economic Policy, 1987; contbr. articles to scholarly jours. Mem. Pakistan Human Rights Commn., Lahore, 1987. Mem. Soc. for Internat. Devel., Pakistan Soc. Devel. Economists, Pakistan Futuristics Inst., Soc. Advancement of Higher Edn. (founding). Club: Gymkhana (Lahore). Home: 11 Saint John's Park, Lahore, Cantonment Pakistan Office: Sayyed Engrs Ltd, 65 Shara Quaide Azam, Lahore-3 Pakistan

HUSSAIN, FAYYAZ, surgeon, educator, social worker; b. Lahore, Punjab, Pakistan, Aug. 29, 1928; s. Mohammed and Zainab Sardar; m. Jabeen Suraiya, Sept. 21, 1959; children: Mahjabeen, Imran, Irfan, Shazia, Lubna. MBBS, King Edward Med. Coll., Lahore, 1952. Diplomate Pakistan Bd. Surgery. Asst. surgeon Pakistan Railways, Lahore, 1952-53; in-charge head Cantonment Gen. Hosp., Lahore, 1953-56; div. surgeon Red Cross, Lahore, 1954-84; dir. S.M. Hosp., Lahore, 1956—; dist. surgeon Red Crescent, Lahore, 1984—; v.p. Islamai Coll., 1965-72; cons. in field. Bd. dirs. Jamiaa Tajveed-ul-Quran, Lahore, 1970—; patron Habib High Sch., 1964—, Cantonment Pub. Sch., 1986—. Mem. Social Welfare Soc. (exec. 1959—), Pakistani Med. Assn., Coll. Gen Practitioners. Club: Service Officers. Home: A/6 Sarfraz Rafiqui Rd, Lahore Pakistan Office: S M Hosp, 264 Ghazi Rd, Lahore Pakistan

HUSSEIN, SADDAM, president Republic of Iraq; b. Tikrit Dist., Iraq, 1937; student College of Law, Egypt, 1961; law degree U. Baghdad, 1971; married Sajida Khair-Allah; 2 sons, 3 daus. Joined Arab Ba'ath (Renaissance) Socialist Party, 1956; participant attempt to overthrow Abdul-Karim Qasem, 1959; second in command Arab Ba'ath Socialist Party; mem. Regional Leadership, 1963; imprisoned 1964-66, escaped 1966; dep. sec. Regional Leadership, Arab Ba'ath Socialist Party, 1966; acting dep. chmn. Revolution Command Council, 1968-69, dep. chmn., 1969-79, chmn., 1979—; dep. sec. Ba'ath Regional Command, 1968-79, sec., 1979—; re-elected mem. Nat. Command, Ba'ath Party, 1965; mem. Nat. Leadership, asst. sec.-gen., 1977-79; pres. Republic of Iraq, 79—; defacto chmn. Revolutionary Council, from 1968; dep. sec. Nat. Command, Ba'ath Party, from 1979 . Decorated 1st degree (civil) Rafidain, 1976. Author polit. and other treatises. Address: Office of President, Baghdad Iraq *

HUSSEIN BIN TALAL, HIS MAJESTY, King of Jordan; b. Amman, Jordan, Nov. 14, 1935; s. Crown Prince Talal and Zein; ed. Victoria Coll., Alexandria, Egypt, Harrow Sch., Eng., also Royal Mil. Acad., Sandhurst, Eng.; m. Princess Dina, 1955 (marriage dissolved); 1 dau., Alia; m. Antoinette Gardiner, 1961 (div. 1972); children: Abdallah, Feisal, Zein and Ayesha (twins); m. Allia Baha Eddin Toukan, 1972 (dec. 1977); children: Haya, Ali; m. Lisa Halaby, June 1978; children: Hamzeh, Hashem, Iman, Raiyah. Succeeded his father, Aug. 1952; came to power, May 1953. Decorated Order Al-Nahda, Order Al-Kawkab, Order Al-Istiqlal, numerous others. Author: Uneasy Lies the Head, 1962; My War With Israel, 1967. Address: Royal Palace, Amman Jordan *

HUSSEINI, HUSSEIN, government official. married; 6 children. Parliamentary rep. Baalbeck-Hermel region Govt. of Lebanon, 1972, elected speaker Ho. of Reps., 1984—, now pres. Nat. Assembly; co-founder High Islamic Shiite Council, 1965-69, mem., 1972—; co-founder Amal and Harakat Al Mahroumeen movements, 1973; sec. gen. Amal, 1978-80; pres. parliamentary com. on hydraulic and electric resources, 1972-74, mem. parliamentary com. of fin. and budget. Office: House of Representatives, Office of Speaker, Beirut Lebanon *

HUSSEINI, ZAFER HILMI, cement company executive; b. Jenin, Palestine, Sept. 10, 1929; s. Hilmi Saleh and Samiha (Ahdab) H.; m. Juhayna Mardam Bey, July 23, 1954; children: Suma, Ramia, Rula. B. Econs., Ripon Coll., 1951; postgrad., Columbia U., 1967. With Arabian Am. Oil Co., Saudia Arabia, U.S., 1952-70; advisor Esso Middle East-Exxon Corp., N.Y.C., 1970-75; sr. v.p. Fluor Arabia Ltd., Dhahran, Saudi Arabia, 1975-76; gen. mgr., chief operating officer Saudi Bahraini Cement Co., Dammam, Saudi Arabia, 1976—. Muslim. Address: Saudi-Bahraini Cement Co, PO Box 2464, Dammam 31451, Saudi Arabia

HUSTAD, THOMAS PEGG, marketing educator; b. Mpls., June 15, 1945; s. Thomas Earl Pegg and John Charles and Dorothy Helen (Anderson) H.; B.S. in Elec. Engring., Purdue U., 1967, M.S. in Indsl. Mgmt., 1969, Ph.D. in Mktg., 1973; m. Sherry Ann Thomas, Jan. 30, 1971; children—Kathleen, John. Vis. asst. prof. Purdue U., West Lafayette, Ind., 1971-72; asst. prof. Faculty of Adminstrv. Studies, York U., Toronto, 1972-74, assoc. prof., 1974-76, assoc. prof., mktg. area coordinator, 1976-77; assoc. prof. mktg. Sch. Bus., Ind. U., Bloomington-Indpls., 1977-82, prof., 1982—, chmn. M.B.A. program, 1983-85 , program chmn. Ind. U. Ann. Bus. Conf., 1983, 84, co-founder Ind. U. Exec. Forum; exec. dir. Ind. U. Internat. Bus. Forum, 1981-85;cons. N. Am. corps., Can. Govt.; condr. seminars for U.S., Can. and Venezuelan industry. Fulbright fellow, 1987. Mem. Am. Mktg. Assn. (award 1973), Product Devel. and Mgmt. Assn. (program chmn. 3d ann. conf., v.p. confs. 1979, pres. elect 1980, pres. 1981, dir. 1982-83, chmn. publ. com. 1982-84, sec./treas. 1984—, Presdl. award 1987), Ancient and Hon. Arty. Co. Mass., Internat. Assn. Jazz Record Collectors, Phi Eta Sigma, Tau Beta Pi, Beta Gamma Sigma. Author: Approaches to the Teaching of Product Development and Management, 1977; editor: International Competition: The American Challenge, 1986; founder, editor: Jour. Product Innovation Mgmt.; contbr. articles to books and profl. jours. Home: 8931 Butternut Ct Indianapolis IN 46260 Office: Indiana U Sch Business Bloomington IN 47405

HUSTED, RALPH WALDO, former utility executive; b. Martinsville, Ill., Apr. 2, 1911; s. Seth and Mary (Church) H.; m. Margaret Walden, Mar. 18, 1937; children: Catherine (Mrs. William R. Burleigh), David W. LL.B., Benjamin Harrison Law Sch., 1936. Bar: Ind. 1935. With Indpls. Power & Light Co., 1929—, sec., counsel, 1957-64, v.p. legal, sec., 1964-73, exec. v.p. adminstrn., 1973-74, pres., chief exec. officer, 1974-75, chmn. bd., chief exec. officer, 1975-76; dir. emeritus Security Savs. Assn., Indpls. Trustee Intercollegiate Studies Inst., Inc., Bryn Mawr, Pa., Liberty Fund, Indpls., Ctr. for Judical Studies, Cumberland, Va. Mem. Ind., Indpls., Am. bar assns. Home: 6230 Breamore Rd Indianapolis IN 46220 Office: 25 Monument Circle Indianapolis IN 46206

HUSTON, HARRIS HYDE, legal consultant; b. Pickaway County, Ohio, July 20, 1907; s. Edwin Minor and Lulu Beatrice (Hyde) H.; m. Hazel Frances Rollins, Dec. 18, 1948; children: Robert Hyde, Linda Rollins (Mrs. Glenn Cartaxo). A.B., Dartmouth Coll., 1929; LL.B., U. Dayton, 1933. Bar: Ohio 1933, D.C. 1970, U.S. Supreme Ct. Asso. Mattern & Sheridan (later Sheridan & Jenkins); later partner Jenkins & Huston, Dayton, Ohio, 1933-40; spl. agt. FBI, 1941-46; asso. dir. surveys and investigations, staff appropriations com. U.S. Ho. of Reps., 1947-48, dir. surveys and investigations, staff appropriations com., 1953-57; dir. tng. Office Spl. Investigations, insp. gen. Dept. Air Force, 1949- 52; spl. asst. to under-sec. for adminstrn. Dept. State, 1953, dep. adminstr. bur. security and consular affairs, 1957-60, acting adminstr., 1961; Am. consul gen., Curacao, Netherlands Antilles, 1962-69, legal cons., 1969—; dir. Huston Collections, 1971—. Decorated comdr. Order Orange Nassau, Netherlands). Mem. Harvard Assocs. Police Sci., Chi Phi. Clubs: Belle Haven Country, ABC (Alexandria, Va.); Nat. Aviation (Washington). Address: 619 29th Rd S Arlington VA 22202

HUSZAGH, FREDRICK WICKETT, law educator, information management company executive, lawyer; b. Evanston, Ill., July 20, 1937; s. Rudolph LeRoy and Dorothea (Wickett) H.; m. Sandra McRae, Apr. 4, 1959; children—Floyd McRae, Fredrick Wickett II, Theodore Wickett II. B.A., Northwestern U., 1958; J.D., U. Chgo., 1962, LL.M., 1963, J.S.D., 1964. Bar: Ill. 1962, U.S. Dist. Ct. D.C. 1965, U.S. Supreme Ct. 1966. Market researcher Leo Burnett Co. Chgo., 1958-59; internat. atty. COMSAT, Washington, 1964-67; assoc. Debevoise & Liberman, Washington, 1967-68; asst. prof. law Am. U., Washington, 1968-71; program dir. NSF, Washington, 1971-73; assoc. prof. U. Mont., Missoula, 1973-76, U. Wis.-Madison, 1976-77; exec. dir. Dean Rusk Ctr., U. Ga., Athens, 1977-82; prof. U. Ga., 1982—; chmn. TWH Corp., Athens, 1982—; cons. Pres. Johnson's Telecommunications Task Force, Washington, 1967-68; co-chmn. Nat. Gov.'s Internat. Trade Staff Commn., Washington, 1979- 81. Author: International Decision-Making Process, 1964; Comparative Facts on Canada, Mexico and U.S., 1979; also articles. Editor Rusk Ctr. Briefings, 1981-82. Mem. Econ. Policy Council, N.Y.C., 1981—. NSF grantee, 1974-78. Republican. Presbyterian. Home: 3890 Barnett Shoals Rd Athens GA 30605 Office: U Ga Law Sch Athens GA 30602

HUTCHENS, TYRA THORNTON, physician, educator; b. Newberg, Oreg., Nov. 29, 1921; s. Fred George and Bessie (Adams) H.; m. Betty Lou Gardner, June 7, 1942; children: Tyra Richard, Robert Jay, Rebecca (Mrs. Mark Pearsall). B.S., U. Oreg., 1943, M.D., 1945. Diplomate: Am. Bd. Pathology, Am. Bd. Nuclear Medicine. Intern Minn. Gen. Hosp., Mpls., 1945-46; AEC postdoctoral research fellow Reed Coll., Med. Sch. U. Oreg., 1948-50; NIH postdoctoral research fellow Med. Sch. U. Oreg., 1951-53; mem. faculty Oreg. Health Scis. U., 1953—, prof., chmn. dept. clin. pathology, 1962-87, prof. emeritus, 1987—, prof. radiotherapy, 1963-71, allied health edn. coordinator, 1969-77; vis. lectr. radiobiology Reed Coll., 1955, 56. Mem. adv. bd. Oreg. Regional Med. Program, 1968-75; mem. statuatory radiation adv. com. Oreg. Bd. Health, 1957-69, chmn., 1967-69; founding trustee Am. Bd. Nuclear Medicine, 1971-77, 82-84, sec., 1973-75, 84-85 ; voting rep. Am. Bd. Med. Specialties, 1973-78, chmn. com. long range planning, 1976-78; mem. sci. adv. bd. Armed Forces Inst. Pathology, 1978-83. Served to lt. (j.g.) M.C., USNR, 1946-48. Charter mem. Acad. Clin. Lab. Physicians and Scientists, Soc. Nuclear Medicine, Am. Coll. Nuclear Physicians; mem. Oreg. Pathologists Assn. (pres. 1968), Pacific N.W. Soc. Nuclear Medicine (pres. 1958), AMA, Coll. Am. Pathologists (bd. govs. 1967-74, pres. 1977-79, chmn. commn. on internat. affairs 1979-83, chmn. planning com. for 1987 World Congress Pathology), Am. Soc. Clin.

Pathologists (bd. registry med. technologists 1967-71), World Assn. of Socs. of Pathology (v.p. 1985-87, bur. of pathology 1981-87, chmn. commn. on world standards 1981-86), World Pathology Found. (pres. 1987—), Assn. Clin. Pathologists (hon.), Italian Soc. Lab. Medicine (hon.), Phi Beta Kappa, Sigma Xi, Alpha Omega Alpha. Home: 7821 SW 51st St Portland OR 97219 Office: Oreg Health Scis U 3181 SW Sam Jackson Blvd Portland OR 97201

HUTCHESON, JERRY DEE, manufacturing company executive; b. Hammon, Okla., Oct. 31, 1932; s. Radford Andrew and Ethel Mae (Boulware) H.; B.S. in Physics, Eastern N. Mex. U., 1959; postgrad. Temple U., 1961-62, U. N.Mex., 1964-65; m. Lynda Lou Weber, Mar. 6, 1953; children—Gerald Dan, Lisa Marie, Vicki Lynn. Research engr. RCA, 1959-62; sect. head Motorola, 1962-63; research physicist Dikewood Corp., 1963-66; sr. mem. tech. staff Signetics Corp., 1966-69; engring. mgr. Litton Systems, Sunnyvale, Calif., 1969-70; engring. mgr. Fairchild Semiconductor, Mountain View, Calif., 1971; equipment engr., group mgr. Teledyne Semiconductor, Mountain View, 1971-74; dir. engring. DCA Reliability Labs., Sunnyvale, 1974-75; founder, prin. Tech. Ventures, San Jose, Calif., 1975—; chief exec. officer VLSI Research, Inc., 1981—. Democratic precinct committeeman, Albuquerque, 1964-66. Served with USAF, 1951-55. Registered profl. engr., Calif. Mem. Nat. Soc. Profl. Engrs., Profl. Engrs. Pvt. Practice, Calif. Soc. Profl. Engrs., Semiconductor Equipment and Materials Inst., Soc. Photo-Optical Instrumentation Engrs., Am. Soc. Test Engrs., Presbyterian. Club: Masons. Contbr. articles to profl. jours. Home: 5950 Vista Loop San Jose CA 95124 Office: VSLI Research 1754 Technology Dr Suite 117 San Jose CA 95110

HUTCHINGS, LA VERE, artist, educator; b. Lewisville, Idaho, Sept. 18, 1918; s. Marion Price and Mellie Grace (Kinghorn) H.; m. Anne Elizabeth Kirkman, Aug. 2, 1940; children—Marianne, Jeanne, Richard, Dorothy, Robert. A.A., Idaho State U., 1940; student Brigham Young U., 1940-41, Chuinard Art Inst., 1954, 55, Art Students League, summer 1970, John Pike Watercolor Sch., spring and summer 1970. Painter, art instr. Armed Forces Inst., Manila, Philippines, 1945-46, Ricks Coll., Idaho Falls, 1968-69, Hutchings Watercolor Workshops, Idaho and Calif., 1967—; painter, owner, operator Hutchings Gallery, Jamestown, Calif., 1979—; mus. collections include: Laguna Beach Mus. Fine Art, Calif., Las Vegas Mus., Nev., Merced Coll. Mus., Calif., Brigham Young U. Mus., Provo, Utah, Caldwell Library, Idaho; shows juried include: Utah Watercolor Soc., Salt Lake City, 1980, Idaho State Art Assn., Twin Falls, 1982, Wyo. State Art Assn., Pinedale, 1984; solo shows include: Brigham Young U., 1983, Merced Coll., 1982. Author: It's Fun to Paint Old Shacks and Barns, 1977; It's Fun to Paint Roads and Rivers, 1982; Make Your Watercolor Sing, 1986. Contbr. articles to newspapers and profl. jours. Pres. O.E. Bell Jr. High Sch. PTA, Idaho Falls, 1958, Toastmasters Internat., Idaho Falls, 1961, Kiwanis of E. Idaho Falls, 1968; bd. dirs. Teton Peaks Council Boy Scouts Am., Idaho Falls, 1953-60. Recipient Purchase award Inland Exhbn. VII, Elliot Block Co., 1971; Chmn.'s award and Okla. Watercolor award Okla. Watercolor Soc., 1981; 1st prize for Landscape Whiskey Painters Am., 1982. Mem. Nat. Watercolor Soc., Watercolor West (v.p. 1978-79), Soc. Western Artists (1st prize for watercolor 1984), Midwest Watercolor Soc. Mormon. Home: PO Box 249 Jamestown CA 95327 Office: Hutchings Gallery PO Box 249 Jamestown CA 95327

HUTCHINSON, ALAN BRADFORD, clergyman; b. Fall River, Mass., Sept. 19, 1927; s. William and Doris (Hart) H.; student Bowdoin Coll., 1945; A.B., Brown U., 1949; B.D., Andover Theol. Sem., 1952; M.A., Columbia, 1959; M.S., Danbury State Coll., 1964; M.S.W., Boston Coll., 1970; Ph.D., Tenn. U., 1975; m. Jean Caryl Cobb, Feb. 14, 1953; m. 2d, Muriel S. Johnson, Sept. 22, 1972; 1 child, Julianna Edith. Ordained to ministry Congl. Ch., 1951; dir. youth work Park Pl. Congl. Ch., Pawtucket, R.I., 1948-51; minister of youth United Ch., Walpole, Mass., 1951-52; pastor Congl. Ch., New Fairfield, Conn., 1952-66; dir. social services Blackstone Valley Community Action Program, Pawtucket, R.I., 1966-72; clin. psychotherapist Providence Mental Health Center, 1972-76, adminstr. outpatient services, 1976-82, adminstr. community support services, 1982—; pastor 1st Universalist Ch., Burrillville, R.I., 1972—; instr. U. R.I., 1975—; chaplain Fed. Correctional Instn., Danbury, Conn., 1957-58. Fellow Am. Orthopsychiat. Assn.; mem. Ballou-Channing Unitarian-Universalist Ministers Assn., No. R.I. Clergy Assn., Am. Correctional Chaplains Assn., Soc. Mayflower Descs. (elder Conn.), Am. Group Psychotherapy Assn., Register Clin. Social Workers, Nat. Assn. Social Workers (clin. diplomate), Acad. Certified Social Workers, Phi Delta Kappa. Clubs: Community (past pres.), Brown University, Bristol Yacht. Home: 3 Brookwood Rd Bristol RI 02809 Office: 520 Hope St Providence RI 02906

HUTCHINSON, CLARENCE HENRY, management consultant, business executive; b. Floodwood, Minn., Apr. 7, 1925; s. Frank W. and Emma C. (Petersen) H.; A.B., Harvard U., 1950, M.B.A., 1955; m. Helen J. Dowgialo, Apr. 29, 1951 (dec. Mar. 1988); children—Charles, Sarah, Karen. Accountant, Honeywell, Inc., Mpls., 1955-59, mgr. fin. planning, 1959-60, mgr. data systems, 1960-62; controller Hexcel Corp., Dublin, Calif., 1962-64, finance dir., treas., 1964-68, v.p. finance, sec., 1968-69; exec. v.p. Desa Industries, Balt., 1969-70; internat. fin. dir. Memorex Corp., Santa Clara, Calif., 1970-72; sr. v.p., treas. Courier Terminal Systems, Inc., Phoenix, 1972; v.p. finance, treas. Data Pathing Inc., Sunnyvale, Calif., 1972-74, v.p., sec., treas., 1974-75, sr. vp., 1975-79; co-founder, dir., exec. v.p. The Info. Group, Inc., Santa Clara, 1985—; dir., treas. Shearmat Structures, Ltd., Winnepeg, Man., Can., 1964-65; dir., pres. Hexcel Structures, Ltd., Winnipeg, 1965-69; treas. Memorex Pacific Corp., Santa Clara, 1971-72; dir., sec. Data Pathing Europa GmbH, Cologne, W.Ger., 1973-79, Data Pathing (U.K.) Ltd., London, 1973-79; asst. sec. Raytek, Inc., Mountain View, Calif., 1979-80. Vice pres. Bloomington (Minn.) Civic Theatre, 1961-62; bd. dirs. Jr. Achievement, Oakland, Calif., 1965-66. Served with AUS, 1943-46. Mem. Planning Execs. Inst. (chpt. sec. 1961-62), Nat. Assn. Accts. (chpt. dir. 1960-62), Fin. Execs. Inst., Security Analysts Inst. San Francisco. Republican. Unitarian. Club: Commonwealth of Calif. Home and Office: 22320 Kendle St Cupertino CA 95014

HUTCHINSON, JOSEPH CANDLER, foreign language educator; b. Hazelhurst, Ga., Jan. 10, 1920; s. George Washington and Lillie Arizona (Rowan) H.; m. June Cruce O'Shields, Aug. 12, 1950 (div. 1980); children—Junie O'Shields, Joseph Candler. B.A., Emory U., 1940, M.A., 1941; Ph.D., U. N.C., 1950; postgrad. U. Paris, summers 1951, 53. Tchr., Tech. High Sch., Atlanta, 1941-42; instr. French, German, Italian, Emory U., Atlanta, 1946-47; instr. U. N.C., Chapel Hill, 1947-50, asst. prof., 1954, assoc. prof., to 1957; asst. prof. Sweet Briar (Va.) Coll., 1950-51, 53-54; asso. prof. Tulane U., New Orleans, 1957-59; fgn. lang. specialist U.S. Office Edn., Washington, 1959-64; acad. adv. hdqrs. Def. Lang. Inst., Washington, 1964-74, Monterey, 1974-77, dir. tng. devel. Def. Lang. Inst. Fgn. Lang. Center, Monterey, Calif., 1977-82, asst. acad. dean, 1982-85; dean of policy, from 1985; vis. prof. U. Va., Charlottesville, 1966, Arlington, 1970, Georgetown U., 1968, Am. U., 1971; cons. Council of Chief State Sch. Officers, 1960, U. Del., 1966, U. Colo., 1968, U. Ill., 1968; U.S. del. Bur. Internat. Lang. Coordination, NATO, 1964-79, 81-82, 86-87. Served with U.S. Army, 1942-46, 51-53. Decorated Bronze Star. Mem. Am. Council on Edn. (task force on internat. edn. 1973), NEA (sec. dept. fgn. langs. 1961-64), Higher Edn. Assn. Monterey Peninsula, Am. Council on Teaching of Fgn. Langs., MLA, Am. Mgmt. Assn., Am. Soc. Tng. and Devel., Monterey Choral Soc., Camerata Singers. Episcopalian. Clubs: Presidio of Monterey Officers and Faculty, Washington Linguistics (v.p. 1970-72). Contbr. articles to profl. jours.; author: Using the Language Laboratory Effectively, School Executives Guide, 1964; The Language Laboratory: Equipment and Utilization in Trends in Language Teaching, 1966, others; editor Dialog on Lang. Instruction, 1986—. Office: Def Lang Inst Fgn Lang Ctr ATFL-DPL Monterey CA 93944

HUTCHINSON, LOREN KELLEY, manufacturing company executive; b. Buffalo, Oct. 23, 1915; s. William L. and Grace May (Kelley) H.; B.A., Ill. Coll., 1941; postgrad. Harvard U., 1954; m. Marjorie Lee Von Tobel, May 14, 1942; children—Loren Kelley, Lynnis Kay, Beth Ellen. Personnel asst. Wilson Packing Co., Chgo., 1941-42; personnel dir. Esquire, Inc., 1945-48; mgr. personnel and labor relations Ill. C. of C., 1948-51; asst. to exec. v.p. Wyman Gordon Co., Worcester, Mass., 1951-54, mgr. indsl. relations, 1954-58, works mgr., 1958-61, mgr. ops. Eastern div., 1961-64, dir. orgn. devel., 1964-65; pres., dir. Croname, Inc., Chgo., 1966-69; pres. DSI Corp., Plymouth, Mich., 1969-71; pres., dir. Southworth Inc., Portland, Maine, from 1971, now chmn. bd.; pres. Integrated Mgmt. Tech. Inc., Falmouth, Maine; incorporator Maine Savs. Bank; chmn. chief exec. officer Page Express, Portland; bd. dirs. Hussey Mfg. Co., Berwick, Maine, Mowatt Sporting Goods Co., Bangor. Bd. dirs. Worcester County Musical Assn., 1953-65, Asso. Industries Maine, Portland Symphony Orch., Jr. Achievement So. Maine, Econ. Resources Council Maine, Central Mass. Symphony Orch.; bd. dirs., campaign chmn. United Fund Greater Portland; chmn. bd. Worcester Orchestral Soc., 1951-65; bd. dirs. Worcester Community Chest and Council, 1954-65, Crusade of Mercy, YMCA; corporator Maine Med. Ctr., Portland; mem. Rep. Nat Com. Served to lt., 1942-45. Mem. Nat. Assn. Metal Name Plate Mfrs. (dir.), Pulp and Paper Machinery Mfrs. Assn. (dir.), Greater Portland C. of C. (dir.), Newcomen Soc., Unitarian. Mason. Clubs: Lake Forest; Harvard (Boston); Chicago Press; Overseas Yacht (N.Y.C.); Portland Country, Cumberland (Portland). Home: 4 Susan Ln Falmouth ME 04105 Office: Foreside Mall PO Box 6100 Falmouth ME 04105

HUTCHINSON, WARNER ALTON, retirement housing executive, writer; b. Syracuse, N.Y., Feb. 21, 1929; s. Warner Alton and Elizabeth (Errickson) H.; BA, UCLA, 1951; M Div., Fuller Theol. Sem., 1955; m. Betty L. Bell, 1979. Ordained to ministry United Ch. of Christ, 1955; traveling sec. Inter-Varsity Christian Fellowship, 1950-52, gen. sec. in New Zealand, 1958-62, Eastern dir. in U.S., 1963-66; with Am. Bible Soc., N.Y.C., 1966-77, Eastern regional sec., 1966-67, Asia sec., 1967-69, exec. sec. for overseas, 1969-71, dep. gen. sec., 1971-72, gen. sec., 1973-77; world service officer for Latin Am. and Asia, United Bible Socs., 1971-76; organizer W.A. Hutchinson, Inc., 1977, pres., 1977-81; dir. Adult Edn. div. Wm. H. Sadlier, Inc., 1980-82; v.p. and pub. B&W Hutchinsons, Inc., 1982-86; cons. Retirement Life Planners, 1986; v.p. 1987—; editor Shepherd Books, Keats Pub. Co. vis. lectr. Fuller Theol. Sem., 1966. Served as chaplain USNR, 1955-58; capt. RES. Mem. Asia Soc., U.S. Naval Inst., Navy League, Naval Res. Assn., Mil. Order World Wars, Religion Publs. Group, Soc. for Scholarly Pub., Overseas Press Club, Ends of the Earth, Phi Beta Kappa. Author: Let the People Rejoice, 1959; Love for Everyday Living, 1978; Strength for Everyday Living, 1978; Ancient Egypt, 1978; Oral Roberts, 1978; Jesus, His Life and Times, 1979; New York, 1979; Famous Bible People, 1981; An Illustrated Life of Jesus from the National Gallery of Art Collection, 1982; Word Processing Made Simple, 1984; Computer Typing Made Simple, 1984; Business Letters Made Simple, 1985; The Complete Displaywriter Handbook, 1986; editor Faith and Inspiration mag., 1977-79; pub. The Living Light iour., 1980-82; others; contbr. articles to profl. jours. Office: 262 S 23d St Philadelphia PA 19103

HUTCHISON, CATHLEEN SMITH, instructional technologist; b. Detroit, June 6, 1949; d. Joseph Donald and Lola Mae (Smith) H.; m. Larry George Fichtner, May 3, 1970 (div. Nov. 1982); 1 son, Erik Matthew Hutchison Fichtner. B.A. in Art History, U. Mich., 1970; M.Ed., Wayne State U., 1982. Various positions with Lee Wards, Taylor, Mich., 1976-78, Chrysler Learning, Detroit, 1978-81; mgr. tng. and devel. Botsford Gen. Hosp., Farmington, Mich., 1981-84; instructional designer Gen. Motors Mktg. Edl. Services, 1984-87; performance technologist Sandia Nat. Labs., 1987—; cons. in field. Co-author: Instructor Competencies: The Standarts, 1988. Mem. Nat. Soc. Performance and Instrn. (v.p. 1988—), Mich. Soc. Instrnl. Tech. (pres. 1985-86), Internat. Bd. Standards for Tng., Performance and Instrn. Profls. (bd. dirs.), Am. Soc. Tng. and Devel., World Future Soc. Club: Detroit Yacht. Office: PO Box 5800 Work Div 3523 Albuquerque NM 87175

HUTCHISON, JOHN MICHAEL, barrister; b. Halifax, Nova Scotia, Can., Mar. 7, 1944; s. John Arthur and Barbara Mary (Wardle) H.; 1 child, Adam Michael Lewis. LLB, U. B.C., Vancouver, 1970. Bar: B.C. 1971, Queen's Counsel 1986. Articled student Sullivan, Smith & Bigelow, Victoria, B.C., Can., 1970-71, assoc., 1971-74, ptnr., 1974-76; ptnr. Sullivan, Smith, Stewart & Gow, Victoria, 1976-79, Smith, Hutchison & Gow, Victoria, 1979-85, Smith Hutchison, Victoria, 1985—; bd. dirs. Walker Systems Corp., pres., bd. dirs. Camosun Coll., Sea Lord Aqua Crops, Inc. Mem. Law Soc. B.C., Can. Bar Assn., Can. Assn. Univ. Solicitors, Can. Inst. Law and Medicine, Am. Trial Lawyers Assn., U.S. Assn. Law and Medicine. Anglican. Clubs: Union, B.C. Rugby Union (chmn. selectors 1985—). Office: Smith Hutchison, 747 Fort St 11th Floor, Victoria, BC Canada V8W 3E9

HUTH, KARL G., physician, educator; b. Germany, Feb. 28, 1933; s. Wilhelm and Ilse (Braune) H.; m. Brigitte Soergel, July 24, 1958; children. MD, U. Heidelberg, 1958. Intern Ludolf-Krehl-Klinik, Heidelberg, Fed. Republic Germany, 1958-60, resident, 1960-68; habilitation U. Giessen, Fed. Republic Germany, 1968-70; head doctor U. Giessen Clinic, Fed. Republic Germany, 1970-73; chief doctor Diakonissen Hosp., Frankfurt, Fed. Republic Germany, 1973—. Author: Ernährung und Diätetik, 1979; co-editor, Lehrbuch der Ernährungstherapie, 1985. Home: Stettenstr 21, 6 Frankfurt 1 Hessen Federal Republic of Germany Office: Diakonissen Krankenhaus, Holzhausenstr 88, 6000 6 Frankfurt Hessen Federal Republic of Germany

HUTH, LESTER CHARLES, lawyer; b. Tiffin, Ohio, Nov. 21, 1924. J.D., U. Notre Dame, 1951. Bar: Ohio 1954. Sole practice, Fostoria, Ohio, 1954—; acting mcpl. judge, Fostoria, 1970, city solicitor, 1954-56, 60-64, police prosecutor, 1964-68; legal counsel to St. Wendelin Parish, Fostoria, 1972—; atty. Selective Service Bd. Appeals, 1956-75. Clk. city council, Fostoria, 1957-58; sec.-treas. Karrick Sch. Handicapped Children, 1956-77; Cub scoutmaster Boy Scouts Am., 1967-68; adviser to Fostoria Family and Child Service, 1977-83. Recipient certs. of appreciation Pres. Lyndon Johnson, 1966, SSS, 1975. Mem. Ohio Bar Assn., Senece County Bar Assn., C. of C. (dir. 1970-71), Fostoria Jaycees (founding pres. 1954). Home: 225 E High St Fostoria OH 44830 Office: 112 E North St Fostoria OH 44830

HUTT, ERIC JOHN VILLETTE, accountant; b. Royston, Eng., May 14, 1915; s. John and Olive Villette (Gillespie) H.; law student London U., 1939; m. Jadwiga de Sulerzyska, Jan. 29, 1949; children—Anthony Villette, Timothy Patrick de Sulerzyski, Clive Karl. Office boy, 1933; jr. accountant, 1934; accountant's articled clk., 1935-39; chief accountant China Engrs. Ltd., Shanghai, 1946-48; mgr. Lowe, Bingham & Thomsons, chartered accountants, Tokyo and Kobe, Japan, 1949-50, partner, 1951-65; adviser, exec. dir. Jardine Matheson & Co., Ltd., Hong Kong, 1966-84; dir. Jardine Fleming & Co., Ltd., Mcht. Bankers, 1970-84, prof., non-exec. dir., fin. cons., 1984—. Served with Brit. Army, 1940-45. Fellow Inst. Chartered Accountants in Eng. and Wales, Huguenot Soc. London; mem. Am. Inst. C.P.A.s (internat. asso.). Clubs: East India, Sports and Schools, St. James St. (London); Hong Kong. Home: 22 Braga Circuit, Kowloon Hong Kong Office: Jeatac Ltd, World Fin Ctr North Tower, Suite 1410, Canton Rd, Kowloon Hong Kong

HUTTENSTINE, MARIAN LOUISE, journalism educator; b. Bloomsburg, Pa., Jan. 26, 1940; d. Ralph Benjamin and Marian Louise (Engler) H.; B.S., Bloomsburg State U., 1961, M.Ed., 1966; postgrad. (NDEA fellow, Newspaper Fund fellow), Rutgers U., 1962-63; Ph.D., U. N.C., 1985. High sch. English, journalism tchr., dept. chmn., 1961-66; asst. prof. Lock Haven (Pa.) U., 1966-73, asso. prof. English, 1973-74; teaching asst., lectr. Sch. Journalism, U. N.C., Chapel Hill, 1974-76; cons., dir. Diener & Assos., Research Triangle Park, N.C., 1975-86; asst. prof. journalism Sch. Communication, U. Ala., Tuscaloosa, 1977—; cons. various publs., Ala., 1977—. Adult leader, vol. worker Luth. Ch., 1962—, Boy Scouts Am. Mem. Assn. Edn. in Journalism and Communication, Internat. Communication Assn., Nat. Fedn. Press Women, Ala. Media Women, Nat. Assn. Female Execs., ACLU, Am. Advt. Fedn., Kappa Tau Alpha. Clubs: Tuscaloosa Advt., Ala. SPJ-SDX. Contbr. papers to profl. lit. Home: K-1 Woodland Trace Tuscaloosa AL 35405 Office: U Ala Dept Journalism Box 1482 Tuscaloosa AL 35487-1482

HUTTER, JAMES RISQUE, lawyer; b. Spokane, Wash., Mar. 20, 1924; s. James R. and Esther (Nelson) H.; m. Patricia Ruth Dunlavy, Aug. 12, 1951; children: Bruce Dunlavy, Gail Anne, Dean James, Karl Nelson. B.S., UCLA, 1947; J.D., Stanford U., 1950. Bar: Calif. 1951, U.S. Supreme Ct. 1965. Assoc. Gibson, Dunn & Crutcher, Los Angeles and Beverly Hills, Calif., 1950-58, ptnr., 1959—; dir. Fifield Manors, Los Angeles, 1955—, v.p., 1964-85, pres., 1985—. Bd. dirs., chmn. fin. com. Congl. Found. for Theol. Studies, Nat. Assn. Congl. Christian Chs., 1961-68; mem. San Marino City Planning Commn., Calif., 1968—, chmn., 1976—. Served to 1st. inf. AUS, 1943-46. Decorated Purple Heart. Mem. State Bar Calif. (com. on corps. 1973-76, exec. com. bus. law sect. 1976-78), ABA, Los Angeles County Bar Assn., Beverly Hills Bar Assn. (bd. govs. 1968-70), Am. Judicature Soc., Town Hall, Phi Delta Phi, Beta Gamma Sigma, Phi Kappa Psi. Clubs: Stock Exchange of Los Angeles, Valley Hunt. Home: 1400 Circle Dr San Marino CA 91108 Office: Gibson Dunn & Crutcher 333 S Grand Ave 48th Floor Los Angeles CA 90071

HUTTER, ROBERT GRANT, lawyer, educator; b. Cleve., May 7, 1948; s. Russell G. and Tresa V. (Ireland) H.; m. Cheryl Felt. B.S.Ch.E., Va. Poly. Inst., 1969; J.D., U. Md., 1973; M.B.A., St. Bonaventure U., 1978. Bar: N.Y. 1980, U.S. Dist. Ct. N.Y. Chem. engr. Westinghouse, Balt., 1969-73; prof. law Alfred U., N.Y., 1974—; ptnr. Sootheran & Hutter, Andover, N.Y., 1981—. Contbr. numerous articles and book revs. to profl. publs. Mem. N.Y. State Bar Assn., Allegany County Bar Assn. (chmn. real estate law com. 1983—). Home: RD 1 Box 81H Wellsville NY 14895 Office: Sootheran & Hutter Attys 15 Main St Andover NY 14806

HUTTO, RUTH BISHOP, nursing adminstrator; b. Harleyville, S.C., May 14, 1927; d. Sidi Hamet and Harriet Elizabeth (Sillivant) Bishop; m. Julius Otey, Oct. 6, 1968; 1 child, Elizabeth. Grad. Med. Coll. S.C., 1951; B.S. in Nursing, Vanderbilt U., 1956; M.A., Columbia U., 1962. Supr. pediatric nursing Med. U. S.C., Charleston, 1956-60; instr., asst. prof. U. Ky. Coll. Nursing, Lexington, 1962-67; chmn. pediatric nursing Med. U. S.C. Coll. Nursing, Charleston, 1967-72, asst. dean, 1972-80, chmn. pediatric nursing, 1980-81, program nurse dir., 1981—. Editor Dimensions, 1985—. Mem. Substance Abuse Com., Charleston County, 1978—; mem. Parent-Child Adv. Bd., Dorchester County, 1982—; mem. Palmetto-Low country Health Systems Agy., Charleston, Berkley & Dorchester Counties, 1981-87; vol. citizens in need of primary nursing skills, Harleyville, S.C., 1968—. Recipient Cert. of Service, Camp High Hope for Exceptional Children, Charleston, 1971, 72, 73, 74, Resolution, S.C. Ho. of Reps. and Senate, 1980; named Career Woman of Yr., Trident Bus. and Profl. Woman's Club, Greater Charleston, 1977. Mem. Internat. Hyperthermia Clin. Soc. (bd. dirs. 1985-87), Clin. Nurse Specialist Group, S.C. League Nursing (bd. dirs. 1984-87, editor newsletter 1984-86, chmn. nominating com. 1986-88), Med. U. S.C. Alumni Assn. (disting. alumni 1974). Methodist. Clubs: Tuesday Afternoon (Harleyville). Home: Rt 2 Box 304 Harleyville SC 29448 Office: Med U SC Med Ctr Clin Nursing 171 Ashley Ave Charleston SC 29425

HUTTON, ANN HAWKES, state official; b. Phila., Feb. 16, 1909; d. Thomas G. and Katharine (Gallagher) Hawkes; m. Leon John H. Hutton, Sept. 23, 1939 (dec.); 1 child, Katharine Ann (Mrs. Charles E. Tweedy III). B.S. in Edn, U. Pa., 1931, J.D., 1934. Dir. advt. Wetherill Paint Co., Phila., Memphis, 1936-38, Caravel Films, N.Y.C., 1938-39; Dir. advt., v.p. Hutton Chevrolet Co., Riverside, N.J., 1949-70; mem. Washington Crossing Park Commn., 1939—, chmn., 1963—; Historian, authority Emanuel Leutze painting Washington Crossing the Delaware; past chmn., now mem. Bucks County Hist.-Tourist Commn., 1960—; commr. Am. Revolution Bicentennial Commn., 1969-73, vice-chmn. council, 1973-76. Author: George Washington Crossed Here, 1948, House of Decision, 1956, Portrait of Patriotism, 1959, The Pennsylvanian, 1962; drama The Decision, 1963, The Year and Spirit of 76, 1972; script for documentary film Washington Crossing the Delaware, 1966; Composer: script for documentary film 1776 Suite From the Decision, 1970; (newspaper column) Now and Then, Intercounty Newspapers. Trustee, former chmn. bd. Historic Fallsington; chmn. bd. Washington Crossing Found.; pres. Hist. Found. Pa. Recipient Nat. Bicentennial medal, 1976, award of merit D.A.R., 1955; Achievement award Commonwealth Pa. for research and furnishing historic Thompson-Neely House, 1955; citation Nat. Camp, Patriotic Order Sons Am., 1959; award Am. Legion Phila., 1960; Freedom Leadership award Freedoms Found. at Valley Forge (1st woman to receive this award), 1960; award Pa. Soc. D.A.R., 1960; award Freedoms Found. for drama The Decision, 1964; Good Citizenship medal Phila.-Continental chpt. SAR, 1967; Exceptional Citizenship award Patriotic Order Sons Am., 1968; Disting. Alumni award Friend's Select Sch., Phila., 1976; Fame award Friendship Fete Phila. and Delaware Valley, 1982; named Distinguished Dau. Pa., 1958; medal of honor D.A.R., 1973; nat. award Nat. Soc. Daus. Founders and Patriots, 1976; Disting. Service award Bucks County Commrs., 1980. Mem. Disting. Daus. Pa. (v.p. 1976-79, pres. 1979-82), Chi Omega, Pi Lambda Theta. Clubs: Bristol Travel; Lost Tree (North Palm Beach, Fla.); Union League (Phila.) (asso.). Home: 6900 N Radcliffe St Bristol PA 19007

HUTTON, EDWARD LUKE, chemical company executive; b. Bedford, Ind., May 5, 1919; s. Fred and Margaret (Drehobl) H.; m. Kathryn Jane Alexander; children—Edward Alexander, Thomas Charles, Jane Clarke. B.S. with distinction, Ind. U., 1940, M.S. with distinction, 1941. Dep. dir. Joint Export Import Agy. (USUK), Berlin, Fed. Republic Germany, 1946-48; v.p. World Commerce Corp., 1948-51; asst. v.p. W.R. Grace & Co., 1951-53, cons., 1960-65, exec. v.p., gen. mgr. Dubois Chems. div., 1965-66, group exec. Specialty Products Group and v.p., 1966-68, exec. v.p., 1968-71; cons. internat. trade and fin. 1953-58; fin. v.p., exec. v.p. Ward Industries, 1958-59; pres., chief exec. officer Chemed Corp., Cincinnati, 1971—, dir.; chmn. Omnicare, Inc., Cincinnati, 1981—; dir. Omnicare, Inc.; chmn., dir. Roto-Rooter, Inc., 1984—; dir. DuBois Germany, Am. States Ins. Co. Co-chmn. Pres.'s Pvt. Sector Survey on Cost Control, exec. com., subcom. Recipient Disting. Alumni Service award Ind. U., 1987. Mem. Internat. Platform Assn., U. Cin. (CBA bd. advisors), Dirs.' Table, AAUP (governing bd. dirs. 1958—), Newcomen Soc. Clubs: Downtown Assn., Econs., Princeton, University (N.Y.C.), Queen City, Bankers (Cin.), Cincinnati. Home: 6680 Miralake Dr Cincinnati OH 45243 Office: Chemed Corp 1200 DuBois Tower Cincinnati OH 45202

HUTTON, IAN, advertising executive; b. Cork, Ireland, Nov. 9, 1942; s. John Noel Lock and Margaret (Barry) H. m. Charity Hamilton, Aug. 26, 1986; children, Tara Mari, Patrick Hugo. Student, St. Mary's Coll., Dublin, Ireland, 1954-59. Sports reporter The Irish Press, Dublin, 1961; copywriter McConnells Advt., Dublin, 1962-63, Youngs Advt., Dublin, 1963-65, S.H. Benson Ltd., London, Eng., 1966, Leo Burnett Ltd., London, 1967-69; assoc. dir. J. Walter Thompson Ltd., London, 1970-75, sr. assoc. dir., 1975-85, creative dir., 1985—. Exhibited film at Met. Mus. of Modern Art, N.Y.C., 1984. Mem. fund raising com. Save The Children; patron: HRH Princess Anne, London, 1986—. Recipient Lion D'or award Cannes, 1978, Lion D'Argent, 1974, 86, Leinster Jr. Championship, Irish Amatuer Boxing Bd., Ireland, 1960. Mem. Design & Art Direction Assn., Creative Circle Assn. Roman Catholic. Club: Mortons (Berkeley Square). Office: J Walter Thompson Ltd, 40 Berkeley Sq, London England WIX 6AD

HUTTON, JACK GOSSETT, JR., psychologist, educator; b. Denver, June 20, 1931; s. Jack Gossett and Margaretta Elizabeth (Lea) H.; student Colo. Coll., 1949-51; B.A., U. Denver, 1953, M.A., 1956; Ph.D., U. Conn., 1968. Asst. dir. div. ednl. measurement and research Assn. Am. Med. Colls., Washington, 1968-71; staff psychologist, profl. exams. div. Psychol. Corp., N.Y.C., 1971-73; ednl. psychologist, asso. prof. Coll. Dentistry, Howard U., Washington, 1973-79, ednl. psychologist, prof. Coll. Dentistry, 1979—; asso. prof. Sch. Edn., Howard U., 1973-77; vis. ednl. specialist Sch. Dentistry, W.Va. U., 1976-83; vis. scholar U. Mich., summer 1968; adj. asst. prof. Sch. Edn., Cath. U., 1969-71. Served with U.S. Army, 1956-58. Mem. Am. Psychol. Assn., Am. Edn. Research Assn., Nat. Council Measurement in Edn., Am. Assn. Dental Schs. (sec. sect. behavioral scis. 1975-76), Behavioral Scientists in Dental Research, AAUP, N.Y. Acad. Scis., Sigma Xi, Psi Chi, Phi Sigma. Contbr. articles to profl. jours. Home: 1101 New Hampshire Ave NW Apt 1018 Washington DC 20037 Office: Howard U Coll Dentistry 600 W St NW Washington DC 20059

HUTTON, RONALD EDMUND, historian, writer; b. Ootacamund, Kerala, India, Dec. 19, 1953; s. Geoffrey Edmund and Elsa Edwina (Hanson) H. BA, Cambridge U., Eng., 1976, MA, 1980; DPhil, Oxford U., Eng., 1980. Fellow Magdalen Coll., Oxford, Eng., 1979-81; lectr. U. Bristol, Eng., 1981—; guest lectr. numerous univs. and profl. socs. Author: The Royalist War Effort, 1981, The Restoration, 1985; contbr. articles to profl. jours. Fellow Royal Hist. Soc. Office: U Bristol Dept History, 13 Woodland Rd, Bristol BS8 1TB, England

HUTZELL, ROBERT RAYMOND, clinical psychologist; b. Des Moines, Dec. 6, 1948; s. Robert Roy and Dorothy Mae (Oldham) H.; m. Vicki Lynn Shinn, Aug. 31, 1969; children: Daisy Lynn, Angela Kathreen. BS with honors and distinction, U. Iowa, 1971; MS, Fla. State U., 1973, PhD, 1975. Cert. health service provider psychology, 1983; cert. psychology peer reviewer, 1987. Trainee, intern Southeastern U.S. VA, 1972-75; clin. psychologist VA, Biloxi, Miss., 1975-76, Knoxville, Iowa, 1976—, dir. Behavioral Health Clinic; dir. psychol. services Mater Clinic, Knoxville, 1983—; adj. faculty U. Iowa, Iowa City, 1978-83; conducts profl. tng. workshops. Mem. editorial adv. bd. The Hospice Jour.; author various books, newspaper column; contbr. articles to profl. jours. and chpts. to books. Recipient Performance award VA, 1978, 81-86. Mem. Am. Psychol. Assn. (Psychologists in Pub. Service cert. of recognition 1983), Midwestern Psychol. Assn., Southeastern Psychol. Assn., Iowa Psychol. Assn. (editor newsletter 1978-86, pres. 1988, Merit award 1986), Nat. Orgn. VA Psychologists (newsletter editor 1984—, trustee 1987—, cert. of recognition 1985), Inst. Logotherapy (diplomate; regional dir. 1984—, Iowa chpt. pres. 1983-87), Iowa Nut Tree Growers Assn. Methodist. Home: Drawer 112 Knoxville IA 50138 Office: VA Med Center Knoxville IA 50138

HUXLEY, ANDREW (FIELDING), physiologist; b. London, Nov. 22, 1917; s. Leonard and Rosalind (Bruce) H.; B.A., Cambridge (Eng.), 1938, M.A., 1941, Sc.D. (hon.), 1978; M.D. (hon.), U. Saar, 1964; D.Sc. (hon.), U. Sheffield (Eng.), 1964, U. Leicester (Eng.), 1967, London U., 1973, U. St. Andrews, Scotland, 1974, U. Aston in Birmingham (Eng.), 1977; LL.D. (hon.), U. Birmingham, 1979, Marseille U., 1979, York U., 1981, U. Western Australia, 1982, NYU, 1982, Oxford U., 1983, U. Pa., 1984, Dundee U., 1984, Harvard U., 1984, U. Keele, 1985, East Anglia U., 1985, Humboldt U., East Berlin, 1985, others; m. Jocelyn Richenda Gammell Pease, July 5, 1947; children—Janet Rachel, Stewart Leonard, Camilla Rosalind, Eleanor Bruce, Henrietta Catherine, Clare Marjory Pease. Research staff Anti-Aircraft Command, 1940-42, Admiralty, 1942-45; fellow Trinity Coll., Cambridge, 1941-60, hon. fellow, 1967—, master, 1984—, dir. studies, 1952-60; demonstrator Cambridge U., 1946-50, asst. dir. research, 1951-59, reader exptl. biophysics, 1959-60, 6th ann. Darwin lectr., 1982; Jodrell prof. physiology U. Coll. London, 1960-69, Royal Soc. research prof., 1969-83, hon. fellow, 1980; emeritus prof. physiology U. London, 1983—; Herter lectr. Johns Hopkins U., 1959; Jesup lectr. Columbia U., 1964; Forbes lectr., 1966; Croonian lectr. Royal Soc., 1967, Florey lectr., 1982, Blackett Meml. lectr., 1984; Fullerian prof. Royal Inst., London, 1967-73; Hans Hecht lectr., Chgo., 1975; Sherrington lectr. Liverpool U., 1976-77; Centenary Colloquium lectr. Berlin Inst. Physiology, 1977; Cecil H. and Ida Green vis. prof. U. B.C., 1980; chmn. Brit. Nat. Com. for Physiol. Scis., 1979. Trustee Brit. Mus. (Natural History), 1981—, Sci. Mus., 1984—. Created knight bachelor, 1974; decorated Order of Merit, 1983; recipient (with A.L. Hodgkin and J.C. Eccles) Nobel prize for physiology or medicine, 1963; Imperial Coll. Sci. and Tech. fellow, 1980. Fellow Royal Soc. (hon.; Copley medal 1973, council 1960-62, 77-79, 80-85, pres. 1980-85), Inst. Biology (hon.), Royal Soc. Can. (hon.), Royal Soc. Edinburgh (hon.), Indian Nat. Sci. Acad. (fgn.); mem. Physiol. Soc. (hon., rev. lectr. on muscular contraction 1973), Brit. Biophys. Soc., Royal Acad. Scis., Letters and Fine Arts Belgium (assoc.), Muscular Dystrophy Group Gt. Britain and No. Ireland (chmn. med. research com. 1974-81, v.p., 1981—), Royal Instn. Gt. Britain (hon.), Anat. Soc. Gt. Britain and Ireland (hon.), Am. Philos. Soc., Brit. Assn. Advancement Sci. (pres. 1976-77), Nat. Acad. Scis. (U.S.) (fgn. assoc.), Agrl. Research Council, Royal Acad. Medicine Belgium (assoc.), Dutch Soc. Scis. (fgn.), Am. Soc. Zoologists (hon.), Royal Irish Acad. (hon.), Nature Conservancy (council). Author: Reflections on Muscle, 1980; editor: Jour. Physiology, 1950-57, chmn. bd. Publs. on analysis of nerve conduction (with Hodgkin), physiology of striated muscle, devel. of interference microscope and ultramicrotome. Office: Trinity Coll, The Master's Lodge, Cambridge CB2 1TQ, England also: Univ College London, Dept of Physiology Gower St, London WC1E 6BT, England *

HUXLEY, HUGH ESMOR, molecular biologist; b. Birkenhead, Eng., Feb. 25, 1924; s. Thomas Hugh and Olwen (Roberts) H.; B.A., Christ's Coll., Cambridge (Eng.) U., 1948, M.A., 1950, Ph.D., 1952, Sc.D., 1964, hon. fellow, 1981; D.Sc. (hon.), Harvard U., 1969, U. Chgo., 1974, U. Pa., 1975. Research student molecular biology unit Med. Research Council, Cavendish Lab., Cambridge, 1948-52, sci. staff, 1954-55; external staff Med. Research Council, dept. biophysics U. Coll., London, 1956-61, Med. Research Council Lab. Molecular Biology, Cambridge, 1962-87, dep. dir., 1977-87; Commonwealth fund fellow dept. biology Mass. Inst. Tech., Boston, 1952-54; fellow Christ's Coll., Cambridge U., 1954-56, fellow King's Coll., 1961-67, fellow Churchill Coll., 1967-87; prof. biology Rosenstiel Basic Med. Scis. Research Ctr., Brandeis U., Waltham, Mass., 1987—. Decorated mem. Order Brit. Empire; recipient Feldberg prize, 1963; Hardy prize, 1965; Louisa Gross Hurwitz prize, 1971; Internat. Feltrinelli prize, 1974; Gairdner award, 1975; Baly medal Royal Coll. Physicians, 1975; Royal medal Royal Soc. London, 1977; E.B. Wilson medal Am. Soc. Cell Biology, 1983; Albert Einstein award World Cultural Council, 1987. Fellow Royal Soc., 1960; mem. Physiol. Soc., Brit. Biophys. Soc., European Molecular Biology Orgn.; hon. fgn. mem. Am. Acad. Arts and Scis., Danish Acad. Scis., Leopoldina Acad., Nat. Acad. Sci. (hon., assoc.). Editor: Progress in Biophysics and Molecular Biology, 1960-66; editorial bd. Jour. Cell Biology, 1959-63, Jour. Molecular Biology, 1962-70, 79—, Jour. Cell Sci., 1966-70. Research, publs. on ultrastructures of straited muscles, especially by electron-microscopy and X-ray diffraction leading to sliding filament theory of contraction (with Jean Hanson; simultaneously proposed by A.F. Huxley and R. Niedergerke): studies on electron microscopy of viruses, ribosomes and other nucleic-acid containing structures. Home: 7 Chaucer Rd, Cambridge England Office: Brandeis U Rosensteil Basic Med Scis Research Ctr Waltham MA 02254 *

HU YAOBANG, Chinese government official; b. Liuyang City, Hunan Province, 1915; m. Li Chao. Head orgn. dept. Communist Youth League, 1935, mem. cen. com., 1936, 49, 1st sec., 1957-64; head orgn. dept. of gen. polit. dept. 18th Corps, 1941, dir. polit. dept., 1949; head polit. dept. 2d Field Army, 1949; vice chmn. Taiyuan Mil. Control Commn., 1949; mem. exec. bd. Sino-Soviet Friendship Assn., 1949-54; dir., head fin. and econs. com. North Sichuan People's Adminstrv. Office, 1950; polit. commissar North Sichuan Mil. Dist., 1950; mem. SW Mil. and Adminstrv. Com., 1950-52; sec. New Dem. Youth League, 1952-57; mem. nat. com. All-China Fedn. Dem. Youth, 1953-58; vice chmn. World Fedn. Dem. Youth, 1953-59; mem. standing com. Nat. People's Congress, 1954-59, re-elected, 1959, 64; mem. exec. com. All-China Fedn. Trade Unions, 1953-57; mem. Cen. Work Com. for Popularization of Standard Spoken Chinese, 1956; vice chmn. Nat. Assn. for Elimination Illiteracy, 1956; mem. 8th Cen. Com. Chinese Communist Party, 1956-67, 11th Cen. Com., 1977, mem. Politburo, 1978, mem. Standing Com., 1980, chmn., 1981-82, mem. Politburo 12th Cen. Com., 1982, mem. Standing Com., 1982-87; mem. standing com. politburo 13th Cen. com., 1987—; acting 1st sec. Shaanxi com. Communist Party, 1965; sec.-gen. Cen. Com., 1978-80, dir. propaganda dept., 1979-80, sec.-gen. secretariat, 1980; 3d sec. Cen. Com. for Inspecting Discipline, 1978-81; gen. sec. Chinese Communist Party, 1980, 82-87. Office: Central Committee of Chinese, Communist Party, Beijing People's Republic of China *

HUYGHE, RENÉ LOUIS, art historian, critic, museum administrator, author; b. Arras, France, May 3, 1906; s. Louis and Marie (Delvoye) H.; m. Lydia Bouthet, Oct. 9, 1950; 1 child, François-Bernard; 1 child by previous marriage, Claire-Hélène. Student, Ecole du Louvre, Paris; Faculty of Letters, Sorbonne, Paris. Mem. staff Musée du Louvre, 1927-29, asst. keeper, 1930-36, head keeper of paintings and drawings, 1937-49; prof. Ecole du Louvre, prof. pyschology of plastic arts coll. de France, from 1950, now hon. prof.; mem. French Mus. Council, 1952—, v.p., 1964-73, pres., 1974—; research prof. Nat. Gallery of Art, Washington, 1967-68; pres. UNESCO Internat. Com. of experts to save Venice; dir. Musée Jacquemart-André, 1974—; dir. art rev. L'Amour de l'Art, 1930—; founder and dir. of rev. Quadridge, 1945—; v.p. Acad. Europeenne; collaborated or organized numerous exhibitions including French Art, London, 1931, Van Gogh and Masterpieces of French Art, Paris, 1937, Modern Painting, Rio de Janeiro, 1945, others; creator film Rubens and His Age (Venice Festival prize); mem. and former pres. Academie Septentrionale. Author: Histoire de l'art contemporain, 1934, Cézanne, 1936, La Peinture française: le Portrait, 2 vols., 1937, Les dessins de Van Gogh, 1937, Les Contemporains, 1939, La Peinture Actuelle, 1945, La Poetique de Vermeer, 1948, Le dessin française au XIXe siecle, 1949, Univers de Watteau, 1950, Gauguin et Noa-Noa, 1951, Le Carnet de Gauguin, 1952, La peinture d'occident, 1952, Dialogue avec le visible, 1955, L'art et l'homme, vols. I & II, 1957, vol. III, 1961, Van Gogh, 1958, Gauguin, 1959, L'art et l'ame, 1960, Peinture française aux XVIIe et XVIIe siecles, 1962, Delacroix ou le combat solitaire, 1963, Les Puissances de l'image, 1965, Sens et destin de l'art, 1967, L'art et le monde moderne, 2 vols., 1970, Formes et forces, 1971, La relève du rèel, 1974, La relève de l'imaginaire, 1976, Ce que je crois, 1976, De l'art a la philosophie, 1980, La nuit appelle l'aurore, 1980, Les Signes du Temps et E'Art Moderne, 1985; (with M. Brion) Le perdre dams Venise, 1987. Decorated Grand Croix Ordre du Merite, Grand Officer Legion d'honneur, Comdr. Ordre de Leopold (Belgium); Comdr. Order of Merit (Italy); Comdr. Merite Culturel, Ordre St. Charles (Monaco); Comdr. Couronne de Chene (Luxembourg); recipient Erasmus prize, 1966. Office: Musee Jacquemart-Andre, 158 Blvd Haussmann, 75008 Paris France

HUYGHEBAERT, JAN, bank executive; b. Brussels, Apr. 6, 1945. BA in Philosophy, Antwerp (Belgium) U., 1965; LLD, Cath. U. Louvain, Belgium, 1968. Attaché Sci. Policy Dept., Brussels, 1970; advisor to Prime Minister, Brussels, 1974-78; alderman Port of Antwerp, 1978-85; pres. Kredietbank N.V., Brussels, 1985—; chmn. bd. Antwerp Gas Distbn. Orgn., 1983-85. Mem. council City of Antwerp, 1976-85; apptd. bd. dirs. Belgian Radio and TV, Brussels, 1977-78; bd. dirs. Kredietbank S.A. Luxembourgeoise. Office: Kredietbank NV, Arenbergstraat 7, 1000 Brussels Belgium

HUYNH TAN PHAT, government official Socialist Republic Vietnam; b. 1913. Formerly editor Thanh-nien; joined Vanguard Youth, 1945; remained in South Vietnam after Geneva Agreement ending anti-French struggle, 1954; sec.-gen. Democratic Party; mem. central com. Nat. Liberation Front, 1964—; pres. Provisional Revolutionary Govt. Republic of South Vietnam, 1969-76, in Saigon, 1975-76; vice premier council of ministers Socialist Republic Vietnam, 1976-82; chmn. State Commn. for Capital Constrn., 1982-83; vice chmn. Council of State, 1982—. Address: Office of Vice Chmn, State Council, Hanoi Socialist Republic of Vietnam *

HWANG, LAURA C.L., bank executive; b. Singapore, Dec. 28, 1949; d. A. Chua Tan and Lily (Ong) Teo; m. Michael Hwang; children: Christopher Wei-Jen, Jonathan Wei-Ming. BA with honours, U. Singapore, 1972. Officer banking Standard Chartered Bank, Singapore, 1973-77; mgr. banking Arbuthnot Latham Asia (Mcht. Banker) Ltd., Singapore, 1977-78, dir., 1978-84, mng. dir., 1984-86; mng. dir. Royal Trust Mcht. Bank Ltd., Singapore, 1986—; chmn. bd. Royal Trust Asset Mgmt. Pte Ltd, Singapore, 1985—; bd. dirs. Royal Trust Nominees Pte Ltd., Singapore, Asia Ltd., Singapore, Royal Trust Securities, Singapore, Liaise (Far East) Ltd., Hong Kong, Royal Trust Hayes Ltd. (formerly Hayes and Co. Ltd.), Hong Kong, Royal Trust Asia Ltd., Hong Kong. Singapore govt. merit scholar Govt. of Singapore, 1968. Mem. Young Pres.'s Orgn., C200. Anglican. Office: Royal Trust Mcht Bank, 50 Raffles Pl, #19-01 Shell Tower, Singapore 0104, Singapore

HWANG, TAI-JU, pediatrics educator; b. Namwon, Chonbuk, Korea, Feb. 5, 1947; s. Geum-Hyun Hwang and Jeong-Soon (Hwang) Yang; m. Yong-Yee Ryee. MD, Chonnam U., Kwangju, Republic of Korea, 1973, PhD, 1983. Intern, then resident pediatrics Chonnam U. Hosp., Kwangju, 1977-81, chmn. dept. pediatrics, 1983—; instr. med. sch. Chonnam U., 1982-85, asst. prof., 1983—. Office: Chonnam Hosp Dept Pediatrics, 8 Hakdong Dong Gu, Kwang Ju Kwangju Republic of Korea

HWANG, YUN-FAN, mechanical engineer; b. Toufen, Miaoli, Taiwan, Jan. 1, 1938; s. Chi-Moy and Rung-Mei (Wun) H.; came to U.S., 1963, naturalized, 1974; m. Chao-Mei Chan, Feb. 22, 1969; children—Sandi, Mark. B.S., Taipei Inst. Tech., Taiwan, 1959; M.S., CCNY, 1965; M.S., NYU, 1971; Ph.D., Pa. State U., 1975. Jr. engr. Chinese Petroleum Corp., Miaoli, Taiwan, 1961-63; project engr. Kentile Inc., Bklyn., 1965-66; mech. engr. Treadwell Corp., N.Y.C., 1966-71; lead acoustics and dynamics engr. Vought Corp., Dallas, 1974-78; research mech. engr. David Taylor Naval Ship Research and Devel. Center, Bethesda, Md., 1978—; tech. cons. in acoustics and vibration. Mem. Acoustical Soc. Am., Sigma Xi. Contbr. articles to profl. jours. Home: 12263 Cliveden St Herndon VA 22070 Office: David Taylor Research Ctr Bethesda MD 20084

HYATALI, SIR ISAAC EMANUEL, chairman elections and boundaries commision Seychelles Republic, former judge; b. Trinidad, Nov. 21, 1917; s. Joseph and Esther H.; m. Audrey Monica Joseph, 1943; 3 children. LL.B., Gray's Inn and Council Legal Edn., London, 1948. Bar: London 1947. Sole practice Trinidad and Tobago, 1947-59; judge Supreme Ct., Trinidad and Tobago, 1959-62, justice of appeal, 1962-72, pres. Indsl. Ct., 1965-72, chief justice, pres. Ct. Appeal, Supreme Ct., 1972-83; justice of appeal, Seychelles Republic, 1983—; chmn. Elections and Boundaries Commn., 1983-86, Am. Life and Gen. Ins. Co. Ltd., Trinidad, 1983—; mem. numerous profl. and civic orgns in Trinidad and Tobago; cons., lectr., arbitrator in field. Editor: West Indian Law Reports, 1961-65. Mem. World Assn. Judges, Council Mgmt., British Inst. Internat. and Comparative Law, World Peace Through Law Ctr. (hon.). Home: 8 Pomme Rose Ave, Cascade St Anns, Port of Spain Trinidad and Tobago Office: Salvaiori Bldg, Frederick St, Port of Spain Trinidad and Tobago also: Am Life and Gen Ins Bldg, 17-19 Pembroke St, Port of Spain Trinidad and Tobago

HYATT, GUY WILLIAM, educator, writer, researcher; b. Swiss, Wis., May 27, 1909. Grad., Lindlawr Med. Coll., St. Andrews Sem., Dequer Inst. Research; 7 hon. degrees. Founder Am. Bible Coll.; past mem. staff Internat. Acad.; nutritional researcher. Served as Aide de Camp Gov.'s staff, Miss. Recipient hon. citation State of Miss. Mem. Royal Geog. Soc. London. Home: Box 331 Pineland FL 33945

HYATT, KENNETH AUSTIN, computer company executive, educator; b. Albany, N.Y., Nov. 18, 1940; s. Leonard John and Charlotte Henrietta (Merz) H.; m. Katharina Judith Schmidt, May 3, 1962; children—Katharina, Kenneth. B.S., Okla. State U., 1969; M.S., Purdue U., 1971; M.B.A., Western New Eng. Coll., 1979, M.S.S.M., 1984, M.P.A., 1985. Enlisted U.S. Air Force, 1958, commd. 2d lt., 1969, advanced through grades to capt., 1972; with Security Service, 1958-69, Systems Command, Alaskan Air Command, 1969-79; corp. supr. systems and evaluation Corp. Computer and Info. Sci. Ctr., Sanders Assocs., Nashua, N.H., 1979-83, corp. mgr. computer support services, 1983-86; course developer edn. support div. Digital Equipment Corp., Maynard, Mass., 1987—. Commr., Billerica Youth Soccer Assn. (Mass.), 1978-79, exec. v.p., 1979-80, publicity dir., 1982-83, coach, 1978-83; mgr. Lowell (Mass.) Jr. Midgets Hockey Team; dir. Lowell Jr. Chiefs Hockey Club; Commr. Met. Boston Hockey League (Midget Open); vice chmn. personnel bd. Town of Billerica, town meeting mem. Mem. Computer Security Inst., Computer Measurement Group, BGS Users Group, SHARE, N.E. Comten Monitor Users Group (treas. 1981-83, dir. 1983—), Res. Officers Assn. (life), Ret. Officers Assn., Purdue Alumni Assn., Okla. State U. Alumni Assn., Western New Eng. Coll. Alumni Assn., Phi Kappa Phi, Pi Mu Epsilon. Club: Naptown Rod and Gun. Lodges: KC, Elks, Masons, Moose, Shriners. Home: 167 Allen Rd Billerica MA 01821 Office: Digital Equipment Co ZK01-3 D-40 Spit Brook Rd Nashua NH 03060

HYBINETTE, GUNNAR KNUT JOHAN, business executive; b. Lidingö, Sweden, Jan. 4, 1920; s. Knut G. E. and Elin S. K. (Strand) H.; B.E., Stockholm Tech. Coll., 1945; postgrad. Stanford U., 1973; m. Ingrid Floré n, Oct. 14, 1961; children—Johan, Catharina, Maria, Knut. Export mgr. Electrolux Sweden, 1950-58; factory mgr. Electrolux Vä stervik-Motala, 1958-65; pres. Bahco-Ventilation, Enkö ping, 1965-79, exec. v.p. Bahco Group, Stockholm, 1972-79, chmn. Bahco Co., Finland, Denmark, Netherlands, France, Ger., Belgium and Eng., 1965-80, chmn., chief exec. officer Bahco Group U.S.A., Atlanta, 1979-84; pres. Scantrade Inc. U.S.A., Atlanta, 1984—. Served with Swedish Army, 1940-45. Decorated knight Order of Wasa (Sweden). Mem. Am. Mgmt. Assn. Lutheran. Club: Rotary (Atlanta). Home: 1648 Shadow Ct Dunwoody GA 30338 Office: PO Box 888788 Atlanta GA 30356

HYDE, ANTHONY, corporate executive, business consultant; b. Windsor, Eng., July 20, 1907; s. Dorsey William and Sybil Marjorie (Cox) H.; A.B. in Econs., Yale U., 1929; m. Katherine Stringer, June 16, 1933 (div.); 1 son, Anthony; m. 2d, Phyllis Elizabeth Reynolds, Jan. 21, 1950 (div.); m. 3d, Pauline Patricia Pickford, Dec. 26, 1963; 1 son, Timothy Alexander David. Reporter, Washington Times, 1929-30; dir. advt. and public relations Washington Gas Light Co., 1930-31, asst. to pres. charge mdsg. and new bus., 1931-33; mem. editorial staff, then promotion dir. Washington Herald, 1933-37; dir. advt. and public relations Phila. Gas Works Co., 1937-39; copywriter Young & Rubicam, Inc., 1939-41; account exec., copywriter Lord & Thomas, Inc., 1941; campaign coordinator OWI, charge info. program on behalf UN, also Am. mem. UN Info. Bd., 1941-42; joint mng. dir. UN Info. Office; dir. info., organizer info. div. Com. Econ. Devel., 1943-45; dep. dir. charge info. and reports Office War Mblzn. and Reconversion, 1945-47; asso. Arthur Newmyer & Assos., counselors, Washington, 1947-48; pres., mng. dir. Tea Bur., Inc., 1948-53; exec. dir. Tea Council U.S.A., 1953-55; staff v.p., charge planning and devel. McCann-Erickson, Inc., 1956-59; exec. v.p. Robert C. Durham Assos., Inc., mgmt. cons., 1959-61; prin. dep. chmn., dir. Armstrong-Warden, Ltd., 1961-62; chmn., dir. successor Smith-Warden, Ltd., London, 1962-68; cons. to bd. Churchman's Ltd., 1969-72; chmn. Tavener Rutledge Ltd., confectionary mfrs., Liverpool, 1971-79; chmn. Forty Plus and successor co. Pauline Hyde Assocs. Ltd., 1979—, Larkfield Ltd., 1980-82; prin. chmn. Sunrise Natural Foods Ltd., 1982-84. Chmn., founder/organizer Democrats Abroad, 1966-81; hon. chmn., 1981—; mem. Dem. Charter Commn., 1973-74, Dem. Nat. Com., 1975-80; del., chmn. del. Democrats Abroad to Dem. Nat. Conv., 1964, 68, 72, 76, 80; U.S. nat jr. saber champion, 1939; mem. U.S. Olympic saber squad, 1939-40, Pilgrims, 1974—. Address: 38 Lower Belgrave St, London SW1W OLN, England

HYDE, CLARENCE BRODIE, II, oil producer; b. Ft. Worth, Oct. 22, 1937; s. Clarence Edgar and Frances (Williams) H.; B.S., Tex. Wesleyan Coll., Ft. Worth, 1961; M.B.A., U. Tex., Austin, 1963; grad. So. Meth. U. Grad. Sch. Banking, 1973; m. Sylvia Flower, June 5, 1960; children—Clarence Brodie III, Brooke Allison, Brett Kinlock, Blair Elizabeth. Vice pres., asst. mgr. lending group, chmn. loan com. Ft. Worth Nat. Bank, 1963-76; ind. oil producer, Ft. Worth, 1976—; pres., chmn. bd. Hyde Oil & Gas Corp. Bd. dirs. Tarrant County chpt. Salvation Army, 1969-79, chmn. bd., 1972-74; trustee Trinity Valley Sch., Ft. Worth, 1970; mgmt. com. Camp Amon Carter, Ft. Worth, 1970-76, adv. mem., 1976—; trustee, mem. exec. com. Tex. Wesleyan Coll., 1971—, also vice chmn. bd., vice chmn. exec. com.; bd. dirs. Big Bros. Tarrant County, 1971; v.p. W.A. Moncrief Radiation Center Ft. Worth, 1971—, Harris Meth. Health Systems, 1983-87; bd. dirs., exec. com. Harris Hosp., Ft. Worth, 1971—; trustee, treas., exec. com. Tarrant County chpt. ARC, 1971-73; bd. dirs., exec. com. Ft. Worth Opera Assn., 1971—, v.p., treas., 1972-74; bd. dirs., exec. com. Hurst-Euless-Bedford Hosp., Ft. Worth, 1973-80; pres. Ft. Worth Arts Council, 1973-75; chmn. Community Pride Campaign, 1972. Named Alumnus of Yr., Tex. Wesleyan Coll., 1985. Mem. Tex. Hosp. Assn. Republican. Methodist. Clubs: Rivercrest Country, Shady Oaks Country, Ft. Worth, Steeplechase, Ridotto, Ft. Worth Petroleum (Ft. Worth). Home: 8 Westover Rd Fort Worth TX 76107 Office: 6300 Ridglea Pl Suite 1018 Fort Worth TX 76116

HYDE, MICHAEL ARTHUR, chemical company executive; b. Kingston, Ont., Can., Apr. 17, 1942; s. Arthur Edwin and Isabell Mary (Moran) H.; m. Monica Jill Hill, Sept. 9, 1964 (div. 1972); children—David Michael, Andrew Tyler; m. Yoko Igaya, May 19, 1981; children—Keri Kazumi, Amanda Izumi. B.Sc. in Engring., Queen's U., Kingston, Ont., 1965. Registered profl. engr., Ont. Tech. mng., construction div. research Dow Chem. Can., Sarnia, Ont., 1971-76, dist. sales mgr. construction, Toronto, 1980-83, nat. sales mgr. constrn. div., Toronto, 1983-84, bus. devel. mgr. constrn. Toronto, 1984-85, mgr. new ventures and diversification, 1986—; dir. research Dow Chem. Japan, Gotemba, Japan, 1976-80; v.p., sec. Mod-Lok Wall Systems Ltd., Vancouver, B.C., Can., 1986—; mem. Fire Test Bd., Ottawa, Ont., 1974-76. Patentee in field. Mem. Ontario Indsl. Roofing Assn. (bd. dirs. 1981-84), Assn. Profl. Engrs., Construction Specs. Can. Conservative. Avocations: swimming, boating, water skiing, cross-country skiing. Home: 22 Lia Crescent, Don Mills, ON Canada M3A 1M7 Office: Dow Chem Can Inc, 3035 Orlando Dr, Mississauga, ON Canada L4V 1L6

HYERA, ASTERIUS MAGNUS, Tanzanian ambassador to U.S.; b. Litembo, Ruvuma, Tanzania, Jan. 19, 1942; s. Magnus Jacob and Benigna Thomas (Hyera) H.; m. Bertha Agnes Alfonse Nyagetera; children—Judith Kishere, Monica Robi, Asteria Benigna, Magnus Ng'ula, Bertha Magori, Christopher Obonyo. Student, St. Francis Coll., Pugu, Tanzania, 1963-64; LL.B., U. East Africa, Dar-Es-Salaam, Tanzania, 1968; LL.M., Columbia U., 1971, cert. in diplomacy, 1971. Commd. fgn. service officer Govt. Tanzania, 1968; with Ministry Fgn. Affairs, Dar-Es-Salaam, Tanzania, 1968-71, Permanent Mission of Tanzania to UN, N.Y.C., 1971-76; dir. legal and internat. orgns. Ministry Fgn. Affairs, Dar-Es-Salaam, Tanzania, 1976-81; spl. asst. for campaign for post of UN sec.-gen. H. E. Salim A. Salim, 1981; ambassador, dep. permanent rep. UN, N.Y.C., 1981-84; Tanzanian ambassador to U.S. Washington, 1984—; A.E. and P. to Mexico; mem. Civil Aviation Bd. Tanzania, 1979-81; mem. workers council Ministry Fgn. Affairs, 1980-81; attended numerous diplomatic confs. Served with Tanzanian Nat. Service, 1968-69. Mem. Chama Cha Mapinduzi. Office: Tanzanian Embassy 2139 R St NW Washington DC 20008

HYMAN, ALBERT LEWIS, physician; b. New Orleans, Nov. 10, 1923; s. David and Mary (Newstadt) H.; m. Neil Steiner, Mar. 27, 1964; 1 son, Albert Arthur. B.S., La. State U., 1943; M.D., 1945; postgrad., U. Cin., U. Paris, U. London, Eng. Diplomate: Am. Bd. Internal Medicine. Intern Charity Hosp., 1945-46, resident, 1947-49, sr. vis. physician, 1959-63; resident Cin. Gen. Hosp., 1946-47; instr. medicine La. State U., 1950-56, asst. prof. medicine, 1956-57; asst. prof. Tulane U, 1957-59, asso. prof., 1959-63; asso. prof. surgery (Med. Sch.), 1963-70, prof. research surgery in cardiology, 1970—, prof. clin. medicine, 1983—, adj. prof. pharmacology, 1974—; dir. Cardiac Catheterization Lab., 1957—; sr. vis. physician Touro Hosp., Touro Infirmary, Hotel Dieu; chief cardiology Sara Mayo Hosp.; cons. in cardiology USPHS, New Orleans Crippled Children's Hosp., St. Tammany Parish Hosp., Covington La. area VA, Hotel Dieu Hosp., Mercy Hosp., East Jefferson Gen. Hosp., St. Charles Gen. Hosp.; electrocardiographer Metairie Hosp., 1959-64, Sara Mayo Hosp., Touro Infirmary, St. Tammany Hosp.; cons. cardiovascular disease New Orleans VA Hosp.; cons. cardiology Baton Rouge Gen. Hosp.; Barlow lectr. in medicine U. So. Calif., 1977; mem. internat. sci. com. IV Internat. Symposium on Pulmonary Circulation, Charles U., Prague. Contbr. over 250 articles to profl. jours. Recipient award for research of the Hadassah, 1980. Fellow ACP, Am. Coll. Chest Physicians, Am. Coll. Cardiology, Am. Fedn. Clin. Research; mem. Am. Heart Assn. (fellow council on circulation, fellow council on clin. cardiology, mem. council on cardiopulmonary medicine, regional rep. council clin. cardiology, chmn. sci. com. of cardiopulmonary council 1981, chmn. cardiopulmonary council, mem. research com. bd. dirs., editorial bd. mem. Circulation Research, Dickinson Richards Meml. Lectr. 1986), La. Heart Assn. (v.p. 1974, Albert L. Hyman Ann. Research award), Am. Soc. Pharmacology and Exptl. Therapeutics, So. Soc. Clin. Investigation (chmn. membership com.), So. Med. Soc., Am. Physiol. Soc., N.Am. Soc. Pacing and Electrophysiology, N.Y. Acad. Scis. Nat. Am. Heart Assn. (vice chmn. research com.), AAUP, Alpha Omega Alpha. Home: 5467 Marcia St New Orleans LA 70124 Office: 3601 Prytania St New Orleans LA 70115

HYMAN, BRUCE MALCOLM, ophthalmologist; b. N.Y.C., May 22, 1943; s. Malcolm A. and Sylvia S. H.; A.B., Columbia U., 1964; M.D., N.Y. U., 1968. Intern in surgery Albert Einstein Coll. Medicine/Bronx Mcpl. Hosp., 1968-69; resident in ophthalmology Manhattan Eye, Ear and Throat Hosp., N.Y.C., 1971-74; pvt. practice medicine specializing in ophthalmology, N.Y.C., 1974—; tchr. attending surgeon Manhattan Eye, Ear and Throat Hosp., 1974—; med. cons. U.S. Seaplane Pilots Assn., 1975—, Health Ins. Plan Greater N.Y., 1977—; ophthalmologist to Hotel Trades Council, Hotel Assn. N.Y.C., 1974—; attending ophthalmologist Roosevelt Hosp., N.Y.C., 1979—, dir. adult outpatient ophthalmology, 1980—; police surgeon N.Y.C., 1977—, dep. chief police surgeon, 1978—; attending ophthalmologist Doctors Hosp., 1979—, Le Roy Hosp., 1979—, St. Luke's Hosp., 1980—; outpatient ophthalmologist N.Y. Hosp., 1975-77; clin. ophthalmologist Columbia Coll. Physicians and Surgeons, 1981—. Served with USPHS, 1969-71. Diplomate Am. Bd. Ophthalmology. Fellow ACS; mem. N.Y. State, N.Y. County med. socs., Am. Acad. Ophthalmology and Otolaryngology. Contbr. articles to profl. jours. Office: 133 E 64th St New York NY 10021

HYMAN, EDWARD SIDNEY, physician, consultant, researcher; b. New Orleans, Jan. 22, 1925; s. David and Mary (Newstadt) H.; m. Jean Simons, Sept. 29, 1956; children—Judith, Sydney, Edward David, Anne. B.S., La. State U., 1944; M.D., Johns Hopkins U., 1946. Diplomate: Am. Bd. Internal

Medicine, Intern Barnes Hosp., Washington U., St. Louis, 1946-47; fellow in medicine Stanford U., San Francisco, 1949-51, asst. resident in medicine, 1950-51, Peter Bent Brigham Hosp., Boston, 1951-53; teaching fellow in medicine Harvard U., Boston, 1952-53; practice medicine specializing in internal medicine, New Orleans, 1953-57; dir. kidney unit Charity Hosp., New Orleans, 1953-55; investigator Touro Research Inst., New Orleans, 1959; dir. Hyman Corp.; mem. staff Sara Mayo Hosp., 1954-79, chief of staff, 1968-70, trustee, 1970-78; mem. staff Touro Infirmary, New Orleans, St. Charles Hosp.; panelist Pres.'s Commn. on Health Needs of Nation, 1952; cons. water quality New Orleans Sewerage and Water Bd., 1978; mem. research adv. com. Cancer Assn. New Orleans, 1976—, La. Bd. Regents, 1983. Contbr. articles to profl. jours. NIH grantee, 1960-81; Am. Heart Assn. grantee, 1962-65. Fellow ACP; mem. Am. Fedn. Clin. Research, Am. Soc. Artificial Internal Organs, Am. Physiol. Soc. Biophys. Soc. (chmn. local arrangements 1971, 77, 81, 87), Am. Soc. Microbiology, AAAS, Pvt. Doctors Am. (co-founder 1968, v.p. 1968—, Dist. Service award 1981), Orleans Parish Med. Soc. (gov. 1972-80), La. State Med. Soc. (ho. of dels. 1970-81). Jewish. Subspecialties: Internal medicine; Biophysics (physics). Current work: Clincial internal medicine, biochemistry, biophysics, nephrology, artificial organs, water quality, government in medicine, cause of death in renal failure, significance of bacteria in urine. Isolated aldosterone, 1949; patentee sheet plastic oxygenator (artificial heart), oil detection device; inventor telephone transmission of electrocardiogram, early data transmission; inventor hydrogen platinum detection of heart shunts, Method for detection of bacteria in urine. Office: 3525 Prytania St Suite 200 New Orleans LA 70115

HYMES, DELL HATHAWAY, anthropologist; b. Portland, Oreg., June 7, 1927; s. Howard Hathaway and Dorothy (Bowman) H.; m. Virginia Margaret Dosch, Apr. 10, 1954; 1 adopted child, Robert Paul; children: Alison Bowman, Kenneth Dell; 1 stepchild, Vicki (Mrs. David Unruh). B.A., Reed Coll., 1950; M.A., Ind. U., 1953, Ph.D., 1955; postgrad., UCLA, 1954-55. Instr., then asst. prof. Harvard U., 1955-60; assoc. prof., then prof. U. Calif.-Berkeley, 1960-65; prof. anthropology U. Pa., 1965-72, prof. folklore and linguistics, 1972-88, prof. sociology, 1974-88, prof. edn., 1975-88, dean U. Grad. Sch. Edn., 1975-87; prof. anthropology and English U. Va., 1987—; bd. dirs. Social Sci. Research Council, 1965-67, 69-70, 71-72; trustee Ctr. for Applied Linguistics, 1973-78. Author: Language in Culture and Society, 1964, The Use of Computers in Anthropology, 1965, Studies in Southwestern Ethnolinguistics, 1967, Pidginization and Creolization of Languages, 1971, Reinventing Anthropology, 1972, Foundations in Sociolinguistics, 1974, Studies in the History of Linguistics, 1974, Soziolinguistik, 1980, Language in Education, 1980, In Vain I Tried to Tell You, 1981, (with John Fought) American Structuralism, 1981, Essays in the History of Linguistic Anthropology, 1983, Vers la Competence Communicative, 1984; assoc. editor: Jour. History Behavioral Scis, 1966—, Am. Jour. Sociology, 1977-80, Jour. Pragmatics, 1977—; contbg. editor: Alcheringa, 1973-80, Theory and Society, 1976—; editor: Language in Society, 1972—. Served with AUS, 1945-47. Fellow Ctr. Advanced Study Behavioral Scis., 1957-58; fellow Clare Hall, Cambridge, Eng.; Guggenheim fellow, 1969; Nat. Endowment for Humanities sr. fellow, 1972-73. Fellow Am. Folklore Soc. (pres. 1973-74); mem. Am. Anthrop. Assn. (exec. bd. 1968-70, pres. 1983), Am. Assn. Applied Linguistics (pres. 1986), Linguistic Soc. Am. (exec. bd. 1967-69, pres. 1982), Am. Acad. Arts and Scis. (council 1979-80), Council on Anthropology and Edn. (pres. 1978), Consortium Social Sci. Assns. (pres. 1984-85). Home: 205 Montvue Charlottesville VA 22901

HYUNG-SANG, CHO, medical educator; b. Seoul, Republic of Korea, Aug. 31, 1928; s. Han-Sung and Park Kee-Bong; m. Kum-Jin Ahn, June 12, 1961; children: Jin-Sook, Hee-Won, Hee Yun. MD, Seoul Nat. U., 1952; PhD, Cath. Med. Coll., Seoul, 1968. Section chief anesthesiology Seoul Red Cross Hosp., 1960-61; assoc. prof. anesthesiology Cath. Med. Coll., Seoul, 1962-68; section chief anesthesiology Sacred Heart Hosp., Seoul, 1968-71; prof. Chung ang U., Seoul, 1971—; supt. U. Hosp. Chungang U., Seoul, 1984-85, Yongsan Hosp., Seoul, 1984-86; dir. Chungang U. Med. Ctr., Seoul, 1986-88. Mem. Korean Soc. Anesthesilogists (pres.). Home: 206-17 4-Ka Myung-Yun Dong, Seoul 110, Republic of Korea Office: Chungang Univ Hosp, 2Ka Pil-Dong, Seoul 110, Republic of Korea

HYYPPÄ, MARKKU TAPANI, neurologist, physician; b. Kajaani, Finland, Oct. 5, 1942; s. Leevi Rafael and Irja (Kukkonen) H.; m. Tuula Harva, 1966 (div. 1978); children: Henrik Juhana, Joonas Jaakkima; m. Vivi-Ann Långvik, 1978; children: Miklos Matias, Sara Cecilia. MD, U. Turku, 1967, D in Med. Sci., 1969, Docent, 1971; Docent in Neurology, U. Helsinki, 1980. Sr. lectr. U. Turku, Finland, 1966-70; asst. prof. in anatomy U. Turku and Oulu, Finland, 1970; postdoctoral fellow MIT, Cambridge, Mass., 1971-72; neurologist U. Turku, Finland, 1972-75; sr. scientist Acad. Finland, Helsinki, 1976-78; asst. prof., chief dept. neurology U. Tampere, Finland, 1978-80; sr. scientist Rehab. Research Centre, Turku, Finland, 1981—; bd. dirs. Psychosomatic Unit Rehab. Research Centre; chief physician Remex Stress Cons. and Mgmt., 1987—. Author: Olen elävä kello, 1981, Kivun kasvot, 1982, Ruumiinkieli, 1987; author: (with others) Uni - varjoko vain?, 1985; editor-in-chief Kollega jour. Med. Student Assn., Turku, 1966. Vice chmn. Soc. Sci. Policy, 1976. Ford Found. fellow, Washington, 1968; Population Council fellow, N.Y.C., 1971; grantee Acad. Finland, 1976-80; recipient Litterature award Otava, 1987. Mem. Internat. Assn. Study Pain, Phys. Soc. Responsibility, Internat. Soc. Psychoneuroendocrinology (adv. bd. 1979-84), Brain Research Soc. Finland, Endocrine Soc. Finland, Sci. Writers Soc. Finland. Office: Rehab Research Centre, SF-20720 Turku Finland

IACHETTI, ROSE MARIA ANNE, educator; b. Watervliet, N.Y., Sept. 22, 1931; d. Augustus and Rose Elizabeth Archer (Orciuolo) Iachetti; B.S., Coll. St. Rose, 1961; M.Ed., U. Ariz., 1969. Joined Sisters of Mercy, Albany, N.Y., 1949-66; tchr. various parochial schs. Albany (N.Y.) Diocese, 1952-66; tchr. Headstart Program, Troy, N.Y., 1966; tchr. fine arts Watervliet Jr. and Sr. High Sch., 1966-67; tchr. W.J. Meyer Sch., Tombstone, Ariz., 1968-71, Colonel Johnston Sch., Ft. Huachuca, Ariz., 1971-78; tchr. Myer Sch., Ft. Huachuca, 1978—, coordinator program for gifted and talented, 1981-85. Ann. chmn. Ariz. Children's Home Assn., Tombstone, 1973-74; trustee Tombstone Sch. Dist. #1, 1972-80; active Democratic Club; mem. Bicentennial Commn. for Ariz., 1972-76, Tombstone Centennial Commn., 1979-80, chmn. Centennial Ball, 1980; pres. Tombstone Community Health Services, 1978-80; mem. Tombstone City Council, 1982-84; governing bd. Southeast Ariz. Area Health Edn. Ctr., 1985—; bd. dirs. S.E. Health Edn. Council, 1985—. Mem. Ariz. Edn. Assn. (so. regional dir. 1971-73), Ft. Huachuca Edn. Assn., Tombstone Dist. 1 Edn. Assn. (pres. 1969-71), Ariz. Sch. Bd. Assn., NEA (del. 1971-73), Ariz. Classroom Tchrs. Assn. (del. 1969-71), Internat. Platform Assn., Tombstone Bus. and Profl. Womens Club, Am. Legion Aux., Tombstone Assn. Arts, Pi Lambda Theta, Delta Kappa Gamma, (pres. 1982-84), Phi Delta Kappa (historian 1979-82, 2d v.p. 1982-83). Home: Round Up Trailer Ranch Box 725 Tombstone AZ 85638 Office: Myer School Fort Huachuca AZ 85613

IACOBUCCI, GUILLERMO ARTURO, chemist; b. Buenos Aires, Argentina, May 11, 1927; s. Guillermo Cesar and Blanca Nieves (Brana) I.; M.Sc., U. Buenos Aires, 1949, Ph.D. in Organic Chemistry, 1952; m. Constantina Maria Gullich, Mar. 28, 1952; children—Eduardo Ernesto, William George. Came to U.S., 1962, naturalized, 1972. Research chemist E.R. Squibb Research Labs., Buenos Aires, 1952-57; research fellow in chemistry Harvard U., Cambridge, Mass., 1958-59, prof. phytochemistry U. Buenos Aires, 1960-61; sr. research chemist Squibb Inst. Med. Research, New Brunswick, N.J., 1962-66; head bio-organic chemistry labs. Coca-Cola Co., Atlanta, 1967-74, asst. dir. corp. research and devel., 1974—; adj. prof. chemistry Emory U., 1975—. John Simon Guggenheim Meml. Found. fellow, 1958. Fellow Am. Inst. Chemists; mem. AAAS, Assn. Harvard Chemists, Am. Chem. Soc., N.Y. Acad. Scis., Am. Soc. Pharmacognosy, Sigma Xi. Contbr. articles on organic chemistry to sci. jours. Patentee in field. Home: 160 North Mill Rd NW Atlanta GA 30328 Office: Coca Cola Co PO Drawer 1734 Atlanta GA 30301

IACOCCA, LIDO ANTHONY (LEE IACOCCA), automotive manufacturing executive; b. Allentown, Pa., Oct. 15, 1924; s. Nicola and Antoinette (Perrotto) I.; m. Mary McCleary, Sept. 29, 1956 (dec.); children—Kathryn Lisa Hentz, Lia Antoinette Nagy. BS, Lehigh U., 1945; ME, Princeton U., 1946. With Ford Motor Co., Dearborn, Mich., 1946-78; successively mem. field sales staff, various merchandising and tng. activities, asst. dirs. sales mgr. Ford Motor Co., Phila.; dist. sales mgr. Ford Motor Co., Washington, 1946-56; truck mktg. mgr. div. office Ford Motor Co., 1956-57, car mktg. mgr., 1957-60, vehicle market mgr., 1960, v.p.; gen. mgr. Ford Motor Co. (Ford div.), 1960-65, v.p. car and truck group, 1965-69, exec. v.p. of co., 1967-69, pres. of co., 1970-78; also pres. Ford Motor Co. (Ford N.Am. automobile ops.); pres., chief operating officer Chrysler Corp., Highland Park, Mich., 1978-79, chmn. bd., chief exec. officer, 1979—. Author: Iacocca: An Autobiography, 1984, Talking Straight, 1988. Past chmn. Statue of Liberty-Ellis Island Centennial Commn. Wallace Meml. fellow Princeton U. Mem. Tau Beta Pi. Club. Detroit Athletic. Office: Chrysler Corp 12000 Chrysler Dr Highland Park MI 48288

IANNUZZI, JOHN NICHOLAS, lawyer, author, educator; b. N.Y.C., May 31, 1935; s. Nicholas Peter and Grace Margaret (Russo) I.; m. Carmen Marina Barrios, Aug. 1979; children: Dana Alejandra, Christina Maria, Nicholas Peter II; children from previous marriage: Andrea Marguerite, Maria Teresa. BS, Fordham U., 1956; JD, N.Y. Law Sch., 1962. Bar: N.Y., U.S. Dist. Ct. (so. and ea. dists.) N.Y. 1964, U.S. Dist. Ct. (no. and we. dists.) N.Y. 1965, U.S. Ct. Appeals (2d cir.) 1965, U.S. Supreme Ct. 1971, U.S. Dist. Ct. Conn. 1978, U.S. Tax Ct. 1978, U.S. Ct. Appeals (5th and 11th cirs.) 1982, U.S. Ct. Appeals (4th cir.) 1988. Assoc. Law Offices of H.H. Lipsig, N.Y.C., 1962, Law Offices of Aaron J. Broder, N.Y.C., 1963; ptnr. Iannuzzi & Iannuzzi, N.Y.C., 1963—; adj. assoc. prof. trial advocacy Fordham U. Author: (novels) What's Happening, 1963, Part 35, 1970, Sicilian Defense, 1974, Courthouse, 1977, J.T., 1984; (non-fiction) Cross-Examination: The Mosaic Art, 1984. Mem. ABA, N.Y. County Bar Assn., N.Y. Criminal Bar Assn., Columbian Lawyers Assn., Lipizzan Internat. Fedn. (pres.). Roman Catholic. Home: 118 Via Settembre, 9 Roma Italy Office: Iannuzzi & Iannuzzi 233 Broadway New York NY 10279 also: Advokatunburo Schumacher, Limmatquai 26, 8001 Zurich Switzerland also: 1253 Phillips Sq, Montreal, PQ Canada

I'ANSON, LAWRENCE WARREN, retired state chief justice; b. Portsmouth, Va., Apr. 21, 1907; s. James Thornton and Emma (Warren) I'A.; m. May Frances Tuttle, Aug. 5, 1933; children—Lawrence Warren, May Frances (Mrs. Peter McCrae Ramsey). A.B., Coll. William and Mary, 1928, LL.D., 1964; LL.B., U. Va., 1931; LL.D., Dickinson Law Sch., 1980; LLD, Elon Coll., 1986. Bar: Va. 1931. Practiced in Portsmouth, 1931-41, commonwealth's atty., 1938-41; judge Ct. of Hustings (now Circuit Ct.), 1941-58; justice Supreme Ct., Va., 1958-81; chief justice Supreme Ct., 1974-81; mem. Jud. Council, 1948-70, chmn., 1974-80; chmn. com. that prepared Handbook for Jurors used in all cts. of record in Va. Mem. Council of Higher Edn. of Va., 1956-59; chmn. Va. Ct. System Study Commn., 1968-71; sponsor Nat. Conf. on Judiciary, 1971; pres., chief exec. officer Beazley Found., Inc., Frederick Found.; chmn. Conf. Chief Justices, 1979-80; pres. bd. Nat. Center for State Cts., 1979-80; chmn. State-Fed. Council; mem. commn. on Future of Va., 1984-85; bd. dirs. Portsmouth Community Trust, 1984—. Trustee, Eastern Va. Med. Sch. Found., 1970-79. Named First Citizen Portsmouth, 1946; recipient William and Mary Alumni medallion; U. Va. Sesquicentennial award, 1969; Lincoln Harley award Am. Judicature Soc., 1973; Disting. Service award Va. Trial Lawyers, 1973; Commonwealth award James Madison U., 1981. Fellow Va. State Bar; mem. ABA (com. to implement standards on jud. adminstrn. 1975-78), Va. Bar Assn. (chmn. jud. sect. 1949), Phi Beta Kappa (pres. chpt. 1981-82), SAR (meritorious service medal 1987), Order of Coif, Pi Kappa Alpha, Omicron Delta Kappa, Phi Alpha Delta. Democrat. Baptist (tchr. I'Anson Bible class 1933-65). Clubs: Harbor, Norfolk, Jesters, Nat. Sojourners, Mason (past dist. dep. Va.), Shriner, Kiwanian (past pres. Portsmouth), Moose, Elks. Home: 214 West Rd Portsmouth VA 23707

IANZITI, ADELBERT JOHN, industrial designer; b. Napa, Calif., Oct. 10, 1927; s. John and Mary Lucy (Lecair) I.; student Napa Jr. Coll., 1947, 48-49; A.A., Fullerton Jr. Coll., 1950; student UCLA, 1950, Santa Monica Community Coll., 1950-51; m. Doris Moore, Aug. 31, 1952; children—Barbara Ann Ream, Susan Therese Shifflett, Joanne Lynn Lely, Jonathan Peter, Janet Carolyn Kroyer. Design draftsman Basalt Rock Co. Inc. div. Dillingham Heavy Constrn., Napa, 1951-66, chief draftsman plant engring., 1966-68, process designer, 1968-82, pres. employees assn., 1967; now self-employed indsl. design cons. Vice-pres., Justin-Siena Parent-Tchr. Group, 1967. Mem. Aggregates and Concrete Assn. No. Calif. (vice-chmn. environ. subcom. 1976-77), Am. Ordinance Assn., Constrn. Specifications Inst., Italian Catholic Fedn., Native Sons of the Golden West. Republican. Roman Catholic. Clubs. Toastmasters, Commonwealth of Calif. Home and Office: 2650 Dorset St Napa CA 94558

IANZITI, GARY JOHN, language educator; b. Napa, Calif., Feb. 25, 1947; arrived in Australia, 1979; s. James Carmine and Imogene (Lockyer) I.; m. Jeanne Claire Rolin, Dec. 21, 1973. BA, U. San Francisco, 1969; MA, U. N.C., 1973, PhD, 1977; D Research, Scuola Normale Superiore, Pisa, Italy, 1987. Research asst. U. N.C., Chapel Hill, 1970-71; assoc. instr. Ind. U., Bloomington, 1972-73; lectr. English U. Pisa, 1976-77; postdoctoral fellow Scuola Normale Superiore, Pisa, 1977-79; research fellow Harvard U. Ctr., Florence, Italy, 1981-82, Am. Acad. Rome, 1986-87; lectr. in Italian U. Wollongong, New South Wales, Australia, 1979-84, sr. lectr. in Italian, 1984—. Author: Humanist Historiography Under the Sforzas, 1988; contbr. articles, book revs. to jours. NDEA fellow, 1971, Fulbright-Hays fellow, 1976, NEH fellow, 1981; recipient Rome prize Andrew Mellon Found., 1986. Mem. Renaissance Soc. Am., MLA. Home: 31 Acacia Ave, Gwynneville 2500, New South Wales Australia Office: U Wollongong, PO Box 1144, Wollongong 2500, New South Wales Australia

IATESTA, JOHN MICHAEL, lawyer; b. Orange, N.J., Dec. 29, 1944; s. Thomas Anthony and Marie Monica I.; m. Paulina Clare Pascuzzi, July 11, 1971. B.S. magna cum laude, Seton Hall U., 1967, J.D. cum laude, 1976, LL.M. in Corp. Law, NYU, 1986; M.S., Fordham U., 1968. Bar: N.J. 1976, U.S. Dist. Ct. N.J. 1976, U.S. Ct. Appeals (3d cir.) 1981, N.Y. 1982, U.S. Supreme Ct. 1985. Law sec. to presiding judge Appellate div. Superior Ct. N.J., Trenton, 1976-77; assoc. Wilentz, Goldman & Spitzer, Woodbridge, N.J., 1977-81, D'Alessandro, Sussman, Jacovino & Mahoney, Florham Park, N.J., 1981-83; corp. counsel Rhone-Poulenc Inc., Monmouth Junction, N.J., 1983—; mem. law com. Nat. Agrl. Chem. Assn., Washington, 1984—. Recipient Book prize, Tchrs. Coll. Columbia U., 1967. Mem. ABA, N.J. Bar Assn., Morris County Bar Assn., Delta Epsilon Sigma, Order of the Cross and Crescent, Kappa Delta Pi. Office: Rhone-Poulenc Inc Black Horse Ln Monmouth Junction NJ 08852

IBACH, DOUGLAS THEODORE, clergyman; b. Pottstown, Pa., July 23, 1925; s. Hiram Christian and Esther (Fry) I.; B.S. in Edn., Temple U., 1950, postgrad. Sch. Theology, 1950-52; M.Div., Louisville Presbyn. Theol. Sem., 1954; m. Marion Elizabeth Torok, Sept. 2, 1950; children—Susan Kay, Marilyn Lee, Douglas Theodore, Grace Louise. Ordained to ministry Presbyn. Ch., 1953; pastor, Pewee Valley, Ky., 1952-55, West Nottingham Presbyn. Ch., Colora, Md., 1955-61, Irwin, Pa., 1961-67, Knox Presbyn. Ch., Falls Church, Va., 1967-72, United Christian Parish Reston (Va.), 1972-87; exec. dir. Camping Assn. of the Presbyteries of Northwestern Pa., Mercer, Pa., 1986—. Youth ministry cons. Nat. Capital Union Presbytery, 1967-86; ecumenical officer Nat. Capital Presbytery, chmn. stewardship com., 1986—; mem. ecumenical relations com. Synod of Virginias, also mem. Interfaith Conf. of Metro Washington; bd. dirs. Reston Inter-Faith, Inc.; dir. Presbyn. Internat. Affairs Seminars. adv. bd. Christmas Internat. House. Served with USNR, 1943-44. Mem. Council Chs. Greater Washington (pres., chmn. instl. ministry commn.), Piedmont Synod U.P. Ch. (dir. youth, camping), Acad. Parish Clergy Assn. Presbyn. Christian Educators, Fairfax County Council Chs. (pres.), Com. 100 Fairfax County. Home: RD 1 Box 584 New Wilmington PA 16142 Office: Camping Assn Presbyteries 100 Venango St Mercer PA 16137

IBRAHIM, ALTAF, textile executive; b. Quelimane, Mozambique, July 7, 1954; came to Pakistan, 1982; s. Ibrahim Hassam and Khatija Tayob; m. Khatija Ismail; 1 child, Mhod Faruk. Degree in Textile Engring., Ecole Superieme des Textiles, Tournai, Belgium, 1976. Dir. Favezal, Quelimane, 1979-80; project dir. Alif Textile, Quelimane, 1981; mng. dir. Alif Textile, Karachi, Pakistan, 1986—. Club: Def. (Karachi). Home: II-Khayaban Haffez, Karachi Pakistan Office: Alif Textile Industries Ltd, 15 Banglore Town, Sharea Faisal Karachi Pakistan

IBRAHIM, ILYAS, civil servant Maldives; B. Male, Maldive Islands, Sept. 18, 1945; s. Ibrahim Maniku and Hawwah (Adam) I.; m. Aishath Nasira, Aug. 12, 1966; m. 2d Aamaal Ali, Sept. 13, 1979. Ed. Majeediyya Sch., Male. With Maldive Civil Service, 1960—, dep. minister defense and nat. security, 1978—, chief of staff nat. security, 1978—, chmn., mng. dir. State Trading Orgn. (Ministry of Trade and Industries), 1978—, minister trade and industries, 1982—; M.P., 1975—; dir. Maldives Shipping Ltd., Maldives Monetary Authority, Maldive Transport & Contracting Co. Sunni Moslem. Office: Ministry of Trade, and Industries Ghazee Bldg, Male Maldives *

IBRAHIM, IZZAT, political official; b. al-Dour Shire, Iraq, 1942. Ed. secondary schs., Iraq. Editor Voice of the Peasant, 1968; head Supreme Com. for Peoples' Work, 1968-70; minister agrarian reform Iraq, 1970-74; v.p. Supreme Agrl. Council, Iraq, 1970-71; head Supreme Agrl. Council, 1971-79; Minister of Agriculture Iraq, 1973-74, Minister of the Interior, 1974-79; vice-chair Revolutionary Command Council, Iraq, 1979—; asst. sec. Regional Command Arab Baath Socialist Party, 1979—; mem. Nat. Command Arab Baath Socialist Party. Office: Revolutionary Command Council, Office of Vice-Chairman, Baghdad Iraq *

IBRAHIM, MOHAMED ABDALLA, banker; b. Cairo, Egypt, Aug. 16, 1938; s. Abdalla Ibrahim and Nefisa (Oaf) A.; m. Fathia Marei Ibrahim, Feb. 10, 1972; children—Yahya, Mona, Nagwa and Dalia (twins). B.Sc. in Acctg., Cairo U., 1959; M.Sc. in Banking Adminstrn., Ein-Shams U., 1964; M.Sc. in Fin., Cairo U., 1968; M.Sc. in Acctg., Calif. State U.-Northridge, 1976. Head auditing dept. Bank Misr, Cairo, 1959-70; acct. Union Bank, Los Angeles, 1971-72; sr. v.p., controller City Nat. Bank, Beverly Hills, Calif., 1973—; treas. Citinat. Devel. Trust, Beverly Hills, 1979—. Mem. Am. Acctg. Assn., Beverly Hills C. of C. Republican. Moslem. Home: 3822 Toland Ave Los Alamitos CA 90720 Office: City Nat Bank 400 N Roxbury Dr Beverly Hills CA 90210

IBRAHIMOV, MIRZA AZHDAROGLU, writer, trade union executive; b. Sarabski, Iran, Oct. 15, 1911; came to USSR, 1918; s. Azhdar and Zohra Ibragimov; m. Primava Sara, July 4, 1938 (dec. 1984); children: Zamira, Levda, Aidyn, Solmar. Student, Leningrad (USSR) State U., 1936. Cert. philologist. Minister Ministry Edn. Azerbaijan, USSR, 1942-44; dep. chmn. Azerbaijan Soviet Socialist Republic Council of Ministers, 1944-48; 1st sec. Azerbaijan Soviet Socialist Republic Writer's Union, 1946-56, 66-72, chmn., 1980—; sec. USSR Writers' Union, 1946-56, 66-72, 80—, chmn. Azerbaijan com. for state prizes; chmn. Azerbaijan Soviet Socialist Republic Presidium of Supreme Soviet, 1954-58; dep. chmn. Presidium USSR Supreme Soviet, 1954-58; academician Azerbaijan Soviet Socialist Republic Acad. Scis., 1944—; chmn. soviet Afro-Asian Solidarity Com., 1977-87. Author: Let the Day Come, 1951 (USSR State prize). Dep. USSR Supreme Soviet, 1937—; mem. Azerbaijan Cen. Com. of Communist Party USSR, 1937—. Recipient Hero of Socialist Labor award USSR Supreme Soviet, 1981. Home: Khagany 19/13 Flat 23, Baku USSR Office: Writers' Union, 25 Khagany Baku, Azerbaijan SSR USSR

IBRU, MICHAEL CHRISTOPHER ONAJIRHEVBE, corporate executive; b. Warri, Bendel, Nigeria, Dec. 25, 1932; s. Peter Epete and Janet (Omotogor) I.; married. Mgr. UAC Nigeria Ltd., Lagos, 1951-66; now dir. The Ibru Orgn., Lagos. Named Outstanding Businessman Nigerian-Am. C. of C. and Industry, 1983; recipient Gold Mercury Internat. award, 1980. Mem. Nigerian Inst. Internat. Affairs (chmn. bd. trustees), Lagos C. of C. and Industry. Mem. Anglican Ch. Office: Ibru Orgn, 33 Creek Road, Apapa, Lagos Nigeria

IBUKA, MASARU, electronics executive; b. Nikko, Japan, Apr. 11, 1908. BS, Waseda U., Tokyo, DSc (hon.), 1979; HHD (hon.), Mindanao State U., Marawi City, The Philippines, 1982. Sr. mng. dir., founder Tokyo Tsushin Kogyo K.K. (former name of Sony Corp.), Tokyo, 1946; pres. Tokyo Tsushin Kogyo K.K. (name changed to Sony Corp. 1958), Tokyo, 1950-71; chmn. Sony Corp., Tokyo, 1971-76, hon. chmn., 1976—; lifetime trustee Japan Com. Econs. Devel., 1967—; chmn. The Railway Tech. Research Inst., 1987—. Inventor modulated light transmission system, 1933. Chmn. bd. Early Devl. Assn., 1969—. Recipient Medal of Honor with Blue Ribbon His Majesty Emperor of Japan, 1960, First Class Order of Sacred Treas., 1978, First Class Order of Rising Sun with Grand Cordon, 1986; named Comdr. First Class of Royal Order of Polar Star His Majesty King of Sweden, 1986. Fellow IEEE (life, Founders medal), mem. Royal Swedish Acad. Engring. Scis. (fgn.), Nat. Acad. Engring. (fgn. assoc.), Japan Inst. Invention and Innovation (pres. 1972—), Japan Audio Soc. (pres. 1979—). Office: Sony Corp, 6-7-35 Kita-Shinagawa, Shinagawa-Ku, Tokyo Japan 141

ICHIKAWA, BANYO, real estate company executive; b. Okazaki, Aichi, Japan, Mar. 21, 1949; s. Hiroshi and Hideko (Shibata) I.; m. Yukiko Nomura, May 18, 1979; children: Hiroko, Masahiro. B.Econs., Doshisha U., Kyoto, 1972. with Ichikawa Co., Ltd., Okazaki, 1972-82; Pres. Ichikawa Co., Ltd., Okazaki, 1982—. Mem. Jr. C. of C. Mem. Liberal Democratic Party. Zyodo-shu. Home: 1-116 Idacho, Okazaki, Aichi 444, Japan

ICHIKAWA, HIDEHIKO, consulting engineer; b. Tokyo, Japan, Mar. 20, 1919; s. Eimei and Tama I.; grad. Tokyo Inst. Tech., 1943; m. Toshiko Kitajima, Apr. 16, 1945; children—Akihiko, Ichikawa, Sumiko, Nakano. Chief engr. Yamadafactory Kobe Steel Works Ltd., 1947-55; asst. mgr. indsl. instrument div. Yamatkae-Honeywell Co., Ltd., Tokyo, 1955-70; factory mgr., dir. Yoshida Electric Co., Ltd., 1971-75; mng. dir. Igarashi, Ichikawa and Partners Cons. Engrs., prodn. control, high speed photography and photonics, Yokohama, 1975—. Served as lt. Japanese Navy, 1941-45. Lic. cons. engr. Mem. Japan Soc. Mech. Engrs., Japanese Cons. Engrs. Assn., Assn. Cons. Engrs., Cons. Engrs. Coop., Kanto Lic. Cons. Engrs. Assn., Showa Econ. Soc., Japan Amateur Radio League. Clubs: Emerald Green, Inagi Radio Control Freight. Home: 1-14-18 Hiyoshi-Honcho, Kohoku-ku, 223 Yokohama Japan Office: 2-45-E111 Hiyoshi-Honcho, Kohoku-ku, 223 Yokohama Japan

ICHIKAWA, MICHIO, information industry developer; b. Kashiwazaki City, Japan, Apr. 23, 1949; parents: Yasuo and Koishi Ichikawa. B of Engring., Yokohama (Japan) Nat. U., 1974. Dept. mgr. Toshiba Corp., Tokyo, 1974-86; asst. mgr. Mitsubishi Corp., Tokyo, 1986—. Buddhist. Club: Century. Home: 1750-25 Suna-Machi 1-chome, Saitama Prefecture, Ohmiya City 330, Japan Office: Mitsubishi Corp, 6-3 Marunouchi 2-chome, Chiyoda-ku Tokyo 100, Japan

ICHIKAWA, YOSHIO, wood trade company executive; b. Koriyama, Japan, Feb. 12, 1914; s. Keisaburo and Eyi I.; law degree U. Tokyo, 1938; m. Shizuko Satoh, May 26, 1946; children—Yoshiro, Shigeo. Mem. staff Ministry of Fin., 1938-48, chief investigator research dept., 1947-54; chief acct. Tobata Chem. Co., Ltd., Tokyo, 1954-74; mng. dir. Kinugasa Co., Ltd., Tokyo, 1964—; mng. dir. Daiwa Shoji Co., Tokyo. Buddhist. Mem. Tokyo C. of C. and Industry. Buddhist. Avocation: travel. Home: 1-1-2-913 Oyada, Adachi-ku, Tokyo 120, Japan Office: 219 Koskudoro Bldg, 10 Ginzanishi-8 chuo-ku, Tokyo 104, Japan

IDE, SATORU, chemical company executive; b. Tokyo, Nov. 20, 1921; s. Makoto and Umeko (Hidai) I.; m. Junko Okumura, Oct. 3, 1951; children: Ken, Kiyoshi. MA in Econs., Tokyo U., 1944. Dir. fin. and adminstrn. Toyo Ink Mfg. Co., Ltd., Tokyo, 1966-69, mng. dir., 1969-73, exec. mng. dir., 1973-75, statutory auditor, 1987—; pres. Toyo Petrolite Co., Ltd., Tokyo, 1975-88, counselor, 1988—. Active Japanese Red Cross Soc., Tokyo. Mem. Nat. Geographic Soc., Nihon Gakushi Kai. Club: Ashigara Shinrin (Shizubka, Japan). Home: 3-14-7 Nishihara, Shibuya-ku, Tokyo 151, Japan Office: Toyo Petrolite Co Ltd, 2-12-15 Shinkawa, Chu O-ku, Tokyo 104, Japan

IDEMA, WILT LUKAS, language educator; b. Dalen, Drenthe, The Netherlands, Nov. 12, 1944; s. Aaldert Jan and Hennie Zwaantina (Buiten) I.; m. Eveline Maria Stuytzand, July 15, 1975; children: Danielle, Aaldert Jan. MA, Leiden U., The Netherlands, 1968, PhD, 1974. Assoc. prof. Chinese lit. Leiden U., 1970-75, prof. of Chinese lit., 1976—; vis. prof. U. Hawaii, 1977. Author: (monographs) Chinese Vernacular Fiction, 1974, Chinese Theater 1100-1450, A Source Book, 1982, The Dramatic Oeuvre of Chu Yu-tun, 1985; translator several books and articles. Grotius Vis. scholar

Am. Com. Edn. Exchange, Amsterdam, The Netherlands, 1987. Mem. European Assn. Chinese Studies (sec. 1982-86), Dutch Assn. Gen. Comparative Lit. Office: Sinological Inst, Arsenaalstr 1, Leiden The Netherlands

IDLER, DAVID RICHARD, biochemist, marine scientist, educator; b. Winnipeg, Man., Can., Mar. 13, 1923; s. Ernest and Alice (Lydon) I.; m. Myrtle Mary Betteridge, Dec. 12, 1956; children: Louise, Mark. BA, U. B.C., Vancouver, 1949, MA, 1950; PhD, U. Wis., 1953; DSc (hon.), U. Guelph, 1987. With Fisheries Research Bd. of Can., 1953-71; dir., investigator in charge of steroid biochemistry Halifax (N.S.) Lab., 1961-69; Atlantic regional dir. research Halifax (N.S.) Lab., Halifax, 1969-71; dir. Marine Sci. Research Lab.; prof. biochemistry Meml. U. Nfld., Can.; prof. biochemistry Meml. U. Nfld., St. John's, 1971-87, J.L. Paton research prof., 1987—. Editor: Steroids in Nonmammalian Vertebrates, 1972; editorial bd.: Steroids, 1963—, Gen. and Comparative Endocrinology, 1966-82, Endocrine Research Communications, 1974—, Can. Jour. Zoology, 1979-82; mem. bd. corr. editors: Jour. Steroid Biochemistry, 1981—. Served with RCAF, 1942-45. Decorated D.F.C. Fellow Royal Soc. Can.; mem. European Soc. Comparative Endocrinologists (founding), Can. Biochem. Soc., Can. Zool. Soc. (v.p. 1985-86, pres. 1987—), Am. Chem. Soc., AAAS, Am. Zool. Soc., Endocrine Soc., N.Y. Acad. Scis. Home: 44 Slattery Rd, Saint John's, NF Canada A1A 1Z8 Office: Meml U Newfoundland, Marine Scis Research Lab, Saint John's, NF Canada A1C 5S7

IDOL, JAMES DANIEL, JR., chemical company executive; b. Harrisonville, Mo., Aug. 7, 1928; s. James Daniel and Gladys Rosita (Lile) I.; m. Marilyn Thorn Randall, 1977. A.B., William Jewell Coll., 1949; M.S., Purdue U., 1952, Ph.D., 1955, D.Sc. (hon.), 1980. With Standard Oil Co., Ohio, 1955-77; research supr. Standard Oil Co., 1965-68, research mgr., 1968-77; mgr. venture research Ashland Chem. Co., Columbus, Ohio, 1977-79; v.p., dir. corp. research and devel. Ashland Chem. Co., 1979—; mem. adv. bd. NSF Presdl. Young Investigators Awards; cons. in field; lectr. chem. engring. dept. Stanford U., 1983, U. Calif., Berkeley, 1986; lectr. Lawrence Berkeley Lab., 1985, 86; mem. adv. bd. Petroleum Research Fund, 1974-76; program coordinator 1st N.Am. Chem. Congress, 1975; indsl. rep. Council for Chem. Research, 1983—, mem. governing bd., 1985—. Contbr. articles to profl. jours; mem. editorial/adv. bd. Indsl. & Engring. Chemistry Jour., 1976-84, Am. Chem. Soc. Symposium Series, 1978-84, Advances in Chemistry Series, 1979-84, Science, 1986-87. Mem. Cleve. Welfare Fedn. Recipient Modern Pioneer award NAM, 1965, Disting. Alumnus citation William Jewell Coll., 1971. Fellow Am. Inst. Chemists (life; bd. dirs. 1981—, vice chmn. 1986, chmn. 1987, Chem. Pioneer award 1968, Mems. and Fellows lectr. 1980); mem. Nat. Acad. Engring., Soc. Plastics Industry, Am. Chem. Soc. (indsl. and engring. chemistry div., chmn. 1971, chem. innovator designation Chem. and Engring. News mag. 1971, Joseph P. Stewart Disting. Service award 1975, Creative Invention award 1975), Am. Mgmt. Assn. (research and devel. council, 1985—), Dirs. of Indsl. Research Assn., Inst. Chem. Engrs., Soc. Plastics Engrs., Indsl. Research Inst. (rep., mem. governing bd. 1985-87), Plastics Pioneers Assn., Soc. Chem. Industry (Perkin medal 1979), Council Chem. Research (indsl. del.), Ind. Acad. Sci., AAAS., Catalysis Soc. (Ciapetti Meml. lectr. 1988), Sigma Xi, Alpha Chi Sigma, Theta Chi Delta, Kappa Mu Epsilon, Alpha Phi Omega, Phi Gamma Delta. Mem. Disciples of Christ Ch. Clubs: Cleve. Athletic, Cosmos, Worthington Hills Country. Lodge: Masons, Shriners. Home: 8008 Park Ridge Ct Worthington OH 43085 Office: PO Box 2219 Columbus OH 43216

IDORN, GUNNAR MORTEN, civil engineer; b. Copenhagen, Jan. 24, 1920; s. Christian Thorvald Idun and Anna Sofie (Hansen) I.; m. Birgit Gertrude Poulsen, Aug. 26, 1922; children: Klaus, Ulla. MSc Civil Engr., Tech. U., Copenhagen, 1943, DSc, 1967. Coast engr. Danish Bd. Maritime Works, 1945-52, Nat. Inst. Bldg. Research, Copenhagen, 1953-60, Danish Acad. Civil Engring., Copenhagen, 1957-61; dir. research Danish Cement Industry, Karlstrup, 1960-76, chief spl. devel., 1976-78; prin. G. M. Idorn Cons. ApS, Naerum, Denmark, 1978-86; pres. G. M. Idorn Cons. A/S, 1986—; lectr. Danish Concrete Inst., 1978-86; cons. to study Nat. Materials Adv. Bd., NRC, Washington, 1977-80; mem. Danish Found. Tech. Research, 1961-67, Danish Council Tech. Research, 1967-73; pres. Research Corp. European Cement Industry, 1972-76; bd. dirs. European Indsl. Research Mgmt. Assn., 1973-77. Author books including Durability of Concrete Structures in Denmark, 1967; authors papers Internat. Congress on Cement Chemistry; co-editor Cement and Concrete Research, 1970—. Mem. Am. Concrete Inst. (hon.), Danish Acad. Tech. Sci. (dir. 1973-75), Danish Concrete Soc., Nordic Concrete Soc., Reunion Internationale les Essais Materiaux, ASTM, Internat. Bd. Forensic Engring. Home: 14 B Tovesvej, DK-2850 Naerum Denmark Office: G M Idorn Cons A/S, Roejelskaer 15, 2840 Holte Denmark

IFEANYI, CHARLES CAMEME (CHIEF), commercial conglomerate executive; b. Ihiala, Anambra, Nigeria, Oct. 14, 1932; s. Ifeanyi Umelogu and Brigid Ifeanyi; m. Beatrice Ihenetu; children—Isidore, Nneka, Chibuzor, Chinyere, Kene, Azuka. B.Sc. Econs. Hons. (Lond), U. Ghana, 1960; Diploma in Bus. Adminstrn., Diploma in Commerce, Institut pour l'Etude des Methodes de Direction de l'Enterprise, Lausanne, Switzerland, 1976. Comptroller, Dept. Customs and Excise, Nigeria, 1974-78; exec. dir. A.G. Lev & Co. (Nigeria) Ltd., 1978—. Mem. council Nigerian Red Cross Soc., Fed. Labour Adv. Council. Mem. Distributive Trade Employers Assn. Nigeria (pres.), Nigerian Employers Consultative Assn. (mem. council). Roman Catholic. Clubs: Peoples of Nigeria (exec. mem.), Lagos Lawn Tennis. Avocations: lawn tennis, swimming. Office: PO Box 159, Iddo House, Iddo, Lagos Nigeria

IFFRIG, GREG FRANK, biologist; b. St. Louis, Aug. 30, 1954; s. Charles Frank and Mary Madeline (Hughes) I.; m. Lynn Kathleen Rothermich, Nov. 24, 1984. BS, S.W. Mo. State U., 1976; MS, U. Mo., 1978. Natural areas coordinator Mo. Dept. Natural Resources, Jefferson City, Mo., 1979-85, dir. adminstrn. div. parks, recreation and historic preservation, 1985-87, dir. ops. Natural Areas Assn., 1987—. Author: (with others) Directory of Missouri Natural Areas, 1985; editor, founder: Natural Areas Jour. 1981—; tech. editor: Terrestrial Natural Communities of Missouri, 1985; contbr. articles to profl. jours. Named on Congl. Record-Interior Com. U.S. Senate for leadership on Irish Wilderness legislation, 1984; Edward K. Love fellow, 1978; recipient Chevron Conservation award, 1988; various fed. and state grants. Mem. Natural Areas Assn. (bd. dirs. 1981—), Mo. Acad. Scis., Mo. Native Plant Soc., The Nature Conservancy (bd. dirs. Mo. chpt. 1979—). Democrat. Roman Catholic. Club: Sierra (bd. dirs. Ozark chpt. 1980-84, sec. 1980-81, Sierran of the Yr. 1983). Avocations: bicycle touring, landscape photography, travel, mountaineering. Home and Office: 3074 E Avalon Dr Springfield MO 65804

IGARASHI, TAKAO, electronic company executive; b. Shiogama, Miyagi, Japan, Aug. 21, 1937; m. Katsuko Ishiwada; children: Elko, Tadashi. Grad., Tohoku U., Sendai, Japan, 1961. Asst. production control Kameido Works Hitachi Ltd., Tokyo, 1961-64, asst. mgr. costing sect., 1964-71, mgr. cost control sect., 1971-74; mgr. acctg. sect. Totsuka Works Hitachi Ltd., Yokohama, Japan, 1974-76; mgr. cost control sect. Yokohama Works Hitachi Ltd., 1976-81, mgr. acctg. dept., 1981-83; mgr. corp. planning and devel. office Hitachi Ltd., Tokyo, 1983—. Home: 1474-5 Maiokacho Totukaku, Yokohama Kanagawa 244, Japan Office: Hitachi Ltd, 4-6 Kanda Surugadai, Tokyo 244, Japan

IGASAKI, TOSHIO, metallurgist, consultant; b. Japan, Jan. 10, 1925; s. Motosuke and Fumiko (Nagamine) I.; B.S. in Metallurgy, Kyoto U., 1947; postgrad. (Fulbright grantee) U. Minn., 1952-54; m. Eiko Ozawa, Nov. 27, 1955; children—Yoko, Tsuyoshi. Research asst. Research Inst., Kyoto U., 1947-51; tech. officer Japanese Air Self Def. Force, 1955-76; cons. Nitta Gelatine Co., Jakarta, Indonesia, 1976-77; v.p. P.T. Intulin, Jakarta, 1977-78; exec. adv. Tech. Coop. Group, Def. Mut. Assn., Tokyo, 1978-80; adviser Komatsu Electronic Metals Co., Ltd., Hiratsuka, 1980—; mem. Research Inst. Nat. Security, Tokyo, 1978—; cons. in field. U.S.Japan Mut. Def. Asst. Program grantee, 1963. Mem. AIME, Japanese-Indonesia Assn. Buddhist. Home: 1959-80 Shinyoshidacho, Kohokuku, Yokohama 223 Japan Office: 2612 Shinomiya, Hiratsuka 254 Japan

IGGULDEN, JOHN MANNERS, manufacturing executive; b. Brighton, Victoria, Australia, Feb. 12, 1917; s. William Alfred and Jessie Lang (Manners) I.; m. Helen Carroll Schapper, Jan. 1942; children: Graham (dec.), Roberta, Kari. Educated pub. schs., Hampton, Victoria. Mng. dir. Bepla Pty. Ltd., Brighton, 1970-74; mng. dir. Bepla Pty. Ltd., Bellingen, New South Wales, 1874-83, chmn. bd., 1983-86; chmn. bd. Nebo Pumps Pty. Ltd., Bellingen, 1982—, Planet Lighting Group Pty. Ltd., Bellingen, 1987—. Author: Breakthrough, 1960, Storms of Summer, 1965, Dark Stranger, 1966, The Promised Land Series, vol. 1, 1986, vol. 2, 1988. Life gov. The Gliding Fedn. Australia, 1965, Port Philip Conservation Council, Victoria, 1972. Australian Nat. Gliding Champion, 1959-60. Presbyterian. Club: Lake Keepit Soaring. Home: Gleniffer Rd Promised Land, 2454 Bellingan, New South Wales Australia Office: Planet Lighting Group Pty Ltd, Tamarind Dr, 2454 Bellingen, New South Wales Australia

IGLESIAS, ENRIQUE V., bank executive; b. Asturias, Spain, 1930. D. in Econs. and Adminstrn., U. de Montevideo, 1953. Tech. dir. Nat. Office of Planning, 1961-65; pres. Cen. Bank, 1967-69; minister nat. def., Uruguay, from 1985, minister fgn. affairs, until 1988; pres. Inter-Am. Devel. Bank, Washington, 1988—. Office: Inter-Am Devel Bank 1300 New York Ave NW Washington DC 20577 *

IGLESIAS PINEDA, CRISTOBAL, newspaper editor; b. Estanzuelas, Usulután, El Salvador, June 15, 1918; s. Cristobal and Josefina (Pineda) Iglesias; m. Ana Trinidad Rivera (div. 1959); children: Romeo, Haydée, Edgard, Roberto; m. Isabel Argueta; children: Jaime, Ana Maria, Martin. Grad. high sch., San Salvador, El Salvador. Reporter La Prensa Gráfica, San Salvador, 1944-45; pvt. sec. Mayor's Office San Salvador, 1946; adminstrv. asst. Honduran Embassy, San Salvador, 1947-48; sec. Ministry of the Interior, San Salvador, 1948-55; pvt. sec. Pres. of Republic of El Salvador, 1956-60; tech. cons. Ministery of the Treasury, San Salvador, 1963-66; editorial chief Diario El Mundo newspaper, San Salvador, 1967-69, exec. dir., 1970—. Author: Memorias de un Escribidor. Hon. pres. Fundación Salvadoreña de Desarrollo de Vivienda Minima, 1985—. Office: El Mundo, 2a Avda Norte 211 Apdo 368, San Salvador El Salvador

IGNACZAK, JÓZEF, mathematician; b. Pabianice, Poland, Jan. 24, 1935; s. Jan and Antonina (Janczak) I.; m. Krystyna Swiatkiewicz, Apr. 5, 1964; children: Anna, Agnieszka. M in Sci., Math., Warsaw U., Poland, 1957; PhD, Polish Acad. Sci., Warsaw, 1960, Habilitated Dozent, 1963. Asst. Polish Acad. Sci., 1957-64; research assoc. Brown U., Providence, 1961-62; asst. prof. Polish Acad. Sci., 1964-72, assoc. prof., 1972-83, prof., 1983—; sr. lectr. Monash U., Australia, 1965-69; reader Ibadan U., Nigeria, 1974-75; prof. Naples U., Italy, 1985, 86. Contbr. articles to profl. jours.; mem. editorial bd. Jour. Thermal Stresses, 1978. Recipient Golden Cross Merit, Polish State Council, 1974, Polonia Restituta Polish State Council, 1983. Mem. Am. Math Soc. Home: ul Miaczynska 54 m 19, 02-637 Warsaw Poland Office: IPPT Polish Acad Sci, ul Swietokrzyska 21, 00-049 Warsaw Poland

IGUCHI, KENJI, film critic, reviewer; b. Hiratsuka, Kanagawa, Japan, June 16, 1949; s. Tohta and Yasue (Tainaka) I.; m. Mayumi Akiyama, Apr. 22, 1978; children: Chihiro, Taku. B in Tech., Shibaura Inst. Tech., Tokyo, 1973. Editor, author: Complete Visual Guidebook of Star Wars, 1980; exec. editor: The Making of Bye-Bye Jupiter, 1984. Mem. Japan Sci. Fiction Writers Club, Motion Picture and TV Engring. Soc. Japan. Club: Ichinohikai (Shibuya, Tokyo). Home: C-106 9-2, Egoto 3-chome, Nakano-ku, Tokyo 165, Japan

IHAMUOTILA, JAAKKO, energy company executive; b. Helsinki, Finland, Nov. 15, 1939; s. Veikko Artturi and Anna-Liisa (Kouki) I.; m. Tuula Elina Turja, 1965; 3 children. M.S. in Engring., U. Tech., Helsinki. Asst. in reactor technics U. Helsinki, 1963-66, acting asst. prof. physics, 1964-66; with Can. Gen. Electric Co., Ltd., Toronto, Ont., 1966; with Imatran Voima Oy, 1966-68; with Valmet Oy, 1968-79, asst. dir., 1970-72, dir. planning, 1972-73, mng. dir., 1973-79, also dir., 1980-82; dir. Neste Oy, Espoo, Finland, 1979—, chmn., chief exec., 1980—; vice chmn. Finnoil Oy, 1980—, Kesoil Oy, 1980—; chmn. Statcon Oy, 1979-81; mem. bd. suprs. Finnish Cultural Found., 1978—, Kansallis-Osake-Pankki, 1980—, Pohjola Ins. Co., 1979—; bd. dirs. Oy Sperry Ab, 1978-81; bd. dirs. Confedn. Finnish Industries, 1980—; mem. Nat. Bd. Econ. Def., 1980—; mem. council U. Tech., Bd. Finnish Employers' Co., 1981—; bd. dirs. Finnish Employers' Gen. Group, 1977—; mem. ICC Commn. on Energy, 1981—, com. Finnish-Soviet Commn. for Econ. Cooperation, 1985—. Mem. Fedn. Finnish Industries (dir. 1980—), Mgmt. Study Group, State Tech. Research Inst., Finnish-Am. C. of C., Finnish-Brit. Trade Assn. Sailship Found. Office: Neste Oy, 02150 Espoo 15 Finland *

IHASHI, NORIHIKO, management consultant; b. Yokosuka-shi, Kanagawa, Japan, Dec. 23, 1940; s. Shinji and Nobuko (Tokuma) I.; m. Mieko Utsunomiya, May 14, 1969; children: Tatsuhiko, Masahiko. Grad., Waseda U., Tokyo, 1963. Cert. profl. engr. Engr. Yamatake Honeywell, Tokyo, 1963-66; trainee, then cons. Japan Productivity Ctr., Tokyo, 1966-70, exec. cons., 1970-84; pres. I.M.C. Corp., Tokyo, 1984—; ptnr., cons. REC Cons. Group, Tokyo, 1986—; researcher prodn. system Chushökigyö Jigyödan, 1984—. Author: Zukai Densanki Nyumon, 1970, Jissen Cost Down Nyumon, 1978. Home: 4-5-4 Uragamidai, Yokosuka Kanagawa 239, Japan Office: IMC Corp, 1-8-1-1 Kajicho, Chiyoda-Ku Tokyo 101, Japan

IIZUKA, HARUMASA, sales representative; b. Gyoda City, Saitama Prefecture, Japan, Dec. 25, 1956; s. Hiroshi and Masako Iizuka. Gen. mgr. Nichi Shinwa Real Estate Co. Ltd., Tokyo, 1982-85; dist. mgr. Terek Co. Ltd., Saitama Prefecture, 1985-86; sales rep. Equitable Seimei Co. Ltd., Tokyo, 1986-88, asst. agy. mgr., 1988—. Home: 2-5-15-403, Urawa-Shi Minami-Honchou, Saitama-Prefecture 336, Japan Office: Equitable Seimei Co Ltd, Higashi-Shinbashi 2-12-7 5F, Mianto-ku, Tokyo 105, Japan

IJDENBERG, MARINA JOHANNA, international civil service organization executive; b. Amsterdam, Netherlands, Dec. 7, 1926; d. Klaas and Helena Suzanna (Schimmel) IJdenberg; grad. Christelijke Hogere Burgersch. B., Utrecht, 1944; 1 dau., Pauline Helena. Asst. to dir. fgn. affairs Internat. Dutch Fair, Utrecht, 1947-53; asst. investment dept. High Authority European Coal and Steel Community, Luxemburg, 1953-59; successively documentalist, prin. asst. to chem. div., fin. analyst Commn. European Communities, Brussels, 1959-74; pres. Brussels sect. of women in Dutch Liberal Party, 1988—; polit. sec. liaison com. Trade Unions and Profl. Orgns., Brussels, 1974-82, adminstr. dir. gen. internal market and indsl. affairs, 1982-86, adminstr. Task Force Small and Medium Sized Enterprises, 1986-87 ; sec., European Civil Service Fedn., Brussels, 1970-87, animator, 1988—. Mem. European Movement, Gen. Assn. Def. Dutch Culture, Dutch Abroad (dir.). Mem. Dutch Reformed Ch. Home: 20 ave de Villequier, 1410 Waterloo, Brabant Belgium

IKAC, NEDELJKO DJURO, marketing specialist; b. Kolarina, Dalmatia, Yugoslavia, July 4, 1939; s. Djuro Marko and Draginja Savo (Olujic) I.; m. Danica Simo Milovanovia (div. 1986); children: Lenka, Tatjana; m. Nevenka Mladjen Ristic. D in Econ. Sci., Faculty Econ. Sci., Belgrade, 1985. Economist Nat. Library Serbia, Belgrade, 1962-69; commercialist Adria Enterprises, Belgrade, 1969-71, Agrooprema Fgn. Trade Enterprise, Belgrade, 1971-72; dir. mktg. Soko. Stark Sweets and Chocolates, Belgrade, 1972-78; cons. General Export Fg. Trade Enterprise, Belgrade, 1978—. Author: Medjunarodni Marketing (International Marketing), 1986; contbr. articles to profl. jours. Mem. Novi Belgrade Community Exec. Council. Mem. Assn. Mktg. Serbia (pres. Belgrade chpt. 1985-87), Orgn. Communist League Gen. Export (sec.). Office: General Export, Narodnih Heroja 43, Novi Beograd 11070, Yugoslavia

IKEDA, MOSS MARCUS MASANOBU, educational administrator, consultant; b. Los Angeles, Sept. 11, 1931; s. Masao Eugene and Masako (Yamashina) I.; BE, U. Hawaii, 1960, MEd, 1962; postgrad. Stanford U., 1961-62; M in Mil. Art and Sci., U.S. Army Command and Gen. Staff Coll., 1975; grad. U.S. Army War Coll., 1976; EdD, U. Hawaii, 1986; m. Shirley Yaeko Okimoto; children—Cynthia Cecile Ikeda Tamashiro, Mark Eugene, Matthew Albert. Tchr., Farrington High Sch., Honolulu, 1962-64; vice-prin. Kailua Intermediate Sch. 1964-65; adminstrv. intern Central Intermediate Sch., Honolulu, 1965-66; vice-prin. Kaimuki High Sch., Honolulu, 1966-67; prin. Kawananakoa Intermediate Sch., Honolulu, 1967-68, Kailua High Sch., 1969-71, Kalaheo High Sch., Kailua, 1972-77; ednl. specialist Hawaii Dept. Edn., Honolulu, 1977-79; ednl. adminstr. Hawaii Dept. Edn., Honolulu, 1979—; frequent speaker on edn.; lectr. U. Hawaii, 1987—. Mem. accrediting commn. for schs. Western Assn. Schs. and Colls. Served with AUS, 1951-57, 68-69, col. Res. ret. Decorated Legion of Merit, Army Commendation medal. Mem. Nat. Assn. Secondary Sch. Prins., Assn. U.S. Army, Res. Officers Assn., Army War Coll. Alumni Assn., Hawaii Govt. Employees Assn., Phi Delta Kappa, Phi Kappa Phi. Home: 47-494 Apoalewa Pl Kaneohe HI 96744 Office: Hawaii Dept Edn 2530 10th Ave Honolulu HI 96816

IKEDA, TSUGUO, construction company executive; b. Saitama, Japan, Nov. 26, 1950; s. Kooshiro and Miyoko Ikeda; m. Tomiyo Murata, Oct. 4, 1976; children: Yudai, Sota. LLB, Rikkyo U., Japan, 1974; MS in Mgmt., Arthur D. Little Mgmt. Edn. Inst., Boston, 1985. Mem. acctg. dept. Sumitomo Constrn. Co. Ltd., Tokyo, 1974-76, fin. controller projects, 1976-82, chief officer dept. constrn. mgmt., 1982-84; gen. mgr. Iraqui br. Sumitomo Constrn. Co. Ltd., Baghdad, 1986—. Home: 3-24-5-505 Ryooke Urawa, Saitama Japan Office: Sumitomo Constrn Co Ltd, 13-4 Araki-Cho, Shinjuku-ku, Tokyo 160, Japan

IKEDA, YUTAKA, electronic equipment manufacturing company executive; b. Kyoto, Japan, Aug. 15, 1949; s. Hiroshi and Miyo (Fujimoto) I.; m. Keiko Isogawa, Mar. 9, 1980; children: Kazuma, Mariko, Masumi. Grad., Kyoto U., 1971. Sales engr. Matsushita Communication Industry, Kyoto, 1968-71; electronic engr. HASC Co., Kyoto, 1971-73; dir. research and devel., DAC Engring. Co., Kyoto, 1973-81; pres. YM Systems, Inc., Kyoto, 1981—. Home: 16-307 2-1 Higashitakenosato, Oharano Nishikyo, 610-11 Kyoto Japan Office: YM Systems Inc, 23-25 Asahi katsura Nishikyo, 615 Kyoto Japan

IKEGAMI, NAOKI, health care educator; b. Tokyo, May 3, 1949; s. Kunie and Fumiko (Yamamoto) I.; m. Yoko Moriya, Apr. 2, 1982; children: Hiroshi, Akiko, Haruko. M.D., Keio U., Tokyo, 1975, D.Med. Sci., 1981; M.A., Leeds U., Eng., 1984. Resident dept. neuropsychiatry Keio U., 1975-76, asst. dept. hosp. and med. adminstrn., 1976-82; asst. prof., 1982-87, assoc. prof 1988—; lectr. Showa U., Tokyo, 1983—. Author: (with others) Handbook on Alcholism, 1982; Alcohol-Related Disorders, 1983; Theory Z Hospital Management, 1984; Health Policy of a Mature Soc., 1987. Mem. editorial bd. Hosp. Adminstrn., 1983—, Internat. Jour. Health Planning and Mgmt., 1985—, Jour. Health Adminstrn. Edn., 1985—. Fellow Japan Soc. Hosp. Adminstrn., Japanese Med. Soc. Alcohol Studies; mem. Japanese Geriatric Soc. Buddhist. Home: Minamisenzoku 2-3-4, Ohtaku, Tokyo 145, Japan Office: Dept Hosp and Med Adminstrn, Keio U Sch Medicine, Shinanomachi 35, Tokyo 160, Japan

IKEGAMI, TOSHIROH, architect; b. Osaka, Japan, Nov. 3, 1948; s. Takeo and Kimiko (Ikawa) I.; m. Junko Takagi, Oct 31, 1982; 1 child, Kei. BArch, U. Osaka, 1974. Lic. architect, Japan. Phys. and social planner Urban Planning Inst., Osaka, 1974-76; chief architect Tadao Ando Architect & Assocs., Osaka, 1976-81; architect Toshiroh Ikegami Architecture Co., Osaka, 1981-86; architect, pres. Urban Gauss, Inc., Osaka, 1986—. Winner 1st Internat. Design Competition, Japan Design Found., 1983. Mem. Japan Inst. Architects, Japan Interior Designers' Assn., Japan Design Network. Home: 6-9-34 Mino-shi, Osaka 562, Japan Office: Urban Gauss Inc, Yasuda Bldg 310 1-8-31, Kyomachibori Nishi-ku, Osaka 550, Japan

IKENBERRY, HENRY CEPHAS, JR., lawyer; b. Cloverdale, Va., Mar. 23, 1920; s. Henry Cephas and Bessie (Peters) I.; m. Margaret Sangster Henry, July 3, 1943; children: Anna Catherine Ikenberry Fawell, Mary Margaret Ikenberry Rauck. B.A., Bridgewater Coll., 1947; J.D., U. Va., 1947. Bar: Va. 1947, W.Va. 1948, D.C. 1948, U.S. Supreme Ct. 1954, U.S. Ct. Claims 1972. Asso. firm Steptoe & Johnson, Washington, 1947-49, 50-53; partner Steptoe & Johnson, 1953-85, of counsel, 1986—; asst. counsel Gen. Aniline & Film Co., N.Y.C., 1949-50; mem. com. on unauthorized practice D.C. Ct. Appeals, 1972-76; dir. 1st Am. Bank, N.A., Washington, Pargas, Inc., 1981-83,. Ruling elder Chevy Chase Presbyn. Ch., Washington, 1970-72; trustee Mary Baldwin Coll., Staunton, Va. Served to lt. comdr. USNR, 1941-46, ETO, PTO. Recipient Alumni citation Bridgewater Coll., 1960; named Ky. col., 1973. Mem. Am., Va. bar assns., Bar Assn. D.C. (chmn. com. on corp. law 1960-61, com. comml. bus. law 1969-72), Raven Soc., Am. Legion, Order Coif, Phi Delta Phi, Tau Kappa Alpha. Clubs: Metropolitan (Washington), Chesapeake Bay Yacht (Easton, Md.); Chevy Chase (Md.); Farmington Country (Charlottesville, Va.). Home: 8101 Connecticut Ave Apt N-308 Chevy Chase MD 20815 Other: Pine Lodge Box 205 Rt 1 Miles River Neck Easton MD 21601 Office: 1330 Connecticut Ave Washington DC 20036

IKENBERRY, STANLEY OLIVER, university president; b. Lamar, Colo., Mar. 3, 1935; s. Oliver Samuel and Margaret (Moulton) I.; m. Judith Ellen Life, Aug. 24, 1958; children: David Lawrence, Steven Oliver, John Paul. BA, Shepherd Coll., Shepherdstown, W.Va., 1956; MA, Mich. State U., 1957, PhD, 1960, LLD (hon.); LLD (hon.), Millikin U., Ill. Coll., Rush U. Instr. Office Evaluation Services, Mich. State U., 1958-60, instr. instl. research, 1960-62; asst. to provost for instl. research, asst. prof. edn. W.Va. U., 1962-65, dean Coll. Human Resources and Edn., assoc. prof. edn., 1965-69; prof., assoc. dir. Ctr. Study Higher Edn., Pa. State U., 1969-71, sr. v.p., 1971-79; pres. U. Ill., Urbana, 1979—; pres. bd. dirs. Appalachia Edn. Lab., 1965-69; bd. dirs. Am. Council on Edn., Harris Bankcorp, Chgo., Franklin Life Ins. Co., Springfield, Pfizer, Inc., N.Y.C. Contbr. articles to profl. jours. Co-chmn. Ill. Gov.'s Commn. on Sci. and Tech., 1982—; trustee, chmn. Carnegie Found. for Advancement Teaching; bd. dirs. Nat. Sci. Ctr. Named hon. alumnus Pa. State U. Mem. Am. Ednl. Research Assn. (bd. dirs.), Am. Assn. Higher Edn. (bd. dirs., Nat. Assn. State Univs. and Land-Grant Colls. (chmn.), Assn. Am. Univs. (exec. com.), Inst. for Ill. (bd. dirs.), Am. Assn. Instl. Research, Nat. Soc. Study Edn. Clubs: Chgo., Econ., Comml., Mid-Am., Tavern (Chgo.); Champaign Country. Office: U Ill Cen Office Office of the Pres Urbana IL 61801

ILACQUA, ROSARIO S., securities analyst; b. Albany, N.Y., Aug. 12, 1927; s. Anthony and Carmela (Gerasia) I.; B.S., Siena Coll., 1950; M.S., Columbia, 1955. With L.F. Rothschild, N.Y.C., 1957-87 , ptnr., 1972-87, Nikko Securities, 1987—. Served with USNR, 1945-46. Chartered fin. analyst. Mem. Nat. Assn. Petroleum Investment Analysts (pres. 1977), N.Y. Soc. Security Analysts, Oil Analysts Group N.Y. (pres. 1972). Club: N.Y. Athletic. Home: 2 Horatio St New York NY 10014 Office: One World Fin Ctr A New York NY 10281

ILASKIVI, RAIMO, mayor; b. Ruokolahti, Finland, May 26, 1928; s. Ragnar Alfred and Elli Aleksandra (Lahtinen) I.; B.Polit. Sci., M.Polit. Sci., U. Helsinki, 1950, Lic. Polit. Sci., 1954, D.Polit. Sci. in Econs., 1958; m. Airi Ellen Uimonen, 1957; 1 child, Ari. Head info. and research div. Finnish Bankers Assn., 1954-60, mng. dir., 1961-79; mng. dir. Indsl. Bank Finland, 1957-79; bd. dirs. Helsinki Stock Exchange, 1964-79; spl. lectr. U. Helsinki, 1952-53, 54-55, sr. lectr., 1959-79; mem. Parliament, 1962-75, chmn. Conservative Party group, 1971-73, 75; presdl. elector, 1968, 78, 82; sec. to prime minister, 1958; mem. Helsinki City Bd., 1967-69; Helsinki City Council, 1969-79; mayor of Helsinki, 1979—; chmn. Assn. Finnish Cities, Helsinki Met. Area Council; dir. Mankala Oy, Helsinki Telephone Co., Finnish Fair Corp., Teolisuuden Voima Oy, Union Bank Finland, Pohjola Ins. Co., Rauma-Repola Oy. Bd. dirs. Hasselby Found., Finnish Nat. Opera. Decorated comdr. 1st class Order White Rose of Finland, Order of Lion; Mil. Medal of Merit of Civil Defense 1st class; comdr. 1st class Order St. Olav (Norway); comdr. 1st class Order Nordstjerna (Sweden); comdr. 1st class Order of Falcon (Iceland); comdr. 1st class Order of Star (Jordan) knight comdr.'s cross Order Merit (Fed. Republic Germany). Author papers, reports in field. Home: 14 Aleksanterinkatu, 01700 Helsinki Finland Office: 2 Katariinankatu, 00180 Helsinki 17 Finland

ILES, PAULINE FRANCES, nursing administrator; b. Kalgoorie, Western Australia, Australia, July 28, 1944; d. Henry Francis and Jean Florence Iles. Grad., Santa Maria Ladies Coll., Western Australia, 1961. Registered gen. nurse, Western Australia. Student nurse St. John of God Hosp., Western Australia, 1962-65; grad. nurse U.K., 1966-68; dir. nursing St. Lukes Pvt. Hosp., Western Australia, 1968-76, St. Pauls Pvt. Nursing Home, Western Australia, 1974-76; dir. nursing, nursing adminstr. St. Annesley Pvt. Nursing Home, Western Australia, 1976-82; dir. nursing, nursing adminstr., mgr. St. Michael's Pvt. Nursing Home, Western Australia, 1982—; dir. nursing St. Michael's Nursing Home, Western Australia, 1987—. Pres. Council on Aging, Western Australia, 1976. Mem. Nursing Homes Assn. (pres. 1972-73, 87, bd. mgmt.), COTA (bd. mgmt.), Australian Assn. Gerontolgoy (bd. mgmt.), Intercare USA, Diversional Therapist Assn. New South Wales, Australian Nursing Homes Assn., Royal Assn. Justices. Mem. Liberal Party Australia. Roman Catholic. Club: Flying Angel British Sailors (Western Australia). Office: Iles Nominees Pty Ltd, 53-57 Wasley St, 6006 North Perth, Western Australia Australia

ILLGEN, JOHN DESMOND, electronic engineer; b. Sydney, Australia, Dec. 14, 1944; s. Lynn William and Patricia (Matthews) I.; m. Susanne Birgitte Nejstgaard, June 25, 1966; children—Michele E., Anne N. M.S. in Elec. Engring. U. Tech. Denmark, 1966. Came to U.S., 1945. Prin. staff engr. Computer Scis. Corp., Falls Church, Va., 1967-73; project mgr. GE Tempo, Santa Barbara, Calif., 1973-79; dir. communications EFFECTS Technology Inc., Santa Barbara, 1979-80; asst. v.p. Kaman Tempo, Santa Barbara, 1980-87, v.p. Calif. Microwave Inc., 1987-88; pres., chief exec. officer Illgen Simulation Techs. Inc., 1988—. Author, editor Tech. Info. Navigation Newsletter, 1977-82; contbr. articles to profl. jours. Chmn., Fairfax County Outdoor Recreation Council, 1969-72; bd. dirs. Youth Soccer Santa Barbara, 1973-74. Mem. IEEE (sr.), Inst. of Navigation, 1980—, Wild Goose Assn. (bd. dirs. 1980—, pres.1987—), Internat. Test and Evaluation Assn. (charter), Old Crows Assn., Armed Forces Communications Electronics Assn. Democrat. Roman Catholic. Clubs: Rotary (pres. 1979-80), Channel City. Home: 7819 Langlo Ranch Rd Goleta CA 93117 Office: Illgen Simulation Techs Inc 351 S Hitchcock Way Santa Barbara CA 93105

ILLMAN, SÖREN ARNOLD, mathematician, educator; b. Helsinki, Finland, May 12, 1943; s. Arne and Hebe Dorotea (Nordström) I.; m. Kerstin Gunhild Anna Johansson, Aug. 25, 1968; children—Erik Jerker, Johanna Kristel. M.S., U. Helsinki, 1966; Ph.D., Princeton U., 1972. Asst. U. Helsinki, 1965-66, prof. math., 1975—; research asst. Acad. of Finland, 1971-72, jr. research fellow, 1972-75; vis. prof. math. Purdue U., West Lafayette, Ind., 1983; vis. prof. Research Inst. Math. Scis., Kyoto (Japan) U., 1986-87; mem. Inst. for Advanced Study, Princeton, N.J., 1974-75; vis. research fellow Institut des Hautes Études Scientifiques, Bures-sur-Yvette, France, 1977, Math. Inst. Oxford U., Eng., 1978, Forschungsinstitut für Matematik, ETH, Zurich, Switzerland, 1982, 85; vis. scholar U. Mich., Ann Arbor, 1983. Contbr. articles to sci. jours. Fulbright grantee, 1967-68; Acad. of Finland grantee, 1982, 86. Fellow Finnish Soc. Scis. and Letters; mem. Finnish Math. Soc. (sec. 1966), Am. Math. Soc. Avocations: music, travel, movies. Home: Johannesbrinken 1B 46-47, Helsinki 12 Finland Office: U Helsinki, Dept Math, Hallituskatu 15, 00100 Helsinki 10 Finland

ILLOUZ, GABRIEL, rheumatologist; b. Mascacara, Algeria, May 12, 1920; arrived in France, 1944; s. Jules and Esther (Monsonego) I.; m. Betsy MacDonald Jolas; children: Frederic, Claire, Antoine. MD, Faculté de Médecine, Paris, 1951. Medecin attaché Hopital Cochin-Université Paris V, 1955-85, Hopital St. Antoine, Paris, 1984—; chargè de cours Faculté La Pitie-Salpetriere, 1963—. Contbr. numerous articles to profl. jours. Served with Med. Corps French Army, 1943-45, ETO. Decorated Croix de Guerre. Mem. French Nat. Council Medicine (rheumatology qualification com.), Ministry of Health High Council on Paramed. Professions, French Nat. Council Rheumatologic Medicine, French Rheumatological Soc., League Against Rheumatism, Soc. Française de Rééducation Fonctionelle, Vets. Med. Corps Freee French Forces (pres.). Club: Francais Libres Paris. Home: 12 Rue Bonaparte, 75006 Paris France

ILTEN, DAVID FREDERICK, chemist; b. Marshalltown, Iowa, July 24, 1938; s. Fred H. and Olga Katherine (Keiper) I.; m. Veronika Maria Thamm, May 18, 1968; children—Paul, Stephan, Eric. B.A., Yale U., 1960; Ph.D. (NIH fellow 1960-64), U. Calif.-Berkeley, 1964. Teaching and research prof. U. Frankfurt (W. Ger.), 1964-68; staff chemist IBM Corp., E. Fishkill, N.Y., 1968-72; teaching and research prof. phys. chemistry Tech. U. Berlin, 1972-74, U. Regensburg, 1974-78; systems analyst chem. application programs and computer-aided ednl. systems Control Data Corp., Frankfurt, 1978—; lectr. univs. Frankfurt, Heidelberg, Stuttgart, Md. Author papers in field. Nat. Merit scholar, 1956; Gen. Motors Corp. fellow, 1956-60, Humboldt fellow, 1964-66. Mem. Am. Chem. Soc., Am. Phys. Soc., Electrochem. Soc., AAAS, N.Y. Acad. Scis., Bunsen Gesellschaft, Gesellschaft Deutscher Chemiker, Verein Deutscher Ingenieure, Sigma Xi. Republican. Lutheran. Clubs: Mory's (Yale U.), Yale of Germany (pres.). Home: An Der Bleiche 47, D-6370 Oberursel 5 Federal Republic of Germany Office: CDC Stresemannallee 30, 6 Frankfurt 70 Federal Republic of Germany

ILYICHEV, LEONID FYODOROVICH, diplomat; b. Krasnodar, U.S.S.R., Mar. 15, 1906. BA, North Caucasian Communist U., Rostov-on-Don, U.S.S.R., 1931; grad. degree, Inst. Red Profs., Moscow, 1937. Factory worker Kosomol Youth Orgn., Krasnodar, U.S.S.R., 1918-27; chmn. Agrl. Inst., Orzhonikidze, U.S.S.R., 1931-34; exec. sec. pubs. Bolshevik, Pravda, Moscow, 1938-44; editor-in-chief Izvestia, Moscow, 1944-48; city editor, editor-in-chief Izvestia and Pravda, Moscow, 1949-52; head dept. Ministry Fgn. Affairs, Moscow, 1953-58; head dept., sec. CPSU Cen. Com., Moscow, 1958-65; dep. minister Ministry Fgn. Affairs, Moscow, 1965—. Author: Materialism and Idealism, 1930, Progress of Science and Technology and the International Relations, 1958, Materialistic Dialectics as the General Theory of Development, 1987. Recipient Lenin prize, U.S.S.R., 1960, Vorovski prize, U.S.S.R., 1963, 11 orders and 36 medals, U.S.S.R. and other countries;. Mem. U.S.S.R. Acad. Scis. (Engels prize 1981). Office: 32-34 Smolenskaya-, Sennaya ploshchad, Moscow USSR

IM, CHHOODETH, government minister; b. Tamoeun, Sangke, Battambang, Cambodia, Sept. 8, 1929; s. Chhem Im and Doeun Dos; m. Natann Im, 1953 (dec. 1975); m. Polee Im, 1978; children: Chuchitr, Cheamchitr, Lekit, Leka. Student, Nat. Inst. Law, Politics and Econ. Studies, 1951-52; diploma, Mil Sch. Adminstrn., France, 1960. Logistical chief, chief G3 sect. in gen. staff, bn. comdr. in Svayrieng province, Khmer liaison officer to Supreme Command Bur. Def. Ministry, Cambodia, 1957-75; engaged in Khmer Resistance Forces, Western Cambodia, from 1977, serves as col., from 1974; dep. chief gen. staff, mem. exec. com. Khmer People's Nat. Liberation Front; minister, mem. coordinating com. for def. Coalition Govt. Dem. Kampuchea, 1982—. Author novels, film screenplays. Mem. Son Sann's faction in Coalition Govt. Dem. Kampuchea. Mem. Nationalist Non-Communist Resistance. Buddhist.

IMADA, HIROSHI, psychology educator; b. Nishinomiya, Japan, May 30, 1934; s. Mequmi and Ikuyo (Sakamoto) I.; m. Setsuko Doi, Mar. 27, 1960; children: Ken, Ryo, Mitsuko. BA, Kwansei Gakuin U., Japan, 1957, MA, 1959, PhD, 1977; PhD, U. Iowa, 1963. Lectr. Kwansei Gakuin U., Nishinomiya, Hyogo, Japan, 1964-68, asst. prof., 1968-74, prof. psychology, 1974—, dep. pres., 1986—. Author: Fear and Anxiety, 1975; co-editor: Behavior Pathology, 1973. Fulbright scholar, 1961-63; Brit. Council scholar, 1968-69. Mem. Japanese Psychol. Assn., Japanese Soc. Animal Psychology, Japanese Psychonomic Soc., Am. Psychol. Assn. (fgn. affiliate). Home: 4-84 Yamada-cho Uegahara, Nishinomiya, Hyogo 662, Japan Office: Kwansei Gakuin, U Uegahara, Nishinomiya, Hyogo 662, Japan

IMBACH, JEAN-LOUIS, chemist; b. Angers, France, Feb. 7, 1936; s. Louis and Edmonde (Lang) I.; m. Michele Rossignol, Aug. 20, 1960; children: Jean-Philippe, Eric, Sophie. PhD, U. Montpellier, France, 1960; postgrad., Eng., U.S. Asst. U. Montpellier, 1960-68; maitre de conf. Inst. d'enseignement Superieur du Benin, Togo, People's Republic of Benin, 1968-71; prof. organic chemistry, dir. bio-organic chem. lab. U. Montpellier, 1971—. Author books; contbr. articles to profl. jours. Recipient Presse prize Ligue Nat. Francaise contre le cancer, 1977, prize Charles Mentzer, 1982. Mem. French Chem. Soc., Internat. Heterocyclic Soc., Am. Chem. Soc., Sigma Xi. Lodge: Rotary. Home: 1108 Rue de le Les Sorbes, 34000 Montpellier France Office: USTL, Pl Bataillon, 34060 Montpellier France

IMBEMBO, ANTHONY LOUIS, surgeon, educator, educational administrator; b. N.Y.C., Nov. 8, 1942; s. Emil Anthony and Theresa (Rippert) I. A.B., Columbia U., 1963, M.D., 1967. Diplomate Am. Bd. Surgery Am. Bd. Thoracic Surgery, Nat. Bd. Med. Examiners. Intern Mass. Gen. Hosp., 1967-68, resident, 1968-73; asst. prof. surgery Johns Hopkins U., 1973-77, assoc. prof., 1977-83, surgeon, 1973-83; prof. surgery, vice chmn. dept. Case Western Res. U., 1983—; dir. dept. surgery Cleve. Met. Gen. Hosp., 1983-88; prof. surgery, chmn. dept. U. Md., 1988—; surgeon-in-chief, U. Md. Hosp., 1988—; cons. Walter Reed Army Med. Ctr., 1982-83; dir. dept surgery Cleve. Met. Gen. Hosp., 1983-88. Johns Hopkins Hosp. grantee, 1976; recipient George J. Stuart award Johns Hopkins U. Sch. Medicine, 1977-84, Dean's Spl. Recognition award, 1983. Fellow A.C.S.; mem. Soc. Univ. Surgeons, Assn. Surg. Edn. (pres. 1982-83), Soc. Surgery of the Alimentary Tract, Internat. Cardiovascular Soc., Assn. Acad. Surgery, N.Y. Acad. Sci., Ea. Assn. Surg. Trauma, Cen. Surg. Assn., Halsted Soc. Home: 13815 Crua Rd Cockeysville MD 21030 Office: U Md Hosp 22 South Greene St Baltimore MD 21201

IMBERT, JEAN, professor; b. Calais, France, June 23, 1919; s. Leon and Maria (Decobert) I.; m. Thérése Chombart, June 5, 1945; children: Jean-Marie, Cécile, Francois, Bruno. Licence, Faculte de Droit de Toulouse, 1943; Doctorat, Faculte de Droit de Paris, 1945. Prof. Faculte de Droit de Nancy, France, 1947-58, Faculte de Droit de Paris, 1958-88; detaché comme Doyen Faculte Droit Phnom-Penh, Cambodia, 1959-61, Recteur Universite Yaoundé, Cameron, 1970-73; dir. des thyseignemento supereurs Nat. Ministry of Edn., Paris, 1976-79. Author: Leprocès de Jèsus, 1981, Histoire des Institutions, 1985; contbr. articles to profl. jours. Home: 16 Rue Marechal Lyautay, 95620 Parmain France Office: Universite de Paris II, 12 Place du Pantheon, 75231 Paris Cedex 05 France

IMBERT, MICHEL ANTONIN, neuroscience educator, researcher; b. Beziers, Herault, France, June 29, 1935; s. Henri Clovis and Marguerite Tiennette (Guiraud) I.; m. Elsa Susana Gomez; 1 child, Diego; m. Sylvia Duchacek, June 26, 1982; 1 child, Dan. Baccalaureat, Lycee P. de Fermat, Toulouse, 1954; Licence es Lettres, Sorbonne, Paris, 1958; Doctorat es Scis., Faculte des Scis., Paris, 1967. Asst. Faculte des Scis., Paris, 1958-67; maitre de conf. U. Paul-Sabatier, Toulouse, France, 1967-72; dep.-dir. Coll. de France, Paris, 1972-81; prof. neuroscience U. Paris XI, Orsay, France, 1982-84, U. Paris VI, Paris, 1984—; dep. sci. dir. CNRS, Paris, 1975-80; exec. sec. Internat. Brain Research Orgn., 1983—; cons. in field. Author: Neurophysiologie Fonctionnelle, 1975, Psychophysiologie Sensorielle, 1982, Vision, 1987, Audition, 1987; chief editor Jour. Physiologie, 1982—; contbr. articles to profl. jours. Served with French Navy, 1960-62. Fulbright fellow, 1965; recipient Prix A. Lacassagne College de France, 1979, Prix Montyon Academie des Scis., 1982. Mem. Assn. des Physiologistes, Internat. Neuropsychological Assn., European Neuroscience Assn. Avocations: jogging; music. Home: Rue des Fosses Saint Jacques 19, 75005 Paris France Office: Univ Pierre et Marie Curie, 4 Place Jussieu, 75230 Paris Cedex 05 France

IMMESBERGER, HELMUT, lawyer; b. Bad Durkheim, W.Ger., Feb. 24, 1934; s. Friedrich Wilhelm and Luise Klara (Schaumloeffel) I.; student U. Mainz, 1953-57, Speyer Coll. Adminstrn., 1959; LL.D., Fed. Acad. Fiscal Mgmt., Siegburg, 1962; m. Doris Pillat, June 24, 1957; children—Jutta, Stephan, Thomas, Petra. With Bad Kreuzhach Taxation Dept. 1961-62; with Kaiserslautern Taxation Dept., 1962-85, adminstrn. dir., 1972-85. Chmn. Christian Democratic Union parliamentary deputation Kaiserslautern Municipal Council, 1978-85, mng. bd., Kaiserlautern Gas Works, Inc., 1986—. Author: Zur Problematik der Abgeordneten im Deutschen Bundestag, 1962; Das Recht der Konzessionsabgaben, 1988; contbr. articles to profl. jours. Named hon. citizen Davenport, Iowa. Home: 72 Rostocker Strasse, D-6750 Kaiserslautern Federal Republic of Germany

IMOH, UNWANA BEN, marketing company executive; b. Abak, Nigeria, May 14, 1948; s. Ben Udo and Akon Ben I.; m. Mary Unwana, Sept. 10, 1983; children: Nsukhoridem, Emine, Erdu. Pres. Pinnacle Holdings Ltd., Lagos, 1984; bd. dirs. A-Z Plastics Ltd., Abak, Nigeria, 1981; mng. dir. Scientific Apparatus Mart Ltd., Lagos, 1981-86; pres. Opulence Internat. Ltd., Drilling and Engring. Ltd., Pinnacle Constrn. Co. Ltd., Dolphin Shipping Lines, Ltd. Patron, CRS Nigeria Youth Club, 1982. Lodge: Rosicrucian (patron 1977), Rotary (v.p. Abak chpt. 1982). Home: 9 Gabaro Close V Island, Lagos Nigeria Office: Pinnacle Holdings Ltd, 170 Awolowo Rd, Ikoyi,, Lagos Nigeria

IMPARATO, ANTHONY MICHAEL, vascular surgeon; b. N.Y.C., July 29, 1922; s. Silverio and Olga (Santilli) I.; m. Agatha Maria Petriccione, Dec. 19, 1943; children: Maria April Imparato Phillips, Karen Elsa Imparato Cotton. A.B., Columbia U., 1943; M.D., NYU, 1946. Diplomate: Am. Bd. Surgery. Intern U.S. Naval Hosp., Bklyn., 1946-47; fellow in anatomy N.Y. U. Med. Sch., 1949-50; successively intern, asst. resident in surgery, resident, chief resident in surgery N.Y. U. Med. Center, 1950-56, mem. faculty, 1956—, prof. surgery, dir. div. vascular surgery, 1975—; cons. Norwalk (Conn.) Hosp., Patterson (N.J.) Gen. Hosp., Manhattan VA Hosp. Author articles in field, chpts. in textbooks. Served as officer M.C. USNR, 46-49, 50. Grantee USPHS, 1976-81. Fellow A.C.S., Am. Coll. Cardiology; mem. Am. Heart Assn. (fellow Stroke Council), Am. Surg. Assn., Soc. for Vascular Surgery (pres. 1984-85), Internat. Cardiovascular Soc., Soc. Clin. Vascular Surgery, Soc. Angiologia Uruguay, Royal Australasian Coll. Surgeons (hon.), Soc. Internat. Chirurgie, N.Y. Regional Vascular Soc. (co-founder, pres. 1982-84), N.Am. Soc. Pacing and Electrophysiology (founder, pres. 1982-84), James IV Assn. Surgeons (dir., treas.), Alpha Omega Alpha. Office: NYU Faculty Practice Area 530 1st Ave New York NY 10016

IMPERATO, PASCAL JAMES, physician, health administrator, author, editor, medical educator; b. N.Y.C., Jan. 13, 1937; s. James Anthony and Madalynne Marguerite (Insante) I.; m. Eleanor Anne Maiella, June 4, 1977; children: Alison Madalynne, Gavin Humbert, Austin Clement. B.S., St. John's U., 1958, D.Sc. (hon.), 1977; M.D., SUNY, Downstate Med. Ctr., 1962; M.P.H. and Tropical Medicine, Tulane U., 1966. Diplomate: Am. Bd. Preventive Medicine, Nat. Bd. Med. Examiners. Fgn. fellow Assn. Am. Med. Colls., Kenya, Tanzania, Uganda, 1961; intern dept. internal medicine L.I. Coll. Hosp., 1962-63, resident dept. medicine, 1963-65; fgn. research fellow Tulane Univ.-U. del Valle, Cali, Colombia, 1965; N.Y. Acad. Medicine/Glorney Raisebeck fellow Tulane U., New Orleans, 1965-66; med. epidemiologist smallpox eradication-measles control program Ctrs. Disease Control/USPHS, Mali, 1966-72; dir. Bur. Infectious Disease Control, N.Y.C. Dept. Health, 1972-74, prin. epidemiologist, dir. immunization program, 1972-74, 1st dep. commr., 1974-77, dir. residency tng. program, 1974-77; chmn. N.Y.C. Swine Influenza Immunization Task Force, 1976-77; med. cons. Africa Bur., U.S. AID, 1974; commr. health N.Y.C., 1977-78; chmn. N.Y.C. Bd. Health, 1977-78; chmn. bd. N.Y.C. Health and Hosps. Corp., 1977-78; chmn. exec. com. N.Y.C. Health Systems Agy., 1977-78; acting health services adminstr. N.Y.C., 1977-78; clin. instr. dept. medicine Cornell U. Med. Coll., N.Y.C., 1972-74, asst. clin. prof., 1974-78, asst. clin. prof. dept. pub. health, 1974-77, assoc. clin. prof., 1977-78, adj. prof., 1979—; assoc. prof. dept. preventive medicine and community health SUNY Downstate Med. Center, 1974-77, lectr., 1977-78, prof. and chmn., 1978—; mem. staff N.Y. Hosp., 1972-78, L.I. Coll. Hosp., 1973—, State Univ. Hosp., 1978—, Kings County Hosp., 1978—; lectr. dept. community medicine Mt. Sinai Sch. Medicine, City U. N.Y., 1974—, dept. health adminstrn. Columbia U. Sch. Pub. Health, 1982—; cons. N.Y. State Edn. Dept., 1982—, Nat. Acad. Scis., 1985, dept. community health services and ambulatory care Brookdale Hosp. Med. Ctr., program for appropriate tech. in health U.S. Aid, 1985—. Author: Doctor in The Land of the Lion, 1964, (with Osa Johnson) Last Adventure, 1966, Bwana Doctor, 1967, The Treatment and Control of Infectious Diseases in Man, 1974, The Cultural Heritage of Africa, 1974, A Wind in Africa, 1975, What To Do About the Flu, 1976, African Folk Medicine, 1977, Historical Dictionary of Mali, 1977, 2d edit., 1986, Dogon Cliff Dwellers: The Art of Mali's Mountain People, 1978, Medical Detective, 1979, (with wife) Mali: A Handbook of Historical Statistics, 1982, The Administration of a Public Health Agency, 1983, Buffoons, Queens and Wooden Horsemen, 1983, (with Greg Mitchell) Acceptable Risks, 1985, (with Robert I. Goler) Early American Medicine, 1987, Arthur Donaldson Smith and the Exploration of Lake Rudolph, 1987, Acquired Immune Deficiency Syndrome: Current Issues and Scientific Studies, 1989, Mali: A Search for Direction, 1989; contbr. articles to profl. jours.; cons. editor: N.Y. State Jour. Medicine, 1983, dep. editor, 1983-86, editor, 1986—; editor Jour. Community Health, 1985—; editorial bd. Explorers Jour., 1979-88. Bd. dirs. Public Health Research Inst., 1977-78, Community Council Greater N.Y., 1977-78, Med. Health and Research Assn., 1977-78, N.Y. Heart Assn., 1983-84, Greater N.Y. Hosp. Assn., 1977-78, Milton Helpern Library Legal Medicine, 1977—; trustee Martin and Osa Johnson Safari Mus., 1964—; mem. adv. bd. Physicians for Social Responsibility, 1983-85; mem. N.Y. State Bd. Medicine, 1985—. Served to lt. comdr. USPHS, 1966-69. Recipient Meritorious Honor award and medal Dept. State, 1971, US AID Meritorious Honor award and medal, 1970, Outstanding Alumnus award Tulane U., 1978, Delta Omega Nat. Merit award, 1978, Frank Babbot award SUNY, 1980, Disting. Alumni Achievement award, and medal SUNY, 1987, Spl. Service award for smallpox eradication USPHS, 1987; Fulbright scholar, North Yemen, 1985. Fellow A.C.P., Royal Soc. Tropical Medicine and Hygiene, Royal African Soc., N.Y. Acad. Medicine, Am. Coll. Epidemiology, Am. Coll. Preventive Medicine; mem. Am. Soc. Tropical Medicine and Hygiene, N.Y. Soc. Tropical Medicine, Kings County Med. Soc., Tanzania Soc., Med. Soc. State N.Y., East African Wildlife Soc., African Studies Assn., Author's Guild, Explorers Club, Delta Omega, Alpha Omega Alpha. Roman Catholic. Office: 450 Clarkson Ave Brooklyn NY 11203

IMPERIALI, GEORGES LOUIS, marketing professional; b. Lausanne, Switzerland, May 2, 1942; s. Alfred R. and Pauline M. (Vietti Violi) I.; m. Sibylle Merz, Apr. 4, 1946; children: Catherine I., Anne Francoise. Lic. Econs. and Commerce Sci., U. Lausanne, 1965, postgrad., 1976. Trainee Novimex GmbH, Dusseldorf, Fed. Republic of Germany, 1966-67; head country group Diethelm & Co. AG, Zurich, 1968; sales mgr. Olivetti SA, Zurich and Bern, Switzerland, 1969-71; asst. to mng. dir. Olivetti SA, Zurich, 1971-75; mktg. mgr. Gretag, Regensdorf, Switzerland, 1976-83; asst. to head photo div., mktg. services mgr. Gretag Aktiengesellschaft, Regensdorf, 1983—. Home: Eggstr 36A, 8102 Oberengstringen, Zurich Switzerland Office: Gretag, Althardstr 70, 8105 Regensdorf Switzerland

IMSENG, RAOUL A., solicitor; b. Brig, Valais, Switzerland, Apr. 8, 1930; s. Josef and Anna (Loretan) I.; J.D., Univs. Zurich, Lausanne and Bern, 1960; m. Anna Zehnder, Nov. 1, 1961; 1 son, Dominik. Substitute, Dist. Ct. Zü rich, 1961-63; adj. Dept. Justice, Canton of Zü rich, 1963-65; dir., mgr. legal dept. Allgemeine Treuhand AG, 1965-78; corp. counsel, sr. v.p. Ringier Ltd., Zü rich, 1979—; dir. J. Henry Schroder Bank AG, Zü rich, Isomat Bau AG, Zü rich, Gustar AG, Zurich, Steigenberger Cons. AG, Zü rich. Served as capt. Swiss Army. Roman Catholic. Hon. mem. Swiss Acad. Ski Club (pub. yearbook). Home: Schönenstrasse 43, 8803 Rüschlikon Switzerland Office: Ringier AG, Dufourstr 23, 8008 Zurich Switzerland

IMURA, TORU, physicist, educator; b. Takamatsu City, Japan, Sept. 25, 1924; s. Kan-ichiro and Haruko I.; B.C., U. Tokyo, 1946; D. Sci., Osaka U., 1957; m. Rie Imura, Nov. 18, 1950; children—Ryo, Sho. Lectr. physics Osaka (Japan) Tech. Coll., 1946-48, prof., 1948-54; asso. prof. physics U. Osaka Prefecture, Japan, 1954-61; asso. prof. physics U. Tokyo, 1961-67; prof. metal physics Nagoya (Japan) U., 1967—, chmn. dept. metallurgy, 1969-70, 73-74, 81-82. Mem. internat. adv. com. 10th Internat. Congress on Electron Microscopy, Hamburg, 1982. Recipient Yamaji award natural sci., 1974; Grand Prix, Internat. Sci. and Tech. Movie Festival, 1978; Chunichi Culture prize, 1983. Mem. Japan Inst. Metals (dir. 1973-77, 84—, v.p. 1981-82, 84-85, pres. 1985-86, 1st. prize Metallographic Exhbn. 1970), Phys. Soc. Japan (dir. 1970-75), Japanese Soc. Electron Microscopy (dir. 1969-71, Seto award 1970), Japan Soc. Promotion of Sci. (judging com. 1981—, internat. judge, Acta Metallurgica gold medal, 1983-86), Eng. Acad. of Japan, Iron and Steel Inst. Japan, Royal Microscopical Soc. (Eng.), Metals Soc. (Eng.), Sigma Xi. Author: Strength of Crystals (in Japanese), 1968. Home: 102 Higashiyama Cooporus 2-58-1, Chikusa-ku, Nagoya City 464, Japan Office: Aichi Inst Tech Yachigusa, Yagusa-cho, Toyota City 470-03, Japan

IN, RACHEL CHIANG, newspaper editor and publisher, researcher; b. China, Mar. 10, 1938, came to U.S., 1960; d. Jen Kwei and Kwei-In (Ling) Chiang; m. Yu-Wei In, June 15, 1960; children: Yee-Liu, Wei-Yee, Thomas, Peggy, Yee-Pao. BA, Tamkang U., China, 1959; MA, CUNY, 1967. Pub., exec. editor Orient Times, N.Y.C., 1979—; mgr. coll. text John Wiley & Sons, N.Y.C., 1967-81; dir. research Editor and Publisher, N.Y.C., 1982-86, Matthew Bender & Co., N.Y.C., 1986—; dir. Overseas Chinese Soc., 1979—; tchr. Chinese. Contbr. articles to profl. jours. Producer benefit concert Com. to Aid Indochinese Refugees, 1979; dir. UN Boat People Rally, 1979; advisor Congl. Adv. Bd., Washington, 1983. Office: Matthew Bender 11 Pennsylvania Plaza New York NY 10001 also: 171 E 84th St #31E New York NY 10028-2049

INABINET, LAWRENCE REDMON, textile company executive; b. Florence, S.C., Jan. 26, 1939; s. Isaac Horace and Ruth (Brunson) I.; student Clemson U., 1957-58; B.A. in History and Econs., Wofford Coll., 1961; postgrad. U. Ga., 1961-62. Dir. personnel, office mgr. Beaunit Textiles, Fountain Inn, S.C., 1967-68; dir. indsl. relations Alice Mfg. Co., Inc., Easley, S.C., 1968—. Bd. dirs. Pickens United Way, 1972—, pres., 1981, 84, 85, v.p., 1983-84, chmn. ARC, 1972-76; adv. com. Tri-County Tech. Coll., 1976—; mem. S.C. State Pvt. Industry Council, 1984-88, S.C. State Job Tng. coordinating Council (gov.'s council), 1988—; chmn. Pvt. Industry Council Pickens, Anderson, Oconee Counties; mem. Republican Nat. Com. Served with USAF, 1962-67; capt. USAFR. Mem. Pickens Area Personnel Assn. (pres. 1975), Indsl. Hygienist Round Table, S.C. Safety and Health Assn., S.C. Textile Mfg. Assn., Easley C. of C. (dir. 1972-76, pres. 1976), Am. Textile Mfg. Assn. (safety and health com.). Home: 2009 Pelzer Hwy Easley SC 29640 Office: PO Box 369 Easley SC 29641

INAGAKI, EIZO, architectural educator. BS, Tokyo U., 1948, PhD, 1961. Prof. Tokyo U., 1973-87, Meiji U., Kawasaki, Japan, 1987—. Co-author: Japanese Architecture and Gardens, 1968, Banister Fletcher's History of Architecture, 1986. Mem. Archtl. Inst. of Japan. Office: Meiji U, Tama-Ku, Kawasaki 214, Japan

INAMORI, KAZUO, chemical executive; b. Kagoshima, Japan, Jan. 30, 1932; s. Kesaichi and Kimi (Tamari) I.; m. Kimi Asako Sunaga, Dec. 14, 1958; children: Shinobu, Chiharu, Mizuho. BS in Chem. Engring., Kagoshima U., 1955. Dir. Kyoto (Japan) Ceramic Co., Ltd., 1959-66, pres., 1966-82; pres. Kyocera Corp. (name formerly Kyoto Ceramic Co., Ltd.), Kyoto, 1982-85, pres., chmn., 1985-86; chmn. Kyocera Corp. (name formerly Kyoto Ceramic Co., Ltd.), 1986—; pres. Kyocera Internat., Inc., Calif., 1969, chmn. bd. Daini-Denden, Tokyo. chmn. Kyoto Community for Econ. Devel., 1985; bd. dirs. Scripps Clinic and Research Found.; pres. Japan-Am. Soc., Kyoto, 1987. Recipient Meml. Productivity award Okouchi Meml. Found., 1972, spl. award Sci. and Tech. Agy. Japan, 1974, Purple Medal Honor Emperor of Japan, 1984. Mem. Swedish Royal Acad. Engring. Scis. (hon.). Office: Kyocera Corp 5-22 Kitainoue-cho, Higashino Yamashinaku, Kyoto Japan

INBAL, ELIAHU, conductor; b. Jerusalem, Feb. 16, 1936; s. Jehuda Joseph and Leah (Museri) I.; m. Helga Fritzsche, 1968; 3 children. Ed. Acad. Music, Jerusalem, Conservatoire National Superieur, Paris. Guest condr. with numerous orchs., including Milan, Rome, Berlin, Munich, Hamburg, Stockholm, Copenhagen, Vienna, Budapest, Amsterdam, London, Paris, Tel Aviv, N.Y.C., Chgo., Toronto, and Tokyo; chief condr. Radio Symphony Orch., Frankfurt, W.Ger., 1974—. Numerous recs. Address: Hessischer Rundfunk, Bertramstrasse 8, 6000 Frankfurt Federal Republic of Germany Address: care Harold Shaw 1995 Broadway New York NY 10023 *

INBAU, FRED EDWARD, lawyer, educator; b. New Orleans, Mar. 27, 1909; s. Fred and Pauline (Boos) I.; m. Ruth L. Major, Sept. 21, 1935 (dec.); children: William Robert, Louise; m. Jane Hanchett Schoenewald, June 27, 1964. B.S., Tulane U., 1930, LL.B., 1932; LL.M., Northwestern U., 1933. Practiced law since 1934; research asst. Sci. Crime Detection Lab., Northwestern U. Sch. Law, 1933-36; asst. prof. law Northwestern U. Sch. Law, 1936-38; dir. Chgo. Police Sci. Crime Detection Lab., 1938-41; trial atty. firm Lord, Bissell and Kadyk, 1941-45; prof. law Northwestern U., 1945—, John Henry Wigmore prof. law, 1974-77, emeritus, 1977—; Pres. Am. Acad. Forensic Scis., 1955-56, Ill. Acad. Criminology, 1951-52, Americans for Effective Law Enforcement, 1966-79, chmn., 1979-82, bd. dirs., 1982—. Author: Criminal Interrogation and Confessions, 3d edit., 1986, Criminal Law for the Police, 1969, Criminal Law for the Layman, 1970, 2d edit., 1977, Scientific Police Investigation, 1972, Medical Jurisprudence, 1971, Evidence Law for Police, 1972, Scientific Evidence in Criminal Cases, 3d edit., 1986, Cases and Comments on Criminal Law, 4th edit., 1987, Cases and Comments on Criminal Procedure, 1974, 2d edit., 1980, Criminal Law and Its Adminstration, 4th edit., 1984, Truth and Deception: The Polygraph

(Lie-Detector) Technique, 2d edit., 1977; editor-in-chief: Jour. Criminal Law, Criminology, and Police Sci., 1967-70, Jour. Police Sci. and Adminstrn., 1973-77. Republican. Home: 222 E Pearson St Chicago IL 60611

INCAPRERA, FRANK PHILIP, physician; b. New Orleans, Aug. 24, 1928; s. Charles and Mamie (Bellipanni) I.; B.S., Loyola U. of South, 1946; M.D., La. State U., 1950; m. Ruth Mary Duhon, Sept. 13, 1952; children—Charles, Cynthia, James, Christopher, Catherine. Intern, Charity Hosp., New Orleans, 1950-51, resident, 1951-52; resident VA Hosp., New Orleans, 1952-54; practice medicine specializing in internal medicine, New Orleans, 1957—; adminstrv. mgr. Internal Medicine Group, New Orleans, 1973—; med. dir. Owens-Ill. Glass Co., New Orleans, 1961-85, Kaiser Aluminum Co., Chalmette, La., 1975-84, Tenneco Oil Co., Chalmette, 1978-84; co-founder Med. Center E. New Orleans, 1975; clin. assoc. prof. medicine Tulane U. Sch. Medicine, 1971-87, clin. prof. medicine, 1987—; mem. New Orleans Bd. Health, 1966-70. Bd. dirs. Methodist Hosp., 1971—, Lutheran Home New Orleans, 1976-80, Chateau de Notre Dame, 1977-82, New Orleans Opera Assn., 1975—; mem. New Orleans Human Relation Com., 1968-70; bd. dirs. Emergency Med. Services Council, 1977-86, pres., La. southeastern region, 1979-81; bd. dirs. New Orleans East Bus. Assn., 1980—, v.p., 1981-83; bd. dirs. Luth. Towers, 1988—, Peace Lake Towers, 1988—; mem. pastoral care adv. com. So. Bapt. Hosp., 1982-83. Served to capt. USAF, 1955-57. Diplomate Am. Bd. Internal Medicine. Fellow ACP, Am. Occupational Medicine Assn., Am. Geriatrics Soc.; mem. AMA, La. (v.p. 1975-76, Orleans Parish (sec. 1972-74) med. socs., New Orleans Acad. Internal Medicine (pres. 1969), La. Occupational Medicine Assn. (pres. 1971-72), La. Soc. Internal Medicine (exec. com. 1975—, pres. 1983-85), New Orleans East C. of C. (dir. 1979-85), Order of St. Louis, Blue Key, Delta Epsilon Sigma. Club: Optimists (dir. 1964-69) (New Orleans). Home: 2218 Lake Oaks Pkwy New Orleans LA 70122 Office: 5640 Read Blvd New Orleans LA 70127

INCHBALD, DENIS JOHN ELLIOT, public relations consultant; b. Ross-on-Wye, Herefordshire, Eng., May 9, 1923; s. Christopher Chantrey Elliot and Olivia Jane (Mills) I.; m. Jacqueline Hazel Jones, Sept. 2, 1955. MA, Jesus Coll., Cambridge U., 1949. Publicity exec. The Daily Telegraph, London, 1950-52; pub. relations exec. Pritchard, Wood & Ptnrs., London, 1952-54; head of publicity Brit. Industries' Fair, London and Birmingham, 1954-56; sr. pub. relations exec. Foote, Cone & Belding, London, 1956-59; dir. pub. relations Foote, Cone & Belding, 1959-68; mng. dir. Welbeck Pub. Relations, London, 1968-76; chmn., mng. dir. Welbeck Pub. Relations, 1976-84, chmn., 1985-88; v.p. Carl Byoir & Assocs., N.Y.C., 1978-86. Contbr., articles to profl. jours. Served as lt. Brit. Royal Navy, 1942-46. Fellow Inst. Pub. Relations (pres. 1969-70), Inst. Practitioners in Advt.; mem. Communications Advt. & Mktg. Edn. Found. (gov. 1969-70), Pub. Relations Cons. Assn. (chmn. 1975-78), Internat. Pub. Relations Assn. Mem. Ch. of Eng. Clubs: Reform, Naval (London). Home: 10 Shardeloes, Amersham, Buckinghamshire HP7 ORL, England

INCLÁN, HILDA MARIANNE, magazine editor, business owner; b. Havana, Cuba, June 4, 1946; came to U.S., 1960, naturalized, 1976; d. Clemente and Rosa Blanca (Guas) Inclán; m. Marcos Gagligarcia, Sept. 2, 1967 (div. 1975); 1 child, Marcos Clemente. BA cum laude in Mass Communications, U. Miami, 1969. Reporter Hollywood (Fla.) Sun-Tattler 48, 1966-67, Ft. Lauderdale (Fla.) News, 1968-70; Latin community writer, daily columnist Miami (Fla.) News, 1970-78; editor-in-chief Intimidades Mag., Virginia Gardens, Fla., 1978-83; editor, owner Ind. Editorial Services, Miami, Fla., 1983-86; pub., editor-in-chief, owner Cruise n' Travel-En Espanol Mag. and Ind. Pub. Co., Inc., Miami, 1984—. Mem. Republican Presdl. Task Force, 1981—, U.S. Senate's Rep. Inner Circle, 1987—. Recipient community service awards from civic orgns. and local schs., local awards for maj. stories on Latin lifestyle and investigative pieces on corruption, Emmy award for documentary on Castro and Drugs, WLTV, 1984. Mem. Women in Communication, Nat. Assn. Female Execs., Mental Health Assn. Dade County, Phi Beta Kappa. Roman Catholic. Club: Coconut Grove Sailing. Office: 10371 SW 44th St Miami FL 33165

INDARAKOSES, MALINEE, auditor, state enterprise officer; b. Bangkok, Thailand, June 4, 1940; s. Chulan and Kwan (Jachakula) Devahastin Na Ayudhaya; children—Chulee, Jiravat. B. in Accountancy, Chulalongkorn U., 1965. C.P.A., Thailand. Sr. auditor Jaiyos & Co., Bangkok, Thailand, 1965-71; chief acct. Muller & Phipps Co., Bangkok, 1971-78; asst. to chief fin. div. Natural Gas Orgn. Thailand, Bangkok, 1978-80; procurement dir. Petroleum Authority Thailand, Bangkok, 1980—; dir. acctg. Petroleum Authority Thailand, Bangkok, 1978-80, dir. procurement, 1980-87; auditor staff, 1987—. Mem. subdiv. Bd. Supervision of Auditing Practice. Budhist.

INFANTE, ISA MARIA, political scientist, educator; b. Santo Domingo, Dominican Republic, Sept. 8, 1942; came to U.S., 1945; d. Rafael Infante and Dolores Nieves; student Woodbury Coll., 1960-61; B.A., U. Calif.-Santa Cruz, 1973; M.A. in Comparative Polit. Systems, Yale U., 1975; postgrad. U. Santa Clara Law Sch. and People's Coll. of Law, 1975-77; Ph.D. in Polit. Sci. (Ford Found. fellow), U. Calif.-Riverside, 1977; 1 child, Ninette Maria. Mgmt. trainee Calif. Savs. and Loan Assn., Los Angeles, 1960-61; asst. fgn. corr. Los Angeles Times, Mexico City, 1961-62; bus. enterprise officer, Los Angeles, 1962-64; regional mgr. advt. Strout Realty, Pasadena, Calif., 1964-66; dir. ops. Branford, Inc., N.Y.C., 1966-68; entrepreneur retail stores, Los Angeles, Lake Elsinore, Calif., Anaheim, Calif.; exec. dir. coll. adult rehab. program U. Calif., Riverside, 1970-71; research asso. U. Calif., Santa Cruz, 1972-73; dir. human resources project SUNY, Binghamton, 1973-75; instr. social scis. div. Riverside (Calif.) Community Coll., 1976; dir. nat. immigration bd. Nat. Lawyers Guild, Los Angeles, 1977; acad. adv. and exec. asst. to provost Antioch Coll. West, Antioch U., San Francisco, 1977-78; sr. devel. officer U.S. Human Resources Corp., San Francisco, 1978; mem. profl. staff Interdepartmental Task Force on Women, White House, Washington, 1978-79; policy fellow and program officer Inst. for Ednl. Leadership/Fund for Improvement of Postsecondary Edn., HEW, Washington, 1978-79; assoc. dean Labor Coll., Empire State Coll., SUNY, N.Y.C., 1979-81; pres. I. Infante Assocs., internat. cons., 1980—; prof. polit. sci., dir. Latin Am. studies dept. Jersey City State Coll., 1983—; cons. to various ednl. orgns. and govt. agys. Pres., Nat. Hispanic Coalition, Washington, 1978-80; notary public, 1980—; mem. Am. Council on Edn., 1980—, Community Bd. 12, Borough of Manhattan, N.Y., 1980—; bd. dirs. Nagle House Co-op, N.Y.C., 1980—, Solidaridad Humana, Inc., N.Y.C., 1980—; trustee Center for Integrative Devel., N.Y.C., 1979. P.R. Legal Defense and Edn. Fund scholar, 1975-77, Pease Barker scholar, 1972-73, Council on Legal Edn. Opportunity scholar, 1975-76. Fellow Am. Polit. Sci. Assn.; mem. Soc. for Internat. Devel., Internat. Polit. Sci. Assn., Am. Ednl. Research Assn., Latin Am. Studies Assn., Univ. and Coll. Labor Edn. Assn., Nat. Women's Polit. Caucus, Nat. Women's Health Network, Nat. Assn. Female Execs. Club: Yale of N.Y.C. Author: (with others) Field Preparation Manual, 1973; contbg. author: Voices From the Ghetto, 1968; The Politics of Teaching Political Science, 1978; Labor Studies Jour., 1981; Black Studies Jour., 1983; Political Affairs, 1984. Address: Route 1 Box 119-I Holladay TN 38341

INFANTES, VÍCTOR, Spanish literature educator; b. Madrid, Jan. 26, 1950; s. Víctor Infantes and Carmen De Miguel; m. Mar Garzón, Oct. 7, 1976 (div. 1987); 1 child, Vitor; m. Nieves Baranda. Documentalist, Sch. Documentation, Madrid, 1979; D in Philology, U. Complutense, Madrid, 1987. Prof. U. Complutense, 1976, Colegio Universitario, Toledo, Spain, 1977-84; sec. U. Complutense Press, Madrid, 1986; E.S. Morby lectr. U. Calif., Berkeley, 1986. Author: Reproducciones Sancho Rayón, 1982, Pliegos Thams Croft, 1983; editor: Juan Caramuel, 1981, Dança de la Muerte, 1982. Mem. Assn. Internat. de Hispanistas, Assn. Hispánica de Literatura Medieval, Assn. Internat. "Siglo de Oro", Printing Hist. Soc., Soc. España de Literatura General y Comparada, Pen Club Internat. Office: Facultad de Filologia, U Complutense, Ciudad Universitaria, Madrid 28040, Spain

INFELD, GREGERS, business executive; b. Copenhagen, Oct. 17, 1950; arrived in Eng., 1984; s. Erik and Sigrid (Vogel-Hansen) I.; m. Vibeke Henriette Pedersen, Apr. 27, 1977; children: Celine, Josephine. BA, Copenhagen Sch. Bus., 1974, 78; MBA, Institut Europeen d'Adminstrn. des Affaires, Fontainebleau, France, 1979. Product mgr. United Wine Import A/S, Denmark, 1971-73, sales mgr., 1973-75; regional mgr. Lego A/S, Denmark, 1975-78; export dir. SEB S.A., France, 1979-84; mktg. dir. Tefal UK Ltd., Slough, Eng., 1984-87, mng. dir., 1987—. Home: Copper Beech, Curson Ave, Beaconsfield, Bucks MP9 2NN, England Office: Tefal UK Ltd, Station Rd Langley, Slough England

INGAGLIO, DIEGO AUGUSTUS, dentist; b. Phila., Dec. 4, 1922; s. Salvatore and Maria Concetta (Giordano) I.; D.D.S., U. Pa., 1947; m. Geraldine Jean Capizzi, July 11, 1948; children—Marie, Francene. With Phila. Mouth Hygiene Dept., 1947-50; asst. clin. dir. Emerson R. Sausser Med. Dental Clinic, Jefferson Hosp., Phila., 1950-51; pvt. practice dentistry, Drexel Hill, Pa., 1953—; staff Suburban Gen. Hosp., Norristown. Editor-in-chief U. Pa. Dental Jour., 1945-47. Served with AUS, 1943-45, 51-53. Fellow Acad. Gen. Dentistry, Acad. Dentistry Internat., Royal Soc. Health; mem. ADA, Pa., Chester-Delaware County dental assns., Am. Internat., Philadelphia County Socs. Clin. Hypnosis, AAAS, Nat. Space Inst., Phila. Physhodontontic Soc. (past pres.), Royal Soc. Hygiene, Am. Assn. Ret. Persons, Nat. Assn. Federally Lic. Firearms Dealers, Nat. Rifle Assn., Omicron Kappa Upsilon, Psi Omega. Clubs: Overbrook, Vespers (Phila.). Address: 801 Roberts Ave Drexel Hill PA 19026

INGERMAN, MICHAEL LEIGH, consultant; b. N.Y.C., Nov. 30, 1937; s. Charles Stryker and Ernestine (Leigh) I.; B.S., George Washington U., 1963; m. Madeleine Edison Sloane; Nov. 24, 1984; children by previous marriage—Shawn Marie, Jenifer Lyn. Health planner, Marin County, Calif., 1969-70, 70-72; regional cons. Bay Area Comprehensive Health Council, San Francisco, 1972-73; hosp. cons. Booz, Allen & Hamilton, San Francisco, 1974; health planning coordinator Peralta Hosp., Oakland, Calif., 1975-76; pres. Discern, Inc., hosp. cons., Nicasio, Calif., 1976-88; assoc. Decision Processes Internat., 1988—; instr. Golden Gate U., 1981—. Capt. Nicasio Vol. Fire Dept., 1976—; dep. coroner Marin County, 1980-83; nat. bd. dirs. Am. Friends Service Com., 1980-81, bd. dirs. Hospice of Marin, 1983—, pres. 1988—; bd. dirs. Friends Assn. Services for the Elderly, 1984—, pres. 1988—. Mem. Marin County Civil Grand Jury, 1977-78; mem. Nicasio Design Rev. Com., 1979-83; bd. dirs. John Woolman Sch., 1980-87. Mem. Am. Hosp. Assn., Calif. Hosp. Assn., Western Hosp. Assn., Healthcare Fin. Mgmt. Assn. Home: 2101 Nicasio Valley Rd Nicasio CA 94946

INGERMAN, PETER ZILAHY, systems consultant; b. N.Y.C., Dec. 9, 1934; s. Charles Stryker and Ernestine (Leigh) I.; A.B., U. Pa., 1958, M.S. in Elec. Engring., 1963; m. Carol Mary Pasquale, Dec. 19, 1970 (div. May 1980). Research investigator U. Pa., Phila., 1958-63; tech. dir. programming research, Westinghouse, Balt., 1963-65; mgr. RCA, Cherry Hill, N.J., 1965-71, staff 1971-72; sr. staff cons., Equitable Life Assurance Soc. of U.S., N.Y.C., 1972-77; ind. cons., 1977—; adj. prof. computer sci. Pratt Inst. Tech., 1968-73; mem. working groups Internat. Fedn. Info. Processing, 1962—; rep. Conf. Data Systems Langs., 1967-71, Am. Nat. Standards Inst., 1960-69. Bd. dirs. Phila. Health Plan, Inc., 1975-77, Crossroads Runaway Program, Inc., 1981-82. C.L.U.; cert. in data processing; cert. in computer programming; cert. systems profl.; cert. emergency med. technician. Fellow Brit. Computer Soc.; mem. IEEE (Sr.), Assn. Computing Machinery, AAAS, N.J. Acad. Scis., Data Processing Mgmt. Assn., Bus. Forms Mgmt. Assn., Mensa, Am. Cryptogram Assn., Am. Guild Organists, Triple Nine Soc., Sigma Xi (life), Upsilon Pi Epsilon. Author: A Syntax-Oriented Translator, 1966, Russian transl., 1969; contbr. papers to publs.; patentee electronic circuits. Office: 40 Needlepoint Ln Willingboro NJ 08046

INGERSLEV, FRITZ HALFDAN BENT, acoustics educator; b. Aarhus, Denmark, July 6, 1912; s. Christian and Helga Victorine (Raeder) I.; m. Else Ingeborg Margrethe Heiberg, May 29, 1948; children: Ib Ulrik, Steen Olaf, Dan Philip, Dorrit Margrethe. M in Elec. Engring., Copenhagen Tech. U., 1936, DSc, 1954. Research asst. Copenhagen Tech. U., 1936-41, asst. prof., 1942-53, prof. acoustics, 1954-82, prof. emeritus, 1982—; engr. acoustics lab. Copenhagen Acad. Tech. Scis., 1941-45, dir., 1945-81. Author: Acoustics in Modern Building Practice, 1949, Measurement of Linear and Nonlinear Distortion in Electrodynamic Loudspeakers, 1953; contbr. articles to profl. jours. Recipient Danish Esso prize, 1952, Chr. Møller Sørensen Found. prize, 1961, Finn Henriksen Found. prize, 1969, medal Groupement Acousticiens de Langue Francaise, 1981. Fellow Am. Acoustical Soc., IEEE; mem. Internat. Inst. Noise Control Engring. (pres. 1974—), Union Internat. Physique Pure et Appliques (sec. 1951-72), UK Inst. Acoustics (hon.), Nat. Acad. Engring. (fgn. assoc.). Home: Vilvordevej 20, DK 2920 Charlottenlund Denmark Office: Tech U, DK-2800 Lyngby Denmark

INGHAM, GEORGE ALEXANDER, sales executive; b. Wakefield, Yorkshire, Eng., Feb. 14, 1936; s. Joseph Stanley and Katherine (Rennie) I.; m. Mavis Wood; children: Veronica Ann, Janet Elizabeth, Martin Graham. Diploma in Mktg. and Econs., Leeds Sch. Commerce, 1959. Ptnr. Family Bus., Horbury, Eng., 1952-53; mgr. sales Granada TV, York, Eng., 1956-57; mgr. regional sales Lincoln Floor Maintenance, Farnborough, Eng., 1957—; bd. dirs. Bridge Mill Autos, Wakefield, Eng. 1984—. Served to sgt. Coldstream Guards, 1953-56. Fellow Inst. Mktg. and Sales Mgmt. Anglican. Club: Century (Ossett, Eng.) (pres. 1983—). Home: Grange View, Healey Rd, Ossett England Office: Lincoln Floor Maintenance, 4 Eelmoor Rd, Farnborough England GU14 7QR

INGIMARSSON, RAGNAR GUDMUNDUR, civil engineer, educator; b. Reykjavik, Iceland, Sept. 10, 1934; s. Ingimar Astvaldur Magnusson and Gudrun Gudmundsdottir; m. Halldora M. Bjarnadottir, Mar. 26, 1960; children—Arna, Ingimar, Bjarni, Ivar. B.Sc., U. St. Andrews (Scotland), 1957, B.Sc. with honors, 1958; Ph.D., U. Mich., 1964. Civil engr. City of Reykjavik, 1958-59; research engr. Bldg. Research Inst., Reykjavik, 1964-71; assoc. prof. civil. engring. U. Iceland, Reykjavik, 1971-73, prof., 1973—, dean Faculty Engring. and Sci., 1979-81; chmn. U. Iceland Bldg. Com., 1978—. Fulbright-Hays grantee, 1959-60. Mem. Assn. Chartered Engrs. in Iceland, ASCE. Lutheran. Lodge: Rotary (Gardar, Iceland). Office: U Iceland, 2-6 Hjardarhagi, 107 Reykjavik Iceland

INGLE, JOHN D., lawyer; b. Indpls., Sept. 15, 1940; s. G. Clyde and Harriet (Neideffer) I.; m. Margaret Messer, Oct. 5, 1976. BS, Ind. U., 1963; JD, Mercer U., 1970; cert., Campbell Coll., 1971. Bar: U.S. Ct. Appeals (4th cir.) 1986. Corr. banking rep. Mcht.s Nat. Bank, Indpls., 1965-67; trust officer 1st Nat. Bank, Hickory, N.C., 1970-73; judge N.C. Dist. Ct., 1973-75; sole practice Hickory, N.C., 1975-80; ptnr. Lovekin & Ingle, Hickory, 1980—; fin. officer USA, BadKreuznach, Fed. Rep. of Germany, 1963-65; park ranger U.S. Park Service, Macon, Ga., 1968-70. Pres. Western Piedmont Humane Soc., Hickory, 1975. Served to capt. Fin. Corps., 1963-65. Mem. N.C. State Bar Assn., Acad. Trial Lawyers, Def. Research Inst. Republican. Presbyterian. Lodges: Masons, Shriners. Office: Lovekin & Ingle 27 1st Ave NE Hickory NC 28603

INGLES, JOSEPH LEGRAND, utility consumer advocate, city official; b. June 15, 1939; s. Vernal Willard and Helen Josephine (Graziano) I.; m. Hazel Jeanette Palmer, Aug. 18, 1962; children—Sally, Christine, Joette, Robert, Michael. B.S., Brigham Young U., 1964; Ph.D., U. Mo., 1968. Research asst. U. Mo., Columbia, 1967-68; grant policy specialist HEW, Washington, 1970-71; asst. prof. govt. and politics U. Md., College Park, 1968-75; dir. human resources Wasatch Front Regional Council, Bountiful, Utah, 1975-77; utility consumer advocate Com. on Consumer Service Utah, 1977—; cons. Ellingson Kilpack Assocs., Salt Lake City, 1972, Bonneville Research Corp., Santa Monica, Calif., 1971, U.S. Dept. Commerce, 1970. Mem. West Bountiful City Council, 1982-88; fellow NDEA, 1964-67; U. Md. grantee, 1969. Fellow Am. Soc. Pub. Adminstrn. (fellowship 1970-71); mem. Nat. Assn. Regulatory Utility Commrs. staff subcom. on consumer affairs, 1982—; mem. gas com. Nat. Assn. State Utility Consumer Advocates, 1983—. Mormon. Lodge: Snowbird Iron Blosam (budget and fin. com. 1987). Home: 1485 N 1100 W West Bountiful UT 84087 Office: Com Consumer Services 408 Heber Wells Bldg PO Box 45802 Salt Lake City UT 84145

INGLIS, BRIAN, writer, journalist; b. Dublin, Ireland, July 31, 1916; s. Claude Cavendish (Inglis) and Vera St John (Blood) I.; m. Ruth Langdon (div.); children: Diana, Neil. BA, Oxford (Eng.) U., 1939; PhD, Dublin U., 1950. Columnist Irish Times, Dublin, 1946-53; editor Spectator, London, 1959-62; presenter TV "What the Papers Say", Manchester, Eng., 1956-86, "All Our Yesterdays", Manchester, Eng., 1962-73; freelance writer. Author: The Hidden Power, 1986, The Unknown Guest, 1987, The Power of Dreams, 1987 and numerous other books. Served with Eng. Royal Air Force, 1946-50. Home: Garden Flat, 23 Lambolle Rd, London NW3 4HS, England

INGRAHAM, EDWARD CLARKE, JR., foreign service officer; b. Mineola, N.Y., Feb. 2, 1922; s. Edward Clarke and Dorothy Hathaway (Sutton) I.; m. Susan Hartman, Jan. 25, 1947; children: John Edward, James William, Elizabeth Ann Ingraham Reed. B.A., Dartmouth Coll., 1943; postgrad., Cornell U., 1957-58. Editorial asst. Moody's Investors Service, N.Y.C., 1946-47; joined U.S. Fgn. Service, 1947; vice consul Cochabamba, Bolivia, 1947-48; 3d sec. embassy La Paz, Bolivia, 1948-50; vice consul Hong Kong, 1950-51, Perth, Australia, 1951-54; consul Madras, India, 1954-56; 2d sec. embassy Djakarta, Indonesia, 1958-60; officer charge Australia-New Zealand affairs State Dept., 1961-62, officer charge Indonesian affairs, 1962-65; assigned Nat. War Coll., 1965-66; chief of embassy polit. sect. Rangoon, Burma, 1966-69; dep. dir. research and analysis for East Asia, State Dept., 1969-71; polit. counselor embassy Islamabad, Pakistan, 1971-74; dir. Office of Indonesian, Malaysian and Singapore Affairs, State Dept., Washington, 1974-77; dep. chief mission Am. embassy, Singapore, 1977-79; diplomat in residence Lake Forest (Ill.) Coll., 1979-80; freedom of info. advisor U.S. Dept. State, 1980—; mem. U.S. del. ANZUS council meeting, Canberra, Australia, 1962, Intergovtl. Group on Indonesia, Amsterdam, Netherlands, 1975, 77. Served with USAAF, 1943-45, ETO. Mem. Am. Fgn. Service Assn. Address: 7700 Sebago Rd Bethesda MD 20817

INGRAHAM, FREDERIC BEACH, lawyer, banker; b. Washington, Feb. 1, 1944; s. David and Laura Hall (Jennings) I.; m. Sarah McJilton Smoot, Mar. 30, 1974; children—David Smoot, Sarah Jennings. B.A., Boston U., 1966; J.D., Fordham U., 1969. Bar: N.Y. 1969. With Morgan Guaranty Trust Co., N.Y.C., 1969—, now v.p.; village justice Laurel Hollow Village Ct., N.Y., 1980—. Home: 1654 Moore's Hill Rd Syosset NY 11791 Office: Morgan Guaranty Trust Co 9 W 57th St New York NY 10019

INGRAHAM, JOHN WRIGHT, banker; b. Evanston, Ill., Nov. 10, 1930; s. Harold Gillette and Mildred (Wright) I.; m. Barbara Gaye Barker, Nov. 8, 1967; children—Kimberly, Elizabeth, Scott. A.B., Harvard U., 1952, M.B.A., 1957; postgrad., NYU Grad. Sch. Bus., 1963-68. Jr. lending positions Citicorp, N.Y.C., 1957-66, sr. lending positions, 1966-70, head instl. recovery mgmt., 1970-78, dep. chmn., credit policy com., 1979—, sr. v.p. oversight N.Am lending, 1979-84, sr. v.p. oversight Latin Am. lending, 1985-87, sr. v.p. oversight global pvt. bank lending and investing, 1988—; bd. dirs. Sprague Techs., Inc., Greenwich, Conn., Ark. Best Corp., Ft. Smith; chmn. audit com. Presto Industries, Houston, 1986-88; vice chmn. bd. Penn Central Corp., Cin., 1978—, chmn. fin. com., bd. dirs.; bd. dirs. Ark. Best Corp., Ft. Smith, 1968-75, 84—; rep. of banking industry before House and Senate coms. and hearings, 1976-78. Trustee Noble and Greenough Sch., Dedham, Mass., 1987—; mem. bus. adv. council to dean U. Ark. Grad. Sch. Bus., Fayetteville, 1985—. Served to lt. USN, 1952-55, Korea. Recipient Disting. Service award Robert Morris Assocs., Phila., 1978. Mem. Fin. Acctg. Standards Bd. (task forces 1974-81), Robert Morris Assocs. (bd. dirs. 1972-75). Republican. Christian Scientist. Clubs: Union (N.Y.C.); Rockaway Hunting, Sleepy Hollow Country (N.Y.); Gulfstream Bath and Tennis (Fla.); Quogue Field; Ocean (Fla.). Home: 950 Park Ave New York NY 10028 Office: Citicorp 399 Park Ave New York NY 10043

INGRAM, DONALD FOLEY WINNINGTON, telecommunications executive; b. Aylmer, Ont., Can., Aug. 23, 1935; s. Foley Winnington and Ruby Louise (Herrics) I.; m. Dawn Marlyn Husser, Mar. 30, 1957; children: Cheryl Lyn, Allan Foley. Grad. high sch., Aylmer. Pres. Wee Lake Farms Ltd., Aylmer, 1965-87; vice-chmn. Amtelecom Group Inc., Aylmer, 1972-85, pres., chief exec. officer, 1985—; also bd. dirs. Amtelecom Group Inc., Aylmer; vice-chmn. Otter/Dorchester Ins. Co., Norwich, Ont., Can., 1975—, also bd. dirs.; owner tobacco farm, Aylmer, 1956-85. Mem. Gideons, Ont. Telephone Assn. (bd. dirs. 1985—), Ont. Flue-Cured Tobacco Growers (mem. mktg. bd. com. 1965-84). Mem. Progressive Conservative Party. Mem. United Ch. of Can. Clubs: K-40 (charter pres.), Kinsmen (Aylmer) (pres. 1967-68). Lodge: Masons. Office: Amtelecom Group Inc, 18 Sydenham St E, Aylmer, ON Canada N5H 1L2

INGRAM, GEORGE, business executive; b. Montclair, N.J., Dec. 10, 1920; s. George and Frances Elizabeth (Watts) I.; m. Olive May Holtz, Feb. 15, 1947; children: Patricia (Mrs. S. K. Bone), George III (dec.), Sara, John. B.S., Yale U., 1942; M.S., Stevens Inst. Tech., 1948. Registered profl. indsl. engr., Pa. Indsl. engr. RCA, 1942-45; cons. mgmt. engr. Stevenson, Jordan & Harrison, Inc., N.Y.C., 1945-51; controller Riegel Paper Corp., 1951-57, Raytheon Co., Lexington, Mass., 1957-60; v.p. Raytheon Co., 1960-61, v.p. fin., 1961-63, sr. v.p., dir., 1963-68; sr. v.p. Champion Internat., Inc., N.Y.C., 1968-69; exec. v.p. Champion Internat., Inc., 1969-72, dir., 1968-72; pres., chief exec. officer, dir. Reed-Ingram Corp., N.Y.C., 1972-77; cons. Reed-Ingram Corp., 1977-83; pres. Dionis Corp., Nantucket, Mass.; chmn. bd., dir. Deerfield Splty. Papers, Inc., 1973-77, Oneida Packaging Products, Inc., 1973-77, Canadian Glassine Co., Ltd., 1973-77; chmn., sec., dir. Arctos Corp., Quaker Hill, Conn., 1980-86; pres., treas., dir. Fitchburg Engring. Corp., Mass., 1980-86; dir. M/A Com, Inc., Burlington, Mass. Trustee Coll. of Wooster, Ohio; nat. bd. dirs. YMCA, also com. on mebership standards. Mem. Fin. Execs. Inst. (past pres. Boston; past chmn. nat. com. securities and exchanges regulation), ASME, Phi Gamma Delta. Republican. Episcopalian. Club: Nantucket Yacht. Home and Office: PO Box 1138 Nantucket MA 02554

INGRAM, ROBERT BRIAN, controller; b. London, Feb. 26, 1945; came to Can., 1947; s. Paul George and Evelyn Mary Joan (Ware) I.; m. Joanne Elizabeth Snowdon, July 11, 1970; children: Paul Charles, Jennifer Lynn. BA in Econs., U. Western Ont., Can., 1969. Internal auditor RCA, Montreal, Que., Can., 1974-76; fin. analyst Allied Chems. Can., Ltd., Montreal, 1976-77, mgr. budgets, 1977-78, asst. treas., 1979-80; asst. treas. Allied Chems. Can., Ltd., Toronto, Ont., 1980-83; treas. Allied Can., Inc., Toronto, Ont., 1983-84, Allied Signal Can., Inc., Toronto, 1985-86; controller Allied Can., Ltd., Toronto, 1987, Allied Chems. Can., Inc., Toronto, 1987-88; pvt. practice Mississauga, Ont., 1988—. Mem. Can. Inst. Chartered Accts., Tax Exec. Inst. Office: Allied Chems Can Inc, 201 City Centre Dr, Mississauga, ON Canada L5B 3A3

INGVAR, DAVID H(ENSCHEN), neurologist, neurophysiologist, educator; b. Lund, Sweden, Feb. 3, 1924; s. Sven and Ingegerd (Henschen) I.; m. Elisabet Ulfsparre, Sept. 14, 1946; children—Christian, Malin, Martin, Anna. M.D., U. Lund, 1950, Ph.D., 1954; D honoris causa, U. Cologne, Fed. Republic Germany, 1988. Research fellow Montreal Neurol. Inst., Que., Can., 1951-53; fellow Nobel Inst. Neurophysiology, Stockholm, 1954-56; research fellow Swedish Med. Research Council, Stockholm, 1956-58; asst. neurologist U. Lund, 1958-66, chief dept. clin. neurophysiology, 1966—, hon. prof., 1974-83, prof. clin. neurophysiology, 1983—. Editor Human Neurobiology, 1981-88; asst. editor EEG Jour., 1974, Acta Neurologica Scandinavia, 1975, Brain Research, 1978. Contbr. articles to profl. jours. Fogarty scholar Nat. Inst. Health, Bethesda, Md., 1981-84. Bd. dirs. Wallenberg Inst., 1983—, Marcus Wallenberg Found. for Internat. Sci. Coop., 1980—. Served as surgeon Swedish Navy, 1948-57. Decorated chevalier Palmes Academiques (France). Mem. Internat. Brain Research Orgn. (Swedish govt. research bd. 1976-82), Social Econ. Bd. Skandinaviska Enskilda Banken, Swedish Soc. Medicine (v.p. 1981-83, pres. 1984-86). Office: Univ Hosp, Dept Clin Neurophysiology, S-221 85 Lund Sweden

INGWERSEN, HENRY WILLIAM, IV, chief of police; b. San Francisco, Mar. 19, 1940; s. Henry William III and Virginia (Carson) I.; m. Carol Jean McCulloch, Aug. 1, 1958; children—Sue Ann, Henry William V. A.A., Coll. of Marin, 1972; B.A. in Adminstrn. of Justice, Golden Gate U., 1974, M.P.A., 1975. Dispatcher, police officer Police Dept., San Rafael, Calif., 1962-70, sgt., 1970-74, lt., 1974, capt., 1974-79, chief of police, 1981—; under-sheriff, Sheriff's Office, County of Marin, Calif., 1979-81; cons. assessment ctr. Office of Josephine County Sheriff, Grants Pass, Oreg., 1980; chmn. adv. com. Santa Rosa Regional Tng. Center, Santa Rosa, Calif., 1978—; cons. Peace Officer Standards and Tngs., Sacramento, Calif., 1982-83; guest lectr. Dominican Coll., San Rafael, 1975-76. Author: Crime Analysis, 1984. Chmn., bd. dirs. Marin Treatment Ctr., San Rafael, 1975—; chmn. Marin County chpt. ARC, San Rafael, 1982-87; bd. dirs. Bay Area Red Cross; mem. exec. council Marin council Boy Scouts Am., San Rafael, 1982-85; consolidation com. Citizens League Marin, Novato, Calif., 1983-85; mem. adv. bd. Marin Cath. High Sch., Kentfield, Calif., 1982-85. Served with USAF, 1958-62. Mem. Marin County Peace Officers Assn. (pres. 1974-75), Calif. Police Chiefs Assn., Calif. Peace Officers Assn. (committeeman

1982-83), Nat. Criminal Justice Assn., Internat. Assn. Chiefs of Police, Marin County Police Chief Assn. (pres. 1987—,office criminal justice planning technical adv. com.), Internat. Police Assn., Calif. Water Fowl Assn. (life). Republican. Lodge: Lions (pres. San Rafael 1980-81); Elks (exalter ruler San Rafael 1981-82; trustee 1984—, chmn. bd. trustees 1987—). Office: City of San Rafael 1400 5th Ave San Rafael CA 94901

INHABER, HERBERT, risk analyst, physicist; b. Montreal, Que., Can., Jan. 25, 1941; s. Samuel and Mollye (Blumenfeld) I.; m. Elizabeth Rose Bowen, Dec. 21, 1964 (div. 1981); m. Reba T. Smith, June 12, 1987. BS, McGill U., 1962; MS, U. Ill., 1964; postgrad., U. Rochester, 1965-67; PhD, U. Okla., 1971. Sci. advisor Sci. Council Can., Ottawa, 1971-72; policy analyst Fed. Dept. Environment, Ottawa, 1972-77; vis. lectr. dept. history sci. and medicine Sch. Forestry and Environ., Yale U., New Haven, 1975; sci. advisor Atomic Energy Control Bd., Ottawa, 1977-80; lectr. physics dept. Carleton U., Ottawa, 1976-80; coordinator Office Risk Analysis, Oak Ridge (Tenn.) Nat. Lab., 1980-84; prin. Risk Concepts Inc., Oak Ridge, 1984-87, pres. A Word to the Wise, Washington, 1987—; exec. scientist NUS Corp., Gaithersburg, Md., 1987—; pres., chief scientist Light Fantastic, Inc., Rockville, Md., 1988—. Author: Environmental Indices, 1976, Physics of the Environment, 1978, Energy Risk Assessment, 1982, What in the World, 1984, (weekly column) Oak Ridger, 1981-86; contbr. articles to Chgo. Tribune, Christian Sci. Monitor, others. Pres. Oak Ridge Friends of the Library, 1983-84. Served with RCAF, 1957-61. Mem. Am. Nuclear Soc., Soc. Risk Analysis (nat. membership chmn., nat. publicity chmn.), AAAS, Am. Phys. Soc., Can. Assn. Physicists, Air Pollution Control Assn., Health Physics Soc., Washington Ind. Writers, Assn. Waste Mgmt. Profls., Mensa, Sigma Xi, Sigma Pi Sigma. Home: 25 Redding Ridge Dr Gaithersburg MD 20878 Office: NUS Corp 910 Clopper Rd Gaithersburg MD 20878

INKLEY, NEIL JAMES, automotive parts executive; b. Ilford, Essex, England, July 27, 1932; s. Leonard James and May Winifred (Neill) I.; m. Katherine Audrey Duthie, Nov. 30, 1957; children: Judith, Michael. BSc in Econs. with hons., U. Coll. Leicester, London U., 1954. Orgn. and methods officer plastics div. I.C.I., Welwyn, Eng., 1959-61; sr. systems analyst Perkins Engines Ltd., Peterborough, Eng., 1961-64; orgn. mgr. Findus Ltd., Cleethorpes, Eng., 1964-71; systems mgr. Leyland (Eng.) Truck & Bus Div., 1971-77; comml. and tech. mgr. Leyland Parts Ltd., Chorley, Eng., 1977-79, warehouse and distbn. mgr., 1979-83, parts sales dir., 1983—; mem. adv. com. Lancashire (Eng.) P.O., 1978—, Lancashire Telecoms. , 1978—; lectr. systems and adminstn. confs., 1964—. Contbr. articles to profl. jours. Served as flight lt. RAF, 1954-59. Fellow Inst. Adminstrv. Mgmt. (nat. chmn. 1978-81, institute medal 1975); mem. Chartered Inst. Transp. Mem. Ch. of England (diocesan sec., mem. Prayer Book Soc.). Home: 6 Knot Ln, Walton-Le-Dale, Preston, Lancashire PR5 4BQ, England Office: Leyland Parts Ltd, Pilling Lane, Chorley, Lancashire PR7 3EL, England

INLOW, RUSH OSBORNE, chemist; b. Seattle, July 10, 1944; s. Edgar Burke and Marigale (Osborne) I.; B.S., U. Wash., 1966; Ph.D., Vanderbilt U., 1975; m. Gloria Elisa Duran, June 7, 1980. Chemist, sect. chief U.S. Dept. Energy, New Brunswick Lab., Argonne, Ill., 1975-78, chief nuclear safeguards br. Albuquerque ops., 1978-82, sr. program engr. Cruise missile systems, 1983-84, program mgr. Navy Strategic Systems, 1984-85, dir. weapon programs div., 1985-88, dir. prodn. ops. div., 1988—, apptd. Fed. Sr. Exec. Service, 1985. Served with USN, 1966-71. Tenn. Eastman fellow, 1974-75. Mem. Am. Chem. Soc., Sigma Xi. Republican. Episcopalian. Contbr. articles to profl. jours. Home: 2024 Monte Largo NE Albuquerque NM 87112

INMAN, LYDIA LUCILLE, retired university dean; b. Collins, Iowa, June 28, 1918; d. Stephen Wall and Florence Iva (Dickson) I. B.S., Iowa State U., 1940, M.S., 1950; Ph.D., U. Minn., 1963. Tchr. home econs. secondary schs., Iowa, Ill., 1940-48; research fellow, instr. dept. household equipment Iowa State U., Ames, 1948-51, asst. prof., 1955-57, assoc. prof., 1957-65, prof., 1965-73, chmn., 1963-66, coordinator resident instrn., 1966-73; vis. instr. dept. home mgmt. Mich. State U., East Lansing, 1951; assoc. prof. dept. household sci. Okla. A&M U., Stillwater, 1951-55; head div. home econs. Northeast Mo. State U., Kirksville, 1973-83, acting dean grad. studies, 1975, dean grad. studies, 1975-83; cons. U. Ariz., 1962. Recipient merit award Dairy Council Greater Kansas City, 1977; General Foods Fund fellow, 1959-60. Mem. Internat. Fedn. Home Econs., Am. Home Econs. Assn., Assn. Adminstrs. Home Econs., Mo. Home Econs. Assn., Am. Vocat. Assn., Mo. Vocat. Assn., Nat. Council Adminstrs. Home Econs., Nat. Assn. Post Secondary Adult Vocat. Home Econs., Mo. State Tchrs. Assn., AAUW, Omicron Nu, Pi Lambda Theta, Delta Kappa Gamma, Sigma Delta Epsilon, Kappa Omicron Phi, Phi Upsilon Omicron, Phi Kappa Phi. Republican. Mormon. Club: Quota Internat. Co-author: (with F. Ehrenkranz) Equipment in the Home, 1973; contbr. articles to profl. jours.

INNIS, PAULINE, author, newspaper company executive; b. Devon, Eng.; came to U.S., 1954; m. Walter Deane Innis, Aug. 1, 1959. Attended U. Manchester, U. London. Author: Hurricane Fighters, 1962; Ernestine or the Pig in the Potting Shed, 1963; The Wild Swans Fly, 1964; The Ice Bird, 1965; Wind of the Pampas, 1967; Fire from the Fountains, 1968; Astronumerology, 1971; Gold in the Blue Ridge, 1973, 2d edit., 1980; My Trails (transl. from French), 1975; (with Mary Jane McCaffery) Protocol, 1977; Prayer and Power in the Capital, 1982, The Secret Gardens of Watergate, 1987, Attention: A Quick Guide to the Armed Services, 1988. Bd. dirs. Washington Goodwill Industries Guild, 1962-66; membership chmn. Welcome to Washington Club, 1961-64; co-chmn. Internat. Workshop Capital Speakers' Club, 1961-64; pres. Children's Book Guild, 1967-68; dir. Ednl. Communications; bd. dirs. Internat. Conf. Women Writers and Journalists; mem. criminal justice com. D.C. Commn. on Status of Women; founder vol. program D.C. Women's Detention Center; chmn. women's com. Washington Opera, 1977-79; mem. Liaison Com. for Med. Edn., 1979—; nat. trustee Med. Coll., Pa., 1980—; bd. dirs. Kahill Gibran Found., 1983—; mem. Edn. Commn. for Fgn. Med. Grads., 1986—. Named Hoosier Woman of Yr., 1966. Mem. Soc. Woman Geographers, Authors League, Smithsonian Assocs. (women's bd.), English-Speaking Union (dir.), Spanish-Portuguese Group D.C. (pres. 1965-66), Brit. Inst. U.S. Clubs: Am. Newspaper Women's (pres. 1971-73), Nat. Press. Home: 2700 Virginia Ave NW Washington DC 20037 also: Skipper's Row Gibson Island MD 21056

INNIS, WALTER DEANE, ret. naval officer, pub. co. exec.; B.S., U.S. Naval Acad., 1932; grad. Naval War Coll., 1948; m. Pauline B. Coleman, Aug. 1, 1959. Commd. ensign USN, 1932, advanced through grades to rear adm.; designated naval aviator, 1936; served in Atlantic Neutrality Patrol, 1941, Mediterranean area, 1942, Aleutians, 1942-43, S.W. Pacific, Saipan, 1944, Iwo Jima, Okinawa, Japan, 1945, Korea and Formosa Strait, 1950-51; exec. officer Naval Air Sta., Dutch Harbor, Alaska, 1943; comdg. officer U.S.S. Bering Strait, 1944-45, exec. officer U.S.S. Philippine Sea, 1950-51; comdg. officer Naval Air Sta., Corpus Christi, Tex., 1946; attended Naval War Coll., 1947-48; faculty Naval War Coll., 1948-50; mem. staff Chief of Naval Ops., Washington, 1951-53; mem. staff comdr.-in-chief Eastern Atlantic (NATO), London, 1953-54; mem. staff sec. def., Washington, 1954-56, mem. U.S. del. Austrian state treaty, Vienna, 1955, mem. staff U.S. ambassador to NATO, Paris, 1956-57; mem. spl. mission from Pres. Eisenhower to Marshall Tito, Yugoslavia, 1955, mem. ops. coordinating bd., Washington, 1954-56; spl. asst. to chief Bur. Aeros., Navy Dept., Washington, 1957-59; mem. staff Sec. of Navy, 1959; cons. Argentine Govt., Buenos Aires, 1959-60; Washington cons. The MITRE Corp., Bedford, Mass., 1962-64; systems analyst Navy Dept., 1964-81; v.p. Devon Pub. Co., Inc., 1981—. Decorated Legion of Merit, Bronze Star. Mem. Ops. Research Soc. Am., Naval Hist. Found., Navy League U.S., Naval Acad. Found., Mil. Order World Wars, Explorers Club, Netherlands-Am. Found., Nat. Hist. Soc., Nat. Trust Hist. Preservation, Halcyon Found., Nat. Soc. Lit. and Arts, Friends of Kennedy Center, VFW, English-Speaking Union, Naval Acad. Alumni Assn., Ind. Soc., Nat. Audubon Soc., Ret. Officers Assn. Republican. Presbyterian. Clubs: Gibson Island (Md.) Yacht Squadron; Army-Navy, Cosmos (Washington). Co-author: Gold in the Blue Ridge, 1973. Author spl. studies for Navy Dept. and Naval War Coll., MITRE Corp. Home: Watergate W 2700 Virginia Ave NW Washington DC 20037 also: Skippers Row Gibson Island MD 21056

INNO, KARL, social scientist; b. Lustivere, Kurista, Estonia, Nov. 14, 1908 (came to U.S. 1950, naturalized 1955); s. Jaan and Marie (Kass) I.; grad. Poltsamaa Gymnasium, 1927; dipl. economist (B.A.), Tartu U., 1932, mag. rer. oec., 1936; m. Erika Plado, Dec. 24, 1933; children—Urve-Hello, Ene-Mall. Pub. auditor Auditing Union of Agrl. Cooperatives, Tallinn, 1932-37; with Tartu U., 1937-44, sr. asst. Sem. Bus. Econs., 1937-38, adj. prof. banking, ins., 1938-40, 1941-44; chief acct. Adminstr. Hdqrs. Textile Industry, Tallinn, 1940-41; chief acct. Tufflite Plastics, Inc., Ballston Spa, N.Y., 1950-64; acct. (auditor) N.Y. State Pub. Service Commn., Albany, 1965-73. Mem. Estonian Assn. of Albany and Schenectady, Inc., Estonian Learned Soc. in Am., Assn. for Advancement Baltic Studies. Author: Tartu University in Estonia during the Swedish Rule 1632-1710, 1972. Author publs. on banking, acctg., edn. and coops.; contbr. articles to profl. jours. on Baltic studies, especially on Estonian problems. Home: Capitol Hill Apts 4-B Elm Ct Rensselaer NY 12144

INNOCENTI, ANTONIO CARDINAL, cardinal Roman Catholic Church; b. Poppi, Fiesole, Tuscany, Aug. 23, 1915. ordained 1938. Consecrated bishop Titular See Aeclanum, 1968; then archbishop Apostolic Nuncio Spain; proclaimed cardinal 1985; prefect Congregation for the Clergy. Address: Citta del Vaticano, Rome Italy *

INNS, HARRY DOUGLAS ELLIS, optometrist; b. Tryconnel, Ont., Can., June 4, 1922; s. Thomas Henry and Eleanor (Ellis) I.; children from previous marriage Suasan Elizabeth, Douglas Michael; m. Helen Lynne Mitchell. Student, U. Toronto, 1946-48; grad., Ont. Coll. Optometry, 1950, OD, 1958. Practice optometry specializing in contact lenses, Brantford, Ont., 1963—. Contbr. articles to profl. jours.; patentee Inns extension disc to facilitate corneal measurements. Served to lt. with RCAF, 1941-45. Fellow Assn. Contact Lens Practitioners Eng., Am. Acad. Optometry, Royal Soc. Health; mem. Internat. Soc. Contact Lens Specialists (congress chmn.), Ont. Optometrical Assn., Can. Assn. Optometrists, Ont. Assn. Optometrists (Edn. Program award 1976, Contact Lens Program award 1978, Internat. Lecture award 1979, Appreciation award 1980, Disting. Service award 1981), Fellow Heraldy Soc. Can. (bd. dirs.); mem. Better Vision Inst., Nat. Eye Research Found., Can. Public Health Assn., Am. Optometric Assn., Brantford C. of C., Internat. Platform Assn., Can. Soc. Safety Engring. Am. Soc. Contact Lens Specialists (sec.), AAAS, Waterloo Alumni Assn., Monarchist League Can., 78th Fraser Highlanders (capt.), Royal Can. Mil. Inst., Royal Can. Air Force Assn. Clubs: Anglican Men's, Kiwanis (Brantford, Ont.). Home: 67 Tutela Heights, Brantford, ON Canada N3T 1A4 Office: 36 King George Rd, Branford, ON Canada N3R 5K1

INOGUCHI, TAKASHI, political scientist, educator; b. Niigata, Japan, Jan. 17, 1944; s. Kokichi and Mitsuko Inoguchi; BA, U. Tokyo, 1966, MA, 1968; PhD, MIT, 1974; m. Kuniko Yokota, Aug. 8, 1976. Assoc. prof. polit. sci. Sophia U., Tokyo, 1974-77, U. Tokyo, 1977—; Japan Found. vis. prof. Grad. Inst. Internat. Studies, Geneva, 1977-78, Australian Nat. U., 1986; Fulbright vis. scholor ctr. Internat. Affairs Harvard U., 1983-84. Grantee Ministry Edn., 1978, 79-81, 81-83, 85-88, 87-90, 88-90. Mem. Japanese Polit. Sci. Assn., Am. Polit. Sci. Assn., Internat. Polit. Sci. Assn., Japanese Assn. Internat. Relations, Internat. Studies Assn. Author: Peking, Pyongyang, Moscow, 1961-66: A Quantitative Analysis of International Relations, 1970; A Comparative Study of Diplomatic Style, China, Britain, Japan, 1978; International Political Economy, 1982; Contemporary Japanese Political Economy, 1983; Introduction to Social Sciences, 1985; The Political Economy of International Relations, 1985; Beyond Free Ride: Japan's New Role in the Changing World, 1987; co-author: Japanese Electoral Behavior, 1986; Politicians with Interest: Japan's Liberal-Democratic Parliamentarians in Action, 1987; States and Societies 1988; editor Leviathan: Japanese Jour. Polit. Sci., 1987—; assoc. editor Internat. Orgn., 1982—; co-editor The Polit. Econ. of Japan, vol. 2, The Changing Internat. Context, 1988; editor Contemporary Polit. Sci. Series, 1988—; assoc. editor other jours. Office: 7-3-1 Hongo, Bunkyo-ku, Tokyo 113, Japan

INOKUCHI, SEIJI, engineering educator; b. Fukuyama, Japan, Jan. 28, 1940; s. Toshio and Yoshiko Inokuchi; married; children: Hiroshi, Akira. B, Osaka (Japan) U., 1962, M in Engring., 1964, D in Engring., 1969. Asst. prof. Osaka U., 1965-69, assoc. prof., 1969-84, prof., 1984—. Recipient Ichimura Prize New Technologie Devel. Found., 1976. Mem. IEEE, Inst. Electronics Info. and Communication System, Info. Processing Soc. Japan. Home: Ishibashi 3-11-3-101, Ikeda 563, Japan Office: Osaka U Faculty Engring Sci, Machikaneyama, Toyonaka 560, Japan

INOUE, EIICHI, scientist, educator; b. Niigata Prefecture, Japan, Feb. 13, 1922; s. Keitaro and Fusa Inoue; BS in Chemistry, Tokyo Inst. Tech., 1945; D in Engring., 1957; m. Sumiko Inoue, Oct. 10, 1949; children: Tan, Atsu. Asst. prof. Salk Inst. for Biol. Studies; assoc. prof. Tokyo Inst. Tech., 1956-61, prof., from 1962, now prof. emeritus also past dir. imaging sci. and engring. lab. and dir. Central Library; prof. Tokai U.; spl. advisor Process Shizai Co., Tokyo. Mem. Chem. Soc. Japan (sci. award), Soc. Photog. Scientists and Engrs. (U.S.) (pres. Tokyo chpt., Kosar Meml. award, fellowship award, hon. mem. award), Soc. Photog. Sci. and Tech. of Japan (past pres., hon. award), Soc. Electrophotography Japan (past pres.), Royal Photog. Soc. Brit., Internat. Com. of Sci. of Photography, Japanese Soc. Printing Sci. and Tech. (past pres.). Buddhist. Clubs: Tokyo Birdie Golf. Co-author series Imaging Science and Engineering; translator (into Japanese): Electrophotography (R.H. Schaffert); also numerous articles and patents. Home: 4-22-32 Seijyo, Setagayaku, Tokyo Japan Office: Process Shizai Co, 7-10-5 Ginza, Chuo-Ku, Tokyo Japan

INOUE, MASAHIKO, securities company executive; b. Osaka, Japan, Jan. 1, 1929; s. Tadamasa and Kaneko (ono) Inoue; m. Kazuko Eto, Jan. 14, 1958; 1 child, Sadahiko. BA in Econs., U. Kyoto, Japan, 1951; student, Harvard U., 1964. Dir. The Sanwa Bank, Ltd., Osaka, 1976-78, sr. mng. dir., 1978-86; pres. Towa Securities Co. Ltd., Tokyo, 1986—; bd. dirs. Sanwa Internat. Fin., Hong Kong, Towa Internat. Ltd., London. Home: 1-1-19 Sekimaci-Minami, Nerima-ku, Tokyo Japan Office: Towa Securities Co Ltd, 1 16 7 Nihonbashi, Chuo-ku, Tokyo Japan

INOUE, MASSAAKI, tire company executive, marketing specialist; b. Tokyo, Oct. 5, 1939; s. Kinnosuke and Yuriko (Hiraswa) I.; m. Noriko Koike, Nov. 23, 1962; children: Shinnosuke, Masaki. BS, Keio U., 1962. Original equipment tire salesman Bridgestone Corp., Tokyo, 1962-67, domestic tire salesman, 1967-71, with off-the-road tire project, 1971-72, regional tire sales mgr. Osaka (Japan) br., 1972-76, tire sales planning mgr., 1976-80, mktg. mgr., 1982—; sr. mktg. dir. Bridgestone Chiba (Japan) Sales Co., 1980-82; chief sec. Cockpit Info. Ctr., Tokyo, 1982—; cons. Japan Mktg. Juku, Tokyo, 1984—. Author lecture series Japanese Mktg. Democrat. Buddhist. Clubs: Kasumigaseki Golf (Ibaragi, Japan); Century Tennis (Tokyo). Home: 1-57-17 Kitakarasuyama, Setagaya-ku, Tokyo 157, Japan Office: Bridgestone Corp, 10-1 Kyobashi 1-Chrome, Chuo-ku, Tokyo 104, Japan

INOUE, RYUICHIRO AKIRA, economist; b. Ashiya, Hyogo, Japan, Feb. 23, 1935; parents: Takashi and Michiko I.; m. Shoko Inoue, Nov. 15, 1942; children: Nami, Dan. B of Econs., Kwansei Gakuin U., Nishinomiya, Japan, 1957. Asst. dir. research div. Japan External Trade Orgn., Tokyo, 1968-71; dir. Japan External Trade Orgn., Paris, 1971-75; dir. internat. econ. affairs div. Japan External Trade Orgn., Tokyo, 1977-80; dir. Japan External Trade Orgn., Amsterdam, The Netherlands, 1981-84; sr. economist Japan External Trade Orgn., Tokyo, 1984—. Author: Foubourg St. Honore, 1977, Open Nation-The Netherlands, 1986, co-author Era of World Enterprise, 1968; co-author, co- editor Era of Soft Industry, 1980; co-author and editor Retail and Wholesale, 1986, Business Group and Enterprises in Asia, 1987; translator Rothschild, 1970. Home: Tobio 4-18-15, 243-02 Atsugi Kanagawa Japan Office: Japan External Trade Orgn, 2-5 Toranomon 2-chome, Minato-ku, Tokyo 105, Japan

INOUE, SHUN, sociologist; b. Sendai, Miyagi, Tohoku, Japan, Sept. 8, 1938; s. Noboru and Tadako (Ishihara) I.; m. Mayako Shigematsu, Mar. 14, 1967. B.A., Kyoto U., 1963, M.A., 1965. Asst. lectr. Kyoto U., 1967-70; lectr. Kobe U. Commerce, Kobe, 1970-72; asso. prof. Osaka Nat. U. (Japan), 1972-80, prof. sociology, 1980—. Mem. Japan Sociol. Assn., Kansai Sociol Assn. Author: The Loss of Meaning in Death, 1973; A Sociology of Play and Games, 1977; Play and Culture, 1981; A Social Psychology of Lies and Lying, 1982; co-author: Introduction to Sociology, 1988; editor: A Sociology of Contemporary Culture, 1987. Home: 3-23-13 Nagaoka, Nagaokakyo-shi, Kyoto 617, Japan Office: Dept Sociology Faculty Human Scis, Osaka Nat Univ, 1-2 Yamadoka Suita-shi, Osaka 565, Japan

INOUE, TAKASHI, food products executive; b. Tokyo, Japan, Aug. 12, 1935; s. Seishiro and Chiyo (Sekimizu) I.; m. Akiko Hirasawa, Feb. 7, 1965; children: Haruko, Naoko, Ken, Makoto. Student, Tokyo U., 1959, D of Agriculture, 1977. Head research group Kirin Brewing Co., Takasaki, 1972-84, gen. mgr. brewing sci. lab., 1984-87, gen. mgr. cen. lab. key tech., 1987—; part-time lectr. Tokyo U. of Agr. and Tech., 1984—. Mem. Inst. Food Technologists, Master Brewers Assn. Am. (corr. chmn. 1985—), Am. Soc. Brewing Chem. Home: 14-3 Tatsumicho, 370 Takasaki, Gunma Japan Office: Cen Lab Key Tech, Kirin Brew Co, 3-Miyaharacho, 370-12 Takasaki, Gunma Japan

INOUE, TAKESHI, psychiatrist; b. Kumamoto, Japan, Sept. 3. 1932; s. Tatsuichi and Shigeye (Matsushita) I.; M.D., Kumamoto U., 1957, Ph.D., 1962; m. Michiko Takeshita, Oct. 8, 1961; children—Hiroko, Takao. Lectr. dept. biochemistry Kumamoto U. Med. Sch., 1957-61; lectr. U. Calif. Med. Sch., San Francisco, 1961-73, postdoctoral fellow, 1968; postdoctoral fellow dept. biochemistry Temple U. Med. Sch., Phila., 1968-70; asst. prof. dept. neuropsychiatry Kumamoto U. Med. Sch. (Japan), 1971-83; dir. Minamata Hosp., 1983-85, dir., 1985—. Mem. Japanese Neurochem. Soc., N.Y. Acad. Scis., Sigma Xi. Home: 1862-4 Tatsudamachi-Yuge,, Kumamoto 862 Japan Office: 4051 Hama, Minamata-Shi, Minamata-Shi 867 Japan

INOUE, YOSHISUKE, educator; b. Nagasaki, Japan, Apr. 21, 1932; s. Arata and Masa I.; children: Mari, Mika, Yumi. BME, Waseda U., 1956; MS (Fulbright scholar), Case Inst. Tech., 1960. Control engr. Yawata Iron & Steel Co. Ltd., Yawata, Japan, 1956-70, asst. mgr. office of pres., 1965-67, mgr. info. info. systems dept., 1968-76; dept. gen. mgr. info systems dept. Nippon Steel, Tokyo, 1976-80, gen. mgr. system devel. office, 1980-86; assoc. prof. bus. adminstrn. St. Andrew's U., Osaka, Japan, 1986—. Mem. Japan Soc. Mech. Engring., Sigma Xi. Anglican. Home: 5-14-4 Kaijin, Funabashi-city 273, Japan Office: St Andrews U, Sch Bus Adminstrn, 276-1 Nishino, Sakai-shi Osaka-fu 588, Japan

INOUYE, DANIEL KEN, U.S. senator; b. Honolulu, Sept. 7, 1924; s. Hyotaro I. and Kame Imanaga; m. Margaret Shinobu Awamura, June 12, 1949; 1 child, Daniel Ken. A.B., U. Hawaii, 1950; J.D., George Washington U., 1952. Jr. asst. pub. prosecutor Honolulu, 1953-54, practice of law, 1954—; majority leader Territorial Ho. of Reps., 1954-58, Senate, 1958-59; mem. 86th-87th U.S. congresses from, Hawaii, U.S. Senate from, Hawaii, 1963—; sec. Senate Democratic Conf.; mem. Dem. Policy Com., Dem. Steering Com., Senate Com. on Appropriations; chmn. subcom. fgn. ops., mem. Commerce Com.; chmn. subcom. on communications Select Com. on Intelligence, 1976-77, ranking mem. subcom. budget authorizations, 1979-84; chmn. Select Com. Indian Affairs; mem. Select Com. on Presdl. Campaign Activities, 1973-74; chmn. Sen. select com. Secret Mil. Assistance to Iran and Nicaraguan Opposition, 1987; dir. Central Pacific Bank. Author: Journey to Washington. Active YMCA, Boy Scouts Am. Keynoter; temporary chmn. Dem. Nat. Conv., 1968, rules com. chmn., 1980, co-chmn. conv., 1984. Served from pvt. to capt. AUS, 1943-47. Decorated D.S.C., Bronze Star, Purple Heart with cluster; named 1 of 10 Outstanding Young Men of Yr. U.S. Jr. C. of C., 1960; recipient Alumnus of Yr. award George Washington U., 1961; Splendid Am. award Thomas A. Dooley Found., 1967; Golden Plate award Am. Acad. Achievement, 1968. Mem. D.A.V. (past comdr. Hawaii), Honolulu C. of C., Am. Legion (Nat. Comdr.'s award 1973). Methodist. Clubs: Lion. (Hawaii), 442d Veterans (Hawaii). Home: 469 Ena Rd Honolulu HI 96814 Office: 722 Hart Senate Bldg Washington DC 20510 *

INSLEY, RICHARD WALLACE, lawyer; business executive; b. Tampa, Fla., Sept. 27, 1918; s. Levin Irving and Sadie Bell (Waddell) I.; m. Eleanor Jane Robinson, Oct. 22, 1945; children: Glen Thomas, Anne Insley McCausland. AB, Trinity Coll., Hartford, Conn., 1946; JD, U. Va., 1970; MBA, Harvard U., 1948. Bar: Mich. 1956. Mem. Richard W. Insley, Atty.-at-Law, St. Joseph, Mich., 1950—; pres. Southwestern Developers Inc., St. Joseph, 1960—, also bd. dirs.; pres. Whinco Inc., Pizza Hut franchisee, St. Joseph, 1969—, also bd. dirs.; v.p., sec. Jan Barb, Inc., Holiday Inn franchisee, St. Joseph, 1970—, also bd. dirs. Trustee Barat Coll., Lake Forest, Ill., 1972-82; mem. U.S. Senate Bus. Adv. Bd., Washington. Served to lt. USN, 1942-45. Decorated Silver Star. Mem. ABA, Mich. State Bar Assn., Berrien County Bar Assn. Republican. Episcopalian. Clubs: Point O'Woods Country, Berrien Hills Country (Benton Harbor, Mich.). Home: 278 Ridgeway Saint Joseph MI 49085 Office: 421 Main St PO Box 63 Saint Joseph MI 49085

INSTONE, JOHN CLIFFORD, manufacturing company executive; b. Phila., Mar. 5, 1924; s. John Leonard and Anna Lena Instone; m. Mary Elizabeth Ketchell, Feb. 12, 1949; children: Linda Jane, John Clifford, Jr. B.S. in Mech. Engring., Drexel U., Phila., 1947. Engr., Proctor Electric Co., Phila., 1947-49; mfg. engr. IRC, Phila., 1949-51; div. gen. mgr. Proctor-Silex Corp. (div. SCM Corp.), Phila. and Mount Airy, N.C., 1951-60; with SL Industries Inc., Marlton, N.J., 1960—; pres., chief exec. officer SL Industries Inc., 1979—; also dir., chmn. bd. New Rochelle Mfg. Co., Inc., N.Y.C., 1984—; dir., chmn. bd. Montevideo Tech., Inc., Minn., 1985—; chmn. bd. SL Auburn, Inc., N.Y.C., SL Internat., Inc. Served to 1st lt. AUS, 1943-45. Mem. Am. Mgmt. Assn. Clubs: Rotary, Elks. Home: 465 Pelham Rd Cherry Hill NJ 08034 Office: SL Industries Inc 3 Greentree Ctr Suite 201 Marlton NJ 08053

INTRILIGATOR, MICHAEL D., economist, educator; b. N.Y.C., Feb. 5, 1938; m. Devrie; children—Kenneth, James, William, Robert. SB in Econs., MIT, 1959; MA, Yale U., 1960; PhD, MIT, 1963. Asst. prof. econs. UCLA, 1963-66, assoc. prof., 1966-72, prof., 1972—, prof. dept. polit. sci., 1981—, dir. Ctr. Internat. and Strategic Affairs, 1982—; dir. Jacob Marschak Interdisciplinary Coll. 1977—,; cons. Inst. Def. Analysis, 1974-77, ACDA, 1968, Rand Corp., 1962-65. Author: Mathematical Optimization and Economic Theory, 1971, also Taiwanese, Spanish and Russian edits., Econometric Models, Techniques and Applications, 1978, 83, Greek and Spanish edits., 1983, (with others) A Forecasting and Policy Simulation Model of the Health Care Sector, 1979; mem. adv. editorial bd. Math. Social Scis., 1983—; assoc. editor Jour. Optimization Theory and Applications, 1979—, Conflict Mgmt. and Peace Sci., 1980—; co-editor: (series) Handbooks in Economics, 1980—, Advanced Textbooks in Economics, 1972—; editor: (with D.A. Kendrick) Frontiers of Quantitative Economics, vol. II, 1974, (with Kenneth Arrow) Handbook of Mathematical Economics, 3 vols., 1981-85; (with Zvi Griliches) Handbook of Econometrics, 3 vols., 1983-86, (with B. Brodie and R. Kolkowicz) National Security and International Stability, 1983, numerous others; contbr. articles to profl. jours. Woodrow Wilson fellow, 1959-60; MIT fellow, 1960-61; recipient Disting. Teaching award UCLA, 1966; Ford fellow, 1967-68; Warren C. Scoville disting. teaching award UCLA, 1976, 79, 82, 84. Fellow Econometric Soc.; mem. Internat. Inst. Strategic Studies, Council Fgn. Relations, others. Office: UCLA Dept Econs Los Angeles CA 90024

INUMA, KAZUMOTO, corporate executive; b. Sendai, Miyagi, Japan, Jan. 24, 1943; s. Kazukiyo and Hiroko Inuma; m. Yoko Inuma, Oct. 6, 1968; children: Kazutake, Kazushige. BS, Tohoku U., Sendai, 1965, MS, 1967, PhD, 1970. With NEC Cen. Research Labs., Kawasaki, Japan, 1970-83; mgr. NEC C&C Systems Research Labs., Kawasaki, 1983-85; asst. gen. mgr. mktg. div. NEC Info. Services, Tokyo, 1985-87; gen. mgr. NEC C&C Info. Tech. Research Lab., Kawasaki, 1987—. Mem. IEEE (Best Paper award 1976), Inst. Electronics, Info. and Communications Engrs., Inst. TV Engrs. Japan. Home: 2-24-14 Sakuragaoka, Setagaya, Tokyo 156, Japan Office: NEC C&C Info Tech Research Lab, 1-1 Miyazaki 4-Crome Miyamae-Ku, Kawasaki, Kanagawa 213, Japan

INZETTA, MARK STEPHEN, lawyer; b. N.Y.C., Apr. 14, 1956; s. James William and Rose Delores (Cirnigliaro) I.; m. Amy Marie Elbert, June 25, 1977; children: Michelle, Margot, Mallory. BBA summa cum laude, U. Cin., 1977; JD, U. Akron, 1980. Bar: Ohio 1980, U.S. Dist. Ct. (no. dist.) Ohio 1980. Legal intern City of Canton, Ohio, 1979-80; assoc. W.J. Ross Co. L.P.A., Canton, 1980-84; asst. gen. counsel Wendy's Internat. Inc., Columbus, Ohio, 1984—; instr. real estate law Stark Tech. Coll., Canton, 1983. Case and comment editor: Akron Law Rev., 1979-80. Instr. religious edn. St. Peter's Cath. Ch.; bd. dirs. Brookside Village Civic Assn., 1985-87, treas., 1986-87; chmn. campaign Earle Wise Appellate Judge, North Canton, Ohio, 1982. Recipient Am. Jurisprudence award Lawyers Coop. Pub. Co., 1978; Dir. of Yr. award North Canton Jaycees, 1982, Presdl. award of honor, 1984; Dist. Dir. award of honor, Ohio Jaycees, 1984. Mem. ABA, Ohio Bar Assn., North Canton Jaycees (bd. dirs. 1981-82, v.p. 1982-83, pres. 1983-84), North Canton C. of C. (bd. dirs. 1983-84). Democrat. Roman Catholic. Home: 1584 Sandy Side Dr Worthington OH 43085 Office: Wendy's Internat Inc 4288 W Dublin-Granville Rd Dublin OH 43017

IONESCU, VASILE VALENTIN, mathematician; b. Buzau, Romania, May 1, 1929; s. Moise and Eugenia (Pavelescu). B of Math., U. Bucharest, 1952. Researcher Mech. Inst., Romanian Acad., Bucharest, 1953-65, prin. researcher, 1965-71; prof. math. U. Craiova, Romania, 1972—. Contbr. articles to profl. jours. Recipient State prize Romanian Socialist Republic, 1963. Home: Stoica Ludescu, Nr 3, Sect I, 78192 Bucharest 32 Romania

IONESCU TULCEA, CASSIUS, educator, research mathematician; b. Bucharest, Rumania, Oct. 14, 1923; naturalized, 1967; s. Ioan and Ana (Caselli) Ionescu T. M.S., U. Bucarest, 1946; Ph.D., Yale, 1959. Mem. faculty U. Bucarest, 1946-57, assoc. prof., 1952-57; research assoc. Yale U., 1957-59, vis. lectr., 1959-61; assoc. prof. U. Pa., 1961-64; prof. U. Ill., Urbana, 1964-66, Northwestern U., 1966—. Author: Hilbert Spaces (in Rumanian), 1956, A Book on Casino Craps, 1980, A Book on Casino Blackjack, 1982; co-author: Probability Calculus (in Rumanian), 1956, Calculus, 1968, An Introduction to Calculus, 1969, Honors Calculus, 1970, Topics in the Theory of Liftings, 1969, Sets, 1971, Topology, 1971, A Book on Casino Gambling, 1976. Recipient Asachi prize Rumanian Acad., 1957. Office: Northwestern U Lunt Bldg Evanston IL 60208

IORDANESCU, RADU EMIL, mathematician, researcher; b. Bucharest, Romania, Aug. 29, 1940; s. Emil Petre and Maria-Maura (Nicolae) I.; m. Florica Nicolae Voinea, June 16, 1986. Diploma in math., U. Bucharest, 1962. Tchr. M. Eminescu High Sch., Bucharest, 1962-64; researcher Inst. Math., Bucharest, 1964-71, prin. researcher, 1971-75; prin. researcher Cen. Inst. Physics, Bucharest, 1975—. Contbr. articles to profl. jours. Recipient Rome Consiglio Nazionale Ricerches award, 1971, Alexander von Humboldt Found. award, 1974. Mem. Soc. Math. Scis. Romania, Am. Math. Soc. Home: Cutitul de Argint 62A, 75212 Bucharest Romania Office: Inst Math, Academiei 14, 70109 Bucharest Romania

IPOUSTEGUY, JEAN, sculptor; b. Dun-sur-Meuse, France, 1920. Studies with Robert Lesbounit, 1938. Painter; one-man shows in sculpture in Europe and U.S. including Galerie Claude Bernard, Paris, 1962-66, Fondation Nationale des Arts graphiques et Plastiques, Paris, 1979, Kunsthalle, Berlin, 1980; Guggenheim Mus., N.Y.C., 1983; group shows include Venice Biennale, 1964, Weiner Festwochen, Vienna, 1981, Seven Dials Gallery, London, 1982; executed monumental sculptures for cities including Berlin, Lyons, Grenoble, Washington (French Embassy), water-colour Galerie Sarver, Paris, 1988. Recipient prize Bright Found., Venice Biennale, 1964; art prize City of Darmstadt, 1968; guest German Acad. Exchange Service, 1973-74; decorated chevalier French Legion of Honor, 1984. Home: 35 rue Chevreul, 94600 Choisy le Roi France

IPPENSEN, CURTIS ALBERT, advertising executive; b. Quincy, Ill., Nov. 23, 1944; s. Curtis Selby and Helen Elizabeth (Bunte) I.; m. Mary Ann Vonderheide, July 30, 1967; 1 dau., Kristin Nicole. B.S. Bradley U., 1966, M.B.A., 1967. Market research analyst Caterpillar Tractor Co., Peoria, Ill., 1967-68, market advt. mgr., 1968-71; account supr. Marsteller, Inc., Chgo., 1971-78; v.p., account supr. Ogilvy & Mather Worldwide, Chgo., 1978-82, v.p., mgmt. supr., 1982-85, sr. v.p., 1985-87, sr. v.p. group dir., 1987—. Committeeman, Boy Scouts Am., Chgo., 1982-84, Crusade of Mercy, Chgo., 1982; v.p. Jaycees, Peoria, Ill., 1970-71; bd. dirs. David Ogilvy Awards, 1980-82. Named Copywriter and Campaigner of Yr. BPAA, 1971. Mem. Am. Mktg. Assn., Zeta Phi. Home: 1156 Wydown Ct Naperville IL 60540 Office: Ogilvy & Mather Worldwide 676 Saint Clair Chicago IL 60611

IPSEN, KNUT, law educator; b. Hamburg, Federal Republic of Germany, June 9, 1935; s. Hans Henning and Ruth (Rickes) I.; m. Heike Becker; children: Bjoern, Goede. Student, U. Kiel, 1959-62, degree, 1967, Habilitation, 1973; D LC, Jagiellonan U., Krakow, Poland, 1986; LLD, 1987. Prof. U. Bochum, Federal Republic of Germany, 1974—, rector, 1979—. Contbr. articles to profl. jours. Conv. agt. Red Cross of Germany, 1986—. Served to maj. German Army, 1956-59. Mem. Union of German Scientists, Union of German Law of Nations, German Soc. of Pub. Law. Home: Nevel Str 59, 04630 Bochum Federal Republic of Germany Office: Ruhr-University Bochum, Universitats Str 50, D-4630 Bochum Federal Republic of Germany

IPSEN, SVEN, engineer; b. Copenhagen, July 7, 1940; s. Hans and Ellen (Senneksen) I.; m. Alice Madsen, Mar. 25, 1967; 1 child, Henriette. BS in Engring., Kobenhavns Teknikum, Copenhagen, 1967. Planning engr. ISS DDRS A/S, Denmark, 1968-80; pres. ISS DDRS A/S (name changed to ISS Servisystem A/S 1987), Copenhagen, 1980—; chmn. bd. ISSELE a.s., ISS Linnedservice a.s., ISS Darenas a.s., ISS Kantineservice a.s., ISS Securitias a.s.; bd. dirs. ISS Data a.s., ISS Internat. Service System Inc., U.S. Mem. World Fedn. Bldg. Service Contracters (bd. dirs.), Nordic Assn. Bldg. Service Contractors (bd. dirs.), Danish Assn. Bldg. Service Contractors, Danish Employers Assn. (bd. dirs. governing body). Office: ISS Servisystem A/S, Rentemestervej 62, 2400 NV Copenhagen Denmark

IQBAL, FATIMA, nurse; b. Shikarpur, Pakistan, Feb. 12, 1946; d. Munshi Khan and Jamila; m. Khurshid Ahmed, (dec.); 1 child, Almas Khurshid Shaiku; m. Khurshid Ahmed Sheikh, Sept. 6, 1972; 5 children. Diploma in Nursing, Islamia Coll., Sukkur, Pakistan, 1965. Home: Sukh Pull, Shikarpur Pakistan

IQBAL, MANZOOR, travel agency executive; b. Dera Gazi Khan, Pakistan, Sept. 12, 1941; s. Sheikh Mohammad Ellahie and Bilquis Manzoor; m. Saira Iqbal, Oct. 29, 1969; children: Nofil Iqbal, Saman Iqbal, Saddam Iqbal. BS, Gordon Coll., 1961. Sales asst. Pakistan Internat. Airlines, Rawalpindi, 1962-70; comml. instr. tng. sch. Pakistan Internat. Airlines, Karachi, 1970-75, mgr. far east, 1975-78; mgr. Tokyo, Japan Pakistan Internat. Airlines, 1978-81; pres. Minahl Internat. Travel Agy., Tokyo, 1981—. Author: Sell-Best, 1970. Club: Fgn. Correspondents.

IRAJ, PARCHAMAZAD, educator, chemistry and solar energy consultant; b. Teheran, Iran, Jan. 13, 1939; s. Mohammad Esmaiil Parchamazad and Akram Jalali; m. Shahin Massoudi, June 14, 1972. BSc in Chemistry, Teheran U., 1961, MSc in Chemistry, 1963; Diploma in Chem. Tech., PhD, Marseille (France) U., 1968. Assoc. prof. then prof. U. Teheran; cons. Ministry of Industry, 1982—, Ministry of Petroleum and petrochemicals, Ministry of Energy, 1981-82. Contbr. articles to profl. jours.; speaker in field. Mem. Chem. Soc. of France, la Coop. Mediterraneenne pur L'Energie Solaire (internat. cen. commn. 1978-82), Internat. Combustion Soc., European Photochemistry Assn. Office: U Teheran, Teheran Iran

IRANI, RAY R., chemical company executive; b. Beirut, Lebanon, Jan. 15, 1935; came to U.S., 1953, naturalized, 1956; s. Rida and Naz I.; m. Joan D. French; children: Glenn R., Lillian M., Martin R. BS in Chemistry, Am. U. Beirut, 1953; PhD in Phys. Chemistry, U. So. Calif., 1957. Sr. research group leader Monsanto Co., 1957-67; assoc. dir. new products, then dir. research Diamond Shamrock Corp., 1967-73; with Olin Corp., 1973-83, pres. chems. group, 1978-80; corp. pres., dir. Olin Corp., Stamford, Conn., 1980-83; exec. v.p. Occidental Petroleum Corp., Los Angeles, 1983-84, pres., chief operating officer, 1984—, also dir.; chmn., chief exec. officer subs. Occidental Chem. Corp., Norwalk, Conn., 1983—; bd. dirs. Am. Petroleum Inst. Author: Particle Size; also author papers in field; numerous patents in field. Trustee St. John's Hosp. and Health Ctr. Found., Natural History Mus. Los Angeles County. Mem. Soap and Detergent Assn., Chem. Mfrs. Assn. (bd. dirs.), Am. Inst. Chemists (hon. fellow award 1983), Am. Chem. Soc., Scientific Research Soc. Am., Indsl. Research Inst., Los Angeles C. of C. (bd. dirs.). Home: 250 Lost District Dr New Canaan CT 06840 Office: Occidental Petroleum Corp 10889 Wilshire Blvd Los Angeles CA 90024 also: Can Occidental Petroleum Ltd, 500 635 8th Ave S W, Calgary, AB Canada T2P 3Z1 *

IRENAS, JOSEPH ERON, lawyer; b. Newark, July 13, 1940; s. Zachary and Bessie (Shain) I.; m. Nancy Harriet Jacknow, 1962; children—Amy Ruth, Edward Eron. A.B., Princeton U., 1962; J.D. cum laude, Harvard U., 1965; postgrad. NYU Sch. Law, 1967-70. Bar: N.J. 1965, N.Y. 1982. Law sec. to justice N.J. Supreme Ct., 1965-66; assoc. McCarter & English, Newark, 1966-71, ptnr., 1972—; trustee Hamilton Investment Trust, Elizabeth, N.J., 1980-83; mem. N.J. Supreme Ct. Dist. Ethics Com., 1984-86, vice chmn., 1986; adj. prof. law Rutgers Sch. Law, Camden, 1985-86, N.J. Bd. Bar Examiners, 1986—. Contbr. articles to legal jours. Chmn. bd. trustees United Hosps. of Newark, 1982-83, trustee United Hosps. Found., 1985—. Fellow Royal Chartered Inst. Arbitrators (London); mem. ABA, Fed. Bar Assn., N.J. Bar Assn., Essex County Bar Assn., Comml. Law League Am., Assn. Trial Lawyers Am. Republican. Jewish. Clubs: Essex (Newark); Princeton (N.Y.C.). Home: 196 Elm Rd Princeton NJ 08540 Office: McCarter & English 550 Broad St Newark NJ 07102

IRFAN, MOHAMMAD, psychiatrist; b. Mansehra, Pakistan, Aug. 10, 1934; s. Abdul Rahim and Misrhim Irfan; married; 4 children. MBBS, King Edward Med. Coll., Lahore, Pakistan, 1959; Diploma in Psychol. Medicine, London, 1970. Pvt. practice psychiatry Dudial, Pakistan; with various hosps. Eng., 1968-70; supt. medicine Govt. Mental Hosp., Dudial, 1970—. Contbr. articles to profl. jours. WHO fellow. Office: Govt Mental Hosp, Dudial, Hazara Pakistan

IRI, MASAO, engineering educator; b. Tokyo, Jan. 7, 1933; s. Jin-ichi and Yasumi (Kuga) I.; m. Yumi Mizoo, Mar. 19, 1960; children—Chika, Masato, Yuka. B.Engring., U. Tokyo, 1955, M.Engring., 1957, Dr. Engring., 1960. Research asst. Kyushu U., Fukuoka, Japan, 1960, asst. prof., 1960-62; assoc. prof. U. Tokyo, 1962-73, prof. math. engring., 1973—, univ. senator, 1986-87, dean faculty engring., 1987—. Author: Network Flow, Transportation and Scheduling, 1969; also 5 books in Japanese and 8 books transl. into Japanese; editor-in-chief Jour. Ops. Research Soc. Japan, 1980-82; adv. editor Networks, 1975—, European Jour. Operational Research, 1981—; assoc. editor Math. Programming, 1976-88; editorial bd. Discrete Applied Math., 1979—, European Jour. Combinatorics, 1981—, Advances in Applied Math., 1982—, Annals of Ops. Research, 1983—, Japan Jour. Applied Math, 1984—, Investigação Operacional, 1985-88, Discreet and Computational Geometry, 1985—; editor monographs in Japanese: Math. Programming, 1980—, New Applied Math., 1973—, Applied Math. series, 1980—, Computer Sci., 1981-83. Recipient Matsunaga prize Matsunaga Found., 1965, New Tech. prize Inst. Chem. Engrs. Japan, 1968. Mem. Math. Programming Soc., Japanese Soc. for Quality Control, Life Support Tech. Soc. (v.p. 1985-87), IEEE (sr. mem. 1984—), Math. Soc. Japan, Linguistic Soc. Japan, Ops. Research Soc. Japan (v.p. 1984-85), Inst. Electronics Info. and Communication Engrs. Japan (Paper prize 1969, 76), Info. Processing Soc. Japan (Paper prize 1988), Soc. Instruments and Control Engrs. Japan, Japanese Acad. of Engring., N.Y. Acad. Sci., Sigma Xi. Internat. Fedn. Operational Research Socs. (v.p. 1983-85). Home: Masago-jutaku 1-201, 4-20 Hongo, Bunkyo-ku, Tokyo 113, Japan Office: U Tokyo Dept Math Engring, 7-3-1 Hongo, Bunkyo-ku, Tokyo 113, Japan

IRISH, GARY GENE, health systems executive; b. Lancaster, Wis., Sept. 17, 1951; s. Clyde Gene and Florence Adele (Haudenshield) I.; m. Karen L. Seinhart, Aug. 18, 1974. B.A., Andrews U., 1973; M.P.H., Loma Linda U., 1975; M.B.A., UCLA, 1980. Asst. health planner Inland Counties Comprehensive Health Planning Council, San Bernardino, Calif., 1975; adminstrv. resident Corona (Calif.) Community Hosp., 1976; health planner Inland Counties Health Systems Agy., Riverside, Calif., 1977-78; dir. resource mgmt. and planning Loma Linda (Calif.) U. Med. Ctr., 1978-82; exec. dir. Loma Linda Gyn-Ob Med. Group, 1982-83; asst. v.p. Adventist Health System/North, Hinsdale, Ill., 1983-85, v.p., 1985-86, v.p. Adventist Health System/North, Eastern and Middle Am., Hinsdale, 1987-88, pres. Glendale Heights Community Hosp., 1988—. Mem. Am. Mktg. Assn., Am. Hosp. Assn., Hosp. Mgmt. Systems Soc., Hosp. Planning Soc., Med. Group Mgmt. Assn. Home: 9340 South Madison Ave Burr Ridge IL 60521

IRISH, LEON EUGENE, lawyer, educator; b. Superior, Wis., June 19, 1938; s. Edward Eugene and Phyllis Ione (Johnson) I.; m. Carolyn Tanner, Aug. 6, 1960; children: Stephen T., Jessica L., Thomas A., Emily A. B.A. in History, Stanford U., 1960; J.D., U. Mich., 1964; D.Phil in Law, Oxford (Eng.) U., 1973. Law clk. to Asso. Justice U.S. Supreme Ct. Byron R. White, 1967; cons. Office Fgn. Direct Investments, Dept. Commerce, 1967-68; spl. rep. sec. def. 7th session 3d UN Conf. Law of Sea; mem. Caplin & Drysdale, chartered, Washington, 1968-85; partner Caplin & Drysdale, 1973-85; prof. law U. Mich. Law Sch., Ann Arbor, 1985—; adj. prof. Georgetown U. Law Center, 1975-85; regent Am. Coll. Tax Counsel; mem. IRS Commr.'s Advisory Group; bd. dirs., vice chmn. Vols. Tech. Assistance. Contbr. articles to legal jours. Mem. Am. Law Inst., ABA, D.C. Bar Assn., Council on Fgn. Relations. Democrat. Episcopalian. Home: 1075 Cedar Bend Dr Ann Arbor MI 48105 Office: U Mich Law Sch Hutchins Hall Ann Arbor MI 48109-1215

IRONS, JEREMY JOHN, actor; b. Cowes, Eng., Sept. 19, 1948; s. Paul Dugan and Barbara Anne (Sharpe) I.; m. Sinead Moira Cusack, Mar. 28, 1978; children: Samuel James, Maximilian Paul. Actor: (stage appearances) including John the Baptist in Godspell, 1973, Mick in The Caretaker, 1974, Petrucio in The Taming of the Shrew, 1975, Harry Thunder in Wild Oats, Royal Shakespeare Co., 1976-77, 86, James Jameson in Rear Column, 1978, The Real Thing, 1984 (Tony award 1984), title role in Richard II, Leontes in Winter's Tale, title role in The Rover, Royal Shakespeare Acad., Stratford-Upon-Avon, Eng., 1986-87, (films) Nijinsky, 1979, The French Lieutenant's Woman, 1980-81, Betrayal, 1982, Moonlighting, 1982, The Wild Duck, 1983, Swann in Love, 1983, The Mission, 1985, Chorus of Disapproval, 1988, Dead Ringers, 1988; (TV appearances) Alex Hepburn in The Captian's Doll, 1982, Charles Ryder in Brideshead Revisited, 1980-81. Address: Hutton Mgmt, 200 Fulham Rd, London England SW10 9PN *

IRUSTA MENDEZ, OSWALDO, management professional; b. La Paz, Bolivia, May 8, 1937; s. Damian and Cinthya (Mendez) I.; m. Mercedes Diaz, May 24, 1957; children: Sylvia, Oswaldo, Miguel. B., San Calixto U., 1955. Sales mgr. Nestle Co., La Paz, 1957-68, Grace and Co., La Paz, 1969-74; gen. mgr. Casa Grace SAm., La Paz, 1975-79, mng. dir., 1980—; bd. dirs. Fabrica Nacional de Vidrios, Baco de la Union. Mem. Soc. Bolivian Cement (v.p.), Andies Confederated C. of C.'s (past pres., permanent cons.), Bolivian C. of C. (dir. 1974, 1st v.p. 1982-84, pres. 1985-87). Clubs: La Paz, Internat. Home: 2005 20 de Octubre Ave No 6, La Paz Bolivia Office: Casa Grace SA, Mercado 1085, No 4784, La Paz Bolivia

IRVINE, JOHN ALEXANDER, lawyer; b. Sault Ste. Marie, Ont. Can., Aug. 10, 1947; s. Alexander and Ruth Catherine (Woolrich) I.; m. Jacquelyn Louise Church, June 13, 1970 (div. 1980); children: John Alexander, Allison Brooks; m. Lynda Kaye Myska Jenkins, May 24, 1981; 1 child, James Woolrich. BS, Auburn U., 1969; JD, Memphis State U., 1972. Bar: Tenn. 1972, Ohio 1982, Tex. 1985. Law clk. U.S. Dist. Ct. (we. dist.) Tenn., 1972-73; asst. dist. atty. gen. 15th Jud. Cir. Tenn., 1973-78; assoc. Glankler, Brown, Gilliland, Chase, Robinson and Raines, Memphis, 1978-81; asst. gen. counsel Mead Corp., Dayton, Ohio, 1981-84; ptnr. Porter & Clements, Houston, 1984-87, prin. Boyer, Norton & Blair, 1987—. Bd. dirs. Make-A-Wish Found. Tex. Gulf Coast, 1985-86. Fellow Tex. Bar Found.; mem. ABA, Tex. Bar Assn., Tenn. Bar Assn., Memphis and Shelby County Bar Assn., Ohio Bar Assn., Dayton Bar Assn., Houston Bar Assn., Memphis State U. Law Sch. Alumnae Assn. (pres. 1975-76, 77-78), U.S. C. of C. (council on antitrust policy 1983—). Republican. Presbyterian. Clubs: Racquet (Memphis); Phoenix (bd. dirs. 1977-78), Houston Met. Racquet, Heritage, Briar, Forum, Texas. Avocations: sports, travel, reading, painting. Office: Boyer Norton & Blair 5 Post Oak Park Houston TX 77027

IRVINE, REED JOHN, media critic, corporation executive; b. Salt Lake City, Sept. 29, 1922; s. William John and Edna Jessup (May) I.; m. Kay Araki, Aug. 14, 1948; 1 son, Donald. A.B., U. Utah, 1942; postgrad., U. Colo., 1943-44, U. Wash., 1949; B.Litt., Oxford U., Eng., 1951. With Gen. Hdqrs. of Allied Occupation of Japan, Tokyo, 1946-48; economist bd. govs. Fed. Res. System, Washington, 1951-63, adviser internat. fin., 1963-77; chmn. bd. Accuracy in Media, Inc., Washington, 1971—; editor AIM Report; syndicated columnist; radio commentator; chmn. Accuracy in Academia, 1985—. Author: Media Mischief and Misdeeds, 1984. Dir. Council Def. of Freedom, Washington, 1970—. Served with USNR, 1942-43, USMC, 1943-46, PTO; to capt. USMCR, 1944-46. Recipient George Washington medal Freedom Found., 1980, Ethics in Journalism award World Media Assn., 1987. Mem. Phi Beta Kappa. Mormon. Club: Nat. Press (Washington). Office: 1275 K St NW Washington DC 20005

IRVINE, ROBIN ELIOT, retired geriatrician, consultant; b. Godalming, Surrey, Eng., Sept. 27, 1920; s. Andrew Leicester and Eleanor Mildred (Lloyd) I.; m. Florence Margaret Walter, July 30, 1947; children—Anne Catharine, Deborah Mary, Andrew Geoffrey, Patricia Margaret, Mary Elizabeth, William Francis, Peter John. M.B., Cambridge U., Eng., 1944, M.A., 1952, M.D., 1955. Registrar, Guys Hosp., London, 1945-52; sr. registrar Royal Victoria Infirmary, Newcastle-on-Tyne, Eng., 1956; asst. physician Sunderland Geriatric Unit, 1956-58; cons. physician Dept. Medicine for Elderly, Hastings, Eng., 1958-85; mem. adv. council Ctr. for Policy on Aging, London, 1964-68; cons. Dept. Health and Social Services, London, 1983-86. Author: (with others), The Older Patient, 1967, 4th edit., 1986. Contbr. chpts. to textbooks. Mem. Hastings Dist. Health Authority, 1982-86, research com. Royal Hosp. and Home for Incurables, London, 1983—. Served to capt. Royal Army M.C., 1945-47. Recipient 1066 award Borough of Hastings, 1978; decorated comdr. Order Brit. Empire. Fellow Royal Coll. Physicians (geriatric, disability, internal medicine coms.); mem. Brit. Geriatrics Soc. (pres. 1981-84), Brit. Med. Assn., Brit. Soc. for Research on Ageing, Med. Disability Soc. Conservative. Roman Catholic. Club: Royal Soc. Medicine (London). Lodge: Catenian Assn. avocations: golf; opera. Home: Dolphin House, Foulon Rd, Saint Peter Port Guernsey, Channel Islands

IRWIN, JAMES BENSON, former astronaut, foundation executive, aeronautical engineer; b. Pitts., Mar. 17, 1930; s. James and Elsie (Strebel) I.; m. Mary Ellen Monroe, Sept. 4, 1959; children: Joy Carmel, Jill Cherie, James Benson, Jan Caron, Joe Chau. B.S., U.S. Naval Acad., 1951; M.S. in Aero. Engring, U. Mich., 1957, D. Astronautical Sci., 1971; D.Sc., William Jewell Coll., 1971, Samford U., 1972. Commd. 2d lt. USAF, 1951, advanced through grades to col., 1971; project officer Wright Patterson AFB, 1957-60; test dir. (ASG-18/AIM-47 armament system), Edwards AFB, Calif., 1961-63; test pilot (F-12 Test Force), Edwards AFB, 1963-65; br. chief (Advanced Systems Hdqrs. Air Def. Command), Colorado Springs, Colo., 1965-66; astronaut NASA, 1966-72. Author: To Rule the Night, 1973, rev. edit., 1982, More Than Earthlings, 1983, More Than an Ark on Ararat, 1985. Founder, pres. evang. found. High Flight, Colorado Springs, Colo., 1972. Decorated NASA Distinguished Service Medal, D.S.M. USAF, City N.Y. Gold Medal, UN Peace medal, City Chgo. Gold medal; order Leopold Belgium; recipient David C. Schilling trophy, 1971, Kitty Hawk meml. award, 1971, Haley Astronautics award AIAA, 1972, John F. Kennedy trophy Arnold Air Soc., 1972, Freedoms Found. Washington medal, 1976, Nat. Citizenship award Mil. Chaplains Assn., 1978, others. Mem. Air Force Assn., Soc. Exptl. Test Pilots. Baptist. Address: High Flight PO Box 1387 202 E Cheyenne Mountain Blvd Colorado Springs CO 80901 *

IRWIN, MICHAEL HENRY KNOX, United Nations official, physician; b. London, June 5, 1931; s. William Knox and Edith Isabel Mary (Collins) I.; m. Miriam Elizabeth Naumann, Nov. 1, 1958 (div. Nov. 1982); children—Christina Susan, Pamela Elizabeth, Diana Jennifer; m. 2d, Frederica Todd Harlow, Apr. 9, 1983. M.B.B.S., St. Bartholomew's Hosp. Med. Coll., London, 1955; M.P.H., Columbia U., 1960. Intern and resident Prince of Wales Hosp., London, 1955-56; med. officer UN, N.Y.C., 1957-61, dep. resident rep. UN Devel. Program, Pakistan, 1961-63; sr. med. officer UN, N.Y.C., 1963-69, med. dir., N.Y.C., 1969-73, dir. div. personnel UN Devel. Program, 1973-76; rep. UNICEF, Bangladesh, 1977-80, sr. adviser UNICEF, N.Y.C., 1980-82, med. dir. UN, UNICEF, UN Devel. Program, N.Y.C., 1982—; sr. cons. Internat. Yr. of Disabled Persons, 1981; cons. Am. Assn. Blood Banks, 1984—. Author: Check-Ups: Safeguarding Your Health, 1961; Overweight: A Problem for Millions, 1964; Travelling Without Tears, 1964; Viruses, Colds and Flu, 1966; Blood: New Uses for Saving Lives, 1967; What Do We Know About Allergies?, 1972; Aspirin: Current Knowledge About an Old Medication, 1983; Can We Survive Nuclear War?, 1984; Nuclear Energy: Good or Bad?, 1984; The Cocaine Epidemic, 1985. Pres. Assistance for Blind Children Internat., 1978-85; mem. exec. bd. Internat. Agy. for Prevention Blindness, 1979-83. Recipient Officer Cross Internat. Fedn. Blood Donor Orgns., 1984. Milbank Meml. Fund fellow, 1959. Fellow Royal Soc. Medicine. Home: 1 W 89th St New York NY 10024 Office: UN New York NY 10017

IRWIN, PETER JOHN, orthopaedic surgeon; b. East St. Louis, Ill., July 7, 1934; s. Peter and Anne (Sokalski) Iwasyszyn; m. Kathryn Swanson, June 15, 1960; children: Kathryn Linda, Mary Elizabeth, Amy Marie, Kenneth John, James Patrick. BS in Biology, St. Louis U., 1955, MD, 1959. Diplomate Am. Bd. Orthopaedic Surgery. Intern, Creighton Meml. St. Joseph Hosp., Omaha, 1959-60; resident orthopaedic surgery U. Ark. Med. Ctr., 1961-65, teaching staff, 1965—; practice medicine specializing in orthopaedic surgery, Fort Smith, Ark., 1965—; mem. staff St. Edward Mercy Med. Ctr., 1965—; mem. staff Sparks Regional Med. Ctr., 1965—, chief of staff, 1979, bd. dirs., 1980-87. Served to lt. comdr. M.C., USN, 1966-68. Fellow Am. Acad. Orthopaedic Surgeons (councillor 1983—), ACS; mem. AMA, So. Med. Assn., Sebastian County Med. Soc., Ark. Orthopaedic Assn. (pres. 1976-77), Mid-Am. Orthopaedic Assn. (founding mem.), Mid-Central States Orthopaedic Soc. (pres. 1979-80), So. Orthopaedic Assn., Am. Orthopaedic Soc. for Sports Medicine, Am. Soc. Sports Medicine, Ark. Hand Club. Office: 1500 Dodson Ave Fort Smith AR 72901

IRWIN, R. ROBERT, lawyer; b. Denver, July 27, 1933; s. Royal Robert and Mildred Mary (Wilson) I.; m. Sue Ann Scott, Dec. 16, 1956; children—Lori, Stacy, Kristi, Amy. Student U. Colo., 1951-54, B.S.L., U. Denver, 1955, LL.B., 1957. Bar: Colo. 1957, Wyo. 1967. Asst. atty. gen. State of Colo., 1958-66; asst. div. atty. Mobil Oil Corp., Casper, Wyo. 1966-70; prin. atty. No. Natural Gas Co., Omaha 1970-72; sr. atty. Coastal Oil & Gas Corp., Denver 1972-83, asst. sec. 1972-83; ptnr. Baker & Hostetler, 1983-87; pvt. practice 1987—. Mem. ABA, Colo. Bar Assn., State Bar Wyo., Arapahoe County Bar Assn., Rocky Mountain Oil and Gas Assn. Republican. Clubs: Los Verdes Golf, Petroleum, Denver Law (Denver). Office: 9960 E Chenango Ave Englewood CO 80111

IRWIN, RICHARD DORSEY, publisher; b. St. Joseph, Mo., Nov. 2, 1905; s. William Herbert and Ida Ferrell (Dorsey) I.; m. Anne Marie Thompson, Feb. 2, 1927; children: Jacqueline Marie Irwin Pipher, Richard Dorsey, Jr. Student, U. Ill., 1924-27; LL.D. (hon.), Ball State U., 1970. Mgr. coll. dept. A.W. Shaw Co., 1928, McGraw-Hill Book Co., 1928-32; hon. chmn., founder Richard D. Irwin, Inc., Homewood, Ill., 1933—; hon. chmn. Dorsey Press, Learning Systems Co., Bus. Publs., Inc., Irwin-Dorsey Internat., Dow Jones-Irwin, Inc.; dir. emeritus 1st Nat. Bank of Harvey; cons. O.P.A., 1943. Mem. Dist. 161 Sch. Bd., Flossmoor, Ill., 1948-54; chmn. bd. Irwin Family Found.; trustee U. Ill. Found., Glenwood Sch. for Boys. Richard D. Irwin Grad. Sch. Mgmt. of Am. Coll., Bryn Mawr, Pa. named for him. Mem. Am. Assn. Collegiate Schs. Bus., Am. Acctg. Assn., Am., Midwest, So. econ. assns., Am. Mktg. Assn., Midwest Bus. Adminstrn. Assn., Am. Bus. Law Assn., Profl. Golfers Assn. (nat. adv. com.), Alpha Kappa Psi, Omicron Delta Epsilon, Beta Gamma Sigma. Clubs: Olympia Fields (Ill.) Country, Flossmoor Country, Chicago Athletic Assn. Home: 1230 Braeburn Rd Flossmoor IL 60422 Office: 1910 Ridge Rd Homewood IL 60430

IRWIN, ROBERT JAMES ARMSTRONG, JR., investment company executive; b. Buffalo, June 27, 1927; s. Robert J.A. and Dorothy (McLean) I.; m. Donna Henwood, Sept. 10, 1966; children: William Baird, Elaine Mitchell, Elizabeth Flora, Robert J.A. IV, Ronald Henwood, Derrick Millet. B.A., Colgate U., 1949; postgrad., U. Buffalo, 1949-50, Babson Inst. Finance, Wellesley, Mass., 1952-53. Exec. trainee Mfrs. & Traders Trust Co., Buffalo, 1950-52; registered rep. Doolittle & Co., Buffalo, 1953-58; with Marine Trust Co. Western N.Y., Buffalo, 1958-66; investment mgmt. officer Marine Trust Co. Western N.Y., 1959-61, v.p. charge investment mgmt. dept., 1961-66; v.p. Marine Midland Banks, Inc., N.Y.C., 1966-69; sr. v.p. Marine Midland Banks, Inc., 1969-71; exec. v.p. Dreyfus-Marine Midland Mgmt. Corp., 1970-72; sr. exec. v.p. Niagara Share Corp., Buffalo, 1972-74; pres. Niagara Share Corp., 1974—, pres., chief exec. officer, 1988—, also bd. dirs.; mem. N.Y. State Comptroller's investment adv. com. for N.Y. State Common Retirement Fund, 1979—; bd. dirs. Kleinwort Benson Investment

Strategies, ASA Ltd.; mem. dirs. adv. council Mfrs. & Traders Trust Co., First Empire State Corp.; bd. govs. Investment Co. Inst.; chmn. of closed end Investment Co. div. of Investment Co. Inst. Bd. dirs. Boys Club Buffalo, Inc., 1953—, v.p., 1964-65; bd. dirs. Buffalo Med. Found., 1975—, Am. Scottish Found.; trustee Baird Found., 1965—, Old Ft. Niagara Assn., Ridley Coll. Found., James H. Cummings Found., 1978—, St. Barnabas Coll. Found. Inc., The Grosvenor Soc.; adv. bd. Dent Neurol. Inst., Buffalo. Clubs: Buffalo (Buffalo), Saturn (Buffalo), Mid Day (Buffalo), Canoe (Buffalo); Royal Canadian Yacht (Toronto); University (N.Y.C.). Home: 101 Meadow Rd Buffalo NY 14216 Office: Niagara Share Corp 344 Delaware Ave Buffalo NY 14202

IRZYK, ALBIN FELIX, army officer; b. Salem, Mass., Jan. 2, 1917; s. Felix and Sophia (Mroczka) I.; A.B., U. Mass., 1940; M.A., Am. U., 1966; grad. Armor Sch., 1949, Command and Gen. Staff Coll., 1950, Nat. War Coll., 1958; m. Laura Evelyn Abbott, May 14, 1946; children—Elizabeth Jane (Mrs. Mize), Albin Felix, Laura Evelyn (Mrs. Osman). Commd. 2d lt. U.S. Army, 1940, advanced through grades to brig. gen., 1963; assigned 3d U.S. Cav., 1940-42; tank battalion comdr., chief staff 4th Armored Div., Europe, 1942-45; mem. staff, faculty Armor Sch., Ft. Knox, Ky., 1947-49, 51-54; staff officer to comdr.-in-chief Pacific, Hawaii, 1954-57; chief Office Internat. Affairs, Dept. Army Gen. Staff, 1958-61; regtl. comdr. 14th Armored Cav., Fulda, Germany, 1961-62; asst chief staff plans, operations and tng. Hdqrs. 7th U.S. Army, Stuttgart, Germany, also Allied Land Forces, Central Europe, Fontainebleau, France, 1962-65; asst. comdt. U.S. Army Armor Sch., Ft. Knox, 1965-67; comdg. gen. U.S. Army Hdqrs. Area Command, Saigon, Vietnam, 1967-68; asst. div. comdr. 4th Inf. Div., Vietnam, 1968-69; comdg. gen., Ft. Devens, Mass., 1970-71. Decorated D.S.C., D.S.M., Silver Star with oak leaf cluster, Legion of Merit with 2 oak leaf clusters, Purple Heart with oak leaf cluster, Air medal with 10 oak leaf clusters; Croix de Guerre and Fourragere (France); Czech War Cross; Chuong My medal (Korea); recipient silver anniversary All American award Sports Illus. mag., 1964, Sir Thomas More award Nat. Council Cath. Men, 1965. Mem. 4th Armored Div. Assn. (pres. 1948-49), European Council Cath. Men (pres. 1964-65), Legion of Valor. Lodge: Rotary. Contbr. articles to profl. jours. Home: 2527 S Flagler Dr West Palm Beach FL 33401

ISAAC, RHYS LLYWELYN, historian, educator; b. Cape Town, Republic South Africa, Nov. 20, 1937; arrived in Australia, 1963; s. William Edwyn and Frances Margaret (Leighton) I.; m. Colleen Margaret Malherbe, Dec. 29, 1962; children: Megan Frances, Lyned Vivienne. BA, U. Cape Town, 1958; MA, U. Oxford, Eng., 1965; BA, Oxon U., 1962. Lectr. history U. Melbourne, Victoria, Australia, 1963-70; sr. lectr. La Trobe U., Melbourne, 1970-78, reader, 1978-85, prof., 1986—; vis. assoc. prof. Johns Hopkins U., Balt., 1975. Author: The Transformation of Virginia, 1740-1790, 1982. Recipient Pulitzer prize for history, 1983; Rhodes scholar Cape Province, 1959. Fellow Acad. Soc. Scis. Australia. Home: 20 Locksley Rd, Ivanhoe 3079, Australia Office: La Trobe U, Bundoora 3083, Australia

ISAAC, WALTER, psychologist, educator; b. Cleve., June 13, 1927; s. Walter Roy and Irene (Pillars) I.; m. Dorothy Jane Emerson, Oct. 14, 1949; children: Susan Irene, Walter Lon. B.S., Western Res. U., 1949; M.A., Ohio State U., 1950, Ph.D., 1953. Predoctoral fellow Sch. Aviation Medicine, U.S. Air Force, Austin, Tex., 1953; research instr. Sch. Medicine U. Wash., Seattle, 1954-56; asst. research psychologist Sch. Medicine UCLA, 1956-57; asst. prof. psychology Emory U., Atlanta, 1957-60; assoc. prof. Emory U., 1960-65, prof., 1965-68; prof. physiol. psychology U. Ga., Athens, 1968—. Served with USNR, 1945-46. Fellow AAAS; mem. Psychonomic Soc., So. Soc. for Philosophy and Psychology, Southeastern Psychol. Assn., Am. Assn. Lab. Animal Sci., Soc. Behavioral Medicine, Nat. Acad. Neuropsychologists, Internat. Neuropsychol. Soc. Home: 180 Chinquapin Way Athens GA 30605 Office: U Georgia Dept Psychology Athens GA 30602

ISAACS, HELEN COOLIDGE ADAMS (MRS. KENNETH L. ISAACS), artist; b. N.Y.C., Jan. 17, 1917; d. Thomas Safford and Martha (Montgomery) Adams; student Miss Hewett's classes, N.Y.C., Miss Porter's Sch., Farmington, Conn., Fontainbleau (France) Sch. Art and Music, 1935, Art Students League, 1936; m. Kenneth L. Isaacs, Mar. 10, 1949; children—Kenneth Coolidge, Anne Isaacs Merwin. Agt., Child's Gallery, Boston; one-woman shows at Child's Gallery, 3 times exhibited in group shows Allied Artists, N.Y., Boston Arts Festival; portraits of various prominent persons; murals in various public bldgs., Boston, Rochester, N.Y., Pittsfield, Mass., Daytona, Fla.; represented in painting and drawing collections Fogg Mus., Cambridge, Mass. Mem. Colonial Dames Am. Clubs: Colony (N.Y.C.); Chilton (Boston). Home: 68 Beacon St Boston MA 02108

ISAACS, KENNETH L., banker; b. Scranton, Pa., June 18, 1904; s. Albert George and Anna Carpenter (Richards) I.; m. Helen Coolidge Adams, Mar. 10, 1949; children: Kenneth C.A., Anne Carpenter Richards Merwin. M.E., Lehigh U., 1925, LL.D., 1965; M.B.A., Harvard U., 1927. Buying dept. Nat. City Co., 1927-30; pvt. investment work 1930-32; asst. to comptroller Cornell U. (specializing on endowment fund investments), 1932-36; with Mass. Investors Trust, 1936-69; formerly chmn., mem. investment mgmt. com. Mass. Investors Trust, Mass. Investors Growth Stock Fund, Inc.; former partner Mass. Financial Services; hon. trustee Suffolk-Franklin Savs. Bank; hon. dir. So. Pacific Co., Phelps Dodge Corp., Gen. Pub. Utilities Corp. Hon. trustee Lehigh U. Republican. Episcopalian. Clubs: Somerset (Boston); Brook (N.Y.C.), Harvard (N.Y.C.), Knickerbocker (N.Y.C.). Home: 68 Beacon St Boston MA 02108 Office: 200 Berkeley St Boston MA 02116

ISAACS, KENNETH S(IDNEY), psychoanalyst, educator; b. Mpls., Apr. 7, 1920; s. Mark William and Sophia (Rai) I.; m. Ruth Elizabeth Johnson, Feb. 21, 1951 (dec. 1967); m. Adele Rella Brodroghy, May 17, 1969; children—Jonathan, James; stepchildren—John, Curtis, Peter and Edward Meissner. B.A., U. Minn., 1944; Ph.D., U. Chgo., 1956; postgrad., Inst. Psychoanalysis, 1957-63. Intern Worcester State Hosp., Mass., 1947-48; trainee VA Mental Hygiene Clinic, Chgo., 1948-50; chief psychologist outpatient clinic system Ill. Dept. Pub. Welfare, 1949-56; research assoc., assoc. prof. U. Ill. Med. Sch., Chgo., 1956-63; practice psychoanalysis Evanston, Ill., 1960—; supr. psychiat. residency program Evanston Hosp., Northwestern U., 1972-81, Northwestern Meml. Hosp.; pres. Chgo. Ctr. Psychoanalytic Psychology, 1984-87; cons. to schs., hosps., clinics, pvt. practitioners and industry; pres. Kenisa Drilling Co., Kenisa Securities Co., Kenisa Oil Co. Author syndicated newspaper column A Psychologist's Notebook; contbr. articles to profl. publs. Served with AUS, 1943-45, ETO. Mem. Am. Psychol. Assn. (bd. dirs. div. psychoanalysis), AAAS, Chgo. Psychoanalytic Soc., Am. Bd. Psychoanalysis (sec. bd. dirs.), N.Y. Acad. Sci., Sigma Xi.

ISAACS, ROBERT WOLFE, structural engineer; b. Clayton, N.Mex., Sept. 22, 1931; s. Robert Phillip and Eva Estella (Freeman) I.; student So. Meth. U., 1949-50, Amarillo Jr. Coll., Tex. Tech U.; B.S. in Civil Engring., UCLA, 1959; m. Ruth Marie Peffley, Jan. 12, 1951; children—Robert Philip, Jeannette Lucille Isaacs Darlington, Charlotte Ruth Isaacs Frye, Rebecca Grace Isaacs Brund. Structural engr. N.Am. Aviation, Rockwell Internat., Los Angeles, 1959—. Asst. scoutmaster, com. mem., fund raiser, Order of Arrow Gt. Western council Boy Scouts Am., 1964—; patron Los Angeles County Mus. Art; active Rep. Party. Served with U.S. Army, 1955. Lic. profl. engr., Tex. Recipient Pride award N.Am Aviation Orgn., 1984; named Pacemaker of Scouting, 1966. Mem. ASCE, Nat. Rifle Assn (life), Calif. Rifle and Pistol Assn. (life), Nat. Muzzleloading Rifle Assn. (endowment life, So. Calif. rep. 1976—), Western States Muzzleloading Rifle Assn. (life, charter, sportsman award 1983), Calif. Muzzleloading Rifle Assn., Colo. State Muzzleloading Rifle Assn., Bakersfield (Calif.) Muzzleloaders, Nat. Assn. Primitive Riflemen, High Desert Muzzleloaders, Santa Fe Trail Rendezvous Assn. (Bourgeous 1988), Piute Mountain Men, Sante Fe Trail Gun, Rockwell Rod and Gun, Burbank Muzzle Loader. Lodge: Masons. Condr. research design and devel. press diffusion bonding of titanium, aircraft design and structure; underwing and overwing inflatable seals (structure liaison B-1B, final mate, asst. checkout B-18). Home: 1028 H-1 Lancaster CA 93534 Office: AF Plant 42 Site 9 Palmdale CA 93550 also: NAm Aircraft Ops Palmdale Facility 2825 E Ave P Palmdale CA 93550

ISAACSON, SIDNEY, pediatrician; b. Bklyn., Mar. 1, 1928; s. Abraham and Florence (Soloff) I.; B.A., N.Y. U., 1949; M.D., Berne U., 1955; m. Harriet Kempler, Dec. 21, 1952; children—Arlene Isaacson Werner, Marsha Lois. Intern Queen's Hosp. Center, 1955-56, resident in pediatrics, 1956, sr. resident, chief pediatrics, 1957-58; practice medicine specializing in pediatrics, Wantagh, N.Y., 1958—; dir. pediatrics Brunswick Gen. Hosp., Amityville, N.Y., 1972-81; clin. asst. prof. pediatrics Cornell Med. Sch., 1973—; attending North Shore Univ. Hosp., Manhasset, N.Y., 1973—; pres. Wantagh Pediatric Assos., P.C., 1971—. Served with M.C., AUS, 1946-47. Diplomate Am. Bd. Pediatrics. Fellow Am. Acad. Pediatricis; mem. AMA, N.Y. State, Nassau County med. socs., Nassau Pediatric Soc. Home and Office: 2975 Jerusalem Ave Wantagh NY 11793

ISABELLE, DIDIER BERNARD, physics educator; b. Paris, Aug. 9, 1934; s. Bernard Etienne and Jacqueline (Beurdeley) I.; m. Rosine Peycelon, July 31, 1958; children—Nathalie, Valerie. Licence es Sciences, Universite de Paris, 1957, Docteur es Sciences, 1961. Fellow, Com. Energie Atomique, France, 1957-61; charge de Recherches Centre National de la Recherche Scientifique, France, 1961-64, maitre de recherches, Orsay, France, 1964-65; prof. physics Universite Clermont Ferrand, France, 1965-86; dir. CERI CNRS, Orleans, France, 1986—; cons. Filmtec S.A., Cournon, France, 1970—. Author: Cours de Physique, 1977; co-author: Traite de Medecine Nucleaire, 1976. Editor: La Recherche en Physique Nucleaire, 1983; co-editor: La Recherche, 1968—. Mem. Soc. Francaise de Physique (nat. com. 1972-74), Soc. Italiana de Fisica, Am. Phys. Soc., N.Y. Acad. Sci. Club: Clermont U. (gen. sec. 1972-84, v.p. 1984—), Yacht Saint Martin (gen. sec. 1978-83). Home: 3E Ave de la Recherche, Scientifique, 45071 Orleans Cedex 2 France Office: CERI CNRS, 3A rue de la Ferollerie, 45071 Orleans Cedex 2 France

ISACOFF, STUART MICHAEL, magazine editor; b. Bklyn., May 20, 1949; s. David and Hannah (Zwirn) I.; m. Adrienne Lisa Kalfus, Jan. 23, 1972; children: Nora Miriam, Rachel Beth. B.A., Bklyn. Coll., 1971, M.A., 1973. Instr., William Paterson Coll., Wayne, N.J., 1977-80; cons. Oxford U. Press, 1978-80; free-lance editor, author, composer, pianist, 1974—; founding editor Keyboard Classics Mag., Katonah, N.Y., 1981—; dir. product devel. Ekay Music, Inc., Katonah, 1982—; dir. arts program Inst. for the New Age, 1980-82; consulting editor Jazz and Keybd. Workshop, Katonah, N.Y., 1986—; composer, cons. Boosey & Hawkes. Author: Gregorian Chants for Recorder, 1975, Dr. Johnson's Piano Method, 1976; contbr.: American Music Before 1865, 1976; editor/composer: From Rags to Jazz, 1976, Easy American Piano Classics, 1978; editor: Miles Davis, 1978, Charlie Parker, 1978, Thelonious Monk, 1978; composer: Skill Builders in 6 vols., 1979, Twelve Jazz Preludes, 1980; author/editor: Jazz Solos for Trumpet, 1984, Jazz Solos for Tenor Sax, 1984, Jazz Solos for Alto Sax, 1984, others; contbr. New Grove Dictionary of Music in the United States, 1984, N.Y. Times. Recipient Deems Taylor award ASCAP, 1987. Mem. Music Critics Assn., Am. Liszt Soc. Martha Baird Rockefeller grantee, 1975-76. Jewish. Office: Keyboard Classics Mag 223 Katonah Ave Katonah NY 10536

ISALY, SHARON MARTIN, interior designer, contractor; b. Columbus, Ohio, July 31, 1946; d. John W. and Patricia M. Martin; student in edn. No. Ariz. U., 1964-66; m. Charles W. Isaly, Nov. 5, 1966; children—Jeffrey Scott, Bradley William. Interior designer John Martin Constrn., Phoenix, 1967-72; interior designer Martin Devel. Co., Missoula, Mont., 1972-79; v.p., ptnr. Security-West Devel. Co., Missoula, 1979-82; dir.; pres., owner SMI Interiors, Missoula; Prospect Assos./Devel. Co., Missoula, 1979-82; v.p. Martin Constrn. Co., Phoenix and San Antonio, 1983-86. Vice-pres. C.W. Isaly Corp., Mesa, Ariz., 1983—, Missoula Civic Symphony, 1977-78; bd. dirs. Missoula Children's Theatre, 1977-78. Mem. Am. Soc. Interior Designers, LWV, Delta Delta Delta. Republican. Methodist. Home: 615 W Lawrence Rd Phoenix AZ 85013 Office: 535 S Dobson Rd Mesa AZ 85202

ISAMU, BABA, construction company executive; b. Oita, Japan, June 13, 1923; s. Gunroku and Kimiko Baba; m. Fumiko Takita, Nov. 3, 1948; children: Shiro, Kyoko Kojima. B in Engring., Osaka (Japan) U., 1945. Cert. architect, cons. engr., value specialist. Mgr. research and devel. Fujita Corp., Tokyo, 1965-75, dir., 1975-85, exec. v.p., 1985—. Author: The Method of Value Engineering in th Construction Industry, 1975, Basics of Construction Value Engineering, 1983, Application of Construction Value Engineering, 1983, Illustration of the Method of Keeping Costs Down in the Construction Industry, 1984. Recipient Presdl. citation Soc. Am. Value Engrs., 1981, Soc. award Associated Gen. Contractors of Japan, 1985. Mem. Internat. Council Bldg. Research, Studies and Documentation, Soc. Japanese Value Engrs. (councilor, Best Paper prize 1973, Promotional Achievment award 1984), Soc. Korean Value Engrs. (adviser), Archtl. Inst. Japan (trustee), Japan Soc. Civil Engrs., Japanese Cons. Engrs. Assn. Club: Tokyo Birdie. Lodge: Rotary. Home: 2-29-21 Irima-cho, Chofu-shi, Tokyo 182, Japan Office: Fujita Corp, 4-6-15 Sendagaya, Shibuya-ku, Tokyo 151, Japan

ISBELL, HAROLD M(AX), writer, investor; b. Maquoketa, Iowa, Sept. 20, 1936; s. H. Max and Marcella E. I.; B.A. cum laude (scholar), Loras Coll., 1959; M.A. (fellow), U. Notre Dame, 1962; grad. U. Mich. Grad. Sch. Bank Mgmt., 1982; m. Mary Carolyn Cosgriff, June 15, 1963; children—Walter Harold, Susan Elizabeth, David Harold, Alice Kathleen. Instr., U. Notre Dame, South Bend, Ind., 1963-64; assoc. prof. St. Mary's Coll., 1969-72; asst. prof. San Francisco Coll. for Women, 1964-69; with Continental Bank & Trust Co., Salt Lake City, 1972-83, v.p., 1977-83, comml. credit officer, 1978-83, also dir. Trustee Judge Meml. Cath. High Sch., Salt Lake City, 1977-84; mem. Utah Council for Handicapped and Developmentally Disabled Persons, 1980-81; bd. dirs. Ballet West, 1983—; founder Cath. Found. Utah, pres. 1984-86, trustee, 1984—; active ACLU, Common Cause. Mem. MLA, Mediaeval Acad. Am. Democrat. Roman Catholic. Club: Alta. Editor and translator: The Last Poets of Imperial Rome, 1971; contbr. to publs. in field of classical Latin lit. and contemporary Am. Lit.

ISBELL, ROBERT, business consultant; b. Anderson, S.C., Nov. 26, 1923; s. Henry Pope and Aileen Annette (Dixon) I.; m. Frances Griffin, Apr. 19, 1953; children: Lyn, Andrea, Eden. A.B. in Journalism, U. S.C., 1948; grad., Sch. Financial Pub. Relations, Northwestern U., 1965, Bank Marketing Grad. Sch., U. Wis., 1973. News editor Elkin (N.C.) Tribune, 1948-50; mng. editor Florence (S.C.) Morning News, 1950-53; pub. relations counsel Tobias & Co., Charleston, S.C., 1954-62; v.p. Bankers Trust of S.C., Columbia, 1963-68, sr. v.p., 1972-76, exec. v.p., 1976-86; pres. Robert Isbell & Co., 1986—; v.p., dir. Phoenix Systems Internat., 1986—; sr. v.p., adminstr. marketing S.C. Nat. Bank, Columbia, 1969-71; mem. faculty Sch. Banking of South, La. State U., summers, 1971-72. Pres. Carolina Carillon, 1968. Served with AUS, 1943-46, PTO. Recipient Silver medal Am. Advt. Fedn., 1966, Laurel award J.B. White Stores, 1969. Mem. Am. Advt. Fedn. (S.C. gov. 1966-67), Pub. Relations Soc. Am. (dir. S.C. chpt. 1969-72, pres. 1972). Episcopalian. Clubs: Summit (Columbia); Beech Mountain (Banner Elk, N.C.). Home: 81 Ridge Lake Dr Columbia SC 29209 Office: 1401 Main St PO Box 11609 Columbia SC 29211

ISCAN, MEHMET YASAR, anthropologist; b. Maras, Turkey, Feb. 17, 1943; came to U.S., 1968; s. Mustafa and Ayse (Yürürdurmaz) I.; m. Walda Mae Engelbrecht, Feb. 14, 1976; 1 dau., Meryem Ayse. BA, U. Ankara (Turkey), 1968; MA, Cornell U., 1973, PhD, 1976. Diplomate Am. Bd. Forensic Anthropology. Asst. prof. anthropology Fla. Atlantic U., Boca Raton, 1977-84, assoc. prof., 1984-86, prof., 1986—; cons. Broward County Med. Examiner's Office, Ft. Lauderdale, Fla., 1981—; chmn. anthrop. scis. Fla. Acad. Sci., 1981-82. Ales Hrdlicka fellow, 1968-69; NSF grantee Cornell Energy Project, 1973-75, 68-69, 86, Smithsonian Inst. grantee, Fla. Atlantic U., 1978—, Deutsche Forschungsgemeinschaft, 1988. Mem. Am. Assn. Phys. Anthropologists, Am. Anthrop. Assn. (biol. anthrop. unit program chmn.), European Anthrop. Assn., Internat. Assn. Forensinc Scis. (chmn. forensic anthropology, 1986-88), Internat. Congress Anthrop. and Ethnol. Scis., Am. Acad. Forensic Scis., Fla. Acad. Scis., Human Biology Council, Internat. Assn. Forensic Scis. (chmn. physical anthrop. sect.), Sigma Xi, (pres. Fla. Atlantic Club 1981-82, 86-88), Dental Anthropol. Assn. (founder, pres. 1986-88). Author: A Topical Guide to the American Journal of Physical Anthropology, 1983, Age Markers in the Human Skeleton; co-author: The Human Skeleton in Forensic Medicine, 1986, Reconstruction of Life from the Skeleton; contbr. over 50 articles to profl. jours., chpts. to books. Office: Fla Atlantic U Dept Anthropology Boca Raton FL 33431-0991

ISELY, HENRY PHILIP, association executive, integrative engineer; b. Montezuma, Kans., Oct. 16, 1915; s. James Walter and Jessie M. (Owen) I; m. Margaret Ann Sheesley, June 12, 1948; children—Zephyr, LaRock, Lark, Robin, Kemper, Heather Capri. Student So. Oreg. Jr. Coll., Ashland, 1934-35, Antioch Coll., 1935-37. Organizer, Action for World Fedn., 1946-50, N.Am. Council for People's World Conv., 1954-58; organizer World Com. for World Constl. Conv., 1958, sec. gen., 1959-66; sec. gen. World Constn. and Parliament Assn., Lakewood, Colo., 1966—, organizer worldwide prep. confs., 1963, 66, 67, 1st session People's World Parliament and World Constl. Conv. in Switzerland, 1968, editor assn. bull. Across Frontiers, 1959—; co-organizer Emergency Council World Trustees, 1971, World Constituent Assembly at Innsbruck, Austria, 1977, Colombo, Sri Lanka, 1978-79, Provisional World Parliament 1st session, Brighton, Eng., 1982, 2d Session New Delhi, India, 1985, 3d Session Miami Beach, Fla., 1987, mem. parliament, 1982—; sec. Working Commn. to Draft World Constn., 1971-77; pres. World Service Trust, 1972-78; ptnr. Builders Found., Vitamin Cottages, 1955—; pres. Earth Rescue Corps, 1984—; sec.-treas. Grad. Sch. World Problems, 1984—; presidium mem. Provisional World Govt., 1987—; pres. World Govt. Funding Corp., 1986—. Author: The People Must Write the Peace, 1950; A Call to All Peoples and All National Governments of the Earth, 1961; Outline for the Debate and Drafting of a World Constitution, 1967; Strategy for Reclaiming Earth for Humanity, 1969; Call to a World Constituent Assembly, 1974; Proposal for Immediate Action by an Emergency Council of World Trustees, 1971; Call to Provisional World Parliament, 1981; People Who Want Peace Must Take Charge of World Affairs, 1982; Plan for Emergency Earth Rescue Administration, 1985; Plan for Earth Finance Credit Corporation, 1987; handbook for provisional world govt. and provisional world parliament, 1988; co-author, editor: A Constitution for the Federation of Earth, 1974, rev. edit., 1977; also author several world legis. measures adopted at Provisional World Parliament. Designer prefab modular panel system of constrn., master plan for Guacamaya project in Costa Rica. Candidate, U.S. Congress, 1958. Recipient Honor award Internat. Assn. Educators for World Peace, 1975, Gandhi medal, 1977. Mem. Soc. Internat. Devel., World Union, World Federalist Assn., World Future Soc., Internat. Assn. for Hydrogen Energy, Global Edn. Assocs., Friends of Earth, Wilderness Soc., Sierra Club, SANE, Global Futures Network, Amnesty Internat., ACLU, Am. Acad. Polit. and Social Sci., Nat. Nutritional Foods Assn., Environ. Def. Fund, Greenpeace, Internat. Studies Assn., War Resistors League, Audubon Soc., Worldwatch Inst., Denver Symphony Soc., Planetary Soc., Nation Assocs. Club: Mt. Vernon Country. Home: 241 Zephyr Ave Lookout Mountain Golden CO 80401 Office: 1480 Hoyt St Suite 31 Lakewood CO 80215

ISELY, MARGARET, nutritional consultant, food stores executive; b. Orion, Ill., Aug. 13, 1921; d. John Henry and Sadie Mae (Durman) Sheesley; m. Henry Philip Isely, June 12, 1948; children—Zephyr, LaRock, Lark, Robin, Kemper, Heather. Student Antioch Coll., 1941-46. Acting dietitian Antioch Coll., Yellow Springs, Ohio, 1942; nutritional cons. Vitamin Cottage, Lakewood, Colo., 1955—; gen. ptnr., mgr. 5 health food stores in Denver area; pres. Nat. Found. for Nutritional Research, Lakewood, 1982—. Mem. Rocky Mountain Nutritional Foods Assn. (pres. Denver 1978-82), Nat. Nutritional Foods Assn. (dir., mem. exec. council 1978-83), Orthomolecular Med. Soc., World Constn. and Parliament Assn. (treas. 1982—, U.S. del. to World Constn. Assembly, Interlaken, Switzerland, 1968, Wolfach, Fed. Republic Germany, 1968, Innsbruck, Austria, 1977, Colombo, Sri Lanka, 1979; U.S. del. to Provisional World Parliament, Brighton, Eng., 1982, New Delhi, India, 1985, Miami Beach, Fla., 1987; mem. Presidium Provisional World Govt., 1987—). Home: 241 Zephyr Ave Golden CO 80401 Office: Vitamin Cottage 8800 W 14th St Lakewood CO 80215

ISHAY, RAM RAYMOND, physician, professional association executive; b. Sousse, Tunisia, May 17, 1931; arrived in Israel, 1955; s. Joseph and Myriam (Haddad) I.; m. Rahel Manor, Dec. 13, 1960; children—Raviv, Roglit. M.D., U. Montpellier, France; postgrad. program health systems mgmt. Harvard U. Bus. Sch., 1974. Head pilot project for integrative medicine in Negev, Israel, 1964; chmn. Sick Funds Orgn., Tel Aviv, 1968-81; pres. Israel Med. Assn., Tel Aviv, 1971-86, editor bull., 1971—; mem. exec. com. Israel Health Council, 1975. Author: Anatomy of Struggle, 1985. Mem. Helsinki Com. on Human Experimentation, 1984. Served to maj. Israeli Army. Mem. Soc. Law and Medicine, Coll. Continuing Med. Edn. (chmn. bd. govs. 1982), Confederation of Intellectual Workers Assns. in Israel (chmn. 1987), World Med. Assn. (council rep. Asia 1986), Israeli Soc. for Med. Ethics (founder). Avocations: painting; carpentry. Office: Israel Med Assn, 39 Shaul Hamelech Blvd, Tel Aviv 64928 Israel

ISHEE, WILLIAM WILLIS, JR., educational administrator; b. Pasadena, Tex.; s. William Willis and Mozelle (Williams) I.; m. Marie Apel, June 1, 1973; 1 child, Jonathan. B.A., U. Houston, 1969; M.Ed., Sam Houston State U., 1972; D.Edn., Tex. A&M U., 1981. Tchr. Spring Br. Schs., Houston, 1969-71, counselor, 1971-74, prin., 1974-75; dir. project Klein Pub. Schs., Tex., 1975-76, dir. personnel, 1976—; bd. dirs. U. Houston Alumni Orgn. Social Sci. Mem. pres.'s council Houston Grand Opera, 1988—, concert master mem. Houston Symphony, 1988—, Ambassador-Houston Ballet, 1987, 88. Mem. Gulf Coast Personnel Adminstrs. (pres. 1984), Tex. Assn. Sch. Personnel Adminstrs. (regional rep. 1985, v.p. 1987-88), Am. Assn. Sch. Personnel Adminstrs. (conf. chmn. 1985-86), Nat. Audubon Soc., Sierra Club, Ctr. Transp. and Commerce, Tex. Hist. Found., Houston Mus. Natural Sci., Mus. Fine Arts. Democrat. Baptist. Avocation: horticulture. Home: 8319 Oak Moss Dr Spring TX 77379 Office: Klein Independent Sch Dist 7200 Spring Cypress Rd Klein TX 77379

ISHIBASHI, FUSAO, cardiologist; b. Yokohama, Japan, Feb. 25, 1922; s. Kotaro and Ichi (Hamazaki) I.; MD, Keio U., 1946, DMS, 1957; m. Kimi Asahina, Jan. 16, 1949; children—Makiko Kikuchi, Yukiko Kimura, Akiko. Intern, Nat. Kurihama Hosp., Yokosuka City, 1946-47; resident in internal medicine Keiyu Hosp., Yokohama City, 1947-49; practice medicine specializing in cardiology; mem. staff Nippon Kokan Hosp., Kawasaki, 1949-81, v.p., 1971-79; mem. staff, dir. Katakura-cho Clinic, Yokohama, 1981—. Speaker World Assn. Med. Info. (chmn. 1979). Mem. Japan Med. Assn., Japan Soc. Internal Medicine, Japanese Circulation Soc. (councillor 1969), Japan Soc. Med. ELectronics and Biol. Engring. Contbr. articles to profl. jours. Home: 602 Katakura-cho, Kanagawa-ku, Yokohama 221, Japan Office: Katakuracho Naika Clinic, 602, Katakuracho, Kanagawaku, Yokohama 221, Japan

ISHIDA, NOBUO, architect, city planning consultant; b. Tokyo, Jan. 3, 1930; s. Shinsuke and Shima Ishida; children: Nina, Motomu. B Engring., Waseda U., Tokyo, 1952, MA in Architecture, 1956. Registered architect. Pres. Ishida Archtl. Office, Tokyo, 1956—; lectr. Toyo U., Tokyo, 1958-59, Internat. Sch. Small & Middle Size Bus. Devel., Tokyo, 1962—, Japan Women's Coll., Tokyo, 1963-76; examiner small and middle size bus. cons. nat. Ministry of Industry and Trade, Tokyo, 1976—; chief examiner of architects nat. bd. exam. Ministry of Constrn., Tokyo, 1980-82; chief architect, cons. Matsuzaka City Redevel. Project, 1965-75; vice chmn. Takaoka City Redevel. Project, 1985—; mem. Toyama (Japan) Prefecture Comm. Devel. Com., 1987—; vice chmn. Koriyama (Japan) Redevel. Project, also 9 other cities. Co-author: The Manual for Self-Diagnosis of Commercial Streets, 1978, The Vital Commercial Street Redevelopment, 1981, The Attractive Commercial Street Redevelopment, 1982. Counsellor Tsurukawa Gakuen Social Welfare Found., Tokyo, 1974—, Found. for Advancement of Garments and Apparel Research, Tokyo, 1982—. Recipient Petit Grand Prix, Nat. Mus. Modern Art, Sao Paulo, 1954, Outstanding Cons. award Chief Sec. of Small & Middle Size Bus. Mgmt. Assn., Tokyo, 1972, Saitama (Japan) Prefectural Gov. award Saitama Prefectional Gov., 1976, Tokyo City Gov. award, 1959. Mem. Archtl. Inst. Japan, Japan Inst. Architects (chief sec. 1984-86), Small & Medium Enterprise Mgmt. Cons. Assn. Japan, City Redevel. Coordinators Assn. Home: 1-24-17-304, Seta Setagaya-Ku, Tokyo 158, Japan Office: Ishida Archtl Office, 4 2 6 Takanawa Minato-Ku, Tokyo 108, Japan

ISHIGURO, KAZUO, novelist, scriptwriter; b. Nagasaki, Kyushu, Japan, Nov. 8, 1954; arrived in Eng., 1960; s. Shizuo and Shizuko (Michida) I.; m. Lorna Anne MacDougall, May 9, 1986. BA in Lit. and Philosophy, U. Kent, Canterbury, 1978; MA in Creative Writing, U. East Anglia, Norwich, 1980. Author: A Pale View of Hills, 1982 (Winifred Holtby award 1983), An Artist of the Floating World, 1986 (Whitbroad Book of Yr. 1986);

scriptwriter TV films A Profile of Arthur J. Mason, 1985 (Best Short Film award Chgo. Film Festival 1985), The Gourmet, 1987. Mem. Labour party.

ISHIGURO, NAOBUMI, banker; b. Dahrien, China, Mar. 24, 1931; arrived in Japan, 1946; s. Tadao and Mitsuko Ishiguro; m. Fumiko Sakamoto, Apr. 11, 1957; children: Naoto, Miki. Bachelor's degree, Osaka (Japan) U., 1954. Mng. dir. Hakkaido Takushoku Bank, Sapporo, Japan, 1984—; Bd. dirs. Sapporo Cable TV, Hokkaido Info. Service, Sapporo. Author: Regional Development Funds, 1964, The Banking, 1975, The Possibilities of Hokkaido, 1980, We Love Hokkaido, 1985. Mem. Hokkaido Devel. Council, Tokyo, 1985; mng. dir. The Hokkaido Keizai Doyukai, Sapporo, 1985; chmn. programming council Japan Broadcasting Assn., Sapporo, 1987. Fellow Money and Banking Soc. Japan. Home: 2-8 Fukuzumi Toyohira-ku, Sapporo, Hokkaido 062, Japan Office: Hokkaido Takushoku Bank, Nishi-3, Ohdhori, Chuo-ku, Sapporo 060, Japan

ISHIHARA, TORU, mathematics educator; b. Kyoto, Japan, Sept. 28, 1942; parents: Arawo Kita and Yoneyo Ishihara; m. Akiko Kanayama, Aug. 3, 1972; children: Yuhko, Keiko. BA, Kyoto U., 1965, MA, 1967, PhD, 1978. Researcher U. Tokushima, Japan, 1968-71, lectr., 1971-73, assoc. prof., 1973-82, prof., 1982—; vis. researcher U. Ill., 1976; reviewer math. reviews, Providence, 1978-87, Zentralblatt fur Math., Berlin, 1985-87. Contbr. articles to profl. jours. Mem. The Math. Soc. Japan, The Am. Math. Soc. Home: Kasuga 3-2-17, Tokushima 770, Japan Office: U Tokushima, Dept Math Comp, Minami-Josanjima 1-1, Tokushima 770, Japan

ISHIHARA, YOSHINORI, pediatrician, hospital director; b. Nagoya, Japan, Jan. 4, 1938; s. Shigenori and Yasuko I.; m. Hiroko Takado, Nov. 4, 1967; children—Takanori, Hironori, Yasunori. Grad., Kyoto Prefectural U. of Med., 1962; postgrad. M.D. course, 1969. Diplomate pediatric cardiologist. Chief of pediatrics Fukui Cardiovascular Ctr., Fukui, Japan, 1967-72; dir. Fukui Ai-iku Hosp., Fukui, Japan, 1972—. Author: Shin-Rinsho-Shonika-Zensho, 1983; contbr. articles to profl. jours. Fellow Fukui Cardiovascular Ctr., Fukui, 1967. Fellow Societas Paediatrica Japonika, Societas Cardiologica Paediatrica Japonika; mem. Japanese Circulation Soc., Japanese Assn. Thoracic Surgery. Club: Fukui North Rotary. Home: 4-7-8 Ninomiya, Fukui 910 Japan

ISHII, BEN, architect; b. Osaka, Japan, Jan. 31, 1950; s. Masakazu and Hisako (Yamamoto) I.; m. Hideko Ise, May 8, 1975; 1 child, Mae. Bachelor's degree, Tokyo Inst. Tech., 1974. Authorized architect. Scholar Prof. Shinohara's Lab., Tokyo, 1974-78; chief designer Ben Ishii Studio, Tokyo, 1978-79; dir. T.I.M.E. Architects, Tokyo, 1980—; instr. Tokyo Design Acad., 1976-83. Prin. works include Take-Up, 1981 (prize 1982), Gyyu Chan Studio, 1984 (prize 1985). Fellow Japan Inst. Architects, Archtl. Inst. Japan; mem. Tokyo Soc. Architects and Bldg. Engrs., Japanese Soc. Comml. Space Designers. Home: 4-18-19-A306 Yoyogi, Shibuya, Tokyo 151, Japan Office: TIME Architects, 4-18-19-B503 Yoyogi, Shibuya, Tokyo 151, Japan

ISHII, BEN TSUTOMU, chemical engineer, educator; b. Tokyo, June 2, 1935; s. Kiyoshi and Nobu (Yoshino) I.; m. Hidie Hideko, Sept. 17, 1965; children: Lily, Ririko. BS, Yokohama Nat. U., Japan, 1959; MS, Tokyo Inst. Tech., 1961, PhD, 1964. Cert. chem. engr. Asst. prof. Tokyo Inst. Tech., 1964-69; assoc. prof. Yokohama Nat. U., 1969-87, assoc. research prof., 1987—; vis. assoc. prof. U. Ariz., Tucson, 1977-78. Author: Basic Transport Phenomena, 1981. Jr. mem. grantee Japan Ministry Edn., 1964, pollution removal grantee Japan Ministry Edn., 1975; McMaster U. fellow, Ont., Can., 1965-67, U. Waterloo fellow, Ont., Can., 1972-74. Mem. N.Y. Acad. Scis., Soc. Math. Biology, Japan Soc. Fluid Mechanics, Japan Soc. Biorheology, Japan Soc. Separation Process Engring. Buddhist. Home: 1839 Hiyoshi-hon-cho, Yokohama koho-ku 223, Japan Office: Yokohama Nat U, Dept of Chem Engring, 156 Tokiwadai Hodogaya-ku, Yokohama 240, Japan

ISHI'I, OSAMU, architect; b. Asuka, Nara, Japan, Mar. 28, 1922; s. Shizutaro and Sadae Ishi'i; m. Ikuko Takeda, May 2, 1952; children: Tomoko, Ryohei. BArch, Yoshino Tech. Sch., Nara, 1940; student, Waseda Tech. Sch., Tokyo, 1940-41. Architect Ohbayashi Corp., Tokyo, 1940-46, Biken Archtl. Design Office, Osaka, Japan, 1956—. Co-author: Ie-Ie, 1984. Served with Japanese Army Air Corps, 1941-45. Recipient Osaka Urban Landscape Architecture prize Osaka Prefecture, 1983, Isoya Yoshida award Isoya Yoshida Meml. Found., 1987. Mem. Archtl. Inst. Japan (Ann. award 1986), Japan Inst. Architects. Buddhist. Home: 1-766, Megamiyama-cho, Koyo-en, Nishinomiya, Hyogo 662, Japan Office: Biken Archtl Design Office, 1-39, 3-chome, Fukushima, Osaka 553, Japan

ISHII, RYUJI, aerodynamicist, researcher; b. Tokyo, June 17, 1941; s. Heiziro and Matsuko I.; m. Naoko Kino, June 5, 1976; children—Hiroko, Yasutaka. B.S., Kyoto U. (Japan), 1965, M.S., 1967, D.Sc., 1974. Research assoc. Kyoto U., 1974—. Mem. AIAA, Japan Soc. Aero. and Space Scis., Japan Soc. Fluid Dynamics. Home: Ukyoku, Umegahata Mikyozaka-cho 8-1, Kyoto 616 Japan Office: Dept Aeronautics, Sakyo-ku Yoshida-Honmachi, Kyoto 606 Japan

ISHIKAWA, HIROSHI, reliability engineering educator; b. Kotohira, Kagawa, Japan, Nov. 29, 1941; s. Asataro and Fusano (Ohnishi) I.; m. Setsuko Kojima, Sept. 26, 1971; children: Chie, Yoko, Emiko. B.Sc., Kyoto U., 1964, M.S., 1966, Ph.D., 1969. Research assoc. Kyoto U., 1969-76; research assoc. Columbia U., N.Y.C., 1973-74, 77-79; assoc. prof. dept. info. sci. Kagawa U., Takamatsu, Japan, 1976-87, prof. 1987—; chmn. conf. organizing com. ICOSSAR '85, 1983, mem. conf. sci. com., 1986, sec.-gen. steering com., ICOSSAR '87, 1986; vice chmn. Com. on Promotion of Tech., Kagawa Prefecture, Takamatsu, Japan, 1985; editorial bd., Internat. Jour. Probabilistic Engrins Mechanics C.M.L pubs., Eng. Co-author: Fatique of Metals and Machine Design, 1977; Introduction to Statistics, 1982; Structural Safety and Reliability, 1984; Linear Algebra, 1985, practice of reliability engring., 1987. Ishikawajima-Harima Heavy Industries Ltd. grantee, 1982. Mem. Japan Soc. Materials Sci. (editorial bd. jour. 1979—), Japan Soc. Mech. Engrs. (reviewer 1980—), ASTM, Internat. Assn. for Structural Safety and Reliability, Japan Soc. Steel Constructions, Shikoku Soc. Materials Sci. (v.p. 1981—), Japan Statis. Soc. Home: 2-4-1 Tokiwa-cho, Takamatsu City, Kagawa 760, Japan Office: Kagawa Univ Dept Info Sci, 2-1 Saiwai-cho Takamatsu, Kagawa 760, Japan Other: Nichimen Am Inc 1185 Ave of the Americas New York NY 10036

ISHIZAKI, HATSUO, civil engineer, educator; b. Tokyo, July 7, 1921; s. Hikaru and Motoko (Ito) I.; B.Eng., U. Tokyo, 1944; Dr.Eng., Kyoto U., 1954; m. Fumiko Suzuki, Oct. 25, 1951; 1 son, Shigeo. Asst. prof. civil engring. Kobe (Japan) U., 1950-53; asst. prof. Kyto U., 1953-59, prof. Disaster Prevention Research Inst., 1959-85, dir. inst., 1969-71, prof emeritus, 1985—. Mem. Japanese Assn. Wind Engring. (chmn. 1979), Archtl. Inst. Japan, Sigma Xi. Author: Wind Resistant Engineering, 1977; editor: Wind Effects on Structures, 1976; regional editor Jour. Wind Engring. and Indsl. Aerodynamics, 1975—. Home: 286 Takasagocho, Byakugoji, Nara 630, Japan Office: Gokasho Uji, Kyoto U, Kyoto 611, Japan

ISHIZAKI, TATSUSHI, physician, parasitologist; b. Tochigi, Japan, Mar. 8, 1915; s. Takaji and Satoko I.; M.D., Tokyo (Japan) U., 1939, Ph.D., 1951; diploma pub. health, Singapore U., 1959; m. Yuriko Sase, Nov. 5, 1946; children—Terumi, Michiharu. With U. Tokyo Sch. Medicine, 1939, sr. asst. dept. phys. therapy and medicine, 1946-55; chief 2d div. dept. parasitology Nat. Inst. Health, Japan, 1953-67, chief dept., 1967-74; lectr. clin. allergy U. Tokyo Sch. Medicine, 1956-71; prof. clin. immunology Dokkyo U. Sch. Medicine, 1973-82, prof. emeritus, 1982—, chmn. clin. profs., 1978-80; panelist Japan-U.S.A. Coop. Study Parasitology, 1965-74. Hon. fellow Am. Coll. Allergists; mem. Japanese Soc. Allergy (exec. com., pres. 1981—), Japanese Soc. Tropical Medicine (hon. fellow, exec. com.), Japanese Soc. Internal Medicine (exec. com.), Japan-German Assn. Protozoan Diseases (pres.), Research, publs. on skin tests for various antigens; standardization of criteria of positive skin test basic phenomena of skin reaction especially mast cell degranulation mechanism analysis of onset of asthma attacks especially related to air pollution, weather; analysis of mechanisms of occupational allergy, others. Home: 34-1 Itabashi 3-chome, Itabashi-ku, Tokyo Japan Office: Dokkyo U Sch Medicine, Mibumachi, Tochigi Prefecture Japan

ISHIZU, SYOHEI, educator; b. Takatuki, Osaka, Japan, Apr. 29, 1955; s. Yutaka and Tomiko Ishizu; m. Reiko Ishizu, Jan. 18, 1981; children: Kenichi, Akira. BS, Hiroshima U., Japan, 1978; MS, Hiroshima U., 1980, PhD, 1985. Asst. prof. Hiroshima U., 1985-88, Tokyo Inst. Tech., 1988—. Mem. Japanese Soc. for Quality Control, Japan Indsl. Mgmt. Assn. Home: 1-304 2000-10 Kosugaya-cho, Sakae-ku, Yokohama 247, Japan Office: Tokyo Inst Tech, 2-12-1 O-Okayama, Meguro-ku, Tokyo 152, Japan

ISLAM, MANZURUL, publications executive; b. Dhaka, Bangladesh, Nov. 14, 1943; s. Abdul and Fatema (Khatun) Quadir; m. Khaleda, Oct. 12, 1969; children: Pial, Kuhel. BA, Notre Dame Coll., Dhaka, Bangaladesh, 1964; higher diploma, Dhaka U., 1965, MA, 1966; PhD, Kennedy-Western U., Calif., 1987. Lectr. English D.N. Coll Nawabganj, Dhaka, Bangladesh, 1965-67, U. Fedn. of Women Coll., Dhaka, 1966-67; sr. lectr. Resdl. Model Coll., Dhaka, 1967; dep. magistrate Govt. of East Pakistan, Dhaka, 1967-68; asst. dir. external services Radio Pakistan Ministry of Info., Karachi, Pakistan, 1968-70; mgr. Oxford U. Press Bangladesh Br., Dhaka, 1970-75; dir. pub., mng. dir. Bangladesh Books Internat. Ltd., Dhaka, 1975-82; pubs. specialist editor King Abdulaziz City of Sci. Tech., Riyadh, Saudi Arabia, 1982—; mem. expert com. Bangla Acad., 1979-81, Asian Cultural Ctr. for UNESCO, Tokyo. Author: Advancement of Publishing, 1987, Publishing Bibliography, 1987, The Book World in Bangladesh, 1987; editor Bangladesh Pubs. Assn. Jour., 1980-82; contbr. articles to profl. jours. Mem. Library Assn. Bangladesh, Bangladesh Pubs. Assn. (exec. 1975-82), Am. Soc. Info. Sci., Stanford U. Alumni Assn., Dhaka U. Alumni Assn. (chmn. 1984-86), Asiatic Soc. Bangladesh. Muslim (Sunni). Lodge: Lions (pres. 1975-76, cabinet sec. 1977-79). Home: KACST Housing CAmpus, PO Box 6086, Riyadh 11662, Saudi Arabia Other: GP JA-28 Rd 1, Mohakhali Dhaka-5 Bangladesh

ISLAM, NURUL, economist; b. Chittagong, Bangladesh, Apr. 1, 1929; s. Abdur Rahman and Mohsena Begum; m. Rowshan Ara; children: Roumeen, Nayeem. MA, Harvard U., 1953, PhD, 1955. Nuffield fellow Sch. Econs., U. London and Cambridge U., 1958; prof. econs. Dhaka U., Bangladesh, 1960-64; dir. Pakistan Inst. Devel., 1965-70; professorial fellow Econ. Growth Ctr., Yale U., New Haven, 1971; chmn. Bangladesh Inst. Devel. Studies, Dhaka, 1971-75; dep. chmn. Ministry of Planning Bangladesh Planning Comm., 1972-75; fellow St. Anthony's Coll. and Oxford U., Eng., 1975-77; asst. dir.-gen. econ. and social policy dept. FAO, UN, Rome, 1977-87; sr. research advisor Internat. Food Policy Research Inst., Washington, 1987—; mem. UN Com. Devel. Planning, 1975-77; chmn. Adminstrv. Com. Coordination of UN System Task Force on Rural Devel., 1977-87. Author: Development and Planning in Bangladesh, 1977, Aid and Influence, 1981, Foreign Trade and Economic Controls in Development: The Case of United Pakistan, 1981, A Short-term Model for Pakistan's Economy: An Econometric Analysis, 1964. Mem. bd. visitors Boston U. Mem. Inst. for Internat. Econs. Office: Internat Food Policy Research Inst 1776 Massachusetts Ave NW Washington DC 20036-1998 also: House #7, Rd #10, Dhanmondi Residential Area, Dhaka Bangladesh

ISLAS-MARROQUIN, JORGE, physician, Mexican Army officer; b. Tulacingo, Hidalgo, Mex., Dec. 15, 1937; s. Teofilo Islas Zarazua and Isabel Marroquin de Islas; m. Ana Maria Ramos Palacios de Islas, June 10, 1962; children—Ana Lourdes, Jorge Carlos. M.D., Escuela Medico Militar, Mexico City, 1960; M.S., U. Nacional Autonoma de Mexico, 1981, Ph.D., 1985. Intern, Hosp. Central Militar, Mexico City, 1961-62; scholar U. Claude Bernard, Lyon, France, 1964-65; asst. prof. Escuela Medico Militar, 1963-69, prof. physiology, 1969—, chief neurophysiol. service, 1969—, chief basic scis., 1982—; prof. neurophysiology Mil. Grad. Med. Sch., 1971—; prof. neurophysiology U. Nacional Autonoma, 1983—. Contbr. articles to med. jours. Serves as col. Mil. Health, Mexican Army, 1982—. Recipient Disting. Service award Mexican Army, 1982, Teaching award, 1983. Mem. Mex. Soc. Physiol. Scis. (treas. 1977-78), Mex. Soc. EEG and Clin. Neurophysiology (pres. 1981-83). Roman Catholic. Avocation: Karate (Black Belt). Home: Alcazar de Toledo 226, 11020 Mexico City Mexico Office: Hosp Mocel, Gelati 33-401, 11850 Mexico City Mexico

ISMAEL, HIROSI HAROLD, government official, surgeon; b. Lelu, Kosrae, Micronesia, Nov. 30, 1936; s. Tara and Kenye (Aaron) I.; m. Mitchigo S. Skilling, Mar. 26, 1965; children: Greeno, Grant, Loto, Paul, Kenye. Cert. nurse, Trust Territory Nursing Sch., Palau, 1959; BS in Surgery and Medicine, Fiji Sch. Medicine, 1964; postgrad. in surgery, Rotura Gen. Hosp., Hamilton Gen. Hosp., New Zealand, 1971. Senator Congress of Micronesia, Pohnpei, Trust Territory Pacific Islands, 1967-79, Congress Federated States Micronesia, Pohnpei, 1979-83; spl. asst. to gov. State of Kosrae, Federated States of Micronesia, 1983-87; v.p. Federated States of Micronesia, 1987—; dr./surgeon Kosrae State Hosp., 1986; chmn. Govtl. Functions; mem. Commn. on Future Polit. Status and Transition, Pohnpei, 1987—; bd. dirs. Telecom., Pohnpei. Chmn. Kosrae Islands Council Polit., Kosrae, Trust Territory Pacific Islands, 1971-74; mem. Micronesian Constl. Conv., Pohnpei, 1975-79. Mem. Trust Territory Pacific Islands Med. Assn. Home: PO Box 1367, Kolonia, Pohnpei 96941, Federated States of Micronesia Office: Office of Pres, PO Box 490, Kolonia, Pohnpei 96941, Federated States of Micronesia

ISMAIL, YAHIA HASSAN, dentist, educator; b. Egypt, Jan. 1, 1938; came to U.S., 1961; s. Hassan Kareem and Horia (Soloman) I.; m. Launa Lutz, Sept. 5, 1968; children: Alan Kareem, Zane Ziad. D.D.S., Cairo U., 1959; M.S., U. Pitts., 1965, D.M.D., 1973, Ph.D., 1973. Instr. Dental Sch. Cairo U., 1959-62; asst. prof. prosthodontics U. Pitts., 1962-68, assoc. prof., 1968-70, prof., 1970—; dir. Prosthodontic Clinic, 1970—, chmn. dept., 1973—; vis. prof., Paris and Marseille, France, Cairo and Alexandria, Egypt, Bengazi, Libya; prof. of implantology and prosthodontics, European U., Brussels; mem. staff VA Hosp., Montefiore Hosp., Univ. Med. Center Hosp., St. Margaret's Hosp. Contbr. articles to profl. jours., textbooks. Bd. dirs. Ridgewood Civic Assn., 1969-73; cubmaster Allegheny Trails council Boy Scouts Am.; coach Youth Soccer League Allegheny County. Fellow Internat. Coll. Dentists, Am. Coll. Dentists, Royal Soc. Medicine; mem. ADA, Internat. Assn. Dentofacial Abnormalities (dir., sec.-treas. 1973-77), Internat. Congress Oral Implantologists (v.p. 1985-86, pres. 1988—), Am. Prosthodontic Soc. (internat. circuite courses humanities citation), Pa. Prosthodontic Assn. (pres.), Prosthodontic Soc. Western Pa. (past pres.), Dental Soc. Western Pa. (past br. pres., bd. dirs.), Am. Coll. Oral Implantations (pres. 1984-86), Am. Coll. Prosthedontists, Am. Assn. Dental Schs., Internat. Assn. Dental Research, Am. Coll. Oral Implantology (pres. 1984-86), Internat. Coll. Oral Implantologists, Royal Coll. Physicians, Omicron Kappa Upsilon. Republican. Club: Univ. Office: U Pittsburgh Sch Dental Medicine Pittsburgh PA 15261

ISMAIL PETRA IBNI AL-MARHUM TUANKU SULTAN YAHAYA PETRA, Sultan of Kelantan; b. 1949; s. Tuanku Yahya Petra; student Sultan Ismail Coll.; m. Tengku Ania, Dec. 4, 1966; 3 children. Named Tengku Mahkota of Kelantan, 1967, sultan, 1979—. Address: Istana, Kota Bharu, Kelantan Malaysia Other: care Press Attache Malaysian Embassy 2401 Massachusetts Ave NW Washington DC 20008 *

ISOZAKI, ARATA, architect; b. Oita, Japan, July 23, 1931; s. Soji and Tetsu Isozaki; m. Noriko (div.); children: Horoshi, Kan; m. Aiko, Feb. 1, 1974. Grad. Archtl. Faculty Univ. of Tokyo, 1954. Staff Kenzo Tange & Urtec, Tokyo, 1954-63; pres. Arata Isozaki & Assocs., Tokyo, 1963—; juror Pritzker Architecture Prize, U.S.A., 1979-84, Concours Internat. de Parc de la Villette, Paris, 1982, The Peak Competition, Hong Kong, 1983, R.S. Reynolds Meml. awards, 1985; ministry of constrn. New Nat. Theater of Japan, 1986. Author: Kukan-e, 1971; Kenchiku-no-Kaitai, 1975; Shuho-ga, Kenshiku-no-Shuji, 1975; Architectural Pilgrimage to World Architecture, 1979—; designer pvt. houses, banks, libraries, schs., mus. Recipient ann. prize Archtl. Inst. Japan, 1967, 70, 75; Artist's Newcomer prize Ministry of Culture, Japan, 1969; Interior award Interior mag., U.S.A., 1983; Mainichi Art award Mainichi Shinbun, Japan, 1984; Royal Gold Medal for Architecture, Eng., 1986. Hon. fellow Acad. Tiberina, AIA; hon. mem. Bund Deutscher Architekten. Office: Arata Isozaki & Assocs, 6-17, Akasaka 9-chome, Minato-ku, Tokyo 107, Japan

ISQUITH, FRED TAYLOR, lawyer; b. N.Y.C., June 6, 1947; s. Santley and Rita (Hoskwith) I.; m. Susan Nora Goldberg, May 23, 1976; children: Fred, Rebecca. BA, Brooklyn Coll. of CUNY, 1968; JD, Columbia U., 1971. Bars: N.Y. 1972, U.S. Dist. Ct. (so. and ea. dists.) N.Y. 1975, U.S. Ct. Appeals (2d cir.) 1975, D.C. 1976, U.S. Supreme Ct. 1983, U.S. Ct. Appeals (8th cir.) 1985, U.S. Ct. Appeals (3d cir.) 1986. Assoc. Reavis & McGrath, N.Y.C., 1971-75, Kaye Scholer et al, N.Y.C., 1975-80; ptnr. Wolf Haldenstein Adler Freeman & Herz, N.Y.C., 1980—; bd. dirs. 103 East 84th St. Corp., N.Y.C., Sheinkopf Communications, Ltd. Mem. ABA, N.Y. State Bar Assn. (com. on legis.), D.C. Bar Assn., Assn. Bar of City of N.Y., Bklyn. Bar Assn. (civil practice law and rules com., legis. com. and fed. ct. coms.). Club: Columbia (N.Y.C.). Office: Wolf Haldenstein Adler et al 270 Madison Ave New York NY 10016

ISRAEL, EDMOND SYLVAIN, bank executive; b. Luxembourg, May 5, 1924; s. Gustave and Erna (Lande) I.; m. Raymonde Bloch, Jan. 6, 1959. With Banque Internat. à Luxembourg, 1946—, dir. gen., bd. dirs.; chmn. bd. dirs. CEDEL S.A., Luxembourg; bd. dirs. Luxembourg Stock Exchange, BNP Luxembourg S.A. Contbr. banking articles to profl. pubs. and spoken at confs. Chmn. Luxembourg Interconfessional Com. Mem. British C. of C. for Belgium and Luxembourg (chmn. luxury chpt., mem. council), Couronne de Chêne (officer nat. order), Mérite Grand-Ducal (commandeur nat. order), Ordrê Civil Militaire Adolphe Nassau (officer). Lodge: Lions. Office: Banque Internat, Luxembourg SA, 2 Blvd Royal, 2953 Luxembourg Luxembourg

ISRAEL, LUCIEN ISIDORE, oncologist, educator; b. Paris, Apr. 14, 1926; s. Jacques and Alice Allegra Israel; M.D., U. Paris, 1956; m. Germaine Bach, Jan. 31, 1949; children—Daniele, Dominique, Guillaume. Chief clinic U. Paris Med. Sch., 1957-62, mem. faculty, 1963—, prof. medicine, 1973—; chief oncology service Univ. Hosp. Lariboisere, 1971-76, Univ. Hosp. Avicenne, 1976—; mem. French-Am. Cancer Agreement Com., 1976-82; dir. Inst. d'Oncologie Cellulaire et Moleculaire Humaine, U. Paris. Served to 1st lt. French Army, 1951-52. Recipient Jean Dagnan Bouveret prize French Acad. Scis., 1974; grantee U.S. Nat. Cancer Inst., 1976-78. Mem. Internat. Assn. Study Lung Cancer, European Orgn. Study Treatment Cancer, French Soc. Respiratory Diseases, Am. Assn. Cancer Research. Author: Conquering Cancer, 1976; La Decision Medicale, 1980; La mé decine et le reste, 1984; Face cachée, 1984; co-editor: Lung Cancer, 1976; contbr. articles med. publs. Home: 36 Mont Thabor, 75001 Paris France Office: Hosp Avicenne, 93000 Bobigny France

ISRAEL, NANCY DIANE, lawyer; b. Fall River, Mass., Apr. 20, 1955; d. David Joseph and Charlotte Millicent (Epstein) I. AB magna cum laude, Harvard U., 1976, JD, 1979. Bar: Mass. 1979, N.Y. 1986. Mem. Hale & Dorr, Boston, 1980-83; atty. Harvard U., Cambridge, Mass., 1983-85, asst. gen. counsel internat. div. Arthur Young and Co., N.Y.C. and Boston, 1985—; chmn. 21st, 22d ann. practical skills seminar, curriculum com., Mass. Continuing Legal Edn., Boston, 1985-86, Ctr. House, Inc., Boston, 1980-86, also bd. dirs. Mem. editorial bd. Mass. Lawyers Weekly, 1988. Mem. energy and environ. issues task force Dukakis gubernatorial campaign, Boston, 1982, southeastern Mass. coordinator, 1974, mem. nat. fin. com. Dukakis Presdl. Campaign, 1987—; bd. dirs. nominating com. Mass. Council for Pub. Justice, Boston, 1971-76; mem. ad hoc com. Coalition for Better Judges, Boston, 1971-72; judge N.E. and Mid.-Atlantic Regionals of Jessup Moot Court Competition, 1988. Named an Outstanding Young Woman of Am., 1986. Fellow Mass. Bar Found. (mem. nominating com. 1988), Am. Bar Found.; mem. Mass. Bar Assn. (computer coll. steering com. 1984-86, del. bd. dels. 1984-87, chmn. young lawyers div. 1986-87, chmn. bus. law sect. 1987-88, commn. on delivery of legal services 1988, exec. com. 1985-86, commn. on professionalism 1985—, chmn. elect young lawyers com. 1987, chmn. young lawyers com. 1988, Silver Gavel award for outstanding leadership 1986), Am. Corp. Counsel Assn. (chmn. nonprofit counsel com. 1983-85, exec. bd. dirs. young lawyers com. 1985—, chmn. young lawyers com. 1988), ABA (exec. council young lawyers div., dist. rep. 1984-86, Mass. del. to ABA Ho. of Dels. 1987—, bd. dirs. continuing legal edn. young lawyers div. 1985-87, Barrister bd. dirs. 1987—, sect. council internat. law sect. 1987—, affiliate outreach team young lawyers div. 1986—), Radcliffe Alumnae Assn., Boston Bar Assn. (bd. dirs. vol. lawyers project 1985—), Women's Bar Assn., Mass. Assn. Women Lawyers, Am. Judicature Soc., Internat. Bar Assn., Internat. Law Soc. (Am. branch), Interests on Lawyers Trust Accounts (mem. implementation com. 1987—). Clubs: Harvard (Boston Schs. and Scholarships com.), Radcliffe, New Bedford Yacht. Office: Office of Gen Counsel Arthur Young & Co 277 Park Ave New York NY 10172

ISRAEL, RICARDO Z(IPPER), educator; b. Santiago, Chile, Oct. 7, 1950; s. Elias M. Israel and Perla A. Zipper; m. Sara Cofré Yãnez, Sept. 24, 1981; children: Daniela, Igal. LLB, U. Chile, Santiago, 1972; MA in Polit. Sci., Essex, Colchester, Eng., 1976, PhD in Polit. Sci., 1981; JD, U. Barcelona, Spain, 1980. Bar: Supreme Ct. Chile, 1981. Sole practice Santiago, 1972-83; prof. U. Chile, 1983—, research dir., 1986—; acad. dir. Ctr. N.Am. Studies, Santiago, 1984—; researcher Ctr. Estudios Desarrollo, Santiago, 1986; cons. Corp. Promocion Univ., Santiago, 1986—; chmn. Chilean Assn. Am. Studies, 1987. Author: Politics & Ideology in Allende's Chile, 1987, Un Mundo Cercano, 1985, Países Socialistas Y Corporaciones Transnacionales, 1984, Democracia Y Liberalismo, 1984; columnist La Epoca mag., Santiago, 1987—; internat. commentator, TV morning news program, Santiago, 1987—. Mem. adv. com. Comm. Nat. Investigacion Sci. Tech., Chile, 1986. Recipient Centennial award Az. State U., Tempe, 1985; Tinker fellow, U. Pitts., 1978, U.N. fellow Cent. Sch. Planning, 1979; Fulbright scholar-in-residence, Wheaton Coll., 1983, Youth for Understanding scholar, Arcadia, Calif., 1967. Mem. Am. Polit. Sci. Assn., Internat. Polit. Sci. Assn., Am. Anthrop. Assn., Soc. Internat. Devel., Chilean Assn. North Am. Studies (pres. 1987—), Assn. Chilena Polit. Sci. (bd. dirs. 1984—). Home: Montecarmelo 30 A-42, Providencia Santiago Chile Office: U Chile Inst Polit Sci, Maria Guerrero 940, Santiago Chile

ISRAELS, MICHAEL JOZEF, lawyer; b. N.Y.C., Sept. 27, 1949; s. Carlos Lindner and Ruth Lucille (Goldstein) I.; m. Maija-Sarmite Jansons, Aug. 31, 1980; children: Aleksandrs Lehman, Peter Carlos. A.B. magna cum laude, Amherst Coll., 1972; J.D., Harvard U., 1975. Bar: N.Y. 1976, U.S. Dist. Ct. (so. and ea. dists.) N.Y. 1976, D.C. 1977, N.J. 1980, U.S. Dist. Ct. N.J. 1980. Assoc. Shearman & Sterling, N.Y.C., 1975-79; sole practice, N.Y.C., 1979-81; ptnr. Courter, Kobert, Laufer & Pease, P.A., Hackettstown, N.J., 1981-83, Fitzpatrick & Israels, Bayonne, N.J., 1983-87; sr. ptnr. Waters, McPherson, McNeill and Fitzpatrick, Secaucus, N.J., 1987—; gen. counsel Kearny (N.J.) Mcpl. Port Authority, 1985—, Jersey City Mcpl. Port Authority, 1986—; Kearny Mcpl. Utilities Authority, 1988—; mem. N.J. Debt. Mgmt. Adv. Com., 1986—; cons. U.S./USSR Trade Council, N.Y.C., 1979, Council on Religion and Internat. Affairs, N.Y.C., 1980. Author: (with Moore, Thomson and Linsky) Report of the New England Conference on Conflicts Between Media and Law, 1977. Contbr. articles to legal jours. Bd. dirs. Community Tax Aid, Inc., N.Y.C., 1976-82, Am. Jewish Com., N.Y.C., 1980-88, Anti-Defamation League N.J., Livingston, 1981—; mem. religious sch. com. Temple Emanu-El, N.Y.C., 1972-84. Mem. ABA (gov. Law Student div. 1974-75), Assn. Bar City N.Y., N.J. Bar Assn., U.S. Assn. for Internat. Migration. Democrat. Clubs: Met. Opera, Harvard (N.Y.C.). Home: PO Box 22 Tranquility NJ 07879 Office: Waters McPherson McNeill Fitzpatrick 400 Plaza Dr Secaucus NJ 07094

ISRANI, KIM, civil engineer; b. Dadu, Pakistan, Dec. 24, 1935; s. Watumal and Vani I.; m. Yashi Israni, May 26, 1964; children: Vijay, Mamta, Sanjay. BS in Engring., Poona U., 1960; MS in Engring., Memphis State U., 1972. Asst. dir. Cen. Water and Power Comm., New Delhi, Ind., 1960-70; civil engr. Pollard Cons., Memphis, 1971-73; design engr. Talbot & Assoc., Orlando, Fla., 1974-75; facilities engr. Dept. Nat. Resources, Des Moines, 1976—. Contbr. articles to profl. jours. Chmn. Indian sect. Internat. Food Fair, Des Moines, 1977-88; dir. Indian dance group Iowa State Fair, Des Moines, 1982-88. Mem. Iowa Assn. Profl., Managerial and Sci. State Employees (bd. dirs. 1986—). Republican. Hindu. Home: 4024 83d St Des Moines IA 50322 Office: Dept Nat Resources Wallace Bldg Des Moines IA 50319-0034

ISSARI, M. ALI, educator, film producer, consultant; b. Esfahan, Iran, Oct. 3, 1921; s. Abbas Bek and Qamar (Soltan) I.; m. Joan Gura Aamodt, 1953; children: Scheherezade, Katayoun, Roxana. B.A., U. Tehran, Iran, 1963; M.A., U. So. Calif., 1968; Ph.D., 1979. Films officer Brit. Embassy, Brit. Council Joint Film Div., Tehran, 1944-50; asst. motion picture officer USIS,

1950-65; cons. to various Iranian Govt. ministries on film and TV devels. 1950-77; liaison officer Am. and Iranian govt. ofcls., 1950-65; prof. cinema Coll. Communication Arts and Scis. Mich. State U., East Lansing, 1969-81; also dir. instructional film and multimedia prodn. Mich. State U., 1969-78; film, public relations adviser to Iranian Oil Operating Cos. in, Iran, 1963-65; spl. cons. on edn. and instructional TV Saudi Arabian Ministry of Info., 1972; tchr. Persian lang. Iran-Am. Soc., Tehran, 1949-59. Producer, dir. over 1000 ednl., instructional and documentary films, 1956-78; freelance film reporter: Telenews, UPI, Iran, 1959-61; project dir., exec. producer: Ancient Iran Film Series, 1974-78; dir. film prodn. workshops, Cranbrook Inst., Detroit, 1973-74; Author: (with Doris A. Paul) A Picture of Persia, 1977, What Is Cinema Vérité?, 1979, Cinema in Iran, 1988; contbr. articles on ednl. communication and audio-visual instruction to periodicals and profl. jours. Founder, exec. sec. Youth Orgn. of Iran, 1951-52; v.p. Rugby Football Fedn., Iran, 1952-53, pres., 1954-55. Recipient Cine Golden Eagle award, 1975, Meritorious Honor award USIA, 1965; decorated Order of Magnum Cap Ord: S.F. Danaie M. Sigillum Denmark, 1960, Order of Cavalieres Italy, 1958, Order of Oranje Nassau Queen Juliana of Holland, 1959, Orders of Kooshesh and Pas HIM Shah of Iran, 1951, 57, Order of Esteghlal King Hussein of Jordan, 1960, Order of Ordinis Sancti Silvestri Papae Pope John 23d, 1959. Mem. Anglo-Iranian Dramatic Soc. (dir. 1943-50), Mich. Film Assn. (cofounder 1972, dir. 1972-73), Middle East Studies Assn. N.Am., Soc. Motion Picture and TV Engrs., Assn. Ednl. Communication and Tech., Delta Kappa Alpha (v.p. 1967). Home: 30856 Agoura Rd #A-1 Agoura Hills CA 91301

ISSLER, HARRY, lawyer; b. Cologne, Germany, Nov. 14, 1935; s. Max and Fanny (Grunbaum) I.; m. Doris Helen Issler, June 1, 1958; children—Adriane P. Schorr, M. Valerie, Stephanie L. B.S., U. Wis., 1955; J.D., Cornell U., 1958. Bar: N.Y. 1958, U.S. Supreme Ct. 1962, U.S. Ct. Mil. Appeals 1967, U.S. Dist. Ct. (so. and ea. dists.) N.Y. 1960, U.S. Customs Ct. 1964, U.S. Tax Ct. 1964; cert. specialist in civil trial advocacy Nat. Bo. Trial Advocacy. Assoc., Wing & Wing, N.Y.C., 1958-60, Fuchsberg & Fuchsberg, N.Y.C., 1960-62; ptnr. Issler & Fein, N.Y.C., 1963-68, Shaw, Issler & Rosenberg, N.Y.C., 1968-70; sole practice, N.Y.C., 1970—; sr. ptnr. Issler & Schrage, P.C., N.Y.C., 1979-84; arbitrator Civil Ct., N.Y. County, 1979—; hearing officer N.Y. State Tax Appeals, 1975-77, Supreme Ct N.Y., N.Y. County Med. Malpractice Panel, 1980—; judge advocate N.Y. State. Served with U.S. Army, 1958-59, N.Y. Army N.G., 1963-88, ret. brig. gen., 1988. Ford Found. scholar, 1951-55. Mem. N.Y. State Bar Assn., Assn. of Bar of City N.Y., Am. Trial Lawyers Assn., N.Y. State Trial Lawyers Assn., Phi Alpha Delta. Club: 42d Infantry Division Officers (N.Y.C.); Officers (U.S. Mcht. Marine Acad.). Home: 1365 York Ave New York NY 10021

ISTEL, JACQUES ANDRE, mayor; b. Paris, Jan. 28, 1929; came to U.S., 1940, naturalized, 1951; s. Andre and Yvonne Mathilde Cremieux I.; m. Felicia Juliana Lee, June 14, 1973; 1 dau. by previous marriage, Claudia Yvonne. A.B., Princeton, 1949. Stock analyst Andre Istel & Co., N.Y.C., 1950, 55; pres. Parachutes Inc., Orange, Mass., 1957-87, Intramgmt. Inc., N.Y.C., 1962-80; chmn. Pilot Knob Corp., 1982—; mayor Town of Felicity, Calif., 1986—; pres. VI World Parachuting Championships, 1962; capt. U.S. Parachuting team, 1956, capt., team leader, 1958; chmn. Mass. Parachuting Commn., 1961-62; lifetime hon. pres. Internat. Parachuting Commn., Fedn. Aero. Internat., 1965—; chmn. Hall of Fame of Parachuting, 1973—; founder Nat. Collegiate Parachuting League, 1957. Author: Coe the Good Dragon at the Center of the World, 1985, Coe le Bon Dragon au Centre du Monde, 1985. Contbr. articles to encys., profl. publs. Trustee Inst. for Man and Sci., 1975-82; bd. dirs. Marine Corps Scholarship Found., 1975-85. Served with USMC, 1952-54; lt. col. Res. Recipient Leo Stevens award, 1958, Diplome Paul Tissandier, 1969. Mem. Nat. Aero. Assn. (dir. 1965-68), Marine Corps Res. Officers Assn. Clubs: Racquet and Tennis (N.Y.C.), Princeton (N.Y.C.). Home: 1040 Fifth Ave New York NY 10028 also: Box 1000 Felicity CA 92283 Office: One Ctr of the World Plaza Felicity CA 92283

ITABASHI, NAMIJI, educational administrator; b. Akita, Japan, Feb. 8, 1908; s. Zenjiro Itabashi and Asa Kurosawa; m. Kazu Moriyama, June 2, 1940; children: Takashi, Toshiko, Mayumi. BA, U. So. Calif., 1937. Clk. Consulate-Gen. Japan, N.Y.C., 1937-42; dep. dir. Japan Broadcasting Assn., Tokyo, 1944-45; pres. Japanese Am. Conversation Inst., Tokyo, 1946—. Recipient Spl. Citation, George Washington U., 1978, Alumni Service awards U. So. Calif., 1980, English Lang. citation Edn. Minister Japan, 1985, Gov. Tokyo, 1985. Mem. Soc. Testing English Proficiency (trustee 1963—), Secretarial Assn. Japan (sec. 1968—). Club: Tokyo Seihoku. Lodge: Rotary. Home: 2-18-7 Kamirenjaku, Mitaka 180, Japan Office: Japanese Am Conversation Inst, Yotsuya 1-21 Shinjuku-ku, Tokyo 160, Japan

ITAGAKI, TAKAO, economist, educator; b. Japan, Aug. 14, 1943; s. Shoichi and Shigeko (Goto) I.; m. Mitsuko Ishizuka, Mar. 27, 1969; 1 child, Shuhei. Bachelor, Kobe U. Commerce, 1966; M.A., Kobe U., 1968; M.A., So. Meth. U., 1976, Ph.D., 1977. Asst. Kobe Gakuin U., 1969-71, instr., 1971-73; lectr. Kinki U., Higashi-Osaka, 1971-72, Kansai U., Suita, 1974, Kobe U., 1981-82; assoc. prof. Kobe Gakuin U., 1973—. Contbr. articles to jours. Recipient research assistantship Dept. Econs., So. Meth. U., Dallas, 1974-77. Mem. Am. Econ. Assn., Can. Econs. Assn., Japan Assn. Econs. and Econometrics, Japan Soc. Internat. Econs., Acad Internat. Bus., Workshop for the Study of Multinat. Enterprises. Home: 12 4 5 chome, Tsutsujigaoka Tarumi Ku, Kobe Hyogo 655, Japan Office: 518 Arise Igawadani-cho, Nishi-ku, Kobe Hyogo 673, Japan

ITKIN, PERRY STEVEN, lawyer; b. Bklyn., Dec. 25, 1944; m. Angela M. Monferrato, Nov. 9, 1978. B.A., Pa. State U., 1966; J.D., Dickinson Sch. Law, 1969. Bar: Fla. 1973, Pa. 1980, U.S. Dist. Ct. (so. dist.) Fla. 1974, U.S. Dist. Ct. (mid. dist.) Fla. 1984, U.S. Ct. Appeals (11th cir.) 1981, U.S. Supreme Ct. 1981. Spl. agt. FBI, 1969-73; assoc. Kirsch and Mills, P.A. Ft. Lauderdale, Fla., 1973-76; ptnr. Gibbs and Itkin, P.A., Ft. Lauderdale, 1976-80; sole practice, Ft. Lauderdale, 1980—, pre. Perry S. Itkin, Lawyer, P.A., 1984—; pres. Rising Sun real Estate Corp., 1988—; city prosecutor City of Margate (Fla.), 1973-74; mcpl. judge Sunrise Mcpl. Ct., 1976. Bd. dirs. Areawide Council on Aging of Broward County (Fla.), Inc., 1974-82, pres., 1981. Recipient Areawide Council on Aging award, 1982; Area Agy. on Aging Advocacy award, 1982. Mem. Am. Arbitration Assn. (panel of arbitrators), Broward County Bar Assn., Pa. Bar Assn., ABA, Fla. Bar, Acad. Fla. Trial Lawyers, Assn. Trial Lawyers Am., Broward County Trial Lawyers Assn., Soc. Former Spl. Agts. FBI. Office: 106 SE 9th St Fort Lauderdale FL 33316

ITÔ, KIYOSI, mathematician; b. Kuwana, Mie, Japan, Sept. 7, 1915; s. Seitaro and Tsuyo (Mizutani) I.; m. Shizue Oizumi, Sept. 23, 1938; children: Keiko, Kazuko, Junko. MS, U. Tokyo, 1938, PhD, 1945; Doctorate (hon.), U. Paris VI, 1981, E.T.H. Zürich, 1987. Statistician Statis. Bur. Govt. Tokyo, 1939-44; assoc. prof. Nagoya U., Japan, 1944-52; prof. Kyoto U., Japan, 1952-67, 75-79, prof. emeritus, 1979—; prof. Aarhus U., Denmark, 1967-69, Cornell U., Ithaca, N.Y., 1969-75, Gakushuin U., Tokyo, 1979-85. Author: Selected Papers of K. Ito, 1986. Recipient Asahi prize Asahi Newpaper Co., Tokyo, 1978, Imperial prize Japan Acad. Sci., Tokyo, 1978, Fujiwara Found. prize, Tokyo, 1985, Wolf Found. prize, Jerusalem, 1987. Home: 17 Ichijoji-Hinokuchi-cho, Kyoto 606, Japan Office: Kyoto U, RIMS, Kyoto 606, Japan

ITO, MASATOSHI, business executive; b. Apr. 30, 1929; m. Nobuko Ito. Grad., Yokohama City U., Japan, 1944. Pres. Ito Yokado Co. Ltd., Japan, 1958—; chmn. Seven-Eleven Japan Co. Home: 25-16 Minamiazabu 1-chome, Minato-ku, Tokyo 106 Japan Office: Ito-Yokado Co Ltd, 1-4 Shiba-Koen 4-chome, Minato-ku, Tokyo Japan *

ITO, SHUNTARO, metal processing company executive; b. Kobe, Hyogo, Japan, Dec. 25, 1939; s. Shigeo and Yoshie (Akimoto) I.; m. Tomiko Hayami, June 6, 1964; children: Yuichiro, Keiko, Kenjiro. BS, Kyoto U., Japan, 1962, MS, 1964; MS, Stanford U., 1971. Indsl. engr. Sumitomo Metal Industries, Osaka, Japan, 1964-70, system analyst, 1971-84, gen. mgr. system, 1984-86, gen. mgr. prodn. control, 1986—. Mem. Japan Soc. Precision Engring. Liberal Democrat. Buddhist. Home: 1-1-5 Ueno-dori Nadaku, Kobe, Hyogo 657, Japan Office: Sumitomo Metal Industries Ltd, Shimaya 5-1-9 Konohana, Osaka 554, Japan

ITO, YOICHIRO, government research scientist, physician; b. Osaka, Japan, Dec. 22, 1928; came to U.S., 1968, naturalized, 1978; s. Taichi and Ai (Kubota) I.; m. Ryoko Tanioka, Dec. 23, 1963; children—Koichi, Shin. M.D., Osaka City U., 1958. Rotating intern U.S. Yokosuka (Japan) Naval Hosp., 1958-59; resident in pathology Cleve. Met. Gen. Hosp., 1959-61, Michael Reese Hosp., Chgo., 1961-63; instr. physiology Osaka City U. Med. Sch., 1963-68; vis. scientist Nat. Heart, Lung and Blood Inst., NIH, Bethesda, Md., 1968-78, med. officer, 1978—. Mem. Japanese Am. Citizens League, Kenshinkai. Recipient 1st place award ann. sci. research presentation at Cleve. Met. Gen. Hosp., 1960, Tech. Excellence award for devel. blood cell separator, 1979; Fulbright exchange scholar, 1959-63; WHO Research Tavel Fund grantee Nat. Inst. Med. Research, London, 1968. Research on innovation in separation sci., including continuous devel. of countercurrent chromatography, cell separation methods; initiated and developed countercurrent chromatography; patentee coil planet centrifuge, rotating-seal-free flow-through centrifuge. Office: NIH 9000 Rockville Pike Bldg 10 Room 5D-12 Bethesda MD 20892

ITO, YOSHIKAZU, chemical products manufacturing company executive. Pres., Toray Industries, Inc., Tokyo. Office: Toray Industries Inc, 2-2 Nihobashi-Muromachi, Chuo-ku, Tokyo Japan *

ITO, YOSHIO, physician; b. Tokyo, June 1, 1918; s. Kazuo and Tome (Nakamura) I.; m. Ichiko Sawada, Dec. 5, 1950; children: Kazuyoshi, Takaaki, Toshiya. MB, Tokyo U., 1941; MD, Tokyo Imperial U., 1949. Resident 2d dept. internal medicine Tokyo U., 1946, instr. internal medicine, 1959-62, assoc. prof., 1962-72, prof., dir. 4th dept. internal medicine, 1972-79; dir. Sanraku Hosp., Tokyo, 1979-86, hon. dir., 1986—; v.p. Japan Heart Found., Tokyo, 1987—. Author: Clinical Pathophysiology of Heart Diseases, 1966, Therapy of Heart Failure, 1970; editor: Clinical Cardiovascular Diseases, 1976. Served to capt. Japanese Army, 1942-45. Mem. Japanese Circulation Soc. (hon., pres. 1978), Internat. Soc. Heart Research (pres. Japanese sect. 1976—), Japanese Assn. Cerebro-Cardiovascular Disease Control (hon., pres. 1979, chief dir. 1975-87), Japan Heart Found. (v.p. 1987—), Internat. Soc. and Fedn. Cardiology (mem. council cardiac metabolism), Internat. Soc. Heart Research (pres.-elect). Buddhist. Home: 1-41-3 Tsurumaki, Setagaya-ku, Tokyo 154, Japan Office: Japan Heart Found 603 Maru, Bldg 2-4-1 Marunouchi, Chiyoda-ku, Tokyo 100, Japan

ITOH, ANRI, urban development planner, architect; b. Tokyo, Jan. 8, 1960; parents Teiji and Hisako (Yamamoto) I. B in Engring., Tokyo U., 1982. Registered architect, Japan. Engr. Kajima Corp., Tokyo, 1982-84, researcher, 1984-85, urban devel. planner, 1985—. Buddhist. Home: 3-7-5-403 Kohinata, Bunkyo-ku, Tokyo 112, Japan Office: Kajima Corp, 1-1-5 Moto-akasaka, Minato-ku, Tokyo 107, Japan

ITOH, JUNJI, business executive; b. Qingdao, China, July 10, 1922; s. Hideo and Fudechiyo Itoh; m. Mizuko Takeoka, 1953; 2 children. Ed. Keio U. With Kanebo Ltd. (formerly Kanegafuchi Spinning Co., Ltd.), 1948—, dir., 1961, mng. dir., 1964, exec. dir., 1966, v.p., 1968, pres., rep. dir., 1968-84, chmn. bd. and rep. dir., 1984—; pres. Kanebo Cosmetics Inc., 1969-81; pres. Kanebo Pharms. Ltd., 1972-84, chmn. bd., rep. dir., 1984—; chmn. bd., rep. dir. Kanebo Fibers 1984-86, Knebo Foods Ltd., 1984-86; pres. Kanebo Synthetic Fabrics Ltd., 1982-83; rep. dir. Nippon Ester Co., Ltd., 1968-83; exec. dir. Japan Fedn. Econ. Orgns., 1968—, Japan Fedn. Employers Assn. (NIKKEIREN), 1968—; bd. dirs. Japan Com. for Econ. Devel., 1970—, vice chmn. bd. Japan Airlines Co., Ltd., 1985-86, chmn. bd., 1986-87. Trustee Keio U., 1970-78, 82—. Decorated Grão Cruz Orden Academico São Francisco (Brazil), Orden do Cruzeiro do Sul (Brazil). Address: Kanebo Ltd, 5-90 Tomobuchi-cho 1-chome, Miyakojima-ku, Osaka 534, Japan

ITOH, MASAO, mechanical engineer, educator; b. Saga, Kyohto, Japan, Jan. 19, 1925; s. Mitsutaka and Yoshi (Saitoh) I.; m. Yasuko Uda, May 10, 1953; children: Masaru, Yumiko Saga. BA in Engring., Osaka U., Japan, 1964, MA and PhD, 1951. Registered profl. engr. Japan. Engr. Shimonoseki Shipyard and Engine Works M.H.I. Ltd., Simonoseki, Japan, 1963-65; chief engring. control sect. tech. adminstrn. dept. M.H.I. Ltd., Tokyo, 1965-75, vice mgr. tech. adminstrn. dept., 1975-79; prof. mech. engring. Ashikaga Inst. Tech., Japan, 1979—. Mem. Soc. Instrument and Control Engring., Japan Soc. Mech. Engrs. Home: 3-14-4 Oyamadai, Tokyo Japan 158 Office: Ashikaga Inst Tech, 268-1 Omai, Ashikaga Japan 326

ITTAH, ALAIN, pediatrician; b. Fes, Maroc, Sept. 1, 1953; s. Marc and Odette (Haziza) I.; m. Florence Scemama, Mar. 10, 1951; children: Jacques, Paola. MD, U. Paris. Intern Hosp. of Paris, 1976; practice medicine specializing in pediatrics Paris; attache de Neo-Natologie, Hosp. of Paris. Contbr. articles to profl. jours. Editor: Carnet de Pediatrie Pratique, 1987. Adminstr. Movement Juif Liberal France Def., 1986. Jewish. Home and Office: 112 Blvd de Courcelles, 75017 Paris France

ITTI, ROLAND, medical professor; b. Mulhouse, Haut-Rhin, France, Oct. 31, 1940; s. Gerard and Erna (Hoch) I.; m. Eliane Heitz, Aug. 8, 1964; children: Emmanuel, Laurent, Isabelle. D. of Scis., Faculte de Scis., Strasbourg, 1966; MD, Faculte de Med., Tours, 1978. Asst. prof. Faculte de Med., Tours, 1968-71, chef de travaux, 1971-80; prof. Faculte de Med., 1980—; chief nuclear med. dept. Trousseau U. Hosp., 1980—. Author: Les Explorations cardio-vasculaires, 1980, Gamma-Cardio, 1982; author films and videos; contbr. numerous articles to profl. jours. Mem. Am. Soc. Nuclear Med., European Soc. Nuclear Med. and Cardiology, French Soc. Nuclear Med. and Cardiology. Home: Chateau de Noire, 37500 Chinon Indre et Loire, France Office: Trousseau U Hosp, 37044 Tours Indre et Loire, France

IVANOV, MIROSLAV, author; b. Jaromer, Czechoslovakia, Apr. 10, 1929; s. Antonin Ivanov-Job and Marie Subrtova; m. Hana Klugova, Dec. 30, 1952; 1 child, Klara. M.A., Charles Univ., 1953. Lectr. Faculty of Philosophy, Prague, 1953-60; editor Hlas Revoluce weekly Prague, 1960-67; freelance writer, Prague, 1967—. Author: Check-mate for the Black, 1965; Mystery of RKZ, 1969; The Secret of the Manuscript of Dvur Kralove, 1970; Death on the Huntman's Hiding Place, 1970; Labyrinth, 1971; Gods Are Gone, 1973; Almost a Detective Story, 1973; Action Wood Grouse, 1974; Czech Pitaval, 1977; A Confidential Report on K.H. Macha, 1977; Wonderful Tales, 1979; Regicide of the Good King Wenceslas, 1979; Fields of Mars, 1981; The Stones Were Burning, 1982; When the Commander Is Dying, 1982; The Fire of the National Theatre or Too Many Accidents, 1983; Symphony of the New World, or On the Sojourn of Antonin Dvořák in New York, 1985, The Assassination of Heydrich, 5th edit., 1987; and others. Recipient literary awards City of Prague, 1960, Union of Antifascist Fighters, 1963, Pubs. Nase Vojsko, 1970; prize winner Ministry of Culture Competition, 1974, Ministry of Nat. Def., 1974; Award of title of Disting. Artist, 1987. Mem. Union of Czechoslovak Writers, Union Czechoslovak Journalists. Home: Podolska 6a, Praha 4, 147 00 Branik Czechoslovakia

IVENS, J(ESSIE) LOREENA, science editor, writer; b. nr. Mt. Carmel, Ill., Apr. 5, 1922; d. Elisher and Gertrude Arletta (McKibben) Moudy; m. Creighton Carl Webb, Dec. 24, 1946 (dec. 1950); m. 2d, Ralph Wilson Ivens, Sept. 30, 1950. B.S., U. Ill.-Urbana-Champaign, 1945, M.S., 1947. Instr. rhetoric U. Ill.-Urbana-Champaign, 1947-48, asst. editor Inst. Aviation, 1950-51; instr. English-journalism Ill. State U., 1948-50; newspaper editor Chanute AFB, Rantoul, Ill., 1951-60; tech. editor Ill. State Water Survey, Champaign, 1960-80, head communications unit, 1980-87, scientist emerita; interim exec. dir. Soc. Ill. Sci. Surveys, 1984. Assoc. editor Man-Made Lakes: Their Problems and Environmental Effects, 1973; author, co-author, editor NSF reports, Water Survey Report, 1977, 81, 83. Served with USNR, 1943-44. Recipient YWCA Achievement award, 1984; Rotary Paul Harris fellow, 1983. Mem. Soc. Tech. Communications, Nat. League Am. Pen Women, AAAS, Women in Communications. Republican. Club: Altrusa International (past pres., past dist. sec.). Home: 802 S Busey St Urbana IL 61801

IVENS, MARY SUE, microbiologist, mycologist; b. Maryville, Tenn., Aug. 23, 1929; d. McPherson Joseph and Sarah Lillie (Hensley) I.; B.S., E. Tenn. State U., 1949; M.S. (NIH research trainee), Tulane U. Sch. Medicine, 1963; Ph.D., La. State U. Sch. Medicine, 1966; postgrad. Oak Ridge Inst. Nuclear Studies, Emory U. Sch. Medicine. Dir. microbiol. and mycol. labs. Lewis-Gale Hosp., Roanoke, Va., 1953-56; research mycologist Ctrs. Disease Control, Atlanta, 1957-60; research assoc. La. State U. Sch. Med., 1963-66, instr. medicine, 1966-72, instr. Microbiology, 1966-72, clin. prof., 1972—; dir. mycology lab, La. State U. Sch. Med., 1963-72; lectr. Sch. Dentistry, La. State U. Med. Ctr., 1968-70; assoc. prof. natural scis. Dillard U., New Orleans, 1972—; assoc. Marine Biol. Lab., Woods Hole, Mass., 1978—; cons. in field. Commr. WHO conf. on center for Mycotic sera 1969; chmn. Gold Medal Award Com. Sigma Xi, 1978; mem. La. assn. defense counsel expert witness bank, 1985—; Bd. dirs. Girl Scouts Council La., Community Relationships Greater New Orleans, Zoning Bd. River Ridge (La.); mem. exec. bd. River Ridge Civic Assn., 1982—, sec., 1982-84; chmn. personnel bd. Riverside Bapt. Ch., River Ridge. Recipient Rosicrucian Humanitarian award, 1981; Macy fellow, MBL, Woods Hole, 1978-79; grantee NSF, NIH; diplomate Am. Bd. Microbiology. Mem. Internat. Soc. Human and Animal Mycology, Med. Mycological Soc. Am., Am. Soc. Microbiology (nat. com. on membership 1983—), AAAS, Nat. Inst. Sci., Sigma Xi. Author articles in field. Home: 408 Berclair Ave New Orleans LA 70123 Office: Dillard U Div Natural Sci New Orleans LA 70122

IVERACH, ROBERT JOHN, lawyer; b. Edmonton, Alta., Can., Dec. 13, 1947; s. David W. and Margaret L. (Ranton) I.; m. Susan Anne Long, May 6, 1977; children—Robert J., Michelle A. B.A., U. Calgary, 1969; LL.B., U. Alta., 1970; LL.M., London Sch. Econs., 1971. Bar: Alta. 1972. Student, atty., Ballem, McDill & MacInnes, Calgary, Alta., 1971-74; ptnr. Fenerty & Co., Calgary, 1974-78; founding ptnr. Bell, Felesky & Iverach, Calgary, 1978—; pres., dir. Sage Resources Ltd., Calgary, 1980—. Co-author: Canadian Income Tax Tips and Traps, 1979. Bd. dirs. Alta. Law Found., 1976-78. Viscount Bennett scholar, 1970. Mem. Law Soc. Alta., Can. Bar Assn. Progressive Conservative. Mem. United Ch. Can. Clubs: Ranchmen's, Petroleum, Professional, Glencoe (Calgary). Office: 350 7th Ave SW, Suite 3400, Calgary, AB Canada T2P 3N9

IVES, RONN BRIAN, artist, educator; b. South Bend, Ind., Apr. 12, 1950; s. Bill H. and Shirley J. (Ryker) I. BFA, U. Ariz., 1975; MFA, U. Ariz., 1978. Freelance artist, Tucson, 1975-79; grad. instr. Intaglio printmaking U. Ariz., Tucson, 1975-77; instr. photography Tucson Mus. Art Sch., 1979; prof. art Old Dominion U., Norfolk, Va., 1979-86; Nat. Endowment Arts grantee, 1982-83. Group shows include: U. Ariz. Mus. Art, Tucson, 1979, Internat. Exhbn., Antwerp, Belgium, 1981, Internat. Invitational Exhbn., San Giorgio, Italy, 1983, San Francisco Art Inst., 1983, Soker-Kaseman Gallery, San Francisco, 1983, Amnesty Internat., Lima, Peru, 1983; Franklin Furnace, N.Y.C., 1983; Va. Mus. Art, Richmond, 1983, 85, 88; represented in permanent collections: San Francisco Art Inst., Erie Art Ctr., Pa., San Antonio Mus. Modern Art, U. Wis., Madison, Mus. Modern Art, N.Y.C., Tyringham Inst., Mass., U. Ariz., Tucson. Contbr. articles to profl. publs.

IVEY, KEVIN JOHN, internist; b. Warwick, Queensland, Australia, Mar. 6, 1939; came to U.S., 1968; s. Albert T. and Rose Anne (Brown) I.; m. Judith G. Kelso, Dec. 31, 1964; children—Thomas, John, Catherine, Mark. M.D., U. Queensland, 1962. Diplomate Eng. Bd. Internal Medicine. Intern, U. Queensland, Brisbane, 1963, resident, 1964; sr. med. resident U. Leeds, Eng., 1965-68; fellow in gastroenterology U. Iowa, Iowa City, 1968-70; clin. lectr. U. Sydney, New South Wales, Australia, 1970-74; assoc. prof. medicine U. Mo.-Columbia, 1975-80; prof. medicine U. Calif.-Irvine, 1980—; chief gastrointestinal research Long Beach VA Med. Ctr., Calif., 1980—; chmn. research and devel. com. 1985-87; mem. VA Merit Rev. Bd. Gastroenterology Research, VA Cen. Office, 1986—, Orange County Philharm. Soc. Author numerous articles. Australian Nat. Health and Med. Research Council grantee, 1972-74; VA grantee, 1976—. Fellow ACP, Royal Australian Coll. Physicians, Royal Coll. Physicians (London); mem. Am. Gastroent. Assn., Am. Fedn. Clin. Research. Clubs: Huntington Harbour Yacht; U. Calif.-Irvine Sailing. also: VAMC Long Beach CA 90822

IVEY, ROBERT CARL, artistic director, educator, choreographer; b. Australia, Aug. 28, 1939; came to U.S., 1951; s. Carl Roy and Virginia (Fulford) I. Student Ga. Southwestern U., 1958-59, Sch. Am. Ballet, 1959, Columbia U., 1959-61, Manhattan Med. Sch., N.Y.C., 1961, Emory U., 1962, Swedish State Theatre Sch., Stockholm, 1968. Soloist Den Norske Opera Ballet, Oslo, Norway, 1964-68, Svenska Riksteatre, Stockholm, Sweden, 1969-75; featured actor Det Norske Theatre, Oslo, 1968-69; choreographer Spoleto Festival USA, Charleston, S.C., 1977-79, choreographer in residence, 1979-83; dir. Robert Ivey Ballet, Charleston, 1979-83; mem. faculty Coll. Charleston, 1979—, choreographer, 1979-83, now prof. dance; asst. dir. Savannah (Ga.) Ballet, 1979-80; choreographer Charleston Opera Co., 1980-83, mem. artistic bd., 1981-88; choreographer Colombia, South Am., 1986; founder E. Cooper Theatre and Theatre Works, Charleston, 1986—. Pres. Charleston Area Arts Council, 1982-86; mem. Govs. Task Force Dance, Columbia, S.C., 1983—; mem. Gov.'s steering com. S.C. Arts Commn., 1983—; toured Soviet Union in cultural exchange, 1987. Recipient choreography award S.C. Arts Commn., 1980, Gov.'s Artistic Excellence award, 1986-87, Gov.'s Outstanding Contbns. award, 1987-88. Mem. Actor's Equity Assn., Charleston Area Arts Council, Screen Actor's Guild. Episcopalian. Office: Robert Ivey Ballet 1632 Ashley Hall Rd Charleston SC 29407

IVY, EDWARD EVERETT, entomologist, consultant; b. Hollis, Okla., Sept. 24, 1913; s. James Thomas and Betty (Minnear) I.; m. Elizabeth Alberta Slater, Feb. 23, 1935 (dec. Mar. 1981); children: James, Betty. BS, Okla State U., 1934; PhD, Tex. A&M U., 1951. Registered profl. entomologist, all 50 states, Can., Mex. Research entomologist USDA, College Station, Tex., 1940-55; salesman pesticides Mich. Chem. Corp., St. Louis, Mich., 1955-63; research entomologist Pennwalt Corp., Phila., 1963-75; cons. in pesticide devel. various nations, 1975—. Contbr. numerous articles to profl. jours. Mem. Entomol. Soc. Am., Am. Registry Profl. Engtomologists, Sigma Xi. Presbyterian. Home and Office: 1771 Broadway Apt 217 Concord CA 95420

IWAI, KATSUHITO, economist, educator; b. Shibuya, Tokyo, Japan, Feb. 13, 1947; parents: Toshiro and Shizue (Watanabe) I.; m. Minae Mizumura. BA, U. Tokyo, 1969; PhD, MIT, 1972. Research economist U. Calif., Berkeley, 1972-73; asst. prof. econs. Yale U., New Haven, Conn., 1973-79, sr. research assoc. Cowles Found., 1979-81; assoc. prof. U. Tokyo, 1981-88, prof., 1988—. Author several books on econs. Office: Faculty Econs, U Tokyo, Bunkyo-ku Tokyo, Japan

IWAMURA, EIRO, steel company executive; b. Sept. 13, 1915; married; 3 children. Ed. Imperial U., Tokyo. With Kawasaki Dockyard Co. Ltd., 1938-56; gen. mgr. steelmaking dept. Chiba Works, 1956-62, gen. mgr. ironmaking dept., 1962-65, exec. v.p., gen. supt. Chiba Works and Welding Rod and Iron Powder Plant, 1975-77; gen. mgr. ironmaking plant constrn. dept. Mizushima Works, 1965-66, dir. bd., asst. gen. supt., 1966-69, mng. dir. tech. dept., tech. devel. dept., overseas tech. assistance dept. and order ctr., 1969-73, sr. mng. dir. tech. dept., subcontract planning dept., 1973-75; pres. Kawasaki Steel Corp., Tokyo, 1977-82, chmn., 1982—. Office: Kawasaki Steel Corp, Chiyoda-Ku, Hibiya Kokusai Bldg, 2-3 Uchisaiwaicho, 2 Chome, Tokyo Japan *

IWANAMI, YUJIRO, publishing company executive; b. Kamakura, Kanagawa, Japan, June 25, 1919; s. Shigeo and Yoshi I.; m. Atsuko; children—Tsutomu, Ritsuko. B.A., U. Tokyo, 1944. Pres. Iwanami Shoten, Pubs., Tokyo, 1949-78, chmn., 1978—. Mem. Japan Book Pubs.' Assn. (councilor), Tokyo Jr. C. of C. and Industry, Internat. House of Japan. Office: Iwanami Shoten Pubs, 2-5-5 Hitotsubashi, Chiyoda-ku, Tokyo 101, Japan

IWASAKI, TSUTOMU, physician, educator; b. Kanagawa, Japan, Sept. 26, 1948; d. Masafumi and Katsu Tagai; m. Yoriko Iwasaki, Nov. 7, 1974; 1 child, Youichi. MD, Gunma (Japan) U., 1973; postgrad., Mayo Grad. Sch. Medicine, 1984; PhD, Shinshu U., Matsumoto, Japan, 1987. Cardiologist Tokyo Met. Geriatric Hosp., 1973-80; research fellow Deborah Cardiovascular Research Inst., Browns Mills, N.J., 1980-81, Mayo Clinic, Rochester, Minn., 1981-84; cardiologist Heart Inst., Japan, 1985-86; asst. prof. Shinshu U. Sch. Medicine, 1987—. Mem. Japan Circulation Soc., Japan Vascular Soc., Sigma Xi. Home: 1433 8 Shimo Okada, Matsumoto Nagano Japan Office: Shinshu U Sch Medicine, Dept Geriatric, Asahi Matsumoto Nagano Japan

IWASAKI, YOICHIRO, plastic company executive; b. Tokyo, Feb. 4, 1929; s. Sakae and Kikue (Uehara) I.; m. Tamako Momma, Nov. 27, 1933; 1 child, Masahiro. BS in Econs., Tokyo U., 1955. With Mitsubishi Rayon Co., Tokyo, 1955—, adminstrv. asst. plastics div., 1987—. Named Hon. Citizen of City of Mobile, Ala. Mem. Licensing Execs. Soc. Home: 8-4 Meguro 4-chome, Meguroku, Tokyo 153, Japan Office: Mitsubishi Rayon Co Ltd, 3-19 Kyobashi 2-chome, Chuo-ku, Tokyo 104, Japan

IWAYAMA, TAJIRO, educator; b. Kyoto, Japan, Jan. 10, 1933; s. Hikoichi and Toku (Fukui) I.; B.A., Doshisha U., 1955, M.A., 1958; M.F.A., State U. Iowa, 1962; m. Ikuyo Takami, Mar. 16, 1960. Research asst. Doshisha U., Kyoto, 1958-63, instr. Am. lit., 1963-65, asst. prof., 1965-70, prof., 1970—, dean acad. affairs, 1977-80, dir. Ctr. Am. Studies, 1983-86, dean Faculty of Letters, 1986— ; dir. Kyoto Am. Studies Summer Seminar, 1981-86 . Fulbright grad. fellow, 1960-62, Am. Council Learned Socs. fellow, 1972-73. Mem. Japanese Assn. Am. Lit. (exec. sec.), MLA, English Lit. Assn. Japan, Japanese Assn. Am. Studies. Author: English Composition Manual, 1978; Saul Bellow, 1982, Invitation to American Literature, 1987, The Gilded Age and American Literature, 1987; editor: East-West Review, 1964-67. Home: 46 Hitsujisaru-cho, Katsura, Nishikyo-ku, Kyoto 615, Japan Office: Doshisha U, Karasuma Imadegawa, Kamikyoku, Kyoto 602, Japan

IYAMUREMYE, ALPHONSE, mathematician; b. Satinskyi, Rwanda, Jan. 25, 1952; arrived in France, 1986; s. Rugangura and Ancilla Nyirabahaya. Lic. in Math., Cath. U. of Louvain, Belgium, 1976; M in Math., U. Laval, Quebec, Can., 1982, PhD in Math., 1986. Asst. prof. Nat. U. of Rwanda, Butare, 1977-80, U. of Brest (France), 1986—. Mem. Am. Math. Soc. Office: U de Bretagne Occidentale, 20 Av le Gorgeu, 29200 Brest Finistere France

IYAYI, MACAULAY, banker; b. Ubiaja, Bendel, Nigeria, Oct. 27, 1948; s. Francis Olfoghe and Felicia Enomere (Esangbedo) I.; m. Patricia Enoyoze Osazuwa, May 7, 1977; 1 child, Osarugue. BS in Econs., U. Ife, Ile-Ife, Nigeria, 1976; MBA, DePaul U., 1981. Supr. New Nigeria Bank Benin City, Bendel, 1970-72; asst. to ops. mgr. Internat. Merchant Bank, Lagos, Nigeria, 1977-78; mgr. Internat. Merchant Bank, Port-Harcourt, Nigeria, 1981-84; asst. gen. mgr. Internat. Merchant Bank, Lagos, Nigeria, 1985—; mng. dir. Alpha Merchant Bank, Port-Harcourt, 1988—; research officer Price Control Bd., Lagos, 1976-77. Fellow Brit. Chartered Inst. Bankers, Nigerian Inst. Bankers; mem. Brit. Inst. Mgmt., Nigerian Inst. Mmgt., Assn. MBA Execs. Office: Alpha Merchant Bank Ltd, Glass House, 188 Awolowo Rd, Ikoyi, PMB 12882 Lagos Nigeria

IZMEROV, NIKOLAY FEDOTOVICH, health administrator; b. Frunze, USSR, Dec. 19, 1927; s. Fedot Fedotovich and Evdokiya Filatovna (Shemilina) I.; m. Natalya Ivanovna dubovskaya; children: Ekaterina, Jana. MD, Med. Inst., Tashkent, USSR, 1952; Hon. degree, Acad. Med. Scis., USSR, 1986. Physician Hosp., Tashkent, USSR, 1952-53; sci. worker Inst. Postgraduate Med. Tng., Moscow, 1954-60; deputy minister Ministry Health RSFSR, Moscow, 1960-64; asst. to dir. gen. World Health Orgn., Geneva, 1964-71; dir. Inst. Industrial Hygiene and Occupational Diseases Acad. Med. Sci., Moscow, 1971-88. Contbr. artilces to profl. jours. Deputy Moscow Soviet of People's Deputies. Recipient Order of the Red Banner of Labor, Medal for Valiant Labor, Supreme Soviet USSR. Mem. Internat. Commn. on Occupational Health, World Health Orgn., Socs. Industrial Hygiene in Bulgaria, Hungary, E. Germany, Czechoslovakia, Ireland. Communist. Home: Kutuzovsky Prospect 35/30R340, 121165 Moscow USSR Office: Inst Indsl Hygiene Occupational, Diseases of USSR, Acad Med Scis, Budennogo Prospekt 31, 105275 Moscow USSR

IZUMIYA, SHYUICHI, mathematician, educator; b. Sapporo, Hokkaido, Japan, July 7, 1952; s. Susumu and Takeko (Tsukuda) I.; m. Megumi Takahashi, May 10, 1977. BSc, Hokkaido U., 1974, MSc, 1977, DSc, 1984. Instr. Nara (Japan) Women's U., 1980-85; asst. prof. Hokkaido U., 1985-87, assoc. prof., 1987—. Mem. Math. Soc. of Japan, Am. Math. Soc., Japan Astronomical Soc. Home: Hiragishi 4-12-5-3, Sapporo 062, Japan Office: Hokkaido U, Dept Math Faculty of Sci, Sapporo 060, Japan

IZURIETA, FABIAN, industrial company executive; b. Quito, Pichincha, Ecuador, Apr. 27, 1946; s. Ricardo and Blanca (Mora Bowen) Izurieta; m. Ana Victoria Teran; children: Diego, Mauricio. Degree in econs., U. Central, Quito, 1969; MBA, Rollins Coll., Orlando, Fla., 1971. With Am. Fed. Savs. and Loan Assn., Orlando, 1970; fin. analyst Standard Brands, Inc., N.Y.C., 1971-73; asst. to pres. Royal Productos Alimenticios, Caracas, Venezuela, 1973, new products mgr., 1973-75; mktg. dir. Fleischman Ecuatoriana, Guayaquil, Equador, 1975-76, gen. mgr., 1976-79; gen. mgr. Unicom Cia. Ltda., Quito, 1979—; bd. dirs. Banco Continental, Equador, 1981—; pres. Johnson Wax, Equador, 1982—; cons. Minister of Industry, Equador, 1983-84; Equadorian del. 26th and 27th Assemblies UN, N.Y.C., 1971, 72. Izquierda Democratica. Roman Catholic. Home: Urb Club Los Chillos, Quito, Pichincha Equador Office: Unicom Cia Ltda, PO Box 8077, Quito, Pichincha Equador

IZZO, LOUIS DOMINIC, psychologist; b. Rochester, N.Y., June 12, 1925; s. Joseph M. and Erminie C. (Pelusio) I.; B.S., U. Rochester, 1953; M.A., 1957; postgrad. U. Mich., 1965-78; m. Helen Theresa Baliski, June 12, 1950; children—Erminie Ann, Joseph Mario, David John, Stephen Anthony. Psychologist, Public Schs. Rochester, 1956-86, initiator Early Detection and Prevention Program, 1957, sr. psychologist program, 1958-69, chief psychologist, program cons. city and county schs. Primary Mental Health Project, 1969—; sr. clin. psychologist Rochester State Hosp., 1958, 59; staff psychologist Center Community Studies, U. Rochester, 1969—; sr. clin. psychologist, asst. chief service, mental hygiene unit Albion State Tng. Sch., Western Reformatory and Prison for Women, 1963-71; pvt. practice hypnotherapy, 1976—; cons. hypnotist, 1979—; pyschol. cons. Bd. Coop. Ednl. Services, 1984—. Served with USAAF, 1945-46; PTO. Mem. Am., N.Y. State, Genesee Valley (pres., 1966-67) psychol. assns., N.Y. Assn. Sch. Psychologists, Rochester Tchrs. Assn., N.Y. State Tchrs. Assn., NEA, Assn. Advance Ethical Hypnosis, Am. Inst. Hypnosis. Author: (with others) New Ways in School Mental Health: Early Detection and Prevention of School Maladaptation, 1975; contbr. articles to profl. jours. Home: 4479 Saint Paul Blvd Rochester NY 14617 Office: 575 Mount Hope Ave Rochester NY 14620 also: 1171 Titus Ave Rochester NY 14617

JAAFAR, MOHAMED ALI, accountant, financial consultant; b. Kota Bharu, Kelantan, Malaysia, June 8, 1924; s. Mohamed Bin Jaafar and Fatimah (Saadiah) Mohamed Ali; m. Siti Fatimah, 1944; m. Sabariah, 1956; children: Rosharumi, Rosmawar, Sabri, Rosnilam, Darma, Atma, Rosdelima, Roslinda. PhD, U. Ga., 1981. Tutor Islah Sch., Kota Bharu, 1949-51; mgr. Coop. Soc., Kelantan, 1951-53; officer IRS, Malaysia, 1954-72; acct. State Econ. Devel. Corp., Terengganu, Malaysia, 1973-80. Mem. Australian Soc. Accts., CPA Assn. Home: Wisma Harumi Kelulut, Marang, Terengganu Malaysia Office: Mohamed Ali & Co, 235-C 1st Floor Jen Bandar, Kuala Terengganu, Terengganu Malaysia

JA'AFAR IBNI AL-MARHUM ABDUL RAHMAN, Sultan Negri Sembilan; b. Klang, Selangor, Malaya, July 19, 1922; m. Tunku Najihah, 1943; 6 children. Student Raffles Coll., Singapore, 1941; L.L.B., Nottingham U., Eng. Officer, Land Office, Seremban, Negri Sembilan, Malaya, 1941-45; asst. dist. officer, Rembau, Negri Sembilan, 1946-47; with State Sec.'s Office, Selangor, 1948; asst. dist. officer of Parit, Perak; asst. state sec. of Ipoh, Perak; dist. officer of Tampin, Negri Sembilan, until 1957; joined Malayan Fgn. Service, 1957; service in Washington, N.Y.C. and London; ambassador to UAR, 1963-65; high commnr. to Nigeria, 1965-67; Yang di-Pertuan Besar of Negari Sembilan, 1967—; Yang di-Pertuan Agong, 1979—; chancellor U. Kemangsaan, Malaysia, 1976—, formerly dep. Paramount Ruler. Address: care Press Attache Malaysian Embassy 2401 Massachusetts Ave NW Washington DC 20008 *

JABALPURWALA, KAIZER ESUFALI, chemical consultant; b. Surat, Gujarat, India, May 4, 1932; came to Can., 1964, naturalized, 1974; s. Esufali G. and Fatema F. (Baxamoosa) J.; m. Sharifa I. Ahmadi, Oct. 23, 1960; children—Sheila, Inez. B.Sc. with honors, Bombay U., 1954, M.Sc. in Phys. Chemistry, 1956, Ph.D. in Phys. and Inorganic Chemistry, 1960. Research asst. Bombay U., India, 1958-61; research assoc. Boston U., 1961-64; tech. mgr. Zochem Ltd., Brampton, Ont., Can., 1964-74; ptnr., exec. dir. G.H. Chems. Ltd., St. Hyacinthe, Que., Can., 1974-83; exec. dir. Jabalpur Industries, Inc., St. Lambert, Que., 1983—, internat. cons., 1983—. Contbr. articles to profl. jours. Patentee in field in U.S.A., Can., U.K. Recipient R.R. Desai gold medal Bombay U., 1961. Mem. Am. Chem. Soc. Chem. Inst. Can., Brit. Chem. Soc., AAAS, N.Y. Acad. Scis., ASTM, Soc. Photog. Scientists and Engrs., TAPPI, Fedn. Socs. Paint Tech., Oil and Colour Chemists Assn. (U.K.), Sigma Xi. Liberal. Mohammedan. Avocation: electronics. Home: 350 Lesperance St, Saint Lambert, PQ Canada J4P 1Y5 Office: Jabalpur Industries Inc, PO Box 94, Saint Lambert, PQ Canada J4P 3N4

JABIN, MARVIN (MARK), real estate developer, lawyer; b. N.Y.C., Mar. 28, 1929; s. Sol and Belle Jabin; BA in Biology and Chemistry, NYU, 1952; BS in Engring., UCLA, 1954, JD, 1957; m. Lelia Honig, May 13, 1952; children: Valerie, Gregory, Anthony, Desiree. Bar: Calif. 1958, U.S. Supreme Ct. 1961; ptnr. Jabin & Jabin, Monterey Park, Calif., 1958—; v.p. CVJ Constrn. Inc., Monterey Park, 1977— ; pres. Jabin Corp., Monterey Park, 1979—; judge protem Alhambra Mcpl. Ct., Calif., 1981-82; asst. prof. bus. law Calif. State U., Los Angeles, 1972-75; dir. Golden Security Thrift & Loan Assn., 1983—. Adv. council Calif. State U., Los Angeles, 1971-76. Served with U.S. Army, 1946-49. Mem. Am. Arbitration Assn. (arbitrator 1963-80), San Gabriel Valley Bar Assn. (pres. 1975), Los Angeles County Bar Assn. (trustee 1975-77), Monterey Park C. of C. (bd. dirs. 1982-85). Lodge: Rotary (bd. dirs. Monterey Park club 1982-83). Office: 701 S Atlantic Blvd Monterey Park CA 91754

JABLONSKI, WANDA MARY, publisher; b. Czechoslovakia; d. Eugene and Mary J.; came to U.S., 1938, naturalized, 1945; BA, Cornell U., 1942; postgrad. Columbia U., 1943; LHD (hon.), St. Lawrence U., 1978. Oil editor Jour. Commerce, N.Y.C., 1943-54; sr. editor Petroleum Week, McGraw-Hill, N.Y.C., 1954-61; founder, owner, editor, pub. Petroleum Intelligence Weekly, N.Y.C., 1961—. Mem. Oxford Energy Policy Club, Council Fgn. Relations, The Com. 200. Home: Bridgehampton NY 11932 Office: PIW 1 Times Sq New York NY 10036

JACINTO, GEORGE ANTHONY, counselor, educator, consultant; b. Gilroy, Calif., Dec. 21, 1949; s. George Peter and Isabelle Agnes (Joseph) J. BS in Criminology-Corrections, Calif. State U.-Fresno, 1974; postgrad. Wash. Theol. Union, 1975, U. Wis., 1980, Boise State U., 1981, postgrad. in social work Fla. State U., 1987—; MEd in Guidance and Counseling-Gen. Personnel Services, Coll. Idaho, 1982. Intern counselor drug and alcohol Mt. Carmel Guild, Paterson, N.J., 1974; dir. recreation program Summer Markham, Toronto, Ont., Can., 1975; pastoral asst. Ch. St. Peter, Toronto, 1975; youth minister Ch. St. Michael, Olympia, Wash., 1976-77; dir. youth ministry St. James Congregation, Franklin, Wis., 1977-80; diocesan youth dir. Cath. Diocese of Boise, Idaho, 1980-83; intern., counselor, grant writer Salvation Army Drug Rehab. Ctr., Boise, 1982; dir. religious edn. St. Andrew Ch., Orlando, Fla., 1983-84; vocat. rehab. counselor DLES, State of Fla., Orlando, 1984-88, sr. vocat. rehab. counselor, 1988—; part-time youth minister Good Shepherd Ch., Orlando, 1985-88; founder Am. Life Planning Assocs., Orlando, 1985—; counselor, career and life planning cons., youth programming cons., youth minister. Active diversion program Union St. Ctr., Olympia, Wash.; campaign leader for children's toys Indo-China Refugee Relief, Milw.; mem. adv. community agys. concerned with youth issues; coordinator community service program for young people, Franklin, Wis. Mem. Am. Assn. Counseling and Devel., Am. Rehab. Counselors Assn., World Future Soc., Nat. Rehabilitation Assn., Fellowship of Reconciliation, Nat. Spiritualist Assn. of Chs., Nat. Assn. Social Workers, Inst. Noetic Scis., New Age Network. Democrat. Home: 923 Bishop Dr Altamonte Springs FL 32701 Office: Vocat Rehab 2520 N Orange Ave Orlando FL 32804

JACKEL, SIMON SAMUEL, food products co. exec., tech. cons.; b. N.Y.C., Nov. 11, 1917; s. Victor and Sadie (Ungar) J.; A.M., Columbia, 1947, Ph.D., 1950; B.S., Coll. City N.Y., 1938; postgrad. U. Ill., 1941-42; m. Betty Carlson, Jan. 22, 1954; children—Phyliss Marcia, Glenn Edward. Head fermentation div. Fleischmann Lab., Stamford, Conn., 1944-59; v.p. research and devel. Vico Products Co., Chgo., 1959-61; dir. lab., research and devel. v.p., dir. lab. and tech. research Quality Bakers of Am. div. Sunbeam Baked Foods, Greenwich, Conn., 1961-84, v.p., research dir., 1980-84; dir. research and devel., mem. operating com. Bakers Research Devel. Service, Greenwich, 1969-84; pres. Plymouth Tech. Services, Westport, Conn., 1951—; dir. hearing aid audiology Jewish Home and Hosp. for Aged, N.Y.C., 1951-76. Mem. sci. adv. com. Am. Inst. Baking, 1970—, mem. sanitation edn. adv. com., 1978-81. Mem. industry adv. com. N.D. State U., 1971-85; chmn. Am. Bakers Assn. tech. liaison com. to U.S. Dept. Agr., 1975-87. Recipient USAAF Exceptional Civilian Service award, 1943; USPHS research grantee, 1947-50. Fellow Am. Inst. Chemists, AAAS; mem. Am. Chem. Soc., Am. Assn. Cereal Chemists (chmn. milling and baking div. 1973-74, chmn. N.Y. sect. 1973-74; Charles N. Frey award 1981; bakery columnist Cereal Foods World 1984—), Am. Soc. Bakery Engrs. (chmn. tech. info. service com. 1979—), ASTM, Am. Bakers Assn. (nutrition com. 1971—, chmn. tech. liaison com. to U.S. Dept. Agr. 1975-87, food tech. regulatory affairs com. 1977—; alt. gov. 1978-87, gov. 1988—), Assn. for Environ. Protection, Ind. Bakers Assn. (cons., food safety com. 1977—, labeling com. 1978—, tech. affairs com. 1978—, chmn. labeling and good mfg. practices com. 1984—), Inst. Food Technologists, Am. Mgmt. Assn., Nutrition Today Soc., Soc. Nutrition Edn., Environ. Mgmt. Assn., N.Y. Acad. Sci., N.Y.C. Chemists Club, Sigma Xi, Phi Lambda Upsilon. Jewish. Author tech. articles; tech. editor Bakery Prodn. and Mktg. Mag., 1968-85; contbr. articles to tech. jours. Patentee in field. Home: 14024 Capitol Dr Tampa FL 33613 Office: 191 Post Rd W Westport CT 06880

JACKLIN, TONY, professional golfer; b. Scunthorpe, July 7, 1944; s. Arthur David J.; m. Vivien Jacklin, 1966 (dec. Apr. 1988); 3 children. Profl. golfer, 1962—; dir. golf Sam Roque Club, Cadiz, Spain. Lincolnshire Open champion, 1961; won Brit. Asst. Profls.' title, 1965; won Dunlop Masters, 1967, 73; first Brit. player to win Brit. Open since 1951, 1969; U.S. Open champion, 1970; first Brit. player to win U.S. Open since 1920 and first since 1900 to hold U.S. and Brit. Open titles simultaneously; Greater Greensboro Open champion, 1968, 72; won Italian Open, 1973, German Open, 1979, Venezuelan Open, 1979, Jersey Open, 1981; Brit. P.G.A. champion, 1982; won 15 other maj. tournaments in various parts of world; capt. Ryder Cup Team, 1983, 85, 87; played in 7 Ryder Cup matches and 4 times for Eng. in World Cup, 3-time capt. Author: Golf With Tony Jacklin, 1969; The Price of Success, 1979; The First Forty Years, 1985. Decorated Order Brit. Empire. Mem. Brit. Profl. Golfers' Assn. (hon. life pres.), European Tour (hon. life). Address: Chestnut Lea, St Mary, Jersey Channel Islands

JACKLIN, WILLIAM THOMAS, county official, educator; b. Chgo., Dec. 26, 1940; s. Robert Theodore and Florence Carrie (Dombrow) J.; m. Bonnie Joy Winquist; 1 child, Laura Carrie. BS, Roosevelt U., 1967; MS in Bus., Ind. U., 1968. Assoc. instr. Ind. U., 1967-69; V.p. DuPage Corp., Lombard, Ill., 1970-73; inst. bus. Coll. DuPage, Glen Ellyn, Ill., 1969—; chief dep. auditor DuPage County, 1973, county auditor, 1973—; v.p. DuPage County Employees Credit Union, 1978-79, pres., 1979-80; fiscal officer DuPage Met. Enforcement Group, 1987—. Announcer CRIS Radio for the Blind. Mem. Ill. Prairie Path, DuPage County Rep. Cen. Com.; sec. York Twp. Rep. Orgn., 1978-80; treas. Highland Hills Assn., 1975-78; chmn. DuPage County com Gerald R. Ford presdl. campaign, 1976; mem. fin. mgmt. project com. Ill. Dept. Commerce and Community Affairs, 1980—; bd. dirs. Lombard Hist. Soc., v.p., 1983-87, pres., 1987—; founding co-chmn. Y. Ill. Conservative Coordinating Council. Mem. Inst. Internal Auditors (govt. and pub. affairs com. 1976-82), Nat. Assn. Accts. (assoc. dir.), Am. Acctg. Assn., Ill. Assn. County Auditors (sec.-treas. 1976-78 v.p. 1978-80, pres. 1980-84), Assn. Govt. Accts., Phi Delta Kappa. Christian Scientist. Lodge: Masons (sec. 1979-80). Home: 41 E 17th St Lombard IL 60148 Office: DuPage Ctr 421 N County Farm Rd Wheaton IL 60187

JACKMAN, MICHELE, management consultant, educator; b. Los Angeles, Aug. 18, 1944; d. Michael and Grace (DeLeo) Pantaleo; m. Jarrell C. Jackman, Sept. 7, 1968; 1 child, Renee Grace. BA in Polit. Sci., U. Calif., Davis, 1966; MSW in Social Policy, Cath. U., 1980; MA in Human Relations Mgmt., U. Okla., 1980. Social worker Los Angeles County, 1966-70; supr., trainer Santa Barbara (Calif.) County, 1970-74; mgr. Drug/Alcohol program U.S. Army, Western Europe, 1974-78; analyst, cons. Office Dep. Chief of Staff Personnel U.S. Army, Washington, 1978-80; trainer, cons. Profit Systems, Internat., Santa Barbara, 1980—; lectr. organizational psychology U. Calif., Santa Barbara; cons. numerous agys., orgns. Co-author: Choices/Challenges Teacher's Guide, 1985; contbr. chpts. to books. Recipient Commdr.'s medal for Disting. Civilian Service U.S. Army, 1977. Mem. Am. Mgmt. Assn., Nat. Assn. Social Workers (chmn. local chpt.), Am. Soc. Tng. and Devel., Nat. Assn. Female Execs., Santa Barbara C. of C. (Bus. award Council of High Edn./Industry 1986). Club: Univ. (Santa Barbara). Lodge: Native Daus. of Golden West. Office: Profit Systems Internat, Tng & Mgmt Systems 17 E Carrillo Suite 45 Santa Barbara CA 93101

JACKSON, ARTHUR GILBERT, drilling company executive; b. Lebanon, Tenn., July 2, 1949; s. Arthur Ilo and Winne Edith (Vaughn) J.; m. Teresa Ann Stacy, Feb. 19, 1987; 1 child, Laura Leah. BS, Vanderbilt U., 1972. Dist. sales rep. Ingersoll-Rand Corp., Elkridge, Md., 1972-75; project dir. Eatherly & Jackson, Lebanon, 1975-76; v.p. Jackson Drilling, Lebanon, 1976-85; pres. Jackson Enterprises, Lebanon, 1985—; v.p. Am. Geosearch, Lebanon, 1984-85; cons. in industry, 1979—; several directorships. Contbr. articles to profl. jours. Mem. Internat. Assn. Air Drilling Contractors, So. Air Drilling Assn. (pres. 1981-86), Ducks Unltd. (founder Wilson County, Tenn. chpt.). Republican. Presbyterian. Office: 204 S Maple St Lebanon TN 37087

JACKSON, BLYDEN, English language educator; b. Paducah, Ky., Oct. 2, 1910; s. George Washington and Julia Estelle (Reid) J.; m. Roberta Bowles, Aug. 2, 1958. AB, Wilberforce U., 1930; AM, U. Mich., 1938, Ph.D. (Rosenwald fellow 1947-49), 1952; LHD (hon.), U. Louisville, 1977; LittD (hon.), Wilberforce U., 1978; Litt.D. (hon.), U.N.C.-Chapel Hill, 1985. Tchr. English, pub. schs. Louisville, 1934-45; asst., then assoc. prof. English Fisk U., 1945-54; prof. English, head dept. Southern U., 1954-62, dean Grad. Sch., 1962-69; prof. English U. N.C., 1969-81; assoc. dean U. N.C. (Grad. Sch.), 1973-76, spl. asst. to dean, 1976-81; Spl. research criticism Negro lit. Author: The Waiting Years; co-author: Black Poetry in America; Asso. editor: CLA Bull; adv. editor: So. Lit. Jour; Contbr. articles to profl. jours. Mem. Coll. Lang Assn. (pres. 1957-59), Modern Lang. Assn. (chmn. 20th century lit. div. 1976), Nat. Council Tchrs. English (Distinguished lectr. 1970-71, chmn. coll. sect. 1971-73, trustee research found. 1975-79), Coll. Lang. Assn. (v.p. 1954-56, pres. 1956-58), Speech Assn. Am., N.C. Tchrs. English, Alpha Phi Alpha. Home: 102 Laurel Hill Rd Chapel Hill NC 27514

JACKSON, BOBBY L., financial corporate executive; b. Jacksonville, Fla., Jan. 15, 1930; s. Walter Drew and Vernie Belle (Knowles) J.; m. Martha Lydia Whiddon, Dec. 23, 1950; children: Debra Lee Danyus, Murray Steven. BS in Bus. Mgmt., Jones Coll., Jacksonville, 1959; BS in Acctg., Jacksonville U., 1974; MBA, U. No. Fla., 1978. CPA, Fla.; cert. assoc. in risk mgmt., Ins. Inst. Am. Asst. credit acctg. supr. Standard Oil of Ky., Jacksonville, 1951-55; staff acct. Humphreys Mining Co., Jacksonville, 1955-62; bus. mgr. Massey Tech. Inst., Jacksonville, 1962-63; chief acct. Jacksonville Shipyards Inc., subs. Fruehauf, 1963-64, corp. controller, 1964—. Mem. Rep. Exec. Com., Jacksonville, 1970-73. Served to cpl. U.S. Army, 1947-48, 1950-51. Mem. Am. Inst. CPAs, Risk and Ins. Mgmt. Soc. (dir. Jacksonville/No. Fla. chpt. 1980-85; pres. 1981), Nat. Assn. Accts. (chpt. pres. 1968-69, Most Valued Mem. award 1963-65, Manuscripts award 1978). Democrat. Baptist. Lodge: Woodmen of World (Fla. state pres. 1969-71). Home: 9178 Tottenham Ct Jacksonville FL 32217 Office: Jacksonville Shipyards Inc 750 E Bay Jacksonville FL 32203

JACKSON, BRUCE GEORGE, lawyer; b. Portland, Oreg., July 15, 1942; s. George William and Sally Marie (Dorner) J.; m. Jane Jackson, Sept. 8, 1972; children—Yvette, Scott. B.S. cum laude, U. Oreg., 1966; J.D., U. Calif.-Berkeley, 1970. Bar: Hawaii 1971, U.S. Dist. Ct. Hawaii 1971. Assoc. Case, Kay & Lynch, Honolulu, 1970-74; ptnr. Curtis W. Carlsmith, Honolulu, 1974-76; sole practice, Honolulu, 1977—; speaker on real property law, land trusts, estate planning, 1977—. Served with N.G., 1960-68. Mem. ABA, Hawaii Bar Assn., Sigma Phi Epsilon (life). Democrat. Clubs: Honolulu, Downtown Exchange (Honolulu). Student editor: Kragen & McNulty on Federal Income Taxation, 1970. Office: Pacific Tower Suite 1132 1001 Bishop St Honolulu HI 96813

JACKSON, DALE EDWARD, security officer; b. Sacramento, Feb. 21, 1950; s. Leonard Franklin and Georgia Lee (Guild) J.; A.A., Am. River Coll., 1971; B.S., U. Calif.-Davis 1973, M.A., 1979; m. Rose Estelle Sherman, Nov. 21, 1982; 1 child, Lindsey Estelle. Police officer City of Roseville, Calif., 1973-77; spl. agt. CIA, Washington, 1977-80; owner, corporate dir. Jackson & Assocs., Investigators, San Francisco, 1980—; splty. gas lab. dir. Liquid Carbonic Corps., San Carlos, Calif., 1980-81; quality program mgr. Hysol div. Dexter Corp., Pittsburgh, Calif., 1981-87; dir. legal and security affairs Hysol AIP Div. Dexter Corp. Pittsburg, Calif., 1987— . Asst. commandant cadets Calif. Cadet Corps San Juan Unified Sch. Dist., Carmichael, Calif., 1968—; chmn. Antioch Community Energy Commn., 1983—; chmn. Antioch City design rev. bd., 1987—. Mem. Am. Chem. Soc., AAAS, Calif. Peace Officers Assn., Peace Officers Assn. Calif., Am. Soc. Quality Control, Am. Soc. Indsl. Security, Asm. Def. Preparedness Assn., Soc. Advancement Materials and Process Engring., U.S. Naval Inst. Republican. Baptist. Club: Lions. Contbr. articles in field to profl. jours. Office: PO Box 312 Pittsburg CA 94565

JACKSON, DANIEL FRANCIS, engineer, educator; b. Pitts., June 11, 1925; s. Daniel F. and Edna (Marzolf) J.; m. Bettina Bush, Dec. 15, 1951. B.S., U. Pitts., 1949, M.S., 1950; Ph.D., State U. N.Y. Coll. Forestry at Syracuse U., 1957. Lectr. U. Pitts., 1949-51; asst. prof. Coll. Steubenville, Ohio, 1951-52; engr. C.E. U.S. Army, Pitts. dist., 1952-53; asst. prof., then asso. prof. Western Mich. U., 1955-59; asso. prof. U. Louisville, 1959-63; prof. civil engring. Syracuse U., 1963-73; dir., prof. div. environ. and urban systems Sch. Tech., Fla. Internat. U., Miami, 1973-78; prof., dir. Inst. Environ. Studies La. State U., Baton Rouge, 1982-86; dir. research Jim Rodgers Pools, Inc., 1978-82; dir. C.C. Adams Center Ecol. Study, 1955-59; asso. dir. Potamological Inst., 1960-63; dir. 1st NATO sponsored Advanced Study Inst., U.S., summer 1962. Author: Algae and Man, 1963, Some Aquatic Resources of Onondaga County, 1964, Some Aspects of Mexomixis, 1967, Algae, Man, and Environment, 1968, Some Endangered and Exotic Species, 1978; filmstrip sets Environmental Pollution, 1969, Man in the Biosphere, 1971; also articles. Pres. Ky. Soc. Natural History, 1961-63; Bd. dirs. Mich. Conservation Clubs, 1955-57. Served with AUS, 1943-46, ETO. Recipient Rotary Internat. award as outstanding tchr. in Ky., 1962; Outstanding Community Leader award for environ. improvement Onondaga County, 1969. Mem. Internat. Limnological Soc., Freshwater Assn. Brit. Empire, Water Pollution Control Fedn., Air Pollution Control Assn., Ecol. Soc. Am., Brit. Ecol. Soc., Limnology and Oceanography Soc., Sigma Xi, Phi Sigma, Nu Sigma Nu, Beta Beta Beta. Home: 3323 Guilford Ct Naples FL 33962

JACKSON, DARYL SANDERS, architect; b. Clunes, Victoria, Australia, Feb. 7, 1937; s. Cecil John and Doreen May (Sanders) J.; m. Kay Parsons, Feb. 12, 1960; children: Timothy, Sara, Olivia, Melissa. BArch, U. Melbourne, 1958; DArch, Royal Melbourne Inst. Tech., 1956. Ptnr. Daryl Jackson-Evan Walker Architects, Melbourne, Australia, 1963-69; prin. Daryl Jackson Pty. Ltd., Melbourne and Canberra, Australia, 1969—; dir. Daryl Jackson Robin Dyke Party Ltd. Author: Daryl Jackson Architecture Drawings and Photographs, 1984; contbr. articles to profl. pubs.; archtl. works include: Lauriston Girls' Sch., Melbourne (Royal Australian Inst. architects Victorian Architecture Awards Bronze medal 1970); Princes Hill High Sch., Melbourne (Royal Auastralian Inst. Architects-Victorian Architecture Awards Bronze medal 1973); City Edge Housing, South Melbourne, Australia (Royal Australian Inst. Architects-Victorian Architecture Awards Bronze medal 1976); State Bank Coll., Baxter, Melbourne (Royal Australian Inst. Architects-Victorian Architecture Awards Bronze medal 1978, Gold medal, 1987); Canberra Sch. Art, Acton, Australia (Royal Australian Inst. Architects-Australian Capital Ter. Architecture Awards Canberra medallion 1981,82, nat. Sir Zelman Cowan award 1981); McLachlan Offices, Barton, Australia (Royal Australian Inst. Architects Australian Capital Ter. Architecture Awards Merit award 1982); Abrahams House, Brighton, Victoria, Australia (Royal Australian Inst. Architects Victorian Architecture Awards Robert Haddon award 1982). Trustee Nat. Gallery Victoria, Melbourne, 1983—. Prize Parliament House Design Competition, 1979. Fellow Royal Australian Inst. Architects (Victorian Architecture Awards citation, 1974, (4) 1976, 1978, 1979; mem. Royal Inst. Brit. Architects, Architecture Assn. London. Office: Daryl Jackson Pty Ltd, 35 Little Bourke St, Melbourne 3000, Australia

JACKSON, DAVID BRADLEY, home builder, developer; b. N.Y.C., Apr. 8, 1945; s. David H. and Sara (Love) Jackson; m. Suzanne Farnsworth, June 17, 1967; 1 son, David B. B.S. Chem. Engring., Lehigh U., 1967. Devel. engr. Hercules, Inc., Wilmington, Del., 1967-68, tech. sales, Cin., 1968-71; market devel. Gen. Electric Co., Pittsfield, Mass., 1971-73; builder, developer, pres. Dave Jackson Homes, Inc., Summit, N.J., 1973—. Patentee: 2 process and product inventions, 1969, 1971. Deacon, Congregational Ch., Short Hills, N.J., 1980-83, trustee, 1976-79. Mem. Builders Assn. Somerset, N.J. (bd. dirs., pres. 1978, Award of Excellence, 1985), Builders Assn. Morris, N.J. (Feibel award 1980, bd. dirs.), N.J. Builders Assn. (bd. dirs., pres. 1984, Builder of Yr. award 1985, Excellence award 1986, named to Hall of Fame 1986), Nat. Assn. Home Builders (bd. dirs.). Office: Dave Jackson Homes Inc 20 Woodmere Dr Summit NJ 07901

JACKSON, DAVID EDWARD PRITCHETT, educator; b. Calcutta, India, Dec. 9, 1941; s. Reginald R.G.P. and Dorothy Elizabeth (Hodgson) J.; m. Margaret Letitia Brown, July 9, 1982. B.A., Pembroke Coll., Cambridge U., 1964, M.A., 1968, Ph.D., 1970. Asst. lectr. U. St. Andrews, Scotland, 1967-68, lectr., 1968-84, sr. lectr., 1984—, chmn. dept. Arabic, 1979-86; research fellow Pembroke Coll., Cambridge U., 1967-70; dir. Sch. Abbasid Studies, U. St. Andrews, 1979—. Joint author: Saladin: The Politics of the Holy War, 1982; contbr. articles to profl. jours. Fgn. Office scholar, Lebanon, 1960-61; Pembroke Coll. Found. scholar, 1963. Fellow Bris. Soc. Middle East Studies; mem. Symposium for Classical Arabic Poetry, L' Union Européenne D'Arabisants et D'Islamisants, Middle East Studies Assn. of Am. Clubs: Hawks, Leander, Oriental, Royal and Ancient Golf. Office: Univ Saint Andrews, Dept Arabic Studies, Saint Andrews, Fife Scotland

JACKSON, DEAN ALBERT, electrical engineer; b. Clarinda, Iowa, Apr. 3, 1921; s. William Newton and Mary Adna (James) J.; m. Nadine Virginia Johnson, Apr. 15, 1948; children—Deborah Ann, Susan Atlee, Sandra Elizabeth, Jennifer Louise, Ted Bradley. B.Sc. in Edn., U. Nebr., 1946, B.Sc. in Elec. Engring., 1952. Registered engr., Wash. Coach, tchr. Superior High Sch., Wyo., 1946-48; coach Multnomah Coll., Portland, Oreg., 1948-49; electrician Commonwealth Elec. Co., Lincoln, Nebr., 1949-52; elec. engr. Reynolds Metals, McCook, Ill., 1952-57; elec. engr. Kaiser Aluminum & Chem. Corp. Spokane, Wash., 1957-65, elec. design supr., 1965-85, staff elec. engr., 1985—. Bd. dirs. Spokane Valley YMCA, Spokane, 1967-68, pres., 1969. Served to 1st lt. C.E., U.S. Army, 1942-46; ETO. Mem. IEEE (sr., bd. dirs. 1970-72, treas. 1972-73, sec. 1973-74, chmn. 1975-76, Spokane Elec. Engr. of Yr. 1977), Lodge: Rotary (bd. dirs. local club 1979-84, treas. 1984-85, sec. 1985-86, pres.-elect 1986, pres. 1987-88). Home: E 10716 21st Spokane WA 99206 Office: Kaiser Aluminum & Chem Corp Trentwood Works Spokane WA 99215

JACKSON, ELMER MARTIN, JR., publishing executive; b. Hagerstown, Md., Mar. 9, 1906; s. Elmer Martin and Blanche Beatrice (Bower) J.; m. Mary W. A. Conard, Aug. 27, 1929 (div.); children: Elmer Martin III, Allen Conard, Pamela Conard; m. Doris C. Grace, Apr. 18, 1972. A.B., St. John's Coll., Annapolis, Md., 1926. Reporter, sports editor, city editor Hagerstown and Annapolis, Md., 1920-30; editor Evening Capital and Md. Gazette, Annapolis, 1933-41; v.p., editor and gen. mgr. Evening Capital and Md. Gazette Newspapers, 1947-69; pres., pub. Anne Arundel Times, 1969—; owner-pub. Worcester Democrat, Pocomoke City, Md.; gen. mgr., editor Capital-Gazette News, also County News, 1961-69; pres. and pub. Carroll County Times, Westminster, Md., Jackson Printing, Inc., Annapolis and St. Michael's, Md., 1975—; owner Scott Book Ctr., Annapolis; bd. dirs. Md. Nat. Bank. Author: The Rat Tat, 1927, Annapolis, Three Centuries of Glamour, 1938; (nature study) The Baltimore Oriole; Maryland Symbols, 1964, (genealogy) Keeping the Lamp of Remembrance Lighted, 1985. Past pres. dist. and state press assns.; mem. evaluating commn. Instns. Higher Learning.; mem. bd. Fed. Council State Govt., Chgo. Alderman, Annapolis, 1932-36; del. Md. Legislature, 1937-41; pres. Anne Arundel Pub. Library Assn., 1945-87, Fine Arts Festival Found.; chmn. Anne Arundel County Econ. Devel. Commn., State Capital Planning Commn.; pres. Md. Gov.'s Prayer Breakfast Soc., 1967-76. Served as comdr. USNR, 1941-47. Named hon. adm. U.S. Naval Acad., 1965; recipient Man of Yr. award Anne Arundel County, 1965, Trustee of Yr. award ALA, Dallas, 1984. Mem. Am. Soc. Newspaper Editors, Newcomen Soc., Md. Hist. Soc. (dir.), Mil. Order World Wars (comdr.), Md. Soc. of SAR (pres. 1985-86), Polit. Sci. Club, Sigma Delta Chi. Democrat. Episcopalian. Clubs: Nat. Press (Washington); Annapolis Athletic (past pres.), Annapolitan (sec.-treas.), Thirteen, Annapolis Yacht, Annapolis Roads Golf and Beach, Naval Academy Officers, Naval Academy Golf, Naval Academy Beach, Young Democratic of Anne Arundel County (past pres.); Army-Navy (Washington); University, So. Md. Soc, Propeller. Lodges: Elks, Civitan (past pres. and dist. gov. internat. club). Home: 219 Claude St Wardour Annapolis MD 21401 also: Rousby Hall Lusby MD 20657 Office: Anne Arundel Times Bldg 208-10 West St Annapolis MD 21401

JACKSON, EUGENE WESLEY, publisher; b. Tulsa, Feb. 23, 1928; s. George Wesley and Ora (Cook) J.; m. Marie-Louise Vermeiren, Jan. 17, 1962; children: Susan Lynne, Geoffrey William. B.A. in Natural Scis., Okla. A. and M. Coll., 1950; postgrad., Tulsa U., 1953-54; M.L.A., Temple U., 1986. Tech. writer Carter Oil Co., Tulsa, 1952-55; med. editor, writer med. jour. Smith Kline & French Labs., Phila., 1956-69; mng. editor Cons. mag., 1961-66, editor, 1966-69; chmn. bd. Springhouse Corp., Pa., 1970—; co-founder, pub. Nursing, 1975-79, 70-78; pub. Nursing Skillbook series, 1975-79, Nursing Photobook series, 1979-81, Nurses' Guide to Drugs, 1981; ptnr. Springhouse Book Co., Springhouse Realty Co., Springhouse Pub. Co. Editor: Common Complaints, 1964; contbr. articles on health and horticulture to consumer mags., 1964-68. Mem. exec. council Conf. Bd., trustee Abington Meml. Hosp., Pa.; mem. pres.'s adv. council Gwynedd-Mercy Coll. Served with M.C., AUS, 1950-52. Mem. Nat. League Nursing, Beta Theta Pi. Baptist. Club: Manufacturers (Dresher, Pa.). Home: Meadowbrook PA 19046 Office: 1111 Bethlehem Pike Spring House PA 19477

JACKSON, GLENDA, actress; b. Birkenhead, Cheshire, Eng., May 9, 1936; d. Harry and Joan J.; m. Roy Hodges (div.); 1 son, Daniel. Ed., West Kirby County Grammar Sch. for Girls. Made stage debut as student in: Separate Tables, Worthing, Eng., 1957; first appeared on London (Eng.) stage at Arts as Ruby in: All Kinds of Men, 1957; appeared in: Hammersmith, 1962, The Idiot, 1963, Alfie, 1963; joined, Royal Shakespeare Co. and; appeared in exptl. Theatre of Cruelty season, L.A.M.D.A., 1964, Stratford season, 1965; played Princess of France in: Love's Labour's Lost; Ophelia in: Hamlet, at Aldwych; played Eva in: Puntila, 1965; reader in: The Investigation, 1965; appeared as Charlotte Corday in: Marat/Sade, 1965, and repeating performance in N.Y. debut at, Martin Beck, 1965 (Variety award as most promising actress); appeared in, U.S. at Aldwych, 1966; as Masha in: Three Sisters at Royal Ct, 1967; as Tamara Fanghorn in: Fanghorn at Fortune, 1967; as Katherine Winter in: Collaborators, 1973; as Solange in: The Maids, 1974; as Hedda Gabler, 1975; as Vittoria Corombona in: The White Devil, 1976; appeared on: stage in Rose, N.Y.C., London, 1980-81, Phaedra, N.Y.C., 1984-85, Strange Interlude, 1985, Macbeth, 1988; appeared in numerous films, 1968—; including Women in Love (Acad. award for Best Actress 1970), Sunday, Bloody Sunday, The Music Lovers, Marat-Sade, Negatives, Mary Queen of Scots, Triple Echo (being reissued as Soldier in Skirts), The Nelson Affair, A Touch of Class (Acad. award for Best Actress 1974), 1973, The Maids, The Romantic Englishwoman, The Incredible Sarah, Nasty Habits, House Calls, Lost and Found, 1979, Health, 1980, Hopscotch, 1980, Stevie, 1981, The Return of the Soldier, 1982, Giro City, Turtle Diary, 1986, Beyond Therapy, Business as Usual; also numerous TV appearances, 1960—; including series Elizabeth R., Patricia Neal Story, 1981, Sakharov, 1984, Strange Interlude, 1988. Office: care Internat Creative Mgmt 8899 Beverly Blvd Los Angeles CA 90048 Address: care Crouch Assocs, 59 Fritch St, London W1 England *

JACKSON, GORDON ALEXANDER, manufacturing executive; b. Melbourne, Victoria, Australia, July 1, 1913; s. William and Annie Rose (Uphon) J.; m. Patricia Winifred Skates, Aug. 10, 1969; children by previous marriage—Diane, Robert, Graeme, Marjory. Music degree, London Coll. Music, 1932. Profl. pianist, Victoria, 1933-45; mng. dir. Klipspringer Pty. Ltd., Victoria, 1950—; chmn. music bd. Australia Council, New South Wales, 1977-83; mng. dir. Corio Meat Packing Co., Victoria, 1965-71, Jackson's Wool and Skin Co., Victoria, 1984—. Mem. Ch. of Eng. Clubs: Athenaeum, Annabels, Victoria Racing. Home: 52 Saint Georges Rd, Toorak, Melbourne, Victoria 3142, Australia Office: Klipspringer Pty Ltd, 37 Cranwell St, Braybrook, Melbourne, Victoria 3019, Australia

JACKSON, GREGORY WAYNE, orthodontist; b. Chgo., Sept. 4, 1950; s. Wayne Eldon and Marilyn Frances (Anderson) J.; m. Nora Ann Echtner, Mar. 17, 1973; children: Eric, David. Student, U. Ill., 1968-70; DDS with honors, U. Ill., Chgo., 1974; MSD, U. Wash., 1978. Practice dentistry specializing in orthodontics Chgo., 1978—; instr. orthodontic dept. U. Ill. Coll. Dentistry, Chgo., 1978-81. Coach Little League Baseball, Oak Brook, Ill., 1986-88. Served to lt. USN, 1974-76. Mem. ADA, Ill. State Dental Soc., Chgo. Dental Soc., Am. Assn. Orthodontists, Midwestern Soc. Orthodontists, Ill. Soc. Orthodontists, Omicron Kappa Upsilon. Evangelical. Club: Oak Brook Polo. Office: 6435 S Pulaski Rd Chicago IL 60629

JACKSON, ISAIAH, conductor; b. Richmond, Va., Jan. 22, 1945; s. Isaiah Allen and Alma Alverta (Norris) J.; m. Helen Tuntland, Aug. 6, 1977; children: Benjamin, Katharine, Caroline. B.A. cum laude, Harvard U., 1966; M.A., Stanford U., 1967; M.S., Juilliard Sch. Music, 1969, D.M.A., 1973. Founder, condr. Juilliard String Ensemble, N.Y.C., 1970-71; asst. condr. Am. Symphony Orch., N.Y.C., 1970-71, Balt. Symphony Orch., 1971-73; assoc. condr. Rochester Philharmonic Orch., N.Y., 1973-87; music dir. Flint Symphony Orch., Mich., 1982-87, Dayton (Ohio) Philharmonic Orch., 1987—; prin. condr. Royal Ballet, Covent Garden, London, 1987, music dir., 1987—; guest condr. N.Y. Philharmonic Orch., N.Y.C., 1978, Boston Pops Orch., 1983, Cleve. Orch., 1983, 84, 86, 87, Detroit Symphony Orch., 1983, 85, San Francisco Symphony, 1984, Toronto Symphony, 1984, Orch. de la Suisse Romande, 1985, 88, BBC Concert Orch., 1987. Recipient First Gov.'s award for arts in Va. Commonwealth Va., 1979. Office: care United Artists 15149 Killion St Van Nuys CA 91411 also: The Royal Ballet, Royal Opera House, London WC2E 9DD, England

JACKSON, JEWEL, state youth authority official; b. Shreveport, La., June 3, 1942; d. Willie Burghardt and Bernice Jewel (Mayberry) Norton; m. Edward James Norman, May 17, 1961 (div. Nov. 1968); children—Steven, June Kelly; m. Wilbert Jackson, Apr. 6, 1969; children—Michael, Anthony. With Calif. Youth Authority, 1965—, group supr., San Andreas and Santa Rosa, 1965-67, youth counselor, Ventura, 1967-78, sr. youth counselor, Stockton, 1978-81, treatment team supr., program mgr., Whittier and Ione, 1981—, affirmative action adv. mem., Sacramento, 1976-78, equal employment adv. mem., 1978-79; speaker U. Pacific Youth Motivational Project, Stockton, Calif., 1985-86. Mem. Women in Criminal Justice-North (co-chair 1974-76), Nat. Assn. for Female Execs., Assn. Black Correctional Workers (chpt. v.p. 1979, editor newsletter 1978-80). Avocations: reading, horseback riding, writing poetry and short stories, designing clothing. Home: PO Box 898 Ione CA 95640

JACKSON, MARY LOUISE, health services executive; b. Phila., June 25, 1938; d. John Francis and Helen Catherine (Peranteau) Martin; m. Howard Clark Jackson III, Dec. 17, 1954; children—Michael, Mark, Brian. Student Bucks County Community Coll., 1977-83. Asst. mgr. retail div. Sears Roebuck & Co., Bensalem, Pa., 1972-77; educator, adminstr., dir. Trevose Behavior Modification Program, Pa., 1975—, leadership tng. workshops, 1979—; salesman Makefield Real Estate, Morrisville, Pa., 1977-78; mortgage fin. cons. Tom Dunphy Real Estate, Feasterville, Pa., 1978-81; weight loss cons., Hulmeville, Pa., 1984—. Writer monthly column The Modifier, 1977—. Mem. Bucks County Bd. Realtors, Hulmeville Hist. Soc. (a founder, charter mem.). Democrat. Presbyterian. Avocations: reading; classical music; speed walking; knitting; fishing. Home: 218 Main St Hulmeville PA 19047

JACKSON, PATRICK JOHN, public relations executive; b. Grand Rapids, Mich., Sept. 5, 1932; s. Ira William and Edythe Jane (Minnema) J.; m. Isobel W. Parke, Oct. 4, 1974; children: Richard, Kevin, Pamela, Roberta, Jennie. Student, Kenyon Coll., 1950-53; M.Ed., Antioch U., 1979. Sports publicity dir. Kenyon Coll., 1951-52; reporter Grand Rapids Press, 1953-54; advt. dir. Beckley (W.Va.) newspapers Corp., 1954-55; v.p. Jackson, King & Griffith, Waynesboro, Va., 1956-59; account exec. Ruder & Finn, N.Y.C., 1958; sr. counsel, co-founder Jackson, Jackson & Wagner, Exeter, N.H., 1959—; editor PR Reporter, 1976—, Who's Who in Pub. Relations, 1976—, Channels, 1982—; adj. prof. public relations Boston U. Sch. Public Communication, 1973-82. Editor: N.H. Conservation Directory, 1970-80. Chmn. Strafford-Rockingham Regional Council, 1977-78; chmn. Southeastern N.H. Regional Planning Commn., 1976-77; mem. Gov.'s Com. on N.H. Future, 1978-79; co-founder, legis. agt. Environ. Coalition, 1972-83; mem. Gov.'s Com. on Forest Resources, 1981-82; founder, lobbyist Statewide Program of Action to Conserve our Environment, 1968—; founder Environ. Found., 1975; dir. Granite State Pub. Radio; mng. trustee Richmond Realty Trust, 1973—; trustee Antioch U., 1981-88; First Amendment Congress, 1980—; chmn. N.H. Agr. Task Force; ; convenor N.Am. Public Relations Council, 1980—; founder, chmn. Epping Planning Bd., 1967-72; pres. Seacoast Region Assn., 1978-82; bd. dirs. N.H. Social Welfare Council, 1982-85, Youth Communication Inc., 1985—; mem. bd. visitors Def. Info. Sch., 1986—. Recipient Communicator of Yr. award Glassboro State U., 1980, Arthur W. Page award U. Tex. 1984, Vern C. Shrantz award Ball State U., 1982, Gold Anvil award, 1986, Learning & Liberty award, 1987. Mem. Public Relations Soc. Am. (pres. New Eng. chpt. 1974-75, nat. dir. 1976-77, nat. sec. 1978, nat. pres. elect 1979, pres. 1980, Lincoln award for public service 1978), Am. Assn. Pub. Opinion Research, Nat. Sch. Pub. Relations Assn., Orgn. Devel. Network, Delta Kappa Epsilon. Quaker. Club: Portsmouth Athanaeum. Home: Tributary Farm Epping NH 03042 Office: Dudley House 14 Front St Exeter NH 03833

JACKSON, PETER MCLEOD, educator; b. Paisley, Scotland, Mar. 29, 1946; s. Andrew and Elizabeth (Young) J.; B.A. in Econs. with 1st class honors, Strathclyde U., 1969; Ph.D., U. Stirling, 1975; m. Janette Ritchie, July 18, 1969; children—Laura Alice, Aileen Susan. Economist, H.M. Treasury, London, 1969-71; lectr. econs. U. Stirling, Scotland, 1971-77; dir. Pub. Sector Econs. Research Centre, U. Leicester, Eng., and head econs. dept., 1977—; lectr. Civil Service Coll., 1972-79; cons. EEC, Royal Inst. Pub. Adminstrn., OECD and various govt. depts.; research dir. Pub. Fin. Found. Mem. East Midlands Planning Council, 1978—, Commn. for Study of Family, 1980—; bd. govs. Blackwood Hodge Mgmt Centre, Neene Coll., 1983—. Colquhoun Club prizewinner, 1969; Social Sci. Research Council grantee, 1977-81; Nuffield Found. grantee, 1978-81; others. Fellow Royal Soc. Arts; mem. Chartered Inst. Pub. Fin. and Accountancy, Royal Inst. Pub. Fin. and Accounting (council), Royal Econ. Soc., Am. Econs. Assn., Royal Inst. Pub. Adminstrn., Royal Commonwealth Soc. Mem. Ch. of Scotland. Author: Public Sector Economics, 1978; Current Issues in Fiscal Policy, 1979; The Political Economy of Bureaucracy, 1981; The Governments and Policy Initiatives, 1981; contbr. articles to profl. jours. Office: Pub Sector Econs Research Centre, Univ Leicester, Leicester LE1 7RH England

JACKSON, RASHLEIGH ESMOND, minister foreign affairs Guyana; b. New Amsterdam, Berbice, Jan. 12, 1929; student Queens Coll., Georgetown, Univ. Coll., Leicester, Eng., Columbia U., N.Y.C.; married; 2 sons, 2 daus. Entered pub. service, 1948; master Queens Coll., 1957; prin. asst. sec. to Ministry of Fgn. Affairs, 1965, sec., 1969-73; permanent rep. to UN, 1973-78; minister fgn. affairs and internat. trade, 1978—; pres. UN Council for Namibia, 1974. Address: Ministry Fgn Affairs, Georgetown Guyana *

JACKSON, ROBERT EUGENE, JR., sugar and real estate executive; b. Memphis, Feb. 26, 1949; s. Robert Eugene and Della Lillian (Sevon) J.; A.A., Palm Beach Jr. Coll., 1970; B.S. in Bus. Adminstrn., U. Fla., 1973, MBA Fla. Atlantic U., 1987. Staff acct. Himes & Himes, C.P.A.s (now Arthur Young), West Palm Beach, Fla., 1973-74; asst. v.p. agrl. cos., treas. real estate cos. Osceola Farms Co., New Hope Sugar Co. and affiliated cos., Palm Beach, Fla., 1974-79, v.p. corp. planning, asst. to gen. mgr. Osceola Farms Co. and New Hope Sugar Co. and related cos., 1981—; pres., gen. mgr., co-owner Tennis Club Internat., 1980-81; v.p., fin. cons. to owner LaCroix Constrn. Co., 1980-81. Adv. bd. Goodwill Industries, West Palm Beach; former bd. dirs. Thrift, Inc., Palm Beach; past treas. Bethesda By the Sea Ch.; active Palm Beach Republican Club. C.P.A. Mem. Am. Inst. C.P.A.s, Fla. Inst. C.P.A.s, Nat. Assn. Accts., East Coast Estate Planning Council, Pi Kappa Alpha. Episcopalian. Clubs: Beach (jr. com. Palm Beach), Kiwanis. Home: 991 N Lake Way Box 2201 Palm Beach FL 33480 Office: 316 Royal Poinciana Plaza Box 1059 Palm Beach FL 33480

JACKSON, ROBERT HENRY, physician, medical administrator; b. Norwalk, Ohio, Oct. 5, 1922; s. Samuel Lloyd and Mona Mae (Zuelch) J.; m. Ann Elisabeth Dornback, Sept. 20, 1958; 1 child, Ann Dornback. BS, Western Res. U., 1947; MD, U. Heidelberg, Fed. Republic of Germany, 1953. Rotating intern St. Luke's Hosp., Cleve., 1953-54; fellow in Urology Mayo Clinic, Rochester, Minn., 1954-55; asst. surg. resident Luth. Hosp., Cleve., 1955-56, Perusse Traumatic Surg. Clinic, Chgo., 1956-57; gen. chmn. Internat. Congress on Neoplastic Diseases, Heidelberg, Fed. Republic Germany, 1973. Author: Joseph Colt Bloodgood: Cancer Pioneer, 1971, The Viral Etiology, Immunology, Immunodiagnosis, Immunotherapy and Immunoprophylaxsis of Human Neoplastic Diseases, 1985. Trustee Presdl. Task Force, Washington, 1984—; mem. Senatorial Com., Washington, 1984—, Nat. Commn. on Health Manpower, Washington, 1965—. Served to brig. gen. U.S. Army, ETO. Named hon. prof. internat. affairs, recipient Jacob Gould Schurman plaque Cornell U., 1961; U. Heidelberg New Univ. dedicated in his honor. Fellow Am. Soc. Abdominal Surgeons; mem. Mayo Clinic Alumni Assn., AMA (founder sect. neoplastic diseases 1971), Am. Assn. Study Neoplastic Diseases (exec. sec. 1960-73, pres. 1974), Mil. Order of the World Wars, Assn. U.S. Army, Res. Officers Assn. (honor roll 1955—), Cleve. Grays, World Med. Assn., Deutsche Medizinische Gesellschaft Von Chgo., Ohio State Med. Assn., Cleve. Acad. Medicine, VFW, U. Heidelberg Med. Alumni in U.S.A., Am. Legion, Cercle D'Etudes sur la Bataille des Ardennes (maj. gen., chargé d'affaires U.S. group, operation France-Luxembourg, 1984—). Avocations: military, woodworking, fishing, boating.

JACKSON, ROBERT HOWARD, lawyer; b. Cleve., Dec. 12, 1936; s. Herman Herbert and Frances (Goldman) J.; m. Donna Lyons, Mar. 22, 1959; children—Karen, Douglas. A.B., U. Ill., 1958; J.D., Case Western Res. U., 1961. Bar: Ohio 1961. Sole practice Cleve., 1961—; fin. trial atty. SEC, Cleve., 1961-66; ptnr. Kohrman Jackson & Krantz, 1969—; lectr. law Case Western Res. Sch. Law, Cleve., 1967-69; bd. dirs. Larizza Industries, Inc. Contbr. articles to legal and lit. jours. Mem. ABA (chmn. subcom. proxy solicitations, shareholders proposals, fed. securities com. 1970-73), Fed. Bar Assn. (chmn. Cleve. chpt. fed. securities com. 1972-73), Internat. Bar Assn., Cleve Bar Assn. Club: Rowfant, Grolier (N.Y.C.). Home: 10 Lyman Circle Shaker Heights OH 44122 Office: 1 Cleveland Ctr 20th Floor 1375 E 9th St Cleveland OH 44114

JACKSON, ROBERT JOHN, industrial engineer; b. Los Angeles, Dec. 24, 1922; s. John M. and Ona Blanche (Hill) J.; m. Ethel K. Beecher, Dec. 1, 1950; children: Kathryn, Bradley, Diane, Margaret, Shirley, Kelly, Riley. AA, Pasadena Coll., 1958. Supr. assembly dept. Lockheed Aircraft Co., Burbank, Calif., 1941-51; time standards engr. Bendix Pacific Co., North Hollywood, Calif., 1951-53; indsl. engr. Walsco Electronic Co., Los Angeles, 1953-55; methods and time standards engr. Lockheed-Calif. Co., Burbank, 1955-69, dir. hours rep., 1969—. Dir. Modal Investment Co., Eagle Rock, Calif., 1955-56. Served with AUS, 1944-46; PTO. Decorated Purple Heart with oak leaf cluster, Bronze Star, Silver Star. Mem. Am. Inst. Indsl. Engrs. Lodge: Masons. Home: 415 N Plymouth Blvd Los Angeles CA 90004 Office: Lockheed-Calif Co 2555 N Hollywood Way Burbank CA 91503

JACKSON, RONALD GORDON, government official; b. Brisbane, Australia, May 5, 1924; s. Rupert Vaughan and Mary (O'Rourke) J.; m. Margaret Alison Pratley, Apr. 5, 1948; children: Ronald Francis, Carolyn Margaret Jackson Huijer. BCom., U. Queensland, 1949; Dr (h.c.), U. New South Wales, 1983. With CSR Ltd., 1941-85, gen. mgr., 1972-82, dir., dep. chmn., 1983-85; chmn. Australian Industry Devel. Corp., 1983—; chmn. Pilbara Iron Ltd., 1972-75, Gove Alumina Ltd., 1972-77, Thiess Holdings Ltd., 1984—, Austek Microsystems Ltd., 1984—, Interscan Internat. Ltd., 1984-87, Austek Microsystems Ltd., 1984-87; counselor Zener Electric Pty. Ltd., 1983—; mem. Pacific adv. council United Techs. Corp., 1984—; lectr. in field, bd. dirs. Res. Bank Australia, Rothmans Holdings Ltd., Rockwell Internat.Pty. Ltd. Mem. vis. com. Grad. Sch. Bus., New South Wales, 1969-73; mem. interim bd. Australian Grad. Sch. Mgmt., 1973-76, chmn. found., 1976-81; bd. govs. Asian Inst. Mgmt., Manilla, 1979—; mem. adv. com. Ctr. for Resource and Environ. Studies, Australian Nat. U., 1984—, chancellor, 1987—; trustee Mitsui Ednl. Found., 1973—, Sydney Hosp. Found. for Research, v.p. Australia/JapanBus. Cooperation Com., 1977; bd. govs. Ian Clunies Ross Meml. Found., 1980—; mem. pres.'s council Nat. Parks and Wildlife Found., 1983—; mem. Police Bd., New South Wales, 1983—, Com. for Devel. Youth Employment, 1983-88; chmn. bd. govs. Arthur Phillip German-Australian Found., 1984—; mem. adv. bd. Salvation Army, 1983—, pres. red shield appeal, Sydney, 1986—, numerous others. Decorated companion and knight Order of Australia, comdr.'s cross Order of Merit Fed. Republic Germany; recipient James N. Kirby Meml. medal Instn. Prodn. Engrs., 1976, John Storey medal Australian Inst. Mgmt., 1978, Vocat. Service award Rotary Club, Sydney, 1984. Mem. Inst. Dirs. Australia (councillor New South Wales br. 1982—), German Australian Chamber Industry and Commerce (councillor 1977—). Clubs: Royal Sydney Yacht Squadron, Union, Royal Sydney Golf, Australian, MIT (Sydney); Queensland. Office: Qantas Internat Ctr, 18-30 Jamison St 24th Floor, Sydney 2000, Australia

JACKSON, (MARY) RUTH, orthopaedic surgeon; b. Jefferson, Iowa, Dec. 13, 1902; d. William Riley and Carolyn Arabelle (Babb) J.; B.A., U. Tex., 1924; M.D., Baylor U., 1928. Gen. intern Meml. Hosp., Worcester, Mass., 1928-29, resident in orthopaedic surgery, 1930-31; intern in orthopaedic surgery Univ. Hosps., U. Iowa, 1929-30; resident in orthopaedic surgery Tex. Scottish Rite Hosp. for Crippled Children, Dallas and asst. at Carrell-Driver-Girard Clinic, Dallas, 1931-32; pvt. practice medicine specializing in orthopaedic surgery, Dallas, 1932—; clin. instr. in orthopaedic surgery Baylor U., Dallas, 1936-43; hon. cons. orthopaedic surgeon Baylor U. Med. Center, Dallas, Parkland Meml. Hosp., Dallas; hon. asst. clin. prof. orthopaedic surgery Southwestern Med. Sch. of U. Tex., Dallas; lectr. in field. Diplomate Am. Bd. Orthopaedic Surgery. Fellow ACS, Internat. Coll. Surgeons; mem. Dallas County Med. Assn., Tex. Med. Assn., So. Med. Assn., AMA, Tex. Orthopaedic Assn., Tex. Rheumatism Assn., Southwestern Surg. Congress, Am. Acad. Orthopaedic Surgeons, Am. Orthopaedic Foot Soc., Am. Assn. for Study Headache, Am. Trauma Soc., Am. Assn. Automotive Medicine, Am. Soc. Contemporary Medicine and Surgery, Western Orthopaedic Assn., Law-Sci. Acad. Am., Pan-Am. Med. Assn. (diplomate sect. orthopaedic surgery), Royal Soc. Medicine (assoc.), Nat. Assn. Disability Examiners, Dallas C. of C., North Dallas C. of C., Kaufman C. of C., Ruth Jackson Soc. Republican. Methodist. Club: Zonta Internat. Author monograph: The Cervical Syndrome, 1956, 4th edit., 1977, Japanese transl, 1967; contbr. articles to profl. jours. Office: 3629 Fairmount Dallas TX 75219

JACKSON, THOMAS FRANCIS, III, lawyer; b. Memphis, Oct. 21, 1940; s. Thomas Francis and Sarah Elizabeth (Farris) J.; children—Thomas Francis, Wythe Macrae Bogy. B.A., Rhodes Coll., 1962; LL.B., George Washington U., 1967. Bar: Tenn. 1967, U.S. Supreme Ct. 1974. Law clk. to chief judge U.S. Dist. Ct., Western Dist. Tenn., 1967-68; assoc. Armstrong, Allen, Braden, Goodman, McBride & Prewitt, Memphis, 1968-72; assoc. Lawler, Humphrey, Dunlap & Wellford, P.C., Memphis, 1972-76, ptnr./owner, 1976-83; sole practice, Memphis, 1983—. Served to lt. USNR, 1962-67. Mem. ABA, Tenn. Bar Assn., Memphis and Shelby County Bar Assn. Republican. Episcopalian. Club: Memphis Country. Home: 507 Williamsburg Ln Memphis TN 38117-3633 Office: 1302 First Tennessee Bldg Memphis TN 38103

JACKSON, WAYNE ROBERT, beverage company executive; b. Adelaide, South Australia, Australia, Apr. 16, 1944; s. Maurice Arnold Jackson and Alice Kathleen (Thompson) Siggins; m. Elizabeth Mary Askwith, Mar. 7, 1968; children: Jane Melinda, Meridie Ann, Anna Louise. Degree in econs., U. Adelaide, 1969; postgrad., Harvard U., 1980. Group mng. dir. Thomas Hardy & Sons Pty Ltd., Reynella, South Australia, 1980—; Mem. Australian Wine and Brandy Corp., 1987. Home: 16 Strathmore Ave, Lockleys, South

Australia 5032, Australia Office: Thomas Hardy & Sons Pty Ltd, Reynell Rd, Reynella, South Australia 5161, Australia

JACKSON, WILLIAM ELMER, JR., packaging company administrator; b. Washington, Pa., Oct. 25, 1935; s. William Elmer and Hazel Celestine (Moore) J.; BS in Indsl. Engring., Okla. U., 1966; MBA in Fin., U. Mo., Kansas City, 1970; children—Randall Lee, Barry Howard. With Sealright Co. Inc., Kansas City, Mo., 1966—, corp. econ. evaluation engr., 1966-69, process engr. central div., 1969-72, profit evaluation specialist, central div., 1972-74, corp. mgr. econ. evaluation, 1974-75, corp. ops. analysis mgr., 1975-78, adminstrv. mgr. central div., 1978-81, mfg. and control mgr. central div., 1981-83, corp. planning and devel., 1983—, chmn. eastern div. operational study project, 1976, chmn. corp. mfg. info. requirements study project, 1978, chmn. western div. operational study project, 1984, Kansas City plant relocation project, 1987, mem. bus. profile study team; sec., treas., dir. Agrl. Tech. Internat. Mktg., Inc., Louisburg, Kans., 1984-85. Com. chmn., merit badge counselor Troop 278 Heart of Am. council Boy Scouts Am., 1972-74; adv. Jr. Achievement of Greater Kansas City, 1974-75; caravan dir. Overland Park Nazarene Ch., 1968-74, ch. bd., 1976-79, 88, ch. treas., 1977-78, fin. com., 1976-78, house com., 1978-79, mem. choir, 1968-81; chmn. adv. bd. mid-mgmt. program Penn Valley Community Coll., Kansas City, Mo., 1980-84, 87; mem. Johnson County Assn. Retarded Citizens. Served with USAF, 1955-59. Mem. Inst. Indsl. Engrs. (sr.), Internat. Platform Assn. Republican. Club: Fishing Club Am. Office: 8300 Ward Pkwy Suite 500 Kansas City MO 64114

JACKSON, WILLIAM GENE, computer company executive; b. Opelika, Ala., Nov. 22, 1946; s. John Willis and Lucy (Jackson) J.; m. Cornelia Turner, Aug. 17, 1969; children—Verzelia Yvett, Gena Nichole, William Gene. B.S. in Mgmt. and Mktg., Syracuse U., 1979, A.A.S. in Mgmt., 1976; postgrad. Pace U. With IBM, 1966—, customer engr. Huntsville, Ala., 1966-72, sr. customer engr., Atlanta, 1972-73, field mgr., Miami, Fla., 1973-75, eastern region ops. analyst Harrison, N.Y., 1975-76, br. mgr., N.Y.C., 1976, region ops. mgr. region 3, Montvale, N.J., 1977-78, employee relations program mgr. personnel, office products div. hdqrs., Franklin Lakes, N.J., 1979, adminstrv. asst. to dir. ops. west, office products div. hdqrs., Franklin Lakes, 1980, IBM corp. service staff, Armonk, N.Y., 1981-82, adminstrv. asst. to pres. customer service div., Franklin Lakes, 1983, region mgr. customer service div., region 7, Southfield, Mich., 1983-84, dir. service support Nat. Service div. Area 4, 1984-87, regional mgr., 1987—. Bd. dirs. spl. affairs Jaycees, Wanaque, N.J., 1978-79. Mem. Am. Mgmt. Assn. Home: 25220 Witherspoon Rd Farmington Hills MI 48018 Office: IBM-NSD Area 4 27800 Northwestern Hwy Southfield MI 48086

JACKSON, WILLIAM KEITH, political science educator; b. Colchester, Essex, Eng., Sept. 5, 1928; arrived in New Zealand, 1956; s. William James and Alice Beatrice (Hill) J.; children: Benjamin Giles, Nigel James, Mathew Guy. Teaching cert., U. London, 1947; BA with 1st honors, U. Nottingham, Eng., 1953; PhD, U. Otago, New Zealand, 1967. From asst. lectr. to sr. lectr. polit. sci. U. Otago, New Zealand, 1956-67; prof. U. Canterbury, New Zealand, 1967—, head polit. sci. dept., 1967-80; election cons., polit. analyst Sta. NZ Radio, Sta. TVNZ. Author: New Zealand, 1969, The Dilemma of Parliament, 1987; editor: Beyond New Zealand, 1980; editorial advisor Politics, Polit. Science, Electoral Studies mags., Jour. Commonwealth and Comparative Studies. Served to sgt. Royal Air Force, 1947-49. Henry Chapman fellow, 1963, Canterbury fellow, 1986; recipient Mobil award Polit Analysis, 1979-80. Mem. Assn. Canadian Studies in Australia and New Zealand, Australasian Polit. Sci. Assn., New Zealand Inst. Internat. Affairs, New Zealand Inst. Pub. Adminstrn., New Zealand Polit. Studies Assn. Office: Univ Canterbury, Dept Polit Sci, Christchurch New Zealand

JACKSON, WILLIAM THOMAS, barrister; b. Nottingham, Eng., Aug. 22, 1926; s. William Thornton and Elizabeth (Martin) J.; m. Anthea June Gillard, July 11, 1953; children: Elizabeth Helen Anthea, Barbara Ann Partridge. MRVCS, Glasgow (Scotland) Vet. Coll., 1948; DVSM, Edinburgh (Scotland) U., 1964; called to the bar, Lincoln's Inn, London, 1975; D in Med. Vet., U. Berne, Switzerland, 1980. Cert. vet. Royal Coll. Vet. Surgeons. Veterinarian W.S. Marshall, Derby, Eng., 1948-53; vet. officer Ministry of Agriculture Fisheries & Food, 1953-71, divisional vet. officer, 1971-87; barrister T. Scott Baker QC, London, 1987, John Phillips QC, London, 1987-88, Chambers John Collins, Lewes, Sussex, Eng., 1988—. Bd. dirs. Raystede Animal Welfare Ctr., Ringmer, East Sussex, Eng., 1987—. Mem. Sussex Vet. Soc. (sr. v.p., pres. 1985-87), Assn. State Vet. Officers, Senate of Bar. Anglican. Home: 19 Ravens Croft, Eastbourne England Office: Chambers John Collins, Westgate Chambers, 144 High St, Lewes England

JACKSON, WILLIAM TURRENTINE, educator; b. Ruston, La., Apr. 5, 1915; s. Brice H. and Luther (Turrentine) J.; m. Barbara Kone, Nov. 28, 1942. A.B., Tex. Western Coll., 1935; A.M., U. Tex., 1936, Ph.D., 1940. Instr. history UCLA, 1940-41, Iowa State U., Ames, 1941-42; asst. prof. Iowa State U., 1944-46, assoc. prof., 1946-48; asst. prof. Am. history U. Chgo., 1948-51; dir. Am. civilization program, asst. prof. Am. history U. Calif. at Davis, 1951-53, assoc. prof. history, 1953-56, prof., 1956—, chmn. dept., 1959-60; vis. prof. Mont. State U., 1941, univs. Mich., 1944, Wyo., 1945, 63, Minn., 1946, Tex., 1947, So. Calif., 1953, 56, Colo., 1961, San Francisco State Coll., 1962, Yale and R.I., 1964, NDEA History Inst., Chadron (Nebr.) State Coll., 1965, La. State U., 1967, U. Ariz., 1968, U. Alta., 1969, U. Nev., 1970, U. Hawaii, 1970, Colo. State U., 1973, Utah State U., 1975; Walter Prescott Webb lectr. U. Tex., 1976; U.S. Dept. State Disting. Am. Specialist lectr. in, Western Europe, 1978; USIA seminar dir. Falkenstein Seminar in Am. Studies, Germany, 1978; cons. hist. sect. Calif. Div. Parks and Recreation, Nat. Park Service, Wells Fargo Bank, U.S. Army Engrs.; cons. hist. sect. Tetra Tech, Inc., Teknekron, Inc., Sci. Applications, Inc.; cons. legal sect. Calif. Atty. Gen., N.Mex. State Engrs. Office; mem. Calif. Gov.'s History Commn.; dir. Nat. Endowment for Humanities Summer Seminar for Coll. Tchrs., 1976-77, 80, 81; hist. cons. Seminar for Secondary Sch. Tchrs., 1983, 84, 86, 87, 88; adv. com. Sacramento Landmarks Commn.; mem. coordinating bd. Calif. Water Resources Center, 1972-81; bd. dirs. Calif. Heritage Council, Calif. Council Humanities; prin. investigator Jackson Research Projects, hist. cons.; David E. Miller lectr. U. Utah. Author: Wagon Roads West, 1953, 65 (awards Pacific Coast br. Am. Hist. Assn., Nat. Inst. Graphic Arts, N.Y.C.), When Grass Was King (Merit award Am. Assn. State and Local History 1956), Treasure Hill, 1963 (Merit award Am. Assn. State and Local History), Twenty Years on the Pacific Slope, 1965, The Enterprising Scot, 1968, Gold Rush Diary of a German Sailor, 1970, Lake Tahoe Water, 1972, Water Policy in Sacramento-San Joaquin Delta, 1977, also numerous hist. monographs and articles.; Bd. editors: Pacific Hist. Rev, 1961-64, 67-70, So. Calif. Quar, 1962—, Arizona and the West, 1968-73, Jour. San Diego History, 1975—, Red River Valley Hist. Rev. Served to ensign USNR, 1942-44. Fulbright research fellow Scotland, 1949-50; Rockefeller Found. fellow Huntington Library, 1953; grantee Am. Philos. Soc., 1955; grantee Social Sci. Research Council, 1956; grantee Am. Hist. Research Center, 1955-56; grantee NSF, 1968-73; grantee Nat. Endowment for Humanities, 1969-70; grantee Humanities Inst., U. Calif., 1971; Guggenheim fellow, 1957-58, 65; Huntington Library fellow, 1972; grantee Am. Council Learned Socs., 1972; recipient Disting. Teaching award Acad. Senate U. Calif. at Davis, 1973-74, Assoc. Students Disting. Teaching award, 1981, Disting. Alumnus award U. Tex.-El Paso. Fellow Calif. Hist. Soc.; mem. Western History Assn. (pres. 1976-77), Am. Hist. Assn. (adv. com. nat. archives 1983-86), Orgn. Am. Historians (mem. com. preservation hist. sites 1960-68, mem. Pelzer award com. 1968-73, Billington Book Prize com. 1982-85), AAUP, Phi Alpha Theta, Pi Sigma Alpha, Theta Xi. Democrat. Methodist. Club: Commonwealth. Home: 702 Miller Dr Davis CA 95616

JACKSON, WILLIAM WARD, chemical company executive; b. Irvington, N.J., Apr. 19, 1913; s. William Henry and Edwina (Ward) J.; m. Rae M. Applegate, Jan. 1, 1943; 1 dau., Hollace D. (Mrs. Tullman). B.S. in Chem. Engring, Newark Coll. Engring., 1936. Prodn., sales positions Celanese Corp. Am. and affiliates, 1932-51; gen. mgr. indsl. chems. dept. Comml. Solvents Corp., N.Y.C., 1951-53; v.p. petrochem. div. Comml. Solvents Corp., 1953-54, v.p. mktg., 1954-72, v.p. mktg. services and purchasing, 1972-75; also dir.; v.p. IMC Chems. Group, 1975-78, corp. cons., 1978—; pres. Ward Jackson Assos., 1978—; pres., dir. Can Carb Ltd., Medicine Hat, Alta., 1975—; dir., mem. exec. com. N.W. Nitro Chem. Corp., 1959-71, Medicine Hat, Alta.; Mem. Aircraft Prodn. Bd., 1942-43; asst. to vice chmn. WPB, 1943-44, aircraft cons., 1943-44; Chmn. bd. Millburn-Short Hills chpt. ARC, 1956-59, dir., 1954-60; bd. dirs. Animal Health Inst. Recipient Certificate of Achievement U.S. Army; Certificate of Service Dept. Commerce. Fellow Am. Inst. Chemists, Soc. Chem. Industry; mem. Am. Inst. Chem. Engrs., Mfg. Chemists Assn., Pharm. Mfg. Assn., Am. Chem. Soc., Fertilizer Inst. Sales Exec. Club, Newcomen Soc. N.Am., Am. Def. Preparedness Assn. (v.p., dir.), Inst. Food Technologists, Drug Chem. and Allied Trade Assn. (past pres., treas., dir., chmn. adv. council, exec. com.), Am. Ordnance Assn. (dir.), N.Y. Bd. Trade (past dir., exec. com.), Armed Forces Chem. Assn., past nat. dir., exec. com., v.p., past pres.). Clubs: Short Hills (N.J.); Union League (N.Y.C.), Racquet and Tennis (N.Y.C.), N.Y. Yacht (N.Y.C.), Canadian (N.Y.C.); Capitol Hill (Washington). Home: 2 Brooklawn Dr Short Hills NJ 07078 Office: 245 Park Ave New York NY 10017

JACKSON-STOPS, GERVASE FRANK ASHWORTH, architectural advisor, historian; b. Northampton, Eng., Apr. 26, 1947; s. Anthony Ashworth and Jean Jackson-Stops. MA, Oxford U., Eng., 1969. Trainee curator Victoria and Albert Mus., London, 1969-71; archivist Nat. Trust, London, 1972-75, archtl. adviser, 1975—; guest curator Treasure Houses Britain exhbn. Nat. Gallery Art, Washington, 1985-86; mem. Historic Bldgs. Council, 1986—; mem. export reviewing com. Ministry Arts, 1987—. Author: The English Country House -- A Grand Tour, 1985, The Country House Garden -- A Grand Tour, 1987; editor: The Treasure Houses of Britain, 1985. Decorated officer Order Brit. Empire. Fellow Soc. Antiquaries London. Mem. Ch. Eng. Clubs: Travellers, Beefsteak (London). Home: The Menagerie, Horton, Northampton NN7 2BX, England Office: Nat Trust, 36 Queen Anne's Gate, London SW1H 9AS, England

JACKY, RICHARD CHARLES, dentist; b. Walla Walla, Wash., June 30, 1935; s. Carl Frederick and Charlotte Mae Danner J.; m. Betty Jean Fields, Sept. 4, 1981; children—Leesa, Tina. B.S., Wash. State U., 1957; D.D.S., Washington U., St. Louis, 1961. Practice dentistry, St. Louis, 1961—; dir. Normandy Bank, St. Louis, 1974—; v.p. Jala Investment Corp., St. Louis, 1966-83. Mem. Am. Dental Assn., Greater St. Louis Dental Assn., Mo. State Dental Assn., Greater North St. Louis Dental Assn. Republican. Roman Catholic. Lodges: Rotary (past pres.), Elks. Home: 5 Manor Ln Ferguson MO 63135 Office: 10 Adams Ave Ferguson MO 63135

JACOB, CHARLES WALDEMAR, investment banker; b. Hamilton, Ohio, Sept. 22, 1943; s. Charles W. and Nancy (Egbert) J.; m. Patricia Suzanne Charlton, June 28, 1969; children—Charles Waldermar, III, Christopher Charlton. B.A., Wesleyan U., Middletown, Conn., 1965; M.B.A., Harvard U., 1967. Mem. fin. staff Ford Motor Co., Dearborn, Mich., 1967-71; dir. fin. analysis corp. staff Rockwell Internat. Corp., El Segundo, Calif., 1971-72; asst. controller automotive ops. Rockwell Internat. Corp., Troy, Mich., 1972-74; corp. controller Chemetron Corp., Chgo., 1974-77; v.p. fin., treas., dir. Flying Tiger Line, Inc., 1977-81; pres. Cunningham, Jacob & Assocs. Inc., Redondo Beach, Calif., 1981—; exec. v.p., dir. Prudential-Bache Trade Services, 1984-88; chmn. econs. and fin. council Air Transp. Assn., 1980; chmn. Bache Pacific Trade Ltd., Hong Kong, Bache Trade Fin. Asia Ltd., Hong Kong; dir. PB Trade Finance, Ltd., London, Bache Pacific Trade Ltd., Hong Kong, Bache Trade Finance Asia Ltd., Hong Kong, PB Internat. Bank, S.A., Luxemburg, PBTC Internat. Bank, N.Y. Mem. Fin. Execs. Inst., Econ. Club Chgo. Episcopalian. Home: The Highlands Seattle WA 98177 Office: 835 Hopkins Way Suite 309 Redondo Beach CA 90277

JACOB, EDWIN J., lawyer; b. Detroit, Aug. 25, 1927; s. A. Aubrey and Estelle R. (Vesell) J.; m. Constance Dorfman, June 15, 1948; children—Louise B., Beth D., Ellen P. A.B. cum laude, Harvard U., 1948, J.D. cum laude, 1951. Bar: N.Y. 1951, U.S. Dist. Ct. (so. dist.) N.Y. 1953, U.S. Dist. Ct. (ea. dist.) N.Y. 1953, U.S. Ct. Appeals (2d cir.) 1954, U.S. Supreme Ct. 1963, U.S. Ct. Appeals (8th cir.) 1981, U.S. Ct. Appeals (10th cir.) 1987. Assoc. Davis Polk Wardwell Sunderland & Kiendl, N.Y.C., 1951-62; ptnr. Cabell, Medinger, Forsyth & Decker, N.Y.C., 1962-69, Lauterstein & Lauterstein, N.Y.C., 1969-72, Jacob, Medinger, & Finnegan, N.Y.C., 1973—. Contbr. articles to profl. jours. Served with USN, 1945-46. Mem. Am. Law Inst., Am. Judicature Soc., Assn. Bar City N.Y. Club: Harvard of N.Y.C. Home: 1 W 72d St New York NY 10023 Office: Jacob Medinger & Finnegan 1270 Ave of Americas New York NY 10020

JACOB, FRANÇOIS, biologist; b. Nancy, France, June 17, 1920; s. Simon and Therese (Franck) J.; M.D., Faculty of Medicine, Paris, 1947; D.Sc., Faculty of Scis., Paris, 1954; D.Sc. (hon.), U. Chgo., 1965; m. Lysiane Bloch, Nov. 27, 1947 (dec. 1984); children: Pierre, Laurent, Odile, Henri. Asst., Pasteur Inst., 1950-56, head dept. cellular genetics, 1960—, pres., dir., 1982—; prof. cellular genetics Coll. of France, 1964—. Recipient Charles Leopold Mayer prize, 1962; Nobel prize in physiology and medicine (with A. Lwoff and J. Monod), 1965. Mem. Académie des Sciences (Paris); fgn. mem. Am. Acad. Arts and Scis., Nat. Acad. Scis. (U.S.), Am. Philos. Soc., Royal Soc. (London), Académie Royale de Médecine de Belgique, Acad. Scis. Hungary, Royal Acad. Scis. Madrid. Author: The Logic of Life, 1970; The Possible and the Actual, 1981, The Statue Within, 1987. Research on genetics bacterial cells and viruses; contbr. to mechanisms of info. transfer (messenger RNA) and genetic basis of regulatory circuits, early stages of the mouse embryo.. Office: Pasteur Inst Dept de Biolog, 25 Rue de D'Roux, 75015 Paris France

JACOB, STANLEY WALLACE, surgeon, educator; b. Phila., 1924; s. Abraham and Belle (Shulman) J.; m. Marilyn Peters; 1 son, Stephen; m. Beverly Swarts; children—Jeffrey, Darren, Robert; m. Gail Brandis; 1 dau., Elyse. M.D. cum laude, Ohio State U., 1948. Diplomate: Am. Bd. Surgery. Intern Beth Israel Hosp., Boston, 1948-49; resident surgery Beth Israel Hosp., 1949-52, 54-56; chief resident surg. service Harvard Med. Sch., 1956-57, instr., 1958-59; asso. vis. surgeon Boston City Hosp., 1958-59; Kemper Found. research scholar A.C.S. 1957-60; asst. prof. surgery U. Oreg. Med. Sch., Portland, 1959-66; asso. prof. U. Oreg. Med. Sch., 1966—; Gerlinger prof. surgery Oreg. Health Scis. U., 1981—. Author: Structure and Function in Man, 5th edit, 1982, Laboratory Guide for Structure and Function in Man, 1982, Dimethyl Sulfoxide Basic Concepts, 1971, Biological Actions of DMSO, 1975; contbr. to: Ency. Brit. Served to capt. M.C. AUS, 1952-54; col. Res. ret. Recipient Gov.'s award Outstanding N.W. Scientist, 1965; 1st pl. German Sci. award, 1965; Markle scholar med. scis., 1960. Mem. Phi Beta Kappa, Sigma Xi, Alpha Omega Alpha. Home: 1055 SW Westwood Ct Portland OR 97201 Office: Oreg Health Scis U Dept Surgery 3181 SW Sam Jackson Park Rd Portland OR 97201

JACOB, THOMAS BERNARD, plastic company executive; b. Salinas, Calif., June 5, 1934; s. Henry E. and Miriam F. J.; 2 children. B.S. in Bus. Adminstrn., Wayne State U., 1960. Br. mgr. Cadillac Plastic and Chem. Co., Toledo, Indpls., Boston, 1961-65; dist. mgr. Cadillac Plastic and Chem. Co., Dallas and Chgo., 1966-72; v.p. field ops. Cadillac Plastic and Chem. Co., 1972-76; exec. v.p. Cadillac Plastic Co., Detroit, 1976-84; pres. Cadillac Plastic Co. Mich./Ohio, 1984—. Served with U.S. Army, 1955-57. Mem. Soc. Plastics Industry, Soc. Plastics Engrs., Nat. Assn. Plastic Distbrs. Clubs: Recess, Renaissance, Bay Point. Office: 26580 W Eight Mile Rd Southfield MI 48034

JACOBI, DEREK GEORGE, actor; b. Oct. 22, 1938; s. Alfred George and Daisy Gertrude (Masters) Jacobi. M.A. with honors, St. Johns Coll., Cambridge, Eng. Artistic assoc. Old Vic Co. (formerly Prospect Theatre Co.), 1976-81; v.p. Nat. Youth Theatre, 1982—. Stage appearances include: Birmingham Repertory Theatre, 1960-63 (first appearance in One Way Pendulum, 1961), National Theatre, 1963-71, Prospect Theatre Co., 1972, 74, 76, 77, 78, Hamlet, 1979, Royal Shakespeare Co., role of Benedick in Much Ado About Nothing, title role in Peer Gynt, Prospero in The Tempest, 1982, 83, title role in Cyrano de Bergerac, 1983; Broadway appearance: Breaking The Code, 1987; TV appearances include: She Stoops to Conquer, Man of Straw, The Pallisers, I Claudius, Philby, Burgess and Maclean, Richard II, Hamlet, Inside The Third Reich; films include: Odessa File, Day of the Jackal, The Medusa Touch, Othello, Three Sisters, Interlude, The Human Factor, Charlotte, The Man Who Went Up in Smoke, Enigma. Recipient BAFTA Best Actor award, 1976-77, Variety Club TV Personality award, 1976, Royal TV Sr. award, 1976, Tony award for Best Actor in Much Ado About Nothing, 1985. Office: care Duncan Heath Assocs, 162-170 Wardour St, Paramount House, London W1, England •

JACOBS, AGNES JACQUELINE EVERINGTON, retired wildlife federation executive; b. Wilkinsburg, Pa., June 17, 1923; d. James Pate and Agnes Kathleen (Scurry) Everington; A.B., Coker Coll., Hartsville, S.C., 1944, LittD (hon.), 1986; M.S, U. S.C., 1961, Ph.D. in Biology, 1968; m. Harold Weinberg Jacobs, May 11, 1947; children—Patricia Francyl, Janet Carolyn, James Cecil. Tchr. pub. schs., Columbia, S.C., 1957-64, 71-73; instructional TV specialist S.C. Dept. Edn., 1968-71; coordinator Inst. Environ. Studies, U. S.C., The Citadel, Clemson U., summers 1972-77; exec. dir. S.C. Wildlife Fedn., Columbia, 1974-83; mem. exec. com. S.C. Gov.'s Overall Recreation Plan Exchange Council, 1975—; charter mem. S.C. Environmental Edn. Assn., 1976—. Lectr. to various civic orgns., garden clubs, Rotary clubs, Scouts; mem. choir St. Michael and All Angels' Ch., Columbia, lay reader, 1980, mem. vestry, 1980-83, sr. warden, 1983; trustee Coker Coll., 1971-77, pres. Alumni Assn., 1975-77; bd. visitors Coker Coll., 1977-80; vice chmn. citizens' environ. planning com. Central Midlands Regional Planning Council, 1976-83; mem. S.C. Coastal Council, 1976-77; mem. citizens' adv. com. Riverbanks Zoo, Columbia, 1979—; mem. Russell Dam Task Force, 1979-83; bd. dirs. Yr. of Coast, 1980; mem. S.C. Forestry Study Group, U.S. Dept. Agr., 1979; Wildlife adv. com. Coll. Agrl. Scis., Clemson U., 1976-82; bd. dirs. Harry R.E. Hampton Wildlife Meml. Fund; co-chmn. Gov.'s Council Natural Resources and the Environment, 1983-85; exec. com. S.C. Marine Sci. Mus., 1986—. Served with USMC Women's Res., 1944-46. Decorated Letter of Commendation; recipient Conservation Educator of Year award S.C. Wildlife Fedn., 1970, F. Bartow Culp award, 1975, Conservationist of Yr. award, 1983; S.C. Conservation of Year award Woodmen of World, 1975; Outstanding Service award Nat. Wildlife Fedn., 1977, Disting. Service award, 1983; Outstanding Alumni award Coker Coll., 1980; S.C. Wildlife and Marine Resource Dept. and Commn.'s Meritorious Service award, 1983; Gov.'s Order of Palmetto, 1983; S.C. Trappers Assn. cert. appreciation, 1983; Environ. Edn. Assn. S.C. citation meritorious service, 1983. NSF fellow, summers 1959-60, 63-65, W. Gordon Belser fellow U. S.C., 1964-65; Belle W. Baruch Found. grantee U. S.C., 1967-68; EPA film grantee, 1980. Mem. AAAS, Am. Inst. Biol. Scis., Assn. Southeastern Biologists, Nat. Assn. Biology Tchrs. (Outstanding Biology Tchr. award for S.C. 1963), S.C. Assn. Biology Tchrs. (pres. 1965), S.C. Acad. Sci. (pres. 1973), S.C. Edn. Assn. (life), Richland County Legal Aux. (charter), Wildlife Soc. (charter mem. S.C. chpt.), S.C. Wildlife Fedn. (life bd. dirs. 1986, trustee Ednl. Found. 1986), Embroiderers' Guild Am. (pres. Millwood chpt. 1986-88, sec. Carolinas Region, 1988—), S.C. State Mus. (chmn., mem. exec. bd. S.C. through the Needle's Eye, 1987), Sigma Xi. Episcopalian. (layreader). Author: Life Science-Teacher's Guide to ITV Courses, 1970; also sci. papers. Producer-tchr ITV Life Science series, 1969-70. Producer films The Loggerhead Turtle Story, 1971, South Carolina Coastal Nesting Birds, 1971, Life in the Coral Reef, 1971, The Russell Dam—A Question of Values, 1977; One Percent, 1980. Home: 5 Northlake Rd Columbia SC 29223

JACOBS, ELEANOR ALICE, retired clinical psychologist, educator; b. Royal Oak, Mich., Dec. 25, 1923; d. Roy Dana and Alice Ann (Keaton) J. B.A., U. Buffalo, 1949, M.A., 1952, Ph.D., 1955. Clin. psychologist VA Hosp., Buffalo, 1954-83; EEO counelor VA Hosp., 1962-79, chief psychology service, 1979-83; clin. prof. SUNY, Buffalo, 1950-83; speaker on psychology to community orgns. and clubs, 1952—; Mem. adult devel. and aging com. NICHD, HEW, 1971-75. Recipient Outstanding Superior Performance award Buffalo VA Hosp., 1958, Spl. Recognition award SUNY, Buffalo, Spl. Recognition award SUNY, 1971; W.L. McKnight award Miami Heart Inst., 1972; Adminstrs. commendation VA, 1974; Dirs. commendation VA Med. Center, Buffalo, 1978; Disting. Alumni award SUNY, Buffalo, 1983; named Woman of Yr. Bus. and Profl. Women's Clubs, Buffalo, 1973. Mem. Am. Psychol. Assn., Eastern Psychol. Assn., N.Y. State Psychol. Assn., Am. Group Psychotherapy Assn., Am. Soc. Group Psychotherapy and Psychodrama, Psychol. Assn. Western N.Y. (Disting. Achievement award 1976), Group Psychotherapy Assn. Western N.Y., Undersea Med. Soc., Sigma Xi. Home: 221 Pleasant Ave N, Ridgeway, ON Canada L0S 1N0

JACOBS, HOWARD ALFRED, accountant; b. San Francisco, Aug. 12, 1923; s. Reuben and Labelle (Fisher) J.; student San Francisco Jr. Coll., 1941; B.C.S., Golden Gate Coll., 1948; cert. indsl. mgmt. Coll. San Mateo, 1969; m. Margot Kahn, June 8, 1945; children—Michael, Stephen, Robert, Donald, Sheryl, Susan, Debra, Denise, David, Richard, Thomas, Michelle. Public acct., San Francisco, 1944-49; asst. to fin. v.p. Lenkurt Elec. Co., San Carlos, Calif., 1949-59; internal auditor Lockheed Aircraft Corp., Sunnyvale, Calif., 1959-66, mgmt. systems specialist, 1966-73, also staff asst. to mgr.; mgr. govt. acctg. Watkins-Johnson Co., Palo Alto, Calif., 1973-88. Served with AUS, 1943. C.P.A., Calif. Mem. Am. Inst. C.P.A.s (life), Calif. Soc. C.P.A.s (life). Clubs: Commonwealth. Lodge: Elks. Home: 1900 Willow Rd Hillsborough CA 94010 Office: 3333 Hillview Ave Palo Alto CA 94304

JACOBS, JIMMIE SPARKMAN, owner, manager real estate; b. Gainesboro, Tenn., Sept. 13, 1932; d. James Merlin and Evelyn Christine (Roberts) Sparkman; B.S., Middle Tenn. State U., 1960; M.A., George Peabody Coll. for Tchrs., 1964, Ed.S., 1968; m. Harold Thomas Jacobs, July 5, 1980; children—Steven M., Victoria C., Teresa J. Tchr. public schs., Nashville, 1960-72; realtor Baker-Harwell Realtors, Inc., Nashville, 1974-76; owner, mgr. real estate, Nashville, 1966-78, Bonita Springs, Fla., 1978—; cons. Bentley Village, life care ctr. Originator team teaching program public schs., Nashville, 1969; active First Bapt. Ch., Bonita Springs, Sunday Sch. dir., 1980-83. Mem. NEA, Tenn. Edn. Assn., Middle Tenn. Edn. Assn., DAR. Republican. Baptist. Author: Eighty-eight Years with Sarah Polk, 1972; The River's Course, 1974. Home: 26756 Hickory Blvd SW Bonita Springs FL 33923

JACOBS, JOSEPH DONOVAN, engineering firm executive; b. Motley, Minn., Dec. 24, 1908; s. Sherman William and Edith Mary (Donovan) J.; m. Virginia Mary O'Meara, Feb. 8, 1937; 1 son, John Michael. B.S. in Civil Engring, U. Minn., 1934. Civil engr., constrn. supr. Walsh Constrn. Co., N.Y.C. and San Francisco, 1934-54; chief engr. Kaiser-Walsh-Perini-Raymond, Australia, 1954-55; founder, sr. officer Jacobs Assocs., San Francisco, 1955—; Chmn., U.S. nat. com. on tunnelling tech. Nat. Acad. Scis., 1977. Recipient Golden Beaver award for engring., 1980; Non-Mem. award Moles, 1981. Fellow ASCE, Instn. Engrs. Australia; mem. Nat. Acad. Engring., Am. Inst. Mining and Metall. Engrs., Nat. Soc. Profl. Engrs., Delta Chi. Clubs: Corinthian Yacht, World Trade, Engineers (San Francisco). Office: 500 Sansome St San Francisco CA 94111

JACOBS, JOSEPH JAMES, lawyer, communications company executive; b. Toronto, Ont., Can., Mar. 18, 1925; came to U.S., 1925; s. Sidney and Hildred Veronica (Greenberg) J.; m. Carole Evelyn Bent, Jan. 22, 1946 (div. 1972); children—Carole Lynn Urgenson, Joseph James III; m. Edna Mae Meincke, Jan. 5, 1973. J.D., Tulane U., 1950. Bar: La. 1950, N.Y. 1951, U.S. Dist. Ct. (so. dist.) N.Y. 1953, U.S. Ct. Mil. Appeals 1953, U.S. Ct. Appeals (2d cir.) 1977, U.S. Ct. Appeals (D.C. cir.) 1980. Assoc. Proskauer, Rose Goetz & Mendelsohn, N.Y.C., 1950-53; asst. gen. counsel, asst. to pres. Am. Broadcasting Co., N.Y.C., 1954-60; gen. atty. Metromedia, Inc., N.Y.C., 1960-61; dir. program and talent negotiations United Artists TV, Inc., 1961-66; atty. United Artists Corp., N.Y.C., 1966-69; v.p., counsel United Artists Broadcasting, Inc., N.Y.C., 1969-71; gen. atty. ITT World Communications Inc., N.Y.C., 1972-74; v.p., legal dir. ITT Communications Ops. and Info. Services Group (formerly U.S. Telephone & Telegraph Corp.), N.Y.C. and Secaucus, N.J., 1974-83, ITT Communications and Info. Services, Inc., Secaucus, 1983—; v.p., gen. counsel U.S. Transmission Systems, Inc., Secaucus, 1984—, ITT World Communications Inc., Secaucus, 1984-88; of counsel Seyfarth, Shaw, Fairweathr & Geraldson, N.Y.C. Bd. editors Tulane Law Rev., 1949, asst. editor-in-chief, 1950. Served with parachute inf. U.S. Army, 1943-46, ETO, PTO, to maj. USAFR ret. Mem. Assn. Bar City of N.Y., Fed. Bar Assn., Order of Coif. Republican. Jewish. Home: 572 Sanderling Ct Secaucus NJ 07094 Office: ITT Communications Services Inc 100 Plaza Dr Secaucus NJ 07094

JACOBS, KAREN LOUISE, medical technologist; b. Kingston, N.Y., May 7, 1943; d. William Charles and Vera Elizabeth (Kelly) Jacobs; BS in Applied Tech., Empire State Coll., 1976; MS in Pub. Service Adminstrn., Russell Sage Coll., 1982. Sr. lab. technician, hosp. lab. supr. City of Kingston (N.Y.) Labs., 1962-68; sr. research asst. Dudley Obs., Albany, N.Y., 1972-75; lab. adminstr. Albany Med. Coll., 1976—, mem. faculty, 1982—; mem. infection control com. and subcoms. on AIDS mgmt. and human immunodeficiency virus precautions Albany Med. Ctr. Infection Control, 1987—;

mem. com. infection control and subcom. universal precautions. Bd. dirs. chpt. Leukemia Soc. Am., 1983. Mem. Clin. Lab. Mgmt. Assn., Blood Banks Assn. of N.Y. State, Am. Soc. Clin. Pathologists, Sierra Club, Earthwatch, Nat. Speleological Soc., Helderburg-Hudson Grotto. Home: 37B Picotte Dr Albany NY 12208 Office: Albany Med Coll Div Oncology 47 New Scotland Ave Albany NY 12208

JACOBS, KEITH WILLIAM, psychologist, educator; b. Ames, Iowa, Feb. 24, 1944; s. Cyril W. and Sylvia Jacobs; B.A., U. No. Iowa, 1968; M.A., Eastern Ill. U., 1972; Ph.D., U. So. Miss., 1975. Adj. instr. psychology Natchez br. U. So. Miss., 1974-75; asst. prof. psychology Loyola U., New Orleans, 1975-79, assoc. prof., 1979-85, prof., chmn. dept., 1985—; lectr. psychology Our Lady of Holy Cross Coll., New Orleans, 1976-80; aux. faculty William Carey Coll. Sch. Nursing, New Orleans, 1979-80. Active ACLU; exec. bd. Oak Harbor Homeowners Assn., 1979-81. Served with U.S. Army, 1968-71. Fellow Am. Psychol. Assn.; mem. Southwestern Psychol. Assn., Midwestern Psychol. Assn., La. Acad. Scis., Southeastern Psychol. Assn., Sigma Xi. Contbr. articles to sci. publs. Home: PO Box 70 Pearlington MS 39572 Office: Loyola U Dept Psychology New Orleans LA 70118

JACOBS, KENT FREDERICK, physician, dermatologist; b. El Paso, Tex., Feb. 13, 1938; s. Carl Frederick and Mercedes D. (Johns) J.; m. Sallie Ritter, Apr. 13, 1971. BS, N.Mex. State U., 1960; MD, Northwestern U., 1964; postgrad., U. Colo., 1967-70. Dir. service unit USPHS, Laguna, N.Mex., 1966-67; pvt. practice specializing in dematology Las Cruces, N.Mex., 1970—; cons. U.S. Army, San Francisco, 1968-70, cons. NIH, Washington, 1983, Holloman AFB, 1972-77; research assoc. VA Hosp., Denver, 1969-70; preceptor U. Tex., Galveston, 1976-77; mem. clin. staff Tex. Tech U., Lubbock, 1977—; asst. clin. prof. U. N.Mex., Albuquerque, 1972—; bd. dirs. First Nat. Bank of Dona Ana County, Las Cruces, N.Mex., 1987—. Contbr. articles to profl. jours. and popular mags. Trustee Mus. N.Mex. Found., 1987—; bd. regents Mus. N.Mex., 1987—. Served to lt. commdr. USCG, 1965-68. Invitational scholar Oreg. Primate Ctr., 1968; Acad. Dermatology Found. fellow, 1969; named Disting. Alumnus N.Mex. State U., 1985. Fellow Am. Acad. Dermatology, Royal Soc. Medicine, Soc. Investigative Dermatology; mem. AMA, Fedn. State Med. Bds. (bd. dirs. 1984-86), N.Mex. Med. Soc., N.Mex. Bd. Med. Examiners (pres. 1983-84), N.Mex. State U. Alumni Assn. (bd. dirs. 1975—), Phi Beta Kappa, Beta Beta Beta. Republican. Presbyterian. Clubs: Mil Gracias (pres. 1972-74), Pres.'s Assocs. Lodge: Rotary. Home: 3610 Southwind Rd Las Cruces NM 88005 Office: 2930 Hillrise Suite 6 Las Cruces NM 88001

JACOBS, LEO HERMAN, real estate investor; b. Des Moines, Nov. 19, 1902; s. Moses and Elizabeth Clara (Byoir) J. Student U. Iowa, 1921-24, U. Calif. So. Branch (now UCLA), 1924-25; A.B., U. So. Calif., 1926. Real estate salesman, 1926-27; pres., dir. Am. Gear and Parts Co., Ltd., San Francisco, 1928-34; owner, mgr. Advance Co., 1935—, bldg. contractor, 1935-75; pres., dir. Laurel Valley Devel. Co., Dallas, 1960-82. Worker, Pres. Birthday Ball, N.Y.C., 1935. Mem. Presidents Club, Old Gold Capital Club, U. Iowa Found., Phi Epsilon Pi. Lodges: Masons (Fifty Yr. award), Shriners.

JACOBS, LOUIS SULLIVAN, architect, educator; s. Morris and Mary Jacobs; B.S. in Architecture and City Planning, Armour Inst. Tech., 1940; M.S. in Indsl. Engring., Ill. Inst. Tech., 1952, Ph.D. curr. comp. in Indsl. Engr., 1958; Sc.D. in Safety, Ind. No. U., 1972, Ph.D. in Human Engring., 1974; M.S. in Profl. Mgmt., 1980. Pres., Louis S. Jacobs & Assos., Architects, Engrs. and Planners, Chgo., 1946—; prof. archtl. engring. Loop Coll., Chgo., 1967-86, coordinator engring., archtl. and tech. services dept. Pub. Service Inst., 1967-75, dept. applied sci., 1975-86; prof. indsl. engring. Ill. Inst. Tech., 1948-58, 67; prof. architecture U. Ill., Chgo., 1967; prof. engring. Chgo. Citywide Coll., 1980. Bd. dirs. Old Town Boys Club, 1951-85; bd. dirs. Eisenberg Chgo. Boys and Girls Club, 1985—; trustee Chgo. Sch. Architecture Found., 1967. Served as lt. USN, 1942-46. Recipient award of merit Office CD, State of Ill., 1957; citation Gov. State of Ill., Office Emergency Services, 1964; citation for Outstanding public services Office of Pres. U.S., U.S. Emergency Resources Bd., 1967; registered profl. engr., Ill., Del., Calif.; registered indsl. engr., safety engr., mfg. engr., Calif.; registered architect, Ill.; cert. hazardous materials mgmt., materials handling; cert. indsl. hygiene, cert. mfr. engr., Robotics, 1980; cert. hazardous control mgr., 1968, mfr. engr., 1968, product safety mgr., 1985, hazardous materials mgr., 1985. Fellow Soc. Am. Registered Architects, Nat. Soc. Profl. Engrs., Systems Safety Soc., Soc. Architects, Ill. Soc. Architects (dir. 1976-78 v.p. 1978-80, pres. 1980-82); mem. AIA, Ill. Soc. Profl. Engrs. (v.p. 1976-83), System Safety Soc. (pres. 1980-85), ASCE, Western Soc. Engrs. (life), Am. Soc. Mil. Engrs., Am. Soc. Safety Engrs., Internat. Materials Mgmt. Soc., Am. Inst. Indsl. Engrs., Soc. for Gen. Systems Research, Standards Engring. Soc., Soc. Mfg. Engrs., Vets. Safety, Constrn. Safety Assn. Am. (v.p. 1976—), Am. Soc. Environ. Engrs. (diplomate), Nat. Safety Mgmt. Soc., Nat. Assn. Fire Investigators, Nat. Fire Protection Assn., Nat. Safety Council, World Safety Orgn. (cert. safety specialist, safety mgr., safety exec. 1986) Mil. Order World Wars, Naval Order U.S., Res. Officers Assn., Tau Beta Pi, Sigma Iota Epsilon, Alpha Phi Mu, Tau Epsilon Phi. Editor: Vector, 1968. Office: 2605 W Pratt Blvd Chicago IL 60645

JACOBS, RICHARD DEARBORN, consulting marine engineer; b. Detroit, July 6, 1920; s. Richard Dearborn and Mattie Phoebe (Cobleigh) J.; divorced; children: Richard, Margaret, Paul, Linden, Susan. BS, U. Mich., 1944. Engr., Detroit Diesel Engine div. Gen. Motors, 1946-51; mgr. indsl. and marine engine div. Reo Motors, Inc., Lansing, Mich., 1951-54; chief engr. Kennedy Marine Engine Co., Biloxi, Miss., 1955-59; marine sales mgr. Nordberg Mfg. Co., Milw., 1959-69; marine sales mgr. Fairbanks Morse Engine div. Colt Industries, Beloit, Wis., 1969-81; pres. R.D. Jacobs & Assocs., cons. engrs., naval architects and marine engrs., Roscoe, Ill., 1981—. Served with AUS, 1944-46. Registered profl. engr., Ill., Mich., Wis., Miss. Mem. Soc. Naval Architects and Marine Engrs. (chmn. sect. 1979-80), Soc. Automotive Engrs., Am. Soc. Naval Engrs., Soc. Am. Mil. Engrs., Soc. Marine Cons., ASTM, Permanent Internat. Assn. Nav. Congresses, Navy League U.S., U.S. Naval Inst., Propeller Club U.S., Nat. Forensic Ctr. Unitarian. Clubs: Country (Beloit); Rockford Polo, Masons. Office: 11405 Main St Roscoe IL 61073

JACOBS, ROBERT, educator; b. Murphysboro, Ill., July 17, 1913; s. Arthur Clarence and Zylphia May (Porter) J.; m. Oma Lee Corgan, Aug. 13, 1939; children: Robert Corgan, Janice Lee Jacobs Friedman, Lawrence James, Linda May (Mrs. Paul Wineberg). B.Ed., So. Ill. U., 1935; M.A., U. Ill., 1939; Ed.D., Wayne State U., 1949. Pub. sch. tchr., adminstr. Wood River, Ill., 1935-42; personnel staff Ford Motor Co., 1945-46; asst. instr. Wayne U., 1946-47; asst. dir. Ednl. Records Bur., N.Y.C., 1947-51; dir. counseling, prof. edn. Tex. A. and M. Coll., 1951-54; ednl. measurements adviser, dep. chief edn. div. U.S. Operations Mission to Ethiopia, FOA, 1954-56; regional edn. adviser S.E. Asia U.S. Operations Mission, Thailand, 1956-58; chief Far East program div. Office Edn., ICA, 1958-61; chief edn. div. Office Ednl. and Social Devel. AID, 1961-62; prof. edn., dean internat. service div. So. Ill. U., Carbondale, 1962-67; prof. emeritus So. Ill. U., 1974—; regional edn. adviser Office Regional Devel. Affairs, Am. embassy, Bangkok, and cons. S.E. Asian Ministers of Edn. Orgn., Bangkok, 1967-74; continuing cons. SEAMEO; ednl. cons., writer, lectr., 1974—; vis. prof., extension lectr. U. Ark., U. Ala., Rutgers U., U. Addis Ababa, George Washington U.; numerous surveys and evaluations edn. programs abroad, including, Korea, Cambodia, Syria, Nigeria, India, Congo, Chile, Colombia; mem. internat. adv. com. Ednl. Records Bur. Served with AUS, 1942-45. Recipient of meritorious service citation ICA, meritorious service citation AID, 1959, meritorious honor award Dept. State, 1968. Mem. NEA, Nat. Soc. Study Edn., AARP, Phi Delta Kappa. Methodist. Home: PO Box 431 Murphysboro IL 62966

JACOBS, SEYMOUR, photographer; b. N.Y.C., Mar. 27, 1931; s. Joseph and Sadie (Weiser) J.; m. Betsy Brubaker (div.); 1 child, Anita. BA, Bklyn. Coll., 1956. French tchr. Bd. Edn., N.Y.C., 1958-78. Photographer Brighton Beach, N.Y. (series in many collections in France and Europe), 1967—. Home: 29 Rue Veron, 75028 Paris France

JACOBS, STANLEY BARRY, nuclear engineer; b. Boston, June 9, 1937; s. Abraham and Jennie Dianne J.; m. Betty Ellen Arth, Mar. 23, 1963; children—Kerry Lynne, Dean Alan. B.Chem. Engring., Rensselaer Poly. Inst., 1958. Registered profl. engr., Mass., N.Y. State, Conn., Calif. Cadet engr. Stone & Webster Engring. Corp., Boston, 1958-60, engr. nuclear div., 1960-67, nuclear engr., 1967-72, project engr., 1971-76, sr. power engr., 1972-76, sr. project engr., 1976, chief licensing engr., 1976-80, asst. engring. mgr., 1980-83, engring. mgr., 1983—, v.p., 1985—. bd. dirs., mem. adv. bd. Ctr. Multiphase Research, Troy, N.Y., 1983—, chair adv. bd., 1986—; mem. Sharon (Mass.) Personnel Bd., 1978-79. Mem. Am. Nuclear Soc. (standards, standards steering, internat. coms.), ASME, Am. Soc. Safety Engrs., Nat. Soc. Profl. Engrs., Mass. Soc. Profl. Engrs., Atomic Indsl. Forum (mem., steering group mem. com. on reactor licensing and safety, chmn. subcom. on standardization, mem. steering group com. on design, constrn. and ops.), Tau Epsilon Phi. Contbr. articles to profl. publs. Home: 32 Spring Ln Sharon MA 02067 Office: 245 Summer St Boston MA 02107

JACOBS, WILFRED EBENEZER, governor general Antigua and Barbuda; b. Grenada, Oct. 19, 1919; ed. Grenada Boys Secondary Sch., Grays Inn, London; m. Carmen Sylva Knight; 1 son, 2 daus. Mem. Exec. and Legis. Councils, St. Vincent, 1946, Dominica, 1948, St. Kitts, 1952-56, Antigua, 1957-60; registrar, additional magistrate St. Vincent, 1946, Dominica, 1947; magistrate St. Kitts, 1949; crown atty. St. Kitts, 1952; atty. gen. Leeward Islands, 1957; legal draftsman, Trinidad and Tobago, 1960; puisne judge, solicitor gen., dir. public prosecutions, Barbados, 1961-66; gov. Antigua, 1967-81; gov.-gen. Antigua and Barbuda, 1981—. Served as capt. St. Kitts-Nevis-Anguilla Def. Force. Decorated knight officer Order Brit. Empire. Fellow Royal Commonwealth Soc. Address: Office of Gov Gen, Saint John's Antigua *

JACOBS, WOODROW COOPER, meteorologist, oceanographer; b. Pasadena, Calif., Sept. 11, 1908; s. William Rozel and Mabelle (Cooper) J.; m. Dorothy Cecelia Quinn, June 15, 1933; 1 child, Marilyn Rozel (Mrs. Wilbur M. Ott). Student, Va. Mil. Inst., 1926-27; A.B., UCLA, 1930; Ph.D. in Meteorology, 1948; M.S., U. So. Calif., 1934; Ph.D., Scripps Instn. Oceanography. With U.S. Weather Bur., San Diego, 1931-36; forecaster fruit-frost service U.S. Weather Bur., Pomona, Calif., 1936-41; research assoc. Scripps Instn. Oceanography, also Carnegie Inst., 1937; chief civilian meteorologist Hdqrs. USAAF, 1941-46; head climatological branch U.S. Weather Bur., Washington, 1946-48; dir. climatology USAF Air Weather Service, Washington, 1948-60; phys. sci. specialist Library of Congress, 1960-61; dir. Nat. Oceanographic Data Center, 1961-67, World Data Center A, Oceanography, 1962-67; dir. environ. data service Environ. Sci. Service Adminstrn., Silver Spring, Md., 1967-70; sr. scientist Ocean Data Systems, Inc., Rockville, Md., 1971—; vis. prof. Mass. Inst. Tech., 1950, U. Chgo., 1956; lectr. meteorology and oceanography Dept. Agr. Grad. Sch., 1942-58; professorial lectr. George Washington U., 1957; USAF mem. two panels Research and Devel. Bd., Dept. Def., 1948-52; com. climatology joint meteorol. com. Joint Chiefs Staff, 1948-58; U.S. del. Internat. Meteorol. Orgn., Toronto, Can., 1947, pres. subcom. agrl. forecasts, 1947-50; mem. commn. climatology World Meteorol. Orgn., 1950-62, chmn. internat. com. exchange data, 1953-60; U.S. del. of Nat. Acad. Scis. to assembly Internat. Union Geodesy and Geophysics, Brussels, 1951, Rome, 1954, Toronto, 1957, Lucerne, 1967; mem. coms. NRC-NSF, 1948—; chmn. interagy. atmospheric scis. oceanography com. on air-sea research, 1963-64; com. on oceanography Smithsonian Instn., 1962-67; working group Intergovtl. Oceanographic Commn., UNESCO, 1962-67; panel mem. Interagy. Com. on Oceanography, 1961-67; adv. council Oceanic Research Inst. of San Diego, 1964—; adv. panel on sea-air interaction program Dept. Commerce, 1964-67; chmn. working group on air-sea inter actions World Meteorol. Orgn., UN, 1964-68; U.S. del. 2d Oceanographic Congress, Moscow, 1966; U.S. mem. Intergovernmental Oceanographic Commn. Com. on Ocean Stas., Paris, 1966; mem. data adv. panel Pres.'s Council on Marine Resources and Engring. Devel., 1967-69; mem. com. on radio frequency requirements for sci. research Nat. Acad. Sci., 1969-70; mem. com. biog. classification Internat. Assn. Phys. and Sci. Oceanography, 1968—; Dept. Commerce mem. Pres.'s Commn. Food from the Sea, 1968-69; adv. bd. Office Critical Tables Fed. Council, 1968-69; U.S. del. planning com. Internat. Indian Ocean Expdn., Paris, 1964. Author: Energy Exchange Between Sea and Atmosphere, 1951, Meteorological Satellites, 1962; co-author: Arctic Meteorology, 1956; also numerous articles in field.; Editor: English edit. Oceanology, Acad. Sci. USSR for scripta technica, Inc, 1962-75; adv. bd.: English edit. Meteorol. and Geoastrophys. Abstracts, 1963—; asso. editor: four publs. Am. Meterol. Soc, 1946-70. Recipient Certificate of Appreciation USAAF, 1946; Distinguished Service award Dept. Commerce, 1970. Fellow Am. Geophys. Union (exec. com. 1947-61, council 1961, sec. sect. meteorology 1947-74, chmn. com. geophys. data), Am. Meterol. Soc. (council 1961-64, chmn. bd. certified cons. meteorologists 1960-62), Washington Acad. Sci.; mem. Internat. Platform Assn., Royal Meteorol. Soc., Md., N.Y. acads. scis., Marine Tech. Soc., Oceanographical Soc. Japan, AAAS, Am. Soc. Limnology and Oceanography, Archeol. Soc. Md., U.S. Navy League (Ormond Beach, Fla.), U.S. Naval Inst. (Annapolis, Md.), SAR, Blue Circle C (UCLA), Sigma Xi, Alpha Tau Omega, Alpha Kappa Psi, Blue Key. Methodist. Clubs: Shawnee Country (Winchester, Va.); Palm Coast Yacht (Fla.); Cosmos (Washington). Lodge: Lions. Home: 234 Ocean Palm Dr Flagler Beach FL 32036 Office: 6309 Bradley Blvd Bethesda MD 20817

JACOBSON, ALLEN FRANK, manufacturing company executive; b. Omaha, Oct. 7, 1926; s. Alma Frank and Ruth Alice (Saalfeld) J.; m. Barbara Jean Benidt, Apr. 18, 1964; children: Allen F., Holly Anne, Paul Andrew. B.S. in Chem. Engring., Iowa State U., 1947. Product engr. tape lab. 3M Co. (Minn. Mining & Mfg. Co.), St. Paul, 1947-50, tech. asst. to plant mgr., Hutchinson, Minn. and Bristol, Pa., 1950-55, tape prodn. supt., Bristol, Pa., 1955-59, plant mgr. tape, 1959-61, plant mgr. tape and AC&S, 1961-63, tape prodn. mgr., 1963, mfg. mgr. tape and allied products, 1963-68, gen. mgr. indsl. tape div., 1968-70, div. v.p. indsl. tape div., 1970-72, exec. v.p., gen. mgr., 1973-75, v.p. European ops., 1975, v.p. tape and allied products group, 1975-81, exec. v.p. indsl. and consumer sector, 1981-84, pres. U.S. ops., 1984-86, chmn., chief exec. officer, 1986—, dir., 1983—; exec. v.p., gen. mgr. 3M Can., Ltd., 1973-75; dir. Valmont Industries Inc., Valley, Nebr., U.S. West Inc., Denver, No. States Power Co., Mpls., Pillsbury Co., Mpls. Recipient Profl. Achievement citation in engring. Iowa State U., 1983, Marston medal Iowa State U., 1986. Avocations: photography; shooting; gardening; golf; reading. Office: Minn Mining & Mfg Co 3M Ctr 220-14W-04 Saint Paul MN 55101 *

JACOBSON, ANNA SUE, financial executive; b. Ft. Smith, Ark., Aug. 13, 1940; d. Ray Bradley and Joy Anna (Person) McAlister, (stepfather) Cleve J. McDonald, Sr.; m. Lyle Norman Jacobson, Nov. 23, 1958; children: Lyle Michael, Daniel Ray, Julie Anne, Eric Joseph. Degree, Coll. for Fin. Planning, 1984. Cert. fin. paraplanner. Office mgr. Twin Cities Lithographic Inst., St. Paul, 1963-66; sec., St. Paul, Mpls., 1971-78; asst. to pres., office mgr. Planners Fin. Services, Mpls., 1978-85, asst. corp. treas., 1987—; fin. paraplanner McAlmont Investment Co., Mpls., 1985—; dir. Planners Fin. Services; mem. bd. advisors Coll. for Fin. Planning, Denver, 1982—; speaker various orgns. Co-creator Paraplanning Profession Advisor. Del., Dem. Farmer Labor Party, St. Paul, 1980; campaign chmn. mayoral election, Roseville, Minn., 1983, county commr., city council election, Roseville, 1980, 84; local chmn. for passage of E.R.A., Minn.; chmn. Am. Lung Assn., St. Paul; past. pres. PTA, Minn. Recipient Volunteerism award Gov. State of Minn., 1981; Cert. of Appreciation, Minn. Bicentennial Com., 1976; mem. exec. council Boy Scouts Am., 1977-81; mem. adv. bd. Sch. Dist. 623, Roseville, Minn., 1978-81; fund raising com. mem. Twin Cities Pub. TV Sta., 1985—. Mem. Internat. Assn. Fin. Planning, Twin Cities Assn. Fin. Planners, Internat. Assn. Bus. and Profl. Women (bd. dirs. 1977-86, pres. 1980-82, named Woman of Yr. 1982), Concordia Acad. Booster Club, Beta Sigma Phi Nu Phi Mu Chpt. Democrat. Lutheran. Avocations: tennis, riding, reading, piano, fencing. Office: McAlmont Investment Co Shelard Plaza N Minneapolis MN 55426

JACOBSON, BARRY STEPHEN, lawyer, administrative judge; b. Bklyn., Mar. 30, 1955; s. Morris and Sally (Ballaban) J. Cert. in drama, Sch. of Performing Arts, N.Y.C., 1973; BA, CUNY, 1977, MA, 1980; JD, Bklyn. Sch. Law, 1980. Bar: N.Y. 1981, U.S. Dist. Ct. (ea. and so. dists.) N.Y. 1981, U.S. Ct. Appeals (2d cir.) 1981, U.S. Supreme Ct. 1984, D.C. 1985, U.S. Ct. Claims 1985, U.S. Ct. Internat. Trade 1985, U.S. Ct. Mil. Appeals 1985. Sole practice Bklyn., 1981; asst. corp. counsel N.Y.C. Law Dept., Bklyn., 1981-84; asst. dist. atty. Borough of Queens, Kew Gardens, N.Y., 1984-85; judge adminstrv. law N.Y. Dept. Motor Vehicles, Bklyn., 1985-86, 87—; assoc. counsel N.Y. State Dept. Health, N.Y.C., 1986; arbitrator N.Y.C. Small Claims Ct., 1986—; gen. counsel Amersfort Flatlands Devel. Corp., Bklyn., 1981-82; arbitrator N.Y.C. Civil Ct. 1987—; adminstrv. law judge N.Y.C. Parking Violators Bur., 1987—; mem. Indigent Defenders Appeal Panel, 1988—. Mem. Roosevelt Dem. Party, Bklyn., 1984—, Kings Hwy. Dem. Party, Bklyn., 1982—; King's County Dem. com., 1986—; gen. counsel, Bklyn. Coll. Hillel, Bklyn. Coll. Student Govts., 1980—, also advisor. Named one of Outstanding Young Men Am., 1983, 85, 86, 87. Mem. ABA, N.Y. State Bar Assn. (spl. com. juvenile justice), Bklyn. Bar Assn. (family ct. com., chmn. young lawyers section), N.Y. County Lawyers Assn. (family ct. com.), Am. Judicature Soc., Bklyn. Coll. Alumni Assn. (gen. counsel student govt. affiliate 1983—, bd. dirs. 1985—), Jaycees (named one of Outstanding Young Men of Am. 1983, 85), NRA, Am. Judges Assn., Phi Delta Phi (hon.). Jewish. Lodges: B'nai B'rith, Hillei (bd. dirs. 1983—, gen. counsel 1987—). Home: 2912 Brighton 12th St Brooklyn NY 11235 Office: NY State Dept Motor Vehicles 350 Livingston St 4th Floor Brooklyn NY 11217

JACOBSON, DAN, writer; b. Johannesburg, South Africa, Mar. 7, 1929; s. Hyman Michael and Liebe (Melamed) J.; m. Margaret Pye, Feb. 13, 1954; children: Simon Orde, Matthew, Jessica. B.A., U. Witwatersrand, Johannesburg, 1949. Journalist and tchr. 1950-54, profl. writer, 1954—; fellow in creative writing Stanford U., 1956-57; vis. prof. English lit. Syracuse U., 1965-66; lectr. Univ. Coll., London, 1975-79; reader in English U. London, 1980—; vis. fellow Humanities Research Centre Australian Nat. U., 1981; vice chmn. lit. panel Arts Council Gt. Britain, 1972-74. Author: The Trap, 1955, A Dance in the Sun, 1956, Price of Diamonds, 1957, The Zulu and the Zeide, 1959, Evidence of Love, 1960, No Further West, 1961, The Beginners, 1966, Through The Wilderness, 1968, The Rape of Tamar, 1970, Inklings, 1973, The Wonder-Worker, 1974, The Confessions of Josef Baisz, 1978, The Story of the Stories, 1982, Time and Time Again: Autobiographies, 1985, Her Story, 1987. Recipient John Llewelyn Rhys award Nat. Book League, 1958, W. Somerset Maugham award Soc. Authors, 1964, H. H. Wingate award Jewish Chronicle, 1978, J.R. Ackerley award for autobiography P.E.N. Club of Gt. Britain, 1986; Soc. Authors travelling fellow, 1986. Address: care Am Heath & Co, 79 St Martins Ln, London WC2N 4AA, England *

JACOBSON, DAVID, rabbi; b. Cin., Dec. 2, 1909; s. Abraham and Rebecca (Sereinsky) J.; m. Helen Gugenheim, Nov. 6, 1938; children: Elizabeth Anne, Dorothy Jean Jacobson Miller. A.B., U. Cin., 1931; Rabbi, Hebrew Union Coll., 1934, D.D., 1959; Ph.D., St. Catherine's Coll., U. Cambridge (Eng.), 1936; LL.D., Our Lady of Lake Coll., 1964. Instr. Hebrew Union Coll., 1933-34; rabbi West Central Liberal Congregation, London, 1934-36, Indpls. Hebrew Congregation, 1936-38, Temple Beth-El, San Antonio, 1938-76; emeritus Temple Beth-El, 1976—; rabbi Temple Mizpah, Abilene, Tex., 1981-86; aux. chaplain, area mil. installations; chaplain Audie Murphy VA Hosp., 1973—; chmn. Rabbinical Placement Commn., 1973-78; chmn. discussion program KSAT-TV, 1956-80, KLRN-TV, 1983. Author: Social Background of the Old Testament, 1942, The Synagogue Through the Ages, 1958; contbr. articles to profl. and gen. publs.; also contbr. to: Universal Jewish Ency, 1939-43. Mem. Tex. Senate Com. Welfare Reform, 1970, Tex. State Ethics Commn., 1971, Tex. State Medicaid Task Force, 1977; mem. com. nursing homes Tex. Dept. Human Resources, 1978-80; pres. San Antonio Soc. Crippled Children and Adults, 1963-66, Goodwill Industries San Antonio, 1956-60, Bexar County chpt. Nat. Tb Assn., 1955-57, Community Welfare Council San Antonio, 1951-53, San Antonio Area Found., 1965-69, Research and Planning Council San Antonio, 1966-67, Tex. Social Welfare Assn., 1967-69, San Antonio Manpower Devel. Council, 1968-76, S.W. region Central Conf. Am. Rabbis, 1969-70, Multiple Sclerosis Soc. San Antonio, 1975-78, Nat. Conf. Social Welfare, 1976-77, Am. Inst. Character Edn., 1976-78, Prevent Blindness Soc., San Antonio, 1980-82; mediator San Antonio Printing Trades and Employers, 1968—; mem. nat. labor panel Am. Arbitration Assn., 1977—, Fed. Mediation and Conciliation Service, 1981—; commr. Housing Authority San Antonio, 1954-58; bd. dirs. Our Lady of Lake U., 1966-76, hon. bd. dirs., 1977—; also chmn. adv. bd. Worden Sch. Social Service of coll., 1958-67; founder U. Ind. Hillel Found., 1938, San Antonio Vis. Nurses Assn., 1952, Community Welfare Council San Antonio, 1944; bd. dirs. S.W. Tex. Meth. Hosp., 1956—, San Antonio Med. Found., 1962—, Alamo council Boy Scouts Am., 1950—, Children's Hosp. Found., 1964—, Keystone Sch., San Antonio, 1960-80, Ecumenical Center for Religion and Health, 1968—, Alamo chpt. Am. Cancer Soc., 1975-83, Hospice of St. Benedict's Hosp., 1977-81, Tex. Council Higher Edn., 1969—, Nat. Jewish Welfare Bd., 1964-72, Alamo chpt. Assn. U.S. Army, 1964-71, Hemis Fair, 1968; life mem. bd. Tex. United Community Services, 1970—; co-chmn. community relations council San Antonio Jewish Fedn., 1978-79; chmn. religion com. United San Antonio, 1980-81, vice chmn. public sector, 1981—; chmn. Bexar County Community Corrections Commn., 1979-81; mem. nat. bd. Goodwill Industries Am., 1965-78; bd. overseers Hebrew Union Coll.-Jewish Inst. Religion, 1966—, bd. govs., 1966-68; bd. govs. Commn. on Social Action of Reform Judaism, 1978—; mem. nat. bd. Nat. Council on Crime and Delinquency, 1972—, Florence G. Heller-Jewish Welfare Bd. Research Center, 1966-70; bd. dirs. Army Med. Dept. Mus. Found., 1985—. Served as chaplain with USNR, 1944-46. Recipient Silver Beaver award Boy Scouts Am., 1958; Aristotle-Aquinas award Cath. Coll. Found. S.A., 1959; Golden Deeds award Exchange Club San Antonio, 1959; Keystone award Boys' Club Am., 1962; Lifetime Achievement award B'nai B'rith, 1964; Nat. Humanitarian award, 1975; Edgar Helms award Goodwill Industries, 1972; shofar award, award San Antonio Transcendental Meditation Soc., 1977; Shofar award, 1984; named Outstanding Jew NCCJ, 1961, Citizen of Year Sembradores de Amistad, 1971. Mem. Central Conf. Am. Rabbis (chmn. com. Judaism and health 1967-72, chmn. nominating com. 1979), Kallah of Tex. Rabbis (pres. 1950-51, chancellor-historian 1977—), Am. Social Health Assn. (dir. 1969-75), Tex. Congress Parents and Tchrs. (hon. life), Sigma Alpha Mu, Pi Tau Pi. Clubs: Rotary (San Antonio), B'nai B'rith (San Antonio) (hon. chmn. 1974), Torch (San Antonio) (pres. 1961), Argyle (San Antonio). Home: 207 Beechwood Ln San Antonio TX 78216

JACOBSON, DENNIS LEONARD, business exec.; b. Stoughton, Wis., May 19, 1945; s. Leonard Harold and Elaine Marie (Folbrecht) J.; B.S. in Bus. Adminstrn. and Econs., U. Wis., 1967; m. Jane Marie McGill, June 3, 1967; children—Timothy Dennis, Darren Todd. Price analyst Caterpillar, Geneva, 1967-71, pricing supr., Peoria, Ill., 1971-73; mgr. pricing Overseas div. Internat. Harvester Co., Chgo., 1973-76, asst. to mng. dir. Internat. Harvester Germany, Neuss/Rhine, W. Ger., 1976-78, mgr. distbr. mktg. Internat. Harvester Agrl. Equipment Europe, Paris, 1978-81, dir. export mktg. Equipment Group, 1978-84; v.p. mktg. Internat. Group Internat. Harvestor, 1984-85, v.p. sales and mktg., Fed. Signal Corp., 1985-86; dir. internat. ops. Outboard Marine Corp., Waukegan, Ill., 1986-88, v.p., corp. officer, 1988—. Pres., parent faculty assn. Am. Internat. Sch., 1977-78. Bd. dirs. St. Therese Hosp., Waukegan, 1987—. Club: Am. Men's. Home: 1420 Lawrence Ave Lake Forest IL 60045

JACOBSON, DONALD THOMAS, managment consultant; b. Powers Lake, N.D., June 5, 1932; s. Martin I. and Gladys E. (Thronson) J.; B.A., Whitman Coll., 1954; M.B.A., Stanford U., 1956; m. Andrea Marie Moore, Aug. 14, 1954; 1 dau., Kathryn E. Hanson. Sales and mktg. mgmt. Guy F. Atkinson Co., Portland, Oreg., 1959-63; sales control mgr. Boise Cascade Corp., Portland, 1964-66; v.p. and dir. research Lund, McCutcheon, Jacobson, Inc., Portland, 1966-74; pres. Mgmt./Mktg. Assocs., Inc., Portland, 1974—; chmn. Oreg. Bus. Workshops, 1974-76; exec. com., dir. Full-Circle, Inc., 1971-77. Served to lt. U.S. Army, 1956-59. Decorated commendation ribbon; recipient Oreg. Econ. Devel. award, 1973; Cert. Mgmt. Cons. Mem. Am. Mktg. Assn. (pres. Oreg. chpt. 1972-73), Am. Mgmt. Assn., Inst. Mgmt. Consultants (cert.; founding mem., founder and pres. Pacific N.W. chpt. 1980-81), Mktg. Research Assn., Nat. Assn. Bus. Economists, Portland Metro. C. of C. (bd. dirs. 1987—, chmn.'s award Outstanding Service, 1987), Met. Chambers Econ. Devel. Council Portland Area (chmn. mktg. task force 1983-85, emerging issues com., 1987—, labor policy com. 1988—, chmn. Tri-Met Task Force 1985—, chmn. transpn. com. 1987—, bd. dirs. 1987—), The Planning Forum (v.p. Oreg. chpt. 1986-87, bd. dirs., 1986—), U.S. Dept. Commerce Nat. Def. Exec. Res. (chmn. Oreg.-Idaho assn. 1969-70), Oregonians for Cost-Effective Govt. (bd. dirs. 1986—), Econ. Roundtable (coordinator 1982-88), Whitman Coll. Alumni Assn. (pres. 1975-77), Stanford U. Bus. Sch. Assn. (pres. Oreg. chpt. 1971-72), Phi Beta Kappa. Republican. Lutheran. Club: University (Portland). Contbr.

articles on mgmt. and mktg. to profl. jours. Home: 2580 SW Buckingham Ave Portland OR 97201 Office: Mgmt/Mktg Assocs Inc 707 SW Washington Portland OR 97205

JACOBSON, EARL JAMES, lawyer, tax leasing executive; b. Chgo., May 10, 1940; s. Benjamin L. and Mary (Urman) J.; m. Donna Jean Breen, Mar. 5, 1983; children—Joan, John. B.A., U. Ill., 1961; M.B.A., U. Chgo., 1963; J.D., Loyola U., Chgo., 1980. Bar: Ill. 1980, U.S. Dist. Ct. (no. dist.) Ill. 1980, U.S. Ct. Internat. Trade 1980, U.S. Ct. Customs and Patent Appeals 1980, U.S. Tax Ct., 1985, U.S. Supreme Ct., 1985. Indsl. salesman Honeywell, Xerox, Chgo., 1964-67; dir. mktg. Mastech Computer, Chgo., 1967-71, Datronic Rental Co., Chgo., 1971-81; v.p. Dearborn Computer Co., Park Ridge, Ill., 1981-82; sr. syndication officer Seattle 1st Nat. Bank, Schaumburg, Ill., 1982-83; v.p. fin. and syndication Hartford Fin. Services, Inverness, Ill., 1983-85; v.p. corp. fin. and corp. counsel Lease Investment Corp., Chgo., 1985-86; dir. equity placement, CIS Corp., Syracuse, N.Y., 1986-87; exec. v.p., gen. counsel Tech. Funding, Inc., Deerfield, Ill., 1987—; pres. MidTech Funding, Inc., Inverness, Ill., 1988—; dir., gen. counsel Info. Systems, Arlington Heights, Ill., 1st Securities, Inc., Chgo., Citifirst, Inc., Chgo. Served with USAF, 1963-69. Mem. ABA, Nat. Assn. Securities Dealers, Equipment Syndication Assn., Ill. State Bar Assn., Chgo. Bar Assn. Club: 20 Plus (Chgo.) (pres. 1980-82). Home: 600 S Dearborn Apt 2102 Chicago IL 60605 Office: Tech Funding Inc 102 Wilmot Rd Suite 500 Deerfield IL 60015

JACOBSON, GLORIA NADINE, college administrator; b. Jewell, Iowa, July 12, 1930; d. Christian Frederick and Amanda M. (Englebart) Larson; B.B.A., U. Iowa, 1974; m. Richard T. Jacobson, July 22, 1951 (dec. Feb. 1988); children—Richard Thomas, Douglas L., William Andrew. Mem. adminstrn. staff U. Iowa, Iowa City, 1950—, asst. to the dean Coll. of Pharmacy, 1981-87, exec. asst., 1987—. Mem. Phi Gamma Nu, Kappa Epsilon. Republican. Lutheran. Home: 415 Ridgeview Iowa City IA 52240 Office: U of Iowa Coll of Pharmacy Iowa City IA 52242

JACOBSON, HAROLD GORDON, radiologist, educator; b. Cin., Oct. 12, 1912; s. Samuel and Regina (Dittman) J.; m. Ruth Enenstein, Aug. 10, 1941; children: Richard, Arthur. B.S., U. Cin., 1934, M.B., 1936, M.D., 1937. Diplomate: Am. Bd. Radiology (trustee 1971-82, chmn. written exams. com. in diagnostic radiology 1973-81, co-chmn., mem., 1981—, treas. 1976-78, v.p. 1978-80, pres. 1980-82, mem. residency rev. com. 1976-82, vice-chmn. 1979-80, chmn. 1980—, exec. com. 1976—). Intern Los Angeles County Gen. Hosp., 1936-38; fellow in pathology Longview Hosp., Cin., 1938; resident Mt. Sinai Hosp., N.Y.C., 1939-41, Associated Hosps. U. Tex., 1941-42; asst. in radiology U. Tex., 1941-42; assoc. radiologist New Haven (Conn.) Hosp.; also instr. Yale U., 1952; asst. chief, asso. radiologist VA Hosp., Bronx, N.Y., 1946-50; chief radiology service VA Hosp., 1950-53, cons., 1958—; asst. clin. prof. N.Y. U., 1952-53, clin. prof., 1953-59, prof. clin. radiology, 1959-64; prof. radiology Albert Einstein Coll. Medicine, 1964-71; prof., chmn. Albert Einstein Coll. Medicine of Montefiore Hosp. and Med. Center, N.Y.C., 1972-85; prof. radiology Albert Einstein Coll. Medicine of Montefiore Hosp. and Med. Center, 1985-86, prof. emeritus, chmn., Disting. Univ. Prof. radiology, 1986—; dir. dept. roentgenology Hosp. for Spl. Surgery, N.Y.C., 1953-55; radiologist-in-chief Montefiore Hosp. and Med. Center, N.Y.C., 1955—; sr. cons. in radiology Nat. Bd. Med. Examiners, 1975—, mem. bd., 1979-83; vis. prof. radiology Inst. Orthopaedics, U. London, 1975—; vis. prof., lectr., UCLA Med. Ctr., 1986, 88, various socs., med. schs., univs. in Israel, Brazil, Finland, Cuba, Eastern Europe; vis. prof., lectr., med. ctrs. Republic of China and guest Chinese Radiol. Soc., 1986; named lectures include Felson Lecture, Carman Lecture, Baylin Lecture, Beeler Lecture, Freedman Lecture, Pfahler Lecture, Chamberlain Lecture, Evans Lecture, Sampson Lecture, Wolf Meml. Lecture, Caffey Lecture, Grubbe Lecture, Myron Melamed Lecture; head del. of radiologists to Republic of China, 1984. Author: (with Clarence Schein, William Z. Stern) The Common Bile Duct, 1967, Neuroradiology Workshop, Vol. III, 1968, (with Ronald O. Murray) Radiology of Skeletal Disorders: Exercises in Diagnosis, 1971, 2d edit., 1977; co-author: Bone Disease Syllabus, 1972, 2d series, 1976, 3d series, 1980, Index for Roentgen Diagnosis, 3d edit, 1975; co-editor in chief: Jour. Internat. Skeletal Soc, 1976—; editorial bd.: Excerpta Medica, 1974—, Jour. AMA, 1979—; coordinator topics in radiology, 1977-79; editor topics in radiology, 1979—; mem. editorial bd. for radiology, 1979—; contbr. articles to profl. jours. Served as maj. M.C AUS, 1942-46. Recipient Gold medal Assn. Univ. Radiologists, 1982, Gold medal Phi Lambda Kappa, 1983, Spl. Excellence award (in lieu of Hon. Doctorate) U. Cin., 1987. Fellow Am. Coll. Radiology (councilor 1960—, bd. chancellors, chmn. com. on radiol. coding 1967—, mem. commn. on credentials 1968—, chmn commn. on affairs Am. Inst. Radiology 1971—, co-chmn. com. on diagnostic coding index and thesaurus 1973—, Gold medal 1978, selected for video taping as living legend in radiology), Royal Coll. Radiologists (London) (hon.); mem. N.Y. Roentgen Soc. (pres. 1959-60, historian 1967—), AMA, N.Y. State Med. Soc., N.Y. Med. Soc., Soc. of Chairmen Acad. Radiology Depts. (mem. exec. council 1972—, pres. 1973-74), Radiol. Soc. N.Am. (pres. 1966-67, mem. bd. censors 1968—, gold medal 1972), Am. Roentgen Ray Soc. (Cert. of Appreciation 1983), Royal Soc. Medicine (hon.), Internat. Skeletal Soc. (co-founder, pres. 1974-75, chmn., mem. exec. com. 1976—), Chinese Radiol. Soc. (hon.), Cuban Radiol. Soc. (hon.), Alpha Omega Alpha (Rigler lectr. 1964, 70, Crookshank lectr. London 1974, Holmes lectr. Boston 1974). Home: 3240 Henry Hudson Pkwy New York NY 10463 Office: Montefiore Med Ctr 111 E 210th St Bronx NY 10467-2490

JACOBSON, HAROLD KARAN, political science educator, research; b. Detroit, June 28, 1929; s. Harold Kenneth and Maxine Anna (Miller) J.; m. Merelyn Jean Lindbloom, Aug. 25, 1951; children: Harold Knute, Eric Alfred, Kristoffer Olaf, Nils Karl. AB, U. Mich., 1950; MA, Yale U., 1952, PhD, 1955. Asst. prof. polit. sci. U. Houston, 1955-57; mem. faculty U. Mich., Ann Arbor, 1957—; assoc. prof. U. Mich., 1961-65, prof., 1965—, Jesse Siddal Reeves prof. polit. sci., 1984—, research scientist, 1977—, chmn. dept., 1972-77, acting chmn., 1981, dir. Ctr. for Polit. Studies, 1986—; vis. prof. Grad. Inst. Internat. Studies, U. Geneva, 1965-66, 70-71, 77-78; World Affairs Center fellow, 1959-60; vis. research scholar European Center Carnegie Endowment for Internat. Peace, Geneva, 1970-71. Author: The USSR and the UN's Economic and Social Activities, 1963, Networks of Interdependence, 1979, 84, (with Eric Stein) Diplomats, Scientists, and Politicians, 1966, (with R.W. Cox and others) The Anatomy of Influence, 1973, (with Dusan Sidjanski and others) The Emerging International Order, 1982, (with David A. Kay and others) Environmental Protection, 1983; Editor: America's Foreign Policy, 1960, 65, (with William Zimmerman) The Shaping of Foreign Policy, 1969; mem. editorial bd. Internat. Orgn., 1968-76, 78—, Am. Jour. Internat. Law, 1979—, Internat. Studies Quar, 1980-85, Jour. Conflict Resolution, 1961-72, Am. Polit. Sci. Rev., 1985—. Mem. U.S. Nat. Commn. for UNESCO, 1980-85. Woodrow Wilson Ctr. fellow, 1984, Ctr. for Advanced Study in Behavioral Scis. fellow, 1988—. Mem. UN Assn. U.S. (bd. dirs. 1980—), Internat. Social Sci. Council, Internat. Studies Assn. (pres. Midwest div. 1969-70, pres. 1982-83), Internat. Polit. Sci. Assn., Council Fgn. Relations, Detroit Com. Fgn. Relations (chmn. 1984-86), Internat. Polit. Sci. Assn. (program chmn.), Am. Polit. Sci. Assn., Midwest Polit. Sci. Assn., Internat. Inst. for Strategic Studies (London), AAUP, AAAS, Phi Beta Kappa, Phi Kappa Phi. Clubs: Cosmos (Washington); Yale (N.Y.C.); de la Fondation Universitaire (Brussels). Home: 2174 Delaware Dr Ann Arbor MI 48103

JACOBSON, HELEN G. (MRS. DAVID JACOBSON), civic worker; b. San Antonio, Tex.; d. Jac Elton and Rosetta (Dreyfus) Gugenheim; B.A., Hollins Coll.; m. David Jacobson, Nov. 6, 1938; children—Elizabeth, Dorothy (Mrs. Sam Miller). News, spl. events staff NBC, N.Y.C., 1933-38. First v.p. San Antonio, Bexar County council Girl Scouts U.S.A., 1957-63; Tex. State rep. UNICEF, 1964-69; bd. dirs. U.S. com. UNICEF, 1970-80, hon. bd. dirs., 1980—; bd. dirs. Nat. Fedn. Temple Sisterhoods, 1973-77, Temple Beth-El Sisterhood, Youth Alternatives, Inc.; bd. dirs. Community Guidance Center, chmn. bd., 1960-63; bd. dirs. Sunshine Cottage Sch. for Deaf Children, chmn. bd., 1952-54; pres. Community Welfare Council, 1968-70; pres. bd. trustees San Antonio Pub. Library, 1957-61; trustee Nat. Council Crime and Delinquency, 1964-70, San Antonio Mus. Assn., 1964-73; bd. dirs. Cancer Therapy and Research Found. South Tex., 1977—, sec., 1977-83; pres. S.W. region Tex. Coalition for Juvenile Justice, 1977-79; chmn. Mayor's Commn. on Status of Women, 1972-74; del. White House Conf. on Children, 1970; mem. Commn. on Social Action of Reform Judaism, 1973-77; chmn. Foster Grandparent project Bexar County Hosp. Dist., 1968-69; sec. Nat. Assembly for Social Policy and Devel., 1969-74; pres. women's com. Ecumenical Center for Religion and Health, 1975-77; mem. criminal justice planning com. Alamo Area Council of Govts., chmn., 1975-77, 1987-88; mem. Tex. Internat. Women's Yr. Coordinating Com., 1977; co-chmn. San Antonio chpt. NCCJ, 1980-84; chmn. United Negro Coll. Fund Campaign, 1983, 84; v.p. Avance; trustee Target 90/Goals for San Antonio. Recipient Headliner award for civic work San Antonio chpt. Women in Communications, 1958; named Vol. Woman of Yr., Express-News, 1959; honoree San Antonio chpt. NCCJ, 1970, Nat. Jewish Hosp., 1978; Nat. Humanitarian award B'nai B'rith, 1975; Hannah G. Solomon award Nat. Council Jewish Women, 1979, San Antonio Women's Hall of Fame, 1986, others. Mem. San Antonio Women's Fedn., Nat. Council Jewish Women, Symphony Soc. (women's com.). Club: Argyle. Home: 207 Beechwood Ln San Antonio TX 78216

JACOBSON, HERBERT LAURENCE, diplomat; b. N.Y.C., Apr. 7, 1915; s. Benjamin Paul and Katherine (Laurence) J.; m. Fiora Ravasini-Osti, May 29, 1949; children—Jesse, Julian. B.A. with honors, Columbia U., 1936; LL.D., Wilfred Laurier U., Ont., Can., 1969. Editor-in-chief World News mag., N.Y.C., 1937-40; head radio dept. MCA, Chgo., 1940-41; dir. gen. radio network Free Terr. Trieste, 1946-52; with U.S. High Commn., Ger., 1953-55, U.S. Embassy, Rome, 1955-57; fgn. bus. mgr. Mondadori Publs., Milan, Italy, 1957-58; export mgr. Squibb of Italy, Rome, 1959-60; regional dir. So. Europe, Cotton Council Internat., 1960-64; dir. Internat. Trade Ctr., UNCTAD/GATT, Geneva, Switzerland, 1964-79; counselor OAS, Washington, 1980-81; counselor UN-ILANUD, Costa Rica, 1981—; lectr. U. Fla. Sch. Journalism, fall 1972. Contbr. articles to newspapers and mags. Recipient Gen. Staff commendation. Served with AUS, 1941-46, MTO. Mem. Phi Beta Kappa.

JACOBSON, LEON ORRIS, physician; b. Sims, N.D., Dec. 16, 1911; s. John and R. Patrine (Johnson) J.; m. Elizabeth Benton, Mar. 18, 1938 (dec.); children: Eric Paul, Judith Ann. B.S., N.D. State Coll., 1935, D.Sc. (hon.), 1966; M.D., U. Chgo., 1939; D.Sc., Acadia U., N.S., 1972. Intern U. Chgo., 1939-40, asst. resident medicine, 1940-41, asst. in medicine, 1941-42, instr., 1942-45, asst. prof., 1945-48, asso. dean, div. biol. scis., 1945-51, asso. prof., 1948-51, prof. medicine, 1951—, Joseph Regenstein prof. biol. and med. scis., 1965—, chmn. dept. medicine, 1961-65, dean div. biol. scis., 1966-75; head hematology sect. U. Chgo. Clinics, 1951-61; mem. Inst. Radiobiology and Biophysics, 1949-54; dir. Franklin McLean Meml. Research Inst., 1974-77; asso. dir. health Plutonium project Manhattan Dist., 1943-45, dir. health, 1945-46; dir. Argonne Cancer Research Hosp., U. Chgo., 1951-67; U.S. rep. 1st and 2d UN Conf. on Peaceful Uses Atomic Energy, Geneva, 1955, 58, WHO conf. Research Radiation Injury, Geneva, 1959; cons. biology div. Argonne Nat. Lab.; mem. adv. com. on isotope distbn. AEC, 1952-56; mem. nat. adv. com. radiation USPHS, 1961, mem. com. radiation studies, cons. hematology study sect.; mem. com. cancer diagnosis and therapy NRC, 1949-55; mem. bd. sci. counselor Nat. Cancer Inst., 1963-67; mem. nat. adv. cancer council, nat. cancer adv. bd. NIH, 1968-72; chmn. sci. adv. bd. Council for Tobacco Research; lectr. Internat. Soc. Hematology and Internat. Congress Radiology, Eng., France, Norway, Sweden, 1950, 5th Internat. Cancer Congress, Paris, 1950, Internat. Soc. Hematology, Argentina, 1952, Paris, 1954, others. Author book on erythropoietin; contbr. chpts. on specialized items to various med. books, articles to med. jours.; Book editor: Perspectives in Biology and Medicine, 1979-83. Recipient Janeway medal, 1953; Robert Roesler de Villiers award Leukemia Soc.; Borden award med. scis. Assn. Am. Med. Colls., 1962; Modern Med. and Am. Nuclear Soc. awards, 1963; John Phillips Meml. award, 1975; Theodore Roosevelt Rough Riders award State of N.D., 1977; Lincoln Laureate State of Ill., 1979; Kennecott lectr., 1963. Mem. A.C.P. (master), Am. Soc. Clin. Investigation, Assn. Am. Physicians, Soc. Exptl. Biology and Medicine, Central Soc. Clin. Research, Am. Assn. Cancer Research, Internat. Soc. Hematology, AMA, Nat. Acad. Sci., Central Clin. Research Club, AAAS, Radiation Research Soc., Am. Soc. Exptl. Pathology, Sigma Xi, Theta Chi, Nu Sigma Nu, Blue Key, Alpha Omega Alpha. Home: 5801 Dorchester Ave Chicago IL 60637 Office: 5841 S Maryland Chicago IL 60637

JACOBUS, CHARLES JOSEPH, lawyer, title company executive, author; b. Ponca City, Okla., Aug. 21, 1947; s. David William and Louise Graham (Johnson) J.; m. Heather Jeanne Jones, June 6, 1970; children—Mary Helen, Charles J. B.S., U. Houston, 1970, J.D., 1973. Bar: Tex. 1973; cert. specialist in residential and comml. real estate law Tex. Bd. Legal Specialization. Sole practice, Houston, 1973-75; staff counsel Tenneco Realty, Inc., Houston, 1975-78; chief legal counsel Speedy Muffler King, Deerfield, Ill., 1978-79; v.p., gen. counsel Tenneco Realty, Inc., 1979-83; v.p. Commerce Title Co., Houston, 1983-85, sr. v.p., gen. counsel Charter Title Co., 1986—; ptnr. Jacobus Boltz & Melamed Attys. at law; dir. Park Tower Nat. Bank, Houston; adj. faculty Coll. Architecture and Environ. Design Tex. A&M U., 1986—; adj. prof. U. Houstoninstr. advanced real estate law State Bar of Tex. Author: Texas Real Estate Law, 5th edit., 1989; Real Estate Law, 1986; co-author, Texas Real Estate, 4th edit., 1987, Ohio Real Estate, 2d edit., 1989, Calif. Real Estate, 1989; editor-in-chief Tex. Real Estate Law Reporter. Chmn. Planning and Zoning Commn., Bellaire, Tex., 1976-77; bd. dirs. Tax Increment Fin. Dist., Bellaire, 1984—. Mem. ABA (chmn. brokers and brokerage com.), Houston Bar Assn. (chmn. real estate sect. 1987-88), Tex. Bar Assn. (faculty advanced real estate law courses), U. Tex. Mortgage Lending INst. (faculty), Am. Coll. Real Estate Lawyers, Houston Real Estate Lawyers Council, Real Estate Educator's Assn. (pres. 1987-88), Tex. Land Title Assn., Nat. Assn. Corp. Real Estate Execs. (chpt. v.p.), Am. Land Devel. Assn. (bd. dirs., Real Estate Educator of Yr. 1986, Outstanding Real Estate Educator in Tex. 1986), Chaine des Rotisseurs, Internat. Wine and Food Soc. (treas. Houston chpt.). Republican. Roman Catholic. Lodge: Knights of the Vine (Master Vintner Houston chpt.). Home: 5223 Pine St Bellaire TX 77401 Office: Charter Title Co 4265 San Felipe Suite 350 Houston TX 77027

JACOBY, JAMES JOSEPH, lawyer; b. N.Y.C., Feb. 19, 1932; s. Alexander and Adelaide (Auerbach) J.; m. Susan Goldberger, Apr. 7, 1971; children—Paul, Jonathan, Peter. B.A., Fordham U., 1953, LL.B., 1959. Bar: N.Y. 1960, U.S. Tax Ct. 1976. Assoc. H. Howard Babcock, N.Y.C., 1960-71; counsel Bush & Schlesinger, 1971-73; ptnr. Schlesinger & Jacoby, 1973-79, Sive Paget & Riesel, P.C., 1979-88, Esanu Katsky Korins & Siger, N.Y., 1988—; Vice pres. Madison Sq. Boys Club Inc., 1971—, trustee, 1961—. Served to 1st lt. USAF, 1953-55. Mem. ABA, N.Y. Bar Assn., N.Y.C. Bar Assn. Club: New York Athletic. Office: 500 Fifth Ave New York NY 10110

JACOBY, MONTE HERRMANN, foundation administrator; b. Alton, Ill., May 23, 1931; s. Philip William and Ruth Mae (Herrmann) J.; m. Nancy Ann Horn, Oct. 16, 1954; 1 child, William Arthur. B.A., DePauw U., 1953. Employment mgr. Olin Corp., East Alton, Ill., 1953-62, dir. univ. relations, Stamford, Conn., 1962-74, dir. edml. and charitable trust, 1974-81, dir. external pub. relations, 1981-86, exec. dir. The Deafness Found., 1987; industry v.p. Coll. Placement Council, Bethlehem, Pa., 1972; mem. minority edn. com. NRC, 1975-78; mem. industry adv. com. Ind. Coll. Funds Am., N.Y.C., 1980-83. Author papers in field. Mem. corp. adv. com. Opportunities Industrialization Ctr., Stamford, 1975-76; mem. vol. staffing com. U.S. Navy Dept., Washington, 1972; chmn. devel. com., trustee Xavier U. La., New Orleans; pres. bd. dirs. Boys Town Ill., Grafton, 1965; bd. dirs. Yerwood Youth Ctr., Stamford, 1970, Boys Clubs Am., Stamford, 1970, Nat. Alliance Bus., Washington, 1978, Liberation House, drug treatment ctr., Stamford. Recipient Disting. Service award Alton Jaycees, 1965; Chancellor's Merit award Atlanta U. Ctr., 1972. Mem. So. Coll. Placement Assn. (life mem.; industry v.p. 1973), Am. Soc. Engring. Edn., Am. Sociol. Soc., Coop. Edn. Assn., U.S. C. of C. (edn. com. 1978-79), Conn. Engring. and Tech. Soc. (exec. com. 1978), Sigma Alpha Epsilon. Republican. Presbyterian. Club: Woodway Country (Darien, Conn.). Avocations: travel, water sports, youth work. Home: 350 Hycliff Terr Stamford CT 06902 Office: Deafness Research Found 9 East 38th St New York NY 10016

JACOVER, JEROLD ALAN, lawyer; b. Chgo., Mar. 20, 1945; s. David Louis and Beverly (Funk) J.; m. Judith Lee Greenwald, June 28, 1970; children—Aric Seth, Evan Michael, Brian Ethan. BSEE, U. Wis., 1967; JD, Georgetown U., 1972. Bar: Ohio 1972, Ill. 1973, U.S. Ct. Appeals (7th cir.) 1974, U.S. Ct. Appeals (Fed. cir.) 1983. Atty. Ralph Nader, Columbus, Ohio, 1972-73, Willian, Brinks & Olds, Chgo., 1973—; lectr. Mallinckrodt Coll., Wilmette, Ill., 1977-78. Mem. Evanston Environ. Control Bd., 1983-86; asst. pack leader Northeast Ill. Council Boy Scouts Am., 1982-84. Mem. Am. Patent Law Assn. (com. chmn. 1980-86, co-editor jour. 1980-81), ABA, Decalogue Soc. Lawyers, Patent Law Assn. Chgo. (treas. 1983-84), Am. Techion Soc. (v.p. 1985-87). Jewish. Club: Nippersink Community (Genoa City, Wis.) (bd. dirs. 1978-86, pres. 1987). Home: 1409 Lincoln St Evanston IL 60201 Office: Willian Brinks & Olds 1 IBM Plaza Suite 4100 Chicago IL 60611

JACOVITCH, JOHN, physicist, nuclear engineer; b. Hemphill, W.Va., Feb. 8, 1930; s. Nicolai and Domnica (Nikitoi) J.; m. Delores French; children—John David, Michael Alan, Daniel Nicolas. B.S., Roanoke Coll., 1958; postgrad., Vanderbilt U., 1958-59; M.S., Lynchburg Coll., 1968. AEC fellow Vanderbilt U., Oak Ridge Nat. Labs., 1958-59; scientist Edgerton Germeshausen & Grier, Inc., Las Vegas, Nev., Goleta, Calif., 1959-62; nuclear research physicist Naval Civil Engring. Lab., Port Hueneme, Calif., 1962-63; radiol. engr. Atomic Internat., Canoga Park, Calif., 1963-65; health physicist, project engr. Babcock & Wilcox Co., Lynchburg, Va., 1965-70; health physicist United Nuclear Corp., Wood River Junction, R.I., 1970-71; mgr. health physics U. Mo. Research Reactor Facility, Columbia, Mo., 1971-76; cons., Columbia, 1976-78; asst. prof. med. radiology U. Ill. Med. Center, Chgo., 1978-80; project engr. Wis. Electric Power Co., Milw., 1980-84, radiation safety officer, clin. asst. prof. Tulane Med. Ctr., New Orleans, 1985-86; health physicist Precision Castparts Corp., Portland, Oreg., 1986—. Contbr. articles to profl. jours. Served with USN, 1947-51. Mem. Internat. Radiation Protection Assn., Health Physics Soc., Am. Assn. Physicists in Medicine, AAAS, Sigma Pi Sigma. Office: 222 SW Harrison St Portland OR 97201

JACOX, JOHN WILLIAM, engineering and consulting company executive; b. Pitts., Dec. 12, 1938; s. John Sherman and Grace Edna (Herbster) J.; 1 child, Brian Erik. BSME, BS in Indsl. Mgmt., Carnegie Mellon U., 1962. Mfg. engr. Nuclear Fuel div. Westinghouse Elec. Co., Pitts., 1962-64; research engr. Continental Can Co. Metal R&D Ctr., Pitts., 1964-65; dataprocessing sales engr., IBM, Pitts., 1965-66; mktg. mgr. nuclear products MSA Internat., Pitts., 1966-72; v.p. Nuclear Cons. Services, Inc., Columbus, Ohio, 1973-84; v.p. NUCON Internat., 1981-84; bd. dirs. NUCON Europe Ltd., London, 1981—; pres. Jacox Assocs., Inc., 1984—; cons., lectr. Nat. Ctr. for Research in Vocat. Edn., 1978-84 ; author, presenter, session chmn. DOE/Harvard Nuclear Air Cleaning Confs., 1974—; lectr. Harvard Sch. Pub. Health Air Cleaning Lab., 1986—; co-chmn. program subcom. Tech. Alliance Cen Ohio, 1984-85, vice chmn., chmn.-elect dir. subcom., 1986-87, chmn. bd. trustees, 1986; program com. World Trade Devel. Club; mem. legis. services com. Coop. edn. adv. com. Otterbein Coll., 1978-82. Mem. ASME (code com. nuclear air and gas treatment, main exec. com., chmn. subcom. field test procedures), Am. Nuclear Soc. (pub. info. com.), N.Y. Acad. Scis. (life), Ohio Acad. Sci. (life), Inst. Environ. Scis., Electric Overstress-Electrostatic Discharge Assn., ASHRAE, Inc., Air Pollution Control Assn., Am. Nat. Standards Inst., Columbus Area C. of C. (tech. roundtable 1983), ASTM (F-21), ASM, Air Force Assn. (life), Mensa, Nat. Rifle Assn. (life), Sun Bunch (pres. 1980-81). Club: Capitol. Home: 5874 Northern Pine Pl Columbus OH 43229 Office: 1445 Summit St Columbus OH 43229

JACQUEMART, ANDRE, physician; b. Paris, Nov. 12, 1916; s. Jean and Albeau J.; m. Christiane Dubernard, Oct. 30, 1959; children: Francoise, Frederic, Anne Marie, Philippe, Christian. MD, FAculty of Medicine, Paris, 1949. Gen. practice medicine Antony, France. Served with French Army, 1933-45. Roman Catholic. Home: 67 Ave Aristide Briand, 92160 Antony France

JACQUILLAT, THIERRY, beverage company executive; b. Versailles, Yvelines, France, July 29, 1938; s. Henry and Simonne (Armand) J.; m. Marie-Annick Waldruche de Montremy, July 1, 1963; children: Matthieu, Aude, Emery, Agathe. B., Lycee Carnot, Paris, 1957; M. Bus., Ecole des Hautes Etudes Commerciales, Paris, 1960. Asst. to mgmt. Pernod Cy, Creteil, France, 1963-68, adminstrv. mgr., 1968-71, 1st sec., 1971-74; 1st sec. Pernod Ricard Cy, Paris, 1974-77, pres. 1977—; chmn. Arts Affaires, Paris, 1968—, Campbell Whisky Holding, London, 1977—, Austin Nichols, N.Y.C., 1980—;bd. dirs. Slivam, Paris, 1984—, Ramazzotti, Milano, 1985, Soginnove, Paris, Inra, Paris, Credit Comml. de France, 1986 . Served to lt. French Marine Corps, 1960-62; Algeria. Decorated Croix de la Valeur Militaire. Roman Catholic. Office: Pernod Ricard Cy, 142 Blvd Haussmann, 75008 Paris France

JADA, SIVANANDA SIVAPPA, research chemist; b. Bellary, India, June 14, 1948; came to U.S., 1979; s. Sivappa S. and Parvatamma N. J.; m. Sushma Tammanagowda, Sept. 4, 1978; children: Nivedita, Ajit. BSc in Chemistry, Karnatak U., Dharwar, India, 1969, MSc in Organic Chemistry, 1971; PhD in Polymer Chemistry, USSR Acad. Scis., Moscow, 1977. Research assoc. U. Ala., 1979-81, Case Western Res. U., Cleve., 1981-83; sr. research assoc. Atlanta U., 1983-84; sr. research chemist Research and Devel. Ctr. Manville Corp., Denver, 1984—. Contbr. articles to profl. jours.; patentee in field. Recipient award Ministry Edn. India-USSR, 1973; scholar Govt. India. Fellow The Am. Inst. Chemists; mem. Am. Chem. Soc., Materials Research Soc., Internat. Union Pure and Applied Chemistry, N.Y. Acad. Sci.

JADALLAH, SAMI JAMIL, legal consultant; b. El-Bireh, Palestine, Jan. 1, 1945; came to U.S., 1962; s. Jamil Ramadan and Muftiah (Wahdan) J.; m. Alma Abdulhadi, Nov. 11, 1981; children: Jamil, Laila, Diala. BA, Ind. U., 1972, M in Pub. Affairs, 1974, JD, 1977. Asst. to dir. Sch. of Pub. and Environ. Affairs U. Ind., Gary, 1972-74, asst. to assoc. dean Sch. of Pub. and Environ. Affairs, 1974-76; legal assoc. Shearman & Sterling, N.Y.C., 1977-79; gen. counsel SOGEX/PEGEL Arabia, Riyadh, Saudi Arabia, 1979-81; fgn. legal advisor Dr. Ali Omair, Riyadh, Saudi Arabia, 1981-82; gen. counsel HAZAR Group of Cos., Riyadh, Saudi Arabia, 1982—; mng. dir. HAZAR S.A., Geneva, Switzerland, 1985—; co-sec. Bell Helicopter Arabia Ltd., Riyadh, 1985—; bd. dirs. Snoopy Ice Cream & Cookie Co., San Francisco, Hazar Indsl. Devel. and Internat. Market. Chmn. N.W. Ind. Muscular Dystrophy Fund Drive, 1971. Mem. (founding) United Palestinian Appeal (bd. dirs. 1978—). Muslim. Home: chemin sur la Gare, 1261 Borex/Vaud Switzerland Office: Hazar SA, 145 rue de Lausanne, 1202 Geneva Switzerland

JAECKEL, MONIKA, sociologist, researcher; b. Tokyo, May 31, 1949; d. Theodor and Margaretha (Kasch) J. Diploma in Sociology, Johann Wolfgang Goethe U., 1974. Researcher Psydata, Frankfurt, Fed. Republic Germany, 1974-75; sr. researcher Deutsches Jugend-institut, Munich, 1976—. Author: Wet wenn nicht wit, 1981; co-author: Mutter Zwischen Beruf und Familie, 1983, Schwesternstreit, 1984; co-editor: Mutter im Zentrum, 1985; contbr. articles to profl. publs.; editor Beitrage zur Feministischen-Theorie und Praxis, 1978-80. Mem. Com. Family Research, Internat. Sociol. Assn., Sozialwissenschaftliche Forschung und Praxis fur Frauen (bd. trustees 1978-80). Office: Deutsches Jugendinstitut, Friebadstrasse 30, 8000 Munich 90 Federal Republic of Germany

JAEGER, LEONARD HENRY, former public utility executive; b. Bklyn., Oct. 6, 1905; s. Leonard and Marie (Ziegler) J.; m. Mary Elizabeth Fallon, Dec. 15, 1951. Grad., Pace Coll., 1926; postgrad., N.Y. U., evenings 1926-30. Accountant Southeastern Power & Light Co., 1926-30; with Commonwealth & So. Corp., 1930-42, 46-49, asst. comptroller, 1948-49; treas. So. Co., Atlanta, 1949-70; v.p. finance So. Co., 1957-70, dir., 1966-70, adv. dir., 1970-75; exec. v.p. So. Co. Services, Inc., 1963-67, dir., vice chmn. bd., 1967-70. Served to capt. AUS, 1942-45. Mem. Fin. Execs. Inst., N.Y. Soc. Security Analysts, N.Y. U. Alumni Assn., Pace Alumni Assn., Edison Electric Inst. (mem., past chmn. investor relations com.). Republican. Lutheran. Home: PO Box 21495 Sarasota FL 34238

JAEGER, SHARON ANN, educator, poet, publisher; b. Douglas, Ariz., Jan. 15, 1945; d. Paul and Catherine (Simon) Jaeger. B.A. summa cum laude, U. Dayton, 1966; M.A. in English, Boston Coll., 1971; D.A. in English, SUNY-Albany, 1982. Asst. to editor-in-chief Foundation Mag., N.Y.C., 1974-76; records specialist, faculty sec. Sch. Nursing U. Alaska, Anchorage, 1978; co-instr. creative writing, instr. writing ctr. Rensselaer Polytech. Inst., Troy, N.Y., 1978-79; tutor writing workshop SUNY, Albany, 1979-80; co-editor Sachem Press, Old Chatham, N.Y., 1980—; editor Intertext, Anchorage, 1982—; Fulbright lectr. U. Nova de Lisboa and U. de Aveiro,

Portugal, 1983-84; poetry readings throughout country, 1979—; coordinator Jawbone Reading Series, Albany, 1981-82; co-instr. writers' workshop Appalachian Writers Assn., Johnson City, Tenn., July 1983; instr. creative visualization workshops Toronto, N.Y.C; vis. asst. prof. Haverford Coll., 1987-88; vis. lectr. U. Pa., 1988; asst. to exec. dir. Peter Lang Pub., 1988. Contbr. poetry to anthologies, periodicals (1st place award McKinney Literary Competition, 1979, Best of Issue award Western Poetry Quar., 1978); Author: (poetry) Filaments of Affinity, 1988; contbr. articles and book revs. to profl. jours. Vol. DeWitt Nursing Home, N.Y.C., 1973-75. Recipient Alpha Sigma Tau Honor Key award U. Dayton, Ohio, 1966; Fulbright lectr., Portugal, 1983-84; Austrian Govt. scholar U. Salzburg, summer 1966; research fellow U. Pa., Phila., 1982-83; Presdl. fellow SUNY, 1979-82. Mem. Comparative Lit. Assn. of Students (pres. U. Pa. 1982-83), Poetry Soc. Am., Acad. Am. Poets, Am. Literary Translators Assn., Am. Comparative Lit. Assn., Modern Lang. Assn., Internat. Soc. for History of Rhetoric, Soc. for Critical Exchange, Rhetoric Soc. Am., Northeast Modern Lang. Assn., Associated Writing Programs, Am. Studies Assn., Fulbright Alumni Assn.

JAEGLY, PIERRE MICHEL, securities company executive; b. Rixheim, Alsace, France, Oct. 5, 1937; s. Charles and Sophie Marie (Schmid) J.; m. Monique Andree Pincemaille, June 29, 1963; children: Alexandre T., Isabelle M.S. M of Law and Econs., U. Strasbourg, France, 1962, postgrad. in econs., 1963-64; cert. in English, U. McGill, Montreal, Quebec, Can., 1966. Fin. analyst Greenshields, Inc., Montreal, 1964-67; trainee, then asst. fin. analyst Quebec Deposit and Investment Fund, Montreal, 1967-69; fin. analyst Eurofin., Paris, 1969-70; sr. fin. analyst Merril Lynch, Geneva, 1970-73; v.p., mgr. security research Merril Lynch, Geneva and Paris, 1973-76; v.p., mgr. internat. sales Merril Lynch, Paris, 1976-79; v.p. fin. services Banque Societe Fin. European, Paris, 1979-83; sr. v.p. Cedel S.A., Luxembourg, 1983—; bd. dirs. Canagex Internat. Fund, Montreal and Luxembourg. Contbr. articles and papers to profl. publs. Initiator, organizer André Malraux Exhibition, Nat. Library of Luxembourg, 1986; founding mem., v.p. Assn. to Support Radio Tele Luxembourg Orch., Luxembourg, 1987. Mem. Assn. Internat. Bond Dealers, N.Y. Soc. Security Analysts, Can. Investment Dealers Assn. (cert.). Rassemblement pour la Republique. Roman Catholic. Clubs: Internat. Bankers, Cercle Munster (Luxembourg). Home: 10 Ave Guillaume, 1650 Luxembourg Luxembourg

JAFFE, ANDREW MARK, editor; b. Atlanta, Aug. 2, 1938; s. Henry Leslie and Diana (Gaines) J.; divorced; 1 child, Christopher. BA, Pomona Coll., 1960; MS, Columbia U., 1962. Newsman AP, Los Angeles, 1964-66; corr. Newsweek mag., Atlanta, 1966-69; African bur. chief Newsweek mag., Nairobi, Kenya, 1969-76; bur. chief Newsweek mag., Miami, 1976-77; bus. editor Los Angeles Herald Examiner, 1978-84; v.p. Spl. Expdns., N.Y.C., 1984-85; editor Adweek/SouthEast, Atlanta, 1985—; instr. UCLA Extension, 1979-84, Atlanta Portfolio Ctr., 1987-88. Author: (with others) Alaska: Southeast to McKinley, 1986; contbg. editor Atlanta mag., 1987-88. Bd. dirs. Atlanta Virtuosi, 1986-88. Served to 1st lt. U.S. Army, 1962-64, Korea. Mem. Sigma Delta Chi. Club: Overseas Press. Office: Adweek Mag 75 Third St NW Atlanta GA 30365

JAFFÉ, ANDREW MICHAEL, art history educator, museum director; b. London, June 3, 1923; s. Arthur Daniel and Marie Marguerite (Strauss) J.; m. Patricia Ann Milne-Henderson. Student Eton Coll., 1937-42, King's Coll., 1945-47, Courtauld Inst. Art, 1949-50; Litt.D., U. Cambridge. Began as reader history of western art U. Cambridge, prof. history of western art, 1973—, dir. Fitzwilliam Mus., 1973—. Author: Van Dyck's Antwerp Sketchbook, 1966; Rubens, 1967; Jordaens, 1968; Rubens and Italy, 1977. Mem. art panel Nat. Trust, mem. Wessex regional com., pres. Cambridge Ctr. Served to lt. comdr. Royal Naval Res., 1950. Decorated officer Orde de Lé opold (Belgium); Commonwealth Fund fellow U.S., 1951-53; King's Coll. fellow Cambridge U. Fellow Royal Soc. Arts; mem. Eastern Arts Assn. (council). Clubs: Beefsteak, Brooks's, Turf (London). Avocation: viticulture. Office: Fitzwilliam Mus, Trumpington St, Cambridge CB2 1QG, England

JAFFE, EUGENE DONALD, business administration educator, researcher; b. N.Y.C., Jan. 9, 1937; arrived in Israel, 1976; s. Isidore Ira and Sadye (Holstein) J.; M. Liora Mayerfeld, Aug. 15, 1965; children: Iris, Nurit. BS in Econs., U. Pa., 1958, PhD, 1965; MBA, NYU, 1961. Asst. prof. St. John's U., N.Y.C., 1966-75, assoc. prof., 1970-76; assoc. prof. Coll. Administrn., Tel-Aviv, 1976-77; assoc. prof., dir. mgmt. tng. ctr. Bar-Ilan U., Ramat-Gan, Israel, 1977—; cons. Litton Industries, N.J., Famous Schs., Inc., N.Y., Hayden Pub. Co., N.J., Israel Nat. Lottery. Author, editor 3 books and profl. articles; mem. editorial bd. Jour. Global Mktg. Recipient scholarship award Automatic Retailers Am., 1963-64, Winifred Fisher award Adult Edn. Council, N.Y., 1975; Found. Econ. Edn. bus. fellow, N.Y., 1968. Mem. Am. Mktg. Assn., European Internat. Bus. Assn., Acad. Internat. Bus., U. Pa. Alumni Club. Home: 15 Havradim St, 42651 Ramat-Poleg, Netanya Israel Office: Bar-Ilan U, PO Box 1530, 52100 Ramat-Gan Israel

JAFFE, LEONARD MAURICE, financial planner, consultant; b. Kankakee, Ill., June 25, 1934; s. Benjamin Harry and Henrietta (Kleinhammer) J.; m. Sandra Gayle Barnbaum, Nov. 3, 1957; children: Loryn Hope, Melissa Suzanne. BS, U. Ill., 1957; cert., Coll. Fin. Planning, 1982. Owner Snowite Laundry, Kankakee, 1960-72; v.p. John Shannon Assocs., Chgo., 1972-83; sr. assoc. Capital Analysts, San Diego, 1983-87; prin. C.I.T.E. Fin. Services, San Diego, 1987—; Past pres. Ill. Laundry Assn., 1965. Contbr. mag. articles on fin. planning. Mem. seminar com. San Diego Cancer Soc., 1986; Rep. precinct capt., south suburbs Chgo., 1972-76; mem. Automotive Service Council. Mem. Internat. Assn. Fin. Planning (bd. dirs. 1982-83), Inst. Cert. Fin. Planners, San Diego C. of C. (seminar com. 1983—). Club: Univ. of San Diego (chmn. Speaker's Forum). Lodge: Rotary (North San Diego). Home: 14683 Woodhue Ln Poway CA 92064

JAFFE, NORA, artist; b. Urbana, Ohio, Feb. 25, 1928; d. Harry Jefferson and Margaret Elizabeth (McNab) Miller; m. Joseph Jaffe, Jan. 19, 1951; children: Lenore A., Kenneth A. One person shows, Village Art Center, N.Y.C., 1963, Sachs Gallery, N.Y.C., 1965, Gallery Lasson Modern Art, London, 1970, Open Studio Gallery, Rhinebeck, N.Y., 1978, Vasar Coll., Poughkeepsie, N.Y., 1979, Pastoral Gallery Art, Easthampton, N.Y., 1983; exhibited in group shows, Mus. Modern Art, N.Y.C., 1961, 64, Pa. Acad. Fine Arts, 1964, 67, 68, David Stuart Galleries, Los Angeles, 1969, Va. Mus. Fine Arts, Richmond, 1970, Orpheus Ascending, Stockbridge, Mass., 1971, New Sch. Art Centre, N.Y.C., 1973, Albin Ziegler Gallery, N.Y.C., 1973, Grad. Center CUNY, 1978, A.I.R. Gallery, N.Y.C., 1983-84, Montclair State Coll., N.J., 1986; represented in permanent collection, Pa. Acad. Fine Arts, Phila., Finch Coll. Mus., N.Y.C., MacDowell Colony, Pan Am. Bldg., N.Y.C., Univ. Art Mus., U. Calif., Berkeley, Bklyn. Mus. MacDowell Colony resident, 1969, 70. Mem. N.Y. Artists Equity Assn. Home: 285 Central Park W New York NY 10024

JAFFE, PAUL LAWRENCE, lawyer; b. Phila., June 24, 1928; s. Albert L. and Elsie (Pelser) J.; children: Marc David, Richard Alan, Peter Edward. B.A., Dickinson Coll., 1947; J.D., U. Pa., 1950. Bar: Pa. Sole practice Phila.; sr. ptnr. Mesirov, Gelman, Jaffe, Cramer and Jamieson (and predecessors), 1959—. Trustee Fedn. Jewish Agencies Phila.; trustee Moss Rehab. Hosp., pres., 1977-80, chmn. bd., 1980-84, hon. chmn. bd., 1984—; trustee, mem. exec. com. Union Am. Hebrew Congregations; chmn. United Law Network, 1987—. Mem. ABA, Pa. Bar Assn., Phila. Bar Assn. Jewish (pres. congregation 1974-77). Clubs: Locust, Union League, Lawyers (Phila.); Loveladies Tennis. Home: 1326 Spruce St Philadelphia PA 19107 Office: 123 S Broad St Philadelphia PA 19109

JAFFE, SYLVIA SARAH, art collector, former medical technologist; b. Detroit, May 16, 1917; d. Sam and Rose (Rosman) Turner; B.S. in Med. Tech., U. Wis., 1940; m. David Jaffe, Nov. 8, 1942. Med. technologist Watts Hosp. Lab., Durham, N.C., 1940-45; research hematology technologist in leukemia Sloan Kettering Meml. Hosp. Lab., N.Y.C., 1946-47; chief med. technologist in hematology Arlington (Va.) Hosp. Lab., 1948-55; chief technologist in diagnostic hematology Georgetown U. Hosp., Washington, 1959-70; collector 19th century and 20th century art, 1970—. Mem. Col. Williamsburg (Va.) Found., hon. citizen. Mem. Am. Soc. Med. Technologists, Am. Soc. Clin. Pathologists (assoc.), Am. Women in Sci., Corcoran Gallery Art, Pa. Acad. Fine Arts, Sierra Club, Nat. Wildlife Fed., World Wildlife Fund., Nat. Audubon Soc., Nat. Trust Hist. Preservation, The Washington Print Club, U. Wis. Alumni Assn., Boston Mus. Arts, Nat. Mus. Women in Arts (charter), Nat. Wildlife Fedn., Sierra Club, Greenpeace, Audubon Soc., Wilderness Soc. Democrat. Jewish. Club: Pioneer Women. Contbr. articles to profl. socs. Address: 1913 S Quincy St Arlington VA 22204

JAFFRY, HASAN FATIMA, gynecologist/obstetrician; b. Agra, Uttar Pradesh, India, June 20, 1946; came to Pakistan, 1947; s. Mukhtar Raza and Rubab Bano (Jaffry) J.; m. Asad Ali, Jan. 12, 1974; children: Satian, Ali Mohsin. MBBS, Fatima Jinnah Med. Coll., Lahore, 1968. Anesthetist Jinnah Postgrad. Med. Ctr., Karachi, Pakistan, 1970; registrar Jinnah Postgrad. Med. Ctr., Karachi, 1972-74, sr. registrar, 1981-84, asst. prof. ob.-gyn., 1984—. Fellow Coll. Physicians and Surgeons Pakistan; mem. Soc. Ob.-Gyn. Karachi. Home: Sadar, Karachi Pakistan Office: Jinnah Postgrad Med Ctr, Sadar, Karachi Pakistan

JAFREE, SAYYID MOHAMMED JAWAID IQBAL See GEOFFREY, IQBAL

JAFRI, JAMALUDDIN, federal agency administrator; b. Payakumbuh, West Sumatra, Indonesia, Dec. 8, 1934; s. Jamaluddin and Fatimah Jafri; m. Tasmin Tamin, Mar. 2, 1958; children: Dita Ardonni, Dita Irwandi, Dita Aries Sanadha, Myra Herlinda. Student, U. Wis., 1955-56; grad. mid. mgmt. course, Bogor, 1973; grad., Nat. Sch. Adminstrn., Jakarta, Indonesia, 1978; insinyur, U. Andalas, Padang, Indonesia, 1978. Office chief Dept. Agr., Pasaman, Indonesia, 1955, Bukittinggi, Indonesia, 1960-64; office chief Dept. Agr., Padang, 1966-78, dir. regional office, 1970-78; dir. prodn. devel. Dept. Agr., Jakarta, 1978-83; sec. Directorate Gen. Agr., Jakarta, 1983-86, dir. pub. relations, 1986-87; agrl. attache Indonesia Indonesian Embassy, Rome, 1987—; chmn. Farmer's Coop. West Sumatra, Bukittinggi, 1964-68; advisor Farmers Assn. West Sumatra, Padang, 1975-78. Author: Agricultural Economics, 1960; editor-in-chief: (newspaper) Agr. and Devel., 1975-78, (bulletin, periodical) Agr., 1986. Vice chmn. Functional Group, West Sumatra, 1971-78; mem. Ho. of Reps., Jakarta, 1977-78; mem. Constn. Assembly Rep. Indonesia, Jakarta, 1978-82. Recipient Comdr. Award Sumatra Armed Forces, 1973, Satya Lencana Pembangunan award Pres. Rep. Indonesia, 1976, Satya Lencana Karya Setya Kelas II award Gov. West Sumatra, 1978. Mem. Indonesian Agronomies Assn., Indonesian Engrs. Assn. Moslem. Club: Jakarta Golf. Home: Jl Palapa Ii #8, Ps Minggu, 12520 Jakarta, Selatan Indonesia

JAGANNATHAN, RANGANATHAN, biochemist; b. Mettur Dam, Tamil Nadu, India, Jan. 28, 1958; s. Ranganathan Srinivasan and Lakshmi (Rangaswamy) Giridhar; m. Nalini Ramaswamy, Apr. 8, 1987. BS, New Sci. Coll., Hyderabad, India, 1978; MS, Inst. Sci., Hyderabad, India, 1980; PhD, U. Bombay, 1987. Research fellow Found. for Med. Research, Bombay, 1980-83, in-charge instrumentation, 1982—, research student, 1983-87, leader biochemistry group, 1986—, research officer, 1987—; participant drug trial for leprosy WHO, 1986-87. Fellow Indian Assn. Leprologists; mem. Internat. Leprosy Assn. Hindu. Home: 1-B, Purnima, Ridge Rd, Bombay 400006, India Office: Found for Med Research, 84A-R.G. Thadani Marg World, Bombay 400018, India

JAGER, ROBERT ANTONIE, aeronautic executive; b. Surabaya, Java, Indonesia, Apr. 7, 1923; came to Netherlands, 1934; s. Coenraad Cornelis Frederik and Franç oise Wilhelmina (Berghuis) J.; m. Clara Maria Theresia Van Berckel, Oct. 8, 1948; children—Tom Coenraad Maria, Gemma Wilhelmina Maria, Claire-Anne Marie, Brigitta Augusta Maria, Martina Elizabeth Maria. Student, Royal Netherlands Naval Coll., 1946-47. Dir. naval air engring. and maintenance Royal Netherlands Navy, 1971-74; prin. tech. officer of bd. Nat. Aerospace Lab., Delft, Netherlands, 1975-85; mng. dir. aerospace North Atlantic Technologies Internat. BV (NORATECH), Netherlands, 1986—; cons. U.S. A/C Industry, Calif./Netherlands, 1975-77; nat. coordinator Agard/NATO, Netherlands, 1976-85; internat. sec. Group for Aero. Research and Tech. in Europe (GARTEUR), Netherlands, 1978-80; internat. sec. European Transonic Wind Tunnel (ETW), 1978-85; project mgr. Indonesian/Netherlands co-operation in aero. research and edn., 1980-85. Served to capt. RNLN, 1948-74. Decorated knight Royal Order of Orange-Nassau, (Netherlands), 1960, decorated officer, 1985. Mem. Royal Netherlands Assn. Aeros. Roman Catholic. Home: Ysvogelplein 8, 2566VS The Hague Netherlands Office: NORATECH, Kapelweg 3, 2587 BH The Hague The Netherlands

JAGGER, MICK (MICHAEL PHILIP JAGGER), rock performer; b. Dartford, Kent, Eng., July 26, 1943; s. Joe and Eva Jagger; m. Bianca Perez Morena de Macias, May 12, 1971 (div. Nov. 1979); 1 dau., Jade; other children: Karis, Elizabeth Scarlett, James Leroy Augustine. Student, London Sch. Econs., 1962-64. Mem., lead singer, occasional guitarist Rolling Stones, 1962—, tour of Europe, 1970, 73, 76, 82, U.S., 1966, 69, 72, 75, 78, 81, Australia, 1973; film appearances include Performance, 1969, Ned Kelly, 1970, Gimmie Shelter, 1970, Sympathy for the Devil, 1970, Ladies and Gentlemen, The Rolling Stones, 1974, Let's Spend the Night Together, 1983. Composer: (with Keith Richards) She's So Cold, (I Can't Get No) Satisfaction, Brown Sugar, Honky Tonk Woman, Jumpin' Jack Flash, Sympathy for the Devil, Get Off My Cloud, Paint it Black, 2000 Light Years from Home, Star Star, Have You Seen Your Mother, Baby (Standing in the Shadows), Mother's Little Helper, Ruby Tuesday, Lady Jane, The Citadel, You Can't Always Get What You Want, Fool to Cry, Start Me Up, As Tears Go By, Wild Horses, many others; albums include: The Rolling Stones, 1964, The Rolling Stones II, 1965, The Rolling Stones Now, 1965, December's Children, 1965, 12x5, 1965, Out of Our Heads, 1965, Aftermath, 1966, High Tide & Green Grass, 1966, Between the Buttons, 1967, Flowers, 1967, Got Live If You Want It, 1967, Her Satanic Majesty's Request, 1967, Beggars Banquet, 1968, Let it Bleed, 1969, Through the Past Darkly, 1969, Get Yer Ya Yas Out, 1970, Sticky Fingers, 1971, Hot Rocks, 1972, More Hot Rocks, 1972, Exile on Main Street, 1972, Goat's Head Soup, 1973, It's Only Rock and Roll, 1974, Metamorphosis, 1975, Black and Blue, 1976, Love You Live, 1977, Some Girls, 1978, Emotional Rescue, 1980, Tatoo You, 1981, Still Life, 1982, Under Cover, 1983, Dirty Work, 1986; solo albums: She's The Boss, 1985, Primitive Cool, 1987, solo singles include Just Another Night of You, Let's Work, (with David Bowie) Dancin' in the Streets. Address: care Rascoff/Zysblat Orgn 110 W 57th St New York NY 10019

JAGGER, PETER JOHN, religious organization administrator, executive; b. Leeds, Yorkshire, England, Jan. 31, 1938; s. Willie and Annie (Pullen) J.; m. Margaret Thompson, Mar. 12, 1960; children: Mark, Catherine. MA, Lambeth U., 1971; M. of Philosophy, U. Leeds, Eng., 1976; PhD, U. Leeds, 1987. Ordained priest, 1969. Curate All Saints Ch., Leeds, 1968-71; vicar Bolton cum Redmire, Yorshire, 1971-77; warden, chief librarian St. Deinol's Library, Hawarden, Deeside, Clywd, Wales, 1977—. Author: Christian Initiation 1552-1969: Rites of Baptism and Confirmation since the Reformation Period, 1970, Being the Church Today: A Collection of Sermons and Addresses by Bishop Henry de Candole, 1974, The Alcuin Club and its Publications: An Annotated Bibliography 1897-1974, 1975, Bishop Henry de Candole: His Life and Times 1895-1971, 1975, A History of the Parish and People Movement, 1978, Clouded Witness: Initiation in the Church of England in the Mid-Victorian Period, 1850-1875, 1982, Gladstone: Politics and Religion A Collection of Founder's Day Lectures delivered at St. Deinol's Library, Hawarden, 1967-1983, 1984; contbr. articles to various periodicals. Dir. self supporting ministry course St. Deiniol's Library; regional rep. Lambeth Diploma of Theology, mem. Brit. Library Nat. Preservation Adv. com., 1985-88, Archbishop of Canterbury's Lambeth Diploma com. Fellow Royal Hist. Soc.; mem. Alcuin Club, Theol. Coll. Prins. Conf. Conservative. Anglican. Home and Office: St Deiniol's Library, Hawarden, Deeside, Clwyd CH5 3DF, Wales

JAGOW, CHARLES HERMAN, lawyer, finance consultant; b. Winona, Minn., Jan. 23, 1910; s. Walter Paul and Anna Marie (Thode) J.; m. Alice MacFarlane, Aug. 3, 1940 (dec. 1967); children—Paul M., Richard C. Student LaCrosse (Wis.) State Tchrs. Coll., 1928-30; A.B. cum laude, U. Wis., 1932, LL.B. cum laude, 1934; LL.M., Columbia U., 1936. Bar: N.Y. 1937. Assoc., Cravath, Swaine & Moore, N.Y.C., 1936-52; atty. Met. Life Ins. Co., N.Y.C., 1952-75, assoc. gen. counsel, 1957-75, v.p., 1967-75; dir. corp. debt financing project Am. Bar Found., Chgo., 1975-81; cons. in corp. fin., N.Y.C., 1975—; counsel Am. Assn. Gifted Children, 1975-85; project dir. Mortgage Bond Indenture Form, English text, 1981, Japanese text, 1982. Elder Presbyn. Ch. Mem. Assn. Life Ins. Counsel, ABA, Assn. Bar City N.Y., Order of Coif, Phi Kappa Phi, Delta Sigma Rho. Home: RD 3 Smalley Corners Rd Carmel NY 10512 Office: 510 E 23d St 1F New York NY 10010

JAHIEL, RENE INO, physician; b. Boulogne S/Seine, France, Mar. 29, 1928; s. Richard and Cecile (Lwovsky) J.; French Lycees, Baccalaureat, 1944; B.A., N.Y. U., 1946; M.D., Downstate Med. Coll., SUNY, 1950; Ph.D., Columbia U., 1957; m. Deborah Berg, May 8, 1955; children—Abigail, Richard, Beth. Intern, Montefiore Hosp., N.Y.C., 1950-51; resident Mt. Sinai Hosp., N.Y.C., 1952, fellow virology, 1952-55; exptl. immunologist Nat. Jewish Hosp., Denver, 1957-59; asst. attending pathologist, exptl. pathology Mt. Sinai Hosp., 1959-61; asst. prof. public health Cornell U. Med. Coll., 1961-66; research asso. prof. preventive medicine NYU, 1967-70, research prof., 1970-76, research prof. medicine Sch. Medicine, 1976—; tchr. met. leadership program U. Coll., NYU, 1969-73; physician Assn. for Help Retarded Children, 1982-88, Young Adult Inst., 1984—, Assn. for Children with Retarded Mental Devel., 1988—; cons. Nat. Ctr. for Health Services Research, 1983-85. Bd. dirs. N.Y. Scientists Com. Public Info., 1974-79, Physicians Forum, 1975-84; mem. interferon adv. com. Am. Cancer Soc., 1985—; mem. nat. bd. Com. for Nat. Health Service, 1976-79, Coalition for a Nat. Health Service, 1980-85. Served to lt. USNR, 1955-57. USPHS Research grantee, 1966-79. Mem. Tissue Culture Assn., AAAS, N.Y. Acad. Scis., Am. Public Health Assn. (chmn. com. on health services research 1980-87, governing council 1983-85), Am. Soc. Info. Sci., Soc. for Social Study of Sci., Assn. Health Services Research. Author sci. research articles on tissue culture, virology, interferon, preventive medicine, health policy, health services research, sociology of knowledge. Home: 100 Bleecker St New York NY 10012

JAHN, BILLIE JANE, nurse; b. Byers, Tex., Dec. 12, 1921; d. Thomas Oscar and Molly Verona (Kennemer) Downing; student Scott and White Sch. Nursing, 1941-42, U. Mich., 1973-75; B.S. in Nursing, Wayne State U., 1971; M.S., East Tex. State U., 1976, Ph.D., 1982; m. Edward L. Jahn, Dec. 6, 1942; children—Antoinette R., James T., Thomas L., Edward L., Janette E. Staff nurse Warren Meml. Hosp., Centerline, Mich., 1957-61; supr. nursing service Mich. Dept. Mental Health, Northville, 1962-71, Franklin County (Tex.) Hosp., 1972-74; instr. nursing Paris (Tex.) Jr. Coll., 1975-80; nurse educator VA, Waco, Tex., 1981-82; exec. v.p., dir., sr. nursing cons. Dos Cabezas, Inc., Mt. Vernon, Waco and Temple, Tex., 1981—; adj. faculty U. Tex.-Arlington, 1985—; mem. dept. phys. medicine and rehab. Scott and White Hosp., Temple, Tex., 1985—; head nurse dept. physc. med. and rehab.; cons. East Tex. State U., Texarkana, 1978—. adj. faculty U. Tex.-Arlington. Vol., ARC, 1971—; den mother Boy Scouts Am., 1960-62; sec. PTA, Warren, Mich., 1960-62; v.p., Temple, Tex., 1957-58. Mem. AAAS, Nat. League Nursing, Nat. Assn. Rehab. Nurses (rev. bd. Rehab. Nursing Inst. 1986—), Tex. League Nursing, AAUP, Nat. Assn. Female Execs., Am. Assn. Curriculum and Supervision, Phi Delta Kappa, Kappa Delta Pi.

JAIDAH, ALI MOHAMMED, petroleum company executive; b. Doha, Qatar, 1941; B.S. in Econs., London U., 1965, M.S., 1966. Head econs. div. dept. petroleum affairs Ministry of Fin. and Petroleum, State of Qatar, 1966-71, dir. petroleum affairs, 1971-76; Qatar gov. for Orgn. Petroleum Exporting Countries, 1976, sec. gen., 1977-78, participant Qatari dels.; mng. dir. Qatar Gen. Petroleum Corp., Doha, 1979-85, also dir.; mem. exec. office Orgn. Arab Petroleum Exporting Countries, 1976; head of delegation, OPEC, OAPEC and other confs. Recipient Silver Medallion award Pres. of Austria. Contbr. articles on petroleum econs. to profl. publs. Office: Qatar Gen Petroleum Corp, PO Box 3212, Doha Qatar *

JAIN, ADISH, engineer; b. Delhi, India, Nov. 3, 1939; came to U.S., 1966; s. Kishori Lal and Kapoori Devi Jain; m. Asha Jain, June 4, 1966; children: Sam, Cindy. BSME, U. Delhi, 1961; MSME, U. Minn., 1963; MBA, U. Wis., 1977. Registered profl. engr., Wis. Lectr. Indian Inst. Tech., New Delhi, 1963-66; project engr. White Farm Equipment, Mpls., 1967-72; sr. project engr. Waukesha (Wis.) Engine, 1972-77; project mgr. Deere & Co., Waterloo, Iowa, 1977-80, mgr. engring. dept., 1981—. Pres. Indo-American Club, Milw., 1970-71; chmn. Energy Conservation Commn., Cedar Falls, 1980-84. Mem. Soc. Automotive Engrs., Am. Soc. Mech. Engrs., Soc. Mfg. Engrs., Beta Gamma Sigma. Jain. Club: Indo-Am. (pres. 1970-71). Home: 910 Juanita Ave Cedar Falls IA 50613 Office: John Deere Product Engring Ctr 6725 Deere Rd Waterloo IA 50704

JAIN, HARSH VARDAN, engineering company executive; b. Kotah, Rajasthan, India, Oct. 15, 1943; s. N.K. and S. (Singh) J.; m. Sudha Kaushik; children: Uday, Ajay. B of Tech. in Mech. Engring. with honors, Indian Inst. Tech., Bombay, 1965. Grad. trainee Birds-Heilgers Group, Calcutta, 1965-67; mktg. trainee, then mktg. mgr. IBM World Trade Corp., Calcutta, New Delhi, Madras, Bombay, 1967-78; sr. mgr. bus. systems div. Nelco-Tata Group, Bombay, 1978-80; sr. exec. v.p. Indian Tool Mfrs. Ltd., Bombay, 1980-83; spl. dir. TI Engring., Madras, India, 1983-87; chmn. bd., mng. dir. Hersh Techs. Pvt. Ltd., Madras, 1987—; bd. dirs. Steel Pipes of India Ltd., Banglore; corp. adv. STI Group, Indore, India, 1987—, STP Ltd., Calcutta, 1987—; cons. Rap and Sachs Ltd., Hosur, India, 1987—. Mem. Am. Mgmt. Assn. Club: Madras. Home: GI Anderson Gardens, 30 Anderson Rd, Madras 600006, India Office: Hersh Techs Pvt Ltd, 9C JP Towers, 7/2 NH Rd, Madras 600034, India

JAIN, PREM CHAND, stock broker; b. Calcutta, India, Dec. 2, 1926. Bd. dirs. Delhi Stock Exchange, 1959—, hon. gen. sec., 1963-65, pres., 1965-66, 68-69, 79-81, 85-87. Home: 32 Hanuman Rd, New Delhi 110002, India Office: Delhi Stock Exchange Assoc Ltd, 3 & 4 4B Asaf Ali Rd, New Delhi 110002, India

JAIN, RAJ KRISHAN, offshore structural engineer; b. Jammu Tawi, Jammu and Kashmir, India, Nov. 7, 1939; came to Eng., 1975; s. Charanjit Lal and Shanti Devi Jain; m. Snehlata Jain, Feb. 23, 1966; children—Mudit, Mohit. B.A., Jammu and Kashmir U., 1961; M.Sc., U. Roorkee, 1963, Ph.D., 1966. Chartered engr., U.K. Vis. lectr. Cranfield Inst. Tech., Eng., 1971-73, sr. research officer, 1975-78; lectr. U. Roorkee, India, 1965-71, 73-75; prin. engr. Vickers Offshore (P & D) Ltd., Brrow-in-Furness, Eng., 1978-81; engring. specialist RJBA Holland B.V., Rijswijk, Holland, 1981-82; sr. project engr. Brown & Root (U.K.) Ltd., London, 1983—; mgr. Pipeline Engring, 1985-86. Mem. editorial bd. Applied Ocean Research Jour., 1981—. Contbr. 30 articles to profl. jours. Commonwealth Acad. fellow, 1971-72. Fellow Inst. Marine Engrs., Inst. Math. and Its Applications; mem. ASME, Royal Inst. for Naval Architects, Soc. for Underwater Tech. Hindu. Club: Selsdon Bridge (Croydon); Jain Assn. U.K. (gen. sec.). Avocations: painting; swimming; gardening. Home: 61 Upper Selsdon Rd, Sanderstead, Surrey CR2 8DJ, England Office: Brown & Root Vickers Ltd, 125 Collier's Wood, London SW19 2JR, England

JAIN, SUSHIL KUMAR, optometrist; b. Pratapgurh, India, Sept. 20, 1955; came to U.S., 1971; s. Nemichand Ratanlal and Hemlata (Salgia) J.; m. Asha Khushranglal, Dec. 2, 1981; children: Ankush, Nishant. BS, Ky. State U., 1976; D of Optometry, So. Coll. Optometry, Memphis, 1981; MS, Old Dominion U., 1984. Clin. intern Nat. Naval Med. Ctr., Washington, 1980, Naval Regional Med. Ctr., San Diego, 1981; optometric physician Sewells Pt. Clinic Navy Base, Norfolk, Va., 1981-84; optometric physician, dept. head U.S. Navy Hosp., Yokosuka, Japan, 1984-87, Camp Pendleton, Calif., 1987—; chmn. tri-service spl. edn. med. bd. U.S. Navy, Japan, 1985-87, eye hazard bd. Marine Corps Base, Camp Pendleton, 1987—. Serves as lt. cmdr. USN, 1981—. Named Kentucky Colonel, Ky. State Gov., 1977. Fellow Am. Coll. Optometric Physicians; mem. Am. Optometric Assn., Coll. Optometrists in Vision Devel. Mem. Jain Ch. Lodge: Lions (Memphis) (charter pres. 1978-79). Office: US Naval Hosp Marine Corps Base Camp Pendleton CA 92055

JAIN, VIJAY PRAKASH, marketing executive; b. Meerut, Uttar Pradesh, India, Aug. 13, 1944; arrived in Denmark, 1972; s. Sumat Prasad and Pushpa Devi (Lata) J.; m. Karen Nielsen, July, 18, 1970; children: Camilla, Anja. Diploma, Sch. World Trade, Vienna, Austria, 1968; MBA, U. Western Ont., London, Can., 1971. Researcher York U., Toronto, Can., 1971-72; lectr. Sch. Commerce, Naestved, Denmark, 1972-76; dir. Lemvig-Fog & Jain Pvt. Ltd., Copenhagen, 1974-79; mng. dir. Silkotex Aps, Silkeborg, Denmark, 1981—; lectr. Sch. Internat. Mktg. and Export, Herning, Denmark, 1980—. Author: Eksport, 1982. Bd. dirs. Internat. Student Ctr.

Mem. Soc. for Intercultural Relations. Home and Office: Silkotex Aps, Vestergade 72, 8600 Silkeborg Denmark

JAIS, RICHARD BENJAMIN, audit company executive; b. Algiers, Algeria, Jan. 1, 1930; s. Jacques Jacob and Irma (Tubiana) J.; m. Rosy Barraud, Aug. 5, 1961; children: Philippe Richard, Stéphane Edouard. Degree in commerce, U. Algiers, 1953. Cert. interpreter Eng. and Spanish. Audit asst. Price Waterhouse Paris, Algiers, 1954-57; audit mgr. Arthur Andersen, Paris, 1957-70; bus. mgr. Hewlett Packard, Paris, 1970; v.p. fin. Comex SA Internat., Marseille, France and Paris, 1970-73; pres. bd. dirs. Continentale D'Audit SA, Marseile and Paris, 1973—; fin. cons. Profigecc Corp., Marseille, 1975—, DSA Internat., Paris, 1984—, Monaco-Cannes, 1988. Mem. French CPA Orgn., Intenat. Audit Group, World Wide Orgn. Mem. Conservative Party. Club: Diplomatique (Zurich). Lodge: Rotary. Office: Continentale d'Audit, 370 Ave Prado, 13008 Marseille France also: 1 Villa Beausejour, 06400 Cannes France

JAKAB, IRENE, psychiatrist; b. Oradea, Rumania; came to U.S., 1961, naturalized, 1966; d. Odon and Rosa A. (Riedl) J. MD, Ferencz József U., Kolozsvar, Hungary, 1944; lic. in psychology, pedagogy, philosophy cum laude, Hungarian U., Cluj, Rumania, 1947; PhD summa cum laude, Pazmany Peter U., Budapest, 1948; Drhc, U. Besançon (France), 1982. Diplomate Am. Bd. Psychiatry. Rotating intern Ferencz József U., 1943-44; resident in psychiatry Univ. Hosp., Kolozsvar, 1944-47; resident in neurology Univ. Hosp., 1947-50; resident internal medicine Univ. Hosp. for Internal Medicine, Pecs, Hungary, 1950-51; chief physician Univ. Hosp. for Neurology and Psychiatry, Pécs, 1951-59; staff neuropathol. research lab. Neurol. Univ. Clinic, Zurich, 1959-61; sect. chief Kans. Neurol. Inst., Topeka, 1961-63; dir. research and edn. 1966; resident psychiatry Topeka State Hosp., 1963-66; asst. psychiatrist McLean Hosp., Belmont, Mass., 1966-67; assoc. psychiatrist McLean Hosp., 1967-74; prof. psychiatry U. Pitts. Med. Sch., 1974—, co-dir. med. student edn. in psychiatry, 1981—; dir. John Merck Program, 1974-81; mem. faculty dept. psychiatry Med. Sch., Pecs, 1951-59; asst. Univ. Hosp. Neurology, Zurich, 1959-61; assoc. psychiatry Harvard U., Boston, 1966-69, asst. prof. psychiatry, 1969-74, lectr. psychiatry, program dir. grad course mental retardation, 1970-87. Author: Dessins et Peintures des Aliénés, 1956, Zeichnungen und Gemälde der Geisteskranken, 1956; editor: Psychiatry and Art, Proc. 4th Internat. Colloquium of Psychopathology of Expression, 1968, Art Interpretation and Art Therapy, 1969, Conscious and Unconscious Expressive Art, 1971, Transcultural Aspects of Psychiatric Art, 1975; co-editor: Dynamische Psychiatrie, 1974; editorial bd.: Confinia Psychiatrica, 1975-81; contbr. articles to profl. jours. Recipient 1st prize Benjamin Rush and Gold medal award for sci. exhibit, 1980, Bronze Chris plaque Columbus Film Festival, 1980, Leadership award Am. Assn. on Mental Deficiency, 1980; Menninger Sch. Psychiatry fellow, Topeka, 1963-66. Mem. AMA, Am. Psychol. Assn., Am. Psychiat. Assn., Société Medico Psychologique de Paris, Internat. Rorschach Soc., N.Y. Acad. Scis., Internat. Soc. Psychopathology of Expression (v.p. 1959—), Am. Soc. Psychopathology of Expression (chmn. 1965—, Ernst Kris Gold Medal award 1988), Royal Soc. of Medicine (affiliate), Internat. Soc. Child Psychiatry and Allied Professions, Deutschsprachige Gesellschaft für Psychopathologie des Ausdruckes (hon.), Deutschsprachige Gesellschaft fur Psychopathologie des Ausdrucks (Prinzhorn prize 1967). Home: 228 Parkman Ave Pittsburgh PA 15213 Office: U Pitts Med Sch 3811 O'Hara St Pittsburgh PA 15213

JAKES, MILOS, government official; b. Cesky Krumlov, Czechoslovakia, Aug. 12, 1922. Mem. Communist Party, 1945—, chmn. Control and Auditing Commn.; mem. Central Com. secretariat, 1977—, chmn. commn. on econ. policy; mem. Presidium, 1981—; gen. sec. Communist Party, Czechoslovakia, 1987—. Office: Communist Party Czechoslovakia, nabr Ludvika Svobody 12, 125 11 Prague Czechoslovakia *

JAKHAR, BAL RAM, member India Parliament; b. Panjkosi, Punjab, India, Aug. 23, 1923; s. Chaudhri Rajaram and Shrimati (Pato Devi) J.; m. Shrimati Rameshwari, Feb. 27, 1937; children: 3 sons, 2 daughters. BA with honors, Forman Christian Coll., 1945. Mem. Punjab Legis. Assembly, Chandigarh, Punjab, India, 1972-77; dep. minister Cooperation Irrigation and Power, Chandigarh, 1972-77; mem. opposition, speaker Punjab Legis. Assembly, 1977-79; mem., speaker House of the People (Lok Sabha), New Delhi, 1980—. Author: People, Parliament and Administration, 1982. Mem. Commonwealth Parliamentarian Assn. Home: 20 Akbar Rd, New Delhi India Office: Parliament House, Parliament St, New Delhi India

JAKOBER, BEN PETER, sculptor; b. Vienna, Austria, July 31, 1930; s. Henry and Olga (Kann) J.; m. Yannick Vu, Oct. 22, 1972; children—Reza, Maima. Exhibitions include Fiac Paris, Galerie Littman Basle, Galerie Brachot Brussels, Fund. March, Belfort Mus., Palais Beaux Arts, Brussels, La. Mus., Recklinghausen Mus., Mannheim, Vienna, Biennale de Venezia; works in collections include: Mus. Modern Art, Vienna, Guiliano Gori, Pistoia, Colombe D'Or St Paul de Vence, Musé e d'Art Moderne, Brussels, Musée Español de Arte Contemporaneo, Madrid. Served to lt. Brit. Army, 1948-50. Home: Sa Bassa Blanca, Malpas Alcudia, Mallorca Spain

JALON, MARC R.D., information and communications manager; b. Leuveh, Flanders, Belgium, May 15, 1953; s. Jules and Jeanne (Vandeput) J. Lic. Applied Econs., U. Louvain, 1977. Acct. Sperry, Belgium, 1978-80, supr. ranks and adminstrn., 1980-84, with pricing and contracts, 1984-86, 1984-86; pricing mgr. Unisys, Brussels, Belgium, 1986—. Home: De Wamaelaar 19, B-8337 Blankerberge Belgium Office: Unysis, Terhulpseteenweg 177 Bus 1, B-1170 Brussels Belgium

JALONICK, GEORGE WASHINGTON, IV, interior and exterior landscape company executive; b. Dallas, Apr. 30, 1940; s. George Washington III and Dorothy Elizabeth (Cockrell) J.; m. Mary Lytle McDonough, Oct. 14, 1966; 1 dau., Mary Clare. B.B.A., U. Tex.-Austin, 1963. Asst. to pres. S.W. Airmotive Co., Dallas, 1963-69; owner Motion Picture Editors, Inc., Dallas, 1969-74; dir. retail sales Lambert Landscape Co., Dallas, 1974-75; owner Adam Whitney Inc., Dallas, 1978—. Bd. dirs. SW Family Inst., 1988—, Am. Heart Assn., 1973-76, Boys Clubs of Dallas, 1974—, Cystic Fibrosis Found., Dallas, 1975-81, Hope Cottage Children's Bur., Inc., Dallas, 1973-79, Dallas Summer Musicals, 1984—; bd. dirs. Am. Lung Assn., 1987—; mem. U. Tex. at Dallas Devel. Bd., 1980—, Aerospace Heritage Found., 1988—; mem. chancellor's council U. Tex., 1983—, Southwest Family Inst., 1987—. Episcopalian. Clubs: Brook Hollow Golf, Idlewild, Terpsichorean. Home: 5712 Redwood Ln Dallas TX 75209 Office: Adam Whitney Inc 2231 Valdina St Dallas TX 75207

JAMAL, MOEZ AHAMED, bank executive; b. Mombasa, Kenya, June 15, 1955; s. Ahamed and Shamsultan (Kalyan); m. Nadia Eboo, June 23, 1979; children: Nijhad, Shazia. BA in Economics with honors, Manchester U., 1976; MBA, NYU, 1979. V.p. Lloyds Bank, N.Y., 1979-85, Credit Suisse, London, 1985—. Moslem. Club: R.A.C. (Pall Mall). Home: 3 The Fairway, New Malden Surrey KT3 4SP, England

JAMAL, MUHAMMAD, business educator; b. New Delhi, Dec. 28, 1946; arrived in Can., 1970; s. Hakim Muhammad and Amtul Qayyum (Khan) Idris; m. Saleha Baig, Oct. 10, 1974; children: Memuna Amna, Muddathhir Karim, Mubashir. BA in Social Studies, Punjab U., Lahore, Pakistan, 1965, MA in Social Scis., 1967; MA in Indsl. Sociology, U. B.C., Vancouver, Can., 1972, PhD in Mgmt., 1976. Asst. research officer Punjab U., Lahore, Pakistan, 1968-70; asst. prof. mgmt. Concordia U., Montreal, Que., Can., 1976-80, assoc. prof. mgmt., 1980—; participant NATO Program on Behavioral Medicine, Castera-Verduzan, France, 1981; vis. prof. mgmt. People's Univ. China, Beijing, 1987; prin. speaker Islamic Countries Conf. on Statis. Scis., Lahore, 1988. Contbr. 3 chpts. to books and 20 articles to profl. jours.; presented 25 papers to nat. and internat. confs. Speaker Islamic Circle N.Am., Montreal, 1980-87. Grantee Province of Que., 1980, 85, 87, Social Scis. and Humanities Research Council, 1987—; recipient Bus. Faculty Research award Seagram Found., Montreal, 1979. Mem. Acad. of Mgmt., Am. Psychol. Assn., Can. Assn. Admistrv. Scis., Islamic Soc. N.Am. Mem. Liberal Party. Muslim. Home: 4876 Felix McLernan, Pierrefonds, PQ Canada H8Y 3K1 Office: Concordia U Loyola Campus, 7141 Sherbrooke St W, Montreal, PQ Canada H4B 1R6

JAMEEL, FATHULLA, Maldives minister external affairs; b. Male, Maldives; s. Mohamed and Shareefa Jameel; m. Aishath Fathulla, Jan. 1, 1970. B.A., Al-Azhar U., Cairo; diploma edn. Ein-Shams U., Cairo. Tchr., Majeediyya Sch., 1969-73; under sec. Ministry External Affairs, Male, Maldives, 1973-76, dep. to head Dept. External Affairs, 1976-77, permanent rep. to UN, 1977-78, minister external affairs, 1978—. Office: Ministry Foreign Affairs, Male Maldives *

JAMES, ALICE HOWRY, educator; b. Evanston, Ill., Apr. 9, 1918; d. Henry Burney and Edyth (Wornall) H.; AB, U. Louisville, 1939, MEd, 1974, EdD, U. Louisville, 1987; m. Thomas James II, July 15, 1941 (dec.); children—Thomas III, Edyth MacMillan, David Buchanan. Tchr., St. Mark's Presch., Louisville, 1959-61; asst. dir., tchr. Crescent Hill Meth. Presch., Louisville, 1961-66; kindergarten tchr. Louisville Bd. Edn., 1966-75; kindergarten tchr. Jefferson County Bd. Edn., Louisville, 1975-79; assoc. prof. early childhood edn. Jefferson Community Coll., Louisville, 1979—. Chmn., Peterson-Dumesnil Restoration Com., 1978; mem. Crescent Hill Community Council Edn. Com., 1979; bd. dirs. Home of the Innocents, 1980-86; mem. career devel. com. Head Start, 1980, chmn. policy council, 1983-84; bd. dirs. Peterson-Dumesnil Found., 1983—, Community Coordinated Child Care, pres. 1987—. Mem. Am. Assn. Community Coll. Early Childhood Educators, Nat. Assn. Edn. Young Children, Ky. Assn. Edn. Young Children, Louisville Assn. for Children Under Six, LWV, Phi Delta Kappa. Episcopalian. Clubs: Pendennis Club, Louisville Country. Home: 240 S Peterson Ave Louisville KY 40206 Office: Jefferson Community Coll 109 E Broadway Louisville KY 40202

JAMES, EARL EUGENE, JR., aerospace engineering executive; b. Oklahoma City, Feb. 8, 1923; s. Earl Eugene and Mary Frances (Godwin) J.; m. Barbara Jane Marshall, Dec. 15, 1945 (dec. Feb. 2, 1982); children—Earl Eugene III, Jeffrey Allan; m. 2d, Vanita L. Nix, Apr. 23, 1983. Student Oklahoma City U., 1940-41; B.S., U. Okla., 1945; postgrad. Tex. Christian U., 1954-57; M.S., So. Meth. U., 1961. Asst. mgr. Rialto Theatre, 1939-42; with Consol. Vultee Aircraft Co., San Diego, 1946-49; with Convair, Ft. Worth, 1949—, group engr., 1955-57, test group engr., supr. fluid dynamics lab., 1957-81, engring. chief Fluid Dynamics Lab., 1981—. Asst. dist. commr. Boy Scouts Am., 1958-59; adviser Jr. Achievement, 1962-63; mem. sch. bd. Castleberry Ind. Sch. Dist. (Tex.), 1969-83; chmn. bd. N.W. br. YMCA, 1971. Served to lt. (j.g.) USNR, 1942-46; PTO. Fellow AIAA (assoc.); mem. Air Force Assn. (life), Gen. Dynamics Mgmt. Assn., Nat. Mgmt. Assn., Okla. U. Alumni Assn. (life), Tex. Congress Parents and Tchrs. (hon. life), Pi Kappa Alpha, Alpha Chi Sigma, Tau Omega. Methodist. Democrat. Clubs: Squaw Creek Golf, Camera. Lodge: Elks. Author/editor over 1000 engring reports. Office: Fluid Dynamics Lab Mail Zone 5850 Box 748 Fort Worth TX 76101

JAMES, EDWARD FOSTER, educator; b. Hagerstown, Md., Mar. 17, 1927; s. Herbert Amory and Lavinia Grayson (Foster) J.; B.A., U. Md., 1954, M.A., 1955; Ph.D. (K.C. fellow), Catholic U. Am., 1969. Lectr., Univ. Coll., U. Md., College Park, 1955-60, asst. prof. English, 1963—, asst. prof. English and secondary edn., 1971-81, head dept. English, U. Md. Eastern Shore, 1970-71: vis. scholar Md. State Coll., 1968-69; cons. Md. Dept. Edn., 1979—; ordained priest Eastern Orthodox Ch., 1975; pastor Orthodox Syro-Chaldean Mission, Washington, 1981—. Served with U.S. Army, 1945-47, 50-51. Mem. Md. Council Tchrs. English Lang. Arts (exec. bd. 1978-80, Tchr. of Yr. award 1979), Nat. Council Tchrs. English, Southeastern Conf. Linguistics, Md. Assn. Tchr. Educators, Washington Linguistics Club, Md. Assn. Depts. English, Phi Kappa Phi, Phi Delta Kappa, Sigma Tau Delta. Contbr. articles to profl. jours.; editorial bd. Md. English Jour., 1975-80, African Directions, 1977; research on Frederick Douglass. Office: U Md English Dept College Park MD 20742

JAMES, FRANCIS EDWARD, JR., investment counselor; b. Woodville, Miss., Jan. 5, 1931; s. Francis Edwin and Ruth (Phillips) J.; m. Iris Senn, Nov. 3, 1952; children: Francis III, Barry, David. B.S., La. State U., 1951; M.S., Rensselaer Poly. Inst., 1966, Ph.D., 1967. Commd. 2d lt. USAF, 1950, advanced through grades to col., 1972; prof. mgmt. and statistics, :hmn. dept quantitative studies Air Force Inst. Tech., Wright Patterson AFB, 1967-71; dir. grad. edn. div. mgmt. programs Air Force Inst. Tech., 1972-74; pres. James Investment Research, Inc., Xenia, Ohio, 1974—; investment counsel to Citizens Heritage Bank, Ohio., State Bank Ohio, Citizens Fed. Savs. & Loan Ohio, Bank One Richmond, Ind.; cons. math. modeling. Author: A Matrix Solution for the General Linear Regression Model; contbr. articles to profl. jours. Mem. Rensselaer Council. Decorated Legion of Merit, D.F.C., Air medal, Joint Services Commendation medal, Meritorious Service medal; recipient Outstanding Acad. Achievement award Rensselaer Poly. Inst., 1965. Mem. Am. Statis. Assn., Mil. Ops. Research Soc., Am. Fin. Assn., Investment Counsel Assn. Am., Mktg. Technicians Assn., Soc. Logistics Engring. (Eckles award 1973, tech. chmn.), Sigma Iota Epsilon, Epsilon Delta Sigma. Lodges: Masons; Rotary. Home: 2604 Lantz Rd Xenia OH 45385 Office: James Investment Research Inc Box 8 Alpha OH 45301

JAMES, GEORGE THURA-RAJA-SINGAM, museum curator; b. Kendong, Negri Sembilan, West Malaysia, Apr. 3, 1912; s. Visuvanathar Sathalingam and Hannah Ponnammah (Christian) J.; Royal Soc. of Health cert. for Public Health Insps. in Malaysia, 1936; diploma for curators Mus. Assn., London, 1949; intern cert. Cleve. Mus., 1949; m. Manonmani May Vadivelu, Sept. 3, 1955; children—Perinpanayagam, Inparani, Inparajah. Asst. supr. Rural Health, Singapore, 1936; asst., Public Health Mus., Med. Coll., Singapore, 1937-42; asst., Public Health Mus., Med. Faculty, Singapore, 1945-54; sr. public health inspector, tng. and health edn. Ministry of Health, Singapore, 1955-67, ret., 1967; hon. curator Nat. U. Social Medicine and Public Health Mus., Singapore, 1967—; admiralty health inspector, Nicobar, 1941. Served with local defense forces, 1939-45. Recipient commendation for service to Allied cause World War II, 1947; Brit. Council scholar for study in U.K., 1948-49; Carnegie travel award for tour U.S. mus., 1949; recipient Italian Acad. award, 1984. Fellow Royal Soc. Health (life), Mus. Assn. (life), Royal Soc. Arts (life) Anglican Welfare Council. Author: The Design for a National Museum of Health, 1979. Home: 49 Gentle Rd, Singapore 1130, Singapore

JAMES, HERB MARK (HERBERT GEORGE), foundation and insurance executive; b. Trail, B.C., Can., Jan. 30, 1936; s. George William and Violet Ethyl (Corbin) J.; student bus. adminstrn. Simon Fraser U., 1965-69; m. Patricia Helen Boyd, Nov. 1, 1958; 1 son, Brad Mark. Founder, Internat. Sound Found., Ottawa, Can., 1967—, Blaine, Wash., 1975—; mem. bus. adv. bd. U.S. Senate, 1981—; mem. Can. Internat. Devel. Agy.; founder Better Hearing Better Life projects, Fiji, Kenya, Cayman Islands, Nepal, Costa Rica, Pakistan, Guatemala. Musician B. Pops Orch. Govt. of Can. grantee, 1973-83. Mem. Blaine C. of C. Clubs: Masons, Shriners, Demolay. Home: RR 2 PO Box 95, Port Moody, BC Canada V3H3E1 Office: USA Am Bldg PO Box 1587 Blaine WA 98230

JAMES, J. PETER COMPTON, communications company executive; b. East Hadden, Northampton, Eng., Nov. 23, 1931; s. Leslie Compton and Dorothy Joyce (Castell) J.; m. Julie Suzanne Garner, Oct. 14, 1957; children: Mark Compton, Sarah Ann, John Compton, Thomas Compton, Peter Compton. Student, All Saints Sch., Bloxham, Eng., 1945-50, St. Catherine's, Oxford, Eng., 1952-55. Salesman Underwood Bus., Northampton, Eng., 1956; br. mgr. Underwood Bus., Reading, Eng., 1956-58; mng. dir. Poplar-Wood, Ltd., Reading, Eng., 1958-65, Midland Bus., London, Northampton, 1965-79, MBM Computers, London, Northampton, 1969-79; chmn., mng. dir. DataTrade, Northampton, Eng., 1980—; owner The Wendover Kennel of Irish Setters and Labradors. Vice chmn. Kennel Club, London, 1987—, gen. com. mem., 1982—. Mem. Lloyd's of London (underwriting mem. 1979—). Club: Irish Setter Assn. (Eng.) (com. mem.), Wig and Pen. Home: Wendover House, Gayton NN7 3HL, England Office: DataTrade Ltd, 38 Billing Rd, Northampton NN1 5DQ, England

JAMES, MARION RAY, editor, publisher; b. Bellmont, Ill., Dec. 6, 1940; s. Francis Miller and Lorraine A. (Wylie) J.; m. Janet Sue Tennis, June 16, 1960; children—Jeffrey Glenn, David Ray, Daniel Scott, Cheryl Lynne. B.S., Oakland City Coll., Ind., 1964; M.S., St. Francis Coll., Fort Wayne, Ind., 1978. Sports and city editor Daily Clarion, Princeton, Ind., 1963-65; English tchr. Jac-Cen-Del High Sch., Osgood, Ind., 1965-66; indsl. editor Whirlpool Corp., Evansville and LaPorte, Ind., 1966-68, Magnavox Govt. and Indsl. Electronics Co., Fort Wayne, 1968-79; editor, pub. Bowhunter mag., Fort Wayne, 1971—; instr. Ind.-Purdue U., Fort Wayne, 1980—. Author: Bowhunting for Whitetail and Mule Deer, 1975, Successful Bowhunting, 1985; editor: Pope and Young Book World Records, 1975, Bowhunting Adventures, 1977. Recipient Best Editorial award United Community Service Publs., 1970-72; named Alumnus of Yr., Oakland City Coll., 1982, to Hall of Fame, Mt. Carmel High Sch., Ill., 1983. Mem. Outdoor Writers Assn. Am., Fort Wayne Assn. Bus. Editors (Fort Wayne Bus. Editor of Yr. 1969, pres. 1975-76), Alpha Phi Gamma, Alpha Psi Omega, Mu Tau Kappa. Club: Toastmasters (Able Toastmaster award). Home: 11513 Brigadoon Ct Fort Wayne IN 46804 Office: Bowhunter Mag 3720 S Calhoun St Fort Wayne IN 46807

JAMES, MILDRED HANNAH, hypnotist; b. Hopewell, Va., Oct. 18, 1918; d. Charles and Fannie (Enoch) Feldman; student Sch. Tech. Hypnosis, Ethical Hypnosis Tng. Center, Am. Inst. Hypnosis, Am. Guild Hypnotherapists; m. Albert W. James, Dec. 31, 1965; children by previous marriage—Sheila, Leslie, Andrea, David, Valerie, Kelly. Apprentice in hypnosis, 1959-60; practicing hypnotist, 1961—; pres., chmn. bd. Mildred H. James, Inc., Kent, Wash., 1976—; lectr., condr. seminars. Mem. Am. Inst. Hypnosis, Am. Guild Hypnotherapists, Hypnotists Union. Author weight reduction methods and smoking control methods; producer cassette tapes. Address: 322 Hibiscus Trail Melbourne Beach FL 32951

JAMES, P(HYLLIS) D(OROTHY) (MRS. C. B. WHITE), author; b. Aug. 3, 1920; d. Sidney Victor and Dorothy Amelia (Hone) J.; m. Connor Bantry White, 1941 (dec. 1964); 2 daughters. Grad., Cambridge Girls High Sch. Adminstr. Nat. Health Service, 1949-68; prin. Home Office Brit. Civil Service, 1968, with Police Dept., 1968-72, Criminal Policy Dept., 1972-79; assoc. fellow Downing Coll., Cambridge, 1986. Author: Cover Her Face, 1962, A Mind to Murder, 1963, Unnatural Causes, 1967, Shroud for a Nightingale, 1971; (with T.A. Critchley) The Maul and the Pear Tree, 1971, An Unsuitable Job for a Woman, 1972, The Black Tower, 1975, Death of an Expert Witness, 1977, Innocent Blood, 1980, The Skull beneath the Skin, 1982, A Taste for Death, 1986. Decorated OBE, 1983. Office: care Elaine Greene Ltd, 31 Newington Green, London N16 9PU, England *

JAMES, THOMAS NAUM, cardiologist, educator; b. Amory, Miss., Oct. 24, 1925; s. Naum and Kata J.; m. Gleaves Elizabeth Tynes, June 22, 1948; children—Thomas Mark, Terrence Fenner, Peter Naum. B.S., Tulane U., 1946, M.D., 1949. Diplomate Am. Bd. Internal Medicine (bd. govs. 1982-88), Bd. Cardiovascular Diseases. Intern Henry Ford Hosp., Detroit, 1949-50, resident in internal medicine and cardiology, 1950-53, mem. staff, 1959-68; practice medicine specializing in cardiology Birmingham, Ala., 1968-87; mem. staff U. Ala. Hosps., 1968-87; instr. medicine Tulane U., New Orleans, 1955-58, asst. prof., 1959; prof. medicine U. Ala. Med. Ctr., Birmingham, 1968-87, prof. pathology, 1968-73, assoc. prof. physiology and biophysics, 1969-73, dir. Cardiovascular Research and Tng. Center, 1970-77, chmn. dept. medicine, dir. div. cardiovascular disease, 1973-81, Mary Gertrude Waters prof. cardiology, 1976-87, Disting. prof. of univ., 1981-87; prof. medicine and pathology, pres. U. Tex. Med. Br., Galveston, 1987—; mem. adv. council Nat. Heart Lung and Blood Inst., 1975-79; pres. 10th World Congress Cardiology, 1986; mem. cardiology del. invited by Chinese Med. Assn. to, People's Republic of China, 1978. Author: Anatomy of the Coronary Arteries, 1961, The Etiology of Myocardial Infarction, 1963; Mem. editorial bd.: Circulation, 1966-83; mem. editorial bd.: Am. Jour. Cardiology, 1968-76; assoc. editor, 1976-82; mem. editorial bd.: Am. Heart Jour, 1976-79; Contbr. articles on cardiovascular diseases to med. jours. Served as capt. M.C. U.S. Army, 1953-55. Mem. ACP (gov. Ala. 1975-79, master 1983), AMA, Am. Clin. and Climatological Assn., Assn. Am. Physicians, Am. Soc. Clin. Investigation, Assn. Univ. Cardiologists (pres. 1978-79), Am. Heart Assn. (pres. 1979-80), Am. Coll. Cardiology (v.p. 1970-71, trustee 1970-71, 76-81, First Disting. Scientist award 1982), Am. Soc. Pharmacology and Exptl. Therapeutics, Soc. Exptl. Biology of Medicine, Am. Coll. Chest Physicians, Central Soc. Clin. Research, Internat. Soc. and Fedn. Cardiology (pres. 1983-84), So. Soc. Clin. Investigation, Am. Fedn. Clin. Research, Phi Beta Kappa, Sigma Xi, Omicron Delta Kappa, Ala. Acad. Honor, Alpha Omega Alpha, Alpha Tau Omega, Phi Chi. Presbyterian. Clubs: Cosmos, Mountain Brook. Office: U Tex Med Br Office of Pres 301 University Blvd Galveston TX 77550

JAMES, WALTER, retired computer information specialist; b. Mpls., June 8, 1915; s. James Edward and Mollie (Gress) Smoleroff; B.Ch.E., U. Minn., 1938, postgrad, 1945-60; m. Jessie Ann Pickens, Dec. 27, 1948; 1 son, Joel Pickens. Process designer Monsanto Chem. Co., St. Louis, 1940-45; instr. math U. Minn., Mpls., 1945-60, extension div., 1950—; researcher computer based applied math. 3M Co., St. Paul, 1960-68; info. systems planner State of Minn., St. Paul, 1968-85; ret., 1985. Mem. Am. Math. Assn., AAAS, Sigma Xi. Contbr. articles to profl. jours. Home: 6228 Brooklyn Dr Brooklyn Center MN 55430

JAMES, WILLIAM HALL, economics educator; b. North Providence, R.I., July 20, 1910; s. John William and May (Hall) J.; student U. Lausanne, 1928-29; B. Phil., Brown U., 1933; M.A., Yale U., 1946, Ph.D., 1953; LL.D., U. New Haven, 1976; m. Virginia Stowell, June 24, 1950; 1 dau., Hillery Stowell. Tchr., New Canaan (Conn.) Bd. Edn., 1933-36; teaching prin. Easton (Conn.) Bd. Edn., 1936-42, 1946-47, supervising prin., 1947-53, supt. schs., 1953-58; supt. schs. Branford (Conn.) Bd. Edn., 1958-66; staff Commn. Higher Edn., Hartford, Conn., 1966-77, dir. accreditation and scholarships, 1966-77, ret., 1977; cons. Greater New Haven State Tech. Coll., 1977-78, Conn. Bd. Higher Edn., 1980-81; adj. prof. history So. Conn. State Coll., New Haven, 1947-49, adj. prof. econs., 1981—; adj. prof. internat. relations, Eurasian affairs and history Western Conn. State Coll., Danbury, 1949-58; adj. prof. ednl. adminstrn. U. Bridgeport (Conn.), 1958; adj. prof. econs. U. New Haven, West Haven, Conn., 1979—; lectr. in field. Mem. North Branford (Conn.) Commn. Econ. Devel., 1980—, chmn., 1981—. Served to maj. USAAF, 1942-46. Recipient Disting. Friend of Greater New Haven State Tech. Coll. award, 1984. Mem. NEA, Conn. Edn. Assn., Conn. Assn. Pub. Sch. Supts., Conn. Assn. Advancement Sch. Adminstrn., Am. Assn. Sch. Adminstrs., Yale Post-Doctoral Seminar Group (pres. 1968-69), Conn. State Employees Assn., Conn. Council Higher Edn. (treas. 1971-77), Am. Assn. Higher Edn., Royal Can. Geog. Soc., SAR, Numerical Control Soc., PTA. Clubs: Rotary (sec.-treas. Schoolmaster's U.S. 1965-69), Am. Legion (post comdr. Easton 1948-49), Exchange. Author: The Monetarists and the Current Crisis, 1975. Home: 373 Reeds Gap Rd Northford CT 06472

JAMES, WILLIAM WESLEY, JR., utility executive; b. Gulfport, Miss., Feb. 24, 1936; s. William Wesley and Mamie (Swanner) J.; m. Beverly Elaine Banderet, Oct. 28, 1952; children—William Wesley, Cheryl Elaine, Carl Byron, Troy Lee. B.E.E., Miss. State U., 1958. Registered profl. engr., Fla. With Fla. Power & Light Co., Miami, 1957-77, systems ops. mgr., 1969-72, supr. distbn., 1972-73, mgr. apprentice tng., 1973-77; vice gen. mgr. Big Rivers Electric Corp., Henderson, Ky., 1977-80; dir. ops. Seminole Electric Coop., Inc., Tampa, Fla., 1981-82; dir. engring. and ops. Wabash Valley Power Assn., Indpls., 1982-86, pres., gen. mgr. Northeastern REMC, Columbia City, Ind., 1986— ; mem. faculty Manatee Jr. Coll., Bradenton, Fla., 1959-69, U. Miami, 1970-77. Coach basketball and football Boys' Club, Brandenton, 1958-64; football coach Pop Warner League, Miami, 1970-77; youth basketball coach Suniland, Miami, 1974-77; mem. gen. adv. bd. tech. edn. Manatee Jr. Coll., 1959-69, Manatee Profl. Guidance Bd., Pub. Schs., Bradenton, 1961-68, council Manatee County PTA, 1964-67; mem. adv. com. Henderson (Ky.) Community Coll., 1978-81, U. Evansville (Ind.) Ctr. Mgmt. Edn., 1979-81; mem. ofcl. bd. 1st Meth. Ch., Bradenton, 1959-69. Named Ky. col., 1980. Mem. Ind. Soc. Profl. Engrs., Nat. Soc. Profl. Engrs., IEEE, Ind. Engring. Soc., Gt. Lakes Electric Consumer Assn. (transmission task force 1982—, bd. dirs. 1983—, resolutions com. 1982—). Office: 10 Governor's Dr PO Box 171 Columbia City IN 46725

JAMESON, SANFORD CHANDLER, educator; b. Toronto, Ohio, Feb. 12, 1932; s. Sanford Frank and Dorothy Lee (Robinson) J.; BS, Miami U., Oxford, Ohio, 1954; MA, Case Western Res. U., 1960; m. Joan Sheridan, June 29, 1963; children: Jennifer Joan, Julie Jo. Asst. dir. admission Case Western Res. U., 1957-60; assoc. dir. admissions Carleton Coll. Northfield, Minn., 1960-63; asst. regional dir. Coll. Entrance Exam. Bd., Evanston, Ill., 1963-66, asst. dir. internat. edn. Central office, N.Y.C., 1966-69, asso. for internat. edn., 1969-71, dir. internat. edn., 1971—; chmn. Nat. Council Evaluation Fgn. Ednl. Credentials, 1974-78; chmn. liaison group for internat. ednl. exchange, 1986-88. Served as lt. USNR, 1954-57. Mem. Assn. Coll. Admission-Counselors, Nat. Assn. Fgn. Student Affairs (bd. dirs., chmn. admission sect., pres. 1976-77), Am. Assn. Collegiate Registrars and Admission Officers, Nat. Liaison Com. Fgn. Student Admissions (chmn. 1972-74, sec. 1974-87), Internat. Sch. Service (bd. dirs. 1974-81, 83—, chmn. 1988—), SAR, Soc. Mayflower Descendants, Soc. of the Cin., Sigma Alpha Epsilon. Presbyterian (elder). Clubs: Mason (32 deg.), Shrine. Author, editor workshop reports in field. Home: 5609 Springfield Dr Bethesda MD 20816 Office: 1717 Massachusetts Ave Washington DC 20036

JAMIESON, CRAWFORD WILLIAM, surgeon; b. Kettering, Northantshire, Eng., Sept. 28, 1937; s. Crawford John and Elizabeth (McAulay) J.; m. Gay Jane Gillibrand, Nov. 18, 1961; 1 child, Crawford Philip. M.B., B.S. with honours in Surgery, Guy's Hosp., U. London, 1960; M.S., U. London, 1970. Surg. registrar Addenbrookes Hosp., Cambridge, Eng., 1964-68; research fellow Tulane U., New Orleans, 1968-70; asst. dir. surg. unit St. Mary's Hosp., London, 1970-72, hon. cons. surgeon, 1982—; hon. cons. surgeon Hammersmith Hosp., London; sr. lectr. surgery U. London; cons. surgeon St. Thomas' Hosp., London; Hunterian prof. Royal Coll. Surgeons Eng., 1970; vis. prof. Tulane U., 1983, Royal Adelaide Hosp., Australia, 1984; organizing chmn. Internat. Vascular Symposium, London, 1981-86. Author: The Surgical Management of Vascular Disease, 1981; chmn. editorial bd. Brit. Jour. Surgery. Contbr. articles to profl. publs. Fellow Internat. Cardiovascular Soc., Royal Coll. Surgeons (Eng.), Assn. Surgeons Gt. Britain; mem. Vascular Surg. Soc. Gt. Britain and Ireland (sec.-treas. 1976-79), Surg. Research Soc. Gt. Britain. Mem. Ch. of Scotland. Home: 19 Gladstone St, London SE1 6EY, England Office: The Consulting Rooms, York House, 199 Westminster Bridge Rd, London SE1 7UT, England

JAMIESON, FRANCES JEAN KENTOR, psychologist; b. Denver, Apr. 8, 1922; d. Charles and Hazel (Dietrich) Kentor; AB, U. Denver, 1943; MA, Stanford, 1950; postgrad. U. Calif. at Berkeley, 1959-60, Nova U., 1977-82; m. Robert Howard Jamieson, Nov. 2, 1946 (dec. June 1953); 1 dau., Nancy Rose. Supr. attendance Office Edn., Modesto, Calif., 1944-46; tchr. pub. schs., Stockton, Calif., 1943-44; prin. Mountain View Sch., Stanislaus County, Calif., 1948-49; supr. guidance, Richmond, Calif., 1949-56, tchr., Sacramento, 1956-58; dean girls, head English dept., Crockett, Calif., 1958-60; coordinator psychol. services Monterey County Office Edn., Salinas, Calif., 1960-64; pvt. practice as psychologist, Sacramento, 1956-58, Salinas, 1963-68, South San Francisco, 1976—; psychologist Diagnostic Sch. for Neurologically Handicapped Children No. Calif., San Francisco, 1968-70, dir. ednl. and psychol. services, 1970-77, asst. supt., 1977-79; psychologist, 1979-87 . Sec. Monterey County Democratic Central Com.; mem. Calif. Dem. Com., 1966-68. Mem. Am. Personnel and Guidance Assn., NEA, Council for Exceptional Children, Nat., Calif. assns. parliamentarians, Calif. Assn. for Measurement and Evaluation in guidance, Calif. Employees Assn., Calif. Fedn. Bus. and Profl. Women's Clubs (state pres. 1973-74), Am. Legion Aux., San Francisco Bus. and Profl. Women's Club, Phi Lambda Theta. Presbyn. (deacon). Clubs: Order Eastern Star, White Shrine, South San Francisco Democratic (pres.). Home: 1031 Cherry Ave #50 San Bruno CA 94066-2342

JAMIESON, SCOTT ALLAN, orthodontist; b. Detroit, Oct. 27, 1947; s. Douglas James and Allana Maria (Minifie) J.; m. Claudia Jane Grzemski, July 29, 1972; children: Jeffrey Allan, Jody Ann, Jayme Allana, Jillian Amanda. DDS, Northwestern U., 1972, MS, 1974; BA, Aquinas Coll., 1982. Staff orthodontist Northwestern U., Chgo., 1976-77; orthodontics assoc. H.T. Perry, Jr., Elgin, Ill., 1976-77; pvt. practice orthodontist, Marquette, Mich., 1977—; lectr. Northwestern U., 1982—. Eucharist minister St. Peters Cathedral, Marquette, 1980—; pres. Marquette Sch. Bd., 1986-87, Rotary Internat., 1984—. Served to lt. comdr. USNR, 1972-74. Decorated Commendation of Achievement medal U.S. Army, 1976. Mem. ADA, Mich. Dental Assn., Superior Dist. Dental Soc. (pres. 1983-84), Am. Assn. Orthodontists, Gt. Lakes Soc. Orthodontists, Mich. Soc. Orthodontists (pres. 1985-86), Acad. Dental Materials, Mich. Cleft Lip and Palate Assn., Mich. State Bd. Dentistry. Republican. Roman Catholic. Avocations: cross-country skiing, fishing, hunting, woodworking.

JAMIL, AHMAD KHAN, physician; b. May 12, 1939; s. Hakim Fazal Ahad; m. Taslim Sattar, Mar. 28, 1968; children: Nasir, Seema. MB, BS, U. Peshawar, Pakistan, 1965. Med. officer Lady Reading Hosp., Peshawar, Pakistan, 1967-68; med. officer Nat. Health Service, England, 1968-72, anesthetist, 1972-75; med. officer, anesthetist Nat. Iranian Oil Co., Iran, 1976-80; gen. practice medicine Pakistan, 1980—. Contbr. articles to med jours.; inventor paediatric endotracheal tube, catheter mount, laryngotracheal toilet, humeral epicondyle holder, also others. Served to capt. Pakistan Army, 1965-67. Recipient Tamgha-i-Jang Indo Pak War award Pakistan army. Mem. Pakistan Med. Assn. Home: Jamil Manzil, Hakim Fazal Ahad Rd, Takht Rhai Pakistan

JAMIL, ANWAR AHMED, educator, researcher; b. Delhi, India, Feb. 14, 1946; s. Ahmed and Jamila Noor. BSc, Karachi U. Pakistan, 1969, MSc in Applied Math., 1972, MSc in Pure Math., 1973, MPhil, 1976. Lectr. U. Karachi, 1973-78, asst. prof., 1978-84, assoc. prof., 1984—; jr. assoc. ICTP, Trieste, Italy. Pres., founder Assn. Physically Handicapped Adults, Karachi, 1976, treas. 1977-83, joint sec., 1984-85. Mng. editor Karachi Jour. Math. Contbr. articles to profl. jours. Recipient Gold medal Higher Secondary Edn., 1967. Mem. Am. Math. Soc. Home: 77 Darul-Aman Soc, Road No 6, Karachi 5 Pakistan Office: Univ Karachi, Dept Math, Karachi Pakistan

JAMISON, JOHN AMBLER, retired circuit judge; b. Florence, S.C., May 14, 1916; s. John Wilson and Elizabeth Ambler (Fleming) J.; m. Mildred Holley, Sept. 22, 1945. LL.B. cum laude, Cumberland U., Lebanon, Tenn., 1941; postgrad., George Washington U., 1943-44, also Indsl. Coll. Armed Forces, 1961; J.D., Samford U., 1969, LL.D. (hon.), 1983. Bar: S.C. 1941, Va. 1942, U.S. Supreme Ct. 1945. Atty. Va. Div. Motor Vehicles, 1947-54; practiced law Fredericksburg, Va., 1954-72; substitute judge Stafford and King George County Cts. and Fredericksburg Municipal Ct., 1956-72; judge 15th Jud. Circuit Va., 1972-87, chief judge, 1976-78, 84-86; Counsel, dir. Nat. Bank of Fredericksburg, 1968-73, 87—. Mem. adv. bds. Va. Gov.'s Hwy. Safety Commn., 1956-62, Cumberland Sch. Law, 1980—; pres. Fredericksburg Rescue Squad, 1960-62, now hon. life mem.; chmn. bd. Fredericksburg Area Mental Hygiene Clinic, 1962-63; hon. chmn. Fredericksburg Area Bicentennial Commn., 1975-77; charter mem. Thomas Jefferson Inst. for Religious Freedom, 1975; bd. visitors Coker Coll., Hartsville, S.C.; bd. dirs. Rappahannock Area Devel. Commn., 1960-66. Served from ensign to comdr. USNR, 1941-46; comdg. officer Richmond Naval Res. Div. 1948-54; mem. Res. 1946-76, ret.; naval aide to govs. Va. 1954-72. Recipient award S.C. Confederate War Centennial Commn., 1965, Cross of Mil. Service UDC. Mem. ABA, Va. Bar Assn., S.C. Bar Assn., 15th Jud. Circuit Bar Assn. (pres. 1959-60, 69-70), Am. Judicature Soc., Am. Law Inst., Res. Officers Assn., Mil. Order World Wars, Naval Res. Assn., Nat. Soc. S.A.R., S.C. and Va. Hist. Socs., Jamestowne Soc., Am. Legion (post comdr. 1951-52), Cumberland Law Sch. Alumni Assn. (nat. pres. 1978-79, dean's council 1980-87, dean's cabinet 1987—, Disting. Alumnus award 1986), Jud. Conf. Va., Cumberland Order Jurisprudence, Hon. Order Ky. Cols., Blue Key, Sigma Delta Kappa. Episcopalian (past vestryman, warden, lay reader). Lodges: Masons, Shriners, Jesters, Kiwanis. Home: 509 Hanover St Fredericksburg VA 22401 Office: PO Drawer 29 Fredericksburg VA 22404

JAMISON, M. HENRY, chemical company executive; b. Somerville, Mass., Oct. 28, 1921; s. Harry and Sarah (Serabian) J.; m. Anna Jo Byrd, Dec. 26, 1948; children: Nancy Ellen, Carol Lee. BS in ChemE, U. Ala., 1946, MS in ChemE, 1947; MBA in Mktg., U. Chgo., 1949. Chem. sales W.R. Grace-Dearborn Div., Chgo., 1950-52; specialty sales mgr. Celanese Chem. Co., N.Y.C., 1952-60; mgr. corp. mktg. devel. Sun Oil Co., Phila., 1960-62; mktg. research and devel. mgr. Phillips Petroleum Co., Bartlesville, Okla., 1962-82; Mktg. research and develop. mgr. Saudi Basic Industries Corp., Riyadh, Saudi Arabia, 1983. Served with USN 1942-46, PTO. Recipient J.A. Burrows award Okla. State U., Stillwater, 1967. Mem. Chem. Mktg. Research Assn., Comml. Devel. Assn., Am. Mktg. Assn., Am. Chem. Soc., European Chem. Market Research Assn. Republican. Congregationalist. Home: 3408 Willowood Dr Bartlesville OK 74006 Office: Saudi Basic Industries Corp, PO 5101, Riyadh 11422, Saudi Arabia

JAMISON, MAX KILLIAN, lawyer, retired university general counsel; b. Santa Cruz, Calif., July 27, 1918; s. Max B. and Millie L. (Killian) J.; m. Mary Kathryn Thurman, Apr. 15, 1953; children—Max Killian, Michael Thurman, Matthew Robert. A.B., U. Calif., Berkeley, 1941; J.D., U. Calif., San Francisco, 1945. Bar: Calif. 1945. Assoc. Jamison and Jamison, Porterville, Calif., 1945-50; assoc. Hanna and Morton, Los Angeles, 1950-62; ptnr. McCutchen, Black, Verleger & Shea, Los Angeles, 1963-81; gen. counsel Hastings Coll. Law U. Calif., San Francisco, 1986—; mem. City Council, Porterville, Calif., 1948-50; mem. state and local govt. com. Los Angles C. of C., chmn. city subcom., 1970-71. Chmn. fin. com., exec. com., bd. dirs. Hastings Coll. Law, 1964-85; active Boy Scouts Am.; life mem. Okla. Zoo Assn., Los Angeles Zoo Assn.; mem. Audubon Soc., Calif. Wetlands and Waterfowl Program stewardship com.; mem. UN Day Dinner Com. Served with U.S. Army AC, 1940-41. Recipient Outstanding Alumni award Hastings Coll. Law, 1978. Fellow Am. Coll. Trial Lawyers; mem. ABA, Los Angeles County Bar Assn., Am. Judicature Soc., Patent Lawyers Assn., Theta Delta Chi. Republican. Episcopalian. Clubs: Ducks Unlimited; Bear River; California (Los Angeles); Lakeside Golf (North Hollywood, Calif.). Lodge: Elks. Home: 37879 Upper Rd P O Box 92 Angelus Oaks CA 92305 Office: 310 E Colorado Glendale CA 92105

JAMISON, SUSAN CLAPP, librarian; b. Pitts., Mar. 21, 1929; d. Harlan Luther and Irene Julia (Krause) Clapp; m. Robert Beatty Jamison, Dec. 19, 1947; children: Linda Jamison Larkin, Stephen Robert. BA in History and English, Coll. Staten Island, CUNY, 1971; M.A. in Am. Studies, U. Del., 1972, Am. History, 1974; MLS U. Md., 1979. Bus. asst. Dr. Robert L. Jacobson, 1960-71; real estate sales Walter Reno Watson Agy., Staten Island, N.Y., 1960-63; tchr. Dover High Sch. (Del.), 1973-75; adj. prof. Wilmington Coll., New Castle, Del., 1975—; asst. dir. Dover Pub. Library, 1980-85; dir. Corbit-Calloway Meml. Library, Odessa, Del., 1975—; grant writer Del. Humanities Forum, Wilmington, 1979-81; mem. speakers bur., 1982-83, evaluator, 1978—; pres. Central Del. Library Consortium, 1982-85. Author: The Face of a Town: the Corbit-Calloway Meml. Library, 1979; author 8 books and programs Yesterday & Today, series 1979-81; contbr. articles to profl. jours; editor and project dir., Six Tricentennial Views of Kent County, 1983-85; author, advisor A Legacy from Del. Women, 1987. Active in Odessa Women's Club, Del., 1975—; host of open house Christmas In Odessa, 1976—; founder, chmn. Septemberfest, 1982; art chmn. Del. Fed. Women's Clubs, 1980-82; publicity chmn. Kent County Tricentennial Commn., Dover, 1983. Recipient Facts on File award for reference pub. ideas, 1985. Mem. Kent Library Network (v.p. 1982-84, pres. 1984-85), Del. Library Assn. (pres. pub. library div. 1979-81, pres. 1985-86), ALA, Del. Folklife Assn. (treas. 1987—). Home: Starr-Lore House Main St Odessa DE 19730 Office: Corbit-Calloway Meml Library 2d and High Sts Odessa DE 19730

JAMORA, SYLVIA JACINTO, dermatologist; b. Manila, Nov. 5, 1939; d. Carmelo Pongco and Concepcion (Sayoc) Jacinto; m. Eduardo Magno Jamora, Jan. 2, 1965; children: Marie Therese, Gary, Maria Jasmin, Jennifer, Marietta. MD, U. Philippines Coll. Medicine, 1962. Adj. resident Dept. Internal Medicine Philippines Gen. Hosp., Manila, 1962-63, asst. resident, 1963-64; resident NYU-Bellevue Med. Ctr. Dept. Dermatology, N.Y.C., 1964-67; instr. Dept. Internal Medicine Philippine Gen. Hosp., Manila, 1967-72; dir. Philippine Dermatol. Soc., Manila, 1970-74, 79-80, pres., 1975-76, 77-78; founder, treas. J&J Med. Clinics, Inc., Makati, 1976—; clin. prof. Dermatology, Skin and Cancer Found., Inc.; cons. dermatologist Med. Ctr. Manila, 1967-87, U.S. Embassy, 1968—, Cardinal Santos Meml. Hosp., Mandaluyong, 1975—, St. Martin de Porres Charity Hosp., San Juan, 1980—, Can. Embassy, 1986—. Editor, founder Philippine Jour. Dermatology and Dermatologic Surgery, 1979; contbg. editor Diseases of the Skin, 1977, 82, 88, Textbook of Pediatrics and Child Health. Pres. White Plains Ladies' Assn., Quezon City, 1976-77; mem. Manila chpt. Zonta Internat., 1976-84, Manila Mahikari Okiyomesho Ctr., 1984—. Recipient Enrile Award of Distinction Philippine Bd. Med. Examiners, 1962. Fellow Am. Acad. Dermatology; mem. Internat. Soc. Dermatol. Surgery (mem. adv. bd. Philippines 1978—), Pacific Dermatol. Assn., Am. Soc. Dermatol. Surgery, Soc. Investigative Dermatology, Philippine Bd. Dermatology (chmn. 1970-74, 79-81), Skin and Cancer Found. Inc. (pres., co-founder, exec. dir. 1984—), Dermatology Found. (Century mem. 1982—), Am. Coll. Cryosurgery (corr. mem. 1978—), Internat. Soc. Pediatric Dermatology, NRC of Philippines (assoc. mem. 1977—), Philippine Med. Assn. (life), Philippine Soc. Cryosurgery (v.p. 1985—). Roman Catholic. Clubs: Makati Sports (Manila); Valley Golf (Cainta); Palicpican Sports and Country (Ternate). Office: Skin Clinic, 1311 Batangas St, Makati Philippines

JAN, ALI RAZA, physician; b. Rawalpindi, Pakistan, Aug. 11, 1936; s. Aziz Ahmed and Iqbal Begum; m. Shamin Ara, May 20, 1961; children: Hassan Raza, Ahmed Raza, Aliya Raza. MB BS in Gynecology-Midwifery honors, Nishtar Med. Coll., Pakistan, 1960. Med. officer Cen. Govt. Hosp., Rawalpindi, 1960-61, resident med. officer, 1961-62; practicing medicine specializing in gen. medicine Rawalpindi, 1963—; med. adviser Pakistan Atomic Energy Commn., 1964—, Oil and Gas Devel. Corp., Rawalpingi, 1966—; med. dir. Aziz Nursing Home, Rawalpingi, 1970—, Diagnostic Ctr., Rawalpindi, 1986—; panel physician Am. Embassy, Islamabad, Pakistan, 1981—; techm. med. adviser to U.S. immigrants, Islamabad, 1981—. Mem. Pakistan Med. Assn. Lodge: Lions (med. adviser Rawalpingi). Home: 36-A Satellite Town, Tawalpindi Pakistan Office: Aziz Nursing Home, Saidpur Rd, Rawalpindi Pakistan

JANACEK, BEDRICH, organist; b. Prague, Czechoslovakia, May 18, 1920; s. Bedrich Frantisek and Marie (Rausova) J.; soloist examination in organ idem, State Conservatory of Music, Prague, 1942, master class for organ, 1945-46, diploma ex., 1946; Choir Master degree, Royal High Music Sch., Stockholm, 1961; m. Elisabet Wentz, Jan. 1, 1951. Organist various concerts, Europe, U.S.A., 1942—, including Royal Festival Hall, London, other concert halls in Eng., Belgium, Czechoslovakia, Germany, Italy and Sweden; also soloist with orchs.; also recs.; tchr. organ State Conservatory of Music, Prague, 1946-48; parish musician Cathedral Parish, Lund, Sweden, 1965-85. Recipient City of Lund cultural prize, 1980. Composer organ compositions and choral works including 2 cantatas with orch., compositions for brass and organ. Home: Kyrkogatan 17, Lund Sweden

JANAS, LUDOVIC JOSEPH, computer specialist, management consultant; b. Lodz, Poland, Aug. 31, 1926; s. Wojciech and Apolonia (Tengowska) J.; BA with honors, Univ. Coll., Cork, Ireland, 1951; postgrad. Birkbeck Coll., U. London, 1955-60; children—Caroline, Anne, Lucille, Michael, Karen, Nicola. Statistician N. Brit. & Mercantile Ins. Co. Ltd., London, 1952-60; chief programmer Comml. Union Assurance Co. Ltd., London and Exeter, Eng., 1960-64; with Wiggins Teape Ltd., London, 1964-72, group systems mgr., 1970-72; dir. computing and mgmt. services King's Coll. Hosp., London, 1972-73; Phoenix Assurance plc, Bristol, Eng., 1973-86, data processing mgr., 1973-83, mgmt. services mgr., 1984-86; computer mgr. Sun Alliance Group, 1984-86; exec. IBM Computer Users Assn., 1986-87; cons. in field. Fellow Royal Statis. Soc., Brit. Computer Soc.; mem. Brit. Inst. Mgmt., Royal Inst. Philosophy, Brit. Ins. Assn. (computer research panel and data protection com.), Assn. Brit. Insurers, Confedn. Brit. Industry (data protection com.). Home: Wint Hill House, Wint Hill, Banwell, Avon BS24 6NN, England

JANČAR, DRAGO, writer, editor; b. Maribor, Slovenia, Yugoslavia, Apr. 13, 1948; s. Anton and Rozalija (Trantura) J.; m. Olga Čerič, Aug. 15, 1970; 1 child, Mateja. Law degree, U. Maribor, 1971. Journalist Večer, Maribor, 1971-74; free-lance writer Maribor, 1974-79; dramaturgist Viba Film, Ljubljana, Yugoslavia, 1979-80; editor Slovene Lit. Soc., Ljubljana, 1980—, Nova Revija, Ljubljana, 1983. Author: (novels) Galley Slave, 1978 (award 1979), Polar Lights, 1984, (short stories) Death at Mary-of-the-Snows, 1984, (plays) The Great Brilliant Waltz, 1984 (award 1985), Daedalus, 1987, After Godot, 1988. Recipient Prešeren Found. prize, 1979, Sterija prize Yugoslav Theatre Festival, 1982; Fulbright fellow, Washington, 1984. Mem. Slovene Writers Assn. Home: Mivka 32, 61 000 Ljubljana, Slovenia Yugoslavia Office: Slovenska Matica, Trg Osvoboditve 7, 61 000 Ljubljana, Slovenia Yugoslavia

JANECEK, LENORE ELAINE, insurance specialist, consultant; b. Chgo., May 2, 1944; d. Morris and Florence (Bear) Picker; M.A.J. in Speech Communications (talent scholar), Northeastern Ill. U., 1972; postgrad. (Ill. Assn. C. of C. Execs. scholar) Inst. for Organizational Mgmt., U. Notre Dame, 1979-80; M.B.A., Columbia Pacific U., 1982; cert. in C. of C. mgmt. U. Colo., 1982; m. John Janecek, Sept. 12, 1964; children—Frank, Michael. Adminstrv. asst., exec. dir. Ill. Mcpl. Retirement Fund, Chgo., 1963-65; personnel mgr. Profile Personnel, Chgo., 1965-68; personnel rep. Marsh Instrument Co., Skokie, Ill., 1971-73; restaurant mgt. Gold Mine Restaurant and What's Cooking Restaurant, Chgo., 1974-76; pres., owner Secretarial Office Services, Chgo., 1976-78; founder, pres. Lincolnwood (Ill.) C. of C. and Industry, 1978-87; pres. Lenore E. Janecek & Assocs., Lincolnwood, 1987—; rep. 10th dist. U.S. C. of C., 1978—. Mem. mktg. bd. Niles Twp. Sheltered Workshop; pres. Lincolnwood Sch. Dist. 74 Sch. Bd. Caucus; bd. mem., officer, founder Ill. Fraternal Order Police Ladies Aux.; bd. dirs., officer Lincolnwood Girl's Softball League, PTA; bd. dirs. United Way, 1982-83; mem. sch. curriculum com. Lincolnwood Bd. Edn. Recipient Disting. Grad. of Yr. Nat. Honor Soc., 1985. Mem. Am. C. of C. Execs., Ill. Assn. C. of C. Execs., Women in Mgmt. (local officer), Nat. Assn. Female Execs., Am. Notary Soc., Ill. LWV, Nat. Council Jewish Women, Hadassah. Jewish. Home: 6707 N Monticello St Lincolnwood IL 60645 Office: 4433 W Touhy Suite 550 Lincolnwood IL 60646

JANES, ROBERT HARRISON, JR., surgeon; b. Little Rock, Nov. 13, 1939; s. Robert Harrison and Fahy Helen (Mathers) J.; B.S., U. Ark., 1965, M.D., 1965; m. Patricia Mayes, June 30, 1962; children—Robert, Clayton, Matthew. Intern surgery U. Ark. Hosps., Little Rock, 1965-66, resident surgery, 1966-70; practice medicine, specializing in surgery Holt-Krock Clinic, Fort Smith, Ark., 1972—; mem. staff Sparks Regional Med. Center, chief surgery, 1977-78, 1982-83; mem. staff St. Edwards Mercy Med. Center; instr. surgery U. Ark., Little Rock, 1969-70, asst. clin. prof. surgery, 1976—. Pres. Sebastian County (Ark.) unit Am. Cancer Soc., 1975-76, bd. dirs. Ark. div., pres. Ark. div., 1978-79, 81-82, nat. bd. dirs., 1982—; bd. dirs. Ft. Smith Symphony, 1979-83 , treas., 1980-82, pres., 1982-83; bd. dirs. Broadway Theatre League Ft. Smith, 1981-84. Served to maj., M.C., USAF, 1970-72. Diplomate Am. Bd. Surgery. Fellow ACS (commn. on cancer 1983—, vice chmn. 1987—), Southwestern Surg. Congress, Western Surg. Assn., 1987—; mem. AMA, Western Sug. Assn., Ark. Med. Soc., Lambda Chi Alpha. Methodist (adminstrv. bd. 1974-77). Clubs: Hardscrabble Country, Fort Smith Racquet; Red Apple Country (Eden Isle, Ark.); Oaklawn Jockey (Hot Springs, Ark.). Contbr. articles to profl. jours. Home: 3707 Old Oaks Ln Fort Smith AR 72903 Office: 1500 Dodson Ave Fort Smith AR 72901

JANGER, ALLEN ROBERT, research organization executive; b. Chgo., Sept. 5, 1932; s. Max and Myrtle Florence (Levy) J.; A.B., U. Chgo., 1952; postgrad. (English Speaking Union scholar) London Sch. Econs., 1955-56; m. Inez Kurn, Sept. 11, 1960; children—Edward, Matthew, Michael. Research assoc. The Conf. Bd., N.Y.C., 1960-65, dir. info. services, 1965-68, sr. research specialist, 1968-75, sr. research assoc. orgn. devel. research, 1975-81, dir. mgmt. research, 1981-82, exec. dir. mgmt. system group, 1982-86, dir. internat. council on orgn. and mgmt., 1984—. Served with U.S. Army, 1957-59; ETO. Author: Matrix Organization of Complex Businesses, 1979, Organization of International Joint Ventures, 1980, External Challenges to Management Decisions, 1981, The Organizing of a Financial Services Company, 1988, (series) The Conference Board Management Outlook. Home: 19 Buena Vista Dr Hastings on Hudson NY 10706 Office: 845 3d Ave New York NY 10022

JANICKI, ROBERT STEPHEN, pharmaceutical company executive; b. Manette, Wash., Dec. 7, 1934; s. Stephen Walter and Elizabeth Caroline (Gorman) J.; m. I. Jane Betcher, Aug. 18, 1956; children: Robert, Beth, David. B.S., Grove City Coll., 1956; M.D., Temple U., 1961. Diplomate: Nat. Bd. Med. Examiners. Intern U.S. Naval Hosp., Phila., 1961-62; resident in occupational medicine USN, 1962-63; assoc. dir. clin. research Dow Pharms., Indpls., 1966-68; assoc. med. dir. Neisler div. Union Carbide Corp., Sterling Forest, N.Y., 1968-69; assoc. med. dir. regulatory affairs Abbott Labs., North Chicago, Ill., 1969-70; dir. clin. research pharm. products div. Abbott Labs., 1970-71, v.p. med. affairs pharm. products div., 1971-79, v.p. research pharm. products div., 1979-83, corp. v.p. research and devel. pharm. products div., 1983—. Contbr. articles profl. to jours. Served to lt. comdr., M.C. USN, 1961-66. Fellow Am. Coll. Clin. Pharm.; mem. Am. Soc. Clin. Pharmacology and Therapeutics, N.Y. Acad. Scis., Inst. Medicine Chgo., Coll. Physicians of Phila., Sigma Xi, Alpha Omega Alpha. Home: 801 Hawthorne Ln Libertyville IL 60048 Office: Abbott Labs 14th St Sheridan Rd North Chicago IL 60064

JANICKI, RYSZARD BOGUSLAW, computer science educator, researcher; b. Wroclaw, Poland, Nov. 24, 1951; s. Walenty and Helena (Kuznicka) J.; M. Maria Anna Maroszek, Oct. 14, 1975; children: Marek, Maciej. MSc, Warsaw Tech. U., 1975; PhD, Polish Acad. Scis., 1977, D.Habil., 1980. Demonstrator Inst. Math. Warsaw Tech. U., Poland, 1975-77, asst. prof., 1977-81, assoc. prof., 1981-86; vis. prof. Aalborg U. Ctr., Denmark, 1984-86, McMaster U., Hamilton, Ont., Can., 1986-87, assoc. prof. dept. computer sci. and systems, 1987—. Cons. Inst. Orgn. for Machine Industry, Warsaw, 1976-81; sr. vis. research fellow U. Newcastle Upon Tyne, Computing Lab., Eng., 1982; mem. Sci. Council Inst. Math. Warsaw Tech. U., 1980-86. Contbr. articles to profl. jours. on theoretical computer sci. (awards Polish Minister of Sci. High Edn. and Tech., 1978, 81). Mem. Assn. for Computing Machinery, Polish Math. Soc., Am. Math. Soc., European Assn. for Theoretical Computer Sci. Roman Catholic. Avocations: travelling, books, films, yachting. Office: McMaster U, Dept Computer Sci and Systems, 1280 Main St W, Hamilton, ON Canada L8S 4K1

JANIW, WOLODYMYR, university rector; b. Lwiw, Ukraine, Nov. 21, 1908; s. Osyp and Eleonore (Bilecka) J.; Licentiate in Philosophy, U. Lwiw, 1934; Ph.D., Friedrich Wilhelms U., Berlin, 1944; Dr. phil. habil., Ukrainian Free U., Munich, W. Ger., 1949; m. Sophie Moyseowycz, Sept. 27, 1939. Editor, Ukrainian Students Monthly, 1932-34, Nash Klych, weekly, Lwiw, 1933; in exile, 1939—; mem. faculty Ukrainian Free U., 1946—, prof. psychology and sociology, 1956—, rector, 1968-86; gen. sec. Shevchenko Sci. Soc., 1952-68, v.p., 1968-85, pres. 1985-87; mem. sci. council Arbeits und Förderungsgemeinschaft der Ukrainischen Wissenschaften, 1963—, pres., 1979, trustee, 1973-79. Mem. Ukrainian Nat. Com., 1941; founder, 1st pres. Ukrainian Christian Movement, 1953. Decorated comdr. St. Gregory Pontifical Order Vatican, 1964; named hon. citizen Winnipeg, Man., Can., 1971. Mem. gen. council Union Catholique Internat. de la Presse, 1957-72; bd. dirs. Fedn. Internat. des Hommes Catholiques Unum Omnes, 1967—; chief Ukrainian dels. 2d and 3d congresses Cath. Laymen, Rome, 1957, 67. Mem. Berufsverband der Deutschen Psychologen, Acad. Internat. des Scis. et des Lettres, Deutsche Gesellschaft Psychologie, Soc. Sci. Theologica Ucrainorum, Inst. d'études slaves, La Real Acad. Hispano-Americana, Freier Deutscher Autorenverband, PEN-Club, World Literary Acad. Author: Outline of Ukrainian Civilization, 2d edit., 1961; Religion in the Life of the Ukrainian People, 1966; Studies and Materials on Modern Ukrainian History, 1970 (in Ukrainian), Vol. II, 1983; Ukrainische Freie Universitä t, 1976, also author 4 vols. of Ukrainian poetry. Home: 29 rue des Bauves, 95200 Sarcelles France Office: 15 Peinzenauerstrasse, 8000 Munich 80 Federal Republic of Germany

JANJUA, BRIAN, pharmaceutical company executive; b. Rawalpindi, Punjab, Pakistan, Aug. 25, 1948; s. Anthony P. and Josephine (Raja) J.; m. Phillipa Drago, Dec. 27, 1975; children: Shane, Adrian. BA, Punjab U., Lahore, 1971; MBA, Inst. Bus. Adminstrn., Karachi, Pakistan, 1978. Tchr. Burn Hall Sch., Abbottabad, Pakistan, 1969-71; sales rep. State Life Ins. Corp. of Pakistan, Karachi, 1972-73; mktg. research cons. Nasiruddin & Assocs. Ltd., Karachi, 1974-75; account exec. Asiatic Advt. Ltd., Karachi, 1976-77, Internat. Advt. Ltd., Karachi, 1978-79; mgr. sales Bayer Pharma Ltd., Karachi, 1980-83; gen. mgr., chief exec. officer for Pakistan W. Woodward Pak Ltd., Karachi, 1983—. Active Contraceptive Social Mktg. Project in Pakistan, Karachi. Mem. Pakistan Mgmt. Assn., Mktg. Assn. Pakistan. Home: 249 Catholic Colony No 1, Karachi 74800, Pakistan Office: W Woodward Pakistan Ltd, F 275 SITE, Karachi Pakistan

JANKLOW, MORTON LLOYD, lawyer, literary agent; b. N.Y.C., May 30, 1930; s. Maurice and Lillian (Levantin) J.; m. Linda Mervyn LeRoy, Nov. 27, 1960; children: Angela LeRoy, Lucas Warner. A.B., Syracuse U., 1950; J.D., Columbia U., 1953. Bar: N.Y. 1953, D.C. 1959, U.S. Supreme Ct 1959. Sr. partner Janklow & Traum, N.Y.C., 1967—; chmn., chief exec. officer Morton L. Janklow Assocs., Inc. (lit. agy.), 1977—; bd. dirs. Orbis Communications, Inc., N.Y.C.; bd. dirs., mem. finance com. McCaffrey & McCall, Inc., N.Y.C., 1962-87; chmn. exec. com. Harvey Group, Inc., N.Y.C., 1968-71, Cable Funding Corp., N.Y.C., 1971-73; mem. exec. com. Sloan Commn. Cable Communications, 1970-71; Andrew Wellington Cordier fellow Columbia U. Sch. Internat. Affairs; vis. lectr. Radcliffe Coll., Columbia Law Sch., NYU; bus. and fin. adv. bd. NYU Press and NYU Sch. Arts, 1977—; life mem. Harlan Fiske Stone Fellowship of Columbia U. Law Sch.; founder Morton L. Janklow Program for Advocacy in Arts, Columbia U. Law Sch. Bd. dirs., exec. com., devel. chmn. City Center Music and Drama, 1971-75; bd. dirs. Film Soc., Lincoln Ctr., 1972-75, Am. Cinematheque, 1971-75; bd. govs. Jewish Mus., 1969-75; dir., chmn. Janklow Found.; trustee Mr. and Mrs. Harry M. Warner Found., 1965—, Jorja and Sidney Sheldon Found.; mem. Council of Friends, Whitney Mus. Am. Art, 1973-82, also mem. com. on paintings and sculptures; bd. advisors Princeton U. Art. Mus.; mem. adv. bd. Guggenheim Mus.; adv. council Sch. Arts, NYU; mem. Ind. Com. on Arts Policy; bd. advisors Columbia U. Jour. Art and the Law. Served with AUS, 1953-55. Mem. Assn. Bar City N.Y. (membership com. 1967—), N.Y. County Lawyers Assn., N.Y. State, Am., Fed. Communications bar assns., Am. Judicature Soc., Council on Fgn. Relations. Home: 32 E 64th St New York NY 10021 Office: 598 Madison Ave New York NY 10022

JANKOVIC, BRANIMIR (MIODRAG), educator, lawyer; b. Valjevo, Yugoslavia, Nov. 13, 1920; s. Miodrag and Ljubica (Ivkovic) J.; m. Bordjoski, Mar. 27, 1944; 1 child, Nada. JD, PhD, U. Belgrade, Yugoslavia, 1950. Prof. internat. law U. Sarajevo, Yugoslavia, 1948-60; prof. U. Belgrade, 1960—; adj. prof. Fla. State U., Tallahassee, 1974-84; mem. legal adv. council Yugoslavian Govt., 1967-69. Author: Contemporary International Law Topics, 1953, An Introduction to Contemporary Public International Law, 1953, International Law (essays), 1953, Manual of Public International Law, 1958, 60, International Law, Belgrade, 1970, 73, 81, Public International Law, New York, 1984; contbr. articles to profl. jours. Rep. Commn. of UN on Human Rights, 1967-74; mem., vice chmn. UN Spl. Bd. Legal Experts, 1967—; pres. Yugoslav Permanent Conf. Rectors, 1967-70; mem. exec. conf. European Permanent Conf. Rectors, Geneva, 1968-71; mem. Fed. Council Edn. and Culture, 1966-72; mem. Yugoslav Nat. Commn. of UNESCO, 1967-75; dep. Yugoslav Fed. Assembly, 1966-69. Decorated Order of Republic of Yugoslavia. Mem. Internat. Law Assn. (London), Am. Soc. Internat. Law. Office: 165 Jove Ilica Str, Belgrade Yugoslavia

JANKOW, ROBERT, career continuation and hi-tech product distribution consultant; b. N.Y.C., Oct. 4, 1941; arrived at Switzerland, 1964, dual U.S.-Swiss citizen; s. Jack Aaron and Sylvia (Levenson) J.; m. Anne-Marie (Jankow) Knecht, June 8, 1969; children: Joel, Danielle. BS, Rensselaer Poly. Inst., 1962; MS, Swiss Fed. Inst. Tech., Zurich, 1965, PhD, 1968. Research chemist Geigy Chem. Corp., Ardsley, N.Y., 1963-64; sr. applications engr. Cary Instruments div. Varian Assocs., Monrovia, Calif., 1968-71; asst. gen. mgr. Orbisphere Labs., Geneva, 1971-73; pres., founder, dir. Instrumatic S.A., Geneva, 1973-86; pres. Dr. R. Jankow-Consultants, Geneva, 1986—; v.p. Geneva, D.B.M. Europe, 1987—; cons. Charles River Data Systems, Boston, 1987—; bd. dirs. Internat. Growth Funds Mgmt., Neuchatel, Switzerland. Author: Polarization Spectra of Non-Aromatic Compounds, 1968; also articles in English, French, German and Japanese profl. jours. Pres. Am. Students Assn., Zurich, 1967-68; mem. honor com. Amis Suisse de Pugwash, Geneva, 1982-85. Swiss Fed. Inst. Tech. fellow, 1965-68; postgrad. fellow NYU, 1969. Mem. Schweizer Elektronik Verein, Swiss-Am. C. of C., Brit. Am. C. of C., Swiss Chem. Soc., Ohio Gun Collectors' Soc. Club: Geneva Yacht. Office: DBM Europe (Switzerland), 45 rue de Lausanne, CH 1201 Geneva Switzerland

JANNE, ERKKI JUHANI, biochemist, educator; b. Kotka, Finland, Oct. 16, 1941; s. Erkki Anders and Tuovi Tellervo (Kunnas) J.; m. Sirpa Sylvikki Kotilainen, Nov. 28, 1964; children—Sami Pekka, Paivi Tellervo, Marja Sylvikki. M.D., U. Helsinki, 1966, D.Med. Scis., 1967. Instr. U. Helsinki, Finland, 1964-72, assoc. prof. biochemistry, 1974-87, acting chmn. dept. biochemistry, 1978-81; prof. biotech. U. Kuopio, Finland, 1988—; vis. scientist U. Chgo., 1969-71; vis. scholar U. Wash., Seattle, 1983; med. adviser, med. dir. Ciba Geigy, Helsinki, 1968—. Contbr. numerous articles, chpts. on basic biochemistry and cancer research to profl. jours. Editorial adviser or referee for 15 internat. biochemistry and cancer research jours. Mem. Biochem. Soc. (London). Office: U Kuopio Dept Biochemistry, PO Box 6, SF-70211 Kuopio Finland

JANNEN, ROBERT LAWRENCE, communications company executive; b. N.Y.C., May 3, 1927; s. John and Emma (Wilson) J.; m. Dolores Shegelski, Dec. 22, 1945; children—Robert, Judith Jannen Perry. B.S. in Chem. Engring., Tri-State U., 1950, LL.D., 1975; M.B.A., UCLA, 1961. Engr., C.F. Braun Co., Los Angeles, 1950-52; sales mgr. Fansteel Metall. Corp., Chgo., 1952-55, AMF Corp., Los Angeles, 1955—; pres. Leach Corp., Los Angeles, 1959-75, also dir.; pres. John Blue Co., Huntsville, Ala., 1975—, R.L. Jannen Cons. Co.; pres., dir. Subscription TV Inc., N.Y.C., 1975—, Burnley Corp., Huntsville; lectr. numerous univs.; chmn. bd. Corona Corp. Corona Calif., also dir.; bd. dirs. Othy Corp., Warsaw, Ind., dir. LRE Inc., Munich, Germany, Leach Corp., Los Angeles, Ashlock Mfg., San Francisco, Levin and Son, Los Angeles. Contbr. numerous articles to trade publs.; patentee in field. Pres., West Covina (Calif.) Little League, South Hills Homeowners Assn.; exec. council Boy Scouts Am.; bd. dirs. Huntsville Boys Club, 1978—; trustee, chmn. bd. Tri-State U., Multiple Sclerosis Soc. Served with AUS, 1943-46. Certified profl. mgr. Mem. Farm Equipment Mfrs. Assn., Nat. Fertilizer Inst., Nat. Fertilizer Solutions Assn., Electronic Engrs. Assn., Internat. Rocket Soc., Am. Mktg. Assn., Sales Execs. Club, C. of C. of Los Angeles, Newcomen Soc., U. Calif., Tri-State U. Alumni Assns., Skull and Bones, Tau Sigma Psi. Republican. Clubs: Huntsville Country, Los Angeles Athletic, Masons, Elks, Moose. Home: 6775 Grandola Dr Las Vegas NV 89103 Office: PO Box 1607 Huntsville AL 35807

JANOVER, ROBERT H., lawyer; b. N.Y.C., Aug. 17, 1930; s. Cyrus J. and Lillian D. (Horwitz) J.; B.A., Princeton U., 1952; J.D., Harvard U., 1957; m. Mary Elizabeth McMahon, Oct. 23, 1966; 1 dau., Laura Lockwood. Admitted to N.Y. State bar, 1957, U.S. Supreme Ct. bar, 1961, D.C. bar, 1966, Mich. bar, 1973; practice law, N.Y.C., 1957-65; cons. Office of Edn. HEW, 1965, legis. atty. Office of Gen. Counsel, HEW, 1965-66; asst. gen. atty. Mgmt. Assistance Inc., N.Y.C., 1966-71; atty. Ford Motor Credit Co., Dearborn, Mich., 1971-74; mem. firm Freud, Markus, Slavin, Toohey & Galgan, Troy, Mich., 1974-79; sole practice law, Detroit, 1979—, Bloomfield Hills, Mich., 1982—. Bd. dirs. Oakland Citizens League, 1976—, v.p., 1976-79, pres., 1979—; bd. dirs. Civic Searchlight, 1979—. Served to 1st lt. U.S. Army, 1952-54. Mem. Mich. State Bar, Am., N.Y. State, Detroit bar assns., Bar Assn. D.C., Assn. Bar of City of N.Y. Clubs: Players (Detroit), City (Bloomfield Hills), Harvard (N.Y.C.). Home: 685 Ardmoor Dr Birmingham MI 48010 Office: 860 West Long Lake Rd Suite 200 Bloomfield Hills MI 48013

JANOWITZ, GUNDULA, opera singer; b. Berlin, Aug. 2, 1937; d. Theodor and Else (Neumann) J.; married; 1 dau. Ed., Acad. Music and Performing Arts, Graz, Austria. Debut with Vienna State Opera (Austria); now mem. Vienna State Opera, Deutsche Oper, Berlin; appearances with Deutsche Oper, Berlin, 1966, Met. Opera, N.Y.C., 1967, Teatro Colón, Buenos Aires, Argentina, 1970; Munich State Opera (W.Ger.), 1971, Grand Opera, Paris, 1973, Covent Garden Opera, 1976, La Scala, 1978; concert appearances in maj. cities throughout the world; appeared at Bayreuth, Aix-en-Provence, Glyndebourne, Spoleto, Salzurg, Munich festivals; rec. artist Deutsche Grammophon, EMI, Decca. Office: care Wiener Staatsoper, 1010 Vienna, Opernring 2 Austria *

JANOWSKI, THADDEUS MARIAN, architect; b. Cracow, Poland, Aug. 16, 1923; came to U.S., 1960, naturalized, 1972; s. Stanislaw and Maria (Kijak) J.; m. Zofia K. Owinski, Apr. 19, 1949 (div.); 1 child, Barbara Margaret. MCP in Architecture, Poly. Acad., Cracow, 1949; MArch, U. Ill., 1962; PhD (hon.), Inst. Three Dimensional Perception, 1987. Chief architect Miastoprojekt Cracow, 1949-58; chief cons. So. Poland K.U.A., Warsaw, 1958-60; lectr. Poly Acad. Cracow, 1947-50, 1958-60; instr. U. Ill., 1960-62; assoc. prof. U. Man., Can., 1962-65, Iowa State U., Ames, 1965-71; prof. Syracuse U., N.Y., 1971—; pres. Inst. Three Dimensional Perception, Inc., 1985; chief architect for Saudi royal family estates, Ga., 1983—. Numerous exhbns. in U.S. and Europe, 1961—; built over 6 million sq. ft. constrn. commns. include Interstate Farm Devel., Des Moines, 1967, Settlement of town houses, East Des Moines, 1969. Co-author: Sacred Art in Poland, 1955; The Urban Scale, 1968. Patentee in field. Recipient numerous prizes nat. or internat. competitions including prize Polish Embassy bldg., Peking, China, 1955, 1st prize Polish Pavillion, Brussels, Belgium, 1956, 1st prize astronomy obs. and planetarium Warsaw, 1956, award exptl. bldg., Moscow, 1959, 1st prize sch. bldgs., Poland, 1960, prize Red Rock Hill Devel., San Francisco, 1961, 2d prize campus, Dublin, Ireland, 1964, 1st prize Olympic Stadium, Banff, Can., 1962, 2d and 3rd prizes fall out shelters Office Civil Defense, 1964, 2d prize, 1966; 1st prize Bicentennial medal Iowa, 1972; 1st prize for U.S. Stamp Copernicus Quincentennial; 1st prize and commn. for monument commemorating victims of Katyn Massacre, Toronto, 1979, Syracuse, N.Y., 1985. Mem. Assn. Polish Architects, Assn. Painters, Sculptors and Artists in Poland, Assn. Scientists Hist. Armament, Canadian Assn. U. Tchrs., Nat. Rifle Assn.

JANSEN, HANS PETER, shipping executive; b. Neuss, Fed. Republic Germany, Sept. 2, 1929; s. Peter and Sofia (Effenberger) J.; m. Gerda Jansen Hummelt, May 1, 1956; children: Jan Joerg, Petra Gertraud, Gepa Marion. Grad., Comml. Coll., Dusseldorf, Fed. Republic Germany, 1949; PhD in Bus Adminstrn., Kennedy Western U., 1987. Trainee Gesellschaft fur Getreidehandel AG, Dusseldorf, 1949-51, mgmt. asst., 1951-56; gen. mgr. Deutsche Tradax GmbH, Hamburg, Fed. Republic Germany, 1956-68; chief exec. Hens Futter GmbH, Grossauheim, Fed. Republic Germany, 1968-72, Rhenania GmbH, Mannheim, Fed. Republic Germany, 1972-87; mem. exec. bd. Kuehne and Nagel, AG, Luxemburg, 1988—; mem. mgmt. bd. Kuehne and Nagel Internat., AG, Pfäffikon, Switzerland, 1988—; bd. dirs. several German cos. Author: Development of Container Shipping, 1986. Editor Archiv East German Genealogists, Herne, Fed. Republic Germany, 1955—. Club: Rotary (pres. 1983-84). Office: Kuehne and Nagel Internat AG, C-8808 Pfaffikon Switzerland

JANSEN, ISABEL, civic worker; b. Phlox, Wis., May 26, 1906; d. Mose A. and Clara K. J.; RN, Marquette U., Milw., 1927. Surg. asst. to prof. oral and maxillofacial surgery Marquette U., 1927-52; ret., 1954; chmn. Antigo Freedom Com., 1960—. Recipient Liberty award Congress of Freedom, Inc., annually 1972-78, Keeper of the Flame award Woman Constitutionalist, 1974, cert. of appreciation Nat. Police Officers Assn. Am., 1973, Spl. award for Service to Nursing Marquette U. Nurses Alumni Assn., 1987. Roman Catholic. Research on heart deaths in Antigo, Wis., 1974; research on cancer deaths in Antigo, 1930-80; inventor Jansen Ray Pen, 1947. Home: 608 Gowan Rd Antigo WI 54409

JANSHEKAR, HOSSEIN, company executive, biotechnologist, consultant; b. Teheran, Iran, Dec. 30, 1947; came to Switzerland, 1973; s. Mohammad Janshekar and Safieh Mohtaj. B.Sc. in Chem. Engring., Arya-Mehr U. of Tech., Teheran, 1972; D. Tech. Scis., Inst. Biotech., Swiss Fed. Inst. Tech., Zurich, 1979; BBA, 1988. Lab. asst. Lab. of Imperial Air Force Hosp., Teheran, 1971-72; research scientist Biochem. Bioenviron. Research Ctr., Teheran, 1972-73; research assoc., dept. biotech. Swiss Fed. Inst. Tech., Zurich, 1974-79, project mgr., 1979-82; asst. v.p. Petrogenetic AG, Zurich, 1982-85; pres. Petrotec Systems AG, Zurich, 1985-86; vice chmn. Inst. Biotech., Zurich, 1986-88; mgr. SRI Internat., Zurich, 1988—; bd. dirs. Petrotec Holdings AG, Zurich, Jojoba Mgmt. AG, Biel, Switzerland; dir. European br. Centurion Capital Corp., Zurich, Switzerland. Contbr. articles to profl. jours. Served to lt. Iranian Air Force, 1971-72. Mem. Swiss Soc. for Microbiology, Fachgruppe fü r Verfahrens und Chemieingeneiur Technik, Am. Chem. Soc., Amnesty Internat. Avocations: tennis; skiing; swimming; jogging. Home: Grosswiesenstrasse 167, 8051 Zurich Switzerland Office: SRI Internat, Pelikanstrasse 37, 8001 Zurich Switzerland

JANSSENS, MARK HENDRIK LEO, sales executive; b. Antwerp, Belgium, Jan. 31, 1943; s. Leo Janssens and Octavy De Maeyer; m. An Hoppenbrouwers, Mar. 25, 1966; children: Dieter, Jeroen, Sofie. Degree in electronics and nuclear physics engring., RHIK, Mol, Belgium, 1965. Tech. dept. Kinshasa (Zaire) U., 1966-69; lab. supr. Zairese Telecom, Kinshasa, 1969-71; devel. engr. Bell Telephone Mfg. Co., Antwerp, 1972-73; sales engr. Hewlett Packard Belgium, Brussels, 1973-80, sales mgr., 1980-83, support mgr., 1983-84, software mgr., 1984-85; sales mgr. internat. Delaware Computing, Antwerp, 1985—. Home: De Gilmanstraat 17, 2100 Deurne Belgium Office: Delaware Computing, Noordersingel 28, 2200 Borgerhout Belgium

JANSSON, JOHN PHILLIP, architect, consultant; b. Phila., Nov. 27, 1918; s. John A. and Isabelle (Ericson) J.; B.Arch., Pratt Inst., 1947; postgrad. SUNY, 1949; m. Ann C. Winter, Apr. 8, 1944 (div. Oct. 1970); children—Linda Ann, Lora Joan; m. 2d, Elizabeth Clow Peer, Jan. 21, 1978 (dec. May 1984). Architect for various firms, 1949-54; pvt. practice architecture, N.Y.C., 1949—; cons. mktg. of products, materials and services to bldg. and constrn. industry, 1949—; exec. v.p. Archtl. Aluminum Mfrs. Assn., N.Y.C., 1954-58; mgr. market devel. Olin-Metals Div., N.Y.C., 1958-62; dir. Pope, Evans & Robbins, cons. engrs., 1970-82; partner Morris Ketchum, Jr. and Assocs., Architects, 1964-68; exec. dir. N.Y. State Council on Architecture, 1968-73, Associated 1973-74; dir. Gruzen and Partners, Architects Planners, Engineers, 1972-74; pres. Bldg. Constrn. Tech., 1975-78; v.p. The Ehrenkrantz Group, Architects Club: Planners, 1974-82; dir. U.S. trade mission leader to Nigeria, Dept. Commerce, 1981; cons. N.Y. State Pure Waters Authority, 1968-69; chmn. N.Y. State Architecture-Constrn. Interagy. Com., 1968-74; sec. N.Y. State Gov.'s Adv. Com. for State Constrn. Programs, 1970-71. Mem. N.Y. State Citizens Com. Pub. Schs., 1952-55; v.p. citizens adv. com. Housing Authority, Town Oyster Bay, N.Y., 1966-68; bd. dirs. Bldg. Industry Data Adv. Council, 1976-78, Park-Ten Coop., 1981-82; instr. Outward Bound, Hurricane Island, Rockland, Maine, 1982—; media specialist The Image Ctr. Am's. Cup, 1987. Served to capt. USMCR, 1943-46. Registered architect, N.Y.; lic. Nat. Council Archtl. Registration Bds. operator/navigator passenger-carrying vessels, U.S. Coast Guard. Mem. AIA (architects in govt. com. 1971-77), Am. Arbitration Assn., Constrn. Specification Inst., Nat. Inst. Archtl. Edn., BRAB Bldg. Research Inst., Nat. Inst. Bldg. Scis., Archtl. League N.Y., N.Y. Bldg. Congress, N.Y. State Assn. Architects (dir.), Soc. Archtl. Historians, Nat. Trust for Historic Preservation, Mus. Modern Art, Victorian Soc. Am., Associated Council Arts, Am. Mgmt. Assn., Soc. Mil. Engrs., Soc. Mktg. Profl. Services, Soc. Value Engrs., Mcpl. Art Soc. N.Y.C. Club: Orient Yacht. Home: 138 Spa Dr Annapolis MD 21403 also: 154 Beacon Ln Jupiter FL 33469

JANSSON, KURT GUNNAR, United Nations official; b. Norrmark, Finland, Nov. 20, 1915; s. Edvin Gustav and Maria Matilda (Hinke) J.; M.A., Helsinki U., 1938, Dr. Polit. Sci., 1986; m. Eva Kyrohonka, June 2, 1943; children—Olli Tiitola, Hannele Gripenberg, Heidi Ross, Harri, Simone. Dir. gen. Vocat. Rehab. Agy. Finland, 1945-51; chief Rehab. unit UN, N.Y.C., 1953-59, chief regional social affairs office, Beirut, 1959-62, asst. dir. socialpolicy div., N.Y.C., 1962-64, dep. dir., 1964-69, dir., 1969-72, resident rep. UN devel. program, Pakistan, 1972-75, Nigeria, 1975-77, UN asst. sec. gen. and spl. rep. UNICEF, Cambodia, 1980-81, UN asst. sec. gen. emergency ops. in Ethiopia, 1984-85. Chmn., Bd. Rehab. Cons., World Vets. Fedn., Paris, 1959—; sec. gen. World Land Reform Conf., Rome, 1968; sec. gen. World Conf. Social Welfare Ministers, N.Y.C., 1966. Served with Finnish Army, 1939-44. Decorated officer Freedom Cross, comdr. Order of White Rose of Finland. recipient Lasker award, 1965, Internat. Rehab. award World Vets Fedn., 1962. Mem. Internat. Devel. Assn., Social Policy Assn. Finland, Econs. Assn. Finland. Author: Selective Placement in Industry, 1952; Technical Cooperation Among Developing Countries, 1979; Technical Cooperation for Disability Prevention and Rehab., 1981; The Ethiopian Famine: An Inside View, 1986. Home: 79 Ave Maurice Donat, 06700 Saint Laurent-du-Var France

JANTUNEN, KAUKO ILMARI, physician; b. Ruokolahti, Finland, Aug. 27, 1941; came to U.S., 1970, naturalized, 1978; s. Heimo and Helvi Sivia (Teppana) J.; M.D., U. Helsinki (Finland), 1967; m. Irene Marcarelli, Sept. 29, 1985; children—Pertti Tapio, Timo Juhani, Frank Kari, David Jabez. Gen. practice medicine, Kiihtelysvaara, Finland, 1967-69, Pajala, Sweden, 1969-70; intern St. Luke's Hosp., Fargo, N.D., 1970-71; practice family medicine, New York Mills, Minn., 1971-75, Lake Worth, Fla., 1975—; staff Drs. Hosp. Diplomate Am. Bd. Family Practice. Fellow Am. Acad. Family Physicians; mem. AMA. Pentecostal. Address: 1622 S Dixie Hwy Lake Worth FL 33460

JANTZEN, J(OHN) MARC, educator; b. Hillsboro, Kans., July 30, 1908; s. John D. and Louise (Janzen) J.; m. Ruth Patton, June 9, 1935; children: John Marc, Myron Patton, Karen Louise. A.B., Bethel Coll., Newton, Kans., 1934; A.M., U. Kans., 1937, Ph.D., 1940. Elementary sch. tchr. Marion County, Kans., 1927-30, Hillsboro, Kan., 1930-31; high sch. tchr. 1934-36; instr. sch. edn. U. Kans., 1936-40; asst. prof. Sch. Edn., U. of Pacific, Stockton, Calif., 1940-42; assoc. prof. Sch. Edn., U. of Pacific, 1942-44, prof., 1944-78, prof. emeritus, 1978—, also dean sch. edn., 1944-74, emeritus, 1974—, dir. summer sessions, 1940-72; condr. seminars; Past chmn. commn. equal opportunities in edn. Calif. Dept. Edn.; mem., chmn. Commn. Tchr. Edn. Calif. Tchrs. Assn., 1956-62; mem. Nat. Council for Accreditation Tchr. Edn., 1969-72. Bd. dirs. Ednl. Travel Inst., 1965—. Recipient Hon. Service award Calif. Congress of Parents and Tchrs., 1982; Paul Harris fellow Rotary Found., 1980. Mem. Am., Calif. edn. research assns., Calif. Council for Edn. Tchrs., Calif. Assn. of Colls. for Tchr. Edn. (sec.-treas. 1975-85), N.E.A., Phi Delta Kappa. Methodist. Lodge: Rotary. Home: 117 W Euclid Ave Stockton CA 95204

JANULAITIS, M. VICTOR, consulting company executive; b. Augsberg, Ger., Sept. 25, 1945; came to U.S., 1948, naturalized, 1953; s. Vytautas P. Janulaitis; m. Carol L. George, Nov. 23, 1968; children—Victoria C., Michael G. B.S., Loyola U., Chgo., 1967; M.B.A., U. Chgo., 1971. C.P.A., Ill.; cert. mgmt. cons.; cert. data processor. With IBM, Chgo., 1967-71, Touche Ross & Co., Chgo., 1971-78; v.p. Damon Corp., Boston, 1978-79; part-time instr. Harvard U. Grad. Sch., 1979-80, ind. cons., 1979-80; v.p. Western ops. Index Systems, Los Angeles and Boston, 1979-82; founder, chief exec. officer Positive Support Rev., Inc., Los Angeles, 1982—; chmn. UCLA Grad. Sch. Mgmt. Assocs. Program, 1986-88, mem. adv. bd. Author: (with others) Managing the System Development Process, 1980. Treas. adv. bd. Malibu Sch., Calif., 1982, 84. Mem. Am. Inst. C.P.A.s, Ill. Soc. C.P.A.s, Am. Prodn. and Inventory Control Soc. (bd. dirs.), Soc. Mgmt. Info. Systems (So. Calif. chpt.), Inst. Mgmt. Cons. (Los Angeles chpt.). Office: Positive Support Rev Inc 10880 Wilshire Blvd Los Angeles CA 90024

JANURA, JAN AROL, apparel manufacturing executive; b. Chgo., May 12, 1949; s. Harold Charles and Violet Mary J.; B.S., Colo. State U., 1971; M.A., Fuller Theol. Sem., 1973. Area dir. Young Life Campaign, Seattle, 1973-76; chief exec. officer, dir. Carol Anderson, Inc., Los Angeles, 1977—; chief fin. officer Fresh Retail Chain, 1988—, Outdoor Videos Inc., 1988—; pres. Los Angeles Electric Motorcar Co., 1979-80; bd. dirs. Western Leadership Found., Starr Leadership Found., SW Leadership Found., NW Fellowship; mem Presl. Task Force, 1986; founder Janura Library, 1986. Mem. Rep. Nat. Com., 1986, Rep. Presdl. Task Force, 1984-86; trustee Janura Library, Glendale, Colo. Weyerhaueser fellow, 1972-73; recipient Salesman of Yr. award, 1983, 84. Clubs: Snowcreek Athletic, Los Angeles Athletic, Wash. Athletic, N.Y. Athletic, Admirals (life), Solomon Hill Hunt, Scootney Farms Hunting. Office: 5770 Anderson St Vernon CA 90058

JANUSZEWSKI, BODO, psychology educator; b. Oppeln, Oberschlesien, Germany, Feb. 16, 1943; s. Josef and Lucia (Loch) J.; m. Ingeborg Kriegs, June 11, 1971; children: Ingo, Till. DSc in Natural Resources, U. Cologne, Fed. Rep. of Germany, 1975. Cert. Psychologist. Educator Inst. of Spl. Edn., Cologne, 1975-78, asst. prof., 1978-80; asst. prof. dept. spl. edn. U. Cologne, 1980—; instr. Initial Tng. of Tchrs., Kiel. Fed. Rep. of Germany, 1976-78; tchr. dept. spl. edn. U. Dortmund Fed. Rep. Germany, 1980—; cons. in field. Author: Evaluation of Special Trainings of Teachers, 1975; contbr. articles to profl. jours. Served to lt. German Army, 1963-65. Fellow Examination Bd. for Tchrs. in Spl., Vocat. and Acad. Edn., Commn. for the Reform of Studies Spl. Edn.; mem. German Assn. for Group Therapy and Group Dynamics, German Assn. Ednl. Sci., German Assn. for Psychology, Assn. for Gestalt Theory, World Assn. for Ednl., Research, Internat. Assn. Group Therapy, The World Edn. Fellowship. Office: U Köln, Frangenheimstr 4, D-5000 Köln 41 Federal Republic of Germany

JANZEN, NORINE MADELYN QUINLAN, medical technologist; b. Fond du Lac, Wis., Feb. 9, 1943; d. Joseph Wesley and Norma Edith (Gustin) Quinlan; BS, Marian Coll., 1965; med. technologist St. Agnes Sch. Med. Tech., Fond du Lac, 1966; MA, Central Mich. U., 1980; m. Douglas Mac Arthur Janzen, July 18, 1970; 1 son, Justin James. Med. technologist Mayfair Med. Lab., Wauwatosa, Wis., 1966-69; supr. med. technologist Dr.'s Mason, Chamberlain, Franke, Klink & Kamper, Milw., 1969-76, Hartford-Parkview Clinic, Ltd., 1976—. Substitute poll worker Fond du Lac Dem. Com., 1964-65; mem. Dem. Nat. Com., 1973—. Mem. Nat. Soc. Med. Technologists (awards com. 1984-87, chmn. 1986-88), Wis. Assn. Med. Technologists (chmn. awards com. 1976-77, 84-85, 86-87, treas. 1977-81, pres.-elect 1981-82, pres. 1982-83, dir. 1977-84, 85-87, Mem. of Yr. 1982, numerous service awards, chair ann. meeting 1987-88), Milw. Soc. Med. Technologists (pres. 1971-72; dir. 1972-73), Communications of Wis. (originator, chmn. 1977-79), Southeastern Suprs. Group (co-chmn. 1976-77), LWV, Alpha Delta Theta (nat. dist. chmn. 1967-69; nat. alumnae dir. 1969-71), Alpha Mu Tau. Methodist. Home: N 98 W 17298 Dotty Way Germantown WI 53022 Office: Hartford-Parkview Clinic 1004 E Sumner St Hartford WI 53027

JAPENGA, JACK WALLACE, radiologist; b. Chgo., June 22, 1928; s. Jacob Martin and Theresa Alberta (Jaax) J.; Ph.B., U. Chgo., 1949, M.D., 1953; m. Laurena Booker, Nov. 1, 1952; children—William Martin, Ann Theresa, Charles Albert, Diana. Intern, USPHS Hosp., San Francisco, 1953-54; resident in radiology U. Chgo., 1956-59; practice medicine specializing in radiology, Covina, Calif., 1959—, also med. seminar dir.; mem. staffs Magan Med. Clinic, Covina, Calif., San Dimas (Calif.) Community Hosp. (hon.), Foothill Presbyn. Hosp., Glendora, Glendora Community Hosp.; chmn. pub. health commn. County of Los Angeles, 1975-81. Served with USPHS, 1953-56. Mem. Am., Calif. (ho. of dels., mem. polit. action com.), Los Angeles County (pres. Foothill Dist.) med. assns., Am. Coll. Radiology Am. Fedn. Physicians and Dentists (pres. Calif. council), Glendora Radiol. Assn. Inc. (past pres.; dir.), Am. Thermographic Soc. Republican. Home: 2452 N Cameron St Covina CA 91724 Office: 210 S Grand St Glendora CA 91740

JAQUENOUD, PAUL GUSTAVE, anesthesiologist; b. Lyon, France, Feb. 26, 1924; s. Pierre Richard and Marguerite Françoise (Besson) J.; m. Alice Marcelle Haeffely, Mar. 20, 1947 (dec. Jan. 1979); children: Pascal, Christine, François, Thierry; m. Paula Janie Vidal-Michel, Apr. 27, 1985. MD, U. Marseille, France, 1950. Head experimental surgery lab. U. Marseille, 1950-55; asst. anesthesiologist Marseilles Hosp., 1950-70; lectr. anesthesiology U. Marseilles, 1950-76; practice medicine specializing in anesthesiology Monticelli Hosp. Ambrose Pare Hosp., Marseille, 1970—; sworn expert Ct Appeals, Aix-en-Provence, France, 1974—. Author: Questions to my Anesthetist, 1980; co-author: Pharmacology of the Nervous System, 1955, Lectures on Anesthesiology, 1956, 3d edit. 1964. Served with med. corp Swiss Army, 1944-45. Mem. Profl. Union French Anesthesiologists (pres. 1954-64), European Assn. Anesthesiologists (pres. 1960), French Soc. Anesthesiologists, Assn. French Anesthesiologists, French Soc. Anesthesia and Critical Care, Swiss Soc. Anesthesia. Roman Catholic. Lodge: Lions. Home: 122 rue Ct Rolland-Amboisel, 13008 Marseille France Office: Clinique Monticelli, 88 rue Ct Rolland, 13008 Marseille France

JAQUES, WILLIAM EVERETT, physician, educator; b. Newbury, Mass., July 11, 1917; s. Arthur Wellington and Helen Alice (Colby) J.; student U. N.H., 1935-38; M.D., C.M., McGill U., 1942; m. Betty Charlene Mansfield, Mar. 30, 1968; children—William, Roberta Gail, Alice Penelope, Judith Anne, Pamela Jane, Arthur William, David Everett. Intern, Bridgeport (Conn.) Hosp., 1943-44, resident in pathology, 1946-47; resident in pathology Mass. Meml. Hosp., Boston, 1947-49; instr. Harvard U. Med. Sch., 1949-53; resident Children's Med. Center, Boston, 1949-50, asst. pathologist, 1950-51; asso. pathologist Peter Bent Brigham Hosp., Boston, 1951-53; asso. prof. pathology La. State U., 1953-57; prof., chmn. dept. pathology U. Okla. Med. Sch., 1957-65; mem. staff Univ. Hosp., Oklahoma City, 1957-65; vis. prof. Nat. Def. Med. Center, Taipei, Taiwan, 1965-66; prof., chmn. dept. pathology U. Ark. Med. Center, 1966-74; dir. pathology Nat. Center Toxicology Research, Jefferson, Ark., 1971-74; clin. prof. pathology U. Okla., Tulsa, 1974-81, Okla. Coll. Osteo. Medicine and Surgery, Tulsa, 1975-81; prof. pathology Am. U. of Caribbean, Plymouth, Montserrat, W.I., 1981-84, dean med. scis., 1982-84; clin. prof. pathology U. South Fla., Tampa, 1984—. Mem. exec. com. Okla. div. Am. Cancer Soc.,

1959-65. Served with Armed Forces, 1943-46. Mem. AMA, Am. Assn. Pathologists and Bacteriologists, Am. Soc. Exptl. Pathology, Am. Assn. Med. Colls., Internat. Acad. Pathology, Am. Coll. Angiology, Am. Soc. Coloposcopy, Am. Legion, Sigma Xi, Alpha Omega Alpha. Co-author: Introduction to Colopscopy, 1960; contbr. articles to profl. jours. Home: PO Box 2000 Sarasota FL 34230

JAQUITH, GEORGE OAKES, ophthalmologist; b. Caldwell, Idaho, July 29, 1916; s. Gail Belmont and Myrtle (Burch) J.; B.A., Coll. Idaho, 1938; M.B., Northwestern U., 1942, M.D., 1943; m. Pearl Elizabeth Taylor, Nov. 30, 1939; children—Patricia Ann Jaquith Mueller, George, Michele Eugenie Jaquith Smith. Intern, Wesley Meml. Hosp., Chgo., 1942-43; resident ophthalmology U.S. Naval Hosp., San Diego, 1946-48; pvt. practice medicine, specializing in ophthamology, Brawley, Calif., 1948—; pres. Pioneers Meml. Hosp. staff, Brawley, 1953; dir., exec. com. Calif. Med. Eye Council, 1960—; v.p. Calif. Med. Eye Found., 1976—. Sponsor Anza council Boy Scouts Am., 1966—. Gold card holder Republican Assos., Imperial County, Calif., 1967-68. Served with M.C., USN, 1943-47; PTO. Mem. Imperial County Med. Soc. (pres. 1961), Calif. Med. Assn. (del. 1961—), Nat., So. Calif. (dir. 1966—, chmn. med. adv. com. 1968-69) socs. prevention blindness, Calif. Assn. Ophthalmology (treas. 1976—), San Diego, Los Angeles ophthal. socs., Los Angeles Research Study Club, Nathan Smith Davis Soc., Coll. Idaho Assos., Am. Legion, VFW, Res. Officers Assn., Basenji Assn., Nat. Geneal. Soc., Phi Beta Pi, Lambda Chi Alpha. Presbyn. (elder). Clubs: Cuyamaca (San Diego); Elks. Office: 665 S Western PO Box 511 Brawley CA 92227

JARAMILLO, IGOR ALFREDO, pharmaceutical executive; b. Quito, Pichincha, Ecuador, July 16, 1954; arrived in Switzerland, 1986; s. Fidel Nicanor and Melida Rosario (Buendia) J.; m. Magdalena Pilar Pazy Mino, Nov. 18, 1977; children: Gabriela, Fidel. BS, Mejia Inst., Quito, 1972; MD, Cen. U., Quito, 1979, cert. tchr. semiology, 1980. Med. dir. Publitec, Quito, 1979-80; product mgr. Ciba-Geigy Ecuatoriana S.A., Quito, 1980-83, mgr. mktg., 1983-85; dep. zone mgr. Ciba-Geigy A.G., Basle, Switzerland, 1986—, product coordinator servipharm, 1987-88. Editor: Vademecum Pharma Special, 1980. Mem. Med. Fedn. Ecuador, Pichincha's Commerce Chamber. Avocations: music, reading, writing. Home: Starenstrasse 37, 41003 Bottminngen Basel Land, Switzerland Office: Ciba-Geigy AG, Mission Strase 62, 4002 Basel Switzerland

JARMAN, MICHAEL, chemist; b. Wolverhampton, Staffordshire, Eng., Apr. 17, 1940; s. Richard Ralph and Phyllis Noel (Riddoch) J. PhD, U. Cambridge, 1966; DSC, U. London, 1984. Postdoctoral scientist, sr. lectr. Inst. Cancer Research, Sutton, Surrey, Eng., 1965-85, reader in chemistry, 1985—, vice-chmn. acad. bd., 1984-87, mem. mgmt. com., 1984-87; mem. editorial bd. Anti-Cancer Drug Design, 1986—. Contbr. numerous articles to profl. jours.; patentee in field. Fellow Royal Soc. Chemistry (Interdisciplinary award 1986); mem. Assn. Cancer Research, Brit. Mass Spectrometry Soc. Office: Inst Cancer Research, Cotswold Rd, Sutton, Surrey SM2 5NG, England

JARMAN, RICHARD NEVILLE, arts administrator; b. Sawbridgeworth, Hertfordshire, Eng., Apr. 24, 1949; s. David Gwyn and Pauline (Lane) J. BA in English, Oxford (Eng.) U., 1971. Publicity officer Sadlers Wells Opera, London, 1971-74; asst. to adminstrv. dir. English Nat. Opera, London, 1974-76; touring officer dance Arts Council Gt. Britain, London, 1976-77; free-lance mgr. London, 1977-78; artistic asst. Edinburgh Internat. Festival, Scotland, 1978-82, adminstr., 1982-84; gen. adminstr. London Festival Ballet, 1984—. Mem. Soc. West End Theatres. Home: 7 Legard Rd, Highbury, London N51 DE, England Office: London Festival Ballet, 39 Jay Mews, London SW7 2ES, England

JARNIEWICZ, JERZY JAN, English philologist, educator, poet; b. Lowicz, Poland, May 4, 1958; s. Leszek and Janina (Platak) J.; m. Anita Biernacka, Sept. 3, 1981; children: Magdalena, Agnieszka. MA in English Literature, U. Lodz, Poland, 1982; postgrad., U. Lodz, 1984. Lectr. in English Literature U. Lodz, 1982—; Brit. Council vis. scholar U. Sheffield, Eng., 1987; vis scholar Worcester Coll., U. Oxford, Eng., 1984-85. Author (poetry): Korytarze, 1984; translator Polish and English poetry in numerous literary publs.; contbr. literary articles to mags. including The Cambridge Quarterly, Isis, Akcent, Odra, Pismo, LnSw. Recipient Poetry Award Young Writers Assn., Lodz, 1977. Mem. Association des Createurs de la Culture, La Soc. des Auteurs Polonais. Home: Mysliwska 19/21 m 5, 93-519 Lodz Poland Office: Instytut Filologii Angielskiej, U Lodz, Kosciuszki 65, 90-514 Lodz Poland

JAROSZCZYK, TADEUSZ, research engineer, manager; b. Grezow, Poland, Dec. 10, 1938; came to U.S., 1981; s. Alesander and Zofia (Trojanek) J.; m. Dorota-Barbara Pieczara, Sept. 15, 1960; children—Malgorzata, Thomasz-Michal. Prodn. technician, Technicum of Mech. Engring.-Poland, 1956; Mech. Technician, Mil. Officers Sch. in Engring.-Poland, 1960; M.Sc. in Mech. Engring., Mil. Acad. Tech.-Warsaw, 1970; Ph.D., Mil. Acad. Tech., 1975. Process technician Warsaw Tool Assn., Poland, 1956-57; chief repair shop Mil. Service, Poland, 1960-65; mgr. filtration lab. Mil. Acad. Tech., Warsaw, 1970-77; mgr. filtration lab. Radom Inst. Tech., Poland, 1977-79; mgr. filtration and ventilation lab. Central Inst. Occupational Safety & Health, Warsaw, 1979-81; research engr. Nelson Industries, Inc., Stoughton, Wis., 1982—, mgr. air and filtration research, 1987—; air and oil filtration expert Polish Central Engrs. Assn., 1975-81. Co-author: Oil, Fuel and Air Filtration for Piston Engines, 1977; Filtration-Principles and Practices, 2d Edit., 1986. Contbr. articles to profl. jours. Inventor in field. Served to lt. col. Polish Army, 1957-77. Recipient 2d Degree Individual award Minister Sci., Higher Edn. and Tech., Warsaw, 1979; 3d Degree award, Minister Nat. Def., Warsaw, 1975. Mem. Soc. Automotive Engrs. Avocations: travel, history. Home: 1231 Furseth Rd Stoughton WI 53589 Office: Nelson Industries Inc Hwy 51 W Box 600 Stoughton WI 53589

JARRATT, SIR ALEXANDER ANTHONY, financial executive; b. Jan. 19, 1924; s. Alexander and Mary Jarratt; m. Mary Philomena Keogh, 1946; 3 children. BCom., U. Birmingham, Eng., 1949; LLD (hon.), U. Birmingham, 1982; DSc (hon.), U. Cranfield, 1973; DUniv., U. Brunel, 1979. Asst. prin. Ministry of Power, 1949, prin., 1953, treas., 1954-55; prin. pvt. sec. to Minister of Power, 1955-59, asst. sec. oil div., 1959-63, under-sec. gas div., 1963-64, with cabinet office, 1964-65; sec. Nat. Bd. for Prices and Incomes, 1965-68, dep. sec., 1967; dep. under-sec. of state Dept. of Employment and Productivity, 1968-70; dep. sec. Ministry of Agriculture, 1970; mng. dir. IPC, 1970-73; chmn., chief exec. IPC and IPC Newspapers, 1974; chmn. Reed Internat., 1974-85, Smiths Industries plc, 1985—; also bd. dirs.; dep. chmn. Prudential Corporation plc, 1987—, Midland Bank, 1980—; bd. dirs. ICI, Thyssen-Bornemisza Group; chancellor U. Birmingham, 1983—; mem. Ford European adv. council, 1983—; mem. council Confdn. Brit. Industry, 1972—, mem. pres.'s com., 1983-86, chmn. econ. policy com., 1972-74, employment policy com., 1983-86; chmn. Henley: The Mgmt. Coll., gov. Ashridge Mgmt. Coll., v.p. Inst. of Mktg., panel mem. Internat. Ctr. for Settlement of Investment Disputes; chmn. adv. bd. Inst. Occupational Health. Served Brit. mil., 1942-46. Decorated Knight, 1979, CB, 1968. Mem. Advt. Assn. (pres. 1979-83), Indsl. Soc. (chmn. 1975-79), Periodical Publishers Assn. (pres. 1983-85). Club: Savile. Office: Smiths Industries plc, 765 Finchley Rd, Childs Hill, London NW11 8DS, England *

JARRE, MAURICE ALEXIS, composer; b. Lyons, France, Sept. 13, 1924; s. André and Gabrielle (Boullu) J.; m. Dany Saval, Jan. 30, 1965 (divorced); children: Stephanie, Jean-Michel; m. Laura Devon, Dec. 30, 1967 (divorced); m. Khong Fiu Fong, Dec. 6, 1984. Composer symphonic music including Mouvements en relief, Polyphonies conertantes, Passacaille à la mémoire d'Honegger, Mobiles, Armide; film scores include Hotel des Invalides, La Tete contre les Murs, Eyes without a Face, Crack in the Mirror, Sundays and Cybele, The Longest Day, Lawrence of Arabia (Acad. award), The Collector, Is Paris Burning?, Weekend at Dunkirk, Dr. Zhivago (Acad. award), Nights of the Generals, The Professionals, Grand Prix, Five Card Stud, Pancho Villa, Isadora, The Damned, Ryan's Daughter, Ash Wednesday, The Life and Times of Judge Roy Bean, The Mackintosh Man, The Effect of Gamma Rays on Man-in-the-Moon Marigolds, Island at the Top of the World, Mandingo, Shogun, Posse, Winter Kills, The Black Marble, Taps, Firefox, Young Doctors in Love, The Year of Living Dangerously, Dreamscape, A Passage to India (Acad. award), Witness, Top Secret, Mad Max Beyond Thunderdome, Solarbabies, The Mosquito Coast, Tai-Pan, No Way Out, Julia & Julia, Moon Over Parador, Gorillas in the Mist. Chevalier, Legion of Honor (France), comdr. of Arts and Letters (France). Office: care M Kohner 9169 Sunset Blvd Hollywood CA 90069 *

JARRETT, JOHN C., II, obstetrician, gynecologist; b. Cleve., Dec. 25, 1950; s. John Crow and Mary Louise (Gilmore) J.; m. Cynthia L. Jarrett, Aug. 12, 1973 (div. Mar. 1986); children: Jennifer, Jay, Casey. BA, Princeton U., 1973; MD, Case Western Res. U., 1977. Diplomate Am. Bd. Ob-Gyn. Resident in ob-gyn. U. Mich., Ann Arbor, 1977-81; instr. ob-gyn. U. Ill., Chgo., 1981-83, asst. prof. ob-gyn., 1983-84; asst. prof. ob-gyn. Ind. U., Indpls., 1984-85; ob-gyn. Pregnancy Initiation Ctr., Indpls., 1985—, also bd. dirs. Contbr. articles to profl. jours. Fellow Am. Coll. Ob-Gyns.; mem. Am. Fertility Soc., Soc. Reproductive Endocrinologists, Soc. Assisted Reproductive Tech., Soc. Reproductive Surgeons, Cen. Assn. Ob-Gyns (Prize award 1983), Alpha Omega Alpha, Am. Diabetes Assn. (Citation 1983). Home: 10720 Downing Carmel IN 46032 Office: Pregnancy Initiation Ctr 8091 Township Line Rd Suite 110 Indianapolis IN 46260

JARRETT, PAUL EUGENE, consultant surgeon; b. Blackburn, Lancashire, U.K., Feb. 18, 1943; s. Maurice Eugene and Doris Mabel (Lake) J.; m. Ann Wilson, Apr. 1, 1966; children—Michael. B.A., Cambridge U., 1963, M.B., 1966, B.Chir., 1966, M.A., 1967. Diplomate Coll. Obstetricians. Intern, St. Peter's Hosp., Chertsey, 1966-67, St. Thomas's Hosp., London, 1967; resident in surgery Royal Hosp., Wolverhampton, 1970-72, St. Thomas Hosp., 1972-76; sr. surg. registrar St. Thomas's Hosp., London, 1974-77; cons. surgeon Kingston Hosp., Surrey, Eng., 1977—; hon. clin. tutor St. Thomas's Hosp., London, 1978—, Westminster Hosp., London, 1978—; cons. day surgery The Chest Hosp., Athens, 1983—; dir. You and Your Health Ltd., Wimbledon, Surrey, 1980—. Contbr. articles to profl. jours., chpts. to books. Trustee Princess Alice Hospice, Esher, Surrey, 1984—. Fellow Royal Coll. Surgeons; mem. British Med. Assn., Can. Med. Assn., European Soc. Cardiovascular Surgery, Assn. Surgeons Gt. Britain, The Venous Forum. Mem. Ch. of England. Avocations: antique surg. instruments; gardening; golf. Office: Kingston Hosp Dept Surgery, Galsworthy Rd, Kingston-upon-Thames, Surrey KT2 7QB, England

JARUZELSKI, WOJCIECH, army officer, Polish government official; b. Kurow, Lublin, July 6, 1923; m. Barbara Jaruzelski; 1 child, Monika; grad. Gen. Karol Swierczewski Acad. Gen. Staff. Served with Polish Armed Forces in USSR and Poland, 1943-45; various Sr. Army posts, 1945-65; chief of Central Polit. Dept. of Armed Forces, 1960-65; dep. minister of Nat. Def., 1962-68, minister, 1968-83; supreme comdr. armed forces during Wartime, 1983—; chmn. Nat. Def. Com., 1983—, premier, 1981-85, chmn. Council of State, 1985—, chief gen. staff, 1965-68, brig. gen. 1956, div. gen., 1960, gen. arms, 1968, gen. of army, 1973; mem. Polish United Workers' Party Central Com., 1964—, mem. Polit. Bur., 1971—; 1st sec., 1981—; dep. to Seym, 1961—; v.p. Chief Council of Union of Fighters for Freedom and Democracy, 1972—; chmn. Mil. Council Nat. Salvation, 1981-83; mem. presidium All-Poland Com. Nat. Unity Front, 1981-83; provisional mem. Nat. Council Patriotic Movement for Nat. Rebirth, 1982-83, mem., 1983—. Decorations include Order of Builders of People's Poland, Order of Banner of Labour (1st class), Knight's Cross of Order of Polonia Restituta, Silver Cross of Virtuti Militari and Cross of Valour, Medal of 30th Anniversary of People's Poland, Order of Red Banner (USSR), Order of Lenin, also others. Office: Office of Council of State, Warsaw Poland

JARVI, NEEME, conductor; b. Tallinn, USSR, June 7, 1937; came to U.S., 1980; s. August and Elss Jarvi; m. Liilia Jarvi, Sept. 2, 1961; children: Paavo, Kristjan, Maarika. Diploma in Music and Conducting, Leningrad (USSR) State Conservatorium, 1960. Conductor Estonian Radio Symphony Orch., 1960-63, chief conductor, 1963-76; chief conductor Estonian State Opera, 1963-76, Estonian State Symphony, 1976-80, Gothenburg (Sweden) Symphony Orch., 1981—; prin. conductor, music dir. Scottish Nat. Orch., Glasgow, 1984-88; prin. guest conductor Birmingham (Eng.) Symphony Orch., 1980-83; guest conducted with N.Y. Philharm. Orch., Boston Symphony Orch., Phila. Orch., Chgo. Symphony, Concertgebow, London Philharmonic, London Symphony, all Scandinavian Orchs., several operas at Met. Opera House, N.Y.C. Recs. include complete symphonies of Sibelius, Stenhammar, Berwald, Dvorak, Gade, Svendsen, Brahms, R. Strauss, Glasounov, Eduard Tubin, Schostakovitch, Prokoffiev, many others. Recipient First Prize in Conducting Accademia Nazionale di Santa Cecilia, 1971. Office: care Ronald Wilford Columbia Artists Mgmt 165 W 57th St New York NY 10019

JAUHO, PEKKA ANTTI, physicist, educator; b. Oulu, Finland, Apr. 27, 1923; s. Antti Arvid and Sylvi Matilda (Pajari) J.; m. Kyllikki Jauho, Apr. 1, 1948; children: Antti, Pekka. MS, U. Helsinki, Finland, 1948, PhD, 1950; D of Tech. (hon.), U. Tech., Helsinki, 1986; D Honoris Causa, U. Oulu, 1983. Actuary Ins. Co Kansa, Helsinki, 1951-54, Ins. Co. Varma, Helsinki, 1954-55; assoc. prof. physics U. Tech., Helsinki, 1955-57, prof., 1957-70; gen. dir. Tech. Research Ctr., Helsinki, 1979-87; mem. staff Acad. Finland, Helsinki, 1987—; pres. Finnish Acad. Tech., Helsinki, 1971-77; mem. com. Scientific Cooperation, Paris, 1966-69. Author: Atomic and Nuclear Physics, 1959; contbr. numerous articles to profl. jours. Chmn. Huhtamaki Co., 1986, bd. dirs., 1971—; bd. dirs. Wartsila Co., Helsinki, 1982—. Served to maj. Air Force of Finland, 1941-44. Named Chevalier de Legion D'Honneur, 1975, Commandeur Les Palmes Academiques, 1985, Commandeur of the Lion of Finland y Grave, 1986, Commandeur of the Finnish White Rose, 1976. Mem. Internat. Union Acads., Finnish Acad. Scis., Scientific Soc. Finland, ESA, Rilem (hon.), Bd. of Nordita, Am. Nuclear Soc. Liberal. Lutheran. Home: Menninkaisentie 6 L, Espoo Finland 02110

JAUNAUX, YVES, physician; b. Reims, Champagne, France, July 23, 1944; s. Robert and Jeanne (Hoyet) J.; m. Thérèse Blonde, June 12, 1974; children: Anne, Laure. MD, U. Reims, 1971. Physician various hosps., Reims, 1962-70, Exercice Libéral, La Ferte Gaucher, 1970—; Co-dir. Avenir et Liberté (newspaper), 1985, L'Essentiel de L'Actualite Politique et Parlementaire (newspaper), 1986; v.p. Club Avenir et Liberté, 1983-87, sec. gen., 1987—. Maire Adjoint La Ferte Gaucher, 1983—. Named Chevalier de l'Ordre du Mérite, 1987. Mem. Conseil Dept. L'Ordres des Med. Rassemblement pour la République. Roman Catholic. Office: Avenir et Liberte, 18 ave de la Marne, 92600 Asnieres France

JAVACHEFF, CHRISTO VLADIMIROV See CHRISTO

JAVID, NIKZAD SABET, prosthodontics educator, dentist; b. Kashan, Iran, May 24, 1934; s. Salam and Pika (Farhang) Javid-S.; m. Mahnaz Zolfaghari, Oct. 22, 1942; children—Nikrooz, Behrooz, Farnaz. D.M.D., U. Tehran, Iran, 1958; cert., U. Chgo., 1970; M.Sc., Ohio State U., 1971; M.Ed., U. Fla., 1981. Asst. prof. U. Tehran, 1959-69, prof., dean, 1975-79; asst. prof. Ohio State U., 1971-73, assoc. prof., 1973-74; assoc. prof. removable prosthodontics U. Fla., 1974-75, prof., 1980—; pvt. practice dentistry specializing in prosthodontics, Gainsville, Fla., 1980—; cons. in field. Author books, including: Stress Breaker in Partial Denture, 1966, Cleft Palate Prosthetics, 1968, Complete Denture Construction, 1974, (with Sara Nawab) Essentials of Complete Denture Prosthodontics, 1987; contbr. numerous articles to profl. jours. Named Outstanding Clin. Instr. of Yr. Student Dental Council, Columbus, Ohio, 1973. Fellow Internat. Coll. Dentists, Internat. Coll. Prosthodontics, Am. Coll. Prosthodontics, Am. Acad. Maxillofacial Prosthetics, Royal Soc. Health (Eng.); mem. Iranian Dental Assn. (dir. 1975-78), ADA, Internat. Assn. Dental Research (sec.-treas. Iran div. 1978). Lodge: Lions. Home: 3865 NW 38th Pl Gainesville FL 32605 Office: U Fla JHMHC Box J-435 Gainesville FL 32610

JAVIER, AILEEN RIEGO, pathologist; b. Fabrica, Negros Occidental, Philippines, Apr. 4, 1948; d. Filemon Yanson and Alicia Vazquez (Alteros) R.; m. Mark Anthony Navarro Javier, July 15, 1972; children: Martha Francesca, Nadine Ruth. BS, U. Phillipines, 1967, MD, 1972. Diplomate Philipine Bd. Pathology. Instr. pathology U. Philipines, Manila, 1972-76, asst. prof., 1976-80, sr. lectr., 1987—; cons. Lung Ctr. Philipines, Quezon City, 1982-86, med. specialist, 1987—; med. specialist Philipine Children's Ctr., Quezon City, 1981-82, cons. 1986; cons. Polymedic Gen. Hosp., Rizal, Philipines, 1984-86, dept. chmn. 1987—; med. specialist Nat. Kidney Inst., Quezon City, 1984-87; cons. 87—, Bur. Research and Labs, Manila, 1987—; v.p. Philipine Blood Coordinating Council, 1987—. Active Goodwill Industries, Quezon City, 1981. Fellow Philipine Soc. Oncologists; mem. Internat. Acad. Pathology, Philipine Soc. Pathologists (treas. 1985-87., pres. 1987-88). Baptist. Office: Lung Ctr of Philipines, Quezon City Philipines

JAWARA, DAWDA KAIRABA, president of Gambia; b. Barajally, Gambia, May 16, 1924; s. Almamy and Mama (Fatty) J.; diploma tropical vet. medicine U. Edinburgh (Scotland), 1957; LL.D. (hon.), U. Ife (Nigeria), 1978; DS (hon.) Colo. State U., 1986. Vet. officer, Gambia, 1954-60; leader People's Progressive Party, Gambia, 1960—; minister edn., Gambia, 1960-61, premier, 1962-65, prime minister, 1966-70, pres., 1970—; v.p. Senegambia Confedn., 1982—. Chmn., Permanent Inter-State Com. for Drought Control in the Sahel, 1977, 79; hon. procurator Afro-European Dialogue of Peutinger Collegium, 1978. Recipient decorations from Senegal, Mauritania, Lebanon, Liberia, Nigeria, Guinea, China; created knight bachelor, 1966; knight grand cross Order St. Michael and St. George, 1974; recipient Peutinger gold medal, 1979, Agricola gold medal, 1980. Mem. Royal Coll. Vet. Surgeons, Commonwealth Vet. Assn. (pres. from 1967). Office: President's Office, Banjul The Gambia

JAWOROWSKI, ANDRZEJ EDWARD, physicist, educator; b. Lublin, Poland, Dec. 28, 1942; came to U.S. 1978; s. Edward and Anna Bogumila (Grudzien) J.; m. Bozena Helena Nalecz, Aug. 15, 1965; 1 child, Peter Andrew. M.S. in Physics, U. Warsaw, 1966, Ph.D., 1974. Instr. physics, U. Warsaw, 1966-68, sr. lectr., 1968-74, asst. prof., 1974-78; sr. research assoc. SUNY-Albany, 1978-83; assoc. prof. physics, semicondr. group leader dept. physics Wright State U., Dayton, Ohio, 1983—; research assoc. Inst. Nuclear Research, Swierk, Poland, 1967-74; head of program Inst. Physics, Polish Acad. Scis., Warsaw, 1976-77; cons. Mobil Solar Energy Co., Waltham, Mass., 1980-83, 85-86; cons. Universal Energy Systems, Dayton, 1985—. Contbr. articles to profl. jours. Recipient Ministry of Sci. Sch. Acad. Rank and Tech. prize, Warsaw, 1975, Award of Pres. of U. Warsaw, 1975,77. Mem. European Phys. Soc., Am. Phys. Soc., Polish Phys. Soc. (sec. Warsaw dept. 1975-77), Electrochem. Soc., Materials Research Soc. Office: Wright State U Dept Physics Dayton OH 45435

JAY, DAVID JAKUBOWICZ, management consultant; b. Danzig, Poland, Dec. 7, 1925; s. Mendel and Gladys Gitta (Zalc) Jakubowicz; came to U.S., 1938, naturalized, 1944; B.S., Wayne State U., 1948; M.S., U. Mich., 1949, postgrad., 1956-57; postgrad. U. Cin., 1951-53, Mass. Inst. Tech., 1957; m. Shirley Anne Shapiro, Sept. 7, 1947; children—Melvin Maurice, Evelyn Deborah. Supr. man-made diamonds Gen. Electric Corp., Detroit, 1951-56; instr. U. Detroit, 1948-51; asst. to v.p. engring. Ford Motor Co., Dearborn, Mich., 1956-63; project mgr. Apollo environ. control radiators N.Am. Rockwell, Downey, Calif., 1963-68; staff to v.p. corporate planning Aerospace Corp., El Segundo, Calif., 1968-70; founder, pres. PBM Systems Inc., 1970-83; pres. Cal-Best Hydrofarms Coop., Los Alamitos, 1972-77; cons. in field, 1983—. Pres., Community Design Corp., Los Alamitos, 1971-75; life master Am. Contract Bridge League. Served with USNR, 1944-46. Registered profl. engr., Calif., Mich., Ohio. Fellow Inst. Advancement Engring.; mem. Inst. Mgmt. Sci. (chmn. 1961-62), Western Greenhouse Vegetable Growers Assn. (sec.-treas. 1972-75), Tau Beta Pi. Jewish. Patentee in air supported ground vehicle, others. Home: 13441 Roane Circle Santa Ana CA 92705

JAY, DENNIS WANG-HONG, dental surgeon, business executive; b. Hong Kong, Mar. 5, 1941; arrived in Can., 1961; s. Kai-Chu and Kwan-Yee (Wong) J.; m. Mary Delorita Allain, Sept. 4, 1971; children: Denise Elizabeth, Juliana Ka-Ching, Andrew Philip. BSc, U. Montreal, Can., 1966; DDS, McGill U., 1970. Pvt. practice dental surgery Saint John, N.B., Can., 1970-79; chief dept. dentistry St. John Gen. Hosp., 1972-79, founder cleft palate team, 1975-79; pres. Brimark Holdings Ltd., Strathmore, Alta., Can., 1979—, Kai Yee Holdings Ltd., 1980—, Triple Luck Holdings Ltd., 1980—, Dennis Jay Import & Export Enterprises Inc., Strathmore, 1987—, Kayson Investment Ltd., Calgary, Alta., 1987—; mem. Saint John Gen. Hosp. Med. Adv. Com., 1972-79; mem. planning com. dental div. N.B. Regional Hosp., 1978-79. L.J.A. Amoyt scholar Loyola Coll., U. Montreal, 1964. Mem. Can. Dental Assn., Alta. Dental Assn., Calgary Dental Soc., Calgary Aquarium Soc., Calgary Entrepreneurs Info. Exchange Assn., Phi Lambda Rho. Office: 115 2d Ave, PO Box 1522, Strathmore, AB Canada T0J 3H0 also: Import-Export, PO Bag 2000, Strathmore, AB Canada T0J 3H0

JAY, FRANK PETER, editor, educator; b. Bklyn., Feb. 12, 1922; s. Frank G. and Harriet Ann (Niffer) J.; m. Jayne Marie Charles, Aug. 15, 1947; children—Jennifer, Christopher, Alison, Angela, Jonathan, Melissa, Bryan, Nicole, Matthew. A.B., Fordham U., 1943; M.A., Columbia U., 1946. Mem. faculty Fordham U., 1946—, prof. English, 1948—; editor-in-chief reference books Funk & Wagnalls, N.Y.C., 1963-65; exec. editor Funk & Wagnalls, 1968-73; editor-in-chief reference books Reader's Digest, N.Y.C., 1965-66; editor-in-chief IEEE Dictionary, 1975—; sec. com. terminology IEEE. Author: Jack: The Story of a Pretty Good Donkey, 1970, also articles, short stories; editor-in-chief: The New Internat. Year Book, 1963, 64, 65, Internat. Everyman's Ency., 20 vols, 1970. Served with USAAF, 1942-43. Mem. Internat. Platform Assn., Kappa Delta Pi. Clubs: Overseas Press (N.Y.C.), Princeton (N.Y.C.); Manhasset Country (N.Y.). Home: 3 Huntington Rd Port Washington NY 11050

JAY, JAMES ALBERT, insurance company executive; b. Superior, Wis., Aug. 24, 1916; s. Clarence William and Louie (Davies) J.; student pub. schs., Mpls.; m. Margie Hoffpauir, Dec. 23, 1941; 1 son, James A. Franchise with The Stauffer System of Calif., 1946-49; Ala. dist. mgr. Guaranty Savs. Life Ins. Co., Montgomery, Ala., 1949-51, state mgr. La., 1951—, dir., 1952—, La. gen. agent, 1964—; La. gen agt. Gen. United Life Ins. Co. of Des Moines (merged with Lincoln Liberty Life Ins. Co., Des Moines, with All Am. Life Ins. Co., Chgo. 1984), 1969—. Com. chmn. Attakapas council Boy Scouts Am., Alexandria, La., 1955, council commr., 1961-62, commr. Manchac dist., 1967—. Served as cpl. USMC, 1942-45, PTO. Decorated Purple Heart. Mem. Nat., Baton Rouge life underwriters assns., Gen. Agts. and Mgrs. Conf., Internat. Platform Assn. Methodist. Elk. Home: 5919 Clematis Dr Baton Rouge LA 70808 Office: 2279 Main St Baton Rouge LA 70802

JAY, KATHLEEN FELAN, material management professional; b. Muskegon, Mich., Aug. 10, 1957; d. Joseph D. and Clara Sue (Swiatecki) Felan; m. Bernard Raymond Jay, Aug. 19, 1987; 1 child, Raymond. AA in Internat. Trade, Siena Heights Coll., 1976, BA in Bus. Mgmt., 1982. Claims clk. Social Security Adminstrn., Dayton, Ohio, 1976-80; sec. Office Civilian Personnel Ops., Randolph AFB, 1982-83; program dir. Tex. Luth. Coll., Sequin, 1983-84; supply cataloger Cataloging and Standardization Ctr., Battle Creek, Mich., 1984—. Ukrainian Prof's. Assn. scholar Cen. Mich. U., 1978, Internat. Devel. scholar Cen. Mich. U., 1978. Mem. Siena Heights Coll. Alumni Assn. Roman Catholic. Home: 1361 Capital Ave SW Battle Creek MI 49015

JAYARAM, SUSAN ANN, professional secretary; b. Stockton, Calif., Nov. 23, 1930; d. George Leroy and Violet Yvonne (Rushing) Potter; m. M. R. Jayaram, July 2, 1960. Student Pasadena Coll., 1951-52; Woodbury Coll., 1961; A.A., Long Beach City Coll., 1979. Cert. profl. Sec. Sec. to mgr. First Western Bank, Los Angeles, 1953-56; sec. to pres. Studio City Bank (Calif.), 1957-60; sec. to exec. vice-pres. Union Bank, Los Angeles, 1962-81; sec. to vice chmn. Imperial Bank, Los Angeles, 1981-82; personal sec. to Howard B. Keck, chmn. W.M. Keck. Found., 1982—. Sec., bd. advisors Citizens for Law Enforcement Needs, 1972-74; dir. Los Angeles/Bombay Sister City Com.; mem. Jeffery Found. Mem. DAR (Susan B. Anthony chpt.), Jeffery Found., Assistance League So. Calif., Freedoms Found. at Valley Forge (Los Angeles chpt.), U.S. Navy League (Beverly Hills, Orange County Councils) League of the Americas (pres. 1988—). Republican. Club: Los Angeles (dir., sec. 1967-81). Editor: Angeles Club Panorama, 1979-80; California Clarion, 1978-80. Office: HB Keck 555 S Flower St Los Angeles CA 90071

JAYAWARDENA, NEVILLE UBESINGHE, banker; b. Hambantota, Sri Lanka, Feb. 25, 1908; s. Diyonis Ubesinghe and Podinona (Gajaweera) J.; m. Gertrude Mildred Wickremasinghe (dec.); children: Lalith Roxley, Ainsley Nimal, Yasodha Neiliya; m. Amybelle Millicent de Silva, Sept. 21, 1961. BS in Econs. with honors, London Sch. Econs., 1932. With Govt. Clerical Service; staff asst. Dept. Commerce and Industry, 1932; commr. commodity purchase, commr. war risks ins., dir. gen. war supplies during World War II, senator, 1957-62, additional controller fin. and supply (econs.); mem. Nat. Planning Council, 1958-61; examiner in econs. Civil Service Examination; successively controller exchange, dep. gov., gov. Cen. Bank, dep. gov., 1950, gov., 1953; founder, pres. Mercantile Credit Ltd., 1956—; chmn. Sampath Bank Ltd., Union Assurance Ltd.; chmn., bd. dirs. Mercantile Fin. Services Ltd., Mercantile Fin. Brokers Ltd., Mercantile Stock Brokers Ltd., Mercantile Lloyds Leasing Ltd., Mercantile Brokers Ltd., Colombo, Mercantile Shipping Co. Ltd., Mercs-Ballast-Nedam (Ceylon) Ltd., Lanka Carbons Ltd., Lanka Carbons Ltd.; pres. Allied Investments Ltd., Premier Investments Ltd., Allied Trust Ltd., Allied Holdings Ltd., Genuine Gems (Ceylon) Ltd., Colombo Agys. Ltd., Mercantile Tours (Ceylon) Ltd., Polychems. Ltd., Mercs Convs. (Lanka) Ltd., Premier Engrs. (Metalock) Ltd.; sr. ptnr. Allied Floral Enterprises; bd. dirs. Exotica Resorts Lanka Ltd., Mercantile Mcht. Bank Ltd., Nasio Chems. Ltd., Vavasseur Trustees Ltd., Vavasseur Shipping Agys. Ltd., Ceylon Career Apparel Ltd., Katunayake, Sri Lanka, Omega Holdings Ltd., Associated Hotels Ltd., Colombo, Union Carbide Lanka Ltd., Eveready Battery Co. Lanka (pvt.) Ltd., Ruhunu Hotels and Travels Ltd. Fellow Royal Statis. Soc.; mem. Royal Asiatic Soc., Sri Lanka Assn. for Advancement Sci., Cen. Cultural Fund. Home: 18 Cambridge Pl, Colombo 7 Sri Lanka Office: Mercantile Credit Group Cos, 55 Janadhipathi Mawatha, Colombo 1 Sri Lanka

JAYDOS, ROBERT ANTHONY, architect; b. Chgo., Feb. 5, 1938; s. Anthony Walter and Angeline Rita J.; BArch., U. Ill., 1968; children by previous marriage—Robert Anthony, Christine Marie, Shari Anne. Designer, Perkins & Will, Chgo., 1968-69; designer, asst. job capt. Loebl, Schlossman, Bennett & Dart, Chgo., 1969-71; draftsman Graham, Anderson, Probst & White, Chgo., 1971-72; job capt. Marshall Lieb & Assos., Chgo., 1972-73; pres., design cons. Smith & Jaydos Inc., Elk Grove Village, Ill., owner, operator Jaydos & Assocs., Architects, Elk Grove Village, 1973-80, pres., 1980—, Jaydos and Assocs., Architects, Ltd. Served with USAF, 1955-59. Mem. Easter Seals Com., 1983. Registered architect, Ill., Nebr., Iowa, Ohio; lic. comml. pilot. Mem. Nat. Council Archtl. Registration Bds., U. Ill. Alumni Assn. (life), Art Inst. Chgo. Club: Rotary. Office: Jaydos & Assocs Architects Ltd 414 N Orleans Chicago IL 60610

JAYEWARDENE, JUNIUS RICHARD, president of Sri Lanka; b. Colombo, Ceylon, Sept. 17, 1906; s. E.W. and Agnes Helen Jayewardene; m. Elina B. Rupesinghe, 1935; 1 child. Student Royal Coll., Univ. Coll. Law Coll. of Colombo. Mem. Colombo Municipal Council, 1940, State Council, 1943; hon. sec. Ceylon Nat. Congress, 1940-47; mem. Ho. of Reps., 1945-77, leader, 1953-56; minister of fin., 1947-53, of agr. and food, 1953-56, of fin., info., broadcasting, local govt. and housing, 1960; dep. leader of opposition, 1960-65; minister of state, parliamentary sec. to minister def., external affairs and planning, 1965-70; leader opposition, 1970-77; prime minister of Sri Lanka, 1977-78; minister of aviation, 1978, pres. of Sri Lanka, 1978—; minister of def. and plan implementation, 1979—, minister of higher edn., Janatha estate devel., state plantations, 1981—, minister of power, from 1982, minister of energy, 1982—; del. numerous internat. confs. Hon. trustee Anakarika Dharmapala Trust; hon. treas. United Nat. Party, 1947-48, v.p., 1953, sec., 1972, leader, 1973-75, 75—. Author: Some Sermons of the Buddha; Buddhist Essays; (speeches) In Council; Buddhism and Marxism; Selected Speeches. Address: Office of Pres, Colombo Sri Lanka

JEAN, (BENOIT GUILLAUME MARIE ROBERT LOUIS ANTOINE ADOLPHE MARC D'AVIANO), Grand Duke of Luxembourg; b. Berg Castle, Luxembourg, Jan. 5, 1921; s. Felix, Prince of Bourbon-Parma and Prince of Luxembourg and Charlotte, Grand-Duchess of Luxembourg; ed. Luxembourg and Ampleforth Coll. (Gt. Brit.), Laval U. (Que., Can.), 1940-42; Dr. Hon., U. Strasbourg (France), 1957, Miami U., Oxford, Ohio, 1979; m. Princess Josephine-Charlotte of Belgium, Apr. 9, 1953; children—Marie Astrid, Henri (hereditary grand duke), Jean, Margaretha, Guillaume. Mem. Luxembourg Council of State, 1951-61; lt.-rep. of Grand Duchess, 1961-64; grand duke of Luxembourg, 1964—. Chief scout of Luxembourg, 1945—; mem. Internat. Olympic Com., 1946—. Served as capt. Irish Guards, Brit. Army, 1942-45; col. Luxembourg Army, 1945, gen., 1964. Decorated Croix de Guerre (Luxembourg, France, Belgium and Netherlands); Silver Star (U.S.). Home: Chateau de Berg, Colmar-Berg Luxembourg Office: Grand Ducal Palace,, Luxembourg *

JEANMART, CLAUDE RENE GUSTAVE, chemical engineer; b. Paris, Nov. 18, 1933; s. Constant Jules Henri and Marie Celine Therese (Flamant) J.; m. Raymonde Mireille Andree Ponce, Aug. 1, 1955; children—Marie-Christine, Philippe, Thierry. B.Sc., Ecole Nationale Superieure de Chimie de Paris, 1955, Ing.D., 1961. Research engr. Centre de Recherches Rhone-Poulenc, Vitry sur Seine, 1961-68, head dept., 1968-76, planning mgr. Rhone Poulenc Chimie Fine, Paris, 1977-79; research mgr. Alimentation Equilibree Commentry AEC, Paris, 1979-82; sci. adviser Rhône-Poulenc Group, Paris, 1982-87, deputy sci. mgr., 1987—. Patentee in field. Served as lt. French Army, 1956-58. Recipient Carrion prix Societe d'Encouragement pour l'Industrie Nationale, 1983, correspondant de l'Académie des Scis., 1987. Mem. Societe Francaise de Chimie, Am. Chem. Soc. Home: 16 rue des Lievres, 91800 Brunoy France Office: Rhone Poulenc SA, 25 Quai Paul Doumer, 92408 Courbevoie Cedex France

JEANNE, PIERRE PAUL, chief financial officer; b. Montigny, France, May 29, 1932; s. Louis and Anne-Marie (Malherbe) J.; 1 child, Katherine. Grad. econs., Conservatoire National des Arts et Metiers, Paris, 1985. Asst. chief acct. Selection Du Reader's Digest, Paris, 1960-68, controller, 1968-83, chief fin. officer, 1983—. Served with French Army, 1952-56. Home: 28 Residence Bel Ebat, La Celle Saint Cloud, 78170 Yvelines France Office: Reader's Digest France, 5-7 Ave Louis Pasteur, 92220 Bagneux France

JEANNERET, MICHEL, French educator; b. Lausanne, Switzerland, Mar. 6, 1940; s. Edmond and Lore (Marks) J.; m. Marian Elizabeth Hobson, Nov. 10, 1941; 1 child, Marc. Licence es Lettres, U. Neuchâtel, Switzerland, 1963; MA, U. Cambridge, 1967; D. Lettres, U. Neuchâtel, 1969. Research fellow Gonville and Caius Coll., Cambridge, Eng., 1967-69; prof. ordinaire U. Geneva, 1971—, v. dean faculty letters, 1977-82, head French dept., 1978—; vis. fellow, U. Princeton, 1988; vis. prof. U. Calif., Irvine. Author: Poésie et Tradition Biblique, 1969, La Lettre Perdue, 1978, La Follia Romantica, 1984, Des Mets et des Mots, 1987. Home: 8 Ave Des Amazones, 1224 Geneva Switzerland Office: Faculte Des Lettres, U Geneva, 1211 Geneva 4, Switzerland

JEANNIN, YVES PHILIPPE, educator; b. Boulogne, Seine, France, Apr. 11, 1931; s. Raymond and Suzanne (Du Chatelet) J.; m. Suzanne Belle, Apr. 4, 1956; children: Philippe, Sylvie. Ingenieur, Ecole Nationale Superieure de Chimie de Paris, 1954; MD, U. Paris, 1962. Asst. U. Paris, 1956-63; postdoctoral fellow USAEC, Chgo. and Ames (Iowa), 1963; lectr. Toulouse (France) U., 1964-74; prof. U. Paris, 1974—. Author: Chimie Physique, 1960. Mem. Acad. Scis. (corr.), Internat. Union Pure and Applied Chemistry (pres.-elect). Home: 22 Rue Henri Heine, Paris France Office: U P Et M Curie, 4 Place Jussieu, Paris France

JEANSSON, BO LARS GOSTA, telecommunications executive; b. Molndal, Sweden, Aug. 24, 1943; came to Malaysia, 1984; s. Gosta Olav and Norma Kristina (Gustavsson) J. Student, Edn. Lundsberg Boarding Sch., Sweden, 1961-64, Wangfeldts Symnasium, Gothenburg, Sweden, 1976-77. Various positions Nordisk Ressebureau AB, Gothenburg, 1964, AB Gotaverken, Gothenburg, 1965, AB Papyrus, Molndal, Sweden, 1967, AB Syntes, Nol, Sweden, 1967-74; engaged in fin. and adminstrn. Weko AB, Grabo, Sweden, 1974; with purchasing Telefon AB LM Ericsson, Molndal, 1975; mgr. logistic Philips/LM Ericsson Joint Venture, Riyadh, Saudi Arabia, 1978-82; mgr. logisitcs and purchasing Telefon AB LM Ericsson, Saudi Arabia, 1982-84; mgr. logistics Electroscon Network Engring. S/B, Kuala Lumpur, Malaysia, 1984-88, Ericsson Network Engring. Pte. Ltd., Sinapore, 1988—. Mem. Molndal Assessemnt Bd., 1977-78. Mem. SIF Trade Union (chmn. Molndal 1977-78), Swedish Purchase Mgrs. Club. Mem. Liberal Party. Home: No 7 Swiss Club Lane, Singapore 1128, Singapore Office: Ericsson Network Engring Pte Ltd, 510 Tromson Rd #18-00 SLF Complex, Singapore 1129, Singapore

JEANTELOT, CHARLES JEAN, French diplomat; b. Rabat, Morocco, Jan. 12, 1925; came to France; s. Marie-Joseph Charles Jeantelot and Lucienne Campredon; m. Jeanne Nora La Martina, Dec. 11, 1946; children: Charles, Bernard. BA, Lycée Gouraud, Rabat, 1943; diplôme d'Arabe, Institute des Hautes Etudes Marocaines, Rabat, 1946; licence en droit, Faculteé de Droit, Hanoi, Vietnam, 1952. Secrétaire d'Ambassade Govt. of France, Rabat, 1956-65, Jeddah, Saudi Arabia, 1965-67; conseiller d'Ambassade Govt. of France, Tripoli, Libya, 1970-74; consul gen. Govt. of France, Tananarive, Madagascar, 1976-79; ammbassador Govt. of France, Aden, Yemen, 1979-83, Khartoum and Muscat Sultanate of Oman, Sudan, 1984. Served with French Army, 1944-45. Decorated Croix de Guerre, commdr. de l'Order du Mérite Nat., officier de la Legion d'Honneur (all France). Roman Catholic. Home: 12 rue de Chabrol, Paris Xe France 75010 Office: Ministère des Affaires Etrangèeres, 37 Quai d'Orsay, Paris France 75007

JEBSEN, ATLE, ship owner; b. Bergen, Norway, Nov. 10, 1935; s. Kristian Stange and Sigfried (Kjerland) J.; 3 children. BA in Econs., Queens Coll., Cambridge, Eng., 1959, MA, 1961. Chartering clk. broker A/S Kristian Jebsens Rederi, Dregger/Bergen, Norway, 1962-65, dir., 1965—, mng. dir., 1967—, chmn., chief exec. officer Jebsen-Group's, 1967—; chmn., 1984—; chmn. bd. dirs. Den Norske Krigsforsikringen for Skib, Oslo, Bedriftsforsamling Elkem A/S; chmn. Jebsens Drilling. Mem. Norwegian Shipowners Assn. (pres. 1982-83). Office: A/S Kristian Jebsens Rederi, Sandbrugt 5, PO Box 4145, 5015 Dreggen/Bergen Norway

JEBSEN, PETER MENTZ, textile executive; b. Kristiansand, Norway, June 21, 1930; s. Erik G. and Margit (von Erpecom) J.; m. Turid Kelvenberg; children: Tom Erik, Janicke, Peter M. Jr., Christian. BA, Dartmouth Coll., 1955; MBA, Amos Tuck Sch., 1956. Purchasing mgr. Hoie Fabrikker A.S., Norway, 1956-58, prodn. planning mgr., 1958-59, pres., 1965-71; asst. purchasing mgr. Milliken Inc., N.Y.C., 1960-62, purchasing mgr., 1962-64, div. sales mgr., 1964-65; pres. Norion A.S., Norway, 1971-85, Hoie-Arne A.S., Mosby, Norway, 1985—; chmn. bd. Bergen Bank, Kristiansand, 1972—, Strong Plast A.S., Kristiansand, 1986—, Hoie Finans A.S., Kristiansand, Tedeco A.A., Oslo, 1978—, Tekstilservice A.S., Oslo, 1973—; bd. dirs. Ernst Hotel A.S., Norgesplaster A.S. Served as sgt. Royal Norwegian Air Force, 1951-52. Office: Hoie-Arne AS, 4710 Mosby Norway

JECKLIN, LOIS U., art corporation executive, consultant; b. Manning, Iowa, Oct. 5, 1934; d. J.R. and Ruth O. (Austin) Underwood; m. Dirk C. Jecklin, June 24, 1955; children—Jennifer Anne, Ivan Peter. Student State U. Iowa, 1953-55, 60-61, 74-75. Residency coordinator Quad City Arts Council, Rock Island, Ill., 1973-78; field rep. Affiliate Artists, Inc., N.Y.C., 1975-77; mgr., artist in residence Deere & Co., Moline, Ill., 1977-80; dir. Vis. Artist Series, Davenport, Iowa, 1978-81; pres. Vis. Artists, Inc., Davenport, 1981-88; pres., owner Jecklin Assocs., 1988—; cons. writer's program St. Ambrose Coll., Davenport, 1981, 83, 85; mem. com. Iowa Arts Council, Des Moines, 1983-84; panelist Chamber Music Am., N.Y.C., 1984, Pub. Art Conf., Cedar Rapids, Iowa, 1984; panelist, mem. com. Lt. Gov.'s Conf. on Iowa's Future, Des Moines, 1984. Trustee Davenport Mus. Art, Nature Conservancy Iowa; mem. steering com. Iowa Citizens for Arts, Des Moines, 1970-71; bd. dirs. Tri-City Symphony Orchestra Assn., Davenport, 1968-83; founding mem. Urban Design Council, HOME, City of Davenport Beautification Com., all Davenport, 1970-72. Recipient numerous awards Izaak Walton League, Davenport Art Gallery, Assn. for Retarded Citizens, Am. Heart Assn., Ill. Bur. Corrections, many others; LaVernes Noyes scholar, 1953-55. Mem. Am. Council for Arts, Ptnrs. for Livable Places, Ann. Coll. Univ. Community Arts Adminstrs., Nat. Assembly Local Arts Agys., Crow Valley Golf Club. Republican. Episcopalian. Club: Outing. Lodge Rotary. Home and Office: 2717 Nichols Ln Davenport IA 52803

JEE, JUSTIN SOONHO, accountant; b. Pusan, Korea, June 29, 1951; came to U.S., 1976; s. Hanwoong and Boksoo (Park) J.; m. Ahyung Lee, May 2, 1976. BS, U. Korea, 1976; BS in Acctg., U. Minn., 1980; MBA, San Diego State U., 1984. CPA, Minn.; cert. mgmt. acct. Tax acct. Midway Nat. Bank, St. Paul, 1981-83; fin. analyst Medical, Inc., Inver Grove Heights, Minn., 1984-87; sr. staff acct. Internat. Trade Adminstrn., Import Adminstrn., U.S. Dept. Commerce, Washington, 1987—; cons. Bus. Devel. Ctr., San Diego, 1984. Mem. Am. Inst. CPA's, Minn. Soc. CPA's, Inst. Cert. Mgmt. Accts. (cert.), D.C. Inst. CPA's. Home: 10315 Bushman Dr Oakton VA 22124 Office: US Dept Commerce ITA Import Adminstrn Room 3087B 14th St and Constitution Ave Washington DC 20230

JEFFARES, ALEXANDER NORMAN, academic advisor; b. Dublin, Ireland, Aug. 11, 1920; s. Cecil Norman and Agnes (Fraser) J.; m. Jeanne Agnes Calembert; 1 child, Felicity Anne Jeffares Sekine. MA, U. Oxford, Eng., 1946, D Philosophy, 1948; PhD, U. Dublin; Doctorate (hon.), U. Lille, France, 1975. Prof. English lit. U. Edinburgh, S. Australia, 1951-56; dept. chmn., prof. English lit. U. Leads, Eng., 1957-74; prof. English lit. U. Stirling, Scotland, 1974-86; mng. dir. Academic Adv. Services, Ltd., Crail, Scotland, 1977—; bd. dirs. Colin Smythe, Ltd., Eng. Author: History of Anglo Literature, 1982, A New Commentary on Yeat's Poems, 1986; (with A. Kamm) An Irish Childhood W.B. Yeats, 1988, A Jewish Childhood, 1988; (poems) Brought Up in Dublin, 1987, Brought Up to Leave, 1987. Vice-chmn. Muckhart Community Council, Scottish Arts Council. Fellow Royal Soc. Lit., Royal Soc. Edinburgh (v.p.), Australian Acad. Humanities, Trinity Coll. (hon.); mem. Arts Council London, Royal Commonwealth Soc., Scottish Pen, Boon Trust Scotland (pres.). Anglican. Club: Athenaeum (London). Home: Craighead Cottage, Crail KY103XN, Scotland

JEFFERDS, JOSEPH CROSBY, JR., industrial machinery distributing company executive; b. Charleston, W.Va., June 24, 1919; s. Joseph Crosby and Agnes Atkinson (Arbuckle) J.; B.S. in Mech. Engring., MIT., 1940; Sc.D. (hon.), W.Va. Inst. Tech., 1969; m. Olivia Polk Evans, May 15, 1943; children—Joseph C. III, Marion Jefferds Sinclair, Olivia Polk, Robert Grosvenor. Trainee, Bethlehem Steel Co. (Pa.), 1940; v.p., dir. Kanawha Drug Co., Charleston, 1946-85; pres. Jefferds Corp., Charleston, 1947—. Mech. Equipment Service Co., Charleston, 1952—; bd. dirs. United Bankshares Inc., Bell Atlantic Corp. Mem. W.Va. Bd. Edn., 1957-65, pres., 1963; trustee W.Va. Coll. Grad. Studies Found., W.Va. Inst. Tech. Found., Montgomery, Highland Hosp., Charleston; trustee U. Charleston. Served from 2d lt. to lt. col. AUS, 1941-46. Mem. Charleston Area C. of C. (pres. 1972), ASME, Def. Preparedness Assn., Am. Inst. Indsl. Engrs. Republican. Episcopalian. Clubs: Charleston Rotary (past pres.); Edgewood Country (past pres.). Author: A History of St. John's Episcopal Church, 1976; Captain Matthew Arbuckle. Home: 3 Scott Rd Charleston WV 25314 Office: PO Box 757 US Rt 35 Saint Albans WV 25177

JEFFERSON, DAVID ROWE, college dean, educator, financial planner; b. Hillsdale, Mich., June 18, 1931; s. Howard Bonar and Genevieve (Rowe) J.; m. Anne Morgan, June 22, 1957; children: David Rowe Jr., Peter Hamilton. BA, Harvard U., 1953; MDiv, Yale U., 1956; postgrad., Edinburgh (Scotland) U., 1954-55, NYU, 1958-60. CLU; chartered fin. cons., notary public, justice of the peace. Assoc. dir. YMCA Student Hostel, Edinburgh, 1954-55; exec. sec., chaplain Student Christian Movement of Oeens and Nassau, Edinburgh, 1956-58; asst. prof. philosophy and sociology, dir. admissions C.W. Post Coll., Edinburgh, 1958-63; dean admission, asst. prof. sociology Dickinson Coll., Carlisle, Pa., 1963-69; headmaster Worcester (Mass.) Acad., Carlisle, Pa., 1969-70; dean of students Bradford (Mass.) Coll., Carlisle, Pa., 1971—; pres. Ctr. for Fin. Planning, Portsmouth, N.H., 1983—; sr. devel. officer Joslin Diabetes Ctr., Boston, 1988—; sr. devel. officer Joslin Diabetes Ctr., Boston, 1988—; sr. planner Fin. Perspectives Planning, Boston, 1988—; trainer New England Vol. Employment Service Team, Boston, 1976—. Author: Guide to 2 Year Colleges, 1972; editor: Guide to Private Two-Year Colleges in New England, 1972; also numerous newspaper articles. Trainer New Eng. Vol. Employment Service Team; lay reader, sr. warden local Episc. Ch.; mem. planning bd. Town of Hampton Falls, N.H., 1984-87; vestryman St. John's Episc. Ch., Portsmouth, 1987—. Mem. Nat. Assn. Estate Planning Councils (state chmn., regional dir. 1986—), N.H. Estate Planning Council (v.p. 1985, pres. 1987—), Am. Soc. CLU's and Chartered Fin. Cons., N.H. Soc. CLUs and Chartered Fin. Consultants (bd. dirs. 1987—), Internat. Assn. Fin. Planners, Hasty Pudding Inst. 1770, Pi Gamma Mu. Republican. Clubs: Harvard U. (N.Y.C.); Iroquois, Harvard Faculty (Cambridge, Mass.); Worcester, Harvard U. Faculty (Worcester). Lodges: Masons (32 degree), Rotary. Home: 4 Oak Dr PO Box 128 Hampton Falls NH 03844 Office: Ctr for Fin Planning PO Box 1177 Hampton NH 03842

JEFFERY, IVAN LEE, manufacturing executive; b. Coldwater, Mich., May 13, 1946; s. George W. and Mary C. (Rendell) J.; B. degree in bus. adminstrn., Mich. State U., 1969; m. Wilhelmina Stunz, Jan. 8, 1977; children by previous marriage—Trinka Kathleen, Clifford Thomas. Owner, founder, Navi Industries, Bronson, Mich., 1969-73; plant supt. Aluminum Alloys, Inc., Sinking Spring, Pa., 1973-74, gen. mgr., 1977-79; gen. mgr. Crescent Brass Mfg. Corp., Reading, Pa., 1974-77, v.p., gen. mgr., 1979-81, pres., 1981—, also dir.; pres. Callowhill Brass, Inc., 1986; Bronson Devel. Corp., 1972-73; dir. Aluminum Alloys, Inc.; mem. industry sector adv. com. on nonferrous ores and metals U.S. Dept. Commerce. Trustee, Bronson Bd. Edn.; guest lectr. Parsons. Sch. Design, N.Y.C., 1985—. Mem. Am. Foundrymen's Assn., Non-Ferrous Foundrymen's Soc. (alternate dir., pres. Eastern Pa. mgmt. group, Nat. v.p., 1987—). Home: RD 1 Box 166-C Birdsboro PA 19508 Office: Crescent Brass Mfg Co 7th and Spruce Sts Reading PA 19603

JEFFERY, ROGER E., newspaper editor; b. Saltash, Cornwall, Eng., Feb. 16, 1943; s. Jack and Joan (Ashfield) J.; m. Susan Nixon; 1 child, Lisa. Editor Evening Trib., Nuneaton, Warwickshire, Eng., 1974—. Home: 81 Kingsbridge Rd, Nuneaton Warwicks, England Office: Evening Trib, Whitacre Rd, Nuneaton, Warwicks CV11 6BT, England

JEFFETT, NANCY PEARCE, tennis administrator, foundation executive; b. St. Louis, July 16, 1928; d. Charles Frederick and Lillian (Schaefer) Pearce; m. Frank A. Jeffett, Dec. 29, 1956; children—Wiliam F., Elizabeth. B.S. in Edn., Washington U., St. Louis, 1951. Co-founder Tyler (Tex.) Tennis Assn., 1954; chmn. jr. devel. com. Tex. Tennis Assn., Dallas, 1963—, chmn. Virginia Slims Dallas Tennis tournament, 1970—, MCB Internat. Teams, U.S. and Gt. Britain, 1973—; chmn., pres. Maureen Connolly Brinker Tennis Found., Dallas, 1968—; mem. Women's Internat. Profl. Tennis Council, 1974-87; chmn. Davis Cup Tie, U.S. vs. Mex., 1965; capt. U.S. Fedn. Cup Tennis Team, 1983; chmn. Wightman Cup and Fedn. Cup Com., 1976-87. Mem. bd. YMCA, Tyler, 1956, Dallas, 1962, Crystal Charity Ball. Recipient Caswell award Tex. Tennis Assn., 1970; Service Bowl award U.S. Tennis Assn., 1970; World Championship Tennis Service to Tennis award, 1983; named Tex. Mus. Tennis Hall of Fame, 1983. Mem. Jr. League Dallas, The All-England Club of Wimbledon, Dallas Tennis Assn. (dir.), Tex. Tennis Assn. (dir.), U.S. Tennis Assn. (exec. com.), Lawn Tennis Assn. U.S., All Eng. Lawn and Crocquet Club. Republican. Episcopalian. Home and Office: Maureen Connolly Brinker Tennis Found 5419 Wateka Dr Dallas TX 75209

JEFFORDS, EDWARD ALAN, lawyer; b. Rector, Ark., Nov. 28, 1945; s. Roy Ezra and Sylvia Belle (Dickinson) J.; A.A., Victor Valley Coll., 1967; student U. Wis. Mgmt. Inst., 1977; B.A., SUNY-Albany, 1978; J.D., Baylor U. Sch. Law, 1985; m. Judith Ann Williams, Nov. 25, 1981; 1 son by previous marriage, Dana Alan. Bar: Tex., U.S. Dist Ct. (we. dist., so. dist.) Tex., U.S. Ct. Appeals (5th cir.). Editor, Auburn (Wash.) Globe-News, 1967; fine arts editor Tacoma News-Tribune, 1967-72; exec. dir. Ozark Inst., Eureka Springs, 1973-82; asst. atty. gen. State of Tex.; exec. editor Baylor Law Rev., 1984-85. Served with USAF, 1963-67. Mem. Travis County Bar Assn., ABA, Tex. Trial Lawyers Assn., Assn. Trial Lawyers Am., Am. Judicature Assn., Order of Barrister, State Bar Coll., Delta Theta Phi.

JEFFREDO, JOHN VICTOR, aerospace engineer, manufacturing company executive, inventor; b. Los Angeles, Nov. 5, 1927; s. John Edward and Pauline Matilda (Whitten) J.; m. Elma Jean Nesmith, (div. 1958); children: Joyce Jean Jeffredo Ryder, Michael John; m. Doris Louise Hinz, (div. 1980); children: John Victor, Louise Victoria Jeffredo-Warden; m. Gerda Adelheid Pillich. Grad. in aero. engring. Cal-Aero Tech. Inst., 1948; AA in machine design, Pasadena City Coll., 1951; grad. electronics The Ordnance Sch. U.S. Army, 1951; AA in Am. Indian Studies, Palomar Coll., 1978; postgrad. U. So. Calif., 1955-58; MBA, La Jolla U., 1980, PhD in Human Relations, 1984. Design engr. Douglas Aircraft Co., Long Beach and Santa Monica, Calif., 1955-58; devel. engr. Honeywell Ordnance Corp., Duarte, Calif., 1958-62; cons. Honeywell devel. labs., Seattle, 1962-65; supr. mech. engr. dept. aerospace div. Control Data Corp., Pasadena, Calif., 1965-68; project engr. Cubic Corp., San Diego, 1968-70; supr. mech. engring. dept. Babcock Electronics Co., Costa Mesa, Calif., 1970-72; owner, operator Jeffredo Gunsight Co., Fallbrook, Calif., 1971-81; chief engr. Western Designs, Inc., Fallbrook, 1972-81, exec. dir., 1981, chief exec. officer, 1988—; owner, operator Western Designs, Fallbrook, 1981-87; pres. JXJ, Inc., San Marcos, Calif., exec. dir., 1981—, mgr. Jeffredo Gunsight div. 1981—, chief engr. JXJ, Inc., 1987—; owner, mgr. Energy Assocs., San Diego, 1982-86; pres. Jeffredo Internat., 1984—; engring. cons. Action Instruments Co., Inc., Gen. Dynamics, Alcyon Corp., Systems Exploration, Inc. (all San Diego), Hughes Aircraft Co., El Segundo, Allied-Bendix, San Marcos; bd. dirs. Indian World Corp. Author: Wildcatting; contbr. articles to trade jours. and mags.; guest editorial writer Town Hall, San Diego Union; patentee agrl. frost control, vehicle off-road drive system, recoil absorbing system for firearms, telescope sight mounting system for firearms, breech mech. sporting firearm, elec. switch activating system, 33 others. Mem. San Diego County Border Task Force on Undocumented Aliens, 1979-80, 81-82; chmn. Native Californian Coalition, 1982—. Served with U.S. Army, 1951-53. Recipient Superior Service commendation U.S. Naval Ordnance Test Sta., Pasadena, 1959. Mem. Am. Soc. for Metals, Nat. Hist. Soc., Nat. Rifle Assn. (life), San Diego Zool. Soc., Sierra Club, Nat. Wildlife Fedn., The Wilderness Soc., Rocky Mountain Elk Found. Avocations: sculpture, chess, music, conservation, travel. Home: 1629 Via Monserate Fallbrook CA 92028 Office: 133 N Pacific St Suite D San Marcos CA 92069

JEFFREYS, ELYSTAN GEOFFREY, geologist, oil company executive; b. N.Y.C., Apr. 26, 1926; s. Geoffrey and Georgene Frances Theodora (Littell) J.; m. Pat Rumage, May 1, 1946; children: Jeri Lynn, David Powell; m. 2d, Peggi Villar, Feb. 28, 1975. Geol. Engr., Colo. Sch. Mines, 1951, grad. Econ. Evaluation and Investment Decision Methods, 1972. Registered profl. engr., Miss.; registered land surveyor, Miss. Ptnr. G. Jeffreys & Son, 1951-53, Jeffreys and Launius, 1953-55; instr. structural geology U. So. Miss., 1955; pvt. practice petroleum exploration, 1954-77; exploration mgr. Arrowhead Exploration Co., Mobile and Brewton, Ala., 1977-83; cons. geologist, 1964—; pres., chmn. bd., chief exec. officer Major Oil Co., Jackson, Miss., 1961-84; pres., chief exec. officer The Jeffreys Co., Inc., Mobile, Ala. Trustee Nat. Eye Found. Served with 281st Combat Engrs., U.S. Army, 1944-46, ETO. Mem. Miss. Geol. Soc., New Orleans Geol. Soc., Am. Assn. Petroleum Geologists, Gulf Coast Assn. Geol. Socs. (treas. 1960, cert. of service 1971), Soc. Petroleum Engrs. AIME, Soc. Petroleum Evaluation Engrs., Am. Assn. Petroleum Landmen, Ind. Petroleum Assn. Am., Assn. Petroleum Landmen of Ala., Soc. Ind. Profl. Earth Scientists, English Speaking Union, Mobile-Bristol Soc. (treas.), Pi Kappa Alpha. Clubs: Athlestan; Capital City Petroleum, Bienville. Lodges: Masons (32 degree), Shriners. Home: 1810 Old Government St Mobile AL 36606

JEFFREY-SMITH, LILLI ANN, biofeedback specialist, educator, administrator; b. Bedford, Ind., 1944; d. Charles Constantine and Adelai (Malon) Jeffrey-Smith. Grad. Ind. Bus. Coll., 1963; B.S., Ind. U., 1973; grad. Psychosomatic Medicine Clinic, Berkeley, Calif. (accredited by Albert Einstein Coll. Medicine); PhD in Behavioral Sci., Kennedy-Western U., 1988. Cert. biofeedback specialist. Project assoc., stress mgmt. clinician City of Indpls., 1973-79; cons. Airport Med. Clinic, Indpls., 1981; outreach coordinator Abbot-Northwestern Hosp., Mpls., 1981; dir. biofeedback dept. Sister Kenney Inst., Mpls., 1979-81, Noran Neurol. Clinic, Mpls., 1981-83; instr., dir. Biofeedback Tng. and Treatment Ctr., Edina, Minn., 1979—; pres. Biofeedback Research and Devel. Co. Ltd., Edina, 1983—; cons. to biofeedback depts. St. Joseph Hosp., Mankato, Minn., 1984—, Lakeview Clinic, Waconia, Minn., 1983, Psychiat. Clinic of Mankato, 1983—, Fairview Ridges Hosp., Burnsville, Minn., 1987—. Author, narrator health and wellness tape series. Mem. Republican Presdl. Task Force, 1984—, NSC, 1985; co-chmn. Mayor's Handicapped Task Force, Indpls., 1975; founder, pres. Miss Wheel Chair of Ind., Inc. Named Hon. Lt. Gov., State of Ind., 1978; given Key to the City of Indpls., 1973, Flag of the City of Indpls., 1975. Mem. Am. Inst. Stress, N.Y. Acad. Sci., AAAS, Edina C. of C., Minn. Women's Network, Biofeedback Soc. Am., Biofeedback Soc. Minn., Am. Assn. Control Tension, Am. Assn. Behavioral Therapists, Am. Assn. Biofeedback Clinicians, Nat. Assn. Women Bus. Owners, Soc. Open Focus and Tng. Research, Assn. Trainers in Clin. Hypnosis, Internat. Stress and Tension Control Assn., Minn. Assn. Rehab. Providers, Nat. Assn. Exec. Women, Internat. Platform Assn. Avocations: music; stamp collecting; shooting; poetry. Office: Biofeedback Tng & Treatment Ctr 6545 France Ave S Southdale Med Bldg Suite 158 Edina MN 55435

JEGHERS, HAROLD JOSEPH, internist, educator; b. Jersey City, Sept. 26, 1904; s. Albert and Matilda (Gerckens) J.; m. Isabel J. Wile, June 21, 1935; children: Harold, Dee, Sanderson, Theodore. B.S., Rensselaer Poly. Inst., 1928; M.D., Western Res. U., 1932; D.Sc. (hon.), Georgetown U., 1975, Coll. Medicine and Dentistry of N.J., 1976. Intern 5th med. service Boston City Hosp., 1933-34, resident, 1935-37; physician-in-chief Boston City Hosp. (5th Med. Service), 1943-46, cons. physician, 1946-66; instr. to asso. prof. medicine Boston U. Sch. Medicine, 1935-46; prof. and dir. dept. medicine Georgetown U. Sch. Medicine, 1946-56; prof., dir. dept. medicine N.J. Coll. Medicine and Dentistry, Jersey City, 1956-66, emeritus, 1966—; med. dir. St. Vincent Hosp., Worcester, Mass., 1966-78, emeritus, 1979—; prof. med. edn. Office Med. Edn. Research and Curriculum Devel., Northeastern Ohio Univs. Coll. Medicine, 1977-86 ; cons. med. edn. St. Elizabeth Hosp., Youngstown, Ohio, 1977—, Cleve. Health Scis. Library, Case Western Res. U. and Cleve. Med. Library Assn., 1979-86; prof. Tufts U., 1966-74; dir. med. ward service Jersey City Med. Ctr., 1958-66; dir. Tufts med. service Boston City Hosp., 1969-71; cons. medicine Georgetown U. Sch. Medicine, 1957-59; rep. from A.C.P. to div. med. scis. NRC, 1950-53. Author articles and sects. in books.; developer: Jeghers Med. Index System. Recipient Laetare award Guild of St. Luke, Boston, 1958; Distinguished Alumni award Case Western Res. U. Sch. Medicine, 1974. Fellow A.C.P., Am. Soc. for Clin. Investigation; mem. A.M.A., Am. Fedn. for Clin. Research, So. Soc. for Clin. Research (v.p. 1948-49), Assn. Am. Physicians, Mass. Med. Soc., Sigma Xi.

JEHAN, SARDAR, forensic pathologist; b. Madras, India, June 1, 1932; s. Mohiudeen Sheriff and Mumtaz Begum; m. Syed Mohammed Kabiruddin; children: Shameem Fathimah, S.M. Naseerudin, Naseem Fathimah, S.M. Baseerudin. MBBS, Madras Med. Coll., 1957; Diploma in Criminology, U. Madras, 1965, Diploma in Med. and Forensic Jurisprudence, 1974. Civil asst. surgeon Madras Govt., 1958-64; tutor in forensic medicine U. Madras, 1965-68; lectr. in forensic medicine, pathology dept. U. Malaya, Kuala Lumpur, 1968-71; clin. attachment U. Glasgow, Scotland, 1972; clin. specialist in legal medicine Gen. Hosp. Kuala Lumpur, 1972-74; head dept. pathology Gen. Hosp. Kuala Lumpur, West Malaysia, 1974-76; cons. legal medicine Malaysian Govt., Kuala Lumpur, 1974-80; forensic pathologist Malaysian Govt., Kuching, Sarawak, East Malaysia, 1980—; vol. Med. Mission for Haj Pilgrimage, Mecca, Medina, Saudi Arabia, 1972; rural med. vol. Perkim, West Malaysia, 1973-80, Perkis, East Malaysia, 1980-87. Contbr. articles to med. jours. Home: Meranti Roadway Rd, Kuching Sarawak, Malaysia

JEHANGIR, ALAM, surgeon; b. Lahore, Pakistan, Aug. 1, 1934; s. Abdul Majid and Iqbal (Begum); m. Rehana Jehangir, Mar. 2, 1963; children: Sarah Zarah, Shahreyar, Fehreyar. M Medicine and Sci., King Edward Med. Coll., Lahore, Pakistan, 1956, MS, 1960. Research asst. Pakistan Med. Council, Lahore, 1957-58; registrar surgery Mayo Hosp., Lahore, 1959-61, vis. surgeon, 1961-63; surg. specialist Services Hosp., Lahore, 1965-71; chief med. officer Water and Power Devel. Authority, Lahore, 1972-78; cons. surgeon Lahore, 1979—; asst. prof. surgery King Edward Med. Coll., Lahore, 1961-63. V.p. Pakistan Soc. Planned Parenthood, Lahore, 1981—, project dir., 1986—. Recipient Common Wealth scholarship British Council, 1962-63. Fellow Royal Coll. Surgeons (England and Scotland); mem. Pakistan Soc. Surgeons, Pakistan Med. Assn. (pres. Lahore chpt. 1978-80). Clubs: Punjab, Gymkhana. Home: 15-B Ahmed Block, New Garden Town, Lahore Pakistan Office: 2-Golf Rd, Lahore Pakistan

JEITSCHKO, WOLFGANG KARL, chemistry educator; b. Prague, May 27, 1936; came to Germany, 1975; s. Karl Friedrich and Agnes (Maier) J.; m. Marieluise Fichtner, July 19, 1964; children: Andreas Wolfgang, Thomas David, Peter Oliver. Student Techhochschule, Wien 1956-62, Dr. Phil., U. Wien, 1964. With Metallwerke Plansee AG, Reutte/Tyrol, 1962-64; post doctoral fellow U. Pa., Phila., 1964-66; research assoc., lectr. U. Ill., Champaign-Urbana, 1967-69; with cen. research dept. DuPont Co., Wilmington, Del., 1969-75; prof. U. Giessen, Germany, 1975-79; ordinary prof. U. Dortmund, Germany, 1979-82; ordinary prof., dir. U. Muenster, Germany, 1982—. Mem. Am. Chem. Soc., Am. Crystallographic Assn., Gesellschaft Deutscher Chemiker, Deutsche Gesellsch. Metallkd.. Contbr. articles to profl. jours. Office: Anorganisch-Chemisches Inst Univ, Wilhelm-Klemm-str 8, D-4400 Muenster Federal Republic of Germany

JELEN, JAROSLAW ANDRZEJ, mathematician, researcher; b. Nowy Targ, Cracow, Poland, Sept. 14, 1943; came to Can., 1984; s. Henryk and Maria (Cieslewicz) J.; m. Alicja Barbara Solecka, Feb. 13, 1971; 1 child, Marek. MS in Math., U. Wroclaw, Poland, 1969; PhD, Acad. Mining and Metallurgy, Cracow, Poland, 1978. Programmer, computer factory, Wroclaw, 1969-71; research scientist Petroleum Inst., Cracow, 1971-78; asst. prof. U. Cracow, 1979-84; research scientist Nova Husky Research Co. Ltd., Calgary, Alta., Can., 1985. Contbr. articles to profl. jours. Co-inventor in area of oil and gas exploitation. Mem. Am. Math. Soc., Solidarity (Poland). Roman Catholic. Avocations: downhill skiing, swimming, hiking. Home: 35 Sanderling Hill NW, Calgary, AB Canada T3K 3B6

JELINEK, YESHAYAHU ANDREW, historian, educator; b. Prievidza, Czechoslovakia, July 16, 1933; s. Vojtech and Regina (Rosenthal) J.; m. Miriam Funt, Feb. 14, 1948; children: Noa'ah, Ori, Hadas. BA, Hebrew U., 1961, MA, 1963; PhD, Ind. U., 1966. Vis. asst. prof. U. Denver, 1966-67, U. Minn., Mpls., 1967-69; sr. lectr. U. Haifa, Israel, 1969-77; vis. lectr. Columbia U., N.Y.C., 1975; vis. assoc. prof. Denison U., Granville, Ohio, 1978-79; assoc. prof. history Ben Gurion U. Negev, Beer-Sheva, Israel, 1980—; sr. researcher Ben Gurion Research Inst., Kiriat Sdeh Boker, Israel, 1980—. Author: The Parish Republic: Hlinka's Slovak People's Party, 1939-45, 1976; The Lust for Power: Nationalism, Slovakia, and the Communists, 1918-1948, 1983; contbr. articles to profl. jours. Served with Israeli Army, 1951-53. Recipient award Inst. Contemporary Jewry, Jerusalem, 1961; fgn. student fellow Inds. U., Bloomington, 1963-66; sr. research fellow Columbia U., N.Y.C., 1975; recipient awards Meml. Found. Jewish Culture, 1979-84. Mem. Am. Assn. Advancement Slavic Studies, Assn. Jewish Studies, Czechoslovak History Conf., Assn. Slovak Studies. Office: Ben Gurion Research Inst, Kiriat Sdeh Boker 84993, Israel

JELKILDE, STIG, agricultural development adminstrator; b. Copenhagen, July 9, 1941; s. Ib Thejll and Else (Hammelev) Jelnes; m. Estrid Soekilde, July 15, 1966 (div. Aug. 1985); children—Leif, Johanne, Ida Kirstine. B.Sc., Frederiksborg Statsskole U., Denmark, 1960; M. Sc. (hon), Royal Vet. and Agr. U., Denmark, 1969. Assoc. expert FAO, Paraguay, 1969-71; asst. to country rep., Columbia, 1971-73, World Food Programme project officer, Central Am., 1973-76, asst. rep., Columbia, 1976-80, dep. rep., Ecuador, 1980-82; agr. coordinator Danagro Adviser, Denmark, 1982-84; agr. devel. adminstr. World Agro Consult, Denmark, 1984—, I. Krü ger A/S, Denmark, 1985, Cowiconsult, Denmark, 1987—. Mem. Danish Singing Soc., 1984—. Served to 1st lt. Royal Danish Lifeguard, 1961-63. Mem. Assn. Danish Univ. Grads. in Agr. Liberal. Lutheran. Home: Azaleaparken Roskildevej 53, lej 2 208, DK-2000 Copenhagen F Denmark Office: World Agro Consult, Roskildevej 53 LEJ 2 208, DK-2000 Copenhagen F Denmark

JELKS, EDWARD BAKER, archeologist, educator; b. Macon, Ga., Sept. 10, 1922; s. Oliver Robinson and Lucille (Jarrett) J.; m. Juliet Elizabeth Christian, Aug. 12, 1944; 1 son, Edward Christian. B.A., U. Tex., 1948, M.A., 1951, Ph.D., 1965. Archeologist Smithsonian Instn., 1950-53, Nat. Park Service, 1953-58; research scientist U. Tex., Austin, 1958-65; assoc. prof. anthropology So. Meth. U., Dallas, 1965-68; prof. anthropology Ill. State U., Normal, 1968-84; prof. emeritus Ill. State U., 1984—; dir. Midwestern Archeol. Research Ctr., 1981-84; active archeol. field research Tex., La., Ill., Va., Mo., Nfld., Micronesia. Co-author: Handbook of Texas Archeology, 1954, Trick Taking Potential, 1974, The Joachim De Brum House, Likiep, Marshall Islands, 1978; author: Archaelogical Explorations at Signal Hill, Newfoundland, 1973; editor: Historical Dictionary of North American Archaeology, 1988. Served with USN, 1942-44. Recipient Outstanding Contributions to Field of Va. Antiquities ann. award, 1982, Clarence H. Webb award, 1984, J.C. Harrington medal Hist. Archaeology, 1988; Smithsonian Instn. research fellow, 1968. Fellow AAAS; mem. Tex. Archeol. Soc. (pres. 1957-58), Soc. Profl. Archeologists (pres. 1976-77, grievance coordinator 1987-88), Soc. Hist. Archaeology (pres. 1968-69), Am. Soc. for Conservation Archaeology (v.p. 1975-76), Pan Am. Inst. Geography and History (chmn. archaeology work group 1982—), Soc. for Am. Archaeology, Delta Chi. Home: 605 N School St Normal IL 61761

JELLICOE, GEORGE PATRICK JOHN RUSHWORTH, business executive, government official; b. Apr. 4, 1918; s. Earl Jellicoe and Florence Gwendoline (Cayzer) J.; m. Patricia Christine O'Kane, 1944 (div. 1966); 4 children; m. Philippa Dunne, 1966; 3 children. Student, U. Cambridge; LLD (hon.), U. Southampton. 1st sec. Diplomatic Service, Washington, Brussels, Baghdad; then Lord-in-Waiting 1961; joint parliamentary sec. Ministry of Housing and Local Govt., 1961-62; minister of state Home Office, 1962-63; first lord of the admiralty 1963-64; minister of def. Royal Navy, 1964; dep. leader opposition House of Lords, 1967-70, leader, 1970-73; Lord Privy Seal and minister-in-charge Civil Service Dept., 1970-73; chmn. Med. Research Council, 1982—; chmn. Davy Corp. plc, 1985; bd. dirs. Warburg and Co., Sotheby and Co., Morgan Crucible, Tate and Lyle; chancellor Southampton U., 1984—. Chmn. Brit. Adv. Com. on Oil Pollution of the Sea, 1968-70, 3d Internat. Conf. of Commerce and Industry, 1979-82, East European Trade Council, 1986—, Anglo-Hellenic League, 1978-86; pres. Nat. Fedn. Housing Socs., 1965-70, mem. parliamentary and sci. com., 1980-83; gov. Ctr. for Environmental Studies, 1967-70; hon. page to King George VI. Served Brit. mil., World War II. Decorated Knight Comdr. Order of Brit. Empire, 1986. Club: Brooks. Home: Tidcombe Manor, Tidcombe near Marlborough, Wilts England Office: Onslow Square, London SW7, England *

JELSMA, EDWARD RICHARD, transportation consultant; b. Enid, Okla., Mar. 15, 1915; s. Edward Darwin and Orilla (Hackathorn) J.; B.S., Okla. State U., 1937, M.S., 1938; postgrad. Stanford, 1939-40; diploma internat. law U.S. Naval War Coll.; diploma Mind Control Inst.; Ph.D. (hon.), Colo. Christian Coll., 1973; m. Marjorie Marie Crain, Feb. 12, 1948 (dec. June 1984); children—Schuyler, Richard, Lisa; m. Erika M. Jelsma, 1985. Asst. to tax counsel Standard Oil Co. Calif., San Francisco, 1940-41; dep. fiscal dir. Bur. Ordnance, U.S. Dept. Navy, Washington, 1946-48, asst. fiscal dir. dept., 1948-49; engaged in citrus industry, 1949—; profl. mem. Interstate and Fgn. Commerce Com., U.S. Senate, 1949-55; dir. bur. transport econs. and stats. ICC, 1955-58; admitted to ICC bar, 1958; pres. E.R. Jelsma & Assocs., transp. cons., 1958—; pres. Skyland Farms, Agro Energy Corp., 1980-82; grad. asst. Okla. State U., 1937-38; instr. Northwestern State Coll., 1938-39, Am. U., 1946-49; guest lectr. U. Louisville, 1942-43. Pres., Sylvan Shores Assn., Mt. Dora, 1973-82; chmn. Lake County Republican Exec. Com., 1985-88. Served from ensign to lt. comdr., USN, 1941-52, ret. Mem. State of Fla. Res. Officers Assn. (v.p. 1982-83, pres. Fla. chpt. 1983-84). Club: Mason (32 deg.). Author: Minimum Wage Legislation, 1938. Office: 1811 Morningside Dr Mount Dora FL 32757

JEMNITZ, JÁNOS, historian; b. Budapest, Hungary, Nov. 27, 1930; s. Sándor Jemnitz and Julia Weisz; divorced; children: Katalin, Anna. Diploma, Eötvös Lorund U., Budapest, 1953. Cons. MTA Történettudományi Intézet; mem. internat. consultive bd. Internationaler Tagung der Historiker der Arbeiterbewegung, Vienna, Austria, 1980—. Author: A Hábouru Veszélye és a II Int., 1966, The Danger of War and the II International, 1972, A Nemzetközi Munkásmozgalom, 1914-1917, 1975; co-editor: Karl Kautsky...und Südosteuzopa, 1986. Home: XII Arnyas u 1/a, Budapest Hungary Office: MTA Történettudományi Intézet, I Uri u 51-53, Budapest Hungary

JENEFSKY, JACK, wholesale executive; b. Dayton, Ohio, Oct. 27, 1919; s. David and Anna (Saeks) J.; m. Beverly J. Mueller, Feb. 23, 1962; 1 child, Anna Elizabeth; 1 stepchild, Cathryn Jean Mueller. BSBA, Ohio State U., 1941; postgrad. Harvard Bus. Sch., 1943; MA in Econs., U. Dayton, 1948. Surplus broker, Dayton, 1946-48; sales rep. Remington Rand-Univac, Dayton, 1949-56, mgr. AF account, 1957-59, br. mgr. Dayton, 1960-61, regional mktg. cons. Midwest region, Dayton, 1962-63; pres. Bowman Supply Co., Dayton, 1963—. Selection adv. bd. Air Force Acad., 3d congl. dist., chmn., 1974-82; chmn. 3d. dist. screening bds. Mil. Acad., 1976-82; coordinator Great Lakes region, res. assistance program CAP, 1970-73. Served from pvt. to capt. USAAF, 1942-46; CBI, maj. USAF, 1951-53; col Res. Mem. Air Force Assn. (comdr. Ohio wing 1957-58, 58-59), Res. Officers Assn. (pres. Ohio dept. 1956-57, nat. council 1957-58, chmn. research and devel. com. 1961-62), Dayton Area C. of C. (chmn. spl. events com. 1970-72, chmn. research com. on mil. affairs 1983—), Miami Valley Mil. Affairs Assn. (trustee 1985—, pres. bd. trustees 1987—), Ohio State U. Alumni Assn. (pres. Montgomery County, Ohio, 1959-60), Nat. Sojourners (pres. Dayton 1961-62). Jewish. Club: Harvard Bus. Sch. Dayton (pres. 1961-62). Lodge: Lions. Home: 136 Briar Heath Circle Dayton OH 45415 Office: Bowman Supply Co PO Box 1404 Dayton OH 45401

JENKINS, BRUCE ARMAND, manufacturing company executive; b. Lansing, Mich., June 4, 1933; s. George H. Jenkins and Margaret E. (Hoeflinger) Tinlin; m. Peggy A. Unruh, July 22, 1967; children: David, Mark. With Gen. Motors Corp., Lansing, 1953-83, supr. tech. tng., 1984-86; pres. Advanced Tech. Seminars, Inc., Eagle, Mich., 1986—; chmn. bd. Allied Tech. Tooling, Inc., Potterville, Mich., 1987—. Author: Automotive Plastics, 1985, Plastics Repair, 1986, Cast Plastic Tooling Techniques, 1986; contbr. numerous articles to profl. jours. Pastor Foursquare Gospel Ch., Eagle, 1983—. Served to 1st lt. U.S. Army, 1950-1961. Republican. Office: Advanced Tech Seminars Inc PO Box 42 Eagle MI 48822 also: Allied Tech Tooling Inc 570 E Main St Potterville MI 48876

JENKINS, CHARLES FRANKLIN, educator; b. Kansas City, Mo., Sept. 20, 1926; s. Festus Earl and Winnifred Chasteen (Nicholson) J.; m. Evelyn M. Jenkins, May 28, 1988. A.A., Kansas City Jr. Coll., 1945; B.A., U. Mo., 1948, M.A., 1951, postgrad. summers, nights 1951-52, 72-74; postgrad. summers Cornell U., 1953, 54; Ed.S., Central Mo. State U., 1971; Ed.D., U. Kans., 1979. Tchr. sci. and math. Raytown (Mo.) Jr. High Sch., 1951-54, Paseo High Sch., Kansas City, Mo., 1954-58; tchr. math Basehor (Kans.) Jr. High Sch., 1964-68, Old Mission Jr. High Sch., Shawnee Mission, Kans., 1968-77; tchr. sci. Raytown High Sch., 1977-78, Lewis Middle Sch., Excelsior Springs, Mo., 1978-79; spl. edn. tchr., homebound program Kansas City (Mo.) Public Schs., 1979—. Served with AUS, 1946-47. Mem. Nat. Council Tchrs. Math, Research Council Diagnostic and Prescriptive Math, NEA (life), Assn. Supervision and Curriculum Devel., Phi Delta Kappa. Democrat. Methodist. Home: 15 E Pocahontas Ln Kansas City MO 64114 Office: Kansas City Public Schs Bd Edn Bldg 1211 McGee St Kansas City MO 64106

JENKINS, CLARA BARNES, educator; b. Franklinton, N.C.; d. Walter and Stella (Griffin) Barnes; BS, Winston-Salem State U., 1939; MA, N.C. Ctl. U., 1947; EdD, U. Pitts., 1965; postgrad., N.Y.U., 1947-48, U. N.C.-Chapel Hill, 1963, N.C. Agrl. and Tech. State U., 1971; m. Hugh Jenkins, Dec. 24, 1949 (div. Feb. 1955). Tchr. pub. schs., Wendell, N.C., 1939-43, Wise, N.C., 1943-45; mem. faculty Fayetteville State U., 1945-53, Rust Coll., Holly Spring, Miss., 1953-58; asst. prof. Shaw U., 1958-64; prof. edn. and psychology St. Paul's Coll., Lawrenceville, Va., 1964—; vis. prof. edn. Friendship Jr. Coll., Rock Hill, S.C., summer 1947, N.C. Agrl. and Tech. State U., 1966-83. Former mem. bd. dirs. Winston-Salem State U. Notary pub., N.C.; United Negro Coll. Fund Faculty fellow, 1963-64; Am. Bapt. Conv. grantee, 1963-64. Mem. AAUP, Nat. Soc. for Study Edn., NEA, AAUW, Am. Hist. Assn., Va. Edn. Assn., Am. Acad. Polit. and Social Sci., AAAS, Internat. Platform Assn., Assn. Tchr. Educators, History Edn. Soc., Doctoral Assn. Educators, Am. Assn. Higher Edn., Am. Soc. Notaries, Acad. Polit. Sci., Am. Psychol. Assn., Soc. Research in Child Devel., Am. Soc. Notaries, Marquis Biog. Library Soc., Jean Piaget Soc., Philosophy of Edn. Soc., Soc. Profs. Edn., Am. Soc. Notaries, Phi Eta Kappa, Zeta Phi Beta, Phi Delta Kappa, Kappa Delta Pi. Episcopalian. Home: 920 Bridges St Henderson NC 27536 Office: St Paul's Coll Lawrenceville VA 23868

JENKINS, E. CYNTHIA, state legislator; b. Nashville, July 21, 1924; d. Stephen Alexander and Mayne Hampton (Young) Burnley; B.A., U. Louisville, 1945; M.L.A., Pratt Inst., 1966; postgrad., Columbia U.; m. Joseph D. Jenkins, Apr. 17, 1949; 1 son, Joseph D. Librarian, Bklyn. Public Library, 1960-62; br. librarian Queensborough Public Library, Jamaica, N.Y., 1962—; mem. N.Y. State Assembly, 1982—. Founder, Social Concern Vendor Agy., Social Concern Home Attendant Program; elected Dem. dist. leader 29th Assembly Dist., 1978—; charter mem. Women's Legis. Caucus; founder, pres. Social Concern Nat. Credit Union; charter mem. Queens Women's Polit. Caucus; founder SE Queens Regular Dem. Club: charter mem. Queens chpt. Top Ladies of Distinction. Recipient service citation Negro Bus. and Profl. Women, Jamaica chpt. Mem. N.Y. Black Librarians Caucus (founder), ALA (council), N.Y. Library Assn., Alpha Kappa Alpha (award, Epsilon Pi Omega chpt.). Methodist. Editor, contbr. Forum mag.; contbr. to Handbook on Black Librarianship. Home: 174-63 128 Ave Jamaica NY 11434 Office: 226-18 Merrick Blvd Laurelton NY 11413

JENKINS, E(THEL) VALERIE, retired media specialist; b. Amherst, Ohio, Sept. 7, 1913; d. Frank A. and Ethel E. (Dute) Eppley; student Hiram Coll., 1932; B.A., Baldwin-Wallace Coll., 1936; postgrad. Western Res. U., 1936, 41, 66, State U. Iowa, 1938-39, Ohio State U., 1960; M.A., Kent State U., 1962; m. William J. Jenkins, Aug. 13, 1944 (div. May 1964). Dir. dramatics Baldwin-Wallace Coll., Berea, Ohio, 1936-38; tchr. English and speech St. Elmo (Ill.) High Sch., 1939-42; tchr. English, speech, dir. dramatics Clearview-Lorain (Ohio) High Sch., 1942-57, librarian, 1949-57; library coordinator Amherst (Ohio) Pub. Schs., 1957-80, drama dir., 1957-60, 75-77; instr. Kent State U., 1963-66; instr. speech Cleve. State U., 1966-70; lectr. costumes for theatre; owner, operator children's theatre, also costume rental; cons. Amherst Pub. Library Bldg. Program, 1972-73. Founder Workshop Players, Inc., 1948, trustee, 1948—, pres., 1948-49, 56-58, 60, 75-80, now vol. worker; mng. dir. Workshop Theatre, 1980—; mem. bd. Amherst Pub. Library, 1962—, pres., 1963-65, 83-85. Recipient Amherst Gallery Success for Alumni, 1987, Alumni Merit award Baldwin-Wallace Coll., 1986, Community Improvement award Amherst C. of C., 1987; Paul Harris fellow Rotary Internat., 1985. Mem. Nat., Ohio (life) edn. assns., Am. Theatre Assn., ALA, Ohio Ednl. Library Media Assn. (dir. NE chpt. 1974-76), Amherst Tchrs. Assn. (pres. 1962-64), Delta Kappa Gamma, Phi Mu. Republican. Congregationalist. Home: 439 Shupe Ave Amherst OH 44001

JENKINS, GEORGE HENRY, photographer, educator; b. Shanghai, China, Oct. 24, 1929 (parents Am. citizens); s. Clarence O. and Efransinia M. (Pomorenkoff) J.; grad. N.Y. Inst. Photography, 1952; student Purdue U., 1952-55; student Ind. U., 1955-58, B.B.A., Ind. No. U., 1972; M.Ed., Wayne State U., 1976, Ph.D., 1985; Ph.D., Columbia Pacific U., 1984; m. Madge Marie Vickroy, Aug. 19, 1967. Photographer, Ft. Wayne (Ind.) Jour.-Gazette, 1952-55; computer programer Gen. Electric Co., Ft. Wayne, 1955-61; data processing mgr. Columbia Record Club subs. CBS, Terre Haute, Ind., 1961-63; adminstrv. coordinator Capital Record Club, Scranton, Pa. and Toronto, Ont., Can., 1963-64; mktg. systems analyst Xerox Corp., Detroit, 1964-66; dir. systems and data processing Nicholson File Co., Anderson, Ind., 1966-69; hosp. adminstr. Wayne County Gen. Hosp., Eloise, Mich., 1969-78; asst. prof. bus. Western Washington U., Bellingham, 1978-80; asst. prof. Lima (Ohio) Tech. Coll., 1980-83; assoc. prof. Findlay (Ohio) Coll., 1983—; freelance photographer, 1969—, writer/producer, 1984—. Chmn. supervisory bd. Eloise Credit Union, 1972-76. Served with USAF, 1948-52. Cert. data processor, data educator, systems profl. Mem. Photog. Soc. Gt. Britain, Photog. Soc. Am., Assn. System Mgmt., Human Factors Soc., Am. Inst. Indsl. Engrs., Data Processing Mgmt. Assn. of Lima (pres. 1984-85). Presbyterian. Clubs: 8-16 Film and Video Movie Makers (Detroit), Detroit Yacht, Lima. Lodge: Elks. (Lima, Ohio). Home: 710 W Main St Cairo OH 45820 Office: Findlay Coll Findlay OH 45840

JENKINS, ORVILLE WESLEY, retired religious administrator; b. Hico, Tex., Apr. 29, 1913; s. Daniel Wesley and Eva (Caldwell) J.; m. Louise Cantrell, June 29, 1939; children—Orville Wesley, Jannette (Mrs. John Calhoun), Jeanne (Mrs. David Hubbs). Student, Tex. Tech U., 1929-34; B.A., Pasadena Coll., 1938; student, Nazarene Theol. Sem., 1946-47; D.D., So. Nazarene U., 1957. Ordained to ministry Ch. of Nazarene, 1939; pastor Dinuba, Calif., 1938-42, Fresno, Calif., 1942-45, Topeka, 1945-47, Salem, Oreg., 1947-50, Kansas City, Mo., 1959-61; supt. West Tex. Dist. Ch. of Nazarene, 1950-59, Kansas City Dist., 1961-64; exec. sec. dept. home missions Ch. of Nazarene, Kansas City, 1946-68; gen. supt. Ch. of Nazarene, 1968-85. Former trustee So. Nazarene U. Home: 2309 W 103d St Leawood KS 66206 Office: 6401 Paseo Kansas City MO 64131

JENKINS, ROBERT ELLSWORTH, JR., ecologist; b. Lewistown, Pa., Sept. 30, 1942; s. Robert Ellsworth and Ellen Magdalena (Wesner) J.; AB, Rutgers U., 1964; PhD, Harvard U., 1970; m. Diane Alyce St. Pierre, Nov. 4, 1964; children: Heather Elizabeth, Robert Ellsworth III. Mem. staff Nature Conservancy, Washington, 1970—, v.p. sci. programs, 1972—; co-founder Center Applied Research in Environ. Scis., 1971; founder, dir. State Natural Heritage Programs, 1974—; sci. advisor WNET Nature, 1986—. Mem. Conservation sect. U.S. com. Internat. Biol. Program, 1970-75; mem. Fed. Com. Research Natural Areas, 1970—, U.S. Nat. Commn. for UNESCO, 1974-76; research asso. Smithsonian Instn., 1971-73; mem. bd. Rare Animal Relief Effort, 1974-76; mem. U.S. com. for CODATA, 1987—, parks and preserves com. U.S./Soviet Environ. Protection Agreements; mem. natural areas com. U.S. Man and Biosphere Program, 1978—; adv. council Ctr. for Plant Conservation, 1984—; mem. sci. adv. bd. Stanford Inst. for Conservation Biol., 1984—; councellor Xerces Soc., 1985—; mem. U.S. Nat. Commn. for CODATA, 1987 ; adv. com. Can. Nat. Biol. Survey, 1986—; chmn. commn. on Biol. Diversity and Survey of Assn. of Systematics Collections, 1986—. Bd. dirs. Mass. Planned Parenthood League, 1970-73, bd. gov's. Soc. for Conservation Biology, 1988—. Recipient Conservation award Am. Motors Corp., 1978; Henry Rutgers scholar, 1963-64; Richmond fellow, 1965-69; research fellow Orgn. Tropical Studies, 1966; NCN Species Sarvival Commn. rep, 1984-87, regional mem., 1988-91Demographic fellow Population Council, 1969-70. Fellow AAAS (council 1972-73); mem. Am. Inst. Biol. Scis. (council 1970—), Ecol. Soc. Am., Wildlife Soc., Soc. for Conservation (mem.-at-large, bd. govs.), Nature Conservancy, Zero Population Growth (founder, dir. Mass. 1969-70). Home: RFD 6 Box 335 Warrenton VA 22186 Office: 1800 N Kent St Arlington VA 22209

JENKINS, ROGER LANE, marketing educator; b. June 16, 1946; m. Basia Matthews; children—Sean Kirk, Sasha Nicole. B.S. in Bus. Adminstrn., Berea (Ky.) Coll., 1968; M.B.A., E. Tenn. State U., 1970; Ph.D., Ohio State U., 1976. Acct., Shell Oil Co., Tenn., 1965-66; asst. to treas. Berea Coll., 1966-68; auditor Kemper Ins., Chgo., 1967, 68; internat. acct. Eastman Kodak, 1969-76; instr. acctg. E. Tenn. State U., 1970-73; asst. dir. grad. bus. programs Ohio State U., 1973-76, asst. prof. mktg., 1977-78; asst. prof. U. Tenn., Knoxville, 1978-80, asso. prof., 1980-86, prof., 1987—, now also dean grad. bus. programs. Warren Wilson scholar, 1963-65; James S. Kemper scholar, 1966-68; Albert Herring fellow, 1976. Mem. Am. Mktg. Assn., So. Mktg. Assn., Midwest Mktg. Assn., Acad. Mktg. Sci. (program co-chmn. 1982—, program chmn. 1984, pres. 1986—, trustee grad. mgmt. council 1986—, vice chmn. 1987, chmn. bd. trustees 1988—), Assn. Consumer Research, Am. Inst. Decision Sci. (mktg. book rev. editor 1979-80), Acad. Internat. Bus. (pres., bd. dirs.), Dogwood Arts Festival. Home: 3933 Topside Rd Knoxville TN 37920 Office: U Tenn 721 Stokely Mgmt Ctr Knoxville TN 37996

JENKINS, ROY HARRIS, member British Parliament, writer; b. Nov. 11, 1920; s. Arthur and Hattie J.; m. Jennifer Morris, 1945; 2 sons, 1 dau. ed. Abersychan Grammar Sch., also Balliol Coll., Oxford (Eng.) U.; numerous hon. degrees. Mem. staff Indsl. and Comml. Fin. Corp., 1946-48; Labour Party mem. Parliament, 1948-77, Social Democratic mem., 1982-87; chancellor Oxford U., 1987—; parliamentary pvt. sec. to sec. state commonwealth relations, 1949-50; gov. Brit. Films Inst., 1955-58; mem. com. mgmt. Soc. Authors, 1956-60; chmn. Fabian Soc., 1957-58; mem. council Britain in Europe; dep. chmn. Common Market campaign, 1961-63; dir. fin. ops. John Lewis Partnership Ltd., 1963-64; minister of aviation, 1964-65; sec. state for home dept., 1965-67; chancellor of exchequer, 1967-70; dep. leader Labour party, 1970-72; home sec., 1974-77; pres. Commn. European Communities, 1977-81; privy Councillor; a founder, first leader Social Democratic Party, 1981. Served with Royal Arty., 1942-46. Recipient Charlemagne prize, 1972; Robert Schumann prize, 1972; prix Bentinck, 1978; decorated Order of Merit (Luxembourg), 1976; grand cross Order of Charles III (Spain), 1980. Mem. Am. Acad. Arts and Scis. (hon. fgn.). Author: Mr. Attlee: An Interim Biography, 1948; New Fabian Essays, 1952; Pursuit of Progress, 1953; Mr. Balfour's Poodle, 1954; Sir Charles Dilke: A Victorian Tragedy, 1958; The Labour Case, 1959; Asquith, 1964; Essays and Speeches, 1967; Afternoon on the Potomac, 1972; What Matters Now, 1972; Nine Men of Power, 1974; Partnership of Principle, 1985; Truman, 1986.

JENNEKENS, JON HUBERT, international energy agency executive; b. Toronto, Ont., Can., Oct. 21, 1932; s. Hubert Joseph and Laura Cecelia (Thorvaldson) J.; m. Norah Margaret Magee, June 6, 1954; children: Sandra Ellen, Jon Darren, Jennifer Norah. R.M.C., Royal Mil. Coll., Kingston, Ont., Can., 1954; BSc with honors, Queens U., Kingston, Ont., Can., 1956. Nuclear ops. engr., dir. regulation Atomic Energy of Can. Ltd. and Atomic Energy Control Bd., Ottawa, Ont., 1958-87; also pres., chief exec. officer Atomic Energy Control Bd., Ottawa, Ont.; dep. dir. gen. of safeguards Internat. Atomic Energy Agency, Vienna, Austria, 1987—. Served to 1st lt. Royal Can. Elec. and Civil Engrs., 1954-58, Korea and Can. Decorated officer of the Order of Canada. Fellow Can. Acad. Engring.; mem. Assn. Profl. Engrs. Ont. (cert.). Home: Wegelergasse 6-6, A 1400 Vienna Austria Office: Internat Atomic Energy Agy, Wagramerstrasse 5, Postfach 100, A-1400 Vienna Austria

JENNER, WILLIAM ALEXANDER, meteorologist, educator; b. Indianola, Iowa, Nov. 10, 1915; s. Edwin Alexander and Elizabeth May (Brown) J.; AB, Cen. Meth. Coll., Mo., 1938; certificate meteorology U. Chgo., 1943; MEd, U. Mo., 1947; postgrad. Am. U., 1951-58; m. Jean Norden, Sept. 1, 1946; children—Carol Beth, Paul William, Susan Lynn. Instr. U. Mo., 1946-47; research meteorologist U.S. Weather Bur., Chgo., 1947-49; staff Hdqrs. Air Weather Service, Andrews AFB, Md., 1949-58, Scott AFB, Ill., 1958-84, dir. tng., 1960-84. Mem. O'Fallon (Ill.) Twp. High Sch. Bd. Edn., 1962—, sec., 1964-71, pres., 1971-83, 1985-87; pres. St. Clair County Regional Vocat. System Bd., 1986—; vice chmn. southwestern div. Ill. Assn. Sch. Bds., 1987—; comdr. 507 th Fighter Group Assn. Inc., 1987—; mem. O'Fallon Planning Commn., 1973-84, sec., 1979-81, sub-div. chmn., 1978-84; alderman City of O'Fallon, 1984—. Served with AUS, 1942-46. Recipient Disting. Service award O'Fallon PTA, 1968, Disting. Service award City of O'Fallon, 1985, Merit cert. St. Clair County, 1987; Exceptional Civilian Service award Dept. Air Force, 1984; Jenmer Award established by Air Weather Service, 1984. Fellow Am. Meteorol. Soc.; mem. Am. Psychol. Assn., Wilson Ornithological Soc., Am. Philatelic Soc., Am. Philatelic Congress, Am. Meteorol. Soc., AAAS, Nat. Soc. Study Edn., N.Y. Acad. Scis., Am. Legion, Phi Delta Kappa, Psi Chi. Clubs: Masons, Shriners, O'Fallon Sportsmen's, Toastmasters Internat. Home: 307 Alma St O'Fallon IL 62269

JENNINGS, ALSTON, lawyer; b. West Helena, Ark., Oct. 30, 1917; s. Earp Franklin and Irma (Alston) J.; m. Dorothy Buie Jones, June 12, 1943; children: Alston, Eugene Franklin, Ann Buie. A.B., Columbia U., 1938; J.D., Northwestern U., 1941. Bar: Ark. 1941. Practiced law Little Rock, 1947—; spl. agt. intelligence unit Treasury Dept., 1946; asso. Wright, Harrison, Lindsey & Upton, 1949-51, mem., 1951-60; mem. Wright, Lindsey, Jennings, Lester & Shults, 1960-65, Wright, Lindsey and Jennings, 1965—. Bd. dirs. Community Chest Greater Little Rock; mem. adv. bd. Salvation Army, Pulaski County. Served to lt. USNR, 1941-45. Fellow Am. Bar Found.; mem. ABA, Ark. Bar Assn., Pulaski County Bar Assn. (past pres.), Internat. Assn. Ins. Counsel (pres. 1972-73), Am. Coll. Trial Lawyers (regent 1975-79, treas. 1979-80, pres.-elect 1980-81, pres. 1981-82). Home: 5300 Sherwood Little Rock AR 72207 Office: 200 W Capitol Ave Little Rock AR 72201

JENNINGS, EDWARD HARRINGTON, university president; b. Mpls., Feb. 18, 1937; s. Edward G. and Ruth (Harrington) J.; children: William F., Steven W. B.S., U. N.C., 1959; M.B.A., Western Res. U., 1963; Ph.D. (NDEA fellow 1966-69), U. Mich., 1969. Engr. Deering Milliken Co., Spartanburg, S.C., 1959-61, Merck & Co., West Point, Pa., 1963-65; mem. faculty U. Iowa, 1969-75, v.p. fin., 1975-79; vis. prof. U. Der es Salam, Tanzania, 1971-72; pres. U. Wyo., Laramie, 1979-81, Ohio State U., Columbus, 1981—. Co-author: Fundamentals of Investments, 1976; contbr. articles profl. jours. Mem. Am. Fin. Assn., Western Fin. Assn., Midwest Fin. Assn. Lutheran. Office: Ohio State U 190 N Oval Mall Columbus OH 43210 *

JENNINGS, ELIZABETH, poet, critic; b. Boston, Lincs, U.K., July 18, 1926; d. H. C. Jennings. M.A., St. Anne's Coll., Oxford U. Asst. Oxford City Library (Eng.), 1950-58; reader Chatto & Windus Ltd., 1958-60; free-lance writer, 1960—. Author books of poetry: Poems, 1953; A Way of Looking (Somerset Maugham award 1956), 1955; A Sense of the World, 1958; Song for A Birth or Death, 1961; Recoveries, 1963; The Mind has Mountains (Richard Hillary Prize 1966), 1966; (for children) The Secret Brother, 1966; Collected Poems, 1967; The Animals' Arrival, 1969; Lucidities, 1971; Relationships, 1972; Growing Points, 1975; Consequently I Rejoice, 1977; (for children) After the Ark, 1978; Moments of Grace, 1979; Celebrations and Elegies, 1982; Criticism: Every Changing Shape, 1961; Seven Men of Vision, 1976; Moments of Grace, 1979; Selected Poems, 1979; In Praise of Our Lady, 1982; Extending the Territory, 1985; A Quintet, 1985; Collected Poems, 1986 (W.H. Smith award 1987); author translation of Michelangelo's Sonnets, 1961; contbr. to New Yorker, So. Rev. Poetry, Botteghe Oscure, Daily Telegraph, Encounter, New Statesman, Observer, Scotsman, Country Life, Listener and others; editor: Batsford Book of Religious Verse, 1982. Recipient Arts Council prize for Poems, 1953, Arts Council award, 1981. Office: care David Higham Assocs Ltd. 5-8 Lower John St, London W1R 4HA, England

JENNINGS, JEFFREY HOWELLS, lawyer; b. Pitts., Feb. 16, 1919; s. Elroy Jeffrey and Bertha Marie (Howells) J.; m. Patricia Walmsley, Oct. 26, 1945; children—Randolph, Sharon, Thomas, Andrea, Alison. A.B., Columbia U., 1941, J.D., 1944. Bar: N.Y. 1944. Assoc. to counsel Columbia U., N.Y.C., 1944-55; asst. U.S. atty. Eastern Dist. N.Y., 1961-66; now sole practice, Smithtown, N.Y.; librarian Old Mill Sch., N.Y.C., 1973. Prin. clk. Smithtown Hwy Dept., 1961. Recipient Cross of Honor Order of DeMolay, 1972. Mem. Columbia U. Secondary Sch. Com., Friends Assn. for Higher Edn., Smithtown C. of C. (pres. 1959-60), Phi Delta Phi. Republican. Quaker. Clubs: Dramatists Guild (N.Y.C.). Works include: Battle of the Andes, The Classmate, 1934; Laws into Song, The Fossil, 1963; Manhattan 2, New Oberammergau Players, 1982, India Or Bust, The Countersign, 1987. Home: 1348 Bridgewater Ct Wichita KS 67209 Office: 11 Rainbow Dr Hauppauge NY 11788

JENNINGS, MARCELLA GRADY, rancher, investor; b. Springfield, Ill., Mar. 4, 1920; d. William Francis and Magdalene Mary (Spies) Grady; student pub. schs.; m. Leo J. Jennings, Dec. 16, 1950 (dec.). Pub. relations Econolite Corp., Los Angeles, 1958-61; v.p., asst. mgr. LJ Quarter Circle Ranch, Inc., Polson, Mont., 1961-73, pres., gen. mgr., owner, 1973—; dir. Giselle's Travel Inc., Sacramento; fin. advisor to Allentown, Inc., Charlo, Mont.; sales cons. to Amie's Jumpin' Jacks and Jills, Garland, Tex. investor. Mem. Internat. Charolais Assn., Los Angeles County Apt. Assn. Republican. Roman Catholic. Home and Office: 509 Mt Holyoke Ave Pacific Palisades CA 90272

JENNINGS, MARIANNE MOODY, lawyer, educator; b. Johnstown, Pa., Sept. 11, 1953; d. James L. and Jennie (Ure) Moody; m. Terry H. Jennings, Nov. 5, 1976; children: Sarah Anne, Claire Elizabeth. B.S. in Fin., Brigham Young U., 1974, J.D., 1977. Bar: Ariz. 1977, U.S. Dist. Ct. Ariz. 1977. Law clk. Fed. Pub. Defender, Las Vegas, 1975; U.S. Atty., Las Vegas, 1976, Udall, Shumway, Bentley, Allen & Lyons, Mesa, Ariz., 1976; asst. prof. bus. law Ariz. State U., Tempe, Ariz., 1977-80, assoc. prof., 1980-83, prof., 1983—, assoc. dean, 1986-88. Bd. dirs. Ariz. Girls Ranch, Inc.; gubernatorial appointee Ariz. Corp. Commn., 1984-85. Bd. dirs. Ariz. Pub. Service, Inc., 1987—. Named Outstanding Undergrad. Bus. Prof., Ariz. State U., 1980, 85; recipient Provost Research Incentive Fund Ariz. State U., 1982, 83, Burlington Northern Found. Teaching Excellence award, 1986. Mem. Ariz. Bar Assn., Am. Bus. Law Assn., Pacific Southwest Bus. Law Assn., Faculty Women's Assn., Beta Gamma Sigma. Republican. Mormon. Author: (with Michael Litka) Business Law, 1983; Business Strategy for the Political Arena, 1984; Real Estate Law, 1985, Law for Business, 1985, Business and the Legal Environment, 1988. Office: Ariz State U Coll Business Tempe AZ 85287

JENNINGS, MICHAEL GLENN, author, advertising agency executive; b. Buena Vista, Va., Apr. 17, 1931; s. Glen Edward and Vaughnye Mae (Bays) J.; student Va. and N.J. schs.; m. Susan Berger, Oct. 25, 1975; children by previous marriage—Marc Emery, Jason Glenn, Dana Michael. Advt. copywriter Hicks and Greist, 1948-51; promotion copywriter Louisville Courier-Jour., 1955-56; disc jockey Sta. WKLO, Louisville, 1955-56; house organs editor Home Life Ins. Co., N.Y.C., 1956-58; creative dir. Burke, Charles & Guignon, Ltd., Great Neck, N.Y., 1958-61; pres. Michael Jennings & Colleagues, Williston Park, N.Y., 1961-64; producer, host radio program Michael Jennings' Kaleidoscope, Sta. WLIR, L.I., 1964-65; advt. mgr. Aeolian Pianos, Inc., 1965-68; promotion dir. G.P. Putnam Sons, pubs., 1968-69; v.p., creative dir. Douglas Samuel Advt., Inc., West Caldwell, N.J., 1983-85; autonomous affiliate Douglas Samuel Advt. Inc., West Caldwell, N.J., 1986-87 ; pres. Michael Jennings Advt., Hewitt, N.J., 1987—; author: (novel) There Was a Young Lady From Windmere, 1973; (children's novels) Mattie Fritts and the Flying Mushroom, 1973, Mattie Fritts and the Cuckoo Caper, 1976, The Bears Who Came to Breakfix, 1977; (young adult nonfiction) Tape Recorder Fun: Be Your Own Favorite Disc Jockey, 1978; Robin Goodfellow and The Giant Dwarf, 1981; co-author (play): The Briar Patch, 1982; (screenplay) No Halos in Hell, 1983. Actor, dir. Antrim Players, Suffern, N.Y., 1975-79; narrator Island Lyric Opera, Garden City, N.Y., 1978-79; theatre reviewer Sta. WRKL, Rockland County, N.Y., 1980-81. Served with USAF, 1951-55. Mem. Authors Guild, Dramatists Guild Address: 1584 Macopin Rd West Milford NJ 07480

JENNY, HANS HEINRICH, college administrator; b. Ennenda, Switzerland, Apr. 11, 1922; came to U.S., 1947, naturalized, 1957; s. Sebastian and Gertrude (Peter) J. B.A., Ecole Supérieure de Commerce, Lausanne, Switzerland, 1942; postgrad. U. Lausanne, 1942-43; Lic. rer. pol., U. Bern, Switzerland, 1947, Dr. rer. pol., 1950; postgrad. George Washington U. Law Sch., 1947, Yale U., 1948-49. Instr. dept. econs. Coll. of Wooster, Ohio, 1949-51, asst. prof., 1951-54, assoc. prof., 1954-59, prof., 1959-62, dir. instl. research, 1962-66, v.p. budgetary affairs, 1966-69, v.p. fin. and bus., 1969-81; exec. v.p. Chapman Coll., Orange, Calif., 1982-88, dean Sch. Bus. and Mgmt., 1983-85; mem. staff Nat. Commn. on Financing of Postsecondary Edn., 1971-72, Pres.'s Commn. on Philanthropy and Pub. Needs, 1974-75. Author: The Golden Years, 1970; The Turning Point, 1972; The Consolidated Net Worth of Private Colleges, 1973; The Bottom Line, 1978; Financial Viability in Postsecondary Education, 1979; Institutional Financial Assessment, 1979; Another Challenge: Age 70 Retirement in Higher Education, 1979; Retirement Plans in Transition, 1986; Hang-Gliding, or Looking for an Updraft: A Study of College and University Finance in the 1980s-The Capital Margin, 1980. Bd. dirs. Nat. Ctr. Higher Edn. Mgmt. Systems, Cummins Mid-Am. Inc. Mem. North Cen. Assn. Colls. and Schs. (commr.), Assn. Instl. Research (treas. 1979-82), Inst. for Mgmt. Scis., Nat. Assn. Coll. and Univ. Bus. Officers (chmn. benefits and personnel coms. 1985-88). Lodge: Rotary.

JENS, ARTHUR MARX, JR., insurance company executive; b. Winfield, Ill., June 26, 1912; s. Arthur M. and Jeanette Elizabeth (Vinton) J.; m. Elizabeth Lee Shafer, Aug. 14, 1937; children—Timothy Vinton, Christopher Edward, Jeffrey Arthur. B.S., Northwestern U., 1934; J.D., Kent Coll. Law, Ill. Inst. Tech., 1939. Bar: Ill. 1939. Ins. underwriter, claim mgr. Continental Casualty Co. and Royal Globe Group, Chgo., 1934-39; sec., asst. treas. TWA, Kansas City, Mo., 1939-47; v.p., pres., chmn. bd. Fred S. James & Co. Inc., Chgo., 1947-76, hon. chmn. bd.; dir. Airline Service Corp. and all TWA subs., Comml. Resources Corp.; founder, dir. 6 First Security Banks of DuPage County; chmn. Jenson Corp. Life gov. Central DuPage Hosp.; mem. Ill. Gov.'s Panel on Racing. Mem. Ill. State Bar Assn., ABA, Nat. Assn. Ins. Agts. and Brokers (dir.). Republican. Presbyterian. Clubs: Chgo. Golf (past pres.), Mid-Day (trustee), Chgo. Club (Room 19); Thunderbird Country (Palm Springs, Calif.). Contbr. articles to air transp. and ins. jours. Home: 22 W 210 Stanton Rd Glen Ellyn IL 60137 Office: 230 W Monroe St Chicago IL 60606

JENS, ELIZABETH LEE SHAFER (MRS. ARTHUR M. JENS, JR.), civic worker; b. Monroe, Mich., Jan. 25, 1915; d. Frank Lee and Mary (Bogard) Shafer; student Kalamazoo Coll., 1932-34, U. Wis., summer 1935; B.S., Northwestern U., 1936; postgrad. Wheaton Coll., summer 1965; L.P.N., Triton Coll., 1969; m. Arthur M. Jens, Jr., Aug. 14, 1937; children—Timothy V., Christopher E., Jeffrey A. Gray Lady, Hines, (Ill.) Hosp., 1948-49, 51-53; vol. Elgin (Ill.) State Hosp., 1958-72; writer Newsletter Vol. Planning Council, 1960-62; mem. Family Service Assn. Du Page County; vol. coordinator, chmn. bd. dirs., treas. Thursday Evening Club, social club for recovering mental patients Du Page County, 1966—; vol. FISH orgn., 1973-84. Bd. dirs. Du Page County Mental Health Soc., 1962-68, sec., 1963-64, 65-68, chmn. forgotten patient com., 1963-68, chmn. new projects, 1965-68; co-chmn. Glen Ellyn unit Central Du Page Hosp. Assn. Women's Aux., 1959-60; bd. dirs. chmn. com. on pesticides, Ill. Audubon Soc., 1963-73; mem. Ill. Pesticide Control Com., 1963-73, Citizens Com. Dutch Elm Disease, Glen Ellyn, 1960; bd. dirs. Natural Resources Council Ill., 1961-67, sec., 1961-64; bd. dirs. Du Page Art League, 1958-68, chmn. bd., 1961-63, chmn. new bldg. com., 1968-75; bd. dirs. mem. planning com., publicity chmn. Du Page Fine Arts Assn., 1965-67; bd. dirs. Friends Library Glen Ellyn, 1967-68, Rachel Carson Trust for Living Environment 1971-74; bd. dirs. Du Page Mental Health Assn., 1973—, sec., 1973-75, pres., 1980-81, chmn. community liaison, 1981—, chmn. action group, 1976—; mem. Du Page Subarea adv. council Suburban Cook County-Du Page County Health Systems Agy., 1977-83; bd. dirs. Du Page County Comprehensive Health Planning Agy., 1976, DuPage County Bd. of Health, 1987—; mem. DuPage County Mental HealthAdv. Bd., 1977—; mem. com. on midlife and older women Ill. Commn. on Status of Women, 1978-85; bd. dirs., publicity chmn., DuPage County Council Vol. Coordinators, 1977-78; bd. dirs., membership chmn. Homemakers Equal Rights Assn. in DuPage County, 1979-84; publicity chmn. Homemakers Coalition for Equal Rights, 1984—, pres. 1986—; mem. ERA Ill. Bd., 1987—; mem. DuPage County Health Planning Com., 1984—; mem. Community Care Coalition of DuPage County, 1988—; mem. pub. relations com. Bethlehem Ctr. Food Bank of DuPage County, 1987—; tour guide Stacy's Tavern-Glen Ellyn Hist. Mus., 1986—; chmn. Grass Roots Com. to Pass Ill. Marital Property Act, 1982—. Hon. mention in Nat. Sonnet contest, 1967; Vol. of Year, Ill. Mental Health Assn., 1975; Service award Ill. Rehab. Assn., 1980; named DuPage County Outstanding Woman Leader in Arts and Culture, W. Suburban YWCA, 1984. Mem. Wilderness Soc., Humane Soc. U.S., W. Suburban Humane Soc., Nat. Trust for Hist. Preservation, Du Page County Hist. Soc., Glen Ellyn Hist. Soc., Nat. Audubon Soc., Nat. Writers Club (monthly meeting chmn. Midwest chpt. 1973-74, 4th award Ann. Mag. Con. test 1978), Defenders of Wildlife, Theosophical Soc. Am., Nature Conservancy Ill. (hon.), NAACP, Chgo. Art Inst. (life), Ill. Assn. Mental Health (dir. 1966-68), Amnesty Internat., Pi Beta Phi. Writer column Mental Health and You for Press Publs., 1969—, Life Newspapers, 1982—, Pioneer Newspapers, 1984, Herald Newspapers, 1986—; author: The Jewelled Flower: The True Account of a Courageous Young Man's Life and Death By His Own Hand, 1987. Home: 22 W 210 Stanton Rd Glen Ellyn IL 60137

JENS, WALTER, philologist, author, critic; b. Hamburg, Germany, Mar. 8, 1923; s. Walter and Anna (Martens) J.; m. Inge Puttfarcken, 1951; 2 children. Ed. Hamburg U., Freiburg im Breisgau U.; D.Phil (hon.). Asst. Hamburg U. and Tubingen U. (W.Ger.), 1946-50; dozent Tübingen U., 1950-56, prof. classical philology and rhetoric, 1956—; dir. Inst. für Allgemeine Rhetorik, 1967—. Author: (novels) Nein—Die Welt der Angeklagten, 1950, Der Blinde, 1951, Vergessene Gesichter, 1952, Der Mann, der nicht alt werden wote, 1955, Das Testament des Odysseus, 1957, Der Fall Judas, 1975; Die Stichomythie in der frühen griechischen Tragö die, 1955; Hofmannsthal und die Griechen, 1955; (essays) Statt einer Literaturgeschicht, 1957, Moderne Literatur—moderne Wirklichkeit, 1958, Die Götter sind sterblich, 1959; Deutsche Literatur der Gegenwart, 1961; Zueignungen, 1962; Herr Meister, 1963; Euripides-Blchner, 1964; Von deutscher Rede, 1969; Am Anfang der Stall, am Ende der Galgen, 1972; Fernsehen-Themen und Tabus, 1973; Republikanische Reden, 1976; Eine deutsche Universität, 500 Jahre Tübinger Gelehrtenrepublik, 1977; Zur Antike, 1978; Die Orestie des Aischylos, 1979, Ort der Handlung ist Deutschland, 1981, Die kleine grosse Stadt Tü bingen, 1981; In Sachen Lessing, 1983; Kanzel und Katheder, 1984; Momos am Bildschirm, 1984, Dichtung und Religion, 1985, Deutsche Lebenstaufe, 1987; (TV plays) Die Verschwörung, 1969, Der tödliche Schlag, 1974; (libretto) Der Ausbruch, 1975, Roccos Erzahlung, 1985; (drama) Der Untergang, 1982; Die Friedensfrau, 1986; editor: Warum ich Christ bin, 1979; In letzter Stunde, 1982. Recipient Lessingpreis der Hansestadt Hamburg, 1968, TV prize Trade Union German Employees, 1976; Heine-Preis der Stadt Düsseldorf, 1981; Adolf Grimme Preis des Deutschen Volkshochschulverbands, 1984. Mem. German PEN (pres. 1976-82), Berliner Akademie der Künste, Deutsche Akademie für Sprache und Dichtung, Acad. der Künste der DDR.

JENSEN, ALTON DEAN, architect; b. Centerfield, Utah, May 9, 1927; s. Alton H. and Arvilla (Roylance) J.; m. Anita Heaton, Mar. 14, 1953; children: Bradly Dean (dec.), Dale Alton, Ryan Heaton. Cert. Archtl. Drafting, Utah Tech. Coll., 1950. Registered architect Utah, Nev., Ariz., Colo., Idaho, Wyo., Oreg., Calif., Nebr., Mont., N.D., S.D., Minn., Wash.; cert. architect Nat. Council Archtl. Registration Bds. Chief draftsman, office mgr. Miles E. Miller, Salt Lake City, 1950-54; chief draftsman Robert L. Spingmeyer, Salt Lake City, 1954-58; assoc. Donald H. Panushka & Assocs., Salt Lake City, 1958-62; pvt. practice architecture Salt Lake City, 1962—; chmn. graphic arts dept adv. com. Utah Tech. Coll., Salt Lake City; mem. master plan com. Salt Lake City Internat. Airport, 1979-81; mem. airport plan com. Wasatch Front Regional Council, Salt Lake City, 1979—. Mem. Utah Pilots Assn., Silver Wings, Quiet Birdmen. Republican. Mormon. Home: 268 U St Salt Lake City UT 84103 Office: 646 S 900 E Salt Lake City UT 84102 also: 3390 Wynn Rd Suite D Las Vegas NV 89102

JENSEN, BO GREEN, writer, critic; b. Copenhagen, Denmark, Dec. 18, 1955; s. Harald Jensen and Birthe (Green) Kylbo; m. Lili Elbek, Aug. 6, 1976. Student, U. Copenhagen, 1980. Vis. fellow in Am. Studies Yale U., New Haven, 1981-82; lit. critic Weekendavisen Berlingske Aften, Copenhagen, 1981—; visiting prof., writer-in-residence, Dept. Scandinavian Studies U. Minn., Mpls., 1988—; pub.'s reader Forlaget Centrum, Aarhus, Denmark, 1983-85; bd. dirs. Writers' Union of Denmark, Copenhagen, 1987. Editor Borgens Forlag A/S, 1986—; author (poetry): Requiem and Mass, 1981, The Absolute Game, 1981, The Constant Angel, 1982, Mondo Sinistro, 1983, The Apocalypse Testament, 1984, The Meaning of Places, 1985, The Gate of Earth, 1986, Somewhere in Uncertainty, 1987, Tangled Up in Blue, 1988; (books) The Dance Through the Summer, 1981, In the Course of the Year, 1983, The Colossus of Amager, 1984, So as not to Wither to Death, 1985, A Mural of Reptiles, 1985, As Far as We Can Tell the Sky is Blue, 1985, The Noise of Reality, 1987; (non-fiction) In Search of White Noise-Rock Notes 1978-83, 1983, De Profundis and the Meaning of Suffering-A Book on Oscar Wilde, 1984, The Insight of Distance-Essays on Literature 1980-84, 1985, Images on the Voyage-25 Movies of the 80's, 1987, Wittness to the Signature-An Album of Essyas, 1988; translations of works including Eliot, Hemingway, West, Cohen. Fulbright scholar Copenhagen, 1981; Danish Funding of Arts grantee, 1983; recipient The Critics' award, 1986. Mem. Tidsskrift for Rymisk Musik, Filmavisen Tusind Øjne, Assn. Edn. Writers, Danish Assn. Critics, Danish P.E.N., Danish Acad. Appreciation Crime Fiction, Danish Fulbright Soc. Home: Sonder Blvd 34, V 1720 Kobenhavn Denmark Office: Weekendavisen Berlingske Aften, Gammel Mont 1, K 1147 Kobenhavn Denmark

JENSEN, DALLIN W., lawyer; b. Afton, Wyo., June 2, 1932; s. Louis J. and Nellie B. Jensen; m. Barbara J. Bassett, Mar. 22, 1958; children—Brad L., Julie N. B.S., Brigham Young U., 1954; J.D., U. Utah, 1960. Bar: Utah 1960, U.S. Dist. Ct. Utah 1962, U.S. Ct. Appeals (10th cir.) 1974, U.S. Ct. Appeals D.C. 1980, U.S. Supreme Ct. 1971. Asst. atty. gen. Utah Atty. Gen., Salt Lake City, 1960-83, solicitor gen., 1983—; alt. commr. Upper Colo. River Commn., 1983—; mem. Colo. River Basin Salinity Adv. Council, 1975—; spl. legal cons. Nat. Water Commn., Washington, 1971-73; mem. energy law center adv. council U. Utah Coll. Law, 1976—. Edit. bd. Rocky Mountain Mineral Law Found., 1983-85. Author: (with Wells A. Hutchins) The Utah Law of Water Rights, 1965. Contbr. articles on water law and water resource mgmt. to profl. jours. Served with U.S. Army, 1955-57. Mem. Ch. Jesus Christ Latter-day Saints. Home: 3565 S 2175 E Salt Lake City UT 84109 Office: Utah Atty Gen 1636 W N Temple #300 Salt Lake City UT 84116

JENSEN, DAVID LYNN, mathematician; b. Brigham City, Utah, Sept. 8, 1941; s. Jacob Lynn and Florence (Tanner) J.; B.S., Utah State U., 1964, M.S., 1972; m. Marva Myler, June 21, 1963 (div.), m. 2d Margaret Prantner, Mar. 23, 1983. Lab. technician Thiokol Chem. Corp., Brigham City, 1961-64; computer programmer Utah State U. Computer Center, Logan, 1964-65; mathematician, computer programmer USAF Logistics Command, Hill AFB, Utah, 1965-68; instr. data processing Weber State Coll., Ogden, Utah, 1968-69; data analyst Reentry and Environ. Systems Div., Gen. Electric Co., Hill AFB, 1969-71; mathematician Advanced Tech. Ctr., Calspan Corp., Buffalo, 1972-83; research data analyst Sigma Systems Tech., Inc., Buffalo, 1983—. Program chmn. exploring com. Lake Bonneville council Boy Scouts Am., Ogden, 1969-71, program chmn. exploring com. Bird Haven Dist., 1969-71, tng. chmn. exploring com. Greater Niagara Frontier council, Buffalo, 1973-76, recipient Scouters Tng. award, 1971. Mem. Am. Statis. Assn., Sigma Xi. Mormon. Home: 40 Nancy Ln North Tonawanda NY 14120 Office: Sigma Systems Tech Inc PO Box 634 5813 Main St Williamsville NY 14221

JENSEN, ELWOOD VERNON, biochemist; b. Fargo, N.D., Jan. 13, 1920; s. Eli A. and Vera (Morris) J.; m. Mary Welmoth Collette, June 17, 1941 (dec. Nov. 1982); children: Karen Collette, Thomas Eli; m. Hiltrud Herborg, Dec. 21, 1983. A.B., Wittenberg U., 1940, D.Sc. (hon.), 1963; Ph.D., U. Chgo., 1944; D.Sc. (hon.), Acadia U., 1976. Faculty U. Chgo., 1947—, assoc. prof. biochemistry Ben May Lab. Cancer Research, 1954-60, prof., 1960-63, Am. Cancer Soc. research prof. physiology, 1963-69, dir. Ben May Lab., 1969-82, dir. Biomed. Ctr. Population Research, 1972-75, prof. physiology, 1969-73, 77-84, prof. biophysics, 1973-84, prof. biochemistry, 1980—, Charles B. Huggins disting. service prof., 1981—; research dir. Ludwig Inst. for Cancer Research, 1983-87; scholar-in-residence Fogarty Internat. Ctr. NIH, 1988; Vis. prof. Max-Planck-Inst. für Biochemie, Munich, Germany, 1958; mem. chemotherapy rev. bd. Nat. Cancer Inst., 1960-62, bd. sci. counselors, 1969-72; mem. Nat. Adv. Council Child Health and Human Devel., 1976-80; mem. adv. com. biochemistry and chem. carcinogenesis Am. Cancer Soc., 1968-72, council for research and clin. investigation, 1974-77; mem. assembly life scis. NRC, 1975-78; mem. com. on sci., engring. and public policy Nat. Acad. Scis., 1981-82; mem. research adv. bd. Clin. Research Inst. of Montreal, 1987—. Editorial-adv. bd. Perspectives in Biology and Medicine, 1966—, Archives of Biochemistry and Biophysics, 1979-84; editorial adv. bd. Biochemistry, 1969-72, Life Scis, 1973-78, Breast Cancer Research and Treatment, 1980—; assoc. editor: Jour. Steroid Biochemistry, 1974—; contbr. articles to profl. jours. Guggenheim fellow, 1946-47; recipient D.R. Edwards medal, 1970, La Madonnina prize, 1973, G.H.A. Clowes award, 1975, Papanicolaou award, 1975, prix Roussel, 1976, Nat. award Am. Cancer Soc., 1976, Amory prize, 1977, Gregory Pincus Meml. award, 1978, Gairdner Found. award, 1979, Lucy Wortham James award, 1980, Charles F. Kettering prize, 1980, Nat. Acad. Clin. Biochemistry award, 1981, Pharmacia award, 1982, Hubert H. Humphrey award, 1983, Rolf Luft medal, 1983, Renzo Grattarola award, 1984, Fred C. Koch award, 1984, Axel Munthe award, 1985. Mem. Nat. Acad. Scis. (council 1981-84), Am. Acad. Arts and Scis., Am. Soc. Biol. Chemists, Am. Chem. Soc., Am. Assn. Cancer Research, Endocrine Soc. (pres. 1980-81), AAAS, Am. Gynec. and Obstet. Soc. (hon.). Clubs: Quadrangle, Chicago Literary, Cosmos. Office: Fogarty Internat Ctr Nat Institutes Health Bethesda MD 20892

JENSEN, ERIK HENNING, travel company executive; b. Aarhus, Denmark, Oct. 18, 1933; s. Thorvald and Doris Johanne (Moller) J.; m. Jytte Kaja Nielsen, Mar. 26, 1955 (dec. 1964); children: Jan Henrik, Niels Bo; m. Jacqueline Christiane Louise Henriksen, May 5, 1970; 1 child, Helene Christane. Navigator/traffic mgr. Flying Enterprise, Copenhagen, 1961-65; mgr. traffic/planning Conair Ltd., Copenhagen, 1965-67; dir. Spies Travels, Copenhagen, 1967—, pres., chief exec. officer, 1986—; also bd. dirs. Spies Travels; bd. dirs. Conair Ltd., Copenhagen, 1975—, Simon Spies Ltd., Hotel Mercur Ltd., Mercur Film Ltd., Spies Destination Service Ltd., Spies Found., 1983—. Served to capt. Danish Air Force, 1952-61. Home: 10 Parkvaenget, 2680 Solrod Strand Denmark Office: Spies Travels, 41 Nyropsgade, DK-1625 Copenhagen Denmark

JENSEN, HANS BISGAARD, sales executive; b. Hundslund, Denmark, June 28, 1941; s. Peter Bisgaard and Erna (Knudsen) J.; m. Ulla Nielsen; children: Peter, Mette, Lise Lotte Bisgaard. Degree in Mech. Engring, Odense (Denmark) Tech. Inst., 1965; Diploma in Specialized Bus. Studies, Copenhagen (Denmark) Handelskole, 1976. Tech. engr. Anhydro A/S, Copenhagen, 1966-70, sales engr., 1970-76; sales mgr. Humudan A/S, Aalborg, Denmark, 1976-77, gen. mgr., 1977-79; sales mgr. T-T Industriteknik, Odense, 1979-84, T-T Plastic Machinery, Odense, 1984—. Office: T-T Plastic Machinery A/S, Bredstedgade 25, DK-5000 Odense Denmark

JENSEN, HANS PETTER, geotechnical consulting company executive; b. Oslo, Oct. 13, 1942; s. Bernhard H. and Elsa (Guberg) J.; m. Astrid Kvamme; children: Eivind, Anders, Petter. BCE, Purdue (Ind.) U., 1966, MCE, 1967. Teaching/research asst. Purdue U., Lafayette, Ind., 1966-67; civil engr. Noteby, Oslo, 1967-69; civil and soils engr. Noteby, Stavanger, Norway, 1969-72, mgr. br. office, 1972-76; exec. engr. Noteby, Oslo, 1976-79; mgr. soils div., ptnr. Noteby, 1979—; lectr. univs. Contbr. numerous articles on soil mechanics and found. engring. to profl. publs. Norwegian Soc. Found. Engrs. grantee, 1985. Mem. ASCE, Norwegian Soc. Profl. Engrs. (bd. dirs. 1974-76, 86—), Norwegian Soc. Soils and Found. Engrs., Norwegian Soc. Chartered Engrs. Clubs: Oslo Yacht (bd. dirs. 1982-86), Royal Yacht (Oslo). Office: Noteby Wald Thranesgate, 75 PO Box 9810, ILA 0 132 Oslo 1 Norway

JENSEN, HANS-ERIC, consultant, surgeon; b. Copenhagen, July 23, 1928; s. Georg and Anna Marie (Eriksen) J.; m. Tove Nielsen, Mar. 29, 1972; children—Tom, Frank, Jeanette, Michael. M.D., Univ. Copenhagen, 1955, Ph.D., 1965. Resident in surgery Kommunehosp., Copenhagen, 1955-62, sr. resident, 1965-71, chmn. 1971-87 , resident Bispebjerg Hosp., Copenhagen, 1962-64; research fellow Michael Reese Hosp., Chgo., 1964-65; cons. surgeon, 1987—; vis. prof., U.S.A., Japan, Israel, Sweden, Argentina, Italy, 1974-84. Mem. editorial bd. Acta Chirurgica Scandinavia, Brit. Jour. Digestive Surgery. Contbr. articles to profl. jours. Served with Danish Red Cross 1951. WHO fellow, 1967. Mem. Danish Surg. Soc., Soc. Internat. Surgery, Nordic Surg. Soc. (sec. 1980-83, pres. 1983-85), Collegium Internationale Chirurgiae Digestivae, Internat. Sci. Com. (pres. elect World Congress 1988). Avocations: tennis; golf. Home: Bellevue Krogen, 2930 Klampenborg Denmark Office: Kommunehosp, O Farimagsgade, 1399 Copenhagen Denmark

JENSEN, HANS-PETER, neurosurgeon; b. Leipzig, Ger., Nov. 7, 1921; s. Agathon and Anneliese (von Lackum) J.; student U. Leipzig, 1942-44; M.D., U. Frankfurt, 1949, cert. in neurosurgery, 1955; m. Reta-Ingeborg Pauls, 1953; children—Nora-Ingeborg, Birgit-Christiane, Jens-Peter, Jens-Michael. Resident in neurology and neurosurgery Univ. Hosp. Frankfurt and Univ. Hosp. Wü rzburg, 1949-55; research fellow in neurosurgery Children's Meml. Hosp., Chgo., 1959-60; privat dozent in surgery and neurosurgery U. Wü rzburg, 1959-70; prof. neurosurgery U. Kiel, 1971—; dir. Neurosurg. Univ. Hosp. Kiel, 1971—. Mem. German Soc. Neurosurgery (pres.), German Soc. Surgery, German Soc. Neurology, Internat. Soc. Pediatric Neurosurgery, Royal Soc. Medicine (London), Am. Acad. Neurol. Surgery, Congress Neurol. Surgeons, Panafrican Assn. Neurol. Scis. Clubs: Lions, Masons (32 deg.). Author: Grundriss der gesamten Chirurgie, 1960; Traumatologie in der chirurgischen Praxis, 1965; Paediatrische Neurochirurgie, 1967; Praktische Anatomie-Kopfband Lanz-Wachsmuth, 1985; editor Neuropaediatrie, Jour. Pediatric Neurobiology, Neurology and Neurosurgery, Hippokrates. Home: 23 Karolinenweg, 2300 Kiel Federal Republic of Germany Office: 8 Weimarer Strasse, 2300 Kiel Federal Republic of Germany

JENSEN, HARLAN ELLSWORTH, veterinarian, educator; b. St. Ansgar, Iowa, Oct. 6, 1915; s. Bert and Mattie (Hansen) J.; m. Naomi Louise Geiger, June 7, 1941; children: Kendra Lee Jensen Belfi, Doris Eileen, Richard Harlan. D.V.M., Iowa State U., 1941; Ph.D., U. Mo., 1971. Diplomate: Charter diplomate Am. Coll. Vet. Ophthalmologists (v.p. 1970-72, pres. 1972-73). Vet. practice Galesburg, Ill., 1941-46; small animal internship New Brunswick, N.J., 1946-47; small animal practice Cleve., 1947-58, San Diego, 1958-62, Houston, 1962-67; faculty U. Mo., Columbia, 1967-85; chief opthalmology, prof. Vet. Sch. U. Mo., 1967-80, prof. emeritus Vet. Sch., 1980—, assoc. prof. ophthalmology Med. Sch., 1972-80, now cons. vet. opthalmology Med. Sch.; cons. in vet. ophthalmology to pharm. firms; guest lectr., prof. opthalmology U. Utrecht (Netherlands) Vet. Sch., 1973; tchr., lectr. various vet. meetings; condr. seminar World Congress Small Animal Medicine and Surgery, 1977. Author: Stereoscopic Atlas of Clinical Ophthalmology of Domestic Animals, 1971, Stereoscopic Atlas of Ophthalmic Surgery of Domestic Animals, 1974; co-author: Stereoscopic Atlas of Soft Tissue Surgery of Small Animals, 1973, Clinical Dermatology of Small Animals, 1974; contbr. articles to profl. jours. Recipient Gaines award AVMA, 1973. Mem. Am. Vet. Radiology Soc. (pres. 1956-57), Am. Vet. Ophthalmology Soc. (pres. 1960-62), Farm House Frat., Sigma Xi, Phi Kappa Phi, Phi Zeta, Gamma Sigma Delta. Baptist. Club: Rotary (pres. Pacific Beach, Calif. 1960-62, pres. Columbia 1977-78). Home: 6810 Overlook Dr Fort Myers FL 33919

JENSEN, HELEN, musical artists mgmt. co. exec.; b. Seattle, June 30, 1919; d. Frank and Sophia (Kantosky) Leponis; student public schs., Seattle; m. Ernest Jensen, Dec. 2, 1939; children—Ernest, Ronald Lee. Co-chmn., Seattle Community Concert Assn., 1957-62; sec. family concerts Seattle Symphony Orch., 1959-61; hostess radio program Timely Topics, 1959-60; gen. mgr. Western Opera Co., Seattle, 1962-64, pres. 1963-64; v.p., dir., mgr. public relations Seattle Opera Assn., 1964—, preview artists Coordinator, 1981-84; bus. mgr. Portland (Oreg.) Opera Co., 1968, cons., 1967-69; owner, mgr. Helen Jensen Artists Mgmt., Seattle, 1970—. First v.p. Music and Art Found., 1981-84, pres. 1984-85. Recipient Cert., Women in Bus in the Field of Art, 1973; award Seattle Opera Assn., 1974; Outstanding Service award Music and Art Found., 1984; award of distinction Seattle Opera Guild, 1983. Mem. Am. Guild Mus. Artists, Music and Art Found., Seattle Opera Guild (pres., award of distinction 1983), Ballard Symphony League (sec.), Seattle Civic Opera Assn. (pres. 1981-84), Portland Opera Assn., Portland Opera Guild, Seattle Civic Opera Assn. (pres. 1981-89), 200 Plus One, Aria Preview, Lyric Preview Group, Past Pres. Assembly (pres. 1977-79, parliamentarian 1987-88), Pres.'s Forum (program vice chmn. 1987-88), North Shore Performing Arts Assn. (pres. 1981). Clubs: Helen Jensen Hiking, Kenmore Community. Home: 19029 56th Ln NE Seattle WA 98155 Office: 716 Joseph Vance Bldg Seattle WA 98101

JENSEN, JERRY KIRTLAND, industrial engineer, operations manager; b. Chgo., Sept. 27, 1947; s. Harry Dybdahl and Violet May (Nowak) J. BS, Cornell U., 1969, M in Indsl. Engring., 1971. Cert. in prodn. and inventory mgmt. Pres., Jensen's Cinema 16, Western Springs, Ill., 1970—; indsl. engr. Gen. Foods, Chgo., 1970-72, sr. indsl. engr., 1972-73, prodn. scheduling supr., 1973-74, prodn. control mgr., 1974-76; mgmt. systems specialist Beatrice Cos., Chgo., 1976-77, operating services project mgr., 1977-79, mgr. indsl. engring., 1980-84, mgr. mfg. services dir. Louver Drape, Inc. div. Home Fashions Inc., Memphis, 1984-85, dir. ops., 1985—; v.p., sec. Country Residential, Inc., Western Springs and Crystal Lake, Ill., 1978-86. Author: (with Dr. Joel Ross) Productivity, People and Profits, 1981; contbr. Productivity Improvement: Case Studies of Proven Practice, 1981. Film festivals chmn. Western Springs Recreation Commn., 1969-70, 73-84; active Theatre of Western Springs, 1983—, Theatre Memphis, 1984—, Germantown Theatre, 1985— (bd. dirs., treas. 1987, 2d v.p. 1988). Mem. Am. Prodn. and Inventory Control Soc. (program chmn. Memphis chpt. 1986, v.p. 1986-87, pres. 1987-88), Am. Inst. Indsl. Engrs. (nat. productivity com. 1982-85, v.p. services Chgo. chpt. 1984), Great Lakes English Springer Spaniel Breeders Assn. (pres. 1979-81), English Springer Spaniel Field Trial Assn., Alpha Phi Omega, Beta Theta Pi. Methodist. Clubs: Cornell, Variety. Home: 2828 Treasure Island W Memphis TN 38115 Office: 3970 Delp St Memphis TN 38118

JENSEN, KNUD WERNER KOCH, contracting company executive; b. Odense, Denmark, May 8, 1935; s. Holger and Christine (Koch) J.; m. Inge Pedersen, Nov. 5, 1960; children: Claus, Helle, Per. ME, Odense Maskinteknikum U., 1958; diploma in acctg., Tietgenskolen Comml. Sch., 1965. Registered profl. engr., Denmark. Engr. Haustrups Fabriker, Odense, 1960-67; chief sec. A/S Phoenix Contractors, Vejen, Denmark, 1967-69, dep. dir., 1969-72, vice dir., 1972-73, mng. dir., 1974—. Home: Brombaergangen 5, DK-6600 Vejen Denmark Office: A/S Phoenix Contractors, V. Alle 1, DK-6600 Vejen Denmark

JENSEN, KURT, computer science researcher, consultant; b. Hjorring, Jutland, Denmark, May 30, 1950; s. Henry Hardi and Willia (Christensen) J.; m. Elsie Heidmann, June 6, 1987. M Computer Sci., Math., Physics, Aarhus U., Denmark, 1976; PhD in Computer Sci., Aarhus U., 1980. Asst. prof. Aarhus U., 1976-81, assoc. prof. computer sci., 1981—; systems designer Meta Software, Cambridge, Mass., 1988—; cons. on impact of computers on working conditions; cons. Danish Research Libraries, 1984-86; mem. steering com. European Petri Net Workshops, 1985—. Contbr. articles to profl. publs.; referee internat. sci. jours. Mem. Danish Nat. Team Orienteering (Danish champion three times). Office: Aarhus U, Ny Munkegade 116, DK 8000 Aarhus C Denmark

JENSON, NORMAN CARLTON, JR., music educator, church organist, choir master, musical theatre director; b. Glendale, Calif., Nov. 3, 1937; s. Norman Carlton and Mildred (Erickson) J.; m. Carolyn Keyser, Aug. 10, 1968; children—Jennifer Lynn, Lisa Ann. B.A., Occidental Coll., 1959; M.Mus., Ariz. State U., 1970. Music tchr. Wilson Jr. High Sch., Pasadena, Calif., 1963-65, Pasadena High Sch., 1965-69, Coronado High Sch., Scottsdale, Ariz., 1971-72; prof music Scottsdale Community Coll., 1972—; organist Sepulveda (Calif.) Community Methodist Ch., 1953-55, St. James Presbyterian Ch., Tarzana, Calif., 1955-56, North Hollywood (Calif.) First Presbyn. Ch., 1956-60, 63-67; organist, choirmaster Camp Smith Protestant Chapel, Pearl Harbor, Hawaii, 1960-63, First Congregational Ch., Pasadena, 1968, First Presbyn. Ch., Phoenix, 1970-72, Scottsdale United Presbyn. Ch., 1972-81, Mountain View Presbyn. Ch., Scottsdale, 1981-83; organist 2nd Ch. of Christ Scientist, Scottsdale, 1986—; dir. musical theater Calif. and Ariz.; founding dir. Scottsdale Masterworks Chorals; guest choral condr., choral adjudicator, guest organist. Active fin. fund drive Scottsdale YMCA, 1983, dir. Family Camp, Pasadena YMCA, 1984. Served to lt. USNR, 1960-63. Named one of two American choral condrs. to participate J.S. Bach Acad., Stuttgart, W.Ger., summer 1980. Mem. Am. Choral Dirs. Assn., Am. Guild of Organists, Music Educators Nat. Conf., Ariz. Music Educators Assn., Ariz. Choral Dirs. Assn., Phoenix Fedn. Musicians, YMCA. Republican. Presbyterian. Home: 8513 E Edward Ave Scottsdale AZ 85253 Office: Scottsdale Community Coll 9000 E Chaparral Rd Scottsdale AZ 85256-2699

JENTSCH, WERNER, mathematician, educator; b. Leipzig, Germany, July 14, 1918; s. Paul and Margit (Hirsch) J.; m. Erika Scheller, Apr. 5, 1950; children: Thomas, Jörg. PhD, Hochschule für Elektrotechnik, Ilmenau, German Dem. Republic, 1959; DSc Rer. Nat., U. Halle, German Dem. Republic, 1976. Tchr. univ. level Leipzig, German Dem. Republic, 1950-55; sci. collaborator Hochschule Elektrotechnik, Ilmenau, 1955-61; tchr. univ. level Martin-Luther-Universität, Halle, 1961-78, tchr. emeritus, 1978—; dir. sci. staff U. Halle, 1965-72. Contbr. numerous articles to profl. jours. Mem. Am. Math. Soc., Mathematische Gesellschaft der German Dem. Republic, Gesellschaft für Angewandte Mathematik und Mechanik. Home: Heinrich-Zille Strasse 13A, 4020 Halle Saale German Democratic Republic Office: Martin Luther Univ, Universitatsplatz 6, Sektion Mathematik, 4020 Halle German Democratic Republic

JENTZ, GAYLORD ADAIR, lawyer, educator; b. Beloit, Wis., Aug. 7, 1931; s. Merlyn Adair and Delva (Mullen) J.; m. JoAnn Mary Hornung, Aug. 6, 1955; children: Katherine Ann, Gary Adair, Loretta Ann, Rory Adair. B.A., U. Wis., 1953, J.D., 1957, M.B.A., 1958. Bar: Wis. 1957. Pvt. practice law Madison, 1957-58; from instr. to asso. prof. bus. law U. Okla., 1958-65; vis. instr. to vis. prof. U. Wis. Law Sch., summers 1957-65; asso. prof. to prof. U. Tex., Austin, 1965-68; prof. U. Tex., 1968—, Herbert D. Kelleher prof. bus. law, 1982—, chmn. gen. bus. dept., 1968-74, 80-86. Author: (with others) Business Law Text and Cases, 2d edit, 1968, 1978, Tex. Uniform Comml. Code, 1967, rev. edit., 1975, West's Business Law: Text and Cases, 2d edit., 1983, 3d edit., 1986, 4th edit., 1989, West's Business Law: Alternate UCC Comprehensive Edition, 3d edit., 1987, Tex. Family Law, 6th edit., 1987, Business Law Today, 1988; dep. editor Social Sci. Quar., 1966-82, mem. editorial bd., 1982—; editorial staff, dep. editor Am. Bus. Law Jour, 1967-69, editor-in-chief, 1969-74, adv. editor, 1974—; contbr. articles to profl. jours. Served with AUS, 1953-55. Recipient Outstanding Tchr. award Tex. U. Coll. Bus., 1967, Jack G. Taylor Teaching Excellence award, 1971, Joe D. Beasley Grad. Teaching Excellence award, 1978, CBA Found. Adv. Council award, 1979, Grad. Bus. Council Outstanding Grad. Bus. Prof. award, 1980, James C. Scorboro Meml. award for Outstanding Leadership in Banking Edn. Colo. Grad. Sch. Banking, 1983. Mem. Southwestern Fedn. Adminstrv. Disciplines (v.p. 1979-80, pres. 1980-81), Am. Arbitration Assn. (nat. panel 1966—), Am. Bus. Law Assn. (pres. 1971-72, Faculty award of excellence 1981), So. Bus. Law Assn. (pres. 1967), Tex. Assn. Coll. Tchrs. (pres. Austin chpt. 1967-68, exec. com. 1969-70, state pres. 1971-72), Wis. Bar Assn., Omicron Delta Kappa, Phi Kappa Phi. (pres. 1983-84). Home: 4106 North Hills Dr Austin TX 78731 Office: U Texas Coll Bus Adminstrn CBA5.202 Austin TX 78712

JEPSON, ROBERT SCOTT, JR., international investment banking specialist; b. Richmond, Va., July 20, 1942; s. Robert Scott and Inda (Hodges) J., B.S., U. Richmond, 1964, M.Commerce, 1975; LLD (hon.), Gonzaga U., 1986; DCS, U. Richmond, 1987; HHD (hon.), Hamline U., 1988; m. Alice Finch Andrews, Dec. 28, 1964; children—Robert Scott, John Steven. With Va. Commonwealth Bankshares, Richmond, 1966-68; v.p. corp. fin. Birr Wilson & Co., Inc., San Francisco, 1968-69; with Calif. Capital Mgmt. Corp., Irvine, 1970-73; pres. Calcap Securities Corp., Los Angeles, 1970-73; v.p., dir. corp. fin. Cantor Fitzgerald & Co., Beverly Hills, Calif., 1973-75; dir. corp. planning and devel. Campbell Industries, San Diego, 1975-77; v.p., mgr. merger and acquisition div. Continental Ill. Bank, Chgo., 1977-82; sr. v.p., group head U.S. Capital Markets Group, 1st Nat. Bank Chgo., 1983—; chmn. bd. Jepson Corp., Chgo., Signet Armorlite, Inc., San Marcos, Calif., Emerson Quiet Kool Corp., Woodbridge, N.J., Air-Maze Corp., Bedford Heights, Ohio, Hedstrom Corp., Bedford, Pa., Gerry Sportswear Corp., Seattle, Atlantic Industries, Inc., Nutley, N.J., Jepson-Burns Corp., Winston-Salem, N.J., Farwest Garments, Inc., Seattle, Jepson Vineyards Ltd., Ukiah, Calif., Trans-Aero Industries, Inc., Los Angeles, Denman Tire Corp., Warren, Ohio; vice chmn. bd. Hill Refrigeration, Trenton, N.J.; asst. prof. fin. Nat. U., 1976. Trustee, Gonzaga U., Spokane, Wash., 1982—; bd. trustees , Hamlin U., St. Paul, Minn., 1987. Served to 1st lt. M.P., Corps, AUS, 1964-66. Mem. Omicron Delta Kappa, Alpha Kappa Psi. Republican. Clubs: Mid-Am., Chgo. Home: 65 Hills & Dales Rd Barrington Hills IL 60010 Office: The Jepson Corp 360 W Butterfield Rd Elmhurst IL 60126

JERNDAL, JENS, foundation executive, consultant; b. Goteborg, Sweden, Jan. 5, 1934; came to Spain, 1968; s. Ebbe and Ingrid M. (Forsberg) J.; children: C. Patrick, J.O. Mathias, J.T. Christofer. MS, Stockholm U., 1958; BA, Uppsala U., 1959; Diploma, Internat. Coll. Acupuncture, Colombo, Sri Lanka, 1982; MD, 1987. Attaché Royal Swedish Ministry Fgn. Affairs, 1960-62; embassy sec. Royal Swedish Embassy, Copenhagen, 1962; 1st sec. Royal Swedish Embassy, Karachi, Pakistan, 1964, Royal Swedish Ministry Fgn. Affairs, 1965-68; investment broker Real Lanzarote SA, Las Palmas, Spain, 1968—; expert del. U.N. High Commr. for Refugees, Geneva, 1966-67; pres. Cosmosophical Found., Stockholm, 1977—, Dragon's Head Centre of Holistic Medicine, Spain, 1982—; lectr. in astrology and alternative medicine. Author: Indonesien, 1958; contbr. articles to profl. jours. Fgn. lang. transmission mgr., broadcaster for Radio Sweden, 1956-57; rep. Assn. Swedish Citizens Residing Abroad, Canary Islands, 1972-75. Decorated Knight of Royal Order of Dannebrog His Majesty the King of Denmark, 1963. Mem. Astrol. Assn. Britain, Am. Fedn. Astrologers, Acupuncture Found. Sri Lanka, Medicina Alternativa (life, vis. lectr.), Commonwealth Inst. Acupuncture and Natural Medicines (founding). Office: Dragon's Head Centres, of Holistic Medicine, PO Box 248, Arrecife de Lanzarote Spain

JERNE, NIELS KAJ, scientist; b. London, Dec. 23, 1911; s. Hans Jessen and Else Marie (Lindberg) J.; m. Ursula Alexandra Kohl, 1964; 2 children. Grad. U. Leiden, U. Copenhagen; hon. degrees U. Chgo., U. Copenhagen, U. Basel, U. Rotterdam, Columbia U. Research worker Danish State Serum Inst., Copenhagen, 1943-55; chief med. officer WHO, Geneva, 1956-62; prof. biophysics U. Geneva, 1960-62; chmn. dept. microbiology U. Pitts., 1962-66; prof. exptl. therapy J.W. Goethe U., Frankfurt, 1966-69; dir. Basel Inst. for Immunology, 1969-80; prof. Inst. Pasteur, Paris, 1981-82; Contbr. articles to profl. jours. Recipient Marcel Benoist prize, Berne, 1979, Paul Ehrlich prize, Frankfurt, 1982; shared Nobel prize for medicine, 1984. Mem. Am. Philos. Soc., Acad. des Sciences de l'Inst. de France, mem. Am. Acad. Arts and Scis., U.S.A. Nat. Acad. Scis., others. Office: Basel Inst of Immunology, CH-4058 Basel Switzerland other: Chateau de Bellevue, Castillon-du-Nord, Gard 30210, France *

JERNIGAN, EDDIE DEAN, brokerage house executive; b. Sparta, Tenn., Mar. 18, 1956; s. Edward Martin and Johonnie Margaret (McCoin) J.; m. Sandy Gale, Apr. 5, 1986. BS, Middle Tenn. State U., 1978. Account exec. Thomson McKinnon Securities, Nashville, 1980-82; commodity broker Maduff and Sons, Inc., Nashville, 1982-84, Donaldson, Lufkin, Jenrette Co., N.Y.C., 1984-85; sr. v.p. investments Prudential- Bache Securities, Inc., Nashville, 1985-88; v.p. Thomson McKinnon Securities Inc., 1988—. Editor Jernigan's Cotton Sheet Newsletter, 1986; contbr. articles to profl. jours. Mem. Am. Cotton Shippers Assn., Western Cotton Shippers Assn., So. Cotton Assn., Tex. Cotton Assn., Am. Agrl. Editors Assn., Am. Security Council. Presbyterian.

JEROPOULOS, DOROS ANTONIADES JAMES, shipping agency executive; b. Larnaca, Cyprus, Oct. 11, 1936; s. James and Ellie (Vassiliou) Antoniades; m. Sophie Theodosiou, Dec. 28, 1958 (div. 1969); children: Sotiris, Antonis; m. Elisabeth Christodoulou, May 30, 1971. Diploma in Bus. Studies, Am. U., Beirut, Lebanon, 1957. Jr. co-owner S. Ch. Jeropoulos and Co., Limassol, Cyprus, 1958-61; dir. S. Ch. Jeropoulos and Co., Limassol, 1961-73, mng. dir., 1973—; exec. chmn. Jeropoulos Holding Ltd., 1982—; mng. dir. Jeropoulos Travel and Tours, Limassol, 1978; chmn. D.A.S. Shipowners Ltd., Honduras, 1979—, Titania Trading Co., Limassol, 1981—, D.A. Toys Ltd., Limassol, 1984—, Uni Fortrans Internat. Forwarders, Nicosia, Cyprus, 1984—; bd. dirs. Plaza Hotel Enterprises Ltd., Limassol, Cyprus Airways Ltd., Nicosia, Covotsos Textiles Ltd., Limassol. Editor: (book) T/ments and Feeder Service, 1987. Pres. nat. exec. council Cyprus Scouts Assn., Limassol, 1986; vice chmn. Cyprus Port Authority, 1979-88; chmn. cultural com. Municipality of Limassol, 1986. Recipient Internat. Trade Promotion award Chamber Trade, 1980, Leipzig Golden medal Leipzig Fair Authority, 1982. Mem. Internat. Mgmt. Assn., Cyprus Shipping Assn. (pres. 1982-83), Cyprus Productivity Centre (guest lectr.), Cyprus Industrialist and Employers Fedn. Democrat. Greek Orthodox. Clubs: Aris (chmn. 1985—), Sporting (founder 1966, Limassol). Home: 15A Alasias, Limassol Cyprus Office: PO Box 278, Limassol Cyprus

JERRITTS, STEPHEN G., computer company executive; b. New Brunswick, N.J., Sept. 14, 1925; s. Steve and Anna (Kovacs) J.; m. Audrey Virginia Smith, June 1948; children: Marsha Carol, Robert Stephen, Linda Ann; m. 2d, Ewa Elizabet Rydell-Vejlens, Nov. 5, 1966; 1 son, Carl Stephen. Student, Union Coll., 1943-44; B.M.E., Rensselaer Poly. Inst., 1947, M.S. Mgmt., 1948. With IBM, various locations, 1949-58, IBM World Trade, N.Y.C., 1958-67, Bull Gen. Electric div. Gen. Electric, France, 1967-70, merged into Honeywell Bull, 1970-74; v.p., mng. dir. Honeywell Info. Systems Ltd., London, 1974-76; group v.p. Honeywell U.S. Info. Systems, Boston, 1977-80; pres., chief operating officer Honeywell Info. Systems, 1980-82, also bd. dirs.; pres., chief exec. officer Lee Data Corp., 1983-85, also bd. dirs.; with Storage Tech. Corp., 1985—, pres., chief operating officer, 1985-87, vice-chmn. bd. dirs., 1988—; bd. dirs. First Bank, Mpls., 1980-83. Bd. dirs. Guthrie Theatre, 1980-83, Charles Babbage Inst., 1980—; trustee Rensselaer Poly. Inst., 1980-85. Served with USNR, 1943-46. Mem. Computer Bus. Equipment Mfrs. (dir. exec. com. 1979-82), Assoc. Industries Mass. (dir. 1978-80). Clubs: Wellesley (Mass.) Country; Minneapolis. Home: 650 College Ave Boulder CO 80302 Office: Storage Tech Corp 2270 S 88th St Louisville CO 80028

JERSILD, THOMAS NIELSEN, lawyer; b. Chgo., Dec. 12, 1936; s. Gerhardt S. and Martha M. (Beck) J.; m. Colleen Gay Campbell, June 15, 1963; children: Karen, Paul. BA, U. Chgo., 1957, JD, 1961. Bar: Ill. 1961, U.S. Dist. Ct. (no. dist.) Ill. 1961. Ptnr. Mayer, Brown & Platt, Chgo., 1969—. Editor: U. Chgo. Law Rev., 1959-61. Vice chmn. Ill. Sec. of State's Corp. Acts Adv. Com. Mem. ABA, Fed. Energy Bar Assn. (former chmn. crude oil and natural gas liquids com.), Chgo. Bar Assn. (sec., corp. law com., former chmn. pub. utility law com.), Ill. Bar Assn. (corp. and securities law sect.), Eastern Mineral Law Inst. (coal com.), Legal Club Chgo. (sec., treas. 1976-77), Law Club Chgo. Clubs: University, Attic (Chgo.). Office: Mayer Brown & Platt 190 S LaSalle St Chicago IL 60603

JERVIS, JANIS WILLIAMS, public service organization executive; b. Wilmington, N.C., Apr. 5, 1924; d. R. Saunders and Thelma J. (Pickard) Williams; m. Frederick Martin Jervis, Sept. 23, 1947; children—Bruce Martin, Ellen Day, Jane Winfield. B.A., U. N.C., 1947; postgrad. U. N.H., 1947-49. Freelance writer, Durham, N.H., 1960-71; co-founder, seminar leader, dir. publs., exec. dir. Ctr. for Constructive Change, Durham, 1971—; mgmt. cons., 1974—; treas., dir. Delphi Mgmt. Systems, Durham, 1981-85. Trustee, Gruber Found., 1981—; active City/Town Planning Forums, 1975-84. Saul O. Sidore Found. grantee, 1979-80. Author: Change: Piecemeal or Comprehensive, 1975; contbr. numerous articles to profl. jours. Office: Ctr Constructive Change 16 Strafford Ave Durham NH 03824

JESPERSEN, KNUD JESPER VINGGAARD, history educator; b. Eilskov, Denmark, Feb. 8, 1942; s. Lauritz Nikolaj and Kathrine (Vinggaard) J.; m. Karen Marie Madsen, Nov. 26, 1965; children—Kjeld, Dorthe, Henrik. M.A. in History, Odense U. (Denmark), 1971, D. Phil., 1977. Archivist State Archives, Odense, 1969-71; asst. prof. history Odense U., 1971-75, prof., 1975—; vis. scholar Cambridge U., 1978; adv. Ministry Edn., Denmark, 1980—, vis. prof. Yale U., 1989. Author: Rostjenestetaksation og Adelsgods, 1977, Odense bys History, 1984, Guldendals Danmarkshistorie 1648-1730, 1989. Contbr. numerous articles to profl. jours. Editor (yearbook) Danish Nobility, 1980—. Served to 1st lt. Danish Army, 1961-63. Fellow Royal Danish Hist. Soc.; mem. Danish Com. Mil. History, Danish Foreign Policy Soc. Liberal. Lutheran. Home: Teglbakken 46, 5690 Tommerup Denmark Office: Odense U Dept History, Campusvej 55, DK 5230 Odense M Denmark

JESS, PER, surgeon; b. Copenhagen, Aug. 6, 1945; s. Svend Richard and Gudrun (Jess) Olsen; m. Lisbeth Johansen, Dec. 7, 1984; m. Kristine Hansen, Dec. 21, 1973 (div. May 1979); children: Tine, Mia. M.D., U. Copenhagen, 1972. Registrar, County Hosp., Roskilde, 1972-75; registrar in surgery Bispebjerg Hosp., Copenhagen, 1975-81, sr. registrar, 1982—; sr. registrar County Hosp., Roskilde, 1981-82; mem. faculty U. Copenhagen, 1983—. Contbr. articles to profl. jours. Mem. Danish med. group Amnesty Internat., 1976—. Served to lt. Med. Corps Denmark, 1976-77. Grantee Danish Research Council, 1979, Roskilde Research Council, 1982. Mem. Danish Soc. Gastroenterology, Danish Sc. Surgery, Scandinavian Soc. Surgery. Clubs: Olstykke Bicycling. Avocations: Bicycling. Office: Bispebjerg Hosp, Dept D, 2400 Copenhagen NV Denmark

JESSERAMSING, CHITMANSING, ambassador; b. Mahebourg, Mauritius, Aug. 25, 1933; s. Jeewoonarain and Banitha (Bindah) J.; m. Usha Seereeram; children—Devindra, Janita, Anjali. B.A. with honors, Delhi U., 1957, M.A. with honors, 1959; Diploma in Diplomatic Studies, Canberra U., 1966, Queen's Coll., Oxford U., 1967; M.A., Georgetown U., 1974. Prin. Islamic Cultural Coll., Mauritius, 1961-62; edn. officer English Dept. Royal Coll., Curepipe, 1962-66; diplomatic officer Prime Minister's Office Govt. of Mauritius, 1967-68; 1st sec. Mauritius embassy, Washington, 1968-79, minister-counsellor, charge d'affaires, 1979-81, ambassador to U.S., also accredited to Can., Brazil, Argentina, Cuba, Trinidad and Tobago, Jamaica, Barbados, Mex., 1982—; high commr. to Can. 1984—. Mem. Royal Coll. Philos. Soc. (founder, pres. 1962-66). Club: International (Washington). Home: 6604 Kenhill Rd Bethesda MD 20817 Office: Embassy of Mauritius 4301 Connecticut Ave NW Suite 134 Washington DC 20008

JESSUP, JOE LEE, educator, management consultant; b. Cordele, Ga., June 23, 1913; s. Horace Andrew and Elizabeth (Wilson) J.; m. Genevieve Quirk Galloway, Aug. 29, 1946; 1 child, Gail Elizabeth. B.S., U. Ala., 1936; M.B.A., Harvard U., 1941; LL.D., Chung-Ang U., Seoul, Korea, 1964. Sales rep. Proctor & Gamble, 1937-40; liaison officer bur. pub. relations U.S. War Dept., 1941; spl. asst. and exec. asst. Far Ea. div. and office exports Bd. Econ. Warfare, 1942-43; exec. officer, office deptl. adminstrn. Dept. State, 1946; exec. sec. adminstr.'s adv. council War Assets Adminstrn., 1946-48; v.p. sales Airken, Capitol & Service Co., 1948-52; assoc. prof. bus. adminstrn. George Washington U., 1952, prof., 1952-77, prof. emeritus, 1977—, asst. dean Sch. Govt., 1951-60; pres. Jessup and Co., Ft. Lauderdale, Fla., 1957—; bd. dirs. Giant Food, Inc., Washington (audit comm. 1974-75), 1971-75, Am. Equity Investors, Inc., 1986-87, Hunter Assn. Labs, Fairfax, Va., 1964-69 (exec. comm. 1966-69, exec. v.p. 1967, gen. mgr. 1969), coordinator air force resources mgmt. program, 1951-57; del. in gen. 10th Internat. Mgmt. Conf., Sao Paulo, Brazil, 1954, 11th Conf., Paris, 1957, 12th Conf., Sydney and Melbourne, Australia, 1960, 13th Conf., Rotterdam, Netherlands, 1966, 14th Conf., Tokyo, 1969, 15th Conf., Munich, Germany, 1972; mem. Md. Econ. Devel. Adv. Commn., 1973-75. Mem. nat. adv. council Center for Study Presidency, 1974; mem. Broward Bd. Trustees Philn. Orch. Fla., 1986—; mem. Chaine des Rotisseur, 1987—; mem. Civil Service Commn., Arlington County, Va., 1952-54; trustee Tng. Within Industry Found., Summit, N.J., 1954-58. Served from 2d lt. to lt. col. AUS,

1941-46. Decorated Bronze Star; recipient cert. of appreciation Sec. of Air Force, 1957. Mem. Acad. Mgmt. Clubs: Harvard (N.Y.C.); University (Washington); Coral Ridge Yacht; Tower (Ft. Lauderdale). Home: 2801 NE 57th St Fort Lauderdale FL 33308

JESSUP, WARREN T., patent lawyer; b. Eureka, Calif., Aug. 1, 1916; s. Thurman W. and Amelia (Johnson) J.; m. Evelyn Via, Sept. 13, 1941; children: Thurman W., Paul H., Stephen T., Marilyn R. Jessup Huffman. B.S., U. So. Calif., 1937; J.D., George Washington U., 1942. Bar: D.C. 1941, Calif. 1947, U.S. Dist. Ct. (cen., so., no. dists.) Calif. 1947, U.S. Ct. Appeals (Fed. cir.) 1947, U.S. Supreme Ct. 1947. Engr. Gen. Electric Co., 1937-38, patent dept., 1938-42; mem. patent div. USN, 1944-46; patent counsel 11th Naval Dist., 1946-50; mem. Huebner, Beehler, Worrel & Herzig, 1950-56; ptnr. Herzig & Jessup, 1957-59; individual practice law 1959-68; mem. firm Jessup & Beecher, Sherman Oaks, also, Los Angeles, 1968-85, Jessup Beecher & Slehofer, Westlake Village, Calif., 1985—; instr. patent law, grad. div. Law Sch., U. So. Calif.; instr. bus. law U. Calif. at Los Angeles. Author: Patent Guide for Navy Inventors, 1950; Contbr. to: Ency. of Patent Practice and Invention Mgmt. Chmn. citizens adv. com. Point Mugu State Park, 1973; mem. Ventura County Mental Health Adv. Bd., 1977-82, chmn., 1979. Served from ensign to lt. comdr. USN, 1942-46; comdr. Res. Mem. Patent Law Assn. Los Angeles (pres. 1974-75), NSPE, Am. Intellectual Property Law Assn., Conejo Valley Bar Assn. (pres. 1987), Conejo Valley Hist. Soc. (bd. dirs. 1971-83), Order of Coif, Tau Beta Pi, Eta Kappa Nu, Phi Kappa Phi, Phi Delta Phi. Baptist. Office: Jessup Beecher & Slehofer 875 Westlake Blvd Suite 205 Westlake Village CA 91361

JESTER, ROBERTS CHARLES, JR., engineering services company executive; b. Atlanta, July 12, 1917; s. Roberts Charles and Lynwood (Waters) J.; children: Rita (Mrs. Charles B. Jones, Jr.), Carol (Mrs. John M. Sisk, Jr.), Janelle (Mrs. Michael C. Patty). B.S., U. Ga., 1940; grad., Advanced Mgmt. Program, Harvard, 1957. Chief clk. Ga. R.R., 1936-40; project mgr. Mich. Design & Engring. Co., 1941-42; partner Allstate Engring. Service Co., Dayton, Ohio, 1943-45; pres. Allstates Engring. Co., 1945-54; chmn., chief exec. officer Allstates Engring. Co. Inc., Allstates Design & Devel. Co. Inc., Trenton, N.J., 1954—; dir. N.J. Nat. Bank. Bd. dirs., vice chmn. Greater Trenton Symphony Assn.; bd. dirs. George Washington council Boy Scouts Am.; bd. govs. Hamilton Hosp.; mem. lay adv. bd. St. Francis Hosp.; trustee YMCA, Trenton. Mem. Greater Trenton C. of C. (bd. dirs.). Republican. Presbyterian. Clubs: Mason (Shriner, Jester), Engineers, Trenton Country (past pres.); Metropolitan (N.Y.C.); Pitts. Athletic; Little Egg Harbor Yacht (N.J.). Office: 367 Pennington Ave Trenton NJ 08608

JETER, KATHERINE LESLIE BRASH, lawyer; b. Gulfport, Miss., July 24, 1921; d. Ralph Edward and Rosa Meta (Jacobs) Brash; m. Robert McLean Jeter, Jr., May 11, 1946. B.A., Newcomb Coll. of Tulane U., 1943; J.D., Tulane U., 1945. Bar: La. 1945 U.S. Dist. Ct. (we. dist.) La. 1948, U.S. Tax Ct. 1965, U.S. Supreme Ct. 1971, U.S. Dist. Ct. (ea. dist.) La. 1975, U.S. Ct. Appeals (5th cir.) 1981, U.S. Dist. Ct. (mid. dist.) La. 1982. Assoc. Montgomery, Fenner & Brown, New Orleans, 1945-46, Tucker, Martin, Holder, Jeter & Jackson, Shreveport, 1947-49; ptnr. Jeter, Jackson and Hickman and predecessors, Shreveport, 1980—; judge pro tem 1st Jud. Dist. Ct., Caddo Parish, La., 1982-83; mem. adv. com. to joint legis. subcom. on mgmt. of the community. Pres. YWCA of Shreveport, 1963; hon. consul of France; Shreveport; pres. Little Theatre of Shreveport, 1966-67; pres. Shreveport Art Guild, 1974-75; mem. task force crim justice La. Priorities for the Future, 1978; pres. LWV of Shreveport, 1950-51. Recipient Disting. Grad. award Tulane Law Sch., 1983. Mem. La. State Law Inst. (mem. council 1980—, adv. com. La. Civil Code 1973-77, temp. ad hoc. com. 1976-77), Public Affairs Research Council (bd. trustees 1976-81, exec. com. 1981—, area exec. committeeman Shreveport area 1982), ABA, La. Bar Assn., Shreveport Bar Assn. (pres. 1986), Nat. Assn. Women Lawyers, Shreveport Assn. for Women Attys., C. of C. Shreveport (bd. dirs. 1975-77), Order of Coif, Phi Beta Kappa. Baptist. Contbr. articles on law to profl. jours.; editor Tulane Law Rev., 1945. Home: 3959 Maryland Ave Shreveport LA 71106 Office: 401 Edwards St Suite 905 Shreveport LA 71101-3146

JETHMAL, PISHU, travel agent; b. Gaya, India, Apr. 30, 1944; arrived in Singapore, 1948; s. Jethmal Pritamdas and Devi Jethmal; m. Jyoti Shamdasani, Dec. 17, 1965; children: Geetanjali, Mansha, Karishma. Grad. high sch., Singapore. Chmn. P. Jethmal Travel Ltd., Singapore, 1961—, also bd. dirs.; chmn. P. Jethmal Cargo Ltd., Singapore, 1976—, also bd. dirs. Mem. Nat. Assn. Travel Agts. Singapore, Skal Club Singapore, Singapore Indian C. of C., Sindhi Merchants Assn. Hindu. Clubs: Am. (Singapore), Chinese Swimming (Singapore). Lodge: Lions (dir. 1975). Office: P Jethmal Travel Ltd, 1 Colombo Ct #05-07, 0617 Singapore Singapore

JETT, RICHARD JAMES, bank executive; b. South Gate, Calif., May 7, 1940; s. Artie Richard and Evelyn Clara (Tuksbre) J.; m. Deborrah C. Wiesman, July 14, 1975 (div. Sept. 1982); m. Michelle Diane Hall, Oct. 25, 1984; children: Sandi, Teri, Richi. Diploma in retail banking, U. Va. Collector Dial Fin., Alhambra, Calif., 1960-62; v.p. 1st Interstate Bank, Los Angeles, 1962-79; exec. v.p. Citrus State Bank, Covina, Calif., 1979-82; pres., chief exec. officer Empire Bank, N.A., Ontario, Calif., 1982—, also bd. dirs.; Bd. dirs. Haven Escrow Co., Inc., Covina, Calif. Mem. Am. Bankers Assn. (advisor 1979-83,), Am. Inst. Banking (bd. dirs. 1983—), Independent Bankers Assn. So. Calif. (bd. dirs. 1984—), Calif. Bankers Assn. (bd. dirs. 1985-87, 88—), Covina C. of C. (pres. 1986-876, named Dir. of Yr. 1984). Republican. Lutheran. Lodges: Lions, Masons. Home: 646 Chaparro Rd Covina CA 91724 Office: Empire Bank NA 800 N Haven Ave Ontario CA 91764

JETTKE, HARRY JEROME, government official; b. Detroit, Jan. 2, 1925; s. Harry H. and Eugenia M. (Dziatkiewicz) J.; B.A., Wayne State U., 1961; m. Josefina Suarez-Garcia, Oct. 22, 1948; 1 dau., Joan Lillian Jettke Sorger. Owner, operator Farmacia Virreyes/Farmacia Regina, Toluca, Mex., 1948-55; intern pharmacist Cunningham Drug Stores, Detroit, 1955-63; drug specialist, product safety specialist FDA, Detroit, 1963-73; acting dir. Cleve., U.S. Consumer Product Safety Commn., 1973-75, compliance officer, 1975-78, supr., investigations, 1978-82, regional compliance officer, 1982-83, sr. resident, 1983—. Served with Fin. Dept., U.S. Army, 1942-43. Drug specialist FDA. Mem. Am. Soc. for Quality Control (sr., chmn. Cleve. sect. 1977-78, cert. quality technician, cert. quality engr.), Asociación Nacional Mexicana de Estadistica y Control de Calidad, policy com. Cleve. Fed. Exec. Bd., 1985. Roman Catholic. Home: 25715 Yoeman Dr Westlake OH 44145 Office: US Consumer Product Safety Commn One Playhouse Sq 1375 Euclid Ave Cleveland OH 44114

JEUFROY, ODILE, psychiatrist; b. Rabat, Maroc, France, Nov. 21, 1940. Physique Chemistry Biologie, Faculté de Scis., Rabat, 1958. Resident in psychiatry Clinique de Quissac, Gard and Remoulins, France, 1969-71; physician dir. Bourneville Centre, Montpellier, France, 1971-74; practice medicine specializing in psychiatry and psychoanalysis Montpellier, 1974—. Mem. Ecole de la Cause Freudienne. Home and Office: 16 Ave D Assas, 34000 Montpellier France

JEWERS, KENNETH, government scientist; b. London, Sept. 24, 1931; s. James and Margaret Ann (Harvey) J.; m. Iris Dorothy Thornton, Apr. 2, 1960; 1 son, Kevin Conrad. BSc, U. Sheffield, 1954, PhD, 1958. Scientist Shell Internat., London, 1957-60; sr. scientist Tropical Products Inst., London, 1960—; prin. scientist Tropical Research and Devel. Inst. (now Overseas Devel. Natural Resources Inst.), London, 1983—; expert Med. U., Bangkok, 1962-64, SEATO prof., 1965-67; vis. scientist Wellcome Research, Beckenham, Eng., 1976-77; chmn. I.J.K. Cosywarm Enterprises, London, 1977—, I.J.K. Leisure, London, 1981—, Bus. Centre Piccadilly Ltd., 1988; rapporteur 2d Joint FAO/WHO/UNEP Internat. Conf. on Mycotoxins, Bangkok, 1987. Author: Naturally Occuring Antitumor Agents, 1972, Recent Developments in Cancer Chemotherapy, 1981; patentee in field. Mem. Econ. and Medicinal Plants Assn. (chmn. 1978-81). Home: 49 Homemead Rd, Bickley, Kent BR2 8AX, England Office: Overseas Devel Natural Resources Inst, 56/62 Gray's Inn Rd, London WC1X 8LU, England

JEWITT, ANTHONY JOHN, business information company executive; b. London, Oct. 7, 1935; s. John and Ellen Margaret (Tatlock) J.; m. Janet Julia Smith, July 26, 1958; children—Marie Julia Ann, Jennie Ann Louise, Catherine Jane. P.M.D., Harvard U., 1969. Trainee, Brit. Petroleum, London, 1954-58; dir. Reed Employment Ltd., London, 1960-69; group chmn. ICC Info. Group, London, 1969—; dir. Marcom Systems Ltd., Twickenham, Eng., S.I. Mgmt., Crowthorne, Eng. Contbr. articles to profl. jours. Served to capt. Brit. Army, 1958-60. Fellow Chartered Inst. Secs. (assoc.), British Inst. Mgmt., Inst. Mktg. Mem. Ch. of England. Club: St. James (London). Home: 13 Pelling Hill, Old Windsor, Berkshire SL4 2LL, England Office: ICC Group Plc, 16/26 Banner St, London EC1Y 8QE, England

JEWKES, GORDON WESLEY, diplomat; b. Nov. 18, 1931; s. Jesse Jewkes; m. Joyce Lyons, 1954; 2 sons. Grad., U. Newark-on-Trent, Eng. With Gen. Register Office, 1950-63, CS Pay Research Unit, 1963-65; joined HM Diplomatic Service, 1968, CO, later FCO, 1968-69; consul (comml.) HM Diplomatic Service, Chgo., 1969-72; dep. high commr. HM Diplomatic Service, Port of Spain, Trinidad and Tobago, 1972-75; fin. officer and head fin. dept. FCO HM Diplomatic Service, 1975-79; consul-gen. HM Diplomatic Service, Cleve., 1979-82, Chgo., 1982-85; gov. Falkland Islands, 1985—, also high commr. Brit. Antarctic Terr., 1985—. Office: Fgn and Commonwealth Office, London SW1A 2AH, England *

JHA, SHYAM CHANDRA, marketing executive; b. Ghoghardiha, Bihar, India, Feb. 6, 1959; came to France, 1984; came to Switzerland, 1988; s. Kuldev and Shanti Jha; m. Lalita Rani Singh, Sept. 6, 1984. BTech, Indian Inst. Tech., New Delhi, 1983. Mgr. project Schlumberger Co., Melun, France, 1983-85, Hewlett-Packard Co., Eybens, France, 1985-88; mgr. European product Hewlett-Packard Co., Geneva, 1988—. Author: State of India's Environment, 1983; contbr. articles to sci. jours. Home: 15 rue du Trabli, CH-1236 Cartigny Switzerland Office: Hewlett-Packard SA, 150 route du Nant d'Avril, CH-1217 Meyrin 2 Geneva Switzerland

JHABVALA, RUTH PRAWER, author; b. Cologne, Germany, May 7, 1927; d. Marcus and Eleonora (Cohn) Prawer; m. C.S.H. Jhabvala, 1951; 3 children. M.A.; D.Litt. (hon.) London U. Lived in India, 1951-75, U.S., 1975—. Author: (novels) To Whom She Will, 1955; Nature of Passion, 1956; Esmond in India, 1958; The Householder, 1960; Get Ready for Battle, 1963; Like Birds, Like Fishes, 1964; A Backward Place, 1965; A New Dominion, 1971; Heat and Dust, 1975; In Search of Love and Beauty, 1983; Three Continents, 1987; (short story collections) A Stronger Climate, 1968; An Experience of India, 1970; How I Became a Holy Mother, 1976; Out of India (selected stories), 1986; (film scripts) The Householder, 1963, Shakespeare Wallah, 1965; The Guru, 1969; Bombay Talkie, 1971; Autobiography of a Princess, 1975; Roseland, 1977; Hullabaloo over Georgie and Bonnie's Pictures, 1978; Jane Austen in Manhattan, 1980; Quartet, 1981; Heat and Dust, 1983; the Bostonians, 1984; Room With A View, 1986 (Acad. award for screenplay); Recipient Booker award for best novel, 1975; Guggenheim fellow, 1976; Neill Gunn. Internat. fellow, 1979; Mac Arthur fellow, 1984-89. Home: 400 E 52d St New York NY 10022 Other: care John Murray, 50 Albemarle St, London W1, England

JHUNJHUNWALA, RAVIN KUMAR, refractory specialist; b. Barang, India, Sept. 29, 1952; s. Jugal Kishore and Sushila Devi (Modi) J.; m. Sheela Gupta, Dec. 11, 1975; children: Rashmi, Shilpa. B in Commerce, Ravenshaw Coll., Cuttack, Orissa, India, 1971; M in Chem. Engring., Soc. Engrs., London, 1975; postgrad. exec. edn. program Harvard U., 1982. Exec. trainee Orissa Industries Ltd., Rourkela, India, 1971-72, works mgr., 1974-82, industry chief exec., 1982—; tech. trainee Harbison Walker Internat. div. Dresser Industries, Inc., Pitts., 1972-73. Author tech. papers. Mem. Indian Inst. Indsl. Engrs., Soc. Engrs. U.K., All India Mgmt. Assn. (governing council 1984—), Indian Inst. Ceramics, Am. Ceramic Soc., Rourkela Profl. Assn., Rourkela Cultural Trust, Assn. Indian Engring. Industries. Lodge: Lions. Avocations: fgn. langs., reading. Office: Orissa Industries Ltd, Uditnagar, Orissa India

JIAHUAN LUO, ambassador; b. Macao, China, July 10, 1928; arrived in Sierra Leone, 1985; s. Ergang Luo and Wanfen Chen; m. Wenjun Qian; 1 child, Shihua. Master's degree, U. Nanking, 1951. 3d sec. Chinese Embassy to Gt. Britain, London, 1964-67, 1st sec., 1978-83; counselor Chinese Fgn. Ministry, Beijing, 1983-85; Chinese ambassador to Sierra Leone Freetown, 1985—. Home: Beijing China Office: Embassy of Peoples Republic China, PO Box 778, 29 Wilberforce Loop, Freetown Sierra Leone

JIANG, KONG-YANG, aesthetics and literary theory educator; b. Wansien, China, Jan. 23, 1923; s. Kwang-She Jiang and Fu-San Yu; m. Zhi-Zhen Pu, Dec. 25, 1948; children—Pu, Hong, Lian, Yu. B.A., Central Polit. U. of China, 1946. Banker Farmer's Bank of China, Chengkiang, 1946-48; editor and translator HaiKwang Library, Shanghai, 1948-51; prof. Fudan U., Shanghai, 1951—. Author: Introduction to Literature, 1957; Beauty and Its Creation, 1980; Image and Type, 1980; Classical German Aesthetics, 1980; Essays on the Musical Aesthetical Thinkings in the pre-Qin Dynasties, 1986; Critical Essays on Aesthetics and Literature, 1986. Editor-in-chief Dictionary of Aesthetics, 1983; Aesthetics and Art Criticism, 1984. Mem. Research Soc. of Aesthetics (chmn. 1980—), Chinese Soc. Aesthetics (vice chmn. 1983—). Home: The 9th Dormitory, No 14, Fudan U, Shanghai Peoples Republic of China Office: Fudan U, Dept Chinese Lit, Shanghai Peoples Republic of China

JIANG, PAUL YUN-MING, foreign language educator, author; b. Taipei, China, Dec. 4, 1939; came to N.Z. and Australia, 1966; s. Chung-san and Yi-mei (Chung) J.; m. Anna Chiu, Feb. 22, 1969; children—Roland, Eugene. B.A., Nat. Taiwan U. (China), 1961; M.A., Fujen U. (China), 1964; Ph.D., Auckland U. (N.Z.), 1975. Lectr. Auckland U., 1966-71, sr. lectr., 1972-78; vis. prof. Chengchi U., Taiwan, 1973-74, head Chinese Dept. Macquarie U., Sydney, Australia, 1979—, acting head Sch. Modern Langs., 1985-86; vis. research prof. Nat. Taiwan U., 1983-84. Author: Criterion of Truth, 1972, The Search for Mind: Ch'en Pai-sha, Philosopher-Poet (Pacific Culture Found. award 1980), 1980, A New Interpretation of Neo-Confucianism, 1987, Ch'en Nsien-chang, 1988; contbr. to newspapers and profl. jours.. Served to 2d lt. Chinese Air Force, 1964-65. N.Z. Govt. grantee, 1973; Macquarie U. Research grantee, 1979-85; Pacific Cultural Found. grantee, 1980, ROC Nat. Govt. grantee, 1972-73, 83-84, 87-88. Fellow Oriental Soc. Australia, Internat. Soc. Chinese Philosophy, Am. Council Learned Soc. and Internat. Conf. Chu Hsi, Internat. Biographical Assn.; mem. Asian Studies Assn. Australia, Australian Assn. Chinese Culture (chmn. 1982-85). Avocations: piano; bridge. Office: Macquarie U, Chinese Sect, North Ryde, New South Wales 2113, Australia

JIANG, ZILONG, editor, writer; b. Cang County, He-Bei, People's Republic of China, July 2, 1941; s. Junshan and Wei Jiang; m. Qinglian Zhang, June 1, 1968; children: Xiaozhun, Wei. Diploma secondary profl. sch., China Ocean Charting Sch., 1962; student, China Luxun Lit. Inst., Beijing, 1980. Sec., dir. workshop Tianjin (People's Republic of China) Heavy-Duty Machinery Factory, 1965-82; editor, writer, permanent vice chmn. Tianjin Writer Assn., 1982—; publ. cons. to 7 provinces. Author: Snake God (Tianjin Luxun Lit. prize 1986), All Colours of the Rainbow (1st prize for novelette), Pioneer (nat. novelette prize 1980), Yan and Zhao Sad Melody (3d nat. novelette prize), A New Year Call (nat. short story No. 1 prize, 1982), Diary of a Factory Secretary (nat. short story prize), Minute of Qiao Director on the Official Post (nat. short story 1st prize 1979); cons. editorial bd. People Lit. Served as cartographer Chinese Navy, 1962-65, dir. regiment armyman com. Recipient 6 nat. awards for important lit., 11 lit. awards of provinces and cities, Honor award Tianjin Luxun Lit. and Art, 1982. Mem. China Writer Assn. (bd. dirs.), Tianjin Lit. Artist Com. Home: 10 6 Bldg Jieyuan Li, Miyun Rd, Tianjin Peoples Republic of China Office: Tianjin Writer Assn, 163 Xinhua Rd, Tianjin People's Republic of China

JILANI, ATIQ AHMED, industrialist; b. Amroha, India, Feb. 1, 1948; came to U.S., 1970; s. Siddiq Ahmed and Nasima (Khatoon) J.; m. Khalida Bano Naqvi, Dec. 25, 1975; children: Hussain, Ibrahim. BE, NED Engring. Coll., Karachi U., 1969; MS, Tuskegee Inst., Ala., 1971; cert. in mgmt., Purdue U., 1978, Northwestern U., 1980, U. Pa., 1982. Registered profl. engr., Ill. Script writer Karachi (Pakistan) TV, 1967-70; mem. research staff AEC, Tuskegee, Ala., 1970-71; design engr. Lummus Industries, Columbus, Ga., 1971-73; product engr. Borg-Warner Corp., Chgo., 1974-78, mgr. engring. Chgo. Marine Containers div. Sea Containers, Broadview, Ill., 1978-80; v.p. operations Borg-Erickson Corp., Chgo., 1980-81, chief operating officer, v.p., gen. mgr. 1981-85; pres., chief exec. officer, Circuit Systems Inc., 1985-87, chmn. bd. dirs., 1986—; cons. in industry and agr. UN, including work in South Asia, 1981. Contbr. articles to profl. jours.; patentee (U.S. and internat.) in field agrl. equipment. Mem. Rep. Precinct Com., York Twp., Du Page County, Ill., 1988—; organizer Voter registration campaign for Asian-Am. voters in Du Page County, 1987—. Recipient Asian Human Services of Chgo. Honor award 1988. Mem. Inst. Printed Circuits, Assn. Energy Engrs. (charter), Thinkers Forum (pres. 1967-70). Home: PO Box 3212 Oak Brook IL 60521

JIMÉNEZ, JOSÉ DE JESÚS, physician, baseball researcher; b. Santiago, Dominican Republic, May 28, 1937. M.D., U. Santo Domingo, 1960. Intern, Ottawa (Ont., Can.) Gen. Hosp., 1961-62; resident in medicine, 1962-63; fellow in cardiology Phila. Gen. Hosp., 1963-64, resident in cardiology, 1964-65; resident in medicine Grad. Hosp., Phila., 1965-66; resident in internal medicine Albert Einstein Hosp., Phila., 1966-67; chief dept. cardiology Jose María Cabral Hosp., Santiago, 1967-72; prof. Cath. U. Madre y Maestra, Santiago, 1973—; chief of internal medicine New José María Cabral U. Hosp., Santiago, 1977—; research Latin Am. baseball players. Author: Baseball Archives, 1977; A Life Dedicated to Science; contbr. articles to med. jours. Mem. ACP, N.Y. Acad. Scis., Am. Coll. Physicians, N.Y. Acad. Sci., Am. Soc. Baseball Research. Office: Máximo Gómez 34, Santiago Dominican Republic

JIMENEZ, MENARDO R., SR., real estate executive, advertising executive; b. Manila, Dec. 6, 1932; m. Carolina Gozon; children: Menardo Jr., Joel, Laura, Carmen. BS in Commerce, Far Ea. U., Manila, 1952. CPA, The Philippines. Chmn. Majent Mgmt. and Devel. Corp., M.A. Jimenez Enterprises, Inc.; pres. Mont-Aire Realty and Devel. Corp.; pres., chief exec. officer Republic Braodcasting System, Inc.; pres. Justitia Realty and Mgmt. Corp., GMA Mktg. and Prodns., Inc.; chmn., trustee Kapwa Ko Mahal Ko Found., Inc.; treas., bd. dirs. Medicard Philippines, Inc.; chmn. Prison Fellowship Philippines, Inc; bd. dirs. Prison Fellowship Internat.; pres. Alta Power Prodns., Inc. Recipient cert. of appreciation Supreme Council, 1975, Sining, Inc. trophy, 1975, Presdl. Merit award Fin. Execs. Inst. Philippines, 1976, cert. of appreciation Narcotics Found. Philippines, Inc., 1977-78, Model Businessman and Civic Leader of Yr. trophy Fame Mass Media Coordinating Services, 1978, Outstanding Business Exec. in Field Nation Bldg. Spl. award, 1978, cert. of appreciation Asian Fedn. Advt. Assns., 1978, plaque of appreciation Kapisanan Ng Mga Broadcasters Sa Pilipinas, 1979, plaque of appreciation GMA Radio-TV Arts, 1979, plaque of appreciation Rotary Club of Dagupan, 1979, Outstanding Citizen for Yr. in field of broadcasting award of distinction Olongapo News, 1979, citation of honor as disting. community achiever of New Soc. Philippine Research Soc. for Community Devel., 1980, cert. of appreciation Integrated Bar of Philippines, 1980, plaque of appreciation and recognition Kapisanang Ng Mga Broadcasters Sa Pilipinas, 1981. Mem. Philippine Inst. CPA's, Internat. Advt. Assn., Inc., Chamber Internat. Trade, Manila Overseas Press Club, Am. Philatelic Soc., U.S. Possessions Philatelic Soc., Philippine Numismatic and Antiquarian Soc. Clubs: Manila Polo, Met., Inc. (Manila) (chmn., trustee). Office: Republic Broadcasting System Inc, Saggitatrius Bldg 2d Floor, 3116 Metro Manila The Philippines

JIMENEZ-TORRES, CARLOS FEDERICO, physician; b. Aquada, P.R., Oct. 19, 1921; s. Carlos Jimenez and Pura Torres; student U. P.R., 1936-39; M.D., George Washington U., 1943; postgrad. radiology U. Pa., 1948-49; m. Domitila Ferrer, June 18, 1949; children—Lorraine, Carlos Federico, Luis Javier, Pura Elaine, Janet Arlene. Intern, Fajardo Dist. Hosp., 1943-44; resident Presbyn. Hosp., Phila., 1949-51; physician VA Center and Hosp., San Juan, P.R., 1946-48; practice medicine specializing in radiology, Ponce, P.R., 1952—; instr. radiology U. Pa. Sch. Medicine, 1950-51; lectr. radiology U. P.R. Sch. Medicine, 1952—; asso. clin. prof. radiology Cath. U. P.R. Sch. Medicine, 1979—; cons. radiology Ponce Med. Center. Bd. dirs., past treas. Liceo Ponceno. Served with AUS, 1944-46. Diplomate Am. Bd. Radiology. Mem. Am., Pan Am., P.R. med. assns., Am. Coll. Radiology, P.R., Inter-Am. radiol. socs., Radiol. Soc. N.Am., Am. Legion, USCG Aux., U.S. Power Squadron. Roman Catholic. Clubs: KC, Lions (past dist. zone chmn., past pres. Ponce), Ponce Yacht (past commodore). Home: 16 Universidad St Ponce PR 00731 Office: Lorraine Building Ponce PR 00731

JIN, SHIBAI, comparative educator, translator; b. Kai Yuan, Lian Ning, People's Republic of China, June 22, 1925; s. Xi-Jiu Jin and Xiu-Xian Chang; m. Ying Zhao, Oct. 1946; children: Aiguang, Wei, Pei, Ning. BA in Econs., Nat. N.E. Univ., Shenyang, People's Republic of China, 1948; postgrad., Harbin (People's Republic of China) Inst. Fgn. Langs., 1950. Translator, researcher Ministry Edn. China, Bejing, 1952-63; researcher Inst. Edn. Research, Bejing, 1964-73, China's Inst. Sci. Technol. Info., Bejing, 1974-79; research fellow, prof. Cen. Inst. Ednl. Sci., Bejing, 1979—. Author: China's Normal Education, 1982, Comparative Education in China, 1983, China's Education and its Problems, 1984. Mem. Comparative Edn. (sec.-gen. 1979-86), Soc. China (vice chmn. 1986-87). Office: Nat Inst Ednl Research, 10 Bei Huan Xi Rd, Beijing People's Repbulic of China

JINASENA, RANJIT TISSAWEERA, finance executive; b. Colombo, Sri Lanka, June 4, 1945; s. Tissaweera Siriwardene and Lily Margaret (Fernando) J.; m. Nilanthani Priyadarshani de Mel, Jan. 27, 1975; children: Suren, Chanaka. Student, Loughborough U. Tech., Eng., 1965; diploma in mgmt., Aquinas U., Colombo, 1968. Dir. fin. Jinasena Group of Cos., Colombo, 1967—. Anglican. Club: Ceylon Motor Sports (Colombo) (pres.). Home: No 69/3 Kynsey Rd, 8 Colombo Sri Lanka Office: Jinasena Group of Cos, #4 Hunupitiya Rd, 2 Colombo Sri Lanka

JINNETT, ROBERT JEFFERSON, lawyer; b. Birmingham, Ala., May 9, 1949; s. Bryan Floyd Jr. and Elizabeth Coleman (Borders) J.; m. Doreen S. Ziff, Aug. 2, 1975; children: Brynn Leigh, Maren Alexandra. BA, Harvard U., 1971; JD, Cornell U., 1975. Bar: N.Y. 1976, U.S. Dist. Ct. (no. dist.) N.Y. 1976, U.S. Dist. Ct. (so. dist.) N.Y. 1978, U.S. Dist. Ct. (ea. dist.) N.Y. 1979. Law clk. N.Y. State Ct. Appeals, Albany, 1975-77; assoc. Rogers & Wells, N.Y.C., 1977-82; assoc. LeBoeuf, Lamb, Leiby & MacRae, N.Y.C., 1983-86, ptnr., 1986—. Contbg. author: High Tech Real Estate, 1985. DAAD fellow U. Heidelberg, Fed. Republic Germany, 1971-72; recipient 3d Nat. Prize, Nathan Burkan Meml. Comp. ASCAP, 1974. Mem. ABA, Nat. Assn. Corp. Dirs. Episcopalian. Office: LeBoeuf Lamb Leiby & MacRae 520 Madison Ave New York NY 10022

JI PENGFEI, government official People's Republic of China; b. Linyi, Shanxi Province, China, 1910; m. Xu Hanbing. Student Cen. Party Sch., Inst. Marxism-Leninism, 1937; grad. Mil. Med. Coll., Xi'an. Joined Communist Party, 1931; on Long March in Med. Dept., Red Army, 1935; dep. polit. commissar Army Corps, 3d Field Army, 1950; ambassador People's Republic of China to German Dem. Republic, 1953-55; council mem. Inst. Fgn. Affairs, 1955; vice minister fgn. affairs, 1955-71, acting minister fgn. affairs, 1971-72, minister fgn. affairs, 1972-74; mem. 10th Cen. Com., Chinese Communist Party, 1973, mem. Standing Com., 1975-78, sec. gen. Standing Com., 1975-79, mem. 11th Cen. Com., 1977, mem. Presidium, Standing Com., 12th Cen. Com., 1982; mem. polit. and legal affairs group Cen. Com., 1978—; dir. Internat. Liaison Dept., Cen. Com., 1979-82; sec.-gen. standing com. Nat. People's Congress, 1975-79; vice-premier State Council, 1979-82, sec.-gen., 1980-81, state councilor, 1982-88, in charge Hong Kong affairs, 1984—. Office: care State Council, Beijing People's Republic of China *

JIWKOW, WASIL, violin maker; b. Jakimovo, Bulgaria, Dec. 12, 1926; s. George and Todora J. Master Diploma for stringed instrument making with Master Manachil Crastew, Sofia, Bulgaria, 1951. Internat. exhbns.; Concours International de Quatuor a Cordes, Liege, Belgium, 1957, 60, 63, 69, 72, Societa Filarmonica Ascolana, Mostra Internazionale di Luteria, Viola Moderna, Ascoli, Italy, 1959, Concours Internat. for Stringed Instruments, Poznan, Poland, 1967, The Violin Soc. of Am. Internat. Bicentennial Exhbn. and Competition, Phila., 1976; exhibited 24 original instruments (violins, violas, celloes) at Arts Acad., Interlochen, Mich., 1975. Recipient numerous certs. and first prizes, including: 2d prize for violin, Poznan,, 1972, 1st prize for best making and style Quartet Competition, Liege, Belgium; Diploma for best making and tone, Phila., 1976, diploma for workmanship, viola, La Jolla, Calif., 1978. Office: Artistic Atelier for Violin Making, Muller-Strasse 26, 8000 Munich 5 Federal Republic of Germany

JOACHIM, MIROSLAV VACLAV JAN, communications engineer; b. Praha, Czechoslovakia, Jan. 1, 1919; s. Karel and Frantiska (Hrdlickova) J.; grad. Tech. U., Praha, 1946, cert. in Radio Engring. with honors, 1946, Dr. Tech. Scis., 1947; postgrad. M.I.T., summer 1948; m. Nadezda Huskova, Apr. 26, 1951; children—Zoja, Olga. Asst., Tech. U., Praha, 1945-51; chief of sect. Ministry of Post and Telecommunications, Praha, 1951-61, sr. counsellor for sci., 1977—; sr. counsellor Internat. Telecommunication Union, Geneva, 1961-75; dir. research inst. Federal Ministry of Posts and Telecommunications, Praha, 1975-77; Informatique A, Conservatoire Nat. des Arts et Métiers, Paris, 1972, sr. counsellor for sci., 1977-82; ambassador Internat. Amateur Radio Club, Geneva. Mem. Central Radio Club Praha. Author: Radio in Aviation, 1945; Long Term Predictions of Ionospheric Propagation, 1978; Search for Extra-Terrestrial Intelligence, 1985; inventor in field of radio direction finding. Home: Podbelohorska 43/2881, 150 00 Prague 5, Czechoslovakia

JOANNOU, GEORGE CHRISTOPHER, diversified business executive; b. Iran, Mar. 17, 1937; s. Christopher H. and Eva (Sadafi) J.; m. Dina Soubra, June 16, 1979; children: Christopher A., Ariane P., Jason K., Adam A., Rhea A.N. AA, Alborz Coll., Tehran, Iran; student, Hunter Coll., 1960. Sales mgr., Iran Lufthansa, Tehran, 1956-59; sales mgr., Europe, Iran, Frankfurt, Fed. Republic Germany Lufthansa, 1959-61, sales mgr., N.Y., Alitalia, N.Y., 1961-63; interline sales mgr. TWA, N.Y.C., 1963-66; gen. mgr. sales and services on loan to Saudi, Jeddah TWA, 1957-58; regional dir. SE Asia TWA, Bangkok, Thailand, 1968-72; founder, chmn. CAMS Group, London and Coral Springs, Fla., 1972—. Recipient U.S. Travel Service award People to People Program of Pres. Kennedy, 1963, Civil Aviation award Govt. Saudi Arabia, 19685. Mem. Pacific Area Travel Assn. (cofounder Thailand chpt.). Home: CAMS Group Dina Indsl Plaza 3561 NW 126th Ave Coral Springs FL 33065

JOAQUIM, RICHARD RALPH, hotel executive; b. Cambridge, Mass., July 28, 1936; s. Manuel and Mary (Marrano) J.; B.F.A., Boston U., 1955, Mus. B., 1959; m. Nancy Phyllis Reis, Oct. 22, 1960; 1 dau., Vanessa Reis. Social dir., coordinator summer resort, Wolfeboro, N.H., 1957-59; concert soloist N.H. Symphony Orch., Vt. Choral Soc., Choral Arts Soc., Schenectady Chamber Orch., 1957-60; coordinator performance functions, mgr. theatre Boston U., 1959-60, asst. program dir., 1963-64, dir. univ. programs, 1964-70; gen. mgr. Harrison House of Glen Cove; dir. Conf. Service Corp., Glen Cove, N.Y., 1970-74, sr. v.p., dir. design and devel.; v.p. Arltec, also mng. dir. Sheraton Internat. Conf. Center, 1975-76; v.p., mng. dir. Scottsdale (Ariz.) Conf. Center and Resort Hotel, 1976—; pres. Internat. Conf. Resorts, Inc., 1977, chmn. bd., 1977—; pres. Western Conf. Resorts; concert solist U.S. Army Field Band, Washington, 1960-62. Creative arts cons., editorial cons., concert mgr. Commr. recreation Watertown, Mass., 1967—; mem. Spl. Study Com. Watertown, 1967—, Glen Cove Mayor's Urban Renewal Com., Nat. Com. for Performing Arts Ctr. at Boston U., Jacob K. Kavits Fellows Program Fellowship Bd. Bd. dirs. Nat. Entertainment Conf.; trustee Boston U., 1983—, Hotel and Food Adminstrn. Program Adv. Bd., Boston U., 1986—. Served with AUS, 1960-62. Mem. Assn. Coll. and Univ. Concert Mgrs., Am. Symphonic League, Am. Fedn. Film Socs., Assn. Am. Artists, Am. Personnel and Guidance Assn., La Chaine des Rotisseurs, Knights of the Vine, Nat. Alumni Council Boston U. Clubs: The Lotos (N.Y.); The Arizona (Phoenix). Office: 7700 McCormick Pkwy Scottsdale AZ 85258

JOB, WILLIAM JAMES, architect; b. Glen Innes, New South Wales, Australia, Apr. 12, 1929; s. George Charles and Phyliss Clara (Stephenson) J.; m. Judith Ann Macsonald, Feb. 13, 1954; children: Sally, Michael, Timothy. Engring. Degree, Sydney (Australia) Tech. Coll., 1952; Architecture Degree, New South Wales U., 1955. Design engr. Colgate Palmolive Pty. Ltd., Sydney, 1948-54; architect Fowell Mansfield, Sydney, 1955-57; assoc. ptnr. Bligh Jessup and Bretnall, Brisbane, Queensland, Australia, 1957-59; chmn. William Job & Assocs. Pty. Ltd., Brisbane, 1960—; bd. dirs. Bartlett Researched Securities Ltd.; chmn. South Brisbane Hosp., Supa Corp. Pty. Ltd., V.R.C. Printing Pty. Ltd. Bd. dirs. Brisbane River Authority, 1987—, Brisbane Coll. Advance Edn., 1982; chmn. Commonwealth Games Ceremonal Div., Mt. Gravatt Coll. Advance Edn., 1978-82. Fellow Royal Australian Inst. Architects, Australian Inst. Mgmt.; mem. Order of Australia. Mem. Ch. of Eng. Clubs: Queensland Cricketeers (pres. 1980-84), Brisbane Golf, Tattersalls. Home: 12 View St, Coorparoo Queensland 4151, Australia Office: William Job & Assocs Pty Ltd, 49 Park Rd, Milton Queensland 4064, Australia

JOCELYN, HENRY DAVID, classical scholar, educator; b. Bega, NSW, Australia, Aug. 22, 1933; s. John Daniel and Phyllis Irene (Burton) J.; m. Margaret Jill Morton, Oct. 22, 1958; children: Daniel Luke, James Edmund. BA, U. Sydney, 1955, U. Cambridge, 1957; PhD, U. Cambridge, 1963. Lectr. Latin U. Sydney, 1960-64, sr. lectr. Latin, 1964-66, reader Latin, 1966-70, prof. Latin, 1970-73; prof. Latin U. Manchester, Eng., 1973—. Author: The Tragedies of Ennius, 1967; co-author: Regnier de Graaf on the Human Reproductive Organs, 1972; contbr. articles to profl. jours. Fellow Brit. Acad. Home: 4 Clayton Ave, Manchester M20 0BN, England Office: U Manchester, Manchester M13 9PL, England

JOCIC, DUSAN, electrical engineer, consultant; b. Belgrade, Yugoslavia, Sept. 7, 1935; came to U.S., 1963; s. Zivojin Petar and Vukosava (Stojkovic) J.; m. Coral Shirley Walker, July 2, 1966. A.S., Pierce Coll., 1985. Design engring. mgr. quality control Belfuse Inc., Jersey City, 1968-74; dir. quality assurance Vanguard Electric Co., Inglewood, Calif., 1974-75; mgr. prodn. Ferrodyne Corp., Venice, Calif., 1975-76; research and devel. assoc. Litton Guidance/Control Systems, Woodland Hills, Calif., 1976-85; mem. tech. staff def. electronics ops. Autonetics Marine Systems div. Rockwell Internat., Anaheim, Calif., 1985—; cons. Encore, San Jose, Calif., 1983—. Patentee in field. Sustaining mem. Republican Nat. Com., Washington, 1980—; mem. Rep. Senatorial Club, 1980, Rep. Congl. Com., 1980. Mem. IEEE (sr. mem., adviser to exec. bd. 1984, sec. 1986—), IEEE Magnetic Soc. (Los Angeles chpt.), Internat. Power Conversion Soc. Serbian Orthodox. Home: 342 Maui Dr Placentia CA 92670 Office: Rockwell Internat Tech Staff D/379-060 031-GE 22 3370 Miraloma Ave PO Box 4921 Anaheim CA 92803-4921

JODRY, BERND, banker; b. Pforzheim, Germany, Nov. 9, 1943; s. Hans Ferdinand and Marcelle P. (van Schoeland) J.; m. Mechtild Aenne Koehntopp, Apr. 13, 1973; 1 dau., Jasmin Silja. B.A. in Bus. Adminstrn., Betriebswirtschafts-Akademie, Frankfurt, 1965. Asst. dep. gen. mgr. B. Grimm & Co., Bangkok, Thailand, 1965-68; mgr. Elfein GmbH, Frankfurt, West Germany, 1969; rep. Bank of Am., Frankfurt, Germany/Austria Bank Am. Travelers Cheques, Frankfurt, 1969-85, regional mgr. mktg. Germany, Switzerland, Austria, Frankfurt, 1973-85; regional mgr. mktg. Germany, South Africa and Malta, Frankfort, 1985-87, regional mgr. mktg. Germany and Malta, 1988— ; v.p., registered mgr. BankAm. Cheque Corp., San Francisco. Mem. Nat. Assn. Security Dealers (registered rep. 1968). Club: Royal Bangkok Sports. Home and Office: Lerchenstrasse 4, D-4598 Cappeln Federal Republic of Germany

JOE, GREGORY MARTIN, lawyer; b. San Francisco, June 2, 1949; s. Martin and Donna Joe. B.A., U. Calif.-Berkeley, 1972, Credential, 1973; J.D., U. Calif.-San Francisco, 1976. Bar: Calif. 1977, U.S. Dist. Ct. (no. dist.) Calif. 1977. Sole practice, Oakland, Calif., 1978—; legal adviser Nat. Ski Patrol System, East Bay Ski Patrol, Oakland, Calif., 1980—; legal counsel Tau Kappa Epsilon-Nu, Berkeley, Calif., 1982—. Recipient Service award Nat. Ski Patrol System, 1976, 81, 86. Mem. ABA, Calif. Young Lawyers Assn., Nat. Ski Patrol System, Soc. for Preservation Early Am. Art, Tenn. Squire Assn., Tau Kappa Epsilon (trustee 1975—), Phi Delta Kappa. Home: 21 Alta Ave Piedmont CA 94611 Office: 590 Merritt Ave Suite 4 Oakland CA 94610

JOERGES, CHRISTIAN HARALD, lawyer, educator; b. Weissenfels, Germany, Sept. 27, 1943; s. Harald and Maria (Heyden) J.; m. Annette Rothenberg, Mar. 20, 1972; children: Johanna, Charlotte. Student in law, Frankfurt (Fed. Republic of Germany) U., 1962-66, JD, 1971; student, Inst. for Internat. and Fgn. Trade Law, Washington, D.C., 1966-67, Netherlands Inst. for Advanced Study, 1985-86. Asst. Law Sch., Frankfurt U., 1972-73, docent, 1973-74; prof. law U. Bremen, Fed. Republic of Germany, 1974—, co-dir. Ctr. for European Legal Policy, 1982-87; prof. European U. Inst., Florence, Italy, 1987-88. Author, editor books and articles in law jours. Recipient Walter Koeb Gedachtuis prize U. Frankfurt, 1971. Office: U Bremen FB6, PO Box 33 0440, 28 Bremen 33 Federal Republic of Germany

JOESOEF, DJOENAEDI, pharmaceutical executive; b. Surakarta, Central Java, Indonesia, June 6, 1933; s. Hong Sian and Bong Tjao (Tjin) Joe; m. Juniati Joesoef, Apr. 8, 1956; children—Edijanto, Rijanto, Lisa, Rachmadi. Sales exec. Eng Thay Hoo Drugstore, Surakarta, Indonesia, 1950-56; mng. dir. Kongdang Sewu Pharm./Wholesale Co., Surakarta, 1956—; pres., dir. PT Konimex Pharm. Lab., Surakarta, 1967—, PT Sinar Intermark, 1982—; chmn. Viva Cosmetics Ltd., Surabaya, 1984—, PT Surya Multi Indopack, Surabaya, 1983—; commr. PT Altron Electronics Hirepurchase. Vice chmn. Panti Kosala Health Found., Surakarta, 1982—; sponsor Sri Bengawan Table Tennis Club, 1983. Lodge: Rotary. Home: 96-98 jl Urip Sumoharjo, Surakarta, Central Java Indonesia Office: PT Konimex Desa Sanggrahan, Kabupaten Grogol, Kecamatan Sukoharjo, Central Java Indonesia

JOHA, EDWIN GEORGE, business services company executive; b. Voorburg, Netherlands, July 19, 1945; s. Jasper Gijsbert and Goswina Anna (Botke) J.; m. Renee Frederica Dousi, Sept. 30, 1977; children—Eric Alexander, Aimee Celeste. Ing., Inst. Tech. Rotterdam, 1967; Bus. Admin., Nijenrode, 1968. Mktg. engr. Sigri GmbH, Meitingen, 1970-71; client service exec. A.C. Nielsen B.V., Amsterdam, 1971-76, project mgr., 1978-82; internat. mktg. mgr. A.C. Nielsen Internat. Inc., Northbrook, Ill., 1982—; area mgr. Stork Bepak B.V., Utrecht, 1976-78. Served with Netherlands Army, 1968-70. Office: AC Nielsen Internat, Deimerhof 2, Diemen 1112 XL, The Netherlands

JOHANN, GERD KARL, psychology educator, researcher; b. Ludwigshafen, Rheinland Pfalz, Fed. Republic Germany, Aug. 8, 1953; s. Philipp and Elfriede (Bauder) J. Diploma in Psychology, Erziehuugswisseuschaftliche Hochschule, Landau, Fed. Rep. Germany, 1982. Evaluator Hochschulmodellversuch Betriebspadagogik, Landau, 1982-83; lectr. Erziehuugswisseuschaftliche Hochschule, Landau, 1982—; cons. BASF, Ludwigshafen, 1982, Kaufhof AG, Cologne, Fed. Republic Germany, 1984-85, Bildungswerk der Fraukeuthaler Wirtschaft, Frankenthal, 1986—, Rationalisierungs Com. der Deutscheu Wirtschaft, 1986—. Contbr. articles to various jours. Friedrich-Ebert-Stiftung scholar, Bonn, 1980. Club: TC-BASF (Ludwigshafen). Home: Von Stein Strasse 54, 6700 Ludwigshafen Rheinland Pfalz Federal Republic of Germany Office: EWH, 6740 Landau Rheinland Pfalz Federal Republic of Germany

JOHANNES, HELGI (JONSSON), writer; b. Reykjavik, Iceland, Sept. 5, 1926; s. Jon and Jonina (Johannesdottir) Matthiasson; m. Margret Guttormsdottir, Dec. 31, 1969; children—Jon Gauti, Guttormur Helgi. Grad. Sch. Commerce, Reykjavik, 1949. Sailor, 1949-52; sec. Icelandic Parliament, 1952-62; archivist Reykjaviks City Archive, 1971-73; freelance writer, 1973—. Books include: Any Weather Whatever, 1957; Looked upon the Frozen Snow, 1958, The Painters House, 1961, The White Sails, 1962, Black Ceremony, 1965, The Carousel, 1969, Phantoms Assemble to a Conference, 1971, Sailor in Peace and at War, 1976, Gifts You are Offered, 1976, A Boy from the East Coast, 1977, 2d vol., 1978; Aiming for the Sky, 1979, The Composer, 1980, Head of Police Force during the British and American Occupation of Iceland in the Second World War, 1981, Valur Gislason and the Theater, 1981, 211 Comic Tales, 1982, Heard and Seen, 1983; The Story of Communications in Iceland, 1986; (radio play) An Island in the Ocean, 1975; translator: The Unknown Soldier (v. Linna), 1971, Our Honor and Power (Nordahl Grieg), 1977. Columnist Morgunbladid, 1975—. Contbr. short stories to anthologies including World Prize Stories, 1956. Grantee Icelandic Govt., 1956—, Icelandic Cultural Ministry, 1972. Recipient 1st prize short story Eimreidin Mag., 1955; award Icelandic Nat. Broadcasting Sta., 1971. Mem. Icelandic Writers Found. (mem. adversary com. 1975, lit. prize 1976, 80, 88).

JOHANNES, RALPH, architectural educator; b. Free City Danzig, Oct. 24, 1929; s. Wilhelm and Carla (von Luebbers) J.; m. Ursel Elsner, Feb. 10, 1967; children: Christian, Astrid, Nils Wilhelm. Grad., Hochschule fuer bildende Kuenste, Berlin, 1958; postgrad., Regent-Poly. Inst., London, 1960, Pratt Inst., N.Y.C., 1961. Mem. staff H. Heide, architect, Berlin, 1958-59, Emberton, Franck & Tardrew, Architects, London, 1959-60, A.M. Gear & Assocs., Architects, London, 1960-61; spl. asst. dept. interior design Pratt Inst., N.Y.C., 1961; research asst. Hochschule fuer Gestaltung, Ulm, Fed. Republic Germany, 1962; lectr. architecture Folkwangschule fuer Gestaltung, Essen, Fed. Republic Germany, 1963-73; prof. architecture Essen U., 1973—. Author: Danzig in memoriam, 1971, Von Bergford ueber Bergford, 1979; contbr. articles to German and Brit. archtl. jours. Fulbright scholar, 1961-62. Mem. Architektenkammer Nordrhein-Westfalen, Archtl. Assn. London., Design History Soc. London. Home: 30 Ruestermark, D-4300 Essen 1 Federal Republic of Germany Office: U Essen, Fachbereich Architektur Bio-, und Geowissenschaften, Universitaets D-4300 strasse 15, 4300 Essen 1 Federal Republic of Germany

JOHANNISON, LARS, hotel company executive; b. Stockholm, Feb. 2, 1938; s. Stig A.C. and Britt (Winblad von W.) J.; m. Britta Gabrielle du Rietz, Feb. 28, 1972; 1 child, Brita Charlotte. Student, Hotel & Restaurant Sch., Stockholm, 1955-59, Cornell U., 1966. Trainee Grand Hotel de Malte, Paris, 1959-60; chef Tore Wretman Restaurants, Stockholm, 1960-62; head waiter Savoy Hotel, Malmö, Sweden, 1962-65; conf. mgr. Hotel Foresta, Stockholm, 1965-67, restaurant mgr., 1967-71; owner, mgr. Trädgårdshotellet, Åtvidaberg, Sweden, 1972—; cons. SAS Internat. Hotels, Oslo, 1984. Author: Cookbook for Schlemmertopf, 1979; contbr. articles to Restauranger & Storkök, 1974—. Mem. Hotel Sales Mktg. Assn., Relais & Chateaux, M. Sandahl Found. (treas.). Club: Åtvidaberg Golf. Office: Trädgårdshotellet, PO Box 178, 597 00 Åtvidaberg Sweden

JOHANNISSON, ELIZABETH INGRID, medical educator; b. Ronneby, Sweden, Sept. 15, 1934; d. Axel Folke and Ingeborg (Bjö rksten) J.; M.D., Karolinska Inst., 1963, Ph.D., 1968; 1 child, Anders Erik Thorell. Asst. dept. pathology Karolinska Hosp., Stockholm, 1959-65, assoc. prof. hormone lab., 1966-68; assoc. prof. WHO Research and Tng. Ctr. on Human Reproduction, Karolinska Inst., 1968-72, med. officer WHO Human Reproduction Unit, Geneva, 1972-74; assoc. prof. Centre de Cytologie, Hopital cantonal, Geneva, 1974-82; assoc. prof., chief cytology service dept. ob-gyn U. Basle, 1983-85; sec. gen. Internat. Com. for Research in Reprodn., Geneva, 1986—; med. cons. WHO. Fellow Internat. Acad. Cytology; mem. Swedish Soc. Endocrinology, Internat. Soc. Andrology (exec. bd. 1985—), Swedish Soc. Pathology and Clin. Cytology, N.Y. Acad. Scis., AAAS, Internat. Soc. Andrology (exec. bd.), Internat. Fedn. Fertility Socs. (exec. bd.), Ednl., Sci., and Cultural Orgn. (U.N.). Co-editor: WHO Current Problems in Human Fertility Control, 1974; assoc. editor Internat. Jour. Andrology; contbr. articles to profl. jours.

JOHANSEN, EIVIND HERBERT, corporate executive, former army officer; b. Charleston, S.C., Mar. 7, 1927; s. Andrew and Ruth Lee (Thames) J.; m. Dolores E. Klockmann, June 9, 1950; children: Chris Allen, Jane Elizabeth. B.S., Tex. A&M U., 1950; M.S., George Washington U., 1968; postgrad., Harvard U., 1955, Army Command and Gen. Staff Coll., 1963, Naval War Coll., 1967, Advanced Mgmt. Program, U. Pitts., 1971. Quartermaster officer U.S. Army, 1950-79, advanced through grades to lt. gen., 1977; strategic planner Office Joint Chiefs of Staff, 1968-69, group comdr., 1969-70; army dir. distbn. 1970-72, army dir. materiel, 1972-75; comdg. gen. Army Aviation Systems Command, St. Louis, 1975-77; army dep. chief staff for logistics Washington, 1977-79; ret. 1979; pres., chief exec. officer Nat. Industries for Severely Handicapped, Inc., 1979—; mem. exec. council, chmn. mgmt. improvement com. Fed. Exec. Bd., St. Louis, 1975-77; bd. advs. Am. Def. Preparedness Assn., St. Louis, 1975-77, tech. and mgmt. adv. bd., Washington, 1977-79; chmn. Army Logistics Policy Council, 1977-79; bd. advs. Army Logistic Mgmt. Coll., 1978-79, Army Mgmt. Engring. Coll., 1978-79. Contbr. articles to profl. jours. Mem. Pres.' Com. for Purchase from Blind and Other Severely Handicapped, Washington, 1973-74, chmn., 1975; mem. Pres.'s Com. on Employment of Handicapped; bd. dirs., chmn. ind. ops. com. Mo. Goodwill Industries, 1975-77; chmn. Jr. Achievement Youth Program, St. Louis, 1975-77; sponsor Air Explorer Post, Boy Scouts Am., 1975-77; bd. dirs. Q.M. Found., 1979-88. Decorated D.S.M., Legion of Merit with two oak leaf clusters, Bronze Star, numerous others; recipient Tex. A&M Disting. Alumnus award. Mem. Assn. U.S. Army (bd. advisors St. Louis 1975-77), Am. Helicopter Soc., Army Aviation Assn. Am., Ret. Officers Assn., Nat. Rehab. Assn., Tex. A&M Alumni Assn. Washington (exec. bd. 1974, 78-79, pres. 1975), George Washington U. Alumni Assn., U. Pitts. Alumni Assn., Harvard U. Alumni Assn. Club: Toastmasters. Home: 6310 Windpatterns Trail Fairfax Station VA 22039

JOHANSEN, HANS CHRISTIAN, economic historian, educator; b. Aarhus, Denmark, June 27, 1935; s. Vilhelm and Clara (Andersen) J.; m. Kirstine Madsen; children: Jens, Hanne. MA in Econ., U. Aarhus, 1963, PhD, 1968. Sr. lectr. U. Aarhus, Denmark, 1964-70; prof. U. Odense, Denmark, 1970—. Author books and articles on internat. econ. and social history. Mem. Danish Royal Acad. Sci., Norwegian Acad. Sci. Home: Anne Maries Alles 4a, DK-5250 Odense SV Denmark Office: U Odense, Campusevej, DK-5230 Odense M Denmark

JOHANSSON, BENGT WILHELM, cardiologist, educator; b. Lund, Sweden, Feb. 28, 1930; s. Nils V. and Ulla E. (Karlsson) J.; m. Ulla Margareta Petersson, June 5, 1954; 1 child.; m. Anita Christian Olsson, Oct. 27, 1982. MB, U. Lund, 1957, MD, 1966. Intern, Malmö (Sweden) Gen. Hosp., 1957-59, also resident in cardiology, asst. med. officer, 1957-67, mem. med. staff, 1957—, registrar, 1967-74, head sect. cardiology, 1974—; practice medicine specializing in cardiology, Lund, 1957—, Malmö, 1957—; former dist. med. officer Limmared, Sweden; mem. faculty dept. medicine U. Lund, 1967—. Contbr. numerous articles on cardiovascular physiology and research to sci. jours. Served to lt., M.C., Swedish Army, 1948-66. Mem. Am. Coll. Cardiology, Swedish Soc. Cardiology, Internat. Coll. Angiology, Swedish Soc. Internat. Medicine, Physiol. Assn. Lund, Internat. Hibernation Soc., Am. Geriatrics Soc., Swedish Assn. Med. Physics and Technics, Swedish Soc. Med. Scis., Malmo Assn. for Head Physicians, Swedish Med. Assn., Lund Med. Assn., Malmo Med. Assn., Danish Cardiac Soc., AAAS. Club: Travellers. Lodges: Rotary, Masons. Office: Malmö General Hospital, Section Cardiology, S 214 01 Malmö Sweden

JOHANSSON, KURT ENAR, philosopher; b. Sundsvall, Sweden, Nov. 2, 1927; s. Folke Knut Erik and Olga Viktoria (Bostedt) J.; m. Tamara Stepanovna (div. 1969); 1 child, Enar Folke. PhD, U. Stockholm, 1983. Lectr. philosophy Åbo Acad., Finland, 1967—. Author: Aleksej Gastev Proletarian Bard of the Machine Age, 1983. Decorated Finlands Lejons Orden riddarteckent av I klass Office of Pres. of Finland. Clubs: Svenska Klubben (Åbo, Finland), Juvenalorden (Uppsala, Sweden). Home: Tavastg 30 E 40, 20700 Åbo Finland Office: Åbo Acad - Russian Inst, Fänriksgatan 3, 20500 Åbo Finland

JOHANSSON, STEN ROLAND, sociologist; b. Morjärv, Sweden, Jan. 20, 1939; s. Holmfrid and Helga Julia (Lejon) J.; m. Lena Lundberg, Aug. 24, 1964; children: Herman, Helga. Student, U. Oreg., 1961-62; fil kand, Uppsala U., 1963, fil lic, 1967. Research asst. dept. sociology Uppsala (Sweden) U., 1963-66; expert on living conditions Swedish Ministry Labor and Housing, Stockholm, 1967-72; prof. social policy Swedish Inst. for Social Research, Stockholm, 1973-82; advisor Office Swedish Prime Minister, Stockholm, 1982-83; dir. Gen. Stats. Sweden, Stockholm, 1983—. Author: On the Level of Living Survey, 1970, When Is the Time Ripe?, 1975, Towards a Theory of Social Reporting, 1979, The Cause of Poland Is Ours, 1984. Mem. Swedish Sociol. Assn. (bd. dirs. 1973-75), Scandinavian Sociol. Assn. (chmn. 1971-73), Internat. Statis. Inst. Mem. Social Democratic Party. Office: Statistics Sweden, Karlavagen 100, S-115 81 Stockholm Sweden

JOHLER, JOSEPH RALPH, physicist; b. Scranton, Pa., Feb. 23, 1919; s. Joseph Jacob and Lillian (Dietzel) J.; B.A., Am. U., 1941; B.S.E., George Washington U., 1950; m. Nora Stella Callahan, Sept. 16, 1953; children—Dennis Ralph, Mark Stephen, Paul Norman, Annette Diane. Ballistic mathematician Ballistic Research Lab., Aberdeen Proving Grounds, Md., 1942-45; with Nat. Bur. Standards, Washington, 1946-51, electronic engr. Boulder Labs., 1951-65, chief electromagnetic theory sect., 1961-65; program leader, electromagnetic theory program Environmental Sci. Services Adminstrn., Inst. Telecommunication Scis. and Aeronomy, U.S. Dept. Commerce, Boulder, 1965-70, physicist, project scientist Office Telecommunications 1970-72, chief nav. and D-Region Sci. sect., 1972-76; pres. Colo. Research and Prediction Lab., Boulder, 1976-86; cons. Johler Assocs., 1986—. Served with USNR, 1944-46. Research Nat. Bur. Standards Disting. Authorship award, 1963, 66. Mem. AAAS, Am. Geophys. Union, Am. Math. Soc., Sci. Research Soc. Am., Internat. Union Radio Sci., IEEE (sr. mem., life mem.), Internat. Radio Consultative Com., Soc. Indsl. and Applied Math., Wild Goose Assn. (Gold Medal of Merit award 1982). Contbr. articles to profl. jours. Home: 16796 W 74th Pl Golden CO 80403

JOHN, ERHARD RUDOLF JOSEF, educator, consultant; b. Gablonz, Germany, Oct. 14, 1919; s. Josef and Emma Maria (Haschke) J.; m. Erika Ursula Tauchnitz, Apr. 23, 1924; childreN; Eva-Maria, Matthias, Constanze, Klaus-Peter. Student, Karls U., Prague; grad., Staatsexamer Tech. U., Dresden, German Dem. Republic, 1952; PhD, Humboldt U., Berlin, 1956; Dr. phil. habilitation, Karl Marx U., Leipzig, German Dem. Republic, 1962. Oberschullehrer Oberschule, Thum, German Dem. Republic, 1949-50; dir. Landesvolkshochschule, Meissen, German Dem. Republic, 1951-54; aspirant Humboldt U., 1954-56; oberassistent Karl Marx U., 1956-62, dozent, 1962-64, prof., 1964-85, prof. emeritus, 1986—. Author: Probleme Ästhetik, 1967, 15 books on asthetics and culture theory; editor, co-author numerous books and articles in field. Bd. dirs. trade unions, Berlin, 1967-82. Served with German armed forces, 1939-45. Decorated Vaterländischer Verdienstorden i. Bronce, Berlin, 1979; named Verdienter Aktivist, Berlin, 1971. Mem. Kulturbund (bd. dirs.), Gewerkschaft Wissenschaft (bd. dirs.), Internat. Soc. Aesthetics, Urania Soc. Popular Scis., Inst. Aesthetics and Theory of Culture (founder, bd. dirs., dir. subsect., leader numerous research teams)., Klub d. Intelligenz. Home: Wilhelm-Wild-Strasse 11, 7031 Bezirk Leipzig German Democratic Republic Office: Karl-Marx-U, Karl-Marx-Platz 9, 7010 Leipzig German Democratic Republic

JOHN, LEONARD KEITH, aerospace and mechanical engineer, consultant; b. Lahore, Pakistan, Apr. 10, 1949; came to Can., 1975; s. Edwin Kenneth William and Olive (Khairullah) J.; m. Yvonne Anna Lee-Anan, Dec. 20, 1980; children: Sarah Ashley, Jason William. Full Tech. Cert., Harrow Coll. Tech. and Art, Middlesex, Eng., 1971; B.S. with honors, Hendon Coll., London, 1975; M.Engring., U. Toronto, 1978. Chartered engr., U.K.; registered profl. engr., Ont. Aeronautical apprentice Westland Helicopters Ltd., Hayes, Middlesex, Eng., 1965-70, research and devel. engr., 1970-71; devel. engr. Westland Helicopters/Hendon, Hayes and Hendon, Eng., 1971-75; sr. devel. engr. non-metallics The de Havilland Aircraft Co. Can., div. Boeing of Can. Ltd., Downsview, Ont., 1975-80; group leader composite structure devel. 1980-85, chief advanced composites and nonmetallics, 1985—; pres. 620688 Ont. Inc., Toronto, 1985—. Contbr. articles to profl. jours.; patentee in field. Inventor Graphite Fibre Violin, violin type mus. instruments; violins exhibited Planete Composite, Bordeaux, France, 1985, Ontario Sci. Centre, Toronto, 1988, Sec. of State Exhibit, Bravo Canada, Toronto, Quebec City and Vancouver, 1988. Recipient F. H. Baldwin award Can. Aeros. and Space Inst., 1982. Mem. Instn. Mech. Engrs. (Eng.) (mem. aerospace industries div. 1984—), Assn. Profl. Engrs. Province Ont., Soc. for Advancement Material and Process Engring. (outstanding service award 1979). Mem. Ch. of England. Avocations: flying; travel; music.

JOHN, PRINCE, The Grand Duke of Avram, Marquis of Mathra, Earl of Enoch, Viscount Ulom, Lord Rama, cardinal, archbishop, Earl Marshall; b. Kalgoorlie, West Australia, Mar. 12, 1944; s. John Charlton and Phyllis Grace (Wood) Rudge; D.Litterarum 1977, D.Sc., 1978, 85, M.B.A., 1978, D.Phil., 1979, D.C.L., 1980, 81, D.B.A., 1981, D.D., 1982; hon. degrees: D.S.T., D.C.L., D.Eng.; m. Maureen Agnes Markham; children—Mary-Ellen, Charles, Stephanie. Mng. dir. Mary-Ellen Mines Pty. Ltd., Tasmania, 1969-86, Aaron Pty. Ltd., 1971-86, Aabec Investments Pty. Ltd., 1971-86; chmn. Royal Australian Exchange; gov. Royal Bank of Avram, 1979—; prof. bus. adminstrn. Royal Coll. Dirs., 1980—; prof. sci. Royal Australian Inst. Colls., 1981—; chief herald Australian Heraldic Archival Register, 1986—; Earl Marshall The Royal Coll. of Heraldy, 1986—, Coll. of Arms of Noblesse, 1987—. Served to adm. Australian Navy, 1979—, Grand Master of Orders of the Avram, 1979, St. Mark, 1985, The Ankh, 1986, Continental Ch. Cross, 1985, The Most Sacred Order of the Holy Wisdom, 1986, The Most Sacred Lamb, 1986; adminstr. of following orders: Serene Order of

Leonard, 1986, Illustrious Order of Merit, 1986, The Black Swan, 1986, Royal Order, 1986. Created Earl of Enoch, 1976, Duke of Avram, 1979, Marquis of Mathra, 1980, The Viscount Ulom, 1981, The Lord Rama, 1981, chevalier, 1981, knight of bountiful endeavours, 1976; created knight of sword, 1971, knight of merit, 1976, royal knight, 1975, chevalier of honour, 1979; decorated grand knight Order Leonard, 1979; knight grand cross Order Sacred Sword and Lance, 1981; knight of Veritas, 1981; knight grand cross The Royal roder, 1986; knight grand cross of justice, 1985; knight comdr. grand cross Order of St. Mark, 1985; Continental Gold Ch. cross, 1985; grand knight cross Order of The Ankh, 1985, The Order of the Holy Cross of Jerusalem, 1986, Grand Croix Order Souverain des Chevaliers du Saint-Sepulcre Byzantin, 1986, Magnus Cruz Ordo Supremus et Militaris Sancti Stephani Martyr, 1986, Knight Grand Cross Order of Aeterna Lucina, 1986, Knight Grand Star Illustrious Order of Merit, 1986; created Cardinal Archbishop, The Royal See of the Continent of Australia, 1982—; chartered scientist, chemist, engr., Australia. Fellow Royal Coll. Dirs., Royal Australian Inst. Colls.; mem. Royal Soc. Tasmania (life), The Grand Council of Confederation of Chivalry. Clubs: Masons, Apex (1st peer pres. 1976-77), Rosicrucians, Order Mondial des Gourmets Degustateurs Rotisseurs, other learned clubs, orgns., socs. Contbr. articles on philosophy, ethics, theology, sci. Home: Ormiston Palace, Strahan, 7468 Tasmania Australia

JOHN PAUL II, HIS HOLINESS POPE (KAROL JOZEF WOJTYLA), bishop of Rome; b. Wadowice, Poland, May 18, 1920; s. Karol and Emilia (Kaczorowska) W. Student, Jagiellonian U., Krakow; studied in underground seminary, Krakow, during World War II; Doctorate in ethics, Pontifical Angelicum U., Rome, 1948; Doctorate in theology, Catholic U. of Lublin, Poland; Dr. (hon.), J. Guttenberg U., Mainz, W. Ger., 1977. Ordained priest Roman Cath. Ch., 1946; prof. moral theology Jagiellonian U.; prof. ethics Cath. U. of Lublin, 1954-58, dir. ethics inst., 1956-58; aux. bishop of Krakow 1958, archbishop of Krakow, 1964-78; great chancellor Pontifical Theol. Faculty, Krakow; created cardinal by Pope Paul VI, 1967; elected Pope Oct. 16, 1978, installed, Oct. 22, 1978. Author of: books, poetry, plays, including The Goldsmith's Shop; Play Easter Vigil and Other Poems, 1979, Love & Responsibility, 1960, The Acting Person, 1969, Foundations of Renewal, 1972, Sign of Contradiction, 1976, Redemptor Hominis; Encyclical Redemptor Hominis, 1979; contbr. articles on philosophy, ethics and theology to jours. Address: Palazzo Apostolico, The Vatican Vatican City *

JOHNS, JASPER, artist; b. Augusta, Ga., May 15, 1930; s. Jasper and Jean (Riley) J. Student, U. S.C., 1947-48. One-man exhbns. include, Leo Castelli Gallery, N.Y.C., 1958, 60, 61, 63, 66, 68, 76, 81, 84, Minami Gallery, Tokyo, 1965, 75, Galerie Rive Droite, Paris, 1959, 61, Galleria D'Arte Del Naviglio, Milan, Italy, 1959, Ileana Sonnabend, Paris, 1963, Columbia Mus. Art (S.C.), 1960, Jewish Mus., N.Y.C., 1964, White-chapel Gallery, London, 1964, Pasadena Mus. (Calif.), 1965, Smithsonian Instn. Nat. Collection Fine Arts, 1966, Arts Council Great Britain, 1974-75, Whitney Mus. Am. Art, 1977, Kunsthalle, Cologne, 1978, Centre Pompidou, Paris, 1978, Hayward Gallery, London, 1978, Seibu Mus., Tokyo, 1978, San Francisco Mus. Modern Art, 1978, Kunstmuseum, Basel, 1979, Des Moines Art Ctr., 1983, St. Louis Art Mus., 1985, Mus. Modern Art, 1986, Kunsthalle, 1986, Leo Castelli Gallery, 1987; represented in permanent collections, Mus. Modern Art, Albright-Knox Art Gallery, Buffalo, Tate Gallery, London, Moderna Museet, Stockholm, Stedelijk Mus., Amsterdam, Holland, Whitney Mus., N.Y.C., Kunstmuseum, Basel, Centre Pompidou. Recipient 1st prize Print Biennale Ljubljana, Yugoslavia, prize IX Sao Paulo (Brazil) Bienal, Skowhegan Medal for Painting Skowhegan Sch. of Painting and Sculpture, Skowhegan Medal for Graphics, Mayors award of Honor for Arts and Culture City of N.Y., Gold Medal for Graphic Art, Am. Acad. Inst. of Arts and Letters, Wolf Prize for Painting, Wolf Found. Mem. Nat. Inst. Arts and Letters, Am. Acad. Arts and Scis. Address: care Leo Castelli Gallery 420 W Broadway New York NY 10012 *

JOHNS, WILLIAM HOWARD, psychiatrist; b. Hamilton, Ohio, Apr. 18, 1941; s. Howard William and Martha (Sleigh) J.; m. Catherine Marie O'Keefe, May 30, 1982; children: Howard William II, Stephanie Marie. AB, Princeton U., 1963; MS in Anatomy, U. Cin., 1968; DO, Kirksville (Mo.) Coll. Osteo. Medicine, 1973; postgrad., Topeka Inst. for Psychoanalysis, 1984—. Instr. anatomy Kirksville Coll. Osteo. Medicine, 1967-73; intern Grandview Hosp., Dayton, 1973-74; resident neurology Cleve. Clinic Hosp., 1974-77; asst. prof. neurology Ohio U. Coll. Osteo. Medicine, Athens, 1977-78; pvt. practice in neurology Dayton, Ohio, 1978-82; resident psychiatry The Menninger Found., Topeka, Kans., 1982-85, psychiatrist, 1985—; clin. asst. prof. neurology Wright State U. Med. Sch., Dayton, 1979-82, Ohio U. Coll. Osteo. Medicine, Athens, 1979-82, W.Va. Sch. Osteo. Medicine, Lewisburg, 1979-82. Mem. Am. Psychiat. Assn., Am. Acad. Neurology. Home: 517 Danbury Ln Topeka KS 66606 Office: The Menninger Found PO Box 829 Topeka KS 66601

JOHNSEN, TROND, finance company executive; b. Stavanger, Norway, Nov. 23, 1952. BA, Handelsakademiet, Oslo, 1977; MBA, Ariz. State U., 1978; B in Mktg., Communications, IFM U., Oslo, 1987. Asst. mgr. mktg., controller, mgr. acctg. Agro Fellesslakteri A/L, Stavanger, 1979-82; fin. dir. Trallfa A/S, Bryne, Norway, 1982-84; fin. mgr. Novenco AS, Oslo, 1984-86; fin. dir. Skatron AS, Tranby, Norway, 1986—; advisor NKS, Oslo, 1985—. Mem. Nat. MBA Orgn. (bd. dirs. Stavanger chpt. 1982-84). Home: Blakstadmarka 42B, N-1378 Asker Norway

JOHNSON, ALAN ARTHUR, physicist, educator; b. Beckenham, Eng., Aug. 18, 1930; came to U.S., 1962; s. Frederick W. and Dorothy (Tew) S.; m. Elizabeth Ann Banks, June 22, 1958 (div. Dec. 1982); children: Stephen Graham, Michael Andrew, David Nicholas, Brian Philip, Susan Christine. B.Sc. with spl. honours in Physics, Reading (Eng.) U., 1952; M.A. in Physics, U. Toronto, 1954; Ph. D. in Metal Physics, U. London, Eng.; diplomate, Imperial Coll., London, 1960. Sci. officer Royal Naval Sci. Service, Eng., 1954-56; lectr. metallurgy Imperial Coll. Sci. and Tech., U. London, 1960-62; dir. research Materials Research Corp., Orangeburg, N.Y., 1963-65; prof. phys. metallurgy Bklyn. Poly. Inst., 1965-71, head dept. phys. and engring., metallurgy, 1967-71; prof. materials sci., chmn. dept. Wash. State U., 1971-75; dean Grad. Sch., U. Louisville, 1975-76, prof. materials sci., 1975—; cons. to govt. and industry, 1960—. Editor: Water Pollution in the Greater New York Area, 1971; Contbr. 100 articles to profl. jours.; Editor in chief: Internat. Jour. Ocean Engring, 1968-75; assoc. editor, 1975—; editorial adv. bd.: Resource Mgmt. and Optimization, Ency. Environ. Sci. and Engring. Fellow Am. Soc. Metals (nat. nominating com. 1980-81, chmn. Louisville chpt. 1981-82, chmn. metals engring. inst. com. 1982-83), Inst. of Metals, Inst. of Physics, Council of Engring. Instns. (chartered); mem. Sigma Xi, Tau Beta Pi, Phi Kappa Phi. Office: U Louisville Ernst Hall Room 311 Louisville KY 40292

JOHNSON, ARNOLD IVAN, civil engineer; b. Madison, Nebr., June 3, 1919; s. Casten Henry and Awilda May (Reeves) J.; B.S.C.E., U. Nebr., 1949, A.B., 1950, postgrad., 1950-54; m. Betty Lou Spencer, June 3, 1941; children—Robert Arnold, Bruce Gary, Carmen Sue Johnson Mark. With U.S. Geol. Survey, 1948-79, asst. chief Office Water Data Coordination, Washington, 1971-79; water resources cons. Woodward-Clyde Cons., Denver, 1979-84; pres. A. Ivan Johnson, Inc. Cons., Arvada, Colo., 1984—; faculty affiliate Colo. State U., 1969-70; bd. dirs. Renewable Natural Resources Found., 1971-81; pres. Internat. Commn. Ground Water, 1972-75, Internat. Commn. Remote Sensing and Data Transmission, 1980-87; v.p. U.S. nat. commn. Internat. Union Geodesy and Geophysics, 1976-79. Served with USNR, 1942-44. Recipient Award of Merit Dept. Interior, 1962, Meritorious Service award, 1977; Engr. of Yr. award Profl. Engrs. in Govt., 1969; registered profl. engr., Colo., D.C. Fellow ASCE, ASTM (hon., William T. Cavanaugh Meml. award 1988), Am. Water Resources Assn. (pres. 1972, rep. to Nat. Acad. Sci. 1971-79); mem. Am. Geophys. Union (life, sec., sect. on hydrology 1973-77, EOS editor 1984—), Assn. Engring. Geologists, Internat. Assn. Hydrological Scis. (hon. pres. 1987—), Internat. Soc. Soil Sci., Internat. Soc. Soil Mechanics and Found. Engring., Am. Soc. Photogram and Remote Sensing; Internat. Assn. Hydrogeology, Assn. Geohydrologists Internat. Devel., NSPE (chpt. pres. 1970-71), Archaeol. Soc. Am., Bibl. Archaeol. Soc. Author, editor 100 reports and books in field.

JOHNSON, BENJAMIN LEIBOLD, education specialist; educator, education training analyst; b. Norborne, Mo., Nov. 23, 1950; s. Murrell Faxton and Chlora Pauline (Naylor) J.; B.A., Central Mo. State U., 1971, B.S., 1974, M.S., 1976. Tchr., Raytown and Independence (Mo.) Public Schs., 1974-76; with Wayne Regan, Inc., Realtors, Shawnee, Kans., 1976; tchr., chmn. dept. social studies, English, French, Breckenridge (Mo.) Public Schs., 1979-80; career intern edn. specialist Ft. Sill, Okla., 1980-82, tng. analyst/edn. specialist, 1982-85; edn. specialist/instr. U.S. Army Engrs. Sch., Fort Belvoir, Va., 1985—. dept. chmn. social studies, English and French, also edn. specialist. Served with USNR, 1976-79. Mem. Assn. Am. Geographers, Nat. Council Social Studies, Am. Acad. Polit. and Social Scis., Nat. Space Inst., Nat. Council Tchrs. English, Am. Congress on Surveying and Mapping, Naval Enlisted Res. Assn., Assn. Supervision and Curriculum Devel., Assn. U.S. Army, Am. Sq. Dance Soc., Acad. Sci. Fiction, Fantasy and Horror Films Nat. Rifle Assn., N.Am. Darting Assn. Lodges: Masons, Scottish Rite; Order DeMolay. Home: 7519 Republic Ct Apt 201 Alexandria VA 22306

JOHNSON, BRAD HART, urban and regional planner, transportation systems planner; b. Dowagiac, Mich., Oct. 2, 1951; s. Irving Julius and Marjorie June (Hart) J.; m. Rosemary Christoff, June 23, 1979. AS, Kalamazoo (Mich.) Valley Community Coll., 1976; BS, Mich. State U., 1978. Regional planner Cheyenne-Laramie County Regional Planning Office, Wyo., 1978-80; city planner City of Longmont, Colo., 1980; transp. planner County of Kalamazoo, 1980-81; transp. program dir. Pikes Peak Area Council of Govts., Colorado Springs, Colo., 1982-86; transp. mgr. Planning Research Corp. (now P&D Techs.), Colorado Springs, 1986-87, sr. transp. planner, sr. project mgr., 1987—; com. mem. Transp. Research Bd., Washington, 1983-86. Contbr. tech. reports to profl. publs. Served with USAF, 1970-74. Recipient Letter of Appreciation, Pikes Peak Area Council Govts., 1986, Letter of Appreciation, Transp. Adv. Com., 1986; named One of Outstanding Young Men of Am., 1986. Mem. Urban and Regional Info. Systems Assn. (past chmn. transp. spl. interest group). Home: 130 E Kelly Rd Woodland Park CO 80863-8358

JOHNSON, BRUCE, engineering educator; b. Hawarden, Iowa, Sept. 4, 1932; s. York and Dorothy Ellen (DeBruce) J.; m. Dorothy Jane Rylander, Aug. 27, 1955; children: Sharon Lee, Kristen Kay. B.S. in Mech. Engring., Iowa State U., 1955; M.S. in Mech. Engring., Purdue U., 1962, Ph.D., 1965. Instr. U.S. Naval Acad., Annapolis, Md., 1957-59, assoc. prof., 1964-70, project dir. model basin, 1968-76, prof., 1970—, Naval Sea Systems Command prof. hydrodynamics, 1975-87, dir. Hydromechanics Lab., 1976-87; instr. Purdue U., 1959-64; chmn. 18th Am. Towing Tank Conf., 1977, U.S. Rep. Info. Com. Internat. Towing Tank Conf., 1975-84, chmn. symbols and terminology group, 1985—. Author: (with T. Gillmer) Introduction to Naval Architecture, 1982; editor: (with B. Nehrling) Proc. of 18th Am. Towing Tank Conf, 1977; contbr. articles to profl. publs. Trustee Bauman Bible Telecasts, 1970—. Served with USN, 1955-59. Ford Found. grantee, 1962-64; recipient award for excellence in engring. teaching Western Electric Fund, 1971. Mem. ASME, Am. Soc. for Engring. Edn., Soc. Naval Architects and Marine Engrs. (chmn. Chesapeake Sailing Yacht Symposium 1985, 87), Am. Soc. Naval Engrs. (chmn. scholarship com. 1983—, nat. council 1986-88), Soc. Naval Architects Japan. Methodist. Club: Md. Capital Yacht. Home: 12600 Kilbourne Ln Bowie MD 20715 Office: US Naval Acad Naval System Engring Dept Annapolis MD 21402

JOHNSON, BRUCE ROSS, educator; b. La Porte, Ind., May 18, 1949; s. Egbert Johannes Daniel and Ruth Elvera (Johnson) J. BS, Ball State U., Muncie, Ind., 1971; ME, Valparaiso U., 1975; postgrad. Nat. Coll. Edn., Evanston, Ill., 1974, Beiging Normal U., 1988. Cert. elem. sch. tchr., Ind. Vol. tchr. Peace Corps, St. Vincent, W.I., 1971-72; tchr. South Central Sch., Union Mills, Ind., 1972-76, 77—; missionary tchr. Luth. Ch., Liberia, West Africa, 1976-77; vis. educator U. London, 1974, U. Moscow, 1974, U. Paris, 1974. Contbr. articles to newspapers. Pres. People to People Internat., La Porte, Ind., 1981-83, trustee, Kansas City, Mo., 1983—; bd. dirs. La Porte County Library Leasing Corp., 1988—; mem. ch. council Bethany Luth. Ch., La Porte, 1983—; v.p. Friends of La Porte County Library, 1984, pres. 1986—; chmn. books and coffee series LaPorte County Pub. Library, 1985—; trustee La Porte County Hist. Soc., 1985—; v.p. Ind. Geneal. Soc., 1981-82; pres. Community Concert Assn., La Porte, 1984; mem. Pan Am. Games Com., 1986-87; mem. steering com. La Porte County Spelling Bee, 1979-85, chmn., 1981, 85; chmn. Miss. Valley council People-to-People, 1983—. Named one of Outsanding Young Men Am., 1985, State finalist NASA Tchr.-in-Space project, 1985; Ind. State Tchrs. Assn. scholarship, 1970, Dean Earl A. Johnson Outstanding Service award Ball State U., 1971; Cert. of Merit, Ind. Dept. Edn., 1985. Mem. NEA (life), Ind. State Tchrs. Assn., Phi Delta Kappa. Clubs: Amateur Music (pres. 1982-83) (La Porte), Little Theater (bd. dirs. 1980-83), Lions (bd. dirs. 1983—). Avocations: Performing in musical theater, collecting foreign coins, traveling, gardening. Home: 2012 S Village Rd La Porte IN 46350 Office: South Central Community Schs 9808 S 600 W Union Mills IN 46382

JOHNSON, CECILE RYDEN (MRS. PHILIP JOHNSON), artist; b. Jamestown, N.Y.; d. Ernest Edwin and Agnes E. (Johnson) Ryden; m. Philip Arthur Johnson; children: Pamela Cecile, Stevan Philip. AB, Augustana Coll.; postgrad., Am. Acad. Fine Arts, Art Inst. Chgo., U. Wis., U. Colo., Pa. Acad. Fine Art, Scripps Coll. One-woman shows include Grand Cen. Gallery, N.Y.C., 1965, 67, 69, 71, 73, 75, TWA Paris, 1973, Greenville Mus. Art, Remington Mus., 1980; exhibited with Am. Watercolor Soc., Washington Watercolor Soc., Artist Guild of Chgo., Art Dirs. Annual, Nat. Acad., N.Y.C., Soc. of Illustrators; designed and executed stained glass windows for Nursery Chapel, Augustana, Chgo., 12 paintings on Bermuda for collection Bank of Bermuda, 1964, mural for Bermuda Airport, 1966, 32 paintings for U.S. Naval Art Collection on women in naval service, ofcl. lithographs, nat. fine art com. Lake Placid Olympic Organizing Com., 1980; traveling solo exhibit Am. Univs., 1964-66; designed covers Ford Times, Chgo. Tribune Sunday Mag., others; designed Am. UNICEF Christmas card for 1968; illustration in Motor Boating, Ford Times, Lincoln Mercury Times; designed and executed Memorable Mountains series for skiing mag., 1965-74, folios of ski prints for Aspen, Vail, Snowbird, Lake Tahoe, series of 16 prints for TWA on Paris, London, Rome, 1973, series of paintings and folio prints for Napa Valley Vinters, 1975, Broadmoor Hotel, Colorado Springs, 10 originals and 450 signed prints for Broadmoor West, 1976, mural for 1st Fed. Savings and Loan, St. Paul, Bicentennial painting of St. Paul's Fed. Courts Bldg., silk screen for U.S. Hockey Team, 1976 Olympics; represented in permanent collections Augustana Coll., Gen. Mills, Minn. Mining, Ford Motor Co., Nat. Safety Council, Henderson Coll., Wagner Coll., Skiing mag., Davenport Mcpl. Art Gallery, others; affiliation Grand Cen. Galleries, N.Y.C., others. Recipient awards All Ill. Watercolor, 1953, Ill. Fedn. Music Clubs, 1955, Outstanding Achievement award Alumni Assn. Augustana Coll., 1962, Woman of Achievement award in Art Nat. League Pen Women, 1962, Catherine Lorillard Wolffe gold medal for watercolor, 1965, Disting. Citizen citation Macalester Coll., 1979; named 1st Woman Artist by USN and NACAL Com. Salmagana Club. Mem. Am. Watercolor Soc., Soc. Illustrators, Allied Artists, Knickerbocker Soc., Audubon Art Soc. Lutheran. Featured in film Creating in Watercolor, on ABC Wide World of Sports, 1977, 79, in Am. Artists Mag., Jan. 1983, 87. Studio: One W 67th St New York NY 10023

JOHNSON, CHARLES EDGAR, educator; b. Rochester, N.Y., July 6, 1919; s. Mason Frank and Ethel Clithero (Lyons) J.; B.S., SUNY, Geneseo, 1946; M.A., UCLA, 1948; M.Ed., U. Ill., 1950, Ed.D., 1952; m. Rita Irene Boyd, July 19, 1963. Tchr., Mt. Morris, N.Y., 1946-47, Geneseo, N.Y., 1948-49; asst. prof. U. Kans., Lawrence, 1951-55; assoc. prof. U. Ill., Urbana, 1955-65; prof. edn. U. Ga., Athens, 1965-85, prof. emeritus, 1985—, assoc. dir. Research and Devel. Ctr., 1965-68, dir. Ga. Ednl. Models, 1968-75,Ga. Tchr. Assessment Project, 1976-81; ednl. researcher Spencer Press, Chgo., Grolier Inc., N.Y.C., 1958-62; vis. prof. U. P.R., 1963-64; cons. tchr. edn. Ministry of Edn., Indonesia, 1980, 82. Served with AUS, 1941-46. Recipient Cert. of Merit, U. Ga., 1980. Mem. Am. Edn. Research Assn., Assn. Supervision and Curriculum Devel., Phi Delta Kappa (v.p. U. Ga. chpt. 1986-88), Kappa Delta Pi (tchr. educator award for excellence 1979). Baptist. Clubs: Elks, Masons. Designer competency based tchr. edn. program model and Ga. tchr. performance assessment instruments; contbr. numerous articles in field to profl. jours.; editor Holiday Series, Garrard Pub. Co., Champaign, Ill., 1962—. Home: 245 Pine Forest Dr Athens GA 30606 Office: U Ga Coll Edn 427 Aderhold Hall Athens GA 30602

JOHNSON, CHARLES FOREMAN, architect, architectural photographer, planning, architecture and systems engineering consultant; b. Plainfield, N.J., May 28, 1929; s. Charles E. and E. Lucile (Casner) J.; student Union Jr. Coll., 1947; B.Arch., U. So. Calif., 1958; postgrad. UCLA, 1959-60; m. Beverly Jean Hinnendale, Feb. 19, 1961 (div. 1970); children—Kevin, David. Draftsman, Wigton-Abbott, P.C., Plainfield, 1946-48; architect, cons., graphic, interior and engring. systems designer, 1952—; designer, draftsman with H.W. Underhill, Architect, Los Angeles, 1953-55; teaching asst. U. So. Calif., Los Angeles, 1954-55; designer with Carrington H. Lewis, Architect, Palos Verdes, Calif., 1955-56; grad. architect Ramo-Wooldridge Corp., Los Angeles, 1956-58; tech. dir. Atlas weapon system Space Tech. Labs., Los Angeles, 1958-60; advanced planner and systems engr. Minuteman Weapon System, TRW, Los Angeles, 1960-64, div. staff ops. dir., 1964-68; cons. N.Mex. Regional Med. Program and N.Mex. State Dept. Hosps., 1968-70; prin. Charles F. Johnson, architect, Los Angeles, 1953-68, Sante Fe, N.Mex., 1968—; free lance archtl. photographer, Sante Fe, 1971—. Major archtl. works include: residential bldgs. in Calif., 1955-66; Bashein Bldg. at Los Lunas (N.Mex.) Hosp. and Tng. Sch., 1969, various residential bldgs., Santa Fe, 1973—, Kurtz Home, Dillon, Colo., 1981, Whispering Boulders Home, Carefree, Ariz., 1981, Hedrick House, Santa Fe, 1983, Kole House, Green Valley, Ariz., 1984, Casa Largo, Santa Fe (used for film The Man Who Fell to Earth), 1974, Rubel House, Santa Fe, 1986, Smith House, Carefree, Ariz., 1987, Klopfer House, Sante Fe, 1988. Pres., Santa Fe Coalition for the Arts, 1977; set designer Santa Fe Fiesta Melodrama, 1969, 71, 74, 77, 78, 81; designed Jay Miller & Friends Fiesta float 1970-88 (winner of 20 awards). Mem. Delta Sigma Phi. Club: El Gancho Tennis. Contbr. articles on facility planning and mgmt. to profl. publs.; contbr. archtl. photographs to mags. in U.S., Eng., France, Japan and Italy, contbr. articles on facility mgmt., planning info. systems, etc. to profl. jours. Recognized for work in organic architecture and siting buildings to fit the land. Club: El Gancho Tennis. Avocations: music, photography, collecting architecture books, Frank Lloyd Wright works. Home: 900 Countryclub Circle The Boulders P O Box 6070 Carefree AZ 85377

JOHNSON, CHARLES LENARD, human resources executive; b. Hurlock, Md., Mar. 23, 1942; s. Monroe S. and Rachel E. (Jolley) J.; m. Harriet Arhoda Rock, Aug. 6, 1967; 1 child, Rhonda Charlene. B.S., Morgan State U., 1964; M.A., Antioch U., 1979. Commd. 2d lt. U.S. Army, 1964, advanced through grades to capt., 1966; served in Vietnam, 1966-67; resigned, 1969; employee relations specialist Gen. electric Co., Bridgeport, Conn., 1969-70, mgr. employment, 1970-71, employee relations specialist, Columbia, Md., 1971-73; mgr. employee relations Washington Suburban San. Commn., Hyattsville, Md., 1973-76, mgr. labor relations, 1976-77, asst. to dir. engring., 1980-82; dir. employee/labor relations Johns Hopkins Med. Instns., Balt., 1980-82; v.p. human resources Regional Med. Ctr. at Memphis, 1982-86; pres. C. L. Johnson and Assocs. Cons. to Mgmt., 1986—. Bd. dirs. Memphis Urban League, 1982—, Blue Cross/Blue Shield, Memphis, 1982-83, Alliance for Progress, Memphis, 1982—; mem. health services adv. bd. Memphis State U., 1982—; legis. adv. Rep. Dist. 87, Memphis, 1982—; chmn. personnel com. Howard County Govt., Columbia, 1980-82; community adv. County Exec., Howard County, 1979-82; polit. adv. East Side Democratic Club, Balt., 1980-82.; grad. Leadership Memphis, 1985; active Boy Scouts Am.; mem. allocations com. United Way, 1983—. Democrat. Methodist. Home: 8720 Edney Ridge Dr Memphis TN 38018 Office: CL Johnson and Assocs 8720 Edney Ridge Dr Cordova TN 38018

JOHNSON, CHARLES OWEN, retired lawyer; b. Monroe, La., Aug. 18, 1926; s. Clifford U. and Laura (Owen) J. BA, Tulane U., 1946, JD, 1969; LLB, Harvard U., 1948; LLM, Columbia U., 1955. Bar: La. 1949. Sole practice, Monroe, 1949-50; mem. law editorial staff West Pub. Co., St. Paul, 1953; atty. Office of Chief Counsel, IRS, Washington, 1955-79, chief Ct. Appeals br. Tax Ct. Div., 1968-79. Author: The Genealogy of Several Allied Families, 1961. Served with AUS, 1950-52. Mem. Fed. Bar Assn., La. Bar Assn., Nat. Lawyers Club, Nat. Gavel Soc. (treas.), Soc. Colonial Wars (past dep. gov. D.C. soc.), SAR, S.R. (past pres. D.C. Soc.), Soc. War of 1812 (past pres. D.C. soc.), S.C.V., Soc. Colonial New Eng. (gov. gen. nat. soc.), Sons Union Vets., St. Andrew's Soc. Washington, Royal Soc. St. George, Sons and Daus. of Pilgrims (treas. gen.), Huguenot Soc. S.C., Huguenot Soc. La. (past pres.), Soc. Descs. Jersey Settlers, La. Colonials, Jamestowne Soc., Soc. Descs. Old Plymouth Colony, Order Ams. of Armorial Ancestry (past pres.), Soc. Descs. Colonial Clergy (past chancellor gen.), Hereditary Order Descs. Colonial Govs. (past gov. gen.), First Families of Ga. (chancellor gen.), Order Founders and Patriots of Am. (past gov. D.C. and La. Soc.), Order First Families Miss. 1699-1817 (gov. gen. 1967-69), Mil. Order Stars and Bars (past judge adv. gen.), Soc. Cin., Hereditary Order First Families of Mass. (registrar gen.), Nat. Geneal. Soc., Va. Geneal. Soc., Miss. Hist. Soc., Va. Hist. Soc., Phi Beta Kappa. Clubs: Arts, Army and Navy (Washington). Lodges: Masons, K.T., Shriners, Order Eastern Star. Home: 2111 S Jefferson Davis Hwy #809 Arlington VA 22202-3122

JOHNSON, CHARLES WAYNE, mining engineer, mining executive; b. Vinita, Okla., Feb. 7, 1921; s. Charles Monroe and Willie Mae (Hudson) J.; m. Cleo Faye Wittee, 1940 (div. 1952); m. Genevieve Hobbs, 1960 (dec. Sept. 1985); m. Susan Gates Johnson, Apr. 19, 1986; 1 child, Karen Candace Limon. BE, Kensington U., 1974, ME, 1975, PhDE, 1976. Owner El Monte (Calif.) Mfg. Co., 1946-49; co-owner Anjo Pest Control, Pasadena, Calif., 1946-56, Hoover-Johnson Cons. Co., Denver, 1956-59; pres. Vanguard Chem. Co., Denver, 1957-61, Mineral Products Co., Boise, Idaho, 1957-61; owner Crown Hill Meml. Park, Dallas, 1959-61, Johnson Engring., Victorville, Calif., 1961-86; pres. Astro Minerals, Victorville, 1985-87; owner J&D Mining Co., Victorville, 1977—. Contbr. articles to profl. pubs.; patentee in field. Active Rep. VIP Club. Served with USN, 1941-45. Recipient Outstanding Achievement award East Pasadena Bus. Assn., 1948. Mem. Ch. Ancient Christianity. Office: Johnson Engring Astro Minerals PO Box 641 Wrightwood CA 92397

JOHNSON, CLAYTON ERROLD, poultry company executive; b. DeSota, Wis., Apr. 20, 1921; s. James and Louella (Goodin) J.; student U. Wis., 1940-41, Tex. A. and M. Coll., 1946; m. Betty J. Higenbotham, May 23, 1943; children—Roderick and Ronald (twins), Richard. Pres. Flavor Fresh Brand, Inc., 1949—; Calif. gen. bldg. contractor, 1947—. Served with USAAF, 1942-45. Home: 3002 El Camino Las Vegas NV 89102 Office: 830 E Sahara Las Vegas NV 89104

JOHNSON, CLIFTON HERMAN, historian-archivist, research center director; b. Griffin, Ga., Sept. 13, 1921; s. John and Pearl (Parrish) J.; student U. Conn., 1943-44; BA, U. N.C., 1948, PhD 1959; MA U. Chgo., 1949; postgrad. U. Wis., 1951; m. Rosemary Brunst, Aug. 2, 1960; children: Charles, Robert, Virginia. Tutor, LeMoyne Coll., Memphis, 1950-53, asst. prof., 1953-56, prof., 1960-61, 63-66; asst. prof. East Carolina Coll., 1958-59; asst. librarian and archivist Fisk U., 1961-63; exec. dir. Amistad Research Center, New Orleans, 1966—. Bd. dirs. La. World Expn., 1980-82, Lillie Carroll Jackson Mus., 1978—, Countee Cullen Found., 1981-87, Friends of Archives La., 1978—, La. Folklife Commn., 1982-85. Served with AUS, 1940-45. Mem. So. Hist. Assn., Soc. Am. Archivists, Assn. for Study Negro Life and History, Orgn. Am. Historians, Nat. Assn. Human Rights Workers. Author: (with Carroll Barber) The American Negro: A Selected and Annotated Bibliography for High Schools and Junior Colleges, 1968; editor: God Struck Me Dead: Religious Conversions and Experiences and Autobiographies of Ex-Slaves, 1969. Office: Tulane U Tilton Hall New Orleans LA 70118

JOHNSON, CONRAD FRANÇOIS, gas company executive; b. Iroquois Falls, Ont., Can., Aug. 24, 1935; s. Alexander and Irene (Lariviere) J.; m. Marie Arsenault, Sept. 6, 1958; children: Martin, Dominique, Christine. Diploma, Montreal (Que., Can.) Inst. Tech., 1962; B of Applied Sci. in Engring., Montreal U. Poly., 1968; MBA, U. Me. Ont., London. Assoc. dir. Que. Dept. Edn., Quebec, 1968-70; exec. v.p. Laval Dairy, Quebec, 1970-74; pres., chief exec. officer Montel Inc., Montmagny, Que., 1974-82; v.p. mktg. GazInter-Cite Que., Quebec, 1982-85; v.p. sales GazMetropolitain Inc, Quebec, 1985-87; regional v.p. Metro Gaz Mktg., Quebec, 1987; pres., chief exec. officer CTR/Inc., Quebec, 1987—; pres. SSQ Immobiliere Real Estate, Ste. Foy, Que.; bd. dirs. Mut. Ins. Group SSQ, Ste. Foy, Montel Inc., Montmagny, Place Samuel Hollande Inc., Quebec.; speaker in field. Pres. Eye Sickness Research Found., Quebec, 1984—. Mem. Corp. Profl. Engrs., MBA Assn. Province Que., Quebec Metro C. of C. and Industry (pres. 1980-

81). Club: Garrison (Que.). Home and Office: 1652 Place de Bruyere, Sainte Foy, PQ Canada G1W 3H1

JOHNSON, CURTISS SHERMAN, writer, former publishing exec.; b. Meriden, Conn., Apr. 7, 1899; s. Sherman Foster and Adele (Curtiss) J.; B.S., Wesleyan U., 1921; m. Mary Lawton, Sept. 12, 1922 (dec. 1968); children—Curtiss Sherman, Dorothy L. (Mrs. Robert Pollitt) (dec.); m. Barbara Burleigh, Nov. 1968. Advt. mgr. Manning Bowman & Co., Meriden, 1921-26; v.p. The Silex Co., Hartford, Conn., 1927-28; rep. Curtis Publishing Co., Phila., 1928-32; pres. Curtiss Johnson Publs., Deep River, Conn., 1946-60; v.p. Deep River Nat. Bank; dir. Deep River Savs. Bank. Mem. Conn. Flood Control and Water Policy Commn., Hartford, 1954; mem. staff Gov. of Conn., 1940-46; mem. Conn. Safety Commn. Bd. dirs. Middlesex Meml. Hosp.; trustee Henry Whitfield State Mus.; chmn. Conn. River Mus. Served as lt., inf. U.S. Army, World War I; maj. Conn. State Guard, World War II. Mem. Conn, Editorial Assn. (pres. 1941-43). Author: Three Quarters of a Century, 1949; Politics and a Belly-Full, 1962; The Indomitable R. H. Macy, 1964; America's First Lady Boss, 1965; Deadline, 1969; Raymond E. Baldwin, Connecticut Statesman, 1972; History of Pratt-Read Corporation, 1976. Home: River Rd Essex CT 06426

JOHNSON, DAVID OWEN, supply company executive; b. Portland, Oreg., July 16, 1918; s. Leonard Eric and Margaret Garwood (Pfeuffer) J.; student U. Calif., Berkeley, 1940, U. Oreg., 1960; m. Murel Olive Kelsey, Dec. 6, 1943; children—Mignon Johnson Ervin, Cynthia. Mgr. accounts payable dept. Pacific Nat. Fire Ins. Co., San Francisco, 1936-42; with constrn. dept. Johns-Manville Corp., Los Angeles, 1946-48; founder, pres. Johnson Acoustical & Supply Co., Portland, 1948—; mem. nat. adv. bd. Armstrong Cork Co., 1968-74; chmn. adv. bd. U. Oreg. Grad. Sch. Bus. Conf., 1971. Chmn. bd. local Jr. Achievement, 1969, chmn. bd. govs., 1975-76, nat. Bronze Leadership award, 1982; pres. Portland Chamber Orch., 1958; bd. govs. Shriners Hosp. for Crippled Children, Portland; bd. dirs. Campfire Girls, 1965-67, Builders Exchange Coop., 1964-66, 83-88, Portland Opera Assn., 1985, 86; trustee U. Oreg. Found., 1985-88; West Coast Chamber Orch. Assn., William Temple House; v.p. exec. bd., mem. pres.'s council Columbia-Pacific council Boy Scouts Am. Served to 2d lt. C.E., U.S. Army, 1943-46. Recipient Contractor of Yr. award, 1967, Disting. Eagle award Boy Scouts Am., 1980, Silver Beaver award, 1985; Paul Harris fellow. Mem. Am. Inst. Constructors, Ceilings and Interior Systems Contractors Assn. (nat. pres. 1966-67, DeGelleke award 1982), Asso. Interior Contractors Oreg. (pres. 1976-77), Oreg. Club. (pres. 1964), Oreg. Execs. (pres. 1958), Portland Rose Festival Assn. (dir. 1973-76), Royal Rosarians, Nat. Eagle Scout Assn., Lang Syne Soc., Philalethes Soc. Republican. Mem. Christian Ch. Clubs: University, Arlington, Multnoman Athletic. Lodges: Rotary (pres. Portland 1984-85),Masons (sovereign grand insp. gen. Oreg.), Scottish Rite (supreme council), Shriners. Home: 3434 SW Lakeview Blvd Lake Oswego OR 97035 Office: 2001 NW 19th Ave Portland OR 97209

JOHNSON, DAVID WOLCOTT, psychologist, educator; b. Muncie, Ind., Feb. 7, 1940; s. Roger Wildfield and Francis Elizabeth (Pierce) J.; m. Linda Mulholland, July 7, 1973; children: James, David, Catherine, Margaret, Jeremiah. B.S., Ball State U., 1962; M.A., Columbia U., 1964, Ed.D., 1966. Asst. prof. ednl. psychology U. Minn., Mpls., 1966-69; asso. prof. U. Minn., 1969-73, prof., 1973—; organizational cons., psychotherapist. Author: Social Psychology of Education, 1970, (with Goodwin Watson) Social Psychology: Issues and Insights, 1972, Reaching Out, 1972, 3d edit., 1986, Contemporary Social Psychology, 1973, (with Frank Johnson) Joining Together, 1975, 3d edit., 1987, (with Roger Johnson) Learning Together and Alone, 1975, 2d edit., 1987, Human Relations and Your Career, 1978, 2d edit., 1987, Educational Psychology, 1979, (with Dean Tjosvold) Productive Conflict Management, 1983, Circles of Learning, 1984, 2d edit., 1986, (with R. Johnson) Cooperative Learning, 1984, Cooperation in the Classroom, 1984, (with R. Johnson) Structuring Cooperative Learning, 1987, (with R. Johnson) Creative Conflict, 1987; contbr. over 250 articles to profl. jours.; editor: Am. Ednl. Research Jour, 1981-83. Bd. dirs. Walk-In Counseling Center, 1971-74. Recipient Gordon Allport award Soc. for Psychol. Study of Social Issues, 1981, Helen Plante award Am. Soc. Engring. Edn., 1984, Outstanding Research award Am. Personnel and Guidance Assn., 1988, Nat. Council for the Social Studies Research award. Fellow Am. Psychol. Assn.; mem. Am. Sociol. Assn., Am. Ednl. Research Assn., Am. Mgmt. Assn., Am. Assn. for Counseling and Devel. Democrat. Home: 7208 Cornelia Dr Edina MN 55435 Office: U Minn 330 Burton Hall Minneapolis MN 55455

JOHNSON, DEANNA K., educator, court reporter; b. Aug. 12, 1942, Paragould, Ark.; d. Howard and Agnes (Christian) Nichols; divorced; 1 child, Terri-Anne. Student Oakland City Coll., 1961-62, Acad. Steno Arts, 1973-76, Bay Area Inst. Ct. Reporting, 1976-78, Gadsden State Community Coll., 1983-84. Registered profl. reporter; cert. shorthand reporter, Calif. Exec. sec. various, Calif., 1960-75; ct. reporter Hendersheid & Assocs, San Francisco, 1976-78, DeSouza & Assocs., San Mateo, Calif., 1978-79; agy. owner, ct. reporter Johnson & Assocs., San Leandro, Calif., 1979-80; part-time ct. reporter freelance, Gadsden, Ala., 1980—; dir. Sch. Ct. Reporting, Gadsden State Jr. Coll., 1982—; hon. mem. faculty Ala. Supreme Ct./Jud. Coll., 1984. Honors com. Gadsden State Community Coll., 1983-85, Pres.' Cup selection com., 1983; mem., vessel examiner USCG Aux., 1986—. Author: Deposition Manual, 1985. Editor Under the Bench, 1983-85. Reviewer occupational brief Ct. Reporters No. 202, 1982, 86. Ct. Reporter Pres.'s Council on Mental Health, San Francisco, 1978; guest speaker in field. Mem. Nat. Assn. Female Execs., Ala. Shorthand Reporters Assn. (sec., chmn. pub. relations, various coms. 1983—, pres.-elect, chmn. nominations conv., pub. relations, Ala. del. to nat. conv. 1984-88), Nat. Shorthand Reporters Assn. (conv. planning com., 1985-86, 86-87, 87-88, chmn. Midyear Seminar 1988, Ala. chief examiner, 1983—, sch. evaluator for Bd. Approved Reporter Tng., various coms. 1983—), Nat. Notary Assn., Calif. Ct. Reporters Assn., Ala. Edn. Assn., NEA, U.S. Coast Guard Aux. Republican. Lodge: Internat. Order Job's Daus. (honored queen 1959, sec. 1973-77). Avocations: antiques, boating, reading, knitting, flying. Office: Gadsden State Community Coll 1001 George Wallace Dr Gadsden AL 35999

JOHNSON, DEWEY E(DWARD), dentist; b. Charleston, S.C., Mar. 19, 1935; s. Dewey Edward and Mabel (Momeier) J.; A.B. in Geology, U. N.C., 1957, D.D.S., 1961. Practice dentistry, Charleston, 1964—, assoc. to Stanley H. Karesh, D.D.S., 1970-76. Served to lt. USNR, 1961-63. Mem. Royal Soc. Health, Charleston C. of C. (cruise ship com. 1969), ADA, Charleston Dental Soc., Hibernian Soc., Charleston Museum, Internat. Platform Assn., Charleston Library Soc., S.C. Hist. Soc., Gibbes Art Gallery, Preservation Soc. of Charleston, Navy League of U.S., Phi Kappa Sigma, Sigma Gamma Epsilon, Psi Omega. Congregationalist. Club: Optimist. Home: 142 S Battery Charleston SC 29401 Office: Sergeant Jasper Bldg Charleston SC 29401

JOHNSON, DONALD (DON) WAYNE, lawyer; b. Memphis, Feb. 2, 1950; s. Hugh Don and Oline (Rowland) J.; m. Jan Marie Mullinax, May 12, 1972 (div. 1980); 1 son, Scott Fitzgerald. Student Memphis State U., 1968, Lee Coll., 1968-72; JD, Woodrow Wilson Coll. Law, 1975. Bar: Ga. 1975, U.S. Dist. Ct. (no. dist.) Ga. 1975, U.S. Ct. Appeals (5th cir.) 1976, U.S. Tax Ct. 1978, U.S. Ct. Claims 1978, U.S. Supreme Ct. 1979, U.S. Ct. Appeals (11th, 9th, Fed., D.C. cirs.) 1984. Ptnr. Barnes & Johnson, Dalton, Ga., 1975-77, Johnson & Fain, Dalton, 1977-80; sole practice, Dalton, 1980-85, Atlanta, 1985—. Bd. dirs. Pathway Christian Sch., Dalton, 1978-85, Jr. Achievement of Dalton, 1978-84, bd. dirs. Dalton-Whitfield County Day Care Ctrs., Inc. Mem. Ga. Trial Lawyers Assn. (bd. govs. 1984), Assn. Trial Lawyers Am., Ga. Bar Assn., ABA, Christian Legal Soc. Mem. Ch. of God. Office: 1900 The Exchange Suite 305 Atlanta GA 30339

JOHNSON, DOUGLAS BLAIKIE, engineer, corporate planning counselor; b. Chgo., Sept. 13, 1952; s. Marvin Melrose and Anne Stuart (Campbell) J.; m. Pamela Jane Tomlinson, Aug. 1, 1975; children—Richard Aaron, Lauren Stuart, Diana Blaikie, Scott Nathaniel. B.S.M.E., U. Nebr., 1974; J.D., Seton Hall U., 1980. Bar: Nebr. 1980, U.S. Dist. Ct. Nebr. 1980; registered profl. engr., Nebr. Project engr. Dupont, Cleve., 1974-75; project engr. Exxon Chems., Linden, N.J., 1975-78, cost engr., 1978-80; sr. engr. InterNorth, Inc., Omaha, 1980-82, market planner, 1982-84, corp. planner, 1984-85, bus. mgr., 1985-86; program mgr. Brunswick Corp., Lincoln, Nebr., 1987—. Loaned exec. United Way of Midlands, Omaha, 1982, Midland council Boy Scouts Am., 1984, Jr. Achievement, Cleve., 1974. Mem. ABA, Fed. Energy Bar Assn., Assn. Trial Lawyers Am., Nebr. Bar Assn., Omaha Bar Assn., Sigma Tau, Pi Tau Sigma, Triangle. Republican. Presbyterian. Home: 14705 U Plaza Omaha NE 68137 Office: Brunswick Corp Def Div 4300 Industrial Ave Lincoln NE 68504

JOHNSON, DOUGLAS JAMES, artist; b. Coldwater, Mich., Dec. 20, 1937; arrived in France, 1973; s. Kenneth James and Elsie Ames (Cabeen) J. BFA, Mich. State U., 1959; MFA, Columbia U., 1962. lectr. Bath Acad. Art, Corsham, Eng., 1964-65; art dir. Iran-Am. Soc. Cultural Ctr., Tehran, 1968-73. Exhibited in galleries throughout Europe and the U.S. including Karl Flinker, Paris, Carlton, N.Y., St. Charles, New Orleans, La., Juana Mordo, Madrid, others; represented in numerous pvt. and pub. collections. Recipient Tiffany Found. award, Italy, 1962. Episcopalian. Home: 8 rue des Cordeliers, 04300 Forcalquier France

JOHNSON, EARL, JR., judge, author; b. Watertown, S.D., June 10, 1933; s. Earl Jerome and Doris Melissa (Schwartz) J.; m. Barbara Claire Yanow, Oct. 11, 1970; children: Kelly Ann, Earl Eric, Agaarn Yanovitch. B.A. in Econs., Northwestern U., 1955, LL.M., 1961; J.D., U. Chgo., 1960. Bar: Ill. 1960, U.S. Ct. Appeals (9th cir.) 1964, D.C. 1965, U.S. Supreme Ct. 1966, Calif. 1972. Trial atty., organized crime sect. Dept. Justice, Washington, Miami, Fla. and Las Vegas, Nev., 1961-64; dep. dir. Neighborhood Legal Services Project, 1964-65; dep. dir. OEO Legal Services Program, 1965-66, dir., 1966-68; vis. scholar Center for Study of Law and Soc., U. Calif., Berkeley, 1968-69; assoc. prof. U. So. Calif. Law Center, Los Angeles, 1969-75, dir. clin. programs, 1970-73; prof. law U. So. Calif. Law Center, 1976-82, dir. Program Study Dispute Resolution Policy, Social Sci. Research Inst., 1975-82; assoc. justice Calif. Ct. Appeal, 1982—; co-dir. Access to Justice Project, European U. Inst., 1975-79; vis. scholar Inst. Comparative Law, U. Florence, Italy, 1973, 75; Robert H. Jackson lectr. Nat. Jud. Coll., 1980; adv. panel Legal Services Corp., 1976-80; legis. impact panel Nat. Acad. Scis., 1977-80; faculty Asian Workshop on Legal Services to Poor, 1974; mem. Internat. Legal Ctr., Legal Services in Developing Countries, 1972-75; Founder, bd. mem. Action for Legal Rights, 1971-74; pres., trustee Western Ctr. on Law and Poverty, 1972-73, 76-80; v.p., chmn. exec com. Calif. Rural Legal Assistance Corp., 1973-74; exec. com. Nat. Sr. Citizens Law Ctr., 1980-82; sec. Nat. Resource Ctr. for Consumers of Legal Services, 1974-82. Author: Justice and Reform: The Formative Years of the American Legal Services Program, 1974, 2d edit., 1978, Toward Equal Justice: A Comparative Study of Legal Aid in Modern Societies, 1975, Outside the Courts: A Survey of Diversion Alternatives in Civil Cases, 1977, Dispute Processing Strategies, 1978, Dispute Resolution in America, 1985, California Trial Guide, 5 Vol., 1986, Tex. Trial Guide, 1988; editor: U. Chgo. Law Rev, 1960; mem. editorial bd. Am. Bar Found. Research Jour., 1987—; contbr. articles to books and periodicals. Bd. dirs. Beverly Hills Bar Found., 1972-73, Nat. Legal Aid and Defenders Assn., 1987—; trustee Los Angeles Legal Aid Found., 1969-71; mem. Los Angeles County Regional Planning Commn., 1980-81; bd. visitors U. San Diego Law Sch., 1983-86. Served with USNR, 1955-58. Recipient Dart award for acad. innovation U. So. Calif., 1971; Loren Miller Legal Services award Calif. State Bar, 1977; named So. Calif. Citizen of Week, 1978; Ford Found. fellow, 1960; Dept. State lectr., 1975; grantee Ford Found.; grantee Russell Sage Found.; grantee Law Enforcement Assistance Adminstrn.; grantee NSF. Mem. ABA (com. chmn. 1972-75, mem. spl. com. resolution minor disputes 1976-83), Calif. Bar Assn., Los Angeles Bar Assn. (mem. neighborhood justice center com. 1976-81), Law and Soc. Assn., Nat. Legal Aid and Defenders Assn. (dir. 1968-79), Am. Acad. Polit. and Social Sci., Law and Society Assn., Calif. Judges Assn. (appellate cts. com. 1983—, ethics com. 1985—), Internat. Assn. Procedural Law, Order of Coif. Democrat. Office: State of Calif Ct Appeals 2d Appellate Dist 3580 Wilshire Blvd Los Angeles CA 90010

JOHNSON, EARL DALLAM, aviation and fin. cons.; b. Hamilton, Ohio, Dec. 14, 1905; s. Sidney Cornelius and Marion Esley (Felton) J.; B.A., U. Wis., 1928; grad. Randolph and Kelley Fields, 1931; m. Mytle O. Vietmeyer, Nov. 3, 1932; children—Raud Earl, Susan Lynne, Cynthia Lee. Vice pres., dir. Loom- Sayles & Co., Boston, 1947-50; ; asst. sec. army Dept. Army, Washington, 1950-51, undersec. army, 1952-54, also chmn. bd. Panama Canal, 1952-54, pres. Air Transport Assn. and Air Cargo Inc., Washington, 1954-55; sr. v.p., exec. v.p., pres., vice chmn. bd. Gen. Dynamics Co., N.Y.C., 1955-63; exec. v.p. Delta Airlines, Atlanta, 1963-64; cons. aviation, Greenwich, Conn., 1964—; dir. numerous corps., including Gen. Dynamics, Damson Oil, Menasco Mfg. Co. Ltd.; lectr. in field; Def. Dept. sr. ofcl. on Japanese Peace Treaty. Trustee Air Acad. Found., Colorado Springs, Bataan Meml. Hosp., Albuquerque, Lovelace Med. Found., Albuquerque; past pres. Wings Club, N.Y.C.; past gov. Union League Club, N.Y.C. Served to col. AC, U.S. Army, 1931-33, 1941-45. Mem. Navy League (life), Nat. Security Indsl. Assn., Nat. Transp. Assn., Air Force Assn., Phi Beta Kappa, Pi Kappa Alpha. Clubs: Greenwich Country; Rolling Rock (Ligonier, Pa.); Explorers (N.Y.C.); Club Limited. Home: 36 W Brother Dr Greenwich CT 06830

JOHNSON, EDWARD MICHAEL, lawyer, investment banker; b. Waco, Tex., July 12, 1944; s. Edward James and Anne Margaret (Stuchly) J.; m. Yvonne Margaret Hill, May 7, 1977; children—Hilary Yvonne, Megan Joy, Michael David. BA in Polit. Sci., Southwest Tex. State U., 1967; JD, St. Mary's U. 1970. Bar: Tex. 1971, U.S. Dist. Ct. (we. dist.) Tex. 1972, U.S. Supreme Ct. 1972. Briefing atty. U.S. Dist. Judge John H. Wood Jr., San Antonio, Tex., 1971-72, asst. U.S. atty. Dept. Justice, San Antonio, 1972-76, sole practice, San Antonio, 1976—; sr. atty. Wiley, Garwood, Hornbuckle, Higdon & Johnson, San Antonio, 1980-81; pres. McCabe Petroleum Corp., San Antonio, 1981; chmn., pres. Harvest Investments Corp., San Antonio, 1984—; also dir.; chmn. bd., chief exec. officer Blue Chip Petroleum Corp., San Antonio, 1981-83; gen. ptnr. Med. Mobility Ltd. IV, San Antonio, 1984—; mgr. Med. Mobility Joint Venture, San Antonio, 1984—; exec. cons. Advance Tax Representation, Inc., 1987—; gen. ptnr. Harvest Venture Capital Ltd. I, San Antonio, 1986—; pres. Blue Chip Securities Corp., San Antonio, 1984—. Co-chmn. fund raising com. Am. Heart Assn., San Antonio, 1982-84; bd. dirs. Am. Cancer Soc., San Antonio, 1982-84; chmn. San Fernando Cathedral Endowment Fund, San Antonio, 1986; mem. Gideons Internatl., San Antonio, 1982—; bd. dirs. Tex. Bible Inst., 1984-87, Christian Businessmen's Com., San Antonio, 1981—; mem., speaker Full Gospel Businessmen's Fellowship, 1981—; scoutmaster Alamo area council Boy Scouts Am., San Antonio, 1973-74; founder, chmn. Christian Businessmen's Focus on the Family, San Antonio, 1984-85. Recipient spl. commendation Dept. Transp. 1973, Dept. Air Force HQ, ATC, 1974, Dept. Treasury, 1974; named Outstanding Asst. U.S. Atty. Dept. Justice, 1974, 75, one of Outstanding Young Men Am., 1975, one of Outstanding Young Texans, 1976. Mem. Fed. Bar Assn. (pres. San Antonio chpt. 1975-76; v.p. 1973-74, sec. 1972-73, named outstanding chpt. pres. 1976), Tex. Bar Assn., San Antonio Bar Assn., Fed. Practice Licensing Com. Republican.

JOHNSON, F. ROSS, food products and tobacco company executive; b. Winnipeg, Man., Can., Dec. 13, 1931; s. Frederick Hamilton and Caroline (Green) J.; m. Laurie Ann Graumann; children: Bruce, Neil. BComm, U. Man., 1952; MBA, U. Toronto, Ont., Can., 1956; LLD (hon.), St. Francis Xavier U., Antigonish, 1978, Meml. U. Nfld., 1980. Tchr. U. Toronto, 1962-64; dir. mktg. CGE, Toronto, 1964-66; mgr. mdse. T. Eaton Co., 1966-67; exec. v.p. GSW Ltd., 1967-71; pres. Standard Brands Ltd., Toronto, 1971, pres., chief exec. officer, 1972; v.p. Standard Brands, Inc., N.Y.C., 1973, sr. v.p., dir., 1974, pres., 1975-81, chief exec. officer, 1976-81, chmn., 1977-81, chmn., chief operating officer, 1981; pres., chief operating officer Nabisco Brands, Inc. (formerly Standard Brands, Inc. and Nabisco, Inc.), Parsippany, N.J., 1984-85, vice chmn., 1985-86; pres., chief operating officer R.J. Reynolds Industries Inc. (known as RJR Nabisco, Inc. as of 1986), Winston-Salem, N.C., 1985-87; pres., chief exec. officer RJR Nabisco, Inc., Winston-Salem, N.C., 1987—; dir. Wosk's Ltd., Vancouver, Bank of N.S., Toronto. Mem. adv. council Columbia U. Bus. Sch., N.Y.C.; chmn. bd. N.Y.C. chpt. Nat. Multiple Sclerosis Soc., 1980—. Served to lt., Ordance Corps Royal Can. Army. Mem. Grocery Mfrs. Assn. (dir.), Young Pres.'s Orgn., Phi Delta Theta (pres. 1951). Clubs: Mt. Bruno Country; Brook (N.Y.C.), The Links (N.Y.C.), Blind Brook (N.Y.C.), Econ. (N.Y.C.); Conn. Golf (Easton). Office: RJR Nabisco Inc 1100 Reynolds Blvd RJR World Hdqrs Bldg Winston-Salem NC 27105 *

JOHNSON, FRANCES FLAHERTY, retired educator, career development specialist; b. Hamlet, N.C., Feb. 23, 1916; d. John Lawrence and Mary Elizabeth (Shortridge) Flaherty; m. Clifton Jerome Johnson, Nov. 27, 1940 (dec. 1953); 1 child, Carolyn Johnson Koch. BS, State Tchrs. Coll., Fredricksburg, Va., 1936; MEd, U. N.C., 1958; postgrad. U. Oslo, 1963, U. Vienna, Austria, 1967; student Shetland Islands tradition and crafts, Lerwick, Scotland, 1979. Tchr. Cumberland County Schs., Godwin, N.C., 1936-37; tchr. Aberdeen Schs., N.C., 1937-39, prin., 1939-41; counselor Fayetteville Schs., N.C., 1958-64, Winston-Salem Forsyth Schs., N.C., 1964-65; cons. Dept. Pub. Instrn., Raleigh, N.C., 1965-71; project dir. Dare-Hyde-Tyrrell Schs., Manteo, N.C., 1971-73; vocat. counselor Wake Schs., Raleigh, 1973-74; now ret. contbg. mem. Smithsonian Inst., Washington, 1988— ; active SITES and outreach programs. Mem. Am. Assn. for Adult and Continuing Edn. (del. for people-to-people visit to Soviet Union and to People's Republic China 1983), Am. Assn. for Counseling Devel., Asia Soc. Avocation: traveling.

JOHNSON, FRANK STANLEY, JR., government official; b. N.Y.C., Dec. 24, 1930; s. Frank Stanley and Alice Claire (Stern) J.; m. Lavern Schlemeyer, Aug. 19, 1978; children: Kenneth F. (dec.), Scott D.; stepdaughter: Lisa Lam. B.S. in Mktg. with honors, Ind. U., Bloomington, 1955. Reporter, then edn. editor Newsday, Garden City, N.Y., 1955-59; asst. to pres. Daniel & Florence Guggenheim Found. and Solomon R. Guggenheim Found., N.Y.C., 1959-61; asst. dir., then dir. info. Sci. Research Assos., Inc. (subs. IBM), Chgo., 1962-66; asst. to pres., dir. public affairs Rodman Job Corps Tng. Center (subs. IBM), New Bedford, Mass., 1966-68; mgr. communications IBM Corp., Endicott, N.Y., 1968-69; v.p. Chgo. Bd. Trade, 1969-72; dir. public affairs U.S. Dept. Labor, Washington, 1972-73; dir. public affairs and advt. Gen. Dynamics, Inc., St. Louis, 1974-78; v.p. public affairs Revlon, Inc.; also pres. Revlon Found., Inc., N.Y.C., 1978-81; pres. Frank Johnson & Assocs. Ltd., 1981—; v.p. Newport News Shipbldg. & Dry Dock Co. (Va.), 1981-83; dir. pub. affairs NASA, asst. assoc. adminstr. external relations, 1983-86; asst. postmaster gen. U.S. Postal Service, 1986—; founder, 1st chmn. Internat. Grad. Achievement, Inc., 1960-63. Bd. dirs. Susquenango County (N.Y.) council Boy Scouts Am., 1968-69, St. Louis chpt. Nat. Multiple Sclerosis Soc., 1974-78, Acting Co., Inc., N.Y., 1980—82, Goodwill Industries Am., Washington, 1982-88 , Va. Opera Assn., Norfolk, 1982-84; adv. bd. Adelphi Coll., Garden City, N.Y., 1957-59, trustee Manhattanville Coll., 1982-88 ; adv. bd. European Pub. Relations Roundtable, 1978-82. Served with USMC, 1950-53. Recipient Golden Trumpet award Publicity Club Chgo., 1969, Outstanding Shareholder Communications award Nat. Security Traders Assn., 1969; Best in Industry award Fin. World mag., 1975, 76, 2d best, 1962. Mem. Public Relations Soc. Am. Clubs: Capitol Hill, Nat. Press (Washington); Overseas Press Am. (N.Y.C.), Wings (N.Y.C.). Home: 6639 Madison-McLean Dr McLean VA 22101-2902 Office: US Postal Service 475 L'Enfant Plaza SW Washington DC 20260-3100

JOHNSON, FRANK WALKER, geologist, consultant; b. St. Augustine, Fla., May 22, 1909; s. Frank Henton and Grace Viola (Walker) J.; m. Helen Miller, Oct. 17, 1953 (div. 1979); children—Joseph Miller, Elena Margaret; m. 2d, Miriam Juvonen, Apr. 21, 1979. B.A., U. Nebr., 1934, D.Sc. (hon.), 1979. Various positions as geologist for mus. and oil cos., 1934-58; v.p. exploration research Jersey Prodn. Research Co., Tulsa, 1958-61; dep. mgr. exploration Standard Oil Co. (now Exxon), N.Y.C., 1961-66, sr. exploration advisor, 1966-68; chmn. research adv. com. Exxon's Exploration Research, 1962-68; exploration mgr. Esso Standard Eastern, N.Y.C., 1968-71; cons. geologist, 1972—; vol. Am. Mus. Natural History, N.Y.C., 1972—. Contbr. articles to profl. jours. Recipient N.Y.C. Mayor's Vol. Service award, 1976. Fellow Geol. Soc. Am.; mem. AAAS, Am. Assn. Petroleum Geologists, N.Y. Acad. Sci., Soc. Econ. Paleontologists and Mineralogists, Soc. Vertebrate Paleontology, Petroleum Exploration Soc. N.Y., Am. Geog. Soc. (bd. councillors 1966-76). Republican. Congregational. Club: Explorers (N.Y.C.). Home: 5 W 86th St Apt 8C New York NY 10024

JOHNSON, FRANKLIN RIDGWAY, lawyer, trustee, financial executive; b. Boston, Mar. 23, 1912; s. Howard Franklin and Mary Helena (Morse) J.; m. Hope Gray Lord, June 1, 1940; children: Nathaniel, Samuel, Anne, Rebecca; m. Sarah Q. Shaw, Aug. 16, 1962; m. Mary Compton, June 3, 1985. JD, Northeastern U., 1939; spl. student, Harvard U. Law Sch., 1941-42. Bar: Mass. 1939. Ptnr. Choate, Hall & Stewart, Boston, 1950-56; sr. officer, legal counsel Colonial Mgmt. Assocs., 1956-63, Eaton & Howard, Inc., 1963-65; sr. v.p., gen. counsel Keystone Custodian Funds, Inc., 1965-77; pres., dir. Keystone OTC Fund, Inc., Boston, 1974-77; of counsel Choate, Hall & Stewart, Boston, 1978-80; sole practice law Boston, 1980-83; of counsel Edess & McNally, Inc., Concord, Mass., 1983—; lectr. bus. law Sch. of Mgmt. Boston U., 1981-82; trustee Middlesex Savs. Bank, 1948-87; trustee, chmn. audit com. Pioneer Fund, Pioneer Scout, Pioneer II, Pioneer Three, Pioneer Bond Fund, Pioneer Mcpl. Bond Fund. Mem. Concord Bd. Selectmen, (Mass.), 1951-55, chmn. bd. 1953-55; mem. adv. com. Harvard Law Sch. Study State Securities Regulation, 1954-56. Mem. ABA, Nat. Assn. Securities Dealers (gov. 1971-73), Investment Co. Inst. (gov. 1959-62, 68-71). Republican. Episcopalian. Club Concord (Country). Home: 100 Keyes Rd Apt 216 Concord MA 01742 Office: 7 Main St Box 278 Concord MA 01742

JOHNSON, FRANKLYN ARTHUR, academic administrator; b. Rochester, N.Y., Nov. 6, 1921; s .Robert Barnes and Olyve Cole (Eckler) J.; m. Emily Bernetta Lingle, Aug. 15, 1945 (div. Aug. 1978); children: Franklyn A. Jr., Terri A. Cochran, Sandra C. Baldwin. BA, Rutgers U., 1947; MA, Harvard U., 1949, PhD, 1952; LHD (hon.), Jacksonville U., 1961; DLitt (hon.), Mt. Senario Coll., Ladysmith, Wis., 1971; LLD (hon.), Flagler Coll., St. Augustine, Fla., 1976; DCL (hon.), Drury Coll., Springfield, Mo., 1976; HHD (hon.), Mo. Valley Coll., 1978. Intelligence officer CIA, Washington, 1949-51; asst., assoc. prof. govt. Rollins Coll., Winter Park, Fla., 1952-56; pres., prof. govt. Jacksonville U., Fla., 1956-63, Calif. State U., Los Angeles, 1963-65; asst. sec., dir. Job Corps OEO, Washington, 1965-67; pres., chmn., trustee Wm. H. Donner Found., N.Y.C., 1967-70; dir. Arthur Vining Davis Founds., Coral Gables, Fla., 1970-78; prof. adminstrn. Fla. Atlantic U., Boca Raton, 1970-87; pres., prof. mgmt. S.W. Fla. Coll., Naples, 1987—; trustee Inst. for Am. Univs., Aix-en-Provence, France, 1967—, Eckerd Coll., St. Petersburg, Fla., 1978—; chmn. Southeastern Council Founds., Atlanta, 1975-77; bd. dirs. Fla. Ctr. Mgmt., Sarasota, 1980—. Author: Defence by Committee, 1960, Defence by Ministry, 1980, 1981, One More Hill, 1949, 1987, 1988; also articles on def., civil and mil. relations, adminstrn. Mem. U.S. Com. United World Colls., N.Y.C., 1975-85, Fla. Gov's. Council on Indian Affairs, Tallahassee, 1975-80, exec. adv. council Fla. Atlantic U. (chmn.). Served to lt. U.S. Army, 1942-45, ETO. Decorated Croix deGuerre (France), Silver Star, 5 Bronze Stars, 3 Purple Hearts; recipient George Washingon honor medal Freedoms Found., Valley Forge, 1956, Profl. Achievement award Barry U., Miami, Fla.; named Champion Ind. Higher Edn. in Fla., Ind. Colls. Fla. Fellow Inter-U. Seminar on Armed Forces and Soc.; mem. Can. Inst. Strategic Studies, Phi Beta Kappa, Phi Alpha Theta, Pi Alpha Alpha (pres.), Phi Kappa Phi. Republican. Presbyterian. Home: Box 1873 Bonita Springs FL 33959

JOHNSON, FREDERICK DEAN, former food co. exec., cons.; b. Shreve, Ohio, Feb. 27, 1911; s. Harry H. and Grace Marcella (Cammarn) J.; A.B., Coll. Wooster (Ohio), 1935; m. Haulwen Elizabeth Richey, June 19, 1937; children—Frederick Dean II, Mary Haulwen, Grace Elizabeth. Dir. research Bama Co. (now Bama Products Borden Foods div. Borden Inc.), Birmingham, Ala., 1961-65, dir. research, Houston, 1965-76, dir. product devel. and tech. adviser, 1976-78, cons., 1978—; U.S. del. FAO/WHO Codex Alimentarius Commn. Processed Fruits and Vegetables, 1973, 74, 75. Bd. dirs. Afton Oaks Civic Club, 1967-70, 82—. Mem. Internat. Jelly and Preserve Assn. (chmn. quality control adv. com. 1969-73, chmn. standards com. 1973-76, citation and plaque 1974), Inst. Food Technologists (charter), Am. Chem. Soc. (past sec., chmn. Wooster sect.), AAAS. Republican (precinct chmn. 1981—). Presbyterian (ruling elder). Home: 4546 Shetland Ln Houston TX 77027

JOHNSON, GABRIEL AMPAH, university rector, biology educator; b. Aneho, Oct. 13, 1930; s. William K. K. Johnson and Rebecca A. Ekue-Hettah; m. Louise Chipan, 1960; 4 children. Ed. U. Poitiers (France); D.d.'État; Dr. (hon.), Sherbrooke U., Can., 1979. Teaching asst. U. Poitiers, until 1956; research fellow C.N.R.S., France, 1958-60; dep. dir. edn. Togo, 1959-60, dir. higher edn., 1970-75; asst. prof. Nat. U. of Ivory Coast, Abidjan, 1961-64, assoc. prof., 1965-66, prof., chmn. biology, 1966—, asst. dean Faculty of Scis., 1963-68, founding dir. Nat. Centre for Social Services, 1964-68; founding rector U. Benin, Lome, Togo, 1970—; pres. Nat. Planning

Commn. Togo, 1973; pres. Assn. African Univs., 1977-80; mem. bd. adminstrn. Assn. Partially or Fully French Speaking Univs., 1975—, Pan African Inst. for Devel., 1977—. Contbr. articles to sci. jours. Mem. Central Com. Togo People's Rally, 1976—; founding pres. Africa Club for an Integrated Devel., 1980—. Decorated chevalier Ordre Nationale de la Cote d'Ivoire, 1966, officier Ordre du Mono (Togo), officier Legion d'honneur (France), comdr. Order Cruzeiro do Sul (Brazil); lauréat, Faculty Sci., U. Poitiers, 1954; recipient Medal of Honor, U. São Paolo (Brazil), 1980. Mem. Zool. Soc. France, Biol. Soc. France, Endocrinol. Soc. France. Office: Université du Benin, BP 1515, Lome Togo *

JOHNSON, HARDWICK SMITH, JR., educator; b. Millen, Ga., Aug. 13, 1958; s. Hardwick Smith Sr. and Louise (Joiner) J. B.A., Atlanta Christian Coll., 1981; M.Ed., Ga. So. Coll., 1984; EdS, Ga. State U., 1988, DSc (hon.) Holy Trinity Coll. Cert. spl. edn. educator, Ga.; cert. sch. psychometrist, Ga. Spl. edn. resource tchr. Claxton High Sch., Ga., 1983-86; psychometrist Meriwether County Sch. System, Greenville, Ga., 1986—; free-lance genealogist, Statesboro, Ga., 1980-86; supervising tchr. Ga. So. Coll., Profl. Lab. Experiences, Statesboro, 1984—; cons. Resource Ctr., Greenville, 1986, 1st Families of Ga., Atlanta, 1986. Coordinator Evans County Spl. Olympics, Claxton, 1983-84; organizing club pres. Young Reps. Coweta County. Author: The History of the Johnson Family and Johnson Church, 1976, The Aaron Family, 1986. Named Tchr. of the Year, Council for Exceptional Children, Claxton, 1985; named to Hon. Order Ky. Col., 1986; created knight H.S.H. Robert W. Y. S. Formhals, 1987; named hon. admiral Tex. Navy Gov. of Tex., 1987, lt. col. a.d.c. Gov. of Ga., 1987, citizen State of Okla., citizen Los Angeles, col. Gov. La., lt. col. Gov. Ala. Decorated with Oak Leaf Cluster; recipient Liberty medal, SAR, Meritorious Service award, SAR, Silver Good Citizenship medal, SAR. Fellow Am. Coll. Genealogists; mem. SAR (v.p. chpt. 1985-86, pres. Statesboro chpt. 1986-87, state sec. 1987—, Meritorious Service medal Ga. soc. 1987), Sons of Confederate Vets., Sons of Am. Colonists (nat. v.p. 1986—, gov. Ga. soc. 1987—), Council for Exceptional Children (pres.-elect, v.p. 1985-86), Ga. Assn. Educators (sch. rep. 1985—, pres.-elect 1986-87), NEA (sch. rep.), Ga. Assn. Sch. Psychologists, Continental Soc. Sons Indian Wars (nat. pres.), Jamestowne Soc., Gen. Soc. Colonial Wars, Colonial Order Acorn, First Families Ga. (founding sec./treas. gen.), Nat. Huguenot Soc., Gen. Soc. War 1812, Sons Revolution in State of Ga., Old Guard Gate City Guard-Atlanta, Nat. Soc. Descendants Early Quakers, Order Ams. Armorial Ancestry, Hereditary Order Descendants Loyalists and Patriots Am. Revolution, Descendants Washington's Army at Valley Forge, Kappa Delta Pi (historian 1983—), Phi Delta Kappa (historian 1987—). Republican. Christian Ch. Clubs: St. George's Soc. (Jacksonville, Fla.); Order of St. John of Jerusalem (asst. registrar gen. 1987—); The Old Guard (Atlanta). Lodges: Masons, DeMolay (master councilor 1977-78). Avocations: heraldry, travel, writing, reading. Home: 15 Watson Dr Newnan GA 30263 Office: Meriwether County Sch System PO Box 70 Greenville GA 30222

JOHNSON, HAROLD ARTHUR, manufacturing company exec.; b. Warren, Pa., May 17, 1924; s. Oscar William and Alvina Victoria (Nelson) J.; B.S. in Indsl. Engring., Pa. State U., 1950; m. Alice Meredith Jones, June 15, 1955; children—Mark, Thomas. Draftsman, Pa. Furnace and Iron Co., Warren 1941-43, engr., 1950-52, chief engr., 1952-61, sales and engring. mgr., 1961-63, sec.-treas., 1963-68, v.p., 1968-72, also dir.; exec. v.p., dir. Allegheny Valve Co., Allegheny Coupling Co., Warren, 1972-82, pres., treas., 1982—, also dir.; exec. v.p. Rand Machine Products, Inc., Jamestown, N.Y., 1972—, also dir. Active Warren County Sch. Authorities, 1961—, chmn., 1980—; chmn. Warren County Hosp. Authority, 1971—; exec. com. Boy Scouts Am., 1972-73, pres. 1986-87; former treas. Trinity Episcopalian Ch.; sr. warden, vestryman, trustee Erie (Pa.) Diocese, 1975-81 ; bd. dirs., pres., treas. DeFrees Family Found. Served with AUS, 1943-46. Decorated Bronze Star. Mem. ASME, Truck Trailer Mfrs. Assn. (tank conf. engring. com., chmn. 1961-62), C. of C., Am. Legion (past officer), Tau Beta Pi, Phi Kappa Phi, Phi Eta Sigma, Phi Sigma Kappa. Republican. Clubs: Conewango, Conewango Valley Country, Rotary, Masons, Shriners, Grotto. Contbr. articles in field to profl. jours. Home: 103 Memorial Pl RD Warren PA 16365 Office: 419 3d Ave Warren PA 16365

JOHNSON, HOWARD ARTHUR, SR., research executive; b. London, Ind., Dec. 16, 1923; s. Arthur and Inez (Smiley) J.; A.B., Franklin Coll. Ind., 1949; M.A., Wesleyan U., Conn., 1950; m. Joy Anne Nelson, July 19, 1947; children—Howard A., Kraig N. Physicist U.S. Naval Ordnance Plant, Indpls., 1950-54; operations research analyst Air-Proving Ground Command, Eglin AFB, Fla., 1954-58; chief ops. analysis 3d Air Force in Eng., 1958; dep. chief ops. analysis USAF Europe, Wiesbaden, Germany, 1958-61; dir. operations model evaluation group air force (OMEGA), also sr. mgmt. staff Washington Research Center Tech. Ops., Inc., Washington, 1961-63; sr. staff scientist Spindletop Research, Inc., Lexington, Ky., 1963-66, mgr. comparative effectiveness research div., 1966-67; research dir. Vitro Services div. Vitro Corp. Am., Ft. Walton Beach, Fla., 1967-68; sci. asst. to dir. of test Armament Devel. and Test Center, Eglin AFB, Fla., 1968-73, sr. ops. research scientist Tactical Air Warfare Center, 1973-84; chief scientist, owner Assoc. Cons., 1984—; cons. Supreme Hdgrs. Allied Powers, Europe, 1960-61, Ministry Def., Bonn, Fed. Republic Germany, 1960-61, USAF, 1964-65, U. Ky. Med. Center, 1967, Gulf South Research Inst., 1968-84. Served to capt. USAAF, 1943-45; mem. USAF Res.; mem. Internat. Exec. Service Corps, 1984—. Decorated Air medal. Mem. Ops. Research Soc. Am., Inst. Mgmt. Scis., Am. Statis. Assn., Mil. Ops. Research Soc., Internat. Test and Evaluation Assn., Armed Forces Communications and Electronics Assn., N.Y. Acad. Scis., Washington Operations Research and Mgmt. Sci. Council, Sigma Xi, Phi Delta Theta. Mason (32 deg., Shriner). Co-discoverer isotope of platinum. Author numerous profl. papers. Home: 309 Yacht Club Dr NE Fort Walton Beach FL 32548 Office: PO Box 1682 Fort Walton Beach FL 32549

JOHNSON, HOWARD ARTHUR, JR., operations research analyst; b. Indpls., July 25, 1952; s. Howard Arthur Sr. and Joy (Nelson) J.; m. Teresa Thirsk, Aug. 11, 1979, 1 child, Jaie E. BA in Polit. Sci. and Ops. Research Analysis, U. Kans., 1974; MA in Internat. Studies and Mgmt., U. Wyo., 1984. Ops. research analyst Armament Systems, Inc., Ft. Walton Beach, Fla., 1980-81, EG&G InterTech, Inc., Arlington, Va., 1981-84, dep. to U.S. dir. plans and budgets, Royal Saudi Navy, Saudi Arabian Ministry Def. and Aviation, Riyadh, Saudi Arabia, 1981-82; ops. research analyst FMC Corp., Mpls., 1984-85; ops. research analyst Honeywell, Inc., 1985— sr. prin. systems engr., 1985—; cons. USN, Coronado, 1977-78. Sustaining mem. Rep. Nat. Com., Washington, 1984—. Served to lt. USN, 1974-78. Grad. acad. scholar U. Wyo., 1983-84. Mem. AAAS, Ops. Research Soc. Am., Acad. Internat. Bus., Inst. Mgmt. Scis., Fgn. Policy Research Inst., Mil. Ops. Research Soc., Armed Forces Communications Electronics Assn., Washington Ops. Research Mgmt. Sci. Council, Tau Kappa Epsilon. Home: 10409 Huntington Dr Eden Prairie MN 55344 Office: Honeywell Inc 10400 Yellow Circle Dr Minnetonka MN 55343

JOHNSON, HOWARD WESLEY, former university president, business executive; b. Chgo., July 2, 1922; s. Albert H. and Laura (Hansen) J.; m. Elizabeth J. Weed, Feb. 18, 1950; children: Stephen Andrew, Laura Ann, Bruce Howard. B.A., Central Coll., Chgo., 1943; M.A., U. Chgo., 1947; certificate, Glasgow (Scotland) U., 1946; recipient numerous hon. degrees. From asst. to assoc. prof., dir. mgmt. research U. Chgo., 1948-51, 53-55; asst. to v.p. personnel adminstrn. Gen. Mills, Inc., 1952-53; assoc. prof., dir. exec. programs, assoc. dean Sloan Sch. Mgmt., MIT, 1955-59, prof., dean, 1959-66; pres. MIT, 1966-71; chmn. corp., 1971-83, hon. chmn., 1983—; exec. v.p. Federated Dept. Stores, 1966; now dir.; chmn. Fed. Res. Bank Boston, 1968-69; dir. Hitchiner Mfg. Co., 1961-71, John Hancock Mut. Life Ins. Co., Champion Internat. Corp., E.I. duPont de Nemours & Co., Morgan Guaranty Trust Co.; trustee Putnam Funds, 1961-71; Mem. Pres.'s Adv. Com. on Labor-Mgmt. Policy, 1966-68; chmn. Environ. Studies Bd. Nat. Acad. Scis.-Nat. Acad. Engring., 1973-75; mem. sci. adv. com. Mass. Gen. Hosp., 1968-70; mem. Nat. Manpower Adv. Com., 1967-69, Nat. Commn. on Productivity, 1970-72; trustee Com. Econ. Devel., 1968-71, Wellesley Coll., 1968-86, trustee emeritus, 1986—, Radcliffe Coll., 1973-79; hon. trustee Aspen Inst. for Humanistic Studies, Inst. Def. Analyses, 1971-79; mem. corp. Woods Hole (Mass.) Oceanographic Instn. Trustee WGBH Ednl. Found., 1966-71; mem. corp. Mus. Sci., Boston; overseer Boston Symphony Orch., 1968-72; mem.-at-large Boy Scouts Am.; pres. Boston Mus. Fine Arts, 1975-80, chmn. bd. overseers, 1980-83, chmn. exec. com., 1983-87; trustee Alfred P. Sloan Found., 1982—, Nat. Arts Stabilization Found. (bd. dirs. 1983-87), Henry Francis du Pont Winterthur Mus., 1984-87; bd. dirs. Museo de Arte de Ponce, 1983—. Served with AUS, 1943-46. Recipient Alumni medal U. Chgo., 1970. Fellow Am. Acad. Arts and Scis., AAAS; mem. Council Fgn. Relations, Am. Philos. Soc., Phi Gamma Delta. Clubs: Univ. (N.Y.C.); Somerset, Comml., Tavern, St. Botolph (Boston). Home: Box 140 South Harpswell MA 04079

JOHNSON, JAMES LAWRENCE, telephone company executive; b. Vernon, Tex., Apr. 12, 1927; s. Samuel Lonzo and Adeline Mary (Donges) J.; m. Ruth Helen Zweig, Aug. 5, 1949; children: James Lawrence, Helayne, Barry, Todd. BBA in Acctg., Tex. Tech Coll., 1949. Acct. Whiteside Laundry, Lubbock, Tex., 1949; with Gen. Telephone Co. SW, San Angelo, Tex., 1949-59; asst. controller Gen. Telephone Co. SW, 1953-59, v.p., controller, treas., 1966-69; controller Gen. Telephone Co. Mich., Muskegon, 1959-63; asst. controller telephone ops., then chief acct. consol. ops. GTE Service Corp., N.Y.C., 1963-66; v.p., controller telephone ops. GTE Service Corp., 1969-74; v.p. revenue requirements Gen. Telephone & Electronics Corp., Stamford, Conn., 1974-76; pres. Gen. Telephone Co. Ill., Bloomington, 1976-81; also dir., also group v.p. Gen. Telephone Co. Ill. (No. region); pres. GTE telephone operating group Gen. Telephone & Electronics Corp., from 1981; sr. v.p. GTE Corp., until 1986; pres., chief operating officer, dir. GTE Corp., Stamford, Conn., 1986-88, chmn., chief exec. officer, 1988—; dir. First Fed. Savs. & Loan Assn., Bloomington.; Mem. adv. council Coll. Bus., Ill. State U., Normal. Trustee, adv. council Mennonite Hosp., Bloomington; bd. dirs. Bloomington Unlimited; mem. Wesleyan Assos., Ill. Wesleyan U., Bloomington. Served with USNR, 1945-47. Mem. Nat. Accts. Assn., Fin. Execs. Inst., Ill. Telephone Assn. (dir.), McLean County Assn. Commerce and Industry (dir.). Republican. Methodist. Clubs: Bloomington Country, Crestwicke Country (Bloomington); Woodway Country (Darien, Conn.). Lodge: Rotary. Office: GTE Corp One Stamford Forum Stamford CT 06904 *

JOHNSON, JAMES TERENCE, college president, lawyer, clergyman; b. Springfield, Mo., Oct. 25, 1942; s. Clifford Lester and Margaret Jeanne (Wallace) J.; m. Martha Susan Mitchell, May 2, 1964; children: Jennifer Jeanne, Emily Jill. BA, Okla. Christian Coll., 1964; JD, So. Meth. U., 1967; LLD, Pepperdine U., 1980. Staff counsel, asst. prof. Okla. Christian Coll., Oklahoma City, 1968-72; v.p. Okla. Christian Coll., 1972-73, exec. v.p., 1973-74, pres., 1974—; minister Okla., Tex., 1961—; pvt. practice law Oklahoma City, 1969—; co-founder Enterprise Sq., U.S.A., 1982. Trustee Freedom Found.; bd. dirs. Okla. Ind. Coll. Found. Mem. Okla. Bar Assn., Newcomen Soc., Phi Delta Theta. Mem. Ch. of Christ. Office: Okla Christian Coll Oklahoma City OK 73136

JOHNSON, JAMES WALKER, lawyer; b. Cleve., Aug. 17, 1953; s. John Everett and Jane (Walker) J.; m. Joan Essex, Oct. 24, 1982; 1 child, Robert Everett. BA, Cornell U., 1975; JD, U. Kans., 1978; LLM in Taxation, Georgetown U., 1983. Bar: Kans. 1978, U.S. Ct. Claims 1979, U.S. Tax Ct. 1979, D.C. 1983, U.S. Supreme Ct. 1986. Trial atty. tax div. U.S. Justice Dept., Washington, 1978-84; assoc. Steptoe & Johnson, Washington, 1984—; adj. prof. law Georgetown U., 1987—. Contbr. articles to profl. jours. Mem. ABA (tax sect.). Home: 3312 Camalier Dr Chevy Chase MD 20815 Office: Steptoe & Johnson 1330 Connecticut Ave NW Washington DC 20036

JOHNSON, JOYCE MARIE, psychiatrist, medical epidemiologist; b. Baton Rouge, Jan. 30, 1952; d. Gene Addison and Helen Marie (Kalcik) J.; m. James Albert Calderwood, Mar. 28, 1987. B.A., Luther Coll., Decorah, Iowa, 1972; M.A., U. Iowa, 1974; D.O., Mich. State U., 1980. Cooking instr. Kirkwood Community Coll., Iowa City, Iowa, 1974-76; health planner Iowa Regional Med. Program, Iowa City, 1974-76; intern USPHS Hosp., Balt., 1980-81; med. epidemiologist Hepatitis Labs., Ctrs. Disease Control, Phoenix, 1981-83, AIDS, Ctrs. Disease Control, Atlanta, 1983-84; resident in psychiatry NIMH, 1984-87; staff psychiatrist, 1987—. Med. Perspectives fellow, New Guinea and Thailand, 1978-79; mem. clin. faculty Mich. State U., 1983—, Georgetown U. Med. Ctr., 1988—; vol. physician DoCare, Haiti, 1983, Mex., 1984; speaker community orgns. Recipient Alper award for community service Mich. State U., 1980; Am. Osteo. Assn. scholar 1976-78; Nat. Osteo. Found., fellow, Bangkok, 1981-82; Am. Psychiatric Assn. fellow. 1986. Fellow Am. Osteo. Coll. Preventive Medicine (cert.); mem. Mensa. Office: 5518 Western Ave Chevy Chase MD 20815

JOHNSON, JUDITH LAWSON, commodity broker; b. Memphis, Jan. 12, 1943; d. David Voss and Julia (Larkey) J.; B.A., Smith Coll., 1965; M.A.T., Duke U., 1966. Sales asst. Howard, Weil, Labouisse, Friedrichs, Inc., New Orleans, 1969-72, analyst, Chgo., 1975-77, 1st v.p., commodity sales mgr., New Orleans, 1977—. Mem. Chgo. Mercantile Exchange, N.Y. Futures Exchange, Futures Industry Assn., Nat. Futures Assn. (western bus. conduct com.). Presbyterian. Home: 3009 Constance St New Orleans LA 70115 Office: Howard Weil Labouisse Friedrichs Inc Inc Energy Ctr 1100 Poydras St Suite 900 New Orleans LA 70163

JOHNSON, KEITH, Jamaican ambassador to U.S.; b. Spanish Town, St. Catherine, Jamaica, July 29, 1921; s. Septimus A. and Emily Johnson; grad. Kingston Coll., Jamaica, 1937; postgrad. in demography, Columbia U., 1950-51; m. Pamela B. Rodgers; children—Hope and Marie (twins). With Jamaica Civil Service, 1939-48, statistician, 1942-48; research asst. Bur. Applied Social Research, Columbia U., 1948-49; profl. trainee various positions, then social affairs officer UN population br., dept. social and econ. affairs UN, 1949-62; formerly consul gen. for Jamaica in U.S.; Jamaica's permanent rep. to UN, 1967-73; non-resident ambassador to Republic of Argentina, 1969-73; ambassador to W.Ger., Luxembourg and Netherlands, 1973-81; non-resident ambassador to Israel, 1975-81, to the Holy See, 1980-85; ambassador to U.S., Washington, 1981—and permanent rep. to OAS, 1981—. Chmn. prep. com., rapporteur-gen. UN Conf. on Human Environ. Recipient Jamaica Ind. medal, 1963; Internat. Relations award U.S. and City Coll. chpt. West Indian Students Assn., 1963; Human Relations award West Indian Cultural Soc., Boston, 1965; Humanitarian award West Indian Celebration Com., 1966; Franklin Mint Peace medal, 1967; grand marshall Martin Luther King Jr. Meml. Day Parade, 1968; Comdr. Order of Distinction, Jamaica, 1970; Grand Cross, Fed. Republic Germany, 1981; Grand Cross, Luxembourg, 1981; Grand Cross, Order of Pius IX, Vatican, 1983; Order of Jamaica, 1983. Mem. 369th Vets.' Assn. (hon.); Inst. Sci. Study Population, Soc. Fgn. Consuls, West Indian Students Assn. (pres. 1954-57, chmn. adv. com. 1958—). Address: Embassy of Jamaica 1850 K St NW Suite 355 Washington DC 20006

JOHNSON, KENNETH LEROY, retired air force officer, program management company executive; b. Chgo., Jan. 24, 1922; s. Stanley C. and Nell L. (Lundberg) J.; student Kans. State Coll., 1940-42, U. So. Calif., 1956-57; B.S., U. Omaha, 1959; m. Tran Thi Phuong, July 3, 1946; children—Jeffery John, Candy Ann, James John; children by previous marriage—Kenneth LeRoy, Terri Ann, Jeff J. Commd. U.S. Air Force, 1942, advanced through grades to col., 1960; ret., 1969; contract mgr. Pacific Architects & Engrs. Co., Vietnam, 1970-74; program mgr. Bell Helicopter Internat., Tehran, Iran, 1977-79. Decorated D.F.C. with oak leaf cluster, Purple Heart, Bronze Star, Air medal with seven oak leaf clusters, numerous others. Mem. Nat. Assn. Security Dealers. Republican. Lodge: Masons. Home: 3020 S Sheridan Wichita KS 67217

JOHNSON, KENNETH ODELL, retired engineering executive; b. Harville, Mo., Aug. 31, 1922; s. Kenneth D. and Polly Louise (Wilson) J.; B.S. in Aero. Engring., Purdue U., 1950; m. Betty Lou Jones, Aug. 5, 1950; children—Cynthia Jo, Gregory Alan. Engr., design, quality and production mgmt. Gen. Lamp Co., Elwood, Ind., 1950-51; mem. staff aircraft gas turbine engine design Allison div. Gen. Motors Corp., Speedway, Ind., 1951-66; mem. turbofan aircraft engines plus marine, indsl. gas turbine engine design mgmt. staff Gen. Electric Co., 1966-86, dir. aerospace engring Belcan Corp., Cin., 1986—. Served to capt. USAF, 1942-45. Fellow AIAA (assoc.). Republican. Methodist. Holder over 20 patents in field. Recipient UDF Pioneer & Extraordinary Service award for unducted fan invention, Gen. Electric Co., 1985, cert. recognition NASA, 1987; named to Gen. Electric Aircraft Engines Propulsion Hall of Fame, 1987. Home: 8360 Arapaho Ln Cincinnati OH 45243 Office: Belcan Corp Aerospace Engring 10200 Anderson Way Cincinnati OH 45242

JOHNSON, LAWRENCE ALLAN, SR., chiropractic physician, real estate developer; b. Balt., Feb. 17, 1943; s. Harvey McMullen and Virginia Pauline (Thompson) J.; m. Sunny Lin Malone, Apr. 22, 1967; children: James, Melanie, Lawrence Jr., Jeff, Amanda, Amber, Susanne, Brittany, Courtney. BA magna cum laude, George Williams Coll., 1968; D in Chiropractic Medicine, Nat. Coll., Lombard, Ill., 1972. Pres. Chiropractic Clinics N.Mex., Los Lunas, Belen, Rio Rancho and Albuquerque, 1972—; pres. Ambulance Services N.Mex., Bernalillo and Valencia Counties, 1983-87, Lazy J Enterprises, Bernalillo and Valencia Counties, 1975—. Chmn. Rep. fin. com., Valencia County, 1983-84, 19th precinct chmn., 1985-87, vice chmn. 1980-84. Mem. N.Mex. Physicians of Chiropractic Medicine (charter, pres. 1986), N.Mex. Chiropractic Assn. (sec., treas. 1972-73, 81-82, bd. dirs. 1972-73, 79-83, editor jour. 1972-85, Nat. Excellence jour. award 1980, Outstanding Service 1972-82, founder, editor newsletter 1985—), Bernalillo County Chiropractic Assn. (charter, pres. 1972-74, 79-85), Nat. Coll. Alumni Assn. (field advisor 1983-86, Chiropractor of Yr. 1986, Outstanding Grad. 1982, bd. dirs. 1985—). Roman Catholic. Lodges: Lions (sec., treas. Los Lunas, N.Mex. club 1980, pres. 1981, 86, Lion of Yr. 1981, Outstanding E.M.S. award 1987), Masons, Moose. Home: 4203 Hwy 85 SW Los Lunas NM 87031 Office: Chiropractic Clinic NMex 4205 Hwy 85 SW Los Lunas NM 87031

JOHNSON, LAYMON, JR., budget analyst; b. Jackson, Miss., Sept. 1, 1948; s. Laymon and Bertha (Yarbrough) J.; m. Charlene J. Johnson, Nov. 13, 1982. B in Tech., U. Dayton, 1970; MS in Systems Mgmt., U. So. Calif., 1978. Mem. tech. staff Rockwell Internat., Canoga Park, Calif., 1975-77; sr. dynamics engr. Gen. Dynamics, Pomona, Calif., 1978-83; sr. budget analyst , budget mgr. Northrop Corp., Pico Rivera, Calif., 1983—. Served to lt. comdr. USNR, 1970—. Mem. U.S. Naval Inst., Naval Res. Assn., Res. Officers Assn. U.S., Assn. Mil. Surgeons U.S., Assn. Systems Mgmt., Ops. Research Soc. Am., Los Angeles County Mus. Art, Smithsonian Assos., Nat. Hist. Soc., Archimedes Circle, Tau Alpha Pi. Democrat. Roman Catholic. Office: Northrop Corp Advanced Systems Div 8900 E Washington Blvd Pico Rivera CA 90660

JOHNSON, LEE HARNIE, emeritus dean, educator; b. Houston, Jan. 4, 1909; s. Lee Harnie and Isabelle (Smart) J.; m. Eulalie Woolverton McKay, Oct. 19, 1940 (dec.); children: Lee McKay, William Irving; m. Kate Chamness O'Meallie, Aug. 21, 1976. B.A., Rice Inst., 1930, M.A., 1931; M.S., Harvard, 1932, Sc.D., 1935. Fellow in math. Rice Inst., 1930-31; asst. in civil engring. Harvard, 1932-35; asst. engring. aide U.S. Waterways Expt. Sta., Vicksburg, Miss., 1935-36; asst. to engr. in charge design U.S. Engr. Office, Mobile, Ala., 1936-37; dean engring. and prof. civil engring. U. Miss., 1937-50, dir. def., war tng. program, 1941-45; dean engring., prof. civil engring. Tulane U., 1950-72, emeritus dean, 1972—, W.R. Irby prof. engring., 1972-79; tchr. math Newman High Sch., 1979-87. Author: The Slide Rule, 1947, Nomography and Empirical Equations, 1952, Engineering: Principles and Problems, 1960; Contbr. to engring. jours. Graham Baker and Hohenthal scholar Rice Inst.; Hilton scholar Harvard U.; Lee H. Johnson award for excellence in teaching established in his honor Tulane U. Mem. ASCE, Am. Soc. Engring. Edn., La. Engring. Soc., Phi Beta Kappa, Kappa Delta Phi, Tau Beta Pi, Chi Epsilon, Gamma Alpha, Omicron Delta Kappa. Republican. Presbyterian. Clubs: New Orleans Country (New Orleans), Boston (New Orleans). Home: 211 Fairway Dr New Orleans LA 70124

JOHNSON, LEONARD COSBY, military broker, aviation sales executive; b. Galveston, Tex., Aug. 12, 1926; s. Stuart Asa and Corrie Leavell (Cosby) J.; m. Maire Irene Harkonen, Oct. 2, 1961; children—Harald Martin, Corrie Leavell, Steven Cosby, Leila Anneli. BA, Tulane U., 1956; student Frankfurt U., 1956-58. Mgr., sales rep. Wilson Harrell Co., Europe, Africa, Asia, 1958-78; v.p. Assoc. Brands, Philippines and S.E. Asia, 1978-85; Philippines sales rep. L.J. Elkin Inc., Novato, Calif., 1980-81; cons. mil. brokers, 1981—; regional mgr. Philippines, Hawaii Pacific Assocs. Co., Honolulu, 1984—; mktg. mgr./mil. cons. Pacific Airways Corp., Manila, 1975—. Served with AUS, 1948-52. German Govt. grantee, 1956. Baptist. Clubs: Clark Air Base Aero. Lodges: Elks, Masons, Shriners. Home: 110 Mil Flores Dr, Beverly Hills Subdiv Taytay, Rizal 1901, Philippines Office: Pacific Airways Corp, Poste Restante, Taytay, Rizal 3139, Philippines

JOHNSON, LILLIAN BEATRICE, sociologist, educator; b. Wilmington, N.C., Nov. 8, 1922; d. James Archie and Mary Gaston (Atkins) J. A.A., Peace Coll., 1940; B.R.E., Presbyterian Sch. Christian Edn., 1942; M.S., N.C. State U., 1965, Ph.D., 1972. Dir. Christian edn. First Presbyn. Ch., Pensacola, Fla., 1945-47, Greenwood, S.C., 1947-48, Durham, N.C., 1948-51; club dir. Army Spl. Services, No. Command, Japan, 1951-53; teenage dir. YWCA, Washington, 1953-56, assoc. exec. Honolulu, 1956-59, exec. dir. Tulsa, 1959-62; instr. N.C. State U., 1962-72; asst. prof. Greensboro Coll., 1972-75; mem. faculty sociology dept. Livingston U., 1975—, now prof. Election law commr. State of Ala. Mem. Am. Sociol. Assn., So. Sociol. Soc., Ala.-Miss. Sociol. Assn. (treas.), Nat. Council Family Relations, Ala. Council on Family Relations (v.p. 1981-83), Alpha Kappa Delta (treas. 1984-86). Home: Meadowbrook Dr Livingston AL 35470 Office: Livingston U Livingston AL 35470

JOHNSON, LOUIS ALBERT, writer; b. Wellington, New Zealand, Sept. 27, 1924; s. Alber George and Louisa Murray (Betts) J.; m. Patricia Lucy Mason; children: Cassandra, Mark, Andrew; m. Cecilia Margery Wace Wilson, Dec. 15, 1970; children: Miranda, Lucien. Cert. tchr., New Zealand. Journalist H.B. Herald Tribune, Hastings, New Zealand, 1958-63; editor New Zealand Dept. Edn., Wellington, New Zealand, 1963-68; officer-in-charge Bur. Lit., Papua New Guinea, 1968-69; sr. lectr. Mitchell Coll., Bathurst, New Zealand, 1971-80; Editor New Zealand Poetry Yearbook, 1951-64, Numbers lit. quar., New Zealand, 1953-60. Decorated Officer Brit. Empire Queen's New Year Honours; recipient New Zealand Book award for Poetry, 1975; Writing fellowship Victoria U. of Wellington, 1980; Katherine Mansfield fellow, 1988. Home: 4 Te Motu Rd, Pukerua Bay New Zealand

JOHNSON, LUANNE ELIZABETH, financial planner, seminar moderator; b. Litchfield, Ill., Jan. 28, 1949; d. A. Edward and Margaret Elizabeth (Viner) J. B.A., MacMurray Coll., 1971; lang. arts specialist So. Ill. U.-Edwardsville, 1980. Cert. fin. planner; Lang. Arts Specialist. Elem. sch. tchr. Jacksonville Sch. Dist., Ill., 1971-74, Southwestern Sch. Dist., Piasa, Ill., 1974-83; adminstrv. dir. Computer Learning Source, Inc., St. Louis, 1983-86; pres. LJ Resources, Alton, Ill., 1983-87; fin. analyst G.L. Pittsford and Assocs., 1986-87; seminar moderator Nat. Inst. Fin., South Plainfield, N.J., 1985—, Personal Fin. Seminars, Inc., St. Louis, 1985-86, pres. Ind. Union Coffee Co., Inc., 1987—; bd. dirs. Computer Learning Source, Inc., 1983-86, instr., seminar writer and moderator Dun & Bradstreet Bus. Edn. Services, 1986; chmn. St. Louis Fin. Planner of Yr., 1985-86. Vestry woman St. Paul's Episcopal Parish, Alton, 1982-85, Sunday Sch. tchr., 1981-86. Named Outstanding Tchr. of Yr., PTA Shipman, Ill., 1977; recipient Grand Cross of Color, Internat. Order Rainbow for Girls, 1968. Mem. Internat. Assn. Fin. Planning (bd. dirs. St. Louis chpt. 1985-86), Inst. Cert. Fin. Planners, Nat. Assn. Female Execs., Personal Fin. Mgmt for Women, DAR (state treas. Ill. 1986-87, named Outstanding Jr. Ill. Orgn. 1984), Jr. League Greater Alton (fin. com. 1984-86), Union Station Merchant's Assn. (mem. budget com. 1987—). Lodge: Order Eastern Star. Avocations: antiquing; home renovation; aerobics. Home: 2625 N Meridian Apt 907 Indianapolis IN 46208 Office: 39 Jackson St Suite 135 Indianapolis IN 46225

JOHNSON, MADGE RICHARDS, business owner, fundraiser, consultant; b. Washington, Oct. 4, 1952; d. Benjamin Ellsworth and Virginia (Oliver) Richards; m. Jeffrey Leonard Johnson, June 25, 1977; children: Jared Benjamin, Jessica Lauren. B.S. in Bus. Mgmt., Strayer Coll., 1973; postgrad. in Bus. Adminstrn., Am. U., 1975-77. Nat. govt. sales rep. G.F.C. Mfg. Co., Bklyn., 1972-75; ter. sales rep. John H. Breck, Am. Cyanamid, Wayne, N.J., 1975-77; ter. sales mgr. Drackett Products Co., Cin., 1977-81, E.J. Brach & Sons., Chgo., Annapolis, Md., 1981-87, owner, pres. Madge Johnson Ltd., 1987—. Mem. Nat. Assn. Female Execs., Grocery Mfrs. Reps., Women in Consumer Product Sales. Home and Office: 625 Rolling Dale Rd Annapolis MD 21401

JOHNSON, MARGARET HELEN, welding executive; b. Chgo., June 3, 1933; d. Harold W. and Clara J. (Pape) Glavin; m. Odean Jack Johnson, Nov. 18, 1950; children: Karen Ann, Dean Harold. Student Moody Bible Inst., 1976-78. V.p., sec. Seamline Welding, Inc., Chgo., 1956—, also dir.;

trustee SWCEPS, Chgo., 1963—. Author: Living Faith, 1973, 80, Lord's Ladder of Love, 1976, God's Rainbow, 1982; contbr. articles to religion mags. Mem. Rep. Presdl. Task Force, 1982-88, trustee, 1986-88, renew facilitator 1986-88, co-chairperson 1986-88, life, 1988; charter founder Ronald Reagan Rep. Ctr., 1987, mem. Lake View Neighborhood Group, Chgo.; active Mary, Seat of Wisdom Cath. Women's Club, 1970—, Renew facilitator, 1986-87, co-chairperson, 1986-88; Sunday sch. tchr., 1985. Mem. ASCAP, Fedn. Ind. Small Bus., Internat. Platform Assn., Small Group Community. Roman Catholic. Home: 6 S Seminary Ave Park Ridge IL 60068

JOHNSON, MARILYN, obstetrician, gynecologist; b. Houston, May 7, 1925; d. William Walton and Marilyn (Henderson) J.; B.A., Rice Inst., 1945; M.D., Baylor U., 1950. Intern, New Eng. Hosp. Women and Children, Boston, 1950-51; resident Meth. Hosp., Houston, 1951-53; resident in gynecology M.D. Anderson Tumor Inst., Houston, 1954, fellow, 1955; fellow in gynecol. pathology Harvard Med. Sch., 1952-53; practice medicine specializing in ob-gyn, Houston, 1954-81, Fredericksburg, Tex., 1981—; mem. staffs St. Joseph's, Meml., Meth., Park Plaza, Hill Country Meml. Rosewood, South Austin Community, Comfort (Tex.) Community hosps.; clin. instr. ob-gyn Coll. Medicine, Baylor U., 1954—, Postgrad. Sch. Medicine, U. Tex., 1954—; gynecologist De Pelchin Faith Home, Houston, 1954—, also Rice U., Richmond State Sch.; med. dirs. Birthright, Inc., Houston, 1973—; pro-life public speaker. Bd. dirs. Right to Life, Houston, Found. for Life. Sandoz Labs. grantee, 1973, 75, Delbay Pharm. Co. grantee, 1977. Fellow Am. Coll. Obstetricians and Gynecologists; mem. AMA, Am. Soc. Colposcopic Pathologists, Tex. Med. Assn., Am. Med. Women's Assn., Internat. Infertility Assn., Harris County Med. Soc., Postgrad. med. Assembly S. Tex., Houston Ob-Gyn Soc., Tex. Folklore Soc. Republican. Baptist. Clubs: Zonta; Fredericksburg Rockhounds. Home: 205 S Orange St Fredericksburg TX 78624 Office: 204 W Schubert St Fredericksburg TX 78624

JOHNSON, MARVIN DONALD, brewery executive; b. Willcox, Ariz., Nov. 2, 1928; s. Wellington Lott and Hazel Valentine (Bendure) J.; m. Stella C. Pacheco, Feb. 14, 1953; children: Lynn Anne, Marshall Donald, Karen Marie. BS, U. Ariz., 1950, MS, 1957; Ed.D. (hon.), Lincoln Coll., 1970. Asst. grad. mgr. U. Ariz., 1950-52, dir. student union, 1952-58, dir. alumni assn., 1958-63, v.p. univ relations, 1963-77; adminstrv. v.p. student affairs alumni relations and devel. U. N.Mex., Albuquerque, 1977-85; v.p. corp. affairs Adolph Coors Co., 1985—; dir. Radio Fiesta, Ariz. Pres., Palo Verde Mental Health Assn., Ariz., 1967-69. Editor: Successful Governmental Relations, 1981. Chmn. Tucson Crime Commn., Ariz., 1969-71; pres. Catalina council Boy Scouts Am., 1966, bd. dirs. Gt. S.W. council, 1983-85; bd. dirs. Fund for Tucson, 1960-65, Maxwell Mus., 1977-85, Sta. KNME-TV, 1977-85, N.Mex. div. Am. Cancer Soc., 1978-85, United Way Albuquerque, 1978-79, 83-85; mem. White House Conf. on Youth, 1971, Gov's. Film Commn., Ariz., 1972-77. Recipient Outstanding Alumni award Future Farmers Am., Ariz., 1964; Outstanding Alumni award Ariz. 4-H, 1970; Silver Antelope award Boy Scouts Am., 1975; Super P.R. award Am. Cancer Soc. N.Mex., 1979; N.Mex. Disting. Pub. Service award, 1982. Mem. Pub. Relations Soc. Am., Inst. Ednl. Mgmt. (trustee 1972-76), Nat. Assn. State Univs. and Land Grant Colls. (mem. exec. com. 1973-77), Council Advancement and Support Edn. (trustee 1976-85, nat. chmn. 1980-81), Newcomen Soc. N. Am., Western Athletic Conf. (chmn. council 1978-79), Ariz. Cattle Growers Assn., Lamplighters Ednl. Round Table, Golden C. of C. (pres. 1988, bd. dirs 1986—), Alpha Zeta, Kappa Kappa Psi, Gamma Sigma Delta, Alpha Kappa Psi, Phi Eta Sigma, Sigma Chi (grand trustee 1973-83, internat. pres. 1983-85). Democrat. Methodist. Club: Denver Rotary. Home: 13950 W 30th Ave Golden CO 80401 Office: Adolph Coors Co Golden CO 80401

JOHNSON, MARVIN MELROSE, industrial engineer; b. Neligh, Nebr., Apr. 21, 1925; s. Harold Nighram and Melissa (Bare) J.; m. Anne Stuart Campbell, Nov. 10, 1951; children: Douglas Blake, Harold James, Phyllis Anne, Nighram Marvin, Melissa Joan. B.S., Purdue U., 1949; postgrad., Ill. Inst. Tech., 1953; M.S. in Indsl. Engring, U. Iowa, 1966, Ph.D., 1968. Registered profl. engr., Iowa, Mo., Nebr. Quality control supr., indsl. engr. Houdaille Hershey, Chgo., 1949-52; indsl. engr. Bell & Howell, Chgo., 1952-54; with Bendix Aviation Corp., Davenport, Iowa, 1954-64; successively chief indsl. engr., staff asst., supr. procedures and systems Bendix Aviation Corp., 1954-63; reliability engr. Bendix Aviation Corp. (Pioneer Central div.), 1963-64, cons., 1964—; lectr. indsl. engring State U Iowa, 1963-64; instr. indsl. engring. U. Iowa, 1965-66; asso. prof. U. Nebr., 1968-73, prof., 1973—; AID adv., mgmt. engring. and food processing Kabul (Afghanistan) U., 1975-76; vis. prof. indsl. engring. U. P.R., Mayaguez, 1982-83; NSF trainee U. Iowa, 1964-67. Editor The Johnson Reporter, 1980—. Served with AUS, 1943-46, ETO. Fellow Am. Inst. Indsl. Engrs.; Mem. Am. Soc. Engring. Educators, Am. Statis. Assn., ASME, Ops. Research Soc. Am., Inst. Mgmt. Sci., Sigma Xi, Tau Beta Pi, Pi Tau Sigma, Alpha Pi Mu. Presbyterian. Home: 2507 Ammon Ave Lincoln NE 68507 Office: 175 Nebraska Hall U Nebr Lincoln NE 68588

JOHNSON, NORMA J., specialty wool grower; b. Dover, Ohio, Aug. 30, 1925; d. Jasper Crile and Mildred Catherine (Russell) J.; student Heidelberg Coll., 1943; cert. drafting techniques Case Sch. Applied Sci., 1944; student Western Res. U., 1945-47, Ohio State U., 1951, Muskingum Coll., 1965; A.A., Kent State U., 1979, Buckeye Joint Vocat. Sch., 1979-84; m. Robert Blake Covey, Oct. 7, 1951 (div. 1960); 1 dau., Susan Kay. Instr. arts and crafts Univ. Settlement House, Cleve., 1944; mech. draftswoman Nat. Assn. Civil Aeros., Cleve., 1944-46; mfrs. rep. Nat. Spice House, 1947-49; tchr. econs., home econs., English, math, history, high sch., Tuscarawas County Sch. System, New Philadelphia, Ohio, 1962-69; owner, mgr., operator Sunny Slopes Farm, producer of specialty wools and grains, Dover, Ohio, 1969—. Tchr., Meth. Sunday Sch., 1956-61; chaplain Winfield PTA, 1960; program dir. Brandywine Grange, 1960-62; troop leader Girl Scouts, U.S.A., 1961-70; mem. Tuscarawas County Jail Com., 1981-87. Recipient cert. of merit Tuscarawas County Schs., 1965, Ohio Wildlife Conservation award Tuscarawas County, 1972, 1st and 3d premiums for handspinning fleece, Ohio State Fair, 1984, 8th and 10th premiums, Mich. Stat Fair, 1985. Mem. Mid States Wool Growers, Am. Angus Assn., Club: Nat. Grange. Bldg. designed and constructed interior facilities for the Scheuerhaus. Home and Office: Rt 1 Box 398 Dover OH 44622

JOHNSON, PHILIP CORTELYOU, architect; b. Cleve., July 8, 1906; s. Homer M. and Louise (Pope) J. A.B., Harvard, 1930, B.Arch., 1943. Dir. dept. architecture and design Mus. Modern Art, 1930-36, 46-54, trustee, 1958—. Architect: Lincoln Center, N.Y.C., Glass House, New Canaan, Conn.; co-architect: Seagram Bldg, N.Y.C.; Works include Pennzoil Pl, Houston, IDS Center, Mpls., Niagara Falls (N.Y.) Conv. Center, addition to Boston Pub. Library, Bobst N.Y. U. Library; Author: (with Henry-Russel Hitchcock) Works include Architecture Since 1922, 1932, Mies van der Rohe, 1947, rev., 1953. Recipient Bronze Medallion City of N.Y., 1978; Pritzker prize, 1979; AIA Gold medal, 1978; fellows award R.I. Sch. Design, 1983; Herbert Adams medal Nat. Sculpture Soc., 1984. Mem. Acad. Arts and Letters. Home: Ponus St New Canaan CT 06840 Office: 885 3rd Ave #300 New York NY 10022 *

JOHNSON, PHILIP WAYNE, lawyer; b. Greenwood, Ark., Oct. 24, 1944; s. John Luther and Flora (Joyce) J.; m. Carla Jean Newsom, Nov. 6, 1970; children—Betsy, Carl, Jeff, Laura, Philip. B.A., Tex. Tech U., 1965, J.D., 1975. Bar: Tex. 1975, U.S. Dist. Ct. (no. and we. dists.) Tex. 1976, U.S. Ct. Appeals (5th cir.) 1984, U.S. Supreme Ct. 1984. Assoc. Crenshaw Dupree & Milam, Lubbock, Tex., 1975-80, ptnr., 1980—; dir. Indian Maiden Cosmetics, Lubbock; mem. pattern jury charge and adminstrn. of justice coms. State Bar Tex., 1985—. Bd. dirs., pres. Lubbock County Legal Aid Soc., Tex., 1977-79; bd. dirs., chmn. Trinity Christian Schs., Lubbock, 1978-83, 85—; bd. dirs., pres. S.W. Lighthouse for Blind, Lubbock, 1978—. Served to capt. USAF, 1965-72. Decorated Silver Star, D.F.C. (3); Cross of Gallantry (Vietnam). Mem. Def. Research Inst., ABA, Tex. Bar Assn., Tex. Assn. Def. Counsel (v.p. 1983-85), Lubbock County Bar Assn. (pres. 1984-85), Phi Delta Phi. Home: 2301 60th St Lubbock TX 79412 Office: Crenshaw Dupree & Milam 1500 Broadway Lubbock TX 79401

JOHNSON, PIERRE MARC, former premier Quebec, lawyer, physician; b. Montreal, Que., Can., July 5, 1946; s. Daniel and Reine (Gagné) Johnson; m. Marie-Louise Parent, June 30, 1973; children: Marc Olivier, Marie-Claude. BA, Coll. Jean-Brebéuf, Montreal, 1967; LLB, Univ. de Montreal, 1970; MD, U. de Sherbrooke, 1975. Bar: Que. 1971. Minister labour and manpower Parliament, Que., 1977-80, minister consumer affairs, coops. and fin. instns., 1980-81, minister social affairs, 1981-84, minister justice, intergovtl. affairs, 1984-85; prime minister Province of Que., 1985; leader of official opposition Que. Nat. Assembly, 1985-87, mem. Anjou dist., 1976-87; vis. prof. Osgoode Hall Law Sch. York U., Toronto, Ont., Can., 1987—, Ctr. Research on Pub. Law U. Montreal, Montreal, Que., Can.; Mem. Nat. Assembly for Anjou, 1976; mem. Nat. Exec. Council P.Q., 1977-79; pres. Parti Québécois, 1985-87. Bd. dirs., mem. various coms. Oxfam Can. and Oxfam Que., 1969-76. Mem. Que. Bar, Que. Coll. Physicians and Surgeons. Roman Catholic. Office: 800 Pl Victoria, Tour de la Bourse, CP 204, Montreal, PQ Canada H4Z 1E3

JOHNSON, REX SUTHERLAND, architect; b. London, Aug. 24, 1928; s. Adam Sutherland and Grace (Elizabeth) J.; m. Betty Elsie Manning; children: Mark, Michael. Diploma of Architecture, Nor. Poly., London, 1957, FRIBA, 1968, FCIArb., 1970. Chartered architect. Architect Sir Thomas Bennett of T.P. Bennett & Son, London, 1946-61; jr. ptnr. Oliver Law & Ptnrs., London, 1961-63; ptnr. Ronald Ward & Ptnrs., London, 1963—; bd. dirs. Ronald Ward Internat., London. Architect numerous bldgs. in London and U.K. Chmn. Platt Conservative Soc., Kent., 1978; jr. warden Guild of Freeman City London, 1987. Served with Brit. Royal Navy, 1947-48. Fellow Royal Inst. Brit. Architects (assoc. 1958-68), Chartered Inst. Arbitators; mem. London C. of C. and Industry (council mem.). Conservative. Anglican. Clubs: City, Livery, Caledonian, United Wards of City of London (v.p.). Lodges: Royal Athelstan (past master), Worshipful Co. of Woolmen (ct. mem.), Rotary (past pres. Westminister Pimlico), Worshipful Ct. of Carmen. Home: Whitepines Longmill Ln, Crouch Near Sevenoaks, Kent HT15 8QB, England Office: Ronald Ward & Partners, 29 Chesham Pl Belgrave Sq, London SW1X 8HD, England

JOHNSON, RHONDA LOUISE SWIFT, high school counselor, small business consultant; b. Houston, July 21, 1952; d. Archie Swift and Dorothy Nell (Fitzpatrick) Johnson; m. Clarence Johnson. B.A., Tex. So. U., Houston, 1974, M.A., 1977. Cert. tchr., Tex. Tchr., Aldine Sch. Dist., Houston, 1974—, gifted and talented curriculum developer, 1982, sponsor Literary mag. Nimitz High Sch., 1980—, speech coach Carver High Sch., 1975. Vol., campaign to elect Rodney Ellis to City Council Houston, 1983; orientation coordinator Holman St. Baptist Ch., Houston, 1983—; vol. campaign to elect Anthony Hall for city Council Houston, 1983. Named Tchr. of Month, Aldine Sch. Dist., 1977. Mem. NEA, Tex. State Tchrs. Assn., Nat. Council Tchrs. English, Assn for Secondary Curriculum and Devel., Tex. Assn. for Sch. Counselors. Democrat. Clubs: Houston Urban League, Young Democrats. Office: Nimitz High Sch 2005 W Thorne St Houston TX 77073

JOHNSON, RICHARD ARLO, lawyer; b. Vermillion, S.D., July 8, 1952; s. Arlo Goodwin and Edna Marie (Styles) J.; m. Diane Marie Zephier, Aug. 18, 1972 (div. Jan. 1979); m. Sheryl Lavonne Mader, June 5, 1981; 1 stepson, Chadwick O. Wagner; 1 child, Sarah N. B.A., U.S.D., 1974, J.D., 1976. Bar: S.D. 1977, U.S. Dist. Ct. S.D. 1977. Ptnr. Pruitt, Matthews & Muilenberg, Sioux Falls, S.D., 1977—. Mem. Pub. Defender Adv. Bd., Sioux Falls, 1983—. Mem. Assn. Trial Lawyers Am., S.D. Trial Lawyers Assn., ABA, S.D. Bar Assn., Am. Orthopsychiatric Assn., Phi Delta Phi (pres. 1976-77). Democrat. Lutheran. Lodges: Masons, Shriners. Home: 409 E Lotta Sioux City SD 57105 Office: 141 N Main Ave Suite 801 Sioux Falls SD 57102

JOHNSON, RICHARD FRED, lawyer; b. Chgo., July 12, 1944; s. Sylvester Hiram and Naomi Ruth (Jackson) J.; m. Sheila Conley, June 26, 1970; children—Brendon, Bridget, Timothy, Laura. B.S., Miami U., Oxford, Ohio, 1966; J.D. cum laude, Northwestern U., 1969. Bar: Ill. 1969, U.S. Dist. Ct. (no. dist.) Ill. 1969, U.S. Ct. Appeals (7th cir.) 1977, U.S. Supreme Ct. 1978, U.S. Ct. Appeals (2d cir.) 1980. Law clk. U.S. Dist. Ct. (no. dist.) Ill., Chgo., 1969-70; assoc. firm Lord, Bissell & Brook, Chgo., 1970-77, ptnr., 1977—; lectr. legal edn. Contbr. articles to profl. jours. Recipient Am. Jurisprudence award, 1968. Mem. Chgo. Bar Assn., Ill. State Bar Assn. Club: Union League (Chgo.). Home: 521 W Roscoe St Chicago IL 60657 Office: Lord Bissell & Brook 115 S La Salle St Harris Bank Bldg Chicago IL 60603

JOHNSON, RICHARD TENNEY, lawyer; b. Evanston, Ill., Mar. 24, 1930; s. Ernest Levin and Margaret Abbott (Higgins) J., m. Marilyn Bliss Meuth, May 1, 1954; children: Ross Tenney, Lenore, Jocelyn. A.B. with high honors, U. Rochester, 1951; postgrad., Trinity Coll., Dublin, Ireland, 1954-55; LL.B., Harvard, 1958. Bar: D.C. 1959. Trainee Office Sec. Def., 1957-59; atty. Office Gen. Counsel. Dept. Def., 1959-63; dep. gen. counsel Dept. Army, 1963-67, Dept. Transp., 1967-70; gen. counsel CAB, 1970-73, NASA, 1973-75, ERDA, 1975-76; mem. CAB, 1976-77; chmn. organizational integration Dept. Energy Activation, Exec. Office of Pres., 1977; ptnr. firm Sullivan & Beauregard, 1978-81; gen. counsel Dept. Energy, 1981-83; ptnr. firm Zuckert, Scoutt, Rasenberger & Johnson, 1983-87, Law Offices of R. Tenney Johnson, Washington, 1987—. Served to lt. USNR, 1951-54. Mem. ABA, Fed. Bar Assn., Phi Beta Kappa, Theta Delta Chi. Office: 2300 N St NW Suite 600 Washington DC 20037

JOHNSON, ROBERT GERALD, consultant; b. Omaha, Mar. 13, 1928; s. Enoch and Helen Christine (Peterson) J.; m. Patsy Ruth Green, Feb. 24, 1950; children: Cynthia Marie, Cheryl Leigh, Christina Ruth. A.B., U. Colo., 1951; M.Sc., U. Omaha, 1953; Ed.D., Fla. State U., 1959. Pub. sch. tchr. Omaha, 1951-53; instr. Fla. State U., 1953-55, 57-59; supr. elem. and jr. high sch. Guam, 1955-57; edn. adviser AID, Bangkok, Thailand, 1959-63; dep. chief East South Africa edn. br. AID, Washington, 1963-65; chief East South Africa edn. br. AID, 1965-66, dep. chief edn. div., 1966-67, chief Africa edn. div., 1967-69; asst. dir. edn. AID, Thailand, 1969-72; assigned AID, Washington, 1972-75; chief human resources devel. AID, La Paz, Bolivia, 1975-77, Kingston, Jamaica, 1977-80; cons. AID, 1980—, U.S. Dept. State, 1980; cons. Checci and Co. Cons., Inc., 1984—, v.p., 1986—. Mem. bd. Internat. Sch., Bangkok, 1961-63. Served with AUS, 1946-48. Mem. Am. Fgn. Service Assn., Phi Delta Kappa. Club: Royal Bangkok Sports. Home: 7419 Park Terrace Dr Alexandria VA 22307

JOHNSON, RODNEY DALE, protective services official, photographer; b. Montebello, Calif., May 14, 1944; s. Albert Gottfreid and Maxine Elliot (Rogers) J.; m. Karen Rae Van Antwerp, May 18, 1968; 1 child, Tiffany Nicole. AA, Ela Community Coll., 1973; postgrad. Law Enforcement Spl., FBI, Acad., 1976; BA, U. of La Verne, 1978. Cert. tchr. police sci., Calif. Dep., Los Angeles County Sheriff, 1969-75, dep. IV, 1976-78, sgt., 1978—; fire arms inst., Hacienda Heights, Calif., 1975—; photography instr., Hacienda Heights, 1983—; pres. Wheelhouse Enterprises, Inc., Whittier, 1971-86; instr. State Sheriff's Civil Procedural Sch. Los Medanos Coll., Concord, Calif., 1985—. Creator and actor, Cap'n Andy, 1973-80; song writer for Cap'n Andy theme, 1972. Served as sgt. USMC, 1965-69, Vietnam, master sgt. Res. Recipient Service award Trinity Broadcasting Network, 1979. Mem. Profl. Peace Officers Assn., Sheriff's Relief Assn., Assoc. Photographers Internat. Republican. Mem. Assembly of God. Club: Faithbuilders (pres. 1981—), (Pomona).

JOHNSON, ROGER HARRY, ophthalmologist; b. Madison, Wis., Jan. 29, 1914; s. Harry John and Louise Augusta (Nissalk) J.; m. Elizabeth Louise Hill, July 27, 1940 (div.); children—Roger H., Trygve N., Casey. B.S., U. Wis., 1937, M.D., 1939. Intern U. Oreg., Portland, 1939-40; resident Mayo Clinic, U. Minn., Rochester, 1941-45; practice medicine specializing in ophthalmology, Seattle, 1945—; clin. prof. ophthalmology U. Wash. Contbr. articles to profl. jours. Recipient Roger Johnson annual lecture award Children's Orthopedic Hosp., Seattle, 1984. Fellow Am. Acad. Ophthalmology; mem. AMA, Pacific Coast Soc. Ophthalmology, King County Med. Soc., Interocular Lens Soc. Republican. Home: 4201 NE 33rd St Seattle WA 98101 Office: Doctors Office 414 Cobb Bldg Seattle WA 98101

JOHNSON, ROYAL M., civil service administrative officer, consultant; b. Spokane, Wash., May 31, 1944; s. Ward Willis and Juanita May (Whitmore) J.; m. Anne-Marie Marshall Seale, Feb. 4, 1965 (div. Sept. 1979); children: Veronica Anne, Chad Lewis, Dale Richard; m. Virginia Laverne Pelton, June 15, 1981; stepchildren: Cynthia Conner, David Conner, Debra Conner. AA, Ventura Community Coll., 1971; BA, LaVerne U., 1972; MA, Columbia Pacific U., 1986, postgrad., 1986—. Prodn. dispatcher Naval Missile Ctr., Pt. Mugu, Calif., 1969-71, adminstrv. asst., 1971-74, mgmt. analyst, 1974-75; adminstrv. officer Shasta Lake Ranger Dist., Redding, Calif., 1975-77; program mgr. Shasta-Trinity Nat. Forest, Redding, 1977-79; adminstrv. officer Tongass Nat. Forest, Ketchikan, Alaska, 1979—; Bd. dirs. Royal Assocs., Ketchikan; pres. Opportunity Cons., Anderson, Calif., 1976-79. Author: (pamphlet) Handbook for Redi-Reminder Service, 1970, The Complete, Realistic Self-Hypnosis Program, 1982, The Royal Trust, 1984, (audio cassette) The Outside Assistance Program, 1982. Served with U.S. Army, 1961-64, Korea. Home: PO Box 7158 Ketchikan AK 99901 Office: USDA Forest Service Fed Bldg Ketchikan AK 99901

JOHNSON, SAMUEL CURTIS, wax company executive; b. Racine, Wis., Mar. 2, 1928; s. Herbert Fisk and Gertrude (Brauner) J.; m. Imogene Powers, May 8, 1954; children: Samuel Curtis III, Helen Johnson-Leipold, Herbert Fisk III, Winifred Johnson Marquart. BA, Cornell U., 1950; MBA, Harvard U., 1952; LLD (hon.), Carthage Coll., 1974, Northland Coll., 1974, Ripon Coll., 1980, Carroll Coll., 1981, U. Surrey, 1985, Marquette U., 1986. With S.C. Johnson & Son, Inc., Racine, 1954—; internat. v.p. S.C. Johnson & Son, Inc., 1962-63, exec. v.p., 1963-66, pres., 1966-67, chmn., pres., chief exec. officer, 1967-72, chmn., chief exec. officer, 1972-79, chmn., 1979-80, chmn., chief exec. officer, 1980—; bd. dirs. H.J. Heinz Co., Pitts., Johnson Wax Cos., Eng., Japan, Germany, Switzerland, Can., Australia, France, Egypt, Mex., Deere & Co., Moline, Ill., Mobil Corp., N.Y.C.; chmn. bd. dirs. Johnson Heritage Bancorp, Ltd., Racine, Wis., Johnson Worldwide Assocs., Inc. Chmn. The Mayo Found., Johnson's Wax Fund, Inc., Johnson Found., Inc.; trustee emeritus Cornell U.; founding chmn. emeritus Prairie Sch., Racine; mem. adv. council Cornell U. Grad. Sch. Mgmt.; bd. regents Smithsonian Assn.; mem. Bus. Council. Mem. Chi Psi. Clubs: Cornell (N.Y.C., Milw.); Univ. (Milw.); Racine Country; Am. (London). Home: 4815 Lighthouse Dr Racine WI 53402 Office: S C Johnson & Son Inc 1525 Howe St Racine WI 53403

JOHNSON, SEARCY LEE, lawyer; b. Dallas, Aug. 30, 1908; s. Jesse Lee and Annie Clyde (Searcy) J.; m. Lillian Cox; 1 child, Susan Lee (Mrs. Keyes). A.B., Williams Coll., 1929; LL.B., U. Tex., 1933. Bar: Tex. 1933. Since practiced in Dallas; partner Lawther, Cramer, Perry & Johnson, 1941, then Johnson, Guthrie, White & Stanfield; now sole practic; Legal adv. Gen. Hershey (on vets. reemployment), 1944-45; spl. asst. to U.S. Atty. Gen., organizer, chief Veterans Affairs sect. Dept. Justice, 1945-47. Author: Feast of Tabernacles; Contbr. to: Hildebrand's Texas Corporations, 1942, also articles to legal jours.; Composer: others. The Ballad of the Thresher. Served as lt. comdr. USNR, 1941-45. Decorated Army Commendation award. Mem. Washington Bar Assn., Tex. Bar Assn., Dallas Bar Assn. (spl. prosecutor 1938), Am. Legion, Amvets (charter mem.), ASCAP, Am. Authors and Composers, S.A.R., Am. Judicature Soc., Fellows Tex. Bar, Psi Upsilon. Clubs: Dallas, Dallas Country. Home and Office: 3901 Gillon Ave Dallas TX 75205

JOHNSON, STEPHEN THOMAS, tool engineer; b. Washington, May 31, 1954; s. Glenn Elmer and Marie Veronica (Rando) J.; m. Joan Marie Wagner, Apr. 16, 1983. BMET with honors, Northeastern U., 1978. Draftsman Hollingsworth & Vose, East Walpole, Mass., 1973-74; tech. aide U.S. Army Natick Research and Devel. Command, Natick, Mass., 1975-78; tool designer Boeing Aircraft Co., Renton, Wash., 1978-81, lead propulsion engr., 1981; lead tool designer Sikorsky Aircraft, Stratford, Conn., 1981—. Patentee direct ohmnic heating device. Mem. Am. Soc. Metals, ASME. Home: 1004 Stratford Rd Stratford CT 06497

JOHNSON, THEODORE OLIVER, JR., musician, educator; b. Elkhart, Ind., Oct. 9, 1929; s. Theodore Oliver and Harriet Koehler (Herrold) J.; m. Carol Ann Jolliff, June 22, 1968; children: Karen, Nancy, Steven, David. MusB, U. Mich., 1951, MusM, 1952, DMus Arts, 1959. Mem. music-theory faculty, violinist in faculty string quartet Sch. Fine Arts, U. Kans., 1958-64; mem. music theory and lit. faculty Sch. Music Coll. Arts and Letters, Mich. State U., East Lansing, 1964—; prof. music Coll. Arts and Letters, Mich. State U., 1977—, chair music theory, 1984—. Violist and violinist, Beaumont String Quartet, 1964-80, concertmaster, Lansing Symphony Orch., 1967-69, prin. violist, Lansing Symphony Orch., 1982-86 , concertmaster, Grand Rapids Symphony Orch., 1972-73; dir. music, Bethel Baptist Ch., 1969-82; solo recitalist.; Composer motets; author: An Analytical Survey of the Fifteen Two-Part Inventions by J.S. Bach, 1982; An Analytical Survey of the Fifteen Sinfonias (Three-Part Inventions) by J.S. Bach, 1986. Served in U.S. Army, 1952-55, Korea, Japan. Recipient Stanley award U. Mich. Sch. Music, 1951; Fulbright scholar, Munich 1956-57; U. Mich. Rackham fellow, 1957-58. Mem. Phi Mu Alpha Sinfonia, Phi Kappa Phi, Pi Kappa Lambda, Phi Eta Sigma. Home: 651 Hillcrest Ave East Lansing MI 48823 Office: Mich State U Sch of Music East Lansing MI 48824

JOHNSON, THOMAS EDWARD, stockbroker; b. Statesboro, Ga., June 4, 1938; s. James Bryan and Eunice (Waters) J.; m. Barbara Cecelia Dieringer, Jan. 28, 1983. B.A., Vanderbilt U., 1960; LL.B., Yale U., 1963. Bar: N.Y. 1967. Atty., Simpson, Thacher & Bartlett, N.Y.C., 1966-69; with H.C. Wainwright & Co., N.Y.C., 1969-72, ptnr., 1973-76; dir., v.p. Wainwright Sec. Inc., N.Y.C., 1977-78; v.p. Merrill Lynch Internat., Paris, 1978-83, v.p., mgr., 1983-84, asst. mgr., 1984—; sr. v.p., exec. dir. Lehman Bros., Kuhn Loeb Internat., London, 1983. Served to 1st lt. U.S. Army, 1964-66. Republican. Clubs: Yale, Cercle de l'Union Interallié e. Home: 197 Bld St Germain, 75007 Paris France Office: Merrill Lynch SAF, 96 Ave d'Iena, 75116 Paris France

JOHNSON, THOMAS S., banker; b. Racine, Wis., Nov. 19, 1940; s. H. Norman and Jane Agnes (McAvoy) J.; m. Margaret Ann Werner, Apr. 18, 1970; children: Thomas Philip, Scott Michael, Margaret Ann. A.B. in Econs., Trinity Coll., 1962; M.B.A., Harvard U., 1964. Instr. Ateneo de Manila U. Grad. Bus. Sch., Philippines, 1964-66; spl. asst. to controller U.S. Dept. Def., Washington, 1966-69; with Chem. Bank, N.Y.C., 1969—, pres., dir., 1983—; dir. Pan Atlantic Re, Chem. Banking Corp., Tex. Commerce Bankshares; mem. adv. com. on internat. fin. markets N.Y. Fed. Reserve Bank. Chmn. bd. dirs. Union Theol. Sem.; bd. dirs. Montclair Art Mus. (N.J.), Phelps Stokes Fund, N.Y.C.; trustee Trinity Coll.; v.p., bd. dirs. Cancer Research Inst. Mem. Assn. Res. City Bankers, The Group of 30, Council Fgn. Relations, Bond Club N.Y., Econs. Club N.Y. Democrat. Roman Catholic. Clubs: Montclair Golf; Palm Beach Polo & Country; Harvard Bus.; River (N.Y.C.), The Links; Chgo. Office: Chem Bank 277 Park Ave New York NY 10172

JOHNSON, THOMAS STUART, lawyer; b. Rockford, Ill., May 21, 1942; s. Frederick C. and Pauline (Ross) J. BA, Rockford Coll. 1964; JD, Harvard U., 1967. Bar: Ill. 1967. Pres. Williams & McCarthy, Rockford, 1967—; bd. dirs. John S. Barnes Corp., Rockford, Odin Corp., Rockford. Contbr. articles to profl. jours. Chmn. bd. trustees Rockford Coll., 1986—; chmn. bd. dirs. Ill. Inst. Continuing Legal Edn., Chgo., 1984-86; trustee Emanuel Med. Ctr., Turlock, Cal., 1984-86, trustee Swedish Covenant Hosp., Chgo., 1984-86; treas. Lawyers Trust Fund of Ill., Chgo., 1984-86; chmn. bd. Svenson Charitable Found., 1985—; mem. bd. govs., mem. council Regent's Coll., London, 1985—; dir. benevolence bd. Covenant Ch. Am., Chgo., 1984-86; chmn. Regent's Found. for Internat. Edn., London. Served with U.S. Army, 1965-67. Fellow Am. Bar Found.; mem. ABA (ho. dels. 1982—, chmn. commn. on advt. 1984—), Ill. Bar Assn. (bd. govs. 1976-82), Am. Judicature Soc. (bd. dirs. 1986—). Republican. Clubs: Rockford Country, University, Rockford City. Home: 913 N Main St Rockford IL 61103

JOHNSON, TOD STUART, market research company executive; b. Mpls., June 6, 1944; s. David Z. and Helen R. (Connor) J.; m. Cindy Schwartz, Aug. 28, 1966; children—Scott, Stacey. B.S., Carnegie Mellon U., 1966, M.S.I.A., 1967. Vice pres. Market Sci. Assocs., Inc., Des Plaines, Ill., 1967-71; pres., chief exec. officer NPD Research, Inc., Port Washington, N.Y., 1971—, Home Testing Inst., Inc., Port Washington, N.Y., 1980—, OPOC Computing, Inc., Port Washington, N.Y., 1980—, NPD Group, Port Washington, N.Y., 1982—; chmn., dir. NPD/Nielsen, Inc.; bd. dirs. Advt. Research Found., N.Y.C., sec., 1988. Contbr. articles to profl. jours.; patentee in field. Trustee, Carnegie-Mellon U., Pitts., 1980—, chmn. trustee student affairs com., 1982-85; trustee Council for Arts in Westchester, 1987—; assoc. trustee North Shore U. Hosp., Manhasset, N.Y., 1984—. Mem. Young Pres. Orgn., Am. Mktg. Assn., Am. Assn. Pub. Opinion

Research. Republican. Jewish. Home: 10 Heathcote Rd Scarsdale NY 10583 Office: NPD Group 900 West Shore Rd Port Washington NY 11050

JOHNSON, WALLACE, retired army officer; b. Oklahoma City, Aug. 8, 1939; s. Carroll Wallace and Pauletta (Bibbs) J.; m. Lela Mae Johnson, Dec. 25, 1959; children: Wallace, Steven, Valerie Lynne, Sharon Denise. BS, U. Okla., 1961; MBA, Ala. A&M U., 1973. Commd. 2d lt. U.S. Army, 1961, advanced through grades to lt. col., 1978; exec. officer 101st Ordnance Bn., Heilbronn, W. Ger., 1976-78; surety insp. Office of Insp. Gen., Heidelberg, W. Ger., 1978-79; logistics instr. Command and Gen. Staff Coll., Ft. Leavenworth, Kans., 1979-84; chief materiel and logistics systems div. Army Missile and Munition Ctr. and Sch., 1984-85; sr. program analyst CAS, Inc., 1985-86; mgr. logistics integration Acustar, Inc. Mil.-Pub. Electronic Systems, 1986—; instr. U.S. Army service shcs. Decorated Combat Inf. Badge, Bronze Star, Army Commendation medal, Meritorious Service medal. Mem. Assn. U.S. Army, Am. Def. Preparedness Assn., Internat. Platform Assn., Nat. Space Club, Assn. Unmanned Vehicles. Democrat. Baptist. Club: Jaywalkers of Ft. Leavenworth (v.p. 1980-81). Lodge: Sertoma (pres. 1981-84). Home: 6500 Willow Springs Blvd Huntsville AL 35806 Office: Pentastar Electronic Inc Huntsville AL 35805

JOHNSON, WARREN RICHARD, aerospace company executive, retired marine corps officer; b. Stillwater, Minn., Sept. 25, 1928; s. Seymour Evan Richard and Ethel Christine (Hallen) J.; m. Violet L. Bergquist, June 11, 1950; children—Karen C., Warren R., Matthew E., Paul W. B.A., U. Minn., 1950; student, Indsl. Coll. Armed Forces, 1969-70; M.S.B.A., George Washington U., 1970. Commd. 2d lt. U.S. Marine Corps, 1950, advanced through grades to maj. gen., 1976; served as supply officer First Marine Div. Korea, 1952-53; exec. officer Supply Sch. Co. Camp Lejeune, N.C., 1954-57; served with 3d Marine Div. Okinawa, Japan, 1957-58; at Marine Corps Supply Ctr. Barstow, Calif., 1958-61; at Marine Corps. Hdqrs. 1961-64, marine aide to asst. sec. Navy for installations and logistics, 1965-67; supply officer 9th Marine Amphibious Brigade Vietnam, 1967-68; served at Marine Corps Supply Activity Phila., 1968-69; dir. supply ops. div., dir. tech. ops. div. and dep. chief of staff for ops. 1970-73; comdr. 2d Force Service Regt., Fleet Marine Force Atlantic, 1973-74; comdg. gen. Marine Corps Supply Ctr. Albany, Ga., 1974-76; asst. dep. chief of staff for installations and logistics Marine Corps. Hdqrs. Washington, 1976-77; dep. chief of staff 1977; comdg. gen. Marine Corps Logistics Base Albany, Ga., 1977-80; ret. U.S. Marine Corps, 1980; program dir. Fairchild Republic Co., Farmingdale, N.Y., 1980-87; tech. advisor Grumman Aerospace Corp., Beth Page, N.Y., 1987—; tech. adv. Grumman Aerospace Corp., Bethpage, N.Y., 1987—. Decorated Legion of Merit, Bronze Star. Mem. Marine Corps Assn., U.S. Naval Inst., Am. Def. Preparedness Assn. Lutheran. Home: Tulip Dr Rural Rt #1 Box 149A Huntington NY 11743 Office: Grumman Aerospace Corp Bethpage NY 11714

JOHNSON, WILLIAM CUMMING, JR., civic worker, former educator; b. Memphis, June 26, 1904; s. William Cumming and Evangeline (Harvey) J.; B.S., Princeton U., 1925; E.E., Rensselaer Poly. Inst., 1927; postgrad. in engring. Gen. Electric Co., 1927-30; m. Mayo Crew, Feb. 5, 1926; children—Kenn Harvey, Carel Crew, EveAnne. With Gen. Electric Co., Schenectady, 1927-33; asst. prof. Rensselaer Poly. Inst., 1933-39; asso. prof. Va. Poly. Inst., 1939-43; research and devel. Goodyear Aerospace Corp., Akron, Ohio, 1943-65; asst. prof. Kent State U., 1965-74; vol. Western Res. Hist. Soc., Cleve., 1970-81, trustee, 1982-86 ; registrar Ohio soc. Order Founders and Patriots Am., 1977-81. Mem. AIAA, Ohio Geneal. Soc. (v.p. 1974-80), Phi Beta Kappa, Sigma Xi. Quaker. Developed method for calculation stresses in helicopter rotor blades; patentee airship-enclosed radar. Home: 11687 Vaughn Rd Hiram OH 44234

JOHNSON, WILLIAM HERBERT, emergency medicine physician, aerospace physician, retired air national guard officer; b. Elkhart, Ind., Dec. 12, 1928; s. Herbert John and Lorene Wilhemena (Johnson) J.; m. Ann Marie Bacon, Oct. 17, 1964; children—Ernest Michael, Jennifer Lynn. A.B., Augustana Coll., 1951; M.D., Ind. U., 1958. Intern, Indpls. Gen. Hosp., 1958-59; resident in internal medicine Ind. U. Med. Ctr., Indpls., 1960-61; practice medicine specializing in gen. medicine, East Gary, Ind., 1959-60; asst. surgeon U.S. Steel Co., Gary Works (Ind.), 1959-60; ptnr. Gary Clinic (now Ross Clinic), 1962-69; staff physician student health services Western Mich. U., 1969-74; staff physician Trauma and Emergency Ctr., Bronson Methodist Hosp., Kalamazoo, Mich., 1969—, chmn., 1972-74; asst. clin. prof. medicine Mich. State U. Coll. Human Medicine, East Lansing, 1976-81; past mem. staffs Borgess Med. Ctr., Community Hosp. Assn., Leila Y. Post Montgomery Hosp., Three Rivers Hosp.; med. dir. emergency dept., mem. exec. bd. Elkhart (Ind.) Gen. Hosp., Goshen (Ind.) Gen. Hosp.; med. dir. Emergency Med. System, Elkhart County, Ind.; pres. Elkhart Emergency Physicians, Inc., Emergency Room Physicians, Inc. Pres. Corey Lake Improvement Assn., 1978-80. Served with USAF, 1951-53, 61-62; ret. brig. gen. Air N.G., 1961-85. Decorated Air N.G. Meritorious Service award, USAF Legion of Merit; nominee Malcolm C. Grove award USAF Flight Surgeon of Yr., 1971; recipient Minuteman award State of N.J. Fellow Aerospace Med. Assn. (by-laws com., membership com.); mem. Kalamazoo Acad. Medicine, Mich. Med. Soc., AMA Physician's Recognition award 1983), Am. Coll. Emergency Physicians (pres. Mich. chpt. 1976-78, dir.), Calhoun County Med. Soc., Univ. Assn. for Emergency Medicine, Soc. USAF Flight Surgeons (constn., by-laws com.), Alliance of Air N.G. Flight Surgeons (dir., mem. membership com., chmn. nominating com., past pres.), Assn. Mil. Surgeons U.S., Mich. Assn. of Professions, Res. Officers Assn., Air Force Assn., Augustana Coll. (Ill.) Alumni Bd. Lutheran. Lodge: Elks. Contbg. editor to books, articles to profl. jours.; contbg. editor, mem. editorial bd. Annals of Emergency Medicine, 1972—; mem. editorial bd. Aviation, Space and Environ. Medicine, 1981—, editor book rev. sect., 1984—. Home and Office: 11451 Coon Hollow Rd Three Rivers MI 49093

JOHNSON, WILLIAM K., health physicist, state official; b. St. Joseph, Mo., Feb. 6, 1934; s. Maxwell McCole and Kittie Ellen (Jackson) J.; m. Barbara Ann Terrell, June 23, 1980; stepchildren—Michael Terrell, Stephen M. Terrell. Student, S.W. Mo. State U., 1961-62, Mich. Tech. U., 1975-77, N.E. Mo. State U., 1982-83; B.S., Calif. Pacific U., 1983, Ph.D., 1985. Cert. Nat. Registry Radiation Protection Technologists. Supr. licensing Mo. Div. Ins., Jefferson City, 1969-73; supr. radiation systems Disaster Planning and Ops., Jefferson City, 1973-81; state radiol. def. officer State Emergency Mgmt. Agy., Jefferson City, 1981—; Radiation safety officer Mo. N.G., Jefferson City, 1977—; state coordinator Mo. Nuclear Emergency Team, Jefferson City, 1978—; cons. dir. Radiation Safety Cons., Jefferson City, 1982—. Author emergency procedure publs. Active United Way, Boy Scouts Am. Recipient Silver Beaver award Boy Scouts Am., 1972. Mem. Health Physics Soc. (pub. info. con.). Am. Assn. Physicists in Medicine, Am. Nuclear Soc., Mo. Acad. Scis., Radiol. Def. Officers Assn., Am. Legion. Lodges: Eagles; Masons; K.T. Home: 651 Belmont Dr Jefferson City MO 65109 Office: State Emergency Mgmt Agy Jefferson City MO 65102

JOHNSON, WILLIAM MICHAEL, physician; b. Olean, N.Y., Nov. 20, 1940; s. Loren Edward and Ann Elizabeth (Van Dyke) J.; m. Marlene Elsie Brill, June 26, 1965; children: Michael Scott, Susan Kim, Amy Marlene, Linda Marie. AB, Stanford U., 1963, MD, 1968; MPH, Harvard U., 1970, M in Indsl. Health, 1971. Diplomate Am. Bd. Internal Medicine, Am. Bd. Preventive Medicine. Intern, SUNY-Buffalo Hosps., 1968-69; resident in occupational medicine Harvard Sch. Public Health, Boston, 1969-71; acting dep. dir. div. field studies and clin. investigations Nat. Inst. Occupational Safety and Health Cin., 1971-73; resident in internal medicine U. Ariz. Hosps., Tucson, 1973-75, fellow in pulmonary disease, 1975-77; asst. prof. environ. health, adj. asst. prof. medicine U. Wash., Seattle, 1977-80; commd. lt. col. U.S. Army, 1980, advanced through grades to col., 1986; chief pulmonary disease service Dwight David Eisenhower Army Med. Center, Fort Gordon, Ga., 1983, staff, 1980-83; asst. clin. prof. medicine Med. Coll. Ga., Augusta, 1981-88, assoc. clin. prof. of medicine, 1988—. Contbr. articles on pulmonary disease and occupational cancer to profl. jours. Served as surgeon USPHS, 1971-73. Fellow Am. Coll. Chest Physicians; mem. Am. Thoracic Soc., Soc. Occupational and Environ. Health, N.Y. Acad. Scis. Home: 2948 Foxhall Circle Augusta GA 30907 Office: Dwight D Eisenhower Army Med Center Fort Gordon GA 30905

JOHNSON, WILLIAM POTTER, newspaper publisher; b. Peoria, Ill., May 4, 1935; s. William Zweigle and Helen Marr (Potter) J.; m. Pauline Ruth Rowe, May 18, 1968; children: Darragh Elizabeth, William Potter. AB, U. Mich., 1957. Gen. mgr. Bureau County Rep., Inc., Princeton, Ill., 1961-72; pres. Johnson Newspapers, Inc., Sebastopol, Calif., 1972-75, Evergreen, Colo., 1974-86, Canyon Commons Investment, Evergreen, 1974—; pres., chmn. bd. dirs. Johnson Media, Inc., Winter Park, Colo., 1987—. Alt. del. Rep. Nat. Conv., 1968. Served to lt. USNR, 1958-61. Mem. Colo. Press Assn., Nat. Newspaper Assn., Suburban Newspapers Am., San Francisco Press Club, Beta Theta Pi, Sigma Delta Chi. Roman Catholic. Clubs: Hiwan Country (Evergreen); Oro Valley Country (Tucson), Canada Hills Country; Grand Lake (Colo.) Tennis. Home: 445 W Rapa Pl Tucson AZ 85701 Office: PO Box 409 Winter Park CO 80482

JOHNSON, WILLIAM THOMAS, endodontics educator, endodontist; b. Des Moines, Apr. 11, 1949; s. Gaillard Xenton and Alvah (Monson) J.; m. Georgia Kay Tonn, Aug. 25, 1974. B.A., Drake U., 1971; D.D.S., U. Iowa, 1975, cert. endodontics, 1981, M.S., 1981. Diplomate Am. Bd. Endodontics. Resident U. Iowa, Iowa City, 1979-81, asst. prof., 1981-82; pvt. practice endodontics, Des Moines, 1982-83; asst. prof. endodontics U. Nebr., Lincoln, 1983—; interim chmn. Dept. Endodontics U. Neb. Coll. of Dentistry, 1988; pvt. practice dentistry, Cedar Rapids, Iowa, 1977-79. Contbr. articles to profl. jours. Served to capt. U.S. Army, 1975-77; to maj. Iowa N.G., 1977—. Mem. Am. Assn. Endodontists, ADA, Am. Assn. Dental Schs., Delta Sigma Delta. Lutheran. Avocation: photography. Home: 2831 S 74th St Lincoln NE 68506 Office: U Nebr Med Ctr Coll Dentistry 40th and Holdrege St Lincoln NE 68583

JOHNSON-CHAMP, DEBRA SUE, lawyer, educator; b. Emporia, Kans., Nov. 8, 1955; d. Bert John and S. Christine (Brigman) Johnson; m. Michael W. Champ, Nov. 23, 1979; children: Natalie, John. BA, U. Denver, 1977; JD, Pepperdine U., 1980; postgrad. in library sci. U. So. Calif., 1983—. Bar: Calif. 1981. Sole practice, Long Beach, Calif., 1981-82, Los Angeles, 1981-87; legal reference librarian, instr. Southwestern U. Sch. Law, Los Angeles, 1982-88; adj. prof. law, 1987-88; atty. Contos & Bunch, Woodland Hills, Calif., 1988—. Editor-in-chief: Southern Calif. Assn. Law Libraries Newsletter, 1984-85. Contbr. articles to profl. journs. Mem. law rev. Pepperdine U., 1978-80. West Pub. Co. scholar, 1983; trustee United Meth. Ch., Tujunga, Calif., 1986—. Recipient H. Wayne Gillis Moot Ct. award, 1980, Vincent S. Dalsimer Best Brief award, 1979. Mem. ABA, So. Calif. Assn. Law Libraries, Am. Assn. Law Libraries, Calif. Bar Assn., Southwestern Affiliates, Friends of the Library Los Angeles. Democrat. Home: 5740 Valerie Ave Woodland Hills CA 91367 Office: Contos & Bunch 5855 Topanga Canyon Blvd Suite 400 Woodland Hills CA 91367

JOHNSON-SNYDER, BRENDA FAYE, army officer; b. Fort Leavenworth, Kans., Jan. 13, 1953; d. Hugh Dorsey and Marguerite Elizabeth (Achilles) Johnson; children: Beth Louise, Barbra Marie; m. Lloyd Howard Snyder. Cert. in lang. and humanities Scripps Coll., Claremont, Calif., 1970; cert. in fine arts U.S. Internat. U., San Diego, 1972; AA in Liberal Arts, Fresno City Coll., Calif., 1973; BA in Psychology/Sociology, Calif. State U.-Fresno, 1975; MA in German, Antioch Internat. U., Yellow Springs, Ohio, 1986; postgrad. in linguistics Union Coll., Cin., 1986-87. Cert. educator, counselor, instr. U.S. Army. Commd. lt. U.S. Army, 1976; adjutant/test officer U.S. Army Armed Forces Entrance and Examining Sta., Mpls., 1978-80, promoted to capt., 1980, asst. area club mgr., U.S. Army Command, Grafenwoehr, Fed. Republic Germany, 1982-83, contbg. editor U.S. Army-Trojan, Fort Leavenworth, 1983, spl. edn. instr. U.S. Army-Acad. div., 1983-84, ops., quality control supr. U.S. Army-Vocat. Tng., 1984-85, behavioral sci. research analyst U.S. Army-Dept. Mental Health, 1985-86; fire inspector Fresno (Calif.) Fire Dept., 1986—; co-owner Spacemakers, Inc., 1988—. Lang. instr., cons. German-Am. relations, 1983-86. Author: Men in Power, 1986; co-author: The Trial, 1986; co-editor: (mag.) Stray Shots-Book of Poems, 1983. Cultural arts dir., phys. edn. dir. Mormon Ch., Mpls., 1978-79; mgr. tonemaster Calif., 1988—; campaign coordinator elections Fresno City Council, 1985; bd. dirs., sec. Burn Aware Bd. Decorated Army Commendation medal; Calif. Gov.'s scholar, 1969-75. Mem. Assn. U.S. Army, Nat. Assn. Female Execs., NOW, Jr. C. of C. (speech cons. 1983), Calif. Scholarship Fedn., Cen. Calif. Psychol. Assn., Summit Orgn., Fire Prevention Officers Assn., Mensa, Phi Beta Kappa, Phi Kappa Phi, Alpha Gamma Sigma, Phi Theta Kappa. Avocations: swimming, sailing, skating, dance, tennis.

JOHNSTON, BRUCE GILBERT, civil engineer; b. Detroit, Oct. 13, 1905; s. Sterling and Ida (Peake) J.; m. Ruth Elizabeth Barker, Aug. 5, 1939; children—Sterling, Carol Anne Snow, David. B.S. in Civil Engring. U. Ill., 1930; M.S., Lehigh U., Bethlehem, Pa., 1934; Ph.D. in Sci, Columbia U., 1938. Engaged in engring. constrn. Coolidge Dam, Ariz., 1927-29; with design office Roberts & Schaefer Co., Chgo., 1930; instr. civil engring. Columbia U., 1934-38; charge structural research Fritz Engring. Lab., Lehigh U., 1938-50, asst. dir. lab., 1938-47, dir., 1947-50, mem. univ. faculty, 1938-50, prof. civil engring., 1945-50; prof. structural engring. U. Mich., 1950-68, emeritus, 1968—; prof. civil engring. U. Ariz., Tucson, 1968-70; engr. Johns Hopkins Applied Physics Lab., Silver Spring, Md., 1942-45; chmn. Column Research Council, 1956-62. Author: Basic Steel Design, 3d edit, 1986, also tech. papers.; Editor: Column Research Council Design Guide, 3 edits, 1960-76. Recipient Alumni Honor award for disting. service in engring. U. Ill., 1981, Special Citation award Am. Inst. Steel Constrn., 1988. Hon. mem. ASCE (chmn. structural div. 1965-66, chmn. engring. mechanics div. 1961-62, J.J.R. Croes medal 1937, 54, Ernest E. Howard medal 1974, first Shortridge Hardesty award 1987); mem. Nat. Acad. Engring., Sigma Xi, Phi Kappa Phi, Tau Beta Pi, Chi Epsilon. Methodist. Address: 5025 E Calle Barril Tucson AZ 85718

JOHNSTON, CHRISTINA JANE, real estate executive, mortgage broker, educator; b. Toronto, Ont., Can., June 3, 1952; d. George Elmer and Mary Selina (Northey) J. B.A. with honors, U. Western Ont., London, 1975. Researcher, writer House of Commons, Ottawa, Ont., 1975-77; adminstrv. mgr. sales Marco Beach Realty, Marco Island, Fla., 1977-79; pres., owner Marco Summit Realty, Marco Island, 1979-82; v.p., mortgage broker Windjammer of Marco, Marco Island, 1979—; instr. Realty World Acad., St. Petersburg, Fla., 1979—; pres., mgr. Fla. Sun Realty Co., Sarasota, 1982-86; v.p., mgr. Fla. Home Properties & Comml. Realty, Inc., 1986-87; mgr. 1st So. Trust Realty Corp., 1987—; bd. dirs., chmn. edn. com. Sarasota Bd. Realtors, 1985-86, also mem. realtors polit. action com. 1985—; pres. So. Gulf Council Realty World, 1980-82; bd. dirs. First Fla. region Broker's Council, Realty World, 1982-84; pres. Women's Council of Realtors, Marco Island, 1988—; dir. Marco Island Bd. Realtors, 1987—. Contbr. articles to profl. jours. Pres. Young Progressive Conservatives, Cambridge, Ont., 1968-70; Recipient Office of Yr. award Realty World, 1980, Top Listing Office award, 1981, Spl. award for Prodn., 1981, Million Dollar Sales Awards Marco Beach and Realty World, 1979-81. Mem. Sarasota C. of C., Marco Island C. of C. (chmn. Expo '82). Home: 591 Yellowbird Dr Marco Island FL 33937

JOHNSTON, DENNIS ROY, facility management consultant, corporation interior design company executive; b. Wahoo, Nebr., June 29, 1937; s. Roy Alfred and Wilma Jean (Weidensall) J.; Student U. Nebr., 1955-56, 57-58, U. Colo., 1961-64; m. Dorothy McLay Carr, June 19, 1965; children—Kristin Anne, Ami Carr. City planner Denver Urban Renewal Authority, 1965-69; dir. graphics Haines, Lundberg & Waehler, N.Y.C., 1969-72; sr. v.p., sr. project mgr. LCP Assos., Inc., N.Y.C., 1972—. Mem. Adminstrv. Mgmt. Soc. (cert. of merit), Am. Mgmt. Assn., Fish and Game Assn. Chatham. Republican. Methodist. Home: 3 Sussex Ave Chatham NJ 07928 Office: LCP Assos Inc 25 Tudor City Pl New York NY 10017

JOHNSTON, EDWARD INGRAM, accountant; b. Antrim, U.K., May 27, 1930; s. Samuel William and Ismae Jane (Ingram) J. Sr. leaving cert., Portora Royal, 1946. Chartered acct. Trainee, Ulster Bank, Ltd., Belfast, 1947-54; exec. United Dominions Trust Ltd., Belfast, London, 1954-62; acct. S. B. Quin Knox & Co., Belfast, 1963-66; ptnr. Wright, Fitzsimons, Cameron, Accts., Belfast, 1966-80; chmn. United Dominions Trust (Carplant) Ltd., 1980—; dir. Securicor (Ulster) Ltd., Belfast, 1980—, Citron Estates (Belfast) Ltd., 1980—, U.D.T. Bank Ltd., 1985—; dir. T.S.B. Northern Ireland, PLC, 1986—. Fellow Inst. Chartered Accts. in Ireland.

JOHNSTON, FRANKLIN ELMO, construction executive; b. Manhattan, Kans., Nov. 7, 1944; s. Elmo F. and Florence R. (Nanninga) J.; B.S.E.E., Kans. State U., 1967; postgrad. Tex. A&M U., 1967-68, St. Marys U., 1968-71, U. Kans., 1971-72; m. Barbara L. Goss, Aug. 6, 1971; children—Jennifer Medora, Amanda Beth. Design engr. Robertson, Peters & Williams, Lawrence, Kans., 1971-72, Black & Veatch Cons. Engrs., Kansas City, Mo., 1972-73; mng. ptnr. Goss-Johnston Bldg. Co., Kerrville, Tex., 1973-83, owner, operator, 1983—; cons. elec. engr.; researcher solar energy. Served to capt., design engr., USAF, 1967-71. Recipient Career Builder award Butler Mfg. Co., 1975; Registered profl. engr., Tex., Kans. Methodist. Lodge: Rotary. Office: Goss Johnston Bldg Co PO Box 1562 Kerrville TX 78029-1562

JOHNSTON, GEORGE ELMER, real estate developer; b. Brockville, Ont., Can., Jan. 31, 1927; came to U.S., 1977; s. George Elmer and Jane (Drew) J.; m. Mary Selina Northey, Aug. 1, 1951; children: Christina, Patricia, Shelly, Teri. Grad., Brockville Collegiate High Sch., Ontario, Can. Lic. real estate agt., Fla. Pres., chief exec. officer Williams Shoe Ltd., 1949-65; v.p. J.A. Johnston Co., Ltd., Brockville, Ont., Can., 1951-65; pres., chief exec. officer Jarman Shoes, Cambridge, Ont., Can., 1953-65; chief exec. officer Genesco (Can) Ltd., Cambridge, 1965-67; pvt. practice real estate Cambridge, 1967-68; chmn., chief exec. officer Diversco Holdings Ltd., Cambridge, 1968-74; v.p. Ontario Trust Co., Toronto, Ont., Can., 1972-74; pres., chief exec. officer Windjammer Corp., Marco Island, Fla., 1977—; pres. Johnco Investments Inc., Marco Island, 1977—. Chmn. fund raising campaign Peel Meml. Hosp., 1954-56; bd. dirs. Waterloo Cancer Soc., Ont., 1966-67; chmn. Plebisite Com., Galt., Ont., 1966-67; campaign dir. then chmn. Prog. Conservatives of Ont., Waterloo County, 1968-74; campaign chmn. providence of Ont. Prog. Conservatives of Can. Served with Royal Can. Naval Res., 1944-45. Distinctive Merit award Graphics Club of Can., 1969, Merit award Premier of Ont., 1972, Special Sales award Marco Beach Realty, Inc. 1978, Comml. Salesman of Yr. Marco Beach Realty, 1979. Mem. Marco Island Area Bd. Realtors, Fla. Assn. of Realtors, Nat. Assn. Realtors. Anglican. Clubs: International (assoc.). Home: PO Box 806 Marco Island FL 33969

JOHNSTON, JOHN BENNETT, JR., U.S. senator; b. Shreveport, La., June 10, 1932; m. Mary Gunn, 1956; children: Bennett, Hunter, Mary, Sally. Student, Washington and Lee U., U.S. Mil. Acad.; LL.B., La. State U., 1956. Bar: La. 1956. Formerly mem. firm Johnston, Johnston & Thornton; mem. U.S. Senate from La., 1972—, mem. spl. com. on aging; chmn. Dem. senatorial campaign com., 1975-76; chmn. La. Ho. of Reps., 1964-68, mem. appropriations com., chmn. subcom. energy and water devel., chmn. com. on energy and natural resources, mem. budget com. Served with U.S. Army, 1956-59. Mem. ABA, La. Bar Assn., Shreveport Bar Assn. Democrat. Address: Office of the Senate 136 Hart Senate Bldg Washington DC 20510

JOHNSTON, JOHN WAYNE, educational administrator; b. McAlester, Okla., Oct. 8, 1943; s. Cecil Wayne and Hazel Elena (Robinson) J.; m. Lynda Faith Gee, Feb. 4, 1971 (div.); 1 son, Ian Sean. Student Graceland Coll., 1961-62, William Jewell Coll., 1962-63; B.S. in Journalism, Kans. U., 1964; M.A. in Edn. and Sociology, U. Mo.-Kansas City, 1966; M.A. in Polit. Sci., History and Econs., Goddard Coll., 1972; Ph.D. (hon.), Calif. Western U., 1975; Ph.D. in Social Psychology, Internat. U., 1975. Instr. Central Mo. State U., Independence, 1969-72; founder, chancellor The Internat. U., Independence, 1973—; Editor: Internat. U. Press, 1973—. Bd. dirs. Good Govt. League, Independence, Com. for County Progress, Jackson County, Mo.; asst. varsity soccer coach Ft. Osage High Sch., 1983-87. Republican. Mem. Reorganized Church of Jesus Christ of Latter Day Saints (ordained minister). Lodge: Lions (Independence). Author: Divided for Plunder, 1984; Turmoil in the North, 1984, Crisis in Northern Ireland, 1985, The University of the Future, 1985.

JOHNSTON, JOSEPHINE R., chemist; b. Cranston, R.I., Aug. 9, 1926; d. Robert and Rose (Varca) Forte; student Carnegie Inst., 1945-47; B.S., Mich. State U., 1972, M.A., 1973; postgrad. Mass. Inst. Tech., 1973—m. Howard Robert Johnston, Mar. 7, 1949; 1 son, Kevin Howard. Med. technologist South Nassau Community Hosp., Rockville Centre, N.Y., 1947-50, Mich. State U., East Lansing, 1950-53, dept. pathology Albany (N.Y.) Med. Center, 1953-54; med. lab. supr. Bulova Watch Co., Jackson Heights, N.Y., 1954-57; sr. chemistry technologist Mid Island Hosp., Bethpage, N.Y., 1958-66; faculty specialist Mich. State U., East Lansing, 1966-76; sr. research asso. Uniformed Services Univ., Bethesda, Md., 1976-78, asst. to chmn. dept. physiology, 1978-82, asso. to chmn., 1982—. Mem. Analytical Chem. Soc., Data and Electronic Soc., Internat. Platform Assn. Lutheran. Contbr. articles in field to profl. jours. Office: 4301 Jones Bridge Rd Bethesda MD 20014

JOHNSTON, ROBERT ALAN, banker; b. Melbourne, July 19, 1924; m. Verna Mullin, 1948; 4 children. B.Comm., U. Melbourne. With Commonwealth Bank of Australia, 1940-60; with Res. Bank of Australia, Sydney. 1960—, dep. mgr., then mgr. investment dept., 1964-70, chief mgr. internat. dept., 1970-76, adviser, 1973-82, chief rep., London, 1976-77; exec. dir. World Bank Group, Washington, 1977-79; sec. Reserve Bank of Australia, 1980-82, gov., chmn. 1982—. Served with RAAF, 1943-46. Office: Reserve Bank of Australia, 65 Martin Pl GPO Box 3947, Sydney NSW 2001, Australia

JOHNSTON, ROBERT JAMES, marine engineer; b. Cheboygan, Mich., Apr. 25, 1918; s. Clyde Dolphin and Ruby (Bennett) J.; m. Marcia McColly Timbrook, July 24, 1976; children—Robert James II, John David. B.S. in Mech. Engring., Purdue U., 1940; M.S. in Naval Architecture and Marine Engring., MIT, 1948. Research engr. Indpls. Power and Light Co., 1940-42; pres. Miami (Fla.) Shipbldg. Corp., 1954-60; dir. marine programs Grumman Corp., 1960-72; mgr. hydrofoil tech. David Taylor Naval Research and Devel. Center, Bethesda, Md., 1972-82; pres. Advanced Marine Systems Assocs., Inc., 1982—. Served to capt. USN, 1942-54. Mem. Internat. Hydrofoil Soc. (pres. N.Am. sect. 1979, internat. pres. 1985-87), Soc. Naval Architects and Marine Engrs., Am. Soc. Naval Engrs., Sigma Xi. Clubs: Pelican Bay Country (Daytona, Fla.). Author papers in field; lectr. in field. Home and Office: 199 Surf Scooter Dr Daytona Beach FL 32019

JOHNSTON, RUTH LE ROY, nosologist, med. record adminstr.; b. Elizabeth, N.J.; d. James Archibald and Frances Ione Davis (Austin) Le Roy; BA, Bob Jones U., Greenville, S.C., 1945; postgrad. in medicine Emory U.; m. Earl Benton Johnston, Aug. 19, 1944 (dec.); 1 son, Jonathan Bruce (dec.). Various hosp. positions Atlanta, Asheville, N.C., 1948-55; chief med. record librarian VA Hosp., Richmond, Va., 1955-60, Wood, Wis., 1960, Hines, Ill., 1960-62; supervisory med. classification specialist, nosologist research and stats. Social Security Adminstrn., HEW, Balt., 1962-68; med. record cons. health data service Md. Blue Cross-Blue Shield, Balt., 1970-71; chief med. record adminstr. Good Samaritan Hosp., West Palm Beach, Fla., 1971-74; med. record adminstr. Gorgas Hosp., U.S. C.Z., Panama, 1974-77; library asst. North Palm Beach Public Library, 1978-80; lectr. in field, cons. Mem. Save the Panama Canal Club; 1st vice-chmn. bd. dirs. Paradise Harbour Condominium, 1973; charter mem. Republican Presdl. Task Force. Registered med. record adminstr., nosologist, Fla. Recipient VA and civil service awards, 1960-68. Mem. Va. (treas. 1957-58, pres. 1960), Md. (v.p. 1963), Fla., Am. med. record assns., Internat. Platform Assn., Audubon Soc., Nat. Assn. Fed. Ret. Employees, Am. Assn. Ret. Persons. Home: 100 Paradise Harbor Blvd North Palm Beach FL 33408

JOHNSTON, THOMAS, trust company executive; b. Coatbridge, Lanarkshire, Scotland, Nov. 20, 1946; arrived in The Bahamas, 1971; s. Walter and Agnes Wright Reid (Richardson) J.; m. Hollie Marie Moss, Apr. 21, 1977; children: Paul Walter, Claire Gail, Anne Marie Shannon. Degree in Chartered Acctg., The Inst. of Chartered Accts. of Scotland, Edinburgh, 1970. Chartered acct. Audit sr. Coopers & Lybrand, Nassau, The Bahamas, 1971-74; audit supr. Coopers & Lybrand, Glasgow, Scotland, 1974-75; internal auditor Roywest Trust Corp. (Bahamas) Ltd., Nassau, 1975-78, asst. to gen. mgr., 1978-81; mgr. fin. and adminstrn. Roywest Trust Corp. (Cayman) Ltd., Grand Cayman, 1981-84; controller Roywest Trust Corp. (Bahamas) Ltd., Nassau, 1984-86, treas., 1986—. Presbyterian. Home: Winton Meadows, PO Box N 8918, Nassau The Bahamas Office: Natwest Internat Trust Corp Ltd, PO Box N7788, Nassau The Bahamas

JOHNSTONE, C. BRUCE, investment company executive; b. N.Y.C., Nov. 7, 1940; s. R. Adam and Muriel S. (Smith) J.; m. Helen Louise Lott, Aug. 27, 1963; children—Brent Paul, Reed Evan. A.B. cum laude, Harvard U.,

1962, M.B.A., 1966. Chartered fin. analyst. Vice pres., portfolio mgr. Fidelity Equity Income Fund, Boston, 1972—; portfolio group leader income and growth funds Fidelity Investments,Boston, 1981—, sr. v.p., 1984—; sr. v.p., dir. Fidelity Mgmt. Trust Co., Boston, 1982—; mng. dir. Fidelity Investments, Boston, 1983—. Chmn. Needham Bikeways Com., Mass., 1976-80; soccer and baseball coach Needham Little League, 1979—; class endowment agt. Harvard Coll., 1980—, com. on Harvard U. Resources, 1987—; sect. sec. Harvard U. Bus. Sch., 1971—, class sec., 1986—; pres. elem. sch. PTA, Needham, 1980-82. Served to lt. USNR, 1962-68. Mem. Chartered Fin. Analysts, Boston Security Analysts Soc., Fin. Analysts Fedn., Harvard U. Bus. Sch. Assn. (alumni council mem. 1988—), Harvard Alumni Assn. (dir. 1988—, mem. resources com., 1987—). Clubs: Wellesley Country (Mass.); Harvard Varsity (Cambridge, Mass.); Harvard of Boston (scholarship com.). Home: 827 Charles River St Needham MA 02192 Office: Fidelity Investments 82 Devonshire St Boston MA 02109

JOHNSTONE, CHAUNCEY OLCOTT, pharmaceutical company executive; b. N.Y.C., Sept. 11, 1943; s. Edmund F. and Janet (Olcott) J.; B.A., Jacksonville U., 1965; m. Patricia E. Porter, May 30, 1971; children—Carolyn Ann, Jessica Olcott. Fin. analyst Dun & Bradstreet, Inc., Jacksonville, Fla., 1965-68; co-founder, v.p. Trinity Industries, Inc., Mount Kisco, N.Y., 1968-77; product mgr. Beiersdorf, Inc., Norwalk, Conn., 1978-81, mktg. mgr., from 1982, v.p. and mem. mgmt. bd., 1984-88, sr. v.p., mem. mgmt. bd. 1988—. Bd. dirs. Wilton (Conn.) chpt. ARC, 1976-81; charter mem. Wilton Vol. Ambulance Corps, 1976—; corp. mem. Dublin Sch., N.H., 1986—. Club: Wilton Riding (Conn.). Home: 19 Hillbrook Rd Wilton CT 06897 Office: Beiersdorf Inc BDF Plaza PO Box 5529 Norwalk CT 06856

JOHNSTONE, L(ARRY) CRAIG, diplomat; b. Seattle, Sept. 1, 1942; s. Jack Robert Johnstone and Evelyn (Ecker) Steger; m. Janet G. Buechel, Aug. 14, 1976; children—Alexa, Christopher, Meredith. B.A., U. Md., 1964, postgrad., 1965; postgrad., Harvard U., 1970-71. Joined fgn. service Dept. State, 1967; intern Inst. Internat. Edn., Vietnam, 1965; dist. sr. adviser U.S. Mil. Assistance Command, Vietnam, 1966-67; dir. for evaluations U.S. Mil. Assistance Command, Saigon, Vietnam, 1968-70; fellow Council Fgn. Relations, N.Y.C., 1970; polit.-mil. officer Am. embassy, Ottawa, Ont., Can., 1972-73; dep. dir. secretariat staff Dept. State, Washington, 1974-75, program officer Sinai support mission, 1975; chief econ. sect. Am. embassy, Kingston, Jamaica, 1976-77; Asian affairs officer Am. embassy, Paris, 1978-79, polit.-mil. officer, 1980-81; dir. for Central Am. Dept. State, Washington, 1981-83; dep. asst. sec. Bur. Inter-Am. Affairs, Dept. State, Washington, 1983-85; U.S. ambassador to Algeria Algiers, 1985—. Recipient Arthur Fleming award Am. Jr. C. of C., 1969, Superior Honor award Dept. State, 1983, 84; Inst. Politics fellow Harvard U., Cambridge, Mass., 1971. Mem. Am. Fgn. Service Assn. (William R. Rivkin award 1975). Episcopalian. Home and Office: US Ambassador to Algeria Dept State Washington DC 20520 *

JOHNSTON-THOMAS, PAMELLA DELORES, physician; b. Westmoreland, Jamaica, W.I., May 11, 1947; came to U.S., 1976; d. Wellesley and Hyacinth Ida (Muir) Johnston; m. Earl Alfonso Thomas, Apr. 9, 1977; children—Ramogi Odhiamo, Monifa Jamila. M.D., U. W.I., 1974. Intern, Brookdale Hosp., Bklyn., 1976-77; resident in Surgery Cath. Med. Centre, Queens, N.Y., 1978-79; attending physician N.Y.C. Transit, N.Y.C., 1983-86; asst. med. dir. 1986—. attending physician Brookdale Hosp., Bklyn., 1979-83. Mem. Am. Occupational Med. Assn., N.Y. Occupational Med. Assn., Am. Pub. Health Assn., N.Y. Pub. Health Assn.

JOICEY-CECIL, JAMES DAVID EDWARD, stockbroker; b. Sevenoaks, Kent, Eng., Sept. 24, 1946; s. Edward Wilfrid George and Rosemary Lusia (Bowes-Lyon) Joicey-Cecil; m. Jane Susanna Brydon Adeley, Apr. 5, 1975; children—Katherine Mary, Susanna Maud. Student Eton Coll., 1959-65. Chartered acct. Whinney Murray & Co., London, 1965-72; ptnr., stockbroker James Capel & Co., London, 1972—. Fellow Inst. Chartered Accts. in Eng. and Wales; mem. London Stock Exchange. Clubs: Annabels (Berkeley Square); City. Home: 49 Clapham Common South Side, London SW4 9BX, England Office: James Capel & Co, James Capel House, 6 Bevis Marks, London EC3A 7JQ, England

JOLLES, GEORGES EDGAR RENÉ, scientist; b. Vienna, Austria, Apr. 10, 1929; s. Henri and Marguerite (Weinber) J.; m. Bernadette Bergeret, July 4, 1959; children: Charles, Francoise, Brigitte. Lic. es Scis., Ecole Superieure de Chimie, Lyons, France, 1950; PhD, U. Paris, 1953; postgrad. U. Louvain, 1953-54, U. Wis., 1954-55. Research assoc. Rhone-Poulenc Group, Paris, 1956-70, dir. pharm. research, 1970-76, research dir. health div., 1976-82, sci. dir., 1982—; mem. French Nat. Research Council, 1970-80. Author: Histochimie Normale et Pathologique, 1969, Drug Design, Fact or Fantasy?, 1984, Immunostimulants, Now and Tomorrow, 1986; contbr. articles to profl. jours.; patentee in field. Recipient Galien award Medecine Mondiale, 1973; named Knight of French Nat. Order Merit. Mem. Am. Chem. Soc., Internat. Soc. Chemotherapy, Soc. Chimique de France, Societe de Chimie Biologique, N.Y. Acad. Scis. Roman Catholic. Home: 1 Allée des Pins, 92330 Sceaux France Office: 20 Ave Raymond Aron, 92165 Antony France

JOLLES, PAUL RODOLPHE, food corporation executive; b. Berne, Switzerland, Dec. 25, 1919; s. Leo and Ida (Hegnauer) J.; m. Erna Ryffel, May 28, 1956; children: Alexander, Claudia, Adrian. BA, U. Lausanne, U. Berne, 1941; MA, Harvard U., 1942, PhD, 1945; D. Econs. (hon.), U. Berne, 1972. Diplomat, Swiss embassy, Washington, 1943-49; civil servant Swiss Fgn. Office, Berne, Swiss Ministry Econs., 1949-56; exec. sec., dep. dir. gen. IAEA, UN, N.Y.C., Vienna, Austria, 1957-61; ambassador, del. for trade negotiations Swiss Govt., Berne, 1961-66; state sec. Fed. Office Fgn. Econ. Affairs, Berne, 1966-84; chmn. bd. Nestle S.A., Vevey, Switzerland, 1984—; hon. prof. fgn. econ. policy U. Berne, 1985-87. Author: Von der Handelspolitik zur Aussenwirtschaftspolitik, 1983. Contbr. numerous articles to Swiss, fgn. jours. Recipient Freedom prize Schmidheiny Found., St. Gallen, Switzerland, 1984; John Harvard fellow 1942. Mem. Conf. Bd., 1985—; chmn. bd. trustees Art Inst. Berne, 1975-86; bd. dirs. Kustmuseum Berne; trustee Mus. Contemporary Art, Basle. Avocation: contemporary art. Office: Nestle SA, Ave Nestle, 1800 Vevey Switzerland

JOLLIFF, ROBERT ALLEN, corporate executive; b. Wooster, Ohio, Sept. 12, 1943; s. Samuel Martin and Ethel May (Eschliman) J.; m. Marcella Joanne BAttig, AUg. 31, 1968; children: John Douglas, Laura Joanne. BS, Kent State U., 1965; MBA, U. Akron, 1974. Asst. cash mgr. B.F. Goodrich, Akron, Ohio, 1968-73; cash mgr. Aladdin Industries, Nashville, 1973-74; cash mgr. McDermott Inc., New Orleans, 1974-78, treas., 1978—. Trustee Blood Ctr. SE La., New Orleans, 1986—. Served to 1st lt., U.S. Army, 1966-68. Mem. Nat. Assn. Corp. Treas., Winchester Arms Collectors Assn. Republican. Methodist. Lodge: Masons. Office: McDermott Inc 1010 Common St New Orleans LA 70112

JOLLY, CHARLES NELSON, pharmaceutical company executive, lawyer; b. New Brunswick, N.J., Aug. 14, 1942; s. Nelson Frederick and Marie Mercedes (Montemayor) J.; m. Katherine Bonita Phelan, June 4, 1966; children—T. Christopher, Susan Noel. B.S., Holy Cross Coll., 1964; LL.B., George Washington U., 1967. Bar: D.C. 1968, Tenn. 1984. Atty. Swift & Co., 1966-70; atty. Miles Labs., 1970-71, dir. legis. affairs, Washington, 1971-75, assoc. gen. counsel, Elkhart, Ind., 1975-77; bd. dirs., v.p. legal affairs Chattem Inc., Chattanooga. Mem. ABA, Tenn. and D.C. Bar Assns., Proprietary Assn. (dir.), Better Bus. Bur. of Chattanooga (vice chmn., bd. dirs.). Clubs: The Narrows (McConnelsburg, Pa.), Chattanooga Retriever (dir.). Office: 1715 W 38th St Chattanooga TN 37409

JOLLY, DANIEL EHS, dentist; b. St. Louis, Aug. 25, 1952; s. Melvin Joseph and Betty Ehs (Koehler) J.; m. Paula Kay Haas, Oct. 13, 1972 (div. Mar. 1988); 1 child, Farrell Elisabeth Ehs; m. Barbara Lee Lindahl, May 7, 1988. BA in Biology and Chemistry, U. Mo., Kansas City, 1974, DDS, 1977. Resident VA Med. Ctr., Leavenworth, Kans., 1977-78; gen. practice dentistry sect. Newcastle, Wyo., 1978-79; asst. prof. U. Mo., Kansas City, 1979-87; chief restorative dentistry Truman Med. Ctr., Kansas City, 1979-87; dir. dental oncology Trinity Luth. Hosp., 1982-87; clin. assoc. prof., dir. gen. practice residency program Ohio State U. Coll. Dentistry, Columbus, 1987—; bd. dirs. Rinehart Found., U. Mo. Dental Sch., Kansas City, 1985-87; cons. Lee's Summit (Mo.) Care Ctr., 1984-87, Longview Nursing Ctr., Grandview, Mo. 1986-87. Author: (manual) Hospital Dental Hygiene, 1984, Hospital Dentistry, 1985; (booklet) Nursing Home Dentistry, 1986, Dental Oncology, 1986. Mem. regional council Easter Seal Soc., Kansas City, 1985-87, profl. adv. council Nat. Easter Seal Soc., 1986—; bd. dirs. Easter Seal Rehab. Ctr., Columbus, 1988—. Fellow Acad. Dentistry Internat., Am. Soc. Dentistry for Children, Am. Assn. Hosp. Dentists (com. residency edn.), Acad. Gen. Dentistry (spokesperson on dentistry for handicapped, sec. 1987-88, v.p. 1988—); mem. Internat. Assn. Dentistry for Handicapped., ADA (alternate del. 1985-86), Am. Soc. Geriatric Dentistry, Mo. Dental Assn., (chmn. spl. care dentistry com. 1983-87, del. 1984-87), Greater Kansas City Dental Soc. (chmn. spl patient com., mem. constn. and by-laws com., pub. relations com.), Acad. Dentistry for the Handicapped (bd. dirs. 1984—, mem. research com.), SAR, Omicron Kappa Upsilon. Club: Magna Charta Barons. Home: 3429 Riverside Green Dublin OH 43017 Office: Ohio State U Coll Dentistry 305 W 12th Ave Columbus OH 43210

JOLLY, WAYNE TRAVIS, geologist, educator; b. Jacksonville, Tex., Aug. 15, 1940; s. Edward B. and Alfreda J. (Sharp) J. B.F.A., U. Tex., 1963; M.A., SUNY, Binghamton, 1967, Ph.D. (univ. fellow), 1970. Postdoctoral fellow U. Sask., Saskatoon, 1970-71; prof. geology Brock U., St. Catherines, Ont., Can., 1971—; chmn. dept. Brock U., 1980-84; vis. scientist Commonwealth Sci. and Indsl. Research Orgn., Perth, Australia, 1978; vis. prof. U. Western Ont., 1976. Recipient Acad. Excellence award and Tchr. of Yr. award Brock U. Alumni Assn., 1981 NRC Can. grantee, 1971—. Mem. Geol. Soc. Am., Am. Geophys. Union, Geol. Assn. Can. Office: Dept Geol Science, Brock U, Saint Catharines, ON Canada

JONAS, PETER, opera company executive; b. London, Oct. 14, 1946; s. Walter Adolf and Hilda May J. BA with honors, U. Sussex, England, 1968; lt. Royal Acad. Music, Royal No. Coll Music, England, 1971; student, Royal Coll. Mus., London, 1971-73, Eastman Sch. Music, Rochester, N.Y., 1973-74. Asst. to music dir., artistic adminstr. Chgo. Symphony Orch., 1974-76; dir. artistic adminstrn. Orchestral Assn. Chgo., Chgo. Symphony Orch., Chgo. Civic Orch., Chgo., 1977-85; mng. dir. English Nat. Opera, London, 1985—; bd. mgmt. Nat. Opera Studio, London, 1985—; mem. council Royal Coll. Music, 1988—. Club: Athenaeum (Pall Mall). Home: 18 Lonsdale Pl, Barnsbury St, London N1 1EL, England Office: English Nat Opera, London Coliseum, Saint Martins Lane, London WC2N 4ES, England

JONASSEN, GAYLORD D., product development engineer, management consultant; b. East Orange, N.J., Oct. 13, 1932; s. Jonas M. and Alma M. (Stelter) J.; B.S. in M.E., Ariz. State U., 1960; m. Shirley Ann Christophel, June 15, 1956; children—Glenn, Brenda, Devel. engr. Motorola Semiconductor, Phoenix, 1956-60; plant and facilities research and devel. engr. Western Electric, N.Y.C., 1960-65; new products mgr. Deutsch Relays, Long Island, N.Y., 1965-67; new product mktg./sales mgr. Kinemotive Corp., Farmingdale, N.Y., 1967-69; div. mgr. Atlantic Sci. Corp., Plainview, N.Y., 1969-70; exec. v.p., tech. dir. Telecommunications Industries, Inc., Copaigue, N.Y., 1970-73; founder, pres., Internat. Protein Industries, Inc., Hauppauge, 1973-84, chmn. bd., 1973-84; mgmt. cons. Gaylord Jonassen Assocs., 1984-85; systems engring. project mgr. Norden Systems, 1985—. Served with U.S. Navy, 1950-54. Recipient Disting. Achievement award, Coll. Engring. and Applied Sci., Ariz. State U., 1982; ASTM fellow, 1958. Mem. L.I. Assn. Commerce and Industry. Baptist (deacon). Patentee in field. Contbr. articles to various publs. Home: 9 Wood Ln Smithtown NY 11787 Office: 75 Maxess Rd Melville NY 11747

JONATANSSON, ELIAS, industrial engineer; b. Bolungarvik, Iceland, Nov. 16, 1959; s. Jonatan Einarsson and Halla P. Kristjandottir; m. Kristin Gudrun Gunnarsdotti; 1 child, Gunnar Mar. BS in Mech. Engring., U. Iceland, 1983; MS in Indsl. Engring., Oreg. State U., 1986. Engr. VST Cons. Engrs., Reykjavik, Iceland, 1985-88; mgr. project Pols Electronics Ltd., Isafjordur, Iceland, 1988—. Home: Skolastigur 19, 415 Bolungarvik Iceland Office: Pols Electronics Ltd, Sindragata 10, 400 Isafjordur Iceland

JÓNATANSSON, HALLDÓR, utility company executive; b. Reykjavik, Iceland, Jan. 21, 1932; s. Jónatan Hallvarõsson and Sigurrós Gisladóttir; m. Gudrún Dagbjartsdóttir, May 3, 1958; children: Dagny, Rósa, Jórunn, Steinunn. JD, U. Iceland, Reykjavik, 1956; MA, Fletcher Sch. Law and Diplomacy, Medford, Mass., 1957. Sec. Ministry of Justice, Reykjavik, 1957; div. chief Ministry of Commerce, Reykjavik, 1957 65; office mgr. Landsvirkjun, Reykjavik, 1965-71, dep. gen. mgr., 1971-83, gen. mgr., 1983—. Recipient Knights Cross Order the Falcon, Pres. Iceland, 1970; Order Merit Grand Duke of Luxembourg, 1986. Mem. Assn. Icelandic Electric Utilities (dep. chmn.), NORDEL (leading people active in electric energy in Nordic countries) (bd. dirs.). Home: Thinghólsbraut 46, 200 Kópavogur Iceland Office: Landsvirkjun, Nat Power Co, Háaleitisbraut 68, 103 Reykjavik Iceland

JONES, ALAN, university administrator; b. Liverpool, Eng., Dec. 27, 1935; s. Leonard Ellwood and Doris Jones. BSc, U. Liverpool, Eng., 1961; MSc, U. Manchester, Eng., 1967. Experimental officer ICI, Ltd., Billingam, Eng., 1961-63; adminstrv. asst. U. Liverpool, 1965-84, asst. registrar, 1984—. Co-contbr. papers to profl. jour., 1966-70. Mem. Conf. Univ. Admistrs., Royal Soc. Chemists, Musicians Union, Brit. Assn. Ski Instrs. Office: U Liverpool, PO Box 147, Liverpool, Merseyside L69 3BX, England

JONES, ALBERT PEARSON, retired lawyer, former educator; b. Dallas, July 19, 1907; s. Bush and Ethel (Hatton) J.; m. Annette Lewis, Oct. 3, 1936; children—Dan Pearson, Lewis Avery. B.A., U. Tex.-Austin, M.A., 1927, LL.B., 1930. Bar: Tex. 1930, U.S. Ct. Appeals (5th cir.) 1935, U.S. Supreme Ct. 1950. Assoc. Baker & Botts, Houston, 1930-43; ptnr. Helm & Jones, 1943-62; Joseph C. Hutcheson prof. law U. Tex.-Austin, 1962-77, prof. emeritus, 1977—; adj. prof. law U. Houston, 1981; 1st asst. atty. gen. Tex., 1963. Editor-in-chief Tex. Law Rev., 1929-30; pres. Tex. Law Rev. Publs., 1971-74; co-author: Texas Trial and Appellate Procedure, 1974, The Judicial Process in Texas Prior to Trial, 2d edit., Cases and Materials on Employees' Rights, 1970; contbr. articles to profl. jours. Fellow Am. Coll. Trial Lawyers; mem. State Bar Tex. (pres. 1950-51), Houston Bar Assn., Am. Law Inst. (life), Am. Judicature Soc., Phi Beta Kappa, Order Coif, Phi Delta Phi. Democrat. Episcopalian. Clubs: Houston Country. Lodge: Masons. Home: 3195 Del Monte St Houston TX 77019 Office: 2700 America Tower 2929 Allen Pkwy Houston TX 77019

JONES, ALLEN, artist, educator; b. Southampton, Hampshire, Eng., Sept. 1, 1937; s. William and Madeline (Aveson) J.; m. Janet Bowen, Dec. 1964 (div. 1978); children—Thea, Sarah. N.D.D., Hornsey Sch. Art, London, 1959, A.T.D., 1960; student Royal Coll. Art, London, 1960-61. Tchr. lithography, London, 1961-63; guest prof. art UCLA, U. So. Fla., Tampa, Hamburg, Berlin; designer for stage and TV, Eng., Federal Republic Germany, 1968-80. Author: Allen Jones Figures, 1969; Allen Jones Projects, 1971; Allen Jones Waitress, 1972. Exhibited in numerous mus. and galleries internationally, 1961—; represented in pub. and pvt. collections throughout World inc. paintings in Eng. and Fed. Republic Germany, graphic work art council tour, 1978; TV designs for West Deutsche Rundfunk, Cologne, Federal Republic Germany, London Week-End TV; mural and sculpture commns., Switzerland, Eng., U.S.,1984—. Recipient prix des Jeunes Artistes, Paris Biennale, 1963. Mem. Royal Acad. Office: Waddington Galleries, 2 Cork St, London WI, England

JONES, ANABEL RATCLIFF, anesthesiologist; b. Lafayette, Ind., Sept. 6, 1933; d. Frank William and Mary Rovene (Holt) Ratcliff; A.B., Ind. U., 1955, M.D., 1959; m. Wiley A. Jones, Oct. 4, 1975; 1 son by previous marriage, Warren Lee. Intern, Meth. Hosp., Indpls., 1959-60; resident anesthesiology Ind. U. Med. Center, Indpls., 1960-62; staff anesthesiologist VA Hosp., Indpls., 1962-63; practice medicine, specializing in anesthesiology, Lafayette, 1963—; mem. staff St. Elizabeth Hosp., Home Hosp., Purdue U. Hosp.; instr. Ind. U. Med. Center, Indpls., 1962—. Piano accompanist civic chorus, also combined civic vocal groups; mem. governing bd. Lafayette Symphony Orch., 1971-88. Diplomate Am. Bd. Anesthesiology. Mem. Am. Soc. Anesthesiologists, Internat. Anesthesia Research Soc., Ind. Med. Assn., Ind. Soc. Anesthesiologists, AMA, DAR (gen. Lafayette chpt.), Kappa Kappa Kappa, Delta Delta Delta. Methodist. Home: 3301 Cedar Ln Lafayette IN 47905 Office: Life Bldg Lafayette IN 47901

JONES, ANTHONY EDWARD, art institute adminstrator, art historian, painter; b. Mountain Ash, Wales, Eng., Aug. 3, 1944. Student, Goldsmiths Coll. U. London, 1962-63; BA with honors in Art and Design, Newport Coll. Art, Wales, 1966; MFA, Tulane U., 1968; postgrad., Tex. Christian U., Ft. Worth, 1972-78. Grad. teaching asst. Tulane U., New Orleans, 1966-67; instr., artist-in-residence Loyola U., 1967-68; teaching fellow Gloucester Coll. Art, Cheltenham, Eng., 1968-69; instr. Adult Edn. Ctr., Stroud, Eng., 1968-69; lectr., dept. head sculpture Glasgow (Scotland) Sch. Art, 1969-72; chmn. dept. art and art history Tex. Christian U., Ft. Worth, 1972-80; dir. Glasgow Sch. Art, 1980-86; pres. Sch. Art Inst. of Chgo., 1986—; elected to grad. faculty, fellow of Centennial Coll., Tex. Christian U., 1973, tenured, 1975, prof., 1979; vis. prof. U. Wales, 1978; cons. Welsh Arts Council, 1978; chmn. faculty Glasgow Sch. Art, 1980-86; appointed vice chmn. bd. govs., 1983. One-man shows include Nat. Eisteddfod of Wales, 1960-62, U. Southwestern La., 1967, Delgado Mus., New Orleans, 1968, Atelier Chapman Kelley, Dallas, 1968, Loyola U., New Orleans, 1968, Tulane U., 1968; exhibited in group shows at Newport Coll., 1963-66, Arts Council of Wales, 1965-66, Structure 66 Sculpture Competition and Internat. Touring Exhbn., 1966 (major prize winner), Gulf States Open Painting and Sculpture, Mobile, 1967, Newcomb Coll. Spring Exhbn., New Orleans, 1967-68, Tulane U., 1967-68, Art in Wales Today, Cardiff, 1969, Nat. Mus. Wales, 1969, Arlington Mill Gallery, 1970, Compass Gallery, Glasgow, 1970-72, Art Spectrum, Scotland, 1971, Tex. Christian U., 1971-79, McLellan Galleries, Glasgow, 1972, Arts Council of Scotland, 1972, Tex. Fine Arts Assn., Arlington, 1972, Simonne Stern Gallery, New Orleans, 1974, Tex. Fine Arts Assn., Ft. Worth, 1976, Tex. Fine Arts Citation Touring Exhbn., 1975-76, Ark. State U. Invitational, 1975-76, Tex. Wesleyan Coll. Invitational, 1979, Carlin Gallery, Ft. Worth, summer 1979, The Fine Art Soc. Gallery, Glasgow, 1982-84; represented in permanent collections Morrice Curet, Memphis, Raymond Coutiarde, Tunisia, Northwood Inst., Dallas, Lesley Thomas, Rabastens, France, Loyola U., New Orleans, Arts Council of Wales, Arts Council of Scotland, Livingston New Town, Scotland, Ft. Worth Nat. Bank, Sprint Printing Co., Ft. Worth, U. Ark., Tate Gallery, London, Nat. Mus. Wales; contbg. photographer Change and Decay exhbn. Victoria and Albert Mus., London, 1977; contbr. articles to profl. jours. Cons. Royal Commn. on Ancient and Hist. Monuments for Wales, 1977—; contbr. Wales Nat. Bldg. Record, 1977—; cons., contbr. Victoria and Albert Mus., London, 1977. Mem. Am. Crafts Council, Nat. Council of Art Adminstrs., Coll. Art Assn. Am., Tex. Assn. Schs. Art, Com. Higher Edn. Art and Design, Third Eye Arts Centre (bd. dirs. 1983—), Charles Rennie Mackintosh Soc. (vice chmn., com. mem. 1982-86), Com. Prins. Scottish Cen. Insts. Higher Edn., Scottish Edn. Dept. (coordinating com. 1980—), Fulbright Scholars Assn. (U.S.-U.K. Ednl. Commn. 1982—). Office: Sch of the Art Inst of Chgo Office of Pres Columbus Dr & Jackson Blvd Chicago IL 60603 *

JONES, BARRY OWEN, politician; b. Geelong, Australia, Oct. 11, 1932; s. Claud Edward and Ruth Marion (Black) J.; m. Rosemary Hanbury, June 30, 1961; LL.B., Melbourne U., 1965, M.A., 1968; DSc, Macquerie U., 1988. High sch. tchr. Victorian Edn. Dept., 1957-67; history lectr. La Trobe U., Melbourne, 1968-70; ptnr. Norris, Collins & Jones, 1970-78; mem. State Parliament of Victoria, 1972-77, mem. Australian Ho. of Reps, 1977—, minister for sci., 1983—, minister for tech., 1983-84, minister for customs, 1988—. Author: Decades of Decision, 1965; Age of Apocalypse, 1975; Macmillan Dictionary of Biography, 1981; Sleepers, Wake!, 1982. Fellow Royal Soc. Arts, London. Methodist. Home: PO Box 231, Saint Albans, Victoria 3021, Australia Office: Parliament House, Canberra 2600, Australia

JONES, BETTY HARRIS, educator; b. St. Louis, May 25, 1937; d. Homer and Pearl (Fulgham) Harris; A.B., Rutgers U., 1967; M.A., Bryn Mawr Coll., 1968, Ph.D., 1972; m. Calvin Walter Jones, Dec. 2, 1954; children—Christopher Walter, Nicholas Alexander. Instr. in English, Rutgers U., Camden, N.J., 1969-72, asst. prof., 1972—; mem. Nat. Faculty for Humanities, Arts, and Scis., 1983—; bd. dirs. Burlington County Opportunities Industrialization Ctrs.; cons. Phila. Sch. Dist. Grad. collector in English, Bryn Mawr Coll., mem. bd. cons., 1974-76. Contbr. articles to profl. jours. Danforth Found. fellow, 1967-68; Danforth Found. assoc., 1972; Rutgers U. summer fellow, 1975, faculty fellow, 1977; nominee Lindback award for excellence in coll. teaching, 1970, 77; named one of Ten Top Profs. in the Delaware Valley, Phila. Inquirer, 1986; cited for Outstanding Coll. Teaching Gov. N.J., 1986; recipient Outstanding Faculty award for excellence in classroom and disting. service to campus Rutgers U. Alumni Assn. Camden, 1987. Mem. MLA, AAUP, N.J. Coll. English Assn., Nat. Council Tchrs. English, Alumnae Assn. Bryn Mawr Coll. (3d v.p., exec. bd.). Contbr. articles to profl. jours., essay to book. Home: 42 Norman Ln Willingboro NJ 08046 Office: Rutgers U Camden NJ 08102

JONES, BEVERLY ANN MILLER, nursing executive; b. Bklyn., July 14, 1927; d. Hayman Edward and Eleanor Virginia (Doyle) Miller. B.S.N., Adelphi U., 1949; m. Kenneth Lonzo Jones, Sept. 5, 1953; children—Steven Kenneth, Lonnie Cord. Chief nurse regional blood program ARC, N.Y.C., 1951-54; asst. dir., acting dir. nursing M.D. Anderson Hosp. and Tumor Inst., Houston, 1954-55; asst. dir. nursing Sibley Meml. Hosp., Washington, 1959-61; assoc. dir. nursing service Anne Arundel Gen. Hosp., Annapolis, Md., 1966-70; asst. adminstr. nursing Alexandria (Va.) Hosp., 1972-73; asst. adminstr. patient services Longmont (Colo.) United Hosp., 1977—; instr. ARC, 1953-57; mem. adv. bd. Boulder Valley Vo.-Tech Health Occupations Program, 1977-80; chmn. nurse enrollment com. D.C. chpt. ARC, 1959-61; del. nursing adminstrs. good will trip to Poland, Hungary, Sweden and Eng., 1980. Contbr. articles to profl. jours. Bd. dirs. Meals on Wheels, Longmont, Colo., 1978-80; bd. dirs. Longmont Coalition for Women in Crisis; mem. Colo. Hosp. Assn. Task Force on Nat. Commn. on Nursing, 1982; mem. utilization com. Boulder (Colo.) Hospice, 1979-83; mem. council labor relations Colo. Hosp. Assn., 1982-87; mem.-at-large exec. com. nursing service adminstrs. Sect. Md. Nurses' Assn., 1966-69. Recipient Excellence in Human Caring Nightingale award U. Colo. Sch. of Nursing. Mem. Am. Orgn. Nurse Execs. (chmn. com. membership services and promotions, recipient recognition of excellence in nursing adminstrn.), Colo. Soc. Nurse Execs. (dir. 1978-80, 84-86, pres. 1980-81, mem. com. on nominations 1985-86). Home: 8902 Quail Rd Longmont CO 80501 Office: PO Box 1659 Longmont CO 80501

JONES, BRUCE STANLEY, pharmaceutical wholesaling company executive; b. Sydney, New South Wales, Australia, June 25, 1938; s. Stanley Aldred and Elsie May (Wilkinson) J.; m. Jennifer Hepper, Dec. 16, 1959 (div. Sept. 1971); m. Barbara Marie Coyle, June 25, 1988; children—Stephen Mark, Sandra Michelle. Student pub. schs; grad. Ampgs Coll. Adv. Edn., Mt. Eliza, Victoria, 1987. Mgr. Angus & Coote P/L, Sydney, Australia, 1953-66; nat. sales control Australian Services Canteens Orgn., Melbourne, 1966-72; brand mgr. wines Dalgety, Ltd., Melbourne, 1972-74; br. mgr. Burns Philip, Lautoka, Fiji, 1974-75, mdse. controller Fiji Ops., 1976-77, mgr., Burns Philp-Am. Samoa, 1977-79; divisional mgr. mdse. Australian Pharm. Industries Ltd., 1979-82, mng. dir. subs. Co. Chemgoods Pty. Ltd., Brisbane, Queensland, 1982-84, divisional mgr. merchandise franchise groups, 1987—. Co-chmn. Inaugural Ball Com. for 1st Locally Appointed Gov., 1978. Fellow Soc. Sr. Execs.; assoc. fellow Australian Inst. Mgmt. Home: 31 Candowie Crescent, Baulkham Hills NSW 2153, Australia Office: PO Box 123, Wentworthville, New South Wales 2145, Australia

JONES, CAROL LEIGH, organist, music educator; b. Covina, Calif., July 23, 1949; d. Earl Lee and Lucille Elenor (Thompson) J.; m. Robert Frank Zadel, Jan. 29, 1977. Grad. prep. Sherwood Music Conservatory, Chgo., 1964; AA, Saddleback Coll., 1986; student Bob St. John, Pomona, Calif., Bill Thomson, Woodland Hill, Calif., George Wright, Hollywood, Calif. Instr. Gould Music, Covina, 1967-72; product specialist Conn Organ Corp., Oakbrook, Ill., 1972-77; concert organist Conn Keyboards, Inc., Carol Stream, Ill., 1978-79, Yamaha Internat., Buena Park, Calif., 1979-80, Norlin Corp., Lincolnshire, Ill., 1980-81, Kimball Internat., Jasper, Ind., 1981-86; concert artist Gulbransen, Inc., San Diego, 1988—; dir. music edn. Organ Exchange, Inc., San Diego, 1979—; organist, instr. CLJ & Co., Mission Viejo, Calif., 1978—; concert artist Gulbransen Organ, Inc., St. Louis, 1988—; judge Yamaha Electone Festival, Los Angeles, 1980; arranger Hal Leonard Artist Series, 1974. Rec. artist Have You Met Miss Jones, 1970, Conn. Organ Presents Carol Jones, 1977, Second Time Around, 1982. Sherwood Music Conservatory scholar, 1967. Mem. Keyboard World (favorite female organist 1974), Amateur Organist Assn. Internat. (industry dir. 1977-80, panelist conv. 1982-87, western regional dir. 1988—), Am. Theatre Organ Soc., Nat. Assn. Music Mchts. Republican. Roman Catholic.

JONES, CHARLES DAVIS, insurance consultant; b. Abraham, W.Va., Jan. 6, 1917; s. Benjamin Franklin and Mary Catherine (Smith) J.; student Beckley Coll., 1936-37, Concord Coll., 1937-38; A.B., Marshall U., 1947; postgrad. Columbia U., 1947; M.A., N.Y.U., 1956; postgrad. Am. U., 1957; m. Letha Arbell Plumley; children—Charles Davis, Irvin Howard; m. 2d, Margaret Lee Greene, Aug. 4, 1951. With Social Security Adminstrn., 1951-77, field rep., Charleston, W. Va., 1951-54, policy examiner, sect. chief, state ops. officer, Balt., 1954-66, area chief field ops. Bur. Disability Ins., Balt., 1966-71, dir. gen. policy coordination and liaison, 1971-75, chief eligibility policy to Office of Policy and Regulations, 1975-77; disability ins. cons., 1977—; mem. staff sec's. task force on medicaid and related programs HEW, 1969; mem. Social Security Adminstrn. Task Force on Social Security Adminstrn. Regional Orgns. and Functions, 1970. Active Balt. Mus. Art. Served to 1st lt. USAF, 1942-45. Decorated 4 Air medals. Mem. Nat. Assn. of Disability Examiners, Mensa, VFW, Nat. Trust for Historic Preservation, Eighth Air Force Hist. Soc. (life), 96th Bomb Group Assn. (life), Nat. Hist. Soc. Home: 3904 Elm Ave Baltimore MD 21211

JONES, CHARLES J., firefighter; b. Marshfield, Oreg., Jan. 29, 1940; s. Charles J. Cotter and Lois C. (Smith) Meltebeke; m. Carol S. Lund, Jan. 11, 1961 (div. 1966); children: April M., Autumn C.; m. Sharon S. Madsen, Mar. 29, 1969; children: Mary E., Judith A., Kari C. AS in Fire Sci. Tech., Portland Community Coll., 1974; BS in Fire Adminstrn., Eastern Oreg. State Coll., 1983; diploma, Nat. Fire Acad., 1983, 85. Cert. class VI fire officer, Oreg.; lic. real estate agt., Oreg. From firefighter to capt. Washington County Fire Dist., Aloha, Oreg., 1964-74, battalion chief, 1974-81, dir. research and devel., 1981-85, dir. strategic planning, 1986-88; cons. Washington County Consol. Communications Agy., 1983-86, chmn. mgmt. bd., 1982-83; mem. adv. bd. Washington County Emergency Med. Services, 1981-83. Editor local newsletter Internat. Assn. Firefighters, 1970; contbr. articles on fire dept. mgmt. to jours. Active Community Planning Orgn., Washington County, 1979—. Served with USAF, 1957-59. Mem. Oreg. Fire Chiefs Assn. (chmn. seminar com. 1982-83, 89, co-chmn. 1981, 84, 86, 87, 88). Republican. Congregationalist. Club: Pontiac (Portland). Office: Washington County Fire Dist 1 20665 SW Blanton Aloha OR 97007

JONES, CLARENCE ROLLINS, mechanical engineer; b. Ashton, S.C., Nov. 7, 1923; s. Clarence Rollins and Susan (Black) J.; B.S. in Mech. Engring., Clemson A&M Coll., 1947, M.S., 1949; m. Eunice Varn Polk, July 26, 1944; children—Susan Varn, Mary Deborah. Instr., Clemson (S.C.) U., 1947-49; project engr. Patchen & Zimmerman Engrs., Augusta, Ga., 1949-51; owner, cons. engr., Jones Engring. Co. engring., archtl. firm, Augusta; past chmn. bd., pres. Jones & Fellers, architects, engrs. and planners, Mid-South Corp.; past v.p. So. Industries Investment Co., Augusta; pres. Clarence R. Jones, Cons., Ltd., Jones Internat. Ltd.; Am. Internat. Trading Co., Jones Contracting and Trading Co. chmn. HDR Energy Devel. Corp., Savannah Coalport, Inc. Vice chmn. Citizens Adv. Com. City of Augusta, 1963-72; mem. adv. bd. HUD; mem. emergency resources planning com. State of Ga., 1961-65. Past chmn. Greater Augusta Arts Council. Served from pvt. to 1st lt. AUS, 1942-47; PTO. Registered profl. engr. Ga., S.C., N.C., Idaho, Ohio., Ala., Ky., Miss., W.Va., Tex., La., Fla., Va., N.Y., Md., N.J., Tenn., Ill., Ind., Hawaii, Ariz. Mem. Nat. Soc. Profl. Engrs. (past v.p., past vice chmn. profl. engrs. in pvt. practice), ASHRAE, ASME, Soc. Am. Mil. Engrs., Assn. U.S. Army, Ga. Soc. Profl. Engrs. (pres., dir. 1962-—), Augusta Com. of 100 (past dir.), Augusta C. of C. (past chmn. red carpet com.), U.S. Regional Export Expansion Council, World Trade Council. Methodist. Clubs: Masons, Lions (dir. Augusta 1960-—), Augusta Country. Home: 3415 Walton Way Augusta GA 30909

JONES, CLIFFORD AARON, lawyer, international businessman; b. Long Lane, Mo., Feb. 19, 1912; s. Burley Monroe and Arlie (Benton) J.; widowed, 1975; m. Christina Wagner, Dec. 24, 1978. LL.B., U. Mo., 1938, J.D., 1969. Bar: Nev. 1938, U.S. Dist. Ct. Nev. 1939, D.C. 1982, U.S. Ct. Appeals (9th and D.C. cirs.) 1983, U.S. Supreme Ct. 1983. Founder, sr. partner firm Jones, Jones, Close & Brown, Las Vegas, Nev., 1938—; majority leader Nev. Legislature, 1941-42; judge 8th Jud. Dist., Nev., 1945-46; lt. gov., State of Nev., 1947-54; owner, builder, chmn. bd. Thunderbird Hotel, Inc., Las Vegas, 1948-64; founder Valley Bank of Nev., 1953; founder, sec., dir. First Western Savs. and Loan Assn., 1954-66; pres., chmn. bd. Caribbean-Am. Investment Co., Inc., 1960-78; pres., dir. Income Investments, Inc., 1963-65; sr. v.p., dir. First Western Fin. Corp., 1963-66; dir., past pres. Baker & Hazard, 1966—; dir. Barrington Industries, Inc., 1966-70, Internat. Commodities Exchange, 1973—; chmn. bd., pres. Central African Land and Cattle Co., 1974-76. Mem. Clark County (Nev.) Democratic Central Com., 1940-80, chmn., 1948; nat. committeeman from Nev. Dem. Party, 1954; mem. Nev. Dem. State Central Com., 1945-60; 4 time del. Dem. Nat. Conv. Served as lt. col. F.A. U.S. Army, 1942-46, ETO. Mem. ABA (past mem. tax sect.), Am. Coll. Probate Counsel, Nev. Bar Assn., D.C. Bar Assn., Am. Legion, V.F.W., Phi Delta Phi, Kappa Sigma. Clubs: United Nations Lions (Las Vegas), Elks (Las Vegas), Lions (Las Vegas) (past pres.). Office: Jones Jones Close & Brown 300 S 4th St Valley Bank Plaza Suite 700 Las Vegas NV 89101

JONES, CLIFFORD BOWEN, insurance executive; b. Neath, Glamorgan, Wales, May 9, 1920; s. Thomas Henry and Beatrice Maude (Bowen) J.; m. Grace Elizabeth Evans, Mar. 2, 1946; 1 child, Susan Bowen Jones. Certs. in engring., Cardiff Tech. Coll., Swansea Tech. Coll., Birmingham Tech. Coll. Articled engr. then. tech. asst. Borough Gas Dept., Neath, 1938-45; asst. engr. then mgr. Borough Gas Co., Halesowen, Worcestershire, 1945-53; asst. distbn. engr. West Midlands Gas Bd., Dudley, Worcestershire, 1953-58; sr. life underwriter Confedn. Life Ins. Co., London, 1958-85, representing underwriter, 1985—; cons. rep. Confedn. Life Ins. Co. of Can., 1985—. Fellow Life Ins. Assn. G.B. Clubs: Stourbridge Rugby Football, Claverly Cricket, Bridgenorth Rugby Football, Stourbridge Golf. Home: Twelve Noches, Heather Dr, Kinver, Stourbridge, W Midlands DY7 6DR, England Office: Confedn Life Ins Co, 17 Lichfield St, Walsall, West Midlands WS1 1UA, England

JONES, CLYDE ADAM, educator, artist; b. Cobleskill, N.Y., Nov. 10, 1924; s. Lester L. and Myra (Karker) J.; B.F.A., Syracuse U., 1948, M.A., 1954; Ed.D., Pa. State U., 1961. Tchr. art North High Sch., Binghamton, N.Y., 1948-49, 1950-56; instr. ceramics Jr. League of Binghamton, 1950-53; guest instr. ceramics Rehab. Guild, Saranac Lake, N.Y., 1951-54; asst. prof. art edn. Edinboro (Pa.) State Coll., 1956-58; instr. Creative Arts Workshop, Cornell U., Ithaca, N.Y., summer, 1958; asst. prof. child devel. U. Conn., Storrs, 1961-66, asst. dean Sch. Home Econs. and Family Studies, 1976-79, trustee Syracuse U. Library Assocs., 1970, assoc. prof. human devel. and family relations, 1966—; cons. Head Start program, Conn., 1965-66. Mem. Gov.'s Commn. on Status or Women, 1965-67, bd. mem. Greater Mansfield Arts Council, 1986—, mem. governing bd. Nat. Assn. for Creative Children and Adults, 1986—. Served with AUS, 1943-45. Mem. Conn. Assn. for Edn. of Young Children (v.p. 1970-72), New Eng. Assn. for Edn. of Young Children (publs. com. 1980—, editor newsletter 1963-65), Hartford Assn. for Edn. of Young Children (pres. 1967-69), Nat. Assn. for Edn. of Young Children, Soc. for Research in Child Devel., Nat. Soc. for Study of Edn., Nat. Art Edn. Assn. (research trainee 1965), Internat. soc. for Edn. thru Art, Assn. for Childhood Edn. Internat., Conn. Home Econs. Assn. (del., dir. 1978-82), Am. Home Econs. Assn., Phi Delta Kappa. One man shows: Rehab. Guild, Saranac Lake, N.Y., Windham Hosp., Willimantic, Conn., Art Bldg, Pa. State U., Student Union U. Conn.; group shows include: Roberson Meml., Binghamton, N.Y., Erie (Pa.) Art Mus., Munson-Williams-Proctor Inst., Utica, N.Y., Mus. of Fine Arts, Syracuse, Norwich (Conn.) Art Mus., Albany Inst. of History and Art, Essex (Conn.)) Art Assn.; illustrations for history volumes of Sch. of Home Econs. and Family Studies and Sch. of Nursing, U. Conn. Home: 52 Storrs Heights Rd Storrs CT 06268 Office: U Conn Human Devel Ctr Storrs CT 06268

JONES, DONALD GEORGE, surveying company executive, consultant; b. London, Mar. 15, 1930; s. George Henry and Rose May (Drury) J.; m. Elizabeth Ann Cox, Sept. 22, 1962; children—Karen Natalie, Alison Christina, Lucy Ann. Chartered Surveyors degree, Coll. Estate Mgmt., London, 1954. Jr. surveyor for local govt., West Ham, London, 1946-50; surveyor pvt. quantity surveying firm, London, 1950-60; sr. ptnr., chmn. D.G. Jones & Ptnrs., Internat., 1961—. Fellow Royal Instn. Chartered Surveyors. Conservative. Anglican. Office: D G Jones and Ptnrs, Karandokis Bldg, Princess Zena de Tyras St, Suite 17, Nicosia Cyprus also: The Old Palace, The Green, Richmond, Surrey England

JONES, DORIS MAE, court reporting company executive; b. Allentown, Pa., Nov. 24, 1938; d. Michael C. and Ann (Fedor) Hardony; m. Lewis M. Horwitz, Mar. 14, 1964 (div. 1984); children: Monica B., Pamela L. BS, Mich. State U., 1960; postgrad. Cleve. Marshall Law Sch., 1962; cert. Emery Sch., 1975. Ct. reporter Doris O. Wong Assocs., Boston, 1975-79; ofcl. reporter U.S. Dist. Cts., Boston, 1979-81; pres. Doris M. Jones & Assocs., Boston, 1980—. Bd. dirs., sec. Lawrence Extended Day Program, Brookline, Mass., 1977-81; steering com. hospitality program, Episcopal Diocese, Boston, 1984—, co-chair, 1987. Mem. Nat. Shorthand Reporters Assn., Mass. Shorthand Reporters Assn. (sec. 1977-79, bd. dirs. 1977-80), Greater Boston C. fo C. (mem. Execs. Club), Phi Gamma Nu, Delta Zeta. Avocations: reading, traveling, cooking, public speaking. Address: Doris M Jones & Assocs Inc 59 Temple Pl Boston MA 02111

JONES, DOROTHY CAMERON, language professional, educator; b. Detroit, Feb. 5, 1922; d. Vinton Ernest and Beatrice Olive (Cameron) J. B.A., Wayne State U., 1943, M.A., 1944; Ph.D., U. Colo., 1965. Attendance officer Detroit Bd. Edn., 1943-44; tchr. English Denby High Sch., Detroit, 1946-56, 57-58; exchange tchr. Honolulu, 1956-57; instr., asst. prof. English Colo. Women's Coll., Denver, 1962-66; mem. faculty U. No. Colo., Greeley, 1966—; prof. English U. No. Colo., 1974—. Contbr. articles to profl. lit. Served with WAVES USNR, 1944-46. Faculty research grantee, 1970, 76. Mem. Internat. Shakespeare Assn., Central States Renaissance Soc., Patristic, Medieval and Renaissance Conf., Rocky Mountain Medieval and Renaissance Soc., Rocky Mountain MLA, Delta Kappa Gamma, Pi Lambda Theta. Home: 1009 13th Ave Apt 312 Greeley CO 80631 Office: U No Colo Dept English 40 Michener Library Greeley CO 80639

JONES, DOUGLAS SAMUEL, mathematics educator; b. Corby, Northants, Eng., Jan. 10, 1922; s. Jesse Dewis and Bessie (Streather) J.; m. Ivy Styles, Sept. 23, 1950; children: Helen Elizabeth, Philip Andrew. BA, Oxford (Eng.) U., 1947; DSc, Manchester (Eng.) U., 1957, Strathclyde U., Glasgow, Scotland, 1975. Commonwealth fund fellow MIT, Cambridge, Mass., 1947-48; asst. lectr. U. Manchester, 1948-51, lectr., 1951-54; research prof. NYU, N.Y.C., 1955; sr. lectr. U. Manchester, 1955-57; prof. U. Keele, Eng., 1957-64; vis. prof. NYU, 1962-63; Ivory prof. math. U. Dundee, Scotland, 1964—; mem. Univ. Grants Com., U.K., 1976-86, Computer Bd., U.K., 1977-82, Open Univ. Vis. Com., U.K., 1982-87; chmn. Math. Scis. Sub.-Com., U.K., 1976-86. Author: Theory of Electromagnetism, 1964, Theory of Generalized Functions, 1982, Elementary Information Theory, 1979, 7 others; also articles; trustee Quar. Jour. Mechanics and Applied Math., 1980—. Mem. Council of Royal Soc., London, 1973-74, Council of Inst. Math. and Applications, 1982-85, 86—. Served with RAF, 1941-45. Recipient Keith prize Royal Soc. Edinburgh, 1974, Van Der Pol Gold medal Internat. Union Radio Sci., 1981, Naylor prize London Math. Soc., 1987. Fellow Royal Soc. Edinburgh, Royal Soc. London, Inst. Math. and Its Applications (pres. 1988). Home: 1 The Nurseries, St Madoes, Perth PH2 7NX, Scotland Office: U Dundee Dept Math, Dundee DD1 4HN, Scotland

JONES, E. STEWART, JR., lawyer; b. Troy, N.Y., Dec. 4, 1941; s. E. Stewart and Louise (Farley) J.; m. Constance M., Dec. 28, 1968; children: Christopher, Brady, Erin. BA, Williams Coll., 1963; JD, Albany Law Sch., 1966. Bar: N.Y. 1966, U.S. Dist. Ct. (no. dist.) N.Y. 1966, U.S. Supreme Ct. 1970, U.S. Ct. Appeals (2d cir.) 1976, U.S. Dist. Ct. (we. dist.) N.Y. 1987; cert. specialist in civil and criminal trial advocacy. Asst. dist. atty. Rensselaer County (N.Y.), 1968-70, spl. prosecutor, 1974; ptnr. E. Stewart Jones, Troy, N.Y., 1974—; lectr. in field; mem. com. on profl. standards of 3d jud. dept. State of N.Y., 1977-80; mem. merit selection panel for selection and appointment of U.S. magistrate for No. Dist. N.Y., 1981; bd. dirs., trustee Troy Savs. Bank. Contbr. numerous articles to profl. jours. Served with USNG, 1966-72. Fellow Am. Bar Found., Internat. Acad. Trial Lawyers, Am. Bd. Criminal Trial Lawyers, Am. Coll. Trial Lawyers, Roscoe Pound Assn.; mem. N.Y. State Bar Assn. (Outstanding Practitioner award 1980, mem. continuing edn. com. 1977-78, mem. exec. com. of criminal justice sect. 1977—, mem. exec. com. trial lawyers sect. 1981—, mem. spl. com. med. malpractice, other coms.), N.Y. State Trial Lawyers Assn. (dir. 1982—, co-chmn. com. on med. jurisprudence 1973-74, vice chmn. com. criminal law and procedure 1974-76, co-chmn. criminal law sect. 1978), Capital Dist. Trial Lawyers Assn. (dir. 1973-76), ABA (numerous coms.) Calif. Attys. for Criminal Justice, Practising Law Inst., Am. Judicature Soc. (sustaining), Renssealer County Bar Assn., Am. Soc. Law and Medicine, ACLU, N.Y. Civil Liberties Union, Lawyer to Lawyer Consultation (panel), Albany County Bar Assn., N.Y. State Defenders Assn., Nat. Orgn. for Reform of Marijuana Laws, Am. Arbitration Assn., Fed. Bar Council, Upstate Trial Attys. Assn., Inc. Clubs: Schuyler Meadows, Troy Country, Troy, Steuben Athletic, Fort Orange, Wychmere Harbor; Stone Horse Yacht (Harwich Port, Mass.); Equinox Country (Manchester, Vt.). Home: 46 Schuyler Rd Loudonville NY 12211 Office: 28 2d St Troy NY 12181

JONES, EARL, real estate broker, insurance executive; b. Stephens, Ark., Sept. 30, 1934; s. Ceasar and Pearl (Christopher) J.; m. Edna M. Hollis, Dec. 15, 1953 (div. 1971); children: Donna Lynn, Michelle Marie, Carla Ann; m. Annie Lea Wesley, Apr. 18, 1984. Cert., Mich. State U., 1964; BA, Western State U. for Profl. Studies, 1984, MBA, 1984. Lubrication mechanic Grace Motor Sales, Detroit, 1952-53; various positions Chrysler Corp., Detroit, 1953-60; sales mgmt. Great Lakes Life Ins., Detroit, 1960-65; pres. Earl Jones-Commonwealth Agy., Inc., Detroit, 1965—; real estate broker Detroit, 1971—. Recipient Appreciation awards Detroit C. of C., 1972, 73. Mem. Profl. Ins. Agts. Assn., Ind. Ins. Agts. Assn., Detroit Bd. Realtors, Detroit Real Estate Brokers Assn., Met. Detroit Ins. Club. Methodist. Club: Econ. (Detroit). Lodges: Masons, Shriners. Office: 18222 James Couzens Hwy Detroit MI 48235

JONES, EDWARD LOUIS, historian, educator; b. Georgetown, Tex., Jan. 15, 1922; s. Henry Horace and Elizabeth (Steen) J.; m. Dorothy M. Showers, Mar. 1, 1952 (div. Sept. 1963); children: Cynthia, Frances, Edward Lawrence; Lynne Ann McGreevy, Oct. 7, 1963; children Christopher Louis, Teresa Lynne. BA in Philosophy, U. Wash., 1952, BA in Far East, 1952, BA in Speech, 1955, postgrad., 1952-54; JD, Gonzaga U., 1967. Social worker Los Angeles Pub. Assistance, 1956-57; producer, dir. Little Theatre, Hollywood, Calif. and Seattle, 1956-60; research analyst, cons. to Office of Atty. Gen., Olympia and Seattle, Wash., 1963-66; coordinator of counseling SOIC, Seattle, 1966-68; lectr., advisor, asst. to dean U. Wash., Seattle, 1968—; instr. Gonzaga U., Spokane, Wash., 1961-62, Seattle Community Coll., 1967-68; dir. drama workshop, Driftwood Players, Edmonds, Wash., 1975-76. Author: The Black Diaspora: Colonization of Colored People, 1988, Tutankhamon: Son of the Sun, King of Upper and Lower Egypt, 1978, Black Orators' Workbook, 1982, Black Zeus, 1972, Profiles in African Heritage, 1972; editor, pub. NACADA Jour. Nat. Acad. Advising Assn., 1981—, Afro-World Briefs newsletter, 1985—. V.p. Wash. Com. on Consumer Interests, Seattle, 1966-68. Served to 2d lt. Fr. Army, 1940-45. Recipient Outstanding Teaching award U. Wash., 1986, Tyee Inst. Yr. U. Wash., 1987, appreciation award Office Minority Affairs, 1987, acad. excellence award Nat. Soc. Black Engrs., 1987; Frederick Douglass scholar Nat. Council Black Studies, 1985, 86. Mem. Nat. Assn. Student Personnel Adminstrs., Smithsonian Inst. (assoc.), Am. Acad. Polit. and Social Sci., Nat. Acad. Advising Assn. (bd. dirs. 1979-82, Cert. of Appreciation 1982, editor Jour. 1981—, award for Excellence 1985), Western Polit. Sci. Assn. Democrat. Baptist. Office: U Wash Seattle WA 98195

JONES, ELDRED DUROSIMI, educator, consultant; b. Freetown, Sierra Leone, Jan. 6, 1925; s. Eldred Prince William and Ethline Marie (Quinn) J.; m. Birdie Marjorie Pratt, June 23, 1952; children: Essemary, Ethline. BA, Fourah Bay Coll., Freetown, 1947; BA in English Lang. and Lit. with honors, Oxford U., Eng., 1953, MA, 1959; PhD, U. Durham, Eng., 1962; LLD, Williams Coll., Williamstown, Mass., 1985. Prof., head Dept. English Fourah Bay Coll., 1964-74, prin., 1974-85; emeritus prof. U. Sierra Leone, Freetown, 1985—; vis. prof. Leeds U., Eng., 1966; distng. vis. prof. U. N.C., Can., 1972; commonwealth prof. U. Sheffield and Kent, Eng., 1973-74; Margaret Bundy Scott prof. Williams Coll., 1980; cons. Assn. Commonwealth lang. and Lit., Eng., 1964—. Mem. bd. govs., bd. trustees. secondary sch., Freetown, 1955—, chmn., 1986—; cons. mem. Globe Playhouse Trust, London, 1972—; chmn. mng. com. Noma Award for Pub. in Africa. Sr. research fellow Folger Shakespear Library, Washington, 1969; Commonwealth fellow U. Toronto, 1970-71; recipient Criticism Prize First World Festival Negro Arts, Govt. Senegal, Dakar, 1966. Fellow Royal Soc. Arts; mem. Internat. Shakespeare Assn. (mem. exec. com. 1976—), African Lit. Assn., Order of the Republic of Sierra Leone. Anglican. Club: Freetown Jr. Dinner (pres. 1973-76). Office: Sierra Leone Univ Press, PO Box 87, Freetown Sierra Leone

JONES, FARRELL, lawyer; b. Chgo., May 6, 1926; s. Farrell and Kathryn (Crum) J.; BA, Lincoln U., 1950; JD, N.Y. U., 1957; m. Audrey E. Howard, June 16, 1951; children—Joanne Kathryn and Jacqueline Elinor (twins). Social investigator N.Y.C. Dept. Social Services, 1957-58; admitted to N.Y. State bar, 1958; asst. counsel Gov. Harriman's Com. to Rev. N.Y. State Parole System, 1958; field rep. N.Y. State Commn. for Human Rights, 1958-60, sr. field rep., 1960-61, regional dir. L.I. region, 1961-63; exec. dir. Nassau County (N.Y.) Commn. on Human Rights, 1963-70; dep. county exec. Nassau County, 1970-71; asso. dir., clin. asst. prof. div. alcoholism and drug dependence State U. N.Y. Downstate Med. Center, 1971; 1st dep. adminstr. N.Y.C. Human Resources Adminstrn., 1971-74; asst. v.p. Blue Cross and Blue Shield Greater N.Y., 1974-88; sole practice, Port Washington, N.Y., 1988—; bd. dirs. Health Watch Info. & Promotion Services, Bklyn, N.Y. (nat.); cons. N.Y. State Dept. Edn. on Intergroup Relations; cons. L.I. Sch. Dists.; pres. Sci. Mus. L.I., Plandome, N.Y., 1984—; bd. dirs. Am. Com. on Africa. Bd. dirs. Family Service Assn. Nassau County, N.Y.C. Comprehensive Health Planning Agy., 1971-74, Cow Bay Housing, Port Washington, 1975-85; chmn. Nassau County Econ. Opportunity Commn., 1971-72; pres. Nassau County Law Services Com., 1969-71; bd. dirs. Health and Welfare Council of Nassau County, Nassau County Community Econ. Devel. Corp., Nassau Community Health Services Found., 1966-69, Community Health Plan of Suffolk County, N.Y., 1981—, chmn. labor com., 1981—; mem. Nassau County Crime Council, 1966-71; trustee Adelphi U., mem. adv. bd. Sch. Social Work, 1964—, chmn., 1970—; asso. trustee North Shore Hosp., 1970-74; trustee Port Washington Pub. Library, 1976—, Urban League L.I., 1976—; mem. Nassau County Youth Bd., 1964-71; mem. adv. council Hofstra U., 1967-72, v.p., 1971-72. Served with AUS, 1951-53. Recipient Brotherhood award NCCJ, 1982. Mem. One Hundred Black Men (exec. bd. Nassau-Suffolk chpt. 1983-87), Nassau County Bar Assn., NAACP (life mem., pres. Great Neck, Manhasset, Port Washington and Roslyn br. 1983—), Alpha Phi Alpha. Unitarian. Address: 22 Driftwood Dr Port Washington NY 11050

JONES, FRANKLIN ROSS, educator; b. Charlotte, N.C., Jan. 3, 1921; s. William Morton and Olive Ruth (Moser) J.; divorced; children: Franklin Ross, C. Morton, Susan Noel. AB, Lenoir Rhyne Coll., 1941; MA, U. N.C., 1951; DEd, Duke U., 1960. Tchr. schs. N.C., 1944-48; prin. Jr. High Sch., Henderson, N.C., 1948-54; dist. sch. prin. Wake County, N.C., 1954-56; dist. supt. Roxboro (N.C.) schs., 1956-58; chmn. dept. edn. Randolph-Macon Coll., Ashland, Va., 1959-64; dean Sch. Edn. Old Dominion U., 1964-69; founder Child Study Center, 1965, disting. prof., 1969—, social founds. program leader, 1973-77, doctoral program liaison rep., 1974-77, faculty chmn., 1981—; dir. Forest Ridge Corp., 1985; vis. research scholar Duke U., 1967; cons. HEW, State Sch. Systems and Colls.; lectr. in field. Mem. com. White House Conf. Children and Youth, 1968-71, Eastern regional chmn., 1968-71; mem. Va. Gov.'s Com. Implementation, 1971-73. Author: Psychology of Human Development, 1969, 2d edit., 1985, Handbook on Testing, 1972, Understanding the Middlescent Years, 1978, Theory of Adult Development, 1980, Radio series, WTAR, Norfolk, 1973-75. Mem. Norfolk Urban Coalition, 1969-73; chmn. March of Dimes, Person County, N.C., 1956-57; mem. adv. bd. Tidewater Rehab. Center, 1967-69; chmn. Hull Scholarship Fund, 1983-85 ; coordinator U. Joy Fund Drive, 1974—; univ. chmn. United Fund, 1982, 84. Named Eminent Prof. Old Domion U., 1974, Dean's service award, 1984. Mem. Va. Assn. U. Profs. (dir. 1962-64), South Atlantic Philosophy Edn. Soc. (pres. 1966-69, dir. 1969—), Va. Assn. Research in Edn. (disting. research awards 1972, 73, 78), Southeast Psychol. Assn., N.C. Edn. Assn. (pres. North Central chpt. 1951, pres. North Cen. Prins. 1956), Eastern Ednl. Research Assn., Nat. Urban Edn. Assn., Alpha Tau Kappa, Kappa Delta Pi, Phi Delta Kappa, Phi Kappa Phi, Pi Gamma Mu (sec. 1962-64). Club: Harbor (Norfolk). Lodges: Lions, Rotary. Home: 1026 Manchester Ave Norfolk VA 23508

JONES, FREDERIC JOSEPH, Italian studies educator; b. Blaina, Wales, Feb. 28, 1925; s. Joseph John and Winifred (Stephens) J.; m. Mair James, Dec. 28, 1956. BA, MA, Oxford U., 1946, BLitt, 1949; Dr, U. Paris, 1952. Officer Brit. Council, 1947-49; lectr. French and Italian Univ. Coll., Cardiff, Wales, 1953-66; prof. Italian studies U. Wales, Cardiff, 1966—, dean faculty arts, 1972-74. Author: A Modern Italian Grammar, 1960 (Italian Soc. prize 1962), La poesia italiana contomporanea, 1975, The Modern Italian Lyric, 1986, Giuseppe Ungaretti, 1977 (Vallombrosa prize 1978); editor: Andre Gide, Les Caves du Vatican, 1962; contbr. articles on Italian and French lit. and econs. to profl. jours. Recipient award Brit. Acad., 1983, 86; Leverhulme Trust fellow, 1975. Mem. Soc. for Italian Studies (chmn. 1987—), Gt. Britain and Ireland Soc. for Italian Tchrs. Home: 63 Black Oak Rd, Cyncoed, Cardiff CF2 6QU, Wales Office: Univ Coll, PO Box 78, Cardiff CF1 1XL, England

JONES, GEORGE RICHARD, marketing manager; b. Liverpool, Eng., Sept. 20, 1931; arrived in Canada, 1955; s. George and Lillian (Daniels) J.; m. Christine Patricia Kyle, Oct. 2, 1954; children: Stephen Ross, Lois Christine, Philip Rolf, Richard Craig, Andrew Daryl. Cert. in indsl. mgmt., McGill U., Montreal, Quebec, 1965; BA, Carleton U., Ottawa, Ont., 1977. Asst. analytical chemist A.H. Knight Ltd., Liverpool, 1948-49; radar engr. Marconi's Wireless Co., Chelmsford, Eng., 1954-55; mgr. field service Can. Aviation Electronics, Montreal, 1955-67; sales mgr. BRH Assocs., Ottawa, 1967-69; dist. mgr. Hewlett Packard Can. Ltd., Ottawa, 1969-75, br. mgr., 1975-83, mktg. mgr. fed. govt., 1983—; bd. dirs. Ottawa Carleton Econ. Dev. Corp.; chmn. advisory com. St. Lawrence Coll. Kingston, Can. Mem. Neilson Task Force, 1985, Jr. Achievers Can. Served with RAF, 1949-54. Mem. Can. Mfrs. Assn. (comn. chmn. 1985—), Dept. Supply and Services (liaison com. chmn. 1986—), Info. Technol. Assn., Project Mgrs. Inst. (v.p. 1986—), Bd. Trade (mem. hitech com. 1985). Mem. Anglican Ch. Club: Canadian. Home: 24 Bearbrook Rd, Gloucester, ON Canada K1B 3H9 Office: Hewlett Packard Canada Ltd, 2670 Queensview Dr, Ottawa, ON Canada K2B 8K1

JONES, GERRE LYLE, marketing and public relations consultant; b. Kansas City, Mo., June 22, 1926; s. Eugene Riley and Carolyn (Newell) J.; m. Charlotte Mae Reinhold, Oct. 30, 1948; children: Beverly Anne Jones Putnam, Wendy Sue. BJ, U. Mo., 1948, postgrad., 1953-54. Exec. sec. Effingham (Ill.) C. of C., 1948-50; field rep. Nat. Found. Infantile Paralysis, N.Y.C., 1950-57; dir. pub. relations Inst. Logopedics, Wichita, Kans., 1957-58; owner Gerre Jones & Assocs., Pub. Relations, Kansas City, Mo., 1958-63; info. officer Radio Free Europe Fund, Munich, Federal Republic of Germany, 1963-65, spl. asst. to dir. pub. relations, 1965-66; exec. asst. pub. affairs Edward Durell Stone, 1967-68; dir. mktg. and communications Vincent C. Kling & Ptnrs., Phila., 1969-71; mktg. cons. Ellerbe Architects, Washington, 1972; v.p. Gaio Assocs., Ltd., Washington, 1972-73, exec. v.p., 1973-76; exec. v.p. Bldg. Industry Devel. Services, Washington, 1973-76; pres. Gerre Jones Assocs. Inc., Albuquerque, 1976—; sr. v.p. Barlow Assocs., Inc., Washington, 1977-78; lectr. numerous colls. and univs. Author: How to Market Professional Design Services, 1973, 2d edit., 1983, How to Prepare Professional Design Brochures, 1976, (with Stuart H. Rose) How to Find and Win New Business, 1976, Public Relations for the Design Professional, 1980; contbr. articles to profl. jours. Served with USAAF, 1944-45, maj. USAF (ret.). Mem. Internat. Radio and TV Soc., Nat. Assn. Sci. Writers, Am. Soc. Tng. and Devel., AIA (hon.), Sigma Delta Chi, Alpha Delta Sigma, Phi Delta Phi. Republican. Clubs: Kansas City Press; Overseas Press; Deadline (N.Y.C.). Lodge: Masons.

JONES, GLANVILLE REES JEFFREYS, geography educator; b. Velindre, Swansea, Wales, Dec. 12, 1923; s. Benjamin and Sarah (Jeffreys) J. m. Pamela Winship, Sept. 12, 1959; children: Sarah, David. BA in Geography with 1st class honors, U. Wales, 1948, MA, 1949. Asst. lectr. geography U. Leeds, Eng., 1949-52, lectr., 1952-65, sr. lectr., 1965-69, reader hist., geography, 1969-74, prof., 1974—; O'Donnell lectr. U. Wales, 1975; chmn. adv. com. Rescue Archaeology, Yorkshire-Humberside, Eng., 1975-79. Author, editor: (with S.R. Eyre) Geography as Human Ecology, 1966, (with

M.W. Beresford) Leeds and Its Region, 1967; author: Post-Roman Wales in Agrarian History of England and Wales I, 1972; contbr. numerous articles on hist. geography and history of settlement to profl. jours. Recipient Hywel Dda prize U. Wales, 1974. Fellow Soc. Antiquaries; mem. Inst. Brit. Geographers, Brit. Assn. Advancement Sci (pres. sect. H anthropology and archaeology). Home: 26 Lee Ln E Horsforth, Leeds LS18 5RE, England Office: U Leeds, Leeds LS2 9JT, England

JONES, GLENN EARLE, property management executive; b. Greensboro, N.C., May 11, 1946; s. Harold Clifford and AnnaBelle (Goodwin) J. B.S., Cornell U. Sch. Hotel and Restaurant Mgmt., 1968. Asst. to gen. mgr. Warwick Hotel, Houston, 1968-69; Northeastern Ohio sales rep. L.G. Balfour Co., Attleboro, Mass., 1969-72; resident mgr. Chase Park Plaza Hotel, St. Louis, 1972-74; gen. mgr. Holiday Inn, Steamboat Springs, Colo., 1974, Santa Fe Hilton Inn, 1975, Sheraton Inn, New Orleans, 1976-79; pres. Landmark Systems, Inc., New Orleans, 1979—; chmn. Sheraton, So. Regional Owners and Mgrs. Council, 1981—. Mem. com. membership Greater New Orleans Tourist and Conv. Commn.; mem. dist. com. United Fund. Mem. New Orleans Hotel and Motel Assn. (treas.), Cornell Soc. Hotelmen, Am. Hotel Mgmt. Assn. (cert., mem. fund devel. com. Ednl. Inst.). Episcopalian. Home: 636 Lang St New Orleans LA 70131

JONES, GORDON EDWIN, horticulturist; b. Lorraine, N.Y., Feb. 1, 1921; s. Griffith Edwin and Mary Edna (Green) J.; B.S., Cornell U., 1943; M.S., Hofstra U., 1961; m. Thelma Dolores Popp, Dec. 27, 1946; children—Susan D., Thomas E., Robin A., Peter G. Mgr. flower seed div. and trial grounds Robson Seed Co., Hall, N.Y., 1945-56; asst. prof. ornamental horticulture dept. N.Y. State A&T Coll., Farmingdale, 1957-65; dir. Planting Fields Arboretum, Oyster Bay, N.Y., 1958—. Trustee, Planting Fields Found.; bd. dirs. Rhododendron Species Found.; past dist. commr. Boy Scouts Am. Served to capt. U.S. Army, 1943-46; ETO. Recipient Silver Achievement medal Nat. Council award Federated Garden Clubs, 1975; named Man of Year, L.I. Nurserymen's Assn., 1979; Gold Medal of Hort. award N.Y. State Nurserymen's Assn., 1985; Sidney M. Shapiro Meml. Adminstrv. Award, 1987. Mem. Am. Rhododendron Soc. (gold medal, bronze medal), Am. Assn. Bot. Gardens and Arboreta (dir.), Assn. Interpretive Naturalists, Hort. Soc. N.Y. (past dir.), N.Y. Hortus Club (sec.-treas.), Pi Alpha Xi, Alpha Gamma Rho. Club: Oyster Bay Rotary (pres. 1980-81). Editor: Rhododendrons and Their Relatives, 1971; contbr. articles to profl. jours. Home and Office: Planting Fields Arboretum PO Box 653 Oyster Bay NY 11771

JONES, GURNOS, chemistry educator; b. Clydach, Breconshire, Wales, Dec. 12, 1928; s. John Brynley and Sylvia (Rackham) J.; m. Patricia Rose Osguthorpe, Oct. 10, 1953; children: Owen, Glyn. BS, Sheffield U., Eng., 1949, PhD, 1952; DS, U. Keele, Eng. Sci. officer Tropical Products Lab., London, 1954-55; asst. lectr. U. Keele, Staffordshire, 1955-58, lectr., 1958-64, sr. lectr., 1964-68, reader, 1968-85, prof., 1985—. Author, editor: Quinolines vol. 1, 1977, vol. 2, 1982; contbr. more than 100 articles and revs. to sci. jours. Fellow Royal Soc. Chemistry; mem. Am. Chem. Soc., London Climbers Club. Home: The University, 24 Larchwood, Keele Staffordshire ST5 5BB, England Office: U Keele, Chemistry Dept, Keele Staffordshire ST5 5BG, England

JONES, GWYNETH, soprano; b. Pontnewynydd, Wales, Nov. 7, 1936; d. Edward George and Violet (Webster) J.; m. Till Haberfeld, Mar. 7, 1969. Student, Royal Coll. Music, London, Accademia Chigiana, Siena, Italy, Internat. Opera Center, Zurich, Switzerland; Dr. h.c. musica, U. Wales. Mem. Royal Opera, Covent Garden, Eng., 1963—, Vienna (Austria) State Opera, 1966—; also mem. Munich Bavarian State Opera, 1967—. Guest performances in numerous opera houses including Hamburg, Bayreuth, Berlin, Paris, Zurich, Rome, Chgo., San Francisco, Los Angeles, Tokyo, Buenos Aires, Munich, La Scala, Milan, Met. Opera, N.Y.C., Salzburg Festival, Verona; appeared in 50 leading roles including Tosca, Turandot, Leonora in Il Trovatore, Desdemona in Otello, Lady MacBeth, Fidelio, Aida, Senta, Sieglinde, Marschallin, Isolde, Salome, Brunnhilde, Medea, Kundry, Madame Butterfly, Elizabeth/Venus in Tannhauser, Ariadne, Farberin, Elektra, Helena in Aegyptische Helena, Poppea, Santuzza, Hannah Glawari; court singer, Bavaria, Austria; rec. artist for Decca, Deutsche Grammophon, EMI, CBS, films, TV and concert appearances. Decorated dame comdr. Order Brit. Empire. Office: Columbia Artists Mgmt 165 W 57th Suite 7 New York NY 10019 also: Box 8037, Zurich Switzerland *

JONES, H(AROLD) GILBERT, JR., lawyer; b. Fargo, N.D., Nov. 2, 1927; s. Harold Gilbert and Charlotte Viola (Chambers) J.; m. Julie Squier, Feb. 15, 1964; children: Lenna Lettice Mills Jones Carroll, Thomas Squier, Christopher Lee. B.Eng., Yale U., 1947; postgrad., Mich. U., 1948-49; J.D., UCLA, 1956. Bar: Calif. 1957. Mem., ptnr. Overton, Lyman & Prince, Los Angeles, 1956-61; founding partner Bonne, Jones, Bridges, Mueller & O'Keefe, Los Angeles, 1961—. Bd. dirs. Wilshire YMCA, 1969-75. Served with U.S. Army, 1950-52. Fellow Am. Coll. Trial Lawyers, Internat. Acad. Trial Lawyers; mem. State Bar Calif., ABA, Los Angeles County Bar Assn. (past chmn. legal-med. relations com.), Orange County Bar Assn., Wilshire Bar Assn., Am. Bd. Trial Advs. (nat. bd. dirs.1977—, past pres. Los Angeles chpt., nat. pres.-elect 1988), Am. Acad. Forensic Scis., So. Calif. Assn. Def. Counsel. Clubs: Jonathan, Transpacific Yacht (bd. dirs.), Calif. Yacht, Los Angeles Yacht, Newport Harbor Yacht (judge adv.). Home: 818 Harbor Island Dr Newport Beach CA 92660 Office: 3699 Wilshire Blvd 10th Floor Los Angeles CA 90010 also: 801 Civic Center Dr Suite 400 Santa Ana CA 92701

JONES, HOMER WALTER, JR., statistician; b. N.Y.C., Sept. 3, 1925; s. Homer Walter and Margaret (Campbell) J.; M.E., Stevens Inst. Tech., 1947, M.S., 1950; M.B.A., Am. U., 1959; M.S., George Washington U., 1965; m. Shirley Jean Dabbs, June 15, 1957; children—Laura Gwen, Linda Margaret. Cost estimator Standard Oil Devel. Co., Linden, N.J., 1947-51; engr. Wallace and Tiernan Co., Belleville, N.J., 1957-58; math. statistician U.S. Treasury Dept., Internal Revenue Service, Washington, 1959—; ltd. partner Vista Lakes Estates, Alta Vista, Va. Pres., IRS Chess Club, 1968-78; team capt. D.C. Chess League, 1963-86; nat. tournament dir. U.S. Chess Fedn., 1978—, rated expert, 1984—; mem. exec. com. Va. Chess Fedn., 1975-78; organizer Region III Chess Championship, 1974-77, 79; dir. U.S. Jr. Chess Championship, Memphis, 1978; dir. USAF Chess Team Qualification Tournament, 1983—. Mem. and host family Am. Field Service, 1977-78, 87; elder Presbyn. Ch., 1973-76, 78; treas. Performing Arts Assn. of Alexandria, 1985-87. Served with USNR, 1944-45. Recipient Certificate of Award, U.S. Treasury Dept., 1978, 84. Mem. U.S. Chess Fedn. (regional v.p. 1973-76, voting mem. 1973-83), Assn. U.S. Chess Journalists (sec.-treas. 1976-79), Chess Journalists Am., Am. Statis. Assn., Am. Assn. Ret. Persons, DAV, Tau Beta Pi. Editor: Kings File mag., 1974. Asst. editor Va. Chess Fedn. Newsletter, 1976-83, games editor, 1978, 80-82. Home: 607 Pulman Pl Alexandria VA 22305 Office: 1201 E St NW Washington DC 20224

JONES, HUGH MCKITTRICK, architect; b. St. Louis, Oct. 6, 1919; s. Hugh McKittrick and Carroll (West) J.; m. Elizabeth Siddons Mowbray, Sept. 9, 1940 (dec. July 1978); children: Cynthia Siddons Jones Benjamin, Terry West (Mrs. James Henry Eddy, Jr.), Hugh McKittrick III, Timothy Millard.; m. Margaret Twichell Mowbray, Mar. 17, 1984; stepchildren: Burton Twichell Mowbray, Katharine Siddons Mowbray Michie. B.S., Harvard, 1940, B.Arch., 1942, M.Arch., 1947. Registered profl. architect, Conn. Trainee Office Walter Bogner, Cambridge, Mass., 1945-47, Office Douglas Orr, New Haven, 1947-49; architect Jones & Mowbray, New Haven and Guilford, Conn., 1949-54, Office Hugh Jones, Guilford, 1954-87; now ret. cons. Office Hugh Jones; corporator, trustee Guilford Savs. Bank, 1954—, v.p., 1975-77, vice chmn., 1977—; v.p. Envirland Co., 1976—. Mem. Guilford Republican Town Com., 1952-84, now assoc.; mem. Guilford Town Planning Commn., 1953-58, chmn., 1956; mem. Regional Planning Agy., 1961-69; rep. Conn. Ho. Reps., 1963-67; mem. Conn. Commn. to Study Metro Govt., 1965-67, Conn. Gov.'s Task Force on Housing, 1971-73; chmn. Regional Housing Council for S. Central Planning Region, 1974-80; mem. Guilford Land Conservation Trust, 1965—; pres. Guilford Found., 1976-80, bd. dirs., 1977-82, 83—; treas. Guilford Preservation Alliance, 1981—; mem. Guilford Keeping Soc., 1979—. Served to lt. USNR, 1942-46, PTO. Fellow AIA (pres. Conn. chpt. 1962, 63, Nat. dir. 1970-73), Guilford C. of C., Sierra Club, Am. Arbitration Assn. (nat. panel arbitrators 1956—). Home: 265 Dromara Rd PO Box 361 Guilford CT 06437

JONES, JACK ALAN, mechanical engineer, consultant; b. Newark, Apr. 15, 1948; s. James Corbett and Mertel Mathilda (Bergbauer) J. Cert., U. Calif., Santa Barbara, 1969; BSME, Rutgers U., 1970; MSME, Rice U., 1973. Registered profl. engr., N.J. Mech. engr. Bechman Instruments, Irvine, Calif., 1973-74; sr. engr. Garrett A. Research, Torrance, Calif., 1974-79; sr. engr., mem. tech. staff Jet Propulsion Lab., Pasadena, Calif., 1979—; cons. Aerojet Electro Systems, Azusa, Calif., 1985-86. Contbr. articles to profl. jours.; patentee cryogenic refrigeration. Recipient Manned Flight Awareness Honoree award NASA, 1987; NSF fellow, 1970-73; Dirs. Discretionary grantee, 1985-86. Mem. AIAA, ASME, Sigma Xi. Democrat. Office: Jet Propulsion Lab 4800 Oak Grove Dr Pasadena CA 91109

JONES, JENKIN LLOYD, newspaper publisher; b. Madison, Wis., Nov. 1, 1911; s. Richard Lloyd and Georgia (Hayden) J.; m. Ana Maria de Andrada Rocha, July 30, 1976; children: Jenkin Lloyd, David, Georgia; step-children: Maria Alice Rocha, Paulo Rocha. PhB, U. Wis., 1933; various hon. degrees. Reporter Tulsa Tribune, 1933, mng. editor, 1938, editor, 1941-88, pub., 1963—; dir. Newspaper Printing Corp., Tulsa. Author: The Changing World, 1966; writer syndicated weekly column. Served to lt. comdr. USNR, 1944-46, PTO. Recipient William Allen White award Okla. Hall of Fame, 1957; Fourth Estate award Am. Legion, 1970; Freedom Leadership award Freedoms Found., 1969; Disting. Service award U. Wis., 1970; Disting. Service award U. Okla., 1971; Disting. Service award Okla. State U., 1972. Mem. Am. Soc. Newspaper Editors (pres. 1957), Inter Am. Press Assn., U.S. C. of C. (pres. 1969), Internat. Press Inst. Republican. Unitarian. Clubs: So. Hills Country (Tulsa), Summit (Tulsa). Home: 6683 S Jamestown Pl Tulsa OK 74136 Office: Tulsa Tribune Box 1770 Tulsa OK 74102

JONES, JOHN FRANK, lawyer, consultant; b. Carrington, N.D., Feb. 24, 1922; s. Dwight Frank and Veronica Esther (Sheehy) J.; m. Sally Oppegard; children—Janna Jones Bellwin, John M., Jeramy Ridder, Jill Jones Nester, Julie, Jeffrey, J. David. B.S., U. N.D., 1946; M.S. in Organic Chemistry, U. Wis., 1953; J.D., U. Akron, 1956. Bar: Ohio 1956, U.S. Patent Office, U.S. Ct. Appeals. Patent atty. B. F. Goodrich Co., Akron, Ohio, 1956-62; sr. patent atty. Standard Oil Co., Cleve., 1962-70, patent counsel, 1970-81, food and drug atty. Vistron Corp. subs. Standard Oil Co., Cleve., 1968-81, ret., 1981; cons. to Standard Oil Co., Cleve. and Ashland Chem. Co. (div. Ashland Oil Co.), Columbus, Ohio, 1981—, B.F. Goodrich Co. Served with USAAF, 1943-46. Decorated D.F.C., Air medal. Mem. Am. Chem. Soc., Ohio Bar Assn., ABA, Cleve. Patent Law Assn. Republican. Patentee in chem. and polymer fields; contbr. articles on polymer sci. to profl. jours. Home and Office: 2724 Cedar Hill Rd Cuyahoga Falls OH 44223

JONES, JOHN HARRIS, lawyer, banker; b. New Blaine, Ark., Apr. 9, 1922; s. Ira Burton and Byrd (Harris); m. Marjorie Crosby Hart, 1983. A.B., U. Central Ark., 1941; postgrad., George Washington U. Law Sch., 1941-42; LL.B., Yale, 1947. Bar: Ark. 1946, U.S. Supreme Ct. 1963. Communications clk. FBI, 1941-42; practice in Pine Bluff, 1947—; spl. judge Circuit Ct., 1950; chmn. bd. Pine Bluff Nat. Bank, 1964-77, pres., 1966-76; Mem. Ark. Bd. Law Examiners, 1953-59; Republican nominee for U.S. Senate, 1974; Rep. presdl. elector, 1980; v.p., dir. John Rust Found., 1953-60. Served to 1st lt. USAAF, 1943-45. Decorated Purple Heart, Air medal. Mem. ABA, Ark. Bar Assn., Jefferson County Bar Assn. (pres. 1959-60), Am. Judicature Soc., Res. Officers Assn. Mem. Christian Ch. (elder 1963-65, trustee 1965-71, 78-84). Club: Pine Bluff Country. Home: 4001 Cherry St Pine Bluff AR 71603 Office: National Bldg Pine Bluff AR 71611

JONES, JOHN HOWEL, physician, consultant; b. Aberystwyth, Wales, Eng., Mar. 4, 1928; s. John Emrys and Mary (Edwards) J.; m. Sheila Mary Forster, Mar. 19, 1928; children: Elizabeth, Hugh, David. BA, U. Cambridge, Eng., 1949, MB, 1952, BChir, 1952; MD, Cambridge U., 1964. Intern St. George's Hosp., London, 1952-54, 56-58, Brompton Hosp., London, 1958-59, Queen Elizabeth Hosp., Birmingham, Eng., 1959-61, Cen. Middlesex Hosp., London, 1963-65; cons. physician West Midlands Regional Health Authority, Coventry and Rugby, Eng., 1966—; med. officer Great Britain Olympic Team, 1976-84, Eng. Commonwealth Games Team, 1976-84; med. advisor Commonwealth Games Fedn., 1982—. Served as capt. Royal Army Med. Corps., 1954-56. Home: 41 Hillmorton Rd, Rugby, Warwicks CV22 5AB, England

JONES, JOHN MARTIN, JR., lawyer; b. Balt., Dec. 31, 1928; s. John Martin and Nannalee (Rogers) J.; m. Dayle Fort Nesbitt, July 27, 1969; children—David Mallory, Kelly Anne Klein, Jeffrey Wallace Arthur, Kathleen Celeste Silvester; stepchildren—Martha Nesbitt Dewey, William Fort Nesbitt, Howard Scott Nesbitt. AB, U. Md., 1951, LLB, 1953. Bar: Md. Ct. Appeals bar 1953, U.S. Dist. Ct. bar for Dist. Md 1953, U.S. Ct. Appeals bar for 4th Circuit 1954, ICC 1956, U.S. Supreme Ct. bar 1959. Assoc. Piper & Marbury, Balt., 1954-59; ptnr. Piper & Marbury, 1960-86; asst. atty. gen. State of Md., 1959-60; mem. Md. Gov.'s Commn. to Study Tax Laws. Mem. Balt. Area council Boy Scouts Am.; publ. adv. Regional Planning Council, Greater Balt., 1977. Mem. Am. Bar Assn., Md. State Bar Assn., Bar Assn. Balt. City, Am. Judicature Soc., Am. Law Inst., Order of Coif, Delta Theta Phi, Delta Kappa Epsilon. Clubs: Center, Yale of N.Y.C, DKE of N.Y.C, Rule Day; Univ. (Washington). Home: 8025 Strauff Rd Baltimore MD 21204 Office: 25 S Charles St Suite 2222 Baltimore MD 21201

JONES, JOHN MICHAEL, poultry scientist; b. Redditch, Worcs, Eng., Sept. 10, 1939; s. Horace George and Violet Jane (Howell) J. BS with honors, U. Birmingham, Eng., 1962, PhD, 1966. Postdoctoral fellow Lister Inst. Preventive Medicine, London, 1966-69; head poultry tech. group, Agrl. and Food Research Council Food Research Inst., Norwich, Eng., 1969-84; pvt. practice in poultry sci. cons. Norwich, Eng., 1984—; mem. council mgmt. British Poultry Sci. Ltd., 1983—, asst. editor, 1987—. Contbr. articles to profl. jours. Active European Econ. Community S.C.A.R. Agro-Food Working Group on Poultry Meat Quality, 1982-83. Mem. Inst. Food Technologists (profl. mem.), World's Poultry Sci. Assn., Poultry Sci. Assn. Mem. Ch. of Eng. Home and Office: 18 Sywell Close, Old Catton, Norwich NR6 7EW, England

JONES, KENNETH CALLOW, III, financial executive; b. Evanston, Ill., Sept. 27, 1945; s. Kenneth Callow Jr. and Phyllis Rae (Wheelock) J.; B.A., Denison U., 1967; M.Govtl. Adminstrn., U. Pa., 1968; 1 son, Aaron McKennon. Budget analyst positions, dir. crime control program City of Rochester (N.Y.), 1968-71, dir. fed. program rev., 1972, dep. budget dir., 1973; budget officer City of Portland (Oreg.), 1973-78, dir. Office of Mgmt. Services, 1978-80; pres. Performance Mgmt. Assos., 1980-84; dir. mgmt. services HealthLink, Portland, 1984—; columnist The Bus. Jour., 1984-86; arbitrator Portland Better Bus. Bur.; adj. asst. prof. Portland State U., 1976—, Lewis and Clark Coll. Served to 1st lt. USAR, 1968-74. Samuel S. Fels scholar, 1967-68, fellow, 1968. Mem. Am. Soc. Pub. Adminstrn. (v.p. Oreg. chpt., then pres.), Healthcare Fin. Mgmt. Assn., Alpha Kappa Delta, Pi Sigma Alpha, Psi Chi. Club: Portland City. Home: 8500 SW Mapleridge Dr Portland OR 97225 Office: 500 NE Multnomah Portland OR 97232

JONES, LEON HERBERT (HERB), JR., artist; b. Norfolk, Va., Mar. 25, 1923; s. Leon Herbert and Edna May (Curling J.; student William and Mary Coll., 1942-44; m. Barbara Dean, Sept. 14, 1947; children—Robert Clair, Louis Herbert. Marine structural draftsman and designer Norfolk (Va.) Shipbuilding & Dry Dock Co., 1944-46; freelance comml. artist, 1946-49; prin. Herb Jones Realty, Norfolk, 1949-58; owner, mgr. Herb Jones Art Studio, Norfolk, 1958—; one-man shows: Norfolk Mus., 1968, Potomac Gallery, Alexandria, Va., 1979, Salisbury Gallery, 1979, Walter C. Rawls Mus., Courtland, Va., 1967, Virginia Beach Maritime Mus., 1983 Village Gallery, Virginia Beach, Va., 1984, Va. Mus. Marine Scis., 1986-87, Olde Towne Gallery, 1987; group shows include: Chrysler Mus., Norfolk, 1973, 74, SUNY, Buffalo, 1966, Springfield (Mass.) Mus. Fine Arts, 1966, Mariners Mus., Newport News, Va., 1967-73, Va. Mus., Richmond, 1969, 71, Columbia (S.C.) Mus. Art, 1972, Winston-Salem (N.C.) Gallery Contemporary Art, 1970, 72, Norfolk Mus., 1963-69, Vladimir Arts, Winsbach, W. Ger., 1978, 79, Chesapeake Bay Maritime Mus., Md., Mobile Mus. Traveling Show, 1983, Knoxville World's Fair in Fine Arts, 1982, Art Buyers Caravan, Atlanta, 1982, Colonial Wild Fowl Festival, Williamsburg, Va., 1983, Chesapeake Jubilee (Va.) (award of excellence) 1984, Peninsula Fine Arts Festival, Newport News, 1984, Currituck Wildlife Show, N.C., 1984, Medley of Arts, Hampton, Va., 1984, Easton Nat. Wildfowl and Art Exhibit, Easton, Md., 1984; Mid-Atlantic Art Exhibit, Virginia Beach, Va., 1985, Chincoteague Island Easter Festival, Va., 1985, Harborfest Norfolk, Va., 1985, Mid-Atlantic Wildfowl Festival, Hampton Wildlife Festival, 1986 (award), Medley of the Arts, 1986, 87, Mid Atlantic Art Exhibits, 1986, 87; represented in permanent collections: Chrysler Mus., wardroom USS Skipjack, USS Iwo Jima, USS John F. Kennedy, USS Dwight D. Eisenhower, U. Va., Charlottesville, U.S. Treasury Dept., Library of Congress, Washington, Edenton Hist. Commn. (N.C.), also pvt. collections; commd. ltd. edit. print series Ducks Unltd., also Va. Beach Maritime Mus., Boy Scouts Am., Va. Mus. Marine Scis., plaque Chesapeake Bay Bridge and Tunnel Commn. Recipient diploma di merito Universita delle Arti, 1981, Gold Centaur award 1983, three Awards of Excellence Printing Industries of the Virginias, 1988; Cavalier of Arts, Acad. Bedriacense Calvatore, Italy, 1985; Oscar d'Italia, Acad. Italia Calvatore, 1985. Mem. Nat. Soc. Arts and Lit., Tidewater Artists Assn., Internat. Platform Assn., Virginia Beach Maritime Mus. (charter), Corr. Academie Europeene, Nat. Am. Film Inst. Methodist. Home and Office: 238 Beck St Norfolk VA 23503

JONES, MALINDA THIESSEN, telecommunications company executive; b. Perryton, Tex., Jan. 23, 1947; d. Chester Francis Thiessen and Bobbye Pearson (Wallis) Schwalm; m. Hollis Bass Jones, Mar. 21, 1969 (div. 1972); 1 child, Reshad. B.A. in Psychology, U. Mo.-Kansas City, 1975. Research asst. U. Kans. Med. Ctr., Kansas City, 1975-77; owner, mgr. Metro Shampoo Co., Kansas City, Mo., 1977-79; regional mgr. U.S. Telecom, Dallas, 1981-82, staff asst. to pres., Dallas, 1983-84, sr. planner, 1984-85; dir. mktg. Telinq Systems Inc., Richardson, Tex., 1985-86, dir. bus. devel. and corp. communications, 1986—; cons. in field. Editor conf. presentations, bus. plans. Vol. tchr. Sch. for Learning Disability, Operation Discovery, Kansas City, 1973-75; corp. liaison exec. assistance program Dallas C. of C./Dallas Ind. Sch. Dist., 1984; chmn. com. Therapeutic Riding Tex., Dallas, 1985. Recipient Outstanding Contbr. award Dallas Ind. Sch. Dist., 1984. Mem. Nat. Assn. Female Execs., Nat. Mus. Assn. for Women in Arts, Assn. Women Entrepreneurs Dallas. Home: 1122 Overlake Dr Richardson TX 75080 Office: Telinq Systems Inc 1651 N Glenville Dr Richardson TX 75081

JONES, MARGUERITE JACKSON, educator; b. Greenwood, Miss., Aug. 12, 1949; d. James and Mary G. (Reedy) Jackson; m. Algee Jones, Apr. 4, 1971; 1 child, Stephanie Nerissa. BS, Miss. Valley State U., 1969; MEd, Miss. State U., 1974; Specialist in Community Coll. Teaching, Ark. State U., 1983; postgrad. U. Ark. Tchr. English, Henderson High Sch., Starkville, Miss., 1969-70; tchr. creative writing Miami (Fla.) Coral Park, 1970-71; tchr. English, head dept. Marion (Ark.) Sr. High Sch., 1971-78; tchr. East Ark. Community Coll., Forrest City, 1978-79; migrant edn. supr. Marion (Ark.) Sch. Dist., 1979-83; mem. faculty Draughons Coll., Memphis, 1978-83; asst. prof. State Tech. Inst., 1984—; cons. writing projects; condr. workshops for ednl. bus., civic groups; dir. Tng. Inst., The Cathedral of Bountiful Blessings Ch. Mem. Nat. Council Tchrs. English, Ark. Assn. Profl. Educators, Assn. Supervision and Curriculum Devel. Home: 3707 Stallion St Memphis TN 38116 Office: State Tech Inst 5983 Macon Grove Memphis TN 38134

JONES, MARY DAILEY (MRS. HARVEY BRADLEY JONES), civic worker; b. Billings, Mont.; d. Leroy Nathaniel and Janet (Currie) Dailey; m. Harvey Bradley Jones, Nov. 15, 1952; children: Dailey, Janet Currie, Ellis Bradley. Student, Carleton Coll., 1943-44, U. Mont., 1944-46, UCLA, 1959. Owner Mary Jones Interiors. Founder, treas. Jr. Art Council, Los Angeles County Mus., 1953-55, v.p., 1955-56; mem. costume council Pasadena (Calif.) Philharm.; co-founder Art Rental Gallery, 1953, chmn. art and architecture tour, 1955; founding mem., sec. Art Alliance, Pasadena Art Mus., 1955-56; benefit chmn. Pasadena Girls Club, 1959, bd. dirs., 1958-60; chmn. Los Angeles Tennis Patron's Assn. Benefit, 1965; sustaining Jr. League Pasadena; mem. docent council Los Angeles County Mus.; mem. costume council Los Angeles County Mus. Art., program chmn. 20th Century Greatest Designers; mem. blue ribbon com. Los Angeles Music Center; benefit chmn. Venice com. Internat. Fund for Monuments, 1971; bd. dirs. Art Ctr. 100, Pasadena, 1988—; co-chmn. benefit Harvard Coll. Scholarship Fund, 1974, steering com. benefit, 1987, Otis Art Inst., 1975; mem. Harvard-Radcliffe scholarship dinner com., 1985; mem. adv. bd. Estelle Doheny Eye Found., 1976, chmn. benefit, 1980; adv. bd. Loyola U. Sch. Fine Arts, Los Angeles; patron chmn. Benefit Achievement Rewards for Coll. Scientists, 1988; chmn. com. Sch. Am. Ballet Benefit, 1988, N.Y.C.; bd. dirs. Founders Music Center, Los Angeles, 1977-81; mem. nat. adv. council Sch. Am. Ballet, N.Y.C., nat. co-chmn. gala, 1980; adv. council on fine arts Loyola-Marymount U.; mem. Los Angeles Olympic Com., 1984, The Colleagues; founding mem. Mus. Contemporary Art, 1986. Mem. Kappa Alpha Theta. Clubs: Valley Hunt (Pasadena); Calif. (Los Angeles). Home: 10375 Wilshire Blvd Apt 8B Los Angeles CA 90024

JONES, NANCY GEX, broadcast association executive; b. Cin., Feb. 1, 1952; d. Richard Stanley and Mary Kathryn (Brady) Gex; m. Jesse Holman Jones II, Oct. 1, 1983; children: Malia Louise, Hali Kathryn. B.S., Eastern Mich. U., 1976. Account exec. KTRH/KLOL Radio, Houston, 1981-83, sales mgr., 1983; broadcast cons. various radio stas., Tex., 1983-84; pres., owner Broadcast Resources, Inc., Houston, 1984—; exec. dir. Houston Assn. Radio Broadcasters, 1985-88; mgmt. cons., acting gen. sales mgr. Sta. KTRH Radio, 1988—. Publicity chmn. guild bd., bd. dirs. Am. Heart Assn., Houston, 1987—, also mem. communications com. Gulf Coast Council; mem. Houston Ballet Guild, 1984—; chair Houston Ballet Ambassadors II, 1986—; bd. dirs. Houston Zool. Soc., 1985—; mem. victory com. Am. Cancer Com., 1988—. Mem. Tex. Assn. Broadcasters, Radio Advt. Bureau. Avocations: scuba diving; skiing; bicycling; walking. Home: 2406 Locke Ln Houston TX 77019

JONES, NORMA LOUISE, librarian, educator; b. Poplar, Wis.; d. George Elmer and Hilma June (Wiberg) J. BE, U. Wis.; MA, U. Minn., 1952; postgrad, U. Ill., 1957; PhD, U. Mich., 1965; postgrad., NARS, 1978, 79, 80; postgrad. info. sci., Nova U., 1983—. Librarian Grand Rapids (Mich.) Public Schs., 1947-62; with Grand Rapids Public Library, 1948-49; instr. Central Mich. U., Mt. Pleasant, 1954, 55; librarian Benton Harbor (Mich.) Public Schs., 1962-63; asst. prof. library sci. U. Wis., Oshkosh, 1968-70; assoc. prof. U. Wis., 1970-75, prof., 1975—, chmn. dept. library sci., 1980-84, exec. dir. libraries and learning resources, 1987—; lectr. U. Mich., Ann Arbor, 1954, 55, 61, 63-65, asst. prof., 1966-68. Recipient Disting. Teaching award U. Wis.-Oshkosh, 1977. Mem. ALA (chmn. reference conf. 1975—), Assn. Library and Info. Sci. Educators, Spl. Library Assn., Soc. Am. Archivists, Women Librarian Assn., Phi Beta Kappa, Phi Kappa Phi, Pi Lambda Theta, Beta Phi Mu, Sigma Pi Epsilon. Home: 1220 Maricopa Dr Oshkosh WI 54901

JONES, RICHARD CYRUS, lawyer; b. Oak Park, Ill., Oct. 20, 1928; s. Ethler E. and Margaret S. (Stoner) J.; m. Betty Jane Becker; children: Richard C., Carrie, William. PhB, DePaul U., 1960, JD, 1963. Bar: Ill. 1963. Dept. mgr. Chgo. Title & Trust Co., 1947-64; mem. Sachnoff, Schrager, Jones, Weaver & Rubenstein Ltd. and predecessor firms, Chgo., 1964-81; of counsel Sachnoff, Weaver & Rubenstein, Chgo., 1981—; instr. Real Estate Inst., Chgo., 1970—; trustee, sec. Income Properties and Equity Trust, 1974—; trustee, chmn. Ind. Dirs. of Wis. Real Estate Investment Trust, 1980—. Mem. alumni bd. Wayland Acad., 1983-87, trustee, 1986—. Decorated Bronze Star. Mem. ABA, Ill. Bar Assn., Chgo. Bar Assn. (com. chmn. real property law 1970-72, 76—), Chgo. Council Lawyers, Delta Theta Phi. Lodge: Kiwanis (past pres.). Home: 1044 Forest Ave River Forest IL 60305 Office: 30 S Wacker Dr 29th Floor Chicago IL 60606

JONES, RICHARD M., retail executive; b. Eldon, Mo., Nov. 26, 1926; m. Sylvia A. Richardson, 1950; 3 children. B.S. in Bus. Adminstrn., Olivet Nazarene Coll., 1950, LL.D. (hon.), 1983; grad. Advanced Mgmt. Program, Harvard U., 1973. With Sears, Roebuck & Co., 1950—, store mgr., 1963-68; gen. mgr. Sears, Roebuck & Co., Washington and Balt., 1974; exec. v.p.-East Sears, Roebuck & Co., 1974-80, corp. v.p., 1980, vice chmn., chief fin. officer, 1980-85, pres., chief fin. officer, 1986—; dir. Sears Roebuck Found.; bd. of govs. indsl. issuer adv. council Standard & Poor's, Com. for Econ. Devel., Conf. Bd. Chmn. bd. trustees Field Mus. Natural History, Chgo.; bd. dirs. Council for Aid to Edn., Inc., bd. govs. Am. Red Cross, Northwestern Univ. Assocs., Chgo., ARC, Washington, Fishman-Davidson Ctr. adv. bd. Wharton Sch. of U. Pa.; bd. of govs. adv. council J.L. Kellogg Grad. Sch. Mgmt. at Northwestern U. Club: Comml. (bd. of govs.). Office: Sears Roebuck & Co Sears Tower Chicago IL 60684

JONES, ROBERT ALONZO, economist; b. Evanston, Ill., Mar. 15, 1937; s. Robert Vernon and Elsie Pierce (Brown) J.; A.B., Middlebury Coll., 1959; M.B.A., Northwestern U., 1961; m. Kathleen Mary Bush, Aug. 16, 1958; children—Lindsay Rae, Robert Pierce, Gregory Alan, William Kenneth. Sr. research officer Bank of Am., San Francisco, 1969-74; v.p., dir. fin. forecasting Chase Econometrics, San Francisco, 1974-76; chmn. bd. Money Market Services, Inc., Belmont, Calif., 1974-86; chmn. bd. MMS Internat., Redwood City, Calif., 1986—, Market News Service, Inc., N.Y.C., 1987—; dir. Money Market Services, Ltd., London, Money Market Services, Ltd., Hong Kong; dir. Market News Service, Inc., Washington; chmn. bd. trustees Internat. Inst. Econ. Advancement, Incline, Nev., 1982—; instr. money and banking, Am. Inst. Banking, San Francisco, 1971, 72. Councilman, City of Belmont (Calif.), 1970-77, mayor, 1971, 72, 75, 76; dir. San Mateo County Transit Dist., 1975-77; chmn. San Mateo County Council of Mayors, 1975-76; trustee Incline Village Gen. Improvement Dist., 1984-85. Hon. life mem. Calif. PTA; named to Kappa Delta Rho Nat. Hall of Fame. Mem. Nat. Assn. Bus. Economists, San Francisco Bond Club. Republican. Methodist. Author: U. S. Financial System and the Federal Reserve, 1974, Power of Coinage, 1987.

JONES, ROBERT BRYAN, research scientist; b. Chester, Eng., July 28, 1948; s. Robert Caradoc and Eirlys Catherine (Hughes) J.; m. Susan Haddon, July 30, 1970 (div. Nov. 1980). BSc with honors, U. Aberdeen, Scotland, 1971; PhD, U. Hull, Eng., 1976. Sr. scientific officer AFRC Inst. of Animal Physiology and Genetics Research, Edinburgh, Scotland, 1974—. Conrbr. over 90 articles to scientific jours. Mem. Assn. for Study of Animal Behavior, Soc. for Vet. Ethology, World's Poultry Sci. Assn., Internat. Soc. for Comparative Psychology, Internat. Soc. Devel. Psychobiology. Home: 110 Blackford Ave, Edinburgh EH9 3HH, Scotland Office: AFRC Inst of Animal Physiology, and Genetics Research, Roslin EH25 9PS, Scotland

JONES, ROBERT ROLAND, JR., physicist; b. Houston, Sept. 1, 1942; d. Robert R. and Rubye Laura Frances (Burch) J.; children—Regina Renee, Robert R. III. B.S. in Physics, U. Tex.-Austin, 1967, B.A. in Math., 1967; M.A. in Physics, 1970; postgrad. U. Houston, Tex. So. U., 1960-61. Teaching and research asst. U. Tex., Austin, 1967-70; instr. physics and math. Houston Community Coll. and Lockheed Electronics, 1970-72; instr. physics and math. Tex. So. U. and Community Coll., 1972-74; teaching asst. U. Houston, 1974-76; teaching and research asst. Howard U., Washington, 1976-77; sr. engr. assoc. Lockheed Electronics, Inc., Houston, after 1978; owner, operator Trebore Industries, Trebore Medi-Ctr. Recipient Award of Merit, Greater Houston Sci. Fair, 1958; grantee Fisk U., Nashville, 1960; Worthing Scholar, Houston, 1960. Mem. Am. Phys. Soc., Am. Chem. Soc. (cert. of honor and plaque 1965), Sigma Pi Sigma. Republican. Baptist.

JONES, RODDIS STEWART, construction and land development company executive; b. Marshfield, Wis., Jan. 11, 1930; s. Henry Stewart and Sara (Roddis) J.; m. Anne Crook Orum, Jan. 7, 1955; children: Patricia, Jeffrey, Jennifer. BAME, Auburn U., 1952; PMD, Harvard U., 1960; postgrad., U. Wis., Madison, 1959. Lic. realtor, Wash. Project ngr. Marathon Corp., Rothschild, Wis., 1955-57; prodn. supt. indsl. engring., mgr. cost acctg. Roddis Plywood Corp., Marshfield, 1957-60; br. mgr. Weyerhauser Co., Hancock, Vt., Oakland, Calif., Federal Way, Wash., 1960-78; pres., gen. mgr. Roddis Jones Cos., Solarcrete N.W., Investment Bldg. & Devel. Co., Mgmt. Cons. Fin., Prodn. 1978—; pres. Cinn. Pacific Industries, Inc., 1986—. Served as officer USN, 1952-55. Mem. Seattle Master Builders. Republican. Episcopalian. Lodges: Rotary, Elks, Masons. Home: 104 Cascade Key Bellevue WA 98006

JONES, ROGER CLYDE, electrical engineer, educator; b. Lake Andes, S.D., Aug. 17, 1919; s. Robert Clyde and Martha (Albertson) J.; m. Katherine M. Tucker, June 7, 1952; children: Linda Lee, Vonnie Lynette. B.S., U. Nebr., 1949; M.S., U. Md., 1953; Ph.D. U. Md., 1963. With U.S. Naval Research Lab., Washington, 1949-57; staff sr. engr. to chief engr. Melpar, Inc., Falls Church, Va., 1957-58; cons. project engr. Melpar, Inc., 1958-59, sect. head physics, 1959-64, chief scientist for physics, 1964; prof. dept. elec. engring. U. Ariz., Tucson, 1964—; dir. quantum electronics lab. U. Ariz., 1968—, adj. prof. radiology, 1978-86, adj. prof. radiation-oncology, 1986-88, prof. of radiation-oncology, 1988—; guest prof. in exptl. oncology Inst. Cancer Research, Aarhus, Denmark, 1982-83. Served with AUS, 1942-45. Mem. Am. Phys. Soc., Optical Soc. Am., Bioelectromagnetics Soc., IEEE, AAAS, NSPE, Am. Congress on Surveying and Mapping, Eta Kappa Nu, Pi Mu Epsilon. Home: 5809 E 3d St Tucson AZ 85711 Office: U Ariz Dept Elec and Computer Engring Tucson AZ 85711

JONES, RONALD LEE, furniture manufacturing executive; b. Joplin, Mo., Sept. 6, 1942; s. Melvin Levine and Mary Belle (Hackler) J.; m. Nancy Rose Young, June 2, 1962; children: Ronald Jr., Valori Lee, Jennifer Lee, Matthew Lee. BA in Psychology and Bus., Cen. Meth. Coll., Fayette, Mo.; postgrad., So. Meth. U., Baker U. Plant mgr. Duke Mfg. Co., Sedalia, Mo., 1968-72; dep. dir. Mo. Dept. Agriculture, Jefferson City, 1972-74; plant mgr. Ithaca Gun Co., Cameron, Mo., 1974-77; exec. v.p. Chisum Industries, Inc., Tulsa, 1977-79; gen. mgr. Materials Handling div. Hoover Universal, Inc., Memphis, 1979-83; pres. The HON Co., Muscatine, Iowa, 1983-88, also bd. dirs.; pres. HON Industries, 1988—; cons. Draft Systems, Inc., Los Angeles, 1983-86, Sonoco, Inc., Los Angeles, 1985; bd. dirs. Booth, Inc. Author: Industrial Safety for Medium Sized Manufacturing Companies; author articles on mgmt. and human relations. Recipient award Acad. of Excellence State Indsl. Devel. Bd., 1975, Excellence in Mgmt. award, 1976. Mem. Nat. Assn. Office Products (exec. com.). Republican. Mormon (high priest). Office: HON Industries Inc 414 E 3rd St Muscatine IA 52761

JONES, RUSSEL CAMERON, educational administrator; b. Tarentum, Pa., Oct. 18, 1935; s. Frederick Russel and Helena Doris (Elliot) J.; m. Sharon Ann Keillor; children—Amy Sue, Kimberly Nicole, Tamara Melissa. B.S., Carnegie Inst. Tech., 1957, M.S., 1960, Ph.D., 1963. Structural engr. Hunting, Larsen & Dunnels, Pitts., 1957-59; asst. prof. civil engring. M.I.T., 1963-66, assoc. prof., 1966-71; prof., chmn. dept. civil engring. Ohio State U., Columbus, 1971-76; dean Sch. Engring., U. Mass., Amherst, 1977-81; v.p. acad. affairs Boston U., 1981-87, v.p. acad. devel., 1985-87; pres. U. Del., Newark, 1987—. Recipient fellowship NDEA, 1959-62, fellowship ASCE, 1962-63, Collingwood prize ASCE, 1966, Edmund Friedman profl. recognition award ASCE, 1981. Fellow Am. Soc. Engring. Edn., AAAS, ACSE (dir. 1969-71, 72-75, v.p. 1976-77), Royal Soc. for Encouragement of Arts; mem. AAHE, ABET (dir. 1983-86, pres. elect 1986-87, pres. 1987-88), IEEE, Nat. Soc. Profl. Engrs., Sigma Xi, Tau Beta Pi, Phi Kappa Phi, Chi Epsilon, Sigma Nu. Home: 47 Kent Way Newark DE 19711 Office: U Del Office of Pres 132 Hullihen Hall Newark DE 19716

JONES, SALLY DAVIESS PICKRELL, author; b. St. Louis, June 4, 1923; d. Claude Dildine and Marie Daviess (Pittman) Pickrell; student Mills Coll., Oakland, Calif., 1941-43, U. Calif.-Berkeley, 1944, Columbia, 1955-58; m. Charles William Jones, Sept. 2, 1943; 1 son, Matthew Charles. Author: (novel) The Lights Burn Blue, 1947. Mem. UN Women's Guild, Fgn. Policy Assn., Nat. Council Women, Asia Soc., English-Speaking Union, Met. Mus. Art, Internat. Platform Assn. Episcopalian. Address: 311 E 58th St New York NY 10022

JONES, STEPHEN, lawyer; b. Lafayette, La., July 1, 1940; s. Leslie William and Gladys A. (Williams) J.; m. Virginia Hadden (div.); 1 son, John Chapman; m. 2d, Sherrel Alice Stephens, Dec. 27, 1973; children—Stephen Mark, Leslie Rachael, Edward St. Andrew. Student U. Tex. 1960-63; LL.B., U. Okla. 1966. Sec. Rep. Minority Conf., Tex. Ho. of Reps., 1963; personal asst. to Richard M. Nixon, N.Y.C., 1964; adminstrv. asst. to Congressman Paul Findley, 1966-69; legal counsel to gov. of Okla., 1967; spl. asst. U.S. Senator Charles H. Percy and U.S. Rep. Donald Rumsfeld, 1968; mem. U.S. del. to North Atlantic Assembly, NATO, 1968; staff counsel cesure task force Ho. of Reps. Impeachment Inquiry, 1974; spl. U.S. atty. No. Dist. Okla., 1979; spl. prosecutor, spl. asst. dist. atty. State of Okla., 1977; judge Okla. Ct. Appeals, 1982; civil jury instrn. com. Okla. Supreme Ct., 1979-81; adv. com. ct. rules Okla. Ct. Criminal Appeals, 1980; now mng. ptnr. Jones, Bryant & Nigh (formerly Jones, Blakley & Jennings), Enid, Okla.; adj. prof. U. Okla., 1973-76; instr. Phillips U., 1982—. Author: Oklahoma and Politics in State and Nation, 1907-62. Acting chmn. Rep. State Com., Okla., 1982; mem. vestry, sr. warden St. Matthews Episc. Ch. Mem. ABA, Okla. Bar Assn., Garfield County Bar Assn. Clubs: Capitol Hill, Nat. Lawyers (Washington), Beacon, Petroleum (Oklahoma City), Oakwood Country (Enid), Tulsa. Contbr. articles profl. jours. Address: PO Box 472 Enid OK 73702

JONES, STEPHEN PETER, controller; b. Manchester, Eng., Dec. 27, 1954; s. Edward and Irene (Atkinson) Jones; divorced; 1 child, Daniel Restituto Edward. MBA, Nat. U., San Diego, 1988. Fin. analyst Simon Container Machinery, Ltd., Stockport, Eng., 1971-76; group mgmt. acct. Lex Commls. Co., Ltd., Manchester, 1976-77; mgmt. acct. Lex Tillotson Co., Ltd., Burnley, Eng., 1977-78, Manchester, 1978-80; internat. acct. Colgate-Palmolive U.K., Ltd., London, 1980-82; asst. fin. controller Colgate-Palmolive (Caribbean), Inc., Jamaica, Trinidad, Barbados, Guyana, 1982-84; fin. controller Colgate-Palmolive Del Ecuador, S.A., Guayaquil, Ecuador, 1984-85, Colgate-Palmolive (C.A.), Inc., San José, Costa Rica, 1985—. Mem. Inst. Chartered Mgmt. Accts. (assoc.), U.S. C. of C. (econ. com. 1985—). Club: Costa Rica Country (San José). Home and Office: Colgate-Palmolive Inc, Apt 10040, San José Costa Rica

JONES, SUSAN DORFMAN, writer; b. N.Y.C., Oct. 4, 1939; d. Joseph and Sarah (Sorrin) Dorfman; m. William Harry Jones, Sept. 18, 1960; children: Jeffrey Scott, Eric David, Timothy Mark. BA, Syracuse U., 1961. Pres., owner Antiques Corp. Am., 1972-77; communications officer Riggs Bank, Washington, 1978-81; mgr. publs. Potomac Electric Power Co., Washington, 1981-82; sr. mgr. corp. communications MCI Corp., Washington, 1982-83, dir. corp. communications Sears World Trade, Washington, 1983-85; dir. corp. communications and govt. relations Oxford Devel. Corp., Bethesda, Md., 1985-87; free-lance writer, cons., Washington, 1975—; radio personality Sta. 4KQ, Brisbane, Australia, 1962; adj. prof. communications Am. U., Washington, 1978-82. Author, editor, project mgr. corp. ann. reports; writer sch. bd. candidates and home rule campaign speeches, Washington, 1970-76. Treas. playground D.C. Recreation Dept., 1973-79; bd. dirs. March Elem. Sch., Washington, 1969. Recipient 1st place award for columns N.Y. Press Assn., 1961, Gold Quill award Internat. Assn. Bus. Communicators, 1980. Mem. Internat. Assn. Bus. Communicators (treas. 1981), Nat. Assn. Bank Women, Women in Telecommunications, Nat. Press Club, Pub. Relations Soc. Am. Democrat. Jewish. Home and Office: 7300 Burdette Ct Bethesda MD 20817

JONES, THEODORE LAWRENCE, lawyer; b. Dallas, Nov. 29, 1920; s. Theodore Evan and Ernestine Lucy (Douthit) J.; m. Marion Elizabeth Thomas, Feb. 29, 1944; children: Suzanne Lynn, Scott Evan, Stephen Lawrence, Shannon Elizabeth. B.B.A., U. Tex., 1944, J.D., 1948; postgrad., So. Meth. U., 1950-52, Am. U., 1965-66. Bar: Tex. 1948, U.S. Supreme Ct. 1962, D.C. 1988. Asso. Carrington, Gowan, Johnson & Walker, Dallas, 1948-51; gen. counsel W. H. Cothrum & Co., Dallas, 1951-54; practice law Dallas, 1955-56; asst. atty. gen. Tex.; chief div. ins., banking and corp. 1957-60; partner Herring & Jones, Austin, Tex., 1960-61; gen. counsel Maritime Adminstrn., U.S. Dept. Commerce, 1961-63; dep. gen. counsel Dept. Commerce, 1963-64, dep. fed. hwy. adminstr., 1964-66; pres. Am. Ins. Assn., N.Y.C., 1967-86; counsel Hunton & Williams, Washington, 1986—; chmn. interdeptl. com. for bilateral agreements for acceptance of nuclear ship, Savannah, 1962-63; lectr. Fgn. Service Inst., 1962-64; alt. U.S. rep. 11th session Diplomatic Conf. on Maritime Law, Brussels, 1962; advisor U.S. del. 6th session Council, Intergovtl. Maritime Consultative Orgn., London, 1962; mem. maritime subsidy bd. U.S. Dept. Commerce, 1962-63; acting hwy. beautification coordinator, 1965-66; del. White House Conf. on Internat. Cooperation; mem. Property-Casualty Ins. Council, 1976-86, Internat. Ins. Adv. Council, 1980-87; mem. adv. com. Pension Benefit Guaranty Corp., 1977; mem. Time Newstour, Eastern Europe and Persian Gulf, 1981, Mexico and Panama, 1983, Pacific Rim, 1985; bd. dirs. Nat. Safety Council, 1967, Ins. Inst. for Hwy. Safety, 1967-86. Contbr. articles to legal, ins. and fin. jours. Served to lt. (j.g.) USNR, 1944-46. Mem. ABA, D.C. Bar, Fed. Bar Assn. (chmn. nat. speakers bur. 1964), Tex. Bar Assn., Friars, Phi Delta Phi, Beta Gamma Sigma, Phi Eta Sigma. Democrat. Presbyterian. Clubs: Met., Capitol Hill (Washington), Nat. Democratic (Washington), Great Oaks Country (Floyd, Va.), World Trade Ctr. (N.Y.C.). Home: 648 S Carolina Ave SE Washington DC 20003 also: Camp Creek Farm Rt 3 Box 182-B Floyd VA 24091 Office: Hunton & Williams 2000 Pennsylvania Ave NW Suite 9000 Washington DC 20036

JONES, THOMAS ROBERT, social worker; b. Escanaba, Mich., Jan. 3, 1950; s. Gene Milton and Alica Una (Mattson) J.; m. Joy Sedlock. BA, U. Laverne, 1977; MSW, U. Hawaii, 1979. Social work assoc. Continuing Care Services, Camarillo, Calif., 1973-78; psychiat. social worker Camarillo State Hosp., 1980-84; psychotherapist Terkensha Child Treatment Ctr., Sacramento, Calif., 1984—. Mem. Nat. Assn. Social Workers, Soc. Clin. Social Work, Am. Orthopsychiat. Assn., Acad. Cert. Social Workers, Assn. for Advancement Behavior Therapy. Home: 17 Griggs Ln Napa CA 94558 Office: Veterans Home of Calif Yountville CA 94599

JONES, THORNTON KEITH, research chemist; b. Brawley, Calif., Dec. 17, 1923; s. Alfred George and Madge Jones; m. Evalee Vestal, July 4, 1965; children: Brian Keith, Donna Eileen. BS, U. Calif., Berkeley, 1949, postgrad., 1951-52. Research chemist Griffin Chem. Co., Richmond, Calif., 1949-55; western product devel. and improvement mgr. Nopco Chem. Co., Richmond, Calif., 1955; research chemist Chevron Research Co., Richmond, 1956-65, research chemist in spl. products research and devel., 1965-1982; product quality mgr. Chevron USA, Inc., San Francisco, 1982-87, ret. Patentee in field. Vol. fireman and officer, Terra Linda, Calif., 1957-64; mem. adv. com. Terra Linda Dixie Elem. Sch. Dist., 1960-64. Served with Signal Corps, U.S. Army, 1943-46. Mem. Am. Chem. Soc., Forest Products Research Soc., Am. Wood Preservers Assn., Alpha Chi Sigma. Republican. Presbyterian.

JONES, TOM F., communications company executive; b. Wales, Aug. 14, 1938; m. Susan Ann Jones. Student, Cambridge (Eng.) U., 1963, Exeter U., 1979. Dir. Systematic Co., Plymouth, U.K., 1968—; chmn. housing and urban devel. Plymouth City Council, 1980—; bd. dirs. Hosp. Mgmt. Systems Co., Devon, 1983—. Patent in field; contbr. articles to profl. jours. Councillor Plymouth City Council, 1973—; gov. Exeter U., 1978—, Hillside Spl. Sch., Devon, 1978—; chmn. supervisory bd. The Elm Ctr., Devon, 1981—. Served to lt. RAF Res., 1955-81. Fellow Brit. Inst. Mgmt. (membership officer 1965-66); mem. RAF Assn. (Gold Badge award 1965). Mem. Conservative Party. Mem. Ch. of Eng. Lodge: Rotary. Office: Systematic Co, Vine House 34 Regent St, PL4 888 Plymouth United Kingdom

JONES, TREVOR OWEN, automobile supply company executive, management consultant; b. Maidstone, Kent, Eng., Nov. 3, 1930; came to U.S., 1957, naturalized, 1971; s. Richard Owen and Ruby Edith (Martin) J.; m. Jennie Lou Singleton, Sept. 12, 1959; children: Pembroke Robinson, Bronwyn Elizabeth. Higher Nat. Cert. in Elec. Engring., Aston Tech. Coll., Birmingham, Eng., 1952; Ordinary Nat. Cert. in Mech. Engring., Liverpool (Eng.) Tech. Coll., 1957. Registered profl. engr., Wis.; chartered engr., U.K. Student engr., elec. machine design engr. Brit. Gen. Electric Co., 1950-57; project engr., project mgr. Nuclear Ship Savannah, Allis-Chalmers Mfg. Co., 1957-59; with Gen. Motors Corp., 1959-78, staff engr. in charge Apollo computers, 1967, dir. electronic control systems, 1970-72, dir. advanced product engring., 1972-74; dir. Gen. Motors Proving Grounds, 1974-78; v.p. engring., automotive worldwide TRW Inc., Cleve., 1978-80, v.p. transp. electronics group, 1980-85, v.p. sales, mktg., strategic planning and bus. devel., 1985-87; chmn. bd. Libbey-Owens-Ford Inc., 1987—; pres. Internat. Devel. Corp.; vice chmn. Motor Vehicle Safety Adv. Council, 1971; chmn. Nat. Hwy. Safety Adv. Com., 1976. Author, patentee automotive safety and electronics. Trustee Lawrence Inst. Tech., 1973-76; mem. exec. bd. Clinton Valley council Boy Scouts Am., 1975; bd. govs. Cranbrook Inst. Sci., 1977. Served as officer Brit. Army, 1955-57. Recipient Safety award for engring. excellence U.S. Dept. Transp., 1978. Fellow Brit. Instn. Elec. Engrs. (Hooper Meml. prize 1950), IEEE (exec. com. vehicle tech. soc. 1977-81), Soc. Automotive Engrs. (Arch T. Colwell paper award 1974, 75, Vincent Bendix Automotive Electronics award 1976); mem. Nat. Acad. Engring., Engring. Soc. Detroit and Cleve. Republican. Episcopalian. Clubs: Birmingham (Mich.) Athletic; Capitol Hill (Washington); Kirtland Country, Detroit Athletic. Home: 18400 Shelburne Rd Shaker Heights OH 44118

JONES, WALTER HARRISON, chemist; b. Griffin, Sask., Can., Sept. 21, 1922; s. Arthur Frederick and Mildred Tracy (Walter) J.; BS with honors, UCLA, 1944, PhD in Chemistry, 1948; m. Marion Claire Twomey, Oct. 25, 1959 (dec. Jan. 1976). Research chemist Dept. Agr., 1948-51, Los Alamos Sci. Lab., 1951-54; sr. research engr. N. Am. Aviation, 1954-56; mgr. chemistry dept. Ford Motor Co., 1956-60; sr. staff and program mgr., chmn. JANAF-ARPA-NASA Thermochem. panel Inst. Def. Analyses, 1960-63; head propulsion dept. Aerospace Corp., 1963-64; sr. scientist, head advanced tech. Hughes Aircraft Co., 1964-68; prof. aero. systems, dir. Corpus Christi Center, U. W. Fla., Pensacola, 1969-75, prof. chemistry, 1975—; cons. pvt., fed. and state agys.; vis. prof. U. Toronto. Mem. Gov.'s Task Force on Energy, Regional Energy Action Com., Fla. State Energy Office, adv. com. Tampa Bay Regional Planning Council; judge regional and state sci. fairs. Fed. and state grantee; research corp. grantee; ASEE/ONR fellow. NATO Fellow Am. Inst. Chemists; mem. Am. Astron. Soc. (propulsion com.), Am. Chem. Soc. (chmn. Pensacola sect.), N.Y. Acad. Scis., Am. Phys. Soc., AAUP, AAAS, Internat. Solar Energy Soc., AIAA, Combustion Inst. World Assn. Theoretical Organic Chemists, Am. Ordnance Assn., Air Force Assn., Philos. Soc. Washington, Pensacola C. of C., Phi Beta Kappa, Sigma Xi, Pi Mu Epsilon, Phi Lambda Upsilon, Alpha Mu Gamma, Alpha Chi Sigma. Author: (fiction) Prisms in the Pentagon, 1971; contbr. numerous articles tech. jours., chpts. in books. Patentee in field. Home: 2412 Oak Hills Circle Pensacola FL 32514 Office: U West Fla Dept of Chemistry Pensacola FL 32514

JONES, WALTON GLYN, European literature educator; b. Manchester, Eng., Oct. 29, 1928; s. Emrys and Dorothy Ada (North) N.; m. Karen Ruth Fleischer, June 23, 1964 (div. Aug. 1981); children: Stephen, Olaf, Monica, Anna; m. Kirsten Gade, Nov. 30, 1981. BA, Cambridge U., 1952, MA, PhD, 1956. Lectr. Danish U. Coll., London, 1956-63, reader, 1963-73; prof. Scandinavian studies U. Newcastle Upon Tyne, Eng., 1973-86; prof. European lit. U. East Anglia, Norwich, Eng., 1986—; vis. prof. Danish U. Iceland, 1971; prof. lit. Faroese Acad., 1979-81. Author: Johannes Jorgensen, 1964, William Heinesen, 1974, Tove Jansson, 1984, Denmark. A Modern History, 1986; (with others) Danish. A Grammar, 1981. Fellow Royal Norwegian Acad. Scis.; mem. Swedish Lit. Soc. in Finland (hon.), Danish Soc. Authors (corr.). Office: U East Anglia, Norwich NR4 7TJ, England

JONES, WINONA NIGELS, library media specialist; b. St. Petersburg, Fla., Feb. 24, 1928; d. Eugene Arthur and Bertha Lillian (Dixon) Nigels; m. Charles Albert Jones, Nov. 26, 1944; children—Charles Eugene, Sharon Ann Jones Allworth, Caroline Winona Jones Pandorf. AA, St. Petersburg Jr. Coll., 1965; BS, U. South Fla., 1967, MS, 1968; Advanced MS, Fla. State U., 1980. Library media specialist Dunedin (Fla.) Comprehensive High Sch., 1967-76; library media specialist, chmn. dept. Fitzgerald Middle Sch., Largo, Fla., 1976-87; dir. Media Services East Lake High Sch., 1987—. Active Palm Harbor and Pinellas County Hist. Soc. Named Educator of Year, Pinellas County Sch. Bd. and Suncoast C. of C., 1983. Mem. ALA, NEA, AAUW, Fla. Assn. Media in Edn. (pres.), U. So. Fla. Alumni Assn., Assn. Ednl. Communication and Tech. (div. sch. media specialist, coms.), Am. Assn. Sch. Libraries (com.), Southeastern Library Assn., Fla. Library Assn., Assn. Supervision and Curriculum Devel., Fla. State Library Sci. Alumni, U. South Fla. Library Sci. Alumni Assn. (dir.), Phi Theta Kappa, Phi Rho Pi, Beta Phi Mu, Kappa Delta Pi, Delta Kappa Gamma. Democrat. Club: Inner Wheel (Palm Harbor, Fla.) Pilot (Palm Harbor), Civic (Palm Harbor). Lodge: Order of Eastern Star (Palm Harbor) (past worthy matron). Home: 911 Manning Rd Palm Harbor FL 34683 Office: 1300 Silver Eagle Dr Tarpon Springs FL 34689

JONES Y DIEZ ARGUELLES, GASTÓN ROBERTO, educator; b. Cárdenas, Cuba, Dec. 6, 1910; came to U.S., 1963, naturalized, 1971; s. Guillermo Rafael Jones and María de Los Ángeles Diez Arguelles; B.Letters and Scis., Matanzas Inst. Cuba, 1928; Dr. Law, U. Havana (Cuba), 1937; M.A., U. Ala., 1969; m. Dolores Carricarte, May 19, 1950. Practice law, Havana, 1937-60; mcpl. judge, Cuba, 1938-40; cons. atty. Cuban Treasury Dept., 1943-60; instr. dept. fgn. langs. Sacred Heart Coll., Cullman, Ala., 1965-70, St. Bernard Coll., Cullman, 1967-70; asst. prof. U. Ala., Birmingham, 1971-81. Mem. Nat. Bicentennial Com. for celebration of Nat. Fgn. Lang. Discovery Week, 1975-83. Mem. Am. Assn. Tchrs. Spanish and Portuguese (past pres. Ala. chpt., chmn. So. and mountain states regional pub. relations com. 1975-77, chmn. nat. public relations and publicity com. 1977-81), Ala. Assn. Fgn. Lang. Tchrs. (past dir., chmn. com. for advancement fgn. langs. in Ala. 1973-81), Birmingham-Cobán Ala.-Guatemala Partners of Americas (v.p. 1971-81), Sociedad Nacional Hispanica, Cuban Bar Assn. in Exile, Sigma Delta Pi, Omicron Delta Kappa. Roman Catholic. Clubs: Miami Rowing (Outstanding Contbn. award 1985), Coral Gables Country. Lodge: Cuban Rotary in Exile. Contbr. articles to profl. jours. Successfully promoting nat. campaign to make Americans aware of need for fgn. langs. in U.S. Home: 1311 SW 102d Ct Miami FL 33174

JÓNSDÓTTIR, THÓRGUNNUR, writer, translator; b. Reykjavik, Iceland, Dec. 22, 1948; d. Jón Steingrimsson and Thórgunnur Ársaelsdóttir; m. Carl Jeffrey Fehlandt, Oct. 31, 1975 (div. 1985). BA, Akureyri (Iceland) Coll., 1969; postgrad., U. Iceland, 1973-74. Translator Joint Publs. Research Service, Arlington, Va., 1976-82; pvt. practice creative writing 1982—. Contbr. poetry Great Poems of Western World, 1980, World's Great Contemporary Poems, 1981, Am. Poetry Anthology, 1987. Home: Thingholtsstraeti 6, 101 Reykjavik Iceland

JONSSON, GISLI, electrical power engineering educator; b. Reykjavik, Iceland, June 6, 1929; s. Jon and Elin (Gisladottir) G.; m. Margret Gudnadottir, Jan. 9, 1930; children—Elin Gisladottir, Gudni Gislason, Ingunn Gisladottir. M.Sc. in Elec. Engring., Danish Tech. U., Copenhagen, 1956. Elec. engr. Iceland Elec. Authority, Reykjavik, 1956-60; cons. engr., Reykjavik, 1960-61; directing mgr. Mcpl. Elec. Works, Hafnarfjordur, Iceland, 1961-69, Assn. Electricity Systems in Iceland, Reykjavik, 1969-75; prof. elec. power engring. U. Iceland, Reykjavik, 1975—, chmn. engring. dept., 1978-79, electrical engring dept., 1984-85, Engring. Research Inst., 1988—; cons. Elec. State Inspection, Reykjavik, 1981-84; chmn. Assn. Mcpl. Electricity Utility Work's Mgrs., 1963-60. Author: (booklet) Electric Space Heating, 1968; (report) Use of Electric Car in Iceland, 1984, Ripple Control Systems. Mem. Assn. Chartered Engrs. Iceland (chmn. elec. sect. 1971-72), The Consumer Assn. (bd. dirs. 1979-82). Club: Rotary (Hafnarfjordur, pres. 1975-76, Paul Harris fellow). Home: Brekkuhvammur 4, IS-220 Hafnarfjordur Iceland Office: U Iceland, Hjardarhagi 2-6, IS-107 Reykjavik Iceland

JONSSON, HILMAR, librarian, writer; b. Jokulsarhlith, Iceland, May 12, 1932; s. Jon and Jona (Guthlaugsdó ttir) J.; student U. Sorbonne, 1954-55; m. Elisabeth Jensdó ttir, Sept. 5, 1964; children—Jens, Jon Runar, Guthlaug Jona. Librarian, Public Library Reykjavik, Iceland, 1956-58; chief librarian Public Library, Keflavik, Iceland, 1958—. Chmn. Labour Party, Keflavik, 1970—. Mem. Assn. Icelandic Authors, Assn. Icelandic Librarians in Public Libraries (chmn. 1975—). Icelandic I.O.G.T. (grand chief templar). Author numerous books including: Hundabyltingin (novel), 1976; Undirheimarnir risa (essays), 1977; Út Kall i Klúbbinn (play), 1979; contbr. articles to newspapers, jours. Home: 27 Hatun, Keflavik Iceland

JONTRY, RICHARD, psychologist; b. Bklyn., May 5, 1942; s. Henry and Esther (Schor) J.; BA, City U. N.Y., 1964; MA, New Sch., 1966; PhD, Ind. No. U., 1973; m. Sharon Gladson; children: Brie, Ari. Clin. psychology intern N.J. Neuro-Psychiat. Inst., Princeton, 1966-67, research scientist bur. research in neurology and psychiatry, 1967-73; dir. Center Family Interaction, Hatboro, Pa., 1972-74; dir. tng. and edn. bur. substance abuse, div. mental health Del. Dept. Health and Social Services, New Castle, 1974-79; dir. Intercept, Oxford, Pa., 1981—; clin. supr. ARC Counseling Services, So. Chester County Med. Ctr., West Grove, Pa.; adj. prof. Washington Coll., Chestertown, Md., 1980—; cons. Four Winds Alcoholism Rehab. Ctr., N.Mex., 1986—, Family Crises Ctr.; condr. tng. seminars for mental health profls.; mem. Cecil County (Md.) Mental Health and Addictions Adv. Bd., 1970-81, Cecil County Anti-Drug Abuse Action Com., 1980-82, Talbot County (Md.) Sch. Health Curriculum Adv. Com., 1980-82; adv. bd. Lincoln (Pa.) U., 1975-79, NE Regional Support Center, New Haven, 1976-79, Eastern Area Alcohol Tng. Program, Bloomfield, Conn., 1976-79, Johns Hopkins U. Tng. Inst. Alcoholism Counselors, 1976-79; cons. in field. Mem. Internat. Imagery Assn., Assn. Specialists Group Works, Assn. Labor Mgmt. Adminstrs. and Cons. on Alcoholism, Am. Personnel and Guidance

Assn., N.Y. Inst. Gestalt Therapy, Psi Chi. Home: 3413 Monterey Circle Farmington NM 87401 Office: Four Winds Addiction Recovery Ctr 1313 Mission Ave Box 736 Farmington NM 87499

JOPLIN, ALBERT FREDERICK, transportation executive; b. Victoria, B.C., Can., Feb 22, 1919; s. Albert Edward and Emily Eliza (Norford) J.; B.A.Sc. in Civil Engring., U. B.C., 1948; m. Margaret McMorragh-Kavanaugh, May 26, 1947 (dec.); 1 dau., Mary Lynn Barbara; m. 2d, Dorothy Anne Cook, July 29, 1977. With Can. Pacific Ltd., 1947-87 , spl. engr., Calgary, 1962-65, devel. engr., Vancouver, 1965-66, mgr. spl. projects, 1966-68, system mgr. planning and devel., Montreal, Que., 1968-69, dir. devel. planning, 1969-71, v.p. mktg. and sales CP Rail, 1971-74, v.p. operation and maintenance, 1974-76; gen. mgr. Marathon Realty, 1965-66; pres., chief exec. officer Canadian Pacific (Bermuda) Ltd., 1976-84; Shaw Industries, Ltd., Toronto, Ont., Straits Oil and Gas Ltd., pres. Straits Oil and Gas U.S.A. Ltd.; Sydney, Superburn Systems Ltd., Vancouver; chmn., bd. dirs. Leaders Equity Corp., Vancouver. Commr., gen. dir. Can. Pacific Pavilion Expo '86, 1984-87; pres. and chief exec. officer Cen. Ocean Industries Ltd.; active Boy Scouts Can. Served with RCAF, 1941-45. Mem. Assn. Profl. Engrs. B.C. (life), Engring. Inst. Can., Can. Soc. Civil Engrs., Internat. Soc. for Planning and Strategic Mgmt., Vancouver Maritime Arbitrators Assn., Inst. Corp. Dirs. Can., Air Force Officers Assn., Beta Theta Pi. Clubs: Engrs. (Vancouver), Royal Montreal Golf, Traffic, Mount Stephen (Montreal); Canadian Railway; Western Canada Railway; Mid-Ocean, Maritime Museum, Nat. Trust (Bermuda). Lodge: Rotary (Vancouver, B.C.), Order of St. John. Home: 4317 Staulo, Vancouver, BC Canada V6N 3S1 Office: 404-200 Granville St, Vancouver, BC Canada V6C 2R3

JORBERG, LENNART GUSTAV, economics educator; b. Varberg, Sweden, Jan. 26, 1927. Fil Kand, Lund U., Sweden, 1951; Fil Lic, Lund U., 1956, PhD, 1961; postgrad., Harvard U., 1957-58. Asst. dept. econ. history Lune U., 1952-54, lectr., 1961, asst. prof., 1961-70, prof., 1973—, dean faculty social sci., 1977-84; fellow Council Social Scis., Stockholm, 1970-73; vis. prof. Inst. Weltwirtschaft, Kiel, Fed. Republic Germany, 1964, U. Calif., Berkeley, 1965-66. Author: Growth and Fluctuation of Swedish Industry 1869-1912, 1961, A History of Prices in Sweden 1732-1914, 1972; mem. editorial bd. Economy and History, Lund, 1973-80, Explorations in Economic History, 1973-85. Mem. Royal Acad. Scis., Am. Econs. Assn., Econ. History Assn., Internat. Econ. History Assn. (exec. com. 1978—). Office: Dept Econ History, PO Box 7083, S 22007 Lund Sweden

JORDAN, BARBARA SCHWINN, painter; b. Glen Ridge, N.J.; d. Carl Wilhelm Ludwig and Helen Louise (Jordan) Schwinn; grad. N.Y. Sch. Fine and Applied Art (Parsons), N.Y. and Paris; student Grand Central Art Sch., Art Students League, Grand Chaumiere, Academie Julien-Paris, Columbia U., NAD; m. Frank Bertram Jordan, Jr.; children—Janine Jordan Newlin, Frank Bertram III. Illustrator mags. including Vogue, 1930's, Ladies Home Jour., Saturday Evening Post, Colliers, Good Housekeeping, Cosmopolitan, McCall's, American, Town and Country, 1940's-50's. Women's Jour., Eng., Hors Zu, Germany, Marie Claire, France, other fgn. publs., 1950's-60's; portrait painter, including Queen Sirikit, Princess Margaret, Princess Grace; free lance painter, 1970—; one-man shows include Soc. of Illustrators, 1940, 50, Barry Stephens Gallery, 1950, Bodley Gallery, N.Y.C., 1971, 80, Community Coll., West Mifflin, Pa., 1973, Duquesne U., 1973; exhibited in group shows including NAD, 1955, Royal Acad., London, Guild Hall, N.Y., 1981, Summit N.J. Art Ctr., 1981, Meredith Long Gallery, Houston, 1983, Mus. Soc. Illustrators, N.Y., 1985, The Marcus Gallery, Sante Fe, 1985, 86, The Gerald Peters Gallery, Santa Fe, 1985, 86, Brandywine Mus., Pa., 1985, 86, New Britain (Conn.) Mus. Am. Art, 1986, works represented Holbrook Collection, Ga. Mus. Art, Eureka Coll., Ill., New Britain Mus. Am. Art, Mus. of the Soc. of Illustrators, N.Y.C., Brandywine Mus., Pa., Sanford Low Meml. Collection, Del. Art Mus., Wilmington, various pvt. and gallery collections; lectr., instr. illustration Parsons Sch., 1952-54; founder adv. council Art Instrn. Sch., 1956-70. Chmn. art com. UNICEF greeting cards, 1950-61 mem. com. Spence Chapin Sch., Philharm. Soc., 1950's-60's. Winner prizes Art Dirs. Club, 1950, Guild Hall, 1969. Assoc. mem. Guggenheim Mus. Club: Cosmopolitan N.Y. Author: Technique of Barbara Schwinn, 1956; World of Fashion Art, 1968. Home and Studio: Mecox Rd Rural Rt 1 Box 882 Water Mill NY 11976

JORDAN, BRYCE, university president; b. Clovis, N.Mex., Sept. 22, 1924; s. W. Joseph and Kittie (Cole) J.; m. Patricia Jonelle Thornberry, June 10, 1948; children: Julia Cole, Christopher Joseph. Student, Hardin-Simmons U., 1941-42; B.Mus., U. Tex., 1948, M.Mus., 1949; Ph.D., U. N.C., 1956; LLD (hon.), Juniata Coll., 1985. Asst. prof. music Hardin-Simmons U., 1949-51; from asst. prof. to prof. music U. Md., 1954-63; prof. music, chmn. dept. U. Ky., 1963-65, U. Tex., 1965-68; v.p. student affairs U. Tex. at Austin, 1968-70, pres. ad interim, 1970-71; pres. U. Tex. at Dallas, 1971-81; exec. vice chancellor for acad. affairs U. Tex. System, 1981-83; pres. Pa. State U., 1983—; mem. faculty Salzburg (Austria) Seminar Am. Studies, 1960, 602, adv. com. NASA Comml. Programs, 1988—; occasional lectr. Fgn. Service Inst., State Dept., 1962-63; Mem. Yale Council on Music, 1971-73, Nat. Commn. on Higher Edn. Issues, 1982-83; bd. dirs. Mellon Bank Cen., Mellon Bank Corp., Harleysville Mut. Ins. Co., Harleysville Group, Inc., Quaker State Corp. Author: (with Homer Ulrich) Student Manual for Music: A Design for Listening, 1957, Designed for Listening, 1962, also articles, revs.; Assoc. editor: Coll. Music Symposium, 1961-66. Bd. dirs. Dallas Grand Opera Assn., 1973-75, Pa. Economic Devel. Partnership; trustee St. Marks Sch. Tex., 1973-81, Dallas Symphony Assn., 1972-81, Presbyterian Hosp., Dallas, 1976-83; v.p. Dallas Civic Music Assn., 1978-79, pres., 1979-80, exec. com., 1980—; bd. dirs. Dallas County chpt. ARC, 1976-79; div. chmn. United Way of Met. Dallas, 1979; Pa. state chmn. Am. Heart Assn., 1983-84; bd. trustees Com. on Econ. Devel., 1987; mem. Council on Competitiveness, 1987, NASA Comml. Programs Adv. Com., 1988—. Served with USAAF, 1942-46. Named Disting. Alumnus U. N.C., 1985, Hardin-Simmons U., 1987; recipient Pa. State Hon. Alumni award, 1987—. Mem. Coll. Music Soc. (v.p. 1963-65, council 1968—), Am. Musicol. Soc. (chmn. greater Washington chpt. 1958-60), Music Educators Nat. Conf. (pres. Md. br. 1963), Music Tchrs. Nat. Assn., Philos. Soc. Tex., Dallas C. of C. (dir. 1979—), So. Assn. Colls. and Schs. (commn. on colls. 1981-83), Phi Kappa Phi, Pi Kappa Lambda, Phi Mu Alpha. Presbyn. (presiding elder). Home: 639 Kennard Rd State College PA 16801 Office: Pa State U Office of Pres University Park PA 16802

JORDAN, CHARLYN LASKEY, word processing executive, consultant; b. Grand Rapids, Mich., Nov. 25, 1948; d. Donald and Helen Laskey; m. Patrick Michael Jordan, Sept. 1, 1984. Student, Ferris State Coll., 1966-68; BA, Mich. State U., 1972. Cert. secondary tchr., Mich., tchr. vocat. edn., N.J. Mgr. typography dept. Touche Ross & Co., N.Y.C., 1977-79; owner Laskey Word Processing, N.Y.C., 1979—; cons., speaker. Mem. Wang Labs. Photocomposition Users Group (v.p.), Pi Omega Pi. Office: 14 Schoolhouse Rd Amherst NH 03031-1601

JORDAN, DAVID FRANCIS, JR., lawyer; b. N.Y.C., Apr. 18, 1928; s. David Francis Jordan and Frances Marion (J.) Edebohls; m. Bess Vukas, Aug. 4, 1956; children—Melissa Marie, David Francis III, Dennis Paul. A.B., Princeton U., 1950; J.D., NYU, 1953, LL.M. in Taxation, 1970; postgrad. U. Oxford, 1949; grad. Judge Adv. Gen.'s Sch., 1964, Indsl. Coll. Armed Forces, 1973, Command and Gen. Staff Coll., 1968. Bar: N.Y. 1953, U.S. Dist. Ct. D.C. 1953, U.S. Ct. Appeals (D.C. cir.) 1953, U.S. Ct. Mil. Appeals 1953. U.S. Supreme Ct. 1957, U.S. Dist. Ct. (no., so., ea. and we. dists.) N.Y. 1958, U.S. Ct. Appeals (2d cir.) 1958, U.S. Tax Ct. 1958. Law clk. U.S. Ct. Appeals (2d cir.), 1957-58, chief dep., clk., 1958-59; sole practice, Smithtown, N.Y., 1959-63; ptnr. O'Rourke & Jordan, Central Islip, N.Y., 1963-67; asst. dist. atty. Suffolk County, Riverhead, N.Y., 1969-74; law clk. Supreme Ct., Suffolk County, 1975; investigator N.Y. Supreme Ct. Appellate Div. 2d dept., Bklyn., 1976; corp. counsel City of Newburgh, N.Y., 1976-78; acting city mgr., 1978; U.S. magistrate Ea. Dist. N.Y., Bklyn., Uniondale and Hauppauge, N.Y., 1978—; prosecutor 4th JAG Detachment, N.Y.C., 1958-64; mil. judge U.S. Army Judiciary, Washington, 1969-80; lectr. fed. procedure Suffolk County N.Y. Bar Assn., JAGC, 1978—. Adult leader Suffolk County council Boy Scouts Am., St. James, N.Y., 1960s. Served with JAGC, U.S. Army, 1954-57, to col. USAR. Decorated Meritorious Service medal. Mem. ABA, N.Y. State Bar Assn. (mem. fed. constn. com., lectr. fed. procedure 1978—), Suffolk County Bar Assn. (mem. various coms.). Roman Catholic. Lodges: K.C., Elks. Office: US Courthouse 300 Rabro Dr Hauppauge NY 11788

JORDAN, DUPREE, JR., editor, publisher, educator, management consultant, corporate executive; b. Decatur, Ga., May 14, 1929; s. DuPree and Roslyn (Moncrief) J.; A.B., Mercer U., 1947; M.Ed., Emory U., 1954; LL.B., Atlanta Law Sch., 1951, LL.D., 1963, D. Litt., 1971; postgrad. Crozer Theol. Sem., 1948-49, Nat. Inst. Pub. Affairs, summer 1967, Inst. Life-Long Learning, Harvard U., 1979, Inst. Ednl. Mgmt., Harvard U., 1981; m. Margaret Virginia Malone, Dec. 28, 1948; children: Peggy Jordan DeSear, DuPree III, Lyn Jordan Whitworth, Terri Lee Jordan Chesser. Ordained to ministry Bapt. Ch., 1945; pastor Eden Bapt. Ch., Savannah, Ga., 1946-47, Duluth (Ga.) Bapt. Ch., 1954-55; reporter Chester (Pa.) Times, 1948-49; news dir. Sta. WVCH, Chester, Pa., 1948-49; asso. dir. Radio and TV Commn. So. Bapt. Conv., Atlanta, 1949-52, acting dir., 1952-53; tchr. history, speech U. Ga., Atlanta, 1952-55, Bible, English, Westminster Schs., Atlanta, 1954-55; editor, pub., owner West End Star, Atlanta, 1955-66, N. DeKalb Record, Chamblee, Ga., 1956-64, TriCounty Graphic, Atlanta, 1962-64, Piedmont Satellite, 1967-68; pres. Jordan Enterprises, Inc., 1957—, Jordan & Jordan, Advt. and Pub. Relations, 1954—, Fun Products, Inc., 1968-69, Success Publs., Inc., 1969—; pub. Success Orientation, 1969—; partner WE Inc., convenience food stores, 1968-69; dir. pub. affairs So. region Office Econ. Opportunity, Atlanta, 1965-69; news reporter, panelist TV stas., Atlanta, 1955-76; exec. dir. Assn. Pvt. Colls. and Univs. in Ga., 1970-81; dir. Successful Selling Seminars; pres. Ga. Coll. for Leadership Devel., 1969—. Mem. Gov's. Rapid Transit Com., 1963-64. Gov.'s Com. for World's Fair in Atlanta, 1962-64; nat. religious liaison officer OEO, Washington, summer 1968; pres. Christian Council Met. Atlanta, 1973; bd. dirs. Atlanta Girls Club, YMCA, Boy Scouts Am. Named Man of Year radio stas., Atlanta, 1962, 63, West End Jaycees, 1962; recipient Quill award Sigma Delta Chi, 1962, 63, named Ky. col., 1967; mem. hon. staff Gov. Ga., 1962-66, 70-74, 74-78; honored with Rev. Dr. DuPree Jordan, Jr. Day in State of Ga., 1973. Mem. Ga. Press Assn. (bd. mgrs. 1964-65), Nat. Editorial Assn., Nat. Press Club, West End Bus. Men's Assn. (pres. 1962-63), Chamblee-Doraville Bus. Men's Assn. (pres. 1963-64), Fulton County Grand Jurors Assn. (dir. 1961), Ga. State Chamber/Bus. and Industry Assn.; Atlanta, DeKalb County (dir. 1961) chambers commerce, World Future Soc., Pub. Relations Soc. Am., Adminstrv. Mgmt. Soc., Am. Soc. Pub. Adminstrn., Sales and Mktg. Execs. Internat., Soc. Advancement Mgmt., Am. Mgmt. Assn., AIM, Am. Mktg. Assn., Am. Soc. Tng. and Devel., Am., Ga. Socs. assn. execs., Soc. Assn. Mgrs., Am. Assn. Coll. and Univ. Execs., So. Assn. Colls. (State Execs. Council coordinating chmn. 1980), State Assn. Execs. Council, Ga., Internat. assns. bus. communicators, Internat. Soc. Ednl. Planners, Am. Acad. Polit. and Social Sci., Meeting Planners Internat., Nat. Speakers Assn. (profl. awards com. 1980-81, dir., exec. com. 1982-84, sec. bd. 1983-84), Assn. Mgmt. Cons., Internat. Mgmt. Council, Inst. Mgmt. Cons., Mgmt. Consultants, Sigma Delta Chi (dir. 1963), Blue Key, Phi Delta, Alpha Chi Omega, Alpha Psi Omega, Kappa Sigma. Home: 965 Oakhaven Dr Roswell GA 30075 Office: Jordan Internat Enterprises Mail Ctr PO Box 1400 Roswell GA 30077

JORDAN, GEORGE LYMAN, JR., surgeon; b. Kinston, N.C., July 10, 1921; s. George L. and Sally (Herndon) J.; m. Florence Fischer Henszey, June 23, 1945; children: George Lyman III, Florence Elizabeth, Amy Henszey, Jacob Henszey. B.S., U. N.C., 1942; M.D., U. Pa., 1944; M.S. in Surgery, Tulane U., 1949. Diplomate: Am. Bd. Surgery (dir. 1971-77, vice chmn. 1975-77), Am. Bd. Thoracic Surgery. Intern Grady Meml. Hosp., Atlanta, 1944-45; fellow in surgery Tulane U., New Orleans, 1947-49, Mayo Found., Rochester, Minn., 1949-52; practice medicine specializing in surgery Houston, 1952—; instr. surgery Baylor U. Coll. Medicine, Houston, 1952-54; asst. prof. surgery Baylor U. Coll. Medicine, 1954-57, asso. prof., 1958-64, prof., 1964—, disting. prof. surgery, 1978—; dep. chief surgery Ben Taub Gen. Hosp., Houston, 1961-68; chief med. staff Harris County (Tex.) Hosp. Dist., Houston, 1968—; med. adv. HEW, Social Security Adminstrn., Region IV, 1965—; sr. cons. surgery Nat. Inst. Gen. Med. Scis., 1966; mem. surg. research tng. grants com. NIH, 1968-70; adv. Houston chpt. Nat. Found. for Ileitis and Colitis, 1974—; Chmn. commn. on edn. St. Paul's Meth. Ch., 1967-69, mem. adminstrv. bd., 1963—, chmn., 1978, chmn. council on ministries, 1973-75, chmn. pastor-parish relations com., 1977, charge lay leader, 1980-81, trustee, 1984-86, chmn., 1986. Author: (with John M. Howard) Surgical Diseases of the Pancreas, 1960, (with John M. Howard and Howard A. Reber) Surgical Diseases of the Pancreas, 1987; contbr. numerous articles to profl. jours.; editorial bd.: Am. Jour. Surgery, 1968—, Advances in Surgery, 1971-86. Served to capt., M.C. U.S. Army, 1945-47. Fellow A.C.S. (pres. Southeastern Tex. chpt. 1966-67, gov. 1976-82, chmn. bd. govs. 1980-82, exec. com. 1977-82, regent 1982—); mem. Western Surg. Assn. (dist. rep. on exec. com. 1976-80, pres. 1984), Pan-Pacific Surg. Assn.; So. Surg. Assn. (pres. 1984); mem. Am. Surg. Assn. (2d v.p. 1980), Tex. Surg. Soc. (council mem. 1975-78, chmn. council 1978, pres.-elect 1982, pres. 1983), Houston Surg. Soc. (pres. 1980), Am. Assn. Surgery Trauma, Soc. Surgery Alimentary Tract (pres. 1978, chmn. bd. trustees 1979), Univ. Assn. Emergency Med. Services, Am. Assn. Cancer Research (sec. Southwestern sect. 1959-60), Pan Am. med. assns., AMA (residency rev. com. for surgery 1974-80), Harris County Med. Soc., Am. Trauma Soc. (dir. Harris County unit 1974—), Am. Cancer Soc. (dir. Tex. div. 1966-68), Southwestern Surg. Congress, Transplantation Soc., Internat. Cardiovascular Soc., Soc. Univ. Surgeons, Houston Gastroenterol. Soc., Soc. Exptl. Biology and Medicine, N.Y. Acad. Scis., Collegium Internat. Chirurgiae Digestivae, So. Soc. Clin. Investigation, Pancreas Club, Am. Soc. Exptl. Pathology, Assn. Advancement Med. Instrumentation, Phi Beta Kappa, Alpha Omega Alpha. Methodist. Home: 1748 North Blvd Houston TX 77098 Office: Dept Surgery One Baylor Plaza Houston TX 77030

JORDAN, HENRY HELLMUT, JR., mgmt. cons.; b. Heidelberg, Germany, May 31, 1921; came to U.S., 1934, naturalized, 1940; s. Henry H. and Johanna (Narath) J.; m. Hildegarde C. Dallmeyer, Mar. 11, 1942 (dec. 1987); children: Sandra, Michael, Patric, Henry Hellmut. Student U. Cin., 1938-39. Commd. 2d lt. U.S. Army, 1942, advanced through grades to maj., 1956; staff officer Ordnance Corps; ret., 1961; mgr. prodn. and inventory control Sperry Corp., N.Y.C., 1961-66, dir. quality control and field service engring., 1967-68; mgmt. cons. Wright Assos. Inc., N.Y.C., 1969-70; pres. Henry Jordan & Assos., N.Y.C., 1970-74; mng. partner Cons. Services Inc., Atlanta, 1975—; chmn. Center for Inventory Mgmt., Stone Mountain, Ga., 1975—; chmn. bd. Crugers Services Corp., Atlanta. Editorial bd. Jour. Prodn. and Inventory Mgmt.; editor: Production and Inventory Control Handbook, 1986, Cycle Counting for Record Accuracy, 1985, System Implementation Handbook, 1982. Mem. Am. Inst. Indsl. Engrs. (sr.), Inst. Mgmt. Cons. (cert.), Am. Prodn. and Inventory Control Soc. (chmn. curricula and cert. council; Presdl. award of Merit 1974), Am. Radio Relay League. Methodist. Club: Yacht Hilton Head. Home: 941 Carlisle Rd Stone Mountain GA 30083 Office: 400 Perimeter Terr NE Suite 200 Atlanta GA 30346

JORDAN, JOYCE MAE, podiatrist; b. Alton, Ill., Oct. 21, 1949; d. Edward Thomas and Catherine Lutichie (Yates) J.; 1 child, Paul Thomas. B.A., So. Ill. U., 1972; D.P.M., Ohio Coll. Podiatric Medicine, 1983. Recreation supr. Alton Park Recreation Dept., 1968-69; tutor, physics library clk. So. Ill. U., Edwardsville, 1968-72; circulation clk. Alton Telegraph, 1972-73; program dir. MCCADD, Alton, 1973-75; youth program dir. Coordinated Youth Services, Granite City, Ill., 1977-78; extern VA Hosp., Leavenworth, Kans., 1982; preceptor Mobile Foot Health Ctr., Ala., 1983-84; practice medicine specializing in podiatry Am. Podiatry Clinic, New Orleans, 1984—; podiatry cons. Lafon Nursing Home, New Orleans, 1985—, Prayer Tower Nursing Home, New Orleans, 1985—. Mem. La. Podiatry Assn., New Orleans Med. Assn., Nat. Assn. Female Execs., Alpha Kappa Alpha, Kappa Tau Epsilon. Democrat. Baptist. Avocations: singing; painting; collecting foreign artifacts. Home: 6896 Parc Brittany Blvd New Orleans LA 70126 Office: Americare Podiatry Clinic 4335 Elysian Fields Suite 303 New Orleans LA 70122

JORDAN, MICHAEL HUGH, food products company executive; b. Kansas City, Mo., June 15, 1936; m. Kathryn Hiett, Apr. 8, 1961; children: Kathryn, Stephen. B.S. in Chem. Engring., Yale U., 1957; M.S. in Engring., Princeton U., 1958. Cons., prin. McKinsey & Co., Toronto, London, Cleve., 1964-74; dir. fin. planning PepsiCo, Purchase, N.Y., 1974-76; sr. v.p. planning and devel. PepsiCo Internat., Purchase, N.Y., 1976-77; sr. v.p. mfg. ops. Frito-Lay, Dallas, 1977-82, pres., chief exec. officer, 1983-85; pres. PepsiCo Foods Internat., 1982-83; exec. v.p., fin. and adminstrn. PepsiCo Inc., Purchase, 1985-86, pres., 1986, also bd. dirs.; pres., chief exec. officer PepsiCo Inc. Worldwide Foods, Plano, Tex., 1987—; bd. dirs. 1st RepublicBank, Dallas, Melville Corp. Bd. dirs. United Negro Coll. Fund, 1986—. Recipient cert. nuclear engring. Bettis Labs. AEC, Pitts.

JORDAN, RICHARD ALLEN, insurance company executive, lawyer; b. Portsmouth, Ohio, May 19, 1946; s. Clifford Leslie and Roberta Elizabeth (Meade) J.; m. Tracie Marie Stiveson, May 25, 1984; children—Rebecca Christine, Christopher Todd, Amy Elizabeth. B.A., Dartmouth Coll., 1968; J.D., Lincoln U., San Jose, Calif., 1978. Bar: Calif. 1978, U.S. Dist. Ct. (no. dist.) Calif. 1978. Claims supr. Fireman's Fund, San Jose, 1970-77, home office claims supr., San Francisco, 1977-78, dir. claims tng., 1979-81, asst. v.p., Novato, Calif., 1981-84; v.p. Allianz Ins. Co., Los Angeles, 1984-86; v.p. claims, Asbestos Claims Facility, Princeton, N.J, 1986-87; sr. v.p. claims Comml. Union Ins. Cos., Boston, 1987—. Served to 1st lt. U.S. Army, 1968-70. Mem. ABA, Calif. Trial Lawyers Assn., Assn. Trial Lawyers Am., Def. Research Inst., Pacific Claims Exec. Assn. Republican. Congregationalist. Home: 14 Nathanial Dr Amherst NH 03031 Office: Comml Union Ins Cos 1 Beacon St Boston MA 02108

JORDAN, SHARON ANN, clinical social worker, child and family psychotherapist; b. Detroit, July 22, 1953; d. Benneal and Myrtice Marie J. A.B. in Journalism, U. Mich., 1975, M.Urban Planning, 1977, M.S.W., 1979. Social worker, counselor, staff devel. coordinator U. Mich. opportunity program, 1979-84; clin. social worker U. Mich. Children's Psychiat. Hosp., 1984—; mental health profl. Psychiatric Emergency Services U. Mich. Hosp., 1986—; pvt. practice in psychotherapy, 1987—; sr. assoc. Employee Assistance Assn., 1984-87. U. Mich. fellow, 1976-77. Mem. Nat. Assn. Social Workers, Acad. Cert. Social Workers, Am. Ortho-Psychiat. Assn., Nat. Black Child Devel. Inst., Phi Beta Kappa. Office: U Mich Day Hosp Program NI3 A12 Box 0401 Ann Arbor MI 48109

JORDAN, STEVE NICANDROS, housing development company executive; b. Amalias, Greece, Aug. 28, 1918; s. Nicandros Steve and Lucie Nicoletta Marie (Ferigo) J.; m. Dena Callas, Aug. 25, 1946; children—Marilou, Stephanie, Nicolette, Denise, Nicholas. Vice pres. Nat. Gold Mining Corp., Hatch, N.Mex., 1956; pres. S.N. Jordan Assocs., & Co. Indsl. Devel., Las Cruces, 1958-62; with testing div. Douglas Space Exploration Systems, Sacramento, 1962-66; pres., chmn. bd. Calif. Housing Corp., Sacramento, 1966—; pres., chmn. bd. Jordan Mgmt. Co., Sacramento, 1977—; chief exec. officer Cal-Atlas Corp., Sacramento, 1977—; mng. gen. ptnr. 23 real estate partnerships. Pres., Angelic Corp., 1980-87; Sacramento, 1980—. Served with USAAF, 1943-46. Recipient St. Anthony medal Archdiocese Greek Orthodox Ch., 1982; Resolution, State of Calif., Proclamation, City of Sacramento Mem. Nat. Assn. Home Builders, Assn. Builders and Contractors, Urban and Land Inst., Sacramento C. of C., Nat. Fedn. Ind. Bus., Calif. Rural Housing Council (bd. trustees Ch. of the Annunciation). Greek Orthodox. Home: 2600 Eastern Ave Sacramento CA 95821 Office: 3136 Auburn Blvd Sacramento CA 95821

JORDAN, V. CRAIG, endocrine pharmacologist, educator; b. New Braunfels, Tex., July 25, 1947; s. Geoffrey Webster and Sybil Cynthia (Mottram) J.; m. Marion Yvonne Williams, July 29, 1969; children—Helen Melissa Yvonne, Alexandra Katherine Louise. B.Sc. with honors, U. Leeds (Eng.), 1969, Ph.D. in Pharmacology, 1972; D.Sc. in Pharmacology, 1985. Research assoc. Worcester Found. for Exptl. Biology, Shrewsbury, Mass., 1972-73, vis. scientist, 1973-74; lectr. pharmacology U. Leeds, 1973-79; head endocrinology unit Ludwig Inst. for Cancer Research, U. Berne (Switzerland), 1979-80; asst. prof. human oncology and pharmacology U. Wis., Madison, 1978-81, assoc. prof., 1981-85, prof., 1985—, also leader pharmacology group dept. human oncology; bd. dirs. Breast Cancer Research Program, Wis. Clin. Cancer Ctr. Contbr. numerous articles to profl. jours. Served to capt., Intelligence Corps, Brit. Army, 1971-76; Served to capt. Spl. Air Service, 1976-78. Med. Research Council scholar, 1969-72; co-recipient Boston Obstet. Soc. prize, 1974; UICC Internat. Cancer Research Tech. Transfer grantee, 1981; Romnes Faculty fellow, 1984-85. Fellow Am. Inst. Chemists, Royal Soc. Chemistry; mem. Am. Assn. for Cancer Research, Am. Soc. for Pharmacology and Exptl. Therapeutics, Endocrine Soc., Biochem. Soc., Brit. Pharm. Soc., Soc. for Endocrinology. Conservative. Mem. Ch. of England. Research on mechanism of action of antiestrogens as anticancer agts., antiestrogen structure-activity relationships, molecular pharmacology of antiestrogens, metabolism of antiestrogens in animals and man. Office: U Wis 600 Highland Ave Madison WI 53792

JORDAN, WILLIAM REYNIER VAN EVERA, SR., psychotherapist, poet; b. Kansas City, Mo.; s. Russell Clinger and Lois Eleanor (Van Evera) J.; children—William, Michael, Paul. B.S. in Journalism cum laude, U. Fla., 1956; South Asia area specialist U. Pa., 1962; grad. Gen. Staff Coll., 1968; M.A. in Psychology, U. No. Colo., 1979 postgrad. U. So. Fla., 1986—. Served to cpl. U.S. Army, 1947-48, with Mil. Intelligence Res., 1948-51, to 1st lt. inf., 1951-54 re-entered 1957, advanced through grades to col., 1972; chief of plans and analysis psychol. ops. div. Mil. Assistance Command, Vietnam, 1970-71; group ops. officer, later spl. asst. to comdg. officer 902d Mil. Intelligence Group, Washington, 1971-72; ret., 1972; psychotherapist Juvenile Detention, Pensacola, Fla., 1976-77; vol. psychotherapist Colorado Springs Social Services Dept., Colo., 1977-78; psychotherapist Med. Clinic, Saint Petersburg, Fla., 1980-84, Epilepsy Found., Saint Petersburg, 1984—, VA Mental Health Clinic, Bay Pines, Fla. Author: Darkness and Shadows, 1975; More Than Friends, 1978; Heat Lightning, 1984. Leader Rawalpindi council Boy Scouts Am., Pakistan, 1960-62, also troops at Ft. Bragg, N.C., Ft. Leavenworth, Kans., Ft. Holabird, Md., 1964-70; bd. dirs. YMCA, Dundalk, Md., 1969-71, Epilepsy Assn., Pensacola, Fla., 1975-77. Decorated Legion of Merit with oak leaf cluster; Cross of Gallantry with palm (Republic of Vietnam); named Vol. of Yr., Colorado Springs Social Services Dept., 1978. Fellow Internat. Council Sex Edn. and Parenting; mem. Internat. Acad. Behavioral Medicine Counseling and Psychotherapy, Am. Psychol. Assn. (assoc.), Epilepsy Assn. Am. (pres.'s club), Am. Assn. Counseling and Devel.Democrat. Congregationalist. Avocation: photography. Home: 5311 Burlington Ave N Saint Petersburg FL 33710 Office: Suncoast Epilepsy Assn 8800 40th St North Suite 311 Pinellas Park FL 34666

JORGE, NUNO MARIA ROQUE, architect; b. Macau, Portugal, Feb. 9, 1947; s. Adolfo Adroaldo and Edith (Roque) J.; m. Maria de Fátima da Costa Azevedo, Sept. 14, 1975; children: Edith Azevedo, Alexandra Azevedo, Filipa Azevedo. Cert Bus. Mgmt., Inst. Superior de Novas Profissoes, Lisbon, 1972; diploma in architecture, Higher Sch. Fine Arts, Lisbon (Portugal) U., 1974. Architect trainee Ministry do Ultramar, Lisbon, 1972-73; computer programmer, systems analyst Cen. Mecanografico de Exercito, Lisbon, 1973-75; pvt. practice architecture Macau, 1975—; pvt. practice bus. mgr., cons., Macau, 1981—; pvt. practice acct., Macau, 1981—; tech. dir. Sao Tiago Hotel and Tourism Co., Ltd., Macau, 1982—; mng. ptnr. Soc. Geral de Comercio e Industria Ltd., Macau, 1983—. V.p. Portuguese Red Cross, Macau, 1986—; mem. Santa Casa de Misericordia, Macau, 1980—. Served with Portugese mil., 1973-75. Recipient Spl. award for Heritage Preservation, Pacific Area Travel Assn., 1982, Decoration of Profl. Merit, Govt. of Macau, 1984. Mem. Soc. de Geografia de Lisbon (effective 1972—), Macau Assn. Architects in Pvt. Practice (founder, charter mem. 1983—), Portuguese Assn. Acct. (charter mem. v.p., chmn. gen. assembly Macau chpt. 1981—), Macau Mgmt. Assn. (charter mem., advisor 1985—), Portuguese Assn. Architects, Portuguese Assn. Mktg., Alliance Francaise de Macao (charter mem. 1987—). Clubs: Tenis Civil (pres. 1976-77), Macau Trotting, Skal, PATA (treas. Macau chpt. 1983-84). Home: Estrada de D Joao Paulino, # 26 28 30, Macau Republic of China Office: 61 Ave de Amizade, 18th Floor C Cam Fai Coc Bldg, Atterros do Porto Exterior, Macau Republic of China

JORGENSEN, ALFRED H., computer software company executive; b. South Gate, Calif., May 1, 1934; s. Peter Hansen and Anna Christine (Nielsen) J.; A.A., El Camino Coll., 1958; student UCLA, 1958-60; m. Carole Jean Scott, Sept. 3, 1959; children—Mark Alan, Lora Jean. Asso. engr. Litton Industries, Beverly Hills, Calif., 1957-60; engr. Daystrom, Inc., 1960-64; with control systems div. Foxboro Co., Pitts., 1964-67, dist. and regional mgr., 1967-69; with Interactive Scis., Pitts., 1969-72, v.p., 1970-71; v.p. Computeria Inc., 1971, pres., 1971-72; v.p. Interactive Scis. Corp., Braintree, Mass., 1972-77, pres., 1977-80; exec. v.p. Nat. Data Corp., Atlanta, 1980-83;

v.p. Cullinet Software Inc., 1983-85, v.p. systems and computer tech., 1985-87; pres. chief operating officer A.O. Electronics Co., Atlanta, 1987—; bd. dirs. Process Corp., Pitts. Bd. dirs. Mass. Assn. Mental Health, 1977-79, v.p., 1978-79. Served with U.S. Army, 1954-56. Mem. Data Processing Mgmt. Assn., Assn. Iron and Steel Engrs., Instrument Soc. Am., IEEE, Cash Mgmt. Assn., Am. Mgmt. Assn., Nat. Platform Assn. Club: Pearson Yacht (commodore 1984). Home: 4491 Pineridge Circle Dunwoody GA 30338

JØRGENSEN, EBBE GORM, banker; b. Sorø, Denmark, Aug. 25, 1925; s. Jakob and Karen K.M. (Nielsen) J.; m. Gerda Ipsen, Nov. 26, 1955; children Per Gorm and Niels Gorm. BA in Commerce, The Copenhagen Sch. of Econs. and Bus. Adminstrn., 1952. Dep. mng. dir. Prvt. Bank, Copenhagen, 1974—. Office: Privatbanken A/S, PO Box 1000, 2300 Copenhagen S Denmark

JORGENSEN, EIGIL, Danish ambassador to U.S.; b. 1921; m. Alice Jorengen; 1 child. Student, U. Copenhagen. Various positions Danish Ministry Trade and Industry, 1949—; various positions Denmark's Fgn. Service, 1949—; with Marshall plan Danish embassy, U.S.; attaché permanent mission to NATO, Paris; head econ.-polit. div. Danish Ministry Fgn. Affairs; permanent under sec. Prime Minister's Office and sec. to King's Council 1965-73; Danish ambassador to Fed. Republic Germany Bonn, 1973-75; permanent undersec. of state 1975-83; Danish ambassador to U.S. Washington, 1983—. Office: Royal Danish Embassy 3200 Whitehaven St NW Washington DC 20008

JORGENSEN, ERIK HOLGER, lawyer; b. Copenhagen, July 18, 1916; s. Holger and Karla (Andersen) J.; children—Jette Friis, Lone Olesen, John, Jean Ann. J.D., San Francisco Law Sch., 1960. Bar: Calif. 1961. Sole practice, 1961-70; ptnr. Hersh, Hadfield, Jorgensen & Fried, San Francisco, 1970-76, Hadfield & Jorgensen, San Francisco, 1976—. Pres. Aldersly, Danish Retirement Home, San Rafael, Calif., 1974-77, Rebuild Park Soc. Bay Area chpt., 1974-77. Fellow Scandinavian Am. Found. (hon.); mem. ABA, Assn. Trial Lawyers Am., San Francisco Lawyers Club, Bar Assn. of San Francisco, Calif. Assn. Realtors (hon. life bd. dirs.). Author: Master Forms Guide for Successful Real Estate Agreements, Successful Real Estate Sales Agreements, 1982; contbr. articles on law and real estate law to profl. jours. Office: 350 California St San Francisco CA 94104

JORGENSEN, GORDON DAVID, engineering company executive; b. Chgo., Apr. 29, 1921; s. Jacob and Marie (Jensen) J.; B.S. in Elec. Engring., U. Wash., 1948, postgrad. in bus. and mgmt., 1956-59; m. Nadina Anita Peters, Dec. 17, 1948 (div. Aug. 1971); children—Karen Ann, David William, Susan Marie; m. 2d, Barbara Noel, Feb. 10, 1972 (div. July 1976). With R.W. Beck & Assos., Cons. Engrs., Phoenix, 1948—, ptnr., 1954-86; pres. Beck Internat., Phoenix, 1971—. Served to lt. (j.g.) U.S. Maritime Service, 1942-45. Recipient Outstanding Service award Phoenix Tennis Assn., 1967; Commendation, Govt. Honduras, 1970. Registered profl. engr., Alaska, Ariz., Calif., Colo., Nev., N.Mex., N.D., Utah, Wash., Wyo. Mem. IEEE (chmn. Wash.-Alaska sect. 1959-60), Nat. Soc. Profl. Engrs., Am. Soc. Appraisers (sr. mem.), Ariz. Cons. Engrs. Assn., Ariz. Soc. Profl. Engrs., Internat. Assn. Assessing Officers, Southwestern Tennis Assn. (past pres.), U.S. Tennis Assn. (pres. 1987-88, chmn. U.S. Open com.). Presbyterian (elder). Project mgr. for mgmt., operation studies and reorgn. study Honduras power system, 1969-70. Home: 5329 N 25th St Phoenix AZ 85016 Office: RW Beck & Assocs 3003 N Central Phoenix AZ 85012

JORGENSEN, LENNART ANDREW, electric utilities executive; b. Great Falls, Mont., Apr. 17, 1947; s. Lennart Gustave and Thelma Marguerite (Loberg) J.; m. Georgielea Ann Weisgerber, July 22, 1967; children: Eric, Kristopher. Diploma, U.S. Army Air Def. Sch., El Paso, Tex., 1971, 74, U.S. Army Adjutant Gens.' Sch., Indpls., 1972. Engr. Nebr. Pub. Power Dist., Columbus, 1976-80; dir. power City of Colby, Kans., 1980-82; asst. gen. mgr. Clatskanie (Oreg.) People's Utility Dist., 1982—; v.p. Quincy Water Assn., Clatskanie, 1985-87, pres., 1987—, bd. dirs. Cubmaster Boy Scouts Am., Clatskanie, 1983; tng. mgr. USAF MARS Region 5, 1986, emergency coordinator, 1988—; served as staff sgt. U.S. Army, 1966-76. Mem. Am. Pub. Power Assn. (energy services plan com. 1981-82, rates load research com. 1983—, human resources com. 1983—), N.W. Pub. Power Assn., Am. Soc. Pub. Adminstrn., Am. Radio Relay League (emergency coordinator 1976, 85—, 2 Pub. Service awards, 1964, 65, phone activities mgr. 1978), VFW (life, dist. adjutant Columbus, Nebr. Post 1979-80), Am. Legion, Nat. Rifle Assn., Citizens Com.for Right to Keep and Bear Arms (nat. adv. council, citizen of Yr. 1986), Oreg. Mcpl. Fin. Officer's Assn., Internat. Platform Assn., Oreg. State Sheriff's Assn. Club: North American Hunting. Lodge: Kiwanis (bd. dirs. Clatskanie club 1983-84). Home: PO Box 1197 Clatskanie OR 97016-1197 Office: Clatskanie People's Utility Dist PO Box 216 Clatskanie OR 97016-0216

JORGENSEN, PAUL ALFRED, English language educator emeritus; b. Lansing, Mich., Feb. 17, 1916; s. Karl and Rose Josephine (Simmons) J.; m. Virginia Frances Elfrink, Jan. 3, 1942; children: Mary Catherine, Elizabeth Ross Jorgensen Howard. A.B., Santa Barbara State Coll., 1938; M.A., U. Calif. at Berkeley, 1940, Ph.D., 1945. Instr. English Bakersfield (Calif.) Jr. Coll., 1945-46, U. Calif., Berkeley, summer 1946, U. Calif., Davis, 1946-47; mem. faculty UCLA, 1947—, prof. English, 1960-81, prof. emeritus, 1981—; vis. prof. U. Wash., summer 1966; mem. editorial com. U. Calif. Press, 1957-60; mem. Humanities Inst. U. Calif., 1967-69; mem. acad. adv. council Shakespeare Globe Ctr. N.Am. Author: Shakespeare's Military World, 1956, (with Frederick B. Shroyer) A College Treasury, rev. edit, 1967, (with Shroyer) The Informal Essay, 1961, Redeeming Shakespeare's Words, 1962; Editor: The Comedy of Errors, 1964, Othello: An Outline- Guide to the Play, 1964, (with Shroyer) The Art of Prose, 1965, Lear's Self-Discovery, 1967, Our Naked Frailties: Sensational Art and Meaning in Macbeth, 1971, William Shakespeare: The Tragedies, 1985; mem. bd. editors Film Quar, 1958-65, Huntington Library Quar, 1965-83, Coll. English, 1966-70; mem. adv. com. Publs. of MLA of Am, 1978-82. Guggenheim fellow, 1956-57; Regents' Faculty fellow in humanities, 1973-74. Mem. Modern Lang. Assn., Shakespeare Assn. Am. (bibliographer 1954-59), Renaissance Soc. Am., Philol. Assn., Pacific Coast (exec. com. 1962-63). Episcopalian. Home: 234 Tavistock Ave Los Angeles CA 90049

JØRGENSEN, TEIT, photography director; b. Copenhagen, Denmark, Sept. 26, 1947; s. Torben Jørgensen and Merete Bertha Bentzen; m. Lizzie Corfixen, Apr. 25, 1971 (div. 1977); 1 child, Liv; m. Inger Norgaard Madsen. Grad., Helsingør Gymnasium, Helsingør, 1965; postgrad., Delta Foto, Copenhagen, 1965-67; grad. Dir. Photography, Danish Film Sch., 1970. Freelance dir. photography Denmark, 1970—. Dir. photography 80 short films and documentaries, commls., videos, feature films; dir. photography films Tjeunobyll Autumn, 1987 (Gold medal), More Nuclear Power Stations, 1987 (Gold medal). Mem. Danish Assn. Cinematographers, Brit. Kinematograph Sound and TV Soc. Home: Rosenvaengets Alle 14, 2100 Copenhagen O Denmark

JOS, JOSEPH, physician, consultant; b. Paris, Dec. 24, 1928; s. Maurice and Fannie J.; m. Liliane Eisenberger, Apr. 11, 1970; children: Catherine, Philippe. MD, Sch. Med., Paris, 1962; postgrad., Sch. Med., 1963. Intern faculty Necker-Enfants Malades, Paris, 1956-57; resident Hosp. Enfants Malades, Paris, 1957-62; asst. Hosp. Enfants Malades, 1962-69, sr. hosp. lectr., 1962-69, prof., 1970—, cons., 1970—, head dept., 1987—; asst. prof. Faculty Medicine, Paris, 1963-70, assoc. prof., 1970-78, prof., 1987—. Contbr. articles to profl. jours. Recipient Silver medal Faculty Medicine, 1962, Prize of Baron Portal, Nat. Acad. Medicine, 1963. Mem. Soc. Francaise de Pediatrie, European Soc. Pediatric Gastroenterology, Soc. Nat. Gastroenterology, Assn. langue Francaise Etude du Diabete, Internat. Study Group Diabetes in Children, European Assn. Study Diabetes. Club: Etude des Cellules Epitheliales Digestives. Home: Blvd Malesherbes 62, 75008 Paris France Office: Hosp Enfants Malades, 149 rue de Sevres, 75015 Paris France

JOSAFATSSON, SIGVALDI HRAFN, shipping company executive; b. Blonduos, Iceland, Sept. 2, 1948; s. Josafat and Ingibjorg (Petursdottir) Sigvaldason; m. Gudfinna Eggertsdottir, June 24, 1972; children—Thorkell, Edda Gudrun. Ed., Samvinnuskolinn, Bifrost, Iceland, 1967-69. With Samband Line, Reykjavik, 1970-77, mktg. mgr., 1979-84, ops. mgr., 1984—; mgr. Samband Line, Rotterdam, 1988—; with Samband of Iceland, London, 1977-79. Office: Samband Line, Samband House, Reykjavik Iceland

JOSE, PHYLLIS ANN, librarian; b. Detroit, Mar. 15, 1949; d. William Henry and Isobel Eleanor (Mundle) J.; B.A., Mich. State U., 1971, M.A., 1972; M.A. in Library Sci., U. Mich., 1975. Library aide audio-visual div. Dearborn (Mich.) Dept. Libraries, 1973-76, librarian gen. info. div., 1976-77; reference library dir. Oakland County (Mich.) Library, 1977—. Officer Southfield Economic Devel. Corp., 1980—; mem. Southfield Tax Increment Fin. Authority, 1981—; coordinator Southfield Arts Festival, 1984, 85. Mem. ALA, Mich. Library Assn.(ALA cpht. councilor). Presbyterian. Office: 1200 N Telegraph Rd Pontiac MI 48053

JOSE, ROBERT NICHOLAS, writer, cultural counselor; b. London, Nov. 9, 1952; arrived in Australia, 1953; s. Robert Oswald and Pamela Violet (Joynt) J.; m. Madeleine Mary O'Dea. BA with honors, Australian Nat. U., 1973; PhD, Oxford U., 1978. Lectr. in English Australian Nat. U., Canberra, 1978-87; cultural counselor Australian Embassy, Beijing, 1987—. Author: The Possession of Amber , 1980, Rowena's Field, 1984, Feathers or Lead, 1986, Paper Nautilus, 1987. Rhodes scholar, 1973. Mem. Australian Soc. Authors, Assn. Study Australian Lit. Home: 65 Elimatta St, Braddon 2601, Australia Office: Dept Fgn Affairs, Parkes 2601, Australia

JOSEPH, GREGORY PAUL, lawyer; b. Mpls., Jan. 18, 1951; s. George Phillip and Josephine Sheha (Nofel) J.; m. Barbara Joseph, Jan. 19, 1979. B.A. summa cum laude, U. Minn., 1972, J.D. cum laude, 1975. Bar: Minn. 1975, N.Y. 1979, U.S. Dist. Ct. Minn. 1975, U.S. Dist. Ct. (so. and ea. dist.) N.Y. 1979, U.S. Ct. Appeals (8th cir.) 1976, U.S. Ct. Appeals (2d cir.) 1979, U.S. Ct. Appeals (D.C. cir.) 1980, U.S. Supreme Ct. 1983, U.S. Tax Ct. 1987. Sole practice, Mpls., 1975-79, Fried, Frank, Harris, Shriver & Jacobson, N.Y.C., 1979-82; asst. U.S. spl. prosecutor, N.Y.C., Washington, 1981-82; ptnr. Fried, Frank, Harris, Shriver & Jacobson, N.Y.C., 1982—. Author: Modern Visual Evidence, 1984, (supplement 1988); co-author: Evidence in America, 1987. Editor: Emerging Problems Under the Federal Rules of Evidence, 1983; co-editor Sanctions, 1986, 2d rev. edit., 1988; Contbr. articles to profl. jours. Fellow Am. Bar Found.; mem. ABA (chmn. trial evidence com. 1985—), Am. Law Inst., N.Y. State Bar Assn., Minn. State Bar Assn., N.Y. County Lawyers Assn. Home: 40 E 88th St Apt 7C New York NY 10128 Office: Fried Frank Harris Shriver & Jacobson 1 New York Plaza New York NY 10004

JOSEPH, MICHAEL THOMAS, broadcast consultant; b. Youngstown, Ohio, Nov. 23, 1927; s. Thomas A. and Martha (McCarius) J.; m. Eva Ursula Boerger, June 21, 1952. BA, Case Western Res. U., 1949. Program dir. Fetzer Broadcasting, Grand Rapids, Mich., 1952-55; nat. program dir. Founders Corp., N.Y.C., 1955-57; program cons. to ABC, CBS, NBC, Capital Cities, Infinity, Malrite, Cox and the N.Y. Times 1958—; v.p. radio Capital Cities, N.Y.C., 1959-60, NBC, N.Y.C., 1963-65. Creator, owner Hot Hits phrase and format. Mem. Internat. Radio and TV Soc., Nat. Assn. Broadcasters. Roman Catholic. Home: Essex House Towers 160 Central Park S New York NY 10019

JOSEPHSON, BRIAN DAVID, physicist; b. Jan. 4, 1940; s. Abraham and Mimi J.; B.A., Cambridge U., 1960, M.A., Ph.D., 1964; D.Sc. (hon.), U. Wales, 1974; m. Carol Anne Olivier, 1976; 1 dau. Asst. dir. research in physics Cambridge U., 1967-72, reader, 1972-74; vis. faculty Maharishi European Res. U., 1975; prof. physics Cambridge U., 1974—; vis. faculty Maharishi European Res. U., 1975. Recipient Nobel prize in Physics, 1973; fellow Trinity Coll., Cambridge, 1962—; New Scientist award, 1969; Guthrie medal, 1972; van der Pol medal, 1972; Elliott Cresson medal, 1972; Hughes medal, 1972; Holweck medal, 1973; Faraday medal, 1982. Fellow Royal Soc.; mem. IEEE (hon.), Am. Acad. Arts and Scis. (fgn., hon.). Author papers on physics and theory of intelligence; co-editor: Consciousness and the Physical World, 1980. Office: U of Cambridge, Cavendish Lab, Madingley Rd, Cambridge CB3 OHE England *

JOSEPHSON, ERLAND, actor, director; b. June 15, 1923. With Mcpl. Theatre, Helsingborg, 1945-49, Gothenburg, 1949-56, Royal Dramatic Theatre, Stockholm, 1956—; dir. Royal Dramatic Theatre, Stockholm, 1966-75. Film appearances include: Scenes from a Marriage, 1974, Montenegro, 1981, Fanny & Alexander, 1983, After the Rehearsal, 1984, The Unbearable Lightness of Being, 1988; author books including: Cirkel,1946; Spegeln och en portvakt, 1946; Spel med bedrovade artister, 1947; Ensam och fri, 1948; Lyssnarpost, 1949; De vuxna barnen, 1952; Utflykt, 1954; Sallskapslek, 1955; En Berattelse om herr Silberstein, 1957; Kungen ur leken, 1959; Doktor Meyers sista dagar, 1964; Kandidat Nilssons forsta natt, 1964. Office: care Royal Dramatic Theatre, Nybroplan, Box 5037, 102 41 Stockholm Sweden *

JOSET, JACQUES, literature educator; b. Liège, Belgium, July 10, 1943; m. Danièle Solbach, June 1, 1967 (div.); 1 child, Muriel; m. Yolanda Montalvo, June 23, 1984. PhD, U. Liège, 1970. Asst. prof. U. Liège, 1965-72; prof. in Spanish and Latin Am. Langs. and Lits. U. Antwerp, Belgium, 1972—. Author: Juan Ruiz, Libro de buen amor, 1974, La Littérature hispanoaméricaine, 1972, G.García Márquez : coetáneo de la eternidad, 1984, Alonso de Castillo Solórzano, Aventuras del Bachiller Trapaza, 1986, Nuevas investigaciones sobre el "Libro de buen amor", 1988. Recipient Premier Lauréat du Councours award Univ. de Belgique, 1969; Fulbright-Hays scholar, 1987. Mem. Assn. Internat. de Hispanistas, Inst. Internat. Lit. Iberoamericana, Soc. Hispanistes Français, Assn. Hispánica Lit. Medieval. Home: Quai Mativa 54/082, 4020 Liege Belgium Office: U Antwerp, Universiteitsplein 1, 2610 Wilrijk Belgium

JOSEY, E(LONNIE) J(UNIUS), educator, librarian, state administrator; b. Norfolk, Va., Jan. 20, 1924; s. Willie and Frances (Bailey) J.; m. Dorothy Johnson, Sept. 11, 1954 (div. Dec. 1961); 1 dau., Elaine Jacqueline. A.B., Howard U., 1949; M.A., Columbia U., 1950; M.L.S., SUNY- Albany, 1953; L.H.D., Shaw U., 1973; D.P.S., U. Wis., Milw., 1987. Desk asst. Columbia U. Libraries, 1950-52; library tech. asst. central br. N.Y. Pub. Library, N.Y.C., 1952; librarian I Free Library, Phila., 1953-54; instr. social scis. Savannah State Coll., 1954-55, librarian, assoc. prof., 1959-66; librarian, asst. prof. Del. State Coll., 1955-59; assoc. div. library devel. N.Y. State Edn. Dept., Albany, 1966-68; chief Bur. Acad. and Research Libraries, 1968-76, Bur. Specialist Library Services, 1976-86; prof. U. Pitts. Sch. Library and Info. Scis., 1986—; mem. bd. advisors Children's Book Rev. Service, Bklyn., 1972—. Editor, contbg. author: The Black Librarian in America, 1970, What Black Librarians Are Saying, 1972, New Dimensions for Academic Library Service, 1975; co-compiler, co-editor: Handbook of Black Librarianship, 1977; co-editor: A Century of Service: Librarianship in the United States and Canada, 1976, Opportunities for Minorities in Librarianship, 1977, The Information Society: Issues and Answers, 1978, Libraries in the Political Process, 1980, Ethnic Collections in Libraries, 1983, Libraries, Coalitions, And the Public Good, 1987; editorial bd.: Dictionary of Am. Library History, 1974—; mem. editorial adv. bd.: ALA Yearbook, 1975—; spl. advisor: World Ency. Black People, 1974—; contbr. numerous articles to profl. jours. Mem. Albany Interracial Council, 1972-86; mem. exec. bd. Savannah (Ga.) br. NAACP, 1960-66; state youth advisor Ga. Conf., 1962-66; mem. exec. bd. Albany br., 1968-86, treas., 1970-72, 1st v.p., 1981-82, pres., 1982-86, life mem., 1971—, chmn. program com., 1972-76, also trustee; mem. tech. task force Econ. Opportunity Authority of Savannah, 1964-66; bd. dirs. Correta Scott King Award; trustee Minority Edn. and Devel. Agy., Central Islip, N.Y., 1973; bd. mgrs. Savannah Pub. Library, 1962-66; mem. adv. council Sch. Library Sci., N.C. Central U., Sch. Library and Info. Sci., SUNY-Albany, Sch. Library and Info. Sci., Queen's Coll., CUNY; mem. exec. bd. Albany County Opportunity Authority. Served with AUS, 1943-46. Recipient cert. of Appreciation Savannah br. NAACP, 1963, NAACP award Savannah State Coll. chpt., 1964, Merit award for work on econ. opportunity task force Savannah Chatham County, 1966, award for disting. service to librarianship Savannah State Coll. Library, 1967, Jour. Library History award, 1970, N.Y. Black Librarians Inc. award, 1979, N.J. Black Librarians Network award, 1984, Joseph W. Lippincott award, 1980, Disting. Alumnus of Yr. award SUNY Albany Sch. Library and Info. Sci., 1981, Disting. Service award Library Assn. of CUNY, 1982, Martin Luther King Jr. award for disting. community leadership SUNY, Albany, 1984, award for contbns. to librarianship D.C. Assn. Sch. Librarians, 1984, award Kenyan Library Assn., 1984, Disting. Service award Afro-Caribbean Library Assn., Eng., 1984. Mem. ALA (John Cotton Dana award 1962, 64, founder, chmn. Black Caucus 1970-71, mem. council 1970—, exec. bd. 1979-86, v.p./pres.-elect 1983-84, pres. 1984-85, mem. Freedom to Read Found Bd. 1987—, Black Caucus award 1979), Assn. Study Afro-Am. Life and History, AAUP, Am. Acad. Polit. and Social Sci., N.Y. Library Assn. (Disting. Service award 1985), Freedom to Read Found., N.Y. Library Club, ACLU, Internat. Platform Assn., Am. Soc. Info. Scis., Alpha Phi Omega, Kappa Phi Kappa., Sigma Pi Phi. Democrat. Home: 5 Bayard Rd #505 Pittsburgh PA 15213 Office: U Pitts Sch Library and Info Scis Bldg Pittsburgh PA 15260

JOSHI, CHANDRASHEKHAR JANARDAN, physics educator; b. Wai, India, July 22, 1953; came to U.S., 1981; s. Janardan Digambar and Ramabai (Kirpekar) J.; m. Asha Bhatt, Jan. 18, 1982. BS, London U., 1974; PhD, Hull U., U.K., 1978. Research assoc. Nat. Research Council, Can., 1978-81; research engr. UCLA, 1981-83, adj. assoc. prof., 1983-86, assoc. prof.-in-residence, 1986-87, assoc. prof., 1987-88, prof. elec. engring., 1988—; cons. Lawrence Livermore (Calif.) Nat. Lab., 1984, Los Alamos (N.Mex.) Nat. Lab., 1985—. Editor: Laser Acceleration of Particles, 1985; contbr. articles ot profl. jours. Grantee NSF, U.S. Dept. Energy; recipient Queen Mary Prize, Inst. Nuclear Engring., 1974. Mem. AAAS, IEEE, Am. Phys. Soc., N.Y. Acad. Scis. Home: 2004 Pier Ave Santa Monica CA 90405 Office: UCLA 405 Hilgard Ave Los Angeles CA 90024

JOSHI, SEWA RAM, toxicologist; b. Baluana, Punjab, India, Oct. 15, 1933; s. Hariram and Mayadevi (Khindria) J.; came to U.S., 1961, naturalized, 1971; B.Vet. Sci., Punjab U., 1954; M.S., Cornell U., 1963, Ph.D., 1965; m. Surinder Sharma, Aug. 1954; 1 son, Ashok Kumar. State veterinarian Punjab, 1954-55; research assoc. Indian Vet. Research Inst., 1955-61; research assoc. pathology, toxicology Children's Cancer Research Found., Harvard U. Med. Sch., 1965-71; sr. staff fellow Nat. Cancer Inst., NIH, Bethesda, Md., 1971-76; physiologist in pharmacology and toxicology Nat. Center for Drugs and Biologics, FDA, Rockville, Md., 1976—; assoc. prof. Howard U., Washington, 1972-75. Recipient Career Service Recognition award USPHS, 1982. Mem. Soc. Toxicology, Soc. for Study Reprodn., Environ. Mutagen Soc., AAAS, N.Y. Acad. Scis., Sigma Xi. Club: Lake Linganore Country. Co-author: Carcinogenesis-A Comprehensive Survey, vol. 3, 1978. Contbr. tech. articles to profl. jours. Home: 6001 Poindexter Ln Rockville MD 20852 Office: Div Anti-infective Drug Products FDA (HFN-815) Room 12 B16 5600 Fishers Ln Rockville MD 20857

JOSHI, UMASHANKAR JETHALAL, poet, educator; b. Bamana, India, July 21, 1911; s. Jethalal K. and Navalbai B. (Thaker) J.; m. Jyotsna, May 25, 1937; children—Nandini, Svati. M.A., U. Bombay, 1938; Litt.D. (hon.), univs. Bangalor, Jodhpur, Saurashtra, Sardar, Patel, Jadavpur, Visva-Bharati, Jabalpur. Lectr., Sydenham Coll., Bombay, 1938-39; postgrad. tchr. Gujarat Vidyasabha, 1939-46; prof. Gujarati, dir. Sch. Langs., Gujarat U., 1954-70, vice-chancellor, 1966-72; v.p. Indian PEN, 1973-85, pres., 1985—; chmn. Indian Inst. Mass Communication, 1978-80; pres. Nat. Acad. Letters, 1978-82; chancellor Visva-Bharati U., 1979-82. Mem. Indian Parliament, 1970-76. Recipient Sahitya Acad. award, 1973; co-recipient Jnanpith award, 1967. Mem. Gujarat Vidyasabha (hon.), Gujarati Sahitya Parishad (life). Author 10 books of poetry, including: Dharavastra, Saptapadi, 1981; Collected Poems (1931-81), 1981; editor Sanskriti, 1947-84; playwright. Home: 26 Sardar Patel Nagar, Ahmedabad Gujarat 380006, India Office: PEN All-India Ctr, Theosophy Hall, 40 New Marine Lines, Bombay 400020 India

JOSPE, JOSEPH LEWIS, manufacturing company executive; b. Montreal, Que., Can., Oct. 16, 1951; s. Jack David and Miriam (Ripstein) L.; m. Linda Merle Gordon, Sept. 23, 1978; children: Michele Rose, Dara Hannah. BA, McGill U., Montreal, 1972; MS in Econs., London Sch. Econs., 1973; MBA, Harvard U., 1976. Mgr. fin. planning and analysis Bank of Montreal, 1976-78; v.p., sec.-treas. Ideal Security, Inc., LaSalle, Can., 1978—; pres. Lewis, Jospe & Assocs., Montreal, 1978—; chmn. Ouellette Fasteners, Inc., Alexandria, Can., 1987—; sec.-treas. O.J. Ouellette, Inc., LaSalle, 1987—. Mem. Can. Hardware and Houseware Mfg. Assn. (bd. dirs. 1986—, treas. 1987—). Jewish. Home: 3755 Grey Ave, Montreal, PQ Canada H4A 3N8 Office: Ideal Security Inc, 860 90th Ave, LaSalle, PQ Canada H8R 3A2

JOSPIN, LIONEL ROBERT, French politician; b. Meudon, Hauts-de-Seine, July 12, 1937; s. Robert Jospin and Mireille Dandieu; m. Elisabeth Dannenmuller, 1973; 2 children. Ed., Ecole nat. d'administration. Sec., Ministry Fgn. Affairs, 1965-70; prof. Econ. Inst. universitaire de tech. de Paris-Sceaux, also U. Paris XI, 1970-81; nat. sec. Socialist Party, mem. steering com., 1973-75, spokesman on third world affairs, 1975-79, internat. relations, 1979-81, first sec., 1981—; councillor for Paris (18th arrondissement), 1977—, elected Socialist dep. for Paris (27th circ.) to Nat. Assembly, 1981. Avocation: basketball. Office: Parti Socialist, 10 rue de Solferino, 75007 Paris France Other: Parti socialiste 10 rue de Solferino, 10 rue de Solferino, 75007 Paris France *

JOURNEY, DREXEL DAHLKE, lawyer; b. Westfield, Wis., Feb. 23, 1926; s. Clarence Earl and Verna L. Gilmore (Dahlke) Journey Gilmore; m. Vergene Harriet Sandsmark, Oct. 24, 1952; 1 child, Ann Marie. BBA, U. Wis., 1950, LLB, 1952; LLM, George Washington U., 1957. Bar: Wis. 1952, U.S. Dist. Ct. (we. dist.) Wis. 1953, U.S. Supreme Ct. 1955, U.S. Ct. Appeals (4th cir.) 1960, U.S. Ct. Appeals (5th cir.) 1961, U.S. Ct. Appeals (D.C. cir.) 1965, U.S. Ct. Appeals (7th and 9th cirs.) 1967, U.S. Ct. Appeals (1st cir.) 1969, D.C. 1970, U.S. Dist. Ct. D.C. 1970, U.S. Ct. Appeals (2d, 3d, 6th, 8th and 10th cirs.) 1976, U.S. Ct. Appeals (11th cir.) 1981. Counsel FPC, Washington, 1952-66, asst. gen. counsel, 1966-70, dep. gen. counsel, 1970-74, gen. counsel, 1974-77; ptnr. Schiff, Hardin & Waite, Washington, 1977—. Author: Corporate Law and Practice, 1975; contbr. articles to profl. jours. Pres. Am. U. Park Citizens Assn., Washington, 1970-72; trustee Lincoln-Wesmoreland Housing Project, Washington, 1978-79. Served with Mcht. Marine Res. USNR, 1944-46, USNG, 1948-50. Knapp scholar U. Wis., 1952. Mem. ABA, Fed. Bar Assn., Fed. Energy Bar Assn., Nat. Lawyers Club, Phi Kappa Phi, Phi Eta Sigma, Theta Delta Chi. Republican. Congregationalist. Lodge: Masons. Home: 4540 Windom Pl NW Washington DC 20016 Office: Schiff Hardin & Waite 1101 Connecticut Ave NW Washington DC 20036

JOUZEL, SERGE, physician; b. St. Gilles Croix de Vie, Vendeé, France, Jan. 25, 1942; s. Jouzel Camille and Lachese Odette; m. Boitel Annick, Aug. 20, 1966; children: Anne, Bernard, Bénédicte. MD, Medicine Faculty Nantes, France, 1968. Cert. agrl. medicine; cert. geriatric medicine. Intern Untol Hosp., 1966-68; resident La Roche-sur-Yon Hosp., 1966-68; practice gen. medicine, St. Gilles Croix de Vie, 1969—; prin. doctor local hosp., St. Gilles Croix de Vie, 1970. Red Cross doctor, St. Gilles Croix de Vie. Served with French Navy. Roman Catholic. Home and Office: 25 Quai Riviere, 85800 Saint Gilles Croix de Vie Vendee, France

JOVANOVIC, BORISLAV, archaeologist; b. Kavadarci, Yugoslavia, June 22, 1930; s. Radovan and Jelena (Ramadanski) J.; m. Katarina Čuturilo, 1968; 1 child, Tamara. BA, U. Beograd, 1955, PhD, 1966. Assoc. Inst. Archaeology, Beograd, Yugoslavia, 1959-78; dir. Inst. Archaeology, Beograd, 1978-86, sci. counselor, 1986—. Author: Eneolithic Metallurgy in Yugoclavia, 1971, Rudna Glava, Earliest Copper Mining in Central Balkans, 1982. Fellow Deutsches Archaologisches Inst. Office: Inst Archaeology Kn, Mihajlova 35/IV, 11000 Beograd Yugoslavia

JOVANOVIC, SLOBODAN ALEKSA, author; b. Negotin, Serbia, Apr. 23, 1911; s. Aleksa Jovan and Kosara Petar (Ilic) J.; B.A., Belgrade U., 1933, Ph.D., 1956; m. Bojka Jovanovic, Jan. 27, 1949; 1 son, Srdjan. High sch. tchr., Sombor, 1934-35; theatre sec., librarian, Skoplje, 1935-38; theatre sec., librarian, Belgrade, Yugoslavia, 1938-45; dept. chief Nat. Library Serbia, Belgrade, 1945-66. Pres., City of Belgrade Commn. for Lit., Transl., Libraries and Pub. Activities, 1978-82. Decorated Order of Labor with Golden Wreath (Yugoslavia). Mem. Soc. Serbian Librarians (v.p. 1951-54), Sibmas (mem. com. 1962—), Soc. Serbian Lit. Translators (pres. 1963-66, award for life work 1988), Fedn. Yugoslav Lit. Translators (pres. 1966-69), Serbian Shakespearian Soc., Serbian Soc. Comparative Studies Lit., Yugoslav-French Soc., Yugoslav Brit. Soc. Author: Postanak i razvoj francuske i engleske i dejne drame 1850-1914, 1968; Recnik knjizevnih izraza, 1972; A Guide to Yugoslav Libraries and Archives, 1974; editor Bibliotekar, 1949-54; editor in chief Mostovi, 1970-79; editor Leksikon Pisaca Jugoslavije, 1972—. Home: 13 Dositejeva, Belgrade Yugoslavia 11000

JOVANOVIC, VERA MILAN, radiopharmaceutical chemist; b. Jagodnjak, Yugoslavia, Dec. 12, 1932; d. Milan Jovic and Natalija Trbic; m. Boško Jovanovic, May 1, 1960; children: Jasna, Svetlana. BS in Technol. Engring., U. Zagreb, Yugoslavia, 1960; BS in Pharmacy, U. Belgrade, Yugoslavia, 1962, PhD in Pharm. Scis., 1976. Technol. engr. Galenika Pharm. Industry, Belgrade, 1960-61; research radiopharm. chemist Boris Kidrič Inst. Nuclear Scis., Belgrade, 1961—, head dept. radiopharms. control, 1965—. Author: (monographies) Pharmacopoea Yugoslavica, 1972, 87, (with others) various radioisotope textbooks; contbr. articles to profl. jours. Mem. Serbian Pharm. Soc., Serbian Nuclear Medicine Soc. (award for sci. achievement in nuclear medicine 1987), Yugoslavian Nuclear Medicine Soc. Home: Georgi Georgiju Deža 16/25, 11080 Zemun Yugoslavia Office: Boris Kidrič Inst Nuclear Scis, POB 522, Belgrade Yugoslavia

JOVANOVIC, VLADIMIR, law educator; b. Bela Crkva, Vojvodina, Yugoslavia, Nov, 23, 1923; s. Kosta and Marija (Stojadinovic) J.; m. Ljiljana Mikic, Aug. 4, 1952 (dec. 1970); m. Lucija Spirovic, Aug. 1, 1971; 1 child, Marija, 1 stepson, Mirko. Student, Belgrade, Yugoslavia, 1945-50, PhD (hon.), 1956. Asst. Faculty Law, Belgrade, 1951-56, docent, 1956-60, prof. extraordinary, 1960-66, prof. ordinary, 1966—; dir. Inst. Comparative Law, Belgrade, 1979—. Author: Privredno pravo (commercial law), 1961, Menicno i cek. pr. (bill on exchange), 1953, 74, Osiguranje u privredi (ins.), 1963, Samopuravno pravo (sales mgmt.), 1981; contbr. articles to profl. jours. Mem. Assn. Lawyers Economy (exec. bd. 1978). Communist. Home: Gandijeva, 11000 Belgrade SR Serbia Yugoslavia Office: Faculty of Law, Bulevar Revolucije 67, 11000 Belgrade Serbia Yugoslavia

JOVES, LOURDES BALBAS, municipal health officer, physician; b. Sept. 23, 1929; d. Ricardo L. and Mercedes (Corpuz) B.; m. Policarpio N. Joves, Jan. 1, 1958; children: Nora, Policarpio. AA, U. Santo Tomas, Manila, 1949, MD, 1954; MPH, U. Philippines, 1973. Mcpl. health officer Dept. Health, Barcelona, Soraogon, Philippines, 1955-57, Gerona, Tarlac, Philippines, 1957—; scholar Inst. Pub. Health U. Philippines, 1972-73. Named Outstanding Employee in the Field of Nutrition Provincial Nutrition Com., Tarlac, 1984, Outstanding Mcpl. Health Officer Provincial Health Office, Tarlac, 1976 and Asia-Pacific Youth Outreach Devel. Inc., 1985. Fellow Phillipine Acad. Family Physicians; mem. Philippine Med. Assn., Tarlac Med. Soc., Philippine Med. Women's Assn. Roman Catholic. Home: Poblacion 2, Gerona Tarlac III, Philippines Office: Municipal Health Office, Poblacion, Gerona Tarlac 2112, Philippines

JOYCE, BERNITA ANNE, federal government agency administrator; d. Albert A. and Margaret C. Joyce; B.A., Duchesne Coll.; M.B.A., U. Santa Clara, 1968, Ph.D., 1974; m. Kenneth B. Lucas, Aug. 2, 1975. Adminstr., Soc. of Sacred Heart, Menlo Park, Calif. and Seattle, regional adminstr., San Francisco, 1969-71; with Wolfe & Co., C.P.A.s, Washington, 1971-72; fin. dir. Nat. Forest Products Assn., Washington, 1972-74; budget and fiscal officer ICC, Washington, 1974-77, Office Mgmt. and Budget, 1977-80; asst. dir. mgmt. services Bur. Mines, Dept. Interior, 1980-85, asst. dir. Office Policy Analysis, 1985—. Trustee St. Francis Preparatory Sch., Spring Grove, Pa. Author: Financial Viability of Private Elementary Schools. Mem. Am. Inst. CPA's, Sr. Execs. Assn., AAUW, Exec. Women in Govt. (v.p.), Beta Gamma Sigma. Home: 6001 Bradley Blvd Bethesda MD 20817

JOYCE, JAMES DANIEL, clergyman; b. Spencer, Va., Jan. 12, 1921; s. James Garfield and Mary (Taylor) J.; m. Dorothy Beatrice Campbell, Aug. 2, 1946; 1 son, Kevin Campbell. AB in Religion, Johnson Bible Coll., 1945, Lynchburg Coll., 1946; BD, Butler U., 1949; MA in Biblical Theology, Yale U., 1952, PhD, 1958. Ordained to ministry Disciples of Christ Ch., 1943. Pastor Hanover Ave. Christian Ch., Richmond, Va., 1954-59; sr. student leader ecumenical inst. World Council Chs., Geneva, 1960; prof. New Testament and Bible theology Christian Theol. Sem., Indpls., 1961-62; dean grad. sem. Phillips U., Enid, Okla., 1962-74; pastor Bethany Christian Ch., Houston, 1974-80, Covenant Christian Ch., Houston, 1980—; W.E. Garrison lectr. Disciple students Yale U., 1963; Jesse M. Bader lectr. evangelism Drake U., 1968; columnist Christian Jour., 1962-80; bass soloist rec. Joy-ce Sounds, 1977; pres. World Conv. Chrs. of Christ, 1970-74, mem. exec. com., 1974—; lectr. for armed forces in Far East, 1968; adj. prof. speech and creative writing U. Houston and Houston Community Coll., 1981-82; prof. speech and writing Houston Community Coll., 1982—, also head dept. speech; mem. bd. mgrs. Pension Fund Disciples of Christ. Author: The Living Christ in Our Changing World, 1962, The Place of the Sacraments in Worship, 1967. Recipient cert. of merit Methodist Bishop of Korea, 1972. Mem. Am. Assn. Theol. Schs. (exec. com. 1966-72), Theta Phi. Home: 5211 Carew St Houston TX 77096

JOYCE, JOSEPH JAMES, lawyer, soft drink and food company executive; b. Chgo., Sept. 28, 1943; s. Edward R. and Mary E. (Jordan) J.; m. Suzanne M. Sheridan, Aug. 26, 1967; children—Joseph, Michael, Peter, Kevin, Edward. B.S., Xavier U., 1965; J.D. Loyola U., 1968. Bar: Ill. 1968. Mem. Hill, Sherman, Meroni, Gross & Simpson, Chgo., 1968-72; atty. Pepsico., Inc., Purchase, N.Y., 1972-74, trademark counsel, 1974-77, asst. gen. counsel, 1977—, v.p., asst. gen. counsel, 1986—. Contbr. articles to profl. jours. Mem. Ill. Bar Assn., ABA (com. chmn. 1982—), U.S. Trade Assn. (com. chmn. 1979—), Assn. Internationale pour la Protection de la Propieté Industrielle, Licensing Execs. Soc. Westchester-Fairfield Corp. Counsel Assn., Inc., Assn. Inter-Am. de la Propriedad Industrial. Roman Catholic. Office: Pepsico Inc Anderson Hill Rd Purchase NY 10577

JOYCE, WILLIAM ROBERT, textile machinery company executive; b. Springfield, Ohio, Mar. 18, 1936; s. Robert Emmet and Christel Beatrice (Beekman) J.; m. Betty Arlene Provonsha, Aug. 29, 1959; children—Jennifer Lynn, Janet Cathleen. BA in Bus., Calif. Western U., 1982; MBA, Calif. Coast U., 1984. Cert. mfg. engring. technician Soc. Mfg. Engrs., 1975. Mgr. engring. Heinicke Instruments, Hollywood, Fla., 1964-68; div. mgr. Jensen Corp., Pompano Beach, Fla., 1969-72; pres. Textiles Supply, Inc., Gerton, N.C., 1972-80; v.p., gen. mgr. Tex-Fab, Inc., Gerton, N.C., 1980-82; pres. Tex-nology Systems, Inc., Gerton, N.C., 1982—; owner Corrib Enterprises, Automation Cons., Gerton, 1981—. Mem., co-founder Assoc. Woodland Owners N.C.; Upper Hickory Nut Gorge Vol. Fire Dept., Gerton. Served with USAF, 1958-64. Recipient innovative devel. award, 1985, award Optimist Club, 1953-54. Mem. Guild Master Craftsmen (internat. mem.) Nat. Rifle Assn., Soc. Mfg. Engrs., Am. Inst. Design and Drafting, Western Carolina Entrepeneurial Council. Republican. Baptist. Club: Gerton Community Civic. Patentee in field.

JOYNER, WEYLAND THOMAS, physicist, educator; b. Suffolk, Va., Aug. 9, 1929; s. Weyland T. and Thelma (Neal) J.; m. Marianne Steele, Dec. 3, 1955; children: Anne, Weyland, Leigh. B.S., Hampden-Sydney Coll., 1951; M.A., Duke, 1952, Ph.D., 1955. Teaching fellow Duke, 1954, research asso., 1958; physicist Dept. Def., Washington, 1954-57; research physicist U. Md., 1955-57; asst. prof. physics Hampden-Sydney Coll., 1957-59, asso. prof., 1959-63, prof., 1963—, physics chmn., 1968-82, 85—; research asso. Ames Lab. AEC, 1964-65; vis. prof. Pomona Coll., 1965; staff Commn. on Coll. Physics, Ann Arbor, Mich., 1966-67; vis. fellow Dartmouth Coll., 1981; mem. Panel on Preparation Physics Tchrs., 1967-68; nuclear phys. cons. Oak Ridge Inst. Nuclear Studies, 1960-67; NASA-Lewis faculty fellow, 1982-84; pres. Piedmont Farms, Inc., 1958-75; ednl. cons. numerous colls. and univs., 1965-75; pres. Windsor Supply Corp., 1966-82, Three Rivers Farms, Inc., 1971—; mgmt. cons., 1966—; pres. Windsor Seed & Livestock Co., 1969-83; v.p. Software Plus Inc., 1986—, Tidewater F&G, 1982—. Contbr. articles profl. jours. Bd. dirs. Prince Edward Acad., 1971—, exec. com., 1975—; trustee Prince Edward Sch. Electoral Bd., 1979-80. NASA prin. investigator, 1985-87. Fellow AAAS; mem. Am. Phys. Soc., Am. Assn. Physics Tchrs., IEEE, Va. Acad. Sci. (past mem. council, sect. pres.), Am. Inst. Physics (regional counselor, past dir. Coll. Program), Phi Beta Kappa, Sigma Xi, Lambda Chi Alpha. Presbyn. (elder). Home: Venable Pl Hampden-Sydney VA 23943

JRAIGE, WASSIM GEBRAN, manufacturing company executive; b. Beirut, Aug. 26, 1952; parents: Gebran George and Mary Joseph (Barbar) J. BSEE, Am. Univ. Beirut, 1975; MBA, Inst. Europeenne D'Adminstrn. Affaires, Fontainbleau, France, 1981. Cert. elec. engr. Dist. mgr. Westinghouse Elec. Corp., Dubai, United Arab Emirates, 1975-80; area mgr. Raychem Corp., Nicosia, Cyprus, 1981-87; bd. dirs. Vizion Internat., Cyprus. Mem. Alumni Inst. Europeenne D'Adminstrn. Affaires, Alumni Am. U. Beirut. Club: Hiltonia. Home: 5 Prometheus St, 0136 Nicosia Cyprus Office. Raychem Middle East Internat, 21 Akademias Ave, Nicosia Aghlanjia Cyprus

JUAN CARLOS I (DE BORBÓN Y BORBÓN), HIS MAJESTY, King of Spain; b. Rome, Jan. 5, 1938; s. Don Juan de Borbón y Battenberg and Dona Maria de las Mercedes de Borbón y Orleans; m. Princess Sophia of Greece, May 14, 1962; children: Filipe, Elena, Cristina. Student Inst. San Isidro, Madrid, Colegio del Carmen, Gen. Mil. Acad., Zaragoza, U. Madrid; Dr.h.c. (hon.), Strasbourg U., 1979, U. Madrid, Harvard U., 1984; D in Polit. Sci. (hon.) Chulalongkorn U., Bangkok, 1987. Commd. into three armed forces and undertook tng. in each, 1957-59; studied orgn. and activities various govt. ministries; named by Gen. Franco as future King of Spain, 1969; king of Spain, 1975—; capt.-gen. Armed Forces, 1975. Recipient Charlemagne prize, 1982, Bolivar prize UNESCO, 1983. Address: Palacio de la Zarzuela, Madrid Spain *

JUAREZ, ANTONIO, psychotherapist, consultant; b. El Paso, Tex., Nov. 6, 1952; s. Juan Antonio and Amelia (Rivas) J. B.S. in Psychology, U.Tex.-El Paso, 1976, M.A. in Clin. Psychology, 1982; postgrad., N.Mex. State U., 1987—. Caseworker asst. El Paso Mental Health Ctr., 1978-79, caseworker III, 1982-83; clin. specialist S.W. Mental Health Ctr., Las Cruces, N.Mex., 1979-80; therapist, trainer S.W. Community House, El Paso, 1980-81; psychol. cons. El Paso Guidance Ctr., 1981-82, psychotherapist, 1983—, dir. N.E. services; pvt. practice El Paso, 1987—; cons. Citizens and Students Together, El Paso, 1983—, group facilitator Tai Chi Chuan Instr., Sun Valley Regional Hosp., El Paso, Tex., 1988. Published poet. Mem. Latin Am. com. N.Mex. State U., 1985. Served with USAF, 1972-76. Fellow N.Mex. State U., 1981. Mem. U.S.-Mex. Border Health Assn., El Paso Psychol. Assn., Tex. Assn. for Counseling and Devel., Tex. Assn. for Children of Alcoholics, Am. Biographical Inst. Research Assn. Democrat. Roman Catholic. Avocations: martial arts, playing string instruments. Home: PO Box 1493 Santa Teresa NM 88008 Office: El Paso Guidance Ctr 1501 N Mesa St El Paso TX 79901

JUAREZ, MARETTA LIYA CALIMPONG, social worker; b. Gilroy, Calif., Feb. 14, 1958; d. Sulpicio Magsalay and Pelagia Lagotom (Viacrusis) Calimpong; m. Henry Juarez, Mar. 24, 1984. BA, U. Calif., Berkeley, 1979; MSW, San Jose State U., 1983. Lic. clin. social worker. Mgr. Pacific Bell, San Jose, Calif., 1983-84; revenue officer IRS, Salinas, Calif., 1984-85; social worker Santa Cruz (Calif.) County, 1985, Santa Clara County, San Jose, 1985—. Recipient award Am. Legion, 1972. Mem. NOW, Nat. Assn. Social Workers, Nat. Council on Alcoholism. Democrat. Roman Catholic.

JUBANY ARNAU, NARCISCO CARDINAL, archbishop of Barcelona; b. Santa Coloma de Farnes, Spain, Aug. 12, 1913. Ordained priest Roman Cath. Ch., 1939; formerly prof. law Barcelona Sem.; served on Ecclesistical Tribunal; titular bishop of Ortosia, also aux. of Barcelona, 1956; bishop of Gerona, 1964-71; archbishop of Barcelona, 1971—; elevated to Sacred Coll. of Cardinals, 1973; mem. Congregation of Sacraments and Divine Worship, Congregation of Religious and Secular Insts. Address: Calle del Obispo Irutita 5, Barcelona 2 Spain *

JUCEAM, ROBERT E., lawyer; b. N.Y.C., June 16, 1940; s. Benjamin T. and Amelia B. (Spatz) J.; m. Eleanor Pam, May 24, 1970; children: Daniel, Jacquelyn, Gregory. AB, Columbia U., 1961, JD, 1964; LLM, NYU, 1966. Bar: N.Y. 1965, U.S. Dist. Ct. (so. and ea. dists.) N.Y. 1966, U.S. Tax Ct. 1968, U.S. Ct. Appeals (2d cir.) 1967, U.S. Supreme Ct. 1971, U.S. Ct. Appeals (5th cir.) 1978, U.S. Ct. Appeals (D.C. cir.) 1980, U.S. Ct. Appeals (11th cir.) 1987. Law clk. U.S. Dist. Ct., N.Y., 1964-66; assoc. Fried, Frank, Harris, Shriver & Jacobson, N.Y.C., 1966-73, ptnr., 1974—; dir. Nat. Network Def. of the Right to Counsel, Inc., 1985—, Lawyers Com. for Human Rights, 1986—; dir. Am. Immigration Law Found., 1987—; mem. arbitration panel U.S. Dist. Ct. (ea. dist.) N.Y., 1986—. Contbr. articles to legal jours. Trustee Mexican-Am. Legal Def. and Edn. Fund, 1986—. Fellow Am. Bar. Found.; mem. ABA (ho. of dels. 1983—, chmn. com. on immigration sect. litigation 1985-88, mem. com. on immigration sect. administrv. law 1984—, vice-chmn. com. immigration sect. gen. practice , mem. coordinating com. on immigration law 1984-87, mem. com. environ. controls sect. corp. banking and security law, 1983-86), Internat. Bar Assn. (chmn. Sect. Gen. Practice com. bus. migration 1987—), N.Y. State Bar Assn., Assn. Bar City N.Y. (com. on trademarks and unfair competition 1983-86, com. immigration1986—, com. profl. ethics and judicial conduct 1974-77, 81), Am. Judicature Soc. (life), Am. Bar Endowment (com. on profl. ethics and judicial resposibility 1988—), Nat. Conf. Bar Presidents (assoc.), Am. Immigration Lawyers Assn. (pres. 1982-83, bd. govs. 1971—, chmn. N.Y. chpt. 1971-72, gen. counsel 1986—, editor Annual Symposium Handbook 1985—; Edith Lowenstein Meml. award 1981), Am. Arbitration Assn. (comml. panel 1973—), N.Y. County Lawyers Assn., Fed. Bar Assn., Fed. Bar Council, N.Y. Criminal Bar Assn., N.Y. State Trial Lawyers Assn., Nat. Assn. Criminal Def. Lawyers, Alpha Epsilon Pi. Clubs: Columbia, India House (N.Y.C.). Home: 106 Hemlock Rd Manhasset NY 11030 Office: Fried Frank Harris Shriver & Jacobson 1 New York Plaza Suite 2500 New York NY 10004

JUD, RUDOLF, historian; b. Kaltbrunn, Switzerland, Oct. 21, 1923; s. Peter and Agnes (Giger) J.; m. Elisabeth Schmid, Apr. 1, 1950; 1 child, Sibylle. Student, U. Fribourg, Switzerland, 1944-45, 46-49, U. Zürich, 1945-46; Doctorate, U. Vienna, Austria, 1949. Editor, redactor Erasmus (internat. bull. contemporary scholarship), Darmstadt, Fed. Republic Germany, 1947—. Author: Das Linksrheinische Korps des Generals Hotze in Herbst und Winter 1796, 1958, Ordine et Vigilantia, 1965, Freiheit und Recht bei Deutschen Klassikern, 1979, Im Schatten der Wissenschaftlichen Kritik, 1985, Texts for W. Eikel's Calligraphy Cal., 1987, 88. Recipient Johann Heinrich Merck award, Darmstadt, 1957, Palmes Acad., French Govt., 1965, Cross of Merit 1st Class, Fed. Republic Germany, 1983; named Hon. Prof. Austrian Govt., 1965. Mem. Don Suisse Fête Nat. Zürich, A. Paul Weber Soc., Soc. Bibliophiles, Soc. Suisse Préhistoire d'Archéologie, Hugo Obermaier Soc. Address: Alexandraweg 3, D-6100 Darmstadt Federal Republic of Germany

JUDAH, JAY STILLSON, historian, educator; b. Leavenworth, Wash., July 7, 1911; s. Stillson and Maude Alice (Cannon) J.; m. Lucile Elaine Baker, Dec. 2, 1935 (dec. Mar. 1987); children: Jay Stillson Jr., Elaine Judah Keller, Diane Judah Moore; m. Helen Janin Nov. 24, 1987. AB, U. Wash., 1934; Library cert., U. Calif.-Berkeley, 1941; Litt.D., Chapman Coll., 1955. With Pacific Sch. Religion, Berkeley, 1941-69; head librarian Pacific Sch. Religion, 1941-69, prof. history of religion, 1955-69; dir. Bibliog. Ctr., Grad. Theol. Union, Berkeley, 1966-69; head librarian Grad. Theol. Union (Common Library), Berkeley, 1969-76; prof. history of religion Grad. Theol. Union, 1969-76; adj. prof. Pacific Sch. Religion, 1974-79; field faculty Vt. Coll., Norwich U., 1984-85; Nat. v.p. Alliance for Preservation of Religious Liberty, 1978-79. Author: Jehovah's Witnesses, 1964, History and Philosophy of the Metaphysical Movements in America, 1967, Hare Krishna and the Counterculture, 1974; compiler, editor: Index to Religious Periodical Literature, 1949-52, 1952. Guggenheim fellow, 1934; Sealantic Fund fellow, 1957-58. Fellow Internat. Inst. Arts and Letters; mem. Am. Theol. Library Assn. (v.p. 1962-63, pres. 1963-64), Western Theol. Library Assn. (pres. 1954-55), Internat. Assn. Theol. Libraries (sec.-treas. 1955-60). Mem. Christian Ch. (disciples of Christ). Clubs: El Cerrito (Calif.); Tennis (pres. 1958-65); Rossmoor Tennis (pres. 1985-86). Home: 2705 Saklan Indian Dr 8 Walnut Creek CA 94595

JUDD, DOROTHY HEIPLE, educator; b. Oakwood, Ill., May 27, 1922; d. Eldridge Winfield and Mary Luciel (Oliphant) Heiple; B.A., Ind. U., 1944; M.Ed., U. Toledo, 1971; Ed.S., Troy State U., 1976; Ed.D., No. Ill. U., 1981; m. Robert Carpenter Judd, Sept. 19, 1964; children by previous marriage—Patricia Ann Konkoly, Catherine Rafferty, Deborah Brown, Nancy Lee Arrington; stepchildren—Dianna Kay Judd Carlisi, Nancy Carol Judd Wilber, Linda Judd Marinaccio Pucci. Head lang. arts dept. Eisenhower Jr. High Sch., Darien, Ill., 1961-70; instr. devel. edn. Owens Tech. Coll., Perrysburg, Ohio, 1971-73; instr. edn. Troy State U., Montgomery, Ala., also right-to-read coordinator State of Ala., 1975-76; core dept. chair Community Consol. Sch., Dist. 15, Palatine, Ill., 1977-79; asst. prof. curriculum and instrn. No. Ill. U., 1979-83; asst. prof. edn. Southeastern La. U., Hammond, 1984—; pres. R.C. Judd & Assos., Bloomingdale, Ill., 1980-86; pres. Edn. Tng. Service, Inc., Glandale Heights, Ill., 1986—. Mem. Assn. Supervision and Curriculum Devel., Assn. Tchr. Edn., Internat. Council Computers in Edn., Internat. Reading Assn., Nat. Council Social Studies, Nat. Council Tchrs. of English, Pi Lambda Theta, Phi Delta Kappa. Author: Mastering the Micro, 1984, Easy Authoring, 1988; contbg. editor Ednl. Computer mag., 1981-84, Electronic Edn., 1984-88, Acad. Technology, 1987-88; contbr. articles to profl. jours. Home: 1990 Flagstaff Ct Glendale Heights IL 60139

JUDD, JAMES THURSTON, savings and loan executive; b. Hurricane, Utah, Dec. 13, 1938; s. Finley MacFarland and Bessie (Thurston) J.; m. Janis Anderson, July 15, 1960; children: Juliet, Brian. BS, Utah State U., 1961; postgrad., Los Angeles State U., 1962-63, U. Detroit, 1963-64. Cert. flight instr. Fin. analyst automotive assembly div. Ford Motor Co., Detroit, 1961-64; sales mgr. Xerox Corp., Rocester, N.Y., 1966-75; loan mgr. Golden West Fin. Corp. Savs. and Loan, Oakland, Calif., 1975—; pres. Judd Ranch. Chmn. northbay Bringing Entertainment To The Elderly, Saratoga, Calif., 1972—; chmn. Beef for the Poor, Oakland, 1983-87. Mem. Nat. Assn. Real Estate Appraisers, Calif. Assn. Real Estate, Exptl. Aircraft Assn., Simga Nu. Republican. Mormon. Home: 3284 Blackhawk Meadow Dr Danville CA 94526 Office: World Savs and Loan 1901 Harrison St Oakland CA 94612

JUDD, JOHN EDMUND, instrument manufacturing executive; b. New Haven, June 23, 1930; s. Thomas F. and Grace C. (Byrnes) J.; Asso. Sci. in Elec. Engring., U. New Haven, 1954; m. JoAnne Pettrelle, Oct. 4, 1954; children—Robert, Leslie, Bryant. Exptl. test project engr. M.B. Electronics div. Textron, Inc., 1956-62, sales engr., 1962-64, sales mgr. internat. div., 1964-67; gen. sales mgr., products marketing mgr., 1967-72; v.p. Vibra Sciences, Inc., East Haven, Conn., 1973-76; pres. Vibra-Metrics, Inc., Hamden, Conn., 1972-86. Chmn. indsl. adv. council Opportunities Industrialization Center, New Haven, 1970-76; treas. Hamden Figure Skating Assn., 1975-76; mem. Conn. Job Tng. Council. Served with USAF, 1947-50. Mem. Inst. Environ. Scis., Instrument Soc. Am. (sr.), Greater New Haven Mfrs. Assn. (pres., exec. bd.), Vibration Inst., Conn. Bus. and Industry Assn., Nat. Alliance Bus. (vice chmn. New Haven met. council 1979), Greater New Haven C. of C. (bd. dirs.), Greater New Haven Pvt. Industry Council (chmn. 1978-85). Roman Catholic Club: Rotary. Home: 80 Squire Ln Hamden CT 06518 Office: 1014 Sherman Pkwy Hamden CT 06514

JUDD, LEWIS LUND, psychiatrist, educator; b. Los Angeles, Feb. 10, 1930; s. George E. and Emmeline (Lund) J.; B.S., U. Utah, 1954; M.D. cum laude, UCLA, 1956; m. Patricia Ann Hoffman, Jan. 26, 1974; children by previous marriage—Allison Clark, Catherine Anne, Stephanie. Intern, UCLA Sch. Medicine, 1958-59, resident in psychiatry, 1959-60, 62-64, fellow in child psychiatry, 1964-65, asst. prof. depts. psychiatry and psychology, 1965-70, dir. edn., child and adolescent psychiatry dept. psychiatry, 1968; asso. prof. psychiatry U. Calif. at San Diego, La Jolla, 1970, vice chmn., dir. clin. programs dept. psychiatry, 1970-73, dir. drug abuse programs, 1970-73, prof., from 1973, acting chmn. dept., 1974, co-chmn., 1975-77, chmn., 1977-87 ; dir. NIMH, 1988—; chief psychiat. service San Diego VA Hosp., La Jolla, 1972-77; chief psychiat. service U. Calif. Med. Center, San Diego, from 1982, pres. med. staff, chmn. exec. com., from 1982; mem. adv. com. on evaluation drug abuse programs County of San Diego, 1970-73; chmn. clin. projects rev. com. NIMH, 1975-79; guest faculty San Diego Psychoanalytic Inst. Served to capt., M.C., USAF, 1960-62. Fellow Am. Psychiat. Assn.; mem. Soc. Neuroscis., Psychiat. Research Soc., Assn. Acad. Psychiatry, Soc. Research in Child Devel., Am. Coll. Neuropsychopharmacology, So. Calif., San Diego psychiat. socs., Am. Assn. Chmn. Depts. Psychiatry, Alpha Omega Alpha. Contbr. articles to med. jours. Home: 7108 Beechwood Dr Chevy Chase MD 20815 Office: NIMH Office of the Director 5600 Fishers Ln Rockville MD 20857

JUDD, ROBERT CARPENTER, business administration educator; b. Maui, Hawaii, July 6, 1921; s. Robert Augustine and Marguerite (Schoonmaker) J.; m. Dorothy May Heiple, Sept. 19, 1964; children: Dianna Kay (Mrs. Joseph R. Carlisi), Nancy Carol (Mrs. David E. Wilber), Linda Sue (Mrs. Bernard Pucci); stepchildren: Patricia Ann (Mrs. Michael J. Konkoly), Catherine Rafferty, Deborah Rafferty-Brown (Mrs. Herb Brown), Nancy Rafferty (Mrs. Steve Arrington). A.B., U. Chgo., 1942; Ph.D., U. Wis., 1963. Statis. analyst Montgomery Ward & Co., 1943; statis. mgr. Manning, Maxwell & Moore, Inc., 1943-46; market research mgr. R.G. LeTourneau, Inc., 1946-47; instr. statistics Bradley U., 1947-50; spl. risks supr. Continental Casualty Co., 1950-52; asst. to v.p. Mut. of Omaha, 1952-55, Eastern regional mgr. Fed. Life & Casualty Co., 1955-57; asst. prof. econs. and bus., dir. continuing edn. Beloit Coll., 1957-62; asst. prof. bus. orgn. and mgmt. U. Nebr., 1962-63; assoc. prof. mktg. DePaul U., 1963-66, No. Ill. U., 1966-68; prof. ops. analysis U. Toledo, 1968-73, chmn. dept. ops. analysis, 1968-71; v.p. acad. affairs Dyke Coll., 1973-74; prof. Troy State U., Ala., 1974-76; Univ. prof. bus. adminstrn. Gov.'s State U., 1976-85; prof. mgmt. Southeastern La. U., 1984—; vis. prof. mktg. and mgmt. info. Grad. Sch. Bus., Rosary Coll., 1986-87 ; vis. prof. mgmt. U. New Orleans, 1984. Author: Mastering the Micro, 1984, Easy Authoring, 1988; contbr. articles to profl. jours. Fellow AAAS; mem. Am. Mktg. Assn., Ops. Research Soc. Am., Am. Statis. Assn., Delta Sigma Pi, Beta Gamma Sigma, Phi Delta Kappa. Club: Rotary.

JUDE, JAMES RODERICK, cardiac surgeon; b. Maple Lake, Minn., June 2, 1928; s. Bernard Benedict and Cecilia Mary (Leick) J.; m. Sallye Garrigan, Aug. 4, 1951; children—Roderick, John, Cecilia, Victoria, Peter, Robert, Chris. B.S., Coll. St. Thomas, 1949; M.D., U. Minn., 1953. Intern Johns Hopkins Hosp., 1953-54, resident in surgery, 1954-55, 58-61, fellow in cardiovascular research, 1955-56; instr. surgery Johns Hopkins U. and Med. Sch., 1961-62, asst. prof., 1962-64; prof. surgery, chief thoracic and cardiovascular surgery U. Miami Sch. Medicine, 1964-71, clin. prof., 1971—; practice medicine specializing in cardiovascular surgery Miami and Ft. Lauderdale, 1971—. Contbr. articles to med. jours. Trustee Sir Victor Sasson Heart Found., Bahamas, 1973—; mem. Coral Gables (Fla.) Planning Bd., 1973-77. Served with USPHS, 1956-58. Fellow Am. Coll. Chest Physicians, Am. Coll. Cardiology, A.C.S.; mem. Am. Assn. Thoracic Surgery, Am. Surg. Assn., So. Surg. Assn., Soc. Vascular Surgery, Soc. Thoracic Surgeons, Am. Heart Assn., Soc. Univ. Surgeons. Democrat. Roman Catholic. Home: 200 Edgewater Dr Coral Gables FL 33133 Office: 3661 S Miami Ave Miami FL 33133 also: 5601 N Dixie Hwy Fort Lauderdale FL 33334

JUDELL, HAROLD BENN, lawyer; b. Milw., Mar. 9, 1915; s. Philip Fox and Lena Florence (Krause) J.; m. Maria Violeta van Ronzelen, May 5, 1951 (div.); m. Celeste Seymour Grulich, June 24, 1986. BA, U. Wis., 1936, JD, 1938; LLB, Tulane U., 1950. Bar: Wis. 1938, La. 1950. Mem. firm Scheinfeld Collins Durant & Winter, Milw., 1938; spl. agent, adminstrv. asst. to dir. FBI, 1939-44; ptnr. Foley & Judell, New Orleans, 1950—; chmn. bd. Rockwood Nat. Trustee, East Group Properties, 1981—, Sizeler Property Investors, Inc., Greater New Orleans YMCA, Internat. House, 1981—. Mem. ABA, La. Bar Assn., Am. Judicare Soc., Nat. Assn. Bond Lawyers (bd. dirs., pres. 1984-85). Clubs: New Orleans Country, Lawn Tennis, Met. (N.Y.C.); Nacional (Lima, Peru). Office: Foley & Judell 535 Gravier St 8th Floor New Orleans LA 70130

JUDGE, JOHN EMMET, manufacturing company marketing executive; b. Grafton, N.D., May 5, 1912; s. Charles and Lillian (Johnson) J.; m. Clarita Garcia, Apr. 18, 1940; children: Carolyn Judge Stanley, John Emmet, Maureen Judge Barron, Eileen Judge Horowitz, Susan Judge Lloyd. B.S. in Elec. Engring., U. N.D., 1935. Asst. to adminstr. Ruarl Elctrification Adminstrn., 1937-39, Fed. Works Agy., Washington, 1939-42; staff specialist Exec. Office Pres., Washington, 1942; staff Wallace Clark & Co. (mgmt. cons.), N.Y.C., 1943-46; v.p. Morgan Furniture Co., Asheville, N.C., 1946-48; mgr. financial analysis Lincoln-Mercury div. Ford Motor Co., 1949-53, asst. gen. purchasing agt., 1953-55, mgr. mdsg. and product planning, 1955-58, marketing mgr., 1958-60; product planning mgr. Lincoln-Mercury div. Ford Motor Co., Dearborn, Mich., 1960-62; v.p. mktg. services Westinghouse Elec. Corp., Pitts., 1963-67; v.p. mktg. Indian Head, Inc., 1967-68; mktg. cons. 1969—; dir. Capital Corp. of Am. (investments), Intertek Industries, Kratos, Inc., Cashiers Plastics Corp., Cambridge Instruments, Inc.; Mem. adv. com. to U.S. sec. of commerce. Chmn. Birmingham Library Com., 1957; mem. bd. Boysville of Mich., 1957—. Mem. Am. Ordnance Assn., Soc. Advancement Mgmt., N.A.M. (chmn. marketing com.), Am. Soc. M.E., Engring. Soc. Detroit, Nat. Assn. Accountants, Soc. Automotive

Engrs., U. N.D. Alumni Assn. (pres.), Sigma Tau, Alpha Tau Omega. Roman Catholic. Clubs: Detroit Athletic, Economic; Orchard Lake (Mich.). Address: S Lake Shore Dr Harbor Springs MI 49740

JUDGE, ONKAR SINGH, marketing profressional; b. Hoshiarpur, Punjab, India, May 14, 1946; s. Dilbagh and Chanan (Kaur) S.; m. Parminder Kaur, Nov. 16, 1967; children: Ranjay, Madhuvin. Higher nat. diploma in Computer Studies, Slough (Eng.) Coll., 1975, nat. computer ctr. cert. in Systems Analysis, 1975; ordinary nat. diploma in Engring., Highycombe Coll. Arts and Tech., Eng., 1969; BSc in Engring., Baranas Hindu U., India, 1965; sr., Cambridge U.; student, Goethals Meml. Sch., Darjeeling, India. Programmer Coopers Mech. Joints, Slough, 1975; data processing mgr. Brit. Bakels Ltd., Slough, 1975-85; product mgr. Compass Software, London, 1985—. Home: 14 Myrtle Crescent, Slough SL2 5BB, England

JUDSON, LYMAN SPICER VINCENT, author, artist, speech pathologist; b. Plymouth, Mich., Mar. 27, 1903; s. Ernest W. and Fannie Louise (Spicer) J.; m. E. Ellen MacKechnie, 1933 (dec. 1964); m. 2d S. Adele H. Christensen, 1968. A.B., Albion Coll., 1925; postgrad., S.E. Mich. U., 1926, U. Iowa, 1929-30, U. So. Calif., 1927, Harvard, 1942, U. San Francisco, Palma, Mallorca, Spain, 1967; M.S., U. Mich., 1929; legis. scholar, U. Wis., 1931-33, Ph.D., 1933. Various positions as prof. speech communications and dept. chmn., and as dir. pub. relations and/or dir. fund raising and devel. and long-range planning; chief motion picture and visual edn. divs. OAS, 1946-51; producer ednl. motion pictures "Judson Color Jaunts"; served to comdr. USNR, 1942-65; mem. joint bd. USN tng. films, 1944-46; vis. prof. Latin Am. Affairs Assn. Am. Colls.; speech writer for Hon. Christian A. Herter, 1954-57; staff Supreme Allied Comdr. Atlantic; liaison officer staff Supreme Allied Comdr. Europe and European Hdqrs., dir. gen. NATO, 1953-54; spl. mission Vietnam and 7th Fleet, 1966; TV cons. Johnson Found., 1963-64; devel. and fund raising and long-range planning cons. 1965—. Author: Basic Speech and the Voice Science, 1933, The Fundamentals of the Speaker-Audience Relationship, 1934, Modern Group Discussion, 1935, Manual of Group Discussion, 1936, Public Speaking for Future Farmers, 1936, After-Dinner Speaking, 1937, Winning Future Farmers Speeches, 1939, The Student Congress Movement, 1940, The Monroe Doctrine and the Growth of Western Hemisphere Solidarity (co-author), 1941, Voice Science (co-author), 1942, rev. edit., 1965, The Judson Guides to Latin America (co-author), including Let's Go to Columbia, 1949, Let's Go to Guatemala, 1950, Let's Go to Peru, 1951, Your Holiday in Cuba, 1952, Report of Command Information Bureau 47 on Operation Inland Seas, 1959, The Interview, 1966, The Business Conference, 1969, Vincent Judson: The Island Series, 1973, Solution: PNC and PNCLAND, 1973, The AQUA Declaration, 1976, Happy 60th Birthday, 1982, The Shadow(s), 1983. Mem. Boston Athenaeum (Propr.), Explorers Scout Bd., cabinet mem. bed. mem., exec. com. mem., treas. Twin Lakes council Boy Scouts Am., 1972-73; sustaining mem. Rochester Civic Theatre; sustaining mem. Rochester Art Ctr. Fellow Am. Geog. Soc.; mem. Service Corps Retired Execs. (SCORE), Small Bus. Adminstrn., Inter-Am. Soc. Anthropology and Geography, Soc. Am. Archeology, Am. Soc. Agrl. Scis. Am. Acad. Polit. and Social Scis., Pub. Relations Soc. Am., Am. Speech & Hearing Assn., Archeol. Inst. Am. (pres. Winona-Hiawatha Valley chpt.), AAAS, Am. Micros. Soc., Navy League, Explorer's Club (New York, formerly editor of the Explorers LOG), Sigma Xi (Mayo Found. chpt.), Alpha Phi Omega, Delta Sigma Rho (former nat. sec., nat. editor), Tau Kappa Alpha, Pi Kappa Delta, Sigma Delta Chi (Boston prof. chpt.), Sigma Chi (life mem.). Mem. Christ United Methodist Church. Clubs: Rotary (Paul Harris fellow); Cosmos (Washington). Home: Rochester Towers 207 SW 5th Ave Rochester MN 55902

JUENGER, FRIEDRICH KLAUS, lawyer, educator; b. Frankfurt am Main, Ger., Feb. 18, 1930; came to U.S., 1955, naturalized, 1961; s. Wilhelm and Margarete J.; m. Baerbel Thierfelder, Sept. 15, 1967; children: J. Thomas, John F. Referendarexamen (Studienstiftung des deutschen Volkes scholar), J.W. Goethe-Universität, 1955; M.C.L. U. Mich, 1957; J.D. (Harlan-Fiske-Stone scholar), Columbia U., 1960. Bar: N.Y. 1962, Mich. 1970, U.S. Supreme Ct. 1970. Assoc. Cahill, Gordon & Reindel, N.Y.C., 1960-61, Baker & McKenzie, N.Y.C., Chgo., Madrid, 1961-66; assoc. prof. law Wayne State U., Detroit, 1966-68; prof. Wayne State U., 1968-75; vis. prof. Albert-Ludwigs U., Freiburg, Ger., 1972-73, 74, U. Calif., Davis, 1975—; vis. prof. Max-Planck-Institut für ausländisches und internationales Privatrecht, Hamburg, Fed. Republic Germany, 1981-82, U. Jean Moulin, Lyon, France, 1984; lectr. Hague Acad. Internat. Law, 1983, Uruguayan Fgn. Relations Inst., 1987. Author: (with L. Schmidt) German Stock Corporation Act, 1967, Zum Wandel des Internationalen Privatrechts, 1974; editor: Columbia Law Rev, 1959-60; bd. editors Am. Jour. Comparative Law, 1977—; contbr. articles on the conflict of laws, fgn. and comparative law to legal jours. Recipient Faculty Research award Wayne State U., 1971, Disting. Teaching award U. Calif.-Davis, 1985, Gen. Reporter on Judgments Recognition 12th Internat. Congress of Comparative Law, Australia, 1986, Fulbright lecturing award, 1987; Fulbright scholar, 1953-55; Volkswagen Found. research grantee, 1972-73; Fulbright sr. research fellow, 1981-82. Mem. ABA, Am. Fgn. Law Assn., Am. Law Inst., Am. Soc. Internat. Law, Assn. Bar City N.Y., Assn. Can. Law Tchrs., Gesellschaft für Rechtsvergleichung, Internat. Acad. Comparative Law (assoc. mem.), Soc. Pub. Tchrs. of Law. Office: U Calif King Hall Davis CA 95616

JUERGENSMEYER, JOHN ELI, lawyer; b. Stewardson, Ill., May 14, 1934; s. Irvin Karl and Clara Augusta (Johannaber) J.; m. Elizabeth Ann Bogart, Sept. 10, 1963; children—Margaret Ann, Frances Elizabeth. B.A., U. Ill., 1955, J.D., 1963; M.A., Princeton U., 1957, Ph.D., 1960. Bar: Ill. 1963. Mem. faculty extension div. U. Ill., 1961-63, U. Hawaii, 1958-60; mem. firm Kirkland, Brady, McQueen, Martin & Schnell, Elgin, Ill., 1963-64; founder, sr. ptnr. Juergensmeyer, Zimmerman, Smith & Leady, Elgin, 1964-81, Juergensmeyer & Assocs., 1981—; mgr., owner Tollview Office Complex, 1976—; asst. pub. defender Kane County, 1964-67, asst. states atty., 1976-78; spl. asst. atty. gen. State of Ill., 1978-85; hearing officer Ill. Pollution Control Bd., 1971-74; commr. U.S. Nat. Commn. on Libraries and Info. Scis., 1982-88; lectr. Inst. for Continuing Legal Edn., Ill Bar Assn., 1971-73; trustee ALA Endowment Fund, 1979-84; assoc. prof. Judson Coll., Elgin, 1963—. Chmn. Hiawatha Dist. Boy Scouts Am.; v.p. Elgin Family Service Assn., 1967-71; sec. Lloyd Morey Scholarship Fund, 1967-73; commr. Elgin Econ. Devel. Commn., 1971-75; chmn. Elgin Twp. Republican Central Com., 1978-80; adv. bd. Ill. Youth Commn., 1964-68; bd. dirs. Wesley Found. of U. Ill., 1971-75; pres. adv. bd. Elgin Salvation Army, 1973-75. Served to capt. Intelligence Service, USAF, 1958-60. Recipient Anti-Pollution Echo award Defenders of the Fox River, Inc., 1971, Cert. Merit, Heart Fund, 1971, Outstanding Young Man award Jr. C. of C., Elgin, 1967; Princeton U. fellow, 1955-56, Merrill Found. fellow, 1956-58. Mem. Assn. Trial Lawyers Am., ABA, Ill. Bar Assn. (chmn. local govt. com. 1974-75, editor local govt. law newsletter 1973-74), Chgo. Bar Assn. (chmn. local govt. com. 1975-76), Kane County Bar Assn., Am. Arbitration Assn. (arbitrator), Am. Polit. Sci. Assn., Izaak Walton League, Fed. Bar Assn., Phi Beta Kappa, Phi Alpha Delta, Alpha Kappa Lambda. Author: President, Foundations, and the People-to-People Program, 1965. Contbr. to publs. in field. Methodist. Club: Union League (Chgo.). Lodges: Masons, Shriners, Elks, Rotary (pres. 1977-78). Office: 707-A Davis Rd Elgin IL 60120

JUGEL, RICHARD DENNIS, corporate executive, management consultant; b. Winside, Nebr., July 25, 1942; s. Donald Jerome and Ilene Mae (Christensen) J.; m. Marlene Ann Meyer, Jan. 15, 1966; children: Lisa Ann, Lynn Marie. Student, Valparaiso U., 1960-61, Wayne State Coll., 1963. Mgr., dir. Info. Mgmt. Tech., Fargo, N.D., 1968-70; system engr., sales Electronic Data Systems, Dallas, 1970-75; data processing officer Mut. of Omaha, 1975-83; exec. v.p. NewAm. Tech., Inc., Omaha, 1983-85; pres. Richard D. Jugel & Co., Omaha and Fargo, N.D., 1985—; bd. dirs. Mgmt. Info. Solutions, Inc., Houston, 1985—; cons. Distributed Info. Systems Corp., Dallas, 1984—. Emergency coordinator USMC Affiliated Radio Service, Omaha. 1978-82; active disaster communications ARC, Omaha, 1980—. Mem. Data Processing Mgmt. Assn., Nebr. Amateur Radio Emergency Services, Am. Radio Relay League (life), Internat. Platform Assn., NRA. Republican. Lutheran. Clubs: AK-SAR-BEN Amateur Radio (life, pres. 1980) (Omaha). Home: 8014 Taylor Circle Omaha NE 68134 Office: 4510 13th Ave SW Fargo ND 58121-0001

JUGNAUTH, ANEROOD, prime minister of Mauritius; b. Palma, Mauritius, Mar. 29, 1930; m. Sarojini Devi Ballah; 1 son, 1 dau. Ed., Regent Coll., Lincoln's Inn, London. Called to bar, 1954, named Queen's Counsel, 1980. Mem. Legis. Assembly, Mauritius, from 1963, minister of state and devel., 1965-67, minister of labor, 1967, dist. magistrate, 1967, crown counsel, sr. crown counsel, 1971, leader of opposition, 1976, prime minister, 1982—, minister of finance, 1983-84, now also minister of def., internal security, info., external communications, interior, outer islands, justice; pres., co-founder Mouvement Militant Mauricien, 1971—. Office: Office of Prime Minister, Port Louis Mauritius *

JUGUILON, GUADALUPE LAMADRID, physician; b. Philippines, Dec. 12, 1929; d. Filomeno P. and Maria Pilar Bal-locana (Laranang) Lamadrid; m. Crispin Navarro Juguilon, Oct. 20, 1957; children: Marites, John, Jay. AA, U. St. Tomas, Manila, Philippines, 1950, MD, 1955. Cert. Med. Bd. Examination; diplomate Internal Medicine. Resident physician dept. of lab. Baguie Gen. Hosp., Baguie City, Philippines, 1957-60; resident physician dept. of medicine Baguie Gen. Hosp., Baguie City, 1961-70; sr. resident outpatient dept. Baguie Gen. Hosp., Baguie City, Philippines, 1970-74, med. specialist II dept. medicine, 1976-87, head dept. medicine, 1987—; asst. prof. St. Louis Coll. of Medicine, Baguie City, 1978-85; vis. cons. Baguie Med. Ctr., Baguie City, 1977—; head coronary care unit Baguie Gen. Hosp., Baguie City, 1977—, dept. medicine, 1987. editor: newsletter Baguie-Benguet Med. Soc., 1985-86. V.p. Alumniana Agustiniana, Bauguio City, 1985—, Sadiri ti Tagudin, Baguio City, 1986—; treas. Philippine Pub. Health Assn., Baguio City, 1984—; mem. Cath. Women's League, St. John Bosco Parish, Baguio City, 1977-80. Fellow Philippine Coll. of Cardiology, Philippine Acad. of Family Physicians (bd. dirs.), Philippine Coll. of Physicians (pres. no. Luzon chpt. 1985-86), diplomate); mem. (life) Philipine Med. Women's Assn. (pres. 1985-87), Philippine Med. Assn. (outstanding leadership, 1987), Philippine Diabetes Assn. (pres. Baguio-Benguet chpt. 1988), Baguie-Beng Med. Soc., Inc. (pres. 1985-87; outstanding physician, 1987). Lodge: Zonta Internat. (Baguio City). Home: 98 M Roxas St Trancoville, Baguio City 0201, Philippines Office: Baguio Gen Hosp, & Med Ctr, Baguio City 0201, Philippines

JUHÁSZ, GÁBOR DÉNES, physiology educator, researcher; b. Budapest, Hungary, Aug. 30, 1947; s. Dénes and Magdolna (Matykó) J. BA in Biology, Eötuos Lórand U., Budapest, 1970, PhD, 1973. Research asst. Inst. Psychology, Hungarian Acad. Sci., Budapest, 1970-76; research fellow Dept. Comparative Physiology Eötuös Lórand U., 1976—; cons. Dept. Analytical and Gen. Chemistry, Tech. U. Budapest, 1983-87. Contbr. articles to profl. jours. Grantee INSERM, Lyon, France, 1985, NAS, Irvine, Calif., 1975-76. Mem. Hungarian Soc. Physiology (asst. treas., governing council 1980-87). Club: Budapest Riding. Home: X11 Nemetrolgyi ut 82, 1124 Budapest Hungary Office: Eotuos Lorand U, Dept Comparative Physiology, VIII Muzeum Krt 6/a, 1088 Budapest Hungary

JUL, MOGENS HAGNERUP, food scientist; b. Vordingborg, Denmark, Sept. 3, 1914; s. Niels Merrild Hagnerup and Elisabeth Anne (Jacobsen) J.; M.Sc. in Chem. Engring., Tech. U. Denmark, 1937; m. Anna Mae Singer, Aug. 18, 1951; children—Elisabeth Anne, Eric Bartley, Susanne Kathrine. Dir., Danish Ministry of Fisheries Tech. Lab., 1942-48; asso. prof. fisheries industry Danish Tech. U., Copenhagen, 1942-48; chief fisheries technologist FAO, 1948-53; dir. Danish Meat Research Inst., Roskilde, 1953-68; research cons. United Breweries, Hellerup, Denmark, 1965-68; sec. protein advisory group to UN, 1968-71; dir. meat products lab. Danish Ministry of Agr., Copenhagen, 1955-84; asso. prof. food preservation Royal Veterinary and Agrl. U., Copenhagen, 1955-85; dir. Danish Research Inst. for Poultry Processing, Hillerod, 1971-80; cons. World Bank, 1948-49; EEC Commn., 1974-75, 85, UN U., 1978-81; cons. Nordic Council Ministers, 1986-87; leader World Food Program evaluation mission to India, 1975-76, mem., 1981; mem. adv. com. on world hunger problems UN U., 1976-81, chmn., 1979-81; cons. DANIDA, 1981, 84-87, Danish Ministry of Agrl, 1986-88; mem., FAO/DANIDA Dairy Program Evaluation Mission, 1983-84; vice chmn. European collaborative research on food quality and nutritive value, 1980—; mem. agro-food programme com. EEC Standing Com. on Agrl. Research, 1978—; mem. Danish Tech. Research Council, 1960-67, Danish Research Council, 1965-68, Danish Agrl. Research Council, 1967-68; chmn. Danish Tech. Info. Center, 1961-67. Decorated Knight 1st degree Order Dannebrog. Fellow Inst. Food Sci. and Tech. (U.K.), Inst. Food Tech. (U.S.); mem. Internat. Inst. Refrigeration, Danish Food Soc. (hon.), Hon. Soc. Food Sci. (U.S.), Danish Refrigeration Soc., Danish Engring. Soc., Swedish food soc., Danish Acad. Tech. Sci. (hon., v.p. 1958-64). Co-author: Industrial Food Preservation, 1966; Protein and Nutrition Policy in Low-income Countries, 1975; Preservation Technology, 1986; Quality of Pig Meat: Report to the EEC Commission, 1979; Quality of Poultry Meat, 1986; author: Research and Technical Development, 1966, The Quality of Frozen Foods, 1984, Food, Nutrition and Politics in the Nordic Countries, 1988. Home: 18 Hestehavevej, DK 3400 Hillerød Denmark Office: 13 Howitzvej, F DK 2000 Frederiksberg Denmark

JULER, HUMPHREY DESMOND, physician; b. London, June 6, 1918; s. Frank Anderson and Mabel Alicia (Chamberlayne) J.; m. Elizabeth Sheila Lilith Ashe, May 16, 1946 (dec. May 1987); children: Patricia Jane, Peter Rupert, Caroline Andromeda. BA, Cambridge U., 1939, MA, 1940, MB, BChir, 1942. Intern Harefield Hosp., Eng., 1942-43; post-war registrar St. Mary's Paddington Hosp., Eng., 1946-47; medical registrar Dreadnought Seamen's Hosp., Greenwich, Eng., 1947-48; mem. med. staff Chipping Norton War Meml. Hosp., Eng., 1948-83; councillor Charlbury Parish Council, 1959—, Oxfordshire County Council, 1987—. Served as surg. lt. Royal Naval Vol. Res., 1943-46. Fellow Royal Soc. Medicine; mem. Oxford Med. Soc. Club: Marylebone Cricket (London); Swiss Alpine. Home: Crinan Upper House, Market St, Charlbury, Oxfordshire OX7 3PH, England

JULIN, JOSEPH RICHARD, lawyer, educator; b. Chgo., July 5, 1926; s. George Allan and Jennie Elizabeth (Carlsten) J.; m. Dorothy Marie Julian, Oct. 18, 1952; children: Pamela, Thomas, Diane, Linda. Student, Deep Springs Coll., 1944, George Washington U., 1946-49; B.S.L., Northwestern U., 1950, J.D., 1952. Bar: Ill. 1952, Mich. 1960. Assoc. firm Schuyler, Stough & Morris, Chgo., 1952-57; ptnr. Schuyler, Stough & Morris, 1957-59; assoc. prof. law U. Mich., Ann Arbor, 1959-62; prof. law U. Mich., 1962-70, assoc. dean, 1968-70; dean, prof. law U. Fla. Coll. Law, Gainesville, 1971-80; dean emeritus and prof. law U. Fla. Coll. Law, 1980—, Chesterfield Smith prof. law, 1985—; spl. Master U.S. Dist. Ct. 1985—. Author: (with others) Basic Property Law, 1966, 72, 79. Trustee Ann Arbor Bd. Edn., 1966-69, pres., 1968-69. Served with U.S. Army, 1944-46. Fellow Am. Bar Found.; mem. Legal Club of Chgo., Mich. Bar Assn., Ill. Bar Assn., Chgo. Bar Assn., Am. Bar Assn. (chmn. sect. on legal edn. and admissions to the bar 1977-78), Assn. Am. Law Schs. (pres. 1984), Order of Coif., Phi Beta Kappa. Republican. Home: 1657 NW 19th Circle Gainesville FL 32605 Office: U Fla Coll Law Gainesville FL 32611

JULIUS, DAVID IRWIN, retail executive; b. Montreal, Que., Can., May 31, 1943; s. Sam and Ida (Dobrinsky) J.; m. Barbara Graves, Aug. 26, 1964 (div. Sept. 1984); children: Paul Brendan, Jessica Sasha, Rafael Alexander; m. Alice Andreassian, Nov. 18, 1984. BS in Physics with honors, McGill U., Montreal, 1964; PhD in Physics, Cornell U., 1969. Cert. tchr. (habilitation) Univ. Karlsruhe, Fed. Republic Germany, 1973. Research scientist U. Karlsruhe, 1969-74; vis. scientist Weizman Inst. Sci., Rehovot, Israel, 1974-76; programmer-analyst Steinberg, Inc., Montreal, 1976-77; projects adminstr. Miracle Mart Stores, Montreal, 1977-78, dir. info. services, 1978-83, dir. inventory mgmt., 1983—. Contbr. articles to profl. jours. Recipient numerous scholarships McGill Univ., 1960-64, Graduate fellowship Cornell Univ., 1968. Office: The M Stores, 5151 Thimens Blvd, Ville St-Laurent, PQ Canada H4R 2C8

JULL, DAVID FRANCIS, Australian representative; b. Kingaroy, Queensland, Australia, Oct. 4, 1944; s. Alfred Stephen and Olwyn Gwen (Golding) J.; m. Erica Jean Hammond, Dec. 11, 1984; 1 child, Jay Grant. Educated pvt. schs., Brisbane, Australia. Journalist Radio 4BH, Brisbane, 1963-65; dir. news TVQ Channel O, Brisbane, 1965-73, dep. gen. mgr., 1973-75; mem. Ho. Reps. Parliament of Australia, Canberra, 1975-83, 84—; dep. gen. mgr. Queensland Tourist and Travel Corp., Brisbane, 1983-84; chmn. Select Com. on Tourism, 1976-78, Govt. Communications Com., 1977-83; served Joint Com. Fgn. Affairs, 1980—. Recipient Queen's Silver Jubilee Medal, London, 1977. Mem. Commonwealth Parliamentary Assn. Mem. Liberal Party. Mem. Anglican Ch. Clubs: Rugby Union Queensland, Johnsonian. Home: 9 Lochness St, Mansfield, Queensland 4122, Australia Office: Rep Electoral Office, 1961 Logan Rd, Upper Mount Gravait, Queensland Australia

JUMARIE, GUY MICHEL, mathematics educator; b. Guadeloupe, W.I., Mar. 18, 1939; came to Can., 1971; s. Auguste Rosuel and Justine Gertrude (Sinivassin) J.; m. Nadia Eva Arbatchevski, Aug. 4, 1964; 1 child, Catherine Helene. Lic. Math., U. Paris, 1959, Lic. Physics, 1960, Diplome d'Etude Approf., 1961, Dr. in Math., 1962; Ph.D., U. Lille, France, 1972, Dr.Sc.d'Etat, 1981. Research engr. Nord Aviation, Paris, 1962-66, Sud Aviation, Paris, 1966-68; sr. scientist MATRA, Paris, 1968-70; assoc. prof. U. Quebec, Montreal, 1970-75, prof. math., computer sci. and physics, 1975—; invited prof. Ecole Nat. Stats,, Rabat, 1976, Ctr. Internat. Theoretical Physics, Trieste, 1977-86, U. Federale do, Rio de Janeiro, 1982, 84, U. Autonoma de Mex., 1983, U. Stuttgart, 1987; lectr. in field. Author: Subjectivity, Information, Systems, 1986; Relative Information, Theories and Applications, 1988. Contbr. articles to profl. jours. Recipient Silver medal, Societe d'Encouragement pour la Recherche et L'invention, 1975. Mem. Assn. Nationale des Dr Sc d'Etat Fr., ASME, Austrian Soc. fur Cybernetic Studies (fgn. affiliate), Internat. Assn. Cybernetics (scientist). Home: 365 rue de Chateauguay, Apt 252, Longueuil, PQ Canada J4H 3X5 Office: U Quebec, Dept Math and Computer Sci, PO Box 8888 St A M, Montreal, PQ Canada H3C 3P8

JUMPPANEN, VEIKKO KALEVI, mining company executive, consultant; b. Juva, Finland, Apr. 28, 1934; s. Juho Arvi and Ilmi (Parnanen) J.; m. Riitta Kaarina Ahonen, July 7, 1957; children: Tiina-Liisa, Ulla-Maija, Jussi, Paavo. Diploma in Engring., Tech. U., Helsinki, Finland, 1957; diploma, U. Witwatersrand, Johannesburg, Republic South Africa; B of Commerce (hon.), U. South Africa, Pretoria. Asst. mine supt. Okiep Copper Co. Ltd., Cape Province, Republic South Africa, 1968-69; sr. mining engr. CRA Ltd., Melbourne, Australia, 1969-72; mine supr. Railway Co. Ltd., Tasmania, Australia, 1972-75; ops. mgr. Mount Lyell Mining Co., Queenstown, Australia, 1975-78; gen. mgr. Renison Ltd., Tasmania, 1978-83; tech. adviser, cons. P.T. Koba Tin, PT. Lusang Mining, others, Jakarta, Indonesia, 1983—; chief exec. officer Lonrho Uimbabwe Lted. Mining Div. including Independence Mining Ltd. and Corsyn Consol. Mines Ltd., Harare, Zimbabwe, 1983—. Mem. Finnish Inst. Mining and Metallurty, Instn. Mining and Metallurgy (councillor in Zimbabwe 1986-87), South African Inst. Mining and Metallurgy, Australasian Inst. Mining and Metallurgy, South African Mine Mgrs. Assn. (assoc.). Lutheran. Home: 20 Newton Spicer Dr, Harare Zimbabwe Office: Lonrho Zimbabwe, 96 Union Ave, Harare Zimbabwe

JUNCHEN, DAVID LAWRENCE, pipe organ manufacturing company executive; b. Rock Island, Ill., Feb. 23, 1946; s. Lawrence Ernest and Lucy Mae (Ditto) J.; B.S. in Elec. Engring. with highest honors, U. Ill., 1968. Founder, owner Junchen Pipe Organ Service, Sherrard, Ill., 1968—; co-owner Junchen-Collins Organ Corp., Woodstock, Ill., 1975-80; mng. dir. Baranger Studios, South Pasadena, Calif., 1980-81. Named Outstanding Freshman in Engring. U. Ill., 1963-64. Mem. Am. Inst. Organbuilders (bd. dirs. 1986—), Am. Theatre Organ Soc. (Tech. Excellence award 1986), Mus. Box Soc., Automatic Mus. Instrument Collectors Assn., Tau Beta Pi, Sigma Tau, Eta Kappa Nu. Author: Encyclopedia of American Theatre Organs; contbr. to Ency. Automatic Mus. Instruments; composer, arranger over 100 music rolls for self-playing mus. instruments. Office: 280 E Del Mar Suite 311 Pasadena CA 91101

JUNEAU, PIERRE, broadcasting company executive; b. Verdun, Que., Can., Oct. 17, 1922; s. Laurent Edmond and Marguerite (Angrignon) J.; m. Fernande Martin, Mar. 17, 1947; children: Andre, Martin, Isabelle. BA, College Sainte-Marie, Montreal, 1944; student philosophy, Sorbonne, Paris, 1949; licentiate in Philosophy, Institut Catholique, Paris, 1949; LLD (hon.), York U., Toronto, 1973, Trent U., Peterborough, Ont., 1987. With Nat. Film Bd. Can., 1949-66; dist. rep., asst. regional supr. of Que., chief internat. distbn. Nat. Film Bd. Can., Montreal, 1951; asst. head European office Nat. Film Bd. Can., London, 1952-54; sec. Nat. Film Bd. Can., Montreal, 1954-64, sr. asst. to commr. and dir. French Lang. prodn., 1964-66; vice chmn. Bd. Govs., Ottawa, 1966-68; chmn. Can. Radio-TV Commn., Ottawa, 1968-75; minister communications Govt. Can., Ottawa, 1975, adviser to Prime Minister, 1975; chmn. Nat. Capital Commn., 1976-78; under sec. state Govt. Can., 1978-80, dep. minister communications, 1980-82; pres. CBC, Ottawa, 1982—; co-founder Cité libre, periodical, 1949; co-founder, 1st pres. La Federation des Mouvements de jeunesse au Que., early 1950s. Co-founder Montreal Internat. Film Festival, 1950's, pres., 1959-68; former sec., former bd. dirs. Albert-Prevost Psychiat. Inst., Montreal, 1960s; former chmn. bd. Ecole nouvelle St.-Germain; co-founder, bd. dirs. Institut Canadien d'Education des Adultes; bd. dirs. Nat. Arts Centre; bd. govs. U. Ottawa. Decorated officer Order Can. Mem. Royal Soc. Can., Club of Rome. Office: CBC, 1500 Bronson Ave Box 8478, Ottawa, ON Canada K1G 3J5 also: Sta CBW, Box 160, Winnipeg, MB Canada R3C 2H1

JUNEJO, MOHAMMAD KHAN, former prime minister of Pakistan; b. Sindhri, Sanghar, Pakistan, 1932. Educated St. Patrick's Sch., Karachi, Pakistan; Agr. Inst. Hastings, Eng. Pres. Dist. Local Bd. of Sanghar, 1954; mem. West Pakistan Provincial Assembly from Sanghar, 1962; apptd. minister West Pakistan cabinet, 1963-69; minister for rys. Pakistan; 1978-79; mem. Pakistani Nat. Assembly, from 1985, prime minister, 1985-88, minister of def., until 1988; active in health, local govt., coops., works, communications, labor and soc. welfare throughout career; pres. Pakistan; Muslim League, 1985. Lifted state of emergency from Pakistan which was in force for last 20 yrs. Office: Office of Prime Minister, Islamabad Pakistan

JUNG, AI LIEN, physics educator; b. Suzhou, Peoples Republic China, Feb. 13, 1933; s. Chester and Li Yun (Xiao) J.; m. Huo Situ; children: Dan Bing Situ, Dan Qin Situ. BS, Fudan U., Shanghai, Peoples Republic China, 1953; MS, BIAA, Beijing, 1960, PhD, 1978. Tchr., research asst. Beijing Inst. Aeronautics and Astronautics, 1953-55, instr., lectr., 1956-77, assoc. prof., 1978-81, prof., 1985—; vis. scientist MIT, Cambridge, Mass., 1982-84; cons. Chineses Soc. Optical Memory, Beijing, 1985—. Author: Amorphous Semiconductors, 1985 (Prize 1985); inventor positronium in a-Si:H, 1985 (prize 1985). Mem. faculty chorus Beijing Inst. Aeronautics and Astronautics, 1953-56. Fellow Chinese Acad. Soc. Physics; mem. Acad. Soc. Condensed Matter (council 1985—), Chinese Vacuum Soc. Home: BIAA, Faculty Bldg 24 Apt 304, Beijing Peoples Republic China Office: Beijing Inst Aeronautics and Astronautics, Dept Physics, Beijing Peoples Republic China

JUNG, DORIS, dramatic soprano; b. Centralia, Ill., Jan. 5, 1924; d. John Jay and May (Middleton) Crittenden; m. Felix Popper, Nov. 3, 1951; 1 son, Richard Dorian. Ed., U. Ill., Mannes Coll. Music, Vienna Acad. Performing Arts; student of, Julius Cohen, Emma Zador, Luise Helletsgruber, Winifred Cecil. Debut as Vitellia in: Clemenza di Tito, Zurich (Switzerland) Opera, 1955, other appearances with, Hamburg State Opera, Munich State Opera, Vienna State Opera, Royal Opera Copenhagen, Royal Opera Stockholm, Marseille and Strasbourg, France, Naples (Italy) Opera Co., Catania (Italy) Opera Co., N.Y.C. Opera, Met. Opera, also in Mpls., Portland, Oreg., Washington and Aspen, Colo.; soloist: Wagner concert conducted by Leopold Stokowski, 1971; with, Syracuse (N.Y.) Symphony, 1981, voice tchr., N.Y.C., 1970—. Home: 40 W 84th St New York NY 10024

JUNG, RODNEY C., physician, academic administrator; b. New Orleans, Oct. 9, 1920; s. Frederick Charles and Clara (Cuevas) J. B.S. in Zoology with honors, Tulane U., 1941, M.D., 1945, M.S. in Parasitology, 1950, Ph.D., 1953. Diplomate: Am. Bd. Internal Medicine. Intern Charity Hosp. La., New Orleans, 1945-46; dir. Hutchinson Meml. Clinic, 1948; asst. parasitology Tulane U., 1948-50, instr. tropical medicine, 1950-53, asst. prof., 1953-57, asso. prof. tropical medicine, 1951-63, prof. tropical medicine, 1963-73, clin. prof. internal medicine, 1973—, clin. prof. tropical medicine, 1983—, head div. tropical medicine, 1960-63; health dir. City of New Orleans, 1963-70, 79-82; internist in charge Ill. Central Hosp., New Orleans, 1956-70; sr. vis. physician Charity Hosp., 1959—; mem. study sect. on tropical medicine and parasitology Nat. Inst. Allergy and Infectious Disease, 1963-67; mem. Commn. on Parasitic Diseases Armed Forces Epidemiol. Bd., 1967-73; chief communicable disease control, City of New Orleans, 1978; sr. in internal medicine Touro Infirmary. Co-author Animal Agents and Vectors of Disease and Clinical Parasitology; editorial bd.: Am. Jour. Tropical Medicine and Hygiene, 1972—; Contbr. articles to profl. jours. Pres. Irish Cultural

Soc. New Orleans, 1980—; officer res. div. New Orleans Police Dept., 1977-84. Served as lt. (j.g.) M.C. USNR, 1946-48. John and Mary Markle Scholar in med. sci. Fellow ACP; hon. fellow Brazilian Soc. Tropical Medicine; mem. Am., Royal socs. tropical medicine and hygiene, Am. Soc. Parasitologists, La. State Med. Soc., Orleans Parish Med. Soc. , Nat. Rifle Assn., Irish Georgian Soc., La. Mosquito Control Assn., La. Soc. Internal Medicine, Am. Soc. Internal Medicine, New Orleans Acad. Internal Medicine, Am. Def. Preparedness Assn., Irish-Am. Cultural Inst., Nat. Trust. Historic Preservation, La. Landmarks Soc., Naval Inst., New Orleans Mus. Art, New Orleans Opera Assn., La. Wildlife Fedn., Phi Beta Kappa, Sigma Xi, Delta Omega, Alpha Omega Alpha. Presbyterian. Office: 3600 Chestnut New Orleans LA 70115

JUNGBLUTH, CONNIE CARLSON, investment banker; b. Cheyenne, Wyo., June 20, 1955; d. Charles Marion and Janice Yvonne (Keldsen) Carlson; m. Kirk E. Jungbluth, Feb. 5, 1977; 1 child, Tyler. BS, Colo. State U., 1976. CPA, Colo. Sr. acct. Rhode Scripter & Assoc., Boulder, Colo., 1977-81; mng. acct. Arthur Young, Denver, 1981-85; asst. v.p. Dain Bosworth, Denver, 1985-87, George K. Baum & Assocs., Denver, 1987—; bd. dirs. Security Diamond Exchange, Denver. mem. Denver Estate Planning Council, 1981-85, organizer Little People Am., Rocky Mountain Med. Clinic and Symposium, Denver, 1986; adv. bd. Children's Home Health, Denver, 1986—; fin. adv. bd. Gail Shoettler for State Treas., Denver, 1986; bd. advisors U. Denver Sch. Accountancy, 1986—; campaign chmn. Kathi Williams for Colo. State Legis., 1986. Named one of 50 to watch Denver Mag., 1988. Mem. Colo. Soc. CPA's (instr. bank 1983, trustee 1984-87, pres. bd. trustees, 1986-87, bd. dirs. 1987—, chmn. strategic planning com. 1987—, Pub. Service award 1985-87, chmn. career edn. com. 1982-83), Am. Inst. CPA's, Colo. Mcpl. Bond Dealers, MetroNorth C. of C. (bd. dirs. 1987—), Pi Beta Phi. Club: Denver City (bd. dirs. 1987-88).

JUNGER, MARTIN, airline executive; b. Bern, Switzerland, Nov. 23, 1929; m. Myrta Ryf; children: Christine, Beat. D of Econs. and Adminstrn., U. St. Gall. With Swissair, 1958-63, 64—, exec. v.p. planning and fin., 1984—; fin. advisor Ghana Airways, 1963-64; bd. dirs. Union Bank Switzerland, Zurich, Baloise Holding, Basle, Switzerland. Office: Swissair, PO Box 8058, Zurich Switzerland

JUNGHOLM, SVEN JOHAN, financial executive; b. Stockholm, Apr. 16, 1921; s. Karl Johan and Alfhild (Woxell) J.; m. Gunnel Engholm, Dec. 17, 1969; children by previous marriage—Mats, Elena, Ulla. LL.M., U. Stockholm, 1948; M.B.A., Harvard U., 1950. Dir., Skandia Ins., Stockholm, 1952-63, Swedish Employers Confedn., Stockholm, 1963-80; dir. fin. Consulting on Internat. Fin., London, 1980—; His Majesty's impartial investigator on effect of hydro-electric power in Sweden, 1950-52. Author: Foredraginingsteknik, 1962. Served to capt. Swedish Army, 1942-45. Recipient Gold medal Bur. Indsl. Def., Stockholm, 1971, Silver Medal, Crown Princess Margareth's Fund, 1980. Lutheran. Home: Gruwegarden, 13700 Vasterhaninge Sweden

JUNGINGER, HANS-GEORG, manufacturing executive; b. Heidenheim, Germany, Aug. 25, 1939; s. Georg and Anna Barbara (Keck) J.; m. Ingrid Gysin, Mar. 25, 1966; children: Stefan, Susanne. Diploma in physics, Tech. U., Stuttgart, Fed. Republic Germany, 1964; PhD, Tech. U., Braunschweig, Fed. Republic Germany, 1967. Researcher Philips Research, Aachen, Fed. Republic Germany, 1968-79; mgr. factory Philips Heerlen, Netherlands, 1979-81; mgr. plant Philips Apparatefabrik, Krefeld, Fed. Republic Germany, 1981-85; bd. dirs. Grundig AG, Fuerth, Fed. Republic Germany, 1985—. Home: Ebenreuther Strasse 24, 8500 Nueremberg 30 Federal Republic Germany Office: Grundig AG, Kurgartenstr 37, 8510 Fuerth, Bay Federal Republic of Germany

JUNGJOHANN, EUGEN EWALD, child psychiatrist; b. Eckenhagen, Fed. Republic of Germany, Dec. 2, 1930; s. Walter and Berta J.; m. Norma Wagner, July 2, 1960; children: Karin, Mark, Mia. MD, U. Cologne & Freiburg, 1956; degree in psychiatry, U. Wis., Madison, 1965; degree in child psychiatry, U. Düsseldorf, 1972. Cons. psychiatrist State of Wis., Madison, Wis., 1965-66; fellow U. Düsseldorf, Fed. Republic Germany, 1967-69; cons. child psychiatrist Essen, Fed. Republic Germany, 1969-73; dir. Children's Ctr., Aprath, Fed. Republic of Germany, 1974-87, Child Abuse Prevention Ctr., Düsseldorf, 1987—. Author: Retardation. Is It Learned, 1974, An Alternative in Child Psychiatry, 1984; contbr. articles to profl. jours. Fulbright scholar, 1957-59; vis. grantee USSR Ministry of Health, 1972; grantee Stiftung Jugend Marke, 1983, 87. Corr. fellow Am. Psychiat. Assn.; mem. German Soc. of Child Psychiat., Internat. Soc. Child Abuse and Neglect, Internat. Physicians for Prevention of Nuclear War. Home: Kaiser Friedrich Ring 7, 4000 Düsseldorf Federal Republic of Germany

JUNGKUNTZ, RICHARD PAUL, university provost; b. Cleve., Oct. 1, 1918; s. Otto William and Clara Magdalen (Lange) J.; m. Grace Elizabeth Kowalke, Aug. 16, 1943; children—Gay (Mrs. Jeffrey Osborn), Paula (Mrs. Thomas Warren III), Richard, Lisa, Andrea, William (dec.), Laura. B.A., Northwestern Coll., 1939; student, Concordia Sem., 1939-40, Wis. Luth. Sem., 1940-42, Ind. U., 1951; M.A., U. Wis., 1955, Ph.D., 1961. Ordained to ministry Luth. Ch., 1942; pastor St. Matthews Ch., Janesville, Wis., 1942-46, Bethany Ch., Ft. Atkinson, Wis., 1946-49; prof. Northwestern Coll., Watertown, Wis., 1949-61; asst. prof. Concordia Theol. Sem., Springfield, Ill., 1961-65; exec. sec. Commn. Theology and Church Relations of Luth. Ch. Mo. Synod, St. Louis, 1965-70; provost Pacific Luth U., Tacoma, 1970—; acting pres. Pacific Luth U., 1974-75; vis. prof. Concordia Sem., 1970; lectr. Eden Sem., Webster Groves, Mo., 1970; Mem. Commn. Faith and Order of World Council Chs., 1968-77; pres. Lutheran Acad. for Scholarship; chmn. bd. dirs. Christ Sem.-Seminex, St. Louis, 1974-80. Author: Luther's (1519) Lectures on Galatians, 1964, The Gospel of Baptism, 1968, Kasteen Evankeliumi, 1976; Editor: A Project in Biblical Hermeneutics, 1969. Mem. Soc. Bibl. Lit., Luth. Acad. Scholarship, Am. Assn. Higher Edn., Am. Conf. Acad. Deans, Am. Assn. Univ. Adminstrs. Home: 6310 Hillcrest Dr SW Tacoma WA 98499

JUNGNICKEL, DIETER, mathematics educator; b. Berlin, Mar. 20, 1952; s. Heinz and Ilse (Beier) J. Abitur, Gymnasium Steglitz, Berlin, 1971; Dipl. Math., Freie U., Berlin, 1975, Dr. rer. nat., 1976, Habilitation, 1978. Diplomate in Math. Asst. Freie U., Berlin, 1975-78; vis. asst. prof. U. Fla., Gainesville, 1976-77; asst. prof. Technische U., Berlin, 1978-80; prof. math. Justus-Liebig U., Giessen, Germany, 1980—; vis. prof. U. Waterloo, Ont., Can., 1987-88. author: Transversaltheorie, 1982, Graphen, Netzwerke und Algorithmen, 1987; Co-author: Design Theory, 1984. Co-editor: Geometries and Groups, 1981; Combinatorial Theory, 1982. Contbr. articles to profl. jours. Studienstiftung grantee, 1971; European Sci. Program fellow, 1979; recipient 1st prize Bundeswettb Mathematik, 1971, Heisenberg-Stpendium Deutsche Forschungsgem, 1980. Mem. Deutsche Mathematiker-Vereinigung, Am. Math. Soc., Soc. Indls. and Applied Math., Math. Programming Soc., Hochschulverband. Office: Mathematisches Institut, Univ Giebes, Arndstr 2, D-6300 Giessen Federal Republic of Germany

JUNICHIRO, SHIOMI, computer software development company executive; b. Osaka, Japan, June 11, 1944; s. Jyuichi and Haruyo (Shiomi) S.; m. Setsuko Shimizu, Feb. 25, 1979; children: Atsushi, Syuuhei, Mayu. Bachelor's, Osaka Inst. Tech., Osaka City, 1969; Master's, Osaka U., Suita, 1971, postgrad., 1974. Electric communications engr. KDD, Osaka, 1963-69; cons. The Aloha System, Honolulu, 1974-76; pres. Seaon Tech. Trading Co., Osaka, 1977-81, Japan Binal Inc., Osaka, 1981—. Patentee in field. Mem. The Robotics Soc. of Japan. Home: 1 10 29 Tezukayama nishi, Sumiyoshi ku Osaka 558, Japan Office: Japan Binal Inc, 2 1 8 Dojimahama Kita Ku, Osaka 530, Japan

JUNKERMAN, WILLIAM JOSEPH, lawyer; b. N.Y.C., May 5, 1904; s. Otto J. and Margaret Anne (McCarthy) J.; m. Helen Veronica Barrett, June 28, 1930. A.B., NYU, 1925; LL.B., Fordham U., 1928. Bar: N.Y. 1929, U.S. Dist. Ct. (so. and ea. dists.) N.Y. 1929, U.S. Ct. Appeals (1st, 2d and 3d cirs.), U.S. Supreme Ct. 1946. Asst. counsel L.I. State Park Commn., 1929-32; sole practice, N.Y.C., 1932-41; regional atty. CAA, 7th Region, Seattle, 1947-48; mem. Haight, Gardner, Poor & Havens, N.Y.C., 1948-50, gen. ptnr., 1950-80. Served to ensign, 1925, with USN, 1941-46; comdr. USNR. Fellow Am. Coll. Trial Lawyers; mem. Nat. Pilots Assn., Naval Order of U.S., Am. Legion (past comdr.). Clubs: Quiet Birdmen, Wings. Address: 311 W 245th St Fieldston NY 10471

JUNQUEIRA, LUIZ AUGUSTO COSTACURTA, consultant and training company executive; b. Sales Oliveira, Sao Paulo, Brazil, Aug. 27, 1944; s. Affonso and Eunice Junqueira; Asst. Cons. degree in Bus. Adminstrn., Getulio Vargas Found., Rio de Janeiro, Brazil, 1967; m. Keyla Maria Pessolani Wangler, Oct. 15, 1975; children—Rodrigo Denys, Daniela Wangler. Cons., prof. Getulio Vargas Found., Rio De Janeiro, 1967-68; dir., tng. cons. Concisa Social Scis. Cons., Rio De Janeiro, 1968-75; exec. v.p. INCISA Publs., Rio De Janeiro, 1973-75; tng. dir. OPC-Planning and Cons. Co., Rio De Janeiro, 1975-87; pres. C.J. Cons. Co., Rio de Janeiro, 1987—; prof. bus. adminstrn. Moraes Jr. U., 1969-74; speaker 9th Internat. Tng. and Devel. Congress, Rio De Janeiro, 1980. Mem. Brazilian Tng. Soc. (dir. Rio De Janeiro 1979-81), Brazilian Mgmt. Cons. Assn. (affiliate Rio De Janeiro). Roman Catholic. Club: Piraque Navy (Rio De Janeiro). Author: Brazilian Time Management, 1982, 5th edit., 1984; Time Management: A Self Development Program, 2d edit., 1985; Negotiation: Behavior and Techniques, 4th edit., 1985. Home: 333/1403 Av Aquarela Do Brazil, BL 3, 22600 Rio de Janeiro Brazil

JUNTEREAL, FILEMON AVENO, insurance company executive; b. Infanta, Philippines, Jan. 20, 1934; s. Filemon Orozco Juntereal and Pilar (Merana) Aveno; m. Maria Concepcion Sanz Beltran; children: Maria Cecilia, Rene Rafael. BS in Commerce, De La Salle Coll., Manila, 1953; MA, U. Notre Dame, 1958. Prof. Far Eastern U., Manila, 1954-57, De La Salle U., Manila, 1964; statistician Zurich-Am. Ins. Cos., Chgo., 1958-61; mgr. regional group, actuary Afia Worldwide Ins., Manila, Singapore, 1966-74; mgr. regional mktg. Afia Worldwide Ins., Singapore, 1974-78; mng. dir. Monarch Ins. Co. Inc., Manila, 1978—. Univ. scholar U. Notre Dame, 1957, Fulbright Travel scholar, 1957; Smith-Mundt fellow, 1957. Fellow Inst. Internat. Edn.; mem. Actuarial Soc. Philippines, Mgmt. Assn. Philippines, Brit. Inst. Mgmt. Roman Catholic. Clubs: Manila Polo, Manila Yacht. Lodge: Rotary. Home: #20 Hamburg Street, Merville Park, Paranaque Metro Manila 3117, Philippines Office: Monarch Ins Co Inc, Monarch Bldg, 101 Herrera St, Lagazpi Village Metro Manila Philippines

JUNYA, YANO, member House of Representative; b. Osaka, Japan, Apr. 27, 1932; m. Mitsuko Onohara, June 5, 1961; 1 son. MA in Econs., Kyoto U., Japan, 1956. With Obayashigumi Ltd., Osaka, 1956-63; member Osaka Prefectural Assembly, 1963-67, House of Represeantatives, Osaka, 1967—; chmn. Komeito (Clean Govt. Party), Tokyo, 1986—. Chmn. party Cen. Exec. Com., 1986—; dir. Standing Com. Discipline in the Diet. Office: Komeito, 17 Minamimoto-machi, Shinjuku-ku Tokyo 160, Japan

JURASCHECK, FRANÇOIS JACQUES, surgeon; b. Hattstatt, Alsace, France, Oct. 6, 1931; s. Henry and Marthe (Fechner) J.; m. Eva Izsepy; children: Claire, Marc, Anne, Claude. MD, Faculty of Medecine, Strasbourg, France, 1963. Cert. in urology, gen. surgery, labor medicine. Resident Med. Sch., Strasbourg, France, 1961-65, chief of clinic, 1965; asst. City Hosp., Mulhouse, France, 1965-69; chief surgeon City Hosp., Mulhouse, 1969—; cons. in urology, 1962—; dir. surg. activities Nat. Com. of Homologation, France, 1987—. Author: Neuropharmacology of Lower Urinary Tract, 1981; contbr. 96 articles to scholarly jours. Served as capt. with French mil., 1958-61. Recipient Nat. Order of Merit French Govt., 1987. Mem. French Surgeon Assn., French Urol. Assn., Am. Urol. Assn. (corr.), Urodynamics Soc., Internat. Med. Soc. Paraplegia, Soc. Belge d'Urologie (corr.). Roman Catholic. Club: Groupe d'Etudes de Neurourologie lanque francaise. Home: 15 Rue du Markstein, 68100 Mulhouse France Office: Cen Hosp, 87 Ave d'Altkirch, 68051 Mulhouse France

JUREK, BERNARD JAMES, JR., mechanical engineer; b. St. Cloud, Minn., Aug. 19, 1925; s. Ben Joseph and Naomi Louisa (Latteral) J.; B.S. in Mech. Engring., U. Minn., 1946; m. Eileen Mary Dahl, Feb. 25, 1946; children—Thomas Jon, William Robert, Cherilyn Sue, Connie Louise. With Gen. Motors Corp., 1946—, gen. master mechanic Chevrolet Detroit Gear and Axle, 1946-61, gen. supt. prodn. Chevrolet, Warren, Mich., 1961-66, plant mgr., Saginaw (Mich.) Parts Plant, 1966-67, Chevrolet, Bay City, Mich., 1967-72, Chevrolet, Detroit Forge, 1972-77, mgr. R&D, Chevrolet Mfg., Warren, 1977-84, dir. mfg. engring., 1984—; pres. Pyrenees Consulting Corp, 1986—. Active Detroit council Boy Scouts Am. Served with USN, 1943-46. Mem. Soc. Automotive Engrs., Soc. Mfg. Engrs. (cert.). Republican. Baptist. Clubs: Huron River Hunting and Fishing. Lodges: Masons, Shriners. Home: 35675 Congress Rd Farmington Hills MI 48331 Office: Gen Motors Corp Mfg Engring Chevrolet Mfg 30007 Van Dyke St Warren MI 48090

JUST, VOLKER, writer, journalist; b. Gotha, Fed. Republic Germany, Sept. 16, 1937; m. Stephanie Kindermann, May 1, 1979; 1 child, Axel. Licentiatus rerum politicarum, U. Basel, Switzerland, 1963. Market researcher Volkswagen, Wolfsburg, Fed. Republic Germany, 1964-66; mktg. dir. Audi/NSU, Neckarsulm, Fed. Republic Germany, 1966-69; mktg. cons. METRA Internat., Paris, 1969-71; PDG Akademie f. prakt. Absatzwirtschaft, Bernau, Fed. Republic Germany, 1971-78; writer, journalist Uberlingen, Fed. Republic Germany, 1978—. Author: Operations Research in Marketing, 1968; contbr. 30 articles to profl. jours. Club: Bruderkette am Untersberg, (Bad Reichenhall, Fed. Republic Germany). Home and Office: Konstantin-Vanotti-Str 1B, D-7770 Ueberlingen Federal Republic of Germany

JUSTIN, JOSEPH EUGENE, military officer; b. Orange, N.J., June 3, 1945; s. James Fredrick and Elizabeth Ann (McCartney) J.; children: James Kenneth, Joseph Patrick. BS, USAF Acad., 1969; MS, Ohio State U., 1973; MA, U. So. Calif., 1980. Commd. 2d lt. USAF, 1969, advanced through grades to maj., 1980; lead project engr. USAF Avionics Lab. USAF, Wright-Patterson AFB, Ohio, 1970-74; exchange officer USAF Systems Commd. USAF, F.E. Warren AFB, Cheyenne, Wyo., 1974; mgr. guidance improvement program USAF Ballistic Missiles Office, Norton AFB, Calif., 1975-77, chief flight test integration div., 1985—; asst. prof. astronautics USAF Acad., Colorado Springs, Colo., 1977-81; research fellow USAF Hdqrs.-Rand Corp., Santa Monica, Calif., 1981-82; dir. space system studies Hdqrs. USAF, Washington, 1982-85. Mem. AIAA (sr.), Air Force Assn. (life), Air Force War Coll. Assn. (life), USAF Acad. Assn. Grads. (life), Ohio State U. Alumni Assn. (life), USAF Research Assocs. Assn., Naval Inst. Office: USAF Ballistic Missile Office Norton AFB CA 92409

JUSTIN, L(EMBIT) PETER, accountant; b. Tallinn, Estonia, Apr. 4, 1928; came to U.S., 1949, naturalized, 1955; s. Heinrich and Sophia (Malt) Jurgenson; m. Maryellen Wagner, Apr. 26, 1957 (div. 1978); children: Bradford, Janet, Diann, Cristofer; m. Luz Mercedes Arnao, June 7, 1985; children: Eugene, Edward. BA, Columbia U., 1957, MBA, 1959. CPA, Pa. Ptnr. E. Charles Conway and Assocs., Ardmore, Pa., 1955-57; pres. L. Peter Justin and Assocs., Narberth, Pa., 1957—; IRS liaison officer Pa. Soc. Pub. Accts.; dir. Matos Enterprises Ltd., Bryn Mawr, Pa., Dennis Assocs., Inc., Las Vegas; cons. joint com. taxation, U.S. Congress. Mem. Nat. Soc. Pub. Accts., Pa. Soc. Pub. Accts. (pres. 1983-85), Am. Mgmt. Assn. Republican. Club: Vesper (Phila.). Lodge: Lions (pres. Bryn Mawr, Pa. 1982-83, Man of Yr. award 1981, 82, 83). Avocations: boating, skiing, philately. Home: 704 Camp Woods Rd Villanova PA 19085 Office: 2 Bryn Mawr Ave Bryn Mawr PA 19010

JUVELIS, PRISCILLA CATHERINE, antiquarian bookseller; b. Newark, Sept. 2, 1945; d. Steven and Odelite (Canning) Juvelis. B.A., Boston U., 1967. Dir. internat. dept. Harcourt Brace Jovanovich Internat. Corp., N.Y.C., 1971-76; rights dir. The Franklin Library, N.Y.C., 1976-78; owner, pres. Priscilla Juvelis, Inc., Boston, 1980—. Mem. exec. com. Save Venice, Inc. , Boston. Editor, pub.: The Book Beautiful and The Binding as Art, 1983, vols. 1 and 2. Mem. Antiquarian Bookseller's Assn. Am., Mass. and R.I. Bookseller's Assn. (sec. 1983-84, v.p. 1984-86, pres. 1986-88), The Manuscript Soc. (trustee 1987-88). Office: 150 Huntington Ave Boston MA 02115

JUVILER, PETER HENRY, political scientist, educator; b. London, Mar. 26, 1926; came to U.S., 1939, naturalized, 1945; s. Adolphe Adam and Katie (Henry) J.; m. Anne C. Stephens, June 20, 1982; children: Gregory, Geoffry. B.E., Yale U., 1948, M.E., 1949; M.A., Columbia U., 1954, Ph.D., 1960. Project engr. Sperry Gyroscope Co., 1949-52; instr. in politics Princeton U., 1957-58; researcher Law Faculty, Moscow U., 1958-59, 64; instr. Columbia U., 1959-60; assoc. prof. polit. sci. Barnard Coll., Columbia U., 1964-74, prof., 1974—; assoc. Harriman Inst. Columbia U., 1964—; instr. Hunter Coll., 1960-61, asst. prof., 1961-64; mem. acad. council Citizen Exchange Council, 1967-77, trustee, 1971-77, mem. adv. bd., 1977—; mem. com. on Soviet studies Am. Council Learned Socs., 1971-75; co-dir. Columbia U. Center for Study Human Rights, 1986—. Author: Revolutionary Law and Order: Politics and Social Change in the USSR, 1976; editor, contbr.: (with Henry W. Morton) Soviet Policy Making: Studies of Communism on Transition, 1967; co-editor, contbg. author: Foreign Affairs 50-Year Bibliography, 1972; contbr. numerous articles to profl. publs., newspapers, encys. Founding mem. West Kortright Community Centre, Delaware County, N.Y. Served with USN, 1944-66. Mem. AAUP (investigating com. 1970, 74, 77), Am. Polit. Sci. Assn., Am. Assn. Advancement Slavic Studies (publs. com. 1975-78, program com. 1984). Office: Columbia U Barnard Coll 408 Lehman Hall New York NY 10027

JYRKIAINEN, REIJO EINARI, orchestral administrator, composer; b. Suistamo, Finland, Apr. 6, 1934; s. Eino and Vappu Marjatta (Lumikko) J.; m. Rauni Tellervo Savolainen, July 15, 1956; children—Jyri, Mari, Heli, Suvi, Pasi. Cand. phil. Helsinki U., 1963, Licentiate of Philosophy, 1966; Diploma in composition Sibelius Acad., Helsinki, Finland, 1963. Tech. controller Finnish Radio, Helsinki, 1957-66; librarian Helsinki Philharm. Orch., 1966-67, mng. dir., 1971—; head music program Finnish Radio/TV, Helsinki, 1967-71. Composer chamber and electronic music compositions. Vice chmn. Concert Centre, Helsinki, 1980—. Served to ensign Finnish Inf., 1954-55. Mem. Assn. Finnish Symphony Orchs. (vice chmn. 1972—). Office: Helsinki Philharmonic Orch, Finlandia Hall, Karamzininkatu 4, SF-00100 Helsinki Finland

KABADI, UDAYA MANOHAR, physician, endocrinologist; b. Bombay, Maharashtra, India, Jan. 6, 1942; came to U.S., 1971; s. Manohar Bapu and Suniti Manohar (Sumati) K.; m. Mary Udaya Cheruvillil, Aug. 9, 1970; children—Sajit, Rajit. M.B.B.S., Seth G.S. Med. Coll., U. Bombay, India, 1965, M.D., 1970. Diplomate: Am. Bd. Internal Medicine, Intern Jewish Meml. Hosp., N.Y.C., 1971, resident, 1971-72, Beth Israel Med. Center, N.Y.C., 1972-73; asst. physician dept. medicine, 1975-76; fellow VA Med. Center, Bronx, N.Y., 1973-74; attending physician dept. medicine Gouverneur Hosp., N.Y.C., 1975-78, chief walk-in-clinic, 1976-78; staff physician VA Med. Center, Bklyn., 1978-80, chief endocrinology sect., Des Moines, 1980—, research and devel. coordinator, 1981-83 clin. asst. prof. medicine U. Iowa Sch. Medicine, Iowa City, 1980-84, clin. assoc. prof., 1985—; cons. endocrinology Broadlawns Med. Center, Des Moines, 1982—, Iowa Luth. Hosp., 1984—; mem. adv. bd. Central Iowa Diabetes Edn. Center, Des Moines, 1981—. Contbr. articles to profl. jours. Recipient Research Grants VA Research Service, 1981—, Am. Legion, 1981-82. Fellow Royal Coll. Physicians, ACP; mem. Endocrine Soc. Am. Fedn. Clin. Research, N.Y. Acad. Scis., Am. Diabetes Assn., European Assn. Study Diabetes, Am. Assn. Lab. Animal Sci., AAAS. Office: VA Med Ctr 30th and Euclid Sts Des Moines IA 50310

KABAKER, RICHARD ZOHN, lawyer; b. Chgo., Feb. 22, 1935; s. Herman A. and Eve (Horwitz) K.; m. Patricia Lee Florsheim, Sept. 18, 1964; children: Douglas J., Nancy L. BA, U. Mich., 1956, JD, 1959. Bar: Ill. 1959, U.S. Dist. Ct. (no. dist.) Ill. 1960, Ohio 1969, Wis. 1973, U.S. Dist. Ct. (we. dist.) Wis. 1973, U.S. Tax Ct. 1978, U.S. Ct. Appeals (7th cir.) 1960, U.S. Supreme Ct. 1978. Assoc. McDermott, Will & Emery, Chgo., 1960-69, Jones, Day, Cockley & Reavis, Cleve., 1969-71; assoc. prof. law. U. Detroit, 1971-72; asst. prof. U. Wis., Madison, 1972-77; ptnr. Murphy & Desmond, Madison, 1977—; lectr. in field. Author: Wisconsin Estate Planning, 1984; also articles. Editor: Will and Trust Forms, 1981. Chmn. lawyers div. Dane county chpt. capital campaign ARC, Madison, 1984. Smongeski research fellow U. Wis., 1976. Fellow Am. Coll. Probate Counsel (bd. regents 1985—), U. Wis. Found.; mem. Internat. Acad. Estate and Trust Law (internat. exec. com. 1986—), State Bar Wis. (chmn. com. on estate tax apportionment 1983-86), ABA (vice chmn. com. on tax regulations and legis.; joint tenancy 1981-84, chmn. com. on creditors rights in estates and trusts 1986—). Club: Madison. Lodge: Rotary. Home: 5122 Raymond Rd Madison WI 53711 Office: Murphy & Desmond SC PO Box 2038 Madison WI 53701

KABALEVSKY, DMITRYI BORISOVICH, composer; b. St. Petersburg, Dec. 30, 1904; ed. Moscow Conservatory; student N.Y. Myaskovsky and A.B. Goldenweiser. Prof., Moscow Conservatory, 1939—; sec. Union Soviet Composers, 1951—; mem. Communist Party, 1940—, mem. USSR Peace com., 1955—, dep. to USSR Supreme Council, from 1966; mem. council of dirs. Internat. Soc. for Music Edn., 1961—, hon. pres., 1972—; v.p. of the Nationality Soviet of the USSR Supreme Council. Named People's Artist of USSR, 1963; Hero of socialist labour, 1944, 74; recipient Lenin prize; State prize, 1946, 49, 51, 80; R.S.F.S.R. State prize, 1966; decorated Order of Lenin (3), Red Banner of Labour, 1966. Mem. Acad. Pedagogical Scis. Composer: 4 symphonies, 2 string quartets, 4 piano concertos; violin and (2) cello concertos; (cantata) Great Motherland, 1942; (operas) Colas Brugnon, 1937, Under Fire, 1943, Tara's Family, 1950, Nikita Vershinin, 1954, Sisters, 1969; (films) Petersburg Nights, 1933, Shchors, 1939, Marusya's First Year at School, 1948, Mussorgsky, 1950, Volnitsa, 1956, Sisters, 1957, 18th Year, 1958, Gloomy Morning, 1959; 10 Shakespeare sonnets for bass with pianoforte accompaniment, 1953-55, and many other songs and choirs; (symphonic suite) Romeo and Juliet, 1956; (children's cantata) Song of Morning, Spring and Peace, 1957; (operetta) Spring Sings, 1957; (cantata) Lenintsy, 1959; Sonata for Cello and Piano, 1962; (oratorio) Requiem, 1964; author 8 books on music and aesthetics edn. for musicians, teachers and children; about 500 articles. Address: Union of Soviet Composers, 8/10 Neghdanorastr, 103009 Moscow USSR *

KACHELRIES, ROBERT WAYNE, computer consultant; b. Phila., Mar. 22, 1953; s. James Robert and Dolores Mary (Strohm) K.; m. Lynn Anne Fittipaldi, Apr. 15, 1978; children: Thomas Robert, Patricia Lynn. BSEE, Drexel U., Phila., 1976. Contract programmer Keystone Computer Assoc., Ft. Washington, Pa., 1976-78; co-founder, v.p. Adaptive Systems Inc., Newark, Del., 1981-83; founder, Software Resource, West Chester, Pa., 1979—. Patentee automatic reference background monitoring network for a film processor, automatic velocity and position controller for a film processor. Mem. IEEE, ACM. Office: Software Resource 1239 Victoria Ln West Chester PA 19380

KACZMAREK, ZDZISLAW, environmental engineer, scientist, educator; b. Poznan, Poland, Aug. 7, 1928; s. Edward and Klara K.; m. Imelda Kaczmarek, 1950; 3 children. D. Tech. Scis., Poly. U., Warsaw, Poland, 1958. Sci. worker Poly. U., Warsaw, 1947-78, assoc. prof., 1961-67, extraordinary prof., 1967-72, ordinary prof., 1972—, former dir. Inst. Environ. Engring. dept. water and san. engring.; chief of div. State Hydro-Meteorol. Inst., Warsaw, 1957-60, gen. dir. Hydro-Meteorol. Inst., 1963-66; dir. Inst. for Meteorology and Water Economy, Warsaw, 1976-80; chmn. water resources div. Inst. Geophysics, 1981—; chmn. com. water economy Polish Acad. Scis.; first dep. minister of sci. higher edn., and tech., 1972-74; project leader Internat. Inst. Applied Systems Analysis, Austria, 1974-76; dep. chmn. Central Qualifying Commn. for Sci. Personnel, attached to chmn. Council Ministers; chmn. State Council for Environ. Protection. Author numerous sci. publs. Dep. mem. Warsaw com. Polish United Workers' Party, 1955-57, worked in dept. sci. and edn. central com., sr. instr., 1960-63, dep. chief dept., 1966-71; mem. Commn. of Sci. Central Com., Polish United Workers' Party; former mem. gen. bd. Polish Tchrs.' Assn. Decorated Silver and Gold Cross of Merit, Knight's and Officer's Cross, Order of Polonia Restituta and other decorations. Mem. Polish Acad. Scis. (dep. sci. sect. 1971-72, sec. VII dept. 1978-80, sec.-gen. 1981—), Acad. Sci. German Dem. Republic.

KADANKAVIL, KURIAN THOMAS, academic administrator; b. Palai, Kerala, India, June 27, 1936; s. Chacko Chacko Kadankavil and Mariam Kudakachira. BD, Dharmaran Coll., Bangalore, India, 1966; lic. in Philosophy, Gregorian U., Rome, 1968, PhD, 1972; PhD, Fordham U., 1974. Prof. philosophy Dharmaram Vidya Kshetram, Bangalore, 1972, dean dept., 1975-80, dean faculty, 1983-85, pres., 1985-88. Editor-in-chief Jour. Dharma, 1984—. Mem. Indian Philos. Assn., Internat. Fedn. Cath. Univs.

Roman Catholic. Office: Dharmaram Vidya Kshetram, Hosur Rd, Bangalore 560 029, India

KÁDÁR, JÁNOS, Hungarian politician; b. Fiume, now Rijeka, Yugoslavia, May 26, 1912; ed. secondary sch. Mem. Young Communists Workers Fedn., 1931, illegal Communist Party, 1931; an organizer of resistance movement World War II; dep. police chief, 1945; sec. Greater Budapest Party Com., 1945-46; asst. gen. sec. Communist Party, 1947, dep. gen. sec. Hungarian Working People's Party (merger Communist Party and Social Democratic Party), 1948; M.P., Hungary, 1945-51, from 1958; minister internal affairs, 1948; 1st sec. Hungarian Socialist Workers Party, 1956-85, gen. sec., 1985-88, pres., 1988—; prime minister, 1956-58, 61-65; mem. Presdl. Council, from 1965; minister of state, 1958-61; mem. C.C., 1956—; mem. Polit. Com., 1956-88. Decorated Hero of Socialist Labor; Hero of Soviet Union; Order of Lenin; recipient Joliot Curie Gold Medal award; Internat. Lenin Peace award. Author: Firm People's Power: Independent Hungary, 1958; For the Total Victory of Socialism, 1962; On the Road of Lenin, 1964; Patriotism and Internationalism, 1968; For the Socialist Hungary, 1972; Selected Speeches and Articles, 1974; On the Road of the Construction of Developed Socialist Society, 1975; Internationalism, Solidarity, Socialist Patriotism, 1977; For Socialism-For Peace, 1978; Policy of Alliance-National Unity, 1981; Party, Trade Union, Socialism, 1982; The Renewal of Socialism in Hungary, 1986, Válogatott Müvei, 1 kötet, 1957/58 (selected works, vol. 1), 1987. Address: Magyar Szocialista Munkaspart, Szechenyi Rakpart 19, 1054 Budapest Hungary

KADEY, FREDERIC LIONEL, JR., geological consultant; b. Toronto, Ont., Can., June 21, 1918; came to U.S., 1925; s. Frederic Lionel and Catherine Amelia (Davies) K.; m. Brenda Boocook, Oct. 7, 1950; children—Brenda Catherine Kadey King, Frederic Lionel III. B.Sc., Rutgers U., 1941; M.A., Harvard U., 1947. Cert. profl. geologist. Teaching fellow Harvard U., 1946-47; field geol. asst. Sinclair Oil Co., Casper, Wyo.; petrographer, research/devel. dept. U.S. Steel Corp., Pitts., 1947-51; mineralogist Manville Corp., N.J., 1951-66, sect. chief fillers, 1966-71, exploration mgr., Denver, 1972-83; cons. indsl. minerals, Englewood, Colo., 1983—; nat. def. exec. reservist, metals and minerals br. U.S. Dept. Interior, Washington, 1972—. Contbr. chpt. to book, numerous articles in field to profl. jours. Patentee indirect perlite expander. Pres., Chester Twp. Taxpayers Assn., N.J., 1957-61, Chester Twp. Bd. Edn., 1961-68. Served with AUS, 1941-45. Decorated Croix de Guerre (France). Recipient Hal Williams Hardinge award, 1986. Fellow AAAS; mem. Mineral Soc. Am., AIME (Disting. mem. 1981 Soc. Mining Engrs., soc. program chmn. 1981, soc. pres. 1984), Am. Inst. Profl. Geologists (charter, pres. N.Y. State sect. 1967-68), Sigma Xi, Alpha Sigma Phi. Republican. Episcopalian. Address: 7653 S Rosemary Circle Englewood CO 80112

KADHAFI, MUAMMAR MUHAMMAD, See GADHAFI, MUAMMAR MUHAMMED

KADRI, IFTIKHAR MUSTAFA HASAN, architect; b. Ahmedabad, India, Dec. 1, 1929; s. Mustafa Hasan and Karimunnisa Moh Ali (Saleri) K.; B. Engring. with Honors, U. Poona, 1953; m. Vipla, Oct. 16, 1971; children—Isha, Rahul, Manisha. Prin., I.M. Kadri, architect, Bombay, 1960—; mng. dir. Kadri Cons. Pvt. Ltd., archtl. cons., Bombay, 1974—. Hon. architect Govt. of Maharashtra; mem. Govt. of Maharashtra Com. of Experts for Developing New Constrn., Technologies or Materials; mem. joint com. on tall blds. Lehigh (Pa.) U. Maj. works include Otters Club for Aquatics, Bombay, 1972, Ceat Mahal, Bombay, 1973, Hotel Taj Coromandel, Madras, 1974, Fort Aguada and Beach Resort, Goa, 1975; Taj Mahal Hotel, New Delhi, 1977, Kuwait embassy, New Delhi, 1977, Nehru Centre, Bombay, 1977, Hotel Krishna Oberoi, Hyderabed, India, 1983; Agrl. U., Kashmir, India, 1985. Home: 47 Lady Jagmohandas Marg, Bombay 400036, India Office: Shiv Sagar Estate A, Dr Annie Besant Rd, Bombay 400018, India

KADUSHIN, PHINEAS, psychotherapist, researcher; b. N.Y.C., Oct. 18, 1925; s. Max and Evelyn (Garfiel) K. B.A., Columbia U., 1945; rabbi, M.H.L., Jewish Theol. Sem., 1950; M.S. in Psychology, Yeshiva U., 1961. Psychology intern N.J. Dept. Instns. and Agys., Bordentown, 1960-61; sr. psychologist Mental Health Ctr., Perth Amboy, N.J., 1961-66; research assoc. family treatment and study unit dept. psychiatry N.Y. Med. Coll., 1966-70; pvt. practice psychotherapy, N.Y.C., 1971—. Mem. Am. Psychol. Assn. (assoc.), Am. Group Psychotherapy Assn. (assoc.), Eastern group Psychotherapy Assn. (assoc.), Rabbinical Assembly Am. Research on dyadic group therapy, a method of improving the man-woman relationship by therapy in a group of two people previously unknown to each other.

KAEDING, GEORGE FREDERICK, controller; b. Chgo., July 9, 1933; s. Fred John and Marie Lillian (Menard) K.; m. Louise Allen Sprowl, June 18, 1960; children: Peter, James, Marie. BSBA, Bradley U., 1955. Personnel mgr. Phoenix Trimming Co., Chgo., 1958-70, controller, 1970—, sec., treas., 1974—. Mem. Northtown Indsl. Mgmt. Council, Chgo., 1958-70. Served with USAF, 1951-55, USN, 1955-57. Recipient Service award Northtown Indsl. Mgmt. Council, 1966. Republican. Methodist. Lodge: Elks. Office: Phoenix Trimming Co 910 Skokie Blvd Northbrook IL 60062

KAEGBEIN, PAUL FRIEDRICH, professor; b. Dorpat, Estonia, June 26, 1925; s. Paul Heinrich and Elfriede Helene (Meyer) K.; m. Irene Borkowski, July 15, 1950; children: Irene, Christine. PhD in History, Humboldt U., Berlin, 1948. Librarian Humboldt U. Library, Berlin, 1951-52; librarian Technol. U. Library, Berlin, 1952-61, dir., 1962-75; dir. Sch. Librarianship, Cologne, Fed. Republic of Germany, 1975-81; prof. U. Cologne, 1975—; exec. bd. Baltic Hist. Com., Goettingen, 1976—. Author: Deutsche Ratsbuechereien, 1950; co-author: Vier Jahrzehute baltische geschichtsforschung, 1987; editor: Roerig, Fritz: Wirtschaftskraefte im Mittelalter, 1952, 2d edit., 1971, Blumfeldt, Evald, Nigolas Loone: Bibliotheca Estoniae historica 1877-1917, 1987, Bibliothekswissenschaft als spezielle Informations wissenschaft, 1986; contbr. articles to profl. jours. Mem. Internat. Assn. Technol. Univ. Libraries (hon., treas., v.p. 1968-74), German Research Soc. (library com. 1970-75), German Spl. Libraries Assn. (hon., chmn. 1971-79), Found. Prussian Cultural Heritage (chmn. library com.1972-82), Internat. Fedn. Library Assn. (chmn. profl. bd. 1983-85), Beta Phi Mu. Lutheran. Home: 14 Eichenhainallee, Bergisch Gladbach 1, D-5060 North Rhine Westphalia Federal Republic of Germany Office: U Cologne, 33 University St, D-5000 Cologne 41 Federal Republic of Germany

KAEGEL, RAY MARTIN, real estate and insurance broker; b. St. Louis, Dec. 7, 1925; s. Ray E. and Loyola (Mooney) K.; B.S. in Secondary Edn., Washington U., St. Louis, 1948, M.B.A., 1955; m. Daniel Marilyn Dugger, July 2, 1943. Mgr., St. Louis Amusement Co., Inc., 1941-43, 46-52; gen. mgr. Md. Real Estate & Ins. Agy., Inc., Granite City, Ill., 1953-60; pres., gen. mgr., dir. Kaegel Real Estate & Ins. Agy., Inc., Granite City, 1961—; dir. Comfort Air-Conditioning & Heating, Inc., Granite Center. Sec., Granite City Bd. Realtors, 1959-63, 66-77, pres, 1964-65, 79-81, 86-87. Vice chmn. Tri-Cities Area Red Cross, 1972; bd. dirs., v.p. Lighthouse for Blind, St. Louis, 1985-87, vice-chmn. 1987—. Served to lt. (j.g.) USNR, 1943-46. Mem. Nat. (exec. officer's council 1959-77), Ill. assns. real estate bds., Tri-Cities Ind. Ins. Agts. Assn. (pres. 1971-73), Ind. Ins. Agts. Ill., Tri-Cities C. of C., Granite City Multiple Listing Service (sec.-treas. 1971-82, pres. 1982—). Optimist. Home: 14014 Baywood Villages Dr Chesterfield MO 63017 Office: 2001 A Adams Ave Granite City IL 62040

KAEGEL, RICHARD JAMES, journalist, public relations consultant; b. Belleville, Ill., Oct. 27, 1939; s. Raymond C. and Margaret E. (Welch) K.; m. Pamela Lambert, Apr. 11, 1963; children: James, Daniel. B. in Journalism, U. Mo., 1961. Sports writer Daily Tribune, Columbia, Mo., 1962-63; sports editor Press-Record, Granite City, Ill., 1963-65; assoc. editor The Sporting News, St. Louis, 1965-68; exec. sports editor Post-Dispatch, St. Louis, 1968-79; editor The Sporting News, 1979-85; columnist Globe-Dem., St. Louis, 1985-86; founder, pres. Dick Kaegel Assocs., St. Louis, 1987—. Mem. Baseball Writers Assn. Am. Mem. United Ch. Christ. Address: 14 Berrywood Dr Belleville IL 62223

KAFKAS, PETER JOHN, cardiologist; b. Salonica, Greece, Aug. 14, 1929; s. John Andrew and Anna Rika (Naltsa) K.; m. Dec. 10, 1960; children: Barbara, John. MD, U. Salonica, 1960. Intern Evangelismus Med. Ctr., Athens, 1961-62, resident, 1963-64; registrar Brompton Hosp. Brompton Hosp., London, 1965-66; sr. registrar Evangelismos Med. Ctr. Evangelismos Med. Ctr., Athens, 1965-70, cardiologist, assoc. prof. clin. cardiology, 1970-76; cons. cardiologist Higia Hosp., 1977—; asst. prof. clin. cardiology Athens Med. Sch., 1977—. Author: Malignant Pericarditis, 1965, Symptoms and Signs of Cardiac Disease, 1969, Echocardiography, 1972; contbr. articles to profl. jours. Served with Greek Navy, 1953-55. Fellow Am. Coll. Cariology, Internat. Coll. Angiology, Royal Soc. Medicine; mem. Echocardiographic Soc. (pres. 1982—), Greek Cardiologic Soc. (pres. working group on echocardiography 1985-87), Med. Angiologic Soc., Sci. Soc. Evangelismos, Med. Soc. Athens, Higia Hosp. Soc. Home: 7 Pallados Kifisia, Athens Greece Office: 57 Ipsilantou, 115 21 Athens Greece

KAGAMI, KOICHI, warehouse company executive; b. Yokohama, Japan, Jan. 20, 1951; parents Bun-ichi and Yoko (Ohta) K.; m. Chikako Sakurai, Apr. 22, 1984. BA, Keio-gijuku U., Tokyo, 1973, Ricker Coll., Houlton, Maine, 1976. Acct. Mitsui Kanko-kaihatsu, Ltd., Tokyo, 1973-75; clk. Pioneer Valley Arts and Studies Ctr., Northampton, Mass., 1976-77; exec. officer, then exec. v.p. Hiyoshi Corp., Yokohama, 1977—; chief exec. officer Metropolitan Motors Ltd., 1987—. Office: Hiyoshi Corp, 6-66 Sumiyoshi-cho, Yokohama 231, Japan

KAGAN, GEORGE IRWIN, dentist; b Brookline, Mass., Aug. 8, 1939; s. Abraham and Sylvia (Coleman) K. BS in Biol. Psychology, U. Chgo., 1961, BS in Dentistry, 1963; DDS, U. Ill., 1965. Technician Cook County Sch. Nursing, Chgo., 1964-65; intern U. Chgo., 1965-66; staff dentist Chgo. Bd. Health, 1966-68, Stickney Twp. Pub. Health Dist., Burbank, Ill., 1969; dental health care provider State of Ill., 1969-79; gen. practice dentistry, Chgo., 1968—; table clinician Chgo. Dental Soc., 1980-85, Ariz. State Dental Soc., Phoenix, 1983-85. Chmn. counter subversive activeies com. Richard J. Daley Am. Legion Post, 1987-88, historian, 1988—, charter mem., trustee Rep. Presdl. Task Force; mem. Rep. Nat. Com. Served to capt. USAR, 1965-67. Fellow Acad. Gen. Dentistry, Royal Soc. Health; mem. Chgo. Dental Soc., Royal Coll. Dental Surgeons Ont. (licentiate), Ill. State Dental Soc., ADA, Am. Legion, Ill Railway Museum. Club: Senatorial; Ill. Camaro; Mil. Order of the World Wars, Res. Officers Assn. Avocations: railroading, restoration of classic autos, motorsports, touring, history. Office: 1525 E 53d St #516 Chicago IL 60615

KAGAN, SIOMA, educator; b. Riga, Russia, Sept. 29, 1907; came to U.S., 1941, naturalized, 1950; s. Jacques and Berta (Kaplan) K.; m. Jean Batt, Apr. 5, 1947 (div. 1969). Diplom Ingenieur, Technische Hochschule, Berlin, 1931; M.A., Am. U., 1949; Ph.D. in Econs, Columbia U., 1954. Sci. asst. Heinrich Hertz Inst., Berlin, 1931-33; partner Laboratoire Electro-Acoustique, Neuilly-sur-Seine, France, 1933-48; chief French Mission Telecommunications, French Supply Council in N.Am., Washington, 1943-45; mem. telecommunications bd. UN, 1946-47, econ. affairs officer, 1947-48; econs. cons. to govt. and industry; asso. prof. econs. Washington U., St. Louis, 1956-59; staff economist Joint Council Econ. Edn., N.Y.C., 1959-60; prof. internat. bus. U. Oreg., Eugene, 1960- 67, U. Mo., St. Louis, 1967—; faculty leader exec. devel. programs Columbia, Northwestern U., NATO Def. Coll., Rome, others. Contbr. numerous articles profl. publs. Served with Free French Army, 1941-43. Decorated Legion of Honor (France). Recipient Thomas Jefferson award U. Mo., 1984. Fellow Latin Am. Studies Assn.; mem. Am. Econ. Assn., Acad. Polit. Sci., Assn. Asian Studies. Clubs: University (St. Louis); Conanicut Yacht (Jamestown, R.I.). Home: 8132 Roxburgh Dr Saint Louis MO 63105 Office: U Mo Saint Louis MO 63121

KAGAN, STEPHEN BRUCE (SANDY), travel agency executive; b. Elizabeth, N.J., Apr. 27, 1944; s. Herman and Ida (Nadel) K.; m. Susan D. Kaltman, July 3, 1966; children—Sheryl, Rachel. B.S. in Econs., U. Pa., 1966; M.B.A. in Fin., Bernard Baruch Coll., 1969. Chartered fin. analyst. Security analyst Merrill Lynch Pierce Fenner & Smith, N.Y.C., 1966-68; dir. research Deutschmann & Co., N.Y.C., 1968-70; v.p. Equity Sponsors, Inc., N.Y.C., 1970-72; v.p., investment counselor Daniel H. Renberg & Assocs., Inc., Los Angeles, 1972-78; exec. v.p. Ask Mr. Foster Travel Service, Van Nuys, Calif., 1978—. Vice pres. bd. Temple Beth Hillel, North Hollywood, Calif., 1976-83. Mem. Inst. Cert. Fin. Analysts, Beta Gamma Sigma. Home: 13952 Weddington St Van Nuys CA 91401 Office: Ask Mr Foster Travel Service 7833 Haskell Ave Van Nuys CA 91406

KAGEYAMA, HAJIME, agricultural educator; b. Koriyama, Fukushima, Japan, Dec. 27, 1946; s. Yoshiji and Tsuya (Seino) K.; m. Toshiko Abe, July 9, 1976. BA in Agr., Meiji U., 1969. Tchr. agr. Kawagoe (Japan) Agrl. High Sch., 1969—. Mem. program com. Japan Broadcasting Corp., Stebuya, Tokyo, 1977-84. Mem. Japan Soc. for Phys. Culture (archery mgr. 1975-87). Home: Wakita Bil 901, 103 Wakita-cho, Kawagoe 350, Japan Office: Kawagoe Agr High Sch, 5-14 Kosenba-cho, Kawagoe 350, Japan

KAGIRI, PATRICK MBIYU, oil company executive; b. Muranga, Kenya, Apr. 30, 1956; s. Elijah Kagiri and Tabitha (Mumbi) Mbugua; m. Susan Wangui Kagiri, Sept. 1, 1984; children: Kagiri Mbiyu, Mumbi. Acct. MacKenzie Kenya, Ltd., Nairobi, Kenya, 1978-79, group mgmt. acct., 1979-81; bank acct. Mobil Oil Kenya, Ltd., Nairobi, 1981-84, asst. treas., 1984, treas., 1984-85; treas. Kobil Petroleum, Ltd., Nairobi, 1985—; bd. dirs. Keki Enterprises Ltd., Nairobi, 1987—. Recipient CPA Sect. IV prize Kenya Accts. and Secs. Nat. Exam. Bd., 1978, Bus. Adminstrn. prize, 1983. Mem. Inst. CPAs Kenya, Kenya Inst. Mgmt. Mem. Kanu Ch. Clubs: Parklands, Pegasus (Nairobi) (treas. 1987—). Home: PO Box 73978, Nairobi Kenya Office: Kobil Petroleum Ltd, PO Box 30322, Nairobi Kenya

KAHL, ALFRED LOUIS, JR., business administration educator; b. Michigan City, Ind., Oct. 4, 1932; s. Alfred Louis and Marion Carr (Wheeler) K.; m. Lola Latini, Dec. 3, 1955; children—Karen, Kevin. B.Sc., Phoenix U., 1957; B.A., U. Md., 1960; diploma Indsl. Coll. Armed Forces, 1961; M.B.A., U. Pitts., 1962; Ph.D., U. Fla., 1969. Cert. data processor Data Processing Mgmt. Assn.; profl. adminstr. Inst. Chartered Secs. and Adminstrs. in Can. Asst. prof. banking and fin. U. Ga., Athens, 1965-70; prof. commerce U. Tunis (Tunisia), 1970-72; prof., chmn. dept. bus. adminstrn. Mankato State U. (Minn.), 1972-74; assoc. prof. adminstrn. U. Ottawa (Ont., Can.), 1974—, vice chmn. dept. bus. adminstrn., 1976-78, chmn., 1979; cons. in field. Author: (with A. Belkaoui) Corporate Financial Disclosure in Canada, 1978; (with E. Brigham and W. Rentz) Canadian Financial Management: Theory and Practice, 1983; (with J. Riggs and W. Rentz) Essentials of Engineering Economics, 1983; editor: (with others) International Business: The Canadian Way, 1980, rev. edit., 1983; (with M. Crener and B. Dasah) Introduction to Management: A Canadian Perspective, 1981, Process of Management: A Canadian Perspective, 1981; (with W. Rentz) Cases, Readings and Exercises in Canadian Financial Management Theory and Practice, 1983; (with others) Engineering Economics, 1986; (with E. Brigham and W. Rentz) Canadian Financial Management, 2d. edit., 1987; contbr. numerous articles to profl. jours. Fulbright sr. fellow, Burundi, 1977. Fellow Fin. Analysts Fedn.; mem. Acad. Internat. Bus., Acad. Mgmt., Adminstrv. Scis. Assn. Can., Am. Acctg. Assn., Am. Econ. Assn., Am. Fin. Assn., Am. Inst. for Decision Scis., Can. Acad. Acctg. Assn., Fin. Mgmt. Assn., Inst. Indsl. Engrs., Internat. Inst. Forecasters, Micro-Computer Investors Assn., Montreal Soc. Fin. Analysts, Nat. Assn. Bus. Economists, Strategic Mgmt. Soc., Inst. Mgmt. Scis., Beta Gamma Sigma, Alpha Iota Delta, Phi Kappa Phi. Home: 163 Craig Henry Dr, Ottawa, ON Canada K2G 3Z8 Office: U Ottawa Faculty Adminstrn, Ottawa, ON Canada K1N 6N5

KAHL, WILLIAM FREDERICK, college president; b. May 23, 1922; s. William Frederick and Bessie (Glading) K.; m. Mary Carson, Jan. 25, 1964; children: Frederick Glading, Sarah Hartwell. B.A., Brown U., 1945; M.A., Harvard U., 1947, Ph.D., 1955. Lectr. history Boston U., 1947-48, 50; instr. Simmons Coll., Boston, 1948-52; asst. prof. Simmons Coll., 1952-59, asso. prof., 1959-62, prof., 1962-76, provost, 1965-76; pres. Russell Sage Coll., Troy, N.Y., 1976—; dir. Norstar. Author: The London Livery Companies: An essay and bibliography, 1960; contbr. articles to profl. jours. Vice chmn. Hudson River Valley Assn.; bd. dirs. Albany Symphony Orch., Nature Conservancy, Lower East Side Conservancy. Social Sci. Council research grantee, 1957-58. Mem. Am. Hist. Assn., Commn. on Ind. Colls. and Univs. (dir.), Anglo-Am. Hist. Conf. Episcopalian. Home: 29 Old Niskayuna Rd Loudonville NY 12211 Office: Russell Sage Coll Troy NY 12180

KAHN, ANDRÉ S., broadcast company executive; b. Manila, May 6, 1949; m. Rosario Legarda; children: Francesca Linette L., André Renato L. Jr. BSBA, De La Salle U., Manila, 1971. Mgr. advt. Squires Bingham Co., Makati, Metro Manila, 1971-72; exec. v.p. Trans Radio Broadcasting Corp., Makati, Metro Manila, 1971—, Broadcast Electronics Group Inc., Makati, Metro Manila, 1977—, GVM Radio/TV corp., Makati, Metro Manila, 1979—; pres. Media Tech. Konsultants Inc. and Trans Realty Co. Inc., Makati, Metro Manila, 1981—, Media Tech., Makati, Metro Manila, 1982—; v.p J. Romero & Assocs., 1988—. Mem. Philippine Bd. Advt. (chmn. 1986, 87, vice chmn. 1979, 85), Nat. Assn. Broadcasters Philippines (pres. 1979, v.p. radio 1982, exec. v.p. 1983, pres. 1984, chmn. bd. 1985, bd. dirs. 1986, 87), Broadcast Media Council (chmn. rules and enforcement div. 1980, 81, bd. dirs. 1976, 77, 78, 80, 81).

KAHN, FAITH-HOPE, nurse, adminstrator, writer; b. N.Y.C., Apr. 25, 1921; d. Leon and Hazel (Cook) Green; RN, Beth Israel Med. Center, N.Y.C., 1942; student N.Y. U., 1943; m. Edward Kahn, May 29, 1942; children: Ellen Leora, Faith Hope II, Paula Amy. First scrub operating room Beth Israel Hosp., N.Y.C., 1942; supr., operating room Hunts Point Gen. Hosp., 1942; gynecol. reconstrn. procedures researcher Phoenixville (Pa.) Gen. Hosp., 1943, Sydenham Hosp., N.Y.C., 1945; supr. ARC Disaster Field Hosp., Queens, N.Y., 1950-51; adminstr., mgr. team coordinator Dr. Edward Kahn, FACOG, Queens Village, N.Y., 1945—. Inventor, publicity chmn. Girl Scouts U.S.A., 1953; exec. dir. publicity Woodhull Schs., 1956-60; pres., 1961-62; exec. dir. publicity N.Y. Dept. Parks Figure Skating, 1956-70; exec. dir. publicity and applied arts St. John's Hosp., Smithtown, N.Y., 1965-66; state advisor N.Y., U.S. Congressional Adv. Bd., Washington, 1981—; nat. adv. bd. Am. Security Council, 1978—; founder Am. Security Found.; bd. trustees, Am. Police Hall of Fame and Mus., 1983—; mem. Republican Presdl. Task Force, 1986, Statue of Liberty and Ellis Island Centennial Commn., N.Y., 1986—. Recipient citation ARC, 1951, Am. Law Enforcement Officers Assn., Bronze medal Am. Security Council Ednl. Found., 1978, spl. recognition award Center Internat. Security Studies, 1979, Meml. Plate, Patriots of Am. Bicentennial, 1976, Great Seal of U.S.A. Plate, cert. Am. Sons Liberty, 1987, Good Smaritan award, 1987, Justice award Cross of Knights, 1987 Knights of Justice award, 1987; named Knight Chevalier Venerable Order of Michael the Archangel, 1987. Fellow, World Lit. Acad. (life), Acad. Nat. Law Enforcement (hon.); mem. Am. Acad. Ambulatory Nursing Adminstrn., Nurses Assn., Nat. League Nursing, Am. Coll. Obstetricians and Gynecologists, Nat. Assn. Physicians' Nurses, Nat. Critical Care Inst., Assn. Operating Room Nurses, AAAS, Nat. Assn. Female Execs., N.Y. Acad. Scis., Am. Police Acad. (cert. appreciation 1979, 83), Am. Fedn. Police, The Retired Officers Assn., Internat. Platform Assn., Security and Intelligence Found. (cert. appreciation 1986), Internat. Intelligence and Orgnd. Crime Investigators Assn., Smithtown Hist. Soc., Nat. Audubon Soc., NRA. Clubs: Tiyospaye, Paul Revere, Sterlingshire Woman's. Author, editor: The Easy Driving Way for Automatic and the Standard Shift, 1954; (with Edward Kahn) The Pelvic Examination, Outline and Guide for Residents, Internes and Students, 1954; (with Edward Kahn) Traction Hysterosalpingography for Uterine Lesions, 1949; contbr. articles profl. and lay jours. Home: 213 16 85th Ave Hollis Hills NY 11427-1324 Office: 213 16 85th Ave Queens Village NY 11427

KAHN, IRWIN WILLIAM, industrial engineer; b. N.Y.C., Feb. 3, 1923; s. Milton and Clara (Clark) K.; B.S., U. Calif.-Berkeley, 1949; student Cath. U., 1943-44; m. Mildred Cross, May 14, 1946 (dec. May 1966); children: Steven Edward, Michael William, Evelyn Ruth, Joanne Susan; m. 2d, Marajayne Smith, Oct. 9, 1979. Chief indsl. engr. Malsbary Mfg. Co., Oakland, Calif., 1953-57, Yale & Towne Mfg. Co., San Leandro, Calif., 1957-60; sr. indsl. engr. Eitel McCulloch, San Carlos, Calif., 1961-62, Lockheed, Sunnyvale, Calif., 1962-69; v.p. Performance Investors, Inc., Palo Alto, 1969-74; with Kaiser-Permanente Services, Oakland, 1974-76; nat. mgr. material handling Cutter Labs., Berkeley, Calif., 1976-83; sr. mgmt. engr. Children's Hosp. Med. Ctr., Oakland, 1983; sr. indsl. engr. Naval Air Rework Facility, Alameda, Calif., 1983-85, Naval Supply Ctr., Oakland, 1985—; vis. lectr. U. Calif., Berkeley, 1986; tchr. indsl. engring. Laney Coll., Oakland, 1967—, Chabot Coll., Hayward, Calif. Chmn. Alameda County Library Adv. Commn., 1965—. Served with AUS, 1943-46. Registered profl. engr., Calif. Mem. Am. Inst. Indsl. Engrs. (chpt. pres. 1963-64, chmn. conf. 1967 nat. publ. dir. aerospace div. 1968-69), Calif. Soc. Profl. Engrs. (pres. chpt.). Club: Toastmasters (dist. gov. 1960-61). Home: 4966 Elrod Dr Castro Valley CA 94546 Office: Naval Air Rework Facility Alameda CA 94501

KAHN, MARK LEO, arbitrator, educator; b. N.Y.C., Dec. 16, 1921; s. Augustus and Manya (Fertig) K.; B.A., Columbia U., 1942; M.A., Harvard U., 1948, Ph.D. in Econs., 1950; m. Ruth Elizabeth Wecker, Dec. 21, 1947 (div. Jan. 1972); children—Ann Mariam, Peter David, James Allan, Jean Sarah; m. Elaine Johnson Morris, Feb. 12, 1988. Asst. economist U.S. OSS, Washington, 1942-43; teaching fellow Harvard U., 1947-49; dir. case analysis U.S. WSB, Region 6-B Mich., 1952-53; mem. faculty Wayne State U., Detroit, 1949-85, prof. econs., 1960-85, prof. emeritus, 1985—, dept. chmn., 1961-68, dir. indsl. relations M.A. Program, 1978-85; arbitrator union-mgmt. disputes, specializing in airline industry. Bd. govs. Jewish Welfare Fedn. Detroit, 1976-82; bd. dirs. Jewish Home for Aged, Detroit, 1978—. Served to capt. AUS, 1943-46. Decorated Bronze Star. Mem. Indsl. Relations Research Assn. (pres. Detroit chpt. 1956, exec. sec. 1979—; exec. bd. 1986-88), AAUP (past chpt. pres.), Nat. Acad. Arbitrators (bd. govs. 1960-62, v.p. 1976-78, chmn. membership com. 1979-82, pres. 1983-84), Soc. Profls. in Dispute Resolution (v.p. 1982-83, pres. 1986-87). Co-author: Collective Bargaining and Technological Change in American Transportation, 1971; contbr. articles to profl. jours. Home and Office: 4140 2d Ave Detroit MI 48201

KAHN, PAUL MARKHAM, actuary; b. San Francisco, May 8, 1935; s. Sigmund Max and Alexandrina K. (Strauch) K.; m. Linda P. McClure, May 20, 1968. BS, Stanford U., 1956; MA, U. Mich., 1957, PhD, 1961. Asst. actuary Equitable Life Assurance Soc., N.Y.C., 1961-71; v.p., life actuary Beneficial Standard Life, Los Angeles, 1971-75; v.p., actuary Am. Express Life Ins. Co., San Rafael, Calif., 1975-77, P.M. Kahn & Assocs., 1977-. Editor Dictionary of Actuarial and Life Ins. Terms, 1972, 2d edit., 1983, Credibility: Theory and Practice, 1975, Computational Probability, 1980. Fellow Soc. Actuaries (Triennial prize 1961-64), Can. Inst. Actuaries, Conf. Actuaries in Pub. Practice; mem. Am. Acad. Actuaries, Internat. Actuarial Assn., Inst. Actuaries (Eng.), Spanish Actuarial Assn., Swiss Actuarial Assn., German Actuarial Assn., Italian Actuarial Assn., Am. Antiquarian Soc. Clubs: Zamorano (Los Angeles); Roxburghe; Concordia-Argonaut, Comml. (San Francisco); Pacific, Waikiki Yacht (Honolulu). Address: 2430 Pacific Ave San Francisco CA 94115

KAHN, ROBERT IRVING, management consultant; b. Oakland, Calif., May 17, 1918; s. Irving Herman and Francesca (Lowenthal) K.; m. Patricia E. Glenn, Feb. 14, 1946; children: Christopher, Roberta Anne. B.A. cum laude, Stanford U., 1938; M.B.A., Harvard U., 1940; LL.D. (hon.), Franklin Pierce Coll., 1977. Exec. researcher R.H. Macy's, Inc., N.Y.C., 1940-41; controller Smith's, Oakland, 1946-51; v.p., treas. Sherwood Swan & Co., Oakland, 1952-56; prin. Robert Kahn & Assocs. (mgmt. cons.), Lafayette, Calif., 1956—; pres. Kahn and Harris Inc. (investment bankers), San Francisco, 1971—; v.p. Hambrecht & Quist (investment bankers), San Francisco, 1977-80; prin. Pacific Area Corp. Exchange, 1986—; cons. to comdr. gen. U.S. Army and USAF, 1987—; dir. Wal-Mart Stores, Inc., Marc Paul, Inc., Piedmont Grocery Co., Components Corp. Am., Lipps, Inc.; cons. to commdg. gen. Army and Air Force Exchange Service. Publisher: newsletter Retailing Today, 1965—; author: weekly newspaper column Pro and Kahn, 1963-77, 86—; editorial bd.: Jour. of Retailing. Mem. Nat. Eagle Scout Assn., Boy Scouts Am.; past dir. Oakland Council; past bd. dirs. Oakland Area ARC; bd. dirs., officer, mem. exec. com. Unitd Way Bay Area, 1946-81, chmn. allocations, membership, fin., by-laws, and personnel coms.; trustee Kahn Found.; past sec. League to Save Lake Tahoe; founder Lafayette Forward, 1970, sec., 1976—; mem. adv. com. Retail Mgmt. Inst. U. Santa Clara, 1983—. Served with USAAF, 1941-46; with USAF, 1951-52; lt. col. Res. ret. Recipient Mortimer Fleishhacker award as outstanding vol. United Way Bay Area, 1980, Best Article award Jour. Mgmt. Cons., 1984-85; founding mem. Baker Scholar Harvard U., 1939. Mem. Assn. Mgmt. Consultants (pres. 1977), Inst. Mgmt. Consultants (a founder), Nat. Retail Mchts. Assn. (asso. cons. mem.), Mensa, Phi Beta Kappa. Home: 3684 Happy Valley Rd Lafayette CA 94549 Office: PO Box 249 Lafayette CA 94549

KAHN, SANDRA S., psychotherapist; b. Chgo., June 24, 1942; d. Chester and Ruth (Goldblatt) Sutker; m. Jack Murry Kahn, June 1, 1965; children: Erick, Jennifer. BA, U. Miami, 1964; MA, Roosevelt U., 1976. Tchr. Chgo. Pub. Schs., 1965-67; pvt. practice psychotherapy, Northbrook, Ill., 1976—. Host Shared Feelings, Sta. WEEF-AM, Highland Park, Ill., 1983—; author: The Kahn Report on Sexual Preferences, 1981. Mem. Ill. Psychol. Assn., Chgo. Psychol. Assn. (bd. dirs., pres.). Jewish. Office: 2970 Maria Ave Northbrook IL 60062

KAHRMANN, RAINER THOMAS CHRISTIAN, investment banker; b. Arnstadt, Fed. Republic Germany, May 28, 1943; arrived in England, 1974; married; children: Alice, Louise. Licenciate, Univ. Fribourg, Switzerland, 1967, Doctorate, 1968. Corp. fin. officer Dow Chemical Co./Dow Banking Corp., Midland, Mich. and Switzerland, 1969-73; mng. dir., portfolio mgr. EBC AMRO Bank, Ltd., London, 1974—; bd. dirs. Billecart Expansion Holdings, FIMAG AG, Switzerland. Mem. Antiquarian Horological Soc., Brit. Horological Soc. Office: EBC AMRO Bank, 10 Devonshire Sq, London EC2, England

KAIRAMO, KARI ANTERO OSWALD, diversified manufacturing company executive; b. Helsinki, Finland, Dec. 31, 1932; s. Aulis O. and Aino S. (Kulvik) K.; M.S., Helsinki U. Tech., 1959; m. Arja Eeva Sohlberg, June 2, 1957; children—Kristina, Aino-Marja, Juhani. Supt. and project engr. for W. Rosenlew & Co., Pori, 1960-62; project mgr. Metex Corp., tech. div., Helsinki, 1962-64; pres. Finnmetex Ltd., Sao Paulo, S.Am., 1964-65; pres. Madden Machine Co., N.Y.C., 1968-70, v.p., 1965-67; dir. fgn. ops. Nokia Corp., Helsinki, 1970-72, v.p., 1972-77, pres., chief exec. officer, 1977—, chmn., 1986—; Decorated knight, also comdr. of the Order of White Rose (Finland), Order of the Rising Sun, Gold and Silver Star, Japan, 1986; commdr. of 1st class of the Order of the Star of Jordan (Al-Kawkab Al-Urduni), 1987. Dir. Finnish Am. C. of C. (New York) 1967-70, pres. 1969-70, Helsinki, 1972—; dir. Assn. for Finnish Cultural Found., 1977—; dir. Finnish sect. ICC, 1981—. Mem. Confederation of Finnish Industries (exec. com., 1981—, chmn. 1985-87); mem. Finnish Foreign Trade Assn. (chmn.), Finnish Soviet C. of C. (presidium, 1981—); mem. French Finnish C. of C. (adminstrv. council, 1976—); mem. Finnish Section of the European Cultural Found., 1978—. Home: Merihanikka 3, SF-02360 Espoo 36 Finland Office: Nokia Corp, PB 226, SF-00101 Helsinki Finland

KAISER, BO PAUL, consultant in trade promotion, researcher; b. Stockholm, Feb. 5, 1917; m. Gerny Tenström, Jan. 1, 1944; 1 child, Sten. Student, Royal Mil. Acad., 1939, Stockholm Sch. Econs., 1940-43, Stockholm U., 1975-78, Harvard U. Bus. Sch., 1981. Asst. in orgn. dept. Civil Adminstrn. Nat. Def., 1943-45; research mgr. Swedish Gallup Poll, 1946-48, sales mgr., 1949-51, mng. dir., 1952-54; mng. dir. Swedish Retail Research Inst., 1954-58; pres., chief exec. officer Affarsindex AB, Solna, Sweden, 1958-74; spl. cons. A.C. Nielsen Mgmt. Services SA, Lucerne, Switzerland, 1975-80; cons. Unctad-Gatt. Internat. Trade Ctr., Geneva, 1980—; dir. Svenska Johnson's Wax AB, Stockholm; chmn. bd. A.C. Nielsen Co. AB, Stockholm; dir. Marketindex OY, Helsinki; chmn. bd. Marketindex Group, Helsinki. Contbr. articles to profl. jours. Swedish rep. Fedn. Internat. des Societes d'Aviron, 1947-59; mem. exec. com. Swedish Olympic Com., 1956-65; internat. umpire Olympics Helsinki, 1952, European Championships, Copenhagen, 1953, Amsterdam, 1954. Decorated by Pres. Finland, 1953, Swedish Sports Fedn., 1954. Mem. Nat. Index Bd., Internat. C. of C. (commn. on mktg. 1957—), Fedn. Swedish Market Research Insts. (chmn. bd. 1963, 67, 71, 72), European Soc. Opinion and Mktg. Research (Swedish rep. 1964-74), Swedish Rowing Assn. (pres. 1950-55, hon. pres. 1988). Home: Hammarbacken 14, S 182 35 Danderyd Sweden Office: Marketindex AB, Box 1032, S 16421 Kista Sweden

KAISER, EDGAR FOSBURGH, JR., financial institution company executive; b. Portland, Oreg., July 5, 1942; Can. citizen; s. Edgar Fosburgh and Sue (Mead) K.; married; 3 children. BA, Stanford U., 1965; MBA, Harvard U., 1967. With AID, Vietnam, 1967-68; White House fellow asst. to Pres. Johnson, 1968; spl. asst. to sec. interior U.S. Dept. Interior, 1969; mgr. corp. planning and devel. Kaiser Resources, Vancouver, B.C., Can., 1970; v.p., treas. Kaiser Resources Ltd., Vancouver, B.C., Can., 1971-72, exec. v.p. ops., 1972-73, pres., chief exec. officer, 1973-78, chmn. bd., chief exec. officer, 1978-84, chmn. bd., 1971-84; mgr. resources devel. Kaiser Steel Corp., 1970-71, pres., chief exec. officer, 1979-80, chmn. bd., chief exec. officer, 1980-81; chmn., chief exec. officer Bank of B.C., 1984-86; chmn. bd. dirs., pres., chief exec. officer Kaiser Resources Ltd., 1986—; dir. Bell Canada Enterprises Devel. Corp.; past adv.-dir. Pvt. Investment Co. Asia.; past mem. Can. Japan Bus. Cooperation Com., Can.-Korea Bus. Council; mem. Can. com. Pacific Basin Econ. Council; mem. Bus. Council on Nat. Issues, SRI Internat. Council; hon. vice-consul Rep. of Columbia, Vancouver. Trustee, hon. vice consul Republic of Colombia in Vancouver; hon. patron B.C. div. Can. Diabetes Assn.; hon. dir. Vancouver Boys' and Girls' Clubs; bd. govs. Jr. Achievement of B.C., Bus. Council of B.C.; trustee Vancouver Gen. Hosp., Calif. Inst. Tech.; past bd. dirs. Am. Iron and Steel Inst., Internat. Iron and Steel Inst., Stanford U. Alumni Assn., Can. Arthritis & Rheumatism Soc., Vancouver Symphony Soc.; bd. dirs. Man in Motion World Tour Inc., Sadat Peace Found., Diefenbaker Meml. Found. Inc., U. Colo. Found.; chmn. Kaiser Family Found., Kaiser Substance Abuse Found.; founder, mem. adv. com. Denver Broncos Youth Found.; mem. internat. adv. council Gov. Dummer Acad.; vis. com. for grad. sch. Sch. Edn., Harvard U.; mem. internat. council The Salk Inst.; mem. bus. adv. council Faculty Bus., U. Alta.; mem. adv. council Faculty Commerce and Bus. Adminstrn., U. B.C.; past co-chmn. Am. Cancer Soc.; past chmn. Am. Acad. Achievement; patron Vancouver Aquarium. Recipient Golden Plate award Am. Acad. Achievement, 1978, Edgar A. Scholz award B.C. and Yukon Chamber of Mines, 1984, named B.C. Businessman of Yr. Kaiser Resources Ltd., 1979, Mktg. Exec. of Yr. Sales and Mktg. Execs. of Vancouver, 1986. Mem. Coal Assn. Can. (past pres.), Mining Assn. B.C. (v.p. 1973-76), Young President's Orgn., Trilateral Commn., White House Fellows Assn. Home: Vancouver, BC Canada Office: Kaiser Resources Ltd, 1500 W Georgia St 20th Floor, Vancouver, BC Canada V6G 2Z8

KAISER, ROBERT LEE, engineer; b. Louisville, June 28, 1935; s. Harlan K. and LaVerne (Peterson) K.; student U. Louisville, 1953-54, U. Ky., 1958-61; m. Margaret Siler; children—Robin Lee, Robert Lee. Draftsman, designer E.R. Ronald & Assos., Louisville, 1953-54, Thompson-Kissell Co., 1954-56; estimator, engr. George Pridemore & Son, Lexington, Ky., 1956-58; designer, engr., supr. Frankel & Curtis, Lexington, 1958-61; engr. Hugh Dillehay & Assos., 1961-65; owner, engr., operator K-Service, Inc., 1965-74; project engr. Mason & Hanger, Silas Mason Co., Inc., 1974-77; v.p. Webb-Dillehay Design Group, 1977-81; pres. Kaiser-Taulbee Assos., Inc.; sec.-treas. The Triad Engring. Group; energy mgmt. cons., Lexington, 1981—; past chmn., pres. and bd. dirs. Opportunity Workshop Lexington; vis. lectr. mech. engring. and Coll. Architecture, U. Ky. Mem. charter commn. merger Lexington-Fayette County govts.; mem. Gov.'s Task Force on Ednl. Constrn. Criteria, bd. dirs., treas. chpt. Am. Cancer Soc.; trustee Humana Hosp., Lexington. Registered profl. engr., Fla., Ind., Ky., N.Mex., Ariz., Ill. Mem. ASME, Nat., Ky. socs. profl. engrs., Lexington C. of C., ASHRAE (past pres. local chpt.), Assn. Energy Engrs. (pres. local chpt.). Episcopalian. Club: Rotary. Home: 401 Culpepper Rd Lexington KY 40502 Office: PO Box 480 Lexington KY 40585

KAISTHA, KRISHAN KUMAR, toxicologist; b. Sulah, Himachal Pradesh, India, Apr. 6, 1926; came to U.S., 1959, naturalized, 1974; s. Mangat Ram and Tara (Devi) Mahajan K.; m. Swarn L. Kaistha, Feb. 22, 1948; children—Anita Kaistha Mahajan, Vivek, Vinek. B.S. in Chemistry, Punjab U., India, 1947, B.S. in Pharmacy with honors, 1951, M.S., 1955; Ph.D., U. Fla., 1962. Diplomate Am. Bd. Forensic Toxicology; cert. clin. chemist Nat. Registry Clin. Chemistry; cert. clin. lab. specialist Nat. Cert. Agy. Med. Lab. Personnel; registered pharmacist, Ill. Analytical chemist Punjab Govt. Med. Directorate, India, 1952-57, chief pharmacist, 1957-59; research fellow SUNY, Buffalo, 1962-63; head pharm. and phytochem. research lab. Punjab Govt., India, 1964-66; research scientist food and drug directorate Dept. Nat. Health and Welfare, Ottawa, Ont., Can., 1966-69; dir. toxicology labs. Drug Abuse Program Ill. Dept. Mental Health, Chgo., 1969-74; chief toxicologist Ill. Dangerous Drugs Commn., Chgo., 1974-84, acting adminstr., 1981-84; chief toxicologist Ill. Dept. Alcoholism and Substance Abuse, 1984-86; dir., v.p. Tox-Tech, Inc., 1986—; pres., dir. K.K. Bioscience, Inc., 1987—; research assoc. dept. psychiatry U. Chgo., 1969-75. Contbr. numerous research articles to profl. jours. Recipient 1st prize Lunsford-Richardson award, 1962; Gov.'s Economy Incentive award State of Ill., 1973. Fellow N.Y. Acad. Sci., Am. Acad. Forensic Scis., Nat. Acad. Clin. Biochemistry; mem. Am. Acad. Clin. Toxicology, Am. Assn. Clin. Chemists, Am. Soc. Pharmacology and Exptl. Therapeutics, Rho Chi, Phi Kappa Phi, Rho Pi Phi. Home: 542 Ashbury Ave Bolingbrook IL 60439 Office: care IIT Research 10 W 35th St Chicago IL 60616

KAITSCHUK, ROBERT CHARLES, psychologist, travel agency exec.; b. Oak Park, Ill., Sept. 28, 1934; s. Oscar C. and Victoria Marguerite (Schmaus) K.; B.A., Wittenberg U., 1956; M.A., Pepperdine U., 1967. Tchr., Henry Ford II Sch., Chicago Ridge, Ill., 1961-64; counselor, psychologist, div. vocat. edn. West Covina (Calif.) Unified Sch. Dist., 1966-70; prin. Renaissance High Sch., Santa Paula, Calif., 1970-72; personnel mgmt. specialist Ventura County Personnel Dept., Ventura, Calif., 1972-73; vocat. psychologist Calif. Dept. Rehab., Bakersfield dist., 1974-76; psychologist, account exec. Dean Witter & Co., Inc., 1976-77; owner, pres. Elegant Travel, Inc., Mission Viejo, Calif., 1977—; mem. pres. adv. bd. Mission Viejo Nat. Bank, 1982—; mem. Saddleback Community Hosp. Assocs., Laguna Hills, Calif., 1986—. Bd. convocators Calif. Luth. Coll., Thousand Oaks, 1969-77; bd. dirs. Santa Paula Boys Club, 1971-74, Kern County Campfire Girls, 1976-77; v.p. Orange County Assn. for Retarded Citizens, 1978-79. HEW grantee, 1970. Mem. Am. Psychol. Assn., Western Psychol. Assn., Calif. Psychol. Assn., Assn. Retail Travel Agts., Am. Soc. Travel Agts., Soc. Advancement Travel Handicapped. Assn. Calif. Sch. Adminstrs., Benjamin Prince Soc. Wittenberg U. (life), Phi Kappa Psi, Theta Alpha Phi. Republican. Lutheran. Clubs: Rotary (sec. 1978-79, v.p. 1979-80, pres. 1980-81) (Mission Viejo); Mission Viejo Country; Town Hall of Calif. Home: 25751 Knotty Pine Laguna Hills CA 92653 Office: Gateway Ctr 24000 Alicia Pkwy Suite 16 Mission Viejo CA 92691

KAIYALETHE, JOHN KURUVILLA (K.K.), minister; b. Erath, India, May 24, 1936; came to U.S., 1962; s. Kuruvilla Korula and Rachel (Yohannan) K.; m. Tamara Fogel, Sept. 3, 1963; children: Nava, David, Michal. Diploma in Theology, Zion Bible Coll. and Sem., Mulakuzha, India, 1957; ThD, Kingsway Coll. and Sem., 1986; DD (hon.), Jameson Christian Coll. Nat. dir. Sunday Schs. and Youth Dept. Ch. of God, India, 1957-61; sr. pastor Ch. of God, Bombay, 1960-61; free-lance journalist Jerusalem, 1961-62; pres. Internat. Student Fellowship, 1966-71; dir., campus pastor Assemblies of God Campus Ministries, 1967-74, minister, conf. speaker, church growth cons., 1974—; evangelist, conf. speaker; nat. dir. edn. and Sunday schs. India; v.p. U. Minn. Council Religious Advisors. Mem. Presdl. adv. com. Commn. Campus Unrest; mem. Parent Adv. Commn., Mpls. Pub. Schs., 1986—; pioneered adult edn.

KAJIURA, TSUNEO, architectural educator; b. Osaka, Japan, Nov. 16, 1938; s. Kishirou and Misao (Yamamoto) K.; m. Hiroko Kindaichi, Apr. 2, 1965; children: Shinichi, Kajiura. BArch, Tohoku U., Sendai, Japan, 1964; D in Engring., Kyoto (Japan) U., 1966. Archtl. diplomate, Japan. Asst. Osaka City U., 1967-68, lectr., 1968-78, assoc. prof. housing mgmt., residential area planning, 1978—. Author: KANSAI New Airport, 1981, How to Make an Apartment Builing Last a Long Time, 1986; author, editor What to Ask the Condominium Management, 1983. Bd. dirs. West Japan Fedn. Condominium Owners Assn., 1981—. Mem. Japan Archtl. Inst., City Planning Inst. Japan (planning prize 1976), Apartment Maintenance Assn. (bd. dirs. Osaka 1984—). Home: 3-1-21-308 Shinkanaoka, Sakai, Osaka 591, Japan Office: Osaka City Univ, Sugimoto 3-3-138, Osaka 558, Japan

KAKAR, AMAN-UL-MULK, airline executive; b. Pakistan, Feb. 24, 1952; s. Rustam Khan and Begum Mehartaj Kakar; m. Aman Shakila Kakar; three children. MS in Statistics, Gomal U.; LLB, Karachi U. Investigator Inst. Econ. Engring. U. Peshawar, Pakistan, 1976-77; auditor Acct. Gen. Office, Peshawar, 1978—; indsl. engring. analyst, adminstrn. officer Pakistan Internat. Airlines, Karachi, Islamabad, Pakistan, 1979—. Mem. ACMA. Home: Mohallah Babar, Peshawar Pakistan Office: Administrative Officer, Pakistan Internat Airlines, 5 the Mall Rawal Dindi, Punjab 1, Pakistan

KAKATI, DINESH CHANDRA, physician; b. Gauhati, India, Feb. 1, 1941; arrived in Eng., 1969; s. Nara Kanta and Subhandra (Baishya) K.; m. Bhabani Medhi, Mar. 27, 1974; children: Rita, Rishi. MBBS with distinction, Gauhati Med. Sch., 1967; Diploma in Tropical Medicine and Hygiene, Liverpool (Eng.) U., 1970, Diploma in Thoracic Medicine, London U., 1984, Diploma in Cardiac Medicine, 1984; Diploma in Geriatric Medicine, Royal Coll. Physicians, 1985. Sr. house officer Sunderland (Eng.) Health Authority, 1969-70, med. registrar, 1970-72; med. registrar Addinbrook Hosp., Cambridge, Eng., 1972-74, London Hosp., 1974-77; assoc. specialist N.E. Thames region, Hornchurch, Eng., 1977-84, clin. asst., 1984—. Fellow Royal Soc. Health Eng.; mem. Brit. Med. Assn., Royal Coll. Gen. Practitioners (assoc.). Home: 39 Veny Crescent, Hornchurch, London RM12 6TJ, England Office: St Georges Hosp, Suttons Ln, London E6 S56, England

KAKIUCHI, TSUTOMU, architect; b. Wakayama, Japan, Aug. 2, 1947; s. Naruo and Hirako (Kakiuchi) K.; BE in Arch., Osaka Inst. Tech., 1971; BS in Arch., Lawrence Inst. Tech., Mich., 1980. Registered architect, Japan. Designer, Santo Assocs., Inc., Osaka, Japan, 1971-72; designer/estimator Matsumura-gumi Co., Osaka, 1973-79; constrn. adminstr. Azusa Inc., Osaka, 1980-83; pvt. practice architecture, Osaka, 1983—; cons. Azusa, Inc., 1983—, 1986—. owner archtl. cons. Architects, Regional Planning Assn., Kyoto, 1986—. owner archtl. firm Cluster Tech, 1984—. Mem. Archtl. Inst. Japan. Japan Inst. Architects. Buddhist. Office: 22-14 1 chome Naka-Sakurazuka, Toyonaka, Osaka 560, Japan

KAKU, RYUZABURO, precision instruments manufacturing company executive; b. Okazaki, Japan, May 19, 1926; m. Meiko, Dec. 13, 1957; children—Naoko, Toshiro. B., Kyushu U. (Japan), 1954. Pres., Canon Inc., Tokyo. Mem. Tokyo C. of C. Home: #701 2-61-1 Denenchoufu, Ohta-ku, Tokyo 145, Japan Office: Canon Inc, 2-7-1 Nishi-Shinjuku 2 Chome, Shinjuku-ku, Tokyo 160, Japan also: Canon USA Inc One Canon Plaza Lake Success NY 11042 *

KAKULAS, BYRON ARTHUR, neuropathologist; b. Perth, W. Australia, Mar. 29, 1932; s. Arthur Bartholomew and Phyllis (Dimantis) K.; M.B., B.S., St. Mark's Coll., U. Adelaide, 1956; M.D., U. Western Australia, 1964; Didaktora h.c., U. Athens, 1979; m. Valerie Anne Patsoyannis, Feb. 5, 1961; children—Arthur Phillip, Felice Anne, Carolyn Rose. Med. officer Royal Perth Hosp., 1957-63, Mass. Gen. Hosp., Boston, 1963-65; lectr., then reader U. W. Australian Faculty Medicine, 1960-71, Muscular Dystrophy Research Assn. Found. prof. neuropathology, 1971—, dean Faculty Medicine, 1976-78; head dept. neuropathology Royal Perth Hosp., 1967—; bd. dirs. Muscular Dystrophy Research Assn.-Australian Neurol. Found.; exec. com. World Fedn. Neurology Neuromuscular Disease and Rehab. and Restorative Neurology; v.p. Internat. Congress Muscle Disease, 1971, 74, 78; v.p. Vth Internat. Congress Neuromuscular Diseases, 1982; bd. mgmt. Sir Charles Gairdner Hosp., 1977-80, Good Samaritan Industries Inc., 1972-85; pres. Australian Brain Found., 1981-85; med. dir. Neuromuscular Found. and Inst. Western Australia, 1982—; mem. sci. com. Internat. Spinal Research Trust, 1983—. Decorated officer Order Australia; Eli Lilly fellow, 1963-64; C.J. Martin fellow, 1964-65; Fulbright fellow, 1969. Fellow Royal Australasian Coll. Physicians (Rennie Meml. lectr., Bronze medal 1972), Royal Coll. Pathologists Australia, Royal Coll. Pathologists U.K.; mem. Australian and N.Z. Assn. Advancement Sci. (chmn. div. 1983—; Ross meml. lectr. 1977), Australian Med. Assn., Australian Assn. Neurologists (past councillor), Internat. Soc. Greek Neuroscientists (pres. 1985—), Australia-N.Z. Soc. Neuropathology (pres. 1985—), Australian Am. Assn. Greek Orthodox. Club: West Perth Rotary (hon.).Author: Man Marsupials & Muscle, 1982; (with R.D. Adams) Diseases of Muscle, Pathological Foundations of Clinical Myology, 4th ed., 1985; editor: Basic and Clinical Research in Myology, 1973; (with M.R. Dimitrijevic, G. Vrbova) Recent Achievements in Restorative Neurology 2 Progressive Neuromuscular Diseases, 1986. Contbr. articles to med. jours. Home: 59 Dampier Ave, City Beach, Western Australia 6015, Australia Office: Royal Perth Hosp, Dept Neuropathology, Box X2213, Perth, Western Australia 6001, Australia

KALA, RADOSLAW, mathematician, statistician; b. Kowary, Poland, Sept. 17, 1946; s. Czeslaw and Janina (Pawlak) K.; m. Maria Hanna Kaczmarek, July 13, 1974; 1 child, Borys. M.A., Adam Mickiewicz U., 1970, Ph.D., 1975, D.Sc., 1981. Asst. Acad. of Agr., Poznan, Poland, 1970-75, lectr., 1975-83; asst. prof., 1983—, subchief Dept. Math. and Statis. Methods, Poznan, 1981-84, chief, 1984-87. Editor: Biometrical Letters Jour., 1983—; contbr. articles to profl. jours. Recipient 3d prize Ministry of Edn., 1978, 2d prize, 1981, 3d prize, 1983. Mem. Polish Math. Soc. Hugo Steinhaus prize 1979, Polish Biometrical Soc., Am. Math. Soc. Office: Acad Agr Dept Math and Statis Methods, Wojska Polskiego 28, 60-637 Poznan Poland

KALAIDJIAN, BERJ BOGHOS, civil engineer; b. Jerusalem, Mar. 7, 1936; s. Boghos Hovhanes and Shoghagat Kevork (Sahakian) K.; B.C.E., Am. U., Beirut, Lebanon, 1958; m. Sonia Kouyoumdjian, Aug. 19, 1963; children—Shahe, Vatche. Site engr. Consol. Contractors Co., Beirut, 1958-62, project mgr., 1962-64, asst. area mgr., jr. partner, 1964-69; mng. dir., partner Acmecon, Jeddah Saudi Arabia, 1969—, also dir. Club: Armenian Benevolent Union. Home: 27 Belvedere Grove, London SW19 7RQ, England

KALATHAS, JOHN, airline pilot, physicist, oceanographer; b. Athens, Greece, July 24, 1946; s. Panayotis J. and Calypso (George Violaki) K.; m. Catherine Kalathas, July 2, 1973 (div.); 1 child, Hector. BS in Physics, U. Athens, 1968; Diplome D'Etudes Approfondies in Phys. Oceanography, U. Paris, 1969, Diploma De Docteur En Geophysique, 1970. Lic. profl. pilot Oxford, Eng. Air Tng. Sch., 1974. Researcher Inst. Oceanography, Athens, 1971, 74-75, Environ. Pollution Control Project, Athens, 1974-75; pilot Olympic Airways, Athens, 1975—; instr. suba diving Hellenic Fedn. Underwater Activities, 1968—, dep. chief instr., 1975-77. Served with Hellenic Navy, 1971-73. Mem. Hellenic Speleological Soc. Club: Aero Athens. Home: 2 Petrou Dimaki St, GR-106 72 Athens Greece Office: Athens Airport Hellenikon, Athens Greece

KALBFLEISCH, JOHN MCDOWELL, cardiologist, medical educator; b. Lawton, Okla., Nov. 15, 1930; s. George and Etta Lillian (McDowell) K.; m. Jolie Harper, Dec. 30, 1961. A.S., Cameron A&M U., Lawton, 1950; B.S., U. Okla., 1953, M.D., 1957. Diplomate: Am. Bd. Internal Medicine, subsplty. bd. cardiovascular disease. Intern U. Va. Hosp., 1957-58; resident and fellow U. Okla. Med. Center, 1958-61, instr. medicine, 1964-66, asst. prof., 1966-69, assoc. clin. prof., 1970-78; clin. prof. U. Okla. Med. Center (Tulsa br.), 1978—; practice medicine specializing in cardiology Tulsa, 1969—; dir. cardiovascular services St. Francis Hosp., Tulsa, 1975—; mem. physician adv. bd., City of Tulsa, 1978-81; bd. dirs. St. Francis Hosp., exec. com. 1987—. contbr. articles in field to profl. jours. Served with USPHS, 1962-64. Fellow A.C.P., Am. Coll. Cardiology (gov. Okla. 1978-81); mem. Tulsa County Med. Soc., Okla. State Med. Assn., AMA, Am. Heart Assn. (teaching scholar 1967-69), Okla. Soc. Internal Medicine (v.p., pres.-elect 1983-84, pres. 1985-86), Am. Soc. Internal Medicine, AAAS, Am. Fedn. Clin. Research, Am. Inst. Nutrition, Delta Upsilon. Republican. Presbyterian. Office: 6585 S Yale Ave Suite 800 Tulsa OK 74136

KALEN, THOMAS HARRY, banker; b. Balt., Mar. 14, 1938; s. Harry Lawrence and Angela Carolyn (Nockels) K.; B.S., UCLA, 1960; m. Judith L. Cochran, Aug. 29, 1959; children—John Merrill, Bonnie Jean. Account exec. Dean Witter & Co., San Bernardino, Calif., 1966-69; v.p. Chase Investment Mgmt. Co., N.Y.C., 1969-71, Transamerica Corp., Los Angeles, 1971-77, No. Trust Co., Chgo., 1977-82; v.p. Mellon Bank, Pitts., 1982-84; sr. v.p. Boston Safe Deposit & Trust Co., Los Angeles, 1984—. Vice pres., chmn. public relations Calif. Jaycees, 1968; dist. chmn. UCLA Scholarship Soc., 1974-77; chmn. pub. relations com. Mass Transit for Los Angeles, 1976; Mem. adv. bd. Ctr. Entrepreneurial Studies NYU; dir. Venture Capital Studies, NYU, 1983-85. Served with USAF, 1960-66; Vietnam. Named Calif. Outstanding Jaycees, 1968. Mem. Nat. Assn. Security Dealers, Western Pension Conf., Instl. Investor Conf., Pension and Investment Conf. Club: Union League (Chgo.).

KALFUS, ELYSE RUTH, management consultant; b. Norfolk, Va., Sept. 14, 1947; d. Seymour H. and Irene C. (Chernitzer) Chapel; m. Ira F. Kalfus, Dec. 22, 1972 (div. 1977); 1 son, Brian Eric; m. Marshall Gordon, Dec. 12, 1981 (div. 1987); stepchildren—Howard David, Michael Kenneth, Jack Jay, Sheryl Patricia. Student, Norfolk pub. schs. Acctg. clk. Life Ins. Co. Ga., Atlanta, 1970-72; ind. contractor Atlanta Advertiser, Decatur, Ga., 1973-74; bookkeeper William Harvey Rowland & Co., Mableton, Ga., 1974-77; comptroller Sofas & Chairs, Inc., Atlanta, 1977-79; dir. security and distbn. Simon Mktg. Inc., Atlanta, 1979-80, dir. logistics, 1980-85; mgmt., transp. and Logistics, freight rate audit cons., 1979-85; pres. Traffic Mgmt. Cons., Inc., Marietta, Ga., 1985—, TMCI Internat. Ltd., Marietta, 1987—; computer newsletter editor. Mem. Women's Traffic Club Atlanta, Atlanta Computer Users Group (founder; sec.-treas. 1982-85), Council for Logistics Mgmt., Cobb C. of C., Delta Nu Alpha.. Home: 2665 Moss Ln Marietta GA 30067 Office: Traffic Mgmt Cons Inc/TMCI Internat 2130 Kingston Ct Suite B Marietta GA 30067

KALIFF, JOSEPH ALFRED, artist, writer, publishing syndicate executive; b. Fall River, Mass., Apr. 3, 1922; s. George and Marie (Fata) K. Student, Pratt Inst., 1940-41, Brown U., 1942, N.Y. Sch. Indsl. Arts, 1950-51. Free-lance artist, writer 1940-43, and free-lance caricaturist for newspapers and mags., 1945-50; pres. Republic Features Syndicate, N.Y.C., 1950-55, Amusement Features Syndicate, N.Y.C., 1979—; entertainment editor Broadway columnist Bklyn. Daily, 1951-71; mem. bd. judges Miss Universe Contest, 1955, Mrs. Am. Contest, 1951-52, Coll. Queen Contest, 1951-55. Starred in 2 TV programs, Sta.-WPIX; author: nationally syndicated columns Did You Know That?, 1950-52, Magic Carpet Over Broadway, 1950—, It's A Cockeyed World, 1953-79, Karikature Karnival, 1979—, TV and Hollywood Chatter. Served with U.S. Army, 1943-45, ETO. Mem. Caricaturists Soc. Am. (founder, dir. 1950—, pres. 1979—), N.Y. Press Club Assn., Am. Legion. Clubs: Odd Fellows, Circus Saints and Sinners. Home: 224 Highland Blvd Brooklyn NY 11207 Office: 255 W 43d St New York NY 10036

KALIM, MUHAMMAD SIDDIQ, educator, administrator, writer; b. Amritsar, India, Dec. 16, 1921; s. Rahmatullah Chawdhary; m. 1950; 4 children. BA with honours, Univ. Panjab, 1941; MA in English Lit., 1943; MA in English Lit., Birbeck Coll., U. London, 1960. Prof. English Govt. Coll., Lahore, Pakistan, 1954-71, prin., 1972-74, dir. Curriculum Research and Devel. Ctr., Lahore, 1974-80. Author books of poetry and lit. criticism, also books on edn. and culture. Mem. Pakistan Writers Guild, MLA, Am. Ednl. Research Assn. Muslim. Home: 96-K, Gulberg III, Lahore 11 Pakistan

KALIN, IVAN PETROVICH, Soviet government official; b. Moldavian, 1935. Mem. Communist Party Soviet Union, 1955—; grad. Frunze Agrl. Inst., Kishinev and Central Com. Communist Party Higher Sch.; agronomist, dept. chmn., sec. of party com. Viatsa Noue Collective Farm in Orgeev Raion, 1960-63; instr. of party organs dept. of central com. Moldavian Communist Party, sec. party com. for agr. in prodn. adminstrn. in Kalarash; 1st sec. of Kalarash Raion com. Moldavian Communist Party, 1963-67; auditor Communist Party Soviet Union Central Com. Party Higher Sch., 1967-69; mem. central com. Moldavian Communist Party, 1963—; 1st sec. Kalarash Raion agr. dept., 1971-74, chief of agr. and food dept., 1974-76, mem. bur. of central com., 1976—; chmn. presidium Supreme Soviet Moldavian Soviet Socialist Republic, 1980—; dep. and mem. presidium USSR Supreme Soviet, 1980—; candidate mem. central com. Communist Party Soviet Union, 1981—. Office: Moldavian SSR, Council of Ministers, Moscow USSR *

KALINOWSKI, MICHAEL FRANCIS, child and family studies educator; b. Wiesbaden, Germany, July 27, 1947; came to U.S., 1949; s. Frank Stanley and Elizabeth McElroy (Maloney) K.; m. Mary Jane Moran, Jan. 1, 1979; 1 child, Caitlin Elizabeth. Student Am. U., 1965-66, NYU, 1966-67; B.A., Bennington Coll., Vt., 1970; Ed.M., U. Mass., 1972, Ed.D., 1976. Intern UNESCO, Paris, 1970-71; research assoc. ANISA, Amherst, Mass., 1971-74; dir. dept. parents and children, Xavier U., Cin., 1974-75; asst. prof. child and family studies, asst. prof. curriculum and instruction, dir. child devel. labs. U. Tenn., Knoxville, 1976-80; asst. prof. child and family studies, U. N.H., Durham, 1980-84, assoc. prof., 1984—, chmn. dept. family and consumer studies, 1982-85, dir. child and family ctr., 1980-87, dir. Child Study and Devel. Ctr., 1987—; mem. infants and children adv. com. Seacoast Found., 1987—; cons. in field. Co-author: Child Abuse 1976-80, 1982; contbr. articles to numerous publs. Producer, dir., performer over 60 plays in U.S., Haiti. Resident mgr. Ramsey House Mus., Knoxville, 1978-80. Grantee Levi

Strauss Found., 1978, 81, USDA Agl. Experiment Sta., 1980—, N.H. Charitable Fund, 1983, 84, Whiting Found., 1985-86 (pres. 1983-87). Urban Appalachian Program fellow, 1973. Mem. Council Child Devel. Lab. Adminstrs. (pres. 1983—), No. New Eng. Assn. Infant Devel. (v.p. 1982-84), Nat. Assn. Edn. Young Children (program chmn. Tenn. chpt. 1978-79, v.p. Knoxville chpt. 1979-80, program co-chmn. New Eng. chpt. 1983-84, editor New Eng. Curricular series 1986—), Am. Montessori Soc., Nat. Assn. Humane Edn., Nat. Assn. Child Devel. Lab. Schs. (bd. dirs. 1985—). Home: 20 Swaan DrRFD Durham NH 03824 Office: Univ NH Family and Consumer Studies Durham NJ 03801

KALKOFEN, HERMANN ERICH FRITZ, film director, psychology educator; b. Belzig, Brandenburg, Germany, Apr. 18, 1940; s. Hermann Erich Friedrich and Gertrud Henny (Bastine) K.; m. Beatrix Hanke (div. Oct. 1974); 1 child, Dorothea Chistiana. Diploma in Psychology, Georg August U., Göttingen, Fed. Republic Germany, 1964; PhD, Tech. Univ., Braunschweig, Fed. Republic Germany, 1969. Asst. Georg August U., 1964, 1966, lectr. social psychology, 1972—; executive Marplan Co., Frankfurt, Fed. Republic Germany, 1965-66; asst. Tech. U, 1966-68; clin. psychologist Dist. Adminstrn., Stade, Fed. Republic Germany, 1969-70; vis. lectr. Hochschule Fernsehen Film, Münich, Fed. Republic Germany, 1976—; film dir. Inst. Wissenschaftlichen Film, Göttingen, 1970—. Author, dir. or editor various sci. films; contbr. articles to profl. jours. Mem. Deutsche Gesellschaft Semiotik (head film div. 1976, 1978), Deutsche Gesellschaft Psychologie. Office: Inst Wissenschaftlichen Film, Nonnenstieg 72, D-3400 Göttingen Federal Republic of Germany

KALKURA, MURALI DHARA, accountant; b. Arupukotai, Tamil Nadu, India, May 27, 1954; arrived in Zambia, 1985; s. Srinivasa and Sathya Bhama K.; m. Jyothi Kálkura, May 17, 1981; children: Pavithra, Pranava. BSc, Madras Christian Coll., India, 1977. Sub-acct. Madura Coats Ltd., Bangalore, India, 1977-79; asst. acct. Smith, Kline & French Ltd., Bangalore, 1980-81; dep. audit mgr. Bengal Lamps Ltd., Bangalore, 1981-85; acct. mgmt. services Chilanga Cement Ltd., Lusaka, Zambia, 1985—. Mem. Inst. Chartered Accts. (assoc., chartered 1977), Brit. Inst. Mgmt. Home: 37 10th Ave, Ashok Nagar, Madras India

KALLAY, MICHAEL FRANK, II, medical devices company official; b. Painesville, Ohio, Aug. 24, 1944; s. Michael Frank and Marie Francis (Sage) K.; BBA, Ohio U., 1967; m. Irma Yolanda Corona, Aug. 30, 1975; 1 son, William Albert. Salesman, Howmedica, Inc., Rutherford, N.J., 1972-75, Biochem. Procedures/Metpath, North Hollywood, Calif., 1975-76; surg. specialist USCI div. C. R. Bard, Inc., Billerica, Mass., 1976-78; western and central regional mgr. ARCO Med. Products Co., Phila., 1978-80; Midwest regional mgr. Intermedics, Inc., Freeport, Tex., 1980-82; Western U.S. mgr. Renal Systems, Inc., Mpls., 1982—; pres. Kall-Med, Inc., Anaheim Hills, Calif., 1982—. Mem. Am. Mgmt. Assn., Phi Kappa Sigma. Home and Office: 6515 Marengo Dr PO Box 17248 Anaheim Hills CA 92817

KALLENBACK, JAN H. J., business executive; b. Oerebro, Sweden, Aug. 25, 1943; s. Ingvar H. and Asta V. (Neve) K.; m. Ewa B. Brohlen, May 8, 1945; children: Asa, Rolf, Ylva. MSc in Mining, Royal Inst. Tech., Stockholm, 1969. Engr. Bergkonsult AB, Stockholm, 1969-70; mine supt. Boliden AB, 1970-75; gen. mgr. Greenex A/S, Greenland, 1975-77, Gulf Explosives Co. Ltd., United Arab Emirates, 1977-80; export mgr. Nitro Nobel AB, Gyttorp, Sweden, 1980-85; gen. mgr. Hagry Bruk AB, Nora, Sweden, 1985—. Office: Hagby Bruk AB, PO Box 4, 71300 Nora Sweden

KALLICK, SONIA BELLE, nurse, high school teacher; b. Chgo., Mar. 11, 1933; d. Sven and Belle (Damtjernhaug) Aamot; m. Charles Arthur Kallick, Dec. 23, 1956; children: Steven, Karen, Ingrid. RN, Cook County Sch. Nursing, 1953; BS, U. Ill., Chgo., 1956; MA, Lewis U., 1977. RN, Ill.; cert. tchr., Ill. From staff nurse to head nurse Cook County Hosp., Chgo., 1953-56; elem. tchr. Lemont (Ill.) Sch. Dist. 113, 1964-77; high sch. tchr. Lemont Dist. 210, 1977—. Newspaper columnist, 1973-85; author: A Walking Tour of Lemont, 1976. Trustee Chgo. Mural Group, 1976—, Lemont Hist. Soc., 1973—, v.p., 1975-78; v.p. Friends of the Ill. and Mich. Canal, 1982-86, trustee, 1986—; dir. photo project Lemont and Its People, 1986; member, hist. pres. com, Ill. and Mich. Canal Commn., 1987. Recipient Citizens' award, Lemont Bicentennial com., 1976. Mem. Nat. Assn. English Instrs., Assn. Concerned Scientists, Am. Nurses Assn.

KALLSEN, THEODORE JOHN, retired English language educator; b. Jasper, Minn., Mar. 27, 1915; s. Bernhart H. and Irene (Wehrman) K.; m. Marvel J. Stordahl, Aug. 27, 1939; children: Carolyn Irene (Mrs. Harold Pate), Tonya Jo, (Mrs. William Vining, Jr.). B.S., Mankato State U., 1936; M.A., U. Iowa, 1940, Ph.D., 1949. Various teaching positions Minn., Mo., Iowa, 1936-49; asst. prof. integrated studies W.Va. U., Morgantown, 1949-55; prof. English, head dept. Stephen F. Austin State U., Nacogdoches, Tex., 1955-65; prof., dean Sch. Liberal Arts, 1965-76, Disting. prof. English, 1976-80, Disting. prof. emeritus, 1980—; Cons. English curriculum pub. schs. Author: Modern Rhetoric and Usage, 1955, (with D.E. McCoy) Reading and Rhetoric: Order and Idea, 1963, Teachers' Use of Dictating Machines, 1965, Making: Selected Poems, 1981; also traditional and concrete poetry, profl. articles. Served to lt. (j.g.) USNR, 1944-46. Past mem. Nat. Council Tchrs. English, Conf. Coll. Composition and Communication (past mem. exec. com.), AAUP, Tex. Conf. Coll. Tchrs. English, Tex. Coll. English Assn. (past pres.), Modern Lang. Assn., So. Humanities Conf. Clubs: Piney Woods Country (Nacogdoches) (past dir.); East Tex. German-Am. Social (pres. 1974-76). Home: 600 Bostwick Nacogdoches TX 75961

KALMAN, PETER, cardiologist; b. Budapest, Hungary, Feb. 26, 1928; s. Alexander and Ilona (Balog) K.; m. Susan Horanyi, July 7, 1951. M.D., Med. U. Budapest, 1952. Dir. non-invasive lab. Nat. Inst. Cardiology, Budapest, Hungary, 1956-70; head dept. Nat. Med. Inst. Sports, Budapest, 1970-77; head dept. internal medicine and cardiology Tetenyi Hosp., Budapest, 1977—; fellow cardiology Hahnemann Med. Coll., Hosp. Cardiovascular Sect., Phila., 1963; vis. prof. Hahnemann U., Likoff Cardiovascular Inst., Phila., 1981-82. Fellow Am. Coll. Cardiology; mem. Am. Fedn. Aging Research, Internat. Assn. Olympic Med. Officers, European Soc. Cardiology, Hungarian Soc. Cardiology (bd. dirs.), Hungarian Soc. Atherosclerosis (bd. dirs.). Author: Atlas in Phonocardiography, 1973; textbook chpt. on cardiac auscultation, 1986. Home: 29 Hidasz, 1026 Budapest Hungary Office: 12/16 Tetenyi, 1115 Budapest Hungary

KALMAN, RUDOLF EMIL, research mathematician, system scientist; b. Budapest, Hungary, May 19, 1930; s. Otto and Ursula (Grundmann) K.; m. Constantina Stavrou, Sept. 12, 1959; children: Andrew E.F.C., Elisabeth K. S.B., MIT, 1953, S.M., 1954; D.Sc., Columbia U., 1957. Staff engr. IBM Research Lab., Poughkeepsie, N.Y., 1957-58; research mathematician Research Inst. Advanced Studies, Balt., 1958-64; prof. engring. mech. and elec. engring. Stanford U., 1964-67, prof. math. system theory, 1967-71; grad. research prof., dir. Center for Math. System Theory, U. Fla., 1971—; prof. math. system theory Swiss Fed. Inst. Tech., Zurich, 1973—; sci. adviser Ecole Nationale Superieure des Mines de Paris, 1968—; mem. sci. adv. bd. Laboratorio di Cibernetica, Naples, 1970-73. Author: Topics in Mathematical System Theory, 1969; over 120 sci. and tech. papers.; editorial bd.: Jour. Math. Modelling, Math. Systems Theory, Jour. Computer and Systems Scis., Jour. Nonlinear Analysis, Advances in Applied Math., Jour. Optimization Theory and Applications, Systems and Control Letters. Named outstanding young scientist Md. Acad. Sci., 1962; recipient IEEE medal of honor, 1974, Rufus Oldenburger medal ASME, 1976, Centennial medal IEEE, 1984, 1st Kyoto Prize Inamori Found., 1985, Steele prize Am. Math. Soc., 1987; Guggenheim fellow IHES Bures-sur-Yvette, 1971. Fgn. hon. mem. Hungarian Acad. Scis. Office: U Fla Dept Math Gainesville FL 32611 also: ETH-Hauptgebaude, 8092 Zurich Switzerland *

KALMAN, THOMAS PETER, architect; b. Budapest, Hungary, Mar. 11, 1928; came to Can., 1957; s. Marcel Mor and Johanna (Selinko) K.; m. Eva Weisz, June 12, 1949 (div. 1961); 1 dau., Elizabeth; m. Susan Judit Kiss, Mar. 11, 1963; children—Adrien, Nicol. Diploma in Archtl. Engring., Jozsef Nador U. Applied Scis., Budapest, 1950. Prin. architect Thomas P. Kalman, Architect, Toronto, 1964—; dir. G&B Automated Equipment Ltd., Toronto, Logicware, Inc., Toronto. Architect and/or archtl. assoc. archtl. competitions in Hungary Saskatoon Art Gallery, 1952-56, 62 (1st and 2nd place awards). Assoc. author: Oriental Rugs From Canadian Collections, 1975. Mem. Ont. Assn. Architects, Hungarian Budapest, Hungary Assn. Architects, Royal Archtl. Inst. Can., Oriental Rug Society, Inc. (bd. dirs.). Conservative. Jewish. Avocation: carpet, textile and art collector. Home: 603 1/2 Parliament St, Toronto, ON Canada M4X 1F9 Office: Architect, 603 1/2 Parliament St, Toronto, ON Canada M4X 1P9

KALMAZ, EKREM ERROL, environmental scientist; b. Turkey, Jan. 2, 1940; came to U.S., 1962, naturalized, 1979; s. Mehmet and Ayse K.; student Queens U., 1962-63; B.A. in Chemistry, Okla. State U., 1969; M.S. in Environ. Sci. and Engring., U. Okla., 1972, Ph.D. in Engring., 1974; m. Gulgun Durusoy, Oct. 3, 1974; children—Phyllis, Denise. Research asst. Okla. Med. Research Found., Oklahoma City, 1969-72, research asso., 1972-74; postdoctoral research asso. Duke U., 1974-75; postdoctoral fellow NASA L.B. Johnson Space Center, Houston, 1975-76; research asst. prof. dept. engring. sci. and mechanics U. Tenn., Knoxville, 1976-79; sr. environ. scientist Henningson, Durham & Richardson, Inc., engring. cons., Knoxville, from 1979, now sr. research assoc. NRC, Houston; cons. to industry, cons. engrs. and govt. agys. Mem. Am. Chem. Soc., AAAS, Am. Coll. Toxicology, Inst. Environ. Scis. (tech. chmn. water quality impact), Internat. Soc. Ecol. Modeling, N.Y. Acad. Scis., Soc. for Computer Simulation, Am. Inst. Chemists, Sigma Xi. Contbr. articles to profl. jours., chpts. to books. Home: 7036 N Holiday Dr Galveston TX 77550 Office: NASA-Johnson Space Ctr Health Scis Div SD-4 Houston TX 77058

KALMAZ, GULGUN DURUSOY, physician; b. Ankara, Turkey, Jan. 2, 1946; came to U.S., 1974; d. Avni H. and Nazime A. (Ipari) Durusoy; B.A. in Biochemistry, Am. Acad. for Women, Turkey, 1965; M.D., U. Istanbul, Turkey, 1971; postgrad. Duke U. Med. Center, 1974-76; m. Ekrem E. Kalmaz, Oct. 3, 1974; children—Phyllis, Denise. Intern in pediatrics and surgery U. Istanbul Sch. Medicine, 1972-73, resident, 1973-74; practice medicine specializing in hematology, 1973—; research asso. pediatric hematology Zeynep Kamil Children's Hosp., Istanbul, 1973-74; vis. scientist U. Tenn. Meml. Research Center, Knoxville, 1976-78, research asso. dept. med. biology Sch. Medicine, 1978-80; fellow NIH, 1980-83, Shriners Burn Inst., 83-85, dept. internal medicine, div. hematology and oncology U. Tex. Med. Br., Galveston, 85—; mem. staff Univ. Hosp. Recipient Research Service award NIH, 1980-83. Mem. Assn. Exptl. Hematology, Tissue Culture Assn., Sigma Xi. Contbr. articles on hematology to profl. jours. Home: 7036 N Holiday Dr Galveston TX 77550 Office: U Tex Med Br Dept Internal Medicine Div Hematology and Oncology Galveston TX 77550

KALMBACH, GUDRUN, mathematician, educator; b. Grosserlach, Germany, May 27, 1937; d. J Johannes and Elise (Wizemann) K. Ph.D. in Math., U. Gö ttingen, Fed. Republic Germany, 1966. Asst. prof. U. Ill.-Urbana, 1967-69, U. Mass., Amherst, 1970-71, Pa. State U., University Park, 1969-75; prof. math. U. Ulm, Fed. Republic Germany, 1975—. Author: Orthomodular Lattices, 1983; Measures and Hilbert Lattices, 1986; Diskrete Mathematik, 1988; Contbr. articles on algebra, quantum logics and topology to profl. jours. Mem. Am. Math. Soc., A.W.M., D.G.H.K., G.F.P.F. Home: Eberhardistr 60, D-7900 Ulm Federal Republic of Germany Office: U UlmKuhberg, Am Hochstrass 8, D-7900 Ulm Federal Republic of Germany

KALMEIJER, GERARDUS MARIA, communications consultant; b. The Hague, The Netherlands, Jan. 1, 1929; s. Adrianus and Alyda (Beemer) K.; m. Aldegonda Van Dongen, Nov. 9, 1959; children: Inge, Nicole, Gemma. Degree in Econs., U. Melbourne, 1956, U. Rotterdam, 1964; degree in Hosp. Scis., U. Amsterdam, 1977. Cert. in advt. Mng. dir. Intermarco, Hamburg, Fed. Republic Germany, 1964-72, Intermarco Internat., Amsterdam, 1967-72, Foote, Cone & Belding, Amsterdam, 1972-77; cons. Bur. Kalmeijer, Berlicum, The Netherlands, 1978—, Dutch Govt., The Netherlands. Author: Relationships Agency Advertiser, 1986; contbr. articles on communication to profl. publs. Mem. Vereniging Erkende Reclameadves Burs., Genootschap v. Reclame. Roman Catholic. Club: B.Communic (Den Bosch, Netherlands). Home and Office: Plein 29, 5258 TG Berlicum The Netherlands

KALTOFT, JENS, banker; b. Korsoer, Denmark, Sept. 26, 1947; m. Jette Bjoerngaard; children: Peter Rottensten, Martin Rottensten. Trainee Den Danske Bank, Denmark, 1965-68; mgr. Bornholmerbanken, Roenne, Denmark, 1970—. Served to lt. Danish mil., 1968-70. Home: Ellebyvej 13, DK-3700 Roenne Denmark Office: Bornholmerbanken A/S, St Torv 15, DK-3700 Roenne Denmark

KALTSCHMID, JOCHEN HORST, educator; b. Giengen, Ger., Apr. 17, 1933; s. Karl August and Margot (Silberhorn) K.; m. Helga Schumann, Aug. 11, 1961; 1 child, Astrid. Dipl.Hdl., U. Mannheim, 1958, Dr.rer.pol., 1962. Wiss. asst. U. Mannheim, 1962-68; dozent, prof. Paedagogische Hochschule Reutlingen, 1968-73; prof. ednl. sci. U. Heidelberg, 1973—. Author: Menschsein i.d. ind. Gesellschaft, 1965; (with A.F. Caspers) Projektstudien zur Arbeitslehre, 1974, Die Schülerrolle zwischen Anpassung und Emanzipation, 1978, Didaktik d.Erwachsenbildung, 1986, Biographie und Pädagogik, 1988; editor: (with B. Goetz) Erziehungswiss. u. Soziologie, 1977, Sozialisation und Erziehung, 1978, (with R. Arnold) Erwachsenensozialisation und Erwachsenenbildung, 1986. Mem. Deutsche Gesellschaft fuer Erziehungswissenschaft, Ges.z. Foerd. paed. Forschung, Arbeitskreis Universitäre Erwachsenenbildung, Deutsche Schiller-Gesellschaft, Gutenberg-Gesellschaft, Hochschulverband. Home: Danziger Strasse 20, D-6095 Gustavsburg Hessen, Federal Republic of Germany Office: Univ Heidelberg, Erziehungswiss Seminar, Akademiestrasse 3, D-6900 Heidelberg Federal Republic of Germany

KALTWASSER, FRANZ GEORG, library director; b. Nordhausen, Fed. Republic of Germany, Nov. 6, 1927; s. Georg and Mathilde (Menge) K.; m. Sabine Richter, May 17, 1958; children: Tillmann, Stephanie. PhD, U. Munich, Fed. Republic of Germany, 1953. Asst. librarian Bavarian State Library, Munich, 1954-57, 1962-71, dir., 1972—; dir. Coburger Landesbibliothek, Coburg, Fed. Republic of Germany, 1958-61; mem. Bibliotheksausschuss of the Deutsche Forschungsgemeinschaft, 1980-85 (chmn. 1984-85), Beirat of the Deutsche Bibliothek, Frankfurt, 1988—; chmn. Beirat of the Stiftung Preussischer Kulturbesitz, Berlin, 1982—. Contbr. articles to profl. jours. Home: Hartwald Str 7, D-8000 Munich 70 Federal Republic of Germany Office: Bavarian State Library, Ludwigstr 16, D-8000 Munich Federal Republic of Germany

KALUZNIACKI, SOPHIA BARBARA, veterinarian; b. Warsaw, Poland, May 11, 1942; came to U.S., 1952; d. Roman Julius and Stena (Zubrzycki) Kaluzniacki; m. George G. Kulesza, Dec. 27, 1971; 1 child, Christina. Student, U. Ariz., 1960-63, Ariz. State U., 1963-64; D.V.M., Wash. State U., 1968. Asst. prof. U. Ariz., Tucson, 1968-70; staff veterinarian Humane Soc. Ariz., Phoenix, 1970-71; pvt. practice vet. medicine, Green Valley, Ariz., 1971—. Contbr. articles to profl. jours. Adv. bd., sec. Pima County Animal Control, Tucson, 1978—; mem., sec. Ariz. State Bd. Vet. Examiners, Phoenix, 1980—; bd. dirs. Soc. Prevention Cruelty to Animals of Ariz., Inc., Tucson, 1972—; sec. religious edn. bd. St. Luke's Cath. Ch., 1987-88, mem. parish council, co-dir. pre-Sunday sch. religious edn., tchr. kindergarten Sunday sch., lector, eucharistic minister. Mem. AVMA, Ariz. Vet. Med. Assn., So. Ariz. Vet. Med. Assn. Address: Green Valley Animal Hosp 220 E Duval Rd PO Box D Green Valley AZ 85622

KAMALIDENOV, SAKASH, Soviet government official; b. Kazakhstan, USSR, 1938. Ed., Gubkin Petroleum Inst., Moscow. 1st sec., mem. Politburo Cen. Com. Kazakh Komsomol, 1970-83; mem. Cen. Com. Kazakh Communist Party, 1971—, mem. Politburo, 1980—; mem. Politburo of Cen. Com. USSR Komsomol, 1974—; chair com. state security Council Ministers Kazakh Soviet Socialist Republic, 1983—; dep. chmn. Presidium, USSR Supreme Soviet, 1988—. Address: Council Ministers, Alma Ata Kazakhstan, USSR *

KAMANI, PARAG NAVNIT, advocate, business executive, writer; b. Bombay, India, Sept. 11, 1959; s. Navnit Ramji and Susmita Navnit (Shah) K. B.Com. with honors, Sydenham Coll. Commerce and Econs., Bombay, 1979, Govt. Diploma in Bus. Mgmt., 1980; Diploma in Journalism, Bombay Coll. Journalism, 1982; LL.B., Govt. Law Coll., Bombay, 1983. Bar: India 1983. Sole practice, Bombay, 1983—; chmn. Man-Tech Cons., Bombay, 1984—; regional dir. Transnat. Corp. Cons., New Delhi; free-lance writer. Contbg. editor TV & Video World, 1984—. Mem. Internat. Bar Assn., Bar Assn. Maharashtra. Club: Willingdon Sports (Bombay). Home: Kamani House 1st Floor, Dr G Deshmukh Marg, Bombay 400026, India Office: Kamani Chambers, 32 R Kamani Marg, Bombay 400038, India

KAMAREI, AHMAD REZA, biomedical company executive; b. Tehran, Iran, June 5, 1947; came to U.S., 1975; s. Khalil and Ozra (Javadian) K.; m. Zahra Nakhost, Aug. 24, 1971; children—Arzhang, Golbahar. B.S., Coll. Nutrition and Food Sci., Tehran, 1970; M.S., Sch. Agr., Karaj, Iran, 1975; M.S., MIT, 1977, Ph.D. in Food Sci. and Tech., 1982. Food-sci. officer Dept. Foods and Beverages, Shiraz, Iran, 1970-72; asst. mgr. Food Irradiation Ctr., Inst. of Standards, Tehran, 1972-75; vis. scientist Natick R&D Labs., 1975-77; research asst. MIT, Cambridge, 1976-82, research assoc. space foods, 1982-85; v.p. bioprocessing ops. Angio-Med. Corp., Boston, 1985—; vis. research prof. Boston U. Sch. Medicine, 1985—. Contbr. numerous articles to profl. jours.; patentee in field. Mem. Inst. Food Technologists, AAAS, Am. Chem. Soc., Sigma Xi. Office: Angio-Med Corp care Boston U Med Ctr 85 E Newton St Boston MA 02118

KÄMÄRI, JUHA KALEVI, environmental scientist, researcher, consultant; b. Helsinki, Finland, Sept. 10, 1957; s. Jorma Kalle Jalmari and Hertta Aliisa (Vehmersalo) K.; m. Suvi Tuulikki Ojala, June 29, 1979; 1 child, Paula. MS, U. Helsinki, 1983, PhD, 1988. Jr. scientist Internat. Inst. Applied Systems Analysis, Laxenburg, Austria, 1983, research scholar, 1984-85, 87—; research asst. U. Helsinki, 1982-83, researcher, 1983-84; research officer Nat. Bd. Waters, Helsinki, 1984, 85-86; sr. research officer Nat. Bd. Waters and Environment, Helsinki, 1986—; cons. working group on critical loads Nordic Council, Stockholm, 1985—; del. working groups on the environment UN/Econ. Commn. for Europe, OECD, others; sr. research specialist Ministry of the Environment, Helsinki, 1988. Editor: Environmental Impact Models to Assess Regional Acidification, 1988; contbr. numerous sci. articles to profl. jours. Mem. Finnish Limnol. Soc., Water Assn. Finland, Finnish Air Protection Soc. Office: Nat Bd Waters and Environment, P Rautatienkatu 21-B, 00101 Helsinki Finland

KAMATH, PADMANABH MANJUNATH, politics educator; b. Athikaribettu, India, Nov. 22, 1937; s. Manjunath M. and Sundari M. Kamath; m. Sushama Kamath, Apr. 24, 1966; children: Surendra, Suchita. BA with honors, U. Bombay, 1961, MA, 1964, PhD, 1979. Lectr. in polit. sci. Dr. Ambedkar Coll., Mahad, India, 1964-65, S.I.E.S. Coll., Bombay, 1965-72; Montague lectr. in politics U. Bombay, 1972-80, reader in Am. govt. and politics, 1980—; hon. sec. Vidyaprasarak Mandal, Bombay, 1971-76, 85—; vis. lectr. K.C. Coll. Journalism, Bombay, 1977-86; vis. prof. Fla. Internat. U., Miami, 1987. Author: Executive Privilege, 1981, American Foreign Policy: Who Makes It, 1985; editor: Indo-U.S. Relations, 1987. Grantee Fulbright Found., 1976, Am. Council Learned Socs., 1982, Ford Found., 1987. Mem. Am. Polit. Sci. Assn., Indian Assn. for Am. Studies (gen. sec. 1984-85), Indian Inst. Pub. Adminstrn. Home: Devidayal Rd Mulund W, Bombay 400 080, India Office: U Bombay, Bombay 400 098, India

KAMBA, WALTER JOSEPH, university administrator; b. Marondera, Zimbabwe, Sept. 6, 1931; s. Joseph Mafara and Hilda Kamba; m. Angeline Saziso Dube, 1960; children: Dennis Thabo, Mark Adrian, Julian Tendayi. BA, U. Cape Town, Rep. of South Africa, 1954, LLB, 1957; LLM, Yale U., 1963; LLD (hon.), U. Dundee, Scotland, 1982. Lectr. law U. Dundee, 1969-75, sr. lectr., 1975-77, dean faculty of law, 1977-80; vice-prin. U. Zimbabwe, Harare, 1980-81, vice-chancellor, 1981—; bd. dirs. Kingstons Booksellers, Zimbabwe, 1984—. Mem. council U. Zambia, 1981—, UN U., Tokyo, 1983—; mem. Nat. St. John's Ambulance Council, Zimbabwe, 1982-87; trustee Conservation Trust of Zimbabwe, 1981-87; bd. dirs. Electoral Supervisory Commn., Zimbabwe, 1984—; patron Commonwealth Legal Edn. Found., 1986—; former legal advisor Zimbabwe African Nat. Union—Patriotic Front. Decorated Officer dans l'Ordre des Palmes Academiques France, 1982; named Mgr. of Yr. Zimbabwe, 1985. Mem. Internat. Assn. Univs. (v.p. 1985—), Legal Resources Found. (trustee 1984—). Roman Catholic. Office: Univ of Zimbabwe, PO Box MP167, Mt Pleaseant, Harare Zimbabwe

KAMBUROWSKI, JERZY, economics educator; b. Chelm, Poland, Sept. 14, 1953; s. Feliks and Nadzieja (Jakimiuk) K.; m. Grazyna Wiazek, June 4, 1977; children: Marta, Maciej. M in Math., Tech. U., Wroclaw, Poland, 1977, PhD in Economical Sci., 1980; habilitation, Economical Acad., Wroclaw, Poland, 1987, 88. Asst. prof. econs. Wroclaw Tech. U., 1980-88, assoc. prof., 1988—. Contbr. articles to profl. jours. Chief of Solidarity Trade Union at Inst. pf Prodn. Engring. and Mgmt. of Wroctaw Tech. U., 1980-81. Recipient Rector awards Wroctaw Tech. Univ., 1981, 1985, 1986, 87. Mem. Polish Math. Soc., Polish Soc. Operational Research Systems Analysis. Roman Catholic. Home: Zemska 17/26, 54-438 Wroclaw Poland Office: Wroclaw Tech U, Smoluchowskiego 25, 50-327 Wroclaw Poland

KAMDANI, JUSUF, data processing executive; b. Bogor, Indonesia, Jan. 15, 1937. SMA, Canisius Coll., Indonesia, 1956. Adminstrv. clk. Trading Co., Jakarta, Indonesia, 1957-59; salesman Jakarta, Indonesia, 1960-69; dir., founder PT Datascrip Cos., Jakarta, Indonesia, 1970—. Author: Datascrip Management Guide/Systems, 1986. Club: Mercantile. Lodge: Rotary. Office: PT Datascrip, 18 Jl Angkasa, Jakarta 10610, Indonesia

KAMEI, MASAO, electric company executive; b. Kobe City, Japan, Apr. 20, 1916; s. Einosuke and Sei (Kanno) K.; grad. law Tokyo U., 1939; m. Hanae Kano, Nov. 6, 1943; 3 children. Dir. Sumitomo Electric Industries Ltd., Osaka, Japan, 1964—, exec. v.p., 1971-73, pres., 1973-82, chmn., 1982—; exec. dir. Fedn. Econ. Orgns., 1973—, Kansai Econs. Fedn., 1974—; v.p. Japan Fedn. Employers' Assn., 1977—. Commr. Local Govt. System Investigation Council, 1979—; chmn. Japanese Nat. Railways Reform Commn., 1983-87; vice chmn. Japan Productivity Ctr., 1987—; commr. Employment Council, 1986; chmn. Kansai Internat. Airport Co. Ltd., Osaka, 1988—; chmn. Housing and Bldg. Land Council, 1988—. Recipient Disting. Emperor's Blue Ribbon medal, 1976; first class Order of Sacred Treasure, 1986. Home: 34-11 Kyodo 1-chome, Setagaya-ku, Tokyo 156, Japan

KAMEI, YOSHIHIRO, metal processing executive; b. Matsuyama, Ehime, Japan, Dec. 12, 1937; s. Hirokichi and Makiko (Asano) Kamei; m. Takako Nakamura, Mar. 17, 1964; children: Nobuhiro, Sanae. M in Commerce, Waseda U., Tokyo, 1966. Cert. tax acct. Tchr. Ikebukuro High Sch. of Commerce, Itabashi, Tokyo, 1966-68; prof. Dokkyo U., Soka, Saitama, Japan, 1968-70; pres. Kameisanki Co., Matsuyama, Ehime, Japan, 1970—. Host family exchange program, Matsuyama, 1982—. Mem. Japan Soc. for Study Bus. Adminstrn. Lodge: Rotary (chmn. internat. com. Matsuyama 1987). Home: 5-8-50 Kuwabara, Matsuyama, Ehime 790, Japan

KAMEJIMA, KOHJI, control scientist; b. Kyoto, Japan, Feb. 7, 1949; s. Kohichi and Shigeko (Okamoto) K.; m. Michiko Fujii, May 27, 1979; children: Eriko, Kamejima, Kei'ichiroh. BE, Kyoto Inst. Tech., 1971, MS, 1973. Research scientist Cen. Research Lab. Hitachi, Ltd., Kokubunji, Tokyo, 1973-75; research scientist Mech. Engring. Research Lab., Hitachi, Ltd., Tsuchiura, Ibaraki, Japan, 1975—, control scientist, 1973—. Patentee in field. Mem. Am. Math. Soc., Soc. Indsrl. and Applied Math., IEEE, Am. Assn. Artificial Intelligence. Office: Mech Engring Research Lab, Hitachi Ltd, 502 Kandatsu, Tsuchiura, Ibaraki 300, Japan

KAMENKA, EUGENE, historian; b. Cologne, Fed. Republic of Germany, Apr. 3, 1928; arrived in Australia, 1937; s. Sergei and Nadja (Litvin) K.; m. Miriam Mizrahi, 1950 (div. 1964); children: Anat, Eri; m. Alice Erh-Soon Tay, Dec. 18, 1964. BA, U. Sydney, Australia, 1954; PhD, Australian Nat. U., 1964. Research scholar in philosophy Australian Nat. U., Canberra, 1955-57, research fellow in philosophy, 1961-62, research fellow, fellow, sr. fellow, profl. fellow, 1962-74, prof., 1975—; lectr. in philosophy U. of Malaya, Singapore, 1958-59; vis. prof. U. British Columbia, 1986; vis. fellow Trinity Coll., N.Y.C., 1968. Author: The Ethical Foundations of Marxism, 1962, Marxism and Ethics, 1969, The Philosophy of Ludwig Feuerbach, 1970; editor: A World in Revolution?: The University Lectures 1970, 1970, Paradigm for Revolution? The Paris Commune 1871-1971, 1972, Nationalism-The Nature and Evolution of an Idea, 1973, Community as a Social Ideal, 1982, Utopias, 1987; (with Alice E.-S. Tay) Human Rights, 1978,

Justice, 1979, Law-Making in Australia, 1980, Law and Social Control, 1980; (with R. S. Neale) Feudalism, Capitalism and Beyond, 1975; (with Robert Brown and Alice E.-S. Tay) Law and Society-The Crisis in Legal Ideals, 1978; (with Martin Krygier) Bureaucracy, 1979; (with Hon. Mr. Justice F. C. Hutley and Alice E.-S. Tay) Law and the Future of Society, 1979; (with F. B. Smith) Intellectuals and Revolution-Socialism and the Experience of 1848, 1979; (with R. S. Summers and W. Twining) Soziologische Jurisprudenz Und Realistische Utopiae Theorien Des Rechts, 1987; editor, translator: The Portable Karl Marx, 1983. Fellow Acad. Social Scis. in Australia (exec. mem. 1971-74), Australian Acad. Humanities (hon. sec., council 1976-81); mem. Australian Soc. for Legal Philosophy (pres. 1987—). Office: Australian Nat U, History of Ideas Unit, Canberra 2601, Australia

KAMENS, HAROLD, lawyer; b. Passaic, N.J., Apr. 28, 1917; s. Isadore and Esther (Reingold) K.; m. Bernice F., Jan. 11, 1949; children—Roberta Kamens Rabin, Edward A., Elizabeth. J.D., Rutgers U., 1940, B.S. in Acctg., 1945. Bar: N.J. 1941, N.Y. 1981, U.S. dist. ct. 1941, U.S. Ct. Appeals (3d cir.), U.S. Supreme Ct. 1970. Sole practice, Newark, 1946—; lectr. Seton Hall U., Fairleigh Dickinson U., Instn. Continuing Legal Edn. and numerous other profl., bus. groups; chmn. estate planning com. probate sect. N.J. State Bar. Mem. Fed. Bar Assn. (chmn. com. taxation 1976-77), N.J. Bar Assn. (chmn. com. fed. taxation 1967), Essex County Bar Assn. (chmn. 1974-65), Passaic County Bar Assn. (chmn. fed. taxation 1965-75), Assn. Fed. Bar N.J. (v.p. taxation 1977—). Contbr. articles to legal jours.; editor, chief 8 vols. on estate planning techniques; editor Fed. Tax Notes of N.J. Law Jour., 1947—; Office: 76 S Orange Ave South Orange NJ 07079

KAMENSKII, ZAHAR ABRAMOVICH, philosopher, educator, researcher; b. Lougansk, Ukraine, Aug. 25, 1915; s. Abram Zaharovich and Eugenia Lvovna (Berer) K.; m. Lidiya Mihailovlna Gerchikova, June 23, 1941; children: Dmitrii, Lubov. Degree in Philosophy and Literature, Moscow, 1938; postgrad. in Philosophy, Moscow State U., 1941; Doctor of Philosophy, Gosped Inst., Moscow, 1966. Sr. researcher Inst. Philosophy, Acad. Sci., Moscow, 1941-49, 68—; prof. logic Sch N 461 and others, Moscow, 1951-55; sci. editor, head dept. philosophy Soviet Ency., Moscow, 1957-68. Author of numerous books in field; contbr. articles to profl. jours. Served with Soviet Army, 1941-42. Decorated Order Gt. Patriotic War. Mem. Union Soviet Journalists, Club of Moscow Scientists. Home: 26 Petrovka St Apt 107, 103051 Moscow USSR Office: Inst Philosophy, Acad of Sci USSR, Volhonka 14, 121019 Moscow USSR

KAMEYAMA, YUICHI, construction company executive; b. Hekinan, Aichi, Japan, June 29, 1948; s. Masao and Mitsuko Kameyama; m. Mieko Kubota, May 5, 1977; children: Kenichiro, Yumi, Sinji. Bachelor, Nagoya U., Japan, 1971. With Matsumura-Jumi Co., Ltd., Nagoya City, 1971-73; with Hakutake-Kensetsu Co., Ltd., Hekinan City, Japan, 1973-74, mng. dir., 1974-85, pres., 1985—. Named 1st Class Architect Minister Construction, 1974. Mem. Aichi Soc. Architects and Bldg. Engrs. (dir.). Liberal Democratic Party. Buddhist. Home: 23 Sawatari-cho, Hekinan-city, Aichi 447, Japan Office: Hakutake Kensetsu, 1-27 Suma-cho, Hekinan, Aichi 447, Japan

KAMHI, SAMUEL VITALI, diversified manufacturing executive; b. Istanbul, Turkey, Mar. 30, 1922; s. Vitali S. and Suzanne (Kordova) K.; M.Sc. in Mech. Engring., Istanbul Tech. U., 1946; m. Birgit Marianne Waltenburg, May 15, 1963; children—Suzanne, Vili, Madlen. Co-founder Profile Co., Mecidiyekoy, Istanbul, 1952—; chmn. 2 cos., vice-chmn. 14 cos. Profilo Group. Served with Turkish Army, 1946-47. Mem. Mech. Engrs. Assn. Office: Profilo Holding, AS Mecidiyekoy, Istanbul Turkey

KAMIKAWA, ALDEN TANEMITSU, trade association executive; b. Fresno, Calif., Dec. 18, 1940; s. Thomas Taneichi and Miyeko Lorene (Kawamoto) K.; BA, San Francisco State U., 1963, MS, 1968. Vol., Peace Corps, Colombia, 1963-65; counselor U.S. War on Poverty Program, Job Corps, 1965-66; vocat. rehab. counselor Calif. Dept. Rehab., San Jose, 1968-71; asso. dir. manpower devel. and tng. dept. Nat. Assn. Home Builders, Washington, 1971-81, dir. ops., manpower devel. and tng. div., 1982-83; v.p., sec. Home Builders Inst., Washington, 1984—. Participant Pres.'s Jobs-for-Vets. Nat. Com., 1973; mem. com. Job Corps at Work Competition/Expo, Dept. Labor, Washington, 1981. Mem. Am. Rehab. Counseling Assn., Am. Soc. Assn. Execs., Am. Assn. for Counseling and Devel., Am. Vocat. Assn., Japanese Am. Citizens League. Asso. producer film: Build a Better Life, 1977. Home: 1721 P St NW Washington DC 20036 also: 8 Bridge Rd Middlesex Beach DE 19709 Office: Home Builders Inst 15th and M Sts NW Washington DC 20005

KAMIL, LAKSMINDRA USMAN, aircraft industry executive; b. Bandung, Indonesia, June 23, 1953; s. R. Kamil and R. A. Gunawati; m. Naindra Erica, July 17, 1978; children: Nalindra Arrianti Annalia, Ernindra Martiara Daianti. M of Aerospace Tech., Bandung Inst. Tech., 1975; M of Engring., Asian Inst. Tech., Bangkok, 1981. Researcher Indonesian Inst. Aerospace and Space, Jakarta, Indonesia, 1975-77, Pertamina Nat. Oil Co., Jakarta, 1977-78, Agy. for Application and Assessment Tech., Jakarta, 1978—; head market research P.T. Nurtanio, Indonesian Aircraft Industry, Jakarta; internat. sales mgr. P.T. IPTN, Indonesian Aircraft Industry, 1983-87, dep. dir. commerce, 1987—. Mem. AIAA, ASME, Indonesian Aero. and Astronautic Inst., Indonesian Engring. Assn. Office: IPTN Indonesian Aircraft Industries, JL Imam Bonjol 61 14th Floor, Jakarta Pusat, Indonesia

KAMIN, ROBERT YALE, management consultant; b. Lima, Ohio, Oct. 28, 1928; s. Samuel and Elizabeth (Bloom) K.; student Purdue U., 1946-49; B.S. in Econs., U. Pa., 1951; m. Arlene Lonker, May 25, 1951; children—Harriet Ann, Rena Esther, Edward Barry, Pamela Joy. With Neon Products, Inc., Lima, 1951-69, time and motion study engr., 1951-53, prodn. mgr., 1953-55, v.p. mfg., 1955-62, sec.-treas., 1962—; pres. B-K Office Equipment, Inc., 1962—; pres. Robert Y. Kamin Assos.; v.p. Corp. Fin. Assos., Phila., 1972-73; exec. v.p. Kardon Industries Inc., Phila., 1973-79, pres., chief operating officer, 1979-85; pres. Ajax/Acorn Mfg., Inc., a subs. of Kamin Corp., Collegeville, Pa., 1985—. Pres., Jr. Achievement, Lima, 1958-59. Mem. Am. Soc. for Personnel Adminstrn., Assn. Commerce. Lodge: Masons. Author: Supervisory Training in Small Industry, 1962; Modern Shop Management, 1969. Home: 648 Broad Acres Rd Narberth PA 19072 Office: 3930 Germantown Pike Collegeville PA 19426

KAMINSKY, ARTHUR CHARLES, lawyer; b. Bronx, N.Y., Dec. 29, 1946; s. Daniel and Claire (Sternberg) K.; m. Andrea Lynn Polin, Dec. 28, 1969; 1 child, Alexis Kate. BA cum laude with distinction, Cornell U., 1968; JD, Yale U., 1971. Bar: N.Y. 1974, U.S. Dist. Ct. (so. dist.) N.Y. 1975, U.S. Tax Ct. 1977, U.S. Supreme Ct. 1984. Assoc. Paul Weiss Rifkind Wharton & Garrison, 1973-74; ptnr. Taft & Kaminsky, N.Y.C., 1974—; pres. A.C.K. Sports, Inc. (now Athletes and Artists, Inc.), Plandome, N.Y., 1977—, Profl. Sports Investors, Inc., N.Y.C., 1982—; mem. selection com. U.S. Olympic Hockey Team, Mpls., 1980. Co-author: One Goal; A Chronicle of the 1980 U.S. Olympic Hockey Team, 1984; weekly columnist N.Y. Times, 1973-77; intern for 3d congl. dist. N.Y. Adlai E. Stevenson Meml., 1967. Dep. campaign mgr. Lindsay for Pres., N.Y.C., 1972; del. credentials com. Dem. Nat. Conv., Miami, 1972; adminstrv. asst. Rep. Michael Harrington, Washington, 1972-73; pres. Plandome Civic Assn., 1981-82. Recipient Outstanding Sr. award Cornell U., 1968, Friends of Educator award N.Y.C. Teachers Union, 1988; finalist Thurman Arnold moot ct. competition, 1970. Mem. N.Y. State Bar Assn., Assn. Bar City N.Y., Com. Entertainment and Sports, ABA, New Sch. Soc. Research (lectr.), Quill and Dagger, Phi Beta Kappa (hon.). Democrat. Jewish. Club: Friars. Home: 25 Middle Dr Plandome NY 11030 Office: Athletes and Artists Inc 421 Seventh Ave Suite 1410 New York NY 10001

KAMINSKY, LAWRENCE EDWARD, apparel manufacturing executive; b. Fitzgerald, Ga., Nov. 29, 1938; s. Herman Richard and Annie (Cohen) K.; m. Sandra Elizabeth Brown, May 24, 1964 (dec. Aug. 1969); m. Nan Sherry Landsman, May 8, 1977 (div. Jan. 1985); children: David, Samantha, Allison, George. BBA, Emory U., 1961. Pres., chmn. bd., chief exec. officer H.R. Kaminsky & Sons, Inc., Fitzgerald, 1961—; exec. v.p. H-K Corp., 1965-70; pres. Fitzgerald Investors, Inc., 1965-85; bd. dirs. Bank of Fitzgerald, Colony Bancorp. Mem. adv. staff to mayor of Fitzgerald, 1971—; mem. adv. council Ga. 8th Congl. Dist., 1976-82; chmn. Fitzgerald/Ben Hill County chpt. ARC 1978-79; bd. dirs. Alapaha area council Boy Scouts Am.; active Carter Inaugural Com., 1976, presdl. campaign, 1976, Bo Ginn for gov. campaign steering com., Ga.; pres. Fitzgerald Hebrew Congregation, 1972-73. Served with Air NG, 1961-65. Recipient cert. of appreciation Ga. div. adv. council ARC, 1978-79. Mem. Fitzgerald C. of C., Nat. Eagle Scout Assn., Alpha Epsilon Pi (life). Democrat. Clubs: Standard (Atlanta); Spring Hill Country (Tifton). Lodges: Rotary, Elks. Home: Rt 4 PO Box 1265 Tifton GA 31794 Office: N Dixie Hwy Fitzgerald GA 31750

KAMINSKY, RICHARD ALAN, lawyer; b. Toledo, Nov. 15, 1951; s. Jack and Sally (Kale) K. BA, Johns Hopkins U., 1973; JD, U. Mich., 1975. Bar: Ill. 1976, U.S. Dist. Ct. (no. dist.) Ill. 1983. Assoc. Vedder, Price, Kaufman & Kammholz, Chgo., 1976-83; atty. Borg-Warner Corp., Chgo., 1983—. Contbg. chpt. to book. Mem. Chgo. Bar Assn., Ill. Bar Assn., ABA, Ill. State C. of C., Am. Corp. Counsel Assn., Chgo. Vol. Legal Services Found. (vol. atty.). Home: 47 Williamsburg Rd Evanston IL 60203 Office: Borg-Warner Corp 200 S Michigan Ave Chicago IL 60604

KAMISAR, YALE, lawyer, educator; b. N.Y.C., Aug. 29, 1929; s. Samuel and Mollie (Levine) K.; m. Esther Englander, Sept. 7, 1953 (div. Oct. 1973); children: David Graham, Gordon, Jonathan; m. Christine Keller, May 10, 1974. A.B., NYU, 1950; LL.B., Columbia U., 1954; LL.D., John Jay Coll. Criminal Justice, City U. N.Y., 1978. Bar: D.C. 1955. Research assoc. Am. Law Inst., N.Y.C., 1953; assoc. firm Covington & Burling, Washington, 1955-57; assoc. prof. law, then prof. U. Minn. Law Sch., 1957-64; prof. law U. Mich. Law Sch., 1965—; vis. prof. law Harvard, 1964-65; Cons. to Nat. Adv. Commn. Civil Disorders, 1967-68, Nat. Commn. Causes and Prevention Violence, 1968-69. Mem. adv. com. model code pre-arraignment procedure, Am. Law Inst., 1965-75; Reporter-draftsman: Uniform Rules of Criminal Procedure, 1971-73; Author: (with W.B. Lockhart; J.H. Choper and S. Shiffrin) Constitutional Law: Cases, Comments and Questions, 6th edit, 1986, (with W. LaFave and J. Israel) Modern Criminal Procedure: Cases and Commentaries, 6th edit, 1986, (with F. Inbau and T. Arnold) Criminal Justice in Our Time, 1965, (with J. Grano and J. Haddad) Sum and Substance of Criminal Procedure, 1977, Police Interrogation and Confessions: Essays in Law and Policy, 1980; Contbr. articles to profl. jours. Served to 1st lt. AUS, 1951-52. Home: 2910 Daleview Dr Ann Arbor MI 48103

KAMIYAMA, MIKIO, immunochemist, biochemist; b. Kyoto, Japan, Mar. 25, 1936; came to U.S., 1967; s. Seiryo and Tome (Watanabe) K.; m. Minako Toyoguchi, Sept. 30, 1971; children—Eugene, Kay, June. B.S., Kyoto Prefectural U., 1962; D.M.Sc., Ph.D., U. Tokyo, 1967. Postdoctoral fellow Princeton U., 1967-68; research assoc. SUNY-Buffalo, 1969-70; sr. researcher Institut de Puthologie Molé culaire U. Paris, 1971-72, 73-74; vis. lectr. Institut der Physiologische Chemie, U. Marburg., W. Ger., 1972-73; attending staff St. Luke's-Roosevelt Hosp. Ctr. and Columbia U., N.Y.C., 1974-88; dir. Blood Research Inst. St. Michael's Med. Ctr. Newark. Contbr. articles to profl. jours. Mem. Am. Assn. Immunologists, Am. Fedn. for Clin. Research (sr.), N.Y. Acad. Sci., Harvey Soc., Japanese Biochem. Soc. Home: 301 Cathedral Pkwy New York NY 10026 Office: St Luke's-Roosevelt Hosp Ctr 421 W 113th St New York NY 10025

KAMM, JACOB OSWALD, economist; b. Cleve., Nov. 29, 1918; s. Jacob and Minnie K. (Christensen) K.; m. Judith Steinbrenner, Apr. 24, 1965; children: Jacob Oswald II, Christian P. A.B. summa cum laude, Baldwin-Wallace Coll., 1940, LL.D., 1963; A.M., Brown U., 1942; Ph.D., Ohio State U., 1948; LL.D., Erskine Coll., 1971. Asst. econs. Brown U., 1942; instr. Ohio State U., 1945; instr. Baldwin-Wallace Coll., 1943-46, asst. prof., 1947-48, assoc. prof., 1948; prof., dir. Baldwin-Wallace Coll. (Sch. Commerce), 1948-53; econ. cons. to U.S. Post Office, 1951; exec. v.p. Cleve. Quarries Co., 1953- 55, pres., 1955-67, chmn. bd., chief exec. officer, dir., 1967—; chmn. bd., pres., chief exec. officer Electric Furnace Co., 1985—; pres., treas., dir. Am. Shipbldg. Co., 1967-69, pres., 1973-74; dir. Nordson Corp., McDonald Money Market Fund, McDonald Tax-Exempt Fund, Oatey Co., United Screw and Bolt Corp. MTD Products, Inc.; bd. dirs., chmn. Canefco Ltd. Author: Decentralization of Securities Exchanges, 1942, Economics of Investment, 1951, Making Profits in the Stock Market, 3d rev. edit, 1966, Investor's Handbook, 1954; contbg. author: An Introduction to Modern Economics, 1952, Essays On Business Finance, 1953; weekly columnist econ. affairs Cleve. Plain Dealer, 1964-68; contbr. articles to profl. jours. Exec. bd. Lorain County Met. Park Bd., 1961-66; hon. mem. Mental Health Com., 1964-69; mem. St. Luke's Hosp. Assn., 1967—; mem. adv. council Cleve. Mus. Natural History, 1967—; bd. regents State of Ohio, 1969-72, pub. mem. Underground Gas Storage Com. Ohio, 1964-73; chmn. Lorain County Republican Finance Com., 1968-70, mem. exec. com., 1969-70; mem. Ohio Rep. Finance Com., 1969-70; charter life mem. bd. counselors Erskine Coll., 1962—; life fellow Cleve. Zool. Soc., trustee, 1966-77; trustee Fairview Gen. Hosp., 1966-68; trustee Baldwin-Wallace Coll., 1953-78, mem. exec. and investment coms., 1956-78, chmn. investment com., 1974-78, hon. life trustee, 1979—; mem. pres.'s club Ohio State U.; mem. com. grad. edn. and research Brown U., 1977, Red Cross of Constantine. Recipient Alumni Merit award Baldwin-Wallace Coll., 1956, Wisdom award of honor, 1970, Pro Mundi Beneficio medal Acad. Humanities, Sao Paulo, Brazil, 1975, Winston Churchill Medal of Wisdom, 1988; named an Eminent Churchill fellow of the Wisdom Soc., 1988; inducted into the Hall of Excellence for the Ohio Found. of Ind. Colls., 1988. Mem. Am. Econs. Assn., Royal Econ. Soc., Am. Finance Assn., AAUP, Indsl. Assn. North Central Ohio (pres. 1960), Ohio Mfrs. Assn. (exec. com. 1970—, trustee, chmn. bd. trustees 1975-77), Early Settlers Assn. of Western Res. (life mem.), Newcomen Soc. N.Am., Assn. Ohio Commodores, Nat. Alumni Assn. Baldwin-Wallace Coll. (pres. 1961-63), John Baldwin Soc., Ohio Soc. N.Y., Phi Beta Kappa, Phi Alpha Kappa, Delta Phi Alpha, Delta Mu Delta, Beta Gamma Sigma. Methodist. Clubs: Brown University (N.Y.C.); Valley of Cleve. (treas. emeritus), Union (Cleve.); Duquesne (Pitts.); Clifton (Lakewood, Ohio). Lodges: Masons (33 degree), Shriners, Jesters. Home: PO Box 718 Sanibel FL 33957 Office: 435 W Wilson St Salem OH 44460

KAMM, JUERGEN DIETMAR, English literature educator; b. Wuppertal, Fed. Republic Germany, Oct. 11, 1955; s. Guenther and Marianne (Goerlich) K.; m. Sylvia Schaal, July 29, 1983. Dip. teaching, U. Wuppertal, 1982, D in Philosophy with honors, 1986. Fgn. lang. asst. Chalvedon Sch., Basildon, Essex, Eng., 1978-79; tchr. English Gymnasium Am Kothen, Wuppertal, 1980-82; lectr. English lit. U. Wuppertal, Fed. Republic Germany, 1982—; lectr. English lang. and lit. Volkshochschule, Wuppertal and Remscheid, 1980—. Co-author: The English Novel about World War II, 2 vols., 1987; contbr. articles to profl. jours. Served with German army, 1974-75. Recipient Soc. of Friends of Wuppertal U. scholarship, 1986, Original Research prize, 1988. Mem. Internat. Assn. for Study Anglo-Irish Lit. Home: Ibacher Muehle 1, 5630 Remscheid Federal Republic of Germany

KAMMAN, ALAN BERTRAM, communications consulting company executive; b. Phila., Jan. 25, 1931; s. Daniel Lawrence and Sara Belle K.; m. Madeleine Marguerite Pin, Feb. 15, 1960; children: Alan Daniel, Neil Charles. B.C.E., Swarthmore Coll., 1952. With Bell Telephone Co. Pa., Phila., 1952-69; with Arthur D. Little, Inc., Cambridge, Mass., 1969-85; v.p. telecommunications scis. Arthur D. Little, Inc., 1977-81, v.p. corp. staff, 1981-85; pres. Telematix Intern. Ltd., Boston, 1985-87; nat. dir. telecommunications markets KPMG Peat Marwick, Lexington, Mass., 1987—; dir. Modern Gourmet, Inc.; mem. adv. bd. Telecom 75, Telecom 79, Telecom 83. Contbr. articles to telecommunications and computer jours. Bd. dirs. U.S. Council World Communications Yr.; mem. North Country bd. Appalachian Mountain Club. Chosen mem. World Link (orgn. composed of most influential 33,000 people in the world as chosen by World Econ. Forum, Geneva), 1988. Office: Nolan Norton & Co 1 Cranberry Hill Lexington MA 02173

KAMMERER, KELLY CHRISTIAN, lawyer; b. N.Y.C., Nov. 29, 1941; s. William Henry and Edith (Langley) K. B.A., U. Notre Dame, 1963; LL.B., U. Va., 1968. Bar: Va. 1968, N.Y. 1969, D.C. 1969, Fla. 1969. Peace Corps vol., Colombia, 1963-65; Reginald Heber Smith, atty./fellow U. Pa., Washington, 1968-70; atty.-advisor, dep. gen. counsel Peace Corps, Washington, 1970-74; atty.-advisor AID, Dept. State, Washington, 1975-76, asst. gen. counsel, 1976-78, sr. dep. gen. counsel, 1978-82, counselor, 1981-82, dir. congl. relations, 1983—. Recipient Disting. Honor award AID, 1979, Equal Opportunity award, 1982; presdl. rank of Disting. Sr. Exec., 1984. Mem. Inter-Am. Bar Assn., Soc. Internat. Law. Address: 2838 27th St NW Washington DC 20008

KAMMHOLZ, THEOPHIL CARL, lawyer; b. Jefferson County, Wis., Mar. 23, 1909; s. Frederic Carl and Emma (Donner) K.; m. Lura Walker, Apr. 22, 1935 (dec.); children: Carolyn Kammholz Hudson, Robert (dec.). LL.B., U. Wis., 1932. Bar: Wis. 1932, Ill. 1945, D.C. 1964. Asso. Stephens, Sletteland & Sutherland, Madison, Wis., 1932-34, Bogue & Sanderson, Portage, Wis., 1934-35; ptnr. Bogue, Sanderson & Kammholz, Portage, 1935-42; regional counsel War Labor Bd., Chgo., 1943; ptnr. Pope and Ballard, Chgo., 1944-52, Vedder, Price, Kaufman & Kammholz, Chgo., 1952-55, 57—; exec. dir. Chgo. Foundrymen's Assn., 1952; gen. counsel NLRB, Washington, 1955-57; dir. Fosdick Enterprises, Inc.; mem. legal adv. council Mid-Am. Legal Found., 1977—. Co-author: Practice and Procedure Before the NLRB; Contbr. articles profl. jours. Adv. U.S. del. ILO Conf., Geneva, 1954. Mem. ABA, Ill., Wis., Chgo. bar assns., Internat. Soc. Labor Law (U.S. exec. com. 1983—), Am. Arbitration Assn. (adv. council 1982), Wis. Law Alumni Assn. (pres. Chgo. 1953-55), Chgo. Assn. Commerce and Industry (chmn. labor-mgmt. relations com. 1966-68, v.p. govtl. affairs 1968-70, dir., mem. policy com. 1968—, sr. council 1978—), Order of Coif, Delta Sigma Rho, Lambda Chi Alpha. Clubs: North Shore Country (bd. govs. 1971-74), Monroe, Law (exec. com. 1976-80, pres. 1978-79), Metropolitan, University (Chgo.); Kenwood Country (Washington); Portage (Wis.) Country. Home: 1323 Sunview Ln Winnetka IL 60093 Office: Vedder Price Kaufman & Kammholz 222 N LaSalle St Chicago IL 60601 also: 1919 Pennsylvania Ave Washington DC 20006 also: 1 Dag Hammarskjold Plaza New York NY 10017

KAMP, ARTHUR JOSEPH, JR., lawyer; b. Rochester, N.Y., July 22, 1945; s. Arthur Joseph and Irene Catherine (Ehrstein) K.; m. Barbara Hays, Aug. 24, 1968. B.A., SUNY, 1968, J.D., 1970. Bar: N.Y. 1971, U.S. Dist. Ct. (we. dist.) N.Y. 1971, Va. 1973, U.S. Dist. Ct. (ea. dist.) Va. 1973. Atty. Neighborhood Legal Services, Buffalo, 1971; assoc. Diamonstein & Drucker, Newport News, Va., 1972-77; ptnr. Diamonstein, Drucker & Kamp, Newport News, 1977-84, Kamp & Kamp, Newport News, 1984-87, Kaufman & Canoles, 1987— ; v.p., dir. Peninsula Legal Aid Ctr., Inc. Bd. dirs. Hidenwood Presbyn. Ch. PreSch. Served to lt. USAF, 1971-72. Mem. ABA, Newport News Bar Assn. (past bd. dirs., chmn. legal aid com.), Va. Bar Assn. Democrat. Club: Rotary (bd. dirs. Newport News chpt., pres. 1987-88). Office: Kaufman & Canoles 11832 Rock Landing Rd Suite 101 Newport News VA 23606

KAMPELMAN, MAX M., ambassador, lawyer; b. N.Y.C., Nov. 7, 1920; s. Joseph and Eva (Gottlieb) Kampelmacher; m. Marjorie Buetow, Aug. 21, 1948; children: Anne, Jeffrey, Julie, David, Sarah. AB, NYU, 1940, JD, 1945; MA, U. Minn., 1946, PhD, 1951; PhD (hon.), Hebrew U. of Jerusalem, 1982; LHD (hon.), Hebrew Union Coll., 1984, Georgetown U., 1984; LLD (hon.), Bates, 1986; LHD (hon.), U. Minn., 1987, Bar Ilan U., 1987, Jewish Theological Seminary of Am., 1988, N.Y. U., 1988. Bar: N.Y. 1947, D.C. 1950, Md. 1956. Mem. research staff Internat. Ladies Garment Workers Union, N.Y.C., 1940-41; instr. polit. sci. U. Minn., 1946-48; legis. counsel to U.S. Senator Hubert H. Humphrey, Washington, 1949-55; ptnr. Fried, Frank, Harris, Shriver & Kampelman, Washington, 1956-85; sr. advisor U.S. Delegation to UN, 1966-67; ambassador, chmn. U.S. Delegation to Conf. on Security and Cooperation in Europe, Madrid, 1980-83; ambassador, head U.S. Delegation to Negotiations on Nuclear and Space Arms, 1985—; counselor of the U.S. Dept. of State, 1987—; vice chmn. Mayor's Com. on Charter Reform, Mpls., 1947-48; faculty Sch. for Workers U. Wis., summers 1947-48; faculty polit. economy Bennington Coll., Vt., 1948-50; vis. professorial lectr. Dept. Govt. Howard U., 1954-56; vis. prof. polit. sci. Claremont Coll., Calif., summer 1963. Author: The Communist Party vs. The C.I.O.: A Study in Power Politics, 1957, (with Kirkpatrick) The Strategy of Deception, 1963, Three Years at the East-West Divide, 1983; co-author: (with Kirkpatrick) Congress Against the President, 1976; contbr. articles to profl. publs.; moderator Washington Week in Rev. program Eastern Ednl. Network, 1967-70. Pres. Friends of Nat. Zoo, 1958-60, now hon. pres.; hon. vice chmn. Anti-Defamation League B'nai B'rith, 1981—, vice chmn., 1977-81; pres. Am. Friends of Hebrew U., 1975-77, chmn. bd., 1977-80, now chmn. emeritus; co-chmn. U.S. Delegation to observe elections in El Salvador, 1984; chmn. Freedom House, N.Y.C., 1983-85; chmn. emeritus Greater Washington Telecommunications Assn. (WETA-TV); v.p. Helen Dwight Reid Ednl. Found., 1959-85, Jewish Publ. Soc., 1978-85; hon. gov. The Hebrew U. Jerusalem, gov., 1973-85, chmn. Truman Research Inst. for Advancement of Peace, 1983-85; mem. exec. com. Com. on Present Danger, 1976-85; vice chmn. Coalition for a Dem. Majority, 1977-85; overseer Coll. V.I., 1963-80; bd. govs. U. Haifa, 1984-85, Tel Aviv U., 1984-85; bd. advisors Kennedy Inst. Ethics, 1984-85; chmn. Woodrow Wilson Internat. Ctr. for Scholars, 1979-81, bd. trustees, 1979—; trustee Law Cen. Found. NYU, 1978-85; bd. dirs. Georgetown U., 1978-84, Mt. Vernon Coll., 1972-80, U.S. Inst. Peace, 1985-86, Hebrew Immigrant Aid Soc., 1981-85, Am. Peace Soc., 1973-85. Mem. ABA (standing com. on law and nat. security 1979-85), Fed. Bar Assn., Bar Assn. D.C., Am. Polit. Sci. Assn. (treas. 1956-58), D.C. Polit. Sci. Assn. (pres. 1955). Clubs: Cosmos, Army-Navy. Home: 3154 Highland Pl NW Washington DC 20008 Office: Dept State 2201 C St NW Room 7250 S/DEL Washington DC 20520

KAN, DIANA ARTEMIS MANN SHU, artist; b. Hong Kong, Mar. 3, 1926; came to U.S., 1949, naturalized, 1964; d. Kam Shek and Sing-Ying (Hong) K.; m. Paul Schwartz, May 24, 1952; 1 son, Kan Martin Meyer Sing-Si. Student, Art Students League, 1949-51, Beaux Arts, Paris, 1951-52, Grande Chaumiere, Paris, 1951-52. fgn. corr., city editor Cosmorama Pictorial Mag., Hong Kong, 1968; art reviewer Villager, N.Y.C., 1960-69; lectr. Birmingham So. U., N.Y. U., Mills Coll., St. Joseph's Coll., Phila. Mus. Author: White Cloud, 1938, The How and Why of Chinese Painting, 1974; One-man shows, London, 1949, 63, 64, Paris, 1949, Hong Kong, 1937, 39, 41, 47, 48, 52, Shanghai, 1935, 37, 39, Nanking, 1936, 38, Macao, 1947, 48, Bankok, 1947, Casablanca, 1951, 52, San Francisco, 1950, 67, N.Y.C., 1950, 54, 59, 67, 71, 72, 74, 78, Naples, 1971, Elliot Mus., Stuart, Fla., 1967, 73, Bruce Mus., Greenwich, Conn., 1969, Nat. Hist. Mus., Taipei, Taiwan, 1971, N.Y. Cultural Center Mus., 1972, Galerie Barbarella, Palm Beach, Fla., 1972, Hobe Sound (Fla.) Galleries, 1976, 81, Nat. Arts Club, 1979, others; exhibited in group shows, Royal Acad. Fine Arts, London, 1963-64, Royal Soc. Painters, London, 1964, Am. Water Color Soc., N.Y.C., 1966-77, Nat. Acad., N.Y.C., 1967, 69, 70, 74, 75, 76, Nat. Arts Club, N.Y.C., 1964-77, Charles and Emma Frye Mus., Seattle, 1968, Willamette U., Salem, Oreg., 1968, Columbia (S.C.) Mus. Art, 1969, Allied Artists of Am., 1957-77, Audubon Artist, 1974, 76; represented permanent collections, Met. Mus. Art, Phila. Mus. Art, Nelson Gallery, Elliot Mus., Fla., Bruce Mus., Dalhousie U., Atkin Mus., Kansas City, Nat. Hist. Mus., Taipei. Recipient Summer Festival award N.Y.C., 1959, 1st Prize Nat. Art Club, 1982; named Most Outstanding Profl. Woman of Year Washington Sq. chpt. N.Y. League Bus. and Profl. Women's Club, 1971. Fellow Royal Soc. Arts; mem. Pen and Brush Club (dir. 1968, Brush Fund award 1968, Alice S. Buell Meml. award 1969), Nat. Acad. Design (assoc., John Pike Meml. award 1987), Am. Watercolor Soc. (traveling award 1968, Marthe T. McKinnon award 1978, dir. 1975-77), Art Students League, Nat. League Pen Women, Audubon Artists (v.p. 1983), Allied Artists Am. (Barbara Vassilieff Meml. award 1969, Ralph Fabri Meml. award 1975, corr. sec. 1975-78), Catharine Lorillard Wolf Art Club (Anna Hyatt Huntington bronze medal 1970, 74, Gold medal of honor 1982). Clubs: Overseas Press Am., Lotos, The Nat. Arts (N.Y.C.). Home: 15 Gramercy Park S New York NY 10003

KAN, HSIN-CHIA, research scientist; b. Taiwan, Jan. 6, 1952; came to U.S., 1974; s. Tze-Ming and Wei-Hsin (Hsi) K.; B.S. in Physics, Nat. Tsing Hua U., Taiwan, 1974; Ph.D. in Materials Sci., U. Wis., Madison, 1979; m. Ih Chang, Sept. 10, 1977. Research asst. U. Wis., 1975-79; research scientist Eastman Kodak Co., Rochester, N.Y., 1979—. Mem. Soc. Rheology, Sigma Xi. Contbr. articles profl. jours. Office: Research Lab 1669 Lake Ave Rochester NY 14658

KAN, KON CHEONG, architect; b. Singapore, Apr. 15, 1954; s. Kan Yew and Chew Sui Fong. BArch, U. Singapore, 1980. Registered architect, Singapore. Architect Housing and Devel. Bd., Singapore, 1980-81; sr. architect Ong Chin Bee Architects, Singapore, 1981-86; prin. architect KC Kan and Assocs. Architects, Singapore, 1986—. Contbr. monthly articles on archtl. design and geomancy. Mem. Singapore Inst. Architects (corporate, com. mem. 1985-88), Royal Australian Inst. Architects (assoc.), Malaysia Inst. Architects (acad.), Singapore Inst. Mgmt., Nat. U. Singapore Soc. Home: Block 27 Telok Blangah Way, 02-1014, Singapore 0409 Singapore

Office: KC Kan & Assocs Architects, 470 N Bridge Rd, Singapore Fin House 0414, Singapore 0718 Singapore

KAN, PAUL MAN-LOK, computer company executive; b. Canton, China, Feb. 12, 1947; came to Hong Kong, 1947; s. Joseph and Winnie (Mok) K.; m. Maria Chan; children—Katherine, Joanne. M.B.A., Chinese U. of Hong Kong. Cert. data processing Programmer, Govt. Hong Kong, 1967-70; systems analyst Swire Group, Hong Kong, 1970-72; sr. systems analyst, Asiadata, Hong Kong, 1972-74, cons., 1974-76, sr. cons., 1976-78, mktg. mgr., 1978-85, gen. mgr., 1985-87; computer programmer compere TVB (HK) Ltd., Hong Kong, 1983, pres. Champion Group, Champion Technologies Ltd., Chinese Computers Ltd., Chinese Data Processing Co., Ltd., Chinese Paging Co., Ltd., Macintosh Computer Co., Ltd., Lisa Computer Co., Ltd., bd. dirs. Y. S. Kan & Co., Good Time Pub. Ltd., Jockey Daily News, Inside Racing News, Showa Info. Co. (Hong Kong) Ltd., G0-Video Inc., 1987—. Founding chmn. MBA (Chinese U.) Assn., Hong Kong, 1978. Fellow Inst. Data Processing; mem. Brit. Computer Soc., Inst. Mgmt. Services; assoc. Chartered Inst. Transport, Inst. Bankers. Clubs: Royal HK Jockey, Royal HK Golf (Hong Kong). Contbr. articles to profl. jours. Home: PO Box 20003, Hong Kong Hong Kong Office: Champion Group Gloucester, Tower 42/F Landmark, Hong Kong Hong Kong

KAN, YUEN-SHUN WINSTON, architect; b. Hong Kong, Oct. 25, 1941; s. Chi-nam and Pak-yuk (Lau) K.; m. Miao-wah Rosemary Tham, Jan. 31, 1972; children: Yun-lin William, Yun-kuen Patrick. BArch, Melbourne (Australia) U., 1968. Architect Krantz % Sheldon, Perth, Australia, 1967-70, Wong & Tung & Assocs., Hong Kong, 1970-71; architect-in-charge campus devel. Bldgs. Office, Chinese U., Hong Kong, 1971—; design cons. Liu Hok Yan & Assocs., Hong Kong, 1986—. Prin. works include: Karringyip Girls High Sch. and various high-density residential devels., Perth, 1967-70; Mei Foio Sun Chuen Residential Devel., State 4, Hong Kong, 1970-71; structures at Chinese U. Hong Kong including New Acad. Bldg., Basic Med. Scis. Bldg., Sports Centre Complex, Transport and Security Bldg., Univ. Sci. Bldg., Univ. Estate and Maintenance Bldg., Yali Guest House, 1971—; contbr. articles to archtl. publs. Research grantee Univ. Poly. Grants Com. Hong Kong and Govt. of The Netherlands, 1978. Fellow Royal Australian Inst. Architects; mem. Hong Kong Inst. Architects, Royal Inst. Brit. Architects. Home: Apt A Kings Ct, 11th Floor, 11 Man Fuk Rd, ;Kowloon, Hong Kong Hong Kong Office: Bldgs Office, Chinese U Hong Kong, Shatin NT, Hong Kong Hong Kong

KANA, SAID MOHIDINE, financial advisor, petroleum consultant; b. Damascus, Syria, Nov. 3, 1936; s. Mohidine Said and Ramzieh Mohamad (Mahayri) K.; m. Rula Ali Hamwieh, Nov. 11, 1962; children—Rual, Enji, Amr. B.Com., Cairo U., 1960; M.B.A., N.Y. U., 1966, Ph.D., 1970. Chartered acct., Syria. Asst. prof. Fordham U., N.Y.C., 1968-70, Aleppo (Syria) U., 1970-72; mgr. Saba & Co., Dubai, United Arab Emirates, 1972-73; div. chief Arab Fund Econ. and Social Devel., Kuwait, 1973-78; group v.p. B.B. Naft Group, Geneva, Switzerland, 1978-83; pres. Fin. and Cons. Trust (FACT) SA, Geneva, Switzerland, 1983—; fin. advisor Bassatne Holding Co. SA, Luxembourg, 1979-87. Author: Quantitative Analysis, 1971; contbr. articles profl. jours. Syrian Govt. scholar, 1955; Aleppo U. postgrad. scholar, 1963; fellow N.Y. U., 1966; recipient Founders Day award N.Y. U., 1970. Mem. Econ. Scis. Assn., Inst. Chartered Accts. Syria, Am. Acctg. Assn., Arab Soc. Cert. Accts. London. Home: 10 Ave Theodore Vernes, 1290 Versoix, Geneva Switzerland Office: Fin and Cons Trust (FACT) SA, 10a Ave Theodore Vernes, 1290 Versoix, Geneva Switzerland

KANADA, HIROSHI, ladies' accessories company executive; b. Nagano, Japan, Sept. 13, 1928. LLB, Waseda U., Tokyo, 1953. Pres. Kyoai Co., Ltd., Tokyo, 1955—, Kyoai Real Estate Co., Ltd., Tokyo, 1955—, Aurora Fashions Inc., Tokyo, 1955—. Mem. Tokyo Handbags Mfrs. Assn. (bd. dirs.), Tokyo Handbags Wholesalers (v.p.). Lodge: Rotary. Office: Kyoai Co Ltd, 21-6 Yanagibashi, 2-chome, Taito-ku, Tokyo 111, Japan

KANAI, ATSUSHI JAMES, cultured pearls company executive; b. Nagasaki, Kyushu, Japan, May 15, 1915; s. John W. and Asano (Kanai) C.; m. Noriko Indow, May 20, 1952; children—George, Edward. B.A., English Mission, 1935. Pres. Japan Pearl Exporter's Assn., Kobe, 1969—; dir. Japan Pearl Promoting Soc., Tokyo, 1969—. Recipient Blue Ribbon medal, Prime Minister Japan, 1972. Club: Rotary (Kobe, Japan). Home: 2-2 Kitanocho 1-chome, Chuo-ku, Kobe, Hyogu, Honshu 650, Japan

KANAMORI, MASAO, heavy industries company executive; b. Ehime Prefecture, Japan, Dec. 18, 1911; m. Keiko Akamatsu, 1939; 4 children. Ed. Kyushu Imperial U. With Mitsubishi Heavy Industries Ltd., 1935-50, 64—, dir., 1969-71, mng. dir., 1971-75, exec. v.p., 1975-77, pres., 1977-81, chmn., 1981—; with West Japan Heavy Industries Ltd., 1950-52, Mitsubishi Shipbldg. & Engring. Co. Ltd., 1952-64. Recipient Purple Ribbon medal, 1968. Office: care Mitsubishi Heavy Industries Ltd, 5-0-1 Marunouchi, 2-chome, Chiyoda-ku, Tokyo Japan *

KANARI, KISHIRO, capital management company executive; b. Mito, Japan, Nov. 27, 1929; s. Yoshimasa and Haru Kanari; m. Keiko Okazaki, Nov. 18, 1958; children: Satoshi, Hiroshi. BA in Polit. Economy, Waseda U., Tokyo, 1953. Mng. dir. Nippon Kangyo Kakumaru Securities Co., Tokyo, 1973-85; now pres. Kangyo Kakumaru Capital Mgmt. Co. Ltd., Tokyo. Mem. Japan Securities Investment Advisors Assn. (bd. dirs. 1987). Mem. Liberal Democratic Party. Home: 3-40-16, Ooka, Minami-ku, Yokahama 232, Japan Office: Kangyo Kakumaru Capital Mgmt Co Ltd, 1-6-10, Kayabacho, Chuo-ku, Tokyo 103, Japan

KANAZAWA, SHIGEMORI, city planner; b. Tokyo, Japan, May 29, 1951; s. Hidesada and Yoshie (Sonobe) K.; m. Michiko Sakai, Jan. 8, 1981; children: Hideharu, Hideaki. BArch, Kyoto U., Japan, 1975; MArch, Kyoto U., 1978; student, Inst. Univ. Architecture Venice, 1975-76. Planner Nikken Sekkei Ltd., Osaka, Japan, 1978—; lectr. Osaka U., 1986. Co-author: Kyomachiya, 1976, Mizube to Toshi, 1986; contbr. articles, papers to profl. jours. Mem. com. 21st century housing activities plan, Osaka City Govt., 1984, road com. for revitalizing city area, 1985. Mem. Archtl. Inst. Japan, Archtl. Assn. Japan (mem. editorial com., 33rd Young Engr. award., 1986), City Planning Inst. Japan, Japan Assn. Planning Adminstrn. Home: 16-11 Koyoen Nishiyama-cho, Nishinomiya Japan 662 Office: Nikken Sekkei Ltd, 5-21-1 Koraibashi, Higashi-ku Osaka 541, Japan

KANAZIR, DUŠAN, molecular biologist, biochemist, educator; b. Mošorin, Serbia, Yugoslavia, June 28, 1921; s. Todor and Draginja (Stefanovic) K.; m. Mersija Kolakovic; 1 child, Selma. Student, Faculté de Medicine, Paris, 1949; Diploma of Graduation, Faculty of Medicine, Belgrade, Yugoslavia, 1949; PhD in Physiol. Scis., U. Libre, Brussels, 1955. Asst. prof. U. Belgrade, 1957, assoc. prof. Faculty of scis., 1963, prof. Faculty of scis., 1970-87; head lab. biology Inst. Boris Kidrič, Vinča, Yugoslavia, 1950-65, head lab. molecular biology, endocrinology, 1968-74, sci. counselor, 1974—; mem. Fed. Commn. on Nuclear Energy, Belgrade, 1956-65, Fed. Council for Coordiation of Research; expert IAE Agy. Vienna Atomic Ctr., Buenos Aires, 1966-71; counsellor CIBA Sci. Consultation Council, Belgrade, London, 1970-87. Author chpts. to books. V.p. Yugoslav Pugwash Conf., Belgrade, 1959-61, mem., Ljubljana, 1986—, Yugoslav League for Peace, Equality and Independence of People, Belgrade, 1960-65,. Decorated Merit for Nation with Gold Star Presidium of the SFRY, Belgrade, 1965, Brotherhood and Unity with a Golden Wreath, 1976, Commdr. of Legion of Honour Pres. of Republic of France, 1984. Mem. Belgian Soc. Biochemistry, Intern Soc. Cell Biology (exec. bd. 1961-68), European Soc. Radiology (Presidium 1965-68), European Soc. Biochemistry, Intern Jour. of Photochemistry and Photobiology, Japan Jour. of Radiation Research (editor 1980—). Home: Save Kovačeviča 20/III, 11000 Belgrade Yugoslavia Office: Acad Sci & Arts, Knez-Mihailova 35, 11000 Belgrade Yugoslavia

KANCHELI, GUYA ALEXANDROVICH, composer; b. Tbilisi, Georgia, USSR, Aug. 10, 1935; s. Alexander Ivanovich and Agnessa Levanovna (Khechinashvili) K.; m. Valentina Bidzinovna Jikia, Aug. 23, 1946; children: Sandro, Nato. Grad., Georgian State Conservatory, Tbilisi, 1963. musical cons. Rustaveli Theatre, Tbilisi, USSR, 1972—; prime sec. Care Union Georgian composers, Tbilisi, 1984—; sec. Care Union Soviet Composers, Moscow, 1986—. Composer: Seven symphonies, 1967-86; film scores including Children of the Sea, 1964, Don't Grieve!, 1969, The Jug, 1970, The Neighbors, 1971, White Stones, 1972, When Almonds Bloom, 1972, Cranks, 1973, A Captive in the Caucasus, 1975, The Races, 1977, Mimino, 1977, The Quarry, 1979, Tears Dropping, 1982, Amiran's Fairy Tales, 1983, The Blue Mountains, 1985, Kindza-dza, 1986; play scores including The Accusation, 1964, The Good Woman of Setzuan, 1969, Medea, 1971, The Caucasian Chalk Circle, 1975, Easy Money, 1978, Richard III, 1979, As You Like It, 1980, The Centenary, 1981, King Lear, 1987, Electra, 1987; opera Music for the Living, 1983. Dep., State PArliament Georgia, Tbilisi, 1984. Recipient State Prize USSR, 1976, Georgia, 1981. Fellow Care Union Soviet Composers; mem. Care Union Soviet Cinematographists. Office: Care Union of Soviet Composers, Plekhanov 123, 380064 Tbilisi, Georgia USSR

KANDEL, NELSON ROBERT, lawyer; b. Balt., Sept. 15, 1929; m. Brigitte Kleemaier, Feb. 28, 1957; children—Katrin, Christopher, Peter. B.A., U. Md., 1951, LL.B., 1954. Bar: Md. 1954, D.C., U.S. Supreme Ct. Prin. law firm, Balt., 1957—; mem. legal panel ACLU. Trustee Richmond Fellowship Halfway House, Balt. Served with U.S. Army. Mem. ABA, Md. Bar Assn., Balt. Bar Assn. Democrat. Lutheran. Office: 415 One North Charles Baltimore MD 21201

KANDIL, OSAMA ABDEL-MOHSIN, engineering educator, researcher; b. Cairo, Oct. 10, 1944; came to U.S., 1971, naturalized, 1977; s. Abdel-Mohsin Moses and Attiat (Sayed) K.; m. Rawia Ahmed Fouad, Oct. 20, 1968; children—Dalya Osama, Tarek Osama. B.S. with honors, Cairo U., 1966; M.S., Villanova U., 1972; Ph.D., Va. Poly. Inst., 1974. Instr. mech. engring. Cairo U., 1966-70; teaching asst. Villanova U., 1971-72; research asst. Va. Poly. Inst., Blacksburg, 1972-74, asst. prof., 1975-78; assoc. prof. mech. engring. Old Dominion U., Norfolk, Va., 1978-84, prof., 1985—; vis. prof. King Saud U., Riyadh, Saudi Arabia, 1983-84; organizer, chmn. tech. sessions various profl. confs. and speaker in field. Reviewer, AIAA Jour., Jour. Aircraft, NSF, Army Research Office. Contbr. articles to profl. jours. Recipient Morgan award Old Dominion U., 1986; NASA grantee, 1975-78, 78-88, also others. Fellow AIAA (fluid dynamics tech. com. 1983-87); mem. Am. Soc. Engring. Edn., Soc. Engring. Scis., Soc. Indsl. and Applied Math., AAUP, Phi Kappa Phi, Sigma Xi. Home: 7212 Midfield St Norfolk VA 23505

KANDLER, JOSEPH RUDOLPH, financial executive; b. Vienna, Austria, Dec. 13, 1921; came to Can., 1952; s. Franz and Maria Franziska (Stanzel) K.; m. Lubomyra-Melitta Melnechuk, June 15, 1963. D.Rerum Commercialium, Sch. Econs., Vienna, 1949; Chartered Acct., Inst. Chartered Accts. Alta., 1965. Sales exec. Philips, Vienna, 1951; acct. Brown & Root, Ltd. Edmonton, Alta., Can., 1952-54, 56, chief acct., 1957-64; v.p. fin. Healy Ford Ctr. and Assoc. Cos., Edmonton, 1964—; pres. Sentha Investments, Ltd., Edmonton, 1978—. Bd. dirs. Edmonton Symphony, 1969-72, Alta. Cultural Heritage Council, 1973-81, Edmonton Opera, 1982-84, Tri-Bach Festival, 1982-84; founder Johann Strauss Found., Alta., bd. dirs. 1975-84, pres. 1975-78, founder, pres. Johann Straus Found., BC, 1985—; bd. govs. U. Alta., 1982-86, mem. senate, 1973-79, 82-86; mem. adv. com. on cultural and convention ctr. City of Edmonton, 1974-78, vice chmn. 1976-78. Recipient Achievement award for service to community Govt. Alta., 1975. Mem. Inst. Chartered Accts. Alta., Adminstrv. Mgmt. Soc. (pres. 1967-68), Mensa, Edmonton C. of C. (council 1971-75). Roman Catholic. Address: Healy Ford Ctr and Assocs, 10620 Jasper Ave, Edmonton, AB Canada T5J 2A4

KANDLER, OTTO, botanist, editor; b. Deggendorf, Bavaria, Germany, Oct. 23, 1920; s. Karl and Theresia (Katzdobler) K.; m. Gertraud Schafer, Aug. 1, 1953; children—Maya, Barbara, Vera. Dr.rer.nat., U. Munich, 1949; Dr.h.c., U. Ghent (Belgium), 1981, Tech. U. Munich, 1985. Asst., U. Munich (W.Ger.), 1949-53, dozent Univ. Munich, 1953-60, prof. Tech. U. Munich, 1960-68; dir. Bacterial Inst. Dairy Research Sta., Freising, 1957-65; prof. U. Munich, 1968-84, prof. emeritus, 1984—. Editor: Archaebacteria, 1982, Archaebacteria '85, 1986; editor in chief Systematic and Applied Microbiology, 1980—. Senator, Deutsche Forschungsgemeinschaft, Bonn, 1969-75. Recipient Bergey Award, Bergey's Manual Trust, 1982, Hermann Weigmann Medaille, German Soc. Dairy Sci., Kiel, 1984. Mem. Deutsche Akademie der Naturforscher Leopoldina, Bavarian Acad. Sci. Home: Ernst von Romberg Str 13, D-8000 Munchen 50 Federal Republic of Germany Office: Botanisches Institut, der Universitat, Menzinger Str 67, D-8000 Munich 19 Federal Republic of Germany

KANDOU, HEDY HENRIETTE, chemical company executive; b. Surabaya, Indonesia, Mar. 27, 1946; d. M. S. Kandou; m. Agus Subianto, Feb. 3, 1973; children: Grace, Patricia, Fenny. BA, U. Petra, Surabaya, 1971. Tchr. English Surabaya High Sch., 1968-72; instr. English U. Petra, 1972-76; div. mgr. P.T. Tridaya Artha Universal, Surabaya, 1976-78; area products sales mgr. Indofluid Packing & Seal Co., Surabaya, 1978-83; dir. P.T. Duta Tirta Mustika, Surabaya, 1983—; owner, mgr. U.D. Permata Indah, Surabaya, 1985—. Patentee chemistry blending field. Home: Manyar Tirtomoyo II/6, Surabaya 60116, Indonesia Office: PT Duta Tirta Mustika, Darmo Permai Timur III/20, Surabaya 60189, Indonesia

KANE, DANIEL HIPWELL, lawyer; b. Far Rockaway, N.Y., Aug. 18, 1908; s. David and Bertha (Schilling) K.; m. Helen Shirkey, July 30, 1932; children: Ailene (Mrs. Edward Lee Rogers), Daniel Hipwell, Patricia (Mrs. Patrice Hennin), Kevin Kane. B.S., NYU, 1929; J.D., 1931. Bar: N.Y. 1932. Since practiced in N.Y.C.; specializing in patents; sr. partner Kane, Dalsimer, Kane, Sullivan, & Kurucz, 1946—; mem. faculty N.Y.U. Sch. Law, 1947—, adj. prof., 1964—; lectr. Practising Law Inst., 1951—; Vice pres., dir. Dzus Fastener Co., Inc., West Islip, N.Y., 1941—; dir. Pickering & Co., Inc., Plainview, N.Y., 1965—. Author article. Pres. bd. edn. Union Free Sch. Dist. 6, Huntington, N.Y., 1954-55; Trustee William Dzus Fund; bd. dirs. Ukrainian Inst. Am. Mem. Assn. Bar City N.Y., Am. Bar Assn., Am., N.Y. patent law assns., Am. Judicature Soc., Phi Delta Phi. Clubs: NYU (N.Y.C.); Centerport Yacht; Hibernian United Service (Dublin); Ponte Vedra Beach (Fla.). Home: 22 Spring Hollow Rd Centerport NY 11721 Office: 420 Lexington Ave New York NY 10017

KANE, JOHN EWING, economics and finance educator; b. Quitman, Ark., Apr. 2, 1914; s. Robert Lee and Beulah (Jenkins) K.; m. Katherine Edna Miller, Sept. 10, 1939; children—Carolyn, Phyllis Anne. B.S., U. Ark., 1936, M.S., 1939; Ph.D., Am. U., 1950. C.P.A., Ark. Asst. prof. Southwestern at Memphis, 1941-42; economist U.S. Dept. Commerce, Washington, 1942-46; from assoc. prof. to prof. U. Ark., Fayetteville, 1947-55, acctg. v.p. (fin.), 1967-68, prof. econs. and fin., 1959—; exec. v.p. McIlroy Bank, Fayetteville, 1956-58, dir., 1956—; faculty Sch. Banking of South, Baton Rouge, 1967-79, Assemblies of Bank Dirs., Dallas, 1968-74; faculty Southwest Grad. Sch. Banking, Dallas, 1959-79, bd. dirs., 1966-71; chmn. econ. projection panel Ark. State Chamber of Coms. Econ. Projections, 1973—; Ark. rep. Southwest Athletic Conf., Dallas, 1967-73. Editor Ark. Bus. Bull., 1948-50; author: Report to State Legislature on Higher Edn. Financing to 1980, 1968; contbr. to Financial Accounting Theory, 1964, rev. edit., 1973. Bd. dirs., sec.-treas. Northwest Ark. Regional Airport Authority, 1967-69; sec. bd. trustees U. Ark., 1967-68. Served as lt. (j.g.) USN, 1943-45. Research grantee Alcoa Found., 1977-79; recipient Disting. Faculty Service award U. Ark. Alumni Assn., 1975. Mem. SW Social Sci. Assn. (pres. 1965-66), Am. Econ. Assn., Am. Inst. C.P.A.s, Ark. Soc. C.P.A.s, Am. Fin. Assn. Republican. Methodist. Clubs: Fayetteville Country, Fayetteville Town (pres. 1952, 64, 79). Home: 1245 Columbus Blvd Fayetteville AR 72701 Office: U Ark 402 Bus Adminstrn Bldg Fayetteville AR 72701

KANE, JOSEPH CHARLES, management consultant; b. Jackson, Wyo., July 9, 1935; s. Maxwell J. and Ethel M. (Read) K.; A.B., Rutgers U., 1957; M.B.A., U. Pa., 1963; Ph.D., Harvard U., 1974; m. Janet Allis, Aug. 28, 1982. With Gen. Motors Corp., Detroit, 1957-61; cons. McKinsey & Co., Phila., 1961-63; prin. Joseph Kane Assos., N.Y.C., 1963-70; cons. Cambridge Consulting Group, Lexington, Mass., 1970—, prin., 1970—; pres. CMA Products, Stoneham, Mass., 1982—, High Tech Leasing Corp., N.Y.C., 1982—; pres. Charles River Advisors, 1988; lectr. Purdue U., SUNY. Mem. Am. Mgmt. Assn., Nat. Assn. Mgmt. Consultants. Author: To Merge? Why, Why Not, 1972; Small Business: Characteristics of the Successful Entrepreneur, 1982; The Negotiation Process in the Successful Merger Buyout, 1982. Home: 56 Ledgeways Wellesley Hills MA 02181 Office: 33 Bedford St Suite 12 Lexington MA 02173

KANE, MARGARET BRASSLER, sculptor; b. East Orange, N.J., May 25, 1909; d. Hans and Mathilde (Trumpler) Brassler; m. Arthur Ferris Kane, June 11, 1930; children—Jay Brassler, Gregory Ferris. Student, Packer Collegiate Inst., 1920-26, Syracuse U., 1927, Art Students League, 1927-29, N.Y. Coll. Music, 1928-29, John Hovannes Studio, 1932-34; PhD (hon.), Colo. State Christian Coll., 1973. Head craftsman for sculpture, arts and skills unit ARC, Halloran Gen. Hosp., N.Y., 1942-43; 2d v.p. Nat. Assn. Woman Artists, Inc., 1943-45; sec. to exec. bd. Sculptors Guild, Inc., 1942-45, chmn. exhbn. com., 1942, 44; Jury mem. Bklyn. Mus., 1948, Am. Machine & Foundry Co., 1957; com. mem. An American Group, Inc. Work exhibited at Jacques Seligmann Gallery, N.Y., Whitney Ann. Exhbns., all Sculptors Guild Mus. and Outdoor Shows, Nat. Sculpture Soc. Ann. Bas-Relief Exhbn., 1938, Whitney Mus. Sculpture Festival, 1940, Bklyn. Mus. Sculptors Guild, 1938, Bklyn. Soc. Artists, 1942, Lawrence (Mass.) Art Mus., 1938, N.Y. World's Fair, 1939, Sculptors Guild World's Fair Exhbn., 1940, Robinson Gallery, N.Y., 1939, Traveling Mus. and Instns., 1938, Lyman Allyn Mus., 1939, Met. Mus., Internat. Exhbns., 1940, 1949, Roosevelt Field Art Ctr., N.Y.C., 1957, Phila. Mus., N.Y. Archtl. League, Nat. Acad., Penn. Acad., Chgo. Art Inst., Am. Fedn. Arts, Riverside Mus., Montclair Mus., Grand Cen. Art Galleries, Lever House, N.Y.C., 1959-81, Rye (N.Y.) Library, 1962, Lever House Sculptors Guild Ann. Exhbn., 1973-81, N.Y. Bot. Garden, 1981, Sculptors Guild 50th Anniversary Exhbn., Lever House, 1987, Phila. Art Alliance, 1987, also exhbns. of nat. scope, 1938—, solo sculpture exhbn., Friends Greenwich (Conn.) Library, 1962; executed plaque for Burro Monument, Fairplay, Colo.; exhibited N.Y. Bank for Savs., 1968, Mattatuck Mus., Con., 1967, Lamont Gallery, N.H., 1967, Sculptor's Guild 50th Anniversary Lever House, N.Y.C., 1987, Phila. Art Alliance Exhibition Sculpture of the American Scene, 1987; executed: 18 foot carving in limewood depicting History of Man; contbr. articles to mags.; reprodns. in Contemporary Stone Sculpture, 1970, Contemporary American Sculptures. Recipient Anna Hyatt Huntington award, 1942; Am. Artists Profl. League and Montclair Art Assn. Awards, 1943; 1st Henry O. Avery Prize, 1944; Sculpture Prize Bklyn. Soc. Artists, Bklyn. Mus., 1946; John Rogers Award, 1951; Lawrence Hyder Prize, 1952, 54; David H. Zell Meml. Award, 1954, 63; hon. mention U.S. Maritime Commn., 1941 and; A.C.A. Gallery Competition, 1944; Med. of honor for sculpture Nat. Assn. Women Artists, 1951; Med. of honor for sculpture Nat. Acad. Galleries, N.Y.; prize for carved sculpture, 1955; animal sculpture, 1956; 1st award for sculpture Greenwich Art Soc., 1958, 60; 1st award for sculpture Annual New Eng. Exhbns., Silvermine, Conn. Fellow Internat. Inst. Arts and Letters (life); mem. Sculptors Guild (charter), Nat. Assn. Women Artists (2d v.p. 1943-44), Artists Council, U.S.A., Bklyn. Soc. Artists, Greenwich Soc. Artists (council), Pen and Brush, Internat. Sculpture Center, Silvermine Guild Artists, Nat. Trust for Historic Preservation.; Mem. Internat. Soc. Artists (charter). Home and Studio: 30 Strickland Rd Cos Cob CT 06807

KANE, RICHARD, advertising agency executive; b. N.Y.C., Sept. 5, 1928; s. David K. and Eva (Eicholz) Kaplan; m. Racquel Sheps, Oct. 7,1950; children: Brandi, Cindi. Student, U. Mo., 1946-47, CCNY, 1947-48. Copywriter Sta. WDHN, New Brunswick, N.J., 1948, Sta. WHEW, N.Y.C., 1948-50; advt. dir. Rodale Mfg. Co., Emmaus, Pa., 1953-55; pres. Marden-Kane Inc., N.Y.C., 1958—. Served with U.S. Army, 1951-53. Jewish. Club: Friars.

KANE, SAM, meat co. exec.; b. Spisske Podhradie, Czechoslovakia, June 23, 1919; s. Leopold and Bertha (Narcisenfeld) Kannengiesser; grad. Rabbinical Coll. Galanta, 1939; m. Aranka Feldbrand, Jan. 15, 1946; children—Jerry, Harold Ira, Esther Barbara. Came to U.S., 1948, naturalized, 1953. Pres., Sam Kane Wholesale Meat, Inc., Corpus Christi, Tex., 1956—, Sam Kane Meat, Inc., Corpus Christi, 1956—, Sam Kane Packing Co., Corpus Christi, 1962—, Kane Enterprises, Inc., Corpus Christi, 1956—; pres., chmn. bd. Sam Kane Beef Processors, Inc., 1975—; dir. First City Bank Corpus Christi. Pres., Jewish Welfare Appeal, 1962—; pres. Combined Jewish Appeal, 1968, chmn. bd., 1962-64; mem. nat. cabinet United Jewish Appeal; bd. dirs. Tex. Council on Econ. Edn. mem. Gov. Tex. 2000 Commn.; Recipient award chmn. bd. edn. B'nai Israel Synagogue, 1965; Israel Service award, 1966; Koach award State of Israel, 1976; Prime Minister of Israel Peace Medal, 1980; Brotherhood award Corpus Christi chpt. NCCJ, 1984, Torch of Liberty award Anti Defamation League, 1984; named Outstanding Jewish Citizen of Corpus Christi, 1969. Mem. Tex. Council on Econ. Edn. (bd. dirs.), Tex. Taxpayers Assn. Jewish (pres. synagogue 1964-65; Mem. Tex. Taxpayers Assn. Lodge: B'nai B'rith. Home: 27 Hewit Dr Corpus Christi TX 78404 Office: 9001 Leopard St Corpus Christi TX 78409

KANEKO, AKIRA, mathematician, educator; b. Toyohashi, Aichi, Japan; s. Sachie Kaneko; m. Machiko Ohsaki, Apr. 29, 1971; children: Tomoyuki, Kumi. BS, U. Tokyo, 1968, MS, 1970; DSc, U. Tokyo, Japan, 1973. Cert. secondary tchr., Tokyo. Asst. faculty sci. U. Tokyo, 1970-73, assoc. prof. coll. gen. edn., 1973-87, prof. coll. gen. edn., 1987—. Author: Linear Partial Differential Equations with Constant Coefficients, 1976, Introduction to the Theory of Hyperfunctions, 1980. Mem. Math. Soc. Japan, Soc. Math. de France, Am. Math. Soc., Korean Math. Soc. Buddhist. Home: 1-21-15-305, Kitazawa, Setagaya-ku, Tokyo 155, Japan Office: U Tokyo, Coll Gen Edn, Math Dept, 3-8-1 Komaba, Meguro-ku, Tokyo 153, Japan

KANG, CHIN HUAT, pastor; b. Taiping Perak, Malaysia, Oct. 12, 1953; s. Chooi Tit and Siew Mooi (Chong) K.; m. Wai Chee Muck, May 20, 1982. BA, William Jewell Coll., 1982; MDiv, MRE, Golden Gate Bapt. Theol. Sem., 1983-84; D of Ministry, San Francisco Theol. Sem., 1986. Ordained to ministry Gashland Bapt. Ch., 1982. Assoc. pastor Ipoh Bapt. Ch., San Jose, Calif., 1975-76; student pastor Sik Aun Bapt. Ch., George Town, Penang, 1977; pastor Grace Bapt. Ch., Kuala Lumpur, 1978-79; assoc. pastor Southbay Chinese Bapt. Ch., San Jose, 1982-83; pastor Chinese Mission, First Bapt. Ch., Rancho Cordova, Calif., 1983-84; lectr. Bapt. Theol. Sem., Batu Ferringhi, Penang, 1986—; adv. pastor Penang Bapt. Ch., Georgetown, Penang, 1986—; speaker Malaysia Bapt. Conv. Ann. Messagers' Conf., Port Dickson, Malaysia, 1986, Malaysia Bapt. Conv. Youth Conf., Port Dickson, 1987. Contbr. articles to profl. jours. Mem. Pi Gamma Mu. Baptist. Club: Chinese Swimming. Office: Bapt Theol Sem, 40 A D Mk 17, Batu Ferringhi Penang 11100, Malaysia

KANG, EDWARD PAOTAI, biochemist; b. Chung King, China, Aug. 11, 1942; came to U.S., 1961, naturalized, 1977; s. Kang Wai and Kang Ying-Yee Poon; B.S., U. So. Calif., 1966; M.S., Howard U., 1969, Ph.D., 1973; postgrad. U. Md. Pharmacy Sch., 1969-71; m. Nancy Kiang, July 12, 1970; 1 child, Melissa N. Biochemistry investigator Inst. for Med. Research, James F. Mitchell Found., Washington, 1972-73; research asso. ARC Blood Services Labs., Bethesda, Md., 1973-80; sr. scientist, mgr. research and devel. Electro-Nucleonic Inc., Columbia, Md., 1980-86; dir. infectious diseases div., dir. clin. studies United Biomedical, Inc., Lake Success, N.Y., 1986-87; dir. clin. studies, 1987—; instr. Coll. Pharmacy, Howard U., 1971, lectr. chemistry dept., 1972. First aid instr. ARC Safety Services, Montgomery County, Md., 1974-86. Recipient Disting. Alumnus award Howard U. Grad. Sch., 1982. Fellow Am. Inst. Chemists; Mem. Am. Chem. Soc., Internat. Soc. Thrombosis and Haemostasis, Internat. Soc. Blood Transfusion, Am. Assn. Blood Banks, N.Y. Acad. Scis., AAAS, Am. Assn. Clin. Chemistry, Am. Soc. Microbiology, Biochem. Soc. London, Sigma Xi, Rho Chi. Baptist. Contbr. articles to profl. jours. Office: United Biomedical Inc 2 Nevada Dr Lake Success NY 11040

KANG, SEOCK-YOUNG, medical facility administrator; b. Sariwon, Hwanghaido, Republic of Korea, Aug. 10, 1919; s. Pil-Sang and Sun-Bi (Kim) K.; m. Kie-Ock Lee, Nov. 30, 1943 (div.); 1 child, Hong-Bin; m. Jong-Nam Ahn, Mar. 16, 1970; children: Hee-Youn, Tai-Hee. MD, Kumamoto (Japan) Med. Coll., 1943; D in Med. Sci., Seoul (Republic Korea) Nat. U., 1950; PhD, Kyoto (Japan) U., 1956. Asst. dept. pathology Kumamoto Med. Coll., 1943-45, Coll. Medicine Seoul Nat. U., 1945-46; intern Seoul Nat. U. Hosp., 1946-47, resident in Internal medicine, 1947-51; from instr. to prof. Coll. Medicine Seoul Nat. U., 1951-84, chief div. allergy, 1980-84, prof. emeritus, 1984—; mem. internat. adv. bd. Asian Jour. Allergy Clin. Immunology, Bangkok, 1984—; med. advisor Met. Hosp. Armed Forces, Seoul, 1976-86; founder West Pacific Allergy Symposium, 1986. Author: Clinical Allergology Monography, 1984, Allergic Diseases, Diagnosis and Management, 1987, Allergic Diseases, It's Clinical Practice, 1988; mem. editorial bd. Allergy in Practice, Tokyo, 1983—, Jama Korea, Hong Kong, 1986—. Served to lt. Korean Air Force, 1952-53. Recipient prize for med. papers,

1970, med. articles, 1971, Korea Med. Press, Merit medal for Diligence, 1960, Decoration of Nation, 1984, Office Pres. Republic Korea. Mem. Internat. Assn. Allergology and Clin. Immunology, Internat. Assn. Asthmology (nat. del.), Korea-Japan Joint Allergy Symposium (founder, pres. 1983), Korean Soc. History Sci. (v.p. 1975-78), Korean Fedn. Sci Tech. Socs. (council 1978—), Korean Soc. Allergology (pres. 1974—, pub./editor jour. 1974—), Japanese Soc. Allergology (council 1982—), Internat. Coll. Psychosomatic Medicine (dir. Asian chpt. 1984—). Home: 33-98 Myungriun-Dong 1GA, Chongro-ku, Seoul 110-521, Republic of Korea Office: Korean Research Inst Allegology, 451-5 Shingil-Dong, Young Deung Po-ku, Seoul 150-050, Republic of Korea

KANG, SUK-HUN, psychiatric educator; b. Taegu, Republic of Korea, Mar. 13, 1938; s. Shin-Chul Kang and Hae-Soon (Choe) Kang; m. Jum-Hee Park, Dec. 18, 1962; children: Byung-Joon, Joon-Ho, Ji-Hyun. BA, MD, Kyungpook U. Sch. Medicine, Taegu, 1962, DMS, 1975. Diplomate Korean Bd. Psychiatry. Intern Kyungpook U. Hosp., Taegu, 1962-63, resident dept. neuropsychiatry, 1963-67; instr. Kyungpook U. Sch. Medicine, 1970-72, asst. prof., 1972-76, chmn. dept. psychiatry, 1976—, assoc. prof., 1977-82, prof. psychiatry, 1983—, dean academic affairs, 1986-87; chmn. dept. psychiatry Kyungpook U. Hosp., 1976-87, sci. program com. Korean Acad. Psychotherapists, Seoul, Republic of Korea, 1981-87; vis. fellow Mt. Sinai Med. Ctr., N.Y.C., Coll. Physicians and Surgeons Columbia U., N.Y.C., 1978-80. Pub. Dae-Wha, 1985; chief editor Psychotherapy, 1986. Served to lt. Korean Navy, 1967-70. Recipient Acad. Contbn. award Mayor of Opatija, Yougoslavia, 1985. Mem. Am. Transpersonal Psychology Assn. (supporting), 3d Pacific Congress Psychiatry (chmn. sci. program com., Acad. award 1985). Home: Milinae Apt 1-301, Bong-Duk Dong, Taegu 705-023, Republic of Korea Office: Kyungpook U Hosp, 335 Sam-Duk Dong, Taegu 700-412, Republic of Korea

KANG, SUNG KYEW, medical educator; b. Naju, Chonnam, Republic of Korea, Sept. 5, 1941; parents WuonDong and GongRei (Kim) K.; children: Eun-Souk, Hyun-Souk. MD, Chonnam Nat. U., 1967, PhD, 1978. Diplomate Korean Bd. Nephrology, Korean Bd. Internal Medicine. Instr. Chonbuk (Republic of Korea) Nat. U. Med. Sch., 1975-78, assoc. prof., 1978-86, prof., 1986—; vis. prof. SUNY Downstate Med. Ctr., 1983-84. Served to maj. Korean Army, 1972-75. Recipient Chung-Rham award Korean Assn. Internal Medicine, 1983. Mem. Internat. Soc. Nephrology. Office: Chonbuk Nat U Med Sch, 2-20 Kum-Ahm Dong, Chonju, Chonbuk 560-756, Republic of Korea

KANG, YOUNG-GOO, utilities executive; b. Seoul, Republic of Korea, July 6, 1941; s. Jung-Suk and Ei-Ji (Oh) K.; m. Yang-Sook Oh, June 26, 1970; children: Beum-Mo, Seung-Mo. BA, Seoul Nat. U., 1963, MA, 1969. Sales dept. acct., treas. Kukdong Oil Co., Ltd., Seoul, 1965-81; mng. dir. Kukdong City Gas Co., Ltd., Seoul, 1981—. Served to lt. ROTC Korean Army, 1963-65. Office: Kukdong City Gas Co Ltd, 205-205 Kunja-dong, Sungdong-Ku, Seoul 133, Republic of Korea

KANGAS, HEIKKI RISTO JUHANI, transportation administrator; b. Rovaniemi, Finland, July 4, 1946; s. Leevi Heikki Kangas and Suoma Anna-Lisa (Ylipasma) Kolehmainen; m. Ritva Tuulikki Karkkainen, 1970; children: Katja, Krista, Kiril. MS in Engring., U. Oulu, Finland, 1970. Design engr. Rauma-Repola Oy, Lokomo, Tampere, Finland, 1970-73, Kymin Oy, Santasalo Works, Helsinki, Finland, 1973-74; rationalization engr. Rautaruukki Oy Raahe (Finland) Steel Works, 1974-77, mgr. rationalization, 1977-78, transport mgr., 1978—. Author: Locomotive Radio Controlling, 1983, Laser Pointer-Based Control System for Cranes, 1987. Mem. Finnish Tech. Soc., Finnish Rationalization Soc. (bd. dirs. 1976-78), Vuorimiesyhdistys. Office: Rautaruukki Oy, Raahe Steel Works, Raahensalo, SF-92170 Raahe Finland

KANG SHIEN, People's Republic of China government official; b. Huaian County, Hebei Province, 1913. Attended Qinghua U., 1937. Mem. fin. econ. affairs com. N.W. China Mil. Adminstrv. Council, 1950, dir. petroleum adminstrn. bur., 1952; dir. petroleum adminstrn. bur. Ministry of Fuel Industry, 1953-55; asst. minister of petroleum industry Govt. People's Republic of China, 1955-56, vice-minister petroleum industry, 1956-67, criticized and removed from office during Cultural Revolution, 1967, minister of petroleum and chem. industries, 1975-78, minister of state econ. commn., 1978-81, minister of petroleum industry, 1981-82, vice-premier State Council, 1978-82, state councilor, 1982-88; head various govt. delegations abroad. Mem. 11th Cen. Com., Chinese Communist Party, 1977, mem. Presidium, 12th Cen. Com., 1982. Served with 8th Route Army, 1937. Office: care State Council, Beijing People's Republic of China *

KANIA, ARTHUR JOHN, lawyer; b. Moosic, Pa., Feb. 11, 1932; s. Stanley J. and Constance (Jerry) K.; m. Angela Volpe, Apr. 24, 1954; children: Arthur Sandra, Kenneth, Karen, James, Linda, Steven. B.S., U. Scranton, 1953; LL.B., Villanova U., 1956. Bar: Pa. bar 1956. Acct. Peat, Marwick, Mitchell & Co., Phila., 1954-55; ptnr. Davis, Marshall & Crumlish & Kania (now Kania, Lindner, Lasak & Feeney), Phila., 1961—; pres., dir. Greate Bay Hotel Corp. (and affiliated corps.), 1979-81; sec.-treas., dir. Piasecki Aircraft Corp., 202 Data Systems, Newton St. Rd. Assoc.; sec., dir. Indsl. Ops. Corp., Consol. Mortgage Co.; dir. Continental Bank; chmn. bd. dirs. U. Scranton. Mem. chmn.'s adv. com. dept. health adminstrn. Temple U.; mem. Phila. Com. of 70.; Bd. dirs. Piasecki Found.; former vice chmn. bd. trustees Villanova U.; former chmn. bd. trustees Hahnemann Med. Coll., 1978. Mem. Fed. Bar Assn., ABA, Pa. Bar Assn., Phila. Bar Assn. Clubs: Pine Valley (N.J.) Golf; Overbrook (Bryn Mawr, Pa.); Squires Golf (Phila.); Boca Raton (Fla.), Jupiter Hills Golf (Fla.). Home: 1030 Mount Pleasant Rd Bryn Mawr PA 19010 Office: Two Bala Cynwyd Plaza Bala-Cynwyd PA 19004

KANJI, HANSRAJ KALYANJI, trading company executive; restaurant and catering company administrator, real estate executive; b. Visawadar, Gujrat, India, Aug. 8, 1926; s. Kalyanji Kanji and Mewa (Cholera) Rajpopat; m. Sarla Amarsi Mirani, Feb. 5, 1951; children—Sanjay, Parul. Diploma Dawars Coll., 1946. Propr. Raj Trading Corp., Kobe, Japan, 1953-82; fin. dir. Ashoka Co. Ltd., Osaka, 1975, Himalaya Co., Ltd., Kobe, 1975, Taiheiyo Co., Ltd., Kobe, 1976, Raj Trading Corp., Ltd., Kobe, 1982—. Recipient blue ribbon Prime Minister Japan, 1977. Mem. Indian C. of C. (v.p. 1967-69). Club: India (pres. 1966-67). Hindu. Home: 5F/2-2-12 Shinohara Kitamachi, Nada-ku, Kobe 657, Japan Office: Raj Trading Corp Ltd, 12A 119 Itoh-cho, Chuo-ku, Kobe 650, Japan

KANKAANPAA, MATTI, business executive; b. Jyvaskyla, Finland, Nov. 6, 1927; s. Eemil and Aino Amanda (Hakkinen) K.; m. Olga Iris Verio, June 22, 1952; children—Jarmo, Heidi, Kai. M.Sc. in Mech. Engring., U. Tech., 1951. Design engr. Wartsila, Helsinki, 1950-56; staff engr. Beloit Corp., Wis., 1957-63; project mgr. Jaakko Poyry & Co., Helsinki, 1963-67, v.p., 1968-71; dir. paper machine group Valmet Corp., Helsinki, 1971-79, pres., 1980—, chmn., chief exec. officer, 1983—; bd. dirs. Confedn. Finnish Industries, 1985—; chmn. Fedn. Finnish Metal and Engring. Industries, 1985—. Patentee for paper machines. Avocations: music; tennis; golf. Home: Lyokkiniemi 16 C, 02160 Espoo Finland Office: Valmet Corp, Punanotkonkatu 2, 00130 Helsinki Finland

KANKAT, CANEL VACIT, transportation administrator; b. Istanbul, Turkey, May 17, 1942; s. Mehmet Nihat Yilmaz and Nedret (Akca) K.; m. Cansen Ayaz, Apr. 13, 1967 (div. 1973); m. Bülend Bilgiseven, June 17, 1987; 1 child, Ceylan. M in Bus. Adminstrn., U. Istanbul, 1972. Mgr. mktg. Turkey Pan Am, Istanbul, 1964-81; dist. sales mgr. Turkey Cathay Pacific Airways, Dhahran, Saudi Arabia, 1982-83; dist. mgr. sales for Turkey Istanbul, 1986—; mgr. overseas mktg. Intermex, Geneva, 1983-85; sales and station mgr. Tunisair, Istanbul, 1985-86; pres. Assn. Internat. Etudiants en Sci Econ. et Comml., Istanbul, 1967-68. Served as 1st lt. Turkish Navy, 1975-76. Mem. Skal. Home: Ihlamur Yolu 62/15, Tesvikiye, Istanbul Turkey Office: Cathay Pacific Airways, Sivritas Sok 11, Mediciyekoy, Istanbul Turkey

KANNON, KATSUHIRA, architect; b. China, Aug. 1, 1945; s. Seiji and Sumi (Okude) K.; m. Toshiko Nishimura, May 2, 1975; children: Chihiro, Yuto. BA, U. Tokyo, 1969, MA, 1972; MArch, U. Toronto Sch. Architecture, 1979. Registered architect, 1975. Tech. ofcl. Ministry Posts and Telecommunications, Tokyo, 1972-77; teaching asst. U. Toronto, 1978-79; tech. ofcl. Ministry Posts and Telecommunications, Tokyo, 1979-81; dir. design Tokai Postal Bur., Nagoya, Japan, 1981-83, Tokyo Postal Bur., 1983-85; sr. architect Ministry Posts and Telecommunications, Tokyo, 1985-87, prin. architect, 1987—. Prin. works include Nakagyo Post Office, 1976 (award Archtl. Inst. Japan 1979), Atami Post Office, 1984, Den-enchofu Post Office, 1986, Katsushika Post Office, 1987, Mito Cen. Post Office, 1989, Osaka Postal Savs. Hall, 1990. Govt. of Can. scholar, 1977-79. Mem. Archtl. Inst. Japan, Japan Architects Soc. Lodge: Aburatsubo. Home: 2-303 Komaba-1, Meguro-ku, Tokyo 153, Japan Office: Ministry Posts & Telecommunications, 1-3-2 Kasumigaseki Chiyoda-ku, Tokyo 100, Japan

KANO, TERUHIKO, pulp and paper manufacturing engineer, consultant; b. Shizuoka, Japan, Feb. 14, 1928; s. Zenji and Kiyomi Kano; m. Tomiko Kano; children: Keiji, Miki. B, Nihon U., Tokyo, 1951. Registered profl. engr., Tokyo. Sect. chief paper making Daishowa Paper Mfg. Co., Fuji City, Japan, 1955-57, sect. chief constrn. dept., 1957-60, asst. mgr. prodn. control, 1960-63, asst. mill mgr., 1963-68, mgr. research and devel., 1968-71; pres. Daishowa Paper Converting Co., Fuji City, 1971-79; mng. dir. Okura Pulp and Paper Trading Co., Tokyo, 1979-81; dir. mill mgr. Fujikawa (Japan) Paper Co., 1981-84; dir. prodn. dept. LEC, Inc., Tokyo, 1984—. Patentee in field. Mem. city Pollution Control Com., Fuji City, 1965. Home: 4-1-47 Miyazaki Miyamae-Ku, Kawasaki, Kanagawa 213, Japan Office: LEC Inc, 5-7-2 Koishikawa Bunkyo-Ku, Tokyo Japan

KANOH, MINAMI, neuropsychologist, clinical psychologist; b. Hokkaido, Japan, May 19, 1927; s. Osamu and Tomi (Tanaami) K.; m. Kazuko Senba, Oct. 10, 1968; children: Naoto, Ikuo, Tomoh. BA, Hokkaido U., 1951; postgrad., Tokyo U., 1952-55. Lectr. in social psychology Hokkaido U., Sapporo, 1956-66, assoc. prof., 1966-71, prof. clin. psychology and spl. edn., 1971—, dean faculty edn., 1977-81, councillor, 1972-87. Contbg. author: On the Universe of Psychology, 1957, Basic Mechanism of Learning, 1967, Dymanics of Activation and Inhibition in Learning Process, 1982; joint editor Japanese Jour. Ednl. Psychology, 1984-86. Mem. Hokkaido Psychol. Assn. (pres.), Japanese Soc. Psychiatry and Neurology. Home: Katsuraoka 27-5, Otaru, Hokkaido 047-02, Japan Office: Faculty Edn Hokkaido U, Kita Ku Kita 11, Nishi 7 Sapporo, Hokkaido 060, Japan

KANTABUTRA, BUNDHIT, statistician, actuary; b. Lampang, Thailand, Oct. 23, 1916; s. Phya and Khunying Rajavaryekarn; B.S. in Bus. Adminstrn., Far Eastern U., Philippines, 1937; M.S., U. Philippines, 1938; M.B.A., U. Chgo., 1940; grad. War Coll., 1964; DSc (hon.) Kasetsart State U., Bangkok, 1986, D Statis. Sci., Chulalongkorn U., Bangkok, 1988; m. Prapa Kantabutra, Aug. 17, 1942; children: Burin, Jitrapa, Vitit. Asst. sec.-gen. Nat. Econ. Council Thailand, 1959-60; dir. Cen. Statis. Office, Office Prime Minister, Bangkok, Thailand, 1960-63, sec.-gen., 1963-70; founder, prof., chmn. dept. stats. Chulalongkorn U., Bangkok, 1953-63, prof. emeritus, dir. Statis. Computing Ctr., 1963; cons. actuary, 1950—; now founder mem. Kantabutra & Kantabutra, cons. actuaries and statisticians, Bangkok. V.p. Bangkok Music Group, 1968-69. Decorated knight grand cross Most Noble Order of Crown of Thailand, knight comdr. Most Illustrious Order of Chula Chom Klao, also Most Exalted Order of the White Elephant. Fellow Am. Statis. Assn., Actuarial Assn. Thailand; mem. Internat. Statis. Inst., Thai Statis. Assn. (charter pres.), Internat. Assn. Actuaries, Thai Life Assurance Assn. (hon.), Actuarial Assn. Thailand (pres. 1978—). Club: Rotary. Contbr. articles to profl. jours. Home: 182 Soi 49/Sukumvit Rd, Bangkok Thailand Office: 1/7 Convent Rd, Bangkok Thailand

KANTARAT, PANIENG, minister of defense; b. Samut Prakan, Thailand, Apr. 1, 1922; three sons, one dau. Student, Wat Thep Sirin Sch., Bangkok, Royal Thai Army Tech. Sch., Bangkok, Air Command and Staff Coll., Thailand Air Command and Staff Coll., U.S.A., Army War Coll., Bangkok, Nat. Def. Coll., Bangkok, RAF Tchrs.' Flying Tng. Sch., U.K., Fighters' Flying Sch., U.S.A. Pilot officer Lop Buri; air attaché Thai Embassy, London, 1958; dep. chief of staff Thai Army Command, 1962; dir. Directorate of Ops., 1963; dep. chief of Air Staff for Ops. 1971, vice-chief of Air Staff, 1974, chief of Air Staff, 1975, dep. minister of def., 1979-86; minister of def., commdr. in chief Royal Thai Air Force Bangkok, 1986-88. Office: Ministry of Def, Lanamchai Rd, 10200 Bangkok Thailand *

KANTER, DONALD RICHARD, biotechnology, psychobiology researcher; b. Detroit, Jan. 22, 1951; s. Harry Richard and Dorothy May (Kelch) K.; m. Diane Lynn Fickert, July 9, 1971; children—Sean Richard, Donald Mathew, Lauren Marie. B.A., Oakland U., Rochester, Mich., 1976; M.S., Eastern Mich. U., Ypsilanti, 1979; Ph.D., U. Cin., 1983. Instr. lectr. U. Cin., 1978-84; health scis. officer VA Med. Center, Cin., 1980-85; supr. med. affairs Genetic Systems, Seattle, 1985-88; sr. ptnr. BioStat Research, Edmonds, Wash., 1988—; cons. in field, Oakland U. grantee, 1976; NIMH grantee, 1984; VA merit grantee, 1984, Outstanding Contbn. Award, 1985. Mem. AAAS, Am. Psychol. Assn., Sigma Xi. Methodist. Author: (with Karoly et al) Child Health Psychology, 1982; (with Daniel B. Berch) Sustained Attention in Human Performance, 1983; contbr. med. articles to profl. jours. Home and Office: 17207 76th Ave W Edmonds WA 98020

KANTOR, TADEUSZ, painter, theater founder, director; b. Wielopole, nr. Cracow, Poland, Apr. 6, 1915; s. Marian and Helena K.; m. Maria Stangret-Kantor, 1960. Ed., Cracow Acad. Fine Arts. Organized underground theatre, Cracow, during occupation; prof. Cracow Acad. Fine Arts, 1948, 69; founder Cricot 2 Theatre, Cracow, 1955, participant with theatre in festivals: Premio Roma, 1969, 74, Mondial du Theatre, Nancy, 1971-77, Edinburgh Festival, 1972, 73, 76, 80, 8th Arts Festival, Shiraz, 1974-77, Festival d'Automne, Paris, 1977. Dir. numerous plays, including: Cuttle Fish, 1956; In a Little Manor House, 1961; Madman and Nun, 1963; Happening-Cricotage, 1965; Waterhen, 1967; Dead Class, 1975; Ou sont les neiges d'antan, 1978; Wielopole-Wielopole, 1980; exhbns. of paintings: 30th Biennale of Art, Venice, Italy, 1960; L'Art Theatre, Baden-Baden, 1965; São Paulo Biennale, 1967; Happening and Fluxus, Cologne and Stuttgart, 1970; Whitechapel Gallery, London, 1976; Documenta 6, Kassel, 1977; ROSC, 1977; Moderna Museet, Stockholm; Mus. Modern Art, N.Y.C.; Solomon R. Guggenheim Mus., N.Y.C., Foksal Gallery, Warsaw, 1965, 67, 68, 70, 71, 73, 77, Modern Art Gallery Warsaw, 1976, 78, 79; author: Teatr Smierci (Theatre of Death), 1976. Recipient Premio Marzotto, Rome, 1968; prize for painting, Sã o Paulo, 1967; prix Rembrandt, J.W. Goethe-Stiftung Basel, 1978; Grand pix le Theatre des Nations, Caracas, 1978; OBIE prize, 1979, 82; Diploma of Minister of Fgn. Affairs, 1982; 1st prize 20th Edinburgh Festival, 1976. *

KANUK, LESLIE LAZAR, management consultant, educator; b. N.Y.C.; d. Charles and Sylvia (Hoffman) Lazar; m. Jack Lawrence Kanuk; children: Randi Ellen Dauler, Alan Robert. MBA, Baruch Coll., 1964; PhD, CUNY, 1973; PhD (hon.), Mass. Maritime Acad., 1981, Maine Maritime Acad., 1988. Pres. Leslie Kanuk Assocs., mgmt. cons., 1965-78, 81—; Lippert disting. prof. mktg. Baruch Coll., N.Y.C., 1981—; mem. maritime transp. research bd. Nat. Acad. Scis., 1975-78; commr., vice chmn., chmn. Fed. Maritime Commn., 1978-81; chmn. adv. panel on maritime trade and tech. U.S. Congress Office Tech. Assessment, 1982-83; chmn., pres., dir. Containerization and Intermodal Inst., 1981—; panelist NRC-Nat. Acad. Scis., 1975-78; adj. prof. dept. command communications U.S. Army Signal Sch., Ft. Monmouth, N.J., 1967-69; adj. prof. U.S. Mcht. Marine Acad., Kings Point, N.Y., 1970-71; adj. prof. grad. studies program Maine Maritime Acad., 1984—. Author: Upgrading the Low Wage Worker: An Ergonomic Approach, 1967, Environmental and Behavioral Study of U.S. Merchant Marine Officers, 1971, Improving the Efficiency of Maritime Personnel, 1972, Mail Questionnaire Response Behavior, 1974, Toward an Expanding U.S.M.M, 1976, Consumer Behavior, 1978, rev. edits., 1983, 87, Toward a National Transportation Policy, 1981, How To Use Export Trading Companies To Penetrate Foreign Markets, 1983; contbg. editor: Breaking Barriers of Occupational Isolation, 1966, Management of a Seaport, 1972; editor: The American Seafarer monographs, Kings Point, 1974; editorial rev. bd.: Jour. Mktg, 1978; contbr. numerous articles on mgmt., mktg., internat. transp. and export trading. Recipient Connie award Containerization and Intermodal Inst., 1980; Diamond Superwoman award Harpers Bazaar mag., 1980; Person of Yr. award N.Y. Fgn. Freight Forwarders and Brokers Assn., 1981; Person of Yr. award Baruch Fgn. Trade Soc., 1981; Disting. Alumnus award CCNY, 1984; Disting. Alumni award CUNY, 1988; Townsend Harris medal, 1986; AMA Doctoral Consortium fellow, 1971. Mem. Am. Mktg. Assn., Acad. Mgmt., U. S. Council Internat. Bus., Navy League, Beta Gamma Sigma. Office: 46 E 26th St New York NY 10010

KANZAKI, GEORGE AKAKI, industrial engineer, educator; b. Summit, N.J., Oct. 6, 1912; s. Kishiro and Sayeda Kanzaki; m. Katharina Ruehl, Feb. 15, 1955; children: Heikro, Tyrone. ME, Stevens Inst. Tech., Hoboken, N.J., 1934; MS in Indsl. Engring., Arizona State U., 1961; MA, U. Iowa, 1975, PhD, 1980. Registered profl. engr.; cert. mfg. engr. Commd. USAF, 1945, advanced through grades; materials estimator USAF, Nellis AFB, Nevada, 1948-50; mgmt. engring. supr. USAF, Langley AFB, Va., 1950-68; ret. USAF, 1968; indsl. engr. U.S. Army Mgmt. Engr. Tng. Activity, Rock Island (Ill.) Arsenal, 1968-86; prof. indsl. engring. St. Ambrose U., Davenport, Iowa, 1986—; adj. prof. Fla. Inst. Tech., Rock Island, 1976—; asst. prof. U. Iowa, Iowa City, 1984-85. Author, editor: U.S. Army handbook on Mfg. Technology, 1980; contbr. article to profl. jours. Sr. advisor U.S. Congl. Adv. Bd., 1984, 86. Mem. Inst. Indsl. Engrs. (sr.), Soc. Mfg. Engrs., Machine Vision Assn. (sr.), Robotic Inst. Am. (charter), Computer and Automated Systems Assn. (charter), Robotic Internat., Am. Prodn. and Inventory Control Soc., Am. Legion. Club: Rock Island Arsenal Officers. Home: 4327 Royal Oaks Dr Davenport IA 52806 Office: St Ambrose U 518 W Locust St Davenport IA 52803

KAO, CHENG CHI, electronics executive; b. Taipei, Taiwan, Republic of China, Aug. 3, 1941; s. Chin Wu and Su Chin (Wu) K.; m. Susan Lin, July 4, 1970; children: Antonia Hueilan, Albert Chengwei, Helen Siaolan. BS, Taiwan U., 1963; AM, Harvard U., 1965, PhD, 1969. Research fellow Harvard U., Cambridge, Mass., 1969-70; scientist Xerox Corp., Webster, N.Y., 1970-75; mgr. Internat. Materials Research, Inc., Santa Clara, Calif., 1976-78; exec. v.p. President Enterprises Corp., Tainan, Taiwan, 1979-85; pres. Kolyn Enterprises Corp., Los Altos, Calif., 1979—. Contbr. articles to profl. jours. Bd. dirs. Taipei Am. Sch., 1980-82. Mem. IEEE, Chinese Inst. Elec. Engring. (bd. dirs. 1982-85), Sigma Xi. Club: Am. in China (Taipei), Palo Alto Hills Golf and Country. Office: Kolyn Enterprises Corp 4962 El Camino Real Suite 119 Los Altos CA 94022

KAO, RACE LI-CHAN, medical educator; b. Chungking, China, Dec. 1, 1943; came to U.S., 1967, naturalized, 1980; s. Yu-Ho and Tsing (Tsou) K.; m. Lidia Wei Liu, Aug. 18, 1969; children—Elizabeth, Grace. B.S., Nat. Taiwan U., 1965; M.S., U. Ill., 1971, Ph.D., 1972. Research assoc. U. Ill., Urbana, 1972; research assoc. Pa. State U., Hershey, 1972-75, asst. prof. physicology, 1976-77; asst. prof. surgery, physiology, biophysics U. Tex. Med. Br., Galveston, 1977-82, dir. cardiothoracic research, 1977-82; assoc. prof. surgery Washington U., St. Louis, 1982-83; dir. surg. research Allegheny-Singer Research Inst., Pitts., 1983—; prof. physiology and biochemistry Med. Coll. Pa., Phila., 1987—; reviewer, cons. Nat. Heart, Blood and Lung Inst., NIH, 1984—. Contbr. numerous articles in field to profl. jours. Pres., U. Tex. Chinese Assn., 1980. Served with ROTC, Repub. of China, 1965-66. Nat. Taiwan U. Univ. scholar, 1962-65; grantee NIH, 1979—, Tex. Heart Assn., 1979-80, Upjohn Co., 1977-79, Pa. Heart Assn., 1986-87, Mo. Heart Assn., 1982-83. Fellow Am. Heart Assn.; mem. Am. Physiol. Soc., Internat. Soc. Heart Research, Nat. Soc. Med. Research, N.Y. Acad. Sci., AAAS, Nutrition Today Soc. Home: 9382 Doral Dr Pittsburgh PA 15237 Office: Allegheny-Singer Research Inst Surg Research Dept 320 N East Ave Pittsburgh PA 15212

KAPANDJI, ADALBERT IBRAHIM, orthopedic surgeon; b. Paris, Apr. 17, 1928; s. Mehmet Ibrahim and Roberte Jeanne (Chevalier) K.; m. Lydie Mauricette Richard, Oct. 12, 1950; children: Martine, Thierry. MD, Faculty of Medicine U. Paris, 1960. Externe hosps. Pub. Assistance, Paris, 1951-56, interne hosps., 1956-59, asst. hosps., 1960-65; prof. anatomy Nurses Sch. Paris Hosp., 1959-60; chef de clinique Faculty Medicine, Paris, 1960-65; pres. Clinique de L'Yvette S.A., Longjumeau, France, 1965—; prof. articular physiology Physiotherapists Sch. Necker Hosp., Paris, 1959-65, Physiotherapists Staff Sch., Bois-Larris, France, 1968-70. Author: The Physiology of the Joints, 3 vols., 1960 (translated into English, Italian, Spanish, German, Dutch and Japanese). Mem. French Soc. Angeiology, French Soc. Orthopaedics and Traumatoloy, French Soc. Hand Surgery (pres. 1987), Rioplatenese Soc. Anatomy (Argentina). Home: Copernic 7, 91160 Longjumeau France Office: Clinique de L'Yvette, Rt de Cobeil 43, 91160 Longjumeau France

KAPELLA, BOHDAN WOJCIECH, physician; b. St. Etienne, France, Nov. 16, 1943; m. Jablonska Danuta, Sept. 18, 1949; children: Adam, Michel, Jean, Anna. MD, Acad. Medicine Poznan, Poland, 1974, U. Paris, 1981. Resident in surgery Centre Hospitalier Régional de Valenciennes, 1974-79; gen. practice medicine Cucq, France, 1983—. Mem. Franco Polish Soc., Soc. Polish History and Lit., Polonia Scouting Movement. Roman Catholic. Office: Cabinet Med, 33 Ave de la Poste, 62780 Cucq France

KAPIKIAN, ALBERT ZAVEN, epidemiologist, educator; b. N.Y.C., May 9, 1930; s. Zareh Kaloust and Baizar (Bazikian) K.; m. Catherine Firth Andrews, Feb. 27, 1960; children: Albert Kaloust, Thomas Firth, Gregory Baird. BS, Queens Coll., 1952; MD Cornell U., 1956; postgrad. Johns Hopkins U. Sch. Hygiene and Pub. Health, 1961-62. Intern Meadowbrook Hosp., Hempstead, N.Y., 1956-57; commd. med. officer USPHS, 1957, advanced to grade med. dir.; with epidemiology sect. Lab. Infectious Diseases, Nat. Inst. Allergy and Infectious Diseases, NIH, Bethesda, Md., 1957—, head sect., 1967—; research prof. child health and devel. George Washington U. Sch. Medicine and Health Services, 1977—; temporary advisor WHO, 1980—Contbr. articles to profl. jours. Recipient Meritorious Service medal USPHS, 1970, 74, Disting. Service medal USPHS, 1983; Disting. Alumnus award Queens Coll., 1974, Stitt award Assn. Mil. Surgeons, 1974, Kabakjian award Armenian Students Assn. Am., 1974, 87. Contbr. articles to profl. jours. Mem. Infectious Diseases Soc. Am., Am. Epidemiol. Soc., Am. Pub. Health Assn., Soc. Epidemiol. Research, Am. Soc. Microbiology (Behring Diagnostics award, 1987), AAAS. Mem. Armenian Apostolic Ch. Home: 11201 Marcliff Rd Rockville MD 20852 Office: NIH Bethesda MD 20892

KAPILA, VED PARKASH, civil engineer; b. Lopon, India, Dec. 27, 1932; s. Baboo Ram and Amravati (Vasishta) K.; came to U.S., 1963; naturalized, 1977; student Punjab U., India, 1949-51; diploma in civil engring Civil Engring. Sch., Lucknow, Ind., 1951-53; B.S. in Civil Engring., U. Mich., 1964, M.S. in Civil Engring., 1965; M.B.A., Wayne State U., 1970, value engring. orientation, 1970; m. Pushpa Pipat, Nov. 18, 1952; children—Shashi, Rajnish, Rita, Renu. Engring. officer Punjab State Public Works Dept., India, 1953-63; design, engr. Ayres, Lewis, Norris & May, Ann Arbor, Mich., 1964-65; Obenchain Corp., Dearborn, Mich., 1965-66; v.p., chief civil and structural engr. O. Germany, Inc., Warren, Mich., 1966-76; dir. project services and chief planning and scheduling, chief quality assurance, chief client purchasing Hoad Engrs., Inc., Ypsilanti, Mich., 1976-78; pres. Kapila Constrn. Co., Inc., Kapila Contracting Co., Inc., Kapila & Assocs., 1968—. Registered profl. engr. Mich., Ga., Va., Punjab State (India); registered land surveyor, Mich.; licensed builder, Mich.; certified Nat. Council Engring. Examiners. Mem. ASCE, Am. Congress Surveying and Mapping, Am. Concrete Inst., Am. Inst. Steel Constrn., Mich. Soc. Registered Land Surveyors, Am. Soc. Quality Control, Soc. Am. Value Engrs., Nat. Soc. Profl. Engrs. Office: 31333 Thirteen Mile Rd Farmington Hills MI 48018

KAPIOLTAS, JOHN, hotel company executive; b. Akron, Ohio, July 19, 1927; s. Thomas and Giasema (Mihalarou) K. B.A., Kent State U., 1951; cert., Biscayne Hotel Coll., 1952, U. Miami, 1953. Asst. mgr. night auditor Miami Hotels, Miami Beach, Fla., 1951-53; co-owner Ohio Restaurants Corp., Akron, Ohio, 1954-59; resident mgr. The Sheraton Corp., Ind., P.R., Venezuela, Jamaica, 1960-64; gen. mgr. The Sheraton Corp., Middle East, 1964-68, area mgr., 1968-71; v.p. internat. div. The Sheraton Corp., Europe, Africa, Middle East, 1971-74, sr. v.p., 1975-83; pres. Europe, Africa, Middle East and South Asia div. The Sheraton Corp., 1979-83; pres., chief operating officer, dir. The Sheraton Corp., Boston, 1983-85, chmn., pres., chief exec. officer, dir., 1985—; pres. The Sheraton Corp., Europe, Africa, Middle East and India Div., 1979—; pres., chief operating officer, dir. The Sheraton Corp., Boston, 1983—. Served with U.S. Army, 1945-47. Office: The Sheraton Corp 60th State St Boston MA 02109 also: Denham Pl Village Rd, Denham, Uxbridge UBT 5BT, England *

KAPITÁNY, ZSUZSA MARGIT, mathematics researcher; b. Pánd, Hungary, June 4, 1947; s. Gyula and Margit (Nagy) K.; m. László Almási, Apr. 8, 1969 (div. 1977); m. Zoltan Tóth, Nov. 10, 1984; 1 child, Marton. Tchr.'s diploma, Loránd Eötvös U. Scis., Budapest, Hungary, 1970; PhD, Karl Marx U. Econs., Budapest, 1978. Tchr. math and physics Bldg. Indsl. Tech. Sch., Budapest, 1970-73; researcher Inst. Econs. Hungarian Acad. Scis., Budapest, 1973—. Contbr. to books and jours. Office: Hungarian Acad Scis Inst Econs, Budaorsi 45, H-1112 Budapest Hungary

KAPLAN, ARNOLD AARON, physician; b. Chgo., Sept. 26, 1932; s. Al and Belle (Klebansky) K.; m. Barbara Riskin, June 23, 1957. B.S., U. Ill., 1955, M.D., 1960. Diplomate Am. Bd. Internal Medicine. Intern, Jackson Meml. Hosp., Miami, Fla., 1960-61, resident, 1961-63; fellow in nephrology VA Hosp., Miami, 1963-64; practice medicine, Miami, 1964—; staff mem. Parkway Gen. Hosp., 1964—, chief of medicine, 1970-71; staff mem. North Miami Gen. Hosp., 1964—, chief of staff, 1972-73; instr. internal medicine U. Miami. Past bd. dirs. Jewish Community Ctr. N. Dade, also past assoc. chmn. health and phys. edn. com. Recipient Spirit award Jewish Community Ctr., 1981. Mem. AMA, Am. Soc. Internal Medicine, Dade County Med. Assn., Am. Heart Assn., Fla. Med. Assn., Am. Physicians Fellowship, Fla. Heart Assn., Fla. Nephrology Assn. Club: Optimists. Address: 16800 NW 2d Ave North Miami Beach FL 33169

KAPLAN, ARTHUR NORMAN, jewelry store executive; b. Pretoria, South Africa, Oct. 27, 1928; s. Isaac and Hilda (Balzam) K.; m. Berenice Salome Frankel, June 1, 1958; children—Simone Bonita, Lisa Frances. Dir., Balzams Jewellers, Pretoria, South Africa, 1946-63; mng. dir. Coronet Jewellers, Pretoria, 1963-69; dir. Am. Swiss Jewellers, 1969-72; mng. dir., chief exec. Arthur Kaplan Jewellery Holdings Ltd., Pretoria, 1973-87, chmn. bd. dirs., chief exec., 1987—. Fellow Inst. Dirs.; mem. Jewellers Assn. S. Africa (pres.), Jewellery Council S. Africa (vice-chmn.). Jewish. Lodge: Rotary. Home: 258 Lawley St, Waterkloof, Pretoria, Transvaal 0181, Republic of South Africa Office: Arthur Kaplan Jewellers Ltd, 227 Pretorius St, Pretoria 0002, Republic of South Africa

KAPLAN, EDWARD DAVID, lawyer; b. Newburgh, N.Y., Nov. 18, 1929; s. Sidney L. and Lucille C. (Toback) K.; m. Ursula L. Appel, Aug. 23, 1955; children—Karyn Joyce, Gayle Susan. B.A., Middlebury Coll., 1952; LL.B., Bklyn. Law Sch., 1957, J.S.D., 1957. Bar: N.Y. 1957, U.S. Dist. Ct. (so. dist.) N.Y. 1957. Sole practice, Newburgh, N.Y., 1957-68; ptnr. Finkelstein, Kaplan, Levine, Gittlesohn & Tetenbaum, Newburgh, 1968—; legal counsel N.Y. State Jaycees, 1964-65. Pres. Newburgh Area Indsl. Devel., 1975—; faculty Tex. Coll. Trial Advocacy, 1985—. Served with U.S. Army, 1952-54, Korea. Recipient Disting. Service award Newburgh Jaycees, 1965. Mem. Assn. Trial Lawyers Am., N.Y. State Trial Lawyers, N.Y. Bar Assn., Pa. Trial Lawyers, Tex. Trial Lawyers, Jaycees, Orange County Bar Assn. (pres. 1983-84). Jewish. Home: 19 Downing Ave Newburgh NY 12550 Office: Finkelstein Kaplan Levine 436 Robinson Newburgh NY 12550

KAPLAN, JOEL STUART, lawyer; b. Bklyn., Feb. 1, 1937; s. Abraham Larry and Phayne (Moses) K.; m. Joan Ruth Katz, June 19, 1960; children: Andrea Beth, Pamela Jill. BA, Bklyn. Coll., 1958; LLB, N.Y.U., 1961. Bar: N.Y. 1962, U.S. Dist. Ct. (ea. and so. dists.) N.Y. 1964, U.S. Ct. Appeals (2d cir.) 1966, U.S. Supreme Ct. 1979, Fla. 1982, D.C. 1987. Asst. town atty. Town of Hempstead, N.Y.C., 1962-67; ptnr. Jaspan, Kaplan, Levin & Daniels and predecessors, Garden City, N.Y., 1970-83; sole practice, Garden City, 1983—. Chmn., Hempstead Town Public Employment Relations Bd., 1973-81; mem. L.I. Regional Bd. Anti-Defamation League, 1976—; pres. Dist. #1 B'nai B'rith, 1986-87; Rep. candidate N.Y. State Senate, 1974. Mem. ABA, N.Y. State Bar Assn., Nassau County Bar Assn. Home: 973 East End Woodmere NY 11598 Office: 585 Stewart Ave Suite 700 Garden City NY 11530

KAPLAN, LAWRENCE JAY, economics educator; b. N.Y.C., Oct. 28, 1915; s. Harris and Estelle (Wilner) K.; m. Jeanne Leon, June 9, 1946; children—Harriet, Sanford S., Marcia. B.A., Bklyn. Coll., 1937; M.A., Columbia U., 1938, Ph.D., 1958. Chief info. officer Bur. Labor Stats., Dept. of Labor, N.Y.C., 1949-57; dir. planning and research N.Y.C. Dept. City Planning, Dept. Relocation, 1957-65; prof. econs. John Jay Coll. Criminal Justice, N.Y.C., 1965-86, prof. emeritus, 1986—; now lectr. and cons. Author: Elementary Statistics for Economics and Business, 1966; Ins and Outs of On-Track and Off-Track Betting, 1970; Retiring Right: Planning for Your Successful Retirement, 1986. Editor: An Economic Analysis of Crime, 1976. Vice chmn. Profl. Staff Congress-CUNY. Welfare Fund, 1969-86, emeritus, 1986—. Served with mil. intelligence U.S. Army, 1942-45; ETO. Mem. Am. Econ. Assn., Am. Statis. Assn. Democrat. Jewish. Office: John Jay Coll Criminal Justice 445 W 59th St New York NY 10019

KAPLAN, MANFRED HAROLD, trade company executive; b. Bethal, Transvaal, South Africa, Aug. 3, 1928; s. Isaac and Ada (Einbinder) K.; C.T.A., U. Witwatersrand, 1950; m. Pamela Linde, Apr. 11, 1961; 2 children. Dir., Titan Indsl. Corp., Johannesburg, South Africa, 1955-66; founder, mng. dir. Vane Elec. Instrument Group of Cos., Johannesburg, 1966-73; chmn., mng. dir. I.T.S. (Pty.) Ltd. Group of Co., Johannesburg, 1974-84; chief exec. officer Steelex (Pty) Ltd., 1986—. Mem. Profl. Body of Chartered Accts. Clubs: Sports, Masons. Home: 201 Devon Pl, North Ave Riviera 2196, Johannesburg Republic of South Africa Office: PO Box 15763, Doornfontein 2028, Transvaal Republic of South Africa

KAPLAN, MICHAEL DAVID, marketing consultant, writer; b. N.Y.C., Nov. 4, 1940; s. Harry J. and Rose K. Kaplan; m. Barbara Oberstein, Aug. 30, 1964; children: Jeremy Scott, Abigail Sarah. BA, Syracuse U., 1962, postgrad., 1963; postgrad. N.Y.U., 1964. Polit. reporter AP, N.Y.C., 1965-69; v.p. mktg. First Healthcare Corp., Chgo., 1969-74; pres. Resource Dynamics, Inc., Chgo., 1974-79, also bd. dirs.; pres. Randmark Corp., Louisville, 1979-81, also bd. dirs.; pres., chmn. bd. Rand Mgmt. Corp., Louisville, 1981-88, Pavilion Healthcare Centers, 1981-88, chief exec. officer, chmn. bd. dirs. Context, Inc., 1988—,Cen. Dietary Systems, Inc.; lectr. Acad. Gerontol. Edn. and Devel. Author: Comprehensive Guide to Health Care Marketing, 1974; contbr. articles to profl. jours.; contbg. editor Nursing Homes mag., 1978—. Bd. dirs. Kenesth Israel Synagogue, Louisville, Louisville Vaad Hakashruth (pres.). Office: 517 W Ormsby Ave Louisville KY 40203-3017

KAPLAN, MURIEL SHEERR, sculptor; b. Phila., Aug. 15, 1924; d. Maurice J. and Lillian J. (Jamison) Sheerr; B.A., Cornell U., 1946; postgrad. Sarah Lawrence Coll., 1958-60, U. Calif. at Oxford (Eng.), summer 1971, U. Florence (Italy), summer 1973, Art Students League, N.Y.C., summers 1975-85, New Sch., N.Y.C., 1974-78, m. Murray S. Kaplan, June 3, 1946; children—Janet Belsky, James S., Jerrold, Amy Sheerr Eckman. Exhbns. at Women's Clubs in Westchester, 1954-60, Allied Artists Am., 1958-73, Nat. Assn. Women Artists, 1966-78, Bklyn. Museum, 1968, Sculptors Guild, 1972, Bergen County (N.J.) Mus., 1974; 2-person shows: Camino Real Gallery, Boca Raton, Fla., 1980, Norton Art Gallery, Palm Beach, Fla., 1980; represented in permanent collections Jerusalem, Columbia U., Brandeis U., U. Tex.; executed twin 30 foot cor-ten steel sculptures, Tarrytown, N.Y., 1972, 2 large rotating steel sculptures Art Park, Trans-Lux Corp., 1978; art cons., interior designer, 1971-80; sec. commn. to establish art mus. in Westchester, 1956; chmn. Westchester Creative Arts Festival, 1956; tchr. Armory Sch. of Art, 1987. Bd. dirs. Fedn. Jewish Philanthropies, 1956; chmn. 1st WNET, Channel 13 Art Auction; mem. com. art in pub. places, Palm Beach County, Fla., 1984; mem. Com. for the Arts, Palm Beach County, 1985—; art adv. com. Boca Raton Mus. Art, 1987—; tchr. sculpture, Armory Sch., 1987—. Recipient prizes Nat. Assn. Women Artists, 1966, Westchester Women's Club, 1955, 56, Allied Artists Am., 1969, Artists Guild, Palm Beach, 1987, 88. Mem. Art students League N.Y. Nat. Assn. Women Artists, Allied Artists Am., Artists Guild Palm Beach. Democrat. Address: 339 Garden Rd Palm Beach FL 33480

KAPLAN, SAMUEL, pediatric cardiologist; b. Johannesburg, South Africa, Mar. 28, 1922; came to U.S., 1950, naturalized, 1958; s. Aron Leib and Tema K.; m. Molly Eileen McKenzie, Oct. 17, 1952. MB, BcH., U. Witwatersrand, Johannesburg, 1944, MD, 1949. Diplomate: Am. Bd. Pediatrics. Intern Johannesburg, 1945; registrar in medicine 1946; lectr. physiology and medicine U. Witwatersrand, 1946-49; registrar in medicine U. London, 1949-50; fellow in cardiology, research assoc. U. Cin., 1950-54, asst. prof. pediatrics, 1954-61, assoc. prof. pediatrics, 1961-66, prof. pediatrics, 1967-87, asst. prof. medicine, 1954-67, assoc. prof. medicine, 1967-82, prof. medicine, 1982-87; prof. pediatrics UCLA, 1987—; cons. NIH; hon. prof. U. Santa Tomas, Manila. Editorial bd.: Circulation, 1974-80, Am. Jour. Cardiology, 1976-81, Am. Heart Jour, 1981—, Jour. Electrocardiology, 1977—, Clin. Cardiology, 1979—, Jour. Am. Coll. Cardiology, 1983-87. Cecil John Adams fellow, 1949-50; grantee Heart, Lung and Blood Inst. of NIH, 1960-88. Mem. Am. Pediatric Soc., Am. Soc. Pediatric Research, Am. Heart Assn. (med. adv. bd. sect. circulation), Am. Fedn. Clin. Research, Am. Coll. Cardiology, Internat. Cardiovascular Soc., Am. Acad. Pediatrics, Am. Assn. Artificial Internal Organs, Midwest Soc. Pediatric Research (past pres.), Sigma Xi, Alpha Omega Alpha; hon. mem. Peruvian Soc. Cardiology, Peruvian Soc. Angiology, Chilean Soc. Cardiology, Burma Med. Assn. Office: UCLA Sch Medicine Dept Pediatrics Cardiology Los Angeles CA 90024

KAPLAN, SHELDON ZACHARY, international lawyer; b. Boston, Nov. 15, 1911; s. Jacob and Lizzie (Strogoff) K.; m. Megan Vondersmith, May 8, 1947; children: Eldon, Deborah Kaplan Kovach, Daniel, Philip, Rebecca, Abigail Kaplan McKenha. A.B. with honors, Yale U., 1933; postgrad., Harvard U. Law Sch., 1933-34; B.A. in Jurisprudence, Brasenose Coll., Oxford (Eng.) U., 1937; M.A., Oxford (Eng.) U., 1945; Licence en Droit equivalence, U. Nancy, France, 1944; internat. law student, U. Paris and l'Ecole Libre des Sciences Politiques, 1945; Dr. honoris causa, Inca Garcilaso de la Vega U., Lima, Peru, 1970, U. San Martin de Porres, 1979. Bar: Mass. 1940, D.C. 1957, U.S. Supreme Court 1957, also Gray's Inn of London. Research assoc. Elder, Whitman and Weyburn, Boston, 1937-40; sole practice Boston, 1940-42; asst. to legal adviser Dept. State, Washington, 1947-49; staff cons. House Fgn. Affairs Com., 1949-57; ptnr. Dodd, Kaplan & Schmidt, Washington, 1957-58; legal counsel to Govt. Guatemala in U.S., 1960-62, 77-78; gen. counsel Latin Am. and Cen. Am. Sugar Council, 1963-65; counsel Cen. Bank Honduras, 1962-64, Martin & Burt, 1959-62, Wilkinson, Cragun & Barker, Washington, 1962-67, SAHSA, Honduras Airlines, 1963-77; spl. internat. counsel Morrison-Knudsen Co., 1971-74; ptnr. Bechhoefer, Sharlitt & Lyman, Washington, 1975-79; counsel Ward & Mendelsohn, Washington, 1985—; Mem. U.S. Spl. Mission to Costa Rica, 1949, El Salvador, 1950, Europe, 1951, 53, Pakistan, India, Thailand, Indochina, 1953, Latin Am., 1954, Uruguay, 1955, C. Am., 1955, Guatemala, 1957, Europe, 1957; congl. adviser, mem. U.S. del. 10th Gen. Assembly of UN, 1955; del. Govt. Nicaragua 18th and 19th sessions Internat. Sugar Council, London, 1964, 65; Bd. dirs. Glaydin Sch., Leesburg, Va., 1965-70; adv. bd. Campion Hall, Oxford U., 1974-82. Author govt. pub. documents, reports on fgn. affairs.; Contbr. legal and fgn. affairs jours.; Composer popular songs. Rep. candidate for U.S. Congress 8th Congl. Dist., Md., 1974. Served to capt. AUS, 1942-46, E.T.O. Decorated mé daille de la Reconnaissance Française (France); Bronze Star medal U.S.; Orden Del Quetzal (Guatemala); Orden al Merito (Peru). Mem. Nat. Bar Assn. Peru (hon.), Am. Soc. Internat. Law, Brasenose Soc. (Oxford, Eng.), ASCAP, Brit. Sporting Art Trust. Jewish. Clubs: Nat. Steeplechase and Hunt Assn. (N.Y.C.), Mil. Order of Carabao, Oxford and Cambridge (London), Yale (N.Y.C.), Kildare St. (Dublin), Cosmos, Capitol Hill, Army and Navy, Harvard (Washington). Home: 7810 Moorland Ln Bethesda MD 20814-1113 Office: Ward & Mendelsohn 1100 17th St NW Suite 900 Washington DC 20036

KAPLAN, STANLEY ABRAHAM, lawyer, law educator; b. Chgo., July 17, 1910. PhB, U. Chgo., 1931, JD, 1933; LLM, Columbia U., 1935. Bar: Ill. 1934, U.S. Supreme Ct., 1951. Ptnr. Gottlieb and Schwartz, Chgo., after 1934, counsel, to 1978; ptnr. Reuben & Proctor, Chgo., 1978-82; of counsel Isham, Lincoln & Beale, Chgo., 1982-86; sole practice, Chgo., 1986—; prof. law U. Chgo., 1960-78; chief reporter corp. governance project Am. Law Inst., 1980-84. Author: (with Blum) Corporate Readjustments and Reorganizations; editor Legal Ethics Forum of ABA Jour., 1976-85. Served to lt. col. USMCR, 1942-46. Mem. ABA, Ill. State Bar Assn., Chgo. Bar Assn. (bd. mgrs. 1947-49, chmn. securities law com. 1950-51, chmn. corp. law com. 1978-79, Chgo. Council Lawyers, Soc. Am. Law Tchrs., Anti Defamation League (exec. bd. Chgo. div.), Order of Coif, Phi Beta Kappa. Clubs: Standard, Lincoln Park Tennis Assn., Adventurer's, Chgo. Mountaineering. Office: 135 S LaSalle St Suite 1050 Chicago IL 60603

KAPLAN, SYLVIA YALOWITZ KAPLAN (MRS. MILTON I. KAPLAN), librarian, educator; b. Chgo., May 23, 1921; d. Max and Gertrude (Yalowitz) K.; Ph.B., Northwestern U., 1956; M.A. in L.S., Rosary Coll., 1961, postgrad., 1962; postgrad. U. Ill., 1965-69, HEA Inst. on Reclassification, Rosary Coll., 1969, DePaul U., 1970; doctoral candidate (scholar, grad. asst.) U. Pitts., 1980-86; m. Milton I. Kaplan, Apr. 5, 1959. Asst. librarian Argonne Nat. Lab., U. Chgo., 1943-50; chief med. librarian Mcpl. Tb Sanitarium, Chgo., 1953-57; sch. librarian, Gary, Ind., 1957-59; librarian Inst. Applied Research, U. Chgo., 1961-62; chief librarian, instr. med. bibliography Chgo. Med. Sch., 1960-64; librarian Michael Reese Hosp. Sch. Nursing, Chgo., 1964-66; chief librarian Ill. Dept. Mental Health, 1967-70; instr. library sci. Northeastern Ill. State Coll., 1970—; asst. prof. library sci. Eastern Ill. U., Charleston, 1970—. Mem. AAUW, AAUP (officer), Med. Library Assn. (cert.), Am. Assn. Library Schs., Spl. Libraries Assn., Assn. Acad. Librarians, Internat. Assn. Semantics, Hadassah, Internat. Platform Assn. (hon.), Delta Kappa Gamma (hon.; scholar 1979). Democrat. Jewish. Contbr. revs. to profl. jours. Office: Eastern Ill U Dept Library Sci Charleston IL 61920

KAPLANOFF, MARK DEMENTI, educator; b. San Francisco, Feb. 5, 1949; arrived in Eng., 1970; s. Mark and Helen Francis (Salladay) K. BA, Yale U., 1970; BA with honors, Cambridge U., Eng., 1972; MA, Cambridge U., 1975, PhD, 1980. Stone research fellow Peterhouse, Cambridge, Eng., 1975-78; Keasbey fellow Selwyn Coll., Cambridge, 1978-79; asst. lectr. history Cambridge U., 1979-84, lectr. history, 1984—; fellow, asst. dir. studies Pembroke Coll., Cambridge, 1979—; sr. proctor Cambridge U. 1981-82; mem. council of the senate Cambridge U., 1983—; Syndic Cambridge U. Library 1986—. Contbr. articles to profl. jours. Bd. dirs. Friends of the Acad. Library, Phillips Exeter Acad., 1986—. Mem. Am. Hist. Assn., Orgn. Am. Historians, Brit. Assn. for Am. Studies. Republican. Episcopalian. Club: Olympic (San Francisco). Home: 2442 Jackson St San Francisco CA 94115 Office: Pembroke Coll, Cambridge CB2 1RF, England

KAPLUN, SERGE (JOSEF), publisher, media consultant; b. May 13, 1939; s. Sioma B. and Vera (Bernstein) K.; m. Marie-Anne Copponex-Revilliod, Sept. 11, 1962; children: Calire A., Marc P., Colette R. G.C.E.A., Calvin Coll., Geneva, 1958; cert., Interpreters Sch., Geneva, 1961; diploma in Internat. Relations, Postgrad. Inst. HEI, Geneva, 1970. Head personnel Imprimerie Studer SA, Geneva, 1967-69, dir. sales, 1980; press officer World Council Chs., Geneva, 1981; spl. advisor sec.-gen. Internat. Union Child Welfare, Geneva, 1982; cons., dir. Labor et Fides/Triangle, Geneva, 1980-83; external lectr. Librarian High Sch. & IMI, Geneva, 1981—; dir. IBI, Geneva. Author: Marionnettes, 1980; editor: SOEPI. Nat. pres. Jeune Chambre Economique Suisse, 1975. Recipient award UN High Commn. Refugees, 1958. Mem. C. of C. Industry (dir. 1973-83), Jaycees Internat. (v.p. 1976, exec. dir. 1977, Europe Senate Ambassador 1985), Swiss Master Printers (dir. 1970-80), Swiss Pub. Assn., Alumni Assn. HEI Assn. (dir.), SRT-GE (radio TV, dir. 1980—). Roman Catholic. Clubs: Am., CALL (dir.), Mktg. Execs. Home: 14a Place Verte, Geneva Switzerland CH1234 Office: Editions du Tricorne, PO Box 456H, Geneva 4 Switzerland 1211

KAPNICK, HARVEY E., JR., corporate executive; b. Palmyra, Mich., June 16, 1925; s. Harvey E. and Beatrice (Bancroft) K.; m. Jean Bradshaw, Apr. 5, 1947 (dec. 1962); m. Mary Redus Johnson, Aug. 5, 1963; children—David Johnson, Richard Bradshaw, Scott Bancroft. Student, James Miliken U., 1942-44; B.S., Cleary Coll., 1947, D.Sc. in Bus. Adminstrn. (hon.), 1971; postgrad., U. Mich., 1947-48; D.H.L. (hon.), DePauw U., 1979. C.P.A., Ill. Mem. staff, mgr. Arthur Andersen & Co. (C.P.A.'s), Chgo., 1948-56; partner Arthur Andersen & Co. (C.P.A.'s), 1956-62; partner in charge Arthur Andersen & Co. (C.P.A.'s), Cleve., 1962-70; chmn., chief exec. Arthur Andersen & Co. (C.P.A.'s), 1970-79; dep. chmn. 1st Chgo. Corp., 1st Nat. Bank Chgo., 1979-80; pres. Kapnick Investment Co., 1980-84; chmn., pres., chief exec. officer Chgo. Pacific Corp., 1984—; mem. Adv. Com. on Internat. Investment, Tech. and Devel., Adv. Com. for Trade Negotiations. Pres.'s Commn. on Pension Policy, Ill. Fiscal Commn., 1977; Adv. Com. Fed. Consol. Fin. Statements, 1976-78; Chmn. Ill. crusade Am. Cancer Soc., 1972; chmn. campaign Met. Crusade of Mercy, Chgo., 1976; trustee, Meninger Found., Mus. Sci. and Industry, Northwestern U.; bd. dirs. Orchestral Assn., Lyric Opera Chgo., council U. Chgo. Grad. Sch. Bus.; adv. council Stanford Grad. Sch. Bus. Served to 2d lt. USAAF, 1943-46. Mem. Assn. Ohio Commodores, U.S. C. of C. (gov. ops. and mgmt. com.; dir. 1973-76), Ill. C. of C. (dir. 1970-74), ASEAN-U.S. Bus. Council (exec. com. U.S. sect.), Iran-U.S. Bus. Council. Clubs: Met. (Washington); Mid-America (gov. 1971-76, treas. 1974-76), Chgo., Carlton, Univ., Execs., Indian Hill, Econ., Comml. (Chgo.), Naples Yacht, Hole-in-Wall, Port Royal. Home: 1425 Sheridan Rd Wilmette IL 60091 Office: Chgo Pacific Corp 200 S Michigan Ave Chicago IL 60604

KAPNICK, RICHARD BRADSHAW, lawyer; b. Chgo., Aug. 21, 1955; s. Harvey E. and Jean (Bradshaw) K.; m. Claudia Norris, Dec. 30, 1978; children: Sarah Bancroft, John Norris. BA with Distinction, Stanford U., 1977; M Philosophy in Internat. Relations, U. Oxford, 1980; JD with honors, U. Chgo., 1982. Bar: Ill. 1982, U.S. Dist. Ct. (no. dist.) Ill. 1982. Law clk. to justice Ill. Supreme Ct., Chgo., 1982-84; law clk. to Justice John Paul Stevens U.S. Supreme Ct., Washington, 1984-85; assoc. Sidley & Austin, Chgo., 1985—. Mng. editor U. Chgo. Law Rev., 1981-82. Pres. jr. governing bd. Chgo. Symphony Orch., 1986-88. Mem. Order of Coif., Phi Beta Kappa. Republican. Episcopalian. Club: University. Home: 565 Willow Rd Winnetka IL 60093

KAPPENBERG, RICHARD PAUL, neuropsychologist, clinical psychologist; b. Jamaica, N.Y., Feb. 5, 1944; s. John William and Cornelia (Taylor) K.; m. Judith Nakashima, Nov. 26, 1970; children—Erin, Lee. B.A., Fairfield U., 1965, M.A., 1966; Ph.D., U. Hawaii, 1973. Diplomate Am. Acad. Behavioral Medicine, Am. Bd. Med. Psychotherapy, Am. Bd. Vocat. Experts; lic. psychologist, Hawaii; cert. mental health care provider; cert. health care provider in marital and family therapy; cert. disability determination examiner, Hawaii. Dir. rehab. services Salvation Army Men's Soc. Services Ctr., Honolulu, 1967-68; dir. guidance The Acad., Honolulu, 1968-69; counseling intern Counseling and Testing Ctr., U. Hawaii, Honolulu, 1969-70, clin. intern. 1970-72; clin. intern Tripler Army Med. Ctr., Honolulu, 1970-71; psychologist Dept. Army, Schofield Barracks, Hawaii, 1972-73; asst. prof. dept. human devel. U. Hawaii, 1973-79, chmn. dept. human devel., 1980; pvt. practice psychology, Honolulu, 1974—; chief psychologist Rehab. Hosp of Pacific, Honolulu, 1980-86; practicum supr. ednl. psychology Sch. Nursing Social Work, U. Hawaii, 1971-73; cons. psychologist Ctr. Psychol. Service, Tng. and Research, Honolulu, 1970-72, Dept. Indsl. Medicine Kaiser Med. Ctr., 1988; psychologist Model Cities Program, Kuhio Park Terr., Honolulu, 1971; psychologist Met. Counseling Ctr., 1971-72; clin. cons. in psychology div. vocat. rehab. Central sect. State of Hawaii, 1975—; cons. St. Timothy's Preschool, 1978—; neuropsychol. evaluation tng. psychology staff Queen Emma Clinic Queen's Med. Ctr., 1988, neuropsychol. cons., 1987; peer reviewer Office of Civilian Health and Med. Plan for Uniformed Service, 1978—; med cons. in neuropsychology disability determinations Social Security Adminstrn., Honolulu, 1986—; condr. numerous workshops in communication skills for mil. and civilian groups; asst. developer and assessor new criteria for hiring of police officers; chmn. Joint. Com. on Continuing Edn. for Psychologists, 1977, Continuing Edn. for Psychologists Com., 1979, Sunset Legis. and Psychol. Licensing Com., 1980, 81. Contbr. articles to profl. publs. Mem. AAAS, Am. Assn. Marriage and Family Therapists, Am. Acad. Neuropsychology, Am. Psychol. Assn., Western Psychol. Assn., Hawaii Psychol. Assn. (profl. affairs com. 1976, 83-85, conv. com. 1977, pres. 1978, ad hoc com. on lic. legis. 1983, pres.-elect 1988), Hawaii Council on Family Relations (v.p. 1977, 78, 79, 80), Hawaii Assn. Marriage and Family Therapists.

KAPUR, BASANT KUMAR, economist; b. Singapore, Jan. 24, 1950; s. Shiv Nath and Mira Bai (Dhir) K.; m. Renu Wadhawan; 1 child, Sanjeev. BS in Social Sci. with honors, U. Singapore, 1970; MA in Econs., Stanford U., 1973, PhD, 1974. Lectr. U. Singapore, 1974-79; sr. lectr. Nat. Univ. of Singapore, 1979-87, assoc. prof., 1987—. Author: Studies in Inflationary Dynamics, 1986; contbr. articles to profl. jours. Served to lt. inf., Singapore Army, 1975-77. Mem. Econ. Soc. of Singapore, East Asian Econ. Assn. Hindu. Office: Nat Univ of Singapore, Econs Dept, Singapore Singapore

KAPUR, CHITRANJAN, international trading company executive; b. Lahore, Punjab, India, May 14, 1939; came to U.K. 1979; s. Amar Nath and Champa (Bhagat) K.; m. Deepa Chopra, June 7, 1969; children: Gina, Tania. BA magna cum laude, Harvard U., 1960, MBA, 1962; B in Laws, K.C. Coll. Law, Bombay, India, 1966-68. Sr. fin. analyst Hudson Pulp and Paper Corp., N.Y.C., 1962-64; new product mgr., group products mgr. Colgate-Palmolive Pvt. Ltd., Bombay, 1964-68; mng. Export Co. Behshahr Indsl. Group, Tehran, Iran, 1968-70; mng. dir. Technocrat Electronic Controls Pvt. Ltd., New Delhi, India, 1972-75; chief of ops. Bd. Internal Trade, Dar-es-Salaam, Tanzania, 1975-76; mktg. and export dir. Jiroft Agro-Ind. Corp., Tehran, 1976-79; mng. dir. Peacock Products Ltd., Harrow, Eng., 1979—, also dir.; dir. Britten & Crowne Ltd., London, Britanico Ltd., London. Fellow Inst. of Dirs.; mem. English Edn. Soc. New Delhi (treas.), Harvard Alumni Assn. India (sec.-gen.), Provisional World Govt. (fin. minister). Hindu. Clubs: Bombay Gymkhana, Delhi Gymkhana. Avocations: travel, reading, current affairs. Home: D 1/12 Vasant Vihar, New Delhi India Office: Harrow, Peacock Products Ltd, Craigmore, Hill Close, Middlesex HA1 3PQ England

KAPUR, KAILASH CHANDER, industrial engineering educator; b. Rawalpindi, Pakistan, Aug. 17, 1941; s. Gobind Ram and Vidya Vanti (Khanna) K.; m. Geraldine Palmer, May 15, 1969; children—Anjali Joy, Jay Palmer. B.S., Delhi U., India, 1963; M.Tech., Indian Inst. Tech., Kharagpur, 1965; M.S., U. Calif.-Berkeley, 1968, Ph.D., 1969. Registered profl. engr., Mich. Sr. research engr. Gen. Motors Research Labs., Mich., 1969-70; sr. reliability engr. TACOM, U.S. Army, Mich., 1978-79; mem. faculty Wayne State U., Detroit, 1970—, assoc. prof. indsl. engring. and ops., 1973-79, prof., 1979—; vis. prof. U. Waterloo, Can., 1977-78; vis. scholar Ford Motor Co., Mich., summer 1973. Author: Reliability in Engineering Design, 1977; assoc. editor Jour. Reliability and Safety, 1982—; contbr. articles to profl. jours. Grantee Gen. Motors Corp., 1974-77, U.S. Army, 1978-79, U.S. Dept. Transp., 1980-82. Mem. IEEE (sr.), Ops. Research Soc. Am. (sr.), Inst. Indsl. Engrs. (assoc. editor 1980—). Home: 1371 Club Dr Bloomfield Hills MI 48013 Office: Wayne State U Dept Indsl Engring Detroit MI 48202

KAPUSCINSKI, RYSZARD, journalist; b. Pinsk, Poland, Mar. 4, 1932; s. Jozef and Maria Bobka K.; m. Alicja Mielczarek; 1 dau. M.A., Faculty History, Warsaw U. Began career with Sztandar Mlodych, 1951; with Polityka, 1957-61; corr. Polish Press Agy., Africa, Latin Am., 1962-72; with Kultura, 1974-81; dep. chmn. Poland 2000 Com., Polish Acad. Scis., 1981—; vis. prof. Temple U., Phila.; vice chmn. com. research and prognosis, Polish Acad. Scis. Author: Busz po polsku; Czarne gwiazdy; Kirgiz schodzi z konia; Gdyby cala Afryka ... ; Dlaczego zginal Karl von Spreti; Chrystus z karabinem na remieniu; Jeszcze dzien zycia; Etiopia; Cesarz; Wojna futbolowa; Szachinszach. Decorated Gold Cross of Merit, Knight's Cross, Order Polonia Restituta; recipient B Prus, 1975, Internat. prize Internat. Journalists Orng., 1976, State prize (2d class), 1976.

KARABA, FRANK ANDREW, lawyer; b. Chgo., Jan. 23, 1927; s. Frank and Katherine (Danihel) K.; m. Alice June Olsen, June 2, 1951; children: Thomas Frank, Stephen Milton, Catherine Alice. BS with highest distinction, Northwestern U., 1949, JD, 1951. Bar: Ill. 1951. Teaching asso. Northwestern U. Law Sch., 1951-52; law sec. Ill. Supreme Ct., 1952-53; asso. firm Crowley, Barrett & Karaba, Chgo., 1953-60; partner Crowley, Barrett & Karaba, 1960-75, mng. partner, 1975—; dir. A&R Printers, Inc., Caron Internat., Inc., O'Brien Corp., D.L.M. Inc.; Asst. counsel Emergency Commn. on Crime, Chgo. City Council, 1952. Pres. 7th Av. P.T.A., 1964-66; bd. dirs. La Grange Little League, 1964-67, pres., 1968. Served with USNR, 1945-46. Mem. ABA, Ill. Bar Assn., Bar. Assn. (bd. mgrs. 1962-63), Order of Coif. Presbyn. (elder). Clubs: Legal, Law. Home: 812 S Stone Ave La Grange IL 60525 Office: Crowley Barrett & Karaba 111 W Monroe St Chicago IL 60603

KARABAIC, IVO, mechanical engineer, researcher; b. Crikvenica, Yugoslavia, July 25, 1936; s. Anton Suzana (Brnjac) K.; m. Dragica Brodar, Nov. 5, 1960; children—Tomislav, Miroslav. B.S., Faculty of Mech. Engring., 1966, M.Sc., 1976, D. Sc., 1980. Registered profl. engr. Mech. engr., Prvomajska, Zagreb, Yugoslavia, 1966-67, devel. engr., 1967-69; research engr. Prvomajska Inst., Zagreb, 1969-76, head dept., 1976-81; head dept. Rade Koncar, Zagreb, 1981-83, head devel. and research, 1983—; prof. faculty mech. engring. U. Zagreb; cons. in field. Author: Informator, 1982; also articles, conf. proceedings. Mem. Assn. Mech. Engrs., Naval Architects of Croatia. Office: Rade Koncar Fallerovo Set 22, 41000 Zagreb Yugoslavia

KARABTCHEVSKY, ISAAC, music director; b. Sao Paulo, Brazil, Dec. 27, 1934; s. Salomao and Genny (Prouchansky) K.; m. Mria Helena Arnaud Maia Cardoso, Jan. 13, 1968; children—Lucia, Helena. Student Mackenzie Sch., Sao Paulo, 1950-56, Freiburg Sch. Music, Fed. Republic Germany, 1958-62. Music dir. Brazilian Symphony Orch., Rio de Janeiro, 1967—, Opera House Sao Paulo, 1982—. Decorated cruzeiro do sul (Brazil) Ordem do Impiranga, Govt. of Sao Paulo. Avocations: yachting. Office: Orquestra Sinfonica Brasileira, Av Rio Branco 135, Room 918, 20400 Rio de Janeiro Brazil

KARADZHOV, GEORGI EREMIEV, mathematics educator, researcher; b. Trastenik, Pleven, Bulgaria, Mar. 8, 1946; m. Svetlana Vladimirovna Ivanova, May 20, 1973; children: Elena, Valeria. PhD in Math., U. Leningrad, 1973, Acad. Sci., Sofia, Bulgaria, 1987. Asst. prof. Inst. Math., Sofia, 1973-83; assoc. prof. Bulgarian Acad. Scis., Sofia, 1984—. Reviewer Mathematical Reviews, 1981—; contbr. articles to profl. articles. Mem. Am. Math. Soc., Polskie Towarzystwo Matematyczne, Bulgarian Math. Soc. Home: Svoboda 40 78, 1231 Sofia Bulgaria Office: Inst Math, 1113 Sofia Bulgaria

KARAGEORGHIS, VASSOS, archaeologist; b. Trikomo, Cyprus, Apr. 29, 1929; s. George Georghiou and Panayiota Georghiou; student Nicosia, U. Coll., Inst. Archaeology, London U.; Dr. honoris causa, U. de Lyon, U. Göteborg, U. Athens, Birmingham (Eng.) U., Toulouse U., France, Brock U., Can.; m. Jacqueline Girard, Mar. 21, 1953; children—Clio, André . Asst. curator Cyprus Mus., 1952-60, curator, 1960-63; acting dir. Dept. Antiquities, Cyprus, 1963-64, dir., 1964—; vis. research fellow Merton Coll., Oxford U., 1979, sr. research fellow, 1980; vis. fellow All Souls Coll., 1982, Merton Coll., 1988. Mem. governing body Cyprus Research Centre. Fellow Univ. Coll., London. Decorated Chevalier de la Lé gion d'Honneur (France); Order Merit 1st class (Fed. Republic Ger.). Fellow Soc. Antiquaries London (hon.), Royal Soc. Arts, Brit. Acad. (corr.); mem. Soc. For Cypriot Studies, Archaeol. Soc. Athens, Acad. Athens (corr.), Royal Swedish Acad. (fgn.), Academie des Inscriptions et Belles Lettres (fgn. mem.), Accademia dei Lincei (fgn. mem), German Archaeol. Inst. Berlin, Austrian Acad. Scis. (corr.). Author books in English and French on Cypriot archaeology. Archaeol. excavations at Salamis, Kition and several other sites in Cyprus. Office: Cyprus Mus, Dept Antiquities, PO Box 2024, Nicosia Cyprus

KARAGEORGOS, ATHANASSIOS, chemical engineer; b. Athens, Greece, July 24, 1944; s. Constantine and Helen (Papantonopoulou) K. Dipl. Chem. Engr., Nat. Tech. U., Athens, 1968, D. Engring., 1973, postdoctoral degree, 1984. Mgr. research and devel. Papastratos S.A., Piraeus, Greece, 1970-80; plant mgr. Dimes S.A., Magoula of Attika, Greece, 1980-82; sci. adviser Ministry Research and Tech., Athens, 1982—; research fellow lab. phys. chemistry Nat. Tech. U., Athens, 1969-83, asst. prof. stress corrosion cracking of aluminum alloys, 1983—. Author: The Mechanisms in Organic Chemistry, 1970, Inorganic Chemistry, 1979, Organic Chemistry, 1981 (in Greek); contbr. articles to profl. and sci. jours. Served with Greek Army, 1968. Mem. Tech. Chamber Greece, Hellenic Inst. Chem. Engrs., Hellenic Soc. Operational Research, Am. Inst. Chem. Engrs. Greek Orthodox. Lodge: Rotary (sec. gen. 1985-86). Home: 91 Alex Fleming St, 18344 Moschato Greece Office: Ministry Research and Tech, 14 Mesogion St, 11510 Athens Greece

KARAGOZIAN, SERGE VARENACK, physician; b. Romans, France, Nov. 4, 1948; s. Arthur and Lussaper (Boyaojian)k.; m. Martine; 1 child, Igor. B, Lycee Romans, 1967. Diplomate French Bd. Family Practice. Intern Valence Hosp. Ctr., France, 1974; intern rehabilitation Dominique Hosp., Larrey Versailles, France, 1975-76; physician Rockroum Inst., France, 1975; practicing medicine specializing in gen. medicine Valence, France, 1976—, practicing medicine specializing in sports, 1976; cons. L.P.G. System, Valence, 1986—; tchr. Sch. Manual Medicine, Lyon, 1984—. Mem. French Med. Soc., French Orthopedic and Theraputic Soc. Home: Mours, 26540 Saint Eusebe France Office: 1 Ave Victor Hugo, 26000 Valence France

KARAKI, YUKIHIKO, computer educator; b. Ina-city, Nagano, Japan, Jan. 11, 1943; s. Shigeichiro Karaki and Mitsuko Oobayashi; m. Masami Karaki; 1 child, Miho. BA in Culture, U. Tokyo, 1966, MA, 1968, PhD, 1971. Asst. instr. U. Tokyo; lectr. Musashino U. Art, Kodaira, Tokyo, U. Tokyo; asst. prof. Senshu U., Kawasaki, Kanagawa, Japan, prof., 1986—; chmn. Study Meeting of Array Processor, Tokyo, 1980-85; bd. dirs. NSF Supercomputer Group, Boston. Author: The Supercomputer, 1985, Supercomputer Applications, 1985; author, editor jour. Computational Physics, 1984, Present Supercomputers, 1987. Mem. Soc. Computer Sci. (mem. com. computer lang., com. numerical analysis), Phys. Soc. Japan. Home: 7-28-17 Tamagawa-gakuen, 194 Machida Japan Office: Senshu U, 2-1-1 Higashi-mita, Tama-ku, 214 Kawasaki Japan

KARAMATSU, YOSHIKAZU, mathematics educator; b. Matsuyama, Ehime, Japan, Feb. 8, 1937; s. Yoshimasa and Yoshiko (Miyanishi) K.; m. Keiko Inoue, Jan. 5, 1966; children: Michiko, Hironori, Yoko. BS, Sci. U. Tokyo, 1964, MS, 1966. Instr. Sci. U. Tokyo, 1965—; instr. Utsunomiya U., Japan, 1968-70, assoc. prof., 1970-81, prof., 1982—, councilor, 1988—. Author: On Fermat's Last Theorem and the First Factor of the Class Number of the Cyclotomic Fields, 1968, 1980, Introduction to Linear Algebra, Kyoritsu Shuppan, 1983. Mem. Math. Soc. Japan., Math. Soc. Am., Am. Indsl. and Applied Math. Soc. Clubs: Ijikai (Shinjuku), Risokai. Home: 842-1 Hiramatsu-honcho, 321 Utsunomiya, Tochigi Japan Office: Utsunomiya U, 350 Mine-machi, 321 Utsunomiya, Tochigi Japan

KARANJA, JOSPHAT NJUGUNA, government official; b. Feb. 5, 1931. Student, Makerere Coll., Kampala, Uganda, U. Delhi, Princeton U. Lectr. African Studies Fairleigh Dickinson U., Rutherford, N.J., 1961-62; lectr. African and Modern European History U. East Africa, 1962-63; high commr. for Kenya London, 1963-70; vice-chancellor U. Nairobi, Kenya, 1970-79; mem. of parliament Govt. of Kenya, 1986—, v.p., 1988—; bd. dirs. UNITAR; chair, Gen. Accident Ins. Co. (Kenya) Ltd., 1980—. Office: Gen Accident Ins Co (Kenya) Ltd, Icea Bldg Kenyatta Ave, PO Box 42166, Nairobi Kenya *

KARAPOSTOLES, DEMETRIOS ARISTIDES, civil engineer; b. Larissa, Greece, Mar. 2, 1936; s. Aristides Demetrios and Zoi-Lili Aristides (Papadimitriou) K.; m. Toula Haralambos Giagtzoglou, Oct. 24, 1976; children—Zoi-Lili, Aristides. Student Cathedral Sch. St. Paul, 1954, Bethany Coll., W.Va., 1954-56; B.S. in Civil Engring. U. Mich., 1961; degree in civil engring Nat. Tech. U., Athens, 1962. Registered prof. engr.; prof. civil engr. Nat. Tech. U. Athens, 1962. Cons. profl. civil engr., Thessaloniki, 1964-75; assoc. prof. civil engring. Larissa's Inst. Tech., 1975; asst. head hydraulics div. Ministry Pub. Works, Larissa, 1976—. Served to lt. C.E., Greek Army, 1962-64. Fellow ASCE; mem. Tech. Chamber of Greece. Greek Orthodox. Avocations: photography; short-wave radio.

KARASAWA, KOREYOSHI, mechanical engineer; b. Kyoto, Japan, Jan. 19, 1910; s. Junkichi and Shinako Karasawa; m. Karasawa Kazuko, Apr. 29, 1940; 4 daughters. M.Engring., Waseda U., Tokyo, 1936; D.Engring., Kyoto U., Japan, 1955. Chief engr. S. Manchuria Ry. Co., Dairen, China, 1936-46; prof. Osaka City U., Japan, 1950-72, Chubu Tech. Inst., Nagoya, Japan, 1972-82; tech. adviser Hamana Iron Works, Osaka, 1965—. Home: 5-32 Midorigaoka, Itami City 664 Japan

KARASE, CHAKANYUKA, dean of faculty, academic administrator lecturer; b. Marondera, Zimbabwe, June 1, 1952; s. Matipedza Chamunorwa and Sarudzai (Chizengeni) K.; m. Chiedza Karase; children: Matipedza Jr., Tafadzwa. Diploma in Pub. Adminstrn., U. Malawi, 1971; BS, U. Lagos, 1974; M in Pub. Adminstrn., U. Pitts., 1976. Asst. UN Inst. Tng. and Research, N.Y.C., Geneva, 1976-77; lectr. Dept. Polit. Sci. and Pub. Adminstrn. U. Benin, Bendel State, Nigeria, 1977-79; lectr., acting chmn. dept. polit. and adminstrv. studies, acting dean of faculty Studies U. Zimbabwe, Harare, 1979—; V.p. Southern African Univs. Social Sci. Conf., 1976—; chmn. bd. mgmt. Samora Machel Inst., Harare. Contbr. articles to profl. jours. Mem. African Assn. Pub. Adminstrn. and Mgmt., African Polit. Sci. Assn. Home: 224 Enterprise Rd, The Grange, Harare Zimbabwe Office: Univ of Zimbabwe, Dept Polit & Adminstrv Studies, Box MP 167, Harare Zimbabwe

KARASIK, GITA, concert pianist; b. San Francisco, Dec. 14, 1949; d. Monia and Bereni Karasik; pupil of Lev Shorr, Rosina Lhevinne, Karl Ulrich Schnabel. Debut as soloist, San Francisco Symphony, 1958; debut on nat. TV, Bell Telephone Hour, NBC, 1964; N.Y.C. debut Carnegie Hall, 1969; mem. Andy Warhol: Made in China, 1986; solo recitalist, 1972; film score debut Andy Warhol: Made in China, 1986; solo recitalist, guest soloist with major orchs. throughout world, 1955—; tchr. master classes, 1970—; 1st Am. pianist to make ofcl. concert tour of China, 1980; mem. music adv. panel solo artists Nat. Endowment Arts, 1980; interdisciplinary panel 1st D.C. Arts Commn., 1981; mem. Artists for Nuclear Disarmament, Artists to End Hunger. Recipient Solo Artists award Nat. Endowment Arts, 1981-82, Artists award and commd. concerto Ford Found., 1976, Musicians award Rockefeller Found., 1982, 1st prize Xerox/Affiliate Artists Internat. Piano Competition, 1982; winner Young Concert Artists Internat. Auditions, 1969; Solo artist sponsorship Pro Musicis Found., 1978—, Bösendorfer Piano Co., 1976—. Address: care Lee Caplin Prodns 8274 Grand View Los Angeles CA 90046

KARATHANASSIS, ATHANASSIS, research center administrator, educator; b. Volos, Greece, July 7, 1946; s. Eufthimios and Vassiliki K.; m. Helene Papaemmanouil, July 4, 1974; children: Vassiliki, Erasmie. Faculty Letters, U. Thessaloniki, 1969; Masters, Scuola Paleografia e Diplomatica, Venezia, Italy, 1971; Doctorate, U. Thessaloniki, 1976, Faculty Theology, 1987. Assoc. researcher Inst. Ellenico di Venezia (Italy), 1969-72, Inst. Balkan Studies, Thessaloniki, 1974-87; assoc. prof. U. Thessaloniki, 1985-87, U. Athens, 1987—. Author: The Phlanginian School, 1976, The Greek Scholarships, 1982, The Unity of Hellenism, 1985, L'Hellenismne en Transylvanie, 1987, The Metropolitan of Neurokopi, 1987; editor: Fioci di Virtu, 1978; contbr. articles and book revs. to profl. jours. Sec. Dimitcia, Thessaloniki, 1987. Mem. Soc. Greek Historians, Soc. Macedonian Studies, Inst. Patcistik Studies. Home: Theagenus Hacissi 51, 54639 Thessaloniki Greece Office: Inst Balkan Studies, Faculty of Letters, Tsimiski 45, Panepistimioupolis Zografu, 54623 Athens Greece

KARATSU, HAJIME, business educator; b. Tanto, Ryonei, People's Republic of China, Jan. 9, 1919; arrived in Japan, 1935; s. Tsurukichi and Itsuno (Kobayashi) K.; m. Sumako Narumi, Dec. 8, 1945 (dec. Apr. 1973); 1 child, Osamu; m. Natsuko Kimura, Mar. 1, 1975; 1 child, Haruko Ohno. BS in Engring., Tokyo U., 1942. Mgr. Nippon Telegraph & Telephone, Tokyo, 1948-61; mng. dir. Matsushita Communication Indsl. Co. Ltd., Yokohama, Japan, 1961-84; tech. advisor Matsushita Electric Indsl. Co. Ltd., Osaka, Japan, 1984-86; prof. Research and Devel. Inst. Tokai U., Tokyo, 1986—; mem. Indsl. Structural Council of MITI, Tokyo, 1983—; chmn. office automation com. Tokyo Met. Govt. 1984—. Author: System Engineering, 1970, Marketing Science, 1974, Scenario of Japan, 1980, 81, TQC, 1981. Recipient Deming award Japan Union Scientists and Engrs., 1981, Info. Prize Japanese Ministry Internat. Trade and Industry, 1983, Industry Edn. award Japanese Ministry Edn., 1984; named Hon. Citizen State of Tex., 1986. Mem. Japan Ops. Research Inst., Reliability Engring. Assn. Japan; mem. Am. Soc. Quality Control, Inst. 5th Generation Computer Systems. Home: 5-22-2 Denenchofu, Ohta-ku, Tokyo 145 Japan Office: Tokai U, 2-28-4 Tomigaya, Shibuya-ku, Tokyo 151 Japan

KARATSU, OSAMU, large scale integration researcher; b. Tokyo, Apr. 25, 1947; s. Hajime and Sumako (Narumi) K. B.S., Tokyo U., 1970, M.S., 1972, Ph.D. in Physics, 1975. Researcher Nippon Telegraph and Telephone Pub. Corp., Musashino Labs., Tokyo, 1975-79, staff researcher, 1979-83; sr. staff researcher NTT Atsugi Labs., Atsugi, Japan, 1983-86; research group leader NTT LSI Labs, Atsugi, 1987—. Author: Introduction to Very Large Scale Integration Design, 1983; Microelectronics Series, 1985. Mem. Japan Soc. Applied Physics, Am. Phys. Soc., IEEE, Inst. Electronic and Communication Engrs. Japan, Inst. Elec. Engring. Japan. Avocations: playing and listening to classical music. Home: 9-13-8 Arima, Kawasak 13, Japan Office: NTT LSI Labs, 3-1 Morinosato Wakamiya, Atsugi-shi, Kanagawa 243-01, Japan

KARCH, ROBERT E., real estate company executive; b. Bklyn., May 30, 1933; s. Charles H. and Etta R. (Becker) K.; AB, Syracuse U., 1953, MBA, 1958; student in Russian, Army Lang. Sch., Monterey, Calif., 1953-54; m. Brenda Schechter, Sept. 7, 1958; children: Barry S., Karen D., Brian D. With Nationwide Beauty & Barber Supply Co., Syracuse, N.Y., 1956-87, pres., 1966-74, chmn., 1974-87, also dir.; sales mgr. Helen of Troy Corp., El Paso, Tex., 1974-76, v.p. sales and mktg., 1976-79, also dir.; v.p., dir. Bormex Constrn. Inc., 1980-81; pres. BKB Properties, 1978—; ptnr. BKB Ins. Agy., 1987—; instr. investment real estate Acad. Real Estate, 1984-87. Pres. Syracuse Hebrew Day Sch., 1972-73. Served with U.S. Army, 1953-56. Lic. real estate broker, Tex., N.Mex., Colo.; lic. comml. pilot. Mem. Beauty and Barber Supply Inst., Direct Mail/Mktg. Assn., Aircraft Owners and Pilots Assn., Real Estate Securities and Syndication Inst., El Paso Real Estate Investment Club (pres. 1985), Jewish War Vets., El Paso Aviation Assn., El Paso Bd. Realtors (comml. investment div., mem. Exchangers Club, Top Vol. Producer award 1984, 85, 86, Best Real Estate Exchange award 1986), El Paso Apt. Assn. Clubs: Coronado Country, Lancer's. Author: Data Processing for Beauty/Barber Dealers, 1968. Pub. Real Estate Investor's Newsletter, 1982—, Property Mgmt. Newsletter, 1985—. Home: 6016 Torrey Pines El Paso TX 79912 Office: BKB Properties Inc 10622A Montwood Dr El Paso TX 79935

KARES, KAARLO OLAVI, bishop; b. Mikkeli, Finland, Mar. 24, 1903; s. K.R. and Sigrid (Koskinen) K.; m. Aili Mattila; 1 child, Leena. D in Theology (hon.), U. Helsinki, Finland, 1942. Ordained to ministry Luth. Ch., 1928; qualified for prof. eccles. history U. Helsinki;. Curate Lapua, 1928-30; headmaster Christian People's Ednl. Inst., Turku, 1930-60; dean Turku, 1960-62; bishop Diocese of Kuopio, 1962-74. Author: Palava kynttilä, 1936, Heränneen kansan vaellus I-V, 1942-52, Luther, 1945, Päiväkirja, 1958, Kierros auringon Ympäri, 1961, Kallaveden rannalta, 1965, Seuratkaa tähteä, 1974, Olavi Kares kertoo elämastään, 1976, Pohjanmaan lakeusilla ja Auran rannoilla, 1977, Myrskyä ja tyventä, 1978, Värikäs elämän kausi, 1980, Tervaa ja palsamia, 1984. Address: 49 A Linnank, Turku Finland

KARHAUSEN VON BARDENBERG, LUCIEN RICHARD, medical research officer; b. Brussels, Aug. 17, 1927; s. Richard Léon and Jeanne Georgette (van de Kerckhof) K.; m. Annie Cohen-Solal, Oct. 14, 1980 (div. May 1984). MD, U. Brussels, 1952; MS, Harvard U., 1962. Diplomate in internal medicine. Med. officer Inst. Bordet, Brussels U., 1954-56; med. resident Meml. Hosp., Cornell U., N.Y.C., 1956-59; research fellow Sloan Kettering Inst., N.Y.C., 1959-61; asst. prof. Brussels U. Med. Sch., 1962-64; med. research officer Commn. of European Communities, Brussels, 1964-87; fgn. prof. U. Rome La Sapienza, 1988; cons. Italconsult, Saudi Arabia, 1976. Editor several books on pub. health and epidemiology related topics; contbr. numerous articles and papers on clin. medicine, philosophy, philosophy of sci., epidemiology and med. history. Fulbright grantee Dept. State, N.Y.C., 1956-60; recipient Damon Runyon award Damon Runyon Found., N.Y.C., 1958, Squibb Olin award Squibb Med. Found., N.Y.C., 1965. Mem. N.Y. Acad. Scis., Philosophy of Sci. Assn., Assn. Italiana d'Epidemiologia. Home: Quai Bourbon 27, 75004 Paris France Office: Commission of the EC, Plateau du Kirschberg, Luxembourg L2920, Luxembourg

KARIM, SAIYED RABIUL, space planner; b. Calcutta, India, Aug. 14, 1940; s. Syed Fazlul and Syeda Zahanara K. Student, pub. schs., Calcutta, pub. schs., Dhaka, Bangladesh. Mgr. Associated Traders, Dhaka, 1957-58; gen. mgr. Kaar Corp. Ltd., Dhaka, Chittagong, Rangpur, 1959-71; exec. dir. Marna & Co. Ltd., Dhaka, 1972-74, Upodeshok Ltd., Dhaka, 1974-75; mng. dir. Shilpa-o-banijya Ltd., Dhaka, 1975-78, Planners and Consultants Ltd., Dhaka, 1975—; exec. dir. Dauss Internat. Holding Co., Riyadh, Saudi Arabia, PMP Internat. Co., Dhaka, 1986—. Mem. Bangladesh Geog. Soc., Internat. Assn. of Lions Clubs. Clubs: Dhaka Ltd., Tikatuly Sporting (gen. sec. 1954-58). Lodge: Lions (pres. Dhaka Prog., Dist. 315 1986-87). Home: 66 Laboratory Rd, Dhaka 5 Bangladesh Office: Planners and Consultants Ltd, 48 New Elephant Rd, Dhaka 5 Bangladesh

KARIMKUTTICAL, SIMON VARGHESE, association executive; b. Pathanamthitta, Kerala, India, Apr. 28, 1949; s. Varghese Koshy and Thankamma Varghese (Thankamma) K.; m. Daisy Simon, May 25, 1978; children: Phoebe Simon, Paul Simon. Diploma in hotel mgmt., Inst. Hotel Mgmt., Bombay, 1970; BBA, Northwood Inst., 1975, AA in Hotel and Restaurant Mgmt., 1975; postgrad., India Bible and Tng. Inst., Poona, 1977. Cert. hotel administr. Ednl. Inst. Am. Hotel/Motel Assn. Supr. in charge Res. Bank India, Bombay, 1970-72; leading romm steward, trainee asst. mgr. Gulf Hotel-Gulf Air, Doha Qatar, 1972-74; asst. mgr. to dir. aux. enterprises Northwood Inst., Midland, Mich., 1974-75; tng. instr., tng. officer Gulf Hotel, Gulf Air and His Majesty's Palace, Sultantate of Oman, 1976; head dept. mgmt. front office maintenance Inst. Hotel Mgmt., Bombay, 1977-79; assoc. mgr. Asha Handicrafts Assn., Bombay, 1979-80; vice prin. Inst. Hotel Mgmt., Bombay, 1980-86, prin., 1986—; assoc. mgr. Asha Handicrafts Assn., Bombay, 1979-80; mem. Hotel and Restaurant Approval Classification Com., Western Region, India; mem. courses com. Bd. Tech. Exam., Maharashtra, India. Editor Jour. Hospitality Industry. Mem. Nat. Council Hotel Mgmt. and Catering Tech., Indian Inst. Travel and Tourism Mgmt., Hotel and Restaurant Assn. (W.I., sub-com. hospitality, tng. and research). Home: Inst Hotel Mgmt, Veer Sawarkar Marg Dadar, 400 028 Bombay, Maharashtra India Office: Inst Hotel Mgmt Catering, Tech & Applied Nutrition, Veer Sawarkar Marg Dadar, 400028 Bombay, Maharashtra India

KARIOTAKIS, EMMANUEL, surgeon; b. Iraklion, Greece, Jan. 21, 1941; came to France, 1961, naturalized, 1974; s. Constantin and Iokasti (Toupoyanni) K.; m. Regine Loisel, May 22, 1971. M.D., Faculte de Medicine de Paris, 1967, laureat, 1975. Head dept. veinous surgery American Hosp. Paris, Neuilly-sur-Seine, 1980—; cons. French Red Cross, Paris, 1979-87. Contbr. articles to profl. jours. Fellow Association Francaise de Chirurgie, College Francais de Pathologie Vasculaire. Office: Hopital Americain de Paris, 63 Blvd Victor Hugo, Neuilly-sur-Sine 92202 France

KARIUKI, NGENYE, stockbroker, accountant; b. Muranga, Kenya, June 18, 1945; s. Ernest and Bertha (Wanjiku) K.; m. Mary Rose Waroe, Dec. 13, 1975; children—Kariuki, Njeru. B.Commerce, U. Nairobi, Kenya, 1971. Fin. acct. Kenya Engring. Industries, Nairobi, 1971-72; chief acct. Family Planning Assn. Kenya, 1972-74; gen. mgr. Dyer & Blair, Ltd., Nairobi, 1975-79; exec. chmn. Ngenye Kariuki & Co., stockbrokers, Nairobi, 1980—; chmn. Nairobi Stock Exchange, 1979-80, 82—. Dir. Pearl Dry Cleaners Ltd., Nairobi. Commr. Chmn. works and town planning com. Nairobi City Commn., 1988—; mem. Ct. Brokers Licensing Bd. 1984—. Author: How the Nairobi Stock Exchange Works. Dep. chmn. Muranga Coll. Tech., Kenya, 1983—. Mem. Kenya Inst. Mgmt. (exec. council 1984—). Club: United Kenya. Avocations: squash; reading; volleyball; music. Office: Ngenye Kariuki & Co, Muindi Mbingu St, Nairobi Kenya Other: Nairobi Stock Exchange, Stanbank House, Moi Ave, POB 43633 Nairobi Kenya

KARIYA, TAKUYA, regional public officer; b. Nakamura, Kochi, Japan, July 22, 1946; s. Sigehiro and Sadiko K.; m. Mika Kanematsu; children: Yatsuka, Mayumi, Hitomi. Law student, Waseda U., Tokyo, 1971. With Adminstrn. Kochi Prefecture, Nakamura, Japan, 1971-74, Kochi, Japan, 1974-81; chief of charge Adminstrn. Kochi Prefecture, Tosashimizu, Japan, 1981-84; with Adminstrn. Kochi Prefecture, Kochi, Japan, 1984-87, group leader, 1987—. Home: 7-4-2 Hadaminamicho, 780 Kochi Japan Office: Adminstrn Kochi Prefecture, 20-2-1 Marunouchi, 780 Kochi Japan

KARIYA, TETSURO, architect; b. Tokyo, Jan. 20, 1957; s. Toshio and Mitsuko (Hirama) K. BArch, Tokyo U., 1980, MArch, 1982. First class architect, Japan. Architect K. Oikawa & Tetsuro Kariya Architect Studio, Tokyo, 1981-82, Kenzo Tange & Urtec, Tokyo, 1981—, Kenzo Tange Assocs., Tokyo, 1987—. Author: (with others) Semiotic Space in Traditional Town-textures in Japan, 1982, Design Methodology IV, 1982. Mem. Japan Inst. Architects, Tokyo Inst. Architects, Archtl. Inst. of Japan. Clubs: Tosetsukai, Bakayaro-kai (Tokyo). Lodges: Hakureiso, Heda-ryo. Home: 2-14-4 Minami-Ohizumi, Nerima-ku, 178 Tokyo Japan Office: Kenzo Tange Assocs, 7-2-21 Akasaka, Minato-ku, 106 Tokyo Japan

KARL, ALAN GEORGE, corporate executive; b. Chgo., Sept. 16, 1949; s. Francis George and Josephine Rose (Spiotto) K.; student U. Ill., Champaign; BS in Math., Northwestern U.; postgrad. U. Chgo., 1984—. Systems analyst Ill. Bell Telephone Co., Chgo., 1970-73; sr. cons. Applied Info. Devel. Co., Oakbrook, Ill., 1974-78; dir. Smokenders, Inc., 1978-79; sr. cons. Applied Info. Devel. Co., 1979-83; quality assurance cons. Harris Bank, Chgo., 1983-85; dir. quality assurance and security adminstrn. The Options Clearing Corp., 1985-88. Recipient City of Chgo. citation for pub. service, 1977, 79; Achievement award Applied Info. Devel. Co., 1975, 80. Mem. Structured Techniques Assn. (dir.), Mensa. Author computer source library and maintenance system. Home: 260 E Chestnut St Chicago IL 60611

KARL, ANITA KATHERINE, graphic artist, calligrapher; b. N.Y.C., May 27, 1941; d. Otto and Anita Emilie (Herb) Bohnenberger; m. Rolf Karl, Oct. 14, 1961 (div. 1978); 1 child, Anita Korin. BFA, Cooper Union Art Sch., 1961. Staff book designer Alfred A. Knopf, Inc., N.Y.C., 1961-62; freelance book designer Random House/Knopf Inc., N.Y.C., 1962-70; co-founder, ptnr. Compass Projections Studio, Bklyn., 1970—; commns. include: book jacket and calligraphic map design Atheneum Pubs., N.Y.C., 1970—, Random House, Inc., N.Y.C., 1970—, record cover design Shanachie Records, Inc., Ho-Ho-Kus, N.J., 1978—, calligraphy N.Y. Times, 1978—, calligraphic map design Franklin Library, N.Y.C., 1978—, Holt, Rinehart & Winston, N.Y.C., 1980—, Harcourt, Brace, Jovanovich, San Diego, 1982—. Illustrator: From Woman to Woman, 1975; calligrapher: Good King Wenceslas, 1980, Song of the Three Young Men, 1981; artwork selected for group shows Art Dirs.' Club, N.Y.C., 1981, Master Eagle Gallery, N.Y.C., 1981, 83-84, 87, also for books Modern Scribes and Lettering Artists, 1980, Calligraphy Jour., 1981. Co-founder Summer Musical Theater for Young Adults, Inc., 1985. Recipient certs. of excellence Am. Inst. Graphic Arts, N.Y.C., 1969, 75, 87, poster design award Assn. Coll., Univ. and Community Arts Adminstrs., 1979. Avocations: drawing, painting. Office: Compass Projections 20 Henry St Suite 2A Brooklyn NY 11201

KARL, FREDERICK ROBERT, English language educator; b. N.Y.C., Apr. 10, 1927; s. Louis and Edith Ida (Sabloff) K.; m. Dolores Mary Oristaglio, June 8, 1951; children—Deborah, Rebecca, Judith. B.A., Columbia U., 1948; M.A., Stanford U., 1949; Ph.D., Columbia U., 1957. Prof. English, CCNY, 1957-82; prof. English, NYU, N.Y.C., 1982—; Fulbright prof., France, 1965; Am. adviser Conrad edit. Cambridge U., Press, Eng., 1983—. Author: Joseph Conrad: The Three Lives, 1979; American Fictions: 1940-1980, 84; Modern and Modernism, 1985; William Faulkner, American Writer, 1989; gen. editor, volume co-editor: The Collected Letters of Joseph Conrad, Vol. I, 1983, Vol. II, 1986, Vol. III, 1988. Served with USN, 1944-46. Guggenheim fellow, 1966; NEH sr. research fellow, 1978, 88; NYU research fellow, 1984. Mem. MLA, Andiron Club, P.E.N. Office: NYU Dept English New York NY 10003

KARLE, JEROME, research physicist; b. N.Y.C., June 18, 1918; married, 1942; 3 children. B.S., CCNY, 1937; A.M., Harvard U., 1938; M.S., U. Mich., 1942, Ph.D. in Phys. Chemistry, 1943. Research asso. Manhattan project, Chgo., 1943-44, U.S. Navy Project, Mich., 1944-46; head electron diffraction sect. Naval Research Lab., Washington, 1946-58; head diffraction br. Naval Research Lab., 1958, now head lab. for structure matter; mem. NRC, 1954-56, 67-75, 78-87; chmn. U.S. Nat. Com. for Crystallography, 1973-75. Recipient Nobel prize in chemistry, 1985. Fellow Am. Phys. Soc.; mem. Am. Chem. Soc., Crystallograph. Assn. (treas. 1950-52, pres. 1972), Internat. Union Crystallography (exec. com. 1978-87, pres. 1981-84), Am. Math. Soc., AAAS, Nat. Acad. Scis. Office: US Naval Research Lab Structure of Matter Code 6030 Washington DC 20375

KARLOS, ANTHONY CHRIST, broadcasting executive, former retail grocery executive; b. Chgo., Sept. 24, 1912; s. Christ A. and Angeline (Simoulis) K.; m. Demetrea Ganos, June 11, 1944; children: Chris, Dean, Stephanie. Student pub. schs., Chgo. Mgr. family-owned business 1930-37; with Gen. Foods Corp., 1937-43, Grocerland Corp. Inc., Chgo., 1940-78; gen. mgr. Grocerland Corp. Inc., vice chmn. bd., 1961-63, chmn. bd., chief exec. officer, 1963-78, ret.; chmn. bd. dirs., co-founder Century Broadcasting Corp., Chgo., 1964—; co-founder, officer, dir. O'Hare-Chgo. Corp., (O'Hare Inn), 1960-84; co-founder, vice chmn. bd., dir. exec. com. Archer Nat. Bank,

Chgo.; past officer, dir. several corps.; ptnr. in several real estate devels. including high rise office bldgs., indsl. bldgs., shopping ctrs.; former ptnr. Seven Eagles Restaurant, Des Plaines, Ill., Scotch & Sirloin Restaurants; del. 1st Panhellenic Investment Conf., Athens, Greece, 1980. Chmn., co-chmn. numerous fund-raising drives.; past dir. Riveredge Hosp., Forest Park, Ill., 1968; hon. parish council mem. St. Demetrios Greek Orthodox Ch., Chgo.; past mem. nat. bd. trustees City of Hope, Duarte, Calif., med. research fellowship named for Mr. Karlos; hon. trustee Am. Coll. of Greece. Recipient Golden Torch of Hope award for humanitarian ideals City of Hope, 1965, Million Dollar Club award, 1973-74; named Man of Yr. award of merit Ill. and Chgo. Wholesale Grocers Assns., 1961; named to Hall of Fame Carl Schurz High Sch., Chgo., 1985. Mem. Chgo. Wholesale Grocers Assn. (past pres., dir., 1955-62), Chgo. Natural History Mus. (life assoc.), Art Inst. Chgo., Chgo. Symphony Soc., Chgo. Hort. Soc., Chgo. Council Fgn. Relations, United Hellenic Am. Congress (exec. com.), Hellenic Assn. Commerce and Industry of Ill., Order of Ahepa. Clubs: Masons (Chgo.), Execs. (Chgo.). Home: 6747 Minnehaha Lincolnwood Towers IL 60646 Office: Century Broadcasting Corp 875 N Michigan Ave Suite 4145 Chicago IL 60611

KARLSON, BEN EMIL, kitchen design company executive; b. Hedemora, Sweden, Aug. 27, 1934; came to U.S., 1954, naturalized, 1960; s. Emil W.J. and Ester Linnea (Hellman) Karlsson; student bus. mktg. Alexander Hamilton Inst., N.Y.C., 1967, Am. Inst. Kitchen Designers, 1972; grad. Dale Carnegie Inst., 1972; m. Susan Jo Kaupert, Feb. 7, 1958; children—David, Kristine, Thomas. Salesman, Edward Hines Lumber Co., Chgo., 1954-63; v.p., gen. mgr. Lake Forest Lumber Co. (Ill.), 1963-67; pres. Karlson Home Center, Inc., Evanston, Ill., 1967—, Poggenpohl-Midwest/USA, Inc., Evanston, Atag USA Corp., Evanston; dir. tng. U.S. Poggenpohl, Herford, W. Ger., 1981-86 ; pres. Bank Lane Investors, Lake Forest, 1971-72; founder chmn. Evanston Home Show, 1973, 74; judge, Nat. Design Contest, 1974; showroom design cons., Ill., Poggenpohl Kitchens Germany; speaker in field; lectr. on kitchen bus. and design at univs. and convs. Mem. steering com. Covenant Meth. Ch., Evanston, 1968-69; bd. dirs. Evanston Family Counseling Service, 1973-75, Evanston United Community Services, 1974-75, mid-Am. chpt. No. region ARC, 1974; chmn. bus. div. Evanston United Fund, 1974, gen. campaign chmn., 1975. Recipient awards for community service. Cert. kitchen designer. Mem. Nat. Kitchen and Bath Assn. (bd. dirs. 1897—), Evanston Inventure (bd. dirs. 1987—), Am. Inst. Kitchen Designers (pres. 1975-76), Soc. Cert. Kitchen Designers, 1987— (bd. govs., sec. 1987—), Evanston C. of C. (dir. 1973-74, v.p. 1975, pres. 1976), Westmoreland C. of C., Nat. Fed. Ind. Bus., Mid-Am. Swedish Trade Assn. Club: Evanston Rotary (pres. 1984-85). Contbr. kitchen designs to nat. mags. Home: 2311 Central Park Ave Evanston IL 60201 Office: 1815 Central St Evanston IL 60201

KARLSON, KARL EUGENE, surgeon; b. Worcester, Mass., July 20, 1920; s. Karl Johann and Mabel Cecelia (Fisher) K.; m. Gloria E. Anderson, June 24, 1947; children—Karl, Peter, Nancy, Steven, James, Matthew. Student, Bethel Coll., 1938-39; B.S., U. Minn., 1943, M.D., 1944, Ph.D., 1952. Diplomate: Am. Bd. Surgery. Intern U. Minn., Mpls., 1944-45; resident in surgery U. Minn., 1947-51; mem. faculty dept. surgery Downstate Med. Center SUNY, Bklyn., 1951-71; prof. surgery Downstate Med. Center SUNY, 1959-71; prof. med. sci. Brown U., Providence, 1971—; surgeon-in-charge thoracic and cardiovascular surgery R.I. Hosp., Providence, 1971-85; cons. in surgery Miriam Hosp., R.I. Hosp., VA Hosp.; adj. prof. biomed. engring. U. R.I. Contbr. chpts. to med. books, articles to med. jours. Served with USN, 1945-46, 54-56. NIH fellow, 1950-51. Mem. Am. Surg. Assn., Soc. Univ. Surgeons, Soc. Clin. Surgery, Am. Assn. Thoracic Surgery, A.C.S., Soc. Thoracic Surgeons, Soc. Vascular Surgery, Am. Coll. Cardiology, Internat. Cardiovascular Soc., Soc. Internat. de Chirugie. Home: 252 Bowen St Providence RI 02906 Office: 110 Lockwood St Providence RI 02903

KARLSON, LAWRENCE CARL, technology company executive; b. Canora, Saskatchewan, Can., Dec. 29, 1942; s. Carl Louis and Katherine (Novakowski) Kulchyski; m. Margo Thompson, Sept. 28, 1963; children: Graydon, Stephen. Diploma in engring., Ryerson Polytech. Inst., 1963; MBA with distinction, U. Pa., 1980. Mng. dir. Fischer & Porter Party Ltd., Melbourne, Australia, 1973-77; v.p. mktg. Fischer & Porter Co., Warminster, Pa., 1977-78, v.p. mfg., 1978-80, dir., pres. U.S. ops., 1980-83; pres., chief exec. officer Nobel Electronics, Inc., Blue Bell, Pa., 1983-86; pres., chief exec. officer Pharos AB, Blue Bell and Stockholm, 1986—, also bd. dirs.; pres., chief exec. officer Karlson Corp., Blue Bell, 1986—; bd. dirs. Dynisco, Inc., Norwood, Mass., Vidar Systems, Inc., Herndon, Va., ABB Robotics, Inc., New Berlin, Wis.;. Contbr. articles to profl. jours. Bd. dirs. Warminster Gen. Hosp., 1980-86. Griffith Labs. scholar, 1961, Texaco scholar, 1962. Mem. Young Pres.'s Orgn., Union League. Republican. Roman Catholic. Club: Cedarbrook Country (Blue Bell). Home: 1024 Woods Ln Ambler PA 19002 also: Flat 1 Rosebery Ct, 14-15 Charles St, London WIX7HB, England Office: Pharos USA Inc 595 Skippack Pike Suite 300 Blue Bell PA 19422 also: Pharos AB, Sturegatan 32 Box 5226, S-102 45 Stockholm Sweden *

KARLWEIS, GEORGES CHRISTOPH, banker; b. Vienna, Austria, Jan. 25, 1928; came to Switzerland, 1958, naturalized, 1973; s. Oscar and Fernande (Coulon) K.; m. Brigitte Camplez, June 6, 1986. Degree in Law, Faculté de Droit, Paris, 1948. Journalist AGEFI, Paris, 1946-51; v.p. imports, exports Siham, Casablanca, Morocco, 1953-54; commodity trader Ets. Albert Simpere, Paris, 1955-57; vice chmn. La Compagnie Financière Benjamin et Edmond de Rothschild SA, Paris, 1958—, Banque Privée S.A., Geneva, 1964; dir. Banca Privata in Lugano S.A., La Compagnie Financière Benjamin et Edmond de Rothschild S.A., Geneva, Adminstrn. & Gestion S.A., Geneva, N.M. Rothschild & Sons Ltd., London, Rothschild Bank AG, Zurich, Equitas S.A., Geneva, others. Clubs: Golf of Geneva; Golf (Mortefontaine, France); Golf (Cannes-Mougins, France). Home: 3 Chem Palud, 1292 Pregny-Geneve Switzerland Office: Banque Privee SA, 18 rue de Hesse, 1204 Geneva Switzerland

KARM, ROBERT MARCEAU, textile executive; b. Reichenberg, Czechoslovakia, May 11, 1931; s. Robert Jean and ELsa (Wildner) K.; m. Madeleine Daubin, Dec. 24, 1957; children: Jean, Claude. Diploma in textile engring., Ecole Superievre des Industries Textiles de Mulhouse, France, 1952; degree in mech. engr., Fed. Inst. Tech., Switzerland, 1959, D in Sci., 1959. Asst. prof. Fed. Inst. Tech., 1956; with textile machinery constrn. dept. Soc. Alsacienne de Constrns. Mecaniques, France, 1957-59; with diesel engine constrn. dept. SACM Mulhouse, France, 1959-65; product and tech. dir. Martel Catala Selestat, France, 1965—; prof. materials tech. and theoretical mechanics ESITM, France, 1961-65. Patentee in field. Inst. Controle de Gestion fellow, France, 1979. Home: 12 Rue de Paris, 67600 Selestat France Office: Martel Catala, 67600 Selestat France

KARMAL, BABRAK, former president of Democratic Republic of Afghanistan, b. 1929. Ed. Kabul (Afghanistan) U. With Afghan Ministry of Planning, 1957-65; founder Khalq polit. party, Afghanistan, 1965, mem. Parliament, 1965-73, leader Parcham party, 1967-77, dep. leader People's Democratic Party of Afghanistan, 1977-78, dep. prime minister, v.p. Revolutionary Council, 1978, Afghan ambassador to Czechoslovakia, 1978-79; apptd. prime minister of Afghanistan, 1979-81; pres. Revolutionary Council, from 1979, Gen. Sec. cen. com. People's Dem. Party of Afghanistan, 1979-86, mem. Politburo, from 1979; comdr.-in-chief Afghan Armed Forces, 1979-81; reconstituted People's Dem. Party as Nat. Fatherland Front, 1981. Address: Office of President, Da Khalkoo Koor, Kabul Democratic Republic of Afghanistan *

KARNAS, GUY JEAN, psychology educator; b. Etterbeek, Brabant, Belgium, Sept. 15, 1944; s. Marcel Joseph and Rose Jeanne (Jacob) K.; m. Arielle Nadine De Gendt, Sept. 25, 1968; children: Jöelle, Damien. D in Psychology, U. Libre Brussels, 1974. Research asst. Fonds Nat. Recherche Sci., Brussels, 1971-79; research asst. U. Libre Brussels, 1979-81, prof., 1981—; faculty chmn. Psychol. and Pedagological Scis. U. Libre Brussels, 1985—; cons. in field. Author: Simulation etÉtude Différentielle de la Résolution de Probléems, 1976; contbr. articles to profl. jours. Served to cpl. Belgium military, 1970-71. Office: U Libre Brussels, Av Franklin D Roosevelt, 50 (CP122), Brussels 1050, Belgium

KARNES, EVAN BURTON, II, lawyer; b. Chgo.; s. Evan Burton and Mary Alice (Brosnahan) K.; m. Bridget Anne Clerkin, Oct. 9, 1976; children—Kathlen Anne, Evan Burton III, Molly Aileen. A.B., Loyola U., Chgo., 1975; J.D., DePaul U., 1978; student in trial advocacy program, U. Calif. Hastings Coll. Law, 1979. Bar: Ill. 1978, U.S. Dist. Ct. (no. dist.) Ill. 1978, U.S. Ct. Appeals (7th cir.) 1978, U.S. Supreme Ct. 1983. Trial atty. Chgo. Milw. St. Paul & Pacific R.R., Chgo., 1978-81; litigation dept. Baker & McKenzie, Chgo., 1981-87; sr. litigation counsel, Levin & Ginsburg Ltd., Chgo., 1987—; bd. dirs. Triad Communications Inc, Albuquerque, chmn. bd., 1988—. Mem. ABA, Ill. Bar Assn., Fed. Bar Assn., Chgo. Bar Assn., Def. Research Inst., Nat. Assn. R.R. Trial Counsel, Ill. Trial Lawyers Assn., Assn. Trial Lawyers of Am., Blue Key (sec. Loyola U. chpt. 1974-75), Pi Sigma Alpha, Phi Alpha Delta. Club: Union League (Chgo.). Office: Levin & Ginsburg Ltd 180 N LaSalle St 22d Floor Chicago IL 60601

KARO, ARNOLD MITCHELL, physicist; b. Wayne, Nebr., May 14, 1928; s. Henry Arnold and Ethel Leila (Mitchell) Maynard; m. Daniella Thea Cassvan, July 1, 1966; children: Barbara Melissa, Stephen Arnold. BS in Chemistry, Stanford U., 1949, BS in Physics, 1949; PhD in Chem. Physics, MIT, 1953. Teaching fellow MIT, Cambridge, 1949-51; staff physicist Lincoln Lab., Lexington, Mass., 1952; teaching assoc. dept. chemistry U. Utah, Salt Lake City, 1953-54; research assoc. Solid State and Molecular Theory Group, MIT, Cambridge, 1955-58; vis. research scientist European Ctr. Atomic and Molecular Theory U. Paris, Orsay, France, 1975; sr. scientist U. Calif. Lawrence Livermore Nat. Lab., 1958—; cons. in field. Author: (with others) The Lattice Dynamics and Statics of Alkali Halide Crystals, 1979. Contbr. articles to profl. jours. Mem. rev. com. City Pleasanton, Calif., 1973-74. Served with Chem. Corps AUS, 1953-55. Nat. Coffin fellow Gen. Electric Co., 1951-52. Fellow Am. Phys. Soc., AAAS, Am. Inst. Chemistry, N.Y. Acad. Scis.; mem. Calif. Inst. Chemists, (charter), Calif. Acad. Scis., Am. Chem. Soc., Phi Theta Kappa, Phi Lambda Upsilon, Sigma Xi. Presbyterian.

KAROFSKY, PAUL IRWIN, wallcovering distribution executive; b. Boston, Sept. 1, 1943; s. Sydney Bernard and Sylvia (Dulman) K.; m. Lisa Deering Stonberg, June 26, 1966; children: Jody, David. AB, Bowdoin Coll., 1966; MC, Conn. Coll., 1967; Smaller Company Mgmt. Program, Harvard Bus. Sch., 1979. Asst. treas. Northeastern Wallpaper Corp., Boston, 1967-70, exec. v.p., 1971-75, pres., chief exec. officer, 1975—, chmn. bd., 1988—; instr. human relations Weston High Sch., 1983—. Pres. Wellesley-Weston Hot Line, Mass., 1974; class agent Bowdoin Coll., 1978-84, student recruiter, 1984—, regional chmn., 1987—, rep. Alumni Council, 1987—; dir. Commonwealth of Mass. Area Bd. Dept. Mental Health, Newton, 1981; trustee, sec. Hebrew Rehab. Ctr. for Aged, Roslindale, Mass., 1981—; mem. Temple Israel Religious Edn. Com., Boston, 1983—; mem. Gov.'s Entrepreneurial Council, Boston, 1984—; Nat. Assn. Wholesaler Distributors, trustee 1974-76; corporator Grove Hall Savs. Bank, 1985-86, advisory bd. dirs., 1986—. Named Man of Yr., Wallcoverings Mag., Stamford, Conn. Mem. Wallcovering Distbrs. Assn. (pres. 1975-76), Wallcovering Info.; Bur. (v.p. 1975, pres. 1985-86, chmn. Point-of-Sale Mktg. Com. 1986—), New Eng. Wallcovering Distbrs. Assn. (pres.), Young Pres. Orgn. (sec. 1984-85); Assn. Wholesaler Distbrs. (trustee 1974-76). Office: Northeastern Wallpaper Corp 300 Summer St Boston MA 02210

KARPEN, MARIAN JOAN, financial executive; b. Detroit, June 16, 1944; d. Cass John and Mary (Jagiello) K.; A.B., Vassar Coll., 1966; postgrad. Sorbonne, Paris, N.Y. U. Grad. Sch. Bus., 1974-77. New Eng. corr. Women's Wear Daily, Fairchild Publs.-Capital Cities Communications, 1966-68, Paris fashion editor, TV and radio commentator Capital Cities Network, 1968-69; fashion editor Boston Herald Traveler, 1969-71; nat. syndicated newspaper columnist and photojournalist Queen Features Syndicate, N.Y.C., 1971-73; account exec. Blyth Eastman Dillon, N.Y.C., 1973-75, Oppenheimer, N.Y.C., 1975-76; v.p., mcpl. bond coordinator Faulkner Dawkins & Sullivan (merged Shearson Hayden Stone), N.Y.C., 1976-77; mgr. retail mcpl. bond dept. Warburg Paribas Becker-A.G. Becker (merger Becker Paribas and Merrill Lynch), N.Y.C., 1977-79, sr. v.p. and prin., 1977-84; sr. v.p., ltd. ptnr. Bear Stearns & Co., 1984-87, assoc. dir., 1987—, also assoc. bd. dirs.; lectr. fin. seminars, 1978—; mem. bus. adv. council U.S. Rep. Senate. Mem. benefit com. March of Dimes, 1983; mem. Torchlight Ball com. Internat. Games for Disabled, 1984, other benefit coms.; friend vol. Whitney Mus. Am. Art. Recipient Superior Prodn. award Becker Paribas, 1983. Mem. Nat. Assn. Securities Dealers (registered rep.), N.Y. Stock Exchange (registered rep.), N.Y.C. Women's Econ. Roundtable, Am. Soc. Profl. and Exec. Women, AAUW, U.S. Figure Skating Assn., Fishing Club of Am. (angler's honor roll), English Speaking Union. Clubs: Vassar, Skating (N.Y.C. and Boston). Past editorial bd. Retirement Planning Strategist; contbr. articles and photographs to newspapers and mags. Home: 233 E 69th St New York NY 10021 Office: Bear Stearns & Co 245 Park Ave New York NY 10167

KARPICKE, JOHN ARTHUR, systems engineer, experimental psychologist; b. Saginaw, Mich., Nov. 26, 1945; s. Herbert August and Eleanor Louise (Stafford) K.; m. Susan Gail Denyes, Aug. 5, 1972; children—Jeffrey Denyes, Jennifer Denyes. B.S., Mich. State U., 1972; Ph.D., Ind. U., 1976. NIH postdoctoral fellow in psychobiology Fla. State U., Tallahassee, 1976-77; asst. prof. psychology Valparaiso (Ind.) U., 1977-81, research fellow, 1978, 79, 80; mem. tech. staff human factors group Bell Telephone Labs., Indpls., 1981-82; mem. tech. staff system architecture group AT&T Consumer Products Labs., Indpls., 1983-84; mem. tech. staff functional systems design and software group AT&T Consumer Products Labs, Indpls., 1984-85, disting. mem. tech. staff advanced cellular technologies design group, 1985, advanced Voice Techs. group, Indpls., 1986—. Served with USNR, 1969-71; Vietnam. NIMH research grantee, 1979-80; recipient Disting. Tech. Staff award AT&T, 1985. Mem. AAAS, N.Y. Acad. Scis. Contbr. numerous articles to psychology jours. Office: 6612 East 75th St PO Box 1008 Indianapolis IN 46206

KARPILOVSKY, GREGORY, mathematician, educator, researcher; b. Kiev, Ukraine, USSR, Dec. 5, 1940; s. Ilia Aronovich and Roza Gershevna (Kaptournik) K.; m. Helen Swiatlo, June 27, 1976; children: Suzanne, Elliott Michael. BSc with honors, U. Uzhgorod, Ukraine, 1966. PhD, Inst. Radio-electronics, Kharkov, Ukraine, 1970. Asst. prof. Mil. Acad., Kiev, USSR, 1969-70; sr. lectr. Tech. Inst., Astrakhan, USSR, 1971-72; asst. prof. Agrl. Acad., Kiev, 1972-73; tutor U. New South Wales, Sydney, Australia, 1974-77; lectr. La Trobe U., Melbourne, Australia, 1978-83; prof. math. U. Witwatersrand, Johannesburg, Republic of South Africa, 1984—; reviewer profl. jours., 1974—. Author: Commutative Group Algebras, 1983; Projective Representations of Finite Groups, 1985, The Schur Multipiler, 1987, Structure of Blocks of Group Algebras, 1987, The Jacobson Radical of Group Algebras, 1987, The Algebraic Structure of Crossed Products, 1987, Unit Groups of Classical Rings, 1988, Unit Groups of Group Rings, 1988, Topics in Field Theory, 1988, Field Theory: Classical Foundations and Multiplicative Groups, 1988; editor: Group and Semigroup Rings, 1986; contbr. articles to research jours., 1967—. Fellow Internat. Biog. Assn.; mem. Australian Math. Soc., Am. Math. Soc., Confedn. Chivalry. Jewish. Avocations: chess, music, soccer. Home: 14 Leitch Rd, Johannesburg 2193, Republic of South Africa Office: U Witwatersrand, 1 Jan Smuts Ave, Johannesburg 2050, Republic of South Africa

KARPINSKI, JACEK, computer company executive; b. Torino, Italy, Apr. 9, 1927; s. Adam and Wanda (Cumft) K.; m. Eulalia Gryniecka, Mar. 1, 1955 (div. 1975); children—Dorota, Ewa; m. Ewa Stepien, July 11, 1978; children—Adam, Daniel V., Sylvan. Spl. student Harvard U., 1961-62; M.Sc.E.E., Politechnika Warsaw, 1951. System engr. Electronic Systems Mfg., Warsaw, 1951-54; adj. prof. Polish Acad. Scis., Warsaw, 1955-65; head computer lab. Warsaw U., 1965-70; mng. dir. Minicomputer R & D & Prodn., Warsaw, 1970-73; asst. prof. Warsaw Politechnic U., 1973-81; mng. dir. Karpinski Computer Systems, Le Mont, Switzerland, 1983-85; cons. in field of artificial intelligence, 1985—. Author numerous computer systems. Served to lt. Polish Armed Forces, 1941-44. Decorated Cross of Valor (3), Polish Underground Army, 1944, AK Cross, 1944. Mem. IEEE, State Comity for Computers. Roman Catholic. Home: Champ-Soleil, CH-1055 1055 Froideville Switzerland

KARPOV, ANATOLY, chess player; b. Zlatoust, USSR, May 23, 1951; grad. in econs. U. Leningrad, 1978; s. Yevgeny Stepanovich and Nina K.; m. Irina Karpov; 1 son, Anatoly. Began playing chess age 4; youngest chess master in USSR at age 15; world champion, 1975-85. Author: Chess is My Life, 1980, Karpov Teaches Chess, 1987. Address: USSR Chess Assn, Luzhnetskaya 8, Moscow 119270, USSR *

KARR, JOSEPH PETER, podiatrist; b. Chgo., Sept. 7, 1925; s. Vendelin Stephan and Irene (Bielik) Karkoška; m. Marilyn Isabelle Calder, Sept. 1, 1951; children: Joseph Jr., Michael, Paul, Kenneth. D of Surgical Chiropody, Chgo. Coll. Chiropody and Pedic Surgery, 1951; D of Podiatric Medicine (hon.), Ill. Coll. Podiatric Med., 1973. Lic. podiatrist, Ill. Podiatrist Chgo., 1951—; alumni advisor Dr. William M. Scholl Coll. of Podiatric Medicine, Chgo., 1986—. Author: (pamphlet) A Method To Alleviate and Cure the Painful Heel Syndrome, 1978. Served with USCGR, 1943-46. Mem. Am. Podiatric Med. Assn., Ill. Podiatry Soc., Ill. Podiatry Edn. Group, Am. Legion. Roman Catholic. Home: 10624 Kildare Ave Oak Lawn IL 60453 Office: 4008 W 57th Pl Chicago IL 60629

KARSEN, SONJA PETRA, Spanish educator; b. Berlin, Apr. 11, 1919; came to U.S., 1938, naturalized, 1945; d. Fritz and Erna (Heidermann) K. Titulo de Bachiller, 1937; B.A., Carleton Coll., 1939; M.A. (scholar in French), Bryn Mawr Coll., 1941; Ph.D., Columbia U., 1950. Instr. Spanish Lake Erie Coll., Painesville, Ohio, 1943-45; instr. modern langs. U. P.R., 1945-46; instr. Spanish Syracuse U., 1947-50, Bklyn. Coll., 1950-51; asst. to dep. dir. gen. UNESCO, 1951-52, Latin Am. Desk, tech. assistance dept., 1952-53, mem. tech. assistance mission Costa Rica, 1954; asst. prof. Spanish Sweet Briar Coll., Va., 1955-57; assoc. prof., chmn. dept. Romance langs. Skidmore Coll., Saratoga Springs, N.Y., 1957-61, chmn. dept. modern langs. and lits., 1961-79, prof. Spanish, 1961-87, prof. emerita, 1987; Fulbright lectr. Free U., Berlin, 1968; mem. adv. and nominating com. Books Abroad, 1965-67. Author: Guillermo Valencia, Colombian Poet, 1951, Educational Development in Costa Rica with UNESCO's Technical Assistance, 1951-54, 1954, Jaime Torres Bodet: A Poet in a Changing World, 1963, Selected Poems of Jaime Torres Bodet, 1964, Versos y prosas de Jaime Torres Bodet, 1966, Jaime Torres Bodet, 1971, Essays on Iberoamerican Literature and History, 1988; editor: Lang. Assn. Bull., 1980-83; mem. editorial adv. bd.: Modern Lang. Studies; contbr. articles to profl. jours. Decorated chevalier dans l'Ordre des Palmes Academiques, 1964; recipient Leadership award N.Y. State Assn. Fgn. Lang. Tchrs., 1973, 76, 78, Nat. Disting. Leadership award, 1979, Disting. Service award, 1983, 86, Capital Dist. Fgn. Language Disting. Service award, 1987; recipient Spanish Heritage award, 1981, Alumni Achievement award Carleton Coll., 1982; exchange student auspices Inst. Internat. Edn. at Carleton Coll., 1938-39; Buenos Aires Conv. grantee for research in Colombia, 1946-47; faculty research grantee Skidmore Coll., summer 1959, 61, 63-64, 67, 69-70, 73, ad hoc faculty grantee, 71, 78, 85. Mem. AAUP, MLA (del. assembly 1976-78, Mildenberger medal selection com. 1984-86), Am. Assn. Tchrs. Spanish and Portuguese, Nat. Assn. Self-Instructional Lang. Programs (v.p. 1981-82, pres. 1982-83), AAUW, El Ateneo Doctor Jaime Torres Bodet (founding mem.), Nat. Geog. Soc., Instituto Internacional de Literatura Iberoamericana, Asociacion Internacional de Hispanistas, UN Assn. U.S.A., Am. Soc. French Acad. Palms, Fulbright Alumni, Phi Sigma Iota, Sigma Delta Pi. Home: PO Box 441 Saratoga Springs NY 12866

KARSH, YOUSUF, photographer; b. Mardin, Armenia, Dec. 23, 1908; emigrated to Can., 1924; s. Amsih and Bahia K.; m. Estrellita Nachbar, Aug. 28, 1962. Pupil, John H. Garo; numerous hon. degrees including: LL.D., Queen's U., Kingston, Ont., Carleton U.; D.H.L., Dartmouth Coll., Ohio U., Mt. Allison U.; D.C.L., Bishop's U., Lennoxville, Que.; D.H.L., Emerson Coll.; B.Profl. Arts, Brooks Inst.; D.F.A., U. Mass., 1979, U. Hartford, 1980; M.F.A., Tufts U., 1981, Dawson Coll., Montreal, Can., 1981; D.F.A. (hon. degree), Syracuse U., 1986. Opened photog. studio Ottawa, Ont., Can., 1932; vis. prof. photography Ohio U., Emerson Coll.; lectr in field. Author: Faces of Destiny, 1946, Portraits of Greatness, 1959, This Is the Mass, 1958, This Is Rome, 1959, This is the Holy Land, 1960, These are the Sacraments, 1962, In Search of Greatness (autobiography), 1962, The Warren Court, 1965, Karsh Portfolio, 1967, Faces of Our Time, 1971, Karsh Portraits, 1976, Karsh Canadians, 1978, Karsh: A Fifty-Year Retrospective, 1983, paperback edit., 1986; portrait photographer leading nat. and internat. statesmen, corporate execs., polit. and govtl. ofcls., religious leaders including royal families of, Eng., Monaco, Norway, Greece, Pope John Paul II, also leading intellectual and entertainment figures, first one-man show, Nat. Gallery Can., 1959, one man show, Men Who Make Our World, Expo 67, Internat. Ctr. Photography, N.Y.C., 1983, Mus. Photography, Bradford, Eng., 1983, Nat. Portrait Gallery, London, 1984, Edinburgh, Scotland, 1984, People's Republic China, 1985, Helsinki, 1985, Muscarelle Mus. Art, 1987, William and Mary Coll., Williamsburg, Va., 1987, Barbican Ctr., London, 1988, Palais de Tokyo, Paris, 1988, Geneva Inst. Photography, Mus. für Gestahlung, Zürich, Switzerland, 1988, Henry E. Huntington Library and Art Gallery, San Marino, Calif., 1988—, Nat. Gallery, Ottawa, 1988—; exhibited throughout Can., U.S., Europe, Australia, TV appearances; works represented in permanent collections: Mus. Modern Art, N.U.C., Met. Mus. Art, N.Y.C., Art Inst. Chgo., St. Louis Art Mus., George Eastman House, Rochester, N.Y., Nat. Portrait Gallery, London, Nat. Gallery Can., numerous others; photographer ann. poster child: Muscular Dystrophy Assn. Am; 12 photographs used on postage stamps in 13 countries. Decorated Order of Can., Centennial medal, Can. Council medal; recipient U.S. Presdl. citation for service to handicapped, 1971, Achievement in Life award Ency. Brit.; Silver Shingle award Boston U. Sch. Law, 1983; named Master Photog. Arts Profl. Photographers Assn. Can. Fellow Royal Photog. Soc. Gt. Britain; mem. Royal Can. Acad. Arts. Clubs: Dutch Treat (N.Y.C.), Century (N.Y.C.); Rideau (Ottawa). Office: Chateau Laurier, Suite 660, Ottawa, ON Canada K1N 8S7

KARSON, ALLEN RONALD, aerospace company executive; b. Chgo., June 18, 1947; s. Bruno Stanley and Rose Jean (Nowakowski) Kasprzyk; m. Bonnie Jean Pazdziora, Sept. 1, 1968. BS in Acctg., Bradley U., 1970; postgrad. DePaul U., 1972. CPA, Ill. Corp. controller Time Industries, Inc., Chgo., 1973-77; controller U.S. ops. Indal, Inc., Toronto, Ont., Can., 1977; v.p. fin. affairs Rentco Internat., Inc., subs. Fruehauf Corp., The Hague, The Netherlands, 1977-83; pres., chief exec. officer Ideal Aerosmith, Inc., Cheyenne, Wyo., 1983-84, East Grand Forks, Minn., 1984—. Apptd. hon. consul of The Hague, 1985; pres. Bus. Devel. Bd., East Grand Forks, Minn., Econ. Devel. Corp., East Grand Forks, 1985—, East Grand Forks Devel. Authority, 1986—. Mem. Am. Inst. CPA's, Ill. Soc. CPA's, Minn. Soc. CPA's, Planning Execs. Inst., Nat. Assn. Accts. (bd. dirs. Netherlands chpt. 1981-83). Roman Catholic. Lodge: Elks. Office: Ideal Aerosmith Inc Hwy 2 East Grand Forks MN 56721

KARSON, EMILE, international business executive; b. Berlin, Sept. 10, 1921; came to U.S., 1948, naturalized, 1955; s. Bogdan and Zorka (Natowa) Karastoyanoff; m. Lilia Usunowa, Dec. 31, 1944; 1 child, Danielle. LLB, U. Sofia, 1944; LLB, U. Paris, 1946, LLD, 1948; LLM, Yale U., 1951, JSD, 1953; postgrad. U. So. Calif., 1953-54, U. Pa., Harvard U., 1978. Dir. 2 documentary films shown at Cannes and Venice film festivals, 1947; internat. lawyer World Bank, Washington, 1951-55; subs. coordinator Lockheed Aircraft Internat., Los Angeles, 1955-63; dir. European treas.'s office Litton Industries, Inc., 1964-69; corp. treas. Continental Grain Co., N.Y.C., 1969-72; v.p. fin. and adminstrn. Loctite Corp., Newington, Conn., 1972-80; founder, chief exec. INTECH (internat. high tech. venture capital), Washington, 1981—; vis. prof. law U. P.R., 1957; lectr. Naval War Coll., Fgn. Service Inst., U. So. Calif., Ind. U. Mem. Rep. Assocs., 1954-56; cons. Dept. State, 1983, tech. cos.; adv. bd. Genetics Unique Fund, 1985-87. Fellow French Govt., 1945-48. Mem. State Bar Calif., Bar. U.S. Supreme Ct., World Affairs Council, Washington Internat. Trade Assn., MIT forum, Balt.-Washington Venture Group Clubs: Harvard, Harvard Bus. Sch., Yale (Washington). Home: 8821 Belmart Rd Potomac MD 20854

KARTAWINATA, KUSWATA, plant ecologist, researcher; b. Garut, West Java, Indonesia, June 3, 1936; s. Kartawinata and Utasih (Madnaseh) Suhari; m. Jenny Ardantiningsih Sulaeman, Mar. 11, 1971. B.S., Acad. Biology, 1959; B.Sc. with honors, U. Singapore, 1964; Ph.D., U. Hawaii, 1971. Asst. botanist Herbarium Bogoriense, Bogor, 1959-62; instr. U. Hawaii, Honolulu, 1965-71; program mgr. Biotrop, Bogor, 1972-74; sr. scientist Herbarium Borgoriense, Bogor, 1974-78, head, 1978-84; program specialist in ecological scis. UNESCO, Jakarta, Indonesia, 1984—; mem. commn. on ecology Internat. Union for Conservation Nature and Natural Resources, Glands, Switzerland, 1979—, Plant Conservation Adv. Group, Internat. Union for

Conservation of Nature and World Wildlife Fund; mem. editorial bd. Blumea, 1984. Author: (with others) Indonesian Timber, 1979; Keruing, 1983, Pengantar Ekologi, 1985; editor Reinwardtia, 1974—. Contbr. articles to profl. jours. Mem. Ecol. Soc. Am., Brit. Ecol. Soc., Assn. Tropical Biology, N.Y. Acad. Scis., Internat. Assn. Plant Taxonomists, Tropical Grassland Soc. Australia, Sigma Xi. Moslem. Home: Jalan Merak 24, Bogor, 16161 West Java Indonesia Office: UNESCO Regional Office Sci & Tech, Jalan Thamrin 14, 10240 Jakarta Indonesia

KARTUSH, JACK MICHAEL, ear surgeon, educator; b. Detroit, May 18, 1952; s. Sam and Jean (Klein) K.; m. Christine Ann Ostrowski, June 21, 1984; children: Alison, Julia. BS with high honors, Mich. State U., 1974; MD, U. Mich., 1978. Intern in gen. surgery St. Joseph's Hosp., Ann Arbor, 1978, resident in gen. surgery, 1978-80; resident in otolaryngology U. Mich. Hosp., Ann Arbor, 1980-84, fellow in otology and neurotology, 1984-85; asst. prof. otology U. Mich., Ann Arbor, 1985-87; staff physician, dir. otology VA Hosp., Ann Arbor, 1984-87; staff physician specializing in ear and facial paralysis Mich. Ear Inst., Farmington Hills, Mich., 1987—; nat. lectr. on facial paralysis. Contbr. articles to profl. jours. and textbooks. Nat. Hearing Assn. grantee, 1984, Deafness Research Found. grantee, 1986. Fellow Am. Acad. Otolaryngology (facial paralysis study group); mem. AMA, Am. Neurotology Soc., Pan-Am. Assn. Otolaryngology. Office: Mich Ear Inst 27555 Middlebelt Farmington Hills MI 48018

KARTZKE, KLAUS WILHELM, transportation executive; b. Berlin, Mar. 5, 1922; s. Georg and Erna (Hopfe) K.; m. Ingelore Gramm, Aug. 14, 1954; children: Thomas, Suzanne. Student, U. Berlin, 1940-41; BA with first honors, Dickinson Coll., 1949; MBA, U. Pa., 1950; Dr. rer. pol., U. Mainz, Fed. Republic Germany, 1955. Asst. mgr. fin. econ. dept. Adam Opel AG, Russelsheim, Fed. Republic Germany, 1951-56; mgr. fin. econ. dept. Adam Opel AG, 1956-57, asst. to supply mgr., 1958-62, asst. supply mgr., 1962-68, dir. supply, 1968-82, exec. dir. supply passenger cars Europe, 1982-86, mem. bd. mgmt., 1968-86, mem. bd. suprs., 1987—. Contbr. articles to profl. jours. Served to lt. German Army, 1941-47. Mem. Fedn. German Cs. of C. (vice chmn. credit com. 1974-88), Assn. German MBAs, Phi Beta Kappa. Mem. Evangelical Ch. Lodge: Lions (pres. 1987-88). Home: Haydnstrasse 15, 6200 Wiesbaden Hessen Federal Republic of Germany Office: Adam Opel AG, Darmstadterstrasse, 6090 Russelsheim Hessen Federal Republic of Germany

KARVETTI, RITVA-LIISA, science administrator; b. Helsinki, Finland, Apr. 7, 1929; d. Viljo Johannes and Vilma Lydia (Levela) Aro; m. Mauri P. Karvetti, May 9, 1953; children: Satu, Paivi, Juha-Matti. BA, Ea. Wash. U., 1951; MSc, U. Helsinki, 1952, DSc, 1979. Nutritionist Med. Bd. Finland, Helsinki, 1952-53; researcher Red Cross Finland, Helsinki, 1953-55; lectr. Coll. Nursing, Salo, Finland, 1955-72, Tech. Coll., Turku, Finland, 1966-72; researcher Rehab. Research Ctr. Social Ins. Instn., Turku, 1972—; sr. lectr. U. Turku, 1985—. Contbr. articles on human nutrition, food data collecting methods, nutrition edn. and weight reduction to profl. jours. Mem. Internat. Fedn. Univ. Women (v.p. 1980-886, pres. 1986—), Finnish Fedn. Univ. Women (pres. 1974-77). Lutheran.

KARWOSKI, RICHARD C(HARLES), painter, educator; b. Bklyn., Oct. 3, 1938; B.F.A., Pratt Inst., 1961; M.A., Columbia U. Tchrs. Coll., 1963, postgrad., 1969—; doctoral equivalency CUNY, 1974; postgrad. N.Y.U., 1975. Prof. art and advt., dir. Grace Gallery, N.Y.C. Tech. Coll., 1969-80; one-man shows include: Gallery East, East Hampton, N.Y., 1979, 80, 81, 82 (2), 83, 84, Verzyl Gallery, Northport, N.Y., 1980, 81, 82, 83, 84; numerous group shows, the most recent being: Nat. Arts Club, N.Y.C., 1982, Adelphi U. (First prize), 1982, Riverside Art Center, San Bernadino, Calif., 1982, Nassau Community Coll. Firehouse Gallery, 1982, Prints: U.S.A. (Purchase award), N.Y.C., 1982, Guild Hall Mus., 1985, Nancy Stein Gallery, 1985, Parsons Sch. Design, 1987, Kade Gallery Warner Coll., 1987; represented in permanent collections, including: Newark Mus., Butler Inst. Am. Art, Youngstown, Ohio, Everson Mus., Syracuse, N.Y., Detroit Inst. Fine Art, U. Pa., Phila., Ark. Fine Arts Center, Little Rock, Chase Manhattan Bank N.Y.C., others; also numerous pvt. collections; panelist Heckscher Mus., Huntington, N.Y., 1978; commencement speaker High Sch. Art and Design, N.Y.C., 1979; guest artist Heckscher Mus., 1980 (2), Parris Mus., Southampton, N.Y., 1981, 82, Guild Hall Mus., 1984, Newark Mus., 1986, 87,; vis. artist Huntington Twp. (N.Y.) Art League, 1981, 82, guest panelist, 1981; lectr. Bayard Cutting Arboretum Oakdale, N.Y., 1981; TV, radio appearances. Mem. adv. commn. Art and Design High Sch. Recipient Pres.'s award Okla. Watercolor Soc., 1984. Mem. Guild Hall, Parrish Mus., Heckscher Mus., Ky. Watercolor Soc., Audubon Soc. of Artists, Soc. Am. Graphic Artists, Mid West Watercolor Soc., Pa. Soc. Watercolor Painters, Am. Film Inst., Smithsonian Assos., U. City N.Y. Profl. Staff Congress, N.Y. State United Tchrs., Inc., AAUP, Kosciuszko Found., Whitney Mus. Am. Art, N.Y./Artist Equity Assn. (dir. 1982-84), Nat. Arts Club (salzman award 1985), Salamagundi Club. Author: Water Color Bright and Beautiful, 1988, Subject of revs., articles; contbr. articles, illustrations to various publs., including jacket painting: The Intimate Hour, 1979, pubs. to the Artists Magazine and the American Artist Magazine. Office: 300 Jay St Brooklyn NY 11201

KASAI, GEORGE JOJI, retired microbiologist, virologist, consultant, researcher; b. Los Angeles, Apr. 8, 1917; s. Araji and Kichino (Miura) K.; m. Tama Katako, July 7, 1946; children—Margaret L. Kasai Freeburg, Elizabeth J. Kasai Collins, Patricia J. A.A., Los Angeles Jr. Coll., 1936; S.B., UCLA, 1942; S.M., U. Chgo., 1945, Ph.D., 1952. Research asst., bacteriologist dept. microbiology U. Chgo., 1945-52; spl. fellow Zoller Dental Clinic U. Chgo., 1950, research assoc. in oral bacteriology, 1952-64, research assoc. cholera reseach, asst. prof., 1964-69; supervisor microbiologist in bacteriology Camp Zama, Sagami-Ono, Japan, 1969-75; immunology subsect Brooke Army Med. Center, Ft. Sam Houston, Tex., 1975--87; Cons. Swiss Serum and Vaccine, Berne, 1967, WHO Cholera Panel, Geneva, 1967, John Hopkins Hosp., Balt., 1967; Joint investigator, epidemiology Vibrio parahemolyticus, Indonesia, 1972-73. Contbr. articles to profl. jours. Recipient Spl. recognition Swiss Serum and Vaccine Inst., Berne, 1967, Commendation award Japanese Ground Self Def. Forces, Tokyo, 1975, Outstanding award Dept. Army, 1973, 80, 84; Sigma Xi fellow, 1967; AAAS fellow, 1967. Mem. Am. Soc. Microbiology, Soc. Gen. Microbiology, AAAS, N.Y. Acad. Sci., Sigma Xi. Subspecialties: Virology (medicine); Microbiology. Current work: Viral serology; enzyme immuno assay; serology of infectious diseases; clinical virology (viral identification); electron microscopy. Home: 4807 El Gusto San Antonio TX 78233

KASAMATSU, PATRICIA PLANTE, English educator; b. Washington, Jan. 23, 1958; d. Charles Larry and MaryAnn (Vandergrift) Plante; m. Susumu Kasamatsu, May 28, 1983; 1 child, Taiyo Charles. BA, U. Va., 1980. Instr. English YMCA, Kitakyushu, Japan, 1980—, coordinator bus. program, 1983—; instr. English Meiji Gakuen, Kitakyushu, 1985—; pres., co-founder P&C Translation Service, 1987—. Cons. Kitakyushu Mcpl. Govt., 1983—; cons. Kitakyushu Internat. Trade Fair Com., 1980, 83, 86—; mem. com. Kitakyushu Internat. Advancement Council, 1987. Home: 1-23-2 Kikugaoka Kokuraminami, Kitakyushu, Fukuoka F803, Japan

KASATKINA, NATALYA DMITRIYEVNA, ballet dancer, choreographer; b. Moscow, June 7, 1934; Dmitriy A. and Anna A. Kardasheva Kasatkin; student Bolshoi Theatre Ballet Sch., Moscow; m. Vladimir Vasilyev, 1956; 1 son. Joined Bolshoi Theatre Ballet Co., 1954, leading roles include: Frigia in Spartacus, Fate in Carmen, The Possessed in Rites of Sacred Spring; choreographer: Vanini Vanini, 1962, Geologist, 1964, Rites of Sacred Spring, 1965, Tristan and Isolde, 1967, Preludes and Fugues, 1968, Our Yard, 1970, The Creation of the World, 1971, Romeo and Juliet, 1972, Prozrienie, 1974, Gayane, 1977; wrote libretto and produced operat Peter 1, 1975, Cosi fan Tutte (with V. Vasilyov), 1978. Recipient State Prize of USSR. Home: St Karietny Riad, h 5/10, B 37, Moscow 103006, USSR Office: State Acad Bolshoi Theatre USSR, 1 Ploshchad Sverdlova, Moscow USSR *

KASBERGEN, HENDRIK P., insurance company executive; b. Rotterdam, The Netherlands, Jan. 19, 1944; s. J. and R.M. (Kok) K.; married; children: Sander, Jasper. M in Law, U. Amsterdam, The Netherlands, 1974. Claims handler London and Lancashire Ins. Co., Amsterdam, 1964-69; mem. staff Polak Schoute Expertise, Amsterdam, 1969-74; asst. to dir. Jacobs and Brom, Amsterdam, 1974-75; co-dir. Neerlandia van 1880 Ins. Co., The Hague, Netherlands, 1975-84; gen. mgr. Covema Verz. Mij., Rotterdam, 1984—, Agro Lloyd Ins. Co., Rotterdam, 1987—. Contbr. articles to profl. jours. Bd. dirs. Mus. v.d. Bollenstreek, Lisse, The Netherlands. Mem. Techn. Bur. Bevordering Schadeprev. (bd. dirs.), Federatie Onderl Verz. Mijen. Home: Jan Steenstraat 23, 2162 BL Lisse The Netherlands Office: Covema Verz. and Agro Lloyd, Calandstraat 15, Rotterdam 3016 CA, The Netherlands

KASCHAK, LILLIAN ANNE, fin. fund exec.; b. Plymouth, Pa.; d. Stanley and Mary Christine (Sinkiewicz) Javer; student Wyo. Sem., Dean Sch. Bus., 1946-47, Wilkes Coll., 1952-53; m. Joseph V. Kaschak; 1 son, Thomas J. Sr. clk. Prudential Ins. Co., Kingston, Pa., 1953-58; with advt. dept. Wyoming Valley Distbg. Co., Wilkes-Barre, Pa., 1968-69; adminstrv. mgr. Keystone Welfare & Pension Funds, Wilkes-Barre, 1969-82; with Sheetmetal Workers Welfare Fund, Wilkes-Barre, 1982—; partner Kaschak & Slesinski, 1977—. Mem. Eastern Pa. Adminstrs. Assn. (sec.-treas. 1975-79), Tri-County Personnel Assn. (publicity chmn. 1976-78), Madam Curie Soc. Roman Catholic. Clubs: Quota (membership chmn. 1972-79), Wyoming Valley Ski. Home and Office: 306 Stephanie Dr Plymouth PA 18651

KASER, MICHAEL CHARLES, economist; b. London, May 2, 1926; s. Charles Joseph and Mabel Lucina Ella (Blunden) K.; m. Elizabeth Anne Mary Piggford, 1954; children: Gregory Matthew, Benet, Thomas, Lucy. BA, Cambridge U., 1946, MA, 1950. Economist St. Anthony's Coll., Oxford, Eng., British Ministry of Works, 1946-47, Fgn. Office, 1947-51, United Nations Econ. Commn. Europe, 1951-63; lectr. U. Oxford, Eng., 1963-72, dir. Inst. Russian, Soviet and East European studies, reader econ., 1972—; professorial fellow St. Anthony's Coll. Contbr. numerous articles to profl. jours. Mem. coordinating council Area Studies Assn. Mem. Brit. Assn. Soviet Slavonic and East European Studies (pres.), Royal Econ. Soc. (council), Royal Inst. Internat. Affairs Council. Roman Catholic. Home: 7 Chadlington Rd, OX2 6SY Oxford England Office: St Antony's Coll, OX2 6JF Oxford England

KASH, FRANCYS KAYGEY, civic worker, service organization executive; b. Sioux City, Iowa, Feb. 25, 1921; d. Jacob David and Ida (Schwab) Maron; student pub. schs., Sioux City; m. Louis Kash, Dec. 17, 1939; 1 dau., Leslie Jo Kash Brodie. Dir., Columbia Savs. and Loan Assn., Beverly Hills, Calif., 1976-81; v.p. 1st Pacific Bank, 1981-83; public affairs/cultural cons. Los Angeles County, 1983—. Vice pres. B'nai B'rith Women, Washington, 1965-76, mem. exec. bd., 1958, treas., 1963-65, internat. pres., 1976-78, chmn. constitution-policy com., 1982-86, former chmn. Anti-Defamation League planning com., life mem. exec. com., hon. life mem. Commn.; former commr. Hillel, B'nai B'rith Youth Orgn.; guest lectr. U. Calif. Extension, Los Angeles, 1977; mem. exec. com. western region, U.S. Com. for UNICEF, 1966; mem. Los Angeles City Human Relations Commn. Adv. Com., 1963—; chair JFC Greater Los Angeles Bd. Govs., 1987—; del. to U.N. End Decade Cof., Nairobi, 1985; mem. Calif. Atty. Gen. Constl. Rights Adv. Com., 1962-64; bd. govs. Jewish Fedn. Council Greater Los Angeles, 1984—. Named Woman of Achievement, N.Y. Women's Div. of Anti-defamation League, 1976; recipient B'nai B'rith Women Dove of Peace award, 1987, Outstanding Service award State of Israel, 1973, Los Angeles Mayor award, 1976-77. Mem. Jewish Fedn. Council (bd. dirs. 1958-76, pres. women's conf. 1960-61, bd.dirs. exec. com. 1987—), Sisterhood Congregation Mogen David (life), JFC, GLA (bd. dirs, exec. com. Lodge: B'nai B'rith Internat. (bd. govs., adm. com.). Home: 9311 Alcott St Los Angeles CA 90035

KASHANI, JAMAL MOEYED, research scholar, writer, freelance journalist; b. Calcutta, India, Mar. 1, 1918; s. Jalaleddin Moeyed-Ol-Islam and Khanum (Shirazi) K.; m. Lily Mazandi, July 16, 1940; children: Jaleh, Bejan. BA in Econs. with hons., U. Calcutta, 1937; diploma Mil. Acad., Tehran, Iran, 1941. Adminstr. Iran's Oil Industries, Abadan, 1939-68; corr. McGraw-Hill, Dawn Kerachi, Tehran, 1958-77; gen. mgr., dep. editor Iran Tribune, Tehran, 1868-74. Author: Iran's Men of Destiny, 1986, Poets of Iran, 1988, Persian Short Stories, 1988; translator Masonic ritual from English to Persian; dep. editor: Iran Tribune mag., 1968. Recipient cert. for disting. service Iranian Oil Consortium, medal for services to sports from Shah of Iran, 1956. Mem. Iran Soc., Amnesty Internat. Muslim. Lodge: Masons. Home: 3 Sloane Ct E, London Chelsea SW3 4TQ, England

KASHFI, MANSOUR SEID, petroleum geologist, consultant; b. Tehran, Iran, May 21, 1939; s. Mostafa Seid and Khadejeh (Abghari) K.; m. Mahroo Hoghoughi, Oct. 4, 1975; children: David, Karl; B.S., Tehran U., Iran, 1962; M.S., Mich. State U., 1967; Ph.D., U. Tenn., 1971; Cert. petroleum geologist. Teaching asst. U. Tenn., Knoxville, 1967-71; sr. geologist Nat. Iran Oil Co., Tehran, 1971-78; assoc. prof. Pahlavi U., Shiraz, Iran, 1978-81; exploration mgr. Petroleum Corp. Jamaica, Kingston, 1981-82; chief petroleum geologist, The Navajo Nation, Window Rock, Ariz., 1982-84; cons. geologist, Associated Resource, Tulsa, 1984—. Author: Evolution of Oil Industry in Iran and the Middle East, 1981; contbr. articles to profl. jours. Recipient Pahlavi medal Late Shah of Iran, Tehran, 1963. Mem. Am. Assn. Petroleum Geologists, Geol. Soc. Am. Home: PO Box 472921 Garland TX 75047

KASHIMA, TOMOYOSHI, cardiologist, educator; b. Kagoshima, Japan, July 6, 1937; s. Hitoshi and Yasuko (Murata) K.; m. Naoko Odawara, June 7, 1964; children: Junko, Keiko, Tomoko. MB, Kagoshima U., 1963, MD, 1968. Instr. Kagashima U. Sch. Medicine, 1968-81, asst. prof., 1981-82, assoc. prof., 1982-85, prof., 1985, prof., dean Sch. Nursing and Allied Med. Scis., 1986—. Fellow Internat. Coll. Angiology; mem. Japanese Med. Assn., Japanese Curculation Soc., Japanese Soc. Medicine. Home: 4-28-2 Murasakibaru, Kagoshima 890, Japan Office: Kagoshima U Sch Nursing Allied Med Scis, 1208-1 Usuki-cho, Kagoshima 890, Japan

KASHIWAGI, YUSUKE, bank executive; b. Dalian, China, Oct. 17, 1917; s. Hideshige and Kiyo (Yamada) K.; m. Kazuko Sohma, Nov. 1, 1946; children: Mariko, Shigeo, Yoriko, Shigesuke. LLB, Tokyo Imperial U., 1941. Dir. gen. internat. fin. bur. Japan Ministry Fin., Tokyo, 1966-68, v.p. fin., 1968-71, spl. advisor to the minister, 1971-72; dep. pres. Bank Tokyo, 1973-77, pres., 1977-82, chmn. bd., 1982—; bd. dirs. Sony Corp., Tokyo, Meiji Seika Kaisha, Tokyo; mem. exec. com. Trilateral Commn., Tokyo, 1973—; advisor Internat. Fin. Corp., Washington, 1979—; vice-chmn. bus. and industry adv. com. Orgn. for Econ. Coop. and Devel., Paris, 1985-88, chmn. 1988—. Author: Gekidohki no Tsuuka Gaikoh (Monetary Diplomacy in Turbulent Times), 1972, Watashi no Rirekisho (My Memoirs), 1987. Mem. Com. on Fgn. Exchange and Other Transactions, Com. on Fin. Systems Research, Office Trade Ombudsman Adv. Council. Club: Tokyo. Home: 11-16 Nishi-Azabu 1-chome, Minato-ku, 106 Tokyo Japan Office: Bank Tokyo Ltd, 3-2 Nihombashi Hongokucho, 1-chome, 103 Chuo-ku Tokyo, Japan

KASHTANOV, SERGUEI MIKHAILOVICH, historian, researcher, educator; b. Leningrad, USSR, Jan. 29, 1932; s. Mikhail Filippovich and Inna Sergeevna Kashtanov; m. Ljubov Zakharovna Milgotina, Oct. 29, 1960; children: Natalia, Olga, Pavel. Grad., Moscow Inst. Hist. and Archival Studies, Moscow, 1954; DSc, Inst. of History of USSR, Acad. Scis., Moscow, 1968. Jr. research worker Inst. History of Acad. Scis., Moscow, 1956-67, sr. research worker, 1968—; prof. Krupskaja Pedagogical Inst., Moscow, 1972-76, Inst. Hist. and Archival Studies, 1987—. Author: Socio-Political History of Russia, from the end of the XVth to the first half of the XVIth Century, 1967, Essays on Russian Diplomatics, 1970, Russian Diplomatics, 1988. Office: Inst History of USSR of Acad Scis, Ulitsa Dmitria Uljanova 19, 117036 Moscow USSR

KASINDORF, BLANCHE ROBINS, educational administrator; b. N.Y.C., May 18, 1925; d. Samuel David and Anna (Block) Robins; B.A., Hunter Coll., 1944; M.A., N.Y.U., 1948; postgrad. Cornell U., 1946-50; m. David Kasindorf, July 1, 1960. Tchr. pub. schs., Bklyn., 1945-56; instr. Bklyn. Coll., 1956-57; asst. in research for Puerto Rican study Ford Found. and N.Y.C. Bd. Edn., 1956-57; asst. prin. N.Y.C. Pub. Schs., 1957-59; research asso. ednl. programming and stats. N.Y.C. Bd. Edn., 1959-63, coordinator spl. edn. liaison div. child welfare for Bur. Curriculum Research, 1963-64; jr. prin., integration coordinator Bklyn. Sch. Dist. 44, 1964-65; prin. Pub. Sch. 8, Bklyn., 1965-87; cons. to numerous social agys. Mem. NEA, Council Exceptional Children, N.Y.C. Elementary Sch. Prins., Council Supervisory Assns. Contbr. to profl. publs.; also editor instructional materials. Home: 1655 Flatbush Ave Brooklyn NY 11210 Office: PS 8 37 Hicks St Brooklyn NY 11201

KASKE, GERHARD, chemical company executive; b. Parchwitz, Ger., Nov. 7, 1925; s. Hermann and Martha (Kerger) K.; m. Jutta-Alessa von Hinü ber, Apr. 16, 1966; children—Gerold-Ulrich, Tordis-Almut, Burghard-Orgwin. Diploma in physics Freie U. Berlin, 1957; Dr.Eng., Tech. Hochschule, Hannover, Ger., 1964. Plant supr. Chemische Werke Huls AG, Marl, Ger., 1957-65, dept. mgr./dept. dir., 1966-70, exec. dir., 1971—; mng. dir. Katalysatoren Werke Hüls, Marl, 1975—; supervisory bd. Salzgewinnungsgesellschaft Westfalen, Ahaus-Graes, Ger., 1975-86, Ethylen Rohrleitungs GmbH, Marl, 1983—, Recycling Chemie Niederrhein GmbH, Goch, Ger., 1985—. Co-author: Liegnitz-History of a Silesian Town, 1979; contbr. articles to profl. jours.; patentee in chem. engring. Pres. Fed. Soc. Liegnitz, Wuppertal, Ger., 1976—. Mem. German Assn. Mineral. Sci. and Coal Chemistry (pres. Ruhr area), German Physics Assn., Assn. German Chemists. Office: Huls AG, Postfach 1320, D-4370 Marl Federal Republic of Germany

KASKE, KARLHEINZ, engineer, physicist; b. Essen, Fed. Republic Germany, Apr. 19, 1928; m. Christine Holhorst. Dip. in physics, U. Aachen, PhD. With Wernerwerk für messtechnik Karlsruhe, 1950, in charge of power stateion automatization plant, 1967; with Coal Bd., Aachen area, 1953-60; also lectr. Bergshule, Aachen; Siemens cons. Fuji Electric, Tokyo, 1967; mem. reorganization com. for Siemens Co., 1968; mgr. meter mfg. plant Siemens Co., Nuremburg, 1969; mgr. measuring and processing tech. section Siemens Co., 1973, vice chmn. exec. bd., 1973, chmn. exec. bd., 1981. Office: Siemens Capital Corp 767 Fifth Ave New York NY 10153 also: Siemens AG, Wittelsbacherplatz 2, D-8000 Munich 2 Federal Republic of Germany *

KASLICK, JESSICA HELLINGER, psychiatric social worker; b. N.Y.C., Nov. 9, 1945; d. Joshua and Joan (Nathan) Hellinger; student Elmira Coll., 1963-65; B.A., N.Y. U., 1967; M.S., Columbia U., 1969; m. Ralph S. Kaslick, Oct. 24, 1976. Staff, Mt. Sinai Med. Center, N.Y.C. - Dept. Social Work, Child and Adult Psychiat. Service, 1969—, preceptor of med. students, 1970—, preceptor of social work students, 1978—, psychiat. social worker, 1969—. Bd. dirs. Columbia U. Sch. Social Work Alumni Assn., 1977-79. Recipient Alpha Delta Kappa award in sociology, 1967; Vol. Service award, United Hosp. Fund, 1968; DAR Citizenship award, 1963, others. Mem. Nat. Assn. Social Workers, Acad. Cert. Social Workers, Soc. Clin. Social Workers. Contbr. chpts. to books.

KASLÍK, VÁCLAV, producer, conductor, composer; b. Czechoslovakia, Sept. 28, 1917; s. Hynek and Pavla Kaslik; ed. Faculty of Philosophy, Charles U., Prague Conservatory and Conductor's Master Sch. m. Ruzeme Stucesova, Aug. 25, 1942; children—Jiri, Pavel, Ivan. Condr., E.F. Burian Theatre, Prague, 1940-41; asst. dir. Nat. Theatre, Prague, 1941-43, chief opera dir., 1961-65, opera dir., 1966—; chief opera ensemble Opera of May 5th, 1945-48; condr. Smetana Theatre, Prague, 1952-62; condr., Munich and Berlin, Ger., N.Y.C., Moscow, Vienna, Austria, Venice, Italy, Ottawa, Can., Covent Garden, London, Eng.; composer: (operas) Robbers' Ballad, 1944; Calvary, 1950; Krakatit, 1960; (ballets) Don Juan, 1939; Janosik, 1951; Prague Carnival, 1952. producer works for film and TV. Recipient Nat. orders composing and prodn., including Klement Gottwald State prize, 1956; Honored Artist of Czechoslovakia, 1958. Office: Nat Theater, Divadelni 6, 110-00 Prague Czechoslovakia Address: Kaslik Vaclav Prahai Ossr, Soukenicka 11 Czechoslovakia *

KASM, ABDEL RAUF AL-, former prime minister of Syrian Arab Republic; b. Damascus, 1932. Ed., Damascus U. Sch. of Arts, Istanbul U., Geneva U.; D. Arch. Formerly tchr. architecture, dean Sch. of Fine Arts, head archtl. dept. Sch. Civil Engring., Damascus U., 1970-77, rector, 1977-79; engring. practice, 1964-77; gov. of Damascus, 1979-80; prime minister of Syrian Arab Republic, 1980-87; mem. Baath party regional command, 1979, Central Command of Progressive Nat. Front, 1980; head Nat. Security Bur., 1987—; hon. prof. Geneva U., from 1975. Address: Office of Prime Minister, Damascus Syria *

KASPAROV, GARRI KIMOVICH, chess player; b. Baku, USSR, Apr. 13, 1963. Named Azerbaidzhan Champion, 1975, USSR Jr. Champion, 1975, Internat. Master, 1979, Internat. Grandmaster, 1980, World Jr. Champion, 1980, USSR Champion, 1981; challenged Anatoly Karpov to become youngest ever World Champion in 1985; defended title in 1986. Office: care USSR Chess Fedn, Luzhnetskaya 8, Moscow 119270, USSR *

KASPÉ, VLADIMIR, architect; b. Harbin, Manchuria, May 3, 1910; s. Joseph and Maria (Zaitchik) K.; m. Maria Schapiro, Sept. 27, 1941. B, Anders Liceo, Harbin, 1926; Degree in Architecture, Ecole des Beaux-Arts, Paris, 1935, U. Nat. Mexico, 1946. Owner archtl. office Mexico City, 1943—; tchr. various univs., Mexico City, 1943—. Co-author: Arquitectura Como Un Todo, 1986; contbr. articles to profl. jours. Recipient medal French Soc. Architects, 1939, Palmes Academiques, Paris, 1957. Mem. Soc. D'Architectes Diplomes Par le Govt. Francais, Soc. Arquitectos Mexicanos.

KASPER, HORST MANFRED, lawyer; b. Dusseldorf, Germany, June 3, 1939; s. Rudolf Ferdinand and Lilli Helene (Krieger) K. Diplom-Chemiker, U. Bonn., 1963, Dr. rer. nat., 1965; J.D., Seton Hall U., 1978. Bar admittee: N.J. 1978, U.S. Patent Office, 1977. Mem. staff Lincoln Lab., M.I.T., Lexington, 1967-69; mem. tech. staff Bell Telephone Labs., Murray Hill, N.J., 1970-76; asso. Kirschstein, Kirschstein, Ottinger & Frank, N.Y.C., 1976-77; patent atty. Allied Chem. Corp., Morristown, N.J., 1977-79; sole practice, Warren, N.J., 1980-83; with Kasper and Weick, Warren, 1983—. Mem. ABA, N.J. Bar Assn., Internat. Patent and Trademark Assn., Am. Patent Law Assn., N.J. Patent Law Assn., Am. Chem. Soc., Electrochem. Soc., Am. Phys. Soc., AAAS, N.Y. Acad. Scis. Contbr. numerous articles to profl. jours.; patentee semicondr. field.

KASPERCZYK, JÜRGEN, business executive; b. Pitschen, Germany, Mar. 4, 1941; arrived in Luxembourg, 1980; s. Gerhard Max and Edith Clara (Utta) K.; m. Katrin Schimbke, Apr. 25, 1968; children: Martin, Kristina. MSc in Mining Engring., Tech. U., West Berlin, 1968, PhD in Chem. Engring., 1970. Research scientist Bergbauforschung GmbH., Essen, Fed. Republic Germany, 1968-72; mgr. coking plant Rhodesian Iron and Steel Co., Ltd., Redcliff, Rhodesia, 1972-74; project mgr. Exploration und Bergbau GmbH., Düsseldorf, Fed. Republic Germany, 1974-76; tech. mgr. Hansen Neuerburg GmbH., Essen, 1976-78; mng. dir. CARBOMINA Rohstoffhandel GmbH., Essen, 1978-80; pres., chief exec. officer ENSCH S.är.l., Luxembourg, 1980—. Contbr. papers to tech. mags., internat. confs. Clubs: Golf Grand-Ducal (Luxembourg), Cercle Munster (Luxembourg). Lodge: Old Tablers. Office: ENSCH Sarl, 12-14 Bd d'Avranches PO Box 2132, L-1021 Luxembourg Luxembourg

KASPRICK, LYLE CLINTON, food and beverage company executive; b. Angus, Minn., Aug. 23, 1932; s. Max Peter and Mary (Taus) K.; B.S. in Bus. Adminstrn. magna cum laude, U. N.D., 1959; m. Harriet Susan Lydick, July 14, 1953; children—Susan, Michael, John; m. 2d, Kathleen M. Westby, June 4, 1977; 1 stepdau., Kristin Westby. Tax mgr. Arthur Andersen & Co., Mpls., 1959-69; v.p. Search Investments Corp., Mpls., 1969-77; financial v.p., treas. Tropicana Hotel and Country Club, Las Vegas, 1970-72; chief operating officer Key Pharms., Inc., Miami, Fla., 1972-76, dir., 1976-86; dir. Search Investments Corp., 1973-77, Mo Am Co Corp., 1975-76; v.p. MEI Corp., Mpls., 1977-86; v.p. MEI Diversified, Inc., Mpls., 1986—; dir. IVAX Industries, Inc., Miami, Fla., 1987—. Speaker before profl. and civic groups. Del. Republican Party dist. and city convs., 1964, 66, 68, 70. Served with USN, 1951-55. C.P.A., Minn., N.D. Mem. Am. Inst. C.P.A.'s, Minn. Soc. C.P.A.'s, Nat. Assn. Accountants, Am. Legion. Republican. Roman Catholic. Lodge: KC. Home: 7105 Heatherton Trail Minneapolis MN 55435 Office: IVAX Corp Miami FL 33100

KASS, EDWARD HAROLD, epidemiologist; b. N.Y.C., Dec. 20, 1917; s. Hyman A. and Ann (Selvansky) K.; m. Fae Golden, 1943 (dec. 1973); children: Robert, James, Nancy; m. Amalie Moses Hecht, 1975; stepchildren: Anne, Robert, Thomas, Jonathan, Peter. AB with high distinction, U. Ky., 1939, MS, 1941; PhD, U. Wis., 1943; MD, U. Calif., 1947; MA (hon.),

Harvard U., 1958; DSc (hon.), U. Ky., 1962. Diplomate: Am. Bd. Pathology, Am. Bd. Microbiology, Am. Bd. Preventive Medicine. Grad. asst., instr. bacteriology U. Ky., 1939-41; research asst., instr. U. Wis. Med. Sch., 1941-43, immunologist dept. phys. chemistry, 1944, grad. asst. dept. pathology, 1944-45; intern Boston City Hosp., 1947-48, resident, 1948-49, dir. Channing lab., dept. med. microbiology, 1963-77; research fellow Thorndike Meml. Lab., 1949-52, asst. physician, 1951-58; sr. fellow in virus diseases NRC, 1949-52; instr. in medicine Harvard U. Med. Sch., Cambridge, Mass., 1951-52, assoc. in medicine, 1952-55, asst. prof., 1955-58, assoc. prof. bacteriology and immunology, 1958-62, assoc. prof., 1968-69, prof., 1969-73, William Ellery Channing prof. medicine, 1973-88, emeritus, 1988—; assoc. dir. bacteriology Mallory Inst. Pathology, 1957-63; dir. Channing lab. and sr. physician Brigham Women's Hosp., Boston, 1977—; vis. prof. Hebrew U.-Hadassah Med. Sch., Jerusalem, 1974; vis. prof. community medicine St. Thomas Hosp., London, 1982-83; vis. prof. med. microbiology Royal Free Hosp., London, 1982-83; lectr. London Sch. Hygiene and Tropical Medicine; cons. in field. Author 12 books; editor: Jour. Infectious Diseases, 1968-79, Revs. Infectious Diseases, 1979—; mem. editorial bd. various profl. jours.; contbr. articles to med. jours. Recipient Pub. Service award NASA, Nat. Heart, Lung and Blood Inst. award, Pioneer in Antibiotic Therapy award; Oxford U. Macy faculty scholar, 1974-75. Fellow Am. Coll. Epidemiology, ACP (Rosenthal award), Coll. Am. Pathologists, Am. Heart Assn., N.Y. Acad. Scis., Am. Coll. Nutrition, Royal Soc. Medicine (London), Royal Coll. Physicians (London), Infectious Diseases Soc. Am. (sec. 1962-68, pres. 1970, Bristol award 1980); mem. Inst. Medicine (sr.), Nat. Acad. Scis., Internat. Epidemiol. Assn. (treas. 1977-81), Internat. Congress for Infectious Disease (pres. 1983-85), Mass. Infectious Diseases Soc. (pres. 1985-88), Mass. Soc. Pathologists, New England Soc. Pathologists, Soc. Exptl. Biology and Medicine, Am. Acad. Arts and Scis., AAAS, Am. Epidemiol. Soc., Am. Fedn. Clin. Research, German Soc. Internal Medicine (hon.), AMA, Am. Pub. Health Assn., Am. Soc. Clin. Investigation, Am. Soc. Microbiology, Soc. Epidemiol. Research, Am. Soc. Nephrology, Am. Thoracic Soc., Assn. Am. Physicians, Am. Physicians Fellowship (pres. 1985—), Mass. Infectious Diseases Soc. (pres. 1985—), Infectious Disease Soc. Mex. (hon.), Pan Am. Infectious Diseases Soc. (hon.), Japanese Soc. for Infectious Diseases (hon.). Phi Beta Kappa, Sigma Xi, Alpha Omega Alpha. Jewish. Club: Harvard (Boston, N.Y.C.). Home: Todd Pond Rd Lincoln MA 01773 Office: Harvard U Med Sch 180 Longwood Ave Boston MA 02115

KASSEBAUM, JOHN PHILIP, lawyer; b. Kansas City, Mo., Oct. 24, 1932; s. Leonard Charles and Helen Nancy (Horn) K.; m. Nancy Josephine Landon, June 8, 1955; children: John Philip, Richard L., William A., Linda J. Johnson m. 2d, Llewellyn Hood Sinkler, Aug. 4, 1979; stepchildren: G. Dana Sinkler, J. Marshall, Huger II, Llewellyn H. Jensen. AB, U. Kans., 1953; JD, U. Mich., 1956. Bar: Kans. 1956, N.Y. 1979, U.S. Ct. Appeals (2d, 4th, 10th, D.C. cirs.), U.S. Tax Ct., 1976, U.S. Supreme Ct., 1971. Ptnr. Kassebaum & Johnson, N.Y.C. and Wichita, 1970—; spl. asst. atty. gen. Kans., 1970. Chmn. Gov.'s Adv. Commn. Kans. Instl. Mgmt., 1961-69, Skowhegan (Maine) Sch. Painting and Sculpture; bd. dirs., pres. Carolina Art Assn. and Gibbes Art Gallery, Charleston, S.C.; pres. Spoleto Festival U.S.A., Charleston; treas. Am. Arts Alliance, Washington; curator of ceramics Spencer Mus. Art, U. Kans., 1960—; bd. dirs. Nat. Inst. for Music Theater. Mem. Assn. Bar City N.Y., ABA, Assn. Trial Lawyers Am., Kans. Trial Lawyers Assn., Kans. Assn. Def. Counsel, Fedn. Ins. Counsel. Republican. Episcopalian. Author: Kassebaum Collection, Vol. I, 1981. Home: 59 Meeting St Charleston SC 24901 Office: 575 Madison Ave New York NY 10022 also: 125 N Market St Wichita KS 67202

KASSEBAUM, NANCY LANDON, U.S. senator; b. Topeka, July 29, 1932; d. Alfred M. and Theo Landon; children: John Philip, Linda Josephine, Richard Landon, William Alfred. BA in Polit. Sci, U. Kans., 1952; MA in Diplomatic History, U. Mich., 1956. Mem. Maize (Kans.) Sch. Bd.; mem. Washington staff Sen. James B. Pearson of Kans., 1975-76; mem. U.S. Senate from Kans., 1979—, mem. fgn. relations com., commerce, sci. and transp. com., budget com., select com. on ethics. Republican. Episcopalian. Office: US Senate 302 Russell Senate Bldg Washington DC 20510 *

KASSEL, TICHI WILKERSON, publisher; b. Los Angeles; d. Albert Clarence and Beatrice (Velderrain) Noble; ed. Sacred Heart Convent, Mexico, U. Mexico; HHD, Columbia Coll., 1976; m. Arthur M. Kassel, Aug. 23, 1983; children—William Wilkerson Jr., Cynthia Wilkerson. Publisher, editor-in-chief Hollywood Reporter, pres. Hollywood Reporter Corp. Author: (with Marcia Borie) The Hollywood Reporter: The Golden Years, 1984. Mem. exec. com. Los Angeles Mayor's Com. Internat. Visitors and Sister Cities, 1966—; founder Internat. Festival Adv. Council, 1971—; named ofcl. hostess, Los Angeles, 1974; mem. adv. com. Hollywood Festival of the Arts, 1987—; bd. dirs. Friends of U. So. Calif. Libraries, Inst. Advance Planning, Bd. Edn. for Sr. Adults, Los Angeles Music Ctr.; exec. bd. dirs. Bilingual Children's TV; sponsor Make It on Your Own, 1976, Hollywood Reporter Key Art awards, 1971—; founder, sponsor Mkgt. Concept awards, 1981—; active Motion Picture Country Home, Motion Picture and TV Relief Fund, Los Angeles Orphanage; chair Beverly Hills/Cannes Sister Com., 1987—; mem. adv. com. Hollywood Festival of the Arts, 1987—. Recipient Treasury Dept. award, 1966, Nat. Theatre Owners award, 1967, cert. Am. Women in Radio and TV, 1968, Disting. Philanthropic Service award Nat. Jewish Hosp., Denver, citation Will Rogers Hosp., citation O'Donnell Meml. Research Labs., citation Montague Library and Study Ctr., letter Program Youth Opportunity Hubert H. Humphrey, 1968, Golden Flame award Calif. Press Women, 1970, Women of Year award Girl Fridays of Show Bus., 1972, Personal Mgrs. Industry award, 1976, Bronze plaque Mayor Los Angeles, 1972, citation Los Angeles City Council, Award of Excellence Imperial Bank, Shofar award United Jewish Appeal, 1976, ShoWest commendation, 1977-86, Officier de l'Ordre des Arts et des Lettres Govt. of France, 1988. Mem. Printing Industry Am., Cinema Circulus (bd. dirs.), Women of Motion Picture Industry (chair) Am. Women in Radio and TV (bd. dirs.), Calif. Press Women, Nat. Acad. TV Arts and Scis., UN Assn., Internat. Newspaper Promotion Assn., Western Publs. Assn., Dames des Champagne, Calif. Thoroughbreeders Assn., Hollywood C. of C. (bd. dirs. 1972—, Star on Walk honor 1975), Women in Film (founder, pres. emeritus), Los Angeles Film Industry Council (dir.), Delta Kappa Alpha. Office: Hollywood Reporter 6715 Sunset Blvd Hollywood CA 90028

KASSIM-LAKHA, ZUL, diamond mining company executive; b. Kampala, Uganda, Jan. 26, 1938; came to Belgium, 1973; s. Gulam-Husein and Shirin (Jetha) K.; m. Nazli Javeri, Dec. 14, 1969; children: Shirin, Rehmet. MA with honors in Econs., Cambridge U.; diploma in law, Gray's Inn, London. Corp. exec. U.D.T. Fin., London, 1960-62; ptnr. Dunford Hall Mktg. and Advt., Nairobi, Kenya, 1964-69; dir. B. Green Diamonds, Ltd., Hong Kong, 1970-73; mng. dir. Aldiaem S.P.R.L., Antwerp, Belgium, 1974—. Mem. Diamant Beurs. Moslem. Club: Nairobi Mil. and Naval (London).

KASSLER, HASKELL A., lawyer; b. Boston, Feb. 8, 1936; s. Harry and Natalie (Steinberg) K.; m. Mary Elizabeth Kelligrew, May 30, 1965; children—Marion Adelaide, Sarah Elizabeth. B.A., Tufts U., 1957; J.D., Boston U., 1960. Bar: Mass. 1960, U.S. Dist Ct. Mass. 1961, U.S. Dist. Ct. (no. dist.) Miss. 1964, U.S. Dist. Ct. (so. dist.) La. 1965, U.S. Ct. Appeals (5th cir.) 1965, U.S. Ct. Appeals (1st cir.) 1969, U.S. Supreme Ct. 1967. Assoc. Poster, Wilinsky & Goldstein, Boston, 1960-64; sole practice, 1964-66, 69-71; asst. dir. Vol. Defenders Com., Inc., Boston, 1967-68; ptnr. Richmond, Kassler & Feinberg, 1971-76, Richmond, Kassler, Feinberg & Feuer, 1976-79; ptnr. Kassler, Feinberg & Feuer, P.C., Boston, 1979-81; ptnr. Kassler & Feuer, 1981—; regional counsel New Eng. Region, Am. Jewish Congress, 1965-67; counsel Civil Liberties Union Mass. 1968-70; asst. prof. criminal justice Northeastern U., Boston, 1969-76; chmn. Mass. Judicial Nominating Council, 1987—. Trustee, U. Mass. 1977-81, U. Mass. Bldg. Authority, 1980-81; selectman Town of Brookline, 1971-74, mem. town meeting, 1959-84; mem. Local Redistricting Rev. Commn., 1984—. Fellow Am. Acad. Matrimonial Lawyers (chpt. bd. mgrs. 1980-81, v.p. 1981-82, pres. 1984—); mem. ABA, Am. Trial Lawyers Assn., Mass. Bar Assn., Norfolk County Bar Assn. Home: 17 Kilsyth Rd Brookline MA 02146 Office: 85 Devonshire St Boston MA 02109

KASSOFF, MITCHELL JAY, lawyer, educator; b. N.Y.C., June 11, 1953; s. Justice Edwin and Phyllis (Brafman) K.; m. Gwendolyn Jones, Mar. 3, 1979; children: Sarah, Jonathan. BS in Pub. Acctg. magna cum laude, SUNY-Albany, 1975; JD, U. Va., 1978. Bar: N.Y. 1979, N.J. 1983, U.S. Supreme Ct. 1982, U.S. Ct. Appeals (D.C. cir.) 1979, U.S. Tax Ct. 1979, U.S. Ct. Internat. Trade 1981, U.S. Ct. Customs and Patent Appeals 1979, U.S. Dist. Ct. (so., ea., no. and we. dists.) N.Y. 1979, U.S. Dist. Ct. N.J. 1983. Atty. Herzfeld & Rubin, P.C., N.Y.C., 1978-82, Tannenbaum, Dubin & Robinson, N.Y.C., 1982; asst. prof. taxation Pace U., N.Y.C., 1979—; sole practice, N.Y., 1982, N.J., 1983—. Contbr. articles to profl. jours. Mem. ABA, N.Y. State Bar Assn., Queens County Bar Assn. Home: 2 Foster Ct South Orange NJ 07079

KASTEN, ROBERT W., JR., U.S. senator; b. Milw., June 19, 1942; s. Robert W. and Mary (Ogden) K.; m. Eva Jean. B.A., U. Ariz., 1964; M.B.A., Columbia U., 1966. With Genesco, Inc., Nashville, 1966-68; dir., v.p. Gilbert Shoe Co., Thiensville, Wis., 1968-75; mem. Wis. Senate, Madison, 1972-75, mem. joint fin. com., 1973-75, chmn. joint survey com. on tax exemptions, 1973-75; mem. 94th-95th congresses from 9th Wis. Dist., U.S. Senate, 1980—; mem. 100th Congress Com., appropriations com., budget com., commerce, sci. and transp. com., small bus. com. Mem. Milw. Soc. for Prevention of Blindness; regional dir. Milw. Coalition for Clean Water. Served to 1st lt. USAF, 1967-72. Named Jaycee of Yr., 1972; named Legis. Conservationist of Yr. Wis. Wildlife Fedn., 1973, Conservationist of Yr. Wis. Wildlife Fedn., 1986; One of Best Legislators Senate Rep. Class of 1980, Nat. Jour., 1985. Mem. Nat. Audubon Soc., Sigma Nu, Alpha Kappa Psi. Office: US Senate 110 Hart Senate Bldg Washington DC 20510

KASTNER, GEORGE T., university educator, consultant; b. Rumenia, Buckaresti, Venezuela, June 23, 1947; s. Andreas and Katalina (Hershkovitz) K.; m. Raquel Kirzner, Feb. 23, 1968; children: Cecilia, Cynthia, Claire. BS summa cum laude in Indsl. Engring., Technion-Israel Inst. Tech., Haifa, 1971, MS, 1973; postgrad., Case Western Res. U., 1973-74; PhD, U. N.C., 1980. Prof. IESA, Caracas, Venezuela, 1974—, prof., dir., 1982—; pres. REDITUS, Caracas, Venezuela, 1983—; cons. HESHET Cons., Haifa, Israel, 1970-73, Arthur D. Little Internat., Cambridge, 1985—; mng. dir. Arthur D. Little de Venezuela, C.A. Caracas, 1988—; rep. CERA, Caracas and Los Angeles, 1984-87. Contbr. articles to profl. jours. GMA Found. scholar, 1971. Mem. Ops. Research Soc. Am., ORSIS, Inst. Mgmt. Scis., Am. Soc. Quality Control. Jewish.

KASTURI, HIJJAS BIN, architect; b. Singapore, Sept. 26, 1936; arrived in Malaysia, 1966; s. Kasturi Bin Idris and Putih Binte Hussein; m. Elizabeth Wilson (div. 1969); children: Suyani, Khayyam, Serina; m. Angela Jane Longworth, Aug. 11, 1973; children: Mulaika, Bilqis. BArch, U. Melbourne, Australia, 1965, diploma in town and regional planning, 1966. Head design and architecture sch. Mara Inst. Tech., Selangor, Malaysia, 1966-70; sr. ptnr. Akitek Bersekutu Malaysia, Kuala Lumpur, 1970-77; chmn. Hijjas Kasturi Assocs. SDN, Kuala Lumpur, 1977—, Komputa Bina Sendirian Berhad, Kuala Lumpur, 1982—; external examiner Mara Inst. Tech., 1984-85; external examiner, faculty advisor U. Sci. of Malaysia, Penang, 1984—. Prin. works include several office bldgs., sports ctr., recreational club, Malaysia. Bd. dirs. Nat. Gallery Art, Kuala Lumpur, 1977—. Recipient award for archtl. competition Malaysian Inst. Architects and Malayan Banking, 1979. Fellow Royal Australian Inst. Architects; mem. Pertubuhan Akitek Malaysia (corp.), Royal Inst. Brit. Architects (assoc.), Pertubuhan Perancang Malaysia. Clubs: Bankers (Kuala Lumpur) (bd. govs.); Selangor Yacht (vice commodore). Office: Hijjas Kasturi Assocs SDN, Jalan Sultan Ismail, 50250 Kuala Lumpur, Selangor Malaysia

KATASE, TAKAFUMI, construction engineering company executive; b. Osaka, Japan, Nov. 9, 1930; s. Shigehisa and Satsuki K.; m. Tomoko Tanaka, Nov. 3, 1955; children: Yukiko, Hirofumi. M Engring., Kyoto U., 1953; diploma, Rys. Tng. Ctr., Tokyo, 1954, Fgn. Affairs Tng. Ctr., Tokyo, 1968; D in Engring., Nagoya U., 1986. Registered cons. civil engring. Chief new line sect. constrn. div. Japanese Nat. Rys., Tokyo, 1971-73, dir. installations Tokyo-South div., 1973-75, gen. dir. Osaka constrn. div., 1978-81; gen. dir. ry. Banana-Kinsyasa Installations Orgn., Kinshasa, Zaire, 1976-78; instr. Osaka U., 1978-81; dir. Osaka Terminal Bldg. Co. Ltd., 1979-81; dir., chief engr. Ibara Ry. Co. Ltd., Japan, 1986—; exec. mng. dir. Chuo Fukken Cons. Co. Ltd., Osaka, 1986—; mem. steering com. OECF Adv. Com. on Tunneling, Paris, 1969-70, Internat. Symposium on Ry. Cybernetics, Paris, 1968-70; mem. cons. group Osaka/Kyoto/Kobe High Speed Transit System, Osaka, 1978-81. Author: Planning and Design of Shinkansen, 1968, Kinshasa Diary of Railroader (award Japan Soc. Civil Engrs. 1986), 1980; inventor SEC Cement Mortar Mixing Method, 1980. Founder Nat. Fedn. Soft Tennis, Zaire, 1978. French govt. scholar, 1962; recipient Nat. Order of Merit, Republic of Zaire, 1983. Mem. Japan Assn. Civil Engring, Japan Soc. Soil Mechanics (pres. Kansai div.), Japan Ry. Engring. Assn., Japan Metropole Congress, Internat. Fedn. Cons. Engrs., Assn. Japanese Cons. Engrs., Japan Internat. Civil Engring. Assn. (Ozawa award 1983). Lodge: Rotary. Office: Chuo Fukken Cons Co Ltd, 3-5-26 Higashi Mikuni, Yodogawa-Ku Osaka 532, Japan

KATAYAMA, KAZUHIRO, physician, researcher; b. Hiroshima, Japan, Mar. 16, 1953; s. Hyakuroku and Miwako (Imazu) K.; m. Rieko Shiota, May 27, 1984; 1 child, Motofumi. Student, Yamaguchi U. Sch. Medicine, 1972-78, MD, 1978. Intern, then reisdent Yamaguchi U. Hosp., 1978-83; chief cardiovascular div. Shuto Gen. Hosp., Yanai City, Japan, 1983-84; research fellow U. Calif., San Diego, 1984-86, Yamaguchi U. Sch. Medicine, 1986—. Mem. Japanese Circulation Soc., Japanese Med. Engring. Soc., Japanese Med. Assn. Home: 3-5-7 Higashi Obayama, 755 Ube City Japan Office: Yamaguchi U Sch Medicine, 1144 Kogushi, 755 Ube City Japan

KATAYAMA, N., heavy electrical equipment manufacturing company executive. Chmn., Mitsubishi Electric Corp., Tokyo. Office: Mitsubishi Electric Corp, 2-3 Marumouchi, 2-chome, Chiyoda-ku, Tokyo 100, Japan

KATAYAMA, SADAO, economics educator, economist; b. Kyoto, Japan, July 7, 1930; s. Tetsuji and Yoshie (Hirata) K.; m. Kazuko Tsuchida, June 15, 1969; children—Tomoko, Eri. B. Econs., Shiga U., Hikone, Japan, 1953; M. Econs., Kobe U. (Japan), 1955, D. Econs., 1967. Lectr., Jr. Econ. Coll., Shiga U., 1958-64, assoc. prof. Faculty Econs., 1964-72, prof. money and banking, 1972—, dir. Research Inst. for Bus. and Econs., 1975-82, dean Faculty Econs., 1986—. Author: Historical Analysis of the American Dollar (in Japanese), 1967, International Currency (in Japanese), 1983; translator into Japanese: Indian Currency and Finance (J. M. Keynes), 1977; The Evolution of the International Monetary System (B. Tew), 1979. Fulbright sr. research scholar U. Ga., 1976-77. Mem. Royal Econ. Soc. (U.K.), Am. Econ. Assn., Japan Soc. Monetary Econs., Japan Soc. Internat. Econs. Home: 15-22, Daiwa 1-chome, Takatsuki 569, Japan Office: 1-1, Banba 1-chome, Hikone 522, Japan

KATCHADURIAN, KATCH JULIAN ADRIAN, banker; b. Jerusalem, Apr. 28, 1933; arrived in Bahrain, 1983; m. Adrine Katchadurian; children: James, Lisa Tanya. BBA, Pace U., 1963, MBA, 1966. Various positions Intra-Bank, Beirut, Lebanon, 1952-56; area adminstr., asst. cashier Bank of Am., N.Y.C., 1956-66, asst. v.p. corp. relations, 1966-71; v.p. U.S. and Can. Allied Bank Internat., N.Y.C., 1971-73, sr. v.p., div. head, 1973-81, sr. v.p., head corp. fin. group, 1981-82; gen. mgr., chief exec. officer Bahrain Middle East Bank, Manama, 1983—; chmn. BMB Cons. Ltd., Bahrain, BMB Property Services, Bahrain, BMB Trade and Investment Bank, Geneva, Switzerland. Served with U.S. Army.

KATES, HENRY E., life insurance company executive; b. Denver, Feb. 18, 1939; s. I. Allen and Dorothy K.; B.S. in Fin., U. Colo., 1960; children—Dorianne, Bradley; m. Alison Selover, Sept. 12, 1987. Agt., Mut. Benefit Life, Newark, 1960-67, gen. agt., 1967-81; pres. Mut. Benefit Fin. Service Co. (subs.), Providence, 1981-85; exec. v.p. Mut. Benefit Life Ins. Co., 1985-87, pres., 1987—. Trustee Holiday Corp., RKO pictures, Carnegie Hall, U. of Colo. Found., Lincoln Ctr. Theaters, Newark Mus., Am. Council for the Arts. Mem. Newark C. of C. Author: Body Language in Sales, 1980. Club: Boys and Girls. Home: 435 E 52d New York NY 10022 Office: Mut Benefit Life Ins Co 520 Broad St Newark NJ 07102 also: Mut Benefit Life Ins Co 520 Broad St Newark NJ 07101

KATHERINE, ROBERT ANDREW, chemical company executive; b. Phila., May 26, 1941; s. John and Winifred Irene (Smith) K. B.S.Ch.E., Drexel Inst. Tech., 1964, M.B.A., 1968; P.M.D., Harvard U. Grad. Sch. Bus., 1977. Plant mgr. synthetic phenol plastics div. Allied Chem. Corp., 1964-66; asst. to dir. Far East sales Air Products & Chems., Phila., 1966-70; product group mgr. corp. devel. P.Q. Corp., 1970-72, div. sales mgr. splty. chems., 1972-74; bus. dir. polymers Hooker Chem. & Plastics div. Occidental Petroleum Corp., Burlington, N.J., 1974-78; v.p., gen. mgr. Ruco div. Hooker Chem. & Plastics div. Occidental Petroleum Corp., 1978-80, v.p., gen. mgr. fabricated products div., 1980-81; pres. The McCloskey Corp., 1981-83, chmn. bd., chief exec. officer, 1983—; chmn. bd. McCloskey Corp. (Calif.), McCloskey Corp. (Oreg.); instr. Villanova U., 1973-75; asst. prof. Phila. Coll. Textiles and Sci., 1969-75. Mem. adv. bd. Modern Paint & Coatings Mag. Bd. dirs. Inter-Sci. Found., UCLA Med. Sch., 1983-86; bd. dirs., chmn. fin. com., exec. compensation com., mem. exec. com. Hahnemann U.; corp. adv. bd. Huntington's Disease of Am. Mem. Soc. Plastics Industry (chmn. vinyl film group, exec. com. plastic bottle inst.), Nat. Paint and Coatings Assn. (bd. dirs., indsl. coatings steering com.), Young Pres. Orgn., Am. Chem. Soc., Am. Mgmt. Assn. (pres.' assn.), Pa. Soc. Republican. Baptist. Clubs: Harvard Bus. Sch. (Phila., N.Y.C.); Union League (Phila.); Aronimink. Home: 4102 Battles Ln Newtown Square PA 19073 Office: 724 W Lancaster Ave Wayne PA 19087

KATHREIN, REED RICHARD, lawyer; b. Cadillac, Mich., Aug. 14, 1954; s. John Anton and Jean Ann (Reeder) K.; m. Margaret Ann McClellan, Aug. 24, 1980; children—Jonathan, Michael, Eric. Student Universidad Nacional Autonomo de Mexico, Mexico City, 1971, 73; B.A., U. Miami, 1974, J.D., 1977. Bar: Ill. 1977, Fla. 1978, U.S. dist. Ct. (no. dist.) Ill. 1977, U.S. Dist. Ct. (so. dist.) Fla. 1982. Clk. Racal-Milgo Corp., Miami, Fla., 1976-77; assoc. W. Yale Matheson, Chgo., 1977-79; assoc. Arnstein, Gluck, Lehr & Milligan, Chgo., 1979-85, ptnr., 1985-88; assoc. David B. Gold P.L.C., San Francisco. Author newsletter Internat. Bus. Council Midamerica Update, 1981-88. Editor-in-chief Lawyer of the Americas, 1976-77. Mem. ABA (sect. internat. law and practice, chmn. pvt. internat. law com. 1984—), Chgo. Bar Assn. (chmn. internat. and fgn. law com. 1983-84), Ill. Bar Assn. (council mem., internat. and immigration law sect.), Internat. Bus. Council MidAm. (vice-chmn. policy com. 1982-86 , bd. dirs. 1983-88, sec. 1985-87, v.p. 1987-88), Phi Kappa Phi., Omicron Delta Kappa, Sigma Alpha Epsilon. Republican. Club: River (Chgo.). Home: 1098 Idylberry Rd San Rafael CA 94903

KATO, GEN, urban planner, educator; b. Fujisawa, Kanagawa, Japan, May 5, 1940; s. Tadashi and Yone (Sueta) K.; m. Hisako Omori, Dec. 22, 1966; children: Oruli, Jun. BArch, U. Tokyo, 1964, MA in City Planning, 1966; MArch, Harvard U., 1967. With Rogers Taliaferro Kostritsky & Lamb, Inc., Balt., 1967-69; project mgr. Kenzo Tange & Urtec, Tokyo, 1969-73; pres. Inst. for Gen. Urban Studies, Tokyo, 1973—; cons. Ministry of Constrn., Japanese Govt., 1979—, Housing and Devel. Corp. Japan, 1979—. Author: A Modern Metropolis, 1976. Recipient City Planning award U. Tokyo, 1964. Mem. City Planning Inst. Japan. Home: 6-40-7 Shimouma, Setagaya-ku, 154 Tokyo Japan Office: Nihon-Toshi-Sogo-Kenkyu-sho, 1-8-3 Hirakawa-cho, 102 Chiyoda-ku Tokyo, Japan

KATO, HIDETOSHI, sociology educator; b. Tokyo, Apr. 26, 1930; s. Yoshihide and Yasue (Ukita) K.; MA, Hitosubashi U., 1953, PhD, 1976; m. Takae Murayama, Oct. 24, 1955; children: Mari, Fumitoshi. Research assoc. Inst. Humanistic Studies, Kyoto U., later asst. prof., then prof. sociology Gakushuin U., Tokyo, also dir. Research Inst. for Oriental Cultures; now dir. Nat. Inst. Multi Media Edn. Ministry Edn., Japan; vis. prof. univs., U.S., Japan; mem. central edn. bd. Ministry Edn. Japan. Vice pres. Futuribles, Paris; exec. dir. Japan Assn. Future Research; mem. UNESCO Nat. Commn. for Japan. Fellow Author 26 books on sociol. issues, also lit. essays. Rockefeller Found., Ford Found., Internat. House. Mem. Japan Assn. Sociology, Internat. Assn. Sociology, East West Communication Inst, PEN. Home: 5-13-39 Shiroganedai, Minato-ku, Tokyo Japan Office: Univ of the Air, Wakaba 2-chome, Chiba City Japan

KATO, HISAO, mathematics educator; b. Ota, Japan, Dec. 26, 1953; s. Sakan and Chiyo (Kubota) K.; m. Kazuko Awano, June 2, 1985; 1 child, Nagisa. BA, U. Tokyo Edn., 1977; D in Math., U. Tsukuba, Ibaraki, Japan, 1982. Asst. researcher U. Tsukuba, Ibaraki, 1982-85; lectr. Hiroshima (Japan) U., 1985-88, assoc. prof., 1988—. Mem. Math. Soc. Japan, Am. Math. Soc. Home: Saeki-ku Rakurakuen, 6-12-22-502, 731-51 Hiroshima Japan Office: Hiroshima U, Higashisenda-Machi, Nakaku, 730 Hiroshima Japan

KATO, KOICHI, government official; b. Tsuruoka, Yamagata, Japan, June 17, 1939; s. Seizo and Onobu (Kudo) K.; m. Aiko Sugiura, July 8, 1967; children: Ariko, Aoi, Ryosuke, Ayuko. BA, Tokyo U., 1964; MA, Harvard U., 1967. With fgn. ministry Taipei, Washington, Hong Kong, 1964-71; mem. Ho. of Reps., 1972—; dep. chief cabinet sec. Govt. Japan, 1978-80, dir. standing com. rules and adminstrn., 1980-81, minister of state for def., 1984-86; dir. agr. and foresty div. Policy Research Council Liberal Dem. Party, 1981-83, acting chmn. Policy Research Council, 1986-87, dir. gen., 1983-84, acting chmn. research commn. on comprehensive agr., 1987—. Office: House Office Bldg Room 711, 2-1-2 Nagata-cho, 100 Chiyoda-ku, Tokyo Japan

KATO, PETER EIICHI, political scientist, journalist, educator, university dean; b. Osaka, Japan, Mar. 13, 1934; s. Sakae and Yukiko (Masunaga) K.; m. Masako Nagatani, Apr. 16, 1961; children—Momoko, Yuri. LL.B., Tokyo U., 1959. Dep. div. head Ministry Home Affairs, Tokyo, 1970-73; fellow Japanese Govt., Sacramento, Calif., 1974-75; prof. Local Autonomy Coll., Tokyo, 1973-76; sr. staff researcher Nat. Inst. Research Advancement, Tokyo, 1976-78; assoc. prof. Tsukuba U., Sakuramura, Japan, 1978-84, prof., 1985—, dean Coll. Internat. Relations, 1985-88; dir. Chusu Inst. Govtl. Studies, Tokyo, 1978—; mem. bd. dirs. Doshikai, Tokyo, 1981-86, Japan Inst. for Strategic Studies, Tokyo, 1988—. Author: Better Week, 1973; Correspondence From the Source, 1977; The Japanese Public Adminstration, 1980; Meet Us Kanryo, 1983; The Revenge of Cities, 1983; Information: The New Wealth of Nations, 1985; editor Chishiki mag., 1982-84. Councillor, Ministry of Home Affairs, Tokyo, 1978. Mem. Japanese Polit. Sci. Assn., Internat. Inst. Adminstrv. Scis., Japanese Soc. Pub. Adminstrn. Club: Gakushikai (Tokyo). Home: 7-1- Higashiarai, 305 Tsukuba Japan

KATO, RYUICHI, pharmacology educator; b. Hokkaido, Japan, Feb. 23, 1930; s. Tamakichi and Taka (Matsuda) K.; m. Nagako Okabe, May 28, 1961; children—Shigetaka, Akiko. M.D., Keio U., 1954, D.Med.Sci., 1961; Ph.D., U. Milan, Italy, 1962. Asst. in psychiatry Sch. medicine Keio U., Tokyo, 1955-57, prof., chmn. dept., pharmacology, 1977—; research fellow U. Milan, 1957-62; vis. assoc. NIH, Bethesda, Md., 1962-64; sect. head Nat. Inst. Hygenic Sci., Tokyo, 1964-71; head biol. dept. Fujisawa Research Lab., Osaka, 1971-77; mem. new drug devel. com. Ministry Health and Welfare, Japan, 1979—. Author: Drug Metabolism and Action, Toxic, 1968. Editor: Microsomes, Drug Oxidations and Drug Toxicity, 1982; Comparative Biochemical Drug Metabolism, 1984. Recipient award Found. Princess Takamatsu Cancer Research, 1982. Mem. Internat. Soc. Study Xenobiotics (pres. 1986-87), Internat. Union Pharmacology (chmn. sect. drug metabolism 1987—), Japan Pharm. Soc. (trustee), Japan Toxicological Soc. (trustee). Roman Catholic. Home: 5-4-24 Osone-cho 1-chome,, Kohoku-ku,, Yokoahama, Kanagawa 222, Japan Office: Dept Pharmacology, Sch Medicine Keio Univ, 35 Shinanomachi, Shinjuku-ku, Tokyo 160, Japan

KATO, YUDAI, director of cinematography; b. Tokyo, Jan. 1, 1943; s. Toshio and Tazu (Murakami) K.; m. Noriko Koike, June 4, 1983; children: Yuki, Shimpei. Diploma, Tokyo Tech. High Sch. Film loader Toho Motion Picture Co., Tokyo, 1961-64, focus puller, 1964-69, chief asst. camerman, operator, 1969-78, dir. photography, 1978-84; free-lance dir. photography Tokyo, 1984—. Recipient Grand Prix for The Kid Brother Montreal World Film Festival, 1987. Mem. Japan Soc. Cinematographers, Nihon Acad. Sho Kyokai. Home: 3-3-4-1416 Hikarigaoka, Nerima-ku, Tokyo Japan 176 Office: Japan Soc Cinematographers, 2-17-4-203 Shinjuku, Shinjuku-ku, Tokyo Japan 160

KATSH, ABRAHAM ISAAC, university president emeritus, educator; b. Poland, Aug. 10, 1908; came to U.S., 1925, naturalized, 1932; s. Reuben and Rachel (Maskilleison) K.; m. Estelle Wachtell, Feb. 20, 1943; children: Ethan, Salem, Rochelle. BS, NYU, 1931, AM, 1932, JD, 1936; postgrad.,

Princeton, 1941; PhD, Dropsie U., 1944, LLD (hon.), 1976; DHL (hon.), Hebrew Union Coll.-Jewish Inst. of Religion, 1964, Spertus Coll. of Jewish Studies, Chgo., 1968; DD (hon.), Christian Theol. Sem., 1970, U. Dubuque; LHD (hon.), Lebanon Valley (Pa.) Coll. Instr. Hebrew NYU, 1934-37; founder, exec. dir. Jewish Culture Found., 1937-44, exec. chmn., 1944-67, instr. edn., 1937-44, asst. prof., 1944-45, asso. prof., 1945-47, prof. edn., 1947-66; prof. Hebrew and Near Eastern studies Grad. Sch. Arts and Scis., 1966-67; dir. Inst. Hebrew Studies, 1962-67, Arabic instr., 1942-43; founder, dir. Library Judaica and Hebraica, 1942, curator, 1952-67, chmn. dept. fgn. langs., 1953-54, chmn. dept. Hebrew culture edn., 1953-67; dir. Hebrew lang. and lit. sect. Wash. Sq. Coll., 1957-66, NYU disting. prof. research, 1967-68, prof. emeritus, 1976—; lectr. New Sch. Social Research; dir. Am. Workshop on Israel Life and Culture, held in Israel sponsored by N.Y. U., 1949-67; pres. Dropsie U., Phila., 1967-76, pres. emeritus, 1976—, disting. research prof. Hebraica, 1967—, disting. research prof., 1976—; vis. scholar Oxford Center for Postgrad. Hebrew Studies, 1977-78; scholar Mishkenot Shaananim, London, 1978-79; lectr. at internat. congress and world congress; U.S. participant Congress Linguistics and Hebrew Scholarship, U. Vienna, 1976; Chmn. Nat. Bd. of License for Tchrs. and Colls. field Hebrew Studies, 1957—; spl. examiner N.Y.C. Bd. Edn. Author: Einstein's Theory of Relativity (Hebrew), 1937, Hebrew in American Higher Education, 1941, Hebraic Contributions to American Life, 1941, Krochmal and the German Idealists, 1948, Hebrew Language, Literature and Culture in American Institutions of Higher Learning, 1950, Education and Racial Prejudices, Democracy and Interfaith, Hebraic Backgrounds of American Democracy, 1951, Judaism in Islam, 1954, Judaic Backgrounds of Islam (Hebrew), 1957, The Bible and the Koran, 1962, The Antonin Genizah Collection in the USSR, 1963, Yiggal Hazon, 1964, The Scroll of Agony (Hebrew), 1964, (English), 1966, Megilat Yessurin (Hebrew), 1966, Chronique d'una Agonie (French), 1966, Dodens Dokument (Swedish), 1967, Buch der Agonie (German); Midrash David Hanagid (Hebrew), vol. I, 1967, vol. II, 1968, Ginze Mishna, 1971, Ginze Talmud, vol. I, 1976, vol. II, 1979; asst. editor charge: Modern Lang. Jour, 1949-74; mng. editor: Jour. Ednl. Sociology, 1948-51; editor-in-chief: Hebrew Abstracts, 1950-70; editor: Bar Mitzvah, 1955-76, Biblical Heritage of American Democracy, 1977; editorial com.: Nat. Study Jewish Edn, 1957; editor: (1978) Jewish Quar. Rev; chmn. editorial bd.: Jewish Apocryphal Literature, 1968-86; contbr. to jours. and encys. Trustee Dropsie U., A.S.O.R.; bd. govs. World Hebrew Acad.; mem. nat. bd. Jewish Nat. Fund Am., 1986. Recipient B'nai Zion Meritorius key, 1944; Founders citation NYU Chair Hebrew Culture Edn., 1953; B'rith Abraham Gold Medal, 1952; Tercentary citation Jewish Book Council Am., 1954; 1st prize Hebrew Acad. Am., 1956; Matz Found. prize, 1956; 1st prize Hebrew Acad. Histadruth Ivrith, 1957; Dropsie Coll. Jubilee citation, 1957; named Ky. Col., 1957; prof. chair named in honor NYU, 1957; recipient Am. Assn. Jewish Edn. award, 1959; Ernest O. Melby award, 1962; Municipality of Haifa Scholarly prize, 1979; established in his honor Abraham I. Katsh prize Hebrew U. Jerusalem, 1981. Mem. N.Y. State Fedn. Fgn. Lang. Tchrs. (dir.), World Congress Hebrew Lang. and Culture (exec. com.), Jewish Book Council Am. (nat. com.), Zionist Orgn. Am. (nat. chmn. 1949-51), Nat. Council Jewish Edn. (exec. com.), Jewish Acad. Arts and Sci. (chmn. exec. bd., pres. 1981—, Commemorative Einstein medal 1986), Nat. Assn. Profs. Hebrew in Am. Instns. Higher Learning (founder, pres. 1951-53, hon. pres. 1953—, Festschrift in his honor 1985), Am. Assn. Jewish Edn. (nat. chmn. bd. licenses), Hadoar Assn. (exec. bd.), Inst. Internat. Edn., Modern Lang. Assn. (chmn. evaluation modern Hebrew materials), Am. Jewish Congress, World Hebrew Congress, Phi Delta Kappa. Home: 45 E 89th St New York NY 10128

KATSORIS, CONSTANTINE NICHOLAS, legal educator, consultant; b. Bklyn., Dec. 5, 1932; s. Nicholas C. and Nafsika (Klonis) K.; m. Ann Kanganis, Feb. 19; children—Nancy, Nicholas, Louis. B.S. in Acctg., Fordham U., 1953, J.D. cum laude, 1957; LL.M., NYU, 1963. Bar: N.Y. 1957, U.S. Dist. Ct. (so. dist.) N.Y. 1959, U.S. Dist. Ct. (ea. dist.) N.Y. 1959, U.S. Tax Ct. 1959, U.S. Ct. Appeals (2d cir.) 1959, U.S. Supreme Ct. 1961. Assoc. Cahill, Gordon, Reindel & Ohl, N.Y.C., 1958-64; asst. prof. Fordham U. Law Sch., N.Y.C., 1964-66, assoc. prof., 1966-69, prof., 1969—; cons. N.Y. State Temporary Commn. on Estates, 1964-67; arbitration panelist N.Y. Stock Exchange, 1971—, Nat. Assn. Securities Dealers, 1968—, 1st Jud. Dept., 1972—; pub. mem. Securities Industry Conf. on Arbitration, 1977—. Mem. sch. bd. Greek Orthodox Parochial Sch. of St. Spyridon, 1975—, chmn. sch. bd., 1983—. Served with U.S. Army, 1963. Recipient Chapin prize Fordham Law Sch., 1957; cert. of appreciation Nat. Assn. Securities Dealers, 1982. Mem. ABA (fed. estate and gift tax com. 1966—, continuing legal edn. and research com. 1966-68), N.Y. State Bar Assn. (sect. on trust and estates 1969—), Assn. Bar City N.Y. trusts, estates and surrogates' cts. com. 1968-70, legal assistance com. 1965-67), Fordham Law Alumni Assn. (bd. dirs. 1972—, Fordham Law Rev. Alumni Assn. (pres. 1963-64). Republican. Greek Orthodox. Contbr. articles to legal jours. Office: 140 W 62nd St New York NY 10023

KATSUMATA, TAMOTSU, advertising executive; b. Kakegawa, Shizuoka, Japan, Oct. 10, 1939; s. Chutaro and Mie (Hirao) K.; m. Mari Myoga, Mar. 9, 1969; children: Izu, Jo. BS, Meiji U., Tokyo, 1961; postgrad., U. Pitts., 1967-68. Pres. Sanseido K.K., Tokyo, 1962-66; v.p. Sun Planning K.K., Tokyo, 1969—; cons. Osada Electric Mfg. Co., Tokyo, 1972—; bd. dirs. Sun Printing K.K., Tokyo. Editor Zoom Up mag., 1972—. Home: 3-8-7 Gorikida, Asao-ku, Kawasaki City,, 215 Kanagawa Japan Office: Sun Planning KK, Sukiya Bldg 5F 6-3-12, Ginza Chuo-ku, Tokyo 104, Japan

KATZ, ABRAHAM, retired foreign service officer; b. Bklyn., Dec. 4, 1926; s. Alexander and Zina (Rabinowitz) K.; children: Tamar, Jonathan, Naomi. B.A. cum laude, Bklyn. Coll., 1948; M.I.A., Columbia U., 1950; Ph.D., Harvard U., 1968. Commd. fgn. service officer Dept. State, 1951; 1st sec. U.S. missions to NATO, OECD, Paris, 1959-64; counselor Am. Embassy, Moscow, 1964-66; dir. office of OECD European Communities and Atlantic Polit. Econ. Affairs, Washington, 1967-74; dep. chief of mission OECD, Paris, 1974-78; dep. asst. sec. for internat. econ. policy and research Dept. Commerce, Washington, 1978-80; asst. sec. internat. econ. policy Dept. Commerce, 1980-81; U.S. rep., ambassador OECD, Paris, 1981-84; pres. U.S. Council Internat. Bus., 1984—. Author: The Politics of Economic Reform in the Soviet Union, 1972. Decorated grand officier Ordre National du Merite (France). Mem. Assn. Advancement Slavic Studies, Am. Fgn. Service Assn., Am. Assn. Comparative Econ. Studies, Council on Fgn. Relations, Atlantic Inst. (gov.). Clubs: Cosmos, B'nai B'rith, Harvard. Office: USCIB 1212 6th Ave New York NY 10036

KATZ, AVRUM SIDNEY, lawyer; b. Melrose Park, Ill., Oct. 10, 1939; s. Joseph George and Bessie Goldie (Ancel) K.; m. Sheela Cara Cooperman, Sept. 1, 1963; children—Julie Anne, Aaron Richard, Michele Sharon. B.S. in Elec. Engring., Ill. Inst. Tech., 1962; J.D., George Washington U., 1966. Bar: Ill. 1966, U.S. Dist. Ct. (no. dist.) Ill. 1967, U.S. Patent Office 1967, U.S. Supreme Ct. 1977, U.S. Ct. Appeals (7th cir.) 1978; examiner U.S. Patent Office. Assoc. Leonard G. Nierman, Chgo., 1966-67; assoc. Fitch, Even, Tabin, Flannery & Welsh, and predecessor firms, Chgo., 1967-70, ptnr., 1971-82; ptnr. Welsh & Katz, Chgo., 1983—. Author (with others) Effective Litigation Against Knockoffs, 1984, Chip, Mask and Program Protection, 1985, Electronics and Computer Patent and Copyright Practice, 1985. Mem. ad hoc com. Lake Forest (Ill.) City Council, 1970. Recipient award of distinction Patent Resources Group, 1983. Mem. ABA, Ill. Bar Assn., Chgo. Bar Assn., Patent Law Assn. Chgo., IEEE, Delta Theta Phi, Tau Beta Pi, Eta Kappa Nu, Sigma Iota Epsilon. Home: 475 Turicum Rd Lake Forest IL 60045 Office: Welsh & Katz Ltd 135 S LaSalle St Room 1625 Chicago IL 60603

KATZ, BERNARD, physiologist; b. Leipzig, Germany, Mar. 26, 1911; s. Max and Eugenie (Rabinowitz) K.; M.D., U. Leipzig, 1934; Ph.D., U. London, 1938, D.Sc., 1943; D.Sc. (hon.), Southampton, 1971, Melbourne, 1971, Cambridge, 1980; Ph.D. (hon.), Weizmann Inst. Sci., 1979; m. Marguerite Penly, Oct. 27, 1945; children—David, Jonathan. Beit Meml. Research fellow, 1938-39; Carnegie Research fellow, Sydney, Australia, 1939-42; asst. dir. biophys. research U. Coll., London, Eng., 1946-50, reader, 1950, prof., head biophysics dept., 1952-78; lectr. univs., socs. Mem. Agrl. Research Council, 1967-77. Recipient Garten prize U. Leipzig, 1934; Feldberg award, 1965; Baly medal Royal Coll. Physicians, 1967; Copley medal Royal Soc., 1967; Nobel prize in medicine-physiology, 1970; created knight, 1969. Fellow Royal Soc. (council 1964-65, v.p. 1965, biol. sec. 1968-76), Royal Coll. Physicians; fgn. mem. Royal Danish Acad. Scis. and Letters, Acad. Nat. Lincei, Am. Acad. Arts and Sci., Nat. Acad. Scis. U.S. (fgn. asso.), Order Pour le Mé rite fü r Wissenschaften und Kü nste (fgn.) Author: Electric Excitation of Nerve, 1939; Nerve, Muscle and Synapse, 1966; The Release of Neural Transmitter Substances, 1969; also articles. Research on nerve and muscle function especially transmission of impulses from nerve to muscle fibers. Office: Univ Coll Dept Biophysics, Gower St, London WC1E 6BT, England *

KATZ, HILDA, artist; b. June 2, 1909; d. Max and Lina (Schwartz) K. Student, Nat. Acad. Design; student (3 awards; New Sch. Social Research scholarship), 1940-41. Author: (under pen name Hulda Weber) poems including numerous anthologies, spl. ltd. edit., 1987-88; contbr.: numerous poems, short stories to books and mags. including Humpty Dumpty's Mag. (publ. for children); one-woman exhbns. include: Bowdoin Coll. Art Mus., 1951, Calif. State Library, 1953, Print Club Albany, N.Y., 1955, U. Maine, 1955, 58, Jewish Mus., 1956, Pa. State Tchrs. Coll., 1956, Massillon Mus., 1957, Ball State Tchrs. Coll., 1957, Springfield (Mass.) Art Mus., 1957, Miami Beach (Fla.) Art Ctr., Richmond (Ind.) Art Assn., 1959, Old State Capitol Mus. La., other exhbns. include: Corcoran Bienniale Library of Congress, Am. in the War Exhbn, 26 mus., Am. Drawing anns. at: Albany Inst., Nat. Acad. Design, Conn. Acad. Fine Arts, Bklyn. Mus., Delgado Mus., Art-U.S.A., 1959, Congress for Jewish Culture, Met. Mus. Art., Springfield (Mo.) Art Mus., Children's Mus. Hartford, Conn., Miniature Printers, Peoria (Ill.) Art Ctr., Pa. Acad. Fine Arts, Originale Contemporate Graphic Internat., France, Bezalel Nat. Mus., Israel, Venice (Italy) Bienniale, Royal Etchers and Painters Exchange Exhibit, Eng., Bat Yam Mus., Israel, Paris, France, 1958, 59, Am.-Italian Print Exchange, numerous libraries, artists socs., invitational exhbns. include, Rome, Turin, Venice, Florence, Naples (all Italy), Nat. Academe Muse, France, Israel, USIA exhbns. in, Europe, S. Am., Asia, Africa; represented spl. collections, U.S. Nat. Mus., 1965, U. Maine, 1965, Library of Congress, 1965-71, Met. Mus. Art, 1965-66, 80, Nat. Gallery Art, 1966, Nat. Collection Fine Arts, 1966-71, 78, Nat. Air and Space Mus., 1970, N.Y. Pub. Library, 1971, 78, U.S. Mus. History and Tech., 1972, Naval Mus., 1972, Ft. Lewis Coll., Durango, Colo., 1980-81, Boston Pub. Library, 1980-81, Israel Nat. Mus., Jerusalem, 1980-81, State Mus. Albany, N.Y., 1980; also represented in permanent collections Balt. Mus. Art, Franklin D. Roosevelt, Fogg Mus., Harvard, Santa Barbara (Calif.) Art Mus., Syracuse U., Colorado Springs Fine Arts Ctr., Pennell Collection, Am. Artists Group Prize at Samuel Golden Coll., U. Minn., Calif. State Library, Pa. State Library, Bezalel Nat. Mus., Archives Am. Art Smithsonian Instn. (art and poetry), Washington, Archives and State Mus. Albany, N.Y. (120 works), Newark Pub. Library, Addison Gallery Am. Art, Bat Yam Municipal Mus., Safed Mus., Israel, Pa. State Tchrs. Coll., Richmond Art Assn., Peoria (Ill.) Art Ctr., Boston Pub. Library, St. Margaret Mary Sch. Art, Musee Nat. d'Art Modern, Yad Vashem Meml. Archives, Jerusalem (poetry), 1987. Represented as artist and poet: Miss. Art Assn. Internat. Water Color Club award 1947, 51, New Haven Paint and Clay Club, purchase award Peoria Art Ctr. 1950, Print Club Albany 1962, also Library of Congress, U. Minn., Calif. State Library, Met. Mus. Art, Pa. State Tchrs. Coll., Art Assn. Richmond, Ind., N.Y. Pub. Library, Newark Pub. Library, St. Margaret Mary Sch. Art Coll., landscape award Soc. Miniature Painters, Gravers and Sculpture, James Joyce award Poetry Soc. Am. 1975; presented spl. commemoration to Yad Vashem Meml. Hist. Site, Jerusalem, 1987; named Dau. of Mark Twain 1970; life fellow Met. Mus. Art; named to Exec. and Profl. Hall of Fame (plaque of honor 1966). Recipient World Order of Narrative Poets; named Membro Honoris Causa dell'Accademia di Scienze, Letteri, Arti Classe Accademica "Nobel", Milan, 1974, 75, Classe Storia Letter-Atura Americana, Milan, 1978, Exec. and Profl. Hall of Fame-Life, 1966; named A Daughter of Mark Twain, 1970; Met. Mus. fellow, 1966. Fellow Internat. Acad. Poets (founder 1977); mem. Soc. Am. Graphic Artists (group prize 1950), Print Club Albany (N.Y.), Boston Printmakers (award 1955), Washington Printmakers (exhbns.), Conn. Acad. Fine Arts, Am. Color Print Soc., Audubon Artists (group exhbns., award 1944), Phila. Water Color Club (group exhbns.), Nat. Assn. Women Artists (award 1945, 47), Print Council Am., Hunterdon Art Center, Internat. Platform Assn., Poetry Soc. Am., Artists Equity N.Y., Authors Guild, Inc., Accademia Di Scienze, Lettere, Arti-Milano, Italy (Consigliere, named hon. mem. as artist 1974, author/poet 1975); Academia Di Scienze. Lettere, Arti, Classe. Address: 915 West End Ave Apt 5D New York NY 10025

KATZ, HILLIARD JOEL, physician; b. Stockton, Calif., May 26, 1918; s. Nelson and Pauline (Landman) K.; m. Jeanette Lillian Gordon, Aug. 18, 1946; children: Stephanie, Steven Nelson, Hilary. A.B., U. Calif. at Berkeley, 1939; M.D., U. Calif. at San Francisco, 1942. Diplomate: Am. Bd. Internal Medicine. Intern U. Calif. Hosps., San Francisco, 1942-43; asst. resident internal medicine U. Calif. Hosps., 1943-44, attending physician, electrocardiographer, 1948—, chief staff, 1964-66, physician charge CCU,, 1966-73; resident, sr. resident in internal medicine San Francisco VA Hosp., 1946-48; practice medicine specializing in cardiology San Francisco, 1948—; clin. instr. medicine U. Calif. Sch. Medicine, San Francisco, 1948-53; asst. clin. prof. U. Calif. Sch. Medicine, 1953-61, asso. clin. prof., 1961-70, clin. prof. cardiovascular div., 1970—; coordinator for transpacific clin. programs, asst. to chancellor for spl. events U. Calif. Sch. Medicine, San Francisco; chmn. Nat. Com. for Emergency Coronary Care, 1974-76; mem. med. adv. com. Calif. Wine Inst. Served to capt. M.C. AUS, 1944-46. Fellow Am. Coll. Cardiology, A.C.P., Am. Heart Assn. (fellow council clin. cardiology 1963, Distinguished Service award 1963, Service Recognition award 1964); mem. Calif. Heart Assn. (dir. 1956-71), San Francisco Heart Assn. (pres. 1955-57, Distinguished Service certificate 1959), Calif. Acad. Medicine (pres. 1965), U. Calif. Sch. Medicine Alumni-Faculty Assn. (pres. 1961-62), Soc. Med. Friends Wine (pres. 1968, bd. govs.), Berkeley Wine and Food Soc., Wine and Food Soc. San Francisco, Confrerie des Chevaliers du Tastevin, Commanderie de Bordeaux de San Francisco, Cercle de l'Union, Phi Beta Kappa, Alpha Omega Alpha. Club: Nautilus. Home: 223 Cherry St San Francisco CA 94118 Office: 450 Sutter St San Francisco CA 94108

KATZ, JEFFREY HARVEY, lawyer; b. Newark, Apr. 16, 1947; s. Jack and Beatrice (Weinstock) K.; m. Sharon R. Davis, Nov. 7, 1971; children: Stacey, Justin. BEngring, Stevens Inst. Tech., 1970; JD, Seton Hall U., 1981. Bar: N.J. 1981, U.S. Dist. Ct. N.J. 1981, U.S. Ct. Appeals (3d cir.) 1984, U.S. Supreme Ct. 1985. Engr. RKO Gen., WOR AM-FM-TV, N.Y.C., 1967-70; mgr., engr. Pub. Service Electric and Gas Co., Newark, 1977, mgr. telecommunications systems, 1977—; prosecutor Township of Springfield, N.J., 1982-85; chmn. Mcpl. Cable TV Adv. Com., Springfield, 1974-76. Trustee Stevens Inst. Tech., Hoboken, N.J., 1971-74, mem. presdl. search and selection com. 1974-75; lt. Police Res., Springfield, 1968—; mem. Gov's. Mgmt. Improvement Program, Trenton, N.J., 1982-83, Bd. Health, Springfield, 1986; committeeman Township Com. Governing Body, Springfield, 1985—; mayor, mem. planning bd. Town of Springfield, 1988; commr. pub. safety, Springfield, 1988. Named One of Outstanding Young Men of Am., U.S. Jaycees, 1971-73, Citizen of Yr., Springfield B'nai B'rith, 1976, Citizen of Yr., Policeman's Benevolent Assn. Local 76, Springfield, 1985. Mem. ABA, IEEE, Soc. Cable TV Engrs., N.J. State Bar Assn., Union County Bar Assn., Internat. Platform Assn., Jewish War Vets. of U.S. Republican. Jewish. Office: 182 Meisel Ave Springfield NJ 07081

KATZ, JEFFREY IVAN, urologist; b. N.Y.C., Aug. 21, 1943; s. David and Rebecca (Shapiro) K.; B.A., Pa. State U., 1965; M.D., U. Bologna (Italy), 1970; m. Ethelinda Spiegel, Sept. 29, 1973; children—David, Jennifer. Intern, N.Y. Med. Coll., 1971-72; resident in surgery Mt. Sinai Hosp., Miami, Fla., 1972-73, resident in urology Albert Einstein Med. Coll., Bronx, N.Y., 1973-76; practice medicine specializing in urology, West Orange, N.J., 1976—; mem. staff St. Barnabas Med. Center, Livingston, N.J., chief urology, 1984—; med. staff Irvington (N.J.) Gen. Hosp., Kessler Inst. Rehab., West Orange. Diplomate Am. Bd. Urology. Fellow ACS; mem. N.J. Med. Assn., Essex County Med. Assn., AMA, Am. Assn. Clin. Urologists, Am. Urology Assn., N.J. Urology Assn. Jewish. Research in field. Office: 101 Old Short Hills Rd W Orange NJ 07052

KATZ, JOSEPH LOUIS, chemical engineer, educator; b. Colon, Panama, Aug. 4, 1938; naturalized, 1970; s. Adolfo and Margarita (Eisen) K.; m. Liliane Capelluto, Apr. 10, 1965; children: Daniel P., Alan R. B.S., U. Chgo., 1960, Ph.D., 1963. Amanuensis U. Copenhagen Chem. Lab. III, 1963-64; mem. tech. staff N. Am. Aviation Sci. Center, Thousand Oaks, Calif., 1964-70; asso. prof. chem. engring. Clarkson Coll. Tech., Potsdam, N.Y., 1970-75; prof. Clarkson Coll. Tech., 1975-79; prof. chem. engring. Johns Hopkins U., Balt., 1979—; chmn. dept. Johns Hopkins U., 1981-84; dir. Energy Research Inst., 1981-83; prof. U. Aix-Marseille, France, 1976; vis. prof. M.I.T., Cambridge, 1977. Recipient John W. Graham Research prize, 1975, Md. Chemist of Yr. award, 1982; John Simon Guggenheim Meml. Found. fellow, 1976-77. Fellow Am. Phys. Soc., AAAS; mem. Am. Inst. Chem. Engrs., Am. Chem. Soc., Sigma Xi. Home: 5600 Greenspring Ave Baltimore MD 21209 Office: Johns Hopkins Univ Dept Chem Engring Baltimore MD 21218

KATZ, JULIAN, gastroenterologist, educator; b. N.Y.C., Apr. 3, 1937; s. Abraham M. and Fay (Sher) K.; m. Sheila Moriber, Aug. 18, 1963; children—Jonathan Peter, Sara Katherine. A.B., Columbia U., 1958; M.D., U. Chgo., 1962. Diplomate: Am. Bd. Internal Medicine. Intern U. Chgo. Hosps., 1962-63; resident in medicine Duke U., 1963-65; fellow in gastroenterology Yale U., 1965-67; practice medicine specializing in gastroenterology, internal medicine Phila., 1969—; prof. medicine, lectr. in physiology and biochemistry Med. Coll. Pa., 1970—, also lectr. local and nat. groups; chief clin. gastroenterology Med. Coll. Pa. Editor profl. jours.; Contbr. articles to profl. jours. and books. Served with USN, 1967-69. Fellow ACP, Am. Coll. Gastroenterology; mem. Am. Coll. Gastroenterology, Am. Soc. Study Liver Disease, Am. Gastroenterological Assn., others. Home: 701 Dodds Ln Gladwyne PA 19035 Office: Gastrointestinal Specialists 555 City Ave Bala-Cynwyd PA 19004

KATZ, LAWRENCE MARSHALL, educational administrator; b. Norfolk, Va., May 6, 1954; s. Carl J. and Juliet A. Katz; m. Marilyn Spitalny, July 12, 1981. Student Hebrew U., 1974-75; B.A., Columbia U., 1976; M.A., Jewish Theol. Sem., 1978; postgrad. John Carroll U., 1979-81. Fellow in Jewish ednl. leadership Cleve. Bur. Jewish Edn., 1978-80, dir. community services, 1980-82; ednl. dir. Joint Religious Sch., Vineland, N.J., 1982-85; asst. dir. Cin. Bur. Jewish Edn., 1985—. Mem. Council for Jewish Edn., Assn. for Supervision and Curriculum Devel., Jewish Educators Assembly, Am. Assn. Instrnl. Media Specialists, Coalition for Alternatives in Jewish Edn., Judicia Hist. Philatelic Soc. Jewish. Home: 7445 Elbrook Ave Cincinnati OH 45237 Office: 1580 Summit Rd Cincinnati OH 45237

KATZ, MARTHA LESSMAN, lawyer; b. Chgo., Oct. 28, 1952; d. Julius Abraham and Ida (Oiring) Lessman; m. Richard M. Katz, June 27, 1976; 1 child, Julia Erin. AB, Washington U., St. Louis, 1974; JD, Loyola U., Chgo., 1977. Bar: Ill. 1977, U.S. Dist. Ct. (no. dist.) Ill. 1977, Calif. 1981, U.S. Dist. Ct. (so. dist.) Calif. 1981, U.S. Dist. Ct. (no. dist.) Calif. 1982. Assoc. Fein & Hanfling, Chgo., 1977-80, Rudick, Platt & Victor, San Diego, 1981-82, 84—; asst. sec., counsel Itel Corp., San Francisco, 1982-84. Mem. ABA (corp. banking and bus. law, taxation sects.), Ill. Bar Assn., San Diego County Bar Assn., Lawyers Club San Diego, Phi Beta Kappa. Jewish. Office: Rudick Platt & Victor 1770 4th Ave San Diego CA 92101

KATZ, MICHAEL JEFFERY, lawyer; b. Detroit, May 11, 1950; s. Wilfred Lester and Bernice (Ackerman) K. BE with honors, U. Mich., 1972; JD, U. Colo., 1976; cert., U. Denver Grad. Sch. Bus. and Pub. Mgmt., 1985. Bar: Colo. 1978. Research atty. immigration specialist Colo. Rural Legal Services, Denver, 1976-77, supervising atty. migrant farm lab., 1977-78, ind. contractor Colo. Sch. Fin., 1978-79; sole practice Denver, 1978-86; assoc. Levine and Pitler P.C., Denver, 1986-88; gen. counsel Grease Monkey Internat., Inc., Denver, 1988—; lectr. on incorporating small bus. and real estate purchase agreements Front Range Coll., 1986—, real estate and landlord/tenant law, various seminars, 1980—; of counsel Levine & Pitler, P.C., Englewood, Colo., 1985—. Contbr. Action Line column Rocky Mountain News. Mem. Denver Bar Assn. (law day com. 1985—, real estate com. 1980—, pro bono services 1984—), Assn. Trial Lawyers Am., U.S. Yacht Racing Assn. Club: Dillon Yacht (Colo.). Office: Grease Monkey Internat PO Box 5926 1660 Wynkoop #1160 Denver CO 80217

KATZ, RICHARD, architect; b. Chgo., Dec. 19, 1948; s. Jules and Esther (Zuckerstein) K.; m. Susan Rae Ehrlich, Aug. 28, 1977; 1 child, Rachel Elaine. BArch in Design, U. Ill., Chgo., 1974. Registered architect, Ill., Wis. Prin. R. Katz and Assocs., Inc., Oak Park, Ill., 1980—; cons. various law firms, 1980—; faculty mem. Triton Coll., River Grove, Ill., 1986. Mem. research ctr. Frank Lloyd Wright Home and Studio Found., Oak Park, Ill., 1987. Mem. AIA, Constrn. Specifications Inst., Am. Numismatic Assn. Jewish. Office: R Katz & Assocs 1103 Westgate 304 Oak Park IL 60301

KATZ, ROGER MARTIN, infosystems engineer; b. Jamaica, N.Y., Oct. 25, 1945; s. Joseph Morton and Helen (Bodner) K.; m. Gila Iris Slavin, Feb. 14, 1985; children: Adam, Karin. B.E.E. cum laude, Rensselaer Poly. Inst., 1967, M.E., 1968, Ph.D., 1974. Mem. faculty Rensselaer Poly. Inst., Troy, N.Y., 1967-72; mem. staff Mitre Corp., McLean, Va., 1972-82; sect. head Sperry Corp., Great Neck, N.Y., 1982-85; advanced systems engr. Norden Systems, Norwalk, Ct., 1986, mgr. project, Singer Co., Little Falls, N.J., 1987— ; owner Precision Techniques, Westbury, N.Y., 1983—; cons. to U.S. Congress, Office Tech. Assessment, 1983. Contbr. articles to profl. jours. Recipient Wynant James Williams award Rensselaer Poly. Inst., 1967. Mem. AAAS, Armed Forces Communications and Electronics Assn., IEEE, Sigma Xi, Tau Beta Pi, Eta Kappa Nu. Address: 11 Meadow Rd Old Westbury NY 11568

KATZ, SAUL, banker, former government official; b. Boston, Sept. 7, 1915; s. Samuel James and Frances Edna (Wolk) K.; m. Dorothea Anne Cronin, Nov. 16, 1942; children—Stephen E., Cynthia A., Jacqueline A. Student liberal arts Boston Coll., 1934-37, J.D., 1941; student U.S. Naval War Coll., 1964-65; M.S. in Internat. Law, George Washington U., 1965. Bar: Mass. 1941, U.S. Supreme Ct. 1956. Commd. ensign U.S. Navy, 1942, advanced through grades to capt., 1972; assoc. gen. counsel Dept. Navy, Washington, D.C., 1972-80; spl. counsel to adminstr. GSA, Washington, D.C., 1980-85; v.p. Fed. Asset Distbn. Assn.; lectr. Royal Navy, London, 1951-52, U. Md., College Park, 1962-64, Naval War Coll., Newport, R.I., 1967, Dept. Def. Mgmt. Coll., Washington, D.C., 1962-82. Decorated Legion of Merit (2), D.S.M., Cross of King George (Greece). Mem. George Washington U. Club. Clubs: Nat. Lawyers (Washington); N.Y. Yacht. Home: 6403 Woodsong Ct McLean VA 22101

KATZ, SUSAN STANTON, lawyer, consultant, lecturer; b. Oil City, Pa., July 14, 1951; d. Alfred Bernard and Dorothy (Fell) Stanton; m. William Katz, Mar. 27, 1977; children: Curren Elizabeth, Andrew Stanton Geller. BSN, Youngstown State U., 1971, BS, 1975; JD, U. Akron, 1978. Bar: Ohio 1979, U.S. Dist. Ct. (no. dist.) Ohio 1979; RN, Ohio. Nurse intensive care Youngstown Hosp. Assn., Ohio, 1971-75; assoc. Andrews, Kurth, Campbell & Jones, Houston, 1978-79; assoc. Harrington, Huxley & Smith, Youngstown, 1979-85, ptnr., 1986-87, of counsel, 1987—; mem. instl. rev. bd. Youngstown Hosp. Assn., 1979—; consultant health care law Western Res. Care System, Youngstown, 1979—, bio-ethics com., 1985—. Mem. Youngstown Jewish Community Ctr., Leadership Youngstown Alumni; bd. dirs. Western Res. Care System Woman's Bd., Ballet Western Res., Temple Rodef Sholom. Mem. ABA, Ohio Bar Assn., Mahoning County Bar Assn. (chmn. med.-legal com. 1985-87), Trumbull County Bar Assn., Soc. Ohio Hosp. Attys., Def. Research Inst., Ohio Civil Trial Lawyers Assn., Am. Arbitration Assn., Nat. Council of Jewish Women, Youngstown C. of C. (investor), Youngstown Jr. League (bd. dirs. 1985—, adminstrv. v.p. 1986-87). Club: Youngstown. Lodge: Temple Rod of Sholon (bd. trustees 1986—). Office: Harrington Huxley & Smith 1200 Mahoning Bank Bldg Youngstown OH 44425

KATZ, WARREN ALLEN, physician, educator; b. Phila., June 20, 1936; s. Milton Sidney and Elizabeth (Abrams) K.;; children: Heidi Sue, Gregory Eric; m. Ellen Susan Paul, June 30, 1974; 1 child, Jamie Leigh. BA, Temple U., 1957; MD, Jefferson Med. Coll., 1961. Diplomate Am. Bd. Internal Medicine, Am. Bd. Rheumatology. Practice medicine specializing in rheumatology Phila., 1966—; chief rheumatology Med. Coll. Pa., Phila., 1974-86, clin. prof. medicine, 1974—; chief rheumatology Presbyn. Med. Ctr., Phila., 1986—, chmn. dept. medicine, 1987—; prof. clin. medicine U. Pa., Phila., 1987—; pres. Arthritis Profl. Services, Haverford, Pa., 1972—; chmn. gov.'s adv. bd. arthritis State of Pa., 1976-86; vice chmn. bd. dirs. Moss Rehab. Hosp., Phila., 1985—; v.p., med. dir. Medfit Am. Inc., Phila., 1988—. Author, editor: Rheumatology Diagnosis and Management, 1973, 2d edit., 1988; med. editor: AIMplus mag., N.Y.C., 1986—; contbr. chpts. to books and Ency. Brittanica. Mem. Arthritis Found., Atlanta, 1966—, pres. Phila. chpt., 1976-78. Served to maj. USAFR, 1963-70. Fellow Am. Rheumatism

Assn., ACP (life), Phila. County Med. Soc., Fedn. Clin. Research. Republican. Jewish. Office: Presbyn Med Ctr 39th and Market Sts Philadelphia PA 19104

KATZ, WILLIAM DAVID, psychologist, psychoanalytic psychotherapist, educator, metal health consultant; b. N.Y.C., Sept. 14, 1915; s. Charles and Esther (Dann) K. AB, Bklyn. Coll., 1940; MA, NYU, 1942, PhD, 1953. Fellow and diplomate Am. Bd. Med. Psychotherapy, Am. Acad. Behavioral Medicine (fellow). Clin. intern Hillside Hosp., 1950-53; pvt. practice as cons. psychologist and psychotherapist, N.Y., 1942—; staff psychotherapist Palms West (Fla.) Hosp. and Wellington Regional Med. Ctr. (Fla.); cons. psychologist Human Relations Guidance Ctr., 1946-56; exec. dir. Civic Ctr. Clinic, Bklyn. Assn. Rehab. Offenders, Inc., 1951-55, Play Research Inst., Inc., 1953-57; psychotherapist Group for Community Guidance Ctrs., 1955-57; psychotherapist Mental Health Inst., 1957-59, assoc. dir., 1957, exec. dir., 1958; clin. assoc. Psychol. Service Center, N.Y.C., 1968—; supr. psychotherapy Met. Ctr. Mental Health, N.Y.C., 1969—; asst. prof. psychology L.I. U., 1958-64, assoc. prof., 1964-70, prof., 1970-82, prof. emeritus, 1982—, asst. chmn. psychology dept., 1963-72, 74-76, acting chmn., 1966, 75; prof. U.S. Army Chaplain Ctr. and Sch., Fort Wadsworth, 1970-77; psychotherapist Counseling & Psychotherapy Assocs., 1986-87. Assoc. editor Am. Imago, 1978, Am. Psychol. Assn., 1950—; contbr. articles to profl. jours. Recipient Cross of Honor, La Fundacion Internat., Eloy Alfaro, 1964. Fellow Am. Internat. Acad. (cert. and medallion 1957), Assn. Applied Psychoanalysis (exec. sec. 1963-67, 78-79, pres. 1968-69, 74-75; mem. AAAS, Am. Acad. Polit. and Social Scis., Interam. Soc. Psychology, Am. Acad. Psychotherapists, AAUP, Soc. Clin. and Exptl. Hypnosis, Council Psychoanalytic Psychotherapists, Am. Psychol. Assn., N.Y. State Psychol. Assn., N.Y. Soc. Clin. Psychologists, Bklyn. Psychol. Assn. (pres. 1971-72), N.Y. Acad. Scis., S.I. Mental Health Soc., Nat. Register Health Services Provider in Psychology, Bklyn. Assn. Mental Health, Richmond County Psychol. Assn. (pres. 1975), NYU Alumni Assn., Psi Chi, Alpha Phi Omega, Tau Delta Phi. Lodges: KP, Masons, Shriners. Home: 116 Village Walk Dr Royal Palm Beach FL 33411

KATZ, WILLIAM MICHAEL, author; b. N.Y.C., Mar. 18, 1940; s. Herbert and Sylvia (Dulberg) K.; m. Jane Louise Reckseit, Dec. 11, 1966; children: Sharon Elizabeth, Abigail Eve.; BA, U. Chgo., 1961; MS, Columbia U., 1962; Officer CIA, Washington, 1962-63; asst. to dir. Hudson Inst., Harmon, N.Y., 1964-65; mem. editorial staff N.Y. Times, 1965-70, staff editor N.Y. Times Mag., 1968-70; author books including North Star Crusade, 1976, Death Dreams, 1979, Ghostflight, 1980, Visions of Terror, 1981, Copperhead, 1982, Surprise Party, 1984, Open House, 1985, Facemaker, 1988; After Dark, 1988; TV dramas include Nicky's World, 1974; Nightmare at 43 Hillcrest, 1974.

KATZEN, LAWRENCE B., physician; b. Miami Beach, Fla., June 11, 1949; s. Harry H. and Rose (Nash) K.; m. Jane Dormer, Mar. 26, 1976; children—Janine Toba, Harrison Craig. B.S., U. Miami (Fla.), 1970, M.D., 1974. Diplomate Am. Bd. Ophthalmology. Intern, Washington Hosp. Ctr., 1974-75; practice medicine specializing in emergency medicine, Salisbury, Md., 1975-77; resident in ophthalmology Washington Hosp. Ctr., 1977-80; fellow in ophthalmic plastic and reconstructive surgery U. Ill. Hosp./Michael Reese Hosp. Med. Ctr., Chgo., 1980-81; practice medicine specializing in ophthalmology and oculoplastic surgery, Miami Beach and Lake Worth, Fla., 1981—; clin. asst. prof. Bascom Palmer Eye Inst., U. Miami Sch. Medicine, 1983—; mem. staff Ann Bates Leach Eye Hosp., Miami, Parkway Med. Ctr., Miami, JFK Meml. Hosp., Lake Worth, Fla. U. Miami scholar, 1966-67. Fellow Am. Soc. Ophthalmic Plastic and Reconstructive Surgery; mem. Am. Acad. Ophthalmology, AMA, Palm Beach County Med. Soc., Fla. Med. Assn. Jewish. Contbr. articles to profl. jours. Office: 2601 N Flagler Dr West Palm Beach FL 33407 Address: 16400 NW 2d Ave North Miami Beach FL 33169

KATZIR, EPHRAIM, biochemist, educator, former President of Israel; b. Kiev, Russia, May 16, 1916; s. Yehuda and Tsila Katchalski; m. Nina Gotlieb, 1938 (dec. Mar. 12, 1986); 2 children. MSc, Hebrew U., Jerusalem, 1937, PhD, 1941; PhD (hon.), Brandeis U., U. Mich., Harvard U., Northwestern U., Hebrew U., McGill U., Thomas Jefferson U., Oxford U., Weizmann Inst., Hebrew Union Coll., Jerusalem, Eidgenossische Technische Hochschule, U. Miami, Fla., Technion, Israel Inst. Tech., Haifa, U. Buenos Aires, 1986. Prof. biophysics, head dept. biophysics Weizmann Inst. Sci., Rehovot, Israel, 1951-73, prof., 1978-87; prof. emeritus, 1987—; head dept. biotech. Tel-Aviv U., Ramat Aviv; chief scientist Ministry of Def. of Israel, 1966-68; pres. State of Israel, 1973-78; first incumbent Herman F. Mark chair in polymer sci. Poly. Inst. N.Y., 1979, hon. prof., 1975; contbr. author numerous papers to profl. jours. Recipient Tchernikhovski prize, 1948; Weizmann prize, 1950; Israel prize natural scis., 1959; Rothschild prize natural scis., 1961; Linderstrø m-Lang Gold medal, 1969; Hans Krebs medal, 1972; Alpha Omega achievement medal, 1979; Underwood Prescott award, MIT, 1982; Japan prize Sci. and Tech. Found. of Japan; Enzyme Engrng award, 19887. Mem. Israel Acad. Scis. and Humanities, Biochem. Soc. Israel, Israel Chem. Soc., Nat. Acad. Scis. (U.S.), Leopoldina Acad. Sci. (E.Ger.), Am. Soc. Biol. Chemists (hon.), The Royal Soc. London (fgn.), Am. Acad. Arts and Scis. (fgn. hon.). Office: Weizmann Inst Sci, Rehovot 76100 Israel

KATZMAN, GEORGE, international marketing specialist, educator; b. N.Y.C., Feb. 2, 1920; s. Hyman and Helen (Slotnick) K.; m. Ellen Delyse Shure, Sept. 23, 1951; children: Richard Alan, Susan Lea. BA in Internat. Relations, Fla. Internat. U., 1975, MS in Internat. State U. of Fla., 1976. Bus. Lic. real estate broker. Project engr., mgr. Am. Measuring Instruments Corp., Long Island City, N.Y., 1951-53; owner, operator non-ferrous plant, Miami, Fla., 1954-63; mktg. specialist, Miami, 1964-77; self-employed mktg. agt., 1961-76; adj. prof. internat. relations of Europe, Fla. Internat. U., Miami, 1975—; pres. European Mktg. Corp., Miami, Transatlantic Realty Corp., Miami, Fla., 1980—; Am. cons. Pouey, Inc., Paris, 1973—; lectr. on bus. mgmt., mktg., internat. relations, fgn. policy. Author: (monograph) Marketing in Western Europe: Guidelines for the American Businessman. Mem., lectr. S.E. Fla. Holocaust Commn., Fla. Internat. U., 1983-84. Served with U.S. Army, 1943-46, ETO. Democrat. Home and Office: 850 NE 178th Terr North Miami Beach FL 33162

KATZMANN, GARY STEPHEN, lawyer; b. N.Y.C., Apr. 22, 1953; s. John and Sylvia (Butner) K. AB summa cum laude, Columbia U., 1973; MLitt, Oxford U., 1976; MPPM, JD, Yale U., 1979. Bar: Mass. 1982, U.S. Dist. Ct. Mass. 1983, U.S. Ct. Appeals (1st cir.) 1983, D.C. 1984, U.S. Ct. Appeals (2d cir.) 1987. Law clk. to judge U.S. Dist. Ct. (so. dist.) N.Y., N.Y.C., 1979-80, U.S. Ct. Appeals (1st cir.), 1980-81; research assoc. ctr. criminal justice Harvard U. Law Sch., Cambridge, Mass., 1981-83; chief appellate atty., asst. U.S. atty. U.S. Atty.'s Office, Mass., 1983—. Editor law jour. Yale U. Mem. ABA, Phi Beta Kappa. Office: US Attys Office 1107 JW McCormack POCH Boston MA 02109

KAUFFMAN, BRUCE WILLIAM, lawyer, former state supreme court justice; b. Atlantic City, Dec. 1, 1934; s. Joseph Bernard and Lilyan (Abraham) K.; m. Rita Marie Wisneski, Dec. 31, 1971; children—Bradley Leonard, Marjorie Beth, Robert Andrew, Lauri Ann, Christine Lynne. B.A., U. Pa., 1956; LL.B., Yale, 1959. Bar: N.J. bar 1960, Pa. bar 1961, U.S. Supreme Ct. bar 1965, D.C. 1982. Law clk. to judge N.J. Superior Ct., Trenton, 1959-60; assoc. Dilworth, Paxson, Kalish, Levy & Dilks, Phila., 1960-65, ptnr., 1966-80, chmn. litigation dept., 1975-80; justice Supreme Ct. of Pa., 1980-82; chmn., sr. ptnr. Dilworth, Paxson, Kalish & Kauffman, Phila., 1982—; chmn. Jud. Inquiry and Rev. Bd., 1984—; mem. com. of censors U.S. Dist. Ct., Eastern Pa., 1976-80; del. Pa. Constl. Conv., 1967-68; chmn. Montgomery County Govt. Study Commn., 1973-74; mem. Civil Service Commn., Lower Merion Twp., 1978-80, 82—, chmn., 1985—; mem. adv. com. to U.S. Commn. on Civil Rights, 1985—; pres. Merion Park Civic Assn., 1966-68. Trustee Phil. Coll. Art; bd. dirs. Alzheimer's Disease and Related Disorders Assns., Inc. Fellow Am. Coll. Trial Lawyers, Am. Law Inst.; mem. Am., Pa., Phila. bar assns., Am. Judicature Soc., Juristic Soc., Lawyers' Club Phila., Yale Law Sch. Assn. (v.p. 1985), Pa. Soc., USCG Aux., Pi Sigma Alpha, Phi Gamma Mu, Phi Beta Kappa, Order of Coif. Clubs: Union League, Locust, Yale. Office: 2600 Fidelity Bldg Philadelphia PA 19109

KAUFMAN, HARVEY, telecommunications equipment company executive; b. Boston, Nov. 10, 1931; s. Hyman M. and Sophie (Spear) K.; A.B., Harvard U., 1953. Product mgr. Gen. Electric Co., Auburn, N.Y., 1964-69, mgr. overseas bus. devel., Syracuse, N.Y., 1969-72; eastern regional mgr. NEC Telephones, Inc., Glen Cove, N.Y., 1972-77, dir. large systems mktg., Melville, N.Y., 1977-79; v.p. applications engring. Telecom Plus Internat., Inc., Long Island City, N.Y., 1979-83, v.p. strategic planning and product mgmt., 1984-87, exec. dir. mktg. Siemens Info. Systems Inc., Tel Plus Communications Inc., 1987—. Past bd. dirs. Internat. Center of Syracuse, Lynchburg Soc. Engring. and Sci. Served with Signal Corps, U.S. Army, 1953-55. Mem. IEEE. Club: Harvard of The Palm Beaches; Harvard of N.Y.C. Home: 2000 S Ocean Blvd 17C Boca Baton FL 33432 Office: 5500 Broken Sound Blvd Boca Raton FL 33487

KAUFMAN, HARVEY ISIDORE, neuropsychologist; b. Virginia, Minn., May 13, 1937; s. Carl and Marcia (Borkon); m. Glenda Kaufman, Oct. 16, 1971; children: Jason Alexis, Justin Bram. BA, U. Minn., Duluth, 1959, BA cum laude, 1960; MA, U. Minn., Mpls., 1961; PhD, Marquette U., 1967. Felleow and diplomate Am. Bd. Neuropsychology, Am. Bd. Med. Psychotherapists. Psychology supr. Winnebago (Wis.) Mental Health Inst., 1971-75; dir. outpatient services Health Care Ctr., Fond du Lac, Wis., 1975-81; neuropsychologist Sharpe Clinic, Fond du Lac, 1983—, St. Mary's Hosp., Milw., 1986—. Fellow dept. neurology U. Wis. Med. Sch., 1981-82. Mem. Am. Psychol. Assn., Wis. Psychol. Assn., Nat. Acad. Neuropsychologists, Am. Soc. Clin. Hypnosis, Internat. Soc. Clin. Hypnosis, Internat. Neuropsychol. Soc. Home: 409 Berkley Place Fond du Lac WI 54935 Office: Sharpe Med Ctr 92 E Division St Fond du Lac WI 54935

KAUFMAN, IRA GLADSTONE, judge; b. N.Y.C., Dec. 13, 1909; s. Joseph and Esther K.; m. Lillian Kaufman, June 25, 1939; children—Harvey David, Sylvia Kaufman Delin. BS, NYU, 1933, JsD, 1936; BSc in Bus. Adminstrn. (hon.), Cleary Coll., Ypsilanti, Mich., 1976. Bar: Mich. 1939. Sole practice, Detroit, 1939-59; judge of probate Wayne County Probate Ct., Detroit, 1958-84, presiding judge, 1962-63, 66-67, 72-73, 77-85; chief judge pro tem Wayne County Probate and Juvenile Ct., 1981-85; Moot Ct. judge U. Detroit, 1966-72; lectr. Life pres. Adat Shalom Synagogue; trustee Children's Hosp. of Detroit, chmn. devel., 1980-83, hon. chmn. ann. concert 1983, chmn. ad hoc com. alcoholism Detroit United Communities Services, 1967-68; chmn. Detroit Com. Fgn. Relations, 1974-76, Mental Health Com., 1960-70; trustee Mich. Cancer Found., 1973, hon. life trustee emeritus, 1985; trustee Detroit Inst. Tech., 1962, Park Community Com., 1979; pres. Inter-Agy. Council on Alcoholism, 1957; pres., chmn. bd. Met. Soc. for Blind, 1966-70, bd. dirs., 1960—; mem. Gov.'s Com. Mental Health Statute Rev. Commn., 1970-72, Mich. Soc. Mental Health, 1960—; hon. mem. Children's Charter Mich., 1965-75; exec. bd. League Handicapped-Goodwill 1970—; bd. overseers Dropsie Coll., 1973-75; bd. dirs. Hebrew Free Loan Soc. Detroit, Jewish Nat. Fund Bd.; v.p. United Hebrew Schs. Detroit, 1947-58; founding sec. Midrasha Coll. Hebrew Studies, 1948-58; nominating com. Mich. Cancer Found.; pres. Adat Shalom Synagogue, 1947-53, founder cemetary, 1948. Mem. Mich. Probate and Juvenile Ct. Assn. (exec. bd. 1969-72, pres. 1970-71), Mich. Bar Assn., Detroit Bar Assn., Fed. Bar Assn., ABA, U.S. Air Force Assn. (ann. installing officer 1983-84). Clubs: B'nai B'rith (hon. pres. Tikvah Lodge 1974), Knollwood Country, Savoyard. Club: Valley of Detroit. Lodges: Masons (33 degree; sovereign prince), Shriners, Jesters. Contbr. biog. sketches of Mich. judges to Jewish Hist. Soc. publ., 1983-84. Address: 7409 Locklin Rd Union Lake MI 48085

KAUFMAN, JAMES MARK, lawyer; b. Oklahoma City, Feb. 28, 1951; s. Milford James and Frances Aileen (Knight) K.; m. Vicki Jane Johnston, Aug. 18, 1973 (div. June 1985); m. Katheryn Ann Kidd, Nov. 29, 1985; children—Nathan Jay, Kaitlin Ann, Jordan Paige. B.B.A., U. Okla., 1973, J.D., 1976. Bar: Okla. Supreme Ct. 1976, U.S. Dist. Ct. (we. dist.) Okla. 1976, U.S. Ct. Appeals (10th cir.) 1977, U.S. Supreme Ct. 1983. Intern, assoc. Carson-Trattner, Oklahoma City, 1975-77; assoc. firm Cheek, Cheek & Cheek, Oklahoma City, 1977-81, McKinney, Stringer & Webster, Oklahoma City, 1981-84; mem. firm Kaufman & Cheek, Oklahoma City, 1984—. Mem. Okla. Bar Assn., Oklahoma County Bar Assn., ABA, Def. Research Inst., Sigma Chi. Home: 1000 Stonehenge Dr Edmond OK 73034 Office: Kaufman & Cheek 3030 Northwest Hwy Suite 1511 Oklahoma City OK 73112

KAUFMAN, JESS, communication, financial and marketing consultant; b. Bklyn., June 12, 1920; s. Samuel and Alice (Simon) K.; B.S., N.Y.U., 1949, also postgrad.; m. Selma Helen Bruckner, June 20, 1948; children—Steven, David, Susan. Staff tax dept. G.A. Saxton & Co., N.Y.C., 1938-41; chief acct. 3d Naval Dist., 1943-46; comptroller, asst. treas. Hytron div. CBS, N.Y.C., 1946-48; v.p. mktg. Executone, Inc., Long Island City, N.Y., 1948-81; cons. Weinrich-Zitzmann-Whitehead Inc. Fin. Services, 1981-84; pres. Kaufman Assocs. Internat., cons. firm, 1981—; chmn. bd., chief exec. officer Express Telecom Inc., 1983-84; guest lectr. Grad. Sch. Pub. Health, N.Y.U., Grad. Sch. Pub. Health, Columbia U., N.Y.C., Grad. Sch. Pub. Health, Yale U., New Haven, Conn., Army Surgeon Gen. Inst. for Research, Washington, Sch. of Architecture, Stanford (Calif.) U., Am. Hosp. Assn. Inst. on Elec. and Mech. Engring. Design for Hosps., Chgo.; cons. communications and med. electronics AID, industry interface Exec. Br. of U.S. Govt.; participant Nat. Conf. on Internat. Econ. and Social Devel., Washington, HEW Confs. on biology and engring. in medicine, White House Conf. on Health; vis. lectr. hosp. communication systems and health care to various hosp. assns. Participant Gov.'s Conf. on Aging, State of N.Y.; bd. dirs. Producers Council, Inc., Washington. Served with USN, 1941-43. Decorated Purple Heart; elected to Student Hall of Fame, N.Y.U., 19—. Fellow Am. Pub. Health Assn., AAAS, Royal Soc. of Health; mem. Assn. of Mil. Surgeons of U.S., Internat. Hosp. Fedn., Am. Hosp. Assn., AMA, Fgn. Policy Assn., Am. Mgmt. Assn., Pub. Health Assn. of N.Y., Alpha Phi Sigma, N.Y.U. Alumni Assn. (mem. fund campaign com.). Contbr. articles on hosp. communications to profl. publs. Home: 220 Loines Ave PO Box 702 Merrick NY 11566

KAUFMAN, KAREN LYNN, construction company executive; b. Akron, Ohio, Mar. 19, 1948; d. William B. and Edith (Gruber) Rogovy; div.; children—Amanda, Jonathan. Student U. Akron, 1966-68, Tex. Tech U., 1968-69, U. Calif.-Riverside, 1977-80; B.S., U. San Francisco, 1981. Lic. contractor, Calif. Project mgr. Bilsan Corp., Riverside, 1977-79; housing specialist County of Riverside, 1979-80; project mgr. Lewis Homes of Calif., 1980-81; cons. Williams & Burrows, Belmont, Calif., 1982-83; scheduling cons. LAX Terminal 1, Sheraton Grandé Hotel, Los Angeles; project mgr. Hyperion Energy Recovery System Site Utilities, Los Angeles, Morley Constrn. Co., 1983-86; owner, mgr. Amajon, Sunnymead, Calif., 1982-87; project mgr., Modtech, Inc., Perria, Calif., 1988—. Mem. Bldg. Industry Assn., Nat. Assn. Home Builders, Community Assns. Inst., Comml. Indsl. Council. Democrat. Jewish. Club: Aero Club of So. Calif.

KAUFMAN, PHYLLIS CYNTHIA, lawyer, author, theatrical producer; b. Phila., Nov. 4, 1945; d. Harry and Gertrude (Friend) K. BA cum laude, Brandeis U., 1967; JD, Temple U., 1974. Bar: Pa. 1974, U.S. Dist. Ct. (ea. dist.) Pa. 1974. Sole practice entertainment law, Phila., 1977—; exec. producer Playhouse in the Park, Phila., 1979; dir. entertainment Caesar's Hotel-Casino, Atlantic City, N.J., 1980-81; v.p. entertainment Sands Hotel-Casino, Atlantic City, 1981-83; v.p. Kanadus Entertainment Inc., Toronto, 1982—. Co-author: No-Nonsense Financial, Real Estate, Career and Legal Guides, 1985—; assoc. editor Temple Law Quarterly. Bd. dirs. Phila. Coll. Performing Arts, 1977-85, Creative Artists Network, 1986—. Ford Found. grantee, 1965-67. Mem. Phila. Bar Assn. Democrat. Office: 1500 Locust St Suite 3805 Philadelphia PA 19102

KAUFMAN, STEPHEN E., lawyer; b. N.Y.C., Feb. 16, 1932; s. Herbert and Gertrude Kaufman; m. Marina Pinto, June 22, 1967; children: Andrew H. and Douglas P. BA, Williams Coll., 1953; LLB, Columbia U., 1957. Bar: N.Y. 1958, U.S. Ct. Appeals (2d cir.) 1958, U.S. Dist. Ct. (so. and ea. dists.) N.Y. 1960, U.S. Supreme Ct. 1963. Asst. U.S. Atty. U.S. Attys. Office, So. Dist., N.Y., 1964-69, chief of criminal div., 1964-69; pres. Stephen E. Kaufman, P.C., N.Y.C., 1976—; bd. dirs. Mich. Energy Resources, Monroe, Shearson High Yield Fund Inc., Shearson Govt. and Agys. Inc., Shearson Daily Dividend Inc. and other Shearson funds. Bd. dirs. Trinity Sch., N.Y.C., Police Athletic League, N.Y.C. Fellow Am. Coll. Trial Lawyers; mem. ABA, N.Y. State Bar Assn., Assn. of Bar of City of N.Y. Office: 277 Park Ave New York NY 10172

KAUFMANN, ETIENNE ALAIN, gynecologist, obstetrician; b. Strasbourg, Alsace, France, Aug. 11, 1938; s. Robert Simon and Yvonne (Geismar) K.; children: Vanessa, Delphine, Julien. Student, U. Strasbourg France, 1958-68, Doctorat D'Etat, 1967, Cert. Spl. Study in Obstetrics, 1970; Cert. Spl. Study in Gynecology, 1972. Externe Univ. City Hosp., Strasbourg, 1965-68; asst. Cantonal Maternity Menarisio, Switzerland, 1968-70, Ospedale Civico Lugano, Switzerland, 1971; 1st asst. Kant. Frauenspital Chur, Switzerland, 1972; chef clinique Hopital Cantonal Fribourg, Switzerland, 1972-78; practice medicine specializing in ob/gyn Strasbourg, 1978—. Mem. French Soc. Gynecology (adj.). Home: 4 Ile de Muhlmatt, 67400 Illkirch France Office: 10 Ave d'Alsace, 67000 Strasbourg France

KAUFMANN, JAMES A., physician; b. Detroit, Dec. 15, 1923; s. Adolph and Dena (Lieberman) K.; children—Nancy Hope, Robert Scott. Student Vanderbilt U.; M.D., U. Tenn., 1947. Diplomate Am. Bd. Internal Medicine. Intern, Emory U. Service, Grady Meml. Hosp., Atlanta, 1947-48; resident in medicine Tufts U. Service, Pratt Diagnostic Hosp., New Eng. Med. Ctr., Boston, 1949-50, U. Louisville Service, Louisville Gen. Hosp., 1950-51; instr. Emory U. Sch. Medicine, 1952-57, assoc. in medicine, 1957—; practice medicine specializing in internal medicine, Atlanta; mem. staff Crawford W. Long Meml. Hosp.; pres. Kaufmann Diagnostic Clinic; cons. in medicine South Fulton Hosp., 1963-80, Psychiat. Inst. Atlanta, 1963—, Atlanta Fulton County Recreational Authority, 1979—; mem. staff Gov. Jimmy Carter, 1970-74, Gov. George Busbee, 1974-82. Contbr. articles in field to profl. jours. Chmn. bd. trustees Kaufmann Found., 1960-72; mem. southeastern regional bd. Anti-Defamation League, 1964—, vice chmn., 1981-84, chmn., 1984—; nat. vice chmn. Soc. Fellows, 1976—; active Am. Jewish Com., 1953—; active Democratic party Ga., 1960—, Fulton County Dem. party, 1960—, Century Club of Fulton County Dem. party, 1976—, mem. fin. com. Dem. Nat. Com., 1972—, vice chmn. Sam Nunn for Senate Com., 1972, treas. Senator Herman Talmadge Campaign Com., 1974; mem. Com. to Reorganize Comptroller Gen.'s Office, 1963-64; mem. Am. Israel Pub. Affairs Com., 1978—; mem. governing bd. Fulton County Heart Council, 1958-64; dir. med. program Ga. Gen. Assembly, 1970—; chmn. Council on Govtl. Affairs, 1970; mem. employment security agy. advisory council Ga. Dept. Labor, 1978—; sponsor Ga. Med. Polit. Action Com., 1970—; active Atlanta Symphony, 1965—, Nat. Jewish Welfare Bd., 1978—; mem. spl. gifts com. Atlanta Med. Heritage, 1981; chmn. physicians' div. United Way, 1981; bd. dirs. Civic Theater Atlanta, 1970; mem. patron's soc. Crawford W. Long Meml. Hosp., 1970—; trustee Ga. State U. Found., Morehouse Sch. Medicine; mem. Gov.'s Council Profl. Liability. Recipient Pres.'s award Morehouse Sch. Medicine, 1984; Outstanding Community Service award Christian Council Met. Atlanta, 1983, numerous others. Fellow Am. Coll. Chest Physicians (nat. com. on hypertension 1959-66), Am. Coll. Cardiology (chmn. host com. for annual meeting 1986-88), Internat. Coll. Angiology; mem. ACP (life), Am. Soc. Internal Medicine (Disting. Internist award 1984), AMA, Med. Assn. Ga. (chmn. legis. com. 1973—, chmn. legis. council 1973—, speaker of the ho. 1986—, chmn. state com. on quackery 1970-77, mem. exec. com. 1979—, chmn. com. on physician/lawyer liaison 1983-84, Disting. Service award 1988), So. Med. Assn., Med. Assn. Atlanta (trustee), Ga. Diabetes Assn., Atlanta Lung Assn., Ga. Health Network (case cons. 1987-88), Ga. Lung Assn., DeKalb County Med. Soc., Nat. Tb Assn. (pres. 1956), Atlanta Tb Assn. (med. adv. bd. 1953-59, bd. dirs. 1959-63), Nat. Assn. Disability Examiners, Am. Heart Assn. (council clin. cardiology 1968—), Ga. Heart Assn., Am. Assn. for Respiratory Therapy, Am. Physicians Fellowship for Israel, Ga. Soc. Internal Medicine, Ga. Rehab. Assn., Ga. Soc. Respiratory Therapy, Am. Diabetes Assn., Am. Geriatric Soc., Am. Cancer Soc., Ga. Thoracic Soc., Am. Thoracic Soc., Am. Acad. Polit. and Social Sci., Jewish Hist. Soc. Am. (honor historian 1976—), NAACP (life, exec. bd. 1978—, co-chmn. polit. action com. Atlanta 1978—, Humanitarian award 1987), Ga. C. of C. (state/nat. affairs task force 1982), Atlanta C. of C., Cobb County C. of C., Emory U. Alumni Assn. (bd. dirs.), U. Tenn. Coll. Medicine Alumni Assn., Lamplighter Soc. (Emory U.), Atlanta Bot. Soc., Zeta Beta Tau. Clubs: Atlanta Press, Commerce, Georgian, Stadium, Temple, Presidents (U. Tenn.). Lodge: B'nai B'rith (pres. Gate City lodge 1964-65, Silver mem. youth services Pres. club 1977—). Home: 2660 Peachtree Rd NW Apt 11E Atlanta GA 30305 Office: Kaufmann Diagnostic Clinic 565 W Peachtree St NE Atlanta GA 30308

KAUFMANN, MARK STEINER, banker; b. N.Y.C., Dec. 3, 1932; s. Milton L. and Elsa S. (Steiner) K.; B.S. cum laude in Bus. Adminstrn., Lehigh U., 1953; m. Carole Richard, June 16, 1957; children—Jon Richard, Susan Helen. Vice pres., dir. mktg. Standard Fin. Corp. N.Y.C., 1958-64; sr. v.p., dir. Milberg Factors, Inc., N.Y.C., 1964-73; dir. corp. devel. Chase Manhattan Bank, N.Y.C., 1973-87, sr. v.p., 1987—; dir. Chase Manhattan Capital Corp., Wall St. Planning Group. Past treas. bd. trustees Calhoun Sch., N.Y.C.; trustee Temple Israel, N.Y.C. Served as 1st lt. USAF, 1953-55. Recipient Human Relations award Anti-Defamation League, 1973, Human Relations award Am. Jewish Com., 1987. Mem. Am. Arbitration Assn., Beta Gamma Sigma, Lambda Mu Sigma, Pi Gamma Mu, Omicron Delta Kappa. Club: Old Oaks Country (dir.). Home: 124 W 79th St New York NY 10024 Office: Chase Manhattan Bank 1 Chase Manhattan Plaza New York NY 10081

KAUFMANN, MAX RICHARD, chemical company executive; b. Zurich, Switzerland, July 15, 1943; s. Franz Xaver and Rosa (Huerzeler) K.; m. Hanna Spycher, May 6, 1972; children—Christian Alexandre, Thomas Claudio. Chem. Engr., Swiss Fed. Inst. Tech., Zurich, 1967, Ph.D. in Natural Scis., 1971; grad. Gen. Mgmt. Program, Centre Europeen D'Education Permanente, Fontainebleau, France, 1973-76; grad. Mktg. Mgmt. Program, Columbia U., N.Y.C., 1977. Mktg. planner Sandoz Ltd., Basel, Switzerland, 1971-72, salesman Produits Sandoz S.A., Nantes, France, 1973-76, strategic planner Sandoz Inc., Hanover, N.J., 1977-78, sales mgr. Sandoz S.A., Sao Paulo, Brazil, 1978-82, sales mgr. for Scandinavia, Gothenburg, Sweden, 1982-85, with corp. strategy dept. Sandoz Ltd., Basel, 1985-88, mng. dir. Sandoz S.A., Bruxelles, Belgium, 1988—; asst. tchr. Swiss Fed. Inst. Tech., 1968-71; spl. corr. Chemische Rundschau, 1968-71. Contbr. articles to profl. jours. Mem. Swiss Chemists Assn. Roman Catholic. Office: Sandoz SA, 226 Chaussée de Haecht, B-1030 Brussels Belgium

KAUNDA, KENNETH DAVID, president Republic of Zambia; b. Lubwa Mission, Chinsali, No. Rhodesia, Apr. 28, 1924; s. David and Helen Kaunda; ed. Lubwa Tng. Sch., Munali Secondary Sch.; numerous hon. degrees; m. Betty Banda, Aug. 24, 1946; children—Panji, Wazamanzana, Nqeaweze, Tilyenji, Masuzyo, Kaweche, Musata, Kambarage Cheswa. Tchr., Lubwa Tng. Sch., 1943, headmaster, 1944-47; sec. Chinsali Young Men's Farming Assn., 1947; welfare officer Chingola Copper Mine, 1948-49; tchr. sch., 1948-49; founder, sec. Lubwa br. African Nat. Congress, 1950, dist. organizer, 1951. provincial organizer, 1952, sec.-gen. for No. Rhodesia. 1953; broke away to form Zambia African Nat. Congress, 1958; pres. United Nat. Independence Party, 1960—; minister local govt. and social welfare No. Rhodesia, 1962-64, prime minister, 1964; pres. Pan-African Freedom Movement for East, Central and South Africa, 1963; 1st pres. Zambia, 1964—; chancellor U. Zambia, 1966—; chmn. Mining and Indsl. Devel. Corp. of Zambia, 1970—. Chmn. Orgn. of African Unity, 1970; chmn. Non-aligned Nations Conf., 1970-73. Decorated Order of Collar of Nile, Knight of Collar Order Pius XII; Order of Queen of Sheba, others; recipient Quaide Azam Human Rights Internat. prize, Pakistan, 1976; Jawaharlal Nehru award Internat. Understanding. Author: Black Government, 1961; Zambia Shall be Free, 1962; (with Colin Morris) A Humanist in Africa, 1966; Humanism in Zambia and its Implementation, 1967; Letter to My Children, 1977; Kaunda on Violence, 1980. Address: care State House, PO Box 135, Lusaka Zambia Other: Univ of Zambia, PO Box 31338, Lusaka Zambia *

KAUR, PRABHJOT, poet; b. Langarlal, India, July 6, 1927; d. Nidhan Singh; student Khalsa Coll. Women, 1941-45, Punjab U., 1945-47; m. Brig Narenderpal Singh, 1948; 2 daus. Books poetry: Suprne Sadhran, 1949, Do Rang, 1951, Pankhru, 1956, Lala, 1958, Bankapasi, 1958, Pabbi, 1962, Waddarshi Sheesha, 1972, Madhiantar, 1974, Chandra Yug, 1978; short stories: Kinke, 1952, Aman de Na, 1956, Zindgi de Kujh Pal, 1982, Ishq Sharh Ki Nata, 1984; mem. legis. council State of Punjab, 1966-72; mem. central com. of UNESCO, Nat. Writers Com. of India; rep. India at numerous internat. lit. confs. Named Rajya Kavi (Poet Laureate), Punjab

Govt., 1964; recipient honours of Sahitya Shiromani, 1964, Padma Shri, 1967; Sahitya Akademi award, 1964, Golden Laurel leaves United Poets Internat. Phillippines, 1967, Grand Prix de la Rose de la France, 1968, Most Disting. Order Poetry World Poetry Soc., 1974, N.I.F. Cultural Award, 1981, Josh Internat. Award, Kenya, 1982. Nominated by govt. India to Gen. Council of Nat. Sahitya Akademi, 1978, exec. bd., 1978, 83. Address: D-203 Defence Colony, New Delhi 110024 India *

KAVANAGH, NOEL JOSEPH, economics educator; b. Dublin, Ireland, Nov. 3, 1932; s. Thomas and Eileen (Morgan) K. B in Commerce, MA, Trinity Coll., Dublin, 1959. Research officer Bd. of Trade, Newcastle, Eng., 1960-63; mem. faculty Dept. Indsl. Econs. and Bus. Studies Birmingham (Eng.) U., 1963—; cons. in field. Contbr. articles to profl. jours. Club: Sr. Common Room (Birmingham U.) (mem. com. 1987—). Office: Birmingham U, Dept Indsl Econs and Bus Studies, Ashley Blvd, Birmingham B15 2TT, England

KAVESH, ROBERT A., economist, educator; b. N.Y.C., Sept. 12, 1927; s. Samuel and Pearl (Berlin) K.; m. Ruth Freidson, June 24, 1951 (div. 1980); children: Richard, Laura, Andrew, Joseph. B.S., N.Y. U., 1949; M.A., Harvard U., 1950, Ph.D., 1954. Asst. prof. econs. Dartmouth Coll., 1953-56; bus. economist Chase Manhattan Bank, N.Y.C., 1956-58; prof. econs. and finance Grad. Sch. Bus. Adminstrn., NYU, 1958-74, Marcus Nadler prof. finance and econs., 1974—, chmn. dept. econs., 1968-83; dir. Del Labs., Inc., Greater N.Y. Mut. Ins. Co., Ins. Co. Greater N.Y., Apple Bank Savs., Energy Fund, Inc.; mem. Savs. Banks Econ. Forum, 1975—; mem. econ. adv. bd. U.S. Dept. Commerce, 1968-70; mem. investment adv. com. N.Y. State Comptroller, 1976-86; pres. The Money Marketeers, 1983-84; cons. economist Bank Julius Baer, Zurich. Author: Businessmen in Fiction, 1955, How Business Economists Forecast, 1966, Methods and Techniques of Business Forecasting, 1974; also articles.; Asso. editor: Bus. Economics, 1965—. Bd. dirs. Thomas A. Edison Coll. N.J., 1973-78. Served with U.S. Navy, World War II. Recipient Danforth Found. prize disting. teaching, 1968, Madden Meml. award for profl. achievement NYU, 1979, Gt. Tchr. award NYU, 1983. Fellow Nat. Assn. Bus. Economists (council 1973-76); mem. Am. Fin. Assn. (exec. sec.-treas. 1961-79), Regional Sci. Assn. (past sec.), Am. Econ. Assn. Home: 110 Bleecker St New York NY 10012 Office: 100 Trinity Pl New York NY 10006

KAVOSH, HAMID, airline pilot; b. Shiraz, Iran, Mar. 8, 1955; s. Kumarse and Robabeh (Rastegari) K.; m. Farzaneh Kasra, Dec. 1, 1979; children: Morvarid, Maryam. Diploma, Saboriyhan Sch., Shiraz, Iran, 1975. Comml. rated pilot Imperial Aero Club, Shiraz, 1973-74; with Iran Asseman Airlines, 1977—; instrument rated pilot Teheran, 1977; airline transport pilot Miami, Fla., 1978-84; tng. and standardization mgr. 1980-87, pilot F-27 Friendship, 1984-85, pilot DA-20 Falcon, 1985-87, pilot F-28 Fellowship, 1987—. Home: 54 Gisha Nasr Ave 32 St, 14489 Teheran Iran Office: Iran Asseman Airlines, Mehrabad Airport, Teheran Iran

KAWAGUCHI, HARRY HARUMITSU, psychologist; b. Watsonville, Calif., Oct. 14, 1928; s. Kikuzo and Kino (Tanaka) K.; B.A., U. Tex., 1953, M.A., 1957; m. Meredith Ferguson, Apr. 22, 1977. Clin. psychologist Austin (Tex.) State Hosp., 1961-73; pvt. practice clin. psychology, Austin, 1973—; cons. Tex. Vocat. Rehab. Assn., Tex. Com. on Alcoholism. Bd. dirs. Salvation Army Youth Center. Mem. Tex. Psychol. Assn., Assn. Advancement of Psychology, Am. Psychol. Assn., Council for Nat. Register for Health Service Providers in Psychology, Internat. Platform Assn. Democrat. Episcopalian. Home: 5009 Westview Dr Austin TX 78731 Office: 1600 W 38th St Suite 400-7 Austin TX 78731

KAWAGUCHI, MEREDITH FERGUSON, lawyer; b. Dallas, Feb. 5, 1940; d. Hugh William Ferguson and Ruth Virginia (Perdue) Drewery; m. Harry H. Kawaguchi, Apr. 22, 1977. B.A., U. Tex., 1962, M.A., 1968; J.D., So. Meth. U., 1977. Bar: Tex. 1977. Legal examiner gas utilities div. Tex. Railroad Commn., Austin, 1977-84, legal examiner oil and gas div., 1984—; cons. in law, lectr. to profl. confs. Author position paper Tex. Energy Natural Resources Adv. Council. Mem., Sorority Adv. Council, Austin, 1980—, Japanese-Am. Citizens League, Houston, 1981—, Exec. Women in Tex. Govt., Austin, 1984. Recipient Cert. of Recognition, Tex. Railroad Commn., 1982, Outstanding Service award, 1987. Mem. ABA, Tex. Bar Assn., Travis County Bar Assn. (oil gas and mineral law sect.), Travis County Women Lawyers Assn., Internat. Platform Assn. Home: 5009 Westview Dr Austin TX 78731 Office: Tex Railroad Commn 1701 N Congress Austin TX 78711-2967

KAWAI, RYOICHI, manufacturing company executive; b. Tokyo, Japan, Jan. 18, 1917; s. Ryosei and Chieko (Kuwata) K.; m. Junko Tajima, Feb. 10, 1976; children by previous marriage—Kiyoko, Yoshiaki, Makoto, Naoyuki. B.Econs., Tokyo Imperial U., 1939. With Nissan Auto Co., Ltd., 1939; mgr. Machine Export sect. Machine Trade Bur., 1950-52, 3d Section, Guidance Dept., Small Enterprises Agy., 1953-54; pres. Komatsu Ltd., Tokyo, 1964-82, chmn. bd., 1982—; pres. Nippon Hana-no-kai Found., 1970—; mem. Export Ins. Council, Ministry Internat. Trade and Industry, 1982—; mem. com. on fgn. exchange and other transactions, Fin. Ministry, 1983—, operational council of JETRO, 1984—, mem. tax commn., 1984—, Fiscal System Council Fin., 1985—, IMB Japan Adv. Council, 1986—; chmn. Japan-Turkey Econ. Com. of Keidanren, 1986—, Com. on Pvt. Initiative of Keidanren, 1986—; pres. Japan-China Econs. Found., 1986—. Commandeur de l'ordre de Leopold II, Govt. Belgium, 1974. Office: Komatsu Ltd, 3-6, Akasaka 2-chome, Minato-Ku, Tokyo 107, Japan

KAWAKAMI, HIROSHI, corporation executive; b. Hamamatsu, Japan, Jan. 5, 1942; s. Genichi and Tamiko K.; m. Toshiko Nagai, Mar. 20, 1966; children: Iwao, Yoshitsugu. Grad. in Sci. and Engring., Nihon U., 1965. Dir. Yamaha Corp. (formerly Nippon Gakki Co., Ltd.), 1977, mng. dir., 1979, v.p., 1981, pres., 1983. Home: 21-10 Hirosawa-cho 3-chome, Hamamatsu Shizuoka 432, Japan Office: Yamaha Corp, 10 1 Nakazawa-cho, Hamamatsu 430, Japan

KAWAKATSU, HISASHI, marketing educator; b. Nagoya, Japan, Jan. 18, 1931; s. Sakuji and Atsuko K.; m. Ayako, June 19, 1956; children: Hisaaki, Hisabumi. M Sociology, Hitotsubashi U., Tokyo, 1953. Research specialist Tokyo Broadcasting System, 1953-55, comml. mgr., 1956-60, dir. sales promotion, 1970-81, research dir., 1981-86; prof. Sanno Jr. Coll., 1986—; lectr. Sanno Inst. Bus. Adminstrn., 1964—, econs. dept. Keio U., 1981—. Author: Informationology, 1971, Creativity, 1981, Time Management, 1978; Introduction to Advertising, 1986; Personal Organization, 1986, High Sensitive Service, 1987, How to Get Yes in Presentation, 1988. Mem. Japan Mktg. Assn. (dir.), Japan Soc. Advt. Home: 1-23-4 Higashiyama, Meguro-ku, 153 Tokyo Japan

KAWAKATSU, KENJI, bank executive; b. Jan. 16, 1924. Grad., Tokyo U., 1947. With Sanwa Bank Ltd., 1948—, mng. dir., 1976, now chmn., pres. Home: 31-601 Akasoka 6-chome, Minatoku, Tokyo 107 Japan Office: Sanwa Bank Ltd, 1-1-1 Otemachi Chiyada-ku, Tokyo Japan *

KAWAMITSU, ISAO, publishing company executive; b. Tokugun, Taiwan, July 12, 1944; s. Takeji and Mitsuyo (Sawada) K.; m. Sachiko Katayama, Mar. 3, 1983. LLB, Toyo U., Tokyo, 1967. Assoc. mgr. adminstrv. dept. Reader's Internat. Co., Tokyo, 1968-69; with sales dept. Nikkel Sales Ctr. Inc., Tokyo, 1969-73; with sales dept. Nikkel-McGraw-Hill Subscription Sales Co., Tokyo, 1973-81, assoc. mgr., 1981-83, mktg. mgr. fgn. publs. dept., 1983—. Avocations: lure fishing; deep-sea fishing. Home: 1-1-3-1105 Oyata, Adachi-ku, Tokyo 120, Japan Office: Nikkei Bus Publs Subscriptions, 1-14-6 Uchikanda Chiyoda-ku, Tokyo Japan

KAWAMORI, KAZUSIGE, communications company executive; b. Ibaraki, Japan, May 14, 1936; s. Ichirou and Ryou (Yamawaki) K.; m. Ayako Nakane, May 8, 1964; 1 child, Yoko Sigeki. Gen. affair sect. chief Teregram & Telephone Office, Tahara, Aichi, Japan, 1980-83, 1983-85, 1985—. Home: 1512-15 Nishiakuragawa, 510 Yokkaichi Japan Office: Teregram & Telephone Office, 3-39 Kouseidoориminami, 444 Okazaki Aichi, Japan

KAWANA, KOICHI, educator, artist; b. Asahikawa, Hokkaido, Japan, Mar. 16, 1930; came to U.S., 1952, naturalized, 1971; s. Kiichi and Toki (Takeda) K. B.S., Yokohama Mcpl. U., (Japan), 1951; A.B., UCLA, 1955, M.A., 1959, M.F.A., 1964; Ph.D., Pacific Western U., 1979. Lectr. landscape design, Japanese art history UCLA, 1962—, univ. research artist, 1964-66, lectr. art, 1966, asst. prof. art in residence, 1966, sr. artist dept. architects and engrs., 1968-70, design cons., archtl. assoc., 1970-73, prin. archtl. assoc., 1973—; pres. Environ. Design Assocs., 1966-82, chmn., 1982—; v.p. Kapa Co., 1969—. Contbr. articles to profl. jours. Recipient Seikyoju rank and awarded artist name Yocho, Adachi-shiki Sch. Floral Design, 1961; recipient Design award Progressive Architecture, 1972, Gold medal Accademia Italia della Arti e del Lavoro, Henry Shaw medal Trustees of Mo. Bot. Garden, 1987; winner Nat. Soc. Interior Designers competition, 1961; decorated Order of Merit, Mil. and Hospitaller Order St. Lazarus of Jerusalem. Mem. Am. Soc. Interior Designers, So. Calif. Hort. Inst., Japan Am. Soc. So. Calif. (council 1965—Disting. Service award, Victor M. Carter Diamond award 1980), Los Angeles County Mus. Art, Far Eastern Art Council, Pi Gamma Mu, Pi Sigma Alpha. Home: 633 24th St Santa Monica CA 90402 Office: U Calif 601 Westwood Plaza Los Angeles CA 90024

KAWANO, IETOSHI, electronics and software engineer; b. Shimane Prefecture, Japan, July 6, 1941; s. Shosuke and Asako (Gotoh) K.; m. Machiko Giga, Nov. 22, 1969; children—Masatoshi, Hiroshi. BSEE, U. Kyoto, 1964, MS in Electronics, 1966. Engr. Totsuda Works, Hitachi Ltd., Yokohama, Japan, 1966-78, sr. system engr., 1978-86, deputy chief engr., 1986—. Contbr. articles to prof. jours. Patentee in field. Mem. IEEE (paper referee Design Automation Conf. 1980—), Inst. Elec. and Communications Engrs. Japan (paper referee 1977—). Club: Fuji Heigen Golf. Avocations: personal computing, radio amatuer. Home: 1160-12-402 Moro-Oka-Cho, Kohoku-ku, 222 Yokohama Japan Office: Totsuka Facility Hitachi Ltd, 216 Totsuka-cho Totsuka-ku, 222 Yokohama Japan

KAWAR, GHASSOUB FADDOUL, shipping agency executive; b. Amman, Jordan, Nov. 28, 1949; s. Faddoul Jamil and Najla (Jabbour) K.; m. Maha Saeed Jiryes, Feb. 3, 1980; children: Faddoul, Ramez. BS, Am. U., Beirut, 1972; diploma in shipping, London Sch. of Fgn. Trade, 1979. Tchr. Ministry of Edn., Manameh, Bahrain, 1972-74; assistance mgr. Amin Kawar & Sons, Aqaba, Jordan, 1974-76, Aqaba, 1976-78; mgr. Aqaba Shipping Co., Amman, 1979-83; gen. mgr. Amin Kawar & Sons, Amman, 1983—. Club: Am. U. Beirut. Lodge: Rotary. Office: Aqaba Shipping Co Pvt Ltd, 24 Sharif Abdel Hamid Sharaf St, Shmeisani PO Box 5350, Amman Jordan

KAWASHIMA, MASAO, communications and computers co. exec.; b. Kanagawa Prefecture, Japan, Jan. 14, 1929; s. Takashi and Kiyo (Takada) K.; m. Miyako Kinoshita, Dec. 2, 1956; children: Shoichiro, Keiko, Nobuko, Sugimoto. B.Engring. in Electronics, U. Osaka (Japan), 1952, D. Engring., 1962. pres. Fujitsu Inst. of Computer Sci., Tokyo, 1987—, also dir. Fellow IEEE; mem. Inst. Electronics and Infos. Japan, Inst. Elec. Engrs., Inst. TV Engrs. Buddhist. Author works in field; patentee in field. Home: 54 Minami-Kibogaoka, Asahi-ku, Yokohama 241-00, Japan Office: Fujitsu Ltd, 1-6-1 Marunouchi, Chiyoda-Ku, Tokyo 100, Japan

KAWATA, TADASHI, academic adminstrator, educator; b. Tochigi-ken, Japan, June 22, 1925; s. Junichiro and Tei (Mitsugi) K.; B.A. in Econs., U. Tokyo, 1948, Ph.D., 1968; vis. scholar Harvard U., 1955-57, 85; m. Sadako Niimura, May 22, 1952; children—Atsushi, Shin, Chiharu. From lectr. to prof. internat. relations U. Tokyo, 1951-72; prof. internat. relations Sophia U., Tokyo, 1972—, dean Faculty Fgn. Studies, 1981-84; dir. Inst. Am. and Can. Studies, 1987—; prof. emeritus U. Tokyo, 1987—; vis. prof. Universidad Nacional Federico Villarreal, Lima, Peru, 1969, El Colegio de México, 1973-74; lectr. Internat. Seminar Fgn. Service, Salzburg, Austria, 1971; vis. fellow U. Essex, 1985. Served with Japanese Army, 1945. Mem. Internat. Peace Research Assn. (council 1965-71), Peace Studies Assn. Japan (pres. 1975-77), Japan Peace Research Group (dir. 1966-72), Japan Assn. Internat. Econs. (exec. com. 1965—), Japan Assn. Internat. Relations (pres. 1982-84), Sci. Council Japan (exec. com. 1988—), Yomiuri Internat. Econ. Soc. (council 1971—). Author: International Relations, 1958; Modern International Economics, 1967; War Economy and Peace Research, 1969; Challenge of Asia, 1969; Economics of Peace, 1972; The North-South Problem, 1977; Independence of the Third World and Japan, 1977; Political Economy of International Relations, 1980; Economic Friction, 1982, rev. edit., 1986; (with Twu Jaw-Yann) Modern International Society and Economy, 1983; Towards International Political Economy, 1988; mem. editorial com. The Developing Economies, 1965-83. Home: 1-15-11, Arima Miyamae-ku, Kawasaki-shi Kanagawa 213, Japan

KAWECKI, LEON STANLEY, artist; b. nr. Chojnice, Poland, July 2, 1921; s. Adam and Elizabeth (Link); came to U.S., 1952, naturalized, 1956; grad. State Coll. Graphic Arts Poznan (Poland), 1939; student Pitts. Art Inst., 1952-54, Otis Art Inst., 1964, Calif. Inst. Arts, 1966-67, Art Center Coll. Design, 1968, U. Calif. at Irvine, 1968-71; m. Jacqueline Salamey, Apr. 25, 1953; children—Raymond Mark, Steven James, Daniel Noel, Barbara Rachelle. Comml. artist Fuller Label & Box Co., Pitts., 1952-57; packaging designer Standard Packaging Corp., Pitts., 1957-60; art dir. Mead Packaging, Los Angeles, 1960—; exhibited in shows in Warsaw, Poland, Dusseldorf, Germany, Pasadena, Calif., Los Angeles, Mexico City; designer U.S. Bicentennial Commemorative medal Freedom Founders, Polonus Commemorative medal, 1979 Internat. Philatelic Exhbn., Commemorative medal John Paul II - A Son of Poland, Polish-Am. Numis. Assn., commemorative medal 300th Anniversary Relief of Vienna-King John III, Polish Am. Numis. Assn., commemorative medal King John III Sobieski Savior of Christianity, Polish Am. Congress, 1983, commemorative medal 600th Anniversary Coronation and Marriage of King and Queen Jagiello Polish Am. Numismatic Assn. Chgo., 1985, commemorative medal 175th Anniversary Birth Frederic Chopin Assn., 1985, commemorative medal Polish Am. Hist. Assn., 1988, Polonia award Fine Arts and Service, Polish Am. Congress, 1988. Supporting mem. Pitts. Symphony Orch., 1957-58; exec. officer Ariz.-Calif. Nat. Copernicus Com., 1971-73. Served with Polish Armed Forces, 1939-47. Recipient Silver medal All-Polish Scholastic Exhbn., 1936; Grand award U. Pitts., 1960; Gold and Silver medals Folding Box Internat. competition, 1963; Silver medal U.S. Folding Box competition, 1966; Gold medal 500th anniversary Copernicus celebration Adler Planetarium, Chgo., 1973; Silver medal 500th anniversary Copernicus Celebration, Warsaw, Poland, 1973; Grand Prix, World Folklore Philat. Exhbn., Chgo., 1978, award of excellence for exhibit Orange County Advt. Fedn., 1978, State Order Cultural Merit, Polish Ministry Arts and Culture, 1978, hon. medal and diploma 50th anniversary Regional Mus., Chojnice, Poland. others. Mem. Pasadena Arts League, Fountain Valley Arts Assn. (founding), Am. Philatelic Soc., Nat. Soc. Art Dirs., Art Dirs. Club Los Angeles, Polonus Philatelic Soc., Polonus Philatelic Soc. (hon.). Club: Town Hall of Calif. Research in coins and crowns of Poland from 14th to 18th century. Address: 6400 Valley View St Buena Park CA 90620

KAY, ERNEST, editor, publisher; b. Darwen, Lancashire, Eng., June 21, 1915; s. Harold and Florence (Woodall) K.; grad. Spring Bank Sch., Darwen, 1929; recipient 9 hon. doctorates; m. Marjorie Peover, Aug. 12, 1941 (dec. Feb. 1987); children—John Michael, Richard Andrew, Belinda Jean. With various newspapers in U.K., 1929-52; mng. editor Evening News, London, 1952-56; editor, pub. John O'London's Lit. Weekly, 1957-66, Dictionary Internat. Biography, London and Cambridge, 1967—; dir. gen. Internat. Biog. Centre, Cambridge, 1972—; author: Great Men, 2d edit., 1960; Isles of Flowers, 2d edit., 1964; Pragmatic Premier: An Intimate Portrait of Harold Wilson, 1967; The Wit of Harold Wilson, 1968; contbr. various newspapers, mags.; cons. in field of pub. Chmn. Cambridge Symphony Orch. Trust, 1979-83. Recipient Gold medal Internat. Poets Laureate, 1966; Gold medal Haile Selassie of Ethiopia, 1968; key to N.Y.C., 1975, to New Orleans, 1978, to Los Angeles, 1981; named hon. citizen New Orleans, 1982. Life fellow Royal Soc. Arts; fellow Royal Geog. Soc. Mem. Labour Party. Quaker. Club: Nat. Arts (N.Y.C.). Home: Westhurst, 418 Milton Rd, Cambridge CB4 1ST England Office: Internat Biog Centre, Cambridge CB2 3QP, England

KAY, HELEN (MRS. HERBERT J. GOLDFRANK), author; b. N.Y.C., Oct. 27, 1912; d. Hyman and Terese (Herman) Colodny; student public schs. Washington, writer workshops N.Y.U., Bank State Coll.; m. Herbert John Goldfrank, Dec. 25, 1933; children—Lewis Robert, Deborah, Joan. Editorial research Time mag., N.Y.C., 1936, Fortune mag., 1937, Labor Press, SMCWA News, 1943-44, CIO News, 1945. Bd. dirs. Learning to Read Through the Arts at the Guggenheim, 1980. Mem. Authors League, PEN, Soc. Children's Book Writers. Author: Snow Birthday, 1955; One Mitten Lewis, 1955; City Springtime, 1957; A Pony for the Winter, 1959; Lincoln, A Big Man, 1958; Abe Lincoln's Hobby, 1961; How Smart Are Animals, 1963; The Secrets of the Dolphin, 1964; A Stocking for a Kitten, 1965; Picasso's World of Children, 1965, reprinted, 1977; An Egg is for Wishing, 1966; Man and Mastiff, 1967; Apes, 1970; The First Teddy Bear, 1985; The Staff of the Shepherd, 1983; many others. Address: 375 Nannyhagen Rd Thornwood NY 10594

KAYES, PATRICK JOHN, transportation company executive; b. Zomba, Malawi, June 22, 1936; s. Cyril Bernard and Mary Elizabeth (Carroll) K.; m. Michèle Adrienne Marie Ameels, Oct. 29, 1960; children: Guy Patrick, Nicolette Madeleine, Craig Bernard, Julia Michèle. Transport mgr. Chirunga Estates, Ltd., Zomba, 1956-60; depot mgr. Bulwark Transport, Harare, Zimbabwe, 1960-63; exec. mgmt. trainee Swift Transport Services Ltd., Harare, 1963; assemply supt. Booth Pty. Ltd., Sydney, Australia, 1964-66; ops. mgr. United Tanker Services Pty. Ltd., Sydney, 1966-68; gen. mgr.'s asst. McGlashan Transport Pty. Ltd., Burunga, 1968-69; designate mgr. Containerbase Fedn., London, 1969-70; mng. dir. Collings and Stevenson Ltd., London, 1970—; external dir. Chirunga Estates Ltd., Tyrelsoles Ltd., Limbe, Malawi. Served as cpl. British Army, 1954-56. Fellow Chartered Inst. Transp., Inst. Dirs., British Inst. Mgmt. Roman Catholic. Club: Royal Automobile (London). Office: Collings and Stevenson Ltd, Green Ln, Hounslow, Middlesex TW4 6BZ, England

KAYLAN, HOWARD LAWRENCE, musical entertainer, composer; b. N.Y.C., June 22, 1947; s. Sidney and Sally Joyce (Berlin) K.; m. Mary Melita Pepper, June 10, 1967 (div. Sept. 1971); 1 child, Emily Anne; m. Susan Karen Olsen, Apr. 18, 1982. Grad. high sch., Los Angeles. Lead singer rock group The Turtles, Los Angeles, 1965-70, Mothers of Invention, Los Angeles, 1970-72; radio, TV, recording entertainer various broadcast organizations, Los Angeles, 1972—; screenwriter Larry Gelbart, Carl Gotleib prodns., Los Angeles, 1979-85; producer children's records Kidstuff Records, Hollywood, Fla., 1980—; singer, producer rock band Flo and Eddie, Los Angeles, 1976—; singer, producer The Turtles (reunion of original band), Los Angeles, 1980—; actor, TV and film Screen Actors Guild, Los Angeles, 1983—; v.p. Flo and Eddie, Inc., Los Angeles, 1972—; background vocalist various albums for Bruce Springsteen, T. Rex, Blondie, Andy Taylor, Psychedelic Furs, John Lennon, Ozzy Osbourne. Contbr. articles to Creem Magazine, Los Angeles Free Press, Rockit Magazine, Phonograph Record; screenwriter motion picture Death Masque, 1985; actor motion picture Get Crazy, 1985; performed at the White House, 1970. Recipient 6 gold and platinum LP album awards while lead singer, 1965—, cert. achievement State of Calif., 1982, Fine Arts award Bank of Am., Los Angeles, 1965. Mem. AFTRA, Screen Actors Guild, Am. Fedn. Musicians, AGVA. Democrat.

KAYNE, JON BARRY, industrial psychologist; b. Sioux City, Iowa, Oct. 20, 1943; s. Harry Aaron and Barbara Valentine (Daniel) K.; m. Bunee Ellen Price, July 25, 1965; children: Nika Jenine, Abraham; m. 2d Sandra Kay Fossbender, Jan. 5, 1985; 1 child, Shay-Marie Kathryn. BA, U. Colo., 1973; MSW, U. Denver, 1975; PhD, U. No. Colo., 1978. With spl. services Weld County Sch. Dist. 6, Greeley, Colo., 1975-77; forensic diagnostician Jefferson County (Colo.) Diagnostic Unit, 1977-78; assoc., dir. mktg. 1 Dow Ctr., assoc. prof. psychology Hillsdale (Mich.) Coll., 1978-87; pres. Jon B. Kayne, P.C., Hillsdale, 1980-87; chmn. bd. dirs., chief exec. officer Am. Internat. Mgmt. Assocs., Ltd., Denver, 1984-87; v.p. continuous edn. and profl. studies, prof. bus. adminstrn. and psychology Bellevue (Neb.) Coll., 1987—. Chmn. bd. dirs. Domestic Harmony, 1979-82; dir. religious sch., Greeley, 1975-77; candidate for sheriff of Boulder County, 1974. Served with USAR, 1962. Mem. Am. Psychol. Assn., Am. Soc. Clin. Hypnosis, Am. Statis. Assn., Internat. Neuropsychol. Soc., Mich. Soc. Investigative and Forensic Hypnosis (chmn. bd., pres. 1982), N.Y. Acad. Scis., Phi Delta Kappa, Psi Chi, Alpha Gamma Sigma. Office: Bellevue Coll Galvin Rd at Harvell Dr Bellevue NE 68005

KAYS, B. THOMAS, dentist, educator; b. Kansas City, Mo., July 2, 1944; s. Benjamin C. and Mary C. (Shelton) K.; m. Claudia Johnson, Aug. 14, 1982; children—Mary Trinette, B. Charles, Tadd Wright McKellar. B.S., The Citadel, 1966, M.Ed., 1981; D.D.S., U. Iowa, 1970. Gen. practice dentistry, Charleston, S.C., 1972—; asst. clin. prof. Med. U. S.C., Charleston, 1972—. Bd. dirs. Omega Ins. Co., Psi Omega Found. Served to capt. USAF, 1970-72. Fellow ADA (Outstanding Charleston Dentist of Yr. 1986), Am. Coll. Dentists (pres. 1986-87), Internat. Coll. Dentists; mem. S.C. Dental Assn. (v.p. 1984-85, pres. 1986—, directing sec. 1983-84), Coastal Dist. Dental Soc., Charleston Dental Soc., Omicron Kappa Upsilon, Psi Omega (nat. pres. 1983-84). Republican. Episcopalian. Avocations: sailboat racing; photography. Home: 1657 Seignious Dr Charleston SC 29407 Office: 1040 Savannah Hwy Charleston SC 29407

KAYSONE PHOMVIHAN, Laotian prime minister; b. Savannakhet-Province, Laos, 1920; attended U. Hanoi (Vietnam). Joined Free Lao Front (Neo Lao Issara) nationalist movement in exile, Bangkok, 1945; attended 1st resistance congress; minister of def. Free Lao Front resistance Govt., 1950; comdr.-in-chief of Pathet Lao forces, 1954-57; mem. People's Party of Laos, 1955, Lao Patriotic Front (Neo Lao Hak Sat), 1956, vice chmn., 1959, vice chmn. Central Com., 1964; prime minister of Laos, 1975—; gen. sec. Central Com., Lao People's Revolutionary Party. Decorated Order of Lenin. Author: To Build a Peaceful, Independent and Socialist Laos, 1978. Office: Chairman Council of Ministers, Vientiane Laos *

KAZAN, ELIA, theatrical, motion picture director and producer, author; b. Constantinople, Turkey, Sept. 7, 1909; s. George and Athena (Sismanoglou) K.; m. Molly Day Thacher, Dec. 2, 1932 (dec.); children: Judy, Chris, Nick, Katharine; m. Barbara Loden, June 5, 1967 (dec.); 1 child, Leo; m. Frances Rudge, June 28, 1982. A.B., Williams Coll., 1930; postgrad., Yale U., 1930-32; M.F.A., Wesleyan U., Middletown, Conn., 1955. Co-founder Actors Studio. Actor with, Group Theatre, 1932-39; dir. stage plays, 1940-55, including, Skin of Our Teeth, Harriet, Jacobowsky and the Colonel, All My Sons, Deep Are the Roots, A Streetcar Named Desire, Death of a Salesman, Camino Real, Tea and Sympathy, Cat on a Hot Tin Roof, The Dark at the Top of the Stairs, J.B (Antoinette Perry award for direction 1958), Sweet Bird of Youth, After the Fall, But for Whom Charlie, The Changeling; numerous motion pictures, 1944—, including, A Tree Grows in Brooklyn, Boomerang, Gentlemen's Agreement (Acad. award for best direction 1947), Pinky, Panic in the Streets, A Streetcar Named Desire, Zapata, Man on a Tight Rope, On the Waterfront, (1954 Acad. Award for best direction), East of Eden, Baby Doll, A Face in the Crowd, Wild River, Splendor in the Grass, America, America, The Arrangement, The Visitors, The Last Tycoon; author: America, America, 1962, The Arrangement, 1967, A Life, 1988; producer, dir. film, 1968, The Assassins, 1972, The Understudy, 1974, Acts of Love, 1978, The Anatolian, 1982, Elia Kazan, A Life, 1988. Recipient D.W. Griffith award Dirs. Guild Am., 1987.

KAZANOWSKI, ALBIN D(ANIEL), cost analysis consultant; b. Terryville, Conn., Aug. 22, 1926; s. Matthew H. and Mary M. (Sosinski) K.; m. Mary A. Kotuli, July 24, 1949; children—Carol K., Matthew D. Student, MIT, 1944-45; B.S. in Chem. Engring., Northeastern U., Boston, 1951; M.B.A., Harvard U., 1953; cert. cost analyst, Inst. Cost Analysis, 1982. Systems ops. research analyst Kaiser Aluminum & Chem. Corp., Spokane, 1953-60; mgmt. cons. United Research Inc., Beverly Hills, Calif., 1960-62; sr. tech. specialist, supr., sr. mem. tech. staff ops. analysis group advanced systems Space Div. Rockwell Internat., Downey, Calif., 1962-80; mgr. The Aerospace Corp., Los Angeles, 1980—; cons. design and analysis of biomed. expts.; cost analysis cons. Nat. Research Council; lectr. local univs. and Colls. Served with USAF, 1946-47. Fellow AAAS, Inst. for Advancement of Engring., AIAA (assoc.); mem. Ops. Research Soc. Am., Inst. Cost Analysis, Sigma Xi. Republican. Roman Catholic. Clubs: Harvard Bus. Sch. (Los Angeles). Home: 21869 Woodland Crest Dr Woodland Hills CA 91364 Office: PO Box 92957 Los Angeles CA 90009

KAZANTZIDES, SAVAS, manufacturing company executive; b. Athens, Greece, Sept. 30, 1962; s. Elias Savas Kazantzides and Fifi Anne Katsa. BS, Am. U. Greece, 1984; MBA, Kennedy Western U., Calif., 1987. Asst. sales mgr. Viokaz S.A., Athens, 1983, sales mgr., 1984, mktg. mgr., 1986, pres., 1987—. Recipient First Prize for Best Research, Nat. Orgn. Youth, 1980,

First Nat. Metal with 4x100 Relay Team, Greek Fedn. Track and Field, 1978. Mem. Greek Fedn. Scuba Diving. Conservative. Greek Orthodox. Club: Nautical of Greece. Home: 21 Terpsichoris Str, 175 62 P Faliro Athens Greece Office: Viokaz SA, 5 P Mela Str, 121 31 Athens Greece

KAZI, AFROZE, physician; b. Karachi, Sindh, Pakistan, Apr. 13, 1936; d. Mahomed Hassan and Sharafunissa Kazi; m. Imamali Kazi, Jan. 4, 1958; children: Shahzad, Naveed, Samira Junejo. Degree in intersci., D.J. Sci. Coll., Karachi, 1954; MBBS, U. Karachi, 1961. Intern dept. ob-gyn Civil Hosp., Karachi, 1961-62; med. officer population welfare div. Govt. Pakistan, Karachi, 1968-75, dep. dir. population welfare div., 1976-86, dir. population welfare div., 1986—; bd. dirs. Nat. Research Inst. Fertility Control, Karachi, 1986—. Mem. Soc. Ob-gyn Pakistan, Profl. Womens Club. Home: D-78 Block IV, Kehkashan, Karachi, Sindh Pakistan Office: Nat Research Inst Fertility Control, Block 36-A, Pak Sect, Shahrah-E-Iraq, Karachi Pakistan

KAZI, GULZAR HUSSAIN, airline executive; b. Chakwal, Punjab, Pakistan, Oct. 10, 1942; s. Fazal Hussain and Safoor K.; m. Firazat Gulzar, Nov. 2, 1969; children: Mubashir, Mudassir, Ayesha, Muzammil. BS, Govt. Coll., Lahore, Pakistan, 1962; MPA, Punjab U., Lahore, 1964. Asst. mgr. West Pakistan Road Transport Corp., Lahore, 1965-67; orgn. and methods officer Pakistan Internat. Airlines, Karachi, 1967-78, mgr. indsl. engring., 1978-82, gen. mgr. manpower planning, 1982-83, gen. mgr. indsl. relations, 1983-84, gen. mgr. customer service planning, 1984-86, gen. mgr. flight service, 1986—. Guest speaker U. Karachi, 1982-87, Nat. Inst. Pub. Adminstrn., 1984-86. Mem. Am. Mgmt. Assn., Brit. Inst. Mgmt., Am. Inst. Indsl. Engrs., Chartered Inst. Transport. Lodge: Old Ravians (exec. com. 1977). Home: 58/P/2 P E CH S, Karachi, Sind Pakistan Office: Pakistan Internat Airlines, PIA Bldg, Karachi, Sind Pakistan

KAZIMIERCZUK, MARIAN KAZIMIERZ, electrical engineer, educator; b. Smolugi, Poland, Mar. 3, 1948; came to U.S., 1984; s. Stanislaw and Stanislawa (Tomaszewska) K.; m. Alicja Nowowiejska, July 5, 1973; children: Andrzej, Anna. MS, Tech. U. of Warsaw, Poland, 1971, PhD, 1978, DSc, 1984. Instr. elec. engring. Tech. U. of Warsaw, Poland, 1972-78, asst. prof., 1978-84; project engr. Design Automation, Inc., Lexington, Mass., 1984; vis. prof. Va. Poly. Inst., Blacksburg, 1984-85, Wright State U., Dayton, Ohio, 1985—. Contbr. numerous articles to profl. jours.; patentee in field. Recipient Univ. Edn. and Tech. award Polish Ministry of Sci., 1981, 84, 85, Polish Acad. Sci. award 1983. Mem. Assn. Polish Engrs., Polish Soc. Theoretical and Applied Elec. Scis. Roman Catholic. Home: 35 Old Yellow Springs Rd Apt F Fairborn OH 45324 Office: Wright State U Dept Elec Systems Engring Dayton OH 45435

KAZIN, ALFRED, writer; b. Bklyn., June 5, 1915; s. Charles and Gita (Fagelman) K.; m. Caroline Bookman, May 23, 1947 (div.); 1 son, Michael; m. Ann Birstein, June 26, 1952 (div.); 1 dau., Cathrael; m. Judith Dunford, May 21, 1983. B.S.S., CCNY, 1935; A.M., Columbia U., 1938; Litt.D., Adelphi U., 1965, U. New Haven, 1976, Hebrew Union Coll., 1982, CCNY Grad. Ctr., 1986, SUNY, 1987. Lit. editor New Republic, 1942-43, contbg. editor, 1943-45; contbg. editor Fortune Mag., 1943-44; lectr. Black Mountain Coll., fall 1944; vis. prof. U. Minn., summer 1946, 50; lectr. Harvard U., 1953; William Allan Neilson research prof. Smith Coll., 1954-55; Berg prof. lit. NYU, 1957; prof. Am. studies Amherst Coll., 1955-58; vis. prof. CCNY, 1962; Beckman prof. U. Calif., 1963; Disting. prof. English, SUNY-Stony Brook, 1963-73; Disting. prof. English Grad. Ctr., CUNY, 1973-85; William White prof. English, U. Notre Dame, 1978-79. Writer-in-residence, Am. Acad. in Rome, 1975; author: On Native Grounds, 1942, A Walker in the City, 1951, The Inmost Leaf, 1955, Contemporaries, 1962, Starting Out in the Thirties, 1965, Bright Book of Life, 1973, New York Jew, 1978, An American Procession, 1984, A Writers America, 1988; co-author: Introduction to the Works of Anne Frank, 1959; General Introduction to Dell Edition of the Novels of Theodore Dreiser, 1960; others.; editor: The Viking Portable William Blake, 1946; editor: F. Scott Fitzgerald, The Man and His Work, 1951, Moby-Dick, 1956, Introduction to Selected Stories of Sholem Aleichem, 1956, The Open Form: Essays For Our Time, 1961, The Selected Short Stories of Nathaniel Hawthorne, 1966; co-editor: The Stature of Theodore Dreiser, 1955; co-editor: Emerson: A Modern Anthology, 1958; The Ambassadors (James), 1969; contbr. articles to newspapers, mags. Guggenheim fellow, 1940, 1947; Rockefeller fellow study of trade-union and Army popular edn. movements in Gt. Britain, 1945; NEH sr. fellow Ctr. Advanced Study Behavioral Scis., Stanford, 1977-78; Recipient George Polk Meml. award for criticism, 1966; Brandeis U. Creative Arts award, 1973; Hubbell medal MLA, 1982. Mem. Nat. Inst. Arts and Letters, Am. Acad. Arts and Scis., Phi Beta Kappa (hon., recipient orator award Harvard U., 1987). Office: English Dept CUNY 33 W 42d St New York NY 10036

KAZMAYER, ROBERT HENDERSON, business analyst, publisher; b. Rush, N.Y., 1908; s. Jacob and Viola (Darron) K.; m. Clara V. Rapp, July 29, 1936 (div.); 1 child, Robert L.; m. Ida L. Wright, Nov. 18, 1955 (dec. Nov. 1970); m. Doris McMichael Sanderson, Aug. 29, 1988. Student, U. Rochester, 1929-31, Colgate-Divinity Sch., 1931-34; LL.D., Salem Coll., Salem. W.Va., 1956. Ordained deacon M.E. Ch., 1932; ordained elder 1934; held pastorates at Indian Falls, 1930-31; Lewiston M.E. Ch., Rochester, N.Y., 1931-34, Monroe Av M.E. Ch., 1934-38; left ministry to devote full time to writing, lecturing 1939; travelled annually in Central and South Am., Australia, Far East, Eng., much of continental, 1929-41; in 22 months following Pearl Harbor, travelled numerous states addressing over 400 audiences, lecturing on Germany, Russia, Japan, internat. politics; Rochester Town Hall of the Air, WHEC; three years as radio ch. editor WSAY; originator of Kazmayer Seminar Tours; Lectured throughout, U.S., Can., Europe, the East;. Pub. newsletter for U.S., Brit. businessmen Things To Watch and Watch For; Author: Out of the Clouds, 1944, New Strength for America; speeches; contbr. to We Believe in Prayer; Conducted: Pastor's Exchange in Christian Advocate, 1935-36. Recipient L'Accueil De Paris Conseil Municipal Paris, 1956; George Washington Honor medal Freedoms Found., 1961. Life mem. Acad. Polit. Sci., 1952; charter mem. Anglo-Am. Goodwill Assn. (Brit.), Authors League; mem. Am. Acad. Polit. and Social Sci. Methodist. Clubs: Union League (Chgo.); Adventurers (Chgo., N.Y., London); Overseas Press (N.Y.C.). Lodges: Masons (33d degree), Rotary (Paul Harris fellow). Home and Office: 1625 Ariana Lakeland FL 33801

KAZMI SYED, IRSHAD ALI, physician; b. Hissar, India, Jan. 24, 1938; s. Roshan Ali and Aqleem-un-Nissa Kazmi Syed; m. Mumtaz Jahan, Oct. 4, 1958; 4 daughters, 2 sons. BA, Punjab (Pakistan) U., 1966; MBBS, Punjab U., 1968, MA, 1970; LLB, Multan U., Punjab, 1977. Med. officer Malaria Eradication Program, Punjab, Dist. Council Muzaffargarh, Punjab, Ali Clinic, Alipur, Punjab. Sec. gen. Alipur Citizens' Assn., Punjab, 1970, Muslim Edn. Propagation Soc., Alipur, 1980; v.p. Muslim Edn. Soc. Alipur, 1980; chmn. Local Zakat Com. Alipur, 1980. Mem. Pakistan Med. Assn. (pres. Alipur br. 1987—), Islamic Med. Assn., Patients Welfare Soc. (pres. 1975—). Club: Civil (life). Home: Jatoi Rd Alipur, Alipur Dist Muzaffar Garh, Alipur Pakistan Office: Ali Clinic, Jatoi Rd, Alipur Pakistan

KAZOR, WALTER ROBERT, mechanical engineer; b. Avonmore, Pa., Apr. 16, 1922; s. Steven Stanley and Josephine (Lestic) K.; B.S. in Mech. Engring., Pa. State U., 1943; M.S., U. Pitts., 1953, M.Letters in Econs. and Indsl. Mgmt., 1957; m. Gloria Rosalind Roma, Aug. 10, 1946; children—Steven Edward, Christopher Paul, Kathleen Mary Jo. Research engr. Gulf Oil Corp., Pitts., 1946-57; with Westinghouse Electric Corp., 1957-84, quality assurance mgr. breeder reactor components project, Tampa, Fla., 1977-81, mgr. nuclear service center, Tampa, 1981-84; pres. Integrated Quality Systems Corp., Mgmt. Quality Assurance Cons., St. Petersburg, Fla., 1984-86; quality assurance specialist in nuclear waste mgmt. Sci. Applications Internat. Corp., Las Vegas, 1986-88; sr. cons. quality assurance F&M Tech. Services, Inc., Dallas, 1988—; cons., guest lectr. in field. Bd. dirs. New Kensington (Pa.) council Boy Scouts Am., 1958-62. Served with USNR, 1944-46. Registered profl. engr., Pa. Mem. ASME, Am. Soc. Quality Control. Republican. Roman Catholic. Club: Lions (past pres. clubs). Author, patentee in field. Office: F&M Tech Services 2525 Walnut Hill Ln Dallas TX 75229

KAZUYUKI, KITAJIMA, petrowholesaler; b. Tokyo, Aug. 21, 1949; s. Yagoroo and Ikeda (Sueko) K.; m. Miyamoto Mariko, 1977; children: Yuriko, Hisanao. B.Law, Keio U., Tokyo, 1973. Mem. adminstrv. staff Embassy of Japan, Singapore, 1973-75; mng. dir. Hokutoh Sekiyu Co. Ltd., Tokyo, 1976—. Home: 3-13-22-106 Kamiyouga, Setagaya Ward, Tokyo Japan 158 Office: Hokutoh Sekiyu Co Ltd, 3-38-12 Hongoh, Bunkyo Ward, Tokyo 113, Japan

KEAN, HAMILTON FISH, lawyer; b. N.Y.C., Mar. 1, 1925; s. Robert Winthrop and Elizabeth Stuyvesant (Howard) K.; m. Ellen Shaw Garrison, Mar. 25, 1950 (div. 1976); children—Leslie K. McKim, Elizabeth Stuyvesant II, Lloyd Garrison, Lewis Morris; m. Alice Kay Newcomer, July 6, 1981 (dec. 1986). A.B. cum laude, Princeton U., 1949; J.D., Columbia U., 1954. Bar: N.Y. 1954, N.J. 1955. Asst. counsel Waterfront Commn. N.Y. Harbor, 1954; law sec. N.J. Supreme Ct., 1954-55; asst. U.S. atty. N.J. Dist., 1955-57; ptnr. Clapp and Eisenberg and predecessors, Newark, 1957-62; pvt. practice law, trustee various funds and orgns. N.Y.C., 1963—; lectr. law Rutgers U. Sch. Law, 1960; lectr. environ. law SUNY at Purchase, Westchester Community Coll., 1974-76; supervising atty. clin. program environ. law NYU Sch. Law, 1972-76; bd. mem., sec. Environ. Planning Lobby, 1972-78; dir. Livingston Nat. Bank, 1982-84, chmn., 1984; dir. Realty Transfer Co., 1st Jersey Nat. Bank. Bd. dirs. Morris County Urban League, 1956-61; mem. Urban Crisis Task Force, 1976; bd. dirs. Youth Counseling League, 1969—, pres., 1979-83; bd. dirs. Citizens Com. for Children N.Y., 1971—, pres., 1972-77; chmn. Joint Action for Children, 1976; trustee Natural Resources Def. Council, 1975—, treas., 1973-76; bd. dirs. Fountain House, 1973—, pres., 1975-78; mem. Adv. Council to N.Y. State Office Mental Health, 1979-83; mem. Mental Health Services Council, 1983—; trustee Coro Found., 1979-85; mem. N.Y. State Mental Hygiene Planning Council, 1981—; trustee Alice and Hamilton Fish Library, 1981—; bd. mgrs. State Communities Aid Assn., 1982—, pres., 1985—; mem. adminstrv. bd. Lab. Ornithology (Cornell U., 1982-87; trustee Hancock Shaker Village, 1986—. Served to 2d lt. U.S. Army, 1943-46. Decorated Purple Heart. Mem. ABA, N.Y. State Bar Assn. (chmn. conf. on pub. interest law 1975), Assn. Bar City N.Y., Columbia Law Sch. Alumni Assn. (treas. 1958-62). Clubs: Century Assn., Knickerbocker, Princeton, Atrium, Millbrook Golf and Tennis. Office: 120 E 56th St New York NY 10022

KEAN, JOHN VAUGHAN, lawyer; b. Providence, Mar. 12, 1917; s. Otho Vaughan and Mary (Duell) K.; A.B. cum laude, Harvard, 1938, J.D., 1941. Admitted to R.I. bar, 1942; with Edwards & Angell, Providence, 1941—, partner, 1954-87; of counsel, 1987—. Chmn., Downtown Providence YMCA, 1964-67. Bd. dirs. Greater Providence YMCA, 1964-76. Served to capt. AUS, 1943-46, 50-52, brig. gen. Decorated Legion of Merit. Mem. Am., R.I. bar assns., N.G. Assn., Res. Officers Assn., Assn. U.S. Army, R.I. Army N.G. (brig. gen. 1964-72). Episcopalian. Clubs: Harvard R.I. (pres. 1964-66), Agawam Hunt, Hope, Providence Art, Turks Head; Army and Navy (Washington); Sakonnet Golf (Little Compton, R.I.). Home: 518 W Main Rd Little Compton RI 02837 Office: 2700 Hospital Trust Tower Providence RI 02903

KEAN, THOMAS H., governor of New Jersey; b. N.Y.C., Apr. 21, 1935; m. Deborah Bye; children: Thomas, Reed, Alexandra. A.B., Princeton; M.A., Columbia. Tchr. history and govt.; mem. N.J. Assembly, 1967-77, speaker, 1972, minority leader, 1974; acting gov. 1973, gov., 1981-89. Office: Care Carl Golden 112 State House Trenton NJ 08625

KEANEY, WILLIAM REGIS, engineering and construction services executive, consultant; b. Pitts., Nov. 2, 1937; s. William Regis Sr. and Emily Elizabeth (Campi) K.; m. Sharon Lee Robinson, Feb. 23, 1956; children: William R., James A., Robert E., Susan Elizabeth. BBA in Mktg. and Internat. Mktg., Ohio State U., 1961. Sales engr. Burdett Oxygen Co., Cleve., 1961-64, A.O. Smith Co., Milw., 1964-66; pres. W.R. Keaney & Co., Columbus, Ohio, 1966-71, Power Equipment Service Corp., Columbus, 1971-80, Gen. Assocs. Corp., Worthington, Ohio, 1980—; cons. Mannesmann, Houston, 1984-85, TVA, Knoxville, 1984-86, Power Authority of N.Y., White Plains, 1985-86, Utility Power Corp., Atlanta, 1985-86; mem. various task forces in the field. Vol. Cen. Ohio Lung Assn., Columbus, 1984-86. Mem. ASME (subgroups on nonferrous alloys, strength/nonferrous alloys), Am. Welding Soc., Welding Research Council. Democrat. Methodist. Club: Mil. Vehicle Collectors (Ohio). Lodge: Masons. Home: 1314 Oakview Dr Worthington OH 43085 Office: Gen Assocs Corp PO Box 762 Worthington OH 43085

KEARNEY, PATRICIA MICHAL, natural sciences educator, poet, consultant; b. Leisenring, Pa., Oct. 11, 1930; d. John Joseph and Marguerite Costello (Gettings) Kearney; m. George Kehoe Brennen, Dec. 29, 1976 (div. Feb. 1987). B.A., Seton Hill Coll., 1952; postgrad. in medicine U. Pitts., 1954-55, in law Duquesne U., 1955-58, in arts and scis., 1964-65, in microbiology Ill. Inst. Tech., 1977—. Instr. sci Allegheny Gen. Hosp. Sch. Nursing, Pitts., 1952-54, 56-59, adminstrv. asst. to dir., 1959-60, chmn. sci. dept., 1959-60; instr. chemistry dept. Pa. State U., East McKeesport, 1961-64, 66-74; instr. biology dept. Olive Harvey Coll., Chgo., 1974-79, asst. prof. biology, 1979-88; asst. prof. microbiology Daley Coll., Chgo., 1988—; developer and tchr. correlated sci. Rochester Hosp. Sch. Nursing, 1969-72; cons. integrated scis. Westmoreland County Community Coll., Youngwood, Pa., 1972-73; developer computer program anatomy and physiology NSF, Chgo., 1981-83. Reviewer American Biology, 1982-83; author poems in: Anthology of the Verse of American Youth, 1949; America Sings, Annual Anthology of College Poetry, 1949, 50, 51; Voice of America, Anthology of Anthologies of College Poetry, 1953; A Goodly Heritage, Poems of Pennsylvania, 1968; The Family Treasury of Great Poems, 1981; Our 20th Century's Greatest Poems, 1982. Pres., co-founder Community Singers, Scottdale, Pa., 1966-69; vol. organizer Primary Gubernatorial Campaign, Greensburg, Pa., 1966; candidate del. to Dem. nat. conv., 35th Senatorial Dist., Pa., 1972; active Call to Action, Chgo., 1981—. Ctr. for Disease Control grantee, 1971, 81; Argonne Nat. Lab. grantee, 1978; AAAS grantee, 1983-84; recipient Mastery Tchr. award Olive Harvey Coll., 1981; Silver Poet award World Book Co., 1986. Mem. Am. Soc. Microbiology, Nat. Assn. Female Execs., Cornell U. Ornithology Labs., Assn. Women Sci., Pa. Elected Women's Assn., Mensa, Chgo. Colloquium Latin Am., N.Y. Acad. Scis., AAAS, Internat. Platform Assn., Indian Council Fire, Irish Am. Cultural Inst. Democrat. Roman Catholic. Home: 10432 S Prospect Ave Chicago IL 60643

KEARNEY, RICHARD JAMES, marketing cons.; b. Kansas City, Mo., Aug. 25, 1927; s. Emmett Leo and Irene Elizabeth (Ruddock) K.; B.S. in Chem. Engring., U. Mich., 1951; m. Caroline Hamilton Archer, Sept. 19, 1953; children—Caroline Hamilton, Richard James. Chem. purchasing agt. Hercules, Inc., Wilmington, Del., 1954-62; chmn. bd., pres., sr. v.p. Kearney Chems. Inc., Tampa, Fla., 1962-80; sr. v.p. Royster Chems., Inc., Tampa, 1980-82; mktg. cons., Tampa, 1982—. Served with USNR, 1945-46, to 1st lt. AUS, 1951-53, Korea. Mem. Am. Chem. Soc., Pershing Rifles, Scabbard and Blade Honor Soc., Decorative Arts Soc., Tampa Art Mus. Soc., Sigma Chi. Episcopalian. Clubs: U. Mich. Pres.'; Tampa Yacht and Country, Bath, Tower. Office: Caroline Kearney Antiques 4301 El Prado Blvd Tampa FL 33629

KEARNEY, RICHARD MARIUS, philosopher, educator; b. Cork, Ireland, Dec. 8, 1954; s. Kevin Victor Charles and Ann Lelia (Kinmouth) K.; m. Anne Denise Bernard, July 7, 1980; children: Simone, Sarah. BA with 1st class honors, Univ. Coll., Dublin, 1976; MA with 1st class honors, McGill U., 1977; PhD with 1st class honors, U. Paris, 1980. Prof. philosophy Univ. Coll., Dublin, 1981—; vis. prof. Boston Coll., 1987. Author: Poetique du Possible, 1984, Dialogues with Contemporary Continental Thinkers, 1984, Modern Movements in European Philosophy, 1986, Transitions, 1987, The Wake of Imagination, 1988; editor Crane Bag, 1977, Irish Rev., 1977—. Nat. U. Ireland travelling scholar, 1987. Mem. Royal Irish Acad. (com. mem. 1985—), Irish Philos. Assn. (com. mem. 1981—). Roman Catholic. Home: 19 Mt Eden Rd, Donnybrook, Dublin 4 Ireland Office: Univ Coll Dublin, Philosophy Dept, Dublin 4 Ireland

KEARNS, DAVID TODD, business products and systems company financial services executive; b. Rochester, N.Y., Aug. 11, 1930; s. Wilfrid M. and Margaret May (Todd) K.; m. Shirley Virginia Cox, June 1954; children—Katherine, Elizabeth, Anne, Susan, David Todd, Andrew. B.S., U. Rochester, 1952. With IBM Corp., 1954-71, v.p. mktg. ops., data processing div., until 1971; with Xerox Corp., Stamford, Conn., 1971—; group v.p. for info. systems Xerox Corp., 1972-75; group v.p. charge Rank Xerox and Fuji Xerox, 1975-77, exec. v.p. internat. ops., 1977, pres., chief exec. officer, 1977-82, also dir., pres., chief operating officer, 1977-82, pres., chief exec. officer, 1982-85, chmn., chief exec. officer, 1985—; bd. dirs. Rank Xerox Ltd., Time Inc., Fuji Xerox., Chase Manhattan Corp., Dayton Hudson Corp.; chmn. Pres.'s Commn. on Exec. Exchange. Bd. visitors Grad. Sch. Bus., Duke U.; bd. dirs. U. Rochester; trustee Stamford Hosp., Inst. Aerobics Research; bd. dirs. Jr. Achievement; bd. trustees Nat. Urban League. Served with USNR, 1952-54. Mem. Bus. Roundtable, Council on Fgn. Relations, Com. Exec. Exchange (chmn., pres.). Office: Xerox Corp Stamford CT 06904

KEATING, FRANK J., paper company executive; b. Phila., Jan. 2, 1928; s. Joseph Gerald and Alice (Quinn) K.; student Londonderry Coll., No. Ireland; m. Susan R. Keating; children—Carolyn M., Mary E., Frank J., Brian, Leah R. With Daring Paper Co. div. Kardon Industries, Inc. Phila., 1946-71, successively truck loader, shipping clk., asst. shipper, shipper, prodn. scheduler, prodn. mgr., asst. to gen. mgr. United Container Co., 1957-58, asst. to pres. Daring Paper Co., 1958-60, v.p., gen. mgr., 1960-71, exec. v.p., also v.p. parent co., exec. v.p. Morris Sales Service Corp., KFC Fibre, Inc.; now pres. Keating Fibre Inc., Keating Fibre Internat., Inc., Converters Internat. Inc. Mem. Chester County Conservation Com. Served with USNR, 1944-46. Mem. Am. Mgmt. Assn., Downingtown C. of C., Pa. Water Pollution Control Assn., Am. Paper Inst., Fibre Box Assn., TAPPI, Nat. Council Stream Improvement, Montgomery County C. of C., Internat. Platform Assn. Clubs: Whitemarsh Valley Country; Phila. Aviation Country. Office: Whitemarsh Plaza 15 Ridge Pike Conshohocken PA 19428

KEATING, KATHLEEN IRWIN, research educator; b. Jersey City, N.J., Mar. 7, 1938; d. William Richard and Alda Vogt (Madden) Irwin; m. Martin John Keating, Dec. 21, 1962; 1 child, Sean Michael. B.A., Cornell U., 1960; M.S., William Paterson Coll., 1970; M.Ph., Yale U., 1972, Ph.D., 1975. Tchr. pub. schs. Dumont, N.J., 1962-68; researcher Yale U., Haskins Lab., New Haven, 1970-75; assoc. prof. research Rutgers U., New Brunswick, N.J., 1974—, N.J. Agrl. Expt. Sta., New Brunswick, 1975—. cons., lectr. in field. Contbr. to research publs. Grantee NSF, EPA, others. Mem. AAAS, Ecol. Soc. Am., Internat. Soc. Applied and Theoretical Limnology, Internat. Soc. Chem. Ecologists, Soc. Environ. Toxicology and Chemistry, Crustacean Soc., N.J. Acad. Sci., N.Y. Acad. Sci., ASTM, Am. Soc. Limnology and Oceanography, Sigma Xi. Home: 6 Webb Ct Park Ridge NJ 07656 Office: Cook Campus Rutgers U New Brunswick NJ 08903

KEATING, LARRY GRANT, electrical engineer, educator; b. Omaha, Jan. 15, 1944; s. Grant Morris and Dorothy Ann (Kauffold) K.; m. Barbara Jean Merley, Dec. 21, 1968. LLB, Blackstone Sch. Law, 1968; BS, U. Nebr., 1969; BS summa cum laude, Met. State Coll., 1971; MS, U. Colo., Denver, 1978. Chief engr. broadcoast electronics 3 radio stas., 1965-69; coordinator engring. reliability Cobe Labs., Lakewood, Colo., 1972-74; quality engr. Statitrol Corp., Lakewood, Colo., 1974-76; instr. electrical engring. U. Colo., Denver, 1976-78; assoc. prof. Met. State Coll., Denver, 1978-84, chmn. dept., 1984—; cons. Transplan Assocs., Boulder, Colo., 1983-84. Co-author: (book) South Santa Fe Corridor, 1985. Served to 1st lt. U.S. Army, 1962-70. Recipient Outstanding Faculty award U. Colo., Denver, 1980, Outstanding Alumnus award Met. State Coll., 1985. Mem. IEEE (sr.), Instrument Soc. Am. (sr.), Robotics Internat. (sr.), Am. Soc. Engring. Edn., Nat. Assn. Radio and Telecommunications Engrs. (cert. 1st class)., Eta Kappa Nu, Tau Alpha Pi, Chi Epsilon. Home: 6455 E Bates Ave 4-108 Denver CO 80222 Office: Met State Coll 1006 11th St Campus Box 29 Denver CO 80204

KEATINGE, RICHARD HARTE, lawyer; b. San Francisco, Dec. 4, 1919; m. Betty West, Apr. 20, 1944; children: Richard West, Daniel Wilson, Nancy Elizabeth. A.B. with honors, U. Calif., Berkeley, 1939; M.A., Harvard U., 1941; J.D., Georgetown U., 1944. Bar: D.C. 1944, N.Y. 1945, Calif. 1947, U.S. Supreme Ct. 1964. Sr. economist, sr. indsl. specialist WPB, Washington, 1941-44; practice law N.Y.C., 1944-45, Washington, 1945-47, Los Angeles, 1947—; sr. ptnr. Keatinge, Pastor & Mintz (and predecessor firms), 1948-79, Reavis & McGrath, 1979—; spl. asst. atty. gen., State of Calif., 1964-68; public mem. Adminstrv. Conf. of U.S., 1968-74. Mem.: Georgetown Law Jour, 1943-44. Mem. Calif. Law Revision Commn., 1961-68, chmn., 1965-67; trustee Coro Found., 1965-73; bd. trustees, mem. exec. com. U. Calif. Berkeley Found., 1973-87, chmn. bd. trustees, 1983-85. Fellow (life) Am. Bar Found., Am. Coll. Tax Counsel; mem. ABA (bd. govs. 1978-79, mem. ho. of dels. 1974-81, 82—, mem. council 1961-64, 65-69, 74-78, 82—, chmn. adminstrv. law sect. 1967-68, mem. standing com. on resolutions 1973-74, chmn. com. on sales, exchanges and basis taxation sect. 1963-65, mem. council econs. of law practice sect. 1974-75, mem. commn. on law and economy 1976-78, vice chmn. 1977-78, mem. spl. com. on housing and urban devel. law 1968-73, vice chmn. adv. commn. on housing and urban growth 1974-77, nat. sec. Jr. Bar Conf. 1949-50), State Bar Calif. (del. conf. of dels. 1966-67, 77—, mem. exec. com. public law sect. 1976-78), Los Angeles County Bar Assn. (chmn. taxation sect. 1966-67, mem. fair jud. election practices com. 1978-79, mem. exec. com. law office mgmt. sect. 1977-85, mem. housing and urban devel. law com. 1971-80, mem. arbitration com. 1974—, mem. new quarters com. 1979-80), Assn. Bus. Trial Lawyers (bd. govs. 1974-79, pres. 1978-79), Inter-Am. Bar Assn., Internat. Bar Assn., Am. Judicature Soc., Am. Law Inst., Am. Arbitration Assn. (nat. panel of arbitrators 1950—), Com. to Maintain Diversity Jurisdiction, Lawyers Club Los Angeles, Phi Beta Kappa. Home: 220 S San Rafael Ave Pasadena CA 91105 Office: 700 S Flower St 6th Fl Los Angeles CA 90017

KEATS, GLENN ARTHUR, manufacturing company executive; b. Chgo., July 1, 1920; s. Herbert J. and Agnes H. (Streich) K.; m. Olga Maria Loor Hurtado, Feb. 13, 1946; children—Maria Susana Keats Eggemeyer, Allwyn Dolores Keats Gustafson. BS in Commerce, Northwestern U., 1941. Sales exec. Keats-Lorenz Spring Co., Chgo., 1947-56; controller, auditor Plantaciones Ecuatorianas, S.A., Guayaquil, Ecuador, 1956-58; co-founder, sec.-treas. Keats Mfg. Co., Evanston, Ill., 1958—; bd. dirs. Bullock Keats, Ltd., Eng. Sec. Hispanic Soc. Chgo., 1965—. Served to lt. comdr. USN, 1941-47. Mem. Spring Mfrs. Inst., Northwestern U. Alumni Assn., Sigma Nu. Republican. Lutheran. Club: Evanston Golf. Home: 368 Woodland Rd Highland Park IL 60035 Office: 1227 Dodge Ave Evanston IL 60202

KEAVENEY, ARTHUR PETER, educator; b. Galway, Ireland, July 8, 1951. BA, U. Galway, 1972, MA, 1975; PhD, U. Hull, Eng., 1978. Doctoral fellow U. Wales, Aberystwyth, 1978-79; lectr. U. Kent, Canterbury, Eng., 1979—. Author: Sulla the Last Republican, 1983, Rome and the Unification of Italy, 1987; contbr. numerous articles to profl. jours. Office: Univ Kent, Darwin Coll, Canterbury CT2 7NY, England

KEAY, PETER LYLE, aviation systems manager; b. Edinburgh, Scotland, Oct. 7, 1944. BSc, U. Edinburgh, 1966. Airline analyst Brit. Aerospace, London, 1966-70, market devel., 1970-74; sr. cons. Alan Stratford & Assocs., London, 1974-1976; sr. economist Brit. Airports, London, 1976-78, systems policy mgr., 1984—; mktg. mgr. Brit. Airports Internat., London, 1978-82; traffic mgr. Heathrow Airport, London, 1982-84. Mem. Royal Aero. Soc. Club: Royal Overseas (London). Office: Brit Airports-Mercury House, N Hyde Rd, Hayes, London England

KEBBLISH, JOHN BASIL, retired coal company executive, consultant; b. Gray, Pa., Jan. 14, 1925; s. Joseph and Catherine (Benya) K.; m. Ruth L. Mueller, Oct. 14, 1955; children: John J., Heather R. BS in Mining Engring., Pa. State U., 1947, BS in Elec. Engring., 1948. With Consol. Coal Co. (and subs. cos.), various locations, 1948-71; pres. Consol. Coal Co. (Pocahontas Fuel Co. div.), Bluefield, W. Va., 1966-70; v.p. Consol. Coal Co., Pitts., 1970-71; exec. v.p. The Pittston Co., N.Y.C., 1971-73; pres., chief exec. officer Ashland Coal, Inc. (Ky.) (subs. Ashland Oil, Inc.), 1974—; v.p., exec. officer Ashland Oil, Inc., 1976-87, also bd. dirs., now exec. cons. Served with AUS, 1944-46. Office: Ashland Coal Inc 2205 Fifth St Rd Huntington WV 25701

KECK, ROBERT CLIFTON, lawyer; b. Sioux City, Iowa, May 20, 1914; s. Herbert Allen and Harriet (McCutchen) K.; m. Ruth P. Edwards, Nov. 2, 1940 (dec.); children: Robert, Laura E. Simpson, Gloria E. Sauser; m. Lauryne E. George, June 20, 1987. A.B., Ind. U., 1936; J.D., U. Mich., 1939; L.H.D., Nat. Coll. Edn., 1973. Bar: Ill. 1939. Since practiced in Chgo; mem. firm Keck, Mahin & Cate, 1939—, partner, 1946—; sec., dir. Methode Electronics, Inc.; bd. dirs. Schwinn Bicycle Co., Ill. Masonic Med. Ctr. Chmn. bd. trustees Nat. Coll. Edn., 1955—; trustee Sears Roebuck

Found., 1977-79. Served with USNR, 1943-45. Fellow Am. Coll. Trial Lawyers; mem. ABA, Fed. Bar Assn., Ill. Bar Assn., Chgo. Bar assn. Seventh Fed. Circuit (past pres.), Phi Gamma Delta. Republican. Methodist. Clubs: Westmoreland Country (Wilmette);Metropolitan, Chgo.; Biltmore Forest Country (Asheville, N.C.); Glen View (Golf, Ill.). Lodge: Masons. Office: Keck Mahin & Cate Sears Tower 83d Floor Chicago IL 60606

KEEFE, GEORGE EVANS, retired publishing company executive, financial cons.; b. Lawrenceville, N.J., Nov. 28, 1909; s. David and Sabina (Mulligan) K.; B.A., U. Pa., 1930; m. Ruth A. Brockmann, Dec. 16, 1933; children—Ruth K. Clary, David B. With Dun & Bradstreet, Inc. as dist. mgr. Pitts. and Richmond, Va., gen. reporting and service mgr., N.Y.C., 1931-57, v.p., N.Y.C., 1960-68, sr. v.p., 1968-75; chmn., dir. Moody's Investors Service Inc., N.Y.C., 1970-75; pres. dir. Nat. Credit Office, Inc., N.Y.C., 1957-60. Home: 46 Wordsworth Rd Short Hills NJ 07078

KEEFE, ROGER MANTON, former banker, financial consultant; b. New London, Conn., Feb. 26, 1919; s. Arthur T. and Mabel (Foran) K.; m. Ann Hunter, June 4, 1949; children: Christopher Hunter, Matthew Foran, Michael Devereux, Susan Ann, Robin Mary, Victoria Morrill. Student, Coll. St. Gregory, Downside Abbey, Eng., 1936-37; B.A. in History and Internat. Relations, Yale, 1941. With Chase Manhattan Bank, N.Y.C., 1945-71; sr. v.p. charge div. financing devel. and tech. services Chase Manhattan Bank, 1966-71; exec. v.p. Conn. Bank & Trust Co., Hartford, 1971-76; vice chmn. Conn. Bank & Trust Co., 1976-80, CBT Corp., Hartford, 1976-83; chmn. exec. com. CBT Corp., 1980-83, Conn. Bank & Trust Co., 1980-83; pres. R.M. Keefe Assocs., Inc., 1983—; dir. Callahan Mining Co., Maritime Ctr. Mem. exec. council Yale Class of 1941, 1962—, treas., 1966-71, mem. bd. edn., Norwalk, Conn.; mem. Nat. Rep. Fin. Com., 1961—, also treas. adv. fin. com.; mem. N.Y. State Rep. Fin. Com., 1961-69; trustee St. Thomas More Corp., 1962—, treas., 1964-69; trustee Greens Farms Acad., 1978—, Fairfield U., 1982—; bd. dirs. St. Joseph's Med. Ctr., 1978—. Served to maj. AUS., World War II, ETO. Decorated Silver Star, Bronze Star with cluster, Purple Heart., Knight of St. Gregory. Mem. Fin. Execs. Inst., Assn. Res. City Bankers, Am. Arbitration Assn., Southwestern Area Commerce and Industry Assn. (dir. 1978). Clubs: Yale (N.Y.C.); Wee Burn Country, Harbor, Norwalk Yacht; Internat. (Washington). Home: Nathan Hale Rd Wilson Point South Norwalk CT 06854

KEEGAN, JAMES JOSEPH, financial executive, investment banker; b. Phila., Sept. 6, 1947; s. George Washington and Kathyrn Margaret (Eckels) K.; m. Martha Jana Pettinga, Apr. 27, 1984. BBA in Acctg., Tex. Christian U., 1969; MBA in Internat. Fin., U. Mich., 1970. CPA, Colo. Supervising sr. acct. Peat Marwick Mitchell, Denver, 1974-79; pvt. practice acctg., Englewood, Colo., 1979-81; pres. Trinity Securities, Englewood, 1981-83, Keegan Capital Devel., Englewood, 1983—; advisor C.C.R. Video Corp., Hollywood, Calif., Rocky Mountain Water Works, Colorado Springs, Colo., 1984-87, Ingot Mgmt., Vancouver, Can., 1986-88, Reel Treasures Entertainment, Inc., Dallas, 1986-88, The Sugarless Co., Los Angeles, 1986-88. Mgmt. adv. services com. Colo. CPA-Small Bus. Adv. Council, 1984-85; vol. Internat. Golf Tournament, 1986; bd. dirs. Colo. Coalition Econ. Growth; mem. rules and course rating coms. Colo. Golf Assn. Served to capt. USAF, 1971-74. Mem. Am. Inst. CPA's, Colo. Soc. CPA's, C. of C. (mem. pres. council, 1981-82), Colo. Golf Assn. (committeeman 1986—), Fellowship Christian Athletes. Republican. Roman Catholic. Home: 8101 E Dartmouth Ave Unit 36 Denver CO 80231 Office: Keegan Capital Devel 5445 DTC Pkwy Suite 910 Englewood CO 80111

KEEGAN, JANE ANN, insurance executive, consultant; b. Watertown, N.Y., Sept. 1, 1950; d. Richard Isidor and Kathleen (McKinley) K. BA cum laude, SUNY-Potsdam, 1972; MBA in Risk Mgmt., Golden Gate U., 1986. CPCU. Comml. lines mgr. Lithgow & Rayhill, San Francisco, 1977-80; risk mgmt. account coordinator Dinner Levison Co., San Francisco, 1980-83; ins. cons., San Francisco, 1983-84; account mgr. Rollins Burdick Hunter, San Francisco, 1984-85; account exec. Jardine Ins. Brokers, San Francisco, 1985-86; ins. cons., San Francisco, 1986-87, ins. adminstr. Port of Oakland, 1987—. Vol. San Francisco Ballet vol. orgn., 1981—, Bay Area Bus., Govt. ARC disaster conf. steering com., 1987-88; mem. Nob Hill Neighbors Assn., 1982—. Mem. Soc. Chartered Property Casualty Underwriters (spl. events chairperson 1982-84; continuing profl. devel. program award 1985, 88), Risk and Ins. Mgr. Soc. (dep.). Democrat. Roman Catholic. Home: 1635 Clay St Apt 1 San Francisco CA 94109

KEEHN, NEIL FRANCIS, aerospace executive; b. Massillon, Ohio, Oct. 24, 1948; s. Russell Earl and Mary (Danner) K. B.S. in Math., Ariz. State U., Tempe, 1970, postgrad. in elec. engring., 1970. Mem. tech. staff Tech. Service Corp., Santa Monica, Calif., 1972-74, Hughes Aircraft, El Segundo, Calif., 1974-77; program mgr. TRW Inc., Redondo Beach, Calif., 1977-79; mgr. advanced concepts Mil. Space Systems div. Sci. Applications Inc., El Segundo, 1979-80; pres. Strategic Systems Scis., Santa Monica, 1980—. Mem. IEEE (vice chmn. aerospace def. systems panel 1972-76, chmn. 1976-79), AIAA (chmn. mil. space strategy and doctrine com.), U.S. Strategic Inst., Internat. Inst. for Strategic Studies. Contbr. articles to profl. jours.; patentee in digital signal processing.

KEELEY, ROBERT VOSSLER, ambassador; b. Beirut, Sept. 4, 1929; s. James Hugh and Mathilde Julia (Vossler) K.; m. Louise Schoonmaker, June 23, 1951; children: Michael M., Christopher J. A.B., Princeton U., 1951, postgrad., 1951-53; postgrad. (Princeton fellow in pub. affairs), 1970-71; postgrad. (Nat. Inst. Pub. Affairs fellow), Stanford U., 1965-66. With Fgn. Service, Dept. State, Washington, 1956—; officer in charge Congo (Leopoldville) external affairs Washington, 1963-64; officer-in-charge Congo (Brazzaville), Rwanda and Burundi affairs 1964-65; polit. officer Athens, Greece, 1966-70; detailed Woodrow Wilson fellow Princeton U., 1970; dep. chief mission Kampala, Uganda, 1971-73; alt. dir. E. African affairs Washington, 1974; dep. chief mission Phnom Penh, Khmer Republic, 1974-75; dep. dir. Interagency Task Force for Indochina Refugees, 1975-76; ambassador Mauritius, 1976-78; dep. asst. sec. for African Affairs Dept. State, Washington, 1978-80; ambassador to Zimbabwe 1980-84; sr. fellow Ctr. for Study Fgn. Affairs, Fgn. Service Inst., Washington, 1984-85; ambassador to Greece 1985—. Served to lt. (j.g.) USCGR, 1953-55. Mem. Am. Fgn. Service Assn. Club: Cosmos (Washington). Home: 3814 Livingston St NW Washington DC 20015 Office: Dept of State US Ambassador to Greece Washington DC 20520 *

KEENAN, DANIEL JOSEPH, automotive executive; b. Joliet, Ill., Feb. 18, 1929; s. Daniel Francis and Agnes Elizabeth (Webb) K.; student Kent State U., 1962-64, U. Detroit, 1964-74; B.S. in Bus. Adminstrn. and Mgmt., W.Va. State Coll., 1976; m. Elizabeth Therese Rapp, June 20, 1953; children—Daniel P., Therese A., Melanie M., Timothy M. Prodn. supr. Gen. Motors Corp., Chgo., 1954-57; prodn. control supt. Chrysler Corp., Twinsburg, Ohio, 1957-64, div. material mgr., Detroit, 1964-65, prodn. control mgr., 1965-69; ops. mgr. Hoover Universal, Ann Arbor, Mich., 1969-70; corp. prodn. control mgr. Am. Motors Co., Detroit, 1970-78; corp. mgr. material handling engring. and equipment Volkswagen of Am., Warren, Mich., 1978-81; prodn. control mgr., corp. mgr. material handling engring. Chrysler Corp., Highland Park, Mich., 1982—. Mem. Soc. Packaging and Handling Engrs., Am. Prodn. and Inventory Control Soc. Office: 12000 Lynn Townsend Dr Highland Park MI 48203

KEENAN, MICHAEL EDGAR, advertising agency executive; b. Columbus, Ohio, Mar. 15, 1934; s. Edgar Charles and Kathryn Ellen (Dowden) K.; children: Margaret, Matthew, Emily, Jennifer, Andrew, Martha. AB, Duke U., 1955. With research dept. Compton Advt., N.Y.C., 1957-60; mktg. exec. Foote, Cone & Belding, N.Y.C., 1960-62, Lennen & Newell, N.Y.C., 1962-64; v.p., dir. consumer products div. Fuller & Smith & Ross, N.Y.C., 1964-70; chmn., chief exec. officer Keenan & McLaughlin Inc., N.Y.C., 1970-82; chmn. plans bd. Stan Merritt, Inc., N.Y.C., 1983-84; sr. v.p., mng. dir. Western Internat. Media Corp., N.Y.C., 1984—; lectr. mktg. NYU, 1960-64; cons. FTC, Washington. Served with CIC, AUS, 1955-57. Mem. Am. Assn. Advt. Agys. (chmn. N.Y. council), Nat. Agri-Mktg. Assn. (past pres.), Rear Guard (treas.). Club: Thursday (N.Y.C.) (past pres.). Home: 1641 3d Ave Apt 22C New York NY 10128 Office: Western Internat Media Corp 551 Fifth Ave New York NY 10017

KEENE, CLIFFORD HENRY, medical administrator; b. Buffalo, Jan. 28, 1910; s. George Samuel and Henrietta Hedwig (Yeager) K.; m. Mildred Jean Kramer, Mar. 3, 1934; children—Patricia Ann (Mrs. William S. Kneedler), Martha Jane (Mrs. William R. Sproule), Diane Eve (Mrs. Gordon D. Simonds). A.B., U. Mich., 1931, M.D., 1934, M.S. in Surgery, 1938; D.Sc., Hahnemann Med. Coll., 1973; LL.D., Golden Gate U., 1974. Diplomate Am. Bd. Surgery, Am. Bd. Preventive Medicine (occupational medicine). Resident surgeon, instr. surgery U. Mich., 1934-39; cons. surgery of cancer Mich. Med. Soc. and Mich. Dept. Health, 1939-40; pvt. practice surgery Wyandotte, Mich., 1940-41; med. dir. Kaiser-Frazer Corp., 1946-53; instr. surgery U. Mich., 1946-54; med. adminstrv. positions with Kaiser Industries and Kaiser Found., 1954-75, v.p., 1960-75; v.p., gen. mgr. Kaiser Found. Hosps. and Kaiser Found. Health Plan, 1960-67; med. dir. Kaiser Found. Sch. Nursing, 1954-67; dir. Kaiser Found. Research Inst., 1958-75; pres. Kaiser Found. Hosps. Health Plan, Sch. Nursing, 1968-75, dir., 1960-75; chmn. editorial bd. Kaiser Found. Med. Bull., 1954-65; lectr. med. econs. U. Calif.-Berkeley, 1956-75; mem. vis. com. Med. Sch., Stanford U., 1966-72, Harvard U., 1967-71, 79-85, U. Mich., 1973-78; Mem. Presdl. Panel Fgn. Med. Grads. (Nat. Manpower Commn.), 1966-69. Contbr. papers to profl. lit. Bd. visitors Harvard Bus. Adv. Council, 1972, Charles R. Drew Postgrad. Med. Sch., 1972-79; trustee Amman Civil Hosp., Jordan, 1973, Community Hosp. of Monterey Peninsula, 1983—. Served to lt. col. M.C. AUS, 1942-46. Recipient Disting. Service award Group Health Assn. Am., 1974; Disting. Alumnus award U. Mich. Med. Center, 1976; Disting. Alumnus Service award U. Mich., 1985. Fellow ACS; mem. Am. Assn. Indsl. Physicians and Surgeons, Nat. Acad. Scis., Inst. Medicine, Calif. Acad. Medicine, Frederick A. Coller Surg. Soc., Calif., Am. med. assns., Alpha Omega Alpha (editorial bd., contbr. to Pharos mag. 1977—). Home: 3166 Del Ciervo Rd PO Box 961 Pebble Beach CA 93953 Office: Kaiser Center 300 Lakeside Dr Oakland CA 94666

KEENE-BURGESS, RUTH FRANCES, army official; b. South Bend, Ind., Oct. 7, 1948; d. Seymour and Sally (Morris) K.; m. Leslie U. Burgess, Jr., Oct. 1, 1983; children: Michael Leslie, David William, Elizabeth Sue. BS, Ariz. State U., 1970; MS, Fairleigh Dickinson U., 1978; grad., U.S. Army Command and Gen. Staff Coll., 1986. Inventory mgmt. specialist U.S. Army Electronics Command, Phila., 1970-74, U.S. Army Communications-Electronics Materiel Readiness Command, Fort Monmouth, N.J., 1974-79; chief inventory mgmt. div. Crane (Ind.) Army Ammunition Activity, 1979-80; supply systems analyst Hdqrs. 60th Ordnance Group, Zweibruecken, Fed. Republic Germany, 1980-83; chief inventory mgmt. div. Crane (Ind.) Army Ammunition Activity, 1983-85, chief control div., 1985; inventory mgmt. specialist 200th Theater Army Material Mgmt. Ctr., Zweibruecken, 1985—. Mem. Federally Employed Women (chpt. pres. 1979-80), Nat. Assn. Female Execs., Soc. Logistics Engrs., Assn. Computing Machinery, Am. Soc. Public Adminstrn., Soc. Profl. and Exec. Women, Assn. Info. Systems Profls., AAAS, NOW. Democrat. Jewish. Home: 4916 W Pinchot Ave Phoenix AZ 85031 Office: 200th TAMMC Attention AEAGD-MMC-VS APO New York NY 09052

KEENEY, EDMUND LUDLOW, physician; b. Shelbyville, Ind., Aug. 11, 1908; s. Bayard G. and Ethel (Adams) K.; m. Esther Cox Loney Wight, Mar. 14, 1950; children: Edmund Ludlow, Eleanor Seymour (Mrs. Cameron Leroy Smith). A.B., Ind. U., 1930; M.D., Johns Hopkins U., 1934. Diplomate Am. Bd. Internal Medicine. Intern Johns Hopkins Hosp., 1934-37, vis. physician, instr. internal medicine, 1940-48; practice medicine, specializing internal medicine San Diego, 1948- 55; dir. Scripps Clinic and Research Found., La Jolla, 1955-67; pres. Scripps Clinic and Research Found., 1967-77, pres. emeritus, 1977—; med. cons. Aerojet Gen. Corp.; dir. research on fungus infections OSRD, 1942-46; cons. U.S. Navy, 1948—, VA, 1954—. Author: Practical Medical Mycology, 1955, Medical Advice for International Travel; contbr. articles on allergy, immunology and mycology to med. jours. Bd. dirs. U. San Diego, Allergy Found. Am. Fellow A.C.P.; mem. A.M.A., Am. Soc. Clin. Investigation, Am. Acad. Allergy (pres. 1964), Western Assn. Physicians, Calif. Med. Assn., Western Soc. Clin. Research, Phi Beta Kappa, Alpha Omega Alpha, Beta Theta Pi. Republican. Presbyn. Clubs: El Dorado Country, La Jolla Country, Fox Acres Country. Lodge: Rotary. Home: 338 Via del Norte La Jolla CA 92037 Office: 10666 N Torrey Pines Rd La Jolla CA 92037

KEENEY, WILLIAM EDWIN, JR., aerospace engineer; b. Clarinda, Iowa, Aug. 22, 1930; s. William Edwin and Dorothy LaVerne (Enerson) K., B.B.A., U. Nebr., 1952, B.E.E., 1958; m. L. Eileen Faull, Oct. 3, 1980. With AC Electronics div. Gen. Motors, Milw., 1959-67, successively as systems engr., engring. supr., systems engring. group head; with Perkin-Elmer Corp., Wilton, Ct., 1967-77, successively as spacecraft cabin analyzer program mgr., test equipment sect. mgr., systems integration sect. mgr., systems engring. dept. mgr., solid state sensor camera program mgr.; dir. govt. orbital payloads Harris Corp., Melbourne, Fla., 1977-81; v.p. engring. Indsl. Drive div. Kollmorgan Corp., Raford, Va., 1981-87, Electro-Tec Corp., Blacksburg, Va., 1987—; asst. prof. U. Notre Dame, South Bend, Ind., 1954-56. Mem. Danbury (Conn.) City Council, 1973-77; bd. dir. Assn. Religious Communities, Danbury; chmn. com. Conn. council Boy Scouts Am. Served to lt. USN, 1952-56. Mem. IEEE, Smithsonian Instn., Air Force Assn. Democrat. Presbyterian. Lodge: Kiwanis (pres.). Book reviewer Jour. Astronautical Scis., 1976—. Home: Jefferson Forest Dr Blackburg VA 24060 Office: 1600 N Main St Blacksburg VA 24060

KEESEE, THOMAS WOODFIN, JR., financial consultant; b. Helena, Ark., Feb. 11, 1915; s. Thomas Woodfin and Sarah Gladys (Key) K.; m. Patricia Peale, Apr. 6, 1940 (div. Dec. 1951); m. Patricia Hartford, June 26, 1953; children: Allen P.K., Thomas Woodfin, III, Anne H. B.A., Duke U., 1935; J.D., Harvard U., 1938. Bar: N.Y. bar 1939. Asso. firm Simpson, Thacher & Bartlett, N.Y.C., 1938-42; asst. to pres. Sperry Gyroscope Co., Inc., Gt. Neck, N.Y., 1942-46; with Bessemer Securities Corp., N.Y.C., 1946-80; pres., chief exec. officer Bessemer Securities Corp., 1970-76, dir., 1969-80; pres., chief exec. officer Bessemer Trust Co., 1970-76; bd. dirs. ITT Corp., N.Y.C., Am. Guarantee & Liability Ins. Co., Chgo., JWP,Inc., (N.Y.), Zurich Holding Co. Am., Research Properties, Inc., Durham, N.C., Zurich Reins. Co., Rayonier Forest Resources, King Ranch, Inc. ; trustee, chmn. investment com. Nat. Health and Welfare Retirement Assn., 1966-75; chmn. bd., pres. Phipps Houses, 1949-70, bd. dirs.; U.S. adv. bd. Zurich Ins. Co.; gov. Real Estate Bd. N.Y. Inc., 1964-66. Mem. endowment investment com. Duke U., also trustee emeritus; trustee Mianus River Gorge Conservancy; chmn. pres.'s council Nat. Audubon Soc., chmn. 1979-83; pres. The Cisqua Sch., Bedford, N.Y., 1962-67; trustee Allen-Stevenson Sch., N.Y.C., 1950-57; sr. warden St. Matthews Protestant Episc. Ch., 1968-73; bd. visitors Duke U. Sch. Forestry and Environ. Studies; mem. achievement bd. Internat. Council Bird Preservation, Cambridge, Eng. Mem. N.Y. State Bar Assn., Harvard Law Sch. Assn., Pilgrims Soc., Phi Beta Kappa, Sigma Chi. Clubs: Harvard, Knickerbocker, Racquet and Tennis, Board Room (N.Y.C.) (pres. 1976-86); Bedford Golf and Tennis; Clove Valley Rod and Gun (Millbrook, N.Y.); Cosmos (Washington). Home: RD 3 Sarles St Mount Kisco NY 10549

KEESLING, FRANCIS VALENTINE, JR., lawyer, management consultant; b. San Francisco, Mar. 3, 1908; s. Francis Valentine and Haidee (Grau) K.; m. Mary Heath, Mar. 20, 1937; 1 child, Francis Valentine III. Grad., Phillips Acad., Andover, Mass.; A.B., Yale U., 1930; LL.B., Stanford U., 1933. Bar: Calif. 1934. Practice in San Francisco, 1934-55; with West Coast Life Ins. Co., San Francisco, 1936-77; pres. West Coast Life Ins. Co., 1963-68, chmn. bd., 1968-73, dir., 1954-77; gen. counsel, dir. Hexol Inc., 1973—; cons. Met. Parking Corp., 1980—; chief liaison and legis. officer nat. hdqrs. SSS, Washington, 1940-45, spl. adv. to dir., 1945-65; Washington rep. City and County of San Francisco, 1948-55. Mem. welfare com. City and County of San Francisco, 1946-47; mem. San Francisco Bay Area Council; past chmn. task force alcohol and drugs Gov.'s Com. on Traffic Safety; past mem. adv. com. on alcoholism Calif. Dept. Pub. Health; sr. council, past pres. San Francisco YMCA; bd. dirs., past pres. Calif. Traffic Safety Found. Served from lt. to col. U.S. Army. Decorated D.S.M. Mem. Assn. Life. Ins. Counsel (exec. com., pres. 1956-57), Am. Life Conv. (legal sect., past state v.p., del. ho. dels. Am. Bar Assn. 1962-63, past v.p. Calif. and Nev.), Health Ins. Assn., Am., Calif., San Francisco bar assns., San Francisco Art Assn. (past pres.), Calif. Ins. Fedn. (past pres.), Chi Psi, Phi Delta Phi. Clubs: Villa Taverna, Bankers, Pacific Union (San Francisco). Lodge: Masons. Home: 60 San Rafael Ave Belvedere CA 94920 Address: 1000 California St San Francisco CA 94108

KEFALAS, ANTHONY PANAYIOTIS, journalist, economist; b. Athens, Greece, Apr. 8, 1941; s. Pandelis A. and Alexandra (Peratiti) K.; m. Manolia Moyrtzopoulou, Jan. 22, 1964 (div. 1973); children: Alexandra, Isabella, Pandelis; m. Lily Kyriazi, Jul. 20, 1977. BSc in Econs, London Sch. Econs., 1963, MSc in Econs., 1965; PhD in Econs., Wayne State U. and U. Mich., 1970. Instr. Wayne State U., Detroit, 1967-68, Mich. State U., Oakland, 1968-69; asst. prof. Oakland U., 1969-71; research assoc. Ctr. Planning and Econ. Research, Greece, 1972-75; chief editorial writer, analyst Express, Greece, 1975-86; assoc. editor Kerdos, Greece, 1987-88; chief editor Agora, Greece, 1987-88; assoc. editor Oikonomikos Tahydromos, Athens, 1988—; advisor Ministry Fin., Ministry Nat. Economy, Greece, 1978-80; cons. Nat. Retail Mchts. Assn., Greece, 1976—, Citibank, 1986—, Nat. Council Free Enterprise, Greece, 1986-88; corr. Bus. Internat., Greece, 1985—; prof. European campus U. Md., Greece, 1987—. Contbr. articles to profl. publs. Mem. Am. Econ. Assn., Royal Econ. Assn. Club: Athenian Circle (Athens). Lodge: Hellenic (London). Office: Lambrakis Pub House, Oikonomikos Tahydromos, 9 Panepistimioy St, 10245 Athens Greece

KEFALIDES, NICHOLAS ALEXANDER, physician, educator; b. Alexandroupolis, Greece, Jan. 17, 1927; came to U.S., 1947, naturalized; s. Athanasios and Alexandra (Aematidou) K.; m. Eugenia Georgia Kutsunis, Nov. 24, 1949; children—Alexandra Jane, Patricia Ann, Paul Thomas. B.A., Augustana Coll., Rock Island, Ill., 1951; B.S., Univ. Ill.-Chgo., 1953, M.S. in Biochemistry, 1956, M.D., 1956, Ph.D. in Biochemistry, 1965; M.S. (hon.), U. Pa., 1971; doctorate (hon.) U. Reims, France, 1987. Asst prof medicine, Univ Ill. Coll Medicine, Chgo., 1964-65; asst prof medicine, U. Chgo., 1965-69, assoc prof medicine, 1969-70; assoc prof medicine and biochemistry, U. Pa., Phila., 1970-74, prof medicine, 1974—, prof. biochemistry and biophysics, 1975—. Contbr. chpts. to books, articles to profl. jours. Served as surgeon USPHS, 1957-60.; Recipient Borden Research Found. award, 1956; Guggenheim fellow, 1977. Mem. AAAS, Am. Assn. Pathologists, Am. Soc. Clin. Investigation, Am. Soc. Biol. Chemists, Am. Soc. Cell Biology. Office: Connective Tissue Research Inst 3624 Market St Philadelphia PA 19104

KEHOE, SUSAN, communications and training company executive, consultant; b. Cleve., Dec. 5, 1947; d. John William and Mary Margaret (Swicia) Kehoe; m. Gerald Nicholas, May 15, 1970 (div.); children—Patricia, Mark. B.A., U. Detroit, 1970; M.A., Oakland U., 1980, Ph.D., 1983. Cert. secondary tchr., Mich. Trainer ESL Utica Community Schs., Mich., 1974-78; coordinator program Oakland Univ., Rochester, Mich., 1980-83; adj. prof. mktg. Wayne State Univ., Detroit, 1983-85, U. Mich., Ann Arbor, 1984-85; pres., owner The Kehoe Group, Birmingham, Mich., 1983—; trainer, program designer Gen. Motors, Detroit, 1984—; trainer, cons. Nat. Steel, Ecorse, Mich., 1984—; trainer, speech coach AM Gen., Livonia, Mich., 1984—; presenter Nat. Reading Conf., 1981, 83, Internat. Reading Assn., 1982, Am. Edn. Research Assn., 1982, Conf. on Coll. Composition, 1984; mktg. com. Detroit Symphony Orch. Mem. Pub. Relations Soc. Am. (membership chair). Club: Econ. of Detroit. Avocations: art, travel, music. Home: 3858 Lincoln West Birmingham MI 48010 Office: PO Box 242 Franklin MI 48025

KEICHER, WERNER ALEX, lawyer; b. Biel, Switzerland, Dec. 21, 1944; s. Walter Heinrich and Alice (Spielmann) K.; m. Gunny Lassbo, Feb. 28, 1975; children—Helena, Susanne. Dr. Iur, U. Zurich, 1975. Mem. bd. Gen. Trust Co., Vaduz, Liechtenstein. Club: Lions. Author: Die Privatrechtliche Stiftung im Liechtensteinischen Recht, 1975. Home: Eichengasse 8, Vaduz, Liechtenstein FL-9490 Office: Gen Trust Co, Aeulestrasse 5, Vaduz FL-9490 Liechtenstein

KEILER, JOEL IBERT, lawyer; b. Bklyn., Nov. 25, 1936; s. Bernard Benjamin and Dorothy (Kabakow) K.; m. Mary Eskridge, Apr. 21, 1961; children—Kenneth Charles, Leslie Susan. B.A., Bklyn. Coll., 1957; J.D., Duke U., 1960. Bar: D.C. 1961, Mass. 1967, Fla. 1973. With Office of Solicitor, Dept. Labor, Washington, 1961-63; field atty. NLRB, Los Angeles, 1963-67, Boston, 1967-68; assoc. firm Arent, Fox, Kintner, Plotkin & Kahn, Washington, 1968-72; sole practice, Washington, 1972—. Mng. editor: Duke Law Jour., 1960; contbr.: The Developing Labor Law. Mem. Hunters Woods Village Council, Reston, Va., 1982—, Reston Sports Council, 1983—. Served to lt. USCG, 1960-63. Mem. ABA. Clubs: River House Rowing (Miami, Fla.); Reston Tennis Assn. Home: 2512 Farrier Ln Reston VA 22091 Office: 1424 K St NW Suite 400 Washington DC 20005

KEILLER, JAMES BRUCE, college dean, clergyman; b. Racine, Wis., Nov. 21, 1938; s. James Allen and Grace (Modder) K.; diploma Beulah Heights Bible Coll., 1957; B.A., William Carter Coll., 1963, Ed.D. (hon.), 1973; LL.B., Blackstone Sch. Law, 1964; M.A., Evang. Theol. Sem., 1965, B.D., 1966, Th.D., 1968; M.A. in Ednl. Adminstrn., Atlanta U., 1977; EdS in Ednl. Adminstrn., Ga. State U., 1987; grad. tax cons. Nat. Tax Tng. Sch.; postgrad. Atlanta Law Sch.; m. Darsel Lee Bundy, Feb. 8, 1959; 1 dau., Susanne Elizabeth. Ordained to ministry Internat. Pentecostal Assemblies, 1957; pastor Maranatha Temple, Boston, 1957-58, Midland (Mich.) Full Gospel Ch., 1958-64; v.p. acad. dean Beulah Heights Bible Coll., Atlanta, 1964—, trustee, 1964—; nat. dir. youth and Sunday sch. dept. Internat. Pentecostal Assemblies, 1958-64, dir. world missions, Atlanta, 1964-76, youth commn., 1958-64, missions com., 1964-76, exec. bd., 1964-76, missionary editor Bridegroom's Messenger, 1964—; dir. global missions Internat. Pentecostal Ch. of Christ, 1976—, mem. exec. com., 1976—; mem. exec. bd. Mt. Paran Christian Sch. Mem. Republican Presdl. Task Force; mem. Nat. Rep. Senatorial Com., Am. Tax Reduction Movement, So. Ctr. Internat. Studies. Named Alumnus of Year, William Carter Coll., 1965. Fellow Coll. of Preceptors; mem. So. Accrediting Assn. Bible Colls. (exec. sec.), Christian Mgmt. Assn., Soc. Pentecostal Studies, Acad. Polit. Sci., Ind. Order Foresters, Am. Inst. Parliamentarians, Am. Bd. Master Educators (cert.), Evang. Theol. Soc. Republican. Club: Kiwanis (lt. gov. Ga. dist. 1986-87). Home: 892 Berne St SE Atlanta GA 30316 Office: 906 Berne St SE Atlanta GA 30316

KEISER, HENRY BRUCE, lawyer, publisher; b. N.Y.C., Oct. 26, 1927; s. Leo and Jessie (Liebeskind) K.; B.A. with honors in Econs., U. Mich., 1947; J.D. cum laude, Harvard U., 1950; m. Jessie E. Weeks, July 12, 1953; children—Betsy Cordelia Keiser Smith, Matthew Roderick. Admitted to N.Y. bar, 1950, D.C. bar, 1955, Fla. bar, 1956, U.S. Supreme Ct bar, 1954; trial atty. CAB, Washington, 1950-51; head counsel alcoholic beverages sect. OPS, 1951-52; legal asst. to Judge Eugene Black, Tax Ct. U.S., 1953-56; practice in Washington, 1956—; founder, chmn. bd., pres., Fed. Pubs., Inc., 1959-85; chmn. bd. Gene Galasso Assos., Inc., Washington, 1963—; founder, chmn. Crown Eagle Communications Ltd., London, 1978-84; chmn. bd. The Arkhon Corp., Cherry Hill, N.J., 1983—; chmn. Empire Carriages, London, 1984—; chmn. bd., pres. Keiser Enterprises, Inc., Washington, 1985—; chmn. Lion Internat., London, 1985—; chmn. bd. U.S. Telemktg., Inc., Atlanta, 1986—; chmn. bd. Phila. Inst., 1986—; chmn., sec. adv. com. on Constrn. Contract Document Reform, HUD, 1983-85; dir. Nat. Bank of Commerce, Washington, 1983-84; mem. adv. cabinet Southeastern U.,1965-75; judge, bd. of contract appeals, AEC, 1965-75; profl. lectr. Dept. Agr., 1960-77, George Washington U., 1961-79, U. San Francisco, 1965-82, Coll. William and Mary, 1966-75, Calif. Inst. Tech., 1967-72, U. So. Calif., 1973-74, U. Denver, 1975-85, Air Force Inst. Tech., 1975-76, U. Santa Clara, 1975-81, Trustee Touro Coll., 1979—. Served to 1st lt. Judge Adv. Gen. Corps, USAF, 1952-53; maj. Res. (ret.). Lord of Tuxford (hereditary), Nottinghamshire, Eng. Fellow Am. Bar Found., Nat. Contract Mgmt. Assn.; mem. Am. (council pub. contract law sect. 1972-75, fellow 1987—), N.Y., Fla., D.C. (dir. 1965-66, chmn. adminstrv. law sect. 1964-65) bar assns. Jewish. Clubs: Cosmos, Nat. Press, Army Navy, Harvard (Washington); Crockford's (London). Home: 7200 Armat Dr Bethesda MD 20817 Office: 2828 Pennsylvania Ave Washington DC 20007

KEITH, JOCELYN MARGARET, nurse, educator; b. Mt. Gambier, Australia, Aug. 18, 1938; arrived in N.Z., 1938; d. Mervyn Roy and Gwyneth Marion (Pascoe) Buckett; m. Kenneth James Keith, May 13, 1961; children: Judith Mary, John Perry, Susan Elizabeth, Benjamin James Roy. BA, Victoria U., Wellington, N.Z., 1980, BA with honors, 1981; diploma in community health, Otago U., Dunedin, N.Z., 1982. RN, N.Z. Staff nurse Wellington (N.Z.) Hosp. Bd., 1960; pub. health nurse Dept. Health, Wellington, 1960-61; dist. nurse Community Health Services, Wellington, 1977—; lectr. in community health Wellington Sch. Medicine, U. Otago, 1986—; mem. adv. com. Nursing Council N.Z., Wellington, 1986—.

Contbr. articles to profl. jours. Mem. parliamentary watch com. Nat. Council Women, Wellington, 1986—. Decorated Comdr. Brit. Empire, 1987. Mem. N.Z. Nurses Assn. (nat. pres. 1984-86), Pub. Health Assn., N.Z. Inst. Health Adminstrs., N.Z. Fedn. Univ. Women. Anglican. Home: 70 Raroa Rd, Wellington 5, New Zealand Office: Wellington Sch Medicine, Wellington 5, New Zealand

KEITH, KENNETH JAMES, law commissioner, educator; b. Auckland, New Zealand, Nov. 19, 1937; s. Patrick James and Amy Irene (Witheridge) K.; m. Jocelyn Margaret Buckett, May 13, 1961; children: Judith Mary, John Perry, Susan Elizabeth, Benjamin James Roy. LLB, New Zealand U., Auckland, 1961; LLM, Victoria U., Wellington, New Zealand, 1964, Harvard U., 1965. With legal office Dept. of External Affairs Govt. of New Zealand, Wellington, 1960-62; lectr. law Victoria U., 1962-73, prof., 1974—; assoc. legal officer UN, N.Y.C., 1968-70; dir. New Zealand Inst. Internat. Affairs, Wellington, 1972-74; dep. pres. Law Commn. Govt. of New Zealand, Wellington, 1986—; vis. prof. Osgoode Hall Law Sch., Toronto, Canada, 1981-82; judge Western Samoan Ct. of Appeal, Apia, 1982—, Cook Island Ct. of Appeal, Rarotonga, 1982—; mem. Royal Commn. of Electoral system, Wellington, 1985-86, legislation adv. com., Wellington, 1986—. Author: Advisory Jurisdiction of International Court, 1971, A Code of Procedure of Administrative Tribunals, 1972; editor (book) New Zealand Defense Policy, 1972. Council mem. Victoria U., 1982-85. Mem. New Zealand Law Soc., Internat. Inst. Strategic Studies, New Zealand Inst. of Internat. Affairs. Anglican. Office: Law Commn, PO Box 2590, Wellington New Zealand

KEITH, KENT MARSTELLER, corporate executive, lawyer; b. N.Y.C., May 22, 1948; s. Bruce Edgar and Evelyn E. (Johnston) K.; m. Elizabeth Misao Carlson, Aug. 22, 1976. BA in Govt., Harvard U., 1970; BA in Politics and Philosophy, Oxford U., Eng., 1972, MA, 1977; JD, U. Hawaii, 1977. Bar: Hawaii 1977, D.C. 1979. Assoc. Cades, Schutte, Fleming & Wright, Honolulu, 1977-79; coordinator Hawaii Dept. Planning and Econ. Devel., Honolulu, 1979-81, dep. dir., 1981-83, dir., 1983-86; energy resources coordinator State of Hawaii, Honolulu, 1983-86, chmn. State Policy Council, 1983-86; chmn. Aloha Tower Devel. Corp., 1983-86; project mgr. Mililani Tech. Park Oceanic Properties Inc. 1986-88; v.p. pub. relations and bus. devel., 1988—. Author: Hawaii: Looking Back from the Year 2050, 1987; contbr. articles on ocean law to law jours. Pres. Manoa Valley Ch., Honolulu, 1976-78; mem. platform com., Hawaii Dem. Conv., 1982, 84, 86; trustee Hawaii Loa Coll., 1986—, vice chmn. 1987—. Rhodes scholar, 1970; named one of 10 Outstanding Young Men of Am., U.S. Jaycees, 1984. Mem. Am. Assn. Rhodes Scholars, Internat. House of Japan, Nature Conservancy. Clubs: Plaza, Harvard of Hawaii (Honolulu) (bd. dirs. 1974-78, sec. 1974-76). Home: 2626 Hillside Ave Honolulu HI 96822 Office: Oceanic Properties PO Box 2780 Honolulu HI 96803

KEKST, GERSHON, public relations consultant; b. Peabody, Mass., Oct. 12, 1934; B.S., U. Md., 1956; children—Ilana, Michele, David, Joseph Jacob. Founder, pres. Kekst & Co., corp. and fin. pub. relations counsel, N.Y.C., 1970—; dir. Loral Corp. Bd. govs. Weizmann Inst. Sci.; trustee Brandeis U. Served with U.S. Army. Mem. Pub. Relations Soc. Am. (counsellors sect.), Am. Acad. Polit. and Social Sci. Clubs: N.Y. Economic, Harmonie (N.Y.C.). Office: Kekst & Co 437 Madison Ave New York NY 10022

KELAIDITIS, ANESTIS, construction company executive; b. Cairo, Egypt, Feb. 28, 1948; s. Stylianos and Anastasia (Christodoulou) K.; m. Stefania Zaglaras, July 2, 1977; 1 child, Stylianos. Diploma in Civil Engring., Nat. Tech. Univ. Athens, 1971; student Mgmt. Tng. and Devel. program Urwick Mgmt. Ctr., London, 1985. Site engr. Edok S.A.-Eter S.A., Agrinion, Greece, 1972-73, GETEM S.A., Piraeus, Greece, 1973-74; market survey and tenders staff Hydrotechnic S.A., Athens, 1974-75; site engr. Odon & Odostro Maton S.A., Saudi Arabia, 1975-79, bridge engr., 1979-80, project mgr., 1980-85; comml. mgr. Itihad Al Tatwir Wal Tanmia Al Saoudia Ltd., Saudia Arabia, 1986—. Greek Orthodox. Avocations: boy scouts, photography, painting. Home: 88 Rovertou Galli-Kato Heliopolis, 16346 Athens Greece Office: Itihad Al Tatwir Wal, Tanmia Al Saoudia Co Ltd, PO Box 8825, Riyadh 11492, Saudi Arabia

KELALIS, PANAYOTIS, pediatric urologist; b. Nicosia, Cyprus, Jan. 17, 1932; came to U.S., 1960, naturalized, 1969; s. Peter and Julia (Petrides) K.; m. Barbara Wilson, Apr. 8, 1970. Student, U. Edinburgh, 1950-51; M.B.B.Ch., U. Dublin, 1957; M.S. in Urology, Mayo Grad. Sch. Medicine, 1964. Resident in urology Mayo Grad. Sch. Medicine, Rochester, Minn., 1960-64; asst. to staff Mayo Clinic, 1964, cons. urology, 1965—, head sect. pediatric urology, 1975—, chmn. dept. urology, 1982—; prof. urology Mayo Med. Sch., 1975—, Anson L. Clark prof. pediatric urology, 1985—. Editor: Clinical Pediatric Urology, 2 vols., 1976, 2 ed., 1985; contbr. numerous sci. articles to profl. jours., chpts. in books. Hon. consul Republic of Cyprus. Recipient Edward J. Noble Found. award, 1964; decorated knight Order of St. Andrew. Fellow ACS; mem. Am. Assn. Genito-Urinary Surgeons, Internat. Soc. Urology, Am. Urol. Assn., Soc. Pediatric Urology (pres.), Am. Acad. Pediatrics (pres., chmn. urology sect.), Royal Soc. Medicine, Soc. Univ. Urologists; hon. mem. Sociedad Latino Americana de Urologia Infantile, Assn. Francaise d'Urologie, Hellenic Urol. Soc.; corr. mem. Sociedad Argentine de Urologia; mem. Sigma Xi. Office: Mayo Clinic Rochester MN 55901

KELLAM, LUCIUS JAMES, JR., petroleum distributing company executive; b. Belle Haven, Va., Sept. 25, 1911; s. Lucius James and Carrie Hargis (Polk) K.; m. Dorothy Douglass, Sept. 12, 1936; children—Dorothy Douglass Kellam Patterson, Lucius James III. Student Trinity Coll., Hartford, 1931-35, D.Sc. (hon.), 1972. Treas., Sturgis Oil Co., Belle Haven, 1935-38, pres., 1938-46; pres., dir. Kellam Energy, Inc., Belle Haven, 1946—; pres. Shore Savs. and Loan Assn., Belle Haven, 1961-70, chmn. bd., 1970-81; pres. Kellam Propane Gas Co., Inc., Belle Haven, 1956-83; dir. First Va. Bank, Tidewater; chmn., Lucius J. Kellam, Jr. Bridge and Tunnel Commn., 1960—; active Va. Safety Council of Accomack County, 1951-75, Delmarva Adv. Council, 1964-71, pres., 1970-71; active indsl. com. Coastal Plains Regional Commn., 1977-81; bd. dirs. Tidewater Regional Health Planning Council, 1968-76; bd. dirs., 1st v.p. Ocean Hwy. Assn., 1954-70, Va. Travel Council, 1963-66; bd. dirs. Va. Travel Devel. Council, 1967-86, Va. Outdoor Found., 1969-74; active Accomack County Democratic Central Com., 1947-73, Va. Dem. Fin. Com., 1965; del. Dem. Nat. Conv., 1960; trustee Old Dominion U. Ednl. Found., Norfolk, Va., St. James Sch., Hagerstown, Md., Eastern Va. Med. Sch. Found., Norfolk, Mus. Fine Arts, Richmond, 1971-86, Va. Mus. Fine Arts Found., 1987; trustee, mem. exec. com. Northampton-Accomack Meml. Hosp., 1938—, treas., 1964-67, pres., 1967-68. Served to 1st. USNR, 1943-46. Named Man of Yr. Va. C. of C., 1965, Eastern Shore Ruritan Clubs, 1966; recipient Spl. Travel award Va. Travel Council, 1966; Disting. Service award Eastern Shore C. of C., 1967. Mem. Tidewater Automobile Assn. (bd. dirs. 1941—, v.p. 1964-76, pres. 1977-79), Internat. Bridge Tunnel and Turnpike Assn. (bd. dirs. 1962-64), Delta Psi. Clubs: Eaterns Shore Yacht and Country (Melfa, Va.); Princess Anne Country (Virginia Beach, Va.); Commonwealth, Downtown (Richmond, Va.); Harbor (Norfolk); St. Anthony (N.Y.C.); Rotary (pres. 1936). Home: Mount Pleasant Belle Haven VA 23306 Office: Kellam Distbg Co Inc US Route 13 Belle Haven VA 23306

KELLEHER, BRYAN JOHN, company director; b. Caulfield, Australia, Jan. 17, 1924; s. J. Kelleher; m. Mary Teresa Clare, May 18, 1946; 2 children. B.Commerce, Melbourne U., 1950, B.A., 1952. Officer Australian Dept. Navy, 1941-59; sr. research officer Australian Fed. Dept. Labour, Melbourne, 1960-64; sr. insp. Commonwealth Pub. Service Bd., Melbourne, 1964-70; controller indsl. relations Hdqrs. Dept. Postmaster Gen., Melbourne, 1970-74, dep. asst. dir.-gen., 1974-75; mgr. indsl. relations dept. Australian Postal Commn. Hdqrs., Melbourne, 1975-82; dir. Australian Natives Assn. Ins. Co.; Adam Lindsay Gordon 150th Anniversary lectr. Meml. Cottage, Ballarat, Victoria, 1983. Author: The A.N.A.—Its Aims and Influence on the Australian scene, 1963; (with Bruce C. Kelleher) A.N.A.—Some Background Notes for Chairmen, 1970; The A.N.A.—A Forum to Advance Australia, 1980; Federation and Constitutional Reform, 1981; Some National Questions, 1982; Australian Poetry and the A.N.A., 1983; More National Questions—The A.N.A.'s Viewpoint, 1984. Sec. Chadstone (Victoria, Australia) Australian Natives Assn., 1953—, bd. dirs. 1972—, chief pres., Victoria, 1973-74, trustee, 1978—, fed. pres., 1978—, rep. to 5th plenary session Australian Constl. Conv., Adelaide, 1983; life gov. Old Colonists Assn., Victoria, 1974—; chmn. bd. Australian Natives Assn. Permanent Bldg. Soc., 1981-82. Served with 2d Australian Imperial Force, 1942-46. Decorated Queen Elizabeth Silver Jubilee medal. Mem. Royal Hist. Soc. Victoria (life), Econ. Soc. Australia, Henry Lawson Meml. and Lit. Soc. (sec. 1983—, editor The Lawsonian 1984—). Home: 47 Bowen St, 3148 Chadstone, Victoria Australia Office: Australian Natives' Assn, 114-124 Albert Rd, 3205 South Melbourne Australia

KELLEHER, KATHLEEN, insurance marketing specialist; b. Suffern, N.Y., May 3, 1951; d. John James and Carol (Re) K. BA, Fairleigh Dickinson U., 1973. CLU, chartered fin. cons. Ins. sales adminstr. Blyth Eastman Dillon & Co., 1977-79; product mktg. assoc. Dean Witter Reynolds, N.Y.C., 1980-82; mgr. product mktg. annuities and ins. dept. Kidder, Peabody & Co., 1982-85; v.p. nat. sales mgr. ins. Paine Webber, 1985—. Mem. Am. Mgmt. Assn., Internat. Fin. Planners. Republican. Club: Coll. of Ridgewood. Home: 321 Mill Rd Saddle River NJ 07458 Office: Paine Webber 1285 Ave of the Americas New York NY 10020

KELLER, GEORGE MATTHEW, oil executive; b. Kansas City, Mo., Dec. 3, 1923; s. George Matthew and Edna Louise (Mathews) K.; m. Adelaide McCague, Dec. 27, 1946; children: William G., Robert A., Barry R. BS in Chem. Engring., MIT, 1948. Engr. Standard Oil Calif. (now Chevron Corp.), San Francisco, 1948-63, fgn. ops. staff, 1963-67, asst. v.p., asst. to pres., 1967-69, v.p., 1969-74, dir., 1970—, vice-chmn., 1974-81, chmn., chief exec. officer, 1981—; bd. dirs. First Interstate Bancorp., First Interstate Bank Calif., Boeing Co.; SRI Internat. Trustee Notre Dame Coll., Belmont, Calif., Am. Enterprise Inst., Com. for Econ. Devel. Served to 1st lt. USAAF, 1943-46. Mem. Bus. Council, Bus. Roundtable, Trilateral Commn., Council Fgn. Relations, Nat. Petroluem Council. Office: Chevron Corp 225 Bush St San Francisco CA 94104 *

KELLER, GLEN ELVEN, JR., lawyer; b. Longmont, Colo., Dec. 21, 1938; s. Glenn Elven and Elsie Mildred (Hogsett) K.; m. Elizabeth Ann Kauffman, Aug. 14, 1960; children—Patricia Carol Michael Ashby. B.S. in Bus., U. Colo., 1960; J.D., U. Denver, 1964. Bar; Colo. 1964, U.S. Dist. Ct. Colo. 1964, U.S. Ct. Appeals (10th cir.) 1982. Assoc. Phelps, Hall & Keller and predecessor Phelps & Hall, Denver, 1964-67, ptnr., 1967-73; asst. atty. gen. State Colo., Denver, 1973-74; judge U.S. Bankruptcy Ct., Dist. Colo., 1974-82; ptnr. Davis, Graham & Stubbs, Denver, 1982—; lectr. law U. Denver, 1977-81; adj. prof., 1987—; mem. ct. adminstrn. com. Jud. Conf. U.S. Mem. Colo. Bd. Health, 1968-74, pres., 1970-74; pres., dir. The Westernaires, Golden, Colo., Jefferson County R-1 Sch. Bd. Mem. Denver Bar Assn., Colo. Bar Assn., ABA, Nat. Conf. Bankruptcy Judges. Republican. Club: Law (Denver). Office: PO Box 185 Denver CO 80201

KELLER, JAIME ROBERTO, theoretical chemist, physicist; b. Mexico D.F., Mex., Nov. 10, 1936; s. Arturo and Rosario (Torres) K.; m. Christina Pérez, Dec. 20, 1967; children: Cristina, Alejandro, Roberto. BS in Chem. Engring., Universidad Nacional Autonoma de Mex., 1950; PhD in Physics, U. Bristol, 1971. Registered profl. engr., Mex. Project engr. Indsl. Quimica Pensalt, Mex., 1959-61; tech. dir. Derivados Macroquimicos, Mex., 1961; lectr. chemistry Universidad Nacional Autonoma de Mex., 1961-72, prof., 1972-76, head theoretical chemistry dept., 1974-76, prof. physics, 1976—, mem. academic council. Contbr. numerous articles to sci. jours.; editor: Amorphous and Liquid Normal, Transition and Rare Earth Metals, 1978, Density Functional Therapy, 1980, The Mathematics of the Physical Space Time, 1981, Future Trends in Material Sciences, 1988; developer chem. industry processes. Recipient Andres Manuel del Rio prize Mexican Chem. Soc., 1980, Nat. prize Govt. of Mex., 1981, Juan Salvador Agraz prize Alumni Nat. Autonomous U. Mex., 1982; named Disting. Catedra Jose Gomez-Ibanez lectr. Wesleyan U., 1982. Mem. Am. Physics Soc., Societa Italiana di Fisica, European Phys. Soc., Internat. Soc. Quantum Biology, Sociedad Quimica de Mex., Sociedad Mexicana de Fisica, Acad. de la Investigacion Cientifica de Mex., Acad. Européenne, Hydrogen Energy Soc., Mexican Nat. Research System. Roman Catholic. Home: 64 Fuente de la Juventud, Mexico City Mexico Office: Faculty de Quimica, Ciudad Universidad, U Nacional Autonoma de Mex, Mexico City Mexico

KELLER, KENNETH HARRISON, university professor; b. N.Y.C., Oct. 19, 1934; s. Benjamin and Pearl (Pastor) K.; m. Dorothy Robinson, June 2, 1957 (div.); children: Andrew Robinson, Paul Victor; m. Bonita F. Sindelir, June 19, 1981; 1 son, Jesse Daniel. A.B., Columbia U., 1956, B.S., 1957; M.S. in Engring., Johns Hopkins U., 1963, Ph.D., 1964. Asst. prof. dept. chem. engring. U. Minn., Mpls., 1964-68, assoc. prof., 1968-71, prof., 1971—, assoc. dean Grad. Sch., 1973-74, acting dean Grad. Sch., 1974-75, head dept. chem. engring. and materials sci., 1978-80, v.p. acad. affairs, 1980-85, pres., 1985-88; cons. in field; mem. cardiology adv. com. NIH, 1982-86. Editor chem. engring. sect.: Jour. Bioengring, 1975-79. Mem. adv. com. program for Soviet emigre scholars, 1974-82; bd. govs. Argonne Nat. Lab., 1982-85; bd. dirs. Walker Art Ctr., 1982-88, Mpls. Inst. Fine Arts., 1980-88. Served from ensign to lt. USNR, 1957-61. NIH Spl. fellow, 1972-73; vis. fellow Woodrow Wilson Sch. of Pub. and Internat. Affairs, Princeton U., 1988-89. Mem. Am. Soc. Artificial Internal Organs (pres. 1980-81), Am. Inst. Chem. Engrs. (Food and Bioengring. award 1980), Internat. Soc. Artificial Organs, N.Y. Acad. Scis., Am. Council for Emigré s in the Professions (dir. 1972-80), Mpls. C. of C. (bd. dirs.), Phi Beta Kappa, Sigma Xi (nat. lectr. 1978-80). Office: U Minn 151 Amundson Hall 421 Washington Ave SE Minneapolis MN 55455

KELLER, MARGARET GILMER, educator; b. Harrisburg, Pa., July 11, 1922; d. Charles Greenawalt and Mary Ellen (Sullivan) Gilmer; m. George Henry Keller III, July 13, 1940; children: Mary Ellen, Margaret Marie, George Henry. AB, Trinity Coll., 1933, AM, Columbia U., 1934; cert. 1942, cert. State Tchrs. Coll., Bloomsburg, Pa., 1934; Acting chmn. history dept., Trinity Coll., Washington, 1935-36, chmn. classical dept., Convent Sacred Heart, 1936-37, Steelton (Pa.) High Sch., 1937-41, adj. prof. English dept., Rutgers U., 1946—, mem. dean's adv. com. U. Coll.,1968, also advisor to women's clubs U. Coll., chmn. classical dept., Glen Rock (N.J.) High Sch., 1956-59, chmn. fgn. lang. dept, 1959—. Active Am. Cancer Soc., Community Chest ARC, Girl Scouts U.S.A.; mem. nominating bd. Ridgewood (N.J.) Nursing Service, 1959-60; Republican county committeeman; trustee Trinity Coll. (life), 1963-67, 1974—, chmn. 75th Anniversary Fund, 1974-75. Honored by Rutgers U., 1953, 61, 65, 71, 82, 87, Newman Province of N.J., 1963, Nat. Jaycees, 1973, Middle States Assn. Comm. on Secondary Schs., 1970, 74; recipient Robert Ax citation Glen Rock High Sch., 1971, Case Inst., 1976, Alumnae Service award Trinity Coll., 1977, 87, Pres.'s medal, 1982; Outstanding Tchr. of Yr., Rutgers U., Newark, 1982. Mem. NEA, N.J. Edn. Assn., Am. Classical Soc., AAUW (former dir.), Archeol. Inst. Am., MLA, Suprs. Assn. N.J. (sec. 1973-76), Am., N.J., Mid-Atlantic States classical socs., AAUP, Chaplain's Aid Assn., Trinity Coll. Alumni Assn. (nat. pres. 1963-67, recipient Nat. Achievement award, 1987), Rutgers Alumni Assn. (hon., advisor), Phi Chi Theta (hon.), Alpha Sigma Lambda (hon., advisor). Clubs: Newman (adviser Rutgers U.), Univ. Coll. Women (hon. Rutgers U.), Coll. Home: 200 Phelps Rd Ridgewood NJ 07450 Office: Rutgers U New Brunswick NJ 08901

KELLER, MICHAEL ALAN, librarian, educator, musicologist; b. Sterling, Colo., Apr. 5, 1945; s. Ephraim Richard and Mary Patricia (Warren) K.; m. Constance A. Kyle, Sept. 3, 1967 (div. Aug. 1979); children—Kristen J., Paul B.; m. Carol Lawrence, Oct. 6, 1979; children: Laura W., Martha M. B.A., Hamilton Coll., 1967; M.A., SUNY-Buffalo, 1970, postgrad., 1970—; M.L.S., SUNY-Geneseo, 1972. Asst. librarian for reference and cataloging SUNY Music Library, Buffalo, 1970-73; acting undergrad. librarian Cornell U., Ithaca, N.Y., 1976, music librarian, sr. lectr., 1973-81; head music library U. Calif.-Berkeley, 1981-86; assoc. univ. librarian for collection devel. Yale U., 1986—; instr. Stanford U., 1984; cons. Colgate U., Hamilton, N.Y., 1976, Rutgers U., New Brunswick, N.J., 1982, Brown U., Providence, 1983, U. Alta., Edmonton, Can., 1983, NYU, 1984, Los Angeles Music Ctr. Operating Co., 1985-87, City of Ferrara, Italy, U. Pitts., Villa I Tatti-Biblioteca Berenson, Florence, Italy; mem. Bibliog. Commn., Repertoire Internat. de la Presse Mus. de XIXve Siecle, 1981-84; chmn. music program com. Research Libraries Group, 1982-86; reviewer NEH, 1982-88, panelist, 1979—; chmn. Assoc. Music Libraries Group; mem. Joint Com. on Retrospective Conversion in Music, Research Libraries group, collection mgmt. devel. com., 1986—. Author: MSS on Microfilm in Music Library at SUNYAB, 1971; (with Duelder) Music Reference and Research Materials; an annotated bibliography, 1988; contbr. articles to profl. jours. Firefighter, rescue squad mem. Cuyuga Heights Vol. Fire Co., N.Y., 1980-81. Recipient spl. commendation Nat. Music Clubs, 1978, Berkeley Bronze medal U. Calif.-Berkeley, 1983; NDEA Title IV fellow SUNY-Buffalo, 1967-70; Cornell Coll. Arts and Scis. research grantee, 1973-81, U. Calif.-Berkeley humanities research grantee, 1983-84, Council on Library Resources grantee, 1984, Librarian Assoc. U. Calif. grantee, 1985-86, NEH grantee, 1986. Mem. ALA, AAUP, Music Library Assn. (bd. dirs. 1975-77, fin. com. 1982-83, editorial com. index and bibliography series 1981-85), Internat. Assn. Music Libraries, Am. Musicol. Soc. (com. on automated bibliography 1982-83, council 1986-88), Conn. Acad. Arts Scis. (bd. dirs.), Ctr. Research Libraries (mem. adv. com. 1988—). Home: 106 Oliver Rd New Haven CT 06515 Office: Sterling Meml Library New Haven CT 06520

KELLER, OSWALD LEWIN, JR., chemist, researcher; b. N.Y.C., May 24, 1930; s. Oswald Lewin and Katherine Doris (Leiding) K.; m. Dona Claire Guild, Oct. 9, 1953; children—Christopher, Claire, Elaine, Elizabeth. B.S., U. of South, 1951, Ph.D., MIT, 1959. Research staff mem. Oak Ridge Nat. Lab., 1960-65, dir. transuranium lab., 1965-74, 84—, dir. chem. div. 1974-84; mem. Nuclear physics panel Nat. Acad. Scis., 1969-72; chmn. bd. visitors dept. chemistry U. Tenn., Knoxville, 1983-84, mem. dept. energy transplutonium program com., 1966-74, 1980-87, mem. sci. alliance faculty adv. com., 1985; exchange scientist U.S. Nat. Acad. Sci. and Acad. Scis. USSR, 1972; invited speaker Robert A. Welch Found, 1969, 75, 78. Contbr. articles to profl. jours. Served with U.S. Army, 1954-56. Fellow Rockefeller Found., MIT, 1951. Fellow AAAS; mem. Am. Chem. Soc. (councillor 1984-86), Am. Phys. Soc., Phi Beta Kappa. Home: 101 Morgan Rd Oak Ridge TN 37830

KELLER, THOMAS WHITNEY, retired building supply company; b. Hinsdale, Ill., July 26, 1921; s. Raymond L. and Mildred (Whitney) K.; B.A., Duke, 1946; m. Marcia E. Marland, Sept. 6, 1951; children—Peter J., Mark T., Marcia E. II, Scott R. With E.A. Keller Co., La Grange, Ill., 1946-71, sec., 1949-71; pres. TriCounty Land Corp., Lemont, Ill.; owner Keller Plantations, Holland, Mich., 1971—; dir. adv. bd. La Grange State Bank, 1979; past dir. Edgewood Bank, La Grange. Mem. Village of La Grange Parking Commn., 1957-77; former mem. asso. bd. La Grange Community Meml. Gen. Hosp.; former bd. dirs. West Suburban YMCA. Served with AUS, 1942-45. Mem. Am. Legion, Sigma Chi. Methodist. Clubs: Spring Lake Country, Masons, Kiwanis. Home: 15346 Leonard Rd Spring Lake MI 49456

KELLER, WILLIAM MARTIN, corporate executive; b. Wilkes-Barre, Pa., Oct. 26, 1916; s. Roy S. and Alice (Obrien) K.; m. Mary Anne Davis, Oct. 25, 1938; children: Anne Elizabeth Hufford, William Martin III. A.B., Syracuse U.; grad., Harvard U. Bus. Sch.; LL.D. in Internat. Relations, U. Liberia, W. Africa. Indsl. engr. Montgomery Ward & Co., Armstrong Cork Co., Inc.; mgr. indsl. engring., plant mgr., gen. factories mgr., v.p. mfg., v.p. mktg., v.p., gen. mgr. reinforced plastics div., v.p. internat. Owens-Corning Fiberglas Corp., N.Y.C.; U.S. Dept. State Diplomatic rep. to Liberi; pres. W.M. Keller Assocs.; bus. cons. Former chmn. bd. trustees Cherry Lawn Sch., Darien; trustee Council Chs. and Synagogues. Decorated Star of Africa Republic of Liberia). Mem. Pa. Soc. Clubs: Mason (N.Y.C.) (Shriner), Elk (N.Y.C.), Kiwanian. (N.Y.C.), Pinnacle (N.Y.C.), N.Y. Athletic (N.Y.C.) (life); Harvard Business (Denver); Kissing Camels Golf (Colorado Springs, Colo.), Garden of Gods (Colorado Springs, Colo.); Metropolitan (Washington). Home: 2221 Hill Circle Rd Colorado Springs CO 80904

KELLERMAN, AHARON, geography educator; b. Haifa, Israel, Aug. 25, 1945; s. Jehuda Ludwig and Lea Lilli (Zimmer) K.; m. Michal Bergman, July 1, 1973; children: Tovy, Miriam, Noga. BA, U. Haifa, 1969; MA, Hebrew U., Jerusalem, 1973; PhD, Boston U., 1977. Cert. high sch. tchr. Instr. Boston U., 1975-76; vis. asst. prof. U. Miami, Coral Gables, Fla., 1976-77; lectr. U. Haifa, 1977-81, sr. lectr., 1981-87, assoc. prof., 1987—; Chmn. geography dept. Univ. Haifa, 1986—; vis. lectr. Univ. Md., College Park, 1982-83, 84, 85, 87. Contbr. articles to profl. jours. Meml. Found. for Jewish Culture grantee, N.Y.C., 1974-75, Hecht Found. grantee, Haifa, 1984. Mem. Israeli Geog. Soc. (nat. council mem. 1983—, chmn. urban geography sect. 1986—), Assn. Am. Geographers. Jewish. Office: U Haifa, Dept Geography, Haifa 31999, Israel

KELLERMANN, JAN JEHESKEL, physician; b. Bratislava, Czechoslovakia, June 19, 1926; s. Julius and Martha (Gutfreund) K.; M.D., Leopold Franzens U., Innsbruck, Austria, 1955; m. Erika Schwartz, Apr. 26, 1949. Intern, Tel Hashomer Govt. Hosp., Israel, 1955-57, resident, 1960; asso. prin. investigator, prin. investigator Social Rehab. Adminstrn., HEW, Washington, 1969-73, Public Health Service, Cin., 1967-70; head cardiac evaluation and rehab. inst. Chaim Sheba Med. Center, Tel Hashomer, Israel, 1968—; assoc. prof. Sackler Sch. Medicine, Tel Aviv U., 1978-85, chmn. med. rehab., 1983—, prof., 1985—; mem. expert adv. panel for cardiology WHO, 1981; fgn. dir. Internat. Sch. Cardiology, Ettore Majorana, Erice, Sicily; guest lectr. and/or vis. prof. various univs. including Ben Gurion U. of Negev, 1983—; chmn. subcom. allied health professions Council Higher Edn., 1984—; sci. adviser Fondazione Clinica del Lavoro, Paria, 1984. Internat. fellow Am. Heart Assn., 1985. Fellow Am. Coll. Cardiology, Am. Coll. Chest Physicians, Am. Heart Assn.; mem. Internat. Soc. Cardiology (exec. mem. council cardiac rehab.), Israel Med. Assn., Israel Heart Soc. Coauthor or editor 7 books; sr. editor Advances in Cardiology, Bibliotheca Cardiologia. sect. editor Jour. Cardiology, 1977; editor (with Denolin): Critical Evaluation of Cardiac Rehabilitation, 1977; Comprehensive Cardiac Rehabilitation, 1982; editor-in-chief Cardiology, 1979; series editor Advances in Cardiology, 1981—, Bibliotheca Cardiologica, 1981—; contbr. articles to profl. jours. Home: 1 Haseytim St, Ramat Gan Israel Office: Cardiac Rehab Inst, Chaim Sheba Med Center, Tel Hashom Israel

KELLETT, WILLIAM HIRAM, JR., architect, engineer, educator; b. Bryan, Tex., Oct. 15, 1930; s. William Hiram and Elizabeth (Minsky) K.; m. Christiane Maria Binsch, Feb. 2, 1962 (div.); children: Elizabeth Julia, Rene Janine, Kira Lorraine; m. 2d Ann Robertson Wilkins, Dec. 11, 1971; children: Robert Lynn, Patricia Ann. A.A., Victoria Coll., 1954; B. Arch., Tex. A&M U., 1960, M.Arch., 1967. Registered architect, engr. Elec. technician W.E. Kutzschbach Co., Bryan, 1950-51; engring. technologist Johnston & Davis, Victoria, Tex., 1952-54; mech. elec. systems designer Hall Engring. Co., Bryan, 1955-62, Environments, Inc., Bryan, 1962-74; pres. Mech. & Elec Cons., Bryan, 1974-76; owner, operator William H. Kellett, Cons. Engrs., Bryan, 1976—; prof. environ. design, architecture and bldg. constrn., constrn. sci. Tex. A&M U., College Station, 1962-88; with Consulting Engineer, Bryan; bd. dirs. Geranium Junction. Staff editor: Arch. Plus. Vice chmn. City Charter Com., Bryan, 1969; chmn. Bd. Equalization, 1969-70; vice chmn. City Floodwater Mgmt. Commn.; pres. Mayor's Com. on Spl. People. Named Outstanding State Handicapped Employee. Mem. AIA, Illuminating Engrs. Soc., Constrn. Specifications Inst., AAUP, ASHRAE, Refrigeration Engrs. and Tech. Assn., Nat. Soc. Profl. Engrs., Assn. Plumbing Engrs., Tex. Soc. Profl. Engrs., Phi Theta Kappa, Tau Beta Pi, Tau Sigma Delta. Home: 1000 Esther Blvd Bryan TX 77802 Office: Consulting Engineer 806 Oak Bryan TX 77802

KELLEY, JAY HILARY, engineer; b. Greensburg, Pa., Mar. 9, 1920; s. Augustine Bernard and Ellen Marie (Bates) K.; m. Catherine Jane Holway, May 10, 1949; children: Leonard, Christine, Catherine, Mary, Gerard, Patrick, Joyce, Michele, Sheila. BS, Pa. State U., 1942, MS, 1947, PhD, 1952; postdoctoral, U. Pitts., 1952-60. V.p. Calora Coal Co., Mammoth, Pa., 1946-50; sta. mgr. and sr. engr. Joy Machinery Co., Saltsburg, Pa., 1952-57; sr. engr. Westinghouse Electric Co., Pitts., 1957-62; tech. specialist White House Sci. Staff, Washington, 1962-65; prof., dir. Rutgers U., New Brunswick, N.J., 1965-66; mgr. advanced programs and tech. Ford Motor Corp., Phila., 1966-69; pres. Elders Ridge Co., Greensburg, Pa., 1964—; dean, disting. prof. minerals coll. W.Va. U., Morgantown, 1970-87, prof. emeritus, 1987—; engring. cons. Kelastic/Urbdata Engrs., Greensburg, 1967—; adj. prof. Drexel U., Phila., 1968-69; pres., v.p., bd. dirs., trustee Engring. Index, 1965-79. Patentee in field; contbr. articles to profl. jours. Chmn. Buffalo Creek Disaster Commn., Charleston, W.Va., 1973, W.Va. Coal Mine Inspection Bd., Charleston, 1970-78; gen. chmn. Nat. Safety Council, Chgo., 1978-79. Served as 1st lt. U.S. Army, 1943-46, ETO. Mem. IEEE, Soc. Mining Engrs. of AIME, Ops. Research Soc. Am., Am. Mfg. Congress, Engring. Found. (bd. dirs., chmn. project com). Roman Catholic. Clubs: Cosmos (Washington); Youngstown (Ohio). Home: 300 Maple Dr Greensburg PA

15601 Office: W Va Univ Coll of Mineral and Energy Resources Morgantown WV 26506 also: Urbdata Ltd 307 S Pennsylvania Ave Greensburg PA 15601

KELLEY, MAURICE LESLIE, JR., gastroenterologist, educator; b. Indpls., June 29, 1924; s. Maurice Leslie and Martha (Daniel) K.; m. Carol J. Povec, Feb. 11, 1967; children: Elizabeth Ann, Mary Sarah. Student, U. Vt., Va. Ply. Inst., Princeton U., 1943-45; M.D., U. Rochester, 1949. Intern, resident Strong Meml. Hosp., Rochester, N.Y., 1949-51; Bixby fellow in medicine Strong Meml. Hosp., 1953-56; fellow in gastroenterology Mayo Clinic, Rochester, Minn., 1957-59; asst. prof. medicine U. Rochester, 1959-64, assoc. prof., 1964-67; practice medicine specializing in gastroenterology Rochester, N.Y., 1959-67; assoc. prof. clin. medicine Dartmouth Med. Sch., 1967-74, prof. clin. medicine, 1974—; chmn. sect. internal medicine Hitchcock Clinic, 1972-74, chmn. sect. gastroenterology, 1974; mem. staff Strong Meml. Hosp., Hitchcock Clinic, Mary Hitchcock Meml. Hosp.; cons. Canandaigua VA, Rochester Gen., Genesee hosps., VA. Med. Ctr., White River Junction. Contbr. articles to profl. jours., chpts. to books. Served with AUS, 1942-45; M.C. USAF, 1951-53. Fellow ACP (gov. for N.H. 1974-78), Am. Gastroenterol. Assn.; mem. Am. Soc. Gastrointestinal Endoscopy, AMA (chmn. sect. gastroenterology 1970-71), Am. Physiol. Soc., Alpha Omega Alpha. Home: 15 Ledge Rd Hanover NH 03755 Office: 2 Maynard St Hanover NH 03755

KELLEY, MICHAEL CURTIS, mktg. exec.; b. Montemorelos, Nuevo Leon, Mex., May 13, 1947 (parents Am. citizens); s. Horace Agard and Rosayle Montana (Guild) K.; B.A. with honors, Andrews U., Berrien Springs, Mich., 1968; M.S. in Nuclear/Phys. Chemistry (NSF fellow), U. Calif., Berkeley, 1969; children from previous marriage: Sean Michael, Ryan Carlos; m. Ivonne Ruiz, Aug. 10, 1985. Missionary, Mex., 1969-71; instr. Colegio Linda Vista, Chiapas, Mex., 1969-71; instr., asst. prof. chemistry and physics Atlantic Union Coll., South Lancaster, Mass., 1971-78; owner, mgr. computer info. systems cons. co., 1972-78; project leader Digital Programming Services, Inc., Waltham, Mass., 1977-78; project leader software devel. Wang Labs., Lowell, Mass., 1978-79, sales mgr. for Latin Am., 1980-82, area mktg. mgr., 1982-84, dir. mktg. Ams. area, 1984; gen. mgr. Wang Panama, 1984-85; area dir. Latin Am. and Caribbean Wang, 1985— . No. Worcester County campaign coordinator for McGovern for Pres., 1972. Mem. Am. Chem. Soc., Am. Fedn. Info. Processing Socs. Office: Wang Labs 5835 Blue Lagoon Dr Miami FL 33126

KELLEY, NEIL DAVIS, applied meteorologist; b. Clayton, Mo., Jan. 8, 1942; s. Davis Franklin and Louise Minnie (Zager) K.; divorced; BS in Meteorology, St. Louis U., 1963; MS, Pa. State U., 1968. Mem. staff Meteorology Research Inc. Altadena, Calif., 1963-66; field supr. Exxon Research and Engring., Linden, N.J., 1967; instr. meteorology Pa. State U., 1969-71; chief of capability devel. Research Aviation Facility, Nat. Ctr. for Atmospheric Research, Boulder, Colo., 1972-77; prin. scientist Solar Energy Research Inst., Golden, Colo., 1977—. Recipient spl. award Nat. Ctr. Atmospheric Research, 1974; outstanding award Solar Energy Research Inst., 1982. Mem. Instrument Soc. Am., Am. Meteorol. Soc., AAAS, AIAA, Am. Theater Organ Soc., IES, Sigma Xi. Lodge: Elks. Contbr. articles to profl. jours. Office: Solar Energy Research Inst 1617 Cole Blvd Golden CO 80401

KELLEY, WILLIAM LEWIS, engineering and construction company executive; b. Seattle, June 4, 1932; s. Lewis Philips and Sarah Maurine (Middleton) K.; m. Mae Lee Brown, Feb. 17, 1955; children: Michael W., Katherine M., Patrick L. B.S. in C.E., U. Wash.-Seattle, 1955, B.S. in Indsl. Engring., 1955; M.S. in C.E., Stanford U., 1962. Registered profl. engr., Calif., Wash., Ala. Proj. engr. Kaiser Engrs., Venezuela, 1963-65; resident engr. Seattle City Light, Seattle, 1965-68; project mgr. Tippetts, Abbott McCarthy Stratton, Morocco, 1968-71; regional mgr. Internat. Engring. Co., Inc., San Francisco, 1972-74, v.p., 1974-81, exec. v.p., 1981-85; sr. v.p. internat. ops. Morrison-Knudson Engrs., Inc., San Francisco, 1985—. Author: Overseas Marketing Strategy; contbg. author Project Management Handbook; appeared in La Poudre Déscampetten, 1971; patentee apparatus and method for schedule monitoring and control. Mem. NSPE, ASCE, U.S. C. of C., Tau Beta Pi, Zeta Mu Tau, Phi Kappa Sigma. Republican. Methodist. Club: Engineers of San Francisco. Home: 8 Candlestick Rd Orinda CA 94563

KELLEY, WILLIAM NIMMONS, physician, educator; b. Atlanta, June 23, 1939; s. Oscar Lee and Will Nimmons (Allen) K.; m. Lois Faville, Aug. 1, 1959; children: Margaret Paige, Virginia Lynn, Lori Ann, William Mark. M.D., Emory U., 1963. Intern in medicine Parkland Meml. Hosp., Dallas, 1963-64; resident Parkland Meml. Hosp., 1964-65; sr. resident medicine Mass. Gen. Hosp., Boston, 1967-68; clin. asso., sect. on human biochem. genetics NIH, 1965-67; teaching fellow medicine Harvard U. Med. Sch., 1967-68; asst. prof. to prof. medicine, asst. prof. to asso. prof. biochemistry, chief div. rheumatic and genetic diseases Duke U. Sch. Medicine, 1968-75; Macy faculty scholar Oxford U., 1974-75; prof., chmn. dept. internal medicine, prof. dept. biol. chemistry U. Mich. Med. Sch., Ann Arbor, 1975—; mem. metabolism study sect., 1978-81, bd. dirs. adv. council, 1986-87; bd. govs. Am. Bd. Internal Medicine, 1978-86, chmn., 1985-86; mem. exec. com. Am. Bd. Med. Spltys., 1980-82; mem. adv. council Nat. Inst. Arthritis, Diabetes and Digestive and Kidney Diseases, 1984-86, Nat. Inst. Diabetes and Digestive and Kidney Diseases, 1968-87. Author: (with J.B. Wyngaarden) Gout and Hyperuricemia, 1976, (with I.M. Weiner) Uric Acid, 1979, (with Harris, Ruddy and Sledge) Textbook of Rheumatology, 1981, 2d edit., 1985; contbr. articles to med. jours. Recipient C.V. Mosby award, 1967, John D. Lane award USPHS, 1969, Geigy Internat. prize rheumatology, 1969, Research Career Devel. award USPHS, 1972-75, Heinz Karger Meml. Found. prize, 1973; Disting. Med. Achievement award Emory U., 1985; Mead Johnson scholar, 1967; Clin. scholar Am. Rheumatism Assn., 1969-72; Josiah Macy Found. scholar, 1974-75. Fellow Inst. of Medicine, ACP (trustee Mich. chpt. 1975—); mem. Inst. Medicine, Nat. Acad. Scis., Am. Soc. Clin. Investigation (editorial bd. 1974-79, pres.-elect 1982-83, pres. 1983-84), So. Soc. Clin. Investigation, Central Soc. for Clin. Research (pres. elect 1985-86, pres. 1986-87), Am. Soc. Biol. Chemists (editorial bd. 1976-81), Am. Fedn. Clin. Research (nat. council 1977-80, exec. com. 1975-80, nat. sec.-treas. 1976-78, pres. 1979-80, chmn. publs. com. Clin. Research 1976-78), Assn. Am. Physicians, Assn. Profs. Medicine (nominating com. 1978-79, sec.-treas. 1987—), Am. Rheumatism Assn. (chmn. membership com., program com., research com., dir. 1975-76, exec. com. 1976—, editorial bd. 1972-78, sec.-treas. 1982-85, pres.-elect 1985-86, pres. 1986-87), AAAS, Am. Soc. Human Genetics, Am. Soc. Nephrology, Am. Soc. Internal Medicine (trustee Mich. chpt.), Central Rheumatism Soc. (pres. 1978-79), Sigma Xi, Alpha Omega Alpha. Home: 521 Hillspur Rd Ann Arbor MI 48105 Office: Univ Mich Med Ctr 3105 Taubman Box 0368 Dept Internal Medicine Ann Arbor MI 48109

KELLEY-CRESCI, MARILYN V., bookkeeping service owner; b. Tucson, Jan. 13, 1937; d. Marion and Lovetta (Merchant) Adkins; children: Russell D., Wanda L. (dec.), James H.; m. Frank V. Cresci, Sept. 13, 1986. Student Heald Bus. Sch., 1977, Regional Occupational Ctr., 1981. Bookkeeper Barbary Coast, San Jose, Calif., 1980-82, Argon Steel, San Jose, 1982-83, Indsl. Chimney, Hayward, Calif., 1984-85; owner Marilyn's Bookkeeping Service, Union City, Calif., 1983—; corp. sec.-treas. Rod's Trucking, Inc., Newark, Calif., 1985—; corp. v.p., sec. Newark Wreckers, 1987—; bookkeeper R&D Resume Services, Fremont, Calif. 1983—. Fellow Nat. Assn. Female Execs. Republican. Episcopalian. Lodge: Order of Demolay (pres. mother's club 1979-80). Avocations: fishing, camping. Address: 118 Madrone Way Union City CA 94587

KELLNER, RICHARD GEORGE, computer scientist; b. Cleve., July 10, 1943; s. George Ernest and Wanda Julia (Lapinski) K.; BS, Case Inst. Tech., 1965; MS, Stanford U., 1968, PhD, 1969; m. Charlene Ann Zajc, June 26, 1965 (div. 1988); children: Michael Richard, David George. Staff mem. Los Alamos (N.M.) Scientific Lab., 1969-79, Los Alamos Nat. Lab., 1983—; co-owner, dir. software devel. KMP Computer Systems, Inc., Los Alamos, 1979-84; mgr. spl. projects KMP Computer Systems div. 1st Data Resources Inc., Los Alamos, 1984-87; with microcomputer div., 1988—; owner ComPuSpeed, 1986—; co-owner Computer-Aided Communications, 1982-84; cons., 1979—. Mem. AAAS, IEEE, Assn. Computing Machinery, Math. Assn. Am., Soc. Indsl. and Applied Math., Am. Math. Soc. Home: 4496 Ridgeway Dr Los Alamos NM 87544 Office: Los Alamos Nat Lab PO Box 1663 MSK488 Los Alamos NM 87545

KELLOGG, BRUCE MICHAEL, real estate investor, agent; b. Buffalo, Jan. 3, 1947; s. Harlan Wood and Hilma Moore (Yarrington) K.; m. Diane Linda Mancuso, Dec. 25, 1979; children—Jeremy, Catherine, Michael, Elizabeth, David, Allison. B.S.E.E., Rutgers U., 1969; M.B.A., Golden Gate U., 1976. Securities investor, Wilmington, N.C., 1970-73; real estate investor, San Jose, Calif., 1973—; assoc. ERA Hill and Assocs., San Jose, 1987—. Mem. Tri-County Apt. Assn., Calif. Apt. Assn. Nat. Apt. Assn., San Jose Bd. Realtors, Calif. Assn. Realtors, Nat. Assn. Realtors, Republican. Roman Catholic. Contbr. articles to profl. jours. Office: 1510 Parkmoor Ave San Jose CA 95128

KELLOGG, FREDERICK (R.), historian; b. Boston, Dec. 9, 1929; s. Frederick Floyd and Stella Harriet (Plummer) K.; A.B., Stanford U., 1952; M.A., U. So. Calif., 1958; Ph.D., Ind. U., 1969; m. Patricia Kay Hanbery, Aug. 21, 1954 (dec. 1975); 1 dau., Kristine Marie Calvert. Instr., Boise State U., 1962-64, asst. prof., 1964-65; vis. asst. prof. U. Idaho, 1965; asso. prof. Boise State U., 1966-67; instr. history U. Ariz., 1967-68, asst. prof., 1968-71, asso. prof., 1971—. Founder, chmn. Idaho Hist. Conf., 1964. U.S.-Romania Cultural Exchange Research scholar, 1960-61; Sr. Fulbright-Hays Research scholar, Romania, 1969-70. Recipient Am. Council Learned Socs. Research grant, 1970-71; Internat. Research and Exchanges Bd. Sr. Research grant, 1973-74. Mem. Am. Hist. Assn., Am. Assn. Advancement Slavic Studies, Am. Assn. Southeast European Studies. Mng. editor Southeastern Europe, 1974—; contbr. articles to academic publs. Office: U Ariz Dept History Tucson AZ 85721

KELLOGG-SMITH, PETER, educator, inventor, sculptor; b. N.Y.C., Apr. 21, 1920; s. Jewell and Margaret (Shearer) Kellogg-Smith; A.B., St. John's Coll., Annapolis, Md., 1943; postgrad. M.I.T., 1952; M.A., Putney Grad. Sch. Tchr. Edn., 1962; postgrad. Chesapeake Biol. Lab., Solomons, Md., 1968, Md. Inst. Coll. Art, 1975-78; studied yacht design under Franz Plunder, sculpture under Etienne Desmet, Italy, also Reuben Kramer and Arthur Benson, Balt.; children—Peter von Pein, Lee von Pein Schreitz, Ruth Bueneman, Cynthia K. Dax. Tchr. math and sci. Ojai (Calif.) Valley Sch., 1944-46; organizer, acting head Happy Valley Sch., Miners Oaks, Ojai, 1946-47; yacht broker, designer, Chestertown, Md. 1947-61; asst. head Gunston Sch., Centerville, Md., 1950-57; tchr. Abano (Turkey) Grapho-English, 1956; founding headmaster, tchr. Key Sch., Annapolis, Md., 1958-62; founding headmaster, dir. oceanography Bay Country Sch., Arnold, Md., 1962-71; founding dir. Bay Country Inst., 1971-77; tchr. sculpture Acad. Arts, Easton, Md., 1973-76; vis. seminar leader Md. Inst. Coll. Art, 1976-77. Mem. Assn. World Edn., Chesapeake Bay Found., Chestertown Arts League (past pres.), Md. Fedn. Arts (chmn. sculpture), St. John's Coll. Alumni Assn. (pres. Annapolis chpt. 1984-86, 88—). Democrat. Episcopalian. Address: 202 Divinity Ln Arnold MD 21012

KELLOW, JAMES HARRY, transportation company executive; b. Hot Springs, Ark., June 30, 1939; s. Russell Peter and Margaret Elizabeth (Henry) K.; m. Nancy Elaine Womack, Sept. 21, 1974; 1 child, Patrick Clifton. AA, U. Md., 1964; BBA, Memphis State U., 1966, MA, 1969. Asst. dir., sr. research assoc. Bur. Bus. and Econ. Research Memphis State U., 1970-72; dep. dir. Memphis Housing Authority, 1972-77; dir. fin. and adminstrn. Port of Corpus Christi, Tex., 1977-79; pres. Louisville and Jefferson County Riverport Authority, 1979-84; exec. dir. Detroit and Wayne County Port Authority, 1984—, Gt. Detroit Fgn. Trade Zone, Inc., 1986—; co-gen. mgr. Detroit Windsor Port Corp., 1986—, pres., 1988—; bd. dirs. Am. Assn. Port Authorities, 1986-87, Assn. Internat. Great Lakes Ports. Mem United Way Corpus Christi, 1979, chmn. allocation com., 1979; mem. Leadership Detroit, 1985—, Mich. Dist. Export Council, 1985—; treas. Bd. Commrs., Glenview, Ky., 1984. Mem. Inland Rivers Ports and Terminals (1st v.p. 1984), Nat. Assn. Fgn. Trade Zones, Detroit Econ. Club. Episcopalian. Club: Propeller of U.S. Port of Detroit (pres. 1988—). Home: 765 Balfour Grosse Pointe Park MI 48230 Office: Detroit Wayne County Port Auhtority 200 Rennaisance Suite 650 Detroit MI 48243

KELLY, ARTHUR LLOYD, management and investment company executive; b. Chgo., Nov. 15, 1937; s. Thomas Lloyd and Mildred (Wetten) K.; B.S. with honors, Yale U., 1959; M.B.A., U. Chgo., 1964; m. Diane Rex Cain, Nov. 25, 1978; children: Mary Lucinda, Thomas Lloyd, Alison Williams. With A.T. Kearney, Inc., 1959-75, mng. dir., Dusseldorf, W.Ger., 1964-70, v.p. for Europe, Brussels, 1970-73, internat. v.p., London, 1974-75, ptnr., dir., 1969-75, mem. exec. com., 1972-75; pres., chief operating officer, dir. LaSalle Steel Co., Chgo., 1975-81; pres., chief exec. officer, dir. Dalta Corp., Chgo., 1982—; mng. ptnr. KEL Enterprises Ltd., Chgo., 1983—; vice chmn., bd. dirs. ARCH Devel. Corp., Chgo., 1986—; dir. Snap-on Tools Corp., Kenosha, Wis., Twin Disc Inc., Racine, Wis., Georgetown Industries, Inc., Charlotte, N.C., Cimline, Inc., Elk Grove Village, Ill., Crosspoint Venture Ptnrs., Palo Alto, Calif., DataCard Corp., Minnetonka, Minn., Bankhaus Trinkaus & Burkhardt KGaA, Dusseldorf, Fed. Republic of Germany, Northern Trust Corp., Chgo., ,Internet Systems Corp., Chgo., chmn. vis. com. div. phys. scis. U. Chgo., also mem. council Grad. Sch. Bus.; mem. adv. council Ditchley Found., Oxford, Eng.; bd. dirs. Chgo. Council Fgn. Relations (mem. exec. com.), Am. Council on Germany, N.Y.C. Mem. Young Pres.'s Orgn., World Bus. Council, Beta Gamma Sigma. Clubs: Chgo., Racquet, Casino (Chgo.), Brook, Yale (N.Y.C.). Office: 135 S La Salle St Suite 1117 Chicago IL 60603

KELLY, DENNIS RAY, sales executive; b. Olympia, Wash., Aug. 20, 1948; s. William E. and Irene (Lewis) K.; m. Pamela Jo Kresevich, Mar. 16, 1974. BA, Cen. Wash. U., 1972; postgrad., U. Wash., 1977-78. Sales rep. Bumble Bee Sea Foods, Seattle, 1972-74; retail sales mgr. Pacific Pearl Sea Foods, Seattle, 1974-76; regional sales mgr. Castle & Cooke Foods, Seattle, Phila., and N.Y.C., 1976-80; v.p. sales mktg. Frances Andrew Ltd., Seattle, 1980-82; regional sales mgr. Tenneco West, Seattle, 1982-85; sales and mktg. mgr. for western U.S. David Oppenheimer, Seattle, 1985—. Alumni advisor Cen. Wash. U., Ellensburg, 1979-87, alumni bd. dirs., 1986—, fund drive chmn., 1988, mem. sch. community group bd.; mem. Statue of Liberty Ellis Island Found.; chmn. annual fund drive Cen. Wash. U. Mem. New Zealand-Am. Soc., Mfrs. Reps. Club Wash. Republican. Home: 7234 237 Ave NE Redmond WA 98053

KELLY, DONALD PHILIP, holding company executive; b. Chgo., Feb. 24, 1922; s. Thomas Nicholas and Ethel M. (Healy) K.; m. Byrd M. Sullivan, Oct. 25, 1952; children: Patrick, Laura, Thomas. Student, Loyola U., Chgo., 1953-54, De Paul U., 1954-55, Harvard U., 1965. Mgr. tabulating United Ins. Co. Am., 1946-51; mgr. data processing A.B. Wrisley Co., 1951-53; mgr. data processing Swift & Co., 1953-65, asst. controller, 1965-67, controller, 1967-68, v.p. corporate devel., controller, 1968-70, fin. v.p., dir., 1970-73; fin. v.p., dir. Esmark, Inc., Chgo., 1973; pres., chief operating officer Esmark, Inc., 1973-77, pres., chief exec. officer, 1977-82, chmn., pres., chief exec. officer, 1982-84; pres. Kelly, Briggs & Assocs., Inc., Chgo., 1984-86; chmn. BCI Holdings Corp., Chgo., 1986-87; chmn., chief exec. officer E-II Holdings Inc., Chgo., 1987; chmn. bd. dirs. Beatrice Co., Chgo., 1988—. Trustee Michael Reese Hosp. and Med. Center, Chgo., Com. for Econ. Devel., Washington, Mus. Sci. and Industry, Chgo.; mem. Conf. Bd. N.Y.; trustee Coll. Bus. Adminstrn., U. Notre Dame. Served in USNR, 1942-46. Mem. Fin. Execs. Inst. Clubs: Chgo. (Chgo.), Comml. (Chgo.), Econ. (Chgo.). Office: Beatrice Co 2 N LaSalle St Chicago IL 60602

KELLY, EAMON MICHAEL, university president; b. N.Y.C., Apr. 25, 1936; s. Michael Joseph and Kathleen Elizabeth (O'Farrell) K.; m. Margaret Whalen, June 22, 1963; children: Martin (dec.), Paul, Andrew, Peter. BS, Fordham U., 1958; MS, Columbia U., 1960, PhD, 1965. Officer in charge Office of Social Devel., Ford Found., N.Y.C., 1969-73; officer in charge program related investments Ford Found., 1974-79; exec. v.p. Tulane U., New Orleans, 1979-81, pres., 1981—; dir. policy formulation div. Econ. Devel. Adminstrn., Dept. Commerce, Washington, 1968; spl. asst. to adminstr. SBA, Washington, 1968-69; spl. counselor to sec. Dept. Labor, 1977; bd. dirs. So. Edn. Found., Hibernia Nat. Bank, La. Land and Exploration Co., Met. Area Com., Nat. Captioning Inst.; mem. com. for econ. devel. U.S. Ho. Reps., Washington. Contbr. articles to profl. jours. Pres. city council, councilman-at-large City of Englewood, N.J., 1974-77; bd. dirs. Nat. Urban Coalition. Humphrey fellows Nat. Adv. Council. Mem. AAUP, Nat. Assn. Ind. Colls. and Univs. (dir.). Democrat. Roman Catholic. Home: 2 Audubon Pl New Orleans LA 70118 Office: Tulane Univ Office of the President New Orleans LA 70118

KELLY, EDMUND JOSEPH, lawyer, investment banker; b. Mount Vernon, N.Y., May 18, 1937; s. Hugh Joseph and Catherine (Rice) K.; m. Joan Anne Fee, Nov. 18, 1961; children: Kathleen Anne, Edmund Murphy, Thomas More, Mary Fee, Michael McNaboe. A.B. cum laude, Coll. of Holy Cross, 1959; J.D. (James Kent scholar), Columbia U., 1962. Bar: N.Y. 1962. Gen. counsel Office of Sec. of Air Force, Pentagon, Washington, 1962-65; assoc. White & Case, N.Y.C., 1965-70; ptnr. White & Case, 1971-84; vice chmn. Dominick & Dominick Co., N.Y.C., 1984—; bd. dirs. Fed. Paper Bd. Co., Inc., Montvale, N.J.; bd. dirs., mem. exec. com. Chgo. Pneumatic Tool Co., N.Y.C., 1980-86; lectr. Practicing Law Inst., Am. Mgmt. Assn. Author: The Takeover Dialogues, A Discussion of Hostile Takeovers, 1987; editor Columbia Law Rev., 1961-62; contbr. articles to legal jours. Air Force mem. Armed Services Procurement Regulation Com., 1964-65. Clubs: The Board Room (N.Y.C.); Scarsdale Golf. Home: 48 Hampton Rd Scarsdale NY 10583 Office: 90 Broad St New York NY 10004

KELLY, ERIC DAMIAN, lawyer, city planner; b. Pueblo, Colo., Mar. 16, 1947; s. William Bret and Patricia Ruth (Ducy) K.; m. Viana Eileen Rockel, 1980; children: Damian Charles, Eliza Jane, Valissitie Christina Heeren, Douglas Ray Heeren. BA, Williams Coll., 1969; JD, U. Pa., 1975, M of City Planning, 1975. Bar: Colo. 1975, U.S. Dist. Ct. 1976, U.S. Tax Ct. 1976, U.S. Ct. Appeals (10th cir.) 1986. Chief citizens' participation unit EPA, Region III, Phila., 1971-72; project planner Beckett New Town, N.J., 1972-73; v.p., project mgr. Rahenkamp Sachs Wells & Assocs., Inc., Denver and Phila., 1973-76; sole practice, Pueblo, 1976-83; pres. Kelly & Potter, P.C., Pueblo, Albuquerque and Santa Fe, 1983—; adj. asst. prof. U. Colo. Coll. Architecture and Planning, 1976—, land use seminars Fed. Publs., Inc., 1976-84; instr. grad. sch. bus. U. So. Colo., 1986—; pres. Color Radio, Ltd., 1979—; sec., bd. dirs. Lodging Service Corp., 1980—; bd. dirs. Mar Tec Broadcasting Corp., Pueblo Growth Corp., Wildflower, Inc. Author: Land Use Controls, 1976-80, 82; editor, prin. author: The Roadtripper, 1969; contbr. articles to profl. planning and legal jours. Bd. dirs. Broadway Theatre League, Pueblo, 1976-77, Pueblo Beautiful Assn., 1978-82, Better Bus. Bur., 1988; trustee Sangre de Cristo Arts and Conf. Ctr., 1981—, chmn. 1986; trustee Christ Congl. Ch., 1982-83. Served with U.S. Army, 1969-71. Named Outstanding Student, Am. Inst. Planners, 1976. Mem. Am. Inst. Cert. Planners (charter), Am. Planning Assn., Urban Land Inst., ABA, Colo. Bar Assn., Denver Bar Assn., Pueblo County Bar Assn., Williams Coll. Alumni Assn. (class sec. 1969-74, regional sec. 1980-82, class agt. 1985—). Democrat. Club: Pueblo Country. Lodge: Rotary (local dir. 1988, v.p. 1988—). Office: 200 E Abriendo Ave Pueblo CO 81004

KELLY, FREDERICK THOMAS, marketing and sales executive; b. N.Y.C., July 28, 1943; s. Robert Frederick and Catherine Josephine (Gurry) K.; m. Barbara Ann Poggi, Aug. 14, 1966; children: Susan, Lynda, Laurie, Scott. BS, Hofstra U., 1966; MS, Am. U., 1970. Programmer, instr. IBM, Gaithersburg, Md., 1966-70; mgr. tech. tng. Pace Applied Tech., Arlington, Va., 1970-72; mgr. tech. programs Wiley Systems, Bethesda, Md., 1972-73; mgr. resource devel. Comsat Labs., Clarksburg, Md., 1973-80; dir. electronic mail and Intelpost, Comsat Gen., Washington, 1980-85; dir. nat. accounts Comsat Tech. Products, 1986-87; regional dir. sales data network div. Contel/ASC, 1988—. Co-author: Strategy of Computer Selection. Mem. Nat. Capital Area Computer Measurement Group (past v.p.), Computer Measurement Group (past treas.). Office: 2700 Prosperity Ave Fairfax VA 22031

KELLY, GREGORY MAXWELL, mathematics educator; b. Sydney, New South Wales, Australia, June 5, 1930; s. Owen Stephen and Rita Margaret (McCauley) K.; m. Constance Imogen Datson, Nov. 5, 1960; children: Dominic John, Martin Paul, Catherine Louise, Simon Matthew. BSc, U. Sydney, 1951; BA, Cambridge (Eng.) U., 1953, PhD, 1957. Lectr. pure math. U. Sydney, 1957-60, sr. lectr., 1961-65, reader, 1965-66, prof., 1973—; prof. U. New South Wales, Sydney, 1967-73. Author: An Introduction to Algebra and Vector Geometry, 1972, Basic Concepts of Enriched Category Theory, 1982; editor Jour. of Pure and Applied Algebra., 1971—; contbr. over 60 articles to acad. jours. Fellow Australian Acad. Sci.; mem. Australian Math. Soc., Am. Mathematical Soc., Cambridge Philos. Soc., SE Asian Math. Soc. Home: 319 Mona Vale Rd, Saint Ives NSW 2075, Australia Office: U Sydney, Dept Pure Math, 2006 Sydney Australia

KELLY, JOHN HUBERT, diplomat; b. Fond du Lac, Wis., July 20, 1939; s. James Daniel and Clarice L. Kelly; 1 child, David Snowdon. BA, Emory U., 1961; advanced studies cert., Georgetown U., 1982. Vice consul Am. Consulate, Adana, Turkey, 1965-66; Am. consul Am. Consulate, Songkhla, Thailand, 1968-69, third sec. Am. Embassy, Ankara, Turkey, 1966-67; second sec. Am. Embassy, Bangkok, Thailand, 1968-69; first sec. Am. Embassy, Paris, 1976-80; U.S. ambassador Am. Embassy, Beirut, 1986—; fgn. service Dept. of State, Washington, 1972-76, dep. exec. sec., 1980-81, dep. asst. sec. of state, 1982-85. Adv. council mem. Una Chapman Cox Found., 1982-86. Mem. Council on Fgn. Relations, Am. Fgn. Service Assn. Office: care State Dept Am Embassy Beirut 2201 C St NW Washington DC 20520

KELLY, JOHN JAMES, lawyer; b. Rockville Centre, N.Y., July 4, 1949; s. John James Sr. and Eleanor Grace (Vann) K.; m. Clara Sarah Gussin; 1 child, John James III. AB in Govt., Georgetown U., 1971, JD, 1975. Bar: Pa. 1976, D.C. 1979, U.S. Dist. Ct. D.C. 1980, U.S. Claims Ct. 1982, U.S. Ct. Appeals (D.C. cir.) 1980, U.S. Ct. Appeals (fed. cir.) 1982. Law clk. to judge U.S. Dist. Ct., Washington, 1975-77; assoc. Corcoran, Youngman & Rowe, Washington, 1977-80; assoc. Capell, Howard, Knabe & Cobbs, Washington, 1980-83; assoc. Loomis, Owen, Fellman & Howe, Washington, 1983-86; ptnr., 1986—; mem. Jud. Conf. Fed. Cir., Washington, 1988. Contbr. articles to legal publs. Mem. D.C. Bar, Pa. Bar Assn., ABA, Fed. Bar Assn. Democrat. Roman Catholic. Club: Metropolitan. Office: Loomis Owen Fellman & Howe 2020 K St NW Washington DC 20006

KELLY, JOHN LOVE, public relations executive; b. N.Y.C., Jan. 30, 1924; s. Joseph John McDermott and Mary Florence Keenan (Love) K.; m. Helen M. Griffin Hanrahan, June 28, 1952; children: Janet Ann Kelly Alegi, J. Scott. BS, St. Peter's Coll., 1951. Buyer exec. tng. program Macy's, N.Y.C., 1951-53; mktg. exec. Sanforized div. Cluett Peabody Co., N.Y.C., 1953-58; advt. account exec. Batton, Barton, Durstine & Osborn, N.Y.C., 1958-59; advt. mgr. Am. Cyanamid Co., N.Y.C., 1959-64; dir. advt. Fiber div. FMC Corp., N.Y.C., 1964-84; v.p., dir. public relations and communications Avtex Fibers Inc., N.Y.C., 1976—; bd. dirs. Kelhan Ltd. Cath. co-chmn. Peekskill area NCCJ, 1961-64, bd. dirs. Westchester County, 1969-79, nat. bd. dirs., 1966-69; trustee Mercy Coll., Dobbs Ferry, N.Y., 1965-69; trustee emeritus St. Peter's Coll.; councilman Town of Cortlandt (N.Y.), 1962-66, mem. Simon Wiesenthal Ctr., Am. Conf. for Irish Studies, Zoning Bd., 1971-74, mem. Bd. Ethics, 1975-79; mem. Cardinal's Com. of Laity, 1961-71; mem. Greater N.Y. Area council Boy Scouts Am., 1971-79. Mem. Public Relations Soc. Am., Assn. Nat. Advertisers, Public Relations Club N.Y., Man-made Fiber Producers Assn. (chmn. pub. relations com., edn. and pub. relations subcoms.), Bd. Trade N.Y. (textile sect., v.p. 1954-60), Am. Israel Friendship League, Am. Irish Hist. Soc., Internat. Platform Assn., St. Peter's Coll. Alumni Assn. (bd. dirs. 1959-65), Hudson Valley Gaelic Soc. Democrat. Roman Catholic. Clubs: The Univ., Garrison Golf. Home: 21 Furnace Woods Rd Cortlandt NY 10566 Office: 1185 Ave of Americas New York NY 10036

KELLY, JOHN TERENCE, architect; b. Elyria, Ohio, Jan. 27, 1922; s. Thomas Alo and Coletta Margaret (Conrad) K.; B.Arch., Carnegie Mellon U., 1949; M.Arch., Harvard U., 1951, M.Landscape Architecture (Charles Eliot Norton fellow), 1952. Prin., John Terence Kelly, architect, Cleve., 1954—; vis. critic, lectr. U. Mich., U. Cin., Case Western Res. U., McGill U. Bd. dirs. Nova. Served with inf. AUS, 1943-46. Fulbright fellow, Munich, Germany, 1953. Recipient Cleve. Arts prize in Architecture, 1968, Hist. Bldg. award Architects Society of Ohio, 1986. Mem. AIA (nat. com. on design), Am. Inst. Landscape Architects, Am. Inst. Planners, Am. Soc. Planning Ofcls., Western Res. Hist. Soc. Home: 2646 N Moreland Blvd Cleveland OH 44120 Office: 13125 Shaker Sq Cleveland OH 44120

KELLY, PAUL KNOX, investment banker; b. Boston, Feb. 18, 1940; s. Thomas Joseph and Rita Patricia Kelly; m. Nancy Lee Belden, July 17, 1978; 1 child, 3 stepchildren. A.B. in English, U. Pa., 1962; M.B.A. in Fin, Wharton Sch., 1964. Investment analyst bond dept. Prudential Ins. Co. Am., 1964-65; asst. treas. Comml. Credit Co., 1965-68; v.p. First Boston Corp., N.Y.C., 1968-75; partner, mem. mgmt. com., dir. Prescott, Ball & Turben, Cleve., 1975-77; sr. v.p., dir. Butcher & Singer, Inc., 1977-78; exec. v.p., mem. exec. com., dir. Blyth Eastman Dillon & Co., N.Y.C., 1978-80; mng. dir. Merrill Lynch White Weld Capital Markets Group, N.Y.C., 1980-82; exec. v.p., dir. Dean Witter Reynolds, Inc., 1982-84; pres., dir. Quadrex Securities Corp., 1984-85, Peers & Co., 1985—; bd. dirs. THT Lloyd's Inc., Hydrox Corp., Ltd. (N.Z.), Chgo. Sun-Times Corp., Fidelco Indsl. Distbn. Corp. Clubs: Union (Cleve.); Chagrin Valley Hunt; Princeton (N.Y.C.). Home: 16 Edgemarth Hill Rd Westport CT 06880 Office: 1133 Ave of the Americas New York NY 10036

KELLY, PETRA KARIN, mem. West German Bundestag, political activist; b. Günzberg, Fed. Republic Germany, Nov. 29, 1947; came to U.S., 1960, returned to Europe, 1970; s. John E. Kelly (stepfather) and Marianne (Birle) Lehmann Kelly. B.A. cum laude, Sch. Internat. Service, Am. U., Washington, 1970; M.A., U. Amsterdam. Vol. Robert F. Kennedy presdl. campaign, 1968; then worked as vol. for Hubert H. Humphrey; research asst. Europa Inst., Netherlands, 1970-71; internship EEC Commn., Bourse de Recherche, Brussels, 1972, adminstrv. counsel secretariat, 1973-83; co-founder Die Grunen (Green Party), Fed. Republic Germany, 1979—, mem. exec. bd., 1980-82, speaker, 1983; elected to Bundestag as rep. of Die Grunen, 1st team in Parliament, Fed. Republic Germany, 1983-87, 2d team in Parliament, 1987; speaker Green Fraction in Parliament, 1983-84; mem. fgn. relations com., disarmament com., subcom. on European questions; adminstr. social affairs and health at economic and social com., 1972-83. Author: (with Jo Leinen) Life Principles: Okopax-The New Strength, 1983; Um Hoffhung Kämpfen, 1983; Hiroshima, 1984; Liebe gegen Schmerzen, 1986, Tibet: Ein vergewaltigtes hand, 1988; mem. editorial bd. Forum. Founder Grace P. Kelly Assn. for Promotion of Cancer Research for Children, Nuremberg, Fed. Republic Germany, 1973. Recipient Women Strike for Peace prize, 1983, Alternative Nobel prize, 1982; Woodrow Wilson fellow Am. U. Mem. Fed. Assn. Citizens for Environ. Protection, Darmstädter Signel and Humanistische Union, White Rose Found., Bertrand hummell Found., Elmwood Inst. Address: care Die Grunen, Bundeshaus, 5300 Bonn 1 Federal Republic of Germany

KELLY, ROBERT VINCENT, JR., metal company executive; b. Phila., Sept. 29, 1938; s. Robert Vincent and Catherine Mary (Hanley) K.; m. Margaret Cecilia Taylor, Feb. 11, 1961; children: Robert V. III, Christopher T., Michael J., Tasha Marie. BS in Indsl. Mgmt., St. Joseph's U., Phila., 1960; postgrad., Roosevelt U., 1965-66. Gen. foreman prodn. Republic Steel Corp., Chgo., 1963-68; supt. prodn. Phoenix Steel Corp., Phoenixville, Pa., 1969-73; gen. supt. ops. Continental Steel Corp., Kokomo, Ind., 1973-77; gen. mgr. Mac Steel div. Quanex Corp., Jackson, Mich., 1977-81; corp. v.p. Quanex Corp., Houston, 1979-82; pres. steel and bar group Quanex Corp., Jackson, 1982—; pres. La Salle Steel Co., Hammond, Ind., 1985—, Arbuckle Corp., Jackson, 1984—. Leader, com. mem. Boy Scouts Am., Jackson. Served to lt. USN, 1960-63. Mem. Am. Mgmt. Assn. (pres.), Inst. Indsl. Engrs., Assn. Iron and Steel Engrs., Am. Soc. for Metals, USN Inst. Clubs: Jackson Country. Home: 1734 Metzmont Dr Jackson MI 49203 Office: Quanex Corp Steel and Bar Group 1 Jackson Sq Jackson MI 49201

KELLY, SHANNON LYNN, stockbroker; b. Monterey, Calif., Sept. 10, 1956; d. Leonard Howard and Joni Dorothy (Twitchell) Higginbotham; m. Brian Andrew Kelly, Sept. 12, 1982. A.A., U. South Fla., 1974-76; B.A., U. Hawaii, 1979. Outer islands mgr. Gatliff Corp., Honolulu, 1979-81; stockbroker Paine Webber Jackson & Curtis, Honolulu, 1981—, also dir.; freelance poetry writer. Recipient Golden Poet award Am. Poetry Assn., 1987. Mem. Investment Soc. Hawaii (bd. dirs.). Republican, Honolulu Bd. Raltors.

KELLY, THOMAS JOSEPH, librarian service exec.; b. N.Y.C., Sept. 23, 1938; s. Daniel Paul and Margaret Catherine (Kelly) K.; BA, Manhattan Coll., 1961; MBA, Columbia U., 1964. Dir. client relations Quantum Sci. Corp., N.Y.C., 1964-67; library cons. Callaghan & Co., Wilmette, Ill., 1968-70; pres. Associated Library Service, Inc., N.Y.C., 1971—. N.Y. State Coll. scholar, 1956. Mem. ALA. Democrat. Roman Catholic. Office: 1556 3rd Ave New York NY 10128

KELLY, WILLIAM (EAGER), psychoanalyst; b. Nashville, Mar. 17, 1914; s. Charles Peck and Alice (Eager) K.; student Antioch Coll., 1932-34; B.S. in Edn., U. Va., 1938, M.D., 1945; m. Martha L. Parks, June 6, 1953; children: Susie Eager Kelly Sayegh, Penelope Ellen Bayley, Benjamin Alexander. Intern, Kings County Hosp., Bklyn., 1945-46; resident psychiatrist U. Va. Hosp., 1946, Inst. Pa. Hosp., Phila., 1948-50; sr. research psychiatrist VA Hosp., Coatesville, Pa., 1950-51; asst. vis. physician Phila. Gen. Hosp., 1951-59; staff psychiatrist Lakeland Mental Hosp., Camden, N.J., 1951-55; practice medicine specializing in psychiatry, Phila., 1951-83; mem. staff Jefferson Hosp., 1951-71; sr. attending staff Inst. Pa. Hosp., 1951-78, pres. staff, 1968-70, cons., 1978-87, hon. cons., 1987—; attending physician VA Hosp., Phila., 1955-66; cons. neuropsychiatrist Graterford Penitentiary, 1954-58; asst. cons. neuropsychiatrist Devereaux Schs., 1956-58; asst. neurologist Wills Eye Hosp., Phila., 1959-71; cons. psychiatry Valley Forge Gen. Hosp., 1965-74; staff psychiatrist Coatesville (Pa.) VA Hosp., 1974-77, dir. profl. edn., 1977-79, asso. chief of staff for edn., 1979-83; staff psychiatrist Western State Hosp., Staunton, Va., 1985—; instr. psychiatry U. Pa. Med. Sch., 1951-54; instr. neurology Jefferson Med. Coll., 1951-71, clin. prof. psychiatry, 1974-84, hon. prof. psychiatry, 1984—; asst. clin. prof. psychiatry Med. Coll. Pa., 1971-74; grad. psychoanalysis Phila. Assn. Psychoanalysis, 1964, mem., 1966—, dir. extension sch., 1967-73, mem. faculty, 1970-84, sec., 1976-79, bd. dirs., 1976-84; vis. scholar dept. behavioral medicine and psychiatry U. Va. Sch. Medicine, 1985—. Served to capt. M.C., AUS, 1946-48. Diplomate Am. Bd. Psychiatry and Neurology. Fellow Am. Psychiat. Assn., Phila. Psychiat. Soc., Phila. Coll. Physicians, ACP, Am. Coll. Psychiatrists, Am. Coll. Psychoanalysts; Am. Psychoanalytic Assn., AMA, Internat. Psychoanalytic Assn., Va. Psychoanalytic Soc. Editor: Barriers to the Efficacy of Psychiatric Treatment, 1981; The Changing Role of Rehabilitation Medicine in the Management of the Psychiatric Patient, 1983; Alzheimer's Disease and Related Disorders, 1984; Posttraumatic Stress Disorder and the War Veteran Patient, 1985. Home and Office: 2750 Leeds Ln Charlottesville VA 22901

KELMAN, BRYAN NIVISON, company director; b. Sydney, Australia, Dec. 8, 1925; s. William Nivison and Jeannie Craig (Ballantyne) K.; m. Winsome Barclay Shand, July 3, 1952; children—Christopher, Jill (dec.), John. B.Engring., Sydney U., 1949. Chmn., mng. dir. Ready Mixed Concrete U.K., London, 1964-66; sr. exec. officer CSR Ltd., Sydney, 1968-72, dep. gen. mgr., 1972-82, dir., 1973—, chief exec., 1983-87; chmn. Australian Commercial Disputes Centre, Sydney, policy council Australian Meat & Livestock Industry; dir. Macquarie Bank, Sydney, Australian Wool Corp., Melbourne, Fletcher Challenge Ltd., Auckland, New Zealand, Jennings Indsl. Ltd., Melbourne, Homestate Gold of Australia. Chmn. Trade Devel. Council, Canberra, 1978-81; active N.S.W. Art Gallery Trust, Sydney, 1983—, Econ. Planning Adv. Council, Canberra, 1983—, Bus. Council Australia, Melbourne, 1983—. Decorated comdr. Order of Brit. Empire, Order of Australia, 1986. Fellow Australian Acad. Tech. Scis., Inst. Engrs. (hon.); mem. Inst. Quarrying, Inst. Dirs. Presbyterian. Clubs: Union, Australian (Sydney); Melbourne; Queensland (Brisbane). Avocations: trout fishing; golf. Address: 15 Bangalla St, Turramurra New South Wales Australia 2000

KELSO, LOUIS ORTH, investment banker, economist; b. Denver, Dec. 4, 1913; s. Oren S. and Nettie (Wolfe) K.; m. Betty Hawley (div.); children: Martha Jennifer Kelso Brookman, Katherine Elizabeth Balestreri; m. Patricia Hetter. BS cum laude, U. Colo., 1937, LLB, 1938; DSc, Araneta U., Manila, 1962; LLD, Tusculum Coll., Tenn., 1986. Bar: Colo. 1938, Calif. 1946. Assoc. Pershing Bosworth, Dick & Dawson, 1938-42; ptnr. Brobeck, Phleger & Harrison, 1946-58; sr. ptnr. Kelso, Cotton, Seligman & Ray, 1958-70; mng. dir. Louis O. Kelso, Inc., San Francisco, 1970-75; chmn. Kelso & Co., Inc. (mcht. bankers), San Francisco, Newport Beach and N.Y.C., 1975—; also dir. Kelso & Co., Inc. (mcht. bankers), San Francisco; assoc. prof. law U. Colo., 1946; pres. Kelso Inst. Study Econ. Systems, San Francisco; econ. policy advisor ESOP Assn. Am., Washington, 1983—. Author: (with Mortimer J. Adler) The Capitalist Manifesto, 1958, The New Capitalists, 1961, (with Patricia Hetter) Two-Factor Theory The Economics of Reality, 1967, (with Patricia Hetter Kelso) Democracy and Economic Power: Extending the ESOP Revolution, 1986. editor-in-chief Rocky Mountain Law Rev, 1938; contbr. articles to profl. jours. Bd. dirs. Inst. Philos. Research, Chgo.; founding trustee Crystal Springs Sch. Girls, Hillsborough, Calif. Served to lt. USNR, 1942-46. Mem. ABA, Calif. Bar Assn., San Francisco Bar Assn., San Francisco Com. Fgn. Relations. Clubs: Pacific-Union, Bohemian, Villa Taverna (San Francisco); Chicago. Address: 505 Sansome St Suite 1005 San Francisco CA 94111

KELTY, PAUL DAVID, physician; b. Louisville, Oct. 2, 1947; s. William Theadore and Mary Frances (Hinton) K.; m. Connie Darlene Wilkerson, Apr. 16, 1983. B.E.E., U. Louisville, 1970; M.S., Ohio State U., 1971; M.D., U. Louisville, 1978. Mem. tech. staff Bell Labs., Whippany, N.J., 1970-72; design engr. Gen. Electric Co., Louisville, 1972-74; intern St. Mary's Med. Center, Evansville, Ind., 1978-79, resident in ob-gyn, 1979-82; practice medicine, specializing in ob-gyn, Corydon, Ind., 1982—; clin. instr. Dept. Ob-Gyn U. Louisville (Ky.) Sch. Medicine, 1987— . Mem. AMA, Am. Fertility Soc., Am. Inst. Ultrasound in Medicine, N.Y. Acad. Scis., Sigma Xi, Phi Kappa Phi, Tau Beta Pi, Sigma Tau, Sigma Pi Sigma, Eta Kappa Nu, Gamma Beta Phi, Omicron Delta Kappa. Roman Catholic. Home: 1355 Park Ave Corydon IN 47112 Office: 2000 Edsel Ln Corydon IN 47112

KEMAL, YASAR, author; b. Adana, Turkey, 1923; s. Sadik and Nigar Gokceli; student primary; sch.; m. Thilda Serrero, 1952; 1 child, Rasit. Works include novels, short stories, articles. Author: (novels translated into English) Memed My Hawk, 1961; The Wind from the Plain, 1963; Anatolian Tales, 1968; They Burn the Thistles, 1973; Iron Earth, Copper Sky, 1974 (1st prize 14th Internat. Theatre Festival 1966); The Legend of Ararat, 1975; The Legend of the Thousand Bulls, 1976; The Undying Grass, 1977; The Lords of Akchasaz, Part 1: Murder in the Ironsmiths Market, 1979 (Madarali award Best Turkish Novel 1973); The Saga of a Seagull, 1981; The Sea-Crossed Fisherman, 1985, The Birds Have Also Gone, 1987; journalist. Imprisoned for polit. views, 1971, later released under gen. amnesty. Recipient Prix Mondial Cino del Duca, Paris, 1982, The Sedat Simavi Award for Lit., Istanbul, 1985; named Comdr. de la Légion d'Honneur de France, Paris, 1984. Mem. Turkish Writers Union (past pres.). Address: PK 14 Basinkoy, Istanbul Turkey

KEMLER, RAPHAEL LEONARD, thoracic surgeon; b. Hartford, Conn., Oct. 24, 1918; s. Louis Elliot and Esther (Wedeen) K.; m. Joan Ruth Rosen, Dec. 28, 1950; children—David Samuel, Louise Leah. B.A., Yale U., 1939, M.D., 1943. Diplomate Am. Bd. Surgery, Am. Bd. Thoracic and Cardiovascular Surgery. Intern in surgery, Barnes Hosp., St. Louis, 1943-44, resident in gen. surgery, 1944-45, 47, resident in thoracic surgery, 1947-48, fellow in thoracic surgery, 1948-49; practice medicine specializing in cardiovascular and thoracic surgery, Hartford, Conn., 1950—; asst. in surgery, Washington U. Sch. Medicine, 1944-47, asst. in thoracic surgery, 1947-49; asst. clin. prof. surgery U. Conn. Sch. Medicine, 1973-86, assoc. clin. prof., 1987—; active staff, attending thoracic surgeon Cedarcrest Hosp., 1949-76, McCook Meml. Hosp., 1955-68, attending thoracic surgeon and dir. cardiovascular and thoracic surgery Mt. Sinai Hosp., Hartford, corporator, 1987—; attending thoracic surgeon John Dempsey Hosp., Farmington, Conn.; assoc. thoracic and cardiovascular surgeon, Hartford Hosp., sr. attending thoracic surgeon, dir. thoracic surgery New Britain Gen. Hosp.; courtesy staff St. Francis Hosp.; cons. thoracic surgery U.S. VA Hosp., Middlesex Meml. Hosp., Winsted Meml. Hosp., Meriden Hosp., New Britain Meml. Hosp., Conn. Valley Hosp., Bristol Hosp., Rockville Gen. Hosp., Charlotte Hungerford Hosp., Bradley Meml. Hosp., Newington Children's Hosp., Backus Hosp., Laurel Heights Hosp., Manchester Meml. Hosp.; mem. adv. bd. Security Bank & Trust Co., West Hartford, Conn., 1979. Contbr. writings to profl. publs. in field, papers to profl. confs. Bd. dirs. Greater Hartford Community Council, 1975-77, Greater Hartford Jewish Fedn., 1977-81, 85—, chmn. physicians div., 1980, life trustee; bd. dirs. Emanuel Synagogue, pres., 1970-72, life mem.; rep. to Assembly Yale Alumni, 1978-80. Mem. Exec. Com. Yale Alumni in Medicine, 1980-84, nat. fund chmn., 1986—. Served to lt. (j.g.) USNR M.C., 1945-47. Fellow Am. Coll. Chest Physicians, Am. Coll. Cardiology, Am. Coll. Angiology; mem. AMA, Am. Thoracic Soc., Conn. State Med. Soc., Conn. Thoracic Soc. (pres. 1971-72), Hartford Med. Soc. (pres. 1970-71, Loving Cup award 1982), Hartford County Med. Assn. (bd. dirs. 1980—, pres.-elect 1987-88, pres. 1988-89), Am. Assn. Thoracic Surgery (sr.), Hartford County Lung Assn. (bd. dirs. 1959-65), Am. Heart Assn. Greater Hartford (bd. dirs. 1958-63), Soc. Thoracic Surgeons (founding, sr.). Democrat. Jewish. Clubs: Tumblebrook Country (Bloomfield, Conn.), Hartford. Home: 65 Norwood Rd West Hartford CT 06117 Office: 1000 Asylum Ave Hartford CT 06105

KEMMERER, DONALD LORENZO, economics educator; b. Manila, Dec. 24, 1905; s. Edwin Walter and Rachel (Dickele) K.; m. Mirjane Strong, Nov. 27, 1934; children: Jane S., Edwin Walter II. A.B., Princeton U., 1927, A.M., 1931, Ph.D., 1934. Asst. sec. to fin. adv. commns. to Chile, 1925, Poland, 1926, China, 1929; instr. econs. Lehigh U., 1934-37; assoc. U. Ill., 1937-39, asst. prof., 1939-45, assoc. prof., 1945-49, prof. econs., 1949-73, emeritus, 1973—, dir. Ctr. for Econ. Edn., 1981-83; vis. prof. NYU, summer 1952, U. Melbourne, Australia, 1958; cons. Kabul U., Afghanistan, 1959; Fulbright prof. U. Montpellier, France, 1960, U. Munich, 1964; econ. adviser Pa. R.R., 1945, Investors Mgmt. Co., 1950-57; dir. mut. funds Anchor Corp., 1957-75; chmn. bd. Univ. Fed. Savs. and Loan Assn., 1972-75; Cons. European Productivity Agy., 1955; v.p. Economists Nat. Com. Monetary Policy, 1957-67, pres., 1967-70; mem. U.S. Assay Com., 1967. Author: Path to Freedom, 1940, (with E.L. Bogart) Economic History of American People, 1942, rev., 1947, (with E.W. Kemmerer) ABC of Federal Reserve System, 12th edit., 1950, (with R.H. Blodgett) Comparative Economic Development, 1956, (with C.C. Jones) American Economic History, 1957, rev. edit., 1959, John E. Rovensky, Banker and Industrialist, 1977; contbr. articles to profl. jours. Econ. adviser Republican platform planning com., 1944; pres. Lincoln Ednl. Found., 1958-84; bd. dirs. Am. Econ. Found., 1977-83, Am. Inst. Econ. Research, 1977-79, 81-87. Mem. Midwest Econ. Assn. (2d v.p. 1950), Am. Econ. Assn., Am. Hist. Assn., Orgn. Am. Historians, Bus. History Conf. (pres. 1976), Econ. Hist. Assn., Com. Monetary Research and Edn. (pres. 1970-80), Univ. Profs. for Acad. Order (pres. 1972, treas. 1978-84), Phi Beta Kappa, Beta Gamma Sigma. Clubs: Mont Pelerin, Am. Alpine, Champaign Country; Princeton (N.Y.C., Chgo.). Lodge: Rotary. Home: 1006 W Armory Ave Champaign IL 61821

KEMMIS, PETER ARTHUR JOHN BETTY, publishing executive; b. London, Aug. 11, 1936; s. Frederick Arthur and Margaret Myrtle (Morris) B.; m. Sarah Margaret Mason, Apr. 1, 1967; children: Lucy, Karen, Adam. BA, Cambridge (Eng.) U., 1957. Editorial dir. B.T. Batsford Ltd., London, 1968-74, mng. dir., 1974—. Chmn. Barnes Liberals, London. Fellow Royal Soc. Arts; mem. Pub.'s Assn. Democrat. Roman Catholic. Office: BT Batsford Ltd, 4 Fitzhardinge St, London W1H 0AH, England

KEMP, HILDA THIGPEN, educator; b. Henderson, N.C., Oct. 16, 1927; d. Zeno E. and Carrie B. (Wilkins) Thigpen; m. Jerahn T. Kemp, June 7, 1952 (div.); children—Jerahn T. III, Jeannette, Jon. B.S., St. Paul's Coll., 1950; M.S., Ind. U., 1970. Tchr., N.C. Pub. Schs., 1951-52, Palmer Inst., Sedalia, N.C., 1952-53, Warrenton, Ga., 1953-55; tchr. Monroe County Community Schs., Bloomington, Ind., 1969—. Mem. NEA, MCCSC (chairperson found., discussion council), Ind. Tchrs. Assn., Monroe County Edn. Assn. (discussion council), Delta Sigma Theta. Episcopalian. Club: Order Eastern Star. Home: PO Box 1184 Bloomington IN 47402

KEMP, JUNE, employment specialist, educator; b. Homestead, Pa., Dec. 16, 1933; d. Patrick H. and Gladys Naomi (Pifer) Cloherty; adopted d. William P. and Grace Kemp; m. Raymond Vargay, Apr. 21, 1953 (div. 1965); 1 child, Rose Marie. B.A. in Sociology, Fla. Internat. U., 1976, B.A. in Religion, 1978, M.P.A., 1980. Sec. U.S. Air Force, various bases, 1959-84; adj. prof. Miami-Dade Community Coll., Fla., 1980-82; equal employment opportunity staffing specialist U.S. Air Force, Homestead AFB, Fla., 1984—. Leader, cons. Girl Scouts U.S.A., 1952—; lay asst. St. Peter's Luth. Ch., Miami, Sunday sch. tchr., 1974-85, mem. ch. council, women's group, 1988—; bd. dirs. Dade Hire the Handicapped Com., 1985-86. Recipient Outstanding Employee of Yr. award Homestead AFB, 1980, 84 (lectr. 1986—); Fed. Employee of Yr. award Fed. Exec. Bd., 1984. Mem. Am. Soc. Pub. Adminstrn., Am. Bus. Women's Assn. (community Service award 1982), AAUW, Nat. Assn. Retired Fed. Employees, Federally Employed Women, Air Force Assn., Nat. Assn. Female Execs., Irish Soc. of South Fla., Fla. Internat. U. Alumni Assn. (chmn. profl. devel., 1987—, mem. long range planning com.). Phi Lambda Pi. Republican. Lutheran. Club: Toastmasters. Lodge: Lions (vol. tour guide 1988). Avocation: Irish history. Home: 11350 SW 45th St Miami FL 33165

KEMP, MAURY PAGE, financial executive; b. El Paso, Tex., Nov. 25, 1929; s. Roland Gordon and Nora (Henderson) K.; m. Jean Jones, Mar. 30, 1955; children: Diane, Maury Page Jr. BBA, U. Tex., El Paso, 1952. Founder, chmn. Kemp Ford, Inc., El Paso, 1957—, Kemp Group, Inc., El Paso, 1967—, Kemp Chrysler Plymouth, Palm Springs, Calif., 1986—, Kemp Nissan, Palm Springs, 1986—, Kemp Mitsubishi, Palm Springs and El Paso, Tex., 1986—, Kemp Volkswagon-Audi, El Paso, 1987—, Kemp Volkswagon, Audi, Daihatsu, El Paso, 1987—; past owner Main Lincoln-Mercury, San Antonio, Mesilla Valley Lincoln-Mercury, Las Cruces, N. Mex., Selby Motors, Tucson, various car dealerships in Colo., Ariz., N. Mex., Tex., 1964-84; founder Triangle Elec. Supply Co., El Paso, 1986—. Past pres. bd. trustees El Paso Mus. Art; bd. dirs El Paso Indsl. Devel. Bd., Tex. Ind. Coll. Fund, El Paso Renaissance 400, El Paso Arts Alliance, El Paso Cancer Treatment Ctr.; past bd. dirs. United Fund, El Paso Boys Club, El Paso Symphony Assn., Goodwill Industries, El Paso Better Bus. Bur.; mem. vestry St. Clement's Episc. Ch., El Paso. Served with U.S. Army, 1952-54. Recipient Bus. Leadership and Achievement award U. Tex., El Paso, 1980, Outstanding Student award, 1985. Mem. Nat. Automobile Dealers Assn. (past alternate chmn.), Tex. Automobile Dealers Assn. (past dir.), Ford Dealers Advt. Fund (past chmn.), El Paso New Car Dealers Assn. (pres.), Employers Assn. El Paso. Clubs: El Paso Country, Coronado Country, The El Paso, Northwood Country (Dallas); Thunderbird Country (Rancho Mirage, Calif.); The Argyle (San Antonio). Office: Kemp Ford Inc PO Box 1946 El Paso TX 79950

KEMP, TORBEN PETER, philosopher, educator; b. Vindum, Jutland, Denmark, Jan. 24, 1937; s. Svend Carl Hartvig and Birgitte Augusta (Gøtzsche) K.; m. Inge Genefke, July 9, 1965. Grad. in Theology, U. Aarhus, Denmark, 1964; Doctorate in Theology, U. Copenhagen, 1973. Assoc. prof. philosophy U. Copenhagen, 1972—, dept. head, 1979-81, vice-chmn. dept., 1981-84, head Ctr. Philosophy of Tech., 1986-87 ; U. Copenhagen del. to Inter-Univ. Ctr., Dubrovnik, Yugoslavakia, 1979— ; pres. Nordic Inst. for Philosophy, 1980—, Acad. Applied Philosophy, 1986-88 ; mem. collective bd., co-founder Filosofisk Forum, Copenhagen, 1980—; Waerner-prof. U. Gothenburg, Sweden, 1987-88; Author: Sprogets Dimensioner, 1972; Theorie de l'Engagement, 2 vols., 1973; Traek af Nutidens Taenkning, 1977; Marxismen i Frankrig, 1978; Døden og Maskinen, 1981; (with P. Ph. Druet and G. Thill) Technologies et Societes, 1980, Éthique et Médecine, 1987. Recipient Rosenkjaerprisen, Danish Radio, 1972. Office: Univ Copenhagen Dept Philosophy, Njalsgade 80, DK 2300 Copenhagen Denmark

KEMP, WILLIAM, chemistry educator; b. Glasgow, Scotland, Aug. 15, 1932; s. William and Cecilia (Rutherford) K.; m. Louisa Jennette McLelland, June 28, 1957; children: Ian, Gillian, Derek. BSc, Glasgow U., 1953, PhD, 1956. Tech. officer ICI, Ardrossan, Scotland, 1956-58; lectr. in chemistry Paisley (Scotland) Coll. Tech., 1958-60, Heriot-Watt U., Edinburgh, Scotland, 1960—; assessor Scottish Vocat. Edn. Council, 1970—; cons. Chem. Consultancy Services, Edinburgh, 1980—. Author: Practical Organic Chemistry, 1967, Qualitative Organic Analysis, 1986, NMR in Chemistry, 1986, Organic Spectroscopy, 1987; contbr. numerous articles to chem. jours. Fellow Royal Soc. Chemistry. Home: 1 Braidmount View, Edinburgh EH10 6JL, Scotland Office: Heriot-Watt U, Chemistry Dept Riccarton-Currie, Edinburgh EH14 4AS, Scotland

KEMPE, ROBERT ARON, venture management executive; b. Mpls., Mar. 6, 1922; s. Walter A. and Madge (Stoker) K.; m. Virginia Lou Wiseman, June 21, 1946; children: Mark A., Katherine A. BS in Chem. Engring., U. Minn., 1943; postgrad. metallurgy, bus. adminstrn., Case Western Res. U., 1946-49 Various positions TRW, Inc., Cleve., 1943-53, div. sales mgr., 1953; v.p. Metalphoto Corp., Cleve., 1954-63, pres., 1963-71, pres. Allied Decals, Inc., affiliate, Cleve., 1963-68; v.p., treas. Horizons Research Inc., 1970-71; pres. Reuter-Stokes, Inc. (subs. of GE Corp.), 1971-87; pres. Kempe Everest Co., Hudson, Ohio, 1987—; bd. dirs. Horizon Research Inc., Bicron Corp., Centrak Corp. Served to lt. (j.g.) USNR, 1944-46, PTO. Mem. Am. Nuclear Soc. (vice chmn. No. Ohio sect.), Am. Soc. Metals. Sigma Chi. Club: Chemists (N.Y.C.); Country of Hudson (Ohio). Contbr. articles to profl. jours. Patentee in field. Home: 242 E Streetsboro St Hudson OH 44236 Office: Kempe Everest Co 10 W Streetboro St Hudson OH 44236

KEMPER, MARLYN J., information scientist; b. Balt., Mar. 26, 1943; d. Louis and Augusta Louise (Jacobs) Janofsky; m. Bennett I. Kemper, Aug. 1, 1965; children—Alex Randall, Gari Hament, Jason Myles. B.A., Finch Coll., 1964; M.A. in Anthropology, Temple U., Phila., 1970; M.A. in Library Sci., U. S. Fla., 1983; D. in Info. Sci., Nova U., 1986. Dir., Hist. Broward County Preservation Bd., Hollywood, Fla., 1979-87; automated systems librarian Broward County Main Library, Ft. Lauderdale, Fla., 1983-86; asst. prof., dir. info. sci. doctoral program Nova U., Ft. Lauderdale, 1987—. Pub. info. officer Broward County Hist. Commn., 1975-79. Vice chmn. Broward County Library Adv. Bd., 1987—. Recipient Judge L. Clayton Nance award, 1977; Broward County Hist. Commn. award, 1979. Mem. ALA, IEEE, Am. Soc. for Info. Sci., Spl. Libraries Assn., Assn. Computing Machinery, Info. Industry Assn., Beta Phi Mu, Phi Kappa Phi . Author: A Comprehensive Documented History of the City of Pompano Beach, 1982 A Comprehensive History of Dania 1983, Hallandale, 1984, Deerfield Beach, 1985, Plantation, 1986, Davie, 1987, Networking: Choosing A Lan Path to Interconnection, 1987, A Comprehensive History of Davie, 1987; author weekly columns Ft. Lauderdale News, 1975-79; contbr. articles to Microcomputer Environment: Management Issues and articles to profl. jours. Vice chmn. Broward County Library, 1987—. Home: 2845 NE 35th St Fort Lauderdale FL 33306 Office: Nova U Info Sci Dept Parker Bldg 3301 College Ave Fort Lauderdale FL 33314

KEMPER, WALKER WARDER, JR., dentist, educator; b. Indpls., Aug. 26, 1924; s. Walker Warder Sr. and Margaret Louise (Mast) K.; m. Janet Morene Cottingham, June 10, 1950 (div. Oct. 1973); children—Walker Warder III, Todd Geller; m. Stephanie Ann Brean, June 24, 1978; stepchildren—Jeffrey L., Michael L., Scott L. B.S., Butler U., 1949; D.D.S., Ind. U., 1953, M.Sci. Dentistry, 1965. Clin. instr. Ind. U., Indpls., 1953-65; practice dentistry specializing in prosthodontics, Indpls., 1953—; dentistry prof., Ind. U., 1979-87; chief dental sect. St. Vincent Hosp. and Health Care Ctr., 1976-86, exec. com., 1976-86; mem. Ind. State Bd. Dental Examiners, 1971-77; dental dir. Marquette Manor Retirement Home, Indpls., 1975—; Peerview Inc. of Ind. Active in Ind. U. Century Club, Indpls., 1968—, Butler U. Pres.'s Club, 1966—; bd. dirs. Little Read Door Cancer Soc., 1970-74, Paul Coble Post, Am. Legion; chmn. Boys State, 1978-79. Served to staff sgt. USAF, 1943-46. Mem. ADA, John F. Johnston Soc. (pres. 1982, exec. com. 1977-86), Ind. State Dental Assn., Indpls. Dist. Dental Assn. (pres. 1970-71, Honor Dentist of Yr., 1988), Am. Coll. Dentists (pres. Ind. sect. 1988-89), Am. Acad. Crown and Bridge, Am. Acad. Dental Medicine, East Africa Hunters Assn., Safari Club Internat. (prt. (pres. 1982-83 Ind. chapt.), Game Conservation Internat. (Game Coin) (life), Adult Firecrafter, Phi Delta Theta, Omicron Kappa Upsilon (Dental hon.), Psi Omega. Republican. Methodist. Clubs: Meridian Hills Country, Columbia (Indpls.). Avocations: big game hunting, fishing, scuba diving, swimming, skiing, golfing. Home: 7574 N Morningside Dr Indianapolis IN 46240 Office: 8402 N Harcourt Rd Suite 404 Indianapolis IN 46260

KEMPF, PAUL STUART, optics company executive; b. Dubuque, Iowa, Apr. 25, 1918; s. Fred Ferdinand and Vera Content (Smith) K.; m. Dorothea Ruth Guenther, Dec. 16, 1943 (div. June 1966); 1 son, Karlton Guenther; m. Pilar M. Moreno, Dec. 1967; children: Karlos Alberto, Karla Pilar. Student, Iowa State Coll., 1936-37; B.A. cum laude, U. Iowa, 1941; M.B.A. with distinction, Harvard U., 1947. Asst. to mgr. indsl. relations Inland Steel Co., 1947-51; mgr. indsl. relations Inland Steel Products Co., 1951-54; dir. indsl. relations Pacific Mercury Electronics, 1954-56, Hoffman Electronics, 1956-57; v.p. personnel and indsl. relations Crane Co., 1957-59; dir. corp. indsl. relations Hughes Aircraft Co., 1959-64; pres. Western Optics, Inc., 1964-72, Metron Optics Inc., 1972—, Metron Marker Co., 1977—; instr.

UCLA, 1957. Served to lt. USNR, 1942-45. Recipient award for unusual and valuable contbn. to personnel adminstrn. Los Angeles Mchts. and Mfrs. Assn., 1956. Mem. Am. Chem. Soc., Soc. Photo-optical Instrumentation Engrs., Harvard Bus. Sch. Assn., Phi Beta Kappa, Theta Xi. Republican. Methodist. Office: PO Box 690 Solana Beach CA 92075

KEMPNER, ROBERT MAX WASILII, lawyer, political scientist; b. Freiburg, Germany, Oct. 17, 1899; came to U.S., 1939, naturalized; s. Walter K. and Lydia (Rabinowitsch) K.; m. Lydia Hahn (Benedicta Maria); children: Lucian Walter, Andréo Franklin. Student of law, polit. sci., pub. adminstrn., criminology, univs. of Berlin, Breslau, Freiburg (Germany); student of law, polit. sci., pub. adminstrn., criminology (Dr. of Law and Pub. Adminstrn.); student, U. Pa.; PhD (hon.), U. Osnabrück. Asst. to state atty. Berlin, 1926, judge mcpl. ct., 1927; superior govt. counselor (chief legal adviser of Prussian police system of 76,000 men; recommended suppression of Nazi party and prosecution of Hitler for high treason, fired and expatriated by Hitler; Ministry of Interior, Berlin; judge civil service tribunal Ministry of Interior, 1928-33; lectr. German Acad. Politics Sch. Social Work, Police Inst., Berlin, 1926-33; counselor internat. law and migration problems 1934-35; Pres. and prof. polit. sci. Fiorenza Coll., Florence, Italy, and Nice, France, 1936-39; research asso. and asst. Inst. Local and State Govt., U. Pa. (research on machinery of European dictatorships under Carnegie and Carl Schurz grants), 1939-42; expert to Fed. courts, espionage and fgn. agt. trials; expert cons. Dept. Justice, OSS and to sec. of War on legal, polit., police and intelligence techniques of European dictatorships and fgn. orgns. in, 1942-45; U.S. staff prosecutor in Nuremberg trials against Goering, Frick et al; research dir. U.S. prosecution, 1945-46; dep. U.S. chief of counsel for war crimes, chief prosecutor of German Reich cabinet mems., state secs. and diplomats Nuremberg investigation of Holocaust, 1946-49; expert cons. in internat. law; atty. indemnification matters and prosecution of war criminals 1951—; cons. Reichstag fire trial, 1960; cons. to Israel Govt. in Eichmann case, 1961; vis. prof. Erlangen; lectr. schs., colls., univs. and pvt. orgns. Author several books, primarily on Germany, 1931—, The Judgment in The Wilhelmstrassen Case, 1950, German Police Administration, 1953, Eichmann and Accomplices, 1961, SS Under Crossexamination, 1964, 80, The Warren Report in German Language, 1964, Edith Stein and Anne Frank-Two of Hundred thousand, 1968, The Third Reich under Crossexamination, 1969, The Murder of 35,000 Berlin Jews, 1971, American Courts in Germany, The Missed Hitler Stop, 1983, Memoirs: Prosecutor of an Epoch, 1983, The Kempner Bibliography, 1987; contbr. to profl. jours. Decorated German Grand Cross of Merit with star Fed. Republic Germany, Cross of Polonia Restituta.; recipient medal with Star and Schulterband, Fed. Republic Germany; medal Charles U., Prague, Carl von Ossietzky medal, Wilhelm Leuschner medal. Fellow U. Jerusalem.; Mem. Am. Polit. Sci. Assn., Am. Soc. for Internat. Law, German Bar. Home: 112 Lansdowne Ct Lansdowne PA 19050

KEMPTON, ALAN GEORGE, microbiologist; b. Toronto, Can., Aug. 21, 1932; s. Albert Edward and Velma Pearl (Williams) K.; m. Suzanne Philp, Aug. 13, 1955; children—Alan Scott, Kathryn Suzanne. B.S.A., U. Toronto, Ont., Can., 1954, M.S.A., 1956; Ph.D., Mich. State U., 1958. Research officer Agr. Can., Swift Current, Sask., Can., 1958-60; chemist U.S. Army, Natick, Mass., 1960-64; chief bacteriologist Can. Packers Ltd., Toronto, Ont., Can., 1964-66; prof. biology U. Waterloo, Ont., 1966—; cons. food industry. Bioadsorption patentee; contbr. articles to profl. jours. Served to lt. Royal Can. Navy Res., 1950-56, to capt. Royal Can. Armored Corps, 1958-60. Fellow AAAS; mem. N.Y. Acad. Scis., Soc. Indsl. Microbiology, Can. Soc. Microbiologists, Can. Coll. Microbiologists. Home: 117 Moccasin Dr, Waterloo, ON Canada N2L 4C2 Office: U Waterloo, University Ave, Waterloo, ON Canada N2L 3G1

KEMPTON, GRETA M., artist; b. Vienna, Austria; d. H.K. and Josephine K.; student Nat. Acad. Design, Art Students League, N.Y.C., 1930; 1 dau., Daisy Dickson. One woman shows include: Corcoran Gallery Art, Washington, 1949, Canton (Ohio) Art Inst., 1964, Coll. of Wooster, 1963, Akron Art League, 1962, Circle Gallery, Cleve., 1963, Truman Library, Independence, Mo., 1987, others; group shows: NAD, N.Y.C., Dowling Coll., Oakdale, N.Y., Human Resources Center, Albertson, N.Y., L.I. U.; represented in permanent collections: White House, Washington, Truman Library, Independence, Mo., U.S. Supreme Ct., Washington, Dept. Interior, Smithsonian Inst. Portrait Gallery, Treasury Dept., Washington, Pentagon, Valentine Mus., Richmond, Va., Georgetown U., Washington, Nat. Acad. Design, U.S. Capitol, numerous others. Fellow Royal Soc. Arts (London); mem. Soc. Arts and Letters (life); Nat. Arts Club, Corcoran Gallery (life), European Acad. Arts, Scis. and Humanities (corr.), Accademia Italia, Salmagundi Club. Address: 14 E 75th St New York NY 10021

KENAGA, EUGENE ELLIS, entomologist, ecologist; b. Midland, Mich., July 15, 1917; s. Ivan Arthur and Margaret Lena (Supe) K.; m. Joan Elisabeth Bailey, Oct. 12, 1940 (div.); m. Kathleen Virginia Walker, Oct. 20, 1979; children—Dennis K., Marcia B. Davis, David E. B.S., U. Mich., 1939; M.A., U. Kans., 1940; Ph.D., Tokyo U. Agrl., 1977. Entomologist, Dow Chem. Co., Midland, 1940-44, 46-54, group leader, 1954-66, environ. toxicologist, 1966-84, assoc. scientist, 1960-79, research scientist, 1979-82; mem. U.S. del. to U.S.-USSR Sci. Exchange Program Symposium, Tbilisi, Ga., USSR, 1976; mem. sci. rev. panel Nat. Library of Medicine, 1985-88; mem. adv. coms. WHO, 1971, EPA, 1975-82, 1987-88; Internat. Union Pure and 71, cons. in field; environ. cons., 1982-88; pres. Mich. Natural Resources Council, 1972-73. Author: Commercial and Experimental Insecticides, 1957-85; Birds, Birders and Birding in the Saginaw Bay Area, 1984; Avian and Mammalian Wildlife Toxicology, 1979, 81, Ancestors and Descendants of Charles Supe and Caroline Rademacher, 1987, Descendants of Johanes Goräge and John Kenege Sr. and Related Families, 1988; contbr. articles to profl. publs. Patentee in field. Founding pres. Midland Nature Club, 1953-55; Chippewa Nature Ctr., Midland, 1966-70; pres. Mich. Nat. Resources Council, 1972-73. Served to lt. USN, 1946-48. Recipient award creative advances Am. Chem. Soc., 1985. Mem. Soc. Environ. Toxicology and Chemistry (founding pres., Service award 1982; Founders award 1985), Am. Inst. Biol. Scis. (bd. dirs. 1981-83), Mich. Audubon Soc. (pres. 1962-64), Am. Ornithologist Union, Entomol. Soc. Am. (emeritus), Wilson Soc. Republican. Methodist. Club: Explorers' (N.Y.C.).

KENDAL, FELICITY, actress; b. Sept. 25, 1946; d. Geoffrey and Laura K.; 1 son. Ed. at 6 convents in India. First stage appearance in A Midsummer Night's Dream, 1947; grew up touring with parents' theatre co., appearing in such plays as Midsummer Night's Dream, Twelfth Night, The Merchant of Venice, Hamlet, India and Far East; London debut as Carla in Minor Murder, Savoy Theatre, 1967; other stage appearances include: Henry V, The Promise, Leicester, Eng., 1968, Back to Methuselah, Nat. Theatre, A Midsummer Night's Dream, Much Ado about Nothing, Regent's Park, London, 1970, Kean, Oxford, Eng., 1970, London, 1971, Romeo and Juliet, 1972; 'Tis Pity She's a Whore, 1972, The Three Arrows, 1972, The Norman Conquests, London, 1974, Once Upon a Time, Bristol, Eng., 1976, Arms and The Man, Greenwich, Eng., 1978, Clouds, London, 1978, Amadeus, Othello, On the Razzle, 1981, The Second Mrs. Tanqueray, The Real Thing, 1982, Made in Bangkok; TV appearances include: four series of The Good Life, Solo, Twelth Night, 1979, The Mistress; also plays, serials; films: Shakespeare Wallah, 1965, Valentino, 1976. Named Most Promising Newcomer, Variety Club, 1974, Best Actress, 1979; recipient Clarence Derwent award, 1980. Office: care Chatto & Linnit, Princes of Wales Theatre, Coventon St, London W1 England *

KENDALL, DONALD MCINTOSH, food products company executive; b. Sequim, Wash., Mar. 16, 1921; s. Carroll C. and Charlotte (McIntosh) K.; student Western Ky. State Coll., 1941-42; LL.D., Stetson U., 1971; m. Sigrid Ruedt von Collenberg, Dec. 22, 1965; children—Donna Lee Kendall Warren, Edward McDonnell, Donald McIntosh, Kent Collenberg. Spl. field rep. Pepsi-Cola Co., 1947-48, mgr. fountain sales, 1948-49, br. plant mgr. fountain sales, 1949-50, spl. rep., 1950-52, v.p. nat. accounts fountain sales, 1952-57, pres. Pepsi Cola Internat., 1953-63, pres. Pepsi-Cola Co., 1963-65 (merger with Frito-Lay 1965), PepsiCo, Inc., 1965—, pres., chief exec. officer, 1965-71, chmn. bd., chief exec. officer, 1971-86, also bd. dirs., dir., chmn. exec. com., 1986—; dir. Pan Am. Airways, Atlantic Richfield, Investors Diversified Services Mut. Fund Group. Chmn., NOVA Pharm., Lorimar-Telepictures, Nat. Alliance Businessmen, 1969-70, dir., 1970-78. Chmn., Nat. Center for Resource Recovery, Inc. 1970-76, dir., from 1976—; chmn. Emergency Com. for Am. Trade, 1969-76, mem., 1976—; dir. U.S.-USSR Trade and Econ. Council. Chmn., Am. Ballet Theatre Found., 1973-77, chmn. exec. com., 1977-83. Served to lt. AC, USNR, 1942-47. Mem. Internat. C. of C. (trustee council), C. of C. U.S. (dir., vice-chmn. 1980-81, chmn. 1981-82). Clubs: Blind Brook, Links, Lyford Cay, River, Round Hill. Office: Pepsico Inc Purchase NY 10577 *

KENDALL, JULIE ELLEN, information systems educator, researcher; b. Grand Rapids, Mich., Oct. 24, 1952; d. Vernon Ellsworth and Emma M. (Mattson) Tukua; m. Kenneth Edward Kendall, June 11, 1976. BA, U. Minn., 1976; MA, U. Wis., Milw., 1978; PhD, U. Nebr., 1984. Instr. U. Nebr., Lincoln, 1981-85, lectr., 1985-86; asst. prof. George Mason U., Fairfax, Va., 1986—. Author: Systems Analysis and Design, 1988; contbr. articles to profl. jours. Cons. Milw. Blood Ctr., 1977, Youth Service System, Lincoln, Nebr., 1980, ARC, Omaha, 1983-84; theatre critic U. Nebr., 1985. Mem. Acad. Mgmt., Inst. Decision Scis., Inst. Mgmt. Scis. Office: George Mason U Dept Decision Scis Fairfax VA 22030

KENDALL, KENNETH EDWARD, information systems educator, researcher; b. Buffalo, June 12, 1948; s. Edward J. and Julia A. (Bebenek) K.; m. Julie Ellen Tukua, June 11, 1976. BS, Canisius Coll., 1969; MBA, SUNY-Buffalo, 1970, PhD, 1974. Research assoc. SUNY-Buffalo, 1972-74; asst. prof. U. Minn., Mpls., 1974-76; U. Wis.-Milw., 1976-78; assoc. prof. mgmt. info. systems U. Nebr., Lincoln, 1978-86; prof. George Mason U., 1986-88, Rutgers U., Camden, N.J., 1988—; cons. ARC, 1969-74, 79—, Milw. Blood Ctr., 1977; dir. Expert System Research Ctr., 1986-88. Author: Systems Analysis and Design, 1988; contbr. chpts. to books, articles to profl. jours. Critic U. Nebr. Theatre. Grantee U. Minn., 1975, U. Wis., 1977, U. Nebr., 1981, 83. Mem. Inst. Mgmt. Scis., Ops. Research Soc. Am., Decision Scis. Inst. (publs. com. 1980-82), Soc. Info. and Mgmt. Avocations: microcomputers, photography, theatre, flying. Office: Rutgers U Sch Bus Camden NJ 08102

KENDALL, LLOYD DAVID, data processing company executive; b. LeCenter, Minn., Nov. 28, 1936; s. Roy Victor and Dorothy Marie (Poehler) K.; B.S. in Fgn. Service, Georgetown U., 1965; m. Janice Marie Gay, Apr. 4, 1980; children: Michael Henry, Kristin Marie. Mng. editor Nat. Inst. Municipal Law Officers, Washington, 1959-68; exec. v.p. Autocode, Inc., Washington, 1968-70, Autocomp, Inc., Bethesda, Md., 1970-75; dir. info. services Aspen Systems Corp. (subs. Am. Can Co.), Germantown, Md., 1975-76; v.p., gen. mgr. Informatics Gen. Corp., Rockville, Md., 1976-85, sr. staff, 1977-85; pres. publ. systems div. Sterling Software, Inc., 1985-86; v.p. bus. devel. Syntek Engring. & Computer Systems, Inc., 1986-88; pres. ATLIS Pub. Services, Inc., 1988—. Served with USAF, 1955-59. Recipient Outstanding Mgmt. award Informatics Gen. Corp., 1982. Mem. NRA, Nat. Trust Hist. Preservation, Nat. Geographic Soc., Minn. State Soc. Washington, D.C., Data Processing Mgmt. Assn., Nat. Assn. Watch and Clock Collectors, Graphic Communications Assn. Republican. Lutheran. Editor: Law and Computer Technology, 1968; assoc. editor Mcpl. Law Jour., Mcpl. Law Court Decisions, Mcpl. Law Ordinance Review, 1964-68. Home: 1312 Deep Run Ln Reston VA 22090 Office: 6110 Executive Blvd Rockville MD 20852

KENDALL, RICHARD HALE, investment company executive; b. Indpls., Mar. 24, 1930; s. Max L. and Elberta (Hodson) K.; A.B., Earlham Coll., 1952; M.B.A., Ind. U., 1953; m. Ann Woolley, Sept. 6, 1953; children—Michael F., Thomas H. Bus. mgr. Friends United Meeting, Richmond, Ind., 1953-59; v.p., treas. Honeggers & Co., Inc., Fairbury, Ill., 1959-68; v.p. Heath Tecna Corp., Kent, Wash., 1968-71; chmn. bd., treas., dir. Maplehurst Farms, Inc., Indpls., 1971-82; pres., chief exec. officer, treas., dir. Advanced Mktg. Systems Corp., Indpls., 1971-82; sec., dir. Sr. Trust Corp., Indpls., 1971-82; past pres., dir. Master Dairies, Inc.; chmn. bd., chief exec. officer, treas., dir. Maplehurst Deli-Bake, Inc., 1971-82; chmn. bd., chief exec. officer, dir. Maplehurst Deli-Bake/South, Inc., Carrollton, Ga., 1977-82; pres., dir. MW Investments, Inc., 1984-87; pres., chief exec. officer, dir. Ind. Fin. Investors, Inc., Indpls., 1983—; chmn. bd. Key Services Inc.; dir. Matchware Computer Services Ltd., 1984-87; Mem. nat. export expansion council U.S. Dept. Commerce, 1969-71; mem. spl. levy tax com. State Wash., 1970-71; bd. dirs. Greater Indpls. Progress Com., 1977; sec. Indpls. Econ. Devel. Commn., 1983—; bd. dirs. Ind. Soc. to Prevent Blindness, 1983—; bd. visitors Guilford Coll., 1983-86; chmn. adminstrn. and orgn. Highline Coll., 1970-71; trustee Earlham Coll., 1977-86, also mem. exec. com.; trustee Friends United Meeting, 1974-87; advisory council Conner Prairie Pioneer Settlement, 1977-78; dir., fin. com. Friends World Com. for Consultation, 1977-80; bd. dirs. Ind. Salvation Army, 1982-85, Central Ind. Blood Ctr. 1982—, Ruth Lilly Ctr. for Health Edn., 1982—, Friends Ednl. Fund for Negroes, 1981—. Mem. Milk Found. Indpls. (dir. 1971-83), Ind. State C. of C. (dir. small bus. council), Midwest Dairy Products Assn. (dir., v.p. pres. 1981-82). Clubs: Rotary (bd. dirs Rotary Found., Indpls.), Indianapolis (pres., dir.), Meridian Hills Country, Lake Wales Country (Fla.), Athletic, Riviera. Home: 7505 N Central Ave Meridian Hills Indianapolis IN 46240 Office: 151 N Delaware St, Suite 425 Indianapolis IN 46204

KENDALL, ROBERT LLEWELLYN, contractor; b. Mishawaka, Ind., May 3, 1923; s. Harold E. and Jessie (Pettengill) K.; student pub. schs., Cadillac, Mich.; m. Betty Louise Powers, July 23, 1943; children—Stephen, Jane, Kay, Holly, David, Roberta. Owner, Kendall Constrn. Co., Cadillac, 1945-63, Cadillac Lumber Co.; pres. Robert Kendall, Inc.; v.p. Hungerford Constrn. Co., Jackson, Mich. Mayor, Cadillac, 1953-55; mem. Wexford County Bd. Suprs., County Social Welfare Bd., County and City Planning Bds.; chmn. Bd. Edn., 1948-50; pres. Mich. Extended Care Bldg. Corp.; dir. phys. plant services, mem. adminstrv. staff Chelsea Community Hosp, to 1986; mgr. Robert L. Kendall and Assocs., 1986—. Served from pvt. to capt. USAAF, 1942-45; ETO. Mem. C. of C. (pres. 1958-60), Am. Soc. Hosp. Engring., Am. Soc. Profl. Cons. Am. Legion. Presbyterian (deacon). Club: Elks. Home: 340 Edward St Jackson MI 49201 Office: Chelsea Community Hosp 775 S Main St Chelsea MI 48110

KENDALL, WILLIAM DENIS, medical electronic equipment company executive; b. Halifax, Yorkshire, Eng., May 27, 1903; came to U.S., 1923, naturalized, 1957; s. Joe Willie and Sarah Alice (Fell) K.; m. Margaret Burden, May 22, 1952. Student, Halifax Tech. Coll., 1966-69; Ph.D., Calif. Western U., 1974. Chartered engr. Asst. chief insp. Budd Mfg. Co., 1929; dir. mfg. Citroen Motor Co., Paris, France, 1929-38; mng. dir. Brit. Mfg. & Research Co., mfr. aircraft cannons and shells, Grantham, Eng., 1938-45; cons. to Pentagon on high velocity small arms, 1940-45; exec. v.p. Brunswick (N.J.) Ordnance Plant, 1952-56; dir., v.p. operations Mack Trucks Co., 1952-55; pres., dir. Am. Marc, Inc., Los Angeles, 1955-61; pres. Dynapower Systems and Dynapower Medonics, Los Angeles, 1961-73; chmn., chief exec. Kendall Med. Internat., Inc., Los Angeles, 1973—; chmn. Steron Products Inc., 1983—; partner rheumatoid arthritis clinic, London; dir. A.M. Byers Co., Pitts. Mem. Churchill's War Cabinet Gun Bd., 1941-45, M.P., Grantham div. Kesteven and Rutland, 1942-50; councillor Grantham Town Council, 1945-52; Bd. govs. Kings Sch., Grantham, 1942-52. Served with Royal Fleet Aux., 1919-23. Decorated chevalier Oissam Alouite Cherifien; honoured by King George VI for heroic conduct in World War II; freeman City of London, 1942—; mem. Worshipful Co. Clockmakers. Fellow Royal Soc. Arts (London), Inst. Mech. Engrs., Inst. Automotive Engrs. Mem. Religious Soc. Friends (Quaker). Clubs: Mason (Pacific Palisades, Cal.) (32 deg., Shriner), Riviera Country (Pacific Palisades, Cal.); United British Service (Lowestoft, Eng.), Royal Norfolk and Suffolk Yacht (Lowestoft, Eng.). Home: 1319 N Doheny Dr Los Angeles CA 90069

KENDERDINE, JOHN MARSHALL, retired army officer, petroleum engineer; b. Ft. Worth, Dec. 6, 1912; s. Robert Leonard and Caroline (Raab) K.; m. Su Anne Carroll, Feb. 26, 1937; children—James Marshall, Su Carroll. B.S. in Petroleum Engring, Tex. A. and M. Coll., 1934; grad., Army War Coll., 1953, Advanced Mgmt. Program, Harvard, 1959, Exec. Decision Inst., 1961. Registered profl. engr., Tex. Petroleum engr. Gulf Oil Corp., 1934-37; br. mgr. Norvell-Wilder Supply Co., Midland, Tex., 1938-41; commd. 1st lt. AUS, 1941, advanced through grades to brig. gen., 1962; mil. logistician in France, Germany and U.S., World War II; spl. asst. to administr. War Assets Adminstrn., 1946; mil. staff and command assignments 1947-60; joint petroleum officer Europe, 1961; exec. dir. supply operations Def. Supply Agy., 1962-65; comdr. Def. Indsl. Supply Center, Phila., 1965-66, Def. Personnel Support Center, Phila., 1966-67; ret.; v.p. Scott Paper Co., 1967-70; chmn. C.F. Adams, Inc., Ft. Worth, 1970—; pres. Black Jack Oil Co. Contbr. articles to profl. jours. Decorated Legion of Merit, Commendation ribbon with 3 oak leaf clusters, D.S.M. Mem. Am. Logistics Assn., Assn. U.S. Army, Flight Safety Found., Armed Forces Communications and Electronics Assn. (dir. 1965), Commerce and Industry Council Phila., Phila. C. of C. (dir. 1966), Airline Passengers Assn. (adv. bd.). Clubs: Union League, Petroleum, Century II. Home: 3212 Chapparral Ln Fort Worth TX 76109 Office: C F Adams Inc PO Box 253 Fort Worth TX 76101

KENDIG, EDWIN LAWRENCE, JR., physician, educator; b. Victoria, Va., Nov. 12, 1911; s. Edwin Lawrence and Mary McGuire (Yates) K.; m. Emily Viginia Parker, Mar. 22, 1941; children: Anne Randolph (Mrs. R.F. Young), Mary Emily Corbin (Mrs. T.T. Rankin). B.A. magna cum laude, Hampden-Sydney Coll., 1932, B.S. magna cum laude, 1933, D.Sc. hon., 1971; M.D., U. Va., 1936. House officer Med. Coll. Va. Hosp., Richmond, Bellevue Hosp., N.Y.C., Babies Hosp., Wilmington, N.C., Johns Hopkins Hosp., Balt., 1936-40; instr. pediatrics Johns Hopkins U., 1944; practice medicine specializing in pediatrics Richmond, 1940—; dir. child chest clinic Med. Coll. Va., 1944—, prof. pediatrics, 1958—; mem. staff St. Mary's Hosp., Richmond, 1966—, chief of staff, 1966-67; mem. staff Chippenham Hosp., Stuart Circle Hosp.; cons. diseases of chest in children; William P. Buffum orator Brown U., 1979; Abraham Finkelstein Meml. lectr. U. Md., 1983; Derwin Cooper lectr. Duke U. 1984; Bakwin Meml. lectr., NYUúBellevue, 1986. Lectr., throughout the world; contbr. numerous articles on diseases of chest in children to profl. publs.; editor: Disorders of Respiratory Tract in Children, 1967, 72, 77, (with V. Chernick) Disorders of Respiratory Tract in children, 4th edit., 1983, (with C.F. Ferguson) Pediatric Otolaryngology, 1967; contbg. editor: books Current Pediatric Therapy, Gellis and Kagan, 10 edits., Antimicrobial Therapy, Kagan, 3 edits., Practice of Pediatrics, Kelley, Practice of Pediatrics, Maurer, Allergic Diseases of Infancy, Childhood and Adolescence, Bierman and Pearlman; mem. editorial bd. Pediatric Pulmonology; editorial adv. bd. Pediatric Annals; former mem. editorial bd. Pediatrics. Chmn. Richmond Bd. Health, 1961-69; bd. vistors U. Va., 1961-72; former mem. bd. dirs. Va. Hosp. Service Assn.; former ofcl. examiner Am. Bd. Pediatrics; mem. White House Conf. on Children and Youth, 1960; dir. emeritus Dominion Nat. Bank; pres. alumni adv. com. U. Va. Sch. Medicine, Charlottesville, 1974-75; past bd. dirs. Maymont Found., Richmond.; bd. dirs. Children's Hosp., Sheltering Arms Hosp. Recipient resolution of recognition Va. Health Commr., 1978; recipient Obici award Louise Obici Hosp., 1979, Bon Secours award St. Mary's Hosp., 1986; named an Outstanding Alumnus Sch. Medicine U. Va., 1986. Mem. Am. Acad. Pediatrics (past pres. Va. sect., chmn. sect. on diseases of chest, mem. exec. bd. 1971-78, nat. pres. 1978-79, Abraham Jacobi Meml. award with AMA, 1987), Va. Bd. Medicine (past pres.), Richmond Acad. Medicine (pres. 1962, chmn. bd. trustees 1963), Va. Pediatric Soc. (past pres.), Am. Pediatric Soc., AMA (pediatric residency rev. com.), So. Med. Assn., So. Soc. Pediatric Research, Internat. Pediatric Assn. (standing com., Internat. Pediatrics Assn. medal 1986), Med. Soc. Va. (editor Va. Med. Jour. 1982, resolution of recognition), Soc. of Cincinnati, Raven, Phi Beta Kappa, Alpha Omega Alpha, Tau Kappa Alpha, Kappa Sigma, Omicron Delta Kappa. Episcopalian. Clubs: Commonwealth, Country of Va; Farmington (Charlottesville). Home: 5008 Cary St Rd Richmond VA 23226 Office: Med Coll Va 5801 Bremo Rd Richmond VA 23226

KENDREW, JOHN COWDERY, former college president, molecular biologist; b. Oxford, Eng., Mar. 24, 1917; s. Wilfrid George and Evelyn May Graham (Sandberg) K.; B.A., Trinity Coll., Cambridge U., 1939, M.A., 1943, Ph.D., 1949, Sc.D., 1962 (hon. fellow 1972). With Ministry Aircraft Prodn., 1940-45; sci. adv. allied air comdr. in chief, SE Asia, 1944; dep. chmn. Med. Research Council Lab. for Molecular Biology, Cambridge U., 1947-75; fellow of Peterhouse, Cambridge U., 1947-75 (hon. fellow 1975); reader Davy-Faraday Lab., Royal Instn., London, 1954-68; dir.-gen. European Molecular Biology Lab., Heidelberg, Germany, 1975-82; pres. St. John's Coll., Oxford U., 1981-87 (hon. fellw 1987); editor-in-chief Jour. Molecular Biology, 1959-87. Mem. council UN U., 1980-86, chmn., 1983-85. Decorated knight bachelor and comdr. Order Brit. Empire; recipient (with Max Perutz) Nobel prize in chemistry, 1962. Fellow Royal Soc., 1960; fgn. asso. Nat. Acad. Scis. (U.S.); fgn. hon. mem. Am. Acad. Arts and Scis.; hon. mem. Am. Soc. Biol. Chemists; mem. Brit., Am. biophys. socs., Internat. Orgn. Pure and Applied Biophysics (pres. 1969), Internat. Council Sci. Unions (sec. gen. 1974-80, pres. 1983-88). In work with myoglobin, determined structure of a protein in general outline (1957) and atomic detail (1959); observed alpha-helix arrangement of the polypeptide chain, thereby confirming Pauling's earlier description. Home: Guildhall, 4 Church Lane, Linton, Cambridge CB1 6JX, England

KENDRICK, JAMES EARL, computer consulting company executive; b. Indpls., Sept. 12, 1940; s. John William and Mable E. (Colman) K.; B.A., Butler U., 1963; m. Carrie L. Fair, July 19, 1969; children: Carrie F., Leslie F., John F. Exec. dir. Knox County Econ. Opportunity Council, Barbourville, Ky., 1965-66; research scientist N.Y. U., 1967-68; mgr. Volt Info. Scis., Washington, 1968-71, Nat. Urban Coalition, 1972-74; pres. Kendrick & Co., Washington, 1974—. Recipient Rural Service award OEO, 1968; citation Washington chpt. Am. Soc. Tng. and Devel., 1971. Mem. Inst. Mgmt. Consultants (bd. dirs. Washington chpt.), CEO Club, Internat. Assn. Bus. Communicators, Soc. Profl. Mgmt. Cons., Met. Washington Bd. Trade, Sigma Delta Chi. Author: Community Energy Workbook, 1974; National Urban Agenda Survey, 1974; (video) Americans on the Move, 1984; (software) Help for PC DOS, 1985; contbr. articles to profl. jours. Episcopalian. Home: 1412 Dale Dr Silver Spring MD 20910 Office: Kendrick & Co 800 18th St NW Washington DC 20006

KENDRICK, PETER MURRAY, television company executive; b. Winchester, Mass., Oct. 8, 1936; s. Wallace Dolloff and Esther (Burke) K.; m. Grace Terry, June 17, 1967; children—Caroline, Timothy. BS in Bus. Adminstrn., Babson Coll., 1962. Office mgr. Am. Hosp. Supply Corp., Chgo. and Charlotte, N.C., 1962-65; registered rep. Hayden, Stone & Co., 1966-69; gen. mgr. Continental Cablevision, Concord, N.H. and Jackson, Mich., 1969-74; pres. New Eng. Cablevision, Portland, Maine, 1974-79; chmn. bd. New Eng. Cablevision, 1980; pres. Home Theater Network, Portland, 1977—; chmn. bd. Envirologic Data Corp., Portland, 1984-86; vice chmn. bd. dirs., pres., treas. Internat. Cablevision, Inc., Portland, Maine, 1987—; chmn. bd. Kendrick Corp., Portland, 1986—; chmn. bd. The Film Channel, Inc., Portland, 1987—. Trustee North Yarmouth Acad., Yarmouth, Maine, chmn. ann. giving campaign, 1986-87. Served with USAF, 1956-59. Recipient Highest Programming award Cable TV Nat. Assn., 1973, 86. Mem. New Eng. Cable TV Assn. (v.p. 1972, pres. 1975), Mich. Cable TV Assn. (v.p. 1973). Clubs: Portland Country, Portland Yacht. Home: Landing Woods Ln Falmouth Foreside ME 04105 Office: 465 Congress St Portland ME 04101

KENDRICK, RICHARD LOFTON, university administrator, consultant; b. Washington, Nov. 19, 1944; s. Hilary Herbert and Blanche (Lofton) K.; m. Anne Ritchie, Mar. 5, 1966; children—Shawn Elizabeth, Christopher Robert. BS in Bus. and Mktg., Va. Poly. Inst., 1971; postgrad. U. Ky., 1978-80. Adminstr., U.S. Army Security Agy., Washington, 1965-69; with credit, sales and adminstrv. depts U.S. Plywood-Champion Internat., Pa., N.C. and Va., 1971-77; purchasing dir. James Madison U., Harrisonburg, Va., 1977-78, fin. officer, 1978-85 ; cons. Systems and Computer Tech. Corp., Malvern, Pa., 1986; dir. fin. services, Hillsborough Community Coll. System, Tampa, Fla., 1986-87, agt. Mass Mut. Life Ins., Harrisonburg, Va., 1987-88; treas. U. Ark., Fayetteville, 1988—; credit cons. to plywood and lumber industry; cons. to higher edn.; home builder, designer World War II dioramas. Leader, treas. Boy Scouts Am., Harrisonburg, 1977-86; mem. Ashbury United Meth. Ch., 1975-77. Served with U.S. Army, 1965-69. Recipient New Idea award U.S. Plywood-Champion Internat., 1972; named Profl. Pub. Buyer, Nat. Inst. Govt. Purchasers, 1977. Mem. Am. Mktg. Assn., Nat. Assn. Accts., Nat. Assn. Coll. and Univ. Bus. Officers, Fin. Officers of State Colls. and Univs., So. Assn. Coll. and Univ. Bus. Officers, Internat. Platform Assn. Methodist. Clubs: Exchange (Harrisonburg). Home: 2200 Hummingbird Ln Fayetteville AR 72701 Office: U Ark 205 Administration Bldg Fayetteville AR 72701

KENEALLY, THOMAS MICHAEL, author; b. Australia, Oct. 7, 1935; s. Edmund Thomas and Elsie Margaret (Coyle) K.; m. Judith Mary Martin, Aug. 21, 1965; children—Margaret Ann, Jane Rebecca. Ed. St. Patrick's Coll., Strathfield, N.S.W. Author numerous novels including: Bring Larks and Heroes, 1968, A Dutiful Daughter, 1971, The Chant of Jimmie Blacksmith, 1972, Blood Red, Sister Rose, 1974, Gossip From the Forest, 1976, Moses the Lawgiver, 1976, Season in Purgatory, 1977, A Victim of the Aurora, 1978, Passenger, 1978, Confederates, 1979, Schindler's List, 1982, Bullie's House, 1985, Ned Kelly and the City of the Bees, 1985, A Family Madness, 1985, The Playmaker, 1987. Pres. Nat. Book Council Australia; mem. Constn. Commn. Australia., literary arts bd. Australia Council. Fellow Royal Soc. Lit. (London); mem. PEN, Australian Soc. Authors (chmn.). Office: care Tessa Sayle Agy, 11 Jubilee Pl, London SW3 3TE, England Other: care Hodder and Stoughton, 47 Bedford Sq, London UC 3DP England

KENIG, NOE, electronics company executive; b. Warsaw, Poland, June 5, 1923; came to U.S., 1974; naturalized, 1980; s. Lazaro Hersz and Felisa (Elenbogen) K.; diploma mech. and elec. engring., Nat. U. La Plata, Buenos Aires, Argentina, 1951; mech. technologist diploma, Nat. Indsl. Sch. Luis M. Huergo, Buenos Aires, 1951; m. Ida Melnik, Apr. 17, 1948; children—Jorge Alberto, Carlos Eduardo. Licensee, Westinghouse Electric Corp., Argentina, 1941-49, Bendix Home Appliance Corp., Argentina, 1949-67; dir. Philco Argentina Corp., 1959-62; asst. pres., group gen. mgr. subs. Nat. Distillers and Chem. Corp., Argentina, 1968-72; with Motorola Inc., Schaumburg, Ill., 1972—, v.p., dir. corp. multinat. ops., 1983, dir. subs., pres. Mex. subs. Office: 1303 E Algonquin Rd Schaumburg IL 60196

KENILOREA, SIR PETER, prime minister of Solomon Islands; b. Takataka, Malaita, Solomon Islands, May 23, 1943; m. Margaret Kwanairara, 1971; 7 children. Diploma in Edn., Tchrs. Coll. in New Zealand. Schoolmaster, King George VI Secondary Sch., 1968-70; asst. sec. fin., 1971; adminstrv. officer, dist. adminstr., 1971-73; lands officer, 1973-74; dep. sec. to cabinet and to chief minister, 1974-75; dist. commr., Eastern Solomons, 1975-76; mem. Legis. Assembly, 1976, 78; chief minister of Solomon Islands, 1976-78; prime minister of Solomon Islands, 1978-81, 84—; dep. prime minister, minister for natural resources; minister of fgn. affairs, 1988—; mem. Nat. Parliament, 1976; apptd. mem. Privy Council. Contbr. articles to polit. and sci. publs. Decorated knight, 1982; recipient Queen's Silver Jubilee medal, 1977, Solomon Islands Independence medal, 1978. Avocations: reading; sports. Address: Office of Dep Prime Minister, Honiara Guadalcanal, Solomon Islands

KENLEY, ELIZABETH SUE, oil company official; b. Kansas City, Mo., Oct. 4, 1945; d. Ralph Raymond and Josephine Allen (Wells) Cummins. B.S., Kans. U., 1968, M.P.A., 1972. Asst. city mgr. Winfield (Kans.), 1968-70; adminstrv. asst. Kansas City (Mo.) Police Dept., 1970; cons., 1973; with E.I. DuPont Co., Kingwood, Tex., 1974—, regional tech. buyer, 1977-79, cons., plant start up, 1979, regional tech. buyer, 1980-82; internat. project buyer Aramco, Houston, 1982-86, quality assurance liaison, 1986—, also supr. refinery and no. area projects unit. Mem. Houston C. of C., Am. Mgmt. Assn. Home: 9632 Briarforest Houston TX 77063 Office: 9009 West Loop South Houston TX 77096

KENNEDY, CARL HUBERT, III, quality assurance specialist; b. Phila., Oct. 17, 1951; s. Carl Hubert Jr. and Doris E. (Rush) K.; m. Deborah A. Foster, Apr. 23, 1977; 1 child, Carl Hubert IV. BS in Biology, Tusculum Coll., 1975; postgrad., Phila. Coll. Textile and Sci., 1976-77. Supr. mfg. Yarrington Mills Corp., Hatboro, Pa., 1975-78, Therisa Friedman and Sons, Phila., 1978-79; supr. processing R.T. French Co., Souderton, Pa., 1979-84, assoc. quality assurance, Rochester, N.Y., 1984-87, sr. auditor quality assurance, 1988—. Chmn. Warwick Twp. Bd. Parks and Recreation, 1983. Mem. Aircraft Owners and Pilots Assn., Inst. Food Technologists. Republican. Roman Catholic. Home: 6 Heatherwood Rd Fairport NY 14450 Office: 1 Mustard St Rochester NY 14609

KENNEDY, CHARLES ALLEN, lawyer; b. Maysville, Ky., Dec. 11, 1940; s. Elmer Earl and Mary Frances Kennedy; m. Patricia Ann Louderback, Dec. 9, 1961; 1 child, Mimi Mignon. A.B., Morehead State Coll., 1965, M.A. in Edn., 1968; J.D., U. Akron, 1969; LL.M., George Washington U., 1974. Bar: Ohio 1969. Asst. cashier Citizens Bank, Felicity, Ohio, 1961-63; tchr. Triway Local Sch. Dist., Wooster, Ohio, 1965-67; with office of gen. counsel Fgn. Agr. and Spl. Programs Div., U.S. Dept. Agr., Washington, 1969-71; ptnr. Kauffman, Eberhart, Cicconetti & Kennedy Co., Wooster, 1972-86, Kennedy and Cicconetti, Wooster, 1986—. Mem. ABA, Fed. Bar Assn., Assn. Trial Lawyers Am., Ohio State Bar Assn., Ohio Acad. Trial Lawyers, Wayne County Bar Assn., Phi Alpha Delta, Phi Delta Kappa. Republican. Club: Exchange (Wooster). Lodges: Lions, Elks. Home: 1770 Burbank Rd Wooster OH 44691 Office: Kennedy and Cicconetti 558 N Market St Wooster OH 44691

KENNEDY, CORNELIUS BRYANT, lawyer; b. Evanston, Ill., Apr. 13, 1921; s. Millard Bryant and Myrna Estelle (Anderson) K.; m. Anne Martha Reynolds, June 20, 1959; children: Anne Talbot, Lauren Asher. A.B., Yale U., 1943; J.D., Harvard U., 1948. Bar: Ill. bar 1949, D.C. bar 1965. Asso. firm Mayer Meyer Austrian & Platt, Chgo., 1949-54, 55-59; asst. U.S. atty. Dept. Justice, Chgo., 1954-55; counsel to Minority Leader, U.S. Senate, 1959-65; sr. mem. firm Kennedy & Webster, Washington, 1965-82; of counsel Armstrong, Teasdale, Kramer, Vaughan & Schlafly, Washington, 1983—; public mem. Adminstrv. Conf. U.S., 1972-82, sr. conf. fellow, 1982—, chmn. rulemaking com., 1973-82. Contbr. articles to law jours. Fin. chmn. Lyric Opera Co., Chgo., 1954; chmn. young adults group Chgo. Council Fgn. Relations, 1958-59; pres. English Speaking Union Jrs., Chgo., 1957-59; trustee St. John's Child Devel. Ctr., Washington, 1965-67, 75-87, pres., 1983-85 ; exec. dir. Supreme Ct. Hist. Soc., 1984-87. Served to 1st lt., AC U.S. Army, 1942-46. Fellow Am. Bar Found.; mem. Am. Law Inst., ABA (council sect. adminstrv. law 1967-70, chmn. sect. 1976-77), Fed. Bar Assn. (chmn. com. adminstrv. law 1963-64). Clubs: Legal Club Chgo., Explorers, N.Y. City, Capitol Hill, Metropolitan (Washington); Chevy Chase (Md.); Sailing of Chesapeake (Annapolis, Md.); Adventurer's (Chgo.). Home: 7720 Old Georgetown Pike McLean VA 22102 Office: Armstrong Teasdale Kramer et al 2000 Pennsylvania Ave NW Suite 6100 Washington DC 20006

KENNEDY, DAVID BURL, physician; b. Indpls., Jan. 26, 1950; s. Robert Dean and Esther Evelyn (Stephani) K.; m. Barbara Anne Ehrgott, Jan. 6, 1973; children—Elizabeth Anne, Jeffrey Townsend. B.S., Ind. U., 1972, M.D., 1975. Diplomate Am. Bd. Psychiatry and Neurology. Intern, resident Ind. U. Med. Ctr., Indpls., 1975-78; cons. psychiatrist Psychiat. Clinics of Ind., Anderson, 1977, Four County Mental Health Ctr., Logansport, Ind., 1980-86; med. dir. Tipton Psychiat. Program, Tipton County Meml. Hosp., 1986—; staff psychiatrist Regional Mental Health Ctr., Kokomo, Ind., 1978-80; pres. David B. Kennedy, M.D., Inc. and Kennedy Clinics, Indpls. and Kokomo, 1980—; asst. clin. prof. psychiatry Ind. U. Sch. Medicine, Indpls., 1978—; mem. adv. bd. Profl. Communications, Inc., Teaneck, N.J., 1984. Mem. AMA, Ind. State Med. Assn., Marion County Med. Soc., Am. Psychiat. Assn., Ind. Psychiat. Soc., Phi Beta Kappa. Club: Columbia, Skyline (Indpls.). Avocations: boating; computers. Office: 4954 E 56th St Indianapolis IN 46220

KENNEDY, DAVID TINSLEY, lawyer, labor arbitrator; b. Richmond, Va., Mar. 6, 1919; s. David Tinsley and Lilian Brady (Butcher) K.; m. Jean Elizabeth Stephenson, Nov. 26, 1949; children—David T. III, Thomas D., Michael F. J.D., U. Va., 1948. Bar: Va. 1948, W.Va. 1949, U.S. Dist. Ct. (so. dist.) W.Va. 1949, U.S. Ct. Appeals (4th cir.) 1963. Atty., Dist. 29, United Mine Workers Am., Beckley, W.Va., 1949-61; ptnr. Thornhill, Kennedy & Vaughan, Beckley, 1962—; arbitrator Coal Arbitration Service, Washington, 1970—; dir. Raleigh County Nat. Bank, Beckley. Mem. Raleigh County Dem. exec. com., 1980-86, chmn. 1986—. Served to lt. col. U.S. Army, 1942-46, PTO. Mem. W.Va. State Bar, Va. State Bar, Assn. Trial Lawyers Am., ABA. Roman Catholic. Home: 102 Mollohan Dr Beckley WV 25801 Office: Thornhill Kennedy & Vaughan PO Drawer 1008 Beckley WV 25802

KENNEDY, DONALD, university president; b. N.Y.C., Aug. 18, 1931; s. William Dorsey and Barbara (Bean) K.; m. Jeanne Dewey, June 11, 1953; children: Laura Page, Julia Hale. AB, Harvard U., 1952, AM, 1954, PhD, 1956; DSc (hon.), Columbia U., Williams Coll., U. Mich., U. Ariz., U. Rochester, Reed Coll. Mem. faculty Syracuse U., 1956-60; mem. faculty Stanford U., 1960-77, prof. biol. scis., 1965-77, chmn. dept., 1965-72; sr. cons. Office Sci. and Tech. Policy, Exec. Office of Pres., 1976; commr. FDA, 1977-79; v.p., provost Stanford U., 1979-80, pres., 1980—; bd. overseers Harvard U., 1970-76; bd. dirs. Health Effects Inst., Clean Sites Inc., Calif. Nature Conservancy. Author: (with W. H. Telfer) The Biology of Organisms, 1965; also articles.; editor: The Living Cell, 1966, From Cell to Organism, 1967; editorial bd. Jour. Exptl. Zoology, 1965-71, Jour. Comparative Physiology, 1965-76, Jour. Neurophysiology, 1969-75, Science, 1973-77. Fellow Am. Acad. Arts and Scis., AAAS; mem. Nat. Acad. Scis., Am. Physiol. Soc. Office: Stanford U Office of Pres Stanford CA 94305 *

KENNEDY, EDWARD MOORE, U.S. senator; b. Boston, Feb. 22, 1932; s. Joseph Patrick and Rose (Fitzgerald) K.; children: Kara Anne, Edward Moore, Patrick Joseph. A.B., Harvard U., 1956; postgrad., Internat. Law Sch., The Hague, Netherlands, 1958; LL.B., U. Va., 1959. Bar: Mass. 1959, U.S. Supreme Ct. 1963. Asst. dist. atty. Suffolk County, Mass., 1961-62; mem. U.S. Senate from Mass., 1962—, chmn. judiciary com., 1979-81, ranking Dem. mem. labor and human resources com., 1981—, also mem. armed service and joint econ. coms. Author: Decisions for a Decade, 1968, In Critical Condition: The Crisis in America's Health Care, 1972, Our Day and Generation, 1979, (with Mark O. Hatfield) Freeze: How You Can Help Prevent Nuclear War, 1979. Pres. Joseph P. Kennedy, Jr. Found., from 1961; trustee Children's Hosp. Med. Ctr., Boston, John F. Kennedy Library, Boston Symphony, John F. Kennedy Ctr. for Performing Arts, Robert F. Kennedy Meml. Found., Boston Coll., Mass. Gen. Hosp. Served with AUS, 1951-53. Named one of 10 outstanding young men U.S. Jaycees, 1967. Office: 113 Russell Senate Bldg Washington DC 20510 *

KENNEDY, EVELYN SIEFERT, foundation executive; b. Pitts., Nov. 11, 1927; d. Carmine and Assunta (Iacobucci) Rocci; BS magna cum laude, U. R.I., 1969, MS in Textiles and Clothing, 1970; m. George J. Siefert, May 30, 1953 (div. 1974); children: Paul Kenneth, Carl Joseph, Ann Marie; m. Lyle H. Kennedy, II, Oct. 12, 1974 (div. Feb. 1986). With Pitts. Public Schs., 1945-50; with Goodyear Aircraft Corp., Akron, Ohio, 1950-54; clothing instr. Groton (Conn.) Dept. Adult Edn., 1958-68; pres. Sewtique, Groton, 1970, Sewtique II, New London, Conn., 1986; v.p. Kennedy Capital Advisors, Groton, 1973-85, Kennedy Mgmt. Corp., Groton, 1974-85, Kennedy InterVest, Inc., Groton, 1975-85; pres., exec. dir. P.R.I.D.E. Found., Inc., Groton, 1978—; clothing cons. Coop. Extension Service, Dept. Agr.; internat. lectr. on clothing for disabled and elderly; adj. faculty U. Conn., Eastern Conn. State Coll., St. Joseph Coll.; hon. prof. Univ. R.I., assoc. prof., 1987—; fed. expert witness Care Label Law, FTC, 1976; mem. Major Appliance Consumer Action Panel, 1983—. Regional adv. council SBA active corps Execs., Hartford, 1985—; bd. dirs. Easter Seal Rehab. Center Southeastern Conn.; bus. adv. council U. R.I., 1979—, trustee, 1985—; active LWV; mem. Groton Vocat. Edn. Adv. Council. Recipient award of distinction U. R.I., 1969, Small Bus. Adminstrn. Adv. of Year, 1984; named Woman of Yr. Bus. and Profl. Women's Club, 1977, Conn. Home Economist of Yr., 1987. Mem. Internat. Sleep Council (consumer affairs rep.), Nat. Assn. Bedding Mfrs., Conn. Home Economists in Bus. (founder 1977, Women of Yr. 1987), Nat. Home Economists in Bus. (chmn. internat. relations, nat. fin. chmn. 1986), Am. Home Econs. Assn., Coll. and Univ. Bus. Instrs. of Conn., Fashion Group, Omicron Nu, Phi Kappa Phi. Democrat. Roman Catholic. Clubs: New London Zonta, Bus. and Profl. Women's (Outstanding Women of Year 1977). Author: Dressing With Pride, 1980, Clothing Accessibility: A Lesson Plan to Aid the Disabled and Elderly, 1983. Office: 71 Plaza Ct Groton CT 06340

KENNEDY, HAROLD EDWARD, lawyer, corporate executive; b. Pottstown, Pa., Oct. 18, 1927; s. Freeman S. and Alice (Brehm) K.; children from previous marriage: Kathleen, Nancy, Harold, Robert, Ellen, Anne, Susan; m. Eleanor Henry, Jan. 9, 1960. Student, Colgate U., 1945-47; LL.B., Syracuse U., 1952. Bar: N.Y. 1952, U.S. Dist. Ct. (no. dist.) N.Y. 1954, U.S. Supreme Ct. 1956, U.S. Dist. Ct. (so. dist.) N.Y. 1962. Ptnr. Taylor & Kennedy, Amsterdam, N.Y., 1952-59; sr. assoc. Kissam & Halpin, N.Y.C., 1959-60; exec. v.p., gen. counsel Foster Wheeler Corp., Livingston, N.J., 1960—, also bd. dirs.; trustee Compass Group Mut. Funds. Editor Syracuse Law Rev., 1952. Trustee First Presbyn. Ch., Orange, N.J., 1973-76, St. Barnabas Med. Ctr., 1986—, Kessler Inst. for Rehab., 1987—; bd. visitors Syracuse U. Coll. of Law, 1987—; bd. dirs. N.J. Alliance for Action, 1986—. Served with USAAF, 1945-47. Mem. ABA, Machinery and Allied Products Inst., N.Y. State Bar Assn., Order of Coif. Club: Baltusrol Golf (Springfield, N.J.). Office: Foster Wheeler Corp Perryville Corp Park Clinton NJ 08809-4000

KENNEDY, (JOE) JACK, JR., lawyer, state legislator; b. Abingdon, Va., June 11, 1956; s. J. Jack Sr. and Bobbie Lee (Porter) K.; m. Susan Maura Muir, June 30, 1979; children: J. Jack III, Jillian Susanne. BS, Clinch Valley Coll. of U. Va., 1977; cert. in internat. study, U. London, 1977; studies with Va. atty., 1978-81; MA In Polit. Sci., East Tenn. State U., 1982. Bar: Va. 1982, U.S. Dist. Ct. (we. dist.) Va. 1982, U.S. Ct. Appeals (4th cir.) 1982, U.S. Tax Ct. 1982, U.S. Ct. Claims 1982, Supreme Ct. Va. 1982. Mem. Va. Ho. of Dels., Richmond, 1988—. Campaign mgr. U.S. Rep. Rick Boucher, 1984; chmn. City of Norton Dem. com., 1982—, 9th congl. dist. Dem. com., 1985—; del. Dem. Nat. Conv., 1984, 88, mem. platform com. Dem. Nat. Conv., 1988; state chmn. Va. Assn. Local Dem. Chairs, 1986-87; envoy to Carribean Islands of Grenada, Jamaica and Trinidad, U.S. Youth Council, 1985. Named one of Outstanding Young Men Am., 1985, 86, Outstanding Young Dem. Va., 1985. Mem. ABA, Va. Bar Assn., Wise County Bar Assn., Va. Trial Lawyers Assn., Va. C. of C., Wise County C. of C. (v.p. pub. affairs), Nat. Rifle Assn. (life), Phi Sigma Kappa. Baptist. Lodges: Moose, Kiwanis. Home: 699 Fox Run Rd SE Norton VA 24273

KENNEDY, JACK LELAND, lawyer; b. Portland, Oreg., Jan. 30, 1924; s. Ernest E. and Lera M. (Talley) K.; m. Clara C. Hagans, June 5, 1948; children: James M., John C. Grad., Southwestern U., Los Angeles; J.D., Lewis and Clark Coll., 1951. Bar: Oreg. 1951. Since practiced in Portland; partner firm Kennedy, King & Zimmer, 1971—; trustee Northwestern Coll. Law, Portland; dir. Profl. Liability Fund, 1979-82. Contbr. articles to legal jours. Bd. overseers Lewis and Clark Coll. Served with USNR, 1942-46. Recipient Disting. Grad. award Lewis and Clark Coll., 1983. Fellow Am. Coll. Trial Lawyers, Am. Bar Found., Oreg. Bar Found. (charter); mem. ABA (Ho. of Dels. 1984—), Oreg. State Bar (bd. govs. 1976-79, pres. 1978-79), Multnomah Bar Assn. Republican. Clubs: City (Portland); Columbia River Yacht. Home: 1281 SW Davenport St Portland OR 97201 Office: Kennedy King & Zimmer 1211 SW 5th Ave Portland OR 97204

KENNEDY, JAMES HARRINGTON, editor, publisher; b. Lawrence, Mass., Feb. 20, 1924; s. James H. and Margaret Helen (Hyde) K.; m. Sheila Conway, July 1, 1950; children: Kathleen, Brian, Kevin, Gail, Patricia, Maureen, Constance. BS, Lowell Textile Inst., 1948; MS, MIT, 1950. Mgmt. trainee Chicopee Mfg. Corp., Manchester, N.H., 1950-51; mng. editor Textile World McGraw Hill Pub. Co., Greenville, S.C., 1951-54; dir. communications Bruce Payne & Assocs., Westport, Conn., 1954-58; pres. James H. Kennedy & Co., Westport, 1958-70; editor, pub. Cons. News, Fitzwilliam, N.H., 1970—, Exec. Recruiter News, 1980—. Founder Fitzwilliam Conservation Corp., pres., 1970-72; chmn. Fitzwilliam Sq. Dances, 1970—; mem. Fitzwilliam Planning Bd., 1970-72; trustee Am. Liquid Trust, Greenwich, Conn., 1975-78. Served to capt., inf. AUS, 1942-46. Mem. Fitzwilliam Hist. Soc., Acad. Mgmt., N.Y. Bus. Press Editors, Phi Psi. Republican. Roman Catholic. Clubs: Fitzwilliam Swimming (pres. 1978-84), Nat. Press. Address: Templeton Turnpike Fitzwilliam NH 03447

KENNEDY, JOHN XAVIER, investment banker; b. Chgo., June 10, 1918; s. R. Emmet and Bernadine (Galvin) K.; m. Mary Ann Luke, Nov. 6, 1948; children: J. Luke, Mark, Matthew, Pete, Paul, Kristine. Student, Northwestern U., 1946-47; cert. fin., U. Pa., 1964. With United Air Lines, Chgo., 1937-41, 46; with Stifel, Nicolaus & Co., Inc., Chgo., 1946-53, bond salesman, 1946-51, buyer, 1951-53; with White Weld & Co., Chgo., 1953-72, mcpl. bond buyer, 1953-58, mgr. revenue bonds, 1959-63, v.p., 1964-72; v.p. fixed income securities F.S. Moseley & Co., 1972-74; pres. U.S. Securities Corp., 1974-76; v.p. John Nuveen & Co., 1977-78, Paine, Webber Jackson & Curtis, 1979, Securities Corp. Iowa, 1979-84; v.p., mgr. bond dept. Amalgamated Bank, Chgo., 1984; salesman Coldwell Banker, 1985, Cossitt & Co., 1986—; v.p., bd. dirs. Stanley Luke Farm, Inc. Mem. devel. bd. Sisters of St. Joseph, La Grange, Ill.; mem. corp. support DePaul U., 1965-66. Served with USAF, 1942-45. Decorated Air medal. Mem. Securities Industry Assn. (chmn. mcpl. securities com. Cen. States 1965, mem. mcpl. fed. legis. com. 1969-71, mcpl. securities com. 1972), Mcpl. Fin. Forum, Washington, Bond Club Chgo., Mcpl. Bond Club Chgo. (past bd. dirs.). Home: 10101 5th Ave La Grange IL 60525 Office: 126 W Calendar LaGrange IL 60525

KENNEDY, KAEL BEHAN, lawyer; b. Chgo., Sept. 1, 1941; s. W. McNeil and Dot (Behan) K.; m. Pam Wilt, Aug. 29, 1964; 1 child, Mark Wilt. BS, Loyola U., 1963; JD, U. Iowa, 1966. Bar: Iowa 1966, Ill. 1967, U.S. Dist. Ct. (no. dist.) Ill. 1967, (we. dist.) Mo. 1971, (ea. dist.) Mo. 1975, (so. dist.) Tex. 1977, (so. dist.) N.Y. 1978, Dist. S.C. 1982, U.S. Ct. Apls. (7th cir.) 1967, (8th cir.) 1973, (5th cir.) 1980, Mich. 1987, U.S. Dist. Ct. (ea. and we. dists.) Mich. 1987, U.S. Ct. Appeals (6th cir.) 1986. Assoc. Pope, Ballard, Shepard & Fowle, Chgo., 1966-73; ptnr. Pope, Ballard, Shepard & Fowle, Chgo., 1973-79, Katten, Muchin, Zavis, Pearl & Galler, Chgo., 1979-85, Varnum, Riddering, Schmidt & Howlett, Grand Rapids, 1986-88, Matkov, Salzman, Madoff and Gunn, Chgo., 1988—; lectr. in field; instr. Arthur Andersen & Co., St. Charles, Ill., 1983, Ill. Inst. Continuing Legal Edn., Chgo., 1983, 84, Nat. Inst. Trial Adv., Chgo., 1986, 87, 88, Mich. Bar Assn., 1987. Co-author: Antitrust Consent Decree Manual, 1978, Expediting Pretrials and Trials of Antitrust Cases, 1979, Antitrust Law and Mgmt. Govt., 1988. Editorial staff CCH Corp. Law Guide, 1963, 64. Bd. dirs. Lawyers Com. for Civil Rights Under Law, Chgo., 1983, 84; committeeman Deerfield Twp. Rep. Com., Highland Park, Ill., 1982-84; cooperating counsel ACLU, Chgo., 1967-72. Mem. ABA, Ill. Bar Assn. (council antitrust law sect.), Mich. Bar Assn. (council antitrust law sect.), Chgo. Bar Assn., Am. Soc. of Assn. Execs., Mich. Soc. of Assn. Execs. Clubs: University, Legal, Nat. Lawyers, Chgo., Macatawa Bay Yacht. Home: 3920 N Lake Shore Dr Chicago IL 60613 Office: Matkov Salzman Madoff and Gunn 100 W Monroe St # 1500 Chicago IL 60603

KENNEDY, MARC J., lawyer; b. Newburgh, N.Y., Mar. 2, 1945; s. Warren G. K. and Frances F. (Levinson) K.; m. Debra L. Shaw, Apr. 19, 1986; 1 child, Michael L. BA cum laude, Syracuse U., 1967; JD, U. Mich., 1970. Bar: N.Y. 1971. Assoc. Davies, Hardy, Ives & Lawther, N.Y.C., 1971-72, London, Buttenweiser & Chalif, N.Y.C., 1972-73, Silberfeld, Danziger & Bangser, N.Y.C., 1973; counsel Occidental Crude Sales, Inc., N.Y.C., 1974-75; v.p., gen. counsel Internat. Ore & Fertilizer Corp., N.Y.C., 1975-82; asst. gen. counsel Occidental Chem. Corp., Houston, 1982; v.p., gen. counsel Occidental Chem. Co., Tampa, Fla., 1982-87, v.p., gen counsel agrl. products group, 1987—; faculty mentor Columbia Pacific U., Mill Valley, Calif., 1981—. Trustee Bar Harbor Festival Corp., N.Y.C., 1974-87; bd. dirs. Am. Opera Repertory Co., 1982-85; mem. com. planned giving N.Y. Foundling Hosp., 1977—; Explorer post advisor Boy Scouts Am., 1976-78. Mem. ABA (vice-chmn. com. internat. law, liaison young lawyers sect. 1974-75, chmn. sub-com. proposed trade barriers to the importation of products into U.S. 1985—), Am. Corp. Counsel Assn., Internat. Bar Assn., Maritime Law Assn., N.Y. State Bar Assn., Assn. Bar City N.Y. (admiralty law com. 1982-83). Club: Clearwater Yacht. Home: 240 Windward Passage #803 Clearwater FL 34630 Office: Occidental Chem Corp Agrl Products Group 4830 W Kennedy Blvd Tampa FL 33609

KENNEDY, NEIL RICHARD, advertising executive; b. Rochford, Eng., Mar. 6, 1946; s. Walter and Vera Nancy (Harford) K.; m. Georgina Theresa Tolhurst (dec. 1979); children: Caroline Jane, Angus Harford, Elizabeth Theresa, James Richard David; m. Johanna Gesina Woudstra. Grad., U. Uppingham, 1961, postgrad., 1963. Prodn. trainee Colman Prentis & Varley Ltd., London, 1963-65; dep. mng. dir. Childs Greene Assocs. Ltd., London, 1965-76; vice chmn. BSB Dorland Advt. Ltd., London, 1977—. Mem. Inst. Practitioners in Advt., Inst. Mktg., Internat. Advt. Assn., Mktg. Soc. Mem. Conservative Party. Mem. Ch. of Eng. Clubs: Royal Burnham Yacht (commodore 1983-85), Royal Thames Yacht. Home: Stokes Hall, Althorne, Essex CM3 8DS, England Office: Dorland Advt Ltd, 121-141 Westbourne Terr, London W2 6JR, England

KENNEDY, ROBERT DELMONT, petrochemical company executive; b. Pitts., Nov. 8, 1932; s. Thomas Reed and Lois (Smith) K.; m. Sally Duff, Jan. 28, 1956; children: Robert Boyd, Kathleen Tyson, Thomas Alexander, Melissa Kristine. B of Mech. Engring., Cornell U., 1955. With Union Carbide Corp., 1955—, indsl. engr. Nat. Carbon Div., Dayton and Cleve., 1955-59, sales mgr., product mgr., Chgo., 1959-66, mgr. mktg., N.Y.C., dir. internat. mktg., 1964-71, dir. mktg., Europe, 1971-75, sr. v.p., 1975-77, pres. Linde Div., N.Y.C., 1977-81, corp. exec. v.p., 1982-85, pres., chief operating officer chemicals and plastics, 1985-86, chmn., pres., chief exec. officer, 1986—. Past trustee Am. Episcopal Ch., Europe, New Hampton Sch.; moderator Aspen Inst. Program Humanistic Studies, 1979—. Mem. Chem. Mfrs. Assn. (chmn., exec. com.). Republican. Avocations: golf, fishing, boating. Office: Union Carbide Corp 39 Old Ridgebury Rd Danbury CT 06840

KENNEDY, ROGER, JR., insurance company executive; b. Jacksonville, Fla., Sept. 1, 1937; s. Roger and Ella Amanda (Balkcom) K.; A.A., U. Fla., 1959, B.S., 1961; M.Div., Southwestern Bapt. Theol. Sem., 1982; m. Carol Ann Davis, Dec. 14, 1957; children—Roger III, (dec.), Kalen Amanda. Life agt. Penn Mut. Ins. Co., Tampa, Fla., 1961-63, dist. mgr., Memphis, 1963-65, gen. agt. in tng., home office officer, Phila., 1965-66, gen. agt., Houston, 1966-68, Tampa, 1968-78; pres., gen. agt. Kennedy Corp., 1974-78; mgr. The Prin. Fin. Group (formerly The Bankers of Iowa) Tampa Agy., 1982—. Mem. Council of 100-Fla.; past pres. U. Fla. Alumni, Tampa, now mem. Pres.'s council and exec. com.; pres. Nat. Alumni U. Fla.; past pres. Girls Clubs of Tampa; chmn. bd. Prison Crusade Inc., Profl. and Mgmt. Outreach; deacon First Bapt. Ch. of Tampa, 1988—; project bus. instr. Jr. Achievement. Served with Green Berets, U.S. Army, 1955-57. Winner Tex. Cup as outstanding agy. in Tex., 1966; Dixie Cup as outstanding agy. in South, 1973; Amos Alonzo Stagg Assoc. award Fellowship Christian Athletes. CLU, Chartered fin. cons. Mem. Gen. Agts. and Mgrs. Assn. (bd. dirs. 1986—, past pres. Tampa), Nat. Mgmt. Achievement awards 1974-78, 86-88), Life Underwriters Polit. Action Com., Nat. Assn. Life Underwriters, Am. Soc. C.L.U.s (Golden Key), Internat. Platform Assn., Pi Sigma Epsilon. Republican. Clubs: Rotary of Tampa, Palma Ceia Golf & Country. Home: 801 Roxmere Rd Tampa FL 33609 Office: 1408 N Westshore Blvd Suite 600 Tampa FL 33607

KENNEDY, THOMAS PATRICK, communications consultant, financial executive; b. N.Y.C., Oct. 13, 1932; s. Andrew Francis and Marie P. (Scullen) K.; BS, St. Peter's Coll., 1958; postgrad. Seton Hall U., 1959; m. Mary P. Drennan, Jan. 14, 1956 (dec.); children—Thomas Patrick, Kevin M., Michael J., Mary P., Deborah A. Accountant, Haskins & Sells, CPA's, N.Y.C., 1953-54, 55-57; staff Emerson Radio & TV, N.Y.C., 1957-58; various exec. positions CBS, N.Y.C., 1958-67; with Ford Found., N.Y.C., 1967; dir. fin. Pub. Broadcasting Lab., N.Y.C., 1967-69; with Children's TV Workshop Sesame St., N.Y.C., 1969-80, v.p. fin. and adminstrn., 1969-78, treas. 1969-78, sr. v.p., 1978-80; pres. Tomken Mgmt., Ltd., 1980—, chmn. bd., 1983—; chmn. bd., chief exec. officer Effie Techs. Inc., 1984—; v.p., corp. fin. Jersey Capital Mkts Group, Inc., 1987-88; chmn., chief exec. officer Corp. Strategies Group, Inc., 1988—; cons. in field. Bd. advisers Franciscan Communication Ctr.; bd. dirs. Home Monitor Inc., Corporate Strategies, Inc., Cleat Capitol Resources, Inc., Home Energy Savings, Inc.; bd. dirs., exec. dir. Ctr. for Non-Broadcast TV. Served with C.E., U.S. Army, 1954-55. Mem. Fin. Exec. Inst., Internat. Radio and TV Soc., Inst. Broadcast Fin. Mgmt., Nat. Assn. Accountants, Internat. Broadcast Inst., Internat. Inst. Communication, Internat. Assn. Fin. Execs., Am. Assn. Ind. Investors. Roman Catholic. Home: 40 Leonardville Rd Belford NJ 07718 also: Riverview Hist Plaza 45 Newark St Hoboken NJ 07030

KENNEDY, WALTER JEFF, JR., lawyer; b. Kansas City, Kans., May 18, 1928; s. Walter Joseph and Emily (Knecht) K.; m. Norma Jeanne Buie, June 4, 1949 (dec. Mar. 1984); children—Kathleen Kim, Nancy Jo; m. Geraldine M. Rieke, May 30, 1986. A.A., Kansas City Jr. Coll., 1952; A.B., Kans. U., 1954, J.D., 1956. Bar: Mo. 1956, Kans. 1956, U.S. Ct. Appeals (8th and 10th cirs.), U.S. Ct. Claims, 1971, U.S. Tax Ct., 1959, U.S. Dist. Ct. (we. dist.) Mo. 1956, U.S. Dist. Ct. Kans. 1956, U.S. Supreme Ct. 1970. Assoc. Davis, Thompson, Fairchild & Van Dyke, Kansas City, Mo., 1956—; sole practice, El Dorado, Kans., 1957-61; mem. legal staff Farmland Industries, Kansas City, Mo., 1961-63; assoc. Hoskins, King, McGannon, Hahn & Hurwitz, Kansas City, Mo., 1963-68, ptnr., 1968—. Served with USN, 1945-50; PTO. Mem. ABA, Mo. Bar Assn., Mo. Bar Assn. Corp. (banking and bus. orgns. com. 1984-86), Kans. Bar Assn., Lawyers Assn. Kansas City, Kansas City

Bar Assn. Club: Milburn Country (Overland Park, Kans.). Author articles. Office: Commerce Trust Bldg Suite 1100 Kansas City MO 64106

KENNEDY-MINOTT, RODNEY, international relations educator, former ambassador; b. Portland, Oreg., June 1, 1928; s. Joseph Albert and Gainor (Baird) Minott; children—Katharine Pardow, Rodney Glisan, Polly Berry. A.B., Stanford U., 1953, M.A., 1956, Ph.D., 1960. Instr. history Stanford U., 1960-61, asst. prof., asst. dir. history of western civilization program, 1961-62, asst. dir. summer session, 1962-63, dir. summer session, 1963-65; assoc. prof. Portland State U., 1965-66, assoc. prof., assoc. dean instrn. Calif. State U., Hayward, 1966-67, prof., 1967-77, head div. humanities, 1967-69; ambassador to Sweden and chmn. Swedish Fulbright Com. 1977-80; adj. prof. Monterey Inst. Internat. Studies, Calif., 1981; exec. v.p. Direction Internat., Washington, 1982-83; sr. research scholar Hoover Instn., 1981-82, 85—; chmn. Alpha Internat., N.Y.C., 1983—; Congl. staff mem., 1965-66; sr. fellow Ctr. Internat. and Strategic Affairs, UCLA, 1986—; lectr. in field. Author: Peerless Patriots: The Organized Veterans and the Spirit of Americanism, 1962; The Fortress That Never Was: the Myth of Hitler's Bavarian Stronghold, 1964; The Sinking of the Lollipop: Shirley Temple v. Pete McCloskey, 1968, The Far North: Tension Point, 1988. Mem. citizen's adv. council Dominican Coll.; mem. adv. council Pacific Rim Studies, Dominican Coll., San Rafael, Calif.; bd. dirs. Inst. Internat. Studies. Served with U.S. Army, 1950-52. Mem. Am. Hist. Assn., Orgn. Am. Historians, World Affairs Council No. Calif., Internat. Studies Assn., Swedish-Am. C. of C. Clubs: Marines Meml. Assn. (San Francisco), Multnomah Athletic (Portland, Oreg.). Office: The Hoover Instn RM231 LHH Stanford CA 94305

KENNELLY, JOHN JEROME, lawyer; b. Chgo., Dec. 11, 1918; s. Joseph Michael and Anna (Flynn) K.; m. Mary Thompson, Mar. 21, 1949. Ph.B., Loyola U., Chgo., 1939, LL.B., 1941. Bar: Ill. 1941, U.S. Dist. Ct. (no. dist.) Ill. 1941, U.S. Ct. Appeals (7th cir.) 1946, U.S. Supreme Ct. 1956. Sole practice, Chgo., 1946—. Served with USN, 1941-46. Fellow Internat. Acad. Trial Lawyers (past chmn. aviation sect.); mem. Chgo. Bar Assn. (bd. mgrs. 1965-67), Ill. State Bar Assn., ABA (aviation com. chmn. 1981-82), Inter-Am. Bar Assn., Ill. Trial Lawyers Assn. (pres. 1968-69), AIAA, Assn. Trial Lawyers Am., Am. Judicature Soc., Law Sci. Acad. Am., World Assn. Lawyers, Am. Coll. Trial Lawyers, Internat. Acad. Law and Sci., Internat. Soc. Barristers, Am. Soc. Internat. Law, Am. Bar Found. Clubs: Butterfield Country (Hinsdale, Ill.); Beverly Country (Chgo.). Author: Litigation and Trial of Air Crash Cases, 1969; contbr. articles to profl. jours. Office: 111 W Washington St Suite 1449 Chicago IL 60602

KENNERLY, DAVID HUME, photographer, writer, producer; b. Roseburg, Oreg., Mar. 9, 1947; s. Orlie Alden and Joanne (Hume) K.; m. Susan Allwardt, 1967 (div. 1969); m. Mel Harris, Oct. 30, 1983; 1 child, Byron Hume; student Portland State Coll., 1965-66. Photographer, Oreg. Jour., 1966, The Oregonian, 1967, UPI, Los Angeles, 1967-68, N.Y.C., 1968-69, Washington, 1969-70, Saigon, 1971-72; contract photographer Life and Time mags., S.E. Asia, 1972-74; personal photographer Pres. of U.S., Washington, 1974-77; photographer Time mag., Washington, 1977—; dir. photography Philip Morris mag., N.Y., 1987—. Author: Shooter, 1980; co-writer, exec. producer (teleplay), Shooter, 1987; co-writer, dir., producer (script for Am. Film Inst.) Bao Chi, 1987; exec. producer The Taking of Flight 847-The Uli Derickson Story, 1988 (Emmy award nomination 1988). Recipient Pulitzer Prize Columbia U., 1972; 2 1st place awards World Press Photo, 1976, spl. citation Nat. Press Photographers, 1976, Olivier Rebbot award Overseas Press Club, 1985, Front Page award N.Y. Newspaper Guild, 1985-86, 5 Emmy award nominations Nat. Acad. TV Arts and Scis.; directing fellow Am. Film Inst., 1984-86. Mem. White House Press Photographers Assn., Writers Guild Am. Office: care Toren Tanner Mainstain & Hoffer 10866 Wilshire Blvd 10th Floor Los Angeles CA 90024

KENNET, LORD (WAYLAND HILTON YOUNG), politician, writer; b. Eng., Aug. 2, 1923; s. 1st Baron Kennet and Kathleen (Bruce); m. Elizabeth Ann Adams, 1948; 6 children. Student, U. Cambridge, Eng. With fgn. office Brit. Govt., London, 1946-47, 49-51; del. parliamentary assemblies WEU and Council of Europe, London, 1962-65; parliamentary sec. Ministry of Housing and Local Govt., London, 1966-70; opposition spokesman Fgn. Affairs and Sci. Policy, London, 1971-74; chief whip Social Democrat Party House of Lords, London, 1981-83; spokesperson on fgn. affairs and def. Social Dem. Party, London, 1981—; chmn. Adv. Com. on Oil Pollution of the Sea, 1970-74, CPRE, 1971-72, Internat. Parliamentary Confs. on the Environment, 1972-78; dir. Europe Plus Thirty, 1974-75; mem. European Parliament, 1978-79. Author: (as Wayland Young) The Italian Left, 1949, The Deadweight, 1952, Now or Never, 1953, The Montesi Scandal, 1957, Still Alive Tomorrow, 1958, Strategy for Survival, 1959, The Profumo Affair, 1963, Eros Denied, 1965, Thirty-Four Articles, 1965, Existing Mechanisms of Arms Control, 1965; (with Elizabeth Young) London's Churches, 1986; (as Wayland Kennet) Preservation, 1972, The Futures of Europe, 1976, The Rebirth of Britain, 1982; polit. pamphlets and articles on defence, disarmament, environment, multinational companies. Home: 100 Bayswater Rd, London W2 England Office: House of Lords, Social Democrat Party, London England

KENNEY, H(ARRY) WESLEY, JR., producer, director; b. Dayton, Ohio, Jan. 3, 1926; s. Harry Wesley and Minnie Ruth (Keeton) K.; m. Kay Ann Snure (div. 1964); children: Nina, Harry Wesley III, Kara; m. Heather North, May 22, 1971; 1 child, Kevin. BFA, Carnegie Inst. Tech., 1950. Dir. Fights at St. Nicks, Rocky King Detective, Night Beat Dumont Network, N.Y.C., 1950-57; producer, dir. TV shows True Story, Modern Romances NBC, N.Y.C., 1957-61; freelance dir. Omnibus, N.Y.C., 1958; dir. theater prodn. My Three Angels Totem Pole Playhouse, 1955; dir. theater prodn. The King and I Melody Fair Summer Theatre, Niagra Falls, 1959; dir. theater prodn. Twelfth Night Antioch, Yellow Springs, Ohio, 1962; dir. TV series The Doctors NBC, N.Y.C., 1964-66; exec. producer, dir. TV series Days of Our Lives NBC, Los Angeles, 1967-77; dir. TV series All in the Family CBS, Los Angeles, 1974, dir. pilots The Jeffersons, Filthy Rich, Ladies Man, exec. producer TV series The Young and the Restless, 1981-86; producer, dir. (spl.) Miss Kline, We Love You ABC, 1974; exec. producer TV series General Hospital ABC, Los Angeles, 1987—. Served with USN, 1943-46. Recipient 7 Emmy awards Acad. TV Arts and Scis. 1973, 78, 79, 82, 83, 84, 86, Emmy award nominations Acad. TV Arts and Scis., 1972-88. Mem. Dirs. Guild Am., Producers Guild Am., Actors Equity, Omega Delta Kappa. Home: 12996 Galewood St Studio City CA 91604

KENNEY, JOHN MICHEL, architect; b. N.Y.C., Oct. 22, 1938; s. John Peter and Madeline Loretta (Fuller) K.; m. Sharon Hill, July 4, 1956 (div. 1982); children—John Michel, James Brian, Dion Patrick. A.A.S., Orange County Community Coll., 1966; student Columbia U., 1969. Registered architect, N.Y., N.J., Conn., Pa., Del. Vice pres., ptnr., dir. health facilities Perkins & Will Architects, White Plains, N.Y., 1968-81; pres. Architecture for Health Sci. & Commerce, P.C., White Plains, 1981—. Vice chmn. Orange County Dem. Coms., N.Y., 1968; chmn. Dem. Com., Middletown, N.Y., 1966-68; co-chmn. Robert Kennedy Presdl. Election Primary, Orange/Sullivan County, 1968. Mem. Nat. Council of Archtl. Registration Bds., N.Y. Soc. Hosp. Planning, Am. Assn. Hosp. Planners, N.Y. Acad. Scis. Democrat. Avocations: skiing; sailing; travelling. Office: Arch for Health Sci & Commerce 7-11 S Broadway White Plains NY 10601

KENNEY, WILLIAM FITZGERALD, lawyer; b. San Francisco, Nov. 4, 1935; s. Lionel Fitzgerald and Ethel Constance (Brennan) K.; m. Susan Elizabeth Langfitt, May 5, 1962; children—Anne, Carol, James. B.A., U. Calif.-Berkeley, 1957; J.D., Hastings Coll. Law, 1960. Bar: Calif. 1961. Assoc. firm Miller, Osborne Miller & Bartlett, San Mateo, Calif., 1962-64; ptnr. Tormey, Kenney & Cotchett, San Mateo, 1965-67; pres. William F. Kenney, Inc., San Mateo, 1968—, Kennetex, Inc., Dallas, 1981—; gen. ptnr. All-Am. Self Storage, 1985—. Trustee San Mateo City Sch. Dist., 1971-79, pres., 1972-74; pres. March of Dimes, 1972-73; bd. dirs. Boys Club of San Mateo, 1972—. Served with U.S. Army, 1960-62. Mem. State Bar of Calif. (taxation com. 1973-76), San Mateo County Bar Assn. (dir. 1973-75), Calif. Assn. Realtors (legal affairs com. 1978—), San Mateo C. of C. (bd. dirs. 1987—), Self Service Storage Assn., Western region (bd. dirs. 1988—). Republican. Roman Catholic. Club: Rotary (pres. 1978-79). Lodge: Elks (exalted ruler 1974-75). Home: 221 Clark Dr San Mateo CA 94402 Office: William F Kenney Inc 120 N El Camino Real San Mateo CA 94401

KENNICOTT, JAMES W., lawyer, consultant; b. Latrobe, Pa., Feb. 14, 1945; s. W.L. and Alice (Hayes) K.; m. Lynne Dratler Finney, July 1, 1984. AB, Syracuse U., 1967; JD, U. Wyo., 1979. Bar: Utah 1979, U.S. Dist. Ct. (Utah dist.) 1983. Sole practice Park City, Utah, 1979-87; ptnr. Kennicott & Finney, Park City, 1987—; judge pro-tem 1988—; third circuit judge, Park City, 1988—; prin. Ski Cons., Park City, 1969—; cons. Destination Sports Specialists, Park City, 1984—. Trustee Park City Hist. Soc., 1980, Park City Museum Bd., 1983; trustee, pres. Park City Library Bd., 1985. Mem. ABA (real property, probate and trust law sects.), Utah State Bar Assn. (real propert sect.), Utah Library Assn, ALA. Home: PO Box 2339 Park City UT 84060 Office: 1647 Shortline Rd Park City UT 84060

KENNY, JOHN EDWARD, computer analyst; b. Buffalo, Oct. 28, 1945; s. Thomas Edmund and Dorothy Elizabeth (Krull) K.; A.A.S., Erie Community Coll., 1972. Systems analyst Nat. Fuel Gas, Buffalo, 1969-70; programmer Westwood Pharm., Buffalo, 1972-73; programmer Service Systems Corp., Clarence, N.Y., 1974-77, Carborundum, Niagara Falls, N.Y., 1973-74; analyst, programmer A, Marine Midland Bank N.A., Buffalo, 1977-83; sr. analyst, programmer, project leader Empire of Am., FSA, Buffalo, 1983-85, applications project supr., 1985—; tchr. programming langs. Advanced Tng. Center, Buffalo. Mem. Republican Presdl. Task Force; mem. Town of Tonawanda Conservative Com., 1980—; vice chmn. Town of Tonawanda Conservative Com. Mem. Erie County Conservative Party Executive Com., U.S. Jr. C. of C., Am. Inst. Banking, Assn. Systems Mgmt., Kenton Jr. C. of C., Internat. Platform Assn., Smithsonian Assocs., Assn. Computing Machinery, Nat. Geographic Soc., U.S. Golf Assn. (assoc.). Conservative. Roman Catholic. Club: Glen Oak Golf. Lodges: K.C., Lions, Internat. Order Alhambra. Home: 212 McKinley Ave Kenmore NY 14217 Office: 626 Commerce Dr Amherst NY 14150

KENNY, LUIS FEDERICO, lawyer; b. Buenos Aires, June 24, 1955; s. Luis and Elena Dolores (Padilla-Quirno) K.; m. Scodina Hull, Aug. 14, 1982. Grad., Buenos Aires Law Sch., 1976; Grad. in Banking Law, El Salvador U., Buneonos Aires, 1981; postgrad., London Sch. Econs., 1983. Mgr. money marketing Promotora de Finanzas, Buenos Aires, 1975-77; jr. ptnr. Estudio Padilla, Attys., Buenos Aires, 1977-80, sr. ptnr., 1980—; chief legal adviser Banco de Ultramar SA, Buenos Aires, 1978-82; legal advisor Sudamtex SA, Buenos Aires, 1978-80; European rep. U.S. Med. Exports Co., Inc., N.Y.C., 1982-84; bd. dirs. Banco de Ultramar SA, Themegrade Ltd., London, Sears Roebuck Argentina SA, Buenos Aires. Mem. Argentine Com. Bank Lawyers, Argentine Bank Assn., Buenos Aires Bar Assn. Roman Catholic. Clubs: Jockey, Circulo de Armas (Buenos Aires). Office: Estudio Padilla, Av de Mayo 749 3d Floor, 1115 Buenos Aires Argentina

KENT, FREDERICK HEBER, lawyer; b. Fitzgerald, Ga., Apr. 26, 1905; s. Heber and Juanita (McDuffie) K.; m. Norma C. Futch, Apr. 25, 1929; children: Frederick Heber, Norma Futch K. Lockwood, John Bradford, James Cleveland. LLB, J.D., U. Ga., 1926. Bar: Ga. 1926, Fla. 1926. Since practiced in Jacksonville, Fla.; ptnr. Carlton, Fields, Ward, Emmanuel, Smith, Cutler & Kent, P.A. (and predecessor firms); chmn. bd. Kent Theatres, Inc.; pres. Kent Enterprises, Inc., Kent Properties, Inc. Chmn. local ARC, 1934, 1950; pres. Jacksonville's 50 Years of Progress Assn., 1951; bd. dirs. YMCA, pres., 1946-50; bd. dirs. Jacksonville Community Chest-United Fund, 1955-59, pres., 1958-59; chmn. Fla. State Plant Bd., 1955-56; bd. control (regents) Fla. Instns. of Higher Learning, 1953-58, chmn., 1955-56; bd. dirs. Riverside Hosp. Assn., 1956-76, pres., 1964-65; chmn. State Jr. Coll. Council, 1962-72; mem. adv. com. Fla. Higher Edn. Facilities Act, 1963, 64; chmn. bd. trustees Fla. Community Coll., Jacksonville, 1965-71; mem. Select Council on Post High Sch. Edn. in Fla., 1967, Fla. Gov.'s Commn. for Quality Edn., 1967; trustee Bolles Sch., Jacksonville, 1954-65, Theatre Jacksonville, 1966-76; chmn. Fla. Quadricentennial Commn., 1962-65; mem. Jacksonville City Council, 1933-1937; mem. Fla. Democratic Exec. Com., 1938-40. Served as lt. USNR, 1942-45. Recipient Distinguished Service award U.S. Jr. C. of C., 1933, Ted Arnold award Jacksonville C. of C., 1961; Fred H. Kent campus Fla. Community Coll. at Jacksonville named in his honor, 1974. Mem. Internat. Bar Assn., ABA, Fla. Bar Assn., Jacksonville Bar Assn., Jacksonville C. of C., Am. Judicature Soc., Soc. Colonial Wars, Am. Legion, Sigma Alpha Epsilon, Delta Sigma Pi. Republican. Clubs: Rotary (pres. 1958-59), Timuquana Country, Florida Yacht, Seminole, Friars, Ye Mystic Revellers, Ponte Vedra, River, Sawgrass Country. Home: 2970 St Johns Ave Jacksonville FL 32205 Office: PO Box 4700 Jacksonville FL 32201

KENT, GEOFFREY CHARLES, diversified company executive; b. Clevelys, Feb. 2, 1922; s. Percy Whitehead and Madge K.; m. Brenda G. Conisbee, 1955. Ed. Blackpool Grammar Sch. In various advt. and mktg. positions Colman, Prentis & Varley, Mentor, Johnson & Johnson, 1947-58; advt. mgr. John Player & Son, 1958, mktg. dir., 1964, asst. mng. dir., 1969, chmn., mng. dir. and dir. Imperial Group, 1975; chmn. chief exec. Imperial Group PLC, 1981—; dir. Team Lotus Internat. Ltd., 1974; chmn., chief exec. Courage Ltd., 1978-81; dir. Lloyds Bank PLC, Lloyds Bank Internat. Served to flight lt. RAF, 1939-46. Mem. Brewers' Soc. (dir.). Office: Imperial Group PLC, 1 Grosvenor Pl, London SW1X 7HB, England *

KENT, JILL ELSPETH, government official; b. Detroit, June 1, 1948; d. Seymour and Grace (Edelman) K.; m. Mark Elliott Solomons, Aug. 20, 1978. BA, U. Mich., 1970; JD, George Washington U., 1975, LLM, 1979. Bar: D.C. 1975. Mgmt. intern U.S. Dept. Transp., Washington, 1971-73; staff analyst Office Mgmt. and Budget, Exec. Office of Pres., Washington, 1974-76; legis. counsel U.S. Treasury Dept., Washington, 1976-78; dir. legis. reference div. Health Care Financing Administrn., Washington, 1978-80; sr. Budget Examiner Office Mgmt. and Budget, Exec. Office Pres., Washington, 1980-84; chief Treasury, Gen. Services, OMB, 1984-85; dep. asst. sec. for departmental fin. and planning U.S. Dept. Treasury, 1985-86; dep. asst. sec. for dept. fin. and mgmt., 1986-88; asst. sec. of the Treasury, 1988—; pres. S&K Properties Investment Partnership, Washington, 1979—; lectr. D.C. Pub. Schs.; participant charter exec. devel. program Office Mgmt. and Budget, 1984. Recipient Adminstrs. award Health Care Financing Adminstrn., 1980; named one of Top 40 Performers, Management mag., 1987. Mem. ABA, D.C. Bar Assn., Pres's. Council on Mgmt. Improvement. Republican. Jewish. Home: 5300 27th St NW Washington DC 20015 Office: US Dept Treasury Washington DC 20220

KENT, MICHAEL ANTHONY, lawyer; b. Auckland, New Zealand, Feb. 10, 1948; s. Kurt and Gerda (Goldstein) Kent-Koplowitz; m. Chana Oppenheimer, Mar. 18, 1973. LLB with honors, Law Faculty Auckland, 1971. Assoc. Joseph Jeshurun and Co., Haifa, Israel, 1977-80; ptnr. Kent & Meirom Law Office, Kibbutz Yifat, Israel, 1981—; council mem. Law Research Found., Auckland, 1971. Editor Law Jour. U Auckland, 1971. Mem. Kibbutz Yifat, 1972—. Mem. Israel Bar Assn., Internat. Bar Assn. Mem. Labour party. Jewish. Home: Kibbutz Yifat 30069, Israel Office: Kent & Meirom Law Offices, Doar Yifat, Kibbutz Yifat 30069, Israel

KENTON, FRANK JOSEPH, geology firm executive; b. Uniontown, Pa., June 22, 1950; s. Frank Joseph and Jean (Centofanti) K.; m. Maureen Evelyn Rooker, Aug. 16, 1980; children—Frank Joseph, Gabriel William. B.A., Whittier Coll., 1972. Registered geologist, Oreg., Calif., cert. engring. geologist, Calif., Oreg. Staff geologist Leighton & Assocs., La Habra, Calif., 1972-74, Irvine, Calif., 1977-79, sr. geologist, 1979-80, project geologist, 1980-85, chief engring. geologist, 1985-87, assoc., chief engring. geologist, 1987—; ranch mgr. Windfield Manor, Fargo, N.D., 1976-77; v.p. Silver Queen Mining and Refining, Inc., Mojave, Calif., 1980-86; breeder quality Appaloosa show, race horses, 1980—. Mem. Assn. for Engring. Geologists, Am. Inst. Profl. Geologists (cert.), Carmel (Calif.) Friends of Photography. Home: 4911 Leeds St Simi Valley CA 93063 Office: Leighton & Assocs 790 Hampshire Rd Suite H Westlake Village CA 91361

KENYHERCZ, THOMAS MICHAEL, pharmaceutical company executive; b. Youngstown, Ohio, Jan. 6, 1950; s. William Stephen and Goldie Elizabeth (Matica) K.; BS, Youngstown State U., 1971; MS, U. Cin., 1973, PhD in Analytical Chemistry (Lowenstein Schubert Twitchell fellow), 1975; postdoctoral fellow in bioanalytical chemistry, Kissinger fellow, Purdue U., 1975-77; m. Linda Jane Kostyshak, Mar. 20, 1973. Scientist, sr. scientist, mgr. prodn. support labs. Ortho Pharm. Corp., Raritan, N.J., 1977-80; dir., product devel., quality assurance and regulatory affairs Janssen Pharmaceutica Inc., Piscataway, N.J., 1980-85; pres. Kross, Inc., Hillsborough, N.J., 1985—. Coach basketball St. Mary's Sr. High Sch., 1979-83. Recipient SBIR research award EPA for studies of marine contamination, 1987. Active Ctr. for Creative Living, Religious Sci. Ch. Princeton. Mem. Am. Mgmt. Assn., Am. Assn. Clin. Chemists, Am. Chem. Soc., Electrochem. Soc., Parenteral Drug Assn., Pharm. Mfrs. Assn., Drug Info. Assn., Regulatory Affairs Profl. Soc., Am. Soc. Pharmacognosy, Western Electroanalytical Theoretical Soc., Licensing Execs. Soc., Aquinas Inst. Byzantine Catholic. Mem. editorial bd. Jour. Automated Chemistry, 1975—.

KENYON, FRANK EDWIN, psychiatrist, educator; b. Rock Ferry, Eng., Feb. 4, 1929; s. Fred and Winifred (Dobson) K.; m. Eileen Elizabeth Wright, Apr. 2, 1955; children—Richard, Julia. M.A., Cambridge U., 1954, M.D., 1966. House physician Nat. Health Service, Manchester, Eng., 1954-55; sr. house officer, registrar, sr. registrar Bethlem Royal and Maudsley hosps., London, 1958-64; cons. psychiatrist Warneford Hosp., Oxford, Eng., 1964-84; Lord Chancellor's med. visitor, 1983—; clin. lectr. Oxford U. Mem. parole bd. Eng. and Wales, 1979-82. Author: Psychiatric Emergencies, 1968; Successful Sex, 1978; Feeling Healthy, 1978; The Dilemma of Abortion, 1986; contbr. articles to profl. publs. Served to capt. RAMC, 1955-57. Decorated Gen. Service medal, 1954. Fellow Royal Coll. Psychiatrists (examiner 1976-80, bronze medal 1964), Royal Coll. Physicians. Office: The Priory Clinic, 23 Banbury Rd, Oxford OX2 6NN, England

KEOGH, JEANNE MARIE, librarian; b. Toledo, Sept. 20, 1924; d. Thomas Leroy and Agnes Mary (Wenzler) K. BA, Mary Manse Coll., 1946; BLS, Western Res. U., 1947. Asst. librarian tech. dept. Toledo Pub. Library, 1946-54; tech. librarian Libbey Owens Ford Co., Toledo, 1954-83; librarian Libbey Owens Ford Co. (now subs. Pilkington Group), Toledo, 1983—. Established library Riverside Hosp. Nursing Sch., Toledo, 1950-51; gray lady ARC, Toledo, 1966-70; mem. Transp. Safety Info. com., 1972—; mem. fin. com. Mary Manse Coll., Toledo, 1972-75; chmn. bd. Ecumenical Library Toledo, 1976—. Mem. Ohio Library Assn., Cath. Library Assn., Spl. Libraries Assn. (chmn. 1960-70, 72-74, scholarship com. 1968-74, chmn. Detroit conf. hospitality com. 1970, chmn. metals/materials div. 1977-78, metals/materials div. Honors award 1987), Mary Manse Coll. Alumni Assn. (bd. dirs. 1971-76, pres. 1972-73). Club: Quota (Toledo). Office: Libbey Owens Ford Co 1701 E Broadway Toledo OH 43605

KEOUGH, DONALD RAYMOND, beverage and entertainment company executive; b. Maurice, Iowa, Sept. 4, 1926; s. Leo H. and Veronica (Henkels) K.; m. Marilyn Mulhall, Sept. 10, 1949; children: Kathleen Anne, Mary Shayla, Michael Leo, Patrick John, Eileen Tracy, Clarke Robert. BS, Creighton U., 1949, LLD (hon.), 1982; LLD (hon.), U. Notre Dame, 1985. With Butter-Nut Foods Co., Omaha, 1950-61; with Duncan Foods Co., Houston, 1961-67; v.p., dir. mktg. foods div. The Coca-Cola Co., Atlanta, 1967-71, pres. div., 1971-73; exec. v.p. Coca-Cola USA, Atlanta, 1973-74; pres. Coca-Cola USA, 1974-76; exec. v.p. The Coca-Cola Co., Atlanta, 1976-79, sr. exec. v.p., 1980-81, pres., chief operating officer, dir., 1981—; chmn. bd. dirs. Coca-Cola Enterprises Inc., Atlanta, 1986—, Columbia Pictures Entertainment Inc., 1988—; bd. dirs. IBM World Trade Ams. Group, Nat. Service Industries, Inc. Mem. pres.'s council Creighton U.; trustee Spelman Coll., The Lovett Sch., Agnes Scott Coll.; chmn. bd. trustees U. Notre Dame. Served with USNR, 1944-46. Clubs: Capital City, Piedmont Driving, Commerce. Office: The Coca-Cola Co 1 Coca-Cola Plaza NW Atlanta GA 30313

KEOUGH, JAMES GILLMAN, JR., minister; b. Reading, Pa., June 2, 1947; s. James Gillman Sr. and Nora (Deturck) K.; m. Dawn Eileen Wiest, Sept. 17, 1976; children: Cynthia Ann, James Michael, Wendy Sue, Danielle Lynn, Erin Mae, Bevin Leigh. BA in History Edn., Messiah Coll., Grantham, Pa., 1970; MDiv, Lancaster (Pa.) Theol. Sem., 1973; D of Ministry, Ashland (Ohio) Theol. Sem., 1980. Ordained to ministry United Ch. Christ, 1973. Minister St. Luke's United Ch. Christ, Kenhorst, Pa., 1972-75, Congl. Ch., Winchester, Va., 1975-78, 1st Congl. Ch., Newton Falls, Ohio, 1978-82, Cen. Congl. Ch., Middleboro, Mass., 1982-85; sr. minister 1st Congl. Ch., Pontiac, Mich., 1985—. Author: Teaching Prayer in the Local Parish, 1980. Mem. adv. council Pontiac Schs., 1987—; pres. Somebodycares, Pontiac, 1983—; active Dem. Century Club; Dem. candidate Mich. Ho. Reps., 1988. Mem. Nat. Assn. Congl. Christian Chs., Southeast Mich. Congl. Ministerium, Pontiac Ministers Assn. Lodge: Kiwanis. Home: 3062 St Jude Dr Drayton Plains MI 48020 Office: 1st Congl Church 65 E Huron St Pontiac MI 48059

KEOWN, LAURISTON LIVINGSTON, JR., industrial psychologist, consultant; b. Balt., Feb. 24, 1942; s. Lauriston Livingston and Gladys May (Dykes) K.; m. Patje Alexandra Susemihl, Aug. 7, 1962 (div. 1977); children: Christina, Cassandra, Lauriston, Clayton; m. Nancy Ann Hastie, Mar. 18, 1978. BA cum laude, U. Balt., 1965; MS, U. Alta., 1970, PhD, 1977. Chartered psychologist, Alta. Lectr. Nippissing Coll., Laurentian U., North Bay, Ont., Can., 1968-69; chief systems analyst Dept. Youth, Edmonton, Alta., Can., 1969-71, research dir., 1971-72; dir. planning and research Dept. Culture, Youth and Recreation, Alta., 1972-74; dir. planning and devel. Dept. Recreation, Parks and Wildlife, Alta., Edmonton, 1974-75; asst. dir. Transp. Safety Alta. Transp. Dept., 1975-87; dir. Motor Transp. Bus. and Statis. Analysis, Alta. Transp. and Utilities, 1987—; cons. R. Dehaas Assocs., Edmonton, 1979-80, Draherin Group, Edmonton, 1980-82. Author: (with others) Evaluation of Traffic Safety Programs, 1980; contbr. articles to profl. jours. Mem. Alta. Planning Bd., 1974-82, bd. dirs. Alta. Royal Can. Mounted Police Hist. Celebrations Commn., 1974-75; exec. bd. Traffic Records Commn., Nat. Safety Council, 1978—. Indsl. psychology scholar Lamond Dewhurst & Assocs., U. Alta., 1966. Mem. Am. Assn. Motor Vehicle Adminstr., Can. Conf. Motor Transp. Adminstrs., Alta. Psychologists Assn. Episcopalian. Home: PO Box 148, Bon Accord, AB Canada T0A 0K0 Office: AB Transp, Twin Atria Bldg, 4999-98 Ave, Edmonton, AB Canada T6B X3

KEOWN, NANCY ANN, statistician; b. Trochu, Alta., Can., Apr. 15, 1957; d. Bruce Gerald and Norma Daisy (Pierce) Hastie; m. Lauriston Livingston Keown, Jr., Mar. 18, 1978; children: Christina, Cassandra, Lauriston, Clayton. BS in Math. and Stats., U. Alta., 1980, MBA, 1987. Statis. asst. Alta. Transportation, Edmonton, 1977-78; research tech. Alta. Energy and Natural Resources, Edmonton, 1979; farm safety officer Alta. Workers' Health, Safety and Compensation, Edmonton, 1980-82; research officer Alta. Social Services and Community Health, Edmonton, 1982-87; data adminstr. Alta. Govt. Telephones, Edmonton, 1987—. Author monographs: Stress Management for Rural Residents, 1980; Health and Social Service Manpower in Alberta, 1983; Status Report on Child Care Workers, 1984; Survey of Health and Social Service, Personnel Working in Alberta, Annual. Mem. Am. Math. Soc. Anglican. Home: Box 148, Bon Accord, AB Canada T0A 0K0

KEPLEY, THOMAS HOWARD, securities company executive; b. Salisbury, N.C., Jan. 31, 1933; s. Thomas Oscar and Helen Gould (Gantt) K.; B.S., U. N.C., 1955; certificate of honor in investment banking Northwestern U., 1959; certificate of achievement N.Y. Inst. Finance, 1969; m. Elizabeth Ann Doscher, Nov. 25, 1961; children—Thomas Howard, Elizabeth Anne Gilmore. With McCarley & Co., Inc., mems. N.Y. Stock Exchange, Am. Stock Exchange, Asheville, N.C., 1956-58, Columbia, S.C., 1958-79, mgr. S.C. bond dept., 1958-64, v.p., 1964-72, exec. v.p., bd. dirs., 1972-79, merged with Interstate Securities Corp., 1979, v.p., pres.'s adv. bd., 1979-86, dir., 1965—; sr. v.p. Chapin Davis, Inc., 1986-87; chmn. bd. dirs., pres. H.W. Bischoff Transp. Co., Columbia, Charleston, S.C., 1968-74; dir. Computerecords, Inc., Columbia, Happy Folks, Inc., 1971-81. Chmn., Sports-A-Rama, 1969; mem. U. N.C. Edn. Found., Ram's Club, 1981—, Columbia Com. of 100, 1965—. Trustee, Incarnation Devel. Found., Columbia, 1973—, sec., 1974, treas., 1975, v.p., 1976, pres., 1977, fin. advisor, 1978; bd. govs., chmn. investment and comml. coms. S.C. Reins. Facility, 1974—; investment adv. S.C. Med. Malpractice, 1975—; fin. adv. Richland County (S.C.), 1982—; adv. bd. Lutheran So. Sem., pres., 1986—; trustee Luth. Theol. So. Sem., 1983—, also co-chmn. future planning com.; vice chmn. bd. dirs. Lutheridge Devel. Found., 1984—; bd. dirs., v.p. Kidney Found. S.C., 1975—; chmn. United Fund Com., 1974, 75; founding mem. S.C. Debutante Ball, Inc., chmn., 1981-82, pres., 1983—, bd. dirs., 1981—. Served with AUS, 1956-58. Recipient George Washington Honor medal Freedom Found., Valley Forge, Pa., 1969, Key to City of Seoul (Korea), 1958. Mem. N.Y. Stock Exchange (allied), Am. Stock Exchange (allied), Nat. Security Traders Assn. (conduct and ethics com. 1973-75), Securities Dealers of Carolinas (sec. 1964-65, v.p. 1971-72, pres. 1972-73, chmn. bd. dirs. 1974—, permanent chmn. conv. chmn. 1975—, permanent chmn. edn. com. 1975—), Columbia C. of C., Hibernian Soc., Navy League (1st v.p., dir. Columbia 1982—, pres. 1984—), U.S. Navy League (pres. S.C. chpt. 1986—), Smithsonian Assos., Kappa Alpha Order. Lutheran (chmn. worship and music com. 1971-72, vice chmn. finance com. 1972, chmn. ch. council 1973-74, pulpit com. 1973-75; audit com. S.C. Synod 1973—). Clubs: Forest Lake Country (Columbia); Sertoma (charter life mem., exec.), Goff Swamp Hunting and Fishing, George Bunch Dove; Masons; Walnut Hill Hunt. Pioneer indsl. devel. bond underwriting. Home: 4765 Heath Hill Rd Columbia SC 29206 Office: South Carolina National Bank Bldg Suite 650 Box 1730 Columbia SC 29202

KEPNER, WOODY, public relations executive; b. Millersburg, Pa., June 30, 1920; s. E. Elwood and Charlotte (Dressler) K.; m. Palma M. Brown, Feb. 10, 1943; children: Linda Louise Kepner Henke, Dawn Annette Kepner Kendrick, Tana Lee Kepner Tracy. Student pub. schs. Freelance reporter Williamsport Grit, Harrisburg Telegraph, Harrisburg Patriot-News, Harrisburg Sunday Courier, 1935-41; reporter, feature and spl. events writer, photo editor, news editor, news bur mgr. Miami (Fla.) Publicity Dept., 1945-53, dir., 1953-57; pres., owner Woody Kepner Assos. Inc., Miami, 1957—. Vice pres. United Fund Dade County, 1963—. Served with USN, 1942-45. Mem. Fla. Pub. Relations Assn., Pub. Relations Soc. Am., Greater Miami C. of C. Clubs: Bankers, Cricket. Home: 6901 SW 120th St Miami FL 33156 Office: 9200 S Dadeland Blvd Suite 300 Miami FL 33156

KER, (ALICE) ANN STEELE, music educator, composer, organist, choir director; b. Warsaw, Ind., Nov. 10, 1937; d. George Arthur and Winifred Pauline (Foster) Steele; m. Charles Arthur Ker, Sept. 8, 1957 (div.); children: Kelly Lynne, Karen Elizabeth, Kristin Ann. Student, DePauw U., 1955-57, Butler U., 1957-58; BME, Ind. U., 1974; MA, Notre Dame U., 1987. Organist 1st Presbyn. Ch., Warsaw, 1969-79; dir. music Cen. Christian Ch., Huntington, Ind., 1980; mem. faculty Huntington Coll., 1975—; dir. music Redeemer Luth. Ch., Warsaw, 1980-87; dir. music ministries, Reformed Ch. of Palos Heights, Ill., 1987—; festival condr. Luth. Circuit Festival Chorus; co-founder, bd. mem. No. Ind. Opera Assn.; mem. Lakeland Community Concert Assn., concert critic, bd. mem., 1976-80, 87—. Composer: Hear This!, 1973, Triptych, 1980, Three Men on Camelback, 1982, One Glorious God, 1982, For Me, O Lord, 1983, Softly, 1983, Ways to Praise, 1983, The House of the Lord, 1984, Jesus the Savior is Born!, 1988. Active Kosciusko Community Hosp. Aux., 1975—. Winner 1st place composition competition St. Francis Coll., 1974. Mem. Internat. League Women Composers, Am. Guild Organists (bd. dirs. 1978-81), Am. Choral Dirs. Assn., Nat. Guild Piano Tchrs., Am. Musicol. Soc., Music Tchrs. Nat. Assn., Am. Guild Engllish Handbell Ringers. Republican. Home: 1607 N Springhill Rd Warsaw IN 46580 Office: Reformed Ch of Palos Heights 6600 W 127th St Palos Heights IL 60463

KERBY, ROBERT BROWNING, communications consultant; b. Waynesboro, Va., Oct. 21, 1938; s. Guy Albert and Josephine (Carpenter) K. B.S. in Bus. Adminstrn., Va. Poly. Inst., 1960; postgrad. U. Richmond, 1964, Va. Commonwealth U., 1965, U. Va., 1968. Rep. mfrs. Josten Co., Owatonna, Minn., 1960-67; gen. sales mgr. Sta. WANV, Waynesboro, 1967; tech. editor Gen. Electric Co., Waynesboro, 1967-72; v.p., chief exec. officer Fishburne Hudgins Ednl. Found., Inc., Waynesboro, 1972-86, 1986—; chmn. Target-2000 com., City of Waynesboro, 1988—; communications consultant, Nat. Assn. Radio and Telecommunications Engrs., Inc., Waynesboro, 1986—; advisor Sovran Bank, Waynesboro, 1982—. Designer, author: (catalogue) Military School, 1981 (1st place award Printers Assn. Va.'s, 1982). 1st v.p. Shenandoah Valley Art Ctr., Waynesboro; bd. dirs., chmn. Waynesboro Redevel. Housing Authority, 1970-72; pres. Alumni Assn. Offices, 1960-71; chmn. publicity Robinson for Congress, 1970; chmn. fund raising and adv. bd. Salvation Army, 1967-68; chmn. Target 2000 Com. City of Waynesboro, 1988. Mem. SAR, Quarter Century Wireless Assn., Am. Radio Relay League. Republican. Methodist. Office: Cons PO Box 991 Waynesboro VA 22980-0723

KÉRÉKOU, MATHIEU (AHMED), president People's Republic of Benin; b. Natitingou, Sept. 2, 1933; ed. Saint Raphael Mil. Sch., France, other French mil. schs., 1968-70. Served in French Army until 1961; joined Dahomey Army, 1961; aide-de-camp to Pres. Maga, 1961-63; participant mil. coup d'état which removed Pres. Christophe Soglo, 1967; chmn. Mil. Revolutionary Council, 1967-68; comdr. Ouidah paratroop unit, dep. chief of staff, 1970-72; leader mil. coup d'état which ousted Pres. Ahomadegbe, 1972; pres., prime minister, minister nat. def. of Benin, 1972—, also head Mil. Revolutionary Govt.; former minister planning, former minister coordination of fgn. aid, info. and nat. orientation. Address: Office of Pres, Porto Novo People's Republic of Benin *

KERFERD, GEORGE BRISCOE, classicist, educator; b. Melbourne, Victoria, Australia, Jan. 20, 1915; s. John Anderson and Lynette Annie (Looker) K.; m. Mariamna Clapiers de Collongues, Dec. 16, 1944; children: George Briscoe, Charlotte Inna. BA with honors, U. Melbourne, 1936; BA, U. Oxford, Eng., 1939, MA, 1943. Lectr. classics U. Durham, Eng., 1939-41, 46-51; lectr. Greek U. Sydney, Australia, 1945-46; sr. lectr. Greek and Latin U. Manchester, Eng., 1951-56; prof. Classics U. Swansea, Eng., 1956-67; prof. Latin U. Manchester, Eng., 1967-73; vis. prof. Princeton U., 1971-72; prof. Greek U. Manchester, Eng., 1973-82, prof. emeritus Greek, 1982—; vis. prof. U. Tex., Austin, 1986. Author: The Sophistic Movement, 1981; editor jour. Phronesis, 1973-79. Mem. Soc. for Promotion of Hellenic Studies (pres. 1983-86). Home: 31 Belfield Rd, Manchester M20 0BJ, England

KERFOOT, WILLIAM BUCHANAN, JR., research corporation executive, consultant; b. S.I., N.Y., Mar. 13, 1944; s. William Buchanan Kerfoot and Marguerite (Myers) Baumgartel; m. Patricia Hoffmann, Aug. 21, 1965; children—Christopher Alexander, Kerry Ann. B.A. in Entomology, U. Kans., 1966; Ph.D. in Biology, Harvard U., 1970. Asst. scientist Woods Hole (Mass.) Oceanographic Instn., 1970-75; dir. Environ. Mgmt. Inst. div., Environ. Devices Corp., Marion, Mass., 1975-78; pres. K-V Assocs., Inc., Falmouth, Mass., 1978—. Bd. dirs. dir. Assn. for Preservation of Cape Cod, Orleans, Mass., 1975—; mem. water resources council Cape Cod Planning and Econ. Devel. Commn., Barnstable, Mass., 1978—; citizens adv. com. Dept. Environ. Engring., Boston, 1979-84; water resources adv. com. Dept. Environ. Mgmt., Boston, 1984; Mass. ocean sanctuaries study group Exec. Office Environ. Affairs, Boston, 1985-87. Recipient IR 100 Indsl. Research award, 1977; NSF postdoctorate award, 1970; U.S. EPA Spcl. Commendation award, 1987; hon. Woodrow Wilson fellow Woodrow Wilson Found., 1966. Mem. Nat. Water Well Assn., ASTM, Film Soc. Woods Hold (treas. 1974-75). Episcopalian. Lodge: Rotary. Office: K-V Assos Inc 281 Main St Falmouth MA 02540 Home: 49 Ransom Rd Falmouth MA 02540

KERMALLY, SULTAN BADRUDIN, management consultant; b. Zanzibar, Tanzania, Nov. 23, 1938; arrived in Eng., 1959; s. Badrudin and Khanubai (Datoo) K.; m. Laura Watt, Oct. 31, 1958; children: Jenny, Susan, Peter. Student, U. St. Andrews, Scotland, 1964-65; BS in Sociology with honours, U. London, 1969; LLB, U. Dundee, Scotland, 1979; cert. in edn., Jordanhill Coll. Edn., Glasgow. Chartered acct., U.K. Free lance mgmt. cons. Eng., 1965-87; program dir. Mgmt. Centre Europe, Brussels, 1986-87, group dir., 1987—; sr. acad. instr. Coll. Further Edn., 1966-73, Coll. Higher Edn. 1973-86 Dundee Coll. Tech.; social sci. tutor The Open U., Eng., 1971-87, mgmt. edn. tutor, 1983-87; free lance cons. Eng., Europe, 1987—. Author: Multiple Choice Economics, 1986; contbr. articles to profl. jours. Fellow Royal Soc. Arts; mem. Inst. Mktg. (diploma). Moslem. Home: Ave d' Oppem 23, 1950 Kraainem Brussels Belgium Office: Mgmt Centre Europe, Rue Caroly 15, 1040 Brussels Belgium

KERMAN, BARRY MARTIN, ophthalmologist, educator; b. Chgo., Mar. 31, 1945; s. Harvey Nathan and Evelyn (Bialis) K.; B.S., U. Ill., 1967, M.D. with high honors, 1970; m. Pamela Renee Berliant, Aug. 18, 1968; children—Gregory Jason, Jeremy Adam. Intern in medicine Harbor Gen. Hosp., Torrance, Calif., 1970-71; resident in ophthalmology Wadsworth VA Hosp., Los Angeles, 1971-74; fellow in diseases of the retina, vitreous and choroid Jules Stein Eye Inst. UCLA, 1974-75; fellow in ophthalmic ultrasonography Edward S. Harkness Eye Inst., Columbia U., N.Y.C. and U. Iowa Hosps., Iowa City, 1975; asst. prof. ophthalmology UCLA, 1976-78, Harbor Gen. Hosp., 1976-78; asst. clin. prof. ophthalmology UCLA, 1978-83, assoc. clin. prof., 1983—, dir. ophthalmic ultrasonography lab., 1976—; cons. ophthalmologist, Los Angeles, 1976—. Served with USAFR, 1971-77. Diplomate Am. Bd. Ophthalmology. Fellow Am. Acad. Ophthalmology; mem. Calif. Med. Assn., Los Angeles County Med. Assn., Los Angeles Soc. Ophthalmology, Am. Inst. Ultrasound in Medicine, Am. Soc. Ophthalmic Ultrasound, Am. Registry of Diagnostic Med. Sonographers (exec. bd.). Contbr. articles to profl. jours. Office: 2080 Century Park E Suite 800 Los Angeles CA 90067

KERMEEN, SHARON KAY, social services worker; b. Caledonia, Mich., Dec. 2, 1938; d. Wayne Earl and Crystal Doreen (Johnson) K. Grad. high sch., Middleville, Mich. Typist clk. Barry County Dept. of Social Services, Hastings, Mich., 1957-69, clerical supr., 1970-72, eligibility examiner, 1970-72, assistance payments worker, 1972—. Mem. cast Hastings Civic Players, 1963. Mem. Mich. State Employees Assn. (sec. treas., v.p.), United Auto Workers, Hastings Bus. and Profl. Women's Club (corr. sec., 2d v.p.). Home: 321 S Broadway Middleville MI 49333

KERN, EUGENE FRANCIS, corporation executive; b. San Francisco, July 23, 1919; s. Eugene F. and Dorothy (Danforth) K.; m. Paula Stevenson, Oct. 3, 1942; children: Eugene, Tay, Kathy S.; m. 2d. Vida Del Fiorentino, June 10, 1964. AB, Stanford U., 1942. Wholesaleman, price clk. Tay Holbrook, Inc., Fresno, Calif., 1946-47, salesman, 1947-49; indsl. sales Tay Holdbrook, Inc., San Francisco, 1949-51, dir., 1951-64, asst. purchasing agt., 1951-57, corp. sec., 1952-64, mgr., 1957-60, gen. sales mgr., 1960-62, exec. v.p., 1961-62, dir. purchases, 1962-63, exec. v.p. sales, 1963-64; pres., dir. Par-Kern Supply, Inc., San Leandro, Calif., 1964—. Dir. San Francisco Employers Council, 1959-66. Served from 2d lt. to maj. AUS, 1942-45. Decorated Bronze Star. Mem. Western Suppliers Assn., No. Calif. Suppliers Assn. (treas. 1961-62, dir. 1961-63), Am. Arbitration Assn. (nat. panel arbitrators), Internat. Platform Assn., Nat. Assn. Wholesalers, Stamford Alumni Assn. Clubs: Olympic, Commonwealth, Stanford Buck. Home: 743 Parkway South San Francisco CA 94080 Office: 888 Carden St San Leandro CA 94577

KERN, PAUL ALFRED, advertising executive, research consultant, realtor associate; b. Hackensack, N.J., Mar. 17, 1958; s. Paul Julian and Edith Helen (Colten) K. BS in Commerce, U. Va., 1980; MBA, U. So. Calif., 1983. Sales rep. Procter and Gamble, Cin., 1980-81; research services mgr. Opinion Research, Long Beach, Calif., 1984; consumer planning supr. Dentsu, Young and Rubicam, Los Angeles, 1984-85; research executive DJMC Advt., Inc., Los Angeles, 1986; realtors assoc. Tarbell Realtors, Santa Ana, Calif., 1988—; bd. dirs. Applicon, Inc., Hillsdale, N.J., Kernakopia, Hillsdale; cons. Venture Six Enterprises, Encino, Calif., 1985—, DFS/Dorland, Torrance, Calif., 1986, IMI Machinery Inc., Charleston, S.C., 1987—. Coach, supr. Little League Football, Alexandria, Va., 1981; active Surf and Sun Softball League (1987 champions). Recipient Most Calls Per Day award Procter and Gamble, 1980. Mem. Profl. Research Assn., Am. Mktg. Assn., Am. Film Inst., Internat. Platform Assn., U.S. Tennis Assn. (Michelob Light 4.5 Team Championship 1982), U. Va. Alumni Assn, Nat. Assn. Realtors, Calif. Assn. of Realtors, S. Bay Bd. of Realtors (Torrance), Carson Bd. of Realtors. Club: Alta Vista Racquet. Home: 516 S Irena Redondo Beach CA 90277

KERNAN, BARBARA DESIND, senior government executive; b. N.Y.C., Jan. 11, 1939; d. Philip and Anne (Feuer) Desind; m. Joseph E. Kernan, Feb. 14, 1973. BA cum laude, Smith Coll., 1960; postgrad. Oxford U., 1963; MA, Harvard U., 1963, postgrad. John F. Kennedy Sch. of Govt. Harvard U., 1983; postgrad. in edn. policy George Washington U., 1980. Editor, Harvard Law Sch., 1960-62; tchr. English, Newton High Sch. (Mass.), 1962-63; editor Allyn & Bacon Pubs., Boston, 1963-64; edn. asso. Upward Bound, Edn. Assos., Inc., Washington, 1965-68; edn. program specialist Title I, Elem. and Secondary Edn. Act, U.S. Office Edn., 1969-73; fellow Am. Polit. Sci. Assn., Senator William Proxmire and Congressman Alphonzo Bell, 1973-74; spl. asst. to dep. commr. for elem. and secondary edn. and dir. dissemination, sch. finance and analysis, U.S. Office Edn., 1975-77, chief program analysis br. div. edn. for disadvantaged, 1977-79, chief grant program coordination staff Office Dep. Commr. for Ednl. Resources, 1979-80; chief priority concerns staff Office Asst. Sec. Mgmt., U.S. Dept. Edn., Washington, 1980-81, dir. div. orgnl. devel. and analysis Office of Dep. Undersec. for Mgmt., 1981-86; sr. exec. service candidate on spl. project to improve status of women Sec. Transp., Washington, 1983-84; assoc. adminstr. for adminstrn. Nat. Hwy. Traffic Safety Adminstrn., Dept. Transp., 1986—. Recipient awards U.S. Office Edn., 1969, 71, 77, U.S. Dept. Edn., 1981-86; scholarships U. Mich., 1956-58, Smith Coll., 1958-60, Harvard U., 1962-63; Am. Polit. Sci. Assn. fellow, 1973-74; Sr. Exec. fellow John F. Kennedy Sch. Govt. Harvard U., 1983.

KERNAN, JOHN T., education systems company executive; b. Balt., Feb. 17, 1946; m. Dianne M. Kernan, May 11, 1973; 1 child, Amy B. BS, Loyola Coll., Balt., 1969. Dir. info. systems McCormick & Co., Balt., 1969-77, Borden Inc., Columbus, Ohio, 1977-79; v.p. product devel. Deltak Inc., Chgo., 1979-82; v.p., gen. mgr. Gill Mgmt. Services, San Jose, Calif., 1983-85; pres. Edn. Systems Corp., San Diego, 1985—. Served to capt. U.S. Army, 1965-73. Home: 11676 Tierra Del Sur San Diego CA 92130 Office: Edn Systems Corp 6170 Cornerstone Ct E San Diego CA 92121

KERNER, FRED, book publisher, writer; b. Montreal, Can., Feb. 15, 1921; s. Sam and Vera (Goldman) K.; m. Jean Elizabeth Somerville, July 17, 1945 (div. Apr. 1951); 1 son, Jon Fredrik; m. Sally Dee Stouten, May 18, 1959; children: David, Diane. B.A., Sir George Williams U., Montreal, 1942. Asst. sports editor Montreal Gazette, 1942-44; news editor Canadian Press, Montreal, Toronto, N.Y.C., 1944-50; asst. night city editor A.P., N.Y.C., 1950-57; editor Hawthorn Books, Inc., N.Y.C., 1957-58, pres., 1965-68; exec. editor Crest-Premier Books, Fawcett World Library, N.Y.C., 1958-63, editor-in-chief, 1963-65; pres. Centaur House, Inc. (pubs.), 1964-80, Paramount Securities Corp., 1965-67, Veritas Internat. Pubs., 1976—, Publishing Projects, Inc., 1967—; editorial dir. book and ednl. divs. Reader's Digest, Can., 1969-75; v.p., pub. dir. Harlequin Enterprises Ltd., 1975-83, editor emeritus, sr. cons. editor, 1984—; v.p. Publitex Internat. Corp. (pubs.), 1968-75; pres. Athabaska House, 1975-77; dir. Nat. Mint, Inc.; panelist various profl. confs.; chmn. Internat. Affairs Conf. Coll. Editors, 1965; mem. exec. com. Fed. Pub. Lending Rights Commn., 1986—. Author: (with Leonid Kotkin) Eat, Think and be Slender, 1954, (with Walter M. Germain) The Magic Power of Your Mind, 1956, (with Joyce Brothers) Ten Days to a Successful Memory, 1957, Stress and Your Heart, 1961; pseudonym Frederick Kerr: Watch Your Weight Go Down, 1962, (with Walter M. Germain) Secrets of Your Supraconscious, 1965, (with David Goodman) What's Best for Your Child and You, 1966, (with Jesse Reid) Buy High, Sell Higher, 1966; pseudonym M.H. Thaler: It's Fun to Fondue, 1968, (with Ion Grumeza) Nadia, 1977, Mad About Fondue, 1986, (with Andrew Willman) Prospering in the Coming Great Depression, 1988; contbg. author: Successful Writers and How They Work, 1958, Words on Paper, 1960, Overseas Press Club Cookbook, 1964, The Seniors' Guide to Life in the Slow Lane, 1986, Chambers's Ency.; books transl. into French, German, Japanese, Portuguese, Spanish and Italian; editor: Love is a Man's Affair, 1958, Treasury of Lincoln Quotations, 1965, The Canadian Writer's Guide, 9th edit., 1985, 10th edit., 1988; chmn. editorial adv. com. Can. Author & Bookman, 1978—, pub., 1986—. Mem. local sch. bd., N.Y.C., 1968-69; chmn. sch. com. Westmount High Sch., 1970-72; mem. sch. com. Roslyn Sch., 1973; chmn. pubs. com. Edward R. Murrow Meml. Fund; judge Dr. William Henry Drummond Nat. Poetry Contest; trustee Gibson Lit. Awards, C.A.A. Lit. awards, Benson & Hedges Lit. awards, CA&B Student Creative Writing awards; bd. govs. Concordia U., 1975-79; hon. life mem. Can. Book Pubs. Council; mem. exec. com. Pub. Lending Rights Commn., 1986—, vice-chmn., 1988—; founding chmn. C.A.A. Fund to Develop Can. Writers, 1983—. Fellow Can. Copyright Inst. (vice chmn.), Acad. Can. Writers (vice chmn., bd. govs. 1986—); mem. Orgn. Canadian Authors and Pubs. (founding dir.), Canadian Authors Assn. (v.p. 1972-80, founding dir. Lit. Luncheons, pres. Montreal br. 1974-75, nat. pres. 1982-83, hon. life), Periodical Writers' Assn. Can., Can. Writers' Found. (bd. govs. 1982—), Mystery Writers Am., Writers' Union Can., Canadian Soc. Profl. Journalists, Nat. Speakers Assn., Authors Guild, Authors League Am., Internat. P.E.N., Nat. Speakers Assn., Am. Acad. Polit. and Social Sci., Can. Assn. Restoration of Lost Positives (pres.), Can. Soc. for the Preservation of the Natural Bowtie (pres.), Alumni Assn., Sir George Williams U. (exec. com. 1970-75, pres. 1971-73), Sigma Delta Chi. Clubs: Advertising, Deadline, Overseas Press, Dutch Treat (N.Y.C.); Toronto Men's Press; Author's (London, Eng.). Home: 25 Farmview Crescent, Willowdale, ON Canada M2J 1G5 Office: PO Box 952 Station B, Willowdale, ON Canada M2K 2T6

KERNS, GERTRUDE YVONNE, psychologist; b. Flint, Mich., July 25, 1931; d. Lloyd D. and Mildred C. (Ter Achter) B.; B.A., Olivet Coll., 1953; M.A., Wayne State U., 1958; Ph.D., U. Mich., 1979. Sch. psychologist Roseville (Mich.) Pub. Schs., 1958-68, Grosse Pointe (Mich.) Pub. Schs., 1968-86; pvt. practice psychology, Grosse Pointe, 1980—; instr. psychology Macomb Community Coll., 1959-63. Mem. Mich., Am. psychol. assns., Mich., Nat. socs. sch. psychologists, NEA, Psi Chi. Home: 28820 Grant St Saint Clair Shores MI 48081 Office: 63 Kercheval Suite 205 Grosse Pointe MI 48236

KERO, TERRENCE EDSEL FLOM, electrical engineer; b. Moose Lake, Minn, Sept. 21, 1940; s. Andrew Felix and Olga (Koskey) Flom. B.E.E., Ga. Inst. Tech., 1964. Electronic engr. Control Data Corp., Mpls., 1964-67; electronic engr. Xerox, Pasadena, Calif., 1967-68, ITT, Van Nuys, Calif., 1968-75; supr. laser communications GTE, Mountain View, Calif., 1975-77, mgr. dept. systems engring., 1977-81, mgr. tech. devel., 1982-84; mgr. systems engring. US Sprint, Burlingame, Calif., 1985-86; dir. system planning U.S. Sprint, 1986—. Contbr. articles to profl. jours. Mem. Optical Soc. Am., Laser Inst. Am. Home: 3735 Belleview Kansas City MO 64111 Office: 9300 Metcalf Overland Park CA 94010

KERR, CHESTER BROOKS, publisher; b. Norwalk, Conn., Aug. 5, 1913; s. Chester M. and Mary (Seymour) K.; children by previous marriage: John Seymour II, Philip, Alexander, Chester Brooks Jr.; m. Joan Paterson Mills, 1964; stepchildren: Edwin S. Mills, Hilary Mills Loomis, Alison Mills. B.A., Yale U., 1936; L.H.D. hon., Johns Hopkins U., 1978. Editor Harcourt, Brace & Co., 1936-40; dir. Atlantic Monthly Press, 1940-41; acting. dir. U.S. Internat. Book Assn., 1946; v.p. Reynal & Hitchcock, 1947; dir. Survey of Am. Univ. Presses, 1948-49; sec. Yale U. Press, New Haven, 1949-59, dir., 1959-79; fellow Berkeley Coll. Yale U., 1950-75; pres. Ticknor & Fields, a Houghton Mifflin Co. N.Y.C., 1979-85; mem. adminstrv. bd. Papers of Benjamin Franklin, 1954-77; dir. Franklin Book Program, 1971-74; cons. univ. presses pub. program Ford Found., 1956-63, 65-67; chief book div. OWI, 1942-45; cons. to asst. sec. state for info., 1951; cons. Library of Congress, 1976-77; mem. exec. com. Nat. Book Com., 1968-75; dir. Nat. Enquiry, 1975-78. Author: A Report on American University Presses, 1949. Vice chmn. Conn. Vols. for Stevenson, 1952; co.-chmn. New Haven McCarthy for Pres. Com., 1968; trustee New Haven Free Pub. Library, 1953-70. Recipient Curtis Benjamin prize, 1978; named to Pubs. Hall of Fame, 1986. Mem. Assn. Am. Univ. Presses (sec.-treas. 1957-59, pres. 1965-67, dir. 1967-68), Am. Book Pubs. Council (dir. 1966-69), Am. Pubs. Assn. (dir. 1975-78, sec. 1976-77), Internat. Assn. Scholarly Pubs. (pres. 1977-80), Books Across-the-Sea (nat. chmn. 1985-87), English-Speaking Union. Clubs: Yale, Publishers Lunch, Grolier (N.Y.C.); Mory's, Lawn, Elizabethan (New Haven). Home: 421 Humphrey St New Haven CT 06511 Office: Ticknor & Fields 52 Vanderbilt Ave New York NY 10017

KERR, DEBORAH JANE, actress; b. Helensburgh, Scotland, Sept. 30, 1921; came to U.S., 1947; d. Arthur Kerr-Trimmer; m. Anthony C. Bartley, Nov. 28, 1945 (div. 1959); children—Melanie, Francesca; m. Peter Viertel, July 23, 1960. Student, Helensburgh schs., Northumberland House Sch., Bristol. Began motion picture career in England in Major Barbara, 1940; appeared in films: Love on the Dole, Hatter's Castle, The Avengers, Perfect Strangers, I See a Dark Stranger, 1947, Black Narcissus (N.Y. Critics award), The Hucksters, Edward, My Son, King Solomon's Mines, Quo Vadis, Thunder in the East, Prisoner of Zenda, Julius Caesar, Dream Wife, Young Bess, From Here to Eternity, The End of the Affair, 1955, Proud and Profane, 1956, The King and I, 1956, Heaven Knows Mr. Alison, 1956 (N.Y. Critics Award), Bonjour Tristesse, 1958, Count Your Blessings, 1959, The Journey, 1959, Beloved Infidel, 1959, The Grass is Greener, 1960, The Sundowners, 1960 (N.Y. Critics award), The Naked Edge, 1961, Chalk Garden, 1964, Night of the Iguana, 1964, Marriage on the Rocks, 1965, Casino Royale, 1967, The Gypsy Moths, The Arrangement; appeared on stage in Heartbreak House, 1943, Gaslight (for Brit. troops in Europe), 1945, Tea and Sympathy, 1954-55, The Day After the Fair, London, 1972-73, U.S. tour, 1973—; appeared in: U.S. tour of Seascape, 1975, Long Day's Journey into Night, Los Angeles, 1977, Candida, London, 1977, The Last of Mrs. Cheney, U.S. and Can., 1978-79, The Day After the Fair, Australia, 1979; appeared on London stage in Overheard, 1981 (Recipient Sarah Siddons award as Chgo. actress of the year.); TV roles in: Witness for the Prosecution, 1982, A Woman of Substance, 1985, Reunion at Fairborough, 1985, Hold the Dream.1986. Office: care Lantz Office 9255 Sunset Blvd Suite 505 Los Angeles CA 90069 *

KERR, ELIZABETH MARGARET, educator, author; b. Sault Ste Marie, Mich., Jan. 25, 1905; d. John Arthur and Katherine Dorothy (Hirth) Kerr. BA, U. Minn., 1926, MA, 1927, PhD, 1941. Instr. English, Tabor Coll., Hillsboro, Kans., 1929-30, U. Minn., Mpls., 1930-37, 38-43, Coll. of St. Catherine, St. Paul, 1937-38; asst. prof. Rockford (Ill.) Coll., 1943-45; instr. Milw. State Coll., 1945-55; assoc. prof. U. Wis., Milw., 1956-59, prof., 1959-70, prof. emeritus English, 1970—. Author: Bibliography of the Sequence Novel, 1950, Yoknapatawpha: Faulkner's Little Postage Stamp of Native Soil, 1969, William Faulkner's Gothic Domain, 1979, William Faulkner's Yoknapatawpha: "A Kind of Keystone in the Universe", 1984. MLA research grantee, 1942, Summer Salary Support grantee U. Wis., Milw., 1959, 1961. Mem. MLA, Dickens Studies, Soc. for Study So. Lit. Democrat. Congregationalist. Home: Fairhaven 435 Starin Rd Whitewater WI 53190

KERR, FRANK JOHN, astronomer, educator; b. St. Albans, Eng., Jan. 8, 1918; s. Frank Robison and Myrtle Constance (McMeekin) K.; m. Maureen Parnell, Jan. 7, 1966; children: Gillian Wheeler (dec.), Ian Kerr, Robin Lowry. B.Sc., U. Melbourne, Australia, 1938, M.Sc., 1940, D.Sc., 1962; M.S., Harvard U., 1951. Research scholar U. Melbourne, 1939-40; mem. staff radiophysics lab. Commonwealth Sci. and Indsl. Research Orgn., Sydney, Australia, 1940-68; vis. prof. U. Md., 1966-68, prof., 1968-87, prof. emeritus, 1987—, dir. astronomy program, 1973-78, acting provost div. math. phys. scis. and engring., 1978-79, provost, 1979-85; vis. scientist Leiden U., 1957; vis. prof. U. Tex., 1964, U. Tokyo, 1967; Mem. NSF Adv. Panel Astronomy, 1969-72, chmn., 1971-72. Co-editor: Procs. Internat. Astron. Union Symposia, 1963, 73; Contbr. numerous articles to profl. jours. Trustee Assoc. Univs. Inc., 1981-84. Fulbright travel grantee, 1950-51; Leverhulme fellow, 1967; NSF research grantee, 1967-83; Guggenheim fellow, 1974-75. Mem. Internat. Astron. Union (pres. commn. 33 1976-79), Am. Astron. Soc. (councillor 1972-75, v.p. 1980-82). Club: Cosmos (Washington). Home: 12601 Davan Dr Silver Spring MD 20904 Office: U Md Astronomy Program College Park MD 20742

KERR, JAMES WILSON, engineer; b. Balt., May 21, 1921; s. James W. and Laura Virgia (Wright) K.; B.S. with honors, Davidson Coll., 1942; M.S., N.Y. U., 1948; postgrad. Freiburg U., 1957-60, Brookings Inst., 1970, 75, Fed. Exec. Inst., 1982; m. Mary Thomas Montgomery, Feb. 25, 1945 (div., dec.); children: April Kerr Miller, Catherine Kerr Wood (dec.), Wilson, Andrew; m. June Walker, Dec. 27, 1977 (div.); m. Janice White Bain, Jan. 19, 1985. Commd. 2d lt. U.S. Army, 1942, advanced through grades to lt. col., 1964; with inf., World War II, Korea; electronic staff, Ft. Bragg, N.C., 1948-51; weapons research, N.M., 1953-57; adviser French Army, 1957-60; staff electronics, Ft. Monroe, Va., 1960-62; research mgr., div. dir. CD, Pentagon, 1962-64, as civilian, 1964-81, asst. assoc. dir. Fed. Energy Mgmt. Agy. for Research, 1981-85; sr. staff Michael Rogers, Inc., Winter Park, Fla., 1986—; dir. Mt. St. Helen's Tech. Office, 1980; v.p. Latherow & Co., Arlington, Va., 1965-86. Advanced English instr. French Army, 1957-60; cons. Am. Nat. Red Cross Mus., 1968-85, Smithsonian Instn. Dept. Postal History, 1966-85, NSF, 1976-85. Vol. fireman N.Y. State, 1946-48, Fairfax County, Va., 1969—; fire commr. Fairfax County, 1975-81, chmn., 1977-81, Orange County, Fla., 1986—, pres., 1987—; active Boy Scouts Am., in U.S., Asia and Europe, 1933—; chmn. library bd., Orangeburg, N.Y., 1946-48. Decorated Bronze Star (4), Purple Heart; recipient Silver Beaver award Boy Scouts Am., 1956; Fulbright selectee, Japan, 1986; registered profl. engr., Calif. Fellow AAAS, Explorers Club; mem. Nat. Acad. Sci. (various coms. 1962-87), Internat. Assn. Fire Chiefs (chmn. research com. 1969-88, chief sci. adviser 1982-86), Fed. Fire Council, Nat. Fire Protection Assn. (chmn. hosp.

disaster com. 1973—), SAR, Black Forest Mardi Gras (Germany), Nat. Communications Club, Pentagon Officers Athletic Club, IEEE (sr.), Phi Beta Kappa, Gamma Sigma Epsilon, Delta Phi Alpha. Presbyn. (elder 1963—). Author: Korean-English Phrase Book, 1951; 19th Century Korea Postal Handbook, 1965. Editor Korean Philately mag., 1971-80, 85—. Contbr. articles to profl. jours. Club: University (Fla.). Home: PO Box 366 Winter Park FL 32790 Office: MR 1 340 Park Ave N Winter Park FL 32789

KERR, JANET SPENCE, pulmonary physiologist, pharmacologist; b. New Haven, Conn., May 30, 1942; d. Alexander Pyott and Janet Blake (Conley) Spence; m. Thomas Albert Kerr, Jr., July 24, 1965; children—Sarah Patterson, Matthew Spence, Timothy Marden. B.A., Beaver Coll., 1964; M.S., Rutgers U., 1969, Ph.D., 1973. Asst. prof. Rutgers U., Camden, N.J., 1973-76; research assoc. U. Pa. Sch. Medicine, Phila., 1976-79; adj. asst. prof. U. Medicine and Dentistry N.J.-Rutgers Med. Sch., New Brunswick, 1979-84; sr. research pharmacologist E.I. duPont de Nemours & Co., Wilmington, Del., 1985—. Contbr. articles to profl. jours. Bd. dirs. Delaware-Raritan Lung Assn., Princeton, N.J., 1983-85; mem. Del. Lung Assn. class agt. Beaver Coll., Glenside, Pa. Busch fellow Rutgers U., 1972. Mem. AAAS, Am. Heart Assn., Am. Fedn. Clin. Research, Am. Physiol. Soc., Am. Thoracic Soc. (council mem. eastern sect. 1984—), N.Y. Acad. Scis., Sigma Xi. Current work: Role of oxidant-derived free radicals in inflammation. Subspecialties: Physiology (biology); Physiology (medicine). Office: E I du-Pont de Nemours & Co Exptl Sta Wilmington DE 19898

KERR, KLEON HARDING, educator, state senator; b. Plain City, Utah, Apr. 26, 1911; s. William A. and Rosemond (Harding) K.; Asso. Sci., Weber Coll., 1936; B.A., George Washington U., 1939; M.S., Utah State U., Logan, 1946; m. Katherine Abbott, Mar. 15, 1941; children—Kathleen, William A., Rebecca Rae. Tchr., Bear River High Sch., Tremonton, Utah, 1940-56, prin. jr. high sch., 1956-60, prin. Bear River High Sch., 1960-71; city justice Tremonton, 1941-46; sec. to Senator Arthur V. Watkins, 1947. Mayor, Tremonton City, 1948-53; mem. Utah Local Govt. Survey Commn., 1954-55; mem. Utah Ho. of Reps., 1953-56; mem. Utah State Senate, 1957-64, chmn. appropriation com., 1959—, majority leader, 1963; mem. Utah Legis. Council. Dist. dir. vocat. edn. Box Elder Sch. Dist. Recipient Alpha Delta Kappa award for outstanding contbn. to edn., 1982, award for outstanding contbrs. to edn. and govt. Theta Chpt. Alpha Beta Kappa, 1982, Excellence Achieved in Promotion of Tourism award, Allied Category award Utah Travel Council, 1988; named Tourism Ambassador of Month, 1986. Mem. NEA, Utah, Box Elder edn. assns., Nat., Utah secondary schs. prins. assns., Bear River Valley. C. of C. (sec., mgr. 1955-58), Phi Delta Kappa. Mem. Ch. of Jesus Christ of Latter-day Saints. Lion, Kiwanian. Author: (poetry) Open My Eyes 1983, Trouble In the Amen Corner, 1985; We Remember, 1983; (history) Those Who Served Box Elder County, 1984, Those Who Served Tremonton City, 1985, Diamonds in the Rough, 1987, Facts of Life, 1987. Home: Box 246 Tremonton UT 84337

KERR, NANCY KAROLYN, pastor, mental health consultant; b. Ottumwa, Iowa, July 10, 1934; d. Owen W. and Iris Irene (Israel) Kerr; student Boston U., 1953; AA, U. Bridgeport, 1966; BA, Hofstra U., 1967; postgrad. in clin. psychology Adelphi U. Inst. Advanced Psychol. Studies, 1968-73; m. Richard Clayton Williams, June 28, 1953 (div.); children—Richard Charles, Donna Louise. Ordained pastor Mennonite Ch., 1987. Pastoral counselor Nat. Council Chs., Jackson, Miss., 1964; dir. teen program Waterbury (Conn.) YWCA, 1966-67; intern in psychology N.Y. Med. Coll., 1971-72; research cons., 1972-73; coordinator home services, psychologist City and County of Denver, 1972-75; cons. Mennonite Mental Health Services, Denver, 1975-78; asst. prof. psychology Messiah Coll., 1978-79; mental health cons., 1979-81; called to ministry Mennonite Ch., 1981, pastor Cin. Mennonite Fellowship, 1981-83, nat. chmn. summer curriculum, coordinator campus peace evangelism, 1981-83, mem. Gen. Conf. Peace and Justice Reference Council, 1983-85; instr. Associated Mennonite Bibl. Sems., 1985; teaching elder Assembly Mennonite Ch., 1985-86; pastor Pulaski Mennonite Ch., 1986—; mem. Tri-County Counseling Clinic, Memphis, Mo., 1980-81; spl. ch. curriculum Nat. Council Chs., 1981; mem. Cen. Dist. Conf. Peace and Justice Com., 1981—. Mem. Waterbury Planned Parenthood Bd., 1964-67; mem. MW Children's Home Bd., 1974-75; bd. dirs. Boulder (Colo.) ARC, 1977-78; mem. Mennonite Disabilities Respite Care Bd., 1981-86. Mem. Am. Psychol. Assn., Soc. Psychologists for Study of Social Issues, Davis County Ministries Assn. (v.p. 1988—). Office: Pulaski Mennonite Ch Box 98 Pulaski IA 52584

KERR, WILLIAM ANDREW, lawyer, educator; b. Harding, W.Va., Nov. 17, 1934; s. William James and Tocie Nyle (Morris) K.; m. Elizabeth Ann McMillin, Aug. 3, 1968. A.B., W.Va. U., 1955, J.D., 1957; LL.M., Harvard U., 1958; B.D., Duke U., 1968. Bar: W.Va. 1957, Pa. 1962, Ind. 1980. Assoc. McClintic, James, Wise and Robinson, Charleston, W.Va., 1958; assoc. Schnader, Harrison, Segal and Lewis, Phila., 1961-64; asst. prof. law Cleve. State U., 1966-67, assoc. prof. law, 1967-68; assoc. prof. law Ind. U., Indpls., 1968-69, 72-74; prof. Ind. U., 1974—; asst. U.S. atty. So. Dist. Ind., Indpls., 1969-72; exec. dir. Ind. Jud. Ctr., 1974-86; dir. research Ind. Pros. Attys. Council, 1972-74; mem. Ind. Criminal Law Study Commn., 1973—, sec., 1973-83; reporter speedy trial com. U.S. Dist. Ct. (so. dist.) Ind., 1975-84; trustee Ind. Criminal Justice Inst., 1983-86; dir. Indpls. Lawyers Commn., 1975-77, Ind. Lawyers Commn., 1980-83; mem. records mgmt. com. Ind. Supreme Ct., 1983-86. Bd. dirs. Ch. Fedn. Greater Indpls., 1979-87. Served to capt. JAGC, USAF, 1958-61. Decorated Air Force Commendation medal; Ford Found. fellow Harvard Law Sch., 1957-58; recipient Outstanding Prof. award Students Ind. U. Sch. Law, 1974, Disting. Service award Ind. Council Juvenile Ct. Judges, 1979, Outstanding Jud. Edn. Program award Nat. Council Juvenile and Family Ct. Judges, 1985. Mem. Ind. State Bar Assn., Indpls. Bar Assn., Phila. Bar Assn., W.Va. Bar Assn., Nat. Dist. Attys. Assn., Am. Judicature Soc., Fed. Bar Assn. (Outstanding Service award Indpls. chpt. 1975), Order of Coif, Phi Beta Kappa. Office: 735 W New York St Indianapolis IN 46202

KERRIGAN, JOHN FRANCIS, literary educator; b. Liverpool, Eng., June 16, 1956; s. Stephen Francis and Patricia (Baker) K. BA, Oxford U., Eng., 1977, MA, 1980. Domus sr. scholar Merton Coll., Oxford, 1977-79, jr. research fellow, 1979-82; research fellow St. John's Coll., Cambridge, Eng., 1982-86; asst. lectr. Cambridge U., Eng., 1982-86; research fellow St. John's Coll., Cambridge, Eng., 1986—; lectr. Cambridge U., Eng., 1986—; dir. studies English St. John's Coll., Cambridge, Eng., 1987—; trustee The Wordsworth Trust, Dove Cottage, Grasmere, 1984—; vis. prof. Meiji U., Tokyo, 1986. Author numerous lit. essays; editor: Shakespeare's Love's Labours Lost, 1982, Shakespeare's Sonnets and A Lover's Complaint, 1986; contbr. articles to scholarly jours. Named Chatterton lectr. Brit. Acad., 1988. Home and Office: St John's College, Cambridge England

KERRY, JOHN FORBES, U.S. Senator; b. Denver, Dec. 11, 1943; s. Richard John and Rosemary (Forbes) K.; m. Julia Stimson Thorne, May 22, 1970; children: Alexandra, Vanessa. B.A., Yale U., 1966; J.D., Boston Coll., 1976. Bar: Mass. 1976. Nat. coordinator Vietnam Vets. Against The War, 1969-71; asst. dist. atty. Middlesex (Mass.) County, 1976-79; ptnr. firm Kerry & Sragow, Boston, 1979-82; lt. gov. State of Mass., 1983-85; U.S. senator from Mass. 1985—. Author: The New Soldier, 1971. Democratic candidate for Congress from, 5th Mass. Dist., 1972; bd. vistors Walsh Sch. Fgn. Service, Georgetown U. Served to lt. (j.g.) SUNR, 1966-69. Decorated Silver Star; decorated Bronze Star with oak leaf cluster, Purple Hearts (3). Roman Catholic. Office: Office of Senate Members 362 Russell Senate Bldg Washington DC 20510 *

KERRY, TREVOR LEWIS, educator; b. Dagenham, Essex, Eng., May 7, 1942; s. Lewis Lloyd and Doreen Jesse (Perry) K.; m. Carolle Anne Stapells, Aug. 31, 1963; children: Andrew John, Adrian Paul. BA, Durham U., 1963; MTh, Nottingham U., 1970, MPhil, 1976, PhD, 1982; licentiate, Brit. Inst. Profl. Photographers, 1972. Asst. tchr. Suttons Sch., Havering, 1966-68; lectr. Bishop Grosseteste Coll., Lincoln, 1968-76; project coordinator Nottingham U., 1976-80; prin. lectr. Charlotte Mason Coll., Cumbria, 1980-81; project coordinator Nottingham U., 1981-83; head applied social scis. Doncaster Met. Inst. Higher Edn., Eng., 1984—; examiner Archchiop's Diploma for Readers, Ch. of Eng., 1980—, Liverpool Univ., 1988. Author: Teaching Bright Pupils, 1981, Effective Questioning, 1982, The New Teacher, 1982, Invitation to Teaching, 1986; editor ednl. series of books; contbr. articles to profl. jours. Fellow Coll. of Preceptors. Avocation: ornithology. Home: 15 Lady Bower Close, North Hykeham, Lincoln LN6 8EX, England Office: Doncaster Met Inst Higher Edn, Waterdale, Doncaster DN1 8EX, England

KERSEY, TERRY L(EE), astronautical engineer; b. San Francisco, June 9, 1947; s. Ida Helen (Schmeichel) K. Houseman, orderly Mills Meml. Hosp., San Mateo, Calif., 1965-68; security guard Lawrence Security, San Francisco, 1973-74; electronic engr. and technician engring. research and devel. dept. McCulloch Corp., Los Angeles, 1977; warehouseman C.C.H. Computax Co., Redondo Beach, Calif., 1977-78; with material ops. and planning customer support dept. Allied-Signal Aerospace Co., Torrance, Calif., 1978—. Participant 9th Space Simulation conf., Los Angeles, 1977, 31st Internat. Astronautical Fedn. Congress., Tokyo, 1980, Unispace 1982 for the U.N., Vienna. Served to sgt. USAF, 1968-72, Vietnam. Mem. AIAA (mem. space systems tech. com. 1981—, mem. aerodynamics com. 1980—, Wright Flyer Project Aerodynamics com. 1980—), Nat. Space Inst., Am. Astronautical Soc., The Planetary Soc., Internat. L5 Soc., Ind. Space Research Group, IEEE Computer Soc. Zen Buddhist.

KERSHAW, THOMAS ABBOTT, restaurant company executive; b. Phila., Dec. 1, 1938; s. Melville Gartside and Florence Frieda (Yackle) K.; B.S. in Mech. Engring., Swarthmore Coll., 1960; M.B.A., Harvard U., 1962. Mem. market devel. staff E.I. duPont de Nemours, Wilmington, Del., 1962-64; production mgr. Data Packaging Corp., Cambridge, Mass., 1964-65; owner Primus Assos., Warren, Vt., 1965-66; market devel. mgr. Bolt Beramek & Newman, Cambridge, 1966-69; pres. Exec. Townhouse Corp., Boston, 1969-81; pres. Hampshire House Corp., 1969—, Bull Finch Pub on Pickering Wharf, 1984—, Bull Finch Enterprises, 1985—. Pres., Beacon Hill Bus. Assn., 1979-84; bd. dirs. Beacon Hill Civic Assn.; Rep. ward chmn., vice chmn. city com., Eagle. Named Restauranteur of Year, Mass. Restaurant Assn., 1984.Chmn. bd. Greater Boston Conv. and Visitors Bur. Mem. Theater Dist. Assn., Harvard Bus. Sch. Assn., Nat. Restaurant Assn. (bd. dirs.), Mass. Restaurant Assn. (v.p.), Boston C. of C. Presbyterian. Clubs: Harvard (Boston, N.Y.C.); Union Boat, Corinthian Yacht. Home: 84 Beacon St Boston MA 02108

KERSJES, ANTON FRANS JAN, conductor; b. Arnhem, Netherlands, Aug. 17, 1923; s. Anton Frans Jan and Elisabeth (Peperkamp) K.; m. Margaretha van de Groenekan, Aug. 9, 1946. First violinist Arnhem Symphony Orch., 1940-41; choir condr., 1945-46, 49; co-founder Kunstmaand Chamber Orch., 1953; condr. Netherlands Ballet Sonia Gaskell, 1953-61, Netherlands Opera Co., 1955-60, Amsterdam Ballet, 1960-62; 1st condr. Amsterdam Philharm. Orch., 1953-83, prin. guest condr., 1983—; condr. Netherlands Philharm. Orch. including Concertgebouw Orch., Orchs. Radio Hilversum; guest condr. Netherlands Opera Co. leader condr.'s class Amsterdam Muzieklyceum, Sweelinck Conservatory, 1969-79; leader condr.'s and opera class, adj. dir. Maastricht Conservatory, 1988—; guest lectr. Rijkshogeschool Maastricht; tours in Europe, Scandinavia, U.K., USSR; condr. over 125 concerts, 5 operas on TV; recs. for E.M.I., H.M.V. Decorated officer Order Orange Nassau; recipient Silver medal City of Amsterdam, Silver medal Concertgebouw. Lodge: Rotary. Office: Beurs van Berlage, Damrak 40a, 1012 LK Amsterdam The Netherlands

KERSTEN, GUNTHER HANS, cardiologist; b. Cologne, Germany, Jan. 10, 1930; s. Friedrich Karl and Mathilde Martha (Scherb) K.; m. Ethel Elaine Brokaw, Feb. 26, 1958; children—Gunther H., Karin E. M.D., U. Cologne, 1956. Intern, Monmouth Med. Ctr., Long Branch, N.J., 1956-57; resident Thomas Jefferson U., Phila., 1958-61, fellow in cardiology, Phila., 1961-62; practice medicine specializing in cardiology; mem. staff Univ. Hosp., Cologne. Contbr. articles to profl. jours. Lutheran. Club: Astoria. Home: 43 Belevedere St, Cologne 5000 Federal Republic Germany Office: 10 Lichhof, 5000 Cologne Federal Republic of Germany

KERSTETTER, WAYNE ARTHUR, criminal justice educator, lawyer; b. Chgo., Dec. 1, 1939; s. Arthur Edward and Lillian (Asplund) K.; B.A., U. Chgo., 1964, J.D., 1967. Bar: Ill. 1968. Asst. commr. N.Y. Police Dept., N.Y.C., 1972-73; supt. Ill. Bur. Investigation, Chgo., 1973-76; assoc. dir. Ctr. for Studies in Criminal Justice, U. Chgo., 1976-78; assoc. prof. criminal justice, dept. criminal justice U. Ill.-Chgo., 1978—; sr. research fellow Am. Bar Found., Chgo., 1982—; cons. U.S. Civil Rights Commn., U. Chgo., ABT Assocs., Univ. Research Assocs., Police Found. Mem. transition team Mayor Washington, Chgo., 1983, Criminal Justice Project of Cook County, 1987. Served with USNR, 1962-64. Research grantee Nat. Inst. Justice, 1976, Chgo. Bar Found., 1979-80, Am. Bar Found., 1983; fellow Ctr. for Studies in Criminal Justice, U. Chgo. Law Sch., 1978—. Mem. ABA. Office: Am Bar Found 750 N Lake Shore Dr Chicago IL 60611

KERSTING, ROBERT EDWARD, lawyer; b. Clinton, Iowa Aug. 26, 1916; s. Augustus Henry and Eva (Schaub) K.; student pub. and pvt. schs.; B.S. in Econs., Northwestern U., 1938, J.D., 1941; m. Dolores June Shoup, Dec. 19, 1978; children—Judith, Linda, Laura, Sheryl, Lynn. Bar: Ill. 1941, Ariz. 1946. Practice law, Chgo., 1941-42, Phoenix, 1946—; pres. Red Rock Ranches and Ariz. Aviation Co., 1945-50; spl. asst. atty. gen. of Ariz., 1954—; test pilot, exec. Howard Aircraft, Chgo., 1942-43; sec.-treas., dir. Savage Industries, Inc., 1947—, Ariz. Welding Equipment Co., 1947—, Savage Mfg. Co., 1948—, Phoenix Irrigation Service, Inc., 1957—, Trust Investment Enterprises, 1959—, Sun States Land and Devel. Co.; chmn. bd., Counsel Sunshine Land & Cattle Corp.; pres., dir., gen. counsel Yavapai Hotels Corp., Western Growth Capital Corp.; dir., gen. counsel Ins. Corp. Am., Queen Creek Land & Cattle Corp.; dir., mem. exec. com. Financial Corp. Ariz.; field counsel Fed. Nat. Mortgage Assn.; pres. Integrity Escrows of Ariz., 1st Western Funding Corp., 1st Tex. Holding Corp.; gen. counsel, mem. exec. com., dir. Investors United Life Ins. Co., Western Nat. Mortgage Corp., Global Machinery Corp., Synthetic Lubricants Corp.; counsel Technopulp AG, Zurich and Madrid, 1974—; mem. Chgo. Bd. Trade, 1940-41. Active ARC; sec., dir. Phoenix Symphony Assn.; treas. Phoenix charter govt. com., 1950; chmn. Phoenix Athletic Commn., 1952. Mem. Ariz. state central com. Democratic party, 1951—, alt. del., nat. conv., 1952, 56; pres. Phoenix Young Democrats Club, 1948, nat. com. Young Democrats of Ariz., 1950; pres. Ariz. Dem. Assn., 1955; del., mem. rules com. Dem. Nat. Conv., 1960; treas. Maricopa County Dem. Central Com. Bd. dirs. McCune Found. Served as chief flight instr. USAAF, also with flight tng. program USN, 1941-45. Mem. Am., Ariz. bar assns., Navy League of U.S., N.U. Alumni Club (pres. 1947), C. of C., Teen-Age C. of C. (dir. 1947), Am. Detective Assn. (pres. 1957—), Phi Gamma Delta, Phi Delta Phi. Episcopalian. Moose. Clubs: 20-30, Phoenix Press, Phoenix Country, Paradise Valley Racquet, Racquet (Palm Springs, Calif.); Executive, Fraternal Order of Police. Home: 18043 N 45th Ave Glendale AZ 85308

KERWIN, LARKIN, Canadian research council administrator, physics educator; b. Quebec, Que., Can., June 22, 1924; m. Maria Guadalupe Turcot, 1950; 8 children. Cert. engring. studies St. Francis Xavier U., 1943, B.Sc. summa cum laude, 1944; M.Sc. magna cum laude, MIT, 1946; D.Sc. magna cum laude, U. Laval, 1949; LL.D. (honoris cause), St. Francis Xavier U., 1970, U. Toronto, 1973, Concordia U., Montreal, 1976, U. Alta., 1983, U. Dalhousie, 1983; D.Sc. (honoris causa), U. B.C., 1973, McGill U., 1974, Meml. U. Newfoundland, 1978, U. Ottawa, 1981, Royal Mil. Coll. Can., 1983, U. Winnipeg, 1983 D.Civil Law h.c., Bihsop's U., 1978. Teaching asst. St. Francis Xavier U., 1944; lab. demonstrator U. Toronto, 1945; research physicist Geotech. Corp., Cambridge, Mass., 1945; lab. asst. physics dept. U. Laval, Quebec, 1946-48, asst. prof., 1948-51, assoc. prof., 1951-56, prof., Chair of Atomic Physics, 1956, dir. Mass. Spectrometry Lab., 1955-66, chmn. dept. physics, 1961-67; dir. Van de Graaf Accelerator Lab., 1961-72, vice-dean faculty of scis., 1967-68, acad. vice-rector, 1969-72; rector, 1972-77; pres., Nat. Research Council Can., 1980—. Author: Atomic Physics, An Introduction, 1963; mem. editorial bd. Interdisciplinary Sci. Revs. Mag., 1981—; contbr. numerous articles to profl. jours. Trustee Nat. Museums of Can., 1980—; adv. council Ottawa chpt. Can. Soc. Weizmann Inst. Sci., 1981—; Canadian rep. Versailles conf. on tech. and employment, 1982; bd. govs. Carleton U., 1983—. Recipient Centenary medal, 1967; knight Equestrian Order of Holy Sepulchre of Jerusalem, 1970, knight comdr., 1972, comdr. with star, 1974, knight grand cross, 1980; Jubilee medal, 1977; Centenary medal of Roumania, 1977; officer Order of Can., 1978, companion, 1980; medal of Laval Alumni, 1978; Ordre du Merite, Société Saint-Jean Baptiste de Que., 1979; Gold medal, Can. Council Profl. Engrs., 1982, officer Order of Quebec, 1987; Outstanding Achievement award Govt. Can., 1987. Fellow Royal Soc. Can., Royal Soc. Arts, AAAS, Am. Inst. Physics; mem. Internat. Union Pure and Applied Physics (pres. 1987—), Association Canadienne Française pour l'Avancement des Sciences (Pariseau medal 1965), Am. Phys. Soc., Can. Assn. Univ. Tchrs., Corp. Profl. Engrs. Que., Sociedad Mexicana Fisica, Can. Assn. Physicists (Gold medal 1969), Assn. Sci. Engring. and Technol. Community of Can., Le Cercle Universitaire de Québec. Office: Nat Research Council of Can, Montreal Rd, Ottawa, ON Canada K1A 0R6

KESER, PAUL DAVID, consultant robotics and automation, retired manufacturing company executive; b. Phila., Sept. 10, 1927; s. Otto August Leo and Madeline (Hoch) K.; m. Jo Anne Griffin, Nov. 11, 1951 (div. 1956); 1 child, William Griffin; m. Nancy Jones, Aug. 15, 1959; children—Paul David, Tonya Marie. Student Temple U., 1947-49. Electronic engr. Shallcross Mfg., Clifton Heights, Pa., 1951-55, Internat. Resistance Co., Burlington, Iowa, 1955-63; sr. devel. engr. Speer Carbon, Niagara Falls, N.Y., 1963-68; mgr., electronic engr. Butler Mfg. Co., Galesburg, Ill., 1969—. Patentee in field. Chmn. camping and conf. operating com. Ill. Synod Luth. Ch. in Am., 1978—; bd. dirs. blood ctr. ARC, 1980—, United Way, 1983—, Ill. So. Wis. Exchange Dist., 1982-85; pres. Galesburg Exchange Club, 1985—. Mem. Soc. Mfg. Engrs. (sr.), Instruments Soc. Am. (sr.), Numerical Control Soc. (sr.), IEEE. Republican. Avocations: bike riding; boating; golf; racquetball. Home: Rural Route 2 Box 248 Galesburg IL 61401

KESISOGLU, GARBIS, publishing company executive; b. Istanbul, Turkey, June 27, 1936; came to Fed. Republic Germany, 1955; s. Serkis and Varvar (Norhadian) K.; m. Mari Demirhekim, Jan. 7, 1977. M.Sc., Tech. U. Munich, Fed. Republic Germany, 1960. Engr. A Kunz & Co., Munich, 1960-64, 1966-68; corr. Hurriyet Newspaper, Frankfurt, Fed. Republic Germany, 1968-71; mng. dir. Ege-Pub. Ltd., Frankfort, 1971-83, Ter-Pub. Ltd., Frankfurt, 1983—. Served to lt. Turkish Army, 1964-66. Mem. Bavarian Journalists, Internat. Airline Passenges Assn. Dallas, Internat. Circulation Mfrs. Assn. Clubs: Press (Munich); Clipper, TWA Ambassador, Six Continents, Brit. Airways Exec. Home: Jakob Latscha Strasse 29, 6072 Dreieich 3 Federal Republic of Germany Office: Ter-Druckerei GMBH, Admiral Rosendahl Str 16, 6078 Neulsenburg 4 Federal Republic of Germany

KESSEL, DAGOBERT GUNTRAM, petroleum science educator; b. Koenigsberg, Germany, May 16, 1935; s. Fritz Karl and Margarete (Bittner) K.; m. Christel Annemarie Brederlow, June 1, 1963; children: Susanne, Barbara, Michael. Diploma in geophysics, Tech. U. Clausthal, Fed. Republic Germany, 1964, PhD in Theoretical Physics, 1968. Research geophysicist Texaco Belgium S.A., Ghent, 1968-71; coordinator reservoir physics Deutsche Texaco AG, Wietze, Fed. Republic Germany, 1971-79, mgr. R. and T. producing, 1979-86; dir., prof. petroleum sci. German Inst. for Petroleum Research Tech. U. Clausthal, 1986—. Contbr. articles to profl. jours. Mem. Soc. Petroleum Engrs., Deutsche Wissenschaftliche Gesellschaft fuer Erodel, Erdgas, Kohle E.V. Lutheran. Office: German Inst Petroleum Research, Walther-Nernst-Str 7, 3392 Clausthal-Zellerfeld Federal Republic of Germany

KESSLER, A. D., business, financial, investment and real estate advisor, consultant, educator, lecturer; b. N.Y.C., May 1, 1923; s. Morris William and Belle Miriam (Pastor) K.; m. Ruth Schwartz, Nov. 20, 1944; children: Brian Lloyd, Judd Stuart, Earl Vaughn. Student U. Newark, 1940-41, Rutgers U., 1941-42, 46, Albright Coll., 1942, Newark Coll. Engring., 1946; MBA, Kensington U., 1976, PhD in Mgmt. and Behavioral Psychology, 1977. Sr. cert. rev. appraiser (CRA), cert. exchangor (CE); registered mortgage underwriter (RMU). Pvt. practice real estate, ins. and bus. brokerage, N.J., Pa., Fla., N.Y., Nev., Calif., Hong Kong, 1946; pres. Armor Corp., 1947-68; pres. Folding Carton Corp., Am., N.Y.C., 1958-68; exec. v.p. Henry Schindall Assocs., N.Y.C., 1966-67; tax rep. Calif. State Bd. Equalization, 1968-69; aviation cons. transp. div. Calif., Dept. Aeros., also pub. info. officer; 1969-71; FAA Gen. Aviation Safety Counselor; broker, mgr. La Costa (Calif.) Sales Corp., 1971-75; chmn. bd. Profl. Ednl. Found., 1975—, Timeshare Resorts Internat., 1975—, Interex, Leucadia, Calif., 1975-82, The Kessler Orgn., Rancho Santa Fe, Calif., 1975—, The Kessler Fin. Group, Fin. Ind. Inst., 1977—; pres. Ednl. Video Inst., 1978—, Fin. Planning Inst., 1975—; treas., exec. bd. dirs. Nat. Challenge Com. on Disability, 1983—; dir. Practice Mgmt. Cons. Abacus Data Systems, 1984—; broker mgr. Rancho Sante Fe (Calif.) Acreage & Homes, Inc., 1987—; mktg. dir. Commercial Real Estate Services, Rancho Sante Fe, 1987—; publisher, editor in chief Creative Real Estate Mag., 1975—; publisher Creative Real Estate Mag. of Australia and New Zealand; founder, editor Moderator of Tape of the Month Club; founder, producer, chmn. Internat. Real Estate Expo; chmn. bd. The Brain Trust, Rancho Santa Fe, Calif., 1977—; fin. lectr. for Internat. Cruise Ships, Cunard Line, Norwegian Am. Cruises, others; adj. faculty, prof. of fin. Clayton U., St. Louis, Calif. Scoutmaster Orange Mountain council Boy Scouts Am., 1955-62; harbor master N.J. Marine Patrol, 1958-67; dep. sheriff, Essex County, N.J., 1951-65. Served with USAF, 1942-45. Decorated D.F.C., Air medal, Purple Heart; named to French Legion of Honor, Order of Lafayette. Mem. Am. Soc. Editors and Publishers, Author's Guild, Internat. Platform Assn., Nat. Speakers Assn., Nat. Press Photographers Assn., Guild Assn. Airport Execs., Aviation and Space Writers Assn., Nat. Assn. of Real Estate Editors (NAAREE), Internat. Exchangors Assn. (founder), Nat. Press Club, Overseas Press Club. Clubs: La Costa Country, Cuyamaca, Rancho Santa Fe Country. Lodges: Masons, Shriners. Author: A Fortune At Your Feet, 1981, How You Can Get Rich, Stay Rich and Enjoy Being Rich, 1981, Financial Independence, 1987, The Profit, 1987; author and inst. "Your Key to Success" seminar, 1988; editor: The Real Estate News Observer, 1975—; fin. editor API, 1978—; fin. columnist Money Matters, 1986—; syndicated columnist, radio and tv host of "Money Making Ideas", 1977; producer (movies) The Flight of the Cobra, Rena, We Have Your Daughters, Music Row; speaker for radio and TV as The Real Estate Answerman, 1975—; host (radio and TV show) Ask Mr. Money. Home: Box 1144 Rancho Santa Fe CA 92067

KESSLER, ALBERT LEON, lawyer; b. Elizabeth, N.J., Mar. 9, 1916; s. Samuel and Lena (Schwartz) K.; m. Bernice Scarr, June 20, 1950; children—Frederic Stuart, Ruth Ellen. B.A., NYU, 1937, LL.B., 1939, LL.M., 1950. Bar: N.J. 1941, U.S. Dist. Ct. N.J. 1941. Atty., Bd. Vets. Housing, Rahway, N.J., 1951-58; spl. counsel vets. loans State of N.J., 1953-69, spl. counsel pub. housing, 1953-67; sole practice, Elizabeth, 1941—; lectr. appellate advocacy Rutgers Law Sch., Newark, N.J., 1954-62. Counsel Union County Democratic Com., Elizabeth, 1951; dist. committeeman Union Twp. Dem. Com., 1980—; fire commr. Union County, 1984-85; mem. Union Twp. Zoning Bd., 1986—; vice chmn. Union Twp. Community Devel. Agy., 1988—; pres. Home for Disabled Soldiers, Menlo Park, 1953-73, N.J. Union YM-YWHA, 1965-68; chmn. East Union County chpt. ARC, 1959-61. Served to capt. U.S. Army, 1942-46, MTO, ETO. Decorated D.S.C., D.S.M.; named Citizen of Yr., Union Twp. Com., 1983, Y Man of Yr. YM-YWHA's of Eastern Union County, 1969 (1st ann. award). Mem. N.J. State Bar Assn., Union County Bar Assn. (trustee 1972-75). Res. Officers Assn. (pres. Elizabeth 1953-54), Am. Legion. Lodges: Masons, B'nai Brith. Home: 934 Lowden Ave Union NJ 07083 Office: 1139 E Jersey St Elizabeth NJ 07201

KESSLER, LAWRENCE W., scientist, scientific instrument company executive; b. Chgo., Sept. 26, 1942; s. Michael C. and Sue (Sniader) K.; m. Francesca Agramonte, Nov. 30, 1985; children: Jeffrey, Brett, Corey, Brandy, Lindsay. BSEE, Purdue U., 1964; MS, U. Ill., 1966, PhD, 1968. Mem. research staff Zenith Radio Corp., Chgo., 1968-74; pres. Sonoscan, Inc., Bensenville, Ill., 1975—; adj. prof. info. engring., U. Ill., Chgo., 1975-78; organizer 7th Internat. Symposium Acoustical Imaging and Holography, 1976, 16th Internat. Symposium on Acoustical Imaging, June 1987; mem. statutory adv. com. FDA, 1973-75. Editor: Procs. Ultrasonics Symposium, IEEE, Inc. 1970; Acoustical Holography, Vol. 7, 1977, Vol. 16, 1988; contbr. articles to tech. jours. Patentee acoustical microscopy, Bragg diffraction imaging, also liquid crystal device. Fellow Acoustical Soc. Am.; sr. mem. IEEE (sec.-treas. sonics and utrasonics div. 1969-71, pres. div. 1971-73, nat. lectr. 1981-82); mem. Am. Inst. Ultrasound in Medicine, Am. Soc. Nondestructive Testing, Sigma Xi, Etta Kappa Nu. Home: 543 Rutgers Ln Elk Grove Village IL 60007 Office: Sonoscan Inc 530 E Green St Bensenville IL 60106

KESSLER, MICHAEL GEORGE, tax fraud investigator; b. Bklyn., Dec. 31, 1951; s. Anthony Vincent and Mildred Marie K.; AA, St. John's U., Jamaica, N.Y., 1971, BS, 1973, MBA, 1978; cert. advanced grad. study Pace U., 1980; m. Eloise Lita Mogel, Mar. 16, 1975; children: Jonathan, Timothy. Cash control officer R. H. Macy's, N.Y.C., 1969-73; sr. auditor Blue Cross-

Blue Shield Greater N.Y., N.Y.C., 1973-78; prin. spl. audit investigator N.Y. State Atty. Gen., N.Y.C., 1978-81, regional chief auditor investigator, 1981-83, asst. chief auditor investigator, statewide tng. officer, 1983-87; chief of investigations, N.Y. State Tax Enforcement, 1987—; auditor in charge Medicare/Medicaid Fraud Control Tng. Program, HEW. Pres. bd. mgrs. The Oaks at LaTourette Condominium; mem. N.Y.C. Community Bd. #3, Staten Island. Recipient cert. achievement Blue Cross Assn., 1974; award of spl. recognition for unique achievement and service Borough Pres., Staten Island; cert. tchr., N.Y. State. Mem. Assn. Internal Auditors, Community Assns. Inst. (bd. dirs.), Am. Soc. Indsl. Security, Nat. Law Enforcement Assocs. Contbg. author HEW audit manual; author investigative auditing workpapers, medicaid fraud report for Nat. Assn. Attys. Gen., 1983. Home: 3 Whitcomb Ave Mount Sinai NY 11766

KESSLER, MILTON, manufacturing executive; b. E. Pitts., Nov. 2, 1917; s. Harry and Rose (Hirsch) K.; m. Justine Levy, Nov. 16, 1947; children—Ronald N., Kathyann, Wendy, Brian. Pres., Kessler Products Co., Inc., Youngstown, Ohio, 1940—, Kessler Inc., Youngstown, 1955—, Dover Molded Products (Ohio), 1958—, Youngstown Kitchens, 1975—, Anderson (S.C.) Textile, 1974—; chmn. bd. Space Links, Youngstown, 1975—, Youngstown Thermal Inc., 1981—, Thermal Resources Ohio, Thermal Resources St. Louis, Thermal Resources Balt. Bd. dirs. Heritage Manor, Youngstown, 1960. Mem. Am. Mgmt. Assn., Young Pres. Orgn., Youngstown C. of C., Soc. Plastics Industry, Soc. Plastics Engrs. Republican. Jewish. Clubs: Squaw Creek Country (dir. 1977), B'nai B'rith, Masons (32d degree). Inventor in field. Home: 6690 Harrington St Boardman OH 44512 Office: 302 McClurg Rd Youngstown OH 44512

KESTER, PATRICIA ANNETTE, clinical psychologist, educator; b. Colorado Springs, Colo., Aug. 9, 1945; d. James Douglas and Lucille Erma (Townley) K.; B.A., U. Tex., Austin, 1967; M.Ed., U. Houston, 1973; Ph.D., U.S. Internat. U., 1978. Social worker Okla. Dept. Public Welfare, Oklahoma City, 1967-68, Tex. Dept. Public Welfare, Houston, 1968-69, Harris County Child Welfare, Houston, 1969-71; tchr. Houston Ind. Sch. Dist., 1971-72; counselor Tex. Research Inst. for Mental Sci., Houston, 1973-74; research assoc. dept. psychiatry SUNY, Stony Brook, 1974-76; psychol. intern Mercy Hosp., San Diego, 1977-78; lectr. dept. psychology U. Calif., San Diego, 1979; postdoctoral fellow Garrard Ctr. for Psychology, La Mesa, Calif., 1979-80; pvt. practice clin. psychology, La Mesa, Calif., 1980-82, Orange, Calif., 1980-88, La Jolla, Calif., 1982—; adj. asst. prof. Chapman Coll., Orange, 1979-84. Bd. dirs. Who Cares, community mental health ctr., Houston, 1973-74. NIH fellow, 1974-76; NIMH grantee, 1975-76. Mem. Am. Psychol. Assn., Calif. Psychol. Assn., Calif. Assn. Marriage and Family Therapists, Am. Assn. Sex Educators and Therapists, Acad. San Diego Psychologists, San Diego Soc. Sex Therapy and Edn. (pres. 1986-87), Soc. Scientific Study Sex (local chpt. chair 1985-86, Western Region conf. chair 1986). Contbr. articles to profl. publs. Home: PO Box 278 La Jolla CA 92038 Office: 8950 Villa La Jolla Dr Suite 2200 La Jolla CA 92037

KESTLER, MAXIMILIANO, television company executive, lawyer, educator; b. San Felipe, Guatemala, June 6, 1919; s. Maximiliano and Silda (Farnes) K.; m. Maria Teresa Amparo Morán, June 25, 1955; children: Maximiliano, Eduardo Cristián. Atty. and Notary, U. San Carlos, Guatemala, 1950; cert. internat. law, Internat. Tng. Centre, Strasbourg, France, 1975. Prof. law and social sci. U. San Carlos, 1952-56, U. Rafael Landivar, 1961-64, U. Francisco, Marroquin, Guatemala, 1966-79; vice-minister fgn. affairs Guatemala, 1961-66; pres. Radiotelevisión Guatemala-Channel 3, Guatemala City, 1981—; advisor various Guatemalan fin. instns.; rep., chief ambassador Mission of Guatemala to UN, 1966; dir. Sch. Internat. Relations Guatemala Ministry Fgn. Affairs, 1974—. Author: Introduction to Guatemalan Constitutional Law, 1950 (Gold Medal 1951). Mem. Com. to Eradicate Illiteracy in Guatemala. Recipient Civil Order Merit Govt. of Spain, 1962, Grand Cross Republic of Chile, 1963, Estrella Brillante Republic of China, 1961, Grand Cross of Disting. Service Govt. Peru, 1965, Order Aztec Eagle, Govt. Mexico, 1966, Order San Silvestre Pope John Paul II, 1981. Mem. Guatemalan Assn. Internat. Law (exec. dir. 1964—), Phi Delta Phi. Home: 4th Ave 20-44, Zone 14, Guatemala City Guatemala Office: Canal 3-Radio-TV Guatemala, 30 Avenida 3-40, Zona 11 Apartado 1376, Guatemala City Guatemala

KESWICK, SIMON LINDLEY, financial executive; b. May 20, 1942; s. Sir William Keswick; m. Emma Chetwode, 1971; 4 children. Student, Eton Coll., Eng., U. Cambridge, Eng. Chmn. Jardine Matheson Ins. Brokers Ltd., 1978-82; mng. dir. Jardine Matheson and Co., Hong Kong, 1982, chmn., 1983—; chmn. Jardine Mathson Holdings Ltd., 1984—; chmn. Hong Kong Land Co., 1983—, Hong Kong and Shanghai Banking Corp., 1983—; past bd. dirs. Fleetways Holdings Ltd., Australia, Greenfriar Investment Co. Ltd., Matheson and Co. Ltd. Mem. the Queen's Body Guard for Scotland, Royal Co. of Archers, 1982—. Clubs: White's, Turf, Union (Sydney). Office: 35 Mount Kellett Rd, Hong Kong Hong Kong *

KETCHUM, ALTON HARRINGTON, retired advertising executive; b. Cleve., Oct. 8, 1904; s. Wesley H. and Velma M. (Davis) K.; m. Robyna Neilson, Apr. 27, 1940; 1 dau., Deborah (Mrs. Harvey Lambert). B.A., Western Res. U., 1926. Spl. corr. United Press, 1926-27; editorial, advt. work Penton Pub. Co., Powers-House Co., Nesbitt Service Co., 1927-33; with McCann-Erickson, Inc., 1934-62, beginning as copy writer, successively copy group head, v.p., creative supr. internat. div., 1948-62; v.p. Infoplan div. Interpublic, Inc., 1962-64; corporate adminstrv. staff Interpublic, 1964-69; mng. dir. Harrington's Hist. Resources, 1970—; Spl. asst. Petroleum Adminstrn. for War, 1943-44; supr. nat. campaign to explain Am. econ. system sponsored by Advt. Council, 1948-51; spl. rep. USIA, India, 1954, cons., 1956—, mem. exec. res., 1957-60. Designer People's Capitalism exhibit, 1956, Golden Key Exhibit for Dept. Commerce, 1956; Author: Follow the Sun, 1930, The Miracle of America, 1948, The March of Freedom, 1951, Let Freedom Ring, 1952, Uncle Sam: The Man and The Legend, 1959, The Green Bough, 1984; editor: Bull. Inst. Mktg. Communications, 1965-69, Principles and Practices of Marketing Communications, 1966; mem. internat. editorial bd. World Govt. News, 1949-52. Organizer Westchester-Fairfield (Conn.) com. Am. Assn. for UN, 1946; mem. Historic Dist. Commn., Greenwich; Mem. Greenwich (Conn.) Aux. Police. Recipient awards Freedoms Found., 1949, 61, award of merit USIA, 1956; medal for outstanding service to advt. Advt. Fedn. Am., 1961; Ohio Gov.'s award for achievement, 1965. Mem. Assn. Am. Geographers, Am. Acad. Polit. and Social Sci., Am., Greenwich hist. socs., India-Am. League (pres. 1960-64), Hist. Assn. Gt. Britain, Nat. Planning Assn., S.A.R., Company Mil. Historians. Home: 333 Cognewaug Rd Cos Cob CT 06807

KETCHUM, MILO SMITH, civil engineer; b. Denver, Mar. 8, 1910; s. Milo Smith and Esther (Beatty) K.; m. Gretchen Allenbach, Feb. 28, 1944; children: David Milo, Marcia Anne, Matthew Phillip, Mark Allen. B.S., U. Ill., 1931, M.S., 1932; D.Sc. (hon.), U. Colo., 1976. Asst. prof. Case Sch. Applied Sci., Cleve., 1937-44; engr. F.G. Browne, Marion, Ohio, 1944-45; owner, operator Milo S. Ketchum, Cons. Engrs., Denver, 1945-52; partner, prin. Ketchum, Konkel, Barrett, Nickel & Austin, Cons. Engrs. and predecessor firm, Denver, 1952—; prof. civil engring. U. Conn., Storrs, 1967-78; emeritus U. Conn., 1978—; mem. Progressive Architecture Design Awards Jury, 1958, Am. Inst. Steel Constrn. Design Awards Jury, 1975, James F. Lincoln Arc Welding Found. Design Awards Jury, 1977; Stanton Walker lectr. U. Md., 1966. Author: Handbook of Standard Structural Details for Buildings, 1956; editor-in-chief Structural Engineering Practice, 1981-84; contbr. engring. articles to tech. mags. and jours. Recipient Disting. Alumnus award U. Ill., 1979. Fellow Am. Concrete Inst. (hon. mem.; dir., Turner medal 1966), ASCE (pres. Colo. sect., hon.), Instn. Structural Engrs. (London), Am. Cons. Engrs. Council; mem. Nat. Acad. Engring., Am. Soc. Engring. Edn., Internat. Assn. Shell and Space Structures, Structural Engrs. Assn. Colo. (pres.), Cons. Engrs. Council Colo. (pres.), Old Saybrook (Conn.) Hist. Soc., Sigma Xi, Tau Beta Pi, Chi Epsilon, Phi Kappa Phi, Alpha Delta Phi. Club: North Cove Yacht. Home: 165 Estes St Denver CO 80226

KETELSEN, JAMES LEE, diversified industry executive; b. Davenport, Ia., Nov. 14, 1930; s. Ernest Henry and Helen (Schumann) K.; children: James V., Lee. B.S., Northwestern U., 1952. C.P.A., Tex., Ill. Accountant Price Waterhouse & Co. (C.P.A.s), Chgo., 1955-59; v.p. finance, treas. J.I. Case Co., Racine, Wis., 1962-68; pres., chief exec. officer J.I. Case Co., 1968-72; exec. v.p. Tenneco Inc., Houston, 1972—; chmn. bd., chief exec. officer Tenneco Inc., 1978—, also dir.; dir. J.P. Morgan & Co., Sara Lee Corp., GTE Corp., Alliance for Free Enterprise, Houston C. of C., Exec. Council on Fgn. Diplomats. Mem. Pres.' Bd. of Advisors on Pvt. Sector Initiatives, Com. for Econ. Devel.; bd. dirs. Am. Petroleum Inst.; trustee Northwestern U., Conf. Bd. Served to lt. USNR, 1952-55. Mem. Nat. Petroleum Council, Bus. Roundtable, Chi Psi. Clubs: River Oaks Country (Houston), Petroleum (Houston). Office: Tenneco Inc 1010 Milam St PO Box 2511 Houston TX 77252 also: Monroe Auto Equipment Co 1 Intarnational Dr Monroe MI 48161

KETNER, KENNETH LAINE, philosopher, educator; b. Mountain Home, Okla., Mar. 24, 1939; s. Louis Elaine and Johnnie Lucille (Hannah) K.; m. Berti Gabriella Zehetmeier, Aug. 24, 1964; 1 child, Kenneth Laine Jr. B.A. in Philosophy, Okla. State U., 1961, M.A., 1967; M.A. in Folklore, UCLA, 1968; Ph.D. in Philosophy, U. Calif., Santa Barbara, 1972. Part-time instr. Okla. State U., 1964-67; teaching asst. U. Calif., Santa Barbara, 1969-70; mem. faculty Tex. Tech U., Lubbock, 1971—; prof. philosophy Tex. Tech U., 1977—, chmn. dept., 1979-81; founder, dir. Inst. Studies in Pragmaticism, 1972—; Charles Sanders Peirce prof. philosophy 1981—. Author: A Critical Study of Stephen C. Pepper's Approach to Metaphysics, 1967, An Essay on the Nature of World Views, 1972, An Emendation of R. G. Collingwood's Doctrine of Absolute Presuppositions, 1973, also articles; editor, compiler: Charles Sanders Peirce: Contributions to The Nation, 4 parts, 1975, 78, 79, 87, Comprehensive Bibliography of Works of C.S. Peirce, 1977, rev. edit., 1986; founder, editor Peirce Studies, 1979—. Asst. prof. philosophy and folklore UCLA, summers 1972, 74; co-organizer C.S. Peirce Bicentennial Internat. Congress, Amsterdam, Netherlands, 1976, Peirce Sesquicentennial Internat. Congress. Served to capt. USAR, 1962-64. Grantee NSF; Grantee Nat. Endowment Humanities; Grantee Am. Council Learned Socs. Fellow Am. Anthrop. Assn., Charles S. Peirce Soc. (pres. 1978); mem. Am. Philos. Assn., Am. Folklore Soc., Semiotic Soc. Am. (editorial bd. jour.), Deutsche Gesellschaft für Semiotik, Tau Kappa Epsilon. Democrat. Taoist. Lodge: Rotary. Home: PO Box 65135 Lubbock TX 79464 Office: Texas Tech U Library 304-K Lubbock TX 79409

KETTIS, PÄR AXEL, government official; b. Norrtalje, Sweden, Dec. 26, 1933; s. Axel Herman and Olga Elisabeth (Nordin) K.; m. Gunilla Lindh-Foster; children: Anna Magdalena, Eva Alexandra, Agneta Elisabeth. Degree in Law, Stockholm U., 1958. Clk. Swedish Parliament, Stockholm, 1957-58; attache Fgn. Ministry, Stockholm, 1959; attache Swedish Embassy, Warsaw, Poland, 1960-62, consellor, 1974-76; 1st sec. Swedish Embassy, Addis Ababa, Ethiopia, 1962-65, Khartoum, Sudan, 1962-65; 1st sec. Fgn. Ministry Polit. Dept. Swedish Embassy, Stockholm, 1965-69, dep. asst. sec., 1977-81; minister Swedish Embassy, Washington, 1982-84; dep. sec. gen. Nordic Council Secretariat, Stockholm, 1974-76; dir. gen. Nat. Def. Radio Communication Inst., Stockholm, 1985—; dep. sec. Fgn. Relations Com., 1966-67. Home: Karlavagen 113, 115 26 Stockholm Sweden Office: Forsvarets Radioansalt, PO Box 301, 161 26 Bromma Sweden

KETTLEWELL, NEIL MACKEWAN, neuroscience educator, researcher, sculptor; b. Evanston, Ill., May 27, 1938; s. George Edward and Barbara Sidney (Kidde) K.; m. Phyllis Ann Miller, Jan. 30, 1965 (div. Sept. 1976); 1 son, Brant Regnar; m. Toni Ann Gianoulias, June 2, 1978. B.S., Kent State U., 1962; M.A., U. Mich., 1965, Ph.D., 1969. Research asst. in psychology U. Mich., 1963-69, programmer, 1966-69, systems analyst time scheduling office, 1967-69; lectr. U. Mont., 1969-70, asst. prof. psychology, 1970-75, assoc. prof., 1976—; cons. in field; sculptor, exhibited numerous nat. galleries; sculptural commns. Franklin Mint, 1981, 82, Cin. Reds, 1981, others; cons. in art mktg. Served with USAR, 1958-66. U. Mich. Presdl. scholar, 1964. Mem. Soc. Neurosci., N.Y. Acad. Scis., Sculptors Internat., Pi Mu Epsilon, Psi Chi, Phi Eta Sigma. Subspecialties: Neuropsychology; Molecular biology. Current work: Ultrastructural synaptic changes in brain as result of experience. Home: 172 Fairway Dr Missoula MT 59803 Office: Dept Psychology U Mont Missoula MT 59801

KEY, HELEN ELAINE, accounting, consulting company executive; b. Cleve., Jan. 16, 1946; d. Maud and Helen (Key) Vance. B.S., W.Va. State Coll., 1968; M.Ed., Cleve. State U., 1977. Tchr. Cleve. Bd. Edn., 1968—; instr. Cuyahoga Community Coll., Cleve., part-time, 1969-78, Dyke Coll., Cleve., part-time, 1979—; pres. H.E. Key & Assos., Cleve., 1983—; treas. BK4W Inc., Cleve., 1981. Mem. Am. Assn. Notary Pubs., Women Bus. Owners Assn., AAUW, NAACP, Cleve. Area Bus. Tchrs., NEA, Pi Lambda Theta, Alpha Kappa Alpha. Democrat. Baptist. Club: Toastmistress (sec. 1978) (Cleve.). Home: 564 Wilkes Ln Richmond Heights OH 44143

KEY, TED, cartoonist; b. Fresno, Calif., Aug. 25, 1912; s. Simon Leon and Fanny (Kahn) K.; m. Anne Elizabeth Wilkinson, Sept. 30, 1937 (dec. July 1984); children: Stephen Lewis, David Edward, Peter Lawrence; m. Bonnie Williams-Cohen, Nov. 17, 1987. BA, U. Calif., Berkeley, 1933. Assoc. editor Judge mag., N.Y.C., 1937-39; radio staff writer J. Walter Thompson Advt. Agy., N.Y.C., 1939-43; cartoonist Hazel Saturday Evening Post, Phila., 1946-70, King Features Syndicate, 1969—; cartoonist, writer The Econs. Press, Inc., Fairfield, N.J., 1957—; screenwriter Walt Disney Prodns., Burbank, Calif., 1970-77. Writer, cartoonist for CBS, NBC, mags., books, newspapers; playwright (radio prodn.) The Clinic (pub. in anthology Best Broadcasts Of 1939-40); creator (cartoon features) Diz and Liz for Jack and Jill mag, 1961-71, (TV series) Hazel; author: Hazel, NBC-TV (4 yrs.), CBS-TV (1 yr.), 1946, Here's Hazel, Many Happy Returns, 1950, If You Like Hazel, 1952, So'm I, 1953, Hazel Rides Again, 1955, Fasten Your Seat Belts, 1956, Phyllis, 1957, All Hazel, 1958, The Hazel Jubilee, 1959, The Biggest Dog in the World, 1960, Hazel Time, 1962, Life With Hazel, 1965, Diz and Liz, 1965, Squirrels in the Feeding Station, 1967, Hazel Power, 1971, Right On Hazel, 1972, Ms. Hazel, 1972, Hazel's Feline Funnies, 1982; story/screenwriter: Million Dollar Duck, The Cat From Outer Space (also wrote novel), Gus; developer: Positive Attitude Posters, 1965—, Sales Bullets, 1960—; cartoons included in New Yorker, Esquire, Look, Life, Ladies Home Jour., McCall's, Good Housekeeping, Better Homes and Gardens, People, Mademoiselle. Served as sgt. Signal Corps AUS, 1943-46. Mem. Nat. Cartoonists Soc. (Best Syndicated Panel award 1977), Writers Guild Am. West. Jewish. Club: Players (N.Y.C.). Home and Office: 1694 Glenhardie Rd Wayne PA 19087

KEYES, MARION ALVAH, IV, manufacturing company executive; b. Bellingham, Wash., May 11, 1938; s. Marion Alvah and Winnefred Agnes (Nolte) K.; B.S. in Chem. Engring., Stanford U., 1960; M.S. in E.E., U. Ill., 1968; M.B.A., Baldwin Wallace Coll., 1981; m. Loretta Jean Mattson, Nov. 17, 1962; children—Marion A., Zachary Leigh, Richard. Lic. cogeneration profl. engr. Teaching asst. dept. math. Stanford U., 1958-59, technician Stanford Aerosol Labs., 1957-59; chem. engr. Ketchikan (Alaska) Pulp Co., 1960-63; dir. engring. Control Systems div. Beloit Corp. (Wis.), 1963-70; gen. mgr. digital systems div. Taylor Instrument Co., Rochester, N.Y., 1970-75; v.p. engring., pres. , Bailey Controls Co., Wickliffe, Ohio, 1975-85; v.p., group exec., Babcock & Wilcox Indsl. Products & Services Group. McDermott Internat., Inc., 1985—. Past bd. advisors Fenn Coll. Engring. Cleve. State U.; bd. dirs. Baldwin Coll., United Cerebral Palsy, Cleve.; past pres., mem. exec. bd. N.E. Ohio council Boy Scouts Am.; pres. Area 5 Boy Scouts Am. Registered profl. engr., Calif., Wis., N.Y., Ill., Ohio. Holder 39 U.S. and over 50 fgn. patents; author over 100 tech. papers. Fellow Tech. Assn. Pulp & Paper Industry, Am. Inst. Chemists; mem. Ohio Acad. Scis. (life), Cleve. Engring. Soc. (bd. dirs.), Employers Resource Council (bd. dirs., exec. com), Am. Assn. Artificial Intelligence, Am. Mgmt. Assn., IEEE, U.S. Automation Research Council, Am. Automatic Control Council (past sec. and dir.) Instrument Soc. Am., Am. Inst. Chem. Engrs., Am. Chem. Soc., Wis. Acad. Arts, Scis. and Letters. Republican. Lutheran. Club: Willoughby Men's Athletic. Editor: A Glossary Of Automatic Control Terminology, 1970. Contbr. articles to profl. jours. Patentee in field. Home: 120 Riverstone Dr Chagrin Falls OH 44022 Office: Babcock & Wilcox 35 River St Chagrin Falls OH 44022

KEYES, WAYNE PORTER, aerospace company executive; b. Oakland, Calif., Sept. 2, 1927; s. William Reed and Ruth Adalaide (Bigelow) K.; m. Helen Jean Padua; children: Leilani, David; children from previous marriage: Nancy Lee, Robert Wayne, Graham Lee, Wanda Claire; stepchildren: Phillip Lawrence Camero, Michael Allen Camero. BS, Coll. Notre Dame, Belmont, Calif., 1971; MS, U. So. Calif., 1974; MS, Stanford U., 1977, PhD, 1982. Enlisted USN, 1945; commd. ensign USN, 1957, advanced through grades to lt., 1961; ret., 1967; with Lockheed Missiles & Space Co., Sunnyvale, Calif., 1967-79, support engr., sr. logistics specialist, 1975-79; mgr. field order adminstrn. Amdahl Corp., Sunnyvale, 1979-81; mgr. development planning STC Computer Research Corp., Santa Clara, Calif., 1981-83; project mgr. Trident II Integrated Logistics Support, Westinghouse Marine div., Sunnyvale, Calif., 1983-85; project mgr. Peacekeeper Integrated Logistics Support, Northrop Electronics div., Hawthorne, Calif., 1985-86, chief systems engr. Acurex Corp., Aerotherm div., Mountain View, Calif., 1986—; nat. def. exec. reserve U.S. Dept. Transp., 1981—; lectr. systems mgmt. U. So. Calif., Los Angeles and Sunnyvale, 1978—. Active Boy Scouts Am. Named an Eagle Scout Boy Scouts Am., 1944; recipient Silver Beaver award Boy Scouts Am., 1986. Registered profl. engr., Calif.; cert. community coll. instr., Calif. Mem. NSPE, Calif. Soc. Profl. Engrs., Inst. Indsl. Engrs., Soc. Logistics Engrs. (Cert. Profl. Logistician award), Soc. Advancement Mgmt., Ret. Officers Assn., Nat. Assn. Uniformed Services, Nat. Eagle Scout Assn., V.F.W., Nat. Rifle Assn., Calif. Rifle and Pistol Assn., Am. Philatelic Soc., Am. Radio Relay League. Republican. Club: Toastmasters (Disting. Toastmaster award). Home: 1024 Oaktree Dr San Jose CA 95129 Office: Acurex Corp 520 Clyde Ave PO Box 7040 Mountain View CA 94039

KEYKO, GEORGE JOHN, watch electronics company executive; b. New Britain, Conn., May 6, 1924; s. John Simonovich and Nellie Ivanovna (Gretcha) K.; B.S., Yale, 1949; m. Anne Romanchuk, Jan. 31, 1948; children—David, Mark. Spl. rep. Lederle Labs., Conn. and N.Y., 1949-52; pres. Teacher Toys, Inc., Conn., 1952-56; sales mgr. Washington Forge, N.J., 1956-60; sales mgr. shaver div. Ronson Corp., Woodbridge, N.J., 1960-63; sales mgr. Caravelle and BEP div. Bulova Watch Co., N.Y.C., 1963-66; v.p. mktg. Technipower div. Benrus Watch Co., Ridgefield, Conn., 1966-68; exec. v.p. Heuer Time & Electronics Corp., Springfield, N.J., 1969, pres., 1970-75; now pres. Lumisphere Inc.; dir. New Products Devel. Assocs, Etilmech, Inc., Novato, calif., Chemical Device Corp., Yorktown Heights, N.Y., Century Mktg., Republic of China, Wet-Lite Corp. Chief timer internat. Ski Racers Assn., 1970-72; vestryman St. Paul's Ch., Westfield, N.J.; Founder Life-Link Assn. Recipient Spl. award from INTREPID 22 - 12 Meter Yacht America's Cup, 1970. Mem. Am. Watch Mfg. Assn., Sports Car Club Am., N.Y. Sales Exec. Club. Republican. Episcopalian. Club: Echo Lake Country (Westfield, N.J.). Home: 931 Kimball Ave Westfield NJ 07090

KEYLOCK, HENRY THOMAS, banking executive; b. Pretoria, Transvaal, Republic of South Africa, Aug. 28, 1942; s. Henry and Helena Hendrina (Brink) K.; m. Carol Ann Bailey, June 29, 1946; children: Bradley, Lawrence, Miles, Dean, Charles, Spencer. Student, U. Cambridge, Eng., 1958-60. Banking officer Standard Bank Ltd., Salisbury, Zimbabwe, 1960-64, Lusaka, Zambia, 1964-68; banking officer NedBank Ltd., Durban, Republic of South Africa, 1969-74, tng. officer, 1975-78; ops. and mgmt. officer NedBank Ltd., Johannesburg, Republic of South Africa, 1978-79, ops. and mgmt. mgr., 1979-85, elec. banking mgr., 1985—. Mem. Progressive Federal Party. Methodist. Home: 5 Sun Gardens 216 Smit St, Fairlands Transvaal 2194, Republic of South Africa Office: NedBank Ltd, 105 West S, Standton, Johannesburg, Transvaal 2195, Republic of South Africa

KEYZER, DIRK JOHAN, surgeon, medical educator; b. Dinxperlo, Netherlands, May 27, 1942; s. Isaac and Christina (Godyn) de Keyzer; m. Elisabeth Johanna Deys, Jan. 25, 1966; children—Ann Caroline, Ies Cor. M.D., U. Utrecht, 1968; Med. Drs., Royal Tropical Inst., Amsterdam, 1970. Resident Univ. Teaching Hosp., Leiden, Red Cross Hosp., The Hague; cardiac house surgeon Univ. Hosp. Utrecht, 1968; gen. house surgeon Red Cross Hosp., The Hague, 1969-70; med. officer Mberesh Hosp., Zambia, 1970-73; house surgeon teaching hosps., The Hague, Leiden, 1973-79; gen., vascular, pulmonary surgeon St. Joseph Hosp., Kerkrade, Netherlands, 1979—; flying dr. Dutch Tourist Bur., The Hague, 1977-79; faculty dept. surgery U. Maastricht, Netherlands, 1982-83. Mem. Royal Med. Assn., Dutch Surg. Assn. Conservative. Avocations: tennis; skiing, travelling. Home: Brewersstreet 1, Simpelveld 6369-EN Netherlands Office: St Joseph Hosp, Wyngracht 45, Kerkrade The Netherlands

KHABIBULAYEV, PULAT, nuclear physicist, science academy administrator; b. Andizhan, Uzbekistan, USSR, Oct. 14, 1936; s. Kabibulla Kirgizbayev and Salia Tashlanova; m. Eleonora Rakhmatdjanovna; children: Dilnoz, Salombek, Dinmukhamed. PhD in physics and Math., V.I. Lenin Cen. Asian State U., Tashkent, USSR, 1960. Dir. Nuclear Physics Inst., Tashkent, 1978—; pres. Acad. Scis. Uzbekistan Tashkent, 1984—; chmn. Abu Raikhan Biruni state prize com. Uzbekistan, Tashkent; prof. physics. Author: Dynamics of Solutions in Inhomogeneous Condensed Media, 1986, other books. Chmn. Supreme Soviet of Uzbek Soviet Socialist Republic, 1985—; chmn. Uzebk Republican Soc. of Knowledge, Tashkent, 1987. Recipient 3 state awards, 1973, 76, 81, Golden medal UN Internat. Orgn. for Intelligence Preservation, 1985, others. Communist. Office: Acad of Scis, Gogolya 70, Tashkent, Uzbekistan USSR

KHACHATURIAN, HENRY, neurobiologist; b. Tehran, Iran, Oct. 19, 1951; s. Shahen and Emma (Babayan) K.; m. Ellen Catherine Quinn, June 24, 1983. B.S., SUNY-Brockport, 1974, M.S., 1976; Ph.D., U. Rochester, 1981. Postdoctoral scholar Mental Health Research Inst., U. Mich., Ann Arbor, 1980-83, research investigator, 1983-87; asst. prof. dept. Anatomy & Neurobiology Health Sci. Ctr. U. Tenn., Memphis, 1987-88, dir. med. embryology, 1987-8—; program dir. Nat. Inst. Mental Health, 1988—; instr. human gross anatomy U. Rochester Med. Sch., 1978-79. Contbr. articles to profl. jours. Recipient John R. Bartlett prize in neurosci. Center for Brain Research, U. Rochester, 1979; Outstanding Research award Sch. Medicine, U. Rochester, 1980; Best Tchr. award U. Rochester, 1980. Mem. Soc. for Neurosci., Internat. Narcotic Res. Assn., N.Y. Acad. Sci. Office: Nat Inst of Mental Health Neurosciences Research Br Div of Basic Scis Room 11-105 Parklawn Bldg Rockville MD 20857

KHADAFY, MOAMMAR, See GADHAFI, MUAMMAR MUHAMMED

KHADDAM, ABDEL HALIM, vice-president of Syrian Arab Republic; b. Lattakia, Syria, 1932; LL.B., Damascus U. Gov. of Damascus, 1964; minister of economy and fgn. trade, 1969-70; dep. prime minister and minister of fgn. affairs, 1970-84, v.p. for mil. and polit. affairs, 1984, now v.p., 1984—; mem. Regional Command, Baath Party, 1971-84. Address: Office of Vice Pres, Damascus Syrian Arab Republic *

KHADDURI, FARID MAJID, mechanical engineer; b. Baghdad, Iraq, Aug. 10, 1945; came to U.S., 1947, naturalized, 1954; s. Majid and Majdia (Dawaff) K.; m. Alicia Basiliko, Nov. 18, 1973; children: Alexandra, Justine. B.A. in Physics, Amherst Coll., 1967; M.S. in Engring. Sci, George Washington U., 1976. Analytical engr. Atlantic Research Corp., Gainesville, Va., 1968-72, sr. design engr., 1972-73; chief engr. Trident I Missile Post Boost Control System, 1973-78; program mgr. MX programs, 1979-81, Trident II Post Boost Control System, 1981-83, mgr. Trident Project Office, 1983-85, mgr. strategic systems, 1985-88, dir., 1988—. Mem. Am. Phys. Soc., ASME. Republican. Club: Kenwood Country (Bethesda, Md.). Current Work: Program management solid rocket propulsion. Subspecialties: Aerospace engineering and technology; Solid rocket propulsion. Home: 5526 Westbard Ave Bethesda MD 20816

KHAIR-EL-DIN, ABD-EL-HAMID MAHMOUD, architectural educator; b. Toukh-Dalakah, Menofiah, Egypt, Feb. 21, 1928; s. Mahmoud Mohammed Khair-el-Din and Aisha Abd-el-Rehim Abou-Nagi; m. Aleya Ibrahim el-Enany, July 21, 1958; children: Gihan, Tarik. BArch with honors, Ain-Shams U., Cairo, 1955; MArch, Cath. U. Am., Washington, 1962, D in Architecture, 1974. Instr. architecture Ain-Shams U., 1955-58; vis. lectr. Assuit U., Egypt, 1963-64; lectr. Coll. Engring. Baghdad U., Iraq, 1965-68; architect, planner Ministry Housing Orgns., Cairo, 1968-69, Tripoli, Libya, 1969-71; asst. prof. Tripoli U., 1974-76, assoc. prof., 1978-79; vis. assoc. prof. Hampton U., Va., 1976-78; assoc. prof. Coll. Architecture and Planning King Saud U., Riyadh, Saudi Arabia, 1979—; cons. El-mousel Univ., Iraq, 1964-65, Diplomatic Quarter Saudi Housing, Riyadh, 1979-81. Editor: El-Omran Archtl. Jour., 1987—; contbr. articles to profl. jours. Egyptian Govt. Grad. Studies scholar, 1958-62. Mem. Internat. Union Architects, Internat. Assn. Housing, Am. Assn. Health Facilities, Egyptian Engring. Architects Syndicate. Republican. Muslim. Home: 55 Abd-el-

Aziz, Saud St, Apt #5, Rhoda, Cairo Egypt Office: King Saud Univ, Coll Architecture, PO Box 57448, Riyadh Saudi Arabia

KHAIRULLAH, ZAHID YAHYA, management sciences and marketing educator, consultant; b. Bombay, India, Sept. 29, 1945; came to U.S., 1972; s. Yahya Gulamhusein and Sugra Abdulhusein (Batliwala) K.; m. Durriya Haider, May 1971; children: Nazifah, Firhana, Sakhiba. B Tech. in Metall. Engring., Indian Inst. Tech., Bombay, 1971; MS in Mech. Engring., SUNY-Buffalo, 1974, MBA in Mgmt. Sci., 1977, PhD in Mgmt., 1982. Jr. officer M/S Spl. Steels, Ltd., Bombay, 1971-72; design engr. M/S Secure Enterprises, Buffalo, 1974-77; asst. prof. mgmt. scis. St. Bonaventure U., N.Y., 1977-82, assoc. prof., chmn. depts. mgmt. sci. and mktg., 1982-85, prof., chmn. depts., 1985-87, prof., dean Sch. Bus., 1987—; research assoc. SUNY-Buffalo, 1979; cons. in field; lectr. various colls. and univs. Contbr. articles to profl. jours. Mem. exec. com., treas. Islamic Soc. So. Tier, Olean, N.Y., 1982—; active So. Tier West Econ. Devel. Task Force, 1982-83, So. Tier West Community Devel. Com. 1988—. Fellow Acad. Mktg. Sci.; mem. Am. Inst. Decision Scis., Inst. Mgmt. Scis., Am. Soc. Ops. Research, Am. Prodn. Inventory Control Soc. (cert. prodn. and inventory mgr., v.p. edn., seminars 1984-85, pres. 1985-87, bd. dirs. Pa.-N.Y. chpt. 1984—), Beta Gamma Sigma (life), Delta Mu Delta (life). Home: 2316 Sheldon Dr Allegany NY 14706 Office: Sch Bus Adminstrn St Bonaventure Univ St Bonaventure NY 14778

KHAKEE, ABDUL, educator, researcher; b. Zanzibar, Aug. 27, 1938; arrived in Sweden, 1961; s. Gulam Mohamed and Nur Banu (Pir) K.; m.Gunilla Hjordis Häggblom, Aug. 29, 1969; children: Anna, Carin. MS, U. Göteborg, Sweden, 1965, PhD in Econs., 1969; PhD in Geography, U. Umeå, Sweden, 1984. Teaching asst. Göteborg Sch. Econs., 1965-69; instr. U. Göteborg, 1966-69; sr. lectr. U. Stockholm, 1970-71; research assoc. Nordic Inst. of Urban & Regional Planning, Stockholm, 1970-71; vis. prof. U. Delaware, Coll. Urban Affairs and Pub. Policy, Newark, 1975-76; sr. lectr. U. Umeå, 1972-79; vis. prof. U. Lisbon, Portugal, 1984-86; assoc. prof. U. Umeaå, Sweden, 1979—; research fellow Swedish Council for Bldg. Research, Stockholm, 1987—; cons. Göteborg Bank, 1965-66; educator Adult Edn. Ctr., Göteborg, 1966-70; research adviser Municipality of Västeras, 1983-87. Author: Development and Planning in Tanzania, 1970, Planning in a Mixed Economy, 1979, Municipal Futures Studies, 1982, Municipal Planning, 1983; contbr. 25 urban planning articles to profl. jours. Mem. Labor Edn. Council, Göteborg, 1966-70, Umeå Men's Choir, 1987—; chmn. Parents' Assn., Umeå, 1980-82. Swedish Council for Social Research grantee, 1969; recipient Swedish Am. Found. award, 1975, Japanese Soc. Research Council, 1977, Jan Wallanders Found. award, 1986-87. Mem. Swedish Econ. Assn., Swedish Assn. Urban and Regional Planners, Assn. for Cultural Econs. Home: Kiselstråket 13, 90242 Umea Sweden Office: U Umeå, University Campus, 90187 Umeå Sweden

KHALEF, BACHIR, physician, physicist, educator; b. Constantine, Algeria, Jan. 2, 1937; arrived in France, 1954; s. Mohand Khalef and Zahra Belmoufok; m. Nicole Auge, July 8, 1962 (div.); children: Francois, Anne, Emmanuelle; m. Evelyne Ritaine. Lic. in Math., Faculte des Scie, Bordeaux, France, 1960, Lic. in Physique, 1961, Diplôme d'Etudes Approfondies, 1966; MD, Faculte de Medecine, 1973. Intern Hosp. Pellegrin, 1969-71; resident Hosp. Haut Leveque, 1971-73; math. monitor Faculte des Scie, Bordeaux, 1960-62; prof. physics Lycee Montaigne, Bordeaux, 1962-73; prof. acupuncture U. Bordeaux, 1979-88; dir. Cabinet Med., Talence, France, 1973—. Author: Approche Mathematique et Thermodynamique de l'Acupuncture, 1978, Vitesse de Reactions Photo Chimique, 1966, Laser en Médecine, 1984, Acupuncture Medecine de L'Energie, 1984. Office: Cabinet Med, les Terrasses, 33400 Talence France

KHALIFA BIN SALMAN AL-KHALIFA, SHEIKH See AL-KHALIFA, SHEIKH KHALIFA IBN SALMAN

KHAMBATTA, HOSHANG JAL, anesthesiology educator, anesthesiologist, researcher; b. Bombay, India, Mar. 30, 1931; came to U.S. 1968, naturalized 1976; s. Jal Faramji and Jer Jal (Unwala) K.; m. Renate Friederike Krause, Jan. 4, 1963; children—Sonja, Gustav. M.B., B.S., Dow Med. Coll., Karachi, Pakistan, 1956; M.D., Nat. Bds. in Med. for Fgn. Grads., 1970. Diplomate in Anaesthesia, Royal Coll. Surgeons, Eng., 1967. Instr. anesthesiology Coll. Physicians and Surgeons, Columbia U., N.Y.C., 1971-73, assoc., 1973-74, asst. prof., 1974-82, assoc. prof., 1982—; asst. attending anesthesiologist Columbia-Presbyterian Med. Ctr., N.Y.C., 1977-82, assoc. attending anesthesiologist, 1982—; vis. prof. Georg August U., Göttingen, Fed. Republic Germany, 1985. Editor Am. Soc. Indian Anesiologists, J. Anesthesia and Analgesia; contbr. articles to profl. jours. Research fellow in anesthesiology Columbia U., 1970-71; NIH grantee, 1973-79; German Research Found. grantee in cardiology U. Göttingen, 1985. Mem. Am. Physiol. Soc., Royal Coll. Surgeons Faculty Anesthesia, Am. Coll. Anesthesiologists, Am. Soc. Anesthesiologists, Soc. Neurosurg., Anesthesia and Neurol. Supportive Care (founding mem.), Soc. Cardiovascular Anesthesiologists. Home: 291 Audubon Rd Englewood NJ 07631

KHAMENEI, HOJATOLESLAM ALI, president Islamic Republic of Iran, religious leader; b. Meshed, Khorassan, 1940; married, 1964; 4 sons, 1 dau. Ed. in Qom; studied under Ayatollah Khomeini. Imprisoned 6 times, 1964-78; former personal rep. of Ayatollah Khomeini to Supreme Def. Council; mem. Revolutionary Council until its dissolution, 1979; Friday prayer leader, Teheran, 1980—; sec.-gen., mem. central com. Islamic Republican Party, 1980—. pres. of Iran, 1981—. 1981. Address: Office of Pres, Tehran Iran *

KHAN, AMANULLAH, physician; b. Jullundhar, India, Mar. 2, 1940; came to U.S., 1964; s. Ahmad Ali and Qamar (Nisa) K.; m. Fran Elise Austin, Dec. 9, 1972; children: Roxanna, Sabrina, Shireen. Licentiate state med. faculty, West Pakistan Med. Sch., 1959; MBBS, King Edward Med. Coll., Lahore, 1963; PhD, Baylor U., 1968. Diplomate: Am. Bd. Allergy and Immunology, Am. Bd. Lab. Immunology. Rotating intern Samaritan Hosp., Troy, N.Y., 1965-66; fellow in hematology and oncology Wadley Insts. of Molecular Medicine, Dallas, 1966-69, chief research fellow, 1969-70, chmn. dept. immunotherapy, 1970—; mem. staffs Morton Cancer and Research Hosp. and Doctor's Hosp., Dallas, Plano (Tex.) Med. Ctr.; adj. prof. Tex. Woman's U., 1975—, N. Tex. State U., 1975—. Author: Immune Regulators in Transfer Factor, 1979, Interferon: Properties and Clinical Uses, 1980, Experimental Hematology Today, 1980, Human Lymphokines, 1982; editor: Jour. Clin. Hematology and Oncology, 1971—; mem. editorial bd.: Exptl. Hematology, 1973-75; contbr. articles to sci. jours. Fellow ACP, Am. Coll. Allergists; mem. Am. Assn. Immunologists, Am. Soc. Clin. Oncology, Am. Soc. Hematology, AMA, Dallas County Med. Soc., Tex. Med. Assn., King Edward Med. Coll. Alumni Assn. (pres. 1974-75, 78-79), Assn. Pakistani Physicians N. Am. (pres. 1983-84). Office: Wadley Insts Molecular Medicine 9000 Harry Hines Dallas TX 75235

KHAN, GHULAM ISHAQ, Pakistan government official; b. 1915; married, 1950; 1 son, 5 daughters. Ed., Islamia Coll., Peshawar, Pakistan, Punjab U. Various government posts Pakistan, 1948-85, chmn. Senate, 1985—, acting pres., 1988—. Address: 2 52d St, Shalimar 6/4, Islamabad Pakistan *

KHAN, IFTIKHAR AHMAD, epidemiologist; b. Umarzai, Pakistan, Dec. 1, 1930; s. Khan Obedullah and Zamaruth (Hafiz) K.; m. Razia Begum; children: Nighat, Jaffer, Farhat. BSc, Islamia Coll. of Peshawar, Pakistan, 1952; MBBS in Medicine and Surgery, Dow Med. Coll., Karachi, Pakistan, 1959; DPH, Pub. Health Coll., Lahore, Pakistan, 1961. Lectr. dept. hygiene Khyber Med. Coll. of Peshawar, Pakistan, 1959-64, asst. prof. preventive medicine, 1961-71, prof., head dept. community medicine, 1971—; dir. community health Univ. of Peshawar, Pakistan, 1970-80; WHO-KAP study on ORS, 1985. Assoc. editor: Synopsis Hygiene and Pub. Health, 1970; editor: Community Medicine, 1988—. Mem. Am. Pub. Health Assn., Pakistan Pub. Health Assn., Expert Panel on Community Health, Pakistan Med. Research Council, Epidemiology and Prevention Internat. Soc. Cardiology. Office: Khyber Med Coll, Peshawar Pakistan

KHAN, MUHAMMAD YUNUS, medical educator; b. Hoshiarpur, Punjab, India, Dec. 19, 1924; arrived in Pakistan, 1947; s. Muhammad Abdullah Khan; m. Sughra Khan; 1 child, Naveed Yunus. MBBS, K.E. Med. Coll., Lahore, Pakistan, 1946; M of Philosophy in Anatomy, Basic Med. Scis. Inst., Karachi, Pakistan, 1961; PhD, Ind. U., Indpls., 1963. Lectr., med. demonstrator Dow Med. Coll., Karachi, 1952-64; asst. prof. anatomy Dow Med. Coll., Jinnah Postgrad. Med. Ctr., Karachi, 1964-70; prof. Jinnah Postgrad. Med. Ctr., Karachi, 1970-86, exec. dir., 1975-77, 83-84; prof. anatomy Coll. Physicians and Surgeons Pakistan, Karachi, 1986—; short-term cons. Eastern Mediterranean Region WHO, 1985-87. Author research papers in field. Research grantee Ford Found., 1968, NIH, 1970, Pakistan Med. Research Council, 1975, Pakistan Sci. Found., 1979. Fellow Coll. Physicians and Surgeons Pakistan. Home and Office: Coll Physicians and Surgeons, Defence Housing Authority, Karachi 46, Pakistan

KHAN, MUZAFFAR ALI, oil company executive; b. Umraoti, India, July 5, 1938; s. Mahboob Ali Khan and Abida Begum; m. Fauzia Khan, Mar. 21, 1973; 1 dau., Zainab. BE Commerce, U. Karachi, (Pakistan), 1959; PhD (hon.) Marquis Scicluna Internat. U. Found. Experience Acctg. clk. Burmah Oil Co., Karachi, Pakistan, 1955-61; acctg. asst. Pakistan Internat. Airlines Co., Karachi, 1961-63; asst. cost acct. Colony Textile Mills, Multon, Pakistan, 1964-65; accounts officer Mitchells' Fruit Farms, Renala, Khurd, 1965-69; mgr. Shishmahal Hosiery Co., Lahore, Pakistan, 1969-70; comptroller Petrolube, Jeddah, Saudi Arabia, 1971—. Contbr. articles to profl. acctg. jours. Fellow Inst. Cost and Mgmt. Accts. of Pakistan, Chartered Inst. Secs. and Adminstrs. (London); mem. Assn. Ins. and Risk Mgrs. in Industry and Commerce (London), Brit. Inst. Mgmt., Am. Mgmt. Assn. (internat.), Inst. Petroleum, European Econ. Assn. (founder), Am. Entrepreneur Assn., Inst. Mktg. Mgmt. Pakistan (assoc.), Inst. Corp. Secs. Pakistan (assoc.). Home: 40th St Alazizyah, Jeddah Saudi Arabia Office: Petromin Lubricating Oil Co, PO Box 1432, Jeddah Saudi Arabia

KHAN, NADEEM KAMAL MUSTAFA, accountant, health science facility administrator; b. Karachi, Sind, Pakistan, July 22, 1952; s. Mohammad Mustafa and Suraiya Mustafa Khan; m. Imrana Afridi, Dec. 16, 1983; children: Usman, Anam. BA, U. Peshawar, Pakistan, 1969-71; BSc in Econs. with honors, U. London, 1971-74. Chartered acct. Trainee acct. to investigation sr. Price Waterhouse and Co., London, 1974-79; sr. Hays Allan, London, 1979-80; asst. fin. mgr. The Aga Khan Hosp. and Med. Coll., Karachi, Pakistan, 1981-82; fin. mgr. The Aga Khan U. Hosp. and The Aga Khan U., Karachi, Pakistan, 1982-87, dir. fin. and info. systems, 1987—, mgmt. and systems devel., 1983-86; mgmt. cons. Hays Allan, London, 1980; lectr. devel. mgmt. skills Aga Khan Health Services Workshop, 1986. Fellow Inst. Chartered Accts. in Eng. and Wales (assoc. 1978). Moslem. Home: 35 K Block 6 PECHS, Karachi 29 Sind Pakistan Office: The Aga Khan U Hosp & Aga Khan U, Stadium Rd PO Box 3500, Karachi 5 Sind Pakistan

KHAN, NAEEM AHMAD, physicist; b. Hoshiarpur, East Punjab, India, Apr. 12, 1928; s. Maqsood Ahmad and Kaneez Fatima Khan; m. Zahida Naeem, May 13, 1960; children: Nazra Naeem, Nudrat Naeem, Maudood Naeem. BA with honors, St. Stephen's Coll., Delhi, India, 1946; MA in Math., U. Sind, Karachi, Pakistan, 1950; MS, U. Karachi, 1955; PhD, U. Manchester, Eng., 1958. Profl. asst. meteorol. dept. Govt. of India, 1946-47; profl. asst. meteorol. dept. Pakistan Meteorol. Dept., 1947-50, asst. meteorologist, 1950, 55-61; sr. sci. officer Pakistan Atomic Energy Centre, Karachi and Lahore, 1961-65; sr. sci. officer/head nuclear physics, dir. Lahore, 1965-66, prin. sci. officer, dir., 1967-69; chief sci. officer, dir. tng. Secretariat Karachi, 1970; chief sci. officer, sec. Secretariat Islamabad, 1970-75, chief sci. officer, dir. research Secretariat, 1975-76; prin. sci. officer, dir. Pakistan Inst. Nuclear Sci. & Tech., Nilore, 1969-70, chief sci. officer, dir., 1970, dir. PINSTECH, 1977-84, chief scientist, 1982; chmn. Pakistan Council Sci. & Indsl. Research, Islamabad, 1984—. Contbr. numerous articles to profl. jours. Fellow Inst. Physics, Phys. Soc., Pakistan Acad. Scis., Islamic Acad. Scis. Office: Pakistan Council Sci and, Indsl Research, PO Box 672, Karachi Pakistan

KHAN, NASSIRUDDIN AZAM, medical school administrator; b. Hazara, Pakistan, Feb. 5, 1928. MD with honors, U. Punjab, Lahore, Pakistan, 1951, MB, BChir. House physician to prof. medicine 1951-52; med. officer N.W. Frontier, Pakistan, 1952-54; postgrad. scholar Eng., 1954-55; registrar Nat. Health Service, Eng., 1955-56; assoc. prof. medicine and pharmacology 1957-62; prof. medicine Khyber Med. Coll., Peshawar, Pakistan, 1962—, head dept. medicine, prin.-dean; hon. physician to Pres. of Pakistan; cons. Pakistan Army; examiner U. Peshawar, U. Sind., U. Karachi, U. Punjab, U. Basrah, Armed Forces Med. Coll., Coll. Physicians and Surgeons Pakistan. Contbr. numerous articles to med. jours. Bd. govs. Pakistan Med. Research Council, Ayub Med. Coll.; bd. studies Quaid-e-Azam U.; convenor bd. studies in medicine, mem. syndicate and senate U. Peshawar. Fellow Royal Coll. Physicians (Edinburgh), Royal Coll. Physicians (London, regional advisor), Am. Coll. Cardiologists, Coll Physicians and Surgeons (Pakistan, mem. council and exec. com.); mem. Pakistan Med. and Dental Council (v.p.), Pakistan Sci. Found., Nat. Formulary Com. Pakistan (past chmn.), Pakistan Med. Assn. Peshawar (past pres.), Pakistan Cardiac Soc. Office: Khyber Med Coll, Office of the Prin and Dean, Peshawar 41126, Pakistan

KHAN, OBAIDULLAH A.Z.M., ambassador, author; b. Barisal, Bangladesh, May 1, 1934; s. Abdul Jabbar and Saleha Khan; m. Jahanara Huqchowdhury, Aug. 31, 1958 (div. 1977); children—Riaz Ahmed, Faiyyaz Ahmed; m. Mahjabeen Khan, Nov. 27, 1977; 1 child, Sumanah. B.A., Dhaka U., 1953, M.A., 1954; Diploma in Pub. Adminstrn., Cambridge U. (Eng.), 1959; fellow Harvard U., 1974-75. Civil servant Govt. of Pakistan, 1957-69, econ. counselor, 1969-71; permanent sec. Govt. of Bangladesh, 1972-82, cabinet minister agr., 1982-84, ambassador to U.S., 1984—; cons. World Bank, Washington, 1975-76, 82. Author poetry: Satnari Har, 1955, Kakhono Rang Kakhonosur, 1970, Kamaler Chokh, 1976, Amikimbodontir Katha Balchhi, 1980, Sahishnu Pratiksha, 1982, Premer Kavita, 1983, Prayer for Rains and Brave of Heart, 1983, Amar Samoy (My Times), 1986; scholarly books including: Poverty Oriented Rural Development, 1976, Rural Development in South Asia, 1979, others. Recipient Bangla Acad. poetry award, 1979, Nat. Poetry award, 1984. Fellow Bangladesh Inst. Devel. Studies, Ctr. Internat. Affairs; Assn. Creative Writers, (pres. 1980-84), mem. Soc. Internat. Devel., Bagladesh Ctr. Devel. Studies. Club: International (Washington). Avocations: reading; classical music. Home: 4 Highboro Ct Bethesda MD 20817 Office: Embassy of Bangladesh 2201 Wisconsin Ave NW Washington DC 20007

KHAN, SHAUKAT ALI, librarian; b. Aligarh, India, July 16, 1938; arrived in Pakistan, 1960; s. Ahmad Ali Khan and Hamida Khatoon; m. Afrida Khanum, Dec. 11, 1972; children: Amir, Yasir, Haris, Azfar. BLS, Muslim U., Aligarh, 1959; MA in Lit., U. Karachi, Pakistan, 1974. Librarian Halim Degree Coll., Kanpur, India, 1959-60, Jinnah Coll., Karachi, 1960-61; asst. librarian Inst. Pub. and Bus. Adminstrn., Karachi, 1961-62; asst. librarian sr. staff library Pakistan Internat. Airlines, Karachi, 1962-64, sr. tech. librarian, 1964-70, tech. publs. officer, 1970-80, asst. mgr. tech. publs., 1980—; dir. studies Special Library Assn., Karachi, 1970-87. Mem. Social Evils Eradication Assn. of Pakistan, Karachi, 1960-70. Fellow Spl. Library Assn. (dir. studies). Home: 1342/8 Azizabad, Karachi, Sind Pakistan Office: Pakistan Internat Airlines, Airport, Karachi, Sind Pakistan

KHAN, ZIA ULLAH, physician; b. Sargodha, Pakistan, Mar. 3, 1944; d. Chaudhry Inayat Ullah and Bibi Aisha; married; children: Wagas Zia, Faisal Zia, Atif Zia. MB BS, Nishtar Med. Coll., 1967. Jr., sr. house surgeon in orthopedics Nishtar Hosp., Multan, Pakistan, 1969-70; med. officer Libyan Health Ctr., Sabratha, 1971-75, dist. health officer, 1975-80; med. officer Aziz Fatima Trust Hosp., Faisalabad, Pakistan, 1980-81; gen. practice medicine Atif Clinic, Faisalabad, 1981—; med. cons. Faisalabad Devel Authority, Nat. Bank of Pakistan, Faiji Fertilizers Orgn., also other banks. Mem. Pakistan Med. Assn. (exec. mem. 1985—). Home: Sargoha Rd, Faisalabad Pakistan Office: Atif Clinic, Styana Rd, Faisalabad Pakistan

KHANDWALLA, PRADIP NAVIN, management educator; b. Bombay, India, Feb. 18, 1940; s. Navin Tuljaram and Sarayubala Kanaiyalal (Munshi) K.; m. Anjali Ishwarlal Shah, July 14, 1968; 1 child, Kalini. B Commerce, U. Bombay, 1960; MBA, U. Pa., 1966; MS, Carnegie-Mellon Inst., Pitts., 1968; PhD, Carnegie-Mellon Inst., 1970. Asst. prof. faculty mgmt. McGill U., Montreal, Que., Can., 1969-73; assoc. prof. McGill U., 1973-77; vis. prof. Indian Inst. Mgmt., Ahmedabad, 1975-77; prof. Indian Inst. Mgmt., 1977-85, Larsen and Toubro chair prof. orgnl. behavior, 1985—; cons. World Bank, Washington, 1978-80, Indsl. Devel. Bank India, Bombay, 1984-85, Gujarat State Fin. Corp., Ahmedabad, 1986-87; bd. dirs. NTC (Gujarat) Ltd., Ahmedabad, Surgiplast Ltd., Ahmedabad, FORE, New Delhi, India, CEE, Ahmedabad, Bhanu Iron and Steel Ltd., New Delhi, Amruta Mills, Ahmedabad, Mudra Communications, Ahmedabad. Author: The Design of Organizations (textbook), 1977, Wild Words (poems), 1982, Fourth Eye: Excellence through Creativity, 1984; editor Vikalpa: The Jour. for Decision Makers, 1981-85; guest editor Internat. Studies of Mgmt. and Orgn.; contbr. papers and articles to profl. publs. Founder, chmn. Bharatiya Youth Forum, Bombay, 1960-64. Recipient Taktasinhji prize Sydenham Coll., Bombay, 1960; Ford Found. fellow, 1966, Can. Council fellow, 1975; recipient Seagram Research award Bronfman Found., Can., 1973. Mem. Inst. Chartered Accts., India. Hindu. Home: 429 IIMA, Ahmedabad Gujarat 380015, India Office: Indian Inst Mgmt, Vikram Sarabbai Rd, Ahmedabad Gujarat 380015, India

KHANNA, PURUSHOTTAM, environmental engineer; b. Sagar, India, July 14, 1942; s. Jyoti Prasad and Yashoda (Mehrotra) K. BE with honors, Jabalpur U., 1964; ME with honors, Roorkee U., 1966, PhD, 1972. Lectr. Roorkee (India) U., 1967-72, reader, 1972-76; prof. IIT, Bombay, 1977-86; dir. Nat. Environ. Engring. Research Inst., Nagpur, India, 1987—; cons. UNICEF, Bhutan, India, 1977-82, UNEP, Kenya, 1983-86, SIDA, India, 1983-84, WHO-UNEP, India, 1986-87. Contbr. articles to profl. jours. Recipient B.P. Poddar Meml. award Bharat C. of C., 1986, Golden Jubilee award IAEC. Fellow Indian Nat. Acad. Engring.; mem. Indian Assn. for Water Pollution Control (life; mem. council 1982-84), Indian Water Works Assn. (IWWA awards 1974, 79, 80). Home: Nehru Marg, Nagpur 440 020, India Office: Nat Environ Engring Res Inst, Nehru Marg, Nagpur 440020, India

KHANTZIAN, EDWARD JOHN, psychiatrist, psychoanalyst; b. Haverhill, Mass., May 26, 1935; s. John Stephen and Nuvart K.; A.B., Boston U., 1958; M.D., Albany Med. Coll., 1963; m. Carol Ann DeAndrus, May 17, 1959; children—Nancy Jo, Susan Joyce, Jane Elizabeth, John Stephen. Intern, R.I. Hosp., Providence, 1963-64; resident Mass. Mental Health Center-Boston Psychopathic Hosp., 1964-67; practice medicine specializing in adult psychiatry, 1967—, specializing in psychoanalysis, Haverhill, Mass., 1973—; chief psychiat. consultation service Cambridge (Mass.) Hosp., 1967-71, dir. drug treatment program, 1971-74, asso. dir. dept. psychiatry, 1976-80, spl. asst. to dir., 1980-82, dir. departmental liaison, 1982-85, prin. psychiatrists for addictions, 1985—, pres. med. staff, 1983-84. dir. drug treatment services Cambridge-Somerville Mental Health and Retardation Center, 1974-76, asso. dir. clin. services, 1976-80; program dir. Drug Problems Resource Center, Cambridge, 1974-76; instr. psychiatry Harvard Med. Sch., Boston, 1967-73, asst. prof., 1973-78, asso. prof., 1978—; prin. collaborator Polydrug Treatment Program, Nat. Inst. Drug Abuse, 1974-76; mem. Drug Rehab. Adv. Bd. Commonwealth Mass., 1973-78, chmn., 1976-78. Served to maj. M.C., U.S. Army, 1967-70. Diplomate Am. Bd. Psychiatry and Neurology. Fellow Am. Psychiat. Assn. (cons. com. drug abuse 1984-86, mem. 1986—); mem. Boston Psychoanalytic Soc. and Inst. (Felix and Helen Deutsch prize 1973), Am. Psychoanalytic Assn., Mass. Psychiat. Soc., North Essex County Med. Soc., Am. Coll. Psychoanalysts, Group for Advancement Psychiatry (chmn. com. on alcoholism and addictions), North Essex Mental Health Assn. (dir., 1st v.p. 1975-77). Editorial rev. bd. Jour. Substance Abuse Treatment, 1984—, Am. Jour. Drug and Alcohol Abuse, 1986—; contbr. articles to profl. jours. Home: 55 King St Groveland MA 01834 Office: 10-12 Phoenix Row Haverhill MA 01830

KHARE, MOHAN, chemist; b. Varanasi, India, May 15, 1942; s. Dwarka Nath and Rampyari Devi Khare Srivastava; came to U.S., 1967, naturalized, 1971; B.Sc., Banaras Hindu U., 1961, M.Sc., 1963, Ph.D., 1967; m. Meena K., Nov. 20, 1973; 1 son, Rohit. Research asso. U. Md., College Park, 1967-69, Oreg. State U., Corvallis, 1969-70; sr. research asso. Cornell U., Ithaca, N.Y., 1970-78; analytical specialist Hydroscience Inc., (subsidiary of Dow Chem. Co.), Knoxville, Tenn., 1978-80; tech. specialist IT Enviroscience subs. IT Corp., Knoxville, 1980-82; research prof. chemistry U. Nev., Las Vegas, 1982-84, mgr. organic div. quality assurance lab. 1982-84; mgr. organic analysis lab. Environ. Monitoring Services Rockwell Internat., Thousand Oaks, Calif., 1984-85; dir. environmental analytical lab. EA Engring., Sci., and Tech., Inc., Sparks, Md., 1985-87; sr. v.p. Recra Environ., Inc., Columbia, Md., 1987—. Mem. AAAS, Am. Chem. Soc., AMS. Contbr. articles to profl. jours. including protocols and standard operating procedures for hazardous waste analytical program. Home: 10189 Maxine Rd Ellicott City MD 21043 Office: Recra Environ Inc 8320 Guilford Rd Columbia MD 21046

KHATAMI, MUHAMMAD, government official; b. Ardakan, Yazd, Iran, Sept. 29, 1943; s. Saied Rohollah Khatamee; married; 2 children. BA in Philosophy, Coll. Lit. and Human Scis., Esfahan, Iran. Tchr., then prof. Theol. Ctr., Qum, Iran; dir. Hamburg Islamic Ctr., 1978-80; mem. parliament Islamic Consultative Assembly Iran, Tehran, 1980-81; minister Ministry Culture and Islamic Guidance, Tehran, 1982—; supr. Keyhan Inst., Tehran, 1980—. Contbr. articles to profl. jours. Served with Iranian Army, 1968-70. Office: Ministry Culture and Islamic, Guidance Baharestan Sq, Tehran Iran

KHATIB, HISHAM MOHAMMED, government official, former power utility administrator; b. Acre, Palestine, Jan. 5, 1936; emigrated to Jordan, 1948; s. Mohammed Hashim and Fahiemh (Tabriey) K.; m. Maha Daher, Aug. 21, 1968; children—Mohammed, Lynn, Issam. B.Sc. in Econs., U. London, 1967, Ph.D. in Engring., 1973; B.Sc., Ain Shams U., 1959; M.Sc., U. Birmingham, 1962. Engr. Jerusalem Dist. Electric Co., 1959-66, chief engr., 1966-74; dep. dir. gen. Jordan Electricity Authority, Amman, 1974-76, dir. gen., 1980-84; minister of energy and mineral resources, 1984—; sr. energy adviser Arab Fund, Kuwait, 1976-80. Trustee Royal Fine Arts Soc., Jordan, 1983. Fellow IIEE; IEE (chartered engr.). Moslem. Club: Rotary. Office: Jordan Ministry of Energy, PO Box 2310, Amman Jordan

KHAYAT, FADY HEKMAT, marketing professional; b. Beirut, Lebanon, July 27, 1957; s. George Sami and Marie (Debai) K.; m. Ann Louise Erickson, Dec. 27, 1980; children: Stephany, Mark. BS in Chem., Purdue U., 1980; MBA, St. Edwards U., 1981. Mgr. Middle East Searle Pharm. Co., Chgo., 1982-87; area mktg. mgr. Cilag Agrl. Products (Johnson & Johnson), Schaffhausen, Switzerland, 1987—. Mem. Am. Chem. Soc. Home: 1409 N Salisbury St West Lafayette IN 47906 Office: Cilag Ag Products, Industriestrasse 24, 7UG 6300 Schaffhausen Switzerland

KHAYYAT, SHIMON LATIF, educator; b. Baghdad, Iraq, Dec. 13, 1938; came to U.S., 1972, naturalized, 1976; s. Haskel and Georgiya (Shabat) K.; BA, Hebrew U., Jerusalem, 1965, MA (Ben Tzvi Inst. scholar 1966-70), 1971; PhD (Meml. Found. Jewish Culture scholar 1974-76), Dropsie U., 1975; m. Vita Glassman, May 13, 1971; children: Haskel, Devorah. Tchr. Arabic, Israel, 1967-70; translator Arabic documents from Ottoman period Council Sephardic Community, Jerusalem, 1969-71; research asst. dept. geography Hebrew U., 1969-70, dept. music, 1972, Truman Inst., 1971-72; asso. prof. Arabic, Hebrew and Syriac, Dropsie U., Phila., 1974-82, chmn. Middle East program, 1975-82; summer tchr. Camp Ramah, Can., 1973, 74. Recipient B'Nai Zion medal, 1973. Mem. Nat. Assn. Profs. Hebrew, Assn. Jewish Studies, Am. Oriental Soc., Profs. for Peace in Middle East. Author: (in Arabic) Iraqi Proverbs, vol. I, 1968, vol. II, 1976, vol. III, IV, 1987; contbr. numerous articles to profl. jours. Home: 504 Grand St Apt H32 New York NY 10002

KHIEU SAMPHAN, Democratic Kampuchean government official; b. Svay Rieng Province, Cambodia, 1932. D.Econs., U. Paris. Former editor L'Observateur, French lang. jour., Phnon Penh; dep. Nat. Assembly in Prince Sihanouk's party, Sangkum Reastr Niyum; served as sec. of state for commerce; left Phnom-Penh to join maquis guerillas; 1967; dep. prime minister, minister of nat. def. Royal Govt. of Nat. Union of Kampuchea, 1970-76; comdr. in chief People's Army of Nat. Liberation of Kampuchea, 1970-76; mem. Polit. Bur., Nat. United Front Kampuchea, 1970-76; pres. of Presidium of State of Democratic Kampuchea, 1976-82, prime minister, 1979-82, v.p. of Democratic Kampuchea in charge fgn. affairs, 1982—. Address: Mission of Dem Kampuchea to UN 747 Third Ave 8th Floor New York NY 10017 *

KHIM, JAY WOOK, high technology company executive, economist; b. Taegu, Korea, Oct. 22, 1940; came to U.S., 1965; s. Joon Mook and Soon E.

(Lee) K.; m. Millie Myung-soon Jean; children: Katheryn, Anthony. BS in Agrl. Econs., Kyung Pook U., Korea, 1963, MA in Agrl. Econs., 1966; postgrad. PhD program in Econs., U. Md., 1965-69, DBA in Mgmt. Sci., 1972; LLD (hon.), Randolph-Macon Coll. Mem. research staff Brookings Instn., Washington, 1967-69; sr. economist NAB, Dept. of Labor, Washington, 1969-72; sr. assoc. Planning Research Corp., Washington, 1972-74; chmn., chief exec. officer JWK Internat. Corp., Washington, 1974—, Internat. Trade and Investment Corp., Washington, 1977—. Author, editor more than 100 research reports, articles for fed. govt. in fields of health, energy, def., transp., housing and internat. affairs. Bd. dirs. George Mason Inst., George Mason U., Fairfax, Va., 1983—; mem. Democratic Nat. Fin. Council, Washington, 1980-84; bd. dirs. League of Korean Ams., Washington, 1983, 84; bd. trustees Fairfax Hosp. Assn., 1986—. Fulbright scholar, 1965, 66; recipient Sam Ill Found. award Korea, 1962, 63. Mem. Young Pres.'s Orgn., Pres. Club of Am. Mgmt. Assn., Nat. Security Assn., Am. Def. Preparedness Assn., Am. Econ. Assn., Fairfax C. of C. (bd. dirs. 1984—). Clubs: Pisces, University, Capital Hill (Washington); Nat. Dem., Internat., Tournament Players, Internat. (Washington); River Bend Country (Great Falls, Va.); Fiarbanks Golf and Country (San Diego). Home: 10900 Tara Rd Potomac MD 20854 Office: JWK Internat Corp 7617 Little River Turnpike Annandale VA 22003

KHINDARIA, BRIJESH KUMAR, journalist; b. Lahore, India, Feb. 9, 1945; s. Sohanlal and Vimla (Dhawan) K. B.A. with honors, St. Stephens Coll., Delhi U., 1964; postgrad. Delhi Sch. Econs., 1965; postgrad. diploma Surrey U., 1968. Staff corr. Reuters News Agy., various locations, 1968-77; freelance corr. Observer London, 1977—, Fairchild Publs., N.Y.C., 1977-84, Guardian, London, 1977-79, Fin. Times, London, 1979-83, Internat. Herald Tribune, Paris, 1983—, Times of India/Econ. Times, 1984—, Economist Publs., 1987, Wall St. Jour. Spl. Projects, 1987—, India Today, 1987—; pres. Diplomatic Forum for Bus., Geneva, 1983—; pres. Integrated Publs., Geneva, 1985—; sr. adv. UN Internat. Bus. Council, N.Y.C., Internat. Bus. Govt. Counsellors, Washington. Author, editor: Enlightenment and Invincibility, 1982. Contbr. Yearbook of Ency. Brittanica, 1981, 82, 83, 85. Named Minister of the Age of Enlightenment, Maharishi European Research U., Seelisberg, Switzerland. Mem. Nat. Union Journalists, Assn. Internat. Journalists Belgium, Assn. Fgn. Corrs., UN Corrs. Assn., Soc. Internat. Devel., Spiritual Regeneration Movement. Hindu. Avocations: audio-visual design; classical Indian music; yoga; teaching meditation. Home: 34 rue Daubin, 1203 Geneva Switzerland Office: Palais des Nations, Salle de Presse, Ave de la Paix, 1211 Geneva 10 Switzerland

KHO, EUSEBIO, surgeon; b. Philippines, Dec. 16, 1933; s. Joaquin and Francisca (Chua) K.; came to U.S., 1964; A.A., Silliman U., Philippines, 1955; M.D., State U. Philippines, 1960; fellow in surgery, Johns Hopkins, 1965-67; m. Grace C. Lim, May 24, 1964; children—Michelle Mae, April Tiffany, Bradley Jude, Jaclyn Ashley, Matthew Ryan. Intern in surgery Balt. City Hosp., 1964-65, resident in gen. surgery, 1965-67; research asso. pediatric surgery U. Chgo. Hosps., 1967-68; resident in gen. surgery, then chief resident U. Tex. Hosp., San Antonio, 1968-70; hosp. surgeon St. Anthony Hosp., Louisville, 1970-72; practice medicine specializing in surgery, Scottsburg, Ind., 1972—; chmn. dept. surgery Scott County Meml. Hosp., 1973—; cons. surgeon Washington County Meml. Hosp., Salem, Ind., also Clark County Meml. Hosp., Jeffersonville, Ind., 1973—; courtesy surgeon Suburban Hosp., Louisville, 1973—; gen. surgeon U.S. Army Hosp., Louisville, 1980—. Served to lt. col. M.C., USAR, 1980—. Diplomate Am. Bd. Surgery. Fellow A.C.S., Am. Soc. Abdominal Surgeons; mem. Am. Coll. Internat. Physicians (founding mem., trustee 1974—), AMA (Physician's Recognition award 1969, 72), Ind., Ky., Philippine med. assns., Internat. Coll. Surgeons, Soc. Philippine Surgeons in Am. (life), Assn. Philippine Practicing Physicians in Am. (life), Assn. Mil. Surgeons of U.S., Res. Officers Assn. of U.S., Mark Ravitch Surg. Assn., Bradley Aust Surg. Soc., N.Y. Acad. Scis. Presbyterian. Clubs: Optimists, Masons. Home: 14 Carla Ln Scottsburg IN 47170 Office: 137 E McClain Ave Scottsburg IN 47170

KHÔI, LÊ THÀNH, economics educator, b. Hanoi, Vietnam, May 3, 1923; came to France, 1947; s. Le Thanh Y and Pham Thi Nghia; m. Tham Thi Hong Anh; children—Le Thi Huong Du, Le Thi Van Dao, Le Hong Nguyen. Ph.D. in Econs., Faculty Law and Econs.-Paris, 1949; Diploma in Internat. Law, Acad. Internat. Law, The Hague, 1950; Diploma Chinese and Vietnamese, Sch. Oriental Lang.-Paris, 1950; Ph.D., Sorbonne, 1968. Asst. prof. Faculte Droit et Sciences economiques, Paris, 1956-62; assoc. prof., Caen, 1962-63; maitre, then dir. research IEDES (Institut d'etude du developpement economique et social), U. Paris I, 1963-71; prof. comparative edn. and econs. edn. U. Paris V, 1971—; UNESCO cons. in field. Author: L'industrie de l'enseignement, 1967, L'education comparee, 1981, Histoire du Vietnam des origines a 1858, 1982, others. Contbr. articles to profl. jours. Mem. Vietnamese Assn. Social Sci. in France, French Speaking Assn. Comparative Edn. (v.p. 1982—). Buddhist. Avocations: collecting Vietnamese art; Chinese and Japanese paintings; Chinese jade. Home: 15 rue Georges Pitard, 75015 Paris France Office: UER Sciences de l'Education, 28 Rue Serpente, 75015 Paris France

KHOMEINI, (AYATOLLAH) RUHOLLAH MUSSAVI, political and religious leader of Iran; b. Khomein, Iran, May 17, 1900; s. Sayed Mustafa and Hajar (Saghafi) Mussavi; married; 1 son, Sayed Ahmed, 3 daus. Tchr., Madresseh Faizieh; leading opponent of Mohammed Reza Shah; led clergy in gen. strike against Govt. of Shah, 1962; arrested, detained, under house arrest, 1963; arrested, 1964, exiled to Turkey; exiled to Iraq, 1965; head theol. sch. in Iraq, 1965-78, expelled by Iraqi govt., 1978; in exile in Neauphe-le-Chateau, France, 1978-79; returned to Iran, 1979; forced resignation of existing govt., apptd. new govt., 1979; returned to City of Qom, 1979; formed spl. militia Army of Guardians of Islamic Revolution, 1979; took control of Iran, Nov. 1979, named polit. and religious leader Islamic Republic of Iran for life, 1979. Shi'ite Muslim. Author 21 books. Office: Madresseh Faizieh, Qom 61 Kuche Yakhachal Ghazi, Qom Iran *

KHORAICHE, ANTOINE PIERRE CARDINAL (HIS BEATITUDE ANTHONY PETER), patriarch of Antioch for Maronites; b. Ain-Ebel, Lebanon, Sept. 20, 1907. Ordained priest Roman Catholic Ch., 1930; consecrated titular bishop of Tarsus and aux. bishop of Sidon of Maronites, 1950; bishop of Sidon, from 1957; elected patriarch of Antioch for Maronites, Beirut, Lebanon, 1975; elevated to Sacred Coll. of Cardinals, 1983. Mem. Congregation of Oriental Chs., Commn. for Revision of Code of Oriental Canon Law. Advocate reconciliation among various Lebanese ethnic and religious groups and withdrawal fgn. troops from Lebanon. Office: Patriarcat Maronite, Dimane Lebanon *

KHORANA, HAR GOBIND, chemist, educator; b. Raipur, India, Jan. 9, 1922; s. Shri Ganpat Rai and Shrimati Krishna (Devi) K.; m. Esther Elizabeth Sibler, 1952; children: Julia, Emilie, Dave Roy. B.S., Punjab U., 1943, M.S., 1945; Ph.D., Liverpool (Eng.) U., 1948; D.Sc., U. Chgo., 1967. Head organic chemistry group B.C. Research Council, 1952-60; vis. prof. Rockefeller Inst., N.Y.C., 1958—; prof. co-dir. Inst. Enzyme Research, U. Wis., Madison, 1960-70, prof. dept. biochemistry, 1962-70, Conrad A. Elvehjem prof. life scis., 1964-70; Alfred P. Sloan prof. biology and chemistry MIT, Cambridge, 1970—; vis. prof. Stanford U., 1964; mem. adv. bd. Biopolymers. Author: Some Recent Developments in the Chemistry of Phosphate Esters of Biological Interests, 1961; Mem. editorial bd.: Jour. Am. Chem. Soc, 1963—. Recipient Merck award Chem. Inst. Can., 1958, Gold medal Profl. Inst. Pub. Service Can., 1960, Dannie-Heinneman Preiz Gö ttingen, Germany, 1967, Remsen award Johns Hopkins U., 1968, Am. Chem. Soc. award for creative work in synthetic organic chemistry, 1968, Louisa Gross Horwitz prize, 1968, Lasker Found. award for basic med. research, 1968, Nobel prize in medicine, 1968; elected to Deutsche Akademie der Naturforscher Leopoldina HalleSaale, Germany, 1968; Overseas fellow Churchill Coll., Cambridge, Eng., 1967. Fellow Chem. Inst. Can., Am. Acad. Arts and Scis.; mem. Nat. Acad. Sci. Office: MIT Dept Biology and Chemistry Room 180511 Cambridge MA 02139 *

KHOSLA, SHEELKUMAR LALCHAND, oil company executive; b. Amritsar, Punjab, India, Sept. 27, 1934; s. Lalchand and Khosla (Premvati) K.; m. Snehlata Snehlata, May 1, 1959; children: 2 sons, 1 daughter. MA in Econs., Bombay U., 1956. Joint sec., fin. adviser India Ministry Petroleum, New Delhi, 1976-81; chmn. Assam State Electricity Bd., India, 1981-82; energy adviser Planning Commn. India, New Delhi, 1983-86; chmn., chief exec. Indian Oil Corp. Ltd., New Delhi, 1986—. Contbr. articles to profl. jours. Club: Panch Shila. Home: K-99 Haus Khas Enclave, New Delhi 110 017, India Office: Indian Oil Corp Core-2, Scope Complex Lodhi Rd, 7 Institutional Area, New Delhi 1100 03, India

KHOSLA, VED MITTER, oral and maxillofacial surgeon, educator; b. Nairobi, Kenya, Jan. 13, 1926; s. Jagdish Rai and Tara V. K.; m. Santosh Ved Chabra, Oct. 11, 1952; children: Ashok M., Siddarth M. Student, U. Cambridge, 1945; L.D.S., Edinburgh Dental Hosp. and Sch., 1950, Coll. Dental Surgeons, Sask., Can., 1962. Prof. oral surgery, dir. postdoctoral studies in oral surgery U. Calif. Sch. Dentistry, San Francisco, 1968—; chief oral surgery San Francisco Gen. Hosp.; lectr. oral surgery U. of Pacific, VA Hosp.; vis. cons. Fresno County Hosp. Dental Clinic.; Mem. planning com., exec. med. com. San Francisco Gen. Hosp. Contbr. articles to profl. jours. Examiner in photography and gardening Boy Scouts Am., 1971-73, Guatemala Clinic, 1972. Granted personal coat of arms by H.M. Queen Elizabeth II, 1959. Fellow Royal Coll. Surgeons (Edinburgh), Internat. Assn. Oral Surgeons, Internat. Coll. Applied Nutrition, Internat. Coll. Dentists, Royal Soc. Health, AAAS, Am. Coll. Dentists; mem. Brit. Assn. Oral Surgeons, Am. Soc. Oral Surgeons, Am. Dental Soc. Anesthesiology, Am. Acad. Dental Radiology, Omicron Kappa Upsilon. Club: Masons. Home: 1525 Lakeview Dr Hillsborough CA 94010 Office: U Calif Sch Dentistry Oral Surgery Div 3d and Parnassus Aves San Francisco CA 94122

KHOURI, FRED JOHN, political science educator; b. Cranford, N.J., Aug. 15, 1916; s. Peter and Mary (Rizk) K.; m. Catherine McLean, June 24, 1964. Student, Union Jr. Coll., Roselle, N.J., 1934-36; B.A., Columbia U., 1938, M.A., 1939, Ph.D., 1953. Instr. Brownsville Jr. Coll. and High Sch., Tex., 1939-40; instr. polit. sci. U. Tenn., 1946-47, U. Conn., 1947-50; asst. prof. Villanova U., Pa., 1951-61, prof., 1964-86; prof. emeritus Villanova U., 1986—; vis. prof. Am. U. of Beirut, Lebanon, 1961-64; mem. Brookings Instn. Middle East Study Group, 1975-76; sr. fellow Middle East Ctr U. Pa., 1978-79, 80-81; lectr. in field. Author: The Arab States and the UN, 1954, The Arab Israeli Dilemma, 1968, 2d edit., 1976, 3d edit., 1985; assoc. editor: Jour. South Asian and Middle Eastern Studies; contbr. to books and profl. jours. Served with U.S. Army, 1941-45. Decorated Order of Cedars Lebanon. Fellow Middle East Studies Assn.; mem. Middle East Inst., Am. Polit. Sci. Assn., Am. Soc. Internat. Law, Internat. Studies Assn., Am. Acad. Polit. and Social Sci., World Affairs Council, Phi Kappa Phi. Democrat. Roman Catholic. Home: 1209 W Wynnewood Rd Apt 310 Wynnewood PA 19096 Office: Villanova Univ Villanova PA 19085

KHOURY, RIAD PHILIP, corporation executive, financial consultant; b. Beirut, May 25, 1935; came to U.S., 1979; s. Philip Mitri and Efrocine (Moujaes) K.; m. Samira Saade, Apr. 24, 1964; children: Philip, Marc, Serge. Graduate studies in fin. and mgmt. Ind. fin. cons. Baghdad, Iraq, 1955-58; ind. fin. investment adviser Jeddah, Saudi Arabia, 1959-61; mgr. Eastern Comml. Bank, Beirut, 1962-65; chief exec. officer United Bank of Lebanon and Pakistan, Beirut, 1965-70; vice chmn., chief exec. officer ADCOM Bank, Beirut, 1971-74; pres. Khoury Assocs. Internat., Annandale, Va., 1980—; banking and fin. cons. Lebanese Ministry Fin., Beirut, 1978-79. Recipient Officier Scientifique De L'ordre Du Merite award Le Merite, Paris, 1964, Cravate D'Honneur award Groupment Philantropique, Brussels, 1965. Home and Office: 6320 Wendy Ann Ct Fairfax Station VA 22039

KHOUW, BOEN TIE, biochemist; b. Tegal, Java, Indonesia, Sept. 4, 1934; came to Can., 1957; s. Bian Hin and Swan Nio (Liem) K.; m. Eugenia Yuen-Chi Yu, Sept. 29, 1967; children—Charlotte, Vivian. B.Sc., Mt. Allison U., 1960; M.Sc., U. Windsor, 1965, Ph.D., 1968. Technician, Fisheries Research Bd., Ellerslie, P.E.I., 1959-62; research scientist Can. Packers, Inc., Toronto, Ont., 1967-73, sr. scientist, 1973-80, tech. group mgr. pharms., 1980-87 , sect. leader biochem. research, 1986-87 ; tech. mgr. Waitaki Internat. Biosciences, Toronto, 1987—; guest lectr. chem. engring. U. Toronto, 1980—. Contbr. articles to profl. jours.; patentee in field. Office: Waitaki Internat Biosciences, 55 Glen Scarlett Rd, Toronto, ON Canada M6N 1P5

KHRENNIKOV, TIKHON NIKOLAYEVICH, composer; b. Eleta, Lietsk region, USSR, June 10, 1913; s. Nikolay and Varvara (Kharlamova) K.; m. Klara Arnoldovna Vax, 1936; 1 child. Ed. Moscow Conservatoire; attended Music Tech. Coll., Moscow, 1929-32. Dir. music Central Theatre of Soviet Army, 1941-54; gen. sec. Soviet Composers' Union, 1948-57, 1st sec., 1957—; dep. to USSR Supreme Soviet, 1962—; mem. com. USSR Parliamentary Group; mem. Central Auditing Com., CPSU, 1961-76; mem. CPSU, 1947—; mem. Santa Cecilia, 1983. Prin. compositions include: Two Piano Concertos, 1933, 71, Five Pieces for Piano, 1933, First Symphony, 1935, Three Pieces for Piano, 1935, Suite for Orchestra from Music for Much Ado About Nothing, In the Storm (opera), 1939, Second Symphony, 1941, incidental music for play Long Ago, 1942, Frol Skobeyev (opera), 1950, Mother (opera), 1956, Concerto for Violin and Orch., 1959, A Hundred Devils and One Girl (operetta), 1961, Two Concertos for Violin, 1964, 76, White Nights (operetta), 1967, Boy Giant (opera for children), 1969, Our Courtyard (ballet for children), 1970, Much Ado About Hearts (chamber opera), 1974, Third Symphony, 1975, Love for Love, (ballet), 1975, Concerto No. 2 for violin and orchestra, 1976, The Hussars' Ballad (ballet), 1980. Recipient State prize, 1942, 46, 51, 67, 79, People's Artist of the R.S.F.S.R., 1955, of the U.S.S.R., 1963; decorated Order of Lenin, 1963, Red Banner of Labour, 1967, Lenin prize, 1973, Gorky prize, 1979. Address: Composers Union of USSR, Ul Nezhdanovoi 8/10, Moscow USSR *

KHUBCHANDANI, INDRU TEKCHAND, colon and rectal surgeon; b. Karachi, India; s. Tekchand and Sarsati Khubchandani; m. Lynne Adderley, July 11, 1965; children—Joya, Mona, Sonya. M.D., Grant Med. Coll., Bombay, India, 1956; postgrad. Royal Coll. Surgeons, Eng., 1960. Diplomate Am. Bd. Colon and Rectal Surgeons. Fellowship in gen. surgery New Eng. Hosp., Boston, 1961-62; residency Temple U. Med. Sch., Phila., 1962-64; chief div. colon and rectal surgery Healtheast Teaching Hosps. Allentown, Pa., 1979—, also program dir. colon and rectal residency, bd. dirs.; bd. dirs. Healtheast, Slate Belt Med. Ctr.; clin. assoc. U. Pa. Mem. editorial bd. Jour. ColoProctology, 1980—; prof. clin. surgery Hannemann U., Phila. Jour. Diseases of Colon and Rectum. Pres. Harry E. Bacon Found., 1985; fund raiser Republican Party. Fellow Royal Coll. Surgeons (Edinburgh); mem. Am. Soc. Colon and Rectal Surgeons (chmn. sci. and comml. exhibits 1979—, Best Paper awards 1970, 81, Rowell award 1985), Assn. Surgeons India, Assn. Colon and Rectal Surgeons India (pres.), Royal Soc. Medicine, NE Soc. Colon and Rectal Surgeons (pres.), Pa. Soc. Colon and Rectal Surgeons (pres.), Internat. Soc. Univ. Colon and Rectal Surgeons (dir. gen. 1980—), Chilean Soc. Coloproctology (hon.), Venezuelan Soc. Colon and Rectal Surgeons (hon.), Sociedad Gallegade De Patologia Digestiva, La Coruna, Spain (hon.). Clubs: Hindu. Lehigh Country, Contemporary, Pa. Soc. Lodges: Rotary, Masons. Office: 1275 S Cedar Crest Blvd Allentown PA 18193

KHURI, NICOLA NAJIB, educator, physicist; b. Beirut, Lebanon, May 27, 1933; came to U.S., 1959, naturalized, 1970; s. Najib N. and Odette (Joujou) K.; m. Elizabeth Anne Tyson, Dec. 9, 1955; children: Suzanne Odette, Najib Nicholas. B.A with high distinction, Am. U. Beirut, 1952; Ph.D., Princeton U., 1957. Asst. prof. Am. U. Beirut, 1957-58, 60-61, assoc. prof., 1961-62; mem. Inst. Advanced Study, Princeton U., 1959-60, 62-63; vis. assoc. prof. Columbia, 1963-64; assoc. prof. Rockefeller U., 1964-68, prof., 1968—; cons. Brookhaven Nat. Lab., 1963-73; mem. Carnegie Panel on U.S. Security and Arms Control, 1981-83; vis. scientist European Ctr. for Nuclear Research, Geneva, Centre d'Etudes Nucleaires, Saclay, France, Max Planck Inst. für Physik, Munich, Fed. Republic Germany. Contbr. articles to profl. jours. Trustee Am. U. Beirut, Brearley Sch., N.Y.C., 1970-79. Fellow Am. Phys. Soc.; mem. Council on Fgn. Relations. Club: Century (N.Y.C.). Home: 4715 Iselin Ave Riverdale NY 10471 Office: Rockefeller U New York NY 10021

KHUSH, GURDEV SINGH, geneticist; b. Rurkee, Punjab, India, Aug. 22, 1935; arrived in Philippines, 1967; s. Kartar Singh and Pritam Kaur (Dosanjh) Kooner; m. Harwant Kaur Grewal, Dec. 31, 1961; children: Ranjiv, Manjeev, Sonia, Kiran. BS in Agr., Punjab U., India, 1955; PhD, U. Calif., Davis, 1960; PhD (hon.), Punjab Agr. U., 1987. Research asst. U. Calif., Davis, 1957-60, asst. geneticist, 1960-67; plant breeder Internat. Rice Research Inst., Manila, 1967-72; plant breeder, head dept. plant breeding Internat. Rice Research Inst., 1972-85, prin. plant breeder, head dept. plant breeding, 1986—; cons. rice breeding programs Burma, Bangladesh, China, India, Indonesia, Iraq, Egypt, Sri Lanka, Bhutan, Kampuchea, Vietnam, Korea, Australia. Author: Cytogenetics of Aneuploids, 1973; editor: Rice Genetics Newsletter; contbr. articles to books and profl. jours. Recipient Borlaug award Coromandal Fertilizers Ltd., Delhi, India, 1977, Japan prize Sci. and Tech. Found., Tokyo, 1987. Mem. Genetic Soc. Am., Am. Soc. Agronomy (fellows award 1987), Indian Soc. Genetics and Plant Breeding (fellows award 1988), Crop Sci. Soc. Philippines (fellows award 1986), Rice Genetics Coop. (sec. 1985—). Office: care Internat Rice Research Inst, PO Box 933, Manila Philippines

KIBAKI, MWAI, minister of health of Kenya; b. Othaya, Kenya, 1931; B.Sc. in Econs., Makerere Univ. Coll., 1960. Nat. exec. officer Kenya African Nat. U., 1960-62; rep. Central Legis. Assembly of E. African Common Services Orgn., 1962; mem. Ho. of Reps., 1963—; parliamentary sec. to treasury, 1963; asst. minister of econ. planning and devel., 1964-66; minister for commerce and industry, 1966-69; minister fin., 1969-70, 78-82; minister fin. and econ. planning, 1970-78; minister of home affairs, 1978-79, 82-88; v.p. Republic of Kenya, 1978-88; minister of health, 1988—. V.p. Kenya African Nat. Union, 1978—. Address: Office of Vice Pres, Nairobi Kenya *

KIBIRIBIRI, PHILIP MWANGI, labor union administrator; b. Nairobi, Kenya, July 3, 1933; s. John Kibiribiri and Lydia Wambui Kringa; m. Lily Waruguru Mwangi, Oct. 2, 1954; children: Kibiribiri, Munyiri, Wambui, Macharia, Muturi, Watrimu, Githaiga. Clk. Med. Dept., Muranga Town, Kenya, 1952-55, Adminstrn., Muranga Town, 1957-60; asst. sec. Muranga Farmers Co-op Union, Muranga Town, 1961-62; gen. sec. Sisal and Coffee Workers Union, Thika Town, Kenya, 1963, West Germany Trade Union Course, Bdnn, Fed. Republic Germany, 1964; orgn. dir. Kenya Plantation and Agrl. Workers Union, Nakuru Town, Kenya, 1965-66, gen. sec., 1967—; vice chmn. gen. Cen. Orgn. of Trade Unions, Nairobi, 1973-81, chmn. gen., 1981—. Mem. Internat. Fedn. of Plantation Agrl. and llied Workers (2d vice chmn. in Africa). Home: Govt Rd Nakuru, 763 Nakuru Kenya Office: KPA Workers Union, Kenyatta Ave, 1161 Nakuru Kenya

KIBLER, ROBERT CARROLL, high technology financial company executive; b. Mathews, Va., Jan. 9, 1927; s. John Lee and Myrtle Wilson (Nash) K.; m. Margia Lee Ivey, June 2, 1956; children—Tommy Wayne, Melissa Cherie. B.S., Am. U., 1951. Dept. comptroller Capital Airlines, Washington, 1951-60; asst. treas. C-E-I-R, Inc., Washington, 1960-68; v.p. fin., Computer Leasing Co., Arlington, Va., 1968-70, v.p., fin., treas., 1973-75; sr. v.p. fin., adminstr., treas. Alcorn Combustion Co., N.Y.C., 1970-73; v.p., treas. Greyhound Computer Corp., Phoenix, 1975-84, Greyhound Capital Corp., Phoenix, 1984-86; v.p., treas., asst. sec. Bell Atlantic Systems Leasing Internat., Inc., Phoenix, 1986—. Mem. Capital Airlines Assn. Served with USAAF, 1945-47. Republican. Methodist. Office: Bell Atlantic Systems Leasing 11811 N Tatum Blvd Phoenix AZ 85028-1601

KIDD, ALAN JOHN, historian, educator; b. London, June 19, 1947; s. Charles James and Ellen Ethel (Barrier) K.; m. Elaine Judith May, Aug. 21, 1969; children: Jonathan, Matthew. BA in History with honors, U. Hull, 1969; MA in History, U. Manchester, 1981. Tchr. Manchester Edn. Com., Eng., 1970-75; lectr. History and Edn. City of Manchester Coll. of Higher Edn., 1975-78; sr. lectr. History Manchester Poly., 1978—. Editor, co-founder Manchester Region History Rev.; author: City Class and Culture, 1985; contbr. articles to profl. jours. Mem. Econ. History Soc., Social History Soc., Nat. Assn. Tchrs. in Further and Higher Edn., Conf. for Reg. and Local Historians. Mem. Labour Party. Mem. Ch. of Eng. Office: Manchester Poly, Lower Ormond St, Manchester England

KIDD, DEBRA JEAN, communications consultant; b. Chgo., May 13, 1956; d. Fred A. and Jean (Pezzopane) Winchar; m. Kim Joseph Kidd, July 22, 1978; 1 child, Jennifer Marie. A.A. in Bus. with high honors, Wright Jr. Coll., 1977. Legal sec. Sidley & Austin, Chgo., 1977-80; investment adminstr. Golder, Thoma & Co., Chgo., 1980-81, exec. asst., 1981-84; sales rep. Dataspeed, Inc., Chgo., 1984, midwestern regional mgr. Dataspeed, Inc., Chgo., 1985; communications cons. Chgo. Communications, Inc., Chgo., 1986—; owner, founder Captain Kidd's Video, Niles, 1981-84. Vol. Am. Lung Assn., Chgo., 1979; vol. tchr. CCD Our Lady Mother of Ch., Norridge, Ill., 1981-83. Mem. Nat. Assn. Female Execs., Nat. Assn. Bus. Women, Nat. Assn. Profl. Saleswomen, Nat. Network of Women in Sales, Bus. and Profl. Women's Club, Phi Theta Kappa. Roman Catholic. Avocations: camping; snow and water skiing; horseback riding; sailing; reading; needlepoint.

KIDD, REBECCA (LOUISE) MONTGOMERY, artist; b. Muncie, Ind., Nov. 29, 1942; d. Joe Bucklyn and Mary Marguerite (Mark) Montgomery; corr. student comml. art, Famous Artists Schs.; cert. of completion corr. course U. Sci. and Philosophy, Waynesboro, Va., 1976; m. Ben Roy Kidd, Apr. 10, 1964; children—Daniel Ben, Diana Piper. Character painter, 1966—; portrait painter and drawer, 1962-81, 83—; painter in oils, pastels; outdoor scene, still life, floral painter, 1969—; children's story illustrator, 1972-74; restorer old houses, 1972-81; adaptor of master's paintings, 1974-82; miniature painter, 1974-82; film illustrator, 1975; Am. Indian painter, 1975-81; trading pin designer, 1977, 78; lithograph printmaker, 1977; monotype printmaker, 1978—; one woman show: Roadside Gallery, Melfa, Va., 1982; group shows include: Roadside Gallery, 1977—, The Gallery, Ct. Plaza, Salisbury, Md., 1977-84, Queens Coll., Cambridge U., 1982. Mem. Quality Edn. Accomack County (Va.), Exec. Com., 1979-80. Mem. Eastern Shore Art League (constn. and bylaws chmn. 1979, dir. 1982), Visual Artists and Galleries Assn., Nat. Mus. Women in Arts (charter), Nat. Trust Historic Preservation (assoc.), Internat. Platform Assn. (merit award and popular choice award 1984 conv.). Subject of articles in several news publs. Address: 9 Lake St Onancock VA 23417

KIDDE, JOHN LYON, multi-industry company executive; b. June 5, 1934. BA, Princeton U., 1959; postgrad., Columbia U., 1955-56. Indsl. research analyst Federated Employers San Francisco, 1956-57; fin. dir. Walter Kidde S.A. do Brasil, Rio De Janeiro, 1959-60; European mgr. Walter Kidde Co., Inc., Paris, 1962-66; joint mng. dir. Walter Kidde Co., Ltd., Northolt, Eng., corp. European mgr., 1966-67; dir. internat. ops. Kidde, Inc., U.S.A., Saddle Brook, N.J., 1967-68, v.p., dir. internat. ops., 1968-87, also bd. dirs. various Kidde Inc. fgn. subs.; gen. ptnr. Claflin Capital I, II, III, & IV, Boston, The Opportunity Fund, Boston.; bd. dirs. Celtic Trust Co. Ltd., Metalbanc, Inc., Miami, Fla., Tortola, Brit. Virgin Islands., Interfin. Inc., N.Y.C., U.S. Investment Pub., N.Y.C. The Futures Group, Glastonbury, Conn., Internat. Resource Group, Inc., Setauket, N.Y., Pasco Internat., Saddle brook, Md., Constrn. Specialties, Cranford, N.J., Canadian Am. Investment Mgmt., Halifax, N.S., Can., Australasia, Inc., Cayman Island, N.C. Savs. and Loan/Guaranty Savs. Bank, Fayetteville, N.C., Essex Life Ins. Co., Inc., West Orange, N.J., Internat. AgriTech Resources, Inc., N.Y.C. Hon. trustee Montclair (N.J.) Art Mus., Pace U., Clara Maass Med. Ctr., Belleville, N.J., Internat. Coll. Cayman Island, Grand Cayman, Charles Hayden Found., N.Y.C.; pres. Community Found. N.J., Albert Payson Terhune Found., Pompton Lakes, N.J.; chmn. bd. trustees Assist Inc., Peterborough, N.H.; mem. adv. bd. Midlantic Nat. Bank/North, West Patterson, N.J. Served with U.S. Army. Home: 154 Oldchester Rd Essex Fells NJ 07021 Office: Kidde Inc Park 80 West-Plaza Two Box 5555 Saddle Brook NJ 07662

KIEFER, ANSELM KARL ALBERT, artist; b. Donaueschingen, Germany, Mar. 8, 1945; s. Albert and Cacilia (Forster) K.; m. Monika Bornebusch, Feb. 9, 1971; children: Daniel, Sarah, Julian. Student State Acad. Arts, Karlsruhe, State Acad. Arts, Dusseldorf. One-man shows include Galerie am Kaiserplatz Karlsruhe, Fed. Republic Germany, 1969, Galerie Michael Werner, Cologne, Fed. Republic Germany, 1973, 74, 75, 76, 77, Galerie im Goethe-Institut/Provisorium, Amsterdam, 1973, Galerie Felix Handschine, Basel, Switzerland, 1973, Galerie t'Venster/Rotterdam Arts Found., The Netherlands, 1974, Bonner Kunstverein, Bonn, Fed. Republic Germany, 1977, Galerie Helen van der Meij, Amsterdam, 1977, 80, Galerie Maier-Hahn, Dusseldorf, Fed. Republic Germany, 1978, Stedelijk Van Abbemuseum, Eindhoven, The Netherlands, 1979, (with George Baselitz) XXXIX Biennale Venedig at German Pavilion, 1980, Mannheimer Kunstverein, Mannheim, Fed. Republic Germany, 1980, Wurttembergischer Kunstverein, Stuttgart, Fed. Republic Germany, 1980, Galerie Paul Maenz, Cologne, 1981, 84, Marian Goodman Gallery, N.Y.C., 1981, 82, Museum

Folkwang, Essen, Fed. Republic Germany, 1981, Whitechapel Art Gallery, London, 1982, Mary Boone Gallery, N.Y.C., 1982, Sonja Henie-Niels Onstad Founds., Oslo, 1983, Anthony d'Offay Gallery, London, 1983, Hans-Thoma-Museum, Bernau/Schwarzwald, Fed. Republic Germany, 1983, Mus. Contemporary Art, Los Angeles, 1983-84, Stadtische Kunsthalle, Dusseldorf, and Musee d'Art Moderne de la Ville de Paris, 1983, Israel Mus., Jerusalem, 1983; group shows include Musee d'Art Moderne, Paris, 1977, Teheran Mus. Contemporary Art, Iran, 1978, Badischer Kunstvereine, Karlsruhe, Fed. Republic Germany, 1979, Royal Acad., London, 1981, Palais des Beaux Arts, Brussels, 1981, Kunsthalle, Dusseldorf, 1981, Galeria Stein, Turin, Italy, 1982, Documenta 7, Kassel, Germany, 1982,St. Louis Art Mus., 1983, Inst. for Art and Urban Researches, Long Island City, N.Y., 1983, Inst. Contemporary Art at U. Phila., 1983, Mus. Contemporary Art, Chgo., 1983, New Port Harbour Mus., New Port Beach, Calif., 1983, Corooran Gallery Art, Washington, 1983, Fondacion S. Moragas, Barcelona, Spain, 1983, Biblioteca Nacional, Madrid, 1984, Stedelijk Mus., Amsterdam, 1984-85, Castello di Rivoli, Torino, 1985, La Grande Halle de la Vilette, Paris, 1985, Mus. Art, Carnegie Inst., Pitts., 1985, Nationalgalerie, Berlin, 1985, Royal Acad., London, 1985, Kunsthalle Basle, Switzerland, 1986; represented in permanent collections Art Inst. Chgo., Los Angeles County Mus. Art, Mus. Contemporary Art, Los Angeles, Mus. Modern Art, N.Y.C., Solomon R. Guggenheim Mus., N.Y.C., Mus. Art, Carnegie Inst., Phila. Mus. Art, Va. Mus., Richmond, Hirshhorn Mus., Smithsonian Instn., Washington, Tamayo Mus., Mexico City, Stadtische Galerie mit Sammlung Ludgie, Aachen, Nationalgalerie, Berlin, Kunsthalle, Bielefeld, Folkwang Mus., Essen, Staatsgalerie moderner Kunst im Haus der Kunst, Munich, Staatsgalerie, Stuttgart (all Fed. Republic Germany), Stedelijk Mus., Stedelijk Van Abbemuseum, Eindhoven, Groninger Mus., Groningen, Mus. Boymans-van Beuningen, Rotterdam (all The Netherlands), Kunsthaus Zurich, Switzerland, Tate Gallery, London, Musé e Nationale d'Art Moderne Centre Georges Pompidou, Paris.

KIEFER, WILLIAM LEE, computer marketing executive; b. St. Louis, Aug. 19, 1946; m. Joyce Ann Cwiklowski, Aug. 15, 1970; children: Jason Lee, William Andrew. AA, St. Louis Community Coll., 1971; BS, U. Mo., St. Louis, 1975. Ins. agt. Liberty Mut. Ins. Co., St. Louis, 1973-75; Dem. dir. elections City of St. Louis, 1975; mktg. specialist GAF Corp., Lincolnwood, Ill., 1976-79; with Microdata Corp., St. Louis, 1979-83, Honeywell, Inc., St. Louis, 1983-85, Harris computer systems div., 1985-86, Computervision Corp., St. Louis, 1986—. Dem. ward committeeman City of St. Louis, 1976-79, mem. ward steering com., 1974-79, campaign mgr., 1974-76. Served with USMC, 1965-69. Mem. Am. Inst. Design and Drafting, Soc. Mfg. Engrs. (program chmn. St. Louis chpt. 1987), Assn. Integrated Mfg., St. Louis Jaycees, North Park Neighborhood Assn. (chmn.), VFW, Am. Legion, U. Mo.-St. Louis Alumni Assn. (v.p.), Alumni Alliance U. Mo. System, U. Mo.-St. Louis Bus. Alumni Assn. (pres. 1980-81). Roman Catholic. Club: St. Louis Engrs. Home: 9472 Yorktown Dr Saint Louis MO 63137

KIEFNER, JOHN ROBERT, JR., lawyer, educator; b. Peoria, Ill., May 31, 1946; s. John Robert and Luna Merle (Froment) K.; m. Harriett E. Kidd, Aug. 3, 1968; 1 son, John William. B.A., Johns Hopkins U., 1968; J.D., Stetson U., 1971. Bar: Fla. 1971, U.S. Ct. Appeals (D.C. cir.) 1971, U.S. Ct. Appeals (11th cir.) 1981, U.S. Supreme Ct. 1979, U.S. Ct. Mil. Appeals 1971, U.S. Tax Ct. 1981, U.S. Dist. Ct. (no. dist.) Fla. 1971, U.S. Dist. Ct. (mid. dist.) Fla. 1981. Staff atty. SEC, Washington, 1971-74, br. chief, 1974-77, regional trial counsel, 1977-82; mem. Robbins, Gaynor, Burton, Hampp, Burns, Bronstein & Shasteen, St. Petersburg, Fla., 1982-86; ptnr. Riden & Goldstein, P.A., St. Petersburg, 1986—; adj. prof. law Stetson U., St. Petersburg, 1982—. Past chmn. Combined Fed. Campaign, 1976-77. Served to capt. U.S. Army, 1968-76. Recipient Cert. of Merit, SEC, 1982; Charles A. Dana scholar, 1970-71. Mem. Fla. Bar Assn., ABA, St. Petersburg Bar Assn., Fla. Acad. Trial Lawyers, Am. Trial Lawyers Assn., Pinella County Trial Lawyers Assn., Fed. Bar Assn., Nat. Assn. Colls. and Univs. (recruitment com.), St. Petersburg Area C. of C., Johns Hopkins U. Alumni Assn. Lutheran. Lodges: Masons, Shriners. Home: 1117 42d Ave NE Saint Petersburg FL 33703 Office: Riden & Goldstein PA 100 2d Ave S City Ctr North Tower Suite 400 Saint Petersburg FL 33701

KIELY, DAN RAY, banking and real estate development executive; b. Ft. Sill, Okla., Jan. 2, 1944; s. William Robert and Leona Maxine (Ross) K.; B.A. in Psychology, U. Colo., 1966; m. J.D., Stanford U., 1969; m. Lucianne Holt, June 11, 1966; children—Jefferson Ray, Matthew Ray. Admitted to Colo. bar, 1969, Va. bar, 1973, D.C. bar, 1970; assoc. firm Holme, Roberts and Owen, Denver, 1969-70; pres. DeRand Equity Group, Arlington, Va., 1973—; pres., chmn. bd. Bankwest Corp. and related banks, Denver.; pres., dir. United Gibraltar Corp. Del., Inc., 1987—; dir. DeRand Corp. and affiliates; trustee DeRand Real Estate Investment Trust; speaker, lectr. in field. Deacon, McLean (Va.) Baptist Ch., 1977-80. Served as officer, USAR, 1969-73. Decorated Legion of Merit; cert. property mgr. Mem. Nat. Bd. Realtors, Inst. Real Estate Mgmt., Nat. Assn. Rev. Appraisers, Internat. Council Shopping Centers, Nat. Assn. Real Estate Investment Trusts, Am. Bar Assn., Colo. Bar Assn., D.C. Bar Assn. Colo. Indsl. Bankers Assn. (bd. dirs.), The Internat. Inst (cert. valuer). Home: 501 E Causeway Vero Beach FL 32963 Office: 2201 Wilson Blvd Arlington VA 22201

KIENER, GEORGES NICOLAS, cosmetic company executive; b. St. Etienne, Loire, France, Dec. 21, 1956; s. Gerard Emile and Ludmilla (Tchegloff) K.; m. Karen Beesley, Sept. 8, 1984; 1 child, William James. Diploma, Inst. Polit. Scis., Strasbourg, France, 1981; MBA, European Inst. Bus. Adminstrn., Fontainbleau, France, 1982. Operational auditor L'Oreal, Paris, 1982-86; adminstrv. and fin. dir. Parfums et Collections subs. L'Oreal, Bonn, Fed Republic Germany, 1986—. Home: Am Rodderberg 20, 5307 Wachtberg-Niederbachem Federal Republic of Germany Office: Parfums Et Collections GMBH, In Der Raste 24, 5300 Bonn Federal Republic of Germany

KIENER, JEROME M., nonferrous metals company executive; b. St. Nabord, France, Oct. 1, 1944; came to U.S., 1977; s. Jean Jacques and Anne-Marie (de Montalembert de Cers) K.; M.S. in Mech. Engring., U. Wis.-Madison, 1969; m. Beatrice Chereil de la Riviere, Oct. 3, 1970; children—Ariane, Florian, Emmanuel, Charles. Internat. sales engr. W. R. Grace & Co., Neuilly-Seine and Epernon, France, 1969-72; market research assoc., comml. dir. Société Metallurgique Le Nickel-SLN, Paris, France, 1972-76; v.p. fin., sec. Le Nickel Inc., N.Y.C., 1977-80, Pitts., 1980-83; corporate mgmt. group Cogema, Velizy, France, 1984—. Roman Catholic. Club: Duquesne (Pitts.). Office: 2 rue Paul Dautier, 78141 Velizy-Villacoublay France

KIENHOLZ, LYN SHEARER, arts projects coordinator; b. Chgo.; d. Mitchell W. and Lucille M. (Hock) Shearer; student Sullins Coll., Md. Coll. Women. Assoc. producer Kurt Simon Prodns., Beverly Hills, Calif., 1963-65; owner, mgr. Vuokko Boutique, Beverly Hills, 1969-75; bd. dirs. Los Angeles Inst. Contemporary Art, 1976-79, Fellows of Contemporary Art, 1977-79, Internat. Network for Arts, 1979—, Los Angeles Contemporary Exhbns., 1980-82; exec. sec., bd. dirs. Beaubourg Found. (now George Pompidou Art and Culture Found.), 1977-81; visual arts adv. Performing Arts Council, Los Angeles Music Center, 1980—; bd. govs. Calif. Inst. Tech. Baxter Art Gallery, 1980-85; adv. bd. dirs. Fine Arts Communications, pub. Images & Issues mag., 1981-85; founder, pres. bd. dirs. Calif./Internat. Arts Found., 1981—; bd. dirs., western chmn. ArtTable 1983—; exec. bd. Sovereign Fund, 1981—; exec. bd. dirs. Scandinavia Today, 1982-83, Arts, Inc., 1987—, Art L.A./87, 1987, Art L.A., 1988; mem. adv. bd. Otis/Parsons Sch. Design, 1983-85, U. So. Calif. dept. fine arts, 1983-85; bd. dirs. UK/LA Festival of Britain, 1986-88; hon. bd. dirs. L'Ensemble des Deux Mondes, Paris, 1986—; mem. Comité International pour les Museés d'Art Moderne, 1985—. Bd. dirs. Arts, Inc., 1987—. Co-host radio program ARTS/L.A., 1987—; contbg. editor Calif. mag., 1984—. Address: 2737 Outpost Dr Los Angeles CA 90068

KIERNAN, BENEDICT FRANCIS, historian, educator; b. Melbourne, Australia, Jan. 29, 1953; s. Peter Brian and Joan Catherine (Silk) K.; m. Chanthou Boua, Dec. 16, 1978; children: Mia-lia Boua, Derry Reuben. BA with honors, Monash U., Clayton, Australia, 1975, PhD, 1983. Tutor in History U. New South Wales, Kensington, Australia, 1975-77; research fellow Australian Inst. Multicultural Affairs, Melbourne, 1983; postdoctoral fellow Monash U., Clayton, 1984-85; lectr. in History U. Wollongong, Australia, 1986, sr. lectr., 1987—; advisor Cambodia Documentation Commn., N.Y.C., 1984—. Author: How Pol Pot Came to Power, 1985; author, editor: (with others) Peasants and Politics in Kampuchea 1942-1981, 1982, Burchett, 1986; contbg. editor Indochina Issues, Washington, 1982-86; editorial bd. Bull. Concerned Asian Scholars, Boulder, Colo., 1983—. Mem. Asian Studies Assn. Australia. Mem. Australian Labor Party. Office: Univ Wollongong, Dept History-Politics, Wollongong, New South Wales 2500, Australia

KIERNAN, JAMES PATRICK, anthropologist, educator, researcher; b. Dundalk, Louth, Ireland, Feb. 6, 1935; arrived in Republic of South Africa, 1967; s. Edward and Bridget (Hernan) K.; m. Ann Mary Murray, June 7, 1977; 1 child, Sarah Siave. BA with honors, U. Dublin, Ireland, 1956; MA in Econs., Victoria U., Manchester, Eng., 1967, PhD, 1973. Cert. social anthropologist. Lectr. Catholic Sem., Cedara, Republic of South Africa, 1961-69; asst. lectr. U. Manchester, 1970-72; lectr. U. Natal, Durban, Republic of South Africa, 1973-75, sr. lectr., 1976-81, prof., 1982—; research fellow U. Manchester, 1979-80; planning cons. dept cooperation and devel. Republic of South African Govt., Durban, 1981-83. Author: Fragmented Priest, 1971; contbr. articles to profl. jours. Mem. Republic of South Africa Assn. Soc. Anthropologists, Assn. Social Anthropologists Great Brit. and Commonwealth, Internat. Assn. History of Religions, African Studies Assn. U.S.A., World Union of Urban Anthropologists. Office: U Natal, King George V Ave, 4001 Durban, Natal Republic of South Africa

KIHARA, YASUSHI, development company executive; b. Fukuoka, Kyushu, Japan, Jan. 22, 1932; s. Katsumi and Haruko (Yamagata) K.; m. Tsugiko Kagayama, Oct. 17, 1960; children: Rie, Yumi. BA in Jurisprudence, Kyushu U., Fukuoka, 1953, MA in Jurisprudence, 1955. Dir. Japan Devel. Bank, Tokyo, 1977-79; sr. exec. dir. Tokyo Urban Devel. Co. Ltd., 1979—, New Urban Energy Supply Co. Ltd., Tokyo, 1983—; chmn. Anadolu-Japan Turizm A.S., Istanbul, 1987—; rep. dir. Urban Techno-Inst., Tokyo, 1985—. Mem. Tokyo Marine Environ. Soc. (bd. dirs. 1979—). Office: Tokyo Urban Devel Co Ltd, Nishishinjuku 6-6-2, Shinju ku, Tokyo 160, Japan

KIHLE, DONALD ARTHUR, lawyer; b. Noonan, N.D., Apr. 4, 1934; s. J. Arthur and Linnie W. (Ljunngren) K.; m. Judith Anne, Aug. 18, 1964; children—Kevin, Kirsten, Kathryn, Kurte. B.S. in Indsl. Engring., U. N.D., 1957; J.D., U. Okla., 1967. Bar: Okla. 1967, U.S. Dist. Cts. (we. and no. dists.) Okla. 1967, U.S. Ct. Appeals (10th cir.) 1967, U.S. Supreme Ct. 1971. Asso., Huffman, Arrington, Scheurich & Kincaid, Tulsa, 1967-71, ptnr., 1971-78; shareholder, dir., officer Huffman Arrington Kihle Gaberino & Dunn, Tulsa, 1978—. Asst. scoutmaster Boy Scouts Am., 1979-86, dist. chmn., 1983-85, cubmaster 1986-88; mem. Statewide Law Day Com., 1982-86, chmn., 1983-85. Served to 1st lt. U.S. Army, 1957-59. Mem. ABA, Okla. Bar Assn. (chmn. constnl. bicentennial com. 1986—), Constitution 200 (exec. com. 1986—), Tulsa County Bar Assn., Sigma Tau, Phi Delta Phi, Order of Coif, Sigma Chi. Republican. Clubs: Tulsa (bd. dirs. 1987—), Southern Hills Country (Tulsa). Home: 4717 S Lewis Ct Tulsa OK 74105 Office: 1000 ONEOK Plaza Tulsa OK 74103

KIHN, HARRY, electronics engineer, manufacturing company executive; b. Tarnow, Austria, Jan. 24, 1912; came to U.S., 1920, naturalized 1927; s. Morris and Sabina K.; m. Minna Schechter, Nov., 1937; children—Michael Allan, Leslie Morris. B.S. in Elec. Engring., Cooper Union Inst. Tech., 1934; M.S. in Elec. Engring., U. Pa., 1952. Devel. engr. Hygrade-Sylvania Co., Clifton, N.J., 1935-38; devel. engr. Ferris Instrument Co., Boonton, N.J., 1938; radio, TV research engr. RCA Mfg. Co., Camden, N.J., 1939-42; electronics computer and TV researcher corp. staff engr. patents and licensing RCA Labs., Princeton, N.J., 1942-75; sr. staff tech. advisor RCA Labs., 1975-77; pres. Kihn Assocs., robotics, nuclear energy, med. electronics cons., 1977—; mem. program rev. com. Office of Nuclear Waste Isolation, Dept. Energy, Washington, 1979—; instr. electronics Rutgers U. Extension. Sr. editor Gov.'s Commn. on Sci. and Tech. Contbr. articles to profl. jours., tech. confs. Patentee in field. Vice pres. Lawrenceville Sch. Bd., 1957-60; bd. dirs. Lawrenceville Adult Sch., 1960-62, George Washington Council Boy Scouts Am.; chmn. Lawrenceville Ednl. Found., 1950-74. Recipient Microminiaturization award Miniature Precision Bearings, Inc., 1958, 2 research awards RCA Corp., 1952-56. Fellow IEEE (life, Centennial medal 1984); mem. N.Y. Acad. Sci., AAAS, Nat. Acad. Sci. (materials adv. bd. 1961-62), Nat. Soc. Profl. Engrs., Mercer Soc. Profl. Engrs. (pres., named Engr. of Yr. 1986-87), Am. Def. Preparedness Assn., Sigma Xi. Lodges: Lions, Rotary. Home: 30 Green Ave Lawrenceville NJ 08648

KIKER, EDWARD BRUCE, lunar mining geologist, educator; b. London, Aug. 1, 1947; (parents Am. citizens); s. Wellborn Clarke and Evelyn (Williams) K. AB, Harvard U., 1970. Natural resources specialist U.S. Army, Ft. Greely, Alaska, 1975-83; dir. High Frontier, Delta, Alaska, 1985-87; mil. analyst space systems U.S. Army Space Inst., Ft. Leavenworth, Kans., 1987—; chief exec. officer Outer Space Indsl. Resources Investigations Systems, Leavenworth, Kans., 1987—; cons. hist. affairs, Delta, 1985—. Contbr. articles on space to profl. jours. Asst. dist. commr. Boy Scouts Am., Delta, 1975-87, scoutmaster; space lobbyist L-5 Soc., Delta, 1975-87. Served to capt. U.S. Army, 1971-75. Recipient Silver Beaver award Boy Scouts Am., 1986, Merit award Boy Scouts Am., 1981, 83; named Eagle Scout Boy Scouts Am., 1962; grantee Sigma Xi, 1969;. Fellow Brit. Interplanetary Soc.; mem. Nat. Space Council, Alaska Acad. Scis. (bd. dirs. 1983—), Am. Legion, Am. Acad. Scis., Soc. Am. Foresters, Am. Forestry Assn., NRA, AAAS, Am. Space Assn., Air Force Assn., Planetary Soc., Space Studies Inst., U.S. Def. Com., Nat. Space Soc.

KIKUCHI, GORO, medical school president; b. Ohe, Yamagata, Japan, Jan. 14, 1920; s. Masagoro and Kiku K.; m. Teruko Kasai, Nov. 18, 1952; children: Akio, Yuriko. MD, Nippon Med. Sch., Tokyo, 1944, PhD, 1951. Instr. Nippon Med. Sch., Tokyo, 1944-51, asst. prof. biochem., 1952-59, guest prof., 1983-86, pres., 1986—; research assoc. U. Chgo., 1955-57, Columbia U., N.Y.C., 1957-59; prof. Tohoku U., Sendai, Japan, 1959-83, emeritus prof., 1983—; guest prof. Saitama Med. Sch., Japan, 1984-86. Author: New Biochemistry, 1966, General Medical Chemistry, 1980; Editor: Jour. Biochemistry, 1971-78. Recipient Promotion of Sci. prize Naito Meml. Found., Tokyo, 1975, Med. Research prize Japan Med. Assn., Tokyo, 1981, Purple Ribbon prize Japanese Govt., 1985. Mem. Japanese Biochem. Soc. (hon., pres. 1978-79), Nat. Com. on Biochemistry, Internat. Union Biochemistry (com. on symposium), Am. Soc. for Biochem. and Molecular Biol. (hon.), N.Y. Acad. Scis. Home: 310-1-18-17 Hayamiya, Nerima Ku, 176 Tokyo Japan Office: Nippon Med Sch, 1-1-5 Sendagi, Bunkyo Ku, 113 Tokyo Japan

KIKUCHI, KIYOAKI, diplomat; b. Miyagi Prefecture, Japan, Dec. 1, 1922; s. Yaemon and Shuku (Arima) K.; m. Fusako Sato; children: Michiko Sano, Atsuko Lichtenberk. BA, LLB, Tokyo Imperial U., 1943; MA, Johns Hopkins U., 1951; LLD (hon.), Mex. Acad. de Derecho Internacional, Mexico City, 1984. Pvt. sec. to fgn. minister Ministry Fgn. Affairs, Tokyo, 1962-64, dep. dir.-gen. Econ. Cooperation Bur., 1971-75, dir.-gen., 1975-78, dep. minister for fgn. affairs, 1979-81; minister counselor Embassy of Japan, Washington, 1969-71; ambassador extraordinary and plenipotentiary Singapore, 1978-79, Mex., 1981-84; permanent rep. Mission Japan to UN, N.Y.C., 1986—. Clubs: Tokyo; Met. (N.Y.C.). Office: Permanent Mission Japan to UN 866 United Nations Plaza New York NY 10017

KIKUCHI, KOKICHI, pathologist, medical educator; b. Maoka, Karafuto, Japan, May 17, 1932; s. Toyokichi and Yoshi K.; m. Yuko Tsuji, Nov. 17, 1962; 1 child, Yuri. MD, Hokkaido U. Sch. Medicine, Sapporo, Japan, 1957, PhD in Medicine, 1962. Instr. Cancer Inst. Hokkaido U. Sch. Medicine, Sapporo, 1962-66, asst. prof. Dept. Pathology, 1966-69, assoc. prof., 1968-71; prof., chmn. Dept. Pathology Sapporo Med. Coll., 1971—, v.p., dean, 1982-86, pres., 1986—, pres. Sch. Allied Health Professions, 1986—; vis. investigator Sloan-Kettering Cancer Inst., N.Y.C., 1966-68; councillor Japanese Cancer Assn., Tokyo, Japanese Immunology Soc., Kyoto, Japan Pathol. Soc., Tokyo, chmn. edn. com. 1984—. Author, editor: Medical Immunology, 2d edit., 1981, Pathology, 3d edit., 1984, New Special pathology, 10th edit., 1985, New General Pathology, 14th edit., 1987, Immunology, Ann. Rev. edit., 1987—. V.p. Orgn. for Hoddaido Internat. Med. and Indsl. Complex, Sapporo, 1987. Recipient Hokkaido Med. prize Hokkaido Prefecture, Sapporo, 1974, Hokkaido Med. Assn. prize, 1974, Princess Takamatsu Cancer Prize, 1988. Mem. Japan Med. Assn. (mem. edn. com. 1986—), Internat. Acad. Pathology, N.Y. Acad. Sci., Hokkaido Med. Cong. (pres. 1986-87). Home: Fushimi 3-7-1, Chuo-ku, Sapporo, 064 Hokkaido Japan Office: Sapporo Med Coll, South 1 West 17, Chuo-ku, Sapporo, 060 Hokkaido Japan

KIKUTAKE, KIYONORI, architect, educator; b. Kurume, Japan, Apr. 1, 1928; s. Kiyoshi and Masue K.; m. Norie Sasaki, 1953; 2 children. B.A., Waseda U. Founder Kiyonori Kikutake & Assocs., 1953, now rep. dir.; prof. architecture Waseda U., 1959—; mem. bd. Archtl. Inst. Japan, 1962—; exec. dir. Tokyo YMCA Inst. Design; vis. prof. U. Hawaii, 1971; del. UNESCO Internat. Conf., Zurich, Switzerland, 1970. Maj. archtl. works include: Shimane Prefectural Mus., 1959; Sky House, 1958; Adminstrn. Bldg. for Izumo Shrine; Tatebayashi City Hall, 1963; Hotel Tokoen, 1964; Miyakonojo City Hall, Pacific Hotel, Chigasaki, 1966; Iwate Prefectural Library, 1967; Shimane Prefectural Library; Hagi Civic Centre, 1968; Kurume Civic Centre, 1969; Expo Tower for Expo 70, Osaka, Japan, 1969; Pasadena Heights, tiered mass housing, 1972; Aquapolis, floating module for ocean, Ocean Expo 75, 1975; Hagi City Hall, 1974; redevel. of Yamaga City Ctr., 1975; Tsukuba Acad. New Town; Pedestrian Deck Network and the Symbol Tower, 1976; Otsu Shopping Centre, 1976; brs. of Kyoto Community Bank, 1971—; Tanabe Mus., Matsue City, 1979; Darumaya-Seibu Dept. Store, 1980; Treasury of Izumo Shrine, 1981; Seibu-Yaow Shopping Centre, 1981; Karuizawa Art Mus., Kuamoto Prefecture Arts and Crafts Centre, 1982; Fukuoka City Hall (Assembly Hall), 1982; Fgn. Pavilion for Expo '85; author: Metabolism, 1960; Taisha Kenchiku-ron (Metabolic Architecture), 1968; Ningen-no-Kenchiku (Human Architecture), 1970; Ningen-no-Toshi (A Human City), 1970; Essence of Architecture, 1973; Floating City, 1973; Kiyonori Kikutake—Works and Methods 1956-70, 1973; Community and Civilization, 1978; Kiyonori Kikutake—Concepts and Planning, 1978; Ningen-no-Kankyo (Human Environment), 1978; Community and City, 1978; Tight Spaces, Macro-Engineering, 1982. Recipient awards, including Arts award Ministry Edn., 1964, Archtl. Inst. Japan award, 1964, Cultural Merit award of Kurume City, 1975, Auguste Perret award UIA, 1978, XXI Mainichi Art awards, 1979. Fellow AIA (hon.; Hawaii chpt. Pan Pacific Archtl. citation 1964); mem. Japan Fedn. Profl. Architects Assns. (v.p. 1982—), Tokyo Profl. Architects' Assn. (v.p. 1982—), Japan Architects' Assn. (v.p. 1982—), Japan Inst. Macro-Engring. (v.p. 1985). *

KILALEA, MARK RODERICK, film producer; b. Gweru, Zimbabwe, Nov. 9, 1951; s. Patrick Garret and Joan (Gannon) K.; m. Jane Margaret Sloan; children: Sarah Jane Tapiwa, Daniel Mark Tendayi. BA in English with honors, Univ. Coll. of Rhodesia and Nyasaland, Salisbury, 1972. Tchr. English and Drama Jameson High Sch., Zimbabwe, 1974-76; head dept. English Marlborough High Sch., Zimbabwe, 1977-78; dir., writer Zimbabwe Broadcasting Corp., Harare, 1978-80; exec. producer Radio 3-Zimbabwe Broadcasting Co., Harare, 1980; mgr. location and prodn. Cannon Marble Arch Prodns., Harare, 1981—; free-lance broadcaster, Harare, 1977-78; dir. Third World Ednl. Prodns., Harare, 1980—. Prodn., location mgr. for such feature films as The Leopard, 1982, King Solomon's Mines, 1984, Quatermain, 1985, Cry Freedom, 1986, Nam, 1987, A World Apart, 1987 (Grand Prix award Cannes Film Festival, 1988), Dry White Season, 1988; TV series Mandela, 1986; concert video Graceland: Paul Simon in Concert. Recipient Osiris award UN, 1982. Mem. Zimbabwe Film TV and Allied Workers Assn. (v.p. 1987-88). Home and Office: 7 Everett Close, Avondale, Harare Zimbabwe

KILANDER, KJELL OLOF, management consultant, educator; b. Sundsvall, Sweden, May 7, 1931; s. Einar and Armida (Hansson) K.; m. Ebba Gustafsson, Apr. 5, 1953 (div. 1982); children—Gunilla, Jan, Monica, Annika. Forest officer Sch. Forestry, Stockholma, 1955, M.Forestry, 1957, Ph.D., 1961. Researcher, Stockholm, 1955-63; research mgr. Skogsarbeten, Stockholm, 1964-65; pres. Kilander Konsult Ab, Stockholm, 1966-69; pres. Fed. of Forest Owners & Subs., Stockholm, 1969-77; pres. Ab Skogsagarinvest & Subs., Stockholm, 1978-79; pres. AB Crema, Stockholm, 1980—; assoc. prof. economy U. Agr., Sweden, 1983—. Contbr. articles to profl. jours. Mem. Swedish Assn. Pulp and Paper Engring., Commonwealth Forestry Assn. (London), Royal Swedish Acad. Forestry and Agr., Royal Swedish Acad. Engring. Sci. Club: Sallskapet (Stockholm). Home: Idrottsvagen 35, S-19170 Sollentuna Sweden Office: AB Crema, Munkbron 11, S-11128 Stockholm Sweden

KILBORNE, GEORGE BRIGGS, investment company executive; b. N.Y.C., Oct. 7, 1930; s. Robert Stewart and Barbara Briggs Kilborne; B.A., Yale U., 1952; m. Lucie Wheeler Peck, Nov. 12, 1960 (div. 1978); children—George Briggs, Kim McNeil, Sarah Skinner. Vice pres. William Skinner & Sons, N.Y.C., 1955-60; pres. Bus. Research Co., Birmingham, Mich., 1961-74, Creative Capital of Mich., Inc., Birmingham, 1962-70; partner Comac Co., 1968-70; chmn., pres. First Citizen Bank, Troy, Mich., 1970-74; engaged in real estate investing and cons., Palm Beach, Fla., 1975-79; mng. dir. corp. acquisitions Bessemer Securities Corp., N.Y.C., 1980-84; pres. Bay Street Corp., Palm Beach, 1984—; pres. Pon Capital Corp., Braintree, Mass., 1987—; chmn. State Bank of Mich., Coopersville, 1966-67, Muskegon (Mich.) Bank & Trust, 1967-68, Bank of Lansing (Mich.), 1968-69; vice chmn. Creative Capital Corp., N.Y.C., 1968-70, Hockey Club of Pitts., 1968-70; dir. Watts Industries, Inc., N. Andover, Mass., 1981-84, Roller Bearing Corp. of Am., West Trenton, N.J., 1987—, Diversified Communications, Portland, Maine, 1982—. Bd. dirs. Oakland (Mich.) unit. Am. Cancer Soc., 1973-74; mem. Republican Com., Dist. 13, Palm Beach County, Fla., 1976-80; mem. Palm Beach County Rep. Exec. Com., 1976-80; bd. dirs. Palm Beach Rep. Club, 1977-80. Served to lt. (j.g.) USN, 1953-55. Recipient Disting. Service award First Citizen Bank, Troy, 1974, Midwest Assn. Small Bus. Investment Cos., 1970. Mem. Nat. Assn. Small Bus. Investment Cos. (gov. 1967-70, mem. exec. com. 1967, pres. Midwest assn. 1970). Clubs: Yale of the Palm Beaches (pres. 1979-80), Bath and Tennis (Palm Beach, Fla.); Wianno (Mass.) Yacht, Wianno; Univ. (N.Y.C.). Office: PO Box 252 Osterville MA 02655

KILBORNE, ROBERT STEWART, retired business executive; b. N.Y.C., Aug. 1, 1905; s. Robert Stewart and Katharine (Skinner) K.; grad. Groton (Mass.) Sch., 1923; Yale, 1923-25; m. Barbara Briggs, Nov. 28, 1925 (dec. 1968); children—Belle (Mrs. Richard S. Taylor), Robert Stewart III (deceased), George Briggs; m. 2d, Jane Lowes Houk, May 2, 1969. Joined William Skinner & Sons (Mass. Common Law Trust), N.Y.C., 1925, pres. Truhu Fabrics Corp. (subs.), 1933, v.p. William Skinner & Sons, 1941, trustee, 1945-61, pres., 1947-61; commr. of conservation N.Y. State Conservation Dept., 1966-70; spl. asst. to gov. on conservation affairs State of N.Y., 1970-75. Mem. industry adv. com. OPA, Washington, 1943-46, OPS, 1951-53; member adv. com. research & devel. br. mil. planning div. Office Q.M. Gen., Washington 1943-49, synthetic br. broad woven fabrics div. Q.M. Assn., Washington, 1951-61; chmn. Saratoga Springs Commn., 1966-72; alternate to gov. N.Y. State for Delaware River Basin Commn., 1966-71; mem. bd. Saratoga Performing Arts Center, 1966-72, Gt. Lakes Commn., 1966-75, Hudson River Valley Commn., 1966-77; commr. N.Y. State Taconic Park Commn., 1963-76; temporary study commn. for future Adirondacks, 1970-71; mem. Bedford Historic Rev. Commn., 1972-78; trustee Arthur Butler Meml. Sanctuary, 1967-78; bd. dirs. Union Theol. Sem., 1950-66, The Equitable Life Assurance Soc. U.S., 1946-77; bd. dirs. Humane Soc. of South Coastal Ga., 1978-83, pres., 1982-83; bd. dirs. Sea Island (Ga.) Property Owners Assn., 1978-81, v.p., 1979, pres., 1980-81. Mem. Am. Cotton Mfrs. Inst., Inc. (dir. 1958-62), Nat. Fedn. Textiles, Inc. (dir. 1949-58, pres. 1954-55), Am. Arbitration Assn., Am. Textile Mfrs. Inst. (hon. dir. 1962—), MAP Internat. (adv. com.), Soc. Mayflower Descs., New Eng. Soc. of N.Y., Nat. Aero. Assn., Coastal Ga. Hist. Soc., Delta Kappa Epsilon. Republican. Presbyterian (elder). Clubs: Wings; Sea Island (Ga.) Cottage; Yale (Atlanta); OX5 Aviation Pioneers. Home: 137 W Cherokee Rd Sea Island GA 31561

KILBOURNE, WILLIAM TRUMAN, oil company executive, lawyer; b. Washington, June 24, 1934; s. Walter Harry and Lillian (Robinson) K.; m. Susan Blodgett Lowe, Apr. 4, 1959 (div. 1980); children: William Truman, Laura Ives, Thomas Lowe; m. Judith Hope Francis, Aug. 26, 1982. BA in Econs., Yale U., 1956; JD, U. Mich., 1962; postgrad. in law, George Washington U., 1965-66. Staff atty. FCC, Washington, 1962-63; of counsel, asst. sec. The Superior Oil Co., Washington, 1963-68; v.p. corp. affairs McIntyre Porcupine Mines Ltd., Toronto, Ont., Can., 1968-72; v.p., sec. legal No. and Cen. Gas. Corp., Toronto, 1972-75; v.p., sec. legal Norcen Energy Resources

Ltd., Toronto, 1975-78, v.p., adminstr., sec., 1978-82; v.p., sec. legal affairs Norcen Energy Resources Ltd., Toronto and Calgary, Alta., 1982—; bd. dirs. Iron Ore Co. Can., Cleve.; dir., sec. Superior Propane Inc., Toronto, Norcen Explorer, Inc., Calgary, Norcen Internat. Ltd., Calgary. Bd. govs. Lakefield (Ont.) Coll. Sch., 1979-87; dir., treas. Centre Stage, Toronto, 1983-87; bd. dirs. Alta. Theatre Projects, Calgary, 1985-87. Served as lt. USNR, 1956-65. Mem. Can. Petroleum Assn., Assn. of Gen. Counsel Alta., Coal Assn. Can. (pres. 1974-76). Progressive Conservative. Mem. Anglican Ch. Clubs: Met., Chevy Chase (Washington); Bohemian (San Francsico); Royal Can. Yacht, Granite, Univ. (Toronto); Petroleum, Glencoe (Calgary). Office: Norcen Energy Resources Ltd, 715 Fifth Ave SW, Calgary, AB Canada T2P 2X7

KILCULLEN, MARY ANN, military officer; b. Tucson, Feb. 11, 1956; d. William Joseph and Phyllis (O'Brien) K.; m. John Edward Martin, June 28, 1985; children: Kirstin Meischel Kilcullen-Martin, Monique Alexandria. BS, Ariz. State U., 1981; field artillery student, Alpha Battery Officer Student Bn., Ft. Sill, Okla., 1985-86. Commd. 2d lt. F.A., U.S. Army, 1981, advanced through ranks to capt., 1984; with Tactical Intelligence, Babenhausen, Fed. Republic of Germany, 1984-85; comdr. Hdqrs. and Headqrs. Battery, 212th F.A. Brigade, Ft. Sill, 1986-88; asst. personnel officer III Corps Artillery. Named one of Outstanding Young Women Am., 1987. Mem. Res. Officer Assn., Assn. U.S. Army, Field Artillery Assn. Democrat. Roman Catholic. Avocations: sailing, water skiing, writing poetry, photography. Home: 7204 SW Drakestone Blvd Lawton OK 73505-7446 Office: Hdqrs and Hdqrs Battery III Corps Artillery Fort Sill OK 73505-6000

KILDEY, GRAHAM THOMAS, architect; b. Brisbane, Australia, Jan. 4, 1947; m. Jan Shellard; children: Brooke Elise, Boyd Thomas. Diploma in Architecture, Queensland Inst. Tech., 1972. Prin., dir. Architects Australia, Brisbane, 1980—, Gapcote Property Ltd., Brisbane, 1980—, M.A.G. Projects Property Ltd., 1980—, Ballada Properties Ltd, 1980—. Assoc. Royal Australian Inst. of Architects. Clubs: Old Cricketers, Royal Qld Golf, Qld Lawn Tennis Assn. Office: 111 Maygar St Windsor, 4030 Brisbane QLD, Australia

KILFEDDER, JAMES ALEXANDER, member of Parliament, Northern Ireland; b. Kinlough, County Leitrium, Ireland, July 16, 1928; s. Robert and Elizabeth K. B.A., Trinity Coll., Dublin. Called to English Bar, Gray's Inn, 1958. M.P. (UU) Belfast West, 1964-66, North Down, 1970—. Mem. (Official Unionist) North Down, Northern Ireland Assembly, 1973-75; Mem. (UUUC) North Down, Northern Ireland Constitutional Conv., 1975-76. Former chief whip and hon. sec. Ulster Unionist Parly Party. Leader Ulster Popular Unionist Party. Mem. Trustee Savs. Banks Party Com. Avocation: walking in the country. Office: Ulster Popular Unionist Party, Belfast Northern Ireland *

KILGORE, DONALD GIBSON, JR., pathologist; b. Dallas, Nov. 21, 1927; s. Donald Gibson and Gladys (Watson) K.; m. Jean Upchurch Augur, Aug. 23, 1952; children: Michael Augur, Stephen Bassett, Phillip Arthur, Geoffrey Scott, Sharon Louise. Student, So. Methodist U., 1943-45; MD, Southwestern Med. Coll., U. Tex., 1949. Diplomate Am. Bd. Pathology, Am. Bd. Dermatopathology, Am. Bd. Blood Banking. Intern Parkland Meml. Hosp., Dallas, 1949-50; resident in pathology Charity Hosp. La., New Orleans, 1950-54, asst. pathologist, 1952-54; pathologist Greenville Hosp. System, S.C., 1956—; dir. labs. Greenville Meml. Hosp., 1972—, Greenville Hosp. System, 1985—; cons. pathologist St. Francis Hosp., Shriners Hosp., Greenville, Easley Baptist. Hosp.; vis. lectr. Clemson U., 1963—; asst. prof. pathology Med. U. S.C., 1968—; pres. Pathology Assocs. of Greenville, 1983—. Bd. dirs. Greenville County United Fund, 1966-74, Greenville Community Council, 1968-71, Friends of Greenville County Library, 1966-74; trustee Sch. Dist. Greenville County, 1970—; bd. govs. S.C. Patient Compensation Fund, 1977—; patron Greenville Mus. Art, Greenville Little Theatre, 1956—; notary pub., S.C., 1966—. Served to capt. USAF, 1954-56. Recipient Disting. Service award S.C. Hosp. Assn., 1976; Paul Harris fellow Rotary, 1988. Fellow Coll. Am. Pathologists (assemblyman S.C. 1968-71), Am. Soc. Clin. Pathologists (councilor S.C. 1959-62), Am. Soc. Dermatopathology; mem. Am. Assn. Blood Banks (life, adv. council 1962-67, insp. committeeman Southeast dist. 1965—), AMA (ho. of dels. 1978—), So. Med. Assn., S.C. Med. Assn., (exec. council 1969-76, 1978—, pres. 1974-75; A.H. Robins award for Outstanding Community Service 1985), Am. Soc. Cytology, Am. Coll. Nuclear Medicine, Nat. Assn. Med. Examiners, S.C. Inst. Med. Edn. and Research (pres. 1974-80), S.C. Soc. Pathologists (pres. 1969-72), Richard III Soc. (co-chmn. Am. 1966-75), Soc. Ancient Numismatics, Am. Numis. Assn. (life.), Blue Ridge Numis. Assn., Royal Numis. Soc. (life), Greenville County Hist. Soc., Mensa, S.C. Congress Parents and Tchrs., Greenville County Dental Soc., Greater Greenville C. of C., Greenville County Hist. Soc., Preservation Soc. of Charleston (life), S.C. Hist. Soc. (life), Friends of Tewkesbury Abbey, Canterbury Cathedral Trust in Am. (life), U.S. Power Squadron, Soc. Med. Friends of Wine, Wine Acad. Am., Soc. Wine Educators, Conf. de la Chaine des Rotisseurs (vice-charge de Missions Greenville chpt.), Les Amis du Vin, Clan MacDuff Soc. Am. (exec. council 1980—), St. Andrews Soc. Upper S.C., Phi Eta Sigma, Phi Chi. Democrat. Presbyterian (ruling elder 1969—). Clubs: Commerce, Poinsett, Torch, Greenville Country, Thirty-Nine (pres. 1981-82), Chandon. Lodge: Rotary (Paul Harris fellow 1988). Home: 129 Rockingham Rd Greenville SC 29607-3620 Office: 8 Memorial Medical Ct Greenville SC 29605

KILGORE, ROBERT MARTIN, lawyer; b. Beckley, W.Va., Jan. 3, 1924; s. Harley Martin and Lois (Lilly) K.; B.S. in Physics, Georgetown U., 1947; postgrad. Columbia, 1947-49; J.D., George Washington U., 1952; m. Helen Hogan, Dec. 14, 1974. Admitted to D.C. bar, 1952, W.Va. bar, 1953; patent examiner U.S. Patent Office, Washington 1951-55, 68-85; counsel Com. on Judiciary, U.S. Senate, 1955-58; asso. firm Powell, Dorsey & Blum, Washington, 1959-61; pvt. practice, Washington, 1961-80; legal cons. Bd. Vet. Appeals, VA, 1966-67. CD dir. Forest Heights, Md., 1956-58; instr. first aid ARC, 1955-76, first aid chmn. D.C. chpt., 1971-75, instr. sailing, 1972-76; pres. 2d Homeowners Assn., 1973-76, P.T.O. Credit Union, 1980. Served from pvt. to lt. AUS, 1943-46. Registered parliamentarian. Mem. Am., Fed., W.Va., D.C. bar assns., DAV, W.Va. State Soc. (v.p. 1956-58), SAR, Patent Office Soc. (exec. com. 1972-80, pres. 1975-77, chmn. bd. govs. jour. 1977-83, Outstanding Service award 1981), Am. Camillia Soc., Nat. Assn. Parliamentarians (unit pres. 1976-78, state treas.), Am. Inst. Parliamentarians (nat. dir. 1974-75, pres. D.C. chpt. 1974-76), Am. Legion, Am. Judicature Soc., Washington Area Intergroup Assn. (chmn. 1971). Democrat. Baptist. Clubs: George Washington U.; Toastmaster (dist. lt. gov. 1972-74). Home: 14827 N Anderson Ct Woodbridge VA 22193

KILGORE, WILLIAM JACKSON, philosopher, educator; b. Dallas, Apr. 30, 1917; s. Rather Bowlin and Clara (Cole) K.; m. Barbara Schmickle, Dec. 4, 1943; 1 dau., Barbara (Sally B.). A.B., Baylor U., 1938; Ph.D., U. Tex., 1958; student, Columbia U., 1949. Prof. philosophy Baylor U., 1949—, chmn. dept., 1959-87, J. Newton Rayzor, Sr. Disting. prof. philosophy, 1976—; asst. prof. philosophy U. Tex., summer 1958; organizer, pres. Centennial Symposium on Ortega y Gasset World Congress of Philosophy, 1983. Author: Alejandro Korn's Interpretation of Creative Freedom, 1958, Una evaluación crítica de la filosofía de Alejandro Korn, 1961, One America, Two Cultures, 1965, An Introductory Logic, 1968, 2d edit., 1979; also articles in English, Portuguese, French and Spanish.; Translator An Introduction to the Philosophy of Understanding of Andrés Bello, 1983. Pres. sect. on ethics and problems of freedom XIII Internat. Congress of Philosophy, Mexico City, 1963; pres. sect. on art and communication Inter-Am. Congress of Philosophy, Brazilia, 1972. Grantee Danforth Found., 1957-58, Am. Council Learned Socs., 1961, 86, Argentine Philos. Soc., 1986; Fulbright grantee, 1984; Mexican Philos Assn. grantee, 1984; hon. prof. Universidad Nacional Pedro Henríquez Ureña, Santo Domingo. Mem. Am. Philos. Assn., Southwestern Philos. Assn. (pres. 1963-64), Am. AAUP (2d v.p. 1968-70, nat. council 1962-65, 68-70, pres. Tex. conf. 1965), Tex. Philos. Soc., Inter-Am. Soc. Philosophy (exec. com. 1977—, pres. 1981-85), Interam. Soc. Psychology, Peruvian Philos. Soc. (hon.), Soc. for Iberian and Latin Am. Thought (pres. 1976). Home: 305 Guittard Ave Waco TX 76706

KILJUNEN, KIMMO ROOBERT, development researcher, writer; b. Rauha, Karelia, Finland, June 13, 1951; s. Veikko Benjamin and Ulla Kaarina (Heikkinen) K.; m. Marja-Liisa Makinen, Jan. 17, 1971; children: Rauha, Veikko, Riikka, Jaakko. MA, Helsinki U., Finland, 1973; M.Phil., Sussex U., Brighton, Eng., 1977, PhD, 1985. Asst. lectr. Inst. Devel. Studies Helsinki U., 1972-73, dir. Inst. Devel. Studies, 1986—; orgn. sec. Finnish UN Assn., Helsinki, 1974-75; Brit. Council fellow Inst. Devel. Studies Sussex U., 1975-78; research fellow Labour Inst. Econ. Research, Helsinki, 1979-81, Acad. Finland, Helsinki, 1981-85; sec. gen. Kampuchea Inquiry Commn., Helsinki, 1980-82, Internat. Peace Bur., Geneva, Switzerland, 1984-85. Author: Finland and New International Division of Labour, 1988; editor: Namibia-The Last Colony, 1981, Kampuchea-Decade of the Genocide, 1984, Mini-NIEO, 1989; contbr.numerous articles to profl. jours., mags., newspapers. City councillor Vantaa, Finland, 1984—. Mem. Finnish Soc. Devel. Studies (vice chmn. Helsinki 1984—), Finnish UN Assn. (pres. Helsinki 1987—), European Assn. Devel., Research and Tng. Insts. (exec. com. Geneva 1987—). Home: Pallastunturinkuja 5A 2, SF-01280 Vantaa Finland Office: Inst Devel Studies Helsinki U, Annankatu 42D, SF-00100 Helsinki Finland

KILLANIN, LORD (MICHAEL MORRIS), author, film producer, honorary life pres. International Olympic Committee; b. July 30, 1914; s. George Henry Morris and Dora Maryan Hall; ed. Eton Coll., Sorbonne, Paris; B.A., Magdalene Coll., Cambridge (Eng.) U., 1935, M.A., 1939; LL.D., Nat. U. Ireland, 1975; D.Litt., New U. Ulster, 1977; m. Sheila Mary Dunlop, 1945; children—Redmond Morris, Deborah Bryden, Michael Morris, John Morris. With London Daily Express, then Daily Mail, 1935-39, war corr. Japanese-Chinese War, 1937-38; polit. columnist Sunday Dispatch, 1938-39; assoc. in prodn. (with John Ford) film The Quiet Man, 1952, also The Rising of the Moon, The Playboy of the Western World, Gideon's Day, Young Cassidy, Alfred the Great; chmn. Chubb Ireland Ltd.; past dir. Irish Shell, Ulster Bank Ltd., Beamish and Crawford Ltd.; chmn. Ulster Investment Bank Ltd., Lombard Ulster Banking Ltd.; dir. Syntex Ireland, Norman Telecom Ireland Ltd., Gallaher (Dublin) Ltd.; mem. Lloyds' of London. Pres., Olympic Council Ireland, 1950-73; mem. Internat. Olympic Com., 1952-80, exec., 1967, v.p., 1968-72, pres., 1972-80, hon. life pres., 1980; former mem. Cultural Relations Com., Nat. Monuments Advisory Council (past chmn.), Irish Sailors and Soldiers Land Trust, Irish Turf Club, Nat. Hunt Steeplechase Com.; chmn. Govt. Commn. on Thoroughbred Horse Industry, 1983-86; chmn. Galway Race Com., 1969-84, Heritage Council, 1980. Served with King's Royal Rifle Corps, 1939-45. Decorated mem. Order of Brit. Empire; Knight of Malta; Order of Sacred Treasure (Japan); German Grand Cross; Order of Grimaldi (Monaco); Finnish Order of Olympic Merit; comdr. Legion of Honor (France); grand officer Italian Order Merit; Cross of Merit (Germany); Polish Order of Merit with Star; grand officer Order of Phoenix (Greece); Knight grand cross Order Civil Merit (Spain); Olympic Order of Merit; Flag of Yugoslavia with ribbon; others. Mem. Royal Irish Acad., French Acad. Sport, Connemara Pony Breeders Soc. (past pres.), Galway C. of C. (past pres.), Inc. Sales Mgrs. Assn. Ireland (past pres.). Clubs: Stephen's Green (Dublin); Garrick, Beefsteak (London); County (Galway); Irish Turf (past steward). Author: Sir Godfrey Kneller-The Life of the 18th Century Painter; (with Michael Duignan) A Shell Guide to Ireland; (with John Rodda) The Olympic Games; My Olympic Years; My Ireland; also newspaper articles; editor, contbg. author: Four Days.

KILLEEN, RICHARD JOHN, artist; b. Auckland, New Zealand, Apr. 10, 1946; s. Sydney John and Freda Joyce (Killip) K.; m. Margreta Chance; children: Samuel, Zahra. BFA, Auckland U., 1966. One-man shows in New Zealand, Australia and U.S.A.; represented New Zealand Sydney Biennale, 1982, 86, Edinburgh Festival, 1984. Travel grantee Queen Elizabeth II Arts Council, 1976; recipient Art award Benson and Hedges, 1976. Home and Office: 41 King George Ave, Epsom Auckland 3, New Zealand

KILLEN, CARROLL GORDEN, electronics company executive; b. Provencal, La., Mar. 22, 1919; s. Carroll Graves and Ella (Crowder) K.; m. Clara Donald Butler, Aug. 15, 1941; children—Carroll Gorden III, Margaret Karen, Lloyd Butler, Sara Elizabeth. Grad., La. State U.; B.S., La. Northwestern State Coll. Electronics engr. Magnolia Petroleum Co., Dallas, 1940-42; electronics engr. Watson Labs., Red Bank, N.J., 1942-45; chief application engr. Sprague Electric Co., North Adams, Mass., 1947-55, mgr. field engring., 1955-60, v.p. mktg. and sales, 1960-73, sr. v.p. mktg. and sales, 1973-85; v.p., gen. mgr. Tansitor Electronics, Inc., Bennington, Vt., 1985—, also dir.; dir. Cera-Mite Corp., Grafton, Wis.; cons. U.S. Dept. Def., Washington, 1949-73, U.S. Dept. Commerce, 1984—; dir. Tantalum Internat. Study Ctr., Brussels, Belgium, 1983-85, mem. exec. com., 1983—; pres. T.I.C., 1984-85. Author: Factors Influencing Capacitor Reliability, 1955. Served to 1st lt. USAF, 1945-47, PTO. Mem. IEEE (chmn. conf. bd. 1971-74, chmn. electro conf. 1976-79), Electronic Industries Assn. (gov. 1976—), Am. Ordnance Assn., Newcomer Soc., Nat. Security Indsl. Assn. (trustee 1980-85), Am. Mgmt. Assn. Republican. Baptist. Club: Sales Execs. Lodge: Masons. Home: 511 Gage St Bennington VT 05201 Office: Tansitor Electronics Inc West Rd PO Box 230 Bennington VT 05201

KILLGORE, ANDREW IVY, former ambassador; b. Greensboro, Ala., Nov. 7, 1919; m. Marjorie Davis Nicholls; children: Elizabeth Nicholls Krieger, Andrew Nicholls, Jane G., Roberta K. McInerney. B.S., Livingston U., 1943; J.D., U. Ala., 1949, Arab language tng. Fgn. Service Inst., 1955-57. Bar: Ala. bar. Selector-analyst U.S. Displaced Persons Commn., 1949-50; displaced populations officer U.S. Displaced Persons Commn., Frankfurt, W.Ger., 1950-51; visa officer Am. embassy, London, 1951-53; evaluator Dept. State, 1953-55; polit. officer Beirut, Lebanon, 1956-57; consul Jerusalem, 1957-59; polit. officer Amman, Jordan, 1959-61; internat. relations officer Dept. State, 1961-62; officer-in-charge Iraq-Jordan affairs, 1962-65; pub. affairs officer USIS, Baghdad, Iraq, 1965-67; polit. officer Dacca, E.Pakistan (now Bangladesh), 1967-70; polit.-econ. officer Arab Region North Directorate, 1970-72; counselor polit. affairs Tehran, Iran, 1972-74; in charge d'affaires Manama, Bahrain, 1974; dep. chief mission Wellington, N.Z., 1974-77; ambassador to Qatar Doha, 1977-80; ret. 1980; pres. The Amrok Corp., Washington, 1980—. Pub. Washington Report on Middle East Affairs. Co-chmn. Am. Citizens Overseas Polit. Action Com.; bd. dirs. Am. sect. Musa Al-Alami of Jericho Found.; pres. Am. Ednl. Trust. Served as lt. (j.g.) USN, 1943-46. Clubs: Army and Navy, Cosmos. Office: 1900 18th St NW Washington DC 20009

KILLHOUR, WILLIAM GHERKY, paper company executive; b. Phila., June 2, 1925; s. William Brelsford and Jean (Gherky) K.; A.B. in Econs., U. Pa., 1947; m. Josephine Quarrier Greenwood, July 12, 1947; children—Daphne S. (Mrs. John David Polys), William Brelsford II, Jean Gherky (Mrs. David Akers), Gilson Engel. Salesman, Quaker City Paper Co., York, Pa., 1947-50; co-founder W.B. Killhour & Sons, Inc., Phila., 1950, salesman, treas., mgr. printing paper div., 1950-61, pres., 1961-84; v.p. sales Killhour Comml. Paper Co., 1984—; mem. Paper Distbn. Council of U.S., 1977-81; past mem. mcht. adv. com. Sorg Paper Co., Scott Paper Co., Howard Paper Mills, Kimberly Clark. Pres., Stafford Sch. PTA, 1959. Served from ensign to lt. (j.g.) USNR, 1944-46; PTO. Mem. Paper Trade Assn. Phila. (pres. 1966), Nat. Paper Trade Assn. (regional dir. 1974—, mem. indsl. paper com. 1972-73, nat. treas. 1977-78, nat. v.p. 1978-80, pres. 1980-81), Susquenhanna Litho Club (pres. 1970), Jr. Execs. Club Graphic Arts of Phila. (dir. 1955-60), St. Andrews Soc. Phila., York Club Printing House Craftsmen, Fearing Family Orgn., Mayflower Soc. Clubs: Merion Cricket, Palmetto (founder, pres. Hilton Head, S.C.), Philadelphia Racquet (chmn. squash racquets com. 1972—), Country of York, Undine Barge; Spanish Wells Golf (Hilton Head, S.C.). Lodge: Masons. Nat. age group champion double sculls, 1982; nat. single sculls champion. 1985; Can. Henley single sculls champion, 1985; world 8-oar crew champion, Toronto, 1985, Sweden, 87; world 4-oar crew champion, 1985, 87; world double sculls bronze, 1985, nat. 8-oar crew age group champion, 1986, nat. 4-oar crew age group champion, 1987, world 4- and 8-oar crew champion, 1987; single scull winner Head of Chattahoochie Regatta, Atlanta. Home and Office: 4 Brams Point Rd Hilton Head Island SC 29928

KILLICK, ANTHONY JOHN (TONY), economist, consultant; b. Crowborough, Eng., June 25, 1934; s. William Albert and Edith (Hoath) K.; m. Ingeborg Nitzsche, Nov., 1958; children: Andrea, Sonia. Diploma in Politics and Econs., Ruskin Coll., 1985; BA in Philosophy, Politics and Econs., Oxford U., 1958. Lectr. econs. U. Ghana, 1961-65; tutor econs. Ruskin Coll., Oxford U., 1965-67; sr. econ. advisor Ministry Overseas Devel., London, 1967-69; econ. advisor Ministry Fin. and Planning, Accra, Ghana, 1969-72; research fellow Harvard U., Cambridge, Mass., 1972-73; vis. prof. U. Nairobi, Kenya, 1973-79; research officer Overseas Devel. Inst., London, 1979-82, dir., 1982-87, sr. research fellow, 1987—; cons. UNIDO, 1969, 81, UNCTAD, 1977-78, 86-87, ILO, 1979, 85-86, World Bank, 1980, 84-85, 86, 88, Govt. Kenya, 1981-84, Govt. Dominican Republic, 1985; mem. Commn. Enquiry into Taxation, Govt. Zimbabwe, 1984-86; hon. research fellow U. Coll., London, 1984—; assoc. Inst. Devel. Studies, U. Sussex, 1986—; vis. fellow Wolfson Coll., Cambridge, 1987-88. Mem. Royal Econ. Soc., Devel. Studies Assn. (pres. 1986-88), Royal Inst. Internat. Affairs. Home: 64 Thundridge Hill, Ware SG12 OUF, England Office: Overseas Devel Inst, Regents Coll Inner Circle, Regents Park, London NW1 4NS, England

KILLORIN, EDWARD WYLLY, lawyer, tree farmer; b. Savannah, Ga., Oct. 16, 1928; s. Joseph Ignatius and Myrtle (Bell) K.; B.S., Spring Hill Coll., Mobile, 1952; LL.B. magna cum laude, U. Ga., 1957; m. Virginia Melson Ware, June 15, 1957; children—Robert Ware, Edward Wylly, Joseph Rigdon. Admitted to Ga. bar, 1956; practice in Atlanta, 1957—; ptnr. firm Gambrell, Russell, Killorin & Forbes, 1964-78; sr. ptnr. firm Killorin & Killorin, 1978—; lectr. Inst. Continuing Legal Edn. Ga., 1967—. Adj. prof. law Ga. State U., 1984—. Chmn., Gov.'s Adv. Com. on Coordination State and Local Govt., 1973, Gov.'s Legal Adv. Council for Workmen's Compensation, 1974-76; bd. regents Spring Hill Coll., 1975-82, trustee, 1981—. Served with AUS, 1946-47, 52-54. Mem. ABA, Internat., Ga. (chmn. jud. compensation com. 1976-77, chmn. legis. com. 1977-78), Atlanta (editor Atlanta Lawyer 1967-70, exec. com. 1971-74, chmn. legislation com. 1978-80) bar assns., Am. Judicature Soc., Lawyers Club Atlanta, Atlanta Legal Aid Soc. (adv. com. 1966-70, dir. 1971-74), Nat. Legal Aid and Defender Assn., Internat. Assn. Ins. Counsel (chmn. environ. law com. 1976-78), Atlanta Lawyers Found., Ga. Bar Found. (life), Ga. Def. Lawyers Assn. (dir. 1972-80), Ga. C. of C. (chmn. govtl. dept. 1970-75, chmn. workmen's compensation com. 1979—), Def. Research Inst. (Ga. chmn. 1970-71), Spring Hill Coll. Alumni Assn. (nat. pres. 1972-74), U. Ga. Law Sch. Assn. (nat. pres. 1986-87) Ga. Forestry Assn. (life, bd. dirs. 1969—, pres. 1977-79, chmn. bd. 1979-81), Am. Forestry Assn., Demosthenian Lit. Soc. (pres. 1957), Sphinx, Blue Key, Gridiron, Phi Beta Kappa, Phi Beta Kappa Assos., Phi Kappa Phi, Phi Delta Phi, Phi Omega. Clubs: Capital City, Peachtree Golf, Commerce (Atlanta); Oglethorpe (Savannah). Roman Catholic. Contbr. articles to legal jours. Home: 436 Blackland Rd NW Atlanta GA 30342 Office: Killorin & Killorin 11 Piedmont Ctr Atlanta GA 30305

KILMAN, JAMES WILLIAM, surgeon, educator; b. Terre Haute, Ind., Jan. 22, 1931; s. Arthur and Irene (Piker) K.; m. Priscilla Margaret Jackson, June 20, 1968; children: James William, Julia Anne, Jennifer Irene. B.S., Ind. State U., 1956; M.D., Ind. U., 1960. Intern Ind.U. Med. Ctr., Indpls., 1960-61; resident surgery Ind.U. Med. Center, 1961-66, asst. prof., 1966-69, assoc. prof., 1969-73; prof. surgery Ohio State U. Coll. Medicine, 1973-; chmn. dept. thoracic surgery Children's Hosp.; attending surgeon Univ. Hosp., Columbus, Ohio; attending staff Children's Hosp., Columbus; pres. staff Children's Hosp., 1978; attending staff Grant Hosp., Riverside Hosp.; cons. surgeon VA Hosp., Dayton; pres. Columbus Acad. Medicine, 1977. Trustee Central Ohio Heart Assn., Acad. Medicine Edn. Found., Children's Hosp., 1978—. Served with USNR, 1951-55. USPHS Cardiovascular fellow, 1963-64. Mem. Columbus Surg. Soc. (pres. 1973-74), Columbus Acad. Medicine (council 1971-73), Am. Surg. Assn., Soc. U. Surgeons, Am. Assn. Thoracic Surgery, Am., Central, Western surg. assns., Soc. Vascular Surgery, Internat. Cardiovascular Soc., Internat. Soc. Surgeons, Chest Club, Cardiovascular Surgery Club, Sigma Xi, Alpha Omega Alpha. Home: 4231 Jackson Pike Grove City OH 43123 Office: 410 W 10th Ave Columbus OH 43210

KILMANN, RALPH HERMAN, business educator; b. N.Y.C., Oct. 5, 1946; s. Martin Herbert and Lilli (Loeb) K.; children: Catherine Mary, Christopher Martin, Arlette; m. Ines Colon, May 28, 1988. B.S., Carnegie-Mellon U., 1970, M.S., 1970; Ph.D., UCLA, 1972. Instr. Grad. Sch. Bus., U. Pitts., 1972, asst. prof., 1972-75, assoc. prof., 1975-79, prof., 1979—, coordinator organizational studies group, 1981-84, 86—, dir. program in corp. culture, 1983—; pres. Organizational Design Cons., Pitts., 1975—. Author: Social Systems Design: Normative Theory and the MAPS Design Technology, 1977, Beyond the Quick Fix: Managing Five Tracks to Organizational Success, 1984; co-author: Methodological Approaches to Social Science: Integrating Divergent Concepts and Theories, 1978, Corporate Tragedies: Product Tampering, Sabotage and Other Catastrophes, 1984, The Management of Organization Design: Vols. I and II, 1976, Producing Useful Knowledge for Organizations, 1983, Gaining Control of the Corporate Culture, 1985, Corporate Transformation: Revitalizing Organizations for a Competitive World, 1987; editorial bd.: Jour. Mgmt., 1983—, Acad. Mgmt. Exec., 1987—, Jour. Organizational Change Mgmt., 1988—; contbr. chpts. to books, articles to profl. jours. Mem. Eastern Acad. Mgmt. (treas. 1975-76, dir. 1983-86), Am. Psychol. Assn., Inst. Mgmt. Scis. (1st prize Nat. Coll. Planning competition 1976), Beta Gamma Sigma. Home: 165 Millview Dr Pittsburgh PA 15238 Office: Joseph M Katz Grad Sch Bus U Pitts Roberto Clemente Dr Pittsburgh PA 15260

KILMARTIN, EDWARD JOHN, theologian, educator; b. Portland, Maine, Aug. 31, 1923; s. Patrick Joseph and Elizabeth Gertrude (Sullivan) K. A.B., Boston Coll., 1947, M.A. in Philosophy, 1948, S.T.L., 1955, M.S. in Chemistry, Holy Cross Coll., 1950; S.T.D., Gregorian U., Rome, 1958. Joined S.J., Roman Catholic Ch., 1941; ordained priest Roman Cath. Ch., 1954; tchr. chemistry Fairfield (Conn.) Prep. Sch., 1950-51; prof. sacramental theology Weston Coll., Sch. Theology, Boston Coll., 1958-77, dean sch., 1960-62; prof. liturg. theology U. Notre Dame, 1977-84, dir. grad. program in liturg. studies, 1980-84; prof. liturgical theology Pontifical Oriental Inst., Rome, 1985—. Assoc. editor: New Testament Abstracts, 1959-67; Author: The Eucharist in the Primitive Church, 1965; also articles on N.T. Mem. Cath. Theol. Soc. Am., Cath. Bibl. Assn. Office: Pontifical Oriental Inst, Piazza S Maria, Maggiore 7, 00185 Rome Italy

KILMARTIN, JOSEPH FRANCIS, JR., business executive, consultant; b. New Haven, Mar. 11, 1924; s. Joseph Francis and Lauretta M. (Collins) K.; student St. Thomas Sem., 1944; B.A., Holy Cross Coll., 1947; m. Gloria M. Schaffer, June 26, 1954; children—Joanne, Diane. Prodn. mgr. A.C. Gilbert Co., New Haven, 1947-49; profl. performer Broadway show Small Wonder, also TV shows Your Hit Parade, Philco Playhouse, Armstrong Circle Theatre, 1949-50; producer NBC-TV, N.Y.C., 1950-53; v.p. sales Cellomatic Corp., N.Y.C., 1953-59; sr. v.p. Transfilm Inc., N.Y.C., 1959-62, MPO Videotronics, N.Y.C., 1962-66; pres. Bus. Programs Inc., Larchmont, N.Y., 1966-75, Greenwich, Conn., 1975—; lectr. in field, cons. Mexican Dept. Agrarian Affairs and Colonization, 1974—. Active fund-raising Community Chest, 1947-49, ARC, 1947-49, Boy Scouts Am., 1958-66, United Fund, 1970-73; mem. Congl. Adv. Bd., Presdl. Task Force, Atlantic Council, Conn. Venture Group. Recipient medal of excellence Mexican Agrarian Affairs and Colonization Dept., 1976; Golden Medallion award in bus. communication Miami Internat. Film Festival, 1978. Mem. Am. Mgmt. Assn., N.Y. Sales Exec. Club, TV Execs. Soc., Pres.'s Assn., Five Hundred Club. Republican. Roman Catholic. Clubs: Larchmont (N.Y.) Yacht; Bonnie Brair Country (bd. govs. 1970-72); Westchester Country; University (N.Y.C.) Home: 30 Bowman Dr S Greenwich CT 06830 Office: 87 Greenwich Ave Greenwich CT 06830

KILONZO, GAD PAUL, psychiatrist; b. Suji, Kilimanjaro, Tanzania, July 1, 1940; s. Paulo Saburi and Kirindi Nakizwa (Kajiru) K.; m. Susan Rachel Frank, Oct. 17, 1972; children: Semkae, Isae, Kajiru, Mrema. BA, Macalester Coll., 1966; MBChB, Makerere U., Kampala, Uganda, 1971; MS in Medicine, U. Daresalaam, Tanzania, 1977. Intern Muhimbili Hosp., Dar es Salaam, Tanzania, 1971-72; med. registrar Ligula Hosp., Mtwara, Tanzania, 1972-73; dist. med. officer Kibondo (Tanzania) Govt. Hosp., 1973-74; med. resident Muhimbili Med. Ctr., Dar es Salaam, 1974-77, head dept. psychiatry, 1985—, sr. lectr., 1986—; cons. psychiatrist, 1982—; resident in psychiatry U. Dar es Salaam, 1977-86; sec. to exec. MSO Forensic Psychiatric Services, Vancouver, 1980-82; supr. Nat. Mental Health Program, Dar es Salaam, 1982—. Assoc. editor: (jours.) The Makererean, 1967-71, Makererean Med., 1968-69. Recipient Award of Merit Forensic Psychiatric Inst., 1980, 81, 82. Fellow Royal Acad. Psychiatry; mem. Med. Assn. Tanzania, African Psychiatry Assn., Mental Health Workers Assn. Tanzania (chmn. 1982—). Club: Kawe (Dar es Salaam). Office: Muhimbili Med Ctr, PO Box 65293, Dar es Salaam Tanzania

KILPATRICK, ROBERT DONALD, insurance company executive; b. Fairbanks, La., Feb. 5, 1924; s. Thomas David and Lula Mae (Crowell) K.; m. Faye Hines, May 29, 1948; children: Robert Donald, Kathleen Spencer, Lauren Douglas Petrovits, Tracy Crowell, Thomas David. B.A., U. Richmond, 1948; postgrad., Harvard U. Grad. Sch. Bus., 1973; received honorary degrees from, Univ. Hartford, Univ. Richmond (Va.), Trinity Coll. (Conn.). With Conn. Gen. Life Ins. Co. (subs. CIGNA Corp.), Hartford, 1954-82, pres., chief exec. officer; also bd. dirs., 1976-82; pres. CIGNA Corp., 1982-85, co-chief exec. officer, 1982-83, chmn., chief exec. officer, 1983—; dir. Allied Signal Inc.; trustee The Conf. Bd., Com. for Econ. Devel. Trustee, vice rector U. Richmond; bd. dirs. Nat. Sci. Ctr. for Communications and Electronics, Com. for a Responsible Red. Budget; sponsors trustee Colgate Darden Grad. Sch. U. Va.; bd. dirs. Assocs. of Harvard U. Grad. Sch. Bus. Adminstrn.; mem. Phila. World Affairs Council; chmn. Corp. Council Winterthur Mus., Phila. Mem. Bus. Roundtable (exec. com., chmn. com. on fed. budget, policy com.). Office: Cigna Corp One Logan Sq Philadelphia PA 19103 *

KILROY, THOMAS FRANCIS, English educator, playwright; b. Callan, Kilkenny, Ireland, Sept. 23, 1934; s. Thomas and May (Devine) K.; m. Patricia Cobey, 1963 (div. 1980); children: Hugh, Lorcan, Desmond; m. Julia Lowell Carlson, Dec. 19, 1981; 1 child, Hannah May. MA, Univ. Coll., Dublin, Ireland, 1957. Coll. lectr. Univ. Coll., Dublin, 1966-74; prof. modern English Univ. Coll., Galway, Ireland, 1978—. Author: The Big Chapel, 1971; author (plays) Death and Ressurection of Mr. Roche, 1968, Talbot's Box, 1977, Double Cross, 1986. Recipient Fiction prize The Guardian, London, 1971. Fellow Royal Soc. Lit. (Heinneman award for lit. 1971); mem. Irish Acad. Letters (AIB Literary prize 1972), AOSDANA (Irish Artists Assn.). Office: Univ Coll, Galway Ireland

KIM, CHAN-YUNG, pediatric educator; b. Masan, Kyon-Nam Do, Korea, Feb. 20, 1928; s. Ki-Tae and Hong-Kum (Oh) K.; m. Jung-Ok Yoo, May 19, 1957; children: Seong-Jin, Hyong-Jin. BS, Seoul Nat. U., Republic of Korea, 1948, MD, 1952, MS, 1961, PhD, 1964. Diplomate Korea Bd. Pediatrics. Asst. prof. then assoc. prof. pediatric dept. Pusan (Republic of Korea) U. Hosp., 1957-70, supt., 1972-74, prof., chmn. pediatric dept., 1971—; assoc. dean coll. of medicine Pusan Nat. U., 1964-66, chmn. nursing div. coll. of medicine, 1971-72, mem. faculty grad. sch., 1976-84; vis. prof. Hosp. for Sick Children Edinburgh, Scotland, 1967-68, London U., 1967-68; dean Coll. of Medicine Pusan Nat. U., 1980-82. Author: (with others) Book of Child Care, 1976, Textbook of Pediatrics, 1984. Active Child Health Service Bd., Pusan City, 1971—, Social and Cultural Com. Bd., Pusan City, 1980-82. Recipient Official Commendation for Child Health Prime Minister Korea, 1963. Fellow Korean Pediatric Assn. (pres. 1979-80); mem. Korean Acad. Tuberculosis, Korean Soc. Nuclear Medicine, Korean Soc. Allergology. Lodge: Rotary. Home: 512 3-ka Seodaeshin-Dong, SeoGu 600 Pusan Republic of Korea Office: Pusan U Hosp Dept Pediatrics, 10 1-ka Ami-Dong, SeoGu 600 Pusan Republic of Korea

KIM, DAE JUNG, politician; b. Hukwang-ri Haewi-myon, Shinangun, Korea, Dec. 3, 1925; s. Un Shic Kim and Soo Keum Chang; m. Cha Yong Ae, 1944 (dec. 1959); children—Hong Il, Kim, Hong Up, Kim; m. Lee Hee Ho, May 10, 1962; 1 child, Hong Gul Kim. Cert. mgmt. course U. Korea, Seoul, 1964; indsl. mgmt. course Kyunghee U., Seoul, 1966; econs. course, 1970; LL.D. (hon.), Emory U., 1983. Pres. Mokpo Marine Corp., Chollanam-do, 1947-54, Mokpo Daily News, 1950-52; mem. Parliament Opposition, Seoul, 1963-72; spokesman major Opposition Party, Seoul, 1963-68; presdl. candidate New Democratic Party, Seoul, 1970-71; co-chmn. Council for Promotion of Democracy, Seoul, 1985—, presdl. candidate, 1987; advisor Robert F. Kennedy Meml., Washington, 1984—, Minn. Ctr. for Treatment of Victims of Torture, 1983. Author: Prison Writings, 1984, With the Conscience to Act, 1985. Served as vice chief Navy Police, 1950-51. Recipient Human Rights award Bruno Kreisky, 1982, Human Rights award N.Am. Coalition for Human Rights in Korea, 1984. Roman Catholic. Avocations: reading, appreciating plays. Home: 178-1 Tongkyo-dong, Mapo-ku, Seoul 121-00, Republic of Korea Office: Party for Peace and Democracy, Dae-Ha Bldg, 14-11 Yoido-dong, Yungdungpo-Ku, Seoul Republic of Korea

KIM, DEWEY HONGWOO, public service consultant; b. Washington, July 4, 1928; s. Henry Cu and Edith (Ahn) K.; B.A. with honors, U. Hawaii, 1950; M.P.A. with highest distinction (Hugh D. Ingersol Outstanding Grad. award), Maxwell Sch., Syracuse (N.Y.) U., 1961; LL.D. (hon.), Myong Ji U., Seoul, Korea, 1981; m. Lila Lee, Mar. 10, 1951; children—Melissa, Dewey Hongwoo, Michael. Personnel officer 14th Coast Guard Dist., 1953-54; with IRS, 1956-68, dir. mgmt. tng., 1966-68; assoc. dean coll. Continuing Edn., U. Hawaii, 1968-70, asst. v.p. acad. affairs, 1970-78, vice-chancellor for community colls., 1978-80, chancellor community colls., 1980-83, chancellor emeritus, 1983—; dir. Pacific and Asian affairs Pub. Adminstrn. Service, 1983—; mgmt. cons., 1960—; dir. 1st Fed. Savs. & Loan Assn., Firstfed of Am., Inc.; pres. Friends of the Ctr. for Korean Studies U. Hawaii, 1987—. Exec. asst. Honolulu Fed. Exec. Bd., 1967; chmn. Hawaii Task Force Police and Pub. Protection, 1970-74; commr. Accrediting Commn. Jr. and Community Colls. Trustee U. Hawaii Found., 1972-82; co-sponsor Dewey and Lila Kim fellowship for univ. faculty in English from Korea to study in U.S.; chmn. adv. council Kapiolani Community Coll., 1985—. Recipient awards IRS, 1958, 59, 67, 68; William E. Mosher fellow, 1960-61. Mem. Am. Soc. Pub. Adminstrn. (pres. Honolulu 1959), Honolulu Fed. Businessmen's Assn., Western Assn. Schs. and Colls. (chmn. and pres. 1981-83), Soc. Fellow Syracuse U. (founding mem. 1986), Phi Kappa Phi.

KIM, E. HAN, finance and business administration educator; b. Seoul, Korea, May 27, 1946; came to U.S., 1966; s. Chang Yoon and Young Ja (Chung) K.; m. Tack Han, June 14, 1969; children—Juliane H., Elaine H., Deborah H. B.S., U. Rochester, 1969; M.B.A., Cornell U., 1971; Ph.D., SUNY-Buffalo, 1975. Asst. prof. Ohio State U., Columbus, 1975-77, assoc. prof., 1979-80; assoc. prof. to prof. fin. and bus. adminstrn. U. Mich., Ann Arbor, 1980-84, Fred M. Taylor Disting. prof., 1984—, chmn. fin. dept., 1988—; vis. assoc. prof. U. Chgo., 1978-79; econ. cons. Govt. of Korea, 1985—. Assoc. editor Jour. Fin., 1979-83, 1988—, Fin. Rev., 1982—; contbr. numerous articles to profl. jours. Mem. Korea-Am. Econ. Assn. (sec. gen. 1985, v.p. 1986), Am. Econ. Assn., Am. Fin. Assn., Western Fin. Assn. Avocation: tennis. Office: U Mich Sch Bus Adminstrn Ann Arbor MI 48109

KIM, EDWARD WILLIAM, ophthalmic surgeon; b. Seoul, Korea, Nov. 25, 1949; came to U.S., 1957; s. Shoon Kul and Pok Chu (Kim) K.; m. Carole Sachi Takemoto, July 24, 1976; children—Brian, Ashley. B.A., Occidental Coll., Los Angeles, 1971; postgrad. Calif. Inst. Tech., 1971; M.D., U. Calif.-San Francisco, 1975; M.P.H., U. Calif.-Berkley, 1975. Diplomate Nat. Bd. Med. Examiners, Am. Bd. Ophthalmology. Intern, San Francisco Gen. Hosp., 1975-76; resident in ophthalmology Harvard U.-Mass. Eye and Ear Infirmary, Boston, 1977-79; clin. fellow in ophthalmology Harvard U., 1977-79; clin. fellow in retina Harvard, 1980; practice medicine in ophthalmic surgery, South Laguna and San Clemente, Calif., 1980—; vol. ophthalmologist Eye Care Inc., Ecole St. Vincent's, Haiti, 1980; core investigator Staar Surg., Monrovia, Calif., 1984-87; chief of staff, South Coast Med. Ctr., 1988-89. Founding mem. Orange County Ctr. for Performing Arts, Calif., 1982; pres. Laguna Beach Summer Music Festival, Calif., 1984. Reinhart scholar U. Calif.-San Francisco, 1972-73; R. Taussig scholar, 1974-75. Fellow ACS, Am. Acad. Ophthalmology, Internat. Coll. Surgeons; mem. Calif. Med. Assn., Keratorefractive Soc., Orange County Med. Assn., Mensa, Expts. in Art and Tech. Office: Harvard Eye Assocs 665 Camino De Los Mares Suite 102 San Clemente CA 92672

KIM, GILL-RYOUNG, otolaryngologist; b. Koesan, Republic of Korea, May 4, 1926; s. Joowhan Kim and Eumjeon Lew; m. Joochoon Song, Nov. 21, 1955; 1 child, Young-Ho. BS, Severance Med. Coll., Korea, 1948, MD, 1955; MS, Yonsei U., 1957; PhD, Toho U., 1961. Diplomate Korean Bd. Otolaryngology. Instr. Korea U., Seoul, 1958-62; instr. Yonsei U., Seoul, 1962-63, asst. prof. medicine, 1963-66, assoc. prof., 1966-69, prof., 1969—, dir. med. library, 1983—, chmn. dept. otolaryngology, 1968-84; med. cons. U.S. Army, Seoul, 1975—. Author: (with others) Textbook of New Otolaryngology, 1969, English-Korean Medical Dictionary, 1973, Special Medical English, 1984; Career of the Jesus Christ, 1983. Recipient Appreciation award U.S. Army, 1987. Mem. Internat. Fedn. Oto-Rhino-Laryngol. Socs. (exec. com. 1977-85, counselor 1985—, spl. awards 1985, 87), Korean Otolaryngological Soc. (chmn. 1978-81), Korean Med. Assn. (bd. dirs. 1972-82), Korean Med. Library Assn. (pres. 1986—), Korean Soc. Logopedics and Phoniatrics (pres. 1980—), Collegium Medicorum Theatri, Collegium Oto-Rhino-Laryngol. Amicitiae Sacrum, Korean-German Med. Soc. (v.p. 1987—). Office: Yonsei U Coll Medicine, 134 Shinchon-dong, Sodaemoon-ku, Seoul 120-749, Korea

KIM, HONG TAE, orthopedic surgeon; b. Gumchun, Chungdo, Korea, Aug. 18, 1939; s. Jong Doo Kim and Bock Soo Sohn; m. Jung Ock Yun, Dec. 9, 1968; 1 child, So Yeon. MD, Kyngbuk U., 1964. Intern in orthopedic surgery Presbyn. Hosp., Daegu, Republic of Korea, 1964-65, resident, 1965-69; practice medicine specializing in orthopedic surgery Daegu, 1969—; chief dept. orthopedic surgery Fatima Hosp., Daegu, 1972—; clin. prof. orthopedics Kyungbuk Nat. U., Daegu, 1976—, Kemyeong U., Daegu, 1985—. Served to capt. M.C. Korean Army, 1969-72. Mem. Korean Med. Assn., Korean Orthopedic Assn., Western Pacific Orthopedic Assn., Daegu Orthopedic Assn. (pres. 1985—). Home: 1022-61 Manchoon-dong, Soosung-ku, Daegu 634, Korea Office: Fatima Hosp, 302 Sinam-dong Dong-ku, Daegu 635, Korea

KIM, HUN JOO, neurosurgery educator; b. Taegu, Kyungbuk, Republic of Korea, Mar. 22, 1947; s. Sung Suk Kim and Kum Hyang Lee; m. Kyung Sook Choi, May 21, 1977; children: Hyun Na, Min Hyun. B, Grad. Sch. Yonsei U., Seoul, Republic of Korea, 1972, M, 1976, MD, 1982. Diplomate Korean Med. Bd., Korean Neurosurgical Bd. Instr. neurosurgery Yonsei U. Med. Coll., 1980-82; asst. prof. Yonsei U. Weon Ju (Republic of Korea) Med. Coll., 1982-86, assoc. prof., 1986—. Served to maj. Korean Army, 1977-80. Med. Coll. Va. Research fellow in neurosurgery, 1983-85. Mem. Korean Neurosurgical Soc. (Grand Prix award 1982), Korean Traumatology Soc. Presbyterian. Clubs: YMCA, Weon Ju Golf. Home and Office: 162 Ilsan Dong, Weon Ju, Kang Weon Do Republic of Korea 220-00

KIM, IH CHIN, pediatrician; b. Seoul, Korea, Aug. 6, 1925; s. Young Whan and Young Ho (Cho) K.; came to U.S., 1953, naturalized, 1965; MD, Seoul Nat. U., 1950; student Yon Sei U., 1944-46; postgrad. U. Pa., 1954-55; m. Helen Fern Wagner, Mar. 15, 1957; children: Catherine Joy Kim Smith, Stephen Thomas. Intern, Transp. Hosps., Seoul and Pusan, Korea, 1950-51; resident in pediatrics Pusan Children's Charity Hosp., 1951-53, Children's Hosp. Phila., 1953-55, fellow in pediatric gastroenterology, 1955-58, research assoc., 1958-67, med. staff, 1963-67; practice medicine, specializing in pediatrics, Easton, Pa., 1965—, Phillipsburg, N.J., 1971—; staff dept. pediatrics Hahnemann Med. Coll. and Hosp., Phila., 1967—, Easton Hosp., 1965—, Warren Hosp., Phillipsburg, N.J., 1966—, chief dept. pediatrics, 1978—; clin. asst. prof. pediatrics Hahnemann Med. Coll., Phila., 1971—. Diplomate Am. Bd. Pediatrics. Fellow Am. Acad. Pediatrics; mem. AMA. Presbyterian. Club: County of Northampton County. Contbr. articles to med. jours. Address: 6 Ivy Court Easton PA 18042 Office: 985 Belvidere Rd Phillipsburg NJ 08865

KIM, JONGSIK, mathematics educator; b. Kwanchon, Korea, May 20, 1939; s. Bu-Young Kim and Hee-Chun Lee; m. Ae-Kyung Park, Dec. 14, 1974; 1 child, Jin-Soo. BS, Seoul (Korea) Nat. U., 1961, MS, 1966; PhD, Purdue U., 1972. Asst. prof. Seoul Nat. U., 1973-79, assoc. prof., 1980-84; prof. %, 1985—; vis. prof. Rutgers U., New Brunswick, N.J., 1976-77; vis. prof. Purdue U., West Lafayette, Ind., 1985; cons. research and devel. Korean Sci. and Engring. Found., Seoul, 1980-82; policy cons. Ministry Sci. and Tech., Seoul, 1981-83; dep. dir. Research Inst. Basic Scis., Seoul, 1987—. Author: Theory pf Partial Differential Equation, 1985; editor: Differential Geometry and Partial Differential Equations, 1986; contbr. articles to profl. jours. Recipient Nat. Medal Magnolia, Pres. Republic Korea, 1987. Mem. Korean Math. Soc. (editor 1975—, gen. sec. 1980-82, v.p. 1984-86, Acad. Prize 1987), Am. Math. Soc., Korean Acad. Council. Home: 104 Hyoshin Villar, 1506-42 Seocho-Dong, Seocho-Ku, Seoul 135, Korea Office: Seoul Nat U Dept Math, Kwanak-Ku, 151 Seoul Korea

KIM, KEITH, freight forwarding company executive; b. Seoul, Korea, Oct. 11, 1935; came to U.S., 1953, naturalized, 1969; s. Rinsuk and S.E. (Chu) K.; A.A., Los Angeles City Coll., 1955; B.A., Los Angeles State Coll., 1957; m. Theresa Lee, Sept. 5, 1968; children—Dominick, Glenn, Matthew. Import mgr. Judson Sheldon Internat. Corp., Los Angeles, 1965-69; import mgr. P.I.E. Transport, Inc., Inglewood, Calif., 1969-70; v.p. Shiloh Internat., Inc., Los Angeles, 1970-76, pres., 1976—; corp. v.p., cons. Dunbar Customs Services, Inglewood, 1973-77; pres. Alpha Cargo Service, 1978—. Lic. customshouse broker U.S. Treasury Dept. Home: 28523 Rothrock Dr Rancho Palos Verdes CA 90274 Office: 1222 E Imperial Ave El Segundo CA 90245

KIM, KYUNG YOUNG, environmental designer; b. Seoul, South Korea, June 5, 1948; s. Eui Jong and Myung Ja (Lee) K.; m. Chun Ok Park; children: Sungmi, Nami. BA, Duksung Womens Coll., 1977; MA, Seoul Nat. U., 1981. Landscape architect Garim Landscape Architecture Co., Seoul, 1980-81, Sammi Co., Seoul, 1981-82; pres. Rami Environ. Art Research Inst., Seoul, 1983—; lectr. Junbuk Nat. U., Junju, 1985—, grad. sch. Hanyang U., Seoul, 1987—; cons. Seoul City. Mem. Korean Inst. Landscape Architects. Home: Hanyang Town 104-HO, 105-8 Samsungdong Gangnamgu, 135 Seoul Republic of Korea Office: Rami Environ Art Research Inst, Youngsung Bldg No 303 108-8, Samsungdong Gangnamgu, 135 Seoul Republic of Korea

KIM, KYUNG-WON, Republic of Korea ambassador to the U.S.; b. Korea, June 12, 1936; married; 2 children. Student, Seoul Nat. U., Korea, 1954-55; B.A. magna cum laude in Polit. Sci., Williams Coll., Mass., 1959, LL.D. (hon.), 1984; Ph.D. in Polit. Sci., Harvard U., 1963. Teaching fellow dept. govt. Harvard U., Cambridge, Mass., 1962-63; asst. prof. polit. sci. York U., Toronto, Ont., Can., 1963-66; Can. Council fellow, 1966-67; assoc. prof. polit. sci. NYU, N.Y.C., 1967-71, sr. fellow Ctr. Internat. Affairs, 1969-71, dir. grad. studies, dept. polit. and internat. studies NYU, 1970-71; prof. polit. sci. Korea U., 1971-75, dir. policy studies Asiatic Research Ctr., 1972-75; mem. Republic of Korea Delegation to the UN, 1973, 75; mem. policy adv. com. for the Prime Minister of the Republic of Korea, 1973-75, spl. asst. to the pres. for internat. affairs, 1975-81, pres.'s spl. envoy to Norway, Sweden, Denmark, Iceland and Finland, 1976; sec.-gen. to the Pres. of the Republic of Korea, 1980-81, permanent observer of the Republic of Korea to the UN, 1981-85; ambassador of the Republic of Korea to the U.S., 1985—. Author: Revolution and International Systems, 1970. Address: Embassy of Korea 2370 Massachusetts Ave NW Washington DC 20008

KIM, SANG-MIN, ophthalmologist, educator; b. Pohang, Kyunbook, Korea, Dec. 15, 1931; s. Tae-Shin and Kyung-Az Kim; m. Ok-Kyu Woo, Dec. 24, 1960; children: Choong-Rak, Jung-Rak, Kyung-Rak. MB, Seoul (Republic Korea) Nat. U., 1958, D of Med. Sci., 1967. Diplomate in opthalmology. From instr. to assoc. prof. opthalmology Cath. Med. Coll., Seoul, 1965-71; assoc. prof. Chosun U., Kwangju, Republic Korea, 1971, Chung Ang U., Seoul, 1971-74; prof., chmn. dept. medicine Kyunghee U., Seoul, 1974—. Author: Elementary Optics, 1977, Spectacle Optics, 1982, Sound Management of the Eye, 1981, (with others) Textbook of Opthalmology, 1986. Served to lt. comdr. Republic Korea Navy, 1958-64. Decorated Nat. medal Merit (Republic Korea); recipient Rose of Sharon Grand prize Lions Internat., 1987. Mem. Korean Opthalmol. Soc. (exec. dir. 1984-86, councillor 1986—), Korean Assn. Prevention Blindness (standing dir.). Lodge: Lions (zone chmn. 1979-80, dep. gov. 1980-81, chmn. eye bank 1982—). Home: 2-406 Daelim Apts, Sangdo-Dong Dongjak-ku, Seoul 156-032, Republic of Korea Office: Kyunghee U Hosp Opthalmology Dept, 1 Hoeki-Dong Dong Daemon-ku, Seoul 130-702, Republic of Korea

KIM, SE JUNG, civil engineer; Seoul, Korea, Feb. 29, 1931; came to U.S., 1968, naturalized, 1973; s. Ki Yong and Soon Dong (Cha) K.; B.S., Seoul Nat. U., 1957; m. Yong Ok Son, Mar. 26, 1961; children—Dohi, Ginny. Civil engr. U.S. Army Corps Engrs., Seoul, 1957-65; project mgr. Ghana State Constrn. Corp., Accra, 1965-68; sr. civil engr. Howard, Needles, Tammen & Bergendoff, N.Y.C., 1968-75; partner Solar Engr. and Builders, Spring Valley, N.Y., 1975-79; sr. civil engr. Tippetts-Abbett-McCarthy-Stratton, N.Y.C., 1979—. Registered profl. engr., N.Y. State. Mem. Nat. Soc. Profl. Engrs., Am. Water Works Assn., Seoul Nat. U. Coll. Engring. Alumni Assn. (pres. N.Y. chpt. 1984). Home: 68 Minute Man Circle Orangeburg NY 10962 Office: Tippetts-Abbett-McCarthy-Stratton 655 3d Ave New York NY 10017

KIM, SO GU, geophysics educator; b. Kimhwa, Kangwon, Korea, Apr. 15, 1942; s. Won Shik and Yonee (Gil) K.; m. Chung Soon Park, Dec. 29, 1973; children: Matthew, Deborah. BS in Physics, Sogang U., 1967; MS in Geophysics, Oreg. State U., 1971; PhD, St. Louis U., 1976. Research asst. St. Louis U., 1972-76; sr. seismic analyst Seismograph Service Corp., Tulsa, 1976-77; sr. researcher Inst. Energy and Resources, Seoul, Korea, 1977-79; guest worker IISEE, Tokyo, 1977, Norwegian Seismic Array (NORSAR), Winter 1986; research assoc. NOAA/CIRES, Boulder, 1978-79; assoc. prof. Hanyang U., Seoul, Korea, 1979-83, prof., head earth and marine scis., 1984—; vis. prof. Hamburg U., Fed. Republic of Germany, Summer 1984, Geophysical Research Inst. U. New Eng., Australia, Summer 1987; cons. Ministry Sci. and Tech., Seoul, 1977-82, Advanced Energy Inst., 1980-81, 1985-86, Korea Ocean Research and Devel., 1984-85; des dir. Inst. Environ. scis., Seoul, 1979-80; instr. Seoul Nat. U., 1979, Sogang U., 1985. Contbr. articles to profl. jours.; author: Seismology, 1983, Elastic Wave Theory, 1988. Recipient award for earthquake disaster/Hongsung, Ministry Sci. and Tech., 1979. Mem. Earthquake Engring. Research Inst., Assn. Geoscientists for Internat. Devel., Internat. Union Geodesy and Geophysics, Sigma Xi. Roman Catholic. Home: 5-301 Woo Sung, Apts Jamsil Songpa-ku, Seoul 138-229, Republic of Korea Office: Hanyang U Dept Earth/Marine, Scis Ahnsansi, Kyong-gi-do 425-170, Republic of Korea

KIM, STEPHEN SOU-HWAN, archbishop; b. Taegu, Korea, May 8, 1922. PhB, Sophia U., Tokyo, 1944; M in Theology, Cath. Coll., Seoul, Republic of Korea, 1950; Dr. in Sociology, Münster U., Fed. Republic Germany, 1964; doctorate, Sogang U., Seoul, 1974, U. Notre Dame, 1977. Ordained priest Roman Cath. Ch., 1951, consecrated bishop, 1966. Pastor Andong parish, Archdiocese of Taegu, Andong, Republic of Korea, 1951-53; sec. to archbishop Archdiocese of Taegu, Taegu, 1953-55; pastor Hwangkeumdong parish, Archdiocese of Taegu, Kimcheon, Republic of Korea, 1955-56; pres. Cath. Shibo weekly newspaper, Taegu, 1964-66; bishop Diocese of Masan, Republic of Korea, 1966-68; archbishop Archdiocese of Seoul, 1968—, cardinal, 1969—; pres. Bishop's Conf. Korea, Seoul, 1971—, del. to synod, Vatican City, 1967, 71, 74, 80, 83-86; pres. Follow-up Com. for Fedn. Asian Bishop's Conf., 1970-73. Home and Office: Archdiocese of Seoul, 1 2ka Myong-dong, Chung-ku, Seoul 100, Republic of Korea

KIM, SUNG SOON, cardiology educator; b. Seoul, Republic of Korea, Nov. 23, 1945; s. Chong Sung and Chung Hyun (Noh) K.; m. Ghi Su Kim; children: Ge Young, Ge Sun. MD, Yonsei U., Seoul, 1970, MS, 1974, DMS, 1979. Intern, then resident Yonsei U. Coll. Medicine Severance Hosp., 1970-75; instr. Yonsei U. Coll. Medicine, 1975-79, assoc. prof. medicine, 1986—; fellow in cardiology St. Louis U. Sch. Medicine, 1979-81, instr., 1979-82; fellow in electrophysiology U. Ill. Hosp., Chgo., 1982-83; instr. Washington U. Sch. Medicine, St. Louis, 1983-84, asst. prof., 1984-86; staff cardiologist Severence Hosp., Seoul, 1975-79, St. Louis U. Hosp., 1981-82; dir. telemetry unit, Jewish Hosp. of St. Louis, 1983-86. Fellow ACP, Am. Coll Cardiology, Council on Clin. Cardiology; mem. Cardiac Electrophysiology Soc., N.Am. Soc. Pacing and Electrophysiology.d. Office: Severance Hosp Cardiology Div, Yonsei U Medicine CPO Box 8044, 120 Seoul Republic of Korea

KIM, WAN HEE, engineering educator, business executive; b. Osan, Korea, May 24, 1926; came to U.S., 1953, naturalized, 1962; s. Sang Chul and Cuck Hyung (Chong) K.; m. Chung Sook Noh, Jan. 23, 1960; children: Millie, Richard K. B.E., Seoul Nat. U., 1950; M.S. in Elec. Engring, U. Utah, 1954, Ph.D., 1956. Research asst. U. Ill., Urbana, 1955-56; research staff IBM Research Ctr., Poughkeepsie, N.Y., 1956-57; asst. prof. Columbia U., N.Y.C., 1957-59; assoc. prof. Columbia U., 1959-63, prof. elec. engring., 1963-78; chmn. Tech. Cons., Inc., N.Y.C., 1962-69; chmn. KOMKOR Am., Inc., N.Y.C., 1970-72; spl. advisor for the pres. and govt. Korea, 1967-79; adviser Korea Advanced Inst. Sci., Seoul, 1971-73; chmn. Korea Inst. Electronics Tech., 1977-81; mem. bd. Korea Telecommunication Electric Research Inst., 1977-81; pres. WHK Engring. Corp. Am., 1982-84, WHK Electronics Inc., 1982-84; chmn., chief exec. officer Industries Assn. Electronic Korea, 1978-81; chmn. WHK Industries Inc., 1984—, AEA Corp.; pres. Asian Electronics Union, 1979-83; pub. Electronic Times of Korea, 1982-83; cons. The World Bank, Washington, other indsl. orgns. Author: (with R.T. Chien) Topological Analysis and Synthesis of Communication Networks, 1962, (with H.E. Meadows) Modern Network Analysis, 1970; pub.: The Dr. Kim Report on Korea, 1988—; also numerous articles. U.S. rep. on U.S.-Japan Scientists Coop. Program.; trustee U.S.-ASIA Inst., Washington, 1984—. Served with Korean Army, 1950-53. Decorated Bronze Star; recipient Achievement medal U.S.-Asia Inst.; Guggenheim grantee, 1964; NSF research grantee, 1958—. Fellow IEEE, Union Radio Scientifique Internat. (mem. U.S. nat. com. Commn. Band C 1963-78), Sigma Xi, Tau Beta Pi. Home: 282 Woodland St Tenafly NJ 07670 Office: 459 Homer Ave Suite 8 Palo Alto CA 94301

KIM, WOO-CHOONG, industrialist; b. Taegu, Republic of Korea, Dec. 19, 1936; s. Yong-Ha and In-Hang (Chun) Kim; m. Hrrja Chung, Apr. 4, 1964; children: Sun-Jeong, Sun-Jae, Sun-Hyup, Sun-Yong. BA in Econs., Yonsei U., Seoul, Republic of Korea, 1960; D in Econs (hon.), Yonsei U., 1985; DBA, Korea U., Seoul, 1986. Founder/chmn. Daewoo Group, Seoul, 1967—; mem. Pacific adv. council of United Technologies Corp. Vice-chmn. Fedn. Korean Industries, Seoul, 1979—, Korean Fgn. Trade Assn., Seoul, 1979—; bd. dirs. Korea-U.S. Econ. Council, Seoul, 1987—, Yonsei Cancer Ctr., Seoul, 1987—. Recipient Indsl. Order Gold Tower Korean Govt., 1972, Yonsei Mgmt. prize, 1976, Order of the Two Niles Sudanese Govt., 1979, Internat. Bus. award Internat. C. of C., 1984. Mem. Korean Fedn. Textile Industries (chmn. bd. dirs. 1986—), Korea Sports Assn. (vice-chmn. 1987—), Korea Baduk Assn. (chmn. bd. dirs. 1987—). Office: Daewoo Corp, 541 Namdaemunno 5-Ga, Chung-ku, Seoul Republic of Korea

KIM, YOON BERM, immunologist, educator; b. Soon Chun, Korea, Apr. 25, 1929; s. Sang Sun and Yang Rang (Lee) K.; m. Soon Cha Kim, Feb. 23, 1959; children: John, Jean, Paul. M.D., Seoul Nat. U., 1958; Ph.D., U. Minn., 1965. Intern Univ. Hosp. Seoul Nat. U., 1958-59; mem. faculty U. Minn., Mpls., 1960-73; assoc. prof. microbiology U. Minn., 1970-73; mem., head lab. ontogeny of immune system Sloan Kettering Inst. Cancer Research, Rye, N.Y., 1973-83; prof. immunology Cornell U. Grad. Sch. Med. Scis., N.Y.C., 1973-83; chmn. immunology unit Cornell U. Grad. Sch. Med. Scis., 1980-82; prof. microbiology, immunology and medicine, chmn. dept. micorbiology and immunology U. Health Scis., Chgo. Med. Sch., 1983—; m. Lobund adv. bd. U. Notre Dame, 1977—. Contbr. numerous articles on immunology to profl. jours. Recipient research career devel. award USPHS, 1968-73. Mem. Assn. Gnotobiotics (pres.), Am. Assn. Immunologists, Am. Soc. Microbiology, Am. Assn. Pathologists, AAAS, Korean Med. Assn. Am., N.Y. Acad. Scis., Reticuloendothelial Soc., Internat. Soc. Devel. Comparative Immunology, Harvey Soc., Internat. Soc. Interferon Research, Chgo. Assn. Immunologists, Assn. Med. Sch. Microbiology Chmn., Sigma Xi, Alpha Omega Alpha. Home: 313 Weatherford Ct Lake Bluff IL 60044 Office: 3333 Green Bay Rd North Chicago IL 60064

KIM, YOUNG SOO, machinery manufacturing company executive; b. Seoul, Korea, Dec. 10, 1940; s. Suk Joo and Soon Keum K.; m. Son Sun Za.; children—Maeng Zoon, Zung A., Kyung A. B.A., Hankuk U. fgn. studies, Seoul, Korea, 1967. Gen. mgr. Hyundai Constrn. Co., Bangkok, Thailand, 1972-75; gen. mgr. Hyundai Am. Corp., Agana, Guam, 1975-78; sr. dir. Hyunda Internat. Inc., Seoul, 1978-79; exec. dir. Korea Heavy Industries and Constrn. Co. Ltd., Seoul, 1979—; exec. dir. Perak Hanjoon Simen, Ipoh, 1980—. Avocations: reading; golf. Home: 1 Tiger Close, Ipoh, Perak Malaysia Other: 187-40 Yunhi-Dong, Sudaemun-Ku, Seoul Korea

KIM, YOUNG-HO, consul; b. Republic of Korea, Dec. 6, 1938; s. Weol-Bong Kim and So-Yeon Kang; m. Sung-Hi Kim; children: Ki-Nam, Do-Hoon, Jeong-Hoon. BA in Commerce, Busan Nat. U., 1963; MA in Internat. Trade, Seong Kyun Kwan U., Seoul, 1972. Asst. chief Osrok head office Office of Supply, Govt. of Republic of Korea, Seoul, 1963-74, dir. Osrok head office, 1981-86; consul Korean consulate gen. Office of Supply, Govt. of Republic of Korea, Hamburg, Fed. Republic Germany, 1974-80, 86—; Rep. UN Escape, Bangkok, 1984, Import Mgmt. Seminar, Canton, People's Republic of China, 1985 South Conference, London, 1987. Office: Korean Cons Gen, Hagedorn Str 53, 2000 Hamburg 13 FRG

KIM, YOUN-SUK ERNEST, economist, educator; b. Kwangju, Korea, Sept. 15, 1934; came to U.S., 1959, naturalized, 1977; s. Jse-Kyu and Young-

Unn (Chung) K.; B.A. in Bus. Adminstrn., Seoul Nat. U., 1958; M.A. in Econs., New Sch., 1967; Ph.D., 1973; m. Y. Hannar, Apr. 24, 1966; children—Y. Herb, Nancy Y., John Y. Statistician, Am. Photog. Corp., 1963-67; econometrician Candeub, Fleissig & Assos., planning cons., Newark, 1968-70; adj. prof. Fairleigh Dickinson U., Teaneck, N.J., 1971-73; mem. faculty Kean Coll., Union, N.J., 1974—, assoc. prof. econs., 1979-84, prof., 1985—; vis. prof. econs. Seoul (Korea) Nat. U., 1987-88. Grantee N.E. Asia Council, Kean Coll., Korea Economic Research Inst., 1987. Mem. Am. Econ. Assn., Western Econ. Assn., Eastern Econ. Assn., Atlantic Econ. Soc., Japan Econ. Seminar, Assn. Asian Studies, Democrat. Contbr. articles to profl. jours.; also books. Home: 102 E Madison Ave Cresskill NJ 07626 Office: Kean Coll Morris Ave Union NJ 07083

KIM, YUNG DAI, research scientist; b. Seoul, Korea, Mar. 24, 1936; came to U.S., 1957, naturalized, 1971; s. Ik S. and Jung H. (Juhn) K.; m. Young S. Chyung, June 17, 1967; children—Jean Ok, Sue Ok. Ph.D., U. Minn., 1968. Vis. scientist Kettering Research Lab., Yellow Springs, Ohio, 1968-69; NIH fellow Northwestern U., Evanston, Ill., 1969-71; NIH research fellow U. Pa., Phila., 1971-73; immunochemist Worthington Biochem. Co., Freehold, N.J., 1973-74; sr. scientist Abbott Labs., North Chicago, Ill., 1974—. Mem. Am. Assn. Immunologists, Am. Chem. Soc., Sigma Xi, Phi Lambda Upsilon. Mem. editorial bd. Cancer Control and Therapy jour.; contbr. articles to profl. jours.; patentee in field. Home: 1728 Virginia Ave Libertyville IL 60048 Office: Abbott Labs North Cancer Researcl Lab D90C Chicago IL 60064

KIMBALL, MARY LEE EVANS, civic leader; b. St. Louis, Jan. 27, 1911; d. Dwight Durkee and Elmira (Lee) Evans; A.B. cum laude, Smith Coll., 1933; M.A., Radcliffe Coll., 1935; diplome d'etudes Univ. (Am. fellow Inst. Internat. Edn., 1936-37) Universite de Paris (France), 1937; diplome Ecole du Louvre, Paris, 1962; postgrad. (predoctoral fellow) U. Conn., 1967-68; M.A., Trinity Coll., 1971, U. Conn., 1971; m. Chase Kimball, June 27, 1942; children—Elmira Lee (Mrs. H. Thomas Byron, Jr.), Helen Chase (Mrs. Robert Z. Brooke), Mary Eliza. Tchr. French, Cambridge Sch., Kendall Green, Mass., 1937-38, Wheaton Coll., 1938-41, Greenwood Sch., Ruxton, Md., 1941-42, Montessori Sch., Calgary, Alta., Can., 1945, Milton Acad., Mass., 1948-52; instr. French, Tufts U., 1952-58; asst. prof. French, Newton Coll. Sacred Heart, 1958-59; asst. prof. French, Stonehill Coll., 1959-64; asso. prof. French, Salem (Mass.) State Coll., 1965; asst. prof. French, U. Mass., Boston, 1965-81. Bd. dirs. Heart Fund, Boston, to 1970; mem. womans bd. Day-Kimball Hosp., Conn.; Milton chmn. Boston Arts Festival, 1957-60. Pres., Milton Womens Republican Club, 1958-60; Milton Rep. Town Com. to 1988; chevalier de l'Ordre des Palmes Acad., 1974. Bd. dirs. French Library Boston, 1972—, Home for Aged Women, 1981—; chmn. UN Council of South Shore, 1983—; mem. corp. Milton Hosp., 1981—. Instr. French, U.S. Army, Whitehorse, Yukon, 1944. Decorated chevalier de l'ordre des Palmes Académiques (France). Mem. LWV (voters' service chmn., internat. relations chmn. Milton 1948-52), Am. Assn. Tchrs. French, Modern Lang. Assn., Alliance Francaise (bd. dirs. 1978—), Am. Hist. Assn., UN Assn. Greater Boston (pres. 1981-84), UN Council South Shore (dir. 1975—), Mass. Soc. Colonial Dames, Fragment Soc. Boston, Colonial Dames Am. Clubs: Chromatic (pres. 1977-87), Smith College (dir. 1955-61, 70-75, pres. Class of 1933, 1973-78), Chilton, Women's City (Boston); Milton Women's (internat. relations chmn. 1958-60, 62-64 garden and conservation chmn. 1960-61), Coll. (Boston), University (Boston), University (Washington). Home: Pomfret Centre CT 06259 Other: 434 Brush Hill Rd Milton MA 02186

KIMBALL, REID ROBERTS, psychiatrist; b. Draper, Utah, June 29, 1926; s. Crozier and Mary Lenore (Roberts) K.; B.S., Brigham Young U., 1949; M.D., U. Utah, 1951; m. Barbara Joy Radmore, Aug. 3, 1962; children—Valery, Michael, Pauline, Karen, Kay. Intern, Thomas D. Dee Hosp., Ogden, Utah, 1951-52; resident Norristown (Pa.) State Hosp., 1952-53, Oreg. State Hosp., Salem, 1953-55, Palo Alto (Calif.) VA Hosp., 1956; practice medicine specializing in psychiatry, Eugene, Oreg., 1957-60, Salem, Oreg., 1960-72, Portland, Oreg., 1972-77; dir. Out-patient Clinic Oreg. State Hosp., Salem, 1956-57; mem. staff Sacred Heart Hosp., Eugene, consultation/liaison psychiatry, 1977—; asst. prof. psychology U. Oreg., Eugene, 1957-65, prof., 1977—; dir. med. edn. Oreg. State Hosp., Salem, 1984—; asst. prof. psychiatry U. Oreg., Portland, 1965, adj. asst. prof., 1982—. Mem. Lane County Community Mental Health Adv. Bd., 1980-81. Served with USN, 1943-45. Mem. Am., Oreg. (chmn. psychiatry sect. 1973-74) med. assns., Lane County Med. Soc., Am. (pres. Oreg. dist. br. 1973-74), North Pacific Psychiat. Assn. (pres. 1988—), Lane County (pres. 1979-80) Psychiat. Assn. (pres. 1979-80), Am. Gerontology Soc. Home: 1963 Stone Crest Dr Eugene OR 97401 Office: 132 E Broadway Suite 303 Eugene OR 97401

KIMBELL, MARION JOEL, engineer; b. McDonough, Ga., Sept. 7, 1923; s. Charles Marvin and Mary (McMillian) K.; B.S. in Civil Engring., U. Houston, 1949, M.Chem. Engring., 1953; m. Judy Weidner, Dec. 18, 1946; children—Nancy, Susan, Candice. Civil engr. U.S. Dept. Interior, Lemmon, S.D., 1954; chief piping engr. M.W. Kellog Co., Paducah, Ky., 1955; nuclear engr. Westinghouse Atomic Power Div., Pitts., 1956-59; control systems prin. engr. Kaiser Engrs., Oakland, Calif., 1959-80; control systems supervising engr. Bechtel Inc., San Francisco, 1980—; control systems tchr. Laney Coll. cons. engr. NASA, Gen. Atomic Co.; advisory bd. Chabot Collage on radiation tech. Served as sgt. U.S. Army, 1943-46. Registered profl. nuclear engr., Calif.; control systems engr., Calif. Mem. Instrument Soc. of Am. (sr. mem. exec. com.). Clubs: Moose. Contbr. articles to profl. jours. Home: 22324 Ralston Ct Hayward CA 94541 Office: Bechtel Inc 50 Beal St PO Box 3965 San Francisco CA 94119

KIMBERLY, WILLIAM ESSICK, investment banker; b. Neenah, Wis., Mar. 19, 1933; s. John Robbins and Elizabeth McFarland (Essick) K.; m. Elena Guajardo, Nov. 27, 1965; children—Essicka Amelia, Ariadne Elena, Dagny Maria. Student Williams Coll., 1951-53, U. Wis., 1953-54. Sr v.p. Kimberly-Clark Corp, Neenah, Wis., 1959-83; prin. W.E. Kimberly Investments, Neenah, 1983-85; pres. Kimberly, Brunell, & Lehmann, Inc., Washington, 1986—; dir. Capitol Video Corp., Washington, Systems Impact Inc., Kimberly Gallery of Art Inc., Washington Emergency and Systems, Inc. Served with USNR, 1956-58. Republican. Episcopalian. Club: Metropolitan (Washington). Avocations: auto racing, music, art, movies. Home: 4082 Ridgeview Circle Arlington VA 22207 Office: Kimberly Brunell & Lehmann Inc 1025 Thomas Jefferson St NW Washington DC 20007

KIMBLE, BARBARA ANN, protective services official; b. Toledo, Mar. 21, 1945; d. George Leroy and Elvera Betty (Rose) Kimble. BA, U. Toledo, 1967; grad. Patricia Stevens Modeling and Career Coll., 1967; postgrad. in Computer Sci., N. Tex. State U., 1986—. Modeling instr. Patricia Stevens Modeling and Career Coll., Toledo, 1966, Barbizon Sch. Modeling, Dallas, 1972; operator Nat. Crime Info. Ctr., FBI, Dallas, 1979-83, investigative communications technician, 1983-84, coordinator, 1983-87; gen. police instr., tech. info. specialist, FBI, Dallas, 1987—; Texette and tour guide Dallas Cowboys, 1971-79. Named Miss Amity, Miss Tex. Universe Pageant, 1971; recipient Performance award, FBI, 1981-85. Mem. Nat. Baton Twirling Assn., Nat. Baton Twirling Judges Bur., Nat. Baton Twirling Tchrs. Assn., Tex. Criminal Justice Info. Users Group. Avocations: sewing, dancing, crocheting.

KIMBLE, GLADYS AUGUSTA LEE, nurse, civic worker; b. Niagara Falls, Can., June 28, 1906; d. William and Florence Augusta Baker (Buckton) Lee; naturalized citizen of the U.S.; RN, Christ Hosp., Jersey City, 1929; BS, Columbia U. Tchrs. Coll., 1938, MA, 1948; m. George Edmond Kimble, Jan. 5, 1952. Nurse, Willard Parker Hosp., N.Y.C., 1931; asst. and supervisory relief nurse Margaret Hague Maternity Hosp., Jersey City, 1931-37; staff nurse, relief supr. Manhattan Eye, Ear and Throat Hosp., 1937-38; sr. staff, asst. nurse supr. Vis. Nurse Service, N.Y.C., 1938-41; sr. public health nurse USPHS, Little Rock, 1941-43; public health supr. Providence Dist. Nursing Assn., 1943-46; edn. dir. Jersey City Public Health Nursing Service, 1946-49, also instr. Seton Hall U., 1947-48; public health nurse cons. U.S. Inst. Inter-Am. Affairs, Brazil, 1949-51; dir. public health dept. Englewood (N.J.) Hosp., 1951-53; nurse coordinator exchange visitor nurse program Overlook Hosp., Summit, N.J., 1964-71. Recipient Appreciation award for service rendered Providence Hosp., 1944; Woman of Yr. award Essex County Bus. and Profl. Women, 1968. Fellow Am. Public Health Assn. (life), mem. Sarasota Geneal. Soc. (charter). Episcopalian. Lodges: Daus. of the Nile, Ladies Oriental Shrine of N. Am. (SAR-I Ct. 79), Royal Order of Jesterettes, Eillim Ives #18, Saratoga. Home: 4540 Bee Ridge Rc Villa 12 Sarasota FL 34233

KIMBLER, LARRY BERNARD, real estate executive, accountant; b. Lucasville, Ohio, Sept. 6, 1938; s. Benjamin F. and Elizabeth L. (Kerr) K.; m. Susanna Hayes, June 20, 1964; children—Beth Ann, Carolyn Sue. B.B.A., U. Cin., 1964; C.P.A., Ohio. Acct. Peat, Marwick, Mitchell & Co., Cin., 1964-68; mgr. acctg. and taxes Andrew Jergens & Co., Cin., 1968-70; exec. v.p. Am. Lakes & Land Co., Houston, 1970-74; from group controller real estate and minerals to gen. mgr. land utilization Internat. Paper Co., 1974-81; pres. Internat. Paper Realty Co., N.Y.C., 1977-81; v.p. corp. real estate GTE, Stamford, Conn., also pres. GTE Realty Corp., 1981—; dir., mem. exec. com. Stamford Econ. Assistance Corp.; past pres. Westchester So. Conn. chpt., NACORE; trustee, treas. Low-Heywood Thomas Sch., Stamford; lectr., speaker in field; mem. adv. bd. Homer Hoyt Inst.; officer, bd. dirs. INdsl. Devel. Research Council; editorial adv. bd. Bldg. Econs. Contbr. articles to profl. jours. Served with AUS, 1956-59. Mem. Am. Inst. Corp. Asset Mgmt. (bd. govs.), Nat. Assn. Corp. Real Estate Execs. (master corp. real estate designation, chpt. pres.), Am. Inst. C.P.A.s, Indsl. Devel. Research Council (dir., Officer Disting. Service award 1983, 87, Master Profl. Designation). Presbyterian. Republican. Home: 28 Nathan Hale Dr Stamford CT 06902 Office: GTE 1 Stamford Forum Stamford CT 06904

KIMBRELL, HORACE WARREN, lawyer; b. Lees Summit, Mo., Apr. 19, 1916; s. Raymond Benefiel and Ruberta Katherine (Magers) K.; m. Ethel Young, Aug. 5, 1956. A.B., U. Kansas City, Mo., 1936, LL.B., 1939; L.H.D. (hon.), City U., Bellevue, Wash., 1982. Bar: Mo. 1939. Since practiced in Kansas City; mem. staff U.S. atty. Western Dist. Mo., 1953-61; asst. gen. counsel Kansas City Life Ins. Co., 1961-72, asst. v.p., exec. adminstr. public affairs, 1972-76, asso. dir. public relations, 1976-78; public speaker and lectr. 1979—. Pres. Goodwill Industries Greater Kansas City, 1952-66, chmn. bd., 1966-76; pres. Goodwill Industries Am., Inc., 1961-66, chmn. bd., 1966-68, nat. ambassador, 1968—; sec. trustees U. Kansas City, 1949—; founder, trustee St. Paul Sch. Theology Methodist, Kansas City, 1958—. Served USNR, 1942-46. First recipient President's award U. Mo. System, 1982; recipient Chmn.'s award for outstanding vol. service Goodwill Industries Am., 1983. Mem. ABA, Fed. Bar Assn. (pres. Kansas City 1958, Earl Kintner award 1981), 8th circuit Bar Assn. (nat. v.p. 1965-67, mem. nat. council 1967—), Kansas City Bar Assn., Kansas City Lawyers Assn., Mo. Bar, Am. Judicature Soc., Nat. Lawyers Club (charter), Am. Soc. Internat. Law, Internat. Platform Assn., Navy League, State Hist. Soc. Mo. (life), World Order Through Law Center (charter). Republican. Methodist (ofcl. bd., Sunday sch. tchr.). Home and Office: 5900 E 129th St Grandview MO 64030

KIMES, BEVERLY RAE, editor, writer; b. Aurora, Ill., Aug. 17, 1939; d. Raymond Lionel and Grace Florence (Perrin) K.; m. James H. Cox, July 6, 1984. B.S., U. Ill., 1961; M.A. in Journalism, Pa. State U., 1963. Dir. publicity Mateer Playhouse, Neff's Mills, Pa., 1962, Pavillion Theatre, University Park, Pa., 1963; asst. editor Automobile Quar. Publs., N.Y.C., Princeton, N.J., 1963-64, assoc. editor, 1965-66, mng. editor, 1967-74, editor, 1975-81; editor The Classic Car, 1981—. Bd. dirs. Auburn-Cord-Duesenberg Mus., Milestone Car Soc.; mem. internat. coordination com. Nat. Automotive History Collection, Detroit Pub. Library. Recipient Cugnot award Soc. Automotive Historians, 1978, 79, 83, 85, 86, Thomas McKean trophy, 1983, 85, 86, Moto award Nat. Assn. Automotive Journalists, 1984, 85, 86. Mem. Internat. Motor Press Assn., Milestone Car Soc. (bd. dirs.), Soc. Automotive Historians (pres. 1987—). Author: The Classic Tradition of the Lincoln Motor Car, 1968; (with R.M. Langworth) Oldsmobile: The First Seventy-Five Years, 1972; The Cars That Henry Ford Built, 1978; (with Rene Dreyfus) My Two Lives, 1983; (with Robert C. Ackerson) Chevrolet: A History from 1911, 1984; The Standard Catalog of American Cars 1805-1942, 1985; The Star and the Laurel: The Centennial History of Daimler, Mercedes and Benz, 1986; editor: Great Cars and Grand Marques, 1976; Packard: History of the Motor Car and the Company, 1979; Automobile Quarterly's Handbook of Automotive Hobbies, 1981.

KIMII, DANIEL NZUKI, accountant; b. Nairobi, Kenya, Aug. 7, 1933; s. Kimii Philip and Mbaika Mbiti; m. Scolastica Leah, Aug. 7, 1955; children: Boniface M. Nzuki, Anthony M Nzuki, Felistas Mutheu. Fin. acct. Pfizer Labs. Ltd., Nairobi, 1961—. Roman Catholic. Home: Box 18244, Nairobi Kenya

KIM IL-SUNG, president Democratic People's Republic Korea; b. Mangyongche, Pyongyang City, Korea, Apr. 15, 1912; s. Kim Hyong Jik and Kama Ban Sok; m. Kim Jung Sook; m. 2d, Kim Song Ae. Founder, Down with Imperialism Union, 1926, Korean Communist Youth League, 1927; prisoner, Kirin, China, 1929-30; founder Korean Revolutionary Army, 1930, Korean People's Revolutionary Army, 1932; joined Communist Party, 1931; leader anti-Japanese People's Revolutionary Army, 1932-45; founder, chmn. Assn. for Restoration of Fatherland, 1936; founder Central Organizing Com. N. Korean Communist Party, 1945; founder, chmn. N. Korean Provisional People's Com. 1946; chmn. Party Central Com. Workers' Party, 1946—, chmn. N. Korean People's Com., 1947; founder Korean People's Army, 1948; founder, head of state, prime minister Dem. People's Republic Korea, 1948-72; pres., head of state, 1972—; chmn. Mil. Commn., supreme commdr. Korean People's Army, 1950-53; sec. gen. Central Com. Workers' Party Korea, 1966—. Author various works. Decorated Marshal Dem. People's Republic Korea, 1950, Hero Dem. People's Republic Korea (3 times), Labor Hero Dem. People's Republic Korea, Order of Freedom and Independence 1st class, Order of Lenin, 1987, numerous others. Address: Presidential House, Pyongyang Democratic People's Republic of Korea *

KIMLICKA, STEFAN, information scientist; b. Topolcany, Czechoslovakia, Nov. 9, 1943; s. Stefan and Stefania (Davidova) K.; m. Zuzana Svitacova, May 18, 1968; 1 child, Matej. Diploma in engring., Slovak Tech. U., Bratislava, Czechoslovakia, 1968; postgrad., Inst. Sci. and Tech. Info., Moscow, 1969; D of Engring., Inst. Economy, Bratislava, 1978; postgrad., Comenius U., Bratislava, 1984. Research worker Cen. Economy Library, Bratislava, 1969-76; research worker Comenius U., 1976-78, vis. lectr. philosophy, 1980-84, head dept. info., 1985-87, mem. state examination commn. for grads., 1981—; chief project Inst. Water Research, Bratislava, 1978-80, Matica Slovenska, Bratislava, 1987—; mem. Experts Commn., Ministry Edn., Bratislava, 1981—; mem. sci. adv. bd. Info. Ctr., Slovak Acad. Scis., Bratislava, 1986—. Recipient Memory medal Matica Slovenska, 1986. Mem. Assn. Slovak Librarians and Informatists (exec. sec. 1976-85, v.p. 1976—). Home: ul Belu Kuna 23, 85103 Bratislava Czechoslovakia Office: Matica Slovenska, na Uviati 52, 82632 Bratislava Czechoslovakia

KIM MAHN JE, former minister of finance South Korea; b. Sunsan, Kyongsangpukto, Korea, Dec. 1934. Degree, U. Denver, 1958; Ph.D. in Econs., U. Mo. Mem. econs. faculty U. Mo., Seoul Nat. U. (Korea); faculty Sogang U., Seoul, 1965-70, prof., 1982—; pres. Korea Devel. Inst., 1971-82; pres. KorAm Bank, 1983-84; minister of fin. South Korea, Seoul, 1983-87; mem. Monetary Bd. Korea, 1975—; mem. Legis. Assembly, 1980—; mem. Deliberations Com. for Promotion of Banking Industry. Office: Deputy Prime Minister, Seoul Republic of Korea *

KIMMEL, CARY ALLEN, electronics marketing executive; b. N.Y.C., Sept. 21, 1943; s. Sam and Helen (Siegal) K.; m. Rita Terese Kinsella, Nov. 24, 1967; children: David Larkin, Robert Lowell, Sarah Catherine. BA, Queens Coll., 1964; postgrad., Air Force Inst. Tech., 1967. Fgn. service res. officer U.S. Dept. State, N.Y.C., 1964; planning analyst U.S. Dept. Navy, Washington, 1964-67; sr. parametric analyst Grumman Aircraft Co., Bethpage, N.Y., 1967-69; fin. mgmt. positions Xerox Corp, Rochester, N.Y., 1969-84; bus. devel. mgr. Xerox Corp., El Segundo, Calif., 1984—; lectr. World Bank, 1988. Author: (with others) World Bank Electronics Industry Handbook, 1988. Named N.Y. Regents scholar, 1960, Fed. Mgmt. Intern, 1965. Mem. Am. Mgmt. Assn. (lectr. 1986). Office: Xerox Corp 701 S Aviation Blvd El Segundo CA 90245

KIMMEL, ROBERT IRVING, design consultant, former state government official; b. Uniontown, Pa., Jan. 28, 1922; s. Andrew Filson and Dorothy Jean (Walker) K.; student Bucknell U., Lewisburg, Pa., 1940-41, 43-44, Washington U., St. Louis, 1942, Pa. State U., 1972; children—Donna Jean, Robert Filson, LuAnna Pat, Kevin Normaine, Gregory Paul. Self-employed entertainer, 1944; mgr. Cassiday Theaters, Midland, Mich., 1945-46; engring. illustrator Dow Chem. Co., Midland, 1946-59; engring. mgr. Radio Communications Co., Bloomsburg, Pa., 1959-64; chief electronics Pa. State Police, Harrisburg, 1964-74, dir. communications div., 1974-79; chmn. Pa. Law Enforcement Telecommunications Planning Com., 1976-79; design cons. Communications Systems Design Assos., Harrisburg, 1979—; v.p. Partnership, Inc., 1980—; mgr. Paxton Herald and Paxton Herald West newspapers, 1981—; cons., lectr. in field. Mem. task force Cultural Center, Harrisburg, 1975-76; head coach Lakevue Midget Baseball Assn., 1976-78; pres. council St. Mark's Lutheran Ch., Harrisburg, 1975-79; bd. dirs. Harrisburg Performing Arts Co., 79, Emergency Health Services Fedn., 1984-86; v.p., bd. dirs. Am. Lung Assn. Cen. Pa., 1987—; instr. Dancers Workshop, 1979—; sec.-treas. Susquehanna Valley Assn., 1984—. Served with USAAF, 1942-43. Recipient various pub. service awards, certs. of merit. Fellow Radio Club Am.; mem. Assn. Pub.-Safety Communications Officers (pres. 1978-79), Pa. Chiefs Police Assn. (life; chmn. frequency adv. com. 1967-79), Engrs. Soc. Pa. (pres. 1978-79), Nat. Assn. Dance and Affiliated Artists (past v.p.), Greater Harrisburg Arts Council (dir.), Internat. Platform Assn. Author papers in field. Developer vehicle location system, elec. security systems. Home: 1002A N 6th St Harrisburg PA 17102 Office: 101 Lincoln St Harrisburg PA 17111

KIMMLE, MANFRED, diversified company executive; b. Vienna, Oct. 12, 1942; s. Bernhard and Else (Hungerland) Schultze-Kimmle; m. Erika Maier, Sept. 28, 1973. D.S., Univ. de Paris-Sorbonne, Paris, 1965; Diplom, Freie Universitat, West Berlin, 1965; M.B.A., Harvard U., 1967, D.B.A., 1972; B.A. (hons.), Muhlenberg Coll., 1962. Exec. trainee Commerzbank, West Berlin, Germany, 1962; sales and systems engr IBM Corp, West Berlin, 1964-65; asst. to pres. Dobelle S.A., Amiens, France, 1965; sr. engagement mgr. McKinsey & Co. Inc., N.Y. and Dusseldorf, 1967-74; v.p., exec. v.p. Thyssen-Bornemisza, Monaco, Amsterdam, N.Y., 1974-80, mem. bd mgmt., 1980—; chief staff Thyssen-Bornemisza Group, Monaco, Amsterdam, N.Y., 1984-86; pres. Thyssen-Bornemisza Group Inc., N.Y., 1985—, TBG Holdings, 1986—. Author: Top Management System, 1972. Contbr. articles to profl. jours. Office: TBG Inc 1211 Ave of the Americas New York NY 10036

KIMN, HA-JINE, mathematics and computer science educator; b. Daegu, Kyungbuk, Korea, May 7, 1939; s. Wankyu and Boksoon (Chung) K.; m. Hak-Shin Koh, Mar. 1 , 1961; children: Sarah, Jihie, Junghan. BS, Seoul Nat. U., Republic of Korea, 1962; MS Diplôme d'Etudes Approfondis, U. Grenoble, France, 1978; PhD, U. St-Etienne, France, 1980. Tchr. Seoul Nat. U. High Sch., 1965-67; lectr. Seoul Nat. U., 1972-76; lectr. Ajou U., Suwon, Republic of Korea, 1974-80, asst. prof., 1980-84, assoc. prof., 1984—, dean student affairs, 1982-84, dir. research and devel. ctr., 1986-88; dir. French-Korean tech. coop. ctr. 1986—; vis. prof. Nat. Inst. for Research in Informatics and Automation, Versailles, France, 1984-85; mem. adv. com. Ministry Sci. and Tech., Seoul, 1981-82. Author: Polynomital Approximation, 1988; contbr. articles to profl. jours. Served as sgt. Korean Army, 1962-65. Recipient Merit prize Suwon Edn. Assn., 1982, Ajou U., 1984. Mem. Korean Math. Soc., Korea Info. Sci. Soc., Am. Math. Soc., Soc. Indsl. and Applied Maths., Soc. Math. Appliquées Industrielles. Presbyterian. Home: Hangang Hyundai Apt 9-304, Huksok 2-dong Tongjak-ku, 156-072 Seoul Republic of Korea Office: Ajou U, Wonchun-Dong, 440-749 Suwon Republic of Korea

KIMPEL, BENJAMIN FRANKLIN, emeritus philosophy educator, writer; b. Racine, Wis., May 9, 1905; s. Benjamin F. and Agnes (Beltz) K. B.A., U. Wis., 1926; fellow anthropology, U. Nebr., 1927-28; Ph.D. (Tew fellow), Yale U., 1932. Ordained to ministry Am. Unitarian Assn., 1937; mem. faculty Kans. Wesleyan U., 1933-36, prof. philosophy, 1935-36; prof. philosophy Drew U., 1938-72, prof. emeritus, 1972—. Author: Religious Faith, Language, and Knowledge, 1952, Faith and Moral Authority, 1953, Symbols of Religious Faith, 1954, Moral Principles in the Bible, 1956, Language and Religion, 1957, Principles of Moral Philosophy, 1960, Kant's Critical Philosophy, 1964, Hegel's Philosophy of History, 1964, Nietzsche's Beyond Good and Evil, 1964, Schopenhauer's Philosophy, 1965, Philosophy of Zen Buddhism, 1966, Philosophies of Life of the Ancient Greeks and Israelites: An analysis of their parallels, 1981, Emily Dickinson as Philosopher, 1981, A Philosophy of the Religions of Ancient Greeks and Israelites, 1983, Stoic Moral Philosophies: Their Counsel for Today, 1984, Moral Philosophies in the Plays by Shakespeare, 1984. Mem. AAUP, Am. Philos. Assn., Beta Beta Beta, Kappa Pi, Pi Gamma Mu, Psi Chi, Phi Sigma Tau, Sigma Phi. Home: North Bennington VT 05257

KIMPORT, DAVID LLOYD, lawyer; b. Hot Springs, S.D., Nov. 28, 1945; s. Ralph E. and Ruth N. (Hutchinson) K.; m. Barbara H. Buggert, Apr. 2, 1976; children—Katrina Elizabeth, Rebecca Helen, Susanna Ruth. A.B. summa cum laude, Bowdoin Coll., 1968; postgrad. Imperial Coll., U. London, 1970-71; J.D., Stanford U., 1975. Bar: Calif. 1975, U.S. Supreme Ct. 1978. Assoc. Baker & McKenzie, San Francisco, 1975-82, ptnr., 1982—. Active San Francisco Planning and Urban Research, 1978—, Commonwealth Club of Calif., 1984—, The Family, 1987—. Served with U.S. Army, 1968-70. Decorated Bronze Star; Fulbright grantee, 1970. Mem. ABA, San Francisco Bar Assn., Phi Beta Kappa. Democrat. Episcopalian. Office: Baker & McKenzie Two Embarcadero Ctr San Francisco CA 94111

KIMURA, TSUTO, architectural design company executive; b. Tokyo, Okubo Shinjuku-ku, Japan, Aug. 15, 1933; s. Norio Honda and Chyo (Kimura) K.; m. Sachiko Sekine, Nov. 10, 1961; children: Takeshi, Sigeru, Shuzo. BS in Architecture, Waseda U., 1958; MArch, U. Ill., 1967. Asst. Waseda U., Tokyo, 1958-60; architect Sta. NHK-TV Broadcasting Ctr., Tokyo, 1960-65; pres. Tsuto Kimura Architects & Assocs., Tokyo, 1968—; research and teaching asst. U. Ill., 1965-67, Waseda U., Tokyo, 1968-77. Prin. works include NHK-TV Broadcasting Complex Bldg., Kamakura Rojuman. Recipient Murano prize Waseda U. Archtl. Dept., 1958, 1st prize Internat. Design Competition, Perugia, Italy, 1971, 3d prize Internat. Design Competition, Vienna, Austria, 1971. Mem. Machida City Planning Deliveration, Koganei City Planning Deliveration, Japan Inst. Architecture, Archtl. Inst. Japan. Office: Tsuto Kimura Architect & Assocs, 6F Plaza Shinoju, 168 Shinjuku Japan also: Mauna Lani Resort Point Condo F-201 Kohala Coast HI 96743

KINCAID, EUGENE D., III, lawyer; b. Uvalde, Tex., Mar. 7, 1941; s. Eugene D. and Lochie M. (Mundine) K. B.A., Baylor U., 1962; J.D., U. Tex.-Austin, 1966. Bar: Tex. 1966. Briefing atty. Tex. Ct. Criminal Appeals, 1967-68; asst. city atty. San Antonio, 1969; atty. Tex. Water Rights Commn., Austin, 1970-71; sole practice, Uvalde, 1971—. exec. v.p. EDK Ranches Inc., AVK Ranch Co. Chmn. Uvalde Housing Authority, 1972-80; mem. Uralde Arts Council. Mem. State Bar of Tex., Border Dist. Bar Assn., Uvalde County Bar Assn. (pres. 1972), Magna Charta Barons, San Antonio Mus. Assn., Pi Sigma Alpha, Sigma Delta Pi. Republican. Anglican. Clubs: Uvalde Country. Office: 243 N Getty PO Box 1769 Uvalde TX 78801

KIND, KENNETH WAYNE, lawyer, real estate broker; b. Missoula, Mont., Apr. 1, 1948; s. Joseph Bruce and Elinor Joy (Smith) K.; m. Diane Lucille Jozaitis, Aug. 28, 1971; children: Kirstin Amber, Kenneth Warner. B.A., Calif. State U.-Northridge, 1973; J.D., Calif. Western U., 1976. Bar: Calif. 1976, U.S. Dist. Ct. (ea. dist.) Calif. 1976. Mem. celebrity security staff Brownstone Am., Beverly Hills, Calif., 1970-76; tchr. Army and Navy Acad., Carlsbad, Calif., 1975-76; real estate broker, Bakersfield, Calif., 1978—; sole practice, Bakersfield, 1976—; lectr. mechanic's lien laws, Calif., 1983—. Staff writer Calif. Western Law Jour., 1975. Served as sgt. U.S. Army, 1967-70. Mem. ABA, VFW, Nat. Order Barristers. Libertarian. Office: 1715 Chester Ave Suite 300 Bakersfield CA 93301

KINDEL, JAMES HORACE, JR., lawyer; b. Los Angeles, Nov. 8, 1913; s. James Horace and Philipina (Butte) K.; children: William, Mary, Robert, John. A.B., UCLA, 1934; LL.B., Loyola U., Los Angeles, 1940. Bar: Calif. 1941; C.P.A., Calif. Pvt. legal practice Kindel & Anderson, Los Angeles, Woodland Hills and Newport Beach, Calif., 1945—; ret. partner Coopers-Lybrand; officer, dir., part-owner R.J. Noble Co. (road and asphalt contractors), Orange, Calif., 1950—; part-owner sand and gravel and poultry bus., Guatemala; part owner Sunnymead Poultry Ranch, Calif., Tex. Trustee UCLA Found. Mem. ABA, Los Angeles Bar Assn., Orange County Bar

Assn., State Bar Calif., Am. Inst. C.P.A.s, Phi Delta Phi, Theta Xi. Clubs: Chancery, California (Los Angeles); Reform (London). Home: 800 W 1st 2405 Los Angeles CA 90012 Office: 555 S Flower St Los Angeles CA 90071 also: 1301 Dove St Suite 1050 Newport Beach CA 92660

KINDRICK, ROBERT LEROY, academic administrator, educator; b. Kansas City, Mo., Aug. 17, 1942; s. Robert William and Waneta LeVeta (Lobdell) K.; B.A., Park Coll., 1964; M.A., U. Mo., Kansas City, 1967; Ph.D., U. Tex., 1971; m. Carolyn Jean Reed, Aug. 20, 1965. Instr., Central Mo. State U., Warrenburg, 1967-69, asst. prof., 1969-73, assoc. prof., 1973-78, prof. English, 1978-80, head dept. English, 1975-80; dean Coll. Arts and Scis., also prof. English, Western Ill. U., Macomb, 1980-84; v.p. acad. affairs, prof. English, Emporia State U., Kans., 1984-87; provost, v.p. academic affairs, prof. English, Eastern Ill. U., Charleston, 1987—. Chmn. bd. dirs. Mo. Com. for Humanities, 1979-80. Pres. Park Coll. Young Dems., 1963; v.p. Mo. Young Dems., Jefferson City, 1964; campus coordinator United Way, Macomb, Ill., 1983; mem. study com. Emporia Arts Council, 1985-86. U. Tex. fellow, 1965-66; Am. Council Learned Socs. travel grantee, 1975; Nat. Endowment for Humanities summer fellow, 1977; Mediaeval Acad. Am. grantee, 1976; Mo. Com. Humanities grantee, 1975-84; Assn. Scottish Lit. Studies grantee, 1979. Mem. Mo. Assn. Depts. English (pres. 1978-80), Mo. Philological Assn. (founding pres. 1975-77), Medieval Assn. Midwest (councillor 1977—, ex officio bd. 1980—, v.p. 1987-88, exec. sec. 1988—), Ill. Medieval Assn. (founding exec. sec. 1983—), Mid-Am. Medieval Assn., Rocky Mountain MLA, Assn. Scottish Lt. Studies, Early English Text Soc., Société Rencesvals, Medieval Acad. N.Am. (exec. sec. com. on ctrs. and regional assns.), Internat. Arthurian Soc., Sigma Tau Delta, Phi Kappa Phi. Club: Rotary (editor Warrensburg club). Author: Robert Henryson, 1980; A New Classical Rhetoric, 1980; editor: Teaching the Middle Ages, 1981—; editor Studies in Medieval and Renaissance Teaching, 1975-80; contbr. articles to profl. jours. Home: 400 S 6th Mattoon IL 61938 Office: Eastern Ill U Office of Provost Old Main St Charleston IL 61920

KINDS, HERBERT E(UGENE), educator; b. Cleve., Feb. 25, 1933; s. Levander and Esther (Johnson) K. B.S. (Tyng scholar), Williams Coll., 1951-55; postgrad. Harvard U., 1955-58, Case Western Res. U., 1972, 80-81, LHD (hon.) Natchez Jr. Coll., 1968. Instr. Natchez (Miss.) Jr. Coll., 1958-68, registrar, 1967, dean, 1968; tchr. Cleve. Pub. Schs., 1968—; owner Kinds Tutorial Service, 1972—; instr. med. sci. Cuyahoga Community Coll., 1975-81, instr. chemistry. Deacon Mt. Herodon Bapt. Ch.; mem. Cleve. City Club, 1968, Comdr.'s Club for Disabled Am. Vets.; nat. assoc. Smithsonian Instn. Named one of Outstanding Young Men of Am., 1967. Mem. Math. Assn. Am., Am. Chem. Soc., Am. Fedn. Tchrs., Cleve. Mus. Art, Internat. Platform Assn., The World of Poetry, Case Western Reserve U. (fellow), Phi Beta Kappa. Clubs: Williams of N.Y., Williams of Northeastern Ohio. Home: 9023 Columbia Ave Cleveland OH 44108

KINDT, JOHN WARREN, lawyer, educator, legal and managerial consultant; b. Oak Park, Ill., May 24, 1950; s. Warren Frederick and Lois Jeannette (Woelffer) K.; m. Anne Marie Johnson, Apr. 17, 1982. AB, Coll. William and Mary, 1972; JD, U. Ga., 1976, MBA, 1977; LLM, U. Va., 1978, SJD, 1981. Bar: D.C. 1976, Ga. 1976, Va. 1977. Advisor to Gov. of Va., 1971-72; congl. asst. to Congressman M. Caldwell Butler, 1972-73; cons. White House staff, 1976-77; asst. prof. U. Ill., 1978-81, assoc. prof., 1981-85, prof., 1985—; cons. 3d UN Conf. on Law of the Sea; lectr. U. Ill. Exec. MBA Program. Author: Marine Pollution and the Law of the Sea, 4 vols., 1986; contbr. articles to profl. jours. Caucus chmn., del. White House Conf. on Youth, 1970; co-chmn. Va. Gov.'s Adv. Council on Youth, 1971; mem. Athens (Ga.) Legal Aid Soc., 1975-76. Rotary fellow, 1979-80; Smithsonian ABA/ELI scholar, 1981; sr. fellow London Sch. of Econs., 1985-86. Mem. Am. Soc. Internat. Law, Assn. Trial Lawyers Am., ABA, D.C. Bar Assn., Va. Bar Assn., Ga. Bar Assn., Environ. Law Soc. Home: 801 N Brookside Ln Mahomet IL 61853 Office: U Ill 1206 S 6th St 350 Commerce West Champaign IL 61820

KING, ALGIN BRADDY, college dean, marketing educator; b. Latta, S.C., Jan. 19, 1926; s. Dewey Algin and Elizabeth (Braddy) K.; m. Joyce Heisick, Aug. 21, 1976; children: Drucilla Ratcliff, Martha Louise. B.A. in Retailing and Polit. Sci. (W.T. Grant Retailing scholar) cum laude, U. S.C., 1947; M.S., NYU, 1953; Ph.D., Ohio State U., 1966. Exec. trainee Sears, Roebuck & Co., 1948-48; instr. retailing U. S.C., 1948-51; chief econ. analysis br. dist. OPS, 1951-53; exec. dir. Columbia (S.C.) Mchts. Assn., 1953-54; asst. prof. Tex. A&M U., 1954-55; mem. faculty Coll. William and Mary, 1955-72, prof. bus. adminstrn., 1959-72, dir. Bur. Bus. Research, 1959-63, assoc. dean Sch. Bus. Adminstrn., 1968-72; prof., dean Sch. Bus., Central Conn. State Coll., Avon, 1972-73; prof., head dept. bus. and econs. James Madison U., 1973-74; prof., dean Sch. Bus., Western Carolina U., Cullowhee, 1974-76; prof. mktg. and mgmt. Christopher Newport Coll., Newport News, Va., 1976—, dean sch. bus. adminstrn. and econs., 1977-87; chmn. dept. mktg., sch. bus. and econs. Towson State U., 1987—; pres. Bus. and Adminstrv. Cons. Ltd. (mgmt. and mktg. cons.); teaching asst. Ohio State U., 1963-64; professorial lectr. George Washington U.; mgmt. cons. CSC, U.S. Army. Author: (with others) Hampton Waterfront Economic Study, 1967, The Source Book of Economics, 1973, Management Perceptions, 1976; also chpts. in books, articles. Mem. finance resource group Conn. Council Higher Edn., 1972-73; mem. U.S. Senatorial Bus. Adv. Bd. Mem. U.S. Sales and Mktg. Execs. Club, Am. Marketing Assn., Acad. Mgmt., Am. Inst. Decision Scis., Phi Beta Kappa. Independent. Methodist. Lodges: Masons, Rotary.

KING, ARNOLD KIMSEY, JR., clergyman, nursing home executive; b. Durham, N.C., May 7, 1931; s. Arnold Kimsey and Edna May (Coates) K.; m. Marjorie Jean Fisher, June 22, 1952; children: Leslie Diane, Carole Jean, Arnold Kimsey III, Julia Paige. BA, U. N.C., 1955; M in Divinity, Duke U., 1959; DD, Am. Bible Inst., 1971. Ordained deacon Methodist Ch., 1956, elder, 1959; lic. hotel adminstr., nursing home adminstr. N.C. Enlisted U.S. Air Force, 1951, served as staff sgt., various assignments in psychol. training, bus. adminstrn., mgmt.; minister, organizer Aldersgate Methodist Ch., Chapel Hill, N.C., 1955-61; assoc. pastor Edenton St. Methodist Ch., Raleigh, N.C., 1961-64; pastor Ahoskie (N.C.) United Methodist Ch., 1964-70; pastor Woodland (N.C.) United Methodist Ch., 1970-74; sec. N.C. Annual Conf., United Methodist Ch., Raleigh, 1972-74; asst. adminstr. Methodist Retirement Homes Inc., Durham, 1974-75, adminstr., Durham, 1975-88; statistician, pub. N.C. Ann. Conf. of United Meth. Ch., 1988—; bd. dirs. Equity Homes Inc., Equity Retirement Housing, Marriott Vacation Resorts, Marriott's Swallowtail at Sea Pines; vis. prof. Methodist studies Southeastern Bapt. Theol. Sem., Wake Forest, N.C. Mem. N.C. Commn. on Health Services Mem. Young Democrats Club, N.C. Gov.'s Com. on Aging, United Fund, Am. Cancer Soc.; councilman Town of Woodland, 1972-74; trustee, mem. exec. com. Goodwill Industries, Durham, 1974-78; theol. adv. to UN Internat. Yr. of Handicapped. Named Tar Heel of Week, Raleigh (N.C.) News and Observer, 1969. Mem. N.C. Bd. Examiners of Nursing Home Adminstrs., N.C. Hist. Assn. (past pres. United Methodist Conf.), Am. Acad. Med. Adminstrn., Am. Coll. Health Care Adminstrs., Am. Assn. Non-Profit Homes for Aging, N.C. Assn. Non-Profit Homes for Aging, Am. Hotel and Motel Assn., Paralyzed Vets. Am., Nat. Paraplegia Found., Methodist Found., N.C. Conf. Bd. Ministerial Tng. and Qualifications, N.C. Conf. Bd. Evangelism (past pres., v.p.), Mensa, Lambda Chi Alpha. Lodges: Kiwanis, Rotary, Optimists, Masons, Shriners. Contbr. to U.S. Air Force manuals; contbr. articles to profl. jours.; contbr. N.C. Christian Advocate Weekly, 1973—; lectr. to profl. confs. Home: 5315 Yardley Terr Durham NC 27707

KING, CHARLES ROSS, physician; b. Nevada, Iowa, Aug. 22, 1925; s. Carl Russell and Dorothy Sarah (Mills) K.; m. Frances Pamela Carter, Jan. 8, 1949; children—Deborah Diane, Carter Ross, Charles Conrad, Corbin Kent. Student, Butler U., 1943; B.S. in Bus., Ind. U., 1948, M.D., 1964. Diplomate Am. Bd. Family Practice. Dep. dir. Ind. Pub. Works and Supply, 1949-52; salesman Knox Coal Corp., 1952-59; rotating intern Marion County Gen. Hosp., Indpls., 1964-65; family practice medicine Anderson, Ind., 1965—; sec.-treas. staff Community Hosp., 1969-72, pres. elect, dir., chief medicine, 1973—, bd. dirs., 1973-75; sec.-treas. St. John's Hosp., 1968-69, chief medicine, 1972-73, chief pediatrics, 1977—; dir. Rolling Hills Convalescent Ctr., 1968-73; pres. Profl. Ctr. Lab., 1965—; vice chmn. Madison County Bd. Health, 1966-69, chmn., 1986—; chmn. bd. dirs. First Nat. Bank Madison County, Anderson. Bd. dirs. Family Service Madison County, 1968-69, Madison County Assn. Mentally Retarded, 1972-76; chmn. bd. dirs. Anderson Downtown Devel. Corp., 1980—. Served with AUS, 1944-46. Recipient Dr. James Macholtz award Spl. Olympics, 1986—. Fellow Royal Soc. Health, Am. Acad. Family Practice (charter); mem. AMA (Physician's Recognition award 1969, 72, 75, 78, 81, 84, 87), Ind. Med. Assn., Pan Am. Med. Assn., Am. Acad. Gen. Practice, Madison County Med. Soc. (pres. 1970), 8th Dist. Med. Soc. (sec.-treas. 1968), Anderson C. of C. (bd. dirs. 1979-82), Indpls. Mus. Art (corp. mem.), Phi Delta Theta (pres. Alumni Assn. 1952), Phi Chi. Methodist. Club: Anderson Country (bd. dirs. 1976-79). Home: 920 N Madison Ave Anderson IN 46011 Office: 1933 Chase St Anderson IN 46014

KING, CHARLES THOMAS, ret. educator; b. Coatsville, Pa., July 19, 1911; s. John Henry and Estella (Orr) K.; B.S., West Chester State Coll., 1932; Ed.M., Temple U., 1944; Ed.D., Rutgers U., 1957; m. Dorothy Eckman, Nov. 30, 1933; children—Marilyn Mae, Kenneth Alan, Donald Edwin. Tchr., West Pottsgorve Twp. Sch., Stowe, Pa., 1933-35, Haverford Twp. Sch., Havertown, Pa., 1935-38; dir. elem. health and phys. edn. Havertown Twp. Sch., 1938-42; prin. Llanerch Sch., Havertown, 1942-45; supervising prin. West Pottsgrove Twp. Sch., 1945-47; prin. Glenwood and Short Hills Schs., Millburn, N.J., 1947-51; asst. to supt., 1951-59, asst. supt., 1959-62, supt., 1962-74; mem. state adv. council on Handicapped 1968-72; mem. state cert. appeals com., 1972-74. Pres., Millburn (N.J.) Community Council, 1954-56; bd. dirs. Millburn Public Library, 1962-74; chmn. N.J. Council Econ. Edn., 1972-74. Mem. Essex County Supts. Roundtable (chmn. 1965-66), Phi Delta Kappa (emeritus; chpt. pres. 1959-60), West Chester State Coll. Alumni Assn. (chpt. pres. 1981-83; Disting. Alumni award 1982). Congregationalist (deacon). Club: Rotary (pres. 1957-58). Home: 115 Hobart Ave Short Hills NJ 07078

KING, EMMETT ALONZO, III, business executive insurance consultant; b. Norfolk, Va., June 9, 1942; s. Emmett S. and Mary Lee (Sutton) K.; m. Yvonne J. Bullock, Apr. 5, 1965 (div. 1979); children: Andre, Jacqueline; m. Yvonne Levelle Kier, Oct. 19, 1980; stepchildren: Richard, Roland. Student, Mary-Hardin-Baylor Coll., 1967, Coll. of Ins., 1971. Benefits rep. EBS Mgmt. Cons., Inc., N.Y.C., 1968; sr. group adminstr. group ins. sales office Conn. Gen. Life Ins. Co., N.Y.C., 1968-70; successively group adminstr., account exec., asst. v.p., v.p., mgr. employee benefits dept. Bayly, Martin & Fay, Inc., N.Y.C., 1971-83; sr. cons., nat. account exec. Graycliffe Associates, Inc., N.Y.C., 1983-84; account exec. Hartford Ins. Cos., N.Y.C., 1984-86; nat. account exec., sr. cons. GAB Bus. Services, Inc., Parsippany, 1986-88; dir. mktg. Total Plan Adminstrs., Inc., Cranford, N.J., 1988—; vis. lectr. Princeton U.; 3-time judge Ala. Jr. Miss. Program; hon. trooper Ala. State. Charter mem. Tri-W Black Families, Inc., 1979—. Served with U.S. Army 1961-67. Named hon. Ala. state trooper. Mem. Nat. Ins. Industry Assn. (charter), 100 Black Men Inc., Am. Spl. Risks Assn., Group Ins. Assn. Greater N.Y., Self Ins. Inst. Am., N.Y.C. C. of C. Office: Total Plan Adminstrs Inc 14 Commerce Dr Cranford NJ 07016

KING, ERIKA IRENE, painter, specialist in collage; b. Phila., May 8, 1942; d. Ernest R. and Hildegard (Saul) Herbster; m. William Donald King, Aug. 17, 1972 (div. June 1978). Student Earlham Coll., 1960-62, Kunst Gewerbeschule, Lucerne, Switzerland, 1962-63, Ecole des Beaux Arts, Paris, 1963-64. Dir., Grove House Art Gallery, Miami, Fla., 1972-74; ptnr., dir. Miller and King Gallery, Miami, 1974-77; art columnist Lowe Mus. Mag., 1982-85; represented by galleries and art cons., N.Y.C., Miami, Chgo., Detroit, Atlanta, Washington, Boston, Dallas, 1977-85. One-man shows include Galeria El Bosco, Madrid, 1966, Woodstock Gallery, London, 1967; exhibited in group shows N.Y.C., San Francisco, Miami, New Orleans, Chgo., Caracas, Washington, Atlanta, 1970-85; represented in numerous pub. and pvt. collections. Mem. Artists Speak for Peace, Miami, bd. dirs. Mets., Coral Gables, Fla., 1977-80, Lowe Mus., 1980-82. Mem. Met. Mus. and Art Ctrs (various art awards), Miami Ctr. for Fine Arts, Whitney Mus. Am. Art., Nat. Found. Women in Arts. Democrat. Clubs: Grove Isle, Ensign Bitters (Coconut Grove, Fla.). Avocations: foreign languages; boating. Home and office: Box 715 Coconut Grove FL 33133

KING, FRANCIS HENRY, novelist; b. Adelboden, Switzerland, Mar. 3, 1923; s. Eustace Arthur Cecil and Faith Mina (Read) K. M.A., Oxford U., 1948. Drama critic Sunday Telegraph, London, 1978—. Author: To the Dark Tower, 1946; Never Again, 1947; An Air That Kills, 1948; The Dividing Stream (Somerset Maugham award), 1951; The Dark Glasses, 1954; The Widow, 1957, The Man on the Rock, 1957, So Hurt and Humiliated, 1959; The Custom House, 1961; The Japanese Umbrella (Katherine Mansfield Short Story prize), 1964; The Last of the Pleasure Gardens, 1965; The Waves Behind the Boat, 1967; The Brighton Belle, 1968; A Domestic Animal, 1970; Flights, 1973; A Game of Patience, 1974; The Needle, 1975; Hard Feelings, 1976; Danny Hill, 1977; The Action, 1978; Indirect Method, 1980; Act of Darkness, 1983; Voices in an Empty Room, 1984; One is a Wanderer, 1985, Frozen Music, 1987, The Woman Who Was God, 1988; (poetry) Rod of Incantation, 1952; (biography) E.M. Forster and His World, 1978; gen. editor: Introducing Greece, 1956; Japan, 1970. Decorated comdr. Brit. Empire. Fellow Royal Soc. Lit.; mem. Soc. Authors Internat. PEN (pres. 1986—). Office: Sunday Telegraph, 181 Marsh Wall, London E14 9SR, England

KING, GEORGE RALEIGH, manufacturing company executive; b. Benton Harbor, Mich., May 13, 1931; s. Maurice Peter and Opal Ruth (Hart) King; m. Phyllis Stratton, Apr. 10, 1950; children—Paula King Zang, Angela King Moleski, Philip. Student Adrian Coll., 1950-51. Cert. purchasing profl. exec. status. With Kirsch Co., Sturgis, Mich., 1951—, data processing trainee, 1951-53, data processing mgr., 1953-59, asst. purchasing agt., 1959-62, purchasing agt., 1962-68, asst. dir. purchasing, 1968-71, dir. purchasing, 1971—. Author: Rods & Rings, 1972. Elder, 1st Presbyterian Ch., Sturgis, 1970; pres. Sturgis Civic Players, 1972. Recipient citation Boy Scouts Am., 1966, Jr. Achievement, 1967; nominated candidate for adminstr. Fed. Procurement Policy, Reagan Adminstrn., Washington, 1980. Mem. Am. Purchasing Soc. (pres. 1979-81), Nat. Assn. Purchasing Mgmt., Southwestern Purchasing Assn. Clubs: Klinger Lake Country, Exchange (pres. Sturgis 1959, dist. gov. dist and nat. clubs 1961). Masons, Elks. Home: 906 S Lakeview Sturgis MI 49091 Office: Kirsch Co 309 N Prospect St Sturgis MI 49091

KING, GUNDAR JULIAN, educational administrator; b. Riga, Latvia, Apr. 19, 1926; came to U.S., 1950, naturalized, 1954; s. Attis K. and Austra (Dale) Kenins: m. Valda K. Andersons, Sept. 18, 1954; children—John T., Marita A. Student, J.W. Goethe U., Frankfurt, Germany, 1946-48; BBA, U. Oreg., 1956; MBA, Stanford U., 1958. Asst. field supr. Internat. Refugee Orgn., Frankfurt, 1948-50; br. office mfr. Williams Form Engrng. Corp., Portland, Oreg., 1952-54; project mgr. Market Research Assocs., Palo Alto, Calif., 1958-60; asst. prof., assoc. prof. Pacific Lutheran U., 1960-66, prof., 1966—, dean Sch. Bus. Adminstrn., 1970—; vis. prof. mgmt. U.S. Naval Postgrad. Sch., 1971-72, San Francisco State U., 1980, 87-88. Author: Economic Policies in Occupied Latvia, 1965. Contbr. articles to profl. publs. Mem. Gov.'s Com. on Reorgn. Wash. State Govt., 1965—; mem. study group on pricing U.S. Commn. Govt. Procurement, 1971-72; pres. N.W. Univs. Bus. Adminstrn. Conf., 1965-66. Served with AUS, 1950-52. Fulbright-Hayes scholar Thailand, 1988. Mem. AAUP (past chpt. pres.), Am. Mktg. Assn. (past chpt. pres.), Assn. Advancement Baltic Studies (pres. 1970), Western Assn. Collegiate Schs. Bus. (pres. 1971-71), Alpha Kappa Psi, Beta Gamma Sigma. Home: PO Box 44401 Parkland WA 98444 Office: Pacific Lutheran U Tacoma WA 98447

KING, HENRY HAYES, JR., holding company executive; b. Shreveport, La., July 12, 1932; s. Henry Hayes and Vashti Estell (Bullock) K.; m. Beverly Ann Farmer, June 16, 1956; children: Beverly Lynn, Thomas Bradford, David Earl. B.A., La. State U., 1956; postgrad., South Tex. Coll. Law, 1962; grad., Advanced Mgmt. Program, Harvard U. Grad. Sch. Bus., 1976. With Tex. Eastern Transmission Corp., Houston, 1958-76, dir. employee relations, 1971-72, dir. pub. relations, 1972-73, gen. mgr. human relations, 1973-74, gen. mgr. corp. adminstrv. staff, 1974, v.p. corp. adminstrv. staff, 1974-76; v.p. adminstrn. Tex. Eastern Corp., Houston, 1976-80, sr. v.p., chief adminstrv. officer, 1980-82, exec. v.p., 1982-84, pres., chief operating officer, 1984-87, vice chmn. bd., also dir.; dir. Tex. Commerce Bancshares. Bd. dirs. Jr. Achievement, Greater Houston Conv. and Visitors Council, Tex. Research League, Bus. Council for Internat. Understanding, Assocs. Harvard Bus. Sch., Mus. Fine Arts, Pvt. Sector Initiatives, Houston Grand Opera, Gas Research Inst.; chmn. Jr. Achievement Southeast Tex. Served to capt., inf. U.S. Army, 1956-58. Mem. Am. Compensation Assn., Am. Mgmt. Assn., Am. Soc. Personnel Adminstrn., Houston Personnel Assn., Interstate Natural Gas Assn. Am., Public Relations Soc. Am., La. State U. Found., Rice U. Assocs., Houston C. of C. Republican. Methodist. Clubs: Astrodome, Houston, Houston Ctr., Harvard Bus. Sch. of Houston. Office: Tex Eastern Transmission Corp 1 Houston Ctr PO Box 2521 Houston TX 77252 *

KING, JACK A., lawyer; b. Lafayette, Ind., July 29, 1936; s. Noah C. and Mabel E. (Pierce) K.; m. Mary S. King, Dec. 10, 1960; children—Jeffrey A., Janice D., Julie D. B.S. in Fin., Ind. U., Bloomington, 1958, J.D., 1961. Bar: Ind. 1961. Ptnr. Ball, Eggleston, King & Bumbleburg, Lafayette, 1961-70; judge Superior Ct. 2 of Tippecanoe County (Ind.), 1970-78; assoc. gen. counsel Dairyland Ins. Co., 1978, v.p. and assoc. gen. counsel, 1979, v.p., gen. counsel and asst. sec., 1980-85; v.p. and counsel Sentry Ctr. West, 1981-85; asst. gen. counsel Sentry Corp., 1979-85; v.p., gen. counsel, and asst. sec. Gt. S.W. Fire Ins. Co., 1980-85, Gt. S.W. Surplus Lines Ins. Co., 1981-85; v.p. and gen. counsel Dairyland County Mut. Ins. Co. Tex., 1980-85; v.p.-legal and asst. sec. Scottsdale Ins. Co. and Nat. Casualty Co., 1985—; bd. dirs. Ariz. Joint Underwriting Plan, 1978-81, mem. exec. com., 1980-81; mem. Ariz. Property & Casualty Ins. Commn., 1985-86, vice chmn., 1986; mem. Ariz. Study Commn. on Ins., 1986-87. Bd. dirs. Scottsdale (Ariz.) Art Ctr. Assn., 1981-84. Mem. ABA, Ind. Bar Assn., Maricopa County Bar Assn. Cons.: The Law of Competitive Business Practices, 2d edit. Office: 8370 E Via de Ventura Scottsdale AZ 85258

KING, JAMES LAWRENCE, JR., mathematics educator; b. Detroit, Mar. 20, 1935; s. James Lawrence and Olive Lenore (Vibbard) K.; m. Gloria Herrera; 1 child, Gloria Lynn. BS in Physics, Wayne State U., 1960, BS in Math., 1962, MA in Math. Stats., 1965, postgrad. First aid medic Great Lakes Steel, Ecorse, Mich., 1956-65; instr. Wayne State U., Detroit, 1960-62, 65; sci., math. tchr. Yeshivath Beth Yehudah Schs., 1960-65; sr. mathematician Gen. Motors Corp., Warren, Mich., 1965-67; tchr. math., sci. Los Angeles Unified Schs., 1967-68; prof. math., student advisor Los Angeles S.W. Coll., 1968—; numismatist, 1974—. Bass-baritone concert choir Wayne State U., 1956-64. Served with USN, 1952-56, USNR, 1956-64. Grantee NSF, 1969. Mem. Am. Numismatic Assn. (cert.), Nat. Geographic Soc., Math. Assn. Am. Republican. Club: Interval Internat. Time Share. Office: Los Angeles SW Coll 1600 W Imperial Hwy Los Angeles CA 90047

KING, JOSEPH CLEMENT, physician, health care management consultant; b. Colorado Springs, Colo., Aug. 20, 1922; s. Charles Clement and Gladys (Ascher) K.; B.S., Tulane U., 1944, M.D., 1946; m. Margie Freudenthal Leopold, Apr. 2, 1947; children—Leopold Ascher, Jocelyn King Tobias. Instr. zoology Tulane U., 1941-42; rotating intern Michael Reese Hosp., Chgo., 1946-47, resident in internal medicine, 1947-50; assoc. with Dr. Sidney Portis, Chgo., 1950-51; practice medicine specializing in internal medicine, Chgo., 1953-77, Palm Springs, Calif., 1977-79; attending staff Louis A. Weiss Hosp., Chgo., 1953-77, hon. staff, 1979—; attending staff Desert Hosp., 1977-79; med. dir. Life Extension Inst., Chgo., 1979-80; dir. employee health services Continental Ill. Nat. Bank, Chgo., 1980-87; exec. cons. health care mgmt. Coopers & Lybrand, Chgo., 1987-88; asst. to assoc. clin. prof. internal medicine Northwestern U. Med. Sch., Chgo., 1954-67; clin. asst. prof. medicine Abraham Lincoln Sch. Medicine U. Ill., 1973-77; clin. asst. prof. preventive medicine and community health Northwestern U. Med. Sch., 1980—; asst. prof. preventive medicine Rush Med. Coll., 1986—. Served to capt. M.C., AUS, 1944-46, 1951-53. Diplomate Am. Bd. Internal Medicine. Fellow ACP, Am. Occupational Med. Assn.; mem. Chgo. Soc. Internal Medicine, Chgo. Med. Soc., Am., Ill., Riverside County, Calif. med. assns., Am. Heart Assn., Chgo. Heart Assn. (bd. govs.), Am. Rheumatism Assn., Assn. Bank Med. Dirs., Am. Cancer Soc. (v.p. Chgo. unit), Cen. States Acad. Occupational Medicine, Am. Occupational Med. Assn. (bd. govs.), Tulane Med. Alumni Assn. (past dir.), Medic Alert (mem. midwest adv. bd.), Chgo. Assn. Commerce and Industry (mem. occupational medicine com.), Ill. State C. of C. (health care cost mgmt. task force), Phi Beta Kappa, Beta Mu, Alpha Omega Alpha. Club: Med. Dirs. Chgo. (past pres.). Contbr. numerous articles in field to med. jours. Office: 10524 Sunningdale Dr Rancho Mirage CA 92270

KING, JOSEPH JERONE, association executive; b. Spokane, Wash., Sept. 27, 1910, s. Joseph Jerone and Alice (Halferty) K., B.A. with gr. distinction, Stanford U., 1935; M.A., Duke U., 1937; m. Irma Kathleen Martin, Aug. 22, 1937; children—Sally Jo (Mrs. John S. Thompson), Nikki Sue (Mrs. Dennis Ring), Cindy Lou (Mrs. Richard Mullen). Instr. econs. Black Mountain Coll., 1937-38; numerous adminstrv. positions Farm Security Adminstrn., U.S. Dept. Agriculture, Portland, 1939-51; Oreg. state dir. Christian Rural Overseas Program, 1950-51; sr. civilian for indsl. relations Puget Sound Naval Shipyard, 1951-58; public affairs dir. Assn. Wash. Industries, Olympia, 1958-78, exec. cons., 1978—; Western mgr. Inst. Applied Econs., 1981—. Mem. President's Assos., Central Wash. U., mem. Gov.'s Council for Reorg. Wash. State Govt.; mem. adv. council Coll. Edn. Washington State U.; dir. manpower Statewide Public Edn. Mgmt. Survey; mem. Gov.'s Commn. on Employment of Physically Handicapped; mem. adv. council, dept. econs. and bus. adminstrn. Central Wash. U., 1973—, Coll. of Edn., mem. exec. com. Rural Edn. Ctr.; mem. profl. edn. adv. council Wash. State Dept. Public Instrn., 1977—, chmn. community edn. adv. council, 1981—; chmn. adv. com. for Anderson Landing Wildlife Project, Kitsap County (Wash.) Bd. Commrs.; pres. bd. State-Wide Project Bus. Liaison with Edn.; mem. Spokane Bd. Scholastic Excellence: bd. dirs. Paul Linder Found. for Edn. in Cen. Kitsap, Spokane Bus. Assisting Scholastic Excellence, Moses Lake Agrl. Edn. Found. Served with USAAF, 1944. Recipient Outstanding Service awards DAV, Assn. Wash. Bus., Golden Bell award Washington Assn. Sch. Adminstrs.; named hon. citizen City of Vancouver (Wash.), hon. Wash. adm., hon. Wash. gen. Mem. Am. Soc. Pub. Adminstrn., Am. Legion (hon. life mem.), Phi Beta Kappa, Pi Gamma Mu. Clubs: Washington Athletic, Kitsap Country, Elks, Masons (Shriner). Author: Winning, Printings, 1961. Home: Ioka Beach-Hood Canal 11655 Ioka Way NW Silverdale WA 98383

KING, PETER TIAN-LUNG, physician; b. Shanghai, Republic of China, May 9, 1947; arrived in Hong Kong, 1958.; s. Gordon S. and Sunny (Moh) K. BS, Fordham U., N.Y.C., 1970; MD, Temple U., Phila., 1974. Diplomate Am. Bd. Internal Med., Am. Bd. Internal Med. subspecialty Cardiovascular Diseases. Intern Pacific Med. Ctr., San Francisco, 1974-75; resident UCLA and VA Med. Ctr., Sepulveda, Calif., 1975-80; fellow in cardiology UCLA and VA Med. Ctr., 1978-80; attending cardiologist Hong Kong Adventist Hosp. Heart Ctr., 1980—, dir. intensive care unit, cardiac rehab. program, cardiopulmonary lab., 1981-83. Author, editor: Cardiac Rehabilitation for Nurses, 1982. Fellow ACP, Am. Coll. of Chest Physicians. Club: Rotary. Office: Prince's Bldg Suite 1508, 10 Charter Rd Central, Hong Kong Hong Kong

KING, PHILLIP, sculptor; b. Kheredine, Tunisia, 1934; s. Thomas John and Gabrielle Clemence (Liautald) K.; m. Lilian Odelle, 1957; 1 child, Anthony. Grad., Cambridge U., 1957; student, St. Martin's Sch. Art, London, 1957-58. Tchr. St. Martin's Sch. Art, 1959, 69—, Bennington (Vt.) Coll., 1964; prof. sculpture Royal Coll. Art, London, 1980—; asst. to Henry Moore, 1959-60; trustee Tate Gallery, 1967-69. One-man exhbns. in Eng., U.S., France, Fed. Republic of Germany, Italy, Japan, The Netherlands, Switzerland; exhibited in group shows at Eng., U.S., Spain, Fed. Republic of Germany, Italy, France, The Netherlands, Sweden, Norway, Belgium, Japan, Czechoslovakia, Switzerland. Served with Brit. Army, 1952-54. Decorated comdr. Order Brit. Empire, 1974; recipient 1st prize Socha Piestanskysch Parkov, Piestany, Czechoslovakia; named Peter Stuyvesant travel bursary, 1965; Boise scholar, 1960. Mem. Assn. Royal Acad. Art. Address: Rowan Gallery, 11 Bruton Place, London W1X 7AB, England

KING, PHILLIP KENNETH, sculptor; b. Tunis, Tunisia, May 1, 1934; s. Thomas John and Gabrielle Laurence (Liautard) K.; m. Lilian Odelle, July 22, 1957 (div. June 1987); 1 child, Antony (dec.). MA, U. Cambridge, Eng., 1957; student, St. Martin's Sch. Art, London, 1957-59. Asst. to Henry Moore Hertfordshire, Eng., 1957-59; prof. of sculpture Royal Coll. Art, 1980-88, royal acadamician, 1988—; trustee Tate Gallery. One-man shows include: Whitechapel Gallery, London, 1968, Brit. Pavilion, Venice Biennale, 1968, Tour of European Mus., 1974-75, Arts Council Tour Provincial Mus.

in Eng., 1975-76, Hayward Gallery, London, 1981, Nishimura Gallery, Tokyo, 1987; group exhibitions include: Brit. Sculpture, Madrid and Bilbao, 1961, Walker Art Ctr., Minn. and touring U.S., 1965, Stedelijk Mus., Amsterdam and touring mus. in Europe, 1966, Carnegie Inst., N.Y.C., 1967, Brit. Council exhibit touring mus. in Japan, 1982, Fondation Cartier, France, 1985, Rotunda Gallery, Hong Kong, 1986, Symposium in Krefelk, Federal Republic of Germany, 1987; represented in pub. collections: Art Gallery of New South Wales, Sydney, Falleris d'Art Moderne, Turin, Los Angeles County Mus., Louisiana Mus. Modern Art, Denmark, Musee Nationale d'Art Moderne, Centre George Pompidou, Paris, Mus. Modern Art, N.Y.C., Nat. Mus. Art, Osaka, Japan, Tate Gallery, London, Ulster Mus., Belfast, Tel Aviv Mus., Israel. Mem. Royal Acad. Arts (assoc.). Mem. Ch. of Eng. Office: Mayor Rowan Gellery, 31a Bruton Pl, London W1X 7AB, England

KING, RICHARD, retired investment company executive; b. Boston, Feb. 3, 1913; s. Stanley and Gertrude Louisa (Besse) K.; m. Gillet Epps, Nov. 5, 1949. B.A., Amherst Coll., 1935; postgrad. Harvard U., 1936. With Socony Vacuum Oil Co., N.Y.C., 1937-42; exec. dir. Darien Housing Authority, Conn., 1946-52; officer Whiteford Plastics Co., N.Y.C., 1951-52; v.p., pres., dir. Electric Indicator Co., Stamford, Conn., 1952-67; v.p., dir. Edo Corp., College Point, N.Y., 1960-68; sr. v.p., Wright Investors Service, Bridgeport, Conn., 1967-80; ret., 1980. Bd. dirs. Rockledge Found., Inc., Darien; trustee U.S. Naval Acad. Found., 1971—. Served to lt. comdr. USN, 1942-46, ATO. Clubs: Wee Burn Country (Darien); Amherst, Harvard (N.Y.C.). Home: Shennamere Rd Darien CT 06820

KING, ROBERT AUGUSTIN, engineering company executive; b. Marion, Ind., Sept. 3, 1910; s. Roy Melvin and Estella Bernice (Sheron) K.; m. Johanna A. Akkerman, July 19, 1975; children: Robert Alexander, Sharon Johanna, Estella Regina; children by previous marriage: Hugh Melbourne, Mary Elizabeth. B.S. in Chem. Engring, U. Okla., 1935. Chief chemist Phillips Petroleum Co., Borger, Tex., 1935-43; sr. process engr. E. B. Badger & Sons, N.Y.C. and London, 1944-53; dist. mgr. Stone & Webster, N.Y.C., 1954-56; mng. dir. Badger Co., The Hague, Netherlands, 1957-64; pres. King-Wilkinson, Inc., Houston, 1965-84; also dir. King-Wilkinson, Inc.; pres. Robert A. King Inc., 1985—. Mem. Am. Inst. Chem. Engrs., Am. Chem. Soc., Inst. Petroleum (London). Democrat. Episcopalian. Clubs: Petroleum, Warwick (Houston); Chemists (N.Y.C.); American (London). Home: 11026 Braes Forest Houston TX 77071 Office: 8300 Bissonnet Suite 260 Houston TX 77074

KING, ROBERT BRUCE, remote sensing specialist; b. Woking, Eng., Sept. 10, 1937; s. William James and Edith Florence (Dudman) K.; m. Jamela Abrahams, June 15, 1964; 1 child, Reyahn. B.Sc., U. Natal, 1959; Ph.D., U. Edinburgh, 1968. Engring. geologist Kantey & Templer, Cape Town, 1960-64; sr. sci. officer Overseas Devel. Natural Resources Inst., Surbiton, Eng., 1964-74, officer grade 7, 1974—; sr. research fellow U. Dar es Salaam, 1976-79, assoc. prof. geography, 1979-81. Author: Land Systems N. Zambia, 1976; Land Resources Rukwa Region, 1979; Remote Sensing Manual, 1984; Land Resource Survey of Toledo Dist., Belize, 1986. Fellow Geol. Soc. London, Remote Sensing Soc.; mem. Instn. Geologists, Am. Soc. Photogrammetry and Remote Sensing, Brit. Geomorphological Research Group. Islam. Home: Kerry Stables, 4 Lammas Ln, Esher, Surrey KT10 8NY, England Office: ODNRI, Central Ave, Chatham Maritime, Chatham, Kent ME4 4TB, England

KING, ROBERT LUCIEN, lawyer; b. Petaluma, Calif., Aug. 9, 1936; s. John Joseph and Ramona Margaret (Thorson) K.; m. Suzanne Nanette Parre, May 18, 1956 (div. 1973); children—Renee Michelle, Candyce Lynn, Danielle Louise, Benjamin Robert; m. Linda Diane Carey, Mar. 15, 1974 (div. 1981); 1 child, Debra Robin; m. J'an See, Oct. 27, 1984; 1 child, Jonathan Fielding. A.B. in Philosophy, Stanford U., 1958, J.D., 1960. Bar: Calif., N.Y. 1961. Asst. U.S. atty. U.S. Atty's. Office (so. dist.), N.Y.C., 1964-67; assoc. Debevoise & Plimpton, N.Y.C., 1960-64, 67-70, ptnr., 1970—; lectr. Practising Law Inst., N.Y.C., NYU Labor Forum, N.Y.C., 1983, NYU Sch. Continuing Edn., N.Y.C., 1970s. Dir. Nat. Scholarship Service and Fund for Negro Students, N.Y.C., 1983—. Fellow Am. Coll. Trial Lawyers; mem. ABA, Assn. Bar City N.Y., Calif. Bar Assn. Democrat. Home: 235 W 71st St Apt 81 New York NY 10023 Office: Debevoise & Plimpton 875 3d Ave New York NY 10022

KING, RONALD LEE, accountant, government agency official; b. Scottsbluff, Nebr., Aug. 23, 1941; s. Fred and Dorothy Eldean (Lang) K.; m. Bouala Phannavong Oudomvilay Phasiboribounbane, Dec. 7, 1974; children—Donald, Naransra, Terry. Student Oceanside-Carlsbad Coll., 1961-62; B.S. in Acctg., Golden Gate U., 1966. C.P.A., Calif. Office mgr. Nat. Auto Supply, San Francisco, 1963-66; acct. GAO, San Francisco, 1966-68, supervisory auditor, Saigon, Vietnam, 1969-72, Bangkok, 1973-75, Washington, 1975-80, GAO evaluator, 1980-83, group dir., 1983—, agy. rep. constrn. sector, Nat. Metric Council, Washington 1979—, Fed. Constrn. Council, 1983—; mem. conf. planning com. Adv. Bd. on Built Environment, Nat. Acad. Sci., Washington, 1981-83. Served as cpl. USMC, 1959-63. A.P. Giannini Found. scholar, 1965. Mem. Am. Inst. C.P.A.s, Calif. Soc. C.P.A.s, Assn. Govt. Accts. Democrat. Lutheran.

KING, RUTH ALLEN, management consultant; b. Providence, Oct. 8, 1910; d. Arthur S. and Wilhelmina H. (Harmon) Allen; grad. Tefft Bus. Inst., Providence, 1929; 1 dau., Phyllis King Dunham. Sec. to atty., Providence, 1929; stenographer N.Y. Urban League, N.Y.C., 1929-75; sec. adminstrn., adminstrv. asst., placement officer, asst. dir. Nat. Urban League Skills Bank, to 1975; founder/sec. The Edges Group, Inc., 1969—; Named Affirmative Action Pioneer, Met. N.Y. Project Equality, 1975; Ruth Allen King Scholarship Fund established, 1970; EDGES Ruth Allen King Ann. Excalibur award established, 1978; recipient Ann Tanneyhill award for commitment to Urban League Movement, 1975; Recognition award NCCJ, 1975; spl. citation Gov. of R.I. and Providence Plantations, 1981, citation Medgar Evers Coll., 1983; Ruth Allen King Appreciation Day proclaimed in her honor, Providence, Mar. 9, 1981, N.Y.C., 1975; citation R.I. Ho. of Reps., 1981; plaque Urban League R.I., 1981; Woman of Yr. award Suffolk (N.Y.) chpt. Jack and Jill of Am., 1982; numerous others. Mem. N.Y. Personnel Mgmt. Assn., Council Concerned Black Execs., Julius A. Thomas Soc. (charter), NAACP (life). Home and Office: 185 Hall St Apt 1715 Brooklyn NY 11205

KING, SHELDON SELIG, medical center administrator, educator; b. N.Y.C., Aug. 28, 1931; s. Benjamin and Jeanne (Fritz) K.; m. Ruth Arden Zeller, June 26, 1955 (div. 1987); children: Tracy Elizabeth, Meredith Ellen, Adam Bradley. A.B., NYU, 1952; M.S., Yale U., 1957. Adminstrv. intern Montefiore Hosp., N.Y.C., 1952, 55; adminstrv. asst. Mt. Sinai Hosp., N.Y.C., 1957-60; asst. dir. Mt. Sinai Hosp., 1960-66, dir. planning, 1966-68; exec. dir. Albert Einstein Coll. Medicine-Bronx Municipal Hosp. Center, Bronx, N.Y., 1968-72; asst. prof. Albert Einstein Coll. Medicine, N.Y.C., 1968-72; dir. hosps. and clinics Univ. Hosp., assoc. clin. prof. U. Calif., San Diego, 1972-81; acting head div. health care scis., dept. community medicine U. Calif. (Sch. Medicine), 1978-81; assoc. v.p. Stanford U., 1981-85, clin. assoc. prof. dept. community, family and preventive medicine; mem. adminstrv. bd. Council Teaching Hosps., 1981-86, chmn. adminstrv. bd., 1985; preceptor George Washington U., Ithaca Coll., Yale, U. Mo., CUNY; chmn. health care com. San Diego County Immigration Council, 1974-77; adv. council Calif. Health Facilities Commn., 1977-82; chmn. ad hoc bd. advs. Am. Bd. Internal medicine, 1985—; bd. trustees Calif. Hosp. Assn., 1978-81. Mem. editorial adv. bd.: Who's Who in Health Care, 1977; mem. editorial bd. Jour. Med. Edn, 1979-84. Bd. dirs. Hosp. Council San Diego and Imperial Counties, 1974-77, treas., 1976—, pres., 1977—; bd. dirs. United Way San Diego, 1975-80, Brith Milah Bd.; active Accreditation Council for Grad. Med. Edn., 1987—, Prospective Payment Assessment Commn., 1987—. Served with AUS, 1952-55. Fellow Am. Coll. Health Care Execs., Am. Pub. Health Assn., Royal Soc. Health; mem. Am. Hosp. Assn. (gov. council Met. sect. 1983-86, council on fin. 1987, house of dels. 1987—), Calif. Hosp. Assn. (trustee 1978-81), Am. Podiatric Med. Assn.(Project Council 2000 1985-86), Hosp. Research and Devel. Inst. Inc., Inst. of Medicine. Home: 7 Bay Tree Ln Los Altos CA 94022 Office: Stanford Univ Hosp C-204 Stanford CA 94305

KING, THOMAS JEREMY (TOM), politician; b. June 13, 1933; s. J.H. King; m. Jane Tilney, 1960; 2 children. MA, U. Cambridge. With E.S. and A. Robinson Ltd., Bristol, Eng., 1956, div. gen. mgr., 1964-69; PPS to Minister for Posts and Telecommunications, 1970-72, Minister for Indsl. Devel., 1972-74; front bench spokesman for Ministry of Industry, 1975-76, Ministry of Energy, 1976-79; minister for local govt. and environmental services 1979-83; sec. of state Dept. of Environment, 1983, Dept. of Transport, 1983, Dept. of Employment, 1983-85; sec. of state for No. Ireland 1985—; chmn. sale Tilney Co. Ltd., 1971-79; vice-chmn. Conservative Parliamentary Industry com., 1974. M.P. from Bridgwater, 1970—. Served to capt. mil. service, 1951-53, Tanzania and Kenya. Decorated PC, 1979. Office: House of Commons, London SW1, England *

KING, WALTER FRANCIS, III, physicist, acoustician; b. Attleboro, Mass., Jan. 24, 1932; s. Walter Francis and Alby (Doyle) K.; m. Christian Magdefrau, Dec. 19, 1963; children—Marcus F., Jennifer. A.B. in Physics, Brown U., 1959; Ph.D. in Physics, Pa. State U., 1969. Radar field engr. Sperry Gyroscope Co., Great Neck, N.Y., 1960-62; project engr. AEG, Berlin, 1963-64; research asst. dept. physics Pa. State U., 1964-68; asst. prof. physics Tech. U. Denmark, Lyngby, 1969-70; research assoc. ARL Pa. State U., 1970-75; sr. scientist Dept. Turbulence Research, Deutsche Forschungs- und Versuchsanstalt für Luft-und Raumfahrt, Berlin, 1975—; mem. Fed. Noise Control Com., Germany, 1976-77. Contbr. articles to profl. jours. Served with U.S. Army, 1951-53. Mem. Acoustical Soc. Am., Deutsche Gesellschaft fur Luft und Raumfaht. Office: DFVLR Dept Turbulence Research, Muller-Breslau St 8, 1000 Berlin 12 Federal Republic of Germany

KING, (JACK) WELDON, photographer; b. Springfield, Mo., Jan. 19, 1911; s. Clyde Nelson and Mary Blanche (Murphy) K.; B.A., Drury Coll., 1934, Mus.B., 1934. Chief still photographer African expdns. including Gatti-Hallicrafters Expdn., 1947-48, 12th Gatti Expdn., 1952, Wyman Carroll Congo Expdn., 1955, 13th Gatti Expdn., 1956, 14th Gatti Expdn., 1957; also freelance photog. expdns., Africa, 1960, 66, 76-77; trips for GAF Corp. to S.Am., 1962, 63, 77-78, Australia and N.Z., 1972-73; Alaska, 1982, Europe, 1983, also numerous assignments throughout contiguous states U.S. Served as photographer with Coast Arty. Corps, U.S. Army, 1941-42; PTO; Japanese prisoner of war, 1942-45. Decorated numerous service ribbons and battle stars. Mem. Space Pioneers, Am. Theatre Organ Soc., Humane Soc. U.S., Friends Animals, Animal Protection Inst. Am., African Wildlife Leadership Found., World Wildlife Fund, Am. Defenders of Bataan and Corregidor, Am. Ex-Prisoners War, Lambda Chi Alpha. Democrat. Roman Catholic. Contbr. to numerous art books including Africa is Adventure, 1959, also French and German edits.; Primitive Peoples Today, 1956; Africa: A Natural History, 1965; South America and Central America, 1967; Animal Worlds, 1963; Living Plants of the World, 1963; The Earth Beneath Us, 1964; Living Trees of the World; The Life of the Jungle, 1970; Living Mammals of the World. Contbr. photographs to mags., encys., textbooks. Address: 1234 E Grand Ave Springfield MO 65804

KINGHAM, RICHARD FRANK, lawyer; b. Lafayette, Ind., Aug. 2, 1946; s. James R. and Loretta C. (Hoenigke) K.; m. Justine Frances McClung, July 6, 1968; 1 child, Richard Patterson. BA, George Washington U., 1968; JD, U. Va., 1973. Bar: D.C. 1973, U.S. Dist. Ct. D.C. 1974, U.S. Ct. Appeals (D.C. cir.) 1974, U.S. Ct. Appeals (8th cir.) 1977, U.S. Supreme Ct. 1977, U.S. Ct. Appeals (5th cir.) 1980. Editorial asst. Washington Star, 1964-68, 69-70; assoc. Covington & Burling, Washington, 1973-81, ptnr., 1981—; lectr. law U. Va., Charlottesville, 1977—; mem. com. on issues and priorities for new vaccine devel. Inst. Medicine Nat. Acad. Scis., 1983—. Articles editor U. Va. law rev., 1972-73; contbr. articles to profl. jours. Served with U.S. Army, 1968-69. Mem. ABA, Food and Drug Law Inst., Soc. Vertebrate Paleontology, Order of Coif. Republican. Episcopalian. Home: 2432 Tracy Pl NW Washington DC 20008 Office: Covington & Burling 1201 Pennsylvania Ave NW PO Box 7566 Washington DC 20044

KING-JEFFERS, SHARON WINDSOR, lawyer; b. Chelsea, Mass., Mar. 17, 1940; d. Edward Windsor King and Mildred Bowman (Bannar) Moldenhauer; m. Leland Roland Jeffers, Apr. 20, 1968; children—Sean Edward, Lance Thomas. B.S.L., Western State U., Fullerton, Calif., 1974, J.D., 1975. Bar: Calif. 1978. Legal research supr. 1st Am. Title Ins. Co., Santa Ana, Calif., 1978-79; sole practice, Norco, Calif., 1979-80, assoc. practice, 1981-82; sole practice, Riverside, Calif., 1982—; selected participant Leadership Am. '88; steering com. Leadership Calif. Editorial staff Western State U. Law Rev., 1973-75. Trustee Chaffey Community Coll., Alta Loma, Calif., 1977-82, sec. 1977-79, v.p., 1979-80, pres., 1980-82; trustee Charter Grove Psychiat. Hosp., Corona, Calif., 1982—, pres., 1984-86; adv. bd. Charter Med. Network, 1983; past pres. Corona Music Theater Assn.; former bd. dirs., pres., charter mem. vol. Aux. Kellogg Psychiat. Hosp., others; mem. Inland Empire Cultural Arts Found., Riverside, San Bernardino, 1983; mem. Child Care Action Task Force, Riverside. Recipient Am. Jurisprudence award in criminal law Bancroft-Whitney Co., 1972; Calif. Legal Secs. scholar, 1973. Mem. State Bar Assn. Calif., Riverside County Bar Assn. (estate planning, probate, trust sect., pub./bar relations, medical/legal liaison and law and media coms., family law sect., chmn. speakers bur., participant Leadership Am. '88, also steering com., liasion), Nu Beta Epsilon. Republican. Roman Catholic. Clubs: Toastmasters Internat., USAF Acad. Parents Assn. (Inland Empire) (treas. 1987-88, v.p. 1988—). Lodge: Soroptomists (co-chmn. intercommunity com. Riverside chpt. 1983-84, del. 1984-86, chmn. women helping women com. 1985, chmn. gold key com. 1987-88, v.p. 1988, pres. 1988-89). Office: 4255 Main St Suite 3 Riverside CA 92501

KING OF WARTNABY, LORD (JOHN LEONARD), business executive. s. Albert John and Kathleen King; m. Lorna Kathleen Sykes, 1941 (dec. 1969); 4 children: m. Isabel Monckton, 1970. Founder Ferrybridge Industries Ltd. and Whitehouse Industries Ltd., subsequently Pollard Ball and Roller Bearing Co. Ltd., 1945, mng. dir., 1945, chmn., 1961-69; chmn. Dennis Motor Holdings Ltd., 1970-72, Babcock Internat. plc, 1972—; chmn. Brit. Airways, 1981—, Nat. Nuclear Corp., Brit. Nuclear Assocs. Ltd., SKF (U.K.) Ltd., Dick Corp. (USA), First Union Corp. (USA); past bd. dirs. Royal Ordnance plc, Clogau Gold Mines, Mill Feed Holdings, Tyneham Investments, Babcock Plant Leasing; mem. Engring. Industries Council, 1975, NEDC Com. on Fin. for Investments, 1976-78, Grand Council and fin. Policy Com., CBI, 1976-78. Chmn. City and Indsl. Liaison Council, 1973-85, Rev. Bd. for Govt. Contracts, 1975-78, Brit. Olympic Appeals Com., 1975-78, Macmillan appeal for Continuing Care, 1977-78, NEB, 1980-81, Alexandra Rose Day Found., 1980-85; mem. com. Ranfurly Library Service; v.p. Nat. Soc. for Cancer Releif; bd. dirs. Royal Opera Trust. Decorated Royal Order of Polar Star (Sweden), 1983; named Freeman, City of London, 1984; recipient Nat. Free Enterprise award, 1987. Clubs: White's, Pratts', Brook (N.Y.C.), Badsworth Foxhounds (MFH 1949-58), Duke of Rutland's Foxhounds (Belvoir) (MFH 1958-72), Belvoir Hunt (chmn. 1972). Office: Babcock Internat Inc 425 Post Rd Fairfield CT 06430 also: Cleveland House, St James's Sq, London SW1Y 4LN, England *

KINGSLEY, BEN, actor; b. Scarborough, Eng., Dec. 31, 1943; s. Rehimtulla Harji and Anna Lyna (Goodman) Bhanji; m. Gillian Alison Macaulay Sutcliffe, July 1, 1978; 1 son, Edmund William MacAulay. M.A. (hon.), Salford U. Assoc. artist Royal Shakespeare Co., Eng., 1968—. Appeared in plays including Hamlet, 1975-76, Othello, 1985-86, Edmund Kean, 1981-83; films include Gandhi, 1981 (Acad. award 1982), Betrayal, 1982, Turtle Diary, 1984, Harem, 1985, Shostakovich-A Testimony, 1987, Pascali's Island, 1987, The Train, 1987, Without a Clue, 1988, Weisenthall, 1988, Murderers Amongst Us, 1988. Recipient Padma Shri award Govt. of India, 1984, Grammy award. 1984; named Best Actor and Best Newcomer Brit. Acad. Film and TV Arts, 1982, Best Actor Standard Film Awards, London, 1983. Mem. Brit. Acad. Film and TV Arts, Acad. Motion Picture Arts and Scis. Address: care ICM Ltd, 388 396 Oxford St, London W1, England

KING-SMITH, ERIC ALFRED, biomedical engineer, consultant; b. Melbourne, Australia, Mar. 3, 1926; came to U.S., 1965; s. Frederick and Irene Victoria (Harlem) K-S.; m. Ruth Ethel Lustig, Aug. 8, 1950 (div. 1980); children—Judith Elaine, Bernard Alan, Naomi Louise; m. Roxie Harriet Freedman, Jan. 7, 1985. B.E.E., U. Melbourne, 1947, M.Eng. Sc., 1949, Ph.D., 1970. Sr. lectr. elec. engring. U. Melbourne, 1958-65; research assoc., spl. lectr. U. Mich., Ann Arbor, 1966-68, NIH spl. fellow in bioengring., 1968-71; new product devel. mgr. Medtronic, Inc., Mpls., 1970-74; electronic design specialist 3M Detection Systems, St. Paul, 1974-76; sr. product devel. specialist 3M Health Care Group, St. Paul, 1976—; adj. prof. mech. engring. U. Minn., Mpls., 1980-84; research collaborator Brookhaven Nat. Labs., 1972-76; bioengring. cons. Dorland's Med. Dictionary, 1970-74. Author: Mudpac Manual, 1962; also articles. Grad. scholar, 1947-48; NIH spl. fellow, 1968-70. Fellow Instn. Elec. Engrs. (U.K.), Instn. Engrs. (Australia) (aero. com. 1955-57); mem. IEEE (sr. mem.; chpt. chmn. 1977-78), Australian Computer Soc. (founding mem.; editor Victoria div. 1962-65, sec. 1961-62); mem. N.Y. Acad. Scis., AAAS, Biol. Engring. Soc. (U.K.), Internat. Soc. Chronobiology, Internat. Continence Soc. Office: 3M Health Care Group Bldg 270-2N-5 3M Ctr Saint Paul MN 55144

KINGTON, BARRY CLARK, investor, consultant; b. Nashville, Sept. 2, 1942; s. William Hayes and Margret Elisabeth (Clark) K.; 1 son, Barry Clark. BS, Murray State U., 1969. Owner coal and oil rights; investor stocks and commodities; bus. cons., Point One Adv. Group, Inc. Bd. dirs. Youth Athletics, 1970-73, County Fair, 1971. Mem. Internat. Soc. Philos. Enquiry, N.Y. Acad. Scis., Triple Nine Soc. (internat. membership officer) Appoloosa Horse Club, Archaeol. Inst. Am., Jaycees (v.p. 1973), Mensa (pres. Evansville area 1986-88), AAAS, Am. Angus Assn., Prometheus Soc., Clubs: Petroleum, Shamrock. Home: Kilmarnock Ln Madisonville KY 42431 Office: PO Box 1111 Madisonville KY 42431

KINMONT, PATRICK DAVID CLIFFORD, consultant dermatologist; b. Newark-on-Trent, Nottinghamshire, Eng., Feb. 28, 1916; s. Patrick and Marie Therese (Clifford) K.; m. Elizabeth Gladys Matilda West, Mar. 25, 1950; children—Patrick William John, Elizabeth Phillipa Ann Kinmont Drysdale. Student Epsom Coll. (Eng.), 1926-34; M.R.C.S., King's Coll. Hosp. (Eng.), 1939, M.B., B.S., 1939; M.D., London U., 1946. Intern, Kings Hosp., London, 1939, resident in dermatology, 1946-47; cons. dermatologist Nat. Health Service, Derbyshire Royal Infirmary, Eng., 1947-73; sr. cons. dermatologist Univ. Hosp., Nottingham, Eng., 1973-79; emeritus cons. dermatologist Nottingham Hosps., 1979—; vis. prof. Pa. State U., Hershey, 1982, Kuwait U., 1979-80, 81; vis. lectr. U. Chgo., 1973; hon. lectr. Sydney U., Australia, 1967, Melbourne U., Australia, 1967, Adelaide U., Australia, 1967, Dacca U., Bangladesh, 1967, Damascus U., Syria, 1967. Author: (with R.B. Coles) Skin Diseases for Beginners, 1957; also articles. Bd. dirs. Christian Children's Fund, Great Britain, 1982—. Served to maj. Royal Army Med. Corps, 1939-45. Recipient Brit. Empire (Mil) medal, 1945; Army Council Territorial decoration, 1946. Fellow Royal Coll. Physicians; mem. Irish Assn. Dermatologists (hon.), Brit. Assn. Dermatologists, N. Eng. Assn. Dermatologists; internat. mem. Am. Dermatol. Assn., N.Y. Acad. Scis. Mem. Ch. of Eng. Club: Kildare St. and Univ. (Dublin). Avocations: game shooting; fishing; cricket. Home: Ermine House, Fulbeck, Lincolnshire NG32 3JT, England Office: Consulting Rooms, 11 Regent St, Nottingham England

KINN, JOHN MATTHIAS, association executive, consultant; b. N.Y.C., July 25, 1925; s. John M. and Marie A. (Bremme) K.; m. Gloria Anita Thomas, Dec. 26, 1953; children—Robert A., Ian M., Laurel K. B.S. in Elec. Engring., U. Mo., 1949. Cert. assn. exec. Sr. engr. Western Electric Co., N.Y.C., 1950-53; group chief Bell Telephone Labs., Whippany, N.J., 1953-55; assoc. editor Electronics mag., McGraw-Hill, N.Y.C., 1955-59; engring. editor IBM Jour., N.Y.C., 1959-61, mgr. sci. info., 1961-65; dir. edn. IEEE, N.Y.C., 1965-79, cons., 1979-80; v.p. engring. Electronic Industries Assn., Washington, 1980—. Contbr. articles to various books and mags., 1955—. Committeeman Westchester (N.Y.) council Boy Scouts Am., 1960-80. Served with USN, 1943-46; PTO. Mem. IEEE (sr.), Am. Soc. Assn. Execs., Am. Soc. Tng. Dirs., AAAS. Office: Electronic Industries Assn 2001 Eye St NW Washington DC 20006

KINNEAR, JAMES WESLEY, III, petroleum company executive; b. Pitts., Mar. 21, 1928; s. James Wesley and Susan (Jenkins) K.; m. Mary Tullis, June 17, 1950; children: Robin Wood (Mrs. David Bruce Anderson), Susan, James Wesley IV, William M. BS with distinction, U.S. Naval Acad., 1950. With Texaco Inc., 1954—; sales mgr. Texaco Inc., Hawaii, 1959-63; div. sales mgr. Texaco Inc., Los Angeles, 1963-64; asst. to vice chmn. bd. dirs. Texaco Inc., N.Y.C., 1964-65, asst. to chmn. bd. dirs., gen. mgr. marine dept., 1965, v.p. supply and distbn., 1966-70, sr. v.p. strategic planning, 1970-71, sr. v.p. worldwide refining, petrochems., supply and distbn., 1971-72, sr. v.p. world wide mktg., also in charge internat. marine ops. and petrochems., 1972-76, sr. v.p. internat. marine and aviation sales petrochem. dept., marine dept., mktg. and refining in Europe, 1976-78, exec. v.p., 1978-83, also bd. dirs., vice chmn. bd. dirs., 1983-86, pres., chief exec. officer, 1987—; pres. Texaco U.S.A., 1982-84; bd. dirs., mem. Am. Petroleum Inst., Nat. Petroleum Council, Corning Glass Works, Bus. Council of N.Y.; mem. Bus. Round Table. Pres. bd. trustees St. Paul's Sch., Concord, N.H. Served to lt. comdr. USNR, 1950-54. Mem. U.S. Naval Inst. Episcopalian. Clubs: Round Hill (Greenwich, Conn.); Verbank Hunting, Brook (N.Y.C.); Iron City Fishing (Parry Sound, Ont.); Augusta (Ga.) Nat. Golf. Home: 149 Taconic Rd Greenwich CT 06830 Office: Texaco Inc 2000 Westchester Ave White Plains NY 10650

KINNERSLEY, SUSAN VIOLA, health care administrator, nurse; b. Columbus, Wis., May 23, 1951; d. Lester Otto and Lois Viola (Rath) Henning; children: Rebecca Sue, Kenneth Ryan. BS in Nursing, Olivet Nazarene Coll., Kankakee, Ill., 1973; MS, Govs. State U., Park Forest South, Ill., 1977. RN, Ill., Calif., Ind. Nurse Aide Columbus Community Hosp., Wis., 1967-69; nurse aide Riverside Hosp., Kankakee, 1971-73, RN, 1973; RN Palos Community Hosp., Ill., 1973-74; instr. St. Joseph Hosp. Sch. of Nursing, Joliet, Ill., 1974-76; project coordinator Our Lady of Mercy Hosp., Dyer, Ind., 1976-78, asst. dir. nursing, 1978-80, dir. of spl. services, 1980-81; dir. of nursing services Culver Union Hosp., Crawfordsville, Ind., 1981-84, dir. of patient services, 1984, asst. adminstr., 1984-86; dir. nursing, asst. adminstr. AMI-Visalia (Calif.) Community Hosp., 1986—. Adv. bd. Am. Med. Home Care, Crawfordsville, 1984-85, Ivy Tech Assoc. Degree Program, Lafayette, Ind., 1985-86. Mem. Calif. Soc. for Nursing Service Adminstrn., Sigma Theta Tau (Delta Omicron chpt.). Republican. Nazarene. Club: Quota. Avocations: softball, reading. Office: Visalia Community Hosp 1633 S Court St Visalia CA 93277

KINNEY, ABBOTT FORD, radio broadcasting executive; b. Los Angeles, Nov. 11, 1909; s. Gilbert Earle and Mabel (Ford) K.; student Ark. Coll., 1923, 26, 27; m. Dorothy Lucille Jeffers, Sept. 19, 1943 (dec. Jan. 1986); children—Colleen, Joyce, Rosemary. Editor Dermott News, 1934-39; partner Delta Drug Co., 1940-49; pres., gen. mgr. S.E. Ark. Broadcasters, Inc., Dermott and McGehee, 1951—; corr. Comml. Appeal, Memphis, Ark. Gazette, Little Rock, 1935-53; research early aeros. Inst. Aero. Scis., 1941, castor bean prodn., 1941-42. Mem. Ark. Geol. and Conservation Commn., 1959-63; chmn. Ark. Planning Commn.; mem. Mississippi River Pkwy. Commn., Park Commn. Past pres., mem. exec. bd. DeSoto Area council Boy Scouts Am.; chmn. County Library Bd.; mem. past pres. Hosp. Adv. Bd.; mem. bd. McGehee-Dermott Indsl. Devel. Corp., Chicot Fair Assn., Christian Rural Overseas Program. Recipient Silver Beaver award Boy Scouts Am.; honored with Abbott Kinney Day by civic orgns. and schs. S.E. Ark., 1955; named one of Ark.'s 10 Outstanding Community Leaders, 1969. Mem. AIM, Nat. Assn. Radio and TV Broadcasters, Ark. Broadcasters Assn., Ark., S.E. Ark. chambers commerce, Internat. Broadcasters Soc. (editorial adv. bd.), Ark. Hist. Assn., Am. Numis. Assn. Club: Rotary. Home: Dermott AR 71638 Office: SE Ark Broadcasters Inc Dermott AR 71638

KINNEY, JEREMY FOWLER, oil company executive; b. N.Y.C., July 20, 1945; s. Francis Sherwood and Mary Dalton (Fowler) K. B.A., Yale U., 1968; M.B.A., Harvard U., 1973. Assoc. Eastdil Realty, Inc., N.Y.C., 1973-78, v.p., 1978-79; prin. Kinney Myers Interests, Dallas, 1979-81; pres. Kinney Oil Co., Denver, 1982—. Co-chmn. Opera Colo., Denver, 1985-87. Served to 1st lt. USMCR, 1968-71. Mem. Ind. Petroleum Assn. of Mountain States (pub. lands com. 1982-86). Republican. Roman Catholic. Clubs: Racquet and Tennis (N.Y.C.); Denver; Nat. Golf Links Am. (Southampton, N.Y.), Shinnecock Hills Golf (Southampton). Office: Kinney Oil Co 1331 17th St Suite 710 Denver CO 80202

KINNOCK, NEIL GORDON, British government and political leader; b. Mar. 28, 1942; s. Gordon and Mary (Howells) K.; m. Glenys Elizabeth Parry, 1967; 2 children. B.A. in Indsl. Relations and History, Univ. Coll., Cardiff, Wales. Tutor organizer in indsl. and trade union studies Workers Ednl. Assn., 1966-70; M.P. for Bedwellty, 1970-83, for Islwyn, 1983—; parliamentary pvt. sec. to sec. of state for employment, 1974-75; mem. nat. exec. com. Labor Party, 1978—, parly com. Parliamentary Labor Party, 1979—;

leader Labor Party, leader of Opposition, 1983—; chief Opposition spokesman on edn., 1979-83. Mem. editorial bd. Labor Research Dept., 1974—. Author: Wales and the Common Market, 1971; also articles. Mem. Welsh Hosp. Bd., 1969-71; bd. dirs. Fair Play for Children, 1979—, 7:84 Theatre Co. (Eng.) Ltd., 1979—. Mem. Socialist Ednl. Assn., Assn. Liberal Edn. (pres. 1980-82). Address: House of Commons, London SW1 England *

KINOSHITA, SHIGERU, ophthalmologist; b. Osaka, Japan, Mar. 14, 1950; s. Kanezo and Masako K.; m. Junko Mikawa, Apr. 29, 1974; children: Manabu, Makoto. MD, Osaka U., 1974, DSc, 1983. Resident Osaka U. Hosp., 1974-79; research fellow Harvard Med. Sch., 1979-82; instr. Osaka U. Med. Sch., 1982-84, asst. prof., 1984—; dir. eye div. Osaka Rosai Hosp., 1984—. Home: 1-3-11 Kitabatake Abenoku, 545 Osaka Japan

KINOSHITA, SHINJI, cardiologist, educator; b. Otaru, Hokkaido, Japan, Jan. 7, 1931; s. Sakuzo and Torayo (Takahashi) K.; m. Hitomi Sano, Oct. 2, 1962; children—Yorko, Makoto. M.D., Hokkaido U., 1955, D.M.S., 1959. Intern, City of Otaru Hosp., Japan, 1954-55; research assoc. 2d dept. medicine, Sch. Medicine, Hokkaido U., Sapporo, Japan, 1955-68, instr., 1968-76, assoc. prof., 1976-83; prof. Health Adminstrn. Center, Hokkaido U., 1983—, dir., 1986—. Inventor color-vectorcardiograph; contbr. articles to profl. jours. in field including: Circulation, Am. Jour. Cardiology. Fellow Hokkaido Br. Japanese Circulation Soc.; mem. Japanese Circulation Soc., N.Y. Acad. Scis., Am. Heart Assn. (reviewer 1978-81). Home: 4-Jo 3-Chome 3-27, Tonden, Kita-Ku, Sapporo Hokkaido 001, Japan Office: Health Adminstrn Center, Hokkaido Univ, Kita-8 Nishi-5 Kita-Ku, 060 Sapporo Hokkaido Japan

KINRADE, KERRY FRANCIS, insurance executive; b. Los Angeles, Oct. 1, 1936; s. John T. and Claire (Bovee) K.; B.A., UCLA, 1959; M.P.A., U. So. Calif., 1969; m. Linda C. Wolf, May 31, 1969. With State Compensation Ins. Fund, San Francisco, 1960—, supervising mgmt. analyst, 1979-83, claims mgr., 1983—. Bd. dirs. Salem Luth. Home, Oakland, Calif. Mem. Am. Soc. Pub. Adminstrn. Office: 1275 Market St San Francisco CA 94103

KINSELLA, THOMAS, poet, educator; b. Dublin, May 4, 1928; s. John Paul and Agnes (Casserly) K.; m. Eleanor Walsh, 1955, 3 children. With Irish Civil Service, 1946-65, asst. prin. officer Dept. Fin., 1960-65; artist in residence So. Ill. U., 1965-67, prof. English, 1967-70; prof. Temple U., Phila., 1970—; dir. Dolmen Press Ltd., Cuala Press Ltd, Dublin; founder Peppercanister, Dublin, 1972.; publs.: Poems, 1956, Another September, 1958, Downstream, 1962, Nightwalker and Other Poems, 1966, Notes from the Land of the Dead, 1972, New Poems, 1973, Selected Poems 1956-68, 1973, Song of the Night and Other Poems, 1978, The Messenger, 1978, Fifteen Dead, 1979, One and Other Poems, 1979, Butcher's Dozen, 1972, Finistere, 1972; Songs of the Psyche, 1984; Her Vertical Smile, 1984; St. Catherine's Clock, 1987; Out of Ireland, 1987; editor: Selected Poems of Austin Clarke, 1976; (with Sean O'Tuama) Poems of the Dispossessed 1600-1900, 1980; transl. (from Old Irish) The Tain, 1970. Guggenheim fellow, 1968-69, 71-72; recipient Guinness Poetry award, 1958, Irish Arts Council Triennial Book award, 1960, Denis Devlin Meml. award, 1966, 69. Mem. Irish Acad. Letters. Address: 47 Percy Pl, Dublin 4 Ireland Other: English Dept Temple U Philadelphia PA 19122 *

KINSER, RICHARD EDWARD, management consultant; b. Los Angeles, May 14, 1936; s. Edward Lee and M. Yvonne (Withes) K.; m. Suzanne Carol Logan, Mar. 22, 1958. BA in Econs., Stanford U., 1958. Mgr. U.S. Steel Corp., San Francisco, 1958-65; v.p. Booz-Allen & Hamilton, Inc., San Francisco, 1965-78, Washington, 1971-73; sr. v.p., bd. dirs. William H. Clark Assocs., Inc., San Francisco, 1979-81; dep. dir. presdl. personnel The White House, Washington, 1981-83; mng. ptnr. Gould & McCoy, Inc., 1983-86; pres. Kinser & Assoc., N.Y.C., 1986—; bd. dirs. Measurmatic, Inc., San Francisco, Pure Water, Inc., Lincoln, Nebr.; lectr. in field. Bd. dirs. San Francisco Bicentenial Com., 1976, Americans for Oxford; mem. vice-chancellor's adv. com. Oxford U. Fellow Aspen Inst.; mem. World Affairs Council, White House Fellows Commn. (commr.). Republican. Clubs: Bankers, Commonwealth, Economics, Mid-Atlantic. Home: 415 E 54th St New York NY 10022 Office: 405 Lexington Ave #4515 New York NY 10174

KINSINGER, ROBERT EARL, executive; b. Chgo., Aug. 5, 1923; s. Elmer John and Frances Louise (Ballenger) K.; m. Sylvia Kading, May 20, 1950; children: William, Candace, Lisa. A.B., Stanford U., 1948, M.A., 1951; Ed.D., Columbia U., 1958; LL.D., Simpson Coll., 1977; L.H.D., Hahnemann U.; Litt.D., Thomas Jefferson U., 1986. Staff mem. U.S. del. 3d Gen. Assembly UN, Paris, France, 1948; regional field rep., mgr. chpt. and regional blood center ARC, Boise, Ida., 1949-56; lectr. Columbia U., 1956, Queens Coll., 1957; ednl. cons. Nat. League Nursing, 1957-60; dir. health careers project SUNY, 1960-66; program dir. W.K. Kellogg Found., Battle Creek, Mich., 1966-70, v.p., 1970-83; chmn. Ednl. Services for the Professions, Inc., 1983-87; pres. Kinland Properties; cons. in field; vice chmn. adv. council Mich. Comprehensive Health Planning Bd.; chmn. Commn. on Physicians Assts.; bd. dirs. Highlands, Inc.; dir. Jossey-Bass Inc., Pubs.; dir., trustee, mem. exec. com. Fielding Inst.; adv. com. Corp. Community Coll. TV. Author: Education for Health Technicians-An Overview, 1965; co-author: Clinical Nursing Instruction by Television, 1965; Editor: Career Opportunities for Health Technicians, 1971. Chmn. bd. overseers Univ. of the State of N.Y. Regents Coll. Degrees and Regents Coll. Examinations. Served to lt. USNR, World War II. Recipient commn. of honor SUNY, Farmingdale, 1970; Man of Yr. award Nat. Council Community Services, 1971; Honors of Soc. award Am. Soc. Allied Health Professions. Fellow Am. Soc. Allied Health Profls.; mem. AAAS, Am. Assn. Higher Edn., Am. Dietetic Assn. (chmn. adv. com.). Club: Marina West Yacht. Home and Office: 21901 Confidence Rd Twain Harte CA 95383

KINTNER, WILLIAM ROSCOE, political scientist; b. Lock Haven, Pa., Apr. 21, 1915; s. Joseph Jennings and Florence (Kendig) K.; m. Xandree M. Hyatt, June 15, 1940 (dec.); children: Kay Caldwell, Jane Kintner Hogan, Gail Kintner Markou, Carl H.; m. Faith Childs Halterman, Aug. 28, 1987. B.S., U.S. Mil. Acad., 1940; Ph.D., Georgetown U., 1949. Commd. 2d lt. U.S. Army, 1940, advanced through grades to col., 1956; inf. bn. co. Korean War; mem. sr. staff CIA, 1950-52; mem. planning staff NSC, 1954; mem. staff spl. asst. to Pres. 1955; cons. Pres.'s Com. to study U.S. Assistance Program (Draper Com.), 1959; chief long-range plans strategic analysis sect. Coordination Group, Chief of Staff, U.S. Army, 1959-61; ret. 1961; prof. emeritus polit. sci. Wharton Sch., U. Pa., Phila., 1961-85; dep. dir. Fgn. Policy Research Inst., Phila., 1961-69; dir. Fgn. Policy Research Inst., 1969-73, pres., 1976; Am. ambassador to Thailand 1973-75; cons. Dept. Def., NSC, Stanford Research Inst.; fellow Hudson Inst.; sr. adviser Ops. Research Office, Johns Hopkins U., 1956-57; mem. acad. bd. Inter-Am. Def. Coll., 1967-72; mem. Bd. Fgn. Scholarships, 1970-73; civilian faculty adv. com. Nat. War Coll., 1970-72; mem. adv. bd. Naval War Coll., 1985; bd. mem. U.S. Peace Inst., 1986—. Author: The Front is Everywhere, 1950, (with George C. Reinhardt) Atomic Weapons in Land Combat, 1953, The Haphazard Years, 1960, (with others) Forging a New Sword, 1958, Protracted Conflict, 1959, A Forward Strategy for America, 1961, Building the Atlantic World, 1963, (with Joseph Z. Kornfeder) The New Frontier of War, 1962, Peace and the Strategy Conflict, 1967, (with Harriet Fast Scott) The Nuclear Revolution in Soviet Military Affairs, 1969, (with Wolfgang Klaiber) Eastern Europe and European Security, 1971, (with Harvey Sicherman) Technology and International Politics, 1975, (with John F. Copper) A Matter of Two Chinas: The China-Taiwan Issue in U.S. Foreign Policy, 1979, Arms Control: The American Dilemma, 1987; editor: Orbis, 1969-73, 76—; editor, contbr.: Safeguard: Why the ABM Makes Sense, 1969, Soviet Global Strategy, 1987; contbr. articles to profl. jours. Trustee Freedom House, N.Y.C.; mem. bd. Gen. Ch. of New Jerusalem, Bryn Athyn, Pa.; mem. adv. com. World Affairs Council, Phila. Decorated Legion of Merit with oak leaf cluster, Bronze Star with oak leaf cluster. Mem. Council Fgn. Relations, Am. Polit. Sci. Assn., Pa. Soc., Council Am. Ambassadors. Home: 2259 Pennypack Ln Bryn Athyn PA 19009

KINTS, DENIS HENRY LOUIS, physician; b. Cartigny, Somme, France, Oct. 11, 1935; s. Henri and Sophie (Molet) K.; m. Anne Berger, Apr. 14, 1962; 1 child, Isabelle. DMS, Sch. of Medicine, Lille, France, 1965. Diplomate in gen. medicine, 1966. Sole practice gen. medicine Marseille en Bsis, France, 1966-72, Denain, France, 1972—. V.p., auditeur Inst. des Hautes Etudes de la Defense Nationale de la Zone NORD, Valenciennes, France, 1978. Served to col. St. Algiers Army, 1963. Recipient Chevalier Mérite Nat., 1978; decorated Officier des Palmes Académiques, 1984. Mem. Departmental Union Nat. Med. Res. (del. 1985). Roman Catholic. Home: Jules Mousseron, 59220 Denain France Office: IHEDN, 13 place Joffre, 75700 Paris France

KINZIE, JEANNIE JONES, radiation oncologist; b. Great Falls, Mont., Mar. 14, 1940; d. James Wayne and Lillian Alice (Young) Jones; m. Joseph Lee Kinzie, Mar. 26, 1965 (div. Sept. 1982); 1 child, Daniel Joseph. Student, Oreg. State U., 1960; BS, Mont. State U., 1961; MD, Washington U., St. Louis, 1965. Diplomate Am. Bd. Radiology. Intern. in surgery U. N.C., Chapel Hill, 1965-66; resident in therapeutic radiology Washington U., St. Louis, 1968-71, instr. in radiology, 1971-73; asst. prof. in radiology Med. Coll. of Wis., Milw., 1973-75; asst. prof. in radiology U. Chgo., 1975-78, assoc. prof. in radiology, 1978-80; assoc. prof. of radiation oncology Wayne State U., Detroit, 1980-85; prof. radiology U. Colo., Denver, 1985—; dir. radiation oncology U. Hosp., Denver, 1985—; bd. dirs. Rocky Mountain Oncology Soc.; cons. Denver Vets. Hosp., Denver Gen. Hosp., Rose Med. Ctr., FDA Ctr. for Devices and Radiologic Health; sci. adv. bd. Cancer League of Colo.; examiner Am. Bd. Radiology; cons. Food and Drug Adminstrn., 1987—; adv. physician Colo. Med. Found. 1988—. Assoc. editor Internat. Jour. Radiation Oncology Biology and Physics; contbr. articles to profl. jours.; chpts. to books. Bd. dirs. Denver unit Am. Cancer Soc., 1986—. NIH grantee, 1973-75; Am. Coll. Radiology fellow, 1984. Mem. Denver Med. Soc., Colo. Med. Soc., Colo. Radiol. Soc., Rocky Mountain Oncology Soc., Am. Coll Radiology, Soc. Head and Neck Surgeons, AMA, Am. Radium Soc., Am. Soc. Therapeutic Radiologists, Am. Cancer Soc. (bd. dirs. Denver unit). Am. Soc. Clin. Oncology. Republican. Lutheran. Home: PO Box 2585 Evergreen CO 80439 Office: Radiation Oncology Box A031 4200 E 9th Ave Denver CO 80262

KIOULAFAS, KYRIACOS, economics educator; b. Manolates, Samos, Greece, Nov. 21, 1940; parents Emmanouel and Maria Kioulafas; m. Joanne Dikaiou, Aug. 17, 1970; 1 child, Maria. B in Econs., Athens U., 1963, LLB, 1969, postgrad. in math., 1969-71; PhD, Heriot-Wat U., Edinburgh, Scotland, 1976. Unpaid asst. Athens U., 1971-76, lectr., 1977-81, prof., 1977—; sr. researcher Greek Man Power Orgn., Athens, 1971-84, Inst. Econ. and Ind. Research, Athens, 1985—; vis. prof. Greek Forces Acad., Athens, 1977—, Greek Armed Forces Acad., Athens, 1984-85, Greek Nat. Def. Acad., Athens, 1983-85; cons. Greek Tourist Orgn., Athens, 1984—, Greek Advt. Firm, Athens, 1984, Internat. Labor Office, Liberia, 1980. Author: Advertising in Greece, 1981, Greek Traffic, 1983, Structure of Greek Labour Force, 1987; contbr. articles to profl. jours. Pres. Jr. Champer Internat., Athens, 1978-81; gen. sec. Greek Studies Soc., Athens, 1985-87. Served to capt. Greek Air Force, 1963-70. Grantee NATO, 1972-76, Greek Man Power Orgn., 1972-76. Fellow Greek O.R. Orgn., Greek Statis. Orgn., Greek Economist Orgn. Mem. New Democracy Party. Orthodox. Home: Sfacion 6-8/10439, Athens Greece Office: Athens U, Pesmatgoglou 8, Athens Greece

KIOULPAPAS, TASSOS, food service company executive; b. Athens, Greece, Apr. 26, 1943; s. Emil and Anastasia (Marselou) K.; m. Sofia Kaneti, Apr. 26, 1980; children: Elisabeth, Emil. Degree in Econs., Athens U., 1967; grad., Ecole Hautes Etudes Commerciales, Paris, 1971. Pres. Xenex Ltd., Athens, 1969—; chmn. bd. Floca-Goody's Group of Cos., Athens, 1985—. Mem. Food Service Cons. Internat. (treas. 1987-88), Confrerie Chaine Rotisseurs. Club: Yacht of Greece (Piraeus). Office: Xenex Ltd, 124 Kifissias Ave, 115-26 Athens Greece

KIPP, EGBERT MASON, mgmt. cons.; b. Angola, Nov. 27, 1914; s. Ray Bassett and Letitia Mary (Mason) K.; (parents Am. citizens); B.S., Iowa Wesleyan Coll., 1934, D.Sc. (hon.), 1961; M.S., Boston U., 1935; Ph.D., Pa. State U., 1939; m. Pauline Sylvia Lougee, Dec. 24, 1935; children—David Alden, Richard Mason, Rebecca Weldon. Chief lubricants div. Alcoa, New Kensington, Pa., 1947-59; dir. research and devel Foote Mineral Co., Exton, Pa., 1957-59; asst. to mgr. product devel., research and devel. Sun Oil Co., Marcus Hook, Pa., 1959-60, mgr. basic research, 1960-62, asso. dir. research and devel., 1962-70; mgmt. cons. in sci. and tech., tribology, Paoli, Pa., 1971—; lectr. confs. in field; plenary lectr. 3d Internat. Conf. Metal Working Lubricants, Esslingen, W. Ger., 1981; guest lectr. coll. engring., Pa. State U., College Station, 1987—. Mem. Am. Soc. Lubrication Engrs. (pres. 1946, chmn. long range planning com. 1967-70), Pitts. Chemists Club (pres. 1952), Am. Assn. Cons. Chemists and Chem. Engrs., Am. Assn. Small Research and Devel. Cos., Am. Chem. Soc., Am. Inst. Chemists (Honor award Phila. chpt. 1965), Pa. Inst. Chemists (pres. 1974-75), Research and Mgmt. Group Phila. (pres. 1975). Methodist. Author: People Aspects of Research and Development Custom Building Your Management Career, 1967; also tech. and mgmt. articles; patentee in field of lubricants.

KIRALY, ISTVÁN, literature educator; b. Ragály, Borsod, Hungary, July 15, 1921; s. István and Ilona (Joó) K.; m. Mária Landler, Nov. 11, 1954; children: Katalin, Julia. PhD, U. Budapest, 1944. Tchr. Middlesch., Debrecen, Hungary, 1945-46, Hungarian Ednl. Council, Budapest, 1946-48; prof. U. Budapest, 1949—. Author: Mikszáth Kálmán, 1952, Ady Endre, vols. 1 and 2, 1970, Kosztolányi Dezső, 1985, Kultura és politika, 1987. Mem. Hungarian Parliament, 1971-85. Mem. Hungarian Acad., Finno-Hungarian Soc. (v.p. 1965—). Home: Kossuth Lajos tér 18, 1055 Budapest Hungary Office: Univ ELTE, Pesti Barnabés u 1, 1051 Budapest Hungary

KIRBY, DIANA CATHERINE, nurse, army officer; b. Guttenberg, Iowa, Jan. 22, 1951; d. Albert Edward and Bernadette Lucretia (Berns) Cherne; BS in Nursing, U. Iowa, 1973; MS in Edn., U. So. Calif., 1977; MS in Nursing, U. Md., 1987; lic. pilot; m. Fred W. Kirby, Nov. 24, 1981. Mem. nursing staff Mercy Med. Ctr., Dubuque, Iowa, 1973-74; commd. 1st lt. Nurse Corps, U.S. Army, 1974, advanced through grades to maj., 1984; service in W. Ger.; community health nurse William Beaumont Army Med. Center, 1978-80, Ft. Leonard Wood, Mo., 1980-82, Ft. Meade, Md., 1987; chief community nursing Dewitt Army Community Hosp., Ft. Belvoir, Va., 1987—. Mem. Am. Nurses Assn., Iowa Nurses Assn., Nat. League Nursing, Am. Nurses Found., Assn. Mil. Surgeons U.S., Nat. Trust for Hist. Preservation, Am. Philatelic Soc., Sigma Theta Tau. Roman Catholic. Address: 6833 Silver Ann Dr Lorton VA 22079

KIRBY, DOROTHY MANVILLE, social worker; b. Burke, S.D., Oct. 23, 1917; d. Charles Vietz and Gail Lorena (Coonen) Manville; m. Sigmund Kirby, July 11, 1941 (div. 1969); children; Paul Howard, Robert Charles. BA, Wayne State U., 1970, MSW, 1972. Cert. social worker, Mich. Pvt. practice social work Allen Park, Mich., 1973—; conduct seminars on stress, personal effectiveness and communication for various orgns., hosps. and bus. Subscription chmn. Allen Park Symphony Orchestra, 1985-86. Mem. Am. Group Psychotherapy Assn., Nat. Assn. Social Workers (clin.), Nat. Assn. Marriage and Family Counseling, Mich. Assn. Marriage and Family Counseling (sec. 1982), LWV (pres. Allen Park 1965-66). Presbyterian. Lodge: Soroptimists. Home and Office: 15720 Wick Rd Allen Park MI 48101

KIRBY, JACK ARTHUR, lawyer; b. Willard, Ohio, Feb. 27, 1941; s. Arthur Norris and Kathryn Elizabeth (Bell) K.; m. Candace Huber, Mar. 1, 1969; 1 dau.; Victoria Huber. Student, Va. Mil. Inst., 1959-60; B.A., Denison U., 1963; J.D., Washington and Lee U., 1970. Bar: Pa. 1971. Mem. rev. counsel staff estate planning dept. Girard Bank, Phila., 1970-72; mem. examinations dept. estate planning and taxation Am. Coll. Life Underwriters, Bryn Mawr, Pa., 1975-79; assoc. Harvey, Pennington, Herting & Renneisen Ltd., Phila., 1979-86; sole practice, Ardmore, Pa., 1986—; adj. asst. prof. bus. law Drexel U., 1978; ad hoc lectr. on estate and tax planning to civic and charitable groups; spl. counsel Am. Soc. Farm Mgrs. and Rural Appraisers, U.S. Ho. of Reps. Ways & Means Com., 1977. Served with USN, 1964-67, to lt. comdr. JAGC, USNR, 1973-75. Mem. Phila. Bar Assn., Pa. Bar Assn., ABA. Republican. Clubs: Overbrook Golf, Rittenhouse. Author: Estate Planner's Kit, 1978. Contbr. articles to profl. jours. Home: 1516 County Line Rd Rosemont PA 19010 Office: PO Box 778 Bryn Mawr PA 19010

KIRBY, KELVIN JEFFERSON, mechanical engineer; b. Birmingham, Eng., Mar. 18, 1961; s. Maurice William and Joyce Dorothy (Green) K.; m. Nicola Jane Thombs, Aug. 27, 1984. BS in Engring., Lanchester Poly. U., 1983, MS in Info. Systems and Tech., 1988. Engr. Land Rover U.K. Ltd., Birmingham, 1979-82, Gaydon Tech. Ltd., Warwick, Eng., 1982-83; tng. officer Austin Rover Group, Coventry, Eng., 1983-85; tng. exec. Jaguar Cars PLC, Coventry, 1985—; bd. dirs. Electronic Security Systems Ltd., Stratford-Upon Avon; cons. Metrotec. Devel. U.K. Ltd., Stratford-Upon Avon, 1982—. Mem. Instn. Mech. Engrs. (assoc.). Conservative. Mem. Ch. of England. Home: 2 Lincoln Close Wellesbourne, Warwick CV35 9JE, England Office: Jaguar Cars, Sandy Lane, Coventry CV6 3GB, England

KIRCHER, JOHN JOSEPH, law educator; b. Milw., July 26, 1938; s. Joseph John and Martha Marie (Jach) K.; m. Marcia Susan Adamkiewicz, Aug. 26, 1961; children: Joseph John, Mary Kathryn. BA, Marquette U., 1960, JD, 1963. Bar: Wis. 1963, U.S. Dist. Ct. (ea. dist.) Wis. 1963. Sole practice, Port Washington, Wis., 1963-66; with Def. Research Inst., Milw., 1966-80, research dir., 1972-80; with Marquette U., 1970—, prof. law, 1980—; chmn. Wis. Jud. Council, 1981-83. Author: (with J.D. Ghiardi) Punitive Damages: Law and Practice, 1981; mem. editorial bd. Def. Law Jour. and Products Liability Law Rev.; contbr. articles to profl. jours. Recipient Teaching Excellence award Marquette U., 1986, Disting. Service award Def. Research Inst., 1980, Marquette Law Rev. Editor's award, 1988. Mem. ABA, Am. Law Inst., Wis. Bar Assn., Wis. Supreme Ct. Bd. Atty.'s Profl. Competence, Am. Judicature Soc., Assn. Internationale de Droit des Assurances. Roman Catholic. Lodge: Scribes. Address: 1103 W Wisconsin Ave Milwaukee WI 53233

KIRCHGAESSLER, KLAUS-UWE, medical sociologist; b. Augsburg, Fed Republic Germany, Sept. 1, 1955; s. Klaus and Elisabeth (Reiter) K.; m. Bettina Stankewitz, Aug. 22, 1987. MD, U. Giessen, Fed. Republic Germany, 1984, Doctorate in Medicine, 1986. Lectr. in med. sociology U. Giessen, 1984—; adv. WHO European Office, Copenhagen, 1984, 87. Author: Diagnose U. Deutung, 1986; contbr. articles to profl. jours. Deutsche Forschungs-Gemeinschaft research grantee, 1987—. Mem. European Soc. Med. Sociology, German Soc. Sociology. Roman Catholic. Office: U Giessen, Friedrichstrasse 24, 6300, Giessen Federal Republic of Germany

KIRCHMAN, CHARLES VINCENT, lawyer; b. Washington, June 28, 1935; s. Floyd Vincent and Dorothy Johanna (Johnson) K.; m. Erika Ottilie Knoeppel, July 4, 1959; children: Mark C., Eric H., Charles E. BA, U. Md., 1959; JD, George Washington U., 1962. Bar: D.C. 1962, Md. 1970. Security specialist Adj. Gen.'s Office, U.S. Army, 1962-64; sole practice, Washington, 1964-70, Wheaton, Md., 1970-73; ptnr. Andrews & Schick, Waldorf, Md., 1973-77; sole practice, Wheaton, Md., 1977—. Mem. adv. bd. Immigration Reform Law Inst. Served with AUS, 1953-56. Mem. Am. Trial Lawyers Assn., D.C. Bar Assn., Md. Bar Assn., Charles County Bar Assn., Am. Arbitration Assn. (nat. panel), Md. Hist. Soc. Democrat. Club: Manor Country. Home: 14801 Notley Rd Silver Spring MD 20904 Office: 11141 Georgia Ave Wheaton MD 20902

KIRCHNER, JAMES WILLIAM, electrical engineer; b. Cleve., Oct. 17, 1920; s. William Sebastian and Marcella Louise (Stuart) K.; m. Eda Christene Landfear, June 11, 1950 (dec. May 1977); children—Kathleen Ann Kirchner Stewart, Susan Lynn Kirchner Boundane. B.S. in Elec. Engring., Ohio U., 1950, M.S., 1951. Registered profl. engr., Ohio. Instr. elec. engring. Ohio U., Athens, 1950-52; mgr. liaison engring. Lear Siegler Inc., Maple Heights, Ohio, 1952-64; coordinator engring. services Case Western Res. U., Cleve., 1964-72, gen. mgr. Med. Ctr. Co. (CWRU), 1972—. Mem. Portage County Republican Exec. Com., 1961-62; treas. PTA, Aurora, Ohio, 1963-65, v.p., 1965-66; mem. The Ch. in Aurora, 1956—. Served with USAAF, 1942-45, PTO. Mem. Cleve. Soc. Profl. Engrs. (bd. dirs. 1969-71), Nat. Soc. Profl. Engrs., Ohio Soc. Profl. Engrs., Cleve. Engring. Soc. (chmn. environ. com. 1976), IEEE (sr.), Air Pollution Control Assn., Am. Soc. Engring. Edn. Home: 140 Aurora Hudson Rd Aurora OH 44202 Office: 2250 Circle Dr Cleveland OH 44106

KIRCHNER, RICHARD JAY, educator; b. Schenectady, Feb. 17, 1930; s. Richard Jacob and Leah (Williams) K.; B.S., U. Wis., 1952, M.S., 1955, postgrad., 1956; Ed.D., Mich. State U, 1962; m. Barbara Ann Crane, Feb. 2, 1952; children—Richard Alec, Barbara Jayne, Carolyn Diane, Robert Jay, Kathleen Kay. Instr. wrestling and track coach St. Cloud (Minn.) Tchrs. Coll., 1955-56; asst. prof., coaching staff Central Mich. U., Mt. Pleasant, 1956-62, prof. recreation, chmn. dept., 1962-87, with Office of Dean sch. edn., health and human services, 1987-88, chmn. pres.'s adv. com.; camp program dir., camp dir. Elkton-Pigeon-Bayport Sch. Camp, Caseville, Mich., 1962; municipal recreation dir. Petoskey (Mich.), 1963, cons., 1964-74; vice chmn. citizens adv. com. Recreation Services div. Mich. Dept. Conservation, 1966-67. Pres. Mt. Pleasant Intermediate Sch. PTA, 1968-69; chmn. tech. planning com. Mt. Pleasant Recreation Commn. Served to capt. USMCR, 1952-54. Mem. AAHPER (v.p. Mich. 1966-67, v.p. Midwest dist. 1973-74), Nat Recreation and Parks Assn., Am. Assn. Leisure and Recreation (nat. pres. 1976-77, nat. accreditation council 1978-83, vice chmn. 1979-81, chmn. 1981-83), Am. Camp Assn., Mich. Soc. Arts, Sci. and Letters, Mich. Soc. Gerontology, Outdoor Edn. and Camping Council (charter), Mich. Recreation and Parks Assn. (v.p. 1968-70), Phi Eta Sigma, Phi Epsilon Kappa, Phi Delta Kappa. Home: 6953 Riverside Dr Mount Pleasant MI 48858

KIRDAR, EDIB E., civil engineer; b. Izmir, Turkey, Dec. 25, 1931; s. Emin and Nuzhet K.; came to U.S., 1959, naturalized, 1977; B.S. in Civil Engring., Robert Coll., Istanbul, Turkey, 1955; postgrad. Ariz. State U., 1959-68; m. Zeynep Keymen, Jan. 28, 1961; children—Leyla, Murad. Mgr. Office Internat. Affairs, Salt River Project, Phoenix, 1959—; mem. Am. Spl. Study Program, Dept. State visit Middle East, 1977; mem. U.S. Delegation to UN Conf. Hungary, 1985; U.S. Agy. Internat. Devel. cons. to Pakistan, 1985. Pres., Scottsdale Community Players, 1973; bd. dirs. Ariz. Teen Talent Search Inc. Recipient cert. of service Salt River project Employees Recreational Assn., 1969, 72. Mem. ASCE, Am. Water Resources Assn., Am. Public Works Assn., Western Snow Conf., Ariz. Water Resources Com., World Affairs Council Phoenix (v.p. 1985-86), Phoenix Com. on Fgn. Relations. Republican. Moslem. Lodges: Lions (pres. Tempe), Moose (dir. 1978, Rookie of Yr. award 1979); Papago Toastmasters (pres. 1969, 75, Able Toastmasters cert. and speech awards). Contbr. tech. articles on hydrology, runoff forecast, reservoir ops., computer modeling to profl. jours. Office: Salt River Project PO Box 52025 Phoenix AZ 85072-2025

KIRIAKOPOULOS, GEORGE CONSTANTINE, dentist; b. Derby, Conn., June 3, 1926; s. Constantine Elias and Rose (Yerontakis) K.; A.A., U. Paris (France), 1947; A.B., Bklyn. Coll., 1950; D.D.S., Columbia, 1954; m. Virginia Demos, June 3, 1956; 1 dau., Stephanie. Pvt. practice gen. dentistry, Fort Lee, N.J., 1955—; assoc. dir. dept. dentistry St. Giles Hosp., Bklyn., 1955-60; attending dept. oral surgery Lenox Hill Hosp., N.Y.C., 1956-60, adj. oral surgeon, 1960-64; assoc. prof., then prof. dept. pedodontics Columbia, 1956—; attending in dentistry Presbyn. Hosp., 1986—. Served with AUS, 1943-46. Decorated Bronze Star, Silver Star, D.S.M.; recipient Medal of Meritorious Service, Lenox Hill Hosp., 1964. Fellow Royal Soc. Health; mem. ADA, Am. Assn. Hosp. Dentists, N.Y. State Dental Soc., Columbia U. Alumni Assn., Psi Omega. Greek Orthodox (pres. Parish Council, Cathedral St. John, Tenafly, 1980—). Author: Your Child's Teeth - the Layman's View, 1966; Who Wants to Be a Dentist?, 1968; The Modern Thermopylae—Battle of Crete, May 1941, 1978; Portrait of a Cretan Hero, 1978; Cyprus and the Polish Connection, 1980; Ten Days of Destiny, 1985, Paperback edit., 1986, others. Home: 2205 Mackay Ave Fort Lee NJ 07024 Office: 415 West St Fort Lee NJ 07024

KIRK, CARMEN ZETLER, data processing executive; b. Altoona, Pa., May 22, 1941; d. Paul Alan and Mary Evelyn (Pearce) Zetler. BA, Pa. State U., 1959-63; MBA, St. Mary's Coll. Calif., 1977. Cert. in data processing. Pub. sch. tchr. State Ga., 1965-66; systems analyst U.S. Govt. Dept. Army, Oakland, Calif., 1967-70; programmer analyst Contra Costa County, Martinez, Calif., 1970-76; applications mgr. Stanford (Calif.) U., 1976-79; owner Zetler Assocs., Palo Alto, Calif., 1979—; cons. State Calif., Sacramento, 1985—. Author: (tech. manuals) Comparex, 1982-83. Vol. Stanford Med. Ctr. Aux., 1985—. Office: Zetler Assocs PO Box 50395 Palo Alto CA 94303

KIRK, DENNIS DEAN, lawyer; b. Pittsburg, Kans., Dec. 13, 1950; s. Homer Standley and Maida Corena (Rouse) K. A.A., Hutchinson Community Jr. Coll., 1970; B.S. with distinction, No. Ariz. U., 1972; J.D., Washburn U., 1975. Bar: Kans. 1975, U.S. Dist. Ct. Kans. 1975, D.C. 1977, U.S. Ct. Appeals (D.C. cir.) 1978, U.S. Supreme Ct. 1979, U.S. Ct. Appeals (5th cir.) 1981, U.S. Dist. Ct. Md. 1984, U.S. Tax Ct. 1984, U.S. Claims Ct. 1984, U.S. Ct. Appeals (fed. cir.) 1984, U.S. Ct. Mil. Appeals 1984. Trial atty. ICC, Washington, 1975-77; assoc. Goff, Sims, Cloud, Stroud & Walker, Washington, 1977-82; sole practice, Washington, 1982—; dir., v.p. law Collegiate Challenge, Inc., Vienna, Va., 1984; dir., pres., Law Facilities, Inc., Washington, 1982—. Vol. parole and probation officer Shawnee County, Kans., 1973-74; mem. Citizens' Adv. Task Force Group, Md. Nat. Park and Planning Commn., 1978-80; mem. citizens' task force on gen. plan amendments study Fairfax County Council, Va., 1981-82; mem. Seven Corners Task Force, Fairfax County, 1981-82, chmn. transp. and housing subcoms.; pres. Seven Springs Tenants' Assn., College Park, Md., 1976-80, Ravenwood Park Citizens' Assn., 1981-82; dir. Greenwood Homes, Ic., Fairfax County Dept. Housing and Community Devel., 1983—; mem. Gala Com. Spotlight the Kennedy Ctr., Pres.' Adv. Com. on the Arts, 1986-87; founding chmn., charter mem. Mason Dist. Jaycees, 1984-86; sec., gen. counsel, bd. dirs. U.S. Assocs. for the Cultural Triangle in Sri Lanka, 1983—; commr. Consumer Protection Commn., Fairfax County, 1982—; mem. Mason Dist. Rep. Com., 1981—; Ravenwood precinct chmn. Republican Orgn., Falls Church, Va., 1982-87; active Fairfax County Young Reps. Named to Honorable Order Ky. Cols. Mem. ABA, Assn. Trial Lawyers Am., Specialized Carriers and Rigging Assn., Regional Distbn. Carriers Conf., Nat. Rifle Assn. (life), Am. Fed. Musicians (life), Phi Kappa Phi, Phi Alpha Delta. Methodist. Lodge: Masons (life), Shriners (life). Avocation: music. Home: 6315 Anneliese Dr Falls Church VA 22044 Office: Dennis Dean & Kirk National Pl N Suite 1213 1331 Pennsylvania Ave NW Washington DC 20004

KIRK, ROBERT LEONARD, aerospace executive; b. Charleston, W.Va., Jan. 4, 1929; s. William Edward and Lillian (Dunnigan) K.; m. Elise Kuhl, July 2, 1955; 3 children. B.S. in Engring., Purdue U., 1952. Engr. Rockwell Internat., 1955-58, Litton Industries, Inc., Calif., Wash., Switzerland, 1958-67; v.p. ITT, N.Y.C., 1967-77; pres., chief exec. officer LTV Aerospace and Def. Co., Dallas, 1977-86; pres., chief operating officer The LTV Corp., Dallas, 1986—; pres., chief exec. officer Allied Signal Aerospace Co., Arlington, Va.; former dir. Planning and Research Corp., First City Bank of Dallas. Trustee Falcon Found., Ctr. for Strategic and Internat. Studies; bd. dirs. U.S. Air Force Acad. Found.; former com. chmn. Tex. Sci. and Tech. Council; chmn. exec. coalition Nat. Initiative for Tech. and Disabled. Served with USN, 1952-55. Recipient Disting. Pub. Service award HHS. Fellow AIAA (assoc.); mem. Aerospace Industries Assn. (chmn. bd. govs. 1986), S.W. Research Inst. (trustee), Am. Def. Preparedness Assn. (bd. dirs.). Office: Allied-Signal Aerospace Co 1000 Wilson Blvd Arlington VA 22209 *

KIRK, ROBIN RICHARD, accountant; b. Oamaru, Otago, N.Z., May 18, 1940; s. Robert C. and Hilda Mary (Notman) K.; m. Colleen Shirley Kirk, Mar. 30, 1961 (dec.); children—Peter Robert, Dierdre Joy. B.A., Victoria U., 1978. Sr. Supr. Post Office, N.Z., 1955-79; acct. N.Z. Coop. Dairy Co., Hamilton, 1980—. Mem. bd. rep. N.Z. Jaycees, 1968-72. Recipient prize in pub. adminstrn. Civil Service Inst., 1976. Mem. N.Z. Inst. Pub. Adminstrn., Inst. Internal Auditors. Presbyterian. Address: 17 Powells Rd, Hamilton, Waikato 2001, New Zealand

KIRK, ROGER, foreign service officer; b. Newport, R.I., Nov. 2, 1930; s. Alan Goodrich and Lydia Selden (Chapin) K.; m. Madeleine Elizabeth Yaw, Apr. 20, 1954; children: Marian, Sarah Kirk Love, Julia Kirk Thompson, Alan. A.B., Princeton U., 1952; postgrad., Johns Hopkins U. Sch. Advanced Internat. Studies, 1953. Joined Fgn. Service, 1955; adminstrv. asst. Am. embassy, Moscow, USSR, 1949-50, 51; mem. staff Exec. Secretariat, Dept. State, Washington, 1955-57; staff asst. Office Sec. State, 1960-61, Office Soviet Affairs, 1962-63; polit. officer Rome, Italy, 1957-59, Moscow, 1963-65, New Delhi, India, 1965-67, Saigon, Vietnam, 1968-69; internat. relations officer Bur. East Asian Affairs, 1969-71; assigned Sr. Seminar, 1971-72; dep. asst. dir. Internat. Relations Bur., ACDA, 1972-73; ambassador to Somalia, Mogadiscio, 1973-75; dep. dir. Bur. Intelligence and Research, Dept. State, 1975-78; resident rep. U.S. Mission to IAEA, 1978-83; permanent U.S. rep. to UN Indsl. Devel. Orgn., 1980-83; sr. dep. asst. sec. Bur. Internat. Orgn. Affairs, Dept. State, 1983-85; U.S. ambassador to Romania Bucharest, 1985—. Served to lt. USAF, 1952-55. Episcopalian. Office: Am Embassy-Bucharest AmCon Gen APO New York NY 09213

KIRK, RUSSELL AMOS, writer, lecturer, foundation president; b. Plymouth, Mich., Oct. 19, 1918; s. Russell Andrew and Marjorie (Pierce) K.; m. Annette Yvonne Courtemanche, Sept. 19, 1964; 4 children. B.A., Mich. State U., 1940; M.A., Duke U., 1941; D.Litt., St. Andrews U., Scotland, 1952; hon. degrees include; Litt.D., Boston Coll., St. John's U., Loyola Coll., Balt., Gannon Coll., Central Mich. U., Albion Coll., Grand Valley Coll.; L.L.D., Park Coll., Niagara U., Pepperdine U.; L.H.D., Le Moyne Coll.; D.Journalism, Olivet Coll., 1977. Pres., Ednl. Reviewer Found., 1960—, Marguerite Eyer Wilbur Found., 1979—; vis. prof. various univs.; Fulbright lectr., Scotland, 1987; dir. social sci. program Ednl. Research Council Am., 1979-85. Contbr. to scholarly and popular publs., U.S., Can., Gt. Britain, Australia, Italy, Norway, Austria, including Sewanee Rev., Contemporary Rev., Dublin Rev., Yale Rev., Jour. History of Ideas, Annals of Am. Acad., N.Y. Times mag., Fortune, Wall St. Jour., History Today, Gen. Edn., The Critic, Kenyon Rev., Nat. Rev., The Month, Southwest Rev., Commonweal, Christianity Today, Queen's Quar., America, Chronicles of Culture, Analysis, Center mag., The World & I; founder quar. jour.: Modern Age; editor quar.: Univ. Bookman; Author: John Randolph of Roanoke, 1951, 64, 78, The Conservative Mind, 1953, 73, 78, 86, St. Andrews, 1954, A Program for Conservatives, 1954, 88, Academic Freedom, 1955, Beyond the Dreams of Avarice, 1956, The Intelligent Woman's Guide to Conservatism, 1957, The American Cause, 1957, Old House of Fear, 1961, 63, The Surly Sullen Bell, 1962, Confessions of a Bohemian Tory, 1963, The Intemperate Professor, 1965, A Creature of the Twilight, 1966, Edmund Burke, 1967, 88, Political Principles of Robert A. Taft, 1967, Enemies of the Permanent Things, 1969, 84, Eliot and His Age, 1972, 84, Roots of American Order, 1974, 78,The Princess of All Lands, 1979, Decadence and Renewal in Higher Learning, 1979, Lord of the Hollow Dark, 1979, Portable Conservative Reader, 1982, Reclaiming a Patrimony, 1983, Watchers at the Strait Gate, 1984, The Wise Men Know What Wicked Things Are Written on the Sky, 1987; also critical intros. and prefaces to reprints standard scholarly works. Recipient Ingersoll prize for scholarly writing, 1984; Guggenheim fellow.; sr. fellow Am. Council Learned Socs.; Constl. fellow NEH; disting. fellow Heritage Found. Address: Piety Hill Mecosta MI 49332

KIRK, VIRGINIA, psychologist, retired; b. Kirksville, Mo., Dec. 22, 1895; d. Sherman and Harriet Rose (White) K.; B.A., Drake U., 1917; postgrad. U. Nanking (China), 1921-22; B.N., Yale U., 1927, M.S., 1930; Ph.D., U. Chgo., 1949. Research asst. Yale Psycho-Clinic, New Haven, 1930-31; dir. nursing Emma Pendleton Bradley Home, Riverside, R.I., 1931-35; asst. in ednl. psychology Columbia U., N.Y.C., summer 1935; research assoc. Williamson County Child Guidance Study, Franklin, Tenn., 1935-42; instr. Sch. Medicine, Vanderbilt U., Nashville, 1943-47, asst. prof., 1947-53, assoc. prof., 1953-60, asso. clin. prof. emerita, 1961—; pvt. practice clin. psychology, 1948-73, part-time, 1973-76; cons. psychologist sponsored Center of Research, Vanderbilt U. Hosp., 1963-73; cons. clin. psychologist Family and Children's Service, Nashville, 1953-73; mem. childhood and adolescence com. Nashville Mental Health Assn., 1975-76. Recipient Disting. Alumni Service award Drake U., 1965; lic. psychologist, Tenn.; cert. clin. psychologist, Va.; diplomate in clin. psychology Am. Bd. Profl. Psychology. Fellow Am. Psychol. Assn.; mem. Tenn. (honors award 1976), Midwestern, Southeastern psychol. assns., Am. Assn. Mental Deficiency, N.Y. Acad. Scis., Tenn. Acad. Sci., Canby Robinson Soc. of Vanderbilt Med. Sch. (life), AAAS. Author: (with E.S. Robinson) Introduction to Psychology, 1935; also articles. Club: Yale of Mid. Tenn. Address: Apt 404 The Towers 4343 Lebanon Rd Hermitage TN 37076

KIRKBRIDE, CHALMER GATLIN, chemical engineer; b. nr. Tyrone, Okla., Dec. 27, 1906; s. Zachariah Martin and Georgia Anna (Gatlin) K.; m. Billie Lucille Skains, Apr. 13, 1939; 1 son, Chalmer Gatlin Jr. B.S.E., U. Mich., 1930, M.S.E., 1930; Sc.D., Beaver Coll., 1959; Eng. D., Drexel U., 1960, Widener U., 1970. Chem. engr. research dept. Standard Oil Co., Whiting, Ind., 1930-34; dir. tech. service Am. Oil Co., Texas City, Tex., 1934-41; chief chem. engring. devel. Mobil Oil Co., Dallas, 1942-44; Disting. prof. Tex. A&M U., 1944-47, cons. chem. engr., 1944-47; sci. cons. to sec. of War Bikini atomic bomb tests, 1946; v.p. charge research and devel. Houdry Process Corp., Marcus Hook, Pa., 1947-52; pres. and chmn. bd. Houdry Process Corp., Phila., 1952-56; dir. Houdry Process Corp., 1948-62, Catalytic Constrn. Co., 1952-56; exec. dir. comml. devel., research, engring. and patent depts. Sun Oil Co., Phila., 1956-60; v.p. comml. devel., research, engring. and patents Sun Oil Co., 1960-70, corp. dir., 1963-70; now pres. Kirkbride Assocs., Inc. div. Amoco Chems. Co., Chgo.; pres. Avisun, Phila., 1959-60; dir. Avisun (now div. Amoco Chems. Co., Chgo.), 1959-68, Sunolin Chem. Co., 1957-68; exec. producer motion picture The Seeds of Evil, 1972; Dir. Coordinating Research Council, 1958-70; pres. Co-ordinating Research Council, 1965-67; Mem. Pres. Nixon's Task Force on Oceanography, 1969; mem. adv. panel on sea grant programs NOAA Dept. Commerce, 1970-74; petroleum specialist Fed. Energy Agy., 1974-75; sci. adviser to adminstr. ERDA, 1975-77, cons. engr., 1978—; pres. Kirkbride Assocs. Inc., 1979—. Author: Chemical Engineering Fundamentals, 1947; Contbr. articles to profl. jours. Trustee Widener U., Chester, Pa., 1956-72, hon., 1972—, vice chmn. bd. trustees, 1959-71; chmn. bd. dirs. Riddle Meml. Hosp., 1965-67, dir., 1965-71. Served as 2d lt. Chem. Warfare Res., 1935-40. Recipient Disting. Pub. Service award U.S. Navy, 1968; Engring. Centennial medal Widener U., 1970; George Washington award Phila. Engring. Club, 1971; Dedicated Kirkbride Hall of Sci. and Engring. Widener U., 1965; elected to Nat. Acad. Engring., 1967. Fellow Am. Inst. Chem. Engrs. (pres. 1954, Profl. Progress award 1951, Founders award 1967, Fuels and Petrochem. award 1976, named Eminent Chem. Engr. 1983); mem. Am. Chem. Soc., Am. Petroleum Inst., Alpha Chi Sigma, Phi Lambda Upsilon, Tau Beta Pi. Clubs: Army-Navy (Washington). Office: 4000 Massachusetts Ave NW Suite 805 Washington DC 20016

KIRKELIE, GREGORY EVAN, lawyer; b. Santa Monica, Calif., Mar. 30, 1942; s. George Evan and Margaret Allen (Moody) K.; m. Beverly Anne Ward, Aug. 7, 1967; children—Carrie Ann, Daniel Evan. B.A. cum laude, Calif. State U.-Northridge, 1964; J.D., U. So. Calif., 1970. Bar: Calif. 1970, U.S. Dist Ct. (cen. dist.) Calif 1970. Ptnr. Ervin, Cohen & Jessup, Beverly Hills, Calif., 1970-80; v.p. legal and gen. counsel Factors Etc., Inc., Bear, Del., 1978-80; prin. Kirkelie Bus. Parks, Chatsworth, Calif., 1981—. Bd. dirs. Los Angeles Bapt. City Mission Soc., 1972—, Eastern Coll., St. Davids, Pa., 1982—. Served to lt. (j.g.) USNR, 1964-67. Mem. ABA, Calif. Bar Assn., Los Angeles County Bar Assn., Order of Coif. Republican. Baptist. Address: 10951 Oso Ave Chatsworth CA 91311

KIRKHAM, DON, soil physicist, educator; b. Provo, Utah, Feb. 11, 1908; s. Francis Washington and Martha Alzina (Robison) K.; m. Mary Elizabeth Erwin, Sept. 2, 1939; children: Victoria, Mary Beth, Don Collier. Clarinetist diploma, McCune Sch. Music and Art, Salt Lake City, 1926; student, U. Utah, 1925-27; A.B. with honors in physics, Columbia U., 1933, A.M. in Physics, 1934, Ph.D., 1938; Erediplom, U. Ghent, Belgium, 1958; D.Agrl. Scis. (hon.), Royal Agrl. U., Ghent, 1963. Asst. in physics Columbia U., 1934-38; instr., asst. prof. math. and physics, also asso. Agrl. Expt. Sta., Utah State U., 1937-40; hydraulic engr. Soil Conservation Service, Dept. Agr., 1940; civilian physicist Bur. Ordnance, U.S. Navy, 1940-46; asso. physics George Washington U., 1946; mem. faculty Iowa State U., Ames, 1946—; Curtiss Disting. prof. agr., prof. agronomy and physics Iowa State U., 1959-78, prof. emeritus, 1978—; Fulbright prof., The Netherlands, 1950-51, Guggenheim fellow, Belgium, 1957-58; lectr. U. Vienna, Austria, 1958, Ireland, 1960; lectr. Göttingen (Germany) U., 1974; land reclamation adviser Turkish Govt., 1959; Ford Found. land reclamation cons. UAR; also lectr. Alexandria (Egypt) U., 1961; guest prof. Hohenheim-Stuttgart U., 1982; sect. chmn. Internat. Soil Structure Symposium, Belgium, 1958; panelist IAEA, Vienna, 1960; lectr., Yugoslavia, Bulgaria, 1964; mem. U.S. AID Univ. Study Team, Argentina, summer 1965; panelist on land reclamation FAO, Egypt, 1974-77; council Internat. Sodic Soil Symposium, Budapest, 1964; soil physics del. to internat. congresses and symposia, Armenia, 1969, Moscow, 1971, New Delhi, 1971, Belgium, 1973, Madras, India, 1973; sect. chmn. 7th congress Internat. Soil and Tillage Orgn., Uppsala, Sweden, 1976. Author: (with W.L. Powers) Advanced Soil Physics; contbr. numerous articles to books, sci. jours.; assoc. editor: Jour. Water Resources Research, 1965-71; cons. editor: Soil Science. Dir. Iowa Water Resources Research Council, 1964-73; Active Boy Scouts Am.; mem. Utah N.G., 1925-27. Co-recipient Internat. Wolf prize in Agr., Israel, 1984; recipient Gov.'s medal for sci. achievement in Iowa, 1985, Merit Honor award U. Utah, 1987. Fellow Am. Phys. Soc., Am. Soc. Agronomy; mem. Am. Geophysics Union (award most meritorious paper sci. hydrology 1952), Soil Sci. Soc. Am. (chmn. soil physics 1950, Stevenson award 1951, 25th anniversary honor lect. 1961, del. to internat. meetings in Bucharest 1964, hon. mem.), Am. Math. Assn., Netherlands Soc. Agrl. Research, Internat. Soil Sci. Soc. (U.S. v.p. 1957-59), Iowa Acad. Soc. (most meritorious paper math. 1948, physics 1949), Internat. Soil Tillage Orgn. (hon. 1982), S.A.R. (v.p. Iowa 1966), Internat. Soc. Soil Sci. (hon. 1986), Am. Water Research Assn. (hon. 1986), Sigma Xi (honor lectr. U. Iowa chpt. 1959), Phi Kappa Phi, Gamma Sigma Delta. Republican. Mem. Ch. of Jesus Christ of Latter-Day Saints (missionary Germany 1927-30, pres. Hamburg dist. 1930). Home: 2109 Clark Ave Ames IA 50010

KIRKHAM, FRANCIS ROBISON, lawyer; b. Fillmore, Utah, Aug. 23, 1904; s. Francis W. and Alzina (Robison) K.; m. Ellis Musser, July 9, 1929; children: James F., Elizabeth (Mrs. James Stillman, Jr.), Katherine (Mrs. Geoffrey Hallam Movius), Eugene R. A.B., George Washington U., 1930, LL.B., 1931. Bar: D.C. 1931, Calif. 1936. Law clk. Chief Justice Charles E. Hughes, 1933-35; with firm Pillsbury, Madison & Sutro, San Francisco, 1936—; partner Pillsbury, Madison & Sutro, 1940—; gen. counsel Standard Oil Co., Calif., 1960-70; Mem. atty. gen.'s nat. com. to study antitrust laws, 1953-55, mem. commn. on Revision Fed. Ct. Appellate System, 1973. Author: (with Reynolds Robertson) Jurisdiction of the Supreme Court of the U.S. Drafted for Supreme Court Revision of General Orders in Bankruptcy, 1936, 39. Recipient Alumni Achievement award; George Washington U., 1970; Alumni Merit Honor award U. Utah, 1976. Fellow Am. Coll. Trial Lawyers, Am. Bar Found.; mem. ABA (chmn. anti-trust law sect. 1961), San Francisco Bar Assn., State Bar Calif., Am. Law Inst., Am. Judicature Soc., Am. Soc. Internat. Law, Order of Coif, Delta Theta Phi. Clubs: Pacific Union (San Francisco), Bohemian (San Francisco), San Francisco Golf (San Francisco), Stock Exchange (San Francisco). Home: 3245 Pacific Ave San Francisco CA 94118 Office: Pillsbury Madison & Sutro 225 Bush St San Francisco CA 94104-2105

KIRKMAN, HADLEY, anatomist, researcher; b. Richmond, Ind., Mar. 14, 1901; s. Madison Lee and Leila Piety (Hadley) K.; m. Gladys L. Tracy, Apr. 5, 1942; 1 dau., Tracy Leigh Kirkman-Liff. A.B., Iowa U., Iowa City, 1925; student, Bradley U., Peoria, Ill., 1923-24; M.S., U. Chgo., 1929; Ph.D., Columbia U., 1937. Acting asst. prof. zoology Ohio U., 1928-29; instr. anatomy N.Y. Med. Coll., 1929-32, Columbia U., 1934-36, Stanford (Calif.) U., 1936-38, asst. prof., 1938-43, assoc. prof., 1943-59, prof., 1949-65, active prof. emeritus, 1965—. Contbr. numerous articles to profl. jours. NSF, sr. fellow, 1957-58; USPHS, spl. fellow, 1958-59; research grantee Am. Cancer Soc., Jane Coffin Childs Meml. Fund, Yale U., USPHS, 1948-76. Fellow N.Y. Acad. Scis., AAAS; mem. Am. Assn. Anatomists, Am. Assn. Cancer Research, AAUP, Gamma Alpha, Sigma Xi. Democrat. Home: 623 Cabrillo Ave Stanford CA 94305 Office: Stanford University Room 8 Old Anatomy Bldg Stanford CA 94305

KIRKPATRICK, ALLEN, lawyer; b. Pitts., Dec. 5, 1919; s. Allen and Elizabeth Moorehead (Hamilton) K.; m. Susette Silvester, Sept. 2, 1944; children—Allen, Susette, Sally, Richard. B.S. in Elec. Engring., MIT, 1943; LL.B., U. Va., 1948. Bar: D.C. 1948, Md. 1967, U.S. Ct. Claims 1950, U.S. Ct. Customs and Patent Appeals 1950, U.S. Ct. Appeals (1st, 2d, 4th, 5th, 6th and 9th cirs.), U.S. Supreme Ct. 1951. Examiner, U.S. Patent Office, Washington, 1948-50; assoc. Cushman, Darby & Cushman, Washington 1950-54, ptnr., 1954—. Served to lt. (j.g.) USNR, 1943-46. Fellow Am. Coll. Trial Lawyers; mem. ABA, Am. Patent Law Assn., Bar Assn. D.C., D.C. Bar Assn. Republican. Clubs: Chevy Chase, Metropolitan (Washington). Office: Cushman Darby & Cushman 1615 L St NW Washington DC 20036

KIRKPATRICK, ANNE SAUNDERS, systems analyst; b. Birmingham, Mich., July 4, 1938; d. Stanley Rathbun and Esther (Casteel) Saunders; m. Robert Armstrong Kirkpatrick, Oct. 5, 1963; children: Elizabeth, Martha, Robert, Sarah. Student, Wellesley Coll., 1956-57, Laval U., Quebec City, Can., 1958, U. Ariz., 1958-59; BA in Philosophy, U. Mich., 1961. Systems engr. IBM, Chgo., 1962-64; systems analyst Commonwealth Edison Co., Chgo., 1981—. Treas. Taproot Reps., DuPage County, Ill., 1977-80; pres. Hinsdale (Ill.) Women's Rep. Club, 1978-81. Club: Wellesley of Chgo. (bd. dirs. 1972-73). Home: 524 N Lincoln Hinsdale IL 60521 Office: Commonwealth Edison Co 72 W Adams Room 1122 Chicago IL 60603

KIRKPATRICK, EVRON MAURICE, foundation executive; b. nr. Raub, Ind., Aug. 15, 1911; s. Omer and Lenna Mae (Hain) K.; m. Jeane D. Jordan, Feb. 20, 1955; children: Thomas Reed (dec.), Mary Ellen, Ann Maureen, Douglas J., John E., Stuart A. BA with high honors, U. Ill., 1932, AM, 1933; PhD, Yale U., 1939; LLD, Ind. U., 1977. Instr. polit. sci. U. Minn., 1935-39, asst. prof., 1939-43, assoc. prof., 1943-48, prof., 1948, chmn. social sci. div., 1944-48; asst. research dir. research and analysis br. OSS, 1945; asst. research dir. and projects control Officer Research and Intelligence, Dept. State, Washington, 1946, intelligence program adviser, 1947, chief external research staff, 1948-52, chief psychol., intelligence and research staff, 1952-54, dep. dir. Office Research and Intelligence, 1954; exec. dir. Am. Polit. Sci. Assn., 1954-81; editorial adviser in polit. sci. Henry Holt & Co., 1952-60, Holt Rinehart, and Winston, 1960-68; chmn. bd. trustees Orgn. Pub. Research Inc., 1955—; lectr. Howard U., 1957-61; cons. Nat. Ednl. TV, 1963-65; professorial lectr. Georgetown U., 1959-84; mem. Pres.'s Commn. on Registration and Voting Participation, 1963-64, Commn. on Presdl. Campaign Debates, 1963-64, Presdl. Task Force on Career Advancement, 1966; mem. nat. adv. com. on accreditation and instnl. eligibility U.S. Dept. Edn. Author: The People, Politics and the Politician, 1941, American Government, 1942, Survey of American Government, 1943, (with A.N. Christensen) Running the Country, 1946, Target: The World Communist Propaganda Activities in 1955, 1956, (with Jeanne Kirkpatrick) Elections-U.S.A., 1956, Year of Crisis: An Analysis of Communist Propaganda Activities in 1956, 1957; contbr.: Man and Society, 1938, Essays on the Behavioral Study of Politics, 1962, Perspectives, 1963, Foundation of Political Science, 1977, The Past and Future of Presidential Debates, 1979; editor: World Affairs; mem. editorial adv. bd.: The Atlantic Community; contbr. articles to profl. jours. Trustee Nat. Ctr. Edn. Politics, Library Assocs., Georgetown U., 1979—; trustee Helen Dwight Reid Ednl. Found., 1960—, treas., 1964-72, pres., 1972—; dir. Govtl. Affairs Inst., 1954-64; mem. adv. com. on fgn. affairs So. Regional Edn. Bd., 1952-56; chmn. trustees Inst. Am. Univs., France, 1958—; bd. advisers Hubert H. Humphrey Inst., 1978—; bd. dirs. James Madison Found., 1985—, U.S. Inst. Peace, 1985—; resident scholar Am. Enterprise Inst., 1981-87. Mem. Nat. Arbitration Assn. (bd. arbitrators 1943-47), Internat. Polit. Sci. Assn. (mem. council 1955-67, exec. com. 1958-64), Am. Polit. Sci. Assn., Nat. Acad. Scis. (mem. div. behavioral scis. NRC 1963-66, mem. com. internat. relations in behavioral NRC 1966-70), U.S. Dept. Edn. Accreditation and Instnl. Eligibility (nat. adv. com. 1987—), Am. Peace Soc. (pres.), Phi Beta Kappa, Pi Sigma Alpha (mem. exec. com. 1958-80, pres. 1974-76). Home: 6812 Granby St Bethesda MD 20817 Office: 4000 Albemarle St NW Washington DC 20016

KIRKPATRICK, FORREST HUNTER, management consultant; b. Galion, Ohio, Sept. 4, 1905; s. Arch M. and Mildred (Hunter) K. Student, U. Dijon, 1926; A.B., Bethany Coll., 1927, LL.D., 1949; A.M., Columbia U., 1931, profl. diploma, 1934, 36; postgrad., U. London, U. Pitts., U. Pa., U. Cambridge, U. Oxford; LL.D., Coll. Steubenville, 1958, Drury Coll., 1968; Hum.D., Wheeling Coll., 1981. Dean, prof. Bethany Coll., 1927-40, 46-52; gen. mgr. personnel adminstrn. RCA, 1941-46, edn. cons., 1946-60; vis. prof. or lectr. N.Y. U., U. Pitts., Columbia U., U. Akron, U. Wis., Cornell U., 1938-54; asst. to chmn. Wheeling-Pitts. Steel Corp., 1952-64, v.p., 1964-70, vis. prof. W.Va. U., 1970-80; adj. prof. Bethany Coll., 1970-87; dir. Sharon Tube Co., Banner Fibreboard Co. Cons. Am. Council on Edn., 1938-45, War Manpower Com., 1942-44, Dept. State, 1944, U.S. Civil Service, 1945, Post Office Dept., 1953, HEW, 1970; mem. ednl. program com. USAF, 1948-51; mem. mission to Sweden Dept. Labor, 1962, mem. manpower adv. com., 1963-68; dir. Blue Cross & Blue Shield of W.Va., 1955-85. Mem. W.Va. Commn. Higher Edn., 1964-70, Edn. Com. of the States, 1973-77, Humanities Found. of W.Va., 1972-77, W.Va. Water Resources Bd., 1975-83, State Bldg. Commn., 1983—; bd. govs. W.Va. U., 1957-69; bd. dirs. Wheeling Symphony Soc., Inc., 1950-81, Wheeling Country Day Sch., 1953-64, 70-73, Northern Panhandle Behavioral Health Center, 1974-84; trustee Ohio Valley Med. Center, Inc., Wheeling, 1954-87. Mem. Indsl. Relations Research Assn. (life), Nat. Assn. Mfrs. (dir. 1965-70), Acad. Polit. Sci. (life), Am. Personnel and Guidance Assn. (life), NEA (life), AAUP (emeritus), Am. Mgmt. Assn. (emeritus), Nat. Vocat. Guidance Assn., Nat. Alliance Businessmen (met. chmn. 1971-72), Beta Gamma Sigma, Beta Theta Pi, Alpha Kappa Psi, Kappa Delta Pi, Phi Delta Kappa. Clubs: University (N.Y.C. and Pitts.); Fort Henry, Wheeling Country (Wheeling); Duquesne (Pitts.); Soc. Friends of St. George (Windsor Castle). Home: Tally Ho Apts 931 National Rd Wheeling WV 26003 Office: PO 268 Wheeling WV 26003

KIRKPATRICK, JEANE DUANE JORDAN, political scientist, government official; b. Duncan, Okla., Nov. 19, 1926; d. Welcher F. and Leona (Kile) Jordan; m. Evron M. Kirkpatrick, Feb. 20, 1955; children: Douglas Jordan, John Evron, Stuart Alan. AA, Stephens Coll., 1946; AB, Barnard Coll., 1948; MA, Columbia U., 1950, PhD, 1968; postgrad. (French govt. fellow), U. Paris Inst. de Sci. Politique, 1952-53; LHD (hon.), Mt. Vernon Coll., 1978, Georgetown U., 1981, U. Pitts., 1981, U. West Fla., 1981, U. Charleston, 1982, St. Anselm's, 1982, Hebrew U., 1982, Betheny Coll., 1983, Colo. Sch. Mines, 1983, St. John's U., 1983; Loyola Coll., 1985, Hebrew Union Coll., 1985, Universidad Francisco Marroquin, Guatemala, 1985, Coll. of William and Mary, 1986. Research analyst Dept. State, 1951-53; research asso. George Washington U., 1954-56, Fund for the Rep., 1956-58; asst. prof. polit. sci. Trinity Coll., 1962-67; assoc. prof. polit. sci. Georgetown U., Washington, 1967-73; prof. Georgetown U., 1973—; Leavey prof. in founds. Am. freedom, 1978—; sr. fellow Am. Enterprise Inst. for Pub. Policy Research, 1977—; mem. cabinet U.S. permanent rep. to UN, 1981-85; co-chmn. task force presdl. election process 20th Century Fund; cons. Am. Council Learned Socs., Dept. State, HEW, Dept. Def., intermittently 1955-72; vice chmn. com. on v.p. selection Democratic Nat. Com., 1972-74, mem. nat. commn. party structure and presdl. nomination, 1975; mem. credentials com. Dem. Nat. Conv., 1976; mem. internat. research council Center for Strategic and Internat. Studies. Author: Foreign Students in the United States: A National Survey, 1966, Mass Behavior in Battle and Captivity, 1968, Leader and Vanguard in Mass Society: The Peronist Movement in Argentina, 1971, Political Woman, 1974, The Presidential Elite, 1976, Dismantling the Parties: Reflections on Party Reform and Party Decomposition, 1978, The Reagan Phenomenon, 1983, Dictatorships and Doublestandards, 1982; Legitimacy and Force (2 vols.), 1988; editor, contbr.: Elections USA, 1956, Strategy of Deception, 1963, the New Class, 1978, The New American Political System, 1978; contbr. articles to Publius; others. Trustee Helen Dwight Reid Ednl. Found., 1972—; trustee Robert A. Taft Inst. Govt., 1978—; mem. bd. curators Stephens Coll. Recipient Disting. Alumna award Stephens Coll., 1978, B'nai B'rith Humanitarian award, 1982, award of the Commonwealth Fund, 1983, Gold medal VFW, 1984, French Prix Politique, 1984, Dept. Defense Disting. Pub. Service medal, 1985, Spl. award from the Mayor N.Y.C., 1985, Presdl. medal of Freedom, 1985, others; Earhart fellow, 1956-57. Mem. Internat. Polit. Sci. Assn. (exec. council), Am. Polit. Sci. Assn., So. Polit. Sci. Assn. Office: Am Enterprise Inst 1150 17th St NW Washington DC 20036

KIRKPATRICK, ROBERT HUGH, marketing executive; b. Kingston, N.Y., Mar. 3, 1954; s. Oscar Hugh and Ann (Page) K.; m. Debra Cook, Oct. 25, 1986; 1 child, Page. BA in Polit. Sci. with high honors, SUNY, Oneonta, 1977; M in Pub. and Pvt. Mgmt., Yale U., 1979. Policy analyst edn. com. N.Y. State Assembly, 1977; mgr. mktg. Cummins Engine Co., Columbus, Ind., 1980-81, mgr. mktg. ops., 1982-83, dir. electronics mktg., 1984-86; dir. bus. devel. Service Products Co. subs. Cummins Engine Co., Columbus, Ind., 1987—; cons. in field, New Haven, 1978-79. Contbr. articles to bus. jours. Trustee SUNY, Albany, N.Y., 1975-76; pres. Columbus Arts Guild, 1981-82; treas. Sans Souci, Inc., Columbus, 1983-85; mem. city transp. commn., Oneonta, N.Y., 1973-74. Club: Yale (Indpls.) (treas. 1981-85). Home: 3973 N Wood Lake Dr Columbus IN 47201 Office: Cummins Engine Co Box 3005 Columbus IN 47202

KIRONDE-KIGOZI, SAMS SENDAWULA, data processing executive; b. Mityana, Uganda, Oct. 17, 1943; s. Samson Kironde and Solome (Nalukwago) Birabwa; m. Alice Norah, Jan. 18, 1970 (dec. June 1975); children: Solome Nampala, Don Wassanyi; m. Flavia Nakawombe, Feb. 25,

1984; children: Andrew Joseph Sempala, Isaac Philip Kisitu. Cert. edn., Makerere U., Kampala, Uganda; Dip. TH candidate, Trinity Coll., Bristol, Eng.; MABS, Covenant Sem., St. Louis, 1980; DTh candidate, Internat. Bible Inst. and Seminary, Orlando, Fla., 1985—. Tchr. Namutamba Sch., Kampala, Uganda, 1966; depot mgr. Brooke Bond Ltd., Kamuli, Uganda, 1966-71; ter. mgr. Wrigley Co. E.A., Kampala, 1971-72; asst. pastor Redeemed Ch., Kampala, 1971-73; computer operator Sauer Computers, St. Louis, 1977-79; data processing mgr. Anheuser-Busch, Inc., Sylmar, Calif., 1980—. Exec. sec. Com. on Uganda, Inc., Van Nuys, Calif. 1978—; sec. Uganda Human Rights League, Washington, 1982-83; chmn. Ugandan Com. Dem. Assn., Los Angeles, 1982-84. Home: 6541 Kester Ave Van Nuys CA 91411 Office: Anheuser Busch 15420 Cobalt Sylmar CA 91342

KIRSCH, DANIEL LAWRENCE, medical device company executive, medical device designer and consultant; b. Bklyn., Nov. 20, 1954; s. Robert J. and May (Vichengrad) K. Student CUNY-Queens Coll., 1972-74, Los Angeles City Coll., 1975-76; BS, Los Angeles Coll. Chiropractic, 1976-79; PhD in Neurobiology, City U. Los Angeles, 1980-81. Assoc. dir. Nat. Acad. Acupuncture, N.Y.C., 1973-75; exec. dir. Nat. Electro-Acutherapy Found., Glendale, Calif., 1976-79; clin. dir. Electro-Acuptherapy Med. Ctr., Laguna Beach, Calif., 1979-80, Electro-Acuptherapy Pain Ctr., Palm Springs, Calif., 1980-81; chmn., chief exec. officer Electromed. Products, Inc., Hawthorne, Calif., 1981—; dean, grad. sch. electromedical scis. City U. Los Angeles, 1985—; vis. clin. dir. Ctr. for Pain and Stress, Columbia Univ., N.Y., 1985; Author: The Complete Clinical Guide to Electro-Acutherapy, 1978; editor Am. Jour. Electromedicine, 1984—; contbr. articles to profl. jours. Patentee Alpha-Stim. Mem. Los Angeles Better Bus. Bur., 1982—, Sell Overseas Am., Woodland Hills, Calif., 1982—. Mem. Health Industry Mfrs. Assn., AAAS, Internat. Electromedicine Inst. (chmn. adv. bd. 1982-83), Nat. Inst. Electromed. Info. (chmn. adv. bd. 1983-84), N.Y. Acad. Scis., AAUP Republican. Jewish. Home: PO Box 2486 Malibu CA 90265 Office: PO Box 2486 Malibu CA 90265

KIRSCH, LAURENCE STEPHEN, lawyer; b. Washington, July 20, 1957; s. Ben and Bertha (Gomberg) K.; m. Celia Goldman, Aug. 19, 1979. BAS, MS, U. Pa., 1979; JD, Harvard U., 1982. Bar: D.C. 1982, U.S. Ct. Appeals (3d cir.) 1983, U.S. Dist. Ct. D.C. 1985, U.S. Ct. Appeals (D.C. cir.) 1985, U.S. Supreme Ct. 1987. Law clk. to presiding judge Pa. Dist. Ct., Phila., 1982-83; vis. asst. prof. law U. Bridgeport (Conn.) Law Sch., 1983-84; assoc. Cadwalader, Wickersham & Taft, Washington, 1984—; chmn. steering coms. Superfund. Editor-in-chief Indoor Pollution Law Report, 1987—; contbr. articles to profl. jours. Mem. ABA, Fed. Bar Assn., AAAS, Air Pollution Control Assn. (indoor air quality com.), Environ. Law Inst., Nat. Inst. Bldg. Scis. (indoor air quality com.), Am. Soc. Testing and Measurement (indoor air quality com.), Phi Beta Kappa. Home: 5911 Gloster Rd Bethesda MD 20816 Office: Cadwalader Wickersham & Taft 1333 New Hampshire Ave NW Washington DC 20036

KIRSCHENBAUM, WILLIAM, corporate executive; b. N.Y.C., Dec. 12, 1944; s. Benjamin and Fannie (Mintzer) K.; m. Clarissa Wald, June 17, 1979; 1 child, Benjamin. BA, CCNY, 1965; postgrad. CUNY, 1969. Asst. to sr. v.p. Ogden Corp., N.Y.C., 1968-70; ptnr. Palm State Properties, Ft. Lauderdale, Fla., 1970-74; mgr. ea. region Booz Allen Acquisition Services, N.Y.C., 1974-78; mng. dir. corp. fin. Neuberger & Berman, N.Y.C., 1978-82; pres. Unicorp Am. Corp., N.Y.C., 1982-83, also bd. dirs.; chmn. bd. dirs. Hamilton Savs. Bank, Hamilton, Carter, Smith, Inc., Bankers and Shoppers Ins. Co. subs. Travellers Ins. Co.; mem. exec. com. of bd. dirs. Bankers & Shippers Ins. Co. Bd. dirs. Am. Jewish Congress, 1972-83, Com. for Present Danger, 1978—, Jewish Conciliation Bd. Am., 1979—; mem. nat. young leadership cabinet United Jewish Appeal, 1978-80; bd. dirs. Com. for Econ. Growth of Israel, 1977—, Nat. Jewish Coalition, 1985—, Associated Builders and Owners of Greater N.Y., 1986—; chmn. bd. N.Y. Adv. Bd. Starlight Found., 1986-87. Mem. N.Am. Soc. Corp. Planning (N.Y. dir. 1977-80), Assn. Corp. Growth, Blue Key, Pi Sigma Alpha. Club: City Athletic. Home: 1020 Park Ave New York NY 10028

KIRSCHNER, ERNST, manufacturing executive; b. Gablonz, Federal Republic Germany, Sept. 27, 1929. Sales mgr. before 1964; with Susa-Werke, Heubach, Fed. Republic Germany, 1964—. Office: Susa-Werke, D-7072 Heubach Federal Republic of Germany

KIRSCHNER, RONALD ALLEN, osteopathic plastic surgeon, educator; b. N.Y.C., Jan. 18, 1942; s. Hyman C. and Eleanor (Pinkus) K.; m. Olivia Barbara Schlesinger, June 27, 1964; children: Andrew Scott, Julie Renee. AB, NYU, 1962; DO, Phila. Coll. Osteo. Medicine, 1966, MS in Otolaryngology, 1972. Disting. Practioner Am. Acad. Practice. Intern Le Roy Hosp., N.Y.C., 1966-67; resident Grandview Hosp., Dayton, Ohio, 1967-68; resident Phila. Coll. Osteo. Medicine, 1970-72, asst. prof., 1972-74, assoc. prof., 1974-76, clin. assoc. prof., 1976-85, clin. prof., 1985—; dir. neurosensory unit, 1973-76; NIH fellow Armed Forces Inst. Pathology, Washington, 1971; practice medicine specializing in plastic surgery, Bala Cynwyd, Pa., 1976—; attending physician, cons. Presbyn.-U. Pa. Med. Ctr., 1987—, Hosp. of Phila. Coll. Osteo. Medicine, chmn. laser and dndoscopy com., 1987—; attending physician Suburban Gen. Hosp., chief ear, nose and throat and plastic surgery, 1976—, chmn. div. surgery, 1983—; attending physician, cons. Del. Valley Med. Ctr., 1985—; v.p., chief med. adv. Courtlandt Group, 1979-85, exec. v.p., 1985-86, also dir. research and edn., 1986; otolaryngologist Pa. Hearing Assn., 1986—; preceptor Xanar Laser Div., Johnson & Johnson, 1982; design cons. Pilling, Inc., 1982-87, Inframed Inc., 1985—, Sigma Dynamics Inc.; otologic cons. Nat. Childrens' Hearing Aid Bank; pres. Kirschner Design Group, Inc., 1987—; dir. head and neck YAG laser protocol Cooper Lasersonics, 1983—; chmn. med. symposium internat. conf. on Applied Laser Electro Optics, 1986, 87; cons. Bur. Vocat. Rehab., Imunodiagnostics Lab., Allergy Mgmt. Systems Inc. Served with M.C., USN, 1968-70; lt. comdr. Res. Recipient award for disting. teaching Lindbach Found., 1973, Legion of Honor, Chapel of Four Chaplains, 1982; Survivor of Yr. award, 1984; diplomate Am. Osteo. Bd. Otolaryngology. Fellow Pan Am. Allergy Assn., Phila. Acad. Facial Plastic Surgery, Phila. Laryngologic Soc., Am. Soc. Lasers in Medicine and Surgery, Am. Auditory Soc., Am. Acad. Otolaryngology-Head and Neck Surgery, Soc. Ear, Nose, and Throat Advances in Children, Am. Acad. Cosmetic Facial Plastic Surgery (assoc.), Soc. Photo Optical Engrs., Osteo. Coll. Ophthalmology and Otorhinolaryngology, Osteo. Coll. Otorhinolaryngology and Ophtalmology, Am. Acad. Cosmetic Surgery; mem. Am. Osteo. Assn. (editorial cons. Jour. 1977—, editorial referee 1980—), Philadelphia County Osteo. Med. Assn. (chair laser com.), Centurian Club of Deafness Research Found., Internat. Assn. Logopedics and Phoniatrics, Midwestern Biolaser Inst., Inst. for Applied Laser Surgery (pres.), Laser Inst. Am. (chmn. lasers 1987-88, Outstanding Service award 1986), Pa. Osteo. Med. Assn. (chmn. com. otolaryngology 1984—, chmn. com. promotion of research 1985—), Am. Acad. Osteopathy, Survivors Club of Phila. Coll. Osteo. Medicine (pres. 1981-82), Internat. Soc. for Optical Engring., AAAS, N.Y. Acad. Scis., Am. Soc. Liposuction Surgery, Laser Assn. Am. (sec. 1985—), Am. Assn. Advancement Med. Instrumentation, Am. Soc. Cosmetic Surgeons, Pa. Hearing Aid Soc. (otologist), Pan Am. Assn. Otolaryngology and Bronchoesophagology, Pa. Acad. Opthalmology and Otolaryngology, Platform Assn. Am., Pa. Osteo. Med. Soc., Lambda Omicron Gamma (pres. 1981-82, Disting. Service award Caduceus chpt. 1982). Jewish. Clubs: Variety, NYU, Vesper. Lodges: Masons, Shriners. Med. editor Med. Portfolio, 1980-85; guest editor Surg. Clinics of N.Am., 1984; monthly columnist Photonics Spectra, 1987—; mem. editorial bd. Pa. Osteo. Med. Jour., Laurin Publs., 1987—; articles to med. jours.; developer various med. instruments. Office: 2 Bala Cynwyd Plaza Suite IL17 Bala-Cynwyd PA 19004

KIRWAN-TAYLOR, PETER ROBIN, investment banker; b. Virginia Water, Surrey, England, Jan. 18, 1930; came to U.S., 1981; s. William John Kirwan-Taylor and Hélène Charlotte (de Berqueley Grant Richards) Kemble; m. Julia Ogden, 1952 (div. 1965); children: Antonia, Charles, Laura; m. Michele Eads Clarke, 1966 (div. 1970); 1 child, Hélène; m. Nancy Ann Norman, Oct. 1, 1970; 1 child, John. Student, Trinity Coll., Cambridge, Eng., 1950-51. Mgr. Peat Marwick Mitchell & Co., London, 1951-59; dir. Hill Samuel & Co., London, 1960-70, English Property Corp., London and N.Y. C., 1970-76; pres. Maxwell Cummings & Sons, Montreal, Can., 1976-81; vice chmn. Danville Resources Inc., N.Y.C., 1981-85; bd. dirs. The Prospect Group, Inc., N.Y.C., 1986—; bd. dirs. Adobe Resources, N.Y.C., Adacorp, Inc., Dallas, Landmark Land Co., Inc., Carmel, Calif., London United Investments PLC, Abermin Corp., Vancouver, B.C.; chmn. Am. Gold Resources, Denver. Fellow Inst. Chartered Accts. Home: 160 E 72nd St New York NY 10021 Office: The Prospect Group Inc 667 Madison Ave New York NY 10021

KISEKKA, SAMSON, prime minister of Uganda: b. 1913. Physician, prime minister of Uganda, 1986—. Chief spokesman for Nat. Resistance Army. Office: Office of the Prime Minister, Kampala Uganda *

KISER, NAGIKO SATO, librarian; b. Taipei, Republic of China, Aug. 7, 1923; came to U.S., 1950; d. Takeichi and Kinue (Sooma) Sato; m. Virgil Kiser, Dec. 4, 1979 (dec. Mar. 1981). Secondary teaching credential, Tsuda Coll., Tokyo, 1945; BA in Journalism, Trinity U., 1953; BFA, Ohio State U., 1956, MA in Art History, 1959; MLS, cert. in library media, SUNY, Albany, 1974. Cert. community coll. librarian, Calif., cert. jr. coll. tchr., Calif., cert. secondary edn. tchr., Calif., cert. tchr. library media specialist and art, N.Y. Pub. relations reporter The Mainichi Newspapers, Osaka, Japan, 1945-50; contract interpreter U.S. Dept. State, Washington, 1956-58, 66-67; resource specialist Richmond (Calif.) Unified Sch. Dist., 1968-69; editing supr. CTB/McGraw-Hill, Monterey, Calif., 1969-71; multi-media specialist Monterey Peninsula Unified Sch. Dist., 1975-77; librarian Nishimachi Internat. Sch., Tokyo, 1979-80, Sacramento City Unified Sch. Dist., 1977-79, 81-85; sr. librarian Camarillo (Calif.) State Hosp., 1985—. Editor: Short Form Test of Academic Aptitude, 1970, Prescriptive Mathematics Inventory, 1970, Tests of Basic Experience, 1970. Mem. Calif. State Supt.'s Regional Council on Asian Pacific Affairs, Sacramento, 1984—. Library Media Specialist Tng. Program scholar U.S. Office Edn., 1974. Fellow Internat. Biographical Assn.; mem. ALA, AAUW, Calif. Library Assn., Calif. Media and Library Educators Assn., Asunaro Shoogai Kyooiku Kondankai Lifetime Edn. Promoting Assn. (Japan), The Mus. Soc., Internat. House of Japan, Matsuyama Sacramento Sister City Corp., Japanese Am. Citizens League, UN Assn. U.S., Ikenoboo Ikebana Soc. Am. Mem. Christian Science Ch. Office: Camarillo State Hosp Profl Library 1878 S Lewis Rd Camarillo CA 93011

KISH, JOSEPH LAURENCE, JR., management consultant; b. Bklyn., July 13, 1933; s. Joseph Lawrence and Grace Veronica (Skippon) K.; m. Elissa Anne Lucadamo, Oct. 16, 1955; children: Grace Edna, Joseph Robert, Frances Caroline. BA in Econs., Bklyn. Coll., 1955; postgrad. in bus., NYU, 1955-56. Mgmt. analyst N.Y. State Dept. Welfare, Albany, 1956-59; systems analyst Lockheed Electronics Co., Plainfield, N.J., 1959-61; corp. mgr. Olin Mathieson Chem. Corp., N.Y.C., 1961-66; pres. Iron Mountain, Inc., N.Y.C., 1966-76; v.p. Fenvessy Assos., N.Y.C., 1976-81; pres. Acumen, Inc., Raritan, N.J., 1981-83; v.p. Fenvessy & Schwab, Inc., N.Y.C., 1983-86; exec. v.p. Data Port Mgmt. Corp., N.Y.C., 1986—; professorial lectr. Am. U.; adj. prof. NYU, Columbia U.; comml. arbitrator Am. Arbitration Assn. Author: Paperwork in Transition, 1965, Microfilm in Business, 1966, Business Forms Design and Administration, 1972, Micrographics, 1980, Greater Efficiency in the Small Office, 1982, Word Processing in the Transitional Office, 1983; contbr. more than 400 articles on bus. mgmt. to tech. jours. Bd. Mgrs. Ships-A-Shore Condominium Assn., Cape Cod, Mass., 1981—; hon. com. awards dinner Am. Cancer Soc., 1980—. Served with inf. AUS, 1956-58. Recipient Grillo award Adminstrv. Mgmt. Soc., 1980-81. Mem. Am. Mgmt. Assn. (Silver medallion), Assn. Mgmt. Cons., Nat. Micrographics Assn., Inst. Mgmt. Cons., Assn. Records Mgrs. and Adminstrs., Am. Legion. Republican. Roman Catholic. Club: N.Y. Athletic. Lodge: Elks. Home: 717 Mountain Ave Westfield NJ 07090 Office: Data-Port Mgmt Corp World Trade Center New York NY 10048

KISHABA, TOMOKAZU, physician; b. Naha, Okinawa, Feb. 16, 1942; s. Chorin and Kayo Kishaba; M.D., Kyoto (Japan) U., 1966; m. Ayako Nakamoto, Apr. 19, 1969; children—Waka, Yuka, Chica, Taka. Intern, Phila. Gen. Hosp., 1970-71; resident in medicine D.C. Gen. Hosp., 1971-74; fellow in infectious diseases U. Louisville Med. Sch., 1974-76; asst. chief sect. internal medicine Okinawa Chubu Hosp., 1976—. Diplomate Am. Bd. Internal Medicine, Am. Bd. Infectious Diseases. Mem. Japanese Soc. Internal Medicine, Japanese Soc. Infectious Diseases, Japanese Soc. Chemotherapy, Am. Soc. Microbiology. Author articles in field. Home: 1944 Hiyane, Okinawa City, Okinawa 904-21, Japan Office: Okinawa Chubu Hosp, 208-3 Miyasato Gushikawa City, Okinawa 904-22, Japan

KISHPAUGH, ALLAN RICHARD, mechanical engineer; b. Dover, N.J., Aug. 31, 1937; B.S. in Mech. Engring., N.J. Inst. Tech., 1967; m. Maryann M. Bizub, July 31, 1965. Engring. technician Stapling Machines Co., Rockaway, N.J., 1956-65; design engr. Airoyal Engring. Co., Livingston, N.J., 1965-66; project engr. Simautics Co., Fairfield, N.J., 1966-67; design engr. Pyrofilm Resistor Mfg. Co., Cedar Knolls, N.J., 1967-68; sr. engr., project mgr. Packaging Systems div. Standard Packaging Corp., Clifton, N.J., 1968-77; sr. machine design engr. Travenol Labs., Round Lake, Ill., 1977-79; dir. engring. TEC, Inc., Alsip, Ill., 1979-80; mgmt. cons., machine developer, Palos Heights, Ill., 1980—; owner Ark Internat., 1981—. Councilman, Borough of Victory Gardens (N.J.), 1969-71, council pres., 1971, police commnr., 1970-70, chmn. fin. com., 1970; pres. Pompton River Assn., Wayne, N.J., 1976-77; mem. Wayne Flood Control Commn., 1976-77; past deacon, elder, Sunday sch. tchr. and supt. local Presbyn. chs. Served with Air N.G., 1960-61, 62-65, with USAF, 1961-62. Registered profl. engr., N.J., Ill. Mem. ASME (vice chmn. N.J. sect. 1973-74, numerous other regional offices, food, drug and beverage com. 1983-88), Nat. Soc. Profl. Engrs., Midwest Soc. Profl. Cons. (bd. dirs. 1986, 87), Ill. Soc. Profl. Engrs. (chpt. officer 1984—), Chgo. Assn. Commerce and Industry. Patentee mechanism for feeding binding wire, wirebound box-making machine, method packaging granular materials, others in field. Address: 6118 W 123d St Palos Heights IL 60463

KISNER, JACOB, poet, editor, publisher; b. Chelsea, Mass., Apr. 30, 1926; s. Louis and Sarah (Kotel) K.: student Calvin Coolidge Coll., 1945-46, Burdett Coll., 1943-45, Harvard Extension, 1944-48; m. Gladys Selma Feinstein, May 29, 1947; 1 dau. Lesley Kisner Cafarelli. Sunday dept. writer Boston Globe, 1943-45; local news editor Jewish Advocate, Boston, 1945-46; founder, editor, pub. Dorchester (Mass.) Herald, 1946-47; trade reporter Fairchild News Service, Boston, 1948-49; sr. proof-reader Rec. and Statis. Corp., Boston, 1950-54; editor Crossroads, Toronto, Ont., Can., 1964-67; Am. editor View, 1967—; research dir. N.Y. bur. Moneytree Publs., N.Y.C., 1972—; free lance writer, 1943—; philatelic journalist; discussion moderator Great Books Found., Boston, 1948-51; judge of poetry contests, Rochester, N.Y., also N.Y. Poetry Forum, 1969—; N.Y. State dir. and N.Y.C. chmn. World Poetry Day Com., 1971—; v.p., incorporator N.Y. Poetry Forum, 1973-75; founder postmaster Park Ave Local Post, 1978—; author plays: First Came Paula, 1954, Speak of the Devil, 1955, The Monkey's Tail, 1956; author TV plays: The Late Mr. Honeywell, 1957, A World Apart, 1957; author: (poetry) I Am Hephaestus, 1966, numerous pub. articles, revs., research on stamps and postal hist.; contbr. poetry to various lit. jours. and anthologies. Recipient World Peace award Ky. State Poetry Soc., 1970, Gold Medal award Internat. Poets' Shrine, 1971, Radio award sta. WEFG, 1970, Spl. Citation award Poetry Pageant, 1970. Mem. Acad. Am. Poets, Wilson MacDonald Poetry Soc. Can. (exec. com. 1967-77, v.p. 1977—). Am. Philatelic Soc., Trans-Miss. Philatelic Soc., Soc. Philatelic Ams., Soc. Israel Philatelists, Am. Revenue Assn., Confederate Stamp Alliance, United Postal Stationery Soc., Scandinavian Collectors Club, Perfins Club, Am. Philatelic Research Library. Address: 254 Park Ave S Penthouse F New York NY 10010

KISS, LASZLO, biochemist; b. Debrecen, Hungary, Oct. 11, 1943; s. Laszlo and Szende Gizella (Pongor) K.; grad. L. Kossuth U., 1968, Ph.D., 1972, candidate Degree of Academy, 1980; m. Irene Arky, July 11, 1970; children—Orsolya, Gergely. Research fellow, Research Inst. for Medicinal Plants, Budapest, Hungary, 1968-73; sci. fellow Biochem. Inst., L. Kossuth U., Debrecen, Hungary, 1973-80, head enzymology research group, 1980—, asoc. prof., 1984—, instr. biochemistry sec. Red Cross orgs. of L. Kossuth U., 1979—. Mem. Hungarian Chem. Soc., Hungarian Biol. Soc., Assn. Hungarian Biochemists. Mem. Calvinist Church. Contbr. research articles to profl. publs. Office: Biochem Inst, L Kossuth Univ, H-4010 Debrecen Hungary

KISS, STEPHEN PAUL, manufacturing company executive; b. Feldebro, Heves, Hungary, June 24, 1924; s. Istvan and Maria (Fazekas) K. Student U. Gregoriana, Rome, 1945-47; student in econs. U. Innsbruck (Austria), 1947-50, student in civil engring., 1955. Mgr., Frobisher Ltd., Somalia, 1956-60; ptnr. Buy Am. Co., Frankfurt, W.Ger., 1961-65; owner, Italced Srl., Rome, Italy, 1965-77; owner, mgr. Faced Srl., Nepi, Italy, 1977—; lectr. on surface bonding cement, dry stacking mortarless bldg. techniques, USSR, London, others Roman Catholic. Address: Zona Industriale, SS Cassia Km 36 4, Nepi 01036 Italy

KISSA, ERIK, chemist; b. Abja, Estonia, Apr. 7, 1923; came to U.S., 1951, naturalized, 1956; s. Mats and Selma (Wilson) K.; M.S., Tech. U. Karlsruhe (Germany), 1951; Ph.D., U. Del., 1956; m. Selma Alide Tamm, Sept. 6, 1952; children—Erik Harold, Karl Martin. Research chemist E. I. du Pont de Nemours & Co. Inc., Wilmington, Del., 1951-67, sr. research chemist, 1967-74, research assoc. Jackson Lab., 1974-86, sr. research assoc., 1986—; UN tech. expert, India, 1978, 79, China, 1982, Korea, 1986, 87. Fellow Am. Inst. Chemists; mem. Am. Chem. Soc., AAAS, Internat. Assn. Colloid and Interface Scientists, Fiber Soc. Lutheran. Clubs: Du Pont Country, Del. Camera. Editor: (with W. G. Cutler) Detergency Theory and Technology, 1987; contbr. numerous articles, chpts. on surface chemistry of textiles, dyes and analytical chemistry to profl. publs.; U.S., fgn. patentee in field. Home: 1436 Fresno Rd Wilmington DE 19803 Office: EI DuPont de Nemours & Co Jackson Lab Wilmington DE 19898

KISSEL, WILLIAM THORN, JR., sculptor; b. N.Y.C., Feb. 6, 1920; s. William Thorn and Frances A. (Dallett) K.; grad. Choate Sch., 1939; B.A., Harvard U., 1944; postgrad. (Fellow), Pa. Acad. Fine Arts, 1951-53; grad. Barnes Found., 1953. Rinehart Grad. Sch. Sculpture, Balt., 1958; m. Barbara Eldred Case, June 17, 1943 (dec. June 8, 1978); children—William Thorn III (dec.), Michael C. Exhibited sculpture Lever House, N.Y.C., N.A.D., N.Y.C., Balt. Sculptor's Exhibit, York, Pa., Beverly, Mass., Gloucester, Woodmere Gallery, Germantown, Pa.; represented in pvt. collections, U.S.; executed large granite meml., Montclair, N.J., also many animal sculpture studies and commns. Served as pilot, lt. (j.g.) USNR, 1942-45. Recipient Mass. Sculptor's award Regional Exhibit, Beverly, Mass., 1958; Speyer award, NAD, 1966, 68, Am. Artists Profl. League award, 1966. Fellow Am. Artists Profl. League; mem. Nat. Sculpture Soc., Mcpl. Art Soc. N.Y.C., Soc. of Cincinnati. Republican. Episcopalian. Home: 223 Valley Rd Owings Mills MD 21117

KISSICK, LUTHER CLEVELAND, JR., retired air force officer, free-lance writer; b. Mount Hope, Kans., Feb. 21, 1919; s. Luther Cleveland and Irma LouAnna (Fisher) K.; m. Phyllis Anne Traver, Nov. 13, 1946. Student, Kans. State U., 1941; BA in Polit. Sci., Syracuse U., 1957; MA in Internat. Relations, USAF Inst., 1958. Enlisted USAF, 1941; commd. 2d. lt. AUS, 1942; advanced through grades to col. USAF, 1963; air combat intellegence officer 23d Fighter Group 14th Air Force, Republic of China, 1942-45; chief J-2 policy Hdqrs. Far East Command/UN Command, Tokyo, 1954-57; comdr. Def. Liasion Ministry of Nat. Def., London, 1963-66; ret. USAF, 1969; commodity specialist Goodbody & Co., Tampa, Fla., 1969-70; internat. mktg. profl. Fla. Citrus, Tampa, 1971-72; account exec. B.C. Christopher, Hutchinson, Kans., 1973-76; freelance writer, cons. Mount Hope, 1977—. Author: Guerrilla One, 1982. Organizer U.S. wheat mktg. program to China Wheat Growers Assn., Hutchinson and Mt. Hope, 1976-80. Decorated Bronze Star (2), Purple Heart, Legion of Merit (2), Air Medal, Chinese Wings. Mem. Flying Tigers, Ret. Officers Assn., RAF Club. Lodge: Masons. Home and Office: Rural Rt 1 Box 54 Mount Hope KS 67108

KISSICK, WILLIAM LEE, physician, educator; b. Detroit, July 29, 1932; s. William Leslie and Florence (Rock) K.; m. Priscilla Harriet Dillingham, June 16, 1956; children: William, Robert-John, Jonathan, Elizabeth. B.A., Yale U., 1953, M.D., 1957, M.P.H., 1959, Dr.P.H., 1961. Intern Yale-New Haven Med. Center, 1957-58; resident Montefiore Hosp. and Med. Center, N.Y.C., 1961-62; program office Div. Community Health Service, 1962-63; spl. asst. to asst. sec. for health U.S. Dept. HEW, 1964-65; dir. Office Program Planning Evaluation, Office of Surgeon Gen., USPHS, 1966-68; exec. dir., nat. adv. commn. health facilities Office of the Pres., Washington, 1968; prof., chmn. dept. community medicine Sch. Medicine U. Pa., 1968-71, George S. Pepper prof. public health and preventive medicine, 1971—, prof. research medicine, 1976—, prof. health care systems Wharton Sch., 1971—, prof. health policy and mgmt. Sch. Nursing, 1978—; chmn. interdisciplinary health policy and planning curriculum U. Pa. (Wharton Sch.), 1980—; dir. Center for Health Policy U. Pa., 1981—; fellow, mem. exec. com. Nat. Center for Health Care Mgmt.; dir. health policy Leonard Davis Inst. Health Econs.; vis. prof. community medicine Guy's Hosp. Med. Sch.; vis. prof. dept. social sci. and adminstrn. London Sch. Econs. and Polit. Scis.; vis. prof. Inst. European Health Services Research, Leuven U., 1974-75; cons. N.C. Dept. Planning, Nat. Center Health Services Research, Health Resources Adminstrn., Benedum Found., WHO, Appalachian Regional Commn., HealthEast, Smith Kline-Beckman, Pew Meml. Trust, Health Systems Group, Allegheny Health Services, Health Resources Adminstrn., VA, Colonial Penn Group, Ctr. Disease Control; mem. Accrediting Commn. on Edn. for Health Services Adminstrn., 1980-86; chmn. com. on med. affairs Yale U. Council, 1980-86, fellow Yale Corp., 1987—; mem. Mayor's Commn., 1981-83; mem. com. on medicine and soc. Coll. Physicians of Phila., 1983-88 ; mem. council on med. socs. Am. Coll. Physicians, 1983-87. Editor: Dimensions and Determinants of Health Policy, 1968. Contbr. articles to profl. jours. Bd. dirs. Met. Collegiate Center Germantown, Yale Alumni Fund; trustee Appalachian Regional Hosps., 1969-76. Served with USPHS, 1962-68. Fellow Yale Corp. Mem. AAAS, Am. Coll. Preventive Medicine, Am. Public Health Assn., Pa., Phila. Coll. Physicians, Assn. Health Services Research, Assn. Tchrs. Preventive Medicine, Med. Adminstrs. Conf., Physicians for Social Responsibility, Nat. Assn. Pub. Health Policy, Nat. Health Policy Forum. Home: Ellet Lane Philadelphia PA 19119

KISSINGER, HENRY ALFRED, former secretary of state, international consulting company executive; b. Fuerth, Germany, May 27, 1923; came to U.S., 1938, naturalized, 1943; s. Louis and Paula (Stern) K.; m. Ann Fleischer, Feb. 6, 1949 (div. 1964); children—Elizabeth, David; m. Nancy Maginnes, Mar. 30, 1974. A.B. summa cum laude, Harvard U., 1950, M.A., 1952, Ph.D., 1954. Exec. dir. Harvard Internat. Seminar, 1951-69; mem. faculty dept. govt., Ctr. for Internat. Affairs Harvard U., 1954-69; dir. def. studies program Harvard Internat. Seminar, 1958-69, assoc. prof. govt., 1959-62, prof., 1962-69; faculty Ctr. Internat. Affairs, Harvard U., 1960-69; asst. to Pres. for Nat. Security Affairs, 1969-75; Sec. of State 1973-77; faculty Georgetown U., 1977—; founder, chmn. Kissinger Assocs., Inc., N.Y.C.; contbg. analyst ABC News, 1983—; chmn. Nat. Bipartisan Commn. on Central Am., 1983-84; mem. internat. adv. com. Chase Bank. ; study dir. nuclear weapons and fgn. policy Council Fgn. Relations, 1955-56; dir. spl. studies project Rockefeller Bros. Fund, Inc., 1956-58; cons. Ops. Research Office, 1950-61; cons. to dir. Psychol. Strategy Bd., 1952; cons. Ops. Coordinating Bd., 1955, Weapons Systems Evaluation Group, 1959-60, NSC, 1961-62, ACDA, 1961-68, Dept. State, 1965-69. Author: Nuclear Weapons and Foreign Policy, 1957, A World Restored: Castlereagh, Metternich and the Restoration of Peace, 1812-22, 1957, The Necessity for Choice: Prospects of American Foreign Policy, 1961, The Troubled Partnership: A Reappraisal of the Atlantic Alliance, 1965, White House Years, 1979, For the Record, 1981, Years of Upheaval, 1982, Observations: Selected Speeches and Essays, 1984; Editor: Problems of National Strategy: A Book of Readings, 1965, Confluence, An Internat. Forum, 1951-58; Contbr. to profl. jours. Trustee Met. Mus. Art, N.Y.C., 1978—. Served with AUS, 1943-46. Recipient citation Overseas Press Club, 1958, Woodrow Wilson prize for best book fields of govt., politics, internat. affairs, 1958, Distinguished Pub. Service award Am. Inst. Pub. Service, 1973, Nobel Peace prize, 1973, Presdl. Medal of Freedom, 1977, Medal of Liberty, 1986; Guggenheim fellow, 1965-66. Mem. Am. Polit. Sci. Assn., Council Fgn. Relations, Am. Acad. Arts and Scis., Phi Beta Kappa. Clubs: Metropolitan (Washington); Century, River (N.Y.C.), Bohemian (San Francisco). Office: Kissinger Assocs Inc 350 Park Ave 26th Floor New York NY 10022

KISSINGER, WALTER BERNHARD, automotive test and service equipment manufacturing company executive; b. Furth, Germany, June 21, 1924; came to U.S., 1938, naturalized, 1939; s. Louis and Paula (Stern) K.; m. Eugenie Van Drooge, July 4, 1958; children: William, Thomas, Dana Marie, John. B.A., Princeton U., 1951; M.B.A., Harvard U., 1953. Asst. to v.p. fgn. operations Gen. Tire & Rubber Co., Akron, Ohio, 1953-56; pres. Advanced Vacuum Products Co., Stamford, Conn., 1957-62; exec. v.p., dir. Glass-tite Industries, Providence, 1960-62; asst. to pres. Jerrold Corp., 1963-64; exec. v.p., Chmn. exec. com., dir. Jervis Corp., Hicksville, N.Y., 1964-68; chmn., pres., chief exec. officer Allen Group Inc., Melville, N.Y., 1969—. Served to capt. AUS, 1943-46, 50. Decorated Commendation medal. Club: Princeton of New York. Office: The Allen Group Inc 534 Broadhollow Rd Melville NY 11747

KISSLING, FRED RALPH, JR., insurance agency executive; b. Nashville, Feb. 10, 1930; s. Fred Ralph and Sarah Elizabeth (FitzGerald) K.; m. Mary Jane Gallaher; children: Sarah Fitzgerald, Jayne Kirkpatrick. BA, Vanderbilt U., 1952, MA, 1958. Spl. agt. Northwestern Mut. Life Ins. Co., Nashville, 1953-58, gen. agt., Lexington, Ky., 1962-80; gen. agt. New Eng. Mut. Life Ins. Co., 1981-87; mgr. life dept. Bennett & Edwards, Kingsport, Tenn., 1958-62; pres. Employee Benefit Cons., Inc., Lexington, 1961—; ptnr. Kennington Assocs., 1967—; pub. Leader's mag., 1973—, editor, 1981—. Author: Sell and Grow Rich, 1966; editor: Questionnaire in Pension Planning, 1971, Questionnaire in Estate Planning, 1971. Adv. bd. Salvation Army, Lexington, 1971—, chmn., 1988—; gen. chmn. United Way of Blue Grass, 1975, bd. dirs., 1975-78, 80-83; trustee, chmn. bd. Lexington Children's Theatre, 1979-81, pres., 1981-83. Mem. Am. Soc. CLU's (chpt. pres. 1969-70, 80-81, regional v.p. 1971-73), Ky. Gen. Agts. and Mgrs. Assn. (pres. 1965-66), Million Dollar Round Table (life mem., v.p., program chmn. 1976), Assn. for Advanced Underwriting (bd. dirs. 1976-84, sec.-treas. 1979-80, v.p. 1980-81, pres. 1982-83), Am. Soc. Pension Actuaries (bd. dirs. 1971-78, pres. 1974), Nat. Assn. of Estate Planning Councils (bd. dirs. 1986—), Sigma Chi (national sec., treas. 1987-88). Clubs: Lexington, Lexington Polo; Iroquois Hunt. Lodges: Masons, Shriners. Office: 98 Dennis Dr Lexington KY 40503

KIST, NICOLAAS CHRISTIAAN, civil engineer; b. S.I., N.Y., Aug. 8, 1928; s. Herman Jacob and Ernestine Clara (Nickenig) K.; m. Nancy Prichard Jones, Apr. 24, 1954; children—Cornelia Helena, Johanna Claire, Susanna Maria. M.S. in Civil Engring., Technische Hogesch., Delft, Netherlands, 1953. Registered profl. engr., Ill. Jr. and field engr. Chgo. Bridge and Iron, Chgo., 1957-59, project mgr., Italy, 1959-60, constrn./sales/engring. service mgr., Netherlands, 1960-67, internat. engr. standards coordinator, Oak Brook, Ill., 1967-68, asst. dir. corp. nuclear quality assurance, 1968-72; pres. N.C. Kist & Assocs., Inc., Naperville, Ill., 1972—; speaker, cons. in quality assurance/quality improvement; internat. speaker quality auditing. Served to lt. (j.g.) USN, 1953-57. Mem. Am. Soc. Quality Control (regional councilor 1981-85), Am. Arbitration Soc. (arbitrator 1979), ASME, ASCE, Royal Soc. Engrs. (Netherlands). Republican. Methodist. Avocations: backpacking, art history, travel, observing nature. Home: 900 E Porter Ave Naperville IL 60540 Office: N C Kist & Assocs Inc 127-A S Washington Naperville IL 60540

KISTNER, DAVID HAROLD, biology educator; b. Cin., July 30, 1931; s. Harold Adolf and Hilda (Gick) K.; m. Alzada A. Carlisle, Aug. 8, 1957; children—Alzada H., Kymry Marie Carlisle. A.B., U. Chgo., 1952, B.S., 1956, Ph.D., 1957. Instr. U. Rochester, 1957-59; instr., asst. prof. biology Calif. State U., Chico, 1959-64; assoc. prof. Calif. State U., 1964-67, prof., 1967—; research asso. Field Mus. Natural History, 1967—, Atlantica Ecol. Research Sta., Salisbury, Zimbabwe, 1970—; dir. Shinner Inst. Study Interrelated Insects, 1968-75. Author: (with others) Social Insects, Vols. 1-3; editor: Sociobiology, 1975—; contbr. articles to profl. jours. Patron Am. Mus. Natural History; life mem. Republican Nat. Com., 1980—. Recipient Outstanding Prof. award Calif. State Univs. and Colls., Los Angeles, 1976; John Simon Guggenheim Meml. Found. fellow, 1965-66; grantee NSF, 1960—, Am. Philos. Soc., 1972, Nat. Geog. Soc., 1988. Fellow Explorers Club, Calif. Acad. Scis.; mem. Entomol. Soc. Am., Pacific CoastEntomol. Soc., Kans. Entomol. Soc., AAUP, AAAS, Soc. Study of Evolution, Am. Soc. Naturalists, Am. Soc. Zoologists, Soc. Study of Systematic Zoology, Internat. Soc. Study of Social Insects, Chico State Coll. Assos. (charter), Council Biology Editors. Home: 3 Canterbury Circle Chico CA 95926

KISYNSKI, JAN MARIA, mathematics educator; b. Warsaw, Poland, June 24, 1933; s. Jerzy and Jadwiga (Lubek) K.; m. Krystyna Pawlak, Jan. 14, 1967 (dec. 1979); children: Maciej, Jacek. MS, U.M. Curie-Sklodowska, Lublin, Poland, 1955, PhD, 1960; habilitation, Inst. of Math., Polish Acad. Sci., 1964. Asst. U. M. Curie-Sklodowska, Lublin, 1955-59; asst. U. Warsaw (Poland), 1959-61, lectr. thru ord. prof., 1969-85; ord. prof. math. Tech. U., Lublin, 1985—; asst. thru lectr. Inst. Math., Polish Acad. Sci., 1961-69; cons. Inst. Nuclear Research, 1972-76; mem. Redaction Com. of Studia Mathematica, 1971—, Redaction Com. of Commentationes Mathematicae, 1975—. Contbr. articles to profl. jours. Recipient Golden Cross of Merit Polish State Council, 1975, Cavalier Cross Polonia Restituta, 1980, medal of 40th Anniversary of People's Poland, 1984. Fellow Sci. Soc. Warsaw; mem. Polish Math. Soc., Am. Math. Soc., Trade Union of Polish Tchrs. Roman Catholic. Home: Tymiankowa 56m 4, 20-542 Lublin Poland Office: Tech Univ of Lublin, J Dabrowskiego 13, 20-109 Lublin Poland

KITA, MORIO, writer, physician; b. Tokyo, May 1, 1927; s. Mokichi and Teruko K.; m. Kimiko Yokoyama, April 3, 3, 1961; 1 child, Yuka. MD, Tohoku U., Sendai, Japan, 1960. Asst. Keio U., Tokyo, 1953-57; intern Tohoku U., Sendai, 1952-53; resident Keio U., Tokyo, 1954-64. Author: Yoru To Kiri No Sumide, 1960, The House of Nire, 1964, Kagayakeku Aoi Sora No Sitade, 1985; numerous others. Mem. Nippon Bungeika Kyokai. Home: 6-16-5 Matsubara Setagaya, Tokyo 101, Japan Office: care Japan Fgn Rights Ctr, Akimoto Bldg 1-38 Kanda Jinbocho, Chiyoda-Ku, Tokyo Japan

KITADA, HITOSHI, mathematics educator; b. Tokyo, Feb. 15, 1948; s. Minoru and Rie (Nakahara) K.; m. Keiko Toda, Mar. 22, 1980. BSc, U. Tokyo, 1973, DSc, 1979; MSc, Osaka City U., 1975. Tech. officer dept. statis. and info. Ministry Health and Welfare, Tokyo, 1975-77; asst. dept. pure and applied scis. U. Tokyo, 1977-82, assoc. prof. math., 1982—. Office: U Tokyo Dept Math, Komaba, Meguro-ku, 153 Tokyo Japan

KITADA, SHINICHI, biochemist; b. Osaka, Japan, Dec. 9, 1948; came to U.S., 1975; s. Koichi and Asako Kitada; M.D., Kyoto U., 1973; M.S. in Biol. Chemistry (Japan Soc. Promotion Sci. fellow 1975-76), UCLA, 1977, Ph.D., 1979. Intern, Kyoto U. Hosp., 1973-74, resident physician Chest Disease Research Inst., 1974-75; research scholar lab. nuclear medicine and radiation biology UCLA, 1979—. Mem. Am. Oil Chemists Soc., N.Y. Acad. Scis., Sigma Xi. Author papers in field. Home: 478 Landfair Ave Apt 5 Los Angeles CA 90024 Office: 900 Veteran Ave Los Angeles CA 90024

KITADAI, REIICHIRO, architect; b. Tokyo, July 15, 1926; s. Shigehiro and Rinko Kitadai; m. Junko Yamazaki Kitadai, Jan. 10, 1953; children: Miwako, Yukiko. MS, U. Tokyo, 1948. Pres., cons. GKK Architects & Engrs., Tokyo, 1950—; advisor Ministry of Constrn., Tokyo, 1962-63, Ctr. for Fire Sci. and Tech., Sci. U. Tokyo, 1975—; councilor Japan Architecture Dissemination Ctr., Tokyo, 1986—. Designer: All Nippon Airway Tng. Ctr., 1980. Cons. Tokyo Girl's Med. Coll., 1980—. Recipient Archtl. Design award Kanagawa Prefecture, 1963. Mem. Archtl. Inst. Japan, Japan Inst. Architects (pres. 1988—). Clubs: Hodogaya Country (Yokohama, Japan); Golden Spa (Tokyo). Lodge: Rotary. Home: 3-19-6 Sengoku, Bunkyo-ku, Tokyo 112, Japan Office: 2-8-8 Shinjuku, Shinjuku-Ku, Tokyo 160, Japan

KITAGAWA, AUDREY EMIKO, lawyer; b. Honolulu, Mar. 31, 1951; s. Yonoichi and Yoshiko (Nagaishi) K. B.A. cum laude, U. So. Calif., 1973; J.D., Boston Coll., 1976. Bar: Hawaii, 1977, U.S. Dist. Ct. Hawaii, 1977. Assoc., Rice, Lee & Wong, Honolulu, 1977-80; sole practice, Honolulu, 1980—. Exec. editor Internat. Law Jour., 1976. Mem. Historic Hawaii Found., 1984. Mem. Hawaii Bar Assn., ABA, Assn. Trial Lawyers Am., Japan-Hawaii Lawyers Assn. (v.p. 1982—), Law Office Mgmt. Discussion Group, Hawaii Lawyers Care, Phi Alpha Delta. Republican. Club: Honolulu. Office: 820 Mililani St Suite 615 Honolulu HI 96813

KITAJIMA, YOSHITOSHI, printing company executive; b. Tokyo, Aug. 25, 1933; s. Orie and Toshiko Kitajima; B.Econs., Keio U., Tokyo, 1958; m. Kiyoko Sumitomo; children—Yoshinari, Motoharu, Naoko. With Fuji Bank, Ltd., from 1958; exec. dir., from 1970 with Dai Nippon Printing Co., Ltd., Tokyo, 1963—, exec. v.p., 1975-79, chmn. bd., 1979—, also dir.; pres. Hokkaido Coca-Cola Bottling Co., Ltd. Mem. Fedn. Econ. Orgns. Clubs: Toyko Am., Tokyo Rotary. Office: Dai Nippon Printing Co Ltd, 1-1, Ichigaya-Kagacho 1-chome, Shinjuku-ku, 162 Tokyo Japan

KITAMURA, TOSHINORI, psychiatrist; b. Yokohama, Kanagawa, Japan, Oct. 16, 1947; s. Masanori and Kikuko (Matsumoto) K.; m. Fusako Oami, Mar. 17, 1973. M.D., Keio Gijuku U. Sch. Medicine, Tokyo, 1972. Psychiatrist, Inst. Psychiatry, Tokyo, 1973-76; hon. research fellow U. Birmingham (U.K.), 1976-80; clin. instr. Keio Gijuku U., Tokyo, 1980-83, lectr., 1983; chief sect. mental health for elderly NIMH, Ichikawa, Japan, 1983—; vis. lectr. Keio Gijuku U., 1986—; head Group for Research Assessment in Psychiatry, Tokyo, 1981—; mem. com. Med. Selection Japanese Astronauts, 1987—, com. Psychiatric Diagnostic Criteria Japan, 1987—, com. Guideline for Psychiatric Treatment, 1987—. Contbr. articles to profl. jours. Mem. Royal Coll. Psychiatrists, British Council Japan Assn. Home: 2-8-15-501 Sendagaya, Shibuya-ku, Tokyo 151, Japan Office: NIMH, 1-7-3 Konodai, Ichikawa, Chiba 272, Japan

KITAYAMA, TAKAO, development planning and project management company executive; b. Kobe, Hyogo, Japan, Sept. 13, 1941; s. Mitsugu and Asako (Ando) K.; m. Keiko Kitayama, Apr. 17, 1950; children: Tetsuko, Shin. Exec. v.p. Hamano Inst., Tokyo; cons. Issey Miyake Design Studio, Tokyo, 1984—, Todao Ando Archtl. Assocs., Osaka, 1980—, Shiro Kuramata Design Office, Tokyo, 1980—, Toshiyuki Kita Design Office, Osaka, 1983—, Cassina Japan, Tokyo, 1982—. Projects include: From 1st Bldg. (Japan Archtl. Acad. award), Axis Bldg. (Mainichi Newspaper Design award), Rose Garden Bldg., Kobe, Step Bldg., Takamatsu, Japan, Festival Bldg., Okinawa, Japan, PortoPia '81 Fashion Live Theater, numerous others. Home: 1 25 12 Seta, Setagayaku Tokyo 158, Japan Office: Hamano Inst, 1 9 7 Nishi Azabu Minatoku, 106 Tokyo Japan

KITAYENDO, DIMITRI GEORGIEVITCH, orchestra conductor; b. Leningrad, USSR, Aug. 18, 1940; s. George Ivanovitch and Anna Dmitrievna (Zahkarova) K.; m. Margaret Nikolaevna Vorobjova. Student, Conservatory Mus., Leningrad, 1958-63; postgrad. opera and symphony conducting, Moscow Conservatory, 1963-66; diploma in conducting with honors, Acad. Music and Beaux Arts, Vienna, 1967. Asst. condr. opera and ballet Stanislavsky, Nemerovitch and Dantchenko Theatres, Moscow, 1968-69, prin. condr., 1970-76; chief condr., music. dir. Moscow State Philharmony Orch., 1976—; prof. conducting Moscow State Tchaikovsky Conservatory of Music, 1967—; guest condr. symphony orchs. USSR, Europe, U.S.A., opera houses Berlin, Vienna, Copenhagen, Cologne; mem. jury 1st Toscanini Competition in Conducting, Parma, Italy, 1985. Recipient 2d prize Herbert von Karajen Competition, Fed. Republic Germany, 1969. Communist. Office: Moscow State Philharmony, Groky St 31, 104050 Moscow USSR

KITBUNCHU, MICHAEL MICHAI CARDINAL, archbishop of Bangkok; b. Samphran, Thailand, Jan. 25, 1929. Ordained priest Roman Catholic Ch., 1959; rector met. sem., Bangkok, 1965-72; consecrated archbishop of Bangkok, 1973; elevated to Sacred Coll. of Cardinals, 1983 (1st cardinal from Thailand); titular ch., St. Laurence in Panisperna. Mem. Congregation for Evangelization of Peoples. Address: 51 Assumption Cathedral, Bangrak, Bangkok 10500, Thailand *

KITCHEN, CHARLES WILLIAM, lawyer; b. Cleve., July 17, 1926; s. Karl K. and Lucille W. (Keynes) K.; m. Mary Applegate, July 22, 1950; children—Kenneth K., Guy R., Ann Kitchen Campbell. B.A., Western Res. U., 1948; J.D., 1950. Bar: Ohio 1950, U.S. Dist. Ct. Ohio 1952, U.S. Ct. Appeals (6th cir.) 1972, U.S. Supreme Ct. 1981. Ptnr., Kitchen, Messner & Deery and predecessor, Cleve., 1950—, mng. ptnr., 1972—. Mem. Citizens League, Greater Cleve. Growth Assn.; vice chmn. Regional Council on Alcoholism, 1981-85, chmn., 1985-86. Served with A.C., U.S. Army, 1944-45. Fellow Am. Coll. Trial Lawyers (life del. 8th Ohio Jud. Conf.); mem. Am. Arbitration Assn. (panelist 1961—), Cleve. Assn. Civil Trial Attys. (pres. 1971-72), Ohio Assn. Civil Trial Attys. (pres. 1975-76, Greater Cleve. Bar Assn. (chmn. med.-legal com. 1974-75, chmn. lawyers assistance program 1981-83, trustee 1984-87), Ohio Bar Assn. (Ho. of Dels. 1977-80), ABA, Def. Research Inst., Internat. Assn. Def. Counsel (med. malpractice com. 1982—, def. counsel com. 1986—), Am. Judicature Soc., Am. Soc. Hosp. Attys. of Am. Hosp. Assn., Am. Legion, Order of Coif, Beta Theta Pi, Phi Delta Phi. Presbyterian. Club: Westwood Country (Rocky River, Ohio). Lodge: Masons. Home: 28949 Turnbridge Rd Bay Village OH 44140 Office: Kitchen Messner & Deery 1100 Illuminating Bldg 55 Public Sq Cleveland OH 44113

KITCHEN, LAWRENCE OSCAR, aircraft/aerospace corporation executive; b. Ft. Mill, S.C., June 8, 1923; s. Samuel Sumpter and Ruby Azalee (Grigg) K.; m. Brenda Lenhart, Nov. 25, 1978; children by previous marriage: Brenda, Alan, Janet. Ed., Foothill Coll. Aero. engr. U.S. Navy Bur. Aeronautics, Washington, 1946-58; staff asst. to asst. chief bur. U.S. Navy Bur. Aeronautics, 1958; with Lockheed Missiles & Space Co., Sunnyvale, Calif., 1958-70; mgr. product support logistics Lockheed Missiles & Space Co., 1964-68, dir. fin. controls, 1968-70; v.p.-fin. Lockheed-Ga. Co., Marietta, 1970-71; pres. Lockheed-Ga. Co., 1971-75; pres. Lockheed Corp., Burbank, Calif., 1975-76, pres., chief operating officer, 1976-85, chmn. bd. dirs., chief exec. officer, 1986—; bd. dirs. Security Pacific Nat. Bank, Security Pacific Corp., PacTel Personal Communications. Mem. nominating com. Aviation Hall of Fame. Served with USMC, 1942-46. Mem. Nat. Def. Transp. Assn., AIAA, Nat. Assn. Accountants, Navy League, Am. Def. Preparedness Assn., Soc. Logistics Engrs., Air Force Assn., Assn. U.S. Army. Clubs: Burning Tree, North Ranch, Lakeside Golf, Wings. Office: Lockheed Corp 4500 Park Granada Blvd Calabasas CA 91399 *

KITE, JOSEPH HIRAM, JR., microbiologist, educator, researcher; b. Decatur, Ga., Nov. 11, 1926; s. Joseph Hiram and Lulie (Hatch) K.; m. Jane Pascale, Aug. 6, 1970. A.B., Emory U., 1948; M.S., U. Tenn., 1954; Ph.D., U. Mich., 1959. Med. technician in bacteriology Communicable Disease Ctr., Atlanta, 1950-51, VA Hosp., 1951-52; research assoc. U. Buffalo, 1958-59, instr., 1959-63; asst. prof. bacteriology and immunology SUNY-Buffalo, 1963-68, assoc. prof. microbiology, 1968-72, prof. microbiology, 1972—. Contbr. articles to med. jours., chpts. to med. textbooks. Served with AUS, 1945-46. Mem. Am. Assn. Immunologists, Am. Soc. Microbiology, Tissue Culture Assn., AAAS, N.Y. Acad. Scis. Methodist. Subspecialties: Immunology (medicine); Microbiology (medicine). Current work: Autoimmune diseases; teaching medical, dental and graduate students; research in mechanisms of autoimmune disease and regulation of immune response. Home: 108 Chasewood Ln East Amherst NY 14051 Office: Dept Microbiology Med Sch SUNY Buffalo NY 14214

KITHIER, KAREL, physician, pathology educator; b. Prague, Czechoslovakia, Dec. 6, 1930; came to U.S. 1968, naturalized, 1978; s. Karel and Marie (Bohackova) K.; m. Viktorie Svecova, May 6, 1961; 1 child, Karel. M.D., Charles U., Prague, 1962, Ph.D., 1967. Research scientist Research Inst. for Child Devel., Prague, 1967-68, Child Research Ctr. of Mich., Detroit, 1968-71, Mich. Cancer Found., Detroit, 1972-74; asst. prof. pathology Wayne State U Sch. Medicine, Detroit, 1974-78, assoc. prof. pathology, 1978—; chief, clin. immunology Detroit Receiving Hosp. and Univ. Health Ctr., Detroit, 1978—, assoc. head clin. chemistry, 1978—; staff pathologist VA Med. Ctr., Allen Park, Mich., 1976—. Contbr. articles to profl. jours. Fellow Nat. Acad. Clin. Biochemistry; mem. Am. Assn. Cancer Research, Am. Assn. Immunologists, Am. Assn. Clin. Chemists, Internat. Soc. Oncodevelopmental Biology and Medicine. Avocation: fishing. Office: Wayne State U Sch Medicine 540 E Canfield St Detroit MI 48201

KITTL, PABLO, materials scientist; b. Buenos Aires, Argentina, Nov. 18, 1934; s. Erwin and Georgina (Duclout) K.; Licenciado en Fisica, Facultad de Ciencias de San Luis, Universidad de Cuyo, San Luis, Argentina, 1965; Revalidation, U. Chile, Santiago, 1980. Prof. spl. physics Facultad de Ciencias de San Luis, Universidad de Cuyo, 1963-64; researcher Instituto de Investigaciones y Ensayes de Materiales, U. Chile, 1965-80, chief Electron Microscopy Lab., 1980—; prof. Facultad de Ciencias Fisico Matematicas, Universidad de Chile, 1980—; vis. prof. UCLA, 1973, dept. material scis. Fed. U. Sao Carlos (Brazil), 1978. Recipient award, Latin Am. Jour. of Met. and Materials, 1987. Mem. Am. Acad. Mechanics. Contbr. articles on materials sci. to profl. jours. Home: Torrealba 85, Vina de Mar Chile Office: Instituto de Investigaciones y Enrayes de Materiales, y Enrayed de Materiales, Casilla 1420, Santiago Chile

KITTRIE, NICHOLAS N(ORBERT NEHEMIAH), legal educator, international consultant, author; b. en route Bilgoraj, Poland, Mar. 26, 1930; came to U.S., 1944; s. S.K. Kronenbergh and Perla F. (Ver Standig) K. (parents Brit. citizens); m. Sara Yudovic de Burak, June 1, 1962; children: Orde Felicien, Norda Nicole, Zachary McNair. Student, U. Cairo, 1946, U. London, 1947; LLB, U. Kans., 1950, MA, 1951; postgrad., U. Chgo., 1954-55; LLM, Georgetown U., 1963, SJD, 1968. Bar: Kans. 1953, D.C. 1958, U.S. Supreme Ct. Research asst. U. London, 1947; instr. Western civilization dept. U. Kans., 1948-50; legal analyst Kans. Govt. Research Ctr., 1951-54; asst. to dir. legis. service Am. Bar. Assn., 1955-56; project dir. Am. Bar Found., 1956-58; research assoc. Yale Law Sch., 1958; legal asst. to U.S. Senator Wiley 1959; counsel to U.S. Senator Estes Kefauver, antitrust and monopoly subcom. U.S. Senate, 1959-62; ptnr. DeGrazia & Kittrie, Washington, 1962-67; prof. criminal and comparative law Washington Coll. Law, Am. U., 1963—, dir. Inst. for Advanced Studies in Justice, 1970-78, dean, 1977-79, Mooers scholar and prof. law, 1983—; dean Sch. Justice, Washington, 1969-71; dir. Inst. Law and Policy, 1980—; lectr. U. Ottawa, summer 1966; research scholar Univs. Warsaw and Berlin, summers 1967, 68; research assoc. Ctr. Studies Criminal Justice U. Chgo., 1967-68; dir. Law and Policy Inst., Jerusalem, summers 1970-76, Inst. Law and Mass Media, 1978—; vis. fellow Inst. Advanced Legal Research U. London, 1973-74, Nat. Inst. Justice U.S. Dept. Justice, 1979-80; vis. prof. London Sch. Econs., 1974; cons. Pres.'s Commn. Marijuana and Drug Abuse, 1972, v.p.'s commn. to combat terrorism, 1985; permanent rep. of AIDP to UN Social and Econs. Council, 1975—; mem. task force on role of psychology in criminal justice Am. Psychol. Assn., 1975-76; dir. 1st Washington Devel. Corp., Bank of Chios, Athens, Greece; dir., gen. counsel Liberty House Investments; v.p. Nickal Corp.; chmn. KVK Communications Ltd. Author: International Legal Responsibility for Colonial People, 1951, Survey of Adminstration of Criminal Justice, 1956, (with others) The Mentally Disabled and the Law, 1959, The Right to be Different: Deviance and Enforced Law, 1971, The Comparative Law of Israel and the Middle East, 1971, The Real Estate Settlement Process and Its Cost, 1972, Crescent and Star: Arab-Israeli Perspectives on the Middle East Conflict, 1972, The Juvenile Drug Offender, 1972, Medicine, Law and Public Policy, 1975, Sanctions, Sentencing and Corrections, 1981, The Tree of Liberty: Rebellion and Political Crime in America, 1986, The Uncertain Future: Gorbachev's Eastern Bloc, 1988; chmn. editorial bd. Jour. Criminology, 1973-75, Justice mag., 1973-75; mem. editorial bd. Law and Human Behavior, 1976-80; mem. editorial adv. bd. The Washington Times; mem. exec. bd. Paragon House Pubs.; sr. cons. U.S. News and World Report Books; contbr. articles to profl. jours. Vice chmn. UN Alliance for Crime Prevention and Criminal Justice, 1976—, sci. com. U. Messina, Italy; mem. senate Am. U., 1964-72. Served with Brit. Middle East Command, 1944-45. Raymond fellow U. Chgo., 1954-55; sr. fellow NEH, 1973-74. Mem. Am. Soc. Criminology (pres. 1975), AAAS (council 1972—), Internat. Assn. Penal Law (Am. sect. v.p., sec.-gen. 1975—), Internat. Assn. Comparative Pub. Law (dir. 1976—), Am. Soc. Pub. Adminstrn., Am. Judicature Soc., Am. Soc. Internat. Law, Internat. Inst. Space Law, ABA, Inter-Am. Bar Assn., Kans. Bar Assn., D.C. Bar Assn., Phi Delta Phi, Pi Sigma Alpha. Clubs: Rose Haven Yacht (dir.), Cosmos. Home: 6908 Ayr Ln Bethesda MD 20817 also: Ramsbridge Farm Leesburg VA 22075 Office: Law Sch American Univ 4400 Massachusetts Ave NW Washington DC 20016

KITZINGER, UWE, college president; b. Nuremberg, Germany, Apr. 12, 1928; m. Sheila Helena Elizabeth Webster, Oct. 4, 1952; children—Celia, Tessa, Nell, Polly, Jenny. B.A., M.A., 1953; B.Litt., M.Litt., 1956, 1980; LLD (hon.), 1986. Sec. econ. sect. Council of Europe, Strasbourg, 1951-58; lectr. U. Saar, 1954-56; fellow Nuffield Coll., Oxford U., 1956-76; advisor to v.p. ext. relations EEC, Brussels, 1973-75; dean INSEAD, Fontainbleau, 1976-80; dir. Oxford Ctr. Mgmt. Studies, 1980-84; pres. Templeton Coll., Oxford, Eng., 1984—; founding chmn. Com. on Atlantic Studies; founding chmn. Internat. Assn. Macro-Engring. Socs., 1987—; mem. Brit. Acad. Com. of Ency. Brit., 1969—; adv. bd. Pace U., N.Y.C., 1981—, Berlin Sci. Ctr., 1983—. Founding editor Jour. Common Market Studies, 1961—; author: German Electral Politics, 1960; The Challenge of the Common Market, 1961; Diplomacy and Persuasion, 1973. Pres., Oxford Union, 1950; council mem. OXFAM, 1981. Mem. Major Projects Assn. (chmn. 1981-87), Royal Inst. Internat. Affairs (council). Clubs: Reform, Royal Thames Yacht, Oxford Univ., Cambridge Univ. Office: Templeton Coll, Oxford OX1 5NY, England

KIVIMAKI, MIKKO ANTERO, steel company executive; b. Mantta, Finland, Jan. 1, 1939; s. Julius Evert and Eva (Enegren) K.; m. Pirjo-Riitta Marjukka Kolehmainen, July 1, 1972; children—Markus, Tuomas. LL.M., Helsinki U., 1965. Lawyer, Rautaruukki Oy, Helsinki, Finland, 1967-68, sec. bd., 1968-72, asst. dir., 1972-76, adminstrv. dir., 1976-80, v.p., 1980-82, pres., 1982—, chmn., 1985—; mem. supervisory bd. Kansallis Bank, Sampo, Indsl. Mut. Ins. Co.; mem. gen. assembly Confedn. of Finnish Industries. Mem. Internat. Iron and Steel Inst. (exec. com.), Finnish Employers Assn. (council), Fedn. Finnish Metal and Engring. Industries, Employers' Assn. Finnish Metal Industries, Oy Koneisto Ab. Home: Kontiontie 1 B, SF-02110 Espoo Finland Office: Rautaruukki Oy, Fredrikinkatu 51-53, SF-00100 Helsinki Finland

KIYOHARA, MICHIYA, electrical machine company executive; b. Tokyo, Nov. 22, 1919; s. Sadao and Sute K.; m. Keiko Ishiguro, Jan. 3, 1948; children—Toshiko, Tatsuya. Diploma, Kyoto U. (Japan), 1942; D.Engring. (hon.), Nagoya U. (Japan), 1977. Engr., Osaka Radio Co. (Japan), 1946-50; prof. elec. engring. Osaka Indsl. U., 1950-51; engr. DAIHEN Corp. 1951-85, exec. v.p., 1983-85; pres. DAIHEN Tech. Inst., Japan, 1984—; prof. Osaka U., 1955-59, 69-76, Nagoya, 1978-83; study mem. nat. standard com. Japan, 1955-76; lectr. robotics Welding Inst. symposium, London, 1983. Author: Argon Arc Welding, 1955; Arc Welding Equipment, 1967; Fusion Welding Equipment, 1978; patentee arc welding. Recipient Blue Ribbon prize Emperor of Japan, 1981. Mem. Japan Light Metal Welding Soc. (bd. dirs. 1975-83), Internat. Welding Soc., High Temperature Soc. (bd. dirs., auditor 1977-83), Japanese Welding Soc. (bd. dirs. 1979-82). Mem. Liberal Democratic Party. Shintoist. Office: Daihen Corp, 2-1-11 Tagawa Yodogawa-ku, Osaka 532, Japan

KIZHAKEMURI, DOMINIC CHACKO (D.C. KIZHAKEMURI), publisher; b. Kottayam, Kerala, India, Jan. 12, 1914; s. Chacko Dominic and Aleamma K.; m. Ponnamma Deecee; children—Tara, Meera, Ravi. Tchr., Kottayam, 1930-42; founding mem. SPCS writers coop. soc., Kottayam, 1945, sec., 1965-73; propr. D.C. Books, Kottayam, 1974—; mng. ptnr. Current Books, Kairalee Mudralayam, Kottayam, 1978—. Author: Elivaanam, Kuttichool, 1948; Methranum Kothukum, 1950; Karuppum Veluppum, 1948, 55; Enne Veruthe Vidaruth, 1986; Mukhya Manthri Muthal, 1987. Gen. sec. Kairali Children's Book Trust, Kottayam, 1980—. Columnist Kumkumom, 1984—, Manorajyan, 1984—. Pres., Kerala Freedom Fighters Assn., 1984—; chmn. Kottayam Citizens' Council, 1986—. Decorated Tamrapatra (India). Mem. Malayalam Book Devel. Council, Ofcl. Lang. Com. of Kerala, 1976—. Mem. Authors Guild India. Office: DC Books, Good Shepherd St, PO Box 214, Kottayam Kerala 686001, India

KJARTANSSON, KRISTJAN GEORG, soft drink bottling company executive; b. Reykjavik, Iceland, June 22, 1934; s. Halldor and Else (Nielsen) K.; grad. Comml. Coll. Iceland, 1956; student U. Iceland, 1956-60; m. Iounn Bjornsdottir, Sept. 28, 1957; children—Edda Birna, Halldor, Bjorn. Gen. mgr. Elding Trading Co. Inc., 1960-65; gen. mgr., v.p. Verksmidjan Vifilfell, Coca-Cola Bottlers in Iceland, 1965—; bd. dirs. various cos.; trustee Reykjavik Savs. Bank. Mem. Independence Party. Office: Box 1383 Reykjavik, Reykjavik Iceland

KJELLBERG, JAN WILLIAM, refractory and mineral company executive; b. Uppsala, Sweden, Jan. 13, 1938; s. Jonas Mark and Birgit (Hedenstedt) K.; m. Inga Birgitta Sjulander, June 27, 1964; children—Carl, Anders, Eva, Ann. Bergsingenjor, Royal Inst. Tech., Stockholm, 1964. Research engr., Sandvik, Sandviken, 1964-67, sales mgr., 1967-73; sales dir. Norrbottens Jarnverk, Lulea, 1973-76; pres. Jarnforadling, Halleforsnas, 1973-76, Acierex/Jarnforadling, Stockholm, 1978-79, Forshammar Group, Goteborg, 1979—. Home: Sveagatan 11, 41314 Goteborg Sweden Office: Svenska Forshammar AB, PO Box 8913, S-40273 Goteborg Sweden Other: Forshammar Group, Molndalsvegen 22, S-40020 Gotheborg Sweden

KLADNIG, WOLFGANG FRIEDRICH, chemist, educator; b. Vienna, Austria, July 24, 1944; s. Friedrich Otto and Hermine Maria (Preisinger) K.; m. Ingrid Rauchmann, June 9, 1984; 1 child, Viktoria Katherine. Dipl.Ing., Tech. U. Vienna, 1970, Ph.D., 1972. Asst. prof. Tech. U. Vienna, 1970-74; vis. scientist Imperial Coll., London, 1973; scientist dept. phys. chemistry IVIC, Caracas, Venezuela, 1974-77, indsl. cons., 1977; fellow, asso. scientist dept. chem. engring. Worcester (Mass.) Poly. Inst., 1977-79; project mgr., engr. chem. plants Voest Alpine AG, Linz, Austria, 1979-81, project mgr. product planning, 1981-84, mgr. research and devel., materials scis., siderurgical div., dept. engring. ceramics, 1984-87; ceramics devel. engr., Ruthner Research Ctr., Vienna, 1987—; lectr. U. Linz, 1987—. Mem. Verein Osterr Chemiker, Austrian Soc. Chem. Industry, Gesellschaft Deutscher Chemiker, Dechema, Catalysis Soc., Am. Chem. Soc., N.Y. Acad. Scis., Austrian Venezuelan Soc., Sigma Xi. Roman Catholic. Contbr. articles to profl. publs.; patentee in field. Home: 106/10/4 Krottenbachstr, 1190 Vienna Austria

KLAGES, CONSTANCE WARNER, management consultant; b. N.Y.C.; d. Ernest Frederick and Elsie (Roedler) K.; m. R. James Lotz, Jr., Apr. 26, 1975. B.A., Dickinson Coll., 1956. Asst. personnel dir., personnel asst. Internat. Internat. Edn., N.Y.C., 1956-62; employment supr., salary asst. Sperry Rand Corp., N.Y.C., 1962-65; research and survey mgr. Commerce & Indsl. Assn., Inc., N.Y.C., 1965-66; v.p., assoc., research dir. Battalia Lotz & Assn., Inc., N.Y.C., 1966-75; exec. v.p., treas. Internat. Mgmt. Advisors, Inc., N.Y.C., 1975—. Vol. membership com. Sutton Area Community Elmhurst Gen. Hosp., N.Y.C., 1976; bd. advisors Dickinson Coll., 1980-84, trustee, 1984—. Mem. Nat. Assn. Corp. and Profl. Recruiters, Dickinson Coll. Alumni Council. Office: Internat Mgmt Advisors Inc 767 3d Ave New York NY 10017

KLAHR, SAULO, scientist, educator; b. Santander, Colombia, June 8, 1935; came to U.S., 1961, naturalized, 1970; s. Herman and Raquel (Konigsberg) K.; m. Carol Declue, Dec. 29, 1965; children—James Herman, Robert David. B.A., Colegio Santa Librada, Cali, Colombia, 1954; M.D., U. Nat., Bogota, Colombia, 1959. Intern Hosp. San Juan de Dios, Bogota, 1958-59; resident U. Hosp., Cali, 1959-61; mem. faculty Washington U. Sch. Medicine, St. Louis, 1966—; prof. medicine Washington U. Sch. Medicine, 1972-86, Joseph Friedman Prof. of Renal Disease, 1986—, dir. renal div., 1972—; asso. physician Barnes Hosp., 1972-75, physician, 1975—; established investigator Am. Heart Assn., 1968-73; mem. adv. com. artificial kidney chronic uremia program USPHS, 1971—; bd. dirs. Eastern Mo. Kidney Found., 1973-75, chmn. med. adv. bd., 1973-74; research com. Mo. Heart Assn., 1973-80, chmn., 1980-81; sci. adv. bd. Nat. Kidney Found., 1978—, chmn., 1983-84, chmn. research and fellowship com., 1979-81, v.p., 1986—; mem. gen. medicine B study sect. USPHS, 1979-83, chmn. gen. medicine B study sect., 1981-83; mem. cardiovascular and renal rev. group FDA, mem. VA Merit Rev. Bd. Nephrology, 1984-87, chmn. 1986-87. Author articles, chpts. in books; editor: Contemporary Nephrology, Chronic Renal Disease, Nutrition and the Kidney; mem. editorial bd. Am. Jour. Nephrology, Am. Jour. Physiology and Renal and Electrolyte, Kidney and Body Fluids in Health and Disease, Am. Jour. Kidney Diseases, Internat. Jour. Pediatric Nephrology; assoc. editor Jour. Clin. Investigation. USPHS postdoctoral fellow, 1961-63. Fellow ACP; mem. Am. Soc. Nephrology (councilor 1980-81, sec.-treas. 1981-84, pres.-elect 1984-85, pres. 1985-86), Internat. Soc. Nephrology (councillor 1987, mem. mgmt. com. 1987), Am. Soc. Clin. Investigation, Am. Physiol. Soc., Biophys. Soc., N.Y. Acad. Scis., Am. Soc. Renal Biochemistry and Metabolism (pres. 1982-84), Central Soc. Clin. Research, Soc. Exptl. Biology and Medicine, Am. Assn. Physicians, Soc. Gen. Physiologists, Sigma Xi. Home: 11544 Ladue Rd Saint Louis MO 63141

KLAJBOR, DOROTHEA M., lawyer, consultant; b. Dunkirk, N.Y., Dec. 2, 1915; d. Joseph M., Sr., and Susan R. (Schrantz) K.; student George Washington U., 1949-52; J.D., Am. U., Washington, 1956. Admitted to D.C. bar, 1957; successively legal asst., legis. atty., atty., 2d asst. to Chief U.S. Marshal, civil rights compliance officer Dept. of Justice, Washington, 1938-70; supr. Town of Dunkirk, N.Y., 1973-76; mem. N.Y. State Liquor Authority, Buffalo, 1976-82. Bd. dirs. Center for Women Govt., Albany, N.Y., 1978-82, Dunkirk Sr. Citizens Ctr., 1983; mem. Chautauqua County Task Force on Aging, 1972-73, Town of Dunkirk Indsl. Devel. Agy., 1972-76, Chautauqua County Planning Bd., 1973-76, No. Chautauqua County Intermcpl. Planning Bd., 1974-76, Chautauqua County Overall Econ. Devel. Planning Bd., 1974-76, Literacy Vols., 1972-76, West Dunkirk Vol. Fire Dept., 1973—; adv. bd. Dunkirk Sr. Citizens, 1974-76; mem. women's div. N.Y. State Democratic Com. Mem. Am. Bar Assn. (life), Fed. Bar Assn., D.C. Bar, Women's Bar Assn. D.C., AAUW, Nat. Lawyers Club, Cath. Daus. Am., No. Chautauqua Club Assocs. (life), Dunkirk Hist. Soc. (life), Kappa Beta Pi. Democrat. Roman Catholic. Clubs: Chautauqua County Dem. Women's (treas. 1974-76), Zonta Internat. (chmn. com. on status of women; Industry Person of Yr. award 1980, Calista Jones award for advancement rights of women 1984), Town of Dunkirk Dem. Home: 91 Forest Pl Fredonia NY 14063

KLANICZAY, TIBOR, literary historian, educator; b. Budapest, Hungary, July 5, 1923; s. Gyula and Gizella (Heyszl) K.; m. Maria Bessenyei, 1949; 2 sons, 1 dau. Dr. h.c. (hon.), U. Tours (France). Lectr., Eotvos Lorand U., Budapest, 1949-57; dep. dir. Inst. Lit. Studies, Hungarian Acad. Scis., 1956-83; vis. prof. Sorbonne, Paris, 1967-68, U. Rome, 1975-79; dir. Ctr. Renaissance Research, Budapest, 1970—; dir. Inst. Lit. Studies, Hungarian Acad. Scis., 1984—. Author: Zrinyi Miklos, 1954, 64; Reneszansz es Barokk, 1961; (with others) History of Hungarian Literature, 1964, Marxizmus es Irodalomtudomany, 1964; co-author, editor: A magyar irondalom tortenete I II, 1964; A mult nagy korszakai, 1973; La crisi del Rinascimento e il Manierismo, 1973; A Manierizmus, 1975; Hagyomanyok ebresztese, 1976; Renaissance und Manierismus, 1977; Pallas magyar ivadékai, 1985, Renesans, Manieryzm, Barok, 1986; editor periodical Irodalomtorteneti Kozlemenyek, 1958-80; mem. adv. bd. Revue de Litterature Comparee, Paris, Can. Rev. Comparative Literature. Gen. sec. Internat. Assn. Hungarian Studies, Budapest. Decorated officier Ordre des Palmes Académiques; cavaliere dell'Ordine al Merito della Republica Italiana; recipient Kossuth prize, 1955; Labour Order of Merit. Fellow Mediaeval Acad. America; mem. Acad. Scis., Internat. Assn. Comparative Lit. (dir.), Federation des Sociétés et des Institutes pour l'Etude de la Renaissance, Federation Internationale des Langues et Litté ratures Modernes, Associazione Internazionale per gli Studi di Lingua e Letteratura Italiana (mem. consiglio direttivo).

KLARSKOV, FINN, advertising executive; b. Copenhagen, May 10, 1940; s. Hans and Anna (Christensen) K.; m. Kirsten Kofoed; children: Marianne, Christian. B in Mktg., U. Handelshøjkolen, Copenhagen, 1969. Prin. FBK Reklamebureau, Copenhagen, 1970—. Contbr. articles to profl. jours. Office: FBK Reklamebureau, Nyhavn 38, DK-1051 Copenhagen K Denmark

KLASKY, CHARLES M., writer, director, producer; b. Hollywood, Calif., June 14, 1949; s. Maurice Leonard and Molly (Rudnick) K.; m. Amy Vangsgard, September, 1986. BA, Occidental Coll., 1971; MA, Calif. State U., 1974; postgrad., Ea. Mont. Coll., 1975. Writer, producer Dave Bell & Assocs., Hollywood, Calif., 1978-80; writer Walt Disney Ednl. Media Co., Burbank, Calif., 1981-82; writer/media producer Ednl. Devel. Specialists, Lakewood, Calif., 1981-82, Calif. State U. Consortium, Long Beach, 1982-83, Times Mirror TV, Long Beach, 1982-83; exec. producer Montage Communications, Hollywood, 1982-83; dir. media tng. Cal Fed Ind., Los Angeles, 1983—; prof., lectr. UCLA, others, 1980—; conductor seminars in field. Contbr. articles to profl jours.; author 52 pub. books; writer, producer, dir. 94 TV programs; producer nat. media campaign for disabled. Recipient 2 Silver awards Vision Arts and Scis., N.Y. Film Festival, 1979, Gold award Chgo. Film Festival, 1979, others. Mem. Internat. TV Assn. (3 Silver Angel awards 1984), Nat. Acad. TV Arts and Scis. (2 Emmy awards 1979), Info. Film Producers Assn.

KLASNIC, JOHN CHARLES (JACK), graphic arts company executive; b. McKeesport, Pa., Nov. 11, 1939; s. Stephen Andrew and Helen Lucille (Domarski) K.; m. Kathleen Frances Carroll, June 24, 1967; 1 child, Kathleen Jackie. BS in Printing Mgmt., Carnegie-Mellon U., 1962; Acctg. cert. U. Balt., 1976. Chief estimator King Brothers, Balt., 1963-66; branch mgr. Am. Bank, Norfolk, Va., 1966-67; plant mgr. Waverly Press, Balt., 1967-73; asst. v.p. mfg., Port City Press, Pikesville, Md., 1973-76; pres. Klasnic and Assocs., Inc., White Hall, Md., 1976—; instr. Catonsville (Md.) Community Coll., 1977—; instr. Printing Industries Md., Balt., 1979—, Printing Industries, P.C., Washington, 1981-86. Author: In Plant Printing Handbook, 1981, Printing Handbook, 1984, How to Kill an Inplant, 1986; contbr. over 750 articles to profl. jours., lectr. to profl. seminars. Fund raiser numerous charities, Balt. County, 1968—; adviser Md. Penitentiary Rehab. Program, Balt., 1979—; mem. PTA Hereford Mid. Sch., Freeland, Md., 1980—. Served with U.S. Army, 1962-63. Named In-Plant Reprodns. and Electronic Pub. 1987 Industry Leader of Yr.; named Dean of In-Plant Cons.; recipient numerous awards for excellence in graphic arts. Fellow In-Plant Mgmt. Assn.; mem. Assn. Graphic Arts Cons. (pres. 1983-85), Printing Industry Am., Graphic Arts Tech Found., Nat. Assn. Printers and Lithographers, Am. Legion Democrat. Roman Catholic. Home: 18925 Vernon Rd White Hall MD 21161

KLATSKIN, BERTRAM, oral surgeon; b. N.Y.C., Feb. 11, 1916; s. Archibald and Celia (Golubowski) K.; m. Ruth Weiner, Nov. 20, 1941; children: Andrew, Lois Klatskin Kolstad, Beth Klatskin Sidebotham. A.B. with honors, Cornell U., 1937; D.D.S., Columbia U., 1941. Diplomate: N.Y. State Bd. Oral Surgery. Intern in oral surgery Morrisania City Hosp., Bronx, N.Y., 1941-42; resident Sea View Hosp., S.I., N.Y., 1942-43; gen. practice dentistry S.I., 1943-61, pvt. practice oral surgery, 1961-82; mem. staff Sea View Hosp., 1943-84, chief oral surgery, 1950-84, dir. dental services, 1973-84, also mem. exec. bd., v.p. med.-dental staff and med. bd., 1976-80, pres., 1980-84, dep. dir. med. affairs, 1979-84, dir. emeritus dental services, 1984—; assoc. attending oral surgeon S.I. Hosp., 1970-72, attending oral surgeon, 1972-82, mem. exec. bd., 1974-77; also mem. tumor bd., asst. attending oral surgeon Columbia-Presbyn. Med. Center, 1972-74, assoc. attending oral surgeon, 1974-82; oral surgery staff Columbia U. Dental Sch., 1943-82, St. Vincents Med. Center, Richmond Meml. Hosp.; clin. prof. oral and maxillofacial surgery Columbia U. Dental Sch., 1976-82; clin. prof. oral and maxillofacial surgery U. Colo. Dental Sch., 1985—; lectr. community and profl. groups; malpractice cons. N.Y. State Supreme Ct.; mem. dist. bd. Health Systems Agy.; dental cons. nursing homes.; mem. Emergency Med. Service Com., N.Y.C. Health and Hosps. Corp. Council of Med. Bd. Pres., 1980-84. Contbr. articles to profl. jours. Mem. Sea View Community Adv. Bd.; mem. exec. bd. S.I. unit Am. Cancer Soc., 1967—, vice chmn., 1975-77, honoree, 1978. Served as maj. AUS, 1953-55. Fellow Am. Coll. Dentists, Internat. Assn. Oral Surgeons, Royal Soc. Health, Am. Assn. Oral and Maxillofacial Surgeons; mem. Am. Dental Assn. (life), N.Y. State Second Dist. Dental Soc. (trustee 1964), Richmond County Dental Soc. (pres. 1963, Man. of Yr. 1984), Colo. Dental Assn., Denver Dental Soc., N.Y. State Soc. Oral Surgeons, Am. Dental Soc. Anesthesiology, Met. Conf. Hosp. Dental Chiefs, Am. Assn. Hosp. Dentists, Clin. Soc. Sea View Hosp. (pres. 1975-80), Columbia Dental Alumni Assn., DAV, Omicron Kappa Upsilon, Alpha Omega (pres. 1968-70). Club: Cornell. Lodge: Masons. Home: 6495 Happy Canyon Rd #7 Denver CO 80237 Office: Sea View Hosp 460 Brielle Ave Staten Island NY 10314

KLAUS, FRANCOIS, ballet dancer; b. Cannes, France. Student with Julie Sedova and Mariko Besobrazova. Former dancer with Stuttgart Ballet and Ballet of Munich State Opera (W.Ger.); prin. dancer Hamburg Ballet, 1972—; John Neumeier (dir. of Hamburg Ballet) created for him such roles as Schumann (Meyerbeer-Schumann), Oberon (A Midsummer Night's Dream), Prince Desire (The Sleeping Beauty), Quant (The Age of Anxiety), King Arthur (Saga of King Arthur) and leading roles in Saint Matthew Passion and Mozart 338, Mahler's 3d Symphony; repertoire includes Petrucchio (The Taming of The Shrew), Romeo, Mercutio and Tybalt (Romeo and Juliet), Gunther and Drosselmeier (Nutcracker), The King (in John Neumeier's version of Swan Lake), Don Juan and Albrecht (Giselle); guest dancer, Stuttgart, Munich, Frankfurt, Vienna, Florence, Paris, Stockholm, Monte Carlo, and Australia. Address: care Press Relations, Ballet de, Hamburg Staatsoper, Gr Theaterstrasse 34, D-2000 Hamburg 36 Federal Republic of Germany

KLAUS, TERFLOTH, ambassador; b. Dusseldorf, Fed. Republic Germany, May 20, 1929. JD, U. Bonn, Fed. Republic Germany, 1953. Chief de cabinet European Communities Commn., Brussels, 1970-73; ambassador to Burma Rangoon, 1973-75; spokesman Fgn. Ministry, Bonn, 1975-77; ambassador to Tunisia Tunis, 1977-80; ambassador to Pakistan Islamabad, 1980-84; ambassador to Finland Helsinki, 1984—. Office: German Embassy, Frederikinkatu 61, Helsinki Finland

KLAUSMEIER, HERBERT JOHN, psychologist, educator; b. Boonville, Ind., Nov. 4, 1915; s. Henry P. and Catherine E. (Heilmann) K.; m. Iyla T. Johnson, Aug. 18, 1946; children—Thomas Wayne, Connie Alice. B.S., Ind. State U., 1940, M.S., 1947; Ed.D., Stanford, 1949. Sch. tchr. 1936-38, 40-41, 46-47; asst. prof., asso. prof. psychology and edn. U. No. Colo., 1949-52; asst. prof. ednl. psychology U. Wis., Madison, 1952-54; assoc. prof. U. Wis., 1954-57, prof., 1958—, V.A.C. Henmon prof. ednl. psychology, 1968-86, prof. emeritus, 1986—; assoc. dir. Wis. Research and Devel. Center for Cognitive Learning, 1964-67, dir., 1967-72, also originator individually guided edn., sch. improvement research method, sch. self-improvement process. Author or co-author: Teaching in the Secondary School, 1953, 3d edit, 1968, Teaching in the Elementary School, 1956, 4th edit, 1974, Psychology in Theory and Practice, 1959, Analyses of Concept Learning, 1966, Conceptual Learning and Development: A Cognitive View, 1974, Individually Guided Motivation, 1975, Learning and Human Abilities: Educational Psychology, 1961, 4th edit, 1975, Faciliating Student Learning, 1975, Individually Guided Elementary Education, 1977; Cognitive Development of Children and Youth: A Longitudinal Study, 1978, Cognitive Learning and Development: Information-Processing and Piagetian Perspectives, 1979, Learning and Teaching Concepts: A Strategy for Testing Applications of Theory, 1980, Improvement of Education through Research: Five Longitudinal Case Studies, 1983, The Renewal and Improvement of Secondary Education: Concepts and Practices, 1983, A Process Guide for School Improvement, 1985, Developing and Institutionalizing a Self-Improvement Capability, 1985, Local Scholl Self-Improvement: Processes and Directions, 1987; editor: Leadership Series in Individually Guided Education 1976, 77. Served with USNR, 1941-46. Recipient Alumni Disting. Service award Ind. State U., 1962; Disting. Research award Wis. Edn. Research Assn., 1976; Leadership award Assn. Individually Guided Edn., 1976; Disting. Friend of Edn. award Wis. Sch. Adminstrs., 1982, Am. Edn. Research, Service award, 1985; Phi Delta Kappa biennial award for outstanding research, 1985. Fellow Am. Psychol. Assn. (pres. Rocky Mountain br. 1951-52, pres. ednl. psychology div. 1970-71); mem. Am. Edn. Research Assn., others. Home: 10 Colony Circle Madison WI 53717

KLEBE, GISELHER, composer; b. Mannheim, Fed. Republic of Germany, June 28, 1925; s. Franz and Gertrud (Michaelis) K.; m. Lore Schiller, Sept. 10, 1946; children: Sonja, Annette. Grad. in music, Konservatorium, Berlin, 1951. Berufung an die musikakademie Detmold als Dozent fur Komposition und Theorie, 1957; ernennung zum professor für Komposition 1962; pres. Akademie der Künste, Berlin, 1986, Abt. Musik d. Dramatiker-Union, Berlin, 1986. Bühnenwerke: 12 Opern u.a.: Die tödlichen Wünsche, nach Balzac, 1959, Jakobowsky und der Oberst, nach Werfel, 1965, Die Fastnachtsbeichte, nach Zuckmayer, 1983, 5 Ballete; Orchesterwerke: u.a. Die Zwitschermaschine, 5 sinfonien, Orpheus, Konzert für Orgel u. Orchester, BegrüBung Salutations, Konzert für Clarinette und Orchester, Lied für Orchester; Kammermusik: u.a. 3 Streichquartette Römische Elegien f. Sprecher, Klav, cembalo u. KontrabaB, Elegia appasionata für Klaviertrio, Berlioz-Variationen für Orgel und Schlagzeug, Al Rovescio für Flöte, Harfe, Klavier und Metallidiophone, Alborada für Harfe solo, Der dunkle Gedanke für Klarinette und Klavier, Veränderung der Klaviersonate op. 27,2 von Ludwig van Beethoven in Sonate für Horn und Klavier; Kirchenmusikalische werke: u.a. Stabat mater, Messe Gebet einer armen Seele für Chor und Orgel, Choral und Tedeum, Orgerwerke, Notturno für Orchester, 1987, Konzert fü Harfe und Orchester, 1988, Soiree für Posaune und Kammerensemble, 1987. Recipient Berliner Kunstpreis, 1952, Kompositionspreis der Unesco, 1954, GroBer Kuntspreis des Landes Nordrhein-Westfalen, 1959, Premio Marzotto für die Vereinigung Europas, 1964, Bundesverdienstkreuz 1. Klasse, 1975. Mem. Freie Akademie der Künste Hamburg, Akademie der Künste Berlin, Akademie der Schönen Künste München, Ehrendirektor des Internationalen Harfenzentrms. Address: Bruchstrasse 16, 4930 Detmold 1, Federal Republic of Germany Office: Hochschule für Musik Detmold, Allee 22, 4930 Detmold Federal Republic of Germany

KLEE, KARL HEINZ, lawyer; b. Innsbruck, Austria, June 9; s. Ernst and Anna Barbara (Richter) K.; LL.D., U. Innsbruck, 1953; m. Charlotte Haslwanter, Jan. 19, 1961; 1 dau., Katharina. Admitted to bar, 1960, since practiced in Innsbruck; dir. organizing com. Alpine Ski World Championships; pres. Alpbacher Bergbahn Gesellschaft. Mem. Austrian Olympic Com., 1965, v.p., 1969, hon. mem., 1977; pres. Austrian Ski Fedn., 1966, Austrian Ski Pool, 1971; sec. gen. XII Olympic Winters Games, Innsbruck, 1973-78. Recipient Golden Badge of Honor, Republic of Austria and Land of Styria; hon. ring City of Innsbruck; Coubertin medal; decorated knight Royal Swedish Order Polar Star; comdr. Order Nat. duMerite (France). Mem. Tyrolean Bar Chamber (exec. com.), Internat. Ski Assn. Club: Innsbruck Panathlon (pres.). Home: 16 Gartenweg, A6064 Rum Austria Office: 38 Maria Theresienstrasse, A6020 Innsbruck Austria

KLEEB, STÉPHANE, film director; b. Mar. 17, 1955; m. Bette Solheim; children: Maja, Wim, Matthis. SAWI, Schweiz. Ausbildungszentrum fur Werbung und Info., Biel, Switzerland, 1975; LIFS, London Internat. Film Sch., 1978. Free-lance film technician, asst. cameraman Switzerland, 1976-80; free-lance cameraman various TV and film productions, Switzerland, 1981-88, dir., 1981—. Film author and dir.: What Are You Going to Do with the Old Dummies, 1978, Time to Weep, Time to Laugh, 1981, Fridolin the Window Cleaner (TV series), 1984-87. Mem. Swiss Film Technician Orgn., Pro Litteris.

KLEEMAN, ROBERT HERBERT, dentist; b. Bklyn., Feb 4, 1931; s. Louis and Rae (Schwartz) K.; grad. Pennington Sch., 1949; B.S., L.I.U., 1952; D.D.S., Loyola U., 1956; postgrad. in oral surgery N.Y.U., 1956-57; m. Florence Million, Dec. 3, 1982; 1 son by previous marriage, Robert Joseph. Intern oral surgery Queens Gen. Hosp. Center, 1957-58, attending dentist, 1958-63; practice dentistry specializing in oral surgery, Riverdale, N.Y., 1959-82; attending dentist St. Agatha Home for Children, 1958-62; guest lectr. spl. radiation procedure course Queens Gen. Hosp. Center, 1958-62; corp. exec. Beta Internat., Inc., Interglobal Investment Ltd. Scenic prodn. designer Actors Conservatory Theatre, Ardsley, N.Y., Harrison (N.Y.) Players, Inc. Fellow Am. Endodontic Soc.; mem. ADA, Am. Dental Soc. Anesthesiology, Internat. Acad. Orthodontics, Am. Soc. Dentistry for Children, Am. Sch. Health Assn., Royal Soc. Health, Am. Orthodontic Soc., N.Y. Artists Equity Assn., Am. Theatre Assn., Am. Philatelic Soc., New Rochelle Art Assn. Exhibited XIII Internat. Dental Congress in Cologne, Germany, 1962, Art Exhibit Bronxville Theater, 1963, Art Exhibit YM-YWHA of Mid-Westchester, 1978, Lake Worth Art Soc., 1988. Address: Berkshire G 151 West Palm Beach FL 33417

KLEID, WALLACE, lawyer; b. Balt., June 25, 1946; s. Max E. and Bess (Hubberman) K.; m. Loryn Sari Lesser, July 1, 1979; children: Micah Saul, Matthew Brett; 1 dau. by previous marriage, Kathy Jill. BA, U. Md., 1967; JD, U. Md.-Balt., 1971. Bar: Md. 1972, U.S. Ct. Mil. Appeals 1973, U.S. Dist. Ct. Md. 1972, U.S. Supreme Ct. 1975, U.S. Ct. Appeals (4th cir.) 1975, D.C. 1982. Law clk. State's Atty. Baltimore County, Md., 1970-72, asst. state's atty., 1972-77; sole practice, Balt. and Towson, Md., 1972-85; ptnr. Floam & Kleid, Balt., Towson, 1985—; mem. Rape Adv. Commn., Baltimore County, 1974-75; presenter testimony on rape Md. Gen. Assembly, 1975; cons. TV program Women and the Law, 1976-77; lectr. in field. Bd. dirs. Colonial Village Neighborhood Assn., Balt., 1969-75, Citizens Dem. Club, Balt., 1972-75; Cheswolde Neighborhood Assn., Balt., v.p., 1981-84, pres., 1984-86, bd. dirs. 1986—. Served to sgt. U.S. Army Res., 1968-74. Recipient Civilian award Balt. County Police Dept., 1975. Mem. ABA (gen. practice sect., vice-chmn., liaison to nat., state, and local bar leaders gen. practice sect. 1987-88, mem. conterace planning subcom. 1988—, chmn. subcom. on assocs. employment agreements 1978-88), Assn. Trial Lawyers Am., Baltimore County Bar Assn. (lawyer referral com. 1976-78, chmn. ins. trust 1980-87, vice chmn. 1988—), Balt. City Bar Assn. (workmens compensation com., family law com.), Fed. Bar Assn., Md. State Bar Assn. (chmn. spl. com. to establish gen. practice sect. council 1988—, chmn. gen. practice sect. 1985-87, sect. council 1988, cons. spl. com. on regulation of lawyers' trust and fiduciary accounts 1987, atty. grievance commn. 1982—, Md. Criminal Def. Assn., Nat. Def. Attys. Assn., Md. State Atty.'s Assn., Md. Trial Lawyers Assn., Nat. Dist. Attys. Assn., D.C. Bar Assn., Zeta Beta Tau. Democrat. Jewish. Home: 6228 Benhurst Rd Baltimore MD 21209 Office: 1118 N Calvert St Baltimore MD 21202

KLEIMAN, ARTHUR, magazine editor; b. N.Y.C., May 28, 1950; s. Alex and Betty (Silverberg) K.; m. Kathleen Roszkowski, Aug. 2, 1980; 1 child, Jeffrey Adam. B.S.E.E., Hofstra U., 1974; B.S. in Elec. Engring., RCA, 1971. Editor, editorial dir. Gernsback Pub., N.Y.C., 1974—. Mem. IEEE. Home: 1332 Allen Dr Seaford NY 11783 Office: Gernsback Pub Inc 200 Park Ave S New York NY 10003

KLEIMAN, BERNARD, lawyer; b. Chgo., Jan. 26, 1928; s. Isadore and Pearl (Wikoff) K.; m. Gloria Baime, Nov. 15, 1986; children—Leslie, David. B.S., Purdue U., 1951; J.D., Northwestern U., 1954. Bar: Ill. bar 1954. Practice law in assn. with Abraham W. Brussell, 1957-60; dist. counsel United Steel Workers Am., 1960-65, gen. counsel, 1965—; partner Kleiman, Cornfield & Feldman, Chgo., 1960-75; prin. B. Kleiman (P.C.), 1976-77, Kleiman and Whitney (P.C.), 1978—; mem. collective bargaining coms. for nat. labor negotiations in basic steel, aluminum and can mfg. industries. Contbr. articles to legal jours. Served with U.S. Army, 1946-48. Mem. Am., Ill., Chgo., Allegheny County bar assns. Office: 1 E Wacker Dr Chicago IL 60601 also: 5 Gateway Center Pittsburgh PA 15222

KLEIMAN, GARY HOWARD, radio station executive, consultant; b. Phila., Jan. 24, 1952; s. Leon and Martha (Rubin) K.; m. Annette Suzanne Vranich, Sept. 23, 1978; children: Aaron Jay, Jared Adam. Diploma Am. Acad. Broadcasting, Phila., 1969, Pa. State Fire Sch., Media, 1969; BS, Temple U., 1972. Cert. radio mktg. cons. Gen. mgr. Sta. WFEC, Harrisburg, Pa., 1974-75; local sales mgr. Sta. WYSP-FM, Phila., 1976-79; pres. A.S.K. Advt., King of Prussia, Pa., 1976-80; v.p., gen. mgr. Sta. WGLU-FM, Johnstown, 1980-82, Sta. WAJE, Edensburg, Pa., 1982-84, Sta. WSBY-WQHQ-AM-FM, Salisbury, Md., 1984-86; mgr. Sta. WJDY, Salisbury, 1986-87; pres. Ideas Unltd. Mktg. and Advt. Co., Salisbury, 1986—; gen. mgr. Sta. WACS-FM, Schenectady, N.Y., 1988—; media cons., Sta. WMDT TV, Salisbury, Md., 1988; dir., tchr. Am. Acad. Broadcasting, Phila., 1976-79. Contbr. articles to profl. publs. Active campaigner Cambria County Democratic Com., 1982-84; com. chmn. Salisbury Revitalization, 1984—; bd. dirs. Salisbury Regional Urban Design Action Team, 1984—, Deers Head Hosp. Found., 1987—; co-sponsor projects Lower Shore Easter Seals, Salisbury, 1985, Am. Cancer Soc., 1984-85, Kidney Found., 1985, Epilepsy Assn., 1985; promotion coordinator Salisbury Festival com., 1985, 87, 88, vice-chmn., 1985-88; mem. exec. com. Lower Shore chpt. March of Dimes, 1984—; bd. dirs. Am. Heart Assn., 1987-88, Johnstown Area Regional Industries, 1981-84. Recipient numerous awards from local civic orgns., 1981—. Mem. Downtown Salisbury Assn., Salisbury Area C. of C., Salisbury Jaycees (Jaycee Springboard award 1985), Johnstown Jaycees. Democrat. Jewish. Club: Salisbury State Coll. Athletic. Avocations: photography, camping, skiing, softball, volleyball. Home and Office: 115 Tall Timber Dr Fruitland MD 21826 also: Sta WMDT TV 202 Downtown Plaza Salisbury MD 21801

KLEIN, BERNARD, publishing company executive; b. N.Y.C., Sept. 20, 1921; s. Joseph J. and Anna (Wolfe) K.; m. Betty Stecher, Feb. 17, 1946; children: Cheryl Rona, Barry Todd, Cindy Ann. B.A., CCNY, 1942. Founder, pres. U.S. List Co., N.Y.C., 1946—; founder, pres., chief editor B. Klein Pubs., Inc., Coral Springs, Fla. and Rye, N.Y., 1953—; cons. direct mail advt. and reference book pub. to pubs., industry, 1950—. Author: all biennials Ency. of American Indian, 1954—; Guide to American Directories. Served with AUS, 1942-45, ETO. Mem. Direct Mail Advt. Assn. Lodge: Masons.

KLEIN, CHARLES HENLE, lithographing co. exec.; b. Cin., Oct. 5, 1908; s. Benjamin Franklin and Flora (Henle) K.; student Purdue U., 1926-27, U. Cin., 1927-28; m. Ruth Becker, Sept. 23, 1938; children—Betsy (Mrs. Marvin H. Schwartz), Charles H., Carla (Mrs. George Fee III). Pres., Progress Lithographing Co., Cin., 1934-59, Novelart Mfg. Co., Cin., 1960—; dir. R.A. Taylor Corp. Founding mem. Chief Execs. Forum. Clubs: Losantiville Country, Queen City, Bankers (Cin.). Home: 6754 Fairoaks Dr Amberley

Village Cincinnati OH 45237 Office: 2121 Section Rd Amberley Village Cincinnati OH 45237

KLEIN, DAVID, foreign service officer; b. N.Y.C., Sept. 2, 1919; s. Sam and Fannie H. (Falk) K.; m. Anne L. Cochran, Mar. 14, 1953; children—Peter S., Steven C., John W., Barbara J., Richard L., Suzanne G. B.A., Bklyn. Coll., 1939; M.B.A., Harvard U., 1947; M.A., Columbia U., 1952; postgrad., U. Md., 1964-66; grad., Nat. War Coll., 1966. Fgn. service officer 1947—; vice consul Lourenco Marques, 1947-49; 3d sec., econ. officer Rangoon, Burma, 1949-51; Russian lang. and area studies Dept. State, 1951-52; 2d sec., consular/econ. officer Moscow, 1952-54; Regensburg-Soviet studies 1954-55; polit./econ. officer Berlin, 1955-57; 1st sec., polit. officer Bonn, Germany, 1957-60; Soviet desk Dept. State, 1960-62; sr. mem. for European affairs Nat. Security Council, 1962-65; counselor econ. affairs Moscow, 1966-67; counselor polit. affairs 1967-68; polit. adviser Berlin, 1968-71, U.S. minister to, 1971-74; asst. dir. ACDA, Washington, 1974-75; exec. dir. Am. Council on Germany, 1975-88, dir., 1975—; exec. dir. John J. McCloy Fund, 1975-88; pres. German Am. Partnership Program, 1976-85; spl. asst. for fgn. affairs for pres. Fairleigh Dickinson U., N.J., 1986—; instr. govt. and politics U. Md., 1969-71; chmn. bd. Zeiss Avionics, Calif. Author: The Basmachi, a Study in Soviet Nationalities, 1952. Bd. dirs. Deutsches Haus, N.Y. U., 1977—; vice chmn. bd. trustees Mercer County Community Coll., West Windsor, N.J., 1978-84; mem. adv. bd. Byrnes Internat. Ctr., U. S.C., 1987— Served to col. AUS, 1941-46. Decorated Legion of Merit; recipient superior service award Dept. State, 1964; Baker scholar Harvard Bus. Sch. Mem. Harvard Bus. Club (v.p. Washington 1965-66), Am. Fgn. Service Assn., Council on Fgn. Relations. Unitarian. Clubs: Century (N.Y.), Univ. (N.Y.). Home: 6535 CMTP Kittansett La Jolla CA 92037 office: Fairleigh Dickinson U Hackensack NJ

KLEIN, ERNEST JOSEPH, aerospace engineer; b. Winnipeg, Manitoba, Can., Jan. 12, 1928; s. Jacob Albert and Pauline Josephine (von Zeltner) K.; m. Helen Julie Humenik, June 6, 1956 (div. 1974); m. Traute Wollenberg, Oct. 30, 1982. BSc, U. Manitoba, Winnipeg, 1953; postgrad., U. Ottawa, Can., 1957, Cambridge U., Eng., 1962; Cert. in Engring. Mgmt., George Washington U., Washington, 1967; postgrad., Pacific We. U., Los Angeles. Registered profl. engr., Manitoba, Ont. Can. Ops. engr. Can. Broadcasting Corp., Winnipeg, 1952-53; signals engr. Can. Nat. Railways, Winnipeg, 1953-54; design approvals engr. Dept. Nat. Def., Ottawa, 1955-57; standard labs. engr. Transport Can. (Regs.), Ottawa, 1957-58, systems engr. (Telecom), 1958-60, research and devel., 1960-61; project engr. research and devel. Transport Can. (Regs.), London, 1961-65; mem. sci. staff Bellcomm (Bell Labs.), Washington, 1966-70; pres., chief exec. officer Ketas Cda/Ketek, Winnipeg, 1975—. Patentee in field; contbr. articles to profl. jours. Mem. AIAA, IEEE (sr.), Can. Aeronautics and Space Inst., Assn. Profl. Engrs. Ontario, Winnipeg C. of C. (pub. fin. com. 1982—, chmn. energy com. 1987—). Office: Ketas Can Inc/Ketek Inc, Box 2550, Winnipeg, MB Canada R3C 4B3

KLEIN, ERNST STEFAN, journalist, editor; b. Danderyd, Sweden, Nov. 24, 1937; s. Oskar and Gerda (Koch) K.; m. Helena Lundgren, Apr. 29, 1961; children: Pernilla, Paul. Editorial writer Expressen, Stockholm, 1962, editor editorial page, 1968-75, U.S. corr., 1975-77, fgn. editor, 1977—. Author: Jimmy Carter, 1977. Vice pres. Swedish Liberal Youth, 1961-63. Home: Skogsliden 12, S182 74 Stocksund Sweden Office: Expressen Gjorwellsgatan, 30 S 105 16 Stockholm Sweden

KLEIN, GEORGE DEVRIES, geologist; b. Den Haag, Netherlands, Jan. 21, 1933; came to U.S., 1947, naturalized, 1955; s. Alfred and Doris (deVries) K.; m. Chung Sook Kim Chung, May 23, 1982. BA, Wesleyan U., 1954; MA, U. Kans., 1957; Ph.D., Yale U., 1960. Research sedimentologist Sinclair Research Inc., 1960-61; asst. prof. geology U. Pitts., 1961-63; asst. prof. to assoc. prof. U. Pa., 1963-69; prof. U. Ill., Urbana, 1970—; vis. fellow Wolfson Coll. Oxford U., 1969; vis. prof. geology U. Calif., Berkeley, 1970; vis. prof. oceanography Oreg. State U., 1974, Seoul Nat. U., 1980, U. Tokyo, 1983; CIC vis. exchange prof. geophys. sci. U. Chgo., 1979-80; vis. research prof. geophysics U. Utrecht, 1988; chief scientist Deep Sea Drilling Project Leg 58, 1977-78; continuing edn. lectr.; asso. Center Advanced Studies U. Ill., 1974, 83. Author: Sandstone Depositional Models for Exploration for Fossil Fuels, 3d edit, 1985, Clastic Tidal Facies, 1977, Holocene Tidal Sedimentation, 1976; mem. editorial bd. Geol. Soc. Am. Bull., 1973-74, assoc. editor, 1975-81; cons. editor: McGraw-Hill Ency. of Sci. and Yearbook, 1977—; chief cons. adv. editor: CEPCO div. Burgess Pub. Co, 1979-81; series editor: Geol. Sci. Monographs, Internat. Human Resources Devel. Corp. Press, Inc., 1981-87, Sedimentary Geology, Prentice-Hall Inc., 1988—; mem. editorial bd. Sedimentary Geology, 1985— Elsevier; mng. editor Sedimentology, Earth Scis. Revs., 1987—. Recipient Outstanding Paper award Jour. Sedimentary Petrology, 1970; Erasmus Haworth Disting. Alumnus award in geology U. Kans., 1980; Outstanding Geology Faculty Mem. award U. Ill. Geology Grad. Student Assn., 1983; NSF grantee. Fellow AAAS, Geol. Soc. Am. (chmn. div. sedimentary geology 1985-86), Geol. Assn. Can.; mem. Am. Geophys. Union, Am. Inst. Profl. Geologists, Soc. Exploration Geophysicists, Soc. Econ. Paleontologists and Mineralogists, Internat. Assn. Sedimentologists, Am. Assn. Petroleum Geologists, Sigma Xi. Office: Dept Geology Univ Ill 245 Natural History Bldg 1301 W Green St Urbana IL 61801-2999

KLEIN, GEORGE ROBERT, periodical distribution company executive; b. Washington, Pa., Sept. 28, 1909; s. George Ruttman and Virginia R. (Hickey) K.; m. Mary Elizabeth Fisher, Jan. 28, 1939. BA, Ohio Weslyan U., 1930; BS, MIT, 1932. Pres. George R. Klein News Co., Shaker Heights, Ohio, 1940—. Chmn. bd. trustees Ch. of the Saviour, United Meth., 1960—; vice chmn., trustee St. Luke's Hosp., 1965—; v.p. bd. mgrs. Cen. YMCA, 1946-71; trustee Christian Residences Found., 1965—, Goodwill Industries Cleve., 1967-70, Ch. of the Saviour Found., 1962—, N.E. Ohio Conf. Meth. Ch., 1965—, Cleve. Zool. Soc., 1970—, Mus. Arts Assn., 1973—, Play House Found., 1972—, Ohio Weslyan U., 1971—, Univ. Circle Found., 1974—; trustee, pres. Cleve. Play House Theatre; mem. Welfare Fedn. Manpower Commn., 1971-74; pres. Ohio Weslyan U. Assocs., 1960-62. Served with USN, 1943-46. Mem. Nat. Bur. Ind. Pubs. and Periodical Distbrs. Assn. (past pres.), Mid-Am. Periodical Distbrs. Assn. (past pres.), Mag. Distbrs. Research Project Group (past pres.), Nat. Council Periodical Distbrs. Assn. (past dir.), Ind. Periodical Distbrs. Great Lakes (past pres.), Cleve. Engring. Soc., Sigma Pi Sigma, Pi Mu Epsilon, Omicron Delta Kappa. Clubs: Canterbury Golf; Skating; City (Cleve.); Rowfant; University; Marco Polo; Union. Lodge: Kiwanis. Home: 23699 Shaker Blvd Shaker Heights OH 44122

KLEIN, HELMFRIED ERNST, psychiatrist; b. Bachmehring, Fed. Republic of Germany, May 10, 1945; s. Ernst C. and Luitgard (Rudolph) K.; m. Marita Eisenmann, Mar. 12, 1977; children: Julian, Silvan. MD, U. Munich, PhD, 1970. Gen. practice medicine Fed. Republic of Germany, 1974-76; asst. prof. medicine NYU, 1976-77; staff physician Psychiatric Clinic, U. Munich, 1977-84, prof. psychiatry, 1987; dir. Arzt für Nervenheilkunde, Psychotherapie, Fachklinik für Psychiatrie und Neurologie, Regensburg, Fed. Republic of Germany, 1984—. Author books, contbr. articles on psychiatry to various publs. Mem. various profl. orgns. Office: Fachklinik Psychiatrie, und Neurologie, Universitatstrasse 84, 8400 Regensburg Federal Republic of Germany

KLEIN, HENRY, lawyer; b. N.Y.C., Oct. 6, 1949; s. Leo Herman and Florence (Silver) K.; m. Ann Laura Hallasey, July 30, 1972; children—Lauren Jennifer, Benjamin Jason. B.A., SUNY-Albany, 1971; J.D., U. San Diego, 1975. Bar: Calif. 1975, U.S. Ct. Customs and Patent Appeals 1976. Trademark atty. U.S. Patent Office, Washington, 1975-77; ptnr. Ladas & Parry, Los Angeles, 1978—. Mem. San Diego Law Rev., 1974-75; editor-in-chief Trademark Soc. Newsletter, 1977. Mem. U. San Diego Civil Legal Clinic, 1974, Civil Rights Research Council, San Diego, 1974, Calif. Pub. Interest Research Group, San Diego, 1975. N.Y. State scholar, 1967-71; Tex. State legal scholar State of Tex., 1972; recipient Am. Jurisprudence award Bancroft-Whitney Co. and Lawyer Co-Op. Pub. Co., Lubbock, Tex., 1972; Patent Trademark Spl. Achievement awards U.S. Dept. Commerce, Washington, 1976, 77. Mem. U.S. Trademark Assn. (v.p. 1976, pres., chmn. 1977), Los Angeles Patent Law Assn., Phi Delta Phi. Republican. Jewish. Home: 6134 Cabrillo Ct Alta Loma CA 91701

KLEIN, JOSEPH MARK, mining company executive; b. N.Y.C., Nov. 9, 1921; s. Erwin Wolffe and Ada (Black) K.; m. Betty Evelyn Northington, Dec. 24, 1948; children: Kathryn Ann, Elizabeth Ellen, Joseph Mark, Timothy Northington. Certificate in fgn. trade, Am. Grad Sch. Internat. Mgmt., 1946. Vice pres. internat. ops. Clary Corp., San Gabriel, Calif., 1948-60; dir. Clary Corp., 1967-70; dir. internat. ops. Remington Rand Corp., N.Y.C., 1961-62; pres. NBC Internat. Ltd.; v.p. NBC News, N.Y.C., 1962-66; exec. v.p., dir. Cyprus Mines Corp., Los Angeles, 1966-79; chmn. bd. Hawaiian Cement Corp., 1969-79; pres., dir. Pluess-Staufer Industries, Inc., Los Angeles, 1979—; dir. Mission Ins. Group, Inc.; mem. Pres.'s Export Expansion Council, 1971-74; Vice-chmn. bd. trustees Am. Grad. Sch. Internat. Mgmt., 1975-83, chmn. bd. trustees, 1983-88, chmn. exec. com., 1988—. Served to capt. U.S. Army, 1940-46. Decorated Silver Star, Bronze Star, Purple Heart; recipient Jonas B. Mayer Outstanding Alumni Assn. award Am. Grad. Sch. Internat. Mgmt., 1974, So. Calif. Alumni Assn. award, 1974. Mem. Am. Inst. Mining Engrs., Newcomen Soc., Town Hall, Ret. Officers Assn., Mil. Order Purple Heart (Ariz. comdr. 1949-50, comdr. Hollywood chpt. 1987—), Am. Legion (vice commdr. 1988—). Republican. Presbyterian. Clubs: California, Riviera Country. Lodge: Elks. Home: 1071 Villa View Dr Pacific Palisades CA 90272 Office: 845 Via de la Paz Suite 487 Pacific Palisades CA 90272

KLEIN, KAUNER HARRO, economist; b. Sonthofen, Fed. Republic of Germany, Aug. 20, 1942; arrived in Colombia, 1983; s. Werner and Hermine (Rauner) K.; m. Ursula Elly Gueler, July 8, 1971; children: Christoph, Marilene, Johann, Beatriz. Betriebs-und Marktwirtschaftler, Akademie f. Betriebswirtschaft, 1968. Mgr. prodn. Polygram Internat., Hamburg, Fed. Republic of Germany, 1968-75; mgr. internat. advt. Beiersdorf AG, Hamburg, 1975-76; mgr. mktg. Madrid, 1976-83; gen. mgr. Cali, Columbia, 1983—; Bd. dirs. Comfenalco, Cali, Fedy, Cali. Mem. Colombo-Aleman C. of C. Roman Catholic. Club: Country, Farallones (Cali). Lodge: Rotary. Office: BDF Colombia SA Autopista, Yumbo Km 3, AA 8112 Cali Valle, Colombia

KLEIN, LAWRENCE ROBERT, economist, educator; b. Omaha, Sept. 14, 1920; s. Leo Byron and Blanche (Monheit) K.; m. Sonia Adelson, Feb. 15, 1947; children: Hannah, Rebecca, Rachel, Jonathan. B.A., U. Calif.-Berkeley, 1942; Ph.D., MIT, 1944; M.A., Lincoln Coll., Oxford U., 1957; LL.D. (hon.), U. Mich., 1977, Dickinson Coll., 1981; Sc.D. (hon.), Widener Coll., 1977, Elizabethtown Coll., 1981, Ball State U., 1982, Technion, 1982, U. Nebr., 1983; Dr. honoris causa, U. Vienna, 1977; Dr.Ed., Villanova U., 1978; Dr. (h.c.), Bonn U., 1974, Free U. Brussels, 1979, U. Paris, 1979, U. Madrid, 1980. Faculty U. Chgo., 1944-47; research assoc. Nat. Bur. Econ. Research, 1948-50; faculty U. Mich., 1949-54; research assoc. Survey Research Center, 1949-54, Oxford Inst. Stats., 1954-58; faculty U. Pa., Phila., 1958—, prof., 1958—, Univ. prof., 1964—, Benjamin Franklin prof., 1968—; vis. prof. Osaka U., Japan, 1960, U. Colo., 1962, CUNY, 1962-63, 82, Hebrew U., 1964, Princeton U., 1966, Stanford U., summer 1968, U. Copenhagen, 1974; Ford vis. prof. U. Calif. at Berkeley, 1968, Inst. for Advanced Studies, Vienna, 1970, 74; cons. Canadian Govt., 1947, UNCTAD, 1966, 67, 75, 77, 80, McMillan Co., 1965-74, E.I. du Pont de Nemours, 1966-68, State of N.Y., 1969, AT&T, 1969, Fed. Res. Bd., 1973, UNIDO, 1973-75, Congl. Budget Office, 1977—, Council Econ. Advisers, 1977-80; chmn. bd. trustees Wharton Econometric Forecasting Assocs., Inc., 1969-80, chmn. profl. bd., 1980—; trustee Maurice Falk Inst. for Econ. Research, Israel, 1969-75; adv. council Inst. Advanced Studies, Vienna, 1977—; chmn. econ. adv. com. Gov. of Pa., 1976-78; mem. com. on prices Fed. Res. Bd., 1968-70; prin. investigator econometric model project Brookings Instn., 1963-72, Project LINK, 1968—; sr. adviser Brookings Panel on Econ. Activity, 1970—; mem. adv. com. Inst. Internat. Econs., 1983; coordinator Jimmy Carter's Econ. Task Force, 1976; mem. adv. bd. Strategic Studies Center, Stanford Research Inst., 1974-76. Author: The Keynesian Revolution, 1947, Textbook of Econometrics, 1953, An Econometric Model of the United States, 1929-1952, 1955, Wharton Econometric Forecasting Model, 1967, Essay on the Theory of Economic Prediction, 1968, An Introduction to Econometric Forecasting and Forecasting Models, 1980; Author-editor: Brookings Quar. Econometric Model of U.S.; Ecometric Model Performance, 1976, Lectures in Econometrics, 1983; Editor: Internat. Econ. Rev, 1959-65; asso. editor, 1965—; Editorial bd.: Empirical Econs, 1976—. Recipient William F. Butler award N.Y. Assn. Bus. Economists, 1975; Golden Slipper Club award, 1977; Pres.'s medal U. Pa., 1980; Alfred Nobel Meml. prize in econs., 1980. Fellow Econometric Soc. (past pres.), Am. Acad. Arts and Scis., Nat. Assn. Bus. Economists; mem. Am. Philos. Soc., Nat. Acad. Scis., Social Sci. Research Council (fellow 1945-46, 47-48, com. econ. stability, dir. 1971-76), Am. Econ. Assn. (John Bates Clark medalist 1959, exec. com. 1966-68, pres. 1977), Eastern Econ. Assn. (pres. 1974-76). Office: Dept of Economics/Fin U of Pa Philadelphia PA 19104 *

KLEIN, MARTIN I., lawyer; b. N.Y.C., Nov. 12, 1947; m. Diane Levbarg. B.A., Lehigh U., 1969; J.D., Am. U., 1972. Bar: N.Y. 1973, Fla. 1978, Calif. 1981, D.C. 1981. Mem. profl. staff U.S. Senate Com. on Labor and Pub. Welfare, 1969-72, legis. aide U.S. Senator Jacob K. Javits, 1969-72; ptnr., head creditors' rights dept. Dreyer & Traub, N.Y.C., 1980—; lectr. Am. Law Inst.-ABA Com. on Continuing Profl. Edn., 1975—, The Practising Law Inst., 1975—, Mathematica, 1981—; adj. assoc. prof. law Benjamin Cardozo Sch. Law, Yeshiva U., 1980—; lectr. Columbia U. Sch. Law, 1980—; mem. med. malpractice mediation panel appellate div. Supreme Ct. State N.Y. 1980—; mem. law com. bd. dirs. Jewish Guild for the Blind; trustee, treas, Cen. Synagogue, N.Y.C., 1986—; arbitrator, N.Y.C. Small Claims Ct. Contbr. articles on fin., real estate and comml. law to profl. jours. Del. White House Conf. on Youth, 1971. Mem. ABA, N.Y. State Bar Assn., Fla. Bar. Assn., Calif. Bar Assn., D.C. Bar Assn., N.Y. County Lawyers Assn. (mem. com. on bankruptcy), Am. Arbitration Assn. (mem. comml. panel). Office: Dreyer & Traub 101 Park Ave 39th Floor New York NY 10178

KLEIN, PAULA SCHWARTZ, metals broker, public relations and development executive; b. Chgo., Oct. 16, 1941; d. Arthur A. and Rosalyn (Davidson) Schwartz; student Mich. State U., 1959-60; B.A., Governors State U., 1974, M.A., 1975; m. Sanford David Klein, Dec. 18, 1960 (div. 1981); children—Gregory Scott, Julie Ann. Mem. editorial staff Okinawa Morning Star, Machinato, 1960-63; exec. dir. Bloom Twp. Com. on Youth, Chicago Heights, Ill., 1975-81; dir. fund devel. and pub. relations South Chgo. Community Hosp., 1981-84; v.p. South Chgo. Health Care Found., 1982-84; dir. devel. and pub. relations Chgo. Crime Commn., 1985-88; broker Universal Metals, Chgo., 1988—. Mem. Calumet Area Indsl. Commn. Mem. Nat. Soc. Fund Raising Profls., Nat. Assn. Prevention Profls., So. Suburban Youth Service Alliance, Criminal Def. Consortium, Nat. Assn. Hosp. Devel., Twp. Ofcls. Ill., Youth Network Council, Sierra Club. Jewish. Home: 1908 N Dayton Chicago IL 60614 Office: Universal Scrap Metals 2201 W Fulton St Chicago IL 60612

KLEIN, PETER MARTIN, lawyer, transportation company executive; b. N.Y.C., June 2, 1934; s. Saul and Esther (Goldstein) K.; m. Ellen Judith Matlick, June 18, 1961; children: Amy Lynn, Steven Ezra. A.B., Columbia U., 1956, J.D., 1962. Bar: N.Y. 1962, D.C. 1964, U.S. Supreme Ct. bar 1966. Asst. proctor Columbia U., 1959-62; asst. counsel Mil. Sea Transp. Service, Office Gen. Counsel, Dept. Navy, Washington, 1962-65; trial atty. civil div. U.S. Dept. Justice, N.Y.C., 1966-69; gen. atty. Sea-Land Service, Inc., Menlo Park, N.J., 1969-76; v.p., gen. counsel sec. Sea-Land Service, Inc., 1976-79, Sea-Land Industries, Inc., Menlo Park, 1979-84; asso. gen. counsel R.J. Reynolds Industries, Inc., Winston-Salem, N.C., 1978-84; sr. v.p., gen. counsel, sec. Sea-Land Corp., N.J., 1984—, dir., 1988—; mem. adv. com. on pvt. internat. law Dept. State, 1974—; mem. U.S. delegation UN Conf. on Trade and Devel., UN Commn. on Internat. Trade Law, 1975-76, trade regulation adv. bd. Bur. Nat. Affairs, 1986-88. Trustee Jewish Edn. Assn. Met. N.J., 1973-76; trustee Temple B'nai Abraham of Essex County, N.J., 1973—, v.p., 1976-81, pres., 1981-83; mem. Essex County Dems. Com., 1986-88. Served with USN, 1956-59, Antarctica. Mem. Am. Maritime Assn. (dir., chmn. coms. on law and legis. 1974-78), Am. Polar Soc., ABA, Navy League U.S. (life mem.), Fed. Bar Assn., N.Y. State Bar Assn., D.C. Bar Assn., Internat. Bar Assn., Maritime Law Assn., U.S. Club, Nat. Press. Home: 22 Sandalwood Dr Livingston NJ 07039 Office: Sea-Land Corp PO Box 800 Iselin NJ 08830

KLEIN, ROBERT DALE, lawyer; b. Balt., July 29, 1951; s. James Robert and Madeline Margaret (Horak) K.; m. Patricia Kay Purvis, May 6, 1978; children—Morgan Elizabeth, Patrick Jameson, Evan Robert. Student U. Durham, Eng., 1971-72; B.S., MIT, 1973; J.D., Columbia U., 1976. Bar: Md. 1976, U.S. Dist. Ct. Md. 1977, U.S. Ct. Appeals (4th cir.) 1978, U.S. Dist. Ct. D.C. 1983, D.C. 1983. Assoc., Piper & Marbury, Balt., 1976-84, ptnr., 1984-87; ptnr. Digges, Wharton and Levin, 1987—. Author: Maryland Civil Procedure Forms: Practice, 1984; editor Def. Line Jour., 1983-84; contbr. articles to profl. jours. Alfred P. Sloan Found. scholar, 1969-73. Mem. ABA, Md. State Bar Assn., Balt. Bar Assn. (chmn. com. on long range planning 1986-87, chmn. product liability law com. 1987-88, chmn. spl. com. on video 1983-84, chmn. standing com. on pub. relations 1984-86), Md. Assn. Def. Trial Counsel (bd. dirs. 1984—, v.p. 1985-86, pres. 1986-87), D.C. Bar Assn., Def. Research Inst. (exceptional performance award 1987), Chi Phi (sec. Beta chpt.). Roman Catholic. Home: 1501 Near Thicket Ln Baltimore MD 21153 Office: Digges Wharton and Levin 225 Duke of Gloucester St Annapolis MD 21401

KLEIN, ROBERTA PHYLLIS, writer; b. Columbus, Ohio, Dec. 26, 1934; d. Arthur Ezra and Anne Dorothy (Shrut) Krum Sternberg; m. Joseph Klein, Jan. 25, 1953 (div. 1969); children—Kenneth, Wendy, Ronald, Karyn, Valerie; m. Joseph Klein, Mar. 17, 1970. Student U. Pitts., 1952-53, Miami-Dade Community Coll., Miami, 1964-65, U. Miami, 1975-76. Copywriter, account exec. Azen and Assocs., Ft. Lauderdale, Fla., 1977-80; exec. editor Fla. Designers Quar., Miami, 1978-83; editor-in-chief On Design mag., 1983-84; dir. Sunshine State Bank, South Miami, Fla., 1978-85; design writer Sunshine Mag., Ft. Lauderdale News/Sun Sentinel, 1984-85; contbg. editor So. Accents Mag., Atlanta; contbg. writer Fla. Real Estate Mag., 1987—; stringer Money Mag.; lectr. Purdue U., Ill., Inst. Bus. Designers, Miami, Orlando, Am. Soc. Interior Designers, Miami, Atlanta, Jacksonville, 1980-83. Contbr. feature articles to mags. Active Am. Heart Assn., Miami, Miami City Ballet Guild, Fla. Film Festival, Miami Internat. Book Fair, Fla., Miami, Zool. Soc., Miami. Recipient Editorial awards Am. Soc. Interior Designers, Miami/Ft. Lauderdale, 1978, Inst. Bus. Designers, Fla. chpt., Miami, 1979, Interior Design Guild, Miami, 1981; Editorial/Pictorial award AIA, Miami/Ft. Lauderdale chpt., 1980, Addy awards, 1977, 85, Greater Miami C. of C. Democrat. Jewish. Avocations: tennis; fishing; cooking; concerts; theatre. Home and Office: 6000 Alton Rd Miami Beach FL 33140

KLEIN, SNIRA L(UBOVSKY), Hebrew language and literature educator. came to U.S., 1959, naturalized, 1974; d. Avraham and Devora (Unger) Lubovsky; m. Earl H. Klein, Dec. 25, 1975. Tchr. cert., Tchrs. Seminar, Netanya, Israel, 1956; B. Rel. Edn., U. Judaism, 1961, M in Hebrew Lit., 1963; BA, Calif. State U., Northridge, 1966; MA, UCLA, 1971, PhD, 1983. Teaching asst. UCLA, 1969-71, vis. lectr., 1985—; instr., continuing edn. U. Judaism, Los Angeles, 1971-76, instr., 1975—. Mem. Assn. for Jewish Studies, Nat. Assn. of Profs. of Hebrew, World Union of Jewish Studies. Jewish. Office: U Judaism 15600 Mulholland Dr Los Angeles CA 90077

KLEINER, HANSPETER, editor; b. Zurich, Switzerland, Feb. 22, 1936; s. Edwin Mathias and Eva Celestina (Balmelli) K.; m. Elisabeth Raymonde Guillais; children: Thierry Edwin, Nicole Cathrine. BA, U. Florence, Italy, 1961; MA, U. Zurich, 1962. Polit. editor Neue Zürches Zeitung, Zurich, 1962-77; editor-in-chief Schweizerische Depeschenagentur (Swiss News Agy.), Bern, 1977-88; media cons. 1988—; lectr. Fribourg (Switzerland) U., 1981-85. Author: (text) Auswahlkriterien, 1981; editor: Neuordnung der Altersvorsorge, 1971. Community pres. Town of Schwerzenbach, Switzerland, 1975-77, local Dem. del., 1971-77. Served with Swiss Temporary Army, 1955—. Mem. Swiss Assn. Journalists, Zurich Press Assn. (bd. dirs. 1973-77). Lodge: Rotary.

KLEINLEIN, KATHY LYNN, career counseling executive; b. S.I., N.Y., May 2, 1950; d. Thomas and Helen Mary (O'Reilly) Perricone; m. Kenneth Robert Kleinlein, Oct. 30, 1983. B.A., Wagner Coll., 1971, M.A., 1974; M.B.A., Rutgers U., 1984. Cert. secondary tchr., N.Y., N.J., Fla. Tchr. English, N.Y.C. Bd. Edn., S.I., 1971-74, Matawan (N.J.) Bd. Edn., 1974-79; instr. English, Middlesex County Coll., Edison, N.J., 1978-81; med. sales rep. Pfizer/Roerig, Bklyn., 1979-81, mgr. tng. ops., N.Y.C., 1981-87; dir. sales tng. Winthrop Pharms. div. Sterling Drug, N.Y.C., 1987-88, Reuters Info. Systems, N.Y.C., 1988—; pres. dir. sales tng., Women in Transition, career counseling firm; personnel mgmt. officer U.S. Army Res., N.J., 1981-86; dir. sales tng. and devel. Sterling Drug, Inc. div. Winthrop Pharms., N.Y.C.; cons. Concepts & Producers, N.Y.C., 1981-85. Trainer United Way, 1982-83, mem. polit. action com., 1982—; mem. Republican Presdl. Task Force, Washington, 1983—. Served to Capt., U.S. Army, 1974-78. First woman in N.Y. Army N.G., 1974; first woman instr. Empire State Mil. Acad., Peekskill, N.Y., 1976. Mem. Nat. Soc. Pharm. Sales Trainers, Sales and Mktg. Execs., Am. Soc. Tng. and Devel., N.J. Assn. Women Bus. Owners, LWV, Matawan C. of C., Alpha Omicron Pi. Republican. Roman Catholic. Club: Atlantis Divers (N.Y.C.). Home: 93 Idolstone Ln Matawan NJ 07747 Office: Reuters Info Systems 1700 Broadway St New York NY 10019

KLEINPETER, SIDNEY HARRISON, communications consultant, airport design consultant, electrical engineer; b. Alexandria, La., Oct. 21, 1942; s. Harrison Moore and Gladys Agnes (Gremillion) K.; m. Elaine Marie Latiolais, Sept. 27, 1965 (dec. June 1970); children: Elicia Louise, Kyle Alan; m. Roberta C. Rogers, Aug. 4, 1972. BSEE, La. Tech. U., Ruston, 1965, MSEE, 1968. Registered profl. engr., Alaska, Tex., La. Assoc. engr. LTV Aerospace Corp., Dallas, 1965-66; assoc. instr. La. Tech. U., 1966-68; systems engr. LTV Electrosystems, Greenville, Tex., 1968-69; sr. engr. Rockwell Internat., Richardson, Tex., 1969-80, ARCO Oil and Gas Co., Anchorage, 1980-84; inventor of DRAMIS system drilling rig alarm, monitor and info. system; airport navigational systems, insrument landing systems, satellite TV systems design, installation, computer systems design and installation cons. Pathfinders Co., Anchorage, 1984—; chief engr. KATB FM radio sta.; v.p., bd. dirs. Air Cushions Guides Inc.; Anchorage del. Rep. Party dist. conv., 1984, 86, 88; Anchorage precinct committeeman, 1986—; assemblyman City of St. Paul, Tex., 1978-80. Mem. Nat. Rifle Assn. (v.p. 1984-85). Club: Christian Sportsman (Anchorage) (v.p. 1983-84). Pub.: ENTELEC Conf. Procs., 1983,84, DRAMIS, Automatic Test of Navigational Aids, Satellite TV in the Oil Industry. Home and Office: Pathfinders Co 6002 Doncaster Dr Anchorage AK 99504

KLEINROCK, LEWIS JAMES, investment company executive; b. Scranton, Pa., May 26, 1932; s. Harry and Mary (Ryan) K.; m. Judith Mae Powell, Mar. 14, 1952; children: David (dec.), Linda (dec.), James; m. Mary Virginia Barry, Dec. 15, 1984. B.A., Williams Coll., 1953; postgrad., Law Sch., Yale U., 1953-54; M.B.A., Harvard U., 1959. Systems analyst Esso Standard Oil Co., Bayonne, N.J., 1959-60; investment counselor Lehman, Pa., 1960-62; investment asso. Utilities and Industries Corp., N.Y.C., 1962-63; dep. dir. investment research Chase Investors Mgmt. Corp., N.Y.C., 1963-73; dir. investment research John Hancock Mut. Life Ins. Co., Boston, 1973-79; sr. v.p., head portfolio mgmt. John Hancock Mut. Life Ins. Co., 1980-82; pres., chief exec. officer Independence Investment Assocs., 1982—; dir., chmn. fin. com. John Hancock Variable Life Ins. Co., 1981-82; dir. John Hancock Venture Capital Fund. Served with USMC, 1954-57, summer 1958. Mem. Boston, N.Y. Soc. Security Analysts, Fin. Analysts Fedn., Inst. Chartered Fin. Analysts. Home: 11 Hough Rd Belmont MA 02178 Office: One Liberty Sq Boston MA 02109

KLEINSCHMIDT, WILLIAM EDWARD, business consultant, educator; b. Highland Park, Ill., Feb. 5, 1951; s. Edward Ernst and Marie Jeannette K. BBA, U. Miami, 1973, MS, 1975, cert. in acctg., 1975, doctoral candidate, 1978—; MBA, Barry U., 1979. Computer office mgr. U. Miami (Fla.), 1971-75; pres. Kleinschmidt Enterprises, 1976-78; instr., coordinator bus. seminars, spl. asst. to v.p. bus. affairs, spl. asst. to controller Barry U., Miami Shores, Fla., 1977-80; asst. dir., adult edn. program Miami Edn. Consortium-Embry Riddle Aero. U., Daytona Beach, Fla., 1977-78; co-owner Kleinschmidt Teletypewriter Communications Co. Author: (with E. Tomeski) Study Guide for Fundamentals of Computers in Business, 1979, Fundamentals of Computers in Business (acknowledgements), 1979, Essentials of Computers in Business, 1980, Study Guide for Essentials of Computers in Business, 1980. Co-founder, co-chmn. ann. bus. conf. Barry U., 1978-80; asst. mgr. local polit. election Dade County, 1972-73; vol. com. dir. United Way, Dade County, 1974-75, Archbishop's Charities Drive, 1969-73. Recipient Pres.'s Appreciation cert. Barry U., 1978, numerous other awards and citations; North Shores Optimist Club scholar, 1969. Mem. Am. Acctg. Assn., AAUP, Fla. Inst. CPA's, Gold Coast Unltd.. Orchid Soc., U. Miami Gen. Alumni Assn., Barry U. Gen. Alumni Assn., Armed Forces Communications and Electronics Assn., Assn. Systems Mgmt., Cath. Forensic League. Miami Shores C. of C., Beta Alpha Psi. Lodges: KC, Fraternal Order Police Booster State of Fla. Address: PO Box 2644 Miami Beach FL 33140

KLEINSCHUSTER, STEPHEN JOHN, university dean; b. Bath, Pa., June 3, 1939; s. Stephen John and Elizabeth (Morro) K.; m. Karen Kreutzer, June 25, 1966; children: Stephan, Luke. Student, Baylor U. Coll. Med., 1962; BS, Colo. State U., 1963, MS, 1966; PhD, Oreg. State U., 1970; postdoctoral fellow, U. Chgo., 1971. Lectr. Community Coll. of Denver, 1972; asst. prof. Met. State Coll., Denver, 1971-73; affiliate prof. Col. State U., Ft. Collins, 1973; asst. prof. Colo. State U., Ft. Collins, 1973-75, assoc. prof., 1975-77; assoc. prof. Utah State U., Logan, 1977-81, prof., dept. head, 1981-83; prof., dean U. of N.H., Durham, 1983-85, Rutgers U., New Brunswick, N.H., 1985—; bd. dirs. Utah State U. Animal Tumor Program, 1977-83, Vet. Sci. Tissue Culture Facility, 1978-83, Inst. for Marine and Coastal Studies (interim) New Brunswick, 1985—; mem. NASLUGC Div. Agriculture Com. on Biotechnology, 1985—. Author over 60 articles in profl. field. Mem. State of Utah Adv. Council on Sci. & Tech., Logan, 1983, N.J. State Agrl. Adv. Com., 1985, N.J. Action Group for Agr. in the Classroom, 1985; chmn. N.J. State Agrl. Devel. Com., 1984. Recipient NASA Achievement award US/USSR Biosatellite Project, 1977, Cancer Research Commendation, State of UT, 1982, various cancer research grants NIH, 1975-85. Mem. AAAS, Am. Assn. Anatomists, Am. Soc. Zoologists, N.Y. Acad. Sci., Council Agrl. Sci. and Tech. Roman Catholic. Office: Rutgers U Cook Coll Office of the Dean Lipman Dr New Brunswick NJ 08903

KLEINSORGE, WILLIAM PETER, metallurgical engineer; b. San Francisco, Feb. 10, 1941; s. William P. Kleinsorge; m. Kathryn Deane Vincent, Nov. 14, 1966; children—Elizabeth Louise, Victoria Anne. B.S. in Metall. Engring., U. Nev.-Reno, 1964. Registered profl. engr., S.C., Calif. Welding engr. Mare Island Naval Shipyard, Vallejo, Calif., 1965-69, Charleston-Naval Shipyard, 1969-70; supervisory welding engr. U.S. Naval Ship Repair Facility, Republic of the Philippines, Subic Bay, 1970-72; head welding engr. Charleston Naval Shipyard, 72-79; metall. engr. U.S. Nuclear Regulatory Commn., Atlanta, 1979—; cons. in field. Served with U.S. Army N.G., 1965-72. Mem. Am. Soc. Metals, Am. Welding Soc., Am. Soc. Mil., Engrs. Lodge: Mason.

KLEMEN, MICHAEL CARL, data processing executive; b. Vienna, Austria, June 26, 1954; s. Alexander and Hilde Klemen; m. Doris Preiss, Sept. 29, 1982; 1 child, Christoph. MA, U. Trade, Vienna, 1977. Asst. to v.p. fin. Austrian Travel Agy., Vienna, 1972-79; mgr. data processing Linotype GESMBH, Vienna, 1979-80; mng. dir. Linotype Miete GESMBH, Vienna, 1980-81; mgr. fin. Mergenthaler Linotype GMBH, Frankfurt, Fed. Republic of Germany, 1981; project mgr. organisation Austrian Airlines, Vienna, 1981-84; div. mgr. Softlab Gesmbh, Vienna and Munich, 1985-88; mgr. div. Software AG, Vienna, 1988—; cons. Touropa Austria, Kuwait Airways. Contbr. articles to profl. jours. Office: Software AG, Schottenfeldgasse 69, 1070 Vienna Austria

KLENNER, HERMANN, legal researcher; b. Erbach, Germany, Jan. 5, 1926. Grad., U. Halle, German Dem. Republic, 1949, U. Berlin, German Dem. Republic, 1952. Prof. U. Berlin, German Dem. Republic, 1956-60, Berlin Acad. Scis., German Dem. Republic, 1967—. Author: Marxism and Human Rights, 1982, From the Law of Nature to the Nature of Law, 1984; editor: (books) Hegel's Philosophy of Law, 1987, Kant's Philosophy of Law, 1988. Recipient Püfendorf medal, 1983, Hegel medal Acad. Scis., 1984. Mem. Internat. Assn. Philosophy of Law (exec. com. 1967-87). Office: Acad of Scis, 1080 Otto-Nuschke Str 10 22/23, 1080 Berlin German Democratic Republic

KLEPPE, CARL-GEORG, advertising and public relations consultant; b. Koenigsberg, Germany, Jan. 6, 1928; s. Wilhelm Wilson and Ella (Knorr) K.; Abitur, Ratsgymnasium Gladbeck, 1947. Reporter Westfalenpost, Gladbeck, 1947-48, Westfaelische Rundschau, Gladbeck, 1948-51, city editor, Bottrop, 1951-53; asst. Schnupp Advt., Wiesbaden, 1954-57, advt. and pub. relations cons., 1958-60; advt. and pub. relations cons. Carl-Georg Kleppe, Wiesbaden, 1961-72, Muenster, 1972—. Office: Am Schlossgarten 4, 4400 Muenster Federal Republic of Germany

KLETSCHKA, HAROLD DALE, cardiovascular surgeon, biomedical company executive; b. Mpls., Aug. 26, 1924; s. Herbert Leland and Emma Elizabeth (Kopf) K. A.S., Brainerd (Minn.) Jr. Coll., 1943; B.S., U. Minn., 1946, M.B., 1947, M.D., 1948; LL.B., Blackstone Sch. Law, Ill., 1970; grad, Air War Coll., 1972. Diplomate: Am. Bd. Surgery, Am. Bd. Thoracic Surgery. Intern Kings County Hosp., Bklyn., 1947-49; asst. resident surgery Univ. Hosp., Ann Arbor, Mich., 1950-51; resident gen. surgery State U. N.Y. Downstate Med. Center, 1953-54, chief resident thoracic surgery, 1952-53, 54-55; thoracic and gen. surgeon Bratrud Clinic, Thief River Falls, Minn., 1951-52; asst. chief, acting chief neurosurgery 3275th and 2349th USAF hosps., Parks AFB, Calif., 1955-56; asst. chief thoracic surgery 3275th and 2349th USAF hosps., 1956, chief thoracic surgery, 1956-57; founder, chief USAF Cardiovascular Research Center, 1957-58; practice medicine specializing in thoracic and cardiovascular surgery San Francisco and San Jose, Calif., 1958-59; thoracic surgeon VA Hosp., Syracuse, N.Y., 1959-60; chief thoracic surgery 1960-67; asst. prof. surgery SUNY Upstate Med Center, Syracuse, 1959-67; cons. thoracic surgery SUNY Upstate Med Center, 1959-67, USAF med service liaison officer for surgeon gen., 1964-67; dep. comdr., chief hosp. services 102d TAC Hosp., Phalsbourg Air Base, France, 1961-62; mil. cons. to surgeon gen. USAF; surgeon Hdqrs. Command USAF, 1965-73; aerospace med. cons. to dir. Aerospace Med. Services, Malcolm Grow USAF Med. Center, 1965-73; thoracic surgeon VA Hosp., Houston, 1967-68, Montgomery, Ala., 1968-72; dir. cardiopulmonary labs. VA Hosp., 1970-72; co-founder, incorporator, 1st chmn. bd., pres., chief exec. officer Bio-Medicus, Inc., Minn., 1972—; mem. Nat. council on U.S.-USSR Health Care, Citizen Exchange Corps, N.Y.C., 1976—; mem. exec. com. Council for U.S.-USSR Health Exchange, Boston, 1976—. Contbr.: chpt. to Progress in Surface and Membrane Science, 1973; Bd. editors: Minn. Medicine, 1960-82, editor charge spl. issue, 1966; contbr. articles to profl. jours.; collaborator liturg. mus. composition dedicated to Cardinal Spellman: Pater Noster, 1961, internat. TV performance, 1962. Campaign mgr. Ind. Republican candidate Dist. 43B, Minn. Ho. of Reps.; mem. nat. adv. bd. Am. Security Council.; mem. Reagan-Bush '84 Election Com., Reagan Presdl. Campaign Task Force, Reagan Nat. Adv. Bd.; spl. advisor U.S. Congl. Adv. Bd. Recipient Bausch & Lomb Hon. Sci. award, 1941, IR-100 award for devel. Rafferty-Kletschka artificial heart, 1972, Worldwide Symbolic grad. Air War Coll., 1973, 1st pl. award Med./Analytical div. Plastics World, 1976, 1st prize in Med. div. 8th Bachner award competition, 1976; named to Wisdom Hall of Fame, 1979; Winston Churchill Medal of Wisdom, 1988. Fellow A.C.S.; mem. Am. Heart Assn. (council on basic scis., council on cardiovascular surgery), Am. Med. Writers Assn., Internat. Platform Assn., AAUP, Air Force Assn., U. Minn. Alumni Assn., Am. Soc. Artificial Internal Organs, Twin City Thoracic and Cardiovascular Surg. Soc., VFW, European Soc. Artificial Organs, Internat. Soc. Heart Transplantation; European Acad. Arts, Scis. and Humanities, Clarence Dennis Soc. Club: K.C. (4 deg.). Home: 1925 Noble Dr Minneapolis MN 55422

KLIBANOV, ALEXANDER MAXIM, chemistry and biotechnology educator, researcher; b. Moscow, July 15, 1949; U.S., 1977, naturalized, 1983; s. Maxim and Eugenia (Tomas) K.; m. Margarita Romanycheva, Apr. 21, 1972; 1 child, Tanya. M.S., Moscow U., 1971, Ph.D., 1974. Research chemist Moscow U., 1974-77; postgrad. research chemist U. Calif.-San Diego, 1978-79; asst. prof. applied biological sci. dept. MIT, Cambridge, 1979-83, assoc. prof., 1983-87, prof., 1987-88, prof. chemistry dept., MIT, 1988—, E.L. Doherty prof., 1981; cons. in field. Contbr. over 100 articles to profl. jours.; mem. editorial bd.; Applied Biochemistry and Biotech, 1981—, Advances Biochem. Engring./Biotechnol., 1985—, Chimicaoggi, 1986—. Numerous research grants. Mem. Am. Chem. Soc., Am. Soc. Biol. Chemists. Jewish. Research on enzyme stability and stblzn., immobilized enzymes and cells, enzymes as catalysts in organic chemistry, enzymes for wastewater treatment. Home: 61 W Blvd Rd Newton MA 02159 Office: MIT Bldg 16-209 Cambridge MA 02139

KLIMESZ, HENRY ROMAN, economist, marketing consultant; b. Gorlice, Poland, June 26, 1926; came to U.S., 1959, naturalized, 1964; s. Jan Siegmund and Louise Klimesz; B.A., Central Sch. Planning and Stats., Warsaw, 1952, M.Econ., 1957; M.B.A., Temple U., Phila., 1965; M.A., U. Pa., 1975. Internat. trade specialist Varimex Ltd., Warsaw, 1950-54; market analyst, editor Polish Chamber Fgn. Trade, Warsaw, 1954-58; export sales mgr. Tiona Petroleum Co., Pennsauken, N.J., 1961-66; assoc. prof. econs. Atlantic Community Coll., Mays Landing, N.J., 1967-80; research assoc. Warsaw U., 1980-82, 83-85; internat. mktg. cons., 1985—; assoc. prof. econs. and bus. Westminster Coll., New Wilmington, Pa., 1982-83. Senatorial scholar, 1965-67. Mem. Am. Econ. Assn., Acad. Internat. Bus., Polish Inst. Arts and Scis., Rencontres Creatives Internationales. Republican. Roman Catholic. Author: Poland's Trade Through the Black Sea in XVIII Century, 1970; co-author: Statistical Guide for Foreign Trade Executives, 1957; editor Rynki Zagraniczne, 1957-58. Address: 170 Lakeside Rd Ardmore PA 19003

KLINAR, PETER, sociology educator; b. Mar. 22, 1934; s. Peter and Helena (Cerk) K.; m. Sonja Perlic, Oct. 6, 1962; 1 child, Ales. MA in Polit. Sci., Faculty Sociology Polit. Sci. and Journalism, Ljubljana, Yugoslavia, 1967, PhD, 1974. Judge Celje Dist. Ct., Yugoslavia, 1957-61; from asst. to prof. sociology Faculty Sociology Polit. Sci. and Journalism, Ljubljana, 1961—, head dept. sociology, 1966-68, 70-73, 81-83, vice dean, 1968-70, 75-77, dean, 1983-85. Author: International Migration, 1976, Class and Stratificetion Structure, 1979, International Migration in Crisis, 1985; editor sociology publ., 1980-87. Mem. commn. Research Assn. Slovenias, 1978—, Socialist Alliance of Slovenian, 1968—. Recipient State Order for Research Work, Pres. Yugoslavia, 1980. Mem. Slovenian Sociol. Assn. (pres. 1980-83, award 1984), Imigration Internat. Sociol. Assn. Home: Ilirska 4, 61000 Ljubljana Yugoslavia Office: Faculty Sociology Polit Sci, and Journalism, Kardeljeva Pl 5, 61000 Ljubljana Yugoslavia

KLINE, DAVID GELLINGER, neurosurgery educator; b. Phila., Oct. 13, 1934; s. David Francis and Lois Ann (Gellinger) K.; m. Carol Anne Loewen, Mar. 1, 1958 (div.); children: Susan, Robert, Nancy. A.B. in Chemistry, U. Pa., 1956, M.D., 1960. Diplomate Am. Bd. Neurol. Surgery (sec.-treas. 1978-83, chmn. 1983-84, adv. bd. 1984-90). Intern U. Mich., Ann Arbor, 1960-61; resident in gen. surgery U. Mich., 1961-62, teaching assoc. in neurosurgery, 1964-67; research investigator Walter Reed Army Inst. Research and Walter Reed Gen. Hosp., 1962-64; instr. La. State U. Med. Sch., New Orleans, 1967-68; asst. prof. La. State U. Med. Sch., 1968-70, assoc. prof., 1970-73, prof., 1973—, chmn. dept. neurosurgery, 1971—; cons. USPHS Health Center Hosp., New Orleans VA Hosp., Kessler AFB Hosp.-Lederle Labs.; vis. investigator Delta Regional Primate Center, Covington; mem. Am. Bd. Med. Specialists, 1978-86, mem. residency rev. com., 1977-84. Contbr. articles to sci. jours., also mem. editorial bds. Served with M.C. AUS, 1962-64. Recipient Frederick Coller Surg. prize, 1967; numerous grants. Mem. Am. Acad. Neurol. Surgery, Soc. Neurol. Surgeons (treas. 1986—), So. Neurol. Surgery Soc. (sec. 1976-79, pres. 1985-86), Am. Assn. Neurol. Surgeons (bd. dirs. 1985—), Soc. Univ. Neurosurgeons, Congress Neurol. Surgeons, Assn. Acad. Surgery, Surg. Biol. Club II, Soc. Univ. Surgeons, A.C.S., Sunderland Club (pres. 1981), Am. Bd. of Neurol. Surg. (sec.-treas. 1978-83, chmn. 1984), Phi Beta Kappa, Kappa Sigma, Phi Chi. Episcopalian (vestry and lay reader). Home: 307 Fairway Dr New Orleans LA 70124 Office: Med Center La State U 1542 Tulane Ave New Orleans LA 70112

KLINE, FRED WALTER, communications company executive; b. Oakland, Calif., May 17, 1918; s. Walter E. and Jean M. Kline; m. Verna Marie Taylor, Dec. 27, 1952; children—Kathleen, Nora, Fred Walter. B.A. in Calif. History, U. Calif.-Berkeley, 1940. With Walter E. Kline & Assocs. and successor Fred Kline Agy., Inc., from 1937; chmn. bd., pres. Kline Communications Corp., Los Angeles, 1956—; pres. Capitol News Service. Commr. Los Angeles County Fire Services Commn., Calif. Motion Picture Devel. Council; former fed. civil def. liaison; developer state-wide paramedic rescue program; Calif. chmn. Office of Asst. Sec. Def.; mem. Calif. Com. for Employer Support of Guard and Res. Served with USAAF, World War II; brig. gen. Calif. Mil. Dept. Recipient Inter-Racial award City of Los Angeles, 1963, named Man of Yr., 1964. Mem. Acad. Motion Picture Arts and Scis., Radio and TV News Assn. So. Calif., Pub. Relations Soc. Am., Calif. Newspaper Pubs. Assn., Cath. Press Council (founding mem.), Pacific Pioneer Broadcasters, Footprinters Internat., Am. Mil. Govt. Assn. (past pres.), Navy League, Calif. State Police Officers Assn., Internat. Assn. Profl. Firefighters (hon. life), Peace Officers Assn. Los Angeles County (life), Internat. Assn. Chiefs of Police, Internat. Assn. Fire Chiefs, Calif. Fire Chiefs Assn., Fire Marshals Assn. N.Am., Nat. Fire Protection Assn., Nat. Fin. Writers Assn., Hollywood C. of C., Nat. Fire Sci. Acad., Calif. State Mil. Forces, Calif. Pubs. Assn., So. Calif. Cable Club. Sigma Delta Chi. Clubs: Greater Los Angeles Press, Media (Los Angeles), Sacramento Press. Columnist Calif. newspapers. Office: 6340 Bryn Mawr Dr Los Angeles CA 90068

KLINE, GEORGE LOUIS, educator, writer; b. Galesburg, Ill., Mar. 3, 1921; s. Allen Sides and Wahneta (Burner) K.; m. Virginia Harrington Hardy, Apr. 17, 1943; children: Brenda Marie, Jeffrey Allen, Christina Hardy (Mrs. Francis C. Hanak). Student, Boston U., 1938-41; A.B. with honors, Columbia Coll., 1947; M.A., Columbia U., 1948, Ph.D., 1950. Instr. philosophy Columbia U., 1950-52, 53-54, asst. prof., 1954-60; vis. asst. prof. U. Chgo., 1952-53; assoc. prof. philosophy and Russian Bryn Mawr Coll., 1960-66, prof. philosophy, 1966—, Milton C. Nahm prof. philosophy, 1981—, chmn. dept., 1977-82; lectr. Free U., West Berlin, Heidelberg U., Fed. Republic Germany, London Sch. Econs. and Polit. Sci., Marburg U., Mid East Tech. U., Ankara, Turkey, Oxford (Eng.) U., Queens U., Belfast, Trinity Coll., Dublin, U. Belgrade, Yugoslavia, U. Zagreb, Yugoslavia, U. P.R., Uppsala U., Sweden; participant internat. confs. Austria, Can., Denmark, France, Fed. Republic Germany, The Netherlands, Italy, Mex., Scotland. Author: Spinoza in Soviet Philosophy, 1952, reprint, 1981, Religious and Anti-Religious Thought in Russia, 1968; co-author: Continuity and Change in Russian and Soviet Thought, 1955, Marx and the Western World, 1967, Phenomenology and Existentialism, 1967, rev. edit., 1969, Hegel and the Philosophy of Religion, 1970, Sartre: A Collection of Critical Essays, 1971, Hegel and the History of Philosophy, 1974, Dissent in The USSR: Politics, Ideology, and People, 1975, Speculum Spinozanum, 1977, Western Philosophical Systems in Russian Literature, 1979, Vico and Marx: Affinities and Contrasts, 1983, Nineteenth Century Religious Thought in the West, 1985, Spinoza nel 350 anniversario della nascita, 1985, Handbook of Russian Literature, 1985, Hegel and Whitehead: Contemporary Perspectives on Systematic Philosophy, 1986, George Lukacs and his World: A Reassessment, 1987; works translated into numerous foreign languages; translator: History of Russian Philosophy (V.V. Zenkovsky), 2 vols, 1953, Boris Pasternak: Seven Poems, 1969, 2d edit., 1972, Joseph Brodsky: Selected Poems, 1973; co-translator: A Part of Speech (Joseph Brodsky), 1980; editor: Soviet Education, 1957, Alfred North Whitehead: Essays on his Philosophy, 1963; editor, contbr.: European Philosophy Today, 1965; co-editor, contbr.: Russian Philosophy, 3 vols, 1965, 2d edit., 1969, reprint, 1976, 84, Explorations in Whitehead's Philosophy, 1983, Philosophical Sovietology, 1988; co-editor: Jour. Philosophy, 1959-64, cons. editor, 1964-78; cons. editor Ency. Philosophy, 1962-67, Studies in Soviet Thought, 1962—, Jour. Value Inquiry, 1967—, Process Studies, 1970—, Soviet Union, 1975-80, Philosophy Research Archives, 1975—, Jour. History of Ideas, 1976-86, Slavic Review, 1977-79, Soviet Studies in Philosophy, 1987—; cons. editor philosophy: Current Digest of Soviet Press, 1961-64; contbr. numerous articles to nat. and internat. jours. Served with USAAF, 1942-45. Decorated D.F.C; Cutting traveling fellow Paris, 1949-50; Fulbright fellow Paris, 1950, 79; Ford fellow Paris, 1954-55; Rockefeller fellow USSR and East Europe, 1960; Nat. Endowment for Humanities sr. fellow, 1970-71; Guggenheim fellow, 1978-79. Mem. Am. Philos. Assn., Soc. Ancient Greek Philosophy, Metaphys. Soc. Am. (councillor 1969-71, 78-82, v.p. 1984-85, pres. 1985-86), Internat. Soc. Metaphysics, Philosophy Edn. Soc. (pub. Rev. Metaphys., dir. 1966—), Soc. Phenomenology and Existential Philosophy, Am. Assn. Advancement Slavic Studies (dir. 1972-75), Hegel Soc. Am. (councillor 1968-70, 74-78, v.p. 1971-73, pres. 1984-86), Internationale Hegel-Vereinigung, Soc. Advancement Am. Philosophy, Soc. Study History of Philosophy, P.E.N., Soc. Philosophy of Creativity (chmn. Eastern div. 1976-78), Phi Beta Kappa. Home: 632 Valley View Rd Ardmore PA 19003 Office: Thomas Library Bryn Mawr Coll Bryn Mawr PA 19010

KLINE, JAMES EDWARD, lawyer; b. Fremont, Ohio, Aug. 3, 1941; s. Walter J. and Sophia Kline; m. Mary Ann Bruening, Aug. 29, 1964; children: Laura Anne, Matthew Thomas, Jennifer Sue. BS in Social Sci., John Carroll U., 1963; JD, Ohio State U., 1966. Bar: Ohio 1966. Assoc. Eastman & Smith, Toledo, 1966-70; ptnr. Eastman, Stichter, Smith & Bergman, 1970-84, Shumaker, Loop & Kendrick, 1984—; corp. sec., Sheller-Globe Corp. 1977-84; adj. prof. Coll. Law U. Toledo, 1988—; bd. dirs. Diversified Material Handling, Inc., Security Funding, Inc., Essex Devel. Group, Inc. Trustee Kidney Found. of Northwestern Ohio, Inc., 1972-81, pres., 1979-80; bd. dirs. Crosby Gardens, Toledo, 1974-80, pres., 1977-79; trustee Toledo Symphony Orch., 1981—; bd. dirs. Toledo Zool. Soc., 1983—, Toledo Area Regional Transit Authority, 1984—, pres. 1987—; bd. dirs. Home Away From Home, Inc. (Ronald McDonald House NW Ohio), 1983-88; trustee Lourdes Coll., 1988—. Fellow Ohio Bar Found.; mem. ABA, Ohio State Bar Assn. (corp. law com. sec. 1973-76, vice chmn. 1977-82, chmn. 1977-82, 83-86), Toledo Bar Assn., Nat. Assn. Corp. Dirs., Toledo Area C. of C. Roman Catholic. Clubs: Inverness, Toledo. Home: 5958 Swan Creek Dr Toledo OH 43614 Office: 1000 Jackson Blvd Toledo OH 43624

KLINE, JOHN ANDREW, osteopathic physician, pathologist; b. Lancaster, Pa., Jan. 2, 1930; s. Ellis Preston and Lola Imogene (Welchans) K.; m. Gloria Charollotte Ziliak, June 13, 1955; children—Kevin A., Stephan M., Gayle T.; m. 2d. Jane Ann Moore, July 27, 1974. B.S., Franklin and Marshall Coll., 1951; D.O., Phila. Coll. Osteopathy, 1955. Gen. practice, Cumberland (Maine) Ctr., 1956-60; resident in pathology Osteo. Hosp. Maine, Portland, 1960-62, Flint (Mich.) Osteo. Hosp., 1962-63; assoc. pathologist Chgo. Coll. Osteopathy, 1963-64; chmn. dept. pathology Waterville (Maine) Osteo. Hosp., 1964-67; chmn. dept. pathology Grand Rapids (Mich.) Osteo. Hosp., 1967-74; assoc. pathologist Kirksville (Mo.) Coll. Osteo. Medicine, 1974-78, prof., dept. chmn., 1978-80; pathologist Grim Smith Hosp., Kirksville, Mo., 1980-88; prof., chmn. Dept. Pathology W.Va. Sch. Osteo. Medicine, 1988—; dir. Dillavou, Tran & Kline Nat. Lab., Reference Labs. N.E. Mo., Inc. Chmn. Coalition for Mandatory Spl. Edn., Mich., 1970-72; mem. Mo. Mental Health Commn., 1982-86, sec., 1983-84, chmn., 1984-85. Pres. Adair Co. Unit of Am. Cancer Soc., 1987-88, bd. dirs. Mo. div., 1987-88. Named Citizen of Yr., Mich. Council for Exceptional Children, 1972; Citizen of Yr., Kent County (Mich.) Assn. for Mentally Handicapped, 1972. Mem. Am. Osteo. Assn. Am. Coll. Osteo. Pathologists (past pres.), Mo. Assn. Osteo. Physicians and Surgeons, N.E. Mo. Assn. Osteo. Physicians and Surgeons, Am. Registry Pathology (Armed Forces Inst. Pathology). Republican. Methodist. Lodge: Masons. Contbr. articles to profl. jours. Home: 3 Woodland Ln Kirksville MO 63501 Office: Grim Smith Hosp 1211 S Franklin St PO Box 917 Kirksville MO 63501

KLINEDINST, THOMAS JOHN, insurance company executive; b. York, Pa., June 29, 1918; s. David Philip and Mary M. (Moulson) K.; m. Betty Ann Broeman, Feb. 22, 1941; children—Thomas John, Kit Helton, Charles B., Mary Ashmore. B.S., U. Va., 1939. Spl. agt. Fidelity & Deposit Co., Balt., 1939-41; mgr. bond dept. Thomas E. Wood, Inc., Cin., 1941-50, v.p., 1950-66, exec. v.p., 1966-68, pres., 1969—, chmn., chief exec. officer, 1987—; pres. CORVA, Cin., 1967-70; dir. 1st Nat. Cin. Corp., 1st Nat. Bank, Cin., Hennegan Co., Cin., Pres. St. Francis Hosp., 1962-75, Providence Hosp., Cin., 1968-77, Cin. Mus. Festival Assn., 1965-67, Cin. Symphony Orch., 1973-77; mem. Cin. Hosp. Council, 1976—, pres., 1980; treas. Cin. Inst. Fine Arts, 1983—, Cin. Better Bus. Bur., 1983-88; trustee Hamilton County Hosp. Commn., 1977—. Recipient Founders Day award Xavier U., Cin., Seminary Guild award Franciscan Friars, Cin., 1972, Heritage award Franciscan Sisters, N.Y.C., 1982, Disting. Service award Providence Hosp., 1976. Mem. Ohio Med. Profl. Liability Assn. (pres. 1983—), Nat. Assn. Casualty and Surety Agts., Ohio Ind. Agts. Assn. (chmn. malpractice com. 1976). Republican. Roman Catholic. Clubs: Queen City Commonwealth, Cin. Country (Cin.); Ocean Reef (North Key Largo, Fla.). Office: Thomas E Wood Inc 1500 Carew Tower Cincinnati OH 45202

KLING, SIEGBERT A., agricultural irrigation equipment manufacturing company executive; b. Gross-Friedrichsdorf, Germany, Feb. 14, 1939; came to U.S., 1956, naturalized, 1965; s. Herman and Ella Gertrude (Heldt) K.; student Suomi Coll., 1957-59; M.A., U. Munich (W.Ger.), 1966; m. Aug. 20, 1977; children—Tyson Charles (dec.), Lindsey Lee. Internat. advt. coordinator for central Europe, Batten, Barton, Durstine & Osborn, N.Y.C., 1963-69; dir. advt. and public relations, exec. Credit Union League, Des Moines, 1969-77; internat. ops. dir. Reinke Mfg. Co., Inc., Deshler, Nebr., 1980—; chmn., dir. World Trade Council, 1980—. Hon. bd. dirs. Iowa Ednl. Broadcast System, 1976—. Served with U.S. Army, 1959-63. Recipient various advt. awards. Mem. Midwest Internat. Trade Assn., Am. Legion, Izaak Walton League. Lutheran. Home: 840 Olive Hebron NE 68370 Office: Reinke Mfg Co Inc PO Box 566 Deshler NE 68340

KLINGAMAN, ROBERT L., golf professional; b. 1914. DBA magna cum laude, Thompson Coll., 1936; cert., Cades CPA sch., Phila., 1942; D of Golf, John Marshall Coll., 1950; LLB, Am. Sch. Law, Chgo., 1954, LLD, 1954; RPA, Sorensen Sch. of Architecture, 1956. Previously acct. York, Pa.; propr. Dr. Bob Klingaman's Master Golf Sch. Author 20 books on golf including Master Golf, 1939; architect several golf courses. Recipient Lifetime Testimonial Golf Writers Assn. Am., 1987, gold plaque Austad's. Mem. Golf Writers Assn. Am. (life). Club: Honey Run Golf (York). Lodges: Shriners, Masons (32 degree), Zeredatha. Home: 739 Elm Terr York PA 17404

KLINGEN, HELMUT, mathematician; b. Viersen, Federal Republic Germany, Dec. 16, 1927; s. Michael and Emma (Hertzer) K.; m. Anita Steinert, Dec. 22, 1962; children: Christoph, Philipp. Dr.rer.nat., U. Goettingen, Fed. Republic Germany, 1954, Dr. habil., 1957. Assoc. prof. U. Goettingen, 1957-59, U. Marburg, Fed. Republic Germany, 1960, U. Heidelberg, Fed. Republic Germany, 1961; prof. U. Freiburg, Fed. Republic Germany, 1962—; vis. asst. prof. U. Calif., Berkeley, 1958-59; vis. prof. Inst. Advanced Study, Princeton U., 1965-66, Tata Inst. Fundamental Research, Bombay, 1968. Contbr. numerous articles to profl. jours. Mem. Am. Math. Soc., Deutsche Mathematiker Vereinigung. Home: 22 R Booz Str, D-7802 Merzhausen bei Freiburg Federal Republic of Germany Office: Math Inst U, Albertstr 23 b, D-7800 Freiburg Federal Republic of Germany

KLINGENSMITH, ARTHUR PAUL, state agency administrator, consultant; b. Los Angeles, May 23, 1949; s. Paul Arthur and Hermine Elinore (Wacek) K.; m. Donna J. Bellucci, Apr. 26, 1976 (div. Jan. 1981). AA in Social Sci., Indian Valley Jr. Coll., 1976; BA in Indsl. Psychology, San Francisco State U., 1979; MA in Indsl. Psychology, Columbia Pacific U., 1980. Enlisted USAF, Biloxi, Miss.; advanced through grades to staff sgt. USAF; instr. radio ops. USAF, Biloxi, 1968-72; air traffic control operator USAF, Hamilton AFB Novato, Calif., 1972-74; resigned USAF, 1974; elec. technician Calif. Dept. Transp., Oakland, 1975-78; right of way agt. Calif. Dept. Transp., San Francisco, 1978-85; sr. right of way agt. Calif. Dept. Transp., Sacramento, 1985-87, computer researcher, 1985-87. Bd. dirs. Kentfield Med. Found. Mem. Internat. Right of Way Assn. (instr. 1982—), Am. Arbitration Assn., Marin County Bd. Realtors, Assn. Humanistic Psychology, Nat. Assn. Housing and Redevel. Officials, Inst. Noetic Sci., Am. Mgmt. Assn. Republican. Office: APK Enterprises PO Box 574 Sausalito CA 94966

KLINGER, JURGEN, physicist, educator; b. Reichenberg, Bohemia, Czechoslovakia, Oct. 12, 1939; came to France, 1967; s. Edgar and Marie (Augsten) K.; m. Yvette Theiler, May 5, 1971; children: Werner, Yves, Sylvie. MS, Tech. U., Munich, 1966; DSc, U. Grenoble (France), 1974. Asst., U. Grenoble, 1967-76, asst. prof. geophysics, 1977—; chmn. organizing com. NATO Workshop in Ices in Solar System, Nice, France, 1984; mem. sci. com. 7th Internat. Symposium on Physics and Chemistry of Ice. Chief editor: Ices in the Solar System. Contbr. articles to profl. jours. Mem. Bur. Internat. Commn. Snow and Ice, Internat. Glaciol. Soc., Soc. française de Physique, Soc. française des specialistes en Astronomie, Deutsche Gesellschaft für Polarforschung. Participant Comet Simulation experiment, Deutsche Gesellschaft fuer Luftund Raumfahrt, Cologne. Office: Lab Glaciologie du CNRS, BP96, F38402 Sainte Martin D'Heres France

KLINK, KARIN ELIZABETH, medical communications company executive, writer; b. N.Y.C., Nov. 12, 1937; d. Nils Gustaf and Mary Josephine (Crowley) Hernblad; m. Fredric J. Klink, Nov. 28, 1958 (div. Apr. 1979);

children: Christopher Frederick, Charles Gustaf. BA in Geology, Barnard Coll., 1958; MFA in Film Making, Columbia U., 1963; MS in Counseling and Art Therapy, U. Bridgeport, 1977; grad. cert. in corp. video Fairfield U., 1983. Film editor, writer Eye Gate House, N.Y.C., 1966-68; sr. editor Starting Tomorrow, N.Y.C., 1968-70; dir. creative therapies Hall-Brooke Hosp., Westport, Conn., 1978-83; mgr. editorial devel. New Eng. Advt. Assn., Norwalk, Conn., 1984-85; editorial dir. Logical Communications, Norwalk, 1985; pres. Creative Word & Image, Rowayton, Conn., 1985—; cons. audio-visual specialist in Wetlands, Norwalk Schs., 1985; free-lance writer, editor for various cos., Conn., 1984—. Artist; exhibited in various shows; author films, filmstrips and videotapes; designer, animator The Stage Evolves, 1964; writer, photographer slide tape, 1985. Sec. bd., aerial photographer Preserve the Wetlands, Rowayton, 1983—; bd. dirs. Arts Inst., Silvermine Guild, New Canaan, Conn., 1984—. Mem. Women in Communications, Inc., Am. Art Therapy Assn. (profl.), Silvermine Guild Artists (artist mem., various awards), Rowayton Art Ctr. (artist mem., bd. dirs.), So. Conn. Art Therapy Assn. (art therapist, pres. 1982-83). Democrat. Episcopalian. Avocations: drawing; painting; aerial photography; sailing; painted Easter egg in White House collection at Smithsonian Inst. Home and Office: 13 Sammis St Rowayton CT 06853

KLINKENBIJL, JEAN HENRI, mechanical engineer; b. Tiel, Gelderland, The Netherlands, Jan. 17, 1928; s. Wouter and Bertha Klinkenbijl; m. Bernardina Mulder, Aug. 25, 1955; children: Jeanine, Monique, Brigitte, Jean. Student, Secondary Modern Sch., Amsterdam, The Netherlands, 1945; mech. engr., Tech. Coll., Amsterdam, 1949. Asst. sales mgr. Imprimex, Amsterdam, 1951-56; asst. mgr. Nederlandse Machinehandel Mij., Amsterdam, 1956-68; mgr. Heesen-ICA B.V., Hertogenbosch, 1968—. Served to capt. The Netherlands mil., 1949-51. Home: Brabantlaan 55, Vught, 5262 GX Noord Brabant The Netherlands Office: Heesen-ICA BV, Hervensebaan 15, 5232 JL Hertogenbosch The Netherlands

KLINKMULLER, ERICH, economist; b. Berlin, Oct. 21, 1928; m. Christa Edelbauer, June 11, 1964; children—Andreas, Veronika. Dr. rer. pol., Free U. Berlin, 1959. Research fellow Harvard U., 1959-60; asst. prof. econs. Free U. Berlin, 1960-66; lectr. econs. U. Calif., Santa Barbara, 1966-67; prof. econs. U. Ariz., Tucson, 1967-68; assoc. prof. econs. St. Louis U., 1968-70; prof. econs. Free U. Berlin, 1970—. Author: Cooperation Between CMEA Countries, 1960; Interdisciplinary Research Among the Social Sciences in the U.S. and Elsewhere, 1986. Contbr. articles to profl. jours. Mem. Am. Econ. Assn., Verein fur Socialpolitik, Assn. Comparative Econ. Studies. Home: 34A Bahnhofstrasse, Lichterfelde, 1-45 Berlin Federal Republic of Germany Office: Free Univ Berlin, 55 Garystrasse, 1-33 Berlin Dahlem Federal Republic of Germany

KLINT, STEEN, chemical company executive; b. Copenhagen, Denmark, Jan. 10, 1951; arrived in Can., 1954; BS, U. Western Ont., Canada, 1978. Sales mgr. Tricil, Sarnia, Ont., Can., 1982; plant mgr. Tricil, Charlottetown, Can., 1986. Mem. Liquid Indsl. Control Assn. (treas. 1984-86, bd. dirs.), Nat. Solid Waste Mgmt. Assn., Chem. Waste Transp. Council, Air Pollution Control Assn. Office: Tricil Ltd, PO Box 2518, Charlottetown, Prince Edward Island CAN C1A 8C2

KLIORE, ARVYDAS JOSEPH, radio scientist; b. Kaunas, Lithuania, Aug. 5, 1935; came to U.S., 1949, naturalized, 1955; s. Bronius Joseph and Antonia (Valaitis) K.; B.S., U. Ill., 1956; M.S., U. Mich., 1957; Ph.D., Mich. State U., 1962; m. Birute Anna Ulenas, Sept. 3, 1960; children—Saule Andrea, Rima Birute. Research engr. Armour Research Found., Chgo., 1956-58, sr. scientist, 1962-65; mem. tech. staff, research scientist Jet Propulsion Lab., Calif. Inst. Tech., Pasadena, 1965-87, sr. research sci., 1987—; lectr. UCLA, 1963-64. Recipient NASA medal, 1972, also several Group Achievement awards. Mem. Internat. Com. for Space Research, Am. Astron. Soc. (a founder div. for planetary scis.), Am. Geophys. Union, AAAS, Planetary Soc., Am. Lithuanian Commn. (council), Sigma Xi. Roman Catholic. Club: Bačka Athletic. Contbr. radio sci. articles to profl. jours. Office: Calif Inst Tech Jet Propulsion Lab 4800 Oak Grove Dr Pasadena CA 91109

KLIPPERT, RICHARD HOBDELL, JR., engineering executive; b. Oakland, Calif., Jan. 25, 1940; s. Richard Hobdell and Carol Ione (Knight) K.; m. Penelope Ann Barker, Sept. 5, 1979; children—David, Deborah, Candice, Kristina. BS in Bus., Oreg. State U., 1962; postgrad. in polit. sci. U. Calif.-Berkeley, 1968-69, in polit. sci. and mgmt. George Washington U., 1972-73; grad. Naval War Coll., 1973. Commd. ensign USN, 1962, advanced through grades to comdr., 1971, ret., 1982, expert: Antisubmarine Warfare; mem. Combat Search and Rescue, Southeast Asia, 1964-67; exec. officer H.S. Squadron, 1974; mem. Flag Staff, 1974-79; chief engr. Light Airborne Multipurpose System MK-III, Washington, 1979-82; sr. engr., mgr. IBM, Boulder, Colo., 1982-83, engring. mgr., 1983-84, mgr. HH-60 systems engring., 1984-85, mgr. V-22 engring., 1985-88, program mgr. Document Mgmt. Systems Integration, 1988—. Author: The Moon Book, 1971. Contbr. papers to tech. lit. Decorated Silver Star, Navy Commendation; recipient Outstanding Achievement and Golden Circle awards IBM, 1986. Mem. Soc. Naval Engrs., Soc. Automotive Engrs., Naval Inst., Sigma Chi. Republican. Avocations: golf, tennis, photography, bridge. Home: Box 615 Niwot CO 80544-0615 Office: IBM Diagonal Hwy Boulder CO 80301

KLIPSTEIN, ROBERT ALAN, lawyer; b. N.Y.C., Sept. 23, 1936; s. Harold David and Hyacinth (Levin) K. A.B., Columbia U., 1957, J.D., 1960; LL.M. in Taxation, NYU, 1965. Bar: N.Y. 1960, U.S. Supreme Ct. 1964. Practice law, N.Y.C., 1961—; assoc. Saxe Bacon & O'Shea, 1961, Rosenman, Colin, Kaye, Petschek & Freund, 1962-63; law sec. to justice N.Y. County Supreme Ct., 1963-64; assoc. Bernays & Eisner, 1965-70; ptnr. Eisner, Klipstein & Klipstein, 1971-77; ptnr. Danziger, Bangser, Klipstein, Goldsmith, Greenwald & Weiss, 1977—; arbitrator City of N.Y. Small Claims Ct., 1971—. Served with U.S. Army, 1960-62. Mem. ABA, N.Y. State Bar Assn., Assn. Bar City of N.Y., N.Y. County Lawyers Assn., Am. Immigration Lawyers Assn., Westchester County Bar Assn., Am. Judges Assn. Club: Univ. Glee (N.Y.C.). Home: 401 E 74th St New York NY 10021 Office: 230 Park Ave New York NY 10169

KLITZING, KLAUS VON, institute administrator, physicist; b. Schroda, June 28, 1943; s. Bogislav and Anny (Ulbrich) von K.; m. Renate Falkenberg, May 27, 1971; children—Andreas, Christine, Thomas. Diploma, Tech. U. Braunschweig, 1969; Ph.D., U. Wuerzburg, 1972, Habilitation, 1978. Faculty mem. Tech. U., Munich, W.Ger., 1980-84; dir. Max Planck Inst. for Festkőrperforschung, Stuttgart, W.Ger., 1985—. Recipient Schottky prize Deutsche Phys. Gesellschaft, 1981, Hewlett Packard prize European Phys. Soc., 1982, Nobel prize in physics Royal Swedish Acad. Sci., 1985. Office: Max Planck Inst, fur Festkörperforschung, Heisenbergstr 1, D-7000 Stuttgart 80 Federal Republic of Germany

KLITZSCH, HANS EBERHARD, geologist, educator; b. Remda, Fed. Republic Germany, Aug. 18, 1933; s. Paul Rudolf and Hertha Margarete (Grü newald) K.; m. Ingrid Meissner, Aug. 30, 1958 (div. 1974); children—Michael, Barbara; m. Eva Marie Michaelis, July 20, 1977; 1 child, Christina. Diploma, Free U. Berlin, 1957, Dr.rer.nat., 1958. Engring. geologist USGS, Heidelberg, W.Ger., 1957-58; oil geologist DEA-Libya, Tripoli, 1959-64, exploration mgr., 1964-67; lectr. Tech. U. Berlin, 1967-69, prof. geology, 1969—; leader spl. project on arid areas, 1981—. Editor: Research in Egypt and Sudan, 1984, 87. Contbr. articles to profl. jours. Fellow Geol. Soc. Africa (hon.); mem. Petroleum Exploration Soc. Libya (dir. 1965-66), Am. Assn. Petroleum Geologists, Geologische Vereinigung, Deutsche Geologische Gesellschaft, Explorers Club. German Research Found. grantee, 1969—. Office: Technische Universitaet Berlin, Sekr BH 2, Ernst-Reuter-Platz 1, Berlin 12, Federal Republic of Germany

KLOCK, JOSEPH PETER, JR., lawyer; b. Phila., Mar. 14, 1949; s. Joseph Peter and Mary Dorothy (Fornace) K.; m. Susan Marie Girsch, Mar. 17, 1979; children: Susan Elizabeth, Kathleen Marie, Robert Charles, Peter Joseph II. BA, LaSalle Coll., 1970; JD, U. Miami, Fla., 1973. Bar: Fla. 1973, Pa. 1973, D.C. 1978. Ptnr. Steel, Hector & Davis, Miami, Fla., 1977—; exec. chmn. Steel, Hector & Davis, Miami, 1983—; adj. prof. U. Miami Law Sch., 1974—; bd. dirs. Nat. Beverage Corp., Premier Hotel Corp., Bayfront Park Mgmt. Trust. Trustee The Carrollton Sch., Belen Jesuit Prepatory Sch., Miami Children's Hosp. Fellow Am. Bar Found; mem. ABA, Fla. Bar (chmn. civil procedure rules com. 1979-82), Pa. Bar Assn., D.C. Bar Assn., Dade County Bar Assn., Monroe County Bar Assn., Palm Beach County Bar Assn., Bar Assn. City N.Y., Am. Law Inst., Am. Bar Found., Iron Arrow Hon. Soc., Phi Alpha Delta, Phi Kappa Phi, Omicron Delta Kappa. Democrat. Roman Catholic. Clubs: Surf (Miami Beach, Fla.); Governors, Brickell, Executive, City (Miami). Home: 5095 SW 82d St Miami FL 33143 Office: Steel Hector & Davis 4000 Southeast Fin Center 200 S Biscayne Blvd Miami FL 33131

KLOCKHAUS, RUTH IRMGARD, university teacher, researcher; b. Berlin, Aug. 17, 1923; m. Wolfgang Klockhaus. PhD, Erlangen-Nürnberg U., 1966. Prof. Erlangen-Nürnberg U., Fed. Republic of Germany, 1980—. Author: Einstellung zur Wohnumgebung, 1975; (with B. Habermann-Morbey) Psychologie des Schulvandalismus, 1986, (with A. Trapp-Michel) Vandalistisches Verhalten Jugendlicher, 1988. Mem. Deutsche Gesellschaft für Psychologie. Home: Westtorgraben 13, D 8500 Nürnberg 80 Federal Republic of Germany

KLODZINSKI, JOSEPH ANTHONY, data communications executive, consultant; b. Chgo., Aug. 19, 1942; s. Joseph Fabian and Haline Ann (Bieganski) K.; m. Mary Margaret Osten, Nov. 19, 1966; children: Joseph II, Catherine Ann, Patricia Ann. BBA, Loyola U., Chgo., 1964; MEd, Boston U., 1968; MBA, Northwestern U., 1971. Packaging engr. Westvaco, Chgo., 1969-72; regional mgr. MacMillan, Chgo., 1972-74; fin. applications cons. IC Systems Corp., Schaumburg, Ill., 1974-77; mgmt. info. systems salesman Honeywell, Chgo., 1977-80; mgmt. info. systems and communications cons. Intertel, Chgo., 1980-82; dist. sales mgr. UDS/Motorola, Chgo., 1982—. Contbr. articles to profl. jours. Mem. parish council Ch. of Holy Spirit, Schaumburg, 1980-85. Served to capt. U.S. Army, 1965-69, Vietnam. Decorated Bronze Star; named Pacesetter, Honeywell Mktg. Mgmt., 1978, Top Sales Mgr., IC Systems Corp., 1975-76, Top Sales Mgr., MacMillan, 1974; fellow Lions Clubs Internat. Found., 1984. Mem. Am. Numismatic Assn. (life), co-founder Australian Numismatic Assn. (Sydney), Oceanic Navigation Research Soc. Roman Catholic. Lodges: K.C., Elks, Lions (pres. Schaumburg 1980-82, DG cabinet No. Ill. zone chmn. 1982-86, dep. dist. gov. 1986—, DG awards 1983-88). Home: 1419 Chalfont Dr Schaumburg IL 60194 Office: UDS/Motorola 3801 W Lake Ave Glenview IL 60025

KLOFT, HANS, historian, educator; b. Düsseldorf, Germany, Apr. 10, 1939; s. Johannes and Mathilde (Jüntgen) K.; m. Gertraud Zimmermann, Nov. 21, 1971 (div. 1988); m. Beate Jaecker, Aug. 1988; 1 child, Katharina. PhD, U. Köln, Fed. Republic Germany, 1968. Asst. prof. Rheinisch-Westfälische Technische Hochschule Aachen, Fed. Republic Germany, 1968-71, akademic rat, 1971-73, akademic oberrat, 1973-77; ordentlicher prof. U. Bremen, Fed. Republic Germany. Author: Liberalitas Principis, 1970, Einführung Geschichte, 1973, Prorogation, 1977; editor: Ideologie und Herrhaft, 1979, Fürsorge und Sozialmassnahmen, 1988. Fellow: Wittheit Bremen, Historikerverband, Mommsen Gesellschaft. Roman Catholic. Home: Wernigeroderstr 36, 2800 Bremen Federal Republic of Germany Office: Univ Bremen, Achterstrasse, 33 Bremen Federal Republic of Germany

KLOHN, FRANKLIN JAMES, JR., clinical psychologist, educator; b. Galion, Ohio, Aug. 8, 1951; s. Franklin J. and Ruth (Dorchester) K.; m. Lisa Smith Klohn; 1 child, Katherine Susanne. BS, U. Dubuque, 1974; MS, Central Mo. State U., Warrensburg, 1978; PhD, Calif. Sch. Profl. Psychology, Fresno, 1984. Psychologist IV, coordinator psychol. services Galesburg Mental Health Ctr., Ill., 1984-85; instr. Carl Sandburg Coll., Galesburg, 1978-85; asst. prof. dept. orthopaedics U. S.C. Sch. of Medicine, 1988—; cons. psychologist vocat. rehab. dept., 1986—; ind. practice, 1986—; coordinator psychological services child and adolescent program William S. Hall Psychiat. Inst., 1985-87; dir. pain therapy Ctr. of Columbia Richland Meml. Hosp., 1987—. Cons. North East Iowa council Boy Scouts Am., Dubuque, 1971-76; mem. youth com. Trinity Cathedral, 1986—. Mem. Am. Psychol. Assn., Assn. Advancement of Behavior Therapy, Assn. Advancement Psychology, Assn. Behavior Analysis, Southeastern Psychol. Assn. Episcopalian. Home: 5005 Village Creek Dr Columbia SC 29210 Office: Pain Therapy Ctr of Columbia One Richland Med Park Suite 220 Columbia SC 29203

KLOHS, MURLE WILLIAM, consulting chemist; b. Aberdeen, S.D., Dec. 24, 1920; s. William Henry and Lowell (Lewis) K.; student Westmar Coll., 1938-40; B.Sc., U. Notre Dame, 1947; Riker fellow, Harvard U., 1950; m. Dolores Catherine Borm, June 16, 1946; children—Wendy C., Linda L. Jr. chemist Harrower Lab., Glendale, Calif., 1947, Rexall Drug Co., Los Angeles, 1947-49; sr. chemist Riker Labs., Inc., Los Angeles, 1949-57, dir. medicinal chemistry, Northridge, Calif., 1957-69, mgr. chem. research dept., 1969-72, mgr. pharm. devel. dept., 1972-73, mgr. tech. liaison and comml. devel., 1973-82; cons. chemist, 1982—. Served to lt. USNR, 1943-46. Mem. Am. Chem. Soc., N.Y. Acad. Scis., Am. Pharm. Assn., Soc. Econ. Botany, Am. Pharmacognosy Soc. Club: Adventures (Los Angeles). Contbr. articles to profl. jours. Home and Office: 19831 Echo Blue Dr Lake Wildwood Penn Valley CA 95946

KLONOFF, HARRY, psychologist; b. Winnipeg, Man., Can., July 29, 1924; s. Abraham and Ida (Aronovitch) K.; m. Mary Plosker, Aug. 16, 1948; children: Hillary, Pamela, Melanie. B.A., U. Man., 1949; M.A., U. Toronto, 1951; Ph.D. (research fellow), U. Wash., 1954. Head dept. psychology Shaughnessy Vets. Hosp., Vancouver, B.C., Can., 1955-61, Shaughnessy Hosp., 1961-77; head div. psychology dept. psychiatry U. B.C., Vancouver, 1961-82; prof. U. B.C., 1970—; head dept. psychology Health Scis. Centre Hosp., 1981-82; head sect. psychology Vancouver Gen. Hosp., 1970-78. Contbr. articles on psychology and psychiatry to sci. publs., chpts. in books. Served with AUS, 1944-46. Nat. Health Med. Research Council grantee, 1968—. Mem. Am. Psychol. Assn., Can. Psychol. Assn., Western Psychol. Assn., B.C. Psychol. Assn. (pres. 1957-58), AAAS, Internat. Neuropsychology Soc., Gerontol. Soc., Assn. Am. Med. Colls., Can. Mental Health Assn. Home: 4533 Belmont Ave, Vancouver, BC Canada V6R 1C5 Office: 7-2255 Westbrook Mall, University of British Columbia, Vancouver, BC Canada V6T 2A1

KLOPF, GORDON JOHN, college dean, educational consultant; b. Milw., Jan. 10, 1917; s. Milton and Lillian (Spiegler) K. B.S., U. Wis., 1939, M.A., 1941, Ph.D., 1950; postgrad., U. Mich. Tchr., counselor pub. schs. Burlington, Wis., 1939-41; counselor men's activities, instr. speech Wayne U., 1942-47; coordinator student's activities summer insts. for sch. counselors U. Wis., Madison, 1947-51; prof. tng. personnel, guidance workers serving with AUS, U.S. Dept. State, Am. Council on Edn. project Tokyo U., Kyoto U., Kyushu U., Japan, 1951-52; dean students coll. for tchrs. SUNY, 1952-59; ednl. specialist in guidance U.S. Dept. State, Japan, 1954; assoc. prof. edn., dept. guidance, student personnel adminstrn. Tchrs. Coll., Columbia U., N.Y.C., 1958-64; asst. to pres., chmn. guidance programs Bank Street Coll. Edn., N.Y.C., 1964-69, dean of faculties, 1965-80, provost, 1970-80, dean Ctr. for Leadership devel., dir. Sch. and Gen. Ledership and Supervision Program, disting. specialist in ednl. leadership, 1980—; pres. Gordon J. Klopf, ednl. cons., N.Y.C., 1983—; cons. to Japanese colls., high schs. in student guidance, 1951-52, 1954; cons. U.S. Office Edn., Washington, 1964-81. P.R. Dept. Instrn., 1965—, Mendoza Found., Ministry of Edn., Venezuela, 1971-80. Author: Student Leadership and Government, 1949, rev., 1955; Planning Student Activities in the High School, 1950; College Student Government, 1960, Teacher Education In a Social Context, 1967, Perspectives On Learning, 1967, New Careers in the American School, 1968, New Careers and Roles in Education, 1968, Teams for Learning, 1969; The Principal and Staff Development in the School, 1976; author-Editor: Education Before Five, 1977; co-author: Mentoring, 1982, The School Principal and Special Education, 1982; co-author numerous other works in field. editor: Operational Studies in Guidance, 1962, Orientation, 1963, Encounter and Dialogue, 1963, Student Personnel Work in the Future, 1966, Jour. Research and Devel. in Edn., Vol. 5, No. 3, 1972; editor, chmn. The Role and Preparation of the Counselor in the Secondary School, 1963; adv. editor Brit. Young Children's Ency., 16 vols., 1970. Past chmn. adv. council U.S. Student Assn.; nat. chmn. Project Follow Through, 1967-68; trustee U.S. Com. for UNICEF, 1971-81, chmn. edn. com., 1975-80; trustee, sec. Bklyn. Children's Mus., 1980—; bd. dirs. Daytop Inc., 1973—. Hampton Day Sch.; pres., bd. trustees Am. Assn. Colls. Tchr. Edn., 1977-81; v.p. Elem. Sch. Ctr., N.Y.; sec. Nat. Orgnl. Adv. Council for Children; chairperson long range planning Morning Side Gardens Housing Corp., N.Y. Mem. N.Y. State Deans Assn. (research chmn., past v.p.), Am. Personnel and Guidance Assn., Western N.Y. Personnel and Guidance Assn. (past pres.), AAUP, Am. Coll. Personnel Assn., Buffalo World Hospitality Assn. (past chmn.), NEA, Phi Delta Kappa. Address: 70 LaSalle St New York NY 10027

KLOPSCH, HEINZ PETER, mathematician, educator; b. Wrzesnia, Poland, Nov. 25, 1941; came to Germany, 1945; s. Siegfried Karl Adolf and Frieda Katharine (Leptien) K.; m. Sylke Alma Krutzfeldt, Mar. 30, 1967; children—Ingolf, Benjamin. Dr.rer.nat., U. Kiel, 1968, Dr.rer.nat. habil., 1977. Research fellow U. Calif.-Berkeley, 1968-69; asst. prof. U. Kiel, W.Ger., 1969-77, univ. lectr. math., 1977—. Contbr. articles to profl. jours.Mem. Deutsche Mathematiker-Vereinigung, Am. Math. Soc. Home: Projensdorfer Str 70, 2300 Kiel 1 Federal Republic of Germany Office: Math Seminar U Kiel, Olshausen Str 40, 2300 Kiel 1 Federal Republic of Germany

KLOS, ELMER, film director; b. Brno, Czechoslovakia, Jan. 26, 1910; s. Rudolf and Marie K.; student Faculty of Law Charles U., Prague; m. Anne Vopalka, 1935; 2 children. Dir., Short Film Studios, 1946-47; head creative art staff, scriptwriter Barrandov Feature Film Studio, 1948-74; prof. film and TV faculty Prague U., 1956-70; dir. films: Kidnapped, 1952, Death is Called Engelchen, 1963, Obzalovany, 1964, The Shop on the High Street, 1965, Desire called Anada, 1969. Recipient State prize 2d class, 1960, Gold prize Moscow Internat. Film Festival, 1963, State prize, 1964, Grand Prix Karlovy Vary Internat. Film Festival, 1964, U.S. Acad. award Oscar, 1965, N.Y. Film Critics award, 1967, Selznik prize U.S., 1966. Mem. Czechoslovk Union of Film Artists (pres. 1963-66). Address: Strahovska 203, Hradcany, Prague 1 Czechoslovakia *

KLOSKOWSKA, ANTONINA, sociology educator; b. Piotrkow, Poland, Nov. 7, 1919; d. Wincenty and Cecylia (Szretter) K. M.A. in Sociology, Lodz U. (Poland), 1948, Ph.D. in Sociology, 1950; Docent, Central State Commn. (Poland), 1954. Asst. Lodz U., 1946-48, sr. asst., 1948-52; adj. prof. Polish Acad. Scis., Lodz, 1952-54, docent, 1954-66; prof. extraordinary U. Lodz, 1966-73; prof. ordinary Warsaw U. (Poland), from 1977; pres. Inst. Sociology Council, Warsaw, 1981-84. Author: Machiavelli, 1954; Kultura masowa, 1964; Z historii i socjologil kultury, 1969; Socjologia kultury, 1981, others. Active League Polish Women, 1965, Polish Women Council, Lodz and Warsaw, Mem. Polish Acad. Scis., Polish Sociol. Assn. Office: Univ of Warsaw, Inst Sociology, Karowa 18, Warsaw 00-364 Poland *

KLOSKOWSKI, VINCENT JOHN, JR., educator, school administrator, author; b. Sept. 30, 1934; s. Vincent and Mary Kloskowski; m. Gerri K.; 1 son, Vincent John III. B.S. with honors, Seton Hall U., N.J., 1960, M.A., 1971; postgrad. Newark State Coll., 1960-62, Trenton (N.J.) State Coll., 1961-64; M.Ed. (Asian Found. scholar), Rutgers U., 1964; Ph.D., U. Western Ont., 1971; postdoctorate Harvard U., 1975, Appalachian State U., 1979; Ed.D. in Ednl. Adminstrn., Nova U., Fla., 1976. Substitute tchr. South River (N.J.) High Sch., 1958-60; tchr. Madison Twp. (N.J.) Public Schs., 1960-64; co-adj. mem. staff Rutgers U., 1961-64; remedial specialist North Brunswick (N.J.) Public Schs., 1964-65; vice prin. Jamesburg (N.J.) High Sch., 1965-66; asst. supt., child study coordinator, curriculum coordinator, fed. coordinator urban funding Public Schs. Jamesburg, 1966-77, prin. elem., jr. high sch. and spl. edn. bldg., 1966-77; ednl. specialist N.J. Dept. Edn., 1977—; cons. to para-profls. Mercer County Community Coll., Trenton, 1972; pvt. practice ednl. counseling, 1973—; speaker ann. conf. on incoming students Seton Hall U., Jamesburg Public Schs. In-Service Program, Middlesex County Child Study Team, PTA Jamesburg Pub. Schs., 1970, 72, Middlesex County Curriculum Council, East Brunswick Vocat. Sch., Holy Innocence Soc., Avenel, N.J., St. Catherines PTA, Clayton, N.J.; panelist child study devel. Madison Twp. Public Schs.; participant Internat. Reading Assn., Somerville, N.J., 42d Summer Sch. Conf. Sch. Adminstrn., Harvard U., Scott Foresman New Programs in Reading, Freehold, N.J., Ann. Reading Inst., Rutgers U., McGraw-Hill-Sullivan Reading Program, Hightstown, N.J., use of para-profls. in public schs. N.J. State Dept.-Middlesex County Community Coll., Edison; cons. Setting Up Pvt. Spl. Edn. Facility, South Brunswick, Ednl. Cons. Service N.J., 1971—, reading techniques for para-profl. Mercer County Community Coll., Trenton, 1971; merit badge counselor Boy Scouts Am.; mem. alumni resource bank counsel, mem. staff and adv. bd. transition program Rutgers U. Coll. Kettering Found. fellow. Mem. Acad. Fellows (speaker nat. confs.), Am. Assn. Sch. Adminstrs., N.J. Assn. Sch. Prins., NEA (life), N.J., Middlesex County, Jamesburg edn. assns., Nat. Ednl. Assn. Sch. Prins., N.J. Classroom Tchrs. Assn., N.J. Assn. Retarded Children, Internat., N.J. reading assns., Middlesex County Audio-Visual Assn., Am. Soc. Notaries, Phi Delta Kappa, Alpha Epsilon Mu, Kappa Delta Pi. Author: Didacticism-Montessori and the Special Child, 1969; Amish School System and Special Education; asst. editor Seton Hall U. Newspaper and Coll. Yearbook, 1959-60; book reviewer Narod Polski, nat. Polish-Am. newspaper, 1976—. Home: 41 Daily St South River NJ 08882

KLOSS, GENE (ALICE GENEVA GLASIER), artist; b. Oakland, Calif., July 27, 1903; d. Herbert P. and Carrie (Hefty) Glasier; m. Phillips Kloss, May 19, 1925. A.B., U. Calif., 1924; student, Calif. Sch. Fine Arts, 1924-25. Illustrator: The Great Kiva (Phillips Kloss), 1980; One-man shows Sandzen Meml. Gallery, Lindsborg, Kans., Albany Inst. History and Art, 1953, Tulsa, Scottsdale, Ariz., Albuquerque, 1956, Findlay Galleries, Chgo., 1957, Mus. N.Mex., 1960, W. Tex. Mus., 1964, Mus. Arts and Scis., Grand Junction, Colo., 1967, Mus. Okla., 1970, Brandywine Galleries, Albuquerque, 1971, Bishop's Gallery, 1972, Gallery A, Taos, N.Mex., 1973, Gallery Graphics, Carmel, 1973, Wichita (Kans.) Art Assn., 1974, Pratt Graphic Center, N.Y.C., 1976—, Muckenthaler Cultural Center, Los Angeles, 1980, Mus. of Tex. Tech U., 1984; exhibited in Three Centuries Art U.S., Paris, 1938; exhibited 3-man show, Pratt Graphic Center, N.Y., 1975; represented in collections, Library Congress, Carnegie Inst., Smithsonian Instn., N.Y. Pub. Library, Met. Mus., Pa. Acad. Fine Arts, Chgo. Art Inst., Corcoran Gallery, Washington, San Francisco Mus., Honolulu Acad. Fine Arts, Dallas Mus., Mus. N.Mex., Tulsa U., Kans. State Coll., Pa. U. John Taylor Arms Meml., Met. Mus., Peabody Mus., Mus. Tokyo, Auchenback Found. for Graphic Arts, San Francisco, Nat. Gallery, U. N.Mex. Mus., Copley Library, La Jolla, Calif., others; executed 1953 membership prints for, Albany Print Club and for Soc. Am. Graphic Artists, gift plate for, Print Makers of Calif., 1956; exhibited with, Audubon Soc., 1955; etcher, painter in oil, watercolor. Recipient Eyre Gold medal Pa. Acad. Fine Arts, 1936; asso. mem. award Calif. Soc. Etchers, 1934; honorarium Cal. Soc. Etchers, 1940, 41, 44; 3d award oils Oakland Art Gallery Ann., 1939; Purchase prize Chgo. Soc. Etchers, 1940; best black and white Tucson Fine Arts Assn., 1941; 1st prize Print Club, Phila., 1944; Purchase prize Library Congress, 1946; 1st prize prints N.Mex. State Fair, 1946; Ann. Exhibit Meriden, Conn., 1947; Open award Calif. Soc. Etchers, 1949-51; Henry B. Shope prize Soc. Am. Etchers, 1951; hon. mention, 1953; 1st prize prints Arts and Crafts Assn., Meriden, Conn., 1951; 1st prize Chgo. Soc. Etchers, 1952; Phila. Sketch Club prize, 1957; Fowler purchase prize Albany Print Club, 1959; purchase prize, 1961; Annoymous prize NAD, 1961. N.A. Mem. NAD, Soc. Am. Graphic Artists, Print Club of Albany, Phila. Water Color Club, MBLS (adv.).

KLOTSCHE, CHARLES MARTIN, real estate development company executive; b. Milw., Jan. 30, 1941; s. J.M. and Roberta; BA in Econs., Babson Coll., 1962; MBA in Fin., U. Wis.-Milw., 1968; m. Christine, Feb. 13, 1972; children: Lyna, Kelly. Pres., Sante Fe Equities, Inc., 1978—; chmn. bd. First Equity Corp., 1980—; pres. N. Am. Yachtshares, Inc., 1981—, Pan Am. Publs., Inc., 1982—, Trans Pacific Investments Inc., 1986—; chmn. bd., chief exec. officer Klotsche Properties, Inc., 1983—; adv. dir. Bank of Santa Fe. Bd. dirs. N.Mex. Spl. Olympics for Mentally Retarded, Orch. Santa Fe, Santa Fe Assn. Retarded Citizens, St. Elizabeth Shelter; pres. Santa Fe Bus. Community for Arts, 1986—. Served with Officer Corps USMC, 1964-67. Recipient 3 nat. awards for excellence Nat. Assn. Homebuilders. Mem. U.S. Mortgage Brokers Assn., Nat. Assn. Realtors, Urban Land Inst., N.Mex. Gen. Contractors Assn., Rocky Mountain Outdoor Writers and Photographers Assn., Internat. Assn. Resort Developers, Timesharing Internat. Republican. Lutheran. Lodge: Rotary. Author: The Encumbered Perceptive and the Intrepid, 1978, The Real Estate Revolution, 1979, Real Estate Investing, A Practical Guide to Wealth Building Secrets, 1980, Real Estate Syndications, The Complete Handbook, 1983, Real Estate Development and Finance Handbook, 1986, The Omega Point, 1988. Office: PO Box 68 Tesuque NM 87574

KLUCINA, JOHN LOUIS, economist, publisher, business executive; b. New Orleans, Nov. 14, 1935; s. John J. and Emma Betty (Manzie) K.; student Bradley U., Peoria, Ill., 1951-52, So. Ill. U., Carbondale, 1952-53, Boston U., 1955, LaSalle Inst., Chgo., 1970, Cornell U., 1975-76, Wharton Sch., U. Pa., 1976, 77, 80; m. Marie Elizabeth Schrider, Oct. 24, 1970; children—John Jaie, Mathew Michael, MariBeth. Account exec. Gottschaldt & Assos. Advt., Miami, Fla., 1960-61, Keyes, Maddon & Jones, Chgo., 1961-63, Martin E. Janis & Co., Chgo., 1963; pres., chief operating officer Klucina Assos., Toledo, 1963-65; account supr. Talifarro Assos., Tampa, Fla., 1965-66; sports editor Perry Newspapers, Inc., West Palm Beach, Fla., 1966-68; asst. city editor Knickerbocker News-Union Star, Capital Newspaper Group div. Hearst Corp., Albany, N.Y., 1970-72, state editor, 1972-73, bur. chief, 1973-74, regional editor, 1974-75, bus./econs./fin. and labor editor, 1975-86, Knickerbocker News, 1986-87; bus., econs. labor writer Times-Union, Sunday Times-Union and Knickerbocker News, 1986-87; pres., chief operating officer Mohawk Printing and Publ. Co., Inc., Capital-Examiner, 1987—, others. Trustee, Capital Newspapers Employee Pension Fund; past pres. parish council St. Helen's Ch., Niskayuna, N.Y.; treas. Little League, Niskayuna, N.Y.; state dir. U.S. Wrestling Fedn.; fin. dir. World Cup of Wrestling, 1987; treas. Adirondack Three Style Wrestling Assn., Albany, 1984-88. Served with AC, USN, 1955-59. Mem. Pub. Relations Soc. Am., Indsl. Relations Research Assn., Newspaper Guild (past pres., mem. exec. bd., council v.p., chief negotiator), Sigma Delta Chi (past chpt. pres., past nat. regional dir.). Club: Colonie Golf. Home: 79 Molly Ct Orchard Park Niskayuna NY 12309 Office: 715 State St Schenectady NY 12307

KLUCK, CLARENCE JOSEPH, physician; b. Stevens Point, Wis., June 20, 1929; s. Joseph Bernard and Mildred Lorraine (Helminiak) K.; m. Joan Catherine Larkin, May 26, 1955; children: Paul Bernard, Annette Louise Kluck Winston, David John, Maureen Ellen. BS in Med. Sci., U. Wis., 1951, MD, 1954. Resident San Joaquin Hosp., French Camp, Calif., 1955-56; asst. instr. medicine Ohio State U., Columbus, 1958-60; physician, chief of medicine Redford Med. Ctr., Detroit, 1960-69; practice medicine specializing in internal medicine Denver, 1969-83; med. dir. Atlantic Richfield Co., Denver, 1983-85; corp. med. dir. Cyprus Minerals Co., Englewood, Colo., 1985—; bd. dirs. Climbo Catering, Detroit, 1967-69, Met. Labs., Denver, 1970-81; pres., bd. dirs. Pack Investments, Inc., Denver, 1985—. Contbr. articles to profl. jours. Served to capt. U.S. Army, 1956-58. Recipient Century Club award Boy Scouts Am., 1972. Fellow Am. Occupational Med. Assn.; mem. Am. Acad. Occupational Medicine, Rocky Mountain Acad. Occupational Medicine (bd. dirs. 1985-88), Denver Med. Soc. (bd. dirs. 1973-74, council mem. 1981—), Colo. Med. Soc. (del. 1973-74, 81—), Am. Mining Congress Health Commn., Am. Soc. Internal Medicine, Colo. Soc. Internal Medicine. Roman Catholic. Clubs: Flatirons (Boulder, Colo.); Metropolitan. Home: 5245 E Oxford Ave PO Box 5277 Englewood CO 80155-5277 Office: Cyprus Minerals Co 7200 S Alton Way Englewood CO 80112

KLUETING, HARM, historian, lecturer; b. Iserlohn, North Rhine-Westphalia, Fed. Republic of Germany, Mar. 23, 1949; s. Hermann Ernst and Esther Hanna Lydia (Grabow) K.; m. Edeltraud Dreher, Mar. 15, 1971. PhD in Slavic Philology, Ruhr U. Bochum, Fed. Republic of Germany, 1974; MA in History, U. Cologne, Fed. Republic of Germany, 1978, habilitation in modern history, 1984. Lectr. dept. history U. Cologne, 1984—; chair dept. early modern history U. Osnabruck, Fed. Republic of Germany, 1985-87. Author: Säkularisation im Herzogtum Westfalen, 1980, Lehre von der Macht der Staaten, 1986, also 49 other books and articles, over 100 revs. Mem. Internat. Commn. for History Reps. and Parliamentary Instns., Westfalen Hist. Commn., Deutsche Gesellschaft für Erforschung 18 Jahrhunderts. Home: Linckensstrasse, D 4400 Munster Federal Republic of Germany Office: U Cologne Dept History, Albertus Magnus Platz, D 5000 Cologne Federal Republic of Germany

KLUG, AARON, biological chemist; b. Aug. 11, 1926; s. Lazar and Bella (Silin) K.; m. Liebe Bobrow, 1948; 2 children. B.Sc., U. Witwatersrand; M.Sc., U. Cape Town; Ph.D., Cambridge U; D.Sc. (hon.), U. Chgo., 1978, Columbia U., 1978; Dr. (hon.), U. Strasbourg, 1978; Dr. Fil. (hon.), U. Stockholm, 1980. Jr. lectr., 1947-48; research student Cavendish Lab., Cambridge U. (Eng.), 1949-52, Rouse-Ball research student Trinity Coll., 1949-52, colloid sci. dept., 1953; Nuffield research fellow Birkbeck Coll., London, 1954-57, dir. virus structure research group, 1958-61; mem. staff Med. Research Council Lab. Molecular Biology, Cambridge U., 1962—, joint head div. structural studies, 1978-86; Leeuwenhoek lectr. Royal Soc., 1973; Dunham lectr. Harvard U. Med. Sch., 1975; Harvey lectr., N.Y.C., 1979; Lane lectr. Stanford U., 1983. Contbr. articles to sci. jours. Recipient Heineken prize Royal Netherlands Acad. sci., 1979, Louisa Gross Horwitz prize Columbia U., 1981, Nobel prize in chemistry, 1982; Gold medal of Merit, U. Cape Town, 1983; Copley medal Royal Soc., 1985. Fellow Royal Soc.; mem. Am. Acad. Arts and Scis. (fgn. hon.), Nat. Acad. Scis. (fgn. assoc.). Office: Med Research Council, Lab of Molecular Biology, Cambridge CB2 2QH, England *

KLUNZINGER, THOMAS EDWARD, writer, reapportionment specialist, actor; b. Ann Arbor, Mich., Sept. 11, 1944; s. Willard Reuben and Katherine Eileen (McCurdy) K.; B.A. cum laude in Advt., Mich. State U., 1966. Copywriter Campbell-Ewald Advt. Co., Detroit, 1966-70; travel cons. Moorman's Travel Service, Detroit, 1973-74; media dir. Taylor for Congress campaign, East Lansing, Mich., 1974; communications specialist House Republican Staff, Lansing, Mich., 1975-80; trustee Meridian Twp., Ingham County, Mich., 1980-84; vice chmn. Econ. Devel. Corp., 1982-84; compliance officer The Eyde Co., Lansing, 1985-88, writer Power Assocs., Plymouth, 1988— . Mem. Ingham County Republican Com., 1976—, sec., 1987-88, Mich. Rep. State Com., 1981-85. Mem. Dramatists Guild, Am. Numismatic Assn., Mich. Numismatic Soc., Zero Population Growth, Mensa. Author: Chester!, 1981; Heavy Lady, 1983; Double Standards, 1985; A Villa in Unadilla, 1985, Losing It, 1987, The Wizards of Kyshtym/Deine Kleine Beine, 1988. Address: PO Box 16231 Lansing MI 48901

KLUSEN, ERNST, ethnomusicologist; b. Düsseldorf, Fed. Republic of Germany, Feb. 20, 1909; s. Ernst and Katharina (Korbmacher) K.; m. Gertrud Arnold, Apr. 5, 1935 (dec. 1960); children: Ernst A., Gertrud Klusen Leutz; m. Margarete Schilling, July 11, 1961 (dec. 1980). MA in Music, Univ., Cologne, Fed. Republic of Germany, 1933; PhD in Musicology, Univ., Bonn, Fed. Republic of Germany, 1939. Instr. Coll., Krefeld, Fed. Republic of Germany, 1933-38; instr. Oberstudienrat Coll., Viersen, Fed. Republic of Germany, 1938-61; prof. Pedagogical Acad., Neuss, Fed. Republic of Germany, 1961-69; prof. ordinarius Pedagogical Acad. Rhineland, Cologne, 1969-76, prof. emeritus, 1976; dean dept. Pedagogical Acad., Neuss, Fed. Republic of Germany, 1970-72; pres. Nat. Com. of Internat. Folk Music Council, 1975-79. Author: Volkslied: Fund und Erfindung, 1969, Elektronische Medien und musikalische Laienaktivitat, 1980, Deutsche Lieder, 1987. Bd. dirs. Sch. Adulteral Edn., Viersen, 1947-61. Recipient Rheinlandtaler award Landschaftsverband, 1977, Benedictspreis award Town of Mönchengladbach, 1978, Stadtehrenplakette Town of Krefeld, 1981. Mem. Arbeitsgemeinschaft Rheinische Musikgechichte (pres. 1975-77, hon. mem. 1977—), Com. of Song Research of German Folklore Soc. (pres. 1972-82). Roman Catholic. Lodge: Lions (pres. local chpt. 1972-73). Home: Im grünen Winkel 18, D 4060 Viersen 1 Federal Republic of Germany

KLUTZNICK, PHILIP M., lawyer, former government official; b. Kansas City, Mo., July 9, 1907; s. Morris and Minnie (Spindler) K.; m. Ethel Riekes, June 8, 1930; children: Bettylu, Richard (dec.), Thomas Joseph, James Benjamin, Robert, Samuel. Student, U. Kans., 1924-25, U. Nebr., 1925-26; LLB, Creighton U., Omaha, 1929, LLD (hon.), 1957; DHL (hon.), Dropsie Coll., 1954, Hebrew Union Coll.-Jewish Inst. Religion, 1957, Coll. Jewish Studies, 1968; LLD (hon.), Wilberforce (Ohio) U., 1959, Chgo. Med. Sch., 1968, Yeshiva U., 1974, Brandeis U., 1974, Roosevelt U., 1981, U. Ill.-Chgo., 1983; LHD (hon.), Governor's State U., 1983; LLD (hon.), Northwestern U., 1984, DePaul U., 1984. Admitted to bar, 1930. U.S. commr. Fed. Pub. Housing Authority, 1944-46; hon. dir. Mortgage Guaranty Ins. Corp., Milw., JD, 1930; Mem. U.S. dels. to UN, 1957, 61, 62; U.S. rep., rank of ambassador, to ECOSOC, 1961-63; mem. President's Adv. Com. on Indo-Chinese Refugees; sec. commerce Washington, 1980-81. Bd. dirs. Nat. Jewish Welfare Bd., Exec. Service Corps; founder Inst. Jewish Policy Planning; nat. council Boy Scouts Am.; chmn. exec. com. Dearborn Park; trustee Gen. Marshall Found.; hon. bd. dirs. Creighton U., Roosevelt U., Lyric Opera Chgo.; trustee Com. Econ. Devel.; pres. emeritus World Jewish Congress, 1977— ; vice chmn. Leadership Greater Chgo.; bd. govs. Chgo. Symphony. Recipient Ralph Bunche peace award, 1981; named to Chgo. Bus. Hall of Fame, 1985. Mem. UN Assn. U.S.A. (gov.; sr. dir.), Chgo. Assn. Commerce and Industry (adv. com.), Lambda Alpha, Zeta Beta Tau (hon.), B'nai B'rith (hon. internat. pres.). Clubs: Cosmos, Army-Navy (Washington); Standard, Carlton, Commercial, (Chgo.). Office: 737 N Michigan Ave Suite 920 Chicago IL 60611

KNABE, WOLFGANG KARL, social scientist, government official; b. Dusseldorf, Fed. Republic Germany, Dec. 29, 1950; s. Josef and Ruth (Forner) K.; m. Edith Maria Fluck, May 19, 1978. Ph.D., U. Cologne, 1977. Scholar, Fritz-Thyssen-Found., Cologne, 1976-77; asst. prof. Sociology U. Augsburg, Fed. Republic Germany, 1979-82; officer in charge Bavarian Diet, head dept. sect. Bayerischer Landtag Maximilianeum, Munich, Fed. Republic Germany, 1982-85; socio-cultural scientist Bavarian Acad. Sci., Swabian Research Council, 1986—. Author: Untersuchungen ü ber die Grundlagen der Maria-Religion (U. Cologne valde laudabile), 1978; contbr. articles to profl. jours.; research in social and polit. minorities in Iran, Afghanistan, Middle India, Sri Lanka and Latin Am. (research project participant). Town councilor, 1984. Home: Ahrenstr 19, 8900 Augsburg 21 Federal Republic of Germany

KNAEBEL, JOHN BALLANTINE, mining consulant; b. Denver, Jan. 1, 1906; s. Ernest and Cornelia (Park) K.; student Cornell U., 1924-28; field geology Northwestern U., summer 1928; B.S. in Engring., Stanford U., 1929, E.M., 1930; m. Joy James, 1931 (div. May 1956); children—Jeffrey James, Stephen Park; m. 2d, Nelle M. McNulty, Mar. 14, 1958; 1 stepson, Terrence Patrick McNulty. Mining engr. Cananea Consol. Copper Co., Mexico, summer 1929; with U.S. Bur. Mines, 1930-33; mgr. East Mindanao Mining Co., Philippines, 1933-36; cons. engr., Western U.S., Can., C.Am., Mex., 1937-38; mng. dir. Amparo Mining Co., Ltd., Can., 1938-40; successively supt., asst. mgr., asst. to v.p., asst. mgr. Western Mines, U.S. Smelting, Refining & Mining Co., N.Mex., Utah, Western U.S., 1940-46; engr.-in-charge Anaconda Brit. Guiana Mines, Ltd., also mng. dir. Mineração Gurupi, S.A., Brasil (Anaconda Copper Mining Co. subs), 1946-50; gen. mgr. N.Mex. ops. Anaconda Co., 1951-56, Anaconda Co., 1955—, asst. to v.p.-in-charge mining ops., 1956-58; cons. engr., 1958; pres., mng. dir. Anaconda Iron Ore (Ont). Ltd., Can., 1959-71; v.p., gen. mgr. Anaconda Co. (Can.), Ltd., Western div., 1962-71; v.p. Anaconda Am. Brass, Ltd., Western Exploration div., 1963-71; gen mgr. new mines dept. Anaconda Co., 1963-71, v.p., 1964-71; mining cons., 1971—. Named Mining Man of Yr., Mining World mag., 1956; recipient William Lawrence Saunders Gold medal for disting. achievement in mining AIME, 1959; Daniel C. Jackling award Soc. Mining Engrs.-Am. Inst. Mining Engrs., 1972. Mem. N.W., N.Mex. (dir. 1952-57, pres. 1956), Colo., Ariz. mining assns., Am. Mining Congress (Western bd. govs. 1955-57), Geol. and Mining Soc., AIME (Disting. Mem. 1975), Soc. Econ. Geologists, Tucson C. of C. (dir., mem. exec. com. 1964), Ariz. Acad. Public Affairs, Can. Inst. Mining and Metallurgy, Assn. Profl. Engrs. B.C., Assn. Profl. Engrs. Ont., Am. Forestry Assn., Nat. Geog. Soc., Nat. Wildlife Fedn., Aircraft Owners and Pilots Assn., Quiet Birdmen, Internat. Wood Collectors Soc., Sigma Xi, Sigma Gamma Epsilon. Contbr. articles and tech. papers on mining to profl. publs. Home and Office: PO Box 1329 Winston OR 97496

KNAKE, BARRY EDWARD, management consulting executive, industrial psychologist; b. Chgo., Oct. 1, 1946; s. Louis Edward and Betty Agnus (Ryden) K.; m. Rita Kaye Watson, Feb. 7, 1967; children: Sean, Ryan, Julene. BA, Eastern Wash. U., 1969, MS, 1971. Grad. teaching fellow Eastern Wash. U., Cheney, 1969-70; personnel analyst City of Seattle, 1972-74; psychology instr. So. Seattle Community Coll., 1973; personnel psychologist U.S. Office Personnel Mgmt., Seattle, 1974-81; pres. KMB Assocs., Seattle, 1981—. Contbr. articles on personnel mgmt., testing, job analysis, affirmative action, job element testing to profl. jours. Mem. Seattle Urban League Employment Com., Seattle, 1983—; mem. Gov.'s Com. on Employment of Handicapped, Olympia, 1980—. Mem. AAAS, Am. Psychol. Assn. (assoc.). Home and Office: 6730 13th Ave SW Seattle WA 98106

KNAPEN, HUGO, sales executive; b. St. Truiden, Limburg, Belgium, Feb. 9, 1950; s. Georges and Germaine (GeLenne) K.; m. Godelieve Sterken, Sept. 9, 1975. Chemistry Degree, Terbiest, Belgium, 1971; postgrad. Limburg U. Ctr., 1978; sales courses, Zurich and Hamburg Asst. coordinator research Janssen Pharm., Beerse, Belgium, 1973-75; product mgr. VEL, Leuven, 1979-82; mng. dir. Heyer Belgium, St. Truiden, Belgium, 1983—. Working mem. AntiGif Centre, Brussels, 1983—. Mem. Syndicate Kamer Bouw, Antwerp Mycological Soc. Roman Catholic. Avocations: shooting; tennis; motorcycling; music. Home: Nachtegaal 27, 3813 Zepperen, Limburg Belgium Office: Heyer Belgium, Meiveldlaan, 3800 St Truiden, Limburg Belgium

KNAPP, ANDREAS KARL, psychology professor; b. Halle, Saale, Germany, Jan. 4, 1948; s. Heinz-Jochen and Maria (Muller) K.; m. Edeltraut Lorenz, May 30, 1968. Diploma in psychology, U. Technol., Braunschweig, Fed. Republic Germany, 1973, MA, 1974, Doctorate, 1975. Lectr. Tchrs. Coll., Landau, Fed. Republic Germany, 1974-80; prof. U. Technol., Darmstadt, Fed. Republic Germany, 1980-83; prof., lab. dir. Johannes-Gutenberg U., Mainz, Fed. Republic Germany, 1983—. Author 3 books; editor 2 book series, 1 jour.; contbr. articles to profl. jours. Grantee German Sci. Found., Bonn, Fed. Republic Germany, 1978-80, 86—, NATO Sci. Affairs div., Brussels, 1986-88, Fulbright Commn., Washington and Bonn, 1985. Mem. German Assn. Psychology, Am. Psychol. Assn. Office: Johannes Gutenberg U, Dept Psychology, Saarstrasse 21, 6500 Mainz Federal Republic of Germany

KNAPP, ARTHUR BERNARD, archaeologist, educator; b. Akron, Ohio, Sept. 6, 1941; s. Arthur Cecil and Regina Gertrude (Davis) K.; m. Christina Mary Monsarrat Sumner, Jan. 28, 1984; stepchildren: Katherine, Joanna. BA magna cum laude, U. Akron, 1967; MA, U. Calif., Berkeley, 1973, PhD, 1979. Teaching asst. dept. Near Ea. Studies U. Calif., Berkeley, 1973-75, acting instr., 1976-79, lectr. in archaeology, ancient history, 1979-83; nat. postdoctoral research fellow Dept. Archaeology U. Sydney, Australia, 1984-87; research affiliate Dept. Anthropology U. Sydney, 1987—; hon. research assos. Sch. History, Philosophy, Politics Macquarie U., Sydney, 1984-87; archaeol. fieldworker in Israel, Cyprus and Jordan, 1974, 82-86. Editor: Prehistoric Production and Exchange, 1985; Author: Copper Production and Divine Protection, 1986, Ancient Western Asia and Egypt, 1988; editor: Prehistoric Production and Exchange, 1985; founding editor Jour. Mediterranean Archaeology, 1988; contbr. articles to scholarly jours. Grantee Ford Found., 1972, Australian Inst. Nuclear Sci. and Engring., 1984-86, Ministry of Sci. and Tech. Commonwealth Govt. Australia, 1984-87; Fulbright fellow, 1987-88. Mem. Am. Oriental Soc., Am. Schs. Oriental Research, Assn. Field Archaeology, Current Anthropology (assoc.), Soc. Am. Archaeology.

KNAPP, CLEON TALBOYS, publisher; b. Los Angeles, Apr. 28, 1937; s. Cleon T. and Sally (Brasfield) K.; m. Elizabeth Ann Wood, Mar. 17, 1979; children: Jeffrey James, Brian Patrick, Aaron Bradley, Laura Ann. Student, UCLA, 1955-58. With John C. Brasfield Pub. Corp. (purchased co. in 1965, changed name to Knapp Communications Corp. 1977); now pub. Bon Appetit mag., Archtl. Digest, Home mag., Los Angeles, 1958—; chief exec. officer Bon Appetit mag., Archtl. Digest, Home mag., 1965—, chmn. bd.; chmn. Knapp Press, Rosebud Press; owner Wilshire Mktg. Corp., Wood Knapp Home Video; organizer, dir. Wilshire Bancorp. Trustee UCLA Found.; bd. dirs. Damon Runyon-Walter Winchell Cancer Fund. Mem. Mag. Pubs. Assn. (bd. dirs.). Office: Knapp Communications Corp 5900 Wilshire Blvd Los Angeles CA 90036

KNAPP, HORST HERBERT, publisher, journalist; b. Vienna, Austria, Apr. 10, 1925; s. Josef and Hermine (Sengelin) K.; student Vienna U., 1946-48, 51-54; m. Elfriede Naschold, Aug. 11, 1962; children—Karina, Arno. Editor, UP, 1946-50; freelance econ. journalist, 1950-60; pub., editor-in-chief Finanznachrichten, Vienna, 1960—; lectr., leader seminars in group dynamics, 1954-60; lectr. vienna Diplomatic Acad., 1973-74; mem. informal econ. adv. staffs, chancellors Klaus and Kreisky; mem. council of econ. advs. to Minister Fin., 1983-84. Recipient Renner award in journalism, 1968; Körner award for social sis., 1972; Ausch award for econs., 1980; Vienna Order of Merit, 1986. Mem. Club Econ. Journalists (founding). Author: Wirtschaftsfibel, 1967; Gesellschaftsfibel, 1973; Wirtschaftswissen knapp gefasst, 1976; Angebot sucht Nachfrage, 1984. Office: 1 Bankgasse, Vienna 1010, Austria

KNAPP, PHILIP BERNARD, inventor, lecturer, consultant; b. N.Y.C., Aug. 6, 1923; s. Litman Victor and Sophie (Klien) K.; m. Harriet D. Kramer, Mar. 11, 1952; children—John A., Joshua E., Josiah A. Student Manhattan Sch. Music, 1946-51; B.S., Clayton U., 1985, M.B.A., 1985, PhD in Bus., 1986. Mgmt. cons. Bruce Payne and Assoc., N.Y.C., 1957-60; nat. mgr. mktg. cons. Lybrand, Ross Bros and Montgomery, N.Y.C., 1962-65; v.p. Stewart Dougall and Assocs., N.Y.C., 1965-67; pres. Aptek Industries, Inc., Carle Place, N.Y., 1967-73, Hortigro, Inc., Lynbrook, N.Y., 1976-82, Apredel, Inc., Amityville, N.Y., 1974—; prof. SUNY, Farmingdale, 1985-87, lectr. in concept devel., process of invention, 1983-84; prof. engring. mgmt. Cooper Union, 1986-87; lectr., panelist N.Y. Soc. Profl. Inventors, Farmingdale, 1984; dir. indsl. design lab. Pratt Inst., Bklyn., 1966-67, instr., cons., 1964-67. Author: The Process of Invention; Consultants Guide To Acquisitions. Holder 28 U.S. and fgn. patents, created over 50 inventions. Designer, craftsman contemporary furniture. Active Le Bourget Soc., Amityville. Served with U.S. Army, 1943-45, ETO. Mem. N.Y. Soc. Profl. Inventors (charter mem.; chmn. legal com. 1983-86, chmn. fin. com. 1983-86, pres. 1987—), Fedn. Am. scientists, N.Y. Acad. Scis., AAAS, DAV. Avocations: fishing; vegetable gardening. Home: 116 Stuart Ave Amityville NY 11701 Office: Apredel Inc 116 Stuart Ave Amityville NY 11701

KNAPP, TILLMANN WILHELM, engineering company executive; b. Wiesbaden, Germany, Feb. 28, 1941; s. Wilhelm and Norgard (Melzer) K.; m. Elke Walther, Mar. 24, 1970; 1 son, Helge. M.S. in Engring., Wiesbaden Tech. Sch., 1961. Tech. asst. Beer Maschinenbau, Wiesbaden, 1961-69; tech. mgr. Kindler u. Schiermeier, Munich, Fed. Republic Germany, 1969-70, Beckman Instruments, Munich, 1970-72; mgr. research and devel. Ratisch Instrument, Munich, 1972-73; mng. dir. J.U.M. Engring., Munich, 1973-85, pres., 1985—. Mem. Soc. Automotive Engrs. Home: Keferloherstrasse 89, 8000 Munich 40 Federal Republic of Germany Office: JUM Engring GmbH, Ingolstaedter Strasse G1P, 8000 Munich 45 Federal Republic of Germany

KNAPP, VIKTOR, legal educator; b. Prague, Czechoslovakia, Dec. 18, 1913; s. Rudolf and Elisabeth (Slivova) K.; m. Marta Knappova, Mar. 28, 1958. JD, Charles U., Prague, 1936, PhD, 1949; D honoris causa, U. Montpellier, France, 1980. Sole practice Prague, 1936-45, civil servant, 1945-48; asst. prof. law Charles U., 1948-51, prof., 1951—; dir. Inst. State and Law Czechoslovak Acad. Scis., Prague, 1958-71, researcher, 1971—; vis. prof. Karl Marx U., Leipzig, German Dem. Republic, 1951-52, U. Sorbonne, Paris, 1966-67, U. Regensburg, Fed. Republic Germany, 1967-68; prof. Internat. Faculty Comparative Law, Strasbourg, France, 1961—. Author: Ownership in the People's Democracy, 1952, Applicability of the Cybernetic Methods in Law, 1963, Philosophical Problems of Czechoslovak Law, 1967, Legal Science, 1978; editor Vol. I International Encyclopedia of Comparative Law; contbr. numerous articles to profl. jours. Decorated Order of Labour (Czechoslovakia). Mem. Czechoslovak Acad. Scis., Internat. Acad. Comparative Law. Home: Nad Patankou 8, CS-160 00 Prague 6 Dejvice, Czechoslovakia

KNAPP, WILLIAM BERNARD, cardiologist; b. Paterson, N.J., Oct. 26, 1921; s. Joseph and Mary (Cannon) K.; m. Jeannette C. Zarnowiecki, Jan. 31, 1948; children: William, Thomas, Bernadette, Richard, Suzanne. Diplomate Am. Bd. Internal Medicine. Attending physician Cook County Hosp., Chgo.; assoc. clin. prof. medicine Loyola U., Chgo.; chmn. medicine Little Co. of Mary Hosp., 1960-80; chmn. Holy Cross Hosp., Suburban Hosp., Hinsdale, Ill., 1976-81; practice medicine specializing in cardiology; chmn. S.W. Hosp. Planning, Chgo.; established 1st coronary care unit in Ill., 1965. Bd. dirs. Retirement Village, Civic Assn., Geneva Lake, Wis., 1970—; dir. water safety patrol, Geneva Lake, 1970—. Served with U.S. Army, 1943-46. Recipient Research award Ill. Inst. Medicine; 1st Professorial Chair Cardiology named in honor Loyola U., Chgo., 1985 . Fellow Am. Coll. Cardiology, Am. Coll. Chest Physicians, Am. Coll. Angiology, Chgo. Inst. Medicine; mem. N.Am. Soc. Pacing and Electrophysiology, AMA, ACP, Ill. Med. Soc., Chgo. Med. Soc., Inst. Medicine Chgo., Blue Key Honor Soc. Roman Catholic. Clubs: Butterfield Country (Oak Brook, Ill.); Big Foot Country; Beverly Country (Chgo.); Tracer; Whitehall. Office: 3900 W 95th St Evergreen Park IL 60642

KNAPPENBERGER, DON J., lawyer; b. Kansas City, Kans., June 30, 1950; s. Joseph F. and Opal S. (Schlickau) K.; m. Karen L. Knappenberger. B.S. cum laude, Kans. State U., 1972; J.D., Washburn U., 1975. Bar: Kans. 1975, U.S. Dist. Ct. Kans. 1975. County atty. Stafford County, Kans., 1975-80; ptnr. Gates & Knappenberger, St. John, Kans., 1975-82; sole practice, St. John, 1982—. Sec. Stafford County Fair, 1977-78; instr. Outreach, Great Bend., Kans.; mem. Stafford County Republican Central Com., 1975—. Mem. Kans. Bar Assn., ABA, St. John Bus. Assn., St. John Jaycees, Stafford County Hist. Soc. Lutheran. Club: Stafford County Country. Home: 115 S Monroe Saint John KS 67576 Office: PO Box 245 Saint John KS 67576

KNASS, DAVID ANTHONY, pharmaceutical executive; b. Wrexham, Clwyd, Wales, Sept. 7, 1950; s. Alfred and Beatrice Margaret (Ellis) K.; m. Marilyn Derbyshire, Feb. 1, 1975; children: Gareth, Kathryn, Jenny. BS in Pharmacy with honors, Manchester U., Eng., 1972. clin. tutor, lectr. Manchester U., 1978-83; chmn. Stockport & Dist. Br. PSGB, 1987—. Research and devel. pharmacist Imperial Chem. Industries, Macclesfield, Eng., 1973-75; staff pharmacist Christie Hosp. & Holt Radium Inst., Manchester, 1975-80; prin. pharmacist Tameside Gen Hosp., Ashton-U-Lyne, Eng., 1980-83; dist. pharm. officer Oldhamn, Stockport and Tameside & Glossop Health Authorities, Manchester, 1983—. Mem. Pharm. Soc., Guild Hosp. Pharmacists, Hosp. Pharmacist Group, U.K. Clin. Pharmacy Assn. Mem. Ch. of Eng. Home: 10 Clifton Dr, Marple, Stockport SK6 6PP, England Office: Tameside & Glossop Health, Authority, Greenfield St, Hyde, Stockport SK14 1DB, England

KNAUER, VELMA STANFORD, savings and loan executive; b. Pottstown, Pa., July 4, 1918; d. Chester Miller and Pearl Fretz (Miller) Stanford; student public schs.; m. Joseph Daniel Knauer, Feb. 17, 1940; children—Joseph Daniel, Susan Velma Knauer Metz. With U.S. Axle Co., Inc., Pottstown, 1936-45; with First Fed. Savs. & Loan Assn., Pottstown, 1953—, controller, 1953—, asst. treas., 1953-62, asst. sec., 1962-75, treas., 1976—. Mem. Am. Soc. Profl. and Exec. Women. Home: 970 Feist Ave Pottstown PA 19464 Office: Box 1 High and Hanover Sts Pottstown PA 19464

KNAUER, WILLIAM JEROME, JR., ophthalmologist, educator; b. Jacksonville, Fla., Aug. 7, 1924. Student U. Fla., 1942-44; M.D., George Washington U., 1948. Diplomate Am. Bd. Ophthalmology, 1953. Intern Emory U., Atlanta, 1948-49; resident Johns Hopkins Hosp. Wilmer Eye Inst., Balt., 1949-52, 54-56; pvt. practice ophthalmology, Jacksonville, Fla., 1956—, chief dept. ophthalmology St. Vincent's Med. Ctr., Jacksonville, 1961-75, chief med. and dental staff, 1975-76, presently mem. staff; mem. staff Riverside Hosp., Jacksonville; mem. courtesy staff Bapt. Meml., St. Luke's, Univ. hosps., Jacksonville; instr. ophthalmology U. Fla., Gainesville. Bd. dirs. Young Life, 1969-71; vestryman St. Mark's Episcopal Ch., 1957-70; bd. dirs. Mental Health Assn., 1959-62; trustee Bartram Sch., 1972-74; exec. com. United Fund; mem. Com. 100 and 2 per cent Club, Jacksonville. Fellow Am. Bd. Ophthalmology, Am. Acad. Ophthalmology and Otolaryngology, ACS, Soc. Eye Surgeons; mem. Am. Soc. Contemporary Ophthalmology, Duval County Med. Soc. (sec. 1958), Fla. Med. Assn., AMA, So. Med. Assn., Internat. Glaucoma Congress, Duval County Soc. Ophthalmology (pres. 1958), Fla. Soc. Ophthalmology, Found. for Sight (chmn., bd. dirs.), Assn. Cryosurgery, Am. Intraocular Lens Implant Soc., U.S. Eye Study Club (pres. 1973), Soc. Cons. Clin. Ophthalmologists, Contact Lens Assn. Am., Smith-Reed Russell Soc., William Beaumont Soc., Sigma Alpha Epsilon. Clubs: Rotary (bd. dirs. 1982-84), Ye Mystic Revelers (capt. 1974, king 1980), Fla. Yacht, Timuquana Country (bd. govs. 1967-69), Ponte Vedra, River, Tournament Players Championship Assn. Contbr. articles to med. jours. Office: 2535 Riverside Ave Jacksonville FL 32204

KNAUF, JANINE BERNICE, educator; b. Rochester, N.Y., Apr. 10, 1945; d. William Charles and Ila May (Hauss) Knauf; S.B., M.I.T., 1967; M.B.A., Rutgers U., 1971; M.Ph., Columbia U., 1979, Ph.D., 1981; 1 son, Christopher Robert Burgess. Research engr. Northrop/Norair, Hawthorne, Calif., 1965-66; sci. research engr. Rockwell Internat., Los Angeles, 1967-68; acct. Knauf and Knauf, Rochester, 1968-69, 76, 78; lectr. mgmt. dept. Poly. Inst. N.Y., 1972-73; asst. prof. info. systems Rutgers U., Newark, N.J., 1973-80; computer cons. Keefe, Bruyette & Woods, Inc., N.Y.C., 1978—; asst. prof. acctg. Fla. State U., Tallahassee, 1980-85; v.p. Knauf and Knauf, PC, Pittsford, 1985—. C.P.A., Fla., N.Y. Mem. Soc. Women Engrs., Internat. Platform Assn., AIAA, Am. Woman's, Am. Inst. C.P.A.s, Am. Women's Soc. C.P.A.s, N.Y. Soc. C.P.A.'s, Fla. Inst. C.P.A.s, Am. Acctg. Assn., Aircraft Owners and Pilots Assn., Beta Gamma Sigma, Sigma Gamma Tau.

KNAUF, TASSILO ERICH, education educator; b. Weilheim, Germany, Mar. 9, 1944; s. Walter and Anneliese (Kloos) K.; m. Anne Ehrenhold, Oct. 11, 1968; 1 child, Helen. Dr.Phil., U. Hamburg, 1973. Collaborator, U. Goettingen, Fed. Republic Germany, 1970-74; vice dir. Adult Coll., Salzgitter, Fed. Republic Germany, 1975-76; asst. prof. U. Bielefeld, Fed. Republic Germany, 1976-80, U. Bremen, 1980-81; prof., dean dept. U. Essen, 1981—. Author: Die Braunschweiger Stadtpfarrkirchen, 1974; Kloster Luene, 1974. Editor: Handlungsorientiertes Lernen, 1979; Handbuch Zur Unterrichtsvorbereitung, 1979. Co-editor: Jour. Arbeiten Und Lernen, 1980-83. Home: Am Gottesberg 61, D-4800 Bielefeld Federal Republic of Germany Office: U Essen Universitaetsstr, D-4300 Essen Federal Republic of Germany

KNAUSS, ROBERT LYNN, legal educator, university dean; b. Detroit, Mar. 24, 1931; s. Karl Ernst and Loise (Atkinson) K.; m. Angela Tirola Lawson, Feb. 21, 1973; children by previous marriage: Robert B., Charles H., Katherine E.; 1 stepson, Ian T. Lawson. A.B., Harvard U., 1952; J.D., U. Mich., 1957. Bar: Calif., Tenn., Tex. Assoc. Pillsbury, Madison & Sutro, San Francisco, 1958-60; prof. law U. Mich., 1960-72; v.p. U. Mich. (Office Student Services), 1970-72; dean, prof. law Vanderbilt U., Nashville, 1972-79; vis. prof. Vt. Law Sch., South Royalton, Amos Tuck Sch. Bus. Adminstrn., Dartmouth Coll., Hanover, N.H., 1979-81; disting. univ. prof. law U. Houston Law Center, 1981—, dean, 1981—; cons. spl. studies security markets SEC, 1962-63; rapporteur, panel on capital formation Am. Soc. Internat. Law, 1967-71; dir. Houston Natural Gas, 1975-85, Mexico Fund, 1985—; gen. ptnr. Equus Ltd., 1984—, Allwaste, Inc., 1988—. Editor: Small Business Financing, 4 vols., 1966, Securities Regulation Sourcebook, 1970-71, (with others) Cases and Materials on Enterprise Organizations, 1987; contbr. articles to profl. jours. Regent Nat. Coll. Dist. Attys., 1981—. Served to lt. (j.g.) USNR, 1952-55. Mem. ABA, Calif. Bar Assn., Tenn. Bar Assn., Tex. Bar Assn., Am. Law Inst., Order of Coif. Home: 2004 Milford St Houston TX 77098 Office: U Houston Law Ctr Univ Park Houston TX 77004

KNECHT, PETER FRANZ, anthropologist; b. Zurich, Switzerland, Apr. 11, 1937; s. Walter Knecht. Licentiate Theology, U. Gregoriana, Rome, 1963; M in Sociology, Tokyo U., 1973. Asst. prof. Nanzan U., Nagoya, Japan, 1979-86, assoc. prof., 1986—. Editor jour. Asian Folklore Studies, 1980—; contbr. articles to profl. jours. Mem. Japanese Ethnological Soc. (trustee 1986-88), European Assn. Japanese Studies, Assn. Asian Studies. Office: Nanzan U Dept Anthropology, 18 Yamazato-cho, Showa-ku 466 Nagoya Japan

KNEISEL, WILLIAM JOHN, investment banker; b. Boston, Aug. 11, 1947; s. John J. and Ann (Henningsen) K.; m. Anne Hooper, June 21, 1970; children: John Ames, Tyler Dillon. BA, Dartmouth Coll., 1969; MBA, Harvard U., 1974. Asst. cashier Citibank NA, N.Y.C., 1969-72; assoc. Morgan Stanley and Co., N.Y.C., 1974-78, v.p., 1979-80, prin., 1981-82, mng. dir., 1983—; bd. dirs. Henningsen Foods, Inc., White Plains, N.Y., 1985—. Mem. Bond Club N.Y. (treas. 1984). Roman Catholic. Clubs: Racquet and Tennis, Manchester Yacht, Essex County. Office: Morgan Stanley Internat, 1A Wimple St, London England

KNEITEL, THOMAS STEPHEN, writer, consultant, editor; b. Bklyn., Jan. 28, 1933; s. Seymour Holtzer and Ruth Florence (Fleischer) K.; m. Judith Gibson, Apr. 26, 1961; children: Robin, Kerry, Kathleen, David, Karin, Terri, Skip (dec.), Sandi. Student, U. Miami, Fla.; B.A., M.A., N.Y. U.; Ph.D., Columbia U. Announcer Sta. WTTT, Miami, 1951-52; exec. United Artists Corp., N.Y.C., 1954-59; mng. editor Ziff-Davis Publishing Co., N.Y.C., 1959-60; film writer U.S. Army Signal Corps Pictorial Center, N.Y.C., 1960-61; editor Horizons Publs., Oklahoma City, 1961-62; editorial dir. Cowan Pub. Corp., N.Y.C., 1962-82; v.p., editor Popular Communications Mag., N.Y.C., 1982—. Author: numerous books including 103 Simple Transitor Projects, 1962, CB'ers SSB Handbook, 1977, Registry of Government Radio Frequencies, 1979-87, Air-Scan Directory, 1979, 80, 81, 84, Energy-Scan Directory, 1980, Radio Station Treasury, 1986, Tomcat's Big CB Handbook, 1988, Tune in on Telephone Calls, 1988, Guide to Embassy and Espionage Communications, 1986, also numerous articles, contbr. to Ency. Americana, 1979. Decorated Knight Imperial Order Constantine. Fellow Am. Soc. Psychical Research; mem. SSB Network, Soc. Quarter Century Wireless Assn., Wireless Pioneers, Assn. Old Crows, Army Signal Corps Assn., Armed Forces Communications and Electronics Assn., Aircraft Owners and Pilots Assn., Tau Epsilon Phi, Ordo Templi Orientis. Home: PO Box 381 Smithtown NY 11787 Office: 76 N Broadway Hicksville NY 11801

KNELSON, NELDA LORAIN RIFE, mental health technician, writer; b. Pierce County, N.D., June 16, 1915; d. Herbert Edward and Katie Marie (Christianson) Rife; m. Henry W. Knelson, Sept. 16, 1931 (dec.); children: John Henry, Nelda May (Mrs. James W. Daley), James Douglas. Student, Sauk Valley Coll., 1968-75; PhD (hon.), U. Internat. Found. Mental Health Sci., 1985. Numerous positions various orgns., Dixon, Ill., 1937-47; survey worker, real estate salesperson Hurd Realtors, Dixon, 1948-50; mental health supr. and technician Dixon Devel. Ctr., 1964-83; lyricist Dixon, 1983—. Author: (poetry) Out of the Inkwel, 1959, Out of the Fire, 1960, Out of The Mist, 1968; (juvenile book) Tiger the Autobiography of a Cat, 1975; songs for audio-tapes: Love Letters in Winter, Montanna Mountain, Bicenntennial, Picture Postcard, 1987. Active Girl Scouts U.S. and Boy Scouts Am.; mem. Lee County (Ill.) Hist. Soc.; pres. Lee County Home Extension, 1957-59; trustee Rep. Presdl. Task Force. Mem. Women in the Arts (charter), World Wildlife Fund., Smithsonian Assocs. Home: 2016 W 1st St Dixon IL 61021

KNEPPER, EUGENE ARTHUR, realtor; b. Sioux Falls, S.D., Oct. 8, 1926; s. Arlie John and May (Crone) K.; B.S.C. in Acctg., Drake U., Des Moines, 1951; m. LaNel Strong, May 7, 1948; children—Kenton Todd, Kristin Rene. Acct., G.L. Yager, pub. acct., Estherville, Iowa, 1951-52; auditor R.L. Meriwether, C.P.A., Des Moines, 1952-53; acct. govt. renegotiation dept. Collins Radio Co., Cedar Rapids, Iowa, 1953-54; head acctg. dept. Hawkeye Rubber Mfg. Co., Cedar Rapids, 1954-56; asst. controller United Fire & Casualty Ins. Co., Cedar Rapids, 1956-58; sales assoc. Equitable Life Assurance Soc. U.S., Cedar Rapids, 1958-59; controller Gaddis Enterprises, Inc., Cedar Rapids, 1959-61; owner Estherville Laundry Co., 1959-64; sales assoc., comml. investment div. mgr. Tommy Tucker Realty Co., Cedar Rapids, 1961-74; owner Real Estate Investment Planning Assocs., Cedar Rapids, 1974—; controlling ptnr. numerous real estate syndicates; cons. in field, fin. speaker; guest lectr. Kirkwood Community Coll., Cedar Rapids, Mt. Mercy Coll., Cedar Rapids, Cornell Coll., Mt. Vernon; creative financing instr. Iowa Real Estate Commn.-Iowa Assn. Realtors. Patron Cedar Rapids Symphony, 1983—, treas., mem. exec. com., bd. dirs.; bd. dirs. Oak Hill-Jackson Outreach Fund, 1970-83, pres., 1973-74; bd. dirs. Consumer Credit Counseling Service Cedar Rapids-Marion Area, 1974-80, pres., 1974-80. Served with USNR, 1945-46. Recipient Storm Manuscript award, 1976. Mem. Nat. Assn. Realtors (state mcpl. legis. com., subcom. on multi-family housing), Iowa Assn. Realtors (pres. comml. investment div. 1973, 80, named life mem.; state legis. com., savs. and loan formation feasibility com., mcpl. and county legis. com.),Nat. Assn. Accountants, Nat. Inst. Real Estate Brokers (membership chmn. Iowa 1972-73, regional v.p.), Real Estate Securities and Syndication Inst. (small group investment council, steering com. 1985, vice chmn. regional officers and state officers devel. com.; gov. Iowa div.), Cedar Rapids Bd. Realtors, Internat. Platform Assn., Internat. Inst. Valuers. Methodist. Clubs: Cedar Rapids Optimist (past chmn. boys work com.); Eastern Iowa Execs. (dir., pres. 1981-82). Contbr. articles to profl. jours. Home: 283 Tomahawk Trail SE Cedar Rapids IA 52403 Office: 1808 IE Tower Cedar Rapids IA 52401

KNEPPERS, LEONARDUS CORNELIS M., company executive; b. Amsterdam, The Netherlands, Apr. 29, 1943; s. Cornelis L. and Tonny (Detering) K.; m. Ineke Admiraal, Aug. 22, 1975. Student, Rotterdam, 1968; Degree in Bus. Adminstrn., Haarlemmermeer Coll., The Netherlands, 1965. Fin. mgr. Amro Bank, Amsterdam, 1968-69; comml. mgr. Tradax/Cargill Group, Amsterdam, 1969-72; v.p. Gen. Cosmetics, Amsterdam, 1972-78; mng. dir. Raaco, Denmark, 1978-79, Rolykit Holland, Minden Germany, Barcelona, Spain, 1979-83; pres. YPMA Netherlands, Zwanenburg, 1983—, Dutch Pottery, The Netherlands, Portugal, YPMA, Antwerp, Belgium; mng. dir. Intertrend Ltd, Amsterdam, 1983—; cons. PT. Tempo, Jakarta, Indonesia, 1975-79, Krka, Ljubliana, Yugoslavia, 1976-78. Patentee in field. Mem. Soc. Kring. Home: Russenweg 22, 1861 JP Bergen The Netherlands Office: Ypma Internat BV, PO Box 114, 1160 AC Zwanenburg The Netherlands

KNESS, RICHARD MAYNARD, tenor; b. Rockford, Ill., July 23, 1937; s. Harry William and Helen Loretta (Curran) Kniess; m. Joann Danielle Grillo, July 23, 1967; 1 son, John Richard; children by previous marriage: Paul Richard, Kristin Elaine. B.A., San Diego State U., 1958. pres. Danielle Maynard Assos., Inc. Appeared with more than 60 opera cos., Europe, U.S., Middle East and Mexico, 1967-78; resident dramatic tenor, Met. Opera, N.Y.C. Opera, San Francisco, San Diego, San Antonio, Seattle, Cin., Hartford, Hawaii, Houston, Boston, Milw., 1967—, appeared with numerous symphony orchs., N.Y.C., Phila., Pitts., Cin., Washington, Atlanta, 1967—, leading dramatic tenor, Met. Opera Assn., N.Y.C., 1977—, co-dir. with wife internat. opera co., The Ambassadores of Opera and Concert World Wide, 1979—; Royal Command Performance for King and Queen of Thailand. Served with U.S. Army, 1958-63. Recipient Grammy award for best classical rec., 1967. Republican. Clubs: Lions, N.Y. Athletic. Office: 240 Central Park S Suite 3N New York NY 10019

KNIEHL, HANS JOACHIM, construction company executive; b. Biberach/Riss, Germany, July 6, 1933; married. Diploma in Internat. Relations, Bologna Ctr., Johns Hopkins U., 1959; diploma Bus. Adminstrn., U. Munich, 1958; MA in Econs., Northwestern U., 1960; PhD in Econs., U. Munich, 1966. Program coordinator planning dept. Ford Co., Cologne, Fed. Republic Germany, 1961-65; gen. adminstrn. dept. mgr. Mauser Werke GmbH, Cologne, 1965-67; advisor Spindler Werke KG, Hilden, Fed. Republic Germany, 1968; dir. mgmt. Dyckerhoff & Widmann AG, Munich, Fed. Republic Germany, 1969; dep. mem. bd. dirs. Dyckerhoff & Widmann AG, 1970-77, mem. bd. dirs., 1977—, chief fin. officer, 1976—. Office: 1 Erdinger Landstrasse, D 8000 Munich 81 Federal Republic of Germany

KNIGHT, DOUGLAS MAITLAND, educational administrator, corporation executive; b. Cambridge, Mass., June 8, 1921; s. Claude Rupert and Fanny Sarah Douglas (Brown) K.; m. Grace Wallace Nichols, Oct. 31, 1942; children: Christopher, Douglas Maitland, Thomas, Stephen. A.B., Yale U., 1942, M.A., 1944, Ph.D., 1946; LL.D. (hon.), Ripon Coll., Knox Coll., Davidson Coll., 1963, U. N.C., 1965, Emory U., 1965, Ohio Wesleyan U., 1970, Center Coll., 1973; L.H.D. (hon.), Lawrence U., 1964, Carleton Coll., 1966; Litt.D. (hon.), St. Norbert Coll., Wake Forest Coll., 1964. Instr. English, Yale U., 1946-47, asst. prof., 1947-53; vis. asst. prof. English, U. Calif.-Berkeley, summer 1949; Morse Research fellow 1951-52; pres. Lawrence Coll., Appleton, Wis., 1954-63, Duke U., Durham, N.C., 1963-69; div. v.p. ednl. devel. RCA, N.Y.C., 1969-71; div. v.p. edn. services RCA, 1971-72, staff v.p. edn. and community relations, 1972-73, cons., 1973-75, pres. RCA Iran, 1971-72, dir., 1971-73; pres. Social Econ. and Ednl. Devel., Inc., 1973—, Questar Corp., 1976—; U.S. del. SEATO Conf. Asian Univ. Pres., Pakistan, 1961; nat. commn. UNESCO, 1965-67; chmn. Nat. Adv. Commn. Libraries, 1966-68; adviser Imperial Orgn. for Social Service of Govt. Iran. Author: Pope and the Heroic Tradition, 1951, (poetry) The Dark Gate, 1971; editor, contbr. The Federal Government and Higher Education, 1960, Iliad and Odyssey, Twickenham edit., 1967, Medical Ventures and the University, 1967, Libraries at Large, Tradition, Innovation and the National Interest, 1970. Former mem. corp. MIT; bd. dirs., chmn. Woodrow Wilson Nat. Fellowship Found.; bd. dirs. Catalyst, 1961-73, Near East Found., 1975-84, Internat. Schs. Services, 1976-82, Solebury Sch., 1975-83; trustee Questar Library of Sci. and Art, 1982—. Mem. Am. Assn. Advancement of Humanities (dir. 1979-83), Phi Beta Kappa. Clubs: Grolier, Century Assn. (N.Y.C.); Cosmos (Washington); Elizabethan, Berzelius (New Haven). Home: RFD 3 Box 278 Stockton NJ 08559 Office: Questar Corp PO Box 59 New Hope PA 18938

KNIGHT, HARRY W., management and financial consultant; b. Sedalia, Mo., Apr. 20, 1909; s. Harry William and Florence (Lay) K.; m. Agnes Berger, Sept. 15, 1934; children: Kirk Lay, Harry William. AB, Amherst Coll., 1931; postgrad., Harvard U. Grad. Sch. Bus. Adminstrn., 1931-32; MA, Northwestern U., 1940. With Harris Trust Co., Chgo., 1932-33; sales adminstr. Bauer & Black, 1934-36; fin. dir. City of Winnetka, Ill., 1937-40; city mgr. Two Rivers, Wis., 1941; chief budget sect. War Prodn. Bd., Washington, 1942; asst. chief program control div., munitions assignment bd. Combined Chiefs of Staff, Washington, 1942-45; fin. dir. UNRRA, 1945; sec. fin. com. 3d Council Meeting UNRRA, London, 1945; v.p. Booz, Allen & Hamilton, Inc., 1945-66; chmn. bd. Knight, Gladieux & Smith, 1966-73, Hillsboro Assocs., Inc., N.Y., 1973—, Cigna/Licony, N.Y.; bd. dirs. Shearson Lehman Appreciation Fund and Shearson Lehman Managed Govt. Fund, Cigna/Licony, N.Y.; past bd. dirs. Burlington Industries, Waldorf Astoria, Foxboro and Menlo Venture Capital Fund, Baucroft Racquet Co., other corp. bds. Chmn. Darien Community Fund Dr., 1954; chmn. career conf. Amherst Coll., 1951-54, nat. chmn. capital program, 1962-65, trustee, 1964-81, trustee emeritus, 1981—; pres. Harvard Bus. Sch. Assn., 1960, chmn. golden anniversary, 1958; chmn. adv. council Sch. Internat. Affairs, Columbia U., 1975-82; chmn. Rep. fin. campaign, Darien, 1952; trustee Com. Econ. Devel., 1968—, Hampshire Coll., 1968-76, Hudson Inst., 1973-78. Served to lt. USNR, 1942-45. Recipient Eminent Service medal Amherst Coll. Mem. Fgn. Policy Assn. (bd. dirs. 1955-70), UN Assn. (past treas., gov., now vice chmn.), Delta Kappa Epsilon. Presbyterian. Clubs: Harvard Bus. Sch. (pres. 1970-71), Univ., Sky (N.Y.C.); Wee Burn Country (Darien, Conn.); Jupiter Island; John's Island Country (Fla.); Pine Valley Golf (N.J.); Sharon Park Country (Menlo Park, Calif.). Home: 110 E 57th St Suite 11-H New York NY 10022 also: 1230 Sharon Park Dr Apt 57 Menlo Park CA 94025 also: 400 Beach Rd Vero Beach FL 32960 Office: Hillsboro Assocs 110 E 57th St Suite 11H New York NY 10022

KNIGHT, NORMAN, broadcast executive; b. July 24, 1924; m. Susannah Howard Andre, Aug. 26, 1944; children: Norman Scott, Randolph Howard, Jeffrey Bryant, Robert Andre. LL.D. (hon.), Northeastern U.; D.B.A. (hon.), Nathaniel Hawthorne Coll.; D.C.S. (hon.), Merrimack Coll.; D.H.L. (hon.), Suffolk U. News reporter, scriptwriter Sta. WEW, WIL, WTMV, 1938-41; Announcer, salesman Sta. WTMV, 1942; announcer, promotion mgr., news reporting continuity dir. Sta. KTHS, 1943; announcer Sta. WMC, 1943; announcer, news writer, reporter, salesman Sta. WMMN, 1944; gen. mgr. Sta. WAJR, 1944-46; Eastern dir. sta. relations MBS, 1946-49; v.p. sales, advt. and promotion Sponsor Publs., Inc., 1950-53; gen. mgr. Sta. WABD (now WNYW-TV), 1953-54; exec. v.p., gen. mgr. Yankee Network div. RKO Teleradio Pictures, Inc. (operating Yankee Network WNAC, WRKO, WNAC-TV); also dir. Yankee Network; v.p. RKO Teleradio Pictures, 1954-60; pres. Yankee div. RKO Teleradio Pictures, Inc., 1957-60, Yankee div. RKO Gen., Inc., 1958-60; treas., chmn. Knight Sales, Inc.; chmn., treas. Knight Radio, Inc. (WEZF, WGIR and WGIR-FM), Knight Broadcasting N.H., Inc. (WHEB and WHEB-FM); pres., treas. Knight Communications Corp. (WTAG and WSRS); chmn., treas. Quality Radio Corp. (WSAR), 1960—; chmn. Caribbean Communications Corp. Established complete TV sta.: pub. affairs film unit which produced Brotherhood Series; TV documentaries, 1953-60; Author: others. The Cause of All Mankind. Radio-TV chmn. United Fund Greater Boston, Mass. Cancer Soc., ARC chpt. Met. Boston, Met. Boston chpt. ARC; bus. chmn. Easter Seal Soc.; radio chmn. Salvation Army; dir. Strawberry Banke; bd. dirs. New Eng. Nephrosis Found.; pres., founder New Eng. Kidney Disease Found.; pres. Norman Knight Charitable Found.; trustee Mass. Bd. Regional Community Colls., Agassiz Village Camps, Crippled Children's Non-Sectarian Fund, Boys and Girls Camps, Inc.; mem. nat. council, exec. com. New Eng. council Boy Scouts Am.; exec. com., dir. Rescue, Inc.; exec. com. The Jimmy Fund; exec. com., trustee Children's Cancer Research Found., Dana Farber Cancer Inst.; mem. fin. com. Com. Econ. Devel.; mem. devel. council Boston U.; mem. pres.'s council Boston Coll.; bd. dirs. Freedoms Found.; also nat. co-chmn. Am. Freedom Center. Recipient Americanism award Am. Heritage Com., 1959; named one of ten outstanding young men Boston Jr. C. of C., 1956, Man of Yr. Italian-Am. Police Assn.; award for contbns. radio and TV industry Alpha Epsilon Rho, 1957; Americanism awards various vets. orgns., 1959-60. Mem. Radio-TV Execs. Sec., Young Pres.'s Orgn., Broadcast Pioneers, AIM, Alpha Epsilon Rho. Clubs: Variety (Boston); Broadcasting Execs. New Eng, 100 of Mass. (co-founder, pres., dir.), 100 of N.H. (life), Univ. Office: 63 Bay State Rd Boston MA 02215

KNIGHT, ROBERT EDWARD, banker; b. Alliance, Nebr., Nov. 27, 1941; s. Edward McKean and Ruth (McDuffee) K.; B.A., Yale U., 1963; M.A., Harvard U., 1965, Ph.D., 1968; m. Eva Sophia Youngstrom, Aug. 12, 1966; Asst. prof. U.S. Naval Acad., Annapolis, Md., 1966-68; lectr. U. Md., 1967-68; fin. economist Fed. Res. Bank of Kansas City (Mo.), 1968-70, research officer, economist, 1971-76, asst. v.p., sec., 1977, v.p., sec., 1978-79; pres. Alliance (Nebr.) Nat. Bank, 1979—, now also chmn.; pres. Robert Knight Assocs., banking and econ. cons., Alliance, 1979—; mem. faculty Stonier Grad. Sch. Banking, 1972—, Colo. Grad. Sch. Banking, 1975-82, Am. Inst. Banking, U. Mo., Kansas City, 1971-79, Prochnow Grad. Sch. Banking, U. Wis. Trustee, 1984-85, Knox Presbyn. Ch., Overland Park, Kans., 1965-69; bd. regents Nat. Comml. Lending Sch., 1980-83; chmn. Downtown Improvement Com., Alliance, 1981-84; trustee U. Nebr. Found.; bd. dirs. Stonier Grad. Sch. Banking, Box Butte County Devel. Commn., Nebr. Com. for Humanities, 1986—; mem. fin. com. United Meth. Ch., Alliance, 1982-85, mem. adminstrv. bd., 1987—; Box Butte County Industrial Devel. Bd., 1987—; mem. Nebr. Com. for the Humanities, 1986—; ambassador Nebr. Diplomats. Woodrow Wilson fellow, 1963-64. Mem. Am. Econ. Assn., Am. Fin. Assn., So. Econ. Assn., Nebr. Bankers Assn. (com. state legis. 1980-81, com. comml. loans and investments 1986-87), Am. Inst. Banking (state com. for Nebr. 1980—), Am. Bankers Assn. (econ. adv. com. 1980-83, community bank leadership council), Western Econ. Assn., Econometric Soc. Clubs: Rotary, Masons. Contbr. articles to profl. jours. Home: Drawer E Alliance NE 69301 Office: Alliance Nat Bank Alliance NE 69301

KNIGHT, ROBERT HUNTINGTON, lawyer; b. New Haven, Feb. 27, 1919; s. Earl Wall and Frances Pierpont (Whitney) K.; m. Rosemary C. Gibson, Apr. 19, 1975; children—Robert Huntington, Jessie Valle, Patricia Whitney, Alice Isabel, Eli Whitney. Grad., Phillips Acad., Andover, Mass., 1936; B.A., Yale, 1940; LL.B., U. Va., 1947. Bar: N.Y. bar 1950. With John Orr Young, Inc. (advt. agy.), 1940-41; asst. prof. U. Va. Law Sch., 1947-49; asso. firm Shearman & Sterling & Wright, N.Y.C., 1949-55; partner Shearman & Sterling & Wright, 1955-58; dep. asst. sec. def. for internat. security affairs Dept. Def., 1958-61; gen. counsel Treasury Dept., 1961-62; ptnr. firm Shearman & Sterling, N.Y.C., 1962-80, sr. ptnr., 1980-85; dep. chmn. Fed. Res. Bank N.Y., 1976-77, chmn., 1978-83; counsel to bd. United Technologies Corp., 1974-85; dir. Owens-Corning Fiberglas Corp., Trans-Can. Pipelines, Brit. Steel Corp., Inc., Brit. Steel Canada, Mercator Co., Howmet Turbine Corp.; mem. Intelsat Arbitration Panel, 1971—. Bd. dirs. Internat. Vol. Services; chmn. bd. dirs. U. Va. Law Sch. Found.; bd. dirs. Asia Found. Served to lt. col. USAAF, 1941-45. Mem. ABA, Fed. Bar Assn., Internat. Bar Assn., Inter-Am. Bar Assn., Assn. of Bar of City of N.Y., N.Y. County Lawyers Assn., Internat. Law Assn., Washington Inst. Fgn. Affairs, Council Fgn. Relations. Clubs: Down Town Assn., Pilgrims, India House, Links, Citicorp, World Trade Ctr., River (N.Y.C.); Army and Navy, Metropolitan, City Tavern (Washington); Round Hill (Greenwich, Conn.); Ocean (Ocean Ridge, Fla.). Home: 12 Knollwood Dr Greenwich CT 06830 also: 570 Park Ave New York NY 10021 also: 6767 N Ocean Blvd Ocean Ridge FL 33435 Office: 599 Lexington Ave New York NY 10022

KNIGHT, VICK (RALPH), JR., educational administrator; b. Lakewood, Ohio, Apr. 6, 1928; s. Vick Ralph and Janice (Higgins) K.; B.S., U. So. Calif., 1952; M.A., Los Angeles State Coll., 1956; postgrad. Whittier Coll., 1959-61, Long Beach State Coll., 1960-61, Calif. State Coll.-Fullerton, 1961-64, Claremont Grad. Sch., 1963-65; Ed.D., Calif. Coast U., 1988; m. Beverly Joyce McKeighan, Apr. 14, 1949 (div. 1973); children—Stephen Foster, Mary Ann; m. 2d, Carolyn Schlee, June 6, 1981. Producer-dir. Here Comes Tom Harmon radio series ABC, Hollywood, Calif., 1947-50; tchr., vice-prin. Ranchito Sch. Dist., Pico Rivera, Calif., 1952-59; prin. Kraemer Intermediate Sch., Placentia, Calif., 1959-64; dir. instructional services Placentia Unified Sch. Dist., 1964-65, asst. supt., 1965-71; program dir. World Vista Travel Service, 1970-72; dir. grad. extension La Verne Coll., 1971-73; v.p. Nat. Gen. West Investments, 1971-74; dir. community relations and devel. Childrens Hosp. of Orange County (Calif.), 1974-84; sr. dir. curriculum and edn. services Elsinore Union High Sch. Dist., Lake Elsinore, Calif., 1985-88; pres. Aristan Assocs.; dir. Key Records, Hollywood. Dist. chmn. Valencia council Boy Scouts Am.; chmn. Cancer Soc. Partners of Ams., also chmn. Sister City Com.; chmn. of Community Chest Drives; chmn. adv. com. Esperenza Hosp.; mem. Educare; hon. life mem. Calif. PTA. Bd. dirs. U. Calif.-Irvine Friends of Library, pres., 1975-77; bd. dirs. Muckenthaler Cultural Groups Found.; chmn. bd. William Claude Fields Found. Served with USN, 1946-48. Named One of Five Outstanding Young Men, Calif. Jr. C. of C., 1959; recipient Distinguished Citizen award Whittier Coll., 1960; Educator of Yr. award Orange County Press Club, 1971; Author and Book award U. Calif., 1973; Children's Lit. award Calif. State U.-Fullerton, 1979; Bronze Pelican award Boy Scouts Am. Mem. Nat. Sch. Pub. Relations Assn. (regional v.p.), U.S. (dir.), Calif. (state v.p.), Pico Rivera (pres.) jr. chambers commerce, Audubon Soc., Western Soc. Naturalists, Calif. Tchrs. Assn., NEA, Internat. Platform Assn., ASCAP, Soc. Children's Book Writers, Authors Guild, Authors League Am., Anti-Slubberdegullion Soc., Bank Dicks, Assn. Hosp. Devel., Art Experience, Good Bears of World, Los Compadres con Libros, Blue Key, Skull and Dagger, Les Amis du Vin, Phi Sigma Kappa, Alpha Delta Sigma, E Clampus Vitus, Theta Nu Epsilon. Kiwanian (pres.), Mason. Club: West Atwood Yacht (commodore). Writer weekly Nature Notebook newspaper columns, 1957—; fine arts editor Placentia Courier. Editor curriculum guides: New Math., Lang. Arts, Social Scis., Pub. Relations, Biol. Sci. Substitute Tchrs. Author: (ecology textbooks) It's Our World; It's Our Future; It's Our Choice; Snakes of Hawaii; Earle the Squirrel; Night the Crayons Talked; My Word!; Send for Haym Salomon!; Joby and the Wishing Well; Twilight of the Animal Kingdom; A Tale of Twos; Who's Zoo; A Navel Salute; Friend or Enema?; also math. instrn. units; contbr. articles to various jours. Home: PO Box 4664 Canyon Lake CA 92380

KNIGHT, WILLIAM WILTON, JR., entrepreneur, investor, consultant; b. Emmettsburg, Iowa, Jan. 24, 1922; s. William Wilton and Ellen (Peterson) K.; m. Helen Patten, Dec. 12, 1948 (div. Dec. 1974); 1 child, Karen Lynn; 1 stepchild, Charles Crane; m. Jean Stegall, Nov. 1, 1980. Diploma, Lyons Twp. Jr. Coll., 1941; BS, U. Ill., 1947. Licensed comml. pilot FAA. Service engr. Internat. Harvester Co., Melrose Park, Ill., 1947-48; sales engr., v.p. Patten Industries, Elmhurst, Ill., 1948-83; pvt. practice investment cons. Palos Heights, Ill., 1983—. Mem. adv. bd. Am. Security Council. Served to maj. USMCR, 1942-59, PTO, Korea. Decorated D.F.C. (2) Air medal (7). Mem. Marine Corps Res. Officer's Assn., Res. Officer's Assn. U.S., Mil. Order of World Wars, U. Ill. Alumni Assn., Rep. Nat. Com. (sustaining), Air Force Assn., Aircraft Owners and Pilots Assn., NRA, Am. Legion. Republican. Protestant.

KNIGHTON, GEORGE WILLIAM, nuclear engineer; b. Wilmington, Del., July 9, 1926; s. Isaac L. and Isabel D. (Dobson) K.; B.M.E., U. Del., 1951; m. Ingrid Helene Schneider, Apr. 25, 1953; children—Denise, Donna, Karen, Brian, Janine. Chief condenser design and proposal sect. Foster Wheeler Corp., N.Y.C., 1951-55; sr. mech. engr. Alco Products, Inc., Schenectady, N.Y., 1956-57, project mgr., 1957-60; chief mech. engring. br. U.S. Corps Engrs., Ft. Belvoir, Va., 1960-66, dep. chief engring. div., 1966-69; chmn. Army Reactor Health and Safety Commn., Dept. Army, Washington, 1969-70; project mgr. U.S. AEC, 1971-72; chief environ. projects br. NRC, Bethesda, Md., 1972-78, chief environ. evaluation, 1978-80, chief research and standards coordination br., 1980-82, chief licensing br., 1983-85, dir. project directorate, 1985—. Chmn. bd. edn. Lutheran Weekday Sch., Alexandria, Va., 1966-70; pres. local PTA, 1963-64, sec., 1970-71; pres. Citizens Assn., New Alexandria, Va., 1968-69. Served with AUS, 1944-46. Mem. ASME (vice chmn. nuclear and spl. cycles com. 1974-75), ASTM (sec. E10.02 1972-79, chmn. task group reactor vessel inplace annealing 1970-74). Lutheran (mem. council 1970-71). Home: 6417 10th St Alexandria VA 22307 Office: 7920 Norfolk Ave Bethesda MD 20114

KNILL, WILLIAM SCOTT, newspaper editor; b. Birmingham, West Midlands, Eng., May 28, 1950; s. Edward Francis and Maywa (Stevenson) K.; m. Joyce Gillian Ross, June 5, 1971 (separated); children: Hannah, Faye. Grad., Richmond Coll., Sheffield, Eng., 1968. Reporter Dudley Herald, Worcestershire, Eng., 1967-72; dist. reporter County Express, Dudley and Brierley Hill, West Midlands, Eng., 1972-80; chief reporter County Express, Stourbridge, West Midlands, 1980-82; news editor Stourbridge News, 1982-84; editor Halesowen News & County Express, West Midlands, 1984—. Author: (play) In Brutal Dreams, 1985. Recipient Newspaper Design award Assn. Free Newspapers, 1986, Gold award Dr. Barnardo's Orgn., 1986. Mem. Brit. Homeo. Assn. Buddhist. Home: 91 Enville Rd, Kinver near Stourbridge England Office: Halesowen News, 33 Queensway, Halesowen, West Midlands England

KNOBBS, CLIVE GRAHAM, mining company executive; b. Stockport, Eng., Dec. 28, 1941; s. Henry Knobbs; m. Valerie Joan Perryman, Jan. 19, 1970; 2 children. B. Commerce, U. S. Africa; M.B.L., BSc. Gen. mgr. Duvha Opencast, 1978-79; mng. dir. Rand Mines Chrome Div., 1980-81, Harmony G.M. Co., 1981-82; dep. chair Gold and Uranium Div. Rand Mines (Mining and Services) Ltd., 1982-83, chair, 1983—; chair Blyvooruitzicht Gold Mining Co. Ltd., Dbn. Roodepoort Deep Ltd., E. Rand Proprietary Mines Ltd., Harmony Gold Mining Co. Ltd., La Riviera (Pvt.) Ltd., Pan African Exploration Syndicate (Pvt.) Ltd., Rand Mines Milling and Mining Co. Ltd.; bd. dirs. Pretoria Portland Cement Ltd., Ch. of Mines Services (Pvt.) Ltd., Crown Mines Ltd., Doornfontein Gold Mining Co. Ltd., Geotest (Pvt.) Ltd., Internat. Gold Corp. Ltd., Mine Labour Orgns. (NRC) Ltd., Nuclear Fuels Corp. of S. Africa (Pvt.) Ltd., Rand Refinery Ltd., St. Helena Gold Mines Ltd., The Ch. of Mines Bldg. Co. Ltd., The Gold Mine Mus. (Pvt.) Ltd., The Employment Bur. of Africa Ltd., The Rand Mut. Assurance Co. Ltd., Transvaal Consolidated Land and Exploration Co. ltd., Western Deep Levels Ltd.; alt. dir. Ch. of Mines Tng. Coll., Vaal Reefs Exploration and Mining Co. Ltd. Clubs: Rand, Ch. of Mines Sports, Bedfordview Country. Home: PO Box 62370, Marshalltown 2107, Republic of South Africa Office: Blyvooruitzicht Gold Mining Co, 63 Fox St, Johannesburg 2001, Republic of South Africa *

KNOEBEL, BETTY LOU, food service company executive; b. Hobart, Ind., July 12, 1931; d. Frank O. and Louise C. (Sohn) Burnett; m. F.C. Knoebel, Apr. 27, 1974. Grad., Sch. X-Ray, Methodist Hosp., Gary, Ind., 1950; student, Ind. U., 1952-53. X-ray technician, then various secretarial positions; X-ray technician, asst. adminstr. Melissa Meml. Hosp., Holyoke, Colo.; dir., adminstrv. asst. Nobel/Sysco, Inc., Denver, 1982—; dir. Gen. Mgmt. Corp. Grantee Am. Cancer Soc., 1949-50. Mem. Profl. Women's Assn., Am. Soc. X-Ray Technicians, Colo.-Wyo. Restaurant Assn. (pres. ladies aux. 1978-79). Republican.

KNOEDLER, REINHARD, physicist; b. Stuttgart, Ger., Dec. 23, 1940; s. Walter and Kaethe (Heller) K.; diplom physiker, U. Stuttgart, 1967, dr.rer.nat., 1970; m. Waltraud Ebert, children—Christoph, Sibylle, Andreas, Stefanie. Physicist, Max Planck Inst. Metallforschung, 1967-70; group leader electrochem. tech. Battelle Inst., Frankfurt Main, 1971-80; sr. scientist Asea Brown, Boveri Corp. Research, AG, Heidelberg, 1980-87, group leader, 1987—, on leave at Argonne (Ill.) Nat. Lab., 1981. Mem. Electrochem. Soc. Author papers in field; patentee high energy density batteries. Office: Asea Brown Boveri, Corp Research, 69 Heidelberg Federal Republic of Germany

KNOLL, SIMON, accountant; b. Cologne, Germany, Oct. 5, 1934; came to U.S., 1939, naturalized, 1958; s. Herman and Betty (Feldman) K.; m. Anna Feldman, June 10, 1956 (div. June 1973); children—Sharon, Lawrence, Alan; m. 2d, Judith Steinberg, Nov. 2, 1975; children—Elon, Joseph, David, Daniel. B.B.A., Baruch Coll., 1956. C.P.A., N.Y. Various acctg. firms, 1956-60; staff Henry Warner & Co., N.Y.C., 1960-70, ptnr., 1970-87; ptnr. Knoll, Peller & Co., N.Y.C., 1987—. Mem. Am. Inst. C.P.A.'s, N.Y. State Soc. C.P.A.'s. Mensa. Office: Knoll Peller & Co 225 W 34th St New York NY 10122

KNOLLE, MARY ANNE ERICSON, human resources company executive; b. Kilgore, Tex., Jan. 7, 1941; d. Evert Eric and Frances Leone (Scott) Ericson; children by previous marriage: Clay Claflin, Sunny Claflin; m. John W. Knolle, Mar. 14, 1980; children: Sara Anne, Evelyn. BA, North Tex. State U., 1962; MA, U. Tex., 1968; postgrad., UCLA, 1964-66, U. Houston, 1974-76. Editor co. publs. Gt. S.W. Life Ins. Co., 1962; prof. U. Balt., 1968, Miami (Fla.) Dade Coll., 1968, Savannah (Ga.) State Coll., 1969, U. Houston, 1972-76; dir. pub. relations Alvin (Tex.) Coll., 1970-72; founder, pres. Panorama Programs, Houston, 1972-76; coordinator mgmt. devel. tng. Brown & Root, Inc., Houston, 1970-79; div. founder, mgr. mgmt. and orgnl. devel. systems Diversified Human Resources Group, Inc., Houston, 1979—; founder, pres. Panorama Mgmt. Inst., Houston, 1979—; founder, pres. Panorama Cons., 1980—; cons. moot ct. U. Tex. Law Sch., 1965—. Judge regional speech contest Houston Jaycees. Recipient Blockbuster award United Way, 1979. Mem. Am. Soc. Tng. and Devel., Houston C. of C. (chmn. edn. com.), Alpha Delta Pi (pres. alumnae). Presbyterian. Club: Houston Indoor Tennis. Office: 12307 Broken Arrow Houston TX 77024

KNOORS, JOSEPH, manufacturing company executive; b. Berg a/d Maas, Limburg, The Netherlands, June 2, 1932; m. Mia Coenen, Nov. 24, 1960; children: Karin, Frans. BS in Engring., Higher Tech. Edn., Heerlen, The Netherlands, 1954. Service mgr. Melotte B.V., Maastricht, The Netherlands, 1954-56, sales mgr., 1956-59, mng. dir., 1960—; mng. dir. Hayward Tyler Water Indsl. Products, Luton and Keighley, England, 1978—, Hayward Tyler Process Industry, East Kilbridge, Eng., 1986—. Roman Catholic. Office: Melotte BV/Hayward Tyler Ltd, Fregatweg 50, 6222 NZ Maastricht Limburg, The Netherlands

KNORR, BETTY JEWEL BENKERT (MRS. NEIL MCLEAN KNORR), naturalist; b. Summit, N.J., Aug. 10, 1928; d. William R. and Amelia (Kreutzer) Benkert; grad. high sch.; Ph.D. (hon.), Hamilton State U., 1973, Colo. State Christian Coll., 1973; m. Neil McLean Knorr, Dec. 13, 1946. Licensed bird bander Fish and Wildlife Service, U.S. Dept. Interior, 1957—; banded over 50,000 wild birds of 182 different species; spl. ornithol. research on shorebirds, hummingbirds and blackbirds; other varied research in bird banding; established extensive wildflower preserve and rhododendron gardens at home; engaged in propagation rare native wildflowers donating same to public arboretums, preserves and sanctuaries; vol. tchr., cons. on conservation and nature study, 1948—; tchr. Brookdale Coll.; active many local, state, nat. conservation issues; responsible for sav. wilderness area threatened with destruction and now preserved as part of Cheesequake State Park; organizer nation-wide Project S.N.A.P. to salvage threatened native plants and replant them for ednl. and civic purposes. Active Girl Scouts U.S.A., 1938—; counselor, cons. Boy Scouts Am., 1960—. Mem. Amateur Organists Assn. Internat., Monmouth, Shore organ socs., Eastern Bird Banding Assn., Nat., N.J. Audubon socs., Torrey Bot. Club, Am. Fern Soc. Home: Rural Route 2 Box 459 Easy St Howell NJ 07731

KNORR, ROBERT OTTO, JR., general manager; b. N.Y.C., July 15, 1940; s. Robert O. and Mary (Novhard) K.; B.S. in B.A., Rutgers U., 1962; m. Madeline Nicholes, July 29, 1967; 1 dau., Madeline Lee. Vice pres. fin. Bowmar Ali, Acton, Mass., 1973-75; v.p. fin. Fram Corp., Providence, 1975-79, v.p. mfg., 1980; v.p. mgmt. cons. Auto group Bendix Corp., Southfield, Mich., 1980-82; sr. v.p. ops. Purolator Products, Rahway, N.J., 1982-85; sr. v.p. Sci. Mgmt. Corp., Basking Ridge, N.J., 1986—. Mem. Fin. Execs. Inst. Home: 35 Timberline Way Watchung NJ 07060 Office: Sci Mgmt Corp PO Box 0600 Basking Ridge NJ 07920

KNOTT, THEODORE KENNETH, insurance company executive; b. Niles, Mich., Apr. 8, 1935; s. Kenneth Edward and Mildred Louise K.; B.A., Kalamazoo Coll., 1957; m. Gail Kaiser, Sept. 7, 1957; children—Kimberly, Brett, Leslie, Heather, Kurt. Field rep. Aetna Life Ins. Co., 1961; ins. agt. Charles A. Boyer Inc., Manistee, Mich., 1962-67; pres. Boyer Agy., Manistee, 1967-81, Niagara Ins. Co., B.W.I.; pres., dir. First Ohio Fin. Corp., Celina, Ohio, pres., founder Brokers Placement Inc., Lima, 1988—; exec. v.p. Ohio Reins. Corp.; group v.p. Celina Fin. Corp.; dir. Security Nat. Bank, Manistee, Four Point Travel, Inc., Internat. Mgmt. Co. Past pres. Econ. Devel. Corp., Indsl. Devel. Corp.; bd. dirs. Heartland Syndicate, N.Y. Ins. Exchange. Served with CIC, U.S. Army, 1958-61. Recipient Boss of Yr. award Manistee Jaycees, 1970. Mem. Ind. Ins. Agts. Assn., Profl. Ins. Agts. Assn. Republican. Lutheran. Lodge: Rotary (past pres.). Home: 77 Hawthorn Dr Lima OH 45805 Office: 545 W Market St REET Suite 303 Lima OH 45801

KNOTT, WILEY EUGENE, customer support manager; b. Muncie, Ind., Mar. 18, 1938; s. Joseph Wiley and Mildred Viola (Haxton) K.; B.S. in Elec. Engring., Tri-State U., 1963; postgrad. Union Coll., 1970-73, Ga. Coll., 1987—; 1 child, Brian Evan. Assoc. aircraft engr. Lockheed-Ga. Co., Marietta, 1963-65; tech. publs. engr. Gen. Electric Co., Pittsfield Mass., 1965-77, sr. publs. engr., 1977-79, group leader, 1967-79; specialist engr. Boeing Mil. Airplane Co., Wichita, Kans., 1979-81, sr. specialist engr., 1981-84, logistics mgr., 1984-85, customer support mgr., 1985—; part-time bus. cons., 1972—. Active Jr. Achievement, 1978-79, Am. Security Council, 1975—, Nat. Republican Senatorial Com., 1979-86 , Nat. Rep. Congressional Com., 1979-87, Rep. Nat. Com., 1979-87 , Rep. Presdl. Task Force, 1981-86, Joint Presdl./Congl. Steering Com., 1982-86, Rep. Polit. Action Com., 1979-86. state advisor U.S. Congl. Adv. Bd., 1981-86; adviser Jr. Achievement, 1978-79. Served with AUS, 1956-59. Mem. Am. Def. Preparedness Assn. (life), Am. Mgmt. Assn., Soc. Logistics Engrs., U.S. Golf Assn. PGA Inner Circle, Fraternal Order Police (assoc.), Air Force Assn. (life), Assn. Old Crows, Boeing Mgmt. Club, Nat. Audubon Soc. Methodist.

KNOTTENBELT, HANS JORGEN, economist; b. Bandung, Netherlands, July 19, 1934; s. Anthony and Gertrud Annemarie (Rafflorze) K.; D.Econs., Erasmus U., Rotterdam, Netherlands, 1963; m. Marianne van Berkel, May 21, 1963; children—Karen A.E., Alexander. Researcher, Netherlands Econ. Inst., Rotterdam, 1960-61; sr. cons. Bakkenist, Spits & Co., Rotterdam, 1963-66; product mgr. J. van Nelle Co., Rotterdam, 1966-69; v.p. Netherlands Nat. Tourist Office, The Hague, 1969-74; partner firm Custom Mgmt. B.V., Utrecht, Netherlands, 1974-85; pres. Koninklijke Vereenigde Tapijtfabrieken N.V., Moordrecht, Netherlands 1985-88; ptnr. custom mgmt. firm U. Utrecht, 1988—; cons., lectr. in field. Served with Royal Dutch Marines, 1955-57. Named knight Italian Order of Merit, 1972. Mem. Alumni Assn. Erasmus U. (pres. 1976-79), Netherlands Mgmt. Assn., Netherlands Inst. Mktg., Mars and Mercurius. Club: Rotary. Liberal.

KNOTTS, GLENN R(ICHARD), university administrator; b. East Chicago, Ind., May 16, 1934; s. V. Raymond and Opal Ione (Alexander) K. B.S., Purdue U., 1956, M.S., 1960, Ph.D., 1968; M.S., Ind. U., 1964; Dr. Med. Sci. (hon.), Union Coll., 1975; Sc.D. (hon.), Ricker Coll., 1975. Mem. profl. staff Bapt. Meml. Hosp., San Antonio, 1957-60; instr. chemistry San Antonio Coll., 1958-60; adminstrv. asst. AMA, Chgo., 1960-61, research assoc., 1961-62, dir. advt. eval., div. sci. activities, 1963-69; exec. dir. Am. Sch. Health Assn., Kent, Ohio, 1969-72; vis. disting. prof. health sci. Kent State U., 1969-72, prof., mem. grad. faculty dept. allied health scis., 1972-75, coordinator grad. studies and research, 1975; editor-in-chief, prof. med. journalism U. Tex. System Cancer Ctr. M.D. Anderson Hosp. and Tumor Inst., Houston, 1975-85, head dept. med. info. and publs., 1975-79, dir. div. ednl. resources, 1979-85; dir. devel. U. Tex. Health Sci. Ctr. at Houston, 1985—; prof. U. Tex. Grad. Sch. Biomed. Scis., 1983—; adj. prof. dept. journalism Coll. Communications U. Tex.-Austin, 1984—; vis. prof. health edn. Madison Coll., Va., summer 1965, Union Coll., Ky., summers 1965, 66, 69; vis. prof. health edn. Utah State U., summer 1965; vis. lectr. Ind. U., 1965-66; vis. lectr. pharmacology Purdue U., 1968-69; vis. prof. Pahlavi U. Med. Sch., Iran, summer 1970; adj. prof. allied health scis. Kent State U., 1975—; prof. dept. biomed. communications U. Tex. Sch. Allied Health Scis., Houston, 1976—; prof. dept. behavioral scis. U. Tex. Sch. Pub. Health, 1977—; cons. health scis. communications, 1969—; pres. Health Scis. Inst., 1973—; mem. exec. com. Internat. Union Sch. and Univ. Health and Medicine, Paris, 1969-72. Co-author various texts and filmstrips on health sci.; contbr. numerous articles to profl. jours.; cons. editor: Clin. Pediatrics, 1971—; contbg. editor: Annals of Allergy, 1972—; exec. editor: Cancer Bull., 1976-85; mem. numerous editorial bds. Bd. dirs. Med. Arts Pub. Found., Houston, 1977-80, Art League of Houston, 1986—; mem. adv. bd. World Meetings Inc., 1971—, bd. trustees Mus. Art Am. West, 1987—; trustee Houston Mus. Natural Sci., 1987—. Served with U.S. Army, 1956-58. Recipient Gold medal French-Am. Allergy Soc., 1973. Fellow Am. Pub. Health Assn., Am. Sch. Health Assn. (mem. exec. com. 1968-72, editor Jour. Sch. Health 1975-76 Disting. Service award 1973), Am. Inst. Chemists, Royal Soc. Health; mem. Internat. Union Health Edn., AAHPER, Am. Acad. Pharm. Scis., Am. Med. Writers Assn., Am. Pharm. Assn., AAUP, Am. Chem. Soc., AAAS, AMA, Purdue U. Alumni Assn., Ind. U. Alumni Assn., Union Coll. Alumni Assn., Ricker Coll. Alumni Assn., Sigma Xi, Rho Chi, Sigma Delta Chi, Eta Sigma Gamma, Phi Delta Kappa, Kappa Psi. Republican. Presbyterian. Clubs: Marines Meml. (San Francisco); Univ. Faculty; Doctors, Warwick (Houston). Lodge: Rotary. Home: 2600 Bellefontaine Houston TX 77025 Office: U Tex Health Sci Ctr PO Box 20036 Houston TX 77225

KNOUSE, CHARLES ALLISON, osteopathic physician, pathology educator; b. Plattsburg, Mo., Mar. 14, 1921; s. Charles Albert and Alice Susan May (Trout) K.; m. Iris Christine Ehrenreich, May 21, 1944; children—Thea Christine Knouse Price, Charles Allison, Karen Elizabeth Knouse Brungardt, John Arthur. Grad., Emmettsburgh Jr. Coll., Iowa, 1941; student, U. Chgo., 1941-42; D.O., Kansas City Coll. Osteopathy and Surgery, 1949. Diplomate Nat. Bd. Examiners Osteo. Physicians. Gen. practice medicine Howard City, Mich., 1950-55; asst. to editor Am. Osteo. Assn., Chgo., 1955; gen. practice Seattle, 1956; resident Hosps. Kansas City Coll. Osteopathy and Surgery, 1958-61; mem. faculty Kirksville Coll. Osteopathy and Surgery, Mo., 1961-65; mem. staff Kirksville Osteo. Hosp. 1961-65; prof. pathology, chmn. dept. U. Health Scis., Kansas City, Mo., 1965-68; chmn. dept. pathology Meml. Osteo. Hosp., York, Pa., 1968-78; prof. pathology Ohio U. Coll. Osteo. Medicine, 1978—, dir. lab. services; gen. clinician Ohio U. Osteo. Med. Ctr. (formerly Ohio U. Med. Assocs. Clinic); mem. vis. faculty W.Va. Sch. Osteo. Medicine, 1975-78, U. New Eng. Coll. Osteo Medicine; cons. pathology Nat. Bd. Examiners for Osteo. Physicians and Surgeons. Contbr. articles to osteo. jours. Moderator, chmn. bd. elders 1st Christian Ch., Athens, Ohio. Served with U.S. Mcht. Marine, 1942-44, U.S. Army, 1944-46, ETO. U. Chgo. scholar, 1941. Fellow Am. Osteo. Coll. Pathologists; mem. Am. Osteo. Assn. (lab. surveyor hosp. accreditation, editorial cons. pubs.), Ohio Osteo. Assn., Am. Acad. Osteopathy, AAUP, Am. Assn. Automotive Medicine, Am. Med. Writers Assn., Physicians for Social Responsibility, Psi Sigma Alpha (pres. Grand Council). Mem. Christian Ch. (Disciples of Christ). Home: 85 S May Ave Athens OH 45701 Office: Ohio U Coll Osteo Medicine Grovesnor Hall Athens OH 45701

KNOWLER, LLOYD A., actuary, statistician, educator; b. Hedrick, Iowa, Jan. 30, 1908; s. C.C. and Louise (Wood) K.; B.A., State U. Iowa, 1932, M.S., 1934, Ph.D., 1937; m. Faith M. Stamler, June 30, 1935; children—Mary Louise (Mrs. Murray Adelman), William C. Grad. asst. math., astronomy State U. Iowa, 1932-34, 1935-37, mem. faculty, 1939—, prof. dept. preventive medicine and environ. health, 1946—, prof., chmn. dept. math. and astronomy, 1946-59, prof. dept. math., 1959-65, prof. div. math. scis., 1965—, staff short courses quality control by statis. methods, 1944—; statis. quality control adviser with ICA, Bur. Census in India, 1960-61; instr. math. Hunter Coll., 1937-39; staff short courses, quality control by statis. methods U. Iowa, 1944, Northwestern U., 1945, Purdue U., 1946-59, 62-65, 68-75, U. Ill., 1948-59, 62-65, 68-75, U. Colo., 1950, 51, 53, UCLA, 1956-59, 62-64, U. Mich., 1966; actuary Iowa State Old Age Assistance Commn., 1934-35; cons. actuary, cons. statis. quality control indsl. firms, govt. agys. Bd. dirs. Blue Shield Iowa, 1966—, exec. com., 1968-85, treas., 1978—; mem. joint mgmt. com. Blue Cross and Blue Shield, 1973-85, investment com., 1974—, also chmn. mgmt. liaison com., 1982-84, chmn. mgmt. evaluation and compensation com., 1985-85; trustee Tchrs. Ins. and Annuity Assn., 1958-62; actuarial sci. and statis. cons.; del. Internat. Conf. on Vol. Health Service. Treas., clk. City of University Heights, 1951-53, clk., 1954-60, 62—, investment officer, 1974-75. Recipient Disting. Alumni Achievement award State U. Iowa, 1979; recipient numerous honors and spl. recognitions; registered profl. engr.; cert. quality engr. and reliability engr. Fellow Am. Soc. Quality Control (founding mem.; editorial bd. 1946-54, 60-65; chmn. exam. com. 1985—; Shewhart Medal com. 1950-53, 56-59, chmn. 1964-66; Edward J. Oakley award 1968; reporter panel 1967—, bio-med. steering com. 1967—, publs. mgmt. bd. 1968—; Shewhart medal 1962; 3 scholarships named in his honor State U. Iowa sect.), award by Gov. Branstad of Iowa in recognition of contbns. regarding quality control, 1987, Iowa Acad. Sci. (mng. editor 1971-74), Internat. Actuarial Assn., Am. Soc. Pension Actuaries (ednl. cons. 1971—, ednl. com. 1972-83, dir. 1978-83; cert. pension cons.; enrolled actuary); mem. Am. Math. Soc., Math. Assn. Am. (chmn. Iowa sect. 1952-53), Ops. Research Soc. Quad Cities, Midwestern Actuarial Forum, Am. Acad. Actuaries, Inst. Math. Stats., Am. Soc. Engring. Edn., Biometric Soc., AAUP (sec.-treas. U. Iowa 1946-47, pres. 1952-53), Am. Statis. Assn., Am. Pension Conf., Central Assn. Sci., Math. Tchrs., Am. Soc. Engring. Edn., Soc. Advancement Edn., Phi Beta Kappa (sec.-treas. Hunter Coll. 1938-39, pres. U. Iowa chpt. 1948-49), Sigma Xi (treas. State U. Iowa chpt. 1942-44), Phi Mu Upsilon, Theta Xi (dir. Xi chpt. alumni assn. 1969—). Clubs: Rotary (treas. Iowa City 1968-69, dir. 1969-74, pres. 1973-74, gov. dist. 600 1980-81), Rotary Wheel (v.p. 1982-83, pres. 1983-84, dir. 1984-87); Triangle (Iowa City). Co-author: Basic Skills in Mathematics, 1952; Quality Control Training Manual; Quality Control by Statistical Methods, 1969; contbr. articles actuarial sci. and stats. to profl. jours., reports, pamphlets, manuals. Home: 207 Golfview Ave Iowa City IA 52240

KNOWLES, COLIN GEORGE, academic administrator; b. Southport, Eng., Apr. 11, 1939; s. George Williams and Isabelle (Houghton) K.; m. Mary B. D. Wickliffe, 1961 (dissolved 1980); children: Emma, Samantha; m. Lesley Carolyn Angela Johannes, 1981; 1 child, Marguerite. MInstM, U.K., 1966, FBIM, 1975, FRSA, 1975, MPRISA, 1983; grad., Fontainbleau U., France, 1980; APR, 1987. Co. sec., head pub. affairs Imperial Tobacco Ltd., London, 1960-80; gov. Clayesmore Sch., Dorset, Eng., 1975-85; dir., chmn. Assn. for Bus. Sponsorship of Arts, 1975-84; dir. The Bristol Hippodrome Trust, 1977-81, The Bath Archeol. Trust, 1978-81, The Palladian Trust, 1979-82; chmn. Griffin Assocs. Ltd., London, 1980-83, Concept Communications Ltd., Johannesburg, 1983-84; dir. TWS Pub. Relations Ltd., Johannesburg, 1984-85; dir. pub. relations U. Bophuthatswana, Mmabatho, Southern Africa, 1985—. Mem. Chancellor Duchy of Lancaster's Com. Honour on Bus. and Arts, 1980-81; dir. English Sinfonia Orch. and Midland Sinfonia Concert Soc. Ltd., 1972-80. Named Freeman, City of London, Liveryman, Worshipful Co. of Tobacco Pipe Makers and Tobacco Blenders, 1973, Officer of the Venerable Order of St. John, 1977. Clubs: Carlton, M.C.C. (London). Office: U Bophuthatswana Office Pub Rels, Post Bag X2046 Mafikeng, Republic of Bophuthatswana 8670, Southern Africa

KNOWLES, RICHARD JAMES ROBERT, medical physicist, educator, consultant; b. McPherson, Kans., Aug. 2, 1943; s. Richard E. and Pauline H. (Worland) K.; m. Stephanie R. Closter, May 14, 1970; 1 child, Guenevere Regina. BS, St. Louis U., 1965; MS, Cornell U., 1969; PhD, Poly. U., N.Y., 1979. Diplomate Am. Bd. Sci. in Nuclear Medicine, Am. Bd. Radiology. Chief med. physicist L.I. Coll. Hosp., Bklyn., 1977-81; dir. radiation physics lab. Downstate Med. ctr., Bklyn., 1981-82; sr. med. physicist N.Y. Hosp.-Cornell U. Med. ctr., N.Y.C., 1982—. Author: Quality Assurance and Image Artifacts in Magnetic Resonance Imaging, 1988; contbr. articles to profl. jours. Mem. Am. Phys. Soc., Soc. Nuclear Medicine, Health Physics Soc., Am. Assn. Physicists in Medicine, N.Y. Acad. Scis., Soc. Magnetic Resonance in Medicine, Sigma Xi. Office: NY Hosp-Cornell Med Ctr 525 E 68th St New York NY 10021

KNOWLTON, WILLIAM ALLEN, business executive, consultant; b. Weston, Mass., June 19, 1920; s. Frank Warren and Isabelle (Riese) K.; m. Marjorie Adams Downey, Nov. 27, 1943; children: William Allen, Davis Downey, Timothy Riese, Hollister Knowlton Petraeus. BS, U.S. Mil. Acad., 1943; MA, Columbia U., 1957; grad., Nat. War Coll., 1960; LLD (hon.), Akron U., 1972. Commd. 2d lt. U.S. Army, 1943, advanced through grades to gen., 1976; with 7th Armored Div., World War II, Army Gen. Staff, 1947-49, SHAPE, France, 1951-54; assoc. prof. social scis. U.S. Mil. Acad., 1955-58, supt., 1970-74; bn. comdr. 3d Armored Cav. Regt., 1958-59; mil. attache Tunisia, 1961-63; brig. comdr. Ft. Knox, Ky., 1963-64; with Office Chief Staff U.S. Army, 1964-65; mil. asst. to spl. asst. to sec. and dept. sec. def. Office Sec. Def., 1965-66; sec. Joint Staff, dir. pacification support, dep. asst. chief staff for civil ops. revolutionary devel. support U.S. Mil. Assistance Command, Vietnam, 1966-67; asst. div. comdr. 9th Inf. Div., Vietnam, 1968; sec. gen. staff Office Chief Staff U.S. Army, 1968-70; chief staff hdqrs. U.S. European Command, Stuttgart, W.Ger., 1974-76; comdr. Allied Land Forces Southeastern Europe, Izmir, Turkey, 1976-77; U.S. rep. NATO Mil. Com., Brussels, 1977-80; ret. 1980; cons. on internat. affairs and strategic intelligence R & D Assocs., Marina del Rey, Calif.; sr. assoc. Burdeshaw Assocs. Ltd., 1981—; dir. Aeronca Inc., 1982-86, Chubb Corp., Fed. Ins. Co., Vigilant Ins. Co.; sr. fellow Inst. Higher Def. Studies, Nat. Def. U., 1984—. Contbr.: Ency. Americana and nat. mags. Trustee Davis and Elkins Coll., 1982 . Decorated Def. D.S.M., Army D.S.M., Silver Star with 2 oak leaf clusters, Legion of Merit with oak leaf cluster, D.F.C., Bronze Star with V device, Air medal with 9 oak leaf clusters, Army Commendation medal with oak leaf cluster, knight comdr cross Order Merit W.Ger., officer Legion of Honor France, Vietnamese Nat. Order and Gallantry Cross with palm; recipient George Washington Honor medal Freedoms Found., Valley Forge, 1957-58; named Hon. Pres. Regiment, 40th armor Berlin. Mem. Am. Mil. Inst., 7th Armored Div. Assn. (hon. pres.), Am. Mgmt. Assns., Nat. Assn. Corp. Dirs., Council Fgn. Relations, Acad. Polit. Sci., Soc. Mayflower Descs., Washington Inst. Fgn. Affairs, S.R., Soc. Colonial Wars. Clubs: University (N.Y.C.); Army and Navy (Washington). Home: 4520 4th Rd N Arlington VA 22203

KNOX, JANE WEATHERLY M., oil company executive; b. Scott County, Va., Mar. 8, 1911; d. Joseph Preston and Ida Weatherly; m. Samuel A. Knox, Mar. 1, 1945; children: Samuel A., Joseph Morton, Jimmy Morton (dec.). Student, Clinch Valley Coll.; D in Bus. (hon.), Internat. U. Found., 1987. Mgr. Sears Roebuck Co., Bristol, Tenn., 1940-50; pres. Knox and Sons Oil Co., Wise, Tenn., 1960—, chmn. bd., 1979—. Named First Lady of Yr. Alpha Omega chpt. Beta Sigma Phi., 1987. Mem. Va. Jobbers Assn. (state dir.), DAR (state chmn.), Bus. and Profl. Women's Club (pres.). Presbyterian. Office: PO Box 397 Wise VA 24293

KNOX-DAVIES, PETER SIDNEY, plant pathologist, educator; b. Elandsputte, Transvaal, South Africa, Dec. 7, 1929; s. Edwin Probart and Maud Frances (Thorpe) K.; B.Sc., U. Natal, 1951; M.S., U. Wis., Ph.D., 1959; m. Laetitia Potgieter, Dec. 20, 1972; children—John, Evan, Ula. Lectr., U. Natal, 1951-59, sr. lectr., 1959; sr. lectr. U. Stellenbosch (South Africa), 1962-70, prof., 1970, head dept. plant pathology, 1970—. Fellow South African Soc. Plant Pathology; mem. Internat. Soc. Plant Pathology (council 1968—), Internat. Protea Assn. (hon.), South African Soc. Plant Pathology and Microbiology (pres. 1968-69, 76-79), Am. Phytopath. Soc., Bot. Soc. Am., Brit. Mycol. Soc., Fedn. Brit. Plant Pathologists, Bot. Soc. South Africa. Mem. editorial com. South African Jour. Agrl. Sci., 1976—; contbr. articles to profl. jours. Home: 35 Union Ave, 7600 Stellenbosch Republic of South Africa Office: U Stellenbosch, 7600 Stellenbosch Republic of South Africa

KNUDSEN, KNUD-ENDRE, civil engineer, consultant; b. Oslo, Norway, June 29, 1921; s. Edmund and Therese Marie (Ruud) K.; m. Kari Gulbrandsen, Aug. 14, 1951 (div. Nov. 1981); children—Trond, Lars, Per. M.S. in C.E., Norwegian Inst. Tech., Trondheim, 1946; Ph.D. in Civl Engring., Lehigh U., 1949. Research engr., Lehigh U., 1946-49, asst. prof., 1951-53; mng. dir. Norconsult Ethiopia, Addis Ababa, 1955-59, Norconsult A.S., Oslo, 1961-69, chmn., 1969-71; expert NATO Internat. Staff, Paris, 1959-61; cons. engr. K.E. Knudsen, Oslo, 1969—; pres. Saga Petroleum A.S., Oslo, 1973-79; chmn. bd. reps. Factoring Finans A.S., Oslo, 1980-86, Norsk Skibs Hypthekbank, Oslo, 1980-87; mem. bd. reps. Norsk A/S Philips, 1980—. Contbr. articles to profl. jours. Mem. Royal Norwegian Council for Sci. and Indsl. Resarch, 1976-79; bd. dirs. Fedn. Norwegian Industries, 1976-79; chmn. Commn on Orgn. of Norwegian State Petroleum Affairs, 1970-71. Hon. comsul of Norway to Ethiopia, 1956-59; Decorated knight 1st class Royal Norwegian Order St. Olav. Mem. Norwegian Acad. Tech. Scis. Conservative. Lutheran. Club: Norske Selskab (Oslo). Home: Stjerneveien 18, Oslo 3 Norway

KNUDSEN, MICHAEL CHRISTIAN, advertising executive; b. Copenhagen, Denmark, Jan. 8, 1958; s. Anders Christian and Merete (Wroblewski) K.; m. Anne Clemensen, June 29, 1985. Diploma in strategic planning and orgn. devel., Copenhagen Sch. Econs. and Bus. Adminstrn., 1984, diploma in mktg. mgmt., 1986. Mktg. assoc. Bonnier Publishing, Copenhagen, 1982-84; account exec. Ted Bates AS, Copenhagen, 1984-87; sr. account exec. Ted Bates Advance AS, Copenhagen, 1987—. Home: Frederiksgade 6, 1265 Copenhagen Denmark Office: Ted Bates Advance AS, Landemaerket 29, 1119 Copenhagen Denmark

KNUDSEN, RAYMOND BARNETT, clergyman, association executive, author; b. Denver, Nov. 11, 1919; s. Franklin Ole and Julia (Nielsen) K.; m. Edna Mae Nielsen, Jan. 26, 1940; children: Raymond Barnett, Silas John, Mark Allen, Ann DeLight (Mrs. Arthur James Semotan III). Student, Coll. Emporia, 1937-38, Wheaton Coll., 1938-39; B.A., U. Denver, 1941; Th.M., McCormick Theol. Sem., 1948; postgrad., U. Chgo., 1948; D.D., Burton Coll., 1955, LL.D., 1964; ThD, Miami Bible Inst., 1987. Pastor 8th Ave. Presbyn. Ch., Denver, 1939-40; dir. Martin M. Post Larger Parish, Logansport, Ind., 1941-44; asst. Faith Presbyn. Ch., Chgo., 1945; pastor 1st Presbyn. Ch., Warsaw, Ill., 1946-52, 5th Presbyn. Ch., Springfield, Ill., 1952-63; sr. pastor Webb Horton Meml. Presbyn. Ch., Middletown, N.Y., 1963-70; exec. dir. for donor support Nat. Council Chs. of Christ in U.S.A., 1970-71, asst. gen. sec., 1971-77; pres. Nat. Consultation on Fin. Devel., 1977-85, chmn., 1985—; lectr. philosophy Orange County (N.Y.) Community Coll., 1964-70; instr. Drew U. Sch. Theology, 1978-86, Perkins Sch. Theology So. Meth. U., 1986—; chmn. broadcasting press Synod of Ill., Presbyn. Ch., 1954-60, mem. gen. council, 1954-62; chmn. founding com. Ill. Presbyn. Home, Springfield, 1954; pres. Middletown Council Chs., 1967-69; chmn. Fifty Million Dollar Fund, Hudson River Presbytery, 1964-70; pres. Webb Horton Presbyn. Assos., Counselor Assn., 1954—; v.p. Inst. Activation Research.; cons. Episc. Diocese of Pitts., 1977-85, Orthodox Ch. in Am., 1978—, Christian Meth. Episc. Ch., 1983—, Hawaii conf. United Ch. of Christ, 1983-86, Asbury Hills Camp, 1983-86; cons. Fla. Council of Chs., 1986—, Pitts. Experiment, 1987—, Jesus Fellowship, Inc., 1987—, 1st Bapt. Ch., Washington, 1987—;. Author: The Trinity, 1936, New Models for Financing the Local Church, 1974, 2d edit., 1985, New Models for Creative Giving, 1976, 2d edit., 1985, Models for Ministry, 1976, Developing Dynamic Stewardship, 1977, New Models for Church Administration, 1979, The Workbook, 1978, Christian Stewardship in a Period of Fiscal Change, 1984, Stewardship Enlistment and Commitment, 1986, Let Your Money Do the Talking, 1987, From Commitment? to Commitment, 1987; mem. bd. rev.: Antenna, 1963—; contbr. religious columns to publs.; syndicated newspaper column The Counselor. Mem. Middletown Narcotics Guidance Council, 1969-70; pres. bd. dirs. Occupations, Inc., 1964-69, treas., 1969-71, pres. emeritus, 1976—; bd. dirs. Aid to Retarded Children N.Y., 1963-66, United Presbyn. Student Found., Presbyn. Sr. Services, N.Y.C., 1981-85, Presbyn. Panel, 1981-87; exec. bd. Orange County chpt. Aid Retarded Children; trustee Orange County Workshop for Disabled, 1963, Homemaker Service Orange County; pres. bd. trustees Camp Townsend, 1964-70. Recipient Author citation N.J. Inst. Tech., 1980. Mem. Nat. Temperance League (hon. v.p., chmn. nominating com. 1961-62), Alcohol Edn. Found. (dir.), Counselor Assn. (chmn. bd. 1982—). Clubs: Masons, Rotary (chmn. internat. contacts). Home and Office: 31 Langerfeld Rd Hillsdale NJ 07675

KNUDSON, MELVIN ROBERT, management consultant, business executive; b. Libby, Mont., Oct. 27, 1917; s. John and Serina (Bakken) K.; B.S. in Wood Chemistry, Oreg. State U., 1942; m. Melba Irene Joice, Mar. 5, 1946; children—Mark Bradley, Kevin Marie, Kari Lynne. Mgr. quality control J. Neils Lumber Co., Libby, Mont., 1946-55; mgr. research and devel. St. Regis Paper Co., Libby, 1955-65, div. dir. tech. devel., Tacoma, Wash., 1965-69, div. dir. short and long-range planning, 1969-70; exec. v.p. Property Holding and Devel. Co., Tacoma, 1970-75; exec. v.p. and gen. mgr. U.S. Computers, Inc., Tacoma, 1975-79; corp. mgmt., orgn., univ. governance and adminstrn. cons., 1979—; owner Knudson Travel, Tacoma, 1981—; pres., incorporator, Larex Internat. Corp.; dir. Property Holding and Devel. Co., U.S. Computers; adv. bd. Coll. Engring., Wash. State U., 1967—, chmn., 1971-73. Trustee 1st Luth. Ch., Libby, 1948-56, chmn., 1954-56; trustee Sch. Dist. #4, Libby, 1964-65; trustee Christ Luth. Ch., Tacoma, 1966-71, com. chmn.; trustee Greater Lakes Mental Health Clinic, 1969-73, com. chmn., 1970-73; bd. regents Pacific Luth. U., Tacoma, 1969—, chmn., 1976-81; mem. Steilacoom Improvement Com., 1971-73; chmn. Pacific Luth. U. Pres. Search Com., 1974-75; dir. Wauna Dance Club, 1976-79; dir. Pacific Luth. Univ. "Q" Club, 1976—; bd. dirs. Tenzler Library, Tacoma, 1980-83, Crime Stoppers, 1981-84. Served to lt. col. F.A., Paratroops, U.S. Army, 1941-46. Recipient Disting. Service award Pacific Luth. U., 1986. Mem. Wash. Realtors Assn., Wash. Securities Sales, Am. Governing Bds., Center for Study of Democratic Institutions. Republican. Clubs: Tacoma Country and Golf, Normana Male Chorus (Norwegian Singers Assn. Am.). Patentee high-temperature wood-drying process; developer domestic natural gum. Home: 6928 100th St SW Tacoma WA 98499 Office: 1103 A St Suite 200 Tacoma WA 98402

KNUTESON, KNUT JEFFERY, computer engineer; b. Spanish Fork, Utah, Nov. 1, 1949; s. Harold and Donna Fay (Gardner) K.; m. Kirsti Krogvik, Aug. 25, 1971; children: Kathrine, Knut-Sigurd, Joshua, Kristian, Harold, Marie Elizabeth. Student, Brigham Young U., 1967-72; A in Electronics Tech., Utah Tech. Coll., 1979. Electronics monitor Amund Clausen A/S, Porsgrunn, Norway, 1972-73; electronics technician, librarian Orem (Utah) City Pub. Library, 1977-79; electronics test and lab. technician Gen. Products div. IBM Corp., Tucson, 1979-82; computer systems technician and asst. programmer OmniSoft Corp., Salt Lake City, 1982-83; computer systems technician and cons. World Industries Cons., Inc., Tacoma, 1983-84; engr.-in-charge customer engring. KET Services, Inc., Tooele, Utah and Minnetonka, Minn., 1984—; bd. dirs. OmniSoft, A.M.S., Asociación Civil, Colonia LeBaron, Chihuahua, Mex.; cons. engr. Collier's Pub., 1980—; researcher, compiler Mormon genetic materials. Author religious booklets; compiler indices to Mormon scholarly books. sr. advisor Coll. Reps. Nat. com., 1987—; active neighborhood Crime Watch Pima County Sheriff's Dept., Tucson, 1980-82. Recipient Disting. Leadership award Am. Biog. Inst., 1988, Cert. of Appreciation 2d Amendment Found., 1985-87. Mem. Second Amendment Found. (nat. bd. advisors 1986—), Citizen's Com. for the Right to Keep and Bear Arms (nat. adv. council 1987—, Citizen of Yr. award 1982-87). Libertarian. Mormon.

KNUTZEN, RAYMOND EDWARD, criminal justice educator, consultant; b. Burlington, Wash., July 9, 1941; s. Erwin Edward Knutzen and Lillian Irene (Davis) Mowat; m. Cynthia Louise Neufeldt, Feb. 1, 1969; children: Traci Ann, Michael Edward. AAS with high honors, Everett Community Coll., 1970; BA magna cum laude, Pacific Luth. U., 1971; MA, Wash. State U., 1972. Asst. prof. criminal justice Northeast La. U., Monroe, 1972—. Coordinator Ouchita Valley council Boy Scouts Am., Monroe, 1979. Served with USAF, 1962-66, maj. USAR. Law Enforcement Edn. Program Pacific Luth. U. grantee, 1970-71. Mem. Internat. Assn. of Chiefs of Police, Mensa, Acad. Criminal Justice Sci., La. Justice Educators Assn., Blue Key Soc., Lambda Alpha Epsilon, Alpha Phi Sigma, Omicron Delta Kappa. Republican. Lutheran. Home: 3807 Forsythe Ave Monroe LA 71201-2125 Office: Northeast La U 700 University Ave Monroe LA 71209

KNYPL, EUGENIUSZ TADEUSZ, science information manager; b. Chyrow Poland, May 23, 1939; s. Franciszek Felicjan and Maria (Buczek) K.; m. Maria Anna (Sternal) Nawrocka, Feb. 2, 1968; children—Marta Sylwia; stepchildren: Beata, Nawrocka. M.S. Jagiellonian U., Cracow, Poland, 1962; cert. radiochemistry specialist, Warsaw U., Poland, 1964. Researcher Chemical Works, Oswiecim, Poland, 1962-72; asst. prof., chief info. dept. R & D Ctr. of Rubbers and Vinyl Plastics, Oswiecim, 1973—; lectr. Marx-Lenin Evening U., Bielsko-Biala, Poland, 1980; cons. Inst. Econs. of Chem. Industry, Warsaw, 1983—; panel mem. Internat. Mgmt., Maidenhead, Eng., 1984—. Contbr. articles to profl. jours. Patentee in field. Mem. Polish Tourist and Country Lovers Soc., Warsaw, 1966—. Active Socialistic Youth Union, 1966-74, Solidarity, 1980-81, Guardship of Nature, 1986—; instr. Civil Def., 1968—. Recipient Ministry of Culture and Arts award, 1969, Janek Krasicki award Socialistic Youth Union. 1972, Tech. Achievement award Ministry of Building, 1982, Golden Honour award Chief Tech. Orgn., 1984, R&D award Ministry Chm. and Light Industry, 1987. Mem. Polish Chem. Soc., Chemistry Engrs. Assn., Soc. for Polish-Italian Friendship, Polish Librarian Assn., 'Health Man' Assn. Home: Szpitalna 118/10, 32-602 Oswiecim Poland Office: R & D Ctr Rubbers and Vinyl Plastics, Chemikow, 32-600 Oswiecim Poland

KOBAK, JAMES BENEDICT, management consultant; b. St. Louis, Mar. 4, 1921; s. Edgar and Evelyn (Hubert) K.; m. Hope McEldowney, June 13, 1942; children—James Benedict, John D. (dec.), Thomas M. B.S., Harvard U., 1942; postgrad. in accounting, Pace Coll., 1946-49. C.P.A., N.Y., La., Union S.Africa. Assoc. J.K. Lasser & Co., N.Y.C., 1946-71; partner J.K. Lasser & Co., 1954-64, adminstrv. partner, 1964-71; internat. adminstrv. partner Lasser, Harmood Banner, Dunwoody, N.Y.C., 1964-71; pres. James B. Kobak & Co., Darien, Conn., 1971—; owner Kirkus Revs.; partner James B. Kobak Bus. Models Co., 1972-82; founder Kobak Open; Electronics Pub. Systems, Triad Publs., Gifted and Talented, Human Resource Services Inc., Oceans Mag., Kick Enterprises. Contbr. articles to profl. publs. Chmn. mag. com., mem. bus. com. Nat. council Boy Scouts Am.; co-founder, sec.-treas. John D. Kobak Appalachian Edn. Found., Darien; trustee Hill Sch., Pottstown, Pa. Served to capt., F.A. AUS, 1942-46. Mem. Am. Inst. C.P.A.s, N.Y. State Soc. C.P.A.s, Transvall Soc. Accountants. Presbyterian. Clubs: Harvard (N.Y.C.); Wee Burn Country (Darien); Univ. (Chgo.). Home and Office: 774 Hollow Tree Ridge Rd Darien CT 06820

KOBAYASHI, ATSUMOTO, manufacturing executive, consultant; b. Tochigi, Japan, Mar. 9, 1934; s. Shoji and Hanako (Kobayashi) K.; m. Yoko Gonoi, Dec. 23, 1962; children: Rumi, Masatomo. B in Engring., Tohoku U., Sendai, Japan, 1956. Cert. in engring., safety. Engr. automobile div. Nissan Motor Co., Ltd., Tokyo, 1956-68, mgr. automotive div., 1969-79, mgr. marine div., 1980-83, dep. gen. mgr. textile machinery div., 1984—, leader mgmt. analysis, 1987—; engring. cons., 1965—; safety cons., 1987—. Patentee in field. Mem. Japan Cons. Engrs. Assn., Japan Safety and Health Cons. Assn. Avocation: Shogi (Japanese chess), personal computers. Home and Office: Ogikubo 5-30-17-608, Suginami-ku, 167 Tokyo Japan

KOBAYASHI, EIJI, architect; b. Amakusa, Kumamoto, Japan, Feb. 9, 1947; d. Hiroichi and Tomeno Uehara; m. Kazuko Kobayashi, June 1, 1972; children: Koji, Akiko, Midori. Bachelor's degree, Tokai U., Hiratsuka, Japan, 1971. Designer Saito Architect and Assocs., Tokyo, 1971-72, Ishino & Takano Architects and Assocs., Tokyo, 1972-74; prin. Nakazato & Kobayashi Architects, Nugano, Japan, 1976-79, Eiji Kobayashi Architect and Assocs., Nagano, 1979—. Contbr. articles to profl. jours. Mem. Japan Inst. Architects. Home and Office: 641 Fujimi, Fujimi-machi, Suwa-Gun, 399-02 Nagano, Prefecture Japan

KOBAYASHI, HAJIME MATHEW, industrial planner; b. Chigasaki, Kanagawa, Japan, Sept. 21, 1949; s. Fusajiro and Yoneko (Kadokura) Kobayashi; m. Asako Kuroyanagi, July 1, 1978; children—Mio, Yuri. B.Sc., U. Tokyo, 1971, M.Sc., 1974. Planner planning div. Japan Regional Devel. Corp., Tokyo, 1974, planning indsl. relocation dept., 1976-79, planner Nagaoka Devel. Office, Nagaoka, 1979-83, vice dir. indsl. location promotion div., Tokyo, 1983-86, vice dir. planning div., 1986—; planner land use Nat. Land Agy., Tokyo, 1974-76, mem. com. for fundamental survey and research regarding Nat. Image of Future, 1982-83; co-founder Sight-C; mem. Nogizaka Study Group. Author: Regional Management System in Western Europe, 1980; co-author: Analysis of Venture Business, 1984. Founder sport Gordic (golf played on nordic skis), 1982. Nat. Inst. Research Advancement grantee, 1980. Mem. City Planning Inst. Japan, Internat. New Town Assn., Soc. Researchers of Internat. Devel. Roman Catholic. Clubs: Nagaoka Gordic (sec. 1983—), Chitoseha (Shinnai). Avocations: baseball; surfing; Gordic; samisen; guitar. Home: H-405 30-1 Hisamoto, Takatsu-ku, 213 Kawasaki Kanagawa, Japan Office: Japan Regional Devel Corp, 3-8-1 Kasumigaseki, Chiyoda-ku, 100 Tokyo Japan

KOBAYASHI, HESTER ATSUKO, environmental scientist; b. Honolulu, Oct. 4, 1938; d. Teruo and Kinuyo (Shinkawa) K. B.A., U. Hawaii, 1960, M.S., 1963; M.S. in Pub. Health, UCLA, 1976, D.P.H., 1981. Mgr. Arctic research U. So. Calif., Los Angeles, 1968-72, research assoc., 1973; marine environmentalist Port of Los Angeles, 1972-73; researcher in environ. sci. UCLA, 1976-81; research assoc. in environ. sci. U. Ill., Urbana, 1980-82; environ. researcher BP Am., Cleve., 1982—; cons. EPA, 1984—. Contbr. articles to profl. jours.; patentee in field. Mem. N.J. Inst. Tech. (indsl. adv. bd. Hazardous Waste Mgmt. Ctr.), Am. Soc. Microbiology, Am. Chem. Soc., Soc. Environ. Toxicology and Chemistry, Sigma Xi. Office: BP Am 4440 Warrensville Center Rd Cleveland OH 44128

KOBAYASHI, HIROSHI, history educator; b. Okayama-shi, Japan, June 10, 1951; s. Kazumasa and Masuko (Miyake) K.; m. Miwako Fukunaga, Mar. 1, 1981; children: Nobuhiro Steven, Mariko. BA in Commerce, Waseda U., Tokyo, 1974, MA in Commerce, 1978; MA in History, Ohio State U., 1984. Lectr. in history Nara Bunka Women's Jr. Coll., Yamatotakada, Japan, 1985-86; asst. prof. Nara Sangyo U., Sango-cho, Japan, 1986-87, assoc. prof., 1988—; vis. lectr. U. Malaya, Kuala Lumpur, Malaysia, 1987-88; asst. researcher Marui Corp., Tokyo, 1977-80; research cooperator inst. indsl. mgmt. Waseda U., 1980-82. Fulbright scholar, 1982. Mem. Bus. History Soc. Japan. Buddhist. Home: 2-28-15 Ifuku-cho, Okayama-shi Japan 700 Office: Nara Sangyo U, Tatsuno-kita 3-12-1, Ikomagun Nara Japan 636

KOBAYASHI, KOJI, manufacturing executive; b. Ohtsuki, Yamanashi, Japan, Feb. 17, 1907; s. Tsuneo and Den K.; m. Kazuko Noda, Mar. 10, 1935; children: Teiko Takamatsu, Kimiko Hirano, Noriko Hatori. B, Tokyo Imperial U., 1929, D in Engring., 1939; LLD (hon.), Monmouth Coll. (Ill.), 1968, D in Engring. (hon.), Poly. Inst. N.Y., 1971; D (hon.) Autonomous U, Guadalajara, Mex., 1980. Gen. mgr. Tamagawa plant NEC, Kawasaki, Japan, 1946-49, dir., 1949-56, sr. v.p., 1956-61; exec. v.p., Minato-ku, Tokyo, Japan, 1961-62, sr. exec. v.p., 1962-64, pres., 1964-76, chmn., chief exec. officer, 1976-88, chmn. emeritus, 1988—; bd. dirs. Nippon Avionics Co. Ltd., Tokyo, NEC Home Electronics Ltd., Tokyo, ; hon. mem. Nat. Inst. Higher Edn. in Dublin, Ireland, 1986. Author: Challenges to the Computer Age, 1968, The Problem of Management in the 1970's, 1971, Quality-Oriented Management, C & C is Japan's Wisdom, 1980, The Software Challenge-A Human Perspective, 1982, C & C: Modern Communications—Development of Global Information Media, 1985, My Personal History, 1988. Decorated Comdrs. Cross of Order Merit Polish People's Republic, 1980, Order San Carlos Govt. Republic of Colombia, 1985, Encomienda en la Orden del Merito Civil His Majesty the King of Spanish State, 1986, Grand Cordon Order Rising Sun His Majesty the Emperor of Japan, 1987; recipient Blue Ribbon medal Emperor of Japan, 1964, Golden Plate award Am. Acad. Achievement, 1966, Founders medal, 1984, Spl. UN medal Peace for Internat. Law Enforcement Cooperation Internat. Narcotic Enforcement Officers Assn. UN, 1986. Fellow IEEE (Frederik Philips award, 1977), Internat. Acad. Mgmt.; mem. Indsl. Research Inst. (pres.), Japan Fedn. Employers Assn. (governing dir.), Fedn. Econ. Orgn. (exec. dir.). Club: Club of Rome (Tokyo). Office: NEC Corporation, 33-1 Shiba 5-chome, Minato-ku, 108 Tokyo Japan

KOBAYASHI, NORITAKE, business educator; b. Tokyo, Feb. 23, 1932; s. Daijyo and Makiko (Tadokoro) K.; m. Meiko Mary Margaret Nishino, May 21, 1960; children: Norikazu, Sumiko, Kumiko. AB cum laude, Harvard U., 1953, postgrad., 1953-54; LLB, Keio U., Japan, 1954, PhD, 1973. Lectr. Keio U., Yokohama, Japan, 1956-62, assoc. prof., 1962-73, prof. Grad. Sch. Bus. Adminstrn., 1973—, dir. sch. bus., 1980-83, dean Grad. Sch. Bus. Adminstrn., 1987—; vis. prof. Ind. U., Bloomington, 1968, Asian Inst. Mgmt., Philippines, 1970, Internat. Mgmt. Inst., Geneva, 1974; bd. dirs. Mazda Motor Corp., DIC Degremont Co. Ltd., Ajinomoto Dannone Co. Ltd.; auditor Jusco-Gen. Mills Restaurant Co. Ltd. Author: Joint Venture in Japan, 1967, The World of Japanese Business, 1969, International Business, 1972, Japanese Multinational Enterprises, 1980. Recipient Mgmt. Sci. Pub. Prize Nihon Keiei Kyokai, 1981. Fellow Acad. Internat. Bus.; mem. Comparative Law Assn. Japan, Mgmt. Assn. Japan, Am. Acad. Polit. and Social Sci., Japan-Am. Soc., Keio U. Alumni Assn. Club: Harvard. Home: 9-13 Shirokane 4-chome, Minato-ku, Tokyo 108, Japan Office: Keio U, Grad Sch Bus Adminstrn, 1960 Hiyoshi-Honcho, Kohoku-ku, 223 Yokohama Japan

KOBAYASHI, SUSUMU, data processing executive; b. Kumamoto, Japan, Apr. 3, 1939; s. Senkichiro and Michiko Kobayashi. BS, Tokyo Inst. Tech., 1963. Programmer Osaka (Japan) Gas Co., Ltd., 1963-65, C. Itoh Computing Services Co., Ltd., Tokyo, 1965-67; applications analyst, systems engr. Control Data Far East, Inc., Tokyo, 1967-75; asst. gen. mgr. systems dept. JMA Systems, Inc., Tokyo, 1975-79; dir. Nuclear Data Corp., Tokyo, 1979—. Translator and editor: Fortran 4 (D.D. McCracken), 1968, Lisp 1.5 Primer (C. Weissman), 1970; contbr. articles to electronics mags. Mem. Assn. Computing Machinery, IEEE, Inc., Japan Math. Soc., Japan Info. Processing Soc. Home: 85-2-206 Migawa 2-chome, 310 Mito-shi Ibaraki-ken Japan Office: Nuclear Data Corp, 1-1-71 Nakameguro, 153 Meguro-ku Tokyo Japan

KOBAYASHI, TAIYU, electronics company executive; b. Hyogo Prefecture, Japan, June 13, 1912; m. Nagae Sano, 1938; 2 children. Ed. Kyoto U. Joined Fuji Electric Co., 1935; joined Fujitsu Ltd., 1935, dir., 1964-69, mng. dir., 1969-72, exec. dir., 1972-75, exec. v.p., 1975-76, pres., 1976-81, chmn., 1981—. Recipient Purple Ribbon award with medal of honor, Blue Ribbon award with medal of honor. Mem. Communications Industries Assn. Japan (pres. 1976-78), Japan Electronic Industry Devel. Assn. (pres. 1979—), Engring. Research Assn. of Opto-Electronics Applied System (chmn. 1981—). Office: Fujitsu Ltd, 1-6-1, Chiyoda-ku, Marunouichi, Tokyo Japan *

KOBAYASHI, YOTARO, business products company exeutive; b. London, Apr. 25, 1933; s. Setsutaro and Chizuyo (Shiose) K.; m. Momoyo Matsumoto, Sept. 2, 1963; children: Chiho, Kaku, Maki. BA in Econs., Keio U., Tokyo, 1956; MBA in Indsl. Mgmt., U. Pa., 1958; LHD, S. Peter's Coll., N.J., 1984. With Fuji Photo Co., Ltd., Tokyo, 1958-63, Fuji Xerox Co., Ltd., Tokyo, 1963; resident Rank Xerox Ltd., London, 1963-68; mgr. mktg. planning, dir. Fuji Xerox Co. Ltd., Tokyo, 1968-70, dir., dept. gen. mgr. mktg. ops., 1970-72, mng. dir., gen. mgr. mktg. ops., 1970-76, exec. v.p., 1976-78, pres., 1978—; bd. dirs. Xerox Corp., Stamford, Conn., Iwaki Glass Co. Ltd., Tokyo. Mem. U.S.-Japan Adv. Commn., Tokyo, 1983-84, Posts & Telecommunications Council Ministry Posts & Telecommunications, Tokyo, 1985—, grad. exec. bd. Wharton Sch. U. Pa., 1981-87; cons. Directorate Social Affairs, Manpower and Edn. of Orgn. Econ. Cooperation and Devel., Paris, 1985-86. Mem. Keio U. (bd. trustee), Stanford Grad. Sch. Bus. (adv. council), Asian Inst. Mgmt. (bd. govs.), Keizai Doyu-kai (Japan Assn. Corp. Execs.). Roman Catholic. Club: Tokyo. Office: Fuji Xerox Co Ltd, Kokusai-Sanoh, Bldg 3-5 Akasaka, 3-Chome Minato-Ku, 107 Tokyo Japan

KOBAYSAHI, YUTAKA, airlines executive; b. Tokyo, July 29, 1933; s. Susumu and Mie (Makino) K.; m. Yohko Ii; children: Hajime, Iwao, Nobutaka. LLM in Internat. Law, Keio U., Tokyo, 1956. Mem. mktg. staff sales dept. Japan Air Lines, Tokyo, 1958-61, supt. system-wide scheduling, 1961-65; asst. regional mgr. Germany and Ea. Europe Frankfurt, Fed. Republic Germany, 1965-67; asst. to gen. mgr. internat. passenger sales Tokyo, 1968-69, mgr. interline and agy. mktg. system-wide, 1969-72, asst. gen. mgr. internat. passenger mktg. and sales, 1972-78, dep. gen. mgr. internat. passenger mktg. system-wide, 1978-85, staff v.p. industry affairs, 1985-86, v.p. industry affairs, 1986—. Contbg. author Travel Bus. Mem. Pacific Asia Travel Assn. (bd. dirs. 1985—), East Asia Travel Assn. (bd. dirs. 1985—), Orient Airlines Assn. (mktg. com. 1985—), Japan-Australia Assn., Japan-New Zealand Assn. Home: 27-4 4-chome Zenpukuji, Suginami-Ku, 167 Tokyo Japan Office: Japan Air Lines Head Office, 2-7 3-chome Marunouchi, 100 Chiyoda-ku, Tokyo Japan

KOBDISH, GEORGE CHARLES, lawyer; b. Casper, Wyo., June 30, 1950; s. Richard Matthew and Jo Earl (Uttz) K.; m. Mary Ellen Griffith, Jan. 24, 1969; children—George Charles, Jr., Kelly Rebecca, Kimberlee Nelle. B.B.A. with honors, U. Tex., 1971, J.D., 1974. Bar: Tex. 1974, U.S. Dist. Ct. (no. dist.) Tex. 1975. Asst. atty. gen. State of Tex., Austin, 1974-76; assoc. McCall, Parkhurst & Horton, Dallas, 1976-80, ptnr., 1981—; mem. Tex. Treasurer's Asset Mgmt. Adv. Com., Austin, 1983—, Disting. Service award, 1983. Mem. Nat. Assn. Bond Lawyers, ABA, Dallas Bar Assn. Clubs: 2001, Exchange. Home: 9206 Arbor Branch Dr Dallas TX 75243 Office: McCall Parkhurst & Horton 717 N Harwood Suite 900 Dallas TX 75201

KOBE, DONALD HOLM, physics educator; b. Seattle, Jan. 13, 1934; s. Kenneth Albert and Jeneva Catherine (Holm) K. B.S., U. Texas-Austin, 1956; M.S., U. Minn., 1959; Ph.D., 1961. Vis. asst. prof. Ohio State U., Columbus, 1961-63; research assoc. Quantum Chemistry Group, Uppsala, Sweden, 1964-66; vis. asst. prof. H.C. Oersted Inst., Copenhagen, Denmark, 1966-67, Northeastern U., Boston, 1967-68; prof. No. Texas State U.-Denton, 1968-88, U. North Tex.-Denton, 1988—; Fulbright lectr., Taipei, Taiwan, 1963-64, Nat. Acad. Sci. lectr., Yugoslavia, 1973. Contbr. articles to profl. jours. Fellow Am. Sci. Affiliation; mem. Am. Phys. Soc., Am. Assn. Physics Tchrs., AAAS, Subspecialties: Theoretical physics; Atomic and molecular physics. Current work: I have developed with others a manifestly gauge-invariant formulation of quantum mechanics for the interaction of electromagnetic radiation and charged matter. Home: 1704 Highland Park Rd Denton TX 76205 Office: Univ of North Tex Dept of Physics Denton TX 76203

KOBELT, THOMAS JOHN, business systems company executive; b. Vancouver, B.C., Can., Nov. 21, 1958; s. Jacob R. Kobelt; m. Marilyn Monica Oelke, May 9, 1987. BS, U. B.C., 1980; diploma in Christian Studies, Regent Coll., Vancouver, 1982; MBA, U. Toronto, Ont., Can., 1988. V.p. mktg. Kobelt Mfg., Vancouver, 1980-83, also bd. dirs.; data processing mgr. Glenayre Electronics, Vancouver, 1983-85; software cons. Spicer MacGillivary, Toronto, 1985-86; project mgr. Cantoc Bus. Systems, Toronto, 1986—. Mem. Am. Mgmt. Assn. Mem. Progressive Conservative Party. Baptist.

KOBLENZ, MICHAEL ROBERT, lawyer; b. Newark, Apr. 9, 1948; s. Herman and Esther (Weisman) K.; m. Bonnie Jane Berman, Dec. 22, 1973; children—Adam, Alexander. B.A., George Washington U., 1969, LL.M., 1974; J.D., Am. U., 1972. Bar: N.J. 1972, D.C. 1973, N.Y. 1980, U.S. Dist. Ct. N.J. 1972, U.S. Dist. Ct. D.C. 1973, U.S. Dist. Ct. (so. dist.) N.Y. 1980, U.S. Ct. Appeals (7th cir.) 1976, U.S. Ct. Claims 1973, U.S. Tax Ct. 1973, U.S. Mil. Ct. Appeals 1974. Atty., U.S. Dept. Justice, Washington, 1972-75; lectr. Am. U., 1975-78; spl. asst. U.S. atty. Office of U.S. Atty., Chgo., 1976-78; atty. Commodity Futures Trading Commn., Washington, 1975-77; spl. counsel, 1977, asst. dir., 1977-78; regional counsel, N.Y.C., 1978-80; assoc. Rein, Mound & Cotton, N.Y.C., 1980-82, ptnr., Mound, Cotton & Wollan (and predecessor firms), 1983—. Contbr. articles to legal jours. Mem. bd. appeals Village of Flower Hill, Manhasset, N.Y., 1983-84, trustee, 1984-86; trustee Village of East Hills, 1988—. Recipient Cert. of Appreciation for Outstanding Service U.S. Commodity Futures Trading Commn., 1977. Home: 20 Hemlock Dr East Hills Roslyn NY 11576 Office: Mound Cotton & Wollan 125 Maiden Ln New York NY 10038

KOBZA, DENNIS JEROME, architect; b. Ullysses, Nebr., Sept. 30, 1933; s. Jerry Frank and Agnes Elizabeth (Lavicky) K.; B.S., Healds Archtl. Engring., 1959; m. Doris Mae Riemann, Dec. 26, 1953; children—Dennis Jerome, Diana Jill, David John. Draftsman, designer B.L. Schroder, Palo Alto, Calif., 1959-60; sr. draftsman, designer Ned Abrams, Architect, Sunnyvale, Calif., 1960-61, Kenneth Elvin, Architect, Los Altos, Calif., 1961-62; partner B.L. Schroder, Architect, Palo Alto, 1962-66; pvt. practice architecture, Mountain View, Calif., 1966—. Served with USAF, 1952-56. Recipient Solar PAL award, Palo Alto, 1983, Mountain View Mayoral award, 1979. Mem. C. of C. (dir. 1977-79, Archtl. Excellence award Hayward chpt. 1985, Outstanding Indsl. Devel. award Sacramento chpt., 1980) , AIA (chpt. dir. 1973), Constrn. Specifications Inst. (dir. 1967-68), Am. Inst. Plant Engrs., Nat. Fedn. Ind. Bus. Orgn. Club: Rotary (dir. 1978-79, pres. 1986-87). Home: 3840 May Ct Palo Alto CA 94303 Office: 2083 Old Middlefield Way Mountain View CA 94043

KOÇ, VEHBI, holding company executive; b. Ankara, Turkey, July 20, 1901; s. Haci Mustafa Koçzade and Fatma (Kütükçüzade) Koç; m. Sadberk Koç, 1927; children: Semahat Arsel, Rahmi M., Sevgi Gönül, Suna Kiraç. Hon. doctorate, Eskisehir Anatolian U., 1984. Grocery store owner, pres. Ankara, 1926-28; pres., chmn. Vehbi Koç and Associated Co. Ltd., Ankara, 1937-42, Galata br. Koç Trading Co., Inc., Ankara, 1942-63, Koç Holding Co., Anakara and Istanbul, 1963-84; hon. chmn. Koç Holding A., Istanbul, 1984. Author: My Life Story, 1973, My Reminiscences, My Views and My Advices, 1987. Founder Turkish Ednl. Found., 1967, Family Planning Found., 1985, TUGEV Touris Found., 1985, Vehbi Koç Found., all Istanbul. Recipient model tax payer citation Ankara C. of C., 1972, citation Ministry Edn., 1985, ICC Bus. award Pres. India, 1987. Office: Koc Holding Co, Meelisi Mebusan Cad #53, Findikli, Istanbul Turkey

KOCAOGLU, DUNDAR F., engineering management educator, consultant, researcher; b. Turkey, June 1, 1939; came to U.S., 1960; s. Irfan and Meliha (Uzay) K.; m. Alev Baysak, Oct. 17, 1968; 1 child, Timur. BSCE, Robert Coll., Istanbul, Turkey, 1960; MSCE, Lehigh U., 1962; MS in Indsl. Engring., U. Pitts., 1972, PhD in Ops. Research, 1976. Registered profl. engr., Pa., Oreg. Design engr. Modjeski & Masters, Harrisburg, Pa., 1962-64; ptnr. TEKSER Engring. Co., Istanbul, 1966-69; project engr. United Engrs.,

Phila., 1964-71; research asst. U. Pitts., 1972-74, vis. asst. prof., 1974-76, assoc. prof. indsl. engring., dir. engring. mgmt., 1976-87; prof., dir. engring. mgmt. program, Portland State U., 1987—; pres. TMA-Tech. Mgmt. Assocs., Portland, Oreg., 1977—. Author: Engineering Management, 1981, Management of R&D and Engineering, 1988, Handbook of Technology Management, 1988; series editor Wiley Series in Engring. Mgmt.; editor-in-chief IEEE Transactions on Engring. Mgmt.; contbr. articles on tech. mgmt. to profl. jours. Served to 1t. C.E., Turkish Army, 1966-68. Recipient Centennial medal IEEE, 1984. Mem. Inst., Mgmt. Scis. (pres. Coll. Engring. Mgmt. 1979-81), Am. Soc. Engring. Edn. (chmn. engring. mgmt. div. 1982-83), IEEE Engring. Mgmt. Soc. (sr.; publs. dir. 1982-85), ASCE, Am. Soc. Engring. Mgmt. (dir. 1981-86), Omega Rho (pres. 1984-86).

KOCH, ALEXANDER, sociologist, consultant; b. Hanau, Hesses, Fed. Republic of Germany, Nov. 16, 1932; s. Alexander R. and Alma E.E. (Wetekam) K.; m. Margret A. E. Schrecke, Mar. 22, 1937; children: Christiane M., Ivo A. Maturum Abitur, Hohe Landesschule, Hanau, Hessen, 1953; Comml. Pro, C. of C., Hanau, Hessen, 1955; diploma, U. Frankfurt, 1963. Asst. to personnel dir. Dunlop AG, Hanau, 1963-64, asst. to gen. mgr., 1964-65, personnel mgr., dir., 1965-70; dir. adminstrn. Teves Ltd./ITT, Frankfurt, 1970-74; bd. mem. personnel Braun AG/Gillette, Kronberg, Hessen, 1974-81, Grundig AG, Nuremberg, Bavaria, 1981-87; mgmt. cons. Frankfurt, 1987—; chmn. edn. and tng. com. Fedn. German Employer's Assns., Cologne, 1974—. Contbr. articles on personnel mgmt., social plolitics, tng. and edn., mgmt. technics to profl. jours. Pub. relations mgr. Christian Dem. Union, Hanau. Lodge: Lions. Home: Darmstaedter Str 82, 7 Hessen, D 6450 Hanau Federal Republic of Germany Office: Alexander Koch Cons, Fellner Str 5, 6000 Frankfurt, Hessen Federal Republic of Germany

KOCH, ALWIN GEORGE, engineer, consultant; b. Wisconsin Rapids, Wis., Mar. 7, 1919; s. Alwin G. and Elizabeth (Lusk) K.; B.S., U. Wash., 1949; m. Virginia Murrell, July 11, 1943; children—Mary Elizabeth, Robert James. Sales engr., field rep. Dorr Co., Seattle, 1949-51; dist. engr. Wash. State Dept. Health, Seattle, 1951-72; sr. engr. tech. services unit Wash. Dept. Social and Health Services, 1972-74, dist. engr. for King County, 1974-79; ret., 1979; engring. cons. Chaves & Kearny, Bogata, Colombia, 1968-69, Chaves & Assos., engrs., Bogata, 1974-80; sr. civil and san. engr. Hernando Chaves & Assos., Seattle, 1979-80; cons. engr., Seattle, 1980—. Served to capt. AUS, 1940-46. Registered profl. engr., Wash. Fellow ASCE (life mem.); mem. AAAS, Mensa, Internat. Platform Assn. Home and Office: 6845 32d Ave NE Seattle WA 98115

KOCH, CHARLES DE GANAHL, corporation executive; b. Wichita, Kans., Nov. 1, 1935; s. Fred Chase and Mary Clementine (Robinson) K. B.S. in Gen. Engring, MIT, 1957, M.S. in Mech. Engring., 1958, M.S. in Chem. Engring., 1959. Engr. Arthur D. Little, Inc., Cambridge, Mass., 1959-61; v.p. Koch Engring. Co., Inc., Wichita, 1961-63, pres., 63-71, chmn., 1967-78; pres. Koch Industries, Inc., Wichita, 1966-74, chmn., 1967—; dir. First Nat. Bank Wichita, Squibb Corp. Bd. dirs. Inst. for Humane Studies, Inc., Cato Inst., Citizens for a Sound Economy, Wesley Found., Wichita Collegiate Sch. Mem. Mt. Pelerin Soc. Clubs: Wichita Country, N.Y. Athletic. Office: Koch Industries PO Box 2256 Wichita KS 67201

KOCH, EDNA MAE, lawyer; b. Terre Haute, Ind., Oct. 12, 1951; d. Leo K. and Lucille E. (Smith) K. BS in Nursing, Ind. State U., 1977; JD, Ind. U., 1980. Bar: Ind. 1980, U.S. Dist. Ct. (so. dist.) Ind. 1980. Assoc. Dillon & Cohen, Indpls., 1980-85; ptnr. Tipton, Cohen & Koch, Indpls., 1985—; leader seminars for nurses Ball State U., Muncie, Ind., St. Vincent Hosp., Indpls., Deaconess Hosp., Evansville, Ind., others; lectr. on med. malpractice Cen. Ind. chpt. Am. Assn. Critical Care Nurses, Indpls. "500" Postgrad. Course in Emergency Medicine, Ind. Assn. Osteo. Physicians and Surgeons State Conv., numerous others. Mem. ABA, Ind. State Bar Assn., Indpls. Bar Assn., Ind. Trial Lawyers Assn., Am. Nurses Assn., Ind. State Nurses Assn. Republican. Office: Tipton Cohen & Koch 47 S Meridian St Suite 200 Indianapolis IN 46204

KOCH, EDWARD RICHARD, lawyer, banker; b. Teaneck, N.J., Mar. 25, 1953; s. Edward J. and Adelaide M. (Wunner) K. BS in Econs. magna cum laude, U. Pa., 1975; JD, U. Va., 1980; LLM in Taxation, NYU, 1986. Bar: N.J. 1980, U.S. Dist. Ct. N.J. 1980, U.S. Tax Ct. 1981, U.S. Ct. Claims 1981. Staff acct. Touche Ross & Co., Newark, 1975-77; assoc. Winne, Banta & Rizzi, Hackensack, N.J., 1980-82; tax atty. Allied Corp. (name now Allied-Signal, Inc.), Morristown, 1982-87; asst. v.p. Chem. Bank, N.Y.C., 1987—. Vice chmn. law and legis. com. Athletics Congress, Indpls., 1985—; pres. N.J. Athletics Congress, Red Bank, 1986—. Mem. ABA, N.J. State Bar Assn., Am. Inst. CPA's, N.J. Soc. CPA's, Am. Assn. Attys.-CPA's. Republican. Roman Catholic. Club: N.J. Striders Track (Maywood) (chmn. 1981—). Home: 47 Brandywyne Dr Florham Park NJ 07932 Office: Chem Bank Tax Dept 380 Madison Ave 11th Floor New York NY 10017

KOCHAN, GUENTER, music educator; b. Luckau, Germany, Oct. 2, 1930. Student, Hochschule Musik, Berlin, 1946-50, Acad. Kunste, Berlin, 1950-54. Dozent Hochschule Musik, Berlin, 1951-67, prof., 1967—. Recipient Nat. Prize, German Democratic Republic, 1959, 64, 79, 87. Mem. Acad. Kunste, Verbandes Komponiste. Home: Hohen Neuendorf Veltener Str 13, 1406 Berlin German Democratic Republic

KOCHANOWSKY, BORIS JULIUS, mining consultant; b. Krasnojarsk, Siberia, Russia, May 4, 1905; came to U.S., 1953, naturalized, 1959; s. Julius M. and Maria J. (Borovski) K.; m. Maria E. Chudobba, Sept. 1984; 1 child, Vera. Diplom Ingenieur in Mine Surveying, U. Bergakademie, Freiberg, Ger., 1927, Diplom Ingenieur; in Mining Engring., 1929; Dr. Ingenieur in Mining Engring, U. Bergakademie, Clausthal, Ger., 1955. Coal miner 1923-29; research asso. Coal Bd., Essen, Ger., 1930, U. Bergakademie, Freiberg, 1930-33; asst. to pres., mgr. mining ops., devel. and research Rheinische Kalksteinwerke Co., Germany, 1933-39; mgr. coal mines Switzerland, 1945-46; mgr. asphaltite mine Mendoza, Argentina, 1946-48; prof. engring. and econs. of mining U. Cuyo, San Juan and Mendoza, 1948-53; mem. faculty Pa. State U., 1953—, prof. mining engring., 1961-67, founder, chmn. mineral engring. mgmt. program, 1968-70, prof. emeritus, 1970—; speaker, cons. throughout world. Co-author: Berg und Aufbereitungstechnik, Part I, 1933, Part II, 1935, Neuzeitliche Sprengtechnik, 1966, also numerous articles. Mem. AIME, Am. Soc. Engring. Edn., AAUP. Address: 426 Homan Ave State College PA 16801

KOCIÁNOVÁ, HELENA ELA, economist, researcher; b. Prague, Czechoslovakia, June 29, 1933; d. Pavel Oldřich Chvojka and Maria Terezia (Pivodová) Křivancová; m. Antonin Ladislav Kocián. MS in Econs., Sch. Econ., Prague, 1956. Diplomate in Econs. Statistician Inst. Sci. and Tech. Info., Prague, 1956-57, sr. statistician, 1957-59, profl. worker, 1959-63, sr. profl. worker, 1963-64; research worker Econ. Inst. of Czechoslovak Acad. Sci., Prague, 1964-76, sr. research worker, 1976-87, leading research worker, 1988—; cons. Inst. Sci. and Tech. Info., 1966-72, Sch. Econs., 1980—. Co-author: Economy of Advanced Capitalism and the Scientific-Technological Revolution, 1979 (ann. prize Svoboda pub. house 1980); contbr. articles to profl. jours. Fellow Czechoslovak Sci. Tech. Soc. Office: Econ Inst Czechoslovak Acad Sci, Trida Politickych veznu 7, 111 73 Prague Czechoslovakia

KOCIC, VLAJKO, mathematician, electrical engineer; b. Belgrade, Yugoslavia, Apr. 10, 1953; s. Ljubomir and Nadezda (Djordjevic) K.; m. Paulina Piskulic, July 16, 1977; children—Nikola, Ljubomir. E.E., Faculty Elec. Engring., Belgrade, 1977, M.S. in Applied Math., 1979, Ph.D. in Math., 1981. Asst., dept. math. Faculty Elec. Engring., Belgrade, 1978-85, asst. prof., 1985—; cons. Math. Inst., Belgrade, 1979—; reviewer Math. Revs., Ann Arbor, Mich., 1980—. Contbr. articles to math. jours. Mem. Am. Math. Soc. Avocations: tennis, skiing, swimming. Home: Bulevar Avnoja 82/43, 11070 Belgrade Yugoslavia Office: Faculty of Electrical Engring, Bulevar Revolucije 73, Belgrade Yugoslavia

KOCIKOWSKI, STEFAN, plastics company executive; b. Bagniewo, Poland, Aug. 30, 1924; came to U.K., 1944, naturalized, 1950; s. Paul and Franciszka (Swierczynska) K.; m. Christine Ramlow, July 13, 1947; children—Barbara, Paul, Peter. Student Royal Tech. Coll., Glasgow, 1944-45; diploma in indsl. chemistry Coll. Tech., Northampton, 1962; diploma in plastic technology Brit. Inst. Engring., London, 1964. Chem. asst. Scott Bader Ltd., Wollaston, Eng., 1960-65; project chemist W.R. Grace Ltd., St. Neots, Eng., 1965-67, Mayco Ltd., Ballina, Ireland, 1967-76; research and devel. chemist Flotex Ltd., Ripley, Eng., 1976-78; tech. mgr. Evode Industries Ltd., Swords, County Dublin, Ireland, 1979-85; tech. dir. Hagar Ltd., Ratoath, Ireland, 1985—. Tech. translator Flock quar., 1976—; cons. of plastics and adhesives, 1986—. Inventor field of plastics and polymers. Organist, choir master Dusany Ch., County Meath, 1978—. Cert. Merit for Disting. Achievement, 1987. Fellow Internat. Biog. Assn.; mem. Inst. Polish Engrs. in Gt. Britain (assoc.), Brit. Inst. Engring. Tech. Roman Catholic. Home: Fairyhouse Rd, Piercetown, Dunboyne, County Meath Ireland Office: Hagar Ltd, Porterstown Ln, Fairyhouse Rd, Ratoath, County Meath Ireland

KOCIUBES, JOSEPH LEIB, lawyer; b. Frankfurt, W.Ger., June 16, 1947; came to U.S., 1949; s. Max and Rachel (Ackerman) K.; m. Peggy Ann Roth, May 18, 1969; children: Lisa Roth, Adam Roth. BA, U. Pitts., 1969; JD, Harvard U., 1974. Bar: Mass. 1974, U.S. Dist. Ct. Mass. 1974, U.S. Ct. Apls. (1st cir.) 1975, U.S. Sup. Ct. 1979. Asst. to dean Coll. Arts and Sci., U. Pitts., 1969; dir. health and edn. programs North Shore Community Action Program, Beverly, Mass., 1969-71; asst. dir. Project RAP, Beverly, 1971; assoc. Bingham, Dana & Gould, Boston, 1974-81, ptnr., 1981—, mem. mgmt. com., 1984—; trial teaching advisor Harvard Law Sch., 1979—; mem. adv. council Gov.'s Urea-Formaldehyde Trust Fund, 1986—. Mass. Commn. on the Effects of Indoor Air Pollution, 1987—; bd. dirs. Vol. Lawyers Project, Boston, 1985—. Mem. ABA (litigation sect. task force on uniform securities act 1985), Mass. Bar Assn., Boston Bar Assn. Democrat. Jewish. Club: Harvard (Boston). Home: 187 Nehoiden Rd Newton MA 02168 Office: Bingham Dana & Gould 150 Federal St Boston MA 02110

KOCK, LARS ANDERS WOLFRAM, physician, educator; b. Stockholm, Aug. 29, 1913; s. Gosta and Elsa (Wik) K.; License medicine, Karolinska Institutet, 1941, M.D., 1952; m. Marianne Segerstéen, May 18, 1950; 1 son, Lars Kock. Intern and resident in Stockholm and Stocksund, 1940-54; pvt. practice medicine, specializing in gen. medicine and surgery, Stockholm; house surgeon several hosps., Stockholm, 1940-54; asst. prof. med. history and research Karolinska Institutet, Stockholm, 1953-79, prof., 1982—, med. dir. Swedish Philips Co., Stockholm, 1954-78; dir. Mus. Med. History, Stockholm, 1955—; sr. med. officer Defence Forces Med. Adminstr. Service, Stockholm, 1955-76; fiduciary physician Social Ins. Office, 1976-82. Served with M.C., Swedish Navy, 1945-55. Decorated knight Vasa Order, knight Order North Pole Star, King's Golden Medal with Seraphimer ribbon; recipient Gold Medal for merit Mus. Med. History, Stockholm, 1977. Mem./hon. mem. numerous socs. med. history; mem. Swedish Med. Soc. (150 Silver Jubilee medal 1958, Jubilee prize 1978, hon. sec. sect. med. history 1947-75, pres. 1975—), Friends Mus. Med. History Stockholm (founder, hon. sec. 1952-75, pres. 1975—), Société Internationale d'Histoire de la Médecine (hon. sec. 1964-70), Internat. Acad. History Medicine, Scandinavian Soc. Med. History (pres. 1976-78), Finnish Soc. Med. Scis., Conseil Scientifique du Centre Européen d'Histoire de la Médecine. Author: Resa till Rio, 1947; Resa till Kap, 1949; Kungl, Serafimerlasarettet 1752-1952, 1952; Medicinhistoriens Grunddrag, 1955; Svenska Konungars Sjukdomar, 1963; Kirurgminnen fran Karl Johanstiden, 1964; Olof af Acrel, 1967; Svenska Lakare som Vitterlekare, 1970; Svensk kirurgi-historisk rapsodi, 1978; (memoirs) Läkare och Lekman, 1982; editor: Medicinalväsendeti Sverige 1813-1962, 1963; Dan Vincent Lundberg: Mina Minnen, 1983; editor-in-chief, founder Nordisk Medicinhistorisk Arsbok, 1953—. Contbr. articles to profl. publs. Home: Villa Walhall, Parkgatan 12, 15132 Sodertalje Sweden Office: Rindogatan 21, 11536 Stockholm Sweden

KOCSIS, ZOLTAN, pianist; b. Budapest, Hungary, May 30, 1952; s. Otto and Maria (Matyas) K. Ed. Budapest Music Acad. Asst. prof. Music Acad. Budapest, 1976-79, prof., 1979—; producer archive sect. Hungaroton Rec. Co.; appeared with Dresden Philharmonic Orch. (E.Ger.) and performed in W.Ger., USSR, Austria and Czechoslovakia, 1971; toured with Dezso Ranki and Budapest Symphony Orch., 1971; toured Japan, 1975; recital appearances, Netherlands, Paris, London, Ireland, 1972; concert appearances, Norway, France, Austria, with London Symphony Orch., at Promenade Concerts, London; appeared at Festival Estival, Paris, 1977, Edinburgh Festival, 1978; author numerous publs.; arrangements for piano and 2 pianos. Recipient First prize Beethoven Piano Competition, Hungarian Radio and RV, 1970, Liszt prize 2d degree, 1973, Kossuth prize, 1978. Office: Interconcert Agy, Vorosmarty ter I, 1051 Budapest V, Hungary *

KODAIRA, YUTAKA, architect; b. Urawa, Saitama, Japan, Sept. 29, 1954; s. Masao and Youko K.; m. Takako Kodaira, Oct. 13, 1985; 1 child, Yuuko. BArch, Nihon U., Tokyo, 1978; MArch, U. Fla., Gainesville, 1980, Cert. in Gerontology, 1980. Substitute designer Akabane Archtl. Firm, Yoyogi, Tokyo, 1980; designer Azusa Sekkei, Gotanda, Tokyo, 1980-82; chief designer OAC Archtl. Firm, Sinagawa-ku, Tokyo, 1982-86; pres. ARC PIER Archtl. Firm, Meguro-ku, Tokyo, 1986—. Mem. Japan Inst. Architects, Japan Archtl. Firm Assn. Home: 1-3-16 Ouyaba, 336 Urawa-shi Saitamaken, Japan Office: ARC PIER Archtl Firm, 1-1-65 #406 Nakameguro, 153 Meguro-ku Tokyo, Japan

KODYM, MILOSLAV, psychologist, researcher; b. Sobeslav, Czechoslovakia, Aug. 1, 1930; s. Ruzena Kodymova; m. Miroslava Lintnerova, Sept. 8, 1951; children: Miloslava, Roman. PhD, U. Prague, 1967, CSc, 1971. Tchr. Pedagogic Sch., Ceske Budejovice, Czechoslovakia, 1953-59; mem. faculty Faculty Pedagogy, Ceske Budejovice, 1959-79; sci. worker, dir. Inst. Psychology, Prague, Czechoslovakia, 1979—; chief editor Chechoslovak Psychology, Czechoslovak Acad. Scis., 1979—; pres. sci. bd. pedagogy and psychology, 1982—; chief psychology dept. Faculty Pedagogy, Prague, 1985—. Author: Problem Solving and Performance, 1972, Selection of Talents, 1978, On the Theory of Abilities, 1987; author, editor: Psychological Aspects of Personality Development, 1987. Recipient silver medal Czechoslovk Acad. Scis., 1980, state honors for excellent work, 1985, laureat Acads. Scis. and Social Scis., Moscow-Prague, 1985. Czechoslovak Psychol. Assn. (com. 1982—). Home: Machuldova 596/21, 140 18 Prague 4 Czechoslovakia Office: Inst Psychology Husova, 4 110 00 Prague 1 Czechoslovakia

KOECHLER, HANS, educator; b. Schwaz, Tyrol, Austria, Oct. 18, 1948; s. Hans and Edith (Grabherr) K. Ph.D., U. Innsbruck, 1972. Research asst. U. Innsbruck, 1972-77, asst. prof., 1977-82, prof. philosophy, 1982—; chmn. Com. for Sci. and Politics, Innsbruck, 1972—. Author: The Subject-Object Dialectic, 1974, Skepsis and Social Philosophy, 1978, Philosophy, Law, Politics, 1985, Phenomenological Realism, 1986; editor: (series) Studies in Internat. Relations, 1978—, Sci. and Politics, 1972—, The Crisis of Representative Democracy, 1987, Terrorism and National Liberation, 1988; organizer internat. confs. in fields of human rights and terrorism. Founder, pres. Internat. Progress Orgn., Vienna, 1972—; bd. dirs. Austrian Coll. Soc., 1972—; sec.-gen. Euregio Alpina, Innsbruck, 1973-77; mem. Austrian Peace Research Inst., 1985—. Recipient History medal, Internat. Progress Orgn., 1982. Mem. Austrian Soc. Philosophy (treas.), Inst. Higher Econ. and Social Studies Brussels (hon. mem.), Inst. Diplomatic Relations, Brussels, Internat. Phenomenological Soc., Goerres Soc. Roman Catholic. Clubs: Alpbach. Office: Dept Philosophy, Univ Innsbruck, Innrain 52, A 6020 Innsbruck Austria

KOEHN, PETER, marketing professional; b. Copenhagen, Feb. 24, 1953; s. Hans Henning and Ruth (Haustein) K.; m. Dorota M. Gozik, Sept. 19, 1981. Degree in higher bus., Soenderborg Comml. Sch., Denmark, 1974. Forwarding agent H.K. Samuelsen AS, Soenderborg, 1974-76; mktg. asst. Danfoss AS, Nordborg, Denmark, 1977-82; mktg. mgr. MA Solarium Internat. AS, Soenderborg, 1982-85; dept. sales and mktg. dept. Exhibition Ctr. Herning, Denmark, 1986—; mng. dir. Scan Expo, Herning, 1986—. Home: Lyngens Kvt 68, 7400 Herning Denmark Office: Scan Expo, PO Box 22, 7400 Herning Denmark

KOELZER, GEORGE JOSEPH, lawyer; b. Orange, N.J., Mar. 21, 1938; s. George Joseph and Albertina Florence (Graul) K.; m. Patricia Ann Kilian, Apr. 8, 1967; 1 son, James Patrick. A.B., Rutgers U., 1962, LL.B., 1964. Bar: N.J. 1964, D.C. 1978, N.Y. 1980. Assoc. Louis R. Lombardino, Livingston, N.J., 1964-66, Lum Biunno & Tompkins, Newark, 1971-73, Giordano, Halleran & McOmber, Middletown, N.J., 1973-74; asst. U.S. atty. for N.J., U.S. Dept. Justice, 1966-71; ptnr. Evans, Koelzer, Osborne & Kreizman, N.Y.C. and Red Bank, N.J., 1974-86; ptnr. Ober, Kaler, Grimes & Shriver, Inc., N.Y.C., 1986—; mem. lawyers adv. com. U.S. Ct. Appeals (3d cir.) 1985-87, vice chmn., 1986—, chmn., 1987; mem. lawyers adv. com. U.S. Dist. Ct. N.J., 1984—; permanent mem. Jud. Conf. of U.S. Ct. Appeals for 3d cir.; del. jud. conf. U.S. Ct. Appeals for 2d cir., 1987-88. Recipient Atty. Gen.'s award, 1970. Mem. ABA (sect. litigation, co-chmn. com. on admiralty and maritime litigation 1979-82, mem. council sect. litigation 1985-88, chmn. 9th ann. meeting sect. litigation 1984, dir. div. IV procedural coms. 1982-85, dir. div. I adminstrn. 1988—, mem. nominating com. 1982, 84, 87, advisor standing com. lawyer competence 1986—), Maritime Law Assn. U.S. (ABA relations com., mcht. marine com.), N.Y. State Bar Assn. (admiralty com.), Assn. Bar City N.Y. (admiralty com. 1987—), New York County Lawyers Assn. (admiralty com.), D.C. Bar Assn., N.J. Bar Assn.(chmn. admiralty com. 1985-87), Fed. Bar Assn., Fed. Bar Council, Def. Research Inst. (chmn. admiralty com. 1982-85), Maritime Assn. Port N.Y., Assn. Average Adjusters Gt. Britain, Assn. Average Adjusters U.S., Guild Cath. Lawyers N.Y. Roman Catholic. Clubs: Downtown Athletic, Whitehall, World Trade (N.Y.C.); Nat. Lawyers (Washington); Wig and Pen, Marine, Directors (London); Navesink Country (Middletown); Mid-Ocean (Bermuda). Home: 29 Regent Dr Shrewsbury NJ 07702 Office: 55 Broadway 1 Exchange Plaza New York NY 10006 also: 505 Thornall St 1 Metroplaza Edison NJ 08837

KOENIG, FRANZ CARDINAL, archbishop; b. Rabenstein, Austria, Aug. 3, 1905; D.D.; Ph.D.; hon. degrees univs. Vienna, Innsbruck, Salzburg, Zagreb, Am. univs. Ordained priest Roman Catholic Ch., 1933; prof. high sch.; lectr. U. Vienna, 1946-48, extraordinary prof., from 1948; bishop coadjutor, St. Poelten, 1952; archbishop of Vienna, 1956-85; cardinal, 1958; pres. Secretariat for Non-Believers, 1965-80. Mem. Am. Acad. Arts and Scis. Author: Christus und die Religionen der Erde, 1951; Religionswissenschaftliches Woerterbuch, 1956; Zarathustras Jenseitsvorstellungen und das Alte Testament, 1964; Die Stunde der Welt 1971; Der Aufbruch zum Geist, 1972; Das Zeichen Gottes, 1973; Der Mensch ist fuer die Zukunft angelegt, 1975; Kirche und Welt, 1978; Glaube ist Freiheit, 1981; Der Glaube der Menschen, 1985, Der Weg der Kirche, 1986, Lexikon der Religionen, 1987. Address: Wollzeile 2, 1010 Vienna Austria

KOENIG, ROBERT AUGUST, clergyman, educator; b. Red Wing, Minn., July 14, 1933; s. William C. and Florence E. (Tebbe) K.; BS cum laude, U. Wis., 1955; MA in Ednl. Adminstrn., U. Minn., 1965, PhD, 1973; MDiv magna cum laude, San Francisco Theol. Sem., 1969; postgrad. (John Hay fellow) Bennington Coll., summer, 1965; m. Pauline Louise Olson, June 21, 1962. Supr. music Florence (Wis.) High Sch., 1955-56; dir. instrumental music Chetek (Wis.), public schs., 1958-62; tchr. instrumental music and humanities Palo Alto (Calif.) Sr. High Sch., 1962-65; asst. to minister St. John's Presbyn. Ch., San Francisco, 1964-65; ordained to ministry Presbyn. Ch., 1970; minister Sawyer County (Wis.) larger parish, 1969-74; tchr. gen. music Jordan Jr. High Sch., Palo Alto, 1966-69; instr., Coll. Edn., U. Minn., 1969-71; adminstrv. asst. to pres. Lakewood State Community Coll., White Bear Lake, Minn., 1971-72; asst. to exec. dir. Minn. Higher Edn. Coordinating Bd., St. Paul, 1972, coordinator commn. and personnel services, 1972-74; instr. Inver Hills Community Coll., Inver Grove Heights, Minn., 1974; minister First Presbyn. Ch. of Chippewa Falls (Wis.), 1974-85; sr. pastor Grove Presbyn. Ch., Danville, Pa., 1985-88, First Presbyn. Ch., South St. Paul, Minn., 1988—; mem. study com. Presbytery of Chippewa, 1973-74, mem. ministerial relations com., 1974-77; adj. asst. prof. dept. ednl. adminstrn. U. Minn., Mpls., 1976-77; mem. faculty U. Wis. Extension, Eau Claire, 1977, chmn. 3d Ann. Bibl. Seminar, 1977, mem. faculty Communiversity, 1977-85; mem. internat. coordinating com. of ch. mission Synod of Lakes and Prairies, 1978-79; mem. ministerial relations com. Presbytery of No. Waters, 1977-82, chmn. ministerial relations com., 1981-82, moderator, 1983; chmn. Synod Designation Pastor Plan Cabinet 1982-84; chmn. Presbytery Council, 1982-84; mem. Christian edn. com. Presbytery of Northumberland, 1987-88, mem. Presbytery council, 1987-88; mem. Christian edn. com. Synod of the Trinity, 1987-88, Danville-Riverside Area Ministerial Assn., 1985-88, pres., 1987-88. Bd. dirs. North Central Career Devel. Center, Mpls., 1978-84, chmn. fin. com., 1979-84, bd. dirs. devel. found., 1983-85; pres. Chippewa Valley Ecumenical Housing Assn., 1984-85. Served with U.S. Army, 1956-58; Korea. Lodges: Danville Elks; Wis. Masons (grand chaplain Wis. 1977-80, 83-85). Contbr. articles to profl. jours. Home: 42 Timberwood Dr Danville PA 17821 Office: 332 Bloom St Danville PA 17821

KOENIGSBERGER, DOROTHY MARGARET, historian; b. N.Y.C., Aug. 10, 1938; d. Henry S. and Margaret D. (Milano) Romano; m. Helmut Georg Koenigsberger, July 20, 1961; children: Francesca, Laura (twins). BA, CUNY, Bklyn., 1960; PhD, U. Nottingham, Eng., 1969. Lectr. history Wells Coll., Aurora, N.Y., 1969-71; fellow Soc. for Humanities Cornell U., Ithaca, N.Y., 1971-72; lectr. history The Poly. of N. London, 1975-76; dir. postgrad. studies in humanities, reader in intellectual history, The Hatfield (Eng.) Poly., 1976—. Author: Renaissance Man and Creative Thinking, 1979; author: (with others) Politics and Culture in Early Modern Europe, 1987; contbr. articles to profl. jours. Active Social Dem. Party, Eng., 1984—. Recipient Best 1st or 2d MS Soc. Italian Hist. Studies, 1969. Fellow Royal Hist. Soc. (elected 1980); mem. Soc. for Renaissance Studies (elected 1983), Inst. Hist. Research. Roman Catholic. Home: 41A Lancaster Grove, London NW3 4HB, England

KOEPF, WERNER KARL, marketing professional; b. Erdweis, Austria, Jan. 8, 1942; came to Fed. Republic Germany, 1961; s. Rudolf and Marie (Loew) K.; m. M. Birgitta Ade, Aug. 15, 1967; children: Maximilian, Johanna, Christiane, Angelika. BS in Elec. Engring., St. Poelten, 1961; Diplom Volkswirt, U. Munich, 1966. Sales mgr. German dist. Texas Instruments Corp., Freising, Fed. Republic Germany, 1967-68; ops. mgr. Europe Texas Instruments Corp., Geneva, 1968-70, Slough, Eng., 1970-71; gen. mgr. cen. Europe dist. Texas Instruments Corp., Munich, 1971-76, v.p. distbg. Europe, 1976-82, v.p. mktg. Europe, 1982-85, v.p. internat. systems div., 1985-87, v.p. sci. group, 1987—; pres. Tex. Instruments Internat. Trade Corp., Dallas, 1982-84; chmn. Tex. Instruments Switzerland SA, Zurich, 1982-86, Tex. Instruments Norway, Oslo, 1982-87; bd. dirs. Tex. Instruments Belgium SA, Brussels, 1982-87, Tex. Instruments Spain, Madrid, 1982—. Recipient award for excellency in studies Ministry of Edn., Vienna, Austria, 1961. Roman Catholic. Office: Texas Instruments Deutschland, Haggerty Strasse 1, 8050 Freising Federal Republic of Germany

KOEPPEL, GARY MERLE, writer, publisher, art gallery owner; b. Albany, Oreg., Jan 20, 1938; s. Carl Melvin and Barbara Emma (Adams) K. BA, Portland State U., 1961; MFA, State U. Iowa, 1963. Writing instr. State U. Iowa, Iowa City, 1963-64; guest prof. English, U. P.R. San Juan, 1964-65; assoc. prof. creative writing Portland (Oreg.) State U., 1965-68; owner, operator Coast Gallery, Big Sur, 1971—, Pebble Beach, Calif., 1986—, Maui, Hawaii, 1985—; owner Coast Pub. Co.; editor, pub. Big Sur Gazette, 1978-81; producer, sponsor Maui Marine Art Expo., Monterey Marine Art Expo. Author: Sculptured Sandcast Candles, 1974. Founder Big Sur Vol. Fire Brigade, 1975; chmn. coordinating com. Big Sur Area Planning, 1972-75; chmn. Big Sur Citizens Adv. Com., 1975-78. Mem. Big Sur C. of C. (pres. 1974-75, 82-84), Big Sur Grange, Audubon Soc., Cousteau Soc., Phi Gamma Delta, Alpha Delta Sigma. Address: Coast Gallery PO Box 1501 Pebble Beach CA 93953

KOESTER, BERTHOLD KARL, lawyer; honorary consul Federal Republic of Germany; b. Aachen, Germany, June 30, 1931; s. Wilhelm P. and Margarethe A. (Witteler) K.; m. Hildegard Maria Buettner, June 30, 1961; children: Georg W., Wolfgang J., Reinhard B. JD, U. Muenster, Fed. Republic Germany, 1957. Cert. Real Estate Agt., Ariz. Asst. prof. civil and internat. law U. Muenster, 1957-60; atty. Cts. of Duesseldorf, Fed. Republic Germany, 1960-82; v.p. Bank J. H. Vogeler & Co., Duesseldorf, 1960-64; pres. Bremer Tank-u. Kuehlschifahrts Gesellschaft, Bremen, Fed. Republic Germany, 1969-72; atty., trustee internat. corps., Duesseldorf and Phoenix, 1973-82, Phoenix, 1983—; of counsel Tancer Law Offices, Phoenix, 1978-86; prof. internat. bus. law Am. Grad. Sch. Internat. Mgmt., Glendale, Ariz., 1978-81; with Applewhite, Laflin & Lewis, Real Estate Investments, Phoenix, 1981-86, ptnr., 1982-86, Beucler Real Estate Investments, 1986-88, Scottsdale, Ariz.; hon. consul Fed. Republic of Germany for Ariz., 1982—; chmn., chief exec. officer Arimpex Hi-Tec, Inc., Phoenix, 1981—. Contbr. articles to profl. jours. Pres. Parents Assn. Humboldt Gymnasium, Duesseldorf, 1971-78; active German Red Cross, from 1977. Mem. Duesseldorf Chamber of Lawyers, Bochum (Fed. Republic Germany) Assn. Tax Lawyers, Bonn German-Saudi Arabian Assn. (pres. 1976-79), Bonn German-Korean Assn., Assn. for German-Korean Econ. Devel. (pres. 1974-78), Ariz. Consular Corps, German-Am. C. of C., Phoenix Met. C. of C. Club: Rotary (Scottsdale, Ariz.). Home: 6201 E Cactus Rd Scottsdale AZ 85254

KOESTER, ROBERT JOSEPH, JR., marketing company executive; b. Scranton, Pa., Oct. 23, 1948; s. Robert Joseph and Ann Marie (Wielebinski) K.; 1 child, Robert III; B.S. in mktg., Husson Coll., 1970; M.B.A. in Mktg., U. Scranton, 1977; postgrad. Temple U., Lehigh U.; 1 son, Robert Joseph III. With mktg. dept., Lomma Enterprises Inc., Scranton, 1972-76, asst. mktg. dir., 1973-75, v.p. mktg., 1974-76; dir. coop. edn., contracted edn. and placement Lackawanna Jr. Coll., 1976-77, also, instr. in bus.; dir. coop. edn. Wilkes Coll., Wilkes-Barre, Pa., 1977-82, adj. prof. mktg., 1978-86; dir. community relations Community Med. Center, 1978-82; dir. mktg. Pocono Hosp., East Stroudsburg, Pa., 1983-84; dir. mktg. First Hosp. Corp., 1985-86, pres. RJK Mktg. Assocs., Ltd., 1987—; lectr. mktg. and mgmt.; adj. prof. mktg. Pa. State U., Scranton, 1980-84. Mem. adv. bd. Scranton Salvation Army, mem. Scranton-Lackawanna Health & Welfare Authority. Mem. Am. Mktg. Assn., Acad. Health Care Mktg., Scranton C. of C. (chmn. bus. card exchange com. 1981-82), South Scranton Resident Assn. (pres. 1982-84), Democrat. Lodges: Scranton Kiwanis (bd. dirs. 1974-76, (pres. 1979-80), Elks (lodge officer 1987-88). Home: 225 N Washington Ave Park Plaza Scranton PA 18503 Office: RJK Mktg Assocs Ltd 415 N Washington Ave Scranton PA 18503

KOETZ, AXEL G., management consultant; b. Cologne, Fed. Republic Germany, Apr. 29, 1954; s. Wolfgang and Ursula (Boehm) K. MBA in Econs., U. Cologne, 1977, PhD in Econs., 1981. Asst. prof. U. Cologne, 1977-79; mgr., team mem. econ. research studies Fed. Adminstrn. Insts., Cologne, Bonn, Fed. Republic Germany, 1979-81; mgmt. cons. Kienbaum Mgmt. Cons., Düsseldorf, Fed. Republic Germany, 1981-84, team mgr., 1984-85, br. mgr., 1985-87, v.p., head fin. services and nonprofit orgns. div., 1987—. Author: German Universities with Business/Adminstration Faculties, 1977, Optimal Public Debt, 1981; contbr. articles to profl. jours. Mem. German Assn. MBA Grads. (v.p. 1981-83), German Assn. Strategic Planning (lectr. 1984, 87). Liberal. Home: Bachemer Strasse 2, 5000 Cologne 41 Federal Republic of Germany Office: Kienbaum Unternehmensberatung, Fuellenbachstrasse 8, D-4000 Dusseldorf Federal Republic of Germany

KOFF, DAVID ALAIN, radiologist; b. Paris, Aug. 14, 1954; s. Simon and Judith (Taingiu) K.; m. Nadine Smolarski, Jan. 26, 1983; children: Alexandre, Nicolas. Ednl. Commn. Fgn. Med. Grads., Phila., 1978; cert. radiology, Paris Univ. Rene Descartes, Paris, 1981. Resident Sevres Hosp., Paris, 1978-80; fellow Broussais Hosp., Paris, 1979-81, Ambroise Pare, Paris, 1980. Contbr. articles to profl. jours. Served to capt. French mil., 1982. Mem. Soc. Francaise pour l'Application Ultrasons à la Medecine et à la Biologie, Doppler Club France. Home: 19 Ave Theophile Gautier, 75016 Paris France Office: 15 Charles Duquet, 60100 Creil France

KOFF, HOWARD MICHAEL, lawyer; b. Bklyn., July 25, 1941; s. Arthur and Blanche Koff; m. Linda Sue Bright, Sept. 10, 1966; 1 son, Michael Arthur Bright. B.S., NYU, 1962; J.D., Bklyn. Law Sch., 1965; LL.M. in Taxation, Georgetown U., 1968. Bar: N.Y. 1965, D.C. 1966, U.S. Supreme Ct. 1969, U.S. Ct. Appeals (2d, 3d, 4th, 5th, 7th, 9th and D.C. cirs.), U.S. Dist. Ct. (no. dist.) N.Y. 1981. Appellate atty. Tax Div., U.S. Dept. Justice, Washington, 1965-69; tax supr. Chrysler Corp., Detroit, 1969-70; chief tax counsel Conn. Gen. Life Ins. Co., Hartford, Conn., 1970-77; chief tax counsel Rohm & Haus Co., Phila., 1977-78; ptnr. Dibble, Koff, Lane, Stern and Stern, Rochester, N.Y., 1978-81; pres. Howard M. Koff, P.C., Albany, N.Y., 1981—; lectr. tax matters. Recipient Founders Day award NYU, 1962; Lawyers Coop. award for gen. excellence Lawyers Coop. Pub. Co., 1965. Mem. Fed. Bar Assn. (past pres. Hartford County chpt.), ABA (past chmn. subcom. com. on partnerships tax sect.), Albany County Bar Assn., Estate Planning Council Eastern N.Y., Albany Area C. of C. Republican. Jewish. Clubs: Rotary, Colonie Guilderland N.Y. Charter mem. editorial adv. bd. Jour. Real Estate Taxation; contbr. articles to legal jours. Home: 205 Bentwood Ct W Albany NY 12203 Office: 600 Broadway Albany NY 12207

KOFFORD, CREE-L, lawyer; b. Santaquin, Utah, July 11, 1933; s. Cree C. and Melba (Nelson) K.; m. Ila Jean Macdonald, Sept. 11, 1953; children—Kim, Jane, Bradley, Quinn, Tracy. B.S., U. Utah, 1955; J.D., U. So. Calif., 1961. Bar: Calif. 1962. Ptnr. Munns & Kofford, San Marino, Calif., 1962-68, Munns, Kofford, Hoffman, Hunt & Throckmorton, Pasadena, Calif., 1969—; chmn. bd. Converse Profl. Group, Inc., Pasadena, Calif., Access Controls, Inc., Burbank, Calif., Cannon Safe, Inc., Pico Rivera, Calif., Astro Fab, Inc., Pico Rivera; bd. dirs. Southland Nat. Bank, Arcadia, Calif. Mem. ABA, Calif. Bar Assn., Los Angeles County Bar Assn. Republican. Mormon. Club: Univ. (Pasadena). Home: 1330 Rodeo Rd Arcadia CA 91006 Office: Munns Kofford et al 225 S Lake Ave Penthouse Pasadena CA 91101

KOFORD, STUART KEITH, electronics executive; b. North Hollywood, Calif., Oct. 25, 1953; s. Kenneth Harold and Theresa (Sutton) K.; m. Gail Anne Joerger, Dec. 28, 1985. BSME, Mich. Tech. U., 1976. Engr. Motorola, Schaumburg, Ill., 1976-77, sr. engr., 1977-79; engring. project mgr. Amphenol, Cicero, Ill., 1979-80, mgr. research and devel., 1980-82; mgr. engring. Amphenol, Broadview, Ill., 1982—; pres. Koford Engring., Addison, Ill., 1982. Contbr. articles to profl. jours. Mem. IEEE (program com. Electronic Components Conf. 1979—), Soc. Plastic Engrs., ASME, Electronic Connector Study Group (program chmn. 1982-84). Republican. Roman Catholic. Home: 19W 281 Paul Revere Ln Oak Brook IL 60521 Office: Koford Engring 415 Belden Ave Addison IL 60101

KOGUT, MAURICE DAVID, pediatric endocrinologist; b. Bklyn., July 7, 1930; s. Nat and Etta K.; m. June Patricia Wenzel, May 9, 1959; children: Melissa, Pamela, Stacy. B.A., N.Y. U., 1951, M.D., 1955. Diplomate Am. Bd. Pediatrics, Am. Bd. Pediatric Endocrinology. Pediatric intern and resident Bellevue Hosp., N.Y.C., 1955-57; chief resident in pediatrics Children's Hosp. of Los Angeles, 1959-60, fellow in pediatric endocrinology, 1960-62, head div. endocrinology and metabolism, 1970-80, asso. head dept. pediatrics, 1975-80, program dir. clin. research center, 1967-79; asst. prof. pediatrics Sch. Medicine, U. So. Calif., 1965-68, asso. prof., 1968-73, prof. pediatrics, 1973-80; prof. pediatrics, chmn. dept. of pediatrics Sch. Medicine Wright State U., Dayton, Ohio, 1980—; v.p. for med. affairs Children's Med. Center, Dayton, 1980—. (recipient CINE/65 Golden Eagle film award for med. film 1965). Served as capt. M.C. USAF, 1957-59. USPHS fellow, 1960-62. Mem. Am. Acad. Pediatrics, Am. Acad. Med. Dirs., Soc. for Pediatric Research, Assn. Med. Sch. Pediatric Chairmen, AAAS, AMA, Am. Fedn. Clin. Research, Am. Diabetes Assn., Endocrine Soc., Am. Pediatric Soc., Lawson Wilkins Pediatric Endocrine Soc., Alpha Omega Alpha. Office: Children's Med Center 1 Children's Plaza Dayton OH 45404

KOH, EUSEBIO LEGARDA, mathematics educator; b. Manila, Oct. 4, 1931; s. Enrique Legarda and Felisa Un (Makabuhay) K.; m. Donelita Mesina Viardo, Feb. 21, 1958; children—Eudonette, Elizabeth, Ethel, Denise. B.S. in Mech. Engring. cum laude, U. Philippines, Quezon City, 1954; M.S. in Mech. Engring., Purdue U., 1956; M.S., Birmingham, 1961; Ph.D., SUNY-Stony Brook, 1967. Research engr. Internat. Harvester Co., Chgo., 1956-57; asst. prof. mech. engring. U. Philippines, 1959-64, head dept., 1963-64; assoc. prof. math. U. Regina, Sask., Can., 1970-75, prof., 1975—, head dept. math., 1977-79; guest prof. math. Techn. Hochschule, Darmstadt, Fed. Republic Germany, 1975-76; prof. math. U. Petroleum/Minerals, Dhahran, Saudi Arabia, 1979-81. Contbr. research papers to profl. jours. Pres., Philippine Assn. Sask., 1971, bd. dirs., 1984; editor: Philippine Newsletter, 1985. Colombo Plan scholar Brit. Council, 1960; Travel fellow Nat. Research Council, Fed. Republic Germany, 1975; research grantee Nat. Sci. and Engring. Research Council, 1971—; named Outstanding Prof., U. Philippines Student Union, 1962. Mem. Soc. Indsl. and Applied Math., Am. Math. Soc., Math. Assn. Am., Can. Applied Math. Soc., Philippine Am. Acad. Sci. and Engring. (founding). Avocations: chess, bridge, tennis, golf. Office: Dept of Math and Statistics, Univ of Regina, Regina, SK Canada S4S 0A2

KOH, JOHN TIONG LU, lawyer; b. Ipoh, Perak, Malaysia, July 28, 1955; arrived in Singapore, 1962; s. S.C. Koh and L.K. Li. BA, Cambridge U., 1979, MA, 1982; LLM, Harvard U., 1985. Dep. pub. prosecutor, state counsel Atty. Gen., Singapore, 1980-85; assoc. Milbank, Tweed, Hadley & McCoy, Washington, 1985-86; dep. dir. Comml. Affairs Dept. Singapore, 1986—; barrister-at-law Gray's Inn, London, 1980—; advocate and solicitor Singapore Supreme Ct., 1987—; law lectr. Nat. U. Singapore, 1981-83, 1987; cons. Practice Law Course, Singapore, 1982-84, 87—, Telecommunication Authority Singapore, 1980-83. Asia Found. fellow, 1985-86. Mem. Jud. Legal Officers Assn. (com. mem.). Clubs: Raffles Country, Oxford and Cambridge Soc. Singapore (asst. sec.), Harvard of Singapore. Office: Ministry Fin, Comml Affairs Dept, 8 Shenton Way #42-01, 0106 Singapore Singapore

KOH, KIAN TEE, physician; b. Senggarang, Batu Pahat, Johore, Malaysia, Aug. 10, 1944; s. Kim Cheng and Teo Eng (Teo) Khow; m. Ah Tua Gan, Nov. 1, 1973; children: ChowYong, Chow Yee, Chow Kun, Chow Ping. MB, Nat. Taiwan U., Tapei, 1973. Resident in surgery China Med. Ctr., Taipei, 1973-74; housemanship Gen. Hosp., Kuantan, Pahang, Malaysia, 1974-75; med. officer Gen. Hosp., Johor Baru, Johor, Malaysia, 1975-76, 1977-78, med. officer ear, nose and throat, 1978-80; med. officer Dist. Hosp., Kota Tinggi, Johor, 1976-77; gen. practice medicine Clinic Koh, Johor Baru, 1980—. Author: A Day in General Hospital, 1981. Cons. The Youth United Movement, Johor Baru, 1982—, The Red Crescent Assn., Johor Baru, 1983—, The Basketball Club Assn., Johor Baru, 1984—, The Table Tennis Club Assn., Johor Baru, 1986—. Mem. Malaysian Med. Assn. (life), Writers' Assn. Chinese Medium Malaysia (life), U. Taiwan Alumni Assn. (v.p. 198—), Chinese Assn. Home: #12 Jalan Ungu Tujuh, Taman Pelangi, Johor Baru, 80400 Johor Malaysia Office: Clinic Koh, #3 Jalan Sutera Satu, Taman Sentosa, Johor Baru, 80150 Johor Malaysia

KOH, KYUNG BONG, psychiatry educator; b. Seoul, Republic of Korea, Nov. 10, 1947; s. Joon Sam Koh and Shin Bock Huh; m. Sung Sook Cho, Sept. 25, 1982; children: Jin Young, Jin Woo. MB, Yon Sei U., Seoul, 1974, MS, 1978, PhD, 1988. Diplomate in Psychiatry. Intern, then resident Severance Hosp., Seoul, 1974-79; research fellow Yonsei U. Severance Hosp., Seoul, 1982-83, asst. prof. dept. psychiatry, 1985—; instr., chief dept. psychiatry Yongdong Severance Hosp., Seoul, 1983-85, asst. prof., dir. consultation and liaison dept. psychiatry, 1985—, dir. research, 1986-87. Served as maj. Korean armed forces, 1979-82. Mem. Korean Neuropsychiat. Assn, Korean Psychopharmacological Assn. Office: Yonsei U Severance Hosp, Dept Psychiatry, CPO Box 8044 Seoul Republic of Korea

KOH, TOMMY THONG BEE, foreign service officer, lawyer; b. Singapore, Nov. 12, 1937; s. John Han-kok and Chai-Ying (Sze) K.; m. Siew-Aing Poh, Aug. 5, 1967; children—Wei, Aun. LL.B., Nat. U. Singapore, 1961; LL.M., Harvard U., 1964; diploma in criminology, Cambridge U., 1965; LL.D., Yale U., 1984. Singapore ambassador to UN N.Y.C., 1968-71, 74-84; pres. 3d UN Conf. on Law of Sea, N.Y.C., 1981-82; dean Faculty Law Nat. U. Singapore, 1971-74, prof. law, 1974—; Singapore ambassador to U.S. Washington, 1984—; mem. internat. adv. bd. Harvard Negotiation Jour., Cambridge, Mass., 1985—. Contbr. articles to profl. jours. Recipient Wolfgang Friedman prize Columbia U., 1984; Jackson Ralston prize Stanford U., 1985, Internat. Service award Tufts U., 1987, Jit. Trainor award Georgetown U., 1987, Pub. Service star Singapore Govt., 1971, Meritorious Service medal Singapore Govt., 1979, ann. award for contbr. to world peace Milton Helpern Library of Legal Medicine, N.Y.C., 1982. Office: Singapore Embassy 1824 R St NW Washington DC 20009

KOHEN, MARCEL, physician; b. Istanbul, Turkey, Dec. 29, 1944; arrived in France, 1975; s. Salamon and Berthe (Tchoucran) K.; m. Line Boton, Jan. 5, 1968; 1 child, Betty. MD, Cerrahpsas U., Istanbul, 1971. Diplomate in medicine. Asst. physician Amiral Bristol Hosp., Istanbul, 1971, Hosp. Nat. Health Göztepe, Istanbul, 1973-75; physician Civil Hosp. Strasbourg, France, 1975—. Served with M.C. Turkish Army, 1972-73. Home: 32 Ave des Vosges, 67000 Strasbourg France

KOHL, DORA DIERKS, savings and loan executive; b. Sugar Land, Tex., Aug. 7, 1922; d. Hans Fritz and Elizabeth Amelia (Pilz) Dierks; student pub. schs.; m. Charles William Kohl, Jr., Feb. 27, 1944; 1 son, Charles Johann. With Marshall Canning Co., Sugar Land, 1939-45, Montgomery Ward, Denver, 1945-46; with Liberty County Fed. Savs. & Loan Assn., Liberty, Tex., 1951-85, treas., controller, 1972-77, v.p. personnel, 1977-79, v.p., adminstrv. asst., 1979-85; bookkeeper Black Gold Press, 1985-86; co-owner Trinity Valley Copier Supply, Liberty, 1987—. Sec., Liberty chpt. Am. Cancer Soc. Mem. Am. Savs. and Loan Inst. (pres. Beaumont chpt.), Nat. Soc. Controllers and Financial Officers. Democrat. Presbyterian. Home: 2001 Magnolia St Liberty TX 77575 Office: Trinity Valley Copier Supply 1406 Browning St Liberty TX 77575

KOHL, HELMUT, chancellor Federal Republic Germany; b. Ludwigshafen, Germany, Apr. 3, 1930; s. Hans and Cecile Schnur; student law, polit. sci. and history U. Frankurt; Dr.phil., U. Heidelberg, 1958; m. Hannelore Renner, 1960; children: Walter, Peter. Staff mem. trade assn., 1958; mem. Landtag Rheinland-Pfalz, 1959, chmn. Chistian Democratic Union party Landtag group, 1963, minister pres. Rheinland Pfalz, 1969-76; chmn. Christian Democratic Union party Germany, 1969, chmn. 1973—; chmn. CDU/CSU Parliamentary Party, 1976-82; leader of opposition in Deutsche Bundestag, 1976-82; chancellor of Fed. Republic Germany, Bonn, 1982—. Decorated grand cross 1st class Order of Merit Fed. Republic Germany; Order of Merit of Rhineland-Palatinate. Author: Hausputz hinter den Fassaden, 1971; Zwischen Ideologie und Pragmatismus, 1973; Bundestagsreden, 1978; Neuer Realismus, 1980; Portrait einer Volksparti, 1981. Office: Bundeskanzleramt, Adenauerallee 141, 5300 Bonn 1 Federal Republic of Germany

KOHL, JOHN CLAYTON, emeritus civil engineering educator; b. N.Y.C., June 22, 1908; s. Clayton C. and Margaret (Williams) K.; m. Gladys V. Mitchell, July 10, 1935; children: John Clayton, Atlee Mitchell. Student, Oberlin Coll., 1925-27; B.S.E., U. Mich., 1929; M.A. (hon.), U. Pa., 1973. Registered profl. engr., Pa. With Cin. Union Terminal Co., 1929-30; mem. faculty Carnegie Inst. Tech., 1930-37; with Pitts. Plate Glass Co. and subs. Pitts. Corning Corp., 1937-46; prof. civil engring., dir. Transp. Inst., U. Mich., 1946-66; on leave as asst. adminstr. HHFA, 1961-66; exec. v.p. Am. Transit Assn., Washington, 1966; exec. sec., div. engring. Nat. Acad. Scis.-NRC, 1966-68; sr. asso. Wilbur Smith & Assos., Washington, 1968-70; commr. N.J. Dept. Transp., 1970-74; prof. civil and urban engring. U. Pa., Phila., 1974-76; prof. emeritus U. Pa., 1976—; Trustee Phila., Balt. and Washington, and Del. railroads, 1974-78; sr. vis. fellow Princeton U., 1976-81. Author: (with Atlee M. Kohl) The Smart Way to Buy a Business, 1986; sr. assoc. editor Woodland Pubs., 1986—; contbr. articles to profl. jours. Mem. Mich. Commn. Intergovtl. Relations, 1954-58; vice chmn. truck adv. bd. Mich. Pub. Service Commn., 1957-61; mem. Tristate Transp. Commn. N.Y., 1961-66, 70-74, chmn., 1970-71; mem. Delaware Valley Regional Planning Commn., Phila., 1970-74, chmn., 1973; chmn. Govs. Transp. Com., 1970-73; mem. transp. research adv. com. Dept. Agr., 1957-61; mem. Pres.'s Policy Adv. Com. for D.C., 1963-66; exec. com., chmn. transp. com. Delaware Valley Council, 1976-79; exec. com., co-chmn. transp. com. Penjerdel Council, 1979-82. Served to lt. USNR, 1944-45. Recipient Distinguished Faculty award U. Mich., 1961. Mem. ASCE (pres. Mich. 1956, Civil Govt. award 1979), Am. Soc. Traffic and Transp. (founder mem.), Transp. Research Forum, Transp. Research Bd. (asso.), Tau Beta Pi, Phi Kappa Phi, Chi Epsilon. Home: 200 Aspen Ct Irving TX 75062

KÖHLER, GEORGES J.F., German scientist, immunologist; b. Apr. 17, 1946. Scientist, immunologist Max-Planck Institut fur Immunologie, Stubeweg, Fed. Rep. Germany. Recipient Nobel prize in Medicine and Physiology, 1984, Albert Lasker Med. Research award, 1984. *

KOHLI, MARTIN, sociologist, educator; b. Solothurn, Switzerland, May 8, 1942; arrived in Fed. Republic Germany, 1977; s. Paul and Doris (Christen) K.; m. Freya Dittmann, May 3, 1978. Doctorate, U. Berne, Switzerland, 1972; habilitation, U. Konstanz, Fed. Republic Germany, 1977. Sec. Ministry of Edn., Zurich, Switzerland, 1968-71; asst. prof. U. Konstanz, 1971-77; prof. Free U. Berlin, West Berlin, 1977—. Author: Studium und berufliche Laufbahn, 1973; editor: Soziologie des Lebenslaufs, 1978; contbr. articles to profl. jours.; mem. editorial bd. several profl. jours. Mem. Inst. for Advanced Study, Princeton, N.J., 1984-85. Mem. German Sociol. Soc. (bd. dirs. 1984—), other profl. assns. Office: Inst for Sociology, Hittorfstrasse 16, 1000 Berlin 33 Federal Republic of Germany

KOHLOSS, FREDERICK HENRY, consulting engineer; b. Ft. Sam Houston, Tex., Dec. 4, 1922; s. Fabius Henry and Rowena May (Smith) K.; m. Margaret Mary Grunwell, Sept. 9, 1944; children: Margaret Ralston, Charlotte Todesco, Eleanor. B.S. in Mech. Engring, U. Md., 1943; M.Mech. Engring., U. Del., 1951; J.D., George Washington U., 1949. Mem. engring. faculty George Washington U., Washington, 1946-50; devel. and standards engr. Dept. Def., 1950-51; chief engr. for mech. contractors Washington, 1951-54, Cleve., 1954-55; chief engr. for mech. contractors Honolulu, 1955-56, cons. engr., 1956-61; pres. Frederick H. Kohloss & Assocs., Inc., Cons. Engrs., Honolulu, Tucson, Denver, 1961—. Contbr. to publs. in field. Served with U.S. Army, 1943-46. Fellow ASME, ASHRAE, Am. Cons. Engrs. Council, Chartered Inst. Bldg. Services Engrs., Instn. Engrs. Australia, Soc. Mil. Engrs.; mem. IEEE (sr.), Nat. Soc. Profl. Engrs., Illuminating Engring. Soc. Clubs: Oahu Country (Honolulu). Home: 1645 Ala Wai Blvd Penthouse 1 Honolulu HI 96815 Office: 1001 Bishop St Pauahi Tower Suite 390 Honolulu HI 96813

KOHN, HAROLD ELIAS, lawyer; b. Phila., Apr. 5, 1914; s. Joseph C. and Mayme (Rumm) K.; m. Edith Anderson, Dec. 30, 1946; children: Amy, Ellen, Joseph Carl. A.B., U. Pa., 1934, LL.B., 1937. Bar: Pa. 1938. Pres. Kohn, Savett, Klein & Graf, P.C., Phila.; spl. counsel transit matters City of Phila., 1952-53, 56-62; counsel to gov. State of Pa., 1972; mem. bd. Southeastern Pa. Transp. Authority, 1972-77; mem. Pa. Jud. Inquiry and Rev. Bd., 1973-77; bd. consultors Villanova U. Law Sch. Sec., treas., bd. dirs. Kohn Found.; pres., bd. dirs. Arronson Found., Lavine Found.; bd. dirs. Moss Rehab. Hosp., Phila. Geriatric Ctr.; trustee, mem. exec. com. Phila. Fedn. Jewish Agys.; trustee Temple U.; past mem. exec. com. United Jewish Appeal; past mem. bd. dirs. Phila. Psychiat. Ctr.; past v.p., bd. dirs. Phila. chpt. ACLU. Mem. ABA, Pa., Phila., D.C. bar assns., Internat. Acad. Trial Lawyers, Jud. Conf. 3d Circuit, Am. Law Inst., Order of Coif, Phi Beta Kappa. Home: Philadelphia PA 19106 Office: 1101 Market St Philadelphia PA 19107

KOHN, JUAN DANIEL, steel wire and wire products company executive; b. Ambato, Ecuador, Dec. 5, 1944; s. Camilo and Hilda (Toepfer) K.; m. Alyce Denier (div. 1983); children: Andres, Javier; m. Monica del Carmen Andrade, Sept. 23, 1983; children: Sebastian, Camilo. BS, U. Calif., Berkeley, 1966, MS, 1968. Registered profl. engr., Ecuador. Prodn. mgr. Ideal Industria de Alambre, Quito, Ecuador, 1969-74, gen. mgr., 1974-83; exec. pres. Ideal-Alambrec, Quito, 1983—; bd. dirs. Banco de la Prodn., Quito. Bd. dirs. Ecuadorian Standards Inst., Quito, 1980—, Nat. Council Sci. and Tech., Quito, 1987—, Academia Cotopaxi, Quito, 1976-79, Colegio Alberto Einstein, Quito, 1985-86. Mem. Assn. Entrepreneurs South (pres. 1986—), Quito Chamber of Industries (bd. dirs. 1980-81, 87). Jewish. Home: Ana de Ayala 410, Guapulo, Quito Ecuador Office: Ideal Alambrec, PO Box 3074, Quito Ecuador

KOHN, ROBERT SAMUEL, JR., real estate investment consultant; b. Denver, Jan. 7, 1949; s. Robert Samuel and Miriam Lackner (Neusteter) K.; BS, U. Ariz., 1971; 1 son, Randall Stanton; m. 2d, Eleanor B. Kohn; children: Joseph Robert, Andrea Rene. Asst. buyer Robinson's Dept. Store, Los Angeles, 1971; agt. Neusteter Realty Co., Denver, 1972-73, exec. v.p., 1973-76; pres. Project Devel. Services, Denver, 1976-78, pres., chief exec. officer, 1978-83; pres. Kohn and Assos., Inc., 1979-83, The Burke Co., Inc., Irvine, Calif., 1983-84, ptnr. 1984—. Mem. Bldg. Owners and Mgrs. Assn. (pres. 1977-78, dir. 1972-78, dir. S.W. Conf. Bd. 1977-78), Denver Art Mus., Denver U. Library Assn., Central City Opera House Assn., Inst. Real Estate Mgmt. Republican. Jewish. Club: Newport Beach Tennis. Home: 10 Skysail Dr Corona Del Mar CA 92625 Office: The Burke Co Inc 2111 Bus Center Dr Irvine CA 92715

KOHO, LAURI ANSELM, military officer; b. Kurkijoki, Karelia, Finland, Mar. 23, 1926; s. Antti and Anna (Lajunen) K.; m. Paula Margareta Pettinen, Nov. 7, 1954. Student, Mil. Acad., 1946-47, War Coll., 1958-59, Nat. Def. Coll., 1971. Commd. 2d lt. Finnish Army, 1947, advanced through grades to lt. gen., 1981; asst. mil. attache Finnish Embassy, London, 1961-62; asst. mil. attache for U.S. and Can., mil. advisor Permanent Rep. Finland to UN Finnish Embassy, N.Y.C., 1964-65; asst. mil. advisor Office of Sec. Gen., UN, N.Y.C., 1965-66; advisor UN Middle East Mission, 1967; mil. expert, liaison officer Office of Sec. Gen. UN, N.Y.C., 1968-80; comdg. gen. Cen. Mil. Area, Def. Forces Finland, 1980-81, S.W. Mil. Area, Def. Forces Finland, 1981-86. Decorated Comdr. 1st Class Order of the White Rose of Finland, Comdr. 1st Class Order of the Lion of Finland, Austrian Grand Decoration of Honor in Gold with Star, also various campaign and UN medals. Mem. Internat. Inst. Strategic Studies, U.S. Strategic Inst., Royal United Services Inst. U.K. Lutheran. Lodge: Rotary. Home: Kipparinkatu 3 A 5, SF-53100 Lappeenranta Finland

KOIKE, HISAO, automotive executive; b. Hamamatsu, Japan, Feb. 9, 1921; s. Kuhei and Toki K.; student Fukuroi Bus. High Sch.; m. Midori Omishi, Dec. 4, 1952; Exec. v.p. Yamaha Motor Co. Ltd., Shizuoka, Japan, 1966-71, pres., 1974—; exec. v.p. Nippon Gakki Co., 1971-74. Named Honorable Citizen Cypress City, Calif., 1970. Mem. Iwata C. of C. (chmn.), Japan Marina Assn. (dir.), Japan Boat Industries Assn. (dir.), Japan Automobile Assn. (dir.), Japan Motorcycles Assn. (dir.). Office: Yamaha Motor Co, 2500 Shingai, Iwata City, Shisuoka 438 Japan *

KOIVISTO, MAUNO HENRIK, president Republic of Finland; b. Turku, Finland, Nov. 25, 1923; s. Juho and Hymni Sofia (Eskola) K.; Ph.D., U. Turku, 1956, D.Polit.Sci. (hon.), 1977; D.Comml. Sci. (hon.), Abo Akad., 1978; D.Sociology honoris causa, U. Toulouse (France), 1983; D.Soc.Sci. (hon.), U. Tampere, 1985; D.Polit.Sci. (hon.), U. Helsinki, 1986, LLD, (hon.) U. Prague, 1987; m. Taimi Tellervo Kankaanranta, June 22, 1952; 1 dau., Assi. Mng. dir. Helsinki Worker's Savs. Bank, 1959-67; gov. Bank of Finland, 1968-82; chmn. bd. Postipankki, 1970-82, Mortgage Bank of Finland Oy, 1971-82; gov. for Finland, Internat. Bank Reconstrn. Devel., 1966-69, IMF, 1970-79; bd. adminstrn. Co-op. Union KK, 1964-82; chmn. bd. adminstrn. Co-op. Soc. ELANTO, 1966-82; minister fin., Republic of Finland, 1966-67, 72, dep. prime minister, 1972, prime minister, 1968-70, 79-82, pres., 1982, re-elected, 1988—. Decorated Grand Cross order Finnish White Rose, Order Lenin, and numerous other decorations. Author: Social Relations in Turku Harbor, 1956; Landmarks-Finland in the World, 1985; also 3 books on econs. and social politics. Office: Presdl Palace, 00170 Helsinki Finland

KOIZUMI, SHUNZO, surgeon; b. Kyoto, Japan, Mar. 14, 1946; s. Haruo and Chieko (Ushioda) K.; m. Yoko Yokoe, Aug. 19, 1971; children: Miyuu (dec.), Mitsuteru, Arei. MD, Kyoto U., 1971. Diplomate Am. Bd. Surgery. House staff in medicine Yamagami (Japan) Hosp., Yamato-Takada (Japan) City Hosp.; house staff in anesthesiology Osaka (Japan) Red Cross Hosp., 1972-74; resident Youngstown (Ohio) Hosp. Assn., 1975-76; gen. surg. resident St. Vincent's Med. Ctr., Bridgeport, Conn., 1976-80, chief surg. resident, 1979-80; staff first surg. dept. Kyoto U. Hosp., 1980; surg. cons. for residency dept. abdominal surgery Tenri (Japan) Hosp., 1980—. Editor resident's manual, 1988. Mem. ACS, Japan Surg. Soc., Japan Soc. Med. Edn. Home: 16-1 Ichijoji-Iorino-cho, Sakyo-ku, Kyoto 606, Japan Office: Tenri Hosp, Dept Abdominal Surgery, 200 Mishima-cho, 632 Tenri, Nara Japan

KOJDER, ANDRZEJ, sociologist; b. Grzeska, Poland, Apr. 25, 1941; s. Wladyslaw and Aurelia (Winkiel) K.; m. Ewa Pajestka-Kojder, Dec. 20, 1980; 1 child, Kaja. MA, U. Warsaw, 1969, PhD, 1978. Asst. U. Katowice, 1969-70; researcher U. Warsaw, 1970-72, sr. researcher, 1973-77, asst. prof., 1978—, dep. dir., 1981-87; cons. Research Ctr. for Rehab. of Disabled Persons, Warszawa, 1973-87; chmn. Research Com. for the Sociology of Deviance, 1982-84, 86—; bd. Commn. of Folk Law and Legal Pluralism, 1984—; sec. Research Com. for the Sociology of Law, Warsaw, 1970-82. Editor: L. Petrazycki: On Science, Law and Morality, 1985; contbr. articles to profl. jours. Grantee Ctr. for Comparative Criminology, 1972, Japanese Soc. for the Promotion of Sci., 1977, U. Tokai, 1987. Mem. Solidarity. Home: Lasek Brzozowy 7/14, Warszawa Poland 02-732 Office: U Warsaw, Krakowskie Przedmiescie 26/28, 00380 Warszawa Poland

KOJIMA, SUMIZO, hotel executive; b. Kyoto, Japan, Sept. 5, 1925; s. Ainosuke and Tamao K.; m. Yoshiko Kubo; children: Aitaro, Sadayoshi. Student, Ritsumeikan Comml. Sch., Kyoto, 1944. Dir. The Hokke Club Ltd., Tokyo, 1947-68, mng. dir., 1968-72, v.p., 1973—; v.p. Sakaiminato Marina Hotel Ltd., 1948—; pres. L.&.H. Ltd., Tokyo, 1984—. Mem. Japan-India Bus. Coop. Coms. (del., Japan Jr. Chamber Sr. Club. Lodge: Rotary. Home: 1065-1514 Kamitaga Atami, 413-01 Shizuoka Japan Office: The Hokke Club Co, 2-1-48 Ikenohata, 110 Taito-ku, Tokyo Japan

KOLB, JOSEPH WILBUR, retired educator; b. near Princeton, Ind., Jan. 5, 1902; s. Joseph and Margaret M. (Phillips) K.; A.B., Ind. U., 1926, A.M., 1931; postgrad, Evansville Coll., 1948-52, Ind. State Tchrs. Coll., 1950—, Oakland City Coll., 1952—; m. Mary Elizabeth Wolfe, June 21, 1922; children—Unalea (Mrs. Andrew Robb), Mary Lu (Mrs. Thomas Orr). Tchr., adminstr. pub. schs., Neb., Mo., Ill., Ind., 1923-68. Named Older Hoosier of Yr., Area 13 B. Mem. White House Conf. on Aging; mem. Ind. Joint Commn. on Aged and Aging, Nat., Ind., Gibson County ret. tchrs. assns., Gibson County Council on Aging. Del. Dem. Nat. Conv., 1956, 60, mem. platform com., 1972-74. Mem. NEA, Am. Assn. Ret. Persons, Wabash Valley Assn. Methodist. Mason (32deg. Shriner); mem. Order Eastern Star. Home: 116 N Race St Princeton IN 47670

KOLB, ROBERT FRANK, II, state official; b. Abbeville, S.C., May 25, 1946; s. Hugh Marshall and Bleka Anita (Cherry) K.; B.A. in Econs., Clemson U., 1968, M.Ed. in Personnel, 1978. Area dir. S.C. Employment Security Commn., Liberty, 1968—; instr. bus. and econs. Tri County Tech. Coll., Pendleton, S.C., 1972-80. Bd. dirs., treas. Pickens County (S.C.) Humane Soc., 1974-86; bd. dirs. Easley Pickens County YMCA, 1972—; chmn. Pickens County Republican Party, 1976-81; state credentials chmn. S.C. Rep. Party, 1978-86, mem. state rules com., 1981—; dir. Sunday sch. Liberty (S.C.) 1st Baptist Ch., 1979-82, 85—; past chmn. vocat. adv. com. Pickens County Area Vocat. Ctr. Recipient State of S.C. Service award, 1978. Mem. Liberty C. of C. (pres. 1988—), Internat. Assn. Personnel in Employment Security, S.C. State Employees Assn. (pres. 1987-88), Pickens Area Personnel Assn. (past pres.), U.S. Chess Fedn., S.C. Chess Assn., Liberty Jaycees (internal v.p. 1976-78, pres. 1978-79, chmn. bd. dirs. 1979-80, pres. 1982-83, mem. senate, treas. 1987-88, state v.p. 1988—, chmn. Miss Liberty pageant 1978-84). Club: Capitol Hill. Home: PO Box 146 Chastain Dr Liberty SC 29657

KOLBOOM, INGO, historian, researcher; b. Hohenaspe, Fed. Republic Germany, Feb. 16, 1947; s. Hermann and Agathe (Schmid) K. Licence ès Lettres, U. Paris, 1970; PhD, Tech. U. Berlin, 1982. Lectr., researcher Tech. U. Berlin, 1975-81; lectr. polit. scis. Free U. Berlin, 1982-84, U. Hamburg (Fed. Republic Germany), 1982-84; research fellow German Council Fgn. Policy, Bonn, 1983—; bd. dirs. Comité d'Etudes des Relations Franco-Allemandes (Cerfa), Paris, 1986—, Dokumente Rev. for German-French Dialogue, Bonn, 1986—, Eurocréation, French Office for Cultural and Econ. Itiitatives of Youth in Europe, Pairs, 1987, European Cultural Workshop, Berlin, 1988—. Author: Französische Unterneher 1983, 2d edit., 1987, La Revanche des Patrons, 1986, Deutsch-Französische Sicherheitspolitik, 1986, 2d edit., 1988; editor: Review for German-French Dialoge, Lendemains, Review for French Studies, Berlin, 1975-81, Le couple franco-allemand et la défense de l'Europe, 1986, Frankreich-MenschenLandschaften, 1988; (exhibition) Absolut modern sein, 1986, Deutsche und französische Plakate 1919-39, 1989; free journalist Radio, T.V. Reviews; contbr. articles to profl. jours. Mng. pub. relations dir. German Assn. Romance Studies, 1985-87. Served as lt. inf., German army, 1966-68. Mem. Assn. Transnational Cooperation. Office: Deutsche Gesellschaft Auswärtige Politik, Adenauerallee 131, D-5300 Bonn 1 Federal Republic of Germany

KOLDE, RICHARD ARTHUR, insurance company executive, consultant; b. Pomona, Calif., Jan. 25, 1944; s. Arthur and Rosemary (Decker) K.; m. Lark Holly Defeo, Apr. 30, 1988; children: Nicole Rochelle, Eric Christian. AA, Mt. San Antonio Coll., 1963; BS, U. So. Calif., 1965; AS, Mira Costa Coll., 1979. Asst. mgr., mgr. Lord Rebel Ind., Montclair, Costa Mesa and Carlsbad, Calif., 1971-74; agt. Conn. Mut. Life Ins. Co., San Diego and Carlsbad, 1974-77; pres., owner Investment Assocs., Carlsbad, 1977-82; mng. gen. agt. E.F. Hutton Life Ins. Co., San Diego, 1982—; cons. Hansch Fin. Group, Laguna Hills, Calif., 1984. Bd. dirs. Boys Club Am., Carlsbad, 1980-84, adv. bd., 1984—; bd. dirs. YMCA, Pomona, 1960-64. Served with USAF, 1966-71. Decorated Outstanding Unit award, Small Arms Expert award, Security 1 & 2 Protection of Pres. U.S. award; named Largest Producing Mng. Gen. Agt. in Nation, E.F. Hutton Life Co., 1982, 83. Mem. Nat. Assn. Life Underwriters (legis. officer 1974—), Calif. Assn. Life Underwriters, Internat. Assn. Fin. Planners (Mem. of Yr. award 1977), U.S. Gymnastics Fedn. (coaching credentials, ofcl. judge collegiate level), VFW, Phi Sigma Beta. Republican. Lodge: Rotary.

KOLESON, DONALD RALPH, college dean, educator; b. Eldon, Mo., June 30, 1935; s. Ralph A. and Fern M. (Beanland) K.; children—Anne, David, Janet. B.S. in Edn., Central Mo. State U., 1959; M.Ed., So. Ill. U., 1973. Mem. faculty So. Ill. U., Carbondale, 1968-73; dean tech. edn. Belleville (Ill.) Area Coll., 1982—. Mem. Am. Vocat. Edn. Assn., Am. Welding Assn., Nat. Assn. Two-Year Schs. of Constrn. (pres. 1984-85). Clubs: Masons; Shriners, Jesters.

KOLETTIS, MILTIADES, cardiologist, researcher; b. Island of Kalymnos, Greece, Oct. 26, 1923; s. Theophilos and Vakina (Billiri) K.; m. Agatha Papagiannakaki, Jan. 4, 1959; children: Irene, Theophilos, George. Degree in medicine, U. Athens, Greece, 1948, MD, 1955. Med. diplomate. Intern Evangelismos Hosp., Athens, 1948, 52-53, resident in internal medicine, then cardiology, 1953-57, staff cardiology dept., 1959-65, dir. dept. cardiology, 1986—; assoc. cardiology staff U. Athens, 1966-78; fellow dept. cardiovascular disease Cardiac Lab., Cleve. Clinic, 1968-69; research assoc. dept. Cardiology St. Thomas Hosp., London, 1974-75; assoc. prof. cardiology 7th and 1st Ins. Hosps., Athens, 1977, dir. depts. cardiology, 1978-86. Contbr. approximately 100 articles to Greek and internat. med. jours. Served to lt. med. br. Greek mil., 1948-52. Council of Europe fellow, 1957; Brit. Council scholar, 1958. Mem. AAAS, Royal Soc. Medicine, Greek Soc. Angiology, Greek Cardiac Soc., Athens Med. Assn. Home: 72-74 Aigaiou Pelagous St, 153 41 Attiki Greece Office: Evangelismos Hosp, 45-47 Ipsilantou St, 106 76 Athens Greece

KOLINGBA, ANDRE-DIEUDONNE, head of state Central African Republic; b. Bangui, Central African Republic, Aug. 12, 1936; s. Albert and Cecile (Digo) Nzanga; m. Mireille Kotalimbora, Apr. 29, 1968; children Desire, Guy, Chantal, Arthur, Ernest, Serge, Ginette, Cecile, Andre, Sonia, Thierry, Alexandre, Johanne, Auriele. Formerly signal officer, armored squadron French Army, Brazzaville, Congo; former comdr. Signal Corps, Central African Armed Forces, gen., chief of staff; pres., chief of staff Comité Militaire de Redressement Nat., Central African Republic, 1971—; ambassador to Can., 1975-79; A.E. and P. to Fed Republic Germany, 1979; pres. Central African Republic. (came to office in coup), 1981—, also minister def. and war vets., 1981-83 84—. Decorated Star of Merit. Roman Catholic. Address: Presidence de la Republique, Bangui Central African Republic *

KOLINSKI, RALPH NORBERT, educator; b. Detroit, Mar. 24, 1941; s. Joseph Henry and Margaret (Head) K.; m. Elizabeth Mossakowski, July 3, 1969; children: Emily, Rebecca, John, Laurel. BS, Wayne State U., 1963, MA, 1965, PhD, 1969. Assoc. prof. econs. U. Windsor, Ont., Can., 1966—. Mem. Atlantic Econ. Soc. (exec.), Can. Econ. Assn., Am. Econ. Assn., Pi Gamma Mu, Beta Gamma Sigma. Home: 19904 Anita Harper Woods MI 48225 Office: U Windsor, 401 Sunset, Windsor, ON Canada N9B 3P4

KOLIOPOULOS, JOHN SOTERIOS, modern history educator; b. Votani, Kastoria, Greece, Mar. 10, 1942; s. Soterios Thomas and Melpomeni (Nasiopoulos) K.; m. Christina Kateyanni, Sept. 23, 1962; 1 child, Anna. BA, City College, N.Y.C., 1968; MA, London Sch. Econs., 1969, PhD, 1972. Lectr. Deree Coll., Athens, Greece, 1972-76; asst. prof. U. Thessaloniki, Greece, 1976-79, assoc. prof., 1979-83, prof. modern history, 1983—; vis. prof. Columbia U., N.Y.C., 1980; cons. Anatolia Coll., Thessaloniki, 1981—. Author: Greece and the British Connection, 1935-41, 1977, Brigands with a Cause: Brigandage and Irredentism in Modern Greece, 1821-1912, 1987 (Sir Stephen Runciman award for best book on Modern Greece 1987); editor: History of the Greek Nation (multi-vol. work), 1972-76. Fulbright research grantee, N.Y.C., 1980. Mem. Hist. and Ethnol. Soc. Greece, Greek Folklore and Hist. Archive. Home and Office: Anatolia Coll, PO Box 10143, 541 10 Thessaloniki Greece also: U Thessaloniki, Thessaloniki Greece

KOLKEY, DANIEL MILES, lawyer; b. Chgo., Apr. 21, 1952; s. Eugene Louis and Gilda Penelope (Cowan) K.; m. Donna Lynn Christie, May 15, 1982; children: Eugene, William. BA, Stanford U., 1974; JD, Harvard U., 1977. Bar: Calif. 1977, U.S. Dist. Ct. (cen., no., ea. dists.) Calif., U.S. Ct. Appeals (9th cir.) 1979, U.S. Supreme Ct., 1983. Law clk. U.S. Dist. Ct. judge, N.Y.C., 1977-78; ptnr. Gibson Dunn & Crutcher, Los Angeles, 1978—. Contbr. articles to profl. publs. Co-chmn. and sec. internat. relations sect. Town Hall of Calif., Los Angeles, 1981—; chmn. internat. trade legis. subcom., internat. commerce steering com. Los Angeles Area C. of C., 1983—; mem. adv. council Asia Pacific Ctr. for Resolution of Internat. Bus. Disputes; bd. dirs., sec., treas. Los Angeles Ctr. for Internat. Comml. Arbitration, 1986—; assoc. mem. central com. Calif. Rep. Party, 1983—; mem. Los Angeles Com. on Fgn. Relations, 1983—; mem. Los Angeles World Affairs Council, Rep. Assocs. Mem. ABA, Internat. Bar Assn., Los Angeles County Bar Assn. (exec. com. internat. law sect. 1987—), Chartered Inst. Arbitrators, London (assoc.), Cour Pour L'Arbitrage Internat. en Matiere de Commerce et D'Industrie (Geneva), Wilton Park Alumni of So. Calif. (chmn. exec. com.). Jewish. Office: Gibson Dunn & Crutcher 333 S Grand Ave Los Angeles CA 90071

KOLKOWICZ, ROMAN, political science educator, academic administrator, consultant; b. Poland, Nov. 15, 1929; came to U.S., 1949, naturalized, 1955; s. William and Edwarda (Goldberg) K.; children—Susan, Lisa, Gabriella. B.A., U. Buffalo, 1954; M.A., U. Chgo., 1958, Ph.D., 1964. Sr. staff mem. Rand Corp., Santa Monica, Calif., 1961-66, Inst. Def. analysis, Washington, 1966-70; prof. polit. sci. UCLA, 1970—, dir. Ctr. Internat. Strategic Affairs, 1974-82; co-dir. Project on Arms Control, 1983-85; dir. Project on Politics and War, 1985—; cons. to govt., others. Chmn. fgn. policy platform Calif. Dem. Party, 1972, 76. Served with U.S. Army, 1954-56. Ford Found. grantee, 1975-83; Rockefeller Found. grantee, 1975-77. Mem. Am. Polit. Sci. Assn., Internat. Sociol. Assn., Internat. Polit. Sci. Assn. Author: Soviet Military-Communist Party, 1967; Soldiers, Peasants, Bureaucrats, 1982; National Security and International Stability, 1983; Arms Control and International Security, 1983; Soviet Calculus of War, 1983, Logic of Nuclear Terror, 1987, Dilemmas of Nuclear Deterrence, 1987. Home: 21310 Bellini Dr Topanga CA 90290 Office: Dept Polit Sci UCLA Los Angeles CA 90024

KOLLAER, JIM C., real estate executive, architect; b. Amarillo, Tex., Jan. 5, 1943; s. Walter W. and Margaret M. Kollaer; m. Sally Ann Hawkins, Aug. 6, 1966; 1 son, Andrew N. Student, Amarillo (Tex.) Coll., 1960-62, La. State U., 1962-65; B.Arch., Tex. Tech U., 1969. Lic. architect, Tex.; lic. broker, Tex. Vice pres., dir. urban design RKA Inc. Assoc., Dallas, 1969-75; v.p., dir. mktg. CRS Inc., Houston, 1977-80, sr. planner, 1975-76, assoc., 1976-77; pres. Houston div. Henry Miller Co., Houston, 1980-85; pres. Henry S. Miller/Grubb & Ellis, 1985—, HSM, Inc.; chmn. Tex. Bus. Hall of Fame; dir. HMSCO; cons. and lectr. in field. Sr. fellow Am. Leadership Forum. Named Young Architect of Yr., Dallas, 1974. Mem. AIA, Tex. Soc. Architects, Urban Land Inst., Dallas Bd. Realtors, Tex. Assn. Realtors, Nat. Assn. Realtors, Nat. Assn. Corp. Real Estate Execs., Houston C. of C. (chmn. internat. bus. com. 1982-87), Houston Lyceum. Republican. Presbyterian. Clubs: Dallas, 2001. Office: 2001 Bryan Tower 30th Floor Dallas TX 75201

KOLLAT, DAVID TRUMAN, management consultant; b. Elkhart, Ind., July 7, 1938; s. Walter A. and Mildred E. (Good) K.; children: Lisa, Andra. B.B.A., Western Mich. U., 1960, M.B.A., 1962; D.B.A., Ind. U., 1966. Mem. faculty Ohio State U., Columbus, 1965-72; v.p., then exec. v.p., dir. Mgmt. Horizons, Columbus, 1972-76; v.p. The Limited Stores, Inc., Columbus, 1976-77; exec. v.p. The Limited Stores, Inc., 1977-84; exec. v.p. The Limited Inc., 1984-87, also bd. dirs.; mgmt. cons. Worthington, Ohio, 1987—; bd. dirs. Mast Industries, Cooker Restaurant Corp., Decor Corp. Co-author: Strategic Marketing, 1972, Consumer Behavior, 1978. Served with AUS, 1960-68. Mem. Am. Mktg. Assn. (v.p. 1979-80), Assn. Consumer Research, Beta Gamma Sigma, Omicron Delta Kappa. Home: 6064 Olentangy River Rd Worthington OH 43085

KOLLEGGER, JAMES G., information industry executive; b. Klagenfurt, Austria, Feb. 16, 1942; came to U.S., 1953; s. Willibald K. and Gerda (Baltruschat) Von Fekete; m. Cheryl A. Bales, May 29, 1966 (div. 1976); 1 child, Craig Russell; m. Elaine J. Kenzer, July 7, 1983; 1 child, Eric James. B.S., Boston U., 1964; postgrad., NYU, 1969-71. Asst. mktg. mgr. Structural Clay Inst., Washington, 1966-69; asst. to pres. Heald-Hobson div. MacMillan Info., N.Y.C., 1969-70; pres. EIC-Intelligence, N.Y.C., 1970—; chmn., chief exec. officer Tele/Scope Networks, Inc., 1988—; dir. Environ. Planning Lobby, N.Y.C., 1972-75; council mem. U.S. Govt. Printing Office, Washington, 1982—. Served to capt. U.S. Army, 1964-70. Decorated Army Commendation medal. Mem. Info. Industry Assn. (dir., chmn. policy council 1981-83, dir., named Entrepreneur of Yr. 1986-87), Gateway Info. Providers Group (chmn. 1988—), Assoc. Info. Mgrs. (chmn. 1981-82, dir.), Am. Mgmt. Assn., Info. Systems and Tech. Council, Am. Soc. Info. Sci., Sigma Delta Chi. Republican. Club: Union League (N.Y.C.). Home: 310 W 86th St New York NY 10024 Office: EIC-Intelligence 48 W 38th St New York NY 10018

KOLLER, ARNOLD ALOIS, government minister; b. Appenzell, Switzerland, Aug. 29, 1933; m. Erica Brander, Sept. 23, 1972; 2 children. B in Econs., U. St. Gallen, 1957; LLB, U. Fribourg, 1959, PhD in Law, 1966. Pres. Supreme Ct. Kanton Appenzell Innerrhoden, Switzerland, 1973-86; prof. Swiss, European Comml. and Econ. Law U. St. Sell, Switzerland, 1972-86; minister def. Swiss Govt., 1987—. Mem. Swiss parliament Nat. Council, 1971-86; pres. Christian Dem. party, Centon Appenzell Innerrhoden, 1979-86, Christian Dem. group in Swiss parliament, 1980-84, nat. council Swiss parliament, 1984-85. Served to lt. col. Office: Fed Mil Dept, 30003 Berne Switzerland

KOLLSTEDT, PAULA LUBKE, communication specialist; b. Cin., Aug. 27, 1946; d. Elmer George and Mary Margaret (Kelly) Lubke; m. Stephen Leonard Kollstedt, Jan. 21, 1968; children—Kelly, Lance, Stacey, Jonathan. B.A., Xavier U., 1968, M.Ed., 1982. Cert. secondary tchr., Ohio. Editor, writer Shillito's Dept. Store, Cin., 1966-69; freelance writer, Cin., 1969-74; writer, instr. Prince William County Parks and Recreation Com. (Va.), 1974-75; communications coordinator City of Cin. Recreation Com., 1975-78; cons. Warner Amex Cable Television, Cin., 1982-84, Moellers Assocs., Cin., 1982-84; exec. Communication Specialist Gen. Electric Aircraft Engines, 1984—; speaker Cin. Preschool Coops., 1981, Cin. Women's Conf., 1984, lectr., presenter workshops on self-esteem for parents, 1975-86. Author: Surviving the Crisis of Motherhood, 1982; contbr. articles to newspapers; writer, producer multi-media presentation Communication Cincinnati, (Unique Program award Ohio Parks and Recreation), 1978. Mem. Women in Communications (v.p. programs 1981-82; Gt. Lakes regional 1st pl. award 1984, 86, 87, 88). Recipient Prism awards Pub. Relations Soc. Am., 1983, 85, 86, 87, Bronze Quill award Internat. Assn. Bus. Communicators, 1986, 87, 88. Roman Catholic. Home: 5391 Haft Rd Cincinnati OH 45247 Office: GE Aircraft Engines One Neumann Way MD-C4 Evendale OH 45215

KOLOR, MICHAEL GARRETT, research chemist; b. Bklyn., May 1, 1934; s. Michael Austin and Frances (Nugent) K.; B.S. in Chemistry, Queens Coll. CUNY, 1956; postgrad. Adelphi U., 1958-60; m. Agnes Theresa Fitzpatrick, June 29, 1957; children—Mary Catherine, Michael Francis, Agnes Theresa, Johanna Margaret. Chemist, Nat. Dairy Corp., Oakdale, N.Y., 1956-59; asso. chemist Gen. Foods Corp., Tarrytown, N.Y., 1959-62, research chemist, 1962-65, sr. research chemist, 1965-70, research specialist, 1970-72, sr. research specialist, 1972-79, research scientist, head mass spectrometry lab., 1972—. Mgr., Little League Girls' Softball League. Mem. Am. Soc. for Mass Spectrometry, N.J. Am. Chem. Soc. Mass Spectrometry Group (program chmn. 1968-69). Roman Catholic. Club: Tri-Boro Men's Bowling League. Co-author: Biochemical Applications of Mass Spectrometry, 1972; Supplementary Volume of Biochemical Application of Mass Spectrometry, 1980; Mass. Spectrometry (practical spectroscopy/series, 1979); patentee in field; contbr. articles on chemistry to profl. jours. Home: 71 Margaret Keahon Dr Pearl River NY 10965 Office: 555 S Broadway Tarrytown NY 10591

KOLSON, HARRY, otolaryngologist, educator; b. N.Y.C., Mar. 26, 1915; s. Morris and Jennie (Waldman) K.; m. Ida Burstein, Apr. 27, 1941 (dec. Aug. 1944). B.A., NYU, 1935, D.D.S., 1938, M.D., 1950. Diplomate: Am. Bd. Otolaryngology, Nat. Bd. Med. Examiners. Practice gen. dentistry Jamaica, N.Y., 1938-43; straight surg. intern 3d div. Bellevue Hosp., N.Y.C., 1950-51; asst. resident in surgery 3d div. Bellevue Hosp., 1951-52, Am. Cancer Soc. fellow dept. surgery, 1951-52; resident in ear, nose, throat, head and neck surgery VA Hosp., Bronx, N.Y., 1952-55; asst. chief otolaryngology sect. VA Hosp., 1955-56, chief head and neck surg. sect., 1955-68, chief otolaryngology sect., 1957-68, cons. in otolaryngology, 1968-71; fellow dept. surgery NYU, 1951-52; lectr. bronchoscopy N.Y. Polyclinic Hosp. and Post Grad. Med. Sch., 1955-56, adj. prof., 1956—; instr. dept. head and neck surgery Albert Einstein Coll. Medicine, Bronx, 1955-59; asst. clin. prof. Albert Einstein Coll. Medicine, 1959-65, lectr., 1965-68; asst. vis. surgeon Bronx Mcpl. Hosp. Center, 1955-59, asso. vis. surgeon, 1959-68; asst. clin. prof. otolaryngology Columbia U., 1965-66, asso. clin. prof., 1966-71; prof. clin. otolaryngology Mt. Sinai Sch. Medicine, N.Y.C., 1967-71; cons. Mt. Sinai Hosp. services City Hosp. Center at Elmhurst, 1968-71; prof. otolaryngology N.Y. Med. Coll., 1972—; chief otolaryngology Met. Hosp., N.Y.C., 1972—; chief of staff trainee program VA Hosp., Northport, L.I., N.Y.; chief spl. med. services Suffolk County Health Dept.; chief staff VA Med. Center, Erie, Pa., 1978—; lectr. Fairleigh Dickinson U. Sch. Dentistry, 1964—; vis. prof. Sch. Medicine, Universidad Autonoma de Guadalajara, Mexico, 1974; cons. adv. com. to chief surg. service VA Central Office, Washington, 1969-73. Contbr. articles to med. jours. Served with AUS, 1943-46. Fellow ACS, Am. Acad. Otolaryngology and Ophthalmology, Am. Acad. Facial, Plastic and Reconstructive Surgery, N.Y. Acad. Medicine; mem. AMA, N.Y. State Med. Soc., Queens County Med. Soc., Am. Soc. Maxillofacial Surgeons (constn. and by-laws com., continuing edn. and research com., nominating com., dir., treas. 1973—), Am. Soc. Head and Neck Surgery, Am. Laryngol., Rhinol. and Otol. Soc., Am. Bronco-Esophagological Assn., James Ewing Soc., ADA, N.Y. State Dental Soc., 1st Dist. N.Y. State Dental Soc., L.I. Acad. Odontology, Sigma Epsilon Delta. Republican. Home and Office: 1010 S Ocean Blvd Apt 1711 Pompano Beach FL 33062

KOLSRUD, HENRY GERALD, dentist; b. Minnewaukan, N.D., Aug. 12, 1923; s. Henry G. and Anna Naomi (Moen) K.; m. Loretta Dorothy Cooper, Sept. 3, 1945; children—Gerald Roger, Charles Cooper. Student Concordia Coll., 1941-44; D.D.S., U. Minn., 1947. Gen. practice dentistry, Spokane, Wash., 1953—. Bd. dirs. Spokane County Republican Party, United Crusade, Spokane. Served to capt. USAF, 1950-52. Mem. ADA, Wash. State Dental Assn., Spokane Dist. Dental Soc. Lutheran. Clubs: Spokane Country, Spokane. Lodges: Masons, Shriners. Home: 2107 Waikiki Rd Spokane WA 99218 Office: 3718 N Monroe St Spokane WA 99218

KOLTAI, STEPHEN MIKLOS, mechanical engineer, consultant; b. Ujpest, Hungary, Nov. 5, 1922; came to U.S., 1963; s. Maximilian and Elisabeth (Rado) K.; m. Franciska Gabor, Sept. 14, 1948; children: Eva, Susy. MS in Mech. Engrng., U. Budapest, Hungary, 1948, MS in Econs., MS, BA, 1955. Engr. Hungarian Govt., 1943-49; cons. engr. and diplomatic service various European countries, 1950-62; cons. engr. Pan Bus. Cons. Corp., Switzerland and U.S., 1963-77, Palm Springs, Calif., 1977—. Patentee in field. Charter mem. Rep. Presdl. task force, Washington, 1984—.

KOLVENBACH, PETER HANS, priest, superior Society of Jesus; b. Druten, Netherlands, 1926. Student U. Nijmegan (Netherlands); student theology St. Joseph U., Beirut, Lebanon. Joined Jesuit Order Netherlands; ordained priest Roman Cath. Ch., 1961; prof. linguistics St. Joseph U., Beirut, 1968-81; provincial superior Beirut, 1974-81; rector Pontifical Oriental Inst., Rome, 1981-83; superior-gen. Soc. of Jesus, 1983—. mem. secretariat for promoting Christian Unity. Author various articles and revs. in field of linguistics and spiritual theology. Address: Borgo Santo Spirito 5, 00193 Rome Italy

KOMACHI, HARUHISA, architect; b. Akishima, Japan, Aug. 29, 1946; s. Akihiko and Matsuko (Inoue) K.; m. Chieko Natsume, Mar. 26, 1976; children: Rie, Kaoru, Hiroshi. BArch, Nihon U., Tokyo, 1970. Mem. staff Amemiya Archtl. Design Office, Tokyo, 1972-79; apprentice Arcosanti, Mayer, Ariz., 1974; pres. Komachi Archtl. Design Atelier, Tokyo, 1979—. Mem. Tokyo Soc. Architects and Bldg. Engrs. Home: 236-7 Miyazawa, Akishima, 196 Tokyo Japan

KOMAR, M. HIKMET, manufacturing executive; b. Trabzon, Turkey, May 3, 1929; s. Emin and Mevlude (Elmas) K.; m. Nahide Savda, July 22, 1956 (div. 1963); 1 child, Can Salih; m. Marianne Engberg, Jan. 25, 1965; 1 child, Oya Mine. BA in Econs., Istanbul U., Turkey, 1961. Mktg. mgr. Dizel Makina Ltd., Istanbul, 1952-63; mng. dir. Komar Internat., Stockholm, 1963-67; gen. mgr. Coskunoz A.S., Bursa, Turkey, 1967-80; mng. dir. Yaysan A.S., Bursa, 1980—; bd. dirs. Turkey Tekstil A.S., Hafif Beton A.S., Inegol Kum A.S. Contbr. articles to profl. jours. Served to lt. Turkish armed forces, 1951-52. Mem. Assn. Suppliers Auto Industry, Assn. Businessmen of Bursa, Assn. Spring Research Eng. Lodges: Lions, Nilufer-Bursa. Home: Cekirge C 48/12, Bursa Turkey

KOMATSU, CHIKAHIRO, public relations specialist; b. Hyogo, Japan, Oct. 6, 1933; s. Eijiro and Eiko K.; m. Yoko Isobe, Dec. 15, 1962; children: Sachiyo, Masaaki. MLitt, U. Fgn. Studies, 1957. Mem. staff internat. trade Sumitomo Corp., Osaka, Japan, 1957-64, with staff pub. relations div., 1964-72, dep. mgr. pub. relations div., 1972-77, asst. to gen. mgr., 1977-87; asst. to gen. mgr. planning and coordination div. Sumitomo Corp., Tokyo, 1987—. Mng. editor Sumisho Joohoo, 1964-67, Sunmisho Digest, 1971-73. Chief mgr. Assn. Regional Reagrdence, Toyonaka-shi, Osaka, 1983. Club: Sumitomo (Tokyo and Osaka). Home: Yagumo 3-2-2, Meguro-ku, 152 Tokyo Japan

KOMDAT, JOHN RAYMOND, data processing consultant; b. Brownsville, Tex., Apr. 29, 1943; s. John William and Sara Grace (Williams) K.; m. Linda Jean Garrette, Aug. 26, 1965 (div.); m. Barbara Milroy O'Cain, Sept. 27, 1986; 1 child, Philip August. Student U. Tex., 1961-65. Sr. systems analyst Mass. Blue Cross, Boston, 1970-74; pvt. practice data processing cons., San Francisco, 1974-80, Denver, 1981—; prin. systems analyst mgmt. info. services div. Dept. of Revenue, State of Colo., 1986—; mem. CODASYL End User Facilities Com., 1974-76, allocation com. Mile High United Way. Served with U.S. Army, 1966-70. Mem. AAAS, Assn. Computing Machinery, Denver Downtown Dem. Forum (mem. exec. com.), Mus. Modern Art, Denver Art Mus., Friend of Pub. Radio, Friend of Denver Pub. Library, Colo. State Mgrs. Assn. Democrat. Office: PO Box 10666 Denver CO 80261

KOMLOS, PETER, violinist; b. Budapest, Hungary, Oct. 25, 1935; s. Laszlo and Franciska (Graf) K.; m. Edit Feher, 1960; 2 sons; m. Zsuzsanna Arki, 1984. Ed. Budapest Music Acad. Founded Komlos String Quartet, 1957; 1st violinist Budapest Opera Orchestra, 1960; leader Bartok String Quartet, 1963; extensive concert tours to USSR, Scandinavia, Italy, Austria, W.Ger., Czechoslovakia, 1958-64, to U.S., Can., N.Z., Australia, 1970, Japan, Spain, Portugal, 1971; Far East, U.S., Europe, 1973; recordings include Beethoven's string quartets for Hungaroton, Budapest; Bartok's string quartets for Erato, Paris. Recipient 1st prize Internat. String Quartet Competition, Liè ge, 1964, Liszt prize, 1965, Gramophone Record prize of Germany, 1969, Kossuth prize, 1970, UNESCO Music Council Plaque, 1981; named Eminent Artist, 1980.

KOMMEDAHL, THOR, plant pathology educator; b. Mpls., Apr. 1, 1920; s. Thorbjorn and Martha (Blegen) K.; m. Faye Lillian Jensen, June 2, 1924; children—Kris Alan, Siri Lynn, Lori Anne. B.S., U. Minn., 1945, M.S., 1947, Ph.D., 1951. Instr. U. Minn., St. Paul, 1946-51, asst. prof. plant pathology, 1953-57, assoc. prof., 1957-63, prof., 1963—; asst. prof. plant pathology Ohio Agrl. Research and Devel. Ctr., Wooster, 1951-53, Ohio State U., Columbus, 1951-53; cons. botanist and taxonomist Minn. Dept. Agr., 1954-60. cons. editor McGraw-Hill Ency. Sci. and Tech., 1972-78; editor-in-chief Phytopathology, 1964-67; editor: Procs. IX Internat. Congress

Plant Protection, 2 vols., 1981, corn disease newsletter, 1970-76; sr. editor: Challenging Problems in Plant Health, 1982, Plant Disease Reporter, 1979; Contbr. articles to profl. jours. Guggenheim fellow, 1961; Fulbright scholar, 1968. Fellow AAAS, Am. Phytopathol. Soc. (pres. 1971, publs. coordinator 1978-84, disting. service award 1984); mem. Am. Inst. Biol. Scis., Bot. Soc. Am., Council Biology Editors, Internat. Soc. Plant Pathology (councilor 1971-78, sec.-gen. and treas. 1983-88), Mycol. Soc. Am., Minn. Acad. Sci., N.Y. Acad. Scis., Soc. Scholarly Publs., Weed Sci. Soc. Am. (award of excellence 1968). Baptist. Home: 1666 Coffman St #322 Saint Paul MN 55108 Office: U Minn 495 Borlaug Hall 1991 Buford Circle Saint Paul MN 55108

KON, OI-LIAN, physician; b. Singapore, Sept. 8, 1947; d. Choon-Kooi Kon and Tong-Thye Chen; m. Peter Lam-Hum Hwang, Dec. 21, 1972. B in Medicine and Surgery, U. Singapore, 1971. Diplomate Am. Bd. Internal Medicine. House officer Singapore Gen. Hosp., 1971-72; research fellow McGill U., Montreal, Que., 1972-73; intern Royal Victoria Hosp., Montreal, 1974, resident, 1975-77; research fellow Mayo Clinic, Rochester, Minn., 1978-80; research fellow Meml. U., St. John's, Can., 1980, clin. asst. prof. medicine, 1981-83; sr. lectr. biochemistry Nat. Univ. of Singapore, 1983-85, assoc. prof. biochemistry, 1986—; mem. Internat. Union Biochemistry Com. on Symposia, 1984—; corr. mem. Pub. House of Internat. Council Sci. Unions, 1987—. Editor: Contemporary Themes in Biochemistry, 1986, Integration and Control of Metabolic Processes, 1987, Genes and Proteins: A Laboratory Manual, 1987. Sr. scholar U. Singapore, 1968-70; recipient Oliveiro medal U. Singapore, 1968-70, Silver medal U. Singapore, 1968, 70, Gibbs Gold medal U. Singpore, Yeoh Khuan Joo medal U. Singapore, 1971, Silver medal U. Singapore, 1971; fellow Medical Research Council Can., 1972-73, 78-80. Mem. Endocrine Soc., Singapore Biochem. Soc., Endocrine and Metabolic Soc. Singapore. Office: Nat Univ Singapore, 10 Kent Ridge Crescent, Singapore 0511, Singapore

KONAN-BEDIE, HENRI, economist, politician; b. Dadiékro, Ivory Coast, 1934; m. Henriette Koizan, 1958; 4 children. Student, Poitiers U., France. Civil servant France, 1959-60; counsellor French Embassy, Washington, 1960; founder Ivory Coast Mission to the U.N., 1960; chargé d'affaires Ivory Coast to U.S., 1960, ambassador, 1960-66, ambassador to Can., 1963-66; minister of econs. an fin. Govt. of Ivory Coast, 1966-67; spl. adviser for African affairs Internat. Fin. Corp., 1978-80, pres. nat. assembly, 1980—; mem. Bur. Politique, Parti Démocratique de la Côte d'Ivoire, 1965—; pres. Office Africain et Malgache de la Propriété Industrielle, Banque ouest-africaine de dével.; adminstr. UNESCO Internat. Cultural Funds. Decorated Grand Offidier de l'ordre nat., Ivory Coast, Grand Officier ordre nat. du Mérite, Commdr. Légion d'honneur. Office: Palais de l'Assemblee, B P 1381, Abidjan Ivory Coast *

KONARSKI, FELIKS (REF-REN), author, actor, poet, songwriter; b. Kiev, USSR, Jan. 9, 1907; (parents of Polish nationality); s. Feliks Konarski and Wiktoria (Polecka) Konarska; m. Nina Olenska, Jan. 31, 1931 (dec. Jan. 1983). BA, U. Warsaw, Poland, 1928. Contbg. songwriter Qui Pro Quo Theater, Nowosci Theater, Warsaw, 1926-30; dir. Ref-Ren Theater, Warsaw, 1930-40; dir., pub. affairs officer Theater of 2d Polish Corps, Iraq, Iran, Palestine, Egypt, Italy, 1941-46; dir. Ref-Ren Polish Theater, London, 1947-65, Chgo., 1966—; cons. Polish Nat. Alliance, Chgo., 1983—. Guest author Polish Radio, Paris, 1952; contbg. author Radio Free Europe, Munich, 1960; adj. instr. Alliance Coll., Cambridge Springs, Pa., summers 1958-63; dir. Red Poppies Polish Radio Program, Chgo., 1962—; author: (books) Songs from Ellen's Knapsack (Piosenki z Plecaka Helenki), 1952, Love in my Life (Milosc w moim zyciu), 1967, Elastic Faces (Twarze z gutaperki), 1978, (poetry) Poems Written by the Heart (Wiersze Sercem Pisane) vol. 1, 1972, vol. 2, 1988; also writer, composer numerous songs, musical comedies, and stage revues. Decorated Order of Merit 1st class Polish Govt.-in-Exile, London, 1966, Polonia Restituta Order, 1974; Vets. Cross 1st class Polish Vets. Assn., Toronto, Ont., Can., 1967; Spl. Cultural award Polish Am. Cong., Chgo., 1982. Mem. Union Polish Actors Abroad (hon. pres. 1962—). Office: WPNA Radio 408 S Oak Park Ave Oak Park IL 60302

KONDILIS, FRANCIS NICHOLAS, JR., engineer; b. Tucson, Dec. 10, 1956; s. Francis Nicholas and Barbara Anne (Stahl) K. B.S.E.E., Ariz. State U., 1979; M.S.E.E., U. Md.-College Park, 1982. Registered profl. engr. assoc., Ariz., 1980. Sr. engr. E-O systems Nat. Security Agency, Ft. Meade, Md., 1980-84; program mgr. signal processing systems ESL Inc., Sunnyvale, Calif., 1984—. Served to capt. USAF 1980-84. Mem. IEEE, Nat. Soc. Profl. Engrs., Eta Kappa Nu. Republican. Roman Catholic. Current work: Digital signal processing systems, mgmt. of large high tech. projects, communication and reconnaissance systems. Subspecialties: Optical signal processing; Algorithms. Office: ESL Inc MS 508 PO Box 3510 Sunnyvale CA 94088

KONDO, ASAHI, manufacturing company executive; b. Tokyo, Mar. 30, 1923; parents: Kōichiro and Kiyo Kondo; 1 child, Jun. Degree in jurisprudence, Tokyo U. Pres. Nakayama Kōgyō KK, Osaka, Japan, 1957—; mem. com. Japan Iron and Steel Fedn., 1958—. Home: 6-25-8-1401 Jingumae, Shibuya-ku, Tokyo Japan Office: Nakayama Kōgyō KK, 1-2-133 Nishjima, Nishiyodogawa-ku Osaka Japan

KONDO, MASATOSHI STEPHAN, pharmaceutical executive, educator; b. Asahikawa, Hokkaido, Japan, Feb. 8, 1940; came to U.S, 1984; s. Saburo Mikame and Hanae Kondo; m. Barbara Renate Bunk, Aug. 5, 1964 (div.); 1 child, Mika Naomi. BS, Tokyo U., 1962; PhD, U. Ill., Urbana, 1967; DSc, U. Antwerp, Belgium, 1976. Asst. prof. U. Zurich, Switzerland, 1970-72; prof. U. Antwerp, 1972-82; dir. Yamanouchi Pharm. Co., Tokyo, 1982-84, Bristol-Myers Co., Wallingford, Conn., 1984-88; pres. Strategic Informatica Internat., Wallingford, Conn., 1988—; pres., chief exec. officer Neurotech Labs., Inc, The Woodlands, Tex., 1988—; prof. Yale U., New Haven, Conn., 1985—, U. Conn., Storrs, Conn., 1986—. Author: Microbiology (in Dutch), 1975. Fellow Internat. Agy. for Research on Cancer, WHO, 1976, sr. NATO, 1981; named Leopold II Knight , Kingdom of Belgium, 1980. Mem. AAAS, German Biochem. Soc., Belgian Biochem. Soc., Austrian Biochem. Soc.

KONDZIELA, HENRYK, art historian; b. Tuchola, Poland, Apr. 6, 1931; s. Franciszek and Eleonora Jadwiga (Okonek) K.; M. in History of Art, U. Poznan (Poland), 1955, Ph.D. in History of Art, 1972; m. Stanislawa Chodorowska, July 15, 1957; 1 son, Mariusz. Chief, Monuments-Care Service, Poznan, 1955-72; asst. prof. history of architecture and monuments restoration Tech. U. Poznan, 1972—; dir. Nat. Mus., Poznan, 1978—; permanent cons. Polish State Enterprise for Conservation Cultural Heritage. Polish Ministry Sci. grantee, 1976. Fellow Stowarzyszenie Historyków Sztuki, Towarzystwo Urbanistów Polskich; asso. mem. Internat. Inst. for Conservation, Internat. Council Mus., Internat. Council Monuments and Sites, Stowarzyszenie Konserwatoró w Zabytkó w w Polsce (v.p.). Author: (in Polish with English summary) Stare Miasto w Poznaniu (Old City in Poznan), 1972, 2d edit., 1975. Grantee City of Poznan, 1985, Polish Ministry of Culture, 1987. Home: ul Przemyslowa 49/2, 61-541 Poznan Poland Office: Muzeum Narodowe, Al Marcinkowskiego 9, 61-745 Poznan Poland

KONG, YIM-FAI ALBERT, pediatrician; b. Hong Kong, Dec. 15, 1950; s. Hing Cheung and Lane (Au-Yeung) K.; m. Ming-Yim Susan Chan, Nov. 20, 1978; children: James, Kelvin, Dennis. MBBS, U. Hong Kong, 1973. Med. officer Hong Kong Govt., 1974-79; clin. attachment dept. pediatrics St. Thomas' Hosp., London, 1978; sr. med. officer Princess Margaret Hosp., Hong Kong, 1980-81; officer in charge health service Hong Kong Poly., 1981-84; practice medicine specializing in pediatrics Hong Kong, 1984—; hon. pediatric cons. Hong Kong Bapt. Hosp., 1986—. Fellow Hong Kong Coll. Physicians; mem. Royal Coll. Physicians (diplomate child health, London, Dublin), Hong Kong Med. Assn., Hong Kong Pediatric Soc., Sch. Med. Service Doctors' Assn. Office: Room 1001 Champion Bldg, 301-309 Nathan Rd, N6 Nassau St, G/F, Meifoo, Kowloon Hong Kong

KONIECKO, EDWARD S(TANLEY), biochemist; b. Poland, Mar. 24, 1913; came to U.S., 1959, naturalized, 1966; s. Alexander and Victoria (Czarniecki) K. Food engr., Agrl. U., Warsaw, 1957; M.S. in Food Tech., Acad. Agrl., Warsaw, 1958; M.S. in Econs., Central Sch. Planning and Stats., Warsaw, 1959; Ph.D. in Biochemistry, London Coll. Applied Sci., 1961; postgrad. in Nutrition, Can. U., Guelph, Ont., 1971; Ph.D. in Clin. Nutrition, N.W. London U., 1973. Dir. fin. and acctg. Hdqrs. of State Nutrition, Warsaw, 1950-55; assoc. dir. research Warsaw Dept. Nutrition, 1956-59; chief chemist research and devel. Sugardale Foods, Inc., Canton, Ohio, 1960-76; ind. cons., writer 1976—. Author: Handbook for Meat Chemists, 1979, Nutritional Encyclopedia for the Elderly: A Preventive Medicine Approach, 1981, Handbook for Water Analysis for the Food Industry, 1982, Handbook of Meat Analysis, 1985, also others. Fellow Am. Inst. Chemists; mem. Am. Chem. Soc., AAAS, Assn. Ofcl. Analytical Chemists, N.Y. Acad. Scis. Roman Catholic. Home and Office: PO Box 8341 Canton OH 44711-8341

KONING, JANTINE JACOBA, manufacturing executive; b. Groningen, The Netherlands, Sept. 9, 1950; d. Cornelius and Frederika (Wolters) K.; m. Goeman Martinus, June 25, 1986. BBA, Groningen Sch. Mgmt., 1983, MBA, 1985; postgrad, Northwestern U., 1986-87. Market researcher Douwe Egberts HL, Utrecht, The Netherlands, 1984-85; indsl. engr. Fokker Spl. Products, Hoogeveen, The Netherlands, 1985-86; strategic planner Fokker Aircraft, Amsterdam, The Netherlands, 1986—; bus. planning cons., Woerden, 1987. Contbr. articles to profl. jours. fin. chairperson Ctr. Adult Edn., Groningen, 1982-86. Recipient Unilever Mktg. award Capts. Dutch Industries and Mktg. Profs., Rotterdam, 1986. Mem. Dutch Women's Network, Federatie Nederlandse Vakverenigingen. Mem. Party van de Arbeid. Home: Essenlaan 47, 3442 JG Woerden The Netherlands Office: Fokker Aircraft BV, PO Box 12222, 1100 AE Amsterdam The Netherlands

KONNYU, LESLIE, retired geographer, cartographer, author; b. Tamasi, Hungary, Feb. 28, 1914; s. Joseph and Mary (Polhamer) K.; came to U.S., 1949, naturalized, 1955; diploma Tchrs. Tng. Coll., Hungary, 1933, 44; B.Mus. Edn., St. Louis Mus. and Arts Coll., 1954, diploma cartography, 1957, M.A. in Geography, 1965; m. Elizabeth Gelencser; children—Ernest, Gabriella Konnyu Heizer, Joseph Z. Tchr. elementary sch., Hungary, 1936-42; secondary sch. tchr., Hungary, 1942-44; dir. Refugee Sch., Austria, 1944-49; ch. organist St. Peter's Ch., Jefferson City, Mo., 1949-51; lab. technician Sch. Medicine, Washington U., St. Louis, 1951-55; cartographer Def. Mapping Agy., St. Louis, 1955-73. Dir. Hungarian Radio Program, 1952-58; founder Am. Friends Hungarian Culture, 1959-64; dir. Am. Hungarian Welfare Com., 1956-64; pres. Am. Hungarian Cultural Club, 1967-68; chmn. T.S. Eliot Monument Com., 1972—; chmn. Am. Hungarian Art Hist. Com., 1979—. Recipient Distinguished Community Service award, St. Louis, 1956; certificate merit lit., London, 1972, certificate merit poetry, 1974. Mem. St. Louis Writers Guild (treas. 1968, historian 1974), St. Louis Poetry Center (pres. 1978-80), T.S. Eliot Soc. (dir. 1980), Internat. P.E.N., Mo. Writers Guild, Internat. Poetry Assn., Internat. Acad. Poets, Author 26 books in Hungarian, 1 in French, 1 in German; also author: Bond of Beauty, 1959; Against the River, 1961; A History of American Hungarian Literature II, 1988; Eagles of Two Continents, 1963; Modern Magyar Literature, 1964; John Xantus, Hungarian Geographer in America, 1965. Editor: Historical Highlights of Cartography, 1965, Hungarians in the U.S.A., 1967, Collected Poems, 1968, Condensed Geography of Hungary, 1971, Hungarian Participants in the Art Exhibition of St. Louis World Fair, 1973, Acacias: Hungarians in the Mississippi Valley, 1976, Professional Hungarian Artists Outside Hungary, 1978, St. Louis Hungarian weekly, 1957-58, Am. Hungarian Rev., 1963-74, Gilgamesh, 1980, Hungarian Transylvania, 1982, 50th Literary Album, 1984, Hungarian Bouquet, 1984. Home: 5410 Kerth Rd Saint Louis MO 63128

KONO, MOTOHIKO, movie critic, music producer; b. Tokyo, Nov. 26, 1932; s. Fusao and Yoshiko (Suetaka) K.; m. Setsuko Kurosawa, Jan. 15, 1969; children—Kazuhiko, Masahiko. B.A., Waseda U., Tokyo, 1956. Record producer Nippon Columbia Records, Tokyo, 1956-70; mgr. Warner-Pioneer Records, Tokyo, 1970-72; freelance music producer, Tokyo, 1972—; freelance movie critic, Tokyo, 1974—; radio and TV performer, 1983; dir. Sign of Light & Sounds Sign Design Assn. award 1983. Mem. Japan Film Pen Club, Music Critics Assn. Japan.

KONOPKA, MARY ANN STEPHANY, container mfg. co. exec.; b. Chgo., Jan. 30, 1933; d. Thomas Stephen and Mary Irene (Plucinski) Poltorak; m. Louis Steven Konopka, Nov. 22, 1964 (dec. 1976); stepchildren: Linda Marie Konopka Orseno, Lorraine Louise Konopka Capra. With Continental Group, Inc., West Chicago, Ill., 1952—, project control supr., 1978-83, supr. inventory control, 1983—. Mem. Am. Inventory and Prodn. Soc., Nat. Assn. Female Execs., Am. Soc. Profl. and Exec. Women, U.S. CB Radio Assn. Democrat. Roman Catholic. Club: Northwest Internat. Trade. Home: 526 E Pomeroy St West Chicago IL 60185 Office: Continental Group Inc 1700 Harvester Rd West Chicago IL 60185

KONOWITZ, HERBERT HENRY, manufacturing company executive; b. Brookline, Mass., Feb. 13, 1937; s. Robert Isaac and Sarah (Freedman) K.; m. Linda Phyllis Swartzman, Dec. 20, 1958; children: Cindy Lee, Jeffrey Scott. BSBA, Babson Coll., 1958. V.p. Vita Rest Sales Co., N.Y.C., 1958-63, Lady Linda Covers Inc., N.Y.C., 1963—; pres. Milford Stitching Co. (Del.), 1968—; v.p. Comml. Drapery Contractors, Inc., Silver Springs, Md., 1976-81; dir. Greater Del. Corp., Dover, Del. Nat. Life, Yankee Land, Inc., Reclamation Center, Inc., 1972-75, G.L.K., Inc. Mem. Gov. Del. Council Consumer Affairs, 1971-76; commr. State Lottery Commn., 1978-81; bd. dirs. Job for Del. Grads., Inc., 1979, Health Plan of Del. Chmn. Local Republican Dist. Com., 1971-75; dir. Del. Dept. of Tourism, 1988—; mem. Del. Rep. Central Com., 1971—; vice chmn. Kent County Rep. Com., 1975-79, chmn., 1979-81; v.p. Kent County chpt. Am. Heart Assn., 1974-75, pres., 1975-76; trustee Broadmeadow Sch., 1980-84, Congregation Beth Sholom, 1980-86; mem. parent's council Northfield-Mt. Hermon Sch., 1984-86; county chmn. Gov.'s Election Com., 1984; mem. adv. council Goldey Beacon Coll., 1987. Lodges: Masons, Elks. Home: 55 Beloit Ave Dover DE 19901 Office: Milford Stitching Co S Marshall St Milford DE 19963

KONSKI, JAMES LOUIS, civil engineer; b. N.Y.C., Nov. 4, 1917; s. Herbert D. and Ruby (Louis) K.; children: Alexander, Christina, Marguerite. B.S. in Civil Engring., U. Mo., 1950, M.S. in Civil Engring., 1951. Registered profl. engr., N.Y., Ky., R.I., Kans. registered profl. surveyor. Engr., Bur. Yards and Docks, Washington, 1951; structural engr. Sanderson & Porter, N.Y.C., 1951-52; field engr. Ebasco Services, Inc., Owensboro, Ky., 1952-53; chief structural engr. Berger Assos., Syracuse, N.Y., 1953-54, Endman, Anthony & Hosley (formerly Berger Assos.), Syracuse, 1954-57; pres. Konski Engrs. Profl. Corp., Syracuse, 1957—; prin. Konski Engrs. Internat., 1965—; cons. engr. U.S. Trade Mission to Africa, 1965, to Far East, 1970; speaker Met. Assn. Urban Designers and Environ. Planning Conf., Eng., 1974, Netherlands, 1975. Contbr. articles to profl. jours. Served with USMC, 1939-46; maj. Res. ret. Recipient Honor Award for Disting. Service in Engring., U. Mo., 1986. Fellow ASCE (v.p. 1972-73, nat. dir. 1966-70), Am. Cons. Engrs. Council (past chpt. pres.); mem. Internat. Assn. Bridge and Structural Engrs., Nat. Soc. Profl. Engrs. (past chpt. pres.), Am. Concrete Inst., Prestressed Concrete Inst., Am. Congress Surveying and Mapping, Am. Mil. Engrs., Am. Water Works Assn., Am. Road Builders Assn., Am. Soc. Photogrammetry, League Am. Wheelman (area rep. 1967-77), U.S. Cycling Fedn., Am. Coll. Sports Medicine, Internat. Randonneurs (dir. USA/Can.), Sigma Xi, Tau Beta Pi, Chi Epsilon, Pi Mu Epsilon. Clubs: Onondaga, Cycling (pres. 1967-77). Participant Paris-Brest-Paris Bicycle Race, 1975, 79, 83, 87; dir. Internat. Randonneurs (U.S.). Office: Old Engine House No 2 727 N Salina St Syracuse NY 13208

KONSTANTINOV, MIHAIL MIHAILOV, mathematics educator; b. Sofia, Bulgaria, Mar. 5, 1948; s. Mihail Spirov and Elka Mineva (Hadjimineva) K.; m. Svetlina Nikolaeva Ivanova (div. 1981); 1 child, Mihail; m. Ema Ivanova Vankova. MS in Math., Plovdiv U., Bulgaria, 1982; PhD in Math., Inst. Math. of Bulgarian Acad. Sci., Sofia, 1986. Research scientist Bulgarian Acad. Sci., Sofia, 1979-87; assoc. prof. Higher Inst. Architecture and Civil Engring., Sofia, 1987—; cons. Higher Inst. Mech. and Elec. Engring., Sofia, 1981—. Author: Method of Averaging, 1973, Analysis and Design of Linear Multivariable Systems, 1983; contbr. over 270 articles to profl. jours., 1970—. Served with Bulgarian Army, 1977-78. Mem. Am. Math. Soc., Union Bulgarian Mathematicians, Union Scientists in Bulgaria. Home: 10 Omurtag St, 1124 Sofia Bulgaria Office: Higher Inst Arch & Civil Engring, Dept Math, 1421 Sofia Bulgaria

KONSTANTINOVIČ, ZORAN VLADIMIR, literature educator; b. Belgrade, Yugoslavia, May 6, 1920; arrived in Austria, 1970; s. Vladimir R. and Andja (Milosavljevič) K.; m. Dagmar W. Bestal; 1 child, Vladimir. Doctor degree, U. Belgrade, 1954. Prof. literature U. Belgrade, 1954-70, U. Innsbruck, Austria, 1970—. Author: Phänomenologie und Literaturwissenschaft, 1973, Weltliteratur-Synthesen und Modelle, 1975. Home: Reithmannstrasse 18, Innsbruck Austria Office: U Innsbruck, Dept Literature, Innrain 52, Innsbruck Austria

KONTOGIORGIS, MICHAEL THEODORE, clergyman; b. Boston, May 15, 1948; s. Theodore Michael and Panagiota (Andriopoulos) K.; m. Vicki Betty George, Aug. 27, 1972; children—Kristen, Patricia, Megan. B.A., Hellenic Coll., 1970; M.Div., Holy Cross Greek Orthodox Sch. Theology, 1973, S.T.M., 1974. Ordained deacon Greek Orthodox Ch., 1972, priest, 1973; driving instr. Cleve. Circle Auto Sch., Brookline, Mass., 1969-71; coordinator United Shoppers Assn., Randolph, Mass., 1971-73; asst. to dean Annunciation Greek Orthodox Cathedral of New Eng., Boston, 1973-75; parish priest Holy Trinity Greek Orthodox Ch., Orlando, Fla., 1975—; dir. Greek Orthodox Youth Actionline, Orlando, 1981, Greek Orthodox Altar Boys Workshop, Brooksville, Fla., 1981-83; chmn. Youth Commn., Greek Orthodox Diocese Atlanta, 1981-83; mem. Presbyters Council, Greek Orthodox Archdiocese North and South Am., N.Y.C., 1983—; co-producer, dir. Grecian Echoes radio program, Orlando, 1978; chaplain Orlando Police Dept., 1978-79; bd. dirs. Olympic Village, 1977-84, 1st v.p., 1979-83, pres., 1983-84. Author: The Altar Boy's Guidebook, 1981; editor weekly ch. newsletter Harbinger, 1975—. Named Sakellarios, Greek Orthodox Archdiocese North and S.Am., 1980; recipient Pectoral Cross and plaque for 10th anniversary of ordination Holy Trinity Greek Orthodox Ch., 1983. Mem. Greek Orthdox Clergy Assn. (sec. Atlanta Diocese 1981-83, pres. 1983—), Orthodox Clergy Fellowship North and Central Fla. (sec. 1982—), Holy Cross Greek Orthodox Sch. Theology Alumni Assn. Home: 106 Valencia Loop Altamonte Springs FL 32714 Office: Holy Trinity Greek Orthodox Ch 1217 Trinity Woods Ln Maitland FL 32751

KONTTINEN, MAUNO PELLERVO, thoracic and cardiovascular surgeon; b. Hameenlinna, Finland, Apr. 30, 1944; s. Taisto Ilmari and Helmi Alina (Aalto) K.; m. Seija Tassberg, July 19, 1968; children—Tytti, Tiina, Taru. M.D., U. Helsinki, Finland, 1972. Diplomate Finland Bd. Thoracic and Cardiovascular Surgery. Gen. practice, Espoo City Health Ctr., 1972-75; resident gen. surgery Maria Hosp., Helsinki, 1975-78; resident Helsinki U., Central Hosp., 1978-84, sr. registrar, 1984-87, asst. adminstrv. chief physician, 1987—. Contbr. sci. articles to profl. jours. Mem. Am. Coll. Chest Physicians, Finnish Med. Assn., several domestic and Scandinavian surgical socs. Lutheran. Avocation: music. Home: Kalasaaksentie 4 D 21, 02620 Espoo Finland Office: Helsinki U Cen Hosp, Cen Adminstrn, Stenbackinkatu 9, 00290 Helsinki Finland

KONVITZ, MILTON RIDBAZ, legal educator; b. Safad, Israel, Mar. 12, 1908; came to U.S., 1915, naturalized, 1926; s. Rabbi Joseph and Welia (Ridbaz-Wilowsky) K.; m. Mary Traub, June 18, 1942; 1 son, Josef. BS, NYU, 1928, AM, 1930, JD, 1930; PhD (Sage fellow in philosophy 1932-33), Cornell U., 1933; LittD, Rutgers U., 1954, Dropsie U., 1975; DCL, U. Liberia, 1962; LHD, Hebrew Union Coll-Jewish Inst. Religion, 1966, Yeshiva U., 1972; LLD, Syracuse U., 1971, Jewish Theol. Sem., 1972. Bar: N.J. 1932. Practice law Jersey City and Newark, 1933-46; lectr. on law and pub. adminstrn. NYU, 1938-46; asst. gen. counsel NAACP Legal Def. and Edn. Fund, 1943-46; mem. faculty New Sch. for Social Research, 1944-46; prof. indsl. and labor relations N.Y. State Sch. of Indsl. and Labor Relations, Cornell U., 1946-73; prof. law Cornell U. Law Sch., 1956-73, prof. emeritus, 1973—; mem. Inst. Advanced Study, Princeton, 1959-60; vis. prof. Hebrew U., Jerusalem, 1970; dir. Liberian Codification of Laws project, 1952-80; gen. counsel Newark Housing Authority, 1938-43, N.J. State Housing Authority, 1943-45; Pub. rep. Nat. War Labor Bd. region 2, 1943-46; mem. enforcement commn. and hearing commn. Wage Stablzn. Bd., 1952-53; chmn. nat. com. study of Jewish Edn. in U.S., 1958-59; faculty Salzburg (Austria) Seminar Am. Studies, 1952; panel Fed. Mediation and Conciliation Service, N.Y. Mediation Bd., Am. Arbitration Assn., N.Y. State Pub. Employment Relations, Nat. Mediation Bd. Author: On the Nature of Value: Philosophy of Samuel Alexander, 1946, The Alien and the Asiatic in American Law, 1946, The Constitution and Civil Rights, 1947, Civil Rights in Immigration, 1953, Bill of Rights Reader, 1954, Fundamental Liberties of a Free People, 1957, A Century of Civil Rights, 1961, Expanding Liberties: Freedom's Gains in Postwar America, 1966, Religious Liberty and Conscience, 1968, Judaism and Human Rights, 1972, Judaism and the American Idea, 1978; Founding editor: Industrial and Labor Relations Rev. (vols. 1-5), 1947-52, Liberian Code of Laws (5 vols.), 1957-60, Liberian Code of Laws Revised, 1973—, Liberian Law Reports (27 vols); Mem. editorial bds. of periodicals; chmn. editorial bd.: Midstream Mag; co-editor: Jewish Social Studies; co-founder: Judaism Mag; mem. editorial bd.: Ency. Judaica. Pres. Hebrew Culture Found.; chmn. com. on Jewish studies Meml. Found. for Jewish Culture; nat. comnn. Ramah; commn. reorgn. World Zionist Orgn.; bd. dirs. Am. Histadrut Cultural Exchange Inst.; acad. council Am. Friends Hebrews U.; mem. anti-discrimination com. Anti-Defamation League; bd. advisors Law Students Civil Rights Research Council. Ford Found. Faculty fellow, 1952-53; Guggenheim fellow, 1953-54; Fund for the Republic fellow, 1955; comdr. Order Star of Africa Liberia, 1957; grand band, 1960; fellow Center Advanced Study Behavioral Scis., 1964-65; fellow Nat. Endowment for Humanities, 1975-76; recipient N.Y. U. Washington Sq. Coll. Disting. Alumni award, 1964; Mordecai ben David disting. award Yeshiva U., 1965; Morris J. Kaplun internat. prize for scholarship Hebrew U., 1969; Tercentenary medal Jewish Community of Essex County, N.J., 1954. Fellow Am. Acad. Arts and Scis., Jewish Acad. Arts and Scis., Conf. Jewish Social Studies (dir.), Zionist Acad. Council (exec. com.), Yivo Inst. (acad. council); mem. Am. Philos. Assn., AAUP (council 1961-64), Law and Soc. Assn., Indsl. Relations Research Assn., Internat. Assn. Jewish Law, ACLU (nat. com.), Jewish Publ. Soc. (mem. com. on publs.), Am. Jewish League for Israel (adv. bd.), Order of Coif, Phi Beta Kappa. Home: 16 The Byway Ithaca NY 14850

KONWICKI, TADEUSZ, writer, film director; b. Nowa Wilejka, USSR, June 22, 1926; m. Dunuta Lenica. Ed. Jagellonian U., Cracow, Warsaw U. Partisan, Home Army detachment, 1944-45; mem. Polish Writers Assn., 1949—; editorial staff Nowa Kultura, 1950-57; films directed include: Osatatni dzienlata (Last Day of Summer), 1958, Zaduszki, 1962, Salto, 1965, Jak daleko stad, jak blisko 1972, Dolina Issy, 1982. Author: Wladza, 1954, zonego miasta, 1954, Godzina smutku, 1954, Rojsty, 1956, Dziura w niebie, 1959, Sennik wspolczesny (A Dreambook of our Time), 1963, French version, 1984, Wniebowstapienie, 1967, Zwierzoczlekoupior, 1969, Nic albo nic, 1971, Kronika wyppadkow milosnych, 1974, Kalendarz i klepsydra (The Calendar and the Sand-Glass), 1976, Kompleks polski, 1977, Mala Apokalispsa, 1979, Wschody i zachody Ksiezyca, 1982; film scripts include Zimowy zmierzch (Winter Twilight), Matka Joanna od Aniolow, Faraon, Jowita, Austeria. Recipient State prize, 3d Class, 1950, 54, 1st Class, 1966, knight's cross order of Polonia Restituta, 1954, officer's cross, 1964, medal of 10th Anniversary of People's Poland, 1955, Mondello prize for lit., 1981. Home: Ul Gorskiego 1 m 68, 00-033 Warsaw Poland *

KOO, JORGE LEY, cardiologist; b. Mexico City, Apr. 19, 1936; s. Manuel and Kit Wan (Koo) Ley; m. Judy Beth Wittenberg Bravard, Apr. 3, 1964 (div. 1974); children: Daniel, Monica Frances; m. Maria Teresa Gutierrez, July 3, 1982; children: Sandra Jessica. BS, U. Puebla, 1952, MD, 1958. Cert. cardiologist. Intern Nat. Inst. Neumology, Mexico City, 1961-62; resident in internal medicine Norwalk (Conn.) Hosp., 1962-63; resident Inst. Nat. Cardiology, Mexico City, 1963-65; cardiologist Hosp. Civil de Puebla, Mex., 1966-74, Hosp. Guadalupe, Puebla, Mex., 1966—, Clinic de Prevencion y Diagnostico, Puebla, Mex., 1980—; prof. clin. cardiology U. Puebla, 1966-71, 74-80; pres. Lab. Clinico Guadalupe, Puebla, 1984—. Contbr. articles to profl. publs. Fellow Am. Coll. Cardiology; mem. Mex. Soc. Cardiology, Am. Heart Assn., Mex. Soc. Critical Medicine, Puebla Soc. Cardiology, N.Y. Acad. Scis. Club: Alpha (Puebla). Home: 41 Poniente 916, 72420 Puebla Mexico Office: Clin de Prevencion y Diagnostico, 16 Sur 1308-4, 72000 Puebla Mexico

KOO, PETER HUNG-KWAN, immuno-biochemist, educator; b. Shanghai, China; came to U.S., 1959, naturalized, 1975; s. Yung-Foo and Shun-Wa (Ko) K.; m. S. Alice Ho, Dec. 23, 1967; children: David G., Christopher G. BA, U. Wash., 1964; PhD, U. Md., 1970. Research assoc. Johns Hopkins U., 1970-74, asst. prof. oncology and radiology, 1975-77; staff fellow NIH, Bethesda, Md., 1974-75; asst. prof., assoc. prof. microbiology/immunology Northeastern Ohio Univs. Coll. Medicine, Rootstown, 1977—; adj. assoc. prof., depts. chemistry and biology Kent (Ohio) State U. Research, publs. in field. Deacon, 1st Christian Ch. of Kent, 1978-85, 88—, mem. fin. com., 1982-84; v.p. Am. Cancer Soc. Portage County chpt., 1987—, chmn., 1985—; bd. dirs. Am. Cancer Soc. com. Portage County (Ohio) chpt, Women's Cancer Fund of N.E. Ohio, 1988—. Recipient Cystic Fibrosis Care Fund award 1979, 82, Profl. Edn. Program award, 1986; NIH grantee, 1978-82, Am. Cancer Soc. grantee, 1979, 82, United Way Health Found. grantee, 1982, MEFCOM Found. grantee, 1983—, NSF grantee, 1984—, numerous ednl. grants, 1985—. Mem. N.Y. Acad. Scis., Am. Assn. Immunologists, Johns Hopkins Med. Surg. Assn., AAAS, Am. Chem. Soc., Am. Soc. for Microbiology, Ohio Acad. Sci., Internat. Platform Assn., Sigma Xi. Office: Northeastern Ohio Univ Coll Medicine Rootstown OH 44272

KOONCE, JOHN PETER, investment company executive; b. Coronado, Calif., Jan. 8, 1932; s. Allen Clark and Elizabeth (Webb) K.; B.S., U.S. Naval Acad., 1954; postgrad. U. So. Calif., 1957, U. Alaska, 1961, U. Ill., 1968-69; M.S. in Ops. Research, Fla. Inst. Tech., 1970; postgrad. Claremont Grad. Sch., 1970; m. Marilyn Rose Campbell, Sept. 21, 1952; children—Stephen Allen, William Clark, Peter Marshall. Indsl. engr. Aluminum Co. Am. Lafayette, Ind., 1954-56; electronic research engr. Autonetics Div. N.Am. Aviation, Downey, Calif., 1956-57; systems field engr. Remington Rand Univac, Fayetteville, N.C., 1957-59; project engr. RCA Service Co., Cheyenne, Wyo., 1959-60, project supr., Clear, Alaska, 1960-62, project supr., Yorkshire, Eng., 1962-64, re-entry signature analyst, Patrick AFB, Fla., 1964-66; mem. tech. staff TRW Systems Group, Washington, 1966-68; mgr. ops research systems analysis Magnavox Co., Urbana, Ill., 1968-69; tech. advisor, EDP, to USAF, Aerojet Electro Systems Co., Azusa, Calif., Woomera, Australia, 1969-72; investment exec. Shearson Hammill, Los Angeles, 1972-74; investment exec. Reynolds Securities, Los Angeles, 1974-75; v.p. investments Shearson Hayden Stone, Glendale, Calif., 1975-77; v.p. accounts Paine, Webber, Jackson & Curtis Inc., Los Angeles, 1977-82; pres. Argo Fin. Corp., Santa Monica, Calif., 1982-83, Fin. Packaging Corp., Flintridge, Calif., 1983—; fin. lectr. cruise ship Island Princess; tchr. investments Citrus Coll., Azusa, Calif., Claremont (Calif.) Evening Sch. Vice pres. Claremont Republican Club, 1973, pres., 1974. Chmn., Verdugo Hosp. Assos., 1979. Recipient Merit certificate RCA, 1966. Mem. Nat. Assn. Security Dealers, Internat. Assn. Fin. Planners, Navy League U.S., Naval Acad. Alumni Assn. Clubs: Masons (past master 1987, pres. dist. officers assn.). Kiwanis. Host, commentator, Sta. KWHY-TV, Los Angeles, (weekly) West of Wall Street, 1986-87; contbr. articles to bus. jours. Home: 5228 Escalante Dr La Canada CA 91011 Office: PO Box 711513 Los Angeles CA 90071

KOONCE, KENNETH TERRY, oil company executive; b. Corpus Christi, Tex., June 1, 1938; s. Hubert Allen and Nell Gustine (Lacy) K.; m. Beverly Anne Montgomery, Aug. 6, 1960; children—Diana K. Koonce Walla, Kenneth T., Jr., Kelly M. B.S. in Chem. Engring., Rice U., 1960, Ph.D. in Chem. Engring., 1964. Registered profl. engr., Tex. Research and mgmt. positions Exxon Co. U.S.A. and Exxon Prodn. Research, Houston, 1963-76; prodn. dept. planning coordinator Exxon Co. U.S.A., Houston, 1976-77; western div. ops. mgr. Exxon Co. U.S.A., Los Angeles, 1977-80, western div. mgr., 1980-83; prodn. dept. hdqrs. ops. mgr. Exxon Co. U.S.A., Houston, 1983-85; pres., chief exec. officer Esso Resources Can. Ltd., Calgary, Alta., Can., 1985-88; sr. v.p. Upstream Bus. Exxon Co. U.S.A., 1988—; bd. dirs. Imperial Oil Ltd., Exxon Prodn. Research Co. Contbr. articles to profl. jours.; patentee in field. Pres. Rice U. Engring. Alumni, Houston, 1977; mem. adv. council George Brown Sch. Engring., Rice U., Houston; panel vice chmn. Gulf Coast United Way, Houston, 1984-85; dep. chmn. Calgary United Way, 1986, chmn. 1987; elder Ch. of Christ. Mem. Soc. Petroleum Engrs. (bd. dirs. 1981-84, Sect. Service award 1972), Am. Petroleum Inst., Can. Petroleum Assn. (gov., exec. com.), Tex. State Bd. Profl. Engrs., Tex. Mid-Continent Oil & Gas Assn. (Budget & Exec. Coms. 1988—), Mid-Continent Oil & Gas Assn. (exec. com. 1988—), Nat. Ocean Industries Assn. (Bd., Fin., Govt. & Pub. Affairs Coms. 1988—), Adminstrv. & Devel. Bd. of Inst. for Christian Studies (Austin), Pepperdine U. Bd. of Regents. Republican. Clubs: Calgary Petroleum, Calgary Golf and Country, Ranchmen's, Glencoe (Calgary); Petroleum (Houston), Houstonian. Office: Exxon Co USA PO Box 2180 Houston TX 77252-2180

KOONS, IRVIN LOUIS, design executive, graphic artist; b. Harrisburg, Pa., Mar. 14, 1922; s. Frank and Rose (Silver) K.; m. Leah Fay, Dec. 25, 1949; children: Adam, Jonathan, Joshua. Grad., Pratt Inst., 1942, New Sch., N.Y., 1946; student and instr., Ecole Des Beaux Arts, Fontainebleau, France, 1948-50; student, others schs. in France, Switzerland and Italy, 1947-49. Designer, chief exec. officer Irv Koons Assocs. (subs. Saatchi and Saatchi Compton Worldwide, since 1983), N.Y.C., 1950—; past cultural attache, spl. cons. U.S. Dept. State; dir. 1st internat. packaging exhibition U.S. Info. Agy.; tchr. various art schs.; advisor Inferential Focus Forum; lectr. NYU, U. Pa., Columbia U., U. Tel Aviv, others. Exhibited paintings and drawings in group shows in U.S. and France, represented in several permanent collections; prin. works include Life of Moses series, 1975-78, stained glass wall for Fedn. Jewish Philanthropies, 1975, series coordinated Torah ornaments, 1986; illus. many books and mags. including Ladies Home Jour., Good Housekeeping, Fortune, Seventeen, Sports Illustrated; cons. editor Graphis Packaging, Switzerland, 1970; art critic The Statesman newspaper, India, 1946; contbr. articles on packaging and mktg. to profl. jours. Founder, co-dir. Internat. Design Assistance Commn.; bd. dirs., mem. exec. com. Found. for Future Generations; bd. dirs. Temple Emanuel, Englewood N.J., 1987; trustee Art Ctr. No. N.J., Englewood, 1960-68; contbr. logo and trade mark designs to various non-profit civic orgns. including Am. Cancer Soc., Fedn. Jewish Philanthropies, World Hunger, Sloan-Kettering Meml. Hosp., United Cerebral Palsy, Jewish Theol. Sem., many others. Served with inf. U.S. Army, 1942-46, CBI. Recipient numerous awards including Clio awards, 1976, 77, 81, Gold Clio award, 79, 84, Silver award Variety Store Merchandisers, 1967, Gold award Variety Store Merchandisers, 1970, Gold award Internat. Folding Carton Competition, 1964, Gold award Paperboard Packaging Council, 1974, awards N.Y. Art Dir.'s Club, 1958, 59, 63, 76, 77, 79 (2), awards Am. Inst. Graphic Arts, 1955, 58, 59, 60 (3), 61, 65 (2), 72, awards Package Design Mag., 1963, 64, 65, 66, 67, 68, 70 (3), Gold awards Package Design Council, 1977, 79, 80, Indsl. Design awards, 1968, 75, Package of Yr. award, 1968, Nat. Printing award, 1981, Communication Arts awards, 1960, 64, 66, 67, 71, Best Bottle of Yr. award, 1975, awards Soc. Illustrators, 1959, 68, awards N.J. Art Dir.'s Club, 1962, 65 (3), 68, awards NYU, 1973, 74, many others. Mem. Package Designers Council (Person of Yr. 1982, bd. dirs. 1962—), Indsl. Design Soc. Am., Packaging Inst., Am. Soc. Profl. Cons. Home: 213 Engle St Tenafly NJ 07670 Office: Irv Koons Assocs 625 Madison Ave New York NY 10022

KOORNHOF, PIETER GERHARDUS JACOBUS, ambassador; b. Leeudoringstad, Transvaal, Republic of South Africa, Aug. 2, 1925; married Johanna Louisa Koornhof; children: Gerhard, Johan. BA cum laude, U. S. Africa, Stellenbosch, 1947; D in Philosophy, U. Oxford, 1952. Research officer Ministry of Bantu Admnistrn., Pretoria, Republic of South Africa, 1953; organizer Nat. Party Transvaal, 1956, undersec., 1958; mem. faculty South African Acad. Arts and Scis., 1960, 1978—; dir. cultural infor. Fedn. Afrikaans Cultural Orgns., Johannesburg, Republic of South Africa, 1962; mem. Parliament for Edenvale (later named Primrose), Republic of South Africa, 1964-84; dep. minister Bantu Adminstrn., Bantu Edn. and Immigration, Republic of South Africa, 1968-70; minister of mines, immigration, sport and recreation Republic of South Africa, 1972, minister nat. edn., sport and recreation., 1976-78, minister cooperation and devel., 1978-84, chmn. pres.'s council, 1984-87; South African ambassador to U.S., 1987—; liaison official for immigrants, 1964; mng. dir. Nature Conservation for Nat. Veld Trust S. Africa, 1966; del. Parliamentary Assn. S. Africa to U.S. and Can., 1972, to 13 S. American countries as rep. of S. African Govt., 1974-76, to U.S.A, 1978, to U.S.A. to address symposia in Palm Springs, Calif. and Washington Press Club, 1979, to Republic of China and Hong Kong, 1983. Mem., sec. founding com. Rand Afrikaans U., 1966. Recipient Rhodes scholar Oxford U., 1948, Grand Officers' Cross of Merit award Order of Knights of Malta. Mem. Assn. European Immigration (dir. 1965), S. African Cultural Acad. (co-founder, chmn. 1965). Address: Embassy Republic South Africa 3051 Massachusetts Ave NW Washington DC 20008

KOPEC, ALEKSANDER, mechanical engineer; b. Oct. 12, 1932, Wasowiczowka, Poland; s. Wladyslaw and Aniela Kopec; m. Adela Sudol; 1 child. Grad. Mech. Faculty of Tech., U. Wroclaw, 1957; PhD in Econ. Sci., 1978. Technician Goods Works, Swidnica, 1951-53; technologist, sect. chief, team chief, prodn. mgr., Indsl. Equipment Works, Swidnica, 1957-62; chief engr., then mng. dir. Rolling Stock Works, Swidnica, 1962-67; mng. dir. DOLMEL, elec. machinery plant, Wroclaw, 1967-70; undersec. state Polish Ministry Machine Industry, 1970, 1st state dep. minister, 1973-75, minister, 1975-80, dep. prime minister, 1980-81; pres. Fedn. Sci.-Tech. Orgn. of Socialist Countries, 1980-82, v.p. 1982—; mem. Com. Sci., Tech., and Technol. Progress, 1985—. Mem. Polish Mech. Engrs. and Technicians Assn. (pres. 1975-77, 87—), Chief Tech. Orgn. (pres. 1976-84), World Fedn. Engrs. Orgn. (mem. exec. com.), Central Com. Polish United Workers Party (dep. mem. 1975-80, mem., 1980-81), Internat. Orgn. Coop. in Roller Bearing Industry of Council for Mut. Econ. Assistance (dir.), Com. Econ. Reform. Decorated officer's cross ORP, Order of Banner Labour I and II class, others. Address: 13/15 Senatorska, 00-950 Warsaw Poland

KOPENHAVER, JOSEPHINE YOUNG, painter, educator; b. Seattle, June 9, 1908; d. George Samuel and Blanche Cecilia (Castle) Young; A.B., U. Calif., 1928; M.F.A. (scholar 1936-37), U. So. Calif., 1937; spl. student Claremont Grad. Sch., 1951, 67, Chouinard Art Inst., 1946-47, Otis Art Inst., 1954-55; m. Ralph Witmer Kopenhaver, Apr. 11, 1931. Prof. art Chaffee Jr. Coll., Ontario, Calif., 1946-47, Los Angeles City Coll., 1948-73, Woodbury U., Los Angeles, 1973-76, summer sessions Calif. State U., Los Angeles, 1950, Pasadena City Coll., 1949, Otis Art Inst., Los Angeles, 1959, Pasadena Art Inst., 1948; profl. painter, exhibiting artist, 1933—; work included in exhibits mus. and pvt. galleries U.S. and Mex., 1933—, including Hatfield Galleries, Los Angeles; art juror; represented Archives of Am. Art Oakland (Calif.) Art Mus. Winner first award in oil Los Angeles Art Festival, 1936, various art awards. Mem. Los Angeles Art Assn. (bd. dirs.), Nat. Watercolor Soc. (sec.), Audubon Artists, Artists for Econ. Action, Calif. Tchrs. Assn. Clubs: Los Angeles Athletic, Zeta Tau Alpha. Office: PO Box 10666 Glendale CA 91209 Office: PO Box 10666 Glendale CA 91209

KOPENHAVER, PATRICIA ELLSWORTH, podiatrist. Student, Columbia U., 1950-53; BA, George Washington U., 1954; MA, Columbia U., 1956; Dr. Podiatric Medicine, N.Y. Coll. of Podiatric Medicine, 1963; postgrad., N.Y. Coll. Podiatric Medicine, 1980. Diplomate Nat. Bd. Podiatry Examiners. Practice podiatry Greenwich, Conn., 1964—; mem. staff Laurelton Convalescent Hosp., Greenwich. Publicity dir. Neighbors Club, YWCA, 1968—; Bd. dirs. Monmouth Opera Guild, 1965; trustee Monmouth Opera Festival, 1966, v.p., 1964; mem. Greenwich Arts Council; program chmn. Greenwich Women's Republican Club, 1983-84, 4th dist. rep., 1984-85, 1987—; mem. Greenwich Exchange for Women's Work, 1984; chmn. bd. Greenwich Woman's Club Gardeners, 1986—. Recipient Hosp. Fund award for med. research translations ARC. Mem. Am. Podiatry Assn. (career guidance com.), Conn. Podiatry Assn., Fairfield Podiatry Assn., Am. Woman's Podiatry Assn. (sec.), Am. Assn. Women Podiatrists (charter pres. 1969-78), Acad. Podiatry, Am. Podiatry Council, UN Assn. U.S.A., Acad. Podiatric Medicine, AAUW (chmn. nominating com. 1981, 1st v.p. 1983-84, chmn. fund raising 1984-85, chmn. women's issues 1985), Am. Podiatric Circulatory Soc., NOW, George Washington U., Columbia alumni assns., Fairfield County Alumni Assn. Columbia U., Nat. Fedn. Rep. Women, Bruce Mus., Nature Conservancy, Federated Garden Clubs Conn., Croquet Found. Am., St. Mary Ladies Guild, Greenwich Gardeners Pi Epsilon Chi. Clubs: Soroptimist (vice chmn. program com. 1985—, regional med. scholarship chmn. 1987), Toastmasters, Travel (program com. 1984—, Indian com.), Greenwich Women's (chmn. civic and public affairs com. 1970, program chmn. 1983—, pres. 1985-88, scholarship chmn. 1985—). Home: 2 Sutton Pl S New York NY 10022 Office: 8 Dearfield Dr Greenwich CT 06830

KOPFF, MICHEL, petroleum company executive. Chmn., gen. mgr. Esso S.A.F., Courberoie, France. Address: Esso SAF, Office of Chairman, 6 Ave Andre-Prothin, Courbevoie 92400 France *

KOPP, ELISABETH, Swiss government official; b. Zurich, Dec. 16, 1936; m. Hans W. Kopp; 1 child; Law degree, Zurich Univ., 1960. Mem. City Council, Zumikon, 1970-74; elected pres. City Council, 1974-84; mem. sch. bd., 1972-80; elected Swiss Parliament, 1979-84, mem. Swiss govt. (fed. councillor), 1984—. Avocations: hiking; cooking. Address: Dept of Justice and Police, Bern Switzerland

KOPPE, FRITZ, consumer information administrator; b. Vienna, Austria, Feb. 25, 1929; s. Max Karl and Berta (Fleischer) K.; m. Elfriede Anna Pixner, June 21, 1958; children: Gertrude, Peter. Social worker, Acad. Social Profls., Vienna, 1950; Dr. rer. Pol. (Econs.), U. Vienna, 1954. Drugist W.Neuber A.G., Vienna, Austria, 1943-46; with Nat. Retirement Fund, Vienna, 1951-54; head tng. and press dept. Socialist Youth of Austria, Vienna, 1954-58; broadcasting dir. C. of C. Labour, Vienna, 1958-70; head of staff Minister of Commerce, Vienna, 1970-73; dir. consumer info. Orgn. for Consumer Info., Vienna, 1973—; Internat. Orgn. Consumer Unions rep. at all UN Bodies in Vienna, 1984—. Editor Mar. Trotzdem, 1954-58; contbr. articles to profl. jours. Council mem. Internat. Orgn. Consumer Unions, Den Haag, The Netherlands, 1975— funding mem. Consumer Counncil Austria, 1971—; candidate Socialist Party of Austria for State Parliament, 1960-65; founder Inst. Sci. Politics and Soc., 1969—. Recipient Golden medal of Hon., Rep. of Austria, 1976. Mem. Labour C. of C., Austria Quality Inst. (bd. dirs. 1973—). Office: Verein Fur Konsumenten Info, Mariahilferstrasse 81, A-1060 Vienna Austria

KOPPER, HILMAR, banker; b. Mar. 13, 1935. Mem. bd. mng. dirs. Deutsche Bank AG; chmn. supervisory bd., dep. chmn. supervisory bd., mem. supervisory bd. numerous major cos. Office: Deutsche Bank, Postfach 10 06 01, D-6000 Frankfurt 1 Federal Republic of Germany

KOPRIVICA, DOROTHY MARY, management consultant, real estate and insurance broker; b. St. Louis, May 27, 1921; d. Mitar and Fema (Guzina) K. B.S., Washington U., St. Louis, 1962; cert. in def. inventory mgmt. Dept. Def., 1968. Mgmt. analyst Transp. Supply and Maintenance Command, St. Louis, 1954-57, Dept. Army Transp. Materiel Command, St. Louis, 1957-62; program analyst Dept. Army Aviation System Command, St. Louis, 1962-74, spl. asst. to comdr., 1974-78; ins. broker D. Koprivica, Ins., St. Louis, 1978—; real estate broker Century 21 KARE Realty, St. Louis, 1978—. Mem. Bus. and Profl. Women (pres. 1974-75). Eastern Orthodox. Lodge: Order Eastern Star.

KORANDA, J. TIMOTHY, speech writer; b. Fort Wayne, Ind., July 26, 1950; s. Leroy Frederick and Jean Esther (Weil) K.; B.A., Colgate U., 1971; SB, SM, MIT, 1973; M.B.A., NYU, 1976. Staff writer N.W. Ayer & Son, N.Y.C., 1973-75; broker, investment counselor Bache & Co., N.Y.C., 1975-76; free lance fin. writer, N.Y.C., 1976-78; fin. relations cons. GRM Communications, Inc. div. Carly Ally, also Doremus Inc., N.Y.C., 1976-78; speechwriter Citibank, N.A., 1978-84, AT&T, 1984-85; dir. editorial services RCA, N.Y.C., 1985—; asso. mem. Commodity Futures Trading Commn.; registered mem. Chgo. Bd. Trade; mem. Nat. Democratic Club. Recipient Saturday Rev./World Corporate Communications award. Esquire Corporate Responsibility Advt. award. Mem. Assn. for Symbolic Logic, Econ. History Assn., Phi Beta Kappa. Democrat. Clubs: Copy N.Y., Advt. N.Y. Home: 135-10 Grand Central Pkwy Kew Gardens NY 11435 Office: RCA 30 Rockefeller Plaza New York NY 10112

KORB, KENNETH A., lawyer; b. Boston, Oct. 11, 1932; s. Allan and Mynue (Herbert) K.; m. Jaclyn C. Patricof, June 30, 1962; 1 son, Jason B. BA magna cum laude, Harvard Coll., 1953, JD cum laude, 1956. Bar: Mass. 1956. Law clk. Supreme Jud. Ct. Mass., 1956-57; assoc. Hutchins & Wheeler, Boston, 1957-60; assoc. Kargman & Kargman, Boston, 1960-63; sr. ptnr. Brown, Rudnick, Freed & Gesmer, Boston, 1963—; lectr. Mass. Continuing Legal Edn.; sec., dir., gen. counsel Safety Ins.Co., 1980—; underwriting mem. Lloyd's of London, 1984—. Internat. pres. Soc. Israel Philatelists, 1974-76, bd. dirs. 1976-80. Served with USAR, 1956-62. Mem. ABA, Mass. Bar Assn., Boston Bar Assn. Democrat. Contbr. articles to profl. jours. Home: 24 Helene Rd Waban MA 02168 Office: 1 Financial Place Boston MA 02110

KORBEN, DONALD LEE, counseling psychologist; b. Bklyn., Apr. 4, 1948; s. Abraham and Betty K.; BA, Butler U., 1972; MS, Ind. U., 1973, EdD, 1976. Intern counseling and psychol. services Ind. U., 1974-76; counseling psychologist Counseling Ctr., St. Bonaventure U., 1976—, mem. univ. scholastic evaluation com., 1976—, instl. rev. bd., 1980—, mem. adj. faculty Grad. Sch., 1977-80, chairperson pres.'s council alcohol and drug awareness program, 1982—, counselor, adminstr., dir. Drinking Driver Rehab. Program, 1976—; cons. Proprietory Home Assn. Western N.Y., 1976-80, Alpha Phi Omega; cons., mem. Cattaraugus County Council Alcohol and Substance Abuse, 1980; cons. select com. alcohol and alcohol abuse N.Y. State Senate, 1980, Alpha Phi Omega Nat. Service Orgn., 1984—, Students Against Drunk Driving, 1986—; bd. dirs. Pres.'s Council on Alcohol and Drug Abuse St. Bonaventure Univ., 1981—; instr. Wyo. Sem. Inst. for drug and alcohol abuse, 1984—. Mem. Butler U. Religion Council, 1968-70; vol. Salvation Army, 1966-76, 1984—, Boy Scouts Am., 1966-72, Mental Health Assn. Ind., 1967-70, Nat. Epilepsy Found., 1973-76, 1985—; mem. host com. N.Y. State Spl. Olympics, 1979. Named Outstanding Student of Yr., Butler U., 1970; Outstanding Young Man of Am., Jaycees, 1978; NSF grantee, 1970-71; Ind. U. grantee, 1976. Mem. Am. Psychol. Assn. (mem. div. psychotherapy), Am. Assn. Counseling and Devel., Am. Coll Personnel Assn., Am. Mental Health Counselors Assn., Phi Delta Kappa. Democrat. Jewish. Research on effects of hibernation, factors in assertive tng. with females, others. Home: 757 Main St Olean NY 14760

KORBITZ, BERNARD CARL, oncologist-hematologist, medical educator, medical-legal consultant; b. Lewistown, Mont., Feb. 18, 1935; s. Fredrick William and Rose Eleanore (Ackmann) K.; m. Constance Kay Bolz, June 22, 1957; children—Paul Bernard, Guy Karl. B.S. in Med. Sci., U. Wis.-Madison, 1957, M.D., 1960, M.S. in Oncology, 1962; LL.B., LaSalle U., 1972. Asst. prof. medicine and clin. oncology, U. Wis. Med. Sch., Madison, 1967-71; dir. medicine Presbyn. Med. Ctr., Denver, 1971-73; practice medicine specializing in oncology, hematology, Madison, 1973-76; med. oncologist, hematologist Radiologic Ctr. Meth. Hosp., Omaha, 1976-82; practice medicine specializing in oncology, hematology, Omaha, 1982—; sci. advisor Citizen's Environ. Com., Denver, 1972-73; mem. Cancer Com. Bergan Mercy Hosp., Omaha, 1982—; Meth. Hosp., Omaha, 1977—; dir. Bernard C. Korbitz, P.C., Omaha, 1983—; bd. dirs., pres. Korbitz Langdon, P.C. Contbr. articles to profl. jours. Webelos leader Denver area Council, Mid. Am. Council of Nebr. Boy Scouts Am.; bd. elders King of Kings Luth. Ch., Omaha, 1979-80; mem. People to People Del. Cancer Update to People's Republic China, 1986, Eastern Europe and USSR, 1987; mem. U.S. Senatorial Club, 1984, Republican Presdl. Task Force, 1984. Served to capt. USAF, 1962-64. Fellow ACP, Royal Soc. Health; mem. Am. Soc. Clin. Oncology, Am. Coll. Legal-Medicine, Am. Soc. Internal Medicine, AMA, Nebr. Med. Assn., Omaha Med. Society, Omaha Clin. Soc., Phi Eta Sigma, Phi Beta Kappa, Phi Kappa Phi, Alpha Omega Alpha. Avocations: photography fishing, travel. Home: 9024 Leavenworth St Omaha NE 68114 Office: 8300 Dodge St Suite 226 Omaha NE 68114

KORCÁK, JOSEF, former deputy prime minister of Czechoslovakia; b. Holstejn, Czechoslovakia, Dec. 17, 1921; ed. Sch. Polit. Studies, Central Com. Communist Party Czechoslovakia. Turner, Zbrojovka Brno, Czechoslovakia, 1937-48; regional com. positions Communist Party, 1948-60, mem. Central Com., 1958—, mem. Presidium of Central Com., 1970—; mem. Bur. for Direction Party Work in Czech Lands, 1969; minister of constrn., 1962-63; minister charge central adminstrn. power supply, 1963-68; chmn. Central Com. Czech Nat. Front, 1969-71; prime minister Czechoslovak Socialist Republic, dep. prime minister Czechoslovak Socialist Republic, 1970-87; dep. to Nat. Assembly, 1962-69, to House of People, Fed. Assembly, 1969—, to Czech Nat. Council, 1971—; chmn. Govt. Com. Phys. Fitness and Sports, 1978—. Decorated Order of Republic, 1971, Order Victorious February, 1973, Hero of Socialist Labor, 1981, Klement Gottwald Order for Constrn. of Socialist Homeland, 1981. Address: CSSR, Nabrezi Karla Marxe 8, 147DO Prague 4 Czechoslovakia

KORDÉ, ZOLTÁN, history educator; b. Szeged, Hungary, Apr. 2, 1958; s. Imre and Anna (Mihályi) K. Diploma, József Attila U., Szeged, 1982, PhD, 1986. cert. secondary sch. tchr. Hungarian and French lit., lang. and history. Collaborator sci. research dept. medieval Hungarian history József Attila U., 1982-84, asst. to prof., 1984-87; 1st asst. to prof. JÓzsef Attila U., 1987—. Office: József Attila U, Középkori M Történeti TSZ, Egyetem U 2, 6722-H Szeged Hungary

KORDONS, ULDIS, lawyer; b. Riga, Latvia, July 9, 1941; came to U.S., 1949; s. Evalds and Zenta Alide (Apenits) K.; m. Virginia Lee Knowles, July 16, 1966. AB, Princeton U., 1963; JD, Georgetown U., 1970. Bar: N.Y. 1970, Ohio 1977. Assoc. Whitman & Ransom, N.Y.C., 1970-77, Anderson, Mori & Rabinowitz, Tokyo, 1973-75; counsel Armco Inc., Parsippany, N.J. 1977-84, v.p., gen. counsel, sec. Sybron Corp., Saddle Brook, N.J., 1984—; bd. dirs. Brinkmann Instruments Inc., Westbury, N.Y. Mem. nat. com. Boy Scouts Am., 1982—. Served to lt. USN, 1963-67, Vietnam. Mem. N.Y. Bar Assn., Ohio Bar Assn. Republican. Home: 13 Timberline Rd Ho Ho Kus NJ 07423 Office: Sybron Corp Park 80 W Plaza I Saddle Brook NJ 07662

KORDOSKI, EDWARD WILLIAM, chemist; b. New Britain, Conn., Aug. 15, 1954; s. Edward Joseph and Loretta Barbara (Gorzelanczyk) K.; m. Donna Orischak, July 16, 1977. BS in Chemistry, King's Coll., Wilkes-Barre, Pa., 1977; PhD, U. Md., 1982; MBA, Monmouth (N.J.) Coll., 1986. Teaching asst. U. Md., College Park, 1977-79, research asst., 1979-82; process devel. chemist Ciba-Geigy Corp., Toms River, N.J., 1982-84, sr. process devel. chemist, 1984-87; sr. chemist Ciba-Geigy Corp., Basel, Switzerland, 1987—; mem. Ciba-Geigy mgmt. club, 1982—. Contbr. articles to profl. jours. Mem. Am. Chem. Soc., Delta Mu Delta. Home: Markgraflerstrasse 82, CH-4057 Basel Switzerland Office: Ciba-Geigy Corp, Dyestuffs & Chem Div, K-182 1 03, CH-4057 Basel Switzerland

KOREN, GARY, systems engineer, computerized systems designer; b. Tel Aviv, Israel, July 7, 1949; s. Wolf and Blancha (Amsterdamer) Kornblum; m. Killy Raviv, June 22, 1987. B.S.C. in Indsl. and Mgmt. Engring., Technion Tech. Inst. Design engr. SIMAT Break Presses, Holon, Israel, 1968-69, EGO, Derdiger, Germany, 1969-70; plant engr. ELCO, Ramat Gan, Israel, 1971-72; system analyst Israeli Air Force Inventory Control, 1972-75; program mgr. Israeli Air Force Warehousing, 1975-81; mng. dir., ptnr. Logistica Systems and Computers, Ramat Gan, Israel, 1981—; dir., cons. E.M. Software Industries, Ramat Gan, 1982—, Logistica Inc., N.Y.C., 1984—, Nital, Ramat Gan, 1985—; mgmt. cons. MAMAN, Air Cargo Terminal, Ben Gurion Airport, Israel, 1981—. Served to mg. Air Force, 1972-81. Jewish. Avocation: martial arts.

KOREY-KRZECZOWSKI, GEORGE J. M. KNIAZ, university administrator, management consultant; b. Kielce, Poland, July 13, 1921; came to Can., 1951; s. Antoni-Marian Kniaz and Zofia-Emilia Wanda (Chmielewska) Korczak-Krzeczowski; m. Irene-Marie Latacz, July 15, 1944; 1 child, Andrew George. LL.M., Jagellonian U., Cracow, Poland, 1945; postgrad., Acad. Polit. and Social Sci., Warsaw, Dept. Internat. Law, U. Bucharest, Rumania; LL.D., U. Freiburg, Fed. Republic Germany, 1949; D.Sc. in Econs., U. Tubingen, Fed. Republic Germany, 1950; grad. Inst. Ednl. Mgmt., Harvard U., 1975; recipient 6 hon. doctorate degrees. Dir. Dept. Ministry Culture and Arts, Poland, 1945; v.p. Council Arts and Scis, Kielce, Poland, 1945; press attache Polish embassy, Bucharest; vice-counsul of Poland Polish embassy, cultural counsellor of embassy, 1946; dir., prof. Polish Inst., Bucharest, 1947; consul of Poland Bucharest, 1947, econ. advisor of embassy, 1947; counselor Ministry Fgn. Affairs, Warsaw, 1947; consul of Poland Berlin, 1948-50, Baden-Baden, Fed. Republic Germany, 1948-50; head Econ. and Restitution Mission, 1949-50; asst. supr. indsl. engring. dept. and contract estimating dept. Canadair Ltd., Montreal, Que., Can.; asst. mng. dir., controller Damar Products of Can. Ltd., Montreal, Around-the World Shopped Club (Can.) Ltd., Montreal; v.p., mng. dir. Schlemm Assocs. Ltd.; pvt. practice mgmt. cons; pres. Pan-Am. Mgmt. Ltd.; dean bus., v.p. Ryerson Poly. Inst., 1971, exec. v.p., dean external programs, 1973-77, pres., 1974-75; prof., pres. Can. Sch. Mgmt., Toronto, Ont., 1976—; pres. Northland Open U., 1976-84, Korey Internat. Ltd., Toronto, 1980; disting. vis. prof. bus. adminstrn. Fla. Atlantic U.; prof. bus. adminstrn. Polish U., London; internat. prof. strategic mgmt. IMC, Buckingham, Eng.; former pres. Ryerson Applied Research Ltd.; v.p. and dir. York-Ryerson Computing Ctr.; dir. Can. Ops., Can. Textile Cons.-Ltd., Werner Mgmt. Cons. (Can.) Ltd., indsl. and econ. devel. div. Werner Mgmt. Cons. Inc., N.Y.C.; mng. dir. Werner Assocs., Inc. Author: Siedemnasta Wiosna, 1938, Globorze, 1939, Internationale Rechtsverhaeltnisse Polens im Gebiete des Strafrechts, 1949, Plannung in der Polnischen Landwirtschaft, 1950, Liryki Nostalgiczne, 1974, New Role for the Canadian Economy in the Age of World Food Shortage, 1975, Lunch w Sodomie, 1976, Korey's Stubborn

Thoughts, 1980, University Without Walls, 1980, Tree of Life, 1982; author articles on mgmt., econ. planning, internat. affairs, fgn. markets and mktg.; contbr. to publs. including: Industrial Canada, Can. Textile Jour., Jour. Mktg.; guest lectr. radio and TV. Decorated companion Brit. Inst. Mgmt., knight-grand cross of justice Sovereign Order St. John of Jerusalem; knight Mil. Constantinian Order St. George; knight-comdr. Sovereign Order Cyprus; knight grand cross Mil. Order St. Agatha di Paterno; cross of Polish Home Army, 1939-45; Polish mil. medal for World War II; hon. citizen City of Winnipeg. Fellow Royal Econ. Soc., Royal Soc. Arts, N.Y. Acad. Scis., Can. Internat. Acad. Humanities and Social Scis. (pres.); mem. Inst. Mgmt. Cons. Que. and Ont., Acad. Mktg. Sci. (U.S.), Am. Mgmt. Assn., Acad. Mgmt. (U.S.), Inter-Am. Research Inst., Acad. Internat. Bus., Brit. Inst. Mgmt. (companion), Can. Council Internat. Cooperation (dir.), Can. Inst. Pub. Affairs, European Found. Mgmt. Devel., Internat. Inventors Assn., Polish Inst. (U.K.), Can. Assn. Univ. Bus. Officers, Can. Polish Congress (pres. nat. council 1960-69), other orgns. Roman Catholic. Office: Can Sch Mgmt, 820 Renaissance Plaza, 150 Bloor St W, Toronto, ON Canada M5S 2X9

KOREZLIOGLU, HAYRI, mathematics educator; b. Kula, Manisa, Turkey, Mar. 25, 1930; s. Fethi and Nimet (Gol) K.; m. Leyla Vekilli, June 30, 1954 (div. 1964); children: Cengiz, Deniz;m. Jale Ilden, July 26, 1968; children: Kerem. Erdem, Simla. Licence es Sciences, Faculty of Scis., Paris, 1953; Engring. degree, Ecole Nat. Superieure des Télécommunications, Paris, 1955; Doctorat d'Etat, Faculty of Scis., Paris, 1963. Engr. T.R.T., Paris, 1956-63; researcher Instituto de Fisica Teorica, Naples, Italy, 1963-64; instr. Faculty of Scis., Paris, 1964-65; assoc. prof. Middle E. Tech. U., Ankara, Turkey, 1967-73; prof. math Ecole Nationale Supérieure des Telecommunications, Paris, 1973—; chmn. dept. math. Middle E. Tech. U., 1967-71; chief of probability CNET, Issy-les-Mx/France, 1981-82, chief stochastic systems ENST, Paris, 1983—; me. directing com. Turkish Nat. Research Council, 1972-73. Editor: Processus a deux indices, 1981, Filtering and Control of Random Processes, 1984, Stochastic Analysis and Related Topics, 1988; contbr. articles to profl. jours. Served as 1st lt. Turkish Army, 1965-67. Mem. Soc. Math. of France, Am. Math. Soc., Soc. Bernaoulli, Soc. Mathematiques Appliques et Industrielles. Office: ENST, 46 Rue Barrault, Paris France Home: Le Centaure O5, 48 rue d'Erevan, 92130 Issy Les Moulineaux France

KORGEN, BENJAMIN JEFFRY, physical oceanographer writer; b. Duluth, Minn., Jan. 6, 1931; s. Benne Hanson and Helen Louise (Slattum) K.; B.S., U. Minn., 1956; M.A., U. Mich., 1958; Ph.D., Oreg. State U., 1969; m. Judith Kay Waggoner, Aug. 15, 1959; children—Susan Kay, Jeffry David, James Matthew. Phys. oceanographer U. N.C., Chapel Hill, 1969-74, asst. prof., 1969-74; cons. in oceanography, Sandwich, Mass., 1974-78; cons. Harper & Row Pubs., 1972-74, Thermonetics Corp., San Diego, 1972-74; textbook writer Allyn & Bacon, Boston, 1974-82, Jones & Bartlett, Boston, 1985—; oceanographer U.S. Naval Oceanographic Office, 1978—; adj. asso. prof. Tulane U., 1978—; adv. com. Miss.-Ala. Sea Grant Consortium, 1978-81. Served with USN, 1951-54. U. Mich. grad. fellow, 1957-58; NSF grantee, 1965; Office Naval Research fellow, 1966-69; Office Naval Research-NSF grantee, 1968-69; NSF grantee, 1969-70; U. N.C. Research Council grantee, 1969-72; N.C. Bd. Sci. and Tech. grantee, 1971-72; Naval Oceanographic Office contractee, 1971-73. Mem. Am. Soc. Limnology and Oceanography, Internat. Oceanographic Found., Am. Geophys. Union, AAAS, Geol. Soc. Am., Woods Hole Assocs., Assocs. of Woods Hole Oceanographic Instn., Am. Film Inst., Assocs. of Marine Biol. Lab. Contbr. articles to profl. jours. and popular mags. Home: 219 Loop Dr Slidell LA 70458

KORHONEN, KEIJO TERO, Finnish ambassador to United Nations; b. Paltamo, Finland, Feb. 23, 1934; s. Hannes and Anna (Laari) K.; m. Anneli Torkkila, Aug. 30, 1958; children—Kimmo, Jouni, Teemu. Ph.D. in History, Turku U., Finland, 1963. Asst. in Finnish History, Turku U., 1959-65; held various positions Fgn. Ministry of Finland, Helsinki, 1969-74; prof. polit. history, Helsinki U., 1974-77; minister fgn. affairs of Finland, 1976-77; undersec. polit. affairs Fgn. Ministry, 1977-83; ambassador, permanent rep. of Finland to UN, N.Y.C., 1983—. Author 5 books on Finnish-Soviet/Finnish-Russian fgn. relations. Office: Perm Mission of Finland to UN 2d Floor 866 United Nations Plaza New York NY 10017

KORIYAMA, NAOSHI, English language educator, poet; b. Kikai Island, Japan, Nov. 3, 1926; s. Gensei and Shiho (Kimoto) K.; m. Ruriko Mayeda, Sept. 13, 1954; children: Masayo, Manabu, Takeshi. BA, SUNY, Albany, 1954. Translator U.S. Mil. Govt., Naha, Okinawa, Japan, 1949-50; instr. then asst. prof. English Obirin Jr. Coll., Tokyo, 1956-61; mem. faculty Toyo U., Japan, 1961-67, prof. English, 1967—. Author: (poetry) Coral Reefs, 1957, Plum Tree in Japan and Other Poems, 1959, Songs from Sagamihara, 1967, By the Lakeshore and Other Poems, 1977, Time and Space and Other Poems, 1985. Mem. Poetry Soc. Japan. Home: 2-15-9 Yaei, 229 Sagamihara-shi Kanagawa-ken Japan

KORMES, JOHN WINSTON, lawyer; b. N.Y.C., May 4, 1935; s. Mark and Joanna P. Kormes; m. Frances W. Kormes, Aug. 19, 1978; 1 child, Mark Vincent. B.A. in Econs., U. Mich., 1955, J.D., 1959. Bar: Pa. 1961, D.C. 1961, U.S. Sup. Ct. 1968. With License and Inspection Rev. Bd. Phila., 1972-73; asst. dist. atty. City of Phila., 1973-74, asst. city solicitor, 1974-80; sole practice, Phila., 1961—; moot ct. advisor. Mem. staff Re-Elect the Pres. Com., 1972, Rizzo for Mayor Com., 1971, 75, Phila. Flag Day Assn., 1965—. Served with USAF, 1956-57. Recipient N.Y. Intercoll. Legis. Assembly award, 1954; R.I. Model Congress award, 1954. Fellow Lawyers in Mensa (charter), Internat. Soc. Philos. Enquiry (sr.); mem. Phila. Bar Assn., Phila. Trial Lawyers Assn., N.Y. State Trial Lawyers Assn., Am. Arbitration Assn., Fed. Bar Assn., Pitts. Inst. Legal Medicine, Am. Trial Lawyers Assn., Intertel, Internat. Platform Assn., Internat. Soc. Philos. Enquiry (legal officer 1986—), Delta Sigma Rho. Republican. Clubs: Masons, Shriners, KP, Lions. Home: 1070 Edison Ave Philadelphia PA 19116 Office: 2820 PSFS Bldg 12 S 12th St Philadelphia PA 19107

KORMOS, CHARLES (CAROL), writer, journalist, translator, researcher; b. Lugoj, Banat, Romania, Apr. 10, 1920; s. Gustav and Helen (Löwy) K.; m. Martha Tudic, Jan. 21, 1950 (dec. 1981); 1 child, Diana Lena Kormos Barkan. Student, Vienna (Austria) U. Cert. profl. journalist, Bucharest. Program asst. BBC, European Service, London, 1941-46; fgn. corr. internat. news agys. Bucharest, Romania, 1946-50; English editor Agerpres News Agy., Bucharest, 1947-50; German editor State Pub. House, Bucharest, 1950-52; lathe turner Red Star Works, Bucharest, 1952-53; librarian Dept. Coal Mining, Bucharest, 1953-54; English editor Romania Today Monthly, Bucharest, 1954-80; researcher Mus. of the Diaspora, Tel Aviv, 1983—. Author: Rumania, 1944; (poetry) Pawn and Prophet, 1987; also plays, essays, stories; translator poetry, prose, plays, films, art history. Recipient Creative Writing award Dept. Culture, Jerusalem, 1984. Mem. Voices Israel, Israel Assn. Writers in English. Home: Rh Shimoni 29/18, 69026 Ramat Aviv Israel

KORN, DAVID A., ambassador; b. Wichita Falls, Tex.; s. Thomas A. and Iris E. (Dobson) K.; m. Roberta Cohen. Student, U. Mo., 1951-53; grad., Institut d'Etude Politiques, Paris, 1956; MA, Johns Hopkins U., 1957. Fgn. service officer Dept. State, 1957-81; office dir. for northern Arab affairs Dept. State, Washington, 1972-75; consul gen. Am. Embassy, Calcutta, India, 1975-77; mem. policy planning council Dept. State, Washington, 1977-78, office dir. Arab-Israeli affairs, 1978-81, officer Bur. African Affairs, 1981-82; Chargé d'Affaires Am. Embassy, Addis Ababa, Ethiopia, 1982-85; ambassador to Togo, Lome, 1986—. Author: Ethiopia, The United States and The Soviet Union, 1986; contbr. articles to The World Today. Recipient Meritorius Honor award Dept. State, Washington, 1974, 85, Presidential Meritorius Performance award, Washington, 1985. Mem. Am. Fgn. Service Assn. Home and Office: Ambassador to Togo care Dept State Washington DC 20520

KORN, LESTER BERNARD, business executive, ambassador; b. N.Y.C., Jan. 11, 1936. BS with honors, UCLA, 1959, MBA, 1960; postgrad., Harvard Bus. Sch., 1961. Mgmt. cons. Peat, Marwick, Mitchell & Co., Los Angeles, 1961-66, ptnr., 1966-69; pres., co-founder Korn/Ferry Internat., Los Angeles, 1969-80, chmn. bd., 1980-87; ambassador and U.S. rep. Econ. and Social Council UN, 1987—; alt. rep. 42d UN Gen. Assembly; bd. dirs. Continental Am. Properties, Work Wear Corp., Leisure & Tech. Corp., Josephson Internat., Inc., Music Ctr. Operating Co., Curb Communications Inc., Musifilm Ltd. Bd. dirs. NCCJ; trustee UCLA Found., City of Hope Med. Center; bd. overseers Grad. Sch. Mgmt., UCLA; trustee, founding mem. Dean's Council UCLA; bd. govs. Cedars-Sinai Med. Center; bd. councilors Grad. and Undergrad. Schs. Bus. Adminstrn. and Sch. Bus., U. So. Calif.; spl. advisor, del. UNESCO Inter-gov. Conf. on Edn. for Internat. Understanding, Coop., Peace, 1983; adv. bd. Women in Film Found., 1983-84; chmn. Commn. on Citizen Participation in Govt., State of Calif., 1979-82; bd. dirs. John Douglas French Found. for Alzheimer's Disease; mem. Republican Nat. Exec. Fin. Com., 1985; mem. Pres.'s Commn. White House Fellowships; hon. chairperson 50th Am. Presdl. Inaugural, 1985; co-chmn. So. Calif. region NCCJ; trustee Acad. for Advancement Corp. Governance, Fordham U. Grad. Sch. Bus. Adminstrn. Recipient UCLA Alumni Profl. Achievement award, 1984. Mem. Am. Bus. Conf. (founding mem.), Am. Inst. CPA's, Calif. Soc. CPA's. Clubs: Hillcrest Country, Los Angeles Athletic, Regency (Calif.); Board Room (N.Y.C.). Office: 237 Park Ave New York NY 10017 Office: Korn/Ferry Internat 1800 Century Park E Suite 900 Los Angeles CA 90067

KORNADT, HANS-JOACHIM KURT, psychologist, writer; b. Stargard, Ger., June 16, 1927; s. Kurt Karl and Katharina (Bodenburg) K.; m. Helga Stuhlmann, July 26, 1956 (div.); children—Claus-Ulrich, Tilmann, Nikola, Oliver. Diplom Psychol., U. Marburg, 1952, Ph.D., 1956. Research asst. U. Marburg, 1957; wissenschaftlicher asst. Wü rzburg, 1957-61; dozent Tchr. Tng. Coll., Saarbrü cken, 1961-64, prof., 1964-68; prof. ednl. psychology U. Saar, Saarbrucken, 1968—, dep. dir. Social-Psychol. Research Centre Devel. Planning, 1968—; research in E. Africa, 1965; lectr. Ruhr-U. Bochum, 1968. Mem. wissenschaflicher beirat Fed. Ministry Econ. Coop., 1968—; exec. com. Wissenschaftsrat, 1975-81; chmn. Beirat Hochschulzugangstest der Kultus Minister Konferenz, 1976-86, mem. Kuratorium, 1976— , Beirat Deutsches Inst. Japan-Studien. Author: Thematische Apperzeptions Verfahren, 2d edit., 1979; Situation und Entwickungsprobleme des Schulsystems in Kenya, vol. 1, 1968, vol. 2, 1970; Toward a Motivation Theory of Aggression and Aggression Inhibition, 1974; Lehrziele, Schulleistung und Leistungs beurteilung, 1975; Cross-cultural Research on Motivation, 1980; Aggression and Frustration, 1981; Aggressionsmotiv und Aggressions-Hemmung, 1982; Zur Lage Der Psychologie, 1985. Acad. stipende VW Found., 1977-78; research fellow Japan Soc. Promotion Sci., 1979, Japanese-German Research award, 1988. Mem. German Assn. Psychology (pres. 1982-84), Internat. Council Psychologists, Internat. Soc. Research on Aggression, Internat. Assn. Cross Cultural Psychology. Mem. Free Democratic Party. Home: PO Box 129, D-6705 Deidesheim Federal Republic of Germany Office: Univ Saar, 6600 Saarbrücken Federal Republic of Germany

KORNBERG, ARTHUR, biochemist; b. N.Y.C., Mar. 3, 1918; s. Joseph and Lena (Katz) K.; m. Sylvy R. Levy, Nov. 21, 1943; children: Roger, Thomas Bill, Kenneth Andrew. BS (N.Y. State scholar), CCNY, 1937, LLD (hon.), 1960; MD (Buswell scholar), U. Rochester, 1941, DSc (hon.), 1962; DSc (hon.), U. Pa., U. Notre Dame, 1965, Washington U., 1968, Princeton U., 1970, Colby Coll., 1970; LHD (hon.), Yeshiva U., 1963; MD honoris causa, U. Barcelona, Italy, 1970. Intern in medicine Strong Meml. Hosp., Rochester, N.Y., 1941-42; commd. officer USPHS, 1942, advanced through grades to med. dir., 1951; mem. staff NIH, Bethesda, Md., 1942-52; nutrition sect., div. physiology NIH, 1942-45; chief sect. enzymes and metabolism Nat. Inst. Arthritis and Metabolic Diseases, 1947-52; guest research worker depts. chemistry and pharmacology coll. medicine N.Y. U., 1946; dept. biol. chemistry med. sch. Washington U., 1947; dept. plant biochemistry U. Calif., 1951; prof., head dept. microbiology, med. sch. Washington U., St. Louis, 1953-59; prof., biochemistry Stanford U. Sch. Medicine, 1959—, chmn. dept., 1959-69; Mem. sci. adv. bd. Mass. Gen. Hosp., 1964-67; bd. govs. Weizmann Inst., Israel. Contbr. sci. articles to profl. jours. Served lt. (j.g.), med. officer USCGR, 1942. Recipient Paul-Lewis award in enzyme chemistry, 1951; co-recipient of Nobel prize in medicine, 1959; Max Berg award prolonging human life, 1968; Sci. Achievement award AMA, 1968; Lucy Wortham James award James Ewing Soc., 1968; Borden award Am. Assn. Med. Colls., 1968. Mem. Am. Soc. Biol. Chemists (pres. 1965), Am. Chem. Soc., Harvey Soc., Am. Acad. Arts and Scis., Royal Soc., Nat. Acad. Scis. (mem. council 1963-66), Am. Philos. Soc., Phi Beta Kappa, Sigma Xi, Alpha Omega Alpha. Office: Dept of Biochemistry Stanford U Med Ctr Stanford CA 94305 *

KORNBERG, HANS LEO, biochemist; b. Herford, Germany, Jan. 14, 1928; s. Max and Margarete (Silberbach) K.; B.Sc., U. Sheffield, 1949, Ph.D., 1953, D.Sc. (hon.), 1979; M.A., Oxford U., 1958, D.Sc., 1961; Sc.D. (hon.), U. Cin., 1974; Sc.D., Cambridge U., 1975; D.Sc. (hon.), Warwick U., 1975, Leicester U., 1979, Bath U., 1980, Strathclyde U., 1985; D.U. (hon.), Essex U., 1979; M.D. (hon.), Leipzig U., 1984; m. Monica Mary King, Oct. 6, 1956; children—Julia Margaret, Rachel Elizabeth, Jonathan Paul, Simon Alexander. John Stokes research fellow U. Sheffield, 1951-53; Commonwealth Fund fellow Yale U., U. Calif., Berkeley, Pub. Health Research Inst., N.Y., 1953-55; mem. sci. staff M.R.C. cell metabolism research unit, Oxford, 1955-60; prof. biochemistry U. Leicester, 1960-75; Sir William Dunn prof. biochemistry Cambridge (Eng.) U., 1975—, fellow Christ's Coll., 1975—, Master, 1982—; lectr. Worcester Coll., Oxford, 1958-60; Leeuwenhoek lectr. Royal Soc., 1972; Weizmann Meml. lectr., Rehovot, 1975; mem. Sci. Research Council, 1967-72, chmn. sci. bd., 1969-72; mem. U.G.C. Biol. Sci. Com., 1967-76; U.K. rep. NATO-ASI Panel, 1970-76, chmn., 1974-75; chmn. Royal Commn. on Environ. Pollution, 1976-81; mem. Agrl. Research Council, 1981-84; mem. Priorities Bd. for Research and Devel. in Agr., 1984—. Mng. trustee Nuffield Found., 1972—; gov. Hebrew U. Jerusalem, 1976—; sci. gov. Weizmann Inst. Sci., Rehovot, Israel, 1981—; trustee Marine Biol. Lab., Woods Hole, Mass., 1982-87. Recipient Colworth medal Biochem. Soc., 1963, Otto Warburg medal German Biochem. Soc., 1973; created knight bachelor, 1978; hon. fellow Worcester Coll., Oxford, 1981, Brasenose Coll., Oxford, 1982. Fellow Royal Soc. (council 1975-77), Inst. Biology (v.p. 1970-72), Royal Soc. Arts; hon. mem. Am. Soc. Biochemistry and Microbiology, Am. Acad. Arts & Scis., German Soc. Biol. Chemists, Japanese Biochem. Soc.; mem. Nat. Acad. Sci. (fgn. assoc.), German Acad. Scis. (Leopoldina). Author: (with Hans Krebs) Energy Transformations in Living Matter, 1957; contbr. articles to profl. jours. Office: Univ of Cambridge, Dept Biochemistry, Tennis Court Rd, Cambridge CB2 1QW, England

KORNEL, LUDWIG, educator, physician, scientist; b. Jaslo, Poland, Feb. 27, 1923; came to U.S., 1958, naturalized, 1970; s. Ezriel Edward and Ernestine (Karpf) K.; m. Esther Muller, May 27, 1952; children—Ezriel Edward, Amiel Mark. Student, U. Kazan Med. Inst., USSR, 1943-45; M.D., Wroclaw (Poland) Med. Acad., 1950; Ph.D., U. Birmingham, Eng., 1958. Intern Univ. Hosp., Wroclaw, 1949-50, Hadassah-Hebrew U. Hosp., Jerusalem, 1950-51; resident medicine Hadassah-Hebrew U. Hosp., 1952-55; Brit. Council scholar, Univ. research fellow endocrinology U. Birmingham, 1955-57, lectr. medicine, 1956-57; fellow endocrinology U. Ala. Med. Ctr., 1958-59, successively asst. prof., assoc. prof., prof. medicine, 1961-67; dir. steroid sect. U. Ala. Med. Center, 1962-67, assoc. prof. biochemistry, 1965-67; postdoctoral trainee in steroid biochemistry U. Utah, 1959-61; prof. medicine U. Ill. Coll. Medicine, Chgo., 1967-71; dir. steroid unit Presbyn.-St. Lukes Hosp., Chgo., 1967—; assoc. biochemist Presbyn.-St. Lukes Hosp., 1967-70, sr. biochemist on sci. staff, 1970-71, attending physician, 1967-71; prof. medicine and biochemistry Rush Med. Coll., 1970—; sr. attending physician, sr. scientist Rush-Presbyn.-St. Lukes Med. Cen., 1970—; hon. guest lectr. Polish Acad. Sci., Warsaw, 1965; vis. prof. Kanazawa (Japan) U., 1973, 82, 88. Mem. editorial bd. Clin. Physiology and Biochemistry, 1982—; co-editor: Yearbook of Endocrinology, 1986—; contbr. articles on endocrinology and steroid biochemistry to profl. jours. Recipient Physicians Recognition award AMA, 1969, 73, 76, 81, Outstanding New Citizen award Citzenship Council Met. Chgo., 1970. Fellow Am. Coll. Clin. Pharmacology and Chemotherapy, Nat. Acad. Clin. Biochemistry (bd. dirs. 1982-86), Royal Soc. Health; mem. AMA, AAAS, AAUP, Endocrine Soc., Am. Fedn. Clin. Research, N.Y. Acad. Scis., Am. Physiol. Soc., Cen. Soc. Clin. Research, Am. Acad. Polit. and Social Scis., Fedn. Am. Socs. for Exptl. Biology (nat. corr. 1975—), Sigma Xi. Home: 6757 N LeRoy Ave Lincolnwood IL 60646 Office: Rush Presbyn St Lukes Med Ctr 1653 W Congress Pkwy Chicago IL 60612

KORNFELD, ITZCHAK EHUD, geologist; b. Tel-Aviv, Israel, Feb. 21, 1953; came to U.S., 1962, naturalized, 1968; s. Abraham M. and Helena (Rozdzial) K.; m. Maria Linda Barracca, June 14, 1981; 1 child, Evan Paul. BS, Bklyn. Coll., 1976, MS, 1980. Research scientist in fluid migration and toxic waste. Research Council N.Y., N.Y.C., 1976-78, Bur. Econ. Geology, State of Tex., Austin, 1978-79; cons. EPA, N.Y.C., 1980; sr. geologist Fred C. Hart Assocs., Newark, 1980-81; project mgr. Texaco Inc., New Orleans, 1981-87; cons. scientist, New Orleans, 1987—; mgr. environ. geology Middleberg, Riddle & Gianna, New Orleans; mem. Superfund reconnaissance team assessing groundwater contamination; frequent lectr. Contbr. articles to profl. jours. Coordinator, United Way, New Orleans, 1983—; vol. Sta. WWNO, 1984—; bd. dirs. Congregation Beth Israel, 1983—, Young Leadership Conf., 1984—; mem. reconnaissance team Superfund. Grantee Geol. Soc. Am., 1977, Sigma Xi, 1977. Mem. bd. dirs. Young Leadership Conf. 1984—; pres. Am. Red Magen David for Israel-Ben-Gurion chpt., 1986—. Am. Assn. Petroleum Geologists (regional coordinator cross-sect. com. 1984-85), Am. Geophys. Union, Geol. Soc. Am., New Orleans Geol. Soc. (chmn. computer application com. 1984-87, editor Computer Applications Bulletin 1986—), Internat. Assn. Sedimentologists, Soc. Econ. Mineralogists and Paleontologists. Avocations: music; wine tasting; car racing; gardening. Office: 985 Walker St New Orleans LA 70124-4049

KORNHUBER, HANS HELMUT, neurologist, researcher; b. Metgethen, Germany, Feb. 24, 1928; s. Arnold E. and Gertrud (Wieberneit) K.; children—Karl, Anselm, Johannes, Malte. M.D., U. Heidelberg, 1955; hon. prof. U. Rosario; Dr. med. (hon.), U. Brussels. Docent of neurology and neurophysiology U. Freiburg, 1963-65; research fellow dept. physiology, Johns Hopkins U., Balt., 1965-66; prof. neurology Ulm U., Fed. Republic Germany, 1967—, also head Ctr. Head and Nerve Diseases, senator, head gen. studies program. advisor German Research Council. Author numerous books in field. Contbr. articles to profl. jours. Organizer, Decentralized Rehab. and Home Patient Care. Recipient Hans Berger prize, German EEG Soc., Sci. prize, U. Ulm, Cross of Merit, Fed. Republic Germany. Mem. Belgian Soc. Neurophysiology (hon.), German Physiol. Soc., German Neurol. Soc., German Zool. Soc., German ENT Soc., Chilean Soc. oto-neurology/Ophthalmo-neurology (hon.), Barany Soc. (Hallpike Nylen prize), Humboldt Soc., others. Christian Democrat. Lutheran. Home: Groezingerstrasse 75, 7906 Blaustein Federal Republic of Germany Office: University Clinic, Steinhoevelstrasse 9, D7900 Ulm Federal Republic of Germany

KORNSTEIN, HOWARD PAUL, computer company executive; b. Pitts., May 6, 1940; arrived in Eng., 1972; s. Harry and Sylvia (Rothman) K.; m. Belinda Rosemary; children: Joanna, Abigail. BSc, UCLA, 1963; MSc, U. Surrey, Guildford, Eng., 1973. Sr. eng. 3M, Inc., Los Angeles, 1964-70; cons. Computer Scis. Internat., London, 1970-72; dir. Data Applications Internat., Brussels, 1972-75; tech. mgr. Intel Corp., Swindon, Eng., 1975-83; dir. mktg. Digital Research, Ltd., Newbury, Eng., 1983—, also bd. dirs.; bd. dirs. QA Tng., Ltd., Cirencester, Eng. Mem. editorial bd. Microcomputers and Microsystems, 1983-87, EXE, 1987—. Office: Digital Research Ltd, Oxford House, Newbury, Berkshire England

KOROM, MICHAEL, historian, educator; b. Magyarcsanád, Csongrád, Hungary, July 1, 1928; s. Michael Korom and Margith (Bakai) K.; m. Etelka Kiss, Feb. 15, 1932; children: Michael, Zsuzsanna. Student, L. Eötvös U., Budapest, Hungary, 1948-52, PhD, 1960; candidate in hist. scis., Lomonosov U., Moscow, 1957; D of Hist. Scis., Acad. Sci. Hungary, Budapest, 1976. Sci. researcher Inst. Workers Movement, Budapest, 1952-60; chief chair, docent A. József U., Szeged, Hungary, 1960-67; dir. gen. New Cen. Hungarian Archives, Budapest, 1975-79; prof. L. Kossuth U., Debrecen, Hungary, 1979-83; prof. history L. Eötvös U., 1978—; prof., chief researcher Inst. Polit. Scis., Budapest, 1983—. Author: (with others) A magyarországi munkásmozgalom, 1939-45, 1959, A fasizmus bukása Magyarországon, 1961 (Hungarian Acad. Scis. award 1963), A Kommunista Párt harca a munkásosztály vezette antifasiszta parasztegység megteremtéséért a második világháboru idõszakában, 1964, (with others) Makó, az elsö felszabadult magyar város, 1974, A Hitler-ellenes nemzeti kormány megteremtésének fökérdései Magyarországon, 1975, (with others) A magyar népi demokrácia története, 1944-62, 1978, Magyarország Ideiglenes Nemzeti Kormánya és a fegyverszünet, 1944-45, 1981, Népi demokráciánk születése, 1981, (with others) Magyarorszag felszabadulásának megindulása, 1982, A népi bizottságok és a közigazgatás Magyarországon, 1944-49, 1984, (with others) Isztorijá Vengerszkoj Národnoj Demokrátyi, 1944-75, 1984, A magyar népi demokrácia elsö évei, 1986, A magyar fegyverszünet 1945, 1987, A személyi kultusz néhány kérdése és az európai népi demokráciak, 1987, (with others) Tanulmányok Erdély történetéből, 1988. Chmn. ednl. history bd. Ministry Edn., Budapest, 1965. Mem. Assn. Hungarian Historians (sec. 1964-72). Mem. Hungarian Socialist Worker Party. Home: Torokvesz ut 95-97/c/49, 1025 Budapest Hungary Office: Inst Polit Sci, Ajtosi Durer 19-21, 1146 Budapest Hungary

KOROTKIN, FRED, philatelist, writer; b. Duluth, Minn., Oct. 25, 1917; s. Morris and Ethel (Billert) K. B.A., U. Minn., 1949. Editor Finance & Commerce, and Daily Market Record, Mpls., 1966-67; stamp editor Mpls. Star, 1970-74, White Bear Press, 1976, Minn. Suburban Newspapers, Inc., 1983-85; Writer-instr. Palmer Writers Sch., Mpls.; Mem. philatelic adv. panel Am. Revolution Bicentennial Commn., 1971-74, Am. Revolution Bicentennial Adminstrn., 1974, philatelic advisor, 1974-76; regional rep. Interphil '76, 1974-76. Contbr. revs., articles to popular mags., newspapers. Pres. North High Alumni Assn., Mpls., 1946-47; mem. The Generation After, asso. of Simon Wiesenthal Center for Holocaust Studies, Am. Inst. Cancer Research. Served with U.S. Maritime Service, 1942-43; Served with A. C. U.S. Army, 1943-46. Recipient Distinguished Topical Philatelist award and invited to sign Distinguished Topical Philatelist scroll of honor, 1962, Silver medal for Keeping Posted column in Mpls. Star Am. Philatelic Soc.-Chgo. Philatelic Soc. Conv., 1974. Mem. Am. Topical Assn. (founding pres. chpt. 1957-61, pres. 1968-70, 70-72, dir., nat. adv. com.), Internat. Philatelic Press Club (gov.), Internat. Assn. Philatelic Journalists, Am. Philatelic Soc. (hon., speakers' bur. 1977—, writers unit), New Zealand Stamp Collector's Club Inc. (hon., anonymously donated annual Fred Korotkin Cup for best thematic entry 1966—), Christchurch Philatelic Soc., Inc., Collectors Club N.Y., Manuscript Soc., Statue of Liberty-Ellis Island Found. Inc. (charter), Nat. Com. To Preserve Social Security, Holocaust Survivors Assn. USA (nat. adv. bd.), Keren Or, Inc., Jerusalem Instn. for the Blind, Internat. Platform Assn., People for the Am. Way, DAV (life; comdr. Mpls. chpt. No 1, 1986). Home: 4925 Minnetonka Blvd Minneapolis MN 55416 also: Box 11053 Minneapolis MN 55411

KORPMAN, RALPH ANDREW, physician executive, educator, researcher; b. N.Y.C., Aug. 9, 1952; s. Ralf and Vera Henriette (Terry) K. B.A., Loma Linda U., 1971, M.D., 1974; cert. in exec. mgmt., Claremont Grad. Sch., 1979. Diplomate Am. Bd. Pathology, Nat. Bd. Med. examiners, Am. Coll. Physician Execs. Intern in pathology Loma Linda U. Sch. Medicine, Calif., 1974-75, resident in anatomic pathology and clin. pathology, 1975-78, fellow in hematology, 1978; lead systems designer acad. records Loma Linda U., 1969-74, dir. systems, dept. pathology and lab. medicine, 1974—, asst. prof. Sch. Med., 1979-84, assoc. prof., 1984-87, prof., 1987—; cons., dir. Med. Data Corp., San Bernardino, Calif., 1976-81; chief sci. adv. to pres. and chmn. of bd. HBO & Co., 1981-83; dir. labs. Faculty Med. Lab., Loma Linda, 1979—; pres., chmn. Health Data Scis. Corp., 1983—; dir. various med. corps.; cons. in field; lectr. various confs. Mem. editorial bd. Jour. Clin. Lab. Automation, 1980-85, Software in Healthcare, 1984—, Informatics in Pathology, 1985—. Contbr. articles to profl. jours. Fellow Am. Acad. Med. Dirs., Am. Soc. Clin. Pathologists (Sheard-Sanford award 1975), Assn. Clin. Sci., Coll. Am. Pathologists, Am. Coll. Physician Execs.; mem. Am. Mgmt. Assn., AMA, Am. Soc. Hematology, Assn. Computing Machinery, Calif. Med. Assn., Am. Acad. Med. Dirs., Data Processing Mgmt. Assn., IEEE, MUMPS User Group, N.Y. Acad. Scis., San Bernardino County Med. Soc., Young Pres.'s Orgn., Sigma Xi, Alpha Omega Alpha. Home: PO Box 548 Loma Linda CA 92354 Office: Health Data Scis Corp 268 W Hospitality Ln San Bernardino CA 92408

KORPPOO, SEPPO ILMARI, oil and gas executive; b. Tampere, Finland, June 27, 1948; s. Seppo Tapani and Ilmi (Honkanen) K.; m. Anna Maija Sipilä, June 15, 1974; children: Sanna, Tuomas. MS, Helsinki (Finland) U. Tech., 1975. Cert. naval architect. Project mgr. Wärtsilä, Helsinki, 1974-84; dir. research and devel. Valmet Corp. Helsinki Shipyard, Helsinki, 1984-85; dir. offshore div. Valmet Corp. Helsinki Shipyard, 1985-86; sr. v.p. Wärtsilä Marine Industries, Helsinki, 1987—. Served with Finnish Navy, 1970. Club: RAC (London). Home: Luhtatie 13, 02760 Espoo Finland Office: Wärtsilä Marine Industries, Inc, Munkkisaarenkatu 2, 00150 Helsinki Finland

KORR, IRVIN MORRIS, physiologist, medical educator; b. Phila., Aug. 24, 1909; s. Samuel Pincus and Anna (Goldberg) K.; m. Margot Lindsay, June 13, 1939 (dec. Jan. 1975); 1 child, David L.; m. Janet R. Meneley, June 6, 1986. BA., U. Pa., 1930, MA, 1931; PhD, Princeton U., 1935; DSc (hon.), Kirksville Coll. Osteo. Medicine, 1976. Instr. physiology NYU Coll. Medicine, N.Y.C., 1936-42; sr. physiologist U.S. War Dept., 1942-45; prof. physiology Kirksville Coll. Osteo. Medicine, Mo., 1945-75; prof. biomechanics Mich. State U., East Lansing, 1975-78; prof. med. edn. Tex. Coll. Osteo. Medicine, Ft. Worth, 1978—; co-founder, dir. Ctr. Healthy Aging, Ft. Worth. Author: (with E.L. Hix and K.A. Buzzell) Physiological Basis of Osteopathic Medicine, 1970; Collected Papers of I.M. Korr, 1979. Editor: Neurobiologic Mechanisms in Manipulative Therapy, 1978. Contbr. articles to profl. jours. Bd. dirs. Fed. Correction Inst. Children's Ctr., Fort Worth. Recipient Founder's medal Tex. Coll. Osteo. Medicine, 1982, Kistner award Am. Assn. Colls. Osteo. Medicine, 1983. Fellow AAAS; mem. Am. Physiol. Soc., Soc. Neurosci., Am. Soc. Neurochemistry, Harvey Soc. (life), ACLU, Common Cause, Sierra Club. Home: 740 Oakwood Trail Fort Worth TX 76112

KORRY, EDWARD M., journalist, diplomat, consultant; b. N.Y.C., Jan. 7, 1922; m. Patricia McCarthy, 1950; 1 son, 3 daughters. BA, Washington & Lee U.; postgrad., Advanced Mgmt. Program, Harvard U. Bus. Sch. Sucessively radio news editor London Cable Desk, chief U.N. bur., chief corr. Balkans, chief corr., gen. mgr. Germany United Press, 1942-51, chief European corr., gen. mgr. French Empire, 1951-58; European editor Look Mag., 1958-60; asst. to pres. Cowles Publs. Co., 1960-63; U.S. Ambassador to Ethiopia 1963-67, U.S. Ambassador to Chile, 1967-71; pres. Assn. Am. Pubs., 1972-73, U.N. Assns., 1973-75; cons. U.S. State Dept. and various public service orgns., 1975-76; writer, lectr. 1976-78; vis. prof. govt. Conn. Coll., 1979-81; vis. scholar Ctr. for Internat. Affairs, Harvard U., 1981-83; writer, cons. 1983—. Mem. Council on Fgn. Relations. Home and Office: Chemin des Oisillons 5, 1012 Pully-Lausanne Switzerland

KORTCHNOI, VIKTOR LVOVICH, chess grandmaster; b. Leningrad, USSR, Mar. 23, 1931; s. Lev Merkuryevich and Zelda Gershevna (Asbel) K.; student in history Leningrad U., 1948-54; m. Markaryan, Mar. 23, 1958; 1 son, Igor. Nat. chessmaster, 1950, internat. master, 1954, internat. grandmaster, 1956, champion USSR, 1960, 62, 65, 70, challenged world champion in matches, 1978, 1981; mem. Swiss Olympic chess team; participant Dutch team competition playing for Volmac, Rotterdam. Defected from USSR, 1976. Author: Chess Is My Life, 1977; Persona non Grata (Anti-Chess), 1981. Home: 7 Allmenweg, Wohlen 5610 Switzerland

KORTE, BERNHARD HERMANN, mathematics researcher; b. Bottrop, Germany, Nov. 3, 1938; s. Bernhard F. and Agnes (Schmidt) K.; m. Sabeth Tennholter, Aug. 1, 1966; 1 child, Dagmar. Ph.D. in Math., U. Bonn., 1968, Habilitation, 1970; PhD (hon.) U. Rome, 1987. Research assoc. U. Bonn, Fed. Republic Germany, 1965-70, dir. Institut fur Gellschaftsund Wirtschaftswissenschaften, 1972—; prof. U. Regensburg, Fed. Republic Germany, 1971, U. Bielefeld, Fed. Republic Germany, 1971; prof. Ops. Research U Bonn., 1972—, dir. Inst. Ops. Research, 1972—; disting. sr. fellow RUTCOR Rutgers U., New Brunswick, N.J., 1985—, dir. research Inst. Discrete Math., 1987—. Recipient Grand Officier Cross of the Order of Merit of the Italian Republic, 1986. Contbr. numerous articles to sci. jours. Mem. Am. Math. Soc., Ops. Research Soc. Am., Mathematical Programming Soc., Deutsche Mathematiker Vereinigung. Home: Im Erlengrund 26, 5305 Impekoven, Bonn Federal Republic of Germany Office: Inst Ops Research, Nassestrasse 2, 5300 Bonn 1 Federal Republic of Germany

KÖRTE, GERRIT, automotive executive; b. Hamburg, Fed. Republic of Germany, Feb. 2, 1925; arrived in Denmark, 1980; s. Fokko and Erika Körte; m. Lis Aagaard; children: Jens, Jost, Niels. MS, Tech. U. Karlsruhe, Fed. Republic of Germany, 1952. With constrn., calculation and testing depts. Deutsche Werft, Hamburg, 1952-55; mgr. tech. dept. Esso Tankschiff Reederei, Hamburg, 1956-64; mem. mng. bd. Howaldtswerke Hamburg A.G., 1964-67; mem. exec. bd. Howaldtswerke-Deutsche Werft A.G., Hamburg and Kiel, Fed. Republic of Germany, 1968-80; pres. B&W Diesel A/S, Copenhagen, 1980-84, MAN B&W Diesel Gmbh, Augsburg, Fed. Republic of Germany, 1984—, MAN B&W Diesel A/S, Copenhagen, 1984—; mem. Tech. Beirat Germanischer Lloyd, Hamburg, 1972-78, 84—; mem. Nordic com. Lloyd's Register of Shipping, London, 1981-98, also chmn. tech. com.; chmn. German com., Hamburg, 1984; mem. bd. dels. Fedn. Danish Mech. Engring. and Metalworking Prodn., Copenhagen, 1982; mem. Copenhagen Metal Industry Employers' Fedn., 1982; mem. council Fedn. Danish Industries, Copenhagen, 1983; bd. dirs. various cos. worldwide. Served with German Navy, 1943-45. Fellow Inst. Marine Engrs.; mem. Verwaltungsrat Forschungszentrum des Deutschen Schiffbaus. Club: Kiel Yacht. Office: MAN B&W Diesel A/S, 161 Stamholmen, 2650 Hvidovre, Copenhagen Denmark

KORTH, FRED, lawyer; b. Yorktown, Tex., Sept. 9, 1909; s. Fritz R. J. and Eleanor Marie (Stark) K.; m. Vera Connell, Sept. 12, 1934 (div. Mar. 1966); children: Nina Marie, Fritz-Alan, Vera Sansom (dec.); m. Charlotte Brooks, Aug. 23, 1980. A.B., U. Tex., 1932; LL.B., George Washington U., 1935, LL.D. (hon.), 1960. Bar: Tex., D.C. bars 1935. Sole practice Ft. Worth, 1935-62; ptnr. Wallace & Korth, 1948-51; sole practice Washington, 1964-66; ptnr. Korth & Korth, Washington, 1964—; dep. counselor Dept. Army, 1951-52, asst. sec. army, 1952-53, cons. to sec. army, 1953-60; exec. v.p. Continental Nat. Bank, Ft. Worth, 1953-59, pres., 1959-61; sec. of navy, 1961-63; treas. Ft. Worth Air Terminal Corp., 1953-60; bd. dirs. Fischbach Corp., First Fin. Enterprises, Knickerbocker Life Ins. Co., First Fin. Savs. Bank, Panama Canal Co. Pres. United Fund, Ft. Worth, Tarrant County, 1957-58; bd. dirs. Southwestern Exposition and Fat Stock Show, Ft. Worth, 1953-63, treas., 1960-61; co-executor, co-trustee Marjorie Merriweather Post Estate; mem. nat. council Salk Inst.; trustee Meridian House Internat., Washington, Nat. Def. U. Found. Served as lt. col. Air Transp. Command AUS., 1942-46. Recipient Exceptional Civilian Service award Dept. Army, 1953. Mem. ABA, Tex. Bar Assn., D.C. Bar Assn., Am. Law Inst. (life), Order St. Lazarus, Tex. and Southwestern Cattle Raisers Assn. (treas. 1957-61), Phi Delta Phi, Sigma Phi Epsilon. Democrat. Clubs: Internat. (Washington), Georgetown (Washington), Army-Navy (Washington); Ridglea (Ft. Worth); Argyle (San Antonio); El Paso Country, Coronado Country. Home: 4200 Massachusetts Ave NW 101 Washington DC 20016 also: El Retiro PO Box 13 Ecleto TX 78111 also: 1054 Torrey Pines El Paso TX 79912 Office: 1700 K St NW Suite 501 Washington DC 20006

KORTHALS, ROBERT W., bank executive; b. June 7, 1933. BChemE, U. Toronto, Can., 1955; MBA, Harvard U., 1961. Supt. term financing internat. div. Toronto Dominion Bank, 1967-68, supt. nat. accounts div., 1986-69, asst. gen. mgr. nat. accounts div., 1969-72, v.p. adminstrn., 1972-76, sr. v.p., 1976-78, exec. v.p., chief gen. mgr., 1978-81, pres., 1981—, also bd. dirs.; bd. dirs. Talcorp Ltd., Co-Steel Internat. Ltd., Hayes-Dana Inc., Kidd Creek Mines Ltd., London Life Ins. Co.; chmn., bd. dirs. TD Mortgage Corp. Gov. Cen. Hosp., Toronto; mem. Ont. Econ. Council, Ont. Bus. Adv. Council. Office: Toronto Dominion Bank, Toronto-Dominion Ctr Box 1, Toronto, ON Canada M5K 1A2 *

KORTLANDT, FREDERIK HERMAN HENRI, Slavic languages and comparative linguistics educator; b. Utrecht, The Netherlands, June 19, 1946. BA, U. Amsterdam, 1967, MA, 1969, PhD in Lit., 1972. Asst. prof. U. Amsterdam, 1969-72; prof. Slavic langs. U. Leiden, The Netherlands, 1974—, prof. descriptive and comparative linguistics, 1985—. Author: Modelling the Phoneme, 1972, Slavic Accentuation, 1975; contbr. numerous articles to linguistic jours. Mem. Royal Dutch Acad. Home: Cobetstraat 24, NL 2313 KC Leiden The Netherlands Office: U Leiden Faculty Letters, PO Box 9515, NL-2300RA Leiden The Netherlands

KORWEK, ALEXANDER DONALD, engineering association executive; b. Madison, Ill., Feb. 20, 1932; s. Alexander and Constance (Gulewicz) K.; m. Katherine Moore, Oct. 24, 1954 (div. Nov. 1974); children—Alexander D., Brian P., Lizabeth E.; m. Judith Joy, Jan. 11, 1975; 1 child, Theodore Sofianos. BSBA, Washington U., St. Louis, 1962; MBA, U. Utah, 1967. C.D.P., 1962. Asst. sec., asst. treas. Hoechst (Hystron) Fiber, N.Y.C., 1966-72; v.p. fin. Reeves/Teletape, N.Y.C., 1972-76; prin. A.D. Korwek Cons., North Babylon, N.Y., 1975-77; bus. mgr., chief fin. officer Queens Coll., CUNY, Flushing, N.Y., 1977-79; mng. dir. ASCE, N.Y.C., 1979-81; sec., gen. mgr., chief exec. officer United Engring. Trustees, N.Y.C., 1981—; exec. sec. Engring. Found., N.Y.C., 1981—, Engr. Socs. Library, N.Y.C., 1981—; sec. Daniel Guggenheim Medal Bd., N.Y.C., 1981—, John Fritz Medal Bd., N.Y.C., 1981—. Author: Cost Estimating Relationships, 1967, A Dissertation on Management, 1978; author manuals in field. Commr., Norwalk-Wilton Conv. & Visitors Bur., Conn., 1985. Served with U.S. Army, 1952-54. Recipient award of Appreciation Queen's Coll. Student Body, 1979. Mem. Council of Engr. and Sci. Soc. Execs., N.Y. Soc. Assn. Execs., N.Y. Acad. Sci., ASCE, Assn. for a Better N.Y., N.Y.C. C. of C. Club: Conn. Specialty (pres. Norwalk 1985—). Office: United Engring Trustees Inc 345 E 47th St New York NY 10017

KORYBUT-DASZKIEWICZ, SKARBIMIR MARIA, sales executive; b. Penley, Wales, Apr. 4, 1949; s. Jerzy and Regina (Prejs) K.-D.; m. Ewa Adamczenko, July 21, 1973; children: Anna-Maria, Dorota Ewa. BS in Computing Sci. with honors, North Staffordshire Poly. U., 1972. Programmer Singer Bus. Machines, Nottingham, Eng., 1972-73, G.U.S., Nottingham, 1973-74; systems analyst Rediffusion Computers, Warsaw, Poland, 1974-78; sr. systems analyst Moscow, 1978-85; mgr. software support J.B. Electronics Co., Moscow, 1985-86; mgr. systems sales Rank Xerox EEO, Moscow, 1986—. Mem. Conservative Party. Roman Catholic. Home: 32 Stamford Rd W, Bridgford, Nottingham NG2 6GE, England Office: Rank Xerox EEO, 14-16 Westbourne Grove, London W2 5RH, England

KOSAKA, KEI, department store executive; b. Tokyo, Sept. 28, 1937; s. Takeo and Violette (Hampson) K.; m. Nobuko Kameda, Apr. 7, 1966; children—Sho, Sei. B.A., Colgate U., 1960; M.S., Mich. State U., 1962. Mem. R&D staff Phillips Petroleum Co., Bartlesville, Okla., 1962-64; mem. planning staff AA Chem. Co., Tokyo, 1964-68; mgr. licensing Phillips Petroleum Internat. Ltd., Tokyo, 1968-72, exec., 1972-73, pres., 1974—; exec. Showa Yuka K.K., Tokyo, 1973-74, Fairmont Hotel, Tokyo, 1973-84, pres., 1985—; exec. Komatsu Store, Tokyo, 1982-84, pres., 1985—. Mem. Sigma Xi. Clubs: Tokyo, Hodogaya Country. Home: Minato-Ku, 10-6 Roppongi, 1-Chome, Tokyo 106 Japan Office: Komatsu Store Co Ltd, 9-5 Ginza 6 chome, Chuo-ku, 104 Tokyo Japan

KOSCHORKE, ULRICH M., mathematics educator; b. Königsberg, Ostpreussen, Fed. Republic Germany, Feb. 1, 1941; d. Manfred E. and Emmy (Jellinek) K.; m. Alba Aitken, Dec. 14, 1979; children: Miriam, Raphael. Diplom, Bonn (Fed. Republic Germany) U., 1966, Habilitation, 1973; PhD, Brandeis U., 1968. Asst. prof. math. Rutgers U., New Brunswick, N.J., 1968-74; research mathematician Bonn U., 1971-72, 75-77; asst. prof. CUNY, 1974-75; prof. U.-GH Siegen, Fed. Republic Germany, 1977—; research mem. Inst. Advanced Study, Princeton, N.J., 1980-81. Author: Siegen Topology Symp, 1979, 87, Vector Fields, 1981; contbr. articles profl. jours. Mem. Am. Math. Soc., Deutsche Math. Vereinigung. Home: Auf dem Alten Hof 11, D5902 Netphen 1 Federal Republic of Germany Office: Universitat GH Siegen, Hölderlinstr 3, D59 Siegen Federal Republic of Germany

KOSCIERZYNSKI, RONALD JOHN, educator; b. Detroit, July 18, 1947; s. William Joseph and Jean Mary (Sloncz) K.; m. Barbara Renata, Aug. 19, 1972; children—John Joseph, Anne Marie, Mark Michael, Teresa Rose. A.T., Macomb County (Mich.) Community Coll., 1968; B.S.Ed., Wayne State U., 1970, M.Ed., 1973, Ed.D., 1979. Tchr. electronics Utica (Mich.) Community High Sch., 1972—, chmn. indsl. arts dept., 1981-86, chmn. system-wide indsl. edn., 1975-79, 87—; instr. Macomb County Community Coll., 1977-81; tchr. electronics Hazel Park (Mich.) Adult Edn., 1972-77. Served with AUS, 1970-72. Fin. dir. Our Lady Queen of Apostles Parish, 1978-80. Recipient Paul M. Shilling Disting. Service award Mich. Indsl. Edn. Soc., 1981. Mem. AMVETS (AMVET of yr. Mich., 1982, cmdr. dist. 1 Mich. 1982-83, fin. officer 1984-85, judge advocate 1985-86, 2nd vice commdr. for programs 1986-87, sr. vice comdr. 1987-88, state comdr. 1988—), Mich. Indsl. Edn. Soc. (hon. life, membership dir. 1981-84, treas., 1977-80), Am. Indsl. Arts Student Assn. (chmn. orgnl. com. 1984-87), Am. Polish Engring. Assn., Am. Vocat. Assn., Electricity Electronics Tchrs. Mich., Mich. Occupational Edn. Assn., Mich. Trade and Tech. Educators, Nat. Assn. Indsl. and Tech. Tchrs. Educators, Vocat. Indsl. Clubs Am., Phi Delta Kappa. Club: K.C. Contbr. articles to profl. jours. Office: Utica High Sch 47255 Shelby Rd Utica MI 48087

KOSELLECK, REINHART, historian, educator; b. Görlitz, Fed. Republic Germany, Apr. 23, 1923; s. Arno and Elisabeth (Marchand) K.; m. Felicitas Flimm, 1960; children: Bettina, Felix, Ruprecht, Konrad, Katharina. Student, U. Heidelberg, 1947-53, Bristol U., Eng., 1950; lector for German, Bristol U., 1953-55; habilitation, U. Heidelberg, 1965. Prof. polit. sci. U. Bochum, Fed. Republic Germany, 1966-67; prof. early modern history U. Heidelberg, Fed. Republic Germany, 1967-73; prof. theory of history U. Bielefeld, Fed. Republic Germany, 1973—. Author: Kritik und Krise, 1959, 2d edit., 1969 (translated into Spanish, French, Italian, English), Preussen zwischen Reform und Revolution, 1967, 4th edit, 1987, (translated into Italian), Vergangene Zukunft (translated into English and Italian), 1971.
Mem. Ruenisch Westf Akademie der Wissenschaften Düssldorf, Heidelberger Akademie der Wissenschaften, Historische Kommission bie der Bayerischen Akademie der Wissenschaften, Akademie für Sprache und Dichtung, Darmstadt, Lessing Akademie Wolfenbüttel. Home: Luisen Str 36, 4800 Bielefeld Federal Republic of Germany Office: U Bielefeld, Dept History and Philosophy, Postbox 8640, 4800 Bielefeld Federal Republic of Germany

KOSHOYEV, TEMIRBEK KHUDAIBERGENOVICH, Soviet government official; b. Kirgigstan, 1931. Mem. CPSU, 1952—; grad. Kirghiz Agrl. Inst., 1957. Forester, student, 1950-57; instr. in Central Com. Kirghiz CP, 2nd sec. of com. Kirghiz CP, chmn. exec. com. of peoples' deps., 1st sec. com. Kirghiz CP, 1957-63; mem. auditing com. Kirghiz CP, 1960-61; mem. Cen. Com. Kirghiz CP, 1963—; 1st dep. chmn. exec. com. of Osh Oblast Sov. of Peoples' Deps., 1963-66, chmn., 1966-78; 1st Sec. of Osh Oblast Com. Kirghiz CP, 1978-81; pres. Presidium Kirghiz Supreme Soviet, 1978—; dep. to USSR Supr. Soviet Kirghiz SSR, dep. chmn. of Presidium of USSR Supreme Soviet, 1981-87; mem. Central Auditing Commn. CPSU, 1981—. Office: USSR Supreme Soviet, Oifice of Deputy Chmn, Moscow USSR *

KOSINSKI, JERZY NIKODEM, writer; b. Lodz, Poland, June 14, 1933; came to U.S., 1957, naturalized, 1965; s. Mieczyslaw and Elzbieta (Liniecka) K.; m. Mary H. Weir, Jan. 11, 1962 (dec. 1968); m. Katherina von Fraunhofer, Feb. 15, 1987. M.A. in Polit. Sci, U. Lodz, 1953, M.A. in History, 1955; postgrad., Columbia U., 1958-65; Ph.D. Hon.C. Hebrew Letters, Spertus Coll. Judaica, 1982; LHD, Albion Coll., 1988. Asst. prof. Inst. Sociology and Cultural History, Polish Acad. Scis., Warsaw, 1955-57; Guggenheim Lit. fellow 1967; fellow Center Advanced Studies, Wesleyan U., 1968-69; sr. fellow Council Humanities; vis. lectr. English Princeton, 1969-70; vis. prof. English prose Sch. Drama, Yale; also resident fellow Davenport Coll., 1970-73; fellow Timothy Dwight Coll. Yale U., 1986—. Author: (pseudonym Joseph Novak): The Future is Ours, Comrade, 1960, No Third Path, 1962, (novels) The Painted Bird, 1965 (Best Fgn. book award France), Steps, 1968, Being There, 1971, screenplay, 1978; The Devil Tree, 1st edit., 1973, rev. edit., 1981, Cockpit, 1975, Blind Date, 1977, Passion Play, 1979, screenplay, 1987; Pinball, 1982, The Hermit of 69th Street, 1988; actor in movie Reds. Chmn. bd. Am. Found. for Polish-Jewish Studies, 1987—. Recipient Nat. Book award for Steps, 1969, award in Lit. Am. Acad. Arts and Letters, 1970, Brith Sholom Humanitarian Freedom award, 1974, Best Screenplay of Yr. award for Being There, Writers Guild Am., 1979, Best Screenplay of Yr. award, Brit. Acad. Film and TV Arts, 1981, Polonia Media Perspectives award, 1980, Internat. award Spertus Coll. Judaica, 1982; Ford Found. fellow, 1958-60. Mem. PEN (exec. bd., pres. 1973-75), Nat. Writers Club (exec. bd.), Internat. League for Human Rights (dir.), ACLU (chmn. artists and writers com., mem. nat. adv. council, First Amendment award 1980), Authors Guild. Club: Century Assn. (N.Y.C.). Address: 18-K Hemisphere House 60 W 57th St New York NY 10019

KOSINSKI, LESZEK ANTONI, geography educator; b. Warszawa, Poland, June 13, 1929; came to Can., 1968, naturalized, 1974; s. Jakub and Emilia (Opacka) K.; m. Maria Leokadia Bodakiewicz, Apr. 2, 1951. M.A. in Econs., Central Sch. Planning and Statistics, 1951; M.A., in History, U. Warsaw, 1954; Ph.D., Polish Acad. Scis., 1958, Docent, 1963. Jr. researcher Inst. Town Planning and Architecture, Warsaw, Poland, 1950-54; sr. researcher Inst. Geography, Polish Acad. Scis., 1954-68; prof. geography U. Alberta, Edmonton, Can., 1969—; sec.-gen., treas. Internat. Geol. Union. Autor numerous books including The Population of Europe: A Geographical Perspective, 1970. Editor: (with R.M. Prothero) People on the Move: Studies on Internal Migration, 1975; (with J.I. Clarke and M. Khogali) Population and Development Projects in Africa, 1985. Contbr. articles to profl. jours. Served with Polish Underground, 1943-44. Mem. Can. Population Soc. (pres. 1984-86), Can. Nat. Com. for Geography, Can. Assn. Slavists, Internat. Union for Sci. Study of Population, European Assn. Population Studies, Assn. Population Geographers of India, Assn. Am. Geographers, Can. Assn. Geographers, Population Assn. Am. Avocations: travel; photography; skiing. Office: U Alberta, Dept Geography, Edmonton, AB Canada T6G 2H4

KOSKENVUO, MARKKU JUHANI, epidemiologist, educator; b. Alavus, Finland, June 10, 1945; s. Kaarlo Armas and Inkeri Helena (Låhde) K.; m. Marketta Kuusivaara, Sept. 13, 1970; children: Katja, Leo, Juha, Marina, Ville, Mira. Lic. physician, U. Helsinki, 1972, MD, 1978, docent Pub. Health, 1983. Asst. physician Dept. Pub. Health, U. Helsinki, 1972-77, asst. prof., 1977-80, acting assoc. prof., 1981—; gen. practice medicine Pvt. Health Ctr. of Viherlaakso, Espoo, Finland, 1978—. Contbr. over 70 articles on cardiovascular epidemiology and twin research to profl. jours. Lutheran. Home: Paivaperhontie 4A, 01120 Espoo Finland Office: Dept Pub Health U Helsinki, Haartmanink 3, 00290 Helsinki Finland

KOSKINEN, ESKO HUGO, government official; b. Rauma, Finland, July 22, 1938; s. Hugo and Hellä Johanna (Renvall) K.; m. Anna-Liisa Palkisto, Aug. 25, 1963; children: Hanna, Jussi, Janne. MS, U. Helsinki, 1965, DSc, Licentiate Agrl. and Forestry Scis., 1974; grad., Finnish Inst. Mgmt., 1978. Research chemist Pharm. Mfrs. Star Ltd., Helsinki, Finland, 1959-62; research asst. U. Helsinki, 1962-65, dir. Isotope Lab., Faculty Agr. and Forestry, 1966-71; research mgr. Huhtamäki Ltd., Leiras, Turku, Finland, 1971-74, exec. dir. research, 1974-76, v.p. mktg., 1976-81, v.p. bus. devel. and research, 1981-84; dir. gen. Food Research Program and chmn. project com. on food research Ministry Agr. and Forestry, Helsinki, 1984—, vice chmn. supervisory com. on promotion of food export, 1987—; asst. sec. State Nutrition Council, Helsinki, 1966-67; nutrition research officer Joint Mobile Clinic Program, State Nutrition Council and Social Ins. Instn., Helsinki, 1969-71; v.p. Tehomainos Advt. Ltd., Helsinki, 1977-81; adj. prof. nutrition, U. Helsinki, 1977—; mem. study group on prevention osteoporosis, Nat. Bd. Health, 1986-87; pres. 27th symposium European Nutritionist Group, 1989. Contbr. articles to profl. jours. including Annals Nutrition and Metabolism. Pres. Union Finnish Students Agr. and Forestry, 1967. Fellow Finnish Soc. Food Sci. and Tech. (auditor 1975-86), Fedn. European Nutrition Soc. (mem. adv. bd. 1983—), Soc. Biochemistry, Biophysics and Microbiology Fenniae, Sci. Agrl. Soc. Finland. Lutheran. Home: Martanpenger 1C 29, SF-00240 Helsinki Finland Office: Ministry Agr and Forestry, Food Research Program, Viikki 22 A 313, SF-00710 Helsinki Finland

KOSKINEN, KALEVI, forest industry company executive; b. Karkola, Finland, Sept. 9, 1929. MS, U. Helsinki, Finland, 1954. Sales dir. Koskisen Oy, Jarvela, Finland, 1954-58, chief. exec., 1958-81, 85—, chmn. bd., 1973—. Mem. Karkola Council, 1969-72. Mem. Cen. Assn. Finnish Forest Industries (bd. dirs. 1973-81, 85—), Finnish Sawmill Owner's Assn. Lutheran. Club: Finnish. Home and Office: Koskisen Oy, 16600 Jarvela Finland

KOSLER, ZDENEK, conductor; b. Prague, Czechoslovakia, Mar. 25, 1928; s. Malvina and Vaclav K.; student Acad. Music and Dramatic Arts, Prague; m. Jana Svobodova, 1954. Condr. Prague Nat. Theatre, 1951-58; artistic dir. Olomouc Opera, 1958-62; chief Ostrava Opera, 1962-66; asst. conductor N.Y. Philharmonic Orch., 1963-64, F.O.K. Orch., Prague, 1965-67; chief conductor Berlin Komische Opera, 1966-68, Opera of the Slovak Nat. Theatre, Bratislava, 1971-76; condr. Czech Philharm., 1971-81; artistic dir. Prague Nat. Theatre Opera, 1980-86; numerous concert tours in Japan, 1968—, Great Britain, 1974, 77, Austria, France, Italy and Switzerland, 1976, Can. Recipient award for Outstanding Work, 1958, 1st prize and Gold medal D. Mitropoulos Internat. Competition, N.Y., 1963, Artist of Merit, 1974, Nat. Artist, 1984, Order of Labor award, 1988. Home: Praha 6, Nad Sarkou 35 Czechoslovakia also: Columbia Artists 165 W 57th St New York NY 10019

KOSOVAC, DRAGUTIN, lawyer; b. Sarajevo, Yugoslavia, Jan. 10, 1924; s. Mane and Sofja (Maljkovic) K.; m. Vera Vuckovic, Oct. 10, 1953; children: Milica Babic-Kosovac, Branka. LLB, U. Sarajevo, 1965. V.p. Town Assembly, Sarajevo, 1951-58; minister Govt. of SRB&H, Sarajevo, 1958-60; pres. Sarajevo Dist. Nat. Com., 1962-63; fed. sec. Govt. of Yugoslavia, Belgrade, 1963-67; pres. republic council SRB&H Assembly, Sarajevo, 1967-69, pres. exec. council, 1969-71; mem. staff Presidency of SRB&H, Sarajevo, 1974-76; pres. bd. dirs. Energoinvest, Sarajevo, 1976—. Recipient 4 Nat. awards Pres. of the Republic, AVNOJ award Fedn., 1983, Golden Mercury award Internat. Trade Assn., 1980. Office: Sour Energoinvest, Bratstva Jedinstva 2, 71000 Sarajevo SFRY SRB&H, Yugoslavia

KOST, WAYNE L., business executive; b. Chgo., Feb. 8, 1951; m. Denice Lee Eslinger, Nov. 24, 1979. B.S., Northwestern U., 1973; M.P.A., Syracuse U., 1974. Adminstrv. asst. Chgo. Crime Commn., 1973; staff asso. Va. Mcpl. League, Richmond, 1975-77; dir. inst. affairs Am. Public Works Assn., Chgo., 1977-79; exec. dir. Am. Soc. Quality Control, Milw., 1980-82; sr. v.p. Philip Crosby Assocs., Winter Park, Fla., 1982-85; mng. dir. Crosby Assocs. Internat., Brussels, 1985-87; dir. Can. Region Crosby Assocs. Internat., 1987—; lectr. public adminstrn. Golden Gate U., 1976-78. Bd. dirs. Nat. Council YMCAs, 1970-73, Ill. Commn. on Children, 1969-73; chmn. Gov.'s Com. on Age of Majority, 1972. Gov.'s fellow, 1972. Mem. Am. Soc. Assn. Execs., Nat. Soc. YMCA Youth Govs. Office: 201 W Canton Ave Winter Park FL 32732

KOSTARCZYK, EWA MARIA, neurophysiologist, educator; b. Krakow, Poland, Dec. 27, 1949; d. Stanislaw and Boleslawa (Malina) Kolodziej; 1 child, Alexander Tchorzewski. M of Psychology, Jagellonian U., Krakow, 1973; D of Biology, Polish Acad. Sci., Warsaw, 1980. Asst. Nencki Inst. Exptl. Biology, Polish Acad. Sci., 1977-80, adj. prof. dept. neurophysiology, research assoc., 1980—; assoc. lectr. Inst. Psychology, Jagellonian U., 1984-85, Inst. Physiology, Med. Acad. Warsaw, 1987—. Mem. editorial bd.: Behavioral and Brain Scis. jour., 1985—; contbr. articles to profl. publs. Wellcome Trust research fellow, 1982-84; grantee Polish Acad. Sci., 1977-79, 80, 86. Mem. Polish Physiology Assn., European Neurosci. Assn., Phronesis. Roman Catholic. Office: Polish Acad Sci Nencki Inst, Exptl Biology Pasteur St 3, 02 093 Warsaw Poland

KOSTELANETZ, BORIS, lawyer; b. Leningrad, Russia, June 16, 1911; came to U.S., 1920, naturalized, 1925; s. Nachman and Rosalia (Dimschetz) K.; m. Ethel Cory, Dec. 18, 1938; children: Richard Cory, Lucy Cory. B.C.S., N.Y. U., 1933, B.S., 1936; J.D. magna cum laude, St. John's U., 1936, LL.D. (hon.), 1981. Bar: N.Y. 1936; CPA, N.Y. With Price, Waterhouse & Co., C.P.A.'s, N.Y.C., 1934-37; asst. U.S. atty. So. Dist. N.Y.; also confidential asst. to U.S. atty, 1937-43; spl. asst. to atty. gen. U.S. 1943-46; chief war frauds sect. Dept. Justice, 1945-46; spl. counsel com. investigate crime in interstate commerce U.S. Senate, 1950-51; ptnr. Kostelanetz, Ritholz, Tigue, Fink and predecessors, N.Y.C., 1946—; instr. acctg. N.Y. U., 1937-47, adj. prof. taxation, 1947-69; Mem. com. on character and fitness Appellate div. Supreme Ct. N.Y., 1st dept., 1974—, chmn., 1985—. Author: (with L. Bender) Criminal Aspects of Tax Fraud Cases, 1957, 2d edit., 1968, 3d edit., 1980; Contbr. articles to legal, accounting and tax jours. Chmn. Kefauver for Pres. Com. N.Y. State, 1952. Recipient Meritorious Service award NYU, 1954, John T. Madden Meml. award, 1969; Pietas medal St. John's U., 1961, medal of honor, 1983; Torch of Learning award Am. Friends of Hebrew U. Law Sch., 1979. Fellow Am. Coll. Trial Lawyers, Am. Coll. Tax Counsel, Am. Bar Found.; mem. Internat. Bar Assn., Fed. Bar Assn., ABA (council sect. taxation 1978-81, ho. of dels. 1984—), N.Y. State Bar Assn., N.Y. County Lawyers Assn. (v.p. 1966-69, pres. 1969-71, dir. 1958-64, 66-69, 71-74, chmn. com. judiciary 1965-69), Assn. Bar City N.Y., N.Y. State Soc. C.P.A.s, N.Y. U. Sch. Commerce Alumni Assn. (pres. 1951-52), St. John's U. Law Sch. Alumni Assn. (pres. 1955-57), N.Y. U. Finance Club (pres. 1953-54). Clubs: India House, New York Univ. (N.Y.C.); Nat. Lawyers (Washington). Home: 37 Washington Sq W New

York NY 10011 Office: Kostelanetz Ritholz et al 80 Pine St New York NY 10005

KOSTET, MIKAEL ALF BIRGER, electronic company executive, consultant; b. Mala, Sweden, Feb. 2, 1962; s. Birger Emanuel and Birgitta (Asplund) K. Project team mgr. Swedish Geol. Co., Mala, 1978-85; computer cons. COMTEC, Kristineberg, Sweden, 1983-84, exec., 1986—; antenna system cons. Inventor antenna feed system. Avocation: amateur radio. Home: Folketshusvagen 4, S-920 40 Kristineberg Sweden Office: Kristinebergsstans AB, Kopparvagen 6, S-92040 Kristineberg Sweden

KOSTOULAS, IOANNIS GEORGIOU, physicist, aerospace engineer; b. Petra, Pierias, Greece, Sept. 12, 1936; came to U.S., 1965, naturalized, 1984; s. Georgios Ioannou and Panagiota (Zarogiannis) K.; m. Katina Sioras Kay, June 23, 1979; 1 child, Alexandra. Diploma in Physics U. Thessoloniki, Greece, 1963; M.A., U. Rochester, 1969, Ph.D., 1972; M.S., U. Ala., 1977, Instr. U. Thessaloniki, 1963-65; teaching asst. U. Ala., 1966-67, U. Rochester, 1967-68; guest jr. research assoc. Brookhaven Nat. Lab., Upton, N.Y., 1968-72; research physicist, lectr. UCLA, U. Calif.-San Diego, 1972-76; sr. research assoc. Mich. State U., East Lansing, 1976-78, Fermi Nat. Accelerator Lab., Betavia, Ill., 1976-78; research staff mem. MIT, Cambridge, 1978-80; sr. system engr., physicist Hughes Aircraft Co., El Segundo, Calif., 1980-86; sr. physicist electro-optics and space sensors Rockwell Internat. Corp., Seal Beach and Anaheim, Calif., 1986—. Contbr. articles to profl. jours. Served with Greek Army, 1961-63. Research grantee U. Rochester, 1968-72. Mem. Am. Phys. Soc., Los Alamos Sci. Lab. Exptl. Users Group, Fermi Nat. Accelerator Lab. Users Group, High Energy Discussion Group of Brookhaven Nat. Lab., Pan Macedonian Assn., Save Cyprus Council Los Angeles, Sigma Pi Sigma. Club: Hellenic U. Lodge: Ahepa. Home: 2016 Vanderbilt Ln Apt 7 Redondo Beach CA 90278 Office: Rockwell Internat Co MC OB34 3370 Miraloma Ave PO Box 4192 Anaheim CA 92803

KOSTRZAK, JAN, historian, researcher; b. Józefowo, Kujawy, Poland, Mar. 8, 1946; s. Czeslaw and Regina (Czupryńska) K.; m. Felicja Górecka, Apr. 20, 1968; children: Andrzej-Czeslaw, Anna-Maria. MA in History, U. Nicholas Corpernicus, Torun, Poland, 1972; PhD, Inst. History, Polish Acad. Scis., Warsaw, Poland, 1982. Asst. prof. Inst. Hist., Polish Acad. Scis., 1982—; sec. editorial bd. Sci. Soc. Torun, 1983—. Author: The Origin of Old-Livonian Representative Institutions from the 13th to 15th Centuries, 1985. Recipient various history scholarships, 1984-87. Mem. Sci. Soc. Torun, Polish Hist. Soc. (secondary sec. dist. Torun 1984-87). Roman Catholic. Home: ul Konopnickiej 27 m 8, PL87100 Torun Poland Office: Inst History, Rynek Starego Miasta 29-31, PL00272 Warsaw Poland

KOSTRZEWSKI, JAN KAROL, epidemiologist, researcher; b. Cracow, Poland, Dec. 2, 1915; s. Jan Michal and Maria (Sulikowska) K.; m. Ewa Maria Sobolewska, Sept. 3, 1948; children—Anna, Magdalena, Piotr, Maria. Diploma Med. Faculty Warsaw U., 1945; M.D., Jagiellonian U. Med. Faculty, Cracow, 1948; M.P.H., Harvard, 1958; Doctor Honoris Causa (hon.) Mil. Med. Acad., Poland, 1979, Med. Acad., Lublin, Poland, 1985. Medical diplomate. Asst. in vaccine prodn. Nat. Inst. Hygiene, Warsaw, 1942-51, head dept. epidemiology, 1951-61; vice-minister, chief sanitary insp. Ministry of Health, Warsaw, 1962-67, minister health and social welfare, 1968-72; sec. med. sect. Polish Acad. Scis., Warsaw, 1972-79, v.p., 1980-83, pres., 1984—; prof. epidemiology Warsaw Med. Acad., 1954-58; mem. panel of experts World Health Orgn., Geneva, 1960—; v.p. World Health Assembly, Boston, 1969-70, mem. exec. bd., Geneva, 1973-76, chmn., 1975-76; vice-chmn. internat. commn. global eradication smallpox, WHO, Geneva, 1978-79, chmn. expanded programme immunization, global adv. group, 1978-85; chmn. research strengthening group Spl. Programme for Research and Tng. in Tropical Diseases, 1982-86; Heath Clark lectr. London Sch. Hygiene and Tropical Med., 1986, 87. Author: Health of Polish People Morbidity and Mortality, 1977; (editor and co-author) three books on communicable diseases in Poland; (co-author and co-editor) Epidemiology: A Guide to Teaching Methods, 1973; (chief editor) Jour. Epidemiological Rev., 1953—, Polish Science, 1986—; also numerous sci. papers. Mem., vice chmn. Patriotic movement for nat. rebirth, Warsaw, 1983—; M.P., 1985—. Served to lt. Polish resistance Army, 1944-45, Polish Army, 1948-49. Fellow Indian Nat. Sci. Acad.; mem. Polish Epidemiol. Assn. (mem. exec. com. 1957—), Acad. Med. Scis. (USSR), Academie Nationale de Medecine Paris (corres.), Internat. Epidemiol. Assn. (council mem. 1977-84, pres. 1977-81), Internat. Ctr. for Diarroeal Diseases Research (trustee Bangladesh 1979—, chmn. 1983-84), Societas Medica Polonorum (hon.), Assn. Microbiologists Epidemiologists USSR (hon.), Polish Epidemiol. Assn. (hon.). Roman Catholic. Avocations: sports; photography. Home: Al Roz 10m6, 00556 Warsaw Poland Office: Polish Acad Scis, Palac Kultury I Nauki, Box 24, 00901 Warsaw Poland

KOSTYUK, PLATON GRIGOREVICH, physiologist, Soviet government official; b. Kiev, USSR, Aug. 2, 1924. Grad. in biology, Kiev U., 1946, D Biol. Sci., 1956. Mem. Communist Party Soviet Union, 1947—; prof. biology Kiev U., 1960, head dept. physiology Inst. Veterinary Physiology, 1946-58; head lab. for gen. physiology Bogomolets Inst. Physiology, Ukrainian Acad. Scis., 1958-66, dir., 1966—; corr. mem. Ukrainian Acad. Scis., 1964—, USSR Acad. Scis., 1966—; now chmn. Supreme Soviet, Kiev, Ukrainian Soviet Socialist Republic. Contbr. articles to profl. jours. Decorated Order of Red Banner of Labour. Office: Supreme Soviet Govt, Office Chmn, Kiev Ukrainian SSR, USSR *

KOSUT, KENNETH PAUL, lawyer, corporation executive; b. Houston, Nov. 6, 1949; s. John Marial and Mary Angel (Garcia) K.; m. Susan Marlene Cooper, Sept. 5, 1970 (div. 1977); m. Patricia Rose Coughlin, Jan. 17, 1980 (div. May 1985). B.B.A., U. Houston, 1972; J.D., So. Tex. Coll. Law, 1976. Bar: Tex. 1977, U.S. Dist. Ct. (so. dist.) Tex. 1977, U.S. Supreme Ct. 1986. Contract rep. Aramco Services Co., Houston, 1977-78; atty. Crest Engring. Inc., Houston, 1978-80; v.p., gen. counsel Behring Internat. Inc., Houston, 1980-85, ptnr. Cruver & Evans, 1986-87; ptnr. Evans & Kosut, 1987—. Mem. ABA, Houston Bar Assn., Tex. Bar Assn., Internat. Bar Assn., Houston World Trade Assn. (mem. maritime com.), Republican. Roman Catholic. Clubs: Houstonian, University. Home: 3600 Jeanetta No 1405 Houston TX 77063 Office: 3 Riverway Suite 1776 Houston TX 77056

KOSZELA, BOGDAN, mathematician; b. Lodz, Poland, Apr. 16, 1946; s. Marcin and Maria (Skorynkiewicz) K.; m. Barbara Kowalczyk, Apr. 18, 1968; children: Gregory, Katherine, Ann. M in Math., U. Lodz, 1969; D in Math., Tech. U., Lodz, 1976. Prof.'s asst. Tech. U., Lodz, 1969-76, lectr., 1976—; reviewer math. revs., 1979. Contbr. papers to profl. jours. Recipient Sci. Minister prize, 1977. Mem. Polskie Towarzystwo Matematyczne, Am. Math. Soc. (translator). Home: Pojezierska 7 M 31 Blok 56, 91322 Lodz Poland Office: Politechnika Lodzka, Inst Matematyki, Al Politechniki 11, 90924 Lodz Poland

KOSZEWSKI, BOHDAN JULIUS, internist, medical educator; b. Warsaw, Poland, Dec. 17, 1918; Came to U.S., 1952; s. Mikolaj and Helena (Lubienski) K.; children: Mikolaj Joseph, Wanda Marie, Andrzej Rohdan. MD, U. Zurich, Switzerland, 1946; MS, Creighton U., 1956. Resident in pathology U. Zurich, 1944-46, resident in internal medicine, 1946-50, assoc. in medicine, 1950-52; intern St. Mary's Hosp., Hoboken, N.J., 1953; practice medicine specializing in internal medicine Omaha, 1953—; mem. staff St. Joseph's Hosp., Luth Med. Ctr., Mercy and Meth. Hosps.; instr. internal medicine Creighton U., 1956-57, asst. prof., 1957-65, assoc. prof. internal medicine, 1965—; cons. hematology Omaha VA Hosp., 1957—. Author: Prognosis in Diabetic Coma, 1952; contbr. numerous articles to profl. jours. Served with Polish Army, 1940-45. Fellow ACP, Am. Coll. Angiology (gov. Nebr. chpt.); mem. AAAS, Am. Fedn. Clin. Research, Am. Soc. Hematology, Internat. Soc. Hematology, Polish-Am. Congress Nebr. (pres. 1960-68). Home and Office: 4502 S 42d St Omaha NE 68107

KOTONSKI, WLODZIMIERZ, composer, b. Warsaw, Poland, Aug. 23, 1925; s. Stanislaw and Marianna (Krysiak) K.; m. Jadwiga Chlebowska, 1951; 1 son, Piotr. M.Mus., Warsaw State Higher Sch. Music. With Exptl. Music Studio, Polish Radio and Electronic Music Studio of Westdeutscher Rundfunk, Cologne, 1966-67; assoc. prof. composition, head of electronic music studio, State Higher Sch. Music, Warsaw, 1967-83; prof. in composition Acad. of Music, Warsaw, 1983—; chief music dir. Polish Radio and TV, 1974-76; lectr. on composition, U.S.A., 1978; compositions include orchestral and chamber music, electronic and tape music and instrumental theatre; author: Goralski and Zbojnicki, 1956; Percussion Instruments in the Modern Orchestra, 1967. Music adviser Chmn.'s Com. for Radio and TV, 1977-79. Mem. Polish Composer's Union (dep. chmn. 1965-71), Polish sect. Internat. Soc. Contemporary Music (chmn. 1983-). Recipient Minister of Culture and Art prize 2d class, 1973, Prize of Pres. Polish Radio and TV Com. 1st class, 1979, Gold Cross of Merit, Officer's Cross Order Polonia Restituta. Office: Acad of Music, Okolnik 2, 00-368 Warsaw Poland

KOTTEGODA, SRI RAMACHANDRA, health organization official, physician; b. Tebuwana, Sri Lanka, Nov. 12, 1919; s. Don and Clara Caroline (Wijesinghe) K.; m. Rambukpota Damayanthi, May 12, 1950; children: Indira Savithri, Sripal Mevan, Chandrika Sepali, Samudra Ruvan. BS, U. London, 1942; MBBS, U. Ceylon, 1947; PhD, Oxford U., 1954; DSc (hon.), U. Colombo, Ceylon, 1985. Med. officer Govt. Health Services, Colombo, Ceylon, 1947-49; lectr. in pharmacology U. Ceylon, Colombo, 1949-68; prof. pharmacology U. Colombo, 1968-82, prof. emeritus, 1984%; research fellow Nat. U. Singapore, 1982-86; nat. coordinator health services/research Ministry of Sri Lanka, Kalutara, 1987—; vis. prof. Nat. U. Singapore, 1981; mem. med. ethics com. Ayurvedic Research, Colombo, 1987. Editor Singapore Jour. Obstetrics and Gynaecology, 1983-87. Rockefeller Found. fellow, Cambridge, Mass., 1958; Commonwealth fellow London Univs. Assn., 1967. Fellow of the Faculty of Anaesthetists of the Royal Coll. of Surgeons of Eng., mem. Sri Lanka Assn. for the Advancement of Sci. (pres. 1979), Sri Lanka Acad. Scis. (pres. 1981-82), Physiol. Soc. London, Physiol. Soc. Sri Lanka (various coms.), Brit. Pharmacol. Club: Sinhalese Sports. Home: 19 Welikadawatta, Rajagiriya Sri Lanka Office: Nat Inst Health Scis, Ministry Sri Lanka, PO Box 28, Kalutara Sri Lanka

KOTTLOWSKI, FRANK EDWARD, geologist; b. Indpls., Apr. 11, 1921; s. Frank Charles and Adella (Markworth) K.; m. Florence Jean Chriscoe, Sept. 15, 1945; children: Karen, Janet, Diane. Student, Butler U., 1939-42; A.B., Ind. U., 1947, M.A., 1949, Ph.D., 1951. Party chief Ind. Geology Survey, Bloomington, summers 1948-50; fellow Ind. U., 1947-51, instr. geology, 1950; adj. prof. N.Mex. Inst. Mining and Tech., Socorro, 1970—; econ. geologist N.Mex. Bur. Mines and Mineral Resources, 1951-66, asst. dir., 1966-68, 70-74, acting dir., 1968-70, dir., 1974—; geologic cons. Sandia Corp., 1966-72. Contbr. articles on mineral resources, stratigraphy and areal geology to tech. jours. Mem. Planning Commn. Socorro, 1960-68, 71-78, chmn. 86—; mem. N.Mex. Energy Resources Bd.; chmn. N.Mex. Coal Surface Mining Commn.; sec. Socorro County Democratic party, 1964-68. Served to 1st lt. USAAF, 1942-45. Decorated D.F.C.; decorated Air medal; recipient Richard Owen Disting. Alumni award in Govt. and Industry U. Ind., 1987. Fellow Geol. Soc. Am. (councilor 1980-82, exec. com. 1981-82); mem. Am. Assn. Petroleum Geologists (hon. mem., dist. rep. 1965-68, Disting. Service award, editor 1971-75, pres. energy minerals div. 1987-88), Assn. Am. State Geologists (pres. 1985-86), Soc. Econ. Geologists, AAAS, AIME, Am. Inst. Profl. Geologists (Pub. Service award 1986), Am. Commn. Stratigraphic Nomenclature (sec. 1964-68, chmn. 1968-70), Sigma Xi. Home: 703 Sunset Dr Socorro NM 87801 Office: NMex Bur Mines NMex Tech Socorro NM 87801

KOTUS, JANINA MARIA, mathematician; b. Warsaw, Poland, Nov. 15, 1954; d. Klemens and Zofia (Jankowska) k. MS in Math., Warsaw U., 1979; PhD, Tech. U. of Warsaw, 1983. Asst. Dept. Tech. Physics and Applied Math. Tech. U. of Warsaw, 1982-83, sr. asst., 1983-86, sr. prof., 1987—. Contbr. numerous articles to profl. jours. Recipient Scientific Research award Minister of Sci. and Higher Edn., 1984. Mem. Polish Math. Soc. (Marcinkiewitz award 1979, Young Mathematician prize 1982), Am. Math. Soc. (reviewer 1984—). Office: Tech U of Warsaw, Math Inst, Plac Jednosci Robotniczej 1, 00-661 Warsaw Poland

KOTZEBUE, ROBERT WILLIAM, SR., retired air conditioning company executive; b. Moulton, Tex., Mar. 28, 1909; s. George William and Adelia (Helmcamp) K.; ed. high sch., Frigidaire Air Conditioning Engring. Schs., 1934-36; m. Mary Lou Wanek, May 18, 1929; children—Robert William, Kenneth Lee. Mgr. air conditioning dept. Straus-Frank Co., San Antonio, 1934-41; partner Bell-Kotzebue Co., Inc., wholesale distbrs., San Antonio, 1945-60; owner, operator Kotzebue Distbg. Co., San Antonio, 1960-84, chmn. bd., 1968-84, ret., 1984. Served to capt. C.E., U.S. Army, 1941-45. Registered profl. engr. Tex. Mem. San Antonio Power Squadron (comdr. 1971-72), ASHRAE (life), Nat. Soc. Profl. Engrs. (life), Tex. Soc. Profl. Engrs. Republican. Lutheran. Clubs: Oak Hills Country, St. Anthony. Home: 149 Lou-Jon Circle San Antonio TX 78213

KOUABENAN, DONGO REMI, psychology educator; b. Guiende, Ivory Coast, Sept. 7, 1957; d. Kouame Adou and Prao Adia; m. Edwige Sellaye Kouabenan, Aug. 8, 1971; children: Adou Kouadio Cedric, Affoua Prao Stephanie, Abran Solange Vanessa. M of Psychology, U. Bordeaux II, France, 1979; diploma of Psychology, U. Sorbonne, Paris, 1980; MS in Indsl. Psychology, U. Paris V, 1981; D of Psychology, U. Sorbonne, Paris, 1982. Cert. occupational, work psychologist, Ivory Coast. Prof. psychology, researcher Nat. U. Ivory Coast, Abidjan, 1983—; asst. lectr. Nat. Sch. Adminstrn., Abidjan, 1983—; cons., instr. Univ. Ctr. for Adult Edn., Abidjan, 1985—. Author: Condition d'hygiene et de secutite, 1985; contbr. articles to profl. jours. Mem. Nat. Assn. Psychologists Ivory Coast (gen. sec. 1985-87). Home: Abidjan-Cocody Riviera Golf, Elias 1, Abidjan BP V 34, Ivory Coast Office: Nat U Ivory Coast, Abidjan BP V 34, Ivory Coast

KOUBOURLIS, DEMETRIUS JOHN, real estate investor, educator; b. Rion-Patras, Greece, June 18, 1938; came to U.S., 1959, naturalized, 1972; s. John Antonios and Sophia Sotirios (Iliopoulou) K.; m. Toni Jean Hall, Dec. 28, 1967; children: Sophia C.M. Aadland, Yana D.H., Koren T.D., John D.A., Niki D.A. B.A., Calif. State U., 1963; Ph.D., U. Wash., 1967. Tutor ancient Greek, Italian and English Patras, Greece, 1958-59; tchr. English Greek-Am. Cultural Inst., Patras, 1955-56; teaching asst. U. Wash., Seattle, summer 1966; instr. Slavic lang. U. Colo., Boulder, 1966-67; asst. prof. Slavic lang. and lit. Tulane U., New Orleans, 1967-68, U. N.C., Chapel Hill, 1968-71; asst. prof. fgn. lang. U. Idaho, Moscow, 1971-73; asso. prof. U. Idaho, 1973-75, prof., 1975—; real estate investor, developer, Moscow and Pullman, Wash., owner Moscow Mall, Apts. West, Sound West; U. Idaho rep. to Internat. Research and Exchanges Bd., Ad hoc grantee, 1973-74; Internat. Inst. Math. and Computational Linguistics scholar, Pisa, Italy, 1974, participant exchange lang. tchrs., USSR, 1973. Editorial bd.: Folia Slavica; editorial com.: Slavic and East European Jour.; Author: Soviet Acad. Grammar: Phonology and Morphology, a Computer-Aided Index, 1972, A Concordance to the Poems of Osip Mandelstam, 1974, Topics in Slavic Phonology, 1974; editor: Language Series, 1972—; contbr. articles in field to profl. jours. and books. Mem. Am. Assn. Advancement Slavic Studies, Am. Assn. Tchrs. Slavic and E. European Langs., Am. Council Tchrs. Russian, Assn. Computing Machinery, Assn. Lit. and Linguistic Computing, Pacific Northwest Conf. Fgn. Langs., Western Slavic Assn. Home: NW 1470 Orion Dr Pullman WA 99163 Office: NE 1325 Valley Rd Pullman WA 99163

KOUDELKA, JOSEF, photographer; b. Boskovice, Czechoslovakia, Jan. 10, 1938; s. Josef and Marie (Necasova) K. Degree in Engring., Tech. U., Prague, 1961. Aero. engr., Prague, 1961-67; free-lance photographer Divadlo Theatre mag., Prague, 1961-65; ofcl. photographer Theatre za Branou, Prague, 1965-70; free-lance photographer Magnum photo agy., Paris and N.Y. working in London, 1971-80, in Paris, 1980—; solo photo exhibits Theatre Semafor, Prague, 1961, Gypsies 1961-66, Theatre za Branou, Prague, 1967, Theatre Photography 1965-68, Theatre za Branou, Prague, 1968, Mus. Modern Art, N.Y.C., Carlton Gallery, N.Y.C., 1975, Art Inst. Chgo., 1976, Kunsthaus, Zurich, Tel Aviv Mus, Galerie Delpire, Paris, Stedelijk Mus., Amsterdam, 1978, Musée d'Orange, France, 1979, Camera Obscura, Stockholm, 1980, Galerie le Trepied, Geneva, Carpenter Ctr., Harvard U., Cambridge, Mass., 1981, Hayward Gallery, London, 1984, Nat. Mus. Photography, Bradford, 1985, Galerie Eric Franck, Geneva, 1987, Palais de Tokyo, Paris, 1988, Internat. Ctr. Phonography, N.Y., 1988, Akademie der Kunste, Berlin, 1988; represented in permanent collections Victoria and Albert Mus., London, Arts Council Gt. Britain, London, Ministry of Culture, Brussels, Kunsthaus, Zurich, Stedelijk Mus., Amsterdam, Galerie in Forum Stadtpark, Graz, Austria, Mus. Modern Art, N.Y.C., Phila. Mus. Art. Author: Gypsies, 1975, Exiles, 1988; Grandi Fotografi: Josef Koudelka, 1982; Josef Koudelka, Photo Poche, 1984. Recipient Robert Capa Meml. award Overseas Press Club, 1970; Photography bursary Arts Council Gt. Britain, 1976, Grand Prix National de la Photographie Ministere de la Communication, France; priz Nadar, Paris, 1978; Nat. Endowment Arts grantee, 1980, grantee Centre National des Arts Plastiques, France, 1986. Address: care Magnum Photos, 20 rue des Grand Augustins, Paris 6 France

KOULOUKIS, GEORGE PANAYEOTIS, lawyer; b. Piraeus, Greece, Mar. 31, 1934; s. Panayeotis George and Despina Panayeotis (Tergiotis) K.; B.Law, Athens U., 1957; m. Debby E. Laskaridou, June 15, 1963; children—Evaggelia, Katerina. Admitted to Athens bar, 1959; legal counsel Ionian-Popular Bank Greece, Athens, 1961-75, Hellenic Electric Rys. Corp., Met. subway, Athens, 1961-76, Royal Inst. Co., Athens, 1975—; dir. Aegean Bank Greece. Active Progressive Party Greece, 1959-61. Served to lt. Greek Cav., 1957-59. Mem. Athens Bar Assn. Greek Orthodox. Author: Forced Execution, 1967; specialist in internat. fin. Home: 12 Ardittou St, Athens 407, Greece Office: 17 Navarinou St, Athens 145, Greece

KOURTOGLOU, PRODROMOS JOHN, civil engineer; b. Athens, Feb. 9, 1952; s. John Prodromos and Evanghelia (Marinopoulou) K. Diploma civil engring. Nat. Tech. U., Athens, 1975; M.Sc., U. Birmingham, Eng., 1976. Soils engr. McClelland Engrs., London, 1976; asst., soils lab., Geoerevna SA, Athens, 1977; site officer Greek Corps Engrs., Rhodos, 1977-79; bldg. site dir., cons., Athens, 1979-81; bldg. site dir. Vent S.A., Athens, 1982-83; geotech. investigation site dir. Geomechaniki S.A., Ioannina and Aghion Oros, Greece, 1983-85; sewer network cons. site dir. Vent S.A., Karditsa, Greece, 1985-87. State Found. scholarships, Greece, 1971-75. Mem. Tech. Chamber Greece; assoc. mem. Instn. Civil Engrs., Mem. of Adminstrn., EN.E.K., ASCE. Home: Atlantos 4, GR-175 61 Palaeon Phaleron Greece

KOUSOULAS, DIMITRIOS GEORGE, political science educator, author, businessman; b. Khalkis, Greece, Dec. 22, 1923; came to U.S., 1951, naturalized, 1958; s. George D. and Barbara (Lachnidakis) K.; m. Mary Katris, Jan. 27, 1952; 1 son, George. LL.B., U. Athens, Greece, 1948; M.A. (Fulbright scholar) in Polit. Sci, Syracuse U., 1953, Ph.D., 1956. Fgn. lang. specialist USIA, 1957-60; professorial lectr. Nat. War Coll., George Washington U., 1961-72; asst. prof. Howard U., 1961-64, assoc. prof., 1965-67, prof. govt., chmn. dept., 1967-70; pres. Meridian-West Assocs., 1974—, Woodbridge Nursing Ctr., Inc., 1976—. Author: Greece in World Affairs 1939-53, 1953, Key to Economic Progress, 1958, transl. into 27 langs., Revolution and Defeat: the Story of the Greek Communist Party, 1965, On Government: a Comparative Introduction, 1968, On Government and Politics, 5th edit, 1981, Modern Greece; Profile of a Nation, 1974, Power and Influence: Introduction to International Relations, 1985, Mega-issues of Our Time (in Greek), 1985, KKE, The First Thirty Years (in Greeek), 1987, Political Responsibilities-1964-1974 (in Greek), 1988. Pres. Am. Com. on Cyprus Self-determination, 1964-66; trustee Ahepa Ednl. Found., 1968-76. Served in Greek Armed Forces, 1948-50. Decorated Nat. Resistance medal, knight Royal Order of Phoenix, Golden Cross (Greece). Mem. Am. Acad. Polit. and Social Sci., Acad. Polit. Sci., Am., Internat. polit. sci. assns. Home: 6252 Clearwood Rd Bethesda MD 20817 Office: Howard Univ Washington DC 20001

KOUSSA, HAROLD ALAN, nuclear engineer; b. Central Falls, R.I., June 20, 1947; s. Harold Albert and June Joann (John) K.; m. Marsha Lynn Heidenis, Dec. 1, 1973. B.S., U. R.I., 1969; M.B.A., U. Hartford, 1975; M.S. in Engring. Sci., Rensselaer Poly. Inst., 1977. Reactor engring. asst. Conn. Yankee Atomic Power Co., Haddam Neck, 1969-75, reactor engr., 1975-77; staff nuclear engr. Am. Nuclear Insurers, Farmington, Conn., 1977-79, sr. staff nuclear engr., 1979-81, prin. engr., 1981-82, mgr. ops., 1982—. Mem East Hampton Rep. Town Com., 1982-88; del. Conn. Rep. Conv., 1982, 84, 86; mem. East Hampton Water Pollution Control Authority, 1982—, vice chmn., 1984-85, chmn., 1985—. Engring. duty officer USNR, 1982—. Mem. Am Nuclear Soc., ASME, Am. Mgmt. Assn., Am. Soc. Naval Engrs. Congregationalist. Clubs: Masons, U. R.I. Fast Break. Home: 26 Meadowlark Dr Windsor CT 06095 Office: American Nuclear Insurers 270 Farmington Ave Farmington CT 06032

KOUTNY, MACIEJ, computer science educator; b. Kozy, Poland, Sept. 28, 1958; arrived in Eng., 1985; s. Zenon and Barbara (Jedrzejko) K.; m. Marta Pietkiewicz; 1 child, Aleksandra. MS, Warsaw Tech. U., Poland, 1982, PhD, 1984. Jr. lectr., fellow Inst. Math., Warsaw Tech. U., 1982-86; research assoc. Computing Lab., U. Newcastle Upon Tyne, Eng., 1985-86, lectr., 1986—. Contbr. articles to profl. jours. Roman Catholic. Office: U Newcastle Upon Tyne Comp Lab, Claremont Tower Claremont Rd, Newcastle Upon Tyne England

KOUTROULIS, ARIS GEORGE, artist, educator; b. Athens, Greece, May 14, 1938; came to U.S., 1953; s. George Aris and Julia (Eftimiades) K.; m. Mary Ann Schmid, 1964 (div. 1973); m. Jill Warren, July 4, 1982; 1 dau., Georgina. B.F.A., La. State U., 1961; Master Printer, Tamarind Lithography Workshop, Los Angeles, 1964; M.F.A., Cranbrook Acad. Art, Bloomfield Hills, Mich., 1966. Chmn. bd. Willis Gallery, Detroit, 1970-71; pres. Common Ground of the Arts, Detroit, 1969-72; guest artist Ox-Bow Summer Sch. Art, Saugatuck, Mich., 1973, co-dir., 1975; assoc. prof. art Wayne State U., 1966-75; head painting dept. Ctr. Creative Studies, Detroit, 1975-81, chmn. Fine Arts Dept., 1981—; exhibited one-man shows, Hanamura Gallery, Detroit, 1966, Montgomery Mus. Fine Arts, Ala., 1966, Va. Poly. Inst., 1968, Baton Rouge Gallery, 1968, Wayne State U., 1969, Mich. Council for Arts, 1969, Gertrude Kasle Gallery, Detroit, 1970, Detroit Artists Market, 1973, Klein-Vogel Gallery, Detroit, 1974, Detroit Inst. Arts, 1976, Gloria Cortella Gallery, N.Y.C., 1977, Gallery Renaissance, Detroit, 1980, Haber-Theodore Gallery, N.Y.C., 1980; OK Harris Gallery, N.Y.C., 1980, 81, 82, 83, 85, 87, Mich. Traveling Exhbn., 1981, Cantor/Emberg Gallery, Birmingham, Mich., 1982, Dubins Gallery, Los Angeles, 1984, Nimbus Gallery, Dallas, 1986; exhibited group shows Decorative Arts Ctr., N.Y.C., 1973, Detroit Inst. Arts, 1974, Bykert Gallery, N.Y.C., 1974, Bklyn. Mus., 1977, Brooks Meml. Art Gallery, Memphis, 1977, La. State U. Gallery, 1978, Tyler Sch. Art, Temple U., 1978, Mus. Fine Arts, Springfield, Mass., 1978, Van Doren Gallery, San Francisco, 1978, Consulate Gen. Greece, N.Y.C., 1978, Landmark Gallery, N.Y.C., 1978, Cranbrook Mus. Art, Bloomfield Hills, Mich., 1979, Detroit Inst. Arts, 1980, Mus. Fine Arts Tampa, 1987, 51st nat. mid-yr. exhbn. Butler Inst. Am. Art, Youngstown, Ohio, 1987; represented in pub. collections including Mus. Modern Art, Nat. Gallery Art, Detroit Inst. Arts, Los Angeles County Mus. Art, Cranbrook Mus. Art, Detroit Engring. Soc., Detroit Pub. Library, U. Mich. Art Mus., Anglo-Am. Mus., Amon Carter Mus. Western Art, Ft. Worth, UCLA Grunwald Graphic Arts Found., Ball State U. Art Mus.; represented in corp. collections; commd. Standard Oil Corp., San Ramon, Calif., Arbor Drugs, Inc., Focus Gallery, Bracewell/Patterson, Washington, Mich. Found. for Arts, Detroit Engring. Soc., Art for Detroit, City of Detroit, WDIV-TV4, Detroit, Tampa Mus. Collection. Address: Center for Creative Studies Dept Fine Arts 245 E Kirby St Detroit MI 48202

KOUYOUMJIAN, CHARLES H., financial services, investment company executive; b. Cambridge, Mass., Nov. 20, 1940; s. Housep J. and Victoria M. (Madenjian) K.; B.S. in Bus. Adminstrn., Boston U., 1963; postgrad. Boston Coll., 1969-71; m. Karen L. Dennison, June 19, 1965; children—Joseph, Charles. Dir. purchasing Allis Chalmers Mfg. Co., Boston, 1968; investment broker Hornblower & Weeks Hemphill Noyes Inc., Boston, 1969-71, v.p., resident mgr., Springfield, Mass., 1971-76, regional hdqrs., Boston, 1976-77; v.p., resident mgr. Paine Webber, Inc., Boston, 1977-79, regional sales mgr. Fla. div., 1980-81, dir. Asset Mgmt. Group, nat. hdqrs., N.Y.C., 1982-83, v.p. spl. accounts dept. Boston, 1983-85; pres., chief exec. officer, Empire Nat. Securities, Buffalo, 1985-88, Charles Assocs., 1988—. Mem. camp com. Springfield YMCA, 1973-76; bd. dirs. Health Care Found. Western Mass., 1973-74. Served to capt. USAF, 1963-67. Mem. Boston Options Soc. (chmn.), Springfield C. of C. (dir. 1973-75), Nat. Assn. Securities Dealers (mem. quotation com. 1975-76), Boston Fin. Research Assos., Boston Investment Club, Boston Stockbrokers Club, Securities Industry Assn., Newcomen Soc. U.S. and Gt. Britain, Internat. Assn. Fin. Planning. Clubs: Bond of Boston, Bond of Buffalo. Home: 16 Greenridge Rd Weston MA 02193 Office: Charles Assocs 30 Clematis Ave Waltham MA 02154

KOVACEVIC, ZIVORAD, ambassador; b. Svetozarevo, Yugoslavia, May 30, 1930; s. Ilija Radovan and Dara (Zeljkovic) K.; m. Margita Ilija Kaljevic, July 3, 1958; children: Jelena, Radovan. BA, Sch. of Journalism and Diplomacy, Belgrade, 1952; MA In Polit. Sci., U. Calif., Berkeley, 1960. Dep. sec. gen. The League of Cities of Yugoslavia, 1953-59, sec. gen., 1967-72; dir. The Inst. of Pub. Adminstrn., Belgrade, 1960-63; under sec. Govt. of the Socialist Repub. of Serbia, 1963-67; dep. mayor City of Belgrade, 1972-74, mayor, mem. parliament, 1974-82, cabinet min. in charge of fgn. economic relations, 1982-86; ambassador Socialist Republic of Yugolslavia, Washington, 1987—; mem. panel on urban crisis com. on Sci. and Astronautics House of Reps., U.S. Congress, 1969; pres. Bur. of the Contracting Parties to Barcelona Conv. on the Protection of the Mediterranean, 1983-85. Author books on urbanization in Yugoslavia, international economic relations, others. V.p. Internat. Union of Local Authorities; chmn. of the Environtl. Protection Assn. Recipient numerous Yugoslav decorations and various fgn. states. Mem. Socialist Alliance of Working People of Yugoslavia. Club: Internat. (Washington). Office: Embassy of the Socialist Federal Republic of Yugoslavia 2410 California St NW Washington DC 20008

KOVACEVICH, ROBERT EUGENE, lawyer; m. Yvonne R. Stokke; children: Tawni, Mark, Phillip, Ben. Grad., St. Marins Coll., 1955; JD, Gonzaga U., 1959; LLM in Taxation, NYU, 1960. Bar: Wash. 1960, U.S. Dist. Ct. (ea. and we. dists.) Wash., U.S. Ct. Appeals (9th cir.), U.S. Supreme Ct. Sole practice, Spokane, Wash., 1963-72; ptnr. Kovacevich & Algeo, Spokane, 1972-80; prin. Robert E. Kovacevich, P.S., Spokane, 1980—; speaker in field; instr. fed. taxation Sch. Bus., Gonzaga U., Spokane, 1967-84, instr. M.S. in Bus. program, 1975-84; spl. cons. on IRS, David Brinkley Spl., NBC, 1975; expert witness U.S. Senate Com. on Appropriations, 1976; arbitrator Spokane County Superior Ct., 1985—. Author: Federal Taxation of Non-Competent Indians on Income Generated from Alloted Lands, 1981. Mem. steering com. Deaconess Hosp. Found. Mem. ABA, Spokane County Bar Assn. (ct. arbitrator 1985—), Wash. State Bar Assn. (local adminstrv. com. 1980-81, fee arbitrator 1984—), Estate Planning Council Spokane (past pres.), St. Martin's Coll. of Olympia (trustee 1984—). Club: Spokane. Lodge: Elks (past exalted ruler). Home: S 4603 Pittsburg Spokane WA 99203 Office: 530 Lincoln Bldg Spokane WA 99201

KOVACS, ATTILA LAJOS, cell biologist; b. Kispest, Hungary, Jan. 15, 1947; s. Lajos and Zsuzsanna (D.Szabó) K.; m. Emilia Kultsár, July 16, 1970; children: Zombor, Botond. PhD, Eotvos Lorand U., Budapest, Hungary, 1974; Candidate in biol. sci., Hungary Acad. Sci., Budapest, Hungary, 1983. Asst. Eotvos Lorand U., Budapest, 1970-76, first asst., 1976-84, asst. prof., 1984—. Contbr. articles to profl. jours. Hungarian Scholarship Council scholar, 1979; scholar Norwegian Cancer Soc., 1980, 88. Mem. Hungarian Biol. Soc. Tissue Culture, Cell Biology Group (sec. 1987—), European Cell Biology Orgn., European Tissue Culture Soc., Assn. Hungarian Biochemists, Hungarian Electron Microscopy Group. Home: Allende park 1II7, H-1119 Budapest Hungary Office: Eotvos Lorand Univ, Puskin u3, H-1088 Budapest Hungary Mailing Address: Noreveien 7, Oslo 3 Norway

KOVACS, DENES, violinist; b. Hungary, Apr. 18, 1930; s. Jozsef and Margit (Juhasz) K.; m. Adrienne Izsof, 1955; 1 son, 1 dau. Ed. Budapest Acad. Music. 1st violinist Budapest State Opera, 1951-60; leading violin prof. Budapest Music Acad., 1957—, dir., 1967—; rector Ferenc Liszt Acad. Music, 1971-81, dean string dept., 1981—; concert tours in Europe, U.S., USSR, Iran, India, China and Japan. Named Eminent Artist, 1970; recipient Kossuth prize, 1963; Gold medal of Labor, 1974. Home: Iramja utca 12, Budapest V Hungary *

KOVACS, GAIL LOUISE PATEK, hospital administrator, nurse, biologist; b. Cleve., Feb. 17, 1949; d. Louis Cornelius and Veronica Rose (Skerl) Patek; m. John Joseph Kovacs, June 24, 1972 (div.); 1 child, Jeffrey Joseph. BA in Biology cum laude, Ursuline Coll., 1971; RN, Cleve. Met. Sch. Nursing, 1975; MBA magna cum laude, Cleve. State U., 1982. Med. technologist Cleve. Clinic Found., 1971-72; immunology research asst. Case Western Res. U., Cleve., 1972-73; staff nurse Mt. Sinai Hosp., Cleve., 1975-76; staff nurse Cleve. Met. Gen. Hosp., 1976, infectious disease nurse, 1976-78; assoc. dir. supply services Univ. Hosps of Cleve., 1978-79, asst. dir. material mgmt., 1979, administrv. assoc., 1979-80, assoc. dir. material mgmt., 1980-84, asst. gen. mgr. adminstrn., 1984-87; dir. ops. Meridia Health Ventures, Inc., 1988—; lectr. mgmt., epidemiology and material mgmt. Mem. research bd. advisors Am. Biog. Inst. Recipient Paul Widman Meml. award Ctr. Health Affairs/Greater Cleve. Hosp. Assn., 1985; Cleve. Found. grantee, 1980-81. Mem. Am. Coll. Health Care Execs., Health Care Adminstrs. Assn. N.E. Ohio, Healthcare Fin. Assn., Transplantation Soc. of N.E. Ohio, Health Care Fin. Mgmt. Soc., Health Care Material Mgmt. Soc. (v.p.; Presdl. citation 1985), Internat. Material Mgmt. Soc., Soc. for Hosp. Purchasing and Material Mgmt., N.E. Ohio Soc. for Health Care Material Mgmt., Health Action Council, Beta Gamma Sigma. Roman Catholic. Home: 1450 Blossom Park Ave Lakewood OH 44107 Office: Meridia Health Ventures Inc 6700 Beta Dr Mayfield Village OH 44143

KOVALEV, MIKHAIL VASIL'EVICH, Soviet government official. Dep. minister constrn. Belorussian Soviet Socialist Republic, USSR, 1966-67, dep. min. ind. engring., 1967-68; chair Minsk City Exec. Com. People's Deps., USSR, 1968-78; mem. Cen. Com. Belorussian Communist Party, 1971—; dep. chair Council Ministers, Belorussian Soviet Socialist Republic, 1978-86, chmn., 1986—. Office: Council of Ministers, Minsk Belarussian SSR, USSR *

KOVALEVSKY, JEAN, astronomer; b. Neuilly sur Seine France, May 18, 1929; s. Jean and Hé lène (Pavloff) K.; Licence ès Sci., Ecole Normale Supérieure, Paris, 1952, Agrégation de Mathématiques, 1954, Dr.S., 1959; m. Jeannine Reige, May 18, 1956; children—Jean-Paul, Madeleine, Pierre. Research asst. Paris Obs., 1955-60, Yale U. Obs., 1957-58; chief research and computing service Bur. des Longitures, Paris, 1960-71; dir. Groupe de Recherches de Géodésie Spatiale, Paris, then Grasse, France, 1971-79; dir. Centre d'Etudes et de Recherches Géodynamiques et Astronomiques, Grasse, 1974-82; lectr. Paris U., 1960-73. Served with French Navy, 1952-53, 56. Decorated officer Ordre Nat. du Merite. Mem. Internat. Acad. Astronautics, French Acad. Scis., Internat. Astron. Union, Internat. Com. Space Research (chmn. working group 1965-74), Internat. Assn. Geodesy, Société Astronomique de France (pres. 1970-73), French Nat. Com. Astronomy (chmn. 1973-76). Author: Introduction to Celestial Mechanics, 1967; (with J.J. Levallois) Traité de Géodesie, 1970; editor: L'Astronomie, 1964-70; contbr. articles to profl. jours. Home: La Padovane 8 Rue Saint Michel, 06130 Grasse France Office: Cerga Ave Copernic, 06130 Grasse France

KOVALEVSKY, LEONID, structural engineer, educator; b. Kiev, Russia, Apr. 16, 1916; s. George Paul and Sophia (Doroginski) K.; C.E. in Structural Engring., U. Belgrad (Yugoslavia), 1935-42; Dr.-Ing. in Structural Engring., Technische Hochschule, Munich, Germany, 1950; m. Danica Kosutich, Nov. 6, 1952 (dec. 1976). Came to U.S., 1950, naturalized, 1955. Design engr., Germany, 1942-50, Corbett & Tinghir, Inc., N.Y.C., 1950-53; sr. engr. Erdman & Hosley, Syracuse, N.Y., 1953-56, Daniel, Man, Johnson & Mendenhall & Assos., Los Angeles, 1958-60; structures research specialist space and info. div. Space div. Rockwell Internat. (co. formerly N.Am. Rockwell) Downey, Calif., 1957-58, 61-71, mem. tech. staff B1 div., Los Angeles, 1971-81, N.Am. Aircraft div., 1971-81, now ret.; prof. World Open U. Mem. ASCE. Nat. Mgmt. Assn., Author: (with others) Shel! Analysis Manual, 1966, Analysis of Webs of Partial-Tension-Field Beams Subjected to Lateral Pressure Loadings, 1966; Structural Analysis of Shells, 1972, 2d edit., 1981; contbr. articles on stability, inflatable structures, statistics to tech. publs. Home: 1024 Via Nogales Palos Verdes Estates CA 90274

KOVALIK, OLIVER PETER, physician, psychologist; b. Sabinov, Czechoslovakia, July 12, 1947; came to West Germany, 1979; s. Jan and Helena (Pridavok) K. M.D., Safarik U., Kosice, Czechoslovakia, 1971; PhD in Psychology, Charles U., Prague, Czechoslovakia, 1979. Intern, Derer Gen. Hosp., Bratislava, Czechoslovakia, 1971-72; resident in psychiatry Sch. Medicine, Charles U., Prague, 1973-77; research psychiatrist nervous system research group Inst. Hygiene and Epidemiology, Prague, 1973-79; resident in psychiatry, neurology and psychotherapy Alexian Bros. Hosp. Psychotherapy, Aachen, West Germany, 1980-84, assoc. med. dir., 1984—. Roman Catholic. Avocations: beaux-arts; antiques; music; photography; literature; philosophy. Home: PO Box 970, D-5100 Aachen Federal Republic of Germany Office: Alexianer Krankenhaus, Alexianergraben 33, Postfach 28, D-5100 Aachen Federal Republic of Germany

KOVÁSZNAI, VIKTÓRIA LUKÁCS, art historian, museologist, researcher; b. Budapest, Hungary, Apr. 16, 1942; d. József Kovásznai and Etel Zakar; m. Lajos Lukács, Feb. 4, 1961; 1 child, András. PhD, Eötvös Loránd U., Budapest, 1978. Art historian Hungarian Nat. Gallery, Budapest, 1967—, dir. medal cabinet, 1981. Author: (books) Art at the Turn of the Century, 1979, Czinder, 1980, The Medallic Art of József Reményi, 1980; organizer: (exhbn.) Miklós Borsos, 1976 (quality prize 1976). Recipient Award for Culture Minister of Culture, Budapest, 1986. Fellow Fedn. Internat. de la Medaille; mem. Hungarian Numismatic Soc. (sec. medal sect. 1972). Office: Hungarian Nat Gallery, Pf 31, H-1250 Budapest Hungary

KOVATCH, JAK GENE, artist; b. Los Angeles, Jan. 17, 1929; s. Jack and La Vinia Blanche (Abernathy) K.; m. Carol Jean Wilhelm, Dec. 24, 1967; 1 son by previous marriage, Jason. Student, UCLA, 1946, Chouinard Art Inst., 1947-49, Calif. Sch. Art, Los Angeles, 1949-50, U. So. Calif., 1951, Los Angeles City Coll., 1955-56, Art Students League, N.Y.C., 1972, 75. Student asst. Lynton Kistler Studio, Los Angeles, 1952-53; mem. staff animation dept. Walt Disney Prodns., Inc., Burbank, Calif., 1953; instr. drawing and anatomy Famous Artists Schs., Westport, Conn., 1957-59; tchr. Roger Ludlowe High Sch., Fairfield, Conn., 1959-60; extension instr. N.Y.C. Coll., 1959-60; instr. sculpture Fairfield U., 1967; mem. faculty U. Bridgeport, Conn., 1962—, assoc. prof. dept. design, 1978-88, prof. design, 1988—; fellow Mellon Found.; Vis. Faculty Program Yale U., 1979-80, 81, 82-83; guest lectr. anatomy and figure drawing, 1953—. Stage designer for, Benjamin Zemach, Los Angeles, 1953-54, freelance illustrator, N.Y.C., 1957-58; more than 400 group exhbns., 1949—, latest being, Berkeley Center, Yale U., 1978, Nat. Acad. Galleries, N.Y.C., 1977, 78, 79, Yale U., 1979, De Cordova Mus., Mass., 1978, Am. Acad. and Inst. Arts and Letters, N.Y.C., 1980, Duxbury (Mass.) Complex Mus., 1980, 81, 83, Nat. Arts Club, N.Y.C., 1980-87; rep. permanent collections, Fogg Mus. Art, Cambridge, Mass., Library of Congress, Joseph Hirshhorn Collection, Greenwich, Conn., Fairfield Art Collection, John Slade Ely House Collections, New Haven, Bicentennial Art Collection, Westport (Conn.) Town Hall, Albert Dorne Collection, N.Y.C., also numerous pvt. collections; artist project grant from Conn. Commn. on Arts, Hartford, 1984-85. Mem. selection com. State of Conn. Commn. on Arts, Percent for Art Program, Hartford, 1987-88. Recipient award Boston Mus. Fine Arts, 1954, award Wadsworth Atheneum, Hartford, Conn., 1958, 79; recipient award Mus. Art, Sci. and Industry, Bridgeport, 1962, 63, 65, 66, 75, 77, 79, 81-84, awards Fairfield (Conn.) U. (14) 1973-87, award New Haven Paint and Clay Club, 1976, 78, 81; 100 others. Mem. Boston Printmakers, Artists Equity Assn., Audubon Artists, Conn. Acad. Fine Arts, Greenwich Art Soc., Hudson River Contemporary Artists, Los Angeles Printmaking Soc., Phila. Print Club, Silvermine Guild Artists (trustee 1979-83), Westport-Weston Arts Council. Home: 34 Sasco Creek Rd Westport CT 06880 Office: U Bridgeport Bridgeport CT 06602

KOVATSIS, ANASTASSIOS VASSILIOU, toxicologist, educator; b. Kastoria, Greece, Jan. 12, 1932; s. Vassilios Anastassiou and Kalliopi Panteli (Tsamissi) K.; BS, U. Athens, 1955, MS, 1957; PhD, U. Thessaloniki (Greece), 1968, BM, 1968, MD, 1969; m. Vassilia Paraskeyi Kotsaki, June 16, 1972; 1 dau., Leda-Kalliopi. Supr. biochem. dept. Sanatorium Hosp., Thessaloniki, 1959-60, Maternity Hosp., Thessaloniki, 1960-73; chief asst. dept. legal medicine and toxicology U. Thessaloniki, 1965-77, asst. prof., 1977-78, asso. prof. toxicology, 1978-81, prof., head chair biochemistry and toxicology, 1981—; vis. prof. Coll. Agr. and Vet. Medicine Nihon U., Tokyo, 1980; instr. toxicology U. Gent (Belgium), 1968-69; organizer, gen. sec. Internat. Toxicology Congress, 1980; ofcl. expert on forensic toxicology Ct. of Thessaloniki, 1968—; lectr. U. Kozani, Greece, 1980—. Served with Greek Army, 1957-58. Recipient Silver medal Pharm. Faculty of U. Gent, 1977; Ministry of No. Greece grantee, 1972-73. Mem. Am. Acad. Forensic Sci., Internat. Assn. Forensic Toxicologists, others. Conservative Party. Greek Orthodox. Author: Introduction to Pharmacodynamic and Toxicology, 1974; Pharmacodynamic and Toxicology, vols. I and II, 1973; contbg. author: Analytical Methods in Human Toxicology, 1985. Contbr. numerous articles to profl. jours. Home: 17 Alex Michailidou, Thessaloniki Greece Office: Univ of Thessaloniki, Thessaloniki Greece

KOVELESKI, KATHRYN DELANE, retired educator; b. Detroit, Aug. 12, 1925; d. Edward Albert Vogt and Delane (Bender) Vogt; BA, Olivet (Mich.) Coll., 1947; MA, Wayne State U., Detroit, 1955; m. Casper Koveleski, July 18, 1952; children: Martha, Ann. Tchr. schs. in Mich., 1947-88; tchr. Garden City Schs., 1955-56, 59-88, resource and learning disabilities tchr., 1970-88, ret. 1988. Mem. NEA, Mich. Edn. Assn., Garden City Edn. Assn., Bus. and Profl. Women (pres. Garden City 1982-83, Woman of Yr. 1983-84). Congregationalist. Clubs: Wayne Lit. (past pres.), Sch. Masters Bowling League (v.p. 1984-88), Odd Couples Bowling League (pres. 82-83). Office: 33411 Marquette St Garden City MI 48135

KOWALCZYK, MACIEJ STANISLAW, gynecologist, obstetrician; b. Kraków, Poland, June 8, 1956; s. Bogumil Wieslaw and Teresa Maria (Matowska) K. Degree, Med. Acad., Kraków, 1984; MD, Polish Acad. Sci., Kraków, 1984; postgrad., Inst. Gyn.-Ob, 1988—. Intern Narutowicz Hosp., Kraków, 1984-85; gen. practice medicine Ambulatory First Aid Service, Kraków, 1985—; asst. in ob-gyn Szpital Pokozniczy, Kraków, 1986—, Maternity Amb. for Sch. Tchrs., Kraków, 1987; tchr. Cathedral Normal Anatomy, Med. Acad., Kraków, 1984-86. Mem. commn. Soc. Ins. Inst., Kraków, 1986—. Mem. Polish Gynecol. Soc., Vol. Life Saver's Assn., Soc. Ins. Inst. (commn. 1986—). Roman Catholic. Home: Odrowaža 22/7, Kraków 30009, Poland Office: Szpital Pokožniczy, Siemiradzkiego 1, Kraków 31137, Poland

KOWALCZYK, WOJCIECH JERZY, heavy industry executive; b. Gdansk, Poland, Nov. 25, 1951; s. Jerzy Stefan and Ewa (Trent) K.; m. Malgorzata Teresa Ladynska, Sept. 11, 1976; children—Natalia, Marta. M.S., U. Gdansk, 1976, postgrad., 1979-81; postgrad. Acad. Arts, Gdansk, 1971-74. Dept. export mgr. Zamech, Elblag, Poland, 1977-79; chief info. dept. voivodship com. Polish United Workers Party, Elblag, 1979-81, sec. economy town com., 1982-83; dep. mgr. dir. Mech. Works Zamech, Elblag, 1983—. Editor-in-chief Zamech Mag., 1983—. Contbr. articles to profl. publs. Served with Polish Armed Forces, 1960—. Mem. Polish Assn. for Tourism and Sightseeing (chmn. 1985), Polish Econ. Assn. Altaist. Avocations: music; painting. Home: Boh Monte Casino 1, 82-300 Elblag Poland Office: Mech Works Zamech, Stoczniowa 2, 82-300 Elblag Poland

KOWALEWSKI, ADAM TADEUSZ, architect; b. Wolomin, Poland, Dec. 12, 1940; s. Czeslaw Tomasz and Zofia (Lipinska) K.; m. Malgorzata Anna Zacharzewska, Dec. 8, 1963; 1 son, Michal. M.Arch., Warsaw Tech. U., 1963. Supervising engr. Warsaw Builder Consortium, 1964-66; designer Palle Suenson Study, Copenhagen, 1967-68; team leader Communal Design Office, Warsaw, 1968-72; executing dir. Warsaw Planning Office, 1973-81, chief planner Warsaw Met. Area, 1972-81; UN expert, architect UNCHS (HABITAT) Nairobi, posted in Tripoli, Libya, 1981-85; scientist Polish Acad. Scis., 1986—. Recipient prizes archtl. competitions. Mem. Assn. Polish Architects (v.p. 1978-81), Town Planners Soc. Poland, Internat. Commn. Archtl. Critics (dir. assoc. 1981—), Salzburg Congress on Urban Planning and Devel. Author: Warsaw-Problems of Development, 1981; contbr. chpts. to books, articles to jours. Home: Londyska 15 m 1, 03-921 Warsaw Poland

KOWALSKI, JOHN CHARLES, data processing executive; b. Phila., Sept. 6, 1954; s. John Frank and Mary Ella (Louden) K.; m. Rosemary Rupp, Nov. 2, 1979; 1 child, John Charles. BS, Wharton Bus. Sch., U. Pa., 1980; cert. in cost acctg. Temple U., 1980. Police officer City of Phila., 1974-76; officer mgr., acct. Cen. Safety Equipment Co., Burlington, N.J., 1976-79; data processing mgr. 7-Up Bottling Co., Conshocken, Pa., 1979; asst. controller CSS Internat. Corp., Phila., 1979-80; ptnr. J.D. Assocs., tax, mgmt. and computer cons.; data processing cons. Delphi System Assocs. Inc., 1980-81; data processing mgr. Inolex Chems., Phila., 1981-83, Delphi Systems Assocs. Inc., 1983-86; data processing mgr. LaFrance Corp., Phila., 1987—. Recipient merit commendation Phila. Police Force, 1975. Mem. Assn. Computer and Info. Scis., Data Processing Mgmt. Assn. Democrat. Roman Catholic. Club: Pa. Yacht. Home: 813 Meadowview Ln Mont Clare PA 19453 Office: LaFrance Corp 8425 Executive Ave Philadelphia PA 19153

KOWALSKI, NEAL ANTHONY, transportation executive; b. Cleve., Nov. 30, 1945; s. John Michael and Sally Therese (Maceijewski) K. BA, Cleve. State U., 1971. V.p. Century Lines Inc., Cleve., 1973-88, chief exec. officer, 1988—; v.p. Kealy Trucking Co., Cleve., 1985—, Century Transp. Inc., Cleve., 1986—; pres. Cenjan Inc., Cleve., 1986—. Mem. Cleve. Trucking Assn. Roman Catholic. Club: Traffic (Cleve.). Home: 6924 Ottawa Rd Cleveland OH 44105 Office: Century Lines Inc 3725 Lakeside Ave Cleveland OH 44114

KOWARSKI, ALLEN AVINOAM, endocrinologist; b. Tel Aviv, Dec. 30, 1927; s. Hanoch and Sima (Tkazh) K.; m. Hanna Rose Zas, Mar. 24, 1950; children: David, Ruth. Student, Hebrew U., Jerusalem, 1946-47, MD, 1955; student, U. Lausanne (Switzerland) Med. Sch., 1949-52. Academic physician Hebrew U., 1955-62; instr., fellow Johns Hopkins U., Balt., 1962-68, asst. prof., 1968-72, assoc. prof., 1972—; prof. U. Md., Balt., 1981—. Patentee in field; conbr. over 130 articles to profl. jours.; inventor: the Nonthrombogenic Blood Withdrawal System, the Nonthrombogenic Glucose Monitor. Recipient Hormones in Growth grant NIH, 1979-84, Naturiuretic Hormone grant, NIH, 1983-85, Diabetes grant, NIH, 1985—, Linogliride grant McNeil Pharm., 1984-86, Growth Hormone grant Dupont Critical Care, 1985—. Mem. Am. Pediatric Soc., Soc. Pediatric Research, Lawson-Wilkins Pediatric Endocrine Soc., The Endocrine Soc., Am. Fedn. Clin. Research, Am. Diabetes Assn. (diabetes research award 1983). Office: Univ of Md Sch of Medicine 655 W Baltimore St BRB10-047 Baltimore MD 21201

KOWZAN, TADEUSZ, educator, researcher; b. Wilno, Poland, Nov. 9, 1922; came to France, 1972.; s. Ludwik and Aniela (Zukowska) K.; m. Halina Wolman, May 6, 1950; 1 child, Aniela. PhD, U. Warsaw, 1964, habilitation, 1969. Journalist, theatre critic Poland and France, 1945—; asst. prof. Polish Acad., Warsaw and Paris, 1961-68; assoc. prof. Inst. Arts, Warsaw, 1968-72, U. Lyon II, France, 1972-75; prof. U. Caen, France, 1975—; dir. dept. French and Comparative Lit., 1977-78, 82-83. Author: Jules Renard et son theatre, 1966, Litterature et spectacle, 1970 (Polish Acad. prize 1971), 2nd edit. 1975, Le theatre francais en Pologne, 1972; editor: Analyse semiologique du spectacle theatral, 1976; contbr. articles to profl. jours. French Govt. award, Paris, 1962; Fulbright award, 1987. Mem. Internat. Assn. Semiotics of Performing Arts (dir. counsel 1984—), Internat. Comparative Lit. Assn., Assn. Internationale des Etudes Francaises, Societe d'Histoire du Theatre. Roman Catholic. Home: 2 rue Ledoux, 14000 Caen France Office: U Caen, 14032 Caen, Cedex France

KOYAMA, HIROMI MARIA, bank executive; b. Hyogo ken, Japan, Mar. 21, 1937; d. Hajime and Miiko (Yamamoto) Ichikawa; m. Terutake Koyama Ichikawa, June 26, 1966; children: Akira, Kohei. BA, U. Sacred Heart, Tokyo, 1960. Cert. high sch. English tchr. Asst. to adminstr. Permanent Mission to UN, N.Y.C., 1960-63; tchr. Mrs. Hajime Yasuda English Sch., Tokyo, 1964-67; advisor Banque Internat. a Lusembourg SA, Tokyo, 1986—; auditor Internat. Asset Mgmt. Japan KK, Tokyo, 1988—; part-time advisor English lang. Mitsubishi Paper Co. Ltd., Tokyo, 1965-67. Coordinator, mem. scholarship com. Coll. Women's Assn. Japan, Tokyo, 1980-85. Roman Catholic. Clubs: CWAJ, Nadeshiko Kai (Tokyo). Home: 5-29-8-509 Yoyogi Shibuya, 100 Tokyo Japan Office: Banque Internat a Luxembourg SA, Fukoku Bldg 2-2-2 Uchisaiwai cho, 100 Tokyo Japan

KOYANO, KEIICHIROU, gas company executive; b. Tokyo, Jan. 21, 1953; s. Takaji and Michiyo (Shimizu) K. Student, Nihon U., Tokyo, 1973-77. V.p. Fuji Tubame Co. Ltd., Shizuoka, Japan, 1983—. Home: Ryogaecho 1-4-1, Shizuoka Japan Office: Tubame Co Ltd, Gofukucho 1-4-5, Shizuoka Japan

KOZAK, JOHN W., lawyer; b. Chgo., July 25, 1943; s. Walter and Stella (Palka) K.; m. Elizabeth Mathias, Feb. 3, 1968; children—Jennifer, Mary Margaret, Susanne. BSEE, U. Notre Dame, 1965; JD, Georgetown U., 1968. Bar: Ill. 1968, D.C. 1968. Patent advisor Office of Naval Research, Corona, Calif., 1968-69; assoc. Leydig, Voit & Mayer, Ltd. (and predecessor firms), Chgo., 1969-74, ptnr., 1974—, chmn. mgmt. com., 1982—. Mem. ABA, Am. Intellectual Property Assn., Licensing Execs. Soc., Chgo. Patent Law Assn. Republican. Roman Catholic. Clubs: Law (Chgo.); Meadow (Rolling Meadows, Ill.); Lake Forest Bath and Tennis, Winter (Lake Forest, Ill.). Office: Leydig Voit & Mayer One IBM Plaza Chicago IL 60611

KOZHUHAROV, CHRISTOPHOR, physicist; b. Plovdiv, Bulgaria, Jan. 7, 1946; arrived in Fed. Republic Germany, 1970.; s. Vassil and Nadejda (Aceva) Kojouharov; m. Molly Sue Affleck, Aug. 5, 1983. Mgr inz., Politechnika Slaska, Gliwice, Poland, 1969; Dr. rer. nat., Technische U., Munich, 1974. With Technische Univestität, Munich, 1974-78, GSI, Darmstadt, Fed. Republic Germany, 1979—. Home: Kohlweg 19, 6101 Messel Federal Republic of Germany Office: GSI, Planckstr, 6100 Darmstadt Federal Republic of Germany

KOZINA, THOMAS JOSEPH, gynecologist, obstetrician, educator; b. Milw., June 25, 1930; s. Frank Joseph and Arlene Emily (Skochpol) K.; m. Donna Adamkiewicz; 1 child, Joan Worachek. BS, Marquette U., 1952, MD, 1957. Diplomate Am. Bd. Ob-Gyn. Intern St. Mary's Hosp., Milw., 1957-58, resident in ob-gyn, 1958-60; resident in ob-gyn Mt. Sinai Hosp., Milw., 1960-61; practice medicine specializing in ob-gyn Milw., 1961-78; dir. resident edn. St. Francis Hosp., Milw., 1976-78; assoc. prof. Med. Coll. Wis., Milw., 1978—; chmn. dept. ob-gyn St. Francis Hosp., 1970-78; dir. ob-gyn edn. in family practice Med. Coll. Wis., 1979—. Contbr. articles to profl. jours. Bd. dirs. St. Francis Hosp., 1981-83, Franklin (Wis.) State Bank, 1982—, Mchts. & Mfrs. Bank Holding, Milw., 1984—, Samaitan Health Plan, 1987—. Fellow Am. Coll. Ob-Gyn; mem. AMA, Am. Assn. Gynecol. Laparoscopists, Soc. Tchrs. Family Practice, Milw. Gynecol. Soc., St. Francis/Trinity/St. Luke's Ind. Physician's Assn., Inc. (pres. 1987—), Am. Shetland Sheepdog Assn. (nat. show chairperson 1981-84), St. Francis Ind. Physician Assn. (pres. 1988—). Clubs: Combined Splty. Greater Milw. (pres. 1972-80). Home: 8432 W Ryan Rd Franklin WI 53132 Office: Med Coll Wis 3535 W Oklahoma Ave Milwaukee WI 53215

KOZLOVSKY, YEVGENIY ALEKSANDROVICH, engineer, Soviet government official; b. 1929. Grad. Moscow Geology Inst., 1953; Dr. Tech. Sci., 1973. Chief engr. and head of expdn. in Amur Oblast and Khabarovsk Ter., 1953-65; head of adminstrn. USSR Ministry Geology, 1965-73, dir. sci. research instn., 1973-74; dep. minister of geology USSR, 1974-75, minister geology, 1975—; candidate mem. Central Com. Communist Party Soviet Union, 1976—; dep. to USSR Supreme Soviet, 1979—. Served with Soviet Army, 1945-48. Decorated Order Lenin, Lenin prize, others. Address: USSR Ministry of Geology, Moscow USSR *

KOZLOWSKI, L. DENNIS, manufacturing company executive; b. Irvington, N.J., Nov. 16, 1946; s. Leo Kelly and Agnes (Kozell) K.; B.S., Seton Hall U., 1968; M.B.A., Rivier Coll., 1976; m. Angie Suarez, Mar. 13, 1971; children—Cheryl Marie, Sandra Lisa. V.p. fin. Grinnell Fire Protection Systems div., Providence, 1976-81; v.p., chief fin. officer Ludlow Corp., subs. Tyco Labs., Needham, Mass., 1981-82, pres., chief exec. officer, Grinnell Corp., 1982—; bd. dirs. Whitman and Howard Cons. Engrs., Tyco Labs., Inc., Atlantic Bank and Trust Co.; Better Bus. Bur. of R.I. (chmn., dir.). Home: Runnymede Dr North Hampton NH 03862 Office: Grinnell Corp 3 Tyco Park Exeter NH 03833

KPODO-TAY, DANIEL SYDNEY, architect; b. Anyako, Volta Region Ghana, Oct. 29, 1934; s. Winfred Elliot and Celestina Masa (Adovor) Kpodo-T.; M.S., U. Sci. and Tech., Kumasi, Ghana, 1959-65; m. Charity Mawugbor Doe, Sept. 19, 1959; children—Doris, Divine, Caroline, Celestina. Architect, Ghana Archtl. & Engring. Co., Accra, Ghana, 1965-66; architect-dir. Design & Investigations Co., Accra, 1967; prin. architect Associated Cons., Accra, 1968-77; prin. architect, mng. dir. D.S. Kpodo-Tay & Partners, Accra, Ghana, 1978—. Pres., Old Mawuli Students Union, Ho, Ghana, 1963-75; sr. presbyter Epiphany Presbyterian Ch., Accra, 1978-82. Fellow Ghana Inst. Architects (pres. 1979-80); mem. Inst. Practising Designers (asso.). Clubs: Ghana, Accra Lawn Tennis, Odd Fellows, Masons, Order Foresters. Archtl. designer: Kaneshie Market, Accra, 1972, Mgmt., Devel. and Productivity

Inst., Accra, 1974, Ho Catering Rest House Complex, 1978, Sci. Museum, Accra, 1976, Cocoa Research Inst. Library, Tafo, Ghana, 1975. Home: PO Box 500 8 Fish Close, Teshie-Nungua Estate, Teshie-Nungua, Accra Ghana Office: 45 Labadi Rd, Accra Ghana

KRA, PAULINE SKORNICKI, French educator; b. Lodz, Poland, July 30, 1934; came to U.S., 1950, naturalized, 1955; d. Edward and Nathalie Skornicki; student Radcliffe Coll., 1951-53; B.A., Barnard Coll., 1955; M.A., Columbia U., 1963, Ph.D., 1968; m. Leo Dietrich Kra, Mar. 10, 1955; children—David Theodore, Andrew Jason. Lectr., Queens Coll., City U. N.Y., 1964-65; asst. prof. French, Yeshiva U., N.Y.C., 1968-74, assoc. prof. French, 1974-82, prof., 1982—. Mem. MLA, Am. Assn. Tchrs. French, Am. Soc. 18th Century Studies, Sociètè française d'étude du XVIII siècle, Assn. for Computers and Humanities, Assn. for Literary and Linguistic Computing, Phi Beta Kappa. Author: Religion in Montesquieu's Lettres persanes, 1970; contbr. articles to profl. jours. Home: 109-14 Ascan Ave Forest Hills NY 11375 Office: 500 W 185 St New York NY 10033

KRABBE, ERIK CHRISTIAAN WILLEM, philosopher, educator; b. The Hague, Netherlands, Feb. 16, 1943; s. Dirk Alexander and Anna Elizabeth (Lely) K.; m. Martine Johanna Andrea Vooijs, June 14, 1976; 1 child, Maartje Jacqueline Mathilde. Dr Sci in Philosophy, U. Amsterdam, 1972; PhD in Philosophy, State U. Groningen, Netherlands, 1982. Asst. Inst. Voor Grondslagenonderzoek, U. Amsterdam, Netherlands, 1967-71; asst. dept. philosophy State U. Utrecht, Netherlands, 1971-72; tchr. philos. logic State U. Utrecht, 1972-88, State U. Groningen, Netherlands, 1988—. Author (with E.M. Barth): From Axiom to Dialogue, 1982; contbr. articles to profl. jours. Fellow Netherlands Inst. Advanced Study in Humanities and Social Scis., Wassenaar, 1987-88. Mem. Dutch Research Group on Theory of Argumentation, Internat. Soc. for Study of Argumentaion. Office: State U Groningen, NL 9718 CA Westersingel The Netherlands

KRACH, MITCHELL PETER, fin. exec.; b. Westfield, Mass., Nov. 2, 1924; s. John Joseph and Sophie Mary (Swiatlowski) K.; cert. Mass. Extension U., 1944, Harvard U. Grad. Sch. Bus. Admnstrn., 1966; m. Theresa Florence Sanczuk, May 29, 1957; children—Susan, Gregory, Mitchell, Jonathan, Matthew. Auditor, H.F. Lynch Lumber Co., West Springfield, Mass., 1946-51, dir., 1951-79, sec. bd. dirs., 1951-79, mgr. purchasing, 1951-61, central mgr. purchasing, 1961-71, v.p. purchasing, 1971-76, v.p. purchasing and fin., 1976-79, treas. bd. dirs. 1976-79; treas., chmn. bd. dirs. Nat. Res. Corp., Longmeadow, Mass., 1957—; legal arbitrator bldg. materials. Exec. mem., vice-chmn. bd. govs. Shriners Hosp. for Crippled Children, Springfield, 1980. Cert. purchasing mgr.; notary public; registered and bonded real estate broker, Mass. Mem. Nat. Fedn. Ind. Bus. (nat. adv. council 1978), Nat. Assn. Purchasing Mgmt. (dir. nat. affairs 1965, nat. lumber chmn. 1970-80), Am. Soc. Notaries, Purchasing Mgmt. Assn. W. New Eng. (pres. 1963-64), Purchasing Mgmt. Assn. Worcester, Mfrs. Agts. Nat. Assn. Democrat. Roman Catholic. Clubs: Valley Press, 100 of Mass., Am. Turners, Elks (chmn. bd. trustees), Melha Temple, Masons, Shriners, K.T. Contbr. numerous articles to profl. jours. Home: 33 Forest Glen Rd Longmeadow MA 01106 Office: 1105 Main St West Springfield MA 01089

KRACHT, MANFRED WILHELM, mathematics educator, researcher; b. Essen, Germany, Mar. 31, 1943; s. Wilhelm Alfred and Mathilde Johanna (Eckardt) K. Staatsexamen, U. Muenster, 1968; Dr. rer. nat., U. Duesseldorf, 1971, Habilitation, 1974. Asst. math. U. Duesseldorf, Fed. Republic Germany, 1968-71, dozent math., 1974-75, 76—; asst. lectr. math. and stats. U. Karlsruhe, Fed. Republic Germany, 1971-73; prof. applied math. U. Wuppertal, Fed. Republic Germany, 1975-76. Author: (joint with E. Kreyszig) Methods of Complex Analysis in Partial Differential Equations with Applications, 1988. Contbr. articles to profl. jours. Reviewer Math. Reviews, 1973—, Zentralblatt fuer Mathematik, 1973—. Mem. Deutsche Mathematiker-Vereinigung, Am. Math. Soc. Home: Bocholder Str 120, D-4300 Essen Federal Republic of Germany Office: Inst Math, Univ Duesseldorf, Universitaetsstr 1, D-4000 Duesseldorf Federal Republic of Germany

KRACKE, ROBERT RUSSELL, lawyer; b. Decatur, Ga., Feb. 27, 1938; s. Roy Rachford and Virginia Carolyn (Minter) K.; student Birmingham So. Coll.; B.A., Samford U., 1962; J.D., Cumberland Sch. Law, 1965; m. Barbara Anne Pilgrim, Dec. 18, 1965; children—Shannon Ruth, Robert Russell, Rebecca Anne, Susan Lynn. Bar: Ala. 1965, U.S. Tax Ct. 1971, U.S. Supreme Ct. 1971; individual practice law Birmingham, Ala., 1965—; ptnr. firm Kracke, Thompson & Ellis, 1980—. Mem. Jefferson County Dem. exec. com., 1972—; deacon Ind. Presbyn. Ch., Birmingham, 1973-76, pres. adult choir, 1968—, Housing Agy. Retarded Citizens; pres. Ala. chpt. Nat. Voluntary Health Agys.; trustee, Birmingham Opera Theater; bd. dirs. Jefferson County Assn. Retarded Citizens; bd. dirs., founding pres. Birmingham chpt. Juvenile Diabetes Found. Served with USNR, 1955-61. Mem. Birmingham (exec. com., chmn. law library, law day 1976), Ala., Am. (award merit law day 1976) bar assns., Am. Judicature Soc., Ala. Hist. Assn., Phi Alpha Delta (pres. chpt. 1964-65), Sigma Alpha Epsilon. Democrat. Clubs: Downtown, Relay House. Lodge: Rotary (pres. Shades Valley club; Paul Harris fellow). Editor, Birmingham Bar Bull., 1974—; bd. editors Ala. Lawyer, 1980-86; Contbr. articles to profl. publs. Home: 4410 Briarglen Dr Birmingham AL 35243 Office: Kracke Thompson & Ellis Lakeview Sch Bldg 808 29th St S Birmingham AL 35205

KRAEHE, MARY ALICE, librarian, educator; b. Mpls., Oct. 1, 1924; d. Laurence and Elizabeth (Folds) Eggleston; m. Enno Edward Kraehe, May 25, 1946; children—Laurence Adams, Claudia. B.A., U. Minn., 1945; M.S., U. Ky., 1963. Library asst. U. Ky. Library, Lexington, 1956-64; out-of-print librarian U. N.C., Chapel Hill, 1964-68; out-of-print librarian U. Va. Library, Charlottesville, 1970—, asst. prof., 1974—, African bibliographer, 1976—; book reviewer African Book Pub. Record, 1983—. Author: African Languages, a Guide to the Library Collection of the University of Virginia, rev. edit., 1986. Mem. Archives Libraries Com. (sec. exec. bd. 1981-85, vice chmn. 1986-87, chmn. 1987-88). African Studies Assn., ALA, Va. Library Assn., Southeastern Regional Seminar African Studies, LWV, Colonial Dames, Kappa Kappa Gamma, Beta Phi Mu. Club: Blue Ridge Swim (sec. 1977-83). Home: 130 Bennington Rd Charlottesville VA 22901 Office: U Va Library Collection Devel Dept Charlottesville VA 22903

KRAEMER, SANDY FREDERICK, lawyer; b. Chgo., May 10, 1937; s. Robert O. and Ruth B. (Young) K.; m. Dorothy L. Delabar, June 14, 1964; children—Christina L., Ericka L., Tyler D. B.S., Stanford U., 1960; J.D., Colo. U., 1963. Bar: Colo. 1963. Sole practice Denver, 1964; ptnr Asher & Kraemer, Colorado Springs, Colo., 1964-76; ptnr., pres. Kraemer, Kendall & Bowman, P.C., Colorado Springs, 1977—; dep. atty County of El Paso, Colo., 1976. Author: Solar Law, 1978, supplements, 1980—; contbr. articles to profl. jours.; inventor and patentee games and toys. Mem. bd. regents U. Colo., 1976—, chmn., 1982-83; mem. White House Conf. on Children and Youth, 1970. NSF grantee, 1975, German Marshall Fund grantee, 1979; named Colo. Conservationist of Yr., 1967. Mem. ABA, Colo. Bar Assn., El Paso Bar Assn., World Law Assn., World Peace Through Law (chmn. energy com. Madrid 1979, Berlin 1985). Republican. Lutheran. Home: 2402 Cenesa Ln Colorado Springs CO 80909 Office: Kraemer Kendall & Bowman PC 430 N Tejon St Colorado Springs CO 80903

KRAFT, AUDREY RONA, psychotherapist; b. N.Y.C., Sept. 11, 1949; arrived in The Netherlands, 1974; d. Seymour and Mildred (Krefetz) K. BA cum laude, Boston U., 1971; BA, U. Leiden, The Netherlands, 1976, PhD with honors, 1982. Researcher and clin. psychologist St. Hippolytus Gen. Hosp., Delft, The Netherlands, 1979-85; child and adult psychotherapist Regional Dept. Mental Health, Spijkenisse, The Netherlands, 1984-85; behavioral therapist Delta Psychiat. Hosp., Rotterdam, The Netherlands, 1985—; prof. psychology Webster U., Leiden, 1984—; pvt. practice psychology Amsterdam, The Netherlands, 1984—; postdoctoral researcher Erasmus Univ. Med. Faculty, Rotterdam, Nijmegen U. Psychology Faculty. Contbr. chpts. to book: Directive Therapy with Children and Adolescents, 1985; contbr. articles to psychol. jours. Profl. counselor ACCESS Community Counseling/Info. Service for English-Speaking Persons, The Hague, The Netherlands, 1987. Mem. Dutch Soc. Behavior Therapy, Internat. Soc. Hypnosis (organizer program for 1988 Congress, The Hague), Dutch Soc. Hypnosis, Women's Internat. Network Profls. Jewish. Home: Herengracht 50-C, 1015 BN Amsterdam The Netherlands Office: Delta Psychiat Hosp, Zuiderziekenhuis, Groene Hilledijk 315, 2311 EA Rotterdam The Netherlands

KRAFT, ELAINE JOY, community relations and communications official; b. Seattle, Sept. 1, 1951; d. Harry J. and Leatrice M. (Hanan) K.; m. Lee Somerstein, Aug. 2, 1980; children: Paul Kraft, Leslie Jo. BA, U. Wash., 1973; MPA, U. Puget Sound, 1979. Reporter Jour. Am. Newspaper, Bellevue, Wash., 1972-76; editor Jour./Enterprise Newspapers, Wash. State, 1976; U.S. senator from Wash., 1976-78; mem. staff Wash. Ho. of Reps., 1978-82, public info. officer, 1976-80, mem. leadership staff, asst. to caucus chmn., 1980—; ptnr., pres. Media Kraft Communications; mgr. corp. info., advt. and mktg. communications Weyerhaeuser Co., 1982-85; dir. communications Weyerhaeuser Paper Co., 1985-87; mgr. community relations N.W. region Adolph Coors Co. 1987—. Recipient state and nat. journalism design and advt. awards. Mem. Nat. Fedn. Press Women, Women in Communications, Wash. Press Assn. Home: 14329 SE 63d Bellevue WA 98006 Office: 301 116th Ave #380 Bellevue WA 98004

KRAFVE, ALLEN HORTON, management consultant; b. Superior, Wis., Jan. 26, 1937; s. Richard Ernest and Frances Virginia (Horton) K.; m. Lois Anne Reed, Aug. 15, 1959; children—Bruce Allen, Anne Marie, Carol Elizabeth. B.S. in Mech. Engring., U. Mich., 1958, M.B.A., 1960, M.S. in Mech. Engring., 1961. Asst. prof. mech. engring. San Jose State U. (Calif.), 1961-65; various positions including quality control mgr. Ford Motor Co., Dearborn, Mich., 1965-77; engring. mgr. Kysor/Cadillac, Cadillac, Mich., 1977-82; mgmt. cons., Lake City, Mich., 1982—; bd. dirs. NOC Industries, Cadillac; pres. Lark Homes, Inc., 1979—. Co-author: Reliability Considerations in Design, 1962, internat. conf. paper, 1961. Bd. dirs. Crooked Tree council Girl Scouts U.S.A., Traverse City, Mich., 1983. Mem. ASME, Soc. Automotive Engrs., Am. Soc. Quality Control, Am. Soc. Engring. Edn. Republican. Methodist. Home: 145 Duck Point Dr Lake City MI 49651 Office: Allen H Krafve Cons 2604 Sunnyside Dr Cadillac MI 49601

KRAHEL, THOMAS STEPHEN, account executive; b. Bklyn., Oct. 4, 1947; s. John Frank and Anna (Trusz) K.; m. Jill Susan Friedl, June 12, 1969; children: Bryan Thomas, Audrey Gerda, Leah Ann. PhB, Bklyn. Coll., 1970; MA in Banking and Mgmt. with honors, Adelphi U., 1980. Asst. treas. Chase Manhattan Bank, N.Y.C., 1970-82; sales mgr. Glossit Mfg., Northport, N.Y., 1982-84; mktg. rep. Executone of L.I., Hauppauge, N.Y., 1984-85; account exec. Fin. Mktg. Corp., N.Y.C., 1985-86; acct. exec. UARCO, Inc., N.Y., 1986—; Instr. Dale Carnegie Courses. Co-founder, treas. Tuscany Gardens Assn., Great Neck, N.Y., 1970-80; counselor L.I. Youth Guidance Program. Mem. Mensa, Delta Mu Delta. Republican. Presbyterian. Club: Couples (Greatneck) (pres. 1976-77). Home: 16 West St Northport NY 11768

KRAIPIPADH, PRUTHIGRAI, government official, educator; b. Bangkok, Thailand, Jan. 22, 1930; s. Luang Vidharn and Khaevilai (Tasanasawang) K.; m. Phaitoon Seniwonse, May 9, 1966; children: Pisitpol, Piyaradh. B of Commerce, New South Wales U., Sydney, Australia, 1964; M of Econs., Thammasat U., Bangkok, 1969; PhD, Pacific Western U., Los Angeles, 1979. Exec. sec. Borneo Co. Ltd., Bangkok, 1955-57; with Port Authority of Thailand, Bangkok, 1957—, port specialist, 1980—; part-time dir., lectr. Coll. Profl. Studies, Bangkok, 1975-88. Author: (booklet) Gateway to Thailand, 1969. Bd. dirs. Kraipipadh Inst. Tech., Bangkok. Recipient Port Mgmt. award Japanese Port Bur., 1970, Adminstrv. Staff award Australian Adminstrv. Staff Coll., 1980. Mem. Econs. Assn. Thailand, Brit. Soc. Commerce, Asean Port Authorities Assn. (com. mem.). Buddhist. Club: Royal Bangkok Sport. Home: 1 Soi Patanavej 3, 71 Sukhumvit, Bangkok Thailand Office: Port Authority of Thailand, Klongtoi, 10110 Bangkok Thailand

KRAIROJANANAN, SOMPOP, mathematics educator; b. Songkhla, Thailand, Apr. 1, 1938; s. Chukrai and Van (Kongsakul) K.; m. Suri Manirat, Aug. 9, 1964. BSc with honors in Math., Southampton U., Eng., 1961; MSc in Applied Math., Southampton U., 1963; PhD in Math. Edn., Mich. State U., 1973. Lic. tchr. vocat. and secondary sch., Thailand. Asst. lectr. math. Patumvan Coll. Edn., Bangkok, 1963-66; lectr. applied math. engring. Khonkaen U., Thailand, 1966-67; sr. lectr. math. Liberal Arts Faculty Thammasart U., Bangkok, 1967-70, 73-78; assoc. prof. math. Sci. Faculty Kasetsart U., Bangkok, 1978—; instr. math. and stats., bd. dirs. various secretarial colls. and night schs. for adult edn. Author: 16 math. textbooks; contbr. articles to profl. jours. Thai Govt. scholar, 1958-63; recipient 2d class honors for service in edn. Thailand, 1986. Fellow Royal Inst. for Advancement Sci., Arts and Jurisprudence (assoc.); mem. Am. Math. Soc., S.E. Asian Math. Soc., Math. Soc. Thailand (life), Fgn. Relations Club Kasetsart U. Buddhist. Home: 1129/149 Nakornchaisri Rd, 10300 Dusit Bangkok Thailand Office: Kasetsart U Dept Math, Paholyothin Rd, 10900 Bangkok Thailand

KRAJČOVIČ, RUDOLF, linguistics educator; b. Trakovice, Czechoslovakia, July 22, 1927; s. Rudolf and Mária (Michalová) K.; children: Dana, Peter. MA, Comenius U., Bratislava, Czechoslovakia, 1953, CSc, 1959, PhD, 1984. Asst. lectr. Comenius U., 1950-53, asst. prof., 1953-64, assoc. prof., 1964-86, prof., 1986—; lectr. State Lomonosov's U., Moscow, 1970-71, 75-76, 81—, Internat. Congress Slavists, Sofia 1963, Warsaw 1973, Kiev 1983, Internat. Congress Onomastic Scis., Cracow 1981. Author: Slovak and Other Slavic Languages, 1974, A Historical Phonology of the Slovak Language Heidelberg, 1975, History's Evidence Slovak, 1977, 1980 (Heidelberg Book of Yr. 1983), The Development of the Slovak Language and Dialectology, 1988; contbr. articles to profl. jours. Recipient Stur's award Mus., Modra, Czechoslovakia, 1986, Silver Medal award Comenius U., 1987. Mem. Assn. Slovak Linguists (dep. chmn. 1967-70), Czechoslovak Com. Onomastics, Slovak Com. Onomastics (bd. dirs.), Internat. Com. Slavic Onomastics, Internat. Com. Onomastic Scis., Soc. Linguistica Europae.

KRAKOW, AMY GINZIG, advertising agency executive; b. Bklyn., Feb. 25, 1950; d. Nathan and Iris (Minkowitz) Ginzig; m. Gary Scott Krakow, Nov. 7, 1976. B.A. in Speech and Theatre, Bklyn. Coll., 1971, postgrad. in TV prodn. Promotion mgr. Popular Mechanics, N.Y.C., 1976-77; N.Y. copy mgr. U.S. News and World Report, N.Y.C., 1977-80; promotion mgr.Sta. WINS-Radio, N.Y.C., 1980-82, creator, supervising exec. advt. campaign, , 1981-82; promotion dir. CBS Mags., N.Y.C., 1982-84, The Village Voice, N.Y.C., 1984-85, New York Woman (Am. Express Pub.), 1987—; cons. Silverman Collection, Santa Fe, 1985—; sem. leader Radcliffe Pub. Workshop, 1987; producer Festival of Street Entertainers, N.Y.C., 1984, 85, 87, 88, Albuquerque, 1986. Contbr. articles to consumer and trade mags. including New York, Family Circle, Working Woman, others; producer, artistic dir. Ann. Coney Island Tattoo Festival, 1986, 87, 88, The Psychedelic Festival, 1988. Bd. dirs. Sideshows by the Seashore, Coney Island, U.S.A., Bklyn., 1985—, Bond Street Theater Coalition, 1985—, City Lore, N.Y.C., 1987—. Recipient Addy award, 1985, BPA award, 1981. Creator, producer artistic dir. Annual Coney Island Tattoo Festival 1986, 87, 88, The Psychedelic Festival, 1988. Mem. Advt. Women N.Y., Delta Phi Epsilon (exec. bd. 1984-85). Home: 57 Warren St New York NY 10007 Office: NY Woman 1120 6th Ave New York NY 10036

KRALIK, DUSAN, sculptor; b. Bratislava, Czeckoslovakia, Apr. 20, 1941; s. Stefan and Emilia K.; m. Sona Novatna, Feb. 2, 1963; children: Jursj, Dusan, Barbora. Grad., Acad. Creative Art, Bratislava, 1967. Asst. prof. Comenius U., Trnava, Czeckoslovakia, 1968-74; sculptor Slovak Corp. Creative Arts, Bratislava, 1974—. Prin. works include sculpture in Banska Bysterica (award 1968), for Fed. Assembly, Prague (award 1972). Roman Catholic. Home: Drotarska 4, 811-04 Bratislava Czechoslovakia

KRALL, RONALD LEE, pharmaceutical clinical researcher, neuropharmacologist; b. Balt., June 24, 1947; s. Melvin and Vivian (Lowy) K.; m. Susan Jane Doerner, Nov. 22, 1975; children—Joshua Andrew, Benjamin Eric, Emily Richley. B.A., Swarthmore Coll., 1969; M.D., U. Pitts., 1973. Diplomate: Am. Bd. Neurology and Psychiatry. Intern Los Angeles County Harbor Gen. Hosp., 1973-74; staff assoc. Epilepsy br. NIH, Bethesda, Md., 1974-77; resident, fellow U. Rochester, N.Y., 1977-80, asst. prof., 1980-83; assoc. dir. clin. research Lorex Pharms., Skokie, Ill., 1983-84, dir. clin. research, 1984—; Recipient Commendation Medal USPHS, 1977. Mem. Epilepsy Found. Am. (profl. adv. bd., chairperson profl. adv. bd., bd. dirs. epilepsy services for No. Ill.), Am. Acad. Neurology, Am. Epilepsy Soc., Sleep Research Soc., Clin. Sleep Soc., Am. Soc. Clin. Pharmacology, Sigma Xi. Office: Lorex Pharms Box 163 4930 Oakton St Skokie IL 60077

KRAMER, BARRY ALAN, psychiatrist; b. Phila., Sept. 9, 1948; s. Morris and Harriet (Greenberg) K.; m. Paulie Hoffman, June 9, 1974; children—Daniel Mark, Steven Philip. B.A. in Chemistry, NYU, 1970; M.D., Hahnemann Med. Coll., 1974. Resident in psychiatry Montefiore Hosp. and Med. Ctr., Bronx, N.Y., 1974-77; practice medicine specializing in psychiatry, N.Y.C., 1977-82; staff psychiatrist L.I. Jewish-Hillside Med. Ctr., Glen Oaks, N.Y., 1977-82; asst. prof. SUNY, Stony Brook, 1978-82; practice medicine specializing in psychiatry, Los Angeles, 1982—; asst. prof. psychiatry U. So. Calif., 1982—; ward chief Los Angeles County/U. So. Calif. Med. Ctr., 1982—; mem. med. staff Brotman Hosp., Cedars Sinai Hosp.; cons. Little Neck Nursing Home (N.Y.), 1979-82, L.I. Nursing Home, 1980-82. Reviewer, Am. Jour. Psychiatry, Convulsive Therapy Jour., Hospital and Community Psychiatry; contbr. articles to profl. jours., papers to sci. meetings. NIMH grantee, 1979-80; fellow UCLA/U. So. Calif. Long-Term Gerontology Ctr., 1985-86. Mem. AMA, Am. Psychiat. Assn., AAAS, Internat. Soc. Chronobiology, Internat. Psychiat. Assn. for Advancement of Electrotherapy, Soc. Biol. Psychiatry, Calif. Med. Assn., Los Angeles Med. Assn., Am. Assn. Geriatric Psychiatry, Gerontol. Soc. Am. Jewish. Office: Los Angeles County/U So Calif Med Ctr 1934 Hospital Pl Los Angeles CA 90033 also: PO Box 2681 Beverly Hills CA 90213

KRAMER, EDWARD GEORGE, lawyer; b. Cleve., July 15, 1950; s. Archibald Charles and Katherine Faith (Porter) K.; m. Roberta Darwin, June 15, 1974. BS in Edn., Kent State U., 1972; JD, Case Western Res. U., 1975. Bar: Ohio 1975, U.S. Dist. Ct. (no. dist.) Ohio 1975, U.S. Ct. Appeals (6th cir.) 1980, U.S. Supreme Ct. 1980. Assoc. dir. The Cuyahoga Plan of Ohio, Cleve., 1975-76; exec. dir. The Housing Advs., Inc., Cleve., 1976—; sr. ptnr. Kramer & Tobocman, LPA, Cleve., 1981—; spl. counsel atty. gen. State of Ohio, Columbus, 1983—; pres. Lawyers Services Co., 1987—; alt. consumer rep. FTC, Washington, 1976-77; cons. HUD, Washington, 1978-80, joint select. com. sch. desegregation, Ohio Gen. Assembly, Columbus, 1979; mem. vis. com. Case Western Res. U. Sch. Law, Cleve., 1977-83. Author: (with others) A Guide to Regional Housing Opportunities, 1979, (with Buchanan) Mobile Home Living: A Guide to Consumers' Rights, 1979. Chmn. Ohio Protection and Advocacy System for develepmentally disabled, Columbus, 1978-80; trustee Muscle Disease Soc., Cleve., 1979-81; sec. Cuyahoga County Housing and Econ. Devel. com., Cleve., 1983—; mem. Cleve. Mayor's Com. on Employment of the Handicapped, 1978-79. Named Disting. Recent Grad. Case Western Reserve U. Law Alumni Assn., 1985. Mem. ABA, Cleve. Bar Assn., Fed. Bar Assn., Nat. Audubon Soc., Citizens League, Plantiffs Employment Lawyers Assn., Practicing Law Inst. (assoc.), Wilderness Soc. Democrat. Mem. United Ch. Christ. Club: Cleve. Athletic. Lodge: Masons. Office: Kramer & Tobocman 526 Superior 240 Leader Bldg Cleveland OH 44114

KRAMER, EMMANUEL MARTIN, archeologist; b. Phila., Mar. 18, 1928; s. William Marshall and Sonia Bella K.; B.S. magna cum laude, Temple U., 1950, M.S., 1952; m. Judith Levine, Dec. 22, 1966; children—Henry and Gary (twins), Benjamin. Tchr., Central High Sch., Phila., 1950-52, Roosevelt Jr. High, Phila., 1952-54, Northeast High Sch., Phila., 1954-56, Cheltenham High Sch., Wyncote, Pa., 1956-84; instr. U. of the Arts, 1966, Harvard U., 1972; adj. prof. Beaver Coll., Glenside, Pa., 1976, U. of the Arts; ednl. cons. archeology; lectr. art and archeology. Mem. Cheltenham Twp. Hist. Commn., 1974-79. Served with AUS, 1945-47. William Penn Found. grantee, 1981, 82. Mem. NEA, Soc. Hist. Archeology, Center Am. Archeology, Archeol. Inst. Am., N.Y. Acad. Sci. Author: Observations Concerning Aspects of Religious Archtecture in Western Europe, 1963; contbr. articles to profl. jours. Home: 503 Laverock Rd Glenside PA 19038

KRAMER, FRANK RAYMOND, classicist, educator; b. Baraboo, Wis., Jan. 2, 1908; s. Chris Edward and Mabel (Shaw) K.; m. Hetty Louise Eising, Dec. 20, 1935; children: Bryce Allen, Anita Louise (Mrs. James Cyril Shew). B. Humanities, U. Wis., 1929, M.A. in Greek and Latin, 1931, Ph.D., 1936. Mem. faculty Heidelberg Coll., Tiffin, Ohio, 1938-78; prof. classics Heidelberg Coll., 1944-78; asso. in residence U. Wis., 1948-49, 51-52; vis. prof. Ohio State U., summer 1962, prof. classics, 1978-79; research Am. Sch. Classical Studies, Athens, 1965. Author: Voices in the Valley, Mythmaking and Folk Belief in the Shaping of the Middle West, 1964; also articles. Grantee Wis. Com. Study Am. Civilization, 1948-49, 51-52; Grantee Social Sci. Research Council, 1951. Mem. Am. Philol. Assn., Classical Assn. Middle West and South, Ohio Classical Conf. (pres. 1948-49), Phi Alpha Theta, Eta Sigma Phi. Democrat. Mem. United Ch. Christ. Home: 25 Lincoln Rd Tiffin OH 44883

KRAMER, LEONIE JUDITH, literature educator; b. Melbourne, Victoria, Australia, Jan. 10, 1924; d. A.L. and G. Gibson; m. Harold Kramer; children: Jocelyn, Hilary. Student, Presbyn. Ladies Coll., Melbourne, 1930-41; BA, U. Melbourne, 1945, LLD (hon.), 1983; PhD, Oxford (Eng.) U., 1953; DLitt (hon.), Tasmania U., 1977; LLD (hon.), Australian Nat. U., 1984. Tutor, lectr. U. Melbourne, 1945-49; tutor St. Hugh's Coll., Oxford, 1949-52; lectr., sr. lectr., then assoc. prof. U. New South Wales, Australia, 1958-68; prof. Australian lit. U. Sydney, Australia, 1968—, mem. univs. council, 1974-86; vis. prof., chair Australian studies Harvard U., Cambridge, Mass., 1981-82; chmn. Australian Broadcasting Commn., 1982-83, Darwin Internat. Sch. bd. govs., 1988—; bd. dirs. Australia and New Zealand Banking Group Ltd., Australian Fixed Trusts Group, Western Minig Corp. Ltd., Quadrant Mag. Co. Ltd. Author: Henry Handel Richardson and Some of Her Sources, 1954, A Companion to Australia Felix, 1962, Myself When Laura: Fact and Fiction in Henry Handel Richardson's School Career, 1966, Henry Handel Richardson, 1967, (with Robert D. Eagleson) Language and Literature: A Synthesis, 1976, (with Robert D. Eagleson) A Guide to Language and Literature, 1977, A.D. Hope, 1979; editor: Coast to Coast, 1965, Selected Stories, 1971, Oxford History of Australian Literature, 1981, (with Adrian Mitchell) The Oxford Anthology of Australian Literature, 1985, James McAuley, 1988; editorial advisor: Quadrant mag., Poetry Australia mag., Australian Literary Studies jour. Chmn. bd. dirs. Nat. Inst. Dramatic Art; mem. council Nat. Roads and Motorists' Assn (N.R.M.A). Recipient Britannica Inaugural award, 1986. Sr. fellow Inst. Pub. Affairs, 1988—; fellow Australian Acad. of Humanities, Australian Coll. Edn., Australian Council for Ednl. Standards (v.p.), Australia-Britain Soc. (nat. pres.). Home: 12 Vaucluse Rd, 2030 Vaucluse, New South Wales Australia Office: U Sydney Dept English, 2006 Sydney, New South Wales Australia

KRAMER, PAUL R., lawyer; b. Balt., June 6, 1936; s. Phillip and Lee (Labovitz) K.; m. Janet Amitin, Sept. 1, 1957; children—Jayne, Susan, Nancy. B.A., Am. U., 1959, J.D., 1961. Bar: Md. 1961, D.C. 1962, U.S. Supreme Ct. 1965. Staff atty., dep. dir. Legal Aid Agy., D.C. Fed. Pub. Defender's Office, Washington, 1962-63; asst. U.S. Atty. Dist. Md., 1963-69; dep. U.S. atty. Md., Balt., 1969-83; exec. bd. Balt. Area council Boy Scouts Am., 1970-83, adv. counsel to exec. bd., 1983—; instr. U. Md. Sch. Law, 1975-80; assoc. prof. law Villa Julie Coll., 1976-80; assoc. professorial lectr. George Washington U., 1979; instr. Nat. Coll. Dist. Attys., 1979. Mem. ABA, Fed. Bar Assn. (permanent mem. 4th cir. fed. jud. conf., pres. Balt. chpt. 1973-74, nat. dep. sec. 1981-82, nat. sec. 1982-83, nat. cir. v.p. 1973-81, 85-86, chmn. nat. cir. v.p. 1978-80, mem. nat. council fed. bar assn. 1973—, faculty Fed. Practice Inst. 1981—), Md. Bar Assn., Balt. Bar Assn., Md. Criminal Def. Attys. Assn., Nat. Assn. Criminal Trial Attys., Md. Trial Lawyers Assn., Md. Criminal Def. Atty.'s. Assn. Republican. Jewish. Club: Masons (past master). Home: 6804 Hunt Ct Baltimore MD 21209 Office: 231 St Paul Pl Baltimore MD 21202

KRAMER, REUBEN ROBERT, sculptor; b. Balt., Oct. 9, 1909; s. Israel and Bessie (Silver) K.; m. Perna Krick, June 19, 1944. Grad., Rinehart Sch. Sculpture, 1932, traveling scholar, 1931-33; fellow, Am. Acad. in Rome, 1936. founder Balt. Art Center Children, 1944, dir., 1944-55; instr. Md. Inst., 1957-58; pvt. instr. Exhibited Grand Central Galleries, N.Y.C., 1934, Balt. Mus. Art, 1939-58; exhibited celebration exhbn. for 50 yrs., Balt. Mus. Art, 1978, Exhibited, Internat. Sculpture Show, Phila., 1940, 49, Pa. Acad. Fine Arts, 1949-53, 58, Corcoran Gallery, 1951-58, Am. Jewish Tercentenary Traveling Exhbn., 1954-55; one man shows, Grand Central Galleries, N.Y.C., 1937, Md. Inst., Balt., 1937, Balt. Mus., 1939, 51, 59, 66, Corcoran Gallery, 1960, Am. U., Washington, 1953, (with wife), Western Md. Coll., 1954, Hagerstown Mus., 1955, retrospective Jewish Community Center,

Balt., 1974, Md. Inst. Coll. Art, 1985; commd. to execute wood carving, P.O., St. Albans, W.Va., 1940; 8 ft. bronze statue of Assoc. Justice Thurgood Marshall, Balt. Dept. Housing and Community Devel., 1977; represented in collections, Am. U., Corcoran Gallery, Balt. Mus. Art, Walters Art Gallery, Portland Art Mus., Harvard Law Sch., Govt. House, Annapolis, Md., U. W.Va., also pvt. collections, Martenet, IBM, N. Mailman, Horelick, others.; Indsl. designer, War Dept., 1942-45. Recipient Am. Prix de Rome, 1934-36; 1st prize Balt. Mus. Art, 1940, 48, 51, 53; sculpture award, 1946, 49, 51, 52, 54; 1st prize for Md. Nat. Art Week, 1941; 1st prize Sculptors Guild of Md., 1948; 1st prize Sculptors Guild of Washington, 1952, 54; 1st prize for artistry in craftsmanship Peale Mus., 1949; Drawing prize, 1954; Purchase prize IBM, 1941; Purchase prize Balt. Mus. Art, 1948; Purchase prize Corcoran Gallery Art, 1952; Disting. Alumni award Md. Inst. Coll. Art, 1984; Nat. Inst. Arts and Letters sculpture grantee, 1964; elected to Balt. City Coll. Hall of Fame, 1962; personal archives acquired by Enoch Pratt Library Balt., 1976. Mem. Alumni Am. Acad. in Rome, Artists Equity Assn.

KRAMER, RONALD, manufacturing executive; b. Boston, Feb. 9, 1935; s. Max J. and Loretta C. (Smith) K.; m. Helen A. Kuver, Aug. 14, 1960; children: Daniel, Sarah, Marjorie, Judith. AB, Brown U., 1955; MBA with distinction, Cornell U., 1957. Mgr. sales Gustin-Kramer Inc., Boston, 1960-63; dir. Gustin-Kramer Ltd., Toronto, Ont., Can., 1963-88; chmn. exec. council Johnson Grad. Sch. Mgmt., Cornell U., Ithaca, N.Y., 1980—, mem. univ. council, 1981—. Chmn. Hillcrest Nursery Sch., Toronto, 1973-74; mem. NASP, Brown U., Providence, 1977—. Served to capt. U.S. Army, 1958-60. Named Employer of Yr., Assn. Mentally Retarded, 1977. Mem. Phi Kappa Phi. Jewish. Club: Toronto Cricket. Home: 42 Elgin Ave, Toronto, ON Canada M5R 1G6

KRAMER, WORTH ALAN (LANCE), industrial products company executive; b. Cleve., Sept. 9, 1941; s. Worth Hollis and Alice Farnhum (Hogue) Funk; m. Laura Ann Root, May 25, 1974; children: Courtney, Andrew. BA, Hillsdale Coll., 1966; MBA, So. Ill. U., 1972. Accounts receivable mgr. Monsanto Co., St. Louis, 1972-74; controller Interface Tech., St. Louis, 1974, exec. v.p., 1974-75, pres., 1975-79; v.p. fin. and adminstrn. Smith-Scharff, St. Louis, 1979-82; sec., treas. Watlow Electric Mfg. Co., St. Louis, 1982-88, v.p. fin. and adminstrn., 1988—; mem. small bus. adv. com. Regional Commerce and Growth Assn., St. Louis, 1977-82. trustee Robinwood West Improvement Assn., St. Louis, 1979-82; vestry mem. St. Timothy Episcopal Ch., St. Louis, 1985-86, sr. warden, 1986; bd. dirs. St. Louis Hearing and Speech Ctrs., 1987—. Served to lt. USNR, 1966-71, Vietnam. Decorated Purple Heart, 1968, Bronze Star with Navy Air medal, 1969. Mem. Fin. Exec. Inst., Internat. Execs. Roundtable, Chief Execs. Roundtable (chmn. 1979-80), Fin. Exec. Roundtable (chmn. 1983-84), Alpha Tau Omega. Republican. Club: Greenbriar Hills Country (St. Louis). Home: 2536 Oak Springs Ln Town and Country MO 63131 Office: Watlow Electric Mfg Co 12001 Lackland Rd Saint Louis MO 63146

KRAMM, DEBORAH ANN, data processing executive; b. Pasadena, June 24, 1949; d. Donald F. and Mary (Roach) Coonan; m. Kenneth R. Kramm, Dec. 20, 1969; children: Deidre Lyn, Jonathan Russel. B.A., U. Calif.-Irvine, 1971; M.S., Mich. Tech. U., 1981. Math. asst. NASA-Jet Propulsion Lab., Pasadena, 1967-70; library asst. U. Calif. Irvine Library, 1967-71; research assoc. Mich. Tech. U. Animal Behavior Lab., Houghton, 1971-80; programmer/analyst Shell Oil Co., Houston, 1981-85, corp. auditor EDP, 1985-87, team leader systems analyst, 1987—; chmn. bd. MMARK, Houston, 1983-85. Contbr. articles to profl. jours.; design/program application software: Shell Point-of-Sale Terminal, 1982-85; treas. KFHS Orch., 1986—; Co-leader Boy Scouts Am., Houston, 1981-83. AAUW scholar, 1980; Calif. State scholar, 1967-71. Mem. Nat. Assn. Female Execs., AAUW (pres. br. 1975-81). Club: Shell Data Processors. Home: 5814 Pinewilde Houston TX 77066 Office: Shell Oil Info Ctr 1500 Old Spanish Trail Houston TX 77054

KRANAKIS, EVANGELOS, computer scientist; b. Athens, Nov. 15, 1951; m. Eda Kranakis. BSc in Math., U. Athens, 1973; PhD in Math. Logic, U. Minn., 1980. Teaching asst. U. Minn., Mpls., 1973-76, teaching assoc., 1976-80; asst. prof. Purdue U., West Lafayette, Ind., 1980-82; Gast prof. U. Heidelberg, Fed. Republic Germany, 1982-83; research assoc. Yale U., New Haven, Conn., 1983-85; univ. docent U. Amsterdam, 1985-86; research scientist Ctr. Math. and Computer Sci., Amsterdam, 1986—. Author: Wiley-Teubner Series in Computer Science, Primality and Cryptography, 1986; contbr. articles to profl. jours. Recipient First Prize, Greek Math. Soc., 1972, Teaching award U. Minn., 1978; Minna-James-Heinemann-Stiftung research fellow, 1982-83. Home: Polsbroekstraat 19, 1106 BA Amsterdam The Netherlands Office: Ctr Math and Computer Sci, Kruislaan 413, 1098 SJ Amsterdam The Netherlands

KRANTZ, KERMIT EDWARD, educator, physician; b. Oak Park, Ill., June 4, 1923; s. Andrew Stanley and Beatrice H. (Cibrowski) K.; m. Doris Cole Krantz, Sep. 7, 1946; children: Pamela (Mrs. Richard Huffstutter), Sarah Elizabeth (Mrs. Paul Glaab), Kermit Tripler. BS, Northwestern U., 1945, BM, 1947, MS in Anatomy, 1947, MD, 1948; LittD (hon.), William Woods Coll., 1971. Diplomate Am. Bd. Ob-Gyn. Intern ob-gyn N.Y. Lying-In Hosp., 1947-48; asst. resident, asst. ob-gyn Cornell U. Med. Coll., N.Y. Lying-In Hosp., N.Y. Hosp., 1948-50; fellow, resident in ob-gyn Mary Fletcher Hosp., Burlington, Vt., 1950-51; dir. Durfee Clinic, 1952-55; instr., then asst. prof. U. Vt. Coll. Medicine, 1951-55; asst. prof. U. Ark. Med. Sch., 1955-59; prof., chmn. dept. gynecology and obstetrics U. Kans. Med. Center, 1959—, lectr. history medicine, 1959—, prof. anatomy, 1963—, dean clin. affairs, 1972-74, chief staff, 1972-74, obstetrician and gynecologist in chief, 1959—, assoc. to exec. vice chancellor for facilities devel., 1974-83; cons. in field. Author numerous articles in field. Mem. Nat. Adv. Child Health and Human Devel. Council, NIH, 1974-76. Bowen-Brooks fellow N.Y. Acad. Medicine, 1948-50; recipient Found. award South Atlantic Assn. Obstetricians and Gynecologists, 1950, Found. award Am. Assn. Obstetricians and Gynecologists, 1950, Wyeth-Ayerst Pub. Recognition award 1st Assn. Prof. of Gynecology and Obstetrics; named Outstanding Prof. in Coll. of Medicine Nu Sigma Nu, 1955; Robert A. Ross lectureship award Armed Forces Dist. meeting Am. Coll. Obstetricians and Gynecologists, 1972, Outstanding Civilian Service medal U.S. Army-Dept. Def., 1985; Charles A. Durham Meml. lectr. Ann. Session Tex. Med. Assn., 1978; Markle scholar med. sci., 1957-62. Founding fellow Am. Coll. Obstetricians and Gynecologists (Kermit E. Krantz Lectureship award established 1973, Outstanding Dist. Services award 1978, 82); fellow ACS; mem. Am. Assn. Anatomists, Am. Fedn. Clin. Research, AMA, Am. Med. Writers Assn., Am. Fertility Soc., AAUP, Soc. Exptl. Biology and Medicine, Aerospace Med. Assn., Endocrine Soc., Soc. Gynecologic Investigation, Central Assn. Obstetricians and Gynecologists, N.Y. Acad. Medicine, N.Y. Acad. Sci., Kans. Med. Soc., Assn. Mil. Surgeons U.S. (sustaining), Kans. Obstet. Soc., Sigma Xi, Alpha Omega Alpha. Home: 6711 Overhill Rd Shawnee Mission KS 66208 Office: Univ Kans Med Center Kansas City KS 66103

KRARUP, JAKOB, information scientist, educator; b. Copenhagen, July 21, 1936; s. Georg Schepelern and Agnete (Foght) K.; m. Kirsten Langkilde, Apr. 28, 1961; children—Thomas, Julie. M.Sc., Tech. U. Denmark, 1964, Ph.D., 1967; D.Sc., U. Copenhagen, 1982. Systems analyst Danish Inst. Computing Machinery, Copenhagen, 1958-64; asst. prof. Inst. Math. Stats. and Ops. Research, Tech. U. Denmark, 1964-68, assoc. prof., 1968-71; co-founder, mgr. Spadille, Inc., Hornbaek, 1971-75; assoc. prof. DIKU, U. Copenhagen, 1975-86, prof. ops. research, 1987—; vis. prof. SEMA, Paris, 1968, London Sch. Econs., 1968, 83, U. Calif.-Berkeley, 1969, U. Montreal, 1973, U. Calgary, 1976, Technion, Israel, 1979, EPFL, Lausanne, 1981, 84, Hungarian Acad. Scis., 1983, 84; mem. spl. program panel systems sci. NATO, 1975-79. Editorial bd. European Jour. Operational Research, 1976—, Discrete Applied Math., 1979—, OR Spektrum, 1981—, Advances in Management Studies, 1981—, Annals of Ops. Research, 1983—, Jorbel, 1985—; contbr. articles to profl. jours. Served with Danish Army, 1954-56. Mem. Danish Ops. Research Soc. (pres. 1977-79), Inst. Mgmt. Scis. (council 1979-81), Assn. European Ops. Research Soc. (v.p. 1981-85, pres. 1989—), DAPS Soc. (co- founder, pres. 1978—), Matrafüred Soc. Hungarian Acad. Scis. (hon.). Home: Sommervej 3, DK-3100 Hornbaek Denmark Office: DIKU, Universitetsparken 1, DK-2100 Copenhagen 0 Denmark

KRASLOW, DAVID, newspaperman, author; b. N.Y.C., Apr. 16, 1926; s. Frank and Goldie (Sirota) K.; m. Bernice Schonfeld, Sept. 18, 1949; children: Ellen Anne, Karen Leah, Susan Beth. B.A., U. Miami, Fla., 1948. With Los Angeles Times, 1963-72; Washington corr., news editor Los Angeles Times (Washington Bur.), then chief, 1970-72; asst. mng. editor Washington Star-News, 1972-74; Washington Bur. chief Cox Newspapers, 1974-77; pub. Miami News, 1977—, sports writer, 1947-48; successively sports writer, reporter, Washington corr. Miami Herald, 1948-63. Co-author: A Certain Evil, 1965, The Secret Search for Peace in Vietnam, 1968. Trustee, chmn. acad. affairs com. U. Miami; mem. Orange Bowl Com., Council on Fgn. Relations, N.Y.C.; bd. dirs. United Way of Dade County. Served with USAAF, 1944-46. Recipient George Polk award, 1969; Raymond Clapper award, 1969; Dumont award, 1969; Nieman fellow Harvard U., 1961-62. Mem. InterAm. Press Assn. (bd. dirs., vice chmn. exec. com., chmn. fin. com.), Sigma Delta Chi. Jewish. Clubs: Gridiron, Federal City (Washington); Miami, City, New World Center (Miami). Office: Miami News PO Box 615 Miami FL 33152

KRASNER, OSCAR JAY, educator; b. St. Louis, Dec. 3, 1922; s. Benjamin and Rose (Persov) K.; BS in Pub. Adminstrn., Washington U., St. Louis, 1943; MA in Mgmt. with honors, U. Chgo., 1950; MS in Quantitative Bus. Analysis, U. So. Calif., 1965, DBA in Mgmt., 1969; m. Bonnie Kidder, June 4, 1944; children: Bruce Howard, Glenn Evan, Scott Allan, Steve Leland, Michael Shawn, Bettina Jeanine. Mem. staff Exec. Office of Sec., U.S. Dept. Navy, 1944-56; supervising cons. Bus. Research Corp., Chgo., 1956-57; mem. staff flight propulsion div. Gen. Electric Co., Cin., 1957-61, mgr. VTOL project planning, 1959-61; exec. adviser long range planning space div. N.Am. Rockwell Corp., Downey, Calif., 1962-64, dir. tech. resources analysis exec. offices, 1964-70; pres. Solid State Tech. Corp. Calif., 1968-71; prof. mgmt. Pepperdine U., Los Angeles, 1970—; pres. Rensark Assocs., 1976—; dir. U.S. Innovative Products Corp.; founder XCI Corp., 1984; cons. Active community orgns.; mem. nat. adv. bd. Nat. Congress Inventor Orgns., 1983-84; bd. dirs. Long Beach (Calif.) JCC, 1969-70; founder Internat. Entrepreneurship Ctr., 1988; del. People-to-People Delegation to Peoples' Republic China, 1987. Served with Anti-Aircraft, AUS, 1942-44. Mem. Am. Acad. Mgmt., MBA Internat. (chmn. 1976-77), AIAA, AAAS, World Future Soc., Beta Gamma Sigma. Home: 4709 Autry Ave Long Beach CA 90808 Office: 2151 Michelson Ave Irvine CA 92715

KRASNICK, ARTHUR ROBERT, hotel, restaurant, country club consultant; b. Bronx, N.Y., June 29, 1932; s. Harry and May Krasnick; m. Josephine Flores, May 25, 1963 (div.); children—Allison Maria, Robert John. Student in psychology, CCNY, 1953; postgrad. in hotel mgmt. Lewis Hotel Sch., 1962. Cert. profl. cons. Co-owner, exec. v.p. San Juan Weekly, 1970; dir. restaurant ops. Riviana Foods, Miami, Fla., 1975-76; dir. catering banquets Opryland Hotel, Nashville, 1977-81; internal cons. Coral Gables Country Club, (Fla.), 1982-83; gen. mgr. Emerald Hills Country Club, Hollywood, Fla., 1983—; pres. Associated Food & Beverage Cons.; Miami, 1982—; pres. ARK Mgmt. Cons., Inc., 1986—; dir. Cons. Inc., Miami, 1983—. Mem. Fla. Restaurant Assn., Fla. Hotel Assn. Club: The Jockey (v.p. 1986-87, cons. 1986-87). Home: 950 NW 199 St Miami FL 33169

KRASNO, RICHARD MICHAEL, educational administrator; b. Chgo., Jan. 20, 1942; s. Louis Richard Krasno and Adeline (Glassman) Kaplan; m. Jean Elizabeth Cullander, Sept. 7, 1963; children—Jeffrey Patrick, Eric Peter. B.S., U. Ill., 1965; Ph.D., Stanford U., 1970; Litt.D., Coll. St. Rose, 1983; LL.D., Sacred Heart U., 1984. Asst. prof. U. Chgo., 1970-73; program advisor Latin Am. and Caribbean, Ford Found., Rio de Janeiro, Brazil, 1974-77, program officer Middle East and Africa, N.Y.C., 1978-80; dep. asst. sec. edn. U.S. Govt., Washington, 1980-81; exec. v.p. Inst. Internat. Edn., N.Y.C., 1981-83, pres., chief exec. officer, 1983—; commr. U.S.-Brazil Fulbright Commn., Rio de Janeiro, 1975-77; mem. U.S. del. U.S.-Mex. Bilateral Commn. on Cultural Cooperation, 1980, 84; commr. U.S. Nat. Commn. for UNESCO, Washington, 1983-85. Contbr. numerous articles on internat. edn. to profl. jours. Chmn. internat. transition team Dept. Edn., Washington, 1979-80; trustee Ralph Bunche Inst. on UN, 1986—; trustee Latin Am. scholarship program Am. Univs., Cambridge, Mass., 1980-82, Ctr. for Applied Linguistics, Washington, 1982—. Named Nat. Def. Edn. fellow U.S. Govt., 1967-68; Sr. Fulbright lectr., 1973-74. Mem. Council on Fgn. Relations. Office: Inst Internat Edn 809 UN Plaza New York NY 10017

KRASOVEC, JOZE, theology educator; b. Sodna vas, Yugoslavia, Apr. 20, 1944; s. Jozef and Marija (Flis) K. D of Bibl. Studies, Pontifical Bibl. Inst., Rome, 1976; PhD, Hebrew U., Jerusalem, 1982, ThD, History of Religion, Religious Anthropology Inst. Cath. and Sorbonne, Paris. Prof. O.T., Theol. Faculty, Ljubljana, Yugoslavia, 1976—; researcher, pres. com. for New Slovenian Bible, 1985—. Author: Der Merismus, 1977, Antithetic Structure, 1984, Lexicon of Biblical Names in Slovene, 1984, La Justice (sdq) de Dieu, 1987; contbr. articles to profl. publs. Roman Catholic. Home: Dolnicarjeva 1, 61000 Ljubljana Yugoslavia Office: Theol Faculty, Poljanska 4, 61000 Ljubljana Yugoslavia

KRASS, ALVIN, psychologist, test development company executive; b. Bklyn., Sept. 14, 1928; s. Nathan M. and Nora (Feigels) K.; m. Suzanne Myra Freiwirth, Sept. 5, 1954; children—Peter, Adam, Michael. B.A., Bklyn. Coll., 1951; M.A., NYU, 1952, Ph.D., 1965. Lic. psychologist, N.J.; diplomate Am. Bd. Family Psychology, Am. Bd. Psychotherapy. Staff psychologist Brisbane Child Treatment Center, Allaire, N.J., 1955-58; chief psychologist Monmouth Med. Center, Long Branch, N.J., 1958-62; pvt. practice psychology, Monmouth County, N.J., 1955—; chmn. bd. Key Edn., Inc., Shrewsbury, N.J., 1958—; cons. Monmouth County Parks System, 1977—, N.J. Div. Vocat. Rehab., Red Bank, 1980-82. Author: Mechanisms of the Mind, 1972, also vocat. and learning potential tests. Served with U.S. Army, 1952-54. Recipient Founders' Day award NYU, 1965. Mem. Am. Psychol. Assn., N.J. Psychol. Assn., Am. Acad. Psychotherapists, Monmouth-Ocean County Psychol. Assn. (pres. 1978-79). Jewish. Patentee computer integrated vocat. testing devices. Home: 205 Holland Rd Holmdel NJ 07733 Office: Key Edn Inc 673 Broad St Shrewsbury NJ 07701

KRATZ, HANS LEWIS, financial analyst; b. Jersey City, Sept. 10, 1938; s. John and Anna (Gantenberg) K.; m. Audrey Ann Klein, Nov. 26, 1960; children—Patricia, Kathleen, Denise. B.S. in Econs., St. Peter's Coll., 1960; M.B.A. in Econs. and Fin., Fairleigh Dickinson U., 1968; cert. in consumer credit mgmt. Columbia U., 1975. Mgmt. trainee Chase Manhattan Bank, N.Y.C., 1960-67; asst. cashier Franklin Nat. Bank, N.Y.C., 1967-70; v.p. Mfrs. Hanover Trust Co., N.Y.C., 1970-86; sr. v.p., dir. comml. and consumer loans Independence Savs. Bank, Bklyn., 1987; v.p., mgr. fin. services, Fitch Investors Service, Inc., 1987—. Contbr. articles to profl. jours. Mem. Robert Morris Assocs. (com. chmn. 1980-84, Spl. Service award 1984), Comml. Fin. League (pres. 1977-79), Am. Fin. Services Assn., Am. Assn. Equipment Lessors, Nat. Comml. Fin. Assn. Republican. Roman Catholic. Home: 14 Ilex Pl Aberdeen NJ 07747 Office: Fitch Investors Service Inc 5 Hanover Square New York NY 10004

KRATZER, GUY LIVINGSTON, surgeon; b. Gratz, Pa., Apr. 24, 1911; s. Clarence U. and Carrie E. (Schwalm) K.; m. Kathryn H. Miller, Jan. 27, 1940; 1 son, Guy Miller. Student, Muhlenberg Coll., 1928-31; M.D., Temple U., 1935; M.S., U. Minn., 1945. Diplomate: Am. Bd. Proctology. Intern Harrisburg Hosp., 1935-36; fellow proctology, surgery Mayo Clinic, 1942-46, fellow surgery, 1949-50; asso. surgeon Pottsville Hosp., 1936-41; asso. proctologist Allentown (Pa.) Hosp., 1946—, mem. tumor clinic, 1955—, chief, dept. proctology, 1958—; mem. cons. staff Sacred Heart Hosp., 1946—, chief dept. colon and rectal surgery, 1974—; clin. asso. prof. surgery Milton S. Hershey Med. Center, Pa. State U., 1972-75, clin. prof., 1975—, cons., 1975—; mem. Pa. Bd. Med. Edn. and Licensure, 1984—. Author: Disease of the Colon and Rectum, 1985. Pres. Lehigh Valley chpt., bd. dirs. Am. Cancer Soc. Fellow A.C.S. (pres. S.E. Pa. 1965-66), Am. Proctologic Soc., Internat. Coll. Surgeons; mem. Shelter House Soc., Am. Med. Writers Assn., Pa. Proctologic Soc. (past pres.), Pa. Med. Soc., Am. Med. Authors, Lehigh Valley Med. Soc. (past pres.), Allentown C. of C. (gov.). Club: Lion. Address: 1447 Hamilton St Allentown PA 18102

KRAUCH, CARL HEINRICH, chemist; b. Heidelberg, Ger., Sept. 14, 1931; s. Carl and Maria (Lüders) K.; m. Ursula Kneller, 1958; 1 dau., 3 sons. Ed. Ruprecht-Karl U., Heidelberg, Georg-August U., Göttingen, D of Rerum Naturalium. Head research group radiochem. dept. Max Planck Inst. fü r Kohlenforschung, Mülheim/Ruhr, 1958-67; lectr. U. Cologne, 1965; head research group plastic materials BASF, Ludwigshafen, 1967; prof. Johannes Gutenberg U., Mainz, 1971—; head R&D, dir. Henkel & Cie., GmbH, Dusseldorf, 1971-80, head chem. products div., 1975-80; chmn. Hüls AG, Marl, 1980—; bd. mgmt. VEBA AG, Dusseldorf. Contbr. articles to profl. jours. Address: Vorsitzender des Vorstandes, Huls AG, PF 1320, D-4370 Marl Federal Republic of Germany

KRAUNSOE, NIELS ANTHONY, civil engineer, consultant; b. Southport, Merseyside, Eng., Oct. 13, 1943; arrive in Hong Kong, 1970; s. Edwin Kraunsoe and Gladys (Mc Cubbin) Macquire-Cooper; m. Ann J. Livock; children: James, Emma, Georgina, Victoria, Miranda. Student, Fettes Coll., Edinburgh, 1956-61; Baccalaurea Artis Ingeniaria, MA, Trinity Coll., Dublin, 1966. Engr. W S Atkins & Ptnrs., Epsom, 1966-68, Nuclear Power Group, Somerset, 1968-70, China Light & Power, Hong Kong, 1970-72; chief engr. Binnie & Ptnrs., Hong Kong, 1970-78; project dir. Hong Kong Resort Co., 1979-84; dir., gen. mgr. Rendel Palmer & Tritton, Hong Kong, 1984—; bd. dirs. High-Point CTMS, Hong Kong, Rendel Palmer & Tritton , Hong Kong, Transpn. Planning Assocs., Hong Kong. Bd. mgrs. Discovery Bay Internat. Sch., Hong Kong, 1982—; chmn. adv. com. Constrn. Dept. City Poly. of Hong Kong, 1985—. Fellow Instn. Civil Engrs., British Inst. Mgmt., Instn. Water and Environ. Mgmt., Hong Kong Instn. Engrs. (council 1982—, pres. 1983-87, pres. 1988—). Anglican Christian. Club: Hong Kong. Lodge: Rotary (bd. dirs. 1986—, dir. 1986-88). Office: Rendel Palmer & Tritton, 16 Queens Rd, 1710 New World Tower, Hong Kong Hong Kong

KRAUS, HARRY ARNOLD, marketing communications company executive; b. N.Y.C., Aug. 11, 1936; s. Harry A. and Rosalie Kraus; student Pace Coll., 1954-58, N.Y. U., 1963-65, New Sch., 1966-69; m. Diana Izzi, Apr. 18, 1971; 1 dau., Juliana Margaret; children by previous marriage—Ellen Beth, David Joseph. Vice pres. LHO Inc., N.Y.C., 1969-72; dir. market services Nat. Union Electric Corp., Stamford, Conn., 1962-69; dir. advt. and sales promotion Fedders Corp., Edison, N.J., 1958-62; pres. Modular Mktg. Inc., N.Y.C., 1972—; faculty mem. Inst. Advt. Mgmt.; lectr. and writer in field. Mem. Queens County Republican Com., 1963-65; bd. dirs. Queens Symphony Orch., Alcoholism Council Greater N.Y., Assn. for Classical Music. Recipient Boli awards 1975, 76, 77, 79, Andy awards 1976, 77, 78, 79, John Caples award, 1987. Mem. Direct Mail Mktg. Assn. (Echo award 1980, 81), Council of Sales Promotion Agys., Direct Mktg. Assn. Clubs: Atrium, Friars. Home: 125 W 76th St New York NY 10023 Office: Modular Mktg Inc 1841 Broadway New York NY 10023

KRAUS, JACK CHARLES, real estate corporation executive; b. LaPorte, Ind., June 16, 1947; s. Charles Frederich and Rose (Conforti) K.; m. Deborah Sue Carie, Mar. 13, 1977 (div. 1985) children: Jennifer Louise, Ryan Christopher. AA in Applied Sci., Purdue U., 1978, BS in Tech. with distinction, 1985. Constrn. worker No. Ind. Pub. Service Co., Gary, 1970-72; electrician No. Ind. Pub. Service Co., Bailey, 1972-77; instr., tng. dept. No. Ind. Pub. Service Co., LaPorte, 1977-82, head tng. dept., 1982-84; mgr. No. Ind. Pub. Service Co., Hammond, 1985-88; pres. Real Property Rebates, Inc., LaPorte, 1988—; instr. Purdue U., Westville, Ind., 1985—. Bd. dirs. Lake County Council on Sustance Abuse; coordinator NIPSO Employee Assistance Program. Served as sgt. USMC, 1966-69, Vietnam. Mem. Associated Mgmt. Inst., Purdue Alumni Assn., IEEE, Nat Palm Soc. for No. Ind. Clubs: Cougars (Des Plaines, Ill.). Lodge: Moose. Home and Office: 905 Robert St La Porte IN 46350

KRAUS, NORMA JEAN, business executive; b. Pitts., Feb. 11, 1931; d. Edward Karl and Alli Alexandra (Hermanson) K. B.A., U. Pitts., 1954; postgrad. NYU Grad. Sch. Bus. Adminstrn., 1959-61, Cornell U. Grad. Sch. Labor Relations, 1969-70. Personnel mgr. for several cos., 1957-70; corp. dir. personnel TelePrompter Corp., N.Y.C., 1970-73; exec. asst., speech writer to lt. gov. N.Y. State, Office Lt. Gov., Albany, 1974-79; v.p. human resources, labor relations and stockholder relations Volt Info. Scis., Inc., N.Y.C., 1979—. Co-founder, Manhattan Women's Polit. Caucus, 1971, N.Y. State Women's Polit. Caucus, 1972, vice chair N.Y. State Women's Polit. Caucus, 1978; bd. dirs. Ctr. for Women in Govt., 1977-79. Served to lt. (s.g.) USNR, 1954-57. Pa. State Senatorial scholar, 1950-54. Mem. Women's Econ. Roundtable, Indsl. Relations Research Assn., Employment Mgmt. Assn., Am. Compensation Assn. Democrat. Avocations: politics, women's rights, breeding Persian cats. Office: Volt Info Scis Inc 101 Park Ave New York NY 10178

KRAUS, PANSY DAEGLING, gemology consultant, contributing editor; b. Santa Paula, Calif., Sept. 21, 1916; d. Arthur David and Elsie (Pardee) Daegling; m. Charles Frederick Kraus, Mar. 1, 1941 (div. Nov. 1961). AA, San Bernardino Valley Jr. Coll., 1938; student Longmeyer's Bus. Coll., 1940; grad. gemologist diploma Gemological Assn. Gt. Britain, 1960, Gemological Inst. Am., 1966. Clk. Convair, San Diego, 1943-48; clk. San Diego County Schs. Publs., 1948-57; mgr. Rogers and Boblet Art-Craft, San Diego, 1958-64; part-time editorial asst. Lapidary Jour., San Diego, 1963-64, assoc. editor, 1964-69, editor, 1970—, sr. editor, 1984-85; pvt. practice cons., San Diego, 1985—; lectr. gems, gemology local gem, mineral groups; gem & mineral club bull. editor groups. Mem. San Diego Mineral & Gem Soc., Gemol. Soc. San Diego, Gemol. Assn. Great Britain, Mineral. Soc. Am., Epsilon Sigma Alpha. Author: Introduction to Lapidary, 1987; editor, layout dir.: Gem. Cutting Shop Helps, 1964, The Fundamentals of Gemstone Carving, 1967, Appalachian Mineral and Gem Trails, 1968, Practical Gem Knowledge for the Amateur, 1969, Southwest Mineral and Gem Trails, 1972, revision editor Gemcraft (Quick and Leiper), 1977; contbr. articles to Lapidary jour., Keystone Mktg. catalog. Home and Office: 6127 Mohler St San Diego CA 92120

KRAUSE, CHESTER LEE, publishing company executive; b. Iola, Wis., Dec. 16, 1923; s. Carl and Cora E. (Neil) K. Grad. high sch. In contracting bus, 1946-52. Chief exec. officer Krause Publs., Inc., Iola, pub. hobby periodicals, 1952—. Co-editor: Standard Catalog of World Coins. Mem. Assay Commn., 1961; chmn. bldg. fund drive Iola Hosp., 1975-80; Mem. Village Bd., 1963-72. Served with AUS, 1943-46. Mem. Am. Numis. Assn. (medal of merit, Farren Zerbe award), Central States Numis. Assn. (medal of merit), Canadian Numis. Assn. Club: Lion. Home: 290 E Iola St Iola WI 54945 Office: 700 E State St Iola WI 54945

KRAUSE, ERNST HENRY, aerospace engineer; b. Milw., May 2, 1913; s. Ernst and Martha (Strege) K.; m. Constance Fraser, June 29, 1939 (dec. Nov. 1972); children—Margaret Bird (Mrs. Keith McCormick), Katharine Louise, Carol Marjorie (Mrs. Erik Sorenson), Susan Fraser; m. Betty Lou Davis, Apr. 7, 1974. B.S. in Elec. Engring, U. Wis., 1934, M.S. in Physics, 1935, Ph.D. in Physics, 1938. With Naval Research Lab., Washington, 1938-54; asso. dir. research Naval Research Lab., 1951-54; dir. research Lockheed Aircraft Corp., Van Nuys, Calif., 1954-55; pres., chmn. Systems Research Corp., Van Nuys, 1955-56; v.p., dir. Aeronutronic Systems, Inc., 1956-59; dir. tech. staff Aeronutronic div. Ford Motor Co., 1959-62; with Aerospace Corp., El Segundo, Calif., 1962—; sr. v.p. devel. Aerospace Corp., 1968-78, mgmt. and tech. cons., 1978—. Pres. World Affairs Council of Inland So. Calif., 1968-69. Recipient Distinguished Civilian Service award USN, 1956. Fellow Am. Phys. Soc.; asso. fellow Am. Inst. Aeros. and Astronautics; mem. Sigma Xi, Tau Beta Pi. Home: 3731 Daffadil Ave Corona Del Mar CA 92625

KRAUSE, FRIEDHILDE, librarian; b. Serock, Polannd, Aug. 18, 1928; d. Friedrich Karl and Hildegard (Radetzki) Jonat; m. Werner Krause; children: Maria Krause Bull, Manfred. B in Slavic Philology, Humboldt U., East Berlin, 1951, M in Sci. Librarianship, 1966, PhD, 1970. Vice dir.. German State Library, East Berlin, 1958-76, dir. gen., 1977—; prof. Humboldt U., 1981—. Author: Die slawischen Verbindungen der Kgl. Bibliothek, 1976; editor: Studien zum Buch-und Bibliothekswesen, 1981—, Beiträge aus der DSB, 1986—. Dep. city rep., East Berlin, 1976—. Recipient Nat. Merit Decoration State Council of the German Dem. Republic, 1984, Wilhelm-Bracke Gold medal Union of German Book Traders, 1985. Mem. Internat. Fedn. Library Assn. (mem. standing coms. various sects.), Library Assn. of German Dem. Republic, Pirckheimer Assn. (mem. mng. com.). Office: Deutsche Staatsbibliothek, Unter den Linden 8, 1086 Berlin German Democratic Republic

KRAUSE, HARRY DIETER, lawyer, educator; b. Görlitz, Germany, Apr. 23, 1932; came to U.S., 1951, naturalized, 1954; s. Renatus and Ellen (Abel-

Musgrave) K.; m. Eva Maria Disselnkötter, Aug. 30, 1957; children: Philip Renatus, Thomas Walther, Peter Herbert. Student, Freie Universität Berlin, 1950-51; B.A., U. Mich., 1954, J.D., 1958. Bar: Mich. 1959, D.C. 1959, Ill. 1963, U.S. Supreme Ct 1963. With firm Covington & Burling, 1958-60; with Ford Motor Co., Dearborn, Mich., 1960-63; asst. prof. to prof. law Coll. Law, U. Ill., Champaign, 1963-82, Alumni Disting. prof. law, 1982—; reporter Uniform Parentage Act, 1969-73, Rev. Uniform Adoption Act, 1979-84, Uniform Putative Fathers Act, 1985, Nat. Conf. Commrs. on Uniform State Laws; rapporteur Internat. Acad. Comparative Law, Uppsala, 1966, Teheran, 1974, Budapest, 1978, Caracas, 1983, Sydney, Australia, 1986; cons. on family law and social legislation to numerous fed. and state legis., jud. and exec. commns., cons. and agys.; vis. prof. law U. Mich., 1981, U. Miami, 1987. Author: Illegitimacy: Law and Social Policy, 1971, Family Law: Cases and Materials, 1976, 2d edit., 1983, Kinship Relations, 1976, Family Law in a Nutshell, 1977, 2d edit., 1986, Child Support in America: The Legal Perspective, 1981; law editor: (with R. Walker et. al.) Inclusion Probabilities in Parentage Testing, 1983; bd. editors: Mich. Law Rev., 1957-58, Family Law Quar., 1971—, Jour. Contemporary Health Law and Policy, 1985—, Jour. Legal Edn., 1988—; adv. bd. editors: ABA Jour, 1973-79; contbr. articles to profl. jours. Served with U.S. Army, 1954-56. Guggenheim fellow, 1969-70; assoc. Ctr. Advanced Study U. Ill., 1970, 79; Fulbright prof. U. Bonn, Germany, 1976-77; vis. assoc. Centre Socio-Legal Studies, 1977, vis. fellow Wolfson Coll., Oxford U., 1984; German Marshall Fund U.S. fellow, 1977-78; Hewlett fellow, Australia, 1984; German Acad. Exchange Service fellow, 1985. Mem. Am. Law Inst., ABA (past mem. council sect. family law, com. chmn.), Ill. Bar Assn. (past mem. council sect. on family law, internat. law), Am. Assn. Comparative Study of Law (dir. 1980—), Internat. Soc. Family Law (v.p. 1973-77, exec. council 1977—), Order of Coif. Home: 903 Silver St Urbana IL 61801 Office: Coll Law U Ill Champaign IL 61820

KRAUSE, JÜRGEN, linguistic information science educator, scientist; b. Liebenthal, Germany, Feb. 21, 1944; s. Paul and Erna (Wünsch) K.; m. Ingrid Dettmer, May 21, 1971; children—Wera, Barbara. Dr. in Linguistics, U. Regensburg (W.Ger.), 1975, Dr. Habilitation in Linguistic Info. Sci., 1981. Lectr. non-numerical data processing U. Regensburg, 1971-78, 79-81, prof. linguistic info. sci., 1981—; fellow IBM Sci. Ctr., Heidelberg, W.Ger., 1978-79; cons. Soc. for Info. and Documentation, Frankfurt, W.Ger., 1976-87, Soc. Math. and EDP, 1988—, Fed. Ministry for Research and Tech., Bonn, W.Ger., 1981—. Author: Mensch-Maschine Interaktion, 1982; editor: (with H.J. Niederehe) Mikrocomputer u. Textverarbeitung, 1984; (with B. Endres-Niggemeyer) Sprachverarbeitung in Information und Dokumentation, 1985, Inhaltserschliessung von Massendaten, 1987; exec. editor microfiche publs. Regensburger Mikrofiche Materialien, 1979—; (with P. Hellwig) Sprache und Computer, 1985—; mem. editorial bd. Computer and the Humanities, 1987—; contbr. articles to profl. jours. Mem. Soc. for Advancement Linguistic Data Processing (chmn. 1979-82), Soc. for Linguistic Data Processing (chmn. 1983-85). Office: Dept for Linguistic Info Sci, Univ Regensburg, PO Box 397, 8400 Regensburg 1, Bayern Federal Republic of Germany

KRAUSE, LAWRENCE ALLEN, financial adviser, financial planner; b. Chgo., Oct. 28, 1939; s. Leo and Sylvia Harriet (Bergman) K.; m. Donna Lee Ferkel, Aug. 14, 1971; children—Danielle, Alexis. B.A., State U. Iowa, 1961. Cert. fin. planner. Exec. v.p. Jobs, Inc., Waukegan, Ill., 1961-62; pres. Inventory and Bus. Controls, Waukegan, 1963-66; broker real estate Shoen Realtors, Rockford, Ill., 1967-69; registered rep. Reynolds & Co., San Francisco, 1970-75; dir. fin. planning Sutro & Co., San Francisco, 1975-79; chmn., pres. Lawrence A. Krause & Assocs., Inc., San Francisco, 1979—; pres. KW Securities Corp., San Francisco, 1979—; adj. prof. fin. planning San Francisco State U., 1982-86; mem. adv. com. on fin. planning Golden Gate U., San Francisco, 1982—; mem. faculty U. So. Calif., Los Angeles, 1984; mem. adv. bd. Stanger Register, 1986—. Author: The Money-Go-Round, Sleep-Tight Money; (co-author) Marketing Your Financial Planning Practice; contbr. chpts. to books, articles to profl. jours.; contbg. columnist Los Angeles Times, ABA Jour.; monthly columnist Calif. Bus. mag. Bd. dirs. Am. Cancer Soc., San Francisco, 1980—; bd. govs., bd. dirs. NTL Ctr. Fin. Edn., San Francisco, 1982—. Recipient Fin. Writer's award Fin. Planner mag., 1981; named Nation's Outstanding Fin. Planner for 1980's. Mem. Registry Fin. Planning Practitioners, Internat. Assn. Fin. Planners (San Francisco Fin. Planner of Yr. award 1982, pres. 1980-82, chmn. 1982-83), Inst. Cert. Fin. Planners. Republican. Jewish. Club: Concordia-Argonaut (San Francisco). Office: Lawrence A Krause & Assocs Inc 500 Washington St Suite 750 San Francisco CA 94111

KRAUSE, MARCELLA ELIZABETH MASON (MRS. EUGENE FITCH KRAUSE), educator; b. Norfolk, Nebr.; d. James Haskell and Elizabeth (Vader) Mason; B.S., U. Neb., 1934; M.A., Columbia, 1938; postgrad. summers U. Calif. at Berkeley, 1950, 51, 65, Stanford, 1964, Creighton U., 1966, Chico (Calif.) State U., 1967; m. Eugene Fitch Krause, June 1, 1945; 1 dau., Kathryn Elizabeth. Tchr., Royal (Nebr.) pub. schs., 1930-32, Hardy (Nebr.) pub. schs., 1933-35, Omaha pub. schs., 1935-37, Lincoln Sch. of Tchrs. Coll., Columbia, 1937-38, Florence (Ala.) State Tchrs. Coll., summer 1938, Tchrs. Coll., U. Nebr., 1938-42, Corpus Christi (Tex.) pub. schs., 1942-45, Oakland (Calif.) pub. schs., 1945-83. Bd. dirs. U. Nebr. Womens Faculty Club, 1940-42; mem. Nebr. State Tchrs. Conv. Panel, 1940-; mem. U. Nebr. Reading Inst., 1940; speaker Iowa State Tchrs. Conv., 1941; reading speaker Nebr. State Tchrs. conv., 1941; lectr. Johnson County Tchrs. Inst., 1942; chmn. Reading Survey Corpus Christi pub. schs., 1943; chmn. Inservice Reading Meetings Oakland pub. schs., 1948-57. Mem. Gov.'s Adv. Commn. on Status Women Conf., San Francisco, 1966; service worker ARC, Am. Cancer Soc., United Crusade, Oakland CD; Republican precinct capt., 1964-70; v.p. Oakland Fedn. Rep. Women. Ford Found. Fund for Advancement Edn. fellow, 1955-56; scholar Stanford, 1964; Calif. Congress PTA scholar U. Calif., 1965. Mem. Nat. Council Women, AAUW (dir.), Calif. Tchrs. Assn., Oakland Mus. Assn., U. Nebr. Alumni Assn. (Alumni Achievement award 1984), Californians for Nebr., Ladies Grand Army Republic, 1960, 1986-87 Ruth Assn., Martha Assn. (pres. East Bay chpt. 1979), Sierra DAR (regent), Eastbay DAR Regents Assn. (pres.), Nebr. Alumni Assn. (life, alumni achievement award 1984), Grand Lake Bus. and Profl. Women, Internat. Platform Assn., Eastbay Past Matrons Assn., P.E.O., Pi Lambda Theta (pres. No. Calif. chpt.), Alpha Delta Kappa. Methodist. Mem. Order Eastern Star (past matron). Contbr. articles to profl. jours. Home: 5615 Estates Dr Oakland CA 94618

KRAUSE, ROBERT DALE, former municipal government executive, consultant; b. Port Huron, Mich., July 2, 1923; s. Ernst Karl and Pearl Athena (Bedwell) K.; m. Maxine Ann Driscoll, Jan. 15, 1946. B.A., Western Mich. U., 1948; M.P.A., U. Mich., 1950. Mgmt. analyst AEC, Oak Ridge, 1951-55; personnel dir. City of Kenosha (Wis.), 1955-56; chief classification and pay, Milw. City Service, 1956-65; personnel br. chief AID, Washington, 1965-67; personnel dir. City of Hartford (Conn.), 1967-77; dir. human resources City of Miami (Fla.), 1977-85; cons. to various orgns., 1967-85; lectr. U. Conn., 1972-77, Fla. Internat. U., Miami, 1982-85. Co-chmn. New Eng. Task Force Labor Relations, Hartford, 1969-70; mem. Adv. Com. Personnel and Manpower, Washington, 1971-72; mem. Conn. Adv. Council on Intergovtl. Personnel Act, Hartford, Conn., 1971-75; mem. Task Force, Strategies for Future, Nat. Tng. and Devel. Service, Washington, 1977; mem. adv. com. to dept. pub. adminstrn. Fla. Internat.U., Miami, 1978. Recipient C. H. Cushman award Eastern Region Internat. Personnel Mgmt. Assn., 1982. Named Boss of Yr., Nat. Secs. Assn., Hartford, Conn., 1973. Mem. Internat. Personnel Mgmt. Assn. (pres. 1979, hon. life mem. 1982, Warner W. Stockberger award, 1986), Nat. Pub. Employers Labor Relations Assn. (founder 1972), Am. Soc. Pub. Adminstrs. (chpt. pres. 1965). Democrat. Home and Office: 531 Tibidabo Ave Coral Gables FL 33143

KRAUSEN, ANTHONY SHARNIK, surgeon; b. Phila., Feb. 22, 1944; s. B.M. and Kay S. (Sharnik) K.; m. Susan Elizabeth Park, Sept. 6, 1970; children—Nicole, Allison. Student Germantown Acad., 1949-61; B.A., Princeton U., 1965; M.D., U. Mich., 1969. Intern, Presbyn. Med. Center, Denver, 1969-70; resident St. Joseph Hosp., Denver, 1970-71, Barnes Hosp., St. Louis, 1972-76; with Milw. Med. Clinic, 1976—, head dept. facial plastic surgery, 1984—; mem. staffs Columbia, St. Michael, Children's, St. Mary Hosps., Milw. Pres. Contemporary Art Soc., Milw. Art Mus., 1983, bd. dirs. Friends of Art. Served with U.S. Army Nat. Guard, 1970-76. Fellow Am. Acad. Facial Plastic and Reconstructive Surgery, Am. Acad. Otolaryngology, Soc. Univ. Otolaryngologists, A.C.S.; mem. Nat. Neurofibromatosis Soc. (med. advisor Wis. chpt. 1985—), Wis. Otolaryngological Soc. Clubs: Ivy (Princeton, N.J.); Ausblick Ski (Milw.). Office: 3003 W Good Hope Rd Milwaukee WI 53209

KRAUSS, HENRY FREDERICK, JR., optometrist; b. Sewickley, Pa., Apr. 10, 1952; s. Henry Frederick and Mirella Anna (Guerrieri) K.; m. Sally Winston Miller, July 5, 1975; children—Molly Anne, Henry Neil, Malinda Paige, Michael Winston. B.S., Centre Coll. Ky., 1976; O.D., U. Houston, 1980. Optometrist, owner Eye Care Assocs., Richardson, Tex., 1980—; v.p. ProComp Systems Inc., Albuquerque, 1983-86; ptnr. K-W Distbrs., Dallas, 1983-86, Summit Seminars, Richardson, 1985—. Bd. dirs. Found. for Edn. and Research in Vision, 1988—, Southwest Vision Service Plan, 1982-84. Mem. Am. Optometric Assn., Tex. Optometric Assn. (Young Optometrist of Yr. award 1985), North Tex. Optometric Assn. (pres. 1983-84), Am. Optometric Found., Vision Ednl. Found., Better Vision Inst., Am. Pub. Health Assn. (vision care sect.). Republican. Mormon. Avocations: golf, tennis, photography, horsemanship. Office: Eye Care Assocs 1207 Hampshire Ln #101 Richardson TX 75080

KRAUT, JOEL ARTHUR, ophthalmologist; b. Jersey City, July 21, 1937; s. Alan and Lillian Betty (Kravitz) K.; m. Cathy Jane Kleven, June 30, 1963; children—David Terence, Amy Melissa. A.B. cum laude, Princeton U., 1958; M.D., Columbia U., 1962. Diplomate Am. Bd. Ophthalmology. Intern, Boston U. Med. Ctr., 1962-63; resident in ophthalmology NYU-Bellevue Med. Ctr., N.Y.C., 1963-66; chief ophthalmology USAF Hosp., Tachikawa, Japan, 1966-68; practice medicine specializing in ophthalmology Brookline, Mass., 1968—; clin. assoc., clin. instr. ophthalmology Harvard U. Med., Sch.; clin. instr. ophthalmology Tufts Sch. Medicine, 1968—; asst., surgeon in ophthalmology, dir. Low Vision Ctr., Mass. Eye and Ear Infirmary, 1968—, med. dir. Rehab. Ctr.; dir. physiol. optics dept. opthalmology Tufts-New Eng. Med. Ctr., 1968-73; cons. U.S. 5th Air Force, Japan, 1966-68. Contbr. articles to med. and profl. jours. Chmn. United Way Campaign, 1973; bd. dirs. Boston Aid to Blind, 1987; mem. adv. bd. Mass. Commn. for Blind, 1988. Cane scholar, 1958, St. John-Princeton scholar, 1962; U. Calif. research fellow, 1960. Fellow ACS; mem. Am. Acad. Opthalmology, New Eng. Ophthal. Soc., Mass. Ophthal. Soc., Soc. Geriatric Ophthalmology, Intraocular Lens Soc., New Eng. Lens Implant Soc. (sec. 1979-81, pres. 1981-83), Mass. Med. Soc., Greater Boston Med. Soc., Mass. Soc. Eye Physicians and Surgeons (exec. bd.), Phi Beta Kappa, Sigma Xi. Club: Hazel Hotchkiss Wightman Tennis. Office: 1371 Beacon St Brookline MA 02146

KRAUTBLATT, CHARLES JOHN, electrical engineer; b. College Point, N.Y., Sept. 28, 1950; s. Jack Charles and Catherine (DiDio) K.; m. Ann Florczak, Oct. 12, 1974; 1 child, Kristina Ann. BSEE, DeVry Inst. Tech., Phoenix, 1979. Mem. tech. staff TRW Def. and Space Corp., Los Angeles, 1979-81; dept. mgr. Kyocera Internat., San Diego, 1981-82; pres., tech. dir. EVS Engring., San Diego, 1982-84; cons. San Diego, 1983—. Served as cpl. with USMC, 1967-71. Mem. IEEE, Armed Forces Communications and Electronics Assn., Internat. Computer Cons. of Am. (nominating com. 1986), Calif. Chpt. Internat. Computer Cons. of Am., Air Force Assn., Scripps SR Club, Scripps Civic Assn. Home: 11826 Semillon Blvd San Diego CA 92131 Office: 9842 Herbert St Suite 256 San Diego CA 92131

KRAUTWURST, FRANZ, musicologist, educator; b. Munich, Aug. 7, 1923; s. Ludwig and Maria (Lidl) K.; m. Roswitha Strathmann, 1951; children: Martin, Marianne, Johannes, Renate. PhD, U. Erlangen, Fed. Republic Germany, 1950, Habilitation, 1956. Privatdozent U. Erlangen, 1956-62, univ. dozent, 1962-65, prof. musicology, 1965-80; prof. U. Augsburg, Fed. Republic Germany, 1980—. Author: Die Heilsbronner Chorbücher, 1956, Das Schrifttum zu Musikgeschichte der Stadt Nurnberg, 1964; editor Augsburger Jahrbuch Musikwissenschaft, 1984. Recipient Wissenschafts prize Stadtrat Nurnberg, 1961. Mem. Internat. Musicol. Soc., Gessellschaft Musikforschichte. Mem. Christich-Soziale Union party. Mem. Evangelisch Lutherisch Ch. Home: Im Herrengarten 18, D8520 Buckenhof-Erlangen Federal Republic of Germany Office: U Augsburg, Universitätstrasse 2, D8900 Augsburg Federal Republic of Germany

KRAVITZ, RUBIN, chemist; b. Framingham, Mass., Mar. 22, 1928; s. Abe and Lillian (Cohen) K.; B.S., Northeastern U., 1952; Dr. Pharm., 1982; m. Geraldine Pudaim, Aug. 20, 1950 (dec.); children—Richard Alan, Steven Jay, Stuart Paul; m. 2d, Annabelle S. Durieux, July 16, 1978; 1 dau., Michelle Pearl. Analytical chemist FDA, HEW, Boston, 1956-61, Alcohol and Tobacco Tax div. U.S. Treasury Dept., Boston, 1961-65; supr. phys. testing lab. Plastic div. Am. Hoechst Corp., Leominster, Mass., 1967-78, research chemist Plastic div., 1978-83; sr. devel. engr. EPS, 1983-85; pres. Nat. Plastics Mus. Inc., 1981-85; dir. pres. T.H.E. Hypnosis Ctr., Virginia Beach, Va., 1986—; staff pharmacist MacDonald Army Hosp., Ft. Eustis, Va., 1987; pres., chief exec. officer Cadet Labs., Virginia Beach, Va., 1984—; del. Va. Pharmaceutical Assn., 1988. Cubmaster Boy Scouts Am., Worcester, Mass., 1967-68; trustee, founding pres. Nat. Plastics Ctr. and Mus., 1985—. Served with USAAF, 1946-48. Mem. Assn. Military Surgeons U.S., Soc. Plastic Engrs. (newsletter editor 1969-71, treas. Pioneer Valley sect. 1972-73, v.p. 1973-74, chmn. tech. com. 1973, pres. Pioneer Valley sect. 1975-76, chmn. sect. museum 1979-85, achievement award 1981), ASTM (chmn. compression molding 1969-70, vice chmn. publicity and papers com. D-20 on plastics 1972-76, chmn. subcom. specimen preparation, chmn. sect. plastic furniture, chmn. specimen preparation 1976, chmn. task group Kravitz impact test method 1976, chmn. D 20.12 Olefin Plastics com., mem. exec. com. 1982-85), Assn. Analytical Chemists, Assn. to Advance Ethical Hypnosis, Am. Soc. Research and Clin. Hypnosis. Club: K.P. (chancellor comdr. 1963-64).

KRAW, GEORGE MARTIN, lawyer; b. Oakland, Calif., June 17, 1949; s. George and Pauline Dorothy (Herceg) K.; m. Sarah Lee Kenyon, Sept. 3, 1983. BA, U. Calif.-Santa Cruz, 1971; student, Lenin Inst., Moscow, 1971; MA, U. Calif.-Berkeley, 1974, JD, 1976. Bar: Calif. 1976, U.S. Dist. Ct. (no. dist.) Calif. 1976, U.S. Supreme Ct. 1980. Assoc. Bachan, Skillicorn, Watsonville, Calif., 1976-79, Trepel & Clark, San Jose, Calif., 1979-81; ptnr. Mount, Kraw & Stoelker, San Jose, 1981-88, Kraw & Kraw, San Jose, 1988—; asst. sec. Sysgen, Inc., Fremont, Calif., 1982—. Mem. ABA, Inter-Am. Bar Assn. Clubs: Metropolitan, University (San Jose). Office: Kraw & Kraw 333 W San Carlos River Park Tower 10th Floor San Jose CA 95112

KRAYBILL, RICHARD REIST, chemical engineer; b. Dover, N.H., July 31, 1920; s. Henry Reist and Mary Ruth (Grove) K.; B.Chem. Engring., Purdue U., 1942; M.S., U. Mich., 1943, Ph.D. (Am. Cyanamid fellow, Horace Rackham fellow), 1953; m. Jean Carolyn Gilbert, Aug. 8, 1945; children—Mary, Virginia, Anne, Elizabeth. Lab. asst. Am. Viscose Corp., Parkersburg, W. Va., 1941; asst. research engr. Calif. Research Corp., El Segundo, 1944-46; asst. prof. chem. engring. U. Rochester (N.Y.), 1950-55, assoc. prof., 1955-67; tech. assoc. Eastman Kodak Co., Rochester, 1967-83; sr. lectr. Univ. Coll. Liberal and Applied Studies, U. Rochester, 1978-79; cons. in field. Fellow Am. Inst. Chem. Engrs.; mem. Am. Chem. Soc., Am. Soc. Engring. Edn., Soc. Rheology, Soc. Plastics Engrs. (tech. vols. com. 1971-83; award for best paper 1964), Sigma Xi, Triangle Frat., Alpha Phi Omega, Phi Kappa Phi, Phi Lambda Gamma. Clubs: Pentwater Yacht, Bass Lake Sailing (Pentwater, Mich.); Island Yacht (Clearwater, Fla.); Pentwater Tennis, Shipwatch Tennis (Largo, Fla.). Contbr. articles to profl. jours. Home: 1704 Laurie Lane Belleair FL 34616

KRAYENBÜHL, FRANK FERNAND, architect; b. London, July 4, 1935; arrived in Eng., 1936; s. Hugo Alfred and Elsa Justina (Gross) K. Diploma in architecture, Swiss Tech. U., 1960, D in Tech. Scis., 1963. Pvt. practice architecture Zurich, Switzerland, 1965—; vis. prof. Swiss Tech. U., 1968-69. Prin. works include: Theater of Winterthur, completed 1979 (European Steel Prize 1981), Witikon Nursing Home, Zurich, completed 1983 (Good Bldgs. Zurich 1985), Gross Garage Grüze, Winterthur, completed 1975. Served to lt. col. Tank Corps, Swiss Army, 1955-85. Mem. Bund Schweizer Architekten, Schweizerischer Ingenieur and Architektenverein. Office: Olgastrasse 4, 8001 Zurich Switzerland

KREAGER, EILEEN DAVIS, bursar; b. Caldwell, Ohio, Mar. 2, 1924; d. Fred Raymond and Esther (Farson) Davis. B.B.A., Ohio State U., 1945. With accounts receivable dept. M & R Dietetic, Columbus, Ohio, 1945-50; complete charge bookkeeper Magic Seal Paper Products, Columbus, 1950-53, A. Walt Runglin Co., Los Angeles, 1953-54; office mgr. Roy C. Haddox and Son, Columbus, 1954-60; bursar Meth. Theol. Sch. Ohio, Delaware, 1961-86; adminstrv. cons. Fin. Ltd., 1986—; ptnr. Coll. Adminstrv. Sci., Ohio State U., 1975-80; seminar participant Paperwork Systems and Computer Sci., 1965, Computer Systems, 1964, Griffith Found. Seminar Working Women, 1975; pres. Altrusa Club of Delaware, Ohio, 1972-73. Del. Altrusa Internat., Montreal, 1972, Altrusa Regional, Greenbrier, 1973. Assoc. Am. Inst. Mgmt. (exec. council of Inst., 1979); mem. Am. Soc. Profl. Cons., Internat. Platform Assn., Ohio State U. Alumna Assn., AAUW, Kappa Delta. Methodist. Clubs: Ohio State U. Faculty, Delaware Country. Home: PO Box 214 Worthington OH 43085

KREBS, MARGARET ELOISE, publishing company executive; b. Clearfield, Pa., Apr. 20, 1927; d. Henry Louis and Delia Louise (Beahan) K.; grad. high sch. With Progressive Pub. Co., Inc., Clearfield, 1945—, bus. office mgr., 1956-60, bus. mgr., 1960-63, asst. to pub., 1963-69, asso. pub., 1981—, dir., exec. v.p., 1969-77, pres., 1977—;v.p./sec., dir. Indiana Broadcasters, Inc. (Pa.), Stas. WDAD-AM and WQMU-FM, 1967—; v.p./sec. Clearfield Broadcasters, Inc., Stas. WCPA-AM and WQYX-FM, 1965—, dir., 1971—. Mem. Pa. Newspaper Women's Assn., Clearfield Bus. and Profl. Women's Club (pres. 1952-53, dist. membership chmn. 1952-53), Sigma Delta Chi. Democrat. Roman Catholic. Club: Lake Glendale Sailing (sec. 1966—). Home: 526 Ogden Ave Clearfield PA 16830 Office: 206 E Locust St Clearfield PA 16830

KREBS, WILLIAM DOUGLAS, III, lawyer; b. Milw., May 28, 1917; s. William Douglas and Maybell Elizabeth (Cornish) K.; m. Miriam Elizabeth Sanford, Dec. 27, 1942; children—William Douglas IV, Robert Cornish, Kimberly Marie, Candace Clark. B.A., Ripon Coll., 1938; B.B.A., U. Wis.-Madison, 1947, J.D., 1947. Bar: Wis. 1947, N.Y. 1948. C.P.A., Wis., N.Y. Practice law, Potsdam, N.Y., 1948—. Spl. agt. CIC, 1942-46; asst. dir. security UN Conf. on Internat. Orgn., 1945. Mem. St. Lawrence County Magistrates Assn. (pres. 1972-73), Nat. Counter Intelligence Corps Assn. Christian Scientist, Mensa. Lodge: Lions (1st dist. gov.). Office: 75 Market St Potsdam NY 13676

KREER, IRENE OVERMAN, meeting management executive; b. McGrawsville, Ind., Nov. 11, 1926; d. Ralph and Laura Edith (Sharp) Overman; m. Henry Blackstone Kreer, Dec. 22, 1946; children: Laurene (dec.), Linda Kreer Witt. BS in Speech Pathology, Northwestern U., 1947. Speech pathologist pub. schs. Chgo., 1947-49; staff asst., lectr. Art Inst. Chgo., 1962—; pres. Irene Overman Kreer & Assocs., Inc., Chgo., 1962—; bd. dirs., officer SKK Inc., Chgo., 1962—; frequent lectr. on art, architecture Chgo. area; TV appearances representing Art Inst. edn. programs. Formerly bd. dirs. Glenview (Ill.) Pub. Library; mem. Glenview Community Ch. Mem. Field Mus., Chgo. Architecture Found., Smithsonian Assocs., Nat. Trust for Hist. Preservation, Assoc. Alumnae Northwestern U. (bd. dirs. 1975—), Delta Delta Delta. Republican. Mem. Glenview Community Ch.

KREGER, MELVIN JOSEPH, lawyer; b. Buffalo, Feb. 21, 1937; s. Philip and Bernice (Gerstman) K.; m. Patricia Anderson, July 1, 1955 (div. 1963), children: Beth Barbour, Arlene Roux; m. Renate Hochleitner, Aug. 15, 1975. JD, Mid-valley Coll. Law, 1978; diploma in taxation, U. San Diego, 1985, LLM in Taxation, 1988. Bar: Calif. 1978, U.S. Dist. Ct. (cen. dist.) Calif. 1979, U.S. Tax Ct. 1979. Life underwriter Met. Life Ins. Co., Buffalo, 1958-63; bus. mgr. M. Kreger Bus. Mgmt., Sherman Oaks, Calif., 1963-78, enrolled agt., 1971-78; sole practice North Hollywood, Calif., 1978—. Mem. Nat. Assn. Enrolled Agts. (pres. Los Angeles chpt. 1980-81, chmn. legal com. 1983-86), San Fernando Valley Estate Planning Council, State Bar of Calif., Los Angeles Bar Assn., San Fernando Valley Bar Assn. (probate sect.), Calif. Soc. Enrolled Agts. Jewish. Office: 11424 Burbank Blvd North Hollywood CA 91601

KREIDER, LEONARD EMIL, economics educator; b. Newton, Kans., Feb. 25, 1938; s. Leonard C. and Rachel (Weaver) K.; m. Louise Ann Pankratz, June 10, 1963; children: Brent Emil, Todd Alan, Ryan Eric. Student, Bluffton Coll., 1956-58; BA, Bethel Coll., 1960; student, Princeton U., 1960-61; MA, Ohio State U., 1962, PhD, 1968. Economist So. Ill. U., Carbondale, 1965-70; asst. prof. Beloit (Wis.) Coll., 1970—, prof., 1978, chmn. Dept. Econs. & Mgmt., 1984—, acting v.p. acad. affairs, 1987-88; chief of party, Devel. Assocs., Asuncion, Paraguay, 1970; economist Deere and Co., 1973, Castle and Cooke, San Francisco, 1975-76, AmCore, Rockford, Ill., 1984; cons. corps. and attys. Author: Development and Utilization of Managerial Talent, 1968; contbr. numerous articles, reports to profl. jours. Mem. Nat. Assn. Bus. Economists, Am. Econs. Assn., Am. Assn. Higher Edn., Soc. Internat. Devel. (pres. So. Ill. chpt. 1969), Indsl. Relations Research Assn. (elections com. 1974). Presbyterian. Home: 820 Milwaukee Rd Beloit WI 53511 Office: Dept Econ Mgmt Beloit Coll Beloit WI 53511

KREIFELS, FRANK ANTHONY, lawyer, corporation executive; b. Omaha, Nov. 26, 1951; s. Robert Frank and Mary Ellen (Basan) K.; 1 child, Katherine Joy. BBA in Fin., Creighton U., 1974, MBA in Fin. and Acctg., 1975; J.D., Hamline U., 1977. Bar: Minn. 1978, U.S. Dist. Ct. Minn. 1978, Nebr. 1983. Staff atty. NCR-Comten Inc., St. Paul, 1978-80; gen. counsel, sec. Agriventure Corp., Foxley & Co., Foxley Cattle Co., Herd Co., Flavorland Industries (and all affiliates), Omaha, 1980-85; mem. Ellsworth Law Firm, Omaha, 1985-87, exec. v.p., chief operating officer, Dale Beggs Devel. Co. (and all affiliates), 1987—; cons. Small Bus. Adminstrn., Omaha, 1974; corp. lobbyist Foxley Cattle Co./Herd Co., Omaha, 1981-85; appointed Neb. state reporter Am. Agrl. Law Update, 1985—. Campaign coordinator Nebr. Republican Party, 1982, 84. Smith. Recipient Cert. of Merit, Small Bus. Adminstrn., 1974. Mem. ABA, Am. Corp. Counsel Assn., Am. Agrl. Law Assn., Nebr. State Bar Assn., Phi Alpha Delta. Roman Catholic. Clubs: Omaha Barrister's, Omaha Westroads. Home: 10206 Ohio Dr Omaha NE 68134 Office: Dale Beggs Devel Co The Exchange Bldg 412 S 19th St Omaha NE 68102

KREITLER, THOMAS EDWARD, industrial engineer; b. Monticello, Ill., June 10, 1948; s. Ralph Edward and Frances (Thomas) K. BS in Indsl. Engring., Ill. State U., 1971. Regional sales mgr. Valmont Energy Systems, Valley, Nebr., 1980-81; plant mgr. Garner Industries, Lincoln, Nebr., 1981-83, sales mgr., 1983-84; mgr. quality engring. tooling Brunswick, Lincoln, 1984-86; owner, operator Command Engring., Lincoln, 1987-88; gen. mgr. Chief Command Products div. Chief Industries, 1988—. Patentee in field. Recipient Govs. Sailing Cup, 1982. Mem. Soc. Mfg. Engrs. (sr.), Am. Welding Soc., Lincoln Inventors Assn. (pres. 1987—), Nebr. Water Resources Assn. Roman Catholic. Lodge: Elks. Home: 662 W Lakeshore Dr Lincoln NE 68528 Office: Command Engring 251 Capitol Beach Blvd Lincoln NE 68528

KREITZMAN, SUSAN LINDA, writer; b. N.Y.C., Oct. 27, 1940; arrived in England, 1985; d. Joel David and Rose (Krinsky) Gross; m. Stephen Neil Kreitzman, May 27, 1962; children: Shawm, Aaron. BA, Hofstra U., 1962. Tchr. N.Y.C. Bd. Edn., 1962-65, Cambridge (Mass.) Bd. Edn., 1965-69, Atlanta Bd. Edn., 1969-72; chef Sidney's Just South Restaurant, Atlanta, 1976-77; tchr. Emory U., Atlanta, 1982-84; cons. food Howard Found., Cambridge, Eng., 1982—, Cambridge Nutrition Ltd., Norwich and Norfolk, Eng., 1982—; contbg. food editor Cambridge Scene, 1982—. Author: The Nutrition Cookbook, 1977, Sunday Best, 1981, Garlic, 1984, Deli, 1985, Comfort Food, 1986, Sue Kreitzman's Slim Cuisine, 1987; author, performer (video) Sue Kreitzman's Slim Cuisine, 1987; contbr. articles to profl. jours. and mags.; inventor no-fat saute method, 1987, no-fat mayonnaise, 1987. Jewish. Home and Office: Tiptoft, 54 High St, Burwell Cambs CB5 0HD, England

KREMER, ERHARD KARL, statistics educator; b. Löhnberg, Fed. Republic Germany, Jan. 19, 1953; s. Kurt and Hertha (Fey) K. Diploma, U. Giessen, Fed. Republic Germany, 1977; PhD, U. Hamburg, Fed. Republic Germany, 1979, habilitation, 1983. Group leader Bavarian Reins Co., Munich, 1980-81; prof. stats. U. Hamburg, 1983—; mng. dir. Nonprofit Assn. of Hamburg, 1986—. Author: Introduction to Insurance Mathematics, 1985; contbr. articles to profl. jours. Office: Robert Koch Strasse 14 A, Hamburg Federal Republic of Germany also: U Hamburg Inst Math Scholastics, Bundesstrasse 55, Hamburg Federal Republic of Germany

KREMIN, DANIEL PAUL, educational administrator; b. Bklyn., Sept. 26, 1946; s. Harry and Ruth K.; B.A., Fairleigh Dickinson U., 1967, M.A. (teaching fellow), 1974; M.S., Yeshiva U., 1976, Sp.C., 1977, Ph.D., 1978; m. Diane Joyce Siesel, Mar. 18, 1972; children—Sean, Todd. Tchr., N.Y.C. Bd. Edn., 1967-73; sr. psychologist Columbia Presbyn. Hosp., 1975-76; mem. com. on handicapped N.Y. Bd. Edn., 1977-81, psychologist, 1977-78, clin. coordinator, 1978-79, coordinator learning disabilities identification program, 1979, asst. to regional coordinator, 1979-80, chmn., 1980-81; dir. spl. services Teaneck (N.J.) Public Schs., 1981—. Vol., Whitestone Ambulance Corps, 1977; trustee Temple Sholom, Westbury, N.Y. Fellow clin. psychology Rousso Center, Albert Einstein Coll. Medicine, 1975; recipient Service award Essex County Overbrook Hosp., 1965. Mem. Am. Psychol. Assn., Soc. Pediatric Psychology, Nat. Honor Soc. Psychology, Nat. Assn. Sch. Psychologists, N.Y. State Psychol. Assn., Nassau County Psychol. Assn. Office: 1 W Forest Ave Teaneck NJ 07666

KREMP, HERBERT, journalist; b. Munich, Aug. 12, 1928; s. Johann and Elisabeth Kremp; m. Brigitte Steffal, 1956; 2 children. Ed. Munich U. Reporter, Frankfurter Neue Presse, 1956-57; polit. editor Rheinische Post, 1957-59; dir. polit. dept. Der Tag, Berlin, 1959-61; Bonn corr. Rheinisch Post, 1961-63; editor-in-chief Rheinische Post, 1963-68; editor-in-chief Die Welt, 1969-77, joint editor, 1981—, co-pub., 1981—; chief corr. in Peking, 1977-81, editor-in-chief, 1981—; recipient Konrad Adenauer Prize, 1984. Author: Am Ufer der Rubikon, Eine politische Anthropologie, Die Bambusbrucke: Ein asiatisches Tagebuch, 1979. Address: Godesberger Allee 99, 5300 Bonn 2 Federal Republic of Germany *

KRENTS, MILTON ELLIS, broadcast executive; b. Springfield, Mass., Dec. 22, 1911; s. Morris Joseph and Ethel (Kramer) K.; m. Irma Kopp, May 1, 1938; children—Lawrence, Harold, Elisabeth. B.S., N.Y. U., 1935. Jr. exec. trainee NBC, N.Y.C., 1935-39; dir. radio-TV Am. Jewish Com., 1936-69; TV programming cons. Assn. for Higher Edn. of N.E.A., 1965-68; radio, TV cons. Council Fin. Aid to Edn., 1960-65; communications cons. Revson Found., 1979-80; adv. bd. Nat. Jewish Broadcast Archives, Jewish Mus., N.Y.C., 1987—. Originator, exec. producer: radio and TV series for The Eternal Light, Jewish Theol. Sem., NBC, 1945—; radio cons.: Council for Democracy, 1942-45; radio, TV dir.: Am. Jewish Tercentenary, 1954. Nat. chmn. William E. Wiener Oral History Library, Am. Jewish Commn., 1969-84, dir., 1985—; bd. dirs. NYU Alumni Fedn., 1979-85. Recipient Robert E. Sherwood award, 1958; Faith and Freedom Broadcasting award Religious Heritage Am., 1972; Red Ribbon award Am. Film Festival, N.Y.C., 1983; Nat. Daytime Emmy award, 1983, 86; Alumni Service award and medal NYU, 1984; 40 Yrs. service award NBC-WNBC Radio, 1985. Mem. Pub. Relations Soc. Am., N.Y. U. Alumni Assn. (chmn. communications com. 1980—), Nat. Acad. TV Arts and Scis., Broadcast Pioneers. Home: 141 E 89th St New York NY 10128 Office: 165 E 56th St New York NY 10022

KRENZ, JAN, composer, conductor; b. Wloclawek, Poland, July 14, 1926; s. Otton and Eleonora K.; m. Alina Krenz, 1958; 1 son. Educated Warsaw and Lodz. Condr., Lodz Philharm. Orch., 1945, Poznan Philharm. Orch., 1948-49; dir. and 1st condr. Polish Radio Symphony Orch., Katowice, 1953-67; artistic dir., 1st condr. Grand Opera House (Teatr Wielki), Warsaw, 1967-73; gen. dir. music Bonn Orch., 1978—; concert tours in Hungary, Romania, Czechoslovakia, France, USSR, Germany, Italy, U.K., U.S., Japan, Australia; compositions include: Symphony, 2 string quartets, Nocturnes for Orch., Rozmowa dwoch miast (cantata), Rahpsody for Strings, Xylophone, Tam-Tam, Timpany and Celesta, 1952, Concertino for Piano and Small Symphony Orch., 1952; orchestral transcriptions of works by J.S. Bach, B. Bartok, Szymanowski. Recipient State prize, 1955, 72; prize Minister of Culture and Art, 1955, 63; prize Union of Polish Composers, 1968; Grand prix du Disque, France, 1972; prize of Polish Artists and Musicians Assn., 1974; diploma Ministry Fgn. Affairs, 1980; numerous others. *

KRENZER, ROBERT WAYNE, scientific company executive; b. Springfield, Ill., Aug. 17, 1940; s. John Frank and Edna Iola (Rigsby) K.; Profl. Engr., Colo. Sch. Mines, 1962; M.S., U. Denver, 1966, Ph.D., 1968, M.S.B.A., 1980; m. Patricia Ann Gant, June 24, 1961; children—Deborah Ann, Kurt Wayne. Metallurgist U.S. Steel Corp., Gary, Ind., 1962-63; engr. Hercules Inc., Magna, Utah, and Rocky Hill, N.J., 1963-64; staff Sandia Labs., Livermore, Calif., 1968-72; research specialist, research mgr. Rockwell Internat. Co., Golden, Colo., 1972-84, mgr. spl. projects, 1984-86, program mgr. productivity, 1986—, mem. Rockwell Speakers Bur., 1981—; cons. lasers. Commr. dist. Boy Scouts Am., 1971-72, 76-82, fund drive chmn., 1981, Explorer post adv., 1980-83, exec. com. Outdoor Program, 1986—, mem.-at-large Denver council, 1987—; v.p. Livermore (Calif.) Republican Assembly, 1972; participant Leadership Denver, 1979-80; tour guide Ramses II Egyptian Exhibit, Denver Mus. Nat. History. Joint Honor scholar, 1958; NSF fellow, 1964; ASTM student awardee, 1966. Recipient Rocky Flats Good Citizenship award, 1977; named Rockwell Engr. of Yr., 1976, Rocky Flats Engr. of Yr., 1976. Fellow Am. Soc. Metals (chmn. chpt. 1978, organizer extractive metallurgy chpt. 1980, mem. fellow selection com. 1982-85, council for profl. interests 1983-87); mem. AIME, Nat. Mgmt. Assn., Nat. Eagle Scout Assn., Colo. Mountain Club, Denver C. of C. (energy, transp. and environ. com. 1980-81), Egypt Exploration Soc., Colo. Hist. Soc., Tahosa Alumni Assn. (bd. dirs. 1981—), Sigma Xi, Sigma Phi Epsilon (alumni bd. 1977), Alpha Sigma Mu, Sigma Gamma Epsilon. Club: Elks. Contbg. author book, contbr. articles to profl. publs. Patentee in field. Home: 8426 Quay Dr Arvada CO 80003 Office: PO Box 464 Golden CO 80401

KREPPS, ETHEL CONSTANCE, lawyer; b. Mountain View, Okla., Oct. 31, 1937; d. Howard Haswell and Pearl (Moore) Goomda; R.N., St. John's Med. Center, 1971; B.S., U. Tulsa, 1974, J.D., 1979; m. George Randolph Krepps, Apr. 10, 1954; children—George Randolph, Edward Howard Moore. Nurse, St. John's Med. Center, Tulsa, 1971-75; admitted to Okla. bar, 1979; individual practice law, Tulsa, 1979—; mem. Indian law alumni com. U. Tulsa COll. Law; atty., dir. Indian Child Welfare Program, 1981—; atty. Native Am. Coalition, Inc., Kiowa Tribe Okla., Tulsa Indian Youth Council, Legal Research Okla. Indian Affairs Commn. Chmn., Okla. Indian Child Welfare Orgn., 1981—; tribal sec. Kiowa Tribe Okla., 1979-81. Mem. ABA, Fed. Bar Assn., Tulsa Women Lawyers Assn., AM. Indian Bar Assn., Okla. Indian Bar Assn., Okla. Bar Assn., Tulsa County Bar Assn., Oklahoma County Bar Assn., Am. Indian Nurses Assn. (v.p.), Nat. Indian Social Workers Assn. (pres. 1984—), Assn. Trial Lawyers Am., Phi Alpha Delta, Nat. Native Am. C. of C. (sec. 1980—), Internat. Indian Child Conf. (founder, chair). Democrat. Baptist. Author: A Strong Medicine Wind, 1979; Oklahoma Memories, 1981. Home: 4425 NW 19th Oklahoma City OK 73107 Office: 4010 N Lincoln Suite 200 Oklahoma City OK 74105

KREPS, ROBERT WILSON, research chemist; b. Denver, Feb. 27, 1946; s. Forrest Wilson and Margaret Rose Kreps; student U. Denver, 1964-67; B.S., Iowa State U., 1968; m. Janet Suzanne Graves, May 16, 1968. Staff chemist Cook Paint & Varnish Co., Kansas City, Mo., 1969-70; mgr. battery tech. Farmland Industries, Inc., Kansas City, 1970-72; mgr. quality control Celotex Corp., Charleston, Ill., 1972-73; research chemist Ball Corp., Muncie, Ind., 1973-75; research chemist pigments group SCM Corp., Balt., 1976-78; materials engr. Oceanic div. Westinghouse Electric Co., Annapolis, Md., 1979-80, sr. materials engr., 1980-83; v.p. research and devel. Solson Chem. Inc., Washington, 1984-85; sr. contamination control engr. Northrop Services, Inc., Goddard Space Flight Ctr., Greenbelt, Md., 1984; sr. materials engr. vertical launch system Martin-Marietta Balt. Aerospace, 1985-86, Robert Kreps & Assoc., 1987—. Mem. Am. Chem. Soc. (chmn. membership com. Md. sect. 1979-80, chmn. pub. relations com. 1983-86), Instrument Soc. Am. (exec. council Md. sect. 1980), AAAS, Am. Soc. for Nondestructive Testing, Nat. Assn. Corrosion Engrs., ASTM, AAAS, Inst. Environ. Sci. Column editor Chemtech, 1981—; contbr. articles to profl. jours. Home and Office: 412-B Hidden Brook Dr Glen Burnie MD 21061

KRESS, ELEANOR LADD, educator; b. N.S., Can., Sept. 14, 1919; came to U.S., 1925, naturalized, 1937; d. Philip Putnam and Katherine Fraser (MacKay) Murphy; B.S., Ind. U., 1950, M.S., 1953; Ed.D., Fla. State U., 1960; m. Roy Alfred Kress, Dec. 4, 1969; children—Alexander Ladd, Lisa Ladd Kidder. Classroom tchr., then asst. supt. instrn. Pinellas County (Fla.) schs., 1950-67; assoc. prof. U. Ga., 1967-70, psychology of reading dept. Temple U., Phila., 1970-78; prof. U. S.C., Spartanburg, 1978—; tchr. NDEA seminars, Japan, 1966, Switzerland, 1967. Fellow Linguistics Inst., U. Calif., Berkeley, 1967; Fulbright sr. research fellow, Pakistan, 1983. Mem. Internat. Reading Assn. (dir. 1978-81, pres. Fla. chpt. 1960-61), AAUW (pres. Clearwater chpt. 1964-65), Assn. Childhood Edn. Internat. (pres. Fla. chpt. 1963-64), AAUP, Assn. Supervision and Curriculum Devel., Am. Ednl. Research Assn. Democrat. Club: Altrusa. Author articles in field. Home: 230 Pennsylvania Ave Kutztown PA 19530 also: U SC Spartanburg SC 29303

KRESS, RALPH HERMAN, manufacturing company executive; b. Lawrence, Mass., July 10, 1904; s. Edward and Sadie (Welsh) K.; m. Edna Llewelyn Sheridan, Sept. 9, 1929; 1 son, Edward Sheridan. Student mech. engring. and applied math., Lowell Inst., M.I.T., 1937-39, 42. Salesman Dodge Truck, Lawrence, 1922-34; sales mgr. Chevrolet Truck Sales, Lawrence, 1934-39; engr. GM Chevrolet and Fleet div., Detroit, Boston, Washington, 1939-43; exec. v.p. Dart Truck Co., Kansas City, Mo., 1950-55; mgr. truck div. Letourneau Westinghouse Corp., Peoria, Ill., 1955-62; mgr. truck devel. Caterpillar Tractor Co., Peoria, 1962-69; exec. v.p. Kress Corp., Brimfield, Ill., 1969—. Contbr. articles to profl. jours. Served to maj. U.S. Army, 1943-46. Decorated Legion of Merit. Fellow Soc. Automotive Engrs. (G. Edwin Burks Lecture award 1975); mem. Assn. U.S. Army, Ill. Mining Assn., Western Mining Assn. Republican. Christian Scientist. Club: Rotary. Home: 4444 Knoxville St Peoria IL 61614 Office: PO Box 368 Brimfield IL 61517

KRESSIN, EILEEN KAY, real estate agent; b. Port Washington, Wis., July 1, 1950; d. Harold Frederick and Emma Helen (Nierode) K. B.S., Central Mo. State U., 1974. Directory rep. Southwestern Bell Tel. Co., Kansas City, Mo., 1975-76, directory sales supr., Houston, 1976-78, staff mgr. directory tng., St. Louis, 1978-80, dist. mgr., directory tel. sales, clerical, Kansas City, Mo., 1980-81, div. sales mgr. yellowpages, Oklahoma City, 1981-85; sales assoc. Apple Realty, Inc., Oklahoma City, 1985—. Organist, Holy Cross Lutheran Ch., Oklahoma City, 1982—. Mem. Am. Mktg. Assn. (v.p. 1980), Sales Mgmt. Exec. Assn., Central Mo. State U. Alumni Assn. Republican. Lutheran. Club: Oklahoma City Ski. Office: Apple Realty Inc 11317 S Western Suite 100 Oklahoma City OK 73170

KRETSCHMER, WOLFGANG ERNST, psychiatrist; b. Mergentheim, Fed. Republic of Germany, Feb. 14, 1918; s. Ernst and Luise (Pregizer) K.; m. Marianne Sigel, Apr. 12, 1947; children: Sabine, Stephan. MD, U. Marburg, Fed. Republic of Germany, 1942. Prof. Tübingen, Fed. Republic of Germany, 1958—; scholar State U., Santiago, Chile, 1959-61. Author: Reifung als Grund von Krise, 1972, Psychoanalyse im Widerstreit, 1983. Served to lt. M.C., German Army, 1942-45, Russia. Mem. Deutsche Gesellschaft für Individualpsychologie, Deutsche Gesellschaft für Logotherapie, Real Academia de Medicina (Valencia, Spain chpt. 1969—), Academia de Medicina (Medellin, Columbia 1960—). Home: Spemannstrasse 9, D-7400 Tübingen Federal Republic of Germany

KREUTZER, FRANKLIN DAVID, lawyer; b. Miami, Fla., June 5, 1940; s. Ernst and Elsa (Meitner) K.; m. Judith Sue Jacobs, June 16, 1963; children: Renee Charlotte, Jay Ernst. BBA, U. Miami, 1960, JD, 1964. Bar: Fla. 1964, U.S. Dist. Ct. (so. dist.) Fla. 1965, U.S. Ct. Appeals (5th cir.) 1971, U.S. Ct. Appeals (11th cir.) 1982, U.S. Supreme Ct. 1971. Assoc., Shevin, Goodman & Holtzman, 1964-65; ptnr. Wallace & Kreutzer, P.A., 1966-74; sole practice, Miami, 1974—; participant White House Seminar on Legal Interns, 1963; spl. asst. atty. gen. State of Fla., 1975-78; spl. counsel to comptroller State of Fla., 1975-78; gen. counsel Democratic Exec. Com. Dade County, 1968-70. Mem. City of Miami Pension and Retirement Bd., 1966-68; chmn. Miami Charter Rev. Bd., 1967-81; mem. Dade County Charter Rev. Commn., 1981-82; pres. Greater Miami Hebrew Fla. Loan Assn., 1974-77; pres. S.E. region United Synagogue Am., 1980-84, v.p., 1983-85, chmn. council regional presidents, 1983-85, internat. pres., 1985—; internat. v.p. World Council of Synagogues, 1985—; internat. v.p., exec. com., bd. dirs. Mercaz Conservative Zionism, 1984—; bd. dirs. Jewish Theol. Sem. of Am., 1985—; exec. com. Synagogue Council of Am., 1985—; pres. Temple Zion, 1977-79; bd. dirs. Gen. Council World Zionist Orgn., 1985—; bd. dirs. South Fla. Leukemia Soc., 1968-77; pres. South Fla. chpt. Cystic Fibrosis Found., 1970-74; endowment com. U. Miami, 1974—. Recipient cert. of appreciation City of Miami, 1968; recipient Order Golden Donkey, Dem. Exec. Com. Dade County, 1970. Mem. ABA, Fla. Bar Assn., Fla. Trial Lawyers Assn., Dade County Trial Lawyers Assn., Dade County Bar Assn., Acad. Trial Lawyers Am. (exec. com. 1985), Am. Israel Pub. Affairs Com. (exec. com 1985—), Nat. Jewish Community Relations Adv. Council, Conf. of Pres. of Major Am. Jewish Orgns., Omicron Delta Kappa, Phi Delta Phi. Democrat. Home: 8615 SW 48th St Miami FL 33155 Office: 3041 NW 7th St Suite 100 Miami FL 33125

KREWSON, CHARLES NORMAN, diversified industries exec.; b. Williamsport, Pa., Nov. 22, 1927; s. George Norman and Harriet DeHart (Cawley) K.; B.S., Wharton Sch., U. Pa., 1951; m. Pamela Lee Hudson, June 6, 1953; children—Charles Norman, Patricia, Robert, Katherine, Douglas. With Gen. Electric Co., various locations, 1951-71; v.p. mktg. and internat. devel. Talley Industries, Inc., Mesa, Ariz., 1971-79; pres. Comml. Products Group, 1976-79; group v.p. Gen. Time Corp. subs. Talley Industries, Mesa, 1972, pres., 1973-79, also dir.; chmn., dir. Eastern Time Ltd., Hong Kong, Westclox Can. Ltd., GT Investment Ltd., Can.; chmn., pres. Antilles Industries, Inc.; pres., dir. Talley Internat. Sales Corp.; chmn., pres. Krewson Assocs., Inc., Scottsdale, Ariz., 1978—; dir. Industria Relojera Mexicana S.A. Adv. bd. Fiesta Bowl, 1977—; treas. Valley Presbyn. Ch., Scottsdale, 1981-82. Served with USN, 1945-46. Mem. U.S. C. of C., Nat. Security Indsl. Assn., Am. Def. Preparedness Assn., Phi Gamma Delta, Beta Alpha Psi. Mason (Shriner). Clubs: Arizona (Phoenix); Mountain Shadows Country. Paradise Valley Country, Rotary (Scottsdale). Home: 4138 E Lakeside Ln Scottsdale AZ 85253

KRIEBLE, ROBERT H., corporation executive; b. Worcester, Pa., Aug. 22, 1916; s. Vernon K. and Laura (Cassel) K.; m. Nancy Brayton, Sept. 3, 1939; children: Frederick B., Helen Krieble Fusscas. Student, Haverford Coll., 1935; Ph.D. in Chemistry, Johns Hopkins U., 1939; D.Sc. (hon.), Trinity Coll., Hartford, Conn., 1974. Francis P. Garvin fellow Dept. Chemistry, Johns Hopkins Sch. Higher Edn., 1935-39; research chemist Socony Vacuum Oil Co., 1939-43; various positions with Gen. Electric Co., 1943-56; v.p. Loctite Corp., 1956-64, pres., chief exec. officer, 1964-76, chmn., 1976-80, chmn., chief exec. officer, 1980-86, ret., 1986. Patentee in field of silicones, anaerobic adhesives and petrochems. via air oxidation. Hon. trustee Johns Hopkins U., Balt.; trustee Wadsworth Atheneum, Hartford, Conn.; bd. dirs. Am. Ctr. for Capital Formation- Ctr. for Policy Research, Ctr. Internat. Pvt. Enterprise, Council for Nat. Policy, New Enterprise Assocs., U.S. Bus. and Indsl. Council, Inst. for Ednl. Affairs, Inst. for Polit. Economy, Free Congress Research and Edn. Found., Rockford Inst., Ronald Reagan Presdl. Found., U.S. Bus. and Indsl. Council; chmn. bd. dirs. Inst. for Research on Econs. of Taxation; bd. dirs., vice chmn. Heritage Found.; com. chmn. Council on Trends & Perspectives; vice chmn. Nat. Chamber Found., U.S. C. of C., also chmn. council on trends and perspectives com.; mem. corp. strategic planning council Internat. Mgmt. and Devel. Inst. Recipient Comml. Devel. Assn. Honor award, 1974, Am. Eagle award in Pub. Affairs, 1979, Winthrop-Sears medal - Entrepreneur of Yr. Chem. Industry Assn., 1979, Adhesives and Sealants Council award, 1982. Mem. Phila. Soc., Phi Beta Kappa, Sigma Xi. Clubs: Hartford, University (Hartford); Dauntless (Essex, Conn.); University (Washington). Home: PO Box 507 Old Lyme CT 06371 Office: 15 Lewis St Suite 401 Hartford CT 06103 also: 300 Metropolitan Sq 655 15th St NW Washington DC 20005

KRIEGER, MICHAEL PARIS, neurologist; b. Bay City, Mich., Sept. 13, 1942; s. Maurice Harold and Elinor L. (Kuttner) K.; m. Sherry A. Saunders, Feb. 14, 1983; children—William Harvey, Elizabeth Maurine. A.B., Dartmouth Coll., 1964; M.D., N.Y. Med. Coll., 1968. Diplomate Am. Bd. Psychiatry and Neurology. Resident in internal medicine Meadowbrook Hosp., Long Island, N.Y., 1969-70; resident in neurology Walter Reed Army Med. Ctr., Washington, 1970-73; chief neurology sect. Walson Army Hosp., Ft. Dix, N.J., 1973-75; clin. neurologist, mng. ptnr. Neurol. Assocs. N. Central Ohio Inc., Mansfield, 1975-83; pres., practice medicine specializing in neurology Neurol. Services Inc., Mansfield, 1983—; med. dir. Peoples Hosp. Sleep Disorder Lab., 1986—; chief of staff Peoples Hosp., 1987; cons. neurology, epilepsy Rehab. Ctr. N. Central Ohio, Mansfield, 1967-86; physician, advisor Ohio State Med. Assts. Bd. dirs. Multiple Sclerosis Soc., Mansfield, 1976-78. Served to maj. U.S. Army, 1970-75. Mem. Clin. Sleep Soc., Am. Acad. Neurology, Am. Soc. Internal Medicine, Ohio State Med. Assn., Richland County Med. Soc., Am. Legion. Club: Mens Garden (Mansfield). Avocations: gardening; skiing. Office: Neurol Services Inc 661 Park Ave E Mansfield OH 44905

KRIEGER, PAUL EDWARD, lawyer; b. Fairmont, W.Va., Mar. 30, 1942; s. Paul Julius Krieger and Martha Frances (Graham) Ralph; m. Elizabeth N. Krieger, July 2, 1965; children: Andrew, Thomas. BS in Mining Engring., U. Pitts., 1964; postgrad. Pa. State U., 1964-65; LLB, U. Md., 1968; LLM, George Washington U., 1971. Bar: Md. 1968, D.C. 1973, Tex. 1979, U.S. Patent and Trademark Office, 1970. Faculty research asst. U. Md., 1967-70; assoc. Brumbaugh, Graves, Donohue & Raymond, N.Y.C., 1970-71; ptnr. Lane, Aitken, Dunner & Ziems, Washington, 1971-78; sr. pat. atty. Dresser Industries Inc., Dallas, 1978-79; ptnr. Pravel, Gambrell, Hewitt, Kimball & Krieger, Houston, 1979—; adj. prof. U. Houston Law Ctr., 1985—. Mem. ABA, Am. Pat. Law Assn., State Bar Tex., Houston Pat. Law Assn., N.Y. Pat. Law Assn. Home: 12714 Old Oaks Houston TX 77024 Office: 1177 W Loop S Suite 1010 Houston TX 77027

KRIENKE, CAROL BELLE MANIKOWSKE (MRS. OLIVER KENNETH KRIENKE), realtor, appraiser; b. Oakland, Calif., June 19, 1917; d. George and Ethel (Purdon) Manikowske; student U. Mo., 1937; B.S., U. Minn., 1940; postgrad. UCLA, 1949; m. Oliver Kenneth Krienke, June 4, 1941; children—Diane (Mrs. Robert Denny), Judith (Mrs. Kenneth A. Giss), Debra Louise (Mrs. Ed Paul Davalos). Demonstrator, Gen. Foods Corp., Mpls., 1940; youth leadership State of Minn. Congl. Conf., U. Minn., Mpls. 1940-41; war prodn. worker Airesearch Mfg. Co., Los Angeles, 1944; tchr. Los Angeles City Schs., 1945-49; realtor DBA Ethel Purdon, Manhattan Beach, Calif., 1949; buyer Purdon Furniture & Appliances, Manhattan Beach, 1950-58; realtor O.K. Krienke Realty, Manhattan Beach, 1958—. Manhattan Beach bd. rep. Community Chest for Girl Scouts U.S., 1957; bd. dirs. South Bay council Girl Scouts U.S.A., 1957-62, mem. Manhattan Beach Coordinating Council, 1956-68; mem. Long Beach Area Childrens Home Soc. (v.p., 1967-68, pres. 1979; charter mem. Beach Pixies, 1957—, pres. 1967; chmn. United Way, 1967); sponsor Beach Cities Symphony, 1953—. Mem. DAR (life, citizenship chmn. 1972-73, v.p. 1979, 83—), Colonial Dames XVII Century (charter mem. Jared Eliot chpt. 1977, v.p., pres. 1979-81, 83-84), Friends of Library, Torrance Lomita Bd. of Realtors, South Bay Bd. Realtors, Nat. Soc. New England Women (life, Calif. Poppy Colony), Internat. Platform Assn., Soc. Descs. of Founders of Hartford (life), Friends of Banning Mus., Manhattan Beach Hist. Soc., Manhattan Beach C. of C. (Rose and Scroll award 1985), U. Minn. Alumni (life). Republican. Mem. Community Ch. (pres. Women's Fellowship 1970-71). Home: 924 Highview St Manhattan Beach CA 90266 Office: O K Krienke Realty 1716 Manhattan Beach Blvd Manhattan Beach CA 90266

KRIER, CURTIS GENE, accounting and finance consultant; b. Mpls., Aug. 11, 1948; s. Curtis George and Jeanne (Dale) K.; m. Nancy D. Carlson, Sept. 1980. B.A., U. Minn., 1970, B.S.B., 1978; M.B.A., Mankato State U. (Minn.), 1978. Cert. Am. Inst. Banking. Asst. to bank ops. officer 3d Northwestern Nat. Bank, Mpls., 1972-75; staff acct. Robert G. Engelhart & Co., Burnsville, Minn., 1978-79, House & Nezerka, C.P.A.s, 1979-80; controller Calc-Type, Inc., Mpls., 1980-81; pres. Curtis G. Krier & Co., acctg. and fin. cons., Edina, Minn., 1981-86; v.p. fin. Data Recording Tech. Corp., Mpls., 1986—; treas. Colonial Ch. of Edina . Mem. Nat. Assn. Accts. (sec. bd. dirs. Mpls. Viking chpt. 1982-84). Home: 9211 Lake Riley Blvd Chaska MN 55318 Office: Data Recording Tech Corp 690 Mendelssohn Ave Minneapolis MN 55427

KRIKLER, DENNIS MICHAEL, consultant cardiologist, medical editor; b. Cape Town, Republic South Africa, Dec. 10, 1928; came to Eng., 1966; s. Barnet and Eva (Katz) K.; m. Hanneliese Winterstein, July 3, 1955; children: Shirley Jean, Paul Alan. MB, ChB, U. Cape Town, 1951, MD, 1973. Intern, registrar Groote Schuur Hosp., Cape Town, 1952-56, sr. registrar, 1957-58;; cons. physician Central Hosp., Salisbury, Rhodesia, 1958-66, Prince of Wales's Hosp., London, 1967-73; cons. cardiologist, sr. lectr. cardiovascular diseases Hammersmith Hosp., Royal Postgrad. Med. Sch., London and Ealing Hosp., Southall, Middlesex, Eng., 1973—. Editor, co-author: (with J.F. Goodwin) Cardiac Arrhythmias, 1975; editor, author: Calcium Antagonists, 1980, Amiodarone, 1983; editor: Brit. Heart Jour., 1981—. C.J. Adams Meml. Travelling fellow, 1956; recipient Sir William Osler award U. Miami, 1981; Paul Dudley White fellow and citation internat. achievement Am. Heart Assn., 1984. Fellow Am. Coll. Cardiology, Royal Coll. Physicians (London), Royal Coll. Physicians (Edinburgh); hon. fellow Am. Heart Assn. Council Clin. Cardiology; mem. Brit. Cardiac Soc. (treas. 1976-81), Soc. Francaise de Cardiologie (corr.). Jewish. Avocations: history of medicine, photography. Office: 55 Wimpole St, London W1M 7DF, England

KRIKORIAN, ARAM GIRAIR, consulting company executive; b. Damascus, Syria, May 1, 1949; s. Yervant George and Anahid Helen (Krakirian) K. B.A., Damascus U., 1969-73; cert., U. Chgo., 1974. Asst. gen. mgr. Arab Advt. Agy., Kuwait, 1975-78; client services dir. Impact BBDO, Kuwait, 1979-80; mng. dir. Harlequin Arab World, Athens, Greece, 1981-83; pres., chief exec. officer Consol. Bus. Cons., Athens, 1984—; chmn. Consol. Bus. Cons. Middle East Ltd., Channel Islands, 1984—; lectr. to confs. Exec. sec. Armenian Youth Assn., Damascus, 1970-74. Mem. Inst. Dirs. (assoc.), Armenian Gen. benevolent Assn., Am. Hellenic C. of C., French C. of C. Mem. Armenian Apostolic Ch. Clubs: French Exec., Kuwait Bridge. Avocations: Basketball; bridge; philately. Home and Office: Athanassiou DiaKou 8, 15237 Filothei Greece

KRIKOS, GEORGE ALEXANDER, pathologist, educator; b. Old Phaleron, Greece, Sept. 17, 1922; came to U.S., 1946; s. Alexios and Helen (Spyropoulou) K.; m. Aspasia Manoni, June 22, 1949; children: Helen, Alexandra, Alexios. D.D.S., U. Pa., 1949; Ph.D., U. Rochester, 1959; Ph.D. hon. doctorate, U. Athens, Greece, 1981. Asst. prof. pathology U. Pa. Sch. Dentistry, 1958-61, asso. prof., 1961-67, prof., 1967-68, chmn. dept., 1964-68; asso. prof. oral pathology U. Pa. Grad. Sch., 1962-68, prof. oral pathology, 1968; prof. pathobiology Sch. Dentistry, U. Colo., Denver, 1968-75, chmn. dept. pathobiology, 1968-73, prof. oral biology, 1975-86, clin. prof. oral biology, 1986—, chmn. dept., 1976-77; asst. dean basic sci. affairs Sch. Dentistry, U. Colo., 1973-75, asso. dean oral biology affairs, 1975-76; vis. prof. Sch. Dentistry, U. Athens, 1980-81; mem. dental study sect. NIH, 1966-70; mem. cancer com. Colo.-Wyo. Regional Med. Program, 1970-72; cons. oral pathology Denver VA Hosp., 1970-72. Served with AUS, 1949-54. Mem. Am. Assn. Pathologists, Internat. Assn. Dental Research, Sigma Xi. Home: 350 Ivy St Denver CO 80220 Office: U Colo Sch Dentistry 4200 E 9th Ave Denver CO 80262

KRINGLEN, EINAR, psychiatrist, educator; b. Norway, June 6, 1931; m. Gerd Winge Knutsen. MD, U. Bergen, 1958. Intern Vestfold Sentralsykehus, Tonsberg; resident dept. psychiatry Dikemark Hosp., U. Oslo, 1960-64; research fellow Norwegian Research Council for the Scis. and Humanities, 1965-67; assoc. prof. psychiatry U. Bergen, Norway, 1967-69; prof. clinical psychology U. Bergen, 1969-71; prof. behavioral sci. in medicine U. Oslo, 1976-83, prof. psychiatry and physician in chief Dept. Psychiatry, 1984—; research fellow Nat. Inst. Mental Health, Bethesda, Md., 1965-66, Ctr. Advanced Study in Behavioral Scis., Stanford, Calif., 1974-75. Author several books. Home: Jornstadv 7, 1360 Nesbru Norway Office: Dept Psychiatry, U Oslo, Vinderen, Oslo 3, Norway

KRIPNER, GEORGE MARTIN, lawyer; b. Munich, Bavaria, Fed. Republic of Germany, July 17, 1954; s. Josef and Olga (Wlasjeva) K.; m. Alison Jane Schwartz, May 10, 1975 (div. Mar. 1982). BA, Johns Hopkins U., 1975; JD, U. Balt., 1978. Bar: Pa. 1978, Cts. Mil. Review, 1984, U.S. Ct. Mil. Appeals, 1987. Ptnr. Taylor & Kripner Attys. at Mil. Law, Jacksonville, N.C., 1983—. Bd. dirs. Am. Cancer Soc., Onslow County, N.C., 1986—; Presidio of San Francisco, Korea, Ft. Monmouth, N.J. Served to capt. U.S. Army, 1978-82, Korea. Decorated Meritorious Service medal, 1982, Army Commendation medals, 1980, 81. Mem. ABA, Onslow County Bar Assn., Assn. Trial Lawyers Am. Democrat. Home: 611 Myrtlewood Circle Jacksonville NC 28540 Office: Taylor & Kripner Attys Mil Law 824 Gum Branch Rd Jacksonville NC 28540

KRIPPNER, STANLEY CURTIS, psychologist; b. Edgerton, Wis., Oct. 4, 1932; s. Carroll Porter and Ruth Genevieve (Volenberg) K.; m. Lelie Anne Harris, June 25, 1966; stepchildren—Caron, Robert. B.S., U. Wis., 1954; M.A., Northwestern U., 1957, Ph.D., 1961; Ph.D. (hon.), Univ. Humanistic Studies, San Diego, 1982. Speech therapist Warren Pub. Schs. (Ill.), 1954-55, Richmond Pub. Schs. (Va.), 1955-56; dir. Child Study Ctr. Kent State U. (Ohio), 1961-64; dir. dream lab. Maimonides Med. Ctr., Bklyn., 1964-73; dir. Ctr. Consciousness Studies Saybrook Inst., San Francisco, 1973—; vis. prof. U. P.R., 1972, Sonoma State U., 1972-73, Univ. Life Scis., Bogotá, Colombia, 1974, Inst. for Psychodrama and Humanistic Psychology, Caracas, Venezuela, 1975, West Ga. Coll., 1976, John F. Kennedy U., 1980-82; lectr. Acad. Pedagogical Scis., Moscow, 1971, Acad. Scis., Beijing, China, 1981. Author: (with Montague Ullman) Dream Telepathy, 1973, Song of the Siren: A Parapsychological Odyssey, 1975; (with Alberto Villoldo) The Realms of Healing, 1976, Human Possibilities, 1980; (with Alberto Villoldo) Healing States, 1987; (with Jerry Solfvin) La Science et les Pouvoirs Psychiques de l'Homme, 1986, (with Joseph Dillard) Dreamworking, 1988; editor: Advances in Parapsychological Research, Vol. 1, 1977, Vol. 2, 1978, Vol. 3, 1982, Vol. 4, 1984, Vol. 5, 1987, Psychoenergetic Systems, 1979; co-editor: Galaxies of Life, 1973, The Kirlian Aura, 1974, The Energies of Consciousness, 1975, Future Science, 1977; mem. editorial bd.: Gifted Child Quar., Internat. Jour. Paraphysics, Jour. Humanistic Psychology, Jour. Transpersonal Psychology, Revision Jour., Jour. Theoretical Parapsychology, Jour. Indian Psychology, Psi Research, Metanoia, Dream Network Bulletin, Humanistic Psychologist, Internat. Jour. Psychosomatics, Jour. Creative Children and Adults, InterAm. U. Press; contbr. 500 articles to profl. jours. Mem. adv. bd. A.R.E. Clinic; bd. dirs. Acad. Religion and Psychical Research, Survival Research Found., Aesculapian Inst. for Healing Arts, Hartley Film Found., Inst. for Multilevel Learning, Internat. Horizon Ednl. Audio Recordings, John E. Fetzer Energy Medicine Research Inst., Forest Inst. Profl. Psychology, Humanistic Psychology Ctr. N.Y., Ctr. Transcendence and Transintegration, Ky. Ctr. Psychosynthesis. Recipient Service to Youth award YMCA, 1959; recipient citation of merit Nat. Assn. Gifted Children, 1972, citation of merit Nat. Assn. Creative Children and Adults, 1975, cert of recognition Office of Gifted and Talented, U.S. Office Edn., 1976, Volker Medal South Africa Soc. Psychical Research, 1980. Fellow Am. Soc. Clin. Hypnosis, Am. Psychol. Assn., Soc. Sci. Study Sex; mem. Am. Soc. Psychical Research, N.Y. Soc. Clin. Psychologists (assoc.), Am. Acad. Social and Polit. Sci., AAAS, Am. Ednl. Research Assn., Am. Assn. of Counseling and Devel., Internat. Council Psychologists, Assn. for Study of Dreams, Assn. Anthrop. Study of Consciousness, Assn. Transpersonal Anthropology Internat., Internat. Kirlian Research Assn., Com. for Study Anomalistic Research, Inter-Am. Psychol. Assn., Assn. Humanistic Psychology (pres. 1974-75), Assn. Transpersonal Psychology, Internat. Psychomatics Inst., Internat. Soc. Hypnosis, Internat. Soc. for Study Multiple Personality and Dissociative States, Nat. Assn. for Gifted Children, Sleep Research Soc., Soc. Sci. Exploration, Biofeedback Soc. Am., Council Exceptional Children, Soc. Accelerative Learning and Teaching, Soc. Gen. Systems Research, Swedish Soc. Clin. and Exptl. Hypnosis, Western Psychol. Assn., World Council for Gifted and Talented Children, Internat. Soc. Gen. Semantics, Menninger Found., Nat. Soc. Study of Edn., Parapsychol. Assn. (pres. 1983), Soc. Clin. and Exptl. Hypnosis, Soc. for Sci. Study of Religion, World Future Soc. Home: 79 Woodland Rd Fairfax CA 94930 Office: Saybrook Inst 1772 Vallejo St San Francisco CA 94123

KRISHEN, KUMAR, research technologist; b. Kashmir, India, June 22, 1939; came to U.S., 1964, naturalized, 1976; s. Srikanth and Dhanwate Bhat; B.A. with highest merit in Math. and Physics, Jammu and Kashmir U., India, 1959; B.Tech., Calcutta U., 1962, M.Tech., 1963; M.S. in Elec. Engring., Kans. State U., 1966, Ph.D. with distinction, 1969; m. Vijay Lakshmi Raina, Sept. 12, 1961; children—Lovely, Sweetie, Anjala. Asst. prof. elec. engring. dept. Kans. State U., Manhattan, 1968-69; staff scientist and engr. Lockheed Electronics Co., Inc., Houston, 1969-76; mgr. microwave program NASA, Johnson Space Center, Houston, 1976-78, mgr. advanced microwave programs, 1978-81, coordinator advanced programs expt. systems div., 1981, mgr. advanced programs tracking and communications, 1981-88 ; asst. for tech. and advanced programs, Mission Support Directorate, Johnson Space Ctr., 1988—; lectr. U. Houston Grad. Center, 1980; adj. assoc. prof. Rice U., 1986—; research adv. NRC; coordinator The Krishen Trio Performers, 1969—; established Krishen Found. for Arts and Scis., 1983—. Co-founder, pres., Hindu Worship Soc., 1970-72, 74, 79-80, 83; pres. ICC-CL. Recipient Gold and Silver medals Calcutta U.; Outstanding Performance and Superior Performance awards NASA, 1979, 82, 84, 85, 86, 87; Recipient NASA/JSC Cert. of Commendation, 1987; Govt. India Merit scholar, 1959-61. Sr. Mem. IEEE; mem. Sigma Xi, Phi Kappa Phi, Eta Kappa Nu. Contbr. articles on radar tech. SEN., Communications, Tracking, Robotic Vision, Culture, Poetry, and Human Devel. Home: 4127 Long Grove Dr Seabrook TX 77586 Office: NASA Johnson Space Ctr Code EE Houston TX 77058

KRISHER, BERNARD, foreign correspondent; b. Frankfurt, Germany, Aug. 9, 1931; s. Joseph and Fella (Solnica) K.; m. Akiko Yaginuma, May 1, 1960; children: Deborah, Joseph. B.A., Queens Coll.; postgrad. in advanced internat. reporting program, Columbia U., 1961-62. Staffwriter, then asst. editor mag. N.Y. World-Telegram & Sun, 1955-61; corr. Newsweek, 1963—; bur. chief Newsweek, Tokyo, 1968-80; corr. Fortune, 1981-83; chief editorial advisor Focus Weekly Mag. Shincho-sha Pub. Co., Tokyo, 1981—; contbr. Parade mag., 1984—; hon. research assoc., vis. scholar East Asian Research Ctr., Harvard U., 1978-79; Far East rep. The Media Lab. MIT, 1987—. Author: (with Alan Levy) Draftee's Confidential Guide, 1957, Interview, 1976, The Plus and Minuses of Being Japanese, 1978, Harvard Diary, 1979, How Harvard Sees Japan, 1979, We Who Lived in Japan, 1986. Ford Found. fellow. Mem. Council Fgn. Relations, Signet Soc. Club: Player's. Home: 4-1-7-605 Hiroo, Shibuya-ku, Tokyo Japan (150) Office: Shincho-sha Pub Co, 71 Yarai-cho, Shinjuku-ku, Tokyo Japan

KRISHER, PATTERSON HOWARD, management consultant; b. Oklahoma City, Sept. 14, 1933; s. Sherman and Gladys (Patterson) K.; m. Mary Anne Howard, Nov. 21, 1973; children: Sherman H., Bryan P. B.S. in Indsl. Engring., Okla. State U., 1956; A.M.P., Harvard U., 1971. Cert. mgmt. cons. Plant indsl. engr. Procter & Gamble Mfg. Co., Dallas, 1959-60; mktg. rep. IBM, Dalls, 1960-61; mgmt. cons. Arthur Young & Co., San Francisco, Los Angeles and Dallas, 1961-77; nat. dir. mgmt. services Arthur Young & Co., 1977-83, dir. mgmt. services N.Y.C. Office, 1983-86; gen. ptnr. Leep Assocs., Stamford, Conn., 1986—; pres. LP of Fairfield Co. Inc., 1986—; treas. Inst. Mgmt. Cons., 1984-86; guest instr. U. Tex., Ohio State U.; bd. dirs. Control Mgmt. Systems, Colorado Springs, Colo., Integrity Systems Inc., St. Louis. Contbr. to: Handbook of Business Problem Solving, 1980; mem. editorial bd.: Jour. Mgmt. Cons., 1983-86, Boardroom Reports, 1984—. Chmn. Arthur Young Polit. Action Com., 1978-86; bd. dirs. Homeowners Assn.; mem. vis. com. indsl. engring. dept. Lehigh U., 1984—. Served with USAF, 1956-59. Congregationalist. Clubs: Island Country (Marco Island, Fla.); Sky (N.Y.C.); Burning Tree Country (Greenwich, Conn.) (dir. 1981—). Office: 277 Park Ave New York NY 10172

KRISHNAMOORTHY, MUKKAI SUBRAMANIAM, computer science educator; b. Nagerkoil, Madras, India, Jan. 20, 1948; came to U.S., 1979; s. Mukkai Subramaniam and Parvathi Rajam. M.S., Indian Inst. Tech., Kanpur, 1971, Ph.D., 1976. Asst. prof. Indian Inst. Tech., Kanpur, 1977-80; asst. prof. computer sci. Rensselaer Poly. Inst., Troy, N.Y., 1980-85, assoc. prof., 1985—. Mem. IEEE, Assn. for Computing Machinery, Am. Math. Soc., Soc. Indsl. and Applied Math., Sigma Xi, Pi Mu Epsilon. Research on design and analysis of algorithms for different models of computation. Office: Rensselaer Poly Inst Troy NY 12181

KRISHNAN, RADHA BALA, surgeon; b. Kuala Lumpur, Malaysia, Jan. 4, 1939; s. Radha and Rama (Thilakam) K.; m. Mumtaz Begum, Jan. 13, 1967; children: Mohammed Rafi, Mohd Niraj, Mohd Shanaz. MBBS, Madras (India) Med. Coll., 1963. Gen. practice medicine Kuala Lumpur, 1967—. Fellow Royal Coll. Surgeons, Royal Soc. Health, Internat. Coll. Surgeons; mem. Coll. Gen. Practitioners. Office: 492 Jalan, Ipoh, 51200 Kuala Lumpur Malaysia

KRISHNASWAMY, SUBBANAICKER, association executive; b. Tamilnadu, India, Sept. 25, 1954; s. V. T. Subba Naicker and Subbammal K.; m. Raktima Bhattacharjee, Dec. 13, 1984; 1 child, Rikta. BSc, U. Madurai, 1975; MSc, U. Delhi, 1978; cert. popular studies, Internat. Inst. Population Studies, Bombay, 1979; PhD, Indian Inst. Tech., Bombay, 1985. Research assoc. Indian Inst. Mgmt., Ahmedabad, Gujrat, 1984; sr. research assoc. Spastics Soc. India, Bombay, 1985-86, dir. research, 1986—; mem. research adv. com., cons. Conwest Jain Med. Research Soc., Bombay, 1986—. Contbr. articles to profl. jours. Hindu. Home: 6 KV Block I IIT, Bombay, Maharashtra 400 076, India Office: Spastics Soc India, Upper Colaba Rd, Bombay 400 005, India

KRISTENSEN, LEIF, mathematics educator; m. Florissa Funk De Vries (dec. Jan. 1961); children—Greta Jo, Florissa; m. Sandra Louise Lindquist (div. 1977); children—John, Birgitta. Cand. Mag., Mag. Scient., U. Copenhagen, 1957; Ph.D., U. Chgo., 1961. Assoc. prof. math. U. Aarhus, Denmark, 1961-63, 65, prof., 1965—; vis. prof. U. Calif.-Berkeley, 1964, U. Ill.-Chgo., 1968. Contbr. articles on algebraic topology to profl. jours., 1958—. Fellow Royal Danish Acad. Sci. and Letters; mem. Research Council (1978-86), European Math. Council (sec.-treas. 1978—), Konsistorium of Aarhus U. Home: Vesttoften 2, DK 8250 Egaa Denmark Office: U Aarhus Dept Math, NY Munkegade, DK 8000 Aarhus Denmark

KRISTENSEN, PEDER JOERN, chemical company executive; b. Viborg, Denmark, Dec. 1, 1949; s. Joergen and Gudrun (Pedersen) K.; m. Jette Marianne Koefer, July 5, 1978; children: Michael, Charlotte. Grad. in Chem. Engring., Tech. High Sch. Denmark, Copenhagen, 1974. Registered chem. engr. Research mgr. Finsen Inst., Copenhagen, 1974-76; tech. dir. Danochemo AS, Copenhagen, 1976-85; logistics mgr. Ginge-Kerr AS, Copenhagen, 1985-86; tech. mgr. DS Industries AS, Copenhagen, 1986—. Contbr. articles on cancer research to profl. jours. Home: Blomstermarken 12, 3060 Espergaerde Denmark Office: DS Industries AS, Islands Brygge 24, 2300 Copenhagen Denmark

KRISTY, JAMES E(UGENE), financial management consultant; b. Kenosha, Wis., Sept. 3, 1929; s. Eugene H. and Ann T. Kristy; B.S. in Econs., U. Wis., 1951; M.B.A. in Fin., U. So. Calif., 1964; postgrad. Claremont (Calif.) Grad. Sch.; Ph.D. in Mgmt. and Edn., Columbia-Pacific U., 1981; m. Edith L. Reid, Feb. 19, 1955; children—James R., Ann E., Robert E. Vice-pres., Lloyds Bank Calif., Los Angeles, 1969-71; chief treasury officer Computer Machinery Corp., Los Angeles, 1971-75; sr. v.p., chief fin. officer Century Bank, Los Angeles, 1979; self-employed cons., writer, and lectr., Buena Park, Calif., 1975-78, 80—; mem. faculty Redlands (Calif.) U., Golden Gate U., Los Angeles, at U. Calif., Berkeley, Santa Cruz, Irvine and Riverside, U. So. Calif., Pacific Luth U.; mem. City of Buena Park Fin. Com., 1986—; past dir. Grycner Motors Corp., Madera Mfg. Co. Served as 1st lt. U.S. Army, 1951-53; Korea. Recipient Public Service award SBA, 1971. Author: Analyzing Financial Statements: Quick and Clean, 4th edit., 1984; Price Deflator Software, 1986; Handbook of Budgeting, 1981; (with others) Finance Without Fear, 1983; Analyzing Financial Statements with Electronic Spreadsheets, 1984. Address: PO Box 113 Buena Park CA 90621

KRISTYANTO, HANDOKO, construction company executive; b. Semarang, Middle Java, Indonesia, Feb. 11, 1950; s. Kiswantoro and Minarti Kristyanto; m. Lanny Purwosuwito; children: Davy, Daisy. BS in Electronics, Satya Wacana U., Salatiga, Indonesia, 1973. Sales mgr. P.T. Elnusa, Jakarta, Indonesia, 1973-78, assembling mgr., 1978-80; gen. mgr. P.T. Zest Engring., Jakarta, 1980-83, chmn., 1985—; pres., dir. P.T. Saka Utama Putera, Jakarta, 1983—, chmn. cons., 1985—. Office: PT Saka Utama Putera, Jl Persatuan guru 26, 10160 Jakarta Indonesia

KRIT, ROBERT LEE, development executive; b. Chgo., Apr. 6, 1920; s. Jacob and Tania (Etzkowitz) K.; B.S. in Commerce, DePaul U., 1946; A.B.A., N. Park Coll., 1939; children—Melissa, Margaret, Justin. Dir. Chgo. Herald Am. Mercy Fleet charity drives, 1940-41; asst. exec. dir. cancer research found. U. Chgo., 1947-48; state campaign dir. Am. Cancer Soc., Inc., Chgo., 1948-63; dir. med. devel. U. Chgo., 1963-67; v.p. devel. U. Health Scis./Chgo. Med. Sch. (formerly Chgo. Med. Sch.), 1967—. Moderator, NBC-TV series Tension in Modern Living, Drug Abuse, Aging and Retirement, Health and Devel. Children, Cancer, Bridge For Tomorrow, Healthy Life Style, NBC Ednl. Exchange; host producer TV series Med. Looking Glass, Relevant Issues in Health and Medicine, Coping, Su Salud, Spanish TV series, Chgo. Med. Sch. Reports, radio series; chmn. Ill. Comm. for Nat. Health Agys. Fed. Service Campaigns; mem. adv. bd. Central States Inst. for Addiction Services; v.p. Drug Abuse Council of Ill.; bd. dirs. Lawson YMCA, United Way Lake County, Ill. Found. Dentistry for the Handicapped; vice chmn. North Chgo. Citizens Against Drug & Alcohol Abuse. Served to 1st lt. USAAF, 1942-46. Fellow Inst. Medicine Chgo. (co-chmn. com. on public info., editorial bd. Procs.; Disting. Service award); mem. Chgo. Soc. Fund Raising Execs. (pres. 1964-65), Chgo. Assn. Commerce and Industry (health-in-industry com.), Nat. Acad. TV Arts and Scis. Office: 200 E Randolph Dr Suite 7938 Chicago IL 60601

KROCH, HOWARD MARTIN, banker; b. Manchester, Eng., Sept. 1, 1947; s. Horace John and Gertrude (Segal) K. With Barclays Bank D.C.O., Hamburg, Fed. Republic Germany, 1968-72; merchant banker M.M. Warburg Brinchmann Wirtz, Hamburg, 1972-74, Westbank, Hamburg, 1974-76; merchant banker Hermann & Hauswedell Bank, Hamburg, 1977—, ptnr., 1980—. Clubs: The British (Hamburg)(chmn. 1985), Clipper (Hamburg). Lodge: Anglo-Hanseatic. Office: Herrmann & Hauswedell, Schone Aussicht 8, D2000 Hamburg 76 Federal Republic of Germany

KROEGER, WOLFGANG, nuclear engineer; b. Herne, Fed. Republic of Germany, Aug. 27, 1945; m. Ute Schindler, Aug. 6, 1971; children: Kristina, Anna Katrin. Diploma in Engring., Tech. U., Aachen, Fed. Republic of Germany, 1971; DEng, Tech. U., 1974; habilitation, U. Wuppertal, 1986. Head Inst. Nuclear Safety Research Nuclear Research Ctr., Juelich, Fed. Republic of Germany, 1987—; lectr. dept. safety sci. U. Wuppertal, 1986—. Author: Tschernobyl, 1987; assoc. editor Risk Jour., 1985. Mem. Kerntechnische Gesellschaft, Risk Soc. Office: Nuclear Research Ctr, PO Box 1913, Juelich 517, Federal Republic of Germany

KROENER, WILLIAM FREDERICK, III, lawyer; b. N.Y.C., Aug. 27, 1945; s William Frederick Jr. and Barbara (Mitchell) K.; m. Evelyn Somerville Bibb, Sept. 3, 1966; children—William Frederick, Mary Elizabeth, Evangeline Alberta, James Mitchell. A.B., Yale Coll., 1967; M.B.A., Stanford U., 1971, J.D., 1971. Bar: Calif. 1972, N.Y. 1979, D.C. 1983. Assoc. Davis Polk & Wardwell, N.Y.C. and London, 1971-79, ptnr., N.Y.C., 1979-82, Washington and N.Y.C., 1982—; dir. Indosuez & Ptnrs. N.Am. III N.V. and Mitsubishi Bank Trust Co. of N.Y. Mng. editor Stanford Law Rev., 1970-71. Mem. bd. visitors Stanford U. Law Sch., 1983—. Mem. ABA, N.Y. State Bar Assn., Assn. Bar City N.Y., Fed. Bar Assn., N.Y. Law Inst. Republican. Episcopalian. Clubs: Yale, Wall St. (N.Y.C.); University (Washingon); Kenwood Golf (Bethesda, Md.). Home: 6412 Brookside Dr Chevy Chase MD 20815 also: 404 E 79th St Apt 28-E New York NY 10021 Office: Davis Polk & Wardwell 1575 Eye St NW Suite 400 Washington DC 20005 also: Davis Polk & Wardwell 1 Chase Manhattan Plaza New York NY 10005

KROIZER, ISRAEL, energy company executive; b. Jerusalem, Nov. 30, 1952; s. Jacob and Judith (Havlin) K.; m. Lani Walstein, 1976; children: Gil, Or, Ran. BS in Mech. Engring., Technion, Haifa, 1974, MS in Mech. Engring., 1982. Cert. mech. engr. Engr. Israeli Def. Forces, Jerusalem, 1974-78; project engr. Electra, Jerusalem, 1978-80; proj. mgr. Luz Engring. Corp., Los Angeles, 1983-84; dept. mgr. Luz Industries Israel, Jerusalem, 1980-83, v.p. engring., 1984-86, exec. v.p., 1986-87, pres., 1987—. Recipient Rothschild Industries prize, 1986. Home: 16 Ben-Avi, Jerusalem Israel Office: Luz Industries Israel, PO Box 7929, Jerusalem Israel

KROL, HENRYK EMANUEL, recording executive; b. Gliwice, Poland, Feb. 22, 1952; s. Wilhelm and Ruta Klara (Munter) K.; m. Lidia Boguslawa, Apr. 27, 1985; children: Filip, Paulina. MS, U. Silesia, Poland, 1974, PhD with distinction, 1982. Leader music group Music Studio, Wisla, Poland, 1976—; dir. Profl. Music Studio, Wisla, 1986—; lectr. U. Silesia, 1974-82, adj. assoc. prof., 1982—; cons., mng. acoustics. Mem. Polish Acoustical Soc., Polish Engring. Soc. Clubs: Air, Sailing (Gliwice). Home: 9 Jaskolcza St, Gliwice Poland 44 100 Office: Christian Music Studio, DEOrecordings, PO Box 15, Wisla Poland 43 460

KROL, JOHN CARDINAL, cardinal; b. Cleve., Oct. 26, 1910; s. John and Anna (Pietruszka) K. Student, St. Mary's Sem., Cleve., 1937; J.C.B., Gregorian U., Rome, 1939, J.C.L., 1940; J.C.D., Cath. U. Am., 1942; Ph.D., La Salle Coll., 1961; LL.D., John Carroll U., 1955, St. Joseph U., 1961, St. John U., N.Y., 1964, Coll. Steubenville, 1967, Lycoming Meth. Coll., 1966, Temple U., 1964, Bellarmine-Ursuline Coll., 1968, Drexel U., 1970; D.S.T., Villanova U., 1961; L.H.D., Alliance Coll., 1967, Coll. Chestnut Hill (Pa.), 1975, Holy Family Coll., 1977; D.D., Susquehanna U., 1970; D.Theology, U. Lublin (Poland); HHD, Wheeling Coll., 1984. Priest Roman Catholic Ch., 1937, pvt. chamberlain, 1945, domestic prelate, 1951; parish asst. 1937-38; prof. Diocesan Sem.; also chaplain Jennings Home for Aged, 1942-43; vice chancellor Cleve. Diocese, 1943-51, chancellor of diocese, 1951-53, promoter of justice, 1951-53; consecrated bishop 1953, auxiliary bishop to bishop of Cleve., also vicar gen. Diocese of Cleve., 1953-61; archbishop of Phila., 1961-88; elevated to Sacred Coll. of Cardinals, 1967; undersec. II Vatican Council, 1962-65; mem. Pontifical Commn. Communications Media, 1964-69; chmn. Nat. Cath. Office for Radio and TV, 1963-64, Nat. Cath. Office for Motion Pictures, Cath. Communications Found., 1965-70, Pa. Cath. Conf., 1961—; v.p. Nat. Conf. Cath. Bishops, 1966-71, pres., 1971-74; vice chmn. U.S. Cath. Conf., 1966-71, pres., 1971-74; mem. adminstrv. bd. and com. Nat. Conf. Cath. Bishops/U.S. Cath. Conf., 1983-86; mem. Pontifical Commn. for Mass Media Communications, 1964-69, Sacred Congregation for Evangelization of Nations, 1967-72, Sacred Congregation for Oriental Ch., 1967—, Sacred Congregation for Doctrine of Faith, 1973—; mem. 15 Mem. Council of Cardinals to study and counsel on Vatican finances, 1981; mem. Prefecture of Econ. Affairs of Holy See, 1982; pro.-pres. Extraordinary Synod of Bishops, Rome, 1985. Mem. Pres.'s Nat. Citizens Com. Community Relations; chmn. bd. govs., host 41st Internat. Eucharistic Congress, Phila., 1976; trustee Cath. U. Am., Washington, 1961-71, Nat. Shrine of Immaculate Conception, Cath. League for Religious Assistance to Poland; pres. Center for Applied Research in Apostolate, 1967-70; vice chmn. Com. for Yr. of Bible, 1983; mem. nat. adv. com. Deborah Hosp. Found., 1983; mem. President's Adv. Council for Pvt. Sector Initiatives, 1983-85; mem. council trustees Freedoms Found. at Valley Forge, 1985. Decorated comdr. of cross Order of Merit, Italy; Nat. Order Republic of Chad; recipient gold medal Paderewski Found., 1961; Nat. Human Relations award NCCJ, 1968; Father Sourin award Cath. Philopatrian Inst., 1967; John Wesley Ecumenical award Old St. George's Meth. Ch., 1967; Phila. Freedom medal, 1978; 1st ann. award Angelicum Soc. Am., 1985; Barry award Am. Cath. Hist. Soc., 1985; Copernicus award for advocation of peace throughout world, 1985; Legion of Honor gold medal Chapel of Four Chaplains, 1986; Person of Yr. award Congregation Beth Chaim, Feasterville, Pa., Person the Yr. award Congregation Beth Chaim, Feasterville, Pa., 1985, Shield of Blessed Gregory X Crusader, Nat. Assn. Holy Name Soc., 1986, Bob Hope 5-Star Civilian award Valley Forge Mil. Acad. and Jr. Coll., 1986, Immaculata award Immaculata Coll., 1987. Mem. Canon Law Soc. Am. (pres. 1948-49), Order Sons of Italy (hon.). Office: 222 N 17th St Philadelphia PA 19103 *

KROL, JOSEPH, mechanical and industrial engineer, emeritus educator, underwriter; b. Warsaw, Poland, Jan. 14, 1911; came to U.S., 1956, naturalized, 1962; s. Kazimierz and Feliksa (Tokarzewski) K.; m. Evelyn Swingland, Apr. 15, 1952. MS, Warsaw Inst. Tech., 1937; PhD U. London, 1947. Registered profl. engr., Ga. Tech. officer with directorate ammunition prodn. Brit. Ministry of Supply, London, 1941-45; research scientist U. London, 1946-47; cons. engr., Montreal, Que., Can., 1948-51; assoc. prof. mech. engring. U. Manitoba (Can.), 1951-56; prof. indsl. engring. Ga. Inst. Tech., Atlanta, 1956-79, prof. emeritus indsl. and systems engring., 1980—; underwriting mem. Lloyd's of London, 1985—. Contbr. articles on engring. and mgmt. to profl. jours. Recipient George Stephenson prize, 1951, Centennial medallion Ga. Inst. Tech., 1987. Fellow Inst. Mech. Engrs.; mem. ASME, Engring. Inst. Can., Corp. Profl. Engrs. Que., Am. Econ. Assn., Instrument Soc. Am., AAAS, Am. Statis. Assn., Econometric Soc., Inst. Mgmt. Scis., AAUP, N.Y. Acad. Scis., U.S. Naval Inst., Sigma Xi. Club: Royal Over-Seas League (London). Home: 311 10th St NW Atlanta GA 30318 also: Maison Grande Condominium 6039 Collins Ave Miami Beach FL 33140

KROLIKOWSKI, WERNER, East German political leader; b. Oels, Silesia, Mar. 12, 1928; married, 2 children. Mem. Sozialistische Einheitspartei Deutschlands, 1946—, 1st sec. dist. party br. Ribnitz-Damgarten, 1952, 1st sec. Dresden County, 1960-73, mem. Central Com., 1963—, mem. Politburo, 1971—; mem. Volkskammer, 1963—, mem. com. nat. def., 1971—; sec. for economy Central Com., 1973-76; 1st dep. chmn. Council of Ministers, 1976—; 1st sec. Dresden County com. Sozialistische Einheitspartei Deutschlands. Decorated Vaterländischer Verdienstorden in gold, Medalle für Waffenbrüderschaft in gold, Karl Marx Orden, others. Address: Council of Ministers, Klosterstrasse 47, 102 Berlin German Democratic Republic *

KROLL, BEVERLEY JANE, market research executive; b. Chgo., Jan. 2, 1929; d. Ralph and Agnes Jane (Patton) Layman; m. Harold Kroll, Oct. 26, 1957; children—Jeffrey Joseph, Daniel Ralph. B.A., Nat. Coll., Evanston, Ill., 1970, M.S., 1983. Chief sensory lab. Quartermaster Food & Container Inst., Chgo., 1952-61; pres. Peryam & Kroll Research Corp., Chgo., 1961—. Contbr. articles on sensory methodology to profl. jours. Mem. Am. Mktg. Assn., Mktg. Research Assn. Republican. Club: Lincolnwood (Ill.) Afternoon. Home: 3300 W North Shore Ave Lincolnwood IL 60645 Office: Peryam & Kroll Research Corp 6323 N Avondale Ave Chicago IL 60631

KROMBEIN, KARL VONVORSE, entomologist; b. Buffalo, May 26, 1912; s. Louis Henry and Gertrude (Hoeffler) K.; m. Dorothy Carpenter Buckingham, Dec. 11, 1942; children: Kristin, Kyra, Karlissa. Student, Carnegie Inst. Tech., 1929-31, Canisius Coll., 1931-32; B.S., Cornell U., 1934, M.A., 1935, Ph.D., 1960; Ph.D. in Zoology, U. Peradeniya, Sri Lanka, 1980. Research entomologist Bur. Entomology and Plant Quarantine, Dept. Agr., 1941-51, investigations leader Insect Identification and Parasite Introduction Research br., 1951-65; chmn. dept. entomology Smithsonian Instn., Washington, 1965-71; sr. entomologist Smithsonian Instn., 1971-80, sr. scientist, 1980—; cons. to surgeon gen. USAF, 1972-79, cons. emeritus, 1979—. Author, editor: (with others) Hymenoptera of America North of Mexico-Synoptic Catalog, 1951, Catalog of Hymenoptera in America North of Mexico, 3 vols, 1979; author: Trap-nesting Wasps and Bees: Life Histories, Nests and Associates, 1967; contbr. articles to profl. jours. Served from 1st lt. to maj. AUS, 1942-46, PTO; col. USAF Res. Decorated Legion of Merit, Air Force Commendation medal; named Chief Biomed. Scientist; grantee Am. Philos. Soc., 1952, 55, 59; grantee NSF, 1963; grantee Smithsonian Research Found., 1967, 69, 70, 73; prin. investigator Ceylon Insect Project. Mem. Entomol. Soc. Am. (fellow 1944, governing bd. 1970-72), AAAS (councillor 1970-73), Société Entomologique d'Egypte (hon.), Washington Biologists Field Club (past pres.), Entomol. Soc. Washington (past pres., past editor), Am. Entomol. Soc. (corr.), Sigma Xi, Sigma Phi Epsilon. Unitarian. Club: Cosmos (Washington). Home: 3026 John Marshall Dr Arlington VA 22207 Office: Smithsonian Instn Washington DC 20560

KRUCKS, WILLIAM NORMAN, lawyer; b. Chgo., Oct. 28, 1949; s. William and Lorraine (Rauland) K.; m. Amy Danly, July 10, 1981; children: Kathryn Leigh, Greta Anne. BA, Tulane U., 1972; JD, U. Miss., 1976. Bar: Ill. 1976, Miss. 1976, U.S. Dist. Ct. (no. dist.) Ill. 1976, U.S. Dist. Ct. (no. dist.) Miss. 1976, U.S. Dist. Ct. (cen. dist.) Ill. 1984, U.S. Ct. Appeals (5th and 7th cirs.) 1976, U.S. Supreme Ct. 1980. Assoc. Rooks, Pitts and Poust, Chgo., 1976-83; founding ptnr. Freeborn & Peters, Chgo., 1983—; bd. dirs. Rauland Borg Corp. Editor Miss. Law Jour., 1974-76; contbr. articles to law jours. Atty. Chgo. Vol. Legal Services, 1982—. Named Outstanding Young Man Am., U.S. Jaycees, 1976; recipient Dean Robert T. Farley award U. Miss., 1977. Mem. Ill. Self-Insured Assn., Chgo. Assn. Commerce and Industry, Nat. Council Self-Insured, Better Govt. Assn., Am. Jud. Soc., Tulane U. Alumni Assn., U. Miss. Alumni Assn., ABA, Ill. Bar Assn., Chgo. Bar Assn., Miss. Bar Assn., Workers Compensation Lawyers Assn., Legal Club of Chgo., Phi Delta Phi, Sigma Nu. Republican. Methodist. Clubs: Union League. Home: 344 Locust Rd Winnetka IL 60093 Office: Freeborn & Peters 11 S LaSalle St Suite 1500 Chicago IL 60603

KRUEGER, ALAN DOUGLAS, communications company executive; b. Little Rock, Dec. 24, 1937; s. Herbert C. and Estelle B. Krueger; m. Betty Burns, Apr. 4, 1975; children: (by previous marriage) Scott Alan, Dane Kieth, Kip Douglas, Bryan Lee. Student, U. Ill., 1956, Wright Coll., 1957-58. Project engr. Motorla, Inc., Chgo., 1956-64; service mgr., field tech. rep.

Motorla, Inc., Indpls., 1964-67; pres. Communications Maintenance, Inc., Indpls., 1967-68, Communications Unlimited, Inc., Indpls., 1968—. Methodist. Club: Elks. Home: RR 2 Box 119 Franklin IN 46131 Office: Communications Unlimited Inc 4032 Southeastern Ave Indianapolis IN 46203

KRUEGER, BETTY JANE, telecommunication company executive; b. Indpls., Oct. 4, 1923; d. Forrest Glen and Hazel Luellen (Taylor) Burns; student Butler U., 1948-49; m. Alan Douglas Krueger, Apr. 4, 1975; 1 son by previous marriage—Michael J. Vornehm. Supr., instr. Ind. Bell Telephone Co., Indpls., 1941-54; supr. communications Jones & Laughlin Steel Co., Indpls., 1954-56, Ford Motor Co., Indpls., 1956-64, U.S. Govt., Camp Atterbury, Ind., 1964-66; dir. communications Meth. Hosp. of Ind., Indpls., 1966-79; pres. owner Rent-A-Radio, Inc. of Ind., Indpls., after 1979; sec.-treas. Communications Unltd., Inc. Former pres. Am. Legion Aux.; chmn. for Ind., Girls State U.S.A., 1972-77; probation officer vol., 1973-74; suicide prevention counselor, 1972-73. Recipient award for outstanding community service Ford Motor Co., 1961. Mem. Am. Soc. Hosp. Engring., Am. Hosp. Assn., Nat. Assn. Bus. and Ednl. Radio, Inc., Internat. Teletypewriters for the Deaf, Asso. Public Safety Communications Officers, Inc., Am. Bus. Women. Methodist. Home: RR 2 Box 119 Franklin IN 46131 Office: 4032 Southeastern Ave Indianapolis IN 46203

KRUEGER, BONNIE LEE, editor, writer; b. Chgo., Feb. 3, 1950; d. Harry Bernard and Lillian (Soyak) Krueger; m. James Lawrence Spurlock, Mar. 8, 1972. Student Morraine Valley Coll., 1970. Adminstrv. asst. Carson Pirie Scott & Co., Chgo., 1969-72; traffic coordinator Tatham Laird & Kudner, Chgo., 1973-74; traffic coordinator J. Walter Thompson, Chgo., 1974-76; prodn. coordinator, 1976-78; editor-in-chief Assoc. Pubs., Chgo., 1978—; editor-in-chief Sophisticate's Hairstyle Guide, 1978—, Sophisticates Beauty Guide, 1978—, Complete Woman, 1981—; pub., editorial services dir. Sophisticate's Black Hair Guide, 1983—. Mem. Statue of Liberty Restoration Com., N.Y.C., 1983; campaign worker Cook County State's Atty., Chgo., 1982; poll watcher Cook County Dem. Orgn., 1983. Mem. Soc. Profl. Journalists, Nat. Assn. Female Execs., Am. Health and Beauty Aids Inst. (assoc. mem.), Sigma Delta Chi. Lutheran. Clubs: Sierra, Cousteau Soc. Office: Complete Woman 1165 N Clark St Chicago IL 60610

KRUEGER, JAMES, lawyer; b. N.Y.C., Oct. 27, 1938; s. Carl and Ida (Levey) K.; m. Merry Michael Hill, July 5, 1967; children—Melissa Carlton, James Michael. B.A., UCLA, 1960; LL.B., Loyola U., Los Angeles, 1965. Bar: Hawaii 1966, U.S. Dist. Ct. Hawaii 1966, U.S. Ct. Appeals (9th cir.) 1967, U.S. Tax Ct. 1974, U.S. Supreme Ct. 1982. Assoc. firm Padgett, Greeley, Marumoto & Akinaka, Honolulu, 1967-72; pres. James Krueger Law Corp., Wailuku, Maui, Hawaii, 1973—; speaker, lectr. profl. orgn. convs.; spl. counsel County of Maui, 1974; spl. agt. Internat. Police Congress, Washington. Contbr. articles to profl. jours. Co-founder Nat. Bd. of Trial Advocacy; Gold Trustee Thomas F. Lambert Chair; mem. Commn. Hawaii Ct. Annexed Arbitration, Hawaii State Com. on Lawyer Professionalism, 1988—; del. Hawaii Judicial Conf., 1986—. Fellow Internat. Soc. Barristers, Internat. Acad. Trial Lawyers; mem. ABA (trial techniques com. 1974-76, com. medicine and law, nat. vice-chmn. sect. on tort and ins. practice 1977-81), Assn. Trial Lawyers Am. (gov. 1976-82, state committeeman 1975-76, constl. revisions com. 1977-78, nat. exec. com. 1981-82, amicus curiae com. 1979-80, fed. liaison com. 1980-81, nat. vice chmn. profl. research and devel. com. 1980-81, nat. vice-chmn. publs. dept. 1982-83, nat. vice chmn. edn. policy bd. 1983-84, chmn. Nat. Midwinter Conv. 1988, chmn. Nat. Pub. Relations Com. 1986-88), Hawaii Bar Assn., Fed. Bar Assn., Maui County Bar Assn. (pres. 1975), Melvin M. Belli Soc., Hawaii Acad. Plaintiffs Attys., Am. Coll. Legal Medicine, Am. Soc. Hosp. Attys., Western Trial Lawyers Assn. (pres. 1978-79, v.p. 1977-78, bd. govs. 1982-88), Calif. Trial Lawyers Assn., N.Y. Trial Lawyers Assn., Pa. Trial Lawyers Assn., Tex. Trial Lawyers Assn., NITA Advocates Assn., Phi Alpha Delta. Democrat. Jewish. Clubs: Outrigger Canoe (Honolulu); Transpacific Yacht (Los Angeles); Maui Country. Office: 2065 Main St PO Box T Wailuku HI 96793

KRUG, HARRY EVERISTUS PETER, JR., nuclear engineer; b. Kearney, N.J., Aug. 1, 1932; s. Harry Everistus and Helen (Miliski) K.; m. Madonna Eileen Martin, Nov. 23, 1977 (div. Mar. 1982); children: by previous marriage: Kirk Stanley, Karen Helen, Lynne Allison. B.S., U.S. Mcht. Marine Acad., 1955; M.Nuclear Engring., NYU, 1961. Registered profl. engr., Calif. Fellow engr. Atomic dept. Westinghouse, Pitts., 1961-68; v.p., gen. mgr. NCI, Pitts., 1969-70; nuclear engr. Exxon Nuclear Co., Richland, Wash., 1971; industry mgr. Control Data Corp., Mpls., 1972-73; supr. nuclear engring. Ill. Power Co., Decatur, 1974-75; nuclear engr. U.S. Nuclear Regulatory Commn., Atlanta, 1975—, also mgr. resident inspection program H.B. Robinson Nuclear Plant, expert witness, Bethesda, Md., 1975-85. Contbr. articles to profl. jours. Served to lt. USNR, 1956-58. Mem. Am. Nuclear Soc. (pres. Midwest chpt. 1972), AAAS, N.Y. Assn. Sci. Roman Catholic. Current Work: restructuring of the operating power reactor program, integration of research, lic. and inspection feedback into the inspection program, mgmt. systems analysis. Subspecialties: Nuclear engineering; Management Systems; Applied Mathematics; Artificial intelligence. Home: 241 Rollins Ave Rockville MD 20852

KRUG, JOHN CARLETON (TONY), college administrator, library consultant; b. Evansville, Ind., Nov. 27, 1951; s. John Elmer and Mary Ellen (Moore) K.; m. Anna Marie Waters, July 3, 1983. B.A., Ind. State U., 1972, M.L.S., 1973; Ph.D., So. Ill. U.-Carbondale, 1985. Lic. minister Baptist Ch. Exec. dir. Olney (Ill.) Carnegie Pub. Library, 1973-74; assoc. dean Wabash Valley Coll., Mt. Carmel, Ill., 1974-84; mem. Com. for U.S. Depository State Plan, Springfield, Ill., 1982-84; dir. libraries Maryville Coll., St. Louis, 1984-88; head librarian Bethany (W.Va.) Coll., 1988—; sec. pro-tem Ill. Basin Coal Mining Manpower Council, Mt. Carmel, 1974-79; mem. governing bd. exec. com. Higher Edn. Ctr. Cable TV, 1986-88. Author: Libraries Using/Planning for Microcomputers, 1986; also computer programs. Vice pres. bd. dirs. Wabash Area Vocat. Enterprises, Mt. Carmel, 1979-81; mem. bd. edn. Wabash Community Unit, Mt. Carmel, 1980-83; mem. exec. com. Community Edn. and Arts Assn., Carbondale, 1983-84; mem. visual arts adv. com. Ill. Arts Council, Chgo., 1982-84; pastor Hopewell United Meth. Ch., Bridgeport, Ill., 1976-77; lic. minister Terre Haute 1st Bapt. Ch. (Ind.), 1972—; elder Gateway Christian Ch., 1986-88; bd. dirs. Fair Haven Christian Sch., 1986-88. Conf. speaker Kans. State U., 1982. Mem. ALA, Mo. Library Assn., Nat. Assn. for Preservation and Perpetuation of Storytelling, So. Ill. Learning Resources Consortium (del.), St. Louis Regional Library Network (del. 1985-88), St. Louis Med. Librarians Assn., Evang. Ch. Library Assn., Ch. and Synagogue Library Assn., Gateway Storytelling Guild. Mem. Christian Ch. Home: 203 Richardson Bethany WV 63026 Office: Bethany Coll T W Phillips Meml Library Bethany WV 26032

KRÜGER, GUILLERMO JUAN, film producer; b. Buenos Aires, Mar. 30, 1948; s. Juan Luis and Margarita Maria (Baier) K.; m. Maria Teresa Solá Medina; 1 child, Alexis Luis G. Krüger Solá. BSBA, Georgetown U., 1970. Mgr., producer SRL Film Prodn. Co., Buenos Aires, 1971-74; freelance producer Norlop Thompson, Ecuador, 1976-80; staff mem. Australineas Aereas, Sol Jet, 1980-82; pres. Krüger-Colosimo SA, Buenos Aires and Chile, 1982—. Mem. Asociacion Argentina Productores Cine y Video (v.p. 1987). Home: Montevideo 1875 3, 1021 Buenos Aires Argentina Office: Kruger-Colosimo SA, Angel Carranza 2038, 1414 Buenos Aires Argentina

KRUGER, RUDOLF, opera manager; b. Berlin, Germany, Oct. 30, 1916; came to U.S., 1939, naturalized, 1944; s. Eduard and Julie Eva (Herz) K.; m. Ruth Elizabeth Scallan, Aug. 28, 1951; children: Karen Elizabeth, Philip Edward. Grad., Staatliches Kaiserin Augusta Gymnasium, Berlin, 1935; diploma, Staatsakademie fuer Musik und Darstellende Kunst, Vienna, Austria, 1938; D.F.A. (hon.), Tex. Wesleyan Coll., 1983. Asst. condr. So. Symphony Orch., Columbia Choral Soc., Columbia, S.C., 1939-42; asst. condr. New Orleans Symphony Orch., 1942-45, condr. young people's concerts, 1942-45; asst. condr. New Orleans Opera House Assn. Orch., 1942-45, condr. light opera div., 1943; condr. Mid-Western tour Chgo. Light Opera Co., 1946-47; mus. dir. Jackson (Miss.) Opera Guild, 1948-51, Mobile (Ala.) Opera Guild, 1949-55, New Orleans Light Opera Co., 1949-55; 1st condr. Crescent City Concerts Assn., New Orleans, 1954-55; mus. dir., condr. Ft. Worth Opera Assn., 1955-58, mus. dir., gen. mgr., 1958—; resident mus. dir. Ft. Worth Symphony Orch. Assn., 1963-65; mus. dir., condr. Ft. Worth Ballet Assn., 1965-66; gen. dir. Arlington, Tex., Opera Assn., 1987—; condr. weekly orch. program ABC, MBS, 1943-44; guest condr. Shreveport (La.) Civic Opera, 1962-63, 75, 76-79, Cin. Summer Opera, 1969, New Orleans Opera House Assn., 1969, Dallas Civic Ballet Assn., 1971, P.R. Opera, 1972, State Opera, Hannover, Germany, 1974, Teheran (Iran) Opera, 1976, Conn. Grand Opera, 1979, Philippine Philham. Orch., 1985; dir. opera workshop Tex. Christian U., 1955-58. Served with AUS, 1945-46. Recipient Cert. of Recognition Tex. Fedn. Music Clubs, 1967. Mem. Am. Fedn. Musicians. Episcopalian. Club: Rotarian.

KRUGUER, IGNACIO, international consultant; b. Buenoa Aires, Apr. 5, 1939; s. Jose and Catalina (Lutvak) K. B in Bus. Adminstrn., U. So. Calif., Los Angeles, 1966; MBA, U. So. Calif., 1968. Instr. Los Angeles Bd. Edn., 1967-68; internal auditor Gulf Oil U.S., Los Angeles, 1968-69; mgr. planning Gulf Oil Latin Am., Coral Gables, Fla., 1969-73; v.p. Gulf Oil Latin Am., Coral Gables, 1973-76, Gulf Oil, Houston, 1976-81; pres. Mac Sudamerica S.A., Buenos Aires, 1981—; bd. dirs. Crown Products, Buenos Aires, 1986—, Dapetrol, Buenos Aires, 1984—; dir. UN Devel. Program, Panama, 1985-87. Office: Mac Sudamerica SA, L N Alem 1002 14th floor, Buenos Aires Argentina 1002

KRUIJTBOSCH, EGBERT DIEDERIK, international association executive; b. Wageningen, Netherlands, Aug. 28, 1925; s. Derk Jan and Catharina Gergerdina (Everts) K.; m. Johanna Grietje Thomas, Dec. 1, 1957; 1 child, Annigje. Degree cum laude, Mcpl. U. Amsterdam, 1953; postgrad. Harvard U., MIT, 1957-58. Gen. directorate Programme of Econ. and Mil. Aid, The Hague, 1953-59; first sec. OEEC, 1960-64; coordinator medium term planning Central Planning Bur., The Hague, 1965-66; staff econ. affairs and transp. Rijnmond, Rotterdam, 1966-72; sec. Sci. Council on Govt. Policy, 1972-75; sec. gen. Benelux Econ. Union, Brussels, 1975—. Author: (with C.A. van den Beld and H.J. Middelhoek) De Nederlandse Economie in 1970, 1966; Dublin Port and Docks Board: Studies in Long Term Development of the Port of Dublin, 1971; Management Services in Government, 1974. Served to lt. Netherlands Army, 1948-51. Hon. mem. Groupement Interuniversitaire Benelux des Economistes des Transports, Netherlands C. of C., Belgian Luxemburg C. of C., Netherlands Econ. Soc. Home: Ave Chateau de Walzin 14, Bte 13, 1180 Brussels Belgium Office: Benelux Econ Union, Rue de la Regence 39, 1000 Brussels Belgium

KRUMSKE, WILLIAM FREDERICK, JR., marketing educator, business consultant; b. Chgo., Dec. 17, 1952; s. William Frederick and Harriet Marie (Piwowarczyk) K.; BS, Ill. Inst. Tech., 1974; MS in Bus. Adminstrn., No. Ill. U., 1978; PhD in Mktg., U. Ill., 1987. Salesman, warehouse mgr. Lus-Ter-Oil Beauty Products, Palos Heights, Ill., 1972-74; pub. relations dir. Crouching Lion Inn, Alsip, Ill., 1974; mgr. food and beverage Inn Devel. & Mgmt., Chicago Heights, Ill., 1974-75; v.p., dir. mktg. DeKalb (Ill.) Savs. and Loan Assn., 1975-81; sr. v.p. mktg. Regency Fed. Savs. and Loan Assn., Naperville, Ill., 1981-83; mktg. and research cons., Champaign, Ill., 1983-87; asst. prof. mktg. DePaul U., Chgo., 1987—; cons. in field Oakbrook Terrace, Ill., 1987—; dir. Rock Valley Network, Inc., Rockford, Ill., 1981-82; instr. Coll. Bus., No. Ill. U., 1978-83; mktg. mgr. Jordan Gallagher for State's Atty. campaign, 1976. AMA Doctoral Consortium fellow, 1986, Walter H. Stellner fellow in Mktg., 1985-87; recipient David Kinley Grad. Fellowship award, 1986, William J. Hendrickson award, 1980. Mem. Am. Mktg. Assn., Ill. Savs. and Loan League (mktg. com. 1977-81, chmn. 1979-80), Savs. Instns. Mktg. Soc. Am. 1976-83, Quill and Scroll, Beta Gamma Sigma. Lutheran. Contbr. articles to profl. jours. Home: 17W710 Butterfield Rd Apt 201 Oakbrook Terrace IL 60181 Office: DePaul U Dept Mktg 815A Adminstrn Ctr 243 S Wabash Dr Chicago IL 60604

KRUPER, JOHN GERALD, sales and marketing executive; b. Carbondale, Pa., Feb. 10, 1949; s. John Joseph and Evelyn (Bernosky) K.; B.S. in Bus. Adminstrn. and Accounting, U. Scranton, 1970; postgrad. SUNY, 1974, U. Scranton, 1985; m. Renee Jane Shugg, Aug. 4, 1973; children—Kevin John, Melissa Lynn, Abbey Renee. Store mgr. Endicott Johnson Corp., Schenectady, 1970-71, retail mdse. distbr., Endicott, N.Y., 1971-72, asst. mdse. buyer, 1972-74, full line mdse. buyer, 1974-76, dir. corp. advt. and sales promotion, 1976-79, gen. sales mgr. Ranger div., 1979-81, v.p. merchandising, 1981-84, v.p. branded footwear div., 1984-86; pres. Continental Mktg. Group, Inc., 1986. Served with U.S. Army, 1970. Home: 1406 Spyglass Ln Clarks Summit PA 18411 Office: Suite 111 Park Plaza Scranton PA 18511

KRUPP, MARCUS ABRAHAM, physician; b. El Paso, Tex., Feb. 12, 1913; s. Maurice and Esther (Siegel) K.; m. Muriel McClure, Aug. 9, 1941 (dec. Oct. 1954); children: Michael, David (dec.), Peter, Sara; m. Donna Goodheart Millen, Feb. 28, 1958. A.B., Stanford U., 1934, M.D., 1939. Diplomate: Am. Bd. Internal Medicine. Intern Stanford U. Hosp., Calif., 1938-39; resident in internal medicine Stanford U. Hosp., 1939-42; chief clin. pathology VA Hosp., San Francisco, 1946-50; dir. Palo Alto Med. Research Found., Calif., 1950-86; dir. labs. Palo Alto Med. Clinic, 1950-80; asst. clin. prof. medicine Stanford U., 1946-56, asso. clin. prof., 1956-65, clin. prof., 1965—; mem. med. tech. adv. com. Public Employees Retirement System Calif., 1972—. Editor: (with others) Current Medical Diagnosis and Treatment, ann., 1971-88, Physicians Handbook, 7th-21st edits., 1985. Vice pres. bd. dirs. Calif. Heart Assn., 1974-75; pres. bd. trustees Channing House, Palo Alto. Served to capt. U.S. Army, 1942-46. Recipient Albion Walter Hewlett award Stanford U. Med. Sch., 1987. Fellow ACP; mem. Western Soc. Clin. Research, Calif. Acad. Medicine (pres. 1966), Pacific Interurban Clin. Club (pres. 1977), AAAS, AMA, N.Y. Acad. Scis., Assn. Ind. Research Insts. (pres. 1966-67), Phi Beta Kappa, Alpha Omega Alpha. Home: 195 Ramoso Rd Portola Valley CA 94025 Office: 860 Bryant St Palo Alto CA 94301

KRUPSKA, DANYA (MRS. TED THURSTON), director, choreographer; b. Fall River, Mass., Aug. 13, 1921; d. Bronislaw and Anna (Niementowska) Krupski; m. Edward Hanrihan (div. 1953); 1 child, Brion; m. Ted Thurston, May 27, 1954; 1 child, Tina Lyn. Student, Lankenau Sch. for Girls, Phila.; studied with Ethel Phillips Dance Studio, Catherine Littlefield Ballet Studio, L. Egorova, Paris, Mikhail Mordkin, N.Y.C. and Phila.; studied, Aubrey Hitchens Studio, N.Y.C., Bobby Lewis Dir.'s Studio, N.Y.C. Performed concerts, Phila., 1929-36; also toured, Poland, Roumania, Balkan Countries, Hungary, Vienna, Palestine, joined, Phila. Ballet (Littlefield) for European tour, 1937, Chgo. Opera Season, 1938, Am. Ballet (Ballanchine), N.Y.C., 1938; soloist Broadway prodn.: Frank Fay Show, Radio City Music Hall Ballet; leading role on nat. tour: Johnny Belinda; soloist in: Chouve Souris, 1943; dancer in role of Dream Laurie, 1st nat. co. of Okla., later Broadway co., 1945; asst. to choreographer Agnes de Mille on Rodgers and Hammerstein prodn.: Allegro; then in ballet prodn.: Fall River Legend; then in opera prodn.: Rape of Lucrece; Broadway prodns.: Girl in Pink Tights, Gentlemen Prefer Blonds, Paint Your Wagon; assisted Michael Kidd in Broadway prodn.: Can Can; choreographer Broadway prodn.: Most Happy Fella (Tony award nomination), Seventeen, 1st Shoestring Revue, Carefree Heart, Happiest Girl in the World (Tony award nomination), Her First Roman, 1968, Apollo and Miss Agnes; choreographer Met. Opera prodn.: The Gypsy Baron; choreographer Italian mus.: Rugantino, 1962; choreographer: TV Salute to the Peace Corps, 1965; guest choreographer: Zorba, Nat. Theatre, Reykjavik, Iceland, 1971, Company for Stora Teatern, Gothenburg, Sweden, 1971, Fantastiks, Little Theatre, Gothenburg, 1971, No No Nanette, Malmö Stadsteater, Sweden, 1973, Porgy and Bess, Malmö Stadsteater, Sweden, 1974, Richard Rodger's Prodn. of Rex, Broadway, N.Y.C., 1976, Showboat, Malmö Stadsteater, 1976; dir., choreographer: Bernstein's The Mass, Malmö Stadsteater, 1975, Chicago, Det Danske Teater, Denmark, 1977, Our Man in Havana, Poland, 1977, Cabaret, Helsingborg Stadsteater, Sweden, 1978, Guys and Dolls, Aarhus Teater, Denmark, 1978, Once Upon a Mattress, Nat. Theater Reykjavik, Iceland, 1981, Animalen, Malmö Stadsteater, Sweden, 1985, Papushko, Colonade Theatre, N.Y.C., 1985; producer, dir.; choreographer: The King and I, Malmö Stadstheater, Sweden, 1984, Empress of China, Cin. Playhouse, 1984; dir. mus. prodns., N.Y. City Center; Most Happy Fella, 1959, Showboat, 1961, Fiorello, 1962 (also White House prodn. for gov.'s conf. 1968), Oklahoma, Nat. Theatre, Reykjavik, 1972; choreographer for Buick Hour, 1952, Colgate Comedy Hour, 1953, Omnibus; dir. U.S. Steel Theatre Guild Prodns; Ballets Outlook for Three (Ellington), Pointes on Jazz (Brubeck), Am. Ballet Theatre. Mem. Actors Equity Assn., Soc. Stage Dirs and Choreographers (exec. bd. mem.), Actors Studio (playwrights and dirs. unit). Office: 564 W 52d St New York NY 10019

KRUSE, HANS-JORGEN LUTZ KALODENT, business executive, farmer; b. Copenhagen, Aug. 25, 1938; s. Erik Georg and Kirsten (Holm) K.; m. Else Margrete Andersen, Mar. 21, 1970; children—Jesper, Anne, Katrine. Student Copenhagen schs. Co-founder, v.p. People to People, Scandinavia, 1966-70; pres. Nationwide Orgn. Parttime Agriculturalists, 1975-81, Kalodent, Aps, Esbjerg, Denmark, 1981—; pres. Lutz Resources of Denmark Ltd., 1986—; bd. dirs. Ciminex Ltd., 1988—. Chmn. Mus. Soc. Varde City and Surrounding Country; mem. com. Mus. Found. Varde, 1985—; bd. dirs. Skole og Samfund, Jacobi Sch. Com., 1986—. Contbr. articles profl. jours. Com. mem. Liberal Party of Denmark, Esbjerg, 1972-78. Lutheran. Lodge: Jerne Rotary (pres. 1980-81), Varde Rotary. Home: Elkcerdamvej 17, Varde 6800 Denmark Office: Kalodent, Aps, Frodesgade 90, 6700 Esbjerg Denmark

KRUSSMAN, LOUIS FREDERICK, jewelry company exec.; b. East Orange, N.J., Aug. 25, 1915; s. Leo Frederick and Henriette (de Percin) K.; AB, Fordham U., 1937; m. Alyce Garcin, Feb. 23, 1952; children: Marie Therese Barbara Krussman Shea, Denise Marie Louise. With Trifari, Krussman & Fishel, Inc., N.Y.C., 1937-80, v.p., 1952-64, treas., 1952-73, pres., 1964-78, cons., 1979-80, also dir. Mem. Cardinal's Com. of Laity of Catholic Charities, 1964-85; mem. Cath. Youth Orgn., 1957-82, bd. dirs., 1973-82; bd. dirs. Jewelry Industry Council, 1957-80, Jewelers Vigilance Com., 1967-80; bd. govs. N.Y. chpt. Arthritis Found., 1953-84, v.p., 1960-84; bd. dirs. Fashion Inst. Tech., N.Y.C., 1973-81. Served to capt. USAAC, 1941-45. Recipient Floyd B. Odlum award Arthritis Found., 1970; Brotherhood award NCCJ, 1973; hon. dep. sheriff Westchester County, 1974-82. Mem. Vets. 7th Regt., N.Y.C., Assos. Engr. Corps 7th Regt., N.Y. Srs. Golf Assn. (bd. govs. 1981-85, pres. 1984-85), Westchester Golf Assn. (exec. com. 1979—), Winter Golf League of Advt. Interests (exec. com. 1980—, chmn. admissions com. 1982—). Republican. Roman Catholic. Knight of Malta. Clubs: Westchester Country (gov. 1964—, pres. 1973-74) (Rye, N.Y.); Twenty-Four Karat (pres. 1964, hon. mem. 1983, bd. dirs. 1963-73, 1975-78, chmn. banquet com. 1975-78) (N.Y.C.). Home: Justin Rd Harrison NY 10528 Office: 404 5th Ave New York NY 10018

KRUTECK, LAURENCE R., lawyer, cons.; b. N.Y.C., Dec. 11, 1941; s. Alan R. and Sylvia (Stekler) K.; m. Laura Branigan, Dec. 10, 1980; children—Michael, Sally. B.A., Dartmouth Coll.; J.D., U. Va.; grad. U.S. Army Command and Gen. Staff Coll. Bar: Va. 1966, N.Y. 1967. Ptnr. Kruteck & Leaness, N.Y.C.; bus. mgr., atty. Laura Branigan, Iran Barkley, Lonnie Liston Smith, Don Mattingly; formerly dir., v.p. and gen. counsel Shenandoah Corp., Washington Diplomats Soccer Team, SJR Communications, Inc. Served to col. USAR. Mem. ABA, N.Y. State Bar Assn., Assn. Bar N.Y.C., Va. Bar Assn., Judge Advs. Assn., Res. Officers Assn. Club: Princeton (N.Y.C.). Office: 509 Madison Ave New York NY 10022

KRYN, RANDALL LEE, public relations exec.; b. Chgo., Oct. 12, 1949; s. Chester N. and Beatrice K. Kryn. A.A., Morton Coll., 1970; B.S. in Journalism, No. Ill. U., 1973. Writer and researcher William M. Young & Assocs., Oak Park, Ill., 1977; asst. public relations dir. Oak Park Festival, 1978; founder Oak Park Ctr. of Creativity, 1978, pres., 1978—, pub. relations dir., 1978—; founder, dir. Reality Communication, Oak Park, 1976—; dir. publicity campaigns for communication related orgns., 1976—. Legis. aide to rep. 21st dist. Ill. Gen. Assembly, 1980-83; Rep. candidate for Ill. State Senate, 1982; chmn. 7th Congl. Rep. Council, 1986—; 7th Congl. Dist. Ill. Young Reps., 1982-86. Recipient Golden Trumpet award Publicity Club of Chgo., 1979; named One of 48 Outstanding Young Men of Am. from Ill., Ill. Jaycees, 1980; ambassador for Canberra, Australia, 1982. Mem. Public Relations Soc. Am., Seward Gunderson Soc. (co-founder 1978), Mensa. Author: James Bevel, The Strategist of the 1960s Civil Rights Movement. Home and Office: 1030 Wenonah St Oak Park IL 60304

KRYS, SHELDON JACK, foreign service officer; b. N.Y.C., June 15, 1934; s. Martin and Anna (Jacobowitz) K.; m. Doris M. de Hemptinne, May 24, 1964; children—Wendy M., Madeleine S., Susan Jennifer. N.D., U. Md., College Park, 1955; grad., Nat. War Coll., Washington, 1977. Newscaster Radio Sta. KRSD, Rapid City, S.D., 1955-57; dir., producer Radio Sta. WWDC, Washington, 1957-59; prin. Chris Sheldon Pub. Relations, Washington, 1959-61; cons. to dir. FMCS, Washington, 1961-62; ednl. and cultural affairs officer, dir. reception ctrs. Dept. State, Washington, 1962-64; mgmt. officer Dept. State, London, Eng., 1965-66, spl. asst. to ambassador, 1966 69; dir. personnel Latin Am. Dept. State, Washington, 1969-74; adminstrv. counselor Dept. State, Belgrade, Yugoslavia, 1974-76; fgn. service insp. Dept. State, Washington, 1977-79, exec. dir. Bur. Near Eastern and South Asian Affairs, 1979-83, dep. dir. mgmt. ops., 1983-84, exec. asst. to under sec. for mgmt., 1984-85; ambassador to Trinidad and Tobago Dept. State, 1985—. Blood mobile chmn. Dept. State and AID, 1979-83. Recipient Meritorious Service award, Disting. Honor award, Superior Honor award, Dept. State, Presdl. Meritorious Service award. Mem. Nat. War Coll. Alumni Assn., Am. Fgn. Service Assn. Clubs: City Tavern (Washington); Tranquility Tennis (Trinidad). Office: US Ambassador to Trinidad and Tobago Dept State Washington DC 20520

KRYZA, E. GREGORY, insurance executive, former ambassador, foreign service officer; b. Detroit, Mar. 12, 1922; s. Frank Theodore and Anna Frances (Chapp) K.; m. Alice Larue Henry, Apr. 15, 1983; children: Frank Theodore, Christopher Deniau. Student, Oberlin Coll., 1944-45; B.A., U. Va., 1946; grad., Air War Coll., 1968. Products expediter Bohn Aluminum, Detroit, 1940-42; civilian staff USN, Tangier, Ciudad Trujillo, 1947-50; vice consul Curacao, 1952-54; 3d sec. Am. embassy Brussels, Belgium, 1954-57; 2d sec. Belgrade, Yugoslavia, 1957-59; supervisory adminstrv. officer Dept. State, 1959-63; 1st sec. Nairobi, Kenya, 1963-67; consul Seychelles, 1965-67; counselor Kinshasa, 1968-70, Rio de Janeiro and Brasilia, Brazil, 1970-72; fgn. service insp. 1972-77; exec. dir. Bur. African Affairs, State Dept., 1974; ambassador to Islamic Republic of Mauritania 1977-80; exec. v.p. Am. Fgn. Service Protective Assn., 1981-86; mgr. internat. devel. Blue Cross/Blue Shield Nat. Capital Area; chmn. New Columbia Corp., Washington; sec. State Dept. Fed. Credit Union. Contbr. articles to profl. jours. Pres. Sch. Bd. Am. Sch., Kinshasa, 1968-70. Served to lt. USNR, 1942-47, 50-52, ETO, Korea. Decorated grand officer Order of Merit Mauritania; recipient Meritorious Service award Dept. State, 1965. Mem. Diplomatic and Counselor Officers Ret., Fgn. Service Assn., Assn. Diplomatic Studies (sec.-treas.), Phi Delta Theta. Clubs: Army and Navy, Grads. Office: 550 12th St SW Washington DC 20065

KU, Y. H., engineering educator; b. Wusih, Kiangsu, China, Dec. 24, 1902; came to U.S., 1950; s. Ken Ming Ku and Ching-Su Wang; m. Wei-zing Wang, Apr. 1, 1929; children: Wei-Lien, Wei-Ching, Wei-Wen (Mrs. Chi-Liang Hsieh), Walter, Wei-Chung, Victor, Anna (Mrs. Yuk-Kai Lau). S.B., MIT, 1925, S.M., 1926, Sc.D., 1928; M.A., LL.D., U. Pa., 1972. Prof. elec. engring., head dept. Chekiang U., China, 1929-30; dean engring. Central U., China, 1931-32; pres. Central U., 1944-45; dean engring. Tsing Hua U., China, 1932-37; vice minister Ministry Edn., Republic of China, 1938-44; edn. commr. Shanghai, 1945-47; pres. Nat. Chengchi U., Nanking, 1947-49; vis. prof. MIT, 1950-52; prof. U. Pa., 1952-71, prof. emeritus, 1972—; hon. prof. Jiao-Tong U., Shanghai, 1979—, Xi'an, Southwestern and Northern, 1985—, Northeastern U. Tech. and NW Inst. Telecommunications, 1986—, SE U., 1988—; cons. Gen. Electric Co., Univac, RCA. Author: Analysis and Control of Nonlinear Systems, 1958, Electric Energy Conversion, 1959, Transient Circuit Analysis, 1961, Analysis and Control of Linear Systems, 1962, Collected Scientific Papers, 1971; poems, plays, novels, essays in Chinese Collected Works, 1961; Woodcutter's Song, 1963, Pine Wind, 1964, Lotus Song, 1966, Lofty Mountains, 1968, The Liang River, 1970, The Hui Spring, 1971, The Si Mountain, 1972, 500 Irregular Poems, 1972, The Great Lake, 1973, 1000 Regular Poems, 1973, 360 Recent Poems, 1976, The Tide Sound, 1980, History of Chan (Zen) Masters, 1976, History of Japanese Zen Masters, 1977, History of Zen (in English), 1979, The Long Life, 1981, One Family-Two Worlds (in English), 1982, Poems after Chin Kuan, 1983, Poems after Tao Chien, 1984, 303 Poems after Tang Poets, 1986, Flying Clouds and Flowing Water, 1987, Poems After Wu Wen-Yin, 1988. Recipient Gold medal Ministry Edn., Republic of China; Pro Mundi Beneficio Gold medal Brazilian Acad. Humanities, 1975; Gold medal Chinese Inst. Elec. Engrs., 1972. Fellow Academia Sinica, IEEE (Lamme medal 1972), Instn. Elec. Engrs. (London); mem. Am. Soc. Engring. Edn., Internat. Union Theoretical and Applied Mechanics (mem. gen. assembly), U.S. Nat. Com. on Theoretical and Applied Mechanics, Sigma Xi, Eta Kappa Nu, Phi Tau Phi. Home:

1420 Locust St Philadelphia PA 19102 Office: 200 S 33d St Philadelphia PA 19104

KUAN, WELLINGTON KANG-YEN, management consultant, educator; b. Taipei, Republic China, Jan. 10, 1953; s. Yee-Fah and Kuei-Hsien (Yeh) K. PhD, Northwestern U., Evanston, Ill., 1984. Assoc. prof. Grad. Sch. Mgmt., Tatung Inst. Tech., Taipei, 1984—, acting dean, 1987—; mgmt. cons. Tatung Co., Taipei, 1984—; mem. dissertation com. Pepperdine U., Los Angeles, 1986—. Contbr. articles to profl. jours. Mem. bd. dirs. China Interdisciplinary Assn., Taipei, 1986—. Mem. Acad. Mgmt., Acad. Internat. Bus., Internat. Soc. Planning and Strategic Mgmt., European Found. Mgmt. Devel., Pan-Pacific Bus. Assn. Home: 8 Ln 26 Lienyun St, Taipei 10623, Republic of China Office: Tatung Tech Inst, Grad Sch Mgmt, 40 Chung-Shan N Rd Sec 3, Taipei 10451, Republic of China

KUANG, ZHIQUAN, mathematics professor; b. Guangzhou, Guangdong, Peoples Republic China, Dec. 30, 1935; parents: Ningfa Kuang and Shaorong Li. BS, Peking U., Beijing, 1960. Asst. Inst. Math. Academia Sinica, Beijing, 1960-78, lectr., 1978-81, assoc. prof., 1981—. Contbr. articles to periodicals. Mem. Chinese Math. Soc., Am. Math. Soc. Office: Inst Math Academia Sinica, Beijing Peoples Republic of China

KUBBIG, BERND-WILLI, peace researcher; b. Gehrenrode, Fed. Republic of Germany, July 18, 1950; s. Alfred and Gisela (Drohne) K.; m. Hiltrud Tempka, July 30, 1987. Staatsexamen, U. Marburg, 1976, PhD, 1981. Research fellow Peace Research Inst., Frankfurt, Fed. Republic of Germany, 1979—. Author numerous books and articles on arms control-related issues. Lutheran. Home: Wilhelminenstrasse 6, D-6200 Wiesbaden Federal Republic of Germany Office: Peace Research Inst, (HSFK) Leimenrode 29, D-6000 Frankfurt am Main Federal Republic of Germany

KUBELIK, RAFAEL JERONYM, conductor, composer; b. Bychory, Czechoslovakia, June 29, 1914; s. Jan and Marianne (v. Szell) K.; m. Ludmila Bertlova, 1942 (dec. 1961); 1 child, Martin; m. Elsie Jean Morison, 1963. Degree, Prague Conservatoire Music, Czechoslovakia; D (hon.), Am. Conservatory Music, Chgo. Conductor Czech Philharm. Orch., Prague, 1936, dir. music, 1941-48; dir. music Nat. Opera, Brno, Czechoslovakia, 1939-41, Chgo. Symphony Orch., 1950-53, Covent Garden Opera, London, 1955-58, Symphony Orch. Bavarian Radio, Munich, 1961-79, Met. Opera, N.Y.C., 1973-74. Compositions include various operas, requiems, symphonies, concertos, songs, music for piano and violin; musical recs. include His Master's Voice, Deutsche Grammophon, Orfeo. Named to Grosses Bundesverdienstkreuz, Fed. Republic of Germany, Bavarian Order of Merit, Chevalier de l'Ordre de Daneborg, Denmark, Comtur Istrucao Publica, Portugal, Commandeur de l'Ordre des Arts et Lettres, France; recipient Gold Karl Amadeus Hartmann medal, Munchen Leuchtet City of Munich, Golden Gustav Mahler medal, Vienna, Mahler medal Bruchner Soc. Am., Bruckner medal Italian Assn. Anton Bruckner, Vienna and Genoa, Golden Carl Nielsen medal, Copenhagen, Medal City of Amsterdam, Golden Key City Cleve. Mem. Bavarian Acad. Fine Arts, London Royal Acad. Music, Royal Swedish Acad. Music. Address: 6047 Kastanienbaum, Haus im Sand Switzerland

KUBICKI, BERNARD, cigarette industry marketing executive; b. Quaregnon, Belgium, Mar. 6, 1951; s. Stanislaus and Irene Kubicki; m. Brigitte Opbrouck, Aug. 30, 1986; 1 child, Cédric. Lic. in indsl. and comml. psychology with distinction, Free U. Brussels. Market research Marketing Unit, Brussels, 1977-78; market research mgr. Smith Food Group, Brussels, 1978-82; group product mgr. Unilever, Brussels, 1982-85; mktg. dir. Philip Morris Belgium, Brussels, 1985—. Home: G Hensmansstraat 46, 1600 Sint-Pieters Leeuw Belgium Office: Philip Morris Belgium, Chaussée de la Hulpe 189, 1170 Brussels Belgium

KUBILUS, NORBERT JOHN, information systems executive, educator; b. Newark, Oct. 6, 1948; s. Vity Leo and Ursula Eva (Yarusavage) K.; m. Margaret L. Belfiore, Oct. 10, 1976 (div. 1988); 1 child, Jessica Leigh; m. Linda J. Ferri, July 23, 1988; 1 stepchild, James M. Feigert. ScB cum laude, Seton Hall U., 1970; MS (NSF trainee) Rensselaer Poly. Inst., 1972. Research asst. Rensselaer Poly. Inst., Troy, N.Y., 1971-72; systems programmer, analyst RAPIDATA, Fairfield, N.J., 1972-76, mgr. quality assurance, 1976-78, mgr. corp. support services, 1978-79, mgr. data mgmt. software devel., 1979-80, asst. v.p. ops. adminstrn., 1980-81; v.p. systems devel. and ops. RAPIDATA div. NDC, Fairfield, 1981-83; v.p. info. systems and tech. Ednl. Testing Service, Princeton, N.J., 1983-86, mng. ptnr., Norda Group, Yardley, Pa., 1986—; v.p. mgmt. services Optimal Solutions, Inc., Hoboken, N.J., 1988—; reviewer Reston Pub. Co. (Va.); adj. grad. faculty N.J. Inst. Tech., 1976-84; nat. lectr. Assn. Computing Machinery, 1976-80. Author: Developing Computer-Based Accounts Receivable, 1981, Manager's Guide to Distributed Data Processing, 1982, How to Implement Management Information Systems, 1983, How to Select Small Business Computer Software, 1984; contbr. articles to profl. jours. Treas. Cedar Grove (N.J.) Jaycees, 1977; bd. dirs. Gathering Internat. Families Together, 1983-86. Recipient Physics medal Seton Hall U., 1970, Medal of Honor Am. Biographical Inst., 1986. Mem. Assn. Computing Machinery, Digital Equipment Computer Users Soc. (U.S. exec. bd. 1977-81), Data Processing Mgmt. Assn. (legis. network 1985—, bd. dirs. 1988—, Individual Performance award 1987), Planning Forum, Inst. Cert. Computer Profls. (life, cert. data processor, cert. systems profl., cert. ambassador 1980-82), Am. Mgmt. Assn. (info. systems & tech. council 1985—), Internat. Platform Assn., Sigma Pi Sigma, Upsilon Pi Epsilon. Office: Optimal Solutions Inc 80 River St Hoboken NJ 07030

KUBISTAL, PATRICIA BERNICE, secondary school principal; b. Chgo., Jan. 19, 1938; d. Edward John and Bernice Mildred (Lenz) Kubistal. AB cum laude, Loyola U., Chgo., 1959, AM, 1964, AM, 1965, PhD, 1968; postgrad. Chgo. State Coll., 1962, Ill. Inst. Tech., 1963, State U. Iowa, 1963, Nat. Coll. Edn., 1974-75. With Chgo. Bd. Edn., 1959—, tchr., 1959-63, counselor, 1963-65, adminstrv. intern, 1965-66, asst. to dist. supt., 1966-69, prin. spl. edn. sch., 1969-75, prin. Simpson Sch., 1975-76, Brentano Sch., 1975-87, Roosevelt H.S., 1987; supr. Lake View Evening Sch., 1982—; lectr. Loyola U. Sch. Edn., Nat. Coll. Edn. Grad. Sch., Mundelein Coll.; coordinator Upper Bound Program of U. Ill. Circle Campus, 1966-68. Book rev. editor of Chgo. Prins. Jour., 1970-76, gen. editor, 1982—. Active Crusade of Mercy; mem. com. Ill. Constnl. Conv., 1967-69; mem. Citizens Sch. Com., 1969-71; mem. edn. com. Field Mus., 1971; ednl. advisor North Side Chgo. PTA Region, 1975; gov. Loyola U., 1961-87. Recipient Outstanding Intern award Nat. Assn. Secondary Sch. Prins., 1966, Outstanding Prin. award Citizen's Shc. Com. of Chgo., 1986; named Outstanding History Tchr., Chgo. Pub. Schs., 1963, Outstanding Ill. Educator, 1970, one of Outstanding Women of Ill., 1970, St. Luke's-Logan Sq. Community Person of Yr., 1977; NDEA grantee, 1963, NSF grantee, 1965, HEW Region 5 grantee for drug edn., 1974, Chgo. Bd. Edn. Prins.' grantee for study robotics in elem. schs.; U. Chgo. adminstrv. fellow, 1984. Mem. Ill. Personnel and Guidance Assn., NEA, Ill. Edn. Assn., Chgo. Edn. Assn., Am. Acad. Polit. and Social Sci., Chgo. Prins. Club (pres. aux.), Nat. Council Adminstrv. Women, Chgo. Council Exceptional Children, Chgo. Council Fgn. Relations, Chgo. Urban League, Loyal Christian Benevolent Assn., Kappa Gamma Pi, Pi Gamma Mu, Phi Delta Kappa, Delta Kappa Gamma (parliamentarian 1979-80, Lambda state editor 1982—, mem. internat. communications com.), Delta Sigma Rho, Phi Sigma Tau. Home: 5111 N Oakley Ave Chicago IL 60625 Office: Brentano Sch 2723 N Fairfield Chicago IL 60647

KUBODERA, MASAO, engineer; b. Nirasaki, Yamanshi, Japan, June 21, 1949; s. Masayosi and Kesako Kubodera; m. Yamasita Tomoko, Nov. 7, 1982; children: Yusuke, Kensuke. BS, Tohoku U., Sendai City, Japan, 1973. Engr. Choonpa Kogyo, Ltd., Tachikawa City, Japan, 1973-78; engr. Tokyo Electron, Ltd., Nirasaki City, Japan, 1979-82, sect. mgr., 1982-84, mgr., 1984—. Mem. Japan Soc. Applied Physics, Japan Soc. Precision Engring. Home: 1559-3 Yokkaichiba Isawa-cho, Higashiyatushiro-gun, 406 Yamanashi-ken Japan Office: Tokyo Electron Ltd, 2381-1 Kitagjyo Fujii-Machi, Nirasaki-shi, 407 Yamanashi-ken Japan

KUBOTA, KOICHI, economist; b. Tokyo, Sept. 22, 1930; s. Toyotane and Fumi (Iwanaga) K.; m. Masako Kubota. BA in Econs., U. Tokyo, 1953; MA in Econs., McGill U., Montreal, 1966. Officer Ministry Internat. Trade and Industry, Tokyo, 1953-63; econ. affairs officer UN, N.Y.C., 1968-79; corp. advisor Nippon-Kangyo-Kakumaru Securities, Inc., Tokyo, 1979-81, Kangyo-Kakumaru Research Inst., Inc., Tokyo, 1981—. Contbr. articles to profl. jours. Alcan-Asia scholar, 1961-62; Brofman scholar, 1964. Mem. Am. Econ. Assn. Home: 1-3-27 Jiyugaoka, Meguroku, 152 Tokyo Japan Office: Kangyo-Kakumaru Research Inst Inc, 1-6-10 Nihombashi-Kayabacho, 103 Tokyo Japan

KUBOTA, YOICHI, architectural educator; b. Shimizu, Shizuoka, Japan, Oct. 13, 1951; parents Masao and Michiko K. B in Engring., U. Tokyo, 1975, M in Engring., 1977, DEng, 1980. Registered 1st class archtl. engr. Asst. prof. Saitama U., Urawa, Japan, 1980-87; assoc. prof. city and regional planning Saitama U., Urawa, 1987—; planning and design cons.; part-time instr. Musashino U. Fine Arts, Tokyo, 1986—, U. Tokyo, 1988—; mem. Bd. Rev. on Bldgs., Koshigaya, Saitama, Japan, 1985—; chief sec. bridge design com. Japanese Housing & Urban Devel. Corp., Tokyo, 1987—; vice-chmn. urban design com. Kasukabe, Saitama, 1986—; com. chmn. Saitama Design Council, 1986—. Editor, author: (with others) Design of Streetscape, 1985 (Excellent Sci. Tech. prize 1986); co-author: Knowing Rivers in the City, 1985, Rivers in Tokyo, 1986; contbr. articles to profl. jours. Research grantee Kajima Found., Tokyo, 1982-84, 85-87, Ministry Edn., Japan, 1983, 85-86, 87, Tokyo Found., 1984-87. Mem. Japan Soc. Civil Engrs., City Planning Inst. Japan, Archtl. Inst. Japan, Japanese Inst. Landscape Architects, Man-Environment Research Assn. Club: Internat. Resort Service (Tokyo). Office: Saitama U, 255 Shimo-ohkubo, 338 Urawa Japan

KUBRICK, STANLEY, producer, director, writer; b. N.Y.C., July 26, 1928; m. Christiane Harlan. Ed. high sch. Staff photographer Look mag. Writer, producer, dir. documentaries; feature films include: Killer's Kiss (producer, dir.), The Killing (dir.), Paths of Glory (writer, dir.), Spartacus (dir.), 1960, Lolita (dir.), 1962; producer, dir., writer films: Dr. Strangelove, 1964 (N.Y. Critic award), 2001: A Space Odyssey, 1968 (Oscar award best spl. visual effects), A Clockwork Orange, 1971, Barry Lyndon, 1975, The Shining, 1980; producer, dir., co-writer: Full Metal Jacket, 1987. Address: care Louis C Blau Loeb and Loeb 10100 Santa Monica Blvd Los Angeles CA 90067 *

KUČANDA, DUBRAVKO, English language and linguistics educator; b. Bjelovar, Yugoslavia, Aug. 13, 1950; s. Franjo and Marija (Zebec) K.; m. Ljiljana Pavosevic, Nov. 3, 1979; children: Mirna, Zvončica. BA in English and German, U. Zagreb, Yugoslavia, 1976, MA in Linguisitcs, 1982. Translator, interpreter Industrijsko Poljoprivredni kombinat, Osijek, Yugoslavia, 1975-79; lectr. Pedagoški fakultet U. Osijek, 1979—; vis. prof. dept. English U. Sheffield, Eng., 1983; Maystadt fellow U. Antwerp, Belgium, 1986-87. Contbr. articles to profl. jours. Mem. Linguistics Assn. Great Britain, Internat. Pragmatics Assn., Soc. Linguistica Europea, Društvo za Primijenjenu Lingvistiku SR Hrvatske. Home: Vijenac VI SUK-a 44, 54000 Osijek Yugoslavia Office: Pedagoski Fakultet, J Vlahovica 9, 54000 Osijek Yugoslavia

KUCHARZ, EUGENIUSZ JOZEF LESZEK, physician, educator; b. Katowice, Poland, Jan. 4, 1951; s. Jozef and Bozena Halina (Hadrys) K.; m. Maria Helena Julska, Dec. 18, 1982; 1 child, Patricia Maria. M.D., Silesian Sch. Medicine, Katowice, 1974, Ph.D., 1976, habilitation, 1984, Docent, 1985. Lectr., Silesian Sch. Medicine, Dept. Clin. Chemistry and Labor Diagnostics, Katowice, 1974-82, chmn., 1982—; vis. prof. Med. Coll. Wis., Milw., 1986-88. Author: History of Medical Journals, 1980; Polyglot Medical Dictionary, 1985; Dni Przemijanie, 1987. Founder, editor-in-chief Jour. Med. Scis., 1974—. Contbr. articles to profl. jours. Pres., Silesian Med. Library Council, Katowice, 1984-87. Recipient Brunon Nowakowski award Silesian Sch. Medicine, 1974; Cross of Merit, State Counsil, Warsaw, 1978. Mem. Polish Assn. Esperantists (med. council), Internat. Soc. Internal Medicine, Luctor et Emergo Soc. Amsterdam (hon.), Polish Soc. Internat. Medicine, Internat. Fedn. Clin. Chemistry, Eur. Fedn. Connective Tissue Socs., Polish Biochem. Soc., Polish. Soc. Lab. Diagnostics, Polish Soc. History Medicine and Pharmacy (v.p. 1978-83). Roman Catholic. Home: ul Armii Czerwonej 28/86, 40-004 Katowice Poland Office: Silesian Sch Medicine, Jagiellonska 4, PL-41-200 Sosnowiec Poland

KUCHNER, EUGENE FREDERICK, neurosurgeon, educator; b. N.Y.C., Nov. 19, 1945; s. Morton H. and Edna Estelle (Marks) K.; AB, Johns Hopkins U., 1967; MD, U. Chgo., 1971; m. Joan Ruth Freedman, Sept. 2, 1968; children: Marc Jason, Eric Benjamin. Resident in surgery Yale U. Sch. Medicine, New Haven, 1971-72; resident in neurosurgery Montreal (Que., Can.) Neurol. Inst., McGill U., 1972-76, spine fellow, 1976; neurosurgeon Sch. Medicine, SUNY, Downstate, 1976-79, Stony Brook, 1979—; mem. staff North Shore U. Hosp., Univ. Hosp., Stony Brook, Nassau County Med. Ctr., St. John's Hosp.; cons. in field. Recipient K.G. McKenzie Meml. award Royal Coll. Physicians and Surgeons Can., 1976, Open Scholarship award Johns Hopkins U., yearly, 1963-66, Scholarship award U. Chgo., yearly, 1967-70; NSF fellow, 1968; Blackman-Hoffman Found. fellow, 1969-70. Mem. ACS, Am. Assn. Neurological Surgeons, Congress Neurol. Surgeons, N.Y. Acad. Scis., L.I. Neurosci. Acad., Suffolk Acad. Medicine, Montreal Neurol. Inst. Fellows Soc., N.Y. State Neurosurg. Soc., AMA, N.Y. State Med. Soc., N.Y. State Soc. Surgeons, Am. Epilepsy Soc., Am. Soc. Neuroimaging, Internat. Platform Assn., Assn. Yale Alumni in Medicine, Sigma Xi. Contbr. articles to profl. publs.; specialist in microsurgery, magnetic resonance imaging, spinal trauma, pituitary surgery. Office: Stony Brook Med Ctr PO Box 721 Stony Brook NY 11790-1920

KUCK, KARL HEINZ, cardiologist, educator; b. Aachen, Fed. Republic Germany, Apr. 20, 1952; s. Karl Heinz and Josefine (Piefer) K. MD, U. Cologne, Fed. Republic Germany, 1977. Resident internal medicine dept. Univ. Hosp., Hamburg, 1978-80, resident in cardiology, 1981-84, staff cardiology dept., 1984—, assoc. prof. cardiology, 1985—; fellow in cardiology and electrophysiology U. Limburg, Maastricht, The Netherlands, 1980-81; cons. Medtronic, Maastricht, 1985—. Contbr. articles to profl. jours. Mem. German Soc. Cardiology, N.Am. Soc. Cardiac Pacing and Electrophysiology. Roman Catholic. Home: Heilwig St 108, 2000 Hamburg Federal Republic of Germany Office: Univ Hosp, Martini St 52, 2000 Hamburg Federal Republic of Germany

KUCZER, PETER, architect; b. Lutsk, Russia, Apr. 10, 1949; came to Can., 1965; s. Lipa and Bella (Korostyshevskay) K.; m. Sharon Lipson 1978 (div. Jan. 1981); 1 child, Robyn; m. Sharon Mosher, Feb. 27, 1982; children: Tamara, Aaron, Kratrina, Natasha. B.Sc., Sir George Williams U., Montreal, 1971; postgrad. London U., 1972; B.Environ. Design, N.S. Tech. Coll., 1974, B.Arch., 1976. Mem. staff Arcop Assocs., Montreal, 1973; research and analysis staff Alta. Pub. Works, Edmonton, 1975; pres. Pemik Enterprises, Inc., Montreal, 1976—, Atlantic Center Ltd., 1978—, Corp. Maison St. Paul Inc., 1980—, Maison 360 Notre Dame, 1983—, Condo Marche Ltee, 1982—, Lantern Walk, Inc., West Palm Beach, Fla., 1984—; v.p. New World Constrn. Inc., Montreal, 1977—; sec. treas. Corp. Immobiliere Le Callière Inc., Montreal, 1980—. Architect, developer Le Callière, Montreal, 1979, recipient Beautification award City Montreal, 1982. Mem. N.S. Assn. Architects, Royal Archtl. Inst. Can. Home: 2777 Hill Park Circle, Montreal, PQ Canada H2Y 2AN Office: Pemik Enterprises Inc, 261 Saint Secrement St, Montreal, PQ Canada H2Y 3V2

KUDLOW, LAWRENCE ALAN, economist; b. N.Y.C., Aug. 20, 1947; s. Irving H. and Ruth (Grodnick) K.; m. Judy Pond, July 11, 1987. B.A. in History, U. Rochester, 1969; postgrad., Woodrow Wilson Sch., Princeton U., 1971-73. Staff economist Fed. Res. BanK N.Y., N.Y.C., 1973-75; corp. v.p., chief economist Paine Webber, Jackson & Curtis, N.Y.C., 1975-79; chief economist Bear Stearns & Co., N.Y.C., 1979-81; asst. dir. econ. policy Office of Mgmt. and Budget, Exec. Office of Pres., Washington, 1981-82, assoc. dir. econs. and planning, 1982-83; pres., exec. officer Lawrence Kudlow & Assocs., Washington, 1983-84; pres., chief exec. officer Rodman & Renshaw Econs. Inc., 1984-86, Rodman & Renshaw Capital Group, 1986; chief economist, sr. mng. dir. Bear Stearns & Co., Inc., 1986—. Republican. Office: Bear Stearns & Co Inc 245 Park Ave New York NY 10041

KUDO, EMIKO IWASHITA, former state and county official Hawaii; b. Kona, Hawaii, June 5, 1923; s. Tetsuzo and Kuma (Koga) Iwashita; B.S., U. Hawaii, 1944; M.S. in Vocational Edn., Pa. State U., 1950; postgrad. U. Hawaii, U. Ore., others; m. Thomas Mitsugi Kudo, Aug. 21, 1951; children: Guy J.T., Scott K., Candace F. Tchr. jr. and sr. high sch., Hawaii, 1945-51; instr. home econs. edn. U. Hawaii Tchrs. Coll., Honolulu, 1948-51, Pa. State U., State College, 1949-50; with Hawaii Dept. Edn., Honolulu, 1951-82, supr. sch. lunch service, 1951-64, home econ. edn., 1951-64, dir. home econ. edn., 1964-68, adminstr. vocat.-tech. edn., 1968-76, asst. supt. instructional services, 1976-78, dep. supt. State Dept. Edn., 1978-82; cons. Am. Samoa vocat. edn. state plan devel., 1970-71, vocat. edn. U. Hawaii, 1986, internat. secondary program devel. Ashiya Ednl. System, Japan, 1986-88; state coordinator industry-labor-edn., 1972-76; mem. nat. task force edn. and tng. for minority bus. enterprise, 1972-73; steering com. Career Info. Ctr. Project, 1973-78; co-dir. Hawaii Career Devel. Continuum project, 1971-74; mem. Nat Accreditation and Instl. Eligibility Adv. Council, 1974-77, cons., 1977-78; mem. panel Internat. Conf. Vocat. Guidance, 1978, 80, 82, 86; dir. Dept. Parks and Recreation, City and County of Honolulu, 1982-84 . Exec. bd. Aloha council Boy Scouts Am., 1978-88. Japan Found. Cultural grantee, 1977; Pa. State U. Alumni fellow, 1987. Fellow Pa. State U. Disting. Alumni; mem. Western Assn. Schs. and Colls. (accreditation team mem. Ch. Coll. of Hawaii 1972-73), Am. Vocat. Assn., Hawaii Practical Arts and Vocat. Assn., NEA, Hawaii Edn. Assn., Hawaii State Ednl. Officers Assn., Am., Hawaii home econ. assn., Nat., Hawaii assns. for supervision and curriculum devel., Am. Tech. Edn. Assn., 1 Omicron Nu, Pi Lambda Theta, Phi Delta Kappa, Delta Kappa Gamma. Author handbooks and pamphlets in field. Home and Office: 217 Nenue St Honolulu HI 96821

KUDRYK, OLEG, librarian; b. Rohatyn, Ukraine, Dec. 14, 1912; came to U.S., 1949, naturalized, 1954; s. Theodosius and Olga (Spolitakevich) K.; m. Sophie H. Dydynski, Feb. 5, 1944. Diploma, Conservatory Music, Lviv, 1934; LL.M., U. Lviv, 1937, M.A. in Econ. Sci., 1938; postgrad., U. Vienna, 1945-46; M.A. in L.S., U. Mich., 1960; Ph.D. in Polit. Sci., Ukranian Free U., Munich, 1975. Mgr., legal advisor Coop. Agrl. Soc., Chodoriv, Ukraine, 1938-39; mgr. Import-Export Corp., Cracow, Poland, 1940-44; tchr. Comml. Sch., Ulm, Germany, 1946; adminstr. UNRRA and Internat. Refugee Orgn., Stuttgart, Germany, 1947-49; asst. treas., mgr. Self-Reliance Fed. Credit Union, Detroit, 1953-60; rep., cons. Prudential Ins. Co., Detroit, 1955-60; catalog librarian Ind. U., Bloomington, 1960-63, head order librarian, 1963-70, head acquisitions librarian, 1971-82, spl. projects librarian, asst. to assoc. dean, 1982—; lectr. Ukrainian Free U., 1975—; guest lectr. Ind. U. Sch. Library and Info. Sci., 1965—; mem. exec. bd. Olzhych Research Found., 1985—. Contbr. articles to profl. jours. Grantee Ind. U. Office Research and Advanced Studies Internat. Programs, 1972. Mem. Ukrainian Library Assn. Am. (v.p. 1972-75, exec. bd. 1975—), AAUP (chpt. treas., exec. bd. 1976—), ALA, Assn. Coll. Research Libraries, Am. Econ. Assn., Am. Acad. Polit. and Social Scis., Ukranian Free Acad. Arts and Scis., Shevchenko Sci. Soc. Home: 409 Clover Ln Bloomington IN 47401 Office: Ind U Library Bloomington IN 47405

KUEHN, KLAUS KARL ALBERT, physician, ophthalmologist; b. Breslau, Germany, Apr. 1, 1938; came to U.S., 1956, naturalized, 1971; s. Max and Anneliese (Hecht) K.; m. Eileen L. Nordgaard, June 22, 1961 (div. 1972); children—Stephan Eric, Kristina Annette; m. Lynda O. Hubbs, Oct. 2, 1974. Student, St. Olaf Coll., 1956-57; B.A., B.S., U. Minn., 1961; M.D., 1963. Diplomate Am. Bd. Ophthalmology. Resident in ophthalmology UCLA Affiliated Hosps., 1968-71; practice medicine specializing in ophthalmology, San Bernardino, Calif., 1971—; chief ophthalmology dept. San Bernardino County Med. Ctr., 1979-80; assoc. clin. prof. ophthalmology Jules Stein Eye Inst. and UCLA Med. Ctr., 1978-81. Served to capt. U.S. Army, 1963-64. Fellow Am. Acad. Ophthalmology; mem. AMA, Calif. Med. Assn., Calif. Assn. Ophthalmology (bd. dirs.). Office: 1920 N Waterman Ave San Bernardino CA 92404

KUERBITZ, GUNTHER, optical laboratory scientist; b. Litzmannstadt, Fed. Republic Germany, Feb. 19, 1941. Diploma, U. Muenster, Fed. Republic Germany, 1967; DSc, U. Duesseldorf, Fed. Republic Germany, 1972. Scientist Fraunhofer-Gesellschaft AGD, Muenchen, Fed. Republic Germany, 1967-72; mem. sci. staff U. Dusseldorf, Fed. Republic Germany, 1972-73; scientist Carl Zeiss, Oberkochen, Fed. Republic Germany, 1974-77, leader of electro-optics lab., 1978—. patentee in field. Mem. Deutsche Gesellschaft für Luft-und Raumfahrt, Deutsche Gesellschaft für Angewandte Optik, Deutsche Physikalische Gesellschaft. Home: Helfensteinstr 5, D-7923 Koenigsbronn-Zang Federal Republic of Germany Office: Carl Zeiss, Postfach 1369/1380, D-7082 Oberkochen Federal Republic of Germany

KUESEL, THOMAS ROBERT, civil engineer; b. Richmond Hill, N.Y., July 30, 1926; s. Henry N. and Marie D. (Butt) K.; m. Lucia Elodia Fisher, Jan. 31, 1959; children—Robert Livingston, William Baldwin. B.Engring. with highest honors, Yale U., 1946, M.Engring., 1947. With Parsons, Brinckerhoff, Quade & Douglas, 1947—; project mgr. Parsons, Brinckerhoff, Quade & Douglas, San Francisco, 1967-68; ptnr., sr. v.p. Parsons, Brinckerhoff, Quade & Douglas, N.Y.C., 1968-83, chmn., 1983—, dir., 1968—; vice chmn. OECD Tunneling Conf., Washington, 1970; mem U.S. Nat. Com. on Tunneling Tech., 1972-74. Contbr. 60 articles to profl. jours. Designer more than 120 bridges, 135 tunnels, and numerous other structures in 36 states and 20 fgn. countries most recent: Great Belt Railway Tunnel, Denmark, 1986-88, Ft. McHenry Tunnel, Balt., 1978-85; Rogers Pass Railway Tunnel, B.C., 1981-83. Fellow ASCE, Am. Cons. Engrs. Council: mem. Nat. Acad. Engring., Internat. Assn. for Bridge and Structural Engring., Brit. Tunnelling Soc., Yale Sci. and Engring. Assn., The Moles, Sigma Xi, Tau Beta Pi. Clubs: Yale (N.Y.C.); Wee Burn (Darien, Conn.). Office: One Penn Plaza 250 W 34th St New York NY 10119

KUHARIC, FRANJO CARDINAL, archbishop of Zagreb; b. Pribic, Yugoslavia, Apr. 15, 1919. Ordained priest Roman Catholic Ch., 1945; consecrated titular bishop of Meta and aux. bishop of Zagreb (Yugoslavia), from 1964; apostolic adminstr., 1969, archbishop, 1970, archdiocese of Zagreb, 1970; elevated to Sacred Coll. of Cardinals, 1983; pres. Yugoslav Bishops Conf., 1970; titular ch., St. Jerome of Schiavoni of Croats. Mem. Council for Pub. Affairs of Ch., Congregation Bishops, Congregation Clergy. Address: Kaptol 31, pp 553, 41000 Zagreb Yugoslavia

KUHL, ANNA FAYE, educator, forensic consultant; b. Seattle, Sept. 1, 1941; d. John and Marie Anna (Phillips) Belcher; m. Albert F. Lyle, Jr., Dec. 9, 1960 (div. 1964); children: Robert David, Donna Marie, John Michael; m. Wesley Clarence Kuhl, June 10, 1977. BA in Psychology, Ft. Wright Coll., 1977, MA in Psychology, 1978; PhD in Psychology, Wash. State U., 1981. Therapist Spokane Mental Health Ctr., Wash., 1968-71, 77-80; dir. Domestic Violence Research Bank, Wash. State U., Pullman, 1979-81, lectr. depts. sociology and edn., 1979-81; assoc. prof., chmn. adminstrn. justice San Jose State U., Calif., 1981—; owner Anna F. Kuhl & Assocs., San Jose, 1981—; bd. dirs. Mid.-Peninsula Support Network, San Jose, 1981-84; bd. commrs. Delinquency Prevention Commn., San Jose, 1981-84; bd. dirs. Juvenile justice Commn., 1986—; chmn., bd. dirs. Women and their Children Housing, 1986—. Author: Family Violence: A Textbook, 1988; co-author: Research Methods, Damned If She Does; editor: Western Criminologist, 1986—; contbr. articles to profl. jours. Mem. NOW, 1977—, W.A.T.C.H. (bd. dirs. 1986—), Nat. Coalition Against Domestic Violence, 1977—. Mem. Am. Soc. Criminology (sec. Women's div. 1982-84, chmn. div. on women and crime), Am. Psychol. Assn., Inst. Criminal Justice Ethics, Soc. for Study of Social Problems, Acad. Criminal Justice Scis., Law and Soc. Assn., Phi Kappa Phi, Phi Delta Kappa. Democrat. Mem. Unity Ch. Office: San Jose State U Adminstrn of Justice Dept One Washington Sq San Jose CA 95192

KUHL, MARGARET HELEN CLAYTON (MRS. ALEXIUS M. KUHL), banker; b. Louisville, 1908; d. Joseph Leonard and Maude (Mitzler) Clayton; student Loyola U. Home Study Div., Chgo., 1955—, Buena Vista Coll., Storm Lake, Iowa, summer 1964-65, 66; m. Alexius M. Kuhl, Apr. 21, 1936; children—Carol Lynn Ford Wassmuth, James Michael (adopted). Sales lady, buyer Silverberg, Akron, Iowa, 1924-34; owner dress shop, Fonda, Iowa, 1934-40; librarian, Fonda, 1940-43; bookkeeper, teller First Nat. Bank, Fonda, 1943-44; tchr. speech and drama, librarian asst. Our Lady Good Counsel Sch., Fonda, 1963-69; pres., chmn. bd. Pomeroy State Bank, 1975-83, also dir. Recipient Adult Leadership award Catholic Youth Orgn., 1967, Pro Deo Juventute award, 1969. Mem. Cath. Daus. Am. (dist. dep. 1964-70, state chmn. ecumenism 1970-72, state treas. 1970-72), Diocesan Council Cath. Women (chmn. orgn. and devel. 1964-65), Nat. Council Cath. Women (diocesan pres. 1968-70, diocesan sec. 1966-67; chmn. Women in Community Service Sioux City Diocesan Bd. 1971-72), Women in Community Service (pres. Iowa bd. 1972-73), Legion of Mary (pres. curia 1964-66, 67-70). Clubs:

Sun City (Ariz.) Country, Lakes; Fonda Golf. Home: 4th and Queen Sts Fonda IA 50540

KUHLE, SHIRLEY JEAN, former law enforcement administrator, victimology specialist, crime commissioner; b. Sioux Falls, S.D., Jan. 14, 1936; d. Earl John and Palma Ruth (Knutson) Albertus; m. Donald Eugene Kuhle, June 4, 1954; children—Kim Jean, Kathy Joan, Kenneth John, Kris June. Grad. Realtors Inst., 1969-77; cert. in mgmt. devel. U. Nebr., 1984. Cert. residential specialist; ARC home nursing instr.; cert. advanced victim counseling. Co-owner, asst. mgr. Beltline Tractor Sales, Inc., Lincoln, Nebr., 1960-84; appraiser Nebr. Real Estate Commn., 1974—, broker, 1964—; mem. Nebr. Crime Commn., Lincoln, 1980-87; adminstr. Victim/Witness Unit, Lincoln Police Dept., 1981-87; counselor Homicide Support Group, 1988; trainer victim issues, 1988. Author articles and tng. manuals on victim assistance. Mem. Lincoln/Lancaster County Justice Council, 1981; v.p. Willard Community Ctr., 1982-83; cons. Nebr. Parents Anonymous, 1981, Region VII Rural Domestic Violence Ctr., 1981; pres. Nebr. Task Force Domestic Violence, 1979, 80, 81; pres. Capitol Beach Community Assn., 1979; pres., co-founder Nebr. Coalition Victims of Crime, 1986. Program grantee, Fed. Govt., 1980, 81; recipient admiralship State of Nebr., 1975, Polly Alberto Hurley award, 1986, Liberty Bell award, 1986; Meritorious Service citation City of Lincoln, 1978. Mem. Nat. Orgn. Victims Assistance (life, exec., bd., 1979-84, conf. del.), Police Officers Nebr., Nebr. Sheriffs and Peace Officers Assn., Combined Orgn. of Police Services, Nat. Criminal Justice Assn. (charter). Democrat. Roman Catholic. Home: 930 Manchester Dr Lincoln NE 68528

KUHLER, RENALDO GILLET, museum official, scientific illustrator; b. Teaneck, N.J., Nov. 21, 1931; s. Otto August and Simonne L. (Gillet) K.; B.A., U. Colo., 1961. Curator of history, illustrator exhibit and miniature diorama preparator Eastern Wash. State Hist. Soc. Mus., Spokane, 1962-67; museum illustrator N.C. State Mus. Natural History, Raleigh, 1969—; designer, executor of art work for sci. illustrations, awards, brochures, pamphlets and periodicals Dept. Agr. and Mus., N.C., 1972-74; designer 36 illustrations for Handbook of Reptiles and Amphibians of Florida, Part 1 (Ray E. Ashton), 1981; contbr. many illustrations Atlas of Freshwater Fishes of North America (David Lee). Mem. Nat. Trust Historic Preservation. Democrat. Illustrator: American Firearms and the Changing Frontier (Waldo E. Rosebush), 1962-67. Office: Box 27647 Raleigh NC 27611

KUHLMANN, RALF, marketing professional; b. Wilhelmshaven, Niedersachsen, Federal Republic Germany, Nov. 9, 1948; s. Wilhelm and Else (Lawrenz) K.; m. Kaethe Hoehle, Mar. 10, 1972; children: Kai, Jens. Grad. Ing., Aachen Sch., 1975; Diploma in Ing., TH Berlin, 1978; D in Ing., Th Berlin, 1978. Cert. Engr. Salesman Esso Chemie GmbH Uöln, Fed. Republic Germany, 1978-80, sales rep., 1980-82, sect. head, 1982-84; coordinator Esso Chemie GmbH UKöln, Fed. Republic Germany, 1984-86; mktg. mgr. Exxon Chem. INT, Brussels, 1986—. Home: Sijsjeslann 3, 3078 Everberg Belgium Oince: Exxon Chem Internat, Mechelsesteenweg 363, 1950 Kraainem Belgium

KUHLMEIJER, HEINRICH JOHANNES, business educator; b. Naarden, The Netherlands, Feb. 9, 1916; s. Johannes Kuhlmeyer and Hester Beekman; m. Petronella den Boer, Oct. 30, 1945; children: Hester, Jan, Geertje. MA in Econs., Netherlands Sch. Econs., Rotterdam, 1940, PhD in Econs., 1953. Sec. Govt. Textile Bur., The Hague, The Netherlands, 1945-49; economist Internat. Cotton Adv. Com., Washington, 1949-52; mktg. mgr. C.T. Stork & Co., The Hague, The Netherlands, 1952-58; economist Cotton Council Internat., Paris/Brussels, 1958-60; prof. in bus. adminstrn. Erasmus U., Rotterdam, 1960-81, prof. emeritus, 1981—; vis. prof. U. Mich., Ann Arbor, 1979-80; com. of adv. Trenton State Coll. Author: Managerial Marketing (Dutch, English, Spanish), 1972, 75, 76, Industrial Economics (Dutch), 1982. Mem. Netherlands Inst. Mktg. (hon.), Am. Mktg. Assn., Netherlands Inst. Mgmt. Home: 73 Richard Holstraat, 2551 HN The Hague The Netherlands

KUHN, ANNE NAOMI WICKER (MRS. HAROLD B. KUHN), educator; b. Lynchburg, Va.; d. George Barney and Annie (Hicks) Wicker; m. Harold B. Kuhn. Diploma Malone Coll., 1933, Trinity Coll. Music, London, 1937; A.B., John Fletcher Coll., 1939; M.A., Boston U., 1942, postgrad., 1965-70; postgrad. (fellow) Harvard U., 1942-44, 66-68; hon. grad. Asbury Coll., 1978. Instr., Emmanuel Bible Coll., Birkenhead, Eng., 1936-37; asst. in history John Fletcher Coll., University Park, Iowa, 1938-39; librarian Harvard U., 1939-44; tchr. adult edn. program U.S. Armed Forces, Fuerstenfeldbruck Air Base, Germany, 1951-52; prof. Union Bibl. Sem., Yeotmal, India, 1957-58; lectr. Armenian Bible Inst., Beirut, Lebanon, 1958; prof. German, Asbury Coll., Wilmore, Ky., 1962—, co-dir. coll. study tour to E. Ger. and W. Ger., 1976, 77, 78, co-dir. acad. tours, 1979, 80; dir. acad. tour, Russia, 1981, 85, Scandanavia, 1982, Indonesia, Singapore, 1983, Hong Kong and Thailand, 1983, 85, E.Ger., W.Ger., France and Austria, 1983, Russia and Finland, 1984, 85, Peoples Republic China, 1984, 85, Estonia, Latvia, 1985, Portugal, Spain, France, Ireland, Scotland, Norway, England, 1987; tchr. Seoul Theol. Sem., fall 1978. Author: (pamphlet) The Impact of the Transition to Modern Education Upon Religious Education, 1950; The Influence of Paul Gerhardt upon Wesleyan Hymnody, 1960, Light to Dispel Fear, 1987; transl. German ch. records, poems, letters; contbr. articles to profl. jours. Del. Youth for Christ World Conf., 1948, 50, London Yearly Meeting of Friends, Edinburgh, Scotland, 1948, World Council Chs., Amsterdam, 1948, World Friends Conf., Oxford, Eng., 1952, World Methodist Conf., Oslo, Norway, 1961, Deutscher Kirchentag, Dortmund, Germany, 1963, German Lang. Congress, Bonn, W. Ger., 1974, Internat. Conf. Religion, Amsterdam, Netherlands, Poland, West Berlin, Fed. Republic Germany, 1986, Internat. Missionary Conf., Eng., 1987, Congress on the Bible II, Washington, 1987; participant Internat. Congress World Evangelization, Lausanne, Switzerland, 1974; del., speaker Internat. Conf. on Holocaust and Genocide, Oxford and London, 1988; mem. acad. tour Poland, 1988. Recipient German Consular award, Boston, 1965, Thomas Mann award Boston U., 1967; named Ky. Col., 1978. Fellow Goethe-Institut für Germanisten, Munich, 1966-68, 70-71. Mem. AAUW, Am. Assn. Tchrs. German, NEA, Ky. Ednl. Assn., Lincoln Lit. Soc., Protestant Women of Chapel, Delta Phi Alpha (award 1963, 65). Quaker. Club: Harvard Faculty. Home: 406 Kenyon Ave Wilmore KY 40390

KUHN, CHARLES, industrial executive; b. Cin., Nov. 29, 1919; s. Leo and Vivian (Van Hallenger) K.; student Purdue U., 1938-39; m. Elna Jane Smith, Nov. 17, 1944 (div. 1975); children—James Roland, Karen Jo Ann; m. 2d, Patricia L. McVicar, Nov. 27, 1976 (div. 1980). Vice pres. Fansteel Metall. Corp., 1950-55, Hills McCanna Co., 1955-58; v.p. Dresser Mfg. div. Dresser Industries, Inc., 1958-60, pres., 1960-64, group v.p., dir. parent co., 1964-65; exec. v.p., 1965-68, pres., 1968-70, also chief ops. officer, dir. subs. cos.; pres., dir. Wylain Inc., Dallas, chief exec. officer, 1970-72, chmn. bd., chief exec. officer, 1972-80; chmn. bd., dir. Mich. Gen. Corp., Dallas, 1983—; dir. Lafarge Corp., Dallas, Bay Beer Distbrs., Redondo Beach, Calif. Served with USNR, 1940-42. Mem. Am. Gas Assn., Newcomen Soc. N.Am., Am. Water Works Assn., Pa. Soc., Canadian Gas Assn., Tex. Mid-Continent Oil & Gas Assn. Home: 96 Linda Isle Newport Beach CA 92660 Office: PO Box 400443 Dallas TX 75240

KUHNE, ERIC ALEXIS, hotel executive; b. Geneva, Switzerland, May 18, 1942; s. Charles Francois Xavier and Evelyne Julia (Cavin) K.; m. Marie-Therese Veronique Torrent, Dec. 20, 1971; 1 dau., Ariane Claire. Student Coll. Calvin, Geneva, 1957-60, Ecole Hoteliere, Lausanne, 1961-64. Dir. sales Manhattan Ctr., Brussels, Belgium, 1972-75; dir. mktg. Regent Hotels, Internat., Geneva, 1975-76; dir. sales Ramada Internat., Geneva, 1976-79; dir. sales Hilton Hotels Internat., Geneva, 1979-82; gen. mgr. Ramada Renaissance, Geneva, 1982—; tchr. Hotel Sch., Glion, Switzerland, 1982—. Mem. Swiss Soc. Hoteliers. Club: Kiwanis (Geneva). Home: 7 Avenue des Cavaliers, 1224 Geneva Switzerland Office: Ramada Renaissance Hotel, 19 Ave de Zurich, 1201 Geneva Switzerland

KÜHNEL, HANS, service company executive; b. Lissberg, Hessen, Fed. Republic of Germany, Feb. 4, 1944; s. Rudolph and Frieda (Mann) K.; m. Donna Kühnel, Sept. 11, 1966 (div. Oct. 1983); children: Michael, Susan; m. Elizabeth Kühnel, Mar. 10, 1985; children: Kristie, Tyson. Grad., Bergius U., Frankfurt, Fed. Republic of Germany, 1964. Apprentice Hotel Kaiserhof, Offenbach, Fed. Republic of Germany, 1961-64; waiter Hotelvier Jahreszeiten, Munich, 1966-65, Hotel Lausanne Palace, Switzerland, 1965, Hotel La Bananerai, Ezesurmere, France, 1966; capt., asst. maitre d' Castle Harbour Hotel, Bermuda, 1966-67; asst. maitre d' Inn On Park, Toronto, Ont., 1967; mgr. restaurant Velvet Glove Winnipeg Inn, Can., 1968-69; gen. mgr. Olivers Restaurant, Winnipeg, 1969-70, Discovery Restaurant, Edmonton, Can., 1971-72; pres. The Creperie, Ltd., Edmonton, 1973-75, Your Choice Restaurant Group, Edmonton, 1975—. dir. Edmonton Tourism, 1984-86, Downtown Bus. Assn., Edmonton, 1986-87; mem. Young Pres.'s Orgn. Mem. Can. Restaurant Assn. (bd. dirs. 1984—), Edmonton C. of C. (bd. dirs., v.p. 1987—). Lodge: Rotary.

KUHNER, DAVID ARNOLD, librarian, archivist; b. Columbus, Ohio, Mar. 20, 1921; s. Walter James and Effie Leota (Ranck) K. B.Sc., Ohio State U., 1943; M.Ed., U. Miami, 1951; M.L.S., U. Calif.-Berkeley, 1962. Feature writer Fla. State News Bur., Tallahassee, 1955-61; librarian Stanford U., Calif., 1962-66, John Crerar Library, Chgo., 1966-69; asst. dir. libraries Claremont Colls., Calif., 1970-85, cons. 1985—. Co-editor: Bibliotheca De Re Metallica, 1980. Editor Map of Fla. Industry and Sci., 1961. Contbr. articles to profl. jours. and newspapers. Served to lt. USAF, 1943-46. Mem. ALA (book reviewer 1966-73), Bibliog. Soc. Am., Soc. Am. Archivists. Club: Westerners (Los Angeles). Home: 152 E La Verne Ave Pomona CA 91767 Office: Honnold Library Claremont Colls Claremont CA 91711

KUHNLEIN, URS, molecular biologist, educator, researcher; b. Zurich, Switzerland, Sept. 17, 1940; s. Viktor and Hedwig (Gohner) K.; m. Harriet Veronica Kling, July 29, 1972; children—Letitia, Matthew, Peter. B.Sc. in Exptl. Physics, Fed. Inst. Tech., 1965; Ph.D. in Biology, U. Geneva, 1970. Postdoctoral fellow Stanford Med. Sch., Calif., 1970-72; research biochemist U. Calif., Berkeley, 1972-76; research scholar, sr. scientist B.C. Cancer Research Ctr., Vancouver, 1976-84; assoc. prof. animal sci. McGill U., Montreal, Que., 1985—. Contbr. articles to profl. jours. Nat. Cancer Inst. Can., grantee, 1976-83; Med. Research Council Can. grantee, 1981—; Nat. Sci. and Engring. Research Council Can. grantee, 1985—. Mem. Can. Soc. Animal Sci., Agrl. Inst. Can. Avocations: skiing; mountaineering. Office: Macdonald Coll of McGill Univ, 21 111 Lakeshore Rd, Sainte Anne de Bellevue, PQ Canada H9X 1C0

KUIPER, FRANCISCUS BERNARDUS JACOBUS, language educator; b. The Hague, Netherlands, July 7, 1907; s. Franciscus Bernardus Jacobus and Anna Maria (van Dijck) K.; m. Eduarda Johanna De Jong, Aug. 20, 1934 (div. Dec. 1973); children: Huib, Maarten Joost, Rogier, Els. PhD, Leiden (Netherlands) U., 1934. Latin and Greek tchr. Bataviaas Lyceym, Jakarta, 1934-39; prof. of Sanskrit U. Leiden (Netherlands), 1939-72, prof. emeritus, 1972—; dir. Kern Inst., Leiden, 1961-72. Author: Die Indogermanischen Nasalpräsentia, 1937, Nahali, 1962, Varuna and Vidusaka, 1979, Gopalakelicandrika, 1987; co-founder, co-editor in chief Indo-Iranian Jour., 1957—; contbr. articles to profl. jours. Mem. Linguistic Soc. Am. (hon.), Am. Oriental Soc. (hon.), Danish Acad. Scis. and Letters, Austrian Acad. Scis. Home: Händellaan 19, 2253 BJ Voorschoten The Netherlands

KUIPERS, JACK, mathematician, educator, consultant; b. Grand Rapids, Mich., Mar. 27, 1921; s. Bernard Jacob and Grace (Werkema) K.; m. Lois Belle Holtrop, Mar. 25, 1948; children—Benjamin Jack, Emily Louise, Joel Corneal, Alison Jane, Lynne Marie. A.B., Calvin Coll., 1942; B.S.E.E., U. Mich., 1943, M.S.E., 1958, Info. and Control Engr.'s degree, 1966; postgrad. U. Calif.-Santa Barbara, 1967-70. Asst. to dir. research Electric Sorting Machine Co., Grand Rapids, 1946-50; project engr. Flight Reference and Autopilot Systems, Lear, Inc., Grand Rapids, 1950-53, sr. project engr., analytical design, 1954-59; chief engr. instrument div. R.C. Allen Bus. Machines, In., Grand Rapids, 1953-54; sr. physicist Instrumentation and Control Div. Cleve. Pneumatic Industries, Grand Rapids, 1959-62; lectr. Horace B. Rackman Sch. of Grad. Studies, U. Mich., Ann Arbor, 1962-67, research engr. NASA Apollo Applications Inst. of Sci. and Tech., 1962-67; prof. math. Calvin Coll., Grand Rapids, 1967—; cons. in aerospace tech., math. models. Served with U.S. Army, 1942-46. Mem. Math. Assn. of Am., IEEE, Sigma Xi. Mem. Christian Reformed Ch. Patentee: SPASYN, electromagnetic tracking device and other devels. in field; frequent guest lectr.; contbr. articles to profl. jours. Home: 3085 Baker Park Dr SE Grand Rapids MI 49508 Office: Calvin Coll Dept Math Grand Rapids MI 49506

KUKI, HIROSHI, educational consultant; b. Tokyo, July 16, 1940; s. Kazuyuki and Hanako (Emori) K.; m. Tamae Mizuno. B.A., Waseda U., Tokyo; M.A., U. Hawaii-Honolulu Grad. asst U. Hawaii, 1965-69; research fellow in linguistics B.P. Bishop Mus., Honolulu, 1967; lectr. U. Auckland (N.Z.), 1969-71; study abroad cons. Setagaya Inst. for Study Abroad, Tokyo, 1974—; lectr. Waseda U., 1975—; Columnist Japan Times, 1983-84; author study abroad guides. CWAJ grantee, 1965, NSF grantee, 1967-68. Mem. Nat. Assn. Fgn. Student Affairs, Linguistic Soc. Hawaii (1st sec. treas. 1966). Presbyterian. Clubs: Internat. House of Japan, Tokyo Internat. Players. Office: Setagaya Inst for Study Abroad, 2-31-18, #302, Daizawa, Setagaya-ku, 155 Tokyo Japan

KUKLA, GEORGE JIRI, paleoclimatologist; b. Prague, Czechoslovakia, Mar. 14, 1930; came to U.S., 1971, naturalized, 1980; s. Milos and Jindra (Duskova) K.; R.N.Dr., Charles U., Prague, 1953, 71, Cand. Scis., 1968; m. Helena Kupka, May 19, 1955; children—Susan, Michael. Chief geologist non-metallic prospection Nat. Enterprise, Prague, 1953-58, Ceylon, Argentina, Caribbean, 1956-66; sr. research scientist Archaeol. and Geol. Insts. Czechoslovak Acad. Scis., Prague, 1958-70; sr. research scientist Lamont-Doherty Geol. Obs., Columbia U., N.Y.C., 1971—; vis. prof. paleoclimatology Brown U., Providence, 1972-73, U. Wash., Seattle, 1975, Hebrew U., Jerusalem, 1979, U. Catholique de Louvain, Belgium, 1981; cons. on paleoclimatology satellite meteorology and magnetostratigraphy; project leader Internat. Geol. Correlation Program. NSF sr. fgn. scientist fellow, 1970; research grantee NSF, 1972—, Dept. Energy, 1981—, U.S. Geol. Survey, 1984-86, USAF, 1984—, NASA, 1985—, Battelle, 1988—. Mem. Internat. Union Geol. Scis. (commn.), Internat. Union Quarternary Research, Geol. Soc. Am., Am. Geophys. Union, Am. Meteorol. Soc., Meteorol. Soc. Brazil, Royal Meteorol. Soc. Britain, Nat. Weather Assn. (U.S.), Am. Assn. Quaternary Geology, Deutsche Quartarvereinigung (W. Ger.), Explorers Club. Co-editor jours. including Catena (W. Ger.), 1974—, Quaternary Sci. Revs. (Brit.), 1981—; editor: Periglazialzone, Loess und Paleolithikum der Tschechoslowakei, 1969; The Present Interglacial: How and When Will It End, 1972; World Food Supply in Changing Climate, 1975; Snowwatch 1980, 1981, Snowwatch 1985, 1986; Milankovitch and Climate, 1984. Office: Lamont Doherty Geol Obs Palisades NY 10964

KUKLIN, JEFFREY PETER, lawyer, talent agency executive; b. N.Y.C., Dec. 13, 1935; s. Norman Bennett and Deane (Cable) K.; m. Jensina Olson, Nov. 18, 1960; 1 son, Andrew Bennett; m. 2d, Ronia Levene, June 22, 1969; children—Adam Blake, Jensena Lynne, Jeremy Brett. A.B., Columbia U., 1957, J.D., 1960. Bar: N.Y. 1962, U.S. Supreme Ct. 1965, Calif. 1973. Atty., TV sales adminstrn. NBC-TV, N.Y.C., 1966-67; asst. to dir. bus. affairs CBS News, N.Y.C., 1967-69; atty., assoc. dir. contracts ABC-TV, N.Y.C. and Los Angeles, 1969-73; v.p. bus. affairs and law Tomorrow Entertainment, Inc., Los Angeles, 1973-75; v.p. legal and bus. affairs Billy Jack Enterprises, Inc., Los Angeles, 1975-76; atty., bus. affairs exec. William Morris Agy., Inc., Beverly Hills, Calif., 1976-79, head TV bus. affairs, 1979-81, v.p., head TV bus. affairs, 1981—. Mem. ABA, Acad. TV Arts and Scis., Los Angeles Copyright Soc. Address: 151 El Camino Dr Beverly Hills CA 90212

KUKU, ADEREMI OLUYOMI, mathematics educator; b. Ijebu-Ode, Nigeria, Mar. 20, 1941; s. Busari Adeoye and Abusatu Oriaran (Baruwa) K.; m. Felicia Osifunke Kalesanwo, Dec. 28, 1968; children—Dolapo, Kemi, Yemisi, Solape. B.Sc., U. London, 1965; M.Sc., U. Ibadan, 1968, Ph.D., 1971. Mem. faculty U. Ibadan, 1968—, prof. math, 1982—, head dept., 1983—, dean Postgrad. Sch., 1986—. Vis. prof. U. Bielefeld, W.Ger., 1980, Queens U., Kingston, Ont., Can., 1982. Author: Abstract Algebra, 1980; Axiomatic Theory of Induced Representations of Finite Groups, 1984; contbr. articles to profl. jours. Named Hon. Citizen, Huntsville, Ala., 1968; U.S. State Dept. travel fellow, 1968; Afgrad fellow African Am. Inst., 1970-71; W.Ger. Acad. Exchange awardee, 1982. Vice-chmn. First Congress African Scientists, 1987, Orgn. African Unity scientific com., 1987. Fellow African Acad. Scis., Math. Assn. Nigeria; mem. Sci. Assn. Nigeria (v.p. 1983-84), European Acad. Arts, Scis., Humanities, Internat. Ctr. Theoretical Physics (math. adv. com., 1986—), Internat. Math. Union Commn. Devel. Exchange, 1986—, African Math. Union (pres. 1986—), Nigerian Math Soc. (editor jour. 1981—), Am. Math Soc., Math Assn. Nigeria. Baptist. Clubs: Lions (bd. dirs. 1984—), Ijebu-Ode. Avocations: ballroom dancing; chess; table tennis. Home: 2 Amure St, Kongi Ibadan Oyo Nigeria Office: Univ Ibadan Dept Math, Ibadan Oyo Nigeria

KUKULKA, JOZEF, political science educator; b. Raczyna, Przemysl, Poland, Jan. 3, 1929; s. Jan and Kazimiera (Dziukiewicz) K.; m. Krystyna Bolesta, Feb. 2, 1963; children: Jan, Piotr. High degree, Main Sch. Fgn. Service, Warsaw, Poland, 1953. Asst. Main Sch. Fgn. Service, Warsaw, 1949-53, lectr., 1953-56; doctorant Polish Acad. Sci., Warsaw, 1954-57; lectr. Polish Inst. Internat. Relations, Warsaw, 1962-68, dir., 1977—, extraord. prof., 1977-85, prof., 1985—; secret counsellor Polish Embassy, Paris, 1968-72; supernumerary prof. Inst. Polit. Sci., Warsaw, 1972-77; dir. Inst. International. Relations, Warsaw, 1977—; vice-dean faculty of journalism and polit. sci. Warsaw U., 1975-77. Author: France and Poland after Versailles Treaty 1919-1922, 1970, Political Cooperation between Socialist Countries, 1976, Problems of International Relations Theory, 1978, International Political Relations, 1982. Mem. presidium gen. adminstr. Rural Youth Union, 1958-66; dep. pres. Warsaw com. United Peasant Party, 1959-61, chief com., 1981—; dep. pres. exec. com. Patriotic Movement for Nat. Rebirth, 1984—; dep. pres. com.fgn. affairs Polish Peoples Rep. Diet and secret Polish Group Interparliamentary Union, 1985—. Recipient Gold Cross of Merit Council of the State, 1958, Knightly Cross Order of Polonia Rest. Council of State, 1979, Officer Cross Order of Polonia Restituta, 1984. Home: ul Powsinska 38 m 3, 02-903 Warsaw Poland Office: Inst Stosunkow, Miedzynar, ul Krakowskie Przedm 3, 00-047 Warsaw Poland

KUKWA, LUTZ HELMUT, physician, pharmaceutical company executive; b. Berlin, Aug. 10, 1940; s. Helmut and Elisabeth (Thoma) K.; m. Hildegard Lemmens, Oct. 18, 1964; children: Thomas, Kerstin, Gregor, Christian. Physician, U. Cologne, 1966, MD, 1968. Med. dir. Sanof, Fed. Republic Germany, 1977-81; head corp. mktg. Boehringer, Ingelheim, Fed. Republic Germany, 1982-84; v.p. internat. mktg. Bayer AG, Leverkusen, Fed. Republic Germany, 1984—. Mem. Mktg. Club (sec. Cologne). Office: Bayer AG Leverkusen, D-5090 Leverkusen Federal Republic of Germany

KULECK, WALTER JULIUS, psychologist, consultant; b. Phila., Aug. 25, 1945; s. Walter J. and Alma Kuleck; m. Carol S. Edmonson, June 15, 1968 (div.); 1 child, Julian James; m. Catharine C. Knight, Jan. 2, 1983. BS in Aero. Engring., MIT, 1967, MS in Aero. Engring., 1968; MA in Psychology, U. Mich., 1974, PhD (Ctr. for Creative Leadership fellow), 1976. Lic. psychologist, Ohio. Engr., Vertol div. Boeing, Phila., 1966-71; parts and accessories mgr. West Chester (Pa.) Honda, 1971-72; NIMH trainee, asst. research dir. Inst. for Social Research, U. Mich., Ann Arbor, 1972-76; postdoctoral fellow Ctr. for Creative Leadership, Greensboro, N.C., 1976-77; staff psychologist William, Lynde & Williams, Inc., Painesville, Ohio, 1977-83; pres. Cognitive Processes, Inc., Cleveland Heights, Ohio, 1983-85; sr. sales engr. system div., Keithley Instruments, 1988, export sales mgr., 1988—; founding prin. ProTrane, Detroit, 1984-85; cons. psychologist The Creative Thinking Ctr., Hudson, Ohio, 1983-85, MacArthur Found. Human Devel. Consortium; dir. Innovative Health Systems, Inc., 1984—, v.p. mktg. 1986—; mgr. export mktg. Keithley Instruments Systems Div.; mgmt. psychologist; creativity cons. Bd. dirs. Ch. Growth Ctr., Inc., 1986—. Mem. Am. Psychol. Assn., Cleve. Venture Club (founder), Ruger Collectors' Assn. Republican. Lutheran. Club: Solon Sportsman's (Ohio). Contbr. articles to profl. jours. Office: 3631 Fairmount Blvd Cleveland Heights OH 44118

KULESH, WILLIAM ADAM, insurance executive; b. Bronx, N.Y., Sept. 13, 1929; s. William Adam and Sophia Annastatia (Kurtz) K.; student pub. schs., Bklyn.; m. Catherine Marie Bechler, May 25, 1957; children—Claudia Elizabeth, Christopher John, Terence William. Field underwriter Mchts. Fire Assurance Corp. N.Y., N.Y.C., 46-57; dist. mgr. Kemper Ins. Group, Garden City, N.Y., 1957-59; mgr. Frank E. Wright & Sons Agy., Inc., West Hempstead, N.Y., 1959-64; founder, pres., chief exec. officer Nat. Coverage Corp., Seaford, N.Y., 1964—; mem. Lloyds' of London. Lord of Brampton, Huntington, Cambridgeshire. Served with U.S. Army, 1951-53. Mem. Nat. Small Bus. Assn., L.I. Assn., Internat. Platform Assn., Ind. Ins. Agts. Assn. Russian Orthodox. Clubs: Cherry Valley Country, New Hyde Park Elks. Home: 62 1st St Garden City NY 11530

KULI, AMIEL MICHAEL, airline executive; b. Akron, Ohio, Aug. 5, 1942; s. Amiel Michael and Margaret Emma (Brady) K.; m. Carolyn Elizabeth Phinney, Sept. 26, 1964; children—Michelle Marie, Michael Steven (dec.). Student AG Aviation Acad., Reno, Nev., 1967-68, Akron U., 1969-70, Kent State U., 1971-72. Airline transport pilot, jet capt. Airborne Express, Wilmington, Ohio, 1976-78, chief pilot, dir. flight ops., 1978-79, dir. ops., 1979, v.p. air contract ops., 1979-80, v.p. ops., 1980-83, v.p. govt. affairs, 1983-86; v.p. Air Park Devel.; pres. Sound Suppression, Inc., 1985—; pres. Escort Air, Inc., Akron, Ohio, 1973-76; chief pilot Forest City Enterprises, Cleve., 1970-73. Served with USN, 1960-64, Cuba. Decorated Cuba Crisis medal. Mem. Quiet Birdmen, Nat. Street Rod Assn., Nat. Assn. Fgn. Trade Zones, Am. Legion, VFW (nat. com. 1976). Methodist. Club: Connecting Rods Car (pres. 1986—). Avocations: automobiles; motorcycles; water skiing. Office: Airborne Express Inc 145 Hunter Dr Wilmington OH 45177

KULIČ, VÁCLAV, psychologist, consultant; b. Kostelec, Czechoslovakia, Aug. 30, 1921; s. Václav Kulič and Marie Kuličová; m. Miloslava Piherová, Apr. 29, 1950; 1 child, Jana. Student, Charles U., Prague, Czechoslovakia, 1949; CSc, PhD, Czechoslovak Acad. Scis., Prague, 1969. Tchr. Gymnasium Prague, 1948-61; sci. researcher Comenius Inst. Edn., Czechoslovak Acad. Scis., 1961-81, sci. cons. psychology, 1981—. Author: Error and Learning, 1971, Man, Learning and Automation, 1984, Psychology of Guided Learning, 1988; co-author: Programmed Learning, 1966, Psychology of Successfull Pupil, 1979; contbr. articles to profl. jours. Recipient prize Czechoslovak Acad. Scis., 1966. Mem. Psychol. Assn. of Czechoslovak Acad. Scis., Assn. for Cybernetics of Czechoslovak Acad. Scis. Home: Vinohradska 198, 130 00 Prague Czechoslovakia

KULIKOV, (MARSHAL) VIKTOR GEORGIYEVICH, Soviet army officer; b. July 5, 1921; student Frunze Mil. Acad., Acad. of Gen. Staff, 1948-53. Joined Soviet Army, 1938; comdr. of platoon, 1940, chief of staff tank bn., regiment, brigade, 1941-45; various command posts in tank detachments, 1945-48; comdr. tank regiment, chief of staff tank div., dep. comdr. of army, comdr. of army, 1953-67; comdr. Kiev Mil. Area, 1967-69; comdr.-in-chief Soviet Forces in Ger., 1969-71; chief of gen. staff and 1st dep. minister of def., 1971-77; comdr.-in-chief of Armed Forces of Warsaw Pact, 1977—. Decorated Order of Lenin, Order of the Red Banner (3), others. Address: Ministry of Def, 34 Naberzhnaya M Thoreza, Moscow USSR *

KULKARNI, DILIP, corporate executive; b. Pune, India, Oct. 13, 1950; s. Mahabal and Sheela (Mangaokar) K.; m. Devika Achaladevi, Dec. 6, 1977; children: Mallika, Sangeeta. D in Electronics, S.J. Coll. Engring., Mysore, India, 1974; postgrad., Harvard U., 1987. Jt. mng. dir. Saitex Udyoga Pvt. Ltd., Bombay, 1977-82; pres. Skypak Couriers Pvt. Ltd., Bombay, 1982; chmn. Dilip Holdings Pvt. Ltd., Bombay, 1982-86, Sama Holdings Pvt. Ltd., Bombay, 1986-87; dir. Kopyrite Ltd., Jaipur, India, 1987-88; chmn. Bliss Chems. and Pharms. Ltd., 1988—; bd. dirs. Shibi Capsules, Ltd., Madras, India. Named Spl. Exec. Magistrate, Govt. Maharashtra, 1982. Mem. Young Pres. Orgn., Western India Automobile Assn. Clubs: Leo of North Bombay (pres. 1974-75), Nat. Sports of India, Bombay Presidency Golf, United Services, Madras Gymkhana. Home: 2A Ameya Apts off K Dhuru Rd, Bombay 400028, India Office: Skypak Couriers Pvt Ltd, Skypak House off MV Rd, Andheri (East), Bombay 400 059, India

KULL, RUNAR KAJ ALBIN, dentist; b. Maxmo, Finland, July 1, 1943; came to Sweden, 1946; s. Mickel Albin and Ines Ingegerd (Berg) K.; m. Britt Inger Margareta Leufstadius, Aug. 17, 1968 (div. Mar. 1987); children: Hans, Sara, Lena, Dan, Ida, Jon. DDS, Sch. Dentistry, Umeå, Sweden, 1969. Dentist Västernorrlands Läns Landsting, Ånge, Sweden, 1969-72; dentist, chief staff Jämtlands Lans Länsting, Bräcke, Sweden, 1972-77, Bispgården, Sweden, 1986—; sole practice dentistry Ånge, 1977-86; proprietor Blue Doctor Fishing Shop, Ånge, 1978-86, Bispgården, 1986—. Contbr. articles to sport fishing mags. Recipient Award of Merit, Ballantine's Internat. Photography award, 1983. Mem. Sveriges Tandläkarförbund. Lutheran. Lodges: Rotary, United Ancient Order of Druids. Home:

Forsvägen 37, S-84073 Bispfården Sweden Office: Jämtlands Läns Landsting, Folktandvården Forsvägen 37, S-84073 Bispgården Sweden

KULLBERG, DUANE REUBEN, accounting firm executive; b. Red Wing, Minn., Oct. 6, 1932; s. Carl Reuben and Hazel Norma (Swanson) K.; m. Sina Nell Turner, Oct. 19, 1958; children: Malissa Cox, Caroline Turner. BBA, U. Minn., 1954. CPA, Minn., Ill., Mich., Iowa. With Arthur Andersen & Co. (CPA's), 1954—; ptnr. Arthur Andersen & Co., CPA's, 1967—; mng. ptnr. Arthur Andersen & Co., CPA's, Mpls., 1970-74; dep. mng. ptnr. Arthur Andersen & Co., CPA's, Chgo., 1975-78; vice chmn. acctg. and audit practice Arthur Andersen & Co., CPA's, 1978-80, mng. ptnr., chief exec. officer, 1980—; mem. services policy adv. com. Office U.S. Trade Rep. Trustee Northwestern U., Fin. Acctg. Found., Tax Found. Inc., U. Minn. Found., Art Inst. Chgo.; bd. dirs. Chgo. Council Fgn. Relations, Chgo. Cen. Area Com., Japan-U.S. Bus. Council. Served with AUS, 1956-58. Mem. Am. Inst. CPA's, Ill. Soc. CPA's, Minn. Soc. CPA's, Beta Gamma Sigma (dir.'s table). Republican. Clubs: Chicago, Mid-Am., Attic, Monroe, Commercial (Chgo.); Minneapolis. Home: 2750 Sheridan Rd Evanston IL 60201 also: 12 Gustave-Ador, Geneva Switzerland also: 6444 N 79th St Scottsdale AZ 85253 Office: Arthur Andersen & Co 69 W Washington St Chicago IL 60602

KULLBERG, ROLF EVERT, banker; b. Pohja, Finland, Oct. 3, 1930; s. Harry E. and Svea (Holm) K.; m. Märta Elisabeth Sourander, 1953; children—Hans, Henrik, Tom. M.Soc. Sci., Abo Akademi, 1955. Mem. bd. mgmt. Bank of Finland, Helsinki, 1974—, acting dep. gov., 1979-82, dep. gov., 1982-83, gov., 1983—; mem. supervisory bd. Finnish Fund for Indsl. Devel. Cooperation Ltd., 1979—, Finnish Export Credit Ltd., 1983; gov. Internat Monetary Fund for Finland, 1983—; mem. adv. bd., Indsl. Devel., 1982—; mem. Econ. Council, 1983. Office: Bank of Finland, Snellmaninaukio, 00170 Helsinki Finland

KULOK, WILLIAM ALLAN, venture capitalist; b. Mt. Vernon, N.Y., July 24, 1940; s. Sidney Alexander and Bertha (Lembeck) K.; B.S. in Econs., Wharton Sch., U. Pa., 1962; m. Susan B. Glick, June 26, 1965; children—Jonathan, Brian, Stephanie. Acct., David Kulok Co., N.Y.C., 1962-67; asst. to pres. Syndicate Mags., N.Y.C., 1967-70; founder, 1970, since pres. Kulok Capitol Inc., N.Y.C.; dir. Listcomp Corp., Mail Mgmt. Corp., Mag. Devel. Fund, Lazard Spl. Equities Fund, N.Y. Import/Export Ctr., Inc., Ctr. for Exec. Edn.; lectr. Wharton Sch., U. Chgo., N.Y.U. Pres. N.Y. Soc. Ethical Culture, 1978-80; vice chmn. bd. Ethical Culture Schs., 1979, chmn., 1982-86; C.P.A., N.Y. Mem. Am. Inst. C.P.A.s. Clubs: Rockaway River Country, Sleepy Hollow Country; Tryall Golf and Beach (Jamaica, W.I.). Home: 40 E 84th St New York NY 10028 Office: Waldorf Astoria 301 Park Ave Suite 1855 New York NY 10022

KULPRATHIPANJA, SANTI, chemist; b. Thailand, Sept. 18, 1944; came to U.S., 1968; s. Henglee and Morsul (Gor) Lim; B.S., Chulalongkorn U., 1968; M.S., East Tex. State U., 1970; Ph.D., Iowa State U., 1974; m. Apinya Prasertsintu, Nov. 25, 1974; children—Sathit, Ames, Ann. Research assoc. M.I.T., Cambridge, 1975-78, Mass. Gen. Hosp., Boston, 1976-78, Harvard Med. Sch., 1977-78; sr. research chemist UOP, Inc., Des Plaines, Ill., 1978-81, research specialist, 1981-85; research specialist Allied-Signal Inc., Des Plaines, 1985-88, assoc. scientist Allied-Signal Inc., 1988—. Mem. Am. Chem. Soc., Soc. Nuclear Medicine, Chgo. Soc. Chromatography, Chgo. Catalysis Club, Phi Lambda Upsilon. Contbr. more than 20 articles to tech. jours. More than 45 patents in field of separations. Home: 3920 Winston Dr Hoffman Estates IL 60195 Office: Allied-Signal Inc Engineered Materials Research Ctr 50 E Algonquin Rd Des Plaines IL 60017-5016

KULSTAD, GUY CHARLES, public works official; b. Bend, Oreg., Feb. 28, 1930; s. John Marlyn and Annie Mildred (Boyd) Kulstad Ibison; B.S. in Civil Engring., U. Calif.-Berkeley, 1958; Registered profl. engr., Calif., Oreg., Wash.; registered traffic engr., Calif.; registered land surveyor, Oreg.; cert. community coll. instr., Calif. m. Bonnie Jane Sherman, Aug. 28, 1955; children—Anne Marie Kulstad Hurst, Mark, Alice Kulstad Krause. Engring. aide county rd. dept., Los Angeles, 1951, asst. civil engr., 1953-58; dir. pub. works, Benicia, Calif., 1958-59; dep. dir. pub. works, Solano County, Calif., 1959-65; dir. pub. works, Humboldt County, Calif., 1965—; gen. mgr. gen. Humboldt Bay Wastewater Authority 1975, 82—. Mem. joint liaison com. Mcpl. Pub. Works Officers and Calif. Council of Civil Engrs. and Land Surveyors. Served with AUS, 1951-53. Recipient Outstanding Service award North Bay chpt. Calif. Soc. Profl. Engrs., 1964, Boss of the Year award Arcata Jaycees, Recognition award Humboldt Toastmasters. Fellow ASCE; mem. Nat. Soc. County Engrs. Calif. County Entrs., Nat. Soc. Profl. Engrs., Am. Congress Surveying and Mapping, Calif. Land Surveyors Assn. (surveyor award Humbolt chpt.), Calif. County Engrs. Assn. Clubs: Commonwealth of Calif., Sons of Norway, Toastmasters Internat. Author profl. dissertations. Office: 1106 2d St Eureka CA 95501

KUMAGAI, TAKASHI, engineering company executive; b. Tokyo, May 20, 1931; s. Naoyuki and Yukino (Sumida) K.; m. Kiwako Takeuchi, Mar. 26, 1955; children—Yukihiro, Hideki. B.S., Tokyo U., 1955. Engr. Mamiya Camera Co. Ltd., Tokyo, 1955-64; pres. Shinko Engring. Research Co., 1963—; lectr. automation mechanism Kanagawa U. , 1979—. Contbr. articles to profl. jours. Patentee in field. Group leader Tech. Tour Groupes, 1969—. Mem. Japan Cons. Engrs. Assn. (dir. 1977-79), Japan Indsl. Robot Assn., Japan Soc. Precision Engring., Automation Promotion Assn. (v.p. 1975—). Club: Tsumagoi Yamaha. Home: 4-22-2 Kinuta, Setagaya-ku, Tokyo 157, Japan Office: Shinko Engring Research Co, 6-6-18 Kinuta, Setagaya-ku, Tokyo 157, Japan

KUMAGAI, TAKENOBU, construction company executive; b. Morioka, Iwate, Japan, Jan. 11, 1937; s. Gosuke and Miyuki (Omara) K.; m. Masako Higuchi, Mar. 27, 1963; children: Maoki, Mariko, Seiyu. Grad., Morioka Engring. Sch., 1986. With staff Taisei Constrn. Ltd., Sapporo, Japan, 1956-69; pres. Estimation Cons. Ltd., Sapporo, 1969—. Mem. Bldg. Surveyors' Inst. Japan (bd. dirs. Hokkaido 1982), Japan Inst. Architects, Japan Architects Assn., Assn. Bank Users (bd. dirs. 1985), Assn. Goodwill Tax Payers (bd. dirs. 1986—). Lodge: Rotary.

KUMAHARA, KEISAKU, mathematics educator; b. Sekinomiya, Hyogo, Japan, Nov. 28, 1942; s. Tsutomu and Satoe (Yamane) K.; m. Yoko Tamura, Oct. 6, 1973; 1 child, Mariko. Bachelors degree, Okayama U., Japan, 1965, Masters degree, 1967; Doctorate degree, Osaka U., Japan, 1972. Asst. Osaka U., 1967; assoc. prof. Tottori U., Japan, 1973, prof., 1981. Mem. Math. Soc. Japan, Am. Math. Soc. Home: Koyama-cho Kita 5-225, 680 Tottori Japan

KUMAHOR, PAUL KWASI, accountant; b. Atiavi, Ghana, Oct. 29, 1945; s. Yao and Abla (Sedor) K.; m. Elizabeth Dede-Maneh Jones, Jan. 4, 1975; children: Edem, Esi, Enyonam, Vinyo, Dela. BBA with honors, U. Ghana, 1971. Audit asst. Peat Marwick Cassleton Elliott, Accra, Ghana, 1971-73; sr. auditor Joslyn Layton-Bennet, London, 1974-75, Price Waterhouse, London, 1975-76; audit supr. Price Waterhouse, Lusaka, Zambia, 1977-79, Maputo, Mozambique, 1979-81; audit mgr. Price Waterhouse, Monrovia, Liberia, 1981-83; ptnr.-in-charge for Liberia, Ghana, Sierra Leone Price Waterhouse, Monrovia, 1983—, ptnr. in charge of emerging small businesses Africa, 1988—; ptnr. in charge of practice devel. Anglophone, Africa, 1986—. Mem. Ghana Inst. Chartered Accts. (constl. rev. com.), Internat. Assn. Students of Econs. and Mgmt., Liberian Inst. CPA's (chmn. audit standards com.). Roman Catholic. Club: Siva Sports. Office: Price Waterhouse, PO Box 2085, 197 Ashmun St, Monrovia Liberia

KUMAR, KAPLESH, materials scientist; b. Lucknow, India, Nov. 9, 1947; came to U.S., 1970; s. Shiam and Vidya (Devi) Sunder; m. Savinder Kaur, May 27, 1974; children—Priyadarshini, Ruchira. B.Tech., Indian Inst. Tech., 1969; M.S., Stevens Inst. Tech., 1971; Sc.D., MIT, 1975. Mem. tech. staff Charles Stark Draper Lab., Inc., Cambridge, Mass., 1975-80, chief materials devel. sect., 1980—. Patentee in materials processing. Contbr. articles to profl. publs. Recipient Patent award Charles Stark Draper Lab., Inc., 1982, Invention Disclosure award NASA, 1983. Mem. MIT Sangam Club for India Affairs (pres. 1972-73). Current work: Permanent and soft magnetic materials; structural materials; friction and wear in sliding contacts and surfaces; high temperature superconductors. Subspecialties: Materials; Ceramics.

KUMAR, KRISHNA, physics educator; b. Meerut, India, July 14, 1936; came to U.S., 1956, naturalized, 1966; s. Rangi and Susheila (Devi) Lal; m. Katharine Johnson, May 1, 1960; children—Jai Robert, Raj David. B.Sc. in Physics, Chemistry and Math., Agra U., 1953, M.Sc. in Physics, 1955; M.S. in Physics, Carnegie Mellon U., 1959, Ph.D. in Physics, Carnegie Mellon U., 1964. Research assoc. Mich. State U., 1963-66, MIT, 1966-67, research fellow Niels Bohr Inst., Copenhagen, 1967-69; physicist Oak Ridge Nat. Lab., 1969-71; assoc. prof. Vanderbilt U., Nashville, 1971-77; fgn. collaborator AEC of France, Paris, 1977-79; Nordita prof. U. Bergen, Norway, 1979-80; prof. physics Tenn. Tech. U., Cookeville, 1980-82, Univ. prof. physics, 1983—; lectr. in field; cons. various research labs. Sec., India Assn., Pitts., 1958-59. Recipient gold medal Agra U., 1955; NSF research grantee, 1972-75. Mem. Indian Phys. Soc., Am. Phys. Soc., Tenn. Acad. Scis., Planetary Soc., Sigma Pi Sigma, Sigma Xi. Republican. Hindu. Lodge: Rotary. Author: Nuclear Models and the Search for Unity in Nuclear Physics, 1984; contbr. articles to profl. jours, books. Home: 1248 N Franklin Ave Cookeville TN 38501 Office: Box 5051 Tenn Tech U Cookeville TN 38505

KUMAR, SHIVRAJ, computer consultant; b. Gurgaon, Haryana, India, May 1, 1932; s. Ramji Lal and Jagan Devi; m. Laxmi Kumar, Dec. 13, 1958; children—Kashyap, Jaya, Sanjay. M.Sc., St. John's Coll., Agra, India, 1953. Head Army EDP Team, Hyderabad, India, 1975-78, Personnel Mgmt. Group, New Delhi, 1978-80; zonal mgr. computers Electronics Corp. India Ltd., 1983-87; dir. Usha Computers, 1987—; head examiner Chartered Accts., Delhi, 1982-84; mem. vis. faculty Nat. Productivity Council, Delhi, 1976, Mgmt. Devel. Inst., New Delhi, 1981, ALTC, New Delhi, 1981—. Served to col. Signal Corps, 1980-83. Fellow Instn. Electronics and Telecommunication Engrs.; mem. Computer Soc. India (chmn. 1980-82, chmn. exhbn. com. 1984, chmn. div. 4, 1986-88, sr. life), Instn. Engrs. (com. mem. 1973-74). Hindu. Avocations: photography; light Western music. Home: 210 Munirka Vihar, New Delhi 110067, India Office: Usha-Computers, 3 Cama Place, New Delhi 110 066, India

KUMAR, SUBODH, investment banker; b. New Delhi, India, Jan. 1, 1953; came to Can., 1968; s. Satyaindar and Savitri Devi K. Sudan Sch. Cert., Comboni Coll., 1968; postgrad. St. Michael's Coll., Toronto, 1969; B.A.Sc. with honors in Chem. Engring., U. Toronto, 1973, M.B.A., 1976. Chartered fin. analyst. Chem. design engr. Imperial Oil, Sarnia, 1973-74; research analyst Wood Gundy, Toronto, Ont., 1976, asst. v.p., 1981-85, v.p. 1985-88, dir. 1988—. J.P. Bickell Found. scholar, 1970; U. Toronto masters fellow, 1974. Fellow Inst. Chartered Fin. Analysts; mem. Fin. Analysts Fedn. Office: Wood Gundy Inc, PO Box 274, Toronto Dominion Centre, Toronto, ON Canada M5K 1M7

KUME, TADASHI, business executive; Pres. Honda Motor Co. Ltd., Tokyo. Address: Honda Motor Co Ltd, 1-1 2-chome, Minamiaoyamo, Minato-ku, 107 Tokyo Japan

KUME, YUTAKA, automobile manufacturing company executive; b. Tokyo, May 20, 1921; s. Kinzaburo and Chiyo Kume; m. Aya Yamamoto, Nov. 9, 1947; children: Yoko, Taisuke. B.E. in Aircraft Engring., U. Tokyo, 1944. Joined Nissan Motor Co., Ltd., 1946, gen. mgr. prodn. control and engring. dept. Zama Plant, 1964-71, gen. mgr. Yoshiwara Plant, 1971-73, dir., mem. bd. dirs., gen. mgr. Tochigi Plant, 1973-77, mng. dir., 1977-82, gen. mgr. Tochigi Plant, 1977-78, exec. mng. dir., 1982-83, exec. v.p., gen. mgr. quality adminstrn. div., 1983-85, pres., 1985—. Mem. Japan Fedn. Employers' Assns. (exec. dir.), Japan Automobile Mfrs. Assn., Inc. (vice chmn.), Japan Inst. Indl. Engring. (chmn.), Japan Automobile Fedn., Keidanren Fedn. Econ. Orgns. (chmn. Japan-Greece Econ. Com., com. environment and safety). Avocations: photography, haiku, reading, golf. Home: 571 Unomori, Sagamihara City, Kanagawa Prefecture Japan Office: Nissan Motor Co Ltd, 17-1 Ginza 6-Chome Chuo-Ku, 104 Tokyo Japan

KUMIKAWA, MASA-ICHI, ceramic engineer; b. Osaka, Japan, Dec. 17, 1957; s. Motonobu and Keiko (Ohno) K. B in Engring., Kyoto (Japan) U., 1982, M in Engring., 1984. With Kakogawa (Japan) Works, Kobe Steel Ltd., 1984-87, engr. cold rolling dept., 1984-85, engr. steel sheet dept. and tech. sect., 1985-87; engr. ceramics engring. dept. Murata Mfg. Co. Ltd., Kyoto, Japan, 1987—; cons. Yokaichi plant Murata Mfg. Co., Ltd. Home: 3-13-25 Nagai-cho Higashi, Sumiyoshi-ku Osaka-shi, 558 Osaka Japan Office: Murata Mfg Co Ltd, 2-26-10 Tengin, Nagaokakyo-shi, 617 Kyoto Japan

KUNANUKORNKUL, WANLOP, materials executive; b. Bangkok, July 7, 1952; m. Suthaporn Kunanukornkul. BE, Khonkaen U., Bangkok, 1976. Prodn. engr. United Grain Jute Mill, Saraburi, Thailand, 1976-77; plant engr. Chareon Pokphand Feed Mill, Bangkok, 1977-78; indsl. engr. Warner-Lambert/Adams Ltd., Samutprakarn, Thailand, 1978-80; indsl. engring. mgr. Warner-Lambert/Adams Ltd., Samutprakarn, 1980-81, prodn. planning, inventory control mgr., 1981-83, prodn. services mgr., 1983-85, materials mgr., 1985-88; mgr. materials mgmt. Bristol Myers (Thailand) Ltd., 1988—; cons. Datapro Computer System, Bangkok, 1987—. Mem. Thai Engring. Assn. Democrat. Buddhist. Home: 13/6 Moo Seri-Onnouch, 10250 Prakanong Thailand

KUNCEWICZOWA, MARIA, writer; b. Samara, Russia, Oct. 30, 1897; d. Jozef and Adela Szczepanski; student Warsaw U., Jagellonian U., Cracow, U. Nancy; m. Jerzy Kuncewicz, 1921; 1 son, Witold. Books: Przymierze dzieckiem, Twarz mezczyzny, Milosc Panienska, Dwa Ksiezyce, Dylizans Warszawski, Cudzoziemka, Dni Powszednie Panstwa Kowalskich, Miasto Heroda, Klucze, Zmowa Nieobecnych, 1950, Lesnik, 1954, W Domu i w Polsce, 1958, Odkrycie Patusanu, 1959, Gaj oliwny, 1961, Don Kichote i nianki, 1966, Tristan, 1967; Fantomy, 1971, Natura, 1975, Fantasia Alla Polacca, 1981, Przezrocza, 1985; prof. Polish literature U. Chgo., 1962-70; founder Center Writers in Exile. Recipient Literary prize of Warsaw, 1937, Golden Laurel of Polish Acad. Letters, 1937, Pietrzak prize, 1966, State prize 1st Class, 1974, Medal of Merit, Kosciuszko Found. N.Y., 1972, Medal of Merit Société Europeé ne de Culture Warsaw, 1982. Mem. English-Am.-Polish PEN Club, Centre Writers in Exile (founder). Home: ul Malachowskiego 19, 24-120 Kazimieirz Dolny Poland Office: care Witold Kuncewicz Flint Hill VA 22627

KUNDERA, MILAN, writer, educator; b. Praque, Czecholovakia, Apr. 1, 1929; s. Ludvik and Milada (Janosikova) K.; m. Vera Hrabankova. D.h.c., U. Mich., 1983. Prof., Ecole des Hautes etudes en Sciences Sociales, Paris. Author: The Joke, 1967; Life is Elsewhere, 1969; Laughable Loves, 1969; Farewell Party, 1972; Book of Laughter and Forgetting, 1978; The Unbearable Lightness of Being, 1984; Jerusalem Prix, 1985; Nelly Sachs Preis, 1987; The Art of Novel, 1987; sterreichische Staatsrreis Für Europäische Literatur, 1988. Recipient prix Europe Lit., European Soc., 1981.

KÜNG, HANS, theologian, educator; b. Lucerne, Switzerland, Mar. 19, 1928; Licenciate philosophy Gregorian U., Rome, Italy, 1951; Licenciate theology, 1955; doctorate theology Inst. Catholique and Sorbonne, Paris, 1957; LL.D. (hon.), St. Louis U., U. Toronto; D.D. (hon.), Pacific Sch. Religion, Berkeley, Calif., U. Glasgow, U. Cambridge, Eng.; H.H.D. (hon.), Loyola U., Chgo.; L.H.D. (hon.), U. Mich. Ordained priest Roman Cath. Ch., 1954; mem. practical ministry Cathedral Lucerne, 1957-59; sci. asst. for dogmatic Cath. Theol. Faculty, U. Munster/Westfalen (Germany), 1959-60; prof. fundamental theology Cath.-Theologic Faculty, U. Tübingen (Germany), 1960-63, prof. dogmatic and ecumenical theology, 1963-80, prof. ecumenical theology, 1980—, dir. Inst. Ecumenical Research. 1963—; guest lectr. throughout U.S., Europe, Asia, Africa and Australia. Apptd. by Pope John XXIII as official theol. cons. to 2d Vatican Council, 1962-65. Recipient Oskar Pfister award Am. Psychiat. Assn., 1986. Mem. Am. and German PEN Club. Author: Justification: The Doctrine of Karl Barth and a Catholic Reflection, 1964; The Council, Reform and Reunion, 1961; That the World May Believe, 1963; Structures of the Church, 1964; The Council in Action, 1963; Freedom Today, 1966; The Church, 1967; Truthfulness, 1968; Menschwerdung Gottes, 1970; Infallible? -An Inquiry, 1971; Why Priests?, 1972; Fehlbar? Eine Bilanz, 1973; On Being a Christian, 1976; Signposts for the Future, 1978; Freud and the Problem of God, 1979; The Christian Challenge, 1979; The Church-Maintained in Truth, 1980; Does God Exist, 1980; Eternal Life?, 1984; (with others) Christianity and the World Religions: Paths to Dialogue with Islam, Hinduism, and Buddhism, 1986; also numerous articles. Assoc. editor Jour. Ecumenical Studies, Revue Internationale de Theologie, Concilium; editor Theological Meditations, Ö kumenische Forschungen, Ö kumenische Theologie. Address: Waldhäuserstrasse 23, Tübingen Federal Republic of Germany Office: Eberhard-Karls-Univ of Tübingen, Dept of Cath Theology, Tübingen Federal Republic of Germany

KUNG, PHILIP YUE-FEI, marketing professional; b. Shanghai, Peoples Republic China, July 18, 1947; arrived in Hong Kong, 1948; s. Chia-Lung and Eleanor (Chan) K.; m. Belinda Sue-Wah Yang (div. Dec. 1980); m. Winnie Wan-Nor Har; 1 child, Justin Chi-Hang. BBA, Hardin-Simmons U., 1968, MA in Econs., 1970. Grad. asst. Bur. Econ. and Bus. Research, Abilene, Tex., 1968-70; gen. mgr. Hong Kong Gift Shop, Osaka, 1970; asst. mgr. Kung Brother and Co., Ltd., Hong Kong, 1970-73; asst. regional editor Bus. Internat. Asia/Pacific, Ltd., Hong Kong, 1973-75; pub. mgr. Spicers Internat./Reeds Internat., Hong Kong, 1975; mktg. dir. Levi Strauss Far East, Ltd., Hong Kong, 1975-80; gen. mgr. mktg. Hong Kong Tourist Assn., 1981-86; v.p. travel mktg. Asia, Pacific, Australia region Am. Express, Hong Kong, 1986—; lectr. on mktg. and internat. mgmt. Hong Kong Sue Yan Coll., 1974-77. Mem. Pacific Asia Travel Assn. (com. mem.), SKAL club. Home: 23 Blue Pool Rd Ground Floor, Happy Valley Hong Kong Office: Am Express Internat Inc, One Pacific Place Level 40, #88 Queens Way, Central Hong Kong Hong Kong

KUNG, SHAIN-DOW, molecular biologist, educator; b. China, Mar. 14, 1935, came to U.S., 1971, naturalized, 1977; s. Chao-tzen and Chih (Zhu) K.; grad. Chung-Hsing U., Taiwan, China, 1958; Ph.D., U. Toronto, Can., 1968; m. Helen C.C. Kung, Sept. 5, 1964; children—Grace, David, Andrew. Research fellow Hosp. for Sick Children, Toronto, 1968-70; biologist UCLA, 1971-74; asst. prof. biology U. Md., Baltimore County, 1974-77, assoc. prof., 1977-82, prof., 1982—, acting chmn. dept., 1982-84, assoc. dean arts and sci., 1985-87, prof. botany U. Md., College Park, 1986—; acting dir. Ctr. for Agri. Biotech, 1986-88, dir. 1988—. Author 1 book; editor 2 books; contbr. chpts. to books, articles to profl. jours. Recipient Philip Morris award for disting. achievement in tobacco sci., 1979; named Disting. Scholar, Nat. Acad. Sci., 1981; Fulbright grantee, 1982-83; also grantee NSF, NIH. Mem. Am. Soc. Plant Physiologists, AAAS. Office: U Md Coll Park Ctr for Agri Biotech HJ Patterson Hall College Park MD 20742

KUNG, Z. M. JAMES, banker; b. Shanghai, Peoples Republic China, July 11, 1930; m. Marjorie Kung Woo; 3 children. LLB, Soochow (Peoples Republic China) U., 1950. Chmn., chief mgr. Chekiang First Bank Ltd., Hong Kong; also bd. dirs. Chekiang First Bank Ltd.; Bd. dirs. Dai-Ichi Kangyo Asia Ltd, C.F. Overseas Inc., Unisouth Ltd., Honfirst Securities Ltd., Honfirst Investment Inc., Joint Electronic Teller Services Ltd. Chmn. bd. trustees Chung Chi Coll., Walks for Millions Community Chest, 1984-85; treas. Council of Hong Kong Poly., 1984—; active council Hong Kong Bapt. Coll., 1987—, Grantham Scholarships Fund Com., 1986—, Industry Devel. Bd., 1986-88, Ocean Park Corp. Bd., 1987-88; hon. pres. Chinese YMCA, chmn. 1982-86. Decorated Mem. of the Brit. Empire. Clubs: Hong Kong Overseas Bankers, Hong Kong Country, Kowloon, Royal Hong Kong Golf, Royal Hong Kong Jockey, Pacific, American. Home: 9 Moorsam Rd, Jardine's Lookout Hong Kong

KUNIN, MADELEINE MAY, governor; b. Zurich, Switzerland, Sept. 28, 1933; came to U.S., 1940, naturalized, 1947; d. Ferdinand and Renee (Bloch) May; m. Arthur S. Kunin, June 21, 1959; children—Julia, Peter, Adam, Daniel. B.A., U. Mass., 1956; M.S., Columbia U., 1957; M.A., U. Vt., 1967; several hon. degrees. Newspaper reporter Burlington Free Press, Vt., 1957-58; guide Brussels World's Fair, Belgium, 1958; TV asst. producer Sta. WCAX-TV, Burlington, 1960-61; freelance writer, instr. English Trinity Coll., Burlington, 1969-70; mem. Vt. Ho. of Reps., 1973-78; lt. gov. State of Vt., Montpelier, 1979-82, gov., 1985-87, reelected gov., 1986—; fellow Inst. Politics, Kennedy Sch. Govt., Harvard U., 1983; lectr. Middlebury Coll., St. Michael's Coll., 1984; mem. Vt. Commn. on Adminstrn. of Justice, 1976-77, Vt. Joint Fiscal Com., 1977-78; mem. exec. com. Nat. Conf. Lt. Govs., 1979-80. Author: (with Marilyn Stout) The Big Green Book, 1976; contbr. articles to profl. jours., mags. and newspapers. Mem. exec. com. Dem. Policy Council. Named Outstanding State Legislator, Eagleton Inst. Politics, Rutgers U., 1975. Mem. Nat. Gov.'s Assn. (mem. exec. com.), New England Gov.'s Conf. (chairperson). Democrat. Address: Office of the Gov Pavilion Bldg 5th Floor Montpelier VT 05602 *

KUNISCH, KARL K., mathematics educator; b. Linz, Austria, Sept. 16, 1952; s. Karl Wilhelm August and Johanna Elisabeth (Neuhauser) K.; m. Brigitte Almhofer; children: Katharina, Elisabeth. Diploma, Tech. U. Graz, Austria, 1975, PhD, 1978; MA, Northwestern U., 1975. Asst. prof. Tech. U. Graz, 1976-86, prof., 1986; asst. prof. Brown U., Providence, 1979-80, assoc. prof., 1985; assoc. prof. U. Okla., Norman, 1982-83. Author of numerous research articles. Recipient Pro Scientia, Vienna, 1974-77; grantee Theodor Koerner Found., Vienna, 1979, Fulbright, Vienna, 1978, 85, Max Kade Found, N.Y., 1982-86. Mem. Austrian-Am.-Italian Math. Soc. Office: Tech U Graz, Dep Math, Kopernikusgasse 24, A-8010 Graz Austria

KUNIYUKI, OHTA, advertising executive, interior designer; b. Kyoto, Japan, Apr. 8, 1945; s. Kuniyoshi and Harue Okai O.; m. Miyoko Takayama, Apr. 10, 1971; children: Kunihito, Mami. B in Econs., Doshisha U., Kyoto, 1968. Cert. interior coordinator. With promotion dept. Ministry of Internat. Trade and Industry Matsushita Electric Works, Ltd., Tokyo, 1968-77; mktg. planner Matsushita Electric Works, Ltd., Osaka, Japan, 1978—, mgr. advt. planning sect., 1984—; chief researcher Research and Design Lab., Osaka, 1981-83. Editor: Basic Total Interior, 1979. Club: Uji Lawn Tennis (Kyoto). Home: 17-14 Terayama, Hirono-cho Ugi-shi, Kyoto Japan Office: Matsushita Electric Works Ltd, 1048 Kadoma, Kadoma-shi, Osaka Japan

KUNSTADTER, GERALDINE S., foundation executive; b. Boston, Jan. 6, 1928; d. Harry Herman and Nettie Sapolsky; m. John W. Kunstadter, Apr. 23, 1949; children—John W., Lisa, Christopher, Elizabeth. Student MIT, 1945-48. Draftsman, U. Chgo. Cyclotron Project, 1948; engring. asst. Gen. Electric Corp., Lynn, Mass., 1948-49; chmn., dir. A. Kunstadter Family Found., N.Y.C., 1966—; host family program dir. N.Y.C. Commn. for UN, 1971-86; pres. Nat. Inst. Social Scis., 1979-81. Bd. dirs. Ptnrs. of Ams. Found., Washington, Menninger Clin., Topeka, Atlanta Council, Yale-China Assn., Inst. Current World Affairs, English-Speaking Union, Eliot Feld Ballet, N.Y.C., Ctr. U.S.-China Arts Exchange, N.Y. Regional Assn. Grantmakers, East Side Internat. Community Ctr., Am. Forum; mem. resource council Partners of Ams., Washington, mem. nat. com. U.S.-China relations; mem. Peace Links Leadership Network, Nat. Council of Women (internat. hospitality com.), Overseas Devel. Council, N.Y.-Beijing Friendship City Com.; past mem. coms. MIT; trustee, chmn. bd. Windham Coll., Putney, Vt. Recipient Windham award, 1970, silver medal Nat. Inst. Social Sci., 1981. Club: Am. Women's, Hurlingham, Lansdowne (London).

KUNTZ, HAL GOGGAN, petroleum exploration company executive; b. San Antonio, Dec. 29, 1937; s. Peter A. and Jean M. (Goggan) K.; B.S.E., Princeton U., 1960; M.B.A., Oklahoma City U., 1972; children—Hal Goggan, Peter A. V., Michael B. Line, staff positions Mobil Oil Corp., Dallas, Oklahoma City, New Orleans, 1963-74; co-founder, pres. CLK Corp., New Orleans, Houston, 1974—, IPEX Co., New Orleans, 1975—; pres. Gulf Coast Exploration Co., New Orleans, 1979—, pres. CLK Investments I, II, III and IV, 1979—, CLK Producing, CLK Oil and Gas Co., CLK Exploration Co., 1980—; bd. dirs. Benjamin Franklin Savings and Loan Assn. Mem. Mus. Fine Arts, Houston, 1978—, Houston Opera Soc., 1978—; mem. condrs. circle Houston Symphony, 1980; governing bd. Houston Opera. Served with AUS, 1960-63. Mem. Am. Mgmt. Assn., Nat. Small Bus. Assn., Inter-Am. Soc., Soc. Exploration Geophysics, Am. Assn. Petroleum Geologists, Aircrafts Owners and Pilots Assn., Braeburn C. of C. Republican. Roman Catholic. Clubs: Presidents Council, Petroleum of Houston, University of Houston; Argyle, Order of Alamo (San Antonio), Brae-Burn Country. Office: Suite 1400 1001 Fannin Ave Houston TX 77002

KUNTZ, MARY M. KOHLS, corporate treasurer; b. Chgo., Nov. 25, 1928; d. George William and Myrtle Hansen K.; m. Earl Jeremy Kuntz, July 28, 1957; children: Karen A., Bradford G. Student, Northwestern U., 1946-50. Pvt. practice acctg. Chgo., 1951-63; owner Chgo. Tax Service, 1954-63; controller Gen. Bus. Services, Chgo., 1960-68; v.p., treas. Gen. Tele-Communications, Inc., Chgo., 1968—. Leader Girl Scouts Am., 1968-71; pres.

Wilmette (Ill.) PTA, 1971-75. Mem. Assn. Telemessaging Services Internat., Nat. Soc. Pub. Accts., Chgo. Soc. Clubs. Clubs: Women's Club of Wilmette (bd. dirs. 1975). Office: Gen Tele-Communications Inc 69 W Washington St Chicago IL 60602

KUNZ, EBERHARD, ambassador; b. Neuwurschnitz, Karl-Marx-Stadt, Fed. Republic of Germany, May 11, 1937; s. Max and Liska (Leistner) K.; m. Ingeborg Kunz; 1 child, Andrej. Diploma, Inst. Internal Relations, Moscow, 1964. Vice consul Ministry Fgn. Affairs, Zanzibar, 1965-68; 2d sec. Ministry Fgn. Affairs, Somalia, 1970-73; 1st sec. Ministry Fgn. Affairs, Tanzania, 1976-78; ambassador Ministry Fgn. Affairs, Somalia, 1976-78, Philippines, 1986—. Office: Embassy of German Dem Republic, 2209 Paraiso Rd, Dasmarinas Village, Makati, Metro Manila Philippines

KUNZMAN, MITCHE, art collections executive; b. N.Y.C., Oct. 10, 1950; s. Murray and Ada (Katz) K.; B.F.A., CUNY, 1973; m. Helen A. Adamcio, Apr. 16, 1977. Salesman, Lenem Arts Inc., N.Y.C., 1974-75, East Coast rep., 1975, prin. sales rep. U.S. and Can., after 1975; pres., founder Artifacts Collections N.Y., Inc.; cons. specialist in Rajput and Islamic painting for Phillips Auctions, 1981-82, also Indian miniature paintings. Office: 1273 North Ave New Rochelle NY 10804

KUNZMANN, KARL HEINZ, diplomat; b. Pforzheim, Germany, May 5, 1930; s. Karl and Helene (Krebs) K.; m. Elisabeth Busch, 1955; 1 child, Jutta Kunzmann Burger. Assessor, Dr. Law, Bonn U., 1960. Ambassador United Arab Emirates, 1974-75, Haiti, 1979-82; minister to Peru, 1982-85; head div. Auswartiges Amt, Bonn, Fed. Republic Germany, 1985—. Contbr. articles to profl. jours. Mem. Christian Democratic Party. Evangelist. Office: Auswartiges Amt, Adenauerallee 86, D-5300 Bonn Federal Republic of Geramny

KUO, CHAO-JUNG (C.J.), oil manufacturing company executive; b. Kaohsiung, Taiwan, China, Oct. 12, 1935; s. Chu-Fa and Chien (Tsai) K.; m. Susan Chieu, July 11, 1961; children—Warren, Sherman. B.Sc. in Chem. Engring., Tunghai U., 1959. Process engr. Kaohsiung Oil Refinery, Taiwan, 1961-69; mgr. tech. dept. Bangchak Oil Refinery, Bangkok, Thailand, 1969-81; mgr. mfg. Singapore Petroleum Co. Pte. Ltd., 1981—. Contbr. articles to profl. jours. Served to 2d lt. Taiwan Army, 1959-61. Avocations: reading; golf; music. Home: 16 River Valley Close #05-20, 0923 Singapore Singapore Office: Singapore Petroleum Co Pte Ltd, 6 Shenton Way #42-01 DBS Bldg, 0106 Singapore Singapore

KUO, GLORIA LIANG-HUI, author; b. Kaifeng, Henan, China, July 10, 1926; d. Wen Hsien and Wen Chao (Wang) Kuo. B.A., Nat. Szechuan U., Chengtu, 1948. Journalist, Hsin Ming Evening News, Shanghai, 1948-49; pres. Kuo Liang Hui Enterprise Co. Ltd., Taipei and Hong Kong, 1977—, Internat. art Promotions Ctr., Hong Kong, 1976—; pres. Art of China Monthly, 1985—. Author 34 novels, 20 novelletes, 2 non-fiction books including Debt of Emotion, 1959; The Lock of a Heart, 1962; Green Green Grass, 1963; April Melody, 1964; I'll Cry No More, 1964; When Evening Comes, 1965; Early Puberty, 1967; Their Stories, 1970; Taipei Women, 1980; Appreciating Chinese Art, 1985—. Mem. Chinese Antique Collectors Assn. (exec. dir. 1978—). Avocations: travel; reading; painting; piano playing; singing. Home: 11F, 126-23, Chung Hsiao E Rd, Sec 4, Taipei Taiwan Republic of China Office: Art Promotion Ctr, 124-9, Chung Hsiao E Rd, Sect 4, Taipei 106, Taiwan Republic of China

KUO, NAN-HUNG, government official; b. Tainan, Republic of China, Oct. 23, 1936. BS, Nat. Taiwan U., Taipei, 1958; MS, Nat. Chiao Tung U., Hsinchu, Republic of China, 1960; PhD, Northwest U., 1966. Prof., chmn. dept. electrical engring. Nat. Chiao Tung U., Hsinchu, 1968-72, dean acad. affairs Engring. Coll., 1972-75; dean Engring. Coll. Nat. Chaio Tung U., Hsinchu, 1978-79, pres., 1979—; dir. Dept. Tech. and Vocat. Edn. Ministry Edn., Taipei, Republic of China, 1975-77; supt. Kaohsiung (Republic of China) Jr. Tech. Coll., 1978. Mem. Chinese Nationalist Party. Office: Ministry Communications, 2 Changsha St Sec 1, Taipei 10001, Republic of China

KUO, PING-CHIA, historian, educator; b. Yangshe, Kiangsu, China, Nov. 27, 1908; s. Chu-sen and Hsiao-kuan (Hsu) K.; m. Anita H. Bradley, Aug. 8, 1946. A.M., Harvard U., 1930, Ph.D., 1933. Prof. modern history and Far Eastern internat. relations Nat. Wuhan U., Wuchang, China, 1933-38; editor China Forum, Hankow and Chungking, 1938-40; counsellor Nat. Mil. Council, Chungking, China, 1940-46, Ministry Fgn. Affairs, 1943-46; participated in Cairo Conf. as spl. polit. asst. to Generalissimo Chiang Kai-shek 1943; during war yrs. in Chungking, also served Chinese Govt. concurrently in following capacities: mem. fgn. affairs com. Nat. Supreme Def. Council, 1939-46; chief, editorial and pubs. dept. Ministry Information, 1940-42, mem. central planning bd., 1941-45; tech. expert to Chinese delegation San Francisco Conf., 1945; chief trusteeship sect. secretariat UN, London; (exec. com. prep. commn. and gen. assembly), 1945-46; top-ranking dir. Dept. Security Council Affairs, UN, 1946-48; vis. prof. Chinese history San Francisco State Coll., summers 1954, 58; assoc. prof. history So. Ill. U., 1959-63, prof. history, 1963-72, chmn. dept. history, 1967-71, prof. emeritus, 1972—; sr. fellow Nat. Endowment for Humanities, 1973-74; Pres. Midwest Conf. Asian Studies, 1964. Author: A Critical Study of the First Anglo-Chinese War, with Documents, 1935, Modern Far Eastern Diplomatic History (in Chinese), 1937, China: New Age and New Outlook, 1960, China, in the Modern World Series, 1970; Contbr. to Am. hist. pubs. and various mags. in China and Ency. Brit. Decorated Kwang Hua medal A-1 grade Nat. Mil. Council, Chungking, 1941; Auspicious Star medal Nat. Govt., Chungking, 1944; Victory medal, 1945. Mem. Am. Hist. Assn., Assn. Asian Studies. Club: Commonwealth (San Francisco). Home: 8661 Don Carol Dr El Cerrito CA 94530

KUO, SHIRLEY, Republic of China government official; b. Taiwan, Republic China, Jan. 25, 1930; m. Nieh Wen-ya; 3 daughters. BA, Nat. Taiwan U.; MS, MIT; Phd, Kobe U., Japan. Former dep. gov. Cen. Bank China, from 1979; prof. Nat. Taiwan U., from 1966; minister fin. Republic China, 1988—; Fulbright-Hayes exchange prof. MIT, Cambridge, Mass., 1971-72; vice chmn. Econ. Planning Council, 1973-77, Council Econ. Planning and Devel., 1977-79. Home: 11th-1 Floor, 539 Tunhua S Rd, Taipei Taiwan, Republic of China Office: Ministry Fin, Taipei Taiwan, Republic of China *

KUPCINET, ESSEE SOLOMON, performing arts producer; b. Chgo., Dec. 7; d. Joseph David and Doris (Schoke) Solomon; Ph.B., Northwestern U., 1937; m. Irv Kupcinet, Feb. 12, 1939; children—Karyn (dec.), Jerry S. Asst. to dir. psychology dept. Michael Reese Hosp., Chgo., 1939-41; exec. producer eight Jefferson Award Shows; producer 1st Literary Arts Ball, Cultural Center, Chgo., 1979; talent coordinator Kup's Show, Chgo., 1964-84; producer for spl. events, 1978—. Mem. adv. bd., bd. dirs. Free St. Theater; prodn. chmn. Acad. Honors, 1984-87; chmn. bd. trustees Acad. Sch. Performing Arts, 1984-86, hon. lifetime chair, 1986—; prodn. chmn. Variety Club Telethon, 1984, 85; bd. dirs. Mus. Broadcasting Commn.; exec. com. Chgo. Tourism Council, 1984—; exec. bd. Internat. Theatre Festival, 1985-86; mem. sponsors com. Chgo. Pub. Library, 1985-86. Decorated Knight of Orange Nassau (The Netherlands); recipient Spl. award Jefferson Com., 1976; Cliff Dwellers award, 1975; Emmy award CBS, 1977, 79; Artisan award Acad. Theatre Arts and Friends, 1977; Prime Minister's medal for service to Israel, 1974; Woman of Yr. award Facets Multimedia, 1982, Mass Media award NCCJ, 1988, others; named (with Irv Kupcinet) Mr. and Mrs. Chgo. by Chgo. Acad. for the Arts, 1988, Woman of Yr. Variety Club #26, 1988. Mem. Nat. Acad. TV Arts and Scis. (governing bd., program chmn. 1982—, Govs. award 1986). Jewish. Club: Arts.

KUPER, ADAM JONATHAN, anthropologist, educator; b. Johannesburg, Transvaal, Republic of South Africa, Dec. 29, 1941; s. Simon Meyer and Gerty (Hesselson) K.; m. Jessica Sue Cohen, Dec. 16, 1966; children: Simon, Jeremy, Hannah. BA, U. Witwatersrand, Johannesburg, 1961; PhD, U. Cambridge, Eng., 1966; D (hons.), U. Gothenburg, Sweden, 1978. Lectr. in Social Anthropology Makerere U., Kampala, Uganda, 1967-70; lectr. in Anthropology U. Coll. U. London, 1970-76; prof. African Anthropology and Sociology U. Leiden, The Netherlands, 1976-85; prof. Social Anthropoloby and head Dept. Human Scis. Brunel U., Middlesex, Eng., 1985—. Author: Kalahari Village Politics: An African Democracy, 1970, Anthropologists and Anthropology: The British School, 1922-72, 1973, 2d rev. ed. 1983, Changing Jamaica, 1976, Regionaal Vergelijkend Onderzoek in Afrika, 1977, Wives for Cattle: Bridewealth and Marriage in Southern Africa, 1982, South Africa and the Anthropologist, 1987, The Invention of Primitive Society: Transformations of an Illusion, 1988; editor: The Social Anthropology of Radcliffe-Brown, 1982, The Social Science Encyclopedia, 1985, Current Anthropology, 1985—; contbr. more than 65 articles to profl. jours. Home: 16 Muswell Rd, N10 2BG London Eng Office: Current Anthropology U of Chicago Press Journals Div 5801 S Ellis Ave Chicago IL 60637

KUPERSMITH, JOEL, internist, researcher, educator; b. N.Y.C., Nov. 26, 1939; s. Charles Douglas and Sally (Schulz) K.; m. Judith Rose Friedman, June 15, 1969; children—David Z., Rebecca J., Adam J. B.S., Union Coll., Schenectady, 1960; M.D., N.Y. Med. Coll., 1964. Diplomate: Am. Bd. Internal Medicine, Sub-Bd. Cardiovascular Disease. Intern Kaiser Found. Hosp., San Francisco, 1964-65; resident and chief resident in internal medicine N.Y. Med. Coll., 1967-70; fellow in cardiology Beth Israel Hosp.-Harvard U. Med. Sch., Boston, 1970-72; research assoc. in pharmacology, asst. physician in medicine Columbia-Presbyn. Med. Center, N.Y.C., 1972-74, asst. prof. medicine, 1974-78, dir. electrocardiography and clin. electrophysiology, 1975-77; chief clin. pharmacology Mt. Sinai Sch. Medicine, N.Y.C., 1978-85, assoc. prof. medicine and pharmacology, 1979-85, prof. medicine, 1986—, chief Arrythmia Clinic, 1979-86, chief cardiology div. Beth Israel Med. Ctr., N.Y.C., 1985-86; prof. medicine, chief cardiovascular div. U. Louisville Sch. Medicine, 1986—, V.V. Cooke prof. medicine, 1987—; chief cardiology Humana U. Hosp., Louisville. Contbr. numerous articles to sci. jours. Served with M.C. USN, 1965-67. NIH grantee, 1978—; N.Y. Heart Assn. grantee, 1978-80; Hearst Found. grantee, 1979-87; named to Hon. Order Ky. Cols. Mem. Am. Soc. Clin. Investigation, Am. Soc. Pharmacology and Exptl. Therapeutics, Am. Soc. Clin. Pharmacology and Therapeutics, Am. Fedn. Clin. Research, Humana Heart Inst. Internat. (adv. bd.). Subspecialties: Cardiology; Pharmacology. Current work: Cellular and clinical effects of antirrhythmic drugs; ion sensitive microelectrodes, cellular electrophysiology, antirrhythmic drugs, clinic electrophysiology, electrical cardiac mapping, cardiac arrhythmias.

KUPISIEWICZ, CZESLAW EUGENIUSZ, education educator; b. Sosnowiec, Poland, July 13, 1924; s. Francis-zek and Konstancja (Bialas) K.; m. Regina Zolciak, 1945; 1 child, Jadwiga. MPhil, U. Warsaw, 1951, PhD, 1959, Dr. habil. in Philosophy, 1961. Tchr. jr. high sch. Gorzow, Poland, 1946-47; tchr. jr. high sch. Warsaw, Poland, 1948-51, tchr. sr. high sch., 1951-56; asst. prof. faculty of edn. U. Warsaw, Poland, 1957-68; vice-chmn. Ednl. Experts Com. Poland, 1971-73, chmn., 1987. Author: School Failures, 1964, Foundations of General Didactics, 1973, 9th edit., 1988, Educational Changes, 1978, School Reforms Paradigms, 1985. Recipient Sci. award Ministry of Sci. and Higher Edn., Warsaw, 1974, 78, 86, Warsaw U. award, 1981. Mem. Polish Edn. Soc., Polish Acad. Scis., Polish United Workers Party. Home: Smiala 44B, 01-526 Warsaw 39 92 63, Poland Office: Univ of Warsaw, Faculty of Edn, Szturmowa 1, Warsaw Poland

KUPPERMAN, LOUIS BRANDEIS, lawyer; b. Augusta, Ga., Dec. 16, 1946; s. Herbert Spencer and Mollie (Kleven) K; m. Nancy Ann Coll, Nov. 30, 1967; children—David Evan, Robert Dennis. B.S., Farleigh Dickinson U., 1972; J.D., Bklyn. Law Sch., 1975. Bar: Pa. 1975, U.S. Dist. Ct. (ea. dist.) Pa. 1978, U.S. Ct. Appeals (3d cir.) 1978, U.S. Supreme Ct. 1982. Jud. law clk. to Judge Jacob Kalish Ct. of Common Pleas of Phila. County, 1975-76, to Judge Eugene Gelfand, 1976-77; corp. counsel Health Corp. Am., Wayne, Pa., 1977-78; ptnr. Dilworth, Paxson, Kalish & Kauffman, Phila., 1978-86; mem. firm, chmn. real estate dept. Baskin, Flaherty, Elliott & Mannino, P.C., Phila., 1986—. lectr. Pa. Bar Inst. Author: Real Estate Tax Assessment Appeals, 1987. Chancellor's del. to Phila. Farleigh Dickinson U., 1983, 86. Recipient Disting. Alumnus award Fairleigh Dickinson U., 1983. Mem. ABA, Pa. Bar Assn., Phila. Bar Assn., (chmn. real estate litigation com. 1983-85), Hist. Soc. U.S. Dist. Ct. (ea. dist.) Pa. Club: Racquet of Phila. Home: 424 Charles Ln Wynnewood PA 19096 Office: Baskin Flaherty et al 1800 Three Mellon Bank Ctr Philadelphia PA 19102

KURABAYASHI, IKUSHIRO, pharmaceutical company executive; b. Tokyo, Aug. 14, 1913; s. Genshiro and Sono (Kurabayashi) K.; m. Kiyoka Kawasaki; 1 child, Masahiro Keiko. Phar.B., Tokyo U., 1937. Plant mgr. Takeda Chem. Industries, Ltd., Hikari, Yamaguchi, 1956-65, dir., Osaka, Japan, 1966-72, mng. dir., 1972-74, sr. mng. dir., 1974-76, exec. v.p., 1976-81, pres., 1981—; exec. sec. Kansai Com. for Econ. Devel., Osaka, 1978—; councilor Fed. Econ. Orgn., Tokyo, 1981—; mng. dir. Japanese Chem. Industry Assn., Tokyo, 1981—; permanent com. mem. Kansai Econ. Fedn., Osaka, 1981—. Recipient 6th Order of Merit with Sacred Treas., Japanese Govt., Tokyo, 1940, 5th Order of Merit with Sacred Treas., 1942; Order of Merit on Medicine, Osaka Pref. Gov., 1981. Buddhist. Clubs: Japan Ace Golf (Shiga); Nishinomiya Country (Hyogo). Lodge: Rotary (Osaka). Home: 5-14-10 Motoyama Kita-Machi, Higashinada-ku, Kobe 658 Hyogo Prefecture, Japan Office: Takeda Chem Industries Ltd, 27 Doshomachi 2-chome, Higashi-ku, Osaka 541 Osaka Prefecture, Japan *

KURANARI, TADASHI, Japanese government official; b. Nagasaki, Japan, Aug. 13, 1918. m. Kyoko. Grad. in Law, Tokyo Imperial U., 1941. Formerly with Tokyo Koatsu Co.; mem. Nagasaki Prefectural Govt., 1951-58, past bur. dir.; mem. Japanese Ho. of Reps., 1958—, parliamentary vice minister Econ. Planning Agy., 1963-67, parliamentary vice minister fin., 1967-74, dir. gen., 1974, 76; minister of state for econ. planning, 1974-76, minister fgn. affairs, 1986-87. Mem. Liberal Dem. Party, Japan, former dep. sec.-gen. and chmn. Research Commn. on Tax System and Spl. Research Com. on Internat. Economy, chmn. Council on Anti-Monopoly Problems, 1974-76. Author: Strategy for the Information Society. Recipient Service award Japanese Ho. of Reps., 1983. Address: House of Reps, Tokyo Japan *

KURATA, KUNIO, pharmaceutical company executive; b. Tokyo, July 2, 1931; s. Kunitaro and Toki Kurata; m. Midori Mitsuhashi; children: Kumiko, Atsuko, Sawako. BS, U. Tokyo, 1954, PhD in Biochem., 1970. Scientist Dainippon Pharm. Co., Ltd., Tokyo, 1954-56; researcher Osaka, Japan, 1956-62; researcher Dainabot Co., Ltd., Matsudo, Chiba, Japan, 1962-64, mgr., 1964-69, dir. research, 1964-87, plant master, 1969—; group dir. tech. Tokyo, 1982—; corp. dir. 1984-87, mng. dir., 1987—; lectr. Kitasato U., Tokyo, 1965-68, U. Tokyo, 1980-86. Author numerous books, articles and patents in nuclear medicine and radiochem. Recipient Award of Minister of Sci. and Tech. Adminstrn. Agy., 1962. Mem. Japan Radiol. Soc., Japanese Soc. Nuclear Medicine, Japan Endocrine Soc., Pharm. Soc. Japan, Internat. Soc. Oncodevel. Biology and Medicine. Clubs: Ryugasaki Country (Ibaraki), Clean Eight Country. Home: 9-1 Futaba-cho Tokiwadaira, 270 Matsudo Japan Office: Dainabot Co Ltd, 344 Minoridai, 271 Matsudo, Chiba Japan

KURATKO, DONALD F., business educator, consultant, funeral director; b. Chgo., Aug. 27, 1952; s. Donald W. and Margaret M. (Browne) K.; m. Deborah Ann Doyle, Dec. 28, 1979; 1 child, Christina Diane. B.A. in Econs., John Carroll U., 1974; M.S. in Mortuary Sci. and Adminstrn., Worsham Coll., 1975; M.B.A. in Mktg.-Mgmt., Ill. Benedictine Coll., 1979; D.B.A. in Small Bus. Mgmt., Nova U., 1984. Lic. funeral dir., Ill. Tchr., chmn. bus. dept. Immaculate Conception High Sch., Elmhurst, Ill., 1975-78; prof. bus. Ill. Benedictine Coll., Lisle, 1979-83; prof., coordinator small bus.-mgmt. and entrepreneurship Ball State U., Muncie, Ind., 1983—; funeral dir. Kuratko Funeral Home, North Riverside, Ill., part-time, 1975—; cons. Kendon Associs., Riverside, 1983—; dir. Ind. Cert. Devel. Corp., Indpls.; cons. Small Bus. Devel. Ctr., Muncie C. of C., 1985. Author: Management, 1984; Effective Small Business Management, 1986. Mem. editorial bd. Mid-Am. Bus. Jour., 1985—. Contbr. articles in field to profl. jours. Mem. Small Bus. Council, Muncie, 1984—. Named Tchr. of Yr., Immaculate Conception High Sch., Elmhurst, 1977, Prof. of Yr., Ill. Benedictine Coll., 1981, 83, Prof. of Yr., Ball State U., Muncie, 1984, 85, 86, 87, Outstanding Young Hoosier, Ind. Jaycees, 1985, one of Outstanding Young Men of Am., 1983, 84, named one of Outstanding Young Faculty, Ball Stae U., 1987. Mem. Nat. Acad. Mgmt., Internat. Council for Small Bus., Midwest Bus. Adminstrn. Assn., Midwest Case Writers Assn. Roman Catholic. Avocations: weightlifting, jogging. Home: 3500 S Robinwood Dr Muncie IN 47304 Office: Ball State U Coll Bus Muncie IN 47306

KURCZEWSKI, JACEK MARIA ANTONI, sociology educator; b. Edinburgh, Scotland, Jan. 11, 1943; arrived in Poland, 1946; s. Mieczyslaw and Maria Hanna (Jawornicka) K.; m. Joanna Papierniak, Dec. 19, 1967. MA, U. Warsaw, Poland, 1965, PhD, 1972. Asst. faculty U. Warsaw, 1965-73, adj. faculty, 1973-85, docent, 1985—. Author: Conflict and Solidarnosc, 1981, Dispute and Settlements, 1982, (also editor) Rationing Under Gdansk Agreements, 1985; co-editor: The Polish Sociol. Bull., 1976—, Res Publica, 1987—. Dir. Inst. Social Prevention and Resocialization, Warsaw, 1987—; advisor Solidarnosc, 1981, Anti-Drug Addiction Commn. Experts at Polish Govt., 1985. Mem. Polish Sociol. Assn. (pres. Warsaw chpt. 1976, 80-83, other offices), Inst. Sociology of Law for Europe, bd. dirs. 1976—), Polish Acad. Scis. (mem. sociology com.). Roman Catholic. Home: Mysliwiecka 16 m 4, 00-459 Warsaw Poland

KURFEHS, HAROLD CHARLES, real estate executive; b. Jersey City, Dec. 10, 1939; s. Harold Charles and Matilda Gertrude (Ruschman) K.; B.S. (Oaklawn Found. scholar), St. Peter's Coll., 1962; M.B.A., Wharton Sch., U. Pa., 1964; m. Linda Roberta Lepis, Aug. 1, 1964; children—Harold Charles III, Diane E., Robert C. Product mgr. Am. Brands, Inc., N.Y.C., 1958-62, 64-66; account exec. Benton & Bowles, N.Y.C., 1966-68; account mgr. Wells, Rich, Greene, Inc., N.Y.C., 1968-69; v.p., dir. marketing Meta-Language Products, Inc., N.Y.C., 1969-70; sr. account exec. McCaffrey & McCall, Inc., N.Y.C., 1970-71; dir. advt. Ethan Allen, Inc., N.Y.C., 1972-75; v.p., gen. mgr. retail/franchise div. N.Am. ops. Reed Ltd., Toronto, Ont., Can., 1975-76, also v.p., gen. mgr. fabric div. Reed Nat. Drapery Co., Sanderson, Can., 1975-76; pres. Fairfield Book Co. Inc., Brookfield, Conn., 1977-83, dir. advt. and pub. relations, bd. dirs., mem. mktg. planning bd. Ethan Allen, Inc., Danbury, Conn., 1983-85; comml. investment realtor William Raveis Comml. Investment Real Estate, Danbury, Conn., 1985—; lectr. Western Conn. State U., 1985—. Mem. Co. Mil. Historians, Wharton Grad. Club N.Y., U.S. Naval Inst., Nat. Def. Preparedness Assn., Nat. Rifle Assn. (life), Pi Sigma Phi. Home: 48 Mill Plain Rd Danbury CT 06811 Office: William Raveis Co 66 Bridge St New Milford CT 06776

KURFÜRST, PAVEL, organologist; b. Gottwaldov, Czechoslovakia, June 6, 1940; s. Josef and Zdeňka (Stejskalová) K.; m. Miroslava Krupková; children: Pavla, Michal, Jana. Grad. Faculty Arts, U. Brno, 1976; candidate sci., Acad. Scis., Prague, Czechoslovakia, 1983. Technician Radiocommunications, Prague, 1959-73, Tech. U., Brno, 1973-76; dir. Ethnographic Mus., Brno, 1976-83; asst. dir. Inst. Folk Art, Strážnice, Czechoslovakia, 1983-87; research worker med. faculty U. Brno, 1987—; cons. State Collection Mus. Instruments, Prague, 1979—, Slovak Collection Mus. Instruments, Bratislava, Czechoslovakia, 1978—. Author: Die Letste Entwicklungsphase der Streichlyra in Mitteleuropa, 1986, Brünner Instrumentenbauer des 14.-19. Jahrhunderts, 1980, Die Kurzhalsgeige, 1980, Ala und Harfe mit zwei Resonatoren. Unbekannte Instrumente der Europäzichen Stilmusik des 13. zis 15. Jahrhunderts, 1985; editor: Contributions to the Study of Traditional Musical Instruments in Museum, 1987, Ethnographica, 1976-85; contbr. articles to profl. jours. Mem. Galpin Soc. London. Home: Vinařská 36, 60300 Brno Czechoslovakia Office: Med Faculty U Brno, TŘ Obrancu míru 10, 60200 Brno Czechoslovakia

KURI, ANGEL FERNANDO, electrical engineer; b. Mexico City, Feb. 21, 1950; s. Angel Pablo and Lesbia Eugenia (Morales) K.; m. Leticia Kuri, Apr. 28, 1978; children: Angel, Leticia. Degree in elec. engring., U. Anahuac, Mexico City, 1974; MS, U. Ill., 1976; PhD, Kennedy-Western U., 1987. Acad. tech. Nat. U., Mexico City, 1972-74, researcher, 1976-83; research asst. U. Ill., Urbana, 1974-76; v.p. Micromex, Mexico City, 1983-85; dir. gen. IDET, Mexico City, 1985-87, 1985—; cons. DGSCA UNAM, Mexico City, 1986-87; tech. adv. Computer Sci. Master Program, Mexico City, 1986-87. Recipient 1st Place Nat. Elem. Schs. Mexican Govt., 1962. Mem. IEEE, Soc. Indsl. and Applied Math., Sigma Xi.

KURIEN, BIJI KURIEN, paint company executive; b. Alwaye, Kerala, India, Oct. 20, 1940; s. Vadakumkara Thomas and Annamma (Thomas) K.; m. Jyoti Anne Mathew, June 1, 1967; children: Preeti Ann, Kiron Mary, Vinay Thomas. B in Engring., Sir M. Visveswaraya Coll. Engring., Bangalore, Karnataka, India, 1963; MBA with honors, Indian Inst. Mgmt., Ahmedabad, Gujarat, India, 1968. Jr. engr. Mysore State Electricity Bd., Bangalore, 1963-64; indsl. sales supr. Esso Standard Ea. Inc., Cochin, Kerala, 1964-66; product mgr. Asian Paints India Ltd., Bombay, Maharashtra, 1968-69, br. mgr. Asian Paints India Ltd., Madras, Tamil Nadu, 1969-72; mktg. mgr. Berger Paints India Ltd., Calcutta, West Bengal, 1972-80, chief exec., 1980—; bd. dirs. Pyrene-Rai India Ltd., Bombay, Beepee Coatings Pvt. Ltd., V.V. Nagar, Gujarat, Berger Paints India Ltd. Chmn. Calcutta-I-Care Com., 1985-87; bd. govs. La Martiniere Schs., Calcutta. Mem. Indian Paints Assn. (pres. 1985-86, governing body 1981), Bengal C. of C. and Industry (com. 1984). Mem. Ch. North India. Clubs: Bengal, Saturday (Calcutta). Home: 37 Ahiripukur Rd, Calcutta, West Bengal 700 019, India Office: Berger Paints India Ltd, 32 Chowringhee Rd, Calcutta, West Bengal 700 071, India

KURITA, JIN, architect; b. Shizuoka City, Japan, June 9, 1949; s. Hirokazu and Teruko (Kajiwara) K.; m. Atsumi Okuno, Apr. 10, 1977; children: Yumi, Fumihiko, Tamami. BArch, Nagoya Nat. U., Japan, 1973, MArch, 1975. Registered architect. Pvt. practice architecture Shizuoka City, 1977—; lectr. Fujie Fashion Interior Inst., Shizuoka City, 1986—, Tokai U. Jr. Coll. Author: Another Way of Thinking for Your New Home, 1981. Com. mem. Profl. Consultation Com., Shizuoka City, 1983-86, Shizuoka Mcpl. Cons. Panel, 1983-86. Mem. Japan Inst. Architecture. Club: Kinokai. Home and Office: 606-1 Kita, 420 Shizuoka City Japan

KURIYAMA, KINYA, pharmacology educator; b. Kameoka, Japan, July 11, 1932; s. Haruya and Kouko (Yagi) K.; m. Chieko Imamura, Dec. 7, 1958; children—Takuya, Nagato. M.D., Kyoto Prefectural U. Medicine, 1957, Ph.D., 1963. Asst. prof. dept. pharmacology Kyoto Prefectural U. Medicine, Japan, 1958-63, prof., chmn., 1971—; research assoc. Johns Hopkins U., Balt., 1963-64; research scientist City of Hope Med. Ctr., Duarte, Calif., 1964-68; assoc. prof. U. Loma Linda, Calif., 1968-70; assoc. prof. SUNY-Bklyn., 1970, prof., 1971. Author: Amino Acid Neurotransmitters, 1975. Editor: Sulfur Amino Acids, 1979—. Biochemical Pharmacology, 1981, Japan. Jour. Pharmacology, 1980—, Jour. Neurosci. Research 1980—, Alcohol and Alcoholism, 1980—, Alcohol and Drug Research, 1980—, Neurochem. Research, 1981—, Neurotransmitter Receptors, 1983, Alcohol, 1983—, Devel. Neurosci., 1983—, Clin. Neuropharmacology, 1985—, Behavioral and Brain Sci., 1985—, Asia Pacific Jour. Pharmacology, 1986—, Epilepsy Research, 1986—; editor-in-chief Japanese Jour. Studies Alcohol, 1974—; exec. editor Neurochem. Internat., London, 1980—. Mem. council Internat. Soc. Alcoholism, Chgo., 1980—, Internat. Soc. Neurochem., London, 1981—, Environ. Hadards Search Com., Kyoto, 1973—. Mem. Internat. Soc. for Devel. Neurosci, Japanese Soc. Studies Alcohol, Japanese Soc. Neurochemistry, Japanese Soc. Pharmacology. Home: 69-1 Iwagakakinchi-Cho, Kamigamo, Kita-ku, 603 Kyoto Japan Office: Kyoto Prefectural U of Medicine Dept Pharmacology, Kawaramachi-Hirokoji, Kamikyo-ku, 602 Kyoto Japan

KURJAK, ASIM, gynecologist, obstetrician, professor; b. Kotor Varos, Yugoslavia, Sept. 13, 1942; s. Rasim and Dervisa (Memic) K.; m. Biserka Funduk, Jan. 25, 1943; children: Igor, Alan. MD, U. Zagreb, 1966; PhD, U. Belgrade, 1977. Dir. Health Care Ctr., Kotor Varos, 1966-67; intern dept obstetrics and gynecology U. Zagreb, 1968-80; head Ultrasonic Inst., Zagreb, 1979-, Collaborating Ctr. Ultrasound Developing Countries WHO, Zagreb, 1985—, Dept. Ob/Gyn Dr. Josip Kajfes Teaching Hosp., Zagreb, 1980-; External examiner U. Liverpool, 1980-83. Author 14 books published in Yugoslavia, 1974-86, 16 books publsihed abroad, 1978-86. Recipient Presdl. award, 1975, Il Osimo d'Oro award Italy, 1980, Rudger Boskovic award Yugoslavia 1985. Mem. Assn. Socs. Univ. Profs. and Lectrs. of Yugoslavia (bd. dirs. 1984—), WHO (bd. dirs. postgrad studies ultrasound clin. medicine 1985—, chmn. 1st World Congress ultrasound in developing countries 1986—), Italian Acad. Sci. and Art, Internat. Inst. Malformations. Home: Ljubinkovac Stube 1, 41000 Zagreb Yugoslavia Office: U Zagreb Ultrasonic Inst, Pavleka Miskine 64, Zagreb Yugoslavia

KURMANN, JÜERG HANS, management consultant; b. Basel, Switzerland, May 7, 1953; s. Hans Kurmann and Anne-Marie (Widmer) Blumer; m. Jytte Jensen, Aug. 19, 1983. Degree, U. Basel, Switzerland, 1980. Airfreight mgr. Panalpina World Transport, various locations, 1973-76; sr. cons. Häusermann & Co. AG, Zürich, Switzerland, 1980-82; prin. Jüerg Kurmann & Ptnr., Zürich, 1982-84; mgr. corp. devel. Lumipart AG, Olten, Switzerland, 1984-87; mng. ptnr. CGZ Consulting Group Zürich Inc., 1987-88, A.I.M. Group Zurich Inc., 1988—. Contbr. articles to profl. jours. Home: Regensdorferstrasse 38, 8049 Zurich Switzerland Office: AIM Group Zurich Inc, Aquisitions Investments Mergers, Gartenstrasse 36, 8002 Zurich Switzerland

KURNIATAN, ANAS, civil engineer, educator; b. Padang Panjang, Indonesia, Apr. 9, 1942; s. Dyan and Sukawati K.; grad. in civil engring. Diponegoro U., 1965; m. Sandrawati Kosasih, Jan. 20, 1977; children—Daniel, Anette. Engr., P.N. Nindya Karya, Conefo Project, Jakarta, 1965-66; lectr. Surabaya Inst. Tech., 1967-69; chief dam sect. Selorejo Dam and Karangkates Dam, advisor to gen. supt. civil works Karangkates Dam, dept. public works and energy, govt. Indonesia, Malang, East Java, 1969-72; cons. engr. geotech. engring., P.T. Soiltest and Founds., Jakarta, 1972-78; cons. engr., dir., owner P.T. Geonorma Utama, Jakarta, 1979—; lectr. Christian Indonesian U., Jakarta, 1976—, Tarumanagara U., 1985—. Mem. Indonesian Geotech. Engrs. Assn. (treas.), Internat. Soc. on Soil Mechanics and Found. Engring., S.E. Asian Geotech. Soc., Indonesian Inst. Engrs., Nat. Assn. Indonesian Cons., Indonesian Inst. Structural Engrs. Roman Catholic. Club: Serua. Condr. research in field including expansive/swelling properties of clay. Home: 4 Jalan Dwijaya IV, Jakarta Indonesia

KURNIAWAN, DEWANTO, corp. exec.; b. Palembang, Indonesia, Nov. 15, 1942; s. Soetarto and Maria Kurniawan; student Indonesian schs.; m. Gracie Tasman, Sept. 7, 1963; children—Michael, Florence, Charles, Richard. Pres., dir. P.T. Green ville Real Estate, 1973—, P.T. Galena Tambang, 1975—, P.T. Dewanata Coy Ltd., 1975—, P.T. Dewanta Karsa Internat. Corp., 1975—, P.T. Villa Sari Mas, 1976—, P.T. Tri Karsa Dewantara Corp., 1976—, Dewantara Richwood Indonesia, 1977—, P.T. Pasar Baru Indah Dept. Store (all Jakarta), 1977—, P.T. Wahyu Waruna Watan, P.T. Bluendo Groto; chmn. Lindtan Internat. Corp. Singapore, 1976—; pres., supr. P.T. Brazindon, 1976—; supr. P.T. Bank Indonesia Raya, 1975—; dir. P.T. Sarang Sapta Putra, C.V. Indonesia Jaya Raya, P.T. Grawisa Contractors, P.T. Taman Lina Permai, P.T. Green Garden Ltd., P.T. Cakung Remaja Indah Jaya Housing, P.T. Taman Kedoya Barat Indah, P.T. Star Parama Purnama, P.T. Star Parama Cakrawala, P.T. Delta Samudra, P.T. Manggala Putra Kaloka Manado, P.T. Taman Kota; mem. commissary P.T. Tanjung Sedari Abadi. Home: Blok Y/13 Kepa Duri, Tomang Barat, Jakarta Indonesia Office: PT Green ville Real Estate, Block C3/No 1 J1, Tanjung Duren Barat Complex, Tomang Barat Jakarta, Indonesia

KUROKAWA, KANEYUKI, science administrator; b. Tokyo, Aug. 14, 1928; s. Kanesaburo and Tokiko (Mori) K.; m. Yasuko Nomura, May 22, 1957; children—Michiko, Hiroko. B.S., U. Tokyo, 1951, D.Eng., 1958. Asst., U. Tokyo, 1956-57, asst. prof., 1957-63; tech. staff Bell Labs., Murray Hill, N.J., 1963-65, supr., 1965-75; dep. dir. Fujitsu Labs., Kawasaki, Japan, 1975-79, dir., 1979-85, mng. dir., 1985—; vis. prof. U. Tokyo, 1986—. Author: An Introduction to the Theory of Microwave Circuits, 1969; contbr. articles to profl. jours. Recipient Okabe Meml. prize Inst. Electronics and Communication Engrs. Japan, 1956; progress award Inst. Elec. Engrs. Japan, 1959; cert. of appreciation Internat. Solid State Circuits Conf., 1965. Fellow IEEE; mem. Assn. Computing Machinery, Inst. Electronics and Communication Engrs. Japan. Home: 2-9-7 Nishiwaseda, Shinjuku, 160 Tokyo Japan Office: Fujitsu Labs, 1015 Kamikodanaka, Nakahara, 211 Kawasaki Japan

KUROKAWA, KISHO, architect; b. Aichi Prefecture, Japan, Apr. 8, 1934; s. Miki and Ineko Kurokawa; m. Ayako Wakao; 2 children. B.Arch., Kyoto U., 1957; M.Arch., Tokyo U., 1964. Pres. Kisho Kurokawa Architect & Assocs.; chmn. Urban Design Cons., Inc.; prin. Inst. Social Engring., Inc.; pres. Kurokawa Internat., Inc.; analyst Japan Broadcasting Corp., 1974—; hon. prof. U. Buenos Aires, Argentina, 1985—; vis. prof. Tsinghua U., Beijing, People's Rep. of China; advisor Internat. Design Conf. Aspen, U.S.A., 1974—, Ministry of Constrn.; mem. Archtl. Inst. Japan, City Planning Inst. of Japan, Japan Architects Assn. Author: Prefabricated House, Meatbolism, 1960, Urban Design, 1965, Action Architecture, 1967, Homo-Movens, 1969, Architectural Creation, 1969, The Work of Kisho Kurokawa, 1970, Creating Contemporary Architecture, 1971, Conception of Metabolism, In the Realm of the Future, 1972, The Archipelago of Information: The Future Japan, 1972, Introduction to Urbanism, 1973, Metabolism in Architecture, 1977, A Culture of Grays, 1977, Concept of Space, 1977, Concept of Cities, 1977, Architecture et Design, 1982, Thesis on Architecture, 1982, A Cross Section of Japan, 1983, Architecture of the Street, 1983, Under the Road: Landscape under Roads, 1984, Drawing Collection of World Architecture, 1984, Kisho Kurokawa: Il Futuro Nella Tradizione, 1984, Prospective Dialogues for the 21st Century, 1985, Philosophy of Symbiosis, 1987, New Tokyo Plan 2025, 1987; exhbns. include: Heinz Gallery, Royal Inst. Brit. Architects, 1981, Institut Francais d'Architecture, 1982, Construma by Ministry of Bldg. and Urban Devel., Budapest, Hungary, 1984, Central House for Architects, Moscow, 1984, Mus. Finnish Architecture, Helsinki, 1985, Buenos Aires Biennale of Architecture, Argentina, 1985. Active Urban Culture Council, 1981—, Council Urban Landscaping Nagoya City, 1981—, Rd. and Environ. Council, Japan Hwy. Corp., 1973—, Sci. and Tech. Agy., 1980—, Research Soc. Creation Cultural Environ. in Schs., Ministry of Edn., 1981—, Ministry Internat. Trade and Industry, 1981—, Ministry of Constrn., 1983—, Japanese-Chinese Friendship for 21st Century Com., 1985—; Recipient Takamura Kotaro Design award, 1965; Hiroba prize, 1977, Japan S.D.A. award silver prize Sony Tower, 1977; Chubu Archtl. Award Ishikawa Cultural Ctr., 1978, Store Front Competition Silver prize for head Offices Chubu Gas Group, 1978; Hon. Citizenship, Sofia, Bulgaria, 1979; B.C.S. award Nat. Ethnological Mus., 1979; decorated comdr. Order of Lion (Finland); Recipient Gold medal Acad. Architecture, France, Richard Neutra award State Poly. U., Calif., 1988, others. Hon. fellow AIA, Royal Inst. British Architects, Union Architects Bulgaria; life fellow Royal Soc. Arts U.K.; mem. Japan Architects Assn., Archtl. Inst. Japan, City Planning Inst. Japan, Tokyo Fedn. Profl. Architects, Japan Soc. Futurology, Japan Soc. Ethnology. Avocation: photography. Address: 11F Aoyama Bldg, 1-2-3 Kita Aoyama, Minato-ku, Tokyo Japan

KUROKAWA, YOICHIRO, government official; b. Nishinomiya, Hyogo, Japan, Aug. 8, 1934; s. Saburo and Ryuko (Hashimoto) K.; m. Kimiko Okumura, Aug. 20, 1959. B in Engring., Osaka (Japan) U., 1958. Dir. bldg. dept. Tohoku Regional Postal Service, Sendai, Japan, 1974-75, Kanto Regional Postal Service, Tokyo, 1975-77, Tokyo Regional Postal Service, 1977-79; dep. gen. facility dept. Nat. Space Devel. Agy. Japan, Tokyo, 1979-82; sr. bldg. advisor Bldg. Dept., Ministry of Posts and Telecommunications, Tokyo, 1982-84, dir. constrn. div., 1984-86, dep. dir.-gen., 1986-87, dir.-gen., 1987—. Mem. Archtl. Inst. Japan, Archtl. Assn. Japan. Home: 45-20-305 Ohara-cho, Itabashi-ku, 174 Tokyo Japan Office: Ministry of Posts and Telecommunications, 3-2 Kasumigaseki 1-chome, Chiyoda-ku, 100 Tokyo Japan

KUROKAWA, YOSHITERU, educator, playwright; b. Tokyo, Dec. 7, 1933; s. Kinji and Tsuru (Fukuda) K.; m. Yoko Kurokawa, Apr. 1, 1955; 1 child, Ko. B.A., U. Tokyo, 1955. Lectr., Showa Women's Coll., Tokyo, 1959-62, Hosei U., Tokyo, 1962-64, asst. prof., 1964-66, prof. Am. theater, 1966—; dir. Aristophanes Co. Tokyo, 1981—. Author: A Fool's Death and Other Plays, 1966; Alone in Russia, 1979; Satirical Short Plays, 1980; The Mountain Where We Used to Chase Hares and Other Plays, 1985. Address: 4-24-19 Wakabayashi, Setagaya, 154 Tokyo Japan

KUROSAWA, AKIRA, film director; b. Japan, 1910. Ed., Keika Middle Sch. With Toho Film Co., 1936—. Dir. films including Sugata Sanshiro, Ichiban Utsukushiku, Torano Owofumu Otokotachi, Waga Seishun ni Kunashi, Subarashiki Nichiyobi, Yoidore Tenshi, Shizukanaru Ketto, Norainu, Rashomon, 1950 (1st prize Venice Film Festival, Acad. award), Hakuchi, Ikiru, The Seven Samurai, 1954 (Silver Lion award), Ikimono no Kiroku, Kumonosu Jio, Donzoko, Kakushi Toride no San Akunin, Throne of Blood, 1957, The Hidden Fortress, 1958, The Bad Sleep Well, 1959, Yojimbo, 1961, Sanjuro, 1962, High and Low, 1962, Akahige, Redbeard, 1964, Dodes'ka-den, Derzu Uzala, 1976, Karkerousse, 1977, Kagemusha, 1979 (Golden Palm award, David di Donatello award), Ran, 1985 (Acad. award nomination for best dir.); author: Something Like An Autobiography, 1982. Decorated Order of Yugoslav Flag. Address: 21-6 Seijo 2-chome, Matsubara-cho, Setagaya-ku, 157 Tokyo Japan

KUROYANAGI, TETSUKO, television personality; b. Tokyo, 1934. Student, Tomoe Sch., Tokyo, Tokyo Coll. Music. Actress Nippon Hoso Kyokai Pub. Broadcasting Co., Japan, 1954-71; TV talk show host Asahi Broadcasting Co., 1972—; host Tetsuko's Room, 1975—; also host The Best Ten and Music Plaza. Author: From New York with Love, 1972, Pandas and I, Toto-Chan, The Little Girl at the Window, 1981. Address: care Asahi Hoso-Ashai Broadcasting Co, 2-2-48 Oydo-Minamu, Oyodo-ku, 531 Osaka Japan

KURRELMEYER, LOUIS HAYNER, lawyer; b. Troy, N.Y., July 26, 1928; s. Bernhard and Lucy Julia (Hayner) K.; m. Phyllis A. Damon, June 14, 1952 (div. 1973); children: Ellen Laura, Louis Hayner, Nancy Snow; m. Martina Sophia Kluis, June 14, 1975. AB, Columbia U., 1949, LLB, 1953; MA in Econs., U. N.Mex., 1950. Bar: N.Y. 1953, U.S. Dist. Ct. (so. dist.) N.Y. 1957, U.S. Ct. Appeals (2d cir.) 1957, U.S. Dist. Ct. (ea. dist.) N.Y. 1958, D.C. 1968, U.S. Dist. Ct. D.C. 1968, U.S. Ct. Appeals (D.C. cir.) 1968, U.S. Tax Ct. 1973, U.S. Ct. Claims 1973, U.S. Dist. Ct. Vt. 1983, U.S. Ct. Internat. Trade 1984, U.S. Ct. Appeals (Fed. cir.) 1986. Assoc. Debevoise, Plimpton, Lyons & Gates, N.Y.C., 1953-66; ptnr. Hale Russell & Gray, N.Y.C., 1967-75, counsel, 1976-85; counsel Winthrop, Stimson, Putnam & Roberts, Washington, 1985—. Author: The Potash Industry, 1951; contbr. to CPLR Forms and Guidance for Lawyers, 1963. Asst. transp. adminstr. City of N.Y., 1966-67; v.p. Emerson Sch., N.Y.C., 1960-64, chmn., 1964-69; mem. Prudential Co. Fire Dist. No. 1, Shelburne, Vt., 1977—, chmn., 1977-84. Decorated knight 1st class Royal Swedish Order of North Star. Mem. ABA, D.C. Bar Assn. Home: 45 Clearwater Rd Shelburne VT 05482 Office: Winthrop Stimson Putnam & Roberts 1155 Connecticut Ave Washington DC 20036

KURTIDES, EFSTRATIOS STEPHEN, physician; b. Kilkis, Greece, July 4, 1930; came to U.S. 1955, naturalized 1963; s. Theodore and Agapy (Papadopoulos) K.; m. Elli Hamali, Aug. 17, 1958; children—Pauline, Theodore, Carl, John. Diploma Gymnasium, Kilkis, Greece; M.D., Aristotle U., Thessaloniki, Greece, 1954. Diplomate Am. Bd. Internal Medicine, Am. Bd Hematology. Instr., research fellow Northwestern U. Med. Sch., Chgo., 1961-63; assoc. in medicine, attending physician Northwestern Univ. and Evanston Hosps., Chgo. and Evanston, 1963-66, asst. prof. and sr. attending physician, 1966-76; assoc. prof., chmn. St. Joseph Hosp., Chgo., 1977-79; prof., chmn. Evanston Hosp., Ill., 1979—; bd. dirs. Evanston Hosp., 1980—, Northwestern Infirmary, Student Health Service, 1979—. Contbr. articles to med. jours. Mem. Sch. Bd. Caucus Dist. 65, Evanston, 1963-68. Named Physician of Yr., Evanston Hosp., 1966, 72, 73, 80; recipient Silver Plaque, Evanston Hosp. Medical Staff, 1977. Fellow ACP; mem. AMA, ACS (mem. commn. cancer 1987—), Am. Soc. Hematology, AAAS, Am. Soc. Internal Medicine, Am. Hosp. Assn. (rep. nat. commn. cancer 1987—), N.Y. Acad. Scis., Alpha Omega Alpha. Greek Orthodox. Club: Mich. Shores (Wilmette, Ill.). Avocations: reading; debate; backgammon; bicycling. Office: Dept Medicine Evanston Hosp 2650 Ridge Ave Evanston IL 60201

KURTZ, JOEL BARRY, finance director; b. Bklyn., Aug. 2, 1944; s. Milton and Claire (Diamond) K.; B.B.A., Pace U., 1970; M.B.A., C.W. Post Coll., 1981; m. Judith M. Austin, Aug. 11, 1968; children—Brian, Steven, Stacey. Staff acct. Arthur Andersen & Co., Melville, N.Y., 1970-73; div. controller Elec. Comp. div., Gould Inc., Farmingdale, N.Y., 1973-78; asst. div. controller CBS-Holt, Rinehart & Winston, N.Y.C., 1979-80; controller Siemens Data Switching Systems, formely Databit Inc., Hauppauge, N.Y., 1981-87; dir. fin. Linotype Co., Hauppauge, N.Y., 1987—. Active L.I. Assn., 1981—. Served with U.S. Army, 1966-68. C.P.A., N.Y. Mem. Nat. Assn. Accts. (chpt. pres. 1976-77), N.Y. Soc. C.P.A.s, Am. Inst. C.P.A.s, Am. Mgmt. Assn. Home: 84 Vera Ln Commack NY 11725 Office: 425 Oser Ave Hauppauge NY 11788

KURTZ, KAREN BARBARA, editor, writer; b. Ft. Dodge, Iowa, July 21, 1948; d. Clifford Wenger and Eleanor Marie (Ulrich) Swartzendruber; m. Mark Allen Kurtz, June 25, 1977. AA, Hesston Coll., 1968; BA in Edn., Goshen (Ind.) Coll., 1970; MA in Elem. Edn., Ind. U., 1975. Lifetime cert. elem. tchr. First grade tchr. Fairfield Community Sch., Goshen, 1970-79; asst. editor and advt. copywriter Barth and Assocs., Middlebury, Ind., 1986-87; free-lance writer Kurtz Lens and Pen, Goshen, 1979—; asst. dir.. info. services Goshen (Ind.) Coll., 1987—. Author: Paper Paint and Stuff, 1984; asst. editor: Heritage Country Mag., 1986-87; contbr. articles to various mags. Ch. bd. dirs. Goshen City Ch. of Brethren, 1977, also chmn. stewardship dr., coordinator art in the ch. Mem. NEA, Ind. State Tchr.'s Assn., Fairfield Educators Assn. Republican. Club: Bayview.

KURTZ, MAX, civil engineer, consultant; b. Bklyn., Mar. 25, 1920; s. Samuel and Ida (Malkin) K.; B.B.A., CCNY, 1940; postgrad. Rutgers U., 1943-44; m. Ruth Ingraham, Sept. 9, 1967. Structural engr. Kurtz Steel Constrn. Corp., Mineola, N.Y., 1946-56; pvt. practice cons. engring., Flushing, N.Y., 1956—; condr. seminars on ops. research. Served with U.S. Army, 1943-45. Registered profl. engr., N.Y. Mem. N.Y. State Soc. Profl. Engrs. (Honor award Kings County chpt. 1970), Nat. Soc. Profl. Engrs. Author: Structural Engineering for P.E. Examinations, 3d edit., 1978; Engineering Economics for P.E. Examinations, 3d edit., 1985; Comprehensive Structural Design Guide, 1968; Handbook of Engineering Economics, 1984; Handbook of Applied Mathematics for Engineers and Scientists; editor Kings County Profl. Engr., 1967-71; project editor Civil Engineering Reference Guide, 1986. Home and Office: 33-47 91st St Flushing NY 11372

KURTZ, MAXINE, personnel services executive, lawyer; b. Mpls., Oct. 17, 1921; d. Jack Isadore and Beatrice (Cohen) K. BA, U. Minn., 1942; BS in Govt. Mgmt., U. Denver, 1945, JD, 1962; postdoctoral student, U. Calif., San Diego, 1978. Bar: Colo. 1962. Analyst Tri-County Regional Planning, Denver, 1945-47; chief research and spl. projects Planning Office, City and County of Denver, 1947-66, dir. tech. and evaluation Model Cities Program, 1966-71; personnel research officer Denver Career Service Authority, 1972-86, dir. personnel services, 1986—; expert witness nat. com. on urban problems U.S. Ho. of Reps., U.S. Senate. Author: Law of Planning and Land Use Regulations in Colorado, 1966; co-author: Care and Feeding of Witnesses, Expert and Otherwise, 1974; bd. editors: Pub. Adminstrn. Rev., Washington, 1980-83, 88—; editorial adv. bd. Internat. Personnel Mgmt. Assn.; prin. investigator: Employment: An American Enigma, 1979. Active Women's Forum of Colo.; Denver Dem. Party; chair Colo. adv. com. to U.S. Civil Rights Commn., 1985—. Sloan fellow, U. Denver, 1944-45; recipient Outstanding Achievement award U. Minn., 1971. Mem. Am. Inst. Planners (sec. treas. 1968-70, bd. govs. 1972-75), Am. Soc. Pub. Adminstrn. (nat. council 1978-81, Donald Stone award), ABA, Colo. Bar Assn., Denver Bar Assn., LWV, Pi Alpha Alpha. Jewish. Lodge: Order of St. Ives. Home: 2361 Monaco Pkwy Denver CO 80207 Office: Denver Career Service Authority 414 14th St Denver CO 80202

KURTZ, MYERS RICHARD, hospital administrator; b. Schaefferstown, Pa., June 18, 1924; 1 son, Ronald Hayden. B.S., U. Md., 1958; M.B.A., Ind. U., 1963. Served as enlisted man U.S. Army, 1942-51, commd. 2d lt., 1951; advanced through grades to lt. col. Med. Service Corps, 1965; mem. staff Army Surgeon Gen., Washington, 1963-67; ret. 1967; affiliation adminstr. NYU Med. Ctr., N.Y.C., 1967-69; exec. dir. Ephrata Community Hosp., Pa., 1969-76; supt. Longview State Hosp., Cin., 1976-79; asst. dir. Ohio Dept. Mental Health and Mental Retardation, Columbus, 1979-81; dir. Ohio Dept. Mental Health and Mental Retardation, 1981-82; sr. v.p. Cleve. Met. Gen. Hosp., 1982-83; supt., chief exec. officer Central State Hosp., Milledgeville, Ga., 1983—; adj. asst. prof. dept. psychiatry U. Cin., 1977—. Vice pres., bd. dirs. Coordinated Home Care Agy., Inc., Lancaster County; pres. Lancaster County Hosp. Council; bd. dirs. Pa. Hosp. Assn., Baldwin County United Way, 1986—, Baldwin County Salvation Army; mem. adv. bd. Youth Devel. Ctr., 1984—. Decorated Legion of Merit, Army Commendation medal with oak leaf cluster. Fellow Royal Soc. Health; mem. Am. Coll. Hosp. Adminstrs., Am. Acad. Med. Adminstrs., Am. Hosp. Assn., Milledgeville-Baldwin County C. of C. (bd. dirs. 1984-87, exec. com. 1986—, treas. 1987—), Sigma Iota Epsilon. Lodge: Rotary Internat. Home: 164 Annex Dr Milledgeville GA 31061 Office: Central State Hosp Milledgeville GA 31061

KURTZ, PAUL, philosopher, educator; b. Newark, Dec. 21, 1925; s. Martin and Sara (Lasser) K.; m. Claudine C. Vial, Oct. 6, 1960; children—Valerie L., Patricia A., Jonathan. B.A., NYU, 1948; M.A., Columbia U., 1949, Ph.D., 1952. Instr. Queens Coll., 1950-52; instr. philosophy Trinity Coll., Hartford, Conn., 1952-55; asst. prof. Trinity Coll., 1955-58, assoc. prof., 1958-59; assoc. prof. Vassar Coll., Poughkeepsie, N.Y., 1960-61; vis. prof. New Sch. Social Research, N.Y.C., 1960-65; assoc. prof. Union Coll., Schenectady, 1961-64; prof. Union Coll., 1964-65; vis. prof. U. Besancon, France, 1965; prof. philosophy SUNY-Buffalo, 1965—; moderator TV series. Author: (with Rollo Handy) A Current Appraisal of the Behavioral Sciences, 1964, Decision and the Condition of Man, 1965, The Fullness of Life, 1974, Exuberance, 1977, In Defense of Secular Humanism, 1983, A Skeptics Handbook of Parapsychology, 1985, The Transcendental Temptation, 1986, Forbidden Fruit, 1988; editor: American Thought Before 1900, 1966, American Philosophy in the Twentieth Century, 1966, Sidney Hook and the Contemporary World, 1968, Moral Problems in Contemporary Society, 1969; co-editor: International Directory of Philosophy and Philosophers, 4th edit, 1978-81, Tolerance and Revolution, 1970, Language and Human Nature, 1971, A Catholic/Humanist Dialogue, 1972, The Humanist Alternative, 1973, Idea of a Modern University, 1974, The Philosophy of The Curriculum, 1975, The Ethics of Teaching and Scientific Research, 1977, University and State, 1978, Sidney Hook: Philosopher of Democracy and Humanism, 1983; mem. editorial bd.: The Humanist, 1964-78, editor, 1967-78; mem. editorial bd.: Philosophers Index, 1969—, Question, 1969-81; editor-in-chief: Prometheus Books, 1970—; mem. editorial bd.: The Skeptical Inquirer, 1976—; editor: Free Inquiry, 1980—. chmn. Council on Internat. Studies and World Affairs., 1966-69; trustee Behavioral Research Council, Great Barrington, Mass.; bd. dirs. U.S. Bibliography of Philosophy, 1958-70, Internat. Humanist and Ethical Union, 1968—, Univ. Ctrs. for Rational Alternatives, 1969—; chmn. Com. for Sci. Investigation Claims of Paranormal, 1976—; co-chmn. Internat. Humanist and Ethical Union, 1986— . Served with AUS, 1944-46. Behavioral Research Council fellow, 1962-63; French Govt. fellow, 1965; John Dewey fellow, 1986-87; recipient Bertrand Russell Soc. award, 1988. Mem. Am. Philos. Assn., Acad. Humanism, Am. Ethical Union, Am. Humanist Assn. Home: 660 Le Brun Rd Amherst NY 14226 Office: 700 E Amherst St Buffalo NY 14215

KURTZ, THEODORE STEPHEN, psychoanalyst, educator; b. N.Y.C., Apr. 25, 1944; s. Maxwell Arthur and Evelyn R. (Rosenberg) K.; A.B., Boston U., 1964; M.A., N.Y. U., 1965; postgrad. N.Y. Soc. Freudian Psychologists, 1968-74; m. Maritza J. Zurita, Sept. 12, 1975. Caseworker, N.Y.C. Dept. Social Services, 1965-66; tchr., coordinator classes for emotionally disturbed Northport (N.Y.) Pub. Schs., 1966-70; pvt. practice psychoanalytic psychotherapy, 1968—; prin. Luther E. Woodward Sch. for Emotionally Disturbed Children, Freeport, N.Y., 1970-74; asst. prof. edn. C.W. Post Coll., L.I. U., Greenvale, N.Y., 1974-81; psychol. cons. to pvt. industry, 1971—. Diplomate Am. Inst. Counseling and Psychotherapy; cert. Soc. for Psychoanalytic Psychotherapy. Fellow Am. Orthopsychiat. Assn.; mem. Am. Assn. Marriage and Family Counselors (clin. mem.), Am. Acad. Psychotherapists, Am. Group Psychotherapy Assn., Am. (asso.), Nassau County (exec. bd. 1977-78, chmn. com. on acad. psychology 1977-78) psychol. assns., N.Y. Soc. Clin. Psychologists (asso.), Am. Inst. Profl. Cons.'s (sr.), Am. Soc. Tng. and Devel., Acad. Psychologists in Marital, Sex and Family Therapy, Council Advancement of Psychol. Professions and Scis. Jewish. Contbr. articles to profl. jours. Home: Willow Brook Rd PO Box 529 Cold Spring Harbor NY 11724

KURZ, ANDRZEJ KAROL, publishing executive; b. Bielsko-Biala, Poland, Dec. 28, 1931; s. Stanislaw and Helena (Terlecka) K.; m. Zofia Kawyn; 1 child, Agnieszka. MA in Polish Philology, U. Cracow, Poland, 1953; MA in History, Warsaw (Poland) U., 1955; Doctorate, Inst. Social Sci., Warsaw, 1958. Instr. Jagellonian U., Cracow, 1952-53, Warsaw U., 1953-55; assoc. prof. State Coll. Theatrical Arts, Warsaw, 1966-71, Cracow, 1972—; dir. Lit. Pub. House, Cracow, 1971—; 1st dep. chmn. Radio and TV Com., Warsaw, 1981-82. Author 7 books on theory of polit. history; contbr. articles to profl. jours. 1st sec. Cracow com. Polish United Workers' Party, 1961-65; dep. pres. People's Council City of Cracow, 1973-76, pres. 1980-81. Recipient Minister of Culture and Art award, 1969, 75, 86, Chmn. Radio and TV Com. award, 1987. Club: Kuznica (Cracow). Office: Lit Pub House, ul Dluga 1, 31-147 Cracow Poland

KURZ, JEANNE ANNE WALSH, chiropractor, career advisor; b. Richmond Hill, N.Y., Nov. 19, 1935; d. George Valentine and Catherine Frances (McCann) Walsh; m. E.R.H. Kurz, Sept. 20, 1963; children—Scott George, Laurie Jeanne. A.A.S. in Nursing, Queensborough Community Coll., Bayside, N.Y., 1968-70; B.S., C.W. Post Coll., 1973, postgrad., 1974-76; D.C., Life Chiropractic Coll., Marietta, Ga., 1982. Nurse, Wyckoff Heights Hosp., Bklyn., 1964-66, Southampton Hosp., N.Y., 1968-73; pvt. practice chiropractic, Southampton, N.Y., 1982—; career advisor C.W. Post Coll., Greenvale, N.Y., 1984—. Mem. Internat. Chiropractic Assn., Am. Chiropractic Assn., N.Y. Chiropractic Assn., Pub. Health Assn., Sigma Phi Chi, Phi Theta Kappa, Phi Beta Kappa. Club: Topping Riding (Bridehampton, N.Y.). Avocations: art; archery; aviation; equestrian skills; writing; fencing. Home and Office: Wickapoane Rd Southampton NY 11968-8949

KURZ, JERRY BRUCE, lawyer; b. Chgo., June 21, 1949; s. Jack and Delores Estelle (Koss) K. B.S., U. Okla., 1971; J.D., No. Ill. U., 1979. Bar: Ill. 1980, U.S. Dist. Ct. (no. dist.) Ill. 1980, U.S. Ct. Appeals (7th cir.) 1980, U.S. Tax Ct. 1980, U.S. Dist. Ct. (cen. dist.) Ill. 1983, U.S. Supreme Ct. 1984, U.S. Ct. Appeals (11th cir.) 1986. Tchr., pub. schs., Chgo., 1972-79; ptnr. Hall & Kurz, Chgo., 1980—; dir. Met. Football League, Chgo., 1983—, Free Agt. Scouting Combine, Chgo., 1983—, Minor Profl. Football Assn., 1980—. Served to capt. U.S. Army, 1968-69, Vietnam. Mem. Nat. Assn. Criminal Def. Lawyers, Chgo. Bar Assn., ABA, Assn. Trial Lawyers Am., Phi Alpha Delta. Democrat. Jewish. Home: 3117 Knollwood Glenview IL 60025 Office: Hall & Kurz 7 S Dearborn Suite 1507 Chicago IL 60603

KUSAKA, MASANORI, real estate developer; b. Naruto, Tokushima, Japan, Dec. 20, 1945; s. Souichi and Umeko (Yoshimoto) K.; m. Hatsuko Komatsu, Oct. 21, 1971; children: Tetsuya, Hiroya, Yoko. Grad. high sch., Tokushima. Lic. real estate practitioner. Radio controller Tokushima Prefectural Police Hdqrs., 1965-68; exec. dir. CDC Accts. Co., Ltd., Takamatsu, Japan, 1969-82; pres. Kusaka Kousan Co. Ltd., Takamatsu, 1983—. Mem. Takamatsu Nat. Council, 1985—. Recipient Police Commdr.'s award Tokushima Prefectural Police, 1965. Mem. All Japan Lands and Houses Dealers Soc. Liberal Democrat. Buddhist. Clubs; Royal Hawaiian Ocean Racing (Honolulu); Prestige Country (Kashiwagi). Home: 60 55 947 Hamano cho, Takamatsu 760, Japan Office: Kusaka Kousan Co Ltd, 2 7 14 Kawaramachi, Takamatsu 760, Japan

KUSCH, POLYKARP, physicist, educator; b. Blankenburg, Germany, Jan. 26, 1911; came to U.S., 1912, naturalized, 1923; s. John Matthias and Henrietta (van der Haas) K.; m. Edith Starr McRoberts, Aug. 12, 1935 (dec. 1959); children—Kathryn, Judith, Sara; m. Betty Jane Pezzoni, 1960; children—Diana, Maria. B.S., Case Inst. Tech., 1931, D.Sc., 1956; M.S., U. Ill., 1933, Ph.D., 1936, D.Sc. (hon.), 1961; D.Sc. (hon.), Ohio State U., 1959, Colby Coll., 1961, Gustavus Adolphus Coll., St. Peter, Minn., 1962, Yeshiva U., 1976, Coll. of Incarnate Word, 1980, Columbia U., 1983. Engaged as teaching asst. U. Ill., 1931-36; research asst. U. Minn., 1936-37; instr. Columbia U., 1937-41, assoc. prof. physics, 1946-49, prof., 1949-72, chmn. dept. physics, 1949-52, 60-63, acad. v.p. and provost, 1969-72; engr. Westinghouse, 1941-42; research asso. Columbia U., 1942-44; mem. tech. staff Bell Telephone Labs., 1944-46; prof. physics U. Tex.-Dallas, 1972—, Eugene McDermott prof., 1974-80, Regental prof., 1980-82, Regental prof. emeritus, 1982—. Recipient Nobel prize in physics, 1955, Ill. Achievement award U. Ill., 1975; Fellow; Center for Advanced Study in Behavioral Sciences, 1964-65. Fellow Am. Phys. Soc., A.A.A.S.; mem. Am. Acad. Arts and Scis., Am. Philos. Soc., Nat. Acad. Scis. Democrat. Office: Univ Tex-Dallas PO Box 830688 Richardson TX 75083

KUSHNER, LAURYN BONNIE, plastic manufacturer company official; b. Chgo., July 23, 1955; d. Herman and Rae (Bittenfeld) K. Asst. office mgr. Law Firm of Jenner & Block, Chgo., 1974-78; mgr. Midwest distbn. Supreme Equipment and Systems Corp., Chgo., 1980-85; chief operating officer Thermoform Plastics, Inc., 1986-87; pres. Women Artist's Gallery, 1981.

Chmn. bd. E.P.I.C., Inc., Chgo., 1982. Mem. Nat. Assn. Female Execs., Am. Film Inst., Smithsonian Assocs. Jewish.

KUSIK, CHARLES LEMBIT, chemical engineer; b. N.Y.C., Apr. 24, 1934; s. Charles and Mary (Jackson) K.; B.S., M.I.T., 1956, M.S., 1958; Sc.D., N.Y. U., 1961. Scientist, ops. research group M.I.T., Cambridge, 1961-62; engr. Avco Corp., Wilmington, Mass., 1963-64; mem. profl. staff Arthur D. Little, Inc., Cambridge, 1964—, mgr. metals and energy mgmt. 1980—. Served with U.S. Army, 1962-63. NSF fellow, 1959-61; registered profl. engr., Mass. Mem. Am. Inst. Chem. Engrs., AIME, Am. Mgmt. Assn., N.Y. Acad. Scis., Am. Chem. Soc. Author: (with Kenahan) Energy Use Patterns for Metal Recycling, 1978; (with Makar and Mounier) Availability of Critical Scrap Metals Containing Chromium in the United States, 1980; contbr. articles to profl. jours. Office: 20 Acorn Park Cambridge MA 02140

KUSISTO, OSCAR PERRY, electronics executive; b. Calumet, Mich., Sept. 12, 1915; s. Samuel E. and Sanna (Hakala) K.; student Mich. Coll. Mining and Tech., 1933, U. Mich., 1935-40, Lawrence Tech. Coll., 1941, M.I.T., 1942; m. Dorothy Elizabeth Allison, Jan. 1, 1941; children—Susan Elizabeth, Thomas Perry. Radar Devel. engr., field engrng. supr. Raytheon Mfg. Co., Waltham, Mass., 1942-47; sales engr. Motorola Automotive Products Inc., Detroit, 1947-55, sales mgr., 1955-60, v.p., gen. mgr., 1960-66, pres., 1966—; v.p., gen. mgr. Automotive div. Motorola Inc.; chmn. Motorola Automotive Ltd., Eng.; chmn. emeritus ITA; vice chmn. Autovox Italy; dir. Motorola Inc., Motorola Can. Ltd., Alps-Motorola, Japan; cons. automotive and electronics industries, various internat. cos. Served with USNR, 1932-36. Recipient Commendation award for contbn. to radar devel. U.S. Navy, 1944. Mem. Soc. Automotive Engrs., Am. Radio Relay League. Republican. Congregationalist. Clubs: Recess, Circumnavigators. Pioneer in stereo 8 and quadrophonic 8 industries. Home: 570 Torwood Ln Los Altos CA 94022 Office: Motorola Center Schaumburg IL 60194

KUTASH, IRWIN LAWRENCE, psychoanalyst; b. Bklyn., Apr. 14, 1945; s. Samuel Benjamin and Lee K.; Ph.D., Adelphi U., 1972; cert. in psychotherapy and psychoanalysis Postgrad. Center for Mental Health, 1978; m. Helen Jacobs, Jan. 29, 1967; children—Jeffrey Brian, Abby Victoria, Ross Todd, Steven Brant. Asso. psychologist Central Islip (N.Y.) State Hosp., 1968-72; asso. staff mem. Postgrad. Center for Mental Health, 1972-75; chief alcohol rehab. program, chmn. behavioral sci. council, dir. psychology tng. VA Med. Center, East Orange, N.J., 1975-80; pvt. practice psychotherapy and psychoanalysis, Livingston, N.J., 1972—; clin. assoc. prof. psychiatry and mental health scis. U. Medicine and Dentistry of N.J. 1975—; psychol. cons. N.J. Dept. Human Services, 1975—; sr. supr., tng. analyst, mem. faculty N.Y. Center Psychoanalytic Tng., 1978—; chmn. mental health adv. com. Regional Mental Health Council, 1978—; mem. presdl. task force, nat. adv. council on employee assistance counciling programs, 1978. NIMH grantee, 1972-75. Mem. Am. Psychol. Assn. (pres. section on group psychotherapy, 1988—), N.J. Psychol. Assn., Soc. Psychologists in Pvt. Practice (past pres.), N.J. Acad. Psychology (trustee), N.J. Assn. Advancement Psychology (dir.), N.J. Acad. Psychology (pres.), Am. Group Psychotherapy Assn. Editor, contbg. author: Violence: Perspectives on Murder and Aggression, 1978; The Handbook on Stress and Anxiety: Contemporary Knowledge Theory and Treatment, 1980; Psychotherapist's Casebook: Theory and Technique in the Practice of Modern Therapies, 1986; co-author, developer Criminal Fantasy Technique (psychol. test), 1979; contbr. articles to profl. jours. Home: 4 Ross Rd Livingston NJ 07039 Office: 340 E Northfield Rd Suite 1E Livingston NJ 07039

KUTKA, NICHOLAS, nuclear medicine physician; b. Czechoslovakia, Dec. 17, 1926; s. Vladimir and Agatha (Flenko) K.; m. Anna Cizmar, Aug. 14, 1965; children: Andrew, Gregory. MD, Comenius U., Bratislava, Czechoslovakia, 1951; PhD, Slovak Acad. Scis., Bratislava, 1962. Diplomate internal medicine Postgrad. Edn. of Physicians, 1955, nuclear medicine Am. Bd. Nuclear Medicine, 1973. Asst. prof. inst. physiology Comenius U., Bratislava, 1951; intern, resident in internal medicine Mil. Hosp., Bratislava, 1952-55; chief dept. inst. endocrinology Slovak Acad. Scis., Bratislava, 1956-69; tech. asst. Internat. Atomic Engery Agy., Bogota, Colombia, 1969-70; resident in nuclear medicine Duke U., 1971-73; asst. prof. radiology Baylor Coll. Medicine, Houston, 1973—; dir. nuclear medicine Ben Taub Gen. Hosp., Houston, 1978-81; chief nuclear medicine service VA Med. Ctr., Houston, 1982—; mem. med. staff univ. affiliated hosps. Houston, faculty Sch. Nuclear Medicine Tech.; fellow Internat. Atomic Energy Agy., Rome, 1962-63. Contbr. numerous articles to profl. jours; mem. editorial bd. Endocrinologia Experimentalis. Served with Health Service Czechoslovak Army, 1952-54. Recipient prize in nuclear medicine J.E. Purkyne, 1965. Mem. Harris County Med. Soc., Tex. Med. Assn., Soc. Nuclear Medicine, Am. Coll. Nuclear Physicians, Clin. Ligand Assay Soc. Office: VA Med Ctr Nuclear Medicine Service Houston TX 77030

KUTTNER, BERNARD A., lawyer, former judge; b. Berlin, Ger., Jan. 13, 1934; s. Frank B. and Vera (Knopfmacher); children: Karen M., Robert D., Stacey M. AB cum laude, Dartmouth Coll., 1955; postgrad. U. Va. Law Sch., 1956; JD, Seton Hall U., 1959; postgrad. NYU. Bar: N.J. 1960, N.Y. 1982, D.C. 1982, U.S. Supreme Ct. 1964, U.S. Ct. Mil. Appeals., 1967; cert. civil trial lawyer, N.J., 1982. Assoc. Toner, Crowley, Woelper & Vanderbilt, 1959-62; sole practice, 1962-75; corp. counsel, Irvington, N.J., 1963-66; ptnr. Kuttner, Toner, DiBenedetto & Dowd, Roseland, N.J., 1975-87; sole practice Newark, 1987—; judge N.J. State Div. Tax Apls., 1977-79; instr. civil litigation Montclair State Coll., 1979-82; del. Jud. Conf. N.J. Supreme Ct., 1974-81; vice chmn. Supreme Ct. N.J. Dist. Ethics Com., 1984-85, chmn., 1985-86. Contbr. articles to legal publs. Commr. Essex County (N.J.) Park Commn., 1973-79; appointed bd. on Trial Atty. Certification, N.J. Supreme Ct., 1986. Served to lt. comdr. USNR, 1964-74. Named Outstanding Young Man N.J., N.J. Jaycees 1967. Mem. Inst. for Ethical Behavior (pres. 1985—), ABA (coeditor trial techniques newsletter sect. on tort and ins. practice, chmn. trial techniques com. 1988—, sect. on litigation), D.C. Bar Assn., Irvington Bar Assn. (pres. 1968-70), Essex County Bar Assn. (chmn. 1973-75, com. trial and appellate litigation, judiciary com. 1972-75, treas. 1975-79, pres. 1980-81, products liability com. 1981—), Assn. Trial Lawyers Am., Am. Counsel Assn. Democrat. Jewish. Club: Orange Lawn Tennis. Home: 61 Sagamore Rd Millburn NJ 07041 Office: Kuttner & Affiliates 744 Broad St Newark NJ 07102

KUTZ, ROBERT H., lawyer; b. Brookville, Pa., Oct. 18, 1943; s. Charles M. and Virginia M. (McAuley) K.; children: David P., Robert S. B.A., Allegheny Coll., 1965; J.D., Duquesne U., 1973. Bar: Pa. 1973, U.S. Dist. Ct. (we. dist.) Pa. 1973, U.S. Supreme Ct. 1988; C.L.U. Asst. mgr. Conn. Gen. Life Ins. Co., Pitts., 1968-74; mgmt. employee Aetna Life Co., Pitts., 1975-76; sole practice, Greensburg, Pa., 1973-76, 81—; ptnr. Kutz & Kutz, Greensburg, 1976-80. Mem. Westmoreland Bar Assn., Pa. Bar Assn., ABA. Clubs: University (Pitts); Pike Run Country (Donegal, Pa.). Lodge: Elks.

KUTZIN, MELVIN, infosystems engineer; b. Bronx, N.Y., Dec. 29, 1933; s. Harry and Hilda K.; m. Dorothy Fish, Oct. 29, 1955; children: Michael Scott, Randi. BSEE, Poly. Inst. Bklyn., 1965, MS, 1967. Engr. Bell Telephone Labs., 1957-60; engr. Airborne Instruments Lab., Deer Park, N.Y., 1960-65, program mgr. ECM div., 1965-69; solid state engr. RCA, Somerville, N.J., 1969-71; field application engr. Fairchild Semicondr. Co., Melville, N.Y., 1971-74; dir. microprocessor ops. Schweber Electronics, Westbury, N.Y., 1975-83; v.p. tech. services Diplomat Electronics, Melville, N.Y., 1983-86, dir. computer products, 1986—; internat. lectr. in field; adj. prof. microprocessor NYU Sch. Continuing Edn. Contbr. articles to profl. jours.; developer direct distance dialing, computer designed chip, universal array, early microprocessor, 4 bit parallel processor. Served with U.S. Army, 1955-57. Mem. Soc. Automotive Engrs. (chmn. electronics subcom. on microcomputers 1975—), IEEE. Club: Odd Fellows. Office: Diplomat Electronics 110 Marcus Dr Melville NY 11747

KUWABARA, DENNIS MATSUICHI, optometrist; b. Honolulu, July 20, 1945; s. Robert Tokuichi and Toshiko (Nakashima) K.; m. Judith Naomi Tokumaru, June 28, 1970; children: Jennifer Tomiko, Susan Kazuko. BS, So. Calif. Coll. Optometry, 1968, OD cum laude, 1970. Pvt. practice optometry Waipahu, Honolulu, Hawaii, 1972—; Pres. 1st Study Club for Optometrists, Honolulu, 1982-83; chmn. bd. examiners in Optometry, Honolulu, 1982—; state dir. Optometric Extension Found., Honolulu, 1980—. Served to lt. Med. Service Corps, USN, 1970-72. Named Outstanding Young Person of Hawaii, Hawaii State Jaycees, 1979. Fellow Am. Acad. Optometry; mem. Hawaii Optometric Assn. (pres. 1979-80, Man of Yr. award 1976, Optometrist of Yr. 1983), Am. Optometric Assn., Armed Forces Optometric Soc. Home: 94-447 Holaniku St Mililani Town HI 96789 Office: 94-748 Hikimoe St Waipahu HI 96797 Other: 1441 Kapionali Blvd Suite 710 Honolulu HI 96814

KUWAHARA, MITSUNORI, judicial scrivener and consultant; b. Saseho, Nagasaki, Kyushu, Japan, Sept. 25, 1936; s. Ryoichi and Shizuko Iida K.; m. Kimie Haibara, June 12, 1964; children: Mamie, Koichiro. LLB, Chuo U., Tokyo, 1966. Gen. mgr. law dept. Japan High-rising Housing Co. Ltd., Tokyo, 1967-70; pres. Techunorand Co, Ltd., Tokyo, 1970—; chmn. Kuwahara Firm, Tokyo, 1968—. Mem. Tokyo Jud. Scrivener Assn., Tokyo Cons. on Adminstrv. Papers Assn. Liberal Democrat. Clubs: Do Sports Plaza (Shinjuku, Tokyo); Hayama Mariner (Kanagawa). Home: 1-36-7 Wakamiya, Nakano-ku, Tokyo Japan Office: Kuwahara Firm, Shinjuku Nomura Bldg 9th Floor, 1-26-2 Nishishinjuku, Shinjuku-ku, 163 Tokyo Japan

KUX, DENNIS HENRY, foreign service officer; b. London, Aug. 11, 1931; came to U.S., 1933, naturalized, 1940; s. Lacy and Evelyn (Stern) K.; m. Mary Bower, Apr. 8, 1960; children: Leslie, Sally, Brian. A.B., Lafayette Coll., 1952; M.A., Tufts U., 1955. Internat. economist U.S. Dept. State, Washington, 1955-57; econ. officer U.S. Dept. State, Karachi, Pakistan, 1957-60; comml. and consular officer U.S. Dept. State, Madras, India, 1960-62; Nepal desk officer U.S. Dept. State, Washington, 1962-64, supervisory personnel staffing specialist, 1964-66; polit. officer U.S. Dept. State, Bonn., Ger., 1966-69, Rawalpindi, Pakistan, 1969-71; assigned Army War Coll. U.S. Dept. State, 1971-72; sr. polit. officer for India U.S. Dept. State, Washington, 1972-74; country dir. for India, Nepal and Sri Lanka U.S. Dept. State, 1947-77, assigned Sr. Seminar, 1977-78; polit. counselor U.S. Dept. State, Ankara, Turkey, 1978-80; dep. asst. sec. Bur. Intelligence and Research U.S. Dept. State, Washington, 1981-84; dep. dir. mgmt. ops. U.S. Dept. State, 1984-86; ambassador to Ivory Coast 1986—. Served to 1st lt. AUS, 1952-54. MEM. Assn. Asian Studies; mem. Am. Fgn. Service Assn., Phi Beta Kappa. Office: US Dept State 2201 C St NW Washington DC 20520

KUYPER, JOAN CAROLYN, foundation administrator; b. Balt., Oct. 22, 1941; d. Irving Charles and Ethel Mae (Pritchett) O'Connor; B.A. in Edn., Salisbury State U., 1963; postgrad. Columbia U., 1978; MA in Arts Mgmt. and Bus., NYU, 1988; m. L. William Kuyper, Dec. 20, 1964; children—Susan Carol, Edward Philip. Elem. sch. tchr. Prince Georges County Schs., Md., 1963-68; free lance singer, opera, oratorio, chamber music Amato Opera, N.Y.C., 1967-80; owner, mgr. Privette Artists' Registry, Placement Service for Singers, Teaneck, N.J., 1969-78; exec. dir. Teaneck Artists Perform-Chamber Music Series, 1975-80; program dir. Vols. in Arts & Humanities, Vol. Bur. Bergen County, N.J., 1978-81; dir. Bergen Mus. Art and Sci., 1981-83; cons. Am. Soc. Prevention Cruelty to Animals, 1984, Am. Council for the Arts, 1987; dir. ops. Isabel O'Neil Found. and Studio, 1984-85. Dir. vol. services March of Dimes Birth Defects Found. of Greater N.Y., 1985-88; bd. dirs Pro Arte Chorale and adv. bd. on the arts, Teaneck, 1976-81. Mem. Am. Assn. Mus., Mus. Council N.J., Am. Mktg. Assn., Assn. for Vol. Adminstrn. Democrat. Presbyterian. Clubs: Altrusa (bd. dirs. 1984-86, pres. 1986-88), P.E.O., Phi Alpha Theta. Home: 501 Rutland Ave Teaneck NJ 07666 Office: 233 Park Ave S New York NY 10028

KUZARA, STANLEY ANDREW, real estate executive; b. Dietz, Wyo., Oct. 15, 1906; s. George and Sophia (Mendrick) K.; B.A., U. Wyo., 1929; m. Pauline E. Caywood, June 8, 1935; children—Janet Kuzara Kilpatrick, Richard, Robert. Area dir. Nat. Youth Adminstrn., 1935-42; field dir. ARC, 1942-45; dir. Vets. Info. Center, Colorado Springs, Colo., 1945-49; engaged in real estate, 1950—; propr. Kuzara Agy., Sheridan, Wyo., 1954—; pres. Wymo Oil, Inc., 1958-69. Mem. Sheridan City Planning Commn., 1969-76; hon. dir. N. Am. Indian Found. Named Wyo. Realtor of Yr., Wyo. Assn. Realtors, 1969; Wyo. Citizen of Yr., Wyo. State Elks Assn., 1972. Mem. Wyo. Realtors Assn. (pres. 1964), Nat. Assn. Realtors (regional v.p. 1976), Internat. Assn. Turtles (pres. 1960-83). Clubs: Elks (past exalted ruler, hon. life mem., dist. dep., grand exalted ruler Wyo. N. 1975-76, mem. grand lodge com. credentials 1976-77, Wyoming's Most Disting. Elk 1986-87), Masons, Shriners. Author, pub.: Black Diamonds of Sheridan—A Facet of Wyoming History, 1977. Home: 372 W Loucks St Sheridan WY 82801 Office: 21 S Jefferson St Sheridan WY 82801

KUZELL, WILLIAM CHARLES, physician, instrument company executive; b. Great Falls, Mont., Dec. 13, 1914; s. Charles R. and Theresa (O'Leary) K.; m. Francoise Lavelaine de Maubeuge, Oct. 15, 1945; children: Anne Frances Kuzell Hackstock, Elizabeth Jacqueline, Charles Maubeuge. Exchange student, Lingnan U., Canton, China, 1934-35, U. de Grenoble, summer 1935; BA, Stanford U., 1936, MD, 1941. Diplomate: Am. Bd. Internal Medicine. Clin. prof. medicine emeritus Stanford U., 1986—, research asso. therapeutics, 1948-56, physician in charge arthritis clinic, 1956-59; chief div. rheumatology Presbyn. Med. Center, San Francisco, 1959-85; dir. emeritus Kuzell Inst. for Arthritis and Infectious Disease Research, Med. Research Inst., San Francisco, 1985—; chmn. bd., chief exec. officer Oxford Labs., Inc., Foster City, to 1974; guest lectr. Japan Rheumatism Assn., 1964. Editor: Stanford Med. Bull, 1950-53. Pres., No. Calif. chpt. Arthritis Found., 1971-72, chmn. bd., 1972-80. Served to capt. M.C. AUS, 1942-46. Named Man of Yr. in Medicine Shoong Found. Hall of Fame, 1980; recipient Disting. Service award Arthritis Found., 1981. Fellow ACP, Am. Rheumatis Assn. (pres. No. Calif. chpt. 1953); mem. AMA, Calif. Acad. Medicine, Western Soc. Clin. Research, Japan Rheumatism Assn. (hon.), Sigma Xi, Sigma Nu, Nu Sigma Nu. Clubs: Olympic, Presidio Golf. Home: 25 W Clay Park San Francisco CA 94121 Office: 450 Sutter St San Francisco CA 94108

KUZMAK, LUBOMYR IHOR, surgeon; b. Balyhorod, Ukraine, Aug. 2, 1931; s. Wolodymyr and Lidia (Litynsky) K.; came to U.S., 1965, naturalized, 1968; MD, Med. Acad., Lodz, Poland, 1953; DSc, Silesian Acad. Medicine, Katowice, Poland, 1965; m. Roxana A. Smishkewych, Jan. 22, 1966; 1 dau., Roxolana. Resident, chief resident in gen. surgery Silesian Acad. Medicine, III Surg. Clinic, Bytom, Poland, 1954-61, gen. surgeon head div., asso. prof., 1961-65; resident, chief resident in gen. surgery St. Barnabas Med. Center, Livingston, N.J., 1966-71; practice medicine specializing in gen. vascular and obesity surgery, Newark, 1971—; former chief of surgery Irvington (N.J.) Gen. Hosp.; mem. teaching staff St. Barnabas Med. Center, Livingston; lectr. Diplomate Polish Bd. Gen. Surgery. Fellow Am. Soc. Abdominal Surgeons, Internat. Coll. Surgeons; mem. AMA (Physicians Recognition award 1970-73, 76-79, 79-82, 82-85); Ukranian Med. Assn. N.Am., N.J. Med. Assn., Royal Soc. Medicine, Essex County Med. Assn., Am. Soc. Contemporary Medicine and Surgery, Internat. Platform Assn. Ukranian Catholic. Contbr. articles to profl. jours. Office: 657 Irvington Ave Newark NJ 07106 also: 340 E Northfield Rd Livingston NJ 07039

KVAAL, ERIK, banker; b. Bodo, Norway, Sept. 7, 1931; s. Alf and Ingrid Synnave (Hansen) K.; m. Kari Kaalhus; children: Alf Erik, Hans Petter, Ingrid Tilde, Gustav. Student, Tandheim Handelsgymnas, 1952, Bankakademiet Hoyere avd., 1964. Sec. Hoyre Conservative party, Bodo, 1954; with Bank Norway, 1953-64; asst. chief clk. Norges Banksaudeling, Vardo, 1964-72; mng. dir. Norges Banksaudeling, Hammerfest, 1972-76, Bodo, 1976—. Chmn. Conservative party Youth Orgn., Bodo, 1949-51; bd. dirs. Young Conservative party, Oslo, 1951-53; chmn. Conservative party, Vardo, 1967-72. Lodge: Rotary. Home: Kirkeveien 22, 8000 Bodo Norway Office: Norges Banksaudeling, Dranninopusqt 36, 8000 Bodo Norway

KVARSTEIN, BERNT, urological surgeon; b. Lierne, Norway, Aug. 21, 1930; s. Gunnvald and Gudrun (Berge) K.; M.D., U. Oslo, 1959, Ph.D., 1971; m. Anne-Kari Hegna, June 23, 1955 (dec.); children—Helene, Gunnvald, Bernt Kristian. Intern, Lillehammer Fylkessykehus and Sel and Heidal dists., 1960-61; sci. asst. Inst. of Path. Anatomy, U. Oslo, 1962-63, research fellow Inst. Thrombosis Research, 1965-69; resident and registrar dept. obstetrics and gynecology Univ. Hosp., Oslo, 1964, 69-70, registrar, dept. surgery, 1970-73, sr. registrar div. urology, 1975-78; registrar, sr. registrar dept. surgery Drammen Hosp., Norway, 1973-75; specialist in gen. surgery, 1976, in urology, 1978; surgeon-in-chief Home for Congl. Sisters, Oslo, 1978-79; asst. surgeon-in-chief dept. surgery Akershus Central Hosp., U. Oslo, 1979-82, head sect. of urology, 1982—. Recipient C.R. Bard award, 1982. Mem. Norwegian Med. Assn., Norwegian Surg. Assn., Nordic Surg. Assn., Norwegian Assn. Urology (pres. 1986—), Nordic Urol. Assn., Société Internationale d'Urologie, Internat. Continence Soc., European Assn. Urology. Contbr. articles on endocrinology, cardiovascular surgery, and urology to profl. jours. Address: Lijordv 25, 1343 Eiksmarka Norway

KVASNIČKA, JÁN, political scientist; b. Krompachy, Czeckoslovakia, Nov. 5, 1927; s. Alexander and Mária (Huráková) K.; m. Věra Andělová, May 30, 1953; children: Jan, Lubica. PhD, Comenius U., Bratislava, Czechoslovakia, 1951, DSc, 1975. Prof. Polit. Sci. Comenius U., 1951—; rector Comenius U., 1976-85. Author: Czecholslovakian Legions in Russia: 1917-21, 1963, The Way of Treason, 1983; co-author: October in the Mirror of the Seven Decades, 1987. Recipient Order of Labour Czechoslovakian Govt., 1977. Mem. Slavik Acad. Scis. Office: Comenius Univ of Bratislava, Safarikovo nam 6, 88545 Bratislava Czechoslovakia

KVENVOLD, TONY MARK, electronics executive, consultant; b. Madison, S.D., Oct. 28, 1956; s. Alden Theodor Kvenvold and Dorothy Clara (Verhay) Johnson; m. Wynne Whiting Treanor, June 23, 1979; children: Kristopher, Allyssa. AA, Rochester Community Coll., 1980; BS, Winona State U., 1983. Electronic design engr. Watlow Co., Winona, Minn., 1980-86; pres. Finch Systems, Winona, 1983—; sr. design engr. Quantem Corp., Trenton, N.J., 1986—; Inventor electronic computer chip, 1985. Office: Quantem Corp Box 7599 Trenton NJ 08628

KVERNELAND, OLE BJARNE, advertising executive; b. Oslo, Jan. 30, 1934; s. Bjarne and Hjordis (Almaas) K.; m. Wenche L. Kverneland; children: Hans, Eva, John. Degree, Inst. Practitioners in Advt., London, 1961; degree in media, Inst. for Markedsfaring, Oslo, 1976, degree in prodn., 1978. Trainee Kenyon & Eckhard, Detroit, 1956; media asst. Publisitas, Düsseldorf, Fed. Republic Germany, 1957-58, Lausanne, Switzerland, 1958-59; account exec. D.T.V., London, 1959-62; account exec. Bj. Kverneland A/S, Oslo, 1963—, also mng. dir. Office: Bj Kverneland A/S, Prof Dahls Gt 3, 0355 Oslo 3, Norway

KVIDELAND, REIMUND, educator, folklorist; b. Hoyland, Norway, Jan. 28, 1935; s. Knut and Karen (Foldoy) K.; m. Karin Sivertsen; children: Kristian, Katrin, Elin. Degree, U. Oslo, 1964. Prof. folklore U. Bergen (Norway), 1966—. Author 8 books; founding editor Tradisjon jour; contbr. articles to profl. jours. Mem. Finnish Literary Soc. (corr.), Austrian Soc. Folklore (corr.), Internat. Soc. Ethnology and Folklore (pres. 1987—). Home: Birkelundsbakken 25 A, Paradis 5040, Norway Office: U Bergen Dept Folklore, Olaf Ryesvei 19, Bergen 5007, Norway

KVITASH, VADIM I(SSAY), allergist-immunologist, scientist; b. Odessa, USSR, Mar. 19, 1936; came to U.S. 1974; m. Ivetta Kopilovsky, Apr. 2, 1961; children: Zoya, Sofia. MD, Odessa Med. Sch., 1961; PhD, Mechnikov's Sci. Research Inst. of Virology and Epidemiology, Odessa, 1969. Chief pediatrics Novo-Ivanovsk (USSR) Hosp., 1961-64; postdoctoral researcher Moscow Cen. Inst. Med. Specialization, 1965; postdoctoral researcher exptl., clin., indsl. virology and immunology Mechnikov's Sci. Research Inst. of Virology and Epidemiology, Odessa, 1965-69, research immunologist, 1969-70, chmn. bd. Young Scientists, 1969-74, mem. sci. council, sci. cons., 1970-74; sci., med. cons. systemology lab. Odessa U., 1970-74; med. dir. pediatric depts. Odessa Med. Sch. Hosp., 1970-74; asst. prof. pediatrics Odessa Med. Sch., 1970-74; orderly Mt. Zion Hosp. and Med. Ctr., San Francisco, 1975, research assoc., 1980-82, prin. investigator, 1980-84, resident dept. pathology and lab. medicine, 1981-82; research asst. IMMUNOPATHWAYS LAB., San Francisco, 1976-77, research assoc., 1980-81, sci. dir., founder Balascopy Inst., San Francisco, 1980—; pvt. practice specializing in allergy-immunology San Francisco, 1982—; affiliate sr. scientist Med. Research Inst. of San Francisco, Pacific Presbyn. Med. Ctr., 1985—. Contbr. articles to profl. jours; patentee in field. Named Laureate Best Research Work of Young Scientists, All-Soviet Union Competition, 1968, laureate Best Med. Student Research Work, Ukrainian Soviet Socialist Rep. Competition, 1960; recipient Mechnikov Sci. award, 1966-67, Best Med. Student Research Work award Odessa Med. Sch., 1958-61; Mt. Zion Hosp. and Med. Ctr. research grantee; Internat. award of AIDS research World Fedn. Contraception/Health, 1987. Fellow Am. Coll. Allergists, Am. Coll. Allergy and Immunology (sci. com. basic and clin. immunology, mem. sci. com. computers in medicine); mem. AMA, AAAS, Calif. Med. Assn., San Francisco Med. Soc., San Francisco Soc. Internal Medicine, Am. Acad. Allergy and Immunology, Am. Assn. Clin. Immunology and Allergy, Joint Council Allergy and Immunology, European Acad. Allergology and Clin. Immunology, Pan Am. Allergy Soc., Internat. Corr. Soc. Allergists, Bay Area Huff and Puff Club, Bay Area History Medicine Club, Am. Heart Assn., Am. Assn. Med. Systems and Informatics, Soc. Med. Decision Making, Am. Assn. Artificial Intelligence, Am. Soc. Cybernetics, Assn. Automated Reasoning, Cognitive Sci. Soc., Internat. Soc. for Scis., Assn. Integrative Studies, N.Y. Acad. Sci. Office: 2352 Post St San Francisco CA 94115

KWAK, BYONG-SUN, educational researcher; b. Manchuria, People's Republic of China, Jan. 25, 1942; arrived in Korea, 1945; parents: HoongOon Kwak and Yoonbok Han; m. EunSook Jee, Sept. 15, 1973; children: Daw Young, Dae Hee. Student, Chongjoo Normal Sch., Korea, 1959-62; BA, Seoul Nat. U., 1970, MA, 1973; PhD, Marquette U., 1980. Tchr. elem. sch. Kyongbuk, Korea, 1962-63; tchr. jr. high sch. Seoul, 1970-72; researcher Korean Ednl. Devel. Inst., Seoul, 1973-77, sr. researcher, 1980-83, research fellow, 1984—; cons. UNESCO Bangkok Office, Indonesia, 1984; adv. bd. Presdl. Commn. for Ednl. Reform, Korea, 1985-87; mem. com. Ednl. Ministry for Curriculum, Korea, 1981—; instr. Seoul Nat. U., 1981—; adv. bd. Cen. Council for Edn., Korea, 1988—. Author: book Curriculum, 1983, Korean Primary School, 1986; editor: Toward Improvement of General Education, 1985. Served to sgt. Korean Army, 1963-65;. Recipient Ministry of Edn. award, Seoul, 1981, Nat. medal Pres. of Korea, Seoul, 1986; grantee Fulbright Commn., Washington, 1977-80. Mem. Korean Soc. for Curriculum Studies (chmn.), Ministry of Sci. and Tech. (adv. mem.), Phi Delta Kappa. Office: Korean Ednl Devel Inst, 92-6 Umyeon-Dong Seocho-Gu, 137-140 Seoul Republic of Korea

KWAN, HING-HIN STEPHEN, textile executive; b. Canton, Kwangtung, People's Republic of China, Feb. 28, 1948; arrived in Hong Kong, 1967; s. Ying Biu and Hang Chin (Chan) K.; m. Margaret Wing-Man Lee; children: Evelyne Yik-Yan, Alban Yik-Bun. M in Philosophy, Leeds (Eng.) U., 1974. Mgr. sales Jardine Matheson & Co., Ltd., Hong Kong, 1975-78; mgr. mktg. Jardine Mktg. Services Ltd., Hong Kong, 1978-80; dir., gen. mgr. Kee Shing Indsl. Products Ltd., Hong Kong, 1980-85, mng. dir., 1985—, also bd. dirs. Mem. British Inst. Mgmt., Textile Inst. Home: 84 Waterloo Rd, 12/F, B1, Hong Kong, Kowloon Hong Kong Office: Kee Shing Indsl Products Ltd, 74-76 Kimberley Rd, QPL-KSIP, Holdings Ctr, 3/F, Kowloon Hong Kong

KWARARA, GALEVA, Papua New Guinea government official; b. Kapakapa Village, Central Province, Papua New Guinea, 1942; married; 6 children. Pub. service higher cert., Australian Sch. Pacific Adminstrn., Sydney; student, U. Papua New Guinea. Inspector Tchr.'s Edn. Div., 1972-76; dep. nat. sec. Assn. Tchr. Edn., Melbourne, Australia, 1973; former minister nat. planning and devel., former minister trade and industry Papua New Guinea, Port Moresby, mem. 3d Parliament, 1982—, minister fin. and planning, 1987-88, minister trade and industry, 1988—. Address: Ministry Trade and Industry, Port Moresby Papua New Guinea *

KWASHA, H. CHARLES, cons. actuary; b. Providence, Dec. 2, 1906; s. Barned and Lena (Lisker) K.; A.B., Brown U., 1928; m. Sylvia I. Herman, Aug. 20, 1939; children—Linda Dianne, Bruce Charles, Robert Dexter. Mem. faculty Brown U., 1929, actuary Travelers Ins. Co., 1929-37; head pension dept. Marsh and McLennan, Inc., 1937-44; organized firm, cons. actuarial work H. Charles Kwasha, cons. actuary, 1944; partner Kwasha Lipton, 1947—. Mem. Soc. Actuaries, Sigma Xi, Phi Beta Kappa. Author articles on employee retirement, employee benefit programs. Home: Jockey Club Apt 2204 Miami FL 33161 Office: 10800 Biscayne Blvd Suite 735 Miami FL 33161

KWASNICKI, WITOLD, computer scientist, researcher; b. Bielawa, Wroclaw, Poland, Apr. 5, 1952; s. Mieczystaw Tadeusz and Zofia (Sieminska) K.; m. Halina Gebura, July 20, 1975; children: Jakub, Mateusz. MS in Electronic Engring., Tech. U. Wroctaw, 1976; PhD, Inst. Engring. Cybernetics, Wroctaw, 1980. Asst. Inst. Engring. Cybernetics, 1976-80; sr. researcher Future Research Ctr., Wroclaw, 1980—. Assoc. editor Papers on Sci. of Sci. and Forecasting, 1985-86; contbr. articles to profl. jours. Home: Kietczowska 135/9, 51 315 Wroclaw Poland Office: Tech U Wroctaw, Future Research Ctr, Wyb Wyspianskiego 27, 50 370 Wroclaw Poland

KWEE, MICHAEL CHONG-KOK, financier; b. Samarinda, Indonesia, July 9, 1946; s. Hin Liem and Sau Chun (Yeung) K.; m. Margaret Anne Soden, June 28, 1975; children: Victoria Xiu-Wen, Elizabeth Xiu-Hui. BA in Econs., Le Moyne Coll., Syracuse, N.Y., 1969; MS in Internat. Mgmt., Am. Grad. Sch. Internat. Mgmt., Phoenix, 1970; grad. Program Mgmt. Devel., Harvard U. Bus. Sch., 1978. Investment officer Am. Internat. Group, N.Y.C., 1971-75; asst. v.p. investment Am. Internat. Assurance Co., Ltd., Singapore, 1975-77; v.p. investment Am. Internat. Assurance Co., Ltd., Hong Kong, 1977-81, sr. v.p. fin., 1981-86, dir., 1983-86; pres. Prudential Asset Mgmt. Asia, Ltd., Hong Kong, 1986—; bd. dirs. Prudential Asia Investments Ltd., Hong Kong, Prudential Asia Capital Ltd., Prudential-Bache Capital Funding Asia Ltd., Dragon Seed Co. Ltd., Brunico Ltd., Winton Trading Co. Ltd., Averina Investments Pte. Ltd., The Hour Glass Pte. Ltd. Club: Harvard Bus. Sch. Assn. (Hong Kong). Office: Prudential Asset Mgmt Asia Ltd, 32-F Alexandra House, 18 Chater Rd, Central Hong Kong Hong Kong

KWOCZYNSKI, JAN KAZIMIERZ, cardiologist; b. Sobeslav, Czechoslovakia, May 14, 1915; s. Stanislaw and Maria Eugenia (Jasica) K.; m. Hanna Zyta Sygietynska, June 13, 1958; 1 dau., Marta. Med. diploma U. Warsaw (Poland), 1939; M.D., U. Wroclaw (Poland), 1949. Intern Dist. Mil. Hosp., Warsaw, 1939, 63 Gen. Hosp., Cairo, Egypt, 1942, RAF Hosp., Habbaniya, Iraq, 1943; resident 5 Polish Gen. Hosp., Casamassima, Italy, 1945, Mcpl. Hosp., Warsaw, 1947-54; reader Postgrad. Med. Inst., Warsaw, 1954-60, prof., head cardiology dept., 1973-80; head cardiology dept. Inst. Rheumatology, Warsaw, 1962-70; prof. Ahmadu Bello U., Kaduna, Nigeria, 1970-72; cons. physician St. Luke's Hosp., Malta, 1981; prof. U. Jos (Nigeria), 1982—. Author: Atlas of Electrocardiography, 1957; Electrocardiography, 1972, 77; Cardiology Problems, 1981. Served with M.E. Polish Forces, 1939-45. Decorated Cross for Bravery (Poland); Africa Star, Italy Star, Rockefeller Found. fellow, 1958-59; named knight Order Poland Restituted, 1978; recipient Polish Nat. Sci. prize, 1953. Fellow Am. Coll. Cardiology, Polish Soc. Cardiology (pres. 1973-79 now hon. mem.). Roman Catholic. Home: 118 J Dabrowskiego, M 61 Warsaw 02-598, Poland

KWOK, KA CHEONG ALEX, physician; b. Hong Kong, Aug. 16, 1950; s. Wai Shing Kwok and Shiu Keung Yam; m. Lee Wai Fung Rosa, Dec. 19, 1978; children—Kwok Ching Ying, Daisy, Kwok Chi Ying, Jasmine. Grad. King's Coll., Hong Kong, 1970. B.Medicine and Surgery, U. Hong Kong, 1979. Diplomate med. bd. Intern, resident Queen Elizabeth Hosp., Hong Kong, 1979-80, Queen Mary Hosp., Hong Kong, 1980; med. supt. S. Lantau, Hong Kong, 1980-82; gen. practice medicine, Lantau, 1982—. Mem. Hong Kong Soc. Community Medicine. Home: Sun Wai Village, No 40, 2d Floor, Pui O, Lantau, Hong Kong Hong Kong Office: Grandview Mansion, Mezz Floor, Mui Wo, Lantau Island Hong Kong

KWOK, RUSSELL CHI-YAN, retail company executive; b. Hong Kong, Mar. 9, 1935; s. Lansing and Corinne (Jue) K.; m. Linda Ling-Hui Cheng, Dec. 18, 1965; children: Linnet, Kurt. BS, U. Calif., San Francisco, 1959, PhD, 1963. Sr. organic chemist Eli Lilly & Co., Indpls., 1964-69; research chemist Cutter Labs, Berkeley, Calif., 1969-72; asst. mgr. The Wing On Co., Ltd., Hong Kong, 1972-73, mgr., 1973-82, exec. dir., 1982-84, gen. mgr., 1984—, also bd. dirs. Patentee in field. Vice chmn. Lingnan Coll. Council, Hong Kong, 1984—; supr. Lingnan Dr. Chung Wing Kwong Meml. Middle Sch., Hong Kong, 1984—; mem. Pharmacy & Poison Appeal Tribunal, Hong Kong, 1984—. Mem. Am. Chem. Soc., AAAS, N.Y. Acad. Sci., Pharm. Soc. Hong Kong. Lodge: Rotary (pres. Hong Kong club 1985-86). Home: Wing On Towers, Jardine's Lookout, Boyce Rd #15B, Hong Kong Hong Kong Office: The Wing On Co Ltd, 211 Des Voeux Rd C, Hong Kong Hong Kong

KWONG, BENGIE M.H., electronics company executive; b. Jan. 18, 1948; m. Rosa Y.L. Wong; children: P.W. Kwong, P.Y. Kwong. MBA, Columbia Pacific U., 1982, postgrad., 1988. Mfg. engr., assoc. engr. Ampex Ferrotec Ltd., Hong Kong, U.S., 1970-72; mgr. ops. Data Recall Ltd., Hong Kong, 1972-74; mgr. quality assurance mil programs Fabri-Tek Ltd., Hong Kong, U.S., 1974-79; mgr. indsl. engring., quality assurance, asst. gen. mgr. Atari, Inc., Hong Kong, U.S., 1980-84; gen. mgr. Wong's Electronics Co. Ltd., Hong Kong, U.S., 1984; regional mgr. Wang Pacific Ltd., Asia Pacific, U.S., 1984-87; dir. purchasing Asia/Pacific Wang Pacific Ltd., Hong Kong, 1987—; lectr. Polytechnic of Hong Kong, 1980-81. Bd. dirs. Vocat. Tng. Council, Hong Kong, 1983. Fellow Brit. Inst. Mgmt., Inst. Indsl. Mgrs., Inst. Mfg., Inst. Quality Assurance; mem. IEEE, Engring Soc. Detroit, NSPE, Assn. MBA Execs., Inst. Dirs., Faculty Secs. Adminstrs. (corp. sec.). Office: Wang Pacific Ltd-Wang Labs Inc, 500 Hennessy Rd, 31/F Hennessy Centre, Hong Kong Hong Kong

KWONG, PETER KONG KIT, bishop; b. Hong Kong, Feb. 28, 1936; s. Kwok Kuen and Ching Lan (Chan) K.; Dip.Arts, Chung Chi Coll., 1962; B.D. Kenyon Coll., 1965, D.D., 1986; M.Theology, Colgate Rochester/Bexley Hall, 1971; m. Ha Wai Chung, July 31, 1965; children—Yim Ming, Veronica, Chun Ming, Ernest, Yan Ming, Grace. Ordained to ministry Anglican Ch., 1965; clergy-in-charge Crown of Thorns Ch., Tsuen Wan, Hong Kong, 1965-66; vicar St. James Ch., Wanchai, Hong Kong, 1967-70; curate St. Paul's Ch., Central, Hong Kong, 1971-72; warden Wen Lin Tang, Chinese U. of Hong Kong, 1972-79, asst. lectr., 1972-79; Diocesan sec. Diocese of Hong Kong and Macau of the Anglican Ch., 1979-80, bishop, 1981—. Chmn., Sheng Kung Hui Sec. and Primary schs., 1981—; hon. pres. Hong Kong Juvenile Care Centre, 1981—, Hong Kong Scout Assn., 1981—, Neighbourhood Advice Action Council, 1981—; bd. dirs. Central Hosp., 1981-83, Chinese Christian Chs. Union, 1981—, United Christian Hosp., 1987—; mem. univ. ct. Hong Kong U., 1981—; exec. com. Hong Kong Christian Council, 1980-84; trustee Chung Chi Coll., Chinese U. Hong Kong, Alice Ho Mi u Ling Nethersole Hosp., 1983-85; hon. v.p. Hong Kong Girl Guides Assn., 1981—; pres. Hong Kong council Boys' Brigade, 1982—; mem. basic law drafting com. Hong Kong spl. adminstrv. region People's Republic of China, 1985—, also mem. consultative com. Mem. Christian Assn. for Execs. (patron), Hong Kong Tchrs. Assn. (patron), Council of Chs. of East Asia (hon. treas. 1981-83), Hong Kong Christian Council (chmn. 1983—). Address: 1 Lower Albert Rd, Hong Kong Hong Kong

KWONG, YUNG-HUI, finance company executive; b. Kwantung, China, Jan. 10, 1908; s. Tak Gin and Shee (Au) K.; B.A., Stanford, 1929; C.E., Cornell U., 1932; m. Jean Woon Gin Leung, 1938; children—Wei-June, Wei-Ling, Chun-Chuan, Hsueh-Chuan, Wei-Ching. Mgr., exec. engr. Automotive Parts Mfr. Kiangsi Provincial Govt., Nanchang, China, 1936-38; exec. engr. S.W. Transp. Adminstrn., China Burma Rd., 1938-41; chmn. Jing Hong Trading Corp., Rangoon, Burma, 1942-60; founder, chmn., chief exec. officer, Autocars (Burma) Ltd., Rangoon, 1950-60, Gen. Engring. and Trading Corp., Rangoon, 1951-60, Ensign Motors, Ltd., Rangoon, 1948-60; founder, chmn .China Engrs. Holdings Ltd., Hong Kong, 1961-75; founder, chmn. Intercontinent Finance Corp. Ltd., 1946—, Intercontinent Devel. Corp. Ltd. Mem. China Inst. Engrs., 1933-45. Rotarian (past dir.). Office: Intercontinent Fin Corp, Dominion Ctr, Suite 909, 43-59 Queen's Rd E, Hong Kong Hong Kong

KYDD, GEORGE HERMAN, physiologist; b. Eagle Rock, Va., Aug. 29, 1920; s. George Herman and Nellie Glare (Marshall) K.; m. Mary Louise Penman, Apr. 15, 1944; children: Brenda, Jean, George Herman, Richard Adrian. BS, W.Va. State Coll., 1942; MS, Ohio State U., 1950, PhD, 1955. Research physiologist Aviation Med. Acceleration Lab., Warminster, Pa., 1955-70; assoc. in physiology U. Pa. Sch. Medicine, Phila., 1955-70; with USN Air. Devel. Ctr., Warminster, 1971—, adminstr. phys. sci., 1977—81, research physiologist, 1981—. Served to 1st lt. U.S. Army, 1942-46. Recipient 1st ann. Aerospace award Nat. Med. Assn., 1970. Fellow Aerospace Med. Assn. (mem. sci. program com. 1965); mem. Am. Physiol. Soc., N.Y. Acad. Scis., Aerospace Physiol. Soc. (Fred Hitchcock award 1972), Sigma Xi. Unitarian. Home: 6631 Boyer St Philadelphia PA 19119 Office: US Naval Air Devel Ctr Warminster PA 18974

KYEWSKI, BRUNO ANTON, immunologist; b. Bad Peteratal, Fed. Republic Germany, Nov. 2, 1950; s. Bruno and Maria (Dinger) K. MD, U. Bonn, Fed. Republic Germany, 1975; PhD, U. Freiburg, Fed. Republic Germany, 1980. Postdoctoral fellow Cancer Biology Research Lab. Dept. Radiology Stanford (Calif.) U., 1980-83; staff scientist German Cancer Research Ctr., Heidelberg, Fed. Republic Germany, 1984—. Recipient Henry Kaplan award Organizing Com. Modern Trends in Leukemia Research, Wilsede, Fed. Republic Germany, 1984. Fellow Studienstiftung des Deutschen Volkes. Roman Catholic. Office: German Cancer Research Ctr, Im Neuenheimer Feld 280, D-69 Heidelberg Federal Republic of Germany

KYLE, ALASTAIR BOYD See CUIL DE STRATCLUT, ALECSANDER

KYLE, NOELINE JUNE, historian, educator; b. Kempsey, Australia, Dec. 14, 1940; d. Lawrence Kyle and Kathleen (Clare) Kirkpatrick; div.; children: Susan, Brad Williamson. BA with 1st class honors, U. Newcastle, 1979, PhD, 1983. Lectr. James Cook U., Townsville, Australia, 1984; lectr. edn. U. Wollongong, Australia, 1984—. Author: Tracing Family History in Australia, 1985, Her Natural Destiny: The Education of Women in New South Wales, 1986, We Should've Listened to Grandma, 1988; contbr. articles to profl. jours. Home: 13 Robert St, Corrimed 2518, Wollongong 2500, Australia Office: U Wollongong Faculty Edn, PO Box 1144, Wollongong 2500, Australia

KYLE, ROBERT CAMPBELL, publishing executive; b. Cleve., Jan. 6, 1935; s. C. Donald and Mary Alice (King) K.; m. Barbara Ann Battey, June 8, 1957; children—Peter F., Christopher C., Scott G. B.S., U. Colo., 1956; M.A., Case Western Res. U., 1958; M.B.A., Harvard U., 1962, D.B.A., 1966. Ptnr. McLagan & Co., Chgo., 1966-67; founder, pres. Devel. Systems Corp. (now subs. Longman Group USA), 1967-82, pres. Longman Group USA, Chgo., 1982—; dir. Grubb & Ellis Co., San Francisco, 1976—; bd. dirs. Addison-Wesley-Longman Group Ltd., U.K., 1987—. Author: Property Mamangement, 1979; co-author: Modern Real Estate Practice, 1967, How to Profit form Real Estate, 1988. Mem. Real Estate Educators Assn. (pres. 1981), Internat. Assn. Fin. Planning, Real Estate Securities and Syndication Inst. (dir. book clinic). Clubs: Harvard (N.Y.C.), Economic (Chgo.), Chgo. Yacht, San Diego Yacht. Avocations: Competitive yacht racing; tennis. Home: 935 Private Rd Winnetka IL 60093 Office: Longman Group USA Inc 500 N Dearborn St Chicago IL 60610

KYLIAN, JIRI, choreographer; b. Prague, Czechoslovakia, Mar. 21, 1947. Student of Zora Semberova, from 1962; hon. degree Royal Ballet Sch., London, 1967-68. Dancer, choreographer Stuttgart Ballet (W.Ger.), from 1968; co-artist, choreographer, dir. Netherlands Dance Theatre, 1975-78, artistic dir., choreographer, 1978—; choreographer: Symphony of Psalms, Soldiers' Mass, Sinfonietta, Dream Dances, Children's Games, Transfigured Night, Viewers, Cathédrale Engloutie, Torso, Stoolgame, Symphony in D, November Steps, Glagolitic Mass, Overgrown Path, Intimate Letters, Forgotten Land, Stamping Ground, Dreamtime, Curses and Blessings, Wiegelied, Return to the Stange Land, l'Enfant et les Sortilèges (Hans Christian Andersen Ballet Performance award, 1988), L'Histoire du Soldat, numerous others. Office: Nederlands Dans Theater, Schedeldoekshaven 60, 2511 EN Gravenhage The Netherlands

KYPRIANOU, SPYROS, former President of Republic of Cyprus; b. Limassol, Cyprus, Oct. 28, 1932; s. Achilles and Marie (Araouzou) K.; student higher edn., econs. and commerce City of London Coll., 1950-51; student Gray's Inn, London, 1950-54; diploma in comparative law; m. Mimi Papatheoklitou, Aug. 5, 1956; children: Achilleas, Marcos. Barrister; sec. to Archbishop Makarios, London, 1952-54, Cyprus Ethnarchy, London, 1954-56, 57-59, rep., N.Y.C., 1956-57; minister of justice, 1960; minister of fgn. affairs, 1960-72; individual practice law, 1972-76; participant peace meetings and govtl. formation meetings, 1974-76; organizer Democratic Party of Cyprus, 1976, now leader; mem. Ho. of Reps., 1976—, pres., 1976-77; pres. Republic of Cyprus, 1977-88; participant Com. Ministers of Council of Europe, Strasburg and Paris, pres. Apr.-Dec. 1967; participant numerous internat. confs. Decorated grand cross Order George I Greece; grand cross Fed. Republic Germany; grand star Republic UAR; grand cross Order of Boyaca (Colombia); grand cross Order of Merit (Chile); Order St. Aekaterini Sinai (eccles.); Grand Silver Cross of Austria, Star of Socialist Republic of Romania; Highest medal of Syria; Order of White Lion 1st class (Czechoslovakia); Gt. Star of Friendship of Peoples (E. Ger.); Highest Hon. Distinction of Yugoslavia; Ojaswi Rajanya Nepal Order; Grand Cross of Holy Sepulchre; Order Stara Planina with ribbon (Bulgaria); Highest Honor of Hungary, 1981; Grand Cross Order of Savior (Greece), 1983. Address: Presdl Palace, Nicosia Cyprus

KYRKLUND, BORJE RAGNAR EUGEN, United Nations official; b. Helsinki, Finland, Nov. 16, 1932; s. Ragnar Evald and Gunvor (Sundqvist) K.; m. Tove-Maj Nordstrom, July 13, 1957 (div. Mar. 1974); children—Tua-Li Maria, Ann-Sofi Kristina, Eva-Stina Teresa; m. Jennifer Ann Streeter, May 17, 1976; children—Johanna Kate, Melanie Marika. M.Sc. in Phys. Chemistry, U. Helsinki, 1960. Scientist, Finnish Pulp and Paper Research Inst., Helsinki, 1960-65, head dept., 1966-72; ind. cons. regional Latin Am. projects, aos nat. projects Argentina, Cuba, India, Peru, Hdqrs. FAO, 1971-75; forestry officer FAO, UN, Rome, 1976-79, chief pulp and paper br. Forest Industries div., 1979—. Contbr. articles to profl. jours., chpts. to books. Served to sub-lt. inf. Finnish Army, 1959-60. Mem. Finnish Paper Engrs. Assn., Indian Pulp and Paper Tech. Assn. Office: FAO, Via Delle Terme di Caracalla, 00100 Rome Italy

KYUNO, SHOJI, mathematics educator; b. Ishizuka, Ibaraki, Japan, Jan. 2, 1929; d. Sajuro and Tomi Kyuno. BS, Tohoku U., Sendai, Japan, 1951; DSc, Tsukuba U., Ibaraki, 1981. Lectr. Tohoku Gakuin U., Sendai, 1964-67, asst. prof., 1967-82, prof., 1982—. Organizer Internat. Conf. on Radicals; Theory and Applications, Sendai, Japan, 1988. Mem. Math. Soc. of Japan, Info. Processing Soc. of Japan, Am. Math. Soc. Home: 2 13 59, Izumi 983, Japan Office: Tohoku Gakuin U, Tagajo, Miyagi 985, Japan

KYYRÖ, JYRI, footwear company executive; b. Helsinki, Finland, Aug. 10, 1948; s. Kauko Urmas and Marjatta (Tolvanen) K.; m. Maarit Koski, June 2, 1972; children: Kati, Jukka. MSc in Chemistry, Turko U., 1973. Lab. mgr. Nokia (Finland) Rubber Industries Footwear Div., 1975-78, tech. devel. mgr., 1978-86, prodn. mgr., safety products, 1986-87, devel. mgr. safety products, 1988—. Home: Mustanlahdenk 1B 81, SF 33210 Tampere Finland Office: Nokia Footwear, PO Box 20, SF 37101 Nokia Finland

KYZAR, OLLIE JEANETTE, educator; b. Brookhaven, Miss., Oct. 7, 1933; d. Marcel Wooden and Annie Leona (Brister) Grice; m. Reese Eugene Kyzar, June 16, 1953. B.S. in Edn., Delta State Coll., 1960, postgrad., 1972-74, 79-81, 88—; postgrad. U. So. Miss., 1960-61, 65-66, 69-70, U. Miss., 1961-63. Tchr. English, Fielding L. Wright High Sch., Rolling Fork, Miss., 1960-61; tchr. Fielding L. Wright Elem. Sch., Rolling Fork, 1961-70; homebound tchr. Rolling Fork Elem. Sch., 1970-73, tchr. reading and math., 1973-84, resource tchr. computer assisted instrn., 1984-88, asst. prin., 1988—; evaluator Nat. Council Accreditation Tchr. Edn., Washington, 1982—; mem. supt.'s adv. bd., Rolling Fork, 1981-83; mem. steering com. on sch. evaluation So. Assn. Colls. and Schs., 1962-73. Sunday sch. tchr., former dir. Acteens, mem. Womens Missionary Union, 1st Baptis Ch. Rolling Fork, 1959. Mem. Smithsonian Instn. (assoc.), Nat. Trust Historic Preservation, Fielding L. Wright Tchrs. Assn. (pres. 1966-67), Rolling Fork Assn. Educators (pres. 1977-78, 81-82, Disting. Service award 1978, 82), Miss. Assn. Educators (workshop presenter 1982-84), NEA, Miss. Ednl. Computing Assn., Assn. Supervision and Curiculum Devel., Miss. for Ednl. Broadcasting, Internat. Reading Assn., Miss. Reading Assn., Kappa Delta Pi. Avocations: reading; listening to music; walking; riding bicycle. Home: 105 N 2nd St Rolling Fork MS 39159 Office: Rolling Fork Elem Sch 600 S Pkwy Rolling Fork MS 39159

LAALY, HESHMAT OLLAH, research chemist; b. Kermanshah, Iran, June 23, 1927; came to Germany, 1951, Can., 1967, U.S., 1984; s. Jacob and Saltanat (Afshani) L.; m. Parvaneh Modarai, Oct. 7, 1963; (div. 1971); children: Ramesh, Edmond S.; m. Parivash M. Farahmand, Feb. 7, 1982. BS in Chemistry, U. Stuttgart, Republic of Germany, 1955, MS in Chemistry, 1958, PhD in Chemistry, 1962. Chief chemist Kress Sohne, Krefeld, Republic of Germany, 1963-67; analytical chemist Gulf Oil Research Ctr., Montreal, Que., Can., 1967-70; material scientist Bell-Northern Research, Ottawa, Ont., Can., 1970-71; research officer NRC of Can., Ottawa, 1972-84; pres. Roofing Materials Sci. and Tech., Los Angeles, 1984—; scientist, bd. dirs. Non Smokers Assn. Ottawa, 1982; lectr. profl. assns., U.N. Devel. Programs worldwide. Mem. Chem. Inst. Can., Inst. Roofing and Waterproofing Cons., Single-Ply Roofing Inst., Assn. Profl. Engrs. Ontario, AAAS (Can.), Am. Chem. Soc., ASTM, Internat. Union of Testing and Research Labs. for Material and Structures (tech. com. 1975)), UN Indsl. Devels. Orgns., Internat. Conf. Bldg. Ofcls., Can. Standard Assn., Can. Gen. Standards Bd. Home and Office: 9037 Monte Mar Dr Los Angeles CA 90035

LAANO, ARCHIE BIENVENIDO MAAÑO, cardiologist; b. Tayabas, Quezon, Philippines, Aug. 10, 1939; s. Francisco M. and Iluminada (Maaño) L.; naturalized U.S. citizen; A.A., U. Philippines, 1958, B.S., 1959, M.D., 1963; m. Maria Eleazar, May 2, 1964; 1 dau., Sylvia Marie. Rotating intern Hosp. St. Raphael, New Haven, 1963-64; resident internal medicine, 1964-65; rotating resident pulmonary diseases Laurel Heights Hosp., Shelton, Conn., 1965; affiliated rotating resident Yale-New Haven Med. Center, 1965; resident internal medicine Westchester County Med. Center, Valhalla, N.Y., 1965-66, resident cardiology, 1966-67; resident fellow cardiology Maimonides Med. Center, Bklyn., 1967-68; rotating sr. resident cardiology Coney Island Hosp., Bklyn., 1967-68; fellow internal medicine Mercy Hosp., Rockville Centre, N.Y., 1968-70; med. dir. 54 Main St. Med. Center, Hempstead, N.Y., 1971-76, Bloomingdale's, Garden City, N.Y., 1972—, Esselte Pendaflex Corp., Garden City, 1976—; attending staff Nassau County (N.Y.) Med. Center, Hempstead Gen. Hosp.; practice medicine specializing in cardiology, internal medicine, Nassau County, 1971—; chief med. services, chief profl. services U.S. Army 808th Sta. Hosp., Hempstead, N.Y., 1979—; col. 1st U.S. Army AMEDD Augmentation Detachment, Ft. Meade, Md., 1980—; med. dir. Cities Service Oil Co. (CITGO), L.I. div., 1972—; mem. adv. bd. Guardian Bank, Hempstead; cons. physician ICC, Citgo, Liberty Mut. Ins. Co. Boston, 1972—, U.S. Dept. Transp. Diplomate Am. Bd. Internal Medicine. Fellow Internat.Coll. Angiology, Am. Coll. Angiology, Am. Coll. Internat. Physicians, Internat. Coll. Applied Nutrition, Am. Soc. Contemporary Medicine and Surgery, Acad. Preventive Medicine, Internat. Acad. Med. Preventives, Philippine Coll. Physicians; mem. Am. Coll. Cardiology, AMA, N.Y. State, Nassau County med. socs., Am. Heart Assn., N.Y. Cardiol. Soc., World Med. Assn., Royal Soc. Medicine (London), Nassau Acad. Medicine, Am., N.Y. State, Nassau socs. internal medicine, N.Y. Soc. Acupuncture for Physicians, Am. Geriatrics Soc., Nassau Physicians Guild, Res. Officers Assn. U.S., Assn. Mil. Surgeons, Assn. Philippine Physicians Am. (bd. govs. rep. N.Y. State 1984-86, v.p., chmn. com. nominations and election 1987-88); Assn. Philippine Physicians of N.Y. (founding v.p., pres. 1985-87, pres. emeritus 1988—, chmn. com. on constituion and by-laws, nominations and election, med. coordinator Internat. Games for Disabled Olympics 1984), U.S. Knights of Rizal, U. Philippines Med. Alumni Soc. (pres. class of 1963, 1981—), U. Philippines Med. Alumni Soc. Am. (chmn. bd. 1985—), Phi Kappa Mu (overseas coordinator U. Philippines 1985—). Clubs: Garden City Lions (program chmn. 1975—, chmn. bd. 1978—, pres. 1978-79); West Point Officers, Garden City Country. Home: 80 Stratford Ave Garden City NY 11530 Office: 230 Hilton Ave Suite 106 Plaza 230 Profl Condo Garden City-Hempstead Border NY 11550

LABAEYE, PIERRETTE, otolaryngologist; b. Le Havre, France, Oct. 17, 1932; d. André and Geneviève (Souron) Roze; m. François Labaeye, Oct. 13, 1958; children: Christophe, Vincent. MD, U. Nancy, 1960. Tchr. physiology Nancy's (France) State Hosp., 1957-58, otolaryngologist, surgeon, 1963—; cons. ISIN (engring. sch.), Nancy, 1970, INRS (Inst. for Safety), Nancy, 1970, tchr., 1970, research worker (sci. inst.), 1970. Mem. Sauvegarde de l'art français, Paris, 1978—. Mem. Soc. Française d'Otorhinolaryngology, Soc. Belge d'Otorhinolaryngology, Soc. Otorhinolaryngology de l'Est (pres. 1987-88). Roman Catholic. Club: Cravache du Toulois (Toulouse) (v.p. 1986-87). Home: 6 rue de Manége, 54000 Nancy France Office: Hosp Cen-ORL, 54000 Nancy France

LABARBERA, ANDREW RICHARD, physiology and ob-gyn educator; b. Teaneck, N.J., Oct. 6, 1948; s. Mario Richard and Georgine (Mart) LaB. B.S. cum laude, Iona Coll., 1970; M.Phil., Columbia U. Coll. Physicians and Surgeons, 1974, M.A., 1974, Ph.D., 1975. Instr. dept. biology Iona Coll., 1970; NIH predoctoral trainee, 1971-75; staff assoc. Ctr. Reproductive Scis., Columbia U., N.Y.C., 1975-77; research fellow Mayo Grad. Sch. Medicine, Rochester, Minn., 1977-80; asst. prof. physiology Northwestern U. Med. Sch., Chgo., 1980-86, assoc. prof. physiology 1986-88, asst. prof. ob-gyn, 1985-86, assoc. prof. ob-gyn, 1986-88; dir. R.I.A. labs. Ctr. for Endocrinology, Metabolism and Nutrition, 1980-85; also dir. in vitro fertilization labs Prentice Women's Hosp. and Maternity Ctr., 1985-88; assoc. prof., asst. dir. ob-gyn U. Cin. Coll. Medicine, 1988—; adj. assoc. prof. physiology, 1985-88. Contbr. articles to profl. jours. Bd. dirs. West Wellington Condominium Assn., 1984-85; pres. Sangamon Loft Condominium Assn., 1985-88. Recipient New Investigator award Am. Diabetes Assn., 1982; grantee Population Council, 1972-75, Northwestern U., 1980-81, USPHS-NIH, 1982—, U.S. Dept. Agr., 1986—. Mem. AAAS, Am. Inst. Biol. Sci., Am. Physiol. Soc., Am. Soc. Zoologists, Chgo. Assn. Reproductive Endocrinologists, Am. Fertility Soc., Endocrine Soc., Soc. Expl. Biology and Medicine, Soc. Study of Reproduction (chmn. info. mgmt. com. 1983-85, chmn. membership com. 1987-88), Tissue Culture Assn., Sigma Xi, Beta Beta Beta. Avocation: music. Home: 1168 Eversole Rd Cincinnati OH 45230 Office: U Cincinnati Coll Medicine Dept Ob-Gyn 231 Bethesda Ave Cincinnati OH 45267

LABAT, JOSEPH ERNEST MARC, sugar estate executive; b. Curepipe, Plaines Wilhems, Mauritius, June 4, 1926; s. Theodore Ernest Edouard and Marie Marguerite (Morel) L.; m. Marie Ellen De Chapuiset Le Merle, Dec. 19, 1951; children—Marie-Ellen, Brigite, Jean-Marc, Jean-Pierre, Dominique, Pauline, Vincent, Catherine. Diploma in Sugar Tech. and Agronomy, Coll. Agr., Reduit, Mauritius, 1945-47. Chief agrl. chemist Mon Desert-Alma Sugar Estate, Moka, Mauritius, 1948-49; tech. salesman Piat & Co. Ltd., Port-Louis, Mauritius, 1950-53; chief chemist, asst. factory mgr. Beau Plan Sugar Estate, Pamplemousses, Mauritius, 1954-62, factory mgr., 1963-67, sugar estate mgr., 1968—; chmn. Sugar Transport Ltd., Port-Louis, 1984—; dir. Camarons Hatchery Co. Ltd., Montresor, Mauritius, Camarons Prodn. Co. Ltd., Ferney, Mauritius. Co-author: Official Methods of Control and Analysis for Mauritius Sugar Factories, 1964. Sec. St. Francois d'Assise Ch. Com., Pamplemousses, 1968—. Mem. Mauritius Chamber Agr., Mauritius Sugar Producers' Assn., Societe de Technologie Agricole et Sucriere de Maurice, Royal Soc. Arts and Sci. Mem. Social Democratic Party. Roman Catholic. Clubs: Dodo (Curepipe), Grand Baie Yacht. Avocations: bowling; tennis; volleyball; swimming; boating. Home and Office: Beau Plan Sugar Estate, Pamplemousses Mauritius

LABESSE, JEAN-PIERRE, mathematician, educator; b. Paris, Jan. 4, 1943; s. Marcelin and Fernande (Imbert) L.; m. Therese Dubois-Violette, Apr. 28, 1967; children: Gilles, Sonia. Degree in Math., E.N.S. Ulm, Paris, 1967. Editor, author: Varieétés de Shimura et Fonctions L, 1979. Served with French Army, 1971-72. Mem. Societe Math. de France, Am. Math. Soc., Club Alpin Français.

LABILLE, JEAN-BERNARD, business executive; b. Nogent, France, June 14, 1945; Arrived in Senegal, 1957; s. Bernard and Solange L.; m. Catherine Fournier, July 27, 1973; children: Guillaume, Mathieu, Amanda. Student, Sup de Co., Montpellier, Senegal, 1969. Comml. dir. AFCO, Dakar, Senegal, 1971-75, adj. dir., 1975-80, dir. gen., 1980—. Lodge: Rotary. Home: 55 Hann Residence, BP 2056 Dakar Senegal Office: AFCO, PO Box 2056, Dakar Senegal

LABLANCHE, JEAN-MARC ANDRE, cardiologist, educator; b. Langres, Haute-Marne, France, June 4, 1946; s. Marcel Georges and Paulette (Renard) L.; m. Brigitte Laurence Lespagnol, Nov. 7, 1969; children: Christelle, Catherine. MD, U. Medicine, Lille, France, 1975. Intern, resident U. Hosp. U. Medicine, 1973-77, from asst. prof. cardiology to assoc. prof.,

1977—; lectr. in field. Author books; contbr. articles to med. jours. Served with French Health Corps, 1972-73. Fellow Am. Coll. Cardiology (assoc.); mem. European Soc. Cardiology, Société Française Cardiologie. Roman Catholic. Office: Hopital Cardiologique, Lille, 59037 Nord France

LABONTE, JOVITE, insurance company executive; b. Providence, R.I., Jan. 16, 1933; s. Jovite and Madeleine (Blake) LaB.; m. Jane Ann Lipscomb, Nov. 1, 1958; children: Joanne, David, Tracy. A.B. with honors, Brown U., 1956. Agt. N.Y. Life Ins. Co., Arlington, Va., 1960-62, asst. mgr., 1962-64; regional dir. Alexander Hamilton Life Ins. Co., Grosse Pointe, Mich., 1964-65; v.p. Alexander Hamilton Life Ins. Co., Farmington, Mich., 1965-71; exec. v.p. Gt. Am. Life Ins. Co., Los Angeles, 1971-72, pres., 1972—, chief exec. officer, 1972. Served to 1st lt. USMC, 1956-60. Mem Am. Council Life Ins. (chmn. exec. round table com. 1983-86, bd. dirs. 1984—); mem. Assn. Calif, Life Ins. Cos. (dir. 1982—), Nat. Assn. Life Underwriters. Home: 807 Napoli Pacific Palisades CA 90272 Office: Great Am Life Ins Co 6330 San Vicente Blvd Los Angeles CA 90048

LABOUX, LOUIS ANGE, cardiologist; b. Vertou, France, Feb. 10, 1926; s. Louis Francois and Jeanne Marie (Couprie) L.; m. Colette Olga Templier, July 10, 1953; children: Catherine, Sophie, Francoise, Olivier. BA, St. Stanislas, Nantes, 1945. With Extern Hosp., Nantes, Frances, 1949-50; intern Extern Hosp., Nantes, 1950-54; diploma specialist in serology U. Paris, 1954; diploma specialist in microbiology Pasteur Inst., Paris, 1955; diploma specialist in immunology U. Paris, 1955; lab. chief U. Nantes, 1955-59, asst., 1959-64; practicing medicine specializing in cardiology Paris, 1961—; cardiologist U. Nantes Hosp., 1962—. Contbr. articles to profl. jours. Served to capt. French mil., 1956-60. Fellow French Cardiology Soc.; French Pediatric Cardiology Soc., French Ultrasounds Soc. Roman Catholic. Club: Cardio (La Baule, France, nat. chmn. 1986). Home: 40 Blvd Pasteur, 44100 Nantes France Office: Med Cabinet, 38 Bis Blvd Pasteur, 44100 Nantes France

LABRID, CLAUDE, research institute executive, pharmacologist; b. Neuvic, Correze, France, Jan. 20, 1938; s. Antonio and Fernande (Marin) L.; m. Nicole Lemarchand, Sept. 7, 1963; children—Laurence, Catherine. Licence es Sciences, U. Bordeaux (France), 1965, D.E.A. Biologie, 1967; Docteur es Sciences, U. Clermont-Ferrand, France, 1975. Pharmacologist, Centre Européen de Recherches Mauvernay, Riom, France, 1968-75, head pharmacology CERM Organon, 1976-81; sci. dir. Institut de Recherches Servier, Suresnes, France, 1981-85; dir. sci. devel. Internat. Inst. Research, Neuilly, France, 1986—. Contbr. numerous articles to profl. jours., 1970—. Mem. Internat. Soc. Heart Research, N.Y. Acad. Scis., Société de Chimie Therapeutique, Association Franç aise des Pharmacologistes, Association des Physiologistes, Biochem. Soc., European Soc. Pneumology. Office: IRI Servier, 22 rue Garnier, 92200 Neuilly France

LABSVIRS, JANIS, economist, emeritus educator; b. Bilska, Latvia, Mar. 13, 1907; s. Karlis and Kristina L.; Mag.Oec., Latvian State U., 1930; M.S., Butler U., 1956; Ph.D., Ind. U., 1959. Tchr., Latvia, 1930-36; dir. dept. edn. Fedn. Latvian Trade Unions, 1936-37; v.p. Kr. Baron's U., Extension, Riga, Latvia, 1938-40, also exec. v.p. Filma, Inc., 1939-40; with UNRRA and Internat. Refugee Orgn., Esslingen, Germany, 1945-50; asst. prof. econs. Ind. State U., Terre Haute, 1959-62, assoc. prof., 1963-68, prof., 1969-73, prof. emeritus, 1973—; head dept. public and social affairs Latvian Ministry for Social Affairs, 1938-40; dir. Sch. of Commerce and Gymnasium, Tukums, Latvia, 1941-44. Danforth grantee, 1961; Ind. State U. research grantee, 1966. Mem. Am. Latvian Assn., Am. Assn. Advancement Slavic Studies, Assn. Advancement Baltic Studies, Am. Econ. Assn., Royal Econ. Soc. Lutheran. Author: Local Government's Accounting and Management Practices, 1947; A Case Study in the Sovietization of the Baltic States: Collectivization of Latvian Agriculture 1944-1956, 1959; Atminas un Pardomas, 1984; Karlis Ulmanis, 1987; contbr. articles profl. jours. Home: 3313 Hovey St Indianapolis IN 46218

LABUDDE, ROY CHRISTIAN, lawyer; b. Milw., July 21, 1921; s. Roy Lewis and Thea (Otteson) LaB.; m. Anne P. Held, June 7, 1952; children—Jack, Peter, Michael, Susan, Sarah. A.B., Carleton Coll., 1943; J.D., Harvard U., 1949. Bar; Wis. 1949, U.S. Dist. Cts. (ea. and we. dists.) Wis. 1950, U.S. Ct. Appeals (7th cir.) 1950, U.S. Supreme Ct. 1957. Assoc., Michael, Best & Friedrich, Milw., 1949-57, ptnr., 1958—; dir. DEC-Inter, Inc., Milw. Western Bank, Western Bancshares, Inc., Superior Die Set Corp., Chmn., bd. dirs. Milw. div. Am. Cancer Soc. Served to lt. j.g. USNR, 1943-46. Mem. Milw. Estate Planning Counsel (past pres.), Wis. Bar Assn., Wis. State Bar Attys. (chmn. tax sch., bd. dirs. taxation sect.). Republican. Episcopalian. Clubs: University, Milw., Milw. Country (Milw.); Mason, Shriners. Home: 9000 N Bayside Dr Milwaukee WI 53217 Office: 250 E Wisconsin Ave Room 2000 Milwaukee WI 53202

LACAS, MARIE-LISE CHARLOTTE, psychiatrist, psychoanalyst; b. Paris, Feb. 6, 1933; d. Simon and Simone Thérèse (Lemaire) Mondszain; married; 1 child, Samuel Fernand. Thèse de Médecine, Med. U. Algiers, 1960; lic. de psychologie, Algiers U., Strasbourg and Algiers, 1959. Externe titular Civil Hosp., Algiers, 1953-55, interne titular, 1956-57, 59, interne disposable, 1958; probationer Ste. Française de Psychoanalyse, Paris, 1962-64; analyste membre de l'école Ecole Freudienne de Paris, 1964-79; practice psychoanalysis, Paris, 1962—. Contbr. articles to books and jours. in fields of psychiatry and psychoanalysis. Mem. Ctr. de Formation et de Recherches Psychoanalytiques. Home and Office: 13 Boulevard Raspail, 75007 Paris France

LACASSE, JAMES PHILLIP, lawyer, tax counsel; b. Delta, Colo., Oct. 21, 1948; s. Kyndall and Elizabeth Ann (Harrington) L.; m. Lynda Diane Manly, June 17, 1978; 1 child, Laura Elizabeth. BS in Acctg. with distinction, Ariz. State U., 1970; JD, Coll. of William and Mary, 1973. Bar: Va. 1973. Tax staff Arthur Andersen & Co., Washington, 1973-75; corp. tax coordinator Continental Telecom Inc., Atlanta, 1975-78; internat. tax mgr. R.J. Reynolds Co., Winston-Salem, N.C., 1978-83, western hemisphere treas., 1983-84; sr. tax counsel Sea-Land Corp., Iselin, N.J., 1984-86; dir. taxes Am. Pres. Cos., Ltd., Oakland, Calif., 1986—. Mem. Downtown Crisis Ctr. Winston-Salem, 1983; chairperson social ministry com. St. John's Lutheran Ch., Summit, N.J., 1986. Named one of Outstanding Young Men of Am. U.S. Jaycees, 1983. Mem. ABA, Va. Bar Assn., Tax Execs. Inst. Home: 4 Cavanaugh Ct Piedmont CA 94610 Office: Am Pres Cos Ltd 1800 Harrison St Oakland CA 94612

LACEY, JOHN HUBERT, psychiatrist; b. Loughborough, Leicestershire, Eng., Nov. 4, 1944; s. Percy Hubert and Margaret Sheila (Neal) L.; m. Susan Millicent Liddiard, Feb.7, 1976; children: Emma, Benjamin, Jonathan. B in Medicine and B in Surgery, U. St. Andrews, Scotland, 1969; diploma in obstetrics, Royal Coll. Obstetricians and Gynaecologists, London, 1971; M in Philosophy, London U., 1974; D Med. with commendation, Dundee U., Scotland, 1988. Resident NHS, Dundee, 1969-70, St. Thomas's Hosp., 1970-72, St. George's Hosp., 1972-74; research worker St. George's Hosp. Med. Sch., London, 1974-75, lectr., 1975-78, sr. lectr., hon. cons., 1980—; sr. lectr., hon. cons. Middlesex Hosp. Med. Sch., London, 1978-80; cons. in charge Bulimia Clinic St. George's, London, 1980—; reader U. London, 1988—. Author various books; contbr. articles on eating disorders and gen. psychiatry to profl. jours. Freeman City of London, 1986, Plaisterers' Livery Co., London, 1978. Fellow Royal Coll. Psychiatrists; mem. Brit. Med. Assn., Internat. Coll. Psychosomatic Medicine (sec. 1984—). Club: Athenaeum (London). Home: 5 Atherton Dr, London SW 19, England Office: St George's Hosp Med Sch, Cranmere Terr, Jenner Wing, London, Tooting SW17 0RE, England

LACH, ALMA ELIZABETH, food and cooking writer, consultant; b. Petersburg, Ill.; d. John H. and Clara E. (Boeker) Satorius; diplome de Cordon Bleu, Paris, 1956; m. Donald F. Lach, Mar. 18, 1939; 1 dau., Sandra Judith. Feature writer Children's Activities mag., 1954-55; creator, performer TV show Let's Cook, children's cooking show, 1955; hostess weekly food program on CBS, 1962-66, performer TV show Over Easy, PBS, 1977-78; food editor Chgo. Daily Sun-Times, 1957-65; pres. Alma Lach Kitchens Inc., Chgo., 1966—; dir. Alma Lach Cooking Sch., Chgo.; lectr. U. Chgo. Downtown Coll., Gourmet Inst., U. Md., 1963, Modesto (Calif.) Coll., 1978, U. Chgo., 1981; resident master Shoreland Hall, U. Chgo., 1978-81; food cons. Food Bus. Mag., 1964-66, Chgo.'s New Pump Room, Lettuce Entertain You, Bitter End Resort, Brit. V.I., Midway Airlines, Flying Food Fare, Inc., Berghoff Restaurant, Hans' Bavarian Lodge, Unocal '76, Sweetwater Restaurant, Peer Foods, Univ. Club Chgo.; columnist Modern Packaging, 1967-68, Travel & Camera, 1969, Venture, 1970, Chicago mag., 1978, Bon Appetit, 1980, Tribune Syndicate, 1982, The World & I, 1988. Recipient Pillsbury award, 1958; Grocery Mfrs. Am. Trophy award, 1959, certificate of Honor, 1961; Chevalier du Tastevin, 1962; Commanderie de l'Ordre des Anysetiers du Roy, 1963; Confrerie de la Chaine des Rotisseurs, 1964; Les Dames D'Escoffier, 1982. Mem. U. Chgo. Settlement League, Am. Assn. Food Editors (chmn. 1959). Clubs: Tavern, Quadrangle (Chgo.). Author: A Child's First Cookbook, 1950; The Campbell Kids Have a Party, 1953; The Campbell Kids at Home, 1953; Let's Cook, 1956; Candlelight Cookbook, 1959; Cooking a la Cordon Bleu, 1970; Alma's Almanac, 1972; Hows and Whys of French Cooking, 1974, The World and I, 1988. Contbr. to World Book Yearbook, 1961-75, Grolier Soc. Yearbook, 1962. Home and Office: 5750 Kenwood Ave Chicago IL 60637

LACHANCE, PAUL ALBERT, food science educator, clergyman; b. St. Johnsbury, Vt., June 5, 1933; s. Raymond John and Lucienne (Landry) L.; m. Therese Cecile Cote; children: Michael P., Peter A., M.-Andre, Susan A. B.S., St. Michael's Coll., 1955; postgrad., U. Vt., 1955-57; Ph.D., U. Ottawa, 1960; D.Sc. (hon.), St. Michael's Coll., 1982. Ordained deacon Roman Cath. Ch., 1977. Aerospace biologist Aeromed. Research Labs., Wright-Patterson AFB, Ohio, 1960-63; lectr. dept. biology U. Dayton, Ohio, 1963; flight food and nutrition coordinator NASA Manned Spacecraft Center, Houston, 1963-67; assoc. prof. dept. food sci. Rutgers U., New Brunswick, N.J., 1967-72; prof. Rutgers U., 1972—, dir. grad. program food sci., 1988—, dir. Sch. Feeding effectiveness research project, 1969-72; assigned to St. Paul's Ch., Princeton, N.J.; cons. nutritional aspects of food processing; mem. sci. adv. bd. Roche Chem. div. Hoffmann LaRoche Co.; mem. nutrition policy com. Beatrice Foods Co., 1979-86; mem. religious ministries com. Princeton Med. Center. Mem. editorial adv. bd., Sch. Food Service Research Rev., 1977-82, Jour. Am. Coll. Nutrition, 1986—, Jour. Med. Consultation, 1985—, Nutrition Reports Internat., 1963-83, Profl. Nutritionist, 1977-80; contbr. articles to profl. jours. Served to capt. USAF, 1960-63. Fellow Inst. Food Technologists, Am. Coll. Nutrition; mem. Am. Assn. Cereal Chemists, AAAS, Am. Inst. Nutrition, N.Y. Inst. Food Technologists (chmn. 1977-78), Am. Soc. Clin. Nutrition, N.Y. Acad. Sci., Am. Dietetic Assn., Soc. Nutrition Edn., Am. Public Health Assn., Nat. Assn. Cath. Chaplains, Sociedad Latino Americano de Nutricion, Sigma Xi, Delta Epsilon Sigma. Home: 34 Taylor Rd RD 4 Princeton NJ 08540 Office: Rutgers U PO Box 231 New Brunswick NJ 08903

LACHAUD, GILLES, mathematician, educator; b. Thomery, France, July 26, 1946; s. Pierre and Marcelle (Jouandeau) L.; m. Patricia Giraud, July 23, 1982. B.S., Faculte des Scis., Paris, 1967; Doctorate, U. Paris, 1979. Asst. U. Paris, 1969-81; prof. math. U. Nice, France, 1981-85; dir. research Nat. Ctr. Sci. Research, Marseille, 1985—; dir. Centre International de Rencontres Mathematiques, Marseille, 1985—. Contbr. numerous articles on number theory, automorphic functions and history of math. to profl. pubis. Recipient Prix Paul Rivoire, U. Clermont, 1980. Mem. Soc. Math. France (v.p. 1982-84, counselor 1985-87). Avocation: humanistic psychology. Home: 63 Chemin Joseph Aiguier, 13009 Marseille France Office: CIRM Case 916, Luminy Cedex 9, 13288 Marseille France

LACHENAUER, ROBERT ALVIN, superintendent schools; b. Newark, Apr. 1, 1929; s. Alvin Frederick and Helen Louise (Bowers) L.; m. Patricia McConnell, June 14, 1952; children—Jane, Nancy, Robert. A.B., Montclair State Coll., 1951, M.A., 1956; Ed.S., Seton Hall U., 1983. Cert. sch. adminstr., N.J., sch. bus. adminstr., N.J., tchr., N.J., supr., N.J., secondary sch. prin., N.J. Tchr. Bd. Edn., Union, N.J., 1951-52, 54-57, asst. bd. sec., 1957-61; asst. supt. New Providence Sch. Dist., (N.J.), 1961-76, supt., 1976—; pres. Union County Sch. Bus. Ofcls., 1967-68, Title IV State Adv. Council, Trenton, N.J., 1976-78, Morris-Union Consortium, N.J., 1981-83, Union County Supts. Roundtable, 1983-84; adv. bd. Summit Trust Co., 1971-86. Elder treas. Presbyn. ch., New Providence, 1958-62; treas. New Providence Hist. Soc., 1966-76; pres. United Way, New Providence, 1978. Served as seaman USN, 1952-54. Mem. N.J. Assn. Sch. Bus Officials (pres. 1974-75), Assn. Sch. Bus Officials U.S. (professionalization com. 1974, membership chmn. 1976), N.J. Assn. Ednl. Secs. (adv. bd. 1976—, Outstanding Adminstr. of Yr. 1987). Lodge: Rotary (pres. 1980-81). Home: 81 Penwood Dr Murray Hill NJ 07974 Office: New Providence Bd Edn 340 Central Ave New Providence NJ 07974

LACHS, MANFRED, judge International Court of Justice; b. Stanis, Poland, Apr. 21, 1914; s. Ignacy and Zofia (Hamerski) L.; m. Fin. Halina, July 31, 1946. LL.M., U. Cracow (Poland), 1936, LL.D., 1937; docteur U. Nancy (France), 1939; D.Sc.Law, U. Moscow; LL.D., U. Budapest, 1967, Dr. jur. et sc. pd. (honoris causa); LL.D. (hon.), U. Algiers, U. Delhi, U. Nice, U. Bridgeport, U. Bucharest, U. Brussels, U. New Halifax, N.Y. U., SUNY, U. Southampton, U. Sophia, Howard U., U. Vancouver, U. Helsinki, U. London, U. Cracow, U. Dalhousie, U. Vienna. Prof., Acad. Polit. Scis., Warsaw, Poland, 1949-52; prof. internat. law U. Warsaw, 1952—; legal adviser Polish Ministry Internat. Affairs, 1947-66, ambassador, 1960-66; judge Internat. Ct. of Justice, 1967—, The Hague, Netherlands, pres., 1973-76; chmn legal com. UN gen. assemblies, 1949, 51, 55, vice chmn., 1952; mem. Polish dels. UN Gen. Assemblies, 1946-52, 55-60, 62-66; rep. Poland UN Disarmament Com., 1962-65; rapporteur gen. colloque. Internat. Assn. Juridical Scis., UNESCO, Rome, Italy, 1948, Internat. Law Commn. UN, 1962; chmn. legal com. UN Peaceful Uses of Outer Space, 1962-66; lectr. throughout Europe and U.S.; Dir. Inst. Legal Sci., Polish Acad. Sci., 1961-67. Mem. Permanent Ct. Arbitration, The Hague, 1956—; mem. UN Internat. Civil Service Adv. Bd., 1959-66, UN Internat. Law Commn., 1962-66; adv. council Inst. Air and Space Law McGill U.; council Internat. Inst. Peace and Conflict Research. Recipient award for ednl. achievement Polish Ministry Higher Edn., 1956, award outstanding contbns. devel. rule of law outer space 1962, gold medal, 1966, world jurist award, 1975, Wateler peace prize, Netherlands, 1976, Copernicus prize, 1984, Britannica award, 1987, 1st Class Prize for Sci. Achievements, Polish Acad. Sci., 1988. Fellow UN Inst. for Tng. and Research (hon., sr.); mem. Acad. Moral Scis. of Bologna (corr.), Curatorium Hague Acad. Internat. Law (v.p.), Polish Acad. Scis., Inst. Internat. Law, Institut de France (corr.); hon. mem. Internat. Acad. Astronautics, Mexican Acad. Internat. Law, Indian Soc. Internat. Law, Am. Soc. Internat. Law. Author: War Crimes, 1945; The Geneva Agreements on Indochina, 1954; Multilateral Treaties, 1958: Polish-German Frontier, 1964; The Law of Outer Space, 1964; The Law of Outer Space-An Experience in Law-Making, 1972; Teachings and Teaching of International Law, 1977; The Teacher in International Law, 1982, 2d edit. 1986; The Development and General Trends of International Law of Our Time, 1984; contbr. 120 articles in 11 langs. to profl. jours. Office: Internat Ct of Justice, Peace Palace, The Hague The Netherlands

LACKEY, LARRY ALTON, SR., lawyer, real estate developer; b. Galax, Va., Aug. 24, 1941; s. Alton and Reba Mae (Phipps) L.; B.S. in Accountancy, Southeastern U., 1962, postgrad. in Bus. Adminstrn., 1962; LL.D., (hon.), Midwestern U., 1963; diploma in advanced accountancy La Salle U., Chgo., 1965, LL.B., 1965; Ph.D. in Bus. Adminstrn., Calif. Pacific U., 1977; m. Ilene Jane Minhinnett, June 7, 1963; children—Larry Alton, Teresa Ann, Lisa Marie. Asst. proof dept. Riggs Nat. Bank, Washington, 1958-59, bookkeeper corp. accounts, also comml. accounts teller, 1959, asst. head teller, 1959-60; asst. head teller, then head teller and head note teller, also br. asst. Old Dominion Bank, Arlington, Va., 1960-61; pub. acct., bus. mgmt. analyst, Washington, 1961-68; dir. accounting, treas. W.W. Chambers Co. Inc., undertaking, Washington, 1968-69; exec. v.p., gen. mgr. Old Dominion Casket Co. Inc., Washington, 1969-70; sr. ops. analyst Macke Corp., vending and food service, Washington, 1970-71, asst. dir. corp. taxes, 1970-71; bd. dirs. Hamilton Bank & Trust Co., 1973-75; pub. acct., tax analyst, bus. mgmt. counselor, efficiency analyst firm Mervin G. Hall Co., Oakton, Va., 1971, founder Bus. Mgmt. Services div., fin. analysis, 1971; chmn. bd. dirs. Internat. Moving & Storage Co. Inc.; pres., chmn. bd. dirs. Key Investment Corp.; sec., dir., founder, ALA Corp., nat. automotive system chain, 1975; founder, pres. Bus. Mgmt. Prodns. Inc., 1985—, Westshore Corp., 1985—, Minute Mart Stores Inc., 1986—; founder, ptnr. DeSoto CableVision Inc., 1988—; co-founder, ptnr. Arcadia Village Adult Mobile Home Community, 1988—. Instr. Boyd Sch. of Bus., 1969-71, also trustee; spl. lectr. pub. high schs., Arlington County, Va., 1970-72; spl. cons. Commonwealth Doctors Hosp., Fairfax, Va., 1973—; founder, pres. Bus. Mgmt. Inst., 1978—. Treas., v.p. Camp Springs (Md.) Civic Assn., 1971-73; sec.-treas. Camp Springs Boys Club, 1971-73; baseball asst. Little League, Annandale, Va., 1974-76; trustee Calif. Pacific U., 1977—. Mem. Am. Soc. Internat. Law, Internat. Bar Assn., Nat. Bar Assn., Nat. Lawyers Club, Asia Pacific Lawyers Assn., Am. Soc. Univ. Profs., Annandale Jaycees. Republican. Roman Catholic. Author: How To Start A Small Business, 1971, Greater Achievements Through Greater Knowledge, The People Business...We're In It, Birth of a Small Business—Its Nature and Scope, Recordkeeping for a Small Business, Establishing Its Value and Selling Your Business. Office: PO Box 552 Sarasota FL 33578

LACO, KAROL, Czechoslovakian government official; b. Sobotiste, Oct. 28, 1921. Ed. Faculty Law, Comenius U., Bratislava. Mem. Faculty Law, Comenius U., 1947—, asst. prof., 1952-63, prof., 1963, dean, 1953-56, 57-59, 60-61; dep. to Ho. of Nations, Fed. Assembly, 1968-71; dep. to Slovak Nat. Council, 1968-71; dep. prime minister Czechoslovakia, 1969-88; mem. Czechoslovak Pugwash Com., 1965—; chmn. Govt. Coordination Com. for Nat. Coms., 1970—; dep. Ho. of People, Fed. Assembly, 1971—; head dept. state law U. Komensky, Bratislava, 1978—. Mem. Czechoslovak Acad. Scis., Slovak Acad. Sci. Decorated Order of Labor; recipient Gold medal Comenius U., 1969. Author: THe National Committees, the Core of the Political Basis of People's Democratic Czechoslovakia, 1954; The Social System of the Czechoslovak Socialist Republic, 1960; Constitution of pre-Munich C.S.R. and Constitution of C.S.S.R., Part I, 1966; also textbooks, study aids and articles in profl. jours. Address: Care Fed Assembly, House of People, Prague 1 Czechoslovakia *

LACOMBA, ERNESTO ALEJANDRO, mathematician, educator; b. Mexico City, Dec. 2, 1945; s. Antonio and Catalina (Zamora) L.; m. Ruth Susana Krivorucoff, June 27, 1971; 1 child, Rossana. B.A. in Engring., Poly. Inst., Mexico City, 1966, B.A. in Physics and Math., 1968; Ph.D. in Math., U. Calif.-Berkeley, 1972. Lectr., Poly. Inst., Mexico City, 1966-68; asst. Mexican Oil Inst., 1967-68; asst. prof. U. Brasilia, Brazil, 1972-73; assoc. researcher Universidad Nacional Autónoma de México, Mexico City, 1973-74; vis. researcher U. Dijon, France, 1980-81; vis. prof. U. Barcelona, 1987-88; prof. math. Universidad Autónoma Metropolitana, Mexico City, 1974—, coordinator master's degree, 1976-80, 82-85, research team dir., 1984—. Contbr. articles to profl. jours. Mem. Mexican Com. of Mathematicians to Free Massera, 1978-84. Latin Am. teaching fellow Tufts U., 1972-73; grantee CONACYT, 1976-86 , Ministry Pub. Edn., 1984-86; recipient hon. mention for research OAS, 1985, Research prize Universidad Automoma Met., 1987. Mem. Sociedad Matemática Mexicana (rev. papers editor 1978-84, grant com. 1985), Am. Math. Soc., Math. Assn. Am., Academia de la Investigación Científica, Internat. Math. Union (del. Socidad 1986), Sigma Xi. Jewish. Avocations: baking bread; gardening; hiking; travel; meditation. Home: Jalcomulco 4, Col La Presilla, 10510 Mexico City DF Mexico Office: Univ Autonoma Metropolitana, 09340 Mexico City DF Mexico

LACROIX, ANDRE MARIE ALBERT, industrial control company executive; b. Bone, Algeria, Jan. 27, 1930; s. Robert Achille and Berthe (Servier) L.; m. Jeannine Alice Batlo, Mar. 24, 1956; children—Patrick, Franç oise. Degree in Engring., Ecole Nationale Superieure de Radioelectricite, France, 1957; lic. in sci. Univ. Grenoble (France), 1956. Chief lab. electronics Sogreah, Grenoble, France, 1959-64; chief service electricity/automation C.T.A., Paris, 1964-70; dir. automation studies R.P.T., Lyon, France, 1970-77; dir. automation dept. Euromachines, Decines, France, 1977-83; pres. dir. gen. T.M.A., Decines, 1983—. Home: Parc de Chalin-Le Lulli, 69130 Ecully France Office: TMA, 11 Av Bataillon, Carmagnole Liberte, 69120 Vaulx-en-Velin France

LACROIX, CHRISTIAN MARIE MARC, fashion designer; b. Arles, Bouche du Rhône, France, May 16, 1951; s. Maxime and Jeannette (Bergier) L. Grad., U. Valery, Montpelier, France, 1973. Asst. Hermes Co., Paris, 1978-79, Guy Paulin Co., Paris, 1980-81; chief designer Jean Patou Co., Paris, 1982-87; prin. Christian Lacroix Co., Paris, 1987—. Recipient Golden Thimble award Parisienne, 1986, 88, Council Fashion Designer Am. award, 1987. Roman Catholic. Office: Christian Lacroix, 73 Fauborg St Honore, 75008 Paris France

LACROIX, GUY ROBERT, textile company executive; b. Ottawa, Ont., Can., Aug. 4, 1948; s. Lucien and Cécile (Bélisle) L.; m. Louise L. Roussy, June 14, 1969; children: Guy L., Renée. BBA, Algonquin Coll., Ottawa, 1969. Dir. corp. relations Royal Bank Can., Montreal, Que., 1969-80, Noranda Mines, Toronto, Ont., 1980-83; v.p. human resources Dominion Textile, Inc., Montreal, 1983-87; pres. Dominion Fabrics Co. subs. Dominion Textile, Inc., Montreal, 1987—. Pres. Big Brothers Big Sisters Montreal, 1982-83. Mem. Que. C. of C. (dir. 1986—), Que. Inst. Indsl. Relations (dir. 1986—). Club: University. Office: Dominion Textile, 1950 Sherbrooke W, Montreal, PQ Canada H3H 1E7

LACROIX, JACQUES-MICHEL, physician; b. Libourne, Gironde, France, Mar. 23, 1947; s. Jean and Annette (Lacour) L.; m. Edwige Garcia, Aug. 28, 1970; 1 child, Aude. Doctorat d'Etat, Faculté de Medecine of Bordeaux (France), 1975; diplôme d'Université in Diving and Hyperbaric Medicine, Faculté de Medecine U. Paris, 1979. Profl. cert. in diving medicine, hyperbaric medicine, emergency medicine. Physician Libourne, 1976-80; physician SOS Medecins, Bordeaux, 1980—, pres., 1982-88; pres. Union Nationale SOS Medecins, Bordeaux, 1983-87; attaché Centre Hospitalier Universitaire, Bordeaux, 1980-83; chargé d'enseignement Lab. of Physiology, U. Bordeaux II, 1982—. Contbr. articles to jours. and newspapers. Mem. Fondation SOS Medecins (pres. 1984—), Société Medecine Subaquatique et Hyperbare, Compagnie Nationale Experts Diplômes Ingenieurs Docteurs Sciences, Fedn. Française Etudes et Sports sous Marine (regional physician). Home: Les Mallets, 33750 Nerigean France Office: CGH, 63 bis Rd Bessieres, 75017 Paris France

LACRUZ GUTIERREZ, JOSÉ LUIS, electronic engineer, electrogeophysics engineer; b. Caracas, Venezuela, Nov. 6, 1958; s. Humberto Olivo and Maria Rebeca (Gutierrez) L.; m. Marina Sifuentes, Sept. 14, 1985. BS in Electronic Engring., U. Simon Bolivar, 1983; diploma in Elec. Logging Engring., Schlumberger Tng. Ctr., Medan, Indonesia, 1984, diploma in Geophysics Logging Engring., 1986. Physics trainer U. Simon Bolivar, Caracas, Venezuela, 1980-81, microwaves trainer, 1981-82, quantum physics trainer, 1982-83; jr. field engr. Schlumberger Overseas, Kalimantan, Venezuela, 1983-84; field engr. Schlumberger Overseas, Indonesia, 1984-85; sr. field. engr. Schlumberger Overseas, Kalimantan, 1985-86; gen. field engr. Schlumberger Overseas, Indonesia, 1986—. Author, editor: Field Engineer Cell Book, 1987; author: Oil Well Chemical Pipe Cutters, 1987. Roman Catholic. Clubs: Mediterranee (Maldivas and Malaysa). Home: Calle 12 #2034, El Llano-Tovar, Mérida Venezuela Office: Schlumberger Tech. Services SA, 80 Marine Parade Rd, Pkwy Parade #20-06, 1544 Singapore Singapore

LACY, TERRY GOODWIN, English educator; b. Balt., May 25, 1926; d. Robert and Dorothy H. (Goodwin) L.; m. C. Vernon Cole, July 23, 1948 (div. 1975); children: Marjorie Allen, Robert Spaulding, David Morrell. BA, Smith Coll., 1948; MS, Colo. State U., 1968, PhD, 1972. Pvt. instr. flute Ft. Collins, Colo., 1951-61; instr. tech. journalism Colo. State U., Ft. Collins, 1972-73, asst. prof., 1974-75; instr. English U. Iceland, Reykjavik, 1975—; instr. extension U. Md., Iceland, 1976-77, banking sch., Reykjavik, 1982-83, Comml. Coll., Reykjavik, 1983—; Fulbright-Hays sr. lectr., Reykjavik, 1973. Author: English-Icelandic Dictionary of Business Terms, 1982, Grammar Excersises in Business English, 1986; contbr. articles to profl. jours. Chmn. pulpit com. Foothills Unitarian Ch., Ft. Collins, 1969-70, vice chmn., 1970; Dem. committeewoman, 1972-74; alto Filharmonia chorus, Reykjavik, 1973—; pres. Ft. Collins Bird Club Audubon Soc., Ft. Collins. Ethnic Studies grantee Ford Found., 1970-72. Mem. Nordic Assn. Am. Studies (editorial bd. 1976—), Internat. Assn. Tchrs. English as a Fgn. Lang., Icelandic Assn. English Tchrs. Democrat. Unitarian.

LADD, DONALD MC KINLEY, JR., lawyer; b. Huntington Park, Calif., Oct. 24, 1923; s. Donald McKinley and Rose (Roberts) L.; B.A., Denison U., 1945; J.D., Stanford U., 1950; m. Eleanor June Martin, June 29, 1951; children—Donald, Richard, Cameron. Admitted to Calif. bar, 1950; asso. firm Anderson McPharlin & Conners, Los Angeles, 1951; legal staff Union Pacific RR, Los Angeles, 1953-56; sr. dep. prosecutor City of Pasadena (Calif.), 1956-58; with Office of Dist. Atty., Santa Clara County, Calif.,

1958—, asst. dist. atty., 1971—. Served to capt. USMCR, 1943-46, 51-52. Certified criminal law specialist Calif. Mem. Bay Area Prosecutors Assn., Calif. State Bar, Calif. Dist. Attys Assn., Stanford Law Alumni Assn., Blue Key, Omicron Delta Kappa, Phi Alpha Delta. Clubs: Marines Meml., Am. Commons, English-Speaking Union, Brit. Am. Home: 1034 Golden Way Los Altos CA 94022 Office: Office of Dist Atty Santa Clara County 70 W Hedding St San Jose CA 95110

LADD, EVERETT CARLL, political scientist, author; b. Saco, Maine, Sept. 24, 1937; s. Everett Carll and Agnes Mary (MacMillan) L.; m. Cynthia Louise Northway, June 13, 1959; children: Everett Carll, III, Corina Ruth, Melissa Ann, Benjamin Elliot. A.B. magna cum laude, Bates Coll., 1959; Ph.D. (Woodrow Wilson fellow, Social Sci. Research Council fellow), Cornell U., 1964. Asst. dean students for pub. affairs Cornell U., Ithaca, N.Y., 1963-64; asst. prof. U. Conn., Storrs, 1964-67, assoc. prof., 1967-69, prof. polit. sci., 1969—, dir. Inst. for Social Inquiry, 1968—, co-exec. dir. Roper Ctr. for Pub. Opinion Research, 1977-79, exec. dir., pres. Roper Ctr. for Pub. Opinion Research, 1979—; research fellow Ctr. for Internat. Studies, Harvard U., Cambridge, Mass., 1969-75; mem. exec. council Inter-Univ. Consortium for Polit. and Social Research, 1975-77; adj. scholar Am. Enterprise Inst. Pub. Policy Research, 1978—; adv. editor in social scis. W.W. Norton & Co., 1977—; research assoc. Ctr. for Study Social and Polit. Change, 1986—, Inst. for Study Econ. Culture, 1986—; trustee Nat. Council on Pub. Polls, 1987—. Author: Negro Political Leadership in the South, 1966, Ideology in America: Charge and Response in a City, a Suburb, and a Small Town, 1969, rev. edit. 1986, American Political Parties: Social Change and Political Response, 1970, (with S.M. Lipset) Professors, Unions, and American Education, 1973, Academics, Politics, and the 1972 Election, 1973, The Divided Academy: Professors and Politics, 1975, (with C.D. Hadley) Political Parties and Political Issues: Patterns in Differentiation Since the New Deal, 1973, Transformations of the American Party System: Political Coalitions from the New Deal to the 1970's, 2d edit., 1978, Where Have All the Voters Gone?, 1978, 2d edit., 1982, The American Polity, 1985, 2d edit. 1987; mem. editorial bd.: Pub. Opinion Quar., 1976-82, Polit. Behavior, 1978-84, Politics and Behavior, 1980—, Polity, 1980—, Micro Politics, 1980—, Polit. Sci. Quar., 1982—; cons. editor, mem. editorial bd.: Pub. Opinion mag., 1977—, sr. editor, 1983—; columnist Christian Sci. Monitor, 1987—, cons. pub. opinion research U.S. News, 1986—. Ford Found. fellow, 1969-70; Guggenheim fellow, 1971-72; Rockefeller Found. fellow, 1976-77; Hoover Instn. fellow, 1976-77, 79-80; Center Advanced Study in Behavioral Scis., 1979. Mem. Am. Polit. Sci. Assn., Am. Sociol. Assn., Am. Assn. Public Opinion Research, New Eng. Polit. Sci. Assn. (pres. 1982-83), Acad. Polit. Sci., Phi Beta Kappa, Delta Sigma Rho. Clubs: Cosmos (Washington). Home: 86 Ball Hill Rd Storrs CT 06268 Office: Roper Center PO Box 440 Storrs CT 06268

LADEGAARD, JØRGEN, international mechanical engineering consultant; b. Copenhagen, Apr. 10, 1932; s. Jens Moller and Karen Storck (Simonsen) L.; BSME, MSME, Danish Tech. U., 1958; m. Karin Lind, Mar. 24, 1961. With Danish Acad. Tech. Scis., Copenhagen, 1958-61, Directorate for Sci. Affairs, OECD, Paris, 1961-63, Fedn. Danish Mech. Engring and Metalworking Industries, Copenhagen, 1963-69; mng. dir. Jutland Technol. Inst., Aarhus, Denmark, 1969-87, internat. cons., 1988—. Mem. Instn. Danish Civil Engrs., Danish Acad. Tech. Scis., Danish Acad. of Future Studies. Club: Aarhus Sondre Rotary. Home: 36 Arnakvej, DK-8270 Hojbjerg Denmark

LADIN, EUGENE, communications company executive; b. N.Y.C., Oct. 26, 1927; s. Nat and Mae (Cohen) L.; m. Millicent Dolly Frankel, June 27, 1948; children: Leslie Hope, Stephanie Joy. B.B.A., Pace U., 1956; M.B.A., Air Force Inst. Tech., 1959; postgrad., George Washington U., 1966-69. Cost engr. Rand Corp., Santa Monica, Calif., 1960-62; mgr. cost and econ. analysis Northrop Corp., Hawthorne, Calif., 1962-66; dir. financial planning Communications Satellite Corp., Washington, 1966-70; treas., chief fin. and adminstrv. officer Landis & Gyr, Inc., Elmsford, N.Y., 1970-76; v.p., treas., comptroller P.R. Telephone Co., San Juan, 1976-77; v.p. fin. Comtech Telecommunications Corp., Smithtown, N.Y., 1977—; acting pres. Comtech Antenna Corp., St. Cloud, Fla., 1978-80; chmn., chief exec. officer Telephone Interconnect Enterprises/Sunshine Telephone Co., Balt., Md. and Orlando, Fla., 1980-82; pres. Ladin and Assocs., Cons. and Commodity Traders, Maitland, Fla., 1982-84; pres., chief fin. officer Braintech Inc., South Plainfield, N.J., 1984; sr. v.p. fin., chief fin. officer Teltec Savs. Communications Co., Miami, Fla., 1984—; assoc. prof. acctg. So. Ill. U., East St. Louis, 1960; asso. prof. bus. U. Md., 1969-70; adj. prof. George Washington U., 1969-70; vis. prof. acctg. Pace U., 1970. Served to capt. USAF, 1951-60. Decorated Air Force Commendation medal; recipient Air Force Outstanding Unit award. Mem. Nat. Assn. Accts., Fin. Exec. Inst. Republican. Jewish. Club: Bankers (Miami), Williams Island Country, Turnberry Yacht Country. Home: 20355 NE 34th Del Vista Ct North Miami Beach FL 33180

LAFFERTY, BEVERLY LOU BROOKOVER, physician; b. Newark, Ohio, Aug. 15, 1938; d. Lawrence William and Rosie (Rey) Brookover; B.S., Ohio State U., 1959, M.D., 1963; diplomate Am. Bd. Family Practice; children—Marla Michele, William Brookover, Wesley Voris, Latour Rey. Intern Grant Hosp., Columbus, Ohio, 1963-64; practice medicine, West Union, Ohio, 1964-75, Sun City Center, Fla., 1975-79, Brandon, Fla., 1979—; mem. staff Adams County Hosp., v.p., 1971-72, chief of staff, 1973-75; mem. staff Humana Hosp., Brandon, 1977—, chmn. dept. family practice, 1984-86, hosp. trustee, 1984-87, 88—, chief of staff elect, 1986-88, chief of staff, 1988—. Mem. AMA, Fla., Hillsborough County med. assns., Am. Acad. Family Physicians, Fla. Acad. Family Physicians, Alpha Lambda Delta, Alpha Epsilon Iota, Alpha Epsilon Delta (sec. 1958-59). Mem. Order Eastern Star. Home: 3913 John Moore Rd Brandon FL 33511 Office: 305 S Bryan Rd Brandon FL 33511

LAFORGIA, ANDREA, mathematician, educator, researcher; b. Barletta, Italy, June 20, 1949; s. Michele and Arcangela (Adduci) L.; m. Maria Paola Giovine, Apr. 28, 1975; children—Michela, Serenella. D.Math., U. Torino, Italy, 1973. Fellow Consiglio Nazionale Ricerche, Genova, Italy, 1973-74, Torino, 1974-76, researcher, 1976-84; assoc. prof. math. U. Torino, 1984-87; prof. U. Palermo, 1987—; mem. sci. council Consiglio Nazionale Ricerche, Milano, 1984—. Contbr. articles to profl. jours. Avocations: cooking; bridge. Office: Dept Math, Via Archirafi 34, 90123 Palermo Italy

LÅG, JUL, soil scientist; b. Flesberg, Norway; b. Nov. 13, 1915; s. Torsten and Joran (Brattas) Buind Lå g; widowed; children: Marit, Torleiv. Student, Agrl. U. Norway, 1942, D in Agr., 1949. Prof. Agr. U. Norway, 1949-85 ; rector Agrl. U. Norway, 1968-71; chmn. Agrl. Council Norway, 1972-73. Author several books in Norwegian. Editor: Geomedical Aspects in Present and Future Research, 1980; Basis of Account of Norway's Natural Resources, 1982; Geomedical Research in Relation to Geochemical Registrations, 1984; Geomedical Consequences of Chemical Composition of Freshwater, 1987. Mem. editorial bd. Geoderma, Soil Sci., Alexandria Sci. Exchange, Agrochimica, Ambio. Contbr. articles to profl. jours. Vice chmn. Norwegian Council Parliaments and Scientists, 1969—. Decorated comdrs. Cross Islandic Order Falcon, 1970. Mem. Internat. Soc. Soil Sci. (chmn. group on soils and geomedicine 1986—), Norwegian Acad. Sci. and Letters (pres. 1976-84), Royal Forestry and Agr. Acad. Sweden, Royal Norwegian Soc. Scis. and Letters, Finnish Acad. Sci. and Letters, Danish Acad. Sci. and Letters, Polish Acad. Sci. (Copernicus medal 1974), Soil Sci. Soc. West Germany (corr.), Soil Sci. Soc. Soviet Union (hon.). Avocations: skiing; literature. Office: Agrl U Norway, 1432 As NLH Norway Other: Norske Videnskaps-Akademi, Drammensveien 78, 0271 Oslo Norway

LAGERCRANTZ-OHLIN, ANITA, journalist; b. Stockholm, Feb. 2, 1926; d. Gunnar Fritjoe Lundgren and Barbro (Rålamb) Söderberg; separated; 1 child from previous marriage, Sophie Lagercrantz; 1 child, Ola Thomasson. Reporter Vecko-Revyn Vecko-Journalen, 1974-87; reporter, columnist Femina Svenska Dagbladet and Sköna Hem, Stockholm, 1987—. UN grantee, 1980-81. Home: Djurgardsvagen 128, 11521 Stockholm Sweden Office: Svenska Dagbladel, Ralambso 7, 11521 Stockholm Sweden

LAGERFELD, KARL, fashion designer; b. Hamburg, Germany, 1938; ed. Lycee Montaigne. Fashion stylist with Pierre Balmain, Paris, 1954-58; art mgr. Jean Patou, Paris, 1958-63; free-lance designer asso. with Fendi, 1963—, Chloél, Paris, 1964-83, Paris, Chloe, Paris, 1964-83, Chanel Paris, 1982—; designer Karl Lagerfeld Women's Wear, Inc. and Karl Lagerfeld France, Inc., Paris 1983—; also designer, producer perfume fragrances Chloe, Lagerfeld For Men, KL for Women, KL for men. Decorated Bundesverdienst Kreuz (Fed. Republic Germany). Recipient Munich Fashion prize; Golden Spinning Wheel, 1980; Neiman-Marcus award, 1980. Address: care Karl Lagerfeld France Inc, 144 Ave des Champs-Elysées, 75008 Paris France Other: Chlie by Karl Lagerfeld Goldin Feldman Inc 345 7th Ave New York NY 10001 *

LAGERS, GEORGE HENDRIK, engineering company executive; b. Maastricht, Netherlands, June 15, 1942; s. Frits Jan and Mathilde Philippine (Van Oppen) L.; m. Gerardina Christina Van Haselen, May 16, 1969; children—Frits-Jan, Kees, Roderick. M.Sc., Tech. U., Delft, Holland, 1968. Devel. engr. IHC Gusto, Schiedam, Holland, 1968-72, research and devel. mgr., 1972-77; sr. engr. Marine Structure Cons., Hardinxveld, Holland, 1977-78, mng. dir., 1981—; naval architect Ocean Minerals Co., Mountain View, Calif., 1978-81; guest tchr. Delft Tech. U., 1975-76; dir. Stuyvesant Engring., Metairie, La., 1982-85. Contbr. articles to profl. jours. Mem. Royal Instn. Profl. Engrs. Holland, Soc. Naval Architects and Marine Engrs. Liberal. Roman Catholic. Club: Bataafsch Genootschap (Rotterdam, Netherlands). Office: Marine Structure Consultants, Nyverheidsstraat 54, 3370XE Hardinxveld The Netherlands

LAGERSTEN, KARL HÅKAN, airline executive; b. Ostersund, Sweden, Dec. 5, 1941; s. Karl Einar Birger and Inga-Brita Olivia (Fihnborg) L.; m. Eva Marianne Peterson, July 7, 1984; children: Erik, Johan, Fredrik, Ebba. Student pub. schs., Solna, Sweden. Flight dispatcher Linjeflyg AB, Stockholm, 1965-66, dep. v.p., mgr. ops. control, 1980—; supt. flight ops. Sterling Airways A/S, Copenhagen, 1966-69; dep. supt. ops. control SAS, Copenhagen, 1969-72; head flight ops. office Bd. Civil Aviation, Stockholm/Norrkoping, 1972-80. Home: Ploggatan 8, S-193 oo Sigtuna Sweden Office: Linjeflyg AB, PO Box 550, S-19045 Stockholm-Arlander Sweden

LAGERSTROM, PACO AXEL, scientist; b. Oskarshamm, Sweden, Feb. 24, 1914; s. Paco Harald and Karin (Wiedemann) L. Filosofie Kandidat, U. Stockholm, 1935, Filosofie Licenciat, 1939; postgrad., U. Munster, Germany, 1938; Ph.D. in Math, U. Princeton U., 1942. Instr. math. Princeton U., 1941-44; flight test engr. Bell Aircraft, 1944-45; aerodynamicist Douglas Aircraft, 1945-46, cons., 1946-66; research assoc. in aeros., staff engr. Calif. Inst. Tech., 1946-47, asst. prof. aeros., 1947-49, assoc. prof., 1949-52, prof., 1952-67, prof. applied math., 1967-81, prof. emeritus, 1981—; cons. TRW, 1966-68; vis. prof. U. Paris, 1960-61, Rensselaer Poly. Inst., 1984, Clarkson U., 1986. Contbr. articles to profl. jours. and handbooks. Mem. bd. Coleman Chamber Music, Pasadena, 1950—, pres., 1958-60. Decorated Palmes Académiques France; recipient Patron of Arts award Pasadena Arts Council, 1973; Guggenheim fellow, 1960-61; Fondation des Treilles fellow, France, 1982. Mem. Am. Math. Soc., Assocs. of Caltech. Clubs: The Travellers (Paris); Brook, Knickerbocker (N.Y.C.). Home: 57 San Miguel Rd Pasadena CA 91105 Office: Calif Inst Tech 217-50 Pasadena CA 91125

LAGHARI, JAVAID RASOOLBUX, electrical engineering educator, researcher, consultant; b. Hyderabad, Sind, Pakistan, June 25, 1950; came to U.S., 1980; s. Rasool Bux and Khudeja L.; m. Shahida Parveen, Jan. 11, 1982; 1 child, Zaid. B.Engring., Sind U., Jamshoro, Pakistan, 1971; M.Engring., Middle East Tech. U., Ankara, Turkey, 1975; Ph.D., U. Windsor, 1980. Project engr. Indus Grindery, Hyderabad, 1971-73; asst. exec. engr. Airports Devel. Agy., Karachi, Pakistan, 1975-76; asst. prof. elec. engring. SUNY-Buffalo, 1980-88, assoc. prof., 1988—; assoc. dir. Strategic Def. Initiatives Material Inst., 1985-88; session organizer NATO Advanced Study Inst., Castelvecchio Pascoli, Italy, 1983, Internat. Symposium on Elec. Insulation, Boston, 1988. Contbr. articles to profl. jours. Faculty advisor Pakistan Students Assn., SUNY-Buffalo, 1980—. Merit scholar Govt. Pakistan, Govt. Coll., 1965-67; Govt. Pakistan fellow U. Sind, 1967-71; research scholar Govt. Turkey, Middle East Tech. U., 1973-75; postgrad. scholar Ont. Edn. Ministry, U. Windsor, 1977-80. Mem. IEEE (sr., edn. com., sec. radiation life com., sec. Conf. on Elec. Insulation and Dielectric Phenomena 1985). Avocations: sightseeing; photography. Home: 191 Sprucewood Terr Williamsville NY 14221 Office: SUNY 316 Bonner Hall Dept Elec Engring Buffalo NY 14260

LAGNEVIK, MAGNUS, business administration educator; b. Linköping, Östergötland, Sweden, Mar. 25, 1949; s. A. Harald A. and Gullan I.K. (Aronsson) L.; m. Monica Agneta, Mar. 11, 1948; children: Pi, Anna, Björn. BA in Social Scis., Lund U., 1972, BA in Bus. Adminstrn., 1973, PhD in Bus. Adminstrn., 1976. Asst. prof. Lund (Sweden) U., 1979-83, assoc. prof., 1983—; v.p. interna. programs. MIL Mgmt. Devel. Orgn., Lund, 1981-84; program dir. Strategic Transnat. Exec. Programme, Lund, 1984—. Contbr. articles to profl. jours. Home: Rapsvägen 12, S-240 17 Södra Sandby Sweden Office: Lund Univ, Sch Econs and Adminstrn, PO Box 7080, S-220 07 Lund Sweden

LAGOPOULOS, ALEXANDROS-PHAIDON, urban planning educator; b. Athens, Greece, Jan. 14, 1939; s. Panayiotis and Kyveli (Fahmi) L.; m. Ioulia Fotopoulou (div. 1979); m. Karin Margareta Boklund, 1979. Diploma in Archtl. Engring., Athens (Greece) Nat. Tech. U., 1961; Degree in Urban Planning, Ctr. Recherche d'Urbanisme, Paris, 1969; D IIIe cycle in Social Anthropology, U. Sorbonne, Paris, 1970; PhD in Engring., Athens (Greece) Nat. Tech. U., 1970. Habilitation in Urban and Regional Planning, Athens Nat. Technical U., 1972. Asst. Athens Nat. Tech. U., 1962-64, lectr., 1965-74; prof. Aristotle U. Thessaloniki, Greece, 1974—. Author: Structural Urban Planning, 1973, Treatise on Urban Planning (3 vols.), 1977-81; co-author: (with others) Thessaloniki, 1979; co-editor: The City and the Sign, 1986; mem. editorial committee City and Region jour., 1980—; regular corr. Greece, Espaces Soc. jour., 1987—; contbr. articles to profl. jours. Served to 2d lt. Greek Air Force, 1961-64. Various archtl. awards, Greece, 1964-65; French Govt. scholar Assn. Technique Française, 1968-69; U.S. State Dept. grantee, 1973, U.S. and Greek govts. grantee, Salzburg, Austria, 1973. Mem. Hellenic Semiotic Soc. (v.p. 1979-80, pres. 1981—), Internat. Assn. Semiotic Studies (Greek rep. 1979-87), Internat. Soc. Urban Regional Planners, Soc. Africanistes, Tech. Chamber Greece. Office: Aristotle Univ Thessaloniki, Dept Urban Regional Planning, 54006 Thessaloniki Greece

LAGOS, JAMES HARRY, lawyer, small business advocate; b. Springfield, Ohio, Mar. 14, 1951; s. Harry Thomas and Eugenia (Papas) L.; m. Nike Daphne Pavlatos, July 3, 1976. BA cum laude, Wittenberg U., 1970; JD, Ohio State U., 1972. Bar: U.S. Supreme Ct. 1976, U.S. Ct. Appeals (6th cir.) 1979, U.S. Dist. Ct. (so. dist.) Ohio 1973, U.S. Tax Ct. 1975, Ohio Supreme Ct. 1973. Asst. pros. atty. Clark County, Ohio, 1972-75; ptnr. Lagos & Lagos, Springfield, 1975—; mem. Springfield Small Bus. Council, past chmn., 1977—, Ohio Small Bus. Council, 1980—, past chmn., vice chmn. ; pres. Nat. Small Bus. United, 1982—; del. Small Bus. Nat. Issues Conf., 1984, Ohio Gov.'s Conf. Small Bus., 1984, resource person regulatory and licensing reform com., 1984. Bd. dirs., pres. Greek Orthodox Ch., 1974—; mem. diocese council Greek Orthodox Diocese of Detroit, 1985-86; past chmn. Clark County Child Protection Team, 1974-82, Clark County Young Rep. Club, past pres., sec., treas., 1968-76, chmn. Ohio del. White House Conf. Small Bus., 1985-86. Served as staff sgt. Ohio Air N.G., 1970-76. Recipient Dr. Melvin Emanuel award West Central Ohio Hearing and Speech Assn., 1983, Medal of St. Paul the Apostle Greek Orthodox Archdiocese of North and South Am., 1985; Disting. Service award Springfield-Clark County, 1977; named one of Outstanding Young Men of Am., 1978. Mem. Am. Hellenic Inst. (pub. affairs com. 1979—, bd. dirs.), Am. Hellenic Ednl. Progressive Assn. (past treas), C. of C. (past bd. dirs.), Jaycees (past chmn. several coms. 1973—, Spoke award 1974), ABA, Ohio State Bar Assn., Springfield Bar and Law Library Assn. (past sec., exec. com. 1973—), West Cen. Ohio Hearing and Speech Assn. (bd. dirs., pres., v.p. 1973-84), Alpha Alpha Kappa, Phi Eta Sigma, Tau Pi Phi, Pi Sigma Alpha. Home: 2023 Audubon Park Dr Springfield OH 45504 Office: Lagos & Lagos 31 E High St Suite 500 Springfield OH 45502

LA GUMA, JUSTIN ALEXANDER (ALEX), author, journalist; b. Cape Town, South Africa, Feb. 20, 1925; ed. Cape Tech. Sch., Cape Town, London Sch. Journalism. Mem. Nat. Exec. Coloured People's Congress, 1955—; banned from gatherings, under house arrest, confined in solitary, 1962-66, exiled, 1966; freelance writer, London, 1966—; mem. editorial bd. Afro-Asian Writers' Bur., London, 1968—; author: A Walk in the Night, 1962; And a Threefold Cord, 1965; The Stone Country, 1968; In the Fog of the Season's End, 1972; editor Apartheid (anthology), 1972; Time of the Butcherbird, 1978. Mem. Afro-Asian Writers' Assn. (sec.-gen. 1975—). Address: 36 Woodland Gardens, London N10 3UA, England

LAHHAM, GHASSAN, librarian; b. Damascus, Syria, Oct. 24, 1938; s. Mouhamed Sayah Lahham and Jounaia Hijazl; m. Hayam Hariri, Feb. 18, 1968; children: Nael, Fadi. BA, Cairo U., 1963. Chief of periodical section Damascus U. Library, 1963-65, vice dir., 1966-71; dir. presdl. palace library and archive Presdl. Palace, Dmascus, 1971-83; gen. dir. Syrian Nat. Library, Damascus, 1983—; lectr. Library Sch. in damascus U., 1983—. Mem. Syrian Librarian Assn. (chief 1982—). Home: Nazim Basha 3/2, Damascus 3639, Syria Office: Assad Nat Library, Malki St, PO Box 3639, Damascus Syria

LAHLOU, MICHEL BACHIR, language school executive, researcher; b. Fez, Morocco, Mar. 1, 1942; came to U.S., 1969; s. Outtassi M. and Touriya Lahlou; m. Lydie M. Giry, Jan. 14, 1967; 1 child, Mehdi. Grad. Lycee Michelet, Paris, 1963, Ecole Normale Superieure de St. Cloud, Paris, 1969. Tchr., Ecole Active Bilingue, Paris, 1966-69; prof. UN, N.Y.C., 1969-72; prof. Alliance Francaise, N.Y.C., 1970-73; pres. Phonelab, Inc., Lang. Sch. (teaching fgn. langs. by telephone), N.Y.C., 1974-87; pres. Audio-Lang. and Knowledge Inst., N.Y.C., 1987—; pres. Phonelab Paris: Lang. Sch. by Telephone. Patentee systems of teaching langs. by telephone, 1974. Mem. United Inventors and Scientists Am. Clubs: Sales Exec., William's Univ (N.Y.C.). Office: Phonelab Inc 24 E 39th St New York NY 10016

LAHTINEN, AATOS OSVI, mathematics educator; b. Helsinki, Finland, Oct. 9, 1942; s. Osvi Heikki and Kerttu Annikki (Lehtonen) L.; m. Sirkka-Liisa Virtanen, Aug. 19, 1967; 1 child, Piritta. MSc, U. Helsinki, 1966, PhD, 1972. With U. Helsinki, 1967—, tenure assoc. prof. math., 1977—; bd. dirs. Rolf Nevanlinna Inst., Helsinki. Author: On The Solutions of Delta u-Pu, 1972, Mathematics for Applications, 1987. Grantee Found. for Study Natural Resources, Acad. Finland. Mem. Assn. Univ. Prof. Finland (bd. dirs. 1986—), Finnish Math. Soc. (bd. dirs. 1979—), Finland Council Sci. Socs., Finland Soc. Forestry, Soc. Indsl. and Applied Math. Office: U Helsinki, Hallituskatu 15, 00100 Helsinki Finland

LAI, ALEX CHE WAI, business executive, purchasing specialist; b. Canton, China, Apr. 10, 1952; came to Hong Kong, 1961; s. Ping Kai and Suk Yin (Fung) L.; m. Tam Sau Ling, Sept. 14, 1981; 1 child, Wing Yin. Higher diploma prodn. engring., Hong Kong Tech. Coll., 1972; Indsl. Engr., U. Hong Kong, 1974; higher cert. in mech. engring., Hong Kong Poly., 1976, cert. in works mgmt., 1975. Mgr. quality control/quality assurance Nat. Semicondr., Hong Kong, 1976-78, Mattel Electronics, Hong Kong, 1978-80; mgr. Atari F.E. Ltd., Hong Kong, 1980-84; internat. procurement mgr. CTS, Hong Kong, 1984-85; procurement agt. Xerox Corp., Hong Kong, 1985—; ptnr. Well-House Co., Hong Kong, 1980-83; dir. L.T. Engring. Ltd., Hong Kong; cons. Hip Wo Indsl. Co., Hong Kong. Mem. Inst. Sales Engrs. Avocations: tennis; table tennis; badminton; fishing. Home: Provident Center, Flat C, 21/F Block 2, 23 Wharf Rd, North Point Hong Kong Office: Xerox Corp-Hong Kong, 1213 Peninsula Centre, Kowloon Hong Kong

LAI, CHING-SAN, biophysicist, educator, researcher; b. Keelung, Taiwan, Nov. 27, 1946; came to U.S., 1974; s. Dong-Cheng and Shay (Wu) L.; m. Shan-Lan Liu, Sept. 9, 1972; children: Jennifer, Shawn. BS in Zoology, Taiwan Normal U., Taipei, 1970; PhD in Biophysics, U. Hawaii, 1978. Research assoc. Med. Coll. Wis., Milw, 1979-80, asst. prof. biophysics, 1981-84, assoc. prof., 1985—. Contbr. chpts. to books. NIH grantee, 1982—. Mem. Biophys. Soc., Magnetic Resonance in Medicine. Current work: Electron spin resonance spectroscopy of protein mobility; development of electron spin resonance methodologies for biomedical research. Subspecialties: Biophysics (biology); Biochemistry (biology). Home: 17765 Bolter Ln Brookfield WI 53005

LAI, JENG YIH, surgeon; b. Rep. China, Dec. 5, 1941; came to U.S., 1968; s. Ting-Zo and See-Mae (Lee) L.; m. Su Kao, July 19, 1944; children: Stephen, Christina, Monica. MD, Nat. Taiwan U., 1967. Diplomate Am. Bd. Surgery, Am. Bd. Thoracic Surgery. Intern St. Francis Gen. Hosp., Pitts., 1968-69, resident in gen. surgery, 1969-73; fellow in cardiovascular surgery Rush-Presbyn.-St. Luke's Med. Ctr., Chgo., 1973-74; resident in cardiovascular and thoracic surgery St. Paul Hosp., Dallas, 1974-76; fellow in cardiovascular surgery Tex. Heart Inst., Houston, 1976-77; surgeon cardiovascular and thoracic surgery St. Francis Regional Med. Ctr., Wichita, Kans., 1977—; pvt. practice specializing in cardiovascular and thoracic surgery Wichita, 1981-88; clin. asst. prof. in surgery U. Kans., Wichita. Bd. dirs. Wichita Indochinese Ctr., 1985-86. Served as lt. surgeon China Army, 1967-68. Fellow Am. Coll. Surgeons, Denton A. Cooley Cardiovascular Soc.; mem. AMA, Am. Heart Assn., Med. Soc. Kans., Sedgwick County Med. Soc., Wichita Asian Assn. (pres. 1985-86). Home: 8501 Killarney Pl Wichita KS 67206

LAI, SHIH-TSE JASON, chemistry researcher, educator; b. Chia-yi, Republic of China, Oct. 29, 1951; came to U.S., 1977, naturalized, 1985; s. Chi-Kuei and Yu-Lien (Kao) L.; m. Wei Bamboo Lee, June 25, 1980; 1 child, Shin-Hwa Jeffrey Lee. BS, Nat. Chung-Hsing U., Taichung, Republic of China, 1974; PhD, CUNY, 1983; postgrad., West Coast U. Adminstrn. asst. Tunghai U., Taichung, 1976-77; adjunct lectr. CUNY, Bklyn., 1977-78; research fellow CUNY, Flushing, 1978-83; sr. chemist semicondtr. products div. Rockwell Internat., Newport Beach, Calif., 1983-85; head mass spectrometry lab. Tech. & Ventures div. Baxter Healthcare Corp., Irvine, Calif., 1985—; vis. assoc. prof. Ta-Hwa Inst. Tech., Hsinchu, Republic of China, 1986, 87; seminar speaker Union Chem. Labs., Cen. Police Acad., Nat. Sun Yat-Sen U., Nat. Chung-Hsing U., Republic of China, 1987. Contbr. numerous articles to profl. jours. Coach Tunghai U. Rugby Team, 1976-77; patron Laguna Moulton Playhouse, Laguna Beach, Calif., 1986-87; mem. Orange County Sheriff's Adv. Bd. University fellow, CUNY, 1977; recipient Fellow A scholarship CUNY, 1978-83. Fellow Am. Inst. Chemists; mem. AAAS, N.Y. Acad. Scis., Am. Chem. Soc. (mem. program com. Orange County chpt. 1985-87), Chinese Culture Assn. (pres. CUNY chpt. 1978-80), Friends Orange County Performing Art Ctr., Nat. Chung-Hsing U. Alumni Assn. (v.p. So. Calif. chpt. 1986-88), Taiwan Benevolent Assn. (nat. advisor 1985—, adv. So. Calif. chpt. 1986—, v.p., dir. 1984-86), Asian Am. Alliance Calif. (co-founder, co-chmn.), Am. Soc. Mass Spectrometry, So. Calif. Mass Spectrometry (chmn. program com. 1988—), Fedn. Chinese Student Assn. in USA (bd. dirs. 1978-80), Sigma Xi.

LAIDLAW, HARRY HYDE, JR., entomology educator; b. Houston, Apr. 12, 1907; s. Harry Hyde and Elizabeth Louisa (Quinn) L.; B.S., La. State U., 1933, M.S., 1934; Ph.D. (Univ. fellow, Genetics fellow, Wis. Dormitory fellow, Wis. Alumni Research Found. fellow), U. Wis., 1939; m. Ruth Grant Collins, Oct. 26, 1946; 1 dau., Barbara Scott Laidlaw Murphy. Teaching asst. La. State U., 1933-34, research asst., 1934-35; prof. biol. sci. Oakland City (Ind.) Coll., 1939-41; state apiarist Ala. Dept. Agr. and Industries, Montgomery, 1941-42; entomologist First Army, N.Y.C., 1946-47; asst. prof. entomology, asst. apiculturist U. Calif.-Davis, 1947-53, asso. prof. entomology, asso. apiculturist, 1953-59, prof. entomology, apiculturist, 1960-74, asso. dean Coll. Agr., 1959-64, prof. entomology emeritus, apiculturist emeritus, 1974—; coordinator U. Calif.-Egypt Agrl. Devel. Program, AID, 1979-83. Rockefeller Found. grantee, Brazil, 1954-55, Sudan, 1967. Trustee, Yolo County (Calif.) Med. Soc. Scholarship Com., 1965-83. Served to capt. AUS, 1942-46. Recipient Cert. of Merit, Am. Bee Jour., 1957; Spl. Merit award U. Calif.-Davis, 1959; Merit award, Calif. Central Valley Bee Club, 1974; Merit award West Apicultural Soc., 1980, Gold Merit award Internat. Fedn. Beekeepers' Assns., 1986, 87; NIH grantee, 1963-66; NSF grantee, 1966-74. Fellow AAAS; mem. Am. Genetics Assn., Am. Inst. Biol. Scis., Am. Soc. Naturalists, Am. Soc. Zoologists, Entomol. Soc. Am. (C.W. Woodworth award Pacific br. 1981), Genetics Soc. Am., Internat. Bee Research Assn., Nat. Assn. Uniformed Services, Ret. Officers Assn., Scabbard and Blade, Sigma Xi (treas. Davis chpt. 1959-60, v.p. chpt. 1966-67), Alpha Gamma Rho (pres. La. chpt. 1933-34, counsellor Western Province 1960-66). Democrat. Presbyterian. Club: Commonwealth (San Francisco). Author books, the most recent being: Instrumental Insemination of Honey Bee Queens, 1977; Contemporary Queen Rearing, 1979; author slide set: Instrumental Insemination of Queen Honey Bees, 1976. Home: 761 Sycamore Ln Davis CA 95616 Office: U Calif Dept Entomology Davis CA 95616

LAING, EDWARD ARTHUR, government official, law educator; b. Belize City, Belize, Feb. 27, 1942; came to U.S., 1974; d. Edward Arthur and Marjorie Eunice (Dunn) L.; m. Margery Victoria Fairweather, Apr. 5, 1969; children—Obi, Nyasha. B.A., Cambridge U., 1964, LL.M., 1966; LL.M., Columbia U., 1968. Bar: Eng. 1966, Ill. 1969, Belize 1970, Barbados 1972, D.C. 1985. Assoc. Baker & McKenzie, Chgo. and N.Y.C., 1968-79; sr. lectr. U. West Indies, Barbados and Jamaica, 1970-75; asst. prof. Notre Dame U., Ind., 1974-76; assoc. prof. U. Md., Balt., 1976-81; prof. Howard U., Washington, 1980-85; ambassador to U.S. from Belize, Washington, 1985—; magistrate, crown counsel Belize Govt., 1966-67; faculty Internat. Trade Law Jour., Balt., 1976-81. Author: Introduction to Caribbean Law, 1973; also articles. Ind. advisor Belize C. of C., 1981; 1st pres. Nat. Belize Assn., N.Y., 1981; founder and 1st pres. Consortium for Belizean Devel., Washington, 1985. Recipient scholarship Govt. of Belize, 1961-66; Fulbright Travel grantee, 1967; Ford Found. Research grantee, 1972. Mem. Am. Soc. Internat. Law, Washington Fgn. Law Soc. Avocations: outdoors camping; canoeing.

LAING, GERALD OGILVIE, sculptor; b. Newcastle-Opon-Tyne, Northumberland, England, Feb. 11, 1936; s. Gerald Francis and Enid Moody (Foster) L.; children: Yseult Ogilvie Hughes, Farqohar Piotr, Alexander A.G.V. Student, Royal Mil. Acad., Sandhurst, 1953-55, St. Martin's Sch. of Art, London, 1960-65. Artist-in-residence Aspen Inst. for Humanistic Studies, Colo., 1966; asst. prof. Columbia U., N.Y.C, 1986-87; commr. Royal Fine Art Commn. for Scotland, Edinburg, 1987—. Represented in permanent collections: Victoria and Albert Mus., Scottish Nat. Gallery of Modern Art Mus. Modern Art, N.Y. Whitney Mus., Mpls. Mus., Indpls. Mus., Denver Mus., Univs. of N.Y., Harvard U., Cornell U., Brandeis, P.R., Aberdeen, Strathcyde; author: Kinkell: the Reconstruction of a Scottish Castle, 1985. Served to lt. English Army, 1953-60. Recipient Civil Trust award, Scottisdh Civic Trust, 1971. Mem. Royal Soc. of British Scupltors (assoc.). Episcopalian. Club: Chelsea Arts (London). Lodge: Seaforth. Home: 139 E 66th St New York NY 10021 also: Kinkell Castle, Ross-Shore IV7 8AT, Scotland

LAING, RONALD DAVID, psychiatrist, author; b. Glasgow, Scotland, Oct. 7, 1927; m. Jutta; children: Adam, Natasha, Max. M.D., U. Glasgow, 1951. Intern 1951; conscript psychiatrist Brit. Army, 1951-53; psychiatrist Glasgow Royal Med. Hosp.; tchr. dept. psychol. medicine U. Glasgow, 1953-56; clin. research Tavistock Inst. Human Relations, London, 1956-62; dir. Langham Clinic, London, 1962-65; co-founder Phila. assn. Kingsley Hall, London, 1964; chmn. Phila. Assn. Kingsley Hall, 1964-81; speaker various colls. in, U.S., 1970—. Author: The Divided Self, 1960, The Self and Others, 1961, Sanity, Madness and the Family, 1964; (with David G. Cooper) Reason and Violence: A Decade of Sartre's Philosophy, 1950-60, 1964; (with others) Interpersonal Perception, 1966, The Politics of Experience, 1967, The Politics of the Family, 1969, rev. edit., 1971, Knots, 1970, Self and Others, 1970, The Facts of Life, 1976, Do You Love Me?, 1976, Conversations with Adam and Natasha, 1977, Sonnets, 1979, The Voice of Experience, 1982, Wisdom, Madness and Folly, 1985. Address: care G Aitken, 29 Fernshaw Rd, SW10 London England *

LAINO, JOSEPH FRANCIS, II, educator; b. Springfield, Mass., May 4, 1953; s. Louis Joseph and Victoria Mary (Samay) L.; AA, Springfield Tech. Community Coll., 1975; BA, Am. Internat. Coll., 1975, MA, 1981; MEd, Springfield Coll., 1978. Career counselor, job developer CETA program City of Springfield, Mass., 1975-76; grad. asst. dept. tchr. edn. Springfield Coll., 1976-77; vocat. guidance counselor, dir. Career Ctr., Palmer (Mass.) Public Schs., 1978; tchr., dir. coop. edn. Agawam (Mass.) Public Schs., 1979-85; dropout counselor Chicopee (Mass.) Pub. Schs., 1986—. Mem. Nat. Vocat. Guidance Assn., Nat. Community Edn. Assn., Coop. Edn. Assn., Am. Personnel and Guidance Assn., Am. Sch. Counselor Assn., Am. Vocat. Assn., Mass. Community Edn. Assn., Mass. Sch. Counselors Assn., Mass. Tchrs. Assn., Mass. Vocat. Assn., Mass. Vocat. Guidance Assn., New Eng. Indsl. Arts Tchrs. Assn., Nat. Rifle Assn. Assn. for Supervision and Curriculum Devel., Am. Internat. Coll. Alumni Assn., Springfield Tech. Community Coll. Alumni Assn., Springfield Coll. Alumni Assn., Phi Delta Kappa. Roman Catholic. Clubs: Dante. Lodge: Elks. Home: 135 Magnolia Terr Springfield MA 01108 Office: Bellamy Sch 314 Pendleton Ave Chicopee MA 01020

LAIRD, DORIS ANNE MARLEY, humanities educator, musician; b. Charlotte, N.C., Jan. 15, 1931; d. Eugene Harris and Coleen (Bethea) Marley; m. William Everette Laird Jr., Mar. 13, 1964; children: William Everette III, Andrew Marley, Glen Howard. MusB, Converse Coll., Spartanburg, S.C., 1951; opera cert. New Eng. Conservatory, Boston, 1956; MusM, Boston U., 1956; PhD, Fla. State U., 1980. Leading soprano roles S.C. Opera Co., Columbia, 1951-53, Plymouth Rock Ctr. of Music and Art, Duxbury, Mass., 1953-56; soprano Pro Musica, Boston, 1956, New Eng. Opera Co., Boston, 1956; instr. Stratford Coll., Danville, Va., 1956-58, Sch. Music Fla. State U., Tallahassee, 1958-60, dept. humanities, 1960-68; asst. prof. Fla. A&M U., Tallahassee, 1979—; vis. scholar Cornell U., 1988. Author: Colin Morris: Modern Missionary, 1980; contbr. articles to profl. jours. Soprano Washington St. Meth. Ch., Columbia, S.C., 1951-53, Copley Meth. Ch., Boston, 1953-56, Trinity United Meth. Ch., Tallahassee, 1983—; mem. Saint Andrews Soc., Tallahassee, 1986—; judge Brain Bowl, Tallahassee, 1981-84. Recipient NEH award, 1988; Phi Sigma Tau scholar, 1960. Mem. AAUP, AAUW, Nat. Art Educators Assn., Tallahassee Music Tchrs. Assn., Tallahassee Music Guild, Am. Guild of Organists, DAR (mus. rep. 1984-85), Colonial Dames of 17th Century (music dir. 1984-85). Democrat. Club: University Wy Women's. Avocations: traveling, dancing. Home: 1125 Mercer Dr Tallahassee FL 32312 Office: Fla A&M U Dept Humanities Tallahassee FL 32307

LAJARA, JOSE RAMON, chemist; b. Trubia, Spain, Jan. 31, 1939; s. Jose and Maria L.; m. Lidia Fernandez, Oct. 20, 1969; 4 children. Degree in Chemistry, U. Oviedo, 1961. Tech. supr. Segura-Bartoli, Valladolid, Spain, 1962-64; shift supr. Indsl. de La Soja, Tarragona, 1964-65, refinery supr., 1965-68; plant supt. Cindasa, Tarragona, 1968-69, tech. dir., 1970-78, project and constr. engr., 1978-84; tech. dir., Spanish Oil Seed Processing Plants, Barcelona, Tarragona, Reus, Sevilla, Puebla, 1984-87—, also all Italian ops., 1987—. Contbr. articles on oil extraction to profl. jours. Roman Catholic. Club: Nautico Salou.

LAJMING, WLODZIMIERZ, painter, educator; b. Tczew, Poland, Feb. 7, 1933; s. Mikokaj and Anna (Trzebiatowska) L.; m. Szuba Bogdana, Aug. 18, 1962; 1 child, Ziemowit. Student art schs., Gdynia, Poland, Gdansk, Poland. One-man shows: Sopot, Poland, 1963, Copenhagen, 1965, Gdansk, 1968, 70, Warsaw, Poland, 1969, Worms, Fed. Republic Germany, 1979, Bremen, Fed. Republic Germany, 1980, Bonn, Fed. Republic Germany, 1986; exhibited in numerous group shows, including Ystad, Sweden, 1969, Helsinki, 1972, Gdansk, 1974, Bergen, Holland, 1974, Bremen, 1980; represented in permanent collections Nat. Mus. Gdansk, Nat. Mus. Szczecin, Poland, also pvt. collections; docent, 1988—; prof. High Sch. Fine Arts, Gdansk, 1976-84, dean painting and sculpture sect., 1984-87; prorector sci. works High Sch. Fine Arts, Gdansk. Mem. Internat. Assn. Art, Art Friends Assn. Poland, Polish Art Painters Alliance. Home: Weglarska 1/4 m 20, 80-834 Gdansk Poland Office: Piwna 27 11, Gdansk Poland

LAKAH, JACQUELINE RABBAT, political scientist, educator; b. Cairo, Apr. 14, 1933; came to U.S., 1969, naturalized, 1975; d. Victor Boutros and Alice (Mounayer) Rabbat; m. Antoine K. Lakah, Apr. 8, 1951; children: Micheline, Mireille, Caroline. BA, Am. U. Beirut, 1968; MPh, Columbia U., 1974, cert. Middle East Inst., 1975, PhD, 1978. Asst. prof. polit. sci. and world affairs Fashion Inst. Tech., N.Y.C., 1978—; asst. prof. grad. faculty polit. sci. Columbia U., N.Y.C., summer 1979, vis. scholar, 1982-83, also mem. seminar on Middle East; guest faculty Sarah Lawrence Co.., 1981-82; cons. on Middle East; faculty research fellow SUNY, summer 1982. Fellow Columbia Faculty, 1974, NDEA Title IV, 1974, Middle East Inst., 1975; Rockefeller Found. scholar, 1974. Mem. Am. Profs. for Peace in Mid. East, Internat. Studies Assn., Am. Polit. Sci. Assn., Fgn. Policy Assn., Internat. Studies Assn., Internat. Polit. Sci. Assn. Roman Catholic. Home: 41-15 94th St Queens NY 11373 Office: 7th Ave at 27th St New York NY 10001

LAKE, VICTOR HUGO, former manufacturing company executive; b. Quincy, Mass., Nov. 11, 1919; s. Victor Hugo and Edna Beatrice (Blott) L.; student Lawrence Inst. Tech., 1939-42, U. Maine, 1943; m. Jeannette Elzena Stewart, Apr. 26, 1942; children—Victor Stewart, Valerie Jean; m. 2d, Jacqueline Rose Davis, July 4, 1975. Asst. supt. Taylor Winfield Corp., Detroit, 1938-43; prodn. control mgr. Fed. Machine & Welder Co., Warren, Ohio, 1944-49; with Am. Welding & Mfg. Co., Warren, 1949-82, mgr. materials, 1969-82; ret., 1982. Served with AUS, 1943-44. Mem. Am. Soc. Metals, Trumbull County Indsl. Mgmt. Assn. (pres. 1972-73). Republican. Methodist. Home: 3503 Tiffany Pl New Port Richey FL 34655

LAKSHMANAN, TAVORATH KUNNINANKANDY, physicist, consultant; b. Cannanore, Madras, India, Oct. 31, 1930; came to U.S., 1966; s. Tavorath P. and Janaki (Muliyil) Kunhiraman; m. Eleanore Smyles, Jan. 30, 1964. B.S. with honors, U. Madras, 1949, B.T., 1949; M.A., 1950, M.S., 1950, A.M., Columbia U., 1951, Ph.D., 1966. Prof. physics, dir. grad. research in physics U. Madras, 1956-64, pres. Govt. Coll. and mem. Senate and Acad. Council U. Madras, 1964-66; chief physicist, chief engr. Weston, Schlumberger, Newark, 1966-68; project mgr. RCA, Somerville, N.J., 1968-69; exec. v.p. Robertson and Assocs., Newark, 1970-77; pres. TK Technologies, Matawan, N.J., 1978—; cons., project dir. Frost & Sullivan, N.Y.C., 1978—; seminar leader McGraw-Hill, N.Y.C., 1983—. Contbr. numerous articles in field to profl. jours.; patentee in field of solid state technology. Mem. IEEE, Inst. Physics London, Electronic Industries Assn., Soc. Mfg. Engrs. Office: TK Technologies 3 Waverly Pl Matawan NJ 07747

LAL, DEVENDRA, nuclear geophysics educator; b. Varanasi, India, Feb. 14, 1929; s. Radhe Krishna and Sita Devi (Gupta) L.; m. Aruna Damany, May 17, 1955. BS, Banaras Hindu U., Varanasi, 1947, MS, 1949, DSc, 1984; PhD, Bombay U., 1958. Research student Tata Inst. of Fundamental Research, Bombay, 1949-50, research fellow, assoc. prof., 1950-63, prof., 1963-70, sr. prof., 1970-72; dir. Phys. Research Lab., Ahmedabad, India, 1972-83; sr. prof. Phys. Research Lab., Ahmedabad, 1983—; vis. prof. UCLA, 1965-66, 83-84; prof. Scripps Instn. Oceanography, La Jolla, Calif., 1967—. Editor: Early Solar System Processes and the Present Solar System, 1980. Recipient K.S. Krishnan Gold Medal Indian Geophys. Union, 1965, S.S. Bhatnagar award for Physics Govt. India, 1967, Padma Shri award Govt. India, 1971, award for Excellence in Sci. and Tech. Fedn. of Indian Chamber Com., 1974. Fellow Royal Soc.; mem. Nat. Acad. Scis. (fgn. assoc.), Third World Acad. Scis. (founding mem.), Royal Astron. Soc. (assoc.) Internat. Acad. Aeronautics, Internat. Union of Geodesy and Geophysics (pres. 1984-87), Internat. Assn. Phys. Scis. of the Ocean (pres. 1980-84). Hindu. Office: GRD A 020 Scripps Inst of Oceanography La Jolla CA 92093 also: U Calif-San Diego Scripps Inst Oceanography A-020 La Jolla CA 92093

LALAGAS, KONSTANTINOS, management consultant, government advisor; b. Cavala, Macedonia, Greece, May 8, 1949; s. Georgios and Dimitra (Toulatzis) L.; m. Maria Faleschini, Mar. 28, 1980; 1 child, Corinna-Dimitra. MS in Mining Engring., Mining U., Leoben, Austria, 1973. Project mgr. Soravia-Bau GmbH., Spittal/Drau, Austria, 1975-78, Huta-Hegerfeld AG., Essen, Fed. Republic Germany, 1978-81; company owner Riyadh, Saudi Arabia, 1981-84; mgmt. cons. Beta Co., Riyadh, 1984—; tech. advisor Dep. Ministry of Town Planning, Riyadh, 1985—. Co-author: Standards of Procedure, 1986. Fellow Inst. Profl. Mgrs., Assn. Mining Engrs. Mailing Address: LALAGAS Konstantinos, PO Box 2824, Riyadh, 11461 Saudi Arabia Home: Am Reinbach 5, A-8410 Wildon Styria, Austria Office: Dep Ministry Town Planning, Riyadh Saudi Arabia

LALANNE, JEAN-LOUIS GEORGES, oral surgeon, maxillofacial surgeon; b. Tigne, Maine-et-Loire, France, July 6, 1938; s. Georges Camille and Jeanne-Marie (Tijou) L.; m. Evelyne Marie Belmont, Aug. 28, 1976; 1 child, Arnaud. D in Medicine, U. Tours, France, 1965; Diploma in Oral Surgery, Inst. Stomatology, Paris, 1968. Cert. maxillofacial surgery. Attaché Univ. Hosp., Angers, France, 1969-75, Nantes, France, 1976-79; practice surgery, Angers, 1969—, cons. specialist,, 1969—; pres. Odonto-Stomatological Soc., Nantes, 1974-76. Served to 2d lt. French Health Service, 1965-66. Mem. Soc. D'Odonto-Stomatologie D'Angers (hon. pres. 1976—), Assn. Maxillofacial Surgery (assoc. 1975—). Roman Catholic. Lodge: Rotary. Office: 7 Rue de la Prefecture, 49100 Angers France

LALLY, ANN MARIE, retired educational administrator; b. Chgo., Sept. 23, 1914; d. Martin J. and Della (McDonnell) L. AB, Mundelein Coll., 1935; AM, Northwestern U., 1939, PhD, 1950; postgrad., Chgo. Tchrs. Coll., Chgo. Art Inst., 1935-36. Tchr. Amundsen High Sch., 1935, Lindblom and Von Steuben High Schs., Chgo., 1936-38; chmn. art dept. Schurz High Sch., 1938-40; supr. art Chgo. Pub. Elementary Schs., 1940-48, dir. art Chgo. Public Schs., 1948-57; prin. John Marshall High Sch., 1957-63; supt. Dist. 16, Chgo. Pub. Schs., 1963-64, Dist. 5, 1964-80; lectr. Wright Jr. Coll., 1948; instr. creative drawing Chgo. Acad. Fine Art, 1941; instr. interior design Internat. Harvester Co., 1946-48; lectr. in edn. DePaul U., 1952-74; lectr. in edn. and art U. Chgo., 1956-59; lectr. edn. Chgo. Tchrs. Coll., 1960-62; trustee Pub. Sch. Tchrs. Pension and Retirement Fund Chgo., 1957-71, sec.-treas., 1960-65, pres., 1965-70. Contbr. articles to art and ednl. jours. Charter mem. women's bd. Loyola U., Art Inst. Chgo. Mem. Am. Assn. Sch. Adminstrs., Ill. Assn. Sch. Adminstrs., NEA (life), Ill. Edn. Assn., Dist. Supts. Assn. (pres. 1973-75), Ill. Women Adminstrs. Assn. (award 1979), Nat. Council Adminstrv. Women in Edn. (chmn. profl. relations com. 1958-62), Assn. Supervision and Curriculum Devel., Chgo. Area Women Adminstrs. in Edn. (Outstanding Adminstrn. award 1981), Nat. Art Edn. Assn. (mem. council 1956-60), Western Arts Assn. (pres. 1956-58), Internat. Soc. Edn. in Art, Ill. Art Edn. Assn. (pres. 1955), LWV of Chgo., Chgo. Art Educators Assn. (founder, past v.p., sec. and treas), Ill. Club Cath. Women (bd. dirs. 1981—, rec. sec. 1982-86), Chgo. Pub. Sch. Art Soc., Chgo. Hist. Soc., AAUW (Chgo. chmn. elem. and secondary edn. 1966—, dir.-at-large 1962-66, 78-80, mem. Ill. div. promoting individual liberties task force), Chgo. Area Reading Assn. (bd. dirs. 1963-69), Nat. Assn. Secondary Sch. Prins., Ill. Assn. Secondary Sch. Prins., Chgo. Prins. Assn., Artists Equity Assn. of Chgo., Council on Fgn. Relations, Mundelein Coll. Alumnae Assn. (past pres., chmn. bd., Magnificat medal 1964), Pi Lambda Theta, Delta Kappa Gamma (chmn. legis. com. 1985—). Clubs: Chgo. Woman's (chair legacy com. 1987—), Univ. Guild. Home: 307 Trinity Ct Evanston IL 60201

LALLY, GERASSIMOS HERCULES, civil enginner; b. Alexandria, Egypt, Aug. 27, 1944; s. Hercules Dimitri and Georgia (Lina) L.; m. Panayota Farmacas, Nov. 9, 1968; children: Maira, Tatiana, Hercules-Basil. MCE, Poly. U., Athens, Greece, 1966; M in Econs., Nat. Tech. U. Athens, 1972. Constrn. mgr. Edok Sa Eter Sa, Greece and Libya, 1966-71, coordination mgr., 1972; project area mgr. Edok Sa Eter Sa Enterprise Gen. of Luxembourg, Republic of West Africa, 1972-78; project coordinator Damascus (Syria) Water Supply, 1979-82; chief exec., cons. Edok Sa Eter Sa, Greece, 1983-85; bus. cons. Greece, 1986—; constrn. cons. Encogec Fratolin Spa, Italy, 1979; tendering cons. Bos, France, 1980, Pasotti Spa, Italy, 1987; cons. oil barters Internat. Contracting Group, Middle East; tech. mgr. Vipetva Ind. Devel. Bank, 1988. Candidate mem. Municipality of Voula, Athens, 1986. Mem. Soc. Greek Civil Engrs.-Contractors, So. Am. Mil. Engrs., Internat. Top 500 Bus. Cons., Ctr. Indsl. Devel./European Econ. Community Brussels, Assn. Greek Contractors, Greek Tech. Chamber. Conservative. Christian Orthodox.

LAM, ANNIE YOUNG YING YEE, computer company executive. d. Fu Cheung and Ka Yuk Young; m. Paul Lam Tat Chung, Oct. 27, 1973; 1 child, Mo Yee Lam. B of Social Sci. with honors, Chinese U. Hong Kong, 1972; postgrad., U. Mich., 1982. Exec. officer Hong Kong Govt., 1972-73, 76-78; tax officer (higher grade) U.K. Civil Service, London, 1973-76; sr. personnel officer Royal Hong Kong Jockey Club, 1978-80; Far East personnel mgr. cum Far East mgmt. com. mem. Far East hdqrs. Digital Equip Corp., Hong Kong, 1980-84; mng. dir. Snatch Goal Co., Ltd., Hong Kong, 1984—. Fellow Internat. Biog. Assn.; mem. Brit. Inst. Mgmt., Inst. Personnel Mgmt. Office: Snatch Goal Co Ltd, Room 141 14/F Caxton House, 1 Duddell St, Central Hong Kong Hong Kong

LAM, BILLY, finance company executive; b. Hong Kong, Feb. 27, 1960; s. Muk Kwong and Pui Ha (Wong) L. BS, Queen Mary Coll., London, 1982; MS, London Sch. Econs., 1984. Dir. Shing Fung Fin. Co., Ltd., Hong Kong, 1983—; asst. mgr. Tai Sun Co., Hong Kong, 1983—. Home: 3 Cassia Rd Ground Floor, Yau Yat Chuen Kowloon Hong Kong Office: Tai Sun Co 1301 Fin Bldg, 254/256 Des Veux Rd, Hong Kong Hong Kong

LAM, CHAN F., biomedical engineer, educator; b. Kwangtung, China, Oct. 23, 1943; came to U.S., 1961; s. Wing-Cheong and Choy (Chan) L.; m. Carolina Po Lam, Sept. 18, 1967; children: Shirley, Ken. BS, Calif. State Poly. Coll., 1965; MS in Mech. Engring., Clemson U., 1967, PhD in Elec. Engring., 1970. Asst. prof. dept. biometry Med. U. S.C., Charleston, 1970-75, assoc. prof. dept. biometry, 1975-80, prof., 1980—, dir. ops., chief programming Research Data Processing Ctr., 1971-72, dir. Time Share, Hybrid Computation Lab., 1975-79, dir. Biometry Computer Ctr., 1979-85; dir. Biomed Image and Signal Processing Lab., 1987—; mem. biomed. research tech. rev. com. NIH, 1986-90. Author: Techniques for Analysis and Modeling of Enzyme Kinetic Mechanisms, 1981; contbr. articles, abstracts to publs. Treas. Cooper Estates Civic Club, 1972-74. Research grantee State S.C., 1972-75. Mem. IEEE (sr.; chmn. sect. 1975), Soc. Math. Biology, Pattern Recognition, Assn. Computing Machinery. Home: 1097 Cottingham Dr Mt Pleasant SC 29464 Office: Dept Biometry Med U SC Charleston SC 29425

LAM, CHUN CHOON, statistician, educator; b. Ipoh, Malaysia, Jan. 6, 1944; s. Weng and Choy (Loke) L.; B.Sc. in Math. (Lee's Found. scholar), Nanyang U., Singapore, 1969; M.S. in Stats. (Fulbright-Hays scholar), Ohio State U., 1971, Ph.D. in Stats., 1973; A.M. in Computer Sci., Duke U., 1986; m. Bie Nio Lim, Aug. 19, 1977; 1 child, Sarah. Research scholar Office Aerospace Research, U.S. Air Force, 1970; postdoctoral research fellow dept. computer and info. sci. Ohio State U., Columbus, 1973-74, vis. asst. prof. dept. stats., 1974, vis. prof. dept. stats., 1981; lectr. dept. math. U. Malaya, Kuala Lumpur, Malaysia, 1975-81; asst. prof. div. math. Fayetteville (N.C.) State U., 1982-84; statis. cons., 1970—; now ops. research project analyst TWA, Kansas City. Treas., Logos Presbyn. Ch., Kuala Lumpur, 1980-82. Mem. Malaysian Math. Soc. (hon. treas. 1979-80, editor Bull. 1975-76, 79-80), Am. Statis. Assn., Assn. Computing Machinery, Southeast Asian Math. Soc. Contbr. articles on stats. to profl. jours. Office: Trans World Airlines PO Box 20007 Kansas City MO 64195

LAM, FRANKIE KING-SUN, chemical company executive; b. Hong Kong, Jan. 1, 1961; s. Huen Lam and Lang-Kwai Ng. BA with honors, North Tex. State U., 1982, MA, 1983; MS, Purdue U., 1985, PhD, 1986. Tng. mgr. John Swire and Sons Ltd., Hong Kong, 1986, sr. tng. officer, 1987, asst. mgr. tng., 1987-88; mgr. employee devel. Asia region Dow Chem. Pacific Ltd., Hong Kong, 1988—; adminstr. cash fund IBM China, summer 1985; hon. advisor, bd. dirs. Competitive Edge Tng. Ctr., Hong Kong, 1987—. Author: Supervision Series, 1987, Service, Trust and Loyalty, 1987, Service Excellence, 1987. Active St. John Ambulance Brigade, 1975-80, Meals-on-Wheels for the Elderly, Dallas, 1982-83. E.D. Criddle scholar Purdue U., 1985, Davis Ross scholar; recipient Outstanding Leadership in Internat. Edn. award. Mem. Am. Soc. for Tng. and Devel., Hong Kong Soc. for Tng. and Devel. (instr. 1987—, cert. of Appreciation 1987), Sociology Practice Assn., Am. Sociol. Assn., Inst. Tng. and Devel., North Cen. Sociol. Assn., Population Reference Bur., La Salle Old Boys Assn. (com. 1987), Hong Kong Jr. C. of C., Alpha Kappa Delta, Phi Eta Gamma.

LAMARRE, BERNARD C., engineer; b. Chicoutimi, Que., Can., Aug. 6, 1931; s. Emile J. and Blanche M. (Gagnon) L.; m. Louise Lalonde, Aug. 30, 1952; children: Jean, Christine, Lucie, Monique, Michele, Philippe, Mireille. BASc, Ecole Poly., Montreal, 1952; MSc, Imperial Coll., U. London, 1955; LLD, St. Francis Xavier U., N.S., Can., 1980; D in Engring. (hon.), U. Waterloo, Can., 1983; D in Social Scis. (hon.), U. Concordia, Montreal, 1983; D in Engring. (hon.), U. Montreal, 1985, U. Sherbrooke, Can., 1986, Queen's U., 1987; D in Adminstrn. (hon.), U. Quebec, Chicoutimi, 1987; D in Engring. (hon.), U. Ottawa, Can., 1988. Structural and founds. engr. Lalonde-Valois, Montreal, Que., 1955-58, chief engr., 1958-63; ptnr. Lalonde-Valois, Lamarre Valois, Montreal, 1963-73; chmn., chief exec. officer Lavalin Group, Montreal, 1973—; bd. dirs. La Laurentienne Générale Ins. Co., Can. Gen. Electric, Nat. Bank Can., Polysar Ltd.; former chmn. Can. Devel. Investment Corp. Contbr. articles to profl. jours. Bd. dirs. Royal Victoria Hosp., Montreal, 1979-88; bd. dirs. Montreal Fine Arts Mus., 1979—, chmn. bd., 1982—; mem. corp. Coll. Marie de France, Montreal, 1974—, Coll. Stanislas, 1977—. Decorated officer Order of Can., Order of Que.; recipient Gold medal Nat. Council Engrs. Can., 1985; Athlone scholar, 1952. Fellow Engring. Inst. Can.; hon. fellow Royal Can. Inst. Architects; Mem. Order of Engrs. of Que., ASCE, Prestressed Concrete Inst., Can. Assn. Civil Engrs. Roman Catholic. Clubs: Mont-Royal (Montreal), St. Denis (Montreal), Laval Golf (Montreal). Home: 4850 Cedar Crescent, Montreal, PQ Canada H3W 2H9 Office: 1100 Rene Levesque Blvd W, Montreal, PQ Canada H3B 4P3

LAMB, GEORGE A., university official; b. Pocatello, Idaho, Apr. 3, 1906; s. Luke F. and Mary (Burnell) L.; m. Mary Mellefont, June 25, 1932; children: Mary Anthia Lamb Dorenda, Rose Mary Lamb Malay, Jacqueline Lamb O'Donnell, George Joseph. A.B., U. Portland, 1929, LL.D., 1970; M.S. (Strathcona fellow 1931-32), Yale U., 1932; postgrad., U. Mich., 1932-33. Transp. economist Dept. Agr., 1930-31, 34; teaching fellow U. Mich., 1932-33; mineral economist NRA, 1934-36; transp. economist ICC, 1936-38; economist bituminous coal div. Dept. Interior, 1938-40, chief econs. br., 1940-43, asst. dir. Bur. Mines, 1944-46, dir. Office Coal Research, 1961-63; chief econs. and stats div. Solid Fuels Adminstrn. War, 1943-44; mgr. bus. surveys Pitts. Consol. Coal Co., 1946-61; dir. econ. studies Consol. Coal Co., Pitts., 1963-67; now dir. law enforcement edn., dir. research adminstrn. U. Portland, 1967-88; cons. Nat. Mediation Bd., 1941; mem. Am. Coal Mission to Gt. Britain, 1944; cons. sec. interior, 1950, OPS, 1951-52, cabinet energy study, 1954-56; mem. Am. Coal Team vis. Poland, 1957; U.S. del. ECA Coal Commn., 1959, 60. Contbr. articles to tech. publs. Mem. Am. Statis. Assn., Am. Econ. Assn., AIME, Tau Kappa Epsilon, Beta Gamma Sigma. Roman Catholic. Club: KC. Home: 7908 NE 12th St Vancouver WA 98664 Office: U Portland Portland OR 97203

LAMB, WARREN DAVID, management consultant; b. Wallasey, Cheshire, England, Apr. 28, 1923; came to U.S., 1985; s. David Richard and Rose Marion (Wilkinson) L.; m. Joan Carrington, Nov. 9, 1954 (div. 1975); children: James Marcus, Elizabeth Yolande, Imogen, Timothy Jerome; m. Barbara Mallory, Oct. 6, 1985. Diploma, Laban Ctr. for Movement Study, Manchester, Eng., 1950. Cons. Paton Lawrence & Co., Manchester, Eng., 1950-52; prin. Warren Lamb Assocs., London, Claremont, Calif., 1952—. Author: Posture and Gesture, 1965, Management Behaviour, 1969, Body Code: The Meaning in Movement, 1979. Served with the Brit. Navy, 1941-46, Mediterranean. Fellow Inst. Mgmt. Cons.; mem. Action Profilers Internat. (pres.), The Laban Guild (pres.). Home: 1517 Marjorie Ave Claremont CA 91711

LAMB, WILLIS EUGENE, JR., physicist, educator; b. Los Angeles, July 12, 1913; s. Willis Eugene and Marie Helen (Metcalf) L.; m. Ursula Schaefer, June 5, 1939. B.S., U. Calif., 1934, Ph.D., 1938; D.Sc., U. Pa., 1953, Gustavus Adolphus Coll., 1975; M.A., Oxford (Eng.) U., 1956, Yale, 1961; L.H.D., Yeshiva U., 1965. Mem. faculty Columbia, 1938-52, prof. physics, 1948-52; prof. physics Stanford, 1951-56; Wykeham prof. physics and fellow New Coll., Oxford U., 1956-62; Henry Ford 2d prof. physics Yale, 1962-72, J. Willard Gibbs prof. physics, 1972-74; prof. physics and optical scis. U. Ariz., Tucson, 1974—; Morris Loeb lectr. Harvard, 1953-54; cons. Philips Labs., Bell Telephone Labs., Perkin-Elmer, NASA.; Vis. com. Brookhaven Nat. Lab. Recipient (with Dr. Polycarp Kusch) Nobel prize in physics, 1955; Rumford premium Am. Acad. Arts and Scis., 1953; Research Corp. award, 1955; Guggenheim fellow, 1960-61; recipient Yeshiva award, 1962. Fellow Am. Phys. Soc., N.Y. Acad. Scis.; hon. fellow Inst. Physics and Phys. Soc. (Guthrie lectr. 1958), Royal Soc. Edinburgh (fgn. mem.); mem. Nat. Acad. Scis., Phi Beta Kappa, Sigma Xi. Office: Dept of Physics U Ariz Tucson AZ 85721

LAMBE, JEFFREY FRANCIS, horticulturalist, greenhouse company executive; b. Newmarket, Ont., Can., Aug. 17, 1943; s. William G.A. and Frances (Adams) L.; m. Barbara Jean St. John, Mar. 1, 1969; children: Robyn Lisa, Mark Jeffrey. BSc, U. Guelph, Ont., Can., 1967. Product mgr. Superior Bulb Co., Mississauga, Ont., 1966-68; owner, mgr. greenhouse bus., Leamington, Ont., 1969-72; salesman Ball Superior, Mississauga, 1972-81, sales mgr., 1982-84, gen. mgr., 1985—; bd. dirs. Canadian Greenhouse Conf., Guelph, 1986—. Mem. Bedding Plants Internat. Office: Ball Superior, 1155 Birchview Dr, Mississauga, ON Canada L5H 3EI

LAMBERG-KARLOVSKY, CLIFFORD CHARLES, anthropologist, archaeologist; b. Prague, Czechoslovakia, Oct. 2, 1937; came to U.S., 1939; s. Carl Othmar von Lamberg and Bettina Karlovsky; m. Martha Louise Veale, Sept. 12, 1959; children—Karl Emil Othmar, Christopher William. A.B., Dartmouth Coll., 1959; M.A. (Wenner-Gren fellow), U. Pa., 1964, Ph.D., 1965; M.A. (hon.), Harvard U., 1970. Asst. prof. sociology and anthropology Franklin and Marshall Coll., 1964-65; asst. prof. anthropology Harvard U., 1965-69, prof., 1969—; curator Near Eastern archaeology Peabody Museum Archaeology and Ethnology, 1969—, mus. dir., 1977—; asso. Columbia U., 1969—; trustee Am. Inst. Iranian Studies, 1968—, Am. Inst. Yemeni Studies, 1976-77; dir. research Am. Sch. Prehist. Research, 1974-79, 86—; trustee Am. Sch. Oriental Research, 1969-71, 86—, Centro di Richerche Ligabue, 1984; Reckitt archaeol. lectr. Brit. Acad., 1973; dir. archaeol. surveys in Syria, 1965, excavation projects at Tepe Yahya, Iran, 1967-75, Sarazm, Tadjikistan, USSR, 1985, archaeol. surveys in Saudia Arabia, 1977-80, corresponding fellow Inst. Medio and Extremo Orient, Italy. Author: (with J. Sabloff) Ancient Civilizations: The Near East and Mesoamerica, 1979; editor: (with J. Sabloff) The Rise and Fall of Civilizations, 1973, Ancient Civilizations and Trade, 1975, Hunters, Farmers and Civilization, 1979, Archaeoligical Thought In America, 1987; author, gen. editor Tepe Yahya: The Early Periods, 1986. Recipient medal Iran-Am. Soc., 1972; NSF grantee, 1966-75, 78-80; Nat. Endowment for Arts grantee, 1977—; Nat. Endowment for Humanities grantee, 1977—. Fellow Soc. Antiquaries Gt. Brit. and Ireland (sec. N.Am. chpt.), Am. Anthrop. Assn., Am. Acad. Arts Sci. (chmn. USA/USSR archaeol. exchange program), N.Y. Acad. Sci., Prehist. Soc., Soc. Am. Archaeology, Archeol. Inst. Am.; mem. German Archaeol. Inst., Danish Archaeol. Inst., Brit. Archaeol. Inst., Italian Archeol. Inst. Club: Tavern (Boston). Office: Harvard Univ Peabody Museum Cambridge MA 02138

LAMBERSON, JOHN ROGER, insurance company executive; b. Aurora, Mo., Aug. 16, 1933; s. John Oral Lamberson and Golda May (Caldwell) Tidwell; m. Virginia Lee, Aug. 10, 1957; 1 child, John Clinton. BA, U. Calif., Berkeley, 1954. Coach, tchr. Thousand Palms (Calif.) Sch., 1954-55; underwriter trainee Fireman's Fund Ins. Co., San Francisco, 1955; surety mgr. Safeco Ins. Co. (formerly Gen. Ins. Co.), San Francisco and Sacramento, Calif., 1957-61; exec. v.p., chief operating officer Corroon & Black Corp., N.Y.C., 1961—, also bd. dirs., chmn. constrn. industry div., mem. exec. com., aquisition com.; guest lectr. Grad. Sch. Engring. Stanford U., Fails Mgmt. Inst., participant numerous sems. and forums. Mem. Nat. Assn. Heavy Engring. Constructors (bd. dirs. 1985—), Constrn. Fin. Mgmt. Assn. (bd. dirs. 1987—, exec. com.), Assoc. Gen. Contractors Am. (membership devel. com., past chmn. bd. dirs. nat. assoc. mems. council), Assoc. Gen. Contractors Calif. (bd. dirs. 1976, various past coms.), Nat. Assn. Surety Bond Producers (past nat. pres., regional v.p.), Am. Inst. Contractors, Soc. Am. Mil. Engrs., Young Pres.' Orgn. (sem. leader). Clubs: Bankers (San Francisco); Sharon Heights Golf and Country (Menlo Pk., Calif.). Home: 85 Greenoaks Dr Atherton CA 94025 Office: Corroon & Black Corp Wall St Plaza New York NY 10005

LAMBERT, JACQUES EMMANUEL, physician; b. Nice, France, Sept. 28, 1941; s. Pierre Alphonse and Sylvie Felicie (Bosano) L.; m. Mireille Marie-France Duchemin, July 19, 1968; children: Lucille, Laure, Lydiane. PCB, Faculté de Seines, Montpellier, France, 1960; MD, Faculté de Medecine, Monpellier, 1972, postgrad., 1973, postgrad. degree in Head and Neck Pathology, 1987. Gen. practice specializing in ear, nose and throat Millau, France, 1973—. City counsellor Compeyre, France, 1982—. Served as doctor for French Army Res., 1969-70. Roman Catholic. Home: 12520 Compeyre Aguessac France Office: 16 Boulevard de Layrolle, 12100 Millau France

LAMBERT, PETER JAMES, economics educator; b. Newcastle, Eng., May 17, 1946; s. Wilfred Lambert and Sheila Margaret (Oliver) L.; m. Jane Ann Beckwith, Feb. 23, 1977; children: Thomas Benedict, Hugo Jake. BS, Manchester U., 1968; Diploma in Advanced Math., Oxford U., 1969, PhD, 1972; MS, York U., 1977. Lectr. in pure math. Wadham Coll., Oxford, 1970-71, U. Ibadan, Nigeria, 1971-76; lectr. in econs. U. Hull, Eng., 1977-78, U. York, Eng., 1979—; research assoc. Inst. for Fiscal Studies, London, 1984—. Author: Stationary Processes in Time Analysis, 1983, Advanced Math. for Economists, 1985; joint editor Bulletin Econ. Research, 1984—; contbr. numerous articles to profl. jours. Founder Social Dem. Party, London, 1981. Anglican. Office: U York, Heslington, York YO1 5DD, England

LAMBERT, RENE E., gastroenterologist; b. Lyon, France, July 23, 1930; d. Jacques and Valentine (Neuville) L.; m. Claude Mayoux, Apr. 1, 1952; children—Philippe, Olivier, Pierre Gilles, Flavien. M.D., Sch. Medicine, Lyon, 1958. Research fellow Centre National Recherche Scientifique, Lyon, France, 1959-63, dir. Centre d'epidemiologie, 1978-83; assoc. prof. U. Lyon, 1963-74, prof., 1974—; chief gastroenterology unit Hosp. E. Herriot, Lyon, 1974—; dir. research unit INSERM, 1964-83. Author: Les Aspects Recents de l'ulcere Experimental, 1958; La Digestion, 1976; Epidemiologie: Elements pour le Clinicien, 1981, Les Lasers: applications Medicales, 1987. Contbr. articles to profl. jours. Mem. Internat. Soc. Laser Med. Surg., Eluop. Laser Assn., Am. Gastroent. Assn., Brit. Soc. Gastro., Soc. France Endoscopie Digestive, French Soc. Gastro. Home: 1 Rue Boissac, Lyon 69002 France Office: Hosp E Herriot Place d'Arsonval, Lyon 69374 France

LAMBERT, WILLY EDMOND, biochemist, researcher; b. Brugge, Belgium, Mar. 7, 1953; s. Valere and Irene (Noote) L.; m. Patricia Maria Smitz, Aug. 18, 1978; 1 child, Stefanie. Grad. Latin-Greek, St. Lodewyks Coll., Brugge, 1971; BS in Pharmacy, State U. of Gent, Belgium, 1977, PhD, 1981. Asst. researcher State U. of Gent, 1977-85, research assoc., 1985—. Editor: Modern Chromatographic Analysis of the Vitamins, 1985; contbr. articles to profl. jours. Served to capt. med. service Belgian Army, 1980-81. Mem. Am. Assn. for Clin. Chemists, Am. Pharm. Soc., Am. Chem. Soc. Office: State U of Gent, Harelbekestraat 72, B 9000 Gent Belgium

LAMBIN, GERARD, educator; b. Crain, Yonne, France, Apr. 30, 1946; m. Nicole Rouget, Sept. 5, 1970; children: Helen, Pierre. Doctorate, U. Lille III, 1986. Tchr. U. Rennes II, France, 1988—. Contbr. articles to profl. jours. Home: 15 Place des Cigognes, 45160 Olivet Loiret France

LAMBIRD, PERRY ALBERT, pathologist; b. Reno, Nev., Feb. 7, 1939; s. C. David and Florence (Knowlton) L.; m. Mona Sue Salyer, July 30, 1960; children—Allison Thayer, Jennifer Salyer, Elizabeth Gard, Susannah Johnson. B.A., Stanford U., 1958; M.D., Johns Hopkins U., 1962; M.B.A., Okla. City U., 1973. Diplomate Am. Bd. Pathology. Fellow in internal medicine Johns Hopkins Hosp., Balt., 1962-63, resident pathologist, 1965-68, chief resident, 1968-69; med. cons. USPHS, Washington, 1963-65; pathologist Med. Arts Lab., Oklahoma City, 1969—, Presbyn. Hosp., South Community Hosp., 1974—, Nat. Cancer Inst., 1974-81; propr. Lambird Mgmt. Cons. Service, Oklahoma City, 1974—; pres. Ind. Pathology Inst., Inc., 1984-88, chmn. bd. dirs., 1988—; assoc. prof. pathology and orthopedic surgery U. Okla. Coll. Medicine, 1980—; cons. in field. Reviewer Jour. Am. Med. Assn, 1983—; contbr. articles to profl. jours. Pres. Okla. Symphony Orch., 1974-75, Ballet Okla., 1978-79; del. Republican Nat. Conv., 1976, alt. del., 1984; bd. regents Uniformed Services U. Health Scis., 1983-88; mem. task force entitlements and human assistance programs U.S. Ho. of Reps., 1983—; bd. dirs. Commn. on Office Lab. Assessment, 1988—. Served to lt. comdr. USPHS, 1963-65. Recipient Exec. Leadership award Oklahoma City U., 1976; Physician's Recognition award AMA, 1969-86; Outstanding Pathologist award Am. Pathology Found., 1984. Fellow Am. Soc. Clin. Pathologists, Coll. Am. Pathologists, (gov. 1984—), Internat. Coll. Surgeons; mem. AMA (ho. of dels., council on med. service), Okla. Med. Assn. (ho. of dels., trustee, v.p.), Okla. County Med. Soc. (pres.), Okla. Soc. Cytopathology (pres.), Am. Pathology Found. (pres.), Okla. Found. for Peer Rev. (dir.), Arthur Purdy Stout Soc. Surg. Pathologists, Am. Assn. Pathologists, Okla. Assn. Pathologists (pres.), So. Med. Assn., N.Y. Acad. Sci., Am. Soc. Cytology, Okla. Soc. Cytopaths (pres.), Osler Soc., Okla. City Clin. Soc., Johns Hopkins Med. and Surg. Assn., Phi Beta Kappa, Alpha Omega Alpha. Republican. Methodist. Home: 419 NW 14th St Oklahoma City OK 73103 Office: Med Arts Lab 100 Pasteur 1111 N Lee St Oklahoma City OK 73103

LAMBO, THOMAS ADEOYE, psychiatrist, deputy director general WHO; b. Abeokuta, Nigeria, Mar. 29, 1923; s. David Basil and Felicia (Bolawa) L.; M.B., Ch.B., U. Birmingham, 1948, M.D., 1954; postgrad. London U. Inst. Psychiatry; D.P.M., Eng., 1953; hon. degrees Ahmadu Bello U., Nigeria, 1967, Kent (Ohio) State U., 1969, Birmingham U., 1971, U. Benin, 1973, U. d'Aix-Marseilles (France), 1974, L.I. U., 1975, Louvain U., Belgium, 1976, McGill U., Montreal, 1978, U. Jos, Nigeria, 1979, U. Nigeria, Nsukka, 1979, Hacettepe U., Ankara, 1980, Hahnemann U., Phila., 1984, U. Pa., 1985; m. Dinah Violet Adams; children—David, Richard and Roger (twins). House surgeon, house physician, Birmingham, Eng., from 1949; med. officer, Lagos, Zaria, Gusau, 1951-56; cons. psychiatrist U. Coll. Hosp., Ibadan, also asso. lectr. U. Ibadan, 1956-63; specialist Western Region Ministry Health, 1957-60, sr. specialist Neuro-Psychiat. Centre, 1960-63; prof. psychiatry, head dept. psychiatry and neurology U. Ibadan (Nigeria), 1963-71, dean Med. Faculty, 1966-68, vice chancellor, 1968-71; asst. dir. gen. WHO Geneva, 1971-73, dep. dir. gen., 1973—, mem. expert adv. panel on mental health WHO, 1959-71, mem. adv. com. on med. research, 1970-71, chmn. UN Permanent Adv. Com on Prevention Crime and Treatment of Offenders, 1968-71; vice chmn. UN Adv. Com. on Application Sci. and Tech. to Devel., 1970-71; mem. sci. adv. panel Ciba Found., 1966—, Sci. Com. on Advanced Study in Devel. Scis., 1967-71; chmn. West African Exams. Council, 1969-71, African Chairs Tech. in Food Processing, Biotechs. and Nutrition and Health. Decorated officer Order Brit. Empire; Nigerian Nat. Order of Merit; comdr. Order of Niger; recipient Haile Selassie African Research award, 1970. Justice of peace Western State, Nigeria, 1968. Fellow Royal Coll. Physicians (Edinburgh); mem. Sci. Council for Africa (chmn. 1965), World Fedn. for Mental Health (exec. com. 1964—), Internat. Coll. Tropical Medicine (chmn. 1966-70), Internat. Soc. for Study Human Devel. (co-chmn. 1968—), Nigeria Med. Council, Pontificial Acad. Scis., Third World Acad. Scis. (founding mem.), African Acad. Scis. (founding mem.), West African Council for Med. Research, Swiss Acad. Med. Sci. (hon.), Mexican Inst. Culture (fellow mem. corr. in Nigeria). Contbr. articles to med. and sci. jours., also monographs. Address: WHO, 20 Ave Appia, 1211 Geneva 27, Switzerland Other: Chemin des Chataigniers 27, 1292 Chambesy Switzerland *

LAMBORN, KEITH CECIL, textile company executive; b. London, Oct. 18, 1944; s. Henry George and Lilian Ruth Lamborn; m. Elizabeth Helen Dawkins, Oct. 25, 1979; children: Ruth Clare, David Keith, Louise Elizabeth Helen. Grad. pub. schs., London, 1962. Various dirs. textile and furnishing cos., London and Manchester, Eng., 1969-75; sales dir. Richardson Smith Fabrics Ltd., London, 1975-78; mng. dir. Richardson Smith Fabrics Ltd., High Wylombe, Eng., 1978—, Ramm, Son & Crocker Ltd., Ramms Ltd., High Wylombe, 1978—; bd. dirs. various cos. Designer, colourist. Fellow Royal Soc. Art; mem. Inst. Mktg., Inst. Dirs.

LAMBRAKIS, CHRISTOS, publisher; b. Feb. 24, 1934. Ed., LSE. Pub., editor weekly Tachydromos (Courier), 1955—; owner, pub., editor daily Ta Nea (News), 1957—; owner daily To Vima (Tribune), and weeklies Economicos Tachydromos (Econ. Courier), 1957, Omada (The Team), 1958; pub. monthly Epoches, 1963; pres. Greek sect. Internat. Press Inst. Imprisoned, SyrosPrison Island, Nov. 1967. Recipient FIEJ Golden Pen of Freedom award, 1968. Address: Lambrakis Press, Odos Christou Lada 3, Athens Greece *

LAMBRINOPOULOS, ANDREAS, professional society administrator; b. Patras, Achaia, Greece, Oct. 19, 1936; s. Constantinos and Katerina (Leondaritou) L.; m. Eleftheria Sakellaropoulou, May 6, 1967; children: Katerina, Constantinos. Degree in Mech. and Elec. Engring., Tech. U., Athens, Greece, 1960. Telecommunications engr. Hellenic Telecommunications Orgn., Athens, 1962-67, chief engr., 1969-79, subdir., 1980-81; gov. Hellenic Railways Orgn., Athens, 1982-85, dir. gen., 1986-87, pres., dir. gen., 1987—; chmn. bd. Health Fund Hellenic Railways Personnel, Athens. Author: Wire Telecommunications, 1964, Carrier Equipment, 1975. Served to lt. Greek Armed Forces, 1960-62. Siemens scholar, Munich, 1967-68. Mem. Tech. Chamber of Greece. Mem. Panhellenic Social party. Greek Orthodox. Home: 4 Kerkiras (Kastri), 14671 Athens Greece Office: Hellenic Railways Orgn, 1-3 Karolou St, 10437 Athens Greece

LAMBRIS, JOHN DIMITRIOS, immunologist; b. Rodavgi, Greece, June 3, 1954; came to U.S., 1979; s. Dimitrios and Agathi (Phyhogios) L.; m. Rodothea Kokkinou, July 7, 1976; children—Agatha, Dimitrios. B.S., U. Patras, Greece, 1976, Ph.D., 1979. Research asst. Hellenic Anticancer Inst., Athens, Greece, 1976-79; postdoctoral fellow U. N.C., Chapel Hill, 1979-80, research assoc., 1980-81, asst. prof. immunology, 1981-82; vis. prof. Inst. Medical Micro., Mainz, Fed. Republic Germany, 1982-83; asst. mem. Scripps Clinic and Research Found., La Jolla, Calif., 1983-86; mem. Basel Inst. Immunology, 1986-87, adj. prof. San Diego (Calif.) State U., 1987—. Contbr. articles to profl. publs. Grantee Am. Cancer Soc., 1982, NIH, 1984; recipient New Investigator award NIH, 1982. Fellow European Molecular Biology Orgn., Alexander Von Humboldt, Fed. Republic Germany; mem. Am. Soc. Immunologists, British Soc. Biochemists. Current work: Functional and structural characterization of human complement components and complement receptors. Subspecialty: Immunocytochemistry. Home: Waldshuterstrasse 41, 4310 Rheinfelden Switzerland

LAMBSDORFF, OTTO GRAF, government official; b. Aachen, Germany, 1926. Student, U. Bonn, U. Cologne; LLD, 1952. With Free Dem. Party, Aachen, 1951—; chmn. Aachen Dist. Br. Free Dem. Party, 1951-53, elected to German Bundestag, 1972, fed. minister econs., 1977-83, econ. policy spokesman, 1983—. Office: Free Dem Party, Baumscheidtstr 15, Thomas-Dehler-Haus, Bonn Federal Republic of Germany *

LAMEIRO, GERARD FRANCIS, computer network consultant, columnist; b. Paterson, N.J., Oct. 3, 1949; s. Frank Raymond and Beatrice Cecilia (Donley) L.; BS, Colo. State U., 1971, MS, 1973, PhD, 1977. Sr. scientist Solar Energy Research Inst., Golden, Colo., 1977-78; asst. prof. mgmt. sci. and info. systems Colo. State U., Fort Collins, 1978-82, lectr. dept. computer sci., 1983, lectr. dept. mgmt., 1983; pres. Successful Automated Office Systems, Inc., Fort Collins, 1982-84; product mgr. Hewlett Packard, 1984-88; internat. computer networking consultant, 1988—, Ft. Collins. Columnist The HP Chronicle, 1988 —. Mem. Presdl. Electoral Coll., 1980. Recipient nat. disting. Service award Assn. Energy Engrs., 1981. Colo. Energy Research Inst. fellow 1976; NSF fellow 1978. Mem. Assn. for Computing Machinery. Roman Catholic. Contbr. articles in mgmt. and tech. areas to profl. jours. Home: PO Box 9580 Fort Collins CO 80525 Address: 3313 Downing St Fort Collins CO 80526 Office: Hewlett Packard Co 3313 Downing Ct Fort Collins CO 80525

LAMEY, WILLIAM DANIEL ALEXANDER, association executive; b. Antigonish, N.S., Can., Mar. 8, 1953; came to U.S., 1986; s. Willard D. and M. Irene Lamey. BCommerce in Bus. Adminstrn., St. Mary's U., Halifax, N.S., 1974. Dir. Atlantic region Assn. Student Councils, Halifax, 1972-73; adminstrn. mgr. Bank Montreal, New Glasgow, N.S., 1974-75, Halifax, 1975-76; consumer loan mgr. Bank Montreal, Sydney, N.S., 1976-77; exec. dir. Can. Jaycees, Ottawa, Ont., 1977-80, Assn. Kinsmen Clubs, Cambridge, Ont., 1980-86; sec. gen. Jaycees Internat. Inc., Coral Gables, Fla., 1986—; apptd. by Fla. Sec. Commerce as adv. Fla. Vol. Orgn. of Internat. Commerce Execs. Mem. Met. Bd. Trade, Toronto, Ont., 1980-86. Named Hon. Citizen, City Birmingham, Ala., 1978. Mem. Am. Soc. Assn. Execs. (Gold Circle award 1983), Can. Soc. Assn. Execs., Fla. Soc. Assn. Execs., South Fla. Assn. Execs., Jaycees Internat. (life), Coral Gables Jaycees, Greater Miami C. of C., Coral Gables C. of C. Roman Catholic. Office: Jaycees Internat Inc 400 University Dr Coral Gables FL 33134

LAMM, FRANKLIN CHARLES, bus. exec.; b. Reading, Pa., Jan. 9, 1945; s. John Herman and Helen Rosa (Stamm) L.; student Shattuck Sch., Faribault, Minn., 1961-64, Chulalongkorn U., Bangkok, 1967-68, La Escuela de Agricultura y Cria, Venezuela, 1968; B.A., St. Olaf Coll., 1968; M.A., U. No. Colo., 1973; m. Marion Isabella Banks, Sept. 24, 1968; children—Tammy Michelle, Shattuck Franklin, Robin Julie. Child care worker Northwood Treatment Ctr. for Emotionally Disturbed Children, Duluth, Minn., 1965-66; vol. Peace Corps, Campiarito, Venezuela, 1968-71; assoc. headmaster Vershire Sch. (Vt.), 1971-72; learning disabilities specialist Sch. Dist. #51, Grand Junction, Colo., 1973-78; investment property locator Mesa Properties Ltd., Grand Junction, 1978-79; pres., proprietor, dir. Energy Belt Enterprises, Grand Junction, Colo., 1980-86; pres. Energy Belt Property Mgmt., Energy Belt Farm and Ranch, Energy Belt Devel., Inc., Energy Belt Investments, Inc.; learning disabilities specialist, White Mountain Apache Indian Reservation, Whiteriver, Ariz., 1986—. Chmn. N.W. Citizens Task Force, Mesa County, Colo., 1979-82; scoutmaster Boy Scouts Am., 1980-82, 85—. Mem. Kappa Delta Pi. Republican. Mem. Ch. Jesus Christ Latter-Day Saints. Address: Box 697 Grand Junction CO 81502

LAMMES, FRITS BAREND, gynecologist-oncologist, educator; b. Amsterdam, The Netherlands, Mar. 27, 1934; s. Barend Cornelis and Henriette (Leonhard) L.; m. Maria Schëygrond, Apr. 4, 1959; children—Florentine, Rik, Renske, Hester. Ph.D., Leyden U., 1963. Cons., Leyden U. Hosp., The Netherlands, 1968-71; chief dept. gynecology Rotterdam Radio-therapeutic Inst., 1971-82; prof. gynecology Acad. Med. Ctr. Amsterdam, 1982—; mem. Ovarian Tumor Com. The Netherlands, Trophoblastic Tumors Com. The Netherlands. Author: Practical Gynecology, 1984, 3d edit., 1987. Home: Peppinghof 3, 1391 Abcoude The Netherlands

LAMON, HARRY VINCENT, JR., lawyer; b. Macon, Ga., Sept. 29, 1932; s. Harry Vincent and Helen (Bewley) L.; m. Ada Healey Morris, June 17, 1954; children: Hollis Morris, Helen Kathryn. B.S. cum laude, Davidson Coll., 1954; J.D. with distinction, Emory U., 1958. Bar: Ga. 1958, D.C. 1965. Practice in Atlanta, 1958—; mem. firm Hurt, Richardson, Garner, Todd & Cadenhead; dir. Sockwell Enterprises Inc., Atlanta, V.P. Oil, Atlanta; adj. prof. law Emory U., 1960—. Contbr. articles to profl. jours. Mem. adv. bd. Salvation Army, 1963—, chmn., 1975-79, mem. nat. adv. bd., 1976—; mem. Adv. Council on Employee Welfare and Pension Benefit Plans, 1975-79; mem. Pension Reporter adv. bd. Bur. Nat. Affairs; bd. visitors Davidson Coll.; trustee, past pres. So. Fed. Tax Inst. Inc.; trustee Inst. Continuing Legal Edn. in Ga., 1976—. Served to 1st lt. AUS, 1954-56. Recipient Others award Salvation Army, 1979. Fellow Am. Coll. Probate Counsel, Am. Coll. Tax Counsel, Internat. Acad. Estate and Trust Law; mem. Am., Fed., Atlanta bar assns., Am. Law Inst., Am. Pension Conf., So. Pension Conf. (pres. 1972), State Bar Ga. (chmn. sect. taxation 1969-70, vice chmn. commn. on continuing lawyer competency 1982—), Am. Judicature Soc., Atlanta Tax Forum, Lawyers Club of Atlanta, Nat. Emory U. Law Sch. Alumni Assn. (pres. 1967), Practicing Law Inst., ALI-ABA Inst., C.L.U.s Inst., Phi Beta Kappa, Omicron Delta Kappa, Phi Delta Phi, Phi Delta Theta (chmn. community service day 1969-72, legal commr. 1973-76). Episcopalian (vestryman). Clubs: Kiwanis (Atlanta) (pres. 1973-74), Breakfast (Atlanta), Peachtree Racket (Atlanta) (pres. 1986-87), Capital City (Atlanta), Commerce (Atlanta); University (Washington). Home: 3375 Valley Rd NW Atlanta GA 30305 Office: Hurt Richardson et al 999 Peachtree St NE Suite 1400 Atlanta GA 30309-3999 also: 1730 K St NW Suite 1302 Washington DC 20036

LAMONA, THOMAS ADRIAN, engineering, marketing company executive, consultant; b. Los Angeles, Aug. 19, 1925; s. Thomas Adrian and Joy A. (Kirkman) L.; m. Jeanne Muse, May 21, 1953 (div. 1958); m. Joyce Maurer, Dec. 12, 1971. Student San Fernando Valley Jr. Coll., 1945-46, UCLA, 1948, U. So. Calif., 1955. Various positions 1943-54; sales engr. Everlube Corp., North Hollywood, Calif., 1954-57; cons. engring., Newport Beach, Calif., 1957-67, 1973—; sales engr. Lubeco, Compton, Calif., 1963-73; v.p., bd. dirs. Coating Tech. Corp., Glen Ellyn, Ill., 1986-88. Served with U.S. Army, 1951. Recipient Special Service citation Soc. Mfg. Engrs., region VII, 1979. Mem. Standards Engring. Soc. (Los Angeles sect., mem. chmn. 1975-77, program dir. 1977-78, treas. 1978-81, chmn. 1981-82, Spl. Service citiation 1978, cert. in standards engring. 1979, Outstanding Sect. Mem. 1984), Porsche Owner's Club, Calif. Sports Car Club Am. (Los Angeles) (press relations com. 1955-63). Home: PO Box 2195 Newport Beach CA 92663 Office: Coating Tech Corp PO Box 2126 Glen Ellyn IL 60137

LAMONT, ALICE, accountant, consultant; b. Houston, July 19; d. Harold and Bessie Bliss (Knight) L. BS, Mont. State U.; MBA in Taxation, Golden Gate U., 1982. Tchr. London Central High Sch., 1971-80; acct. Signetics, Sunnyvale, Calif., 1980-82, Metcalf, Frix & Co., Atlanta, 1983-84; propr. Alice Lamont Ltd., 1985—. Mem. Atlanta Hist. Soc., High Mus. Art. Mem. AAUW (life), Ga. Soc. CPAs (assoc.), EDP Auditors, Inst. Internal Auditors, English Speaking Union. Episcopalian. Club: Atlanta Woman's (co-chair ways and means com. 1985-86, asst. treas. 1986-88).

LAMONT, CORLISS, philosopher, educator, author; b. Englewood, N.J., Mar. 28, 1902; s. Thomas William and Florence Haskell (Corliss) L.; m. Margaret H. Irish, June 8, 1928 (div.); children: Margaret Hayes (Mrs. J. David Heap), Florence Parmelee (Mrs. Ralph Antonides), Hayes Corliss, Anne Sterling (Mrs. George Jafferis); m. Helen Boyden Lamb, 1962 (dec. July 1975); m. Beth Fennell, July 24, 1986. Grad., St. Bernard's Sch., 1916, Phillips Exeter Acad., 1920; A.B. magna cum laude, Harvard U., 1924; postgrad., New Coll., Oxford (Eng.) U., 1924-25; Ph.D., Columbia U., 1932. Instr. philosophy Columbia, 1928-32, New Sch. Social Research, 1940-42; lectr. intensive study contemporary Russian civilization Cornell U., 1943, Social Studies Workshop on Soviet Russia, Harvard Grad. Sch. Edn., 1944; lectr. Columbia Sch. Gen. Studies, 1947-59, Columbia seminar assoc., 1971—. Editor: Man Answers Death: An Anthology of Poetry, rev. edit., 1952, Dialogue on John Dewey, 1959, Dialogue on George Santayana, 1959, A Humanist Symposium on Metaphysics, 1960, Albert Rhys Williams: In Memoriam, 1962, The Trial of Elizabeth Gurley Flynn by the American Civil Liberties Union, 1968, The Thomas Lamonts in America, 1971, (with Lansing Lamont) Letters of John Masefield to Florence Lamont, 1979, Collected Poems of John Reed, 1985, The John Reed Centenary, 1988; author: Issues of Immortality, 1932, The Illusion of Immortality, rev. edit, 1965, You Might Like Socialism: A Way of Life for Modern Man, 1939, The Peoples of the Soviet Union, 1946, A Humanist Funeral Service, 1947, Humanism as a Philosophy, 1949, The Independent Mind, 1951, Soviet Civilization, 1952, Freedom Is As Freedom Does: Civil Liberties in America, 1956, rev. edit., 1981, The Philosophy of Humanism, rev. edit., 1982, Freedom of Choice Affirmed, 1967, A Humanist Wedding Service, 1970, Remembering John Masefield, 1971, Lover's Credo, 1983, Voice in the Wilderness: Collected Essays of Fifty Years, 1974, Yes to Life: Memoirs of Corliss Lamont, 1981, A Lifetime of Dissent, 1988; Basic Pamphlet Series, 1952—; co-author: syllabus Introduction to Contemporary Problems in U.S, 1929, Russia Day by Day, (with Margaret I. Lamont), 1933; Frequent contbr. to periodicals; speaker radio, TV; vice chmn.: Jour. Philosophy. Bd. dirs. ACLU, 1932-54; pres. Bill of Rights Fund, 1954-69; chmn. Nat. Emergency Civil Liberties Com., 1965—, Nat. Council American-Soviet Friendship, 1943-46; Candidate for U.S. Senate Am. Labor Party, N.Y., 1952, Independent-Socialist Party, 1958; Vice pres., mem. exec. bd. Poetry Soc. Am., 1971-74. Recipient of N.Y. City Tchrs. Union Ann. award, 1955, Gandhi Peace award, 1981, Ethics in Action award, 1984, John Phillips award Phillips Exeter Acad., 1986-87. Mem. AAAS, Acad. Polit. Sci., NAACP, Am. Humanist Assn. (hon. pres. 1974—, John Dewey Humanist award 1972, Humanist of Yr. award 1977), Acad. Am. Poets, P.E.N., Am. Philos. Assn., UN Assn., Phi Beta Kappa. Clubs: Columbia Faculty (N.Y.C.), Harvard (N.Y.C.). Address: 315 W 106th St New York NY 10025

LAMONT, STEVEN MURRAY, marketing executive; b. Toronto, Ont., Can., Dec. 3, 1954; s. Murray Charles and Doreen Barbara (Kennedy) L.; m. Nora Grace McKay, June 23, 1979 (div. Jan. 1987); m. Marilyn Louise Heggen, Feb. 20, 1987. BS, U. Toronto, 1977; MBA, Harvard U., 1979. Sr. engagement mgr. McKinsey & Co., Toronto, 1979-85; v.p. passenger mktg. Can. Pacific Airlines, Vancouver, BC, Can., 1985-86; v.p. U.S. ops. Contour Blind & Shade, Vancouver, 1987-88.

LAMONTAGNE, PAUL, pharmaceutical company executive; b. Quebec City, Que., Can., July 17, 1932; s. Emile and Imelda (Belanger) L.; m. Monik Lockquell; children: Sylvie, Pierre, Martin. Grad. in Indsl. Engring., Can. Inst. Sci. and Tech., Toronto, Ont., 1964. With tech. services mgmt. Goodyear Tire & Rubber Co., Montreal, Que., Can., 1952-67; pres. Vachon Inc., Montreal, 1967-81, Bombardier Inc., Montreal, 1981-83; v.p. tech. services Can. Post, Ottawa, Ont., 1983-85; exec. v.p., chief operating officer Cumberland Drugs Ltd., Montreal, 1985—. Sr. mem. Am. Inst. Indsl. Engrs.; mem. Can. Mktg. Assn., Am. Mgmt. Assn., Montreal C. of C. Home: 1680 de la Mauricie, Duvernay, Laval, PQ Canada H7E 4J1 Office: Cumberland Drugs Ltd, 4700 Prince of Wales, Montreal, PQ Canada H4B 2L3

LAMOTTE, WILLIAM MITCHELL, insurance brokerage company executive; b. Phila., Sept. 3, 1938; s. Ferdinand and June (Mitchell) LaM.;

B.A., Princeton U., 1961; m. Elizabeth Ewing, Sept. 16, 1961; children—William Mitchell, Anne Hilliard, Nicole. Underwriter, Chubb & Son, N.Y.C., 1961-62; various assignments Johnson & Higgins Pa., Inc., Phila., 1962-69, pres. Johnson & Higgins Wilmington, Del., 1969-75, pres. Johnson & Higgins Mo. Inc., St. Louis, 1975-77, Johnson & Higgins Ill. Inc., Chgo., 1977—, dir. parent firm. Vice pres. Boys Clubs Wilmington, 1974-75; bd. dirs. St. Louis Zoo Friends Assn., 1976-77, Lincoln Park Zool. Soc., 1981—; bd. dirs. Chgo. Boys and Girls Clubs, 1983—, pres., 1984. Clubs: Corinthian Yacht (Phila.); Chicago, Chgo. Yacht, Indian Hill. Home: 109 Greenbay Rd Hubbard Woods IL 60093 Office: Johnson & Higgins Ill Inc 500 W Madison St Chicago IL 60606

L'AMOUR, LOUIS DEARBORN, author; b. Jamestown, N.D., 1908; s. Louis Charles and Emily (Dearborn) LaMoore; m. Katherine Elizabeth Adams, Feb. 19, 1956; children: Beau Dearborn, Angelique Gabrielle. Self ed.; LLD (hon.), Jamestown Coll., 1972, N.D. State U., 1981, U. LaVerne, 1981, Pepperdine U., 1984. Appearances on: Great Tchrs. TV program; Author: poems Smoke From This Altar, 1939, Hondo, 1953, The Burning Hills, 1956, Sitka, 1957, The Daybreakers, 1960, Kid Rodelo, Mustang Man, Kilrone, 1966, The Sky-Liners, 1967, The Broken Gun; Matagorda, 1967, Brionne, 1968, Chancy, 1968, Down the Long Hills, 1968 (Golden Spur awards Western Writers Assn.), The Empty Land, 1969, The Lonely Men, 1969, Conagher, 1969, A Man Called Noon, 1970, Reilly's Luck, 1970, Galloway, 1970, North to the Rails, 1971, Under the Sweet-Water Rim, 1971, Tucker, 1971, Callaghen, 1972, Ride the Dark Trail, 1972, Treasure Mountain, 1972, The Ferguson Rifle, 1973, The Man from Skibbereen, 1973, The Quick and the Dead, 1973, The Californios, 1974, Sackett's Land, 1974, War Party, 1975, Rivers West, 1975, Over on the Dry Side, 1975, Rider of Lost Creek, 1976, Where the Long Grass Blows, 1976, To the Far Blue Mountains, 1976, Borden Chantry, 1977, Fair Blows the Wind, 1978, Showdown at Yellow Butte, 1978, The Mountain Valley War, 1978, Bendigo Shafter, 1979, The Proving Trail, 1979, The Iron Marshal, 1979 (Golden Plate award), Shalako, 1980, The Strong Shall Live, 1980, Yondering, 1980, The Warrior's Path, 1980, The Comstock Lode, 1981, Buckskin Run, 1981, The Shadow Riders, 1982, The Lonesome Gods, 1983, The Walking Drum, 1984, Son of a Wanted Man, 1984, Louis L'Amour's Frontier, 1984, Jubal Sackett, 1985, Passin' Through, 1985, Last of the Breed, 1986, The Haunted Mesa, 1987. Served to 1st lt. AUS, 1942-46. Named Theodore Roosevelt Rough Rider by N.D., 1972; recipient Congl. Medal of Honor, 1983, Presdl. Medal of Freedom, 1984; Am. Book award, 1980, Buffalo Bill award, 1981, Disting. Newsboy award, 1981, Nat. Geneal. Soc. award, 1981. Mem. Acad. Motion Picture Arts and Scis., Calif. Acad. Scis., Nat. Acad. Scis. Address: care Bantam Books 666 Fifth Ave New York NY 10019 *Died June 10, 1988.*

LAMOUREUX, GLORIA KATHLEEN, military nursing administrator; b. Billings, Mont., Nov. 2, 1947; d. Laurits Bungaard and Florence Esther (Nielsen) Nielsen; m. Kenneth Earl Lamoureux, Aug. 31, 1973 (div. Feb. 1979). BS, U. Wyo., 1970; MS, U. Md., 1984. Enrolled USAF, 1970, advanced through grades to lt. col.; staff nurse ob-gyn dept. 57th Tactical Hosp., Nellis AFB, Nev., 1970-71, USAF Hosp., Clark AB, Republic Philipines, 1971-73; charge nurse ob-gyn dept. USAF Rgn. Hosp., Sheppard AFB, Tex., 1973-75; staff nurse ob-gyn dept. USAF Rgn. Hosp., MacDill AFB, Fla., 1976-79; charge nurse ob-gyn dept. USAF Med. Ctr., Andrews AFB, Md., 1979-80, MCH coordinator, 1980-82; chief nurse USAF Clinic, Eielson AFB, Alaska, 1984-86, Air Force Systems Command Hosp., Edwards AFB, Calif., 1986—. Named one of Outstanding Women Am., 1983. Mem. Nurses Assn. of Am. Coll. Obstetricians and Gynecologists (sec.-treas. armed forces dist. 1986—), Air Force Assn., Assn. Mil. Surgeons U.S., Bus. and Profl. Women's Assn., Sigma Theta Tau. Republican. Lutheran. Home: 4500 W Rosamond Blvd Space 5 Rosamond CA 93560 Office: AFSC Hosp Edwards Edwards AFB CA 93523-5300

LAMOUREUX, WILLIAM A., poet; b. Montreal, Que., Can., Aug. 15, 1938; s. William C. and Beatrice (Benoit) L.; B.A., Tufts U., 1964; postgrad. Boston U., 1964-65, U. Hawaii, 1974; came to U.S., 1938, naturalized, 1953. Partner, Lamoureux Funeral Home, Gardner, Mass., 1949-76; founder, propr. Librairie Francaise, Santurce, P.R., 1970-73; broker-salesman J.M. Urner Inc., Realtors, Honolulu, 1974-76; broker-salesman Portner & Portner, Inc., Realtors, Hollywood, Fla., 1978-82; right-of-way agent Fla. Dept. Transp., 1978-80; works include: (poetry) La lumiere se retire du bord de la terrasse....., 1960; Comme je traversais le pays des licornes, 1961; Un oranger, supreme emeraude, 1962. Republican. Roman Catholic. Home and Office: 6 Lantana Ln Sewall's Point Stuart FL 34996

LAMPERT, ELEANOR VERNA, employment development specialist; b. Porterville, Calif., Mar. 23; d. Ernest Samuel and Violet Edna (Watkins) Wilson; student in bus., fin. Porterville Jr. Coll., 1977-78; grad. Anthony Real Estate Sch., 1971; student Laguna Sch. of Art, 1972, U. Calif.-Santa Cruz, 1981; m. Robert Mathew Lampert, Aug. 21, 1935; children—Sally Lu Winton, Lary Lampert, Carol R. John. Bookkeeper, Porterville (Calif.) Hosp., 1956-71; real estate sales staff Ray Realty, Porterville, 1973; sec. Employment Devel. Dept., State of Calif., Porterville, 1973-83, orientation and tng. specialist CETA employees, 1976-80. Author: Black Bloomers and Han-Ga-Ber, 1986. Sec., Employer Adv. Group, 1973-80; mem. U.S. Senatorial Bus. Adv. Bd., 1981-84; charter mem. Presdl. Republican Task Force, 1981-88; mem. Rep. Nat. Congl. Com., 1982-88; pres. Sierra View Hosp. League, 1988—; vol. Calif. Hosp. Assn., 1983-86, Calif. Spl. Olympics Spirit Team. Recipient Merit Cert., Gov. Pat Brown, State of Calif., 1968. Mem. Lindsay Olive Growers, Sunkist Orange Growers, Am. Kennel Club, Internat. Assn. Personnel in Employment Security, Calif. State Employees Assn. (emeritus Nat. Wildlife Fedn., Nat. Rifle Assn., Friends of Porterville Library, Heritage Found., DAR (Kaweah chpt. rec. sec. 1988—), Internat. Platform Assn. Clubs: Porterville Women's (pres. 1988—, dist. rec. sec. 1988—), Internat. Sporting and Leisure. Author: Black Bloomers and Han-Ga-Ber.

LAMPERT, S. HENRY, dentist; b. Bklyn., Mar. 10, 1929; s. Joseph and Sadie (Bass) L.; BA, U. Ill., 1950; DDS, NYU, 1954; m. Jacqueline Adler, Mar. 27, 1955; children: Karen Ann, Beth Robin, Judith Ellen. Intern in dentistry Mt. Sinai Hosp., N.Y.C., 1954-55; gen. practice dentistry, Essex Junction, Vt., 1957—; dir. Temporo Mandibular Joint Program, Med. Center Hosp. Vt., Burlington, 1970-76, attending staff 1957—, peer rev. com., 1978—; mem. staff Fanny Allen Hosp., Winooski, Vt., 1961—; assoc. prof. Sch. Allied Health Scis., U. Vt., Burlington, 1963-73, clin. instr. Coll. Medicine, 1974-75, clin. instr. dept. oral surgery, 1986. Sec., Vt. Bd. Dental Examiners, 1973-76, pres., 1976-77; mem. Northeast Regional Bd. Dental Examiners, 1973-84; lectr. in field. Served to capt. AUS, 1955-57. Mem. ADA (standard setting com. of council on nat. bd. exams. 1978-81), Champlain Valley (pres. 1961-62), Chgo. Dental Socs., Acad. Operative Dentistry, Am. Prosthodontic Soc., Fedn. Prosthodontic Orgns., 1973-87, Am. Assn. Dental Examiners, 1973-84, Alpha Omega. Jewish (bd. govs. synagogue 1967-70, 72-73, chmn. bd. edn.). Lodge: Masons. Contbr. articles to profl. jours.; photographs pub. numerous mags., jours. Home: 22 Forest Rd Essex Junction VT 05452 Office: 48 Main St Essex Junction VT 05452

LAMPROPOULOS, GEORGE ATTHANASSIOS, electrical engineering educator; b. Platanos, Pylias, Greece, Aug. 11, 1955; came to Can., 1979; s. Athanassios A. and Maria A. (Matsaka) L.; m. Marlene Lanpropoulos; 1 child, Marie. BS, U. Patras, 1979; MS in Engring., Queen's U., Kingston, Ont., Can., 1982, PhD, 1985. Asst. prof. elec. engring. Royal Mil. Coll., Kingston, 1984—; instr. MACH Inst., Kingston, 1984—; assoc. prof. Laval U., 1987—; pres. Airborne Underwater Geophys. Signals Ltd.; sec. Advanced Study Inst. on Underwater Acoustic Data Processing NATO, 1988. Contbr. articles to profl. jours. Mem. IEEE (exec. com. Kingston chpt. 1987—), Soc. for Indsl. and Applied Math., Tech. Chamber Greece, Kingston Road Runners Assn. Mem. Liberal Party. Home: 64 Ontario St, Kingston, ON Canada K7L 5J4 Office: Royal Mil Coll, Dept Elec Engring, Kinston, ON Canada K7L 2W3

LANCASTER, CARROLL TOWNES, JR., business executive; b. Waco, Tex., Mar. 14, 1929; s. Carroll T. and Beatrice (Hollaman) L.; student U. Tex., 1948-51, 52-53; m. Catherine Virginia Frommel, May 29, 1954; children—Loren Thomas, Barbara, Beverly, John Tracy. Sales coordinator Union Tank div. Butler Mfg. Co., Houston, 1954-56, sales rep., New Orleans, 1956-57, br. mgr., 1957-60; asst. to exec. v.p. Maloney-Crawford Mfg. Co., Tulsa, 1960-62; mktg. cons., sr. asso. Market/Product Facts, Tulsa, 1962-63; market devel. asst. Norriseal Controls div. Dover Corp., Houston, 1963-66; area dir. Arthritis Found., Houston, 1966-69, dir. S.W. div., 1969-70; exec. dir. United Cerebral Palsy Tex. Gulf Coast, 1971-74; exec. dir. Leukemia Soc. Am., Gulf Coast, 1974-76, Lancaster & Assos., 1976—. Christian edn. tchr., 1966-70, supr., 1971, asst. youth football coach, Bellaire, 1967-68, 70-71; mem. Houston-Galveston Area Health Commn. Study Group, 1972-76, co-chmn., 1976; dir., essayist Tex. Low Vision Council, 1976-79, sec.-treas., 1978-81, pres., 1981-85; pres. Bellaire Civic Action Club, 1987-88; del. Houston Interfaith Sponsoring Com., 1979-81; bd. dirs. Council Chs. Greater Houston, 1966-68, v.p., 1968. Served with USNR, 1946-48, 51-52. Recipient award for securing free blood for indigent Harris County Hosp. Dist., 1968. Mem. Am. Mktg. Assn., Huguenot Soc., San Marcos Acad. Ex-students Assn. (pres. 1982-84), SAR, Delta Sigma Phi. Episcopalian (vestryman 1975-78). Home: 4901 Holly St Bellaire TX 77401 Office: PO Box 745 Bellaire TX 77401

LANCASTER-KEIM, MARY LOUISE, public relations executive; b. Brownsville, Tenn., Mar. 9, 1950; arrived in Hong Kong, 1987; d. James L. and Edith (Crihfield) Lancaster; m. Thomas R. Keim, Apr. 16, 1987. Student, Southwestern U., 1968-70, Vanderbilt U., 1970; BS in Sociology, Memphis State U., 1973. Gen. mgr. Paddock Pools, Inc., Memphis, 1976-80; owner, mgr. Buckingham Palate, Inc., Memphis, 1980-83; dir. advt. John Simmons, Inc., Memphis, 1980-83; v.p. A. Brown-Olmstead, Atlanta, 1983-86; creative dir. Hill & Knowlton, Hong Kong, 1987-88; creative dir., group mgr. Burson-Marsteller, Hong Kong, 1988—. Creator, copywriter 30 Epicurean Delights, 1983 (Am. Soc. Orchestral Leagues award 1983); contbr. articles to major daily newspapers and mags. V.p. 3d Tier Memphis Symphony, 1982-83; press. sec. Memphis City Council campaign, 1983; creative cons. Girls Club, Atlanta, 1985-86. Recipient Phoenix award Ga. Pub. Relations Soc. Am., 1986, John W. Hill award, 1988; named Retailer of Yr., Nat. Casual Furniture Assn., Washington, 1981. Mem. Bus. and Profl. Women, Am. C. of C. Hong Kong. Republican. Presbyterian. Club: Ladies Recreation (Hong Kong). Home: 20 B Branksome, 3 Tregunter Path, Hong Kong Hong Kong Office: Burson-Marsteller, 23/F United Ctr, Hong Kong Hong Kong

LAND, DEREK GORDON, journal editor, consultant; b. Scarborough, Yorkshire, Eng., Aug. 18, 1931; s. Donald Poskett and Ethel (Berry) L.; m. Sylvia Teresa Ballard, Aug. 10, 1960; children: Brigid, Peter, Hilary, Stephen. BSc, U. Liverpool, Eng., 1953, PhD, 1956. Sci. officer Rowett Research Inst., Aberdeen, Scotland, 1955-58; sr. sci. officer Ministry of Agr., Fish and Food, Aberdeen, 1959-62, Low Temperature Research Sta., Cambridge, Eng., 1962-64; prin. sci. officer Food Research Inst., Norwich, Eng., 1964-85; prin. Taint Analysis and Sensory Quality Services, Norwich, 1985—; editor-in-chief Internat. Jour. Food Sci. and Tech., London, 1986—; vis. lectr. analytical chemistry, U. East Anglia, Norwich, 1984—. Author: Odor Description, 1968; editor: Progress in Flavor Research, 1979; contbr. sci. papers and chpts. to books. Sr. hon. research fellow psychology U. Birmingham, Eng., 1985—. Fellow Royal Soc. Chemistry, Inst. Food Sci. and Tech.; mem. Nutrition Soc., ASTM, Internat. Standards Orgn. Home: 8 High Bungay Rd, London, Norwich NR14 6JT, England Office: Inst Food Sci and Tech, 5 Cambridge Ct, 210 Shepherd Bush Rd, London W6 7NL, England

LAND, GEORGE AINSWORTH, philosopher, writer, educator, consultant; b. Hot Springs, Ark., Feb. 27, 1933; s. George Thomas Lock and Mary Elizabeth Land; m. Jo A. Gunn, 1957 (dec. 1969); children—Robert E., Thomas G., Patrick A.; m. Beth Smith Jarman, 1987. Student, Millsaps Coll., 1952-54, U. Veracruz, Mexico, 1957-59; numerous hon. degrees U.S. and abroad. Program dir. Woodall TV Stas. of Ga., Columbus, 1951-52; ops. mgr. Lamar Broadcasting, Jackson, Miss., 1952-54; anthrop. research Cora, Huichole and Yaqui tribes, Latin Am. Mexico, 1955-60; dir. gen. Television del Norte (NBC), Mexico, 1960-62; v.p. Roman Corp., St. Louis, 1962-64; chmn. Transolve Inc., Cambridge, Mass., and St. Petersburg, Fla., 1964-68; chief exec., chmn. Innotek Corp., N.Y.C.; also pres. Hal Roach Studios, Los Angeles and N.Y.C., 1969-71; chmn. emeritus Turtle Bay Inst., N.Y.C., 1971-80; vice chmn. Wilson Learning Corp., Mpls., 1980-87; chmn. Leadership 2000, Phoenix, 1986—; pres. Inst. Transformational Research, Honolulu and Buffalo, 1980—; prof. Mankato State U., 1973-74; chmn. Leadership 2000, Phoenix, 1987—; sr. fellow U. Minn., 1982—; cons.-in-residence Synplex Inc., N.Y.C., AT&T, Forest Hosp., Des Plaines, Social Systems Inc., Chapel Hill, N.C., Children's Hosp., Nat. Med. Ctr., Washington; Mem. Nat. Action Com. on Drug Edn., 1974-75; co-chmn. Syncon Conf., So. Ill. U., 1972-74; keynoter Emerging Trends in Edn. Conf., Minn., 1974, 75, Bicentennial Conf. on Limits to Growth, So. Ill. U., 1976, No. States Power Conf., 1975, U.S. Office of Edn., Nat. Conf. Improvements in Edn., 1979, World Conf. on Gifted, 1977, S.W. Conf. on Arts, 1977, World Symposium on Humanity, 1979, Internat. Conf. Internal Auditors, 1977, Four Corners Conf. on Arts, 1977, Chautaugua Inst., 1977, 78, Conf. Am. Art Tchrs. Assn., 1979, Internat. Conf. on Gifted, 1982, Japan Mgmt. Assn., Nat. Conf. of Art Curators, Chgo, 1985, others; keynoter, Nat. Conf. on Econ. Devel., Mex., 1988, Credit Union Roundtable, Tampa, Fla., 1988, Internat. Bihai Conf., Princeton, N.J., 1982, co-chmn. com. on society World Conf. Peace and Poverty, St. Joseph's U., Phila., 1968, Internat. Bahai Conf. Princeton U., 1987; mem. Nat. Security Seminar, U.S. Dept. Def., 1975; cons., keynoter corp. policy strategic seminars The Bell System, AT&T, 1978—; mem. faculty Edison Electric Grad. Mgmt. Inst., 1972-78; lectr., seminarian in transformation theory, strategic planning and interdisciplinary research Menninger Found., U. Ga., Emory U., Waterloo (Can.) U., Office of Sec. HEW, Jamestown (N.Y.) Coll., Hofstra U., U.S. Office Edn., Calif. Dept. Edn., St. Louis U., Coll. William and Mary, Webster Coll., St. Louis, Wash. State Dept. Edn., U. Ky., So. Ill. U., St. John's U., Harvard U., U. South Fla., MIT, U. Veracruz, Children's Hosp. D.C., Gov.'s Sch. N.C., Scottsdale (Ariz.) Ctr. Arts, Humbolt U., East Berlin, AAAS, others; advanced faculty Creative Problem Solving Inst., SUNY, 1965—, S. Conn. Coll.; disting. lectr. Northwestern State U., La., State U. Coll. N.Y., Coll. of the Lakes, Ill.; cons. govt., industry and instns. in U.S. and abroad, including AT&T, IBM, Dow Chem., Dow Corning, DuPont, Hughes, TRW, 3M, Gen. Mills, Gen. Motors, Moore Corp., Branch Corp., Credit Union Nat. Assn., others. Author: Innovation Systems, 1967, Innovation Technology, 1968, Four Faces of Poverty, 1968, (as George T.L. Land) Grow or Die: The Unifying Principle of Transformation, 1973, Creative Alternatives and Decision Making, 1974, The Opportunity Book, 1980, (with Vaune E. Ainsworth) Forward to Basics; contbr. to profl. jours. and gen. mags. Fellow N.Y. Acad. Scis.; mem. AAAS, Soc. Gen. Systems Research, Soc. Study Gen. Process (founding dir.), Am. Soc. Cybernetics (past v.p.), Creative Edn. Found. (colleague), Soc. Am. Value Engrs. (past dir.), World Future Soc., Com. for Future (colleague), Authors Guild, Authors League Am. Club: Lambs (N.Y.C.). Home: 7119 Red Ledge Dr Paradise Valley AZ 85253 Office: Leadership 2000 3602 E Campbell PhoeniAZ 85018

LAND, MARY ELIZABETH, author, composer; b. Benton, La., Sept. 28, 1908; d. Thomas T. and Elizabeth (Langford) Land; student Gulf Park Coll., Gulfport, Miss., 1924-25, Cheyney Trent Sch. Poetry, Calif., 1937, U. Chgo., 1938; m. Edward Timothy Kelly, 1925; 1 dau., Patricia Kelly Stevens; m. 2d, George T. Lock, 1931; 1 son, George T. Lock-Land. Mem. staff La. Conservation Rev., La. Dept. Conservation, New Orleans, 1940-41, Miss. Valley Sportsman, 1948, So. Outdoors Mag., Atlanta, 1959, 60, 61, West Bank Guide, New Orleans, 1962, Sportsman's News, Hot Springs, Ark., 1960; author (with Arthur Van Pelt) syndicated column, Outdoors South, for weekly newspapers Miss., La., 1947, 48; feature writer Fisherman Mag., 1954, R X Sports and Travel Mag., 1971, Down South Mag., 1964, Natchitoches Times, 1970. Named Co-Poet Laureate for Tenn., 1941; recipient Blue Ribbon award Gulf Coast br. Nat. League Am. Pen Women, Merit certificate Nash Motor Co., 1953, 1st Pl. award La. Press Assn., 1969-70, Merit certificate and 2 Keys to City Mayor New Orleans, 1954, Outstanding Contbn. certificate La. Soc. Colonial Dames, 1971, certificate Am. Bicentennial Research Inst., 1973. Mem. Nat. League Am. Pen Women (past br. pres.), Nat. Fedn. Am. Press Women, La. Press Women, Outdoor Writers Assn. Am., La. Outdoor Writers Assn. (charter), Fedn. Musicians. Author: Shadows of the Swamp (poetry), 1940, Mary Land's Louisiana Cookery, 1954 (So. Books award 1956), New Orleans Cuisine, 1968 (2d pl. award Fedn. Am. Press Women 1969), Abode (poetry), 1972, Dreams (poetry), 1977; contbr. conservation articles to mags., poetry to anthologies; composer: You Hang In My Heart, 1959, As Strange As You Are, 1959, Drink Deep, 1959, Piano Cho Cho Zarzosa, 1959, Voice-Allehandra Allegra, 1959. Address: 310 Shearwater Dr Ocean Springs MS 39564

LANDAU, EMANUEL, epidemiologist; b. N.Y.C., Nov. 28, 1919; s. Meyer and Annie (Heller) L.; B.A., CCNY, 1939; Ph.D., Am. U., 1966; m. Davetta Goldberg, Sept. 4, 1948; children—Melanie, Elizabeth. Supervisory analytical statistician Calif. Dept. Public Health, 1957-59, chief biometry sect., div. air pollution, 1959-62; head lab. and clin. trials sect. Nat. Cancer Inst., 1962-65; statis. adviser Nat. Air Pollution Control Adminstrn., 1965-69; epidemiologist Environ. Health Service, 1969-71, chief epidemiologic studies br. Bur. Radiol. Health, 1971-74; project dir. Am. Public Health Assn., 1975—; cons., adv. in field. Served with AUS, 1942-46. Decorated Belgian Fourragere; recipient Superior Service award HEW, 1963. Fellow Am. Public Health Assn., Royal Soc. Health; mem. Soc. Epidemiologic Research, Am. Statis. Assn. (chmn. com. on stats. and environ.). Democrat. Jewish. Club: Cosmos (Washington). Author, editor articles, reports in field. Home: 4601 N Park Ave Apt 208 Chevy Chase MD 20815 Office: Am Pub Health Assn 1015 15th St NW Washington DC 20005

LANDAU, KURT HEINZ, ergonomics educator; b. Griesheim, Fed. Republic Germany, July 22, 1947; s. Heinrich and Katha Landau; m. Anna Regina Hermann, Feb. 4, 1972; children: Nicole, Marc. Diploma in Indsl. Engring., U. Tech., Darmstadt, Fed. Republic Germany, 1971, D of Engring., 1978. Systems analyst U. Grenoble, France, 1971-72, CERN, Geneva, 1972-74; research assoc. Inst. Arbeitswissenschaft, Darmstadt, 1974-79; head ergonomics dept., fgn. relations coordinator Reichsauschuss für Arbeitstudies, Darmstadt, 1979-82; prof. ergonomics and indsl. engring. Offenburg (Fed. Republic Germany) Coll., 1982-83; prof. ergonomics U. Hohenheim, Stuttgart, Fed. Republic Germany, 1983—; dir. Inst. Household Econs., Stuttgart, 1987—; lectr., seminar presenter in field. Contbr. articles, papers, research reports to profl. jours. Mem. Gesellschaft Arbeitswissenschaft, Gesellschaft Klassifikation, Gesellschaft Hauswirtschaft, Biofeedback Gesellschaft, Reichsauschuss für Arbeitstudies Verband, Brit. Ergonomics Soc., Can. Human Factors Assn. Office: U Hohenheim, Schloss Hohenheim, 7000 Stuttgart Federal Republic of Germany

LANDAU, ZBIGNIEW WLADYSLAW, economist educator; b. Warsaw, Poland, Jan. 18, 1931; s. Wladyslaw and Irena (Helfgot) L.; m. Irena Barska, Mar. 17, 1955; 1 child, Anna Malgorzata. Magister, Central Sch. Planning Statistics, 1955, Doctorate, 1960, Doctorate habilitowany, 1964. Asst. Central Sch. Planning and Statistics, Warszawa, 1950-64, asst. prof., 1964-72, dir. main library, 1966-67, extraordinary prof., 1972-80, full prof., 1980—, deputy dir. Inst. Economy, 1978-81, chair econ. history, 1987—; mem. sci. council Pres. Nat. Bank Poland, Warszawa, 1981—. Author: over 30 books and 400 articles; editor-in-chief: Przeglad Bibliograficzny Pismiennictwa Ekonomicznego, Encyclopedy Polish Interwar History. Recipient Sci. award Minister for Higher Edn., 1965, 67, 71, 75, 76, 78, 81, 87, Sci. award Weekly Polityka, 1972, 86, Sci. award Literni Fond, 1978. Mem. Polish Acad. Scis. (com. econ. scis. 1980—), Polskie Towarzystwo Historyczne, Stowarzyszenie Autorow (Soc. des Auteurs). Home: Sokolicz 5 m 39, ol-508 Warszawa Poland Office: Szkola Glowna Planowania Stat, Katedra Historii Gospodarczej, Wisniowa 41, 25-520 Warsaw Poland

LANDÁZURI RICKETTS, JUAN CARDINAL, Archbishop of Lima; b. Arequipa, Peru, Dec. 19, 1913. Ed. U. Arequipa and U. Antonianum, Rome. Ordained to priesthood, 1939; Franciscan Friar. Titular Archbishop of Roina Peru, 1952-62; created Cardinal 1962; now Archbishop of Lima Peru. Decorated Knight-Comdr. Order of Malta; numerous other honors. Office: Arzobispado, Plaza de Armas, Apartado Postal 1512, Lima 100, Peru *

LANDE, ALEXANDER, physicist, educator; b. Hilversum, Netherlands, Jan. 5, 1936; s. Leo and Bella (Berlin) L. BA, Cornell U., 1957; PhD, MIT, 1963. Instr. Princeton (N.J.) U., 1963-66; asst. prof. physics Niels Bohr Inst., Copenhagen, 1968-70; lectr. in physics Groningen (Netherlands) U., 1972-79, prof. physics, 1979—, chmn. Inst. Theoretical Physics, 1976-83. Author and co-author over 30 papers in field. NSF fellow, 1966-67. Mem. Am. Phys. Soc., European Phys. Soc., Netherlands Phys. Soc., AAAS, Sigma Xi, Phi Beta Kappa. Office: Inst Theoretical Physics, Groningen U, Post Bax 800-WSN, 9700 Groningen The Netherlands

LANDEN, ROBERT GERAN, historian, university administrator; b. Boston, July 13, 1930; s. Harry James and Evelyn Gertrude (Geran) L.; m. Patricia Kizzia, July 19, 1958; children—Michael Geran, Robert Kizzia, Jill Arnett, Amy Patricia. A.B., Coll. of William and Mary, 1952; M.A., U. Mich., 1953; A.M., Princeton U., 1958, Ph.D. (Ford Found. fellow), 1961. Asst. prof. social sci. Ball State U., Muncie, Ind., 1959-60; asst. prof. near eastern studies U. Mich., Ann Arbor, 1960-61; asst. prof. history Dartmouth, Hanover, N.H., 1961-66; asst. dean of freshmen Dartmouth, 1963-64, asso. prof. history, 1966-67; prof., head dept. history Va. Poly. Inst. and State U., Blacksburg, 1967-69; prof. history U. S.C., Columbia, 1969-75; asso. vice provost U. S.C., 1971-72, asso. provost, 1972-73; dean U. S.C. (Coll. of Social and Behavioral Scis.), 1972-75; prof. history U. Tex. at Arlington, 1975-77; dean U. Tex. at Arlington (Coll. Liberal Arts), 1975-77; prof. history U. Tenn., Knoxville, 1977-86; dean Coll. Liberal Arts, 1977-85; prof. history, v.p. acad. affairs, provost U. Montevallo, 1986-88; prof. history, dir. programs in the humanities Va. Poly Inst. and State U., Blacksburg, 1988—. Author: Oman Since 1856, 1967, The Emergence of the Modern Middle East, 1970, (with Abid Al-Marayati) The Middle East, Its Governments and Politics, 1972; contbr. articles to profl. jours. and book revs. to hist. publs. Served with AUS, 1953-55. Am. Council of Learned Socs. fellow, 1965-66; Comparative Studies Center Faculty fellow, 1965-66. Fellow Middle East Studies Assn. of N. Am.; mem. Am. Hist. Assn., Middle East Inst., Theta Delta Chi, Phi Kappa Phi, Phi Delta Theta. Roman Catholic. Office: Va Poly Inst and State U Office of Dir Programs in the Humanities Lane Hall Blacksburg VA 24061

LANDERS, NEWLIN JEWEL, contractor; b. North Salem, Ind., July 10, 1906; s. DeLoy and Pearl (Paige) L.; student Skadron Contractor's Sch., 1963; m. Margaret Richhart; children Lawrence, Marlin; m. Vernette Trosper Lum, May 2, 1959. Owner, mgr. Landers Machine Shop, Bell Gardens, Calif., 1940-41; partner Selwyn-Landers Valve Co., Los Angeles, 1942-54; owner Havasu Landing, Needles, Calif., 1955, Navajo Tract, Apple Valley, Calif., 1957—; owner, mgr. Landers (Calif.) Water Delivery, 1953-80, Landers Tank Installations. Mem. Landers Vol. Fire Dept., 1963—, recipient plaque for contbns., 1981. Recipient plaque and badge Sheriff Rangers' Search and Rescue, 1972; honoree community dinner celebrating his founding of city of Landers, 1981. Club: Moose. Patentee high pressure valves. Home: 632 Landers Ln Landers CA 92285 Office: 1105 Landers Ln Landers CA 92285

LANDERS, SANDRA JEAN, retail company executive; b. Roanoke, Va., July 15, 1937; d. James Lilburn and Dorothy Ellen (Newman) Blankenship; 1 child, Michael; m. Brenton Sylvester Mongan, July 3, 1974 (div. 1982); 1 child, Michael; m. Julian Miller Landers, Jr. Student, Va. So. U., 1957. Med. sec. Lewis Gale Hosp., Roanoke, 1961-67; owner, operator Mystic Sea Hotel, Myrtle Beach, S.C., 1974-77, Poindexter Hotel, Myrtle Beach, 1974-77, Sheraton by-the-Sea, Jekyll Island, Ga., 1978-80; owner, pres. Cassandra's Ltd, Roanoke, 1978—, Cassandra's Carousel, Roanoke, 1983—. Bd. dirs. Recreation Dept., Roanoke, 1971-72; pres. Va.'s Jr. Miss Pageant, 1961-76. Recipient Am.'s Jr. Miss State Pageant award 1973. Mem. Bus. Women of Am. (bd. dirs. 1982-83). Republican. Baptist. Club: Roanoke Jr. Woman's (v.p. 1968-73). Home: 5050 Falcon Ridge Rd SW Roanoke VA 24018 Office: Cassandra's Ltd 2121 Colonial Ave SW Roanoke VA 24015

LANDERS, VERNETTE TROSPER, educator, author; b. Lawton, Okla., May 3, 1912; d. Fred Gilbert and LaVerne Hamilton (Stevens) Trosper; A.B. with honors, U. Calif. at Los Angeles, 1933, M.A., 1935, Ed.D., 1953; Cultural doctorate (hon.), Lit. World U., Tucson, 1985; m. Paul Albert Lum, Aug. 29, 1952 (dec. May 1955); 1 child, William Tappan; m. 2d, Newlin Landers, May 2, 1959; children: Lawrence, Marlin. Tchr. secondary schs., Montebello, Calif., 1935-45, 48-50, 51-59; prof. Long Beach City Coll., 1946-47; asst. prof. Los Angeles State Coll., 1950; dean girls Twenty Nine Palms (Calif.) High Sch., 1960-65; dist. counselor Morongo (Calif.) Unified Sch. Dist., 1965-72, coordinator adult edn., 1965-67, guidance project dir., 1967; clk.-in-charge Landers (Calif.) Post Office, 1962-82; ret., 1982; dep. dir. gen. for the Americas Internat. Biog. Ctr., 1987—. V.p., sec. Landers Assn., 1965—; sec. Landers Vol. Fire Dept., 1972—; life mem. Hi-Desert Playhouse Guild, Hi-Desert Meml. Hosp. Guild; apptd. dep. dir. gen. for Ams. Internat. Biog. Centre, Cambridge, Eng., 1987. Bd. dirs., sec. Desert Emergency Radio Service. Recipient internat. diploma of honor for community service, 1973; Creativity award Internat. Personnel Research Assn., 1972, award Goat Mt. Grange No. 818, 1987; cert. of merit for disting. service to edn., 1973; Order of Rose, Alpha Xi Delta, 1978; poet laureate Center of Internat. Studies and Exchanges, 1981; diploma of merit in letters U. Arts, Parma, Italy, 1982; Golden Yr. Bruin UCLA, 1983; World Culture prize Nat. Ctr. for Studies and Research, Italian Acad., 1984; Golden Palm Diploma of Honor in poetry Leonardo Da Vinci Acad., 1984; Diploma of Merit and titular mem. internat. com. Internat. Ctr. Studies and Exchanges, Rome, 1984; Recognition award San Gorgonio council Girl Scouts U.S., 1984, 85; Cert. of appreciation Morongo Unified Sch. Dist., 1984; plaque for contribution to postal service and community U.S. Postal Service, 1984; Biographee of Yr. award for outstanding achievement in the field of edn. and service to community Hist. Preservations of Am.; named Princess of Poetry of Internat. Ctr. Cultural Studies and Exchange, Italy, 1985; community dinner held in her honor for achievement and service to Community, 1984; Star of Contemporary Poetry Masters of Contemporary Poetry, Internat. Ctr. Cultural Studies and Exchanges, Italy, 1984; named to honor list of leaders of contemporary art and lit. and apptd. titular mem. of Internat. High Com. for World Culture & Arts Leonardo Da Vinci Acad., 1987; ABI medal of honor 1987; other awards and certs. Life fellow Internat. Acad. Poets, World Lit. Acad.; mem. Am. Personnel and Guidance Assn., Internat. Platform Assn., Nat. Ret. Tchrs. Assn., Calif. Assn. for Counseling and Devel., Am. Biog. Research Assn. (life dep. gov.), Nat. Assn. Women Deans and Adminstrs., Montebello Bus. and Profl. Women's Club (pres.), Nat. League Am. Pen Women (sec. 1985-86), Leonardo Da Vinci Acad. Internat. Winged Glory diploma of honor in letters 1982), Landers Area C. of C. (sec. 1985-86, Presdl. award for outstanding service), Desert Nature Mus., Phi Beta Kappa. Clubs: Whitter Toastmistress (Calif.) (pres. 1957); Homestead Valley Women's (Landers). Lodge: Soroptimists (sec. 29 Palms chpt. 1962, life mem., Soroptimist of Yr. local chpt. 19, Woman of Distinction local chpt. 1987-88); Whittier (Calif.) Toastmistress (pres. 1957); Homestead Valley Women's (Landers). Author: Impy, 1974, Talkie, 1975, Impy's Children, 1975; Nineteen O Four, 1976, Little Brown Bat, 1976; Slo-Go, 1977; Owls Who and Who Who, 1978; Sandy, The Coydog, 1979; The Kit Fox and the Walking Stick, 1980; contbr. articles to profl. jours., poems to anthologies. Home: 632 Landers Ln PO Box 3839 Landers CA 92285

LANDHEER, RONALD, linguist, educator; b. Epe, The Netherlands, Apr. 27, 1936; s. Hugo and Wilhelmina (Tels) L.; m. Willy-Mia Kluit, Oct. 30, 1961; children: Jeanine, Hajo. PhD, State U. Leiden, 1984. Tchr. French secondary sch., The Hague, The Netherlands, 1963-67; asst. State U. Leiden, The Netherlands, 1967-73, prof. linguistics, 1973—. Contbr. articles to profl. jours., anthologies. Mem. Societas Linguistica Europaea, Vereniging Academici Wetenschappelijk Onderwijs. Home: Duyvendakstraat 30, 2313 PZ Leiden The Netherlands Office: Rijksuniversiteit, Faculty Letters Postbus 9515, 2300 RA Leiden The Netherlands

LANDIS, JOHN WILLIAM, engineering and construction company executive, government consultant; b. Kutztown, Pa., Oct. 10, 1917; s. Edwin Charles and Estella Juliabelle (Barto) L.; m. Muriel Trayes Souders, July 5, 1941; children: Maureen Lucille, Marcia Millicent. BS in Engring. Physics summa cum laude, Lafayette Coll., Easton, Pa., 1939, ScD (hon.), 1960. Registered profl. engr., Calif. Research engr. Eastman Kodak Co., Rochester, N.Y., 1939-43; cons. Navy Dept., Washington, 1946-50; head sci. and engring. dept. Ednl. Testing Service, Princeton, N.J., 1948-50; reactor engr. AEC, Washington, 1950-53; dir. customer relations atomic energy div. Babcock & Wilcox Co., N.Y.C., 1953-55; asst. mgr. atomic energy div. Babcock & Wilcox Co., Lynchburg, Va., 1955-62, mgr. atomic energy div., 1962-65; gen. mgr. Washington ops. Babcock & Wilcox Co., 1965-68; regional v.p. Gulf Gen. Atomic Co., Washington, 1968-69; group v.p. Gulf Gen. Atomic Co., LaJolla, Calif., 1969-70, pres., dir. subs., 1970-74; pres. Power Systems Co., Gen. Atomic Partnership, LaJolla, Calif., 1974-75; sr. v.p., dir., pres. subs. Stone & Webster Engring. Corp., Boston, 1975—; founding dir. Central fidelity Banks, Inc., Richmond, Va.; founding dir. Nat. Materials Property Data Network, Inc., Phila.; chmn. adv. com. on isotopes and radiation devel. and four other adv. coms. AEC, Washington, 1957-70; chmn. coms., co. rep. Atomic Indsl. Forum (now U.S. Council for Energy Awareness), Washington, 1953—; mem. N.Y. State Adv. Com. on Atomic Energy, 1956-59, Va. State Adv. Com. on Nuclear Energy, 1959-68; vice chmn. mgmt. com. Nat. Environ. Studies Project, Washington, 1974—; dir., v.p., pres., chmn. bds. and coms., trustee Internat. Fund, Am. Nat. Standards Inst., N.Y.C., 1957—; dir., chmn. Fusion Power Assocs., Gaithersburg, Md., 1981—; chmn. com. on energy-related atmospheric pollution World Energy Conf., London, 1984—; dir., chmn. com. on protection of environ. U.S. Energy Assn., Washington, 1981—; mem. fusion adv. panel U.S. Ho. of Reps., Washington, 1979—; charter mem. magnetic fusion adv. com. U.S. Dept. Energy, Washington, 1982-84; chmn. internat. research and devel. panel , chmn. civilian nuclear power panel, vice chmn. energy research adv. bd. U.S. Dept. Energy,1984—; advisor Carnegie-Mellon U., Pitts., 1972-73, Pa. State U., State College, 1980-83, U. Calif.-San Diego, 1974-82; vis. and sustaining fellow MIT, Cambridge, 1971—; chmn. bus. adminstrn. adv. bd. U. San Diego, 1972-75. Co-author: Nuclear Engineering, 1957; contbr. articles to profl. and trade jours. Trustee, chmn. Randolph-Macon Woman's Coll., Lynchburg, Va., 1963—; trustee Lafayette Coll., Easton, Pa., 1962—, Va. Poly. Inst. and State U., Blacksburg, 1966-70; bd. dirs. Va. Poly. Inst. Ednl. Found., Blacksburg, 1968—; mem. Va. Adv. Bd. on Indsl. Devel. and Planning, Richmond, 1962-72; bd. dirs. Va. Engring. Found., Charlottesville, 1962-65; trustee Seven Hills Sch., Lynchburg, Va., 1960-65; co-founder Republican Presdl. Task Force, Washington, 1981—; charter mem. Rep. Senatorial Inner Circle, Washington, 1980—; mem. Rep. Pres. Club, Washington, 1983—; mem. Mayor's Com. on Energy, San Diego, 1973-75. Served to lt. USN, 1943-46, ETO. Recipient Gen. of Industry award State of Okla., 1971, George Washington Kidd award Lafayette Coll., 1972, Lehigh Valley Favorite Son award State of Pa., 1976; named hon. citizen City of Dallas, 1973, Winston Churchill Medal of Honor, 1988; Alumni fellow Lafayette Coll., 1984. Fellow Am. Nuclear Soc. (pres. 1971-72, v.p. 1970-71, treas. 1964-68, chmn. coms. 1956—, bd. dirs. 1956-74), ASME; mem. Nat. Acad. Engring., Am. Soc. Macro-Engring. (pres. 1985-88, chancellor 1988—, charter bd. dirs. 1983—), Internat. Assn. Energy Economists, San Diego Hall Sci. (life), Phi Beta Kappa, Sigma Xi, Tau Beta Pi, Pi Delta Epsilon, Omicron Delta Kappa. Republican. Presbyterian. Clubs: Sphex (pres. 1966-67) (Lynchburg); Algonquin (Boston); Princeton (N.Y.C.). Home: 4 Whispering Ln Weston MA 02193 Office: Stone & Webster Engring Corp 245 Summer St Boston MA 02107

LANDON, JOHN WILLIAM, social worker, educator, author; b. Marlette, Mich., Mar. 24, 1937; s. Norman A. and Merle Irene (Lawrason) L. B.A., Taylor U., 1959; M.Div., Northwestern U., Christian Theol. Sem., 1962; M.S.W., Ind. U., 1966; Ph.D. in Social Sci., Ball State U., 1972. Regional supr. Iowa Dept. Social Welfare, Des Moines, 1965-67; acting chmn. dept. sociology Marion (Ind.) Coll., 1967-69; asst. prof. sociology and social work Ball State U., Muncie, Ind., 1969-71; asst. prof. social work, coordinator base courses Coll. Social Professions U. Ky., Lexington, 1971-73, assoc. prof., coordinator Undergrad. Program in Social Work Coll. of Social Work, 1974-85, prof. 1987—, assoc. dean, 1985—; dir. social work edn. Taylor U., Upland, Ind., 1973-74. Author: From These Men, 1966; Jesse Crawford, Poet of the Organ, Wizard of the Mighty Wurlitzer, 1974; Behold the Mighty Wurlitzer, The History of the Theatre Pipe Organ, 1983; The Development of Social Welfare, 1986. Mem. Am. Sociol. Assn., Council on Social Work Edn., Nat. Assn. Social Workers, Am. Acad. Social Sci., Ind. Acad. Social Sci., AAUP, Nat. Assn. Christians in Social Work, Am. Guild Organists. Home: 809 Celia Lane Lexington KY 40504 Office: U Ky Coll Social Work Lexington KY 40506

LANDRENEAU, RODNEY EDMUND, JR., physician; b. Mamou, La., Jan. 17, 1929; s. Rodney Edmund and Blanche (Savoy) L.; M.D., La. State U., 1951; m. Colleen Fraser, June 4, 1952; children—Rodney Jerome, Michael Douglas, Denise Margaret, Melany Patricia, Fraser Edmund, Edythe Blanche. Intern, Charity Hosp., New Orleans, 1951-52, resident, 1952-54, 56-58; practice medicine specializing in surgery, Eunice, La., 1958-—; pres., dir. Eunice Med. Center, Inc., 1960-—; mem. staff Moosa Meml. Hosp., Eunice, 1958—, chief med. staff; vis. staff Opelousas Gen. Hosp., 1958-—; assoc. faculty La. State U.-Eunice; cons., staff Lafayette (La.) Charity Hosp.; cons. staff surgery Savoy Meml. Hosp., Mamou; pres. Eunice Med. Center, Inc.; dir. Acadiana Bank & Trust Co.; mem. La. State Hosp. Bd., 1972—. Mem. Evangeline council Boy Scouts Am.; bd. dirs., Moosa Meml. Hosp., Eunice, 1986—, bd. govs., 1985-91. Served with M.C., AUS, 1954-56. Recipient Physician's Recognition award AMA, 1978-85. Diplomate Am. Bd. Surgery. Fellow Internat. Coll. Surgeons (regional dir.), ACS (local chmn. com. trauma, instr.), Southeastern Surg. Congress, Pan Pacific Surg. Congress; mem. Am. Bd. Abdominal Surgeons, Am. Geriatrics Soc., St. Edmunds Athletic Assn., St. Landry Hist. Soc. (v.p. chpt.), St. Landry Parish Med. Soc. (pres. 1969-71, 85-87), Am. Legion, SCV, SAR, Alpha Omega Alpha. Democrat. Roman Catholic. Club: St. Edmund's High Sch. Scholastic Booster (pres. 1986—). Home: 1113 Williams St Eunice LA 70535 Office: 301 N Duson St Eunice LA 70535

LANDRIEAU, MARCEL, human resources company executive; b. Les Essarts, France, May 24, 1933; s. Marcel and Louise (Herbreteau) L.; m. Colette Ottolini, Mar. 24, 1956 (div. May 1986); children: Pierre-Henri, Laurence, Nicole. Diploma in Engring., Ecole Centrale, Paris, 1956; MS, Calif. Inst. Tech., 1957; PhD in Bus. Econs., U. Aix-Marseille, France, 1972. Asst. to gen. mgr. Monsanto-France, Paris, 1959-62; dir. devel. Monsanto-France, Wingles, 1962-64, plant mgr., 1964-69; dir. mfg. Duclos-SPCA, Septemes, France, 1969-80; pvt. mgmt. cons. Marseille, France, 1980-84; dir. Ecole Superieur Ingenieurs Marseille, 1984-87; sec. gen. IMT, Marseille, 1987-88; mng. dir. ACOPAD, Marseille, 1988—; prof. bus. adminstrn. Inst. d'Adminstrn. des Enterprises, Aix, France, 1972—. Home: La Colombiere, 13109 Simiane France Office: 86 rue Edmond Rostand, 13006 Marseille France

LANDRUM, LARRY JAMES, computer engineer; b. Santa Rita, N.Mex., May 29, 1943; s. Floyd Joseph and Jewel Helen (Andreska) L.; m. Ann Marie Hartman, Aug. 25, 1963 (div.); children—Larry James, David Wayne, Andrei Mikhail, Donal Wymore; m. 2d, Mary Kathleen Turner, July 27, 1980. Student N.Mex. Inst. Mining and Tech., 1961-62, N. Mex. State U., 1963-65; A.A. in Data Processing, Eastern Ariz. Coll., 1971; B.A. in Computer Sci., U. Tex., 1978. Tech. service rep. Nat. Cash Register, 1966-73; with ASC super-computer project Tex. Instruments, Austin, 1973-80, computer technician, 1973-75, tech. instr., 1975-76, product engr., 1976-78, operating system programmer, 1978-80; computer engr. Ariz. Pub. Service, Phoenix, 1980-84, sr. computer engr., 1984-87, lead computer engr., 1987—; instr. computer fundamentals Eastern Ariz. Coll., 1972-73, Rio Salado Community Coll., Phoenix, 1985-86. Mem. Assn. Computing Machinery, Mensa, Phi Kappa Phi. Methodist. Home: 6025 W Medlock Dr Glendale AZ 85301 Office: Ariz Nuclear Power Project PO Box 52034 Phoenix AZ 85072-2034

LANDSBERG, JERRY, management and investment consultant, optical laboratory executive; b. Dallas, June 30, 1933; s. Max and Rose (Hechtman) L.; grad. So. Meth. U., 1954; m. Gloria Zale, Sept. 2, 1956; children—Steven Jay, Jeffrey Paul, Karen Beth, Ruth Ellen. Salesman, Remington Rand div. Sperry Rand, 1955-57; salesman Zale Corp., 1957-59, asst. mgr., 1959-60, mgr., 1960-63, merchandiser, 1963-67; registered rep., security analyst Silberberg & Co., 1967-69; owner Jerry Landsberg & Assos., 1969-72; v.p. Ross Watch Case Corp., gen. mgr. Kenfield jewelry div., Long Island City, N.Y., 1971-75; pres., chief operating officer King Optical Corp., Dallas, 1974-75; chmn., chief exec. officer Richland Optical Labs. Inc.; pres. Jerry Landsberg Assos., Great Neck, N.Y., 1975—; pres. N. Am. Vision Services, Inc., Freeport, N.Y., 1987—, chmn., chief exec. officer Tech-Optics Internat. Corp. Trustee, Village of Kensington, 1967-75, commr. police, 1967-69, commr. pub. works, 1969-75, dep. mayor, 1969-75, mayor, 1973; fin. v.p. Temple Emanuel, Great Neck, 1964-66, trustee, 1964-74; bd. dirs. Great Neck Symphony Soc., 1974—, pres., 1978-81, chmn. bd., 1981—; trustee North Shore Univ. Hosp., 1981—, Am. Friends of Haifa U., 1986—; mem. adv. bd. Adelphi U. Sch. Nursing, 1981-86, chmn., 1986—; trustee Jewish Inst. Geriatric Care, 1979—, treas., 1983-84; bd. dirs. Great Neck Community Fund; v.p. Zale Found.; Great Neck chmn. Fedn. Jewish Philanthropies; active various community drives. Mem. So. Meth. U. Alumni Assn. (dir. nat. bd., pres. N.Y. club). Clubs: U.S. Power Squadron, Masons, Shriners. Office: 59 Hanse Ave Freeport NY 11520

LANDSBERG, MARGARETHA ELIZABETH, linguist, researcher; b. Arnhem, Netherlands, May 31, 1925; came to Israel, 1946; d. Michel and Rosa-Fina (Cohen) Mogendorff; m. Yosef Ajzenberg, 1946 (div. 1951); 1 child, Rena C.; m. Morris Landsberg, Oct. 7, 1959; children—Michael, Ariel. BA, U. Haifa, 1974, MA, 1975; Researcher U. Haifa, Israel, 1973-81; prof. Fairfax U., 1988—; mem. acad. staff Faculty Humanities Fairfax (Eng.) U.; assoc. jour. Current Anthropology, 1980; symposium organizer 11th Internat. Congress Anthrop. and Ethnol. Scis., Vancouver, B.C., Canada, 1983, 12th, Zagreb, Yugoslavia, 1988. Author: Material for a Bibliography of Translinguistic Studies, The Genesis of Language: A Different Judgment of Evidence, Syntactic Iconicity and Freezes: The Human Dimension; contbr. articles to profl. jours. U. Haifa scholar, 1973, 74, 76. Fellow World Lit. Acad.; mem. Internat. Assn. Semiotic Studies, Semiotic Soc. Am., Linguistic Soc. Am., Am. Biographical Inst. Research Assn. (life bd. govs., dep. dir. gen. Internat. Biographical Centre), Internat. Fedn. Univ. Women. Home: 1 Shikmona St, Bat-Galim, Haifa Israel 35 014

LANDUYT, BERNARD FRANCIS, economist, educator; b. Monmouth, Ill., Mar. 22, 1907; m. Meta Louise Bossong, June 2, 1928. B.Ed., Western Ill. Tchrs. Coll., 1929; A.M., State U. Iowa, 1936, Ph.D., 1938; A.M., Columbia, 1943; LL.D., U. Detroit, 1973. Tchr. pub. schs. 1926-31; tchr., prin., pub. high schs. P.I., 1931-35; instr. State U. Iowa, 1937-38; mem. faculty, dept. econ. and bus. adminstrn. U. Detroit, 1938-71, chmn., 1947-63, prof. econs., 1949-71; chmn. U. Detroit (M.B.A. program), 1948-74; asst. dean U. Detroit (Coll. Commerce and Finance), 1958-63, dean, 1963-71, dean emeritus, 1971—, distinguished prof. adminstrn., 1974—; ret.; lectr. Nat. Mgmt. Assn., 1960—, OPM, 1958—; div. mgmt. edn. U. Mich., 1969—, Inst. for Career and Personal Devel. Central Mich. U., 1976—, Chrysler Inst., 1976-78. Author, lectr. in econs. and mgmt.; Co-author: Administrative Strategy, 1961, Administrative Strategy and Decision Making, 1966. Mem. Detroit St. Ry. Commn., 1963-72, pres., 1970-72; mem. Detroit Rapid Transit Commn., S.E. Mich. Transp. Authority, 1967-72. Served as mil. govt. officer USNR, 1942-46; mem. fgn. trade sub-commn. Allied Control Commn. for Italy econ. and agrl. officer U.S. Mil. Govt. Saipan chief salvage sect. U.S. Mil. Govt. Okinawa ret. comdr. USNR. Decorated Bronze Star. Mem. Am. Econs. Assn., Assn. Social Econs., Naval Res. Assn., Navy League U.S., U.S. Naval Acad. Found., U.S. Naval Inst., Res. Officers Assn., Mil. Order World Wars, Alpha Phi Omega, Beta Alpha Psi, Alpha Sigma Lambda, Beta Gamma Sigma, Delta Phi Epsilon, Kappa Delta Pi, Delta Mu Delta, Order of Artus. Roman Catholic. Home: 31698 Southview Birmingham MI 48009

LANDY, BURTON AARON, lawyer; b. Chgo., Aug. 16, 1929; s. Louis J. and Clara (Ernstein) L.; m. Eleanor M. Simmel, Aug. 4, 1957; children: Michael Simmel, Alisa Anne. Student, Nat. U. Mex., 1948; B.S., Northwestern U., 1950; postgrad. scholar, U. Havana, 1951; J.D., U. Miami, 1952; postgrad. fellow, Inter-Am. Acad. Comparative Law, Havana, Cuba, 1955-56. Bar: Fla. 1952. Practice law in internat. field Miami, 1955—; ptnr. firm Ammerman & Landy, 1957-63, Paul, Landy, Beiley & Harper, P.A. and predecessor firm, 1964—; lectr. Latin Am. bus. law U. Miami Sch. Law, 1972-75; also internat. law confs. in U.S. and abroad; mem. Nat. Conf. on Fgn. Aspects of U.S. Nat. Security, Washington, 1958; mem. organizing com. Miami regional conf. Com. for Internat. Econ. Growth, 1958; mem. U.S. Dept. Commerce Regional Export Expansion Council, 1969-74, mem. Dist. Export Council, 1978—; dir. Fla. Council Internat. Devel., 1977—, chmn. 1986-87; mem. U. Miami Citizens Bd., 1977—; chmn. Fla. del. S.E. U.S.-Japan Assn., 1980-82; mem. adv. com. 1st Miami Trade Fair of Ams., 1978; dir., v.p. Greater Miami Fgn. Trade Zone, Inc., 1978—; mem. organizing com., lectr. 4 Inter-Am. Aviation Law Confs.; bd. dirs. Inter-Am. Bar Legal Found.; participant Aquaculture Symposium Sci. and Man in the Ams., Mexico City, Fla. Gov's Econ. Mission to Japan and Hong Kong, 1978; mem. bd. exec. advisors Law and Econs. Ctr.; mem. vis. com. U. Miami Sch. Bus.; mem. internat. fin. council Office Comptroller of Fla.; founding chmn. Fla.-Korea Econ. Coop. Com., 1982—, Southeast U.S.-Korea Econ. Com., 1985—; chmn. Expo 500 Fla.-Columbus Soc., 1985-87; founding co-chmn. So. Fla. Roundtable-Georgetown U. Ctr. for Strategic and Internat. Studies, 1982—; chmn. Fla. Gov.'s Conf. on World Trade, 1984—; gen. counsel Fla. Internat. Bankers Assn.; dir., former gen. counsel Fla. Internat. Ins. and Reins. Assn. Contbg. editor Econs. Devel. Lawyers of the Ams., 1969-74; contbr. numerous articles to legal jours. in U.S. and fgn. countries. Chmn. City of Miami Internat. Trade and Devel. Com., 1984—; dir. and chmn. internat. task force Beacon Council of Dade County, Fla., 1985; bd. dirs. Internat. Comml. Dispute Resolution Ctr.; appointed by Gov. of Fla. to Internat. Currency and Barter Commn. & Fla. Columbus Hemispheric Trade Commn., 1986. Served with JAGC USAF, 1952-54, Korea; to maj. Res. Named Internat. Trader of Yr., Fla. Council Internat. Devel., 1980, Bus. Person of Yr., 1986; recipient Pan Am. Informatica Comunicaciones Expo award, 1983, Lawyer of Americas award U. Miami, 1984; named hon. consul gen. Republic of Korea, Miami, 1983—, recipient Heung-in medal (Order of Diplomatic Service), 1986. Mem. Inter-Am. Bar Assn. (asst. sec.-gen. 1957-59, treas. 11th conf. 1959, co-chmn. jr. bar sect. 1963-65, mem council 1969—, exec. com. 1975—, pres. 1982-84, awarded Diploma de Honor 1987), ABA (chmn. com. arrangements internat. and comparative law sect. 1964-65, com. on inter-Am. affairs 1985-87), Spanish Am. Bar Assn., Fla. Bar Assn. (vice chmn. adminstrv. law com. 1965, vice chmn. internat. and comparative law com. 1967-68, chmn. aero. law com. 1968-69), Dade County Bar Assn. (chmn. fgn. laws and langs com. 1964-65), Internat. Ctr. Fla. (pres. 1981-82), World Peace Through Law Ctr., Miami Com. Fgn. Relations, Instituto Ibero Americano de Derecho Aeronautico, Am. Soc. Internat. Law, Council Internat. Visitors, Am. Fgn. Law Assn. (pres. Miami 1958), Bar of South Korea (hon. mem.), Greater Miami C. of C. (bd. govs. 1986—), Colombian-Am. C. of C. (bd. dirs. 1986—), Phi Alpha Delta. Home: 6255 Old Cutler Rd Miami FL 33156 Office: Penthouse Atico Fin Ctr Miami FL 33131

LANE, ARTHUR ALAN, lawyer; b. N.Y.C., Dec. 2, 1945; s. George and Delys Lane; m. Jane Ficocella, Dec. 30, 1972; 1 child, Eva B. BA, Yale U., 1967; JD, Columbia U., 1970, MBA, 1971. Bar: N.Y. 1971. Assoc. Webster, Sheffield, Fleischmann, Hitchcock & Brookfield, N.Y.C., 1971-72; asst. to div. counsel Liggett & Myers Inc., N.Y.C., 1973; assoc. Wickes, Riddell, Bloomer, Jacobi & McGuire, N.Y.C., 1974-78, Morgan, Lewis & Bockius, N.Y.C., 1979; ptnr. Eaton & Van Winkle, N.Y.C., 1980—. Mem. ABA, Bar Assn. City N.Y. Home: 315 W 70th St New York NY 10023 Office: Eaton & Van Winkle 600 3d Ave New York NY 10016

LANE, CHARLES STUART, publisher, editor; b. Newton, Mass., Feb. 13, 1924. A.A., Boston U., 1949, B.A., 1952, M.A., 1958, doctoral student, Sch. Edn., 1968-69. English tchr. in pub. and pvt. secondary schs. and colls., 25 yrs.; headmaster Dunbarton Acad., Meredith, N.H., 1959-68; curriculum coordinator of English, Winthrop, Mass. 1970-81; pub.-editor, Jour. Print World, Meredith, N.H., 1978—; dir. Old Print Barn, Meredith, 1975—. Photographer nature photos, panoramas. Served with U.S. Army, 1943-46, PTO. Mem. Bostonian Soc., Am. Legion, VFW, Phi Delta Kappa. Subject of Pub. Broadcasting Service Interview, 1982, 84. Home: RFD 2 Box 1008 Meredith NH 03253 Office: Jour Print World 1000 Winona Rd Meredith NH 03253-9599

LANE, CHERYL ANN GROSS, nursing consultant; b. Pitts., Sept. 24, 1948; d. Charles N. and Maryalda (Freund) Gross; Asso. Sci. with honors, Jr. Coll. of Broward County, 1968; B.S. in Nursing, N.C. A. and T. U., 1981; MA in Counseling, Rollins Coll., 1987. m. Timothy Gerald Lane, June 20, 1969; children—Tamala Ann, Wendelyn Joy, Justin Bradley. Staff nurse Broward Gen. Hosp., Fort Lauderdale, Fla., 1968, asst. head nurse, 1969; oncology nurse clinician Bowman Gray Sch. Medicine, Winston-Salem, N.C., 1969-71, dir. cancer center nursing Oncology Research Center, 1971-81; asst. instr. nursing S.E. Mo. State U., 1981-84; oncology nursing cons., 1981—; mem. tumor registry com. N.C. Bapt. Hosp., 1980-81. Mem. N.C. Adv. Council on Cause and Control of Cancer Task Force, 1978. Mem. Am. Cancer Soc. (bd. dirs. N.C. div. 1979-81),Oncology Nursing Soc. (chairperson membership com. 1979-84, v.p. 1984-88), Piedmont Oncology Assn. (chairperson nursing com. 1979-81), Phi Theta Kappa. Roman Catholic. Author: (manual) Cancer Chemotherapy Guidelines, 1978; contbr. articles on nursing care to profl. jours. Home: 255 Madrid Ct Merritt Island FL 32953 Office: 1257 Florida Ave Rockledge FL 32955

LANE, DANIEL MCNEEL, oncologist, biochemist; b. Ft. Sam Houston, Tex., Jan. 25, 1936; s. Samuel Hartman and Mary Maverick (McNeel) L.; m. Carolyn Ann Spruiell, Nov. 28, 1958; children—Linda Ann, Daniel M. Jr., Maury S., Oleta K. MD, U. Tex.-Dallas, 1961; MS, U. Tenn., 1967; PhD, U. Okla., 1973. Head pediatric hematology/oncology U. Okla. Med. Ctr., Oklahoma City, 1966-70; research fellow Okla. Med. Research Found., Oklahoma City, 1969-72, adj. assoc. mem., 1986—; head pediatric hematology/oncology Tulane Med. Sch., New Orleans, 1972-73; head hematology/oncology Oklahoma City Clinic, 1973-79; dir. clin. investigation Presbyn. Meml. Hosp., Oklahoma City, 1975-77; adj. assoc. mem. Okla. Med. Research Fedn., Oklahoma City, 1986—; gen. ptnr. Candy Factory Hist. Preservation Ptnrs., Memphis, 1981—. Fin. chmn. Dunlap for Congress, 1976; head Physicians for Gov. Nigh, 1978; Dem. candidate for Congress, 5th Dist., 1982. USPHS fellow, 1964-66; spl. research fellow Nat. Heart-Lung Inst., 1969-72. Mem. AMA, Am. Soc. Clin. Oncology, Am. Soc. Hematology. Democrat. Episcopalian. Research on plasma lipids and infant nutrition, apolipoproteins, clin. hematology and oncology (chemotherapy); pediatrics (consultative). Home: 1504 Guilford Ln Oklahoma City OK 73120 Office: 3330 NW 56th St #105 Oklahoma City OK 73112

LANE, GEORGE HOLMAN, JR., newspaper publisher; b. Lewisburg, Tenn., Oct. 18, 1945; s. George Holman and Martha Frances (Ross) L.; m. Sue Carol Colbert, Mar. 26, 1976; children—Lee Anna, Cynthia Lynn, Nathan George. Corr. Miami Herald, Ft. Myers, Fla., 1963-64; editor, pub. Northside Citizen, North Ft. Myers, 1964-65; news/photo stringer S.W. Fla., UPI, 1965-75; news reporter/corr. WINK News, Ft. Myers, 1967-74; bur. chief St. Petersburg Times, Punta Gorda, Fla., 1967-74; legis. aide Fla. State Legislature, Ft. Myers and Tallahassee, 1974-75; gen. mgr., advt. dir. Sunshine Newspaper, Arcadia, Fla., 1976; gen. mgr., pub. Desoto Shopping Guide, Arcadia, 1976-83; founder, pub. Desoto County Times, 1983-86; roving editor Sun Coast Media Group (new owners Desoto County Times), 1986—; roving feature writer Tampa Tribune, 1987—; ptnr. Big Red Q Quickprint Ctr., Arcadia, 1981-84. Author: A Pictorial History of Arcadia and Desoto County, 1984; editor hist. papers in Southwest Fla. history, 1980-83. Pres. Southwest Floridiana, Arcadia, 1980—; chmn. Desoto County Republican Com., 1977-84, precinct 10 committeeman, 1980-88, mem. state com., 1980—; chmn. Desoto County Hist. Commn., 1976—; mem. Desoto County Hist. Soc., 1986—; mem. DeSoto High Sch. Adv. Com., 1983—; chmn. Arcadia/DeSoto County Centennial Celebration Com., 1985-87; mem. Main Street Arcadia Com., 1984—, chmn., 1985-87; co-founder, charter v.p. Save Our School Com., 1985-87; chmn. pub. relations com. Fla. Rep. Party, 1984—; mem. citizens adv. com. Desoto Meml. Hosp., 1981-86; bd. dirs. March of Dimes, 1981-86; mem. vestry St. Edmunds Ch., 1978-80. Recipient Disting. Service award DeSoto Historic Commn. Mem. Downtown Assn. Arcadia (pres. 1981-87), Desoto County C. of C. (Citizen of Yr. 1983, pres. 1982-83), Fla. Advt. Pubs. Assn., Fla. Press Assn., Nat. Assn. Advt. Pubs., Charlotte Harbor Area Hist. Soc., Peace River Valley Hist. Soc., Fla. Hist. Soc., Ducks Unltd. Republican. Episcopalian. Clubs: Arcadia Country, others. Lodges: Odd Fellows, Moose, Rotary (pres. 1983-84, outstanding service award 1978-80), Elks. Home: 910 SE Nineth Ln Arcadia FL 33821 Office: PO Box 1776 Arcadia FL 33821

LANE, HELEN, translator; b. Mpls.; arrived in France, 1972; d. Harold Arthur and Ruth De Ette (Warner) Overholt; m. Frank A. Lane (div. 1953); 1 child, Alan Michael. BA, UCLA, 1943, MA, 1953. cert. romance lang. translator. Translator U.S. Civil Service, Los Angeles, 1944-45; instr. UCLA, 1950-57, Goucher Coll., Balt., 1958-59, NYU, NYC, 1959-60; editorial cons. Grove Press., N.Y.C., 1962-72; translator Rouffignac, France, 1972—; European adv. Columbia Translation Ctr., N.Y.C., 1979—. Book translator: Three Marias, 1977, Manifestoes Surrealism, 1980, I the Supreme, 1986, Spanish Ministry of Culture Grant, 1986, Landscapes After the Battle, 1987. Recipient Translation award Pen Am. Ctr., N.Y.C., 1975, 85, Gulbenkian Prize, 1979, UCLA Alumni award, 1983, Nat. Book award, N.Y.C., 1973, 74. Home and Office: Le Veyssou, 24580 Rouffignac, AC Saint Cernin France

LANE, LAURENCE WILLIAM, JR., ambassador, publisher; b. Des Moines, Nov. 7, 1919; s. Laurence William and Ruth (Bell) L.; m. Donna Jean Gimbel, Apr. 16, 1955; children: Sharon Louise, Robert Laurence,

Brenda Ruth. Student, Pomona Coll., 1938-40, LL.D. (hon.); B.J., Stanford U., 1942. Chmn. bd. Lane Pub. Co.; publisher Sunset Mag. and books; also producer Sunset Films, Menlo Park, Calif., from 1930; chmn. bd. Sunset Films, from 1974; U.S. Ambassador to Australia Washington, 1985—; dir. Calif. Water Service Co., Crown Zellerbach Corp., Pacific Gas and Electric Co. Mem. adv. bd. Sec. Interior's Bd. Nat. Parks; mem. adv. council Grad. Sch. Bus., Stanford U.; mem. Pres.'s Nat. Productivity Adv. Com.; former ambassador U.S. Dept. State; mem. Pacific Basin Econ. Council; trustee Colonial Williamsburg Found.; bd. overseers Hoover Instn. War, Revolution and Peace. Served to lt. USNR, World War II, PTO. Recipient Conservation Service award Sec. Interior; named hon. prof. journalism Stanford U. Fellow Coll. of Notre Dame; mem. Newcomen Soc. N.Am., Alaska Bus. Council, Pacific Area Travel Assn. (life; chmn. 1980—), Japan-Calif. Assn., Los Rancheros Vistadores, Advt. Club San Francisco, No. Calif. Alumni Assn., Alpha Delta Sigma. Republican. Presbyterian. Clubs: Bohemian (San Francisco), Pacific Union (San Francisco); Men's Garden (Los Angeles). Home: 880 Westridge Dr Portola Valley CA 94025 Office: US Ambassador to Australia care Dept of State Washington DC 20520 also: Middlefield and Willow Rds Menlo Park CA 94025 *

LANE, WILLIAM W., electronics executive; b. Roanoke, Va., Feb. 25, 1934; s. Melvin V. and Cecile (Lane); m. Ronnie G Lane, Sept. 14, 1978; 1 son, Jonathan D. B.A., Bklyn. Coll., 1956; M.B.A., Cornell U., 1958. Vice pres. Major Electronics Corp., 1959-70, chmn., dir., 1970; v.p., dir. Internat. Transistor Corp., Burbank, Calif., 1971-73; vice chmn., dir. Internat. Chia Hsin, Taipai, Taiwan, 1973-76; chmn., dir. Emerson (H.K. Ltd.), Hong Kong, from 1976, Emerson Radio Corp., North Bergen, N.J., 1974—; pres. Majorette Enterprises, from 1961; chmn. MAJ EXCO Imports Inc., 1977-85; dir. H.H. Scott, Inc. Cardiac Resusitator Corp., Portland, Oreg. Served with AUS, 1958-59. Mem. bus. adv. bd. U.S. Senate. Office: Emerson Radio Corp 1 Emerson Ln North Bergen NJ 07047

LANESE, JILL RENEE, computer and management consultant; b. Neptune, N.J., June 3, 1952; d. William Herman and Blossom Roslyn (Feldman) Epstein; m. Louis Lanese, June 10, 1984. BA, C.W. Post Coll., 1974. Word processing specialist Nat. Produce Co., Inc., Neptune, 1974-78; systems mgr. AT&T, Basking Ridge, N.J., 1978-81; sr. systems mgr. ITT, N.Y.C., 1981-84; info. systems mgr. Breed, Abbott & Morgan, N.Y.C., 1984-86; word processing/data processing dir., advisor Compu-group, N.Y.C., 1985-88; automation cons. Jill Lanese Computer Cons., N.Y.C., 1986-88, pres. ComputerForce Inc., N.Y.C., 1988—. adv., bd. dirs. ComputerPro,N.Y.C., 1987—. Contbr. articles to newspapers, jours., mags. Bd. dirs., pres. Am. Found. for Animals, West End, N.J., 1982—, dir. fundraiser, 1985-88. Mem. Internat. Platform Assn., Doris Day Animal League, Ind. Computer Cons. Assn., Assn. Info. Systems Profls., Assn. for Women in Computing, Nat. Assn. Female Execs, World Wildlife Fund, Greenpeace, Jacques Cousreau Soc., Humane Soc. U.S., Fund for Ethical Treatment to Animals, Internat. Platform Assn. Republican. Avocations: writing, floral and interior design, nutrition, dogs, photography, travel. Home: 8874 24th Ave Brooklyn NY 11214 Office: ComputerForce Inc 298 Fifth Ave New York NY 10001

LANG, DAVID FREDERICK, accountant; b. London, Nov. 24, 1934; s. Herbert Raphael and Ruth (Levi) L.; m. Carole Diamant, Apr. 1, 1962; children: Michael, Paul. Apprentice Handley Page, Ltd., London, 1951-55; acct. with various firms, London, 1957-81; chief acct. The Royal Aero. Soc., London, 1981—. Served with RAF, 1955-57. Mem. Brit. Inst. Mgmt., Chartered Inst. Transport, Chartered Inst. Mgmt. Accts. (diploma 1960). Office: Royal Aero Soc, 4 Hamilton Pl, London W1V 0BQ, England

LANG, DENNIS CHARLES, marine transportation and insurance broker, consultant; b. Los Angeles, July 21, 1941; s. Chester Charles and Alice Marie (Ryan) L.; m. Joan Mary Schadewald, Jan. 11, 1963 (div. Jan. 1976); children: Dennis Charles, Kristine Marie, Michele Renee; m. Susan Jewel Bass, Feb. 7, 1981; 1 child, Tanner Christian. AA, Los Angeles City Coll., 1965; BS in Bus. Adminstrn., U. Calif., Irvine, 1969; postgrad. in law, Western States U., 1971. Spl. agt. Marine Office Am., Los Angeles, 1963-69; v.p., bd. dirs., marine mgr. Robert F. Driver Co., San Diego, 1969-80; br. mgr., v.p. Fred S. James, San Diego, 1980-81; v.p. oil and gas prodn. Emett & Chandler, Houston, 1981-82; exec. v.p., mgr. oil and gas prodn. Republic Hogg Robinson, San Diego, Los Angeles, 1982-83; pres. Dennis Lang, Houston, 1983—; dir. mktg. Am. Trucking Assurance Alliance, Inc., Oak Brook, Ill., also pres. div. Star Services, Inc.; sr. account exec. for Tex. and N.Mex., Carriers Ins. Co., Des Moines; asst. v.p., dir. transp. div. Wm. Rigg Co., Dallas; cons. to ins., oil, and gas industries. Contbr. articles to profl. jours. Mem. Balboa Park Cultural Funding Com., 1976-79; commr. San Diego County Park and Recreation, 1973-76, San Diego Community Coll., 1975-81; unit commr. longhorn council Boy Scouts Am., Ft. Worth, 1987. Served with USN, 1959-63. Named Outstanding Young Man, Chula Vista C. of C., 1972; recipient Disting. Service award Calif. Jaycees, 1972. Mem. Nat. Assn. Ins. Agts., Ind. Ins. Agts. and Brokers Assn. (bd. dirs. 1969-82), San Diego Agts. and Brokers Assn., Nat. Automobile Mktg. Assocs. (bd. dirs.), Navy League, Internat. Platform Assn., Chula Vista (Calif.) Jaycees (v.p., bd. dirs., Outstanding New Jaycee 1970-71, Outstanding Young Man 1972). Mem. Tex. Motor Transp. Assn. (1985-87, vice chmn. Ft. Worth battle 1986-87). Democrat. Methodist. Clubs: Toastmasters (bd. dirs. 1973-76); Propellor of U.S. (I Day chmn. 1969-82). Lodge: Sertoma (bd. dirs. 1973-76). Office: PO Box 683 Colleyville TX 76034

LANG, FRANCIS HAROVER, lawyer; b. Manchester, Ohio, June 4, 1907; s. James Walter and Mary (Harover) L.; m. Rachel Boyce, Oct. 20, 1934; children: Mary Sue, Charles Boyce, James Richard. A.B., Ohio Wesleyan U., 1929; J.D., Ohio State U., 1932. Bar: Ohio 1932. Practice in East Liverpool, 1932-42, 45—; with War Dept., 1942-45; chmn. bd. First Fed. Savs. & Loan Assn., East Liverpool, 1959-82; former pres., bd. dirs. Walter Lang companies.; hon. bd. dirs. 1st Nat. Community Bank East Liverpool, Ohio. Past bd. dirs. YMCA, Mary Patterson Meml.; past pres. Columbiana council Boy Scouts Am. regional com., E. Central region; mem. at large Nat. council, 1968—; bd. dirs. Bd. Global Ministries of United Methodist Ch., 1968-76. Mem. E. Liverpool C. of C. (past pres.), Columbiana County Bar Assn. (past pres.), Ohio State Bar Assn. Methodist. Clubs: Rotarian (past dist. gov.), E. Liverpool Country, Masons (33d degree). Home: Highland Colony East Liverpool OH 43920 Office: Potters Savs and Loan Bldg East Liverpool OH 43920

LANG, GABRIEL, surgeon, educator; b. Strasbourg, France, Mar. 28, 1931; s. Joseph and Maria (Houette) L.; m. Monique Grau, Nov. 24, 1964; children:Christophe, Denis. MD, Strasbourg U., 1961. Externe Civic Hosp., Strasbourg, 1953-55, resident, 1955-63, assistant, 1963-65; assistant prof. Med. Faculty Strasbourg U., 1965-67, dir. dept. sports Med. Faculty, 1975—; sub chief Stephanie Orthopaedic Hosp., Strasbourg, 1967-75, chief med. officer, 1975-80; prof. orthopaedic surgery Sch. Medicine Louis Pasteur U., Strasbourg, 1980—; med. cons. Mutuelle Generale Edn. Nationale, 1970—. Contbr. over 200 articles to profl. jours. Served to col. Health Services, Algeria, 1956-59. Paul Harris fellow, 1980; named Knight French Nat. Merit, 1978, Knight Acad. Palm, 1981. Mem. Internat. Orthopaedic and Traumatologic Soc., French Orthopaedic Soc., Surg. Acad. Paris, Internat. Alpine Surg. Soc. (past pres.), French East Orthopaedic Soc. (past pres.), Polish Orthopaedic Soc., German Dem. Republic Orthopaedic Soc. Roman Catholic. Lodge: Rotary (founding pres. Strasbourg club 1975). Office: Hopital Stephanie, 15 rue de la Lisiere, 67026 Strasbourg France

LANGAAS, ARILD ODD, advertising executive; b. Oslo, Norway, Sept. 21, 1936; s. Kaare and Erna (Bye) L.; married, June 24, 1961; children: Janne, Gitte, Bosse. Photographer Army of Norway, 1956-59; account exec. Bates Advt. Agy., Norway, 1959-64, v.p., 1968-70; product mgr. Unilever Co., Denmark, 1964-68; gen. mgr. Scaneco Young & Rubicam, Norway, 1970—. Recipient more than 45 creative awards for advt. work. Club: Vaalerenga (Oslo). Office: Scaneco Young & Rubicam, Wldmr Thranesg 84B, Oslo Norway

LANGBACKA, RALF RUNAR, theater director and manager; b. Närpes, Finland, Nov. 20, 1932; s. Runar Emanuel and Hulda Emilia (Backlund) L.; m. Birgitta Runa Danielsson, Nov. 5, 1961; children—Thomas, Mats, Nina. M.A., Abo Akademi, Turku, Finland, 1956. Artistic dir. Swedish Theatre, Turku, 1960-63; dir. Finnish Nat. Theatre, Helsinki, 1963-65; artistic dir. Swedish Theatre, Helsinki, 1965-67, Turku City Theatre, 1971-77; prof. arts, Helsinki, 1979-83, 88—; mng. dir. Helsinki City Theatre, 1983-87; freelance dir. in Finland, Sweden and Norway, 1967-71, 77-83; mem. State Drama Commn., 1967-70. Author: Teatterikirja (Theatre Book), 1977; Bland annat om Brecht (On Brecht and Others), 1982, rev. edit., 1983, Möten med Tjechov (Meetings with Chekhov), 1986, Denna langa dag, detta korta liv, dikter (This Long Day, This Short Life, poems), 1988; also articles on theatre and lit. Recipient Critics Spurs award Finnish Critics Assn., 1963; Pro Finlandia medal, Order Finnish White Rose, 1973; named Prof. of Arts, 1979-84, 88-93. Mem. Finnish Theatre Dirs. Assn. (chmn. 1979-83), Finnish Centre of Internat. Theatre Inst. (pres. 1983—). Socialist. Home: Hopeasalmenranta 1B, 00570 Helsinki 57 Finland

LANGBEIN, HERMANN, organization executive; b. Vienna, May 18, 1912; s. Artur L. and Grete (Haas) L.; m. Loisi Turko, Aug. 12, 1950; children: Lisa, Kurt. Student in journalism, Krankenschwester, Vienna. Gen. sec. Internat. Com. Auschwitz, Vienna, 1954-59, Internat. Com. Camps, Vienna, 1961—. Author: Die Stärkeren, 1949, Menschen in Auschwitz, 1970, Viderstand in den nationalsozialistischen Konzentrationslagern, 1980 and other co-authored publications. Recipient Gerechter, Yad Vashem, Jerusalem, 1968. Home: Weigandhof 5, A-1100 Vienna Austria

LANGDON, ROBERT ADRIAN, historian; b. Adelaide, Australia, Sept. 3, 1924; s. Arthur Louis and Doris Dodd (McFarling) L.; m. Iva Louise Layton, Dec. 6, 1958 (dec. 1984); children: Iva Treasure Langdon Carmody, Louise Vivienne. MA, Australian Nat. U., 1987. Journalist Advertiser Newspapers Ltd., Adelaide, 1953-61, Pacific Publs. Pty. Ltd., Sydney, Australia, 1962-68; exec. officer Pacific Manuscripts Bur. Australian Nat. U., Canberra, 1968-86; vis. fellow Pacific and Southeast Asian history Australian Nat. U., 1986—; bd. dirs. Jour. Pacific History, Canberra; mem. adv. com. South Pacific Cultures Fund, Australian govt., 1974—. Author: Tahiti: Island of Love, 1959, 5th edition, 1979, The Lost Caravel, 1975, The Lost Caravel Re-explored, 1988, The Language of Easter Island (with D. Tryon), 1983; contbr. to encycs. and learned publs. Awarded Cruz de Caballero, Orden de Isabela la Catolica, King of Spain, 1980. Mem. Pacific History Assn. (sec.-treas. 1981-83, pres. 1987—), Hakluyt Soc., Polynesian Soc., Soc. Oceanistes, Societe des Etudes Oceaniennes. Home: 15 Darambal St, Aranda 2614, Australia Office: Australian Nat U, Research Sch Pacific Studies, Canberra 2601, Australia

LANGE, BERND PETER, English literature educator; b. Berlin, Mar. 24, 1943; s. Rudolf and Erika (Steinbrink) L.; m. Helgard Stichnote, Jan. 6, 1967; children: Asja, Jessica. PhD, Free U., Berlin, 1969. Asst. lectr. Free U., 1969-74; lectr. Tech. U. Brunswick, Fed. Republic Germany, 1974-82, prof., 1983—. Author: Dickens, 1969, Gattungsstheorie, 1979, Orwell 1982, 1984; editor: Gulliver, 1979—. Mem. German Shakespeare Soc., 18th Century Soc. Home: Dudweilerstr 2, D-3300 Brunswick Federal Republic of Germany Office: Tech U Brunswick, Muehlenpfordtstrasse 22/3, Brunswick Federal Republic of Germany

LANGE, DAVID RUSSELL, prime minister, minister of education and security intelligence service of New Zealand; b. Otahuhu, N.Z., Aug. 4, 1942; s. Eric Roy and Phoebe (Fysh) L.; m. Naomi Joy Crampton, 1968; children: Roy, Bryon, Emily. LLB, U. Auckland, 1966, LLM with honors. Bar: N.Z. 1966. Barrister, solicitor Kaikohe, 1968, Auckland, 1970-77; M.P. for Mangere, N.Z., 1977—, opposition spokesperson on justice, 1978, opposition spokesperson on social welfare, shadow minister of justice, 1979, dep. leader of opposition, 1979-83, leader, 1983-84, shadow minister overseas trade, fgn. affairs, regional devel. and Pacific Island affairs, 1983-84; privy councillor, 1984; prime minister New Zealand, minister in charge security intelligence service, Wellington, 1984—, minister fgn. affairs, 1984-87, minister of edn., 1987—. Mem. Labour Party. Office: Office Prime Minister, Parliament Bldg, Wellington New Zealand

LANGE, JACK D(AMGAARD), physician, publisher, educator; b. Racine, Wis., Oct. 19, 1906; s. Charles B. and Elsie J. (Damgaard) L.; B.S., Northwestern U., 1938, M.D., 1941, M.S., 1942; m. DeLoris Irene Williams, Aug. 27, 1937; children—Gary Richard, Judy Annette (Mrs. William LeMay), Dennis Kent, Diane Pamela. Founder, pres. Lange Med. Pubs., Los Altos, Calif., 1937-87; intern St. Luke's Hosp., Chgo., 1940-41, resident, 1941-42; resident U. Calif. Hosp. at San Francisco, 1942-43; clin. asst. medicine U. Calif. at San Francisco, 1946-48, clin. instr., 1948-50, asst. clin. prof., 1950-57, asso. clin. prof., 1957-70, clin. prof., 1970-81, clin. prof. emeritus, 1981—; assoc. clin. prof. medicine Stanford (Calif.) U. Sch. Medicine, 1964-73, emeritus, 1973—. Bd. dirs. Aid for Internat. Medicine, 1970—. Served to capt. USAAF, 1943-46. Recipient awards of appreciation Haddash Hebrew U., Israel, 1969, U. Udayana, Bali, 1970, U. Saigon, 1974, U. Indonesia, Jakarta, 1974, Chulalongkorn U., Bangkok, 1975, Yonsei U. Coll. of Medicine, Seoul, 1976; San Francisco medal U. Calif., San Francisco, 1979; Disting. Faculty award Alumni Faculty, 1979; named Hon. Prof. Medicine, U. Peruana Cayetano Heredia, Lima, 1980, Hon. Prof. Medicine, U. Chile, Santiago, 1980. Mem. ACP (life), Am. Med. Soc. of Vienna, AMA, Am. Med. Colls., Am. Diabetic Assn., World Med. Assn., N.Y. Acad. Sci., AAAS, Am. Med. Book Pubs. Assn., Explorers Club (life mem.), Gold-Headed Cane Soc., Nu Sigma Nu. Author: (with Joseph J. McDonald and Joseph G. Chusid) Correlative Neuroanatomy and Functional Neurology, 1938-52; (with John Warkentin) Physicians Handbook, 1941-50. Home: 1400 Geary Blvd Apt #1410 San Francisco CA 94109 Office: 2755 Campus Dr Suite 205 San Mateo CA 94403

LANGE, KURT, pediatrician, educator; b. Berlin, Oct. 31, 1906; came to U.S., 1939, naturalized, 1944; s. Georg and Pauline (Neumann) L.; m. Helen Marcus, June 14, 1936; children: Peter, Monica. M.D., U. Berlin, 1930. Intern U. Berlin (Charite); resident in pathology 2d Med. U. Hosp., Berlin; instr. internal medicine U. Berlin, 1931-34; practice medicine specializing in internal medicine Berlin, 1934-38, N.Y.C., 1939—; instr. medicine N.Y. Med. Coll., N.Y.C., 1939-44, Markle Found. fellow, 1944-45; assoc. prof. medicine N.Y. Med. Coll., 1945-62, prof. clin. pediatrics, 1962-71, prof. pediatrics, 1971—, prof. medicine, 1962—; cons. physician Lenox Hill Hosp., N.Y.C., Chenango Meml. Hosp., Norwich, N.Y., Horton Meml. Hosp., Middletown, N.Y.; research asso. pathologist Lenox Hill Hosp., N.Y.C.; vis. physician Met. Hosp., Bird S. Coler Hosp.; dir. renal service N.Y. Med. Coll., 1952-78, Met. Med. Center, 1952-78. Am. editor: Clin. Nephrology. Chief renal service and lab. OSRD, U.S. Army, 1941-48. Recipient 2d award N.Y. State Med. Soc., 1946, hon. mention AMA, 1963, Bronze medal, 1946, cert. of merit, 1961, Hectoen gold medal, 1966; 1st award N.Y. State Med. Soc., 1967; Franz Volhard medal German Nephrology Soc., 1976; Lester Hoenig award Kidney Found. N.Y., 1977. Fellow A.C.P., Am. Coll. Cardiology; mem. Internat. Soc. Nephrology, Am. Soc. Nephrology, N.Y. Soc. Nephrology, Harvey Soc., Soc. Exptl. Biology and Medicine, Soc. Exptl. Pathology, Am. Soc. Pathology, Explorers Club, Alpha Omega Alpha. Home: 519 E 86th St New York NY 10028 Office: 11 E 68th St New York NY 10021

LANGE, WOLF-DIETER, Romance languages and literatures educator; b. Hamburg, Germany, July 7, 1939; s. Arnold and Ursula (Mollweide) L.; m. Elisabeth Bange, Dr. phil., Nov. 23, 1984; children by previous marriage—Oliver, Nikolaus, Tilman. PhD, U. Cologne, Fed. Republic Germany, 1965. Univ. lectr. U. Cologne, 1970-71, prof., 1971; prof., dir. Romanisches Seminar, U. Bonn, Fed. Republic Germany, 1971—, dean Faculty Letters, 1979-81, mem. univ. senate, 1979-85, vice-dir. state examinations, 1985—. Author: El fraile trobador, 1971; editor: Franz. Lit. 19th Century, 3 vols., 1979-80; König Artus, 1980; (lexicon) Roman. Gegenwartslit., 1984—; Franz. Lit. 20th Century, 1986—; (with W. Habicht) Der Lit.-Brockhaus, 3 vols., 1988; In Thnen begegnet sich das Abendland, 1988. Mem. Société Arthurienne, Hispanistenverband, Mediävistenverband, Deutscher Romanisten-Verband. Home: Lyngsbergstrasse 11, D-5300 Bonn 2 Federal Republic of Germany Office: University-Romanisches Seminar, Am Hof 1, D-5300 Bonn Federal Republic of Germany

LANGE-MCGILL, KENNETH HERMAN, statistician, retired government official; b. Tekamah, Nebr., Dec. 29, 1903; s. Herman Morse and Fidelia Luella (Oberst) McGill; m. Mable Catherine Lange, Aug. 27, 1930; 1 child, Kenneth Herman Jr. AB, U. Nebr., 1930; postgrad. U. Chgo., 1930-31; PhD, U. Mich., 1973. Tchr. pub. schs., Nebr., Marr, Ariz., 1923-26, Blackbird, Riverside, 1926-29; Earhart Found. fellow, instr. U. Mich., 1931-34; analyst Pres.'s Trends Studies, Washington, 1931-34; supr. U.S. Census, Washington, 1934, FERA, Washington, 1934; dir. USPHS, Washington, 1935-41; div. chief nat. hdqrs. SSS, Washington, 1941-70, ret., 1970; mem. Am. mission to Greece and Turkey, Dept. State, 1947-48. Recipient U.S. medal for merit Fed. Govt., 1946. Mem. Am. Statis. Assn., Soc. Greek Stats. (Athens), Chinese Assn. Advancement Sci. (Taipei), Royal Soc. Health (London), Phi Beta Kappa (pres. Washington assn. 1967-68), Alpha Kappa Delta. Presbyterian. Clubs: Sertoma (pres. 1966-67, dist. gov. 1968-70) (Washington); Propeller (Athens, Greece). Lodges: Masons, Shriners. Author reports, monographs and articles. Home: Golden Spring Rt 1 Box 53 Decatur NE 68020 Office: Sir John's Hill 3746 Winding Creek Ln Charlotte NC 28226

LANGENSCHEIDT, FLORIAN, publishing executive; b. Berlin, Mar. 7, 1955; s. Karl Ernst and Renate Tielebier-Langenscheidt; m. Gabriele Quandt. PhD, Ludwig-Maximillians-Univ., Munich, 1982; diploma, Harvard U., 1982; MBA, European Inst. Bus. Adminstrn., Fontainebleau, France, 1985. Editorial dir. Langenscheidt Pubs., Inc., N.Y.C., 1983-84; pub. Polyglott Pubs. Co., Munich, 1985—, Humboldt Pubs. Co., Munich, 1985—, Mentor Pubs. Co., Munich, 1985—; co-pub. Baedeker Pubs. Co., Ostfildern and Munich, Fed. Republic Germany, 1985—; bd. dirs. Langenscheidt Pub. Group, Munich and Berlin, Brockhaus, Duden, Meyes, Mannheim; owner, gen. mgr. Majestic Luftschiffahrtsgesellschaft, Munich, 1987—. Author: The Baby, 1975; contbr. articles on music and lit. to profl. pubs., 1978—; dir. concerts of contemporary music, 1974—. Mem. Atlantikbrücke, Bonn, Fed. Republic Germany, 1987. Grantee Studienstiftung des deutschen Volkes, Bonn, 1974. Mem. New Media Com. of the Börsenverein des deutschen Buchhandels. Office: Langenscheidt KG, Neusserstrasse 3, D-8000 Munich 40 Federal Republic of Germany

LANGERON, JEAN-LUC, obstetrician; b. Cholet, France, July 7, 1943; Jean François and Gisèle (Malbec) L.; m. Marie Elisabeth Denis, July 5, 1968; children: Eric, Anne, Olivier. MD, Faculté de Medecine, 1972. Gen. practice medicine Cholet. Mem. Rally for the Republic Party. Roman Catholic. Club: Aéro. Home and Office: 13 Pl Bretonnaise, 49300 Cholet France

LANGE-SEIDL, ANNEMARIE, semiotics educator; b. Munich, Germany, July 4, 1918; d. Florian and Juliane Seidl; m. Wolfgang Lange; 1 dau., Brigitte Schlieben-Lange. Dr.phil., U. Munich, 1946. Lic. coll. educator, Germany. Prof. linguistics and semiotics Fachhochschule München, 1972-88, Tech. U. Munich, 1983—. Author: Approaches to Theories for Nonverbal Signs, 1977, Semiotics in (East and West) Germany and Austria, 1984; editor: Zeichenkonstitution, 2 vols., 1981, Zeichen und Magie, 1988; co-editor Zeitschrift fur Semiotik, 1979—. Recipient Coupe de Lutece, Academie de Lutece, Paris, 1974, 76. Mem. Internat. Assn. Semiotic Studies, Deutsche Gesellschaft für Semiotik, v.p. 1988—, pres. 1977—, exec. dir. 1978-81), Semiotics Soc. Am., Osterreichische Gesellschaft für Semiotik, Regensburger Schriftstellergruppe Internat. (v.p. 1978—), Florian-Seidl-Archiv (pres. 1973—). Home: Uttinger Strasse 10, D 8000 Munich 70 Federal Republic of Germany

LANGFORD, CHARLES DONALD, surgeon; b. Memphis, Tenn., Dec. 23, 1931; s. John Walker and Edna Grace (Rowlett) L.; m. Mary Alice McCrary, June 3, 1956; children: John Murray, James Davis (dec.), Donna Lee, Paul Owens, Devra Grace. BS, La. State U., 1953; MD, La State U. Sch. Medicine, New Orleans, 1957. Diplomate Am. Bd. Surgery. Intern Charity Hosp., New Orleans, 1958, resident in surgery, 1958-61; clin dir. Lafayette (La.) Charity Hosp., 1961-62, clin. instr. surgery, 1969-70; surgical staff mem. Sellers-Sanders Clinic, New Orleans, 1962-63; chief surgery Hong Kong Bapt. Hosp., Kowloon, 1964-69, surgical staff mem., 1970-73; surgical ptnr. Langford and Smith Med. Group, Kowloon, 1973-75, 1976-80, 1981-86; sr. surgical oncology fellow M.D. Anderson Hosp., Houston, 1975-76; emergency room physician Lafayette Gen. Hosp., 1980-81. Am. Cancer Soc. fellow, 1975-76. Fellow Royal Coll. Surgeons, Am. Coll. Surgeons, Internat. Coll. Surgeons; mem. British Med. Soc., Hong Kong Surg. Soc. Home: 4829 Merida Ave Fort Worth TX 76115 Office: Langford and Smith Med Group, 141 Prince Edward Rd #7-L, Edward Mansion, Mongkok, Kowloon Hong Kong

LANGFORD, DEAN TED, electrical products company executive; b. Princeton, Ill., June 19, 1939; s. Claude Robert and Dorothy Aeileen (Tuckerman) L.; 1 child, Douglas T. B.S. in Math. and Assoc. Engrng., U. Ill., 1962. Regional sales mgr. IBM-N.E. Region, Westport, Conn., 1980-81, corp. dir. mgmt. devel., Armonk, N.Y., 1981-82, group dir., communications, Ryebrook, N.Y., 1982-83; v.p. mktg. GTE Communications Systems, Stamford, Conn., 1983-84; pres. GTE Elec. Products, Danvers, Mass., 1984—. Mem. bd. advisers Sch. Engrng., U. Ill.-Chgo., 1984—; mem. adv. bd. Northeastern U., 1984; trustee Civic Edn. Found. Lincoln-Filene Ctr., Tufts U. Club: Salem Country. Avocations: biking, golf, racquetball, squash, skiing. Home: 29 Fairfield Boston MA 02116 Office: GTE Elec Products 100 Endicott St Danvers MA 01923

LANGFORD, JOHN WILLIAM, logistics and systems engineer, educator; b. Carrollton, Ky., Dec. 9, 1932; s. Audley Delbert and Marguerite Bland (Campbell) L.; m. Margery Ann Staley, Jan. 24, 1955; children—Mary Elizabeth, Margaret Carole, Dirk William. B.S. in Indsl. Engrng., Ga. Inst. Tech., 1954; M.S. in Logistics Mgmt., Air Force Inst. Tech., Dayton, Ohio, 1965. Cert. profl. logistician, engr., Va. Commd. lt. U.S. Air Force, 1955, advanced through grades to lt. col., 1980; planning officer U.S. So. Command, Panama Canal Zone, 1968-71; asst. for logistics Hdqrs., U.S. Air Force, Pentagon, 1973-75; advisor to Shah of Iran, Imperial Command Staff, Tehran, 1976-78; ret., 1980; cons. in mgmt., Dept. Energy, Washington, 1980-82; mgr. marine services U.S. Navy, ERC Internat., Vienna, Va., 1982—; cons. edn. Dept. Def., Washington, 1983—; sr. assoc. Bus. Mgmt. Research, Arlington, Va., 1980—; prof. logistics engrng. Fla. Inst. Tech., Melbourne, 1983—, George Mason U., Fairfax, Va., 1983—. Author: Air University Report: Defense Contract Profits, 1965; Air War College Report: Brazil Air Force Logistics, 1975; Author, editor series on logistics and systems engrng. Soc. of Logistics Engrs. newsletter, 1983—; author, seminar Compendium of Quantitative Logistics Mathematical Methodologies, Third Internat. Logistics Congress, Florence, Italy, 1987. Decorated Air Force Commendation medal, Joint Service Commendation medal Dept. Def., Meritorious Service medal. Mem. Smithsonian Instn. (assoc.), Nat. Trust Hist. Preservation (Capital region assoc.), Am. Film Inst., Nat. Contract Mgmt. Assn., Royal Oak Found. (British Nat. Trust), Ky. Historical Soc., Inst. Indsl. Engrs., Soc. Logistics Engrs. (Forrest Waller award, tech. vice-chmn. 1987—), Ret. Officers Assn., U.S. Naval Inst., Ky. Hist. Soc., Royal Oak Found. Republican. Club: Westwood Country (Vienna) Lodges: Masons, Scottish Rites. Avocations: numismatics; military history; foreign languages; golf; woodworking. Home: 1900 Alto Ct Vienna VA 22180 Office: Evaluation Research Corp Internat 1725 Jefferson Davis Hwy Crystal Sq 2 Suite 300 Arlington VA 22202

LANGFORD, ROLAND EVERETT, military officer, environmental scientist; b. Owensboro, Ky., Apr. 11, 1945; s. John Roland and Mary Helen (Cockriel) L.; m. Son-Hee Shin, Dec. 18, 1971; children: John Everett, Lee Shin. AA, Armstrong State Coll., 1965; BS, Ga. So. Coll., 1967; MS, U. Ga., 1971, PhD, 1974; grad., U.S. Army Command and Gen. Staff Coll., 1985; postgrad. in health physics, U. N.C., 1988—. Registered sanitarian, Ariz.; engr.-in-tng., Ariz. Instr. Savannah (Ga.) Sci. Mus., 1971-72, Bainbridge (Ga.) Jr. Coll., 1973-74; asst. prof. chemistry Ga. Mil. Coll., Milledgeville, 1975-77; asst. prof. Ga. So. Coll., Statesboro, 1977-78; commd. capt. U.S. Army, 1978, advanced through grades to major, 1986; chief chemistry sect. U.S. Army Acad. Health Scis., Ft. Sam Houston, Tex., 1978-79; sanitary engr. U.S. Army Environ. Hygiene Agy., Aberdeen Proving Ground, Md., 1979-81; comdr. environ. sanitation detachment Taegu, Republic of Korea, 1981-83; environ. sci. officer Ft. Huachuca, Ariz., 1984-88; panel mem. Comprehensive Assistance to Undergrad. Sci. Edn., NSF, 1975-77; judge Internat. Sci. Fair, San Antonio, Tex., 1979; mem. sci. rev. panel NIH, 1986—. Contbr. articles to profl. jours. Active Boy Scouts Am., Ft. Sam Houston, 1978-79; mem. parish council, lay minister Holy Family Parish, Ft. Huachuca, 1985-88; advisor Med. Explorer Post, Ft. Huachuca, 1986-88. Fellow Am. Inst. Chemists; mem. Am. Acad. Indsl. Hygiene (cert.), Am. Chem. Soc., Nat. Environ. Health Assn. (cert. hazardous waste specialist), Korean Chem. Soc., Royal Asiatic Soc. (bd. dirs. 1982-83), Assn. Mil. Surgeons U.S., Am. Acad. Sanitarians (cert.), Internat.

Platform Assn. Republican. Roman Catholic. Home: 123 Greenmeadow Ln Summerfield Crossing Chapel Hill NC 27514 Office: AMEDD Student Devel US Army Acad Health Scis Fort Sam Houston TX 78234-6000

LANGFORD, WILLIAM FINLAY, mathematics educator; b. Thunder Bay, Ont., Can., Sept. 11, 1943; s. William Everett and Mary Pearl (Finlay) L.; m. Grace Ann Cooper, Aug. 1, 1970; children—Cathena Dionne, Anne Elisabeth. B.Sc., Queens U., 1966; Ph.D., Calif. Inst. Tech., 1971. Asst. prof. math. McGill U., Montreal, Can., 1970-78, assoc. prof., 1978-82; research visitor U. de Nice, France, 1979-80; assoc. prof. U. Guelph, Ont., Can., 1982-87, prof., 1988—; adj. prof. U. Waterloo, Ont., Can., 1983—; vis. prof. U. Houston, 1985, 87, Tianjan (Republic China) U., 1987. Contbr. articles to profl. jours.; mem. editorial bd. Dynamics and Stability of Systems Jour., 1985—. Natural Scis. and Engring. Research Council Can. grantee, 1971—. Mem. Am. Math. Soc., Can. Math. Soc. (dir. 1985—), Can. Applied Math. Soc., Soc. Indsl. and Applied Math. Mem. United Ch. of Can. Avocations: gardening; photography; hiking; skiing. Home: 959 Gordon St, Guelph, ON Canada N1H 6H9 Office: U Guelph, Dept Math and Statistics, Guelph, ON Canada N1G 2W1

LANGHAM, NORMA, educator, author, composer; b. California, Pa.; d. Alfred Scrivener and Mary Edith (Carter) Langham; B.S., Ohio State U., 1942; B. Theatre Arts, Pasadena Playhouse Coll. Theatre Arts, 1944; M.A., Stanford, 1956, postgrad. Summer Radio-TV Inst., 1960; student Pasadena Inst. Radio, 1944-45. Tchr. sci. California High Sch., 1942-43; asst. office pub. info. Denison U., Granville, Ohio, 1955; instr. speech dept. Westminster Coll., New Wilmington, Pa., 1957-58; instr. theatre. California U. of Pa., 1959, asst. prof., 1960-62, assoc. prof., 1962-79, emeritus, 1979—, co-founder, sponsor, dir. Children's Theatre, 1962-79; mem. Calif., Pa. Community Choir; founder, producer, dir. Food Bank Players, 1985, Patriot Players, 1986. Recipient award exceptional acad. service Pa. Dept. Edn., 1975; Appreciation award Bicentennial Commn. Pa., 1976. Henry C. Frick Ednl. Commn. grantee. Mem. Theatre Assn. Pa., Internat. Platform Assn., California U. of Pa. Assn. Women Faculty (founder, pres. 1972-73), AAUW (co-founder California br., 1st v.p. 1971-72, pres. 1972-73; Outstanding Woman of Yr. 1986), Dramatists Guild, DAR, Alpha Psi Omega, Omicron Nu. Presbyn. (elder). Author: (play) Magic in the Sky, 1963; (text) Public Speaking; (play) John Dough (Freedoms Found. award 1968); (plays) Who Am I?, Hippocrates Oath, Gandhi, Clementine of '49, Soul Force, Esther; composer-lyricist (play) Why Me, Lord?; Music in Freedom, The Day the Moon Fell. Home: Box 455 California PA 15419

LANGILL, GEORGE FRANCIS, hospital administrator, educator; b. Ottawa, Ont., Can., Dec. 31, 1946; s. Roy Joseph and Margaret (O'Hara) L.; m. Lorraine Diane Bavazeau, Aug. 10, 1947; children: Norman, Barbara Ann, Kendra, Leonard. BSc with honors, Ottawa U., 1971, MHA, 1973. Adminstrv. coordinator N.S. Dept. Health, 1973-74; asst. exec. dir. Royal Ottawa Hosp., 1974-79; assoc. exec. dir. Rehab. Ctr., Ottawa, 1979-83; chief exec. officer Royal Ottawa Health Care Group, 1983—; adj. prof., part-time lectr. Faculty Adminstrn., Ottawa U., 1979—; mem. faculty health care adminstrn. WHO, Montreal, 1983—; bd. dirs., mem. exec. com. Can. council Rehab. of Disabled, Toronto, 1985—. Contbr. articles to profl. jours. Mem. Ottawa Bd. Trade, 1986. Mem. Can. Coll. Health Service Execs., Am. Coll. Health Execs., Am. Assn. Mental Health Adminstrs. Clubs: L'Cercle (Ottawa); Cedarhill Golf and Country (Nedean, Ont. Can.). Office: Royal Ottawa Health Care, Group, 1145 Carling Ave, Ottawa, ON Canada K1Z 7K4

LANGIN, JOHN MAUGER BARNES, antique dealer; b. Helier, Jersey, England, July 24, 1934; s. Hiram Georges and Marie Eleanor (Mauger) L. Law Dipl., Caen (France) U., 1956. Bar: English 1963. Jersey, Channel Islands, 1966. Adminstr. Rothchild's Entores Ltd., London, 1967-71; antique dealer R.A. Barnes Antiques, London, 1971—. Editor: Rosy is my Relative, 1967. Mem. Antique Dealers Assn. Mem. Conservative Party. Roman Catholic. Office: R A Barnes Antiques, 26 Lower Richmond Rd, London England

LANGRICK, JOHN NIGEL, accountant; b. Wakefield, Yorkshire, Eng., Sept. 25, 1956; s. Peter Roland and Jean Margaret (Wilson) L. BS, U. Nottingham (Eng.), 1978. Chartered acct., Eng., Wales. Audit sr. Price Waterhouse, Nottingham, 1978-82; audit supr. Price Waterhouse, Brussels, 1982-85; audit sr. mgr. Price Waterhouse, Leicester, Eng., 1985-87; asst. gen. mgr. fin. Scarborough (Eng.) Bldg. Soc., 1987—. Com. mem. Am. Club Brussels, 1982-85; treas. Haymarket and Phoenix Theatre Soc., Leicester, 1985-87. Mem. Inst. Chartered Accts. (assoc.). Mem. Ch. of Eng. Club: Time-Out. Home: 4 The Stoneways, Hutton Buscel, Scarborough YO13 9LP, England Office: Scarborough Bldg Soc, 442-444 Scalby Rd, Scarborough YO12 6EQ, England

LANIER, JAMES OLANDA, lawyer, banker, state legislator; b. Newbern, Tenn., Sept. 8, 1931; s. James P. and Robbye S. L.; m. Carolyn Holland, June 1, 1950; children: James E., Kay Lanier Berkley, Amy Lanier Whitnel. BS, Memphis State U., 1955, JD, 1969. Bar: Tenn. 1969, U.S. Ct. Appeals (6th cir.) 1969, U.S. Supreme Ct. 1975. Prin., James O. Lanier & Assocs., Dyersburg, Tenn., 1969—; apptd. dist. pub. defender 29th Jud. Dist. Tenn., 1987—; pres. Freightmasters, Inc., Union City, Tenn., Dyer County atty., 1973-79, 83—; pres., chmn. bd. Dukedom Bank, Dukedom, Tenn., 1979-82; pub. defender 29th Judicial Dist. of State of Tenn., 1987—; chmn., hearing officer Tenn. Malpractice Rev. Bd. Commr. Dyer County Levee and Drainage Dist., Dyersburg; chief referee Dyer County Juvenile Ct., 1984—; mem. Tenn. Ho. of Reps., 1959-63, 69-81, Ho. of Dels., 1983—; chmn. Com. on Legis., 1985—, Tenn. Tollway Authority, 1975-79; statewide campaign coordinator Gov. Lamar Alexander, 1978; chmn. 8th Congl. Dist. Dem. Convention, 1972; dir. Memphis State U. Nat. Alumni Assn., 1976-80; appointed dist. pub. defender 29th Jud. Dist., State of Tenn., 1987—. Mem. Dyer County Bar Assn., Tenn. Bar Assn. (del.), ABA, Am. Trial Lawyers Assn., Tenn. Trial Lawyers Assn., Dyer County C. of C., Sigma Delta Kappa, Kappa Sigma. Methodist. Clubs: Dyersburg Country, Moose. Home: Route 4 Box 349 Dyersburg TN 38024 Office: 208 N Mill Ave PO Box 742 Dyersburg TN 38024

LANITIS, NICHOLAS CONSTANTINE, investments and manufacturing executive, author; b. Limassol, Cyprus, Sept. 15, 1917; s. Constantine Panayi and Thereza (Nicolaides) L.; m. Vanda E.M. Lainas, Aug. 21, 1947; children—Hebe, Vladimir, Thereza, Julia. B.A., Cambridge (Eng.) U., 1939, M.A. (exhibitioner, scholar), Trinity Coll., 1957. Founder, chmn. Lanitis Bros. Ltd., Nicosia, Cyprus, 1943—, Food Products Co., Ltd., Channel Islands, 1986—, Gen. Fin. Corp. Ltd., Bahamas, 1964—, Lanitis Bros. Trading Ltd., Turks and Caicos Islands, 1965—; co-mng. dir. Cyprus Wines and Spirits Co. Ltd., Limassol, 1944-47; dep. controller supplies Govt. of Cyprus, 1940-42. Author: Rural Indebtedness and Agricultural Co-operation in Cyprus, 1944; Our Destiny, 1963; also booklets. Founder, 1st chmn. The Cyprus Employers Fedn., 1960-63, Cyprus Productivity Ctr., 1961-63; founder, 1st sec. Social Progress Soc., 1944-47. Home: Block B, Park Guillemó, Andorra la Vella Andorra Office: 62 Meritxell Ave, PO Box 86 (French PO), Andorra de Vella Andorra

LANKFORD, JOHN LLEWELLYN, energy technology consultant; b. Hampton, Va., Sept. 13, 1920; s. Stephen Foster and Frances (Llewelling) L.; B.S., Va. Poly. Inst., 1942; postgrad. U. Va., 1947-48; m. Mary Louise Charlton, June 29, 1945; children—John Foster, Susan Charlton. With Nat. Adv. Com. for Aeros., Hampton, Va., 1945-52, Westinghouse-Melpar, Alexandria, Va., 1952-53; head gas dynamics lab. Experiment, Inc., Richmond, Va., 1954-58; project mgr. Naval Surface Weapons Center, Washington, 1958-61, cons. Dept. Navy, 1964-76; chief advanced studies NASA, Washington, 1961-64; acting dept. head, lectr. Montgomery Coll., Rockville, Md., 1977-78; cons. energy program U. Md., College Park, 1979-80; cons. energy tech., Silver Spring, Md., 1980—; mentor, advisor, lectr. sci. fair competitions and magnet programs Montgomery County Schs., 1985—. Served with U.S. Army, 1942-45. Decorated Purple Heart. Fellow AIAA (assoc.); mem. AAAS, ASTM. Methodist. Contbr. articles in field to profl. jours. Home and Office: 1717 Marymont Rd Silver Spring MD 20906

LANNAMANN, RICHARD STUART, executive recruiting consultant; b. Cin., Sept. 4, 1947; s. Frank E. and Grace I. (Tomlinson) L.; A.B. in Econs., Yale U., 1969; M.B.A., Harvard U., 1973; m. Margaret Appleton Payne, June 21, 1969; children—Thomas Cleveland, Edward Payne, John Stewart. Investment analyst U.S. Trust Co. N.Y., 1969-71; research analyst Smith, Barney & Co., N.Y.C., 1973-75, 2d v.p., 1975-77, v.p. successor firm research div. Smith Barney Harris Upham & Co., 1977-78; v.p. Russell Reynolds Assocs., Inc., N.Y.C., 1978-83, mng. dir. 1983-86, 87—; sr. v.p. Mgmt. Asset Corp., Westport, Conn., 1986-87. Mem. N.Y. Soc. Security Analysts, Fin. Analysts Fedn., Inst. Chartered Fin. Analysts. Clubs: Riverside (Conn.) Yacht; Links, Yale (N.Y.C.). Home: 25 Cathlow Dr Riverside CT 06878 Office: 200 Park Ave New York NY 10166

LANNES, WILLIAM JOSEPH, III, electrical engineer; b. New Orleans, Oct. 12, 1937; s. William Joseph, Jr., and Rhea Helen (Simon) L.; B.S.E.E., Tulane U., 1959; M.E.E., U.S. Naval Postgrad. Sch., 1966; m. Patricia Anne Didier, Jan. 17, 1961; children—David Mark, Kenneth John, Jennifer Anne. Commd. 2d lt. U.S. Marine Corps, 1959, advanced through grades to maj., 1967, served as electronics officer, ops. officer, until 1970; substation engr. La. Power & Light, New Orleans, 1970-71, utility engr., 1971-76, system relay engr., 1976-77, system substation engr., 1977-79, engring. supr. for substations, 1979-83, substa. engring. mgr., 1983-86, dir. systems engring., 1986—, v.p. systems engring., 1986-88, central engring., 1988—; instr. Delgado Jr. Coll., 1973-74; instr. elec. engring. U. New Orleans, 1979-80; dir. 5th Dist. Savs. and Loan, 1982—. Committeeman New Orleans Area Council, Boy Scouts Am., 1972-76; vol., United Way 1975, 76, 81; treas., PTA 1971; vol. tchr. Confraternity of Christian Doctrine, 1972; mem. bus. adv. council Our Lady of Holy Cross Coll., 1981-86; chmn. engring. adv. council U. New Orleans; bd. dirs. New Life in La.; vol. coach New Orleans Recreation Dept., 1973; mem. La. Employees Com. on Polit. Action, Tulane Univ. Engring. Council. Decorated Bronze Star; Cross of Gallantry Republic S. Vietnam; recipient cert. of merit, Mayor New Orleans, 1964; registered profl. engr., La. Mem. Electric Power Research Inst. (industry advisor), Edison Electric Inst. (systems and equipment com.), Soc. Power Research and Implementation (chmn. 1987—), Southeastern Electric Exchange (substation com. 1977-85), IEEE (sr., profl. mem., outstanding service award, 1976, chmn. New Orleans sect. 1981-82, Edward Freitag award 1988), Power Engring. Soc.(Prize Paper award 1988), Sigma Xi, Eta Kappa Nu. Democrat. Roman Catholic. Club: Park Timbers. Speaker profl. conf.; contbr. articles to publ. Office: 142 Delaronde St New Orleans LA 70174

L'ANNUNZIATA, MICHAEL FRANK, diplomat, international civil servant; b. Springfield, Mass., Oct. 14, 1943; s. Michael Peter and Irene M. (Dufault) L'A.; m. Maria del Carmen Elena Monge, Mar. 3, 1973; children—Michael O., Helen, Frank E. BS., St. Edward's U., Austin, Tex., 1965; M.S., U. Ariz., 1967, Ph.D., 1970. Research chemist Amchem Products, Inc., Ambler, Pa., 1971-72; research assoc. U. Ariz., Tucson, 1972-73; prof., sect. head U. Chapingo, Mexico, 1973-75; research scientist Nat. Inst. Nuclear Research, Mexico City, 1975-77; assoc. officer IAEA, Vienna, Austria, 1977-80, 2d officer, 1980-83, 1st officer, head sci. visits program, 1983-86, sr. officer, head fellowships sect., 1986—; internat. IAEA cons.; vis. lectr. Advanced Sch. Tropical Agriculture, Cardenas, Mexico, 1973, Timiryazev Agrl. Acad., Moscow, 1980, 81, Nuclear Research Inst. in Vet. Medicine, Lalahan, Turkey, 1981, U. Guanajuato, Mex., 1981. Author: (textbooks) Radiotracers in Agricultural Chemistry, 1979, Radionuclide Tracers, Their Detection and Measurement, 1987; author, editor (with J.O. Legg) Isotopes and Radiation in Agricultural Sciences, Vol. 1, 1984, Vol. 2, 1984. Contbr. articles to profl. jours. Recipient hon. teaching diploma, silver plaque Central U. Ecuador, Quito, 1978. Mem.Sigma Xi, Phi Lambda Upsilon, Gamma Sigma Delta. Roman Catholic. Office: IAEA, PO Box 200, Wagramerstrasse 5, A-1400 Vienna Austria

LANSDOWNE, KAREN MYRTLE, retired English language and literature educator; b. Twin Falls, Idaho, Aug. 11, 1926; d. George and Effie Myrtle (Ayotte) Martin; B.A. in English with honors, U. Oreg., 1948, M.Ed., 1958, M.A. with honors, 1960; m. Paul L. Lansdowne, Sept. 12, 1948; chilren—Michele Lynn, Larry Alan. Tchr., Newfield (N.Y.) High Sch., 1948-50, S. Eugene (Oreg.) High Sch., 1952; mem. faculty U. Oreg., Eugene, 1958-65; asst. prof. English, Lane Community Coll., Eugene, 1965-82, ret., 1982; cons. Oreg. Curriculum Study Center. Rep., Cal Young Neighborhood Assn., 1978—; mem. scholarship com. First Congl. Ch., 1950-70. Mem. MLA, Pacific N.W. Regional Conf. Community Colls., Nat. Council Tchrs. English, U. Oreg. Women, AAUW (sec.), Jaycettes, Pi Lambda Theta (pres.), Phi Beta Patronesses (pres.), Delta Kappa Gamma. Co-author: The Oregon Curriculum: Language/Rhetoric, I, II, III and IV, 1970. Home: 15757 Rim Rd LaPine OR 97739

LANSKY, RALPH, law librarian; b. Riga, Latvia, July 18, 1931; s. Johann Georg and Melitta (Brandt) L.; m. Hildegard Krüger, Mar. 26, 1962; children—Brigitte, Annegret, Sabine Lansky. Student law, univs. Cologne and Bonn (W.Ger), 1953-57; Dr. jur., Bonn U., 1960; postgrad Librarians Inst., Cologne, 1960-62. Librarian, Mcpl. and Univ. Library, Frankfurt, 1962-65, Bonn U., 1966-72; dir. library Max Planck Inst. Fgn. and Internat. Pvt. Law, Hamburg, 1972—. Author: Systematik der Rechtswissenschaft in Grundzügen, 1968; Bibliotheksrechtliche Vorschriften, 3d edit., 1980—; Handbuch der Bibliographien zum Recht der Entwicklungsländer, 1981; Grundliteratur Recht, 3d edit., 1984; Bibliographisches Handbuch der Rechts und Verwaltungswissenschaften, 1987—. Mem. Arbeitsgemeinschaft fur juristisches Bibliotheks-und Dokumentationswesen (chmn. 1971-74, bd. dirs. 1974—), Verein Deutscher Bibliothekare. Office: Max Planck Inst, Mittelweg 187, D-2000 Hamburg 13 Federal Republic of Germany

LANSON, YVES, urology educator; b. Orleans, France, Mar. 29, 1944; s. Bernard and Denise (Bidou) L.; m. Hemeray Nomique, 1968; children: Richard, Thomas. MD, Tours Med. U., 1968. Resident specializing in urology Tours (France) Univ. Hosp., 1968-73, chief resident, 1973-78; prof. urology Tours Med. U., 1978—, chmn. dept., 1982—. Office: CHU Tours Blvd, Tonnelle, 37000 Tours France

LANZANO, RALPH EUGENE, civil engineer; b. N.Y.C., Dec. 26, 1926; s. Ralph and Frances (Giuliano) L.; B.C.E., NYU, 1959. Engring. aide Seelye, Stevenson, Value, Knecht, N.Y.C., 1957-58; jr. civil engr. N.Y.C. Dept. Public Works (name changed to N.Y.C. Dept. Water Resources), 1960-63, asst. civil engr., 1963-68; civil engr., 1968-71; sr. san. engr. Parsons, Brinckerhoff, Quade & Douglas, N.Y.C., 1971-72; civil engr. N.Y.C. Dept. Water Resources, 1972-77, N.Y.C. Dept. Environ. Protection, 1978—. Registered profl. engr., N.Y. Mem. ASCE, ASTM, Nat., N.Y. socs. profl. engrs., Water Pollution Control Fedn., Am. Water Works Assn., Am. Public Health Assn., Am. Fedn. Arts (sustaining), U.S. Inst. Theatre Tech., NYU Alumni Assn., Am. Nat. Theatre and Acad., Lincoln Center Performing Arts (asso.), Am. Film Inst., Nat. Rifle Assn. (life), U.S. Lawn Tennis Assn. (life), Nat., Internat. wildlife fedns., Nat. Parks and Conservation Assn., Nat. Geog. Soc., Nat. Audubon Soc., Am. Automobile Assn., Bklyn. Bot. Garden, Am. Mus. Natural History, Chi Epsilon. Home: 17 Cottage Ct Huntington Station NY 11746 Office: 40 Worth St New York NY 10013

LANZINGER, KLAUS, language educator; b. Woergl, Tyrol, Austria, Feb. 16, 1928; came to U.S., 1971, naturalized, 1979; m. Aida Schuessl, June, 1954; children—Franz, Christine. B.A., Bowdoin Coll., 1951; Ph.D., U. Innsbruck (Austria), 1952. Research asst. U. Innsbruck, 1957-67; assoc. prof. modern langs. U. Notre Dame (Ind.), 1967-77, prof., 1977—, resident dir. fgn. study program, Innsbruck, 1969-71, 76-78, 82-85; acting chmn. dept. Modern and Classical Languages, U. Notre Dame, fall 1987. Author: Epik im amerikanischen Roman, 1965. Editor: Americana-Austriaca, 5 vols., 1966-83. Contbr. numerous articles to profl. jours. Bowdoin Coll. fgn. student scholar, 1950-51; Fulbright research grantee U. Pa., 1961; U. Notre Dame summer research grantee Houghton Library, Harvard U., 1975, 81. Mem. MLA, Deutsche Gesellschaft für Amerikastudien, Thomas Wolfe Soc. Home: 52703 Helvie Dr South Bend IN 46635 Office: U Notre Dame Dept Modern Langs Notre Dame IN 46556

LAPAUTRE, MICHELLE WEILLER, literary agent; b. Phila., July 28, 1931; arrived in France, 1957; d. Eugene Wolf and Leah (Green) Weiller; m. René Lapautre, July 26, 1960; children: Catherine, Stéphane. BA, Pa. State Coll., 1953; MA, Middlebury Coll., 1954; PhD, NYU, 1962. Dir. Michelle Lapautre Lit. Agy., Paris, 1961—. Recipient Disting. Alumna award Pa. State U., 1979, Achievement award Middlebury Coll. Alumi Assn., 1984. Mem. Syndicat des Conseils Littéraires Francais (pres.). Home and Office: 6 Rue Jean Carries, 75007 Paris France

LAPERRIERE, ARTHUR JOSEPH LOUIS, ecologist; b. Acushnet, Mass., July 13, 1942; s. Arthur J.L., Jr., and Yvonne Irene (Frennette) LaP.; B.A., U. Mass., 1964; C.P.Q., U. Okla., 1966; postgrad. U. Md., 1966-67; M.S., Iowa State U., 1971; Ph.D. (NASA fellow), U. Alaska, 1976; postgrad. N.Y. Law Sch., 1987—; children—Monique, Arthur. Research asst. Iowa State U., 1969-71; research fellow U. Alaska, 1971-74, research assoc., 1975-77; dir. Ecosystem Monitor, 1974-77; coordinator nat. wetland inventory U.S. Fish and Wildlife Service, Anchorage, 1977-81; pres. Ind. Seafoods, Ltd., 1981-83; sr. environ. scientist Ott Water Engrs., 1983; biologist Alaska dist. C.E., U.S. Army, 1983-86; chief harbor suprvision and compliance N.Y. dist. C.E. U.S. Army, 1986—. Served with USAF, 1964-69. NASA/Alaska Dept. Fish and Game research grantee, 1975-77; U.S. Fish and Wildlife Service/U.S. Nat. Park Service research grantee, 1976-77; Sierra Found. research grantee, 1976-77. Mem. Iowa Acad. Sci., Am. Soc. Photogrammetry, Wildlife Soc., Am. Soc. Wetland Scientists, Sigma Xi, Gamma Sigma Delta. Club: Elks. Contbr. articles profl. jours. Office: US Army Corps Engrs NY Dist 26 Federal Plaza New York NY 10278-0090

LAPICKI, GREGORY, physicist, educator; b. Warsaw, Poland, Feb. 14, 1945; Magister Fizyki, Warsaw U., 1967; Ph.D. in Physics, NYU, 1975. Postdoctoral trainee dept. physics NYU, N.Y.C., 1975-77, research scientist Radiation and Solid State Lab., 1977-78; vis. asst. prof. dept. physics Tex. A&M U., College Station, 1979-80; asst. prof. dept. chemistry and physics Northwestern State U., Natchitoches, La., 1980-81; assoc. prof. dept. physics East Carolina U., Greenville, N.C., 1981-88, prof., 1988—; participant in research, physics div. Oak Ridge Nat. Lab., 1981-87. Contbr. over 40 articles to profl. jours. Nat. Bur. Standards grantee, 1982-84. Mem. Am. Phys. Soc., Sigma Xi. Office: East Carolina U Dept Physics Greenville NC 27858

LAPIDUS, NORMAN ISRAEL, food broker; b. N.Y.C., July 20, 1930; s. Rueben and Laurette (Goldsmith) L.; B.B.A., CCNY, 1952, candidate M.Internat. Relations, 1956; postgrad. N.Y. U., 1957-60; m. Myrna Sue Cohen, Nov. 20, 1960; children—Robin Anne, Jody Beth. Salesman, Rueben Lapidus Co., N.Y.C., 1954-56, pres., 1960—; sales trainee Cohn-Hall-Marx, N.Y.C., 1955; salesman to v.p. Julius Levy Co., Millburn, N.J., 1964-66, pres., 1966—; salesman Harry W. Freedman Co., 1975-76, v.p., treas., 1976-84, pres., 1984—; pres. Julius Levy/Rueben Lapidus and Harry W. Freedman Cos. div. Pezrow Corp., 1985-86; pres. L&H Food Brokers, 1986—. Recipient Leadership Medallion United Jewish Appeal, 1970, 84. Mem. Maplewood (N.J.) Bd. Adjustment, 1975-82; gen. chmn. Maplewood Citizens Budget Adv. Com., 1977-79, chmn. Maplewood United Jewish Appeal Drive, 1975-76, 83-84; vice-chmn. Maplewood First Aid Squad Bldg. Fund Dr., 1978-79; co-founder Citizens for Charter Change in Essex County (N.J.), 1974, mem. exec. bd., 1974—, treas., 1983-84; founder, chmn. Music Theatre of Maplewood; pres. Maplewood Civic Assn., 1983—; bd. mgrs. Essex County unit Am. Cancer Soc., v.p., 1984-87; mem. adv. bd. Essex County Coll., West Essex, N.J. Served with U.S. Army, 1952-54, Korea. Mem. Nat. Food Brokers Assn. (regional dir., recipient cert. exceptionally meritorious service), Nat. Food Service Sales Com., Met. Food Brokers Assn. (chmn. 1982—), Assn. Food Industries (bd. dirs.), Nat. Food Processors Assn., Young Guard Soc., Old Guard Soc., CCNY Alumni Assn., U.S. Navy Inst., Acad. Polit. Sci., Archeol. Inst. Am., Nat. Trust for Historic Preservation, Assn. Food Distbrs., Am. Legion, LWV. Republican. Jewish. Clubs: Lions (bd. dirs.), B'nai B'rith. Active local theatricals. Home: 21 Lewis Dr Maplewood NJ 07040 Office: 11 Dunbar Rd Springfield NJ 07081

LAPIN, SHARON JOYCE VAUGHN, interior designer; b. Lagrange, Mo., July 28, 1938; d. John Nolan and Wilma Emma (Huebotter) Vaughn; BA summa cum laude, U. Wash., Seattle, 1960; m. Byron Richard Lapin, Oct. 14, 1972. Appeared in various Broadway shows, TV commls. and TV shows, 1962-72; owner Sharon Lapin Designs St. Louis. Bd. dirs. St. Louis conservatory and Schs. for Arts, 1977—, v.p., 1982-87 ; chmn. bd. Studio Set, 1978-81, pres., 1975-78, bd. dirs., 1975-83; bd. dirs. Friends of Sci. Mus., 1980—, v.p., 1984-85; pres. Assocs. Bd. Dirs., St. Louis Sci. Ctr., Inc., 1986-87; bd. dirs. Jr. Div., St. Louis Symphony Women's Assn., 1973-75. Mem. AFTRA, Screen Actors Guild, Actors Equity Assn., Am. Soc. Interior Designers, Pi Beta Phi, Mu Phi Epsilon.

LAPITHIS, ARISTIDES GEORGE, ophthalmic surgeon, consultant; b. Lapithos, Cyprus, May 5, 1921; s. George and Evangelia L.; m. Niki Lapithis; children: George Alkis, Petros, Lia. Grad., Pancyprian Gymnasium, Nicosia, Cyprus, 1939; MD, U. Athens, 1952. Tchr. French and English Lapithos Gymnasium, Nicosia, 1939; asst. sec. Cyprus C. of C., Nicosia, 1940-43; clk. agrl. dept. Govt. Cyprus, 1943-45; practice medicine specializing in ophthalmology Athens, Eng., Europe, 1952-59; cons. ophthalmic surgery St. Barnabas Sch. for the Blind, Nicosia, 1959—; hon. opthalmic surgeon St. Barnabas Sch. for the Blind, Nicosia, 1959—; ophthalmologist schs., Nicosia, 1959-85. Contbr. articles to profl. jours. Mem. Com. on Drugs & Poisons, Govt. Cyprus, 1973—, Bd. Govs. Schs. in Nicosia, 1959-81, sec. 1981—, Red Cross, 1959—. Fellow Internat. Soc. Eye Surgeons; mem. Pancyprian Med. Assn. (exec. com. 1973-76, disciplinary council, 1976-87), Med. Assn. Nicosia (bd. hippocrates, 1973-76), Cyprus Ophthal. Soc. (founder, 1970, sec. 1970-78, pres. 1978-86, gen. sec., 1986—), Cyprus Soc. for the Prevention of Blindness (founder, 1970, pres. 1970—), Société Francaise d'Ophtalmologie, Internat. Soc. for the Prevention of Blindness, Internat. Geog. Opthal. Soc., Internat. Strabismological Ophthal. Soc., Internat. Contact Lens Opthal. Soc., Internat. Refractive Surgery Opthal. Soc., Internat. Orthoptic. Opthal. Soc., Internat. History of Medicine Opthal. Soc., Hellenic Opthal. Soc., No. Greece Opthal. Soc., Balcanique Opthal. Soc. Lodge: Rotary. Home: 3 Photiou St River Ct, Block A 5th Floor, Flat 55, Nicosia Cyprus Office: 40 Evagoras Ave, Pantheon Bldg 1st Floor, Flat 2, Nicosia Cyprus

LA POLLA, JAMES JOSEPH, pediatrician; b. Youngstown, Ohio, Feb. 27, 1934; s. Dominic Joseph and Ann Patricia (Page) La P.; A.B., Duke U., 1956, M.D., 1960; m. Genevieve Jacobson, Oct. 20, 1962; children—Jim, Ken, Vincent, Mike. Intern, Univ. Hosp., Cleve., 1961-62; resident in pediatrics Babies and Childrens's Hosp., Cleve., 1962-64; practice medicine specializing in pediatrics, Warren, Ohio, 1966—; med. dir. Children's Rehab. Center, Youngstown Devel. Center for Retarded; dir. Developmental Clinic, Inc. Bd. dirs. Trumbull County Mental Retardation Bd., Trumbull County Bd. Mental Health; pres. Howland Local Sch. Bd., 1977-78; exec. bd. N.E. Ohio Sch. Bds. Assns; mem. Thubull County Bd. Edn. Served to comdr., USNR, 1964-66. Named Man of Year Jaycees, 1970. Mem. Trumbull County Med. Soc. (exec. com.), Ohio Pediatric Soc. Fellow in developmental pediatrics Harvard U. Med. Sch., 1984. (state chmn. 1972), Ohio Med. Assn., AMA, Am. Assn. Mental Deficiency, Theatre Assn. (dir. award 1974), Internat. Platform Assn., Am. Acad. for Cerebral Palsy and Devel. Medicine. Clubs: Trumbull Country, Buckeye, Howland Rotary (pres., dist. gov.), Shriners. Contbr. articles to profl. jours., chpt. in book. Organized 1st state Olympics for mentally retarded. Home: 707 North Rd SE Warren OH 44484 Office: 8048 E Market St NE Warren OH 44484

LAPORTE, CRAIG AISTON, lawyer; b. Worcester, Mass., Apr. 9, 1953; s. Philip A. and Birgit (Ekengren) L.; m. Arndrea S. Bowman, June 20, 1980; children: Stephen Kyle, David Aiston. BS in Broadcasting, U. Fla., 1975; JD magna cum laude, Stetson U., 1983. Bar: Fla. 1983, U.S. Dist. Ct. (mid. dist.) Fla. 1983. Dep., pilot Pasco County Sheriff's Office, New Port Richey, Fla., 1975-81; assoc. Riley & Proly, Port Richey, 1983—. Served to 2d lt. USAF, 1971-75. Pub. Stetson U. Law Rev. Mem. Assn. Trial Lawyers Am., Fla. Trial Lawyers Assn., West Pasco County Bar Assn. (chmn. med.-legal com. 1987—), ABA, Fla. Bar Assn. (personal injury, wronful death litigation designee), Am. Arbitration Assn., Phi Delta Phi. Republican. Office: 11914 Oak Trail Way Port Richey FL 33568

LAPOSKY, BEN FRANCIS, commercial artist; b. Cherokee, Iowa, Sept. 30, 1914; s. Peter Paul and Leona Anastasia (Gabriel) L. Free-lance comml. artist, oscillographic designer, 1938; creator electronic abstractions, Oscillons, 1952; one-man shows include: USIA, France, 1956; group shows include: Cybernetic Serendipity, London, 1968; Computer Art, N.Y.C., 1976; Computer Art Internat., Lawrence Hall of Sci., U. Calif., Berkeley, 1979; others; contbr. articles to art jours. Recipient Gold Medal award N.Y. Art Dirs. Club, 1957. Subject of article Arts Mag., June 1980. Home and Office: 301 S 6th St Cherokee IA 51012

LAPP, ROGER JAMES, consulting pharmacist; b. Buffalo, Jan. 29, 1933; s. Roger Vincent and Georgia James (Saemenes) L.; student Mich. State U., 1952-53; BS in Pharmacy, U. Buffalo, 1957; m. Judith Bure, Mar. 30, 1956; children: Eric Roger, Mark Frederick. Pharmacist intern Nobb Hill Pharmacy, Buffalo, 1956-57; pharm. intern Buffalo Gen. Hosp., 1957, pharm. resident, 1958; pharmacy mgr. Morton Plant Hosp., Clearwater, Fla., 1960-84, dir. profl. services, 1984-86; cons. pharmacist Basic Am. Med. Co., 1986—; pharmacist, Healthcare Prescription Services, 1986—; preceptor Sch. Pharmacy, U. Fla., Fla. A&M U.; tchr. profl. seminars. Mem. Human Rights Advocacy Com. for Pinellas and Pasco Counties (Fla.), 1973-82, chmn., 1973-81; pres. Upper Pinellas Assn. Mental Retardation Assns., 1970-72, bd. dirs., 1969-78; pres. Am. Cancer Soc., Pinellas County, 1979-82, life bd. dirs.; pres. Pinellas Epilepsy Found., 1978-79; v.p. Fla. Assn. Retarded, 1971-75; bd. dirs. Christian Corp Found. for Mentally Disabled, 1983-86, pres., 1985-86; bd. dirs. Bethel Bethany Homes for the Mentally Disabled, 1986—. Served with U.S. Army, 1958-60. Named Man of Yr., Upper Pinellas Assn. Retarded, 1970, Fla. Cons. Pharmacist of Yr. Bethel Bethany Bd. Dirs., 1987—; recipient Nat. Bowl of Hygeia, Fla. Pharm. Assn. and A.H. Robins Co., 1975, Smith award for helping retarded Kiwanis Club, Clearwater Beach, 1978, cert. of merit for public edn. Am. Cancer Soc., 1978, Citizen Health award Clearwater Sun, 1981. Fellow Am. Soc. Cons. Pharmacists, Fla. Soc. Hosp. Pharmacists (pres. 1972-73, chmn. bd. 1973-74, dir. 1970-78, 79-81; Hosp. Pharmacist of Yr. 1975, Fla. Cons. Pharmacist of Yr. 1987), Fla. Pham. Assn. (award for public relations 1981), Pinellas Soc. Pharmacists (pres. 1982, exec. sec. 1983-86, dir. 1979-86), S.W. Fla. Soc. Hosp. Pharmacists (pres., sec., dir., President's award 1982), Christian Pharmacists Fellowship Internat. (dir. 1984—), Fla. Assn. Retarded Citizens (v.p. 1971-75, Brotherhood award 1975, Pres.'s award 1978, sr. v.p. 1979-81, exec. v.p. 1982), Upper Pinellas Assn. Retarded Citizens, Gideons Internat. Republican. Baptist. Author: Antibiotics, 1974, 5th rev. edit., 1984; contbr. articles to profl. jours. Home: 1998 Temple Terr Clearwater FL 34624 Office: 6575 80th Ave N Pinellas Park FL 33565

LAPPANO-COLLETTA, ELEANOR RITA, research, career and educational consultant; b. N.Y.C., Jan. 12, 1930; d. Ernest and Mary Carmella (Spicciato) Lappano; m. Archangelo Colletta, Nov. 18, 1961; children: Mary Elizabeth, John Ernest, Gina Rose. BS in Chemistry, Fordham U., 1951, MS, 1953, PhD in Biology, 1955. Mem. faculty NYU Postgrad. Med. Sch., 1956-58; mem. faculty, research assoc. devel. biology Rockefeller U., N.Y.C., 1958-59; instr. pathology SUNY Downstate Med. Ctr., Bklyn., 1959-60; biochem. cytologist Hosp. for Spl. Surgery, N.Y.C., 1960-62; research assoc. animal behavior Am. Mus. Natural History, N.Y.C., 1962-67; asst. prof. Manhattan Coll., Riverdale, N.Y., 1967-72; assoc. Sloan-Kettering Inst., N.Y.C., 1973-74; asst. prof. pathology N.Y. Med. Coll., Valhalla, 1974-75; analyst mgmt. performance Office Comptroller, City of N.Y., 1977-78; mem. nat. adv. research resources council NIH, 1973-77; devel. scientist personal products div. Lever Bros., Edgewater, N.J., 1979-80; ind. mgmt. cons., Bronx, N.Y., 1980—. Author papers and reports in field. Pres. Pub. Sch. 122 Community Sch. Bd. 10 N.Y.C. Parents' Assn., 1970-72, treas. parents and prins. forum, 1972-73; edn. chmn. Community Coalition for Scatter Site Housing, 1972-74, West Bronx Civic Improvement Assn., 1971-79; bd. dirs. United Owners Assn., Somers, N.Y., 1979-81. NIH grantee, 1957-58; Office of Naval Research fellow 1955. Mem. AAAS, AAUW, Sigma Xi. Home: 3238 Tibbett Ave Riverdale NY 10463 Office: 6035 Broadway Riverdale NY 10471

LAPPIN, ROBERT SIDNEY, lawyer; b. Boston, Oct. 6, 1928; s. Albert S. and Pearl (Cooper) L.; m. Gloria L. Bevscher (div. 1962); 1 child, Jane E. Lappin Griffiths; m. Anne M. Theroux (div. 1982); 1 child, Joshua C. BA, Norwich U., 1951; MBA, Boston U., 1955; LLB, Boston Coll., 1959. Bar: Mass. 1959, U.S. Supreme Ct. 1961, U.S. Tax Ct. 1962, U.S. Ct. Appeals (fed. cir.) 1974. Ptnr. Lappin, Rosen & Goldberg, Boston, 1959-70, sr. ptnr., 1970-82, mng. ptnr., 1982—. Trustee Norwich U., Northfield, Vt. Mem. ABA, Mass. Bar Assn., Boston Bar Assn. Club: New Seabury Country. Home: 180 Beacon St Boston MA 02116 Office: Lappin Rosen & Goldberg 1 Boston Pl Boston MA 02108

LAPSLEY, WILLIAM WINSTON, utility executive; b. Selma, Ala., Jan. 14, 1910; s. Robert Kay and Ethel Bayne (Pearce) L.; m. June Louise English, June 15, 1935 (dec. 1952); children: Lynn (Mrs. George W. Jordan, Jr.), Robert A., Karen (Mrs. John Muir); m. Frances Vivian Visart Lynn, June 14, 1953 (dec. 1987); stepchildren: Charles R., Jon V. B.S., U.S. Mil. Acad., 1935; M.S. in Civil Enging, U. Calif., Berkeley, 1937; grad., Engr. Sch., 1938, Armed Forces Staff Coll., 1947, Army War Coll., 1951. Commn. 2d lt. U.S. Army, 1935, advanced through grades to maj. gen., 1962; various assignments U.S., ETO, Japan, 1935-56; comdg. gen. U.S. Army Eng. Maintenance Ctr., Columbus, Ohio, 1956-58; div. engr. U.S. Army Engr. Div., Ohio River, 1958-60; comdg. gen. 7th Logistical Command, USARPAC, Korea, 1960-61; div. engr. U.S. Army Engr. Div., N. Pacific, Portland, Oreg., 1962-65; comdg. gen. U.S. Army Mobility Command, Warren, Mich., 1965-67; retired 1967; program mgr. fgn. ops. Kaiser Jeep Corp., Taipei, Taiwan, 1967-68; with Consol. Edison Co. N.Y., Inc., 1969—, exec. v.p., 1971-73, pres., 1973-75, trustee, 1973-82. Mem. Miss. River Commn., 1958-60; mem. Bd. Engrs. for Rivers and Harbors, 1958-60, 62—, U.S. del. U.S.-Can. treaty negotiating team joint use Columbia River water, 1961-62. Decorated Bronze Star with oak leaf cluster, Legion of Merit, D.S.M., numerous area and service ribbons. Mem. Assn. U.S. Army, Alumni Assn. U.S. Mil. Acad., Soc. Am. Mil. Engrs., Sigma Xi, Phi Kappa Phi, Tau Beta Pi. Clubs: Sea Pines; Melrose (Daufuskie Island, S.C.). Home: 41 Willow Oak Rd W Hilton Head Island SC 29928

LARA, MAURICIO ANTONIO, civil engineer, consultant; b. San Salvador, Dec. 27, 1933; s. Antonio Jose and Margarita Regina (Garcia O'Meany) L.; m. Anabella Villatoro, Oct. 20, 1962 (div. 1981); children—Ruy, Denis, Fernando. B.C.E., Catholic U. Am., 1956; auditor Escuela de Ingenieros de Caminos, Canales y Puertos, Madrid, 1957, Tech. U. Munich, 1957-58. Structural engr. with Walter Christman, Munich, 1958, Alfred Kunz & Co., Munich, 1959-60; asst. Inst. for Soil Mechanics, Tech. U., Munich, 1958; pvt. cons. engr., San Salvador, 1961—; pres. Mauricio A. Lara Y Associados, Ingenieros-Arquitectos Consultores, San Salvador, 1975—; mem. Salvadoran Bldg. Code Com., 1967, 77, Salvadoran Tech. Assistance Mission to Managua, 1973; prof. structural analysis and design U. El Salvador, 1966, 70; cons. El Salvador Ministry Pub. Works, 1972—. Fellow ASCE; mem. Salvadoran Assn. Structural Engrs. (co-founder, pres. 1972—), Salvadoran Assn. Consultants (pres. 1985-86), ASTM, Am. Concrete Inst., Internat. Assn. Shell and Spatial Structures, Inst. Eduardo Torroja de la Construction y El Cemento, Assn. Tecnica Espanola del Pretensado, Salvadirean Assn. Engrs. and Architects, Central Am. Assn. Cement and Concrete, Concrete Soc., Earthquake Engring. Research Inst. Roman Catholic. Contbr. articles to profl. jours., papers to profl. confs. Office: 3515 Alameda, Manuel Enrique Araujo, San Salvador El Salvador

LARAKI, AZEDINE, prime minister Morocco; b. Fez, Morocco, 1929. Ph.D., Faculty of Medicine, Paris, 1957. Intern various hosps., Morocco; assoc. med. chief Province of Oujda, Morocco; dir. cabinet Minister of Nat. Edn, Morocco, 1958, Minister of Pub. Health, 1959; dir. Avicennes Hosp., head respiratory surgery and pneumology, from 1967; prof. Faculty of Medicine, from 1967; minister nat. edn. Morocco, from 1977, vice prime minister, 1985, now prime minister; v.p. 4th extraordinary session UNESCO, Paris, 1982; v.p. 23d gen. conf. UNESCO, Sofia, 1985. Address: Office of Prime Minister, Rabat Morocco *

LARBERG, JOHN FREDERICK, social work administrator; b. Kansas City, Mo., Jan. 21, 1930; s. Herman Alvin and Ann (Sabrowsky) L.; AA, Kansas City Jr. Coll., 1948; AB cum laude, U. Mo., 1950, postgrad., 1955-56; MSW, Bryn Mawr Coll., 1961; Cert. social worker. With Westinghouse Electric Corp., 1953-56; dir. House of Industry Settlement House, Phila., 1957-61; asst. to exec. dir. Health and Welfare Council, Inc., Phila., 1961-66; sr. staff cons., 1966-73, dir. Washington office, 1971-72; cons. Nat. Assembly for Social Policy and Devel., Inc., N.Y.C.; nat. dir. community and patient services Nat. Multiple Sclerosis Soc., N.Y.C., 1974-81, nat. dir. spl. projects, 1981-82; adminstrv. v.p. Fedn. Protestant Welfare Agys. N.Y., 1982-86; sr. advisor, 1986-87; exec. dir. Am. Assn. State Social Work Bds., 1987—; cons. to exec. com. Commn. on Vol. Service and Action, 1967-76; cons. Met. N.Y. Project Equality, 1968-73, Encampment for Citizenship, 1973-74, Symphony for UN, 1974-77; bd. dirs. Health Systems Agy. of N.Y., 1984-86. Trustee The Riverside Ch., N.Y.C., 1985—. Served with AUS, 1951-53. Mem. Acad. Cert. Social Workers (charter), Nat. Assn. Social Workers (chpt. legis. com. 1968-70, nat. publs. com. 1968-71, nat. legal regulation com. 1987—), Internat. Council Social Welfare (internat. com. of reps. 1980-84, U.S. Commn. Internat. Coucil Social Welfare (bd. dirs. 1983—, exec. com. 1983—), Internat. Fedn. Multiple Sclerosis Socs. (vice chmn. patient services com. 1976-81, chmn. 1981-84, mem. individual and family services com. 1984—, rep. to Rehab. Internat. Med. Commn. 1976-81), Nat. Conf. Social Welfare (program com. 1966-73, chmn. combined asso. groups 1969-70, nat. dir. 1971-73, 83-87), Malignant Hyperthermia Assn. U.S. (bd. dirs. 1984—, nat. pres. 1985—), Am. Acad. Polit. and Social Sci., AAAS, Nat. Urban League (nat. trustee-at-large 1968), Hawk Mountain Sanctuary Assn., Bryn Mawr Social Work Alumni Assn. (pres. 1963-65), Mo. Soc. N.Y., Am. Mus. Natural History, Nat. Audubon Soc., Nat. Wildlife Found., NAACP, Phi Beta Kappa Assn. N.Y. (pres. 1980-82), Omicron Delta Kappa, QEBH, Alpha Phi Omega, Alpha Pi Zeta, Pi Sigma Alpha, Alpha Kappa Psi. Home: 400 E 58th St New York NY 10022 Office: PO Box 5361 FDR Station New York NY 10150

LARCO COX, GUILLERMO, former prime minister of Peru. Nat. senator, pres. senatorial coms. housing and nat. def. Peru Senate, Lima, 1985-87; prime minister Peru, Lima, 1987-88, former minister of the presidency. Address: Office of Prime Minister, Lima Peru *

LARGE, TIMOTHY WALLACE, religious organization administrator; b. Palo Alto, Calif., Feb. 23, 1942; s. Charles Delano Henry and Jean Eleanor (Parker) L.; m. Vickie Lee Olson, Aug. 6, 1978; children: Jonathan Jeffrey, Sarah Jean. BSBA, Menlo Coll., 1964; MBA, U. Santa Clara, 1966; cert., Multnomah Sch. Bible, Portland, Oreg., 1973; M of Div., Talbot Theol. Sem., La Mirada, Calif., 1978. CPA, Calif. Acct. Bramer Accountancy Corp., Santa Fe Springs, Calif., 1974-76; instr. Biola Coll., La Mirada, Calif., 1978; acct. Conservative Bapt. Assn. So. Calif., Anaheim, 1978-83; CPA H. Canaday, P.A., Santa Fe Springs, 1983—; adminstr. Temple Baptist Ch., Perris, Calif., 1985-87; treas. Inst. Evangelico, La Puenta, Calif., 1987—; cons. Exec. Leasing, La Mirada, 1976—. Treas. Founders chpt. Kidney Found. So. Calif., Orange County, 1974-76; chaplain Christian Hosp. Med. Ctr., Perris, 1985—. Served with U.S. Army, 1965-69. Fellow Nat. Assn. Ch. Bus. Adminstrs.; mem. Am. Mgt. Assn., Christian Ministries Mgt. Assn. Republican. Baptist. Home: 26928 Potomac Dr Sun City CA 92381 Office: 14864 Valley Blvd La Puente CA 91744

LARGESS, GEORGE JOSEPH, retired educator; b. Malden, Mass., Oct. 20, 1917; s. James Edmund and Ellen (Hyland) L.; B.S., U.S. Naval Acad., 1939; postgrad. U.S. Naval Postgrad. Sch., 1945; M.S.T., Am. U., 1972; m. Zoe McCombs, Feb. 2, 1942; children—George Joseph, Robert P., Dennis N., Mary Jude, William M. Commd. ensign USN, 1939, advanced through grades to comdr., 1949; comdr. U.S.S. Altair, 1952-53, U.S.S. Keppler, 1957-58; ret., 1961; project engr. Booz-Allen Applied Research, Inc., 1961-68; instr. math. St. Cecilia's Acad., Washington, 1968-69, Bullis Sch., Silver Spring, Md., 1969-70, Md. and D.C. Public Schs., 1970-80; mem. adv. group on electronic warfare U.S. Dept. Def., 1959-61. Pres., Crestwood Citizens Assn., 1960-61, del. D.C. Fedn., 1961-62; pres. Holy Name Soc., 1962-64, treas., 1974-75, del. Archdiocesan Union, 1961-68; pres. Cath. Youth Orgn., 1958-61; leader Capital council Boy Scouts Am., 1953-56; sec. Archdiocesan Union Holy Name Socs., 1968-71; mem. St. Matthew's Cathedral Council, 1968-85, pres., 1984-85; mem. Calvert Sch. Bd., 1968-70. Recipient Holy Name Soc. Appreciation award, 1964, Georgetown U.-D.C. Schs. award, 1980. Mem. Nat. Council Cath. Men, IEEE, Mil. Order World Wars, Washington Ops. Research Council, Math. Assn. Am., Nat. Council Tchrs. Math., Am. Math. Soc., Am. Security Council, John Carroll Soc., Thomas More Soc., Phi Delta Kappa. Club: Serra of Washington (pres., dist. trustee 1981-84, del. Rome conv. 1983, dist. gov. 1988—). Home: 1908 Quincy St NW Washington DC 20011

LARGMAN, KENNETH, strategic analyst, strategic defense analysis company executive; b. Phila., Apr. 7, 1949; s. Franklin Spencer and Roselynd Marjorie (Golden) L.; m. Suzanna Forest, Nov. 7, 1970 (div. Nov. 1978); 1 child, Jezra. Student, SUNY-Old Westbury, 1969-70. Ind. strategic analyst, 1970-80; chmn., chief exec. officer World Security Council, San Francisco, 1980—; dir. US/Soviet Nuclear Weapons and Strategic Def. Experiment: Discovery of Unanticipated Dangers and Possible Solutions . Author: research documents Space Peacekeeping, 1978, Preventing Nuclear Conflict. An International Beam Weaponry Agreement, 1979, Space Weaponry: Effects on the International Balance of Power and the Prevention of Nuclear War, 1981, Defense Against Nuclear Attack: U.S./Soviet Interactions, Moves, and Countermoves, 1985, 2 vols. on U.S./Soviet options in strategic def. race, 1986. Mem. World Affairs Council.

LARIMER, THOMAS RAYMOND, paper company executive; b. Latrobe, Pa., Apr. 13, 1930; s. S. Raymond and Mae (Stickle) L.; married, 1960 (div. Mar. 1976); children: Peter M., Jane E.; m. Angela McDonnell, 1979. BA in Bus., Pa. State U., 1953; MBA, Xavier U., 1965. Salesman Armstrong Cork Co., Lancaster, Pa., 1954-70; product mgr. Philip Carey Co., Cin., 1970-72; group product mgr. Jim Walter Corp., Tampa, Fla., 1972-80; v.p. sales CPM Inc., Claremont, N.H., 1981-85, v.p. mktg. and planning, 1985—; bd. dirs. Kraft and Packaging Papers div. Am. Paper Inst., N.Y.C. Served with U.S. Army, 1950-52. Mem. TAPPI. Republican. Office: CPM Inc 131 Sullivan St Claremont NH 03743

LARIZADEH, M(OHAMMED) R(EZA), business educator; b. Tehran, Iran, Apr. 14, 1947; came to U.S., 1966; s. Hassan and Nosrat (Saremi) L.; m. Dianne Ellen Pincus, Mar. 25, 1973; children: Dariush, Darya Anna. BA in Econs., Bus., UCLA, 1972, cert. in acctg., 1974. Cert. colls. teaching credential, Calif. (life); lic. real estate agent, Calif. Auditor Peat, Marwick & Mitchell, Los Angeles, 1972-74; controller Petromain Constrn. Co., Tehran, 1975-77; v.p. fin. Pilary Marine Shipping Co., Tehran, 1977-79; prof. Iranian Inst. Banking, Tehran, 1975-78; pres. Audicount Acctg. and Auditing Group, Los Angeles, 1984—; prof. bus. and acctg. East Los Angeles Coll., 1980-87, vice-chmn. dept. bus. and acctg., 1987—; prof. acctg. Santa Monica (Calif.) Coll., 1987—; mgmt. cons. L.P. Assocs. Mfg. Co., Los Angeles, 1981—; mng. dir. Barrington Enterprises, Los Angeles; prof. Santa Monica (Calif.) Coll., 1987. Author/translator: Accounting/Auditing, 1975. Mem. Am. Mgmt. Assn., Faculty Assn. Calif. Community Colls., NEA, Am. Fedn. Tchrs., Calif. Tchrs. Assn., Am. Entrepreneur Assn., Nat. Assn. Realtors, Calif. Assn. Realtors, Iranian Student Assn. (pres. UCLA chpt. 1969-70), Iranian Student Assn. (pres. UCLA chpt. 1969-70), Nat. Trust for Hist. Preservation, Smithsonian Assocs., Alpha Kappa Psi.

LARK, RAYMOND, artist, art scholar; b. Phila., June 16, 1939; s. Thomas and Bertha (Lark) Crawford. Student, Phila. Mus. Sch. Art, 1948-51, Los Angeles Trade Tech. Coll., 1961-62; B.S., Temple U., 1961; L.H.D., U. Colo., 1985. Ednl. dir. Victor Bus. Sch., Los Angeles, 1969-71; public relations exec. Western States Service Co., Los Angeles, 1968-70; owner, mgr. Raymond Lark's House of Fine Foods, Los Angeles, 1962-67; exec. sec. to v.p. Physicians Drug and Supply Co., Phila., 1957-61; lectr. Los Angeles Trade Tech. Coll., 1973, Compton (Calif.) Coll., 1972, Nat. Secs. Assn., Hollywood, Calif., UCLA, numerous others. One-man shows include, Dalzell Hatfield Galleries, Los Angeles, 1970-80, Arthur's Gallery Masterpieces and Jewels, Beverly Hills, Calif., 1971, Dorothy Chandler Pavillion Music Center, Los Angeles, 1974, Honolulu Acad. Arts, 1975, UCLA, 1983, U. Colo. Mus., 1984; group exhbns. include, Smithsonian Instn., 1971, N.J. State Mus., Trenton, 1971, Guggenheim Mus., N.Y.C., 1975, Met. Mus. Art, 1976, La Galerie Mauffe, Paris, 1977, Portsmouth (Va.) Mus., 1979, Ava Dorog Galleries, Munich, W. Ger., 1979, Accademia Italia, Parma, 1980, Ames Art Galleries and Auctioneers, Beverly Hills, 1980, Le Salon des Nations at Centre International d'Art Contemporain, Paris, 1983; represented in permanent collections, Library of Congress, Ont. Coll. Art, Toronto, Mus. African and African Am. Art and Antiquities, Buffalo, Carnegie Inst., numerous others; art commns. for tv. and film studios include, All in the Family, Carol burnett Show, Maude, The Young and the Restless, Universal City Studios, Palace of the Living Arts, Movie Land Wax Mus.; author works in field; author and contbr. more than 50 scholarly treatises on art, edn. and the hist. devel. of Black Ams., chpts. to encyclopedias and textbooks, articles to jours., introductions to mus. exhbn. catalogues. Recipient Gold medal Accademia Italia, 1980, also numerous other gold medals and best of show awards, and 3 presdl. proclamations; Nat. Endowment Arts grantee; ARCO Found. grantee; Colo. Humanities Program grantee; Adolph Coors Beer Found. grantee. Mem. Art West Assn. (pres. 1968-70). Address: PO Box 8990 Los Angeles CA 90008

LA ROCCA, ALDO VITTORIO, mechanical engineer; b. Caserta, Italy, Apr. 22, 1926; came to U.S., 1951, naturalized, 1959; s. Vincenzo and Anna (Casagrande) La R.; Dottore Ingegneria Meccanica, Univ. and Poly. Naples, 1950; Ph.D. in Applied Mechanics, Poly. Inst. Bklyn., 1955; m. Elizabeth Müller, Aug. 31, 1955; children—Renato, Dario, Marcello. Research asso. Poly. Inst. Bklyn., 1951-55; with Gen. Electric Co., 1955-72, advanced propulsion specialist Flight Propulsion Lab., Evendale, Ohio, 1955-60, mgr., cons. engring. advanced propulsion, missile and space div., Phila., also Valley Forge (Pa.) Space Tech. Ctr., 1960-72; advanced tech. mgr. Fiat S.p.A. Research Ctr., Turin, Italy, 1972-77, mem. central staff, advanced tech. planner, 1977—, head auto high power laser program, 1979-86; founder, pres. Lara Cons. S.R.L., 1986—; mem. space and energy com. Internat. Acad. Astronautics, 1978—; mem. sci. com. Italian Nat. Research Council, 1976—; sci. cons. high power laser program lectr. seminars Royal Swedish Acad. Scis., Soc. German Engrs., Philips Research Ctr., Eindhoven, Netherlands. Fulbright fellow, 1951-53; recipient Wallenberg Found. award Royal Swedish Acad. Scis., 1984. Assoc. fellow AIAA; mem. Italian Industry Mgrs. Assn., Sigma Xi. Unitarian. Author, patentee in field. Home: 113 Moncalvo, 10024 Moncalieri Italy Office: Viale dei Castagni 4, 10020 Moncalieri, Turin Italy

LAROCHE, KARL, JR., motion picture and television producer, director, film production executive, audio-visual consultant; b. Stamford, Conn., Mar. 2, 1927; s. Karl and Martha (Meisel) LaR.; m. Clarrissa Worcester Dey, III, Nov. 15, 1952; children—Andre John, Michelle Dey. Student, Art Ctr. Sch., Los Angeles, 1947-49; student Personnel Mgmt., Rollins Coll., 1956-57. Staff engr. Sta. WSRR, Stamford, 1943-45; Sta. WSTC, Stamford, 1947; v.p. Fla. Photo, Inc., Miami, 1950-51; staff photographer Fairchild Aerial Surveys, Inc., N.Y.C., 1952-54; motion picture and aerial photographer RCA Service Co., Missile Test Project, Cocoa, Fla., 1954-56, motion picture dir. RCA, 1957-58, adminstr. photog. services Ballistic Missile Early Warning System Project, Riverton, N.J., Thule, Greenland and Clear, Alaska, 1958-60, motion picture dir. RCA Redstone Pictorial Services, Huntsville, Ala., 1960-64, mgr. film prodn. services, 1964-68; v.p., exec. producer Zapel Studios, Inc., Chgo., 1968-70; mgr. film prodn. and services A.B. Dick Co., Niles, Ill., 1970-72; v.p., exec. producer Bill Stokes Assocs., Dallas, 1972; v.p. prodn. and corp. exec. v.p. Continental Film Prodns. Corp., Chattanooga, 1972-83; audio-visual producer, creative staff corporate communications dept. Provident Life & Accident Ins. Co., Chattanooga, 1983—. Bd. dirs. Lutheran Sch., East Ridge, Tenn., 1977—. Served with USNR, 1945-46, inactive res. 1946-54. Mem. Soc. Motion Picture & TV Engrs., Soc. Photog. Scientists & Engrs., Am. Soc. Photogrammetry, Am. Rocket Soc., AIAA, Internat. TV Assn. (pres. Chattanooga chpt. 1987-88, mem. exec. com. 1988—). Republican. Lutheran. Home: 101 Nancy Ln RT 5 Ringgold GA 30736 Office: Provident Cos Corp Communications 1 Fountain Sq Chattanooga TN 37402

LA ROCHEFOUCAULD, BERNARD, institute executive; b. Paris, Aug. 7, 1922; s. Pierre de L.; m. Brigitte Brian, Dec. 15, 1949; children: Edmond, Anne, Sabine, Sophie, Paul. Diploma, Ecole Centrale, Paris, 1947. Dir. Engelhard Industries Ltd., London, 1951-58; pres. Seretes SA, Paris, 1959-70; exec. v.p. Espace Expantion, Paris, 1970-84; pres. Inst. La Boetie, Paris, 1979—; chmn. Fondation des Parcs de France, Paris, 1983—. Mem. City Council Ingrannes, France. Home: Les Tourelles, 45450 Ingrannes, Fay aux Loges France Office: Inst La Boetie, 44 Ave d'lena, 75010 Paris France

LA ROCQUE, MARILYN ROSS ONDERDONK, communications executive; b. Weehawken, N.J., Oct. 14, 1934; d. Chester Douglas and Marion (Ross) Onderdonk; B.A. cum laude, Mt. Holyoke Coll., 1956; postgrad. N.Y. U., 1956-57; M. Journalism, U. Calif. at Berkeley, 1965; m. Bernard Dean Benz, Oct. 5, 1957 (div. Sept. 1971); children: Mark Douglas, Dean Griffith; m. 2d, Rodney C. LaRocque, Feb. 10, 1973. Jr. exec. Bonwit Teller, N.Y.C., 1956; personnel asst. Warner-Lambert Pharm. Co., Morris Plains, N.J., 1957; editorial asst. Silver Burdett Co., Morristown, 1958; self-employed as pub. relations cons., Moraga, Calif., 1963-71, 73-77; pub. relations mgr. Shaklee Corp., Hayward, 1971-73; pub. relations dir. Fidelity Savs., 1977-78; exec. dir. No. Calif. chpt. Nat. Multiple Sclerosis Soc., 1978-80; v.p. public relations Cambridge Plan Internat., Monterey, Calif., 1980-81; sr. account exec. Hoefer Amidei Assocs., San Francisco, 1981-82; dir. corp. communications, dir. spl. projects, asst. to chmn. Cambridge Plan Internat., Monterey, Calif., 1982-84; dir. communications Buena Vista Winery, Sonoma, Calif., 1984-86, asst. v.p. communications and market support, 1986-87; dir. communications Rutherford Hill Winery, St. Helena, Calif., 1987—; instr. pub. relations U. Calif. Extension, San Francisco, 1977-79. Mem. exec. bd., rep-at-large Oakland (Calif.) Symphony Guild, 1968-69; co-chmn. pub. relations com. Oakland Museum Assn., 1974-75; cabinet mem. Lincoln Child Center, Oakland, 1967-71, pres. membership cabinet, 1970-71, 2d v.p. bd. dirs., 1970-71. Bd. dirs. Calif. Spring Garden and Home Show, 1971-77, Dunsmuir House and Gardens, 1976-77, San Francisco Symphony Assn., 1984—; mem. Calif. State Republican Central Com., 1964-66; v.p. Piedmont council Boy Scouts Am., 1977. Mem. DAR (chpt. regent 1960-61, 66-68), U. Calif. Alumni Assn., Public Relations Soc. Am. (chpt. dir. 1980-82; accredited), Sonoma Valley Vintners Assn. (dir. 1984-87), Napa Valley Wine Auction (pub. relations com.), Internat. Wine and Food Soc. (Marin chpt.), Calif. Hist. Soc., San Francisco Mus. Soc., Nat. Trust for Historic Preservation, Smithsonian Assocs., Sonoma Valley C. of C. (bd. dirs. 1984-87), Am. Inst. Wine and Food, W.I.N.O. (San Francisco chpt.), Knights of the Vine (master lady 1985—). Clubs: Commonwealth of Calif.; Mount Holyoke Coll. Alumnae. Author: Maestro Baton and His Musical Friends, 1968; Happiness is Breathing Better, 1976.

LAROSE, GILLES L., architect; b. Montreal, Que., Can., Oct. 4, 1920; s. Paul Joseph Alexandre and Ernestine Marie (Lemieux) L.; m. Lise Favreau, June 5, 1947; children: Marie-Josée Michèle, Joseph Guy Francois. Degree in Architecture, Beaux-Arts Montreal, 1944. Registered profl. architect, Que. Ptnr. Larose & Larose Architects, Montreal, 1952-58, Larose & Larose Laliberté Petrucci, Montreal, 1958-72, Larose, Laliberté & Petrucci, Montreal, 1972-81, Larose & Petrucci, Montreal, 1981-87, Larose, Petrucci & Martel, Montreal, 1987—. Prin. works include Quebec Ct. House, 1979 (first prize), Modern Art Mus. of Montreal, 1983. Regional pres. Que. Liberal Party, v.p. 1966-68, treas. 1968-72; bd. dirs. Assn. for the Progress of the South, 1982-84. Fellow Royal Archtl. Inst. Can.; mem. Que. Order of Architects, Ont. Assn. Architects, Que. Assn. Architects in Pvt. Practice (bd. dirs. 1982-84), Montreal C. of C. Roman Catholic. Club: Richelieu (Longueuil, Que.) (pres. 1952-53). Home: 333 Riverside Dr Apt 401, Saint Lambert, PQ Canada J4P 1A9 Office: Larose Petrucci Martel, Architects, 1255 University St, Montreal, PQ Canada H3B 3B6

LAROSIERE DE CHAMPFEU, JACQUES, bank executive; b. France, Nov. 12, 1929; m. France du Bos, 1960; 2 children. B. Arts and Law, Inst. d'Etudes Politiques, Paris. Inspecteur des fin. Govt. of France, 1958-61, chargé de mission Inspectorate-Gen. of Fin., 1961-63, chargé de mission External Fin. Office, 1963-65, chargé de mission Treasury, 1965-67, asst. dir. Treasury, 1967, dep. dir., head dept. Ministry of Econs. and Fin., 1971-74, pvt. sec. to Minister of Econs. and Fin., 1974, dir. Treasury, 1974-78, chmn. deps. of fin. Group of Ten, 1976-78, inspecteur gen. des fin., 1981—; mng. dir. Internat. Monetary Fund, Washington, 1978-87; gov. Bank of France, 1987—; censeur for Gen. Council Bank of France, 1974-78; v.p. Caisse Nationale des Telecommunications, 1974-78; dir. Renault, Banque Nationale de Paris, Air France, French Railways; chmn. Econ. and Devel. Rev. Com. OECD, 1967-71. Mem. Société Nationale Industrielle Aerospatiale (dir. 1976-78). Office: Banque de France, 1 rue de la Vrillière, 75001 Paris France

LAROUI, ABDALLAH MALKI, history educator, author; b. Azemmour, Eljadida, Morocco, Nov. 7, 1933; s. Mohammed and Rakia (Dahman) L.; m. Latifa Benjelloun, Feb. 18, 1965; 1 child, Isam. Degree in polit. sci., IEP, Paris, 1956; MA in Islamics, U. Sorbonne, Paris, 1961, PhD in History, Paris, 1976. Culturel attaché Moroccan Embassy, Cairo, 1960, Paris, 1961-62; lectr. U. Sorbonne, Paris, 1962-63; assoc. prof. Rabat U., 1964-67, UCLA, 1968-70; univ. prof. Univ. Muhammad V, Rabat, Morocco, 1971—; cons. UNESCO, Paris, Univ. Peace, San Jose, Costa Rica, ALECSO, Tunis, Tunisia. Author: History of the Maghreb, 1970, The Crisis of the Arab Intellectual, 1976, Islam and Modernity, 1986. Mem. Acad. of The Kingdom of

Morocco. Moslem. Office: Acad of The Kingdom, of Morocco, Avenue des Zaers, Rabat Morocco

LAROUNIS, GEORGE PHILIP, manufacturing company executive; b. Bklyn., Mar. 19, 1928; s. Philip John and Helen (Cormentelou) L.; m. Mary G. Efthymiatou, Jan. 13, 1958; 1 child, Daphne H. B.E.E., U. Mich., 1950, postgrad. in Law; J.D., N.Y. U., 1954. Electronics engr. in research and devel. Columbia U. Electronics Research Lab., 1952-54; asso. firm Pennie, Edmonds, Morton, Barrows & Taylor, N.Y.C., 1954-58; fgn. patent atty. Western Electric Co., N.Y.C., 1958-60; asst. dir. Bendix Internat., Paris, 1960; dir. licensing and indsl. property rights Bendix Internat., to 1974; v.p. staff ops. Bendix Europe, 1974-77; also dir. European affiliate; v.p. Bendix Internat. Fin. Corp., Bendix Internat.; v.p., group exec. Bendix Corp., Paris, 1977-82; pres. Bendix Internat. Cons. Corp., 1974-86, Endevco France S.A.; reg. v.p. Allied Automotive Bendix Europe, 1982-85; v.p. Allied-Signal Internat., Inc., 1985—; dir. Bendix France, France, Jurid, Fed. Republic Germany, Bendix España, Spain, Bendix Italia, Italy, Bendix Ltd. U.K. Bd. govs. Orthodox Cathedral in Paris. Served with U.S. Army, 1946-47. Recipient Spl. Disting. Achievement award Bendix Internat. Mem. N.Y., Fed. Patent bar assns., Licensing Execs. Soc., Am. C. of C. in France (dir., pres.), Tau Beta Pi, Eta Kappa Nu. Club: Polo de Paris. Home: 9 Blvd du Chateau, 92200 Neuilly-sur-Seine France Office: 39 Rue Francois Ier, 75008 Paris France

LARRECHE, JEAN-CLAUDE, business marketing educator, consultant; b. St. Louis, Senegal, July 3, 1947; s. Albert Pierre and Odette (Hau-Sans) L.; m. Denyse Gros, Sept. 10, 1971; children: Sylvie, Philippe. Diploma electronics engring., Inst. Nat. Scis. Appliquées, Lyons, France, 1968; MS in Computer Sci., U. London, 1969; MBA, INSEAD (European Inst. Bus. Adminstrn.), Fountainbleau, France, 1970; PhD in Bus., Stanford U., 1974. Asst. prof. INSEAD, 1974-77, assoc. prof., 1977-82, prof. mktg., 1982—, also bd. dirs., dir. European Strategic Mktg. Inst., 1986—; chmn. Strat*x, Veneux, France, 1985—; dir. Reckitt & Colman, London, 1983—, The Mac Group, Boston, 1985—. Author: Markops, 1987, (with others) Industrat, 1987, Markstrat, 1977; contbr. numerous articles to profl. jours. Air France fellow, 1968, Brit. Council fellow, 1968-69, Ford Found. fellow, 1971-74. Mem. Am. Mktg. Assn., Inst. Mgmt. Sci., Assn. Consumer Research, European Mktg. Acad. Roman Catholic. Office: INSEAD, Blvd de Constance, 77305 Fountainbleau France

LARSEN, CHRISTIAN HENNIG GUNNAR RUNDIN, art dealer; b. Stockholm, Mar. 26, 1958; s. Henning and Anna-Lisa (Axén) L. Student econs., Stockholm U., 1982. Mng. dir. Henning Larsen Agys., Stockholm, 1980-81, Larsen Fine Arts, Stockholm, 1986—. Moderata Samlings. Club: Sallskapet (Stockholm). Home: Karlaplan 10 5 Tr, 115 22 Stockholm Sweden Office: Larsen Fine Arts, Karlaplan 10 5 Tr 4th Floor, 11522 Stockholm Sweden

LARSEN, HANS CHRISTIAN TOM, finance executive; b. Aarhus, Denmark, July 25, 1950; s. Joergen Ellemose and Anne-Lise (Pedersen) L.; m. Birte Christoffersen, Mar. 13, 1972; children: Martin, Mette. HD, Handelshojskolen, Copenhagen, 1986. Bank clk. Handelsbanken, Copenhagen, 1970-74; bookkeeper Renholdningsselskabet af 1898, Copenhagen, 1974-79; account mgr. Hartvig Ensen and Co., A/S, Copenhagen, 1979-86; fin. mgr. Hindsgaul Mannequins, A/S, Copenhagen, 1986—. Office: Hindsgaul Mannequins A/S, Maaloev Byvej 19-23, 2760 Maaloev Denmark

LARSEN, LOUIS ROYTER, retired electronics company executive, consultant; b. Phila., July 4, 1916; s. Lauritz and Anna (Royter) L.; m. Eugenia Riddell Jacobs, Oct. 20, 1944; children: Louis Royter, Eric Risor, Peter Christian, Geoffrey Stang. B.S. in Econs., U. Pa., 1949, M.B.A., 1956. Instr. U. Pa., 1949-51; with Sprague Electric Co., North Adams, Mass., 1951-86; controller Sprague Electric Co., 1967-85, cons. internat. div., 1985-86; independent cons. 1986—. Served with USAAF, 1942-45. Mem. Nat. Assn. Accts. Home: Pochet Rd PO Box 745 East Orleans MA 02643 Office: PO Box 1015 Orleans MA 02653

LARSEN, MOGENS KURT, machine sales and manufacturing company executive; b. Copenhagen, Oct. 27, 1930; s. Lars Ejner and Karen Kirsten (Christiansen) L.; m. Sonja Sorensen, Feb. 27, 1953 (div. Aug. 1958); m. Birgit Sorensen, Dec. 27, 1967; 1 child, Liselotte. Grad., Handelshoejskolen, Copenhagen, 1955; Engr., Chem. (Concrete Tech.) Sch., Ulm, Fed. Republic Germany, 1962. Dept. head Lemvigh-Muller & Munch, Copenhagen, 1947-59; sales mgr. A.P. Hjortsoe, Copenhagen, 1959-65; pres. Hadsten (Denmark) Betonvaerk, 1965-69; dept. head F.B. Kroll, Farum, Denmark, 1969-79; area mgr. John Deere Co., Brussels, 1979-84; pres. Sejma, Herning, Denmark, 1984-87; sales mgr. Danyard, Aalborg, Denmark, 1987—; external examiner Specialarbejderskolen, Hoverdal, Denmark, 1972-80. Served to lt. arty., Danish Army, 1951-53. Mem. Fedn. Danish Industries. Mem. Conservative party. Roman Catholic. Home: Skytten 6, DK-9000 Aalborg Denmark Office: Danyard A/S, PO Box 660, DK-9100 Aalborg Denmark

LARSEN, MOGENS TROLLE, humanities educator; b. Svendborg, Denmark, May 20, 1937; s. Svend Trolle and Johanne (Hansen) L.; m. Tove Clausen; children: Hans Peter, Hanne; m. Susanne Bang; children: Marie, Mikkel. Degree, Copenhagen U., 1966, Dr. phil., 1974. Research asst. Oriental Inst. U. Chgo., 1967-68; lectr. Copenhagen U., 1968-86, dir. Ctr. for Comparative Cultural Studies, 1982-86, prof. research, dir. Ctr. Research in Humanities, 1986—; cons. Assyrian Dictionary Project, Chgo., 1968-80. Author: Old Assyrian City-State, 1976; editor: Power and Propaganda, 1979, Centre and Periphery, 1987; editor Jour. Culture and History, 1987—. Hon. research fellow U. Coll., 1980—. Home: 9 Holsteinsgade, DK 2100 Copenhagen 0 Denmark Office: Copenhagen U, Ctr Research Humanities, 80 Njalsgade, DK 2300 Copenhagen Denmark

LARSEN, OIVIND, physician, educator; b. Oslo, Sept. 6, 1938; s. Finn Oivind and Edith (Schie) L.; m. Ingegerd Froyshov, Sept. 27, 1969; children—Anne Sofie, Finn Yngvar. M.D., U. Oslo, 1962, D.Med. Sci., 1968. Intern, Fredrikstad (Norway) Hosp., 1962-63; asst. dist. physician, Hemne, Norway, 1963; practice medicine specializing in preventive medicine, Oslo, 1964—; research fellow med. history Inst. Preventive Medicine, U. Oslo, 1964-70, asst. prof. med. history univ., 1971-76, 77-84, prof., 1985—; prof. preventive medicine U. Tromso (Norway), 1976-77; indsl. med. officer Siemens, Oslo, 1970—. Author: Schiff und Seuche 1795-1799, 1968; (with Arthur E. Imhof) Sozialgeschichte und Medizin, 1975, Legene og samfunnet (Physicians and Society), 1986. Editor: Nir-Nytt, jour. Scandinavian Council Indsl. Physicans, 1975-80, Norsk Bedriftshelsetjeneste, 1980—; Norges leger 1986 (Biographies of physicians in Norway), 1986. Contbr. papers and books on med. history, epidemiology, preventive medicine. Recipient Lederle award, 1968. Mem. Internat. Acad. Med. History, German Soc. History Medicine and Technics, Norwegian Soc. Indsl. Physicians (chmn. 1980-85), Scandinavian Council Indsl. Physicians (chmn. 1983-86), Norwegian Med. Soc. (chmn. 1986—). Home: Sofiegate 5, N-0170 Oslo 1 Norway

LARSEN, OLE STEVENS, cement company executive; b. Odense, Denmark, May 22, 1934; s. Herman and Marie (Rasmussen) L.; m. Else Hansen, Feb. 20, 1960; children—Kent, Pia. B.Sc. in Indsl. Engring., Odense U., 1958. Mgmt. tng. Gen. Elec. Co., 1961-64; v.p. Haustrups Fabrikker, Odense, 1965-70; pres., chief exec. officer Dampa, Tommerup, Denmark, 1970-76, Aalborg Portland, Denmark, 1976-87 ; dir. Danalith A/S, Valby, Denmark, De Danske Betonfabrikker A/S, Albertslund, Denmark, Lehigh White Cement Co., Allentown, Pa., Faxe Kalkbrud A/S, Copenhagen, Aalborg Energy Cons. Inc., Creskill, N.J.; chmn. bd. Danaske I/S, Aalborg, Hasle Klinker-og Chamottestensfabrik A/S, Ronne, Denmark, Densit A/S, Aalborg, Aalborg Portland U.S. Inc., Dover, Del., Aalborg Cement Co., Inc., Dover, Aalborg Exploration A/S. Bd. dirs. Danish Am. Found., Copenhagen, 1976. Served to lt. Denmark Munitions, 1960. Mem. Chief Execs. Orgns., Fed. Danish Industries (bd. dirs. 1983), Acad. Tech. Scis. (fin. com. 1976), Handelsbanken Aalborg (chmn. adv. bd. 1978), Cembureau (liaison com. 1976, head del. 1976, exec. com. 1976). Home: Lerkenfeltvej 3, DK-9200 Aalborg SV Denmark Office: Aalborg Portland, Rordalsvej 44, DK-9100 Aalborg Denmark

LARSEN, RALPH IRVING, environmental research engineer; b. Corvallis, Oreg., Nov. 26, 1928; s. Walter Winfred and Nellie Lyle (Gellatly) L.; B.S. in Civil Engring., Oreg. State U., 1950; M.S., Harvard U., 1955, Ph.D. in Air Pollution and Indsl. Hygiene, 1957; m. Betty Lois Garner, Oct. 14, 1950; children—Karen Larsen Cleeton, Eric, Kristine Larsen Burns, Jan Alan. San. engr. div. water pollution control USPHS, Washington, 1950-54; chief tech. service state and community service sect. Nat. Air Pollution Control Adminstrn., Cin., 1957-61; with EPA and Nat. Air Pollution Control Adminstrn., 1961—, environ. research engr., environ. ops. br., meteorology and assessment div., Research Triangle Park, N.C., 1971—; air pollution cons. to Poland, 1973, 75, Brazil, 1978; condr. seminars for air pollution researchers, Paris, Vienna and Milan, 1975; adj. lectr. Inst. Air Pollution Tng., 1969—; Falls of Neuse community rep. City of Raleigh (N.C.), 1974—. Recipient Commendation medal USPHS, 1979. Mem. Air Pollution Control Assn. (editorial bd. jour.), Research Soc. Am., Conf. Fed. Environ. Engrs., USPHS Commd. Officers Assn. (past br. pres.). Republican. Mem. Christian and Missionary Alliance Ch. (elder). Contbr. numerous articles to profl. jours. Home: 4012 Colby Dr Raleigh NC 27609 Office: MD-80 EPA Research Triangle Park NC 27711

LARSEN, SVEND ERIK, semiotics professor; b. Kolding, Denmark, Sept. 1, 1946; s. Otto and Ulla (Gustafsson) L.; m. Gunna Jensen, Apr. 12, 1973; children: Anne, Peter. MA, Aarhus (Denmark) U., 1972, PhD, 1974; PhD, Odense (Denmark) U., 1987. Cert. in language and literature. Asst. prof. Dept. of Literature Odense U., 1974-76, vice dean, mem. faculty bd., 1975-79, assoc. prof. Dept. Literature, 1976—; dep. Dansk Magisterforening, 1975-79. Author: Sémiologie Littéraire, 1984, Sprogets Geometri 1-2, 1986; editor Billeder-laest og paskrevet, 1983, Actualité de Brøndal, 1987. Mem. Semiotic Soc. Am., Internat. Assn. Semiotic Studies, Deutsche Gesellschaft für Semiotik, Internat. Assn. Comparative Lit. Office: Odense U, Dept Literature, Campusvej 55, DK 5230 Odense M Denmark

LARSON, ALERON HORACE, SR., lawyer; b. Eau Claire, Wis., Dec. 2, 1917; s. Raymond Albert and Inga Juanita (Tauger) L.; m. Peggy Anngene Thurston, Oct. 22, 1943; children—Aleron Horace, Julie Ann, Thomas Eric, Jonathan Hans. B.S., Univ. Wis., 1940, J.D., 1948. Bar: Wis. 1948, Colo. 1966, U.S. Supreme Ct. 1972. Atty.-advisor Dept. State, Tex., Washington, 1948-54, corp. atty., city councilman, Eau Claire, 1954-57; atty. The RAND Corp.-SDC, Santa Monica, Calif., 1957-64; counsel, v.p., dir. Manning Gas & Oil Co., Denver, 1965-78; ptnr. Larson & Larson, Denver, 1967-79; chmn., sec., treas., chief exec. officer Western Petroleum Corp., Denver, 1979-84; sole practice, Denver, 1985—; v.p., counsel, dir. Colfax Nat. Bank, 1966-72. Councilman Eau Claire City Council, 1956-57; vestryman Vail Episcopal Ch. Served to capt. USAF, 1940-44; PTO. Decorated Silver Star, D.F.C., Purple Heart, Presdl. Unit Citation. Mem. Wis. Bar Assn. Lodge: Rotary (Vail-Eagle Valley).

LARSON, ALLAN LOUIS, political scientist, educator; b. Chetek, Wis., Mar. 31, 1932; s. Leonard Andrew and Mabel (Marek) L. B.A. magna cum laude, U. Wis., Eau Claire, 1954; Ph.D., Northwestern U., 1964. Instr. Evanston Twp. (Ill.) High Sch., 1958-61; asst. prof. polit. sci. U. Wis., 1963-64; asst. prof. Loyola U., Chgo., 1964-68; assoc. prof. Loyola U., 1968-74, prof., 1974—. Author: Comparative Political Analysis, 1980, (essay) The Human Triad: An Introductory Essay on Politics, Society, and Culture, 1988; (with others) Progress and the Crisis of Man, 1976; contbr. articles to profl. jours. Norman Wait Harris fellow in polit. sci. Northwestern U., 1954-56. Mem. Am. Polit. Sci. Assn., AAAS, Am. Acad. Polit. and Social Sci., Acad. Polit. Sci., Midwest Polit. Sci. Assn., AAUP, Kappa Delta Pi, Pi Sigma Alpha, Phi Sigma Epsilon. Roman Catholic. Home: 2015 Orrington Ave Evanston IL 60201 Office: Loyola U 6525 N Sheridan Rd Damen Hall - Room 915 Chicago IL 60626

LARSON, JULIA LOUISE FINK, land use planner; b. Bethesda, Md., July 11, 1950; d. James A. and Helen J. (Grubb) Fink; m. Louis C. Larson, May 27, 1978 (div. Dec. 1981). BS, Radford Coll., 1972; MS, Oreg. State U., 1975; postgrad., Ga. State U., 1986-88. Geography tchr. Rappahannock County High Sch., Washington, Va., 1972-73; research asst./sec. Oreg. Natural Area Preserves Adv. Com., 1974-75; energy conservation specialist Oreg. Dept. Energy, Salem, 1976-77; mem. Oreg. Fire Protection Master Planning Com., 1978-79, Oreg. State Environ. Edn. Adv. Com., 1977-80; growth mgmt. planner Salem Fire Dept., 1978-79; land use planner Salem Dept. Community Devel., 1979-83; field rep. Data Research & Applications, Inc., Atlanta, 1983-84; land use coordinator Ga. Mfd. Housing Assn., Atlanta, 1984-86; owner, The Planning Edge, Atlanta, 1986-87; land use planner, EDAW, Inc., Atlanta, 1987—; editor: Summary of 1987 Energy and Environ. Legis., So. States Energy Bd.; cons. contbg. editor: 1979 Sun Calendar; co-editor: 1976 Energy Calendar. Vice-pres. Liberty Jaycee Women, Salem, 1981; land use adv. Northside Neighbors, Salem, 1979. Recipient cert. of appreciation City of Salem, 1983. Mem. Am. Inst. Cert. Planners, Ga. Planning Assn. (editor Ga. Planner, 1986-87), Am. Mgmt. Assn., AAUW (group leader 1987-88, newsletter editor 1987-88, bd. dirs. 1987—), Am. Assn. Geographers, Am. Bar Assn. (student mem.), Am. Assn. Women Law Students, Ga. Assn. Zoning Adminstrs. and Bldg. Ofcls., High Mus. Art, Smithsonian Assocs., Ga. Conservancy, Delta Theta Phi. Avocations: backpacking; writing; wine tasting. Home: 4717 Roswell Rd L4 Atlanta GA 30342

LARSON, MARK EDWARD, JR., lawyer, business executive; b. Oak Park, Ill., Dec. 16, 1947; s. Mark Edward and Lois Vivian (Benson) L.; m. Patricia Jo Jekerle, Apr. 14, 1973; children—Adam Douglas, Peter Joseph, Alex Edward. B.S. in Acctg., U. Ill., 1969; J.D., Northwestern U., 1972; LL.M. in Taxation, NYU, 1977. Bar: Ill. 1973, U.S. Dist. Ct. (no. dist.) Ill. 1973, N.Y. 1975, U.S. Dist. Ct. (so. dist.) N.Y. 1975, U.S. Ct. Appeals (2d cir.) 1975, D.C. 1976, U.S. Ct. Appeals (7th cir.) 1976, U.S. Tax Ct. 1976, U.S. Supreme Ct. 1976, U.S. Dist. Ct. D.C. 1977, U.S. Ct. Appeals (D.C. cir.) 1977, U.S. Dist. Ct. Minn. 1982, U.S. Ct. Appeals (8th cir.) 1982, Minn. 1982, Tex. 1984. Acct. Deloitte Haskins & Sells, N.Y.C., 1973-75, tax cons., Chgo., 1978-81; atty. Haight, Gardner Poor & Havens, N.Y.C., 1976-78; Lindquist & Vennum, Mpls., 1981-83; ptnr., spl. counsel Farnsworth, Martin & Gallagher, Houston, 1983-86; ptnr. Haliah Lange & Thoma, Austin, Tex., 1987—; v.p., gen. counsel Unitex Fin. Group Inc., Austin, Tex., 1986—; adj. prof. U. Minn., Mpls., 1982-83. Contbr. articles to profl. publs. Fin. chmn. Elk Grove Twp. Rep. Party, Ill., 1979-81. Mem. Am. Assn. Atty.-CPA's, ABA, Am. Inst. CPA's, Nat. Assn. Bond Lawyers, Houston World Trade Assn.

LARSON, WILLIAM JOHN, safety engineer; b. Benton, Ill., Mar. 8, 1923; s. Thure Alfred and Ruth Esther (Anderson) L.; student U. Nebr., 1943-44; E.E., U. Mich. and Mich. State U., 1945; B.S.M.E., Ill. Inst. Tech., 1948; m. Ruth Virginia Cannon, Mar. 17, 1945; children—Barbara Lee Larson Biskie, John Philip. Coop. student to safety engr. Hartford Accident & Indemnity Co., 1941-43, 46-57; safety engr. Argonne (Ill.) Nat. Lab., 1957-71, safety engring. supr., 1971—, supr. fire protection and safety engr., 1972-87 ; safety cons. 1987—; compliance officer Dept. of Labor, 1971; safety cons. and instr. Republican precinct committeeman, 1965-71; vol. Joliet Area Community Hospice, 1983—. Served with Signal Corps, AUS, 1943-46. Cert. safety profl.; registered profl. engr. Calif. Mem. Ill. Engring. Council, Am. Soc. Safety Engrs., Am. Soc. Safety Research (trustee 1986—), Indsl. Conf., Nat. Safety Council (life, exec. com. research and devel. sect., chmn. research and devel. sect. 1984-85 4 Cameron awards). Mem. Evangelical Covenant Ch. Adv. bd. Am. Soc. Safety Engrs. Jour., 1967-75, chmn., 1972-75; contbr. numerous articles to safety jours. Home: 2212 Mayfield Ave Joliet IL 60435 Office: Argonne National Lab 9700 S Cass Ave Argonne IL 60439

LARSSON, BO INGVAR, psychoanalyst; b. Lund, Sweden, June 8, 1937; s. Ingvar and Ruth Dagny Elvira (Hansson) L; m. Karin Agneta Frieberg, June 3, 1959 (div. July 15, 1970); children: Bo Patrik, Bo Pontus, Bo Magnus; m. Anita Natt Och Dag, May 31, 1973 (div. May 10 1976); m. Lis Lind. MD, Karolinska Inst., 1965; postgrad., Swedish Psychoanalytic Soc., 1971. Diplomate Swedish Inst. Psychoanalysis. Intern in psychiatry Sankt Göran Hosp., Stockholm, 1965-68; intern in child psychiatry Kungsholmen Child Guidance Clinic, Stockholm, 1968-69; sec. Swedish Psychoanalytical Soc., Stockholm, 1972-74; sci. sec. Swedish Psychoanalytical Soc., 1974-75, pres., 1975-78, chmn. coms., 1979-83, chmn., 1985—; mem. faculty, U. Stockholm, 1965—; cons. Family Counseling Unit, Stockholm, 1970—; organizer 1st Swedish Psychoanalytic Cogress, 1980-82. Author: Report from a Child Guidance Center; founding editor Scandinavian Psychoanalytic Rev., 1978; contbr. articles to profl. jours, chpt to book. Mem. Swedish Med. Assn., Swedish Psychiat. Assn., Swedish Psychoanalytic Soc., Internat. psychoanalytic Assn. (chmn. organizing com. 1979-81). Home: Smedjevagen 12, S-131 33 Nacka Sweden Office: Swedish Psychoanalytical Soc, Vasterlanggatan 60, S-111 29 Stockholm Sweden

LARSSON, INGEMAR TEODOR, marketing executive; b. Vastervik, Smaland, Sweden, Apr. 19, 1936; s. Conrad T. and Rut A.M. (Rosèn) L.; m. Ylva L. Hakansson, June 24, 1962; children: Christina, Peter. Grad., Orebroskolan Vuxna, Orebro, Sweden, 1973. Mgr. shipping Orebro Pappersbruks A.B., 1958-66, sales asst., 1966-70, mgr. sales, 1970-76; divisional mgr. Billingsfors (Sweden) Bruks A.B., 1977-81; mgr. exports Sprinter Pack A.B., Halmstad, Sweden, 1981-85; dir. mktg. Ramstrom Emballage A.B., Sunne, Sweden, 1985-86, now bd. dirs.; mng. dir. Paraflex A.B., Sunne, 1986—. Bd. dirs. Pentec Ch., Karlstad, Sweden. Lodge: Rotary Internat. Home: Lovsjo 9148, 68603 Amtervik, Varmland Sweden Office: Paraflex AB, PO Box 49, 68600 Sunne, Varmland Sweden

LARUFFA, RICHARD ALPHONSE, mechanical engineer; b. Bklyn., Jan. 16, 1944; s. August John and Concetta (Solimine) LaR.; m. Karen Ann Weber, Mar. 23, 1968; children—Erin Corinne, Scott Vincent. B.Engring. Sci., SUNY-Stony Brook, 1966; M.S., Northwestern U., 1967. Cert. value specialist; registered profl. engr., N.J., N.Y. Engr., Boeing Engring. Co., Huntsville, Ala., 1966; project engr. Exxon Research & Engring. Co., Florham Park, N.J., 1967-71; constrn. mgr. Meridian Engring. Co., N.Y.C., 1971-75; sr. v.p. O'Brien Kreitzberg & Assocs., Inc., Sparta, N.J., 1975—. Mem. Sparta Town Council, 1980-84; mayor Sparta Twp., 1983. N.Y. State Regents scholar; NASA fellow Northwestern U., 1966-67. Mem. Soc. Am. Value Engrs. (bd. dirs.), Am. Arbitration Assn., Constrn. Mgmt. Assn. Am., Assn. Energy Engrs., Nat. Soc. Profl. Engrs. Roman Catholic.

LASAGNI, ALBERTO, construction and building company executive, lawyer; b. Reggio, Emilia, Italy, Nov. 22, 1951; s. Sergio and Maria Luisa (Labanti) L.; m. Maura Manghi, Oct. 1986. D.Polit. Sci., U. Florence, 1975; LL.D., U. Modena, 1980; degree Scuola Specializzazione, Bologna, 1984; degree Brit. C. of C. in Switzerland, 1977. Bar: 1983. Export mgr. Lombardini Motori S.p.A., Reggio Emilia, Italy, 1977-79; gen. mgr., owner IMLA Construzioni, Reggio Emilia, 1979—. Editor-in-chief Quale Impresa, 1979—. Pres., Partito Liberale, Reggio Emilia, 1980, regional rep., 1981; rep. Amnesty Internat., Reggio Emilia, 1980. Served with Fin. Corps, Army, 1976-77. Mem. Central Com. Gruppo Giovani Confindustria (v.p. 1982-84), Federazione Regionale Confindustria (regional rep. 1980-84). Liberal. Jewish. Clubs: Orologio (Milan).Lodge: Rotary (Reggio Emilia, Italy). Home: Via Toschi 5, 42100 Reggio Emilia Italy Office: IMLA Construzioni, Via Passo Buole 27, Reggio Emilia Italy

LA SALLE, ARTHUR EDWARD, historic foundation executive; b. New Orleans, Aug. 9, 1930; s. Rene Charles and Jeanne Matilda (Senac) La S.; divorced; children—Carl Alan, Adam David, Jeanne Ambre Victoria. Student Holy Name of Jesus Coll. Founder, pres. Am. R.R. Equipment Assn., Asheville, N.C., 1960—; founder Trains of Yesterday Mus., Hilliard, Fla., 1964-73; owner, restorer Brush Hill mansion, Irwin, Pa., 1973-77; lessee, restorer Springfield mansion, Fayette, Miss., 1977—; founder, pres. Hist. Springfield Found., Fayette, 1977—; cons. Smithsonian Instn., 1959, 75, Japanese Nat. Rys., Tokyo, 1968, Henry Ford Mus., 1975 City of Natchez, Miss., 1985, Old South Soc., Church Hill, Miss., 1985—; cons. in field; lectr. in field. Author: The Marriage of Andrew Jackson at Springfield Plantation; contbr. articles to profl. jours. Mem. Ry. and Locomotive Hist. Soc., Nat. Trust for Historic Preservation, Natchez Hist. Soc., U.S. Naval Inst. Avocations: historical preservation and study; writing; painting. Home and Office: Springfield Plantation Rt 1 Box 201 Fayette MS 39069

LASANTE, JEAN-CLAUDE, consulting company executive; b. Lille, France, Sept. 17, 1934; s. Marius and Yvonne (Delourme) L.; m. Danièle Buchmann, Sept. 17, 1960; children—Carole, Laurence. diploma Ecole Supérieure de Commerce de Paris, 1957. Export mgr. SACM, Paris, 1958-61; chief exec. Paris Survey, 1968-70; pres. Creargie, Paris, 1970-72; chmn. Eurosurvey Group, Paris, 1972-83; pres. Lasante et Assocs., Paris, 1983—; dir. Inst. Supérieur de Gestion, Paris, 1972—, France-Initiative, Paris, 1979-85, Creargie, Paris, 1970—; v.p. Cogefort. Cogiced. Author: Profession: Chasseur de Tetes, 1977. Co-founder Entreprise et Progres, Paris, 1968, Ethic, Paris, 1976. Mem. Aprocerd (pres. 1982—). Clubs: Interallie, Saint Nom (Paris). Home: rue Daumier 14, 75016 Paris France Office: Lasante et Assocs, Avenue Hoche, 29 Paris France

LASDUN, DENYS LOUIS, architect; b. Sept. 8, 1914; s. Norman and Julie (Abrahams) L.; grad. Rugby Sch.; student Archtl. Assn.; D.A. (hon.), U. Manchester, 1966; D.Litt. (hon.), U. East Anglia, 1974, Sheffield U., 1978; m. Susan Bendit, 1954; 2 sons, 1 dau. Practiced with Wells Coates, Tecton and Drake; pvt. practice architecture with Peter Softley, London, 1960—; Hoffman Wood prof. architecture U. Leeds (Eng.), 1962-63; lectr. U.K., U.S., Europe, China, Hong Kong. Mem. adv. council Victoria and Albert Mus., 1973-83; trustee Brit. Mus., 1975-85; mem. Slade Com., 1976—; mem. arts panel Arts Council Gt. Britain, 1980-84. Served with Royal Engrs., 1939-45. Decorated mem. Order Brit. Empire, 1945, comdr. Brit. Empire, 1965, created knight, 1976; recipient Civic Trust awards class I, 1967, group A, 1969; spl. award Sao Paulo Biennale (Brazil), 1969; awards Concrete Soc., 1977; hon. diploma 1st World Biennale of Architecture, Sofia, 1981. Fellow Royal Inst. Brit. Architects (London architecture Bronze medals 1960, 64, Royal Gold medal 1977, London regional award for Nat. Theatre 1978). AIA (hon.), Royal Coll. Physicians (hon.); mem. Academie d'Architecture Paris, Accademia Nazionale di San Luca (Rome), Bulgarian Inst. Architects (hon.). Works include housing and schs.; London hdqrs. Govt. New South Wales (Australia); flats at 26 St. James's Place; Royal Coll. Physicians; U. East Anglia; residential bldg. Christ's Coll. and Fitzwilliam Coll., Cambridge; U. London Law Inst., Inst. Edn., project for Courtauld Inst.; Nat. Theatre and IBM Central London Mktg. Ctr., South Bank; EEC hdqrs. for European Investment Bank, Luxembourg; Hurva Synagogue, Jerusalem, Cannock Community Hosp., Genoa Opera House, office bldg. 6-12 Fenchurch St. Author: Architecture in an Age of Skepticism, 1984; contbr. articles to archtl. jours. Address: 146 Grosvenor Rd, London SW1V 3JY, England *

LASER, CHARLES, JR., oil company executive, consultant; b. Redford Twp., Mich., July 8, 1933; s. J.C. and Gertrude L.; student Mich. Tech. U., 1952-54, Central Mich. U., 1959-60; m. Glenda Johnson, Sept. 30, 1972; 1 dau., Susan Faye. With Retail Credit Co., 1958-60; exec. dir. Saginaw County Republican Com., 1960-65; exec. dir. Rep. Com. D.C., 1967; fin. dir. San Joaquin Republican Party, Stockton, Calif., 1968; owner Laser Advt., Bay City, Mich., 1969-75; exec. v.p. Vindell Petroleum, Inc., Midland, Mich., 1972-75, Geo Spectra Corp., Ann Arbor, Mich., 1977-86; pres. Laser Exploration Inc., Deerfield Beach, Fla. Chmn. Genesee County Republican Com., 1981-82, mem. Broward County Rep. Exec. Com., 1987-88; adv. com. Tall Pines council Boy Scouts Am.; mem. prevention adv. com. Juvenile Justice Deliquency, Fla., Served with U.S. Army, 1954-58. Mem. Deerfield Beach C. of C. (v.p.), World Trade Council (Palm Beach, Fla. chpt.). Clubs: Detroit Econ., Bankers (Boca Raton), Rep. Men's (v.p. Boca Raton chpt.), Gold Coast Venture Capital (Delray Beach chpt.). Lodge: Rotary, Elks. Home: 1523 E Hillsboro St Apt 131 PO Box 8604 Deerfield Beach FL 33441

LASH, LINDA MARIE, car rental company executive; b. Harrisburg, Pa., June 6, 1948; came to Eng., 1977; d. Howard T. and Eva Gladys (Day) L. Student Eckerd Coll., 1966, U. London, 1967; B.A., Syracuse U., 1970. Rental sales agt. Avis Rent-A-Car, Syracuse, N.Y., 1969-71, tng. specialist, Garden City, N.Y., 1971-74, div. tng. mgr., 1974-77, dir. tng., Bracknell, Berkshire, Eng., 1977-80, 82-86, dir. mktg., 1986-87, dir. customer satisfaction, 1987—, dir. tng., Garden City, 1980-82. NSF summer scholar, 1964. Fellow Brit. Inst. Tng. and Devel.; mem. Am. Soc. Tng. and Devel., Bray Preservation Soc., Phi Mu. Methodist. Club: Crockford's (London). Avocations: skiing; traveling. Home: 9 Ferry End Bray, Berkshire SL6 1AS, England Office: Avis Rent-A-Car, Avis House, Station Rd, Bracknell, Berkshire RG12 1HZ, England

LASHLEY, CURTIS DALE, lawyer; b. Urbana, Ill., Nov. 3, 1956; s. Jack Dale and Janice Elaine (Holman) L.; m. Tamara Dawn Yahnig, June 14,

1986. BA, U. Mo., Kansas City, 1978, JD, 1981. Bar: Mo. 1981, U.S. Dist. Ct. (we. dist.) Mo. 1981, U.S. Tax Ct. 1982. Assoc. Melvin Heller, Inc., Creve Coeur, Mo., 1982; ptnr. Domjan & Lashley, Harrisonville, Mo., 1983-86; asst. gen. counsel, spl. asst. atty. gen. Mo. Dept. Revenue, Independence, 1986—; city atty. Adrian and Strasburg, Mo., 1985-86. V.p. Cass County Young Reps., Harrisonville, 1985. Mem. ABA, Assn. Trial Lawyers Am. Republican. Presbyterian. Lodge: Kiwanis (treas. 1985-86). Office: Mo Dept Revenue 16647 E 23d St Independence MO 64055

LASKER, DANIEL JUDAH, historian, educator; b. Flint, Mich., Apr. 5, 1949; arrived in Israel, 1978; s. Arnold A. and Miriam Florence (Price) L.; m. Debora Susanne Dworkin, June 19, 1973; children: Shoshana R., Yonah S., Adina Y., Dov E., Noam Y. Instr. Kirkland Coll., Clinton, N.Y., 1973-75; asst. prof. Kirkland Coll., Clinton, 1976; vis. asst. prof. Ohio State U., Columbus, 1976-77; asst. prof. U. Tex., Austin, 1977-78; lectr. history Ben Gurion U., Beer Sheva, Israel, 1978-81; sr. lectr. Ben Gurion U., Beer Sheva, 1981—; vis. assoc. prof. U. Toronto, 1983-84. Author: Jewish Philosophical Polemics against Christianity in the Middle Ages, 1977; contbr. numerous articles to Jewish and gen. jours. Mem. Assn. for Jewish Studies, World Union Jewish Studies, Soc. for Judaeo-Arabic Studies. Home: 8 Shivta St, Beer Sheva 84804, Israel Office: Ben Gurion U, Dept History, PO Box 653, Beer Sheva 84105, Israel

LASKER, EDWARD, lawyer; b. Chgo., May 15, 1912; s. Albert D. and Flora (Warner) L.; m. Cynthia S. Palmer, Nov. 1963; children by previous marriage: Albert, Lawrence, Steven. Grad., Phillips Exeter Acad., 1929; B.A., Yale U., 1933; LL.B., UCLA, 1955. Bar: Calif. 1955. Engaged as account exec., v.p. charge radio, 1st v.p., gen. mgr. Lord & Thomas, 1933-41; spl. asst. to sec. navy 1941-42, motion picture producer, 1946- 52; counsel firm McKenna Conner & Cuneo, Los Angeles; dir. Philip Morris, Inc., 1961-80, dir. emeritus, 1980-83, mem. adv. bd., 1983-84; dir. Gt. Western Fin. Corp., 1956-85; asst. chief disciplinary referee Calif. State Bar, 1976-77, mem. disciplinary bd., 1978-80. Trustee Pomona Coll., hon. 1985—; del. Democratic Nat. Conv., 1956, 60. Served from lt. (j.g.) to lt. comdr. USNR, 1942-45. Home: 901 Airole Way Los Angeles CA 90077 Office: 444 S Flower St 10th Floor Los Angeles CA 90071

LASKEY, RICHARD ANTHONY, chemical company executive; b. N.Y.C., Oct. 24, 1936; s. Charles Lewis and Gertrude Ann (Stolzenthaler) L.; student CCNY; B.S. in Chemistry, Ohio City Coll., 1958, M.S. in Organic Chemistry, 1959; Ph.D. in Organic Chemistry, Sussex (Eng.) U., 1970; LL.B., U. Chgo., 1972; M.D. (hon.), Med. Coll. S.A., 1975, fellow, 1976; m. Frances M. Pollack, June 29, 1975; children—Victoria Ann, Deborah Lea. Head sec. med. products, lab. mgr. Hydron Labs., North Brunswick, N.J., 1967-73; v.p. biomed. research Datascope Corp., Paramus, N.J., 1973-82; v.p. research Millbrook Labs., Inc., Rochelle Park, N.J., 1982—; cons. in field. Mem. N.Y.C. Aux. Police, 1963-65. Recipient Doctor's award Chgo. Med. Coll., 1975; fellow Am. Acad. Behavioral Sci., 1976; diplomate Am. Bd. Examiners in Psychotherapy. Mem. Md., Idaho med. socs., Nat. Med. Soc., Internat. Coll. Physicians and Surgeons, Am. Psychotherapy Assn., Nat. Psychol. Assn., AAAS, Assn. Advancement Med. Instrumentation, Soc. Research Adminstrs., Nat. Rifle Assn. Biomed. inventor, patentee. Home: PO Box 133 Washington NJ 07882 Office: PO Box 125 Rochelle Park NJ 07662

LASKIN, OSCAR LARRY, clinical pharmacology educator, virologist; b. Phila., Sept. 11, 1951; s. Bernard and Blanche (Friedman) L.; m. Christine Ann Goril, Apr. 4, 1981. Children—Matthew Benjamin, Joshua Christopher, Jennifer Bonnie, Heather Rose. A.B. summa cum laude, Temple U., 1972, M.D. with honors, 1976. Diplomate Am. Bd. Internal Medicine. Intern Johns Hopkins Hosp., Balt., 1976-77, resident in medicine, 1977-79, fellow in medicine, 1979-82, fellow in pharmacology, 1981-82; asst. prof. clin. pharmacology Cornell U. Med. Coll., N.Y.C., 1982-88, asst. prof. pharamacology and medicine, 1982-88; asst. attending physician N.Y. Hosp., 1982-88; adj. assoc. prof. med. and clin. pharmacology, Cornell U. Med. Coll., 1988—; dir. clin. pharmacology, Merck, Sharp, & Dohme Research Labs., 1988—. Contbr. articles to profl. jours. NIH fellow, 1981; clin. scholar Rockefeller Bros. Fund, 1982; Hartford Found. fellow, 1983; recipient research prize Am. Heart Assn., 1975; pharm. Mfrs. Assn. Found. research starter grantee, 1984-86. Fellow ACP, Infectious Disease Soc. Am.; mem. Am. Fedn. Clin. Research, Am. Soc. Microbiology, Am. Soc. Pharmacology and Exptl. Therapeutics (Young Investigator award 1987), Am. Soc. for Clin. Pharmacology and Therapeutics, Alpha Omega Alpha. Research on clin. pharmacology of antiviral drugs, rapid viral diagnosis and therapy of viral diseases especially herpesviruses. Home: 40 Gates Ave Chatham NJ 07928 Office: Merck Sharp & Dohme Research Labs P O Box 2000 Rahway NJ 07065

LASKO, ALLEN HOWARD, pharmacist; b. Chgo., Oct. 27, 1941; s. Sidney P. and Sara (Hoffman) L.; B.S. (James scholar), U. Ill., 1964; m. Janice Marilynn Chess, Dec. 24, 1968; children—Stephanie Paige, Michael Benjamin. Staff pharmacist Michael Reese Hosp. and Med. Center, Chgo., 1964-68; clin. pharmacist City of Hope Med. Center, Duarte, Calif., 1968-73; chief pharmacist Monrovia (Calif.) Community Hosp., 1973-74, Santa Fe Meml. Hosp., Los Angeles, 1974-77; pvt. investor, 1977—. Recipient Roche Hosp. Pharmacy Research award, 1972-73. Mem. Magic Castle, Flying Samaritans, Mensa, Rho Pi Phi. Jewish. Author books: Diabetes Study Guide, 1972; A Clinical Approach to Lipid Abnormalities Study Guide, 1973; Jet Injection Tested As An Aid in Physiologic Delivery of Insulin, 1973. Home: 376 N Hill St Monrovia CA 91016

LASSAK, MAREK (WLODZIMIERZ), mathematician, researcher; b. Bydgoszcz, Poland, July 11, 1948; s. Zdzislaw and Alicja (Osinska) L.; Halina Ewa Magoycz; 1 child, Beata. MS in Math., Nicolas Copernicus U., Torun, Poland, 1971; PhD in Math., Kishinev (USSR) U., 1975. Teaching asst. Inst. Math. and Physics, Acad. Tech. and Agr., Bydgoszcz, 1971-73, asst. prof., 1976—; research fellow Kishinev U., 1974-75; vis. prof. CUNY, 1987—; vis. prof. U. Wash., Seattle, 1986-87; referee Zentralblatt für Math., Berlin, 1983—, Math. Reviews, Providence, 1986—. Contbr. articles to profl. jours. Mem. Polish Math. Soc. (bd. dirs. 1980-86, pres. Bydgoszcz sect. 1980-86), Am. Math. Soc. Office: Acad Tech and Agr Inst Math, and Physics Kaliskiego 7, 85790 Bydgoszcz Poland Mailing Address: The City Coll, Dept Math Convent Ave at 138th St New York NY 10031

LASSEN, ERIK, physician, researcher; b. Randers, Denmark, Jan. 9, 1945; s. Marius Thomassen and Aase (Christensen) L.; m. Lis Mortensen (div. Jan. 1984); children: Niels, Charlotte; m. Anna Marie Kvorning, Mar. 6, 1986; 1 child, Christian Kvorning. MD, Odense U., Denmark, 1976, Gen. Practitioner degree, 1978. Gen. practice medicine Haderslev, Denmark, 1978-80; physician neurol. dept. Holslebro and Viborg, Denmark, 1981-83; physician psychiatry Viborg and Thisted, Denmark, 1983-84; research asst. psycharmacol. research unit Aarhus U., Risskov, Denmark, 1983-84; gen. practice medicine Odder, Denmark, 1985—; tchr. nurse sch. Viborg, 1981-84, nurse sch. Aarhus, 1983-85, univ. sch. for physiotherapy, Aarhus, 1983-85. Author: Lithium Combination Therapy, 1987; contbr. articles, sci. papers on psychopharmacotherapy. Served as sgt. Danish army, 1965-66. Fellow Alm Danshe Laegeforening, Dansk Psychiatrist Soc., Skandinavisk Soc. for Biologist Psychiatry; mem. Dansk Selskab for Almen Medicin, Sveriges Läkarförband. Lodge: Lions. Home: Rosensgade 29, 8300 Odder Denmark Office: Aarhus U, Psychopamacol Research, Unit, Risskov Denmark

LASSEN, JOHN KAI, lawyer; b. Youngstown, Ohio, Mar. 28, 1942; s. Kai Kierulff and Helen Susanne (Elsaesser) L.; m. Marion duPont McConnell, Sept. 26, 1987; children: Christian K., Laura Wick. BA, Yale, 1964; LLB, U. Pa., 1967. Bar: Del. 1971, U.S. Dist. Ct. Del. 1972. Assoc. Lord, Day & Lord, N.Y.C., 1967; assoc. Morris, Nichols, Arsht & Tunnell, 1971-77, ptnr., 1977-83; ptnr. Lassen, Smith, Katzenstein & Furlow, 1984—. Served to lt. USNR, 1967-70. Fellow Am. Coll. Probate Counsel; mem. ABA, Am. Judicature Soc., Del. Bar Assn. (chmn. decedants, estate and trusts, 1979-81), Del. World Affairs Council, Nat. Assn. Bond Counsel, Del. Com. of 100, Soc. Mayflower Descendants, Del. C. of C. Republican. Presbyterian. Clubs: Wilmington, Wilmington Country, Vicmead Hunt, Lincoln. Lodge: Rotary. Home: Crooked Billet PO Box 3712 3510 Kennett Pike Greenville DE 19807 Office: 1220 Market Bldg PO Box 410 Wilmington DE 19899

LASSEN, PETER ERNST, conductor; b. Copenhagen, June 16, 1935; s. Hans Ernst and Ruth (Von Kessler) L.; m. Anne Grethe Frederiksen; children: Marie, Hans Ernst. Conductor Soenderyllands Symphony Orch., Soenderborg, Denmark, 1963-66, Danish Radio Orch., Copenhagen, 1966-70, Royal Theatre, Copenhagen, 1970—; guest conductor Sweden, Norway, Poland, 1966-70, Hamburg State Opera, Fed. Republic Germany, 1988—, U.S., Japan, France, Fed. Republic Germany, German Dem. Republic, 1970-87. Recipient Honorary award Dansk Kapelmesterforening, Denmark, 1987. Mem. Internat. Soc. Contemporary Music (pres.). Home: Duntzfelts Alle 33, 2400 Hellerup, Copenhagen Denmark Office: Det Kongelige Kapel, Holmes Kanal 3, DK-1060 Copenhagen Denmark

LASSERRE, PIERRE RENE JEAN, marine biologist, educator; b. Dax, France, Oct. 30, 1940; s. Rene Jean and Suzanne Dominiquette (Labat) L.; grad. Faculty of Scis., U. Bordeaux, 1963, D.Biology, 1967, D.Sc., 1977; m. Bernadette Lagarde, May 15, 1965; children—Christophe, Francois. Asst. prof., faculty scis. U. Bordeaux, 1965-70, asso. prof., 1972-80, prof. biol. oceanography, 1980—; head dept. oceanography and mariculture, Inst. Marine Biology, Arcachon, France, 1981—; prof. Pierre and Marie Curie U., Paris, 1982—; dir. Roscoff Biology Sta. (France), 1983—; research assoc. Duke U. Marine Lab., Durham, N.C., 1970-71; cons. UNESCO, research, edn., tng. in marine scis. Latin Am. SE Asia, Africa; expert for UNESCO safeguard of lagoon of Venice, 1981; vis. prof. Venezuela, 1978, 80, Mex., 1978, 80, Sweden, 1973; U.S., 1975, 78, 79, Gt. Britain, 1984, 85, People's Republic of China, 1985; convenor internat. workshops and UNESCO conf. Internat. Symposium on Coastal Lagoons, 1981. Recipient various fellowships and grants including from Carlsberg Found., 1966, Fonds National Belge de la Recherche Scientifique, 1972, 73, NSF U.S., 1971, Marine Biol. Lab., Woods Hole, Mass., 1969, Smithsonian Inst. U.S., 1969; Montgomery-Moore fellowship, Bermuda, 1973, European Molecular Biology Orgn., 1979. Mem. Soc. Exptl. Biology (Cambridge, Eng.), Am. Soc. Limnology and Oceanography, Am. Soc. Zoologists, Société Zoologique de France, Nat. Geog. Soc., Sci. Com. on Oceanic Research, Internat. Assn. Ecology, Internat. Assn. Biol. Oceanography (pres. 1982—), Marine Biol. Assn. of U.K. (council). Editor: Cahiers de Biologie Marine; adv. editor to various sci. jours. on coastal oceanography; sci. advisor two TV movies in field; contbr. reports, monographs, articles to profl. publs. Office: U Paris, Sta Biologique de Roscoff, VI and CNRS, 29211 Roscoff France

LASSETTRE, EDWIN NICHOLS, educator, physical chemist; b. Monroe County, Ga., Oct. 26, 1911; s. Carlos E. and Jennie J. (Nichols) L.; m. Ilse R. Sturies, Dec. 22, 1951. BS, Mont. State Coll., 1933; PhD, Calif. Inst. Tech., 1938; DTech (hon.), Royal Inst. Tech., Stockholm, 1977. Mem. faculty Ohio State U., 1937-62, prof. chemistry, 1950-62; group leader, research scientist Manhattan Project, SAM Labs., Columbia, 1944, Carbide and Carbon Chems. Corp., 1945; staff fellow, mem. adv. com. Mellon Inst., Pitts., 1962-67; staff fellow, prof. chem. physics Carnegie-Mellon U., 1967-74, univ. prof. chem. physics, 1974-77, emeritus, 1977—; dir. Center for Spl. Studies, 1971-73; cons. gaseous diffusion plant Oak Ridge Nat. Lab., 1954-67; rev. com. radiol. physics div. Argonne Nat. Lab., 1968-70; del. Argonne Univs. Assn., 1971-74. Mem. editorial bd. Jour. Chem. Physics, 1967-69, Jour. Electron Spectroscopy and Related Phenomena, 1971-75; contbr. articles in field. Fellow Am. Phys. Soc.; mem. Am. Chem. Soc., N.Y. Acad. Scis., Optical Soc. Am., Math. Assn. Am., Am. Math. Soc. Home: 224 E Waldheim Rd Pittsburgh PA 15215

LASSILA, JAAKKO SAKARI, banker; b. Vaasa, Finland, Mar. 27, 1928; s. Elis Yrjö Harald and Tyyne Eufrosyyne (Hynynen) L.; m. Arnevi Kytöniemi, July 10, 1954; children: Sakari, Juhani, Tapani. BBA, Helsinki Sch. Econs. and Bus., Finland, 1950, MBA, 1955, DSc in Econs., 1966. Alternative exec. dir. Internat. Bank for Reconstruction and Devel., Internat. Fin. Corp., Internat. Devel. Assn. (USA), Washington, 1960-62; sec. Bank Finland, Helsinki, 1962-65; dir. Cen. Fedn. Finnish Woodworking Industries, Helsinki, 1965-67; pres. Industrialization Fund Finland Ltd., Helsinki, 1967-70; bd. dirs. Bank Finland, Helsinki, 1970-73; pres. Pohjola Ins. Co. Ltd., Helsinki, 1974-83, Suomi-Salama Mut. Life Assurance Co., Helsinki, 1977-83; chmn., pres. Pohjola and Suomi-Salama, 1980-83; chmn., chief exec. officer Kansallis-Osake-Pankki, Helsinki, 1983—; chmn. bd. dirs. Rauma-Repola Oy, United Paper Mills Ltd., Kajaani Oy, Lassila & Tikanoja Oy, Oy Shell Ab (Finland), Suomen ICI Oy; bd. dirs. Kone Oy, Oy Julius Tallberg Ab; chmn. supervisory bd. Pohjola Group Ins. Cos., YIT-Yhtymä Oy; vice chmn. supervisory bd. Oy Nokia Ab, mem. supervisory bd. The Finnish Export Credit Ltd., Helsinki Stock Exchange Cooperative Soc.; vice chmn. Joint Delegation Finnish Banks. Mem. Finnish Bankers' Assn. (vice chmn.), Internat. C. of C. (vice chmn. Finnish sect.), Cen. C. of C. (chmn.). Office: Kansallis-Osake-Pankki, Aleksanterinkatu 42, 00100 Helsinki Finland

LASSLO, ANDREW, medicinal chemist, educator; b. Mukacevo, Czechoslovakia, Aug. 24, 1922; came to U.S., 1946, naturalized, 1951; s. Vojtech Laszlo and Terezie (Herskovicova) L.; m. Wilma Ellen Reynolds, July 9, 1955; 1 child, Millicent Andrea. MS, U. Ill., 1948, PhD, 1952, MLS, 1961. Research chemist organic chems. div. Monsanto Chem. Co., St. Louis, 1952-54; asst. prof. pharmacology, div. basic health scis. Emory U., 1954-60; prof., chmn. dept. medicinal chemistry Coll. Pharmacy, U. Tenn. Health Sci. Ctr., 1960—; cons. Geschickter Fund for Med. Research Inc., 1961-62; dir. postgrad. tng. program sci. librarians USPHS, 1966-72; chmn. edn. com. Drug Info. Assn., 1966-68, bd. dirs., 1968-69; dir. postgrad. tng. program organic medicinal chemistry for chemists FDA, 1971; exec. com. adv. council S.E. Regional Med. Library Program, Nat. Library of Medicine, 1969-71; chmn. regional med. library program com. Med. Library Assn., 1971-72; mem. pres.'s faculty adv. council U. Tenn. System, 1970-72; chmn. energy authority U. Tenn. Center for Health Scis., 1975-77, chmn. council departmental chmn., 1977, 81; chmn. Internat. Symposium on Contemporary Trends in Tng. Pharmacologists, Helsinki, 1975. Producer, moderator (TV and radio series) Health Care Perspectives, 1976-78; editor: Surface Chemistry and Dental Integuments, 1973, Blood Platelet Function and Medicinal Chemistry, 1984; contbr. numerous articles in sci. and profl. jours.; mem. editorial bd. Jour. Medicinal and Pharm. Chemistry, 1961, U. Tenn. Press, 1974-77; composer (work for piano) Synthesis in C Minor, 1968; patentee in field. Served to capt. M.S.C., USAR, 1953-62. Recipient Sigma Xi Research prize, 1949, Honor Scroll Tenn. Inst. Chemists, 1976, Americanism medal DAR, 1976; U. Ill. fellow, 1950-51; Geschickter Fund Med. Research grantee, 1959-65, USPHS Research and Tng. grantee, 1958-64, 66-72, 82—, NSF research grantee, 1964-66, Pfeiffer Research Found. grantee, 1981-87. Fellow AAAS, Am. Assn. Pharm. Scientists, Am. Inst. Chemists (nat. councilor for Tenn. 1969-70), Acad. Pharm. Scis.; mem. ALA (life), Am. Chem. Soc. (sr.), Am. Pharm. Assn., Am. Soc. Pharmacology and Exptl. Therapeutics (chmn. subcom. pre-and postdoctoral tng. 1974-78, exec. com. ednl. and profl. affairs 1974-78), Sigma Xi (pres. elect U. Tenn. Ctr. for Health Sci. chpt. 1975-76, pres. 1976-77), Beta Phi Mu, Phi Lambda Sigma, Rho Chi. Methodist. Home: 5479 Timmons Ave Memphis TN 38119 Office: U Tenn Health Sci Ctr 26 S Dunlap St Memphis TN 38163

LASTIMOSO, VIRGINIA GARCIA, pediatrician, educator; b. Cebu City, Philippines, Mar. 20, 1949; d. Cosme Balbon and Clarita Aldanese (Garcia) L. BS, U. San Carlos, Cebu City, 1965-69; MD, Cebu (City) Inst. Medicine, 1969-72. Diplomate Philippine Pediatric Soc. Resident Cebu Drs. Hosp., 1974-77; fellow pediatric cardiology Philippine Heart Ctr. Asia, Manila, 1977-80, cons., 1980-81; practice medicine specializing in pediatrics Cebu City, 1981-84; pediatrician Alasasi Nat. Clinic, Riyadh, Saudi Arabia, 1984—; asst. prof. Pediatrics Cebu Inst. Medicine, Cebu Drs. Hosp.; cons. Cebu Inst. Medicine, Chong Hua Hosp. Contbr. paper to profl. jour. (Tangco award, 2nd. pl., 1981). Mem. Philippine Pediatric Soc. (bd. dirs. 1981-83, sec. 1983-84 Cebu chpt.), Cebu Med. Soc. Roman Catholic. Home: 497-H P del Rosario Extension, Cebu City 6401, Philippines

LASZLO, HERBERT, journalist, clipping service executive; b. Vienna, Austria, Apr. 16, 1940; s. Otto and Elfriede (von Furtenbach) von L.; m. Christiane Zirm, Oct. 30, 1972; children—Florian, Sonia; m. Rosina Niedrist; children—Angela, Claudia. Dr. Jur., U. Vienna, 1963. Jr. employee Internat. Werbeges (IWG), Vienna, 1958; sales rep. Austria Olivetti, Vienna, 1962-63; cons. Int. Betriebs-Beratungs Ges. (IBB), Vienna, 1963-66; freelance cons., Vienna, 1966-86; chief editor Bohmann Verlag, Vienna, 1975-80; chief exec. Observer Ges. mbH, Vienna, 1980—; propr. Boersen-Kurier, Vienna, 1985—. Mem. Wiener Journalism Club (pres. 1983-87). Club: Lions (pres. 1986-87) (Vienna). Office: Observer Ges GmbH, Lessinggasse 21, A-1020 Vienna Austria

LATH, PRADEEP KAILASH CHANDRA, accountant; b. Bombay, Maharashtra, India, Nov. 15, 1959; s. Kailash Chandra and Gayatri Devi (Bachuka) L.; m. Bela Kyal. B. Commerce, U. Bombay, 1980, M. Commerce, 1982. Cert. cost acct., India. Acct. Sunil Textile Mills, Bombay, 1978-80; jr. acct. Manjeet Transport Co., Bombay, 1980-82; cost acct. Larson & Toubro Ltd., Bombay, 1982-84, Hempel's Marine Paints (SA) WLL, Dammam, Saudi Arabia, 1984—. Mem. Inst. Costs and Works Accts. India. (assoc.). Mem. Bhartiya Janta Party. Hindu. Home: Flat #10, Walchand Apt, Cross Garden Bhayander (West) Maharasthra 401101, India Office: Hempel's Marine Paints, (SA) WLL, PO Box 1077, Dammam 31431, Saudi Arabia

LATHAM, ALICE FRANCES PATTERSON, public health nurse; b. Macon, Ga., Dec. 18, 1916; d. Frank Waters and Ruby (Dews) Patterson; R.N., Charity Hosp. Sch. Nursing, New Orleans, 1937; student George Peabody Coll. Tchrs., 1938-39; BS in Pub. Health Nursing, U. N.C., 1954; M.P.H., Johns Hopkins U., 1966; m. William Joseph Latham, July 21, 1940 (dec. Apr. 1981); children: Jo Alice (Mrs. Phillip Schmidt), Marynette (Mrs. Charles Stephens), Lauruby Cathleen; m. Sidney Dumas Herndon, Apr. 26, 1985. Staff pub. health nurse assigned spl. venereal disease study USPHS, Darien, Ga., 1939-40; county pub. health nurse Bacon County, Alma, Ga., 1940-41; USPHS spl. venereal disease project, Glynn County, Brunswick, 1943-47; county pub. health nurse Glynn County, 1949-51, Ware County, Waycross, 1951-52; pub. health nurse supr. Wayne-Long-Brantley-Liberty Counties, Jesup, 1954-56 dist. dir. pub. health nursing Wayne-Long-Appling-Bacon-Pierce Counties, Jesup, 1956-70; dist. chief nursing S.E. Ga. Health Dist., 1970-79, organizer mobile health services, 1973—. Exec. dir. Wayne County Home Health Agy., 1968-80; exec. dir. Ware County Home Health Agy., 1970-79, mem. exec. com., 1978-85; mem. governing bd. S.E. Ga. Health Systems Agy., 1975-82; mem. governing bd. Health Dept. Home Health Agy., 1978—, also author numerous grant proposals. Bd. dirs. Wayne County Mental Health Assn., 1959, 60, 61, 81, 82, Wayne County Tb Assn., 1958-62; a non-alcoholic organizer Jesup group Alcoholics Anonymous, 1962-63; mem. adv. council Ware Meml. Hosp. Sch. Practical Nursing, Waycross, Ga., 1958; mem. Altar Guild, St. Paul's Episcopal Ch., 1979—, vestrywoman, 1981-82. Recipient recognition Gen. Service Bd., Alcoholics Anonymous, Inc. Fellow Am. Pub. Health Assn.; mem. Am., 8th Dist. (pres. 1954-58, sec. 1958-60, dir. 1960-62, 1st v.p. 1962), Ga. (exec. bd. 1954-58, program rev. continuing edn. com. 1980-86) nurses assns., Ga. Pub. Health Assn. (chmn. nursing sect. 1956-57), Ga. Assn. Dist. Chiefs Nursing (pres. 1976). Contbr. to state nursing manuals, cons. to Home Health Service Agys. Home: Route 6 Box 46 Brunswick GA 31520

LATHAM, EDWARD MICHAEL LOCKS, timber merchant; b. London, Jan. 7, 1930; s. Edward Bryan and Anne Arnot (Duncan) L.; m. Joan Doris Coubrough, Oct. 15, 1955; children: Richard, Philippa, Sarah. MA, Clare Coll., Cambridge, Eng., 1955. Chmn., James Latham PLC, and associated cos., 1973-87. Pres., Sandringham Assn. Royal Warrantholders, 1982-83; mem. council Royal Warrantholders Assn., London. Mem. European Tropical Timber Assn. (pres. 1981-82), Timber Trade Fedn. U.K. (pres. 1984-85), Nat. Council Bldg. Material Producers (mem. council), Assn. Technique Internat. des Bois Tropicaux (pres.). Address: Trebartha Lodge, Launceston, Cornwall PL15 7PD, England

LATHAM, EUNICE STUNKARD, (MRS. JOHN R., educational administrator; b. N.Y.C., Sept. 4, 1923; d. Horace Wesley and Frances Grace (Klank) Stunkard; B.A., Wellesley Coll., 1945; m. John Ralph Latham, June 9, 1962. Acting dir. div. reports and analysis UNRRA, Washington, Germany and France, 1945-47; editor Unitarian Service Com., N.Y.C., 1947-49; copywriter J. Walter Thompson Co., N.Y.C., 1949-56, Lambert & Feasley, Inc., N.Y.C., 1956-62, Fuller & Smith & Ross, N.Y.C., 1962-65; v.p., creative supr. Lennen & Newell, Inc., 1965-70; headmistress Barnard Sch., N.Y.C., 1970-85, 87—, dir. devel., 1985—. Election dist. capt. Bronx County, 1948-54; committeewoman Bronx County, 1950-62; trustee Barnard Sch., Antoinette Fischer Williams Fund, Barnard Sch. Money Purchase Pension Plan, Baldwin Sch., Bryn Mawr, Pa., Profl. Children's Sch. Mem. Nat. Assn. Prins. Schs. for Girls (councilor), Head Mistresses Assn. of East (pres.), Guild Ind. Schs. N.Y.C. (v.p.), Shakespeare Soc., Soc. Mayflower Descs. Home: PO Box 171 White Creek NY 12057 Office: 554 Fort Washington Ave New York NY 10033

LATHAM, JOSEPH AL, JR., lawyer; b. Kinston, N.C., Sept. 16, 1951; s. Joseph Al and Margaret Lee (Tyson) L.; m. Elaine Frances Kramer, Dec. 19, 1981. B.A., Yale U., 1973; J.D., Vanderbilt U., 1976. Bar: Calif. 1976, U.S. Dist. Ct. (cen. dist.) Calif. 1977, U.S. Ct. Appeals (9th cir.) 1977, U.S. Dist. Ct. (no. and so. dists.) Calif. 1978, Ga. 1980, U.S. Dist. Ct. (no. dist.) Ga. 1981, U.S. Ct. Appeals (5th and 11th cirs.) 1981, U.S. Dist. Ct. (mid. dist.) Ga. 1982, D.C. 1984. Assoc. Paul, Hastings, Janofsky & Walker, Los Angeles and Orange County, Calif., 1976-80, Atlanta, 1980-83; chief counsel to bd. mem. NLRB, Washington, 1983-85; staff director, US Commission on Civil Rights, Washington, 1985-86; ptnr., Paul, Hastings, Janofsky & Walker, Orange County, Calif., 1987-88, Los Angeles, 1988—. Editorial asst. Employment Discrimination Law, 2d edit., 1983; author articles in Litigation ABA Jour., Employee Relations Law Jour.; articles editor Vanderbilt Law Rev., 1975-76. Mem. ABA (labor and employment law sect.), Order of Coif. Republican. Episcopalian. Office: Paul Hastings Janofsky & Walker 555 S Flower St Los Angeles CA 90071

LATHAM, ROBERT ALLEN, veterinarian; b. Milton Junction, Wis., Nov. 20, 1922; s. Robert Allen and Lillian Gertrude (Schmidt) L.; B.S., U. Ill., 1950, D.V.M., 1952; m. LaVonne Marlys Hilmer, July 21, 1979; children—Robert Allen, Timothy John, Benjamin Walter, Katherine Diana. Gen. practice vet. medicine, Carmi, Ill., 1952, Mt. Carroll, Ill., 1952-55, Erie, Ill., 1955—. Trustee Erie Library Dist., 1970-76; mem. Erie Elem. Sch. Bd., 1963-66. Served with USNR, 1942-46. Recipient Merit award Coll. Vet. Medicine, U. Ill. Alumni Assn., 1980. Fellow Ill. Acad. Veterinary Medicine (pres. 1971); mem. AVMA, Ill. State (pres. 1976), Mississippi Valley (pres. 1964) vet. med. assns., Republican. Mem. Christian Ch. (Disciples of Christ). Club: Lions. Editor Ill. State Vet. Med. Assn. Directory of 1977, 79. Home: 1002 6th St Erie IL 61250 Office: 810 Main St Erie IL 61250

LATHROP, MITCHELL LEE, lawyer; b. Los Angeles, Dec. 15, 1937; s. Alfred Lee and Barbara (Mitchell) L.; children—Christin Lorraine Newlon, Alexander Mitchell, Timothy Trewin Mitchell. B.Sc., U.S. Naval Acad., 1959; J.D., U. So. Calif., 1966. Bar: D.C., Calif. 1966, U.S. Supreme Ct. 1969, N.Y. 1981. Dep. counsel Los Angeles County, Calif., 1966-68; with firm Brill, Hunt, DeBuys and Burby, Los Angeles, 1968-71; ptnr. firm Macdonald, Halsted & Laybourne, Los Angeles and San Diego, 1971-80; sr. ptnr. Rogers & Wells, N.Y.C., San Diego, 1980-86, Adams, Duque & Hazeltine, Los Angeles, N.Y.C. and San Diego, 1986—; presiding referee Calif. Bar Ct., 1984-86, mem. exec. com., 1981-88; lectr. law Advanced Mgmt. Research Inc., Practicing Law Inst. N.Y., Continuing Edn. of Bar, State Bar Calif., ABA. Western Regional chmn. Met. Opera Nat. Council, 1971-81, v.p. and mem. exec. com., 1971—, now chmn.; trustee Honnold Library at Claremont Colls., 1972-80; bd. dirs. Music Ctr. Opera Assn., Los Angeles, sec., 1974-80; bd. dirs. San Diego Opera Assn., 1980—, v.p., 1985—; bd. dirs. Met. Opera Assn., N.Y.C. Served to capt. JAGC, USNR. Mem. ABA, N.Y. Bar Assn., Fed. Bar Assn., Fed. Bar Council, Calif. Bar Assn., D.C. Bar Assn., San Diego County Bar Assn. (chmn. ethics com. 1980-82, bd. dirs. 1982-85, v.p. 1985), Assn. Bus. Trial Lawyers, Assn. So. Calif. Def. Counsel, Los Angeles Opera Assos. (pres. 1970-72), Soc. Colonial Wars in Calif. (gov. 1970-72), Order St. Lazarus of Jerusalem, Friends of Claremont Coll. (dir. 1975-81, pres. 1978-79), Friends of Huntington Library, Am. Bd. Trial Advocates, Judge Advocates Assn. (dir. Los Angeles chpt. 1974-80, pres. So. Calif. chpt. 1977-78), Internat. Assn. Def. Counsel, Brit. United Services Club (dir. Los Angeles 1973-75), Mensa Internat., Calif. Soc., S.R. (pres. 1977-79), Phi Delta Phi. Republican. Clubs: California (Los Angeles); Valley Hunt (Pasadena, Calif.); Metropolitan (N.Y.C.). Home: 706 Stafford Pl San Diego CA 92107 Office: 401 West A St 23d Floor San Diego CA 92101 also: 551 Madison Ave 11th Floor New York NY 10022

LATHROP, THOMAS ALBERT, educator; b. Los Angeles, Apr. 18, 1941; s. Donald C. and Ethel M. (Challacombe) L.; B.A., UCLA, 1964, M.A., 1965, Ph.D., 1970; m. Constance Ellen Cook, Aug. 30, 1969; 1 dau., Aline. Mem. faculty romance langs. UCLA, 1964-66, U. Wyo., 1966-68, Transylvania U., 1973-76, Lafayette Coll., 1976-80; assoc. prof. Spanish, Portuguese and linguistics, U. Del., Newark, 1980—; editor Juan de la Cuesta Hispanic Monographs, 1978—; co-editor The Cabrilho Press, 1974—; asst. editor Cervantes Bull. of the Cervantes Soc. Am., 1980—. AID grantee, 1968; Nat. Endowment for Humanities grantee, 1976, 81; Gulbenkian Found. grantee, 1973; Del Amo Found. grantee, 1972. Mem. MLA, Cervantes Soc. Am., Internat. Assn. Hispanists, Am. Council on Teaching of Fgn. Lang., Am. Assn. Tchrs. Spanish and Portuguese. Author: The Legend of the Siete Infantes de Lara, 1972; (with F. Jensen) The Syntax of the Old Spanish Subjunctive, 1973; Espanol - Lengua y cultura de hoy, 1974; The Evolution of Spanish, 1980; Gramática histórica espanola, 1984, De Acuerdo! and Tanto Mejor, 1986; (with E. Dias) Portugal: Lingua e Cultura, 1978, others. Home: 270 Indian Rd Newark DE 19711 Office: Dept Lang Univ Del Newark DE 19716

LATIOLAIS, MINNIE FITZGERALD, nurse, hospital administrator; b. Vivian, La., Dec. 26, 1921; d. Thomas Ambrose and Mildred Surita (Nagle) Fitzgerald; m. Joseph C. Latiolais Jr., July 19, 1947; children—Felisa, Diana, Sylvia, Mary, Amelia, Joseph Clifton III. RN, New Orleans, 1943. Orthopedic surg. nurse Ochsner Clinic, New Orleans, 1943-47, asst. dir. nursing, 1947; supr. Lafayette (La.) Gen. Hosp., 1960-64; adminstrv. asst., supr. operating room Abbeville (La.) Gen. Hosp., 1964-68; gen. mgr., neurol. surg. nurse J. Robert Rivet, neurol. surgeon, Lafayette, 1968-78; hosp. cons. assoc. B.J. Landry & Assos., hosps. cons., Lafayette, 1979—; dir. nursing Acadia St. Landry Hosp., Church Point, 1981-82; supr. supplies, processing and distbn. Univ. Med. Ctr., Lafayette, 1982—; bd. dirs. SW La. Rehab. Assn., 1975—, pres., 1979-80; mem. Mid-La. Health Systems Agy., 1977-82, project rev. chmn., 1978-80; vice chmn. Acadica Regional Clearing House, 1984-86; mem. crafts and practical nurse com. Lafayette Regional Vocat.-Tech. Inst., 1980-84, chmn. 1983-84. Mem. Am. Nurses Assn., La. State Nurses Assn., Lafayette Dist. Nurses Assn. (pres. 1967-69). Roman Catholic. Home: 1121 S Washington St Lafayette LA 70501

LATONI, ALFONSO RAFAEL, sociology and political science educator; b. Coral Gables, Fla., Feb. 9, 1958; s. Alfonso and Olga (Rodriguez) L.; m. Raquel Leonor Brailowsky, Jan. 25, 1984; 1 child, Elena Isabel. B.A. in Polit. Sci., U. P.R., 1979; M.A., Georgetown U., 1981. Research asst. Smithsonian Instn., Washington, 1979; asst. fgn. student advisor Georgetown U., Washington, 1980-81; teaching fellow dept. sociology Boston Coll., 1982-83; prof. sociology Interamerican U. P.R., San German, 1983-86, cons. for planning new courses, 1983—, assoc. dean studies, 1985-86; prof. sociology and political sci. U. P.R., Mayaguez, 1986—; asst. chmn. dept. sociology U. P.R., Mayaguez, 1988—. Mem. Arts and Cultural Workshop, Adjuntas, P.R., 1984—; tchr. Labor inst. for Worker Edn., Mayaguez, 1983; asst. organizer United Elec. Radio & Machine Workers of Am., Boston, 1982. U. P.R. grad. presdl. scholar, 1979; Boston Coll. grantee, 1982, 83. Mem. Am. Sociol. Assn., N.Y. Acad. Scis., Caribbean Studies Assn., Union Radical Polit. Econs., Phi Delta Kappa. Avocations: camping; hiking; reading; gardening; woodwork. Home: Urb Valle Verde C-13 San German PR 00753 Office: U PR Mayaguez Campus Dept Social Sci Mayaguez PR 00709

LATORTUE, GERARD RENE, minister foreign affairs Republic of Haiti; b. Haiti, June 19, 1934; s. Rene A. and Francoise A. (Dupuy) L.; LL.B., U. Haiti, 1955, LL.M., 1956; Degree in Econ. Devel., U. Paris (France), 1960; m. Marlene Zephirin, Sept. 3, 1966; children: Gaielle, Stephanie, Alexia. Economist, Labor Dept., Port-au-Prince, Haiti, 1960-62; prof. econs. U. Haiti, Port-au-Prince, 1961-63; co-founder, co-dir. Institut de Hautes Etudes Commerciales et Economiques, Port-au-Prince, 1961-63; prof. econs. Inter-Am. U. of P.R., San German, 1963-72, chmn. dept. econs. and bus. adminstrn., 1968-72; project mgr. assistance to small-scale industries in Togo, UN Indsl. Devel. Orgn., 1972-74, chief tech. adviser, 1974-77, chief tech. adviser, Ivory Coast, 1977-82, head indsl. planning sect., indsl. ops. div., Vienna, 1982-84; head negotiations br. Policy Coordination div. UNIDO, Vienna, 1984-86; dir. Systems of Consultations div., UN Indsl. Devel. Orgn., from 1986-88, dir. project rev. and appraisal div. UN Indsl. Devel. Orgn., Vienna, 1988—; minister worship, Republic of Haiti, 1987, minister fgn. affairs, 1987-88, minister internat. cooperation and fgn. affairs, 1988. Decorated Ordre Nat. Honneur et Méite, Grand Croix (Haiti), Ordre de l'Etoile Brillante, Grand Cordon (Taiwan, Republic of China), officer Nat. Labor Order (Haiti). Mem. Am. Econ. Assn., Soc. for Internat. Devel., Am. Mktg. Assn., Nat. Planning Assn. Club: Lions. Contbr. chpts. to books. Home: Scheibelreitergasse 8/3, 1190 Vienna Austria Office: Ministry of Fgn Affairs, Port-au-Prince Haiti

LATTA, DIANA LENNOX, interior designer; b. Lahaina, Maui, Hawaii, Aug. 5, 1936; d. D. Stewart and Jean Marjorie (Anderson) Lennox; grad. the Bishop's Sch., La Jolla, Calif., 1954; student U. Wash., 1954-56; m. Arthur McKee Latta, Jan. 26, 1957 (dec.); children—Mary-Stewart, Marion Mckee (Mrs. Marshall V. Davidson). Dir., Vero Beach (Fla.) br. of Wellington Hall, Ltd., Thomasville, N.C., 1970-72; asst. to chief designer Rablen-West Interiors, Vero Beach, 1972-75; design and adminstrv. asst. to pres. Design Studio Archtl. & Interior Design Concepts, Inc., Vero Beach, 1975-82; owner, designer The Designery, Vero Beach, 1983-87; designer's asst. Frank J. Lincoln Interiors, Inc., Locust Valley and Vero Beach, N.Y., 1987—. Mem. Indian River Meml. Hosp. Women's Aux., Vero Beach, 1957-70, chmn. Charity Ball, 1960, v.p., 1962-64; leading actress in Vero Beach Theatre Guild prodns.: The Laughmaker, 1964, Oklahoma, 1966; model for Holly Fashion Show, Vero Beach, 1962-69; mem. adv. bd. Indian River County 4-H Horsemaster's Club, 1973-76; chmn. fund raising, pub. relations com. McKee Jungle Gardens Preservation Soc., Inc., 1st v.p., chmn. fund raising com., bd. dirs., Vero Beach Mut. Concert Assn., 1973-76, chmn. hospitality com. 1974; bd. dirs. Vero Beach Theatre Guild, 1964. Mem. Internat. Platform Assn., Republican Women Aware. Kappa Kappa Gamma. Republican. Episcopalian. Club: Riomar Bay Yacht (club tennis champion 1964, 66, chmn. tennis com. 1964-66). Home: 555 Honeysuckle Ln Vero Beach FL 32963 Office: 6160 North A1A Vero Beach FL 32963

LATTA, JEAN CAROLYN, financial analyst, chemist; b. Chgo., Oct. 11, 1943; d. John Oscar and Katherine Helen (Schnitzer) Latta. BS in Chemistry, U. Ill., 1966; MS in Chemistry, IIT, 1970; MBA, U. Chgo., 1976. chemist, Gillette Co., Chgo., 1966-67; asst. research chemist, 1969-73; product designer Bunker-Ramo Corp., Chgo., 1973-75; staff exec. George S. May Internat. Co., Park Ridge, Ill., 1977; controller, ind. cons. Bayou City Service Co., Houston, 1978; staff acct. Chemtrust Industries, Franklin Park, Ill., 1979; fin. analyst U. Chgo., 1979-84; sr. price/cost analyst Northrop Corp., Pico Rivera, Calif., 1984-85. Patentee in field. Democrat. Roman Catholic. Home: 701 W Imperial Hwy Apt 1105 La Habra CA 90631

LATTIMER, JOHN KINGSLEY, physician, historian, educator; b. Mt. Clemens, Mich., Oct. 14, 1914; s. Eugene and Gladys Soulier (Lenfestey) L.; A.B., Columbia U., 1935, M.D., 1938, Sc.D., 1943; postgrad. Balliol Coll., Oxford (Eng.) U., 1944, Med. Field Service Sch., Paris, 1945; m. Jamie Elizabeth Hill, Jan. 1948; children—Evan, Jon, Gary. Surg. intern Meth.-Episcopal Hosp., N.Y.C., 1938-40; urol. resident Squier Urol. Clinic, Presbyn. Hosp., N.Y.C., 1940-43, dir. Squier Urol. Clinic, 1955-80, dir. urol. service Presbyn. Hosp., 1955-80, also dir. urology Sch. Nursing; staff asst., instr. urology Columbia U. Coll. Physicians and Surgeons, 1940-53, asst. prof. clin. urology, 1953-55, prof. urology, chmn. dept. urology, 1955—; chief urology Babies Hosp., Vanderbilt Clinic, Frances Delafield Hosp., N.Y.C., 1955; cons. urology VA, N.Y.C., 1947-70, USPHS Hosp., S.I., N.Y., Meth. Hosp., Bklyn., Englewood (N.J.), Yonkers (N.Y.) gen. hosps., Harlem, Roosevelt, St. Lukes hosps. (all N.Y.C.); mem. com. surgery in Tb, genito-urinary Tb, VA; cons. to com. on therapy Nat. Tb Assn.; mem. expert adv. panel biology human reprodn. WHO; Am. Urol. Assn. rep. to NRC-Nat. Acad. Scis.; mem. tng. grants com. NIH, 1968-72. Trustee Presbyn. Hosp., 1974-76; cons. Pres.'s Commn. to Examine CIA, 1975, Select Com. on Assassinations, U.S. Ho. of Reps., 1978; trustee Lincoln Group, Springfield, Ill.; lectr. Fords Theater for Nat. Park Service, Washington. Mem. vis. com. arms and armour dept. Met. Mus. Art, N.Y.C., 1981—; bd. dirs. Ft. Ticonderoga Mus. Assn., 1980—. Served from 1st lt. to maj., M.C., AUS, 1943-46; chief urol. sect. gen. hosps. Recipient Joseph Mather Smith prize for research kidney disease Columbia U., 1943; 1st prize for clin. research Am. Urol. Assn., 1950, 60; prize for research on kidney Tb AMA, 1953; honor award for meritorious work in field of Tb, Am. Acad. Tb Physicians, also prizes for sci. exhibits; gold medal alumni assn. Coll. Physicians and Surgeons, 1971; Hugh Young medal for outstanding work in infectious diseases, 1973; Belfield medal Chgo. Urol. Soc.; Summer Meml. lectr. U. Oreg. Med. Sch., 1968; Burpeau medal N.J. Acad. Medicine; Richard Chute lectr., Boston U., 1973; Stoneburner lectr. Med. Coll. Va., 1973; Mayo Clinic vis. prof., 1976; Gold medal Edward Henderson award Am. Geriatrics Soc., 1978; Great medal City of Paris, 1979; Foss gold medal Geisinger Clinic, U. Pa., Hershey, 1979; Ramon Guiteras medal, 1980; Urology medal Am. Acad. Pediatrics, 1987; First urology award Nat. Kidney Found., N.Y.C., 1987; diplomate Am. Bd. Urology. Fellow ACS (chmn. adv. com. urology 1962-64, gov. 1966-73, com. on undergrad. tng. 1967-73, com. to study size and composition of bd. govs., chmn. nominating com. 1977), AMA, Am. Acad. Pediatrics (chmn. com. pediatric urology, pres. sect. urology 1973-75); mem. N.Y. Acad. Medicine (chmn. genito-urinary surg. sect. 1956-57, trustee 1980-86, sr. v.p. 1985-86), Am. Assn. Genito-Urinary Surgeons (pres. 1981-82), Am. Urol. Assn. (pres. 1975-76; chmn. com. on pediatric urology, pres. N.Y. sect. 1966, exec. com. 1967-78, com. on surgery, chmn. rev. and long range planning com. 1980-81, editorial bd. Jour. Urology 1965-69, chmn. com. to gather info. about urology; chmn. coordinating council for urology), Alumni Assn. Presbyn. Hosp. (pres. N.Y.C. 1967-68), Am. Thoracic Soc., AAUP, N.Y. State Pediatrics Soc., Soc. Univ. Urologists (pres. 1969-70), Nat. Inst. Social Scis., St. Nicholas Soc., Assn. Mil. Surgeons, Harvey Soc., Nat. Tb Assn., N.Y., New York County med. socs., Soc. Pediatric Urology (pres. 1961-62), Brit. Assn. Urol. Surgeons (corr. mem.), N.Y. Soc. Surgeons, N.Y. Soc. Professions, Internat. Société d'Urology (pres. 1973-79), Phila. Coll. Physicians and Surgeons (hon.), Assn. Pediatric Urology (pres. 1961), AAAS, Am. Assn. Clin. Urologists, Assn. Am. Med. Colls., Clin. Soc. Genito-Urinary Surgeons (pres. 1983-84), N.Y. Acad. Scis., Assn. Mil. Surgeons, Assn. Mil. Historians (Nuremburg Trials Unit: 1945-46), Soc. War 1812, Mil. Order Fgn. Wars U.S., Order of Founders and Patriots, Arms and Armour Soc., SAR, Soc. Colonial Wars, Civil War Roundtable N.Y. and Washington, Manuscript Soc., Revolutionary War Round Table of N.Y., Am. Legion, 82d Airborne Div. Assn., 101st Airborne Div. Assn., Res. Officers Assn., Am. Order French Croix de Guerre. Club: Met. Contbr. numerous articles on urology and history to various publs., also chpts. in books; contbr. Ency. Brit.; guest editor New Eng. Jour. Medicine, 1965; researcher, writer, historian, speaker on assassinations of Pres. Lincoln and Kennedy. Office: Harkness Pavilion 180 Ft Washington Ave New York NY 10032

LAU, BRIAN KIMKWONG, management consultant; b. Hong Kong, May 3, 1934; s. Yuk Fai and Choi Yung (Mar) L.; m. Cathy Margaret Loudon, June 8, 1963; children—Wendy, Debbie, Vivien. B.Commerce in Acctg., U. New S. Wales, Australia, 1961. Chief acct., sec. Cowells & Hustlers subs. Reid Murray, Sydney, Australia, 1960-62; prin. King & Lau, Brian K. Lau & Assocs., C.P.A.s, Sydney, 1962-67; mgr. acctg. and fin., sec. Esso Standard (Hong Kong) Ltd., 1967-69; mgr. dir. BIC Mgmt. Cons. Ltd., Hong Kong; dir. cos. Decorated Knight Order St. John of Jerusalem (officer-in-charge Commandary Hong Kong); knight hopitalier Grand Priory of Malta. Fellow Hong Kong Soc. Accts.; mem. Australian Soc. Accts. (sr.), Hong Kong Mgmt. Assn., Sales and Mktg. Execs. Club: World Trade Centre (Hong Kong). Home: G/F Estella Ct, 70B Macdonnell Rd, Hong Kong Hong Kong Office: 48 Hennessy Rd, Suite 1403, Shanghai Ind Invt Bldg, Hong Kong Hong Kong

LAU, ELIZABETH MARTINEZ, sales, public relations and marketing executive, researcher; b. Bayamo, Oriente, Cuba, Nov. 17, 1951; came to U.S., 1967; d. Jose Ramon and Roselvi Kathy (Lau) M.; m. Jose Ramon Argiz, Aug. 9, 1952 (div.); m. Justo Ernesto Montero, Nov. 7, 1950. Student Miami Dade Jr. Coll., 1973-75, U. Miami, 1985—. Exec. sec. Union Fin., Miami, Fla., 1972-75; export sales mgr. Inter City Auto Stores, Miami, 1975-80; salesman A.G.E. Paper, Miami, 1982—. Mem. Nat. Assn. Female Execs., Pacific Inst. Alumni Assn. Republican. Roman Catholic.

LAU, HA VAN, diplomat; b. Binh Trithien, Socialist Republic of Vietnam, Dec. 4, 1918; married; 3 children. Served to col. Popular Army of Vietnam, 1945-54; del. to Internat. conf. on Indochina Geneva, 1954; head mission to execute terms of Geneva Accord HaNoi, 1954-73; del. to Internat. conf. on Vietnam Paris, 1968-70; asst. to minister of fgn. affairs Democratic Republic of Vietnam, 1973; ambassador to Cuba 1974-78; permanent representative to UN N.Y.C., 1978-82; vice minister of A.E. Socialist Republic of Vietnam, 1982-84; ambassador to France Paris, 1984—. Office: Embassy of Socialist Republic of Vietnam, 62 Boileau, 75016 Paris France

LAU, MICHAEL MAN-FAI, assistant principal; b. Hong Kong, Feb. 11, 1953; s. Yam Lau and Leen Ho. B.Sc., U. Toronto, 1978; cert. in edn., U. Hong Kong, 1980, adv. diploma in edn., 1983, M.Edn., 1984. Advanced from tchr. to dean of studies, PHC Wing Kwong Coll., Kowloon, Hong Kong, 1978-85; mem. working party on ednl. TV, Edn. Dept., Hong Kong, 1981-82. Head evang. dept. Mei Foo Sun Chuen Alliance Ch., Kowloon, 1979-80, head Christian edn. dept., 1980-82, vice-chmn. bd. deacons, 1983—. Mem. Hong Kong Assn. Sci. and Maths. Edn. Home: 55 4th St, Sect M, Fairview Park, Yuen Long, NT Hong Kong Office: PHC Wing Kwong Coll, 155 Lung Cheung Rd, Kowloon Hong Kong

LAU, TONY KAN-WOON, pilot; b. Hong Kong, Jan. 16, 1944; s. Wai and Pui-Yiu (Leung) L.; m. Mary Wai-Ling Wong, Dec. 18, 1971; children: Carrie Lau Ka-Lai, Christina Lau Ka-Yun. Student, Wah Yan Coll., 1957-62, Hong Kong Tech. Coll., 1962-63. Sr. harbor pilot Hong Kong Pilot's Assn., Ltd., 1971—; adv. mem. Pilotage Adv. Com., Hong Kong Govt., 1979—; mng. dir. United Pilotage Service Investment Ltd., 1986—, Pilot Transp. Ltd., Hong Kong, 1986—. Organizer Internat. Maritime Pilots' Congress of Internat. Maritime Pilots Assn. Mem. Royal Inst. Navigation, Nautical Inst. Office: Hong Kong Pilots Assn Ltd, 122-124 Connaught Rd, Harbour Commercial Bldg 11th Floor, Central Hong Kong Hong Kong

LAUB, GEORGE COOLEY, lawyer; b. Easton, Pa., Jan. 16, 1912; s. Herbert F. and Hannah A. (Cooley) L.; m. Elizabeth Traill Green, Jan. 19, 1939 (dec. Jan. 1986); m. Josephine Ely Greer, June 6, 1987. A.B., Lafayette Coll., 1933, LL.D. (hon.), 1983; LL.B., U. Pa., 1936. Bar: Pa. 1936, since practiced in Easton; legal adviser, mem. men's adv. bd. Easton Home for Aged Women, 1940-80; past dir. City of Easton Authority, Easton Nat. Bank and Trust Co.; mem. Northampton County Bd. Benchers, 1970-72. Bd. dirs. Community Chest, 1943-45, 49-52, drive chmn., 1949, pres., 1951; life trustee Lafayette Coll., 1958—, chmn. wills and trusts program, 1963-76, sec. bd., 1959-82, counsel, 1965-87. Served to 1st lt., Judge Adv. Gen.'s Dept., AUS, 1945-47. Mem. ABA, Pa. Bar Assn., (exec. com. 1952-54), Northampton County Bar Assn. (pres. 1954-55), SAR, Northampton County Hist. Soc., Am. Judicature Soc., Nat. Assn. Coll. and U. Attys., Trout Unltd., Nat. Skeet Shooting Assn., Phi Delta Theta. Presbyterian (pres. bd. trustees 1957-59). Clubs: Phila. Aviation Country, Sunnybrook Golf; Pomfret; Skytop (Pa.); Easton Anglers; The Milk Pond. Home: 12 Pastern Ln Whitpain Farm Blue Bell PA 19422 Office: Laub Seidel Cohen & Hof Easton Dollar Savs and Trust Co Bldg 8 Centre Sq Easton PA 18042

LAUBACH, GERALD DAVID, pharmaceutical company executive; b. Bethlehem, Pa., Jan. 21, 1926; s. Steward Lovine and Bertha (Rader) L.; m. Winifred Isabel Taylor, Oct. 3, 1953 (dec. Oct. 1979); children: Stephen, Andrea, Hilary. Student, Mt. St. Mary's Coll., 1944-45; A.B. in Chemistry, U. Pa., 1947; Ph.D., Mass. Inst. Tech., 1950; D.Sc. (hon.), Hofstra U., 1979; DL (hon., Conn. Coll., 1986. With Pfizer, Inc., Groton, Conn., 1950—, mgr. medicinal products research, 1958-61, dir. dept. medicinal chemistry, 1961-63, group dir. medicinal research, 1963-64, v.p. medicinal products research and devel., 1964-68, dir., 1968—, mem. exec. com., 1969—, pres. pharm. ops., 1969-71; exec. v.p. Pfizer Inc., Groton, Conn., 1971-72, pres., 1972—; dir. CIGNA Corp. of Phila., PMA, Millipore Corp., Bedford, Mass. Contbr. articles to tech jours. Mem. Pres.'s Commn. on Indsl. Competitiveness; mem. council on health care tech. Inst. Medicine, 1987—; mem. council Rockefeller U. Served with USNR, 1944-46. Mem. Am. Chem. Soc., AAAS, Soc. Chem. Industry, Am. Mgmt. Assn., N.A.M. (dir.), N.Y. Acad. Scis., Nat. Acad. Engrs., Chemists Club N.Y. (dir. 1968—, exec. com. 1969—), Bus. Higher Edn. Forum, Food and Drug Law Inst. (bd. dirs.). Home: Lyme CT 06371 Office: Pfizer Inc 235 E 42nd St New York NY 10017

LAUBAUGH, FREDERICK, association executive, consultant; b. Wilkes-Barre, Pa., Feb. 24, 1926; s. Andrew and Mary (Schumacher) L.; widowed; 1 child, Sarah Jane Rommel (dec.). Student comml. art, Murray Art Sch., Wilkes-Barre; student, U. Buffalo Sch. Bus., Niagara U. Sch. Bus. With Nat. Carbon Co., Nat. Lead Co., Bell Aircraft Co., Niagara Falls, N.Y., 1952-56; pres. Lubri-Gas Mideastern, Niagara Falls, N.Y., 1956-59; pres., chmn. Lloyds Labs. of Am., Inc., Niagara Falls, N.Y., 1958-62; Mid-Atlantic sales mgr. Cling-Surface Co., Buffalo, 1962—; multi-mfrs. rep., prin. Laubaugh Assocs., Niagara Falls, N.Y., 1976—; chmn. Prog. Intelligent Grouping, Niagara Falls, N.Y., 1980—; writer, journalist, columnist (Insight) Media Feeder, 1987—; cons., dir. pub. relations Native Am. Ctr., Niagara Falls, 1980-84; cons. Niagara Falls Family YMCA; mktg. exec. La Maison Descartes of Montreal, 1983—; publicist, seminar coordinator; dir. mktg. Perfetti Assocs. Ltd., 1987—. Weekly columnist on pub. affairs and govt., 1985-86. Cons. Unity Park Housing Complex, Niagara Falls, 1985—, Area I Minority Devel., 1986; active Rep. Presdl. Task Force, Washington, 1982—; chmn. Rep. Party dist. 9, Niagara Falls, 1984-85, dist. 2, 1986—; 2d v.p. Niagara Falls Philharm. Orch., 1983—; bd. dirs. Main St. Bus. Assn., 1985—; mem. Niagara Falls Auxiliary Police. Served with USN, 1943-45, 1951. Recipient cert. of service recognition United Way of Niagara Falls, 1983, Human Rights Commn., 1983-84, Nat. Rep. Congl. Com., 1982-85. Mem. Niagara Falls C. of C., Internat. Mktg. Assn., Internat. Platform Assn. Republican. Mormon. Lodges: Kiwanis, Masons. Office: PO Drawer 260 Niagara Falls NY 14304

LAUBE, ROGER GUSTAV, financial consultant; b. Chgo., Aug. 11, 1921; s. William C. and Elsie (Drews) L.; m. Irene Mary Chadbourne, Mar. 30, 1946; children: David Roger, Philip Russell, Steven Richard. BA, Roosevelt U., 1942; student, John Marshall Law Sch., 1942, 48-50; LLB, Nat. Trust Sch., Northwestern U., 1960; cert., Trust Div., Pacific Coast Grad. Sch. Banking, U. Wash., 1962-64. Cert. fin. cons., registered rep. With Chgo. Title & Trust Co., Chgo., 1938-42, 48-50, Nat. Bank Alaska, Anchorage, 1950-72; mgr. mortgage dept. Nat. Bank Alaska, 1950-56, v.p., trust officer, mgr. trust dept., 1956-72; v.p., trust officer, mktg. dir., mgr. estate and fin. planning div. Bishop Trust Co., Ltd., Honolulu, 1972-82; instr. estate planning U. Hawaii, Honolulu, 1978-82; exec. v.p. Design Capital Planning Group, Inc., Tucson, 1982-83; pres., chief exec. officer Advanced Capital Devel., Inc. of Ariz., Tucson, 1983-85, Prescott, 1985—; registered investment advisor, mng. exec. Integrated Resources Equity Corp., 1983—; Pres. Anchorage Estate Planning Council, 1960-62, Charter mem., 1960-72; Charter mem. Hawaii Estate Planning Council, 1972-82, V.P., 1979, PRES., 1980, bd. dirs., 1981-82; mem. Prescott Estate Planning Council, 1986—, pres. 1988. Pres. Anchorage Community Chorus, 1946-72, pres., 1950-72; mem. Anchorage camp Gideons Internat., 1946-72, Honolulu camp, 1972-82, mem. Central camp, Tucson, 1982-85, Prescott, 1985—; mem. adv. bd. Faith Hosp., Glennallen, Alaska, 1960—, Central Alaska Mission of Far Eastern Gospel Crusade, 1960—; sec.-treas. Alaska Bapt. Found., 1955-72; bd. dirs. Bapt. Found. of Ariz., 1985—, mem. investment com.; pres. Sabinovista Townhouse Assn., 1983-85; bd. dirs. Alaska Festival Music, 1960-72, Anchorage Symphony, 1965-72; bd. advisers Salvation Army, Alaska, 1961-72, chmn., Anchorage, 1969-72, bd. advisers, Honolulu, 1972-82, chmn. bd. advisers, 1976-78. Served to 1st lt., JAGD U.S. Army, 1942-48; asst. staff judge adv. Alaskan Command, 1946-48. Recipient Others award Salvation Army, 1972. Mem. Am. Inst. Banking (instr. trust div. 1961-72), Am. Bankers Assn. (Legis. council trust div. 1960-72), Nat. Assn. LIfe Underwriters (nat com. for No. Ariz.), Prescott LIfe Underwriters Assn., Anchorage C. OF C. (mem. awards com. 1969-71), Internat. Assn. Fin. Planners (cert. investment advisor, Anchorage chpt. 1969-72, treas., exec. com. Honolulu chpt. 1972-82, Ariz. chpt. 1982—, Del. to World Congress Australia and New Zealand 1987), Am. Assn. Handbell Ringers. Baptist (exec. com. Alaska conv. 1959-61, dir. music Alaska 1950-72, Hawaii 1972-82, Tucson 1982-85, 1st So. Bapt. Ch. Prescott Valley, 1985—, chmn. bd. trustees Hawaii 1972-81, Prescott Valley 1986—, worship leader Waikiki Ch. 1979-82). Home: 649 Filaree Dr Prescott AZ 86301 Office: Sun Pine Exec Ctr 915 E Gurley Suite 303 Prescott AZ 86301

LAUBER, MIGNON DIANE, food processing company executive; b. Detroit, Dec. 21; d. Charles Edmond and Maud Lillian (Foster) Donaker; student Kelsey Jenny U., 1958, Brigham Young U., 1959; m. Richard Brian Lauber, Sept. 13, 1963; 1 dau., Leslie Viane (dec.). Owner, operator Alaska World Travel, Ketchikan, 1964-67; founder, owner, pres. Oosick Soup Co., Juneau, Alaska, 1969—. Treas., Pioneer Alaska Lobbyists Soc., Juneau, 1977—. Mem. Bus. and Profl. Women, Alaska C. of C. Libertarian. Club: Washington Athletic. Author: Down at the Water Works with Jesus, 1982; Failure Through Prayer, 1983. Home: 321 Highland Dr Juneau AK 99801 Office: PO Box 1625 Juneau AK 99802

LAUBER, VOLKMAR, political science educator; b. Wels, Austria, Dec. 8, 1944; s. Josef and Gertrud (Ruby) L.; divorced; 1 child, Alexander. LLD, U. Vienna, Austria, 1968; LLM, Harvard U., 1970; D in Polit. Sci., U. N.C., Chapel Hill, 1977. Univ. asst. U. Graz Law Sch., Austria, 1971; vis. lectr. U. South Fla., Tampa, 1976-77; asst. prof. W.Va. Wesleyan coll., Buckhannon, 1977-79, 80-82, Johns Hopkins U., Bologna, Italy, 1979-80; prof. polit. sci. U. Salzburg, Austria, 1982—. Author: The Political Economy of France, 1983; contbr. articles to profl. jours. Home: Joh Filzerstrasse 26/56, 5020 Salzburg Austria Office: Inst f Politikwissenschaft, Mühlbacherhofweg 6, 5020 Salzburg Austria

LAUBSCHER, J. M. STEYN, mechanical engineer, consultant; b. Cape Town, Republic South Africa, May 30, 1943; s. Pieter Johannes and Susanna (Steyn) L.; m. Elzaby Helene Wessels, Apr. 8, 1967; children: Adrienne, Pieter, Steyn. BS in Engring. cum laude, U. Pretoria, Republic of South Africa, 1964. Registered profl. engr. Design. engr. Watson Edwards, Inc., Pretoria, 1965-68; sr. engr. Watson Edwards, Inc., Cape Town, 1969-73, dir., 1973-83, mng. dir., 1984—; chmn. WEVS Projects, Johannesburg, Republic South Africa, 1986—; bd. dirs. WEVO Pty Ltd, Johannesburg, 1974—, WEVO Investments, Johannesburg, 1979—. Chmn. sch. com., Gordon's Bay, Cape, 1980-83. Mem. South African Inst. Mech. Engrs., South African Assn. Consulting Engrs. (pres. 1988—). Club: Strand golf (Cape Town). Office: Watson Edwards Inc, 35 Wale St, Cape Town 8000, Republic of South Africa

LAUDE, RENÉ, neuropsychiatrist, artist; b. La Bassee, France, Feb. 25, 1936; s. Robert and Denise (Crescent) L.; m. Michele Maurizi, July 7, 1961; children: Frederic, Olivier, Thorina Rose. MD, Med. Univ. Lille, France, 1961. Now practicing medicine specializing in neuropsychiatry Villepreux, France. Specialist in electronic and cosmologic art; paintings exhibited in one man showin Paris, also Lausanne (Switzerland) Mus., Ecole Superieur Design Industriel show, Paris, 1988; group shows Centre de Congres du Que., 1980-81, Premio Lubian Italie, 1980, Coliseum de N.Y., 1982, 83, 84, Centre Chanot, Clamart, France, 1983, Isetan Mus. Art, 1985, Laforet Mus., 1985, Düsseldorf, Republic of Germany, 1986, 87, 88, Sydney (Australia) Art Fair, 1988, Mus. Aix-en-Provence, France, 1989, many others; included in pvt. collections, France, Can., Fed. Republic Germany, Australia. Mem. Psychiat. Inst. North France (dir. 1968-77). Avocation: bicycling. Home: 1 rue de l'Echiquier, Jovars-Pontchartrain, Paris France Office: 9 rue Henri Dunant, 78450 Villepreux France

LAUDER, RONALD STEPHEN, private investment manager; b. N.Y.C., Feb. 26, 1944; s. Joseph H. and Estee (Josephine) (Lauder) Mentzer; m. Jo Carol Knopf, July 8, 1967; children: Aerin Rebecca, Jane Alexandra. Degree in French lit., U. Paris, 1964; B.S. in Internat. Bus., U. Pa., 1965. With Estee Lauder, S.A., Paris, 1967-83; sales promotion dir. Estee Lauder, Inc., N.Y.C., 1968-69, v.p. sales promotion, 1969-72; exec. v.p. Clinique, 1972-75, gen. mgr., 1972-75, exec. v.p. internat., 1975-78, exec. v.p., 1978-80; chmn. Estee Lauder Internat., Inc., 1980-83; dep. asst. Sec. of Def., Washington, 1983-85; dir. Estee Lauder Inc.; ambassador to Austria Vienna, 1986-87; pvt. investment mgr. N.Y.C., 1987—. Author: Fighting Violent Crime in America, 1985. Mem. N.Y. State Econ. Devel. Bd., 1972-78; fin. chmn. N.Y. State Republican Com., 1979-82; chmn. 500 Club of N.Y. Rep. Com., 1979-83; trustee Mus. Modern Art, 1975—, Mt. Sinai Med. Ctr., 1981—; mem. vis. com., chmn.'s council Met. Mus. Art. Recipient Ordre De Merit, France, 1985, Disting. Pub. Service medal award Dept. Def., 1986; decorated Great Cross of the Order of Aeronautical Merit with White Ribbon, Spain, 1985. Office: 660 Madison Ave Suite 850 New York NY 10021 •

LAUDER, VALARIE ANNE, editor, educator; b. Detroit, Mar. 1, 1926; d. William J. and Murza Valerie (Mann) L.; AA, Stephens Coll., Columbia, Mo., 1944; postgrad. Northwestern U. With Chgo. Daily News, 1944-52, columnist, 1946-52; lectr. Sch. Assembly Service, also Redpath lectr., 1952-55; freelance writer for mags. and newspapers including N.Y. Times, Yankee, Ford Times, Travel & Leisure, Am. Heritage, 1955—; editor-in-chief Scholastic Roto, 1962; editor U. N.C., 1975-80, lectr. Sch. Journalism, 1980—; nat. chmn. student writing project Ford Times, 1981-86; pub. relations dir. Am. Dance Festival, Duke U., 1982-83, lectr., instr. continuing edn. program, 1984; contbg. editor So. Accents mag., 1982-86. Mem. nat. fund raising bd. Kennedy Ctr., 1962-63. Recipient 1st place award Nat. Fedn. Press Women, 1981; 1st place awards Ill. Women's Press Assn., 1950, 1951. Mem. Pub. Relations Soc. Am. (treas. N.C. chpt. 1982, sec. 1983, v.p. 1984, pres.-elect 1985, pres. 1986, chmn. council of past pres., chmn. 25th Ann. event 1987, del. Nat. Assembly 1988—), Women in Communications (v.p. matrix N.C. Triangle chpt. 1984-85), N.C. Pub. Relations Hall of Fame Com., DAR, Soc. Mayflower Desc. (dir. Ill. Soc. 1946-52), Chapel Hill Hist. Soc. (dir. 1981-85, chmn. publs. com. 1980-85), Chapel Hill Preservation Soc. Clubs: N.C. Press (2d v.p. 1983-85, pres. 1985, 1st pl. awards 1981, 82, 83, 84), Univ. Woman's, Women's Press N.C. (3d v.p. 1981-83, 1st pl. awards 1981, 82). Office: U NC Sch Journalism CB 3365 Chapel Hill NC 27599-3365

LAUDERDALE, CLINT ARLEN, diplomat; b. Ackerly, Tex., Sept. 14, 1932; s. Dee Witt and Lenora (Woodell) L.; m. Maria Theresia Huege, Apr. 24, 1954; children: Michael, Stephen, Teresa, Regina. B.A., U. Calif.-Berkeley, 1957; postgrad., U. Mich., 1970-71. Second sec. U.S. Embassy, Brussels, Belgium, 1967-70; adminstrv. officer Dept. State, Washington, 1971-72, dir. recruitment, 1979-80, dep. asst. sec. for personnel, 1980-84, ambassador to Guyana, 1984-87, fgn. service insp., 1987—; adminstrv. officer U.S. Embassy, Bonn, Fed. Republic of Germany, 1972-75; adminstrv. counselor Madrid, 1975-79. Bd. dirs. Brit.-Am. Hosp., Madrid, 1975-78; gen. mgr. U.S.A. Support Activity, Bonn, 1976; mem. Chevy Chase (Md.) Citizens Assn., 1980-82. Served with U.S. Army, 1951-54. Recipient Superior Honor Dept. State, 1978. Mem. Am. Fgn. Service Assn. (1967), Maitland-Lauderdale Soc. Home: 4501 Connecticut Ave Apt 809 Washington DC 20008 Office: Dept of State 2401 E St NW Washington DC 20520 *

LAUDONE, ANITA H., lawyer, business executive; b. 1948; m. Colin E. Harley; children: Clayton T. Harley, Victoria Spencer Harley. B.A., Conn. Coll., 1970; J.D., Columbia U., 1973. Admitted to N.Y. State bar, 1974, practiced in N.Y.C., 1973-79; asst. sec. Phelps Dodge Corp., N.Y.C., 1979-80, sec., 1980-84, v.p., sec., 1984-85. Editor Columbia Law Rev., 1973. Mem. Phi Beta Kappa. Address: 510 North St Greenwich CT 06830

LAUER, GEORGE, environmental consultant; b. Vienna, Austria, Feb. 18, 1936; came to U.S., 1943; s. Otto and Alice (Denton) L.; m. Sandra Joy Comp, Oct. 1, 1983; children by previous marriage—Julie Anne, Robert L. BS, UCLA, 1961; PhD, Calif. Inst. Tech., 1967. Mem. tech. staff N.Am. Aviation, Canoga Park, Calif., 1966-69; mgr. Rockwell Internat., Thousand Oaks, Calif., 1969-75; div. mgr. ERT, Inc., Westlake Village, Calif., 1975-78; dir. Rockwell Internat., Newbury Park, Calif., 1978-85; dir. Tetra-Tech Inc., Pasadena, Calif., 1985-86; pres. Environ. Monitoring and Services, Inc., 1986-88; sr. cons. Atlantic Richfield, Inc., Los Angeles, 1988—. Contbr. articles to profl. jours.; patentee in field. Served with U.S. Army, 1957-59. Fellow Assn. for Computing Machinery; mem. Am. Chem. Soc., Air Pollution Control Assn. Republican. Jewish. Home: 6009 Maury Ave Woodland Hills CA 91367 Office: Atlantic Richfield Inc 515 S Flower Los Angeles CA 90071

LAUER, JAMES LOTHAR, physicist, educator; b. Vienna, Austria, Aug. 2, 1920; came to U.S., 1938, naturalized, 1943; s. Max and Friederike (Rappaport) L.; m. Stefanie Dorothea Blank, Sept. 5, 1955; children: Michael, Ruth. A.B., Temple U., 1942, M.A., 1944; Ph.D., U. Pa., 1948; postgrad., U. Calif., San Diego, 1964-65. Scientist Sun Oil Co., Marcus Hook, Pa., 1944-52; spectroscopist Sun Oil Co., 1952-64, sr. scientist, 1965-77; asst. prof. U. Pa., 1952-55; lectr. U. Del., 1952-58; research fellow mech. engring. U. Calif., San Diego, 1964-65; research prof. mech. engring. Rensselaer Poly. Inst., Troy, N.Y., 1978-85; prof. mech. engring. Rensselaer Poly. Inst., 1985—, cons. Sun Oil Co. Pa., 1978—, Aluminum Co. Can Ltd., 1976—, Exxon Corp., 1982—, IBM Corp., 1983—. Author: Infrared Fourier Spectroscopy—Chemical Applications, 1978; author numerous tech. papers. Active Penn Wynne Civic Assn., 1959-77, Country Knolls Civic Assn., 1978—. Sun Oil Co. fellow, 1964-65, Air Force Office Sci. Research grantee, 1974-86, Army Research Office grantee, 1985—, NASA Lewis Research Center grantee, 1974-86, NSF grantee, 1987—, Office Naval Research grantee, 1979-82. Mem. Am. Chem. Soc., Am. Phys. Soc., Soc. Applied Spectroscopy, Spectroscopy Soc. Can., Optical Soc. Am., Sigma Xi. Jewish. Home: 7 North East Ln Ballston Lake NY 12019 Office: Rensselaer Poly Inst Dept Mech Engring Troy NY 12181

LAUFER-DVORKIN, BATIA, linguist, educator; b. Vilnius, USSR, Dec. 30, 1946; arrived in Israel, 1959; d. Rafael and Luba (Furman) Dvorkin; m. Zvy Laufer, Aug. 6, 1968; children: Alon, Anat, Sigal. BA, Haifa U., Israel, 1970; MA, Leiden U., The Netherlands, 1974; PhD, Edinburgh U., Scotland, 1986. English tchr. pre-acad. unit Haifa U., 1970-72, tchr. fgn. langs. dept., 1974-83, coordinator lang. lab., 1975—, lectr. applied linguistics English dept., 1985—; lectr. applied linguistics Gordon Tchrs. Coll., Haifa, 1980-83. Co-author: Reading Comprehension Course, 1982, Vocabulary Development, 1984; contbr. 19 articles to profl. jours. Fgn. and Commonwealth office scholar, Brit. Council, 1983, grantee, 1984-85. Mem. Internat. Assn. Tchrs. English as a Fgn. Lang., Assn. Internat. de Linguistique Appliquée, Israeli Applied Linguistics Assn. (sec. 1985—). Office: Haifa U English Dept, Mt Carmel, Haifa 31999, Israel

LAUFMAN, HAROLD, surgeon; b. Milw., Jan. 6, 1912; s. Jacob and Sophia (Peters) L.; m. Marilyn Joselit, 1940 (dec. 1963); children: Dionne Laufman Weigert, Laurien Laufman Kogut; m. June Friend Moses, 1980. B.S., U. Chgo., 1932, M.D., 1937; M.S. in Surgery, Northwestern U., 1946, Ph.D., 1948. Diplomate: Am. Bd. Surgery. Intern Michael Reese Hosp., Chgo., 1936-39; resident in gen. surgery St. Marks Hosp., London, Northwestern U. Med. Sch., Cook County Hosp., Hines VA Hosp., 1939-46; faculty Northwestern U., Chgo., 1941-65; from clin. asst. to prof., attending surgeon Passavant Meml. Hosp., Chgo., 1953-65; prof. surgery, history of medicine Albert Einstein Coll. Medicine, N.Y.C., 1965-79, emeritus prof., 1979—; dir. Inst. Surg. Studies, Montefiore Hosp. and Med. Center, Bronx, N.Y., 1965-81; practice medicine specializing in gen. and vascular surgery Chgo., 1941-65, N.Y.C., 1965-81; ret. professorial lectr. surgery Mt. Sinai Sch. Medicine, N.Y.C., 1979—; attending surgeon Mt. Sinai Hosp., N.Y.C., 1979-83; James IV vis. prof., Israel, 1962; cons., lectr. in field; chmn. FDA Classification Panel Gen. and Plastic Surgery Devices, 1975-78; pres. Harold Laufman Assos., Inc. (cons.), 1977—; chmn. Medinvent Inc. Author: (with S.W. Banks) Surgical Exposures of the Extremities, 1953, 2d edit. 1986, (with R.B. Erichson) Hematologic Problems in Surgery, 1970, Hospital Special Care Facilities, 1981, The Veins, 1986; chmn. editorial bd.: Diagnostica, 1974-79; mem. editorial bd.: Surgery, Gynecology and Obstetrics, 1974—, Infection Control, 1980—, Med. Instrumentation, 1972-83, Med. Research Engring, 1972-79; contbr. articles to sci. publs. Chmn. bd. N.Y. Chamber Soloists, 1974-80, Chamber Music Conf. of the East, 1980—. Served to maj. AUS, 1942-46. Fellow ACS; mem. Assn. Advancement Med. Instrumentation (pres. 1974-75, chmn. bd. 1976-77), Am. Assn. Hosp. Cons., Am. Med. Writers Assn. (pres. 1968-69), Am. Surg. Assn., Société Internationale de Chirurgie, Western Surg. Assn., Cen. Surg. Assn., N.Y. Surg. Soc., Soc. Vascular Surgery, Internat. Cardiovascular Soc., Soc. Surgery Alimentary Tract, Surg. Infection Soc. (councillor 1980-84), Chamber Music Conf. and Composers Forum of East (pres. 1975-85, chmn. bd. 1985-86), Sigma Xi, Alpha Omega Alpha, Phi Sigma Delta, Zeta Beta Tau. Jewish. Clubs: Standard (Chgo.); Harmonie (N.Y.C.); Willow Ridge Country (Harrison, N.Y.). Home and Office: 31 E 72d St New York NY 10021

LAUGHLIN, ALLAN DAVID, health sciences facility administrator; b. Melbourne, Victoria, Australia, Aug. 25, 1947; s. Stanley James and Dorothy Allen (Jenkins) L.; m. Brenda Nan Parkinson, Dec. 7, 1969; children: Stephen Paul, Wendy Jane, Jared Andrew, Matthew James. B of Med. Sci., Monash U., Melbourne, 1969, MBBS, 1972. Registered med. practitioner, New Zealand, Australia. Resident Bendigo Base Hosp., Victoria, 1973; med. officer, adminstr. Karachi (Pakistan) Adventist Hosp., 1974-78; med. dir. Auckland (New Zealand) Adventist Hosp., 1979—. Mem. New Zealand Med. Assn. Office: Auckland Adventist Hosp, 188 87 Heliers Bay Rd, 5 Auckland New Zealand

LAUGHLIN, PHILIP MELVILLE, health care company executive; b. Chgo., Feb. 5, 1947; s. Robert Newton and Adelaide (Melville) L.; m. Dorothy Elizabeth Madgey, June 14, 1980; children: Timothy Melville, Robert Newton III. BA cum laude, Yale U., 1969; MBA, Harvard U., 1976. Planner ITT, Rye, N.Y., 1969-70; fin. analyst, mgr. product mktg. Baxter Internat., Deerfield, Ill., 1976-79; gen. mgr. Amsterdam, The Netherlands, 1979-81; gen. mgr. Sydney, Australia, 1981-82, mng. dir., 1982-86, area mng. dir., 1986-88; v.p. ops. Global Bus. Group, Winnetka, Ill., 1988—. Served to lt. USN, 1970-74, Vietnam. Fellow Australian Inst. Dirs.; mem. Australian Med. Devices and Diagnostics Assn. (exec. com. 1987-88), Med. Engring. Research Assn. (founder, mem. exec. com. 1983-86), New South Wales Chamber of Mfrs. (council mem. 1986-88). Clubs: Harvard, Yale (Chgo.). Home: 180 Apple Tree Rd Winnetka IL 60093 Office: Baxter Internat 1 Parkway N PO Box 784 Deerfield IL 60015-0784

LAUN, HERWART HEINRICH HELMUT, manufacturing executive; b. Ulm, Baden-Württemberg, Fed. Republic of Germany, Mar. 4, 1929; s. Heinrich George and Käte (Gugenhan) L.; m. Christine Wehmeyer, Nov. 20, 1973. Student, U. Nürnberg, 1952-54. Professorial asst. U. Erlangen-Nüurnberg, Fed. Republic of Germany, 1955-60; indsl. advisor 1961-63; dir., vorstand Gold Zack-Werke AG, Mettman, Fed. Republic of Germany, 1963-72; gen. mgr. Johannes Kauffmann GmbH, Langenargen, Fed. Republic of Germany, 1972—; advisor J.G. Schrödel. Mem. Arbeitsgemeinschaft der Deutschen Bettfedernindustrie, Vershofen-Gesellschaft and Absatzwirtschaftliche Gesellschaft. Lodge: Rotary. Office: Johannes Kauffmann GmbH, PO Box 4173, D-7994 Langenargen Federal Republic of Germany

LAUNAY, JEAN, science association executive; b. Fougeres, France, Apr. 5, 1939; s. Louis and Amelie (Douard) L.; m. Christine Ledré; children: Sophie, Laurence. MS, U. Rennes, France, 1963; Diplôme d'Etudes Approfandies, U. Paris Sorbonne, 1965. Scientist, geologist Office Recherche Scientifique et Technique Outre Mer, Dakar, Senegal, from 1966, Noumea, New Caledonia, 1966-83; dir. sci. research inst. Abidjan, Ivory Coast, 1984—. Office: Office Recherche Scientifique, et Technique Outre Mer BP V-51, Abidjan Ivory Coast

LAUNER, MICHAEL ANDREW, psychiatry consultant; b. Manchester, Eng., May 29, 1947; s. Ellis and Sylvia (Cohen) L.; 1 child, Jack Simon. L.R.C.P., M.R.C.S., Leeds U., 1970, D.P.M., 1974; M.R.C., Royal Coll. Psychiatrists, 1975; B.A. in English, Open U., 1982. Registered med. practioner, 1971. Psychiatrist, Leeds Gen. Infirmary, 1974-76; sr. registrar Broadmoor Hosp., 1976, Claybury Hosp., 1977; psychiatry cons. Burnley Dist., Lancs, Eng., 1977—, also chmn. Contbr. articles to profl. jours. Advisor Blackburn Samaritans. Mem. Royal Coll. Psychiatrists (N.W. exec. com. 1982-86), Brit. Med. Assn. Jewish. Avocations: football, writing, eating disorders. Office: Burnley Gen Hosp, Casterton Ave, Burnley Lancs BB11 2RF, England

LAUNSTEIN, HOWARD CLEVELAND, finance educator; b. Flushing, Mich., Oct. 15, 1922; s. John Henry and Jennie Grace (Clevel) L.; m. Elizabeth June Snyder, May 22, 1943; children—Robert John, Howard Elmer. Student, Central Mich. U., 1941-43; B.A., Mich. State U., 1947, M.A., 1948; Ph.D., Ohio State U., 1956. Grad. asst. Mich. State U., 1947-48, instr. acctg., 1948-56; asst. prof. State U. Iowa, Iowa City, 1956-58; assoc. prof. Marquette U., Milw., 1958-64, prof. finance, 1964-87, prof. emeritus, 1987—, chmn. dept., 1959-67; ins. agt. Guarantee Mut. Life Ins. Co., Lansing, Mich., 1948-51; instr. C.P.C.U. program, 1954-55, C.L.U. programs, 1959-81; ins. cons. Marquette U., 1958-87; mem. ednl. com. Wis. Real Estate Examining Bd., 1976-78; dir., auditor Red Cedar Coop. Assn., East Lansing, 1949-52. Contbr. chpts. to books, articles to profl. jours. Asst. cub master, treas. Greendale cub pack Boy Scouts Am., Wis., 1960-66; committeeman Boy Scouts, 1963-66; mem. citizens com. bonding issues Greendale Sch., 1959-61; bd. govs., dir. Nat. Inst. Consumer Credit Mgmt., 1965-87; chmn. awards com. Nat. Assn. Ind. Insurers Jour. Ins., 1962-63, 68-69, 72-73; mem. bd. electors Internat. Ins. Hall of Fame, 1970—, John S. Bickley Awards, 1979—. Served with USAAF, 1942-45. Decorated Air medal. Mem. Internat. Ins. Seminars (bd. govs. 1965—, moderator 1965-71, research directorate 1979-85), Am. Finance Assn., Midwest Econ. Assn., Am. Acctg. Assn., Am. Fin. Mgmt. Assn., Am. Risk and Ins. Assn., Beta Alpha Psi, Delta Sigma Pi, Sigma Epsilon, Beta Gamma. Methodist. Home: 7933 Exuma Ave Port Richey FL 34668

LAUREL, SALVADOR HIDALGO, vice president and minister of foreign affairs of Republic of Philippines; b. Penafrancia, Paco Manila, Philippines, Nov. 18, 1928; s. Jose P. and Paciencia (Hidalgo) L.; m. Celia Diaz; 8 children. BA, LLB, U. Philippines; LLM, JSD, Yale U. Mem. Philippine Senate, 1967-73; mem. com. on justice, com. econ. affairs, com. govt. reorganization, and com. on community devel; v.p. Republic of Philippines, 1986—, prime minister, 1986-87, minister of fgn. affairs, from 1986; rep. UN Gen. Assembly, 1986, Inter-Parliamentary Union Conf., Lima, Peru, 1968; head del. first gen. assembly Agean Inter-Parliamentary Orgn., Singapore, 1978. Contbr. articles to legal publs. Founder, chmn. Citizen's Legal Aid Soc. of Philippines. Named Lawyer of Yr., Justice and Ct. Reporter's Assn., 1967, Most Outstanding Legal Aid Lawyer, Internat. Bar Assn., Stockholm, 1976. Mem. Philippines Bar Assn. Office: Office of Prime Minister, Manila Philippines *

LAURENT, CAMILLE PIERRE, educator; b. Janze, France, Sept. 19, 1937; s. Camille Henri and Félicie Louise (Genet) L.; m. Claire M. Meignant (div. 1967); children: Anne, Frédérique; m. Carole Frédérique Penfrat, 1978; 1 child, Noémie. Diplome d'Etudes Superieures, U. Paris Sorbonne, 1959; aggrégation E.N.S., U. St. Cloud, France, 1961. Asst. prof. Bklyn. Coll., 1961-62, U. Nantes, France, 1965-68; asst. prof. U. Nice, France, 1968-71, assoc. prof. faculty of letters, 1971—, chmn. dept. English, 1979-81, 87—; vis. prof. U. Colo., Boulder, 1981-82. Translator novel Of Time and the River, 1984; contbr. articles to learned jours. Fulbright scholar, 1986. Mem. Soc. Americanistes. Home: 387 Route de Bellet, 06200 Nice France Office: U Nice Faculté Lettres, 98 Blvd Carlone, 06200 Nice France

LAURITZEN, JAN, shipping executive; b. Copenhagen, Nov. 13, 1943; s. Knud and Kirsten (Hartwig-Møller) L.; m. Lene Willestofte Larsen, May 17, 1975; children: Jacob, Louise. Degree, Niels Brocks Bus. Sch., Copenhagen, 1966; BS in Econs., U. Copenhagen, 1970, B Commerce in Internat. Trade, 1984. Chartering trainee Transmarine S.A., Paris, 1966, Fletamar S.L, Madrid, 1967; chartering mgr. O. Bjørn Jensen & Co., Copenhagen, 1968; mng. dir. H. Knop A/S Shipowners & Chartering, Copenhagen, 1969-74; shipowner JAL A/S Shipowners, Copenhagen, 1969-74; ops. mgr. OLAU-LINE A/S, Copenhagen, 1974-77; mem. staff DFDS A/S Shipowners & Forwarders, Copenhagen, 1980; mng. dir. DFDS A/S Shipowners & Forwarders, Hamburg, Fed. Republic Germany, 1981-83; mgr. DFDS A/S Shipowners & Forwarders, Copenhagen, 1983—; bd. dirs. maritime Venture A/S, Copenhagen, CUL (U.K.) Ltd., Harwich, Charlottenlund Group (chmn.). Mem. YMCA, Copenhagen. Home: Engbakkevej 6, 2920 Charlottenlund Denmark Office: DFDS A/S, Skt Annae Pl 30, DK-1295 Copenhagen Denmark

LAUTENBERG, FRANK R., U.S. senator; b. Paterson, N.J., Jan. 23, 1924; s. Samuel and Mollie L.; children: Ellen, Nan, Lisa, Joshua. B.S., Columbia U., 1949; D.H.L., Hebrew Union Coll., Cin. and N.Y.C., 1977; Ph.D. (hon.), Hebrew U., Jerusalem, 1978. Founder Automatic Data Processing, Inc., Clifton, N.J., 1953; exec. v.p. adminstrn. Automatic Data Processing, Inc., 1961-69, pres., 1969-82, chief exec. officer, 1975-82, also chmn. bd.; mem. U.S. Senate from N.J., 1982—. Commr. Port Authority N.Y. and N.J., 1978-82; trustee Sch. Bus., Columbia U.; nat. pres. Am. Friends Hebrew U., 1973-74; former gen. chmn., pres. Nat. United Jewish Appeal, 1975-77; bd. govs. Am. Jewish Com.; mem. internat. bd. govs. Hebrew U., Jerusalem; mem. bd. overseers N.J. Symphony Orch.; bd. govs. Am. Jewish Com.; mem. Pres.'s Commn. on the Holocaust; founder Lautenberg Center for Gen. and Tumor Immunology, Med. Sch., Hebrew U., Jerusalem, 1971; v.p. Jewish Community Fedn. Met. N.J., East Orange; mem. fin. council Nat. Democratic Com. Served with Armed Forces, 1943-46, ETO. Recipient Torch of Learning award Am. Friends Hebrew U., 1971, Scopus award, 1975. Mem. Nat. Assn. Data Processing Service Orgns. (pres. 1968-69, dir. from 1974), Patrons Soc. Met. Opera. Office: US Senate Hart Senate Office Bldg Washington DC 20510 *

LAUTH, ROBERT EDWARD, geologist; b. St. Paul, Feb. 6, 1927; s. Joseph Louis and Gertrude (Stapleton) L.; student St. Thomas Coll., 1944; B.A. in Geology, U. Minn., 1952; m. Suzanne Janice Holmes, Apr. 21, 1947; children—Barbara Jo, Robert Edward II, Elizabeth Suzanne, Leslie Marie. Wellsite geologist Columbia Carbon Co., Houston, 1951-52; dist. geologist Witco Oil & Gas Corp., Amarillo, Tex., 1952-55; field geologist Reynolds Mining Co., Houston, 1955; cons. geologist, Durango, Colo., 1955—. Appraiser helium res. Lindley area Orange Free State, Republic of South Africa, 1988, remaining helium res. Odolanow Plant area Polish Lowlands, Poland, 1988. Served with USNR, 1944-45. Mem. N.Mex., Four Corners (treas., v.p., pres., symposium com.) geol. socs., Rocky Mountain Assn. Geologists, Am. Inst. Profl. Geologists, Am. Inst. Mining, Metall. and Petroleum Engrs., Am. Assn. Petroleum Geologists, Helium Soc., N.Y. Acad. Sci. Am. Assn. Petroleum Landman, Soc. Econ. Paleontologists and Mineralogists, The Explorers Club. Republican. Roman Catholic. K.C. Clubs: Durango Petroleum (dir.), Denver Petroleum, Elks. Author: Desert Creek Field, 1958; (with Silas C. Brown) Oil and Gas Potentialities of Northern Arizona, 1958, Northern Arizona Has Good Oil, Gas Prospects, 1960, Northeastern Arizona; Its Oil, Gas and Helium Prospects, 1961; contbr. papers on oil and gas fields to profl. symposia. Home: 2020 Crestview Dr PO Box 776 Durango CO 81302 Office: 555 S Camino del Rio Durango CO 81301

LAUTLIEV, JOHAN MILEV, library director; b. Plodvdiv, Bulgaria, Feb. 1, 1925; s. Mile Milev and Dobra (Vasileva) L.; m. Kunka Slavi Vasileva; children: Silvena Johan, Dobroslava Johan. Student, Secondary Sch. of Econs., Plovdiv, 1940-44, Acad. Social Scis., Sofia, Bulgaria, 1953-58. Fin. inspector Dist. Coop. Union, Plovdiv, 1949-50; chief Cultural Sector of the City Com. of BCP, Plovdiv, 1951-52; sec. City Com. for Bulgarian-Soviet Friendship, Plovdiv, 1953-55, City com. of the Fatherland Front, Plovdiv, 1956-57; dir. City Library, Plovdiv, 1958; journalist, chief of the cultural dept., dep. editor-in-chief Otechesteven Glas/Fatherland Voice, Plovdiv, 1959-76; dir. Ivan Vazov Nat. Library, Plovdiv, 1976—. Author: New Forms of Work in Ivan Vazov National Library, 1983; author and complier Forty-Eight Rembrandt's Engravings, 1987. Pres. City Peace Com., Plovdiv, 1978—, City Council of Culture, Plovdiv, 1983-85; mem. Bur. of the County Section of the Bulgarian Tennis Fedn., 1975—. Mem. Bulgarian Journalists' Union. Mem. Bulgarian Communist Party. Home: 159 Sesti Septemvri St, 4000 Plovdiv Bulgaria Office: Ivan Vazov Nat Library, N Vapcarov 17, 4000 Plovdiv Bulgaria

LAUWERYNS, JOSEPH MARIE, pathologist, educator; b. Ostend, Belgium, Feb. 27, 1933; s. Joseph Gerard and Jeanne Marie (Ampe) L.; M.D., Cath. U. Louvain, 1958, Ph.D., 1962; specialist in clin. pathology, 1963; m. Anne Van Campenhout, Feb. 11, 1961; children—Brigitte, Philippe, Isabelle, Benedicte. Mem. faculty Cath. U. Leuven Faculty Medicine, 1962—, prof. pathology, 1967—, chmn. dept. biomed. research, 1979—, head dept. pathology and histology Vesalius Inst., 1963—; dir. lab. pathology Acad. Ziekenhuizen, Leuven, 1963—. Decorated officer Belgian Royal Order Crown, cmdr. Belgian Royal Order King Leopold; recipient Specia prize, 1958, Schockaert prize, 1962, Aspen prize, 1973, Smith-Kline-R.I.T. prize, 1983-85; Belgian Public Health travel grantee, 1959; fellow Nat. Belgian Research Funds, 1960-63, WHO, 1963. Mem. Belgian Soc. Pathology (pres. 1975-76), Belgian Soc. Electron Microscopy (pres. 1978—), Assn. Belgian Sci. Socs. (dir.), Royal Belgian Acad. Medicine (prize 1970), Internat. Acad. Pathology, European Soc. Pathology, AAAS. Roman Catholic. Chief editor Tijdschrift voor Geneeskunde, 1974—; discoverer intrapulmonary neuroepithelial bodies. Office: 12 Minderbroedersstraat, B-3000 Leuven Belgium

LAUX, RUSSELL FREDERICK, lawyer; b. West New York, N.J., Dec. 30, 1918; s. Frederick and Theresa A. (Noble) L.; m. Ann deFriedberg, Aug. 22, 1962 (dec.); m. Eva DeLuca, Dec. 24, 1985. Student Pace Inst., 1938-40, Fordham U., 1946-48; LLB summa cum laude, N.Y. Law Sch., 1950; postgrad. Pace Coll., 1951, Columbia U., 1955. Bar: N.Y. 1951, U.S. Dist. (so. dist.) N.Y. 1951, U.S. Ct. Appeals (2d cir.) 1951, U.S. Ct. Claims 1952, U.S. Tax Ct. 1952, U.S. Dist. Ct. (ea. dist.) N.Y. 1953, U.S. Ct. Customs and Patent Appeals 1963, U.S. Ct. Mil. Appeals 1963, U.S. Supreme Ct. 1963. Mem. staff N.Y. State Dept. Law, Richmond County Investigations, 1951-54, N.Y. State Exec. Dept. Office of Commr. of Investigations, 1954-57; comptroller-counsel Odyssey Productions, Inc., 1957-59; ptnr. Ryan, Murray & Laux, N.Y.C., 1951-61, Ryan & Laux, N.Y.C., 1961; sole practice, N.Y.C., 1961—. Active Met. Opera Guild. Served with AUS, 1940-46; capt. Judge Adv. Gen. Vet. Corps of Arty., State of N.Y., 1975—; now col. U.S.A.M. Recipient Eloy Alfaro Grand Cross Republic of Panama. Mem. Bronx County Bar Assn. (recipient Townsend Wandell Gold medal), Nat. Acad. TV Arts & Scis., Internat. Platform Assn., VFW, Order of Lafayette, Sons of Union Vets. of Civil War, Soc. Am. Wars, The Nat. Sojourners, Heroes of '76, Navy League, St. Andrews Soc. N.Y., St. George Soc. N.Y., Soc. Friendly Sons of St. Patrick, English Speaking Union, Asia Soc., China Inst. Am., Army and Navy Union U.S.A., Am. Legion, Mid Manhattan C. of C., Reserve Officers Assn. of U.S. (col.), Delta Theta Phi. Presbyterian. Clubs: Lambs, Knights Hospitaller of St. John of Jerusalem, Grand St. Boys', Soldiers', Sailors' and Airmen's. Lodges: Order of Eastern Star, Masons (past comdr. N.Y. Masonic war vets.), Shriners, Knight of Malta. Office: 71 W 23d St Suite 1530 New York NY 10010

LA VALLE, LUKE PAUL, JR., investment counseling co. exec.; b. Bklyn., Apr. 2, 1942; s. Luke Paul and Rose Dorothy (Saia) LaV.; BS, Boston Coll., 1963; MBA, U. Mass., 1964; postgrad. N.Y.U., 1968-69; m. Ann Rita Wagner, Sept. 11, 1971; children: Luke, Michael, David. Asst. portfolio mgr. investment div. U.S. Trust Co. of N.Y., N.Y.C., 1967-69, portfolio mgr., 1969-72, investment officer, 1972-74, sr. investment officer, 1974-80; pres. Am. Capital Mgmt., Inc., N.Y.C., 1980—, also dir.; dir., pres. Benmarl Wine Co., Ltd. Served to 1st lt. M.I. U.S. Army, 1965-67; to lt. col. M.I., USAR. Fellow Fin. Analysts Fedn.; mem. N.Y. Soc. Security Analysts (sr. security analyst), Soldiers, Sailors and Airmens Club (adv. bd.). Republican. Roman Catholic. Clubs: N.Y. Athletic; Westhampton Yacht Squadron (L.I., bd. dir.). Home: 460 E 79th St New York NY 10021 Office: 90 Broad St New York NY 10004

LAVALLEE, RODERICK LEO, industrial products company executive; b. Sutton, Mass., Aug. 10, 1936; s. Roderick L. and Florence (Gagne) LaV.; m. Janice Vivian LaMotte, Sept. 17, 1960; children: Michelle J., Roderick J. BS, U. Mass., 1958; MBA, Rutgers U., 1970. Constrn. mgr. Hill Constrn. Co., Millbury, Mass., 1960-63; mfg. mgr. Am. Can Co., N.Y.C., 1963-68; corp. audit mgr. Pfizer Corp., N.Y.C., 1968-73; corp. mgr. PIC, GTE Sylvania, Stamford, Conn., 1973-74; dir. materials GTE Internat., Burlington, Mass., 1974-80; corp. v.p. Peabody Internat. Corp., Stamford, 1980-84; pres. Peabody World Trade Corp., Stamford, 1984-85; pres., owner PWWT Corp., 1986—. Served to 1st lt. U.S. Army Res., 1959-62. Home: 36 Oak St New Canaan CT 06840 Office: PWWT Corp 84 W Park Pl Stamford CT 06901

LAVELLE, BRIAN FRANCIS DAVID, lawyer; b. Cleve., Aug. 16, 1941; s. Gerald John and Mary Josephine (O'Callagahan) L.; m. Sara Hill, Sept. 10, 1966; children: S. Elizabeth, B. Francis D., Catherine H. BA, U. Va., 1963; JD, Vanderbilt U., 1966; LLM in Taxation, N.Y.U., 1969. Bar: N.C. 1966, Ohio 1968. Assoc. VanWinkle Buck, Wall, Starnes & Davis, Asheville, N.C., 1968-74, ptnr., 1974—; lectr. continuing edn. N.C. Bar Found., Wake Forest U. Estate Planning Inst., Hartford Tax Inst., Duke U. Estate Planning Inst. Contbr. articles on law to profl. jours. Trustee Carolina Day Sch., 1981—, sec., 1982-85; vice chmn. Buncombe County Indsl. Facilities and Pollution Control Authority, 1976-82; bd. dirs. Western N.C. Community Found., 1986— (sec. 1987—); mem. Asheville Tax Study Group, 1981—, chmn., 1984; bd. advs. U.N.C. Annual Tax Inst., 1981—. Served as capt. Judge Adv. Gen. USAF, 1966-67. Mem. N.C. Bar Assn. (bd. govs. 1979-82, councillor tax sect. 1979-83, councillor estate planning law sect. 1982-85), ABA, Am. Coll. Probate Counsel (state chmn. 1982-85, regent 1984—, lectr. continuing edn.), N.C. State Bar (splty. com. on estate planning and probate law 1984—, v. chmn. 1987—). Episcopalian (clk. vestry All Souls Ch.). Clubs: Rotary of Asheville, Biltmore Forest Country. Home: 45 Brookside

Rd Asheville NC 28803 Office: 11 N Market St PO Box 7376 Asheville NC 28802

LAVENDA, BERNARD HOWARD, chemical physics educator, scientist; b. N.Y.C., Sept. 18, 1945; s. Nathan and Selma (Dubnow) L.; m. Fanny Malka, Mar. 6, 1973; children—Marlene Allyn, Jason Isaac. B.Sc., Clark U., 1966; M.Sc., Weizmann Inst., 1967; Ph.D., Free U. Brussels, 1970. Prof., U. Pisa, Italy, 1972-73, U. Naples, Italy, 1975-80, U. Camerino, Italy, 1980—; cons. TEMA, Bologna, Italy, 1978-84, Nuovo Pignone, Firenze, Italy, 1972-73; vis. prof. Inst. de Fisica U. Fed. de Rio Grande do Sul, Porto Alegre Brasil, 1986; assoc. scientist Internat. Ctr. Theoretical Biology, Venice, 1987—. Author: Thermodynamics of Irreversible Processes, 1978; Nonequilibrium Statistical Thermodynamics, 1985. Contbr. articles to profl. jours. Fellow Royal Soc. Chemistry; mem. Am. Math. Soc. Jewish. Avocation: chess. Home: Frazione Sentino 30/A, 62030 Camerino Italy Office: Univ degli Studi de Camerino, 62032 Camerino Italy

LAVER, MICHAEL JOHN, sociology educator, writer; b. London, Aug. 3, 1949; arrived in Ireland, 1983; s. Frederick John Murray and Kathleen Amy (Blythe) L.; m Bríd Goretti O'Connor, June 23, 1976; children: Conor Murray, Katharine Rose. BA with honors, Essex U., Colchester, Eng., 1970, MA, 1971; PhD, Liverpool (Eng.) U., 1981. Lectr. politics Queens U., Belfast, No. Ireland, 1972-73, Liverpool U., 1973-83; prof. politics and sociology Univ. Coll., Galway, Ireland, 1983—; dir. Ctr. for the Study of Irish Elections, Galway, 1983—; vis. prof. Harvard U., Cambridge ,Mass., 1988-89. Editor: (book series) Sage Modern Politics, 1986—, (jour.) Irish Polit. Studies, 1986—; author 5 books; contbr. articles to profl. jours. Mem. Polit. Studies Assn. Britain, Polit. Studies Assn. Ireland (pres.), European Consortium for Polit. Research (workshop, publ. coms. 1986—, exec. com. 1988—). Home: 7 Montpelier Terr, The Crescent, Galway Ireland Office: Univ Coll, Dept Polit Sci, and Sociology, Galway Ireland

LAVERY, JOHN ROBERT, business executive; b. Toronto, Ont., Can., May 13, 1942; s. John Frederick and Mary Margaret (Myles) L.; m. Elaine Joyce Shawlinski, Aug. 9, 1969; children: Shaunna Lyn, Cara Joyce. Mem. audit staff Ernst & Whinney, London, Ont., 1961-62, audit supr., 1965-67, mgr. cons. services, 1971-73; audit sr. Ernst & Whinney, Toronto, 1963-65, sr. cons., 1968-71; ptnr.-in-charge Ernst & Whinney, Winnipeg, Manitoba, Can., 1973-77; chief exec. officer Winpak Ltd., Winnipeg, 1977—, also bd. dirs.; bd. dirs. Monarch Industries, Ltd., Winnipeg, Victorian Order of Nurses, Ottawa, Ont., LGM Graphics, Inc., Winnipeg. Mem. Inst. Chartered Accts. Ont., Inst. Chartered Accts. Manitoba. Home: 78 Pinevalley Dr, Winnipeg, MB Canada R3K 1Y1 Office: Winpak Ltd, 100 Saulteaux Crescent, Winnipeg, MB Canada R3J 3T3

LAVIGNE, MARIE, economics educator; b. Strasbourg, Alsace, France, June 12, 1935; d. Georges and Natalia (Kolomitseff) Behr; m. Pierre Lavigne, July 28, 1956; children—Anne, Anne. M.A. in Econs., U. Strasbourg, 1955, M.A. in Russian, 1956, Ph.D. in Econs., 1960. Asst. prof., sec.-gen. Ctr. on USSR and Eastern Europe, U. Strasbourg, 1959-69; asst. prof. econs. U. Paris, 1969-73, assoc. prof., 1973-74, prof., 1974—, dir. Ctr. for Internat. Econs. of Socialist Countries, 1973—. Author: Les Economies socialistes sovietique et Europeennes, 1959, 3d edit., 1983; Les Relations Economiques Est Ouest, 1979; Economie Internationale des Pays Socialistes, 1985. Decorated Legion of Honor; recipient Silver medal CNRS, 1963. Mem. Assn. Francaise de Science Economique, Am. Econ. Assn., Am. Assn. for Advancement Slavic Studies. Home: 3 rue de Pouy, 75013 Paris France Office: ISMEA, 11 Rue Pierre et Marie Curie, 75005 Paris France

LAW, BERNARD FRANCIS CARDINAL, archbishop; b. Torreon, Mex., Nov. 4, 1931; s. Bernard A. and Helen A. (Stubblefield) L. B.A., Harvard U., 1953; postgrad., St. Joseph Sem., St. Benedict, La., 1953, Pontifical Coll. Josephinum, Worthington, Ohio, 1955. Ordained priest Roman Catholic Ch., 1961, consecrated bishop, 1973; editor Natchez-Jackson diocesan paper, Jackson, 1963-68; exec. dir. U.S. Bishops Com. for Ecumenical and Interreligious Affairs, 1968-71, chmn., from 1975; vicar gen. Diocese of Natchez-Jackson, 1971-73; bishop Diocese of Springfield-Cape Girardeau, Mo., 1973-84; archbishop Archdiocese of Boston Brighton, MA, 1984—; created cardinal 1985; mem. adminstrv. com. Nat. Conf. Cath. Bishops, from 1975; mem. communication com. U.S. Cath. Conf., 1974, mem. adminstrv. bd., from 1975; mem. Vatican Secretariat for Promoting Christian Unity, from 1976; consultor Vatican Commn. Religious Relations with the Jews, from 1976; chmn. bd. Pope John XXIII Med.-Moral Research and Edn. Ctr., St. Louis, 1980-82; ecclesiastical del. of Pope John Paul II for matters pertaining to former Episcopal priests, 1981. Trustee Pontifical Coll. Josephinum, 1974-85, Nat. Shrine of Immaculate Conception, from 1975; bd. regents Conception (Mo.) Sem. Coll., from 1975. Office: Cardinal's Residence 2101 Commonwealth Ave Boston MA 02135 *

LAW, EDWIN B., construction executive; b. Ft. Worth, Aug. 19, 1924; s. Allan B. and Josephine (Parks) L.; m. Margaret Ellen Russell, May 29, 1948 (div.); children—Patrick E., Michael M., Gregory P., Katherine A., James R.; m. Carol J. Settimo, 1979; 1 stepson, P.J. Student Tex. A. and M. Coll., 1940-42; B.S. in Archtl. Engring., U. Tex., 1949; Engr., J.M. Odom Constrn. Co., Austin, Tex., 1947-49; estimator J.W. Bateson Constrn. Co., Dallas, 1949; chief estimator Von Frellick Inc., San Angelo, Tex., 1949-50, Frank E. Blaser Bldg. Co., Wichita, Kans., 1950-52; chief engr. Dondlinger & Sons Constrn. Co., 1953-59; chmn. bd., chief exec. officer Law Co., Inc., 1959-83, chmn. bd. emeritus, cons., 1983—; chmn. bd., chief exec. officer Law West Inc., 1983—; v.p., dir. Law/Kingdon, Profl. Assn. An Organizer, dir. Civic Progress Citizens Assn., 1957-63; organizer Citizens for Commn.-Mgr. Plan, 1959; pres. Greater Downtown Wichita, 1963-64; chmn. Wichita-Sedgwick County Met. Area Planning Commn., 1962-63, mem., 1961-69; chmn. Bd. Zoning Appeals, 1962-63; bd. dirs. local USO, 1957, NCCJ, United Fund of Wichita and Sedgwick County, Inc. Named Kans. Outstanding Jaycee by Jr. C. of C., 1958-59. Served to capt., USMC, 1942-46, 52-53. Mem. Nat., Ariz. assns. profl. engrs., Asso. Gen. Contractors (life nat. dir., pres. Kans. builders chpt. 1974-75), Wichita C. of C. (dir. 1968-70), Cons. Constructors Council Am., Sigma Nu. Republican. Roman Catholic. Clubs: Phoenix Country, Continental Country, Desert Highland Country. Lodge: KC. Office: 8214 E Del Cadena Scottsdale AZ 85258

LAW, GORDON MALCOLM, personnel executive; b. Sheffield, Yorkshire, Eng., Nov. 7, 1932; s. Robert and Elizabeth Black (Cassells) L.; m. Elaine Whittingham, Aug. 31, 1957; children: Helen, Mary, Charlotte. BA, U. Sheffield, 1955. Staff officer Jessop-Saville Ltd., Sheffield, 1957-62; establishment officer Shepherd Bldg. Group Ltd., York, Yorkshire, Eng., 1962-70; gen. mgr. Woolwich Equitable Bldg. Soc., London, 1970—. Author: Personnel Policy and Line, 1975, 2d edit., 1984; contbr. articles to profl. jours. Chmn. Thames Poly. Ct. Govs., Woolwich, London, 1985—; mem. council Nat. Interactive Video Ctr., London, 1986—. Served to cpl. XII Royal Lancers, 1955-57. Named Liveryman, Worshipful Co. Distillers, London, 1976, Freeman, City of London, 1977. Mem. Chartered Bldg. Socs. Inst. (mem. council/edn. com. and corp. planning com. 1983—), Nat. Council for Ednl. Tech. U.K. Conservative. Presbyterian. Home: 6 Hawthorne Close, Bickley Bromley, Kent BR1 2HJ, England Office: Woolwich Equitable Bldg Soc, Equitable House, London SE18 6AB, England

LAW, PHILLIP GARTH, scientist, educator, Antarctic explorer; b. Tallangatta, Victoria, Australia, Apr. 21, 1912; s. Arthur James and Lillian (Chapman) L.; student Ballarat Tchrs. Coll., 1931, Melbourne Tchrs. Coll., 1932; B.Sc., Melbourne U., 1939, M.Sc., 1941, Dr. Applied Sci. (hon.), 1962; Dr.Edn. (hon.), 1977; m. Nel Isabel Allan, Dec. 20, 1941. Tutor in physics Newman Coll., U. Melbourne, 1941-45; lectr. physics U. Melbourne, 1943-48; dir. Antarctic div. Dept. External Affairs, 1949-66; exec. v.p. Victoria Inst. Colls., 1966-77; chmn. Australian Nat. Com. on Antarctic Research, 1966-80; pres. Victorian Inst. Marine Scis., 1978-80. Pres., Geelong Area Victorian Scouts Assn., 1964—; mem. Victorian Com. for Duke of Edinburgh's Award, 1964-80; pres. Grad Union, U. Melbourne, 1971-77; mem. com. for natural scis. Australian Adv. Com. for UNESCO, 1972-77; dep. pres. Sci. Mus. Victoria, 1979-82; trustee Specific Learning Difficulties Assn., 1972—; mem. governing council Melbourne U., 1959-78, La Trobe U., 1964-74, Sci. Mission for Australian Army to New Guinea, 1944. Decorated officer Order of Australia, comdr. Brit. Empire; recipient Founders Gold medal Royal Geog. Soc., award of merit Commonwealth Profl. Officers Assn. Fellow Australian Acad. Sci., Australian Acad. Technol. Scis., ANZAAS, Australian Inst. Physics, Royal Geog. Soc.; mem. Australian New Zealand Sci. Exploration Soc. (pres. 1976-82, patron 1982—), Brit. Schs. Exploring Soc. (patron 1983—), Melbourne Film Soc. (pres. 1972—), Royal Soc. Victoria (pres. 1967-69, councillor). Author: (with John Béchervaise) ANARE, 1957; Antarctic Odyssey, 1983. Contbr. articles to profl. jours. Leader numerous Antarctic expdns., 1949-66. Responsible for establishing Australia's three permanent Antarctic stations.

LAW, SAMMY KOW KAN, hardware company executive; b. Hong Kong, Nov. 22, 1949; s. Wong and Yin Kue (Fung) L.; m. Stella Ol Har Chan, Oct. 21, 1971; children: Firman Ka Man, Wendy Wing Chi, Wenda Wing Shan, Anthony Ka Cheung. Cert. in Secondary Sch. Edn., King's Coll., Hong Kong, 1967. Gen. mgr. Law Wong Kee Hardware Co., Ltd., Hong Kong, 1969-74, mng. dir., 1974—; bd. dirs. Law Wong Kee Investment Co., Ltd., Honduras Investment Ltd., Hong Kong, PSP Contractors & Traders Ltd., Hong Kong. Office: Law Wong Kee Hardware Co Ltd, Franki Ctr 3/F Room 301, 320 Junction Rd, Kowloon Hong Kong

LAWES, FREDERICK JAMES, glass and metal seals company official; b. Cambridge, Eng., June 12, 1942; s. Samuel and Maurita Winifred, June 7, 1965; children: John Paul Frederick, Stuart Gavin Alisdair. Full tech. cert. in engring., Cambridge Coll. Arts and Tech., 1974. Apprentice/skilled man Pye Unicam, Cambridge, 1958-67; instrument maker dept. engring. Cambridge U., 1967-74; product engr. Cathodeon Ltd., Cambridge, 1975-75, product mgr., 1975—. Mem. Brit. Inst. Mgmt., Mech. Inst. Gen. Technician Engrs., Chartered Engring. Inst. (registered technician). Clubs: H.I.B.S. (Impington, Eng.); Lonestantion Tennis (Eng.).

LAWLER, EDWARD JAMES, lawyer; b. Chgo., Sept. 15, 1908; s. Edward James and Sarah Ann (Gahan) L.; m. Elizabeth Falls Dunscomb, Dec. 16, 1939. Ph.B., U. Chgo., 1930; J.D., Harvard U., 1933. Bar: Ill. 1933, Tenn. 1941. Atty., auditor income tax sect. Office Collector of Internal Revenue, Chgo., 1933-34; spl. atty. Office of Gen. Counsel, IRS, 1935-36; sole practice, Chgo., 1937-38; atty. SEC, 1939-41; sole practice, Memphis, 1941-62; ptnr. Lawler, Humphreys, Dunlap & Wellford, 1962-80, of counsel, 1980-82; sole practice, Memphis, 1983—; adv. panel internat. law Dept. of State, 1967-76; dir. Chromasco, Ltd. (Toronto). Served to lt. comdr. USNR, 1942-45; ETO. Decorated Bronze Star. Fellow Am. Bar Found. (chmn. 1966-67); mem. ABA, Internat. Bar Assn., Tenn. Bar Assn., Memphis-Shelby County Bar Assn., Chgo. Bar Assn., Am. Soc. Internat. Law, Am. Law Inst., Am. Judicature Soc., Phi Beta Kappa. Roman Catholic. Clubs: Royal and Ancient Golf (St. Andrews, Scotland), Memphis Hunt and Polo, Memphis Country. Home: 644 S Belvedere Blvd Memphis TN 38104 Office: 1808 1st Tennessee Bldg Memphis TN 38103

LAWLER, ROBERT EUGENE, radiologist; b. Munfordville, Ky., Sept. 14, 1939; s. William Roscoe and Bonnie Katherine (Crouch) L.; B.S., Western Ky. U., 1960; M.D., Vanderbilt U., 1964; m. Lavona Sue Munden, Dec. 17, 1966; children—Robert Eugene, David Michael, Richard Edward, Deborah Elizabeth. Intern, Butterworth Hosp., Grand Rapids, Mich., 1964-65; resident Vanderbilt Hosp., Nashville, 1965-68; practice medicine specializing in radiology, Wuesthoff Hosp., Rockledge, Fla., 1970-84, Radiology Offices, Inc., Rockledge, 1978—; pres. So. Video Systems, Inc., Tampa and Orlando, Fla., 1977-79; treas., pres., chmn. bd. Chinese-Am. Trading Co., Fla., 1986—, J.T.S. Corp., Ga.; v.p. Radiology Offices, Inc., Fla.; asst. producer movie China Run, 1986; exec. producer movie Vietnam Run, 1988; assoc. producer movie The Cu Chi Tunnels, 1988. Served with USAF, 1968-70. Mem. AMA, Fla. Med. Assn., Brevard Med. Soc., Am. Coll. Radiology, Fla. Radiol. Soc., Soc. Nuclear Medicine. Republican. Mem. Ch. of Christ. Inventor of radiol. technique caliper, 1970. Home: 875 N Indian River Dr Cocoa FL 32922 Office: Ctr Health Imaging Inc 40 Fortenberry Rd Merritt Island FL 32952

LAWLIS, PATRICIA KITE, air force officer, computer consultant; b. Greensburg, Pa., May 5, 1945; d. Joseph Powell, Jr., and Dorothy Theresa (Allshouse) Kite; m. Mark Craig Lawlis, Sept. 17, 1976 (div. 1983); 1 child, Elizabeth Marie. B.S., East Carolina U., 1967; M.S. in Computer Sci., Air Force Inst. Tech., 1982; postgrad. Ariz. State U., 1986—. Cert. secondary math. tchr. Employment counselor Pa. State Employment Service, Washington, Pa., 1967-69; math. tchr. Fort Cherry Sch. Dist., McDonald, Pa., 1969-74; commd. 2d lt. U.S. Air Force, 1974, advanced through grades to maj., 1986, data base mgr. Air Force Space Command, Colorado Springs, Colo., 1974-77, computer systems analyst, USAF in Europe, Birkenfeld, Germany, 1977-80, prof. computer sci. Air Force Inst. Tech., Wright-Patterson AFB, Ohio, 1982-86; computer cons. C.J. Kemp Systems, Inc., Huber Heights, Ohio, 1983—; Ada cons., Ada Joint Program Office, Washington, 1984—. State treas. NOW, Pa., 1973-74. Recipient Mervin E. Gross award Air Force Inst. Tech., 1982, Prof. Ezra Kotcher award, 1985. Mem. Assn. Computing Machinery, Computer Soc. of IEEE, Tau Beta Pi (v.p. Ohio Eta chpt. 1981-82), Upsilon Pi Epsilon. Office: Ariz State U Dept Computer Sci Tempe AZ 85287

LAWNICZAK, MACIEJ JAN, educator; b. Poznan, Poland, Oct. 16, 1926; s. Jan and Zofia (Koronowska) L.; M.Engr., U. Poznan, 1951; dr.tech.scis., Agr. Acad. Poznan, 1954, habilitation, 1965; m. Irena Nather, Oct. 30, 1948; children—Ewa, Dobroslawa. Sawmill workman Ostrow Wlkp, 1940-45; adj. prof. Agrl. Acad. Poznan, Poland, 1954-65; head sect. hydro-thermal wood treatment Dept. Wood Tech, Agrl. Acad., Poznan, 1966-71, dir. mech. wood tech. inst. works, 1971-81, head sect. drying and modification of wood, 1981—; lectr. in field. Recipient III degree, Ministry of Higher Edn., 1970, I degree, 1973, 75, 77, 78, II degree, 1979; Knight Cross of Polonia Restiuta Order, 1972. Mem. Wood Tech. Inst. (mem. sci. council 1973—), Poznan Soc. Friends of Scis. (chmn. commn. wood tech. 1978—), Polish Acad. Sci. (chmn. sect. mech. wood tech. 1974—), Union of Polish Tchrs., Assn. of Engrs. and Technicians of Forestry and Woodworking Industry, Polish Foresters Soc. Contbr. articles in field to profl. jours.; editor-in-chief Folia Forestalia polonica, 1982—. Home: 32 m 3 Kosinskiego, 61 522 Poznan Poland Office: 38/42 Wojska Polskiego, 60 637 Poznan Poland

LAWRENCE, ALBERT WEAVER, insurance company executive; b. Newburgh, N.Y., Aug. 4, 1928; s. Claude D. and Janet (Weaver) L.; m. Barbara Corell, June 28, 1950; children: David, Janet, Elizabeth. BSAE in Engring., Cornell U., 1950; postgrad., Rensselaer Poly. Inst., 1975. Ins. agt., exec. 1953—; founder, chmn. A.W. Lawrence and Co. Inc., Schenectady, N.Y., 1954-82; chmn. bd. dirs. United Community Ins. Com., N.Y.C., N.Y., 1982—, Lawrence Agy. Corp., Albany, N.Y., 1982—, Lawrence Ins. Group Inc., Albany, N.Y., 1986—, Lawrence Group Inc., Schenectady, N.Y., 1986—; chmn. adv. bd. Norstar Bank, Schenectady, 1984—; bus. adv. bd. Health Services Agy. N.Y., Albany, 1985—; bd. dirs. Adapt Inc., Hartford, Conn. Bd. dirs. of overseers, grad. sch. of bus. Rensselaer Poly. Inst., Troy, N.Y.; bd. dirs., sec. Schenectady Devel. Corp.; past pres. Schenectady Girls Club, Family and Child Service Schenectady; chmn. Ind. Living for Physically Disabled past chmn. Schenectady United Fund drive, Jr. Achievement Capital Dist.; trustee Russell Sage Coll., Troy, N.Y., Sunnyview Hosp. and Rehab. Ctr., Schenectady, St. Clare's Hosp. Found. Served as corp. AUS, 1946-47. Recipient Sca-Nec-Ta-De Civic award, 1967. Mem. Nat. Assn. Ins. Brokers (bd. dirs.), Schenectady Hist. Soc. (trustee), Nat. Assn. Ins. Brokers (bd. dirs.), Schenectady C. of C. (past pres.). Republican. Mem. Dutch Reformed Ch. Clubs: Wall Street, Mohawk, Mohawk Golf, Curling, Univ., Ft. Orange (Albany); Cornell, N.Y. Athletic (N.Y.C.); No. Lake George Yacht (past commodore). Home: 1601 Baker Ave Schenectady NY 12309 Office: Lawrence Group Inc 108 Union St Schenectady NY 12305

LAWRENCE, CLIFFORD HUGH, historian, educator; b. London, Dec. 28, 1921; s. Earnest William and Dorothy Estèlle (Mundy) L.; m. Helen Maud Curran, July 11, 1953; children: Peter, Clare, Margaret, Felicity, Katherine, Julia. MA, U. Oxford, Eng., 1948, PhD, 1955. Lectr. U. London, 1951-62, reader history, 1962-70, dean arts faculty, 1975-77, head history dept., 1980-85, prof. medieval history, 1970—; bd. gov's. Heythrop Coll., U. London, 1980—; external examiner reading U. Bristol, Nat. U. Ireland, 1971-72. Author: St. Edmund of Abingdon, 1960, The English Church and the Papacy, 1965, Medieval Monasticism, 1984; contbg. writer: History of the University of Oxford, 1984; contbr. articles to academic jours. Mem. com. Inst. for Hist. Research, London, 1975-80, press U.K. Press Council, 1976-80. Served to maj. Brit. army, 1941-46. Fellow Royal Hist. Soc., Soc. Antiquaries. Mem. Alliance Party. Roman Catholic. Home: 11 Durham Rd, London SW20 OQH, England Office: Royal Holloway Bedford, New Colls, Egham Hill, Egham England

LAWRENCE, GARY WRIGHT, plant nematologist, technical supervisor; b. Charlotte, N.C., June 24, 1954; s. Ernest Grey and Opal Pauline (Wright) L.; m. Amanda Minix, Nov. 26, 1977; 1 child, Katherine Pauline. B.A., Greensboro Coll., 1976; M.S., N.C. State U., 1979; Ph.D., La. State U., 1984. Grad. research asst. dept. plant pathology N.C. State U., 1976-78; grad. research asst. dept. plant pathology La. State U., 1979-82; tech. supr. Pennwalt Corp. (AgChem. Div.), Baton Rouge, 1982-85; research nematologist Miss. State U., 1985—. Contbr. articles to tech. jours. Mem. Am. Phytopath. Soc., Soc. Nematologists, Orgn. Tropical Am. Nematologists, Gamma Sigma Delta, Beta Iota Omega. Baptist. Office: Miss State U Dept Pathology and Weed Sci PO Drawer PG Mississippi State MS 39762

LAWRENCE, JOHN KIDDER, lawyer; b. Detroit, Nov. 18, 1949; s. Luther Ernest and Mary Anna (Kidder) L.; m. Jeanine Ann DeLay, June 20, 1981. A.B., U. Mich., 1971; J.D., Harvard U., 1974. Bar: Mich. 1974, D.C. 1978, U.S. Supreme Ct. 1977. Assoc., Dickinson, Wright, McKean & Cudlip, Detroit, 1973-74; staff atty. Office of Judge Adv. Gen., Washington, 1975-78; assoc. Dickinson, Wright, McKean, Cudlip & Moon, Detroit, 1978-81; ptnr. Dickinson, Wright, Moon, VanDusen & Freeman, Detroit, 1981—. Patron, Founders Soc. Detroit Inst. Arts, 1979—; mem. founds. com. Detroit Symphony Orch., 1983—. Served with U.S. Navy, 1975-78. Mem. ABA, State Bar Mich., D.C. Bar Assn., Am. Judicature Soc., Internat. Bar Assn., Detroit Com. on Fgn. Relations, Am. Hist. Assn., Phi Eta Sigma, Phi Beta Kappa. Democrat. Episcopalian. Club: Detroit. Office: Dickinson Wright Moon et al 800 1st National Bldg Detroit MI 48226

LAWRENCE, RALPH WALDO, manufacturing company executive; b. Mineola, N.Y., Sept. 10, 1941; s. Ralph Waldo and Gertrude (Ingles) L.; m. Judith Alice Frost, June 20, 1964; children: Susan, Carolyn. BA, W.Va. Wesleyan Coll., 1963; M in Pub. Adminstrn., Western Mich. U., 1979. Pres. Lawrence Mfrs., Columbus, Ohio, 1970-85; chief automated info. systems contract services Systems Automation Ctr., Columbus, 1980-87, chief plans and mgmt. div., 1987—. Served to capt. U.S. Army, 1963-66. Mem. Data Processing Mgmt. Assn. (pres. Columbus chpt. 1987, program dir. Columbus chpt. 1985). Republican. Presbyterian. Lodge: Masons. Home: 10201 Covan Dr Westerville OH 43081 Office: Systems Automation Ctr PO Box 1605 Columbus OH 43216-5002

LAWRENCE, ROBERT EDWARD, electrical engineer; b. Boston, May 29, 1946; s. Jules P. and Gertrude (Lander) L.; B.S., Rensselaer Poly. Inst., 1968, M.S., 1969, Ph.D., 1972; 1 son, Andrew Jon. Mem. tech. staff Bell Tel. Labs., Whippany, N.J., 1972-74; engr. Vitro Labs., Silver Spring, Md., 1974-77, sr. staff engr., 1978-80; asso. Booz Allen & Hamilton, Bethesda, Md., 1977-78; dir. Litton Amecom, College Park, Md., 1980-86; consulting engr. The MITRE Corp., McLean, Va., 1986—. Founder, bd. dirs. Vitro Fed. Credit Union, 1970; mem. Prince George's County Econ. Devel. Corp., 1985—. NSF fellow, 1970. Mem. Nat. Security Indsl. Assn., IEEE, Armed Forces Communications Electronics Assn. (chpt. v.p., past chpt. treas.), Assn. Old Crows, Sigma Xi, Tau Beta Pi, Eta Kappa Nu. Contbr. articles to profl. jours. Home: 16212 Grist Mill Dr Rockville MD 20855

LAWRENCE, RODERICK JOHN, architect, social science educator, consultant; b. Adelaide, Australia, Aug. 30, 1949; s. Keith and Babette Naomi (Radford) L.; m. Clarisse Christine Gonet, Sept. 30, 1977; children: Xavier Gerard, Adrien Kieth. BS with first class hons., Adelaide U., Australia, 1972; MS, Cambridge (Eng.) U., 1977; PhD, Ecole Poly., Lausanne, Switzerland, 1983. Architect Edwards, Madigan and Torzillo, Sydney, Australia, 1972-74, S. Australian Housing Trust, Adelaide, 1973-76; research fellow St. John's Coll., Cambridge U., Eng., 1975-77; asst. prof. Ecole Poly. Fed., Lausanne, Switzerland, 1978-84; cons. Econ. Commn. Europe, Geneva, 1984—; master tchng. and research U. Geneva, 1984—; vis. prof. U. Quebec, Montreal, Can., 1987; vis. fellow Flinders U., Adelaide, 1985. Author: Le Seuil Franchi..., 1986, Housing, Dwellings, and Homes, 1987; contbr. articles to profl. jours.; mem. editorial bd. Architecture and Behavior, 1980. Nat. Sci Found. Switzerland fellow, 1984. Mem. Internat. Assn. Study of People and their Phys. Surroundings (bd. dirs. 1986—), Environ. Design Research Assn., People and Phys. Environ. Research Soc., Open House Internat. Assn. Office: Univ Geneva, 9 Rte de Troinex Bat F, Case 266, CH 1227 Carouge Geneva Switzerland

LAWRENCE, SANFORD HULL, physician, immunochemist, writer; b. Kokomo, Ind., July 10, 1919; s. Walter Scott and Florence Elizabeth (Hull) L. AB, Ind. U., 1941, MD, 1944. Intern Rochester (N.Y.) Gen. Hosp., 1944-45; resident Halloran Hosp., Staten Island, N.Y., 1946-49; dir. biochemistry research Lab. San Fernando (Calif.) VA Hosp.; asst. prof. UCLA, 1950—; cons. U.S. Govt., Los Angeles County; lectr. Faculte de Medicine, Paris, various colls. Eng., France, Belgium, Sweden, USSR, India, Japan. Author: Zymogram in Clinical Medicine, 1965; contbr. articles to sic. jours. Mem. Whitley Heights Civic Assn., 1952—; pres. Halloran Hosp. Employees Assn., 1947-48. Served to maj. U.S. Army, 1945-46. Recipient Research award TB and Health Assn., 1955-58, Los Angeles County Heart Assn., 1957-59, Pres.' award, Queen's Blue Bookaward, Am. Men of Sci. award; named one of 2000 Men of Achievement, Leaders of Am. Sci. Mem. AAAS, AMA, N.Y. Acad. Scis., Am. Fedn. Clin. Research, Am. Assn. Clin. Investigation, Am. Assn. Clin. Pathology, Am. Assn. Clin. Chemistry, Los Angeles County Med. Assn. Republican. Methodist. Home: 2014 Whitley Ave Hollywood CA 90068 Home: 160 rue St Martin, Paris 75003, France

LAWRENCE, TELETÉ ZORAYDA, speech and voice pathologist, educator; b. Worcester, Mass., Aug. 5, 1910; d. James Newton and Cora Valeria (Hester) Lester; A.B. cum laude, U. Calif., Berkeley, 1932; M.A., Tex. Christian U., 1963; pvt. study voice with Edgar Schofield, N.Y.C., 1936-41, drama with Enrica Clay Dillon, N.Y.C., 1937-40; m. Ernest Lawrence, Oct. 9, 1939; children—James Lester, Valerie Alma. Lic. speech-lang. pathologist. Mem. Am. Lyric Opera Co., 1939—; instr. speech Sch. Fine Arts, Tex. Christian U., Fort Worth, 1959-66, asst. prof., 1966-71, assoc. prof., 1971-75, prof., 1975-76, emeritus, 1976—, speech pathologist specializing voice disorders Speech and Hearing Clinic, 1959—, faculty research leave, Gt. Britain, Western Europe, Hungary, 1968; pvt. practice speech and voice pathology, 1960—. Mem. bd. Sunshine Haven, home for retarded children, 1957-59; gen. chmn. Ft. Worth and Tarrant County, Nat. Retarded Children's Week, 1954; mem. family and child welfare div. Community Council Ft. Worth and Tarrant County, 1955-57, mem. health and hosp. div., 1959-60; mem. women's com. Ft. Worth chpt. NCCJ, 1956-59; exec. v.p. Fine Arts Found. Guild of Tex. Christian U., 1955-56, past exec. sec., past fin. sec. Recipient Faculty Research grant Tex. Christian U., 1961. Fellow Internat. Soc. Phonetic Scis.; mem. Nat. Council Chs. (bd. joint com. missionary edn. Pacific Coast area, 1952-55), United Ch. Women of Ft. Worth (chmn. Christian world missions dept. 1955-57, pres. 1957-59). Ft. Worth Area Council Chs. (v.p. 1955-57, exec. com. 1957-59, bd. dirs. 1959-60), U. Calif. Alumni Assn. (life), Am. Speech-Lang.-Hearing Assn. (life; cert. clin. competence in speech pathology), Tex. Speech-Lang.-Hearing Assn. (cert.), Ft. Worth Council for Retarded Children, Speech Communication Assn. (sec. speech and hearing disorders interest group 1962-63, mem. com. 1961-64), Am. Dialect Soc., Internat. Assn. Logopedics and Phoniatrics, Phonetic Soc. Japan, AAUP (emeritus), Lambda Ma'ams of Lambda Chi Alpha (pres. Ft. Worth 1962-63), Phi Beta Kappa Assn., Ft. Worth, Phi Beta Kappa (Alpha of Calif. chpt.; charter mem., v.p. Delta of Tex. chpt. 1971-73, pres. 1973-74), Delta Zeta, Psi Chi, Sigma Alpha Eta. Republican. Mem. Christian Ch. Clubs: Woman's of Fort Worth, Women of Rotary. Participant, 13th Congress of Internat. Assn. Logopedics and Phoniatrics, Vienna, 1965, 14th Congress, Paris, 1968, 15th Congress, Buenos Aires, 1971, 16th Congress, Interlaken, Switzerland, 1974, 17th Congress, Copenhagen, 1977, 18th Congress, Washington, 1980, 19th Congress, Edinburgh, Scotland, 1983; participant 10th Internat. Congress of Linguists, Bucharest, 1967; participant 6th Internat. Congress of Phonetic Scis., Prague, 1967, 7th Internat. Congress, Montreal, 1971, 8th Internat. Congress, Leeds, Eng., 1975; participant 1st Congress Internat. Assn. Sci. Study Mental Deficiency, Montpellier, France, 1967, Semmelweis Ann. Week, Budapest Acad. Scis., 1968, 3d World Congress Phoneticians, Tokyo, 1976. Author: Handbook for Instructors of Voice and Diction, 1968; contbr. articles to profl. jours. Home: 3860 South Hills Circle Fort Worth TX 76109

LAWS, RICHARD JOHN SINCLAIR, radio commentator; b. Wau, New Guinea, Aug. 8, 1935; came to Australia, 1941; s. Richard Arthur and Agnes Wilson (Sinclair) L.; m. Caroline Rosalie Margaret Cameron-Waller, Nov. 27, 1976; children by previous marriages—Brett, Luke, Joshua, Samuel, Sarah; stepchildren—Gabrielle, Georgina, Nicola, Susan. Student pub. schs., Sydney, N.S.W. Announcer/commentator Radio Sta. 3BO, Bendigo, Victoria, from 1953, 2UE, Sydney, New South Wales, 1957, 2SM, Sydney, 1959, 2GB, Sydney, 1962, 2YE, Sydney, 1964, 2UW, Sydney, 1969, 2GB, Sydney, 1979—; dir. John S. Laws & Assocs., Pty. Ltd., Sydney, 1981—. Author books of poetry: In Love is an Expensive Place to Die, 1970, Results of Love, 1972, Just You and Me Together Love, 1975, Calendar Collection, 1978, Somewhere Remembering, 1984, Biograph Life by Misadventure by Timothy Hall, 1985. Com. mem. McGrath Found., Sydney, 1979, Nat. Australia Day Council, 1985, Nat. Parks and Wildlife Found., 1980, Duke of Edinburgh Study Conf., 1984. Decorated comdr. Order Brit. Empire; recipient Billboard Internat. Award for on-air achievement, 1974, Australian Radio Record award, 1975, Golden tree award, 1976, Radio award for best talkback Personality in Australia, 1977, 78, 79, 80, 81, Grand Pater award for Outstanding service to radio industry, 1983, Pater award for most popular radio personality in New South Wales, 1983, 84, 85. Avocations: reading; photography; tennis; trail biking. also: Radio Station 2UE, 237 Miller St, 2060 North Sydney, New South Wales Australia

LAWS, RICHARD MAITLAND, scientist, government agency director; b. Whitley Bay, U.K., Apr. 23, 1926; s. Percy Malcolm and Florence May (Heslop) Laws; m. Maureen Isobel Holmes, July 6, 1954; children—Richard Anthony, Christopher Peter, Andrew David. B.A., M.A., Ph.D., Cambridge U. Prin. sci. officer Nat. Inst. Oceanography, Godalming, 1954-61; dir. Nuffield Unit of Animal Ecology, Uganda, 1961-67; dir. Tsavo Research Project, Kenya, 1967-68; head life scis. div. Brit. Antarctic Survey, Natural Environment Research Council, Cambridge, 1969-73, dir., 1973-87; master St. Edmunds Coll., Cambridge, 1985— . Co-author: Elephants and Their Habitats, 1975; editor: Scientific Research in Antarctica, 1977; Antarctic Ecology, 1984, Antartic Nutrient Cycles and Food Webs, 1985. CBE, Her Majesty The Queen, 1983. Fellow Royal Soc. Inst. Biology; mem. Am. Soc. Marine Mammals, Zool. Soc. London, Royal Geog. Soc., Brit. Ecol. Soc., Mammal Soc., African Soc. Mammalogists, Wildlife Soc. Home: 3 The Footpath Coton, Cambridge CB3 7PX England

LAWSON, NIGEL, British government official; b. London, Mar. 11, 1932; s. Ralph and Joan (Davis) L.; m. Vanessa Salmon (div. 1980); m. Therese Mary Maclear, 1980; 6 children. M.A., Oxford U. (Eng.). Mem. editorial staff Financial Times, 1956-60, columnist, 1965; city editor Sunday Telegraph, 1961-63; spl. asst. to Prime Minister, 1963-64; broadcaster BBC, 1965; editor The Spectator, 1966-70; regular contbr. Sunday Times and Evening Standard, 1970-71, The Times, 1971-72; fellow Nuffield Coll., Oxford, 1972-73; spl. polit. adviser Conservative Party Hdqrs., 1973-74; M.P., 1974—, Opposition whip, 1976-77, Opposition spokesman on Treasury and econ. affairs, 1977-79; fin. sec. to Treasury, 1979-81; sec. of state for energy, 1981-83; chancellor of exchequer, 1983—. Author: Contributions to Britain and Canada, 1976; The Coming Confrontation, 1976; (with Bruce-Gardyne) The Power Game, 1976; also pamphlets. Address: House of Commons, London SW 1 England

LAWSON, TERRY MEREDITH, law firm administrator; b. Frederic, Wis., Apr. 14, 1943; s. Meredith C. and Edna V. (Johansen) L.; m. Faye E. Nelson, May 21, 1966 (div. 1971); m. Barbara J. Harper, Sept. 1, 1972. B.B.A., U. Wis.-Madison, 1965; M.Pub. Affairs, U. Colo., Denver, 1976. Dir. mgmt. systems U. Colo. Health Sci. Ctr., Denver, 1975-78, controller, 1978, asst. vice chancellor, 1978-81, vice chancellor, 1981-84; v.p. Denver Consortium Group, Evergreen, Colo., 1982—; sec.-treas., dir. Health Data Analysis, Inc., Littleton, Colo., 1983—; exec. dir. law firm Gorsuch, Kirgis, Campbell, Walker and Grover, Denver, 1984—; pres. Terry M. Lawson & Assocs., 1986—; chmn. exec. com. group on faculty productivity and acad. decision-making model Assn. Acad. Health Ctrs., Inc., 1983-84; bd. dirs. Vindform Industries Inc. Mem. Assn. Legal Adminstrs. (bd. dirs. Mile High chpt. 1986-88, editor Mile High Newsletter 1986-87, chmn. publicity com. 1987-88), ABA (assoc., vice chmn. mktg. administrators com.). Republican. Lutheran. Home: 6591 Hwy 73 Evergreen CO 80439 Office: Gorsuch Kirgis Campbell et al 1401 17th St Suite 1100 Denver CO 80217

LAWSON, THOMAS CHENEY, security, information and credit bureau company executive; b. Pasadena, Calif., Sept. 21, 1955; s. William McDonald and Joan Bell (Jaffee) L.; m. Cathy Lee Taylor. Student Calif. State U., Sacramento, 1973-77. Pres., Tomatron Co., Pasadena, 1970—, Tom's Tune Up & Detail, Pasadena, 1971—, Tom's Pool Service, Sacramento, 1975—, Tom Supply Co., 1975—; mgmt. trainee Permoid Process Co., Los Angeles, 1970-75; regional sales cons. Hoover Co., Burlingame, 1974-76; mktg. exec. River City Prodns., Sacramento, 1977-78; prof. automechanics Calif. State U., Sacramento, 1973-75; territorial rep. Globe div. Burlington House Furniture Co., 1978; So. Calif. territorial rep. Marge Carson Furniture, Inc., 1978-80; pres. Ted L. Gunderson & Assos., Inc., Westwood, Calif., 1980-81; pres., chief exec. officer Apscreen, Newport Beach, Calif., 1981—; pres., chief exec. officer Creditbase Co., Newport Beach, 1982—, Worldata Corp., Newport Beach, 1985—. Calif. Rehab. scholar, 1974-77. Mem. Christian Businessmen's Com. Internat., Council Internat. Investigators, Am. Soc. Indsl. Security (cert.), Nat. Pub. Records Research Assn., Personnel and Indsl. Relations Assn. Office: 1701 Westcliff Dr Suite A Newport Beach CA 92660

LAWTON, ERIC, lawyer, photographer, visual artist; b. N.Y.C., Apr. 9, 1947; s. Leo and Vira (Michaels) L. AB, UCLA, 1969, photographic studies, 1980-81; JD, Loyola U., Los Angeles, 1972. Bar: Calif. 1972, U.S. Dist. Ct. (cen. dist.) Calif. 1974, U.S. Ct. Appeals (9th cir.) 1973, U.S. Supreme Ct. 1976. Assoc. West & Girardi, Los Angeles, 1972-76; sole practice Los Angeles, 1976—; guest lectr. UCLA Law Sch., 1986. one-man shows include Los Angeles Children's Mus., 1980-81, Am. Film Inst., 1981, Marc Richards Gallery, Los Angeles, 1986, U. Art Gallery Calif. State U. Northridge, 1987, John Nichols Gallery, Santa Paula, Calif., 1988; exhibited in group shows at Stockholm Art Fair, Sweden, 1986, L.A. Gallery, 1986-87, Artists' Soc. Internat. Gallery, San Francisco, 1986-87, Fla. State U. Fine Arts Gallery and Mus., Tallahassee, 1988, others; spl. film photographer in The Last Day, 1979, Chiva, Getting on in Style, 1980, Child's Play, 1981, others; multi-media prodns. include The Power, 1979, The Tie That Binds, 1981, Large-Screen Photographic Slide Montage with performance of Los Angeles Philharm. Orch., 1986, Floating Stone performance, Japan Am. Theater, Los Angeles, 1987, others; represented in permanent collections including Bibliotheque Nationale, Paris, Los Angeles Children's Mus., Westwood Nat. Bank, Mobius Soc., Los Angeles, Western Bank, Internat. Photography Mus., Oklahoma City, U.S. Library of Congress, Washington, N.Y. Pub. Library, N.Y.C., others; official White House photographer, 1983; record album covers include Gyuto Monks, Tibetan Tantric Choir, Jungle Suite; poster Japanese Boats; contbr. photographs to newspapers and mags. including, N.Y. Times Mag., Chgo. Tribune, Variety, Gente (Italy), Dukas Femina (Switzerland), others. Active organizing com., citizens adv. and cultural and fine arts adv. commns. XXIII Olympic Games, Los Angeles, 1983-84; mem Cultural and Fine Arts Adv. Commn, 1983-84. Recipient award Fla. Nat. '88. Mem. ABA, Los Angeles Trial Lawyers Assn., Los Angeles County Bar Assn., Santa Monica Bar Assn. Office: 2001 Wilshire Blvd 600 Santa Monica CA 90403

LAWTON, JACQUELINE AGNES, retired communications company executive, management consultant; b. Bklyn., June 9, 1933; d. Thomas G. and Agnes R. (McLaughlin) Maguire; m. George W. Lawton, Feb. 14, 1954; children—George, Victoria, Thomas. With N.Y. Telephone, 1954-82, mktg. mgr. govt., edn. and med. Mid State, 1978-81, mktg. mgr. health care, N.Y.C., 1981-82; dist. field market mgr. health care and lodging; region 1 N.E. and Region 2 Mid Atlantic, AT&T-Am. Bell, N.Y.C., 1982-83; Eastern region mgr. personnel, mktg. and sales AT&T Info. Systems, Parsippany, N.J., 1983-86, pvt. practice mgmt. cons., Cornish Flat, N.H., 1986—. Mem. Nat. Assn. Female Execs. Republican. Roman Catholic. Home and Office: PO Box 163 Cornish Flat NH 03746

LAWTON, MICHAEL JAMES, entomologist, pest management specialist; b. Balt., Aug. 6, 1953; s. James William and Mary Eileen (O'Connor) L.; m. Barbara Ann Byron, Dec. 19, 1983. BS, U. Md., 1975. Registered profl. entomologist. Technician, tech. dir. Atlas Exterminating Co., Towson, Md., 1975-78; asst. tech. dir. Western Exterminator Co., Irvine, Calif., 1978-83, tng. and tech. dir., 1984—. Republican. Office: Western Exterminator Co 1732 Kaiser Ave Irvine CA 92714

LAWYER, VIVIAN JURY, lawyer; b. Farmington, Iowa, Jan. 7, 1932; d. Jewell Everett Jury and Ruby Mae (Schumaker) Brewer; m. Verne Lawyer, Oct. 25, 1959; children—Michael Jury, Steven Verne. Tchr.'s cert. U. No. Iowa, 1951; B.S. with honors, Iowa State U., 1953; J.D. with honors, Drake U., 1968. Bar: Iowa 1968, U.S. Supreme Ct. 1986. Home econs. tchr. Waukee High Sch. (Iowa), 1953-55; home econs. tchr. jr. high sch. and high sch., Des Moines Pub. Schs., 1955-61; sole practice law, Des Moines, 1972—; bd. dirs. Micah Corp.; chmn. juvenile code tng. sessions Iowa Crime Commn., Des Moines, 1978-79, coordinator workshops, 1980; assoc. Law Offices of Verne Lawyer, Des Moines, 1981—; co-founder, bd. dirs. Youth Law Center, Des Moines, 1977—; mem. com. rules of juvenile procedure Supreme Ct. Iowa, 1981-87, adv. com. on costs of ct. appointed counsel Supreme Ct. Iowa, 1985—; trustee Polk County Legal Aid Services, Des Moines, 1980-82; mem. Iowa Dept. Human Services and Supreme Ct. Juvenile Justice County Base Joint Study Com., 1984—; mem. Iowa Task Force permanent families project Nat. Council Juvenile and Family Ct. Judges, 1984—; mem. substance abuse com. Commn. Children, Youth and Families, 1985—; co-chair Polk County Juvenile Detention Task Force, 1988. Editor: Iowa Juvenile Code Manual, 1979, Iowa Juvenile Code Workshop Manual, 1980; co-editor 1987 Cumulative Supplement, Iowa Academy of Trial Lawyers Trial Handbook; author booklet in field, 1981. Mem. Polk County Citizens Commn. on Corrections, 1977. Iowa Dept. Social Services grantee, 1980. Mem. ABA, Iowa Bar Assn., Polk County Bar Assn., Polk County Women Attys. Assn., Assn. Trial Lawyers Am., Assn. Family Counseling in Juvenile and Family Cts., Purple Arrow, Phi Kappa Phi, Omicron Nu. Republican. Home: 5831 N Waterbury Rd Des Moines IA 50312 Office: 427 Fleming Bldg Des Moines IA 50309

LAX, PETER DAVID, mathematician; b. Budapest, Hungary, May 1, 1926; came to U.S., 1941, naturalized, 1944; s. Henry and Klara (Kornfeld) L.; m. Anneli Cahn, 1948; children: John, James D. B.A., N.Y. U., 1947, Ph.D., 1949; D.Sc. (hon.), Kent State U., 1976; D. honoris causa, U. Paris, 1979. Asst. prof. N.Y. U., 1949-57, prof., 1957—; dir. Courant Inst. Math. Scis., 1972-80. Author: (with Ralph Phillips) Scattering Theory, 1967, Scattering Theory for Automorphic Functions, 1976, (with A. Lax and S.Z. Burstein) Calculus with applications and computing), 1976, Hyperbolic Systems of Conservation Laws and the Mathematical Theory of Shock Waves, 1973. Mem. Pres.'s Com. on Nat. Medal of Sci., 1976, Nat. Sci. Bd., 1980-86. Served with AUS, 1944-46. Recipient Semmelweis medal Semmelweis Med. Soc., 1975, Nat. Medal Sci., 1986, Wolf Prize, 1987. Mem. Am. Math. Soc. (pres. 1979-80, Norbert Wiener prize), Nat. Acad. Scis. (applied math. and numerical analysis award 1983), Am. Acad. Arts and Scis., Math. Assn. Am. (bd. govs., Chauvenet prize), Soc. Indsl. and Applied Math.; fgn. asso. Académie des Scis. (France). Office: Courant Inst Math Scis 251 Mercer St New York NY 10012

LAX, PHILIP, land developer, space planner; b. Newark, Apr. 22, 1920; s. Nathan and Beckie (Hirschhorn) L.; m. Mildred Baras, Feb. 15, 1948; children: Corinne, Barbara. B.S., NYU, 1940, postgrad., 1941-42. With Lax & Co., Newark, 1942-77; v.p. Lax & Co., 1950-77; pres. Chathill Mgmt., Inc., 1977—. Pres. B'nai B'rith Ctr., Rochester, Minn., 1965-70, now hon. pres.; trustee Rutgers U. Hillel; pres. B'nai B'rith Rutgers U. Hillel Found. Bldg. Corp., 1969—; chmn. United Jewish Appeal, Maplewood, N.J., 1966, 76; mem. N.J. region exec. bd. Anti-Defamation League, mem. nat. community relations bd.; mem. Gov.'s Conf. on Edn., N.J., 1966, Mayor's Budget Com., Maplewood, 1958-59; co-chmn. N.J. Opera Ball, 1977; trustee B'nai B'rith Found., Washington, 1967—, Philip Lax Gallery of B'nai B'rith History and Archives named for him in Philip Klutznick Mus.; co-chmn. B'nai B'rith internat. council, 1979; chmn. B'nai B'rith intern. council, 1980-85, now hon. chmn. B'nai B'rith internat. council; trustee, mem. exec. com. N.J. sect. NCCJ, 1981; trustee Henry Monsky Found., Washington, 1968—; trustee Leo N. Levi Hosp., Hot Springs, Ark., 1968-71, B'nai Brith World Jewish Ctr., Jerusalem, 1982, Nat. Arthrities Hosp., 1976—, N.Y. Statue of Liberty Centennial Found.; hon. trustee Arts Council of Suburban Essex, N.J., 1980; mem. Econ. Devel. Commn., Twp. of Maplewood, 1979—; mem. steering com. to Restore Ellis Island, 1977—; nat. pres. Ellis Island Restoration Commn., 1978—responsible for planning, funding and operating Genealogy Ctr. on Ellis Island; appointed to planning team of Statue of Liberty and Ellis Island by Nat. Park Service, Dept. of Interior ; mem. Statue of Liberty/Ellis Island Centennial Commn., Statue of Liberty-Ellis Island Centennial Commn., Com. of Architecture and Restoration of Statue of Liberty-Ellis Island. Recipient Found. award B'nai B'rith, 1968, Humanitarian award, 1969, Pres.'s Gold medal, 1975; Pro Mundi Beneficio medal Brazilian Acad. Humanities, 1976; Philip Lax chapel at Rutgers U. Hillel named in his honor. Mem. Am. Soc. Interior Designers, Nat. Soc. Interior Designers (trustee 1970-73), Am. Arbitration Assn., Am. Jewish Hist. Com. (v.p.), Am. Jewish Hist. Soc. (trustee 1984), Am. Soc. Israel Philatelists, Phi Alpha Kappa. Clubs: Masons (32 deg.), Shriners, B'nai B'rith (v.p. Supreme Lodge 1968-71, internat. bd. govs. 1971—, mem. exec. com. of internat. council); NYU (N.Y.C.) (founder 1956). Home: 35 Claremont Dr Maplewood NJ 07040 Office: Chathill Mgmt 830 Morris Turnpike Short Hills NJ 07078

LAXALT, PAUL, former U.S. senator; b. Reno, Aug. 2, 1922; s. Dominique and Theresa (Alpetche) L.; m. Jackalyn Ross, June 23, 1946 (div.); children: Gail, Sheila, John, Michelle, Kevin, Kathleen; m. Carol Wilson, Jan. 2, 1976; 1 child, Denise. Student, Santa Clara U., 1940-43; B.S., LL.B., Denver U., 1949. Bar: Nev. bar 1949. Practice in Carson City; partner firm Laxalt, Ross & Laxalt, 1954-62; dist. atty. Ormsby County, 1951-54; city atty. Carson City, 1954-55; lt. gov. Nev., 1962-66, gov., 1966-70; sr. partner Laxalt, Berry & Allison, Carson City, 1970-74; U.S. senator 1974-86; mem. law firm Laxalt, Washington, Perito & Dubuc, Washington, DC, 1987—; gen. chmn. Nat. Rep. Party, 1983-87; pres., gen. mgr. Ormsby House Hotel and Casino, Carson City, 1972-75. Gen. chmn. Nat. Republican Party, 1983—. Mem. Am. Bar Assn., Am. Legion, VFW. Club: Eagles. Office: Laxalt Washington Perito & Dubuc 1455 Pennsylvania Ave NW Suite 975 Washington DC 20004

LAXENAIRE, MICHEL JEAN, medical educator; b. Leintrey, Lorraine, France, Dec. 18, 1928; s. Jean Georges and Mathilde (Tard) L.; m. Simone Aubertin, Aug. 15, 1959 (dec.); 1 child, Nathalie; m. Marie Claire Aug, June 27, 1967; children: Elisa, Lucile. Lic. de Philosophie, U. Nancy, France, 1951, MD, 1960. Intern Univ. Hosp. Nancy, 1955-59; resident in neuropsychiatry Meyer Meml. Hosp., Buffalo, 1957-58; chief of neuropsychiatry clinic Univ. Hosp. Nancy, 1959-62, head med. psychology and psychiatry sects., 1974—; maitre de Conf. Agrégü248 de Neuro-Psychiatrie, 1963; mem. Médecin des Hôpitaux par Intégration, 1966; prof. sans chaire, 1972; chef du service de psychologie med. au C.H.R. de Nancy, 1974. Author: Les processus de changement en psychothérapie de groupe, 1975, Les rencontres psychologiques du médecin, 1980, La nourriture, la Socieétéet le médecin, 1983. Mem. Soc. Médico-Psychologique, Société de Psychiatrie et de Neurologie de Langue Francaise, Soc. Française de Neurologie, Soc. Psychologie Med. de Langue Française (pres.), Groupe Français d'Etudes de Sociometrie (pres.), Soc. Med. de Nancy. Clubs: Alpin Français, Vosgien. Home: Chemin du Val, 54690 Eulmont France Office: Hosp Jeanne d'Arc, BP 303, 54201 Toul France

LAY, KENNETH LEE, diversified company executive; b. Tyrone, Mo., Apr. 15, 1942; s. Omer and Ruth E. (Reese) L.; m. Judith Diane Ayers, June 10, 1966; children: Mark Kenneth, Elizabeth Ayers. BA, U. Mo., 1964, MA, 1965; PhD, U. Houston, 1970. Corp. economist Exxon Corp., Houston, 1965-68; assoc. prof. and lectr. in econs. George Washington U., 1969-73; tech. asst. to commr. FPC, 1971-72; dep. undersec. for energy Dept. Interior, 1972-74; v.p. Fla. Gas Co. (now Continental Resources Co.), Winter Park, Fla., 1974-79, pres., 1979-81; pres. Fla. Gas Transmission Co., Winter Park, 1976-79; pres., chief operating officer Transco Cos. Inc., Houston, 1981-84, Transcontinental Gas Pipe Line Corp., 1981-84; chmn., pres., chief exec officer Houston Natural Gas Corp., 1984-85; pres., chief exec. officer, chief operating officer Enron Corp. (formerly Internorth), Omaha, 1985; chmn. Enron Corp. (formerly Internorth), Houston, 1986—, now also chief exec. officer, dir.; chmn. bd. dirs. Slurry Transport Assn., 1979-81; dir. Nat. Energy Found., Gas Research Inst., Baker Internat., Sun Banks, Fla. Bd. dirs. John Young Museum, Orlando, Fla., 1974-76, Winter Park Library, 1977-78, Central Fla. Funds Drive; mem. U. Central Fla. Found. Served with USN, 1968-71. Decorated Navy Commendation award; N.A.M. fellow; State Farm fellow; Guggenheim fellow. Mem. Am. Econ. Assn., Interstate Natural Gas Assn. Am. (dir.), Young Presidents Orgn., U.S. C. of C. (natural resource com.). Republican. Methodist. Clubs: Winter Park Racquet, Citrus. Office: Enron Corp 1400 Smith St Houston TX 77002 *

LAYBOURN, JAN LIND, tourism director; b. Copenhagen, May 22, 1947; s. Carl Lind Mortensen and Annie (Pedersen) Laybourn; m. Berit Munck Nielsen, July 1, 1947; children: Steffen, Anna. BS in Econs., Copenhagen Sch. Econs. and Bus. Adminstrn., 1970. Asst. mgr. Copenhagen Tourist Assn., 1972-77, mgr., 1977-83, dir. tourism, 1983—. Bd. dirs. Copenhagen Jazz Festival, 1984—; bd. reps. Copenhagen City Centre Assn., 1984—, Copenhagen Erhvervsting, 1984—. Mem. Fedn. Danish Dirs. Tourism (bd. dirs. 1986—). Home: Laestedet 29, 2670 Copenhagen, Greve Strand Denmark Office: Copenhagen Tourist Assn, Noerregade 7a, 1165 Copenhagen Denmark

LAYDER, DEREK, sociology educator, researcher; b. Liverpool, Eng., Apr. 28, 1948; s. Roy Austin and Joan (Peters) L. B.S. in Sociology, Leicester U., 1970; Ph.D. in Sociology, London Sch. Econs., 1976. Tutor Leicester U., 1973-74, lectr. sociology, 1974—. Author: Structure Interaction and Social Theory, 1981; contbr. articles to profl. publs. Social Sci. Research Council scholar London Sch. Econs., 1970-73. Mem. Brit. Sociol. Assn. Home: 21 Byway Rd, Evington, Leicester LE5 5TF, England Office: Leicester U, Dept Sociology, Leicester LE1 7RH, England

LAYNE, JOHN FRANCIS, accountant; b. Milw., Mar. 25, 1928; s. Lawrence E. and Blanche E. (Tetzlaff) L.; A.A., Valencia Jr. Coll., 1971; B.S.B.A., U. Central Fla., 1972; m. Esther A. Ornberg, Mar. 10, 1951; children—Loretta E., John W., Mark L. Enlisted U.S. Air Force, 1948, advanced through grades to chief warrant officer-4, 1964; test controller, systems devel. Air Proving Ground Ctr., Eglin AFB, 1962-65; standardization/evaluation controller USAF, Far East, Okinawa and Vietnam, 1966-70; ret., 1970; acct. Electric Specialty, Orlando, Fla., 1971-74, controller, 1975-77; fin. field rep. Tupperware div. Dart, Orlando, 1978—. Vice pres. Cen. Fla. Assn. Sq. Dancers, 1977-78, pres., 1978-79, Couple of Yr. award, 1984; chmn. 1978 Fla. Sq. Dance Conv.; active Fla. Fedn. Sq. Dancers, 1978-82, pres., 1982-83. Decorated Bronze Star, Honor medal Republic of Vietnam; recipient Excellence award Far East council Boy Scouts Am., 1968, Am. Sq. Dance Soc., 1983. Mem. Nat. Accts. Assn., Nat. Soc. Pub. Accts., Nat. Assn. Enrolled Agts. Office: Tupperware Home Parties 4975 Preston Park Blvd Suite 490 Plano TX 75075

LAYTON, ALLAN PATRICK, economics educator, researcher; b. Brisbane, Australia, Dec. 1, 1954; s. Reginald and Alma Eileen (Bell) L. B of Econs. with honors, Univ. Queensland, 1976, M of Econs., 1979, PhD, 1982. Research fellow Australian Bur. Statistics, Canberra, 1976; teaching fellow Univ. Queensland, Brisbane, 1979-81, LaTrobe U., Melbourne, Australia, 1982; sr. teaching fellow Griffith U., Brisbane, 1983; lectr. in econs. Macquarie U., Sydney, Australia, 1984-87, sr. lectr. econs., 1987; adj. assoc. prof. Columbia U., N.Y.C., 1988; sr. lectr. U. Queensland, Brisbane, 1989—; research specialties include macroecon. policy, econ. growth cycle research, U.S. services sector research; cons. Overseas Telecommunication Commn., Electricity Commn. New South Wales, Sydney County Council, Westmead Pub. Hosp., Econ. Planning and Adv. Council Australia, Canberra, Westpac Banking Corp. Contbr. articles to profl. jours. Research grantee Govt. Australia, 1977. Mem. Econ. Soc. Australia and New Zealand, Australasian Econ. Soc., Assn. Australian Bus. Economists. Office: U Queensland, Brisbane 4067, Australia

LAYTON, GARLAND MASON, lawyer; b. Boydton, Va., Aug. 20, 1925. LLB, Smith-Deal-Massey Coll. Law, 1952; LLD, Coll. of William and Mary, 1962. Bar: Va. 1951, U.S. Dist. Ct. (ea. dist.) Va. 1961, U.S. Supreme Ct. 1968. Sole practice Virginia Beach, Va., 1952—. Served with USMC, 1940-45, PTO. Mem. ABA, Fed. Bar Assn., Nat. Lawyers Club, Va. Beach Bar Assn. Democrat. Methodist. Home: PO Box 5211 Bayside Station Virginia Beach VA 23455 Office: 4809 Baybridge Ln PO Box 5211 Virginia Beach VA 23455

LAYTON, HARRY CHRISTOPHER, artist, lecturer; b. Safford, Ariz., Nov. 17, 1938; s. Christopher E. and Eurilda (Welker) L.; LHD, Sussex Coll., Eng., 1967; DFA (hon.), London Inst. Applied Research, 1972; DD (hon.), St. Matthew U., Ohio, 1970, PhD (hon.), 1970; m. Karol Barbara Kendall, July 11, 1964; children: Deborah, Christopher, Joseph, Elisabeth, Faith, Aaron, Gretchen, Benjamin, Justin, Matthew, Peter. Lectr. ancient art Serra Cath. High Sch., 1963-64, Los Angeles Dept. Parks and Recreation, summer 1962, 63, 64; interior decorator Cities of Hawthorne, Lawndale, Compton, Gardena and Torrance (Calif.), 1960-68; one-man shows paintings; Nahas Dept. Stores, 1962, 64; group shows include: Gt. Western Savs. & Loan, Lawndale, Calif., 1962, Gardena (Calif.) Adult Sch., 1965, Serra Cath. High Sch., Gardena, 1963, Salon de Nations Paris, 1983; represented in permanent collections: Sussex Coll., Eng., Gardena Masonic Lodge, Culver City-Foshey Masonic Lodge, Gt. Western Savs. & Loan; paintings include: The Fairy Princess, 1975, Nocturnal Covenant, 1963, Blindas Name, 1962, Creation, 1962. Elder Ch. of Jesus Christ of Latter-day Saints, Santa Monica, Calif., 1963—. Mem. Am. Hypnotherapy Assn., Gardena Valley Art Assn., Centinell.a Valley Art Assn., Internat. Soc. Artists, Internat. Platform Assn., Am. Security Council, Soc. for Early Historic Archaeology, Am. Councilor's Soc. of Psychol. Counselors, Am. Legion, Alpha Psi Omega. Republican. Clubs: Masons (32 deg.), Shriners, K.T. Home: 3932 McLaughlin Ave Los Angeles CA 90066 Office: Layton Studios 66849 MV Sta Mar Vista CA 90066

LAYTON, IRVING PETER, poet, teacher; b. Neamtz, Rumania, Mar. 12, 1912; came to Can., 1913; s. Moses Lazarovitch and Klara (Moscovitch) L.; m. Faye Lynch, Sept. 13, 1939 (div.); m. Betty Frances Sutherland, Sept. 13, 1946 (div.); children—Max Rubin, Naomi Parker; m. Aviva Cantor, Sept. 13, 1961 (div.); 1 child, David Herschel; m. Harriet Bernstein, Nov. 23, 1978 (div. Mar. 1984); 1 child, Samantha Clara; m. Anna Pottier, Nov. 8, 1984. B.S. in Agr., Macdonald Coll., Can., 1939; M.A., McGill U., Can., 1946; D.C.L., Bishop's U., Can., 1970; D. Lit., York U., Can., 1979; D.C.L. (hon.), Concordia U., 1976. Prof., York U., lectr. Sir George Williams U., Montreal, 1950-68; poet-in-residence, U. Guelph, 1969-70, U. Ottawa, 1978-79; vis. prof. Concordia U., 1978-79; writer-in-residence, U. Toronto, 1981-82. Served to lt. R.C.A., 1942-43. Author: Here and Now, 1945; Now Is the Place 1948; The Black Huntsmen 1951; (with others) Cerberus, 1952; Love the Conqueror Worm 1953; In the Midst of My Fever 1954; The Long Pea-Shooter 1954; The Cold Green Element 1955; The Blue Propeller 1955; The Bull Calf and Other Poems 1956; Music On A Kazoo 1956; A Laughter in the Mind 1958; Red Carpet for the Sun 1959 (Gov.-Gen. Award for English Poetry 1960); The Swinging Flesh 1961; Balls For a One-Armed Juggler 1963; The Laughing Rooster 1964; Collected Poems 1965; Ed. Love Where the Nights Are Long, 1963, Prix Litteraire de Quebec, First Prize 1963, Periods of the Moon (Poems) 1967, The Shattered Plinths (poetry) 1968, The Whole Bloody Bird (prose and poetry) 1969, Selected Poems 1969, Nail Polish 1971, Collected Poems 1971, Engagements: Selected Prose, 1972, Lovers and Lesser Men 1973, The Pole Vaulter 1974, Seventy-Five Greek Poems 1974, The Darkening Fire (Selected Poems, 1945-68) 1975, Il freddo Verde Elemento (Giulio Einaudi, Torino), 1974, The Unwavering Eye; Selected Poems 1969-75, 1979, For My Brother Jesus 1976, The Covenant 1977, Taking Sides (prose) 1977, Selected Poems, New Directions, 1977, The Uncollected Poems of I.L., 1977, The Tightrope Dancer 1978, The Love Poems of Irving Layton (deluxe edition) 1978, Irving Layton, Carlo Mattioli (Edition Trentadue, Milan) 1978, Irving Layton-Aligi Sassu Portfolio, Milan, 1978, Droppings from Heaven 1979, An Unlikely Affair: Layton-Rath Correspondence 1980, For My Neighbours in Hell 1980, The Love Poems of I.L., 1980, in un'etadi ghiaccio (In an Ice Age-Bilingual Selected Poems, 1981), Europe and Other Bad News, 1981, A Wild Peculiar Joy 1982, Shadows On The Ground (portfolio) 1982, The Gucci Bag 1983, co-ed. with L. Dudek of Canadian Poems 1850-1952, 1953, Las Poemas de Amor, 1983, With Reverence and Delight: The Love Poems of Irving Layton 1984, Selected Poems (bilingual Korean, Eng. ed., Seoul, South Korea 1985), Where Burning Sappho Loved (Libro, Athens) 1985, A Tall Man Executes a Jig (Portfolio with Salvatore Fiume), 1986, Waiting for the Messiah, 1985,

Dance with Desire, 1986, Final Reckoning: Poems 1982-86, 1987, Fortunate Exile, 1987, others. Recipient Can. Council Award 1959; his poems have appeared in translation in Roumanian, Polish, Russian, Korean and in Spanish, Italian in Argentine lit. papers and jours.; in 1956 an Am. ed. of his selected poems under the title The Improved Binoculars with foreword by William Carlos Williams, appeared under the imprint of Jargon Press; awarded a Can. Found. fellowship, 1957; recipient Can. Council Spl. Arts award, 1967, Can. Council Arts award 1979-81, Long Term award, Achievement in Life award Encyclopedia Britannica, 1979; nominated for Nobel Prize by Italy and S. Korea 1982. Avocations: freethinking; handball; swimming; chess. Home and Office: 6879 Monkland Ave, Montreal, PQ Canada H4B 1J5

LAYTON, ROBERT GLENN, radiologist; b. Bklyn., Oct. 14, 1946; s. Irving and Charlotte (Bell) L.; m. Judith Helene Bohrer, May 31, 1969; children—Andrew, Julia. B.S., Union Coll., 1968; M.D., Boston U., 1972. Diplomate Am. Bd. Radiology. Resident in radiology, Boston City Hosp., 1972-75; jr. attending radiologist L.I. Jewish Hosp., Hillside, N.Y., 1975-76; staff radiologist Cedars Med. Ctr., Miami, Fla., 1978—; radiologist Highland Park Gen. Hosp., Miami, 1978-84; clin. prof. U. Miami Sch. Med., 1985—. Pres., Michael-Ann Russell Jewish Community Ctr., Miami, 1980-82; bd. dirs. Jewish Community Ctrs. S. Fla., 1982-86; trustee Temple Sinai of North Dade, North Miami Beach, 1982—, v.p., 1985—. Served to maj. USAF, 1976-78. Mem. AMA, Am. Coll. Radiology, Am. Inst. Ultrasound in Medicine, Miami Radiol. Soc., Begg Soc., Alpha Omega Alpha. Jewish. Avocations: contemporary art, tennis, skiing. Home: 21120 NE 23rd Ct North Miami Beach FL 33180 Office: Cedars Med Ctr Dept Radiology 1400 NW 12th Ave Miami FL 33136

LÁZÁR, GYÖRGY, deputy general secretary; b. Isaszeg, Hungary, Sept. 15, 1924; s. Mihály and Etel (Fehér) L.; m. Adél Kiss; 1 son. Tech. draftsman; mem. Communist Party, 1945—; joined Nat. Planning Office, 1948, chief dept. head, 1953, v.p., 1958; minister of labor, 1970-73; dep. prime minister, chmn. State Planning Com., pres. Nat. Planning Office, 1973-75, prime minister of Hungarian People's Republic, 1975-87, mem. Politburo, 1975—, dep. sec. gen., 1987—. Author: Historic Present, 1983. Decorated Labour Order Merit (twice). Address: Hungarian Socialist, Workers' Party Cen Com, Szechenyi takpart 19, 1358 Budapest Hungary *

LAZAR, KENNETH STUART, architect; b. Bklyn., Jan. 24, 1948; s. Henry Charles and Pauline (Seckular) L.; m. Joan Eleanor Cancelleri, Aug. 16, 1970; children: Jeremy Sean, Marc Jonathan. A.A.S., N.Y.C. Community Coll., 1976. Designer, David Kraus, AIA, N.Y.C., 1968-73; project mgr. Wm. Barnum Assocs., Greenwich, Conn., 1973-79; sr. assoc. Van Summern & Weigold, Stamford, Conn., 1979-84; exec. v.p. Van Summern Group, Inc., Stamford, Conn. and N.Y.C., 1984-86; ptnr. Design Collaborative Inc., Stamford, Conn., White Plains and Lake Success, N.Y., 1986-88; prin. Design Ptnrship., Stamford, Conn. and New Rochelle, N.Y., 1988; ptnr. , 1988—. Mem. AIA, Conn. Soc. Architects.

LAZARCIK, GREGOR, educator, financial research co. exec., economist; b. Horna Streda, Slovakia, Mar. 10, 1923; s. Gaspar and Maria (Rehak) L.; B.S., State Coll. (Slovakia), 1945; M.S., Coll. Agr. (Brno, Czechoslovakia), 1948; cert. Swiss Inst. Tech. (Zurich), 1949; A.M., U. Strasbourg (France), 1952; LL.M., LL.D. (fellow), U. Paris, 1953; Ph.D. (fellow), Columbia, 1960; m. Theresa M. Good, Aug. 14, 1971. Came to U.S., 1953, naturalized, 1958. Asst. to mgr. Central Butter Dairy, Lucerne, Switzerland, 1948-49; controller dairy products Agrl. syndicate, Hazebruck, France, 1949-50, with Research Project on Nat. Income, Columbia U., N.Y.C., 1956—, sr. research economist, 1961—; with L.W. Internat. Financial Research, Inc., N.Y.C., 1961—, dir. research, pres., 1962-13 , chmn. exec. com., 1961—, chmn. bd.; lectr. econs. Hunter Coll., CUNY, 1963-64, econs., Columbia U., 1964-68; prof. econs. SUNY, 1968—. Mem. Am. Econ. Assn., Am. Regional Sci. Assn., Assn. for Study Soviet-Type Economies. Roman Catholic. Author: Le Commerce en Matiere Agricole Entre l'Europe de l'Ouest et l'Europe de L'Est, 1959; Czechoslovak National Income and Product, 1947-56, 1962 (co-author); The Performance of Socialist Agriculture, 1963; Scientific Research and its Relation to Earnings and Stock Prices, 1965; Comparison of Agricultural and Nonagricultural Income, 1937, 48-65, 1968; Defense, Education and Health Expenditures and Their Relation to GNP in Eastern Europe, 1978; Economic Growth in Eastern Europe, 1965-82, 1983; Agricultural Output and Productivity in Eastern Europe and Some Comparisons with the USSR and USA, 1985; contbr. to East European Economics Post-Helsinki, 1977. Address: 633 W 115th St New York NY 10025

LAZAREV, ALEXANDRE, conductor; b. Moscow, Sovjettian, USSR, July 5, 1945; m. Tamara Lazareva; 1 child, Tanja. Student, Moscow Conservatory. Conductor Bolshoi Theatre, Moscow, 1973-86, chief conductor and music dir., 1987—; music dir. Duisburg Symphony, Fed. Republic Germany, 1988—. Recipient 1st prize all-Soviet-Union Competition, 1971, 1st prize and Gold medal Herbert von Karajan Competition, West Berlin, 1972. Office: Bolshoi State Acad Theatre, 1 Ploshchad Sverklova, Moscow USSR

LAZARUS, ARNOLD ALLAN, psychologist, educator; b. Johannesburg, Republic of South Africa, Jan. 27, 1932; came to U.S., 1963; s. Benjamin and Rachel Leah (Mosselson) L.; m. Daphne Ann Kessel, June 10, 1956; children: Linda Sue, Clifford Neil. BA with honors, U. Witwatersrand, 1956; MA, U. Witwatersrand, Johannesburg, 1957, PhD, 1960. Diplomate: Am. Bd. Profl. Psychology, Am. Bd. Med. Psychotherapists (fellow), Internat. Acad. Behavioral Medicine, Counseling and Psychotherapy. Pvt. practice clin. psychology Johannesburg, 1959-63, 64-66; vis. asst. prof. dept. psychology Stanford (Calif.) U., 1963-64; prof. psychology Temple U. Med. Sch., Phila., 1967-70; dir. clin. tng. Yale U., New Haven, 1970-72; disting. prof. Rutgers U., New Brunswick, N.J., 1972—; mem. adv. bd. Psychologists for Social Responsibility, 1984—; cons. in field. Author 12 books including, Behavior Therapy and Beyond, 1971, Multimodal Behavior Therapy, 1976, The Practice of Multimodal Therapy, 1981, In the Mind's Eye, 1984, Marital Myths, 1985, Mind Power: Getting What You Want Through Mental Training, 1987; contbr. articles to profl. jours. Recipient Disting. Service award Am. Bd. Profl. Psychology. Fellow Am. Psychol. Assn., Am. Bd. Profl. Psychology (diplomate); mem. Am. Acad. Psychotherapy, Assn. for Advancement Behavior Therapy (past pres.), Assn. for Advancement Psychotherapy, Nat. Acads. Practice in Psychology (disting.). Home: 56 Herrontown Circle Princeton NJ 08540 Office: Rutgers U PO Box 819 Piscataway NJ 08855

LAZARUS, A(RNOLD) L(ESLIE), English language educator, writer; b. Revere, Mass., Feb. 20, 1914; s. Benjamin and Bessie (Winston) L.; m. Keo Smith Felker, July 24, 1938; children: Karie (Mrs. John Friedman), Dianne (Mrs. James Runnels), David, Peter. Student, Coll. William and Mary, 1931-32; B.A., U. Mich., 1935; M.A., UCLA, 1941, Ed.D., 1957. Tchr. Calif. pub. schs., 1945-53; instr. Santa Monica (Calif.) City Coll., 1953-58; lectr. Los Angeles State Coll., 1958-59; assoc. prof. U. Tex., 1959-62; prof. English, dir. tchr. edn. in English Purdue U., Lafayette, Ind., 1962-79; dir. English Curriculum Center, 1963-79; gen. editor Purdue Research Found. Project English Study Units, 1969-79; mem. bd. judges Book-of-the-Month Club Writing Fellowships, 1967-70. Author: Your English Helper, 1953, Adventures in Modern Literature, 1956, 62, 70, Harbrace English Language Series, 1963, Selected Objectives in the Language Arts, 1967, Entertainments and Valedictions, 1970, (with others) A Catalogue of Performance Objectives in English, 1971, The Grosset and Dunlap Glossary to Literature and Language, 1971, 72, 73, A Suit of Four, 1973, (with Victor Jones) Beyond Graustark, 1981, (with H. Wendell Smith) The NCTE Glossary of Literature and Composition, 1983, Some Light: New and Selected Verse, 1988; poems anthologized in Light Year 1984, 85, 86, 87; contbr. poems, stories to lit. jours.; editor: The Indiana Experience, 1977, The Best of George Ade, 1985, The World of George Barr McCutcheon, 1987; editor (with others) Quartet mag, 1962-68; poetry editor, 1968-73; contbg. author New Book of Knowledge, 1967, Foundations of Education, 1967, College English: The First Year, 1968, 73, 78; contbr. articles to profl. jours. Mem. English com. Coll. Entrance Examination Bd. Served with AUS, 1942-44. Recipient Best Tchr. award Purdue Sch. Humanities, 1974; Kemper McComb award, 1976; Ford Found. fellow, 1954. Mem. Nat. Council Tchrs. of English (exec. com. Conf. English Edn. 1966-72), Poetry Soc. Am., Acad. of Am. Poets, NEA, MLA, Coll. English Assn., Phi Beta Kappa. Home: 945 Ward Dr 69 Santa Barbara CA 93111

LAZO, JACQUI FISKE, lawyer; b. Balt., Apr. 4, 1951; d. Guy W. and E. Jacqueline (Strachan) Fiske; m. John Stephen Lazo, Oct. 12, 1974; 1 child, Jacquelyn Kristina. Student Mills Coll., 1969-71; BA with honors, Goucher Coll., 1973; JD with honors, U. Conn., 1978. Bar: Conn. 1978, Pa. 1988. Assoc. Sohcot & Jacks, East Haven, Conn., 1978-81; ptnr. Gallant, Mednick & Gallant, New Haven, 1982-83, Tirola, Herring, Pober & Lazo, Westport, Conn., 1984-87, Buchanan Ingersoll, Pitts., 1987—. Sec., dir. Guilford Nursing and Homemaker Services, 1980-85; vice chmn. Guilford Zoning Bd. Appeals, 1982-85. Mem. ABA, Conn. Bar Assn. (exec. com. real property sect. 1984-87), Phi Beta Kappa. Home: 5128 Pembroke Pl Pittsburgh PA 15232 Office: Buchanan Ingersoll 600 Grant St 58th Fl Pittsburgh PA 15219

LAZZARA, DENNIS JOSEPH, dentist, orthodontist; b. Chgo., Mar. 14, 1948; s. Joseph James and Jacqueline Joan (Antonini) L.; m. Nancy Ann Pirhofer, Dec. 18, 1971; children: Kristin Lynn, Bryan Matthew, Matthew Dennis, Kathryn Marie, David Brady. B.S., U. Dayton, 1970; D.D.S., Loyola U., 1974. M.S. in Oral Biology, 1976, cert. orthdontics, 1976. Practice dentistry specializing in orthodontics, Geneva, Ill., 1976—; mem. dental staff Delnor Community Hosp., Geneva and St. Charles, Ill., 1976—; sec. dental staff Community Hosp., Geneva, 1978-80, v.p., 1980-82, pres., 1982-84, exec. com., 1982-84. Leader Boy Scouts Am., 1988—. Recipient Award of Merit, Am. Coll. of Dentists, 1974, Harry Sicher honorable mention Council on Research, Am. Assn. Orthodontists, 1977. Mem. Am. Assn. Orthodontists, Midwestern Soc. of Orthodontists, Ill. Soc. Orthodontists, ADA, Fox River Valley Dental Soc. (bd. dirs. 1983-86), Blue Key Nat. Honor Soc. Roman Catholic. Avocations: sailing, golf. Office: 1725 South St Box 575 Geneva IL 60134

LAZZARO, ANTHONY DEREK, university official; b. Utica, N.Y., Jan. 31, 1921; s. Angelo Michael and Philomena (Vanilla) L.; m. Shirley Margaret Jones, Dec. 20, 1941; 1 child, Nancy. B.S. in Indsl. Engring, U. So. Calif., 1948; LL.D., Pepperdine U., 1974. Registered profl. engr., Calif. Asst. bus. mgr. U. So. Calif., Los Angeles, 1948-60; asst. bus. mgr., dir. campus devel. U. So. Calif., 1960-65, asso. bus. mgr., dir. campus devel., 1965-71, asso. v.p. bus. affairs, 1971-72, v.p. bus. affairs, 1972-86, sr. v.p. bus. affairs, 1986-88, univ. v.p., 1988—. Editorial cons. College and University Business, 1955-58. Mem. nat. adv. council United Student Aid Funds, N.Y.C., 1973-78, chmn., 1976-77; dir. Republic Fed. Savs. & Loan Assn. and subs. corps., Los Angeles; spl. studies cons. div. higher edn. Office Edn., HEW, 1956-59; Mem. citizens com. Palos Verdes Bd. Edn., 1955-57; mem. Hoover urban renewal adv. com. Community Redevel. Agy., City of Los Angeles, 1960-88. Served to lt. USNR, 1941-46. Mem. Nat. Assn. Coll. and Univ. Bus. Officers (pres. 1979, dir. 1972-80, chmn. goals and programs com. 1978, chmn. large inst. com. 1986, Disting. Bus. Officer award 1986), Western Assn. Coll. and Univ. Bus. Officers (pres. 1972), Soc. Coll. and Univ. Planning, Blue Key, Phi Kappa Phi, Tau Beta Pi. Club: Jonathan (Los Angeles). Home: 4012 Via Largavista Palos Verdes Estates CA 90274 Office: University Park OWH 100 Los Angeles CA 90089

LEAB, DANIEL JOSEF, history educator; b. Berlin, Aug. 29, 1936; s. Leo and Herta (Marcus) L.; B.A., Columbia U., 1957, M.A., 1961, Ph.D., 1969; m. Katharine Kyes, Aug. 16, 1964; children—Abigail Elizabeth, Constance Martha, Marcus Rogers. Instr., asst. prof. history Columbia U., 1966-73, assoc. dean coll., 1969-70, asst. dean univ. faculties, 1971, spl. asst. exec. v.p., 1973-74; assoc. prof. Seton Hall, 1974-80, prof., 1980—; pub., co-editor Am. Book Prices Current; mng. editor Labor History; dir. Bancroft-Parkman; mem. acquisitions com. Eastman House; cons. AEC, 1972-73; lectr. USIS, summers 1970, 72, 75; sr. Fulbright lectr., 1977, 86-87. Fellow Met. Mus. Art. NEH fellow, 1981. Mem. Am. Hist. Assn., AAUP, Orgn. Am. Historians. Clubs: Century, Grolier. Author: A Union of Individuals, 1970; From Sambo to Superspade: the Black and Film, 1975; The Auction Companion, 1981; The Labor History Reader, 1985. Home: PO Box 216 Washington CT 06793

LEACACOS, PETER JOHN, financial executive; b. Cleve., Sept. 1, 1943; s. John Peter and Velia Celeste (De Marco) L.; m. Sophie Lee Morgan, June 5, 1968; children—Justine Catherine, John Peter. Student, Harvard Coll., 1961-62, 64-65; B.A., Wesleyan U., 1970. Area asst. Europe, Latin Am., Internat. Div., Conn. Bank & Trust Co., Hartford, 1970-72; asst. v.p. internat. div. Cleve. Trust Co., 1972-75; dir. project fin., asst. to exec. v.p. fin.-adminstrn., treas. The McKee Corp., Cleve., 1975-77; dir. project fin. and Latin Am. ops. Universal Engring. & Fin. Corp., Swiss Bank Corp. Cons. Group, Geneva, 1977-84; sr. v.p., gen. mgr. York Hannover. Indsl. Devel. AG, Lucerne, Switzerland, 1984-85, mng. dir., chief exec. officer Maritime Chadlers Service N.V., Inter Maritime Group, Geneva, 1985-86, mng. dir, and chief exec. officer, Third World Energy and Counter Trade Corp., Intermaritime Group, 1985-87, mng. dir. and chief exec. officer World Services Corp., Intermaritime Group, Geneva, 1985-87, fin. and comml. advisor, Office Minister-Pres., Govt. of the Republic of Suriname, 1988—; cons. hydroenergy, indsl., agroindsl. projects, Santiago, Chile, 1980—, investment banking and internatl. project devel. fin. cons., 1988—; fin. advisor Copper Tubing Plant, Valparaiso, Chile, 1981—; bd. dirs. Fipro-Rochem Petroleum Reclamation Services Co., Fiprosa Holding Luxembourg. Contbr. articles on project risk mgmt. and financing to profl. jours. Served with USMC, 1965-68, Vietnam. Decorated Navy Commendation medal and Air medal. Anglican. Mem. Swiss-Am. C. of C., Swiss-Chilean C. of C., N.Am.-Chilean C. of C. Clubs: Harvard (N.Y.C. and Switzerland), Internat. (Washington), Alpin Suisse, Am. Internat. Geneva. Home: Chemin des Chevreuils, CH-1261 Genolier Switzerland

LEACH, DAVID JOHN, educational psychologist, lecturer; b. Rochdale, Lancashire, Eng., Mar. 10, 1945; arrived in Australia, 1979; s. Norman and Dorothy (Stephenson) L.; m. Pauline Dorothy Blow, Feb. 21, 1950; children: Stephen Matthew, William James, Hannah Diane. BA with honors, Liverpool (Eng.) U., 1967, cert. in edn., 1968; MEd in Psychology, Sussex U., Brighton, Eng., 1971. Tchr. Liverpool Inst. High Sch., 1968-69; area ednl. psychologist West Sussex Edn. Authority, Sussex, 1971-74; sr. ednl. psychologist, univ. lectr. Hereford and Worcester Edn. Authority and Birmingham U., 1974-79; lect. psychology Murdoch U., Perth, Western Australia, 1979-84, sr. lectr., 1984—; com. mem. Psychologist's Registration Bd., Perth, 1984-87; chmn. Bd. Ednl. and Developmental Psychologists, Australia, 1984-87, assoc. editor jour., 1984-87; cons. various assns. and agys., 1979—. Author: Learning and Behaviour Difficulties in School, 1977; contbr. articles to profl. jours. Fellow British Psychol. Soc.; mem. Australian Psychol. Soc., Australian Behaviour Modification Assn., Australian Assoc. for Direct Instrn. (v.p. 1987—). Office: Murdoch U, South St, 6150 Murdoch, Perth Australia

LEACH, EDMUND RONALD, educator; b. Sidmouth, Eng., Nov. 7, 1910; s. William Edmund Leach; m. Celia Joyce Buckmaster, 1940; children: Louisa, Alexander Bernard. Student, Marlborough Coll., 1923-29; Exhiber., Clare Coll., Cambridge, Eng., 1929; BA, Cambridge U., 1932, MA, 1938; PhD, U. London, 1947. Comml. asst. Butterfield & Swire, Shanghai, People's Republic of China, 1932-37; lectr., reader social anthropology London Sch. Econs., 1947-53; lectr. Cambridge U., 1953-57, reader, 1957-72, prof., 1972-78; fellow Kings Coll., 1960-66, 79—, provost, 1966-79; anthrop. field research in Formosa, 1937, Kurdistan, 1938, Burma, 1939-45, Borneo, 1947, Ceylon, 1954, 56; mem. Social Sci. Research Council, 1968-71; Malinowski lectr., 1959; Reith lectr., 1967; Frazer lectr., 1982. Author: Social and Economic Organization of the Rowanduz Kurds, 1940, Social Science Research in Sarawak, 1950, Political Systems of Highland Burma, 1954, Pul Eliya: A Village in Ceylon, 1961, Rethinking Anthropology, 1961, A Runaway World?, 1968, Genesis as Myth, 1970, Lévi-Strauss, 1970, Culture and Communication, 1976, L'unité de l'homme et autres essais, 1980, Social Anthropology, 1982; (with D.A. Aycock) Structuralist Interpretations of Biblical Myth, 1983; contbr. articles to profl. jours. Trustee Brit. Mus., 1975-80. Decorated knight Order Brit. Empire; fellow Ctr. for Advanced Study in Behavioral Scis. Stanford U., 1961; sr. fellow Eton Coll., 1966-79. Fellow Brit. Acad.; mem. Royal Anthrop. Inst. (v.p. 1964-66, 68-70, 75—, pres. 1971-74, Curl Essay prize 1951, 57, Rivers medal 1958, Henry Myers lectr. 1966, Huxley lectr. 1980), Assn. Social Anthropologists (chmn. 1966-70), Brit. Humanist Assn. (pres. 1970-72), Am. Acad. Arts and Scis. (fgn. hon.). Home: 11 West Green, Barrington, Cambs CB2 5RZ, England Office: British Acad, 20-21 Cornwell Terrace, London NW1 4QP, England

LEACH, JOHN (HUGH) COLIN, college administrator; b. Dublin, Ireland, May 27, 1932; s. Charles Harold and Nora Eunice (Ashworth) L.; m. Susan Cherry Knox, Oct. 5, 1963 (div. Nov. 1974); children—Rosamund Clare, Polly Rebecca, Conrad Benjamin. M.A. (1st class honours), Oxford U., Eng., 1955. Investment analyst Kleinwort Benson, London, 1957-61, Grieveson Grant, London, 1961-65; investment mgr., dir. Schroder Wagg/A.R.I.E.L., London, 1965-78; bursar, adminstr. Pembroke Coll., Oxford, 1979—, curator Univ. Chest, Oxford, 1981—. Revisor: Oxford Dictionary of Quotations, 1979; editor: Helen (Euripides), 1981. Contbr. book revs., fin. and classical articles to various publs. Mem. exec. com. Nat. House-Bldg. Council, London, 1976-79; treas. Soc. for Promotion Roman Studies, London, 1981—; mem. council Consumers' Assn., London, 1975-82; bd. govs. Abingdon Sch., Eng., 1980—. Fellow Soc. Investment Analysts (editor Investment Analyst 1975-79). Mem. Ch. of Eng. Club: Athenaeum (London). Avocations: writing, chess, skiing, composition of Greek and Latin verse, book reviewing. Address: Pembroke College, Oxford OX1 1DW, England

LEACH, MAURICE DERBY, JR., librarian; b. Lexington, Ky., June 23, 1923; s. Maurice Derby and Sallie Eleanor (Woods) L.; m. Virginia Stuart Baskett, Mar. 16, 1953; 1 dau., Sarah Stuart. A.B., U. Ky., 1945; B.L.S., U. Chgo., 1946. Bibliographer Dept. State, 1947-50; fgn. service officer Dept. State (USIS); vice consul, attache Dept. State (USIS), Cairo and Alexandria, U.A.R., Beirut, 1950-59; chmn. dept. library sci. U. Ky., 1959-66; regional program officer Ford Found., Beirut, 1967-68; univ. librarian, prof. Washington and Lee U., Lexington, Va., 1968-85, prof., 1985—; library adviser Nat. Library, Egypt, Lebanon and acad. libraries in Middle East. Contbr. articles to profl. jours. Served with AUS, 1948-49. Mem. English Speaking Union (pres. Lexington br. 1970-75), Va. Library Assn. (pres. 1976), Southeastern Library Assn., Assn. Preservation of Va. Activities (dir. Lexington br.), Rockbridge Hist. Soc. Episcopalian. Club: Rotary. Home: 1 Courtland Center Lexington VA 24450

LEACH, RICHARD MAXWELL (MAX), JR., corporate professional; b. Chillicothe, Tex., June 14, 1934; s. Richard Maxwell and Lelia Booth (Page) L.; m. Wanda Gail Groves, Feb. 4, 1956; children: Richard Clifton, John Christopher, Sandra Gail, Kathy Lynn. BS in Acctg. magna cum laude, Abilene Christian U., 1955. Registered Fin. Planner., CLU. Asst. dir. agys. Am. Founders Ins. Co., Austin, Tex., 1960-62; owner A.F. Ins. Planning Assocs., Temple, Tex., 1962-65; v.p. sales Christian Fidelity Life Ins. Co., Waxahachie, Tex., 1966-67; exec. v.p. Acad. Computer Tech., Inc., Dallas, 1968-69; pres., chief exec. officer Inta-Search Internat., Inc., Dallas, 1969-71; prin., chief exec. officer, fin. cons. Leach and Assocs., Albuquerque, 1971—; chmn. bd. United Quest, Inc., Albuquerque; chmn. bd. Hosanna Inc., Albuquerque; real estate broker; commodity futures broker; exec. dir., bd. dirs. New Heart, Inc., Albuquerque, 1975-85; owner Insta-Copy, Albuquerque, 1973-76, Radio Sta. KYLE-FM, Temple, 1963-64. Editor, author Hosanna newspaper, 1973-74. Gen. dir. Here's Life, New Mexico, Albuquerque, 1976; exec. dir. Christians for Cambodia, Albuquerque, 1979-80. Served with U.S. Army, 1955-57. Mem. Nat. Futures Assn. Home: 3308 June NE Albuquerque NM 87111 Office: 7200 Montgomery Blvd NE Suite 386 Albuquerque NM 87109

LEACH, ROBERT BARRY, food products executive; b. Repton, Eng., Oct. 2, 1937; came to Fed. Republic Germany, 1986; s. Robert Edmund and Jessie (Beech) L.; m. Uta Runge (div.); 1 child, Pamela; m. Helga Erna Gisela Berg; children: Kristofer, Jennifer. MA, U. Frankfurt, Fed. Republic Germany, 1965. Brand promotion mgr. Procter & Gamble, 1966-73; dir mktg. Leo Burnett, Fed. Republic Germany, 1973-75; gen. mgr. Timex, Fed. Republic Germany, 1976-79; exec. v.p. V.P. Schickendanz, Nurenburg, Fed. Republic Germany, 1980-83; v.p. mktg. GTE Sylvania, Danvers, Mass., 1984-86; mem. bd. Hag Gen. Foods A.G., Bremen, Fed. Republic Germany, 1986—. Author: New Applications of Direct Marketing, 1985. Fellow Inst. Linguists, Brit. Inst. Mgmt.; mem. Am. Mktg. Assn., Chgo. Advt. Club (hon.). Anglican. Clubs: East India, Nat. Liberal (London). Office: Hag Gen Foods AG, Hagstrasse, 2800 Bremen Federal Republic of Germany

LEACH, RUSSELL, lawyer; b. Columbus, Ohio, Aug. 1, 1922; s. Charles Albert and Hazel Kirk (Thatcher) L.; m. Helen M. Sharpe, Feb. 17, 1945; children—Susan Sharpe, Terry Donnell, Ann Dunham. B.A., Ohio State U., 1946, J.D., 1949. Bar: Ohio 1949. Clk. U.S. Geol. Survey, Columbus, 1948-49; reference and teaching asst. Coll. Law, Ohio State U., 1949-51; asst. city atty. City of Columbus, 1951-54, sr. asst. city atty., 1954-55, chief counsel, 1956, 1st asst. city atty., 1957, city atty., 1957-63, presiding judge mcpl. ct., 1964-66; ptnr. Bricker & Eckler, 1966-88, ret., chmn. exec. com., 1982-87; vis. ret. judge Columbus mcpl. cts., 1988—. Commr., Columbus Met. Housing Authority, 1968-74; chmn. Franklin County Republican Com., 1974-78. Served with AUS, 1942-46, 51-53. Named One of 10 Outstanding Young Men of Columbus, Columbus Jaycees, 1956, 57. Mem. ABA, Ohio Bar Assn. (council of dels. 1970-75), Columbus Bar Assn. (pres. 1973-74), Am. Judicature Soc., Pres.' Club Ohio State U., Am. Legion, Delta Theta phi, Chi Phi. Methodist. Home: 1232 Kenbrook Hills Dr Columbus OH 43220 Office: Ohio Ct Claims 65 E State St Suite 1100 Columbus OH 43215

LEACH-CLARK, MARY AGNES, educator, counselor of handicapped; b. Wichita, Kans., Aug. 5, 1931; d. Frank N. and May Jean (Hollow) Leach; m. Courtney Clark, June 12, 1954 (div.); children—David Courtney, Bruce Colin, Anne Clark Nelson, Jeffrey Charles. B.S. in Edn., U. Kans., 1954; M.Ed. in Counseling, Wichita State U., 1978. Lic. counselor, Kans., Colo.; cert. nat. counselor, 1983. Tchr. gifted Dist. 110, Overland Park, Kans., 1954-56; activity dir. Booth Meml. Hosp., Wichita, 1978; tchr. personal and social adjustment classes, Wichita, 1979-81; therapist aidance devel. programs, 1980—; elem. sch. counselor Dist. 259, Wichita, 1986—; dist. resource cons. Kans. Resource Tng. Systems, 1986-87; instr. interior design AIM's Community Coll., Greeley, Colo., 1983; art curriculum coordinator Creative Arts Ctr., Greeley, 1983; instr. interior design and piano improvisation Wichita State Free U., 1983-85 ; interior design instr. Marcus Ctr., Wichita State U., 1984—, also workshop dir. interior design Small Bus. Devel. Ctr., 1985—; home bound spl. edn. tchr. Wichita Pub. Schs. Dist. 259, 1983-86; developmental program tchr. in classrooms Adolescent Psychiat. Unit, St. Francis Hosp., Wichita, 1984. Vol., dir. Off-Broadway Lewis St. Troupers, Downtown Sr. Ctr., 1984—. Interior design cons. Kaleidiscope Segment KAKE TV. Mem. Am. Assn. Counseling and Devel., Amer. Personnel and Guidance Assn., Kans. Mental Health Counselors, Kans. Personnel and Guidance Assn., Kans. Author's Club, Alpha Chi Omega. Office: Box 8065 Wichita KS 67208-0065

LEAHY, JEANNETTE (JEANNETTE OLIVER LEAHY TINEN KAEHLER), actress; b. Eau Claire, Wis., Sept. 9, 1927; d. Kenneth A. and Berthe Hortence (Borie) Oliver; student various acting workshops; m. Thomas J. Leahy (dec.); children—Denyse Leahy Karsten Feeney, Thomas J.; m. William J. Tinen, June 15, 1969 (dec.); m. 3d, Wallace W. Kaehler, Jan. 13, 1980. TV personality Jeannette Lee, Sta. WFBM-TV, Indpls., 1950-53; actress Peninsular Players, summer stock theatre, Door County, Wis., 1960—, also radio, TV, stage, film, commls. Vice-pres., Evanston Drama Club, 1961-62; dir. Wilmette Children's Theatre, 1960-65; bd. dirs. Easter Seal Soc., 1970-75. Mem. Actors Equity Union, SAG, AFTRA, Chgo. Unlimited. Republican. Roman Catholic. Clubs: North Shore Country, Michigan Shores, Wilmette-Kenilworth (pres. 1956-57), North Shore Assos. (pres. 1982-83).

LEAHY, MARK JOSEPH, chemical company executive; b. Long Island, N.Y., Dec. 30, 1953; s. Clifford James and Irma Hedwig (Herzig) L. AA, Fullerton (Calif.) Coll., 1975; BSBA, Calif. State U., Fullerton, 1977. Nat. sales mgr. Imaginary Glass Co., Anaheim, Calif., 1973-78; owner, pres. MJL Assocs., Fullerton, 1978-82; sales exec. DuBois Chems., Industry, Calif., 1982-84; pres. Saudi Chem. Industry, Dammam, Saudi Arabia, 1984-87; v.p. DuBois Middle E., Paris, France, 1987—; cons. in field. Recipient Pres. Club award AK Co., Saudi Arabia, 1985, 86. Mem. Am. Bus. Assn., Damman C. of C. (Saudi Arabia). Democrat. Roman Catholic. Home: 534 Juniper St Brea CA 92621 Office: DuBois Mid E Ltd, 74th Ave Des Champs Elysees, 75008 Paris France

LEAHY, PATRICK JOSEPH, U.S. senator; b. Montpelier, Vt., Mar. 31, 1940; s. Howard and Alba (Zambon) L.; m. Marcelle Pomerleau, Aug. 25, 1962; children: Kevin, Alicia, Mark. B.A., St. Michael's Coll., Vt., 1961; J.D., Georgetown U., 1964. Bar: Vt. 1964, U.S. Supreme Ct. 1964, D.C. 1979, U.S. Ct. Appeals (2d cir.). State's atty. Chittenden County, Vt., 1966-75; mem. U.S. Senate from Vt., 1975—; chmn. com. on agrl., nutrition and forestry, mem. com. on approriations, chmn. jud. subcom. tech. and la, mem. judiciary com., vice-chmn. intelligence com., 1985-86, mem. senate jud. com., vice chmn. senate intelligence com., 1985-86. Mem. Nat. Dist. Attys. Assn. (v.p. 1971-74). Office: 433 Russell Senate Office Bldg Washington DC 20510 *

LEANDRI, PIERRE MAURICE, urologist, surgeon; b. Miliana, Algier, France, Dec. 20, 1945; s. Laurent and Suzanne (Blanc) L.; m. Anne Marie Barthas, Aug. 28, 1975; 1 child, Laurianne. MD, U. Toulouse, France, 1969. Cert. surgeon, France, 1976, Urologist, France 1977. Resident U. Hosp. Toulouse, 1969-75, asst. anatomy med. sch., 1971-75, chief clinic urology, 1975-78, asst. surgeon dept. urology, 1975-78; urologist, surgeon Clinique St. Jean Languedoc, Toulouse, 1978—; urology dept. head Clinique St. Jean Languedoc, Touluose, 1980; bd. dirs. Ctr. Research in Urologic Oncology, Toulouse, 1985—. Served as officer surgeon French Peace Corps, 1972-73. Mem. French Urological Assn., French Urological Soc., European Assn. Urology, Am. Urological Assn. (corresponding). Roman Catholic.

LEAR, ERWIN, anesthesiologist, educator; b. Bridgeport, Conn., Jan. 1, 1924; s. Samuel Joseph and Ida (Ruth) L.; m. Arlene Joyce Alexander, Feb. 15, 1953; children—Stephanie, Samuel. MD, SUNY, 1952. Diplomate Am. Bd. Anesthesiology, Nat. Bd. Med. Examiners. Intern L.I. Coll. Hosp., Bklyn., 1952-53; asst. resident anesthesiology Jewish Hosp., Bklyn., 1953-54; sr. resident Jewish Hosp., 1955, asst., 1955-56, adj., 1956-58, assoc. anesthesiologist, 1958-64; attending anesthesiologist Bklyn. VA Hosp., 1958-64, cons., 1977—; assoc. vis. anesthesiologist Kings County Hosp. Ctr., Bklyn., 1957-80; staff anesthesiologist Kings County Hosp. Ctr., 1980-81; vis. anesthesiologist Queens Gen. Hosp. Ctr., 1955-67; dir. anesthesiology Queens Hosp. Ctr. Jamaica, 1964-67, cons., 1968—; chmn. dept. anesthesiology Catholic Med. Ctr., Queens and Bklyn., 1968-80; dir. anesthesiology Beth Israel Med. Ctr., N.Y.C., 1981—; clin. instr. SUNY Coll. Medicine, Bklyn., 1955-58; clin. asst. prof. SUNY Coll. Medicine, 1958-64, clin. assoc. prof., 1964-71, clin. prof., 1971-80, prof., vice-chmn. clin. anesthesiology, 1980-81; prof. anesthesiology Mt. Sinai Sch. Medicine, 1981—. Author: Chemistry Applied Pharmacology of Tranquilizers; contbr. articles to profl. jours. Served with USNR, 1942-45. Fellow Am. Coll. Anesthesiologists, N.Y. Acad. Medicine (sec. sect. anesthesiology 1985-86, chmn. sect. anesthesiology 1986-87); mem. AMA, Am. Soc. Anesthesiologists (chmn. com. on by-laws 1982-83, dir. 1981—, ho. of dels. 1973—, editor newsletter 1984—, chmn. adminstrv. affairs com., 1987—), N.Y. State Bd. Profl. Med. Conduct, N.Y. State Soc. Anesthesiologists (chmn. pub. relations 1963-73, chmn. com. local arrangements 1968-73, dist. dir. 1972-73, v.p. 1974-75, pres. 1976, bd. dirs. 1972—, chmn. jud. com. 1977-81, assoc. editor Bulletin 1963-77, editor Sphere 1978-84), N.Y. State Med. Soc. (chmn. sect. anesthesiology 1966-67, sec. sect. 1977-81), N.Y. County Med. Soc., SUNY Coll. Medicine Alumni Assn. (pres. 1983, trustee alumni fund 1980), Alpha Omega Alpha. Address: Harriman Dr Sands Point NY 11050

LEAR, JOHN, writer, editor; b. nr. Allen, Pa., Aug. 10, 1909; s. Charles D. and Esther M. (Sourbeer) L.; m. Dorothy Leeds, Sept. 26, 1931 (dec. May 1965); m. Marie Nesta, Aug. 28, 1966. D.Sc. (hon.), Dickinson Coll., 1968. Editor Daily Local News, Mechanicsburg, Pa., 1927-28; reporter Patriot, Harrisburg, 1928-34; writer-editor A.P., Phila., Chgo., N.Y.C., Washington, Buenos Aires; roving assignments A.P., Eastern U.S., Can., S.Am., 1934-42; coordinator info. staff gov. P.R., 1942-43; radio news writer Press Assn., N.Y.C., 1943; free lance mag. corr. 1944-48; mng. editor Steelways mag., 1948-49; chief articles editor Collier's mag., 1949-50, assoc. editor, 1950-53; cons. publs. IBM Corp., 1953-54; dir. spl. atomics and automation studies Research Inst. Am., 1954-55; sci. editor Sat. Rev., 1956-71, sr. editor, 1971-72; v.p. Bauer Engring., Inc., 1972; v.p., chief editor Bauer, Sheaffer & Lear, Inc., Chgo., 1972-75; chief editor Keifer & Assos., Inc., 1975-76; Am. corr. New Scientist, London, 1956-62; editorial cons. Russell Sage Found., 1967-68, Inst. for Social Research, U. Mich., 1972-73; columnist King Features Syndicate, 1973; sci. cons. Crown Publishers, Inc., 1974; editorial cons. Rockefeller Found., 1978-82; cons. Office of Tech. Assessment, U.S. Congress, 1975; publs. cons. Acad. Forum, Nat. Acad. Scis., 1976. Author: Forgotten Front, 1942, Kepler's Dream, 1965, Recombinant DNA—The Untold Story, 1978; Contbg. editor: World Press Rev, 1976-84; sci. editor Pa. mag., 1982-83; editor Pa. Press Bur., Pa. Newspaper Pubs. Assn., 1986; columnist The Gettysburg Times, 1986-87. Recipient Albert Lasker Med. Journalism award, 1952. Mem. AAAS (Westinghouse award 1951), Pa. Legis. Corrs. Assn. (assoc.), Sigma Delta Chi (Disting. Pub. Service award 1950, 61). Home: 130 S Madison St Harrisburg PA 17109

LEAR, NORMAN MILTON, writer, producer, director; b. New Haven, July 27, 1922; s. Herman and Jeanette (Seicol) L.; children: Ellen Lear Reiss, Kate B. Lear LaPook, Maggie B.; m. Lyn Davis; 1 child, Benjamin Davis. Student, Emerson Coll., 1940-42, HHD, 1968. Engaged in pub. relations 1945-49. Comedy writer for TV, 1950-54; writer, dir. for TV and films, 1954-59; writer, producer: films Come Blow Your Horn, 1963, Divorce American Style, 1967, The Night They Raided Minsky's, 1968; writer, producer, dir.: film Cold Turkey, 1971; creator, producer: TV shows TV Guide Awards Show, 1962, Henry Fonda and the Family, 1963, Andy Williams Spl., also, Andy Williams Series, 1965, Robert Young and the Family, 1970; developer: TV shows All in the Family, 1971 (4 Emmy awards 1970-73, Peabody award 1977); creator: TV show Maude, 1972; co-developer: TV show Sanford and Son, 1972; developer: TV show Good Times, 1974, The Jeffersons, 1975, Hot L Baltimore, 1975, Mary Hartman, Mary Hartman, 1976, One Day At a Time, 1975, All's Fair, 1976, A Year at the Top, 1977; co-creator: TV show All That Glitters, 1977; creator: TV show Fernwood 2 Night, 1977; developer: TV show The Baxters, 1979, Palmerstown, 1980; creator, developer TV spl.I Love Liberty, 1982; creator a.k.a. Pablo, 1984; exec. producer Heartsounds, 1984, The Princess Bride, 1987. Pres. Am. Civil Liberties Found. So. Calif., 1973—; trustee Mus. Broadcasting; bd. dirs. People for the American Way. Served with USAAF, 1942-45. Decorated Air medal with 4 oak leaf clusters; named One of Top Ten Motion Picture Producers, Motion Picture Exhibitors, 1963, 67, 68, Showman of Yr., Publicists Guild, 1971-77, Assn. Bus. Mgrs., 1972, Broadcaster of Yr., Internat. Radio and TV Soc., 1973; Man of Yr. Hollywood chpt. Nat. Acad. Television Arts and Scis., 1973; recipient Humanitarian award NCCJ, 1976, Mark Twain award Internat. Platform Assn., 1977, William O. Douglas award Pub. Counsel, 1981, 1st Amendment Lectr. Ford Hall Forum, 1981, Gold medal Internat. Radio and TV Soc., 1981. Disting. Am. award, 1984, Mass Media award Am. Jewish Com. Inst. of Human Relations, 1986, Internat. award of Yr., Nat. Assn. TV Program Execs., 1987; inducted into TV Acad. Hall of Fame, 1984. Mem. Writers Guild Am. (Valentine Davies award 1977), Dirs. Guild Am., AFTRA, Caucus Producers, Writers, and Dirs. Office: Act III Communications 1800 Century Park E Los Angeles CA 90067

LEARY, JOHN CHARLES, foreign service officer; b. Hartford, Conn., Feb. 3, 1924; s. Paul Edward and Hannah (Moylan Lynch) L.; m. Nancy Fay Smith, July 8, 1950; children: Suzanne Elizabeth Leary Connolly, Robert Edward, Barbara Jean Leary Jones, Patricia Fay (dec.), John Charles, Margaret Hannah. BA in Internat. Relations, Yale U., 1947, MA in Econs., 1959; postgrad., Wharton Grad. Sch. U. Pa., 1948-49. Joined U.S. Fgn. Service, Washington, 1949; vice consul U.S. Fgn. Service, Cherbourg, France, 1950-52; econ. officer U.S. Fgn. Service, Duesseldorf, Fed. Republic of Germany, 1953-56; cons. U.S. Fgn. Service, Istanbul, Turkey, 1956-58; internat. economist Dept. State, Washington, 1959-63; 1st sec. Chief Fgn. Econ. Br. Am. Embassy, Tokyo, 1964-68; chief gen. comml. policy div. Dept. State, Washington, 1968-72; mem. 15th Sr. Seminar on Fgn. Policy, 1972-73; counselor econ. and comml. affairs Am. Embassy, Ottawa, Ont., 1973-77; minister-counselor, U.S. rep. UN Indsl. Devel. Orgn., Vienna, Austria, 1977-86; consul gen. Am. Embassy, Sao Paulo, Brazil, 1977-86; ambassador Am. Embassy, Grenada, 1986—; chmn. U.S. del. balance of payments com. GATT, 1961-63. Pres. exec. bd. Am. Internat. Sch., Vienna, 1978—. Served to lt. USAF, 1943-45, ETO. Decorated Air medal with 4 oak leaf clusters; recipient Commendable Service award State Dept., 1963. Mem. Am. Fgn. Service Assn., Am. Econ. Assn. Office: Embassy of Grenada care Dept State 2201 C St NW Washington DC 20520 *

LEASE, JANE ETTA, librarian; b. Kansas City, Kans., Apr. 10, 1924; d. Joy Alva and Emma (Jaggard) Omer; B.S. in Home Econs., U. Ariz., 1957; M.S. in Edn., Ind. U., 1962; M.S. in L.S., U. Denver, 1967; m. Richard J. Lease, Jan. 16, 1960; children—Janet (Mrs. Jacky B. Radifera), Joyce (Mrs. Robert J. Carson), Julia (Mrs. Earle D. Marvin), Cathy (Mrs. Edward F. Warren); stepchildren—Richard Jay II, William Harley. Newspaper reporter Ariz. Daily Star, Tucson, 1937-39; asst. home agt. Dept. Agr., 1957; homemaking tchr., Ft. Huachuca, Ariz., 1957-60; head tchr. Stonebelt Council Retarded Children, Bloomington, Ind., 1960-61; reference clk. Ariz. State U. Library, 1964-66; edn. and psychology librarian N.Mex. State U., 1967-71; Amway distbr., 1973—; cons. solid wastes, distressed land problems reference remedies, 1967; ecology lit. research and cons., 1966—. Ind. observer 1st World Conf. Human Environment, 1972; mem. Las Cruces Community Devel. Priorities Adv. Bd. Mem. ALA, Regional Environ. Edn. Research Info. Orgn., Nat. Assn. Female Execs., P.E.O., D.A.R., Internat. Platform Assn., Las Cruces Antique Car Club, Las Cruces Story League, N.Mex. Library Assn. Methodist (lay leader). Address: 2145 Boise Dr Las Cruces NM 88001

LEASE, RICHARD JAY, former police officer, educator, consultant; b. Cherokee, Ohio, Dec. 10, 1914; s. Harold and Mabelle (Fullerton) L.; m. Marjorie Faye Stoughton, Sept. 2, 1939 (div. Apr. 1957); children: Richard Jay II, William Harley; m. Jane Etta Omer, Jan. 16, 1960; stepchildren: Janet Radifera, Joyce Garson, Julia Marvin, Catherine Warren. Student, Wittenberg U., 1932-33; BA, U. Ariz., 1937, MA, 1961; postgrad., Ind. U., 1950, 60, Ariz. State U., 1956, 63-65, 67—; grad., U. Louisville So. Police Inst., 1955. Grad. asst . U. Ariz., Tucson, 1937-38; with Tucson Police Dept., from 1938; advanced from patrolman to sgt., also served as safety officer Pima County Sheriff's Dept., Tucson, 1953, patrol supr., 1953-55, investigator, 1955-56; tchr. sci. pub. schs. Tucson, 1957-59; lectr. dept. police adminstrn. Ind. U., Bloomington, 1960-65; asst. prof. dept. police sci. N.Mex. State U., Las Cruces, 1965—; cons. law enforcement problems HEW, 1960, Indpls. Police Dept., 1962, Harrisburg Community Coll. Police Sci. Dept., 1967, Phoenix Police Dept., 1968—; advisor police tng. programs several small city police depts., Ind., 1960-63, Indpls., 1962; mem. oral bd. for selection chief in Bateville, Ind., 1962, oral bd. for selection sgts. and lts., Las Cruces Police Dept., 1966—. Author: (with Robert F. Borkenstein) Alcohol and Road Traffic: Problems of Enforcement and Prosecution, 1963; cons. editor Police, various research publs. on chem. intoxication tests, psychol. errors of witnesses, reading disabilities, delinquency. Participant numerous FBI seminars; active youth work, philanthropy, among Am. Indians in Southwest; founder awards outstanding ROTC cadets N.Mex. State U., 1967—; founder Wiltberger ann. awards Nat. Police Combat Pistol Matches; scoutmaster Yucca council Boy Scouts Am., 1966—. Served to 1st lt. USMCR, 1942-45, PTO. Fellow Am. Acad. Forensic Scis. (sec. gen. sect.); mem. Internat. Assn. Chiefs of Police, Internat. Assn. Police Profs., Brit. Acad. Forensic Scis., Can. Soc. Forensic Sci., Am. Soc. Criminology, Ret. Officers Assn., Assn. U.S. Army (2d v.p. 1969—), NEA, N.Mex. Edn. Assn., N.Mex. Police and Sheriffs Assn., Internat. Crossroads, NRA (benefactor mem.), Sigma Chi. Lodges: Masons, Elks. Home and Office: 2145 Boise Dr Las Cruces NM 88001

LEATON, EDWARD K., actuarial and consulting company executive; b. Mt. Vernon, N.Y., Oct. 2, 1928; s. Lionel M. and Henrietta (Kline) L.; m. Janet Kemp; children: Edward M., Kenneth (dec. Mar. 1974), William (dec. Aug. 1972), Robert, Thomas, James, Richard. BS in Mech. Engring., Lehigh U., 1949; MBA, Yale U., 1950. Grad. instr. Yale U., 1949-50; from trainee to asst. supt. Gen. Motors Corp., 1950-54; asst. to exec. v.p. Rowe Mfg. Corp., Whippany, N.J., 1955-56, v.p., dir. mfg., 1956-57; cons. Lambert M. Huppeler Co., Inc., N.Y.C., 1957-69, exec. v.p., 1969-74, pres., chief exec. officer, 1974—, chmn., 1978—, also bd. dirs.; pres. Leaton & Huppeler Co., Inc., N.Y.C., 1967-78, vice chmn., 1978—, also bd. dirs.; gen. agt. Leaton-Burns Agy., N.Y.C.; pres. Exec. Programs, Inc. and Analytical Planning Services, Inc. (both N.Y.C.); pres., bd. dirs. G.A.M.C. Contbr. articles to profl. jours.; speaker before numerous internat., nat. and regional orgns.; inductee to Agy. Mgmt. Hall of Fame, 1987. Chmn. coordinating com. ERISA; sr. warden, lay reader St. Paul's Ch.; mem. leadership com. Community Fund. Trustee Gordon (Mass.) Coll., Trinity Sch. for Ministry, The Am. Coll. Mem. Am. Ordnance Assn. (pres. Lehigh Valley post 1948-49), Life Mgrs. Assn. N.Y. (pres., bd. dirs.), Life Underwriters Assn. N.Y.C. (chmn. bd.), Am. Soc. Pension Actuaries (v.p., bd. dirs.), Assn. Advanced Life Underwriters (bd. dirs.), Am. Soc. CLU's, MDRT Found. (pres., bd. dirs.), Am. Mgmt. Assn., Am. Pension Conf., Nat. Assn. Pension Cons. and Adminstrs. (pres., bd. dirs.), Small Bus. Council Am. (bd. dirs.). Clubs: Union League, Yale (N.Y.C.); Country of Darien (gov., trustee), Nutmeg Curling (Darien, Conn.); Mid-Ocean (Tucker's Town, Bermuda). Office: 101 Park Ave New York NY 10178

LEAVITT, CHARLES LOYAL, English language educator, administrator; b. Randolph, Maine, Apr. 30, 1921; s. Charles Warren Franklin and Alice Mable (Sparrow) L.; m. Emily Raymond Stewart, June 12, 1951 (dec. 1966); m. Virginia Louise Kracke, Sept. 6, 1969. BS in Edn., U. So. Maine, 1946; MA in English, Boston U., 1947; PhD in English, U. Wis., 1961; MLS, Columbia U., 1969. Cert. tchr. English and history, elem., secondary, coll. Instr. English, history Endicott Jr. Coll., Beverly, Mass., 1947-48; assoc. prof. English, Lyndon State Coll., Lyndon Center, Vt., 1948-53, 54-55; teaching asst. English, U. Wis., Madison, 1953-54, 55-59; instr. Wayne State U., Detroit, 1959-61; assoc. prof. Montclair (N.J.) State Coll., 1961-68; v.p., sec., dir. edn., bd. mem. Universal Learning Corp., N.Y.C., 1968-69; assoc. dir. admissions Sarah Lawrence Coll., Bronxville, N.Y., 1970-71; dir. continuing edn., asst. dean, prof. Bloomfield (N.J.) Coll., 1971-74; chmn. liberal arts, prof. Coll. of Ins., N.Y.C., 1975-86, prof. emeritus, 1987—; cons. editor Monarch Lit. Guides, N.Y.C., 1963-68. Author Ten Lit. Study Guides, 1964-66. Treas. Youth Community Funds, York Village, Maine, 1946-47; asst. scoutmaster Boy Scouts Am., York Village, 1946-47; v.p. Overseas Neighbors, Montclair, 1974-75; tchr. Adult Sch. of Montclair, 1963-68. Served with USAAF, 1942-45. Named Most Popular Prof., Montclair State Coll., 1967, Prof. of Yr., Coll. of Ins., 1978; yearbook dedications Lyndon State Coll., 1950, Bloomfield Coll., 1974, Coll. of Ins., 1987; Nat. Audubon scholar, Garden Clubs York Village, 1947. Mem. MLA, Coll. English Assn., Internat. Platform Assn., AAUP, Am. Biog. Inst. (nat. bd. advisors 1982-87), Internat. Biog. Assn. Republican. Baptist. Clubs: Princeton of N.Y.C., Faculty of Columbia U.), New Eng. Soc. N.Y.C. Lodge: Kiwanis. Home: 93 Stonebridge Rd Montclair NJ 07042 Office: One Insurance Plaza 101 Murray St New York NY 10007

LEAVITT, JOSEPH, producer, musician, arts adminstrator; b. Chelsea, Mass.; s. Abraham and Mildred (Leavitt) L.; m. Sally Elissa; children: Howard, Joan. Grad., New Eng. Conservatory Music; BA, Am. U., 1954; student seminars, Harvard Bus. Sch.; student, Boston U., Manhattan Sch. of Music. mem. faculty tympani percussion Peabody Conservatory, 1948-49; faculty arts mgmt. U. Md. summer sch., 1974-76; adj. prof. arts mgmt. Goucher Coll., 1977-84; cons. Joseph Meyerhoff Symphony Hall, 1975-81, Pier 6 Pavilion, 1980-81. Successively musician, pianist, prin. musician, dir. ops. and asst. mgr. Nat. Symphony Orch., Washington, 1949-69, gen. mgr. N.J. Symphony Orch., 1969-71, exec. dir., exec. producer all Wolf Trap prodns., Wolf Trap Found. Performing Arts, Vienna, Va., 1970-73, gen. mgr. Balt. Symphony Orch., 1973-81, exec. dir. 1981-84; exec. v.p. Philharm. Orch. of Fla., 1984—; engagements with Boston Pops, Balt. Symphony Orch.; rec. artist: RCA Victor, Westminster, Columbia records; author: The Rhythms of Contemporary Music, 1963, Reading by Recognition, 1960. Mem. adv. com. Fairfax County Council Arts, 1971-73, Balt. Mayor's Com. on Art and Culture; bd. dirs., v.p. Md. Council for Dance, 1976-78; mem. exec. com. Regional Cultural Commn.; field reader Program for Gifted and Talented, HEW; vice chmn. cultural execs. com. Palm Beach County; dir. Fla. Cultural Action and Ednl. Alliances; panelist cultural affairs com. Dade County; mem. cultural execs. com. Broward County. Served with USAAF, World War II. Recipient Louis Sudler award Am. Symphony Orch. League, 1986. Mem. Internat. Assn. Performing Arts Adminstrs. (bd. dirs.). Clubs: University, Boca Pointe Country, Polo (Boca Raton). Home: 5673 Boca Chica Ln Boca Raton FL 33433 Office: 1430 N Federal Hwy Fort Lauderdale FL 33304

LEAVITT, MARTIN JACK, lawyer; b. Detroit, Mar. 30, 1940; s. Benjamin and Annette (Cohen) L.; m. Janice C. (McCrary) Leavitt; children: Michael J., Paul J., David A.; step-children: Dean N., Kellene R. LLB, Wayne State U., 1964. Bar: Mich. 1965, Fla. 1967. Assoc. Robert A. Sullivan, Detroit, 1968-70; officer, bd. dirs. Law Offices Sullivan & Leavitt, Northville, Mich., 1970—, pres., 1979—; bd. dirs. Premiere Video, Inc., Tyrone Hills of Mich., others. Served to lt. comdr., USNR, 1965-68. Detroit Edison Upper Class scholar, 1958-64. Mem. ABA, Mich. Bar Assn., Fla. Bar Assn., Transp. Lawyers Assn., ICC Practitioners. Jewish. Clubs: Meadowbrook Country, Huron River Hunting & Fishing, (bd. dirs.) Traffic, Savoyard, Rolls Royce Owners (bd. dirs.). Home: 20114 Longridge Northville MI 48167 Office: 22375 Haggerty Rd PO Box 400 Northville MI 48167

LEAVITT, MARY JANICE DEIMEL, educator, civic worker; b. Washington, Aug. 21, 1924; d. Henry L. and Ruth (Grady) Deimel; B.A., Am. U., Washington, 1946; postgrad. U. Md., 1963-65, U. Va., 1965-67, 72-73, 78-79, George Washington U., 1966-67; m. Robert Walker Leavitt, Mar. 30, 1945; children—Michael Deimel, Robert Walker, Caroline Ann Leavitt Snyder. Tchr., Rothery Sch., Arlington, Va., 1947; dir. Sunnyside, Children's House, Washington, 1949; asst. dir. Coop. Sch. for Handicapped Children, Arlington, 1962, dir., Arlington, Springfield, Va., 1963-66; tchr. mentally retarded children Fairfax (Va.) County Pub. Schs., 1966-68; asst. dir. Burgundy Farm Country Day Sch., Alexandria, Va., 1968-69; tchr., substitute tchr. specific learning problem children Accotink Acad., Springfield, Va., 1970-80; substitute tchr. learning disabilities Children's Achievement Center, McLean, Va., 1973-82, Psychiat. Inst., Washington and Rockville, Md., 1976-82, Home-Bound and Substitute Program, Fairfax, Va., 1978-84; asst. info. specialist Ednl. Research Service, Inc., Rosslyn, Va., 1974-76; docent Sully Plantation, Fairfax County (Va.) Park Authority, 1981-87, 88—, vol. Honor Roll, 1987; sec. Widowed Persons Service, 1983-85, mem., 1985—. Mem. edn. subcom. Va. Commn. Children and Youth, 1973-74; Den mother Nat. Capital Area Cub Scouts, Boy Scouts Am., 1962; troop fund raising chmn. Nat. Capitol council Girl Scouts U.S.A., 1968-69; capt. amblyopia team No. Va. chpt. Delta Gamma Alumnae, 1969; vol. Prevention of Blindness, 1980—; fund raiser Martha Movement, 1977-78. Recipient award Nat. Assn. for Retarded Citizens, 1975. Mem. AAUW (co-chmn. met. area mass media com. D.C. chpt. 1973-75, v.p. Alexandria br. 1974-76, fellowship co-chmn. Springfield-Annandale br. 1979-80, name grantee ednl. found. 1980, historian 1980-82, cultural co-chmn. 1983-84), Assn. Part-Time Profls. (co-chmn. Va. local groups, job devel. and membership asst. 1981), Older Women's League, Nat. Trust for Historic Preservation, Nat. Mus. of Women in the Arts (charter mem.), Smithsonian Resident Assoc. Program, Delta Gamma (treas. No. Va. alumnae chpt. 1973-75, pres. 1977-79, found. chmn. 1979-81). Roman Catholic. Club: Arlington Hall Officer's. Home: 7129 Rolling Forest Ave Springfield VA 22152

LEBEAU, BERNARD, physician; b. Paris, Nov. 16, 1945; s. Lucien and Madeleine LeBeau; m. Françoise Catry, July 15, 1969; children: Pierre-Yves, Olivier, Eric. MD, Faculté de Médecine de Paris, 1975. Intern Publique, Paris, 1970-75, chief clinic, 1975-78; practice medicine specializing in diseases of the lung, Paris, 1978—; prof. U. Hotel Dieu, Paris, 1978—; researcher in clin. lung oncology. Author: Pneumologie; contbr. articles to profl. jours. Mem. Com. Francais d'Education S., Soc. Francaise Maladies Respiratoires, Assn. Expector (v.p.). Home: 19E ave rue du Maine, 75014 Paris France Office: Hotel Dieu de Paris, 1 Place du Parvis Notre Dame, 75004 Paris France

LEBEAU, CHARLES PAUL, lawyer; b. Detroit, Dec. 11, 1944; s. Charles Henry Jr. and Mary Barbara (Moran) L.; m. Victoria Joy (Huchin), May 15, 1970; children: Jeffrey Kevin, Timothy Paul. AA, Macomb County Community Coll., Warren, Mich., 1967; BA, Wayne State U., 1969; JD, U. Detroit, 1972; postgrad. study, N.Y.U. Sch. Law tax program, 1972-73. Lic. atty., Calif., Mich. Bar: U.S. Tax Ct., U.S. Ct. Internat. Trade., U.S. Supreme Ct., U.S. Dist. Ct. (so. dist.) Calif. Tax atty. Ford Motor Co., Dearborn, Mich., 1973-75; atty. Hoops & Huff, Detroit, 1975-76; tax atty. Miller, Canfield, Paddock & Stone, Detroit, 1976-78; tax mgr. Oceaneering Internat., Santa Barbara, Calif., 1978-79; tax counsel Signal Cos. Inc., Beverly Hills and La Jolla, Calif., 1979-83; tax atty. Gray, Cary, Ames & Frye, San Diego, 1983-84; of counsel James Watts Esq., La Jolla, 1985, Murfey, Griggs & Frederick, La Jolla, 1986; tax atty. (pvt. practice) Charles P. LeBeau Esq., La Jolla, 1987—; lectr. Golden Gate U. grad. tax program, San Diego, 1979—; adj. prof. law U. San Diego, 1982-85, 88—; mem. Law Rev. U. Detroit, 1971, moot court, U. Detroit, 1971-72; lectr. in taxation. Contbr. articles on internat. tax to profl. jours.; monthly tax case commentator Taxes Internat., London, 1981-85. Campaign coordinator United Way, Santa Barbara, 1979. Mem. ABA, Mich. Bar Assn., Calif. Bar Assn., Los Angeles County Bar Assn., San Diego County Bar Assn., Pi Sigma Alpha. Republican. Roman Catholic. Clubs: La Jolla Sunrise Rotary. Home: 1999 Via Segovia La Jolla CA 92037 Office: Charles P LeBeau Esq 4180 La Jolla Village Dr La Jolla CA 92037

LEBECK, ROBERT, photographer, journalist; b. Berlin, Mar. 21, 1929; s. Kurt and Maria (Kuehne) Lebeck; m. Elke Droescher, Nov. 16, 1978; 1 dau. by previous marriage, Anna. Abitur, Donaueschingen, 1948. Photographer, Tageblatt, Heidelberg, 1952-55; editor Revue, Frankfurt, 1955-60; photographer Kristall, Hamburg, 1960-66, Stern, Hamburg, 1966—; work exhibited in public collections, Mus. für Kunst und Gewerbe, Hamburg, Mus. Folkwang, Essen, Stadtmuseum, Munich. Author: Afrika in Jahre Null, 1961; Augenzuege Robert Lebeck, 1984; Romy Schneider, 1986; Begegnungen Mit Grossen der Zeit, 1987; solo exhbn. Tokio-Moskau-Leopoldville, 1962, 30 Jahre Zeitgeschichte, 1984, The Pioneers of Photography 1840-1900-The Robert Lebeck Collection (pub. in catalogue), Palazzo Vecchio, Florence, Italy, 1988; collector of 19th century photography. Served with German Air Force, 1943-45. Home: 79 Grotiusweg, D-2000 Hamburg 55 Federal Republic of Germany Office: Stern Magazin, Warburg Str 50, D-2000 Hamburg 36 Federal Republic of Germany other: 79 Grotius weg, D-2000 Hamburg 55 Federal Republic of Germany

LEBED, HARTZEL ZANGWILL, former insurance company executive, university president; b. Columbia, Pa., Mar. 1, 1928; m. Ann Kronick, June 12, 1956; children: Holly, Jay, Alex. B.S. in Commerce, U. N.C., 1950. With Conn. Gen. Life Ins. Co., Hartford, 1950—; v.p. group sales Conn. Gen. Life Ins. Co., 1971-73; sr. v.p. group pension ops. Conn. Gen. Life Ins. Co., Hartford, 1973-76, exec. v.p. group pension ops. and reinsurance ops., 1976-78, exec. v.p., chief investment officer, 1978-82; exec. v. p. CIGNA Corp., Hartford, 1982-85, pres., 1985-88; interim pres. U. Hartford, 1988—; bd. dirs. Kaman Corp., Catalyst; chmn. bd. Visitors Greenberg Ctr. for Judaic Studies U. Hartford. Bd. dirs. Hartford Jewish Fedn., Greater Phila. 1st Corp.; trustee Mt. Sinai Hosp. Hartford; vice chmn. distbn. com. Hartford Found. Pub. Giving. Served with USN, 1945-47. Mem. Am. Council Life Ins. (exec. com. 1986—), Health Ins. Assn. Am. (exec. com. 1987—, Industry-Labor Council of Phila., Phila. C. of C. (exec. com. 1986—), Phi Beta Kappa. Office: U Hartford Office of Pres West Hartford CT 06117-0395 Home: 54 Kenmore Rd Bloomfield CT 06002 *

LEBEDEFF, DIANE ALEXIS, judge; b. Detroit, June 25, 1943; d. Alexis M. and Vera A. Lebedeff; m. Keith Lonesome; 1 child, Angelica Lebedeff. B.A., U. Mich., 1965, J.D., 1968. Admitted to N.Y. bar, 1969, Mich. bar, 1969; asso. appellate counsel Legal Aid Soc., N.Y.C., 1968-71; atty. div. criminal justice services N.Y. State, 1971-73; atty. N.Y.C. Dept. Rent and Housing Maintenance, 1976-80, gen. counsel, 1976-80, also counsel N.Y.C. Rent Guidelines; housing judge N.Y. Civil Ct., 1980-82, judge, 1983-87; acting justice N.Y. State Supreme Ct, 1988—. Mem. Community Bd. 2, N.Y.C., 1979-80. Mem. Assn. Bar City N.Y., Am. Bar Assn., Nat. Assn. Women Judges, N.Y. State Assn. Women Judges (bd. dirs. 1984-86, sec. 1986-88, v.p. 1988—), N.Y. State Bar Assn., N.Y. Women's Bar Assn. Clubs: Women's City, City (N.Y.C.). Address: 111 Centre St New York NY 10013

LEBENSAFT, ELISABETH, lexicographer; b. Vienna, Austria, Mar. 4, 1943; d. Otto and Elisabeth (Melichar) L. PhD, U. Vienna, 1970. Staff mem. Oesterreichisches Biographisches Lexikon (Austrian Acad. Sci.), 1979—, co-editor, 1980—, v.p. staff council, 1982-86, mem. exhbn. com. Lebendiges Wissen, 1987; sci. contbr. to exhbn. on Era of Franz Josef I, Govt. of Lower Austria, 1987; lectr. Bruckner Symposium, Linz, Austria, 1987. Author: Anordnung und Funktion zentraler Aufbauelemente... A. Schnitzlers, 1972; scriptwriter, co-editor: (TV film) Ferdinand Raimund: Der Bauer als Millionaer, 1973; contbr. articles to profl. jours. Mem. Verein fuer Geschichte der Stadt Wien, Inst. Fuer Wissenschaft u. Kunst Wien. Home:

Zeleborgasse 4/2/1, 1120 Vienna Austria Office: Austrian Acad Sci, Fleischmarkt 22 2 3, Vienna Austria

LE BLANC, JACQUES M., diplomat; b. St. Cyr l'Ecole, France, Feb. 28, 1934; s. Guillaume L. and Jacqueline E. (Saint-Sauveur) Le B. LLB, U. Paris, 1955; cert., French Nat. Sch. for Overseas, Paris, 1958; M in PUb. Law, U. Dakar, Senegal, 1963. 2d sec. French Embassy, Dakar, 1961-64; 1st sec. French Embassy, Peking, Republic of China, 1964-67; head of the Vietnamese desk French Ministry of Fgn. Affairs, Paris, 1967-71; 2d counselor French Embassy, Washington, 1971-75; dep. dir. staff French Ministry of Fgn. Affairs, Paris, 1975-79; dep. head of mission French Representation to UN, Geneva, 1979-83; ambassador to Upper Volta French Embassy, Ouagadougou, Burkina-Faso, 1983-87; ambassador to the Philippines French Embassy, Manila, 1987—. Named to Legion Merit, Govt. France, 1971, Legion d'honneur, Govt. France, 1987. Office: Embassy of France, 6786 Ayala Ave, Makati Metro Manila Philippines

LEBRO, THEODORE PETER, property tax service exec.; b. Fulton, N.Y., Feb. 12, 1910; s. Peter and Mary (Karpala) L.; BS, Syracuse U., 1954; m. Wanda Saffranski, Oct. 16, 1932. Farmer nr. Fulton, 1935-76; various positions restaurants, grocery, Fulton, 1929-54; owner, operator Lebro Real Estate and Ins. Agency, Fulton, 1951—. Bd. dirs. Lee Meml. Hosp.; pres. Catholic Youth Orgn. Fulton, 1976—; dir. Cath. Charities. Served with 35th inf. U.S. Army, 1942-46; PTO. Certified property mgr. Mem. Soc. Real Estate Appraisers, Oswego County Bd. Realtors, N.Y. State Soc. Appraisers (gov.), Assn. County Dirs., V.F.W., Am. Legion, St. Michael's Soc. (pres. 1960—). Republican. Roman Catholic. Clubs: Beaver Meadow, Pathfinders Game and Fish (life). Lodges: KC, Elks. Home: RFD 1 Box 111 Rt 48S Phoenix NY 13135 Office: 316 W 1st St Fulton NY 13069

LE BROCQUY, LOUIS, painter; b. Dublin, Ireland, Nov. 10, 1916; s. Albert le Brocquy and Sybil Staunton; m. Jean Stoney, 1938 (div. 1948); one child; m. Anne Madden Simpson, 1958; 2 children. LittD (hon.), U. Dublin, 1962, LLD (hon.), 1988. Vis. instr. Cen. Sch. Arts and Crafts, London, 1947-54; vis. tutor Royal Coll. Art, London, 1955-58; dir. Kilkenny (Ireland) Design Workshops, 1965-77; mem. adv. council Guiness Pete Awards, 1980-85. One man shows include Leicester Galleries, London, 1948, Gimpel Fils, London, 1947, 49, 51, 55, 56, 57, 59, 61, 66, 68, 71, 74, 78, 83, Waddington, Dublin, 1951, Robles Gallery, Los Angeles, 1960, Gallery Lienhard, Zurich, 1961, Dawson/Taylor Gallery, Dublin, 1962, 66, 69, 71, 73-75, 81, 85-87, Mcpl. Gallery Modern Art, Dublin, 1966, 78, Ulster Mus., Belfast, 1966-67, 88, Gimpel-Hanover, Emmerich Zurich, 1969, 78, 83, Gimpel, N.Y., 1971, 78, 83, Fondation Maeght, 1973, Bussola, Turin, 1974, Arts Council, Belfast, 1975, 78, Mus. Art Moderne, Paris, 1976, Giustiniani, Genoa, 1977, Waddington, Montreal, Toronto, 1978, Maeght, Barcelona, Madrid, Granada, 1978-79, Jeanne Bucher, Paris, 1979, 82, N.Y. State Mus., 1981, Boston Coll., 1982, Westfield (Mass.) Coll., 1982, Palais des Beaux Arts, Charleroi, 1982, Chgo. Internat. Expn., 1986, Festival Ctr., Adelaide, 1988, Nat. Gallery of Victoria, Westpac, Melbourne, 1988, Mus. of Modern Art, Brisbane, 1988, Musée Picasso, Antibes, 1989; represented in permanent collections including Albright Mus., Buffalo, Arts Council, London, Carnegie Inst., Pitts, Chgo. Arts Club, Columbus (Ohio) Mus., Detroit Inst. Art, Dublin Mcpl. Gallery, Etat Francais S.C.A., Ft. Worth Ctr., Found. Brazil Mus., Bahia, Gulbenkian Mus., Lisbon, Guggenheim Mus., N.Y., J.H. Hirshhorn Found., Washington, Kunsthaus, Zurich, Fondation Maeght, St. Paul, Leeds City Art Gallery, Mus. Art Moderne, Mus. Picasso, Antibes, San Diego Mus., Tate Gallery, London, Uffizi, Florence, Ulster Mus., Victoria and Albert Mus., N.Y. State Mus. Named Chevalier de la Legion d'Honneur, 1974. Office: care Gimpel Fils, 30 Davies St, London W1Y 1LG, England

LEBRÓN SAVIÑON, MARIANO JOSE, writer, pediatrician, educator; b. Santo Domingo, Dominican Republic, Aug. 3, 1922. MD, U. Santo Domingo. Intern in pediatrics Children's Hosp., Buenos Aires. Author: Luces d'Eltrópico, Historia de la Cultura Dominicana, (poems) Sonambulo Sin Suenos, Tiempo en la Tierra, (tales) Los Ancianos, (plays) Cuando el Otono Riega las Hojas, Mirtha Primavera; co-author (with Flores and Jimenes) Cosmohombre, Los Trialogos, Infinitestetica; editor Aula Mag. Nat. U. Pedro Henriquez Ureña, (essays) Americalee. Recipient Honoured Professor award Nat. U. Pedro Henriquez Ureña. Mem. Dominican Acad. Medicine (dir. bulletin), Dominican Soc. Pediatrics, Dominican Soc. Odontopediatrics, Dominican Acad. Lang. (pres.), Duarte Inst. (v.p.), Dominican Inst. Spanish Culture, Dominican Athenaeum, Real Spanish Acad. Lang., Belgranian Acad., N.Am. Acad. Spanish Lang., Honduran Acad. Lang., Porto Rican Acad. Art and Sci., Latin Am. Acad. Office: Dominican Acad, Ensanche La Fe, Avda Tiradentes 66, Santo Domingo Dominican Republic

LE BRUN, JACQUES, religious science educator; b. Paris, May 18, 1931; s. Jean and Marguerite (Delvaux) Le B.; children: Jean-Baptiste, Sophie, Mathilde. Agregation des Lettres, U. Paris Sorbonne, 1955, Dr es Lettres, 1971; dip., Ecole Pratique Hautes Etudes, Paris, 1956. Pensionnaire Fondation Thiers, Paris, 1956-58; asst. U. Poitiers (France), 1959-63; research asst. Nat. Ctr. for Sci. Research, Paris, 1963-64; prof. Ctr. Nat. de Télé-Enseignement, Paris, 1964-78; dir. studies Ecole Pratique Hautes Etudes Sorbonne, 1978—. Author: La Spiritualité de Bossuet, 1972, Oeuvres (Fenelon), 1983, Recherches (R. Simon), 1983, Correspondence (Fenelon), 1986. Home: 57 Rue de Paradis, 75010 Paris France Office: Sorbonne Ecole pratique, Hautes Etudes, 5th Sect 45 Rue des Ecoles, 75005 Paris France

LEBRUN, YVAN, neuroliguist, educator; b. Uccle, Belgium, Feb. 13, 1935; s. Leopold and Clemence (Dekoninck) L.; m. Nicole Paulus, 1959; children: Eric, Nanga, Igor. PhD, U. Brussels, 1964. Fellow Belgian Found. for Sci. Research, Brussels, 1960-68; prof. neurolinguistics Vrije U. Brussels, 1968—. Author: Can and May in Present-day English, 1965, Anatomie et Physiologie de l'Appareil Phonatoire, 1968, 2d rev. edit., 1973, Bouw en Werking van het Spraakorgaan, 1968, 2d rev. edit., 1973, The Artificial Larynx, 1973, Intelligence and Aphasia, 1974, Kind en Taal, 1980, Beknopte Afasieleer, 1980, (with C. Leleux) Précis d'Aphasiologie, 1980, Tratado de Afasia, 1983; editor: Linguistic Research in Belgium, 1966, (with R. Hoops) Neurolinguistic Approaches to Stuttering, 1973, and many others; mem. editorial bd. various sci. jours; contbr. articles, papers to sci. jours. Mem. Bur. Internat. Audiophonologie, Internat. Assn. Logopedics and Phoniatrics, Am. Speech, Lang., Hearing, Assn. Office: Vrije U Brussels, Neurolinguistics, Sch Med, Laarbeeklan 103, 1090 Brussels Belgium

LEBRUN MORATINOS, JOSE ALI CARDINAL, archbishop of Caracas; b. Puerto Cabello, Venezuela, Mar. 19, 1919. Ordained priest Roman Catholic Ch., 1943; consecrated bishop of Arado and aux. bishop of Maracaibo (Venezuela), 1956; 1st bishop of Maracay, 1958-62; bishop of Valencia, 1962-72; titular archbishop of Voncaria and coadjutor archbishop of Caracas (Venezuela), 1972; archbishop of Caracas, 1980; elevated to Sacred Coll. of Cardinals, 1983; v.p. Venezuelan Bishops Conf. Mem. Congregation for Cath. Edn. Address: Arzobispado, Apartado 954, Caracas 101-A Venezuela *

LEBURTON, JEAN-PIERRE, electrical engineering educator; b. Liege, Belgium, Mar. 4, 1949; came to U.S., 1981; s. Edmond Jules and Charlotte (Joniaux) L.; m. Lisette Defraisne, Sept.9, 1983. Lic. in Physics, U. Liege, 1971, PhD in Physics, 1978. E.S.I.S. research assoc. U. Liege, Belgium, 1978-79; research engr. Siemens AG, Munich, Fed. Republic Germany, 1979-81; vis. asst. prof. U. Ill., Urbana-Champaign, 1981-83, asst. prof., 1983-87, assoc. prof., 1987—. Contbr. articles and research papers to profl. jours. Mem. IEEE, Am. Physical Soc.

LECAILLON-THIBON, BERNARD, ophthalmologist; b. Pure, France, May 13, 1927; s. Pierre and Nelly (Petitfrere) Lecaillon; m. Gol Evelyne Morchad Zadch, Jan. 31, 1947; children by previous marriage: Catherine, Philippe; 1 child by present marriage: Paul. MD, U. Paris, 1955. Extern Hosp. Paris, 1947-53, asst., 1954-58; practice medicine specializing in ophthalmology Paris, 1955—; asst. Ctr. Hospitalier, Evreux, France, 1950-60; chief of service Ctr. Hospitalier, Perpignan, 1970—; chief researcher ophthalmology 1970-87. Mem. Assn. Sportive Univ. Perpignanaise (v.p.), Assn. Fed. Ophthalmology Practitioners, Internat. Intra Ocular Implant Club. Home: Chemin du mas Donat 35, 66000 Perpignan France Office: 4 Des Jotglars, 66000 Perpignan France

LE CARUYER DE BEAUVAIS, SAMUEL OLIVIER, diplomat; b. Paris, July 3, 1937; s. Jacques and Simone (de Beaufort) Le Caruyer de B.; m. Claude Roehrich, July 28, 1960; children—Gaspard, Camille. Student Coll. St. Louis de Gonzague and St. Jean de Passy, Faculte des Lettres de Paris, Ecole Nat. des Langes Orientales Vivantes. Vice-consul for France, Taipei, 1964, 3d sec., Rangoon, 1964-66, 2d sec., Peking, 1966-68. New Delhi, 1968-70, London, 1970-72, 1st sec., London, 1972-75, 2d counsellor, Peking, 1975-77; fellow Harvard U. Ctr. Internat. Affairs, 1977-78; dep. dir. Asia and Oceanic div. French Ministry Fgn. Affairs, 1978-82; ambassador of France to Bangladesh, 1928-85; dir. cultural exchanges Ministry of Fgn. Affairs, Paris, 1985-87; deputy dir. gen. cultural, sci., tech. cooperation Ministry of Fgn. Affairs, Paris, 1987—. Decorated knight Nat. Order of Merit, 1975. Office: Ministere des Affaires Etrangé, 23 rue La Perouse, 75016 Paris France

LECERF, OLIVIER MAURICE MARIE, construction company executive; b. Merville-Franceville, France, Aug. 2, 1929; s. Maurice and Colette (Lainé) L.; m. Annie Bazin de Jessey, Jan. 11, 1958; children: Christophe, Véronique. Baccalauré at A in Philosophy, 1946; diploma Inst. Polit. Studies Paris, 1950; M. Law, U. Paris, 1950; diploma Indsl. Studies Ctr., U. Geneva, 1960. Asst. mgr. Omnium pour l'importation et l'exportation, Paris, 1951-56; asst. mgr. Ciments Lafarge, Can., 1956-57, and Brazil, 1958-59, asst. mgr. fgn. dept., 1961, adj. comml. dir., Paris, 1962-64, pres., chief exec. officer Lafarge Cement N.Am., Vancouver, B.C., Can., 1965, pres. Lafarge Can. Que., Montreal, 1968, pres. Lafarge Can. Ltd., 1969, gen. mgr. Can. Cement Lafarge, Montreal, 1970, exec. gen. mgr., Paris, 1971-73, chmn., chief exec. officer (now Lafarge Coppée), 1974—, also dir.; dir Credit Commercial de France Compagnie de St Gobain, Ciments Lafarge, COPABIO, Lafarge Corp., Compagnie du Midi, Sabelfie, Compagnie Coppée de Devel. Indsl., others; mem. internat. adv. bd. Volvo, Banque de France, Elf Aquitaine. Bd. dirs. Institut Francais Relations Internationales. Served with inf. French Army, 1950-51; lt. Res. Decorated chevalier de la Legion d'Honneur, commandeur Ordre National du Merite. Mem. Conf. Bd., Indsl. Studies Center, Geneva, Contbr. articles to profl. jours. Home: 8 rue Guy de Maupassant, 75116 Paris France Office: Lafarge Coppee Group, 28 rue Emile Menier, 75116 Paris France

LECHNER, GEORGE WILLIAM, surgeon; b. Denver, July 30, 1931; s. Frank Clifford and Hazel Mae (Elkins) L.; m. Betty Jane Baumbach, Aug. 3, 1952; children: Kathleen Ann, Elaine Marie, Carol Jean, Patricia Louise, James Richard. Student, U. N.Mex., 1948-49; BA, Pacific Union Coll., 1952; MD summa cum laude, Loma Linda U., 1956. Diplomate Am. Bd. Surgery. Intern Pontiac (Mich.) Gen. Hosp., 1956-57; resident in surgery Harper Hosp., Detroit, 1957-58, Wayne State U. Hosp., 1961-64; instr. surgery Wayne State U., 1963-64; practice medicine specializing in gen., vascular and bariatric surgery Kettering, Ohio, 1964—; surg. teaching faculty Kettering Med. Ctr., Dayton, 1967—, also mem. clin. staff; assoc. clin. prof. surgery, assoc. developer. gen. surgery residency, dir. emergency medicine residency Wright State U., 1975-78, also chmn. residency devel. com.; mem. active staff Kettering Med. Ctr. and Sycamore Hosp.; adj. faculty Kettering Coll. Med. Arts; pres. Kettering Med. Room Corp. Active Big Bros./Big Sisters; bd. elders Seventh-Day Adventist Ch., Kettering; trustee, mem. exec. com. Kettering Med. Ctr., 1971-74; pres. Spring Valley Acad. sch. bd., 1973-75, trustee 1973-78. Served with AUS, 1958-61, Japan. Recipient C.V. Mosby award for acad. excellence, 1956; ACS fellow. Mem. AMA, AAAS, Midwest Surg. Assn., Dayton Surg. Soc., Ohio and Montgomery County Med. Socs., Am. Coll. Emergency Physicians, Soc. Tchrs. Emergency Medicine, Univ. Assn. Emergency Med. Services. Republican. Lodge: Rotary. Home: 1928 Burnham Ln Kettering OH 45429 Office: Leiter Rd Miamisburg OH 45342

LECIEJEWICZ, LECH TADEUSZ, archaeology educator; b. Poznan, Poland, Jan. 26, 1931; s. Tadeusz and Ludwika (Ernst) L.; m. Anna Kulczycka, Mar. 31, 1964. Degree in philosophy, Poznan U., 1953; D in Hist. Scis., Polish Acad. Scis., Warsaw, 1958, habilitation, 1967. Asst. Poznan U., 1951-54; asst. Inst History Material Culture Polish Acad. Scis., Poznan, Warsaw, 1954-58; tutor Inst. History Material Culture Polish Acad. Scis., Warsaw, 1958-68, dir. dept. early medieval archaeology, 1968-71; asst. prof. Inst. History Material Culture Polish Acad. Scis., Warsaw, Wroclaw, 1969-73; dir. dept. Oder region archaeology Polish Acad. Scis., Wroclaw, 1971—, assoc. prof. Inst. History Material Culture, 1973-79, prof. of humanistic scis. Inst. History Material Culture, 1979—; lectr. Wroclaw U., 1973-85, prof. ordinary, 1985—; pres. Sci. Council of Polish Acad. Scis. Inst. History Material Culture, 1981-83. Author: Slowianszczyzna Zachodnia, 1976, Normanowie, 1979, Jäger, Sammler, Bauer, Handwerker, 1982, (with E. and S. Tabaczynski) Torcello Scavi, 1961. Recipient Golden Cross of Merit award State Council Polish People's Republic, 1974, State Prize for Scis., 1970. Mem. Union Authors Zaiks, Polish Archeol. and Numismatic Soc. (v.p. 1975-78, J. Kostrzewski award 1985), Polish Hist. Soc., Internat. Union Slavic Archeology, Internat. Union Prehist. and Protohist. Scis. Roman Catholic. Home: Drukarska 6/9, Wroclaw 53-312, Poland Office: Inst History Material Culture, Wiezienna 6, Wroclaw 50-118, Poland

LECKLITNER, MYRON LYNN, nuclear physician; b. Canton, Ohio, June 16, 1942; s. Myron Devoy and Margaret (Koon) L.; m. Carol Vance, Sept. 1979; 1 child, Tonja Ann. B.S. in Acctg. and Economics, Pa. State U., 1964; B.S. in Chemistry and Biology, U. Ala., 1970, M.D., 1974. Diplomate Am. Bd. Nuclear Medicine. Intern Lloyd Noland Hosp., Birmingham, Ala., 1974-75, resident in internal medicine, 1975-77; resident in nuclear medicine, U. Ala.-Birmingham, 1977-79; asst. prof. U. Tex.-San Antonio, 1979-83; assoc. prof. U. South Ala., Mobile, 1983-86, prof., 1986—; dir. diagnostic imaging div., sr. scientist U. South Ala. Cancer Ctr., 1984—. Vis. prof. U. Nuevo Leon, Mex., 1983, U. Oxford, Eng., 1985, 88, Royal Postgrad. Sch. Med., U. London, 1985, and numerous Am. U. Contbr. chpts. to books, articles to profl. jours. Served to capt. U.S. Army, 1964-67. Decorated Bronze Star medal, 1966, Army Commendation medal, 1966, Air medal, 1966. Fellow Am. Coll. Nuclear Physicians (treas. 1988—, chmn. fin. com. 1986-88, vice chmn. membership com. 1985-87, exec. com. 1985—, bd. Regents 1985—, chmn. fin. com. 1986-88, treas. 1988—); mem. Ala. Soc. Nuclear Medicine (pres. 1985-86, mem. fin. com. 1987—). Avocation: photography. Home: 5505 Oak Park Ct Mobile AL 36609 Office: U South Ala Dept Radiology 2451 Fillingim St MSN 301 Mobile AL 36617

LECLER, PIERRE, otolaryngologist; b. Calais, France, Aug. 31, 1947; s. Roger and Jeanne (Courquin) L.; m. Sabine Devulder, Sept. 23, 1978; children: Florent, Eva, Cletient. BAC, St. Pierre Coll., Calais, 1968. Lodge: Lions (Calais). Home: 6 Ave President Wilson, 62100 Calais France Office: 2 Ave President Wilson, Calais France

LECLERC, JACQUES, French ambassador to Kenya; d. Dijon, France, June 5, 1938; s. Frederic Pierre and Marie Louise (Roux) L.; m. Anne Catherine Dubau, Jan. 11, 1964; children—Georges, Philippe. Ed., U. Sciences Politiques, Paris, 1960. First sec. French embassy, Phnom Penh, Cambodia, 1966-67; tech. adviser Ministry of Edn., Paris, 1970-73; chief Mission of Cooperation, French embassy, Ivory Coast, 1973-75; dep. dir. Ministry of Fgn. Affairs, Paris, 1977-81; ambassador of France to Rwanda, Kigali, 1981-83, to Philippines, Manila, 1984-87, to Kenya, Nairobi, 1987—. Office: French Embassy, PO Box 41784, Nairobi Kenya

LECLERCQ, JEAN-PAUL, otolaryngologist; b. Arras, France, Apr. 8, 1926; s. Jean and Yvonne (Petit) L.; m. Christine Bayart, July 28, 1962; children: Jean-marc, Bénédicte. MD, U. Lille, France, 1956. Cert. otolaryngologist. Intern then resident; otolaryngologist Clinique Bon-Secours, Arras, France, 1969—. V.p. local com. Croix Rouge Francaise (medal). Mem. Syndicat des Propriétaires Forestiers de la Somme, Soc. Francaise d'Oto Rhino Laryngologie. Home: 12 rue Jeanne d'Arc, Arras France 62000

LECLERCQ, XAVIER MARIE, airline executive; b. Dournenez, Brittany, France, Apr. 23, 1944; s. René Lucien and Marie Brigitte (Doare) L.; m. Marie-Paul Gratien (dec.); children: Emmanuelle, Ronan; m. Marie Thérèse Restout, June 14, 1978. LLM, U. Rennes, France, 1966, MA in Econ. Sci., 1971. Asst. gen. sec. Chamber of Commerce and Industry, Morlaix, France, 1968-71, gen. sec., 1977—; mgr. Regional transport Bd. Brittany, Morlaix, 1971-76; dir. Brit Air S.A., Morlaix, 1973-77, chmn., gen. mgr., 1977—. Mem. European Regional Airlines, Internat. Civil Airports Assn., Comité des Transporteurs Aériens Complémentaires Français. Office: Brit Air SA, Aerodome de Ploujean, 29204 Morlaix, Brittany France

LE COAT, GÉRARD GEORGE, sociologist; b. Paris, Apr. 14, 1928. BA, U. Paris, 1949; MA magna cum laude, Lausanne, 1955; PhD, U. Wash., 1972. research asst., 1956; asst. profl. com. arts, 1957; assoc. profl. ERAD, 1960; guest prof., Arts and Hunmanities Council, 1967; guest prof. Ghesinyhk, Moscow, 1969; assoc. prof. U. Wash., 1974; coordinator comp. arts prog. 1974-75; guest prof. UCLA, 1975; guest profl., Princeton U., 1976 (Eberhardt Faber lectures); prof. fine art, U. Montreal, 1976-79; guest prof. U. Lausanne, 1979-80; docent, sociology of culture, U. Lausanne, 1980—; dir. research Fond Nat. de la Recherche Scientifique, 1980—; prof. sociology of art, ECAL, Sch. of Art, 1981—; dir. research, Fond Nat. de la Recherche Sci., 1981—; guest prof. Indian Univs. and Art Schs., 1988, U. Tübingen, 1985. Recipient Medal of Merit, Legion of Honr Assn. (Laurels), publs. Author: The Rhetoric of the Arts, 1975, Musique et porteurs de son en Suisse: la situation sociologique, 1981, Culture au quotidien, jeunesse au quotidien, 1985; co-author: France and Africa in the Age of Imperialism: A Double Impact, 1986; editor in chief Can. Art Rev., 1976-77, co-editor, 1978-79; co-editor Revue Musicale de Suisse Romande, 1982—, ECALE, Swiss Art Review, 1987—. Mem. Soc. for Visual Arts, Am. Musicology Soc., Soc. Suisse de Musicologie (dir. com. 1987—), Can. Soc. 18th c. Studies (pres. 1978-79), Can. univs. Art. Assn (co-dir. 1976-79), Can. Soc. for Interdisciplinary Studies (pres. 1978-82). Home: La Rouvenaz, 31 Ave des Cerisiers, 1009 Pully, VD Lausanne Switzerland

LE COCQ, RHODA PRISCILLA, author, educator; b. Lynden, Wash.; d. Ralph B. and Nellie O. (Straks) Le C.; BA, Wash. State U.; MA in Creative Writing, Stanford U.; MA in Philosophy, U. Calif.-Santa Barbara, 1967; PhD, Calif. Inst. Integral Studies, 1970. Radio writer and actress sta. KHQ, Spokane, sta. KOIN, Portland, Oreg., sta. KIRO, Seattle; owner Le Cocq-Luray, N.Y.C.; lit. scout Farrar, Straus & Cudahy, N.Y.C.; public relations dir. art sch. Honolulu Acad. Arts, 1957-58; owner, propr. public relations counseling firm, Honolulu, 1958-61; info. officer Office CD City and County of Honolulu, 1961-63; info. and legis. officer Sacramento County (Calif.) Dept. Social Welfare, 1969-80; research cons. Integral Sci. Found., Inc., 1981-86; instr. U. Hawaii, 1960-61; asst. prof. philosophy extension dept. U. Calif., Davis, 1970-71; assoc. prof. Calif. Inst. Integral Studies, 1972-81; lectr. Bombay, India, 1973, Cultural Integration Fellowship, 1975-80, Regional Assn. Transpersonal Psychology, 1977. Served to lt. USNR, 1942-46, ret. Res., 1970. Recipient cert. for contbn. to East-West Understanding, Cultural Integration Fellowship, 1969, Author Aiding Internat. Understanding, Cambridge, Eng., 1973, photog. and publs. awards NACID, 1974. Mem. Public Relations Soc. Am., Internat. Platform Assn., Smithsonian Assocs., USNR Assn., Audubon Soc., Wash. State U. Alumni Assn., U. Calif. Santa Barbara Alumni Assn., Stanford Alumni Assn., Mensa, Kappa Alpha Theta, Theta Sigma Phi. Clubs: San Francisco Press; Marines Meml. (life) (San Francisco); Commonwealth Club. Author: Heidegger and Sri Aurobindo, 1972; Vision of Superhumanity, 1973; The Mother/Father Pair, 1977; short story Behold A Pale Horse included in several anthologies, dramatized Nat. Gen. Electric Theatre TV, 1957. Mailing Address: Box 37 Corte Madera CA 94925

LECOMTE, DIDIER, property developer; b. Neuilly, France, Feb. 25, 1943; s. Philippe Lecomte and Francoise (D'Esplechin) Swetchine; m. Christine Charrey, June 15, 1968; children: Cedric, Aurélie. Mgr. Gefic, Paris, 1967-73; European ptnr. Jones Lang Wootton, Paris, 1973-81; European mgr. Bourdais, Paris, 1981-84; gen. mgr. Sari, Paris, 1984—; chmn. Sari Counseil, 1988. Home: 15 rue Picot, 75116 Paris France Office: Sari, 4 place de la Defense, 92090 Paris la Defense France

LECOUTEUX, CLAUDE PIERRE, Germanic languages educator; b. Paris, Feb. 8, 1943; s. Maurice and Nicole (Sauvage) L.; m. Corinne Parizy, June 27, 1979; children: Benoît, Anneliese. BA, U. Paris, 1966, prof. agrégé, 1972, Dr Germanic Studies, 1975; Dr ès Lettres, U. Clermont-Ferrand, 1980. Tchr. nat. edn. C.E.S. of Villemomble, France, 1972-74; lectr. U. Paris Sorbonne, 1974-77, master-lectr., 1978-80; prof. Germanic langs. and lits. U. Caen, France, 1981—. Author: Les Monstres..., 1982, Melusine..., 1982, Kleine Texte zur Alexandersage, 1984, Fantomes et Revenants, 1986, Gespenster u. Wiedergänger im Mittelalter, 1987, Les Nains et les Elfes au Moyen Age, 1988. Served with French Air Force, 1964-66. Recipient prix-Strasbourg, Stiftung F.V.S., Hamburg, Fed. Republic Germany, 1983. Mem. Académie Française (laureat), Assn. Germanistes Enseignement Superieur. Roman Catholic. Office: U Caen, Esplanade de la Paix, 14000 Caen France

LEDBETTER, PETER G., aviation company executive; b. Cork, Ireland, Mar. 7, 1944; s. George Edward and Madeline Elisabeth (Hammond) L.; m. Paula Mary Mullen, Aug. 16, 1974; children—Juliet, Katie, Emma, Nicholas. B.A., Trinity Coll., Dublin U., 1967, B.Bus. Studies, 1967; M.B.A., Nat. U. Ireland, Dublin, 1974; grad. Advanced Mgmt. Program, Harvard Bus. Sch., 1983. Chartered Acct. Acct. Coopers & Lybrand, Dublin, 1969-70, mgmt. cons., Dublin and London, 1971-73; fin. exec. ITG Ltd., Dublin, 1974; exec. v.p., dir. GPA Group Ltd., Shannon Airport, Ireland, 1975—. Fellow Inst. Chartered Accts. Anglican. Clubs: Fitzwilliam Lawn Tennis, Kildare Street and Univ., Portmarnock Golf (Dublin); Internat. Lawn Tennis (London). Home: Sonas, Killaloe, County Clare Ireland Office: GPA Group Ltd, Shannon Airport Ireland

LEDBETTER-STRAIGHT, NORA KATHLEEN, insurance company executive; b. Gary, Ind., May 11, 1934; d. Jacob F. and Nora I. (Bollen) Moser; student U. Houston, 1954-58; m. Robert L. Straight, Aug. 9, 1975; 1 dau., Cindy Kathleen Ledbetter Baurax. Vice pres. Hindman Mortgage Co., Inc., Houston, 1960-70, also mng. partner Assocs. Ins. Agy.; corp. sec. N.Am. Mortgage Co., Houston, 1970—; mng. partner N.Am. Ins. Agy., 1970—, now also pres. and mng. officer; ins. counselor Houston Apt. Assn., 1978—, dir. product service council, 1981—; mem. adv. bd. for continuing edn., State Bd. Ins.; v.p., sec. Better Bodies of Tex., Inc. CPCU; cert. Ins. Inst. Am., Soc. Cert. Ins. Counselors. Mem. Ind. Ins. Agts. Am., Soc. Cert. Ins. Counselors, Soc. C.P.C.U.'s, Community Assos. Inst. (dir. 1976-80), Ind. Ins. Agts. Tex., Tex. Assn. Affiliated Agts. (v.p., bd. dirs.), Ind. Ins. Agts. Houston (dir. 1974-78). Republican. Methodist. Author curriculum materials in field. Office: 14825 St Mary's Ln Houston TX 77079

LEDEEN, ROBERT WAGNER, neurochemist, educator; b. Denver, Aug. 19, 1928; s. Hyman and Olga (Wagner) L.; m. Lydia Rosen Hailparn, July 2, 1982. B.S., U. Calif., Berkeley, 1949; Ph.D., Oreg. State U., 1953. Postdoctoral fellow in chemistry U. Chgo., 1953-54; research assoc. in chemistry Mt. Sinai Hosp., N.Y.C., 1956-59; research fellow Albert Einstein Coll. Medicine, Bronx, N.Y., 1959; asst. prof. Albert Einstein Coll. Medicine, 1963-69, assoc. prof., 1969-75, prof., 1975—. Contbr. articles to profl. jours.; deputy chief editor Jour. Neurochemistry. Mem. neurol. scis. study sect. NIH. Served with U.S. Army, 1954-56. NIH grantee, 1963-88; Nat. Multiple Sclerosis Soc. grantee, 1967-74; recipient Humboldt prize, Javits Neurosci. Investigator award. Mem. Internat. Soc. Neurochemistry, Am. Soc. Neurochemistry, Am. Chem. Soc., Am. Soc. Biol. Chemists, N.Y. Acad. Sci. Jewish. Home: 8 Donald Ct Wayne NJ 07470 Office: 1300 Morris Park Ave Bronx NY 10461

LEDERBERG, JOSHUA, university president, geneticist; b. Montclair, N.J., May 23, 1925; s. Zwi Hirsch and Esther (Goldenbaum) L.; m. Marguerite S. Kirsch, Apr. 5, 1968; children: David Kirsch, Anne. BA, Columbia U., 1944; PhD, Yale U., 1947. With U. Wis., 1947-58; prof. genetics Sch. Medicine, Stanford (Calif.) U., 1959-78; pres. Rockefeller U., N.Y.C., 1978—; mem. adv. com. med. research WHO, 1971-76; mem. bd. sci. advisors Cetus Corp., Emeryville, Calif., J.D. Wolfensohn, Inc., N.Y.C., Hoechst-Celanese Corp., N.Y.C.; mem. study sects. NSF, NIH; mem. U.S. Def. Sci. Bd.; cons. NASA, ACDA; bd. dirs. Inst. Sci. Info. Inc., Phila., Procter & Gamble Co., Cin., Ann. Revs., Inc., Palo Alto, Calif. Trustee Revson Found. Inc., Carnegie Corp., Camille and Henry Dreyfus Found.; bd. dirs. Chem. Industry Inst. Toxicology, N.C., N.Y.C. Ptnrship.; mem. Pres.'s Panel on Mental Retardation, 1961-62; mem. nat. mental health adv. council NIMH, 1967-71. Served with USN, 1943-45. Recipient Nobel prize in physiology and medicine for research genetics of bacteria, 1958. Fellow AAAS, Am. Philos. Soc., Am. Acad. Arts and Scis., N.Y. Acad. Medicine (hon.); mem. Nat. Acad. Scis. (past council mem.), Inst. of Medicine), Royal Soc. London (fgn.), N.Y. Acad. Scis. (hon. life), Alpha Omega Alpha (hon.). Office: Rockefeller Univ Office of Pres 1230 York Ave New York NY 10021

LEDERMAN, PETER (BERND), environmental consulting company executive; b. Weimar, Germany, Nov. 16, 1931; came to U.S., 1939, naturalized, 1945; s. Ernst M. and Irmgard R. (Heilbrunn) L.; B.S.E., U. Mich., 1953, M.S.E., 1961, Ph.D.; m. Susan Sturc, Aug. 25, 1957; children—Stuart M., Ellen L. Instr., U. Mich., 1959-61; research engr. Esso Research Labs., Baton Rouge, La., 1961-63; sr. engr. Esso Research & Engring. Co., Florham Park, N.J., 1963-66; asso. prof. chem. engring. Poly. Inst. Bklyn., 1966-72, adj. prof., 1972-75; dir. Ind. Waste Treatment Research Lab., EPA, Edison, N.J., 1972-75, dir. indsl. and extractive processes research, Washington, 1975-76; v.p. Cotrell Environ. Scis. Div., Research Cottrell, Bound Brook, N.J., 1976-80; v.p. hazard/toxic materials mgmt. Roy F. Weston, Inc., Summit, N.J., 1980—; mem. NRC-Nat. Acad. Sci. Rev. Panel, Office Recycled Tech., U.S. Bur. Standards, 1980-83. Mem. exec. bd. Watchung Area council Boy Scouts Am., 1970-86; mem. affirmative action adv. com. New Providence (N.J.) Bd. Edn., 1979-83. Served with AUS, 1953-55. Recipient Silver medal EPA, 1976. Fellow Am. Inst. Chem. Engrs. (chmn. profl. devel. com., chmn. N.J. sect., recipient Larry K. Cecil award 1987); mem. Am. Chem. Soc., AAAS, Am. Soc. Engring. Edn., Nat. Soc. Profl. Engrs., ASME, Am. Acad. Environ. Engrs., NAM, Sigma Xi, Phi Kappa Phi, Phi Lambda Upsilon. Contbr. numerous articles on environ. regulations, solid waste mgmt., hazardous waste mgmt., computer tech. to profl. jours. Home: 17 Pittsford Way New Providence NJ 07974 Office: PO Box 1333 Summit NJ 07901

LEDGER, PHILIP STEVENS, educator, conductor, musician; b. Bexhill-on-Sea, Sussex, Eng., Dec. 12, 1937; s. Walter Stephen and Winifred Kathleen (Stevens) L; m. Mary Erryl Wells, Apr. 15, 1963; children—Timothy, Katharine. M.A., Mus.B., LLD, King's Coll., 1961. Master of music Chelmford Cathedral, 1962-65; dir. music U. East Anglia, 1965-73, dean Sch. Fine Arts and Music, 1968-71; condr. Cambridge U. Mus. Soc., 1973-82; dir. music, organist King's Coll., Cambridge, 1974-82; prin. Royal Scottish Acad. Music & Drama, Glasgow, 1982—; artistic dir. Aldeburgh Festival; dir. Scottish Opera, Glasgow; v.p. Cambridge Festival Assn.; dir. Nat. Youth Orch. Scotland. Editor: Anthems for Choirs 2 & 3, 1973; The Oxford Book of English Madrigals, 1978; composer/editor: The Six Carols with Descants, 1975. Decorated comdr. Order Brit. Empire; John Stewart of Rannoch scholar; recipient Limpus and Read prizes, Royal Coll. Organists; Silver medal Worshipful Co. Musicians. Fellow Royal Coll. Music, Royal Coll. Organists; mem. Royal Acad. Music (hon.). Clubs: Athenaeum, Sette of Odd Volums. Home: 322 Albert Dr, Glasgow G41 5DZ, Scotland Office: Royal Scottish Acad Mus & Drama, 100 Renfrew St, Glasgow G2 3DB, Scotland

LEDOUX, JACK, author, retired race track executive; b. Orlando, Fla., Oct. 4, 1928; s. Leonard K. and Louise (Downs) L.; m. Lenita C. Riles, Sept. 22, 1981; children: Michele, Lance, Stephen, Lola. BS in Journalism, U. Fla., 1950. Sportswriter, columnist Orlando Sentinel-Star, 1948-53; pub. relations dir. Sarasota, Daytona Beach (Fla.) Kennel Clubs, 1953-55; gen. mgr., corp. sec. Sanford-Orlando Kennel Club, 1955-72; gen. mgr., exec. v.p. Black Hills Kennel Club, Rapid City, S.D., 1964-71; pres., co-owner Exec. Travel, Winter Park, Fla., 1977—, Triex Enterprises, Inc., Winter Park, 1977—; ind. editorial columnist, free-lance writer, 1972—; dir. Ctr. Stage. Mem. Fla. Golf Assn. (chmn. adv. com. 1964-65, bd. dirs., pres.), Am. Greyhound Track Operators Assn. (publ. and supervisory com. Am. Greyhound Racing Ency., pub. 1963, nat. pres.), World Racing Fedn. (chmn.), World Greyhound Racing Fedn. (pres.), U. Fla. Alumni Assn. (past pres. Sarasota County chpt.), Sigma Delta Chi, Theta Chi. Democrat. Clubs: Univ., Country. Home: PO Box 2127 Winter Park FL 32790

LEDOUX, PAUL JOSEPH, astronomer; b. Forrieres, Belgium, Aug. 8, 1914; s. Justin and Ida (Delperdange) L.; Lic., Liege U., 1937, Ph.D., 1946; Dr. (hon.), Brussels U., Cath. U. Leuven; m. Aline Michaux, Feb. 14, 1939 (dec. 1977); 1 dau., Jacqueline. Mem. faculty Liege U., 1947-83, chargé de cours, 1956-59, prof., 1959-83; meteorol. adviser Regie des Voies Aeriennes, Belgium, 1947-49; vis. prof. U. Calif., Berkeley, 1963, U. Colo., Boulder, 1970, U. Wash., Seattle, 1972, Columbia U., 1974; chmn. observing programs com. European So. Obs., 1972-74, mem. council, 1975—, pres. council, 1981-84; mem. council Royal Obs. Belgium, 1980—. Served with Belgian and Brit. armies, 1941-46. Fellow Belgian Govt., Franqui Found., Belgian Am. Ednl. Found.; recipient Prix Franqui, 1964; Prix Decennal des Math. Appliquées, Belgian Govt., 1968; Eddington medal, 1972; medaille J. Jansen, Acad. des Scis., Paris, 1976; medaille de l'Observatoire de Nice, 1984. Fellow AAAS; mem. Acad. Royale de Belgique, Acad. Européenne des Sci., Arts et Lettres, Internat. Astron. Union (pres. commn. internat. constn. of stars 1964-67); assoc. Royal Astron. Soc., Acad. Scis. Paris (fgn. assoc.). Author articles. Office: Inst d'Atrophysique, ave de Cointe 5, 4200 Ougree Belgium

LE DUC, ALBERT LOUIS, JR., college official; b. Montgomery, Ala., Feb. 1, 1937; s. Albert Louis and Rachel Nancy (Wineinger) LeD.; student Duke U., 1954-55; B.A., Fla. State U., 1958, M.S., 1960; m. Ellen Heath, June 18, 1960; children—Albert Louis III, Charles Andrew. Civilian mathematician Army Rocket Guided Missile Agy., Huntsville, Ala., 1958, 59; mathematician analyst RCA Service Co., Patrick AFB, Fla., 1960-63, programming leader, 1963-67, project mgr., Eglin AFB, Fla., 1967-69, mktg. adminstr., Cherry Hill, N.J., 1969-71; tech. dir. Ind. U., Bloomington, 1971-77; dir. analysis programming Miami-Dade Community Coll., Miami, Fla., 1977—; part-time instr. Fla. State U., 1958-60, Brevard Engring. Coll., 1961-62, Ind. U., 1972-77. Bd. dirs. Coll. and Univ. Machine Records Conf., 1979-87. Recipient Frank Martin award Coll. and Univ. Machine Records Conf., 1985. Mem. Assn. Computing Machinery (Best Paper award 1973), Profl. Assn. for Computing and Info. Tech. in Higher Edn. (best paper award 1986). Author: The Computer for Managers, 1972. Home: 10321 SW 107th St Miami FL 33176 Office: 11011 SW 104th St Miami FL 33176

LEDUY, ANH, engineering educator; b. Vietnam, Feb. 6, 1946; came to Can., 1965; s. Thach and Tam (BuiThi) LeD.; m. Suzanne Roger, Sept. 24, 1977; children—Isabelle, Dominic. B.S. in Mech. Engring., U. Sherbrooke, Que., Can., 1969, M.S. in Chem. Engring., 1972; Ph.D. in Biochem. Engring., U. Western Ont., Can., 1975. Registered profl. engr., Que. Research asst. CNRC, Univ. Sherbrooke, Que., Can., 1975-77; asst. prof. chem. engring. Universite Laval, Sainte-Foy, Que., 1977-81, assoc. prof., 1981-85, prof., 1985—; mem. grant selection coms.; cons. in field. Presenter symposiums, confs. Contbr. numerous articles to profl. jours. Mem. Order of Engrs. of Que., Am. Soc. Microbiology, Can. Soc. Chem. Engring., Chem. Inst. Can., Can. Soc. Mech. Engring., Engring. Inst. Can., Am. Inst. Chem. Engrs., Can. Soc. Microbiologists, N.Y. Acad. Scis., Genetics Soc. Can. Office: Universite Laval, Dept Chem Engring, Universite Laval, Sainte-Foy, PQ Canada G1K 7P4 Mailing Address: 3011 Regent St Berkeley CA 94705

LEE, AIK-HOE, psychiatrist; b. Kuala Lumpur, Malaysia, Dec. 2, 1952; s. Kah Lee and Peck-Lian Gan; m. Tan Hui-Leng, Nov. 15, 1980; children: Jill, Kenn. MBBS, U. Malaya, Kuala Lumpur, 1977, M in Psychol. Medicine, 1982. House officer Univ. Hosp., Kuala Lumpur, 1977-78; med. officer Gen. Hosp., Malacca, Malaysia, 1978-80; lectr. psychiatry U. Malaya, Malaysia, 1982-85; practice medicine specializing in psychiatry Petaling Jaya, Malaysia, 1985—; cons. Subang Jaya Med. Ctr., Petaling Jaya, 1985—, Tung Shin Hosp., Kuala Lumpur, 1986—. Contbr. articles to profl. jours. Fellow Royal Australian and New Zealand Coll. Psychiatrists; mem. Malaysian Mental Health Assn. (pres. 1986—), Malaysian Med. Assn., Malaysian Psychiat. Assn., Royal Commonwealth Soc. Home: 66 Jalan Tempinis, Bangsar, Kuala Lumpur 59100, Malaysia Office: Lee Specialist Clinic, 29A Jalan 52/2, Petaling Jaya, Selangor 46200, Malaysia

LEE, ALLAN WREN, clergyman; b. Yakima, Wash., June 3, 1924; s. Percy Anson and Agnes May (Wren) L.; m. Mildred Elaine Ferguson, June 16, 1946; 1 dau., Cynthia Ann. B.A., Phillips U., Enid, Okla., 1949; M.A., Peabody Coll. Tchrs., 1953; B.D., Tex. Christian U., 1955, D.D. (hon.), 1968. Ordained minister Christian Ch. (Disciples of Christ), 1949; pastor chs. in Tex. and Wash., 1955-71; gen. sec. World Conv. Chs. of Christ, Dallas, 1971—; mem. gen. bd. Christian Ch., 1971-73; pres. Seattle Christian Ch. Missionary Union, 1964-66, Wash.-No. Idaho Conv. Christian Chs., 1966. Author: Bridges of Benevolence, 1962, Wit and Wisdom, 1963, The Burro and the Bibles, 1968, Under the Shadow of the Nine Dragons, 1969, Reflections Along the Reef, 1970, Disciple Down Under, 1971, Meet My Mexican Amigos, 1972, One Great Fellowship, 1974, Fifty Years of Faith and Fellowship, 1980, Recollections of a Dandy Little Up-to-Date Town, 1985, also articles. Trustee, N.W. Christian Coll., Eugene, Oreg., 1985—; exec. v.p. Plano Dance Theater Bd., 1987—; mem. TV panel Am. Religious Town Hall, 1986—. Recipient Disting. Service citation Children's Home Soc. Wash., 1967, Disting. Service award Bremerton Jaycees, 1959; Jamaica Tourist Bd. citation, 1984. Mem. Disciples of Christ Hist. Soc. (founder, life mem.), Religious Conv. Mgrs. Assn. (v.p. 1980—), Am. Bible Soc. (nat. adv. council 1985—). Club: Seattle Civitan (pres. 1962-64, lt. gov. Orewa dist. 1965). Home: 2112 Stone Creek Dr Plano TX 75075 Office: First City Bank Ctr 100 N Central Expressway Suite 804 Richardson TX 75080

LEE, AMY FREEMAN, artist, educator; b. San Antonio, Oct. 3, 1914; d. Joe and Julia (Freeman) Freeman; grad. St. Mary's Hall, 1931; student U. Tex., 1931-34; student Incarnate Word Coll., 1934-42, Litt.D. (hon.), 1965; m. Ernest R. Lee, Oct. 17, 1937 (div. Jan., 1941). Art critic San Antonio Express, 1939-41; staff art critic radio sta. KONO, 1947-51; lectr. on art humanities dept. Trinity U., San Antonio, 1954-56, San Antonio Art Inst., 1955-56; lectr. art Our Lady of Lake Coll., San Antonio, 1969-71, one man shows, 1947—, including U. Tex., 1970, 73, Tex. Tech. U., 1970, Del Mar Coll., Corpus Christi, Tex., 1970, Southwestern U., Georgetown, Tex., 1971, 79, Pioneer Meml. Library, Fredricksburg, Tex., 1971, U. Tex. Student Union, 1972, Ojo del Sol Gallery, El Paso, 1972, Shook-Carrington Gallery, San Antonio, 1972, 1st Repertory Theatre, San Antonio, 1974, Sol del Rio Galleries, San Antonio, 1976, Oakwell Library, San Antonio, 1976, U. Central Ark., Conway, 1977, NE La. State U., Monroe, 1978, Our Lady of the Lake U., San Antonio, 1978, Univ. Art Gallery, N. Tex. State U., Denton, 1979, L & L Gallery, Longview, Tex., 1980, Meredith Long Galleries, Houston, 1980, Incarnate Word Coll., San Antonio, 1981, St. Mary's Hall, San Antonio, 1981, others, Tex. and Calif.; exhibited works in numerous group shows U.S. and Europe, including Nat. Soc. Painters in Casein, N.Y.C., 1969-79, Tex. Watercolor Soc., San Antonio, 1974-77, Nat. Watercolor Soc., 1978, 79, Silvermine Guild, New Canaan, Conn., 1974-75, Art Mus. S. Tex., Corpus Christi, 1975-76, Nat. Tour Am. Drawings, Smithsonian Instn., 1965-66, S.W. Tex. Watercolor Soc., 1976, 79, Tex. Watercolor Soc., 1980, Silvermine Guild Artists, New Canaan, Conn., 1980, also ann. exhbns. nat. art socs., galleries, confs.; represented in permanent collections. Pres., mem. exec. bd. San Antonio Blind Assn.; jury mem. children's poetry contest San Antonio Library System; chmn. bd. trustees Incarnate Word Coll., San Antonio; bd. dirs., nat. sec., mem. adv. bd. Gulf States Regional Office; nat. trustee, nat. sec. Humane Soc. U.S.; corp. mem. Cambridge Sch., Weston, Mass.; judge San Antonio Public Schs., 1987, lectr in field; bd. dirs. Madonna Neighborhood Centers, Animal Welfare Soc., West Kennebunk, Maine, Chamber Arts Ensemble, San Antonio, San Antonio Choral Soc., Man and Beast, Inc.; fine arts adv. council U. Tex.; pres. Friends San Antonio Public Library, 1969-70; mem. com. on grievance oversight Tex. State Bar, 1979; adv. bd. Council for Livestock Protection, Braintree, Mass.; mem. citizens' adv. bd. St. Peters-St. Josephs Children's Home, San Antonio, 1981—; mem. nat. adv. bd. Amigos de las Americas, Houston, 1981—, adv. bd. Ballet Concerto, San Antonio, Tex. ; mem. adv. council Coll. Architecture and Environ. Design Tex. A&M U., 1981—; mem. Wild Canid Survival and Research Center, St. Louis. Recipient awards, 1960—, including: 1st prize Contemporary Artists Exhbn., San Antonio, 1973; Women in Art award San Antonio Bus. and Profl. Women's Club, 1975; Drought award Local Artists Exhbn., San Antonio, 1977, drawing award, 1978, M.J. Kaplan award Nat. Soc. Painters in Casein and Acrylic, 1978; numerous other art awards; Hon. Stagescrew award, drama dept. San Antonio Coll., 1975; Service award Providence High Sch., San Antonio, 1976; Gold medal Incarnate Word Coll., San Antonio, 1978; Disting. Alumna medal St. Mary's Hall, 1981; Spl. recognition award Tex. Ednl. Theater Assn., 1982; Arts and Letters award Friends of San Antonio Library, 1985; The Joseph Wood Krutch medal Humane Soc. of U.S., 1985; Harold Vagtborg award Council of Research and Acad. Libraries (San Antonio), 1986; named Woman of Distinction, Baylor U., 1967; Tex. Women's Hall Fame, Gov.'s Tex. Commn. for Women, 1984; Amy Freeman Lee AAUW Ednl. Found. Fellowship named, 1973; honored for 45 yrs. of disting. service to Madonna Ctr., San Antonio, 1986, Mem. Am. Fedn. Arts, Nat. Soc. Painters in Casein, Artists Equity Assn., Boston Soc. Ind. Artists (Smith Coll. purchase prize 1950), San Antonio Art League (adv. bd. of presidents, 6th v.p.), Nat. Soc. Arts and Letters, San Antonio Chamber Music Soc. (dir.), Philos. Soc. Tex., Defenders of Wildlife, Am. Anti-Vivisect. Soc. (life), World Fedn. for Protection Animals (life), Nat. Assn. for Advancement Humane Edn., Tex. Art Educators, Woman's Aux. Santa Rosa Hosp. (founder), St. Mary's Hall Alumni Assn., San Antonio Conservation Soc., Poetry Soc. Am., Am. Soc. for Aesthetics, Assn. Internationale des Critiques d'Art, Paris, Contemporary Artists Group San Antonio (dir.), Southwest Watercolor Soc. (purchase prize 1967, Harwood K. Smith award 1969), Tex. Watercolor Soc. (founder, pres., dir., purchase prize 1963, 64, 69, 74, 79, 80), Nat. Watercolor Soc. (Figure painting award 1967), Calif., Los Angeles, San Antonio watercolor socs., Tex. Art Edn. Assn., Coll. Art Assn. Am., Expts. in Art and Tech., Silvermine Guild Artists, S. Tex. Print Soc., Tex. Fine Arts Assn. (adv. council), Tex. Art Alliance, Artists Fellowship of N.Y., Assn. Governing Bds. Univs. and Colls., Internat. Platform Assn., Bus. and Profl. Women's Club (hon.), AAUP, AAUW, Internat. Soc. for Edn. Through Art, Cum Laude Soc. (hon.), Kappa Pi (hon.), Delta Delta Delta, Tau Sigma Delta (hon.), Delta Kappa Gamma (hon.), numerous other groups. Author: Hobby Horses, 1940; A Critic's Notebook, 1943; Remember Pearl Harbor, 1945. Contbg. editor S.A. mag. and Radio Sta. KTSA, San Antonio, 1977. Address: 127 Canterbury Hill San Antonio TX 78209

LEE, BENJAMIN KAI YIU, investment executive; b. Macau, June 2, 1959; s. Cheung Hing and Shui Fun (Woo) L.; m. Rosa Ling, May 3, 1985. BA magna cum laude, Knox Coll., 1981; MBA in Fin., U. Chgo., 1983. Research assoc. Oak Ridge (Tenn.) Nat. Lab., 1980; research analyst Duty Free Shoppers Ltd., Hong Kong, 1981; assoc. Morgan Stanley & Co., N.Y.C., 1983-86; dir. Terramar Corretora, Porto Alegre, Brazil, 1986-87; internat. assoc., product specialist Morgan Stanley & Co., N.Y.C., Hong Kong, 1987—; registered rep. Chgo. Bd. Trade, Chgo. Merc. Exchange, N.Y. Futures Exchange, N.Y. Stock Exchange, Am. Stock Exchange. Recipient award Wall St. Jour., 1981. Mem. Commodity Futures Trading Commn. (associated), Inst. Estudos Empresariais, Phi Beta Kappa.

LEE, CHEE PENG, architect; b. Singapore, Singapore, Nov. 9, 1955; s. Mun Chong and Wai Chong (Lui) L.; m. Pheck-Yan Lee, Aug. 15, 1982; 1 child, Keng-Yin. BArch, Nat. U. Singapore, 1981. Architect Archurban Architects Planners, Singapore, 1981-85; sr. architect Wong and Ouyang and Assocs., Ltd., Singapore, 1985-86, dir., 1986—. V.p. Ang Mo Kio Bo Wen Community Cen. Ceramic Arts Club, Singapore, 1987. Served to lt. Singapore Infantry, 1973-76. Mem. Singapore Inst. Architects (corp. 1983—), Royal Australian Inst. Architects (assoc. 1983—). Home: 7-A Thomson Hills Dr, 2057 Singapore Singapore Office: 250 N Bridge Rd, #13-05 Raffles City Tower, 0617 Singapore Singapore

LEE, CHING-LI, immunochemist; b. Taiwan, China, Mar. 30, 1942; came to U.S., 1970, naturalized, 1978; s. Yuan-chi and Liung-chu (Chang) L.; m. Ming-lea Liao, Jan. 6, 1972; children—Thomas Lee, George Lee, Jenny Lee. B.S., Chung-Hsing U., Taiwan China, 1969; M.S., Wayne State U., 1972, Ph.D., 1975. Research assoc. Mayo Med. Sch., Rochester, Minn., 1975-77; cancer research scientist II Roswell Pk. Meml. Inst., Buffalo, 1977-79, cancer research scientist III, 1979-83, cancer research scientist IV, 1983-86, cancer research scientist V, 1986—; research asst. prof. SUNY, Buffalo, 1981—. Author: Prostate Cancer, 1981, Biochemical Markers for Cancer, 1982. Contbr. articles to profl. jours. Grantee Nat. Cancer Inst., 1978-81, 1984-86, Am. Cancer Soc., 1983-86, 86-88. Mem. Am. Assn. Immunologists, Am. Assn. Cancer Research, Am. Chemical Soc., Biochemical Soc., N.Y. Acad. Scis. Office: Roswell Pk Meml Inst 666 Elm St Buffalo NY 14263

LEE, CHI-WANG, engineering company executive; b. Hong Kong, Apr. 22, 1955; s. Shek Fen Lee and Chi-Kwan Tong; m. Patricia S.W. Leung, Aug. 1982. MusB, U. Portland, 1981. Sales mgr. Wo Kee Engring. Ltd., Hong Kong, 1982-83, dep. gen. mgr., 1983—; dir., owner Sze and Wang Enterprises Ltd., Aloha, Oregon, Hong Kong, 1986—. Mem. Audio Engring. Soc., Inc., Soc. Motion Picture and TV Engrs. Home: 7640 SW 165th Ave Aloha OR 97007 Office: Wo Kee Engring Ltd, 703A Peter Bldg, 58-62 Queens Rd, Hong Kong Hong Kong

LEE, CHUL CHOO, agricultural engineer, educator; b. Seoul, Korea, Sept. 29, 1929; s. Yong Sang and Sung Min (Park) L.; m. Sung Sook Hong; children: Yong Jin, Yong Jae, Yong Joon. BS, Seoul Nat. U., 1954, MS, 1956; MS, U. Minn., 1958, PhD, 1960. Asst. prof. Seoul Nat. U., 1960-66, assoc. prof., 1966-70, prof., head agrl. machinery dept., 1970-73; prof. Indian Inst. Tech., Kharagpu, India, 1973-74; visiting prof. U. Philippines, Los Baños, 1974-75; agrl. engr. Internat. Rice Research Inst., Los Bañ, 1974-75; sr. project engr. Asian Devel. Bank, Manila, 1975—; tech. advisor Nat. Agrl. Cooperative Fed., Office of Rural Devel., Seoul, 1963-70, 1972-73; research advisor Ministry of Agrl., Suwon, Korea, 1966-70; councilor Ministry of Commerce Patent Bur., 1971-72. Author: Agricultural Machinery, 1964; co-author: Agricultural Machinery, 1962, Farm Machinery Yearbook, 1972; co-editor: Farm Machinery Industrial Research Corp. mag., Tokyo, 1972—. Mem. Korean Soc. Agrl. Engrs., Korean Soc. Agrl. Machinery, Korean Soc. Agrl. Engrs. (v.p. 1956-68, dir. 1968-73, chmn. Agrl. Machinery com. 1968-71). Home: 206 Ho 5 Dong Kuek-Dong Apt, 218-1 Kwang-Jang Dong, Seung-Dong-Ku, Seoul Republic of Korea

LEE, CHUNG-KYOON, psychiatrist, educator; b. Seoul, Korea, Jan. 18, 1929; s. Byung-Je Lee and Joon-Sun Chang; m. Byung-Hyun Chang Lee; children: Yong-Jin, Jung-Jin, Kyoo-Jin. MD, Seoul Nat. U., 1952, PhD, 1963. Cert. in Neurology, Psychiatry. Intern and reaident Seoul Nat. U. Hosp., 1954-59, prof. dept. psychiatry, 1969—; adj. prof. NYU, 1980—; adv. Ministry Law Republic Korea, Seoul, 1981-83; bd. govs. Internat. Organ. Psychophysiology, Montreal, Que., Can., 1981—; chmn. sci. com. 3d Pacific Congress Psychiatry, Seoul, 1982-84; pres. Pacific Rim Coll. Psychiatrists, Los Angeles, 1984-86; adv. WHO Western Pacific Region, Manila, 1984-85, 87. Author: Psychiatry, 1978, rev. edit. 1987 (Korean Med. Assn. award 1982), monograph Minn. Multiphasic Personality Inventory, 1967. Recipient Outstanding Leadership award Pacific Rim Coll. Psychiatry, Los Angeles, 1986. Fellow World Assn. Social Psychiatrists, World Fed. Biolog. Psychiatry, Am. Psychiat. Assn., Internat. Soc. Psychoneuroendocrinology, Korean Assn. Social Psychiatry (pres. 1984-86), Korean Soc. Biolog. Psychiatry (pres. 1986—), Korean Neuropsychiat. Assn. (pres. 1969-70, 79-80, pub. jour. 1969-70, 79-80), Korean Med. Assn. (chmn. sci. com. 1982-85, editor jour., 1982-85, Med. Grand Prize, 1987, literary work award, 1982). Office: Seoul Nat U Dept Neuropsychiatry, 28 Yeongundong Jongrogu, Seoul 110-744, Repubic Korea

LEE, CURTIS HOWARD, mechanical engineer, engineer; b. San Francisco, June 7, 1928; s. Lum Quong and Kum Ho (Lee) L.; B.S. with honor, Calif. State Poly. Coll., 1952; postgrad. McGeorge Coll. Law, 1964-67; m. Mildred Lee; children—Melinda, Roberta, Lorie, Sabrina, Kristina. Mech. engr. Buonaccorsi & Assos., cons. engrs., San Francisco, 1953-57, Eagleson Engrs., cons. engrs., San Francisco, 1957-59; 60-63; chief engr. C.S. Hardeman, San Francisco, 1959-60; spl. project engr. A.E. D'Ambly, cons. engrs., Phila., 1963-64; self-employed as cons. engr., Sacramento, 1964-67; chief engr. George W. Dunn & Assos., cons. engrs. San Diego, 1967-69; prin. Dunn-Lee-Smith-Klein & Assocs., San Diego, 1969-87, Curtis H. Lee Cons. Group, Chula Vista, 1987—. Mem. Accrediting Commn. of Assn. of Ind. Colls. and Schs., 1970-76; mem. adv. panel Calif. State Bldg. Standards Commn., 1971-76; mem. San Diego City Bd. Bldg. Appeals, 1974-79; mem. Chula Vista City Bd. Appeals, 1980-88—. Served with AUS, 1947-48. Registered profl. engr., Ariz., Calif., Colo., Fla., Ga., Wash., Nev., N.Mex., Ohio, Oreg., Pa., Tex. Fellow ASHRAE; mem. Am. Arbitration Assn. (mem. nat. panel 1969—, regional adv. bd. 1977—), Am. Acad. Forensic Scis., Nat. Soc. Profl. Engrs. (pres. San Diego chpt. 1972-73, state dir. 1973-74, nat. dir. 1974-76), ASME, Am. Soc. Plumbing Engrs. (charter pres. San Diego chpt. 1970, nat. 3d v.p. 1970-72), Constrn. Specifications Inst. (dir. San Diego chpt. 1974-75, pres. 1976-77, Inst. com. 1978—, named fellow 1983), Am. Soc. Profl. Estimators, Am. Soc. Quality Control, Instrument Soc. Am., Am. Soc. Testing and Materials, Internat. Assn. Plumbing and Mech. Ofcls., Nat. Fire Protection Assn. Office: 492 3d Ave 101 Chula Vista CA 92010-4614

LEE, DANIEL ANDREW, osteopathic physician, optometrist; b. Bklyn., Aug. 20, 1951; s. Jack W. and Lily (Ho) L.; m. Janet Lynne Eng, June 14, 1975 (div. Sept. 1985); children: Jason Matthew, Brian Christopher; m. Kelly Lynne Crego, Sept. 5, 1987. BS in Psychobiology, SUNY, Stony Brook, 1973; BS in Biology, Westminster Coll., 1973; OD, Pa. Coll. Optometry, 1977; DO, Ohio U., 1984. Cert. in low vision proficiency. Instr. Mohawk Valley Community Coll., Rome, N.Y., 1978-80; pvt. practice optometry, Utica, N.Y., 1978-80, Chauncey, Ohio, 1981-84, Dayton, Ohio, 1984—; intern Grandview Hosp., Dayton, 1984, mem. staff, 1984-85, ophthalmology resident, 1985—; cons. Rome Sch. Dist., Cen. Assn. for Blind, Utica, Kernan Sch. for Multiple Handicapped, Utica; speaker various profl. orgns. and confs.; mem. curriculum adv. com. Deer Creek Curriculum Rev. Conf., 1982. Contbr. articles to profl. jours. Mem. adv. bd. ARC, Rome, 1977-80; mem. Mohawk Valley Chinese Cultural Assn., Rome, 1977-80, Dayton Area Chinese Assn., 1985—; nominated People to People Optometry Delegation to People's Republic of China, 1985, India, 1986. Served with USAF, 1977-80, to lt. comdr. USNR, 1981—. Fellow Am. Acad. Optometry; mem. Am. Osteo. Assn. (student rep. nat. com. on colls. 1984), Ohio Osteo. Assn., Am. Acad. Ophthalmology, Dayton Area Chinese Assn., Gold Key, Montgomery county Med. Soc., Ohio State Med. Assn., Am. Soc. Cataract and Refractive Surgery, Beta Beta Beta. Episcopalian. Avocations: hunting, fishing, martial arts, photography, playing mandolin. Home: 590 Neal Rd Saint Paris OH 43072 Office: Grandview Hosp 405 Grand Ave Dayton OH 45405

LEE, DENNIS PATRICK, lawyer, administrative judge; b. Omaha, Feb. 12, 1955; s. Donald Warren and Betty Jean (O'Leary) L.; m. Rosemarie Bucchino, July 28, 1979; children—Patrick Michael, Katherine Marie. B.A., Creighton U., 1977, J.D., 1980. Bar: Nebr. 1980, U.S. Dist. Ct. Nebr. 1980, U.S. Ct. Appeals (8th cir.) 1980. Assoc. Thompson Crounse & Pieper, Omaha, 1980-84; ptnr. Lee Law Offices, Omaha, 1984-87, Silverman & Lee Law Offices, 1987—; atty. Nebr. State Racing Commn., Lincoln, 1984-87, adminstrv. law judge, State of Nebr., 1985—; lectr. Creighton U., Omaha, 1982-85. Author: Law of Conservatorships, 1981; Legal Aspects of Equine Veterinary Practice, 1984; others. Trustee, Holy Name Cath. Ch., Omaha, 1980-84; chmn. nat. enforcement officers com. Nat. Assn. State Racing Commrs., Lexington, Ky., 1984-87. Mem. Nat. Assn. Trial Attys., Comml. Law League Am., ABA, Nebr. Bar Assn., Omaha Bar Assn. (chmn. conservatorship com. 1981—). Democrat. Roman Catholic. Club: Nebr.-Iowa Referees Assn. (v.p. 1981—). Home: 5401 Blondo St Omaha NE 68104 Office: Silverman & Lee 12165 W Center Rd Suite 52 Omaha NE 68144

LEE, EDWARD BROOKE, JR., real estate executive, fund raiser; b. Silver Spring, Md., Oct. 25, 1917; s. E. Brooke Lee and Elizabeth (Wilson) Aspinwall; m. Camilla Edge, Apr. 15, 1944 (div. Feb. 1983); children: Camilla Lee Alexander, E. Brooke III, Kaiulani Lee Kimbrell, Katherine Blair Lee St. John, Richard Henry, Elizabeth Ashe Somerville; m. Deborah Roche, Apr. 30, 1983; children: Samuel Phillips II, Regina Blair. AB, Princeton U., 1940; student, The Infantry Sch., 1942; postgrad. bus. sch., Harvard U., 1957. Cert. real estate broker Md., D.C., Va. Various indsl. positions to nat. account mgr. Scott Paper Co., Phila., 1940-62; comml. broker Shannon and Luchs, Washington, 1962-83, Merrill Lynch Realty, Washington, 1983—; pres. E. Brooke Lee Properties, Inc., Montgomery County, Md., 1979—; fund raiser key gifts Nat. Found. for Cancer Research, Bethesda, Md., 1985—; v.p. Ga. Ave. Properties, Montgomery County, Ga.-Conn., Inc., Montgomery County, Conn. Aspen, Inc., Montgomery County, 1962—; sec.-treas. Brooke Lee Family, Inc., Montgomey County, 1962—. Author numerous sales articles for purchasing mags. Chmn. Drug Action Coalition, Inc., fin. v.p., bd. dirs., 1966-70; rep. candidate for Mayor of Washington, 1982, rep. primary candidate for U.S. Senate, State of Md., 1986. Served to capt. inf. U.S. Army, 1943-45, ETO. Named Realtor Assoc. of Yr., Washington Bd. of Realtors, 1984. Mem. Harvard Bus. Sch. Club (pres. 1962, exec. v.p. 1975), Princeton Club of Washington (sec., bd. dirs. 1970-75), Princeton Club of N.Y., Nat. Account Mktg. Assn. (pres. 1959-62). Republican. Episcopalian. Clubs: Met., Chevy Chase Country (Washington). Lodge: Kiwanis. Home: 208 Primrose St Chevy Chase MD 20815 Office: Nat Found for Cancer Research 7315 Wisconsin Ave Bethesda MD 20814 also: Merrill Lynch Comml Realty 6701 Rockledge Dr Suite 390 Bethesda MD 20817

LEE, FREDERICK KAM-FAI, architect; b. Macau, May 28, 1935; s. Chak Po and Wai Chan (Kwok) L.; m. Pansy Po-Gee, Dec. 9, 1963; children: Edwin, Alan, Anthony. BCE, Cornell U., 1961; MS, Stanford U., 1962.

Architect, engr. T.C. Yuen & Co., Hong Kong, 1962-63; prin. architect, engr. Ping K. Ng., Hong Kong, 1963-68; ptnr. Samuel Tak Lee & Ptnr., Hong Kong, 1968-81; proprietor Frederick K. F. Lee and Assocs., Hong Kong, 1981—; chmn. Fetpa Co., Ltd. Hong Kong, 1978, Fredgisons Investments Inc., Houston, 1983. Mem. Inst. Structural Engrs. (Eng.), Council Engring. Instns. (Eng.), Hong Kong Inst. Engrs. Clubs: Cornell (Ithaca, N.Y.); Stanford (Calif.). Home: 41A Stubbs Rd, D1 10th Floor, Villa Monte Rosa Hong Kong

LEE, FREDERICK YUK LEONG, physician, educator; b. Honolulu, Sept. 18, 1937; s. Harold K.L. and Frances Y. (Sugai) L.; m. Linda Scott Partridge, June 21, 1974; children—Suelin K.O., David K.F., Catherine K.Y.; children by previous marriage—Mark K.C., Michelle Y.C., Monica Y.Y. Student, U. Hawaii, 1955-58; M.D., Tulane U., 1962. Diplomate Am. Bd. Ob-Gyn, Am. Bd. Laser Surgery. Rotating intern Charity Hosp., New Orleans, 1962-63; resident obstetrics and gynecology Charity Hosp., 1966-69, instr., chief resident, 1968-69; mem. faculty Tulane U. Sch. Medicine, 1969-78; John Rock prof. reproductive physiology dept. obstetrics and gynecology 1974-78, clin. prof., 1978—, dir. sec. reproductive physiology, 1975-78, program dir. studies infertility and fertility, 1973-78, dir. ultra-sound unit, 1974-78, acting chmn. dept. obstetrics and gynecology, 1978. Contbr. articles to med. jours. Served to capt. M.C. USAF, 1962-66. Recipient Sidney K. Simon Meml. prize Tulane U. Med. Sch., 1962; fellow USPHS, 1969-70. Fellow A.C.S., Am. Coll. Obstetricians and Gynecologists; mem. La., New Orleans, Conrad G. Collins and Jefferson obstetrics and gynecol. socs., Soc. Gynecol. Surgeons, Am. Fertility Soc., Am. Inst. Ultrasound in Medicine, Central Assn. Obstetricians and Gynecologists, Am. Soc. Laser Medicine and Surgery, Gunecologic Laser Soc., La. Jefferson Parish med socs., Omega Insts. Internat. (bd. dirs.), Sigma Xi. Home: 686 Kiskatom Lane Mandeville LA 70448 Office: 4425 Conlin St Suite 101 Metairie LA 70006

LEE, GILBERT BROOKS, retired ophthalmology engineer; b. Cohasset, Mass., Sept. 10, 1913; s. John Alden and Charlotte Louise (Brooks) L.; m. Marion Corrine Rapp, Mar. 7, 1943 (div. Jan. 1969); children: Thomas Stearns, Jane Stanton, Frederick Cabot, Eliot Frazar. BA, Reed Coll., 1946; MA, New Sch. for Social Research, 1949. Asst. psychologist Civil Service, Psychophysics of Vision, U.S. Naval Submarine Base, New London, Conn., 1950-53; research assoc. Project Mich., Vision Research Labs., Willow Run, 1954-57; research assoc. dept. ophthalmology U. Mich., Ann Arbor, 1958-72, sr. research assoc., 1972-75, sr. engring. research assoc. ophthalmology, 1975-82, part-time sr. engr. ophthalmology, 1982—; sec. internat. dept., 23d St. YMCA, N.Y.C., 1941-42. Contbr. articles to profl. jours.; local organizer, moderator (TV program) Union of Concerned Scientists' Internat. Satellite Symposium on Nuclear Arms Issues, 1986; producer (TV show) Steps for Peace, 1987. Precinct del. Dem. County Conv., Washtenaw County, 1970, 74; treas. Dem. Party Club, Ann Arbor, Mich., 1971-72, 74-79, vice chmn. nuclear arms control com., 1979; chmn. Precinct Election Inspectors, 1968-75; scoutmaster Portland (Oreg.) area council Boy Scouts Am., 1932-39. Served to capt. AUS, 1942-46, 61-62. Mem. Optical Soc. Am., AAAS, Fedn. Am. Scientists, N.Y. Acad. Sci., Assn. Research in Vision and Ophthalmology, Nation Assocs., ACLU, Sierra Club, Amnesty Internat. Home: 901 Edgewood Pl Ann Arbor MI 48103

LEE, HENRY HOCK-PING, automotive trading company executive; b. Hong Kong, Sept. 18, 1930; s. Yan-To and Kin-Sheun (Leung) L.; m. Siu-Kiu Chun; children: Brigitta, Mary, Henry, Judy. Dept. head Christian Children Fund, Inc., Hong Kong, 1961-64; mgr. Unlong br. Wallace Harper Co., Ltd., Hong Kong, 1965, sales mgr. comml. vehicles, 1966-68, gen. sales mgr., 1969-73, gen. mgr., 1974; mng. dir. Harper Motor Group (now Sime Darby Motor Group), Hong Kong, 1975—, also bd. dirs.; bd. dirs. BMW Concessionaires, Ltd., Hong Kong, Wallace Harper and Co., Ltd., Universal Cars, Ltd., Hong Kong. Rep. bd. govs. Hong Kong Bapt. Coll., 1979-86, Council, 1984-86. Mem. Hong Kong Nursing Mgmt. Assn. (hon. advisor 1986—). Baptist. Clubs: Hong Kong, Kowlloon Tong. Office: Sime Darby Motor Group Ltd, 311 Gloucester Rd 34th Floor, Windsor House, Hong Kong Hong Kong

LEE, HI BAHL, nephrology educator; b. Ahndong, Kyongbook, Korea, Jan. 9, 1942; s. Woo Sung and Pil Joo L.; m. Jung Hee Kwon, Jan. 5, 1972; children: Kang Hahn, Kang Nak, Kang Mia. MD, Seoul Nat. U., 1965, MMS, 1967. Diplomate Am. Bd. Internal Medicine. Med. intern We. Pa. Hosp., Pitts., 1968-69; med. resident U. Minn. Sch. Medicine, 1969-70; med. resident Wayne State U. Sch. Medicine, Detroit, 1970-72, nephrology fellow, 1972-74; clin. asst. prof. So. Ill. U. Sch. Medicine, Carbondale, 1974-80; assoc. prof. Kyung Hee U. Sch. Medicine, Seoul, 1980-82; prof., chmn. dept. medicine Soon Chun Hyang U. Sch. Medicine, Seoul, 1982—. Contbr. articles to profl. jours. Served to lt. M.C., Republic of Korea Army, 1965-68. Mem. Am. Soc. Nephrology, Internat. Soc. Nephrology, Korean Soc. Nephrology, Asian-Pacific Soc. Nephrology. Home: 3-202 Hongshil Apt, Samsong Song Kang Nam Koo, Seoul 135 Republic of Korea Office: Soon Chung Hyang U Hosp, 657 Hannam Dong Yongsan Koo, Seoul 140 Republic of Korea

LEE, HIROMICHI, hotel and restaurant executive; b. Yokohama, Japan, Mar. 31, 1959; s. Hai Tien and Yen Shin (Wu) L.; m. Hsiu Ying Yang, Oct. 15, 1984; children: Wei Na, Wei Li. BS, Nat. Taiwan U., 1981. Account exec. Hai Tien Shipping Co. Ltd., Yokohama, 1981-82; mktg. exec. Holiday Inn, Yokohama, 1982-83, dir. sales, 1983-84, gen. mgr., 1984—; chief exec. officer Chun King Restaurant chain, Yokohama, 1987—. Office: Holiday Inn Yokohama, 77 Yamasmita-cho, Naka-ku, Yokohama 231, Japan

LEE, HONKON, government official Republic Korea; b. Kong Joo, Korea, Dec. 7, 1920; s. Kidong and Jinsil (Ahn) L.; grad. Japanese and Am. mil. schs.; m. Haeran, 1946; 3 children; m. 2d, Kwiran, 1954; 3 children. Commnd. maj. Korean Army, 1946, advanced through grades to gen., 1954; supt. Korean Constabulary Acad., commdr. Korean Constabulary, chief gen. staff Dept. Internal Security, 1946-48; mil. attaché Korean Embassy, Washington, 1949, comdg. gen. divs. and corps, 1949-54; chmn. Joint Chiefs Staff, 1954-56; chief of staff, 1956-59; nat. pres. Korean Vets. Assn., 1960-61; ambassador to Philippines, 1961-62, to Eng., Scandinavian countries, Iceland, Malta and African countries, 1962-67; ambassador-at-large, 1967; chmn. Adv. Reform Com., 1969; chmn. Korean Anti-Communist League, 1976—; chmn. Korea-Brit. Soc., 1978—. Decorated Tae-Guk Order Mil. Merit, 1952, with silver star, 1953, Disting. Diplomatic Service Decoration, 1963; 5 decorations from U.S. Pres.; also numerous fgn. decorations. Office: San 5-19, Chang Choong Dong, Chung-Ku, Seoul Republic of Korea *

LEE, HYUN-CHAE, prime minister of Republic of Korea; b. Hong Sung-Gun, Republic of Korea, Dec. 20, 1929; m. Yo-Hin Kim; 4 children. BS, Seoul Nat. U., Republic of Korea, 1953, PhD in Econs., 1969. Instr. Air Force Acad., Seoul, 1953-58; prof. Pusan (Republic of Korea) Nat. U., 1958-61; prof. Seoul Nat. U., 1961—, dean Coll. Social Scis., 1979-80, pres., 1983-85; prime minister Govt. of Republic of Korea, Seoul, 1988—; vis. prof. U. Pitts. Served to capt. Korean Air Force, 1953-58. Decorated Order of Civil Merit Govt. Republic of Korea, 1982. Mem. Korean Econ. Assn. (pres. 1983-85). Home: 106 Samchong-dong, Chongro-Gu, Seoul 110-230, Republic of Korea Office: Office of Prime Minister, 77 Sejongro, Chongro-Gu, Seoul 110-050, Republic of Korea

LEE, IK-HWAN, educator; b. Tasi, Chonnam-do, Korea, Feb. 6, 1943; s. Tongsul and Ch'aesun) L.; m. Yun-Hwan Kim Lee, Feb. 25, 1973; children—Chong-Eun, Kenneth Kisoo. B.A., Seoul Nat. U., 1968, M.Ed., 1971; Ph.D., U. Tex., Austin, 1979. Humanities assoc. U. Tex., Austin, 1975-77, asst., 1975-76, grad. research asst., 1977-79; asst. prof. linguistics Chung-Ang U., Seoul, Korea, 1979-81, Yonsei U., Seoul, 1981-83, assoc. prof., 1983-87, prof. english, linguistics Yonesi University, 1987—; sec. Seoul Workshop Formal Grammar, 1980-84; research planner Linguistic Soc. Korea, 1983-84, sec. Author: Korean Particles, Complement and Questions, 1980; Modern Semantics, 1984; An Introduction to Semantics, 1985; An Introduction to English Grammar, 1987; editor-in-chief The Korean Society of Cognitive Science, 1987—; author, editor Seoul Papers in Formal Grammar Theory vol. 1, 1985, vol. 2, 1988, Harvard Studies in Korean Linguistics, vol. 1, 1985, vol. 2, 1987; contbr. articles to profl. jours. Served with Korean Army, 1971-73. U. Tex. fellow, 1977, travel grantee, 1978; vis. scholar Harvard U., 1984-85; Daewoo Found. grantee, 1981-83, 84-85; Ministry of Edn. Korea grantee, 1983-84. Mem. Linguistic Soc. Korea (editor 1980-82), Linguistic Soc. Am., MLA, English Lit. Soc. Korea, Internat. Circle of Korean Linguistics, Linguistic Soc. of Korea (gen. sec. 1985-86, 88). Home: 414-42 Mangwon-dong, Mapo'ku, Seoul 121-231, Republic of Korea Office: Yonsei U, Dept English, 134 Sinch'on-dong, Seoul 120-749, Republic of Korea

LEE, JENNIFER MARGARET, editor, historian; b. Tamworth, NSW, Australia, July 17, 1953; d. Jeffrey Denison and Hazel May Lee; m. Michael Duncan Daffey, May 22, 1976; children: Eleanor, Bronwen. BA, Australian Nat. U., 1975, MA, 1980. Adminstrv. trainee Australian Pub. Service, Canberra, Australia, 1975-77; archivist Melbourne (Australia) U., 1984-87, editor Meanjin, 1987—. Co-editor: A People's History of Australia, 4 vols., 1988; contbr. articles to hist. publs. Cons. Youth Affairs Council Australia, 1984; pres. Nat. Youth Council Australia, 1977-80. Nat. scholar Australian Nat. U., 1970-75. Home: 15 Maranoa Crescent, Coburg, Victoria 3058, Australia Office: U Melbourne Meanjin, Parkville, Victoria 3052, Australia

LEE, JOHN YUCHU, industrial and specialty chemicals researcher; b. Tai-Ho, An-Huei, China, Jan. 25, 1948; came to U.S., 1971, naturalized, 1981; s. Tzu-Ching and Hua-Yin (Liao) L.; m. Sheila Yunchi Tsai, May 1, 1976; children—Gary Chiaray, Jenny Chianing. B.S., Nat. Cheng-Kung U., Taiwan, 1970; M.S., S.D. State U., 1974; Ph.D., Vanderbilt U., 1978. Teaching asst. S.D. State U., Brookings, 1973-74; grad. asst. Vanderbilt U., Nashville, 1974-78; research assoc. chemistry dept. Tex. A&M U., College Station, 1978-79, Welch research fellow chemistry dept., 1979-80; research chemist Ethyl Corp., Baton Rouge, La., 1980-88; sr. research chemist, 1988—. Contbr. articles to profl. jours. Patentee in field. Active in Chinese Assn. Baton Rouge, 1980—; spl. mem. Chinese Student Assn. Tex. A&M U., College Station, 1978-80; chmn. Chinese Student Assn. Nashville, 1975-76; prin., program dir. Chinese Sch. in Baton Rouge, 1985-86. Served to 2d lt. Chinese Air Force, 1970-71. Fellow Am. Inst. Chemists; mem. AAAS, Am. Chem. Soc., Royal Soc. Chemistry (chartered chemist), Japanese Chem. Soc., S.D. Acad. Sci., Chinese Am. Chem. Assn., Sigma Xi, Phi Lambda Upsilon. Roman Catholic. Clubs: Ethyl Mgmt., Kenilworth (Baton Rouge). Office: Ethyl Tech Ctr PO Box 14799 Baton Rouge LA 70898

LEE, JONG HYUK, accountant; b. Seoul, Korea, May 6, 1941; came to U.S., 1969, naturalized, 1975; s. Jung Bo and Wol Sun Lee; B.A., Sonoma State U., Rohnert Park, Calif., 1971; M.B.A. in Taxation, Golden Gate U., San Francisco, 1976; m. Esther Kim, Jan. 24, 1970. Cost acct., internal auditor Foremost-McKesson Co., San Francisco, 1971-74; sr. acct. Clark, Wong, Foulkes & Barbieri, C.P.A.s, Oakland, Calif., 1974-77; pres. J.H. Lee Accountancy Corp., Oakland, 1977—; instr. Armstrong Coll., Berkeley, Calif., 1977-78. Bd. dirs. Korean Residents Assn., 1974, Multi-service Center for Koreans, 1979, Better Bus. Bur., 1984—; chmn. caucus Calif.-Nev. ann. conf. United Methodist Ch., 1977; commr. Calif. State Office Econ. Opportunity, 1982-86; pres. Korean-Am. Democratic Network; mem. Dem. Nat. Fin. Council; regional chmn. Adv. Council on Peaceful Unification Policy, Republic of Korea. Served with Korean Marine Corps, 1961-64; 1st lt. Calif. State Mil. Res. C.P.A., Calif. Mem. Am. Inst. C.P.A.s, Nat. Assn. Asian Am. C.P.A.s (dir.), Am. Acctg. Assn., Nat. Assn. Accountants, Internat. Found. Employee Benefit Plans, Calif. Soc. C.P.A.s, Oakland C. of C., Korean Am. C. of C., Democrat. Club: Rotary. Author tax and bus. column Korea Times, 1980. Home: 180 Firestone Dr Walnut Creek CA 94598 Office: 369 13th St Oakland CA 94612

LEE, JUNG SANG, nephrologist, nephrology educator; b. Kyunggi-Do, Korea, Jan. 6, 1942; s. WonJun Lee and Yongai Park; m. Esook, Oct. 14, 1971; children: Jin Young, Ju Young. MD, Seoul Nat. U., 1966, MS, 1969, PhD, 1973. Intern Seoul Nat. U. Hosp., 1966-67, resident, 1967-71; asst. Coll. Medicine, 1971-74, lectr., 1974-78, asst. prof., 1979-83, assoc. prof., 1983—, prof., 1988—, dir. Hemodialysis room, 1978—, dir. cen. lab. ctr., 1986—, asst. clin. chief, 1986—, research dean, 1980—. Editor Seoul Med. Jour., 1985—. Fellow Northwestern Meml. Hosp., Chgo., 1976-78; recipient Smith-Kline Dongsin Sci. award Korean Med. Assn., Seoul, 1987. Trustee Korean Soc. Internal Medicine, Korean Soc. Nephrology; mem. Korean Army Med. Soc. (hon.), Soc. Internat. Nephrology, N.Y. Acad. Sci. Home: 26-1202 Hangang Apt, Kangnam-Ku, 135 Seoul Korea Office: Dept Internal Medicine Seoul Nat U Hosp, 28 Yunkun-Dong Chongo-Ku, 110 Seoul Korea

LEE, (KENNETH) KANGHONG, business executive; b. Seoul, Korea, May 22, 1941; s. Ki-Pal and Bok-Nap (Lee) L.; m. Hae-Soon Nam, May 1, 1968; children—Song-Jae, Hyun-Jae. BE, Seoul Nat. U., 1966. Mgr. Far Eastern Transport Co., Ltd., Seoul, 1965-66, Saigon, Vietnam, 1967-68, Korea Shipbuilding and Engring. Corp., Seoul, 1968-70, Victor B. Handel & Bros., Inc., Los Angeles, 1970-71, 71-72; chmn., pres. Clover Co. Ltd., Seoul, 1972—, Clover Co. Dominicana S.A., Panama, 1984-85, chief exec. officer, Miami, 1985—; dir. govt. sponsored trade mission, Los Angeles, Chgo., N.Y. and Vancouver, Mont. Can., 1975. Vice-pres. subcom. commerce and industry Democratic Justice Party of Republic of Korea, 1985. Served with Korean Marines, 1960-63. Clubs: Seoul West Rotary, Army Aviation Assn. Am. Avocations: golf, skiing. Office: Clover Co Ltd, 302-8 Sungsoo-dong-Ku, 133 Seoul Korea

LEE, KYO SEON, housing company executive; b. Icheon, Kyunggi, Republic Korea, June 10, 1935; s. Seon Kab and Bong Hee (Kim) L.; m. Young Sook Chang, Feb. 18, 1967; 1 child, Ho Chul, Jin Hee, Ho Chan. B of Econs., Korea U., 1961. Mgr. Daihan Coal Corp., Seoul, Republic Korea, 1976; v.p. Samchully Housing Co., Ltd., Seoul, 1985-86, pres., 1986—. Served to cpl. Korean Army, 1956-58. Office: Samchully Housing Co Ltd, Chunji Bldg 1022-7, Bangbae-Dong, Seocho-ku, Seoul 137-063, Republic of Korea

LEE, KYUNG-WOOK, surgeon, educator; b. Seoul, Republic Korea, Oct. 27, 1929; m. Jin-Hwa Kim, Nov. 11, 1959; 1 child, Hyun-Joo. Med. graduate, Seoul Nat. U., 1958, MS, 1960, MD, PhD, 1966. Intern Seoul Nat. U. Hosp., 1958-59, resident in surgery, 1959-63, clin. instr. Med. Sch., 1964-66; clin. prof. Kyung-Hee U. Med. Sch., Seoul, 1973-74, Han-Yang U., Seoul, 1977-88; practice medicine specializing in surgery Seoul. Fellow Internat. Coll. Surgeons (treas. Korea sect. 1979-87, gov. 1981-82); mem. Collegium Internat. Chirurgiae Digestivae. Lodge: Rotary (Paul Harris fellow 1980). Home: 238-36 Bokwang Dong, Yongsan-Koo, Seoul 140-220, Republic of Korea

LEE, LANSING BURROWS, JR., lawyer, corporate executive; b. Augusta, Ga., Dec. 27, 1919; s. Lansing Burrows and Bertha (Barrett) L.; m. Natalie Krug, July 4, 1943; children—Melinda Lee Clark Lansing Burrows III, Bothwell Graves, Richard Hancock. B.S., U. Va., 1939; postgrad U. Ga. Sch. Law, 1939-40; J.D., Harvard U., 1947. Corp. officer Ga.-Carolina Warehouse & Compress Co., Augusta, 1947-57, pres., 1957—; admitted to Ga. bar, 1947, since practiced in Augusta. Chmn. bd. trustees James Brice White Found., 1962—; active Internat. Order of St. Luke; sr. warden Episc. Ch., also chancellor, lay reader. Served to capt. USAAF, 1942-46. Fellow Am. Coll. Probate Counsel; mem. Harvard U. Law Sch. Assn. Ga. (pres. 1966-67), Augusta Bar Assn. (pres. 1966-67), Soc. Colonial Wars Ga. Bar Found., Ga. Bar Assn. (former chmn. fiduciary law sect.). Clubs: Augusta Country, Harvard of Atlanta. Home: 2918 Bransford Rd Augusta GA 30909 Office: 904 First Union Bank Bldg Augusta GA 30901

LEE, LILY KIANG, scientific research company executive; b. Shanghai, China, Nov. 23, 1946; came to U.S., 1967, naturalized, 1974; d. Chi-Wu and An-Teh (Shih) Kiang; B.S., Nat. Cheng-Chi U., 1967; M.B.A. (scholar), Golden Gate U., San Francisco, 1969; m. Robert Edward Lee; children—Jeffrey Anthony, Michelle Adrienne, Stephanie Amanda, Christina Alison. Acct., then acctg. supr. Am. Data Systems, Inc., Canoga Park, Calif., 1969-73; sr. acct. Perpheral Equipment div. Pertec Corp., Chatsworth, Calif., 1973-76; mgr. fin. planning and acctg., then mgr. fin. planning and program control Sci. Center div. Rockwell Internat. Corp., Thousand Oaks, Calif., 1976—. Mem. Am. Mgmt. Assn., Nat. Mgmt. Assn., Nat. Property Mgrs. Assn., Nat. Assn. Female Execs. Republican. Baptist. Office: Rockwell Internat Corp PO Box 1085 1049 Camino Dos Rios Thousand Oaks CA 91360

LEE, MARGARET ANNE, psychotherapist; b. Scribner, Nebr., Nov. 23, 1930; d. William Christian and Caroline Bertha (Benner) Joens; m. Robert Kelly Lee, May 21, 1950 (div. 1971); children: Lawrence Robert, James Kelly, Daniel Richard. AA, Napa Coll., 1949; student, U. Calif., Berkeley, 1949-50; BA, Calif. State Coll., Sonoma, 1975; MSW, Calif. State U., Sacramento, 1977. Lic. clin. social worker, marriage and family counselor, Calif.; tchr. Columnist/stringer Napa (Calif.) Register, 1946-50; eligibility worker, supr. Napa County Dept. Social Services, 1968-75; instr. Napa Valley Community Coll., 1978-83; practice psychotherapy Napa, 1977—; bd. dirs. Project Access, 1978-79. Trustee Napa Valley Community Coll., 1983—, v.p. bd. trustees, 1984-85, pres. bd. trustees, 1986, clk., 1988; bd. dirs. Napa County Council Econ. Opportunity, 1984-85, Napa Chpt. March of Dimes, 1957-71, vice chair edn. com. 1987—; vice chmn. edn. com. Calif. Community Coll. Trustees, 1987-88, chmn. edn. com., 1988—, also legis. com. 1985-87. Recipient Fresh Start award Self mag., Mental Health Assn. Napa County, 1983-87, award Congl. Caucuson Women's Issues, 1984. Mem. Nat. Assn. Social Workers, Mental Health Assn. Napa County, Calif. Assn. Physically and Handicapped, Women's Polit. Caucus. Democrat. Lutheran. Lodge: Soroptimists. Home: 15 Camilla Dr Napa CA 94558 Office: 1100 Trancas PO Box 2099 Napa CA 94558

LEE, MARGARET NORMA, artist; b. Kansas City, Mo., July 7, 1928; d. James W. and Margaret W. (Farin) Lee; PhB, U. Chgo., 1948; MA, Art Inst. Chgo., 1952. Lectr., U. Kansas City, 1957-61; cons. Kansas City Bd. Edn., Kansas City, Mo., 1968-86; guest lectr. U.Mo.-Columbia, 1983, 85, 87; one-woman shows Univ. Women's Club, Kansas City, 1966, Friends of Art, Kansas City, 1969, Fine Arts Gallery U. Mo. at Columbia, 1972, All Souls Unitarian Ch. Kansas City, Mo., 1978; two-Woman show Rockhurst Coll., Kansas City, Mo., 1981 exhibited in group shows U. Kans., Lawrence, 1958, Chgo. Art Inst., 1963, Nelson Art Gallery, Kansas City, Mo., 1968, 74, Mo. Art Show, 1976, Fine Arts Gallery, Davenport, Iowa, 1977; represented in permanent collections Amarillo (Tex.) Art Center, Kansas City (Mo.) Pub. Library, Park Coll., Parkville, Mo. Mem. Coll. Art Assn. Roman Catholic. Contbr. art to profl. jours.; author booklet. Home and Studio: 4109 Holmes St Kansas City MO 64110

LEE, MAYA, clinical psychologist, educator; b. Chgo., Sept. 30, 1937; d. Philip Bruno and Renee (Roll) Dispensa; children—Barbara Pauline, Elizabeth Renee, Renee Marie Foss, Kelly Anne. B.A., Gov.'s State U., 1974, M.A., 1975; Ph.D., U.S. Internat. U., 1978. Lic. psychologist, Calif. Intern, San Bernardino County Mental Health (Calif.), 1977-78, psychologist, 1978-80; pvt. practice psychology, San Bernardino, 1980—. Gov.'s State U. grantee, 1973, 74. Mem. Am. Psychol. Assn., Inland Empire Psychol. Assn., NOW. Democrat. Jewish. Home: 1797 N Arrowhead San Bernardino CA 92405

LEE, MICHAEL CHING HSUEH, chemical engineer, scientist; b. Taipei, Taiwan, China, Oct. 3, 1949; s. Yen Hsuan and Pei Chang L.; came to U.S., 1972; Chem. Engr., Nat. Cheng Kung U., 1966, B.S., 1970; M.S. in Chem. Engring., U. Calif.-Berkeley, 1974; Ph.D., in Mech. Engring., 1977; m. Amy Hsuan Yi Hsu, July 20, 1972; children—Benjamin, Josephine, David, John. Jr. project engr. U. Calif., Berkeley, 1977, postdoctoral chem. engr., 1978; sr. research engr. polymers dept. Gen. Motors Research Labs., Warren, Mich., 1978-81, staff research engr., 1981-83, group leader, 1983-86, program mgr., 1986—, sr. staff research engr., 1985—. Contbr. articles to profl. jours. Patentee in field. Recepient McCuen Spl. Achievement award Gen. Motors Research Labs., 1984, Campbell Sci. Achievement award Gen. Motors Research Labs., 1986. Mem. Am. Chem. Soc., SAE, ASME, Sigma Xi. Roman Catholic. Office: Gen Motors Research Labs 30500 Mound Rd Warren MI 48090-9055

LEE, MING CHO, set designer; b. Shanghai, China, Oct. 3, 1930; came to U.S., 1949, naturalized, 1961; s. Tsufa F. and Ing (Tang) L.; m. Elizabeth Rapport; 3 children. B.A., Occidental Coll., 1953, LHD (hon.), 1975; postgrad. in theatre arts, UCLA; student art, Chang Kuo-Nyen, Shanghai; DFA (hon.), Parsons Sch. Design, 1986. Apprentice, asst. designer Jo Mielzinger, 5 Yrs.; art dir., designer in residence San Francisco Opera, fall 1961; prin. designer Juilliard Opera Theatre and Am. Opera Ctr. of Juilliard Sch. Music, 1964—; tchr. set design Yale U. Drama Sch., 1968—, co-chair, 1979—; tchr. theatre program NYU, 1967-69; set designer Yale Repertory Theatre, 1981-82; adj. prof., scene design adviser Yale U., New Haven; cons. in field; former mem. theatre projects com. N.Y.C. Planning Bd.; mem. adv. council U.S.-China Arts Exchange; trustee Nat. Design Archive. First sets designed for theatre, The Internal Machine, Phoenix, N.Y.C., 1958; designer sets: off-Broadway prodns. The Crucible, 1958, Triad, 1958, Walk in Darkness, 1963, Othello, 1964, Gandhi, 1970, Manhattan Project Seagull, 1974, Cuban Swimmer/Dog Lady, 1984; Broadway prodns. The Moon Besieged, 1962, Mother Courage, 1963, 78, Conversation in the Dark, 1963, Slapstick Tragedy, 1966, A Time for Singing, 1966, Little Murders, 1967, Here's Where I Belong, 1968, King Lear, 1968, Billy, 1969, La Strada, 1969, Lolita, 1971, Two Gentlemen of Verona, 1971, Much Ado About Nothing, 1972, All God's Children Got Wings, 1975, The Glass Menagerie, 1975, 83, For Colored Girls, 1976, Romeo and Juliet, 1976, Caeser and Cleopatra, 1977, The Shadow Box, 1977, Angel, 1979, The Grand Tour, 1978, K2, 1983, most recent work Execution of Justice, 1986; prin. designer, N.Y. Shakespeare Festival, 1962-73, designer N.Y. Shakespeare Festival various theatres and touring group shows, including The Merchant of Venice, 1962, The Tempest, 1962, King Lear, 1962, Macbeth, 1962, Anthony and Cleopatra, 1963, As You Like It, 1963, A Winter's Tale, 1963, Twelfth Night, 1963, Hamlet, 1964, 72, Othello, 1964, Electra, 1964, A Midsummer Night's Dream, 1964, Love's Labour's Lost, 1965, Coriolanus, 1965, Troilus and Cressida, 1965, The Taming of the Shrew, 1965, Henry V, 1965, All's Well That Ends Well, 1966, Measure for Measure, 1966, Richard III, 1966, The Comedy of Errors, 1967, Titus Andronics, 1967, Hair, 1967, Henry IV, Parts I and II, 1968, Romeo and Juliet, 1968, Ergo, 1968, Peer Gynt, 1969, Electra, 1969, Cities in Bezique, 1969, Invitation to a Beheading, 1969, The Wars of the Roses (Henry VI, Parts I, II, and III, and Richard III), 1970, Sambo, 1969, 70, Jack MacGowran in the Works of Samuel Beckett, 1970, Timon of Athens, 1971, Two Gentleman of Verona, 1971, The Tale of Cymbeline, 1971, Older People, 1972, Much Ado About Nothing, 1972, Wedding Band, 1972; designer sets: plays King Lear, N.Y.C., 1968, Lolita, 1971, My Love in Philadelphia, 1971, Remote Asylum, Los Angeles, 1971, Henry IV, Part I, Los Angeles, 1972, Volpone, Los Angeles, 1972, Two Gentlemen of Verona, London, 1973, Lear, New Haven, 1973, The Crucible, Arena Stage, Washington, 1967, The Tenth Man, 1968, Room Service, 1968, The Iceman Cometh, 1968, The Night Thoreau Spent in Jail, 1970, Our Town, 1972, Inherit the Wind, 1973, Julius Caeser, 1975, The Ascent of Mount Fuji, 1975, Waiting for Godot, 1976, For Colored Girls, Los Angeles, 1977, Shadow Box, New Haven, 1977, Twelfth Night, Stratford, Conn., 1978, Hamlet, Washington, 1978, Don Juan, Washington, 1978, The Glass Menagerie, Mpls., 1979, Plenty, Washington, 1980, K2, Washington, 1982, Execution of Justice, Washington, 1985, numerous others; ballets for troupes of Jose Limon, Martha Graham, Gerald Arpino, Alvin Ailey including Missa Brevis, 1958, Three Short Dances, 1959, A Look at Lightning, 1962, Sea Shadow, 1963, Adriadne, 1965, The Witch of Endor, 1965, Olympics, 1966, Night Wings, 1966, Elegy, 1967, The Lady of the House of Sleep, 1968, Secret Places, 1968, A Light Fantastic, 1968, Animus,1969, The Poppet, 1969, Myth of a Voyage, 1973, Don Juan, 1973, Whisper of Darkness, 1974, In-Quest of the Sun, 1975, The Leaves Are Fading, 1975, The Tiller in the Fields, 1978, The Owl and the Pussycat, 1978, Dream of the Red Chamber, 1983, Les Noces, 1985, Tangled Night, 1986, Sephardic Songs, Intermezzo; set designer: opera cos., including Peabody Arts Theatre of Peabody Inst., Balt., 1959-63; designer: Peabody Arts Theatre prodns. The Turk in Italy, The Old Maid and the Thief, The Fall of the City, La Boheme, Amahl and the Night Visitors, The Pearl Fishers, Werther, Hamlet; Empire State Music Festival prodns. Katya Kabanova, 1960, Peter Ibbetson, 1960, The Pearl Fishers, 1961; Balt. Civic Opera prodns. Tristan and Isolde, 1962; Opera Co. of Boston prodn. Madama Butterfly, 1961, Turandot, 1983; Met. Opera Nat. Co. prodns. Madama Butteflly, 1965, Marriage of Figaro, 1966; Opera Soc. Washington prodn. Bombarzo, 1967; N.Y.C. Opera prodns. Don Rodrigo, 1966, Julius Caeser, 1966, Le Coq d'Or, 1967, Bombarzo, 1968, Faust, 1968, Roberto Devereaux, 1970, Susannah, 1971, Maria Stuarda, 1972, Contes D'Hoffman, 1972, Anna Bolena, 1973, Idomeneo, 1975, Attila, 1981, Alceste, 1982; Hamburgische Staatsoper prodns. Julius Caeser, Hamburg, Fed. Republic Germany, 1969, Lucia di Lammermoor, Hamburg, 1971; Juilliard Opera Theatre and Am. Opera Ctr. of Juilliard Sch. Music prodns. Katya Kabanova, 1964, Il Tabarro, 1964, Gianni Schicchi, 1964, Fidelio, 1965, The

Magic Flute, 1965, The Trial of Lucullus, 1965, The Rape of Lucrezia, 1967, L'Ormindo, 1968, The Rake's Progress, 1970, Il Giuramento, 1970, also prodns. at Lyric Opera Chgo., Covent Garden, London, Houston Grand Opera, Teatro Colon, Buenos Aires, San Francisco Opera, Dallas Civic Opera, Kennedy Ctr., Washington, Chilean Opera Soc., Santiago, Associated Opera Co. Am.; one-man shows of water colors and design, Los Angeles, N.Y.C., Calif. Water Color Soc., Los Angeles County Art Show, Ohio U., Athens, Capricorn Gallery, N.Y.C., Compass Gallery, N.Y.C., Library and Mus. Performing Arts, N.Y.C., Mus. City of N.Y., Design '70; designer: Mobile Unit, N.Y. Shakespeare Festival, Florence Sutro Anspacher Theatre, N.Y. Shakespeare Festival, Estelle R. Newman Theatre, N.Y. Shakespeare Festival, Garage Theatre, Harlem Sch. Arts. Bd. dirs. Pan Asian Repertory Theatre, Chen and Dancers; mem. citizens cultural adv. com.; mem. nat. adv. bd. Drama League N.Y.; mem. adv. bd. Theatre at Storm King. Recipient 1st Joseph Maharam award for Electra, 1965, Maharam award for Ergo, 1968, Off-Broadway award Show Bus., 1969, Tony award nomination, 1970, Spl. award Nat. Opera Inst., 1980, Tony award for set design for Broadway play K-2, 1983, Outer Critics Circle award, 1983, Drama Desk award, 1983, Maharam award, 1983, Mayor's award of Honor for Arts and Culture, 1984, 1st Qinyun award for Art and Culture China Inst., 1984, Los Angeles Drama Critics Circle award for Traveller in the Dark, 1985, Hollywood Drama-Logue Critics award for Traveller in the Dark, 1985; named Man of Yr., Chinatown Planning Commn., 1986; Guggenheim fellow, 1988—. Mem. United Scenic Artists Local Union 829 (v.p. 1969-71), Mcpl. Arts Soc. (bd. dirs.). Office: care Drama Sch Yale U 205 Park St New Haven CT 06520

LEE, NELDA S., art appraiser and dealer, film producer; b. Gorman, Tex., July 3, 1941; d. Olan C. and Onis L.; A.S. (Franklin Lindsay Found. grantee), Tarleton State U., Tex., 1961; B.A. in Fine Arts, N. Tex. State U., 1963; postgrad. Tex. Tech. U., 1964, San Miguel de Allende Art Inst., Mexico, 1965; 1 dau., Jeanna Lea Pool. Head dept. art Ector High Sch., Odessa, Tex., 1963-68. Bd. dirs. Odessa YMCA, 1970, bd. dirs. Am. Heart Assn., Odessa, 1975; fund raiser Easter Seal Telethon, Odessa, 1978-79; bd. dirs. Ector County (Tex.) Cultural Center, 1979—, Tex. Bus. Hall of Fame, 1980-85; bd. dirs., mem. acquisition com. Permian Basin Presdl. Mus., Odessa, 1978; bd. dirs., chairperson acquisition com. Odessa Art Mus., 1979—; pres. Mega-Tex. Prodns., TV and movie producers; pres. Ector County Democratic Women's Club, 1975. Recipient Designer-Craftsman award El Paso Mus. Fine Arts, 1964. Mem. Am. Soc. Appraisers, Appraisers Assn. Am., Appraisers of Fine Arts Soc., Nat. Soc. Lit. and the Arts, Tex. Assn. Art Dealers (pres. 1978-79), Odessa C. of C. Contbr. articles to profl. jours. Office: Nelda Lee Inc 2610 E 21st St Odessa TX 79761

LEE, RICHARD H(ARLO), lawyer; b. Glen Falls, N.Y., June 5, 1947; s. Donald D. and Jeanne M. (Uthus) L.; m. Mary Ahearn, June 10, 1972; children: Christine Marie Ahearn Lee, Andrea Elizabeth Ahearn Lee. BS with honors, Mich. State U., 1972; JD magna cum laude, Ariz. State U., 1976. Bar: Ariz. 1977, U.S. Ct. Appeals (6th cir.) 1977, U.S. Dist. Ct. Ariz. 1978, U.S. Ct. Appeals (9th cir.) 1981. Law clk. to presiding justice U.S. Ct. Appeals (6th cir.), Cin., 1976-77; assoc. Sparks & Siler, Scottsdale, Ariz., 1977-78; assoc. Murphy & Posner, Phoenix, 1979-82, ptnr., 1983-86; assoc. Storey & Ross, Phoenix, 1986—. Comment and notes editor Ariz. State U. Law Jour., 1975-76. Chmn. Ariz. Canal Diversion Channel Task Force City of Phoenix, 1985-86, aesthetics com., 1986—; state committeeman Ariz. Dems., Phoenix, 1983-84, 1975 Bond Com. City of Phoenix, 1975; mem. City of Phoenix Neighborhood Orgn. Div. Adv. Com., 1974-75; vol. VISTA Crow Indian Tribe, Crow Agy., Mont., 1969-71. Mem. ABA (litigation, real property, gen. practice and bus. law sects.), Am. Bankruptcy Inst., Ariz. Bar Assn. (chmn. com. on continuing legal edn. bankruptcy sect. 1985-87, chmn. bankruptcy sect. 1987-88), Maricopa County Bar Assn., Maricopa County Bankruptcy Law Assn., Ariz. State U. Coll. Law Alumni Assn. (pres. 1981), Ariz. State U. Alumni Assn. (bd. dirs. 1981-82), Kappa Sigma. Home: 331 W Orangewood Phoenix AZ 85021 Office: Storey & Ross 4742 N 24th St Court 1 4th Floor Phoenix AZ 85016

LEE, ROBERT ERNEST, III, clinical psychologist, marriage and family therapist; b. Los Angeles, Nov. 8, 1943; s. Robert Ernest, Jr., and Maria Agnes (Aprea) L.; A.B., Washington and Lee U., 1965; M.A., Princeton U., 1967, Ph.D., 1968; m. Patricia Ann Ball, May 18, 1973; children—Heather Ball, Samantha Morgan. Intern, Merrill-Palmer Inst., Detroit, 1969-70; clin. psychologist VA Hosp., Allen Park, Mich., 1969-76; pvt. practice clin. psychology, Southfield, Mich., 1976—; cons. Family Service of Detroit and Wayne County; mem. adj. faculty Eastern Mich. U.; mem., vice-chmn. Mich. State Bd. Marriage Counselors. Pres. Mich. Psychologists Polit. Action Com., 1977, trustee, 1972-78. Recipient award of merit Detroit Inst. Tech., 1973; performance award VA, 1975, award for profl. achievement Mich. Assn. Marriage and Family Therapy, 1983; lic. psychologist, cert. marriage counselor, Mich. Fellow Am. Orthopsychiat. Assn.; mem. Am. Assn. Marriage and Family Therapy, Am. Psychol. Assn., Assn. Advancement Psychology, Mich. Assn. Marriage Counselors (pres. 1980), Mich. Interprofl. Assn. Marriage, Divorce and the Family, Mich. Psychol. Assn., Mich. Soc. Clin. Psychologists (pres. 1982, treas. 1977-78), Psychologists Task Force (dir.). Republican. Contbr. articles to profl. jours. Office: 28336 Franklin Rd Southfield MI 48034

LEE, ROBERT FRANK, engineering executive; b. Montreal, Que., Can., Apr. 24, 1948; s. Frank and Alison (Huntly) L.; m. Heather Ann MacKenzie, May 3, 1972 (div. Mar. 1987); children: Jeffrey, Peter. B of Mech. Engring., Concordia U., Montreal, 1972. Sales engr. Trane Co., Wis. and Ont., Can., 1972-77; regional mgr. Beaver Engring., Montreal, 1977-78; project mgr. Midland Ross, Montreal, 1978-80, sales mgr., 1980-84; gen. mgr. Valmet Automation Inc., Montreal, 1984—; bd. dirs. Kajaani, Inc., Pointe Claire, Quebec, Valmet- Automation, Inc., Pointe Claire, Quebec, Valmet Sentre, Inc., Toronto, Ont. Contbr. articles to profl. jours. Mem. Ordre Ingenieurs Que., Canadian Pulp Paper Assn., Tech. Assn. Paper Industry. Home: 200 Somervale Gardens, Apt 11, Pointe-Claire, PQ Canada H9R 3H8 Office: Valmet Automation Inc, 179 Place Frontenac, Pointe Claire, PQ Canada H9R 4Z7

LEE, ROBERT GUM HONG, chemical company executive; b. Montreal, Que., Can., May 22, 1924; s. Hai Chong Lee and Toy Kay Yip; m. Maude Toye; children: Peter, Patricia, Cathrine. BS in Engring., McGill U., Montreal, 1947. Research engr. Can. Liquid Air, Ltd., Montreal, 1947—. Coinventor OBM/Q-BOP Oxygen Seel Refining Process, 1967. Bd. dirs. Montreal Chinese Hosp., 1975-82. Mem. Soc. for Cryobiology, Can. Inst. of Mining and Metalurgy (Airey award 1974), Am. Inst. of Mining and Metalurgy, Am. Chem. Soc. Office: Can Liquid Air Ltd, 1155 Sherbrooke St W, Montreal, PQ Canada H3A 1H8

LEE, SHEW KUHN, optometrist; b. Balt., Apr. 24, 1923; s. Mong Har and Gum Tuey (Wong) L.; Dr. Optometry, Ill. Coll. Optometry, 1949; postgrad. Catholic U. Am., 1957, Md. U., 1959; m. Florence Gin Toy, Oct. 29, 1949; children: Wayson Perry, Davin Jeffrey. Pvt. practice optometry, Washington, 1949—. Lectr. D.C. Traffic Safety Sch.; v.p. D.C. Bd. Optometry, 1959-65; mem. D.C. Bd. Examiners in Optometry, 1973-84, sec., 1974; mem. Eye Bank Council; vision research cons. HEW, 1973. Bd. dirs. Eye Bank and Research Found., Washington Hosp. Center. Served with U.S. Army, 1942-45. Decorated Purple Heart, Bronze Star medal with oak leaf cluster; recipient Meritorious Pub. Service award Govt. of D.C., 1965. Mem. Am. Optometric Assn. (pres. joggers 1968—, distinguished service award 1974), Am. Legion (life; citation of merit 1954, post comdr. D.C. 1960), D.C. Optometric Soc. (sec. 1956-57), Lees Assn. (trustee), Chinese Consol. Benevolent Assn. (founder), Flying Optometrist Assn. (dir. 1974—), Beta Sigma Kappa. Lion (charter pres. Chi-Am. 1960, zone chmn. 1961, dep. dist. gov. 1963, hon. mem. Capitol Hill, Washington Host; Extension award 1960, 75, Presdl. Banner award 1975). Research, publs. in field. Home: 2939 McKinley St NW Washington DC 20015 Office: Lee Bldg 813 7th St NW Washington DC 20001

LEE, SHOU-DONG, health science facility administrator; b. Po-Tein, Fukien, Republic of China, Sept. 30, 1946; arrived in Taiwan, 1967; s. Tzer-Shyan and Suk-Chun (Cho) L.; m. Yun-Ching Lin, Mar.8, 1975; children: Jonathan, Amy. MD, Nat. Def. Med. Ctr., Taipei, Republic of China, 1974; postgrad, U. So. Calif., Los Angeles, 1983. Resident dept. medicine Vets. Gen. Hosp., Taipei, 1974-78, mem. staff, 1978-84, dep. chief emergency unit, 1981-82, chief gastroenterology lab., 1984—; mem. staff New Jeddah Clinic Hosp., Jeddah, Saudi Arabia, 1979-80; research fellow Huntington Meml. Hosp., Pasadena, Calif., 1982-83; Assoc. prof. medicine Nat. Yang-Ming Med. Coll., Taipei 1984—. Recipient Service award Exec. Yuan, Taipei, 1987, Outstanding Research award Nat. Sci. Council, Republic of China, 1987. Mem. Chinese Med. Assn., Republic of China Cardiology Soc., Republic of China Gastroent. Soc., Republic of China Soc. of Ultrasound in Medicine, Gastroent. Soc. Ecuador (hon.), Internat. Soc. Antiviral Research. Office: Vets Gen Hosp Dept Medicine, 201 Shih-Pai Rd Sect 2, Taipei 11217, Republic of China

LEE, SIN HANG, pathologist; b. Hong Kong, Nov. 17, 1932; came to U.S., 1963, naturalized, 1976; s. Yat Sun and Siu Tsing (Wong) L.; M.D., Wuhan Med. Coll., China, 1956; m. Kee Hung Hau, Dec. 31, 1958; children—Emil, Karen. Intern, South Balt. Gen. Hosp., 1963-64; resident N.Y. Hosp., 1964-66; bacteriologist Sichuan Med. Coll., Chengdu, China, 1956-61; demonstrator in pathology U. Hong Kong, 1961-63; instr. pathology Cornell-N.Y. Hosp., 1966-67; fellow in pathology Meml. Hosp. for Cancer, N.Y.C., 1967-68; asst. prof. McGill U., Montreal, 1968-71; asso. prof. Yale U., 1971-73, asso. clin. prof., 1973—; guest prof. Wuhan Med. Coll. (China), 1984—; attending pathologist Hosp. St. Raphael, New Haven, Conn., 1973—. Diplomate Am. Bd. Pathology. Mem. Royal Coll. Physicians and Surgeons Can., AAAS, Internat. Acad. Pathology, Am. Assn. Pathologists, Pathol. Soc. Great Britain and Ireland, N.Y. Acad. Scis. Contbr. articles in field to profl. jours.; patentee in field. Office: 1450 Chapel St New Haven CT 06511

LEE, SOO ANN, economist, educator; b. Singapore, Mar. 21, 1939; d. Teck Hock and Cheng Ee (Khoo) L.; m. Choon Neo Koh (dec. Oct. 1977); children: Justin, Liesl; m. Yuan Tsao Lee, Oct. 1, 1955; m. Tsao Yuan, 1982. BA with honors, U. Malaya, Singapore, 1960; MA, Williams Coll., 1961; PhD, U. Singapore, 1969. Asst. sec. Ministry Commerce and Industry, Singapore, 1960; asst. lectr. U. Malaya, 1961-64; lectr. U. Singapore, 1964-70, sr. lectr., 1971-74, assoc. prof. economics, 1974-80, prof., 1981—; advisor Kikkoman Singapore Pte Ltd., 1982—; bd. dirs. United Internat. Securities, Singapore, NTUC Income. Author: Economic Growth in Malaya, 1974, Industry in Singapore, 1974, Singapore Goes Transnational, 1976, Economic Planning and Project Evaluation, 1977. Trustee Nat. Trade Union Cong. Comfort, Singapore, 1970—; hon. v.p. Boys' Brigade, Singapore, 1982—; chmn. bd. govs. Presbyn. English Schs., Singapore, 1970—; hcmn. Presbyn. Welfare Services, Singapore, 1976—. Named Friend of Labour, Nat. Trade Union Cong., 1982; fellow Ford Found., 1960-61, Harvard Yenching Inst., 1976-77; Fulbright Travel grantee, 1968-69. Mem. Econs. Soc. Singapore (v.p.). Avocations: chess, theology, swimming. Home: 11 Victoria Park Rd, 1026 Singapore Singapore Office: Nat U Singapore Dept Bus Policy, 10 Kent Ridge Crescent, 0511 Singapore Singapore

LEE, TAIK M., government official; b. Seoul, Korea, Jan. 25, 1940; s. Jai Young and Kei Kyung (Yun) L.; m. Jane Sumie Nagata, Apr. 15, 1945; children—Jonathan P., Russell P.N., Mark P. B.A., Pepperdine U., 1970; M.S.W., U. Mich., 1972; M.P.A., U. So. Calif., 1982. Div. mgr. Sears, Roebuck & Co., Los Angeles, 1965-71; spl. asst. to asst. commr. HEW, Washington, 1973-74; sr. planner United Way Washington Met. Area, 1974-75; program analysis officer, program mgmt. div. Office of Human Devel. Services, HHS, Washington, 1975-84, coordinator Office of Planning and Evaluation, 1984—; adj. prof. Cath. U. Am. Recipient cert. of appreciation Nat. Head Start Assn., 1977, 80, Outstanding Performance award, 1985; HEW tng. grants, 1971-72; Sales Leadership award Gen. Foods, 1967; Superior Performance award Sears, Roebuck & Co., 1967, 68, 69. Mem. Am. Mgmt. Assn., Am. Acad. Polit. and Social Sci. Presbyterian. Club: Red Carpet. Author: Proactive Leadership, 1973; Performance Indicators, 1978. Home: 12624 Magna Carta Rd Herndon VA 22071 Office: PO Box 1182 Washington DC 20201

LEE, THOMAS TAN YANG, pediatrician; b. Kweichow, Peoples Republic of China, Sept. 11, 1944; m. So Jean Han, Aug. 19, 1971; 1 child, Adrian. MB, BS, U. Hong Kong, 1967; diploma in child health, Royal Coll. Physicians Surgeons, Glasgow, 1971; diploma occupational medicine, Chinese U. Hong Kong, 1987. Trainee pediatrician Queen Mary Hosp., Hong Kong, 1967-71; registrar Royal Hosp. for Sick Children, Glasgow, Scotland, 1971-72; pediatrician Nethersole Hosp., Hong Kong, 1972-73; ptnr., pediatrician Drs. Anderson and Ptnrs., Hong Kong, 1973—; locum cons., pediatrician Mt. Elizabeth Med. Ctr., Singapore, 1985, 87; hon. lectr. dept. nursing Nethersole Hosp., Hong Kong, 1973—, dept. pediatrics U. Hong Kong, 1975—; prin. surgeon St. John Ambulance Brigade, Hong Kong, 1987—. Chmn. med. subcom. St. John Ambulance Assn., Hong Kong, 1985—; mem. St. John Council, Hong Kong, 1986—. Commonwealth scholar Assn. Commonwealth Univs., 1971; named Serving Brother Most Venerable Order St. John Jerusalem, St. John Ambulance, 1987. Fellow Coll. Physicians Hong Kong (assoc.); mem. Australian Coll. Occupational Medicine, British Med. Assn. (v.p. Hong Kong br. 1977), Soc. Physicians Hong Kong (pres. 1977). Clubs: Hong Kong, Royal Hong Kong Jockey. Office: 16A United Centre, Queensway, Hong Kong Hong Kong

LEE, TING HUI, history educator, poet; b. Malaysia, May 5, 1931; s. Chak and Kheng (Tung) L.; MA, U. Singapore, 1958, PhD, 1985; postgrad. Harvard U., 1967; children—Han Yin, Tang Yin. Polit. sec. Ministry of Culture, Singapore, 1959; dy. dir. Polit. Study Centre, Singapore, 1964-68; asst. dir. edn., Singapore, 1969-71; vis. prof. history Nanyang U., Singapore, 1968-69; vis. prof. dept. polit. sci. U. Western Ont., 1971; sr. research asso. Inst. S.E. Asian Studies, Singapore, 1974-75; sr. research officer, Ministry of Def., Singapore, 1976-82; sr. lectr. history dept. Nat. U. Singapore, 1982—; lectr. Marxism-Leninism course for sr. army officers, adminstrs. and educators, 1978-79; mem. curriculum com. Nat. Youth Leadership Tng. Inst., Singapore; adviser Kreta Ayer Edn. Centre, Singapore. Recipient Pub. Service Star, Pres. of Singapore, 1969. Columbia U. fellow, 1959; Lee Found. grantee, 1956-57. Mem. Singapore Assn. Writers (pres.), Island Soc. Singapore (pres.), South Seas Soc. Singapore (v.p.), Theosophical Soc., Ramakrishna Mission, Ti-Sarana Buddhist Assn., Divine Life Soc., Aurobindo Soc. Author numerous books in field, also poetry; editor: Jour. South Seas Soc., Jour. Island Soc., Island Quar., Island Lit. Office: History Dept, Nat Univ of Singapore, Singapore Kent Ridge, 0511 Singapore

LEE, TONG HUN, economics educator; b. Seoul, Korea, Nov. 20, 1931; came to U.S., 1955, naturalized, 1968; s. Chong Su and Yun (Lee) L.; m. Yul Jah Ahn, June 11, 1960; children: Bruce Keebeck, James Keewon. B.S., Yon-Sei U., 1955; Ph.D., U. Wis., 1961. Asst. prof. econs. U. Tenn., Knoxville, 1962-64; assoc. prof. U. Tenn., 1964-67; prof. econs. U. Wis., Milw., 1967—, chmn. dept. econs., 1978-82. Author: Interregional Intersectoral Flow Analysis, 1973; Contbr. articles to profl. jours. NSF grantee, 1965-67, 73-75. Mem. Am. Econ. Assn., Am. Fin. Assn., Am. Statis. Assn., Econometric Soc. Home: 7250 N Wayside Dr Milwaukee WI 53209

LEE, TONY JER-FU, pharmacologist, educator; b. Hualien, Taiwan, Nov. 10, 1942; s. Huo-Yen and Wan L.; m. Mei-shya Su, June 24, 1978; children—Jonathan, Cheryl. B.S., Taipei (Taiwan) Med. Coll., 1967; Ph.D., W.Va. U., 1973. Postdoctoral fellow UCLA, 1973-75; asst. prof. pharmacology So. Ill. U. Sch. Medicine, Springfield, 1975-80, assoc. prof., 1980-87, prof., 1987—. Contbr. articles to profl. jours.; editorial adv. bd. Jour. Pharmacology and Exptl. Therapeutics, Blood Vessels. Am. Heart Assn. grantee; NIH grantee. Mem. Am. Soc. Pharmacology and Exptl. Therapeutics, Electron Microscopy Soc. Am., Soc. Neurosci., High Blood Pressure Research and Stroke councils of Am. Heart Assn. Home: 61 W Hazel Dell Springfield IL 62707 Office: So Ill Univ, Sch Medicine Dept Pharmacology Springfield IL 62702

LEE, TSUNG-DAO, physicist, educator; b. Shanghai, People's Republic of China, Nov. 25, 1926; s. Tsing-Kong L. and Ming-Chang (Chang); m. Jeannette Chin, June 3, 1950; children: James, Stephen. Student, Nat. Chekiang U., Kweichow, China, 1943-44, Nat. S.W. Assoc. U., Kunming, China, 1945-46; PhD, U. Chgo., 1950; DSc (hon.), Princeton U., 1958; LLD (hon.), Chinese U., Hong Kong, 1969; DSc (hon.), CCNY, 1978. Research assoc. in astronomy U. Chgo., 1950; research assoc., lectr. physics U. Calif., Berkeley, 1950-51; mem. Inst. for Advanced Study, Princeton (N.J.) U., 1951-53, prof. physics, 1960-63; asst. prof. Columbia U., N.Y.C., 1953-55, assoc. prof., 1955-56, prof., 1956-60, 63—, Enrico Fermi prof. physics, 1964—, adj. prof., 1960-62; Loeb lectr. Harvard U., Cambridge, Mass., 1957, 64. Editor: Weak Interactions and High Energy Nutrino Physics, 1966, Particle Physics and Introduction to Field Theory, 1981. Recipient Albert Einstein Sci. award Yeshiva U., 1957, (with Chen Ning Yang) Nobel prize in physics, 1957. Mem. Nat. Acad. Sci., Acad. Sinica, Am. Acad. Arts and Scis., Am. Philos. Soc., Acad. Nazionale dei Lincei. Office: Columbia U Dept Physics New York NY 10027 *

LEE, VIN JANG THOMAS, financial company executive, physicist; b. Honan Province, China, Feb. 14, 1937; came to U.S., 1958; s. Tsin-Yin and Hwa-Neu (Mar) L.; m. Y.T. Margaret Nee, Dec. 29, 1963; 1 child, Maxwell. Diploma in ChemE, Ordnance Engring. Coll., Taipei, Taiwan, 1958; MSChemE, U. Notre Dame, 1959; PhD, U. Mich., 1963. Assoc. prof. chem. engring. U. Mo., Columbia, 1965-74; pres. Econo Trading Co., Santa Monica, Calif., 1975-80, Cyberdyne Inc., Santa Monica, 1980—; vis. prof. catalysis and physical chemistry UCLA, 1972-73. Contbr. numerous articles to sci. jours. Mem. Sigma Xi. Lodge: Masons. Office: Cyberdyne Inc 1045 Ocean Ave Suite 2 Santa Monica CA 90403

LEE, WAYNE CYRIL, author; b. Lamar, Nebr., July 2, 1917; s. David Elmer and Rosa Belle (Deselms) L.; m. Pearl May Sheldon, Mar. 17, 1948; children—Wayne Sheldon, Charles Lester. Rural mail carrier, Lamar, 1951-77; instr. Writer's Digest Sch., 1976—; author non-fiction: Scotty Philip, the Man Who Saved the Buffalo, 1975; Trails of the Smoky Hill, 1980; author fiction: Shadow of the Gun, 1981; Guns at Genesis, 1981; Putnam's Ranch War, 1982; The Violent Trail, 1984; War at Nugget Creek, 1985; Massacre Creek, 1985; The Waiting Gun, 1986; Hawks of Autumn, 1986; many others. Served with Signal Corps, U.S. Army, 1945. Named Historian of Year, High Plains Preservation of History Commn., 1981. Mem. Western Writers Am. (pres. 1970-71), Nebr. Writers Guild (pres. 1974-76), Nebr. State Hist. Soc. Found. (dir. 1975—). Republican. Mem. Christian Ch. Club: Toastmasters (pres. 1964-65, 72-73) (Imperial, Nebr.). Home and Office: Lamar NE 69035

LEE, WILLIAM, managing director construction company; b. Shanghai, Republic of China, Jan. 10, 1935; m. Lina Wong Mui Kwan; two children. BSE, Yokohama U., Japan. Chartered profl. engr., U.K. Mng. dir. The China Engrs. Ltd., Tsuen Wan, Hong Kong. Mem. Royal Instn. Naval Architects, U.K., Hong Kong Mgmt. Assn. Clubs: Royal Hong Kong Golf, Royal Hong Kong Jockey, Hilltop Country, Mariners', Club de Recreio. Lodge: Rotary. Office: The China Engrs Ltd, Constrn Equipment Div, 2-12 Lung Tang Rd, Tsing Lung Tau, Tsuen Wan NT Hong Kong

LEE, WILLIAM JOHNSON, lawyer; b. Oneida, Tenn., Jan. 13, 1924; s. William J. and Ara (Anderson) L.; student Akron U., 1941-43, Denison U., 1943-44, Harvard U., 1944-45; J.D., Ohio State U., 1948. Bar: Ohio 1948, Fla. 1962. Research asst. Ohio State U. Law Sch., 1948-49; asst. dir. Ohio Dept. Liquor Control, chief purchases, 1956-57, atty. examiner, 1951-53, asst. state permit chief, 1953-55, state permit chief, 1955-56; asst. counsel, staff Hupp Corp., 1957-58; spl. counsel City Attys. Office Ft. Lauderdale (Fla.), 1963-65; asst. atty. gen. Office Atty. Gen., State of Ohio, 1966-70; adminstr. State Med. Bd. Ohio, Columbus, 1970-85, also mem. Federated State Bd.'s Nat. Commn. for Evaluation of Fgn. Med. Schs., 1981-83; Mem. Flex 1/Flex 2 Transitional Task Force, 1983-84; pvt. practice law, Ft. Lauderdale, 1965-66; acting municipal judge, Ravenna, Ohio, 1960; instr. Coll. Bus. Adminstrn., Kent State U., 1961-62. Mem. pastoral relations com. Epworth United Meth. Ch., 1976; chmn. legal aid com. Portage County, Ohio, 1960; troop awards chmn. Boy Scouts Am., 1965; mem. ch. bd. Melrose Park (Fla.) Meth. Ch., 1966. Mem. Am. Legion, Fla., Columbus, Akron, Broward County (Fla.) bar assns., Delta Theta Phi, Phi Kappa Tau, Pi Kappa Delta. Served with USAAF, 1943-46. Editorial bd. Ohio State Law Jour., 1947-48; also articles. Home: 4893 Brittany Ct W Columbus OH 43229

LEE, WILLIAM MALCOLM, building materials company executive; b. Atlanta, Sept. 25, 1941; s. Clarence Gordon and Florabel (McGoogan) L.; B.A., Emory U., 1963; postgrad. Ga. State U., 1963-64; children—William Malcolm, Elizabeth Shannon; m. Patricia J. Sanders, 1983; 1 stepson, Charles Loren Hicks. Dist. counselor Atlanta Newspapers, Inc., Atlanta, 1963-65; sales rep., sales mgr. GAF Corp., N.Y.C., 1965-69; corp. v.p. Builder Marts of Am., Inc., Greenville, S.C., 1969-82; with Aid/man Computer Systems subs. BMA, 1983—, v.p., 1984-87; founder Lee Resources, Inc., 1988—, editor, publisher People & Profits newsletter. Lay reader, vestry mem. Episcopal Ch. of the Redeemer. Mem. Nat. Lumber and Bldg. Material Dealers Assn., Newsletter Assn., Nat. Retail Mchts. Assn., Greenville C. of C., Nat. Speakers Assn. Republican. Episcopalian. Home: 3 Parish Ct Greenville SC 29607 Office: PO Box 167111 Greenville SC 29606

LEE, WILLIAM MARSHALL, lawyer; b. N.Y.C., Feb. 23, 1922; s. Marshall McLean and Marguerite (Letts) L.; m. Lois Kathryn Plain, Oct. 10, 1942; children: Marsha (Mrs. Stephen Drynck), William Marshall Jr., Victoria C. (Mrs. Larry Nelson). Student, U. Wis., 1939-40; BS, Aero. U., Chgo., 1942; postgrad., UCLA, 1946-48, Loyola U. Law Sch., Los Angeles, 1948-49; JD, Loyola U., Chgo., 1952. Bar: Ill. 1952. Thermodynamicist Northrop Aircraft Co., Hawthorne, Calif., 1947-49; patent agt. Hill, Sherman, Meroni, Gross & Simpson, Chgo., 1949-51, Borg-Warner Corp., Chgo., 1951-53; ptnr. Hume, Clement, Hume & Lee, Chgo., 1953-72; sole practice William Marshall Lee, Chgo., 1973-74; sr. ptnr. Lee and Smith (and predecessor), Chgo., 1974—; v.p., bd. dirs. Power Packaging, Inc. Speaker and contbr. articles on legal topics. Pres. Glenview (Ill.) Citizens Sch. Com., 1953-57; v.p. Glenbrook High Sch. Bd., 1957-63. Served as lt. USNR, 1942-46, CBI. Recipient Pub. Service award Glenbrook High Sch. Bd., 1963. Mem. ABA (sec. sect. patent, trademark and copyright law 1977-80, governing council 1980-84, vice chmn. sect. patent, trademark and copyright law 1984-85, chmn. 1986-87), Ill. Bar Assn., Chgo. Bar Assn., 7th Fed. Circuit Bar Assn., Internat. Patent Law Assn., Am. Intellectual Property Law Assn., Chgo. Patent Law Assn., Licensing Execs. Soc. (treas. 1977-80, pres. 1981-82, internat. del. 1980—), Phi Delta Theta, Phi Alpha Delta. Republican. Clubs: Law, University, Tower (Chgo.), Snow Chase of Chgo. (pres. 1963-64), Sky Soaring. Home: 84 Otis Rd Barrington IL 60010 Office: 150 S Wacker Dr Chicago IL 60606

LEE, WILLIAM T., insurance agency executive; b. Abbington, Pa., Dec. 15, 1934; s. Arthur Dewey and Mary (Byron) Lee; m. Cynthia D. Baltera, Nov. 23, 1957; children—Wiliam T., Deborah A., Richard C., Robert E., David A. BS, LaSalle Coll., 1957. C.L.U.; cert. agy. mgr.; chartered fin. cons. With N.Y. Life Ins. Co., various locations, 1957—, asst. mgr., Allentown, Pa., 1961-64, gen. mgr. Newtown Square, Johnstown, Pa., 1965—, gen. mgr., Pitts., 1986—. Trustee, officer Lee Hosp., Johnstown, 1977—; chmn., Johnstown Marathon, 1981; dir. membership drive YMCA, 1979. Recipient Golden Eagle ward N.Y. Life Ins. Co., 1982; Nat. Mgmt. award. Mem. Greater Johnstown Com. (exec. bd.), Nat Assn. Life Underwriters (bd. dirs. 1969-74), Nat. Committeeman Pitts. Gen. Agts. and Mgrs. Assn. Republican. Roman Catholic. Clubs: Sunnehanna Country, Johnstown Track (pres. 1982). Lodge: Elks (bd. dirs.). Avocations: Running marathons; racquetball; golf. Home: 1708 Parsonage Ln Bethel Park PA 15102 Office: NY Life Ins Co One Oxford Centre Suite 1400 Pittsburgh PA 15219

LEE, YANG-PAL, economist, educator; b. Kyung-Nam, Korea, Sept. 9, 1947; s. Byung-Doo and Kwi-Nam (Kim) L.; m. Yang-Soon Kim, June 23, 1978; children: James Sung-Min, John Jae-Huhn. BS, MIT, 1972; PhD, Stanford U., 1980. Economist The World Bank, Washington, 1980-83; prof. econs., chmn. Grad. Sch. Policy Studies Korea U., Seoul, 1983—; mem. MIT Edn. Council, Cambridge, Mass. and Seoul, 1985—; advisor Korea Devel. Inst., Seoul, 1987-88. Author: (with others) Korean Social Development Study, vols. 16 and 18, 1986, 87. Mem. Royal Econ. Soc. U.K., Am. Econ. Assn., Korean Econ. Assn., Econometric Soc., Smithsonian Instn. Home: 115 Chang-Sung-Dong, Chong-No-Koo, Seoul 110-034 110, Korea Office: Korea U, Dept Econs, 1 Anam-Dong, Sung-Buk-Koo, Seoul 136-701, Korea

LEE, YONG-KAK, health science facility administrator; b. Seoul, Dec. 7, 1924; s. Hyung-Rae Lee and Kap-Sook Hong; m. Chang-Hee Lee, Dec. 19, 1961; children: Won-Jae, Chul-Jae, Kwang-Jae. MD, Seoul Nat. U., 1945; PhD, Catholic U. Med. Coll., Seoul, 1964. Lectr. bacteriology Ewha U., Seoul, 1948-58, assoc. prof. surgery, 1958-62; mem. staff U.S. Marine Corps., 1950-53; resident in surgery Baylor Med. Coll. Surgery, Houston, 1953-58; prof. surgery Catholic U. Med. Coll., 1962-82, chmn. surgery, 1972-85, dir. St. Mary's Hosp., 1981—. Decorated Medal of Freedom Sec. Navy, U.S., 1954; recipient Pres. Citation (U.S.), 1954. Fellow Internat. Coll. Surgeons,

Am. Coll. Surgeons; mem. Korean Med. Assn. (cons. 1985-87), Korean Vascular Surgery Soc. (pres. 1985-87), Korean Transplantation Soc. (pres. 1980—). Home: 43-15 Joosung-Dong, Seoul 140, Republic of Korea Office: St Mary's Hosp, Yoido, Seoul 150, Republic of Korea

LEE, YOUNG-HO, plastic surgeon, plastic surgeon educator; b. Seoul, Korea, Oct. 17, 1932; s. Hyeun-Soo and Jum-Duck L.; m. Sook Yue Jung, May 22, 1960; children: Eun, Ju. MD, Yonsei U., 1958, PhD, 1974. Resident in plastic surgery U. Pitts., 1967-69; fellow in plastic surgery Blodgett Meml. Hosp., Grand Rapids, Mich., 1969-70; asst. prof. Yonsei U. Med. Coll., Seoul, 1973-75, assoc. prof., 1975-78, prof., 1978—, assoc. dean for acad. affairs, 1983-85, chmn. plastic surgery, 1985—; cons. Korean Army Hosps., Seoul, 1974—. Author: Plastic Surgery, 1987. Served to lt. Korean Navy, 1958-61. Recipient Presdl. award Korean govt., 1979. Fellow ACS; mem. Am. Soc. Plastic Surgery (gen. sec. 1982-84), Korean Soc. Plastic Surgery (pres. 1986—). Office: Yonsei U Coll Med, Shin Chon-Dong Suh Dae Moon-Gu, 120 Seoul Korea

LEE, YUAN T(SEH), chemistry educator, consultant; b. Hsinchu, Taiwan, China, Nov. 29, 1936; came to U.S., 1962, naturalized, 1974; s. Tsefan and Pei (Tasi) L.; m. Bernice Wu, June 28, 1963; children: Ted, Sidney, Charlotte. BS, Nat. Taiwan U., 1959; MS, Nat. Tsinghua U., Taiwan, 1961; PhD, U. Calif., Berkeley, 1965. From asst. prof. to prof. chemistry U. Chgo., 1968-74; prof. U. Calif., Berkeley, 1974—, also prin. investigator Lawrence Berkeley Lab. Contbr. numerous articles on chem. physics to profl. jours. Recipient Nobel Prize in Chemistry, 1986, Ernest O. Lawrence award Dept. Energy, 1981, Nat. Medal of Sci., 1986, Peter Debye award for Phys. Chemistry, 1986; fellow Alfred P. Sloan, 1969-71, John Simon Guggenheim, 1976-77; Camille and Henry Dreyfus Found. Tchr. scholar, 1971-74. Fellow Am. Phys. Soc.; mem. Am. Acad. Arts and Scis., Am. Chem. Soc., AAAS, Nat. Acad. Scis. Office: U Calif Dept Chemistry Berkeley CA 94720 *

LEE, ZUK-NAE, psychiatry educator, psychotherapist; b. Hab-Chun, Kyungnam, Republic of Korea, Feb. 5, 1940; s. Sang-Yong and Yeum-Chun Song-Lee; m. Young-Hee Kwon-Lee, May 7, 1968; children: Kyung-Im, Sung-Lim. MD, Kyungpook U., Taegu, Republic of Korea, 1965; Lic. in Philosophy, Zurich U., Switzerland, 1986. Lic. psychiatrist. Intern Korean First Army Hosp., Taegu, 1965-66, resident, 1966-70; dir. Non-San Army Hosp., 1970-71, 102 Korean Army Hosp., Natrang, Vietnam, 1971-72; psychiatric researcher HQ for Research, Seoul, Republic of Korea, 1972-73; teaching staff Chungnam U. Med. Coll., Taechun, Republic of Korea, 1973-74; tng. cand. Jung Inst., Zurich, 1974-78; asst. prof. Kyungpook U. Med. Coll., Taegu, 1978-82, assoc. prof. psychiatry, 1982—. Chief editor: Shim-Song Yon-Gu, 1986. Served to maj. Korean mil., 1982-83. Mem. Korean Acad. Psychotherapists (pres. Taegu br. 1988—), Korean Assn. Psychotherapists (exec. com. 1984—), Korean Soc. Analytical Psychology (tng. analyst 1978—, v.p. 1986—, pres. 1988—), Inst. for Human Sci. (exec. com. 1987—), Korean Neuropsychiatric Assn. (pres. Taegu br. 1988—). Home: 1701-2 Dae-Myung 5-Dong, Taegu 705035, Republic of Korea Office: Kyungpook U Hosp, 335 Samduk-Dong Choong-Gu, Taegu 630, Republic of Korea

LEECING, WALDEN ALBERT, educator; b. Glendale, Calif., Sept. 6, 1932; s. Horace Walden and Leona Belle (Dudek) L.; m. Elizabeth Joan Miller, Aug. 16, 1958; children: Jeffrey Scott, Brian Walden. BA, U. Redlands, 1954; MA, Stanford U., 1956, postgrad., 1973—. Tchr. El Rancho High Sch., Whittier, Calif., 1957-59, Santa Ana (Calif.) High Sch., 1959-66; from instr. to assoc. prof. lang. arts Chabot Coll., Hayward, Calif., 1967-86, prof., 1986—; chmn. speech dept. Author: The Santa Ana Community Players: 1920-27, 1956, (with James Armstrong) The Curious Eye, 1970, Viva la Causa! A Historiographic Survey of Chicano Studies Programs at Five Bay Area Colleges and Universities. V.p. Santa Ana Community Players, 1964-66; asst. organist San Ramon Valley Ch., 1968—. Mem. Nat. Council English Tchrs., AAUP, No. Calif. Forensics Assn., Am. Guild Organists, Stanford Alumni Assn. (life). KRON-NBC Viewer Adv. Council. Republican. Congregationalist. Home: 697 Paradise Valley Ct S Crow Canyon Country Club Danville CA 94526 Office: Chabot Coll 25555 Hesperian Blvd Hayward CA 94545

LEEDS, NANCY BRECKER, sculptor, lyricist; b. N.Y.C., Dec. 22, 1924; d. Louis Julius and Dorothy (Faggen) Brecker; m. Richard Henry Leeds, May 9, 1945; children—Douglas Brecker, Constance Leeds Bennett. Student Pine Manor Jr. Coll. Pres. Roseland Ballroom, N.Y.C., 1977-81. One-woman shows: Andrew Crispo Gallery, N.Y.C., 1979, Jeannette McIntyre Gallery Fine Arts, Palm Springs, Calif., 1987-88; exhibited in group shows at Bond Street Gallery, Great Neck, N.Y., Gallery Ranieri, N.Y.C., 1978, Country Art Gallery, 1984, Nature Conservatory Show, Country Art Gallery, 1985, Bonwit Teller, Manhasset, N.Y., 1985, Jeanette C. McIntyre Gallery, Palm Springs, Calif., 1987. Writer lyrics for musical Great Scot, 1965; lyricist for popular music. Trustee The Floating Hosp., N.Y.C., 1975—, v.p. Mem. ASCAP, The Dramatist Guild, The Songwriters Guild. Avocations: tennis; skiing.

LEEKHA, VED, personnel director; b. Dist. Multan, India, Aug. 23, 1937; m. Darshan Leekha; m. Darshan Gujral, Aug. 8, 1965; 2 children. Personnel officer Ashoka Hotels, New Delhi, 1962-69; sr. personnel mgr. Jaipur Udyog Ltd., Sawaimadhopur, Rajasthan, India, 1970-77; personnel mgr., gen. mgr. Hindustan Copper Ltd., Calcutta, 1977-86, dir. personnel, 1986—. Fgn. trainee sr. mgmt. course Henley Coll., U.K. Mem. Nat. Inst. Personnel Mgmt. Hindu. Home: 3/9 Rajinder Nagar, New Delhi India Office: Hindustan Copper Ltd, Industry House, 10 Camac St, Calcutta India

LEE KUAN YEW, prime minister of Singapore; b. Singapore, Sept. 16, 1923; s. Lee Chin Koon and Chua Jim Neo; m. Kwa Geok Choo, 1950; 2 sons, 1 dau. Student Raffles Coll., Singapore; B.A. (double 1st Law Tripos, star for spl. distinction), Cambridge (Eng.) U., 1949; LL.D. (hon.), Royal U. Cambodia, 1965, Hong Kong U., 1970, U. Liverpool, 1971, U. Sheffield, 1971. Barrister-at-law, hon. bencher Middle Temple, London, 1969; advocate, solicitor, 1951—; rep. Tanjong Pagar constituency, 1955—; prime minister Singapore, 1959—; adv. trade unions, 1952; rep. Singapore to Parliament of Malaysia, 1963-65; founder, sec.-gen. People's Action Party, 1954—; elected to bur. Socialist Internat., 1967. Decorated companion of Honour, 1970, grand cross Order St. Michael and St. George, U.K., 1972; Grand cordon Order of The Nile, Arab Republic Egypt, 1962; grand cross Royal Order, Cambodia, 1966; first class Order of Rising Sun (Japan), 1967; Bintang Adi Pradana (Indonesia), 1973; Order of Sikatuna (Philippines), 1974. Fellow Inst. Politics, Harvard U., 1968; Hoyt fellow Berkeley Coll., Yale U., 1970; hon. fellow Fitzwilliam Coll., Cambridge, 1969. Fellow Royal Australasian Coll. Surgeons (hon.), Royal Australasian Coll. Physicians (hon.). Address: Prime Minister's Office, Istana Annexe, Singapore 0923 Singapore

LEELAPATRA, VIDHYA, travel agency executive; b. Bangkok, Apr. 27, 1938; s. Sia Kwang and Hui Ngek (Sae Kow) Sae Lee; m. Daranee Vungsoonthon; children: Wantanee, Aniwat, Pisawase, Pataya, Pitayakorn. Jr. degree in Econs., Thammasat U., Bangkok, 1961; diploma in commerce, Overseas Chinese Sch., Taipei, Republic China, 1963; cert. in advanced mgmt. studies, Chulalongkorn U., Bankgkok, 1970. Mktg. exec. Shell Co. Thailand Ltd., Bangkok, 1963-75; mgr. mktg. Siam Kraft Paper Co. Ltd., Bangkok, 1975-76; pres. Timas Agy. Co. Ltd., Bangkok, 1976—; mng. dir. Hikari Travel Co. Ltd., Bangkok, 1980—. Bd. dirs. Samaritans of Bangkok, 1981. Club: Royal Bangkok Sports. Lodge: Lions (Rajdhani) (pres. 1979-80). Home: 427 Arkarnsongkroh, Tungmahamek, Bangkok 10120, Thailand Office: Timas Agy Co Ltd, 30/12 Saladaeng Rd, Silom, Bangkok 10500, Thailand

LEEMING, BRIAN WILLIAM, radiologist; b. Christchurch, N.Z., Feb. 14, 1924; came to U.S., 1970; s. Charles Patrick and Agnes Mary (Cunningham) L.; M.B., Ch.B., Otago U., 1951—; m. June Elizabeth Hayes, Jan. 3, 1953; children—Simon, Nicola, Nigel, Rupert, Gregory. Registrar radiology Guys Hosp., London, 1957-58; charge radiologist Hutt Hosp., N.Z., 1959-64; sr. radiologist Auckland Hosp., N.Z., 1965-69; lectr. radiology Harvard Med. Sch., 1970, asst. prof., 1971-78, assoc. prof., 1978—; sr. radiologist Beth Israel Hosp., Boston, 1970—. Served to capt. N.Z. Army, 1954-68. Diplomate Am. Bd. Radiology. Fellow Royal Australasian Coll. Radiologists, Am. Coll. Radiology, Royal Coll. Radiologists U.K., Royal Australasian Coll. Physicians; mem. Mass. Med. Soc., Mass. Radiol. Soc., New Eng. Roentgen Ray Soc. Roman Catholic. Office: 330 Brookline Ave Boston MA 02215

LEEMING, DAVID JOHN, mathematics educator; b. Victoria, B.C., Can., June 8, 1939; s. Kenneth Llewellyn and Mary Alida (Costen) L.; m. Yvonne Elizabeth Muir, June 18, 1966; children: Heather, Graeme, Robert. BSc, U. B.C., 1961; MA, U. Oreg., 1963; PhD, U. Alta, 1969. Instr. math. U. Victoria, 1963-69, prof., 1969—. Mem. Can. Math. Soc., Math. Assn. Am. Home: 2796 Tudor Ave, Victoria, BC Canada V8N 1L7 Office: U Victoria, Dept Math, Box 1700, Victoria, BC Canada V8W 2Y2

LEENEN, H(ENK) J(ACOBUS) J(OSEPHUS), law educator; b. Venlo, Netherlands, July 25, 1929; s. J.A.H. and A. (van Mackelenbergh) L.; LLM, U. Utrecht, 1952, LLD, 1966; 3 children. Jr. staff mem., then dir. Nat. Health Orgn., 1953-70; prof. social medicine and health law faculties medicine and law U. Amsterdam, 1970—; mem. adv. com. on health legis. Regional Office for Europe, WHO; cons. in field. Mem. Nat. Council Health, Assn. Health Law (pres. 1971—, editor-in-chief jour. 1977—), Dutch Congress Pub. Health (hon. pres. 1974). Author: Social Human Rights and Health Care, 1966, Environmental Health Law, 2d edit., 1976, Individual Human Rights in Health Care, 1978, Structure and Functioning of Health Care, 1979, 2d edit., 1981, Health Care and Law, 1981, Health Law for Students, 1981, Trends in Health Legislation, 1986, Administrative Health Law, 1986, Handbook of Health Law, 1988; editorial bd. Internat. Medicine and Law, 1978, health policy Am. Jour. Law and Medicine. Home: 46 Oosterpark, 1092 AN Amsterdam The Netherlands Office: AC Med Ctr, Mei bergdreef 15, 1105 AL Amsterdam The Netherlands

LEEPER, RAMON JOE, physicist; b. Princeton, Mo., Apr. 1, 1948; s. Joe Edd and Jeanne (Gaul) L.; m. Sumiko Yasuda, Dec. 21, 1976; 1 son, Joe Eric. BS, MIT, 1970; PhD, Iowa State U., 1975. Research assoc. Ames Lab., U.S. Dept. Energy, Iowa, 1975-76; mem. tech. staff Sandia Nat. Labs., Albuquerque, 1976-86, supr. diagnostics div., 1986—; guest scientist Argonne Nat. Lab., Ill., 1971-76; invited lectr. NATO Advanced Study Inst., Italy, summer 1983. Contbr. articles to profl. jours., patentee in field. Recipient Outstanding Teaching award Iowa State U., 1973; NDEA fellow, 1971-73. Mem. Am. Phys. Soc., IEEE (session chmn. 1984), Sigma Xi. Republican. Home: 6905 Rosewood Rd NE Albuquerque NM 87111 Office: Sandia Nat Labs Diagnostics Div 1234 Albuquerque NM 87185

LEES, ALAN ROGER, cosmetic company executive; b. Dunbar, Scotland, Aug. 27, 1939; s. Ronald and Mildred Ellen (Mathew) L.; m. Valerie Maureen Jenkins, July 6, 1964; 1 child, Alan Roger. BS in Theoretical Physics, Southampton Engrng. U., 1962; PhD, Am. Univ., Beirut, 1964. Asst. prof. Am. U., Beirut, 1963; program analyst ICT Corp., Johannesburg, Republic of S. Africa, 1964-65; systems analyst IBM, Johannesburg, 1965-66; systems mgr. Honeywell Info. Systems Ltd. U.K., Ilford, Eng., 1966-76, regional mgr., 1976; dir. Uebenthal Securities Ltd., Hadleigh, Eng., 1976-78; prin., dir. House of Regency, Brentwood, Eng., 1978—, Reform Cosmetics Co., Brentwood, Eng., 1980—; dir., ptnr. Natural Beauty Products Ltd., Bridgend, Wales, 1985—, E3 Enterprises, Brentwood, 1980—; internat. mktg. dir. Ueberlees Assn. Bodyreform Ctrs., Cardiff, Wales, 1988—. Mem. Soc. Model Aeronaut. Engrs., Brit. Computer Soc. Home: 45 Westville Rd, Penylan, Cardiff Mid Galm CF2 5DF, Wales Office: Natural Beauty Products Ltd, Unit 5 Kingsway Bldgs, Bridgend Ind Est, Bridgend CF31 35D, Wales

LEESON, JANET CAROLINE TOLLEFSON, cake specialties company executive; b. L'Anse, Mich., May 23, 1933; d. Harold Arnold and Sylvia Aino (Makikangas) Tollefson; student Prairie State Coll., 1970-76; master decorator degree Wilton Sch. Cake Decorating, 1974; grad. Cosmopolitan Sch. Bus., 1980; m. Raymond Harry Leeson, May 20, 1961; 1 son, Barry Raymond; children by previous marriage—Warren Scott, Debra Delores. Mgr., Peak Service Cleaners, Chgo., 1959; co-owner Ra-Ja-Lee TV, Harvey, Ill., 1961-66; founder and head fgn. trade dept. Wilton Enterprises, Inc., Chgo., 1969-75; tchr. cake decorating J.C. Penney Co., Matteson, Ill., 1975; office mgr. Pat Carpenter Assocs., Highland, Ind., 1975; pres. Leeson's Party Cakes, Inc., cake supplies and cake sculpture, Tinley Park, Ill., 1975—; lectr. and demonstrator cake sculpture and decorating; lectr. small bus. and govt. Sec., Luth. Ch. Women; active worker Boy Scouts Am. and Girl Scouts U.S., 1957-63; bd. dirs. Whittier PTA, 1962-70; active Bremen Twp. Republican party. Recipient numerous awards for cake sculpture and decorating, 1970—. Mem. Internat. Cake Exploration Soc. (charter, Outstanding Mem. Ill. 1984), Retail Bakers Am., Chgo. Area Retail Bakers Assn. (1st pl. in regional midwest wedding cake competition 1978, 80, 1st pl. nat. 1982, others), Am. Bus. Women's Assn. (chpt. publicity chmn., hospitality chmn. 1982-83, chmn. membership com. 1988, named Woman of Yr. 1986), Ingalls Meml. Hosp. Aux., Lupus Found. Am. (hot line girl Tuesdays Ill. chpt.) Lutheran. Home and Office: 6713 W 163d Pl Tinley Park IL 60477

LEET, MILDRED ROBBINS, corporate executive, consultant; b. N.Y.C., Aug. 9, 1922; d. Samuel Milton and Isabella (Zeitz) Elowsky; m. Louis J. Robbins, Feb. 23, 1941 (dec. 1970); children: Jane, Aileen; m. Glen Leet, Aug. 9, 1974. B.A., N.Y. U., 1942. Pres. women's div. United Cerebral Palsy, N.Y.C., 1951-52; bd. dirs. United Cerebral Palsy, 1953—, chmn. bd., 1953-55; rep. Nat. Council Women U.S. at UN, 1957-64, 1st v.p., 1959-64, pres., 1964-68, hon. pres., 1968-70; sec., v.p. conf. group U.S. Nat. Orgns. at UN, 1961-64, 76-78, vice chmn., sec., 1962-64, mem. exec. com., 1961-65, 75—, chmn. hospitality info. service, 1960-66; vice chmn. exec. com. NGO's UN Office Public Info., 1976-78, chmn. ann. conf., 1977; chmn. com. on water, desertification, habitat and environment Conf. NGO's with consultative status with UN/ECOSOC, 1976—; mem. exec. com. Internat. Council Women, 1960-73, v.p., 1970-73; chmn. program planning com., women's com. OEO, 1967-72; chmn. com. on natural disasters N.Am. Com. on Environment, 1973-77; N.Y. State chmn. UN Day, 1975; partner Leet & Leet (cons. women in devel.), 1978—; dir. Trickle Up Program, 1979—. Author articles; editor: UN Calendar & Digest, 1959-64, Measure of Mankind, 1963; editorial bd.: Peace & Change. Co-chmn. Vols. for Stevenson, N.Y.C., 1956; vice chmn. task force Nat. Democratic Com., 1969-72; commr. N.Y. State Commn. on Powers Local Govt., 1970-73; chmn. Coll. for Human Services, 1985—; former mem. bd. dirs. Am. Arbitration Assn., New Directions, Inst. for Mediation and Conflict Resolution, Spirit of Stockholm; bd. dirs. Hotline Internat.; v.p. Save the Children Fedn., 1986—; rep. Internat. Peace Acad. at UN, 1974-77, Internat. Soc. Community Devel., 1977—; del. at large 1st Nat. Women's Conf., Houston, 1977; chmn. task force on internat. interdependence N.Y. State Women's Meeting, 1977; mem. Task Force on Poverty, 1977—; chmn. Task Force on Women, Sci. and Tech. for Devel., 1978; U.S. del. UN Status of Women Commn., 1978, UN Conf. Sci. and Tech. for Devel., 1979, co-dir. Trickle Up Program, Inc, 1979—; Brazzaville Centennial Celebration, 1980; mem. global adv. bd. Internat. Expn. Rural Devel., 1981—; mem. Council Internat. Fellows U. Bridgeport, 1982—; trustee overseas edn. fund LWV, 1983—; v.p. U.S. Com. UN Devel. Fund for Women, 1983—; mem. Nat. Consultative Com. Planning for Nairobi, 1984-85; co-chmn. women in devel. com. Interaction, 1985—; mem. com. of cooperation Interam. Commn. of Women, 1986; bd. dirs. Nat. Women's Conf. Com., 1986-87; adv. com. Am. Assn. Internat. Aging, 1986—. Recipient Crystal award Coll. for Human Services, 1983, ann. award Inst. for Mediation and Conflict Resolution, 1985, Woman of Conscience award Nat. Council Women, 1986, Temple award Inst. of Noetic Scis., 1987, Presdl. End Hunger award, 1987, Giraffe award Giraffe Project, 1987; co-recipient Rose award World Media Inst., 1987, Human Rights award UNIFEM, 1987, Pres.' medal Marymount Manhattan Coll., 1988, Leadership award Peace Corps, 1988. mem. AAAS, Women's Nat. Dem. Club. Clubs: Cosmopolitan, NYU. Home: 54 Riverside Dr New York NY 10024 also: 2 Briar Oak Dr Weston CT 06883 Office: 790 Madison Ave New York NY 10021

LEE TENG-HUI, president Republic of China; b. Taipei, Taiwan, Jan. 15, 1923; s. Chin-lung Lee and Ching Chiang; m. Tseng Wen-fui, Jan. 12, 1949; children: Anna, Anny. Student Kyoto Imperial U., Japan, 1946; B.S., Nat. Taiwan U., 1948; postgrad. Iowa State U., 1953; Ph.D., Cornell U., 1968. Mem. faculty Nat. Taiwan U., Taipei, 1958-78; div. chief Joint Commn. on Rural Reconstruction, Taipei, 1970-72; minister without portfolio Exec. Yuan, Taipei, 1972-78; mayor of Taipei, 1978-81; gov. of Taiwan, 1981-84; v.p. Republic of China, 1985-88, pres., 1988—; chmn. Nationalist Party China, 1988—. Author: Agriculture and Economic Development in Taiwan, vol. 1-3, 1983. Recipient award Am. Farm Econ. Assn., 1969. Mem. Kuomintang. Mem. Christian Ch. Avocation: golf. Office: Office of Pres, 122 Chung-ching S Rd, Sec 1, Taipei Republic of China

LEETS, PETER JOHN, merger and acquisition company executive; b. London, Mar. 12, 1946; came to U.S., 1948; s. Earl Edward and Doris Eileen L.; m. Anne E. Shahinian, May 15, 1982. BS in Mktg., Ind. U., 1969. Salesman Ortho Pharm. Corp., Raritan, N.J., 1969-74; account mgr. Revlon Inc., Indpls., N.J., 1974-76; regional dir. Revlon Inc., Cleve., N.J., 1976-79; field sales mgr. Revlon Inc., Bay Village, Ohio, 1979-83; nat. field sales mgr. Binney & Smith, Bethlehem, Pa., 1983-85; v.p., dir. sales Dell Publishing Co., Inc., N.Y.C., 1985-87; exec. v.p., pres. Geneva Corp., Costa Mesa, Calif., 1987—. participant high sch. career day. Vol., Big Bros., Detroit; mgr. Little League, Grand Rapids, Mich. Served with USAR. Mem. Am. Mgmt. Assn., Ind. U. Alumni (life), Delta Chi. Home: 26152 Flintlock Ln Laguna Hills CA 92653 Office: Geneva Corp 575 Anton Blvd Costa Mesa CA 92626

LEFEBURE, ALAIN PAUL, family physician; b. Paris, Nov. 17, 1946; s. Rene Julien and Ginette (Peradon) L.; m. Lucia Lefebure; children: Vincent, Benjamin. RN, Sch. Nursing, Paris, 1970; Dr. Medicine, U. Paris 7, 1978. Male nurse Tenon Hosp., Paris, 1970-71; intern Bichat Hosp., Paris, 1974-76; resident Bretonneau Hosp., Paris, 1976-78; lectr. in pediatrics Claude Bernard Hosp., Paris, 1976-81; practice medicine specializing in family medicine Paris, 1981—. Served with French Army, 1966-67. Recipient Clarinetist Soloist prize Congratulations from the Jury, 1965. Office: 2 rue Pierre Mouillard, 75020 Paris France

LEFEVER, MAXINE LANE, music educator, consultant; b. Elmhurst, Ill., May 30, 1931; d. Thomas Clinton Lane and Georgia Marie (Hampton) L.; m. Orville Joseph Lefever, Aug. 18, 1951 (div.); student Ill. Wesleyan U., 1949-51; BA, Western State Coll., 1958; MS, Purdue U., 1964, postgrad., 1965. Elem. sch. tchr. Leaf River (Ill.) Pub. Schs., 1953-54, Mancos (Colo.) Pub. Schs., 1954-56; elem./jr. high sch. tchr. Cortez (Colo.) Pub. Schs., 1956-60; instr. bands, Purdue U., Lafayette, Ind., 1965-79, asst. prof., 1980—; cons. numerous festivals and contests; pres., dir. Am. Mus. Ambassadors, 1967—. Contbr. articles to profl. jours.; composer percussion ensembles. Hon. mem. U.S. Navy Band. Mem. Inc. Music Educators Assn., Music Educators Nat. Conf., Nat. Band Assn. (exec. sec., citation of excellence), Coll. Band Dirs. Nat. Assn., Percussion Arts Soc., John Philip Sousa Found. (v.p., exec. sec., Star of Order of Merit), Big Ten Band Dirs. Assn., Alpha Lambda Delta, Delta Omicron, Tau Beta Sigma, Kappa Kappa Psi (hon.), Phi Sigma Kappa (hon.). Home: PO Box 2454 2924 Wilshire St West Lafayette IN 47906

LE FEVRE, WILLIAM MATHIAS, JR., brokerage company executive; b. Muskegon, Mich., Dec. 22, 1927; s. William Mathias and Crystal (Atkinson) LeF.; m. Ada Marie Cannon, 1949 (div. 1973); children—Marie L. Keidel, Jeanne L. Van Vlandren, William Mathias III, Suzanne C.; m. Mathilda Bock Maguire, 1976. Grad., Phillips Exeter Acad., 1946; student, U. Mich., 1946-48. Floor ptnr. Arthur Wiesenberger & Co., N.Y.C., 1956-60; assoc. oddlot broker DeCoppet & Doremus, N.Y.C., 1961-64; v.p. Carter, Walker & Co. Inc., N.Y.C., 1964-68, Bruns, Nordeman & Co., N.Y.C., 1969-71; dir. research Sade & Co., Washington, 1972-73, Mack Bushnell & Edelman, N.Y.C., 1973-74; v.p. investment strategy Granger & Co., N.Y.C., 1974-80, Purcell, Graham & Co., N.Y.C., 1980-86; sr. v.p., mkt. strategy Advest Inc., N.Y.C., 1986—; mem. N.Y. Stock Exchange, 1958-64; assoc. mem. Am. Stock Exchange, 1960-62; speaker various colls., univs. and indsl. assns., 1977—. Editor: Monday Morning Market Memo, 1973—; contbr. market commentary radio and TV, 1980—. Mem. Fin. Analysts Fedn. (profl. conduct com. 1977—), N.Y. Soc. Security Analysts, Fin. Analysts Phila., Market Technicians Assn. N.Y., Fin. Symposium. Club: Stock Exchange Luncheon. Home: 132 E 35th St New York NY 10016 also: 78 Grassy Hill Rd Old Lyme CT 06371 Office: Advest Inc 12 E 49th St New York NY 10017

LEFF, ILENE JOAN, management consultant, human resources executive; b. N.Y.C., Mar. 29, 1942; d. Abraham and Rose (Levy) L.; BA cum laude, U. Pa., 1964; MA with honors, Columbia U., 1969. Statis. analyst McKinsey & Co., N.Y.C., 1969-70, research cons., 1971-74, mgmt. cons., N.Y.C. and Europe, 1974-78; dir. exec. resources Revlon, Inc., N.Y.C., 1978-81, dir. human resources, 1981-83, dir. personnel, 1983-86; cons. APM Inc., 1986-88, ind. cons., 1988—; research asst. U. Pa., Phila., 1964-65; employment counselor State of N.J., Newark, 1965-66; tchr., Newark, 1966-69; lectr. Grad. Program in Pub. Policy, New Sch. for Social Research, Coll. Mt. St. Vincent, Wharton Sch., Duke U.; chmn. com. on employment and unemployment, mem. exec. com. Bus. Research Adv. Council, U.S. Bur. Labor Stats., 1980; sr. del. econ. relations and trade Sino-U.S. Conf., 1986. Ops. council Jr. Achievement Greater N.Y., 1975-78; cons. Com. for Econ. Devel., N.Y. Hosp., Regional Plan Assn., Am. Cancer Soc.; vol. for dep. mayor for ops. N.Y.C., 1977-78. Mem. N.Y. Human Resource Planners (treas. 1984), Fin. Women's Assn. N.Y. (exec. bd., 1977-78, 83-84), The Fashion Group (treas. elect). Contbr. issue papers and program recommendations to candidates for U.S. Pres., U.S. Senate and Congress, N.Y. State Gov., mayor N.Y.C.

LEFFERTS, GEORGE, writer, producer, director; b. Paterson, N.J.; s. Morris and Elinor (Jacobs) L.; m. Elizabeth Ruth Schaul; children—Lauren Ruth, Barbara Ellen; m. 2d, Hilary Sares, July 4, 1982; children: Katherine, Rose-Elizabeth. B.A. in Engring. (Nat. Merit scholar, William Rose scholar), Drew U., 1940; B.A. in English, U. Mich., 1942. Exec. producer, writer, dir. NBC, 1947-57; pres. George Lefferts Assocs., 1968—; exec. producer ABC, 1966-67; program cons. ABC, 1981. Exhibited sculpture, Sculpture Gallery, N.Y.C., 1960; producer: series Report from America, U.S. Dept. State, Tactic, Am. Cancer Soc., others; (Recipient Nat. Media award 1961, Fame award 1962, Fgn. Press award 1963, Golden Globe award 1967, Plaudit award Producers Guild 1968, 69, Cine Golden Eagle award 1974, Peabody award 1970, 75, 1st prize San Francisco Film Festival 1970; nominee Humanitas Prize 1988); author: plays Nantucket Legend, 1960, The Boat, 1968, Hey Everybody, 1969; columnist N.Y. Observer, Litchfield County Times, 1984-87 (1st prize New England Journalism award, 1984, 85); also author mag. articles, works on piano method, syndicated columns, others; prodns. include Biographies in Sound (Peabody award 1956), NBC Theatre, (Ohio State award 1955), Kraft Theatre, Armstrong Circle Theatre, Studio One, Lights Out, Frank Sinatra Show; spl. program Pain, 1971, Bravo Picasso!, 1972, What Price Health; program NBC Investigative Reports, 1972 (Albert Lasker award), CBS, Ben Franklin Series (Peabody award 1975, Emmy award 1975), Ryan's Hope, 1977 (Emmy award 1977), Purex Specials, 1966 (Emmy award 1966), The People vs. Jean Harris, 1981; exec. producer, writer, dir., NBC, Spls. for Women; series (Emmy award 1962), 1961 (Golden Globe award 1961); exec. producer: series Breaking Point, 1962-64 (Producers Guild Plaudit award 1963), CBS, Smithsonian Spls., 1974-75, ABC, Wide World of Entertainment, 1973-74, Bing Crosby Prodns., 1962-64; exec. producer: Wolper Prodns., 1974-75, Time/Life Films, 1978-79; original films produced include: series The Living End, 1959, The Stake, 1960, The Teenager, 1965, The Harness, 1972, The Night They Took Miss Beautiful, 1977, Bud & Lou, 1978, Mean Dog Blues, 1979, The Search for Alexander the Great, 1981, Dressed to Kill, 1980; producer: series Hallmark Hall of Fame, 1969-70, Never Say Goodbye, 1987 (Emmy award 1988, Humaintas award nomination 1988), TV play Teacher, Teacher, 1974 (Emmy award 1974). Served with AUS, 1942-45. REcipient New Eng. Journalism award, 1983, 84. Mem. Nat. Acad. TV Arts and Scis., Am. Acad. Motion Picture Arts and Scis., Christopher Morley Knothole Assn. Club: South Bay Cruising (Babylon, (N.Y.). Home: Robbins Rest Fire Island NY 11770

LEFFLER, JOHN SUTTON, financial company executive; b. Cleve., July 29, 1949; s. William Bain and Marjorie Adele (Smith) L.; B.A. with high honors DePauw U., 1971; M.B.A. (Bache scholar), Emory U., 1973; m. Leslie Dyckman McGaughey; children—Elizabeth Adele, Leigh Dyckman, Laura Sutton, John William. Dir. mgmt. adv. services Arthur Young & Co., Atlanta, Portland, Cin., 1973-77; pres., chief exec. officer Leffler Industries Inc., Cin., 1977—; pres. SIB, Inc., Cin., 1985—; dir. various corps. Hon. mem. bd. govs. Emanuel Found. C.P.A., Ohio; cert. mgmt. cons. Mem. Am. Inst. C.P.A.s, Ohio Soc. C.P.A.s.

LEFKOW, MICHAEL FRANCIS, lawyer; b. Chgo., Dec. 9, 1940; s. Frederick Lord and Marjorie Claiborne (Freeman) L.; m. Joan Marilyn Humphrey, June 21, 1975; children: Maria, Helena, Laura. BA, N. Central

Coll., Naperville, Ill., 1962; JD, Northwestern U., 1966. Bar: Ill. 1966, U.S. Dist. Ct. (no. dist.) Ill. 1967, Colo. 1969, U.S. Ct. Appeals (7th cir.) 1971, U.S. Supreme Ct. 1971, Fla. 1982, U.S. Ct. Appeals (fed. cir.) 1986. Gen. counsel Chgo. Welfare Rights Orgn., Chgo., 1969-72, Ill. Welfare Rights Orgn., Chgo., 1972-76, sole practice, Chgo., 1977-78; mng. atty. Prairie State Legal Services, Inc., Wheaton, Ill., 1978-79; supervisory trial atty. EEOC, Miami, Fla., 1979-82; asst. regional labor counsel U.S. Postal Service, Chgo., 1982-85; sole practice Chgo., 1985—; spl. commr. U.S. Dist. Ct. (no. dist.) Ill., 1985—. Chpt. v.p. League United Latin-Am. Citizens, Miami, 1979; mem. Social Concerns Com., Episcopal Diocese S. Fla., Miami, 1981. Mem. Chgo. Council Lawyers (dir. 1972-74, 87), ABA, Chgo. Bar Assn., Nat. Clearinghouse for Legal Services (past dir.), DuPage County Bar Assn., Fed. Bar Assn. Democrat. Episcopalian. Home: 5206 N Lakewood Ave Chicago IL 60640 Office: 53 W Jackson Blvd Suite 1220 Chicago IL 60604

LEFKOWITZ, STANLEY A., metals company executive; b. Phila., Aug. 5, 1943; s. Henry and Ida (Jacobs) L.; B.A., Temple U., 1965; Ph.D., Princeton, 1970; m. Laurie Drake. Staff dir. Citizens' Commn. on Future of City U. N.Y., N.Y.C., 1970-72; exec. asst. to vice-chancellor for urban affairs City U. N.Y., 1971-73; asst. dir. instructional devel. Queens Coll., Flushing, N.Y. 1973-75; exec. asst. to chmn. bd. Mocatta Metals Corp., N.Y.C., 1975—; instr. chemistry Hunter Coll., 1970-73; dir. Iron Mountain Depository Corp.; cons. N.Y. State Temporary Commn. on Powers of Local Govt., 1973, Greenville (N.C.) Govt. Study Commn., 1972; mem. Citizens' Union Com. on State Legis., 1974-75. AEC research asst., 1968-70; McKay fellow, 1967-68. Mem. Am. Phys. Soc., Assn. Princeton Grad. Alumni (treas. 1976-83). Club: Princeton (N.Y.C.). Home: 60 E 8th St New York NY 10003 Office: 4 World Trade Center New York NY 10048

LEFLER, SALLY GENE, organization executive; b. St. Louis, Apr. 8, 1936; d. James I. Lefler and Gene (Heitman) Tripodi. B.A., Lindenwood Coll., St. Charles, Mo., 1957; postgrad. honors program, Am. U., Case Western Res. U., Harvard U. Trainee U.S. Dept. State, 1957-58; tchr., counselor Fairfax Hall Coll. Prep., Waynesboro, Va., 1958-60; buying exec. Famous-Barr, May Co., St. Louis, 1960-63; devel. dir. St. Louis Carondelet YWCA, 1963-66, exec. dir., 1966-70; fin. and devel. cons. Nat. Bd. YWCA of USA, Atlanta, San Francisco and N.Y.C., 1970-73; real estate broker Holiday Builders, St. Simons Isle, Ga., 1973-74; freelance cons., Chgo., Conn., 1975-79; mgmt. cons., N.Y.C., 1979—; dep. support coordinator world conf. World Assn. of Girl Guides/Girl Scouts, London, Eng., 1984; dir. Office Nat. Bd. dirs., Girl Scouts U.S.; mem. Internat. Tng. Inst. World YWCA, nat. bd., 1969; lectr. in field. Author, organizer: A Social History of Art in Missouri, 1969; asst. editor: Administration Manual, Nat. Bd. YWCA, 1974-75. Republican. Mem. Christian Scientist Ch. Club: Press (Brunswick, Ga.). Lodge: Zonta (treas., bd. dirs., sec. St. Louis County chpt.). Avocations: international travel, exploration of cultures through music and the arts. Home: 5 Orchard Hills New Canaan CT 06840

LE FORESTIER, JEAN-PAUL, metal company executive; b. Compiegne, Oise, France, Dec. 30, 1953; s. Paul and Regine (Vannihuse) LeF.; m. Regine Plaut, Sept. 6, 1980; 1 child, Florian. BS in Engr. Materials Sci., Institut Nat. de Sciences Appliquees, Rennes, France, 1977; DEA, U. P. Sabatier, Toulouse, France, 1979. Research engr. CNRS Electronic Microscopy Lab., Toulouse, 1978, CNES French Space Ctr., Toulouse, 1979-80; tech. mgr. metals div. Materials Research Co., Toulouse, 1981-85, ceramic div. mgr., 1985-87, precious metals div. mgr., 1987-88; tech. mgr. Compagnie des Metaux Precieux, Engelhard, 1988—. Mem. St. Francaise Mettalurgie, St. Francaise du Vide. Roman Catholic. Home: 91 Bis Chemin Raynal, 31200 Toulouse France Office: CMP, 72-78 PV Couturier, 94204 Ivry France

LEFRAK, SAMUEL J., housing and building corporation executive, real estate development, finance, oil and gas exploration, music publisher, communications executive; b. N.Y.C., Feb. 12, 1918; s. Harry and Sarah (Schwartz) LeF.; m. Ethel Stone, May 14, 1941; children: Denise, Richard, Francine, Jacqueline. Grad., U. Md., 1940; postgrad., Columbia, Harvard; LL.D., N.Y. Law Sch., 1975, Colgate U., 1979; consulate laureate, Univ. Studies, Rome, 1972. Pres. Lefrak Orgn., 1948—, chmn. bd., 1975—; creator, sponsor, builder Lefrak City, Battery Park City, Gateway Plaza, Newport complex; bd. visitors Columbia U. Sch. Law, 1983; mem. adv. bd. Sta. WHLI, 1955; commr. Landmarks Preservation Commn., N.Y.C., 1966; commr. pub. works Borough Manhattan, 1956-58, comm. Interstate Sanitation Commn., 1958; Saratoga Springs Commn., 1962—; Mem. adv. bd. Chem Bank.; guest lectr. Harvard Grad. Sch. Bus. Adminstrn., 1971, Yale, 1975, N.Y. U., 1977; guest speaker Financial Women's Assn., N.Y., 1975; guest lectr. Princeton U., U. Haifa, 1983, Oxford U., 1984, Pratt Inst., 1987, Harvard U., 1987; featured speaker Instl. Investment Real Estate Conf., 1975; guest lectr. Japanese Govt., Finnish Govt., Union South Africa, Switzerland, 1967; U.S. del. Internat. Conf. Housing and Urban Devel., Switzerland, 1967; dir. N.Y. World's Fair Corp., 1964-65, N.Y. Indsl. Devel. Corp., 1975—; chmn. bd. L.I. Post; pres. N.Y.C. Comml. Devel. Corp., 1967-71, chmn., 1971—; founding mem. World Business Council, Inc., 1970; mem. Pres.'s Com. Employment Handicapped; spl. cons. urban affairs State Dept., 1969; mem. adv. council Real Estate Inst., N.Y. U., 1970—; mem. gov. fin. Pres.'s Club U. Md., 1971, com. N.Y. State Traffic Safety Council, 1966; bd. visitors Sch. Law, Columbia U., 1983; commr. Saratoga-Capital dist. N.Y. State Park and Recreation Commn., 1973; mem. real estate council exec. com. Met. Mus. Art, 1982; mem. N.Y.C. Pub. Devel. Corp., Nat. Energy Council, U.S. Dept. Commerce, Mayor's Com. on Housing Devel., N.Y.C., 1974—; mem. exec. com. Citizen's Budget Com. for N.Y.C., Inc., 1975—; mem. Gov. Cuomo's Adv. Council, 1983, N.Y. State Gov.'s Task Force on Housing, 1974; establish Lefrak Lecture Series, U. Md., 1982; guest lectr. Pratt Inst. and Harvard U.; bd. visitors Sch. of Law Columbia, 1983. Vice chmn.-at-large A.R.C. in, N.Y.; mem. U.S. com. UN Orgn., 1957; chmn. nat. bd. Histadrut, 1967—; mem. Israel Bonds Prime Minister Com., 1980; dir. Ronald McDonald House, 1986; chmn. bldg. com. Saratoga Performing Arts Ctr.; mem. Fifth Ave. Assn.; dir., chmn. real estate div. Greater N.Y. Fund; hon. com. A.A.U.; Queens chmn. United Greek Orthodox Charities, 1973; chmn. Celebrity Sports Night-Human Resources Center, 1973-74, Sports Assn. Hebrew U. of Jerusalem, 1979; patron Met. Mus. Art; sponsor Israel Philharmonic Orch., Jan Groth Exhibit, Guggenheim Mus.; trustee, dir. Beth-El Hosp.; bd. dirs. U.S.O., Citizens Housing and Planning Council, N.Y., 1957—, Interfaith Movement, Diabetics Found., Queens Cultural Assn., Consumer Credit Counseling Service Greater N.Y., Astoria Motion Picture and TV Center Found.; trustee N.Y. Law Sch., Queens Art and Cultural Center, Jewish Hosp. at Denver, N.Y Civic Budget Com.; trustee, med. adv. bd. Brookdale Hosp. Med. Ctr., Pace U.; mem. exec. bd. Greater N.Y. councils Boy Scouts Am.; founder Albert Einstein Sch. Medicine; mem. Bretton Woods Com.; bd. govs. Invest-in-Am. Nat. Council; mem. task force on energy conservation Div. Community Housing, 1981—; mem. com. N.Y. State Traffic Safety Council, 1966; chmn. Scandinavia Today, 1981—; bd. vis. Sch. Law Columbia U., 1983; mem. adv. bd. The Explorer's Club, 1984; mem. Nat. Com. on U.S.-China Relations Inc.; bd. dirs. Inst. Nautical Archaeology; conf. bd. Keynote Address-Annual Fin. Seminar, 1987. Decorated Order St. John of Jerusalem Pope John; Order of Lion of Finland; Order of the North Star of Sweden, Knights of Malta, 1982; recipient Mayor N.Y.C. award outstanding citizenship, 1960; Nat. Boys Club award, 1960; Citizen of Year award B'nai B'rith, 1963; Am. Achievement award, 1984; Distinguished Achievement award, 1967; Man of Year award V.F.W., 1963; Brotherhood award NCCJ, 1964; Chief Rabbi Herzog gold medal; Torah Fellowship citation Religious Zionist Am., 1966; John F. Kennedy Peace award, 1966; Man of Year award Bklyn. Community Hosp., 1967; Builder of Excellence award Brandeis U., 1968; Master Builder award N.Y. Cardiac Center, 1968; Distinguished Citizen award M Club Found. U. Md., 1970; Distinguished Alumnus award U. Md. Alumni Assn., 1970; Disting. Citizen and Outstanding Community Service award United Way, 1986; Am. Achievement award United Way, 1984; Am. Eagle award nat. council Invest-in Am., 1972; Exec. Sportsman award Human Resources Center, 1973; Archtl. award Fifth Av. Assn., 1974; Excellence in Design award Queens C. of C., 1974; Flame Truth award Fund Higher Edn.; elected hon. citizen Md., 1970; Citizen of Yr. award Bklyn. Philharmonic Orch., 1983; dedication of Samuel J. LeFrak Hall U. Md., 1982; LeFrak Lecture Series at U. Md. established, 1982; Comdr. of the Royal Norwegian Order of Merit, presented by King Olav V, 1987; Rough Riders award Boy Scouts Am., 1987. Mem. Sales Execs. Club N.Y. (dir.), United Hunts Racing Assn., Philharmonic Symphony Soc. N.Y., Explorers Club (dir.), Newcomen Soc. U.S., Phi Kappa Phi, Tau Epsilon Phi (established Samuel J. LeFrak scholarship award 1975). Clubs: U. Md. Pres.'s (mem. Gov. N.Y. fin.), Lotos (bd. dirs. 1975—, Merit award 1973), Grand Street Boys, Friars (dir. Found.), Advertising, Economic, Downtown Athletic (N.Y.C.); Town, Turf and Field; Cat Cay (Nassau, Bahamas); Xanadu Yacht (Freeport, Grand Bahamas); Palm Bay (Miami Beach, Fla.); Seawane; Ocean Reef (Key Largo); Sag Harbor Yacht (L.I.). Lodges: Masons, Shriners. Office: LeFrak Orgn Inc 97-77 Queens Blvd Forest Hills NY 11374

LEFTON, NORMAN BARRY, metals company executive; b. St. Louis, Apr. 25, 1934; s. Samuel Israel and Sarah (Offstein) L.; B.S. in Indsl. Engring., U. Ill., 1955; A.M. in Econs. (Woodrow Wilson fellow 1962-63), U. Chgo., 1963, Ph.D. in Econs., 1972; m. Margaret Clare Bennetto Banks, Nov. 1, 1962; children—Simon J., Sarah J. Indsl. engr. Caterpillar Tractor Co., Peoria, Ill., 1955-56; asst. prof. econs. U. Hawaii, Honolulu, 1965-70; cons. Economist Research Corp., U. Hawaii, Honolulu, 1972-74; chmn. bd. Lefton Iron & Metal Co., East St. Louis, Ill., 1976—; adj. assoc. prof. econs. So. Ill. U., Edwardsville, 1985—; adj. prof. Central Mich. U., Inst. of Personal and Career Devel., 1972—; vis. lectr. Hawaii Loa Coll., Kaneohe, 1975; bd. govs. Ill. Council on Econ. Edn., 1985—. Served with C.E., USN, 1956-59. U. Chgo. fellow, 1963-64. Mem. Navy League of U.S., Ret. Officers Assn., Hawaii Econ. Assn., Atlantic Econ. Soc., Nat. Assn. Bus. Economists, Am. Econ. Assn., Southwestern Ill. Indsl. Assn. (v.p. 1986—), Inst. Scrap Iron and Steel (exec. com. 1979-83), Res. Officers Assn. U.S., Greater E. St. Louis C. of C. (bd. dirs.). Republican. Club: Media. Office: 205 S 17th St East Saint Louis IL 62207

LE GALL, JEAN LOUIS, airline executive; b. Paris, Nov. 15, 1940; s. Martial and Andree (Nicot) Le G.; m. Claire Rouxel, May 19, 1942; 1 child, Philippe. Staff airline research design Transports Aëriens Intercontinentaux (T.A.I.), Orly Airport, Paris, 1958-60, 62-63; airport ops. agt. Air Afrique, Fort Lamy, Chad, 1963-66; tng. inspector, freight Air Afrique, Abidjan, Ivory Coast, 1978; with Union de Transports Aëriens (U.T.A.) French Airlines, 1967-78, 79—; sta. mgr. LeBourget, Paris, 1967-70; freight sta. mgr. Lusaka, Zambia, 1971-74; mgr. launching U.T.A.-Peugot airlift Kano, Nigeria, 1974-77; Internat. Air Transports Assn. rep. for U.T.A. Unit Load Devices control Paris, 1979-82, real estate mgr., 1982—; cargo mgr. Roissy Charles de Gaulle Airport, 1982-84; real estate mgr. 1985—. Mem. T.A.I. Assn. (v.p. 1982), Stock Exchange U.T.A. Assn. Clubs: Tennis (bd. dirs. 1983) (St. Germain en Laye); Judo (treas. 1984) (LeBourget). Home: 14 Rue de Fourqueux, 78100 Saint Germaine en Laye France Office: DF/Gestion Immobilière, UTA H2 BP n 7, 93350 Le Bourget Aëroport France

LE GALLIC, YVES, nuclear scientist; b. Callac, France, May 17, 1932; s. Francis and Yvonne (Jezequel) Le G.; D.Sc., U. Paris, 1959; m. Nadia Monnier, Sept. 19, 1953; children—Yann, Joelle. With French Atomic Energy Commn., 1950—, dir. Office Rayonnements Ionisants, Gif-sur-Yvette, 1979—; maitre de confs. Inst. Scis. et Techniques Nucleaires, 1974—; adminstr. Nat. Bur. Metrology, 1972—, Internat. CIS, 1978—; pres. ORIS Industry, CY, 1985—, Internat. CIS, 1985—, Laboratoire CERBA, 1984—; dir. Syncor Internat. Corp. Served with French Army, 1953-57. Decorated chevalier Ordre National du Merite, chevalier Legion of Honor. Mem. French Nuclear Med. Soc., French Soc. Radioprotection, Internat. Com. Radionuclide Metrology, Am. Soc. Nuclear Medicine, Am. Nuclear Soc. Author numerous papers in field. Home: 106 Ave Sadi Carnot, 91160 Saulx les Chartreaux France Office: CEN/Saclay Oris, BP21, 91190 Gif-sur-Yvette France

LE GARS, JACQUES, company executive; b. Tours, France, Sept. 25, 1948; s. Bernard and Helene (Jubien) Le G.; m. Chantal Janicaud, Apr. 28, 1979. Degree in Engring., Ecole Centrale Lyon (France), 1971. Engr., RTC/Philips, Paris, 1972-75, asst. lab. mgr., Evreux, France, 1976-77, lab. mgr., 1978-80; tech. mgr. SEDEPE, Plaisir, France, 1980—; lab. mgr. Philips, Amiens, France, 1979. Patentee microprocessor-based washing machine, 1979, led-based electronic display board, 1984, fault-tolerant hwy. displays, 1984, transflective hwy. displays, 1985. Office: SEDEPE, RN12, Sainte Appoline, 78372 Plaisir Cedex France

LEGER, PAUL-EMILE CARDINAL, archbishop emeritus; b. Valleyfield, Que., Can., Apr. 26, 1904; s. Ernest and Alda (Beauvais) L. Student, Sem. St. Therese; L.Th., Grand Sem. Montreal; J.C.L., Inst. Catholique, Paris, France; S.T.D., Laval U., 1951, U. Ottawa, 1961; Litt.D., Assumption Coll., 1934, LL.D., McGill U., 1960, St. Francis Xavier U., 1961, U. Toronto, 1965, U. Alta., 1967; D.C.L. (hon.), Bishop's U., Lennoxville, Que., 1965; L.H.D., Waterloo Lutheran U., 1969; Dr. honoris causa, U. Montreal, 1974, U. Sherbrooke, 1974, U. Kingston, 1979. Ordained priest Roman Catholic Ch., 1929; consecrated bishop Roman Catholic Ch., Rome, 1950; elevated to Sacred Coll. Cardinals, 1953; with Inst. Catholique, Paris, 1930-31; prof. Issy-les-Moulineaux, 1931-32, asst. master novices, 1932-33; founder, superior Sem. of Fukuoka, Japan, 1933-39; vicar gen., pastor cathedral Diocese of Valleyfield, 1940-47; rector Canadian Coll., Rome, Italy, 1947-50; archbishop of Montreal, Can., 1950-67; resigned for mission fields Africa, 1967-79; archbishop emeritus of Montreal 1979—; chancellor U. Montreal, 1950; nominated as parish priest St. Madelein Sophie Barat's Parish, 1974, resigned, 1975; Papal legate closing Marian Year, Lourdes, France, 1954, St. Joseph's Oratory, Montreal, 1955, Ste. Anne de Beaupré, Quebec, Can., 1958; Mem. Central Commn. preparatory to Vatican II, 1961; mem. Council Commn. on Sacred Theology, 1962, Sacred Consistorial Congregation Rome, 1963; mem. commn. canon law Council Vatican II, 1963; mem. del. Can. bishops Synod of Bishops, Rome, 1967; mem. Council Propagation of Faith, Rome, 1972, Pontifical Commn. Pastoral of Tourism, Rome, 1972; co-pres. Can. Found. for Refugees, from 1979. Decorated knight grand cross Equestrian of Holy Sepulchre of Jerusalem, 1950; bailiff grand cross of honour and devotion Sovereign Order of Malta, 1954; knight grand cross Legion Honour, France, 1958; grand cross of Benemerencia Portugal, 1965; Coeur d'or Milan, 1967; comdr. Order of Valor and Merit Cameroun Republic, 1969; Medal Chomedey de Maissonneuve, 1983; recipient award for service to humanity Royal Bank Can., 1969; Humanitarian award Variety Clubs Internat., 1976; Man of Yr. award Lester B. Pearson Peace Found., 1979; award for exceptional contbns. to human relations Can. Council for Christians and Jews, 1980. Address: PO Box 1500, Sta A, Montreal, PQ Canada H3C 2Z9

LEGGATT, HUGH FRANK JOHN, fine art dealer; b. London, Feb. 27, 1925; s. Henry Alan and Beatrice Grace (Burton) L.; ed. New Coll., Oxford U.; m. Jennifer Mary Hepworth, June 25, 1953; children—Charles, Martin. With Leggatt Bros., fine art dealers, London, 1946—, partner, 1952—, sr. partner, 1962—; chmn., mng. dir. Fine Art Fin. Investment Co. Ltd. Pres. Fine Art Provident Instn., 1960-63; hon. sec. Heritage in Danger, 1974—; chmn. Soc. London Art Dealers, 1966-70; commr. U.K. Museums and Galleries, 1983—. Served with RAF, 1943-46. Club: White's (London). Contbr. articles to profl. jours. Home: Flat 1, 10 Bury St, St James, London SW1Y 6AA, England Office: 17 Duke St, St James, London SW1, England

LEGGERI, MAURIZIO, civil engineer, educator; b. Potenza, Italy, Mar. 16, 1932; d. Luigi and Maria (Carsughi) L.; married; children: Maria Serena, Francesca, Ilaria. D. Engring., U. Bari, Italy, 1957; B.S., U. Naples, Italy, 1964; M.S., U. Potenza, 1983. Mng. dir. Inst. for Popular Houses, Potenza, 1958-61, HP 3000 Users Group, Italy, 1979-81; mng. dir. earthquake damages Municipality of Potenza, 1980-81; owner, operator Archstudio, Potenza, 1965—; pres. Edipass S.p.A., Potenza, 1983—; auditor Banca di Lucania, S.p.A., Potenza, 1984—; tchr. computer application for reinforced concrete U. Basilicata, 1986—. Regional del. Italian Nat. Olympic Com. Editor: Dimensione, 1980—, Polis, 1983—. Mem. Earthquake Engring. Research Inst., Centro Geomorfologia Aerea del Mediterraneo, Earthquake and Civil Engring. Dynamics, Regione Basilicata, Associazione Italiana di Ingegneria Sismica (v.p. 1985), Italy Geol. Assn.. Club: Amateur Radio (pres. Potenza 1977-84). Lodge: Lions (v.p. Potenza 1973). Home: Via Mazzini 23/E, 85100 Potenza Italy Office: Archstudio, Via F, Baracca 175, 85100 Potenza Italy

LEGLER, THEODORE REX, II, army officer, optometrist; b. Harlan, Ky., May 6, 1946; s. Theodore Rex and Mary Jane (Neese) L.; m. April C. Arington, Aug. 26, 1967; children—Melinda Melodie, Sara Cinnamon, Theodore Rex, III. AB in Optometry, Ind. U., 1968, A.B. in Zoology, 1969, O.D., 1971; MA in Health Services Mgmt., Webster U., St. Louis, 1982; grad. U.S. Army Command and Gen. Staff Coll., Fort Leavenworth, Kans., 1984. Diplomate Nat. Bd. Examiners. Commd. 2d lt. U.S. Army, 1968, advanced through grades to lt. col., 1986; chief optometry clinic U.S. Army, Mannheim, Germany and Fort Ord, Calif., 1971-79; chief optical div. U.S. Army Med. Equipment and Optical Sch., Aurora, Colo., 1979-82; chief optometry service, Fort Campbell, Ky., 1982-85; mem. faculty Acad. Health Services, U.S. Army, 1979-85, Regis Coll., Denver, 1979-82; affiliate prof. So. Coll. Optometry, Memphis, 1982-85; chief optometry Service USA Meddac-Berlin, Fed. Republic Germany, 1985—; tech. cons. Surgeon Gen. U.S. Army, 1976-79; affiliate prof. Ind. U. Sch. Optometry, Bloomington, 1982-85. Active regional and nat. level Boy Scouts Am. Recipient Silver Beaver award Boy Scouts Am., 1973. Fellow Am. Acad. Optometry; mem. Am. Optometric Assn. (optometric recognition award 1981-85, 87-88), Ind. Optometric Assn., Armed Forced Optometric Soc. (service award 1979), Assn. Mil. Surgeons U.S., Ind. U. Alumni Assn. (life), Ind. U. "I" Men's Assn., Nat. Rifle Assn. (life), Nat. Eagle Scout Assn. (life), Beta Sigma Kappa, Omega Epsilon Phi (life). Republican. Mem. Ch. of Christ. Avocations: scouting; fishing. Home: 2468 E Blackford Ave Evansville IN 47714 Office: USA Meddac-Berlin PO Box 4716 APO New York NY 09742

LE GOFF, RÉNE JEAN, business machine company executive; b. Paris, Apr. 21, 1944; s. Rene Marie and Pierina Modesta (Bertazzon) LeG.; m. Chantal Marie-France Houillon, July 10, 1965; children—Clotilde, Benedicte. Engr., Institut Industriel du Nord, Lille, France, 1967. Adminstrv. asst. Clement Mfg. Co., Paris, 1969; sales rep., mktg. mgr. IBM France, Paris, 1970-81, br. office mgr., Paris, and Orleans, 1982-84, dir. mktg., Paris, 1985; group dir. IBM-France Diffusion, 1985—; dir. MNS, Paris, SIRE, Paris. Gen. sec. Nat. Union Corp. Clubs, 1977-80; mem. Mcpl. Office of Sports, 1976-82. Served to lt. French Navy, 1967-69. Recipient French Sport medal Minister Youth and Sports, 1983, Disting. Citizen award Mayor of Paris, 1985; chevalier Nat. Order Merit, 1986. Clubs: Racing of France (treas. 1984—), IBM Sporting (pres. 1974—). Roman Catholic. Avocation: basketball. Home: 11 Ave de Diane, Saint Maur, 94100 Val de Marne France Office: IBM France, Tour Descartes, 92400 Courbevoie La Defense 5 France

LEGORRETA, RICARDO VILCHIS, architect; b. México, D.F, México, May 7, 1931; s. Luis and Guadalupe (Vilchis) L.; m. Maria Luisa Hernández de Legorreta, Jan. 14, 1956; children—Lourdes, Lucía, Elisa, Luis, Ricardo, Victor. Architect, Universidad Nacional Autónomo de Mex., Mexico, 1952. Project mgr. Mr. Villagran Office, Mexico City, 1948-55; ptnr., 1955-60; freelance architect, Mexico City, 1961-62; founder, pres. Legorreta Arquitectos, Mexico City, 1963—, L.A. Diseños, Mexico City, 1977—. Author: Los Muros de México, 1978. Recipient Copeeche Cobeepea Quelaconechi, Archtl. Sch., Oaxaca, México, 1983. Hon. fellow AIA, Mexican Soc. Architects. Mem. Tau Sigma Delta. Roman Catholic. *

LEGRAIN, MARCEL CHARLES, physician; b. Paris, Oct. 13, 1923; s. Pierre and Germaine (Mermet) Legrain; m. Colette Bonamy, Dec. 16, 1952; children: Sylvie Anne, Pierre Michel. MD, U. Paris, 1951. Intern Assistance Publique, Paris, 1947-51; research fellow Harvard U., Boston, 1951-52; assoc. prof. Faculty Medicine U. Paris, 1963-73; prof. medicine Pitie-Salpetriere, Paris, 1973-86, Faculty Medicine, Algiers, Algeria, 1986-88; prof. emeritus Faculty Medicine Pitie-Salpetriere, Paris, 1988—; pres. drug licensing com., Paris, 1978-85. Author: Nephriles aigues, 1951, Nephrology, 1987. Decorated Croix de Guerre, Légion d'honneur, Ordre du mérite. Mem. Soc. de Nephrologie (pres. 1973-75), European Dialysis Transplant Assn. (pres. 1978-81). Roman Catholic.

LEGRAND, VICTOR M.G., cardiology educator; b. Stoumont, Liege, Belgium, Oct. 13, 1952; s. Georges LeGrand and Denise Defraiteur; m. Marcelle Siquet, Aug. 17, 1978; children: Delphine, Stephanie, Philippe. MD, U. Liege, Belgium, 1977, PhD in Clin. Scis., 1983. Fellow in internal medicine Univ. Hosp., Liege, 1977-83, 84-86, assoc. prof. cardiology, 1986—; research fellow U. Mich., Ann Arbor, 1983-84. Contbr. more than 25 articles to profl. jours. NATO grantee, 1983. Mem. Belgian Soc. Internal Medicine, Belgian Soc. Cardiology (Van Doren award 1985), European Soc. Cardiology. Home: rue de Fraineux, La Reid, Liege 4881, Belgium Office: C H U, Sart Tilman B33, Liege Belgium

LEGUEY-FEILLEUX, JEAN-ROBERT, political scientist, educator; b. Marseilles, France, Mar. 28, 1928; came to U.S., Aug. 1949; s. E. Feilleux and Jeanne (Leguey) Feilleux Levassort; m. Virginia Louise Hartwell, Sept. 19, 1953; children—Michele, Monique, Suzanne, Christiane. M.A., Ecole Superieure de Commerce, France, 1949; Diplome Superieur d'Etudes Coloniales, U. d'Aix-Marseille, France, 1949; M.A., U. Fla., 1951; Ph.D., Georgetown U., 1965. Lectr. Sch. Foreign Service Georgetown U., Washington, 1957-66; dir. research Inst. World Polit. Georgetown U., 1960-66; asst. prof. St. Louis U., 1966-70, assoc. prof., 1970—, chmn. polit. sci. dept., 1983—; vis. scholar Harvard Law Sch., Cambridge, Mass., 1974-75; chmn. Fulbright Commn. for France Inst. Internat. Edn., N.Y.C., 1974-76; vis. researcher UN, N.Y.C., 1981. Author (with others): Law of Limited International Conflict, 1965. Contbr. chpt. to Implications of Disarmament, 1977. Contbr. articles to profl. jours. Author testimony Pres.'s Commn. on 25th Anniversary of UN, 1970. Recipient Medaille d'Or Institut Comml., France, 1949, Fulbright award U.S. State Dept., 1950, Cert. Disting. Service Inst. Internat. Edn., 1976; named Outstanding Educator Nutshell Mag., 1982; Malone fellow in Jordan, 1988. Mem. UN Assn. (mem. nat. council chpt. and div. pres. 1972-73, steering com. 1973-75), Am. Biog. Inst. (named to Hall of Fame, 1986), Internat. Human Rights Task Force (chmn. 1975-81), Character Research Assn. (pres. 1980-83), Georgetown U. Gold Key Soc., Alpha Sigma Nu, Phi Alpha Theta, Pi Sigma Alpha, Delta Phi Epsilon, Pi Delta Phi. Roman Catholic. Home: 6139 Kingsbury Ave Saint Louis MO 63112 Office: Saint Louis U Political Science Dept 221 N Grand Blvd Saint Louis MO 63103

LEGUM, JEFFREY ALFRED, automobile company executive; b. Balt., Dec. 16, 1941; s. Leslie and Naomi (Hendler) L.; B.S. in Econs., U. Pa., 1963; grad. Chevrolet Sch. Merchandising and Mgmt., 1966; m. Harriet Cohn, Nov. 10, 1968; children—Laurie Hope, Michael Neil. With Park Circle Motor Co. doing bus. as Legum Chevrolet-Nissan, Balt., 1963—, exec. v.p., 1966-77, pres., 1977—, also dir.; partner Pkwy. Indsl. Center, Dorsey, Md., 1965—; v.p., dir. P.C. Parts Co., 1967—; v.p. Westminster Motor Co. (Md.), 1967-72, pres., dir., 1972—; pres. One Forty Corp., Westminster, 1972—; dir., exec. com. United Consol. Industries, 1970-73; dir. Preakness Celebration, Inc., 1988—; dist. chmn. Chevrolet Dealers Council, 1975-77, chmn. Washington zone, 1982-83. Chmn. auto div. Asso. Jewish Charities, Balt., 1966-69; mem. Md. Service Acad. Review Bd., 1975-77, Bus. Adv. Bd. to Atty. Gen., 1985-87; trustee The Legum Found., Balt., 1967—; trustee, treas., mem. exec. com., chmn. fin. com., The Park Sch., Balt., 1979—; mem. pres.'s com. U. Toronto, 1983—; bd. dirs. Assoc. Placement Bur., Balt., v.p., 1972-76; adv. bd. The Competitive Edge, Albuquerque, 1977-81; bd. dirs. Preakness Celebration, Inc., 1988—; mem. investment com. Balt. Hebrew Congregation, 1980—. Recipient award of honor Assoc. Jewish Charities of Balt., 1967, 68; Cadillac Master Dealer award, 1980, 81, 82, 83, 84, 85, 86, 87; Cadillac Pinnacle Excellence award, 1986; Young Pres.'s Orgn. Cert. Appreciation; Nissan Nat. Merit Master award, 1982, 83, 84, 85, 86, 87; Chevrolet Nat. Service Supremacy award, annually 1979-87. Mem. Md. Auto Trade Assn., Young Pres. Orgn. (pres.'s forum 1977—), Greater Balt. Com., The John Hopkins Assocs., Carroll County C. of C., Baltimore County C. of C., Md. Hist. Soc. (exec. com. Library of Md. History 1981—). Clubs: Suburban (Baltimore County); Johns Hopkins Faculty, University of Pa., Center (Balt.); U. Toronto Faculty (hon.). Home: 10 Stone Hollow Ct Baltimore MD 21208 Office: 7900 Eastern Ave Baltimore MD 21224

LEHEL, GYORGY, conductor; b. Budapest, Hungary, Feb. 10, 1926; s. Laszlo and Klara (Ladanyi) L.; m. Zsurzsa Markovits, 1969; 1 son. Ed. Liszt Acad. Music, Budapest, 1942-47; D.Music (hon.), Chgo. Conservatory Coll., 1977; m. Zsuzsa Markovits, Dec. 23, 1969. Chief condr., music dir. Budapest Symphony Orch., 1962—; condr. concerts, Gt. Britain, Ireland, Belgium, France, Italy, USSR, Germany, Yugoslavia, Austria, Japan, Switzerland, U.S., 1950—. Recipient Liszt prize, 1955, 62, Kossuth prize, 1973; named merited artist, 1968. Office: Symphonic Orch, 5-7 Brody Sandor U, 1800 Budapest 8 Hungary *

LEHEL, LASZLO, manager economics department; b. Budapest, Hungary, Aug. 9, 1956; s. Laszlo and Elizabeth Lehel; m. Csilla Jandala, Mar. 9, 1982 (div. Oct. 1983); m. Vera Mendel, June 21, 1986. BS in Econs., Karl Marx

Econs. U., Budapest, 1980, MS in Econs., 1987; PhD in Economics, 1988. System analyser Mogurt, Budapest, 1980-81; bus. economist Medicor, Budapest, 1981-83, Mogurt, Budapest, 1983-84; mgr. econs. dept. Mogurt, 1984—. Mem. Hungarian Econ. Assn., European Econ. Assn., Hungarian Pub. Relations Com., Hungarian C. of C. Home: Vaci ut 56-58, H-1132 Budapest Hungary Office: Mogurt, Vaci utca 38, H-1056 Budapest Hungary

LE HENAFE, JACQUES CÉLESTIN, French territory government official; b. La Rochelle, France, Feb. 14, 1932; s. Julien and FéLicie (Moret) Le H.; m. Jacqueline Carlotti, Sept. 24, 1955; children: Marie-France, Janick, Jacques, Françoise, Pascale, Jean-Yves. Ed., mil. academies, Billom, Autun, Strasbourg. Officer French Armed Forces, 1950-57; adminstrv. sec. prefecture 1959; trainee Nat. Sch. Adminstrn., 1962-64; attaché prefecture 1965; bur. chief Prefet de la Charente-Maritime, 1965-68; superior adminstr. Wallis and Futuna Islands, Mata-Utu, 1986—. Decorated Comdr. Nat. Order of Merit, Overseas Medal, Combattant Cross, Indochina Commemorative Medal, Knight of the Order of Acad. Palms, Officer of the Order of Arts and Letters, Officer of the Sahametrei, Knight of the Order of the Thai Merit. Home: 5 Impasse des Primeveres, 17138 Saint-Xandre France Office: Adminstrn des iles Wallis et, Futuna, Mata-Utu Wallis Island *

LEHEY, GREGORY FRANCIS, computer company executive, microcomputer consultant; b. Melbourne, Victoria, Australia, Sept. 28, 1948; s. Norman George and Audrey Eileen (Herbert) L. m. Doris Margaret Pischke, May 9, 1975 (div. Sept. 1984); m. Yvonne Ködderitzsch, Mar. 22, 1985; 1 child, Yana Dunia. Student, King's Coll., Taunton, Eng., 1962-66, U. Hamburg, Fed. Republic Germany, 1967-68, U. Exeter, Eng., 1969-72. Systems advisor Sperry Univac, Frankfurt, Fed. Republic Germany, 1973-74; systems programmer SPL Internat., Frankfurt, 1974-75, IBAT-AOP, Essen, Fed. Republic Germany, 1975-76, Karstadt AG, Essen, 1976-82; systems specialist Tandem Computers, Frankfurt, 1982-86, support mgr., 1987—; proprietor Lemis, Voerde, Fed. Republic Germany, Rosbach, 1982—. Home: Gruener Weg 2, 6365 Ober-Rosbach Federal Republic of Germany Office: Tandem Computers Inc, Ben-Gurion Ring 164, 6000 Frankfurt 56 Federal Republic of Germany

LEHIGH, GEORGE EDWARD, medical group administrator, management executive; b. Graettinger, Iowa, Feb. 3, 1927; s. Earl F. and Rachel F. (Baker) L.; m. Karla Bair; children: Bruce V., Susan Paige. Student, N.D. State U., 1944-45, W.Va. U., 1945; BA, Buena Vista Coll., 1948; postgrad., Drake U., 1949-50. Tchr. secondary schs., Iowa, 1953-54; prin. secondary schs., Iowa and Minn., 1948-51, 57-58; jr. exec. World Ins. Co., 1951-54; field cons. Profl. Mgmt. Midwest, Waterloo, Iowa, 1954-57; bus. adminstr. Mankato (Minn.) Clinic, 1958-70; adminstr. Austin (Tex.) Diagnostic Clinic, 1970-75, Jackson (Tenn.) Clinic, P.A., 1975-77; exec. adminstr. Thomas-Davis Clinic, P.C., Tucson, 1977-80; dir. adminstrn. law firm Brown, Maroney, Rose, Baker & Barber, Austin, 1980-82; exec. adminstr. Capitol Anesthesiology Assn., Austin, 1982—; pres. A.P.S. Practice Mgmt., Inc., 1984-85; dir., treas. Profl. Health Services, Inc., Tucson, 1977-80. Bd. dirs. Credit Bur., Mankato, 1960-70, pres., 1967. Fellow Am. Coll. Med. Group Adminstrs.; mem. Med. Group Mgmt. Assn., Austin-Cen. Tex. Assn. Legal Adminstrs. (pres. 1981-82), Anesthesia Adminstrn. Assembly (chmn. 1983-85). Republican. Methodist. Office: 3705 Medical Pkwy Suite 570 Austin TX 78705-1097

LEHMAN, HYLA BEROEN, educator, performing artist; b. Story City, Iowa; d. Lewis Bernard and Helene Louise (Hagen) Beroen; student Waldorf Coll.; B.S. in Edn., Drake U., 1939; M.A., U. Iowa, 1947; postgrad. in classical theatre, Athens, Greece, 1978; m. Fredrick Brackin Lehman, Apr. 30, 1942; children—Rolfe Beroen, Rhea Helene. Tchr. theatre arts and English, LaPorte City, Iowa, Des Moines, Alexandria, Va., Los Angeles; mem. faculty dept. theatre Coe Coll., Cedar Rapids, Iowa, 1974-79; artistic cons. Dance Theatre of the Hemispheres, 1979—, performing artist including Elizabethan Twelfth Night, The Nutcracker, Le Chemin de la Croix, Afternoon in an English Garden, Chidambaram Karanas, A Digit of the Moon, others, 1967—, also bd. dirs.; chmn. bd., 1981-86; judge Am. Coll. Theatre Festival; performer, lectr. at various colls. and univs. Mem. Gov.'s Conf. on Edn.; mem. nat. alumni bd. Drake U.; chmn. Linn County unit Am. Cancer Soc.; mem. Nat. Commn. on Future Drake U.; mem. Public Health Nursing Bd. Recipient Disting. Alumni award Waldorf Coll., 1969. Mem. Am. Theatre Assn., AAUW (state pres. 1952-54, state arts chmn. 1950-52; fellowship named in her honor), Phi Mu Gamma (nat. alumnae dir. 1947-50, nat. pres. 1950-52), Phi Theta Kappa, Kappa Delta Pi. Lutheran. Home: 4347 Eaglemere Ct SE Cedar Rapids IA 52403

LEHMANN, HANS PETER, management consultant; b. Vienna, Austria, Oct. 18, 1944; arrived in Eng., 1982; s. Johann and Friederike (Kronfusz) L.; m. Annemarie Soukup, Dec. 23, 1966 (div. 1976); children—Oliver, Mirjam Bettina; m. Gillian Mary Longden, Sept. 23, 1978; children—Peter Michael, Anna Phillippa. B.Sc. with honors (equivalent), U. Vienna, 1966; M.A., U. Natal, 1977; M.D.P., U. South Africa, Pretoria, 1980. Cons., Vienna, 1966-72; dept. mgr. AECI, Ltd., S. Africa, 1973-77; dept. mgr. Standard Bank, S. Africa, 1977-80; mgmt. cons. Deloitte, Haskins & Sells, Zimbabwe, 1980-82, Eng., 1982—. Campaign adviser Austria Conservative Party, Vienna, 1967, 69. Mem. Brit. Computer Soc., Assn. Computing Machinery, Inst. Mgmt. Consultants. Roman Catholic.

LEHN, JEAN-MARIE PIERRE, chemistry educator; b. Rosheim, Bas-Rhin, France, Sept. 30, 1939; s. Pierre and Marie (Salomon) L.; m. Sylvie Lederer, 1965; 2 children. Grad., U. Strasbourg, France, 1960, PhD, 1963; PhD (hon.), U. Jerusalem, 1984, U. Autonoma, Madrid, Spain, 1985, U. Göttingen, Fed. Republic of Germany, 1987, U. Bruxelles, 1987. Various posts Nat. Ctr. Sci. Research, 1960-66; postdoctoral research assoc. Harvard U., Cambridge, Mass., 1963-64; asst. prof. chemistry U. Strasbourg, 1966-70, assoc. prof., 1970, prof., 1970-79; prof. Coll. de France, Paris, 1979—; with Ctr. Nat. Sci. Research, France, 1960-66; asst. prof. U. Strasbourg, France, 1966-69; assoc. prof. U. Louis Pasteur of Strasbourg, 1970, prof. of chemistry, 1970-79; prof. Coll. France, Paris, 1979—; vis. prof. chemistry Harvard U., 1972, 74, E.T.H., Zurich, Switzerland, 1977, Cambridge (Eng.) U., 1984, Barcelona (Spain) U., 1985, Frankfurt U. (Fed. Republic Germany), 1985-86. Contbr. about 307 articles to sci. publs. Recipient Gold medal Pontifical Acad. Scis., 1981, Paracelsus prize Swiss Chem. Soc., 1982, von Humboldt prize, 1983, Nobel Prize for Chemistry, 1987; named to Officer Légion d'Honneur, Chevalier Ordre Nat. du Mérite. Mem. Inst. de France, Deutsche Acad. der Naturforscher Leopoldina, Acad. Nazionale dei Lincei, Nat. Acad. Sci. (fgn. assoc.), AAAS (fgn. hon.), Royal Netherlands Acad. Arts and Scis. (fgn. mem.). Home: 21 Rue d'Oslo, 67000 Strasbourg France Office: Coll France, 11 Place Marcelin Berthelot, 75005 Paris France also: U Louis Pasteur, 4 Rue Blaise Pascal, 67000 Strasbourg France

LEHNER, GERHARD HANS, engineer, consultant; b. Gera, Federal Republic Germany, Feb. 6, 1924; s. Hans Walther and Margarete (Leibinger) L.; divorced; married. Degree in engring. telecommunications, Mil. Engring. Sch., Wetzlar, Fed. Republic Germany, 1942. Engr. Armed Forces Radio Service, Munich, 1945-48, Bavarian Broadcasting Network, Munich, 1948-52, Radio Free Europe, Munich, 1952-55; chief engr., tech. dir. Barclay Records, Paris, 1956-81; sound system installer, cons. Lido, Paris, Moulin Rouge, Paris, Crazy Horse Saloon, Paris. Served with German Army, 1943-45, Russia. Mem. Audio Engring. Soc. (v.p. 1979-80). Home: 63 Rue de Courcelles, 75008 Paris France

LEHNING, UDO, marketing and sales consultant; b. Bremen, W.Ger., July 9, 1938; s. Hans and Kathe (Meyer) L.; student U. Hamburg, 1959-63. Apprentice, AEG Bremen, 1957-59; trainee AEG, Hamburg, 1963-64, asst. to comml. dir. Kiel Sales Office, 1965-66; regional sales rep. Procter & Gamble, No. Germany, 1966-67, media mgr., 1967-70, product mgr., 1970-71; with Glendinning Internat. GmbH, Frankfurt, 1971-75, mng. dir., 1974—; mng. dir., owner Glendinning & Lehning Mktg. and Sales Cons. Co., Frankfurt, 1976—; presenter seminars since 1985. Author: Trade Terms, Marketing and Sales-in view of the German Grocery Trade, 1978; The Turnover Concentration in the Germany Grocery Trade, 1981, Profiles of the Top German Grocery Accounts since 1983. Home: Emser Weg 2, D-6232 Bad Soden Federal Republic of Germany Office: 19 Steinlestrasse, D-6000 Frankfurt-Main 70 Federal Republic of Germany

LEHR, FRANK HENRY, engineer; b. Easton, Pa., Apr. 2, 1925; s. Francis H. and Sadie (Fulse) L.; m. Veronica Shevock, June 24, 1950; children: Diane C., Frank F., Janice S. BS in Engring, Pa. State U., 1950; MS, N.J. Inst. Tech. (name formerly Newark Coll. Engring.), 1956. Registered profl. engr., N.J., N.Y., Pa., Mass., Conn., Ohio. Field engr. C.R.R. of N.J., Jersey City, 1950-51; structural designer Arthur G. McKee & Co., Union, N.J., 1951, 53-54; constrn. engr. Jersey Testing Lab., Inc., Newark, 1954-57; pres. Frank H. Lehr Assocs. (cons. civil engrs.), East Orange, N.J., 1957—. Chmn. Joint Meeting Sewer Commn. Union and Essex Counties, N.J., 1969-76; mem. Summit (N.J.) Bd. Appeals, 1958-75; mem. City Council, Summit, 1962-76, pres., 1970-76; mem. Summit Bd. Sch. Estimates, 1964-69; mayor City of Summit, 1976-80; freeholder Union County (N.J.), 1981-83, chmn., 1983; chmn. N.J. Natural Resources Com. Served to capt. USMCR, 1943-47, 51-53. Fellow Am. Cons. Engrs. Council, ASCE; mem. Union County Soc. Profl. Engrs. (past pres.), Marine Corps Res. Officers Assn., ASTM, Bldg. Ofcls. N.J. Club: Kiwanis (dir. East Orange chpt.). Home: 16 Myrtle Ave Summit NJ 07901 Office: Frank H Lehr Assocs 101 S Harrison St East Orange NJ 07018

LEHR, MAX I., dentist; b. Russia, Aug. 25, 1908; came to U.S., 1923; s. Isaac and Bella (Curshan) L.; m. Nannette G. Hymanson, Oct. 18, 1947; children: Judith Lehr Smith, Les I. DDS, Northwestern U., 1935. Gen. practice dentistry Oak Park, Ill., 1936—. Served to maj. USAF, 1943-45, PTO. Decorated Bronze Star. Mem. ADA, Ill. Dental Soc., Chgo. Dental Soc., Assn. Mil. Surgeons, Pierre Fauchard Acad., Fédération Dentaire Internationale, Jewish War Vets. of U.S., Am. Legion, Alpha Omega. Club: Northwestern of Chgo. Lodge: B'nai B'rith.

LEHRER, STANLEY, magazine publisher; b. Bklyn., Mar. 18, 1929; s. Martin and Rose L.; m. Laurel Francine Zang, June 8, 1952; children—Merrill Clark, Randee Hope. B.S. in Journalism, N.Y. U., 1950; postgrad. in edn, San Antonio Coll., 1952. Editor and pub. Crossroads mag., Valley Stream, N.Y., 1949-50; youth service editor Open Road mag., N.Y.C., 1950-51; mng. editor School & Society, N.Y.C., 1953-68, v.p., 1956-68; pub. School & Society Books, N.Y.C., 1963-86, School & Society mag., N.Y.C., 1968-72; pub. Intellect mag., N.Y.C., 1972-78, editorial dir., 1974-78; pub., editorial dir. USA Today mag., Valley Stream, N.Y., 1978—, Newsview mag., 1979—, Your Health mag., 1980—, The World of Sci., 1980—; cons. Child Care Publs., N.Y.C., 1955. Producer: (WBAI-FM radio program) Report on Eucation, N.Y.C., 1960-61; author: John Dewey: Master Educator, 1959, Countdown on Segregated Education, 1960, Religion, Government, and Education, 1961, A Century of Higher Education: Classical Citadel to Collegiate Colossus, 1962, Automation, Education, and Human Values, 1966, Conflict and Change on the Campus: The Response to Student Hyperactivism, 1970, Leaders, Teachers, and Learners in Academe: Partners in the Educational Process, 1970, Education and the Many Faces of the Disadvantaged: Cultural and Historical Perspectives, 1972; contbr. articles to nat. mags., newspapers and profl. jours. Vice pres. Garden City Park (N.Y.) Civic Assn., 1961-63; treas. Citizens' Com. Edn. Garden City Park, 1962; mem. nat. jr. book awards com. Boys' Clubs Am., 1954; mem. nat. hon. com. for Richard H. Heindel Meml. Fund, Pa. State U., 1979-80. Served with Signal Corps U.S. Army, 1951-53. Recipient Non-fiction awards Midwestern Writers Conf., Chgo., 1948. Mem. New Hyde Park (N.Y.) C. of C. (dir. 1961-62), Titanic Hist. Soc., S.S. Hist. Soc. Am., Soc. Advancement of Edn. (treas. 1953—, trustee 1963—, pres. 1968—), Psi Chi Omega. Home: 82 Shelbourne Ln New Hyde Park NY 11040 Office: USA Today 99 W Hawthorne Ave Valley Stream NY 11580

LEHTONEN, REIJO PÄIVIÖ, electrical cable manufacturing company executive; b. Helsinki, Finland, May 16, 1930; s. Lauri and Rauha (Heinonen) L.; m. Kaarina Peltoniemi, June 23, 1957; children: Eija, Päivi, Jarmo. Diploma in elec. engring., Tech. Coll. Helsinki, 1955; MS in Engring., U. Oulu, 1976. Lab. engr. Oy Stromberg Ab, Helsinki, 1955-56; methods engr. City Elec. Works, Helsinki, 1956-60; sales engr. Sahkoliikkeiden Oy, Helsinki, 1960-61; dir. Sahkolijkkeiden Oy, Helsinki, 1983-87; tech. mgr. Kaapeliteollisuus Oy, Oulu, 1961-67, gen. mgr., chmn., 1967-87; gen. mgr. Nokia Telecommunication Cables, 1987—. Hon. consul Fed. Republic Germany, 1977—; dist. rep. Confedn. Finnish Industries, Oulu, 1982—. Mem. Tech. Soc. Finland, Elec. Engrs. Assn. Finland, IEEE, Oulu C. of C. (chmn. bd. dirs. 1983-86, bd. dirs. 1980—). Lutheran. Lodge: Rotary (pres. 1977-78). Home: Haapanatie 36, 90150 Oulu Finland Office: Nokia Cables, PO Box 269, SF-90101 Oulu Finland

LEIB, THOMAS JAMES, architect; b. Chgo., July 17, 1948; s. John Jacob and Loretta Bernadette L. B.Arch., U. Ill.-Chgo., 1974; M.Arch., Harvard U., 1976. Registered architect, Mass., Conn., N.Y., Ill., N.H., R.I., Vt., Maine, Pa., Ind., Va. Archtl. designer dept. architecture City of Chgo., 1974-75, Perkins & Will, White Plains, N.Y., 1976-77; project architect WZMH Group, Inc., Boston, 1977-85; pres. Thomas J. Leib & Assocs., Architects and Planners, Cambridge, Mass., 1985—; archtl. design instr. Boston Archtl. Ctr., 1977-79; lectr. Wentworth Inst. Tech., Boston, 1981-82, asst. prof. architecture, 1985-86; lectr. Northeastern U., Boston, 1987. Mem. AIA (scholastic scholarship 1973, sch. medal, cert. of merit 1974), Boston Soc. Architects, Mass. State Assn. Architects, Boston Archtl. Ctr., Nat. Trust for Hist. Preservation. Home: 9B Russell St Cambridge MA 02140-1313 Office: Architects and Planners 875 Main St Cambridge MA 02139 Mailing: PO Box 99 Cambridge MA 02138

LEIBLER, ISI JOSEPH, travel company executive; b. Antwerp, Belgium, Oct. 9, 1934; arrived in Australia, 1938; s. Abraham Samuel and Rachel (Akermann) L.; m. Naomi Helen Porush; children: Tamara Karen, Anton Samuel, Gary Zev, Jonathan Ian. BA with honors, Melbourne U., 1957. Chmn. bd., mng. dir. Jetset Tours Pty. Ltd., Melbourne, 1963; pres. Asia Pacific Jewish Assn., Melbourne, 1980—; chmn. Australian Inst. Jewish Affairs, Melbourne, 1983—; pres. Asia Pacific Region World Jewish Congress, Melbourne, 1985—; pres. Exec. Council Australian Jewry, Melbourne, 1978-80, 82-85, 1987—. Contbr. articles to profl. jours. Mem. Victorian Jewish Bd. Deps. (chmn 1977-82), World Jewish Congress (exec. and governing bd. 1978—), Meml. Found. Jewish Culture (bd. govs. 1979—), Australian Union Jewish Students. Home: 116 Kooyong Rd, 316i Caulfield, Victoria Australia Office: Jetset Tours Pty Ltd, 550 Bourke St, 3000 Melbourne Australia

LEIBOWITT, SOL DAVID, lawyer; b. Bklyn., Feb. 18, 1912; s. Morris and Bella (Small) L.; B.A., Lehigh U., 1933; LL.B., Harvard U., 1936; m. Ethel Leibowitt, June 18, 1950 (dec. Aug. 1985); m. Babs Lee Dec. 28, 1986. Admitted to N.Y. bar, 1937, Conn. bar, 1970; pvt. practice, N.Y.C., 1937-84, Stamford, Conn., 1970-78, Milford, Conn., 1978-79; gen. counsel New Haven Clock and Watch Co., 1955-59, pres., 1958-59; pres. Diagnon Corp., 1981-83, vice chmn., 1983-86; chmn. Card Tech. Corp., 1983-85; dir. Data Card Internat. Corp., Hevant, Eng., 1977-79. Pres. Ethel and David Leibowitt Found.; dir. Am. Com. for Weizman Inst. Sci. Recipient Human Relations award, 1969, Ethel Leibowitt Fund Johns Hopkins U. Sch. Medicine, Meml. award Anti-Defamation League, 1971. Mem. Assn. Bar N.Y.C., Am., N.Y. State bar assns., Anti-Defamation League (commr.), Am. Soc. for Technion U. (mem. bd., v.p., Conn. pres.). Clubs: Lotos, Harvard (N.Y.C.); Banyon Country (West Palm Beach, Fla.), Lotus. Lodge: Masons.

LEIDER, GERALD J., motion picture and television company executive; b. Camden, N.J., May 28, 1931; s. Myer and Minnie Leider; m. Susan Trustman, Dec. 21, 1968; children: Matthew Trustman, Kenneth Harold. B.A., Syracuse U., 1953. Theater producer in N.Y.C., London, 1956-59; dir. spl. programs CBS-TV, 1960-61, dir. program sales, 1961-62; v.p. TV ops. Ashley Famous Agy., Inc., N.Y.C., 1962-69; pres. Warner Bros. TV, Burbank, Calif., 1969-74; exec. v.p. fgn. prodn. Warner Bros. Pictures, Rome, 1975-76; ind. producer motion pictures and TV GJL Prodns., Inc., Los Angeles, 1977-82; pres. ITC Prodns., Inc., Los Angeles, 1982-87; pres., chief exec. officer ITC Entertainment Group, Studio City, Calif., 1987—. Producer: Gielgud's Ages of Man, 1958-59; feature motion pictures include The Jazz Singer (with Neil Diamond), 1980, Trenchcoat, 1983; TV films include And I Alone Survived, 1978, Willa, 1979, The Hostage Tower, 1980. Mem. Bd. Visitors Coll. Visual and Performing Arts, Syracuse U. Recipient Arents Alumni medal Syracuse U., 1977; Fulbright fellow U. Bristol (Eng.), 1954. Mem. Acad. Motion Picture Arts and Scis., Acad. TV Arts and Scis., Am. Film Inst. (second decade council), Hollywood Radio and TV Soc. (pres. 1975-76); mem. steering com. The Caucus for Producers, Writers & Dirs. Office: ITC Entertainment Group 12711 Ventura Blvd Studio City CA 91604

LEIFERMAN, IRWIN HAMILTON, industrial and investment executive; b. Chgo., Jan. 8, 1907; s. Beril and Ida (Rosenbaum) L.; m. Silvia Weiner, Apr. 20, 1947. Student, Crane Jr. Coll., 1923, Northwestern U., 1924-29. Purchasing agt. Hamilton-Ross Corp., Chgo. and Kokomo, Ind., 1924-30; pres. Hamilton Industries Co., 1931-64, chmn. bd., 1964—; past pres. Leiferman Investment Co., now cons.; v.p. Comet Prodns., Inc. (TV), 1965—. Mem. industry com. Dept. Labor, 1940; Mem. advisory com. Brandeis U., 1961-62, life mem. bd.; asso. Cancer Research Found. U. Chgo., 1958; mem. Mt. Sinai Hosp., Chgo.; hon. com. Lowe's Gala, 1972; charter mem. WPBT, Channel 2, Miami; co-founder, pres. Silvia and Irwin H. Leiferman Found.; nat. bd. govs., greater Chgo. bd. govs. Bonds for Israel; founder Miami Med. Center, Greater Technion Israel Inst. Tech., 1972; founder Mt. Sinai Hosp., Miami Beach, Fla., 1969, recipient spl. award, 1972; trustee, life mem. Nathan Goldblatt Soc. Cancer Research; patron Royal Ballet Soc. Miami, Lowe's Mus. Miami, Greater Art Center Miami, Philharmonic Soc. Miami; patron Greater Miami Cultural Art Center, hon. gala com., 1972. Recipient spl. awards; War Bond Program Sec. Treasury; War Bond Program U.S. Dept. Labor. Mem. Chgo. Assn. Commerce and Industry, Ill. Mfrs. Assn., Ill. C. of C., Friends Lowes Mus., Am. Contract Bridge League, Jewish Home for Aged Mens Club, Bayshore Service Club. Jewish (mem. 10155 Collins Ave temple). Clubs: Mem. B'nai Brandeis 33154 (life); Executives, Covenant, International, Green Acres, Standard, Bryn Mawr Country (Chgo.); Bayshore Service, Jockey, Brickell Bay, Westview Country (Miami, Fla.). Home: 10155 Collins Ave #1404 Bal Harbor FL 33154 Office: 9550 Bay Harbor Terr Miami Beach FL also: 33 N LaSalle St Chicago IL 60602

LEIFERMAN, SILVIA WEINER (MRS. IRWIN H. LEIFERMAN), artist, civic worker, sculptor; b. Chgo.; d. Morris and Annah (Kaplan) Weiner; m. Irwin H. Leiferman, Apr. 20, 1947. Student, U. Chgo., 1960-61; studied design and painting, Provincetown, Mass. Organizer, charter mem. women's div. Hebrew U. Chgo., 1947; Head Pres. Accessories by Silvia, Chgo., 1964; organizer women's div. Edgewater Hosp., 1954; chmn. bd. Leiferman Investment Corp.; chairwoman spl. sales and spl. events greater Chgo. Com. for State of Israel; originator, organizer Ambassador's Ball, 1956, Presentation Ball, 1963; met. chmn. numerous spl. events Nat. Council Jewish Women, Nathan Goldblatt Soc. Cancer Research, Chgo.; now life mem., trustee; chmn. numerous spl. events North Shore (Ill.) Combined Jewish Appeal; chmn. women's com. Salute to Med. Research City of Hope, 1959; founder Ballet Soc. of Miami; Bd. dirs. Jewish Children's Bur., North Shore Women's Aux., Mt. Sinai Hosp., George and Ann Portes Cancer Prevention Center Chgo., Nat. Council Jewish Women, Fox River (Ill.) Sanitorium, Edgewater Hosp., Greater Chgo. Bonds for Israel, Orgn. of Rehab. and Tng. Exhibited one-woman shows, Schram Galleries, Ft. Lauderdale, Fla., 1966, 67, D'Arcy Galleries, N.Y.C., 1964, Stevens Annex Bldg., Chgo., 1965, Miami (Fla.) Mus. Modern Art, 1966, 72, Contemporary Gallery, Palm Beach, Fla., 1966, Westview Country Club, 1968, Gallery 99, 1969; exhibited group shows, Ricardo Restaurant Gallery, Chgo., 1961, 62, Bryn Mawr (Chgo.) Country Club, 1961, 62, Covenant Club Ill., Chgo., 1963, D'Arcy Galleries, 1965, Internat. Platform Assn., 1967, Miami Mus. Modern Art, 1967, Bacardi Gallery, 1967, Hollywood Mus. Art, 1968, Gallery 99, Miami, Lowe Art Mus., Crystal Ho. Gallery, Miami Beach, 1968; represented in numerous pvt. collections. Bd. dirs. Brandeis U., Art Inst. Chgo., Miami Mus. Modern Art; co-founder, v.p. Silvia and Irwin Leiferman Found.; donor Leiferman award auspices City of Hope; internat. co-chairwoman Ball Masque; mem. pacesetter/trustee com. Greater Miami Jewish Fedn., 1976-77; founder Mt. Sinai Hosp. Greater Miami, Fla.; donor Michael Reese Hosp., 1978; benefactress Miami Heart Inst., 1979, St. Joseph Hosp., 1979, Mt. Sinai Med. Center, 1979. Recipient citations for def. bond sales U.S. Govt., for Presentation Ball State of Israel, 1965; Pro Mundi Beneficio Gold medal Brazilian Acad. Humanities, 1976; numerous awards Bonds for Israel; numerous awards Combined Jewish Appeal North Shore Spl. Gifts; Keys to cities Met. Miami area; named Woman of Valor State of Israel, 1963; donor award Miami Heart Inst. Fellow Royal Soc. Arts and Scis.; mem. Internat. Council Mus., 1st Ann. Cultural Conf. Chgo., Am. Fedn. Arts, Artist's Equity Assn., Fla. Poetry Soc., Miami Art Center, Miami Beach Opera Guild Com., Greater Miami Cultural Art Center, Guild Com. Greater Miami Cultural Art Center, Sculptors of Fla., Royal Acad. Arts, Internat. Platform Assn., Lowe Art Mus., Am. Contract Bridge League, Friends of U. Haifa. Jewish (mem. bd.). Clubs: Standard, Bryn Mawr Country, Covenant, Green Acres, International, Boye, Whitehall, Key (Chgo.); Jockey, Westview Country, Tower (Miami Beach, Fla.); Brickell Bay. Home: 10155 Collins Ave Bal Harbour FL 33154

LEIFLAND, LEIF, ambassador; b. Stockholm, Dec. 30, 1925; s. Sigfrid and Elna (Johanson) L.; m. Karin Kristina, Feb. 20, 1953; children: Karl Gustaf, Christina, Eva. BBL, U. Lund, 1950. With Swedish Fgn. Service, 1951; first sec. Swedish Fgn. Office, Stockholm, 1958; counselor Embassy of Sweden, Washington, 1970; permanent undersec. Stockholm, 1977; ambassador Embassy of Sweden, London, 1982—. Office: Embassy of Sweden, 11 Montagu Pl, London W1H 2AL, England

LEIFMAN, LEV JACOB, mathematician, translator, editor; b. Kiev, Ukraine, Apr. 12, 1929; came to U.S., 1979; s. Jacob Lev and Nina Boris (Tsyrlin) L.; m. Miriam Israel Eidelson, May 16, 1962; children—Jacob, Tatyana. M.Sc., Kiev U., 1952; Ph.D., Moscow U., 1962. Research prof. Ukrainian Inst. Trade, Kiev, 1959-63; assoc. prof. Novosibirsk U., USSR, 1963-67; research prof. USSR Acad. Scis., Novosibirsk, 1963-70; assoc. prof. Inst. Civil Engrs., Novosibirsk, 1971-73, Haifa (Israel) U., 1974-78; translation editor Am. Math. Soc., Providence, 1979—; head and sci. supr. lab. exptl. programming Inst. Automated Control Systems, Novosibirsk, 1964-69; faculty R.I. Coll., 1982—. Author: Netzplantechnik bei begrenzten Ressourcen, 1968, Modelling of Private Consumption, 1972; editor: Network Planning under Restraints on Resources, 1971; series Modelling of Control Processes, 1967-73, Theory of Probability and Math. Stats., 1978-85, Vestnik of the Leningrad U., 1979-84, Procs. of Steklov Inst. Math, 1983-85, Trans. of Moscow Math. Soc., 1983-85, Mathematics of USSR Sbornik, 1984—, Soviet Math.-Doklady, 1985—, Math. of USSR-Izvestiya, 1985—; contbr. numerous articles to profl. publs., chpts. to books. Mem. Internat. Assn. Cybernetics, N.Y. Acad. Scis., Math. Programming Soc., Soc. Inds. and Applied Math. Jewish. Subspecialties: Algorithms; Operations research (mathematics). Current work: Optimization-development and analysis of methods and algorithms; mathematical models and methods in operations research and economics; mathematical models of translation between natural languages and their implementation on computers. Home: 467 Pleasant St Pawtucket RI 02860 Office: PO Box 6248 Providence RI 02940

LEIGH, DAVID ALAN, architect; b. Murray Bridge, Australia, Sept. 23, 1949; s. Alan Henry and Nancy Peace (Watson) L.; m. Josephine Ann O'Dwyer, May 9, 1970; children: Joanna Chandra, Danielle Nancy. Student, Royal Melbourne Inst. Tech., 1969-73; degree in Architecture, South Australian Inst. Tech., Adelaide, 1975. Sr. architect Australian Nat., Adelaide, 1975-81; dir. Snowden-Leigh Assocs., Adelaide, 1981-84, Kean Milne Holden Assocs., Adelaide, 1984-85; mng. dir. David Leigh Architects, Adelaide, 1985—; panel mem. Architect's Advisory Service, Adelaide, 1975—. Mem. Royal Australian Inst. Architects, Full Gospel Businessmen's Fellowship Internat., Onkaparinga Radio Aeromodellers, Southern Soaring League. Mem. Pentecostal Ch. Office: 92 Melbourne St, 5006 North Adelaide Australia

LEIGH, GEOFFREY NORMAN, real estate company executive; b. London, Mar. 23, 1933; s. Morris and Rose Leigh; m. Sylvia King, 1976; 5 children. Attended Haberdasher's Aske's Sch., London, U. Mich. Chief exec. Allied London Properties Plc, 1970—. Clubs: Hurlingham, Carlton, Saville. Office: Allied London Properties, 26 Manchester Sq, London W1M 6EU, England

LEIGH, RUTH R., interior designer; b. N.Y.C., Feb. 19; d. A. Lawrence and Anne (Frieder) Sokolski; m. Murray Stuart Leigh, June 13, 1943 (dec. Jan. 1983); 1 dau., Leslie Susan Leigh Griffith. Student Hunter Coll., 1934-36, U. Pa. Wharton Sch., 1942. Sales dept. mgr., buyer Saks 34th St., N.Y.C., 1935-37; radio commls. WMCA, N.Y.C., 1936-39; interior decorator Roxberg, Inc., N.Y.C., 1937-40; broker Harold N. Sloane Co., ins. brokers,

N.Y.C., 1940-43; br. mgr. Manpower Inc., N.Y.C., 1952-53; interior designer Storr & Co., N.Y.C., 1949—; builder-broker Ruth S. Leigh, N.Y.C., 1965—. Dist. dir. Girl Scouts U.S.A., 1952-54; fund raiser N.Y. Heart Assn., 1955—, Salvation Army, 1960—; mem. chmn.'s com. U.S. Senatorial Bus. Adv. Bd., 1980—; dir. Interfaith Neighbors, 1964-66; dist. liaison officer Black & White Assos. supporting Odyssey House Drug Addicts, 1969-70; trustee Bloomingdale House of Music; mem. U.S. Senatorial Bus. Adv. Bd., 1982—, Republican Senatorial Inner Circle, 1983-85. Mem. Real Estate Bd. N.Y., Unitarian-Universalist Women's Fedn. (dist. pres. 1966-70), Am. Unitarian Assn. (asst. non-govtl. orgn. rep. UN, nat. chmn. UN seminars 1958-62). Unitarian (v.p. bd. trustees 1972, deacon 1974—, chmn. commn. ch. community 1977-80). Home: 945 Fifth Ave New York NY 10021 Office: 127 E 59th St New York NY 10022

LEIGHTON, CHARLES MILTON, specialty consumer products executive; b. Portland, Maine, June 4, 1935; s. Wilbur F. and Elizabeth (Loveland) L.; A.B., Bowdoin Coll., 1957; M.B.A., Harvard, 1960; m. Deborah Throop Smith, Aug. 30, 1958; children—Julia Loveland, Anne Throop. Produce line mgr. Mine Safety Appliances Co., Pitts., 1960-64; instr. Harvard Bus. Sch., 1964-65; group v.p. Bangor Punta Corp., Boston, 1965-69; chmn., chief exec. officer CML Group, Inc., Boston, 1969—; bd. dirs. Smart Names, Waltham, Mass., New Eng. Mut. Life Ins. Co. Past pres. Alumni Harvard Bus. Sch., Cambridge, Mass. Republican. Episcopalian. Clubs: New York Yacht (rear commodore); Chatham (Mass.) Yacht (vice commodore 1957); Harvard of N.Y.C. and Boston, Harvard Bus. Sch. (Boston); Somerset. Home: 33 Liberty St Concord MA 01742 Office: CML Group Inc 524 Main St Acton MA 01720

LEIGHTON, FRANCES SPATZ, writer, journalist; b. Geauga County, Ohio; m. Kendall King Hoyt, Feb. 1, 1984. Student, Ohio State U. Washington corr. Am. Weekly; corr. and Washington editor This Week Mag.; Washington corr. Met. Group Sunday Mags.; contbg. editor Family Weekly; free-lance journalist Metro Sunday Group, Washington; lectr. summer confs. Dellbrook-Shenandoah Coll., Georgetown U., Washington. Author over 30 books on hist. figures, celebrities, Hollywood, psychiatry, the White House and Capitol Hill, 1957—; (with Frank S. Caprio) How to Avoid a Nervous Breakdown, 1969, (with Mary B. Gallagher) My Life with Jacqueline Kennedy, 1969, (with William Fishbait Miller) Fishbait—the Memoirs of the Congressional Doorkeeper, 1977, (with Lillian Rogers Parks) My 30 Years Backstairs at the White House (made into TV mini-series), 1979, (with Hugh Carter) My Life with the Carter Family of Plains, Georgia, 1978, (with Jerry Cammarata) The Fun Book of Fatherhood-or How the Animal Kingdom is Helping to Raise the Wild Kids at Our House, 1978, (with Natalie Golos) Coping with Your Allergies, 1979, (with Ken Hoyt) Drunk Before Noon—The Behind the Scenes Story of the Washington Press Corps, 1979, (with Louis Hurst) The Sweetest Little Club in the World, The Memoirs of the Senate Restaurateur, 1980, (with John M. Szostak) In the Footsteps of Pope John Paul II, 1980, (with Lillian Rogers Parks) The Roosevelts, a Family in Turmoil, 1981, (with June Allyson) June Allyson, 1982, (with Beverly Slater) Stranger in My Bed, 1985 (made into TV movie, 1986), The Search for the Real Nancy Reagan, 1987; Contbr. numerous feature stories on polit., social and govtl. personalities to various publs. Bd. dirs. Nat. Found., from 1963. Recipient Edgar award, 1961. Mem. Senate Periodical Corr. Assn., White House Corr. Assn., Am. News Women's Club, The Writers Club, Nat. Press Club, Writers League Washington (pres.), Smithsonian Associates, Nat. Trust Historic Preservation, Delta Phi Delta, Sigma Delta Chi. Unitarian. Office: 1035 Nat Press Bldg Washington DC 20045

LEIGHTON, LAWRENCE WARD, investment banker; b. N.Y.C., July 1, 1934; s. Sidney and Florence (Ward) L.; m. Mariana Stroock, June 21, 1959; children: Sandra Florence, Michelle Stroock. BSE, Princeton U., 1956; MBA, Harvard U., 1962. Vice pres. Kuhn Loeb & Co., N.Y.C., 1962-69, Clark, Dodge & Co., Inc., N.Y.C., 1970-74, Norton-Simon, Inc., N.Y.C., 1974-78, ltd. ptnr. Bear, Stearns & Co., N.Y.C., 1978-82; mng. dir. Chase Investment Bank, 1983—. Mem. exec. com. Princeton U. Alumni Council, 1975-80; vice chmn. nat. schs. com. Princeton U., 1980—; chmn. Harvard Bus. Sch. Fund of N.Y., 1964-65; mem. nat. fin. com. Pete DuPont for Pres., 1986-88. Served to lt. (j.g.) USN, 1957-60. Clubs: Stanwich (Greenwich, Conn.); Princeton Club of N.Y. (scholarship com. 1970—); Coral Beach and Tennis (Bermuda). Avocations: flying; golf. Home: 1088 Park Ave New York NY 10128

LEIMKUHLER, GERARD JOSEPH, JR., financial holding company executive; b. Phila., June 13, 1948; s. Gerard Joseph and Dorothy Joan (Gaffney) L.; m. Karen Roberta Hall, Oct. 13, 1973; 1 child, Courtney Hall. B.B.A., Temple U., 1970. Mem. Phila. Stock Exchange, 1971-75; v.p. Oxford First Corp., Phila., 1975-82, sr. v.p., 1982-87, exec. v.p., 1987—; sr. v.p., sec. Oxford Communitities, Inc. Oxford Fin. Cos. Inc., Phila., 1985-87, exec. v.p., sec., 1987—; pres. Gen. Acquistions Corp., Phila., 1977—, also dir.; dir. First Fin. Reality Inc., First Homesites, Inc., First So. Corp., Money Mgmt. Inc., Home Security Corp.; corp. sec. Oxford First Corp., Oxford Communities, Inc., Oxford Fin. Cos., Inc. Mem. Newtown Twp. Planning Commn., Delaware County, Pa., 1976-77, 84—; chmn. Newtown Twp. Investment Adv. Bd. Served with U.S. Army, 1970-71. Mem. Nat. Assn. Securitites Dealers, Am. Mgmt. Assn., Urban Land Inst., Mensa. Republican. Roman Catholic. Clubs: Aronimink Golf, Malta Boat, Temple U. Varsity. Home: 306 French Rd Newtown Square PA 19073 Office: Oxford First Corp 7300 Old York Rd Philadelphia PA 19126

LEINBERGER, CHRISTOPHER BROWN, urban development consultant, writer; b. Charleston, W.Va., Jan. 2, 1951; s. Fredrick Arthur and Helen (Brown) L.; m. Madeleine LeMoyne McDougal, Aug. 25, 1973; children: Christopher Jr., Rebecca. BA in Urban Sociology, Swarthmore Coll., 1972; MBA, Harvard U., 1976. Asst. to pres. ARA Food Services, Inc., Phila., 1973-74, 76-77; dir. concept devel. Saga Corp., Menlo Park, Calif., 1977-79; exec. v.p. Robert Charles Lesser & Co., Beverly Hills, Calif., 1979-82, mng. ptnr., co-owner, 1982—. Contbr. articles to profl. jours. and nat. print media including The Wall Street Jour., Los Angeles Times and The Atlantic Monthly. Vice chmn. Swarthmore Coll. Capital Funds Dr., Los Angeles, 1986. Fellow NSF, 1971, NCAA, 1972, Coro Found., 1972-73. Mem. Urban Land Inst. (council mem. 1984—). Democrat. Clubs: Zamarono (Los Angeles); Juan Tomas (Santa Fe, N.Mex.). Home: Las Milpas PO Box 489 Tesuque NM 87574 Office: Robert Charles Lesser & Co 128 E DeVargas St Santa Fe NM 87501

LEINIEKS, VALDIS, classicist, educator; b. Liepaja, Latvia, Apr. 15, 1932; came to U.S., 1949, naturalized, 1954; s. Arvid Ansis and Valia Leontine (Brunaus) L. B.A., Cornell U., 1955, M.A., 1956; Ph.D., Princeton U., 1962. Instr. classics Cornell Coll., Mount Vernon, Iowa, 1959-62, asst. prof. classics, 1962-64; assoc. prof. classics Ohio State U., 1964-66; assoc. prof. classics U. Nebr., Lincoln, 1966-71, prof. classics, 1971—, chmn. dept. classics, 1967—, chmn. program comparative lit., 1970-86, interim chmn. dept. modern langs., 1982-83. Author: Morphosyntax of the Homeric Greek Verb, 1964; The Structure of Latin, 1975; Index Nepotianus, 1976; The Plays of Sophokles, 1982. Contbr. articles to profl. jours. Mem. AAUP, Am. Classical League, Classical Assn. Middle West and South, Am. Philol. Assn. Republican. Home: 2505 A St Lincoln NE 68502 Office: U Nebr Dept Classics Lincoln NE 68588

LEININGER, ELMER, emeritus chemistry educator; b. Milw., Apr. 19, 1900; s. Philip Henry and Louise (Hardtke) L.; B.S., Carroll Coll., 1923; postgrad. U. Wis., 1923-24; M.S., Mich. State U., 1931; Ph.D., U. Mich., 1941; m. Hazel Ann MacNamara, Dec. 30, 1924 (dec. June 1961); 1 dau., Mary Louise (Mrs. Robert Reed); m. 2d, Byrnice L. Dickinson, 1964. Instr. chem. Mich. State U., 1924-30, prof. chemistry, head analytical chemistry sect. 1930-65, prof. emeritus, 1965-87; chem. cons., 1965-87. Sec., dir. Geneva Lake Civic Assn., 1968-76, 79—; bd. dirs., moderator Pilgrim Ch. Mem. Am. Chem. Soc. (chmn., councilor Mich. sect.), Am. Philatelic Soc., Sigma Xi, Alpha Chi Sigma, Phi Lambda Upsilon. Republican. Clubs: Lake Geneva Country; Green Valley (Ariz.) Country. Editorial adv. bd. Analytical Chemistry. Contbr. articles to profl. jours. Deceased, Sept. 15, 1987. Address: 5 Lake Shore Dr RR 1 Box 70 Lake Geneva WI 53147

LEINSDORF, ERICH, orchestra conductor; b. Vienna, Austria, Feb. 4, 1912; came to U.S., 1937, naturalized, 1942; s. Ludwig Julius and Charlotte (Loebl) L.; m. Anne Frohnknecht, Aug. 3, 1939 (div.); children—David, Gregor, Joshua, Hester, Jennifer; m. Vera Graf. Ed., Vienna; Mus.D. (hon.), Baldwin-Wallace Coll., Berea, Ohio, 1945, Rutgers U., 1952; Mus.D. hon. degree, Williams Coll., 1966, Columbia, 1967. Asst. condr. Salzburg Festival, 1934-37; condr. Met. Opera, until 1943, Cleve. Orch., 1943; music dir. Philharmonic Orch., Rochester, 1947-56; dir. N.Y.C. Center Opera, 1956, Met. Opera, 1957-62; music dir. Boston Symphony Orch., 1962-69; Past mem. Corp. for Pub. Broadcasting; past mem. exec. com. John F. Kennedy Center for Performing Arts; bd. dirs. Am. Arts Alliance; mem. Nat. Council on Arts. Guest appearances with maj. orchs. in, U.S., Europe, including, Phila., Los Angeles, St. Louis, New Orleans, Mpls., Concertgebouw, Amsterdam, Israel Philharmonic, San Francisco Opera, Bayreuth, Holland and Prague festival, London, BBC, London Symphony, Orchestre de Paris, Cleve. Orch., Chgo. Symphony, Berlin Philharmonic, N.Y. Philharmonic, Vienna Symphony.; Author: Cadenza, The Composer's Advocate, 1981; contbr. articles to High Fidelity, Daedalus, N.Y. Times; transcriptions of Brahms Chorale Preludes; Records for, RCA Victor, Westminster., Columbia, Decca (London), E.M.I. Fellow Am. Acad. Arts and Scis.; mem. Nat. Endowment Arts. Office: care Dodds 209 E 56th St New York NY 10022

LEIPHOLZ, HORST HERMANN EDUARD, civil engineering educator; b. Plonhofen, Germany, Sept. 26, 1919; emigrated to Can., naturalized, 1969; s. Ernst and Martha (Wohlfeil) L.; m. Ursula Schlag, May 9, 1942; children: Barbara, Gunthara. Diploma in Math., U. Stuttgart, 1958, Dr. in Engring., 1959, Docent, 1962; Dr. Engring. (hon.), U. Waterloo, 1987, Carleton U., 1987. Lectr., prof. U. Stuttgart, W. Ger, 1958-63; prof. U. Karlsruhe, 1963-69; prof. civil engring. U. Waterloo, Ont., Can., 1969-87, assoc. dean grad. studies, 1975-80, chmn. dept. civil engring., 1982-83, dean grad. studies, 1983-86, prof. emeritus, 1987—. Author: Theory of Elasticity, 1968, Theory of Stability, 1970, Direct Variational Methods and Eigen Value Problems, 1977, Stability of Elastic Systems, 1980; contbr. articles to profl. jours. Recipient award CANCAM, 1975. Fellow Am. Acad. Mechanics, Engring. Inst. of Can., Royal Soc. Can., Can. Soc. Mech. Engring.; mem. ASME, Can. Soc. Mech. Engring. (editor trans. 1981-87), Am. Math. Soc., Soc. Engring. Sci., German Assn. for Engring. Math. and Mechanics. Home: 401 Warrinton Dr, Waterloo, ON Canada N2L 2P7 Office: Univ Waterloo, Waterloo, ON Canada N2L 3G1

LEIS, HENRY PATRICK, JR., surgeon, educator; b. Saranac Lake, N.Y., Aug. 12, 1914; s. Henry P. and Mary A. (Disco) L.; m. Winogene Barnette, Jan. 8, 1944; children—Henry Patrick III, Thomas Frederick. B.S. cum laude, Fordham U., 1936; M.D., N.Y. Med. Coll., 1941. Diplomate Am. Bd. Surgery. Intern Flower and Fifth Ave Hosps., N.Y.C., 1941-42, resident, 1943-44, 46-49, attending surgeon, chief breast service, 1960-81; resident in surgery Kanawa Valley Hosp., Charleston, W.Va., 1942-43; attending surgeon, chief breast service Met. Hosp., N.Y.C., 1960-81, emeritus chief breast service, 1982—; attending surgeon Coler Meml. Hosp., N.Y.C., 1960-76; chief breast surgery Cabrini Hosp. Med. Ctr., 1978-85, cons. breast surgery, 1985—; emeritus surgeon Lenox Hill Hosp., N.Y.C., 1980-83, hon. surg. staff, 1984—; hon. surg. staff Drs. Hosp., N.Y.C., Grand Strand Gen. Hosp., Myrtle Beach, S.C., 1985—; attending surgeon Westchester County Med. Ctr., 1977-81, emeritus surgeon, 1982—; clin. prof. surgery U. S.C. Sch. Medicine, Breast Surg. Oncology, Columbia, 1985—; co-dir. breast cancer ctr., cons. in breast surgery Winthrop Univ. Hosp., Mineola, 1971—, William Jennings Bryan Dorn, VA Hosp., Columbia, S.C., 1985—; cons. in breast surgery St. Claires Hosp., N.Y.C., 1979; attending staff Richland Meml. Hosp., Columbia, 1986—, attending surgical staff, 1987—; clin. prof. surgery, 1960-81, emeritus, 1982—, co-dir. Inst. Breast Diseases, 1978—, emeritus, 1978—, chief breast service N.Y. Med. Coll., 1960-81, emeritus, 1982—; cons. in breast surgery SUNY Div. Rehab., 1965—, Med. and Surg. Specialists Plan N.Y.; mem. Am. Joint Com. on Breast Cancer Staging and End Results; v.p. N.Y. Met. Breast Cancer Group, 1975-76, pres., 1977-79; cons. Med. Advs. Selective Service System, N.Y.C. Alumni trustee N.Y. Med. Coll., 1971-76; adv. council Fordham Coll. Pharmacy, 1968—; bd. dirs. Hall Fame and Mus. Surg. History and Related Scis., 1966—. Author: Diagnosis and Treatment of Breast Lesions: The Breast, Management of Breast Lesions. Co-editor: Breast. Hone. editor Internat. Surgery Jour. Mem. editorial bd. Jour. Senolgia, 1982—; mem. editorial bd. Breast: An Internat. Jour. Contbr. numerous articles to profl. jours. Served to capt. M.C., AUS, 1944-46, PTO. Decorated knight comdr. Equestrian Order Holy Sepulchre Jerusalem, knight Mil., Order of Malta, Knight Noble Co. of the Rose; recipient award of Merit Am. Cancer Soc., 1969, cert. and award for outstanding and devoted services to indigent sick City N.Y., 1965, Dr. George Hohman Meml. medal, 1936, N.Y. Apothecaries medal, 1936, Internat. cert. merit for disting. service to surgery, 1970, award of merit N.Y. Met. Breast Cancer Group, 1976, medal of Ambrogino (Italy), 1977, Service award of Honor N.Y. Med. Coll., 1969, medaille d'Honneur (France), medal of City of Paris, 1979. Fellow ACS, Peruvian Acad. Surgery (hon.), Am. Acad. Compensation Medicine, Am. Soc. Clin. Oncology, Am. Assn. Cancer Research, Am. Geriatrics Soc., Indsl. Med. Assn., Internat. Coll. Surgeons (1st v.p. 1973-74, pres. 1977-78, v.p., chmn. council examiners U.S. sect. 1962-68, pres. 1971, Service award of honor 1971), Internat. Paleopathology Assn. (founder), N.Y. Acad. Medicine, N.Y. Council Surgeons, Royal Soc. Health (Eng.); mem. AAAS, AAUP, Am. Cancer Soc. (com. breast cancer), Am. Med. Writers Assn., AMA, Am. Profl. Practice Assn., Assn. Am. Med. Colls., Am. Coll. Radiology (com. mammography and breast cancer), Assn. Mil. Surgeons U.S., Cath. Physicians Guild (pres. N.Y. 1970-78), Gerontol. Soc., Internat. Platform Assn., N.Y. Acad. Scis., N.Y. Cancer Soc., N.Y. County Med. Soc., N.Y. Surg. Soc., Pan Am Med. Assn. (v.p. N.Am. sect. on cancer 1967—), Pan Pacific Surg. Assn. (v.p. 1980, Res. Officers Assn. U.S., Soc. Acad. Achievement (editorial bd. 1969—), Soc. Med. Jurisprudence, Soc. Nuclear Medicine Surg. Soc. N.Y. Med. Coll., WHO, World Med. Assn., Alumni Assn. N.Y. Med. Coll. (gov. 1960—, pres. 1971), Assn. Mil. Surgeons U.S., Catholic War Vets Assn., VFW, Hollywood Acad. Medicine (hon.), Alpha Omega Alpha, Phi Chi; hon. mem. Argentine Soc. Mammary Pathology, Argentina Cardiac and Thoracic Surg. Soc., Ecuador Med. Assn., Mo. Surg. Soc., Venezuela Surg. Soc., Italian Surg. Soc., S.C. Oncology Soc., So. Med. Assn. Club: Ocean Dunes. Lodge: K.C. (4th deg.).

LEISHER, GEORGE LOY, JR., pharmaceutical executive; b. St. Louis, Feb. 11, 1945; s. George Loy and Wilma (Schrumm) L.; A.Bus., St. Louis Jr. Coll., 1966; B.S.B.A., U. Mo., 1967, postgrad. Law Sch., 1968; m. Rebecca Callaham, May 29, 1970. Asst. personnel dir. Edwin Guth Co., St. Louis, 1967-70; dir. indsl. relations Falstaff Brewing Co., St. Louis, 1970-73; dir. personnel and tng. St. Louis County Dept. Police, St. Louis, 1973-76; corp. v.p. personnel and indsl. relations, dir. K-V Pharm. Co., St. Louis, 1976-84; corp. v.p. human resources Orlove Corp. Group, Ft. Lauderdale, Fla., 1984—. Vice pres. Affton Young Republicans, 1963, treas. Mo. Young Republicans, 1966; sec. Mark Twain Residence Jud. Bd., mem. Rep. Presdl. Task Force, 1981; bd. dirs. Goodwill Industries, Galveston, 1971-72; pres., bd. dirs. Deer Creek Improvement Assn., 1985—; bd. dirs. pharmacy task force Southeastern Coll. Osteo. Medicine; prof. bus. econs. Jr. Achievements. Served in U.S. Army, 1969. Mem. Am. Soc. Personnel Adminstrn., Phi Alpha Delta, Indsl. Relations Club St. Louis. Roman Catholic. Club: Optimists. Home: 319 Woodlake Ln Deer Creek Country Club Deerfield Beach FL 33442 Office: 1900 W Commercial Blvd Fort Lauderdale FL 33309

LEISK, JAMES CLARK, petroleum engineer, consultant; b. Waldo, Ark., May 3, 1929; s. William Charles and Julia Evelyn (Fincher) L.; B.S. in Petroleum Engring., La. State U., 1951; m. Anna Glen Gute, June 25, 1955; children—Julia Ann, Catherine Glen. With Union Producing Co., 1953-67, field drilling and prodn. supt., Tinsley, Miss., 1963-67; dist. petroleum engr., then sr. engr. Pennzoil Producing Co., 1967-72; cons. T.W. McGuire & Assocs., Inc., Shreveport, 1972-78, Caddo Oil Co., Inc., 1978-82; ind. petroleum cons., 1982-87; owner Mildred's Cards & Gifts, Bossier City, La., 1987. Served as 2d lt. C.E., AUS, 1951-52. Mem. Soc. Petroleum Engrs., U.S. Power Squadrons, Delta Kappa Epsilon. Republican. Baptist. Home and Office: 4026 Gilbert Shreveport LA 71106

LEISNER, ANTHONY BAKER, publishing company executive; b. Evanston, Ill., Sept. 13, 1941; s. A. Paul and Ruth (Solms) L.; B.S., Northwestern U., 1964, M.B.A., 1983; children—Justina, William, Sarah. Salesman, Pitney Bowes Co., 1976-77; with Quality Books Inc., Lake Bluff, Ill., 1968—, v.p., 1972—, gen. mgr., 1979—; adj. faculty Lake Forest (Ill.) Sch. Mgmt., 1983—, Kellogg Grad. Sch. Mgmt. Northwestern U., Evanston, Ill. Pres. bd. dirs. Lake Villa (Ill.) Public Library, 1972-78; bd. dirs. No. Ill. Library Systems, 1973-78; chmn. Libertarian Party Lake County (Ill.), 1980-81; probation officer Lake County CAP, 1981. Mem. ALA, Ill. Library Assn. (Gerald L. Campbell award 1980), Am. Booksellers Assn., Acad. Mgmt., Am. Mktg. Assn., Internat. Platform Assn., World Future Soc., World Isshin Ryu Karate Assn. Author: Official Guide to Country Dance Steps, 1980; also articles. Home: 1174 Cherry St Winnetka IL 60093 Office: Quality Books Inc 918 Sherwood Dr Lake Bluff IL 60044

LEISTNER, BERND SIEGFRIED, literary scholar, writer; b. Eibenstock, Germany, May 3, 1939; s. Kurt and Gisela (Reichel) L.; m. Maria-Verena Schoch, Aug. 3, 1965; 1 child, Saskia. B in German and History, Karl Marx U., Leipzig, German Dem. Republic, 1962, Dr, 1971; Habilitation, Karl Marx U., German Dem. Republic, 1982. Tchr. Grammar Sch., Mittweida, German Dem. Republic, 1962-67, G. Dimitroff, Leipzig, German Dem. Republic, 1967-71; sr. lectr. U. Skopje, Yugoslavia, 1971-74, Karl Marx U., 1974-76; research worker Inst. for Classical German Lit., Weimar, German Dem. Republic, 1976—, vice-dir., 1978-87. Author: Unruhe um einen Klassiker, 1978, Johannes Bobrowski: Studien und Interpretationen, 1981, Spielraum des Poetischen, 1985; contbr. over 100 articles to profl. jours. Recipient Heinrich Mann prize Acad. Fine Arts German Dem. Republic, 1985. mem. Writers Assn. German Dem. Republic, PEN. Home: Alfred Kaestnerstrasse 1, 7030 Leipzig German Democratic Republic

LEISY, JAMES FRANKLIN, publisher; b. Normal, Ill., Mar. 21, 1927; s. Ernest Erwin and Elva (Krehbiel) L.; m. Emily Ruth McQueen, June 8, 1949; children: James Franklin, Scot, Rebecca. BBA, So. Meth. U., 1949. Field rep., then editor Prentice-Hall, Inc., N.Y.C., 1949-54; editor Allyn & Bacon, Inc., Boston, 1954-56; founder, exec. editor Wadsworth Pub. Co., Inc., San Francisco, 1956-59, v.p., 1959-60, pres., 1960-77, chmn., chief exec. officer, 1977-85; dep. chmn. Internat. Thomson Orgn., Inc., 1978-85; founder, chmn. Sci. Books Internat., Inc., 1981-83; founder, chmn. Linguistics Internat., Inc., 1983-85; bd. dirs. Mayfield Pub. Co., Inc., Franklin, Beedle and Assocs. Author: Abingdon Song Kit, 1957, Let's All Sing, 1958, Songs for Swinging Housemothers, 1960, Songs for Singin', 1961, Songs for Pickin' and Singin', 1962, Beer Bust Song Book, 1963, Hootenanny Tonight, 1964, Folk Song Fest, 1964, Folk Song Abecedary, 1966, Alpha Kappa Psi Sings, 1967, The Good Times Songbook, 1974, Scrooge, The Christmas Musical, 1978, Alice, A Musical Comedy, 1980, Pinocchio, A Musical Play, 1981, Tiny Tim's Christmas Carol, A Musical Play, 1981, The Pied Piper, 1982, The Nutcracker and Princess Pirlipat, 1982, A Visit from St. Nicholas, 1983, Pandora, 1984, Talkin' 'bout America, 1986, Mouse Country, 1987, The Dingaling Circus Holiday, 1987; composer: songs including Keep a Little Christmas In Your Heart, A Little Old Lady in Tennis Shoes, A Personal Friend of Mine, Please Tell Me Why, An Old Beer Bottle. Bd. dirs. Bethel Coll., Ctr. Entrepreneurial Devel., U. Calif.-Santa Cruz; bd. dirs., mem. exec. com. Calif. Council for Econ. Edn., 1968-71; mem. deans council Sch. Bus. Calif. State U., San Jose; mem. Nat. UN Day Com., 1978. Served with USNR, 1945-46. Named to Career Hall of Fame So. Meth. U., 1968; recipient Higher Edn. Achievement award Assn. of Am. Pubs., 1988. Mem. Young Pres.'s Orgn. (bd. dirs. 1970-73), Assn. Am. Pubs. (bd. dirs. 1982-85), ASCAP, So. Meth. U. Alumni Assn. (bd. dirs. 1965-70), Chief Execs. Orgn., World Business Council, Phi Eta Sigma, Alpha Phi Omega, Alpha Kappa Psi (nat. chmn. song com. 1963-71), Kappa Alpha. Club: Bohemian.

LEITCH, ALMA MAY, city official; b. Fredericksburg, Va., Nov. 24, 1924; d. Maurice Andrew Doggett and Nora May (Spicer) L.; grad. James Monroe High Sch., Fredericksburg; various specialized courses U. Va., Va. Poly. Inst. Dep. commnr. revenue City of Fredericksburg, 1946-69, commr. revenue, 1970—; mem. Va. Adv. Legis. Council, 1977-78; mem. subcom. Commonwealth Va. Revenue Resources and Econ. Commn., 1978. Bd. dirs. Fredericksburg chpt. ARC, 1960—, chmn., 1969, Fredericksburg, Stafford and Spotsylvania chpt. treas., 1988—; sec. Democratic Com. Fredericksburg, 1964; pres., bd. dirs. Rappahannock United Way for Fredericksburg, Spotsylvania, and Stafford counties, 1979; mem. Our Town Fredericksburg, Fredericksburg Area Mus. Recipient various service awards; Outstanding Citizenship award Fredericksburg Area C. of C., 1979. Mem. Commrs. Revenue Assn. Va. (pres. 1979-80), Va. Govtl. Employees Assn. (dir.-at-large 1979-80), League No. Va. Commrs. Revenue (pres. 1972), Va. Assn. Local Exec. Constl. Officers (exec. com.), Internat. Assn. Assessing Officers, Va. Assn. Assessing Officers, Hist. Fredericksburg Found., Bus. and Profl. Women's Club. Club: Ann Page Garden (pres. 1980-82, Mary B. Benoit award 1977), Altrusa. Home: 511 Hanover St Fredericksburg VA 22401 Office: City Hall Box 644 Fredericksburg VA 22401

LEITE, SILVIO CARLOS, data processing executive; b. Rio de Janeiro, Sept. 20, 1952; arrived in Switzerland, 1965; s. Sylvio and Sonia (Engelke) L., m. Monika Schwager, May 27, 1976 (div. July 1983); children: Sandra Claudia, Angela Sabrina. Grad. in Comml. and Bus. Adminstrn., High Sch. Zurich, Switzerland, 1972. Stock broker various banks, Zurich, 1972-73; dep. mgr. passenger reservations Swissair, Kloten, Switzerland, 1973-80, system planner/project mgr., 1980—; project mgr. Swissair/Varig, Zurich and Rio de Janeiro, 1982-83, Swissair/Qantas, Zurich, 1983-84, Swissair/TAP, Zurich and Lisbon, Portugal, 1985-88; cons. in field. Roman Catholic. Home: Hardackedstrasse 29, 8302 Kloten Switzerland Office: Swissair/CPMA, PO Box, 8058 Zurich Switzerland

LEITSCH, WALTER, historian, educator; b. Vienna, Austria, Mar. 26, 1926; s. Josef and Antonie (Pedajas) L.; m. Ludmilla Kunčič, Dec. 24, 1940; children: Alexander, Marie Thérèse, Markus Anton. PhD, U. Vienna, 1954; diploma, Inst. for Research of Austrian History, Vienna, 1956. Asst. Inst. Ea. European History, Vienna, 1955-56, asst. prof., 1956-64; ofcl. Ministry of Edn., Vienna, 1964-65; chmn. Inst. Ea. European History, 1965—; full prof. U. Vienna, 1965—. Author: Moskau und die Politik des Kaiserhofes, 1960; co-author: Das Institut für osteuropäische Geschichte, 1983; editor monograph series Wiener Archiv für Geschichte des Slawentums und Osteuropas, 1966—. Recipient hon. gold medal of municipality of Vienna, 1986. Home: Formanekgasse 10, A-1190 Vienna Austria Office: Inst Ost-Suedosteuropaforschung, Liebiggasse 5, 1010 Vienna Austria

LEITZKE, JACQUE HERBERT, corporation president, psychologist; b. Watertown, Wis., Dec. 25, 1929; s. Herbert Wilbert and Ruth Valberg (Stavenow) L.; m. Mary Annis Lacey, June 20, 1950 (div. Nov. 1963); children: Keith Alan, Sari Dawn, Thora Jacquelynne. BS, U. Wis., Madison, 1955; MA, Kent State U., 1958. Lic. psychologist, Wis., Ill., N.Y. Sch. psychologist BCG, N.Y.C., 1959-61; clin. psychologist Winnebago County Guidance Ctr., Neenah, Wis., 1961-64; sch. psychologist Waukegan City (Ill.) Sch. Dist. 61, 1965-66; clin. psychologist Wis., Ill., 1967-78; corp. pres., chief exec. officer Psychometrics Internat. Corp., Watertown, 1979—. Author: Definitively Incorporeal Human Intelligence Itself;originator intelligence test Abecedarian Measure of Human Intelligence, 1979. Trustee Human Intelligence Research Found. Served with USAF, 1948-51. Mem. Am. Psychol. Assn., Mensa. Home: 1153 Boughton St 808 Watertown WI 53094 Office: Psychometrics Internat Corp PO Box 247 Watertown WI 53094

LEJEUNE, JOSEPH GUILLAUME, international industrial development projects consultant; b. Maastricht, Netherlands, Feb. 25, 1914; s. Jan Joseph and Elise Agnes (Koumans) Le J.; m. Anna-Maria-Margaretha Huffener, Mar. 9, 1943. Bach. Philosophy, U. Louvain (Belgium), 1942, D.Criminology and Social Scis.; postgrad. U. Utrecht, 1946-50. Head field research Mgmt. Inst., Netherlands, 1950-56; cons. OEEC, European Prodn. Agy., Paris, 1956-58; cons. govt. Peru Internat. Lab. Office, Geneva, 1960-62; sec. gen. of Com. of Leading European Enterprises and Banks, for coop. with Latin Am., Paris, 1963-65; dir. Report on Spain for OECD, Paris, 1966-68; cons. UN Mission, UN Indsl. Devel. Orgn., UNIDO, Vienna, Austria, 1970-76; cons. assignments with European enterprises and banks for indsl. projects in developing countries, 1958-60, 68-70, 1976—. Contbr. articles on indsl. devel. projects to profl. jours. Served to capt. Dutch Army, 1944-47. Decorated Kruis van Verdienste (Order of Merit) Queen of Netherlands, 1947; Verzetscherdenkingskruis (Order of the Resistance Movement) Netherlands Govt. Mem. Soc. for Internat. Devel., Royal Air Forces Assn. Roman Catholic. Club: Stade Francais (Paris). Home: 6 Sq Castiglione, Resid Tuileries, Le Chesnay, 78150 Yvelines France

LEJINS, PETER PIERRE, criminologist, sociologist, educator; b. Moscow, Russia, Jan. 20, 1909; came to U.S., 1940, naturalized, 1944; s. Peter P. and Olga (Makarova) L.; m. Nora Muller, June 6, 1937. M. Philosophy, U. Latvia, 1930, LL.M., 1933; postgrad., U. Paris, 1934; Ph.D. (Rockefeller fellow), U. Chgo., 1938; LLD (hon.), Eastern Ky. U., 1986. Chair criminal law U. Latvia, 1938-40; prof. sociology U. Md., College Park, 1941-79, prof. emeritus, 1979—; acting dept. chmn. U. Md., 1944-46, 61; dir. Inst. Criminal Justice and Criminology, 1969-79; chmn. bd. dirs. Nat. Criminal Justice Ednl. Devel. Consortium, 1975-76; prof. Sch. Criminology, Fla. State U., 1982-84; cons. area human resources USAF, 1951—; lectr. delinquency and crime Frederick A. Moran Meml. Inst., summers 1956, 57, 63; Mem. exec. com. Correctional Service Assos., 1947-50, Com. for Am. Participation in 2d Internat. Congress Criminology, Paris, 1950; mem. U.S. delegation 12th Internat. Penal and Penitentiary Congress, The Hague, 1950, 1st UN Congress for Prevention Crime and Treatment Delinquents, Geneva, 1955, 2d Congress, London, Eng., 1960; mem. U.S. delegation 3d UN Congress for Prevention Crime and Treatment of Offenders, Stockholm, 1965, 4th Congress, Kyoto, 1970, 5th Congress, Geneva, 1975; ofl. del. various assns. 7th UN Congress on Prevention of Crime and Treatment of Offenders; U.S. corr. to UN in social def. matters, 1965-76; vice chmn. bd. Joint Commn. on Manpower and Tng. in Corrections, 1964-70; U.S. rep. Internat. Penal and Penitentiary Found., 1974—, v.p., 1981—; mem. Task Force Commd. to Study Correctional System, Joint Commn. on Mental Illness and Health, 1956-57; chmn. cons. com. Uniform Crime Reporting, FBI, 1957-58; mem. bd. Criminal Justice Assn., Washington; pres. bd. Md. Prisoners Aid Assn., 1957-60; chmn. Joint Baltic Am. Com., 1961-62, 66; exec. com. corrections sect. United Community Services, Washington; mem. Md. Gov.'s Commn. Prevention and Treatment Juvenile Offenders; mem. exec. bd. profl. council, council research, trustee Nat. Council Crime and Delinquency, 1968-71; also mem. Md. Council; chmn. adv. bd. Md. Children's Center, 1959-65; chmn. research com., adv. council Inst. Criminological Research, Dept. Corrections, D.C.; chmn. adv. bd., mem. governing bd. Patuxent Inst. Defective Delinquents; chmn. subcom. on instns. task force on correction Gov.'s Crime Commn., 1968-70; mem. research and devel. task force Nat. Adv. Commn. Criminal Justice Standards and Goals, Law Enforcement Assistance Adminstrn., 1972-74, Phase II, 1974-76, chmn., 1974-76; vis. prof. Kuwait U., 1973; pres. Am. Assn. Doctoral Programs in Criminal Justice and Criminology, 1976—. Chief editor: Jour. Research in Crime and Delinquency, 1968-69, bd. editors, 1969—. Contbr. articles to profl. jours. and encys. Chmn. Social Survey Com., 1946-47; Chmn. Community Chest Planning Council, 1949-57, both Prince Georges County, Md.; dir. Health and Welfare Council Nat. Capitol area; 1st v.p. Prince Georges County Regional Com.; bd. dirs. Washington Action for Youth, United Planning Orgn., Am. Found., 1977—; chmn. D.C. Commrs. Com. on Youth Opportunity; pres. bd. dirs. Oscar Freire Inst., Sao Paolo, Brazil, 1974-77. Recipient Alumni Profl. Achievement award U. Chgo., 1973; establishment of annual Peter P. Lejins award for outstanding research in corrections, 1987. Fellow Washington Acad. Sci., Internat. Centre Comparative Criminology; mem. Am. Correctional Assn. (dir., mem. exec. com., chmn. com. on research and planning, pres. 1962-63, chmn. research council, E.R. Cass correctional achievement award 1980), Am. Sociol. Soc. (past pres. D.C.), Eastern Sociol. Soc., So. Sociol. Soc., Soc. Advancement Criminology, Nat. Probation Assn., Internat. Soc. Criminology (pres. sci. commn. 1973-80, hon. pres. 1981—, v.p. 1981—), AAUP, Latvian Frat. Assn. (past pres.), Am. Latvian Assn. (pres. 1951-70, now hon. pres.), Free World Latvian Fedn. (pres. 1956-70), Phi Kappa Phi, Omicron Delta Kappa, Alpha Kappa Delta. Clubs: Cosmos (Washington); Faculty (U. Md.) (College Park); Pres. Club (U. Md., U. Chgo.); Lettonia (past pres.). Lodge: Rotary. Home: 7114 Eversfield Dr College Heights Estates MD 20782

LEKBERG, ROBERT DAVID, chemist; b. Chgo., Feb. 2, 1920; s. Carl H. and Esther (Forsberg) L.; m. Sandra Sakal, Oct. 19, 1970; children by previous marriage: Terry Lee, Jerrald Dean, Roger Daryl, Kathleen Sue, Keith Robin. AA, North Park Coll., 1940; BS, Lewis Inst., 1943. Chemist Glidden Co., Hammond, Ind., 1940-43, Wilson Packing Co., Calumet City, Ill., 1943-45, Libby, McNeil & Libby, Blue Island, Ill., 1945-47; chief chemist Dawes Labs., Chgo., 1947-50; owner, pres. Chemlek Labs. Inc., Alsip, Ill., 1950—, Chemlek Labs. Can. Ltd., Windsor, Ont., 1960-66; lobbyist Ill. Indsl. Council. Editor: Indsl. Dist. Assn. Newsletter, 1975—; patentee chem. processes, pollution control used in Mex., Italy and Brazil. Violinist Chgo. Civic Symphony, 1940-42, N.W. Ind. Symphony, 1976—, Chicago Heights Symphony, 1959—, Southwest Symphony, 1970—; officer with U.S. Power Squadron. Mem. Ill. Mfrs. Assn., Ill. Indsl. Council, Chgo. Feed Club. Republican. Club: Dolton Yacht (past commodore). Home: 6624 Linden Dr Oak Forest IL 60452 Office: Chemlek Labs Inc 4040 W 123d St Alsip IL 60658

LEKHANYA, JUSTIN, minister of defense and internal security of Lesotho; s. Mokhosoa Isaac Ernest L. Student St. Francis Mission, Paray Sch., Thaba-Tseka, 1952-54, Roma Coll., 1955-57. Shaft clk., Springs Mines, 1958-59; joined police force, 1960; head Ruling Mil. Council, Lesotho, 1986—, now also minister of def. and internal security. Office: Ministry of Def, Maseru Lesotho *

LELAS, SRDAN, philosophy of science educator; b. Split, Croatia, Yugoslavia, June 21, 1939; s. Ivan and Mary (Polic) L.; m. Jasmina Lučić, Apr. 4, 1964; children: Vedran, Snyežana. BS in Physics, U. Zagreb, Yugoslavia, 1961, MS in Physics, 1969, PhD, 1973. Asst. Faculty Natural Scis., Zagreb, 1962-76, assoc. prof., 1986—; Fulbright fellow Boston U., 1976-77; charter fellow Wolfson Coll., Oxford, Eng., 1986; course dir. Inter-University Ctr., Dubrovnik, Yugoslavia, 1980—; bd. dirs. Faculty Natural Scis., 1983—. Contbr. articles to profl. jours. Mem. Philosophy Sci. Assn., Croatian Phil. Soc., Croatian Soc. Physics. Home: Petrinjska 83, 41000 Zagreb Yugoslavia Office: Faculty Natural Scis, Marulicev TRG 19 PO Box 162, 41000 Zagreb Yugoslavia

LELOIR, LUIS FEDERICO, biochemist, educator; b. Paris, Sept. 6, 1906; ed. U. Buenos Aires; Dr. h.c., univs. Paris, Granada, Cordoba; m. Amelie Zuherbuhler de Leloir, 1 dau. Research chemist Inst. Biology and Exptl. Medicine, Buenos Aires, Argentina, 1946-47; dir. Inst. Biochem. Research, Campomar, 1947—; head dept. biochemistry U. Buenos Aires, 1962—; mem. directory NRC, 1958-64. Recipient Nobel prize for chemistry, 1970. Fgn. mem. Nat. Acad. Scis. (U.S.), Am. Acad. Art and Scis., Am. Philos. Soc.; mem. Argentine Assn. Advancement Sci. (chmn. 1958-59), Nat. Acad. Medicine. Maj. research includes: isolation of glucose diphosphate, 1948, of uridine diphosphate glucose, 1950, of uridine diphosphate acetylglucosamine, 1953, mechanism of glycogen, 1959, of starch biosynthesis, 1960, isolation of dolechol phosphate from liver, 1970. Address: Inst de Investigaciones Bioquímicas, Fundación Campomar, Antonio Machado 151, 1405 Buenos Aires Argentina

LELONG, PIERRE, auditor; b. Paris, May 22, 1931; s. Marcel and Jeanne (Maistrasse) L.; m. Catherine DeMargne; children: Claude Odier, Olivier, Martin, Marc, Antoine. Licencié en droit, U. Paris, 1952; Diplomá, Inst. Politiques, 1952; Ancien éleve de l'Ecole Nat. d'Adminstrn., Paris, 1957. Adminstr. Ministry of Fin. and Economic Affairs, France, 1958-62; advisor economic affairs Prime Minister Pompidou, France, 1962-67; gen. mgr. Agrl. Intervention Bd., France, 1967-68; mem. French Nat. Assembly, France, 1968-74; sec. of state Posts and Telecommunications, France, 1974-75; mem. Ct. of Auditors, Paris, 1975-77; mem. EEC Ct. of Auditors, Luxembourg, 1977-81, pres., 1981-84, mem., 1984—. Recipient Grand Croix de L'ordre de la Couronne de Chene, Luxembourg, 1985; named Chevalier de la Legion d'honneur, France, 1985. Home: 56 Rue del'Eglise, 7224 Walferdange Luxembourg Office: EEC Ct of Auditors, Kirchberg Luxembourg

LELONG, PIERRE JACQUES, mathematician; b. Paris, Mar. 14, 1912; s. Charles and Marquerite (Bronner) L.; m. France Jacqueline Fages, Dec. 22, 1933; children Jean, Henri, Francoise, Martine. ScD, U. Paris, 1941. Prof. U. Grenoble, France, 1943-45, U. Lille, France, 1945-54, U. Paris, 1954-82; prof. emeritus in math. U. Paris VI, 1982—; advisor for edn. and research Pres. de Gaulle, 1959-61; pres. Research Council of Gov., 1962-64. Author books and contbr. sci. articles to profl. jours. Pres. Commn. Math., CNRS, 1962-66; mem. section Council Econs., 1962-66. Mem. Nat. Acad. Sci. France. Home: 9 Place de Rungis, 75013 Paris France Office: U Paris VI, 4 Place Jussieu, 75005 Paris France

LEM, RICHARD DOUGLAS, painter; b. Los Angeles, Nov. 24, 1933; s. Walter Wing and Betty (Wong) L.; B.A., UCLA, 1958; M.A., Calif. State U.-Los Angeles, 1963; m. Patricia Ann Soohoo, May 10, 1958; 1 son, Stephen Vincent. Exhibited in one-man shows at Gallery 818, Los Angeles, 1965; group shows at Lynn Kottler Galleries, N.Y.C., 1973, Palos Verdes Art Gallery, 1968, Galerie Mouffe, Paris, France, 1976, Le Salon des Nations, Paris, 1984, numerous others; represented in permanent collections; writer, illustrator; Mile's Journey, 1983. Served with AUS, 1958-60. Mem. UCLA Alumni Assn. Address: 1861 Webster Ave Los Angeles CA 90026

LEM, STANISLAW, writer; b. Lvov, Poland, Sept. 12, 1921. Student, Jagellonian U. Lvov Med. Inst., Crakow, Poland. Author: (novels) Man from Mars, 1946, The Astronauts, 1951, Magellan's Cloud, 1955, Eden, 1959, The Investigation, 1959, Return form the Stars, 1961, Solaris, 1961, Memoirs Found in a Bathtub, 1963, The Invincible, 1964, His Master's Voice, 1968, A Perfect Vacuum, 1971, Bezsennošč, 1971, Transfer, 1975, The Chain of Chance, 1976, The Mask, 1976, Wizja lokalna, 1982, The Futurological Congress, 1983, Prowokacja, 1984; (stories) The Star Diaries, 1957, Book of Robots, 1961, Robots' Fairy-Tales, 1964, Cyberiad, 1965, Tales of Pirx the Pilot, 1967, Fantastyka i futurologia, 1970, Golem XIV, 1967; (essays) The Dialogues, 1957, 72, 84, Summa Technologiae, 1964, 67, 74, 84; (autobiography) High Castle, 1966; books translated into 25 langs. Mem. Polish Astronautic Soc., Polish Acad. of Scis. (Poland 2000 Com.), Sci. Fiction Research Assn., Sci. Fiction Writers Am. Office: care Zwiazek Literatow Polskich, Krakowskie Przedmiescie 87, 60-079 Warsaw Poland *

LEMASTER, SHERRY RENEE, fund raising administrator; b. Lexington, Ky., June 25, 1953; d. John William and Mary Charles (Thompson) LeM. BS, U. Ky., 1975, MS, 1984. Cert. fund raising exec.; cert. real estate agt. Lab. technician in virology, serology Cen. Ky. Animal Disease Diagnostic Lab., Lexington, 1975-76; grant coordinator, environ. specialist Commonwealth Ky. Dept. for Natural Resources and Environ. Protection, Frankfurt, 1976-78; coordinator residence hall program Murray (Ky.) State U., 1978-80; dean students Midway (Ky.) Coll., 1980-81, v.p. devel., alumnae affairs, 1981-86; dir. devel. Wilderness Road Council Girl Scouts U.S., Lexington, 1986—. Ambassador, U. Ky. Coll. Agr.; career cons. acad. support services U. Ky.; field reader U.S. Dept. Edn., 1987—; chmn. Midway chpt. Am. Heart Assn., 1981, Woodford County chpt., 1983; mem. adminstrv. bd. First United Meth. Ch., Lexington, 1982-84, 87; mem. Council for Advancement and Support Edn., 1981-86, chmn. Ky. conf., 1982; planning com. Nat. Disciples Devel. Execs. Conf., 1984; active East Ky. First Quality of Life Com. Recipient Young Career Woman award Bus. and Profl. Women's Club, Frankfort, 1981; named Ky. col., 1977, hon. sec. state, 1984. Mem. Am. Council on Edn., Nat. Soc. Fund Raising Execs. (bd. dirs. Lexington chpt. 1986), Greater Lexington Area C. of C. (accreditation com. 1982), Advancement Women in Higher Edn. Adminstrn. (former state planning com.), Ky. Assn. Women Deans Adminstrs. and Counselors (editor Newsletter 1981), U. Ky. Alumni Assn. (life), Gen. Fedn. Womens Clubs, P.E.O. (charter), Ninety-Nines Internat. Assn. Women Pilots (vice chmn. Ky. Bluegrass chpt. 1986-87, chmn. and chmn. bd. 1987-88), Lexington Jaycees, N.Y. Found. Ky. Women, Kentuckians N.Y., Pi Beta Phi Nat. Alumnae Assn. (alumnae province pres. 1980-81, sec. bd. dirs. Ky. Beta chpt. 1982-84), Alpha Kappa Psi Alumnae Assn. (charter Murray chpt.). Avocations: pvt. pilot, needlecrafts, swimming, equitation, racquetball. Home: 104 Highview Dr PO Box 4127 Midway KY 40347-4127 Office: Wilderness Rd Girl Scout Council 2277 Executive Dr Lexington KY 40505

LEMAYEV, NIKOLAY VASIL'YEVICH, government official; b. USSR, 1929. D Tech. Scis., Ufa Petroleum Inst. With Novo-Ufa Petroleum Refinery, USSR, 1953-63; mgr. Nizhekamsk Petrochem. Complex, Kazan, USSR, 1963-85; chief Ministry Petroleum Refining and Petrochem. Industry, Moscow, 1985—. Contbr. articles to profl. jours. Mem. Communist Party Soviet Union. Office: Ministry Petroleum Refining, and Petrochem Industry, Moscow USSR *

LEMBCKE, THOMAS CHARLES, clinical social worker, retailer; b. Appleton, Wis., Jan. 31, 1934; s. Clarence Herman and Miriam Isebel (Lewis) L.; B.Mus., Lawrence U., Appleton, Wis., 1956; postgrad. U. Mich., 1956; M.Div., Garrett Evang. Theol. Sem., 1962; M.S. in Social Work, U. Wis., Milw., 1974; children—Karen Sue, James Alan. Ordained to ministry United Methodist Ch., 1962; pastor United Meth. Ch., Bristol, Wis., 1958-61, Cudahy, Wis., 1961-66, Niagara and Goodman, Wis., 1966-68, Kenosha, Wis., 1968-69; exec. dir. Lakeview council Girl Scouts U.S.A., Waukegan, Ill., 1969-73; dir. social services unit Police Dept. Zion (Ill.), 1975-78; pvt. practice psychotherapy, marriage and family counseling, Zion, 1978-85; pres. Bd. Sailing Center, Inc., 1981-85; county coordinator Green River Regional Mental Health/Mental Retardation Bd., Inc., Morganfield, Ky., 1985—; instr. Coll. of Lake County and LWV Seminar on Community Leadership; guest lectr. U. Wis., Milw. and Parkside; planning com. Nat. Conf. on Police Social Work; sec. bd. missions E. Wis. Conf. United Meth. Ch., 1962-68. Bd. dirs. Contact Teleministry Lake County, 1973-76, treas., 1974, instr. group leaders, 1977; chmn. Lake County Alcohol and Drug Abuse Planning and Coordinating Council, 1978; bd. dirs. Zion-Benton Children's Service, 1976; treas. bd. dirs. Teen Center, Niagara, Wis., 1967-68; mem. Lake County Crisis Center for Prevention and Treatment of Domestic Violence. Recipient Thanks Badge, Girl Scouts U.S.A., 1973; cert. social worker, Ill. Mem. Acad. Cert. Social Workers, Nat. Assn. Social Workers, Internat. Primal Assn. Contbr. articles to publs.; organizer, developer police social services program, Zion. Home: PO Box 6152 Saginaw MI 48608-6152 Office: 125 N Poplar St PO Box 96 Morganfield KY 42437 Other: Bd Sailing Center Inc 3232 Sheridan Rd Zion IL 60099

LEMBONG, JOHANNES TARCICIUS, cardiologist; b. Tomini, Indonesia, June 10, 1930; s. Joseph and Maria (Yo) L.; m. Yetty Maria-Paula Tabanan, Sept. 7, 1958; children: Augustinus Budirahmat, Thomas Trikasih. MD, U. Indonesia Med. Sch., Jakarta, 1960; PhD, U. Dusseldorf Med. Sch., Fed. Republic of Germany, 1980. Cert. internist, cardiologist, otorhinolaryngologist, acupuncturist. Lectr. U. Indonesia Med. Sch., Jakarta, 1958-73; guest physician U. Heidelberg Med. Sch., Fed. Republic of Germany, 1973; resident physician Rhön Clin., Bad Kissingen, Fed. Republic of Germany, 1974-77, St. Elisabeth Hosp., Recklinghausen, Fed. Republic of Germany, 1977-79, Roderbirken Clin., Leichlingan, Fed. Republic of Germany, 1979-81; practice medicine specializing in cardiology, Otorhinolarngology Jakarta, 1981—; pres. commissary P.T. Pharos Indonesia Ltd. Pharm. Mfr., Jakarta, 1981—. V.p. Cath. Students Union, Jakarta, 1953; chmn. Students Cons. Council, Jakarta, 1954; dir. Jr. Econ. High Sch., Jakarta, 1953. Mem. Assn. Internists, Assn. Cardiologists. Roman Catholic. Home: Jalan Limo 39, 12210 Jakarta Indonesia Office: Jalan Tanah Abang Dua 67, 10160 Jakarta Indonesia

LEMELIN, ROGER, newspaper publisher; b. Quebec, Que., Can., Apr. 7, 1919; s. Joseph and Florida (Dumontier) L.; hon. degree Laurentian U., Sudbury, Ont., 1976; m. Valeda Lavigueur, Oct. 27, 1945; children: Pierre, Jacques, Diane and Andre (twins), Sylvie. Journalist, Time and Fortune mags., from 1948; creator TV series The Plouffe Family, in Can.; pres. DuBuisson Prodns., from 1960; pres., pub. French daily La Presse, Montreal, 1972-82. Guggenheim Found. fellow; Rockefeller Found. fellow. Mem. Royal Soc. Can., Acad. Goncourt, Can. News Hall Fame. Clubs: Mt. Royal, St. Denis (Montreal); Garrison (Quebec). Author: The Town Below, 1944, The Plouffe Family, 1949, Fantaisies sur les peches capitaux, 1949, In Quest of Spendor, 1952; also articles, revs. Office: La Presse, 7 St James St, Montreal, PQ Canada H2Y 1K9 Home: 4753 Felix St, Cap Rouge, PQ Canada G0A 1K0 *

LEMÉNAGER, JACQUES LOUIS, physician, educator; b. Caen, Normandie, France, Mar. 30, 1918; s. Léon Eugène and Suzanne Estelle (Hébré) L.; m. Jacqueline Béringer, July 6, 1943; children: Anne, Jean-François, Bernard. MD, U. Paris, 1945, prof. agrégé de medecine, 1958. Intern Hosps. of U. Paris, 1947-51; prof. chest diseases Faculté de Medecine, U. Caen, France, 1958-86; chief chest diseases Univ. Hosp., Caen, 1958-86; pres. assn. to aid patients with chronic respiratory failure, Caen, 1976—. Author books on chest disease; contbr. articles to profl. jours. Served with Mil. Health Service, Army of France, 1939-41, 44-45. Decorated chevalier de l'Ordre Nat. du Merite, chevalier de la Legion d'Honneur. Mem. Société de Pneumologie de Langue Française, Société Française de Cardiologie, Société Medicale des Hospitaux de Paris, Internat. Union Against Tuberculosis, L'Academie Nationale de Medecine (corr.). Roman Catholic.

LEMIRE, DAVID STEPHEN, school counselor; b. Roswell, N.Mex., May 23, 1949; s. Joseph Armon and Jeanne (Longwill) L.; B.A., Linfield Coll., 1972, M.Ed., 1974; Ed. S., Idaho State U., 1978; Ed. S.in Ednl. Adminstrn. and Instructional Leadership, U. Wyo., 1988.Cert. sch. counselor, student personnel worker, psychology instr., Calif. Sch. counselor, psychol. technician and tchr. Goshen County Sch. Dist. 1, Torrington, Wyo., counselor Aspen High Sch., Aspen, Colo.; sch. counselor Unita County Sch. Dist., Evanston, Wyo., coordinator research and devel. Lifelong Learning Ctr. 1986—; pres. David Lemire Software Enterprises, Evanston; dir. Inst. for Advanced Study of Thinkology. Mem. Nat. Assn. Sch. Psychologists, Am. Psychol. Assn., Am. Assn. for Counseling and Devel. Editor WACD Jour.; mng. editor Jour. Humanistic Edn.; contbr. articles to profl. jours. Address: PO Box 1325 Laramie WY 82070-1325 Office: U Wyo Box 4285 Laramie WY 82071 also: Creative Self Inst Adminstrv Offices 2390 Riviera St Reno NV 89509

LEMIRE, LAURENT PIERRE ALFRED, journalist; b. Paris, France, Jan. 4, 1961; s. Jean-Pierre and Anna (Kafara) L. Degree in (art), Coll. de France, Paris, 1980; degree in (sci.), Paris VII Jussieu, 1981; degree in (art), Sorbonne, Paris, 1981. Cert. journalist. Journalist Radio Monte Carlo, Paris, 1981-82; parliamentary asst. Assemblée Nationale, Paris, 1983; journalist La Croix Newspaper, Paris, 1983—. Roman Catholic. Home: 38 rue Stephenson, 75018 Paris France Office: La Croix, 3 rue Bayard, 75008 Paris France

LEMKE, CORRINE LARUE, university grants official; b. Sabin, Minn., May 25, 1934; d. Oswald Edward and Ida M. (Krabbenhoft) L. B.A. in Philosophy, Moorhead State U., 1972. Notary pub., Minn. With WDAY radio and TV sta., Fargo, N.D., 1953-67; fin. aid grant coordinator Moorhead State U., 1967—, mem. task force study of changing student mix, 1983-84. Vol. Comstock Hist. House, Moorhead. Recipient cert. Gov. Minn., 1976, 10 yr. service award Moorhead State U., 1980, letter of commendation U.S. Dept. Edn., 1983. Mem. Minn. Assn. Fin. Aid Adminstrs., Midwest Assn. Student Fin. Aid Adminstrs., Minn. Hist. Soc., State Hist. Soc. North Dakota, State Hist. Soc. Wis., Concordia Hist. Inst. of St. Louis, Phoenix Soc. of Moorhead, Concordia Coll. Alumni Assn., Moorhead State U. Alumni Assn. Lutheran. Author pvt. family history publs. Home: 3209 Village Green Dr East Moorhead MN 56560 Office: Moorhead State U Moorhead MN 56560

LEMONDE, NORMAND GERARD, electronics engineer; b. Woonsocket, R.I., July 28, 1937; s. Gerard and Alice (Badeau) L.; student Brown U., 1956-57, Monmouth Coll., 1965-66; divorced; children—Gerard, David, Lisa, Nicole. Devel. engr. ITT Info. Systems, 1961-63; engring. mgr. Electronic Assocs., Inc., West Long Branch, N.J., 1963-75, chief engr., 1981-85; pres. Seaview Group, 1985—; sr. mgr. computer engring. Perkin-Elmer Corp., Tinton Falls, N.J., 1975-81; cons. computer systems engring. Mem. U.S. Senatorial Bus. Adv. Bd. Served with U.S. Army, 1958-61. Recipient Medal of Merit, Republican Presdl. Task Force, 1980. Mem. Bricklin Internat. Owners Club. Patentee in field of computers. Home: 205 Ivins Rd Neptune NJ 07753

LEMP, JOHN, JR., telecommunications engineer; b. Trenton, N.J., Dec. 10, 1936; s. John and Helena M. (Braddock) L.; B.S. in Elec. Engring., Princeton U., 1959; M.S. in Elec. Engring., Poly. Inst. Bklyn., 1968; M.B.A., Colo. State U., 1973; grad. Air Command and Staff Coll., 1974; grad. Indsl. Coll. Armed Forces, 1981; m. Susan N. Rose, 1955; children—John, Thomas K., Carl A., Adam F.H. Project engr. Gen. Devices, Inc., Princeton, N.J., 1959-60; with Bell Telephone Labs., N.J. and Colo., 1962-74; mgr. bus. planning Aeronutronic Ford Corp., Willow Grove, Pa., 1974-76; mgr. research and devel. ITT, Corinth, Miss., 1976-78; lectr. Sch. Bus., Temple U., Phila., 1976, Sch. Bus., U. Colo., 1982—; project leader Nat. Telecommunication and Info. Adminstrn., U.S. Dept. Commerce, Boulder, Colo., 1978-82; dir. Info. Access Systems, Inc., 1981-84. Lemp Devel. Co., Inc., 1975—. Mem. CAP, 1970—; pres. Carolyn Heights Civic Assn., 1972-73; treas. Frazier Woods Civic Assn., 1975-76. Served with USAF, 1960-63; served to col. USAFR, 1973-74, 80-81. Decorated Air Force Commendation medal, Meritorious Service medal; named Outstanding Elec. Engr., Armed Forces Communications & Electronics Assn., 1959; cert. instrument flight instr., FAA. Mem. IEEE (sr.), Armed Forces Communications and Electronics Assn., Assn. Computing Machinery, Inst. Mgmt. Sci., Air Force Assn. Patentee in field; contbr. articles to profl. jours. Home: 3745 23d St Boulder CO 80302 Office: U Colo PO Box 419 Boulder CO 80309

LEMPERT, PHILIP, advertising executive; b. East Orange, N.J., Apr. 17, 1953; s. Sol and Lillian E. L.; B.S. in Mktg., Drexel U., 1974; M.S. in Package Design, Pratt Inst., 1978. Account exec. The Lempert Co., Belleville, N.J., 1974-76, art dir., 1977, creative dir., 1978, v.p., 1978-81, pres., 1981—; adj. prof. Fairleigh Dickinson U., Seton Hall U. Co-chmn. new leadership com. United Jewish Appeal, 1978-80; Drexel U. Alumni ambassador, 1976—; v.p. Sons of Bosses, 1975-77. Pub., editor newsletter The Lempert Report. Recipient 1st prize in graphic Printing Industries N.Y., 1979, 80, 1st prize in packaging Nat. Office Products Assn., 1976, 77, 2d prize, 1978, Art Dirs. award, 1980, 81, 82. Mem. Packaging Inst., Graphic Artists Guild, Nat. Food Brokers Assn. (chmn. food services com.), Am. Mktg. Assn. Republican. Jewish. Clubs: Greenbrook Country, B'nai B'rith. Lodge: Rotary. Office: 202 Belleville Ave Belleville NJ 07109

LENAS, PARIS PROCOPIOU, mechanical engineer; b. Nicosia, Cyprus, Apr. 2, 1936; s. Procopios and Marie (Peonidou) L.; m. Mary Theodoulou, June 1, 1943; children: Pavlina, Marios. Diploma Mech. Engring., London Poly., 1958; postgrad., U. Toronto, 1967, U. Toronto, 1967. Registered profl. engr., Cyprus. V.p., mgr. Lenas & Charalambides, Nicosia, 1960-66, Newform Furniture Co., Nicosia, 1969-74; mng. dir. MKL Ltd., Nicosia, 1969-74; sr. ptnr., pres. GEMAC Cons., Nicosia, 1969—. Mem. Ho. of Reps., Nicosia, 1976-81. Fellow Brit. Inst. of Mgmt.; mem. Cyprus Profl. Engrs., ASHRAE, Assn. Energy Engrs., Brit. Inst. Mgmt. Mem. Democratic Rally Party. Greek Orthodox. Lodges: Rotary (chmn. 1988—), Solon. Home: 4 Metochiou St, Nicosia Cyprus Office: GEMAC, 73 Prodromos St, Nicosia Cyprus

LENCEK, RADO L., Slavic languages educator; b. Mirna, Yugoslavia, Oct. 3, 1921; came to U.S., 1956; s. Ludovik Ivan and Kati (Jaksa) L.; m. Nina A. Lovrencic, May 4, 1946; children—Bibi-Alice, Lena-Maria. Studied Slavic philology, U. Ljubljana, Slovenia, 1940-45, U. Padova, Italy, 1945-46; teaching diploma, Istituto Magistrale, Gorizia, Italy, 1947; M.A. in Linguistics, U. Chgo., 1959; Ph.D. in Slavic Langs., Harvard U., 1962. Asst. prof. Istituto Magistrale Sloveno, Gorizia-Trieste, Italy, 1944-55; editor USIS-Trieste, Italy, 1951-54; asst. prof. U. Ill., Urbana, 1962-65; asst. prof. Slavic langs. Columbia U., N.Y.C., 1965-69, assoc. prof., 1969-74, prof., 1974—; mem. Inst. on E. Cen. Europe; assoc. Averell Harriman Inst. for Advanced Study of the Soviet Union; vis. assoc. prof. NYU, 1969-72; vis. prof. Yale U., 1974, U. Ill., Urbana, 1977; U.S. coordinator for Cooperation Project on Slavistics. Author: Ob Jadranu, Ethnographic Studies, 1947, The Verb Pattern of Contemporary Slovene, 1966, A Bibliographical Guide to Slavic Civilizations, 1966, The Structure and History of Slovene Language, 1982; editor (with others): Xenia Slavica, Gojko Ruzicic Festschrift, 1975, The Dilemma of the Melting Pot: The Case of the South Slavic Languages, 1976, To Honor Jernej Kopitar, 1780-1980, 1982,; (series) Papers in Slovene Studies, 1975-76; contbr. articles in field of Slavic linguistics and cultures to scholarly jours. and proceedings of internat. confs., symposiums. NSF grantee, 1974, 79; Fulbright fellow, 1986. Fellow Am. Council Learned Socs., Bulgarian Acad. Scis.; mem. Am. Assn. for SE European Studies, Bulgarian Studies Assn., Società Filologica Friulana, Slovenska Kulturna Akcija, Linguistic Soc. Am., Linguistic Circle of N.Y., N.Y. Acad. of Scis., Am. Assn. Advancement Slavic Studies, Am. Assn. Tchrs. Slavic and East European Langs., Soc. Slovene Studies (founder, pres. 1973-83). Home: 560 Riverside Dr New York NY 10027 Office: Columbia U 420 W 118th St New York NY 10027

LENDL, IVAN, professional tennis player; b. Ostrava, Czechoslovakia, Mar. 7, 1960. Winner, Italian Jr. Singles, 1978, French Jr. Singles, 1978, Wimbledon Jr. Singles, 1978, Spanish Open Singles, 1980, 81, S.Am. Open Singles, 1981, Can. Open Singles, 1980, 81, WCT Tournament of Champions Singles, 1982, WCT Masters Singles, 1982, WCT Finals Singles, 1982, Volvo Masters, 1983, Can. Open, 1983, French Open, 1984, 86, Monte Carlo Open, 1985, Suntory Cup, 1985, Tournament of Champs, 1985, U.S. Clay, 1985, U.S. Open, 1985, 86, 87, Mercedes Cup, 1985, Australian Indoor, 1985, European Champion, 1985, AT&T Challenge, 1986, Nabisco Masters, 1986,

U.S. Pro Indoor, 1986, Lipton Internat. Players Champ., 1986, Italian Open, 1986, Volvo Internat., 1986. Avocations: golf, hockey. Office: care Jerry Solomon ProServe Inc 888 17th St NW Washington DC 20006 *

LENDVAI, PAUL, communications company executive; b. Budapest, Hungary, Aug. 24, 1929; arrived in Austria, 1957; s. Andor and Edith (Polacsek) L.; m. Margaret Gordon Pollock. Grad., U. Law, Budapest, 1951. Reporter Kossuth Nepe newspaper, Budapest, 1948, Szabad Nep newspaper, Budapest, 1949; dept. chief Magyar Tavirati Iroda (state news agy.), Budapest, 1949-52; mem. editorial bd. Esti Hirlap newspaper, Budapest, 1957; corr. London Fin. Times, Vienna, Austria, 1960-82; head of programs Ea. Europe Austrian Radio and TV, Vienna, 1982-87; dir. Radio Austria Internat., Vienna, 1987—. Author: Eagles in Cobwebs, 1969, Antisemitism in Eastern Europe, 1971, Bureaucracy of Truth, 1981, Hungary, 1986; editor-in-chief Europaeische Rundschau jour., Vienna, 1973—. Recipient Karl Renner prize Jury of Journalists, 1974, Medal of Honor Pres. of Austria, 1974, Great Medal of Honor, 1986. Mem. Internat. Inst. for Strategic Studies, Austrian Soc. Fgn. Relations, PEN of Austria. Office: ORF Ctr, Wuerzburggasse 30, A-1136 Vienna Austria

LENIHAN, BRIAN JOSEPH, Irish government official; b. Dundalk, County Louth, Ireland, Nov. 17, 1930; s. Patrick J. and Ann (Scanlon) L.; m. Ann Devine, 1958; 4 boys, 1 girl. Student, St. Mary's Coll., Athlone, Ireland; BA, U. Coll., Dublin; LLB, King's Inns Coll., Dublin. Bar: Ireland 1952. Parliamentary sec. to Minister for Lands, Dublin, 1961-64; minister justice Ireland, Dublin, 1964-68, minister edn., 1968-69, minister transport and power, 1969-73, minister fgn. affairs, 1973, 79-81, 87—, minister fisheries, 1977-79, minister agr., 1982, now dep. prime minister. Home: 24 Parkview, Castleknock, Dublin Ireland Office: Ministry Fgn Affairs, 80 St Stephen's Green, Dublin 2 Ireland *

LENKO, ALEXANDER, computer systems and security consultant; b. Walbrzych, Poland, 1, 1947; came to Australia, 1949; s. Sina and Dora (Nissenbaum) L.; m. Eva Kuntzman, Aug. 4, 1974; children—Eytan, Talya, Gali, Dana. B.Sc., Monash U., Melbourne, Australia, 1968; B.Sc. with honors, LaTrobe U., Melbourne, 1969; Dipl. Comm. EDP, Royal Melbourne Inst Tech., 1974. Research chemist ICI Australia Ltd., Melbourne, 1970-72; analyst/programmer Gen. Motors Holden, Melbourne, 1972-74; CIG, Melbourne, 1974; EDP auditor Nat. Australia Bank, Melbourne, 1974-83; computer systems and security cons. TANTAL Pty. Ltd., Melbourne, 1983—, also dir.; ptnr. A.L.C.S. Computer Cons., Melbourne, 1984—; dir. Birkalen Integrated Systems Pty. Ltd., Melbourne, 1978—, C. C. Software Pty. Ltd., Melbourne, 1983—, Australian Computer Resource Centre, 1988—. Pres. LaTrobe Jewish Students, Melbourne, 1969, Jewish Grads., Melbourne, 1973-76. Mem. Australian Computer Soc., Inst. Internal Auditors (gov. Melbourne chpt. 1979-86, editor bull. 1982-83), EDP Auditors Assn. Office: ALCS Ptg Ltd, 1/83 Wellington St, Windsor, Melbourne 3182, Australia

LENMAN, BRUCE PHILIP, historian, educator; b. Aberdeen, Scotland, Apr. 9, 1938; s. Jacob Philip and May (Wishart) L. MA in History with 1st class honors, Aberdeen U., 1960; MLitt, U. Cambridge, 1965, LittD, 1986. Asst. prof. U. Victoria, B.C., Can., 1963; lectr. Queen's Coll., Dundee, Scotland, 1963-67, U. Dundee, 1967-72; lectr. U. St. Andrews, Scotland, 1972-78, sr. lectr., 1978-83, reader in modern history, 1983—; James Pinckney Harrison prof. history Coll. William and Mary, Williamsburg, Va., 1988—; mem. econs. and bus. studies panel Scottish Edn. Dept., Edibugh, 1979-81, humanities sub.-com. Council for Nat. Acad. Awards, London, 1985-87. Author: Economic History of Modern Scotland, 1977 (Scottish Arts Council award 1977), The Jacobite Risings 1689-1746, 1980 (Scottish Arts Council award 1980), Scotland 1746-1832, 1981, The Jacobite Clans of the Great Glen, 1984, The Jacobite Cause, 1986. Brit. Acad.-Newberry Library fellow, 1982; John Carter Brown Library fellow, 1984. Fellow Royal Hist. Soc.; mem. Scottish History Soc. (council 1969-72), Am. Soc. for 18th Century Scottish Studies (co-founder), Soc. Antiquaries of Sctoland (council 1968-71), Hakluyt Soc. Clubs: Royal Commonwealth (London); New Golf (St. Andrews). Office: U St Andrews, Dept Modern History, St Katherine's Lodge, The Scores, Saint Andrews KY16 9AL, Scotland

LENNARTSON, JAMES ROGER, mktg. exec.; b. Jamestown, N.Y., June 6, 1933; s. Anders Leo and Elna Signey (Bloomberg) L.; B.S., U. Buffalo, 1956; m. Barbara Ann Wilson, Jan. 25, 1958; children—Jennifer Lynn, James Roger. Asst. account exec. power systems Westinghouse Nuclear Center, Pitts., 1962-63, sr. account exec. nuclear communications, 1963-66, asst. mgr. power systems mktg. communications, 1966-68, mgr. power systems mktg. communications, 1968-72, staff mgr. mktg. communications, 1972—. Mem. Atomic Indsl. Forum, Pitts. Conv. and Visitors Bur., Assn. Nat. Advertisers. Republican. Presbyterian. Club: Rotary. Office: Westinghouse Energy Center Box 355 Pittsburgh PA 15230

LENNON, EDWARD JAMES, editor; b. Portland, Maine, June 25, 1914; s. Edward James and Mary Elizabeth (Dostie) L.; A.B., Anderson (Ind.) Coll., 1949; M.S., U. Wis., 1950, Ph.D., 1952; m. Helen Margaret McDermott, Dec. 26, 1947; children—Keith, Charla. State editor Portland Evening News, 1935-38; asso. editor Internat. Digest, N.Y.C., 1945-46; chmn. dept. communication disorders U. Montreal, 1961-66; editor-in-chief Acta Symbolica, Memphis, 1969-72; dir. tension control summer program CHU, U. Paris VI, 1967—. Served with AUS, 1942-45. Mem. Internat. Stress and Tension Control Soc., Am. Speech-Lang.-Hearing Assn. Republican. Christian Scientist. Club: Shriners. Author: Le Bé gaiement, 1962; also short stories, articles. Home: 1302 George St Brunswick GA 31520 Office: 4 rue Tournefort, 75005 Paris France

LENNOX, DONALD D(UANE), automotive and housing components company executive; b. Pitts., Dec. 3, 1918; s. Edward George and Sarah B. (Knight) L.; m. Jane Armstrong, June 11, 1949; children: Donald D., J. Gordon. BS with honors, U. Pitts., 1947. CPA, Pa. With Ford Motor Co., 1950-69; with Xerox Corp., 1969-80; corp. v.p. and sr. v.p. info. tech. group Xerox Corp., Rochester, N.Y., 1969-73, group v.p. and pres. info. tech. group, 1973-75, group v.p., pres. info. systems group, 1975-80; sr. v.p., sr. staff officer Xerox Corp., Stamford, Conn., 1973-74; sr. v.p. ops. staff Navistar Internat. Corp., Chgo., 1980-81, exec. v.p., 1981-82, pres., chief operating officer, 1982, chmn., chief exec. officer, 1983-87; chmn., chief exec. officer Schlegel Corp., Rochester, N.Y., 1987—; also bd. dirs. Schlegel Corp., Rochester; bd. dirs. Navistar Internat. Corp., Prudential-Bache Mut. Funds, Gleason Corp. Trustee St. John Fisher Coll. Served with AC USN, 1942-45. Decorated D.F.C. with 2 gold stars, Air medal with 4 gold stars. Mem. Rochester Area C. of C. (pres. 1979), Order of Artus, Soc. Automotive Engrs., Beta Gamma Sigma. Republican. Clubs: Country of Rochester, Genesee Valley; Econ. (Chgo.), Chgo.

LENT, JOHN ANTHONY, journalist, educator; b. East Millsboro, Pa., Sept. 8, 1936; s. John and Rose (Marano) L.; children: Laura, Andrea, John, Lisa, Shahnon. B.S., Ohio U., 1958, M.S., 1960; Ph.D., U. Iowa, 1972; cert., Press Inst. of India, Sophia U., Tokyo, Japan, U. Oslo, Guadalajara, Mex., Summer Sch. Dir. public relations, instr. English W.Va. Tech., Montgomery, 1960-62; Newhouse research asst. and asst. to dir. communications research Syracuse (N.Y.) U., 1962-64; lectr. De La Salle Coll., Manila, 1964-65; asst. prof. W.Va. Tech., 1965-66; asst. prof. journalism U. Wis., Eau Claire, 1966-67; asst. prof. journalism, head tchrs.' journalism sequence Marshall U., Huntington, W.Va., 1967-69; vis. assoc. prof. U. Wyo., Laramie, 1969-70; asst. editor Internat. Communication Bull., Iowa City, 1970-72; coordinator mass communication U. Sains Malaysia, Penang, 1972-74; assoc. prof. communications Temple U., Phila., 1974-76, prof., 1976—; Benedum vis. disting. prof., 1987. Founding editor: Berita, 1975—; author: Asian Newspapers Reluctant Revolution, 1971, Asian Mass Communications: A Comprehensive Bibliography, 1975, 78, 88, Third World Mass Media and Their Search for Modernity, 1977, Broadcasting in Asia and Pacific, 1978, Topics in Third World Mass Media, 1979, Caribbean Mass Communications, 1981, Asian Newspapers: Contemporary Trends and Problems, 1982, Global Guide to Media and Communications, 1987, Videocassettes in the Third World, 1988, others; editor books in field; mem. editorial bd. Crossroads, Human Rights Quar., Communications Booknotes, Gazette, Media History Digest, Asian Thought and Society, Philippine Research Bull., Asian Profile, others; mng. editor Witty World; contbr. numerous articles to profl. jours. Awarded Chapel of Four Chaplains' Legion of Honor; Anchor Hocking scholar, 1954-58; U. Oslo scholar, 1962; Fulbright scholar Philippines, 1964-65; recipient Benedum award, 1968; Broadcast Preceptor award (2), 1979, Eberman Disting. Research award, 1988. Mem. Malaysia/Singapore/Brunei Studies Group (founding chmn. 1975-82), World Media Study Group (exec. bd.), Latin Am. Studies Assn., Caribbean Studies Assn., Assn. Asian Studies, Internat. Assn. Mass Communications Research (visual and comic art organizer), Sigma Delta Chi, Sigma Tau Delta, Kappa Tau Alpha, Phi Alpha Theta. Home: 669 Ferne Blvd Drexel Hill PA 19026 Office: Temple U Philadelphia PA 19122

LENTES, DAVID EUGENE, corporate executive; b. Spokane, Dec. 14, 1951; s. William Eugene and Ellen Elsie L.; m. Debra Kay White, May 19, 1973 (div. 1984); children: Janette Adele, Damon Arthur. AA, Spokane Falls Community Coll., 1972; BBA, Gonzaga U., 1975. V.p. Dellen Wood Products, Inc., Spokane, 1972—, also bd. dirs.; v.p. Custom Computer Services, Inc., Spokane, 1980-87, also bd. dirs.; mng. ptnr. Com-Lease, 1980-87, Len-Lease, 1980—; v.p., bd. dirs. DWP Trucking, Inc., 1982-85, Sentel Corp., 1983—, BDR Investment Corp., 1983—; pres., bd. dirs. ASA Mgmt. Corp., 1984—, also Link Internat., Inc., 1985. Treas. Dishman Hills Natural Area Assn., 1970—; elder Bethany Presbyn. Ch., 1980-83; active Spokane Econ. Devel. Council. Mem. Assn. Wash. Bus., Nat. Fedn. Ind. Businessmen, Am. Fedn. Bus., Better Bus. Bur. (Spokane chpt.), U.S. C. of C., Spokane C. of C., Timber Products Mfrs., Hoo-Hoo Internat. Republican. Office: N 3014 Flora Rd Spokane WA 99216

LENTIN, ANTONY, historian, educator; b. Leicester, Eng., May 30, 1941; s. Henry Louis and Ivy (Pollecoff) L.; m. Monica Ruth Laser, Feb. 3, 1967; 1 child, Simon Adam. BA, Clare Coll., Cambridge, 1963, MA, 1967, PhD, 1969. Barrister-at-law, 1982. Asst. lectr. U. Keele, Satfordshire, 1967-69; asst. prof. U. Waterloo, Ontario, 1969-72, assoc. prof., 1972-74; lectr. The Open U., Milton Keynes, 1975-82, sr. lectr., 1982-87, reader, 1987—; cons. Cambridge Law Surgery, 1982—; adj. lectr. in law, Holborn Sch. Law, London, 1982-83, adj. sr. lectr., 1983-84, adj. reader, 1984-85. Author: Russia in the Eighteenth Century, 1973, Guilt at Versailles, 1984; editor: Shcherbatov, 1969, Enlightened Absolutism, 1985. Recipient Lechmere Essay prize The Middle Temple, London, 1978. Fellow The Royal Hist. Soc. Home: 57 Maids Causeway, Cambridge CB5 8DE, England Office: Open Univ, Arts Faculty, Milton Keynes England

LENTZEN, MANFRED, philologist, educator; b. Dormagen, Fed. Republic Germany, July 15, 1940; s. Carl and Wilma (Schiffer) L.; m. Dorothée Brand, Feb. 3, 1978. PhD, U. Cologne, Fed. Republic Germany, 1965; br. phil. habil., U. Cologne, 1970. Research asst. U. Cologne, Fed. Republic Germany, 1965-70, from asst. prof. to assoc. prof., 1970-74; prof. Romance languages and lit. U. Muenster, Fed. Republic Germany, 1974, dir. Inst. Romance Philology, dean dept. 13, 1975-76. Author: Studien zur Dante-Exegese Cristoforo Landinos, 1971, Der spanische Bürgerkrieg und die Dichter, 1985, also others; contbr. numerous articles on Italian, French and Spanish lit. to profl. publs. and jours. Mem. German Dante Soc., Internat. Italian Assn., Internat. Assn. Neo-Latin Studies, Internat. Hispanic Assn. Roman Catholic. Home: Mersmannsstiege 11, 4417 Altenberge Federal Republic of Germany Office: U Muenster, Bispinghof 3 A, 4400 Muenster Federal Republic of Germany

LENZ, SIEGFRIED, writer; b. Lyck, East Prussia, Mar. 17, 1926; ed. U. Hamburg. Cultural bd. Die Welt, 1949-51; freelance writer, 1952—; novels include: Es waren Habichte in der Luft, 1951; Duell mit dem Schatten, 1953; Sozartlich war Suleyken, 1955, 62, Der Mann im Strom, 1957, 58, Brot und Spiele, 1959; Stadtgesprache, 1963; Deutschstunde, 1968; Das Vorbild, 1973; stories include: Jager des Spotts, 1958; Das Feuerschiff, 1960; Einstein uberquert die Elbe bei Hamburg, 1975; plays include: Zeit der Schuldlosen, 1961; Das Gesicht, 1963; Haussuchung, 1967; other publs. include: Der Oeist dir Mirabelle, 1975; Die Fruchen Romane, 1976; Der Augenbinde, 1969; Der Amuesierdoktor, 1972; Lente von Hamburg, 1969; Bezichungen (essays), 1970; Wo Die Moewen schreien, 1976; polit, journalist, broadcast commentary. Served with German Navy, 1943-45. Recipient Gerhart Hauptmann prize, 1961, Bremer Literaturpreis, 1962, German Masonic lit. prize, 1970. Mem. Free Acad. Arts Hamburg. Address: Preusserstrasse 4, D-2000 Hamburg 52 Federal Republic of Germany *

LENZEN, WOLFGANG MATHIAS, philosopher, educator; b. Essen, Fed. Republic Germany, Feb. 4, 1946; s. Josef and Margret (Wess) L.; m. Gertrud Braunmiller, July 17, 1970; children: Stephan, Christoph, Alexander, Barbara, Angelika. PhD, U. Regensburg, Federal Republic of Germany, 1972. Habilitation, U. Regensburg, 1979. Asst. prof. U. Regensburg, 1974-78, lectr., 1979-80; prof. U. Osnabrück, Federal Republic of Germany, 1981—. Author: Theorien d.Bestätigung, 1974, Recent Work in Epistemic Logic, 1978, Glauben, Wissen und Wahrscheinlichkeit, 1980. Home: Immelmannweg 2, D-4500 Osnabruck Federal Republic of Germany Office: U Osnabruck, Katharinenstr 5, D-4500 Osnabruck Federal Republic of Germany

LENZER, IRMINGARD ISOLDE, psychology educator; b. Munich, Fed. Republic Germany, arrived in Can., 1969; d. Johann and Maria (Pfaffinger) L.; children: Alexander, Anna. BA in Psychology, UCLA, 1964; PhD in Psychology, Ind. U., 1969. Asst. prof. psychology St. Mary's U., Halifax, N.S., Can., 1969-73, assoc. prof., 1973-81, prof., 1981—. Grantee Nat. Scis. and Engring. Research Council Can., 1969—, Health and Welfare Can., 1980-82. Mem. N.Y. Acad. Scis., Can. Psychol. Assn. Home: 1232 Edward St, Halifax, NS Canada B3H 3H4 Office: St Mary's U, Dept Psychology, Robie St, Halifax, NS Canada B3H 3C3

LEONARD, EILEEN ANN, motion picture trust fund executive; b. N.Y.C., Oct. 4, 1941; d. Errol Thomas and Marjorie (Cleary) Connelly; m. Wayne Leonard, Jan. 28, 1967 (div. Mar. 1975); 1 dau., Kimberly Anne; m. 2d Kenneth Paul Vensel, Sept. 6, 1980. B.A., Fairleigh Dickinson U., 1963. French sec. French Railroads, N.Y.C., 1964-65; legal sec. W.R. Grace Co., N.Y.C., 1965-67; exec. sec. Internat. Industries, Los Angeles, 1968-70; adminstr. Contract Services Adminstr. Trust Fund, Los Angeles, 1974-76, dir., 1976—. Pub. relations chairperson Los Angeles Basin Equal Opportunity League, 1975-84; bd. dirs. Internat. Inst., Los Angeles, 1983-86, Inroads, Los Angeles. Mem. Dir. Guild Am., Women in Film. Roman Catholic. Home: 12431 Landale St Studio City CA 91604 Office: Contract Services Adminstr Trust Fund 14144 Ventura Blvd Sherman Oaks CA 91604

LEONARD, GRAHAM DOUGLAS, bishop of London; b. Greenwich, Eng., May 8, 1921; s. Douglas and Emily Mabel (Cheshire) L.; student Balliol Coll., Oxford, 1940-41; M.A., 1947; student Nashotah House; D.D., Episcopal Theol. Seminary, 1974; m. Vivien Priscilla Swann, Jan. 2, 1943; children—James Vivian, Mark Meredith. Curate, Vicar of Ardleigh, 1947-52; 1952-55; gen. sec. Nat. Soc. and Sec. Ch. of Eng. Schs. Council, 1955-58; archdeacon of Hampstead, rector St. Andrew Undershaft, 1962-64; bishop Willesden, 1964-73; bishop of Truro, 1973-81; bishop London, Eng., 1981—; dean Her Majesty's Chapels Royal; prelate Most Excellent Order of Brit. Empire; chmn. Ch. of Eng. Bd. for Social Responsibility, 1976-83 ; mem. House of Lords, from 1977 . Served to capt., Royal Army, 1941-45. Co-author: Growing into Union, 1970; The Gospel is for Everyone, 1971; God Alive: Priorities in Pastoral Theology, 1981. *

LEONARD, JOHN-PAUL, auditor, linguist; b. Pasadena, Calif., Oct. 7, 1948; s. Paul Herman and Blanche Alice (Zapotocky) L. BA, UCLA, 1971; MBA, U. Calif., Berkeley, 1980. Claims rep. Social Security, Oakland, Calif., 1973-79; acct. Union Ice Co., San Francisco, 1980-81; auditor Alumax, Inc., San Mateo, Calif., 1981-83, Norton Co., Surrey, Eng., 1983-84, DWM Copeland, Berlin, 1984-86, Emerson Electric, Brussels, 1986—. Mem. Deutsches Inst. Interne Revision. Sufism. Club: Cercle Polyglotte. Home: rue du Ham 65, 1180 Brussels Belgium Office: Emerson Electric, Chaussée de la Hulpe 181, 1170 Brussels Belgium

LEONARD, JOSEPH B., airline company executive; b. 1943. BS, Auburn U., 1967. V.p. ops. services Eastern Air Lines, Inc., Miami, Fla., 1984-85, sr. v.p. ops. services, 1985, exec. v.p. & gen. mgr. airline ops., 1985-86, pres., from 1986, chief operating officer, 1986—, now also exec. v.p., also dir. Office: Eastern Air Lines Inc Miami Internat Airport Miami FL 33148 *

LEONARD, LAWRENCE LE ROY, JR., family counselor, clergyman; b. Bklyn., Nov. 28, 1943; s. Lawrence Le Roy and Elizabeth (Schell) L.; B.A., Pacific Coll., 1972; postgrad. Columbia U., 1975; D.D., Universal Life Ch., 1979, Ph.D., 1980; D.Metaphysics, 1981. Asst. to asso. dir. Fresh Air Fund, N.Y.C., 1973-74; ordained to ministry Universal Life Ch., 1972; family counselor Agy. Child Devel., Human Resources Adminstrn., N.Y.C., 1974-77; regional supr., legal services specialist Day Care Council N.Y., 1977-78; pvt. practice family counseling, St. Albans, N.Y., 1974—; pres. Paper Talk Counseling Service; former chmn. bd. trustees St. Albans Congregation Universal Life Ch.; program coordinator N.Y.C. Community Centers; condr. leadership seminars for Day Care Center dirs. Producer, dir. S.E. Queens Youth Programs; pres. Positive Praise Award Program; mem. Jamaica Polit. Action League; community liaison Neighborhood Council Services; producer Children's Creative Arts Festival, 1975; scoutmaster Neighborhood Services council Boy Scouts Am., 1974; nat. bd. adv. Am. Biog. Inst. Served with USMC, 1963-69. Recipient honors for USO show, French Consul, Marseilles, France, 1965; cert. family counselor Human Resources Adminstrn.; cert. comml. photographer; holder black belt in martial arts. Mem. Nat. Assn. Edn. of Young Children, Day Care Council N.Y., Smithsonian Inst., Nat. Geog. Soc., Martinist Order (asso.), Internat. Platform Assn., Assn. Research and Enlightenment, Planetary Citizens. Club: Rosicrucian Order (10 deg.). Inventor painting instrument; editor, pub. Axis mag., 1968; co-dir. Actors Quarters, San Diego, 1968; art works exhibited Southwestern Coll., Calif., 1970, Lynn Kottler Galleries, N.Y.C., 1971; profl. flutist, composer; author: Self-Mastery, 1982. Home and Office: 179-71 Anderson Rd Saint Albans NY 11434

LEONARD, RAYMOND LOUIS, transportation company executive, musician; b. Miami, Fla., Sept. 8, 1950; s. Talbert Armlon and Lucy Elizabeth (Setzler) L.; m. Janice Taylor, Aug. 25, 1973; 1 son, Raymond Matthew. Student bus. adminstrn. and music, Belhaven Coll., intermittantly, 1968-73. With Leonard Bros. Trucking Co., Inc., Miami, Fla., 1973-84, terminal mgr., 1973-75, regional mgr., 1975-78, dir. govt. sales, 1978-79, exec. v.p., 1979-84, dir., 1973-84; pres. Intermodal Logistics, Inc., South Miami, Fla., 1985—; chmn. bd. Munitions Carriers Conf., Washington, 1983-84, pres., 1982-83, bd. dirs., 1979-84; dir. SLO Transport Corp., Miami. Mem. Mus. Sci. Century Club, Miami, 1986—. Served with U.S. Army, 1970-76. Piano scholar, Belhaven Coll., 1968-70; winner 1st place solo and ensemble awards trumpet and piano, Fla. Band Masters Assn., 1966-68. Mem. Am. Trucking Assn. (sales and mktg. council), Fla. Trucking Assn., Nat. Def. Transp. Assn., Specialized Carriers and Rigging Assn., Traffic Clubs Internat., Fla. C. of C., Zool. Soc. Fla., Delta Nu Alpha, Phi Mu Alpha Sinfonia. Democrat. Presbyterian. Lodge: Miami Rotary.

LEONARDI, ROBERT MATS KENNETH, computer programmer, consultant; b. Västeras, Sweden, Apr. 21, 1964; s. Irmo Natale Felice and Lizzie (Backas) L. Student, pub. schs., Västeras. Programming educator Studietorbuudet Vuxenskolan, Västeras, 1983; chief exec. officer Da Vinci Computing, Västeras, 1983—; programmer Royal Swedish Navy, Stockholm, 1985—; programmer stock calculation and telecommunications programs. Served with Swedish Navy, 1985—. Mem. Jaycees (bd. dirs. 1988—). Home: Rekylgatan 10 VI, S-723 38 Vasteras Sweden

LEONE, ANTONIO, medical manufacturing company executive; b. Bitonto, Italy, May 22, 1937; s. Giuseppe and Maria Concetta (Achille) L.; m. Pia Bairati, July 29, 1967; children—Francesco, Giorgio Giuseppe. Dr. in Electronic Engring., Polytech. Inst., Torino, Italy, 1965. Service mgr. Gen. Electric, Milano, Italy, 1965-68; sales mgr. Philips, Milano, 1968-70; gen. mgr. Kontron, Milano, 1971—, mng. dir., 1979—, v.p., Zurich, Switzerland, 1981—; chmn. Medicaleasing, Milano, 1978—, also dir.; dir. Kontron Instruments, St. Alban, Great Brit., Kontron Cardiovascular, Everett, Mass. Author: Bioengineering Contribution to Preventive Medicine, 1977; Possibility of Advanced Technology in Early Diagnosis, 1977; Clinical Laboratory Testing in Europe, 1979. Mem. Nat. Ctr. for the Hosp. Bldg. and Technique. Roman Catholic. Office: Kontron Instruments SpA, 3 Via Fantoli 16/15, 20138 Milano Italy

LEONG CHEE, KHEONG, food industries executive; b. Kampar, Malaysia, Feb. 23, 1954; s. Leong Pak Lam and Wong Kam Lan Chee Kheong; m. Ho Yin Leng, Jan. 14, 1984; children: Yuting, Thienfoong. Mng. ptnr. Wing Lok Yuen Biscuit Co., Kampar, 1973—, CB Red Label Sdn. Bhd, Kampar, 1978—; chmn. Shiraiton Sdn. Bhd, Ipoh, Malaysia, 1980—; bd. dirs. Kampar Enterprises Sdn. Bhd, Ipoh. Bd. dirs. Lions Internat., Kampar, 1976-78; v.p. A.C.S. Old Pupil Assn., 1985; hon. pres. Chinese Football Assn., Kampar, 1985. Mem. Brit. Inst. Mgmt. Buddhist. Clubs: Perak Shooting, Kampar Recreation, Golf. Office: Wing Lok Yuen Food Industries, 72 Jalan Gopeng, Kampar, Perak 31900, Malaysia

LEONHARDT, RUDOLF WALTER, editor; b. Altenburg, Thuringia, Germany, Feb. 9, 1921; s. Rudolf Emil and Paula Luise L.; m. Ulrike Pauline Zoerb, June 18, 1949; children—Joachim Rudolf, Dorte Susanne, Timm Christopher. State exam., U. Bonn, 1950, Ph.D., 1950. Asst. lectr. U. Cambridge, 1948-50; programme asst. BBC, London, 1950-55; sub-editor DIE Zeit, Hamburg, 1955-57, cultural editor, 1957-73, dep. editor-in-chief, 1973—. Author, translator of and contbr. to many publs., contbr. articles to profl. jours. Mem. PEN Club of W. Ger. Office: Die Zeit, 1 Speersort, D-2000 Hamburg 1 Federal Republic of Germany

LEONIDAS, PIRES GONCALVES, government official; b. Crúz Alta, Brazil, May 19, 1922. Grad., Superior War Coll., Brazil. Sec. econs. and fin. Brazilian Army, vice chief of staff, coop dir.; armed forces attaché Brazilian Embassy, Colombia; comdr. 4th Inf. Brigade, Brazil; chief of staff 1st Army, Brazil; mem., pres. mil. adv. office Castelo Bianco Adminstrn., Brazil; comdr. 3rd Army, Brazil, 1983—; now minister of army Brazil; former liaison U.S. Brazilian Joint Mil. Commn. Office: Ministry of Army, Brasilia Brazil *

LEONOV, LEONID MAKSIMOVICH, writer; b. Moscow, May 31, 1899; ed. Moscow U. Dep. to Surpeme Soviet, 1970; dir. Pushkin Dom (Pushkin House-U.S.S.R. Acad. Scis., Inst. Russian Lit.), 1972; sec. of bd. USSR Union of Writers; books include: Barsuki, 1924; The Thief, 1927; Sotj, 1930; Skutarevsky, 1932; Road to the Ocean, 1936; The Ordinary Man, 1941; Lenushka, 1943; The Fall of Velikoshumsk, 1944; The Golden Car, 1946; Sazancha, 1959; Mr. McKinley's Flight, 1961; Evgenia Ivanovna, 1963; Plays, 1964; Sot', 1968; The Russian Forest, 1973; In the War Years and After, 1974; Moscow Publicistics, 1976. Recipient State prize, 1942, Lenin prize, 1957; decorated Order of Lenin (four times), Hero of Socialist Labour, Hammer and Sickle Gold medal, Order of Red Banner of Labour, Order of Patriotic War, Merited Worker of Arts of R.S.F.S.R. Address: Union of Soviet Writers, 52 Ul Vorovskogo, Moscow USSR *

LEON-PORTILLA, MIGUEL, historian, educator; b. Mexico City, Mexico, Feb. 22, 1926; s. Miguel and Luisa (Portilla) L.; BA, Loyola U., Los Angeles, 1948, MA, 1951; PhD, Nat. U. Mex., 1956; PhD (hon.), So. Meth. U., 1980; DHL (hon.), So. Meth. U., 1980; PhD (hon.) U. Tel Aviv, 1987; m. Ascensión Hernández Treviño, May 2, 1965; 1 dau., Marisa. Sec., Interam. Indian Inst., Mexico City, 1955-58, asst. dir., 1958-60, dir., 1960-66; prof. faculty philosophy Nat. U. Mex., 1957—, dir. Inst. Hist. Research, 1966—; sec.-gen. Internat. Congress Americanists, Mexico City, 1962; disting. lectr. Am. Anthrop. Assn., 1974. Bd. regents Nat. U. Mex., 1976-86; permanent del. of Mexico to UNESCO, Paris, 1987—. Recipient Elias Sourasky prize in humanistic research Mexican Sec. Edn., 1966; Serra award of the Ams., 1978; Nat. prize in social scis. Govt. of Mex., 1981; Gamio award, 1983; Raphael Heliodoro Valle prize in history, 1984; Guggenheim fellow, 1969; Fulbright fellow, 1975. Mem. Mexican Acad. History, Royal Spanish Acad. Lang., Société des Americanistes de Paris, Inst. Different Civilizations, Sociedad Mexicana de Antropología, Am. Anthrop. Assn., El Colegio Nacional México. Author: La Filosofía Nahuatl estudiada en sus fuentes, 4th edit., 1974; Visión de los Vencidos, 4th edit., 1969; Broken Spears-Aztec Account of Conquest of Mexico, 2d edit. 1965; Aztec Thought and Culture, 1964; Le Crepuscule des Azteques, 1965; Trece Poetas del Mundo Azteca, 1967; Pre-Columbian Literatures of Mexico, 1969; Testimonios Sudcalifornianos, 1970; Religión de los Nicaraos, 1972; Time and Reality in the Thought of the Maya, 1972; The Voyages of Francisco de Ortega to California 1932-36, 1972; Historia Natural y Crónica de la Antigua California, 1973; Il Rovescio della Conquista, Testimoniaze Astechev Maya e Inca, 1974; Anthropology and the Endangered Cultures, 1976; New Light on the Sources of Torquemada's Monarchí a Indiana, 1979; Native Mesoamerican Spirituality, 1980; Toltecayotl, Aspectos de la Cultura Nahuatl, 1980; The Natural History of Baja California, 1980; Native Mesoamerican Spirituality, 1980, The Testaments of Culhuacan, 1984, La Vision de los Vencidos, 1984, La Pensée Azteque, 1985, Time and Reality in the Thought of the Maya, 1988; editor: Monarquía Indiana (Father Juan de Torquenada), 1975; Hamnotzejim Jazon, 1976; Culturas en peligro, 1976; Indian Place Names in Baja California, 1977; Los manifiestos en náhuatl de Emiliano Zapata, 1978; Native Mesoamerican Spirituality, Ancient Myths, Discourses, Stories, Doctrines, Hymns, Poems from the Aztec, Yucatec, Quiché-Maya, and Other Sacred Traditions, 1980; The Natural History of Baja California, 1980; Place Names in Nahuatl: Their Morphology, 1981; Mesoamerica Before 1519, 1984; Codex Fejérváry Mayer, 1985; Libro de los Coloquios, 1986; Huehuehtlahtolli, Testimonies of the Ancient Word, 1988. Home: 103 Alberto Zamora, Coyoacan, Mexico City 21, Mexico Office: Inst de Investig Históricas, Ciudad Universitaria, Mexico City 20, Mexico

LEONTE, ARISTIDE VASILE, mathematics educator; b. N. Balcescu, Teleorman, Rumania, Mar. 9, 1939; s. Vasile Tudor and Maria Ilie (Ivana) L.; m. Eufrosina Virgil Danciulescu; children: Laura, Lucian. Diploma in Math., U. Bucharest, Rumania, 1959, D in Math., 1971. Asst. prof. Pedagogical Inst., Craiova, Rumania, 1960-66; asst. prof. Craiova U., 1966-72, prof., 1972—. Mem. Rumanian Math. Soc., Am. Math. Soc. Office: U Craiova, Al Cuza 13, 1100 Craiova Romania

LEONTIEF, WASSILY, economist; b. Leningrad, Russia, Aug. 5, 1906; s. Wassily and Eugenia (Bekker) L.; m. Estelle Helena Marks, Dec. 25, 1932; 1 dau., Svetlana Eugenia Alpers. Student, U. Leningrad, 1921-25; grad. Learned Economist; Ph.D., U. Berlin, 1928; Ph.D. honoris causa, U. Bruxelles, Belgium, 1962, U. York, Eng., 1967, U. Louvain, 1971, U. Paris, 1972, U. Pa., 1976, U. Lancaster, Eng., 1976. Research economist Inst. Weltwirtschaft, U. Kiel, Germany, 1927-28, 30; econ. adviser to Chinese govt. Nanking, 1929; with Nat. Bur. Econ. Research, N.Y.C., 1931; instr. econs. Harvard, 1932-33, asst. prof., 1933-39, asso. prof., 1939-46, prof., 1946-75, dir. econ. project, 1948-72, Henry Lee prof. econs., 1953-75; prof. econs. N.Y. U., 1975—, univ. prof., 1983—; dir. Inst. Econ. Analysis, 1978-85; cons. Dept. Labor, 1941-47, OSS, 1943-45, UN, 1961-62, Dept. Commerce, 1966-82 , EPA, 1975-80 , UN, 1980—. Author: The Structure of the American Economy, 1919-29, 2d edit., 1976, Studies in the Structure of the American Economy, 1953, 2d edit., 1977, Input-Output Economics, 1966, 2d edit., 1986, Collected Essays, 1966, Theories, Facts and Policies, 1977, The Future of the World Economy, 1977, (with Faye Duchin) The Future Impact of Automation on Workers, 1986; Contbr. articles to sci. jours. and periodicals U.S. and abroad. Mem. Commn. to Study Orgn. of Peace, 1978; trustee N.C. Sch. Sci. and Math., 1978; mem. issues com. Progressive Alliance, 1979; mem. Com. for Nat. Security, 1980. Decorated officer Order Cherubim Univ.Pisa, 1953, Legion of Honor (France), 1967; Order of Rising Sun (Japan), 1984; recipient Bernhard-Harms prize econs. West Germany, 1970, Nobel prize in econs., 1973; Guggenheim fellow, 1940, 50. Fellow Soc. Fellows Harvard (sr. fellow, chmn. 1964-75), Econometric Soc., Royal Statis. Assn. (hon.), Inst. de France (corr.); mem. Am. Philos. Soc., Am. Acad. Arts and Scis., AAAS, Internat. Statis. Inst., Am. Econ. Assn., Am. Statis. Assn., Royal Econ. Soc., Japan Econ. Research Center (hon.), Brit. Acad. (corr.), French Acad. Scis. (corr.), Nat. Acad. Scis., Royal Irish Acad. (hon.), Brit. Assn. Advancement Sci. (pres. Sect. F 1976). Mem. Greek Orthodox Ch. Club: Century. Home: New York NY 10011 Office: NYU Inst Econ Analysis 269 Mercer St Room 203 New York NY 10003

LEOPOLD, IRVING HENRY, physician, medical educator; b. Phila., Apr. 19, 1915; s. Abraham and Dora (Schlow) L.; m. Eunice Robinson, June 24, 1937; children—Ellen Robinson, John. BS, Pa. State U., 1934; MD, U. Pa., 1938, DSc, 1943. Diplomate Am. Bd. Ophthalmology (chmn. bd. 1971-72, examiner 1974-81, subcom. impaired vision and blindness 1967-69, task force on ocular pharmacology, 1967-69, cons. 1975-79, assoc. examiner 1974-81). Intern U. Pa. Hosp., 1938-40; fellow, instr. ophthalmology U. Pa. Hosp., U. Pa. Med. Sch., 1940-45; assoc. Hosp. U. Pa., also U. Pa. Med. Sch., 1945-54; research investigator chem. warfare OSRD, 1941-45; mem. faculty U. Pa. Grad. Sch. Medicine, 1946-64, successively assoc., asst. prof., assoc. prof., 1946-55, prof., head dept. ophthalmology, 1955-64; chief dept. ophthalmology Grad. Hosp., 1955-61; dir. research Wills Eye Hosp., 1949-64, attending surgeon, 1952-64, med. dir., 1961-64, cons. surgeon, 1965-73; chmn. sci. adv. com. Allergan Pharms., 1974, exec. v.p., 1975; prof., chmn. dept. ophthalmology Mt. Sinai Sch. Medicine, 1965-75; dir. dept. ophthalmology Mt. Sinai Hosp., N.Y.C., 1964-75; prof., chmn. dept. ophthalmology U. Calif. at Irvine, 1975-85, prof. pharmacology, 1982-87, prof. emeritus ophthalmology, 1985—; clin. prof. ophthalmolgy Coll. Physicians and Surgeons, Columbia, 1964-66; cons. ophthalmologist St. Joseph's Hosp., 1959-64, Albert Einstein Med. Center, 1959-64; Proctor lectr. U. Calif., 1962; Gifford Meml. lectr., Chgo., 1967; Edwin B. Dunphy lectr. Harvard, 1968; Walter Wright lectr. U. Toronto, 1969; Richardson Cross lectr. Royal Soc. Medicine, 1970; Doyne Meml. lectr. Ophthal. Soc. U.K., 1971; DeSchweinitz Meml. lectr., Phila., 1972; Jules Stein lectr. UCLA, 1974; Bedell lectr., Phila., 1975; Edwin B. Dunphy lectr. Harvard, 1975; Francis H. Adler lectr., Phila., 1980, Dwight Towne lectr., Ky., 1979, C.S. O'Brien lectr., New Orleans, 1979; Disting. vis. lectr. Jefferson Med. Coll., 1980, Moorfields Hosp., Eng., 1980, U. Helsinki, Finland, 1980, Third Francis Heed Adler lectr., 1980, 2d ann. Tullos O. Coston lectr., 1981, Sir Stewart Duke-Elder lectr., 1982, Everett R. Viers lectr., Scott and White Clinic and Tex. A&M U. Coll. Medicine, Temple, Tex., 1982, U. Phillipines 1st lectr, 1st Irving H. Leopold ecture Wills Eye Hosp, 1987—. Eye Resident Soc., Eye Referral Ctr., 1982, Royal Soc. Medicine lectr., London, 1985; lectr. Internat. Congress Ophthalmology, Japan, 1978, Phillipine Bd. Opthalmology; cons. Chem. Warfare Service, U.S. Army, 1948-52, 81; surgeon gen. USPHS, 1953—, FDA, HEW, 1963; mem. med. adv. com. Orange County chpt. Multiple Sclerosis Soc., 1979-81; chmn. ophthalmology panel U.S. Pharmacopeia, 1960-70, mem. revision panel, 1970—; chmn. panel drug efficacy in ophthalmology Nat. Acad. Scis.-NRC, 1966-67, 80—; mem. tng. grants com. USPHS, 1952-58, mem. spl. sensory study sect. research neurol. diseases and blindness, 1954-58; mem. field investigating com. Nat. Inst. Neurol. Diseases and Blindness, 1959-61, mem. neurol. project com., 1961-63, chmn. vision research tng. com., 1967-68; mem. adv. bd. Am. Behcet's Found., Inc., 1980, 81; Expert Agree to Ministry of Health, France, 1981-87; curator ophthalmic pharmaceuticals Found. Am. Acad. Ophthalmology, 1983—; mem. nat. adv. eye council panel on cataract sect. Nat. Eye Inst. and HEW, 1981-85; mem. med. research and devel. command-chemical welfare U.S. Army, 1981-85. Editor-in-chief: Survey of Ophthalmology, 1958-62; cons. editor, 1962—; editorial bd.: Am. Jour. Diabetes, 1956-73, Investigative Ophthalmology, 1961-74; assoc. editor: Am. Jour. Ophthalmology, 1974-88, now mem. editorial bd.; assoc. editor Archives of Ophthalmology, 1974-81; cons. Jour. AMA, 1974-81; editorial cons. Jour. Ocular Pharmacology, 1985—; editor: Ocular Inflammation and Therapeutics, 1981. Trustee Seeing Eye Guide. Recipient Zentmayer award, 1945, 49; honor award Am. Acad. Ophthalmology, 1955, Sr. Hon. award, 1984; Edward Lorenzo Holmes citation and award, 1957; Friedenwald medal Assn. Research Ophthalmology, 1960; Disting. Research award U. Calif., Irvine, Calif., 1980; Disting. Research award U. Calif. Alumni Assn., 1980; Physician's award Pa. Acad. Ophthalmology and Otolaryngology, 1981; Sir Steward Duke-Elder award, Lederle Medal and Prize for Research in Glaucoma Internat. Glaucoma Congress VI and Am. Soc. Contemporary Ophthalmology, 17th ann. sci. assembly, Orlando, Fla., 1982. Mem. N.Y. Acad. Medicine, Am. Ophthal. Soc. (Verhoeff Meml. lectr. 1973, Lucien Howe medal 1974), N.Y. Ophthal. Soc., Am. Acad. Ophthalmology and Otolaryngology (chmn. drug com. ophthalmology 1963-74, Edward Jackson Meml. lectr. 1965, honor guest 1971, 75, Philip M. Corboy Perpetual Excellence award 1988, Disting. Service to Ophthalmology award 1988), Am. Soc. Contemporary Ophthalmology (chief cons. editorial bd. 1981), Assn. Research Ophthalmology (trustee, chmn.), Nat. Soc. Prevention Blindness (dir. 1974-81, v.p., exec. com., hon. bd. dirs.), A.C.S., AAAS, Art Alliance Phila., John Morgan Soc., Coll. Physicians Phila., Am. Diabetes Assn., AMA (chmn. residency rev. com. ophthalmology 1970-72, Physician's Recognition award 1980-87), N.Y. Acad. Sci., Pan Am. Assn. Ophthalmology, Pan Pacific Surg. Assn., Royal Soc. Medicine (London), N.Y. State, N.Y. County, Philadelphia County med. socs., Calif., Orange County med. assns., Orange County Soc. Ophthalmology, Am. Med. Student Assn., Los Angeles Research Study Club (dir. 1979-81), Nat. Soc. to Prevent Blindness (hon. bd. dirs. 1986—), Sigma Xi, Alpha Omega Alpha. Clubs: Medical Biochemist, Vesper (Phila.); Big Canyon Country, Balboa Bay (Newport Beach, Calif.); Century Country, Purchase (N.Y.C.). Home: 1484 Galaxy Dr Newport Beach CA 92660 Office: U Calif Dept Ophthalmology Calif Coll Medicine Irvine CA 92717 Other: Allergan Inc 2525 DuPont Dr Irvine CA 92715

LEOPOLD, MARK F., lawyer; b. Chgo., Jan. 23, 1950; s. Paul F. and Corinne (Shapira) L.; m. Jacqueline Rood, June 9, 1974; children—Jonathan, David. B.A., Am. U., Washington, 1972; J.D., Loyola U., Chgo., 1975. Bar: Ill. 1975, Fla. 1976, U.S. Dist. Ct. (no. dist.) Ill. 1975, U.S. Ct. Appeals (7th cir.) 1976, U.S. Ct. Appeals (8th cir.) 1979. Assoc. McConnell & Campbell, Chgo., 1975-79; atty. U.S. Gypsum Co., Chgo., 1979-82, sr. litigation atty., 1982-84; sr. litigation atty. USG Corp., 1985-87, corp. counsel, 1987, sr. corp. counsel, 1987—; legal writing instr. Loyola U. Sch. Law, Chgo., 1978-79. Commr. Lake County, Waukegan, Ill., 1982-84, Forest Preserve, Libertyville, Ill., 1982-84, Pub. Bldg. Commn., Waukegan, 1980-82; chmn. Deerfield Twp. Republican Central Com., Highland Park, Ill., 1984-86 ; vice-chmn. Lake County Rep. Central Com., Waukegan, 1982-84. Recipient Disting. Service award Jaycees, Highland Park, Ill., 1983. Mem. ABA (anti-trust com. 1976—, litigation com. 1980—, corps. com. 1981—), Chgo. Bar Assn. (antitrust com. 1976—, corp. counsel com. 1984—), Pi Sigma Alpha, Omicron Delta Kappa. Republican. Office: USG Corp 101 S Wacker Dr Chicago IL 60606

LEPAGE, ROBERT JEAN, management consultant; b. Forchies-la-Marche, Belgium, Aug. 12, 1932; s. Louis J. and Paula E. (Ruppel) L.; D.Law, Louvain U., 1956; m. Rosita Baugniet, June 6, 1959; children—Marie, Anne. Admitted to bar, 1957; atty. Ct. of Appeals, Brussels, 1958-59; account supr. and mgr. offices in Europe and U.S. for J. Walter Thompson Co., 1959-70; sr. v.p., dir. Spencer Stuart Mgmt. Cons., 1970-84, also gen. mgr., Europe/S.A. and mng. dir. Belgium; sr. officer, mem. corp. exec. com. Korn/Ferry Internat., Los Angeles, also pres. Europe and mng. dir. Benelux, 1984—; chmn. Lepage Cons. Engrs., 1970—. Chmn. Lycee d'Anvers; bd. dirs. Inst. de l'Entreprise, Brussels. Served as officer Belgian Army, 1957-59. Decorated knight Order of Leopold, officer Order of Crown. Mem. Belgian Mgmt. and Mktg. Assn., Mktg. Communications Execs. Internat., Assn. Doctors Law Louvain, Am. C. of C. in Belgium, Brussels C. of C. (bd. dirs.). Clubs: Çercle Gaulois, Beerschot Tennis, De Warande. Home: Tudor Lodge Olmenlaan 7, 2610 Wilrijk Belgium Office: Ave Louise 523, B25, 1050 Brussels Belgium

LEPISTÖ, TIMO VALTER, academic administrator; b. Pori, Finland, Apr. 28, 1937; s. Valter Armas and Evi Helena (Lampela) L.; m. Ritva Nenny Rantanen, June 12, 1960; children: Jyri, Kari. MS, U. Turku, Finland, 1960, PhD, 1966. Lectr. maths. Tech. Coll. Pori, 1962-70; assoc. prof. math. Tampere (Finland) U. Tech., 1970-71; prof. math. U. Oulu, Finland, 1971-77; prof. math. Tampere U. Tech., 1973—, rector, 1985—. Contbr. articles to profl.; bd. dirs. newspaper Aamulehti, 1985—. Served to over lt. Finnish Infantry, 1960-61. Mem. Am. Math. Soc. lodge: Lielahti Rotary. Office: Tampere U tech, PO Box 527, 33101 Tampere Finland

LEPORE, MICHAEL JOSEPH, gastroenterologist, educator; b. N.Y.C., May 8, 1910; s. Joseph and Florence (Melucci) L.; m. Ardean Clough Everett, Sept. 18, 1937; 1 son, Frederick Everett. B.S., N.Y. U., 1929; M.S., U. Rochester, 1931, M.D. with honor, 1934. Diplomate: Am. Bd. Internal Medicine. Intern Duke Hosp., asst. resident in medicine, 1934-37; fellow in medicine Yale U., 1935-36; asst. in medicine Columbia U., 1937-46, instr., 1946-52, assoc. in medicine, 1952-56, asst. clin. prof. medicine, 1956-63; practice medicine specializing in internal medicine and gastroenterology 1937—; cons. in field; dir. Upjohn Gastrointestinal service Roosevelt Hosp., 1962-66, St. Vincent's Hosp. and Med. Center, 1966-75; mem. staffs Englewood (N.J.) Hosp., St. John's Riverside Hosp., Yonkers, N.Y.; attending physician St. Vincent's Hosp. and Med. Center, N.Y.C., Univ. Hosp., Bellevue Hosp. Center; assoc. prof. clin. medicine Sch. Medicine, N.Y. U., 1968-70, prof., 1971—. Author: Death of the Clinician— Requiem or Reveille?, 1981; Contbr. articles to med. jours. Pres. Upjohn Gastrointestinal Found., 1962-79; mem. pres.'s leadership council U. Rochester. Served as lt. col. M.C. AUS, 1942-46. Decorated Army Commendation medal. Fellow A.C.P., N.Y. Acad. Scis., N.Y. Acad. Medicine; mem. AMA, Am. Gastroenterol. Assn., N.Y. Gastroenterol. Assn., Physiol. Soc. Phila., AAAS, Royal Soc. Medicine, Alpha Omega Alpha, Sigma Xi. Office: 36 7th Ave New York NY 10011

LEPRETTE, JACQUES, diplomat; b. Jan. 22, 1920; ed. U. Paris, Ecole Nationale d'Adminstrn.; married. With European div. Ministry Fgn. Affairs, 1947-49; counselor Council of Europe, 1949-52; head polit. div. French Mil. Govt., Berlin, 1952-55; counselor French Embassy, Washington, 1955-59; with African div. Ministry Fgn. Affairs, 1959-61; ambassador to Mauritania, 1961-64; dir. Internat. Liaison Service for Info., 1964-65; minister-counselor, Washington, 1966-71; dir. UN and internat. orgn. affairs Fgn. Office, 1971-74; asst. dir. polit. affairs Central Adminstrn., 1975-76; permanent rep., A.E. and P. from France to UN, 1976-82; ambassador to the European Communities, 1982-85; ambassador of France, 1984. Decorated commandeur Legion of Honor, Croix de Guerre, Bronze Star. Home: 36 Rue Miollis, 75015 Paris France

LEPSCHY, GIULIO CIRO, linguist, educator; b. Venice, Italy, Jan. 14, 1935; s. Emilio and Sara (Castelfranchi) L.; m. Anna Laura Momigliano, Dec. 12, 1962. Dott Lett, U. Pisa, Italy, 1957; Dipl Lic., Scuola Normale Superiore, Pisa, 1958; Perf, Sch. Normale Superiore, Pisa, 1961. Lectr. dept. Italian studies U. Reading (Eng.), 1964-67, reader, 1967-75, prof., 1975—. Author: A Survey of Structural Linguistics, 1970, Saggi di Linguistica Italiana, 1978, Mutamenti di Prospettiva nella Linguistica; (with others) The Italian Language Today, 1977, rev. edit., 1988. Fellow Brit. Acad.; mem. Philol. Soc., Linguistics Assn. Gt. Britain, Cercle Ferdinand de Saussure, Soc. Linguistica Italiana, Soc. Italiana Glottologia. Office: U Reading Dept Italian Studies, Whitekights Reading RG6 2AA, England

LE QUANG DAO, government official; b. Tien Son district, Ha Bac Province, Vietnam, Aug. 8, 1921. Joined Dem. Youth Union, 1938; mem. Communist Party Vietnam, 1940, sec., 1941-45; sec. Communist Party Vietnam, Hanoi, 1945; sec. party com. Communist Party Vietnam, Hanoi-Ha Dong, 1948-49; then permanent mem. regional party com. 3d interzone and dep. head propoganda bd. Party Cen. Com. Communist Party Vietnam, chief propaganda and tng., 1950, dep. commissar Dien Bien Phu campaign, 1954; then dep. chief Gen. Polit. Dept. Vietnam People's Army, maj.-gen., 2958, lt.-gen., 1974; alt. mem. Party Cen. Com., 1960, full mem., 1972, mem. secretariat, 1976; dep. sec. Hanoi Party Com., 1978; sec. for sci. and edn. Party Cen. Com., 1982, head commn. for sci. and edn., 1984—, mem. presidium, 1983; then chmn. Nat. Assembly; now also vice-chmn. State Council. Office: National Assembly, Office of Chmn, Hanoi Socialist Republic of Vietnam *

LE QUESNE, ALFRED LAURENCE, school master; b. London, Nov. 16, 1928; s. Charles Thomas and Florence Eileen (Pearce Gould) LeQ.; m. Dorothy Mary Parks, June 27, 1964; children: Charles, Elizabeth, John. MA with 1st class honors, U. Oxford, Eng., 1951. Asst. master Shrewsbury (Eng.) Sch., 1951-56, 1961-63, 1969—; history lectr. U. Tasmania, Australia, 1957-60; sr. lectr. U. Sydney, Australia, 1964-68. Author: After Kilvert, 1978, Carlyle, 1982, The Bodyline Controversy, 1983. Mem. Ch. of Eng. Home: 22 Saint Johns Hill, Shrewsbury SY1 1JJ, England

LE RALLE-BUARD, CHANTAL MARIE LUCE, physician; b. Alencon, France, Jan. 9, 1950; d. Rene and Marie (Ribault) Buard; m. Eric Le Ralle, Aug. 9, 1975; children: Vincent, Celine, Delphine. B, Laval, France, 1969; MD, Faculty Rennes, France, 1982. Intern Gen. Hosp., Alencon, France, 1976-82; phlebologist Liberal Hosp., Alencon, 1982—. Mem. French Phlebology Soc., Coll. Bas-Normand D'Angeiologie, Logistique Medico-Chirurgicale Internat., Formation et Conseil Assn., Bas-Normand Coll. Angiology. Roman Catholic. Office: 1 Rue de L'Ancienne Mairie, 61000 Alencon, Orne France

LERAY, JEAN, mathematician; b. Nantes, France, Nov. 7, 1906; s. Francis and Baptistine (Pineau) L.; m. Marguerite Trumier, Oct. 20, 1932; children: Jean-Claude, Françoise, Denis. Agregation, Ecole Normale Superieure, Paris, 1926; Dr es Scis., Nat. Ctr. for Sci. Research, 1933; hon. degrees, U. Chgo. and U. Brussels. Prof. math. U. Nancy, France, 1938-41, U. Paris, 1941-47; prof. math. Coll. de France, Paris, 1947-78, prof. emeritus, 1978—. Author: Hyperbolic Equations, 1953, Lagrangian Analysis and Quantum Mechanics, 1981; contbr. articles to profl. jours. Served to lt. French Army, 1939-45. Recipient Malaxa prize Internat. Com., Romania, 1938, Math. prize Wolf Found., Israel, 1979. Fgn. mem. Nat. Acad. Scis. U.S.A., Am. Acad. Arts and Scis., Am. Philos. Soc., Royal Soc. London, Acad. Nazionale dei Lincei (Feltrinelli prize 1971), Acad. Polonaise Scis., Acad. Nazionale Sci. detta dei XL, Inst. Lombardo, Acad. Sci. e Lettere, Acad. Sci., Lettere e Arti Palermo, Nat. Acad. Scis. USSR; mem. Soc. Math. Suisse (hon.), Acad. Royale Belgique (assoc.), Acad. Sci. Torino (corr.), Acad. Scis. Paris, Wissens Akad. Sci. Gottingen. Home: 6 Ave Jean Racine, 92330 Sceaux France Office: Coll de France, 3 Rue d'Ulm, 75005 Paris France

LERCHE, PETER FRITZ, law professor; b. Leitmeritz, Germany, Jan. 12, 1928; s. Fritz Franz and Karoline (Artmann) L.; m. Ilse Peschek, July 23, 1955; children—Wolfgang, Clemens. Dr. Iur., Munich U., 1952. Prof. pub. law U. Berlin, 1960-65, U. Munich, 1965—. Author: Ubermass und Verfassungsrecht, 1961; Werbung und Verfassung, 1967; Rundfunkmonopol, 1970; Verfassungsrechtliche Aspekte der inneren Pressefreiheit, 1974; Kernkraft und rechtlicher Wandel, 1981. Mem. numerous govtl. commns. in legal matters. Mem. Bavarian Acad. Sci., Union German Lectrs. in Pub. Law (1st pres.). Clubs: Hippopotamus, Rotary (Starnberg). Home: 13 Junkersstrasse, Gauting, 8035 Gauting, Bavaria Federal Republic of Germany Office: Univ Munich, 2 Prof Huber Platz, 8000 Munich 22, Bavaria Federal Republic of Germany

LEREBOUR, FLORENT, general practitioner specializing in aeronautic medicine; b. Bobo Dioulasso, Upper Volta, July 19, 1947; s. Claude and Lemoine L.; m. Anne Verry, Mar. 16, 1972; children: Guillaume, Laetitia, Emilie. MD with distinction, U. Paris, 1973. Intern Switzerland Hosp. of Paris, 1972-73; practice medicine specializing in pediatrics Peymeinade, France, 1973—. Served to capt. French Navy, 1973-74. Republican. Roman Catholic. Lodge: Lions. Home: Campagne l'Aven, 06530 Le Tignet France Office: 3 rue Belletrud, 06530 Peymeinade France

LERMAN, JAMES LEW, educator; b. Elizabeth, N.J., May 2, 1946; s. Sam and Lillian (Leibowitz) L.; A.B., Brown U., 1968; M.A., Kean Coll. N.J., 1974, 82; m. Theresa A. Marino, June 24, 1973; 1 child, Michela Nastasya Marino. Tchr. English, Newark Bd. Edn., 1968-71, media specialist, 1971-77, curriculum supr., 1977-78; pres. Metro. Center for Ednl. Devel., N.Y.C., 1974—; dir. Newark Tchr. Ctr., 1978-84; dir. program devel. Newark Bd. Edn., 1984-86; asst. to supt., S. Orange-Maplewood (N.J.) Bd. Edn., 1986—; pres. Ronna L. Waller Ednl. Found., Inc., 1983—; v.p. E. Alma Flagg Scholarship Fund, Inc., 1984-87; adj. faculty Antioch Coll., 1974-75, Bloomfield Coll., 1975-76, Coll. of Mt. St. Vincent, 1977-79, Kean Coll. of N.J., 1983-84. Bd. dirs. (nat.) Frontlash, 1971-73; mem. Newark Preservation and Landmarks Com.; sec. Newark Council for Humanities, 1984-86; v.p. E. Alma Flagg Scholarship Fund, 1984-87. Recipient award, Am. Fedn. Tchrs., 1981, U.S. Dept. Edn., 1982. Mem. Nat. Soc. Study of Edn., Assn. Supervision and Curriculum Devel., Ednl. Media Assn. N.J. (fellow 1975), Phi Delta Kappa. Editor curriculum guides for Newark Bd. Edn., 1977-78; contbr. articles to profl. jours.

LERNER, SANDY RICHARD, art restorer, appraiser, painter, sculptor, lithographer; b. Pa., May 13; s. Jay N. and Sally L.; B.A., Lafayette Coll., Easton, Pa., 1933; J.D., N.Y. Law Sch., 1938; M.F.A., Pratt Inst., pupil Fred Conway, Diego Rivera, others; children—Sandra, Scott Richard. Commd. lt. USAF, 1940, advanced through grades to col., 1946; service in U.S., Europe, Far East; ret., 1964; asst. to dean, tchr. art restoration, orthographic projection, mech. drawing, chemistry paints and pigments Pratt Inst., 1974; adj. prof. art Parson Sch. Design, 1975, New Sch., 1975-78; exec. dir. Art Restoration Tech. Inst., N.Y.C., 1961—, Learning Through Drawing, 1970—; curator Salmagundi Club, 1970, Masonic Grand Lodge Library, 1966; chmn. jury Washington Sq. Art Show, 1960; appraiser Masonic Thrift, 1979, Navy and Coast Guard Art Collection; restorer Shrine of Guadalupe (Mex.), 1980, numerous others; lecturing asst. prof. West Palm Beach Coll. (Fla.); lectr. U. Palm Beach, West Palm Beach, 1987. Prin. works include portraits of Masonic Grand Master Wendell Walker, Grand Master A.J. Punt, Col. of the Regt. 7th Regt., Rainbow Div., Gen. B. Ehrlich, Col. Davis, Gen. Douglas MacArthur, Winston Churchill. Decorated D.F.C., Air medal; honored for restoration Trinity Cathedral; Col. Miss.; hon. dep. Sheriff Ariz.; recipient Lyle Gun, USCG. Mem. Am. Inst. Conservation, Internat. Inst. Conservation, Art Students League (life), Composers, Authors and Artists, DAV (life), VFW, Am. Legion. Republican. Clubs: Masons, Lions, Rotary. Author numerous articles in field. Address: 101 Central Park West #2C New York NY 10023-4204

LERNER, SHELDON, plastic surgeon; b. N.Y.C., Mar. 3, 1939; s. Louis and Lillian L.; A.B. with honors, Drew U., Madison, N.J., 1961; M.D., U. Louisville, 1965. Intern, resident Albert Einstein Coll. Medicine, Bronx-Mcpl. Hosp. Center, 1965-73; practice medicine, specializing in plastic surgery Plastic Cosmetic and Reconstructive Surgery Center, San Diego, 1973—. Served with USPHS, 1968-70. Mem. AMA, Am. Soc. Plastic and Reconstructive Surgeons, Calif. Med. Soc., San Diego County Med. Soc., San Diego Internat. Plastic Surgery Assn. Clubs: Masons, Shriners. Office: 3399 1st Ave San Diego CA 92103

LE ROY LADURIE, EMMANUEL, author; b. Moutiers, France, July 19, 1929; s. Jacques and Leontine (Dauger) L.; m. Madeleine Pupponi, July 9, 1955; children: Francois, Anne. Agrege d'histoire, Ecole Normale Superieure, Paris, 1953, LittD, 1956; doctoral degree (hon.), U. Geneva. Prof. Lycee de Montpellier (France), 1953-57; researcher Ctr. Nat. Recherche Sci., Paris, 1957-60; asst. prof. Faculty des Lettres de Montpellier, 1960-63; master asst. prof. Ecole Pratique des Hautes Etudes, Paris, 1963-65; dir. studies Ecole Pratique des Hautes Etudes, 1965-69; lecturer Faculty des Lettres de Paris, 1969, U. Paris Sorbonne, 1970-71; prof. geography and social scis. U. Paris-VII, 1970-73; prof. history modern civilization Coll. de France, Paris, 1973-88; dir. Bibliotheque Nat., Paris, 1988—. Author: Montaillou, 1978, Carnival in Romans, 1979, Times of Feast, Times of Famine: A History of Climate Since the Year 1000, 1971. Named Chevalier French Legion of Honor; recipient Silver Medal Ctr. Nat. Recherche Sci., 1966. Roman Catholic. Office: care College de France, 11 Place Marcelin Berthelot, 75231 Paris Cedex 06, France *

LESAFFRE, LUCIEN LEON, marketing executive; b. Isle Aumont, France, Sept. 25, 1945; s. Leon and Gisele Marie (Isaac) L.; m. Myriam George; children: Valery, Alexandra, Aldric. Degree in engring., Hautes Etudes Industrielles, Lille, France, 1968; Lic. en Scis., U. Lille, 1969. Prodn. engr. Societe Lesaffre, Marcq-en-Baroeul, France, 1969-71, chief operating officer, 1971-75, chmn., chief exec. officer, 1976—; chmn. Safproducts, Mpls., 1978—; pres. Lesaffre GmbH, Hamburg, Fed. Republic Germany; bd. dirs. Lesaffre Far East, Hong Kong, Union Generale du Nord Ins. Cos., Internat. Malt Co., Milw., SOGAP, Paris, CEPI, Marcq-en-Baroeul; cons. CPA Orgn., Paris, 1982—; bd. dirs., cons. Soders, Fez, Morocco, 1981—. V.p., bd. dirs. Internat. Airport, Lille, 1983—; French consul to Republic of Costa Rica. Recipient Best Export Performance Award Conseillers du Commerce Exterieur, 1980. Mem. Comite des Fabricants de Levure, Orgn. de la Communaute Européenne, Chambre Syndicale Fabricants Levure, Chambre Syndicale Fabricants Alcool, French C. of C. (bd. dirs.), Union Patronale de la Metropole Nord. Home: 141 rue Gabriel Peri, 59700 Marcq-en-Baroeul France Office: Societe Industrielle Lesaffre, 137 rue Gabriel Peri, 59700 Marcq-en-Baroeul France

LESAGE-COURY, ARIANE, biochemist; b. Damascus, Syria, June 13, 1958; arrived in Can., 1987; d. I. and H. Coury. BS, U. Pierre et Marie Curie, Paris, 1981, MS, 1982, PhD, 1984. Research supr. metabolism unit Ctr. Recherche Delalande, Rueil-Malmaison, France, 1984, research supr. biochemistry unit, 1985-87, cons., 1987—; research assoc. dept. psychology U. B.C., Vancouver, Can., 1987—. Contbr. articles to profl. jours. Fellow Groupe Etude Rythmes Biologiques. Club: Paris Country. Office: UBC, 2136 West Mall, Vancouver, BC Canada V6T 1W5

LESAR, HIRAM HENRY, lawyer, educator; b. Thebes, Ill., May 8, 1912; s. Jacob L. and Missouri Mabel (Keith) L.; m. Rosalee Berry, July 11, 1937

(dec. Oct. 1985); children: James Hiram, Albert Keith, Byron Lee; m. Barbara Thomas, Feb. 12, 1987. A.B., U. Ill., 1934, J.D., 1936; J.S.D., Yale U., 1938. Bar: Ill. 1937, Mo. 1954, U.S. Supreme Ct 1960. Asst. prof. law U. Kans., 1937-40, asso. prof., 1940-42; sr., prin. atty. bd. legal examiners U.S. CSC, 1942-44; assoc. prof. law U. Mo., 1946-48, prof., 1948-57; prof. law Washington U., St. Louis, 1957-72, dean Sch. Law, 1960-72; dean, prof. law So. Ill. U., Carbondale, 1972-80, interim pres. univ., 1974, acting pres., 1979-80, disting. service prof., 1980-82, prof. emeritus, 1982—, vis. disting. service prof., 1983—; disting. vis. prof. McGeorge Sch. Law, 1982-83; vis. prof. law U. Ill., summer 1947, Ind. U., summer 1952, U. So. Calif., summer 1959, U. N.C., summer 1961, NYU, summer 1965. Author: Landlord and Tenant, 1957; Contbr. to: Am. Law of Property, 1952, supplement, 1977, also, Dictionary Am. History, Ency. Brit. Bd. dirs. Legal Aid Soc., St. Louis and St. Louis County, 1960-72, pres., 1966-67; mem. Human Relations Commn., University City, Mo., 1966-71, chmn., 1966, 67; bd. dirs. Land of Lincoln Legal Assistance Found., 1972-82; mem. Fed. Mediation and Conciliation Service, other arbitration panels; bd. dirs. Bacone Coll., 1981-87; trustee Lincoln Acad. Ill., 1987—. Served from lt. (j.g.) to lt. comdr. USNR, 1944-46. Named Laureate Lincoln Acad. of Ill., 1985. Fellow Am. Bar Found.; mem. Am. Arbitration Assn., Am. Law Inst., ABA, Fed. Bar Assn., Mo. Bar Assn., St. Louis Bar Assn., Am. Acad. Polit. and Social Sci., Am. Judicature Soc., AAUP, Phi Beta Kappa, Order of Coif, Phi Kappa Phi, Phi Delta Phi (hon.). Baptist. Clubs: University (St. Louis); Nat. Lawyers (Washington); Yale (Chgo.); Jackson Country. Lodges: Rotary, Masons, K.T., Shriners. Home: 11 Hillcrest Dr Carbondale IL 62901

LESATZ, STEPHEN, JR., lawyer; b. Greeley, Colo., Aug. 5, 1937; s. Stephen J. and Rose (Scholz) LeS.; m. LaDonna M. Distel, June 10, 1961; 1 son, Eric S. B.S. in Bus. Adminstrn., U. Denver, 1959, LL.B., 1961. Bar: Colo. 1962, Minn. 1968, Mich. 1969. Assoc. Haskell, Helmick, Carpenter & Evans, Denver, 1962-68, Arthur E. Anderson, LeSueur, Minn., 1968-69; atty. Whirlpool Corp., Benton Harbor, Mich., 1969-74; assoc. gen. counsel Rocky Mountain Energy Co., Denver, 1974-87, Union Pacific Corp., 1987—; prin. Vista Properties, Denver, 1983—. Mem. Denver Art Mus., Denver Mus. Natural History, U. Denver Chancellor's Soc. Mem. ABA, Colo. Bar Assn., Denver Bar Assn. Republican. Congregationalist. Office: 1919 14th St Boulder CO 80302

LESHCHYSEN, ROBERT, financial services executive; b. Toronto, Ont., Can., May 13, 1950; s. Michael and Ruth (Antonyshyn) L.; m. Myroslava Dubyk, Aug. 22, 1981; children: Oleh, Orest. BA, U. Toronto, 1973, MBA, 1975. Mgmt. trainee Can. Imperial Bank of Commerce, Toronto, 1976-80; mgr., direction and monitoring dept. Ont. Share and Deposit Ins. Corp., Toronto, 1980-87; corp. fin. officer Capital Fin. dept Can. Trustco Mortgage Co., Toronto, 1987; chief, spl. support officer Office of Supt. of Fin. Instns., Toronto, 1987—; bd. dirs. UBA Trading Co. Ltd., Toronto, Wellington Wholesale, Toronto; mem. adv. com. Fed. Bus. Devel. Bank. Mem. The Planning Forum, Toronto Soc. Fin. Analysts, Cert. Gen. Accts. of Ont. Progressive Conservative. Ukranian Catholic. Home: 35 Kingsgate Crescent, Etobicoke, ON Canada M9P 3E2

LESLIE, DONALD DANIEL, historian, educator; b. London, July 1, 1922; s. Alfred and Ada (Schneiderman) L.; m. Helga Selz, Mar. 20, 1958; children: Michal, Gial, Jonathan. BSc, London U., 1943; diploma in Chinese, U. Cambridge, Eng., 1951, MLitt, 1954; Dr univ, U. Paris Sorbonne, 1962. Research fellow Hebrew U., Jerusalem, 1958-60, Australian Nat. U., Canberra, 1963-70; assoc. prof. Tel-Aviv U., 1970-71; sr. lectr. history Canberra Coll. Advanced Edn., 1972—. Author: (with A. Porath) Sayings of Confucius, 1960 (Tchernikowsky award 1973), The Survival of the Chinese Jews, 1972, (with J. Dehergne) Juifs de Chine, 1980 (Therouanne award Acad. Francaise 1981), Islam in Traditional China, 1986, other books and articles on Chinese history, philosophy and religion. Served with armed forces 1943-47, ETO, PTO. Home: 18 Haines St, Curtin, Canberra Australia Office: Canberra Coll Advanced Edn, PO Box 1, Belconnen, Canberra Australia

LESLIE, HENRY ARTHUR, banker; b. Troy, Ala., Oct. 15, 1921; s. James B. and Alice (Minchener) L.; m. Anita Doyle, Apr. 5, 1943; children: Anita Lucinda Leslie Cochrane, Henry Arthur. B.S., U. Ala., 1942, J.D., 1948; J.S.D., Yale U., 1959; grad., Sch. Banking, Rutgers U., 1964. Bar: Ala. 1948. Asst. prof. bus. law U. Ala., 1948-50, 52-54; prof. law, asst. dean U. Ala. (Sch. Law), 1954-59; v.p. trust officer Birmingham Trust Nat. Bank, Ala., 1959-64; sr. v.p., trust officer Union Bank & Trust Co., Montgomery, Ala., 1964-73; sr. v.p., sr. loan officer Union Bank & Trust Co., 1973-76, exec. v.p., 1976-78, pres., chief exec. officer, 1978—, dir., 1973—; mem. Ala. Oil and Gas Bd., 1984-85; dir. 1st Fin. Mgmt. Corp., Fed. Reserve Bank. Pres. Downtown Unltd., 1983-84; mem. Ala. Bd. Bar Examiners, 1973-78; chmn. bd. dirs. Ala. Bankers Found., 1971-77; trustee Ala. Assn. Ind. Colls.; bd. dirs. Shakespeare Theatre. Served to capt. AUS, 1942-46; to lt. col. JAGC Res. Decorated Bronze Star. Mem. ABA, Ala. Bar Assn., Montgomery Bar Assn., Ala. Ind. Bankers (chmn. 1983-84), Ala. Bankers Assn. (trust div. pres. 1963-65), Ind. Bankers Assn. Am. (dir. 1983—), Farrah Order Jurisprudence (pres. 1973), Order of Coif Alumni, Newcomen Soc. N.Am., Montgomery C. of C. (dir. 1983-84, pres. 1987-88), Delta Sigma Pi, Phi Delta Phi, Omicron Delta Kappa, Pi Kappa Phi. Episcopalian (past sr. warden). Clubs: Maxwell Officers, Montgomery Country (dir. 1987—), Capital City (dir.), Kiwanis. Home: 3332 Boxwood Dr Montgomery AL 36111 Office: Union Bank & Trust Co Commerce Street Montgomery AL 36104

LESLIE, JOHN ETHELBERT, investment banker; b. Vienna, Austria, Oct. 13, 1910; came to U.S., 1938, naturalized, 1944; s. Julius and Valerie (Lawetzky) L.; m. Evelyn Ottinger Goetz, Mar. 28, 1940 (dec.); m. Miriam Paul Emmet, June 26, 1986. Dr. Jur., U. Vienna, 1932; diploma, Consular Acad. Polit. Sci. and Econs., Vienna, 1934; M.S., Columbia U., 1942. Sec. to judges Fed. Law Cts. Austria, 1934-36; pvt. practice Vienna, 1936-38; sr. auditor Arthur Anderson & Co., C.P.A.s, N.Y.C., 1941-46; prin. R.G. Rankin & Co., tax cons., N.Y.C., 1946-55; with Bache & Co., Inc. (name later Prudential-Bache Securities Inc.), N.Y.C., 1955-82; chmn. bd. Bache & Co., Inc. (name later Bache Halsey Stuart-Shields Inc.), 1969-78; chmn. exec. com. Bache & Co., Inc. (name now Bache Halsey Stuart-Shields Inc.), 1968-69, chief exec. officer, 1970-77; chmn. bd. Bache Group Inc., 1969-78; chmn. policy com. Bache Group and Bache Halsey Stuart Shields, 1978-79; dir. Bache Group, Inc., 1969-82, chmn. emeritus, 1980—; dir. emeritus Prudential Bache Securities; sr. v.p. dir. 920 Fifth Ave. Corp.; hon. consul gen. of Austria in N.Y., 1965—; mem. adv. com. on internat. capital markets N.Y. Stock Exchange, chmn., 1973-75. Hon. trustee Inst. Internat. Edn.; hon. bd. dirs. N.Y.C. Partnership, Inc, bd. dirs. Econ. Devel. Council N.Y.; pres. H.L. Bache Found.; mem. adv. council internat. affairs Sch. Internat. Affairs, Columbia U., 1975-80 trustee Am.-Austrian Found., chmn. exec. com. Decorated cruz Vermelha de Dedicacao Portugal; Gt. Badge of Honor; comdr. Golden Order of Merit; Gt. Silver Cross Honor with star Austria; Golden Star of Merit Vienna; officer Nat. Order Merit France; officer's cross Order of Merit W.Ger.; officer Order of Crown Belgium; recipient cert. of appreciation City N.Y. Mem. Council Fgn. Relations, Soc. Fgn. Consuls in N.Y.C., Austria C. of C. (past chmn., dir.), France-Am. Soc. (v.p., dir.), Alumni Assn. Sch. Bus. Columbia U., Alumni Assn. Diplomatic Acad., Am. Fgn. Service Assn., Fgn. Policy Assn. (hon. dir.), UN Assn.-U.S.A. (past vice-chmn., gov.), Pilgrims of U.S., Am. Acad. Poets (bd. dirs.). Clubs: Union, Wall Street, 25 Limited Luncheon (N.Y.C.); Piping Rock. Home: 920 Fifth Ave New York NY 10021 Office: Prudential Bache Securities One Seaport Plaza New York NY 10292

LESLIE, ROBERT LORNE, lawyer; b. Adak, Alaska, Feb. 24, 1947; s. J. Lornie and L. Jean (Conelly) L.; children—Lorna Jean, Elizabeth Allen. B.S., U.S. Mil. Acad., 1969; J.D., Hastings Coll. Law, U. Calif.-San Francisco, 1974. Bar: Calif. 1974, D.C. 1979, U.S. Dist. Ct. (no. dist.) Calif. 1974, U.S. Ct. Claims 1975, U.S. Tax Ct. 1975, U.S. Ct. Appeals (9th and D.C. cirs.), U.S. Ct. Mil. Appeals 1980, U.S. Supreme Ct. 1980. Commd. 2d lt. U.S. Army, 1969, advanced through grades to maj., 1980; govt. trial atty. West Coast Field Office, Contract Appeals, Litigation Div. and Regulatory Law Div., Office JAG, Dept. Army, San Francisco, 1974-77; sr. trial atty. and team chief Office of Chief Trial Atty., Dept. Army, Washington, 1977-80; ret., 1980; ptnr. McInerney & Dillon, Oakland, Calif., 1980—; lectr. on govt. contracts CSC, Continuing Legal Edn. Program; lectr. in govt. procurement U.S. Army Materiel Command. Decorated Silver Star, Purple Heart, Meritorious Service medal. Mem. ABA, Fed. Bar Assn. Club: Commonwealth (San Francisco). Home: 4144 Greenwood Ave Oakland CA 94602 Office: Ordway Bldg 18th Floor Oakland CA 94612

LESLY, PHILIP, public relations counsel; b. Chgo., May 29, 1918; m. Ruth Edwards, Oct. 17, 1940 (div. 1971); 1 son, Craig.; m. Virginia Barnes, May 11, 1984. BS magna cum laude, Northwestern U., 1940. Asst. news editor Chgo. Herald & Examiner, 1935-37; copywriter advt. dept. Sears, Roebuck & Co., Chgo., 1940-41; asst. dir. publicity Northwestern U., 1941-42; account exec. Theodore R. Sills & Co. (pub. relations), Chgo., 1942; v.p. Theodore R. Sills & Co. (pub. relations), 1943, exec. v.p., 1945; dir. pub. relations Ziff-Davis Pub. Co., 1945-46; exec. v.p. Harry Coleman & Co. (pub. relations), 1947-49; pres. Philip Lesly Co. (pub. relations), Chgo., 1949—; lectr. pub. relations, pub. opinion to bus. and sch. groups. Co-author: Public Relations: Principles and Procedures, 1945, Everything and The Kitchen Sink, 1955; Author: The People Factor, 1974, Selections from Managing the Human Climate, 1979, How We Discommunicate, 1979, Overcoming Opposition, 1984, Bonanzas and Fool's Gold, 1987; bimonthly Managing the Human Climate; also articles in U.S., Brit. mags. and trade publs.; Editor: Public Relations in Action, 1947, Public Relations Handbook, 3d rev. edit, 1967, Lesly's Public Relations Handbook, 1971, rev. edit., 1978, 83. Recipient Gold Anvil award Pub. Relations Soc. Am., 1979; voted leading active practitioner Pub. Relations Reporter Survey, 1978. Mem. Internat. Pub. Relations Assn., Pub. Relations Soc. Am., Phi Beta Kappa. Club: Mid-America (Chgo.). Home: 155 Harbor Dr Chicago IL 60601 Office: 155 Harbor Dr Suite 2201 Chicago IL 60601

LESNIK, MAX, magazine editor; b. Vueltas, Cuba, Sept. 8, 1930; came to U.S., 1961; s. Samuel and Maria Teresa (Menendez) L.; m. Miriam Alvarez, Dec. 29, 1955; children: Miriam Chavez, Vivian. BA, U. Havana, Cuba, 1953. Columnist Bohemia Mag., Havana, 1951-61; Miami corr. Bohemia Mag., 1961-64; radio commentator Cadena Oriental de Radio Network, Havana, 1953-57; with anti-Batista guerrillas 1957-58; program producer Radio Sta. WMIE, Miami, Fla., 1965-67; pub. and editor Replica Mag., Miami, 1967—; pres. Replica Pubs. Inc., Miami, 1967—. Nat. coordinator Cuban People's Party, 1950-56. Home: 5530 Sardina St Coral Gables FL 33146 Office: 2994 NW 7th St Miami FL 33125

LESNY, IVAN ARNOST, neurologist; b. Prague, Czechoslovakia, Nov. 8, 1914; s. Vincenc Ignac and Milada Barbora (Krausova) L.; m. Eva Hyksova, July 22, 1969; children: Peter, Ivan Jr. MD, Charles U., Prague, 1938, DSc, 1965. Jr. lectr. neurology U. Hosp. Motol, Prague, 1947-55, sr. lectr., 1955-68, prof., 1968—; dir. dept. child neurology, 1971—. Author: Child Neurology, 1980. Recipient Folke-Bernadotte award, 1966, Purkynje's medal, 1979, Charles U. Silver medal, 1987. Mem. World Soc. Cerebral Palsy, Am. Soc. Cerebral Palsy, Catalan Soc. Pediatrics, Purkynje Soc. Neurology (hon.), Purkynje Soc. Neurophysiology, EEG Soc. German Dem. Republic, Indian Acad. Pediatrics, Child Neurol. Soc. Can., Internat. Soc. Electro-Stimulation. Office: Charles U, 25 Smeralova, 17000 Prague 7 Czechoslovakia

LESSENCO, GILBERT BARRY, lawyer; b. Balt., June 19, 1929; s. Jacob David and Sarah (Bank) L.; B.S., Johns Hopkins U., 1950; LL.B., Harvard U., 1953; m. Elaine Beitler, Sept. 3, 1952; children—Susan Donna, Amy Gail, Robert Howard. Admitted to D.C. bar, 1953; since practiced in Washington; mem. firm Wilner and Bergson, 1955-60; partner Wilner & Scheiner, 1960—. Mem., treas. Democratic Central Com., Montgomery County, Md., 1970-74; chmn. Internat. Visitors Service Council, 1962; bd. dirs. Jewish Social Service Agy. of Greater Washington, 1978—, pres., 1984-86; bd. dirs. Mental Health Assn. of Montgomery County, 1980—, pres., 1981-82; trustee Meridian House Found. Served to lt. USAF, 1953-55. Named Outstanding Young Lawyer of Yr., D.C. Jr. Bar, 1965. Mem. Phi Sigma Delta (v.p.). Home: 10731 Gloxinia Dr Rockville MD 20856 Office: 1200 New Hampshire Ave NW Washington DC 20036

LESSER, LAURENCE, music conservatory president, cellist, educator; b. Los Angeles, Oct. 28, 1938; s. Moses Aaron and Rosalyne Anne (Asner) L.; m. Masuko Ushioda, Dec. 23, 1971; children—Erika, Adam. AB, Harvard U., 1961; student of Gaspar Cassadò, Germany, 1961-62; student of Gregor Piatigorsky, 1963-66. Mem. faculty U. So. Calif., Los Angeles, 1963-70; mem. faculty Peabody Inst., Balt., 1970-74; mem. faculty New Eng. Conservatory Music, Boston, 1974—, pres., 1983—; former vis. prof. Eastman Sch. Music, Rochester, N.Y.; vis. prof. Toho Gakuen Sch. Music, Tokyo, 1973—; performed with New Japan Philharm., Boston Symphony, London Philharm., Los Angeles Philharm. and Marlboro, Spoleto, Casals, other festivals; guest Lincoln Ctr. Chamber Music Soc., N.Y.C.; rec. artist. Overseer Boston Symphony Orch.; trustee WGBH Ednl. Found.; mem. adv. council Chamber Music Am. Recipient prize Tchaikovsky Competition, Moscow, 1966; Fulbright scholar, 1961-62; Ford Found. grantee, 1972. Mem. Harvard Musical Assn., Phi Beta Kappa, Pi Kappa Lambda, Sigma Alpha Iota. Jewish. Club: Tavern (Boston). Home: 65 Bellevue St Newton MA 02158 Office: New Eng Conservatory Music 290 Huntington Ave Boston MA 02115

LESSING, DORIS (MAY), writer; b. Kermanshah, Persia, Oct. 22, 1919; d. Alfred Cook and Emily Maude (McVeagh) Tayler; m. Frank Charles Wisdom, 1939 (div. 1943); m. Gottfried Anton Nicholas Lessing, 1945 (div. 1949); children: John W., Jean W., Peter L. Ed. in, So. Rhodesia. Author: (novels) The Grass is Singing, 1950, Children of Violence, 5 vols, 1951-69, Retreat to Innocence, 1953, The Golden Notebook, 1962, Briefing For a Descent Into Hell, 1971, The Summer Before the Dark, 1973, The Memoirs of a Survivor, 1975, Shikasta, 1979, Marriages between Zones Three, Four and Five, 1980, The Sirian Experiments, 1981, The Making of the Representative for Planet 8, 1982, The Sentimental Agents in the Volyen Empire, 1983, The Diaries of Jane Somers (Diary of a Good Neighbour, 1983, and If the Old Could ... , 1984, pub. under pseudonymn Jane Somers), The Good Terrorist, 1985, The Fifth Child, 1988, (nonfiction) Prisons We Choose to Live Inside, 1986, The Wind Blows Away Our Words ... and Other Documents Relating to the Afghan Resistance, 1987, (short novel) Five, 1953, (short stories) The Habit of Loving, 1958, A Man and Two Women, 1964, African Stories, 1965, The Temptation of Jack Orkney and Other Stories, 1972, The Story of a Non-Marrying Man, 1972, Collected African Stories, 1973, (play): Play with a Tiger, 1962, (essays) A Small Personal Voice, 1974, (poetry) Fourteen Poems, 1959, also newspaper reports. Recipient Somerset Maugham award, 1954, Prix Medici, 1976, Austrian State Prize for European Lit., 1981, Shakespeare prize (Hamburg), 1982, W.H. Smith Lit. award, 1986. Mem. Nat. Inst. Arts and Letters, Inst. Cultural Research. Office: care Jonathan Clowes Ltd, 22 Prince Albert Rd, London NW1 7ST, England

LESTER, CHARLES TURNER, JR., lawyer; b. Plainfield, N.J., Jan. 31, 1942; s. Charles Turner and Marlyn Elizabeth (Tate) L.; m. Nancy Hudon Simmons, Aug. 19, 1967; children—Susan Hopson, Mary Elizabeth. B.A., Emory U., 1964, J.D., 1967. Bar: Ga. 1966, U.S. Dist. Ct. (no. dist.) Ga. 1967, D.C. 1970, U.S. Ct. Appeals (5th cir.) 1967, U.S. Ct. Appeals (11th cir.) 1982, U.S. Ct. Appeals (10th cir.) 1984. Assoc. Sutherland, Asbill & Brennan, Atlanta, 1970-77, ptnr., 1977—. Mem. Leadership Atlanta, 1980-81; pres. Atlanta Legal Aid Soc., 1979-80. Served to lt. JAGC, USNR, 1967-70. Mem. State Bar of Ga. (pres. young lawyers sect. 1977-78, bd. govs. 1977-78, 1980—, chmn. formal adv. opinion bd. 1987—, exec. com. 1977-78, 1987—), ABA, Atlanta Bar Assn., Am. Judicature Soc., Lawyers Club Atlanta (treas. 1982-83, exec. com. 1982—, 2d v.p. 1986-87, 1st v.p. 1987-88, pres. 1988—), Am. Bar Foun., D.C. Bar Assn. Democrat. Presbyterian. Home: 1955 Musket Ct Stone Mountain GA 30087 Office: Sutherland Asbill & Brennan 1st Nat Bank Tower Atlanta GA 30303

LESTER, HOWARD, lawyer; b. N.Y.C., Jan. 21, 1927; s. Harry and Fay (Aaron) L.; m. Patricia Barbara Briger, Mar. 6, 1956; children—Peter Bruce, Pamela Robin, Prescott Evan. B.A., Bklyn. Coll., 1949; LL.B., Yale U., 1952. Bar: N.Y. 1953. Practice, N.Y.C., 1953—; former mem. Emile Z. Berman and A. Harold Frost; mem. Lester Schwab Katz & Dwyer, N.Y.C., now sr. ptnr.; lectr. Practicing Law Inst., 1962—, mem. adv. com., 1984—; chmn. Joint Conf. Com. on Calendar Congestion and Related Problems 1st and 2d Jud. Depts., 1971-75. Trustee Buckley Country Day Sch., East Hills, N.Y., 1971-75. Served with U.S. Army, 1945-47. Mem. ABA, N.Y. State Bar Assn. (lectr.; chmn. exec. com. trial lawyer sect. 1972-73), Nassau County Bar Assn., Assn. Bar City N.Y. (ins. com. 1963-66, civil ct. com. 1968-71), Fedn. Ins. Counsel (v.p. 1967-68, gov. 1968—, pres. 1972-73, chmn. bd. 1973-74, bd. dirs. found. 1985—), Bklyn.-Manhattan Trial Lawyers Assn. (pres. 1971), N.Y. County Lawyers Assn., Def. Research Inst. (bd. dirs. 1972-77), Def. Assn. City N.Y., Am. Arbitration Assn. (law com. 1977—), Internat. Assn. Ins. Counsel, U.S. C. of C. (steering com. product liability task force 1977—), Am. Bd. Trial Advs. (adv.). Clubs: Glen Oaks, Yale (N.Y.C.); Banyan, Governors (West Palm Beach, Fla.); High Ridge (Hypaluxo, Fla.); Sands Point Bath and Tennis (N.Y.); Corbey Ct. (New Haven.). Home: 7 Via Los Incas Palm Beach FL 33480 Office: Lester Schwab Katz & Dryer 120 Broadway New York NY 10271

LESTER, JOHN JAMES NATHANIEL, II, engineer, environmental analyst; b. Houston, May 7, 1952; s. John James Nathaniel Lester and Margaret Louise (Tisdale) Sharp; m. Leslie Ann Yarab, Oct. 5, 1980. Student, U. Tex., 1970, Lee Coll., 1971; AS, Grossmont Coll., 1979; BA in Behavioral Sci., Nat. U., 1987, postgrad., 1987—. Registered profl. stationary engr.; ordained to ministry Am. Fellowship Ch. Nuclear power specialist USN, various, 1971-77; microbiology lab. technician VA, San Diego, 1978; prin. engring. asst. San Diego Gas & Electric, 1979-85, engring. environ. analyst, 1985-88; owner Calif. Triad Gem & Mineral Co. Logistics dir. and regional bd. mem. Gary Hart Presdl. Campaign, San Diego, 1984; founding mem. Inlet drug crisis ctr., Houston, 1970; vol. Dir. Aid for Guatemalan Refugees and Orphans, Guatemala, 1988. Served with USN, 1971-77. Mem. ASME, IEEE (interim pres. and founding mem. San Diego region Ocean Engring. Soc. 1984-85), Mensa, Assn. Humanistic Psychology, Amnesty Internat., Hunger Project, Earth Stewards, Human Rights Watch, Sierra Club. Democrat. Home and Office: 2588-D El Camino Real Suite 193 Carlsbad CA 92008

LESTER, RICHARD, film director; b. Jan. 19, 1932; s. Elliott and Ella (Young) L.; m. Deirdre Vivian Smith, 1956; 2 children. B.S., U. Pa. TV dir., CBS, 1951-54, dir., TV Goon Shows, 1956; directed: Running, Jumping and Standing Still Film (Acad. award nomination, 1st prize San Francisco Festival 1960); dir.: feature films It's Trad, Dad, 1962, Mouse on the Moon, 1963, A Hard Day's Night, 1964, The Knack, 1964 (Grand Prix, Cannes Film Festival), Help, 1965 (Best Film award, Best Dir. award Rio de Janeiro Festival), A Funny Thing Happened on the Way to the Forum, 1966, How I Won the War, 1967, Petulia, 1968, The Bed-Sitting Room, 1969 (Ghandi Peace prize, Berlin Festival 1969), The Three Musketeers, 1973, Juggernaut, 1974 (Best Dir., Teheran Festival), The Four Musketeers, 1975, Royal Flash, 1975, Robin and Marian, 1976, The Ritz, 1976, Butch and Sundance—The Early Days, 1978, Cuba, 1979, Superman II, 1980, Superman III, 1982, Finders Keepers, 1984. Office: Twickenham Film Studios, St Margarets, Middlesex England

LESTER, ROY DAVID, lawyer; b. Middletown, Ohio, Jan. 16, 1949; s. Edgel Celsus and Norma Marie (Elam) L.; m. Pamela J. Pendorf, Sept. 1, 1987; children: Justin David, Benjamin. BS, Western Ky. U., 1970; JD, U. Ky., 1975. Bar: Ky. 1975, U.S. Tax Ct. 1979, U.S. Dist. Ct. (ea. dist.) Ky. 1976, U.S. Supreme Ct. 1979. Agt. Mut. Benefit Life, Louisville, 1970-72; ptnr. Stoll, Keenon & Park, Lexington, 1975—; bd. dirs. Almahurst Farm, Lexington, Ford's Fitness Systems Internat., Inc., Lexington. Contbr. articles to profl. jours. Bd. dirs., past pres. Lakeview Estates Lake Assn., Lexington, 1982—. Served with USNG, 1970-76. Mem. Fayette County Bar Assn. (auditor 1984), Order of Coif. Republican. Roman Catholic. Club: YMCA (Lexington), Lexington Country, Lafayette. Home: 2060 Norborne Dr Lexington KY 40502 Office: Stoll Keenon & Park 1000 1st Security Plaza Lexington KY 40507

LESTREL, PETE ERNEST, educator, research anthropologist; b. Quito, Ecuador, Feb. 19, 1938; came to U.S., 1948, naturalized, 1954; s. Hans and Berta (Schwab) L.; m. Dagmar Centa Kowalzyk, Apr. 20, 1968; children—Nicole, Valerie. A.B., UCLA, 1964, M.A., 1966, Ph.D., 1975. Engr., N.Am. Aviation, Los Angeles, 1962-65; instr. Santa Monica (Calif.) Coll., 1967-73; asst. prof. anthropology Case Western Res. U., Cleve., 1973-75, cons. dept. anatomy, 1974-75; asst. prof. UCLA Sch. Dentistry, 1977-80, assoc. prof., 1981—; research anthropologist VA Med. Center, Sepulveda, Calif., 1976—. Editorial bd.: Human Biology Jour, 1980-83; contbr. articles to profl. jours., chpts. in books. Fellow Human Biology Council; mem. Am. Assn. Phys. Anthropologists, Am. Assn. Dental Research, Internat. Assn. Dental Research. Democrat. Home: 7327 De Celis Pl Van Nuys CA 91406 Office: 16111 Plummer Ave Sepulveda CA 91343

LESTZ, GERALD SAMUEL, author, editor, publisher; b. Lancaster, Pa., Mar. 29, 1914; s. Jacob Louis and Fannie (Simon) L.; m. Edith Allport, Aug. 2, 1944 (dec. 1957); children—Michael E., Linda Lestz Weidman; m. Margaret E. Gordon, Apr. 24, 1958; stepchildren—Rien Boebel (dec.), Robert G. Dana. B.S., Wharton Sch., U. Pa., 1935. Reporter, Lancaster Ind., Pa., 1935-37, Lancaster New Era, 1937-41; columnist, editorial writer Lancaster New Era, 1946-79; editor Baer's Agrl. Almanac, Lancaster, 1948—; editor, pub. Stemgas Pub. Co., Lancaster, 1975—, Strasburg Weekly News (Pa.), 1986—, ptnr. Barr-Hurst Book Shop, 1987—. Author various books on history of Lancaster, Amish culture. pres. Heritage Ctr. Mus.; past pres. Lancaster Summer Arts Festival; past pres. Demuth Found., Lancaster; active Gov.'s Adv. Council Library Devel., Harrisburg, 1980-84. Served with USAAF, 1942-46. Recipient Connie award Soc. Am. Travel Writers, 1979; Mayor's Red Rose award Mayor Wohlsen, Lancaster, 1979; various news awards. Mem. Pa. Guild Craftsmen (past state pres.). Republican. Jewish. Clubs: Hamilton, Montana. Home: 375 Conestoga Dr Lancaster PA 17602 Office: Stemgas Pub Co Box 328 Lancaster PA 17603

LESZL, WALTER GABRIELE, philosopher, educator; b. Bassano del Grappa, Italy, Aug. 18, 1940; s. Elemer and Ellen (Wegeli) L. BA, U. Southampton, Eng., 1965; PhD, Oxford U., Eng., 1969. Researcher U. Padua, Italy, 1971-73, asst., 1973-79; assoc. prof. philosophy U. Pisa, Italy, 1979—. Author: Logic and Metaphysics in Aristotle, 1970, Aristotle's Conception of Ontology, 1975, Il "De ideis" di Aristotele, 1975; author, editor: I presocratici, 1982. Fellow Ctr. for Hellenic Studies, Washington, 1969-70, Humboldt-Stiftung, Tuebingen, Fed. Republic Germany, 1980. Home: S Maria, 56100 Pisa Italy Office: U Pisa Dept Philosophy, Piazza Torricelli, 56100 Pisa Italy

LE TALLEC, GEORGES ALEXIS, French supreme court judge; b. Dol, France, July 1, 1923; s. Georges Charles and Marie Louise (Le Mee) Le T.; m. Hélène Jeanne Guegan, Sept. 20, 1949; children: chantal, Catherine, Patrick. License en Droit, U. Paris, 1944, D en Droit, 1949. Barrister St. Brieuc, France, 1946-47; magistrate French Ministry Justice, various cities, 1949-59, Nanterre, 1973-78; expert attached to EEC Paris, 1973-83; legal adviser EEC, Brussels, 1959-73; dir. French Patent and Trademark Office, Paris, 1978-83; judge French Supreme Ct., Paris, 1983—; prof. Ecole Superieure Commerce, Paris, 1976-77; mem. adminstrv. council European Patent Orgn., Munich, 1978-83. Author: (with others) Droit European des Affaires, 1984; contbr. numerous articles on community law, French competition law and indsl. property law to profl. jours. Served with French Army, 1945-46. Decorated officier Legion of Honor, officier du Merite National (France); officier Ordre Ouisssam Alaouite (Morocco); titulaire Grosses Silbernes Ehrenzeichen (Austria). Roman Catholic. Office: Cour de Cassation, 5 quai de l'Horloge, 75001 Paris France

LETHER, FRANK DANIEL PETER MARTINUS, public relations executive; b. The Hague, Netherlands, May 4, 1946; s. Peter Daniel and Classina Adriana (Pepers) L. NIMA A in Mktg., Inst. Social Studies, The Hague, 1979, NIMA B in Mktg., 1980. Mgr. inplant printing dept. Dutch Beton Group, Rijswijk, Netherlands, 1963-70, City of Amsterdam, 1970-71; dep. gen. mgr. Dartli Delfland Reprographics, Amsterdam, 1971-73; display supr. Tex. Instruments Amstelveen, 1973-75; mgr. gen. affairs Mgmt. Tng. Ctr., Amsterdam, 1975-76; asst. to sales mgr. Wang Netherlands, Ijsselstein, 1976-77; product mgr. AM Internat., Rijswijk, 1978-80; pub. relations officer Datapoint Netherlands, Gouda, 1980—. Mem. Infopers (sec., bd. dirs.), Dutch Pub. Relations Assn., Internat. Presstr. Newspoort. Home: 34 Paulus Potterstreet, 3751 VB Bunschoten The Netherlands Office: Datapoint Netherlands, 47 Kampenringweg, 2803 PE Gouda The Netherlands

LE THOUS, ROBERT, airline executive; b. Roscoff, France, July 15, 1937; s. Francis and Adele (Perrot) Le T.; children: Herve, Sophie, Luc,

Marie. Grad. secondary sch., Brest, France. Engr. Naval Yard, Brest, 1954-59; instr. glider Civil Aviation Dist., Challes Les Eaux, France, 1958—; instr. aircraft Civil Aviation Dist., Challes Les Eaux, 1959—; instr., examiner glider and aircraft Air Club, Brest, 1962-75; mgr., chief pilot Aeronautics Sch., Brest, 1979-81; gen. mgr. Finist Air, Brest, 1981—. Mem. Nat. Syndicate Industries, Profls. Gen. Aviation. Roman Catholic. Office: Finist Air, Airport 21, 215 Brest France

LETO, JOHN ANTHONY, trucking firm executive; b. Des Moines, Sept. 19, 1962; s. Paul Joseph and Elsa Mae (Domres) L. Student Grand View Coll., 1981-83, Drake U., 1983-85; BBA, Iowa State U., 1988. Treas. City Wide Cartage Inc., Des Moines, 1975-84, pres., 1984-86. Republican. Roman Catholic. Avocations: photography, golf, bowling. Home: 4453 88th St Urbandale IA 50322 Office: City Wide Cartage Inc 1617 NE 51st Ave Des Moines IA 50313

LETO, SALVATORE, laboratory director, andrologist; b. Borgetto, Sicily, Oct. 28, 1937; came to U.S., 1946; s. Antonino and Elisabetta (Armato) L.; m. Margaret A. Smith, Sept. 12, 1964 (div. July 1970); children—Anthony L., Gerald A.; m. Evelyn H. Brady, Dec. 28, 1973. B.S. in Chemistry, CCNY, 1961; Ph.D. in Biology, Georgetown U., 1967, Cert. clin. lab. supr., N.Y. Staff fellow Nat. Inst. Child Health and Human Devel., NIH, Balt., 1967-71; lab. supr. IDANT Corp., N.Y.C., 1971-72, lab. dir., Balt., 1972-73, Washington Fertility Study Ctr., 1973—; cons., 1980—. Author: Clinical Advances in Andrology, vol. 8, 1982, Male Reproduction and Fertility, 1983; contbr. articles to sci. jours. Served in U.S. Army, 1961-63. Mem. Am. Fertility Soc., Am. Soc. Andrology, Am. Physiol. Soc., AAAS, Am. Assn. Tissue Banks, Pan Am. Congress Andrology, Sigma Xi. Democrat. Roman Catholic. Research in andrology, reproductive biology, cryobiology (human sperm cryo-preservation), immuno-infertility, endocrinology of reproduction. Home: 20 Sparrow Hill Ct Baltimore MD 21228 Office: 2600 Virginia Ave Suite 500 Washington DC 20037

LETOURNEAU, JEAN-PAUL, business association executive; b. St.-Hyacinthe, Que., Can., May 4, 1930; s. Eugene and Annette (Deslandes) L.; m. Claire Paquin, Sept. 26, 1956. Counsellor in Indsl. Relations, U. Montreal, Que., 1953; cert. c. of c. adminstrn., U. Syracuse, 1962; cert. advanced mgmt. U.S. C. of C, 1965. Mcpl. sec. Mont St.-Hilaire, Que., 1950-53; personnel mgr. Dupuis Freres (mail order house), 1953; editor Jeune Commerce, weekly tabloid Fedn. Que. Jr. C's. of C., 1953; sec. gen. Montreal Jr. C. of C., 1953-56; asst. gen. mgr. Province Que. C. of C., Montreal, 1956-59, gen. mgr., 1959-71, exec. v.p., 1971—. Author: Quebec, The Price of Independence, 1969, Report on Corporate Social Responsibilities, 1982. Mem. C. of C. Execs. Can. (past pres., mem. council excellence 1986), Corp. Counsellors in Indsl. Relations of Que., Am. C. of C. Execs. Roman Catholic. Club: St.-Denis. Office: 500 Place D'Armes, Suite 3030, Montreal, PQ Canada H2Y 2W2

LETTIERI, DAN JOHN, psychologist; b. Bklyn., May 23, 1942; s. Sesty and Rose (Gulino) L.; student N.Y. U., 1960-62; B.A., U. Calif. at Berkeley, 1964; M.A., U. Kans., 1966, Ph.D., 1970; postgrad. Johns Hopkins U., 1969-70. Psychologist, Suicide Prevention Center, Los Angeles, 1970-71; dir. research NIMH, Center for Studies of Suicide and Suicide Prevention, Rockville, Md., 1971-72, research psychologist Center for Studies Narcotic and Drug Abuse, 1972-73; research psychologist div. research Psychosocial br. Nat. Inst. Drug Abuse, Rockville, Md., 1973-78, chief Psychosocial br., 1978-82, asst. dir. div. epidemiology and statis. analysis, 1982-83; head treatment program Nat. Inst. Alcoholism and Alcohol Abuse, 1983-87; asst. med. investigator Md. Dept. Post Mortem Examiners, 1970; behavioral sci. cons., dep. coroner, Los Angeles, 1968-69. Vocat. Rehab. Adminstrn. trainee, 1966, USPHS trainee in social psychology, 1964-67. Mem. Internat. Assn. Suicide Prevention, Am. Assn. Suicidology (treas. 1975-77), Am. Psychol. Assn., Phi Beta Kappa, Psi Chi. Cons. editor Drugs and Society, Jour. Life Treatening Behavior, 1975—, Criminology; asst. editor Jour. Crisis; contbr. articles to profl. jours. Office: 74140 El Paseo Suite 132 Palm Desert CA 92260

LETTS, HUBERT WINFRED, writer, publisher; b. Inez, Tex., Aug. 18, 1913; s. Henry Frank and Totsy Clara (Spencer) L., Sr.; m. Clarris Lissie Bright, Oct. 9, 1938; children—Betty Louise Letts Arnold, Janet Gail Letts. B.B.A., U. Tex., 1970. Clk., U.S. Post Office, Corpus Christi, 1937-48, supr., supt., 1948-68; office mgr. Carlton Constrn. Co., Texas City, Tex., 1971-72; constrn. supr. Hospitality Mgmt. Corp., Dallas, 1973-74; writer, pub. Home Pub. Co., Corpus Christi, 1975—. Author: West of the Blue Ridge, 1982; Free Market Economics, 1983; Yankee Land to Dixie Land, 1986. Contbr. articles to profl. jours. and newspapers. Candidate for U.S. Congress from 14th Dist., Tex., 1968. Served with U.S. N.G., 1937-40. Mem. Am. Econ. Assn., Assn. for Comparative Econ. Studies, SAR, Portairs Businessmen's Assn. (pres. 1967). Democrat. Lodge: Kiwanis (pres. 1966). Avocation: genealogy. Home and office: 1037 McClendon St Corpus Christi TX 78404

LETTVIN, THEODORE, concert pianist; b. Chgo., Oct. 29, 1926; s. Solomon and Fannie (Naktin) L.; m. Joan Rorimer; children: Rory, Ellen, David. Mus. B., Curtis Inst. Music, 1949; postgrad., U. Pa. vis. lectr., U. Colo., 1956-57; head piano dept. Cleve. Music Sch. Settlement, 1957-68; prof. piano New Eng. Conservatory Music, Boston, 1968-77; prof., dir., doctoral program in piano performance U. Mich. Sch. Music, Ann Arbor, 1977-87; disting. prof. dept. music, dir. doctor of musical arts/artist's diploma program Rutgers U., New Brunswick, N.J., 1987—; concerts, tchr. master classes U. S.E. Mass., summer 1973; mem. faculty Chamber Music Sch., U. Maine, Orono. First appeared as concert pianist, 1931, solo debut with, Chgo. Symphony Orch., 1939, solo, orchestral appearances include, Boston Symphony Orch., N.Y. Philharmonic, Phila. Orch., Cleve. Orch., Chgo. Orch., Washington Nat. Symphony, Pitts. Symphony, Seattle Symphony, Mpls. Symphony, Atlanta Symphony, other Am. orchs., also European orchs.; radio appearance, Bell Telephone Hour, 1948, debut, Ravinia Festival, 1951, apprentice condr., William Steinberg, Buffalo Symphony Orch., 1950-51, concertized, throughout U.S., Can., Europe, Africa, 1952—, recent concert appearances, Pitts., Cin., Atlanta, Boston, N.Y.C., Phila., Chgo., Cleve., Mpls. and Chautauqua, Ravinia, Interlochen and New Coll., Town Hall, Alice Tully Hall concerts, in N.Y.C., Boston Symphony Orch; concert tours, Europe, 1952, 55, 58, 60, 62—, Israel, 1973, Africa and Japan, 1974; also numerous performances with European orchs., summer festivals, TV; asst. artist: Africa and Japan, Marlboro Music Festival, 1963. Recipient award Soc. Am. Musicians, 1933, Naumberg award, 1948, Michaels Meml. award, 1949, Belgian Internat. Music Competition prize. Mem. Am. Fedn. Musicians, Am. Guild Mus. Artists, AAUP (exec. com.), Music Tchrs. Nat. Assn., Am. Liszt Soc., Curtis Inst. Music Alumnae Assn. (bd. dirs.). Home: Bradford NH 03221 also: 12 Bernard Rd East Brunswick NJ 08816 Office: Rutgers U Douglass Campus Music Bldg Brunswick NJ 08903

LEUBERT, ALFRED OTTO PAUL, international business executive; b. N.Y.C., Dec. 7, 1922; s. Paul T. and Josephine (Haaga) L.; m. Celestine Capka, July 22, 1944 (div. 1977); children: Eloise Ann (Mrs. Kevin B. Cronin), Susan Beth (Mrs. Stephen E. Melvin); m. Hope Sherman Drapkin, June 4, 1978 (div. 1982). Student, Dartmouth Coll., 1943; B.S., Fordham U., 1946; M.B.A., N.Y. U., 1950. Account mgr. J.K. Lasser & Co., N.Y.C., 1948-52; controller Vision, Inc., N.Y.C., 1952-53; with Old Town Corp., 1953-58, controller, 1953-54, sec., controller, 1954-56, sec.-treas., 1956-57, v.p., treas., 1957-58; dir. subsidiaries Old Town Corp. (Old Town Internat. Corp., Old Town Ribbon & Carbon Co., Inc.), Mass. and Calif., 1955-58; v.p., controller Willcox & Gibbs, Inc., N.Y.C., 1958-59; v.p., treas. Willcox & Gibbs, Inc., 1959-65, pres., dir., chief exec. officer, 1966-76; founder, pub., pres. Leubert's Compendium of Bus. (Fin. and Econ. Barometers), 1978—; pres. Alfred O.P. Leubert Ltd., 1981-82; chmn., chief exec. officer Solidyne, Inc., 1982; chmn. bd., pres., chief exec. officer, dir. Chyron Corp., 1983—; chmn. bd., chief exec. officer, bd. dirs. Chyron Group (U.K.) Ltd., 1985—; chmn. bd., chief exec officer, dir. CGS Units Inc., CMX Corp. 1988—, Digital Services Corp.; v.p. chmn. bd. dirs. CMX Laser Sytems, Inc.; instr. accountancy Pace Coll., 1955-57. Bd. dirs. United Fund of Manhasset, 1963-69, pres., 1964-65; bd. dirs. Actor's Studio, 1972-76; adv. bd. St. Anthony's Guidance Clinic, 1967-69. Served to 1st lt., inf. USMCR, 1943-46. Decorated Bronze Star; recipient Humanitarian award Hebrew Acad., N.Y.C., 1971. Mem. Nat. Assn. Accts., Am. Inst. CPAs, N.Y. State Soc. CPAs, Fordham U. Alumni Assn., Newcomen Soc. N.Am. Roman Catholic. Club: N.Y. Athletic (N.Y.C.). Home: 1 Lincoln Plaza New York NY 10023 Office: 265 Spagnoli Dr Melville NY 11747

LEUKEFELD, CARL GEORGE, social worker, USPHS officer; b. Lake Forest, Ill., May 14, 1943; s. Karl Frederick and Berta (Link) L.; B.S., Mo. Valley Coll., 1965; M.S.W., U. Mich., 1967; D.S.W., Cath. U. Am., 1975; cert. Harvard Sch. Public Health, 1980; m. Sara Ann Huffstutler, Aug. 13, 1966; children—Sarabeth, Karl Austin, Marianne. Program dir. Boys Club, Pontiac, Mich., 1966; commd. lt. USPHS, 1967, advanced through grades to capt. 1980; mental health officer, Los Angeles, 1967-71; mental health adv., Rockville, Md., 1971-73; staff asst., then spl. asst. Nat. Inst. on Drug Abuse, USPHS, Rockville, Md., 1975-77, dep. dir., acting dir. div. of resource devel., 1978-81, dep. dir., then dir. div. prevention and treatment devel., 1981-82, acting dir., dep. dir. div. clin. research, 1982-86; detailed to Naval Mil. Personnel Command, 1983—, apptd. chief health services officer USPHS, 1984; fellow mental health career devel. program NIMH, 1973-75. Mem. social work career devel. com. USPHS, chair. social work career devel. com., 1982, chairperson social work profl. adv. subcom. 1983; mem. Intra-Agy. Task Force Emergency Preparedness, 1987—. Editor jour. National Health Line, Health and Social Work; cons. editor Jour. Primary Prevention; co-editor books including Responding to AIDS: Psychosocial Initiatives, 1987. Decorated Commendation medal, 1978, 83, Outstanding Service medal, Meritorious Service medal, 1987; recipient Torch award Am. Humanics Found., 1978. Mem. Nat. Assn. Social Workers (chmn. commn. on health and mental health 1985-87), Acad. Cert. Social Workers, AAAS, Council on Social Work Edn., Am. Public Health Assn., Assn. Mil. Surgeons (chmn. med. service corp. sect. 1987), Commd. Officers Assn. USPHS (bd. dirs.), Alcohol and Drug Abuse Problems Am., Tau Kappa Epsilon, Alpha Phi Omega, Pi Gamma Mu. Presbyterian (elder). Home: 13 Sussex Rd Silver Spring MD 20910 Office: 5600 Fishers Ln Rockville MD 20852

LEUNG, BENJAMIN SHUET-KIN, biochemist, educator; b. Hong Kong, June 30, 1938; came to U.S., 1961, naturalized, 1970; s. Frank Yun-Pui and Ken-Yau (Lee) L.; m. Helen T. Hsu, Oct. 19, 1964; children—Kay, Titus, Steven. Student in chemistry and zoology, Hong Kong Baptist Coll., 1960-61; B.S. cum laude in Chemistry and Zoology, Seattle Pacific U., 1963; Ph.D. in Biochemistry, Colo. State U., 1969. Postdoctoral fellow Vanderbilt U., Nashville, 1969-71; dir. Clin. Research Ctr. Lab., Portland, Oreg., 1971-76; from asst. prof. to assoc. prof. dept. surgery Dept. Oreg. Health Service, Portland, 1971-76; sr. research scientist Cedar Sinai Med. Ctr., Los Angeles, 1976-78; assoc. prof. ob-gyn U. Minn., Mpls., 1978-84, prof. ob-gyn, 1984—, research dir. Endocrine Fellowship, 1978—, head div. cell biology and reprodn., 1984—; ad hoc cons. NIH, NCI, NSF, 1972—. Editor: Hormonal Regulation of Mammary Tumors, Vols. I and II, 1982; mem. editorial bd. Oncology and Biotech. News; contbr. articles to profl. jours. Chmn. Dad's Club Bridlemile Sch., Portland, 1975-76; resource person Community Resource Pool of Edina (Minn.), 1980—. Fellow NIH, Ford Found., 1966-71; grantee NIH, NCI, and others, 1971—. Mem. Am. Soc. Biol. Chemists, Endocrine Soc., Am. Assn. Cancer Research, Soc. Gynecol. Investigation, Minn. Chromatography Forum (chmn. program com. 1983-84), Internat. Platform Assn. Republican. Home: 6076 Olinger Blvd Edina MN 55436 Office: U Minn Dept Ob-gyn 420 Delaware St SE PO Box 395 Mayo Minneapolis MN 55455

LEUNG, RODERICK CHI-TAK, architect; b. Kumming, Peoples Republic of China, Aug. 12, 1949; s. Pe Ban and Kit Chong (Fung) L.; m. Julia Dexter Clark, Sept. 5, 1982; children: Emily, Rebecca. BArch, U. Minn., 1975; MArch, MIT, 1978. Architect Skidmore, Owing & Merrill, Chgo., 1975-83, John Portman & Assocs., Atlanta, 1983-84, Cooper Carry & Assocs., Atlanta, 1984—. Mem. AIA Chgo., AIA Atlanta, MIT Alumni Assn.

LEUPENA, TUPUA, government official of Tuvalu. Gov.-gen., Tuvalu, 1986—. Address: Office of Governor-General, Fongafale Tuvalu •

LEURQUIN, BERNARD, government official; b. Bavay, France, Apr. 4, 1933; s. Gaston and Germaine (Fontaine) L.; m. Renée Chambard, Sept. 4, 1958; children: Philippe, Vincent, Francois, Pierre. Govt. commr. Govt. of France, St. Pierre and Miguelon, 1985—. Office: Hotel de la Prefecture, 97500 St Pierre and Miguelon, French Overseas Territory France •

LEUTWILER, FRITZ, banker; b. Ennetbaden, Switzerland, July 30, 1924; m. Andrée Cottier, 1951; 2 children. Ed. Univ. Zurich; hon. degree, U. Berne, 1978, U. Zurich, 1983, U. Lausanne, Switzerland, 1984. Sec. Assn. for a Sound Currency, 1948-52; with Swiss Nat. Bank, 1952-84, dir. 1st dept., 1959-66, dep. gen. mgr. 3d dept., 1966-68, head 3d dept., 1968-74, chmn. governing bd., 1974-84; chmn. bd., pres. Bank for Internat. Settlements, Basel, 1982-84; bd. dirs. Chem. Bank, Prince of Liechtenstein Found.; chmn. Brown Boveri et Cie, 1985—; advisor Roboco Group, 1985—; mediator between Govt. South Africa and fgn. banks. Home: Weizenacher 4, 8126 Zumikon Switzerland •

LEVAILLANT, FRANCOISE, art historian; b. Paris, Sept. 14, 1944; d. Jean and Raymonde (Seguin) L.; m. Pierre-Etienne Will, 1967 (div. 1984); children: Julien, Alexandre. Agregation Lettres, Ecole Normale Supérieure, Paris, 1967; Doctorat d' Etat, U. Paris, 1986. Asst. U. Paris, 1968-71, master-asst., 1971-79; researcher Cen. Nat. de la Recherche Scientifique, Paris, 1979—; cons. to art pubs. Author, editor: (anthology) Andre Masson's Writings, 1976; mem. editorial staff Revue de l'Art, Histoire de l'Art; author numerous exhbn. catalogs; contbr. numerous articles to profl. mags. Mem. Inst. Nat. Histoire Art (sci. com. 1987), Assn. Profs. Histoire Art et Archaelogie Univs. (bur. 1986—0. Office: U Paris 1, 3 Rue Michelet, 75006 Paris France

LE VAN, DANIEL HAYDEN, business exec.; b. Savannah, Ga., Mar. 29, 1924; s. Daniel Hayden and Ruth (Harner) LeV.; grad. Middlesex Sch., 1943; B.A., Harvard U., 1950; student Babson Inst., 1950-51. Underwriter Zurich Ins. Co., N.Y.C., 1951-52; co-owner, dir. Overseas Properties, Ltd., N.Y.C.; dir. Colonial Gas Co. Served with AUS, 1943-46. Clubs: Harvard (N.Y.C.); Harvard (Boston).

LEVARY, REUVEN ROBERT, management sciences educator, researcher; b. Bucharest, Romania, Jan. 6, 1944; came to U.S., 1975, naturalized, 1983; s. Jacob and Carola (Fisher) L.; m. Martha, Merritt, Dec. 16, 1978 (div.); 1 dau., Sarah; m. Esther Feldman, Aug. 13, 1987. B.Sc., Technion, Haifa, Israel, 1969, M.Sc., 1972; M.S., Case Western Res. U., 1976, Ph.D., 1978. Teaching asst. Technion, 1969-72; grad. asst. Case Western Res. U., 1975-77; asst. prof. mgmt. scis. St. Louis U., 1978-81, assoc. prof., 1981-85, prof., 1985—; vis. scientist Ops. Research Ctr., MIT, 1984-85, vis. assoc. prof. Sloan Sch. Mgmt., spring 1985; NASA-ASEE summer faculty fellow Jet Propulsion Lab., 1987; cons. in field. Contbr. articles to profl. jours. Case Western Res. U. travel grantee, 1977; St. Louis U. grantee, 1979; Beaumont Faculty Devel. Fund grantee, 1984; Burlington No. Found. Faculty Achievement award, 1986. Mem. IEEE (sr.), Ops. Research Soc. Am., Inst. Mgmt. Scis., Soc. for Computer Simulation, Omega Rho. Office: Saint Louis U Dept Mgmt Scis Saint Louis MO 63108

LEVAUX, JEAN-FRANCOIS, engineering company executive; b. Liege, Belgium, Jan. 19, 1946; s. Jacques Thoussaint and Jeanine Marie (Beer) L.; m. Suzanne Marie Preud'homme, Oct. 16, 1971; children: David, Isabelle, Marie Noelle. Docteur en Droit, U. Liege, 1969; Licencie en Scis. Econs. Appliquees, U. Louvain, Belgium, 1972. Programme officer ILO, Geneva and Dakar, 1972-74; asst. to sales adminstrn. mgr. Cockerill S.A., Seraing, Belgium, 1974-77, mgr. sales adminstrn., 1977-81; mgr. contracts-export fin. and trading dept. CMI Cockerill Mech. Industries S.A., Seraing, 1981—; dir. Heurbel S.A., Liege. Mem. Assn. Le Grand Liege. Lodge: Rotary. Home: Chemin des Roches 9, B-4920 Embourg Belgium Office: CMI Cockerill Mech Industries SA, Ave Greiner 1, B-4100 Seraing Belgium

LEVAVY, ZVI, accountant; b. Jerusalem, Oct. 1, 1911; came to U.S., 1929, naturalized, 1944; s. Zeev and Esther (Shapiro) Leibowitz; B.C.S., NYU, 1934; m. Berenice Bardin, Nov. 27, 1935; 1 son, Bardin. Sec., Palestine Trust Co., Tel Aviv, 1934-36; sec., chief acct. Palestine Brewery Richon LeZion, 1936-38; comptroller Zionist Orgn. Am., 1940-43; now practicing C.P.A., N.Y.C. Pres., Perth Amboy Zionist Orgn., 1949-50; pres. Jewish Community Council, Perth Amboy, 1963-66; pres. Morris J. and Betty Kaplun Found.; v.p. Perth Amboy Bd. Edn., 1966-74; mem. Perth Amboy Bd. Sch. Estimate, 1966-74; mem. Middlesex County Coll. Found.; trustee Am. Friends Hebrew U.; member bd. govs. Dropsie U., 1976-85; trustee Annenberg Research Inst., 1985. Served with AUS, World War II; ETO. Fellow Jewish Acad. Arts and Scis. (treas.); mem. Am. Inst. C.P.A.s, N.Y., N.J. socs. C.P.A.s. Home: 148 Kearny Ave Perth Amboy NJ 08861 Office: 50 E 42d St New York NY 10017

LEVBARG, DIANE, fashion industry executive; b. Mar, 18, 1950; d. Morrison Levbarg and Ann-Louise Lewis; m. Martin I. Klein, May 23, 1974. Cert. in retail studies Coll. for Distributive Trades, London; student Vassar Coll., 1972. Exec. Trainee Harrods, London, 1970-71; exec. trainee, asst. dept. mgr., asst. buyer Saks Fifth Ave, N.Y.C., 1971-73; asst. buyer, buyer Bonwit Teller, N.Y.C., 1973-75; merchandise mgr. Bloomingdale's, N.Y.C., 1975-82; pres., fashion cons. Diane Levbarg & Assocs. Inc., N.Y.C., 1982—; exec. v.p. Missoni U.S.A.; v.p. Nina Ricci; cons. Daniel Hechter, Christian Dior U.S.A., Bogner U.S.A.; adv. bd. Lab Inst. of Mdsing. V.P., James Beard Affiliate, City Meals-on-Wheels. Named One of 100 Women of Promise, Good Housekeeping. Address: 200 E 72d St New York NY 10021

LEVÉE, DIDIER ALAIN, physician; b. Falaise, Calvados, France, June 29, 1954; s. Jean-Rene and Emilie Strnad; m. Claudine Jacquemoux, July 16, 1976 (div. Feb. 1985); children: Ludovic, Gwenael; m. Evelyne Odile Bazou, May 7, 1985. Degree in medicine, René Descartes Coll., Paris, 1981; degree in stomatology, Pierre and Marie Curie Coll., Paris, 1982. Practice medicine specializing in stomatology Bayeux, France; cons. Caen Hosp., Bayeux Hosp. Mem. Soc. de Stomatologie et de Chirurgie Maxillo-Faciale de France. Club: Porsche de France (Paris). Home and Office: 47 Rue des Bouchers, 14400 Bayeux France

LEVEIN, ULF INGVAR, microcomputer executive; b. St. Kil, Varmland, Sweden, Sept. 3, 1950; s. Ingvar and Ruth (Erikson) L.; m. Birgitta Nilsson, Feb. 26, 1977; children: Magnus, Malena. MS, U. Goteborg-Chalmers U. Tech., Goteborg, 1974. Telescope and computer operator Rao Space Obs., Onsala, Sweden, 1973-75; microcomputer project mgr., educator Chalmers U. Tech., 1975-77; electronic devel. engr. Novametric AB, Askim, Sweden, 1977-80; microcomputer design engr. AB Volvo, Goteborg, 1980-83; chief exec. officer dept. computer and control techniques Volvo Car Corp., Goteborg, 1983—; mgr. dept. prodn. engring. AB Srenska Elektromaqueter, Åmål, Sweden, 1986—; pres. Dalbo Consult AB, Fengersfors, Sweden, 1986—, AB Christinedals Bruk, Fengersfors, 1987—. Inventor spectrophotometer calibration method. Mem. bd. Volvo group microcomputer standard com., 1980-86, chmn., 1985-86. Mem. Quality Technique Engrs. Assn., VME User Group/Trade Assn. Scandinavia (bd. dirs. 1984-86). Lutheran. Avocations: nature studies, cross-country running, amateur radio. Address: Kristinedals Herrgård, S 662 02 Fengersfors Sweden

LEVENSON, ALAN BRADLEY, lawyer; b. Long Beach, N.Y., Dec. 13, 1935; s. Cyrus O. and Jean (Kotler) L.; m. Joan Marlene Levenson, Aug. 19, 1956; children—Scott Keith, Julie Jo. A.B., Dartmouth Coll., 1956; B.A., Oxford U., Eng., 1958, M.A., 1962; LL.B., Yale U., 1961. Bar: N.Y. 1962, U.S. Dist. Ct. D.C. 1964, U.S. Ct. Appeals (D.C. cir.) 1965, U.S. Supreme Ct. 1965. Law clk., trainee div. corp. fin. SEC, Washington, 1961-62, gen. atty., 1962, trial atty., 1963, br. chief, 1963-65, asst. dir., 1965-68, exec. asst. dir., 1968, dir., 1970-76; v.p. Shareholders Mgmt. Co., Los Angeles, 1969, sr. v.p., 1969-70, exec. v.p., 1970; ptnr. Fulbright & Jaworski, Washington, 1976—; lectr. Cath. U. Am., 1964-68, Columbia U., 1973; adj. prof. Georgetown U., 1964, 77, 79-81, U.S. rep. working party OECD, Paris, 1974-75; adv. com. SEC, 1976-77; mem. adv. bd. Securities Regulation Inst., U. Calif.-San Diego, 1975—, vice chmn. exec. com., 1979-83, chmn., 1984-88, emeritus chmn., 1988—; mem. adv. council SEC Inst., U. So. Calif., Los Angeles, Sch. Acctg., 1981-85; mem. adv. com. Nat. Ctr. Fin. Services, U. Calif.-Berkeley, 1985—, U. Iowa; mem. planning com. Ray Garret Annual Securities Regulation Inst. Northwestern U. Law Sch. Mem. bd. editorial advisors U. Iowa Jour. Corp. Law, 1978—; Bur. Nat. Affairs adv. bd. Securities Regulation and Law Report, 1976—; bd. editors N.Y. Law Jour., 1976—; contbr. articles to profl. jours.; mem. adv. bd. Banking Expansion Reporter. Recipient Disting. Service award SEC, 1972; James B. Richardson fellow Oxford U., 1956. Mem. ABA (exec. com., fed. regulatory securities com., former chair subcom. on securities activities banks), Fed. Bar Assn. (emeritus mem. exec. com. securities law com.), Am. Law Inst., Practicing Law Inst. (nat. adv. com. 1974), Am. Inst. CPA's (pub. dir., bd. dirs. 1983—, fin. com. 1984—, chmn. adv. council auditing standards bd. 1979-80, future issues com. 1982-85), Nat. Assn. Securities Dealers (corp. fin. com. 1981-87, nat. arbitration com. 1983-87, gov.-at-large, bd. govs. 1984-87, exec. com. 1986-87, long range planning com. 1987—), numerous adv. coms. Home: 12512 Exchange Ct S Potomac MD 20854 Office: Fulbright & Jaworski 1150 Connecticut Ave NW Washington DC 20036

LEVENSON, CARL, physician; b. N.Y.C., Sept. 21, 1905; s. Aaron and Sarah Sonia (Asheron) L.; B.A., Cornell U., 1927; M.D. (Mack tuition fellow 1927-31), SUNY, Bklyn., 1931; m. Beatrice Magill Levy, Nov. 29, 1976; 1 son, Donald S.; stepchildren—Margaret Levy Shapin, Richard M. Levy (dec.). Intern, Beth Israel Med. Center, N.Y.C., 1932-34; engaged in public relations for med. socs., N.Y.C., 1934-38; gen. practice medicine, N.Y.C., 1934-42; Chester, Pa., 1946-51; chief phys. medicine Chester Hosp., 1947-51, also asso. Grad. Med. Sch., U. Pa., 1947-51; fellow, resident in phys. medicine and rehab. U. Pa. Hosp., 1958-61; med. dir. Moss Rehab. Hosp., Phila., 1961-67; sr. attending physician, chmn. dept. phys. medicine and rehab. Albert Einstein Med. Center, Phila., 1961-71 emeritus, 1971—; clin. prof. Temple U. Med. Coll., 1963-71; clin. prof. rehab. medicine, psychiatry and human behavior Jefferson Med. Coll., Phila., 1979-83, hon. clin. prof. rehab. medicine, psychiatry and human behavior, 1983—; chief rehab. medicine service VA Med. Center, Coatesville, Pa., 1971-83; cons. VA, Dept. Army, 1946-51; bd. govs. Eastern Pa. chpt. Arthritis Found., 1965-79, mem. medicine and sci. com., 1961-80; mem. Montgomery-Bucks County Profl. Standards Rev. Bd., 1974-80; rehab. com. Am. Heart Assn., 1967-70. Served to maj. M.C., AUS, 1942-46. Decorated Army Commendation medal; named to Legion of Honor Chapel of Four Chaplains, 1982; recipient Disting. Service award Arthritis Found., 1967; grantee U.S. Govt., 1964; diplomate Am. Bd. Phys. Medicine and Rehab. (a founder). Fellow ACP, Coll. Physicians Phila., Am. Acad. Phys. Medicine and Rehab., Am. Heart Assn. (council cerebrovascular diseases), Am. Assn. Clin. Scientists, N.Y. Acad. Medicine, N.Y. Acad. Scis., Royal Soc. Health; mem. AAAS, Pa. Acad. Phys. Medicine and Rehab. (pres. 1968-69), Phila. Soc. Phys. Medicine and Rehab. (pres. 1964-65), AMA, Phila. County Med. Soc., Pa. Med. Soc., Am. Congress Rehab. Medicine, Am. Assn. Electrodiagnosis and Electromyography, Internat. Rehab, Medicine Assn., Nat. Assn. VA Physicians (cert. merit 1985), AMA, Phi Delta Epsilon. Republican. Jewish. Contbr. articles to profl. publs. Home: Wyncote House Apt 604 Wyncote PA 19095

LEVENSON, NATHAN S., architect; b. Pitts., Apr. 22, 1916; s. Max and Anne (Ashinsky) L.; BArch, Carnegie Inst. Tech., 1941; m. Bernice K. Klein, Aug. 31, 1947; children: David, Laura. Sr. draftsman various cos., Pitts., 1939-43; pvt. practice architecture, Pitts., 1948-85; tchr. Coll. of Phillipines, 1945-46; substitute prof. archtl. practice Carnegie Tech., 1959; instr. U. Pitts., 1978; pres. Bldg. Inspection Cons. Inc., 1973-88. Bd. dirs. AIA Pitts. Charitable Assn., 1979, Allegheny County Plumbing Bd., 1981-88; pres. bd. dirs. Bower Hill, 1979. Served to 1st lt. C.E., AUS, 1943-46; ETO, PTO. Registered architect, Pa., Ohio, N.J., Ark., Mich., Md., W.Va. Certified fallout shelter analyst, 1970; recipient 1st pl. award Illuminating Engring. Soc., Pitts., 1965. Mem. AIA (regional rep. housing commn. 1972-77, dir. Pitts. chpt. 1982-85, treas. 1980), Pa. Soc. Architects, Nat. Council Archtl. Registration Bds., Electric League Western Pa. (dir. 1984-86), Pitts. Architecture Club (dir. 1979), Clan-Carnegie-Mellon U. (v.p. 1970-72). Democrat. Jewish. Patentee Terrace Town House, multi-housing (U.S. and Israel). Home: 1160 Bower Hill Rd Apt 1110-B Pittsburgh PA 15243 Office: 303 Triangle Bldg Pittsburgh PA 15222

LEVENSON, WILLIAM ISRAEL, retail merchant; b. Balt., Sept. 10, 1920; s. Reuben Hyman and Miriam (Klein) L.; B.S. in Bus. and Public Adminstrn., U. Md., 1943; m. Gloria Waldman, June 12, 1949; children—Judith, Jerrold, Emily. With Md. Drydock & Shipbldg. Co., 1941-42; with Levenson & Klein, Inc., Balt., 1946—, mdse. mgr., 1952-60, v.p., sec., 1960-72, pres., 1972—; retail rep., bd. dirs. United Furniture Action Com., 1976-78; mem. adv. council furniture mktg. curriculum High Point Coll.,

1979-80; chmn. Furniture Industry Liaison Com., 1980. Mem. profl. adv. bd. Sch. Bus. and Mgmt., U. Md., 1983—. Served to lt. USN, 1942-46. Mem. Nat. Home Furnishing Assn. (chmn. govt. affairs com. 1976-78, pres. 1979-80, chmn. exec. com. 1980-81), Nat. Retail Mchts. Assn. (home furnishings bd. dirs. 1972-73), Furniture Retailers Md. (v.p. 1970-79), VFW, Sigma Alpha Mu. Jewish. Office: Levenson & Klein Inc Monument and Chester Sts Baltimore MD 21205

LEVENTHAL, A. LINDA, lawyer; b. Albany, N.Y., June 10, 1943; d. David Henry and Shirley R. (Asofsky) L. BA, SUNY, Buffalo, 1965; JD, Union U., 1968. Bar: N.Y. 1968, U.S. dist. ct. (no. dist.) N.Y. 1968. Ptnr. Rosenblum & Leventhal, Albany, 1968-78; sole practice, Albany, 1978-84, Schenectady, 1978-84; ptnr. Leventhal & Kirsch, Albany, 1984—; ptnr. Taub & Leventhal, Schenectady 1982—; lectr. continuing legal edn., family law sect. seminars N.Y. State Bar Assn., 1981—; bd. dirs. Legal Aid Soc. Northeastern N.Y., Inc. Bd. mgrs., pres. Commons of East Greenbush Condominium. Mem. ABA, N.Y. State Bar Assn., N.Y. State Women's Bar Assn., Nat. Assn. Women Lawyers, Nat. Assn. Female Execs., Nat. Assn. Bus. and Profl. Women. Lodge: Zonta. Home: 420 West Lawrence St Albany NY 12208 also: 9707 E Mountainview Dr Scottsdale AZ 85258 Office: Pieter Schuyler Bldg 600 Broadway Albany NY 12207 also: 115 Clinton St Schenectady NY 12305

LEVEQUE, MICHEL, SR., diplomat; b. Algiers, France, July 19, 1933; s. Raymond and Suzanne (Lucchini) L.; m. Georgette Van de Kerchove, Oct. 25, 1955; children: Valerie, Beatrice, Michel Jr. BS in Law, U. Paris, 1957; diploma, Ecole Nationale France d'outre-Mer, Paris, 1958. Counsellor Ministry of Planning, Ivory Coast, 1960-63; with dept. atomic affairs Ministry of Fgn. Affairs, Paris, 1963-65, with dept. Am., 1967-69, with dept. staff, 1972-74, dep. dir. African affairs, 1982-85; 1st sec. French embassy, Moscow, 1965-67; counsellor Sofia, Bulgaria, 1969-72, Tunis, Libya, 1974-78; ambassador Tripoli, Libya, 1985—; chief research sect. NATO, Brussels, 1978-82. Served as lt. French army, 1958-60. Home: 57 Rue de l'Universite, Paris 7 France Office: French Embassy, PO Box 312, Tripoli Libya

LEVER, WALTER FREDERICK, physician, educator; b. Erfurt, Germany, Dec. 13, 1909; emigrated to U.S., 1935, naturalized, 1941; s. Alexander and Edith (Hirschberg) L.; m. Frances Broughton, 1940 (div. 1969); children: Joan (Mrs. Russell Young), Susan (Mrs. Richard Siskind); m. Gundula Schaumburg, May 10, 1971; children—Insa Bettina, Mark Alexander. Student, U. Heidelberg, Germany, 1928-30; M.D., U. Leipzig, Germany, 1934; M.D. (hon.), Free U. Berlin, 1984. Diplomate Am. Bd. Dermatology (spl. competence certification in dermatopathology). Intern Cologne (Germany) U. Hosp., 1934-35, St. John's Hosp., Bklyn., 1936; resident dermatology Mass. Gen. Hosp., Boston, 1936-38; research fellow Mass. Gen. Hosp., 1938-44; from asst. to asst. clin. prof. dermatology Harvard Med. Sch., 1944-59, lectr., 1959-76; prof. dermatology Tufts U. Med. Sch, 1959-75, prof. emeritus, 1975—, chmn. dept., 1961-75, acting chmn., 1975-78; lectr. dermatology Boston U. Med. Sch., 1978-82; dir. dermatology service Boston City Hosp., 1961-74; dermatologist-in-chief New Eng. Med. Center Hosps., 1959-78, asso. staff mem., 1978-83; bd. consultation Mass. Gen. Hosp., 1959-76, hon. dermatologist, 1976-83; cons. Robert Breck Brigham Hosp., 1949-76; prin. investigator lipid metabolism USPHS, 1951-65, electron microscopy, 1962-75; mem. gen. medicine study sect. NIH, 1959-63; Dohi lectr., Japan, 1963; Pritzker lectr. U. Toronto, 1976; Novy lectr. U. Calif., Davis, 1977, Pinkus lectr. Wayne U., Detroit, 1987. Author: (with Gundula Schaumburg-Lever) Histopathology of the Skin, 6th edit, 1983, Pemphigus and Pemphigoid, 1965, (with Ken Hashimoto) Appendage Tumors of the Skin, 1969, (with Gundula Schaumburg-Lever) Color Atlas of Histopathology of the Skin, 1988; mem. editorial bd.: Archives of Dermatology, 1963-72, Am. Jour. Dermatopathology, 1979—. Fellow Am. Acad. Dermatology (past dir.); mem. Soc. Investigative Dermatology (past dir., past pres., hon. mem.), New Eng. Dermatol. Soc., Am. Soc. Dermatopathology (past pres.), Am. Dermatol. Assn., Deutsche Akademie der Naturforsher Leopoldina; hon. mem. Pacific Dermatol. Assn., Austrian, Brit., Danish, Dutch, Finnish, French, East German, West German, Greek, Indian, Italian, Japanese, Polish, Uruguayan, Venezuelan, Yugoslav Ddermatol. Socs. Lutheran. Home: Im Kleeacker 29, 7400 Tubingen Federal Republic of Germany

LEVERE, RICHARD DAVID, physician, educator; b. Bklyn., Dec. 13, 1931; s. Samuel and Mae (Fain) L.; m. Diane L. Gonchar, Jan. 15, 1978; children—Elyssa C., Corinne G., Scott M. Student, N.Y. U., 1949-52; M.D., SUNY, N.Y.C., 1956. Intern Bellevue Hosp., N.Y.C., 1956-57; resident Bellevue Hosp., 1957-58, Kings County Hosp., 1960-61; asst. prof. medicine SUNY Downstate Med. Center, 1965-69, asso. prof., 1969-73, prof., 1973-77, vice-chmn. dept. medicine, 1975-77, chief hematology/oncology div., 1970-77; asst. prof. Rockefeller U., 1964-65, adj. prof., 1973—; prof., chmn. dept. medicine N.Y. Med. Coll., 1977—; dir. dept. medicine Westchester County (N.Y.) Med. Center. Contbr. in field. Bd. dirs. Leukemia Soc. Am., 1970—, Am. Heart Assn., 1978—. Served to capt. USAR, 1958-60. NIH grantee, 1971-76, 65—. Fellow ACP (Physician Recognition award 1986); mem. Harvey Soc., Am. Soc. Clin. Investigation, Soc. Study of Blood (pres. 1973-74), Soc. Developmental Biology, Am. Soc. Pharm. Exptl. Therapeutics, Alpha Omega Alpha. Home: 5 Seymour Pl W Armonk NY 10504 Office: NY Med Coll Dept Medicine Munger Pavilion Valhalla NY 10595

LEVERENZ, JERRY WALTER, plant physiologist, researcher; b. Miami, Fla., Apr. 12, 1949; s. Frederick Louis and Mary Lou (Beatty) L.; m. Kathryn Ann. Velander, Aug.31, 1974 (div. Oct. 1983). BS, U. Wash., 1971, MS, 1974; PhD, U. Aberdeen, Scotland, 1979. Research asst. U. Wash., Seattle, 1971-74; pvt. gardener Edinburgh, Scotland, 1975-78; research assoc. U. Edinburgh, 1978-81; co-prin. investigator U. Wash., Seattle, 1981-83; guest researcher U. Umeå, Sweden, 1984—. Contbr. articles to profl. jours. Grantee NSF 1981, Swedish Forest and Agrl. Research Council, 1984, 86. Mem. Am. Soc. Plant Physiologists, Scandinavian Soc. Plant Physiologists, Xi Sigma Pi. Home: Vargvagen 171E, 902-38 Umea Vasterboten Sweden Office: University Umeå, Dept Plant Physiology, S-901 87 Umea Vasterboten Sweden

LEVERKUS, C. ERICH, banker; b. Duisburg, Germany, Mar. 15, 1926; s. C. Otto and Paula (Siebert) L.; m. Ingrid Nottebohm, Aug. 18, 1952; children—Juliane Brumberg, Johannes, Joachim, Jakob, Justus. Diploma Volkswirt, Univ. Tuebinger, 1955, Dr. Rer. Pol., 1957. Chmn. Vereinigte Utramarinfabriken AG, Bensheim, Germany, 1957-72; mng. ptnr. Wilhelm Ree Jr., Hamburg, Germany, 1961-86; gen. ptnr. Leverkus & Co., 1987; dir. Schutzvereinigung f. Wertpapierbesitz, Walter Blohm Stiftung, Krankenhaus Alten Eichen, all Hamburg. Author: Nordelbische Pastorenfamilien undihre Nach Kommen, 1973; Beautiful Lakes of the Canadian Rockies, 1979; Alberta's Forestry Trunk Road, 1979. Chmn., Versammlung Eines Ehrbaren Kaufmanns zu Hamburg e.V., 1982. Knight of Justice, Johanniterorden. Club: Rotary (Hamburg-Altona). Lutheran. Office: Leverkus & Co, Schauenburgerstrasse 55, 2000 Hamburg 1 Federal Republic of Germany

LEVESQUE, RENE JULES ALBERT, physicist, university administrator; b. St. Alexis, Que., Can., Oct. 30, 1926; s. Albert and Elmina Louisa (Veuilleux) L.; m. Alice Farnsworth, Apr. 6, 1956 (div.); children: Marc, Michel, Andre. B.Sc., Sir George Williams U., 1952; Ph.D., Northwestern U., 1957. Research assoc. U. Md., 1957-59; asst. prof. U. Montreal, 1959-64, assoc. prof., 1964-67, prof., 1967—, dir. nuclear physics lab., 1965-69, chmn. dept. physics, 1968-73, vice dean arts and scis., 1973-75, dean, 1975-78, v.p. research, 1978-85, v.p. research and planning, 1985-87, pres., 1987—; mem. Atomic Energy Control Bd., Ottawa, Can., 1985-87, pres., 1987—; mem. adv. com. ING project Atomic Energy of Canada Ltd., 1966-69; mem. adv. bd. physics NRC Canada, 1972-74, pres. nuclear physics grant selection, 1973; mem. adv. bd. on TRIUMF, 1979—; v.p. Commn. Higher Studies Que. Ministry Edn., 1976-77, Natural Scis. and Engring. Research Council Can., 1981-87, Atomic Energy Control Bd., 1985—; v.p. bd. dirs. Can.-France-Hawaii Telescope Corp., 1979-80, pres., 1980-81; pres. permanent research com. Conf. Rectors and Prins. Que. Univs., 1979-80; pres. Mouvement Laïc de langue française, 1961. Mem. Can. Assn. Physicists (pres. 1976-77), U. Montreal Faculty Assn. (pres. 1971), Fedn. Que. Faculty Assn. (pres. 1971-72), Interciencia Assn. (v.p. bd. dirs. 1979-80), Assn. Sci., Engring. and Technol. Community Can. (v.p. 1979-80, pres. 1980-81). Office: Atomic Energy Control Bd, 270 Albert St, Ottawa, ON Canada K1P 5S9 also: PO Box 1046 Sta B, Ottawa, ON Canada K1P 5S9

LEVEY, MICHAEL (VINCENT), art historian, author; b. London, Eng., June 8, 1927; s. O.L.H. and Gladys Mary (Milestone) L.; grad. with 1st class honours in English lang. and lit., Exeter Coll., Oxford, 1950; m. Brigid Brophy, June 12, 1954; 1 dau., Katharine Jane. Asst. keeper Nat. Gallery, London, 1951-66, dep. keeper, 1966-68, keeper, from 1968, dep. dir., 1970-73, dir., 1973-86. Slade prof. fine art Cambridge U., 1963-64; Wrightsman lectr. N.Y. U., 1968; hon. fellow Exeter Coll., Oxford, 1973. Served as capt. King's Shropshire Light Inf., attached Edn. Corps, 1945-48. Decorated Lt. Victorian Order; knight batchelor. Fellow Brit. Acad., Royal Soc. Lit.; mem. Ateneo Veneto (fgn.). Author: National Gallery Catalogues, 1956, 59, 71; Painting in XVIIIth Century Venice, 1959, rev. edit., 1980; From Giotto to Cé zanne, 1962; Durer, 1964; Later Italian Pictures in the Royal Collection, 1964; Rococo to Revolution, 1966; Early Renaissance (Hawthornden prize 1968), 1967; Concise History of Western Art, 1968; Painting at Court, 1971; The Life and Death of Mozart, 1971; Art and Architecture in 18th Century France, 1972; High Renaissance, 1975; The World of Ottoman Art, 1976; The Case of Walter Pater, 1978; (exhbn. catalogue) Sir Thomas Lawrence, 1979; Tempting Fate (fiction), 1982; An Affair on the Appian Way, 1985, Giambattista Tiepolo, 1986 (Banister Fletcher fiction prize 1987), others. Editor: Pater's Marius the Epicurean, 1985. Home: 185 Old Brompton Rd, London SW5 0AN, England

LEVI, ARRIGO, journalist; b. Modena, Italy, July 17, 1926; s. Enzo and Ida (Donati) L.; m. Lina Lenci; 1 child, Donatella. PhD in philosophy, U. Bologna, Italy, 1950. Reporter Italia Libera, Buenos Aires, 1943-44; program asst. BBC, London, 1951-55; foreign correspondent Corriere Della Sera, Milan, 1958-67; editor in chief La Stampa, Turin, Italy, 1973-78; columnist Newsweek, U.S., 1972-79, The Times, London, 1979-83; leader write C. Della Sera, 1988—. Author: Journey Amoung the Economists, 1973, Il Potere in Russia, 1977. Mem. council Human Rights Italian Govt., I.I.S.S. (exec. council), Italian Inst. Internal Affairs, Trilateral Commn. Jewish.

LEVI, DORO TEODORO, archaeologist; b. Trieste, Italy, Jan. 6, 1898; s. Levi Eduardo and Tivoli Eugenia; m. Anna Cosadinos, Feb. 8, 1928. D (hon.), U. Athens, 1988. Author: Price for Archaeology Academia Linc, 1963, Festeis e la Civiltoa Minoica Part I, 4 volumes, 1976-77, Part II, 32 volumes, 1981, 87-88. Vol. 1st World War, Florence, 1917. Mem. Pontifical Acad., German Archeol. Inst., Greek Archeol. Soc. Address: 64 Veikou St, Athens Greece Office: Italian Archeol Sch, Parthenonus 23, Athens Greece

LEVI, EDWARD HIRSCH, former attorney general U.S., university president emeritus; b. Chgo., June 26, 1911; s. Gerson B. and Elsa B. (Hirsch) L.; m. Kate Sulzberger, June 4, 1946; children: John, David, Michael. Ph.B., U. Chgo., 1932, J.D., 1935; J.S.D. (Sterling fellow 1935-36), Yale U., 1938; LL.D., U. Mich., 1959, U. Calif. at Santa Cruz, Jewish Theol. Sem. Am., U. Iowa, Brandeis U., Lake Forest Coll., U. Pa., Dropsie U., Columbia U., Yeshiva U., U. Rochester, U. Toronto, Yale U., U. Notre Dame, Denison U., U. Nebr., U. Miami, Boston Coll., Georgetown U., Claremont Ctr. and Grad. Sch.; L.H.D., Hebrew Union Coll., DePaul U., Loyola U., Kenyon Coll., U. Chgo., Bard Coll., Beloit Coll.; D.C.L., N.Y. U. Bar: Ill. U.S. Supreme Ct. 1945. Asst. prof. U. Chgo. Law Sch., 1936-40, prof. law, 1945-75, dean, 1950-62; provost univ. U. Chgo., 1962-68, univ. pres., 1968-75, pres. emeritus, 1975—; Karl Llewellyn Distinguished Service prof. (on leave) U. Chgo. Law Sch., from 1975, Glen A. Lloyd Disting. Service prof., 1977-85, Glen A. Lloyd Disting. Service prof. emeritus, 1985—; atty. gen. U.S., 1975-77; Thomas Guest prof. U. Colo., summer 1960; Herman Phleger vis. prof. Stanford Law Sch., 1978; lectr. Salzburg (Austria) Seminar in Am. Studies, 1980; spl. asst. to atty. gen. U.S., Washington, 1940-45; 1st asst. war div. Dept. Justice, 1943, 1st asst. antitrust div., 1944-45; chmn. interdeptl. com. on monopolies and cartels, 1944; counsel Fedn. Atomic Scientists with respect to Atomic Energy Act, 1946; counsel subcom. on monopoly power Judiciary Com., 81st Congress, 1950; trustee Aerospace Corp., 1978-80; Mem. research adv. bd. Com. Econ. Devel., 1951-54; bd. Social Sci. Research Council, 1959-62, Council Legal Edn. and Profl. Responsibility, 1968-74; chmn. 1969-73; mem. Citizens Commn. Grad. Med. Edn., 1963-66, Commn. Founds. and Pvt. Philanthropy, 1969-70, Pres.'s Task Force Priorities in Higher Edn., 1969-70, Sloan Commn. Cable Communications, 1970, Nat. Commn. on Productivity, 1970-75, Nat. Council on Humanities, 1974-75, dir. Continental Ill. Holding Corp. Author: Introduction to Legal Reasoning, 1949, Four Talks on Legal Education, 1952, Point of View, 1969; editor: (with J. W. Moore) Gilbert's Collier on Bankruptcy, 1936, Elements of the Law, (with R. S. Steffen), 1950. Hon. trustee U. Chgo.; trustee Internat. Legal Ctr., 1966-75, Woodrow Wilson Nat. Fellowship Found., 1972-75, 77-79, Inst. Psychoanalysis Chgo., 1961-75, Urban Inst., 1968-75, Mus. Sci. and Industry, 1971-75, Russell Sage Found., 1971-75, Aspen Inst. Humanistic Studies, 1970-75, 77-79, Inst. Internat. Edn. (hon.), 1969; public dir. Chgo. Bd. Trade, 1977-80; bd. overseers U. Pa., 1978-82; chmn. bd. Nat. Humanities Ctr., 1979-83, trustee, 1978—; bd. dirs. MacArthur Found., 1979-84, William Benton Found., 1980—, Martin Luther King Jr. Fed. Holiday Commn., 1986. Decorated Legion of Honor (France); recipient Learned Hand medal Fed. Bar Council, 2nd. cir., 1976, Fordham-Stein prize Fordham U., 1977, Brandeis medal Brandeis U., 1978. Fellow Am. Acad. Arts and Scis. (pres. 1986—), Am. Bar Found., U. Calif. Humanities Research Inst. (bd. govs. 1988—); mem. Fed. Bar Assn. (Honor award 1975), Am. Philos. Soc., ABA, Ill. Bar Assn. (Award of Honor 1983), Chgo. Bar Assn. (Centennial award 1975), Am. Law Inst. (council), Am. Judicature Soc., Supreme Ct. Hist. Soc., Phi Beta Kappa, Order of Coif. Clubs: Century (N.Y.C.); Chgo. Comml. Quadrangle Mid-Am. (Chgo.); Columbia Yacht. Office: U Chgo 1116 E 59th St Chicago IL 60637

LEVI, HENRY THOMAS, gemologist; b. Nanticoke, Pa., May 5, 1941; s. Henry Louis and Elinor (Stigora) L.; m. Cathy Ann Ellsworth. Student Shenandoah Coll., 1960-62; B.S., Franklin Pierce Coll., 1966; grad. Canadian Jewellers Inst., 1976; diploma Gemnol. Assn. Gt. Britain, 1977, Gemological Inst. Am.; cert. diamontologist, guild gemologist Diamond Council Am. Asst. store mgr. McCrory Corp., N.Y.C., 1966-68; supr. hardgoods Spartan Store, N.Y.C., 1968-70; mgr. Caldors, Peekskill, N.Y., 1970-73; sales mgr. Pomeroys Co., Wilkes-Barre, Pa., 1973-75; owner, gemologist Levi Jewelers, Nanticoke, 1977-80; mgr. Musselmans Jewelers, Stroudsburg, Pa., 1978-80; now mgr. Phila. Diamond Exchange, Interstate Diamond Corp., King of Prussia, Pa. Served with U.S. Army, 1962-68. Mem. Gemological Assn. Gt. Britain, Canadian Gemological Assn., Gemological Assn. Australia, Zimbabwe Gem and Mineral Soc., Jewelers Vigilance Com., Retail Jewelers Am. , Internat. Platform Assn. Agudah Israel Am., Union orthodox Jewish Congregations Am. Jewish. Lodge: B'nai Brith. Editor, Lapidary Jour., 1977, Canadian Gemologist, 1977, Jewellery World, 1977. Home: 50 C Heisz St Edwardsville PA 18704 Office: 103 Prospect St Nanticoke PA 18634

LEVIE, SIMON HYMAN, museum director; b. Dieren, The Netherlands, Jan. 17, 1925; m. Mary Lion; 3 children. PhD in Art History, U. Basel, Switzerland, 1952. Curator Cen. Mus., Utrecht, Holland, 1953-58; asst. Art Hist. Inst. U. Utrecht, 1958-63; dir. Mcpl. Mus. Amsterdam, The Netherlands, 1963-75; dir. gen. Nat. Mus., Amsterdam, 1975—. Mem. ICOM Found. (pres.), Found. Rembrandt Research Project, Vereniging Rembrandt, Council of Europe (mem. adv. com. on art exhbns.). Office: Rijksmuseum, PO Box 50673, 1007 DD Amsterdam The Netherlands

LE VIEN, JOHN DOUGLAS (JACK LE VIEN), motion picture/television producer, director; b. N.Y.C., July 18, 1918; s. Christopher Luke and Rose Jeanette Le V. Chmn. bd. TCA Travel Corp. Am., 1979—; chmn. bd. Electronic Pub. Co., London. Div. News editor: Pathé News, 1946-57; ind. motion picture and TV dir. and producer, 1958—; producer: (TV series) Valiant Years, 1959-60; exec. producer: (film) Black Fox, 1962 (Acad. award); producer and dir.: (films) Finest Hours, 1963-64, A King's Story, 1965, Churchill Centenary, 1974; (TV shows) Other World of Winston Churchill, 1964, The Gathering Storm, 1973, The Amazing Voyage of Daffodil and Daisy, 1974, Cicero, 1975, Where the Lotus Fell, 1976, Flames Over the Sahara, 1977, Children of the Lotus, 1978, Churchill and The Generals, 1980; pres., exec. producer TV movies, Le Vien Internat. Prodns. Ltd., N.Y.C., 1958—; chmn. bd., exec. producer TV shows, Le Vien Films Ltd., London, Eng., 1963—; author: The Valiant Years, 1961, The Finest Hours, 1964, (with Lady Mosley) The Duchess of Windsor, 1979, (with Barrie Pitt) Churchill and The Generals. Served to col. AUS, World War II, ETO; col. Res. Decorated Legion of Merit, Bronze Star; Legion of Honor; Croix de Guerre France). Mem. Brit. Acad. Film & Television Arts. Club: Overseas Press (N.Y.C.). Home: 15 Chesterfield Hill, London W1, England

LEVI-MONTALCINI, RITA, neurologist, researcher; b. Torino, Italy, Apr. 22, 1909. MD, U. Turin, 1940. Resident, assoc. zoologist Washington U., 1947-51, assoc. prof., 1951-58, prof., 1958-81; with Lab. Cellular Biology, Rome, 1981—. Author: My Life and Work, 1988. Recipient Albert Lasker Med. Research award, 1986, Nobel prize Physiology-Medicine, 1986. Mem. AAAS, Soc. Devel. Biology, Am. Assn. Anatomists, Tissue Culture Assn. Office: Lab di Biologia Cellulare, Via 6 Romagnosa, Rome 00196, Italy *

LEVIN, ALVIN IRVING, educator, composer; b. N.Y.C., Dec. 22, 1921; s. David and Frances (Schloss) L.; B.M. in Edn., U. Miami (Fla.), 1941; M.A., Calif. State U., Los Angeles, 1955; Ed.D. with honors, UCLA, 1968; m. Beatrice Van Loon, June 5, 1976 (div. 1981). Composer, arranger for movies, TV, theater Allied Artists, Eagle-Lion Studios, Los Angeles, 1945-65; tng. and supervising tchr. Los Angeles City Schs., 1957-65, adult edn. instr., 1962-63; research specialist Los Angeles Office Supt. Edn., 1965-67; asst. prof. ednl. research Calif. State U., Los Angeles, 1968; asst. prof. elem. edn. Calif. State U., Northridge, 1969-73; self-employed, Northridge, 1973—; founder, pres. Alvin Irving Levin Philanthropic Found., 1973—; ordained to ministry Ch. of Mind Sci., 1975; founder, pres. Divine Love Ch.-An Internat. Metaphys. Ch., 1977—, Meet Your New Personality, A Mind Expansion Program, 1975-77. Bd. overseers Calif. Sch. Profl. Psychology, 1974—; gen. chmn., producer Fiftieth Anniversary Pageant of North Hollywood Park, 1977. Composer: Symphony for Strings, 1984, Tone Poem for Male Chorus and Brass, 1984. Recipient plaque State of Calif., 1977, Golden Merit medal Rep. Presdl. Task Force, 1985. Named to Rep. Task Force Presdl. Commn., 1986. Mem. Nat. Soc. for Study Edn., AAUP, Am. Statis. Assn., Internat. Council Edn. for Teaching, Los Angeles World Affairs Council, Internat. Platform Assn., North Hollywood C. of C. (dir. 1976—), Phi Delta Kappa. Author: My Ivory Tower, 1950; (music-drama) Happy Land, 1971; Symposium: Values in Kaleidoscope, 1973; America, America! (TV series), 1978-79; (docu-drama) One World, 1980; Symphony for Strings, 1984; Tone Poem for Male Chorus and Brass, 1984; (mus. play) A Tale of Two Planets, 1988; compiler and contbr. U.S. Dept. Edn. reports; Adult Counseling and Guidance, 1967, Parent Child Presch. Program, 1967, English Classes for Foreign Speaking Adult Profls., 1967. Home and Office: 9850 Reseda Blvd #314 Northridge CA 91324

LEVIN, BURTON, diplomat; b. N.Y.C., Sept. 28, 1930; s. Benjamin and Ida (Geller) L.; m. Lily Lee, Jan. 4, 1960; children: Clifton, Alicia. B.A., Bklyn. Coll., 1952; M.Internat. Affairs, Columbia U., 1954; postgrad. in Chinese area tng., Harvard U., 1964. Commd. fgn. service officer Dept. State, 1954; counselor/econ. officer Am. Embassy, Taipei, Taiwan, 1954-56, polit. officer, 1969-74; intelligence research specialist Dept. State, Washington, 1956-58, dir. Republic China affairs, 1974-77; polit. officer Am. Embassy, Jakarta, Indonesia, 1959-63; polit. officer Am. Consulate Gen. Hong Kong, 1965-69, dep. chief mission, 1977-78, consul gen., 1981-86; dep. chief mission Am. Embassy, Bangkok, Thailand, 1978-81; ambassador to Burma, 1987—; vis. fellow Stanford U., 1974; vis. lectr. Harvard U., 1986. Mem. Am. Fgn. Service Assn. Clubs: Am.; Hong Kong Country (Hong Kong). Home: 72 Audubon Rd Wellesley Hills MA 02181

LEVIN, CARL, senator; b. Detroit, June 28, 1934; m. Barbara Halpern, 1961; children: Kate, Laura, Erica. BA, Swarthmore Coll., 1956; JD, Harvard U., 1959. Ptnr. Grossman, Hyman & Grossman, Detroit, 1959-64; asst. atty. gen., gen. counsel Mich. CRC, 1964-67; chief appellate defender City of Detroit, 1968-69, mem. council, 1970-73, pres. council, 1974-77; ptnr. Schlussel, Lifton, Simon, Rands & Kaufman, 1971-73, Jaffe, Snider, Raitt, Garratt & Heuer, 1978-79; U.S. senator from Mich. 1979—; past instr. Wayne State U., U. Detroit. Mem. Mich. Bar Assn., D.C. Bar. Democrat. Office: 459 Russell Senate Bldg Washington DC 20510-2302

LEVIN, DAVID HAROLD, lawyer; b. Pensacola, Fla., Nov. 19, 1928. A.B., Duke U., 1949; J.D., U. Fla., 1952. Bar: Fla. 1952. Asst. county solicitor Escambia County (Fla.), 1952; sr. ptnr. Levin, Middlebrooks, Mabie, Thomas, Mayes & Mitchell, Pensacola; chmn. 1st Jud. Circuit Fla. Jud. Nominating Commn., 1976-78; chmn. Fla. Pollution Control Bd., 1971-74. Chmn., Escambia County Cancer Crusade, 1963-65; pres. Escambia County unit Am. Cancer Soc., 1964-65; bd. dirs. W. Fla. Heart Assn., 1966-69; chmn. United Jewish Appeal Escambia County, 1967-68; former mem. human rights commn. W. Fla. Hosp. Mem. Fla. Alumni Assn. (pres. chpt. 1960), U. Fla. Alumni Assn. (dist. v.p. 1961-62), Blue Key. Recipient Good Govt. award Pensacola Jaycees, 1972; Service award Fla. Council for Clear Air, 1974; Francis Marion Weston award Audubon Soc., 1974; commendation Gov. Fla., 1974. mem. Am. Acad. Matrimonial Lawyers (pres. Fla. chpt. 1987-88). Home: 3632 Menendez Dr Pensacola FL 32503 Office: 226 S Palafox St Pensacola FL 32501

LEVIN, EDWARD M., lawyer, govt. adminstr.; b. Chgo., Oct. 16, 1934; s. Edward M. (dec.) and Anne Meriam (Fantl) L. (dec.); m. Joan Davis, Dec. 3, 1961; children—Daniel Andrew, John Davis. B.S., U. Ill., 1955; LL.B., Harvard U., 1958. Bar: Ill. 1958, U.S. Supreme Ct. 1968. Mem. firm Ancel, Stonesifer, Glink & Levin and predecessors, Chgo., 1958, 61-68; draftsman Ill. Legis. Reference Bur., Springfield, 1961; spl. asst. to regional adminstr. HUD, Chgo., 1968-71, asst. regional adminstr. community planning and mgmt., 1971-73; asst. dir. Ill. Dept. Local Govt. Affairs, Chgo., 1973-77; of counsel Holleb, Gerstein & Glass, Ltd., Chgo., 1977-79; chief counsel Econ. Devel. Adminstrn., U.S. Dept. Commerce, Washington, 1979-85; sr. fellow Nat. Gov's. Assn., 1985-86, sr. counsel U.S. Dept. of Commerce, 1987— ; lectr. U. Ill., 1972-73, adj. assoc. prof. urban scis., 1973-79; lectr. Loyola U., 1976-79, No. Va. law Sch., 1988—. Mem. Ill. Nature Preserves Com., 1963-68, Northeastern Ill. Planning Commn., 1974-77, Ill.-Ind. Bi-State Commn., 1974-77; bd. dirs. Cook County Legal Assistance Found., 1978-79; mem. Ill. div. ACLU, 1965-68, 77-79, v.p., 1977-78, Nat. Assistance Mgmt. Assn., 1988—. Served with AUS, 1958-60. Mem. Fed. Bar Assn., Ill. Bar Assn. (Lincoln award 1977), Chgo. Council Lawyers, Washington Council Lawyers, Nat. Assistance Mgmt. Assn. (bd. dirs. 1988—). Club: Arts (Chgo.). Contbr. articles to profl. jours. Home: 3218 Davenport St NW Washington DC 20008 Office: Hall of the States Rm 250 444 N Capitol St Washington DC 20001

LEVIN, FREDRIC GERSON, lawyer; b. Pensacola, Fla., Mar. 29, 1937; s. Abraham I. and Rose (Lefkowitz) L.; m. Marilyn Kapner, June 14, 1959; children: Marci Levin Goodman, Debra, Martin, Kimberly. BSBA, U. Fla., 1958, JD, 1961. Bar: Fla. 1961, U.S. Dist. Ct. (no. dist.) Fla., U.S. Ct. Appeals (5th cir.). Assoc. Levin, Middlebrooks, Mabie, Thomas, Mayes & Mitchell, P.A., Pensacola, 1961—; counsel Fla. Senate, 1981-82. Author: Effective Opening Statements, 1983; contbr. articles to profl. jours. Fellow Acad. Fla. Trial Lawyers (dir. 1977-84), mem. Inner Circle of Advocates, Ala. Trial Lawyers Assn., Tex. Trial Lawyers Assn., Pa. Trial Lawyers Assn. Democrat. Jewish. Home: 3600 Menendez Dr Pensacola FL 32503 Office: Levin Middlebrooks et al 226 S Palafox Pensacola FL 32501

LEVIN, JEANETTE BROOKS, market researcher, travel agent, property management executive; b. Buffalo, Aug. 5, 1930; d. Morris Jacob and Anna Pearl (Orzech) Brooks; m. Frank Levin, July 11, 1954; children: Arnold, Robert, David Susan. Student U. Buffalo, 1950-58, SUNY, Buffalo, 1965-70; lic. real estate broker; cert. Guided Observation Tchr. Program, Cheektowaga (N.Y.) Schs., 1968. Adult edn. tchr. Cleveland Hill Sch., Cheektowaga, 1965-68; founder, owner, prin. Buffalo Survey & Research, Inc., 1965—; property mgmt. agt. Jackson Sq. Apts., Buffalo, 1978—; pres., mgr. Buffalo Survey Travel, 1978—; cons. politics, image-making for candidates, 1974—. Columnist Buffalo Jewish Rev., 1976-80; media pollster Buffalo newspaper and TV; survey on U.S. tourism, 1973. Pres., Temple Shaarey Zedek Sisterhood, Buffalo, 1977-78, Past Pres.'s Council, 1981-83. Honoree Temple Shaarey Zedek Ann. Ball, 1977; recipient citation for ch. worker of week Amherst Bee, 1978, citations for high degree of accuracy in polling Buffalo News, 1971-87, 85-87. Mem. Mktg. Research Assn., Am. Assn. Pub. Opinion Research, Am. Mktg. Assn., Am. Contract Bridge League. Home: 324 Crosby Blvd Eggertsville NY 14226 Office: 1255 Eggert Rd Buffalo NY 14226

LEVIN, MARSHALL ABBOTT, judge, educator; b. Balt., Nov. 22, 1920; s. Harry Oscar and Rose (DeLaviez) L.; m. Beverly Edelman, Aug. 6, 1948; children—Robert B., Susan R. Levin Lieman, Burton H. B.A., U. Va., 1941; J.D., Harvard U., 1947. Bar: Md. 1947, U.S. Dist. Ct. Md. 1947, U.S. Ct. Appeals (4th cir.) 1950, U.S. Supreme Ct. 1953. Bill drafter, legis. asst. Dept. Legis. Reference, Annapolis, Md., 1948-49; research asst. Workers Compensation Commn., City of Balt., 1951, police magistrate, 1951-55, magistrate housing ct., 1955-58; ptnr. Levin & Levin, Balt., 1947-66; sole practice, Balt., 1966-68; ptnr. Edelman, Levin, Levy & Rubenstein, Balt., 1968-71; judge Circuit Ct. for Balt. City, 1971-87; judge, Spl. Master for Asbestos Litigation, Circuit Ct. for Balt. City, 1987—; chmn. Mayor's Com. on Housing Law Enforcement, Balt., 1963; lectr. nationally on sentencing, death penalty, immunities; lectr. Nat. Conf. on Child Abuse, 1976; dir. Legal Aid Soc., Balt., 1979-81; chmn. jud. bd. sentencing State of Md., 1979-83; chmn. Sentencing Guidelines Bd. State of Md., 1983-87; instituted One Trial/One Day jury system, Balt., 1983; prof. grad. sch. U. Balt., 1979—; prof. Nat. Jud. Coll., U. Nev., 1980—, mem. faculty council, coordinator current issues in civil litigation; adj. prof. jud. studies U. Nev., Reno; adj. mem. faculty Harvard U. Sch. Law; mem. vis. faculty trial advocacy workshop, Harvard U. Sch. Law. Contbr. articles to law revs. Served to lt. USNR, 1941-45, ETO. NEH fellow, 1976; recipient spl. award for service to jud. edn. Nat. Jud. Coll., U. Nev., 1984. Mem. Jud. Disabilities Commn., ABA, Md. State Bar Assn. (Leadership award 1984), Balt. City Bar Assn. (commendation 1982). Democrat. Jewish. Home: 6106 Ivydene Terr Baltimore MD 21209 Office: 306 Courthouse E Baltimore MD 21202

LEVIN, PATRICIA OPPENHEIM, educator; b. Detroit, Apr. 5, 1932; d. Royal A. and Elsa (Freeman) Oppenheim; m. Charles L. Levin, Feb. 21, 1956; children: Arthur David, Amy Ragen, Fredrick Stuart. AB in History, U. Mich., 1954, PhD, 1981; MEd, Marygrove Coll., 1973. Reading and learning disabled tchr., cons., Detroit, 1967-76, Marygrove Coll.; coordinator spl. edn., Marygrove Coll., 1976-86; adj. prof. Oakland U., 1987—; edn., curriculum cons. Lady Elizabeth Sch., Jávea (Alicante) Spain, 1988—; dir. Oppenheim Tchr. Tng. Inst., Detroit; conf. presenter. Mem. Mich. regional bd. ORT, 1965-68, 86—; v.p. women's aux. Children's Hosp. Mich.; bd. dirs. women's com. United Community Services, 1968-73; women's com. Detroit Grand Opera Assn., 1970-75; mem. coms. Detroit Symphony Orch., Detroit Inst. Arts; torch drive area chmn. United Found., 1967-70. Mem. Friends of Detroit Pub. Library, NAACP (life), Internat. Reading Assn., Nat. Council Tchrs. of English, Assn. Supervision and Curriculum Devel., Nat. Assn. Edn. of Young Children, Assn. Children and Adults with Learning Disabilities, Mich. Assn. Children with Learning Disabilities (edn. v.p., exec. bd.), Council Exceptional Children, Assn. Gifted and Talented Children Mich., Mich. Assn. Emotionally Disturbed Children, Orton Soc., Phi Delta Kappa, Pi Lambda Theta. Home: 411 S Woodward Apt 709 Birmingham MI 48009 Office: Oakland U 529 O'Dowd Hall Rochester MI 48309-4401

LEVIN, ROBERT DANIEL, lawyer; b. N.Y.C., Feb. 27, 1930; s. Moses H. and Esther (Walzer) L.; m. Gladys Schoen, Apr. 8, 1954; children—Jeffrey, Donna. A.B., Rutgers U., 1951; J.D., Columbia, 1954. Bar: N.Y. bar 1954. Since practiced in N.Y.C.; with firm Demov, Morris, Levin & Hammerling, 1954-85, sr. ptnr., 1963-85; sr. ptnr. Lowenthal, Landau, Fischer & Ziegler, P.C., 1985—. Co-editor: N.Y. Law Jour. Realty Law Digest. Mem. N.Y. State Bar Assn., Bar Assn. City N.Y. (state legislation and real property law com., com. civil ct.), Phi Beta Kappa, Phi Alpha Delta. Home: 12 Varian Ln Scarsdale NY 10583 Office: Lowenthal Landau Fischer & Ziegler 250 Park Ave New York NY 10177

LEVIN, ROGER MICHAEL, lawyer; b. N.Y.C., Oct. 20, 1942; s. Harold F. and Blanche M. (Tarr) L. B.A. in Polit. Sci., U. Chgo., 1964; Fulbright scholar U. Sri Lanka, 1964-65; M.A. with distinction in Polit. Sci. (Woodrow Wilson fellow), U. Calif.-Berkeley, 1966; J.D., NYU, 1969. Bar: N.Y. 1970, D.C. 1982, U.S. Dist. Ct. (so. and ea. dists.) N.Y., 1971, U.S. Ct. Appeals (2d cir.) 1971, U.S. Ct. Appeals (D.C. cir.) 1979, U.S. Customs Ct. 1974, U.S. Tax Ct. 1981, U.S. Ct. Customs and Patent Appeals 1974, U.S. Supreme Ct. 1974. Personal asst. to U.S. rep. Dept. State, Quang Nam Province, South Vietnam, 1966; asst. to dir. Nr. East/South Asia Bur., Office Internat. Security Affairs, Office Sec. of Def., Washington, 1967; assoc. Wien, Lane & Malkin, N.Y.C., 1969-70; ptnr. Levin & Weissman, N.Y.C., 1975—, mng. ptnr., 1982—. Named Best Oralist, Jessup Internat. Law Moot Ct. Regional Competition NYU, 1969. Mem. ABA, N.Y. State Bar Assn. (com. pension, welfare and related plans and ERISA subcom. labor law sect. 1981—), Assn. Bar City N.Y., D.C. Bar, Am. Soc. Internat. Law. Research editor NYU Jour. Internat. Law and Politics. Office: 122 E 42nd St New York NY 10017

LEVINE, BERNARD BENTON, lawyer; b. New Haven, Aug. 27, 1927; s. Charles and Mildred (Schwartz) L.; m. Joan A. Rapoport, Sept. 7, 1952; children—Stefanie, Kalman, Shelley Levine Kraft. B.A., U. Conn., 1950; LL.B., Boston U., 1953; LL.M. in Taxation, NYU, 1954. Bar: Mass. 1953, Conn. 1954, Mo. 1955. Assoc. Stinson, Mag, Thomson, McEvers & Fizzell, Kansas City, Mo., 1954-55; ptnr. Warrick, Levine & Greene, Kansas City, 1958-68, Levine & Green, Kansas City, 1968-81; sole practice, Kansas City, 1981—; instr. real estate, econs. and comml. law; 1985-87. Contbr. articles to legal jour. Bd. govs., past v.p., past bd. dirs. Jewish Geriatric and Convalescent Ctr., Kansas City, Jewish Family and Children's Services, Kansas City; bd. govs., past dir. Hyman Brand Hebrew Acad., Overland Park, Kans.; bd. dirs. Jewish Community Ctr., Kansas City, Am. Jewish Com., Kansas City, William Jewell Fine Arts Guild, Liberty, Mo., pres.; bd. dirs., mem. campaign cabinet Jewish Fedn., Kansas City. Served with U.S. Army, 1946-48. Mem. ABA (property and internat. savs. and loan div.), U.S. Savs. and Loan League, Mo. Savs. and Loan League, Mo. Bar Assn., Kansas City Bar Assn., Lawyers Assn. Kansas City, Conn. Bar Assn., Mass. Bar Assn. Home: 7318 Mercier St Kansas City MO 64114 Office: 1101 Walnut 1402 Mercantile Tower Kansas City MO 64106

LE VINE, DUANE GILBERT, petroleum company executive; b. Balt., July 5, 1933; s. Harry B. and Frances Annette (Culleton) LeV.; m. Patricia J. Allman, Aug. 10, 1957; children: Duane Gilbert, Michele P., William A., James D., Erin A., Megan K. B.S. in Chem. Engring., Johns Hopkins U., 1956, M.S., 1958. With Exxon Research & Engring. Co., 1959—; dir. fuels products research lab. Exxon Research & Engring. Co., Linden, N.J., 1971-74; mgr. gasoline and lube processes div. Exxon Research & Engring. Co., Florham Park, N.J., 1974-76; gen. mgr. Baytown (Tex.) research and devel. site, 1976-78, exec. dir. corp. research sci. labs., 1979-84; mgr. Exxon Corp. Worldwide Environ. Affairs, N.Y.C., 1984—; mem. Nat. Air Pollution Research Adv. Com., 1971-74, Tex. Energy and Natural Resources Adv. Council, 1976-78; mem. com. energy tech. assessment NASA, 1974; participant UN/industry-sponsored conf. on environ. mgmt., Versailles, France, 1984; mem. adv. com. Calif. Inst. Tech., Johns Hopkins U., Rene Dubos Ctr. Fellow Am. Inst. Chemists; mem. Am. Inst. Chem. Engrs., Internat. Combustion Inst., Am. Chem. Soc., Am. Petroleum Inst., AAAS, N.Y. Acad. Scis., Internat. Petroleum Industry Environ. Conservation Assn. (exec. com. 1984—), Sigma Xi, Tau Beta Pi, Phi Lambda Upsilon. Home: RD 2 Woodedge Rd Tewksbury Twp NJ 08833 Office: Exxon Corp 1251 Ave of the Americas New York NY 10020

LEVINE, HAROLD, lawyer; b. Newark, Apr. 30, 1931; s. Rubin and Gussie (Lifshitz) L.; m. Harriet B. Levine; children—Brenda Sue, Linda Ellen Levine Gersen, Louise Abby, Jill Anne Levine Zuvanich, Charles A., Cristina Gussie, Harold Rubin II; m. Cristina Cervera, Aug. 29, 1980. B.S. in Engring., Purdue U., 1954; J.D. with distinction, George Washington U., 1958. Bar: D.C. 1958, Va., 1958, Mass. 1960, Tex. 1972, U.S. Patent Office, 1958. Naval architect, marine engr. U.S. Navy Dept., 1954-55; patent examiner U.S. Patent Office, 1955-58; with Tex. Instruments Inc., Attleboro, Mass., 1959-77, asst. sec., Dallas, 1969-72, asst. v.p. and gen. patent counsel, 1972-77; ptnr. Sigalos & Levine, Dallas, 1977—; chmn. bd. Vanguard Security, Inc., Houston, 1977—; chmn. Tex. Am. Realty, Dallas, 1977—; lectr. assns., socs.; del. Geneva and Lausanne (Switzerland) Intergovtl. Conf. on Revision, Paris Pat. Conv., 1975-76. Mem. U.S. State Dept. Adv. Panel on Internat. Tech. Transfer, 1977. Mem. ABA (chmn. com. 407 taxation pats. and trdmks. 1971-72), Am. Patent Law Assn., Dallas Bar Assn., Assn. Corp. Pat. Csl. (sec.-treas. 1971-73), Dallas-Fort Worth Patent Law Assn., Pacific Indsl. Property Assn. (pres. 1975-77), Electronic Industries Assn. (pres. pat. com. 1972), NAM, Southwestern Legal Inst. on Patent Law (planning com. 1971-74), U.S. C. of C., Dallas C. of C., Alpha Epsilon Pi, Phi Alpha Delta. Republican. Jewish. Club: Kiwanis. Contbr. chpt. to book, articles to profl. jours. Editor: George Washington U. Law Rev., 1956-57; mem. adv. bd. editors Bur. Nat. Affairs, Pat., Trdmk. and Copyright Jour., 1979-87. Office: Sigalos Levine & Montgomery 2700 1st Republic Bank Ctr Tower II Dallas TX 75201

LEVINE, HELEN SAXON (MRS. NORMAN D. LEVINE), medical technologist; b. San Francisco; d. Ernest M. Saxon and Ann S. Dippel; m. Norman D. Levine, Mar. 2, 1935. AB, U. Ill., 1939. Supr. lab. San Francisco Dept. Pub. Health Tb Sanatorium, 1944-46, U. Ill. Health Services, Urbana, 1952-65; research assoc. in immunobiology, zoology dept. U. Ill., Urbana, 1965—. Mem. Pres.'s Council U. Ill. Kranner Art Mus.-Docent. Mem. AAUP, AAAS, Am. Heart Assn., Ill. Acad. Sci., Ill. Pub. Health Assn., Am. Soc. Med. Technologists, Am. Soc. Clin. Pathologists, Sigma Delta Epsilon. Home: 702 LaSell Dr Champaign IL 61822 Office: U Ill Morrill Hall Urbana IL 61801

LEVINE, HYMAN ISRAEL, chemical company executive; b. Bklyn., Aug. 11, 1909; s. Joseph and Dora (Alpert) L.; student Columbia U. Sch. Pharmacy, 1931; m. Gertrude Sendrowitz, Mar. 25, 1944; 1 son, Theodore. Owner, mgr. Adams & Nassau Pharmacy, Bklyn., 1931-46, Chelsea Pharmacy, N.Y.C., 1946-49; pres., founder Ruger Chem. Co. Inc., N.Y.C., 1949—; pres. Amend Drug & Chem. Co. Inc., Irvington, N.J., 1965—, GLS Realty Co., 1971—, A & R Sales Corp., 1974—, 500 Chancellor Ave., 1976—. Served with USAAF, 1941. Mem. Drug, Chem., Allied Trades, Am. Red Mogen David of Israel, A.R.M.D.I. (freedom chpt.). Jewish. Club: B'nai B'rith. Home: 3039 Harwood Dr Deerfield Beach FL 33441

LEVINE, JAMES, conductor, pianist, artistic director; b. Cin., June 23, 1943; s. Lawrence M. and Helen (Goldstein) L. Studied piano with Rosina Lhevinne and Rudolf Serkin, studied conducting with Jean Morel, Fausto Cleva and Max Rudolf;, studied theory and interpretation with Walter Levin; student, Juilliard Sch. Music; hon. degree, U. Cin. music dir. Ravinia Festival, 1973; artistic dir. Met. Opera, 1986; guest lectr. Sarah Lawrence Coll., Harvard U., Yale U. Piano debut with Cin. Symphony, 1953; conducting debut at Aspen Music Festival, 1961; Met. Opera debut, 1971; Chgo. Symphony debut at Ravinia Festival, 1971; regularly appears throughout U.S. and Europe as condr. and pianist, including Vienna Philharm., Berlin Philharm., Chgo. Symphony, Phila. Orch., Boston Symphony, N.Y. Philharm., Wagner Festival at Bayreuth; made Bayreuth debut in new prodn. of Parsifal, 1982; condr. Salzburg Festival premieres including Schönberg's Moses and Aron, 1987, Mahler's Seventh Symphony, Mendelssohn's Elijah; condr. Met. premier prodns. of Verdi's I Vespri Siciliani, Weill's The Rise and Fall of the City of Mahogonny, Stravinsky's La Rossignol, Oedipus Rex, Berg's Lulu, Mozart's Idomeneo and La Clemenza di Tito, Gershwin's Porgy and Bess; subject of documentary for PBS; artistic dir. Met. Opera. Recipient Smetana medal, 1987. Office: Met Opera Assn Met Opera House Lincoln Ctr New York NY 10023 *

LEVINE, MARILYN MARKOVICH, lawyer, arbitrator; b. Bklyn., Aug. 9, 1930; d. Harry P. and Fannie L. (Hymowitz) Markovich; m. Louis L. Levine, June 24, 1950; children: Steven R., Ronald J., Linda J. Morgenstern. BS summa cum laude, Columbia U., 1950; MA, Adelphi U., 1967; JD, Hofstra U., 1977. Bar: N.Y. 1978, U.S. Dist. Ct. (so. and ea. dists.) N.Y. 1978, D.C. 1979, U.S. Supreme Ct. 1982. Sole practice Valley Stream, N.Y., 1978—; contract arbitrator Bldg. Service Industry, N.Y.C., 1982—; panel arbitrator Retail Food Industry, N.Y.C., 1980—; arbitrator N.Y. Dist. Cts., Nassau County, 1981—. Panel arbitrator Suffolk County Pub. Employee Relations Bd., 1979—, Nassau County Pub. Employee Relations Bd., 1980—, Nat. Mediation Bd., 1986—, N.Y. State Pub. Employee Relations Bd., 1984—; mem. adv. council Ctr. Labor and Industrial Relations, N.Y. Inst. Tech., N.Y., 1985—; counsel Nassau Civic Club, 1978—. Mem. ABA, N.Y. State Bar Assn., D.C. Bar Assn., Nassau County Bar Assn., N.J. Bd. Mediation (panel arbitrator), Am. Arbitration Assn. (arbitrator 1979—), Fed. Mediation Bd. (arbitrator 1980—). Home and Office: 1057 Linden St Valley Stream NY 11580

LEVINE, MAX, stock broker, investment banker, pharmacist; b. N.Y.C., July 5, 1920; s. Isidor and Tillie L.; student CCNY, 1937-39; B.S. in Pharmacy, Columbia U., 1949; m. Maxine Hefler Hubbs, Dec. 28, 1979; 1 dau. by previous marriage—Lorie. Pharm. sales rep. Ayerst Labs., A.H. Robins, N.Y.C., 1953-58; exec. Dram Pharms., Inc., 1959-72; stock broker Edwards & Hanley and Sherman, Fitzpatrick U Co., 1970-82; pres. Berine Enterprises, Ltd., Roslyn, N.Y., 1983—; former v.p., dir. Medi-Waste, Inc., West Babylon, N.Y. Served to lt. USAAF, 1941-45, 51-53; ETO, PTO, Korea; lt. col. USAFR, ret. Mem. Mensa, Res. Officers Assn. Club: K.P. Home: 481 Division Ave Hicksville NY 11801

LEVINE, MELVIN CHARLES, lawyer; b. Bklyn., Nov. 12, 1930; s. Barnet and Jennie (Iser) L. BCS, N.Y. U., 1952; LLB, Harvard U., 1955. Bar: N.Y. 1956, U.S. Supreme Ct. 1964. Assoc., Kriger & Haber, Bklyn., 1956-58, Black, Varian & Simons, N.Y.C., 1959; sole practice, N.Y.C., 1959—; devel. multiple dwelling housing. Mem. N.Y. County Lawyers Assn. (civil ct. com., housing ct. com., liaison to Assn. Bar City of N.Y. on selection of housing and civil ct. judge, task force on tort reform). Democrat. Jewish. Home: 146 Waverly Pl New York NY 10014 Office: 271 Madison Ave Suite 1404 New York NY 10016

LEVINE, MICHAEL JOSEPH, insurance company executive, managment consultant; b. Boston, Mar. 23, 1945; s. Sam and Helen Alice (Michelman) L.; m. Margaret Mary Gutierrez, Aug. 6, 1983; 1 child, Samuel Jacob Gutierrez. BA, Boston U., 1967. Supr. underwriting Comml. Union. Ins., Boston, 1969-73; mgr. Harris-Murtagh Ins., Boston, 1973-75, Cohen-Goldenberg Ins. Agy., Boston, 1975-77; v.p. Southwest Underwriters Ins., Deming, N.Mex., 1977-83, pres., 1983-86; pres. Consol. Ins. Cons., Deming, N.Mex., 1985—. V.p. Border Area Mental Health Services, So. N.Mex., 1978—; pres. Deming Arts Council, 1979-81; treas. Luna County (N.Mex.) Crimestoppers, Inc., 1979—. Mem. Mensa, Soc. CPCU's (cert.), Soc. Cert. Ins. Counselors (cert.), Ins. Mktg. Assocs., Luna County C. of C. (v.p. 1981-84), Ind. Ins. Agts. N.Mex. (state dir. 1985—), Southwest N.Mex. Ind. Ins. Agts. (treas. 1981-83, pres. 1983-85). Democrat. Jewish. Lodges: B'Nai Brith, Moose. Home: 1920 S Silver St Deming NM 88030 Office: Pollard Southwest Ins Agy 120 W Pine St Deming NM 88031

LEVINE, RAPHAEL DAVID, chemistry educator; b. Alexandria, Egypt, Mar. 29, 1938; brought to U.S., 1939; s. Chaim S. and Sofia (Greenberg) L.; m. Gillah T. Ephraty, June 13, 1962; 1 child, Ornah T. MSc, Hebrew U., Jerusalem, 1959; PhD, Nottingham (Eng.) U., 1964; DPhil, Oxford (Eng.) U., 1966. Vis. asst. prof. U. Wis., 1966-68; prof. theoretical chemistry Hebrew U., Jerusalem, 1969—, chmn. research ctr. molecular dynamics, 1981—, Max Born prof. natural philosophy, 1985—; Battelle prof. chemistry and prof. math. Ohio State U., Columbus, 1970-74; Brittingham vis. prof. U. Wis., 1973; adj. prof. U. Tex., Austin, 1974-80, MIT, 1980—; Arthur D. Little lectr. MIT, 1978. Author: Quantum Mechanics of Molecular Rate Processes, 1969, Molecular Reaction Dynamics, 1974, Lasers and Chemical Change, 1981, Molecular Reaction Dynamics and Chemical Reactivity, 1986; mem. editorial bds. several well known scientific jours.; contbr. articles to profl. jours. Served with AUS, 1960-62. Ramsay Meml. fellow, 1964-66, Alfred P. Sloan fellow, 1970-72; recipient Ann. award Internat. Acad. Quantum Molecular Sci., 1968, Landau prize, 1972, Israel prize in Exact Scis., 1974, Weizmann prize, 1979; co-recipient Chemistry prize Wolf Found., 1988. Fellow Am. Phys. Soc.; mem. Israel Chem. Soc. (chmn. div. chem. physics and theoretical chemistry). Office: MIT Room 6-215 Cambridge MA 02139 also: Hebrew U of Jerusalem, Mount Scopus, Jerusalem Israel *

LEVINE, RONALD JAY, lawyer; b. Bklyn., June 23, 1953; s. Louis Leon and Marilyn Priscilla (Markovich) L.; m. Cindy Beth Israel, Nov. 18, 1979; children: Merisa, Alisha. BA summa cum laude, Princeton U., 1974; JD cum laude, Harvard U., 1977. Bar: N.Y. 1978, U.S. Dist. Ct. (so. and ea. dists.) N.Y. 1978, D.C. 1980, N.J. 1987, U.S. Supreme Ct. 1982, U.S. Ct. Appeals (2d cir.) 1983, N.J. 1987, U.S. Dist. Ct. N.J. 1987. Assoc. Phillips, Nizer, Benjamin, Krim & Ballon, N.Y.C., 1977-80, Debevoise & Plimpton, N.Y.C., 1980-84; assoc. Herrick, Feinstein, N.Y.C., 1984-85, ptnr., 1985—; gen. counsel Greater N.Y. Safety Council, N.Y.C., 1979-81; arbitrator Small Claims Ct. of Civil Ct. of City of N.Y., 1983-85. Mem. Site Plan Rev. Adv. Bd., West Windsor, N.J., 1986, planning bd., 1987. Mem. ABA (litigation sect.), N.Y. State Bar Assn. (com. on legal edn. and bar admission, 1982—), Assn. of Bar of City of N.Y. (com. on profl. responsibility 1980-83, com. on legal assistance, 1983-86, product liability com. 1987—), Phi Beta Kappa. Home: 6 Arnold Dr Princeton Junction NJ 08550 Office: Herrick Feinstein 2 Park Ave New York NY 10016

LEVINE, STEVEN ALAN, appraiser, consultant; b. Cin., Aug. 28, 1951; s. E. Pike and Beverly Rae (Friedman) L. BA with honors, U. Cin., 1975; postgrad., George Washington U., 1975-77. Appraiser Real Estate Evaluators and Cons., Cin., 1969-75; program asst. U.S. Renegotiation Bd., Washington, 1975; appraiser D.C. Govt., Washington, 1976-77; emergency mgmt. specialist Fed. Emergency Mgmt. Agy., Washington, 1977-80; v.p. Am. Res. and Appraisal Ctr., Cin., 1980-82; prin. Steven A. Levine & Assocs., Cin., 1982—; cons. U.S. Army, 1982—. Author: The Renegotiation of Defense Contracts, Military Installation Real Property Management, Property Tax Relief Measures for the Elderly, Minimal Repair Program Handbook. Coordinator Henry Jackson for Pres., Washington, 1976; mem. Forum for Urban Studies, Washington, 1977; mem. Common Cause, Washington, 1975-78. Served to sgt. USAF, 1969-75. Named to Hon. Order Ky. Cols., Louisville, 1979; named lt. col. aide-de-camp Staff of Gov. of Ga., Atlanta, 1979, lt. col. aide-de-camp Staff of Gov. of Ala., Montgomery, 1983. Mem. Am. Assn. Cert. Appraisers (sr.), Nat. Assn. Realtors, Am. Soc. Pub. Adminstrn. Jewish. Home: 4680 Mission Ln Cincinnati OH 45223 Office: Steven A Levine & Assocs 7536 Reading Rd Suite 6 PO Box 37652 Cincinnati OH 45222

LEVINE, STEVEN JON, lawyer; b. N.Y.C., Sept. 27, 1942; s. Irving I. and Freda S. (Silverman) L.; m. Linda Jane Silberman, Apr. 23, 1967; 1 son, Lawrence Alan. B.S., Syracuse U., 1964; J.D., St. John's U., 1966; M.A., CCNY, 1973; LL.M., NYU, 1978. Bar: N.Y. 1967. Assoc. Augustin J. San Filippo & Steven Jon Levine, P.C. and predecessor, N.Y.C., 1968-78; mem. Vittoria & Parker, N.Y.C., 1978— ; arbitrator N.Y. County Civil Ct. Panel, 1980— ; asst. csl. N.Y. State Senate Judiciary Com., 1977. Author of legal column Tomorrow newspaper. Committeeman, Bronx County, 1970-76; bd. dirs. Jewish Conciliation Bd. Am., 1973—, atty. mem. conciliation panel, 1973—. Mem. ABA, Internat. Bar Assn., N.Y. State Bar Assn., Westchester County Bar Assn., Assn. Bar City N.Y. (sect. vice chmn. matrimonial com. 1977-80), Am. Arbitration Assn. (no-fault, comml. panels 1975—). Office: 235 Main St Penthouse White Plains NY 10601 also: Vittoria & Parker 630 Fifth Ave New York NY 10111

LEVINSON, CHARLES BERNARD, architect; b. Youngstown, Ohio, Dec. 15, 1912; s. Al and Goldye (Davis) L.; m. Doris Mombach, Nov. 10, 1940; children: Ronnie Ann (Mrs. John Shore), Barbara Jean (Mrs. Ronald Stern), Suzanne (Mrs. Ralph Stern). BS in Architecture, U. Cin., 1934. Draftsman Gulf Refining Co., 1934-35; designer Hunt and Allen, 1935-36; pvt. practice architecture Cin., 1936-39, 40—; ptnr. Steelcraft Mfg. Co. div. Prefabricate Bldg. and Bldg. Products, 1940-44, v.p., 1945-51, exec. v.p., 1951-66, pres., 1966-69; v.p. then pres. Bldg. Products div. Knapp Bros. Mfg. Co., 1949-65, Leesburg Realty Co., 1952-76; sec./treas. then v.p./sec. ABCO Tool and Die Co., 1953-70; v.p., sec. Oceanautic Mfg. and Research Co., 1968-70; prof. U. Cin. Coll. Design Archtl. Art, 1970-85; vis. prof. architecture U. Wis., 1973-76, Coll. of the Desert, Palm Springs, Calif., 1976. V.p. Big Bros. Am., Cin., 1957, mem. spl. projects com., 1965, bd. dirs., 1956-66; bd. trustees Big Bros. Assn. Cin., pres., 1953-54, Bob Hope Cultural Ctr., Palm Desert, Calif., 1986—, Cin. Ballet Co.; mem. Nat. Com. Children and Youth, Nat. Com. for Employment of Youth, vice chmn., 1969, bd. dirs. 1962-68; mem. ad hoc adv. steering com. White House Conf. on Children and Youth, 1966-70; bd. dirs. Better Housing League of Cin., 1950—, Jewish Community Ctr., Cin., 1955—, Home for the Jewish Aged, Cin., 1955—, Palm Springs Friends of Los Angeles Philharmonic Orch., 1986—; numerous other civic activities. Mem. AIA, Ohio Soc. Architects. Republican. Jewish. Clubs: Queen City (Cin.), Losantiville Country (Cin.), Desert Island Country (Rancho Mirage, Calif.). Home: 2355 Bedford Ave Cincinnati OH 45208 Office: 1212 Sycamore St Cincinnati OH 45210

LEVINSON, PETER JOSEPH, lawyer; b. Washington, June 11, 1943; s. Bernard Hirsh and Carlyn Virginia (Krupp) L.; m. Nanette Susan Segal, Mar. 30, 1968; children—Sharman Risa, Justin David. A.B. in History cum laude, Brandeis U., Waltham, Mass., 1965; J.D., Harvard U., 1968. Bar: Hawaii 1971, U.S. Supreme Ct. 1975. Summer supr. Harvard Legal Aid Bur., Cambridge, Mass., 1968; research asst. Harvard Law Sch., 1968-69; teaching fellow Osgoode Hall Law Sch., York U. (Can.), 1969-70, research assoc., 1969-70, asst. prof., 1970-71; dep. atty. gen. State of Hawaii, 1971-75; vis. fellow Harvard U., 1976-77; ptnr. Levinson and Levinson, Honolulu, 1977-79; spl. asst. to dir. Office Program Support, Legal Services Corp., Washington, 1979; cons. Select Commn. on Immigration and Refugee Policy, Washington, 1980-81; minority counsel subcom. on immigration, refugees and internat. law com. on Judiciary, U.S. Ho. of Reps., Washington, 1981-85, Minority counsel subcom. Monopolies and Comml. law, 1985—. Trustee, Hawaii Jewish Welfare Fund, 1972-75, chmn. fund drive, 1972; trustee Temple Emanu-El, Honolulu, 1973-75; mem. alumni admissions council Brandeis U., 1978-82. Recipient award of merit United Jewish Appeal, 1974. Mem. Hawaii State Bar Assn. (chmn. standing com. on continuing legal edn. 1972, chmn. standing com. on jud. adminstrn. 1979), ABA, Am. Judicature Soc. Contbr. articles to profl. jours. Office: B351C Rayburn House Office Bldg Washington DC 20515

LEVI-STRAUSS, CLAUDE, educator; b. Brussels, Nov. 28, 1908; s. Raymond and Emma (Levy) Levi-S.; student Lycée Janson-de-Sailly, Paris, 1919-25; Agrégé de Philosophie, Sorbonne, Paris, 1931; D.Litt., U. Paris, 1948; Ph.D. (hon.), U. Brussels, 1962, Oxford U., 1964, Yale U., 1965, U. Chgo., 1967, Columbia U., 1971, Stirling U., 1972, U. Nat. du Zaire, 1973, U. Uppsala, 1977, Johns Hopkins U., 1978, Laval U., 1979, U. Nat. Mexico, 1979, Visva Bharati U., India, 1980, Harvard U., 1986; m. Dina Dreyfus, 1932; m. 2d, Rose-Marie Ullmo, 1946; 1 son, Laurent; m. 3d, Monique Roman; 1 son, Matthieu. Prof., U. Sao Paulo (Brazil), 1935-38; vis. prof. New Sch. for Social Research, N.Y., 1941-45; cultural counsellor French embassy, Washington, 1946-47; asso. curator Musee de l'Homme, Paris, 1948-49; dir. studies Ecole Pratique des Hautes etudes, Paris, 1950-82; prof. Coll. de France, 1959-82; mem. French Acad., 1973. Decorated grand officier de la Legion d'Honneur, 1985, commandeur, Ordre National du Merite, 1971. Corr. mem. Royal Acad. Netherlands, Norwegian Acad., Brit. Acad., Nat. Acad. Scis., Am. Acad. and Inst. Arts and Letters, Am. Philos. Soc., Royal Anthropol. Inst. Gt. Britain, London Sch. African and Oriental Studies. Publs. include: La Vie familiale et sociale des Indiens Nambikwara, 1948, Les Structures elementaires de la parente, 1949 (The Elementary Structures of Kinship, 1969), Race et histoire, 1952, Tristes Tropiques, 1955, complete edit., 1973 (A World on the Wane, 1961), Anthropologie structurale, Vol. 1, 1958, Vol. 2, 1973 (Structural Anthropology, Vol. 1, 1964, Vol. 2, 1977), Le Totemisme aujourd'hui, 1962 (Totemism, 1963), La Pensee sauvage, 1962 (The Savage Mind, 1966), Le Cru et le cuit, 1964 (The Raw and the Cooked, 1970), Du Miel aux cendres, 1967 (From Honey to Ashes, 1973), L'Origine des manieres de table, 1968 (The Origin of Table Manners, 1978), L'Homme nu, 1971 (The Naked Man, 1981), La Voie des Masques, 1975 (The Way of the Masks, 1982), Le Regard éloigné , 1983 (The View from Afar, 1985), Paroles données, 1984, La Potiere jalouse, 1985 (The Jealous Potter, 1987), Anthropology and Myth, 1987; relevant publs. include: Conversations with Levi-Strauss (ed. G. Charbonnier), 1969; by Octavio Paz: On Levi-Strauss, 1970; Claude Levi Strauss: An Introduction, 1972. Home: 2 rue des Marronniers, 75016 Paris France

LEVIT, EDITHE JUDITH, physician, medical association administrator; b. Wilkes-Barre, Pa., Nov. 29, 1926; m. Samuel M. Levit, Mar. 2, 1952; children: Harry M., David B. B.S. in Biology, Bucknell U., 1946; M.D., Woman's Med. Coll. of Pa., 1951; D.M.S., Med. Coll. Pa., 1978. Grad. asst. in psychology Bucknell U., 1946-47; intern Phila. Gen. Hosp., 1951-52, fellow in endocrinology, 1952-53, clin. instr., asso. in endocrinology, 1953-57, dir. med. edn., 1957-61, cons. med. edn., 1961-65; asst. dir. Nat. Bd. Med. Examiners, Phila., 1961-67; assoc. dir., sec. bd. Nat. Bd. Med. Examiners, 1967-75, v.p., sec. bd., 1975-77, pres., chief exec. officer, 1977-86, pres. emeritus, life mem. bd., 1987—; cons. in field, 1964—; council Coll. Physicians of Phila., 1986—; dir. Phila. Electric Co.; bd. mgrs. Germantown Savs. Bank, Phila. Contbr. articles to profl. jours. Bd. dirs. Phila. Gen. Hosp. Found., 1964-70; bd. dirs. Phila. Council for Internat. Visitors, 1966-72; bd. sci. counselors Nat. Library Medicine, 1981-85. Recipient award for outstanding contbns. in field of med. edn. Commonwealth Com. of Woman's Med. Coll., 1970; Alumni award Bucknell U., 1978; Disting. Dau. of Pa. award, 1981; Spl. Recognition award Assn. Am. Med. Colls., 1986; Disting. Service award Fedn. State Med. Bds., 1987; Master A.C.P. Fellow Coll. Physicians of Phila.; mem. Inst. Medicine of Nat. Acad. Scis., AMA, Pa., Phila. County med. socs., Assn. Am. Med. Colls., Phi Beta Kappa, Alpha Omega Alpha, Phi Sigma. Home: 1910 Spruce St Philadelphia PA 19103 Office: 3930 Chestnut St Philadelphia PA 19104

LEVIT, VICTOR BERT, lawyer, foreign representative, civic worker; b. Singapore, Apr. 21, 1930; s. Bert W. and Thelma (Clumeck) L.; m. Sherry Lynn Chamove, Feb. 25, 1962; children: Carson, Victoria. A.B. in Polit. Sci. with great distinction, Stanford, 1950; LL.B., Stanford U., 1952. Bar: Calif. 1953. Assoc. Long & Levit, San Francisco and Los Angeles, 1953-55, ptnr., 1955-83, mng. ptnr., 1971-83; ptnr. Barger & Wolen, San Francisco, Los Angeles and San Diego, 1983—; assoc. and gen. legal counsel U.S. Jaycees, 1959-61; legal counsel for consul gen. Ethiopia for San Francisco, 1964-71; hon. consul for Ethiopia for San Francisco, Ethiopia, 1971-76; guest lectr. Stanford U. Law Sch., 1958—, Haile Selassie I Univ. Law Sch., 1972-76; mem. com. group ins. programs State Bar Calif., 1980—; Mem. Los Angeles Consular Corps, 1971-77; mem. San Francisco Consular Corps, 1971-77, vice dean, 1975-76; Grader Calif. Bar Exam., 1956-61; del. San Francisco Mcpl. Conf., 1955-63, vice chmn., 1960, chmn., 1961-63. Author: Legal Malpractice in California, 1974, Legal Malpractice, 1977, 2d edit., 1983; Note editor: Stanford Law Rev, 1952-53; legal editor: Underwriters' Report, 1963—; Contbr. articles to legal jours. Campaign chmn. San Francisco Aid Retarded Children, 1960; mem. nat. com. Stanford Law Sch. Fund, 1959—; mem. Mayor's Osaka-San Francisco Affiliation Com., 1959-65, Mayor's Com. for Mcpl. Mgmt., 1961-64; mem. San Francisco Rep. Country Cen. Com., 1956-63; assoc. mem. Calif. Rep. Cen. Com., 1956-63, 70-72; campaign chmn. San Francisco Assemblyman John Busterud, 1960; bd. dirs. San Francisco Comml. Club, 1967-70, San Francisco Planning and Urban Renewal Assn., 1959-60, San Francisco Planning and Urban Renewal Assn. Nat. Found. Infantile Paralysis, 1958, Red Shield Youth Assn., Salvation Army, San Francisco, 1960-70, bd. dirs. NCCJ, San Francisco, 1959—, chmn., No. Calif., 1962-64, 68-70; mem. nat. bd. dirs., 1964-75; bd. dirs. San Francisco Tb and Health Assn., 1962-70, treas., 1964, pres., 1965-67; bd. dirs. San Francisco Assn. Mental Health, 1964-73, pres., 1968-71; mem. com. Nat. Assn. Mental Health, 1969-71; trustee United Bay Area Crusade, 1966-74, Ins. Forum San Francisco; bd. visitors Stanford Law Sch., 1969-75; mem. adv. bd. Jr. League San Francisco, 1971-75. Named Outstanding Young Man San Francisco mng. editors San Francisco newspapers, 1960, One of Five Outstanding Young Men Calif., 1961. Fellow ABA (chmn. profl. liability com. for gen. practice sect. 1979-81, council gen. practice sect. 1982-86, sec.-treas. gen. practice sect. 1986-87); mem. San Francisco Bar Assn. (chmn. ins. com. 1962, 73, chmn. charter flight com. 1962-66), State Bar Calif. (com. on group ins. programs 1980—), Consular Law Soc., Am. Arbitration Assn. (arbitrator), World Assn. Lawyers (chmn. parliamentary law com. 1976—), Am. Law Inst. (adviser restatement of law governing lawyers 1986—), Internat. Bar Assn., San Francisco Jr. C. of C. (dir. 1959, pres. 1958), U.S. Jaycees (exec. com. 1959-61), Jaycees Internat. (life, senator), Calif. Scholarship Fedn., U.S. C. of C. (labor com. 1974-76), San Francisco C. of C. (dir.), Phi Beta Kappa, Order of Coif, Pi Sigma Alpha. Clubs: Commercial (San Francisco) (dir.); Commonwealth (quar. chmn.), California Tennis, Tiburon Peninsula, Concordia. Home: 45 Beach Rd Belvedere CA 94920 Office: 650 California St San Francisco CA 94108

LEVITCH, HARRY HERMAN, retail executive; b. Memphis, Dec. 24, 1918; s. Samuel Arthur and Lena (Feingold) L.; LL.B. cum laude, So. Law U. (now Memphis State U.), 1941; m. Frances Wagner, May 31, 1940; 1 son, Ronald Wagner. Mdse. mgr. Perel & Lowenstein, Inc., 18 yrs.; pres. Harry Levitch Jewelers, Inc., Memphis, 1955—, also treas.; past lectr. on diamonds Memphis State U., Shelby State U. Pres. Leo N. Levi Nat. Arthritis Hosp., Hot Springs Nat. Park, Ark.; del. Conf. on Am.'s Cities, Washington, Regional Conf. U.S. Fgn. Policy, Louisville, Conf. of U.S. Dept. State and So. Center for Internat. Studies; bd. dirs. B'nai B'rith Home and Hosp. for Aged, Memphis, West Tenn. chpt. Arthritis Found.; chmn. Internat. Commn. on Community Vol. Services; adv. bd. dirs. Libertyland and Mid-South Fair Assn.; bd. dirs. W. Tenn. chpt. March of Dimes, NCCJ; lt., spl. dept. sheriff Shelby County (Tenn.). Appointee U.S. Holocaust Meml. Council by Pres. Reagan, 1988—. Served with JAGC, USAAF, 1943-46. Recipient Outstanding Civic Service award City of Memphis; Outstanding Leadership award Christian Bros. Coll.; col. a.d.c. Gov. Tenn.; named Hon. citizen Tex., Ala., Ark., New Orleans. Mem. Memphis Area C. of C., Retail Jewelers of Am., Jewelers Vigilance Com., Nat. Assn. Jewelry Appraisers (sr. appraiser), Internat. Soc. Appraisers, Am. Soc. Appraisers, Diamond Council Am. (cert. gemologist), Jewelry Industry Council. Jewish. Clubs: B'nai B'rith (internat. v.p.), Rotary, Summit, Masons, Shriners. Home: 4972 Peg Ln Memphis TN 38117 Office: Harry Levitch Jewelers Inc Clark Tower Suite 111 5100 Poplar Ave Memphis TN 38137

LEVITCH, PETER, health consulting corporation official; b. Bklyn., Oct. 19, 1932; s. Alexander and Anne (Lewin) L.; B.A., Hofstra U., 1954, M.A., 1957; children—Walter, Cynthia, Elenore, Andrew. Textbook coordinator Am. Sch. Book Co., N.Y.C., 1957-59; med. abstractor William Douglass McAdams, N.Y.C., 1959-60; clin. research assoc. Norwich (N.Y.) Pharmacal Co. (Morton-Norwich), 1961-69; dir. regulatory and clin. affairs Ortho Diagnostics Inc., Raritan, N.J., 1969-80; v.p. Oxford Research Internat. Corp., Bloomfield, N.J., 1980-81, Peter Levitch & Assocs. Inc., Somerville, N.J., 1981—; faculty Center for Profl. Advancement, N.J.; adj. asst. prof. Fairleigh-Dickinson U. Served with U.S. Army, 1954-56. Mem. N.Y. Acad. Scis., AAAS, Pharm. Mfrs. Assn. (steering com.), Health Industry Mfrs. Assn. (standards com.). Contbr. research papers to profl. publs., textbooks; profl. lectr. and cons. in field. Home: 685 Burning Bush Rd Bridgewater NJ 08807 Office: Peter Levitch & Assocs Inc PO Box 72 Somerville NJ 08876

LEVITSKY, MELVYN, foreign service officer; b. Sioux City, Iowa, Mar. 19, 1938; s. David and Mollie (Schwartz) L.; m. Joan Daskovsky, Aug. 12, 1962; children: Adam, Ross Josh. BA, U. Mich., 1960; MA, U. Iowa, 1963. Polit. officer Am. Embassy, Moscow, 1972-75; officer in charge Soviet bilateral relations Dept. State, Washington, 1975-78, dep. dir. UN polit. affairs, 1978-80, dir., 1980-82, dep. asst. sec. for human rights and humanitarian affairs, 1982-83; dep. assoc. dir. for broadcasting and dep. dir. Voice of Am. USIA, Washington, 1983-84; U.S. ambassador to Bulgaria 1984-87; exec. sec. and spl. asst. to Sec. Dept. State, 1987—. Recipient Meritorious Honor award Dept. State, 1968; recipient Superior Honor award Dept. State, 1975. Mem. Am. Fgn. Service Assn. *

LEVITT, IRVING FRANCIS, investment company executive; b. Braddock, Pa., July 3, 1915; s. Charles and Frances (Goretsky) L.; m. Florence Chaikin, Oct. 10, 1937; children: Robert Bruce, Linda Ann (Mrs. Stanley Ehrenpreis). B.S. (hon.) in journalism, U. Mich., 1936. Advt. mgr. feature writer Braddock (Pa.) Free Press, 1936-37; advt. mgr. Levitt Bros. Furniture Stores, 1936-38; partner, exec. adminstr. stores in Levitt Bros. Furniture Stores, Braddock, Vandergrift and New Kensington, Pa., 1938-55; exec. asst., v.p. Levinson Steel Co., Pitts., 1942-44; real estate, indsl. devel. 1938—; pres. Lepar, Inc., 1950-80; pres., chmn. bd. Union Screw & Mfg. Co., Pitts.; chmn. bd. Investment Capital Corp., Pitts., 1955—. Radix Orgn., Inc., N.Y., Radix Real Estate, Inc., RRE Enterprises, Inc.; pres. Kirwan Heights Land Co., King Land Co., Ind., Blawnox Realty Co.; chmn. bd. Apollo Industries, Inc., 1959-68; chmn. bd., dir. Apollo Internat. Corp.; pres., dir. Apollo-Peru S.A., Oakland Investment Corp., Pitts.; v.p., dir. Apollo Indsl., Inc., Apollo Investment Co., Pitts.; sr. v.p. Parker-Levitt Corp., Sarasota, Fla., Marble Island, Inc., Vt.; ptnr. Oliver-Smithfield Venture, Pitts., Nineteen Hundred Group Ltd., Sarasota; dir. Comml. Bank & Trust Co., Pitts.; Nuclear Materials & Equipment Corp., Ednl. Audio Visual, Inc., N.Y., London; chmn. bd., dir. Lido Beach Devel. Co., Inc., Sarasota, Fla.; partner One Hundred Kennedy Ltd., Tampa, Fla., SMP, Ltd., Pine Run Devel., Inc., Sarasota, Fla.; Mem. Pitts. Bd. Realtors, New Kensington Indsl. Devel. Corp., Smaller Mfrs. Council. Bd. dirs. Massanutten Mil. Acad., Woodstock, Va., United Jewish Fedn. Finance, Pitts., Irene Kaufman Settlement Bd.; trustee Levitt Found. Pitts., Rodef Shalom Temple, Pitts. Mem. Nat. Sales Exec. Club (dir. 1952-82), Am. Jewish Com., Chautauqua Soc. Clubs: Westmoreland Country (Export, Pa.) (v.p. 1948-83); Metropolis Country (White Plains, N.Y.); Longboat Key Country; Marco Polo (N.Y.C.); Standard (Pitts.) (dir.), Pitts. Athletic Assn. (Pitts.); Belfry New Century (London). Office: 1800 Second St Suite 808 Sarasota FL 34236 also: 230 Park Ave New York NY 10169

LEVONEN, JUHA KALLE OLAVI, retail executive; b. Varkaus, Finland, Dec. 30, 1952; s. Seppo Olavi and Tyyni Margit Anneli (Teikari) L.; m. Maarit Elise Peiju, Dec. 18, 1976; children: Laura, Katri, Kirsti. MSc in Technics, Åbo Akademi, Turku, Finland, 1980. Dev. and sales engr. Exel OY, Helsinki, Finland, 1980-84; sales mgr. Pyrkijä OY, Turku, 1984-85; devel. mgr. Pyrkijän Teollisuus OY, Turku, 1985-87; mng. dir. Turun Kaihdin OY, Lieto, Finland, 1987—. Office: Turun Kaihdin, Teollisuuskuja 1, 21420 Lieto Finland

LEVUN, CHARLES R(ALPH), lawyer; b. Asbury Park, N.J., Sept. 13, 1944; s. Henry David and Esther (Silverman) L.; m. Nancy Gail Berman, June 18, 1967; children: Kari E., Jami A. BS, U. Ill.-Urbana, 1966; JD, U. Chgo., 1970. Bar: Ill. 1970, U.S. Dist. Ct. (no. dist.) Ill. 1970, U.S. Ct. Claims, 1973, U.S. Tax Ct. 1971. CPA, Ill. Assoc. Aaron, Aaron, Schimberg & Hess, Chgo., 1970-75, ptnr., 1975-78; ptnr. Arvey, Hodes, Costello & Burman, Chgo., 1978-87; ptnr. Cox, Goodman, Levun, Cohen & Brett, Chgo., 1988—; adj. prof. grad. tax program IIT-Chgo. Kent Coll. Law, 1985—; cons. Commerce Clearing House Ptnrship. Tax Reporter, 1987—. Mem. fed. tax com. Chgo. Assn. Commerce and Industry; mem. profl. adv. com. Jewish Fedn. Met. Chgo. Served with USAR, 1968-74. Mem. Chgo. Bar Assn. (chmn. div. on partnerships, real estate and other sheltered investments, tax acctg. 1980-81, co-chmn. spl. projects 1981-83), Ill. Bar Assn. (council fed. taxation sect. 1979-86, chmn. council 1984-85, coeditor Fed. Taxation Newsletter 1981-85), ABA (chmn. subcom. spl. allocations of com. partnerships 1982-86, chmn. subcom. on legislation and regulations of com. on Ptnrships., 1986—). Office: 203 N LaSalle Suite 2100 Chicago IL 60601

LEVY, ALAN DAVID, real estate executive; b. St. Louis, July 19, 1938; s. I. Jack and Natalie (Yawitz) L.; grad. Sch. Real Estate, Washington U., 1960; m. Abby Jane Markowitz, May 12, 1968; children—Jennifer Lynn, Jacqueline Claire. Property mgr. Solon Gershman Inc., Realtors, Clayton, Mo., 1958-61; gen. mgr. Kodner Constrn. Co., St. Louis, 1961-63; regional mgr. Tishman Realty & Constrn. Co., Inc., N.Y.C., 1963-69, v.p., Los Angeles, 1969-77; exec. v.p., dir. Tishman West Mgmt. Corp., 1977-88; pres. Tishman West Cos., 1988—; guest lectr. on real estate mgmt. to various forums. Mem. Los Angeles County Mus. Art; chmn. bd. trustees Westlake Sch. Mem. bldg. owners and mgrs. assns. Los Angeles (dir.), N.J. (co-founder, hon. dir.), Inst. Real Estate Mgmt. (cert. property mgr.), Urban Land Inst., Internat. Council Shopping Centers. Contbr. articles on property mgmt. to trade jours. Office: 10960 Wilshire Blvd Los Angeles CA 90024

LEVY, ALAN JOSEPH, journalist, writer; b. N.Y.C., Feb. 10, 1932; s. Meyer and Frances (Shield) L.; m. Valerie Wladaver, Aug. 7, 1956; children—Monica, Erika. A.B., Brown U., 1952; M.S. in Journalism, Columbia U., 1953. Reporter Louisville Courier-Jour., 1953-60; free-lance contbr. Life, Sat. Eve. Post, N.Y. Times, others, 1960—; investigator Carnegie Commn. Ednl. TV, Boston, 1966-67; fgn. corr. Life, N.Y. Times mags., Prague, Czechoslovakia, 1967-71; script and program cons. Vienna's English Theatre, Austria, 1977-82; free-lance author, dramatist, corr. Vienna, 1971—; lectr. on theatre Salzburg Seminar in Am. Studies, Austria, 1981; adj. prof. lit. and journalism Webster U. 1983—; lectr.-in-residence Gritti Palace, Venice, Italy, 1987. Author: Draftee's Confidential Guide, 1957, 2d edit., 1966, Operation Elvis, 1960, The Elizabeth Taylor Story, 1961, Wanted: Nazi Criminals at Large, 1962, Interpret Your Dreams, 1962, 2d edit., 1975, Kind-Hearted Tiger, 1964, The Culture Vultures, 1968, God Bless You Real Good, 1969, Rowboat to Prague, 1972, 2d edit. titled So Many Heroes, 1980, Good Men Still Live, 1974, The Bluebird of Happiness, 1976, Forever, Sophia, 1979, 2d edit., 1986, Treasures of the Vatican Collections, 1983, Ezra Pound: the Voice of Silence, 1983, W.H. Auden: In the Autumn of the Age of Anxiety, 1983, Vladimir Nabokov: The Velvet Butterfly, 1984, Ezra Pound: A Jewish View, 1988; dramatist The World of Ruth Draper, 1982; librettist Just an Accident?, 1983 (Ernst Krenek prize City of Vienna, 1986). Trustee Thomas Nast Found., Landau, Fed. Republic Germany, 1978—. Served with U.S. Army, 1953-55. Recipient New Republic Younger Writer award, 1958, Best Enterprise Reporting award Sigma Delta Chi, 1959; Bernard De Voto fellow Middlebury Coll., 1963; golden Johann Strauss medal City of Vienna, 1981; travel writing awards Pacific Area Travel Assn., 1978, Govt. of Malta, 1985. mem. Am. Soc. Journalists and Authors, Authors Guild and Dramatists Guild of Authors League of Am., Overseas Press Club Am., PEN, Fgn. Press Assn. Vienna, Austrian Soc. Authors, Composers and Music Pubs. Democrat. Jewish. Office: Care Herbert Rosenberg 89 Southlawn Ave Dobbs Ferry NY 10522

LEVY, ARNOLD S(TUART), real estate company executive; b. Chgo., Mar. 15, 1941; s. Roy and Esther (Scheff) L.; m. Eva Cichosz, Aug. 8, 1976; children—Adam, Rachel, Deborah. B.S., U. Wis., 1963; M.P.A., Roosevelt U., 1970. Dir. Neighborhood Youth Corps, Chgo., 1966-68; v.p. Social Planning Assn., Chgo., 1968-70; planning dir. Office of Mayor Chgo., 1970-74; dep. dir. Mayor's Office Manpower, Chgo., 1974-75; sr. v.p. Urban Investment & Devel. Co., Chgo., 1975—; pres. Ritz-Carlton of Chgo., 1984—, Urban Hotels, 1986—, Logan Sq. Bldg. Corp, Market St. Bldg. Corp., UIDC of Washington, Inc.; lectr. at univs. Pres. Ark, Chgo., 1970-72, Parental Stress Services, Chgo., 1978-79; del. Mid-Term Democratic Nat. Conf., Memphis, 1978; v.p. Inst. Urban Life, Chgo., 1983—. Club: Carlton (Chgo.). Home: 535 Park Ave Glencoe IL 60022 Office: Urban Hotels 900 N Michigan Ave Chicago IL 60611

LEVY, CLAUDE MARCEL, pediatrician; b. Tunis, Tunisia, Jan. 19, 1932; Came to France, 1950; s. Hector Daniel and Anna Tina (Valensi) L.; m. Henriette Marie Chazal; children: Anne, Phillipe. MD, Diploma of Specialist Pediatrics, Faculty Medicine, Paris, 1962. Intern Hosp. Paris, 1956-62; chief clinic Faculty of Medicine Paris, 1962-66; practice medicine specializing in pediatrics, cons. Paris, 1962—. Contbr. articles to profl jours. Mem. Soc. Francaise Pediatrie. Jewish. Home and Office: 64 Ave Felix Faure, 75015 Paris France

LEVY, DAVID, deputy prime minister, minister of construction and housing of Israel; b. Morocco, 1938; came to Israel, 1957; married; 11 children. Ed. secondary sch. Active in Histadrut, Likud candidate for sec. gen., 1977, 81, now chmn. Likud party; mem. Israeli Knesset, 1969—, minister of immigrant absorption, 1977-78, minister of constrn. and housing, 1978—, dep. prime minister, 1981—. Office: Ministry of Constrn and Housing, Jerusalem Israel *

LEVY, HAIM, finance educator; b. Jerusalem, Apr. 1, 1939; m. Nili Abramotiz, Apr. 1961; children: Yoav, Moshe, Omri, Haggai. BA, Hebrew U., Jerusalem, 1963, MA, 1966, PhD, 1969. Instr. bus. Hebrew U., 1968-69, sr. lectr., 1971-73, dir. Sch. of Bus., 1973-75, assoc. prof., 1973-76, prof., 1976—; prof. fin. U. Fla., Gainesville, 1983—; vis. prof. Univ. Ill., 1969-70, Univ. Calif., Berkeley, 1970-72, Univ. Fla., 1975-76, 80, Univ. Pa., 1979-80; served on various acad. coms.; cons. in field. Author: Wage Differentials of Employees in Israel, 1957; co-author: Investment and Portfolio Analysis, 1972, The Structure of Revenues of Local Authorities in Israel, 1973, Corporate Investment and Financing Decisions, 1978, The Israeli Stock Market, 1978, Statistics: Decisions and Applications in Business and Economics, 1981, Business Statistics: Fundamentals and Applications, 1983, Portfolio and Investment Selection: Theory and Practice, 1984; co-editor: Financial Decision Making Under Uncertainty, 1977. Recipient various research grants, fellowships. Home: 12 Shahar St, Jerusalem Israel Office: Hebrew U, Jerusalem Israel

LEVY, HERBERT MONTE, lawyer; b. N.Y.C., Jan. 14, 1923; s. Samuel M. and Hetty D. L.; m. Marilyn Wohl, Aug. 30, 1953; children—Harlan A., Matthew D., Alison Jill. A.B., Columbia U., 1943, LL.B., 1946. Bar: N.Y. 1946, U.S. Dist. Ct. (so. dist.) N.Y. 1946, U.S. Ct. Appeals (2d cir.) 1949, U.S. Dist. Ct. (ea. dist.) N.Y. 1949, U.S. Supreme Ct. 1951, U.S. Ct. Appeals (10th cir.) 1956, U.S. Tax Ct. 1973. Assoc. Rosenman, Goldmark, Colin & Kaye, 1946-47, Javits & Javits, 1947-48; staff counsel ACLU, 1949-56; sole practice, 1956-64; ptnr. Hoffman, Gartlir, Hoffheimer, Gottlieb & Gross, 1965-69; sole practice, N.Y.C., 1969—; faculty N.Y. County Lawyers Assn.; former lectr. Practising Law Inst. Exec. com. on law and social action Am. Jewish Congress, 1961-66; chmn., bd. trustees Congregation B'nai Jeshurun, 1988—. Mem. Fed. Bar Council (past trustee), Bar Assn. City N.Y., N.Y. County Lawyers Assn., 1st Amendment Lawyers Assn. Democrat. Club: Businessmen's (N.Y.C.). Author How to Handle an Appeal (Practising Law Inst.), 1968, rev. edit. 1982; also legal articles. Home: 285 Central Park W Apt 12W New York NY 10024 Office: 60 E 42d St Suite 4210 New York NY 10165

LEVY, JEAN-BERNARD, surgeon, educator; b. Joyeuse, Ardeche, France, Apr. 30, 1941; s. Claude Emile and Yvonne Andrée (Lefebvre) L.; m. Francoise Genevieve Isambert, Nov. 4, 1966; children: Catherine, Laurent. MD, M in Human Biology, Broussais-Hotel Dieu, Paris, 1972; M in Philosophy, Sorbonne, Paris, 1987. Resident various hosps., Paris, 1966-72; clinic chief Hotel Dieu, 1972-78; lectr. anatomy Bichat U., Paris, 1972-84; clin. lectr. Univ. Hosp. Ctr. Bichat U., 1982-86; surgeon Enghien les Bains, France, 1978—; com. mem. Surgery and Vascular Pathology Diseases, Paris, 1980—. Author: Gen. Anatomy, 1974, Arterial Disease of Lower Limbs (intermittent claudication), 1977; editor: 79th Surgery Congress, Paris, 1977; contbr. articles to profl. jours. Served with M.C., French mil., 1988—. Recipient Faculty Medicine award, 1972, Acad. Surgery award, 1972, Soc. Encouragement to Progress, 1976; Kemp Benevolent grantee, 1976. Mem. French Assn. Surgery (execution com. 1975-78), Anatomists Assn., French Vascular Pathology Coll., Internat. Soc. Surgery, Vascular Surgery Soc. French Lang., Phlebology Soc. Club: Racing (Paris). Home: 2 Rue de la Bienfaisance, 75008 Paris France Office: Clinique de Girardin, 16 Ave de Girardin, Enghien les Bains, 95880 Val D'Oise France

LÉVY, JEAN-MARC, pediatrician, educator; b. Bischwiller, France, Aug. 26, 1927; s. Arthur and Irene-Rose (Levy) L.; m. Nicole Paulette Rosenstiel, July 4, 1954; children: Michel, Fabiene. MD, U. Strasbourg, 1955. Intern Hospices Civils Strasbourg (France), 1950-55, chief physician pediatric service, 1972—; clinic chief Faculty Medicine U. Strasbourg, 1955-58, prof. agrege pediatrics, 1961-73, prof. without chair, 1973-77, prof. titulaire, 1977—; pres. Conseil Technique Ecole Puericultrices, 1978—. Pres. Assn. Parents et Amis Handicapes Juifs, 1980—, Assn. Regionale Pour Enfants Leucemiques et Cancereux, 1984—. Mem. Société Francaise Pediatrie, Club Europeen Conseil Genetique, Société Francaise Hématologie, Société Francaise Oncologie Pédiatrique. Lodge: Rotary (pres. Strasbourg South 1984-85). Home: 3 Rue Gottfried, 67000 Strasbourg France Office: Pediatric Service Inst, Puericulture CHR-BPN 426, 67091 Strasbourg France

LEVY, JEROME HENRY, ophthalmic surgeon; b. N.Y.C., Sept. 12, 1942; s. Louis and Lee (Boockvar) L.; B.A. magna cum laude, Syracuse U., 1963; M.D., SUNY, Bklyn., 1966; m. Carol Ruth Freisinger, June 20, 1964; children—Linda, David. Intern, Kings County Hosp., Bklyn., 1966-67; resident in ophthalmology Manhattan Eye, Ear and Throat Hosp., N.Y.C., 1968-70, chief resident, 1970-71, attending surgeon, 1971—, coordinator phacoemulsification tng., 1971—, also prin. investigator YAG laser; practice medicine specializing in ophthalmic surgery, Bronx, N.Y., 1971—; attending surgeon Manhattan Eye, Ear and Throat Hosp.; surgeon dir. N.Y. Eye Surgery Ctr. Diplomate Am. Bd. Ophthalmology. Fellow Am. Acad. Ophthalmology and Otolaryngology, Am., Internat. colls. surgeons; mem. AMA, Am. Intraocular Lens Soc., N.Y. Intraocular Lens Implant Soc. (pres.), Contact Lens Soc. Ophthalmologists, N.Y. State, Bronx County med. socs., Ophthalmic Laser Surg. Soc., Manhattan Ophthal. Soc., Phi Beta Kappa, Phi Kappa Phi. Contbr. articles to profl. pubs. Home: 220 E 63d St New York NY 10021 Office: 1101 Pelham Pkwy Bronx NY 10459

LEVY, JOEL HOWARD, research analyst; b. N.Y.C., Jan. 7, 1938; s. David M. and Mildred (Davidoff) L.; m. Renee Fenchel, Aug. 18, 1963; children: Seth Evan, Alissa Cheryl. B of Chem. Engring., City Coll. N.Y., 1960; MS in Chem. Engring., Poly. Inst. Bklyn., 1968; postgrad., Rider Coll. Mgr. devel. Princeton (N.J.) Chem. Research Inc., 1964-71; pilot plant mgr. Hydron Labs., New Brunswick, N.J., 1971-74; mgr. pilot plant Sun Chem. Corp., East Rutherford, N.J., 1974-75; process devel. supr. chem. div. Quaker Oats, Barrington, Ill., 1975-78; mgr. process engring. div. Searle Chem., Skokie, Ill., 1978-80; sr. mktg. research assoc. Allied Corp., Morristown, N.J., 1980—. Served as sgt. USAR, 1961-67. Mem. Am. Inst. Chem. Engrs., Am. Chem. Soc. (chmn. chem., mktg., econs. N.J. sec. 1985-86), Soc. of Plastics Industry (com. on resin stats., exec. com., chmn. nylon resins), European Chem. Mktg. Research Assn., Société de Chimie. Office: Allied Corp Columbia Rd Park Ave PO Box 2332R Morristown NJ 07960

LEVY, JOHN STUART, dentist, clinical consultant; b. New Haven, Dec. 26, 1946; s. Morton Julian and Pearl Ruth (Brodes) L.; m. Beverly Eileen Eden, Nov. 28, 1971; 1 dau., Perri Melissa. B.S., George Washington U., 1968; D.D.S., Georgetown U., 1976. Registered dentist. Postdoctoral fellow Yale U., New Haven, 1976-78; asst. prof. Georgetown U., Washington, 1976—; pres. Levy-D.D.S., P.C., New Haven, 1976—; dir. Resource Group, East Providence, R.I. Contbr. articles to profl. jours. Bd. dirs. Camp Laurelwood, Madison, Conn., 1979-86; chmn. bd. dirs., Jewish Home for Aged, New Haven, 1985—; bd. dirs. Jewish Fedn.; cabinet, mem. United Jewish Appeal Nat. Young Leadership, N.Y.C., 1980—. Served with U.S. Army, 1968-71. Recipient Joseph Borkowski award for professionalism Georgetown U., 1976; Nat. Service award NIH, 1977, 78. Mem. Internat. Assn. Dental Research, ADA. Jewish. Current Work: Flouride-dental enamel studies, biomaterials related to dental applications. Subspecialty: Cariology. Home: 37 Spoke Dr Woodbridge CT 06525

LEVY, MAURICE MARC, physicist; b. Tlemcen, Algeria, Sept. 7, 1922; s. Jean and Noemi (Fisse) L.; m. Francoise Jeanne Spruytte, July 7, 1947 (div. 1961); children—Bernard, Laurent, Marianne; m. Genevieve Marie Villie, July 15, 1962; children—Delphine, Sophie. Licence es Sciences, U. Algiers, Algeria, 1964; Doctorat es Sciences physiques, U. Paris, 1949, DSc (hon.) U. of Lancaster. Mem. staff Centre National Recherche Scientifique, Paris, 1945-53; maitre de conferences U. Bordeaux, France, 1953-54; prof. theoretical physics U. Paris VI, 1954—; pres. European Space Research Orgn., Neuilly, France, 1972-75, Nat. Space Research Ctr., Paris, 1974-76; program dir. UN Univ. Ctr., Tokyo, 1977-83; dir. Nat. Mus. Sci., Tech. and Industry, Paris, 1983-85; pres. City of Sci. and Industry, 1985-87; adviser to pres. Bank of Y.P. Elkann, 1987—. Author books, and articles. Decorated comdr. Order of Merit, officer Legion of Honor; recipient Robin prize French Phys. Soc., 1957. Mem. Am. Phys. Soc., European Phys. Soc. Office: City of Science and Industry, 211 Ave Jean Jaures, 75019 Paris France

LEVY, OLIVIER, lawyer; b. Geneva, Apr. 24, 1949; s. Gabriel and Denise (Bertschy) L.; LL.B., U. Geneva, 1972, advocate, 1975; m. Elena Tanzio, June 4, 1977. Admitted to Swiss bar, 1973; sec. Internat. Revue of Criminology and Tech. Police, 1972-82; atty., chief accident dept. Helvetia-Accidents Ins., Geneva, 1976-85; legal counselor Fédération des Syndicats Patronaux, Geneva, 1985—; jud. chronicler and corr. Press Agy., APLI. Vice pres. Radical and Progressive Youth Party, Geneva, 1972; mem. Central Com., Radical Party Geneva, 1972; mem. com. of Amnesty Internat. in Geneva, 1973. Served with Swiss Army, 1971. Decorated Pro Merito Melitensi Cross, Sovereign Order of Malta (Rome); comdr. Order Polonia Restituta (Polish Republic in exile, London); Medal of City of Nantes (France); Medal Mil. Merit (Chad); laureate fgn. cultural socs.; named hon. citizen State of Tenn., Silver Medal of Paris; Medal of City of Bressuire (France); Assn. Nationale Belge La Grenade, Soc. Suisse d'Héraldique, Soc. Européenne de Culture, Maintenance Héraldique de France; Soc. Genevoise de Droit & de Législation, Assn. Genevoise de Droit des Affaires. Mem. Soc. Public Art Geneva (former exec. com.), Soc. History and Archeology Geneva, Nat. Acad. History France (fgn. assoc.); Societe Suisse de Phaleristique (sec.-gen.), fgn. cultural acads. Home: 10 Rue de Chavant, 1232 Confignon, 1203 Geneva Switzerland Office: care Fedn des Syndicats Patronaux Ruede, Saint-Jean 98, 1211 Geneva 11 Switzerland

LEVY, PAUL, journalist; b. Lexington, Ky., Feb. 26, 1941; arrived in Eng., 1962; s. H.S. and Shirley (Singer) Levy Meyers; m. Penelope Marcus, June 24, 1977; children—Tatyana Sophie Dorothy, Georgia Natasha Alice. B.A., U. Chgo., 1963; postgrad. Univ. Coll. London, 1964-65, Nuffield Coll. Oxford, 1970-71; Ph.D., Harvard U., 1979. Book pages contbr. The Observer, London, 1974-80, food and wine editor, 1980—. Freelance contbr. Wall St. Jour., A La Carte, Times Lit. Supplement, Lit. Rev., N.Y. Times, 1985—; broadcaster BBC, ind. TV stas., 1985—. Author: G.E. Moore and The Cambridge Apostles, 1980; (with Ann Barr) The Official Foodie Handbook, 1985; Out to Lunch, 1986. Editor: Lytton Strachey: The Really

Interesting Question, 1972; (with Michael Holroyd) The Shorter Strachey, 1980; Trustee, co lit. executor The Strachey Trust, 1972—. Recipient Corning prize for food writing, 1981, 82; Glenfiddich Food Writer of Yr. award, 1981, 84, Restaurant Writer of Yr., 1984, Specialist Writer of Yr. award Brit. Press Awards, 1985. Mem. Circle Wine Writers, Guild Food Writers, Soc. Authors, Nat. Union Journalists. Clubs: Groucho, Wednesday. Avocations: being cooked for; drinking better wines. Office: The Observer, 8 St Andrew's Hill, London EL4V 5JA, England

LEVY, PAUL HENRIE, physicist, researcher, consultant; b. San Pedro, Calif., Sept. 14, 1953; s. Abraham Jack and Naomi Anne (Wehmhoner) L.; m. Christine Marie Infante, June 9, 1980; children—Aaron Paul, Alexia P. B.A., U. Calif., San Diego, 1975; Ph.D. candidate, 1975-78. Scientist, Jaycor, San Diego, 1978-80; sr. scientist Sci. Applications Internat. Corp., La Jolla, Calif., 1980-82; dir. electromagnetics technology Physics Internat., San Leandro, Calif., 1982-86; mgr. radiation effects AVCO Research, Wilmington, Mass., 1986-87; program dir. advanced techn. AVCO Research/Textron, Wilmington, 1988—. Contbr. numerous articles to profl. jours. Mem. Am. Phys. Soc., IEEE (editor, reviewer Transcripts Nuclear Sci.), AAAS, AIAA, Phi Beta Kappa. Democrat. Current work: Transient electromagnetic propagation, coupling and scattering; nuclear radiation effects; directed-energy technology. Subspecialties: Electromagnetics; Nuclear physics; Particle physics. Office: AVCO Research/Textron 210 Lowell St Wilmington MA 01887

LEVY, RENE ARMAND, sociology professor; b. Zurich, Switzerland, Jan. 26, 1944; s. Salomon and Gerty (Hasgall) L. PhD, U. Zurich, 1975. Lectr. sociology Sch. for Social Work, Zurich, 1970-76, 77-80; vis. prof. U. Ottawa, Ont., Can., 1976-77; researcher Sociol. Inst., Zurich, 1978-80; prof. extraordinare U. Lausanne, Switzerland, 1980—; mem. Fed. Commn. for Sci. Info. Policy, 1986—. Author: (with others) Die Stellung der Frau in der Schweiz, 1974, Der Lebenslauf als Statusbiographie, 1977, (with others) Politische Aktivierung in der Schweiz 1945-78, 1981, The Social Structure of Switzerland, 1983, Politique en rase-mottes, 1984, Keine Zukunft für lebendige Arbeit? 1988, Quel avenir pur le travial humain? 1988; editor La vie au travail et son avenir, 1988. Mem. Swiss Sociol. Assn. (mem. directing com. 1983), Am. Sociol. Assn., Assn. Internat. Sociologues Langue Francaise. Office: U Lausanne Inst d'anthropologie, et de sociologie BFSH 2, CH-1015 Lausanne Switzerland

LEVY, ROBERT ALAN, economist, b. Washington, Apr. 18, 1946; s. Walter James and Augusta (Sondheimer) L. B.A., U. Pa., 1968; M.B.A., Columbia U., 1972, MEd, 1987. Tchr. elementary sch., N.Y.C., 1968; personnel asst. Beth Israel Hosp., N.Y.C., 1973-76; energy economist, adminstr. W.J. Levy Consultants Corp., N.Y.C., 1976—. Mem. Internat. Assn. Energy Economists, Am. Econ. Assn., Indsl. Relations Research Assn., Assn. Transpersonal Psychology, Internat. Reading Assn. Home: 201 W 77th St New York NY 10024 Office: WJ Levy Cons Corp 30 Rockefeller Plaza New York NY 10020

LEVY, ROBERT I., packaging company executive; b. Chgo., July 21, 1912; s. Charles I. and Celia (Weinshenker) L.; m. Florence Greenblatt, Dec. 17, 1939; children: Maurice Lewis, Burt Samuel. BS in Optometry, OD, No. Ill. Coll., 1933. Pres. optical co. 1933-46; with Milprint, 1947-53, Traver Corp., 1953, Container Corp. Am., 1953-56; pres. Allpak Co., Chgo., 1958—; spl. cons. Allied Paper Co., 1960—; cons. Hipak Industries, Inc., Rolling Meadows, Ill.; bd. dirs. Ampak Co., Irish Jurong Ltd., Kilcoole Co., Wicklow Ireland; treas. Cen. Steel and Wire; v.p. A and S Trading Co. Mem. City of Chgo. Welfare Council, 1963—; adv. council SBA; past trustee Packaging Found., Mich. State U., Lawrence Hall, Chgo.; bd. dirs., past v.p. Chgo. Met. Council Alcoholism; bd. givs. Psychiat. Inst., Northwestern U.; bd. dirs. Cathedral Shelter; past trustee North Shore Congregation Israel; bd. dirs. Congregation Kol Ami; adv. bd. Martha Washington Hosp., C.A.T.C., Salvation Army. Recipient Man of Yr. award Bonds for Israel, 1973. Mem. AIM (pre.'s council 1967-70). Lodge: B'nai B'rith (local pres.). Home: 2800 Lake Shore Dr Chicago IL 60657 Office: 1010 Lake St Oak Park IL 60301

LEVY, ROBERT S., lawyer; b. N.Y.C., May 27, 1932; s. Harry Victor and Betty Ruth (Kaufman) L.; m. Lorna Iris Klein, June 30, 1957; children—Jill Arden, Kenneth Arlan. B.S. cum laude, N.Y.U., 1954, LL.B. cum laude, 1955. Bar: N.Y. 1956, U.S. Dist. Ct. (so. and ea. dists.) N.Y. 1962, U.S. Supreme Ct. 1967, U.S. Ct. Appeals (2d cir.) 1973. Assoc., Nordlinger, Reigelman, Benetar & Charney, N.Y.C., 1955-59; sr. assoc. Reich, Spitzer & Feldman, N.Y.C., 1959-64; sole practice, N.Y.C., 1964—; mem. nat. panel arbitrators Am. Arbitration Assn., N.Y.C., 1961—. Author: Guide to Franchise Investigation and Contract Negotiation, 1967; Woman's Guide to Franchises, 1967; Directory of State and Federal Funds for Business, 1968. Mem. N.Y. State Bar Assn., Phi Beta Kappa. Jewish. Club: Tam O'Shanter (Brookville, N.Y.). Home: 2495 Aron Dr W Seaford NY 11783

LEVY, ROCHELLE FELDMAN, artist; b. N.Y.C., Aug. 4, 1937; d. S. Harry and Eva (Krause) Feldman; m. Robert Paley Levy, June 4, 1955; children: Kathryn Tracey, Wendy Paige, Robert Paley, Angela Brooke, Michael Tyler. Student Barnard Coll., 1954-55, U. Pa., 1955-56; BFA, Moore Coll. Art, 1979. Mgmt. cons. Woodlyne Sch., Rosemont, Pa., 1983-84; sr. ptnr. DRT Interiors, Phila., 1983—; ptnr. Phila. Phillies, 1981—. One-woman shows: Watson Gallery, Wheaton Coll., Norton, Mass., 1977, U. Pa., 1977, Med. Coll. Pa., Phila., 1982, Aqueduct Race Track, Long Island, N.Y., 1982, 68, Phila. Art Alliance, 1983, Moore Coll. Art, Phila., 1984. Pres., League of Children's Hosp., Phila., 1969-70; chmn. bd. trustees Moore Coll. Art, 1988—. Recipient G. Allen Smith Prize, Woodmere Art Gallery, Chestnut Hill, Pa., 1979. Trustee Moore Coll. Art, 1988—; mem. selections and acquisitions com. Pa. Acad. Fine Arts, 1979—; bd. mgrs., 1975—, chmn. exec. com., 1982—. Mem. Allied Artists Am., Artist's Equity, Phila. Art Alliance, Phila. Print Club.

LEVY, ROGER LAURENCE, computer and telecommunications executive; b. Melbourne, Victoria, Australia, Dec. 1, 1948; s. Robert Samuel and Muriel Eileen (Rhook) L.; m. Margaret Mary French, Aug. 25, 1975; children—Jesinta Eileen, Rebecca Mary. Diploma Elec. Engring., Footscray Inst. Tech., Melbourne, 1968, Diploma Electronic Engring., 1969; B.Engring., (1st class honours), U. Melbourne, 1973, M.Engring. Sci., 1975; grad. Internat. Bus. Mgmt., Inst. Internat. Studies, Tokyo, 1982. Chartered electronics engr. Sr. engr. Telecom Australia, Melbourne, 1968-79; chief engr. G. Close & Assocs., Melbourne, 1979-81; gen. mgr. engring. NEC Australia Pty. Ltd., Mulgrave, Victoria, 1981-84, group gen. mgr., 1984-86; chief exec. Labtam Internat. Pty. Ltd., Braeside, Victoria, 1986; mng. dir., Levy Mgmt. Services Pty Ltd., 1986—. Pub. Service Bd. scholar Govt. Australia, 1975. Fellow Australian Inst. Mgmt., Radio and Electronics Engrs. Australia; mem. Am. Mgmt. Inst., IEEE (sr.). Avocations: golf, music, numismatics. Office: Levy Management Services Pty Ltd, 28 Muir St, Mount Waverly 3149, Australia

LEVY, VIVIANE, federal agency administrator, scientist; b. Alexandria, Egypt, Nov. 16, 1932; came to France, 1948; d. Robert and Lily (Riches) L. BS, U. Sorbnne, Paris, 1954; BE, Ecole Nat. Superieure Chimie, Paris, 1954; PhD, Paris U., 1958. Scientist Ctr. Nat. Research Scientific, Paris, 1954-58, French Atomic Energy Authority, Saclay, France, 1958-70; group leader French Atomic Energy Authority, Saclay, 1970-83, head sect., 1983-86, service head asst., 1987—; prof. physical metallurgy Nat. Inst. Sci. and Nuclear Tech., Saclay and Orsay, France 1968-78; mem. expert material group for fusion European Communities, Brussels, 1981—. Co-author: Handbook for Surfaces and Interfaces, 1978, Elements de Metallurgie Physique, 1977; patentee steels for FBR subassemblies; contbr. articles to profl. jours. Recipient Officier des Palmes Accadémiques Prime Minister of France, Oaris 1984. Mem. Soc. France Metallurgie (recipient Prix Rist award 1966), Soc. France Micriscopie Electronique, Soc. France Energy and Nuclear. Jewish. Office: Centre d'études nucléaire, de Saclay DTech/SRMA, 91191 Gif-sur-Yvette France

LEVY, ZE'EV, philosopher, educator, writer, researcher; b. Dresden, Fed. Republic Germany, Jan. 25, 1921; arrived in Israel, 1934; s. John Josef and Paula (Loewendorf) L.; m. Lea Strauss, 1948; children: Tsafrira, Nadav, Salit, Hadass. BA in Philosophy, Tel-Aviv U., 1967, MA, 1969; PhD, Hebrew U., Jerusalem, 1973. Lectr. Study Ctr. Kibbutz Movement, Givat-Haviva, Israel, 1964-71, Tel-Aviv U., 1972-74; sr. lectr. U. Haifa, Israel, 1974-79, assoc. prof. philosophy, 1979—; vis. prof. Univ. Heidelberg, Hochschule für juedische Studien, Fed. Republic Germany, 1983, SUNY-Binghamton, 1987, Queens Coll. CUNY, 1987. Author: The Philosophy of Franz Rosenzweig, 1969 (Lit. award 1970), Spinoza and the Concept of Judaism, 1972, Structuralism, 1976, Science and Values, 1978, Between Yafeth and Shem, 1982 (English translation 1987), Hermeneutics, 1987; cons. editor Sifriat-Poalim Pub. House, Tel-Aviv, 1975—, New Atheneum, Madison, N.J., 1987—; sect. editor Jour. for Ultimate Reality and Meaning, Toronto, Can., 1985—; editor numerous sci. papers in various langs. Served with Israeli Army, active Res., 1948-76. Mem. World Union Judaic Studies, Philos. Assn. Israel (bd. dirs.), Internat. Spinoza Inst., Internat. Inst. Ultimate Reality and Meaning (bd. dirs.). Mem. Mapam Party. Home: Kibbutz Hama'apil, Doar Na Hefer 39845, Israel Office: Univ Haifa, Mount Carmel, Haifa 31999, Israel

LEVY-ALBAREA, ELIANE CLAUDE, opthalmologist; b. Nëvilly, France, Nov. 4, 1936; d. Robert and Jenny Levy; m. André Albarea, Dec. 1967; children: Yael, Jacques. Bachelor's, Lyceé Jules Ferry, Paris, 1955; MD, Fae Paris, 1968. Diplomate French Bd. Opthalmology. Externat Paris Hosp., 1958-64; intern De Region de Paris, 1964-68, adjoint chief service, 1975—; asst. chief service Hosp. Gonesse, France, 1970-75. Contbr. articles to profl. jours. Mem. European Contact Lens Soc. Opthalmologists, French Opthalmologists, Keiasoufractire Surgery Soc., Intraocular Lens Soc. Home and Office: 7 Rue Georges Berger, 75017 Paris France

LEWANDOWSKA, STANISLAWA SLAWOMIRA, educator; b. Wilno, Poland, June 9, 1924; d. Stanislaw and Anna (Milewska) Grzybowska; m. Alexander Zbigniew Lewandowski. MA in Philosophy, U. Warsaw, Poland, 1950. Advisor Ministry of Edn., Warsaw, 1948-49, Ministry of Higher Edn. State Sci. Pub., Warsaw, 1950-54; editor state sci. pub. Orgn. Editorial Staff of "Hist. Quarterly", Warsaw, 1954-68; asst. Polish Acad. Sci., Warsaw, 1968-72, lectr., 1972-79, assoc. prof., 1979-85; prof. Polish Acad. Sci., Inst. History, Warsaw, 1985—. Author: Resistance Movement in Podlasie, 1976 (award of Ministry of Higher Edn. 1982), Polish Underground Press (award Polish Acad. Sci. 1982), Cryptonym "Authentication", 1984. Recipient Golden Cross of Merit award Council of State, 1978, Polonia Restituta award Council of State, 1987; Italian Fgn. Office scholar, 1975, 79. Mem. The Sci. Council of the Warsaw Polish Acad. of Scis. Inst. of History (hist. com. 1980—, editorial com. Modern History 1969-88). Mem. Polish United Workers Party.Roman Catholic. Home: Odynca 19 7, 02 606 Warszawa Poland Office: Polish Acad Sci Hist Inst, Rynek Starego Miasta 29 31, 00 272 Warszawa Poland

LEWANDOWSKI, BOHDAN, Polish diplomat; b. Poland, June 29, 1926; s. Zygmunt and Stefania (Bekier) L.; m. Helen M. Harris, Nov. 7, 1948; separated, 1980; children: Eliza, Nina. Ed. Acad. Polit. Sci.; M.A., Warsaw U., 1972, D (hon.) Kyung Hee U., Seoul. With Ministry Fgn. Affairs, Warsaw, 1945-46; served with Polish consulates, Pitts., Chgo., 1946, Polish Embassy, Washington, 1946-48, head N.Am. sect., 1951-56, dep. dir. dept. for U.K. and Ams., 1956-60; dir. policy planning, 1966-67, dir. gen., 1971-72; rep. Security Council, UN, 1960, permanent rep. Poland, 1960-66, chmn. Econ. 2d Commn. Gen. Assembly, 1962, rep. from Poland to Gen. Assemblies UN, 1950-71, under-sec.-gen., N.Y.C., 1972-82, sr. adviser to adminstr. of devel. program, 1983—; mem. policy bd. Interaction Council N.Y.C. and Milano, 1984—; cons. Aspen Inst. Humanistic Studies, N.Y.C., 1983—; mem. governing council Ctr. Internat. Studies, NYU, 1983—; Regents prof. U. Calif., San Diego, 1984; vis. prof. Diplomatic Acad., Vienna, Austria, winter 1984, 85, 87, Carleton Coll., Northfield, Minn., Spring 1986, Colo. Coll., Colorado Springs, spring 1988. Mem. Polish Assn. for Club Rome. Home: AL Roz 8, 00-556 Warsaw Poland

LEWIN, DAVID, gynecologist, obstetrician, educator; b. Saint-Mande, France, July 28, 1926; s. Zwi and Hélene (Kosmann) L.; m. Yvonne Bourges, Apr. 8, 1950; children: Francois, Noémie. MD, U. Paris, 1958. Asst. Clinique Baudelocque, Paris, 1956-57; dept. head Centre Hospitalier, Poissy, France, 1967—; prof. U. Paris, 1963—; med. expert High Ct. of Justiciary, 1980-87. Author and co-editor Traité d'Obstétrique, 1956. Expert Com. on Midwife Tng., Brussels, 1983-87; mem. Exec. Bd. FIGO Internat. Body, 1984-87, Nat. Council of Midwifes, Paris, 1977-87; pres. Logiciel Med., Poissy, 1972-87. Mem. Soc. Nat. Ob-Gyn (treas.), Syndicat des Gynécologues-Accoucheurs de Paris (sec.), Informatique et Gynécologie-Obstétrique (pres.), Paris Congress of Ob-Gyn. (treas.). Home: 13 Ave des Ursulines, 78300 Poissy France Office: Centre Hospitalier, Rue du champ gaillard, 78303 Poissy France

LEWIN-RICHTER, ANDRES, sales executive, engineer; b. Miranda, Spain, Mar. 22, 1937; s. Richard Lewin-Richter and Elfi Oslander; m. Cristina Vidal-Quadras; children: Ines, Santiago. Degree in Engring., Barcelona Eng. Sch., 1962; MSEE, Columbia U., N.Y.C., 1964; D. in Indsl. Engring., Barcelona Eng. Sch., 1970. Registered profl. engr., Spain. Project engr. J.M. Huber Corp., Macon, Ga., 1965-66; maintenance engr. Resintex, Barcelona, 1967; sales engr. MIDSA, Badalona, Spain, 1967-68; gen. mgr. Embalajes Plásticos S.A., Esplugas, Spain, 1968-72, Hypar S.A., Barcelona, 1972-73, CAIAC Corbero, Espurgas, 1973-75; mgr. sales Siliconas Hispania S.A., Barcelona, 1975—. Home: Reina Cristina 1, 08003 Barcelona Spain Office: Siliconas Hispania SA, Balmes 357, 08006 Barcelona Spain

LEWINS, STEVEN, security analyst, investment advisor, corporate officer; b. N.Y.C., Jan. 22, 1943; s. Bruno and Kaethe L.; m. Rayna Lee Kornreich, July 4, 1968; children: Shani Nicole, Scott Asher. BA, Queens Coll., CUNY 1964, MA in Diplomatic-Econ. History, 1966, postgrad. in bus. adminstrn., 1969-72; postgrad. cert. in public adminstrn. NYCSC, SUNY, 1967. Park ranger-historian Nat. Park Service, Statue of Liberty, N.Y.C., 1964-66; traffic asst. AT&T, White Plains, N.Y., 1966; adminstrv. intern N.Y. State, Albany, 1966-67; asst. to commr. N.Y. State Narcotics Addiction Control Commn., N.Y.C., 1967-69; security analyst Value Line Investment Survey, N.Y.C., 1969-71, assoc. research dir., 1971-74, research dir., directing editor Value Line Investment Survey, 1974-80, v.p. Value Line Data Services, 1975-80 (created Value Line Financial Data Base, 1974); v.p. Arnold Bernhard & Co., 1975-80, dir., 1976-80, mem. exec. com., 1977-80; ptnr. Ray-Lux Products, 1978-80; pres. RayLux Assocs., 1980-81, dir., 1980-86; founder RayLux Fin. Service, 1980 (1st SEC-registered electonic investment adv. service); v.p., unit head investment div. Citibank N.A., 1981-86, v.p. Citicorp Investment Mgmt., Inc., 1986-88, transp. and aerospace Chancellor Capital Mgmt., 1988—; adv. corp. disclosure com. SEC, 1977-78, ICC, 1982—, Dept. Transp., 1982—, Dept. Justice, 1982—, Dept. State, 1986—; registered investment advisor, 1980—; overseas fact-finding visits include Saudi Arabia, Egypt, Jordan, Israel, 1979, Peoples Republic of China, Japan, Hong Kong, 1981, USSR, 1985, 86, Georgia SSR, 1985, Uzbekistan SSR, 1986. Participant U.S.-USSR Pan Am-Aeroflot Aviation Agreement, 1985, Reagan-Gorbachev Summit Preparations, 1986, 87, 88; Citicorp liaison USSR mission to UN, 1982-88, Inst. U.S. and Can., Acad. Scis. USSR, 1985-88, econs. dept. Acad. Scis. USSR, 1988—. Mem. Croton-on-Hudson Narcotics Guidance Council, 1972-75, Cortland Indsl. Com., 1975-77; dist. leader Democratic Party, 1979-83; founding mem. Challenger Found., 1987. Fellow Fin. Analyst Fedn. Mem. N.Y. Soc. Security Analysts (sr. security analyst, membership com., computer applications symposium, airline splinter group, motor carrier splinter group, aerospace splinter group), Bus. Economists Council, Washington Transp. Roundtable, Assn. Computer Users, Internat. Platform Assn., N.Y. Assn. Bus. Economists, Nat. Assn Bus. Economists, Nat. Planetary Soc., Nat. Space Soc., Nat. Air and Space Mus., Tau Delta Phi (pres. 1963, 64, undergrad. of yr. 1963, spl. student recognition 1964, Coll. Distinction medal French 1964). Democrat. Author: Fashoda Crisis of 1898, 1966, Knowing Your Common Stocks, 1979, The Social Overhaul of the USSR, 1986, Economics Can Bind U.S.-USSR, 1986. Speaker security analysis, econs., corp. disclosure, deregulation, air traffic control and safety, fin. data services, U.S. megatrends, USSR Glastnost and Perestroika. Home: 2 Charles W Briggs Rd Croton-on-Hudson NY 10520 Office: Chancellor Capital Mgmt Inc Citicorp Ctr New York NY 10043

LEWINSKY, HERBERT CHRISTIAN, iron and steel company executive; b. Teschen, Austria, Sept. 20, 1928; s. Wilhelm and Emmy (von Schaible) L.; m. Rosmarie Salcher (dec.); children: Brigitte, Peter, Eva; m. Bettina Schulz. LLD, U. Vienna, Austria, 1951. Head bus. dept. Mobil Oil Austria, Vienna, 1951-64, pres., 1967-72; with retail mktg. staff Mobil Oil USA, N.Y.C., 1964-67; pres. Mobil Oil Germany, Hamburg, 1972-75, 78-86; head. div. Mobil Oil Corp., London, 1975-78; chmn., pres. Voest-Alpine AG, Linz, Austria, 1986—. Recipient Gold medal Republic of Austria, 1967. Roman Catholic. Lodge: Rotary. Office: Voest-Alpine AG, PO Box 2, A-4031 Linz Austria

LEWIS, SIR ALLEN, former governor-general of St. Lucia; b. Oct. 26, 1909; s. George Ferdinand Montgomery and Ida Louisa (Barton) L.; m. Edna Leofride Theobalds, 1936; 5 children. Ed., St. Mary's Coll., St. Lucia; LL.B. with honours, U. London, 1941; LLD (hon.) U. West Indies, 1974. Bar: St. Lucia 1931, England 1946. Pvt. practice law, Windward Islands, 1931-59; acting magistrate, St. Lucia, 1940-41; acting Puisne Judge, Windward and Leeward Islands, 1955-56; judge Fed. Supreme Ct., West Indies, 1959-62, British Caribbean Ct. of Appeal, 1962, Ct. of Appeal, Jamaica, 1962-67, acting pres. Ct. of Appeal, 1966, acting chief justice, Jamaica, 1966, Chief justice West Indies Associated States Supreme Ct., 1967-72; chmn. Nat. Devel. Corp., St. Lucia, 1972-74; chancellor U. West Indies, from 1975; gov. St. Lucia, 1974-79, gov.-gen., 1979-80, 82-87. Author: Revised Edition of Laws of St. Lucia, 1957. Mem. legis. council, St. Lucia, 1943-51, Castries Town Council, 1942-56; pres. West Indies Senate, 1958-59; bd. dirs. St. Lucia br. Brit. Red. Cross Soc., 1955-59; active numerous govt. and pub. coms. on edn. and govt.; patron St. Lucia Assn. for Retarded Children, 1975—, St. Lucia Branch, Brit. Commonwealth Ex-Services League, 1975-80, 1983-87. Decorated Coronation medal, 1953; knight bachelor and knight Order of St. John of Jerusalem; Queen's Jubilee medal, 1977; knight grand cross of St. Michael and St. George, knight grand Cross Royal Victorian Order, grand cross Order of Saint Lucia, Order of Andres Bello (Venezuela), 1986. Anglican. Clubs: Golf, Yacht (St. Lucia). Avocations: gardening; swimming. Address: Beaver Lodge, The Morne PO Box 1076, Castries Saint Lucia also: Univ of the West Indies, Mona Campus, Kingston 7 Jamaica

LEWIS, BARBARA ANN, writer, public relations consultant; b. Buffalo, July 8, 1945; d. Earl and Rose (Galante) Spellburg; m. Knoxie Henry Lewis, Sept. 6, 1975 (div. 1982). B.S., Daemen Coll., 1966; postgrad. SUNY, 1967-69. Exec. sec., sci. instr. Erie Community Coll., Buffalo, 1966-69; beauty and fashion dir., v.p. U.S. Universal, 1971-73; originator, pres. Magic of Venus Internat., Inc., Chgo., 1971-73; writer, producer, narrator The Beauty of It All radio show (nationwide), 1973-75; writer charm curriculum Erie Community Coll., 1968-69; author, producer charity benefit play: The City of Hope, 1972; pub. relations cons. Chgo., 1974-76, Houston, 1982—. Syndicated newspaper columnist The Beauty of It All, 1970-73; contbr. articles to profl. jours. Adoptive parent World Vision, Nairobi, Kenya, 1980—; campaigner Whale Protection Fund, 1978—; mem. Middlebrook Community Assn., Houston, 1978—; charter mem. Statue of Liberty-Ellis Island Commn. Named Student Tchr. of Yr., Nat. Bus. Edn. Assn., 1966; recipient Outstanding Achievement in Bus. Edn. award Nat. Assn. Bus. Tchr. Edn., 1966. Mem. Nat. Bus. Edn. Assn., AAUP, N.Y. Assn. Jr. Coll. Tchrs., Am. Fedn. Tchrs., Faculty Senate of Erie Community Coll., Tex. Mariners Cruising Assn., Alumni Assn. Daemen Coll. Roman Catholic. Club: Clear Lake Rowing. Office: 15815 Stonehaven Dr Houston TX 77059

LEWIS, CLYDE A., lawyer; b. Hoquiam, Wash., June 20, 1913; s. J.D. Clyde and Loretta C. (Adelsperger) L.; A.B., U. Notre Dame, 1934; J.D., Harvard U., 1939; m. Helen M. Judge, Sept. 22, 1936 (dec. Sept. 1985); children—Clyde A., John E. Admitted to N.Y. bar, 1940, U.S. Supreme Ct. bar, 1959; mem. Lewis, Wylie, Madonna & Rogers, and predecessor firms, Plattsburgh, N.Y. Comdr. in chief VFW, 1949-50, also served as sr. and jr. vice comdr. in chief, mem. nat. legis. com. Served to maj. USAAF, 1942-45. Decorated D.F.C. with 2 oak leaf clusters, Air medal with 4 oak leaf clusters; USAF Exceptional Service award; Croix de Guerre (France); decorated knight of Malta. Mem. Am. Legion, Am., N.Y. State bar assns., Notre Dame, Harvard alumni assns., U.S. Strategic Inst. Republican. Roman Catholic. Clubs: Capitol Hill, K.C., Elks. Home: 4 Lighthouse Ln Plattsburgh NY 12901 Office: 53 Court St Plattsburgh NY 12901

LEWIS, DALE PAUL, aerospace executive; b. Detroit, Aug. 20, 1932; s. Floyd Berchard and Elizabeth Ann (Hickey) L.; m. Ann. M. Moody, Feb. 12, 1966; children: Leonard Jonathan, Kimberly Ann, Amanda Elizabeth, Christian Floyd. AA, Glendale (Calif.) Coll., 1958. Regional dir. adminstrn. Council Econ. Indsl. Research, Beverly Hills, Calif., 1962-65; dir. EAI Applied Research and Computation Ctr., El Segundo, Calif., 1965-68; pres., chmn. ICX Group, Fed. Republic Germany, U.S., 1968-80; corp. mgr. Corp. Export Group Digital Equipment Corp., Maynard, Mass. and Washington, 1980-85; chmn., pres. Intertech Group, Eng., U.S., 1980—; cons. com. for sci. and tech. Intercosmos Apollo- Soyuz program; mem. adv. com., cons. Computer Systems Tech. U.S. Dept. Commerce, 1972-74. Founding chmn. U.S. Industry Coalition on Tech. Transfer, Washington, 1983-85; co-chmn. Fairfax County Va. Citizens Budget and Econ. Group, McLean. Served to lt. USCG, 1952-56, 58-60. Recipient Pub. Service citation U.S. Dept. Commerce, 1977. Mem. AIAA, Reserve Officers Assn. Roman Catholic. Club: Hamilton, Bermuda, Royal Bermuda Yacht. Home: 18 Whitney Rd Stowe MA 01775 Office: Intertech Group, Washington Mall One, Church St PO Box HM932, Hamilton Bermuda also: Intertech UK Ltd, 3 Princes St, London W1R 7RA, England

LEWIS, DEL F., city manager, consultant; b. Atlanta, Feb. 2, 1937; d. Ira E. and Ruth (Vandyke) Davenport; m. Claude H. Lewis, Aug. 16, 1959; children: Vivian, Alan. BA, Mo. State U., 1962; BBA, Corpus Christi State U., 1976; cert., Savs. and Loan Inst. Research analyst Dempsy-Tegeler, St. Louis, 1958-60; asst. head teller Roosevelt Fed. Savs., St. Louis, 1960-62; buyer Lichensteins, Corpus Christi, Tex., 1962-64; mgr. Bayview Nursing Home, Rockport, Tex., 1964-67; instr. AAUW, Corpus Christi, 1967-84; city mgr. City of Ingleside, Tex., 1984—; bd. dirs. USO, Corpus Christi. Editor: Coll. Humor Mag., 1958; contbg. editor: Charm Mag., 1957. Mem. City Council, 1981-83, mayor pro tem, 1982; past pres. Aux. Osteopathics, Corpus Christi; past state v.p. Aux. Ostepathics, Tex. Named Outstanding Citizen, Ingleside C. of C., Tex., 1984; Fine Art scholar Mo. State U., Kirksville, 1953-57. Fellow Luce Found.; mem. Rotary, AAUW (pres. 1982-86, leadership com. 1982—), Tex. Assn. City Mgrs., Internat. Found. Women, Internat. City Mgmt. Assn., Navy League (bd.d irs. 1986). Republican. Lodge: Eastern Star.

LEWIS, EDWARD EARL, publisher; b. Royal Oak, Mich., Mar. 9, 1926; s. Arthur Earl and Rose Martha (Gerboth) L.; m. Jean Elizabeth Sanborn, Sept. 23, 1952; children—Steven Edward (dec.), Jon Richard, Brian Arthur. B.S., Ball State U., 1959. Newspaper reporter Star, Muncie, Ind., 1944-46, Statesman, Salem, Oreg., 1946-48; editor Jour. Gas City, Ind., 1949-51, Argus, Brighton, Mich., 1953-55; writer Chrysler Corp., Detroit, 1955-58; pub. relations exec. Wyandotte Chems., Mich., 1958-61; advt. mgr. Gelman Instrument Co., Ann Arbor, Mich., 1962-66; founder pub. subsidiary Gelman Instrument Co., 1966, v.p., gen. mgr., 1966-68, pres., gen. mgr., 1968-71; pres.,owner Ann Arbor Sci. Pubs., Inc., 1971-84; founder, pres., chief exec. officer Lewis Pubs. Inc., 1984—; instr. Cleary Coll., Ypsilanti, Mich., 1964; adj. prof. grad. sch. bus. Ea. Mich. U., Ypsilanti, 1988—. Mem. Bd. Edn., Chelsea, Mich., 1968-70; mem. alumni council Ball State U., 1982-85. Served with USNR, 1943-44. Mem. Indsl. Editors Assn. Detroit (pres.), Internat. Council Indsl. Editors, Ann Arbor President's Assn., AMVETS (founding comdr. Salem post 1947). Club: Chelsea. Lodges: Masons, Kiwanis (pres.-elect Chelsea club 1988). Home: 314 E Middle St Chelsea MI 48118 Office: 121 S Main St Po Box 519 Chelsea MI 48118

LEWIS, EVELYN, communications and public relations executive; b. Goslar, Germany, Sept. 19, 1946; came to U.S. 1952, naturalized 1957; d. Gerson Emanuel and Sala (Mendlowicz) L. B.A., U. Ill.-Chgo., 1968; M.A., Ball State U., 1973, Ph.D., 1976. Research analyst Comptroller, State Ill., Chgo., 1977-78; lectr. polit. sci. dept. Loyola U., Chgo., 1977; asst. to commr. Dept. Human Services, Chgo., 1978-81; group mgr. communications Arthur Andersen & Co., Chgo., 1981-84, mgr. worldwide industry program, 1988—; dir. communications and pub. relations Heidrick and Struggles, Inc., Chgo., 1984-88; adj. faculty Roosevelt U. Sch. Bus. Adminstrn., 1988; bd. dirs. Parental Stress. Mem. venture grants com. United Way of Chgo. Mem. Children of the Holocaust, Chgo., 1982; mem. venture grants com. United Way of Chgo.; bd. dirs. Parental Stress Services. Mem. Internat. Assn. Bus. Communicators, Publicity Club Chgo., Council of Communication Mgmt, Nat. Assn. Female Execs., B'nai Brith. Jewish. Club: Metropolitan (Chgo.). Avocations: writing, poetry, bicycling, hiking. Office: Heidrick and Struggles Inc 125 S Wacker Dr Chicago IL 60606

LEWIS, FARRELL WALTER, clinical psychologist; b. Winslow, Ariz., Feb. 9, 1925; s. Walter L. and Ann (Hatch) L.; B.S. in Psychology magna cum laude, Brigham Young U., 1966, M.A. in Sch. Psychology, 1968, Ph.D. in Clin. Psychology, 1971; m. Irene Whiting, June 24, 1946; children—Lynette Lewis Peterson, Karen Priest, Peggy Lewis Kennedy, Kristine Lewis Holladay, DeeAnn Lewis Abaroa, Stephen. Intern clin. psychology Patton (Calif.) State Hosp., 1969-70; postdoctoral fellow clin. child psychology Devereux Found., Devon, Pa., 1971-72; asst. prof. child devel. Brigham Young U., Provo, Utah, 1972-74, adj. assoc. prof. psychology, 1974-84, adj. prof., 1984—; adminstrv. dir. Timpanogos Community Mental Health Center, Provo, 1974-76, dir. children and youth services, 1974-77, dir. community clin. services, 1977-80, dir. outpatient services, 1980-84, dir. psychol. services, 1984—, dir. children's services, 1988—; designated examiner State of Utah. Dir. Civil Def., Navajo County, Ariz., 1960-63; mem. Human Resources Taskforce Utah County, Utah, 1975-76; mem. Mountain Lands Assn. Govts. Task Force for Children's Services, 1976-77, mem. profl. adv. council Div. Mental Health, 1976-83, mem. quality assurance council, 1978-83. Served with AUS, 1943-46. Named valedictorian Coll. Social Sci., Brigham Young U., 1966, outstanding grad. student Grad. Sch., 1971, recipient James E. Talmadge award, 1966. Diplomate Am. Acad. Behavioral Medicine, Am. Bd. Profl. Neuropsychology. Mem. Am., Rocky Mountain, Utah (dir. 1978-84, pres. 1984, founder div. psychologists in public service 1979, pres. 1981) psychol. assns., Am. Soc. Clin Hypnosis, Nat. Acad. Neuropsychologists, Utah Assn. Mental Health Program Dirs. (pres. 1976-77), Holbrook (Ariz.) C. of C. (pres. 1960), Ariz. Hwy. 66 Assn. (pres. 1959), Nat. Soc. Sons of Utah Pioneers (v.p. 1982), Phi Kappa Phi. Club: Rotary. Home: 722 E 2620 N Provo UT 84604 Office: 585 South State Street Provo UT 84601

LEWIS, FRANK LEROY, electrical engineering educator, researcher; b. Wurzburg, Germany, May 11, 1949; s. Frank Leroy and Ruth Evangeline (Shirley) L.; MBA in Elec. Engring. and Physics, Rice U., 1971, MEE, 1971; MS in Aero. Systems, U. West Fla., 1977; PhD in Elec. Engring., Ga. Tech., 1981. Asst. prof. elec. engring. Ga. Inst. Tech., Atlanta, 1981-86, assoc. prof. 1986—; cons. Lockheed-Ga., Marietta, 1983-87. Author: Optimal Control, 1986; Optimal Estimation, 1986; contbr. articles to engring. jours. Served to lt. USN, 1971-77. NSF grantee, 1982, 86, 88; Fulbright Internat. Exchange scholar, 1988. Mem. AAAS, IEEE (sr.), Control Systems Soc. of IEEE, Soc. Indsl. and Applied Math., Sigma Xi (M. Ferst awards 1981, 84). Current work: Generalized state-space systems. Subspecialty: Systems engineering. Home: 1860 Monroe Dr NE Atlanta GA 30324

LEWIS, GERALD RICHARD JOHN BARCLAY, cardiologist; b. Jaipore, India, Nov. 22, 1941; s. John Arthur and Josephine Kate (Wotherspoon) L.; m. Beryl Monica Moody, 1967; children—Deborah Jane, Suzannah Kate, Amanda Joy. Grad. Christ's Coll., 1960, Otago Med. Sch., 1967. Intern, Christchurch Hosp., New Zealand, 1968; house physician, med. registrar North Centerbury Hosp. Bd., Christchurch, 1968-71; cardiology registrar Walsgrave Hosp., Coventry, Eng., 1972; research fellow dept. clin. pharmacology Royal Postgrad. Med. Sch., London, 1974; cardiac research fellow St. Thomas's Hosp., London, 1974-76; cons. cardiologist dept. cardiology Princess Margaret Hosp., Christchurch, 1977-83; now cardiologist Napier Hosp., New Zealand. Nat. Heart Found. fellow, 1975-76. Fellow Royal Australisian Coll. Physicians; mem. Royal Coll. Physicians, London, Cardiac Soc. Australia and N.Z. (sec. treas.), Nat. Heart Found. N.Z. (com. mem.). Office: Napier Hosp, Napier New Zealand

LEWIS, GLADYS SHERMAN, nurse, educator; b. Wynnewood, Okla., Mar. 20, 1933; d. Andrew and Minnie Elva (Halsey) Sherman; R.N., St. Anthony's Sch. Nursing, 1953; student Okla. Bapt. U., 1953-55; A.B., Tex. Christian U., 1956; postgrad. Southwestern Bapt. Theol. Sem., 1959-60, Escuela de Idiomas, San Jose, Costa Rica, 1960-61; M.A. in Creative Writing, Central (Okla.) State U., 1985; m. Wilbur Curtis Lewis, Jan. 28, 1955; children—Karen, David, Leanne, Cristen. Mem. nursing staff various facilities, Okla., 1953-57; instr. nursing, med. missionary Bapt. mission and hosp., Paraguay, 1961-70; vice-chmn. edn. commn. Paraguay Bapt. Conv., 1962-65; sec. bd. trustees Bapt. Hosp., Paraguay, 1962-65; chmn. personnel com., handbook and policy book officer Bapt. Mission in Paraguay, 1967-70; trustee Southwestern Bapt. Theol. Sem., 1974-84, chmn. student affairs com., 1976-78, vice-chmn. bd. 1978-80; ptnr. Las Amigas Tours, 1978-80; writer, conference leader, campus lectr., 1959—. Active Democratic com., Evang. Women's Caucus, 1979-80; leader Girl Scouts U.S.A., 1965-75; Okla. co-chmn. Nat. Religious Com. for Equal Rights Amendment, 1977-79; tour host Meier Internat. Study League, 1978-81. Mem. AAUW, Internat. and Am. colls. surgeons women's auxiliaries, Okla. State, Okla. County med. auxiliaries, Am. Nurse Assn., Nat. Women's Polit. Caucus, 1979-80. Author: On Earth As It Is, 1983; Two Dreams and a Promise, 1984; also religious instructional texts in English and Spanish; editor Sooner Physician's Heartbeat, 1979-82; contbr. articles to So. Bapt. and secular periodicals. Home: 14501 N Western Ave Edmond OK 73013

LEWIS, HARVEY DELLMOND, JR., clergyman, educator; b. Florence, Tex., Jan. 29, 1918; s. Harvey Dellmond and Rosell Hawkins (Whittenberg) L.; m. Marie Frances Fuscia, Feb. 19, 1945; children—Olan Harvey, Rosell Marie Lewis Carr, Frances Ann Lewis Smith. B.A., Baylor U., 1939; Th.M., Southwestern Bapt. Theol. Sem., 1942; D.D. (hon.), Univ. Mary Hardin Baylor, 1980. Ordained to ministry So. Bapt. Conv., 1937. Pastor Calvary Bapt. Ch., Port Acres, Tex., 1946-48, First Bapt. Ch., Cleveland, Tex., 1948-51, First Bapt. Ch., Kerrville, Tex., 1951-55, Harlandale Bapt. Ch., San Antonio, 1955-58, First Bapt. Ch., Mt. Pleasant, Tex., 1958-63, Central Bapt. Ch., Marshall, Tex., 1963-76; v.p. devel. East Tex. Bapt. U., Marshall, 1976-84, dir. planned giving, 1984-85, acting pres., 1985-86; moderator Tryon Evergreen Assn., Bapt. Gen. Conv., 1949-51; trustee San Marcos Bapt. Acad., Tex., 1955-60, East Tex. Bapt. U., 1959-68, 70-77, Mex. Bapt. Bible Inst., San Antonio, 1955-58. Served chaplain USAAF, 1942-46. Mem. Marshall C. of C. Lodge: Masons (32 degree). Home: 3401 Indian Springs Marshall TX 75670 Office: East Tex Bapt Univ 1209 N Grove Marshall TX 75670

LEWIS, HELEN PHELPS HOYT, association executive; b. Lakewood, N.J., Dec. 27, 1902; d. John Sherman and Ethel Phelps (Stokes) Hoyt; m. Byron Stookey, May 11, 1929 (dec. Oct. 20, 1966); children: John Hoyt, Lyman Brumbaugh, Byron; m. Robert James Lewis, Aug. 5, 1971. A.B., Bryn Mawr Coll., Pa.) Coll., 1923; M.A., Union Theol. Sem. of Columbia U., 1925. Bd. mgrs. Christodora Settlement House, N.Y.C., 1927-38; 1st v.p. Christodora Settlement House, 1929-38; nat. bd. YWCA, 1927-30; mem. women's adv. council N.Y. Bot. Garden, 1952—; mem. nursing com. Columbia Presbyn. Med. Center, N.Y.C., 1944-54; trustee Columbia Presbyn. Med. Center, 1969-78, hon. trustee, 1978—; mem. women's aux. Neurol. Inst., N.Y.C., 1939—, chmn., 1949-54; mem. women's exec. com., chmn. com. hosp. auxs. United Hosp. Fund, 1951-64, vice chmn. women's campaign com., 1961-62, chmn. women's subcom. distbn., 1963-65, vice chmn. women's exec. com., 1963-64. Mem. Colonial Dames Am. (dir. 1951-56, chmn. scholarship com. 1949-51, pres.-gen. 1953-56), Daus. Cincinnati. Republican. Presbyterian. Clubs: Darien (Conn.); Garden (pres. 1935-38), Millbrook Garden (past pres.), Garden Club Am; Colony (N.Y.C.) (gov. 1954-76, sec. 1956-59, sec., v.p. 1969-71, pres. 1972-76, chmn. membership com. 1956-71). Address: 580 Park Ave New York NY 10021

LEWIS, HENRY, III, clinical pharmacist, college dean, educator; b. Tallahassee, Jan. 22, 1950; s. Henry and Evelyn L.; m. Rita Ann Lewis, Dec. 24, 1977. Assoc. dir. pharmacy Bayfront Med. Ctr., St. Petersburg, Fla., 1972-74; assoc. dean planning and devel. Fla. A&M U. Coll. Pharmacy, Tallahassee, 1978—, assoc. prof. clin. pharmacy, 1978—; chmn. Tallahassee Leon Met. Planning Orgn.; mem., bd. dirs., Big Bend Hospice. Bd. dirs. C.K. Steele Jaycees, Tallahassee, Leon County chpt. Am. Cancer Soc. (Fla.); bd. dirs. Fla. Endowment Fund for Higher Edn.; elected to Leon County commr. Dist. #1, 1986. Recipient Kappa Psi Meritorious award, 1986, NAACP Black Achievers award, 1987, Fla. A&M U. Centennial medallion, 1988; named Tchr. of Yr., Fla. A&M U., 1976; grantee Grad. and Profl. Opportunities Program, Dept. Edn., 1979-88, Dept. Health and Rehab. Services, 1982-88, Fla. Bd. Regents, 1982-85, Nat. Inst. Health, 1985—. Mem. Am. Pharm. Assn., Fla. Pharmacy Assn., Nat. Pharm. Assn. (pres.-elect 1988), Am. Assn. Colls. Pharmacy, Tallahassee Frontiers Internat., Rho Chi, Alpha Phi Alpha. Contbr. articles to profl. jours. Home: 3020 Wahnish Way Tallahassee FL 32304 Office: Fla A&M U Coll Pharmacy Tallahassee FL 32307

LEWIS, JAMES BERTON, lawyer; b. Lenox, Tenn., Oct. 29, 1911; s. Oscar and Maude (Kirby) L.; m. Irene Fogt, Dec. 9, 1961; children: Edward K., Robert L. Student, Centralia (Wash.) Jr. Coll., 1929-31, Wash. State Coll., 1931; LL.B., Columbus U., Washington, 1940. Bar: D.C. 1942, N.Y. 1954. With Treasury Dept., 1931-34, IRS, 1934-42, 45-48; atty. Office Tax Legis. Counsel, Treasury Dept., 1948-52; spl. asst. to chief counsel IRS, 1952-53; assoc. firm Paul, Weiss, Rifkind, Wharton & Garrison, N.Y.C., 1953-55; partner Paul, Weiss, Rifkind, Wharton & Garrison, 1955-82, of counsel, 1982—; adj. prof. NYU Law Sch., 1962-83; prof. Benjamin N. Cardozo Sch. Law, 1983—; cons. Am. Law Inst. estate and gift tax, income tax projects; mem. adv. group to commr. IRS, 1976, 87. Author: The Estate Tax, 4th edit, 1979, The Marital Deduction, 1984. Served with USNR, 1942-45. Mem. ABA (vice chmn. publns., sect. taxation 1980-83, chmn. 1984-85), Am. Law Inst., N.Y. State Bar Assn., N.Y. County Lawyers Assn., Assn. Bar City N.Y., D.C. Bar Assn. Democrat. Presbyterian. Club: Masons. Home: 320 E 72d St New York NY 10021 Office: 1285 Ave of the Americas New York NY 10019

LEWIS, JAMES EDWARD, retired chemical company executive; b. Ashland, Ky., July 11, 1927; s. Blaine and Hallie Maude (Heal) L.; m. Mary Ann Johnson, Feb. 23, 1952; children—Martha Lewis Innes, Glenna Lewis Knox, Karen. A.B., Centre Coll. Ky., 1950; M.S., Purdue U., 1954, Ph.D., 1956. Pres. Radiochemistry, Inc., 1956-65; dir. research and devel. United Carbon Co., 1965-70, Ashland Oil, Inc., 1970-74; v.p. research and devel. Ashland Chem. Co., Dublin, Ohio, 1974-79; v.p. Ashland Chem. Co., 1979-88; mayor City of Dublin, 1982-86; lectr. in W. Germany, France, Italy, England, Spain, Denmark, Australia, India, U.S., China, USSR, Japan; mem. Ky. Gov.'s Com. on Nuclear Energy and Space Sci., 1961-65, Ky. Atomic Energy and Space Authority, 1961-65; mem. So. Interstate Nuclear Bd., 1963-65; rep. Indsl. Research Inst., 1967—. Contbr. articles to profl. jours. Mem. Dublin Mcpl. Council, 1979-81. Served with U.S. Army, 1944-47. Recipient Preston Carter prize in chemistry, 1950; S. Warfield prize in math., 1950. Fellow AAAS, Am. Inst. Chemists; mem. Am. Chem. Soc., Am. Phys. Soc., Soc. Chem. Industry, Licensing Execs. Soc. Republican. Club: Muirfield Country. Office: 5200 Blazer Pkwy Dublin OH 43017

LEWIS, JAMES LUTHER, savings and loan executive; b. Bridgeport, Ohio, Sept. 29, 1912; s. William Luther and Gwen (Evans) L.; grad. Mercersburg Acad., 1931; B.A., Yale U., 1935; m. Mary Anne Glen, Oct. 26, 1943; children—William Luther II, Gwendolyn. Salesman, asst. sales dist. mgr. Chgo. Pneumatic Tool Co., 1935-43, asst. to pres., 1946-55; v.p., adminstrn. and sales, dir. Van Norman Industries, Inc., 1956; pres. Insuline Corp., 1956-58; v.p. corp. devel. Norris Thermador Corp., Los Angeles, 1959-65; chmn. bd., dir. Am. Savs. & Loan Assn., Reno, 1965—, Sierra Fin. Corp., 1968—; dir. Firth Sterling Steel Corp., 1956-58. Served to lt. USNR, 1943-46. Decorated Purple Heart, Presdl. Unit citation. Presbyterian. Home: 7755 Lakeside Dr Reno NV 89511 Office: 67 W Liberty St Reno NV 89501

LEWIS, JERRY, comedian; b. Mar. 16, 1926; m. Patti Palmer, 1944 (div.); children: Gary, Ronnie, Scotty, Chris, Anthony, Joseph; m. Sandra Pitnick, 1983. Ed., Irvington (N.J.) High Sch. Prof. cinema U. So. Calif.; pres. Jerry Lewis Prodns., Jerry Lewis Films Inc., P.J. Prodns., Inc., Patti Enterprises. Began as entertainer with record routine at Catskill (N.Y.) hotel; formed comedy team with Dean Martin, 1946-56; performed as a single, 1956—; formed Jerry Lewis Prodns. Inc., prod., dir., writer, star, 1956; films include: My Friend Irma, 1949, My Friend Irma Goes West, 1950; At War with the Army, 1951, That's My Boy, 1951, Sailor Beware, 1952, Jumping Jacks, 1952, Scared Stiff, 1953, The Caddy, 1953, The Stooge, 1953, Money From Home, 1954, Three Ring Circus, 1954, You're Never Too Young, 1955, Artists and Models, 1956, Partners, 1956, Hollywood or Bust, 1956, The Delicate Delinquent, 1957, The Sad Sack, 1958, The Geisha Boy, 1958, Rockabye Baby, 1958, Don't Give Up the Ship, 1959, Visit to a Small Planet, 1959, The Bellboy, 1960, Cinderfella, 1960, The Ladies Man, 1961, It's Only Money, 1961, The Errand Boy, 1962, The Nutty Professor, 1963, Who's Minding The Store, 1963, The Patsy, 1964, The Disorderly Orderly, 1964, The Family Jewels, 1965, Boeing-Boeing, 1965, Three On A Couch, 1965, Way ... Way ... Out, 1966, The Big Mouth, 1967, Don't Raise the Bridge, Lower the Water, 1968, Hook, Line and Sinker, 1968, One More Time, 1969, Which Way To the Front?, 1970, Hardly Working, 1979, King of Comedy, 1981, Slapstick, 1982, Smorgasbord, 1983, To Catch A Cop, 1984, How Did You Get In?, 1985. Comdr. Order of Arts & Letters, France, 1984; nat. chmn. Muscular Dystrophy Assn. Recipient most promising male star in TV award Motion Picture Daily's 2nd Ann. TV poll, 1950, (as team), one of TV's 10 money making stars award Motion Picture Herald - Fame poll, 1951, 53-54, 57, best comedy team award Motion Picture Daily's 16th annual radio poll, 1951-53. Mem. Screen Producers Guild, Screen Dirs. Guild, Screen Writers Guild. Office: care Muscular Dystrophy Assn 810 Seventh Ave New York NY 10019

LEWIS, JOHN DONALD, educator; b. Paterson, N.J., Oct. 6, 1905; s. John T. and Mary (Jones) L.; A.B., Oberlin Coll., 1928; M.A., U. Wis., 1929, Ph.D., 1934; postgrad. U. Berlin, 1932-33; m. Ewart R. Kellogg, June 20, 1933 (dec. Dec. 1968); children—David K., Donald E., Ellen; m. 2d, Mary Jane Miller, Jan. 23, 1972; stepchildren—David J. Miller, Leslie J. Miller. Instr. polit. sci. U. Wis., 1930-32, 33-35, lectr., summers 1938, 39; asst. prof. polit. sci. Oberlin (Ohio) Coll., 1935-42, asso. prof., 1942-48, prof. govt., 1948—, chmn. dept., 1948-50, 53-70, prof. emeritus, 1972—; vis. prof. govt. Wesleyan U. (Conn.), 1950-51, U. Mich., summer 1949, U. Minn., summer 1951, Columbia U., summer 1954, U. Calif., Berkeley, summer 1957; Fulbright vis. lectr. Oxford (Eng.) U., 1959-60; vis. prof. Western Res. U., 1966-67, 73-74, Colo. Coll., 1972, Pa. State U., 1974. Mem. N.E. regional com. on faculty fellowships Fund Advancement Edn., Ford Found., 1951-54, cons. com. on utilization coll. teaching resources, 1956-57. Inst. Internat. Edn. fellow, 1932-33; Social Sci. Research Council fellow, 1939-40, mem. com. faculty research fellowships, 1960-63; Guggenheim Found. fellow, 1943-44. Mem. Am. (v.p. 1962-63), Midwest (pres. 1967-68) polit. sci. assns., AAUP, Am. Acad. Polit. and Social Sci., Am. Soc. Legal and Polit. Philosphy (v.p. 1967-69), Am. Council Learned Socs., Phi Beta Kappa. Author: The Genossenschaft-Theory of Otto von Gierke, 1935; Anti-Federalists versus Federalists, 1967; co-author: Democracy is Different, 1941; The Study of Comparative Government, 1949; Against the Tyrant, 1957. Book rev. editor Am. Polit. Sci. Rev., 1956-59, editorial bd., 1960-64; editorial bd. Midwest Jour. Polit. Sci., 1959-62. Contbr. articles to profl. jours. Home: 255 E College St Oberlin OH 44074

LEWIS, JOHN EVAN, airframe mechanic, airframe sheetmetal instructor; b. Phoenix, Apr. 16, 1935; s. Arthur Isaiah and Caroline (Elderege) L.; m. Dorothy Jane Montierth, June 28, 1960 (div. 1970); 1 child, David Patton. Grad. Phoenix Tech. High Sch. Airframe mechanic McDonnel Douglas, Long Beach, Calif., 1967-68, Norman Hardwell Assn., Vietnam, 1970-72; airframe mechanic, instr. Lear Seigler Inc., Vietnam and USAF, 1972-76; airframe on job trainer Bell Helicopter Internat., Effahan, Iran and Amarillo, Tex., 1976-80; airframe mechanic Temporary Engring. Service, Tucson, 1980, Lockheed Aircraft, Jeddah, Saudi Arabia, 1980-85. Patentee in field. Missionary, Ch. of Jesus Christ of Latter-day Saints, N.Z., 1955-58. Served with USMC, 1958-60. Mem. VFW, Am. Legion. Republican. Avocations: hunting, sports, fishing. Lodges: Moose, Elks. Home: 4725 N Camino Aire Fresco Tucson AZ 85705

LEWIS, JOHN HARDING, retired military officer; b. London, May 23, 1922; s. Charles Harding and Dorothy (O'Farrel) L.; m. Joanna Dorothy Rose White, Mar. 29, 1952; 1 child, Brian Hamilton. Student, Warwick Sch. Joined RAF, 1940, advanced through grades to group capt., 1965, served as pilot and flight comdr. transport support squadrons Europe, Middle East, 1943-47, in charge air ops. Antarctic and Falkland Islands, 1949-50, squadron comdr. RAF Coll. Cranwell and Cen. Flying Sch., 1951-53, mem. RAF commissioning and appointments bds. Ministry of Def., 1954-55, leader RAF party with Commonwealth Trans-Antarctic Expdn., 1955-58, sr. personnel officer staff of Air Sec., 1959-61, comdg. officer #511 Squadron, detachment comdr. Cyprus/ Brit. Honduras, 1961-64, U.K. planning officer staff mil. planning office, Seato, 1964-65, served with hdqrs. Far East Air Force, 1965-66, comdg. officer flying tng. sch., 1967-70, dep. chief Brit. comdrs.-in-chief mission to Russian forces in Dem. Republic Germany, 1970-72, ret., 1972; aviation industry cons. MERO-Werke KG, Wurzburg, Fed. Republid Germany, 1973-74; dep. base mgr., mgr. support services Brit. Aerospace Co., Saudi Arabia, 1976-79, head civil engring. handover sect., 1980-82; cons. Security Home Office, London, 1982—; bd. dirs. Video Security, Yorkshire, 1982—. Recipient Air Force Cross with bar, Polar medal. Fellow Royal Geog. Soc. Conservative. Mem. Ch. of England. Clubs: RAF, Antarctic (London). Home: Brook House Burythorpe, Malton Near York YO17 9LJ, England

LEWIS, JONATHAN JAMES, educational administrator; b. Lorain, Ohio, Mar. 31, 1939; s. Llewellyn D. and Kathryn B. (Walker) L.; B.A. in Am. Studies, Bowling Green (Ohio) State U., 1962, M.A. in Am. Studies, 1966; m. Amanda Dudas, 1973; children—Jonathan Evan, Justin Daniel. Editorial trainee Booth Newspapers, Detroit, 1966-67; news reporter Metro-East Journal, East St. Louis, Ill., 1967-68; adminstrv. asst. Cahokia (Ill.) Sch. Dist. 187, 1968-88; bus. mgr. Meramec Valley R-111 Sch. Dist., 1988— . Pres. Cahokia Library Bd.; chmn. City-Wide Hist. Fair, 1973. Mem. Ill. Assn. Sch Bus. Ofcls., Mo. Assn. Sch. Bus. Ofcls., Assn. Sch. Bus. Ofcls., Assn. Supervision Curriculum Devel., Cahokia Khoury League (chmn. 1986-87). Contbr. articles to local newspapers. Home: 803 Joliet Cahokia IL 62206 Office: 126 N Payne Pacific MO 62206

LEWIS, KENNETH, shipping executive; b. N.Y.C., Aug. 23, 1934; b. Nathaniel and Hanna Evelyn (Kotler) L.; A.B., Princeton U., 1955; J.D., Harvard U., 1958; m. Carol Ann Schnitzer, Aug. 3, 1958 (div. 1982); children—Scott, Laurence, Kathleen; m. 2d, Colleen Anne Wesche, Nov. 27, 1983. Admitted to N.Y., Oreg. bars, 1959; law clk. to judge U.S. Dist. Ct., N.Y.C., 1958-59; asso. King, Miller, Anderson, Nash & Yerke, Portland, Oreg., 1959-61; gen. counsel Indsl. Air Products Co., Portland, 1961-63; v.p. to exec. v.p. Lasco Shipping Co., Portland, 1963-79, pres., 1979—; bd. dirs. Britannia Steam Ship Ins. Assn., Ltd., London, 1986—, The Swedish Club, Gothenburg, 1987—, dep. chmn., 1988—. Mem. Port of Portland Commn., 1974-81, treas., 1977, v.p., 1978, pres., 1979; trustee Lewis and Clark Coll., 1974-83; bd. dirs. Columbia River Maritime Mus., 1987—, Oreg. Community Found., 1982—, treas., 1986—; mem. Portland Met. Area Boundary Commn., 1974-74, Portland Met. Mass Transit Dist. Bd., 1973-74; pres. Portland Zool. Soc., 1970, World Affairs Council of Oreg., 1969. Mem. Am., Oreg. Bar Assns., Soc. Maritime Arbitrators, Inc. Democrat. Jewish. Clubs: Multnomah Athletic, Arlington, University, Masons, City (Portland). Home and Office: 3200 NW Yeon Ave Portland OR 97210

LEWIS, LINDA DONELLE, neurologist, educator; b. Columbus, Ohio, Nov. 27, 1939; d. Donald Peter and Ann Elizabeth (Karn) Lewis; B.S., Bethany Coll., 1961, D.Sc. (hon.), 1981; M.D., W.Va. U., 1965; m. Gary Gambuti, Oct. 6, 1979. Practice medicine specializing in neurology, N.Y.C., 1971—; asst. prof. neurology Coll. Physicians and Surgeons, Columbia U., N.Y.C., from 1971, now clin. prof., assoc. dean student affairs, 1979—; cons. in field; mem. N.Y. State Bd. for Profl. Med. Conduct, 1979—. Recipient Outstanding Teaching award Columbia U., 1977. Mem. AMA (nat. com. on med. edn.), N.Y. State Med. Soc. (del.), New York County Med. Soc., Am. Assn. Med. Colls., Am. Acad. Neurology, AAAS. Contbr. articles to sci. jours. Home: 320 Central Park W New York NY 10025 Office: 710 W 168th St New York NY 10032

LEWIS, MARY THERESE, artist; b. Blue Island, Ill., June 21, 1951; d. Christian Henry and Marie Anne (Corcoran) Berns; B.S. in Math. with highest honors, U. Ill., 1974; M.S. in Physics, U. Chgo., 1978; m. Richard W. Lewis, Feb. 16, 1979. Lead engr. research and devel. robotics and artificial intelligence Boeing Mil. Airplane Co., Wichita, Kans., 1978-84; self-employed artificial intelligence engr., 1984-85; artist, 1985—. Mem. Am. Assn. Artificial Intelligence, Internat. Platform Assn., Phi Kappa Phi. Avocation: classical piano. Home and Office: 2221 Inwood Dr Wilmington DE 19810

LEWIS, MURRAY FISHER, lawyer; b. Ithaca, N.Y., June 26, 1931; s. Morris I. and Sydelle (Fisher) L.; m. Carol Penn, Feb. 7, 1957; children—Andrea J., Sheryl L., Patricia B. M.B.A., Cornell U., 1952, J.D., 1955. Bar: N.Y. 1955, U.S. Dist. Ct. (no. dist.) N.Y. 1959. Assoc. Walter J. Wiggins, Ithaca, 1955-56; asst. county atty. Tompkins County, N.Y., 1956-58; sole practice, Ithaca, 1956—; sec., dir. Morris' Men's Wear, Inc., Ames of Ithaca, Inc. Trustee, Tompkins County Hosp. Corp., 1969-75, pres. bd., 1975. Served as lt. U.S. Navy, 1951-57. Mem. ABA, N.Y. State Bar Assn., Tompkins County Bar Assn., Am. Assn. Trial Lawyers, N.Y. State Trial Lawyers Assn., Am. Arbitration Assn. (panel of arbitrators). Republican. Jewish. Clubs: Elks, Masons. Past contbg. editor N.Y. State Trial Lawyers Quar. Home: 102 White Park Pl Ithaca NY 14850 Office: 200 E Buffalo St Suite 101 Ithaca NY 14850

LEWIS, NORMAN, English language educator, writer; b. N.Y.C., Dec. 30, 1912; s. Herman and Deborah (Nevins) L.; m. Mary Goldstein, July 28, 1934; children—Margery, Debra. B.A., CUNY, 1939; M.A., Columbia U., 1941. Instr., lectr CUNY, N.Y.C., 1943-52; assoc. prof. English NYU, N.Y.C., 1955-64; instr. Compton Coll., Calif., summers 1962-64, UCLA, 1962-69; prof. English Rio Hondo Coll., Whittier, Calif., 1964—, chmn. communications dept., 1964-75. Author: (with Wilfred Funk) Thirty Days to a More Powerful Vocabulary, 1942, rev. edit., 1970, Power with Words, 1943, How to Read Better and Faster, 1944, rev. edit., 1978, The Lewis English Refresher and Vocabulary Builder, 1945, Better English, 1948, Word Power Made Easy, 1949, rev. edit., 1978, The Rapid Vocabulary Builder, 1951, rev. edit., 1980, 3d edit., 1988, How to Get More Out of Your Reading, 1951, Twenty Days to Better Spelling, 1953, The New Roget's Thesaurus in Dictionary Form, 1961, rev. edit., 1978, Dictionary of Correct Spelling, 1962, Correct Spelling Made Easy, 1963, rev. edit. 1987, Dictionary of Modern Pronunciation, 1963, New Guide to Word Power, 1963, The New Power with Words, 1964, Thirty Days to Better English, 1964, The Modern Thesaurus of Synonyms, 1965, RSVP-Reading, Spelling, Vocabulary, Pronunciation, elem. texts, I-III, 1966, coll. edit., 1977, See, Say, and Write!, books I and II, 1973, Instant Spelling Power, 1976, R.S.V.P. for College English Power, book II, 1978, book III, 1979, R.S.V.P. with Etymology, book I, 1980, book II, 1981, book III, 1982, R.S.V.P. books I-III, rev. edits., 1982-83, books A-B, 1985-86, Instant Word Power, 1981, Dictionary of Good English, 1987; also numerous articles in nat. mags.

LEWIS, RALPH MILTON, real estate developer, accountant; b. Johnstown, Pa., Nov. 9, 1919; s. Morris and Sarah (Galfond) L.; m. Goldy Sarah Kimmel, June 12, 1941; children: Richard Alan, Robert Edward, Roger Gordon, Randall Wayne. AA, Los Angeles City Coll., 1939; BS, UCLA, 1941; postgrad., U. So. Calif., 1945-48. Bar: Calif. 1952. Pvt. practice acctg. Los Angeles, 1945-55; practice law Los Angeles, 1953-55; founder Lewis Homes, 1957; chmn. bd. Lewis Construction Co., Upland, Calif., 1959—, Lewis Bldg. Co., Las Vegas, 1960—; Republic Sales Co., Inc. Lewis Bldg. Co., Upland, 1956—; dir., v.p. Kimmel Enterprises, Inc., 1959—; mng. partner Lewis Homes of Calif., 1973—, Lewis Homes of Nev., 1972—, Western Properties, Upland, 1972—, Foothill Investment Co., Las Vegas, 1971—, Republic Mgmt. Co., Upland, 1978-86; dir. Gen. Telephone Co. Calif., 1981-86; mem. adv. bd. Inland div. Security Pacific Nat. Bank; instr. U. So. Calif., UCLA, Los Angeles City Coll., 1948-54, Dooley Law Rev. Course, 1953-54; guest lectr. numerous colls., univs. Contbr. articles to mags., jours. Mem., com. chmn. Calif. Commn. of Housing and Community Devel., 1965-67; mem. Calif. Gov.'s Task Force on the Home Bldg. and Construction Industry, 1967; pres. Bd. of Edn. Citrus Community Coll. Dist., Azusa, Calif., 1969, 73, mem., 1967-73; mem. Citizens Planning Council, Los Angeles County Regional Planning Commn., 1972-73, UCLA Found., Chancellor's Assoc.; mem. dean's council UCLA Grad. Sch. Architecture and Urban Planning.; bd. dirs. Regional Research Inst. So. Calif., 1983-84; chmn. land use and planning com. Citizens' Adv. Council, Calif. Senate Housing Com., 1983-84; founding mem. Rancho Cucamonga Community Found., 1987-88. Recipient Humanitarian award NCCJ, 1979; Builder of Year award Bldg. Industry Assn. So. Calif., 1970; named as U. So. Calif.'s 1st Developer in Residence, 1988 at Lusk Ctr. for Real Estate Devel.; recipient Good Scout award Old Baldy council Boy Scouts Am., 1984; recipient (with wife) Builder of Yr. award Profl. Builder mag., 1987; inducted Nat. Housing Ctr.'s Hall of Fame, Washington, 1988. Mem. Am. Bar Assn., Calif. Soc. C.P.A.'s, Nat. Assn. Home Builders (dir.), Calif. Bldg. Industry Assn. (dir., chmn. affordable housing task force 1978-80, named to Hall of Fame 1987), Bldg. Industry Assn. So. Calif. (past treas., pres., dir., Bldg.

Industry Medal of Honor, 1986). Office: Lewis Homes 1156 N Mountain Ave Upland CA 91786

LEWIS, RITA HOFFMAN, plastic products manufacturing company executive; b. Phila., Aug. 6, 1947; d. Robert John and Helen Anna (Dugan) Hoffman; 1 child, Stephanie Blake. Student Jefferson Med. Coll. Sch. Nursing, 1965-67; Gen. mgr. Sheets & Co., Inc. (now Flower World, Inc.), Woodbury, N.J., 1968-72; dir., exec. v.p., treas. Hoffman Precision Plastics, Inc., Blackwood, N.J., 1973—; ptnr. Timber Assocs.; guest speaker various civic groups, 1974—. Author: That Part of Me I Never Really Meant to Share, 1979; In Retrospect: Caught Between Running and Loving. Mem. Com. for Citizens of Glen Oaks (N.J.), 1979—, Gloucester Twp. Econ. Devel. Com., 1981—, Gloucester Twp. Day Scholarship Com., 1984—; chairperson Gloucester Twp. Day Scholarship Found., 1985—; bd. dirs. Diane Hull Dance Co. Recipient Winning Edge award, 1982, Mayor's award for Womens' Achievement, 1987, Outstanding Community Service award Mayor, Council and Com., 1987. Mem. Sales Assn. Chem. Industry, Blackwood Businessmen's Assn. Roman Catholic.

LEWIS, ROBERT DAVID, ophthalmologist, educator; b. Thomasville, Ga., Aug. 27, 1948; s. Ralph N. and E. Margaret (Klaus) L.; m. Frances Elizabeth Golys, Aug. 29, 1970. BS, St. Louis Coll. Pharmacy, 1971; MD, St. Louis U., 1975. Diplomate Am. Bd. Ophthalmology; registered pharmacist. Intern, Cardinal Glennon Hosp. Children, St. Louis, 1975-76; resident St. Louis U., 1976-79; practice medicine specializing in ophthalmology, St. Louis, 1979—; dir. pediatric ophthalmology St. Louis U., 1980-82, 85, asst. prof., 1980-88, assoc. prof., 1988—; dir. pediatric ophthalmology Cardinal Glennon Hosp. for Children, St. Louis, 1980-82, 85; mem. adv. bd. Delta Gamma Found. for Visually Handicapped Children. Recipient St. Louis U. Award for Teaching, 1982. Fellow ACS; mem. AMA, Mo. Med. Assn., St. Louis Med. Soc., Am. Acad. Ophthalmology, Assn. for Research in Vision and Ophthalmology, Contact Lens Assn. Ophthalmology, Internat. Assn. Ocular Surgeons, Am. Intraocular Implant Soc. Office: 10004 Kennerly Rd Saint Louis MO 63128 also: 3915 Watson Rd Saint Louis MO 63109

LEWIS, ROBERT JOHN CORNELIUS KOONS, university library director, consultant Oriental religions and antiquities; b. Washington, Feb. 15, 1938; s. Frank Ashby and Dorothy Elaine (Koons) L.; m. Martha Marie Popejoy, Dec. 22, 1957 (div. 1964); 1 son, Stephen Ashley; m. 2d, Helena Barbara Vaughn Schumacker, Sept. 11, 1968 (div. 1976); children—Matthew, Randolph; m. Marguerita S. Kris, July 28, 1985. B.A. in History of Religion, George Washington U., 1961, M.A. in Secondary Edn., 1966; M.S. in L.S., Cath. U. Am., 1974. Intelligence analyst CIA, Washington, 1958-62; tech. library supr. Bell Aerospace, Tucson, 1968-70; info. officer Ambionics Inc., Washington, 1970-73; law librarian Patton, Boggs & Blow, Washington, 1973-75; research George Washington U., Washington, 1976-78; library dir. Benjamin Franklin U., Washington, 1979—; Oriental art cons. Silverman Galleries, Alexandria, Va., 1978—. Author, compiler: Brief History of the Rose Mount Branch of the Surles (Searles) Lewis Family of Virginia, 1976, collected poems: Quatrains based on the Love Poems of the 6th Dalai Lama and other poems, 1979; Early Branches of the Lewis Family of Warner Hall, 1985. Served with U.S. Army, 1963-65. Awarded title of Gyalwa Karma Lozang Dondrup, Kalu Rinpoche of Darjeeling, 1977. Mem. Assn. Former Intelligence Officers, ALA (pres. com. 1982), D.C. Library Assn., Met. Washington Library Council, Sigma Phi Epsilon. Episcopalian. Clubs: Mahikari of Am., Subud, Theosophical Soc. Home: 14003 Parkvale Rd Rockville MD 20853 Office: Benjamin Franklin U 100 16th St NW Washington DC 22036

LEWIS, ROBERT TURNER, psychologist; b. Taft, Calif., June 17, 1923; s. D. Arthur and Amy Belle (Turner) L.; m. Jane Badham, Mar. 23, 1946; children—Jane, William, Richard. B.A., U. So. Calif., 1947, M.A., 1950; Ph.D., U. Denver, 1952. Lic. psychologist, Calif. Chief psychologist Hollywood Presbyn. Hosp., Los Angeles, 1953-58; dir. psychol. services Salvation Army, Pasadena, Calif., 1958-68; dir. Pasadena Psychol. Ctr., 1964-74; successively asst. prof., assoc. prof. and prof., Calif. State U.-Los Angeles, 1952-83, prof. emeritus, 1984—; assoc. dir Cortical Function Lab., Los Angeles, 1972-84; clin. dir. Diagnostic Clinic, West Covina, Calif., 1983-85; dir. Job Stress Clinic, Santa Ana, Calif., 1985—. Author: Taking Chances, 1979; co-author: Money Madness, 1978; Human Behavior, 1974; The Psychology of Abnormal Behavior, 1961. Served to lt. (j.g.) USNR, 1943-46, PTO. Mem. Am. Psychol. Assn., Calif. State Psychol. Assn., Los Angeles County Psychol. Assn., Nat. Acad. Neuropsychology. Republican. Office: Job Stress Clinic 1200 N Main St #525 Santa Ana CA 92701

LEWIS, SHERMAN RICHARD, JR., investment banker; b. Ottawa, Ill., Dec. 11, 1936; s. Sherman Richard and Julia Audrey (Rusteen) L.; m. Dorothy Marie Downie, Sept. 9, 1967; children: Thomas, Catherine, Elizabeth, Michael. AB, Northwestern U., 1958; MBA, U. Chgo., 1964. With investment dept. Am. Nat. Bank & Trust Co., Chgo., 1961-64; v.p. Halsey, Stuart & Co., N.Y.C., 1964-70, v.p. in charge corp. fin. dept., 1970-73; v.p. C.J. Lawrence & Sons, N.Y.C., 1970; ptnr. Loeb, Rhoades & Co., N.Y.C., 1974-76, ptnr. in charge corp. fin. dept., 1975-76, exec. v.p., bd. dirs., 1976-77, pres., co-chief exec. officer, 1977-78; vice chmn., co-chief exec. officer Loeb Rhoades, Hornblower & Co., N.Y.C., 1978-79; pres. Shearson/Am. Express Inc., N.Y.C., 1979-82, vice chmn., 1983-84; vice chmn. Shearson Lehman/Am. Express Inc., 1984-87, Shearson Lehman Bros. Inc., 1988—, Shearson Lehman Hutton Inc., 1988—. Mem. President's Commn. on Housing, 1981-82, President's Council on Internat. Youth Exchange, 1982—. Served as commd. officer USMC, 1958-61. Mem. N.Y. Soc. Security Analysts. Clubs: Bond, India House, Ridgewood Country, University, Quogue Field. Office: Shearson Lehman Bros Inc Am Express Tower World Fin Ctr New York NY 10285

LEWIS, VERNITA ANN WICKLIFFE, beauty culturist, fast food restaurant executive; b. Chgo., Apr. 6, 1955; d. Kernett Henry and Clara Lillian (Wells) Robinson; m. Lloyd Maurice Wickliffe, Sr., Jan. 31, 1976 (dec. 1982); children—Calvin Earl, Nicole Latrice, Lloyd Maurice Jr.; m. Kenneth Lewis, Feb. 17, 1985. Student William Jones Comml. Bus. Sch., 1971-72; degree Pivot Point Inst., 1982-83; student Prairie State Coll., 1987-88. Lic. cosmetology tchr. Clerk Typist I & II State Dept. Pub. Aid., Chgo., 1972-74, caseworker I, 1975-77, med. caseworker II, 1978-79, med. caseworker III, 1979-83; cosmetology student instr. Lyndon Beauty Acad., Steger, Ill., 1985—; owner Kenny's for Ribs and Pizza, Chgo., 1985—, MS VE's Profl. Skin Care Salon, Park Forest, Ill.; lectr., cons. Huth Jr. High Sch., Matteson, Ill., 1985—; with child devel. pre-school program Prairie State Jr. Coll., 1988—; underwriter drug abuse program Jesse James Lloyd Wickliffe Meml. Scholarship Fund. Recipient 2d and 3rd place trophies Unique Beauty Sch. Competition, 1982, Morris Acad., 1982; 4th and 3rd place trophies Pivot Point Beauty Sch., 1983; Creative Service award Environ. Conservation Commn., 1984. Mem. Nat. Assn. Female Execs., Nat. Hair Dressers and Cosmetologists Assn., Nat. Cosmetology Assn. (educator esthetics div. 1986—), Ill. Cosmetology Assn. (educator aesthetics div. 1986), Nat. Assn. Nail Artists. Democrat. Club: Sno Goffers Ski. Avocations: music; bowling; gardening.

LEWIS, WALTER ALAN, manufacturing executive; b. Colwyn Bay, Wales, Dec. 7, 1936; arrived in Can., 1967; s. Walter and Dorothy (Taylor) L.; m. Carolyn Isabella Oliver, Oct. 25, 1969; children: Keith, Jeffrey. Grad. high sch., Colwyn Bay. Student acct. Fogg Tatlow & Co., Llandudno, Wales, 1954-60; chartered acct. Deloitte Plender Griffiths & Co., London, 1960-63, Thorne Gunn & Co., Toronto, Ont., 1967-68; asst. corp. sec. Quinton Hazell Ltd., Colwyn Bay, 1964-67, controller, 1969-70; gen. mgr. Knape & Vogt Can. Inc., Toronto, 1970—; Treas. Dewi St. Welsh United Ch., Toronto, 1983—. Fellow Inst. Chartered Accts. in Eng., Wales. Club: Unionville. Lodges: Masons, Lions (dir. 1985-86). Office: Knape & Vogt Can Inc, 340 Carlingview Dr, Rexdale, ON Canada M9W 5G5

LEWIS, WALTER LAUGHN, lawyer, former air force officer; b. Charlottesville, Va., Aug. 22, 1924; s. Chauncey DePew and Clarice Undine (Laughon) L.; m. Karen Irvine, Sept. 22, 1956; children—Karen Hotchkiss, Robin Laughn. B.A., U. Va., 1947, J.D., 1950; postgrad. Acad. Internat. Law, The Hague, Netherlands, 1964, George Washington U. Law Sch., 1967-69, LL.M., 1969. Bar: Va. 1949, U.S. Ct. Mil. Appeals 1953, U.S. Supreme Ct. 1953, N.C. 1983. Commd. officer USAF, 1950, advanced through grades to col.; with Judge Adv. Gen.'s dept. 1950-80; dep. dir. internat. law U.S. Air Forces in Europe, 1962-65; mem. Air Force Bd. Rev. (Ct. Mil. Rev.), 1965-67; staff judge adv. Air Force Missile Devel. Ctr., Holloman AFB, N.Mex., 1969-70; legal officer U.S. Embassy, Bangkok, Thailand, 1971-72; chief mil. justice div. Office of Judge Adv. Gen., Washington, 1972-77, dir. USAF Judiciary, 1977-79; vice comdr. Air Force Legal Services Ctr., Washington, 1979-80, ret., 1980; chmn. rules adv. com. U.S. Ct. Mil. Appeals, Washington, 1981—; assoc. Everett & Hancock, Durham, N.C., 1983-84. Served with USAAF, 1943-45. Decorated Legion of Merit with oak leaf cluster, Air Force Commendation medal with 3 oak leaf clusters, Air Medal with four oak leaf clusters. Mem. Inter-Am. Bar Assn., ABA (co-chmn. criminal justice and mil. com., criminal justice sect. 1984-85, standing com. on mil. law, 1986—), Va. Bar Assn., Fed. Bar Assn. (editor issues sect. jour. 1987—), Am. Judicature Soc., Mil. Law Inst. (pres. 1986—), Delta Theta Phi. Presbyterian. Clubs: Nat. Lawyers, Mason, Shriners, St. Andrews Soc. (N.C., Washington) Home: 2674 N Upshur St Arlington VA 22207

LEWIS, WILLIAM ARTHUR, economist, educator; b. St. Lucia, W.I., Jan. 23, 1915; s. George and Ida (Barton) L.; m. Gladys Isabel Jacobs, May 5, 1947; children: Elizabeth Anne, Barbara Jean. Student, St. Mary's Coll., St. Lucia, 1924-29; B.Com., London Sch. Econs., 1937, Ph.D., 1940; M.A. (hon.), Manchester U., 1951, D.Sc., 1973; L.H.D., Columbia U., 1954, Boston Coll., 1972, Coll. of Wooster, 1980, DePaul U., 1981; LL.D., U. Toronto, 1959, Williams Coll., 1959, U. Wales, 1960, U. Bristol, 1961, U. Dakar, 1962, U. Leicester, 1964, Rutgers U., 1965, U. Brussels, 1968, The Open U., 1974, Atlanta U., 1980, U. Hartford, 1981, York U., 1981, Howard U., 1984, Harvard U., 1984; Litt.D., U. West Indies, 1966, U. Lagos, 1974, Northwestern U., 1979; D.Sc., U. London, 1982; D.Social Sci, Yale U., 1983; hon. fellow, London Sch. Econs., 1959, Weizmann Inst., 1962. Asst. lectr., then lectr., reader London Sch. Econs., 1938-48; Stanley Jevons prof. polit. economy U. Manchester, 1948-59; prin., vice chancelor U. West Indies, 1959-63; prof. econs., internat. affairs Princeton U., 1963-83; prin. Bd. Trade, then Colonial Office U.K., 1943-44; mem. Colonial Econ. Adv. Council U.K., 1945-49; dir. Colonial Devel. Corp. U.K., 1950-52; mem. Deptl. Com. on Fuel and Power U.K., 1951-52; econ. adviser Prime Minister of Ghana, 1957-58; dep. mng. dir. UN Spl. Fund, 1959-60; spl. adviser Prime Minister West Indies, 1961-62; dir. Indsl. Devel. Corp., Jamaica, 1962-63, Central Bank of Jamaica, 1961-62; pres. Caribbean Devel. Bank, 1970-73; chancellor U. Guyana, 1967-73; Mem. econ. adv. council NAACP, 1978-80. Author: Economic Problems of Today, 1940, The Principles of Economic Planning, 1949, The Economics of Overhead Costs, 1949, Economic Survey, 1919-39, 1950, The Theory of Economic Growth, 1955, Politics in West Africa, 1965, Development Planning, 1966, Reflections on the Economic Growth of Nigeria, 1967, Some Aspects of Economic Development, 1969, The Evolution of the International Economic Order, 1978, Growth and Fluctuations 1870-1913, 1978, Racial Conflict and Economic Development; editor: Tropical Development, 1970. Decorated Knight Bachelor, 1963; co-recipient Nobel prize in econs., 1979; Corr. fellow Brit. Acad. Mem. Am. Philos. Soc., Royal Econ. Soc. (council 1949-58), Manchester Statis. Soc. (pres. 1956), Econ. Soc. Ghana (pres. 1958), Am. Econ. Assn. (v.p. 1965, Distinguished fellow 1969, pres. 1983); hon. fgn. mem. Am. Acad. Arts and Scis. Address: Princeton Univ 206 Woodrow Wilson School Princeton NJ 08540 •

LEWIS, WILLIAM HEADLEY, JR., manufacturing company executive; b. Washington, Sept. 29, 1934; s. William Headley and Lois Maude (Bradshaw) L.; B.S. in Metall. Engring., Va. Poly. Inst., 1956; postgrad. Grad. Sch. Bus. Adminstrn., Emory U., 1978; m. Carol Elizabeth Cheek, Apr. 22, 1967; children—Teresa Lynne, Bret Cameron, Charles William, Kevin Marcus. Research engr. Lockheed-Ga. Co., Marietta, 1956-57, sr. research engr., 1960-63, research group engr., 1963-72, research and devel. program mgr., 1972-79, mgr. engring. tech. services, 1979-83, dir. engring. Getex div., 1983-86; gen. mgr. Inspection Systems div. Lockheed Air Terminal, Inc., 1986-87; pres., chief exec. officer Measurement Systems Inc., Atlanta, 1987—; chmn. Lockheed Corp. Task Force on NDE, 1980-86; pres., Measurement Systems, Inc., 1987—; mem. Com. to Study Role of Advanced Tech. in Improving Reliability and Maintainability of Future Weapon Systems, Office of Sec. of Def. co-founder, dir. Applied Tech. Services, Inc., SafeTran Corp.; lectr. grad. studies and continuing edn. Union Coll., Schenectady, 1977-82. Served to 1st lt. USAF, 1957-60. Registered profl. engr., Calif. Fellow Am. Soc. for Non-destructive Testing (cert.; nat. dir. 1976-78, chmn. nat. tech. council 1977-78, chmn. aerospace com. 1972-74, nat. nominating com. 1982-83, 1984-85)); mem. Am. Inst. Aeronautics and Astronics, Am. Soc. for Metals, Nat. Mgmt. Assn., Nat. Acad. Scis. (mem. com. on compressive fracture 1981-83). Editor: Prevention of Structural Failures: The Role of Fracture Mechanics, Failure Analysis, and NDT, 1978; patentee detection apparatus for structural failure in aircraft. Home: 1205 W Nancy Creek Dr Atlanta GA 30319 Office: 2262 Northwest Pkwy Suite B Marietta GA 30067

LEWITAS, ALVIN ROY, health services company executive; b. Bklyn., Oct. 17, 1941; s. Jack and Rita (Spilke) L.; m. Holly Lynn McCown, Mar. 31, 1983; children: David, Alison. BA, U. Md., 1967; MBA, George Washington U., 1970. Adminstrv. asst. Michael Reese Hosp., Chgo., 1970-72; exec. v.p. Mile Sq. Health Ctr., Chgo., 1972-76; pres. Lewitas & Co., Inc., Chgo., 1976-86, Total Home Health Care, Chgo., 1983—; cons. Dysfunctioning Child Ctr., Chgo., 1972—; bd. dirs. MWB Inc., Med. Fin. Corp. Caring Home Health Services Inc. Bd. dirs. U. Chgo. Cancer Research Ctr., 1985—. Served with USAF, 1962-66. Mem. Am. Coll. Healthcare Execs. Home: 3240 N Lake Shore Dr Chicago IL 60657 Office: Total Home Health Care 1050 N State St Chicago IL 60610

LEWITH, GEORGE THOMAS, physician, research center administrator; b. Cardiff, Wales, Dec. 1, 1950; s. Frank and Alice (Schallinger) L.; m. Nicola Rosemary Bazely, May 7, 1977; children: Tom, Emily, Henry. MA in Biochemistry, Cambridge U., Eng., 1971, DMB., B.Chir., 1974. Pediatric intern McMaster U., Ont., Can., 1973; rotating intern in gen. medicine Westminster Hosp. and Univ. Coll. Hosp. Groups, London, 1974-78; gen. practice medicine Queensland, Australia, 1979; lectr. Southampton (Eng.) Med. Sch., 1980-83; co-dir. Ctr. for Study Complementary Medicine, Southampton, 1983—; clin. asst. Salisbury Pain Clinic, Odstock Hosp. Author: Modern Chinese Acupuncture, 1980, A Desk Guide to Classical Chinese Acupuncture, 1980, Alternative Therapies: Acupuncture, 1981, The Acupuncture Treatment of Internal Disease, 1985, (with J. Kenyon) Clinical Ecology, 1985; editor: Modern Medicine Supplement on Pain, 1982, Alternative Therapies: Osteopathy, 1982, Homeopathy, 1982, Healing, 1983, Hypnosis, 1984, Naturopathy, 1984, Relaxation, 1986, Pascoe Therapy, 1985; editorial bd. Complementary Medicine; cons. editor Clin. Biomechanics; contbr. numerous articles to med. jours. Past trustee Koestler Found. Recipient numerous research grants. Home: Twillingate Farm Tiptoe Sway, Lymington SO41 6EJ, England Office: Ctr for Study Complementary, Medicine 51 Bedford Pl, Southampton SO1 2DG, England

LEWITT, MILES MARTIN, computer engineering company executive; b. N.Y.C., July 14, 1952; s. George Herman and Barbara (Lin) L.; m. Susan Beth Orenstein, June 24, 1973. BS summa cum laude, CCNY Engring., 1973; MS, Ariz. State U., 1976. Software engr. Honeywell, Phoenix, 1973-78; software engr., architect iRMX line ops. systems Intel Corp., Santa Clara, Calif., 1978; engring. mgr. Intel, Hillsboro, Oreg., 1978-80, 1981—, corp. strategic staff, 1981-82; engring. mgr. Intel, Israel, 1980-81; instr. Maricopa Tech. Coll., Phoenix, 1974-75. Contbr. articles to profl. jours. Recipient Engring. Alumni award CCNY, 1973, Eliza Ford Prize CCNY, 1973, Advanced Engring. Program award, Honeywell, 1976, Product of Yr. award Electronic Products Mag., 1980. Mem. IEEE Computer Soc. (voting mem.), Assn. Computing Machinery (voting mem.). Democrat. Home: 720 SW Brookwood Ave Hillsboro OR 97123 Office: Intel Corp 5200 NE Elam Young Pkwy Hillsboro OR 97123

LEYDET, FRANÇOIS GUILLAUME, author; b. Neuilly-sur-Seine, France, Aug. 26, 1927; s. Bruno and Dorothy (Lindsey) L.; AB, Harvard, 1947, postgrad. Bus. Sch., 1952; postgrad. Johns Hopkins Sch. Advanced Internat. Studies, 1952-53; Bachelier-ès-lettres-philosophie, U. Paris (France), 1945; m. Patience Abbe, June 17, 1955 (div.); step children: Catherine Abbe Geissler, Lisa Amanda O'Mahony; m. 2d, Roslyn Carney, June 14, 1970; step-children: Walter E. Robb IV, Rachel R. Avery, Holly H. Prunty, Mary-Peck Harris. Came to U.S., 1940, naturalized, 1956. Bd. advisers Research Ranch, Elgin, Ariz., Am. Wilderness Alliance; past dir. Marin County Planned Parenthood Assn., Planned Parenthood Center Tucson. Served to 1st lt. French Army, 1947-48. Mem. Nat. Parks Assn., Wilderness Soc., Sierra Club, Nat. Audubon Soc., World Wildlife Fund, Am. Mus. Natural History, Union Concerned Scientists, Environ. Def. Fund, Friends of the Earth, Ariz.-Sonora Desert Mus., Am. Internat., Ariz. Hist. Soc., Common Cause, World Affairs Council No. Calif., Western Writers Assn. Clubs: Commonwealth, Harvard (San Francisco). Author: The Last Redwoods, 1963; Time and the River Flowing: Grand Canyon, 1964; The Coyote: Defiant Songdog of the West, 1977. Editor: Tomorrow's Wilderness, 1963; contbg. editor On Beyond War; contbr. to Nat. Geog. mag. Address: 183 Oak Ave San Anselmo CA 94960

LEYDIG, CARL FREDERICK, lawyer; b. Denver, Jan. 24, 1925; s. Carl F. and Mae V. (Crowley) L.; m. Patricia L. Schwefer, July 2, 1949; children—Gregory F., Deborah A., Gary W., Suzann M. B.S. in Chem. Engring., Ill. Inst. Tech., 1945; J.D. DePaul U., 1950. Bar: Ill. 1950. Atty., Standard Oil Co. (Ind.), Chgo., 1950-54; assoc., ptnr. Leydig, Voit & Mayer, Ltd. and predecessor firms, Chgo., 1954—. Chmn., Young Republicans of Ill., 1953-55; pres. United Fund of Arlington Heights (Ill.), 1964, 65. Served to lt. j.g. USN, 1943-46. Mem. Am. Intellectual Property Law Assn. (dir. 1979-81), ABA, Chgo. Bar Assn., Patent Law Assn. of Chgo. (pres. 1980), Am. Coll. Trial Lawyers. Roman Catholic. Clubs: Univ., Law (Chgo.); Meadow (Rolling Meadows, Ill.), Inverness Golf (Palatine, Ill.), Innisbrook Golf (Tarpon Springs, Fla.).

LEYDORF, FREDERICK LEROY, lawyer; b. Toledo, June 13, 1930; s. Loftin Herman and Dorothy DeRoyal (Cramer) L.; m. Mary MacKenzie Malcolm, Mar. 28, 1953; children—Robert Malcolm, William Frederick, Katherine Ann, Thomas Richard, Deborah Mary. Student, U. Toledo, 1948-49; B.B.A., U. Mich., 1953; J.D., UCLA, 1958. Bar: Calif. 1959. Assoc. Hammack & Pugh, Los Angeles, 1959-61; ptnr. Willis, Butler, Scheifly, Leydorf & Grant, Los Angeles, 1961-81, Pepper, Hamilton & Scheetz, Los Angeles, 1981-83, Hufstedler, Miller, Carlson, Beardsley, Los Angeles, 1983—; lectr., cons. Calif. Continuing Edn. of Bar, 1965—. Contbg. author: California Non-Profit Corporations, 1969; contbr. articles to profl. jours. Chmn. pub. adminstr.-pub. guardian adv. commn. Los Angeles County Bd. Suprs., 1972-73; bd. dirs. J. W. and Ida M. Jameson Found., 1967—, Western Ctr. on Law and Poverty, Inc., 1980-82; mem. legal com. Music Ctr. Found., 1980—; mem. lawyers adv. council Constl. Rights Found., 1982-85; mem. devel. adv. bd. Sch. Bus. Adminstrn., U. Mich., 1984—Served to lt. USNR, 1953-55. Mem. ABA, Los Angeles County Bar Assn., State Bar Calif. (chmn. conf. dels. 1977, Alumnus of Yr. award, conf. of dels. 1983, mem. exec. com. estate planning, trust and probate law sect. 1979-80), Los Angeles County Bar Found. (pres. 1977-79, bd. dirs. 1975-87), Western Pension Confs., Am. Coll. Probate Counsel, Internat. Acad. Estate and Trust Law (v.p. N.Am. 1978-82), Life Ins. and Trust Council Los Angeles (pres. 1983-84), UCLA Law Alumni Assn. (pres. 1982), Los Angeles World Affairs Council, Phi Delta Phi, Phi Delta Theta. Republican. Lutheran. Clubs: Chancery, Jonathan (Los Angeles); Annandale Golf. Home: 2165 El Molino Pl San Marino CA 91108 Office: Hufstedler Miller Carlson Beardsley 355 S Grand Ave 45th floor Los Angeles CA 90071-3107

LEYSON, DATIVO BORCES, economic attache; b. Cebu, Philippines, Dec. 6, 1930; s. Lucio Velayo and Segunda Borces L.; m. Maria Rosario Karasawa Punsalan, Feb. 17, 1962; children—Leo P., Edmond P., Maria Lisa. Student Far Eastern U., Manila, 1952-55. With Armed Forces of Philippines, 1950-70 (ret.); rep. Central Bank of Philippines, Tokyo, 1971—; econ. attaché Philippine Embassy, Tokyo, 1971—. Roman Catholic. Lodge: Knights of Rizal (Tokyo chpt.). Home: #6 Orchid, Talamban Cebu City, Cebu Philippines Office: 11-24 Nampeidaimachi, Tokyo 150, Japan

L'HOIR, JEAN-XAVIER, physician; b. Neuilly/Seine, France, May 24, 1941; s. Georges Auguste Xavier and Marie-Suzanne Henriette (Fournier) L'H.; m. Francine Treger, Mar. 26, 1969; children: Severine-Marie, Anne-Andree-Marie-Suzanne. MD, Faculty Medicine Paris, 1971. Obstetrician-gynecologist Faculty Medicine Paris, 1967-72; resident Assistance Pub., Paris, 1967-71; asst. Region de Paris, 1973-74; chief of ob-gyn. service Rambouillet, France, 1974—. Author: Erytheme Polymorphe et Grossesse, 1971. Mem. French Soc. Study of Fertility, Cirle Gynecologues Accoucheurs, French Soc. Endoscopy, Group for Study of Endometriose, Circle Study Rambolitain Fecomdation (pres. 1985), French Soc. Colposcopy, European Soc. Human Reprodn. Home and Office: 11 Rue Gambetta, 78120 Rambouillet France

LHO SHIN YONG, former prime minister Republic of Korea; b. So. Pyongyang Province, Feb. 28, 1930; LL.B., Seoul Nat. U. Coll. Law; M.A., Ky State U. Joined Ministry of Fgn. Affairs, Republic of Korea, 1955; served in Washington, Ankara, Bangkok, Rome; consul gen., Los Angeles, 1969-72, New Delhi, 1972; ambassador to India, 1973; vice minister Ministry of Fgn. Affairs, 1974; ambassador to UN, Geneva, 1976; minister of fgn. affairs, 1980-82; dir. Agy. for Nat. Security Planning, 1982-85; prime minister, 1985-87. Mem. Democratic Justice Party. Address: Chung Woo Apt 302-69, Ichon Dong #902, Yongsan Gu, Seoul Republic of Korea

LHOTKA, JOHN FRANCIS, physician, educator; b. Butte, Mont., May 13, 1921; s. John Francis and Mary (Backowske) L.; m. Lois Katherine Clysdale, Sept. 21, 1951. B.A., U. Mont., 1942; M.S. in Anatomy, Northwestern U., 1948, M.B., 1949, M.D., 1951, Ph.D., 1953. Asst. in anatomy Northwestern U., 1947-50; mem. house staff Mpls. Gen. Hosp., 1950-51; Stain Commn. fellow Northwestern U., summer 1953; asst. prof. anatomy U. Okla. Med. Sch., 1951-55, asso. prof., 1955-69, prof. anatomical scis., 1969-86, prof. emeritus, 1986—; Active in numis. field, especially medieval coinage of Western Europe. Author: monographs Introduction to East Roman Coinage, 1957, Medieval Bracteates, 1958, Medieval French Feudal Coinage, 1966, (with P.K. Anderson) Survey of Medieval Iberian Coinages, 1963; also articles in field histochemistry. Served to 1st lt. CWS USAAF, 1942-46, PTO. Decorated Royal Yugoslav War Cross; recipient 4 Heath medals, Medal of Merit, Farran Zerbe award, initial Newell award Am. Numis. Assn., Donat Cross 1st class Order St. Lazarus of Jerusalem, Order of Augustan Eagle, silver medal Alta. and Northwest Ters. Royal Can. Life Saving Soc., Jubilee medal Alta. and Northwest Ters. Royal Can. Life Saving Soc., U. Okla. Media Prodn. award. Fellow Am. Numis. Soc. (life mem., patron), Royal Numis. Soc. (life mem., hon.), Swiss Numis Soc. (life mem.), Spanish Numis. Soc., Am. Geriatric Soc., Internat. Acad. Pathology, Royal Soc. Health, London, Am. Inst. Chemists, Augustan Soc.; mem. Am. Numis. Assn. (life), Am. Philatelic Soc. (life), Okla. Acad. Sci. (sr.), Okla. State Hist. Soc. (life), Am. Soc. Herpatology and Ichthyology, Co. Mil. Historians, Orders and Medals Soc. Am., Brit. Mus. Soc., Metro. Mus. (N.Y.), Oriental Inst. Chgo., Nat. Rifle Assn. (life endowment), Am. Def. Preparedness Assn. (life), Am. Assn. Anatomists, Histochem. Soc., Am. Soc. Zoology, Biol. Stain Commn., Am. Security Council, Soc. for Exptl. Biology and Medicine, Am. Chem. Soc., Archeol. Inst. Am., E. African Wildlife Soc. (life), Nat. Wildlife Fedn., Am. Soc. Mil. Insignia Collectors, Tokens and Medals Soc., Sigma Xi, Phi Sigma. Clubs: Oklahoma City, Petroleum. Office: U Okla Health Ctr BSMB (Anatomical Sci) PO Box 26901 Oklahoma City OK 73190

LI, BINGXI, mathematics educator, researcher, academic administrator; b. Guangzhou, Guangdong, People's Republic of China, Dec. 15, 1934; parents: Hung Fan and Wai Lan (Li) L.; m. Dianmei Li, Aug. 5, 1965; 1 child, Jin. BA, Zhongshan U. (Dr. Sun Yat-sen U.), Guangzhou, 1958. Asst. Peking U., Beijing, 1958-63, Zhongshan U., 1963-65; asst., assoc. prof., prof. Jinan U., Guangzhou, 1965—, chmn. math. dept., 1982-84, v.p., 1984—; vis. scholar U. Calif., Los Angeles, 1979-81. Author: Periodic Orbits of Higher Dimensional Dynamical Systems: Theory & Applications (in Chinese); editor: Annals of Differential Equations, 1985—, Mathematics in Practice and Theory, 1983—; reviewer Zentralblatt für Maftematic, 1983—; also research papers. Hon. Gov. Guangdong Welfare Fund for Handicapped, Guangzhou, 1984—; dep. 6th People's Congress Guangdong Province, 1983-88, Guangdong Province, 7th People's Gongress, 1988. Recipient Award of Distinction Commn. Sci. Tech. Guangdong. Mem. Math. Soc. People's Republic of China, Am. Math. Soc., Math. Assn. Am., N.Y. Acad. Scis. Office: Jinan U, Guangzhou, Guangdong People's Republic of China

LI, EDDIE HERBERT, applied physicist, educator; b. Hong Kong, Feb. 6, 1957; s. Kwok-Keung Lee and Julia Yuk-Ying (Yeung) Li. B.S., Washington State Coll., 1979; M.S., Washington U., St. Louis, 1981; Diploma BTM,

Profl. Bus. and Tech. Mgmt., 1986. Chartered physicist. Head Pi Mu Epsilon Tutoring Ctr., Washington, 1978-81; sr. instr. Matteo Ricci Coll., Hong Kong, 1981-82; engr., sci. officer K.K. Co., Hong Kong, 1982-87; chmn. mgmt. bd., computer aids services group Assn. for Engring. and Med. Services, 1986-87, 1987—; researcher Hong Kong Poly., Hong Kong, 1983; sr. instr. Hong Kong Bapt. Coll., 1984—; civil service examiner Govt. of Hong Kong, 1984—; cons. K.K. Co., Hong Kong, 1985-87; mng. ptnr. HAL Computer Cons., Hong Kong, 1987—; lectr. applied math. City Polytechnic of Hong Kong, 1988—. Author: Differential Equations, 1980; Calculus, 1981; Physics, 1986. Fellow Royal Statis. Soc., Inst. of Mgmt. Specialists, Brit. Soc. Commerce, Soc. Comml. Tchrs., Inst. Math. and its Applications (assoc. fellow); mem. Internat. Assn. Math. Physics, Am. Math. Soc., Am. Phys. Soc., IEEE, AIAA, Inst. Physics, Brit. Soc. Commerce, Faculty Tchrs. Commerce, Soc. Comml. Tchrs., Inst. Sci. Tech., Inst. Bus. and Tech. Mgmt., S.E. Asia Math. Soc., Hong Kong Math. Soc., Hong Kong Statis. Soc., Hong Kong Phys. Soc., Hong Kong Assn. Computer Edn. Club: Raffles. Office: HAL Computer Cons, PO Box 50398, Sai Ying Pun Post Office, Hong Kong Hong Kong

LI, HONG-XIANG, mathematics educator, researcher; b. Suqian, People's Republic of China, Mar. 14, 1936; s. Bao-lian Li and Yuan-hua Zhu; m. Lan-fang Yu, Jan. 18, 1963; children: Ying-ying, Xiao-fang. BS, Nanjing (People's Republic China) U., 1962. Diplomate in math. Asst. Shanghai Inst. Railway Tech., 1962-77, lectr., 1978-85, assoc. prof., 1985—, dir. applied math. research, 1983—. Author (with others) : Advanced Mathematics I and II, 1978, 79, (recipient 1st award), Graph Theory with Applications, 1982 (recipient 2nd award); translator book First Order Partial DE, 1983; manuscripts referee Acta Mathematicae Applicatae Sinica, Beijing, People's Republic China, 1983—; math. reviewer Brown U. Press, Providence, R.I., 1984—; editor Higher Mathematics, 1986-87, Jour. of the Shanghai Inst. Railway Tech., 1985—; contbr. articles to profl. jours. Recipient 2nd award Best Sci. and Tech. Books China, 1983, 2nd award Excellent Articles of All Railway Insts. China, 1985, 1st award Excellent Textbooks Nat. Ednl. Com. China, 1987. Mem. Shanghai Math. Soc. (dir.), Am. Math. Soc. Home: 18-303 Lane 443, Taopu West Rd, Shanghai 200333, People's Republic of China Office: Shanghai Inst Railway Tech, 1 Zhennan Rd, Shanghai 200333, People's Republic of China

LI, KERAN, artist, educator; b. Xuzhou, Jiangsu, People's Republic of China, Mar. 26, 1907; s. Li and Li Lishi; m. Zou Peizhu, 1944; 7 children. Student, Shanghai (People's Republic China) Specialized Sch. Fine Arts, 1925; student dept. research, State Acad. Fine Arts at Xihu, People's Republic China, 1930. Tchr. Pvt. Specialized Sch. Fine Arts, Xuzhou, 1932-37; researcher art sect., com. cultural activties Wuhan (People's Republic China) Polit. Dept., 1938-43; lectr. State Specialized Sch. Chongqing, People's Republic China, 1943-46; assoc. prof. State Specialized Sch. Fine Arts at Beijing, 1946-49; prof. Cen. Acad. Fine Arts, Beijing, 1949—; pres. Research Inst. Chinese Paintings, Beijing, 1981—. Author: Collection Of Sketches by Li Keran, 1959, Li Keran on Painting, Chinese Painting by Li Keran, 1983, Selection of Paintings by Keron, 1986. Mem. China Fedn. Literary and Art Circle, Chinese Artists Assn. (vice chmn.), Chinese People's Polit. Consultive Conf., The Acad. Art and Sci. (German Dem. Republic), Beijing Research Inst. Landscape Painting (hon. Pres.), Chinese Internat. Frienship Promotion Assn. (cons.), Chinese Youth Calligraphy and Painting Research Inst., Beijing Social Welfare Found. (hon. pres.). Home: Cen Acad Fine Arts, Beijing People's Republic of China Office: Cen Acad Fine Arts, Beijing People's Republic of China

LI, LI, mathematics educator; b. Xichuan, Henan, People's Republic of Chinca, Feb. 11, 1928; s. Xiaolan Li and Chunhui Gong; m. Yinmei Shao, Aug. 22, 1952; children: Yunni, Yunling, Yunqing. BS, Nat. Peiyang U., Tianjin, People's Republic of China, 1951. Asst. Tianjin U., 1951-55, lectr., 1956-79, assoc. prof., 1980-82, prof., 1983-86; prof. Beijing Poly. U., 1987—; vis. prof. Southwestern Jiaotong U., Chengdu, 1984—, Dalian Poly. U., 1985—, Henan Tchr. U., Xinxiang, 1986—; mem. editorial com. Jour. Applied Math. and Mechanics, Chongqing, 1982—. Author: Theoretical Mechanics, 1957; Contbr. articles to profl. jours. Mem. Chinese Math. Soc., Am. Math. Soc., Chinese Soc. Theoretical and Applied Mechanics (head stability and vibration group, vice-chmn. gen. mechanics div.). Office: Beijing Poly U, Basic Courses Dept, East Suburb, Beijing People's Republic of China

LI, PEI-SHAN, historian, educator; b. Beijing, Republic of China, Mar. 14, 1924; d. Baoling Li and Huizhi Wang; m. Yonghou Yuan, Feb. 5, 1951; children: He Yuan, Jiang Yuan. BS, Cath. U. Peking, People's Republic of China, 1946; postgrad. in biochem., Peking Union Med. Coll., 1948-50; MS, Yenching U., Peking, 1950. Asst. dept. biochem. Beijing Med. Coll., 1950-52, lectr., 1952-54; researcher sci. div. of propaganda dept. Party Cen. Com., Office of Policy Research Academia Sinica, 1954-66, staff dept. biology, 1973-78; dep. dir. Inst. for History and Natural Scis., 1978-87, assoc. prof., 1980—. Co-author, co-editor: A Brief History of 20th Century Science and Technology, 1986; editor: A Hundred Schools Contending, 1985. Mem. Chinese Soc. for History of Sci. and Tech. (gen. sec. 1980-83, v.p. 1983-87, standing com. 1987—), Internat. Union of History and Philosophy of Sci. (accessor 1985—), History of Sci. Soc. of USA, Chinese Soc. for Dialectics in Nature (standing com. 1981—). Communist. Home: No 2B Shatan N St, East Dist Beijing 100009, People's Republic of China Office: Inst History of Natural Sci, 1 Gong Yuan W St, Beijing 100005, People's Republic of China

LI, QIAO, mathematics educator; b. Changzhou, China, Aug. 18, 1938; s. Cui Li and Xuan Liu; m. Zhen Fang Fan, Nov. 5, 1973; 1 child, An An. BSc, FuDan U., Shanghai, 1961. Asst. U. Sci. and Tech. China, Hefei, 1961-78, instr. math., 1978-82, assoc. prof., 1983-86, prof., 1987—. Author: Eight Lectures on Matrix Theory, 1986; translator: Combinatorial Mathematics, 1983, Principles of Combinatorics, 1986; editor Jour. Applied Math. Chinese Univs., 1985—; reviewer Math. Revs., Ann Arbor, Mich., 1984; contbr. articles to profl. jours. Mem. China Math. Soc., Am. Math. Soc., Graph Theory Soc. China (councilor 1985—, com. on combinatorics 1985—), China Soc. Combinatorial Math. (councilor 1988—). Office: U Sci and Tech of China, Dept Math, Hefei 230 039, Peoples Republic of China

LI, SZE BAY ALBERT, educational administrator; b. Hong Kong, 1936; B.A. in Econs., U. Hong Kong, 1962; cert. ednl. supervision, instrn., U. London, 1986. Local officer The Chartered Bank, Hong Kong, 1963-65; prin. Tsung Tsin Coll., Hong Kong, 1965-69; founder, prin. Lok Sin Tong Yu Kan Hing Sch., Kowloon, Hong Kong, 1969—; vice chmn. Hong Kong Subsidized Schs. Provident Fund Bd. Control, 1974-82; vice-chmn. central com. Hong Kong Edn. dept. Community Youth Club, 1977—; founder, chmn. Wong Tai Sin Dist. Community Youth Clubs Com., 1978-81; mem. adv. com. Hong Kong Tech. Tchrs.' Coll., 1979—; vice chmn. Adv. Com. On Jr. secondary Edn. Assessment, 1980—, Central Com. on Secondary Sch. Places Allocation, 1980-81; adviser Hong Kong Tchrs. Assn., 1981—; chmn. Hong Kong Subsidized Secondary Schs. Council, 1982—; founder, chmn. Wong Tai Sin Dist. Sch. Liaison Com., 1983—; mgr. C.M.A. Choi Cheung Kok Prevocat. Sch., 1984—; mgmt. commn. Queen's Coll. Old Boys Assn. Secondary Sch.; supr. John F. Kennedy Centre, 1984—; chmn. schs. mgmt. com. Hong Kong Red Cross, 1985—, Ng Yuk Secondary Sch. Mgmt. com., 1985—. Nat. pres. Hong Kong Jr. C. of C., 1973; Senator Jr. Chamber Internat., 1972—; mem. Juvenile Ct. Adv. Com., Hong Kong, 1975—; hon. sec. Kowloon region Hong Kong Scout Assn., 1975—; founder mem. Hong Kong Youth Cultural and Arts Competitions Organizing Com., 1975—; lay assessor Magistrates' Cts., 1979—; mem. Hong Kong Bd. Edn., 1979-85, Sch. Med. Service Bd., 1985, Hong Kong Exams. Authority, 1979-83; mem. corruption prevention adv. com. Ind. Commn. against Corruption, 1979-81; mem. Wong Tai Sin Dist. Bd., Hong Kong, 1981—; mem. Money Lenders Ordinance Licensing Ct., Hong Kong, 1982—; justice of peace Hong Kong Govt., 1984—; asst. dir. Hong Kong Red Cross, 1985—. Recipient Disting. Service medal Hong Kong Scout Assn., 1987, CYC Bronze medal, 1987; badge of honor Brit. Red Cross, 1983, cert. of appreciation Duke of Edinburgh's Award Scheme, 1984; Brit. Council scholar, 1986. Fellow Soc. Comml. Tchrs. (Eng.), Faculty Corp. Secs. (Eng.), Brit. Soc. Commerce, Brit. Inst. Mgmt., Royal Coll. Preceptors; mem. Hong Kong Mgmt. Assn., Hong Kong Assn. Bus. Edn. (founder, chmn. 1985—). Lodge: Lions (v.p. local club 1977-78). Office: Lok Sin Tong Yu Kan Hing Sch, 3 Fu Yue St, Wang Tau Hom, Kowloon Hong Kong

LI, TU LEUNG, management executive; b. N.Y.C., Nov. 10, 1948; d. Gum Ming and Toa Moy (Wong) Lee; m. Ta M. Li, Dec. 31, 1969; 1 child, Ta Ming. B.S., U. Utah, 1977. Sr. cons. Aetna Ins. Co., Salt Lake City, 1977-78; advt. mgr. Assn. Surg. Technologist, Littleton, Colo., 1978-80; research mgr. MET-Research Co., Lakewood, Colo., 1980-82; pres., chief exec. officer Tatum & Assocs., Littleton, 1982-85; sr. acct. Martin Marietta Data Systems, Colo., 1985—; dir. Asian X-M Ltd, Loveland, Colo. Contbr. articles on computer mgmt. techniques to publs. Sec., Friends of Littleton Library, 1984. Mem. AAUW (bd. dirs. 1983-84). Club: Argonauts Investment (pres. 1982-83) (Littleton).

LIAN, WANG, mathematics educator, researcher; b. Shanghai, Peoples Republic China, Feb. 19, 1933; s. Wang Yu Ming and Liu Zheng Fu; m. Wang Mu-Qiu, July 5, 1958; children: Wang Jie, Wang Wen. BS, Beijing U., 1956. Adj. prof. Inst. Math. Academia Sinica, Beijing, 1956-61, asst. prof., 1962-78, assoc. prof., 1979-85, prof., 1986—; mem. guiding group math. teaching dept. Grad. Sch. Academia Sinica, 1986—. Author: (with others) Stability of Dynamical Systems with Lagging Argment, 1963, (with others) Stability Theory of Motion and its Applications, 1981, (with others) Qualitative Analysis of Nonlinear Ordinary Differential Equation, 1987, (with others) Stability of Discrete Dynamical System, 1987; mem. editorial bd. Chinese Quar. Jour. Math., 1986—, Annuals of Differential Equations, 1985—. Mem. Am. Math. Soc. (reviewer Math. Revs. 1981—). Home: #407 Bldg 935, Zhong Guan Cun, Beijing 100086, Peoples Republic of China Office: Inst Math Acad Sinica, Zhong Guan-Cun, Beijing 100080, Peoples Republic of China

LIANG, JASON CHIA, research chemist; b. Beijing, Peoples Republic China, Feb. 24, 1935; came to U.S., 1978, naturalized 1984; s. Tsang Truan and Shulin (Tang) L.; m. Joan Chorng Chen, June 11, 1960; children: Cheryl, Chuck. BS in Pharm. Chemistry, U. Beijing, 1957; postgrad. Pharm. Research Instn., Beijing, 1961; MS in Organic Chemistry, U. Oreg., 1980. Chemist Beijing Chem. Factory, 1961-71; research chemist Beijing Pharm. Factory, 1971-78; research chemist Tektronix Inc., Beaverton, Oreg., 1980-84, sr. chemist, 1985—; presenter Internat. Pitts. Conf. on Analytical Chemistry and Applied Spectroscopy, 1988. Contbr. articles to profl. jours.; patentee in field. Fellow Am. Inst. Chemists; mem. Am. Chem Soc. (organic chemistry div., paper presenter 1984-87), Internat. Union Pure and Applied Chemistry (affiliate). Office: Tektronix Inc PO Box 500 M/S 50-320 Beaverton OR 97077

LIANG, STEPHEN TSU WEN, naval architect; b. Guanghou (Canton), Guangdong, China, Sept. 21, 1920; came to U.S., 1943; s. Yen-An and Anning (Chow) L.; m. Jane C. Liang, Apr. 20, 1947; children—Louise, Cheryl. B.S., Whampao Naval Acad., Canton, 1941; postgrad Swarthmore Coll., 1943; M.S., MIT, 1946. Registered profl. engr., N.Y., Md. Test engr. Gen. Electric Co., Lynn, Mass., 1947; project engr. Kiangnan Naval Shipyard, Shanghai, 1948-49; design leader Foster Wheeler Corp., Boston, 1950-54; naval architect Bethlehem Steel Co., Quincy, Mass., 1955-56; project mgr. M.W. Kellogg Co., N.Y.C., 1957-64; sr. naval architect David Taylor Naval Ships Research and Devel. Ctr., Carderock, Md., 1965-83, sr. cons., 1984—; cons in marine tech., 1969-73. Contbr. articles to profl. jours. Mem. ASME, Am. Soc. Naval Engrs., Soc. Naval Architects and Marine Engrs. Home: 11028 Rutledge Dr Gaithersburg MD 20878 Office: David Taylor Naval Ships Research and Devel Ctr Carderock MD 20084

LIANG, YOU-YI, pharmacologist, researcher; b. Haikou, Guangdong, China, Sept. 15, 1930; s. Shao-Yu Liang and Hui-Zeng Zhang; m. Huan-Xiong Chen, Feb. 17, 1958; 1 child, Liang Qing. Student Lingnan U., Canton, China, 1949-50, Tsing Hua U., Beijing, China, 1950-52; B.S., Beijing U., 1953; postgrad. radioisotope tng., Acad. Sci., Shanghai, China, 1958. Research asst. Shanghai Inst. Materia Medica, 1953-60, research assoc., 1960, dir. radioisotope lab., 1961-78, dir. toxicology lab., 1978—, sr. researcher, 1983—, dept. chmn. Pharmacology II, 1984—; vis. researcher Louisville U. (Ky.), 1980-82. Author: (with Zhao Hui-Yang) Nuclear Medicine, 1981; mem. editorial bd. Chinese Jour. of Pharmacology and Toxicology, 1985; patentee heavy metals antidote, antibilharzial drug, anthelmintic drug. Mem. Physiol. Scis. Soc. (council 1984—), Chinese Biochemistry Soc., N.Y. Acad. Scis., Sigma Xi. Office: Shanghai Inst Materia Medica, 319 Yueyang Rd, Shanghai 200031 Peoples Republic China

LIAO, KEREN, mathematics educator; b. Xing Ning, Guangdong, People's Rep. China, July 23, 1932; d. Yi-Ren and Feng-Ying Zhu; m. Le-Ping Gu, Dec. 8, 1934; 1 child, Wen-Sui Liao. Student, Peking U. Asst. prof. math. Peking U., Beijing, 1957-60, asst. prof., 1960-83, assoc. prof., 1983-85; assoc. prof. applied math. dept. Shenzhen U., People's Rep. of China, 1985-87, head prof., 1987—. Author: Mathematical Analysis, 1986. Mem. Guangdong Math Soc., Am. Math Soc. Office: Shenzhen U, Applied Math Dept, Shenzhen Peoples Republic of China

LIBERIA-PETERS, MARIA, Netherlands Antilles government official. Prime minister, minister social and labor affairs Netherlands Antilles, Curacao, 1988—. Address: Office of Prime Minister, Curacao Netherlands Antilles *

LIBERMAN, LUIS, banker, economist; b. San Jose, Costa Rica, Aug. 1, 1946; s. Rodolfo and Bluma (Ginsburg) L.; m. Patricia Loterstein, Jan. 25, 1975; children: Vivian, Marcos, Sergio. BA, UCLA, 1968; MS, U. Ill., 1970, PhD, 1972. Economist World Bank, Washington, 1972-75; advisor Nat. Planning Office, San Jose, 1976-77; econ. advisor Pres. of Costa Rica, San Jose, 1976-77; vice-minister Ministry of Fin. Costa Rica, San Jose, 1977-78; pres. Corp. Internat. Fin., San Jose, 1979-82; gen. mgr. Banco InterFin. S.A., San Jose, 1982—; assoc. prof. econs. U. Costa Rica, 1975—; chmn. bd. dirs. Pvt. Investment Corp., Panama, 1986—; economist Consejeros Econs. y Fin. S.A., San Jose, 1979—. Pres. San Jose Jewish Community, 1982-84; mem. fin. com. Nat. Liberation Party, San Jose, 1986—. Mem. Am. Econs. Assn., Coll. Econs. Costa Rica, Costa Rican Bankers Assn. (bd. dirs. 1983—), Plasticos Para la Construccion (bd. dirs. 1984—), San Jose Chamber of Industry, Omnicron Delta Epsilon. Lodge: B'nai Brith. Home: PO Box 652, 1000 San Jose Costa Rica

LIBERMAN, MICHAEL IRA, accountant; b. N.Y.C., Sept. 16, 1944; s. Abraham and Esther (Tabb) L.; m. Eleanor Toby Levine, Feb. 21, 1976; children: Alexander Jean, Randall Evan; children by previous marriage—Debra Sue, Scott Evan. B.S., U. Pa., 1966, M.S., 1967. Pres., Valley Forge Flag Co., N.Y.C., 1975—; sec. treas. and chmn. bd. Valley Forge Fabrics, N.Y.C., 1977—, Anderson Assocs., N.Y.C., 1979—. Adv. bd. Am. Flag Inst., 1977, U.S. Flag Assn., 1982; mem., v.p. L.I. Regional Bd., Anti-Defamation League, 1980, pres, 1988; committeeman, fin. chmn. Great Neck South Zone, Republican Com., 1982; hon. chmn. bd. govs. Bialystoker Synagogue, 1980—. Jewish. Address: Valley Forge Flag Co Inc 935 Northern Blvd Great Neck NY 11028

LIBIN, JEROME B., lawyer; b. Chgo., Oct. 27, 1936; s. Mitchell and Charlotte Libin; m. June Austin, Apr. 12, 1965; 1 child, Nancy Crawford. B.S., Northwestern U., 1956; J.D., U. Mich., 1959. Bar: D.C. 1961, Ill. 1961. Law clk. U.S. Supreme Ct. Justice Charles E. Whittaker, 1959-60; assoc. Sutherland, Asbill & Brennan, Washington, 1961-66, ptnr., 1966—; professorial lectr. in law George Washington U., 1974-80; cons. Am. Law Inst. Internat. Tax Study Project; master of the bench J. Edgar Murdock Am. Inn of Ct. Contbr. articles to profl. jours. Mem. D.C. Tax Revision Commn., 1976-78; mem. Mayor's Revenue Policy Com., 1980-82; counsel Lawyers' Com. for Civil Rights Under Law, 1980—; mem. com. visitors U. Mich. Law Sch. Served with USAFR, 1960-66. Fellow Am. Bar Found.; mem. ABA, D.C. Bar (chmn. taxation div. 1975-77), Am. Law Inst., Internat. Fiscal Assn. (council U.S.A. br.). Home: 3022 P St NW Washington DC 20007 Office: Sutherland Asbill & Brennan 1275 Pennsylvania Ave NW Washington DC 20004

LIBRODO, RAYMUNDO RIGOR, surgeon, health science facility administrator; b. San Carlos, Philippines, Feb. 6, 1937; s. Hipolito Lauron and Mercedes Mondragon (Rigor) L.; m. Cecillia Padilla Regalado, Jan. 7, 1967; children: Remerose, Lucille Christine, Toni Gretchen. AA, U. Santo Tomas, Manila, 1955, MD, 1964; MA in Hosp. Administrn., U. of the Philippines, Manila, 1981. Resident physician Occ. Negros Provencial Hosp., Bacolod City, Philippines, 1965-70; officer-in-charge dept. surgery Valladolid Emergency Hosp., Philippines, 1968; officer-in-charge Gov. V. M. Gatuslao Meml. Hosp., Himamaylan, Philippines, 1985; officer-in-charge Corazon Locsin Montelibano Meml. Regional Hosp., Bacolod City, 1986-87, chief med. profl. div., 1988—; cons. La Carlota City Hosp., Philippines, 1970-72; bd. dirs. Negros Occ. Rehab. Found. Inc., 1987—; over-all chmn. Corazon Locsin Montelibano Meml. Regional Hosp. Civic Action Group, 1986—. Served to capt. Med. Corps Filipino Army, 1972—. Ministry of Health grantee, U. the Philippines, 1981-82. Mem. Negros Occ. Med. Soc. (life)(v.p. 1984), Philippine Med. Soc. (life), Reserve Officers Legion Philippines (life). Democrat. Roman Catholic. Lodge: Lions. Home: #3 PHHC Rd, Montevista Subdivision, Bacolod City, Negros Occ Philippines 6001 Office: Corazon Locsin Montelibano, Meml Regional Hosp, Lacson St, Bacolod City, Negros Occ Philippines 6001

LICH, GLEN ERNST, educator; b. Fredericksburg, Tex., Nov. 5, 1948; s. Ernst Perry and Thelma Olive (Woolfley) L.; m. Lera Patrick Tyler, Sept. 5, 1970; children: James Ernst Lich-Tyler, Stephen Woolfley Lich-Tyler, Elizabeth Erin Lich-Tyler. Student, U. Vienna, Austria, 1969-70; BA, Southwestern U., 1971; MA, U. Tex., 1976; MA, S.W. Tex. State U., 1978; PhD, Tex. Christian U., 1984; grad., U.S. Army Command and Gen. Staff Coll., 1984. Instr. S.W. Tex. State U., 1977-79, U. New Orleans, 1979-80; asst. prof. English and German Schreiner Coll., 1980-87; asst. prof. English and dir. program for regional studies Baylor U., 1987—; adj. faculty U.S. Army Commd. and Gen. Staff Coll., 1987—; vis. fellow Yale U., 1987; guest to study German-Am. cultural exchange Govt. of Fed. Republic of Germany, 1983; cons. in field. Author: The German Texans, 1981; editor: (with Dona B. Reeves) Retrospect and Retrieval: The German Element in Review, Essays on Cultural Preservation, 1978, German Culture in Texas: A Free Earth, 1980, The Cabin Book, 1985, Texas Country: The Changing Rural Scene, 1986; assoc. editor Jour. German-Am. Studies, 1977-80, Yearbook of German-Am. Studies, 1980—; editor: Jour. Am. Studies Assn. Tex., 1988—; contbr. articles to profl. publs. Served with U.S. Army, 1972-75, maj. USAR, asst. attache to Portugal. NEH research grantee, 1978, 86-87; Fed. Republic Germany, 1987, Swiss Humanities Acad., 1988, Tex. Com. Humanities, 1988, Am. Council of Learned Socs., 1988, Embassy of Can., 1988. Mem. MLA, South Cen. MLA (sect. officer 1977—), Am. Studies Assn., Assn. Am. Geographers, Am. Culture Assn., Western History Assn., Popular Culture Assn., Tex. Assn. Mus., Am. Folklore Assn., Am. Assn. Tchrs. German, Nat. Council Tchrs. English, Oral History Assn., Tex. Folklore Soc., Tex. State Hist. Assn., German Studies Assn., Soc. German-Am. Studies (assoc. editor yearbook 1981—), Pi Kappa Alpha. Home: Kirschenwaldchen 9011 Kingswood Pl Waco TX 76712 Office: Baylor U Ctr for Regional Studies CSB Box 696 Waco TX 76798 Summer Home: Sturdy Oak Farm Comfort TX 78013

LICHAL, ROBERT, government official; b. Vienna, Austria, July 9, 1932; married, 1959; 2 children. LLD, 1955. Staff acct. Lower Austrian Provincial Govt., 1950; legal advisor Modling, Zwettl and Baden bei Wein, Austria; vice-chmn. Union Pub. Service Employees, Austria, 1973—; mem. Bundesrat, Austria, 1976-79, Nationelrat, Austria, 1979—; security spokesman Osterreichische Volkspartei; minister of def. 1987—. Mem. Assn. Christian Trade Unionists (chmn. 1985—, v.p.). Office: Ministry of Def, Vienna Austria *

LICHNEROWICZ, ANDRE L., mathematics educator; b. Bourbon l'Archambault, Allier, France, Jan. 21, 1915; s. Jean and Antoinette (Gressin) L.; m. Suzanne Magdelain, Nov. 26, 1942; children: Marc, Jacques, Jérome. Agrégé in math. and sci., École Normale Supérieure, Paris, 1936; ScD, U. Paris, 1939; Doctorate (hon.), U. Waterloo, Can., 1976, U. Liège, Belgium, 1983, U. Coïmlera, Portugal, 1984. Prof. faculty of scis. U. Strasbourg, France, 1941-49; prof. U. Paris, 1949-52; prof. Coll. France, Paris, 1952-86, prof. emeritus, 1986—; mem. Adv. Com. Research Sci. and Tech., Paris, 1959-63, 67-71; pres. Internat. Com. Math. Teaching, 1962-66. Author over 250 papers in field. Decorated Comdr. Order Nat. Merit, 1965, Comdr. Legion d'Honneur, 1977; recipient Fubini prize, 1954, Copernic medal The Polish Acad., 1973. Mem. Acad. Sci. Paris, Acad. Nazionale di Lincei Roma, Acad. Royale de Belgique, Real Acad. de Scis. Madrid, Pontifical Acad. Sci. Home: 6 Ave Paul Appell, 75014 Paris France Office: Coll France, 11 Place Marcelin Berthelot, 75005 Paris France

LICHTIGFELD, ADOLPH, law and philosophy educator; b. Düsseldorf, Germany, Mar. 23, 1904; s. Joshua and Clara (Weisberg) L.; m. Renia Lifschutz, Apr. 10, 1932 (dec. 1980); children: Freddie, Donnie. JD, U. Cologne, 1931; cert. Minister of Religion, U. London, 1939; PhD, U. South Africa, 1953. Gerichts referendar Amts und Landesgericht Düsseldorf, 1931-33, pvt. tutor of law, 1933-35; spiritual head United Hebrew Instns., Germiston, South Africa, 1939-52; prin. South African Jewish Orphanage, Johannesburg, 1952-71; sr. lectr. philosophy U. South Africa, Johannesburg, 1964-68; hon. lectr. U. Witwatersrand, Johannesburg, 1971—; lectr. philosophy U. Western Cape, Cape Town, South Africa, 1982. Author: Philosophy and Revelation in the Work of Contemporary Jewish Thinkers, 1937, Twenty Centuries of Jewish Thought, 2d edition, 1938, Jasper's Metaphysics, 1954, Aspects of Jasper's Philosophy, 2d edition, 1971; contbr. philosophical articles, papers to numerous publs. Served as chaplain, S.A. Def. Forces, 1942-45, NATOUSA. Named hon. life mem. ARCADIA South African Jewish Children's Home, 1986. Home: PO Box 93036, Yeoville Johannesburg Republic of South Africa Office: U Witwatersrand, Dept Philosophy, Johannesburg Republic of South Africa

LICKLE, WILLIAM CAUFFIEL, banker; b. Wilmington, Del., Aug. 2, 1929; s. Charles Harold and Hazel (Cauffiel) L.; m. Renee Carpenter Kitchell, Nov. 24, 1950; children: Sydney Cauffiel Lindley, Garrison duPont, Ashley Morgan O'Neil, Kemble Carpenter Lickle O'Donnell. BA, U. Va., 1951, LLB, 1953. Bar: Va. 1953. Registered rep. Laird & Co., Inc., Wilmington, Del., 1953-55; v.p., dir. Niront & Co. (real estate developers), Wilmington, 1955-56; ptnr. Wheelock & Lickle (realtors), Greenville, Del., 1956-57; registered rep. Laird, Bissell & Meeds, Inc., Wilmington, 1957-73; ptnr. Laird, Bissell & Meeds, Inc., 1962, dir., 1965, exec. v.p., 1967-68, pres., 1968-69, chmn. exec. com., 1969, chmn. bd., chief exec. officer, 1970-73; sr. v.p., dir. Dean Witter & Co. Inc., 1973-77; chief exec. officer, chmn. bd. Del. Trust Co., Wilmington, 1985—, dir. exec. com., 1973—, chmn. trust com., 1979—, vice chmn., 1977-84; bd. dirs. Bessemer Trust Co. N.J., Bessemer Trust Co. N.Y., Bessemer Trust Co. Fla. Dir. United Community Fund Del., 1960-62; dir. treas. Blue Cross-Blue Shield Del., 1963-68; commr. New Castle County (Del.) Airport, 1964-67, New Castle County Trans. Commn., 1967-69; dir. Easter Seal Soc. Del., 1965-75; dir., vice chmn., founder Better Bus. Bur. Del., 1966-72; spl. gifts chmn. Am. Cancer Soc., Del., 1968; trustee Thomas Jefferson U., Phila., 1971-78, Ethel Walker Sch., Simsbury, Ct., 1977-79, Grand Opera House, Wilmington, 1986—; nat. adv. com. Rollins Coll., Winter Pk, Fla., 1973-76; dir. Del. Mus. Natural History, 1974-81; chmn. fin. com. Del. Cancer Network, 1975-77; bus. econ. devel. com. Del. State C. of C., 1979-80; dir. devel. com. Planned Parenthood Palm Beach (Fla.), 1981-85; hon. dir., past dir., treas. Boys' Club Wilmington, 1963—; trustee, dir. emeritus, exec. com., treas., chmn. fin. com. Med. Ctr. Del., 1965—; trustee, chmn. devel. com. Brandywine River Mus., Chadds Ford, Pa., 1982—; dir. Soc. Four Arts, Palm Beach, 1982—; steering com. U. Va. Jefferson Scholars, Charlottesville, 1985—; gov. corp. council Winterthur Mus., Wilmington, 1986—; dir., exec. com., chmn. fin. com. Celebrate '88 Com., Wilmington, 1986—; bd. mgrs. U. Va. Alumni Assn., Charlottesville, 1987—; founder Del. Community Found., 1987—; spl. asst. Gov.'s Econ. Devel., 1987; Del. fin. com. Citizens for Eisenhower, 1956; fin. chmn. Vols. for Nixon, 1960; state coordinator Del. for Goldwater, 1964; treas., exec. com., fin. com. Del. Rep. State Com., 1964-68; chmn. bd. mgrs., race com. Fairhill (Md.) Races, 1975-86; dir., exec. com., treas., chmn. fin. audit com. Breeder's Cup Ltd., Lexington, Ky., 1984—; dir., exec. com. Thoroughbred Racing Communications, 1987—. Mem. SAR, ABA, Va. Bar Assn., Nat. Steeplechase and Hunt Assn. (sr. mem., past steward), Del. Roundtable, Soc. Colonial Wars Wilmington, Kappa Alpha, Phi Alpha Delta. Clubs: Vicmead Hunt (Greenville, Del.) (bd. dirs.); Wilmington Country (Greenville, Del.); Wilmington; Turf (Del. Park, Wilmington) (bd. dirs. 1976-82); Everglades, Seminole Golf, Bath and Tennis (Palm Beach, Fla.); Saratoga Golf and Polo, Reading Room (Saratoga, N.Y.); Rolling Rock (Ligonier, Pa.); Lyford Cay (Nassau, Bahamas). Home: 300 Rockland Rd Montchanin DE 19710 Office: care Del Trust Co 900 Market St Wilmington DE 19801

LIDDELL, JANE HAWLEY HAWKES, civic worker; b. Newark, Dec. 8, 1907; d. Edward Zeh and Mary Everett (Hawley) Hawkes; A.B., Smith Coll., 1931; postgrad. in art history, Harvard U., 1933-35; M.A., Columbia U., 1940; Carnegie fellow Sorbonne, Paris, 1937; m. Donald M. Liddell, Jr., Mar. 30, 1940; children: Jane Boyer, D. Roger Brooke. Pres., Planned Parenthood Essex County (N.J.), 1947-50; trustee Prospect Hill Sch. Girls, Newark, 1946-50; mem. adv. bd., publicity and public relations chmn. N.J. State Mus., Trenton, 1952-60; sec., then v.p. women's br. N.J. Hist. Soc.; women's aux. prodn. chmn. Englewood (N.J.) Hosp., 1959-61; pres. Dwight Sch. Girls Parents Assn., 1955-57; v.p. Englewood Sch. Boys Parents Assn., 1958-60; mem. Altar Guild, women's aux. bd., rector's adv. council St. Paul's Episcopal Ch., Englewood, 1954-59; bd. dir. N.Y. State Soc. of Nat. Soc. Colonial Dames, 1961-67, rep. conf. Patriotic and Hist. Socs., 1964—; bd. dirs. Huguenot Soc. Am., 1979-86, regional v.p., 1979-82, historian, 1983-84, co-chmn. Tercentennial Book, 1983-85; bd. dirs. Soc. Daus. Holland Dames, 1965-82; nat. jr. v.p. Dames of Loyal Legion, USA; bd. dirs., mem. publs. com. Daus. Cin., 1966-72; bd. dirs. Ch. Women's League Patriotic Service, 1962—, pres., 1968-70, 72-74; bd. dirs., chmn. grants com. Youth Found., N.Y.C., 1974—; chmn. for Newark, Smith Coll. 75th Ann. Fund, 1948-50; pres. North N.J. Smith Club, 1956-58; pres. Smith Coll. Class 1931, 1946-51, 76-81, editor 50th anniversary book, 1980-81. Author: (with others) Huguenot Refugees in the Settling of Colonial America, 1985. Recipient various commendation awards. Republican. Mem. Colonial Dames Am. (N.Y.C. chpt.). Clubs: Colony, City Gardens, Church (N.Y.C.); Jr. League Bergen County; Needle and Bobbin, Nat. Farm and Garden; Englewood Woman's, Englewood Field; Hillsboro (Pompano Beach, Fla.). Editor: Maine Echoes, 1961; research and editor asst., Wartime Writings of American Revolution Officers, 1972-75.

LIDDELL, LEON MORRIS, educator, librarian; b. Gainesville, Tex., July 21, 1914; s. Thomas Leon and Minnie Mae (Morris) L. B.A., U. Tex., 1937, J.D., 1937; B.L.S., U. Chgo., 1946; postgrad., Columbia U., 1948. Bar: Tex. bar 1937. Practiced in Gainesville, 1938-39; with claims dept. Hartford Accident & Indemnity Co., 1937-38, Pacific Mut. Life Ins. Co., 1939-41; asst. prof. law, law librarian U. Conn., 1946-47; asst. prof. law U. Minn., 1949-50, asso. prof., 1950-54, prof. law, 1954-60, law librarian, 1949-60; prof. law, law librarian U. Chgo., 1960-74, prof. law, law librarian emeritus, 1974—; prof. law, law librarian Northwestern U. Law Sch., 1974-80. Served from 2d lt. to maj. AUS, 1941-46. Mem. Am. Bar Assn., Am. Assn. Law Libraries, Chgo Assn. Law Libraries (past pres.), Spl. Libraries Assn. Club: Mason. Home: 4718 Hallmark Ln Houston TX 77056

LIDDY, MARIE THERESE, consulting executive; b. Newark, July 27, 1932; d. Joseph A. and Veronica Cecelia (Beston) L.; B.A. in English and Music, Chestnut Hill Coll., Phila., 1967; M.A. in English and Drama, St. Bonaventure U., Olean, N.Y., 1972, M.A. in Theology and Psychology, 1977. Tchr., counselor John Carroll High Sch., Bel Air, Md., 1968-70; instr. English, asso. in counseling St. Bonaventure U., 1970-72; lectr., career adv. Temple U., Phila., 1972-76; co-dir. campus community, counselor, adminstr. LaSalle Coll., Phila., 1977-78; research and devel. Am. Inst. Property and Liability Underwriters, 1978-80; pres., exec. dir. Mainstream Access, Inc., Phila., 1980-83; prin. Mainstream Access Inc., N.Y., 1983—; seminar leader, 1968—. Mem. Interreligious Task Force Soviet Jewry, 1976-81, Phila. Human Relations Commn., 1972-76; co-sponsor Women's Inter Faith Dialogue on Middle East, 1976-78. Mem. Nat. Assn. Female Execs., Am. Soc. Tng. and Devel. Contbr., Insurance (Job Finder series), 1981; contbr. articles to profl. jours. Home: 64 Southgate Rd Mount Laurel NJ 08054 Office: Onc Commerce Square Philadelphia PA 19103

LIDSTONE, HERRICK KENLEY, JR., lawyer; b. New Rochelle, N.Y., Sept. 10, 1949; s. Herrick Kenley and Marcia Edith (Drake) L.; m. Mary Lynne O'Toole, Aug. 5, 1978; children: Herrick Kevin, James Patrick, John Francis. AB, Cornell U., 1971; JD, U. Colo., 1978. Bar: Colo. 1978, U.S. Dist. Ct. Colo. 1978. Assoc. Roath & Brega, P.C., Denver, 1978-85, Brenman, Epstein, Raskin & Friedlob, P.C., Denver, 1985-86; ptnr. Brenman, Raskin, Friedlob & Tenenbaum, P.C., Denver, 1986—; adj. prof. U. Denver Coll. Law, 1985—; speaker in field various orgns. Editor U. Colo. Law Rev., 1977-78; co-author: Federal Income Taxation of Corporations, 6th edit.; contbr. articles to profl. jours. Served with USN, 1971-75, with USNR, 1975-81. Mem. ABA, Colo. Bar Assn., Denver Bar Assn. (legal fee arbitration com.), Denver Assn. Oil and Gas Title Lawyers. Office: Brenman Raskin Friedlob & Tenenbaum 1400 Glenarm Pl Denver CO 80202

LIE, ALVIN LINGPIAO, retail executive; b. Semarang, Jawa Tengah, Indonesia, Apr. 21, 1961; s. Ay Yen and Moa Nio (Siauw) L; m. Inawati Rahardjo, Jan. 8, 1984; children: Audwin Lee, Bryan Lee, Carmelita Lee. Student in mktg., Systematics Bus. Tng. Ctr., Singapore, 1980-82. Mktg. rep. Precision Carbide Tooling Pte. Ltd., Singapore, 1981-82; sales dir. First Regency Devel. Corp., Sarasota, Fla., 1982-84; mktg. dir. Mickey Morse Dept. Store & Supermarket, Semarang, Indonesia, 1984-86, mng. dir., 1986—; mng. dir. P.T. Sarana Sehat, Semarang, 1986—; bd. dirs. P.T. Alegori Advt., Semarang; dir., producer Octave Records, Semarang, 1986—. Producer numerous musical tapes. Chmn. Persani Indonesia Gymnastics Assn., Jawa Tengah, 1986—; sec. gen. Yadora Sports Fund Com., Jawa Tengah, 1986—; treas. Bakom PKB Communication Bd. for Nat. Unity, Jawa Tengah, 1987—, H.I.P.S.I. Indonesian Social Workers' Union, Cen. Java, 1987—. Mem. Assn. Shopping Ctrs. and Supermarkets in Cen. Java (chmn. 1987—), HIPMI Indonesian Young Businessmen's Assn., Jawa Tengah, Head of Tourism and Telecommunication Dept., 1988-91. Lodge: Lions (pres. 1986-88, zone chmn. internat. dist. 307)). Home: 574 JL Kelengan Besar, Semarang, Jawa Tengah 50133, Indonesia Office: Mickey Morse Group, 42 Jl Depok, Semarang, Jawa Tengah 50133, Indonesia

LIEBENOW, ROBERT C., trade association executive; b. Aberdeen, S.D., Sept. 13, 1922; s. Albert C. and Leta V. (Foot) L. Student, No. State Tchrs. Coll., Aberdeen, 1940-42; J.D., U. S.D., 1946. Bar: Ill. bar 1948, D.C. bar 1969. Lawyer First Nat. Bank, Chgo., 1946-52; asst. sec. Bd. Trade, City of Chgo., 1952, sec., 1953-55, exec. sec., 1955, pres., 1956-65; pres. Corn Refiners Assn., Inc., 1965—. Named One of Ten Outstanding Young Men U.S. Jr. C. of C., 1956. Mem. Am. Assn. Cereal Chemists (hon.), Phi Delta Theta Alumni Assn. Clubs: National Press (Washington), Congressional Country (Washington), University (Washington); Union League (Chgo.), Economic (Chgo.). Home: 1213 Colonial Rd McLean VA 22101 Office: 1001 Connecticut Ave NW Suite 1022 Washington DC 20036

LIEBERMAN, EUGENE, lawyer; b. Chgo., May 17, 1918; s. Harry and Eva (Goldman) L.; m. Pearl Naomi, Aug. 3, 1947; children—Mark, Robert, Steven. JD, DePaul U., 1940. Bar: Ill. 1940, U.S. Supr. Ct. 1963. Mem. firm Jacobs and Lieberman, 1954-60; sr. ptnr. Jacobs, Lieberman and Aling, 1960-74; spl. hearing officer U.S. Dept. Justice, 1967-78; hearing officer Ill. Pollution Control Bd., 1973—; sole practice, Chgo. Contbr. articles to legal publs. Served with U.S. Army, 1942-45, PTO. Recipient 1st in State award Moot Ct. Championship, 1940, Gold award Philatelic Exhbn., Taipei, 1981, Gold award World Philatelic Exhbn., Melbourne, 1984, others. Fellow Am. Acad. Matrimonial Lawyers; mem. Ill. State Bar Assn., Chgo. Bar Assn., Appellate Lawyers Assn., Chgo. Philatelic Soc. (pres. 1964-68). Club: Ill. Athletic (Chgo.). Contbr. articles to legal publs. Home: 801 Leclaire Ave Wilmette IL 60091

LIEBERMAN, STANLEY BERTRAM, real estate developer; b. Trenton, N.J., Mar. 31, 1938; s. Abram Herbert and Frieda (Chamowitz) L.; A.B. in Bus. Mgmt., Rutgers U., 1960; m. Jill Gustafson; children—Louis, Jonathan, Rebecca, Kimberly, Wendy, Julie. Sales mgr. Am. Photograph Corp., N.Y.C., 1960-67, Root Photographers, Chgo., 1968-71; pres. Lieberman Inc., Realtors, Buffalo Grove, Ill., 1971—, Video Homes of Am., Inc., Buffalo Grove, 1972—; chmn. bd. Lieberman Group, Ltd.; instr. course Principles of Real Estate, Harper Coll., Palatine, Ill. Police and fire commr. City of Buffalo Grove, 1971-75; founder, pres. Congregation Beth Judea, 1968-70; treas. United Synagogue of Am. Midwest, 1970. Served as 1st lt. U.S. Army, 1960. Mem. N.W. Suburban Bd. Realtors (pres.), Realtors Nat. Mktg. Inst. Lodges: Rotary (past treas.), B'nai B'rith. Home: RFD Box 2415 Long Grove IL 60047 Office: Lieberman Inc Realtors 400 W Dundee Rd Buffalo Grove IL 60089

LIEBERT, WOLFGANG GUENTER, business consultant; b. Berlin, W. Germany, Jan. 9, 1935; s. Herbert Alfred and Grete Klara (Langer) L.; m. Margot Ida Buller, Sept. 18, 1958; children—Martina, Wolfmar. Diploma for Bus. Adminstrn. and Econs., Tech. U., Berlin, 1963. Econ. journalist Berliner Morgenpost, Berlin, 1963-65; head planning-controlling Braas GmbH, Frankfurt, W. Germany, 1966-67; owner, bus. cons. Liebert & Partners, Berlin, 1967—; lectr. micromacro econs. Tech. Coll., Berlin, 1974—. Vice-chmn. Liberal Party, Fed. Com. for Fin. and Taxes, 1975—. Mem. Internat. Symposium on Small Bus. Lutheran. Contbr. articles to profl. jours. Home: 215 Bundesallee, D-1000 Berlin 15 Federal Republic of Germany Office: 13 a Tauentzienstr, D-1000 Berlin 30 Federal Republic of Germany

LIEBERTHAL, MILTON M., medical consultant, gastroenterologist; b. Jewett City, Conn., Oct. 30, 1911; s. Robert Henry and Erna (Bloomfield) L.; m. Naomi Ruth Burd, June 9, 1935; children—David Henry, Kenneth Guy, Gary Burd. A.B., Dartmouth Coll., 1932; M.D., NYU, 1935. Diplomate Am. Bd. Internal Medicine. Intern, Phila. Gen. Hosp., 1935-37, resident in internal medicine and gastroenterology, 1937-39; practice medicine, Phila., 1939-41; practice medicine specializing in gastroenterology, Bridgeport, Conn., 1946-71; dir. investigative gastroenterology Merrell-Nat. Labs., 1972-76; med. cons. Merrell Dow Pharms., Cin., 1977—; clin. prof. medicine U. Cin. Served to maj. M.C., AUS, 1942-45. Fellow ACP; mem. Am. Gastroent. Assn., Am. Soc. Gastrointestinal Endoscopy, Alpha Omega Alpha. Club: Kenwood Country (Cin.). Author: (with H.O. Conn) The Hepatic Coma Syndromes and Lactulose, 1979; The Lighter Side of Life, 1973; contbr. articles to profl. books and jours.

LIEBLING, NORMAN ROBERT, lawyer; b. Chgo., Feb. 17, 1917; s. Louis and Frances (Geller) L.; m. Florence Levinson, Feb. 25, 1950; children: James, Fred. BA, U. Ill., 1937; JD, Harvard U., 1940. Bar: Ill. 1940. Ptnr. Freeman & Liebling, Chgo., 1948-54, Freeman, Liebling, Adelman & Watson, Chgo., 1955-67; sr. ptnr. Liebling, Adelman & Bernstein, Chgo., 1968-81, Liebling, Uriell & Hamman, Chgo., 1976-82, Liebling & Uriell, Chgo., 1982-83, Schuyler, Roche & Zwirner, Chgo., 1984—; bd. dirs. The United Equitable Corp., Lincolnwood, Ill. Spl. asst. to atty. gen. State of Ill., Chgo., 1958-61; bd. dirs. Rosenbaum Found., Chgo., 1982—. Served to capt. U.S. Army, 1942-46, CBI. Mem. ABA, Chgo. Bar Assn., Harvard Law Soc. Ill. (bd. dirs. 1986—). Clubs: Chgo. Athletic, The Plaza, International (Chgo.). Home: 970 Sunset Ave Winnetka IL 60093 Office: Schuyler Roche & Zwirner One Prudential Plaza 130 E Randolph St Chicago IL 60601

LIEBMAN, RONALD STANLEY, lawyer; b. Balt., Oct. 11, 1943; s. Harry Martin and Martha (Altgenug) L.; m. Simma Liebman, Jan. 8, 1972; children: Shana, Margot. BA, Western Md. Coll., Westminster, 1966; JD, U. Md., 1969. Bar: Md. 1969, D.C. 1977, U.S. Dist. Ct. (ea. dist.) Va. 1970, U.S. Dist. Ct. Md. 1970, U.S. Dist. Ct. D.C. 1982, U.S. Ct. Appeals (4th cir.) 1972, U.S. Ct. Appeals (D.C. cir.) 1982, U.S. Ct. Appeals (5th cir.) 1985. Law clk. to chief judge U.S. Dist. Ct. Md., 1969-70; assoc. Melnicove, Kaufman & Weiner, Balt., 1970-72; asst. U.S. atty. Office of U.S. Atty., Dept. Justice, Balt., 1972-78; ptnr. Sachs, Greenebaum & Tayler, Washington, 1978-82, Patton, Boggs & Blow, Washington, 1982—. Author: Grand Jury, 1983; co-editor: Testimonial Privileges, 1983. Recipient spl. commendation award U.S. Dept. Justice, 1978. Mem. ABA, D.C. Bar Assn., Md. Bar Assn. Club: Sergeants Inn (Balt.). Office: 2550 M St NW Washington DC 20037

LIEBMANN, SEYMOUR W., construction consultant; b. N.Y.C., Nov. 1, 1928; s. Isidor W. and Etta (Waltzer) L.; m. Hinda Adam, Sept. 20, 1959; children: Peter Adam, David W. BS in Mech. Engring., Clarkson U. (formerly Clarkson Tech. Coll.), 1948; grad. Indsl. Coll. Armed Forces, 1963, Command and Gen. Staff Coll., 1966, Army War Coll., 1971. Registered profl. engr., N.Y., Mass., Ga. Area engr. constrn. div. E.I. DuPont de Nemours & Co., Inc., 1952-54; constrn. planner Lummus Co., 1954-56; prin. mech. engr. Perini Corp., 1956-62; v.p. Boston Based Contractors, 1962-66; v.p. A.R. Abrams, Inc., Atlanta, 1967-74, pres., 1974-78, also bd. dirs.; founder Liebmann Assocs., Inc., Atlanta, 1979—; bd. dirs. Abrams Industries; mem. nat. adv. bd. Am. Security Council. Author: Military Engineer Field Notes, 1953, Prestressing Miter Gate Diagonals, 1960; contbr. articles to publs. Mem. USO Council, Atlanta, 1968—, v.p., 1978, mem. exec. com., 1975-79; mem. Nat. UN Day Com., 1975; sr. army coordinator, judge Sci. Fair, Atlanta Pub. Schs., annually 1979-88; asst. scoutmaster troop 298 Atlanta area council Boy Scouts Am., 1980-87, Explorer advisor, 1982-86, unit commr., 1985, dist. commr. North Atlanta Dist., Atlanta Area Council, 1988, mem. faculty Commrs. Coll., 1985-87; mem. alumni adv. com. Clarkson Coll. Tech., 1981—, alumni bd. govs., 1983—, Golden Knight award, 1983; mem. exec. com., zoning chmn. neighbor planning unit City of Atlanta, 1982—, chmn., 1988. Served to 1st lt. C.E., AUS, 1948-52, Korea; col. Res. ret. Decorated Legion of Merit, Meritorious Service medal, U.S. Army Res. medal, 1975; elected to Old Guard of Gate City Guard, 1979; recipient cert. of Achievement Dept. Army, 1978, USO Recognition award, 1979, Order of Arrow award Boy Scouts Am., 1983, 87, award Am. Inst. Plant Engrs., 1987. Fellow Soc. Am. Mil. Engrs. (bd. dirs. 1986—, chmn. readiness com. 1986—, program chmn. Atlanta post 1980-81, v.p. 1982, pres. 1983, Nat. award of Merit 1982-83); mem. Soc. 1st U.S. Inf., Res. Officers Assn., U.S. Army War Coll. Found. (life mem.), U.S. Army War Coll. Alumni Assn., Nat. Soc. Profl. Engrs., Ga. Soc. Profl. Engrs., Engrs. Club Boston, Assn. U.S. Army, Def. Preparedness Assn., Am. Arbitration Assn. (panel arbitrators 1979—, constrn. adv. com. 1984—), Atlanta C. of C., Mil. Order World Wars. Republican. Jewish. Clubs: Ft. McPherson Officers; Ga. Appalachian Trail. Lodges: Masons (32 deg.), Shriners, Elks, Civitan. Home: 3260 Rilman Dr NW Atlanta GA 30327 Office: 6520 Powers Ferry Rd Suite 200 Atlanta GA 30339

LIEBOWITZ, LARRY ARNOLD, chemical engineer; b. Bklyn., June 19, 1942; s. Max and Estelle L.; B. Chem. Engring., CCNY, 1960; M. Chem. Engring., N.Y. U., 1963. Engring. group leader MEPCO div. NV Philips, Morristown, N.J., 1963-68; product mgr. Nytronics, Inc., Berkeley Heights, N.J., 1968-71; engring. mgr. KDI Pyrofilm Corp., Whippany, N.J., 1971-75; pres. LAL Technol. Corp., East Brunswick, N.J., 1975—. Mem. Soc. Plastics Engrs. (chmn. elec. and electronic div. 1970-71), Am. Chem. Soc., Am. Ceramics Soc. Pioneer in devel. of monolithic multilayer ceramic capacitors; developer new superior ceramic materials and chip structures and mfg. techniques for electronic capacitors and resistors which allow their use at microwave frequencies, log-slope method of predicting high-frequency performance of electronic devices, early researcher and participant in White House conference on high temperature superconductor materials. Office: Box 412 East Brunswick NJ 08816

LIEDERMANN, HELMUT, ambassador; b. Vienna, Austria, Aug. 10, 1926; s. Hans and Wanda (Klug) L.; m. Margaret Lukas; 1 child, Peter. D of Law, U. Vienna, 1950. Sec. Embassy, charge d'affaires Austrian Embassy, Warsaw, Poland, 1957-62; dep. head personnel Austrian Fgn. Ministry, Vienna, 1963-65; consul gen. Austrian Delegation, Berlin, 1965-71; dept. dir. Ministry for Fgn. Affairs, Vienna, 1971-77; head delegation Conf. on Security and Cooperation in Europe, Geneva, Switzerland, 1973-75; ambassador to Austria Belgrade, Yugoslavia, 1977-81, Moscow, 1981-85; ambassador and exec. sec. Conf. on Security and Cooperation in Europe, Vienna, 1985—. Contbr. articles to newspapers and profl. jours., chpts. to books on internat. law. Lodge: Rotary. Office: Conf Security Cooperation Europe, 1450 Vienna Austria

LIEDMAN, SVEN-ERIC O., historian, educator; b. Karlskrona, Blekinge, Sweden, June 1, 1939; s. Elvir A.I. and K. Maria (Andren) L.; m. Lena Herdendal, Apr. 28, 1963 (div. 1975); children: Mathilda, Oskar; m. Eva-Maria Flöög, Mar. 22, 1975; 1 child, Per. BA, Lunds U., Sweden, 1959, MA, 1961; PhD, Götedorgs U., Sweden, 1966. Cultural editor Sydsvenska Dagbladet, Malmó, Sweden, 1966-68; asst. prof. Lunds U., Sweden, 1968-70, Göteborg U., Sweden, 1970-79; prof., chmn. Göteborg U., 1979—, also dean faculty of humanities. Author: Israel Hwasser, 1972, Surdeg, 1980, Das Spiel der Gegensistze, 1984, Fran Platon Till Regan, 1986. Office: Göteborg U, Dept Hist Ideas Sci, 41298 Göteborg Sweden

LIEF, HAROLD ISAIAH, psychiatrist; b. N.Y.C., Dec. 29, 1917; s. Jacob F. and Mollie (Filler) L.; m. Myrtis A. Brumfield, Mar. 3, 1961; Caleb B., Frederick V., Oliver F.; children from previous marriage—Polly Lief Goldberg, Jonathan F. B.A., U. Mich., 1938; M.D., N.Y. U., 1942; cert. in psychoanalysis, Columbia Coll. Physicians and Surgeons, 1950; M.A. (hon.), U. Pa., 1971. Intern Queens Gen. Hosp., Jamaica, N.Y., 1942-43; resident psychiatry L.I. Coll. Medicine, 1946-48; pvt. practice psychiatry N.Y.C., 1948-51; asst. physician Presbyn. Hosp., N.Y.C., 1949-51; asst. prof. Tulane U., New Orleans, 1951-54, asso. prof., 1954-60, prof. psychiatry, 1960-67; prof. psychiatry U. Pa., Phila., 1967-82, prof. emeritus, 1982—; dir. div. family study U. Pa., 1967-81; dir. Marriage Council of Phila., 1969-81, Ctr. for Study of Sex. Edn. in Medicine, 1968-82; mem. staff U. Pa. Hosp., 1967-81, Pa. Hosp., 1981—. Author: (with Daniel and William Thompson) The Eighth Generation, 1960; Editor: (with Victor and Nina Lief) Psychological Basis of Medical Practice, 1963, Medical Aspects of Human Sexuality, 1976, (with Arno Karlen) Sex Education in Medicine, 1976, Sexual Problems in Medical Practice, 1981, (with Zwi Hoch) Sexology: Sexual Biology, Behavior and Therapy, 1982, (with Zwi Hoch) International Research in Sexology, 1983. Contbr. numerous articles to publs. Mem. La. State Commn. Civil Rights, 1958-67. Served to maj. M.C. U.S. Army, 1943-46. Commonwealth Fund fellow, 1963-64. Fellow Phila. Coll. Physicians, Am. Psychiat. Assn. (life), N.Y. Acad. Scis., AAAS, Acad. Psychoanalysis (charter, past pres.), Am. Coll. Psychiatrists (founding), Am. Coll. Psychoanalysts (charter); mem. Am. Assn. Marriage and Family Therapists, Sex Info. and Edn. Council U.S. (past pres.), Group Advancement Psychiatry (life), Am. Soc. Adolescent Psychiatry, Am. Psychosomatic Soc., Assn. Psychoanalytic Medicine (life), Internat. Acad. Sex Research, Soc. Sci. Study of Sex, Am. Soc. Sex Educators, Counselors and Therapists, Soc. Sex Therapists and Researchers, World Assn. Sexology (v.p.), Soc. Exploration of Psychotherapy Integration (adv. bd.), Sigma Xi, Alpha Omega Alpha, Phi Eta Sigma, Phi Kappa Phi. Clubs: Germantown Cricket (Phila.); NYU, Columbia. Home: 101 S Buck Ln Haverford PA 19041 Office: 700 Spruce St Suite 503 Philadelphia PA 19106

LIEM, CHANNING, political science educator, former diplomat; b. Ulyul, Korea, Oct. 30, 1909; s. Posung and Posun (Yu) L.; m. Popai Lee, Jan. 29, 1940; children: Edith (Mrs. Young Jo Sul), G. Ramsay, Paul L. B.S., Lafayette Coll., 1934; M.A., Princeton, 1943, Ph.D., 1945. Postdoctoral fellow Yale, 1954-55; dir. Korean Ch. and Inst., N.Y.C., 1936-41; cons. Far Eastern affairs U.S. Office Censorship and War Information, N.Y.C., 1942-45; instr. Princeton, 1946-48; Korean affairs adviser U.S. Mil. Gov. in Korea, Seoul, 1948-49; prof. polit. sci. Chatham Coll., 1949-60; prof. polit. sci. State U. N.Y. Coll. of New Paltz, also chmn., prof. polit. sci. Asian studies, prof. emeritus, 1978—; ambassador Republic Korea to UN, 1960-61; spl. envoy to Republic Korea to Southwestern African Republics, Cameroun, Dahomey, Congo, Ivory Coast, Togo, Ghana, Senegal, 1961; adviser Nat. Com. for Def. Democratic Rights, Republic Korea, 1972—. Author: America's Gift to Korea: Life of Philip Jaisohn, 1952, Civilization of East Asia, 1973, The First Korean American, 1984; Contbr. articles to profl. publs.; Editor: Voice of the Korean People. Trustee Korean Edn. Found. Am., 1944-55; hon. chmn. bd. dirs. Philip Jaisohn Found. Recipient Humanitarian award Nat. Achievement Clubs, 1953; Ford faculty fellowship Chatham Coll., 1954-55; citation for meritorious service Republic Korea, 1961. Mem. Am. Polit. Sci. Assn., Internat. Mark Twain Soc. (hon.), Union Overseas Koreans for Democracy and Unification (sr. chmn.). Club: Princeton (N.Y.C.). Home: 252 Old Kingston Rd New Paltz NY 12561

LIEM, TJING HIAN, tobacco company executive; b. Bojonegoro, Jatim, Indonesia, June 27, 1933; s. Tjhiang Swie and Lien Nio (Hwan) L.; m. Siok Hien Liem, aug. 18, 1963. BA, Inst. Tech., Bandung, Indonesia, 1956; MS, Tech. U., Delft, Holland, 1960. Cert. mech. engr. Cryogenic researcher Sulzer Bros. Ltd., Winterthur, Switzerland, 1960-68; tech. dir. Eprimex B.V., Amsterdam, 1968—; v.p. P.T. Bentoel, Malang, Indonesia, 1980—. Contbr. articles to profl. jours.; patentee in field. Lodge: Rotary (v.p. Malang club 1987-88). Home: Semeru 78, Malang 65112, Indonesia Office: PT Per Rokok Tjap Bentoel, Jalan Susanto 2A, Malang 65118, Indonesia

LIEN, BRUCE HAWKINS, minerals and oil company executive; b. Waubay, S.D., Apr. 7, 1927; s. Peter Calmer and LaRece Catherine (Holm) L.; m. Deanna Jean Browning, May 4, 1978. BS in Bus., Wyo. U., 1953. Laborer, ptnr. Pete Lien & Sons, Inc., Rapid City, S.D., 1944-84, bd. chmn., 1984—. Chmn. Community Chest, Rapid City, S.D., 1956; pres., nat. council Boys Club Am., Rapid City, S.D., N.Y.C., 1968; commr. Presdl. Scholars Commn., Washington, 1982. Served to 1st lt. U.S. Army, 1945-47, 50-53. Recipient Disting. Service award S.D. Sch. Mines, Rapid City, 1972, Disting. Service award Cosmopolitan Internat., Rapid City, 1983; named Disting. Alumnus, Wyo. U., Laramie, 1982. Mem. Internat. Lime Assn. (pres. 1973-75), Nat. Lime Assn. (pres. 1973-75, Merit award 1973, bd. dirs.), VFW. Republican. Lutheran. Club: Cosmopolitan (Rapid City, S.D.). Lodges: Masons, Elks. Home: PO Box 440 Rapid City SD 57709 Office: Pete Lien & Sons Inc I 90 & Deadwood Ave PO Box 440 Rapid City SD 57709

LIEN, ERIC JUNG-CHI, pharmacist, educator; b. Kaohsiung, Taiwan, Nov. 30, 1937; came to U.S., 1963, naturalized, 1973; m. Linda L. Chen, Oct. 2, 1965; children: Raymond, Andrew. B.S. in Pharmacy (Frank Shu China Sci. scholar), Nat. Taiwan U., 1960; Ph.D. in Pharm. Chemistry, U. Calif., San Francisco, 1966; postdoctoral fellow in bio-organic chemistry, Pomona Coll., Claremont, Calif., 1967-68. Hosp. pharmacist 862 Hosp. of Republic of China, 1960-61; asst. prof. pharmaceutics and biomedicinal chemistry U. So. Calif., Los Angeles, 1968-72; assoc. prof. U. So. Calif., 1972-76, prof., 1976—, coordinator sects. biomedicinal chemistry and pharmaceutics, 1975-78, coordinator sect. biomedicinal chemistry, 1975-84; cons. Internat. Medication System, Ltd., 1978, NIH, 1971, 82-87, Inst. Drug Design, Inc., Calif., 1971-73, Allergan Pharms., Inc., 1971-72. Editorial bd. Jour. Clin. Pharmacy and Therapeutics, 1979—; referee Jour. Pharmacokinetics and Biopharmaceutics, Jour. Medicinal Chemistry, Jour. Fool Agr. Chemistry, Jour. Pharm. Sci., Pesticide Biochemistry and Physiology; author 3 books; contbr. numerous articles to profl. jours. Merck grantee, 1970; Abbott grantee, 1971-72; NSF grantee, 1972-74, 1976-77; IMS grantee, 1979; others. Mem. Am. Assn. Cancer Research, Acad. Pharm. Scis., Am. Chem. Soc., Sigma Xi, Rho Chi, Phi Kappa Phi. Office: U So Calif Sch Pharmacy 1985 Zonal Ave Los Angeles CA 90033

LIEN, WEN-PIN, cardiologist; b. Taipei, Taiwan, Dec. 29, 1927; s. Kuang-Yen and Ruey (Chang) L.; M.D., Nat. Taiwan U., 1954; D.Med.Scis., Osaka City (Japan) Med. Coll., 1961; m. Su-Ai Liu, Jan. 20, 1955; children—Chao-Ming, Chao-Tsu, Chao-Wen, Chao-Po. Resident dept. internal medicine Nat. Taiwan U. Hosp., 1954-59, attending physician dept. internal medicine, 1959—; fellow in cardiology Baylor U. Coll. Medicine-Tex. Children's Hosp., Houston, 1966-67; mem. faculty Nat. Taiwan U. Med. Sch., 1965—, asso. prof. medicine, 1971-78, prof., 1978—, chmn. dept. internal medicine, 1986—. Fellow Am. Coll. Cardiology, Am. Coll. Chest Physicians; mem. Republic China Soc. Cardiology (pres. 1971—), Asian Pacific Soc. Cardiology, Internat. Soc. Cardiology, Formosan Med. Assn., Chinese Med. Assn., Biomed. Engring. Soc. China, Western-Pacific Assn. Critical Care Medicine. Contbr. articles to med. jours. Home: Shin-Shen South Rd, 12 Lane 120 Sect 1, Taipei 10622, Republic of China Office: 1 Chang-Te St, Taipei 10016, Republic of China

LIENHARD, SIEGFRIED, Indic studies educator; b. St. Veit, Austria, Aug. 29, 1924; s. Georg and Johanna (Nusser) L.; m. Madeleine Lagerfelt, Aug. 30, 1958. PhD, U. Vienna, 1949. Prof. indology Kiel U., Fed. Republic Germany, 1962-67, Stockholm U., 1967—; vis. prof. Coll. de France, 1976; chmn. Scandanavian Inst. for Asian Studies, Denmark, 1985-86. Author: Songs of Nepal, History of Classical Poetry Sanskrit, etc., 1984, Die Legende vom Prinzen Visvantara, 1980, Die Abenteuer des Kaufmanns Simhala, 1985, Nepalese Manuscripts: Nevari and Sanskrit, 1988. Pres. Swedish Orient Soc., Stockholm, 1986—. Fellow Japan Soc. for Promotion of Sci.; mem. Austrian Acad. Scis., Acad. Scis. Turin, Acad. Scis. Göttingen, Royal Swedish Acad. Letters, History and Antiquities, Royal Danish Acad. Scis., Akhila Bharatiya Sanskrit Parishad (disting.). Home: Korsövägen 11, S-18245 Enebyberg Sweden Office: U Stockholm, S-10691 Stockholm Sweden

LIETZ, JEREMY JON, school system administrator; b. Milw., Oct. 4, 1933; s. John Norman and Dorothy (Bernice) L.; m. Cora Fernandez, Feb. 24, 1983; children: Cheryl, Brian, Angela, Andrew, Christopher. BS, U. Wis., Milw., 1961; MS, U. Wis., Madison, 1971; EdD, Marquette U., 1980. Tchr. Milw. Pub. Schs., 1961-63, diagnostic counselor, 1968-71; sch. adminstr. 1971—; Tchr. Madison (Wis.) Pub. Schs., 1964-65; research assoc. U. Wis., Madison, 1965-67; instr. Marquette U., Milw., 1980-82; lectr. HEW

Conf. on Reading, Greely, Colo., 1973, Nat. Assn. Elem. Sch. Principals Conf. on Reading, St. Louis, 1974, Assn. Wis. Schs. Adminstrs. Conf., Stevens Point, Wis., 1982, also various state and nat. orgns.; co-founder, bd. dirs., cons. Ednl. Leadership Inst., Shorewood, Wis., 1980—; dir. Religious Edn. Program, Cath. Elem. East, Milw., 1985-86. Author: The Elementary School Principal's Role in Special Education, 1982; contbr. articles, chpts., tests, revs. to profl. jours. Served with U.S. Army, 1954-56, ETO. Recipient Cert. of Achievement award Nat. Assn. Elem. Sch. Prins., 1974. Mem. AAAS, Assn. Wis. Sch. Adminstrs. (state planning com. 1977-79), Adminstrs. and Suprs. Council (exec. bd. dirs. 1977-79), U. Wis. (Madison) Alumni Assn., Phi Delta Kappa. Home: 2205 N Summit Ave Milwaukee WI 53202 Office: Ednl Leadership Inst PO Box 11411 Shorewood WI 53211

LIETZEN, JOHN HERVY, personnel executive; b. Kansas City, Kans., July 17, 1947; s. Walter E. and Kathleen M. (Griffith) L.; m. Nora R. Massey, June 12, 1966; children: Gwendolyn Therese, Anne Gabrielle, Sarah Kathleen. BS, Mo. Valley Coll., 1974; MS, U. Mo., 1976. With Union Pacific R.R., 1971—; yard condr. Kansas City, Kans., 1971-77; personnel officer Omaha, 1977-78; dir. personnel Cheyenne, Wyo., 1978-79, sr. tng. officer dept. claims, 1979-83, mgr. staffing, 1983-84, mgr. affirmative action, 1984-86; supr. tech. tng. program devel. Omaha, 1986—. Bd. dirs. Berkshire Village, Kansas City, 1976-77; bd. ministries Valley View Meth. Ch., Overland Pk., Kans., 1976-77; pastor and staff relations com. Hanscom Pk. United Meth. Ch., 1980-81, lay leader, 1983; asst. leader Wyo. council Girl Scouts U.S.A., Cheyenne, 1978-79, asst. leader, Omaha, 1980—, bd. dirs. Great Plains Girl Scout Council, 1987—; exec. bd. Nebr. affiliate Am. Diabetes Assn., 1981—, pres. Midlands chpt., 1982-84, mem. planning and orgn. com., 1986-87, co-founder Omaha Insulin Pump Club, 1986; loaned exec. United Way of Midlands, 1984. Mem. Am. Soc. Personnel and Guidance Assn., Adult and Continuing Edn. Assn. Nebr. (planning com. 1982-84), Am. Soc. for Tng. and Devel. Republican. Home: 310 S 51st St Omaha NE 68132 Office: 1416 Dodge St Omaha NE 68179

LIEVRE, HERVE, film director, writer; b. Roanne, France, Jan. 20, 1951. Grad., Ecole Supérieure de Commerce de Paris, 1974; lic. in econs. scis., Sorbonne, Paris, 1975; Dr. in Psychology, U. Paris Dauphine, 1978. Dir., writer, producer feature films Les Bancals, 1983, La Queue de la Comète, 1988; short films including Le Silence et la Nuit, 1978, F.P., 1979, La Mort en Herbe, 1980, La Ligne Blanche, 1985, Les 5 Premières Minutes, 1987, 8 Heures dans la Vie de B. Talar, 1987; documentaries including La Bruche et le Haricot, 1982, Chaudes Aigues, 1984, Perroquet et Enfants, 1985, Le Noir, le Brun et le Blanc, 1985, Imagerie Astronomique, 1986, Stress et Adaptation, 1987; scriptwriter feature films including Le Poulailler, A Coeur Fermé, Quelques Jours sur la Côte, Hilar Combur, Pèrahim, Le Nain Rouge, Raptus, Le Bonheur; writer plays Une Ile, Une Si Jolie Surprise; co-writer TV series Zoofolies, 1986-87. Address: 6 Rue Henri Regnault, 75014 Paris France

LIFSCHULTZ, PHILLIP, financial and tax consultant; b. Oak Park, Ill., Mar. 5, 1927; s. Abraham Albert and Frances Rhoda (Seigel) L.; m. Edith Louise Leavitt, June 27, 1948; children: Gregory, Bonnie, Jodie. BS in Acctg., U. Ill., 1949; JD, John Marshall Law Sch., 1956. Bar: Ill. 1956. Tax mgr. Arthur Andersen & Co., Chgo., 1957-63; v.p. taxes Montgomery Ward & Co., Chgo., 1963-78; fin. v.p., controller Henry Crown & Co., Chgo., 1978-81; prin. Phillip Lifschultz & Assocs., Chgo., 1981—; exec. dir. Dodi Orgn., 1987. Mem. adv. council Coll. Commerce and Bus. Adminstrn. U. Ill., Urbana-Champaign, 1977-78; chmn., Civic Fedn. Chgo., 1980-82; chmn. adv. bd. to Auditor Gen. of Ill., 1965-73; project dir. Exec. Service Corps of Chgo., Chgo. Bd. Edn. and State of Ill. projects, 1980-87. Served with U.S. Army, 1945-46. Mem. Ill. Bar Assn., Chgo. Bar Assn., Am. Inst. CPA's, Ill. CPA Soc., Am. Arbitration Assn. (comml. panel 1983—), Nat. Retail Merchants Assn. (chmn. tax com. 1975-78), Am. Retail Fedn. (chmn. taxation com. 1971). Clubs: Standard, City (bd. govs.). Home: 976 Oak Dr Glencoe IL 60022 Office: 450 E Devon Itasca IL 60143

LIFTON, ROBERT KENNETH, diversified companies executive; b. N.Y.C., Jan. 9, 1928; s. Benjamin and Anna (Pike) L.; m. Loretta J. Silver, Sept. 5, 1954; children: Elizabeth Gail, Karen Grace. BBA magna cum laude, CCNY, 1948; LLB, Yale U., 1951. Bar: N.Y. 1952. Assoc. Kaye, Scholer, Fierman, Hays & Handler, N.Y.C., 1955-56; asst. to pres. Glickman Corp., N.Y.C., 1956-57; pres. Robert K. Lifton, Inc., N.Y.C., 1957-61; chmn. bd. Terminal Tower Co., Inc., Cleve., 1959-63; pres. Transcontinental Investing Corp., N.Y.C., 1961-72, chmn. bd., 1969-72; ptnr. Venture Assocs., 1972—; pres. Preferred Health Care Ltd., 1983—; chmn. bd. dirs. Marcade Group, Inc., 1986—; bd. dirs. Four Winds, Inc.; bd. dirs., treas. Consol. Accessories Corp., 1980—, Caron's Connection, Inc., 1985—; mem. faculty Columbia U. Law Sch., 1973-78, Yale U. Law Sch., 1973-75; guest lectr. Practicing Law Inst., Yale Law Sch., Pace Inst., NYU; founder Nat. Exec. Conf., Washington, Inc. Author: Practical Real Estate: Legal Tax and Business Strategies, 1978; contbr. articles to profl. jours. and handbooks. Mem. McGovern econ. adv. com., 1972-73; chmn. parents com. Barnard Coll., 1976-78; mem. com. of the collection Whitney Mus., 1976-79; trustee Yale Sch. Fund, 1974-77, NYU Real Estate Inst., 1983— (chmn. oversight com. for Masters degree in real estate); chmn. bd. overseers NYU; chmn. bd. dirs. Fund for Religious Liberty, 1987-88; pres. Am. Jewish Congress, 1988—. Served to lt. (j.g.) USNR, Korea. Recipient Achievement award Sch. Bus. Alumni Soc. of CCNY, James Madison award Fund for Religious Liberty, 1987. Mem. Order of Coif. Home: 983 Park Ave New York NY 10028 Office: 275 Madison Ave 32d Floor New York NY 10016

LIGACHOV, EGOR KUZMICH, Soviet political official; b. 1920. Ed. Moscow Inst. Aviation, Communist Party Soviet Union Higher Party Sch. Engr., 1943-49; mem. Communist Party, 1944—; party and local govt. ofcl., Novosibirsk, 1949-55; vice chmn. Novosibirsk Regional Soviet of Working People's Deps., 1955-58; sec. Novosibirsk regional com. Communist Party Soviet Union, 1959-61, dep. dept. head for RSFSR, 1961-65; 1st sec. Tomsk regional com. Communist Party, 1965—; candidate mem. Central Com. Communist Party Soviet Union, 1966-76, mem., 1976—; mem. secretariat, 1983—, Politburo, 1985—; dep. to Supreme Soviet, 1966—; former chmn. commn. for youth affairs Soviet of the Union. Address: Communist Party of Soviet Union, Politburo, Staraya pl 4, Moscow USSR *

LIGETI, GYORGY SANDOR, Austrian composer; b. Dicsoszentmarton, Romania, May 28, 1923; s. Sandor Ligeti and Ilona Somogyi; m. Vera Spitz, 1957; 1 child. Student Budapest Acad. Music, 1945-49. Tchr., Budapest Acad. Music, 1950-56; guest prof. Stockholm Acad. Music, 1961-71; composer-in-residence Stanford U., Calif., 1972; with Electronic Studios, Cologne, Fed. Republic Germany, 1957-59; prof. composition, Hamburg Music Acad., 1973—. Composer: numerous orchestral and instrumental pieces, including: String Quartet #2, 1968, Melodien, 1971, Monument, Selbstportrait, 1976, Le Grand Macabre, 1977, Trio, 1982, Piano Concerto, 1988. Recipient Grawemeyer award U. Louisville, 1986. Address: Himmelhofgasse 34, A-1130 Vienna Austria Other: Movenstrasse 3, D-2000 Hamburg 60 Federal Republic of Germany

LIGHT, ALFRED ROBERT, lawyer, political scientist; b. Atlanta, Dec. 14, 1949; s. Alfred M. Jr. and Margaret Francis (Asbury) L.; m. Mollie Sue Hall, May 28, 1977; children—Joseph Robert, Gregory Andrew. Student Ga. Inst. Tech., 1967-69; B.A. with highest honors, Johns Hopkins U., 1971; Ph.D., U. N.C., 1976; J.D. cum laude, Harvard U., 1981. Bar: D.C. 1981, Va. 1982. Tax clk. IRS, 1967; lab. technician Custom Farm Services Soils Testing Lab., 1968; warehouse asst. State of Ga. Mines, Mining and Geology, 1970; clk.-typist systems mgmt. div., def. contract adminstrv. services region Def. Supply Agy., Atlanta, 1971, research and teaching asst. dept. polit. sci. U. N.C., Chapel Hill, 1971-74; research asst. Inst. Research in Social Sci., 1975-77; program analyst Office of Sec. Def., 1974; asst. prof. polit. sci., research scientist Ctr. Energy Research, Tex. Tech U., Lubbock, 1977-78; research asst. grad. sch. edn., Harvard U., 1978-79; assoc. Butler, Binion, Rice, Cook & Knapp, Houston, summer 1980, Bracewell & Patterson, Washington, summer 1980, Hunton & Williams, Richmond, Va., 1981—. Active First Bapt. Ch. Served to capt. USAR, 1971-85. Grantee NSF, Inst. Evaluation Research, U. Mass., Ctr. Energy Research, Tex. Tech U.; recipient William Anderson award Am. Polit. Sci. Assn.; Julius Turner award Johns Hopkins U. Mem. ABA, Am. Soc. Pub. Adminstrn., Am. Polit. Sci. Assn., Va. State Bar Assn., Richmond Bar Assn., So. Polit. Sci. Assn., Phi Beta Kappa, Phi Eta Sigma, Pi Sigma Alpha. Democrat. Baptist. Contbr. articles to profl. jours. Home: 11406 Yeomans Dr Richmond VA 23233 Office: Hunton & Williams 707 E Main St Richmond VA 23212

LIGHT, CHRISTOPHER UPJOHN, writer, computer musician; b. Kalamazoo, Jan. 4, 1937; s. Richard and Rachel Mary (Upjohn) L.; A.B., Carleton Coll., 1958; M.S., Columbia U., 1962; M.B.A., Western Mich. U., 1967; Ph.D., Washington U., 1971; m. Lilykate Victoria Wenner, June 22, 1963; children—Victoria Mary, Christopher Upjohn. Editor, pub. The Kalamazoo Mag., 1963-66; pres. Mich. Outdoor Pub. Co., Kalamazoo, 1965-68; chmn. fin. dept. Roosevelt U., Chgo., 1975-78; free-lance writer, computer musician, Chgo. Trustee Harold and Grace Upjohn Found., 1967-84. Recipient Mich. Welfare League ann. press award, 1967. Mem. Am. Econs. Assn., Fin. Mgmt. Assn., Soc. Profl. Journalists, Computer Music Assn., Nat. Acad. Rec. Arts and Scis. Contbr. articles to profl. and microcomputer jours. Record albums: Apple Compote, 1983; One-Man Band, 1985, Ultimate Music Box, 1988. Office: PO Box 185 Hickory Corners MI 49060

LIGHT, MARGARET COE, controller, accountant; b. Waterbury, Conn., July 16, 1947; d. John Allen and Margaret (Connick) Coe. Student U. Calif.-Davis, 1965-67; B.A., UCLA, 1969, M.B.A., 1975. C.P.A., Calif. Cert. mgmt. acct. Trust adminstr. Hong Kong and Shanghai Bank, Beverly Hills, Calif., 1969-71; jr. acct. George P. Madok, C.P.A., Los Angeles, 1972-75; sr. acct. Ernst & Whinney, Trenton, N.J., 1976-78; staff acct. Dart Industries, Inc., Los Angeles, 1978-82, audit mgr. Dart & Kraft, Inc., Atlanta, 1982-84; sr. fin. analyst Kraft, Inc., 1984-85, asst. controller fin. planning and analysis Food Service Group, 1985-87; mgr. bus. analysis Kraft-Rosenblum, 1987-88, controller, 1988—; speaker Inst. Internal Auditors, N.Y.C., 1983. Mem. Calif. State Soc. C.P.A.s, N.J. State Soc. C.P.A.s, Nat. Assn. Accts. (dir. N.J. chpt. 1977, Los Angeles chpt. 1980), Am. Inst. C.P.A.s, Ill. Racquetball Assn. (bd. dirs. 1985-87), Beta Gamma Sigma. Episcopalian. Office: Kraft-Rosenblum 2101 91st St North Bergen NJ 07047

LIGHT, MARILYN HAMILTON, organization and business executive; b. Troy, N.Y., July 6, 1930; d. George Howard and Harriet Euphemia (Pattullo) Hamilton; student Russell Sage Coll., 1950-51, Iona Coll., 1972-74; m. Edward W. Light, Feb. 1, 1955 (dec.); 1 child, Gregory Hamilton (dec.). Pvt. sec., dean women Russell Sage Coll., 1949-52; exec. sec., dist. mgr. Gulf Oil Corp., Albany, N.Y., 1952-55; exec. sec. regional exec. office Owens-Ill., Scarsdale, N.Y., 1965-67; with Hypoglycemia Found., 1967—, exec. sec., Scarsdale, 1967-69, exec. dir., 1969-71, pres., exec. dir. Adrenal Metabolic Research Soc. of found., Mt. Vernon, N.Y., 1971—, now Troy, N.Y.; pres. Marilyn Light, Inc., 1979—, Samar Constrn. Inc., 1980—, Profl. Remodelers Inc., 1981—, Oakline Lumber and Millwork, Inc., Watervliet, N.Y., 1983—; mem. faculty dept. continuing edn. Shenedehowa Schs., Clifton Park, N.Y., 1983—; cons. Paine Found., N.Y.C.; advisor N.Y. Inst. for Child Devel., N.Y.C. Vice chmn., bd. dirs. Troy Civic Devel. Assn. Mem. Mensa, Internat. Platform Assn., AAAS, N.Y. Acad. Scis., Hastings Center, Inst. Soc., Ethics and Life Scis., Nat. Assn. for Female Execs. Clubs: Troy (pres., bd. dirs. 1986—), Troy Women's. Author: Hypoglycemia & Me, 1973; Homeostasis Revisited, 1981; Beleaguered Giant, 1982. Editor: Homeostasis Quar., 1971—. Contbr. articles to profl. publs. Home and Office: 153 Pawling Ave Troy NY 12180

LIGHT, WILLIAM ALLAN, mathematics educator; b. Chester, Cheshire, Eng., Apr. 19, 1950; s. Louis John and Mary Goodbrand (Findlay) L.; m. Anita Mary Edwards, July 24, 1971. BSc, Sussex U., Eng., 1971; MA with distinction, Lancaster U., Eng., 1973, PhD, 1976. Cert. in postgrad. edn., Wales. Tutorial fellow U. Lancaster, 1974-76, lectr., 1976-82, 83-87; vis. prof. Tex. A & M U., College Station, Tex., 1982-83, U. Tex., Austin, 1987—; guest prof. U. Kuwait; bd. dirs. NATO Research Team, 1985—. Author: Approximation in Tensor Product Spaces, 1986; contbr. over 40 papers to profl. confs. and jours. Chmn. Lancaster U. Graduate Assn., 1972-73. Grantee Sci. Research Council, Lancaster. Mem. Am. Math. Soc., London Math. Soc. Office: U Lancaster Dept Math, Lancaster LA1 4YL, England

LIGHTMAN, H. ALLEN, marketing executive; b. Gloucester, Mass., Oct. 23, 1925; s. Abraham and Gertrude (Chait) L.; m. Irma Shorell, Feb. 19, 1954; children—Timothy, Harold, Jr., Stacey. Student, Cambridge U., Eng., 1946; B.B.A., U. Miami, Fla., 1949. Acct. exec. Grant Advt., Miami, Fla., 1948-50; advt. dir. Sears Roebuck & Co., Tampa, Fla., 1950-51; acct. exec. Robert Otto Internat., N.Y.C., 1952-53; account exec., field supr. Amos Parish & Co., N.Y.C., 1954-56; acct. exec. Dowd, Redfield & Johnstone, N.Y.C., 1957-59; chmn. bd. dirs. H. Allen Lightman Inc., N.Y.C., 1959—; dir. Irma Shorell Inc., N.Y.C., 1961—; pres. bd. dirs. Ind. Cosmetic Mfg. & Distbrs., N.Y.C., 1972—; v.p. Alfin Fragrances, Inc., 1985—. Author newspaper column: Seen & Heard, 1965-83; producer: Cable TV program Seen & Heard, 1978—. Served as sgt. U.S. Army, 1943-46, ETO. Decorated Purple Heart, Bronze Star (2); Recipient Pub. Relations Gold Key award, 1987. Fellow Winston Churchill Meml. Library, Harry S. Truman Meml. Library; mem. Nat. Fedn. Ind. Bus. (del. 1979), Alpha Delta Sigma (founder, 1st pres. 1947-48), DAV, Am. Legion (vice comdr. 1948-49). Club: The Jockey. Office: 75 East End Ave Suite 11E New York NY 10028

LIGNIER, ERNEST RICHARD, emeritus federal agency administrator, management executive; b. Brussels, July 19, 1927; s. Pierre Jerome and Elsie Edith (Stone) L.; m. Johanna Panthofer, Apr. 17, 1954. With Nat. Housing Soc., Brussels, 1946-87, sr. exec. mgr.; prof. state and city high schs., Huy, Belgium, 1961-62; mgmt. Belgian Bible Inst., Heverlee, 1978—; mem. various state orgns., Brussels. Chmn. Mas Evangelisation Actions, Belgium, 1960, 70, 75, Belgian Scripture Union, 1987—; mem. European Council Scripture Union, Germany, 1987—; elder Free Evang. Ch. Lodges: Order of Leopold (Knight), Order of Crown (Knight). Home: Rue de L'Infante 105, B 1410 Waterloo Belgium

LI GUIXIAN, government official; b. Gaixian, Liaoning, Peoples Republic of China, 1938. Student, U. Sci. and Tech., 1959; student in electron vacuum chemistry, Mendeleyev Chem. Tech. Inst., Moscow, 1960-65. Joined Chinese Communist Party, 1962; with research inst. Ministry of Pub. Security, 1965; engr. then dep. dir. Liaoning Electronics Bur.; vice gov. Liaoning Province, 1982-85; mem. Standing Com., Liaoning Province Communist Party, 1983—, leading sec., 1985; mem. 12th Cen. Com. Chinese Communist Party, 1985; state councillor State Council, 1988—; gov. People's Bank of China, 1988—. Address: Office State Council, Beijing Peoples Republic of China *

LIJNDEN, ALEXANDER FREDERIK (BARON VAN LIJNDEN), bank executive; b. Elburg, Gelderland, The Netherlands, June 12, 1944; s. Godert Alexander Frederick and Annie (van den Bosch) L.; m. Wilhelmina Euphemia M. Schuyt, Mar. 17, 1972; children: Charlotte, Steven. LLB, State U. Utrecht, The Netherlands, 1965. With H. Albert de Bary & Co. N.V., Amsterdam, The Netherlands, 1969-86, mng. dir., 1986—; chmn. Groot Lemmer b.v., The Netherlands, 1977—. Mem. governing bd. Stichting Ziekenhuis Amstelveen, The Netherlands, 1987—. Mem. Amsterdam Stock Exchange. Club: Indsl. (Amsterdam). Office: H Albert Bary & Co NV, Herengracht 448 456, Amsterdam The Netherlands

LIKHACHEV, DMITRIY SERGEYEVICH, Soviet Russian literature educator; b. St. Petersburg, USSR, Nov. 28, 1906; s. Sergey and Vera Likhacheva; m. Zinaida Makarova, 1936; two children. Ed. Leningrad State U. Assoc. Inst. Russian Lit., Pushkin House, USSR Acad. Scis., 1938—, head sect. early Russian lit., 1954—, academician, 1970—; lectr. Kazan State U., 1942-43; prof. Leningrad State U., 1946-53. Author: The Culture of the Russian People from the 10th to the 17th Centuries, 1961; Russian Culture of the Time of Andrei Rublev, 1962; Textology, 1962; The Poetics of Old Russian Literature, 1967; The Artistic Heritage of Old Russia, 1971; The Evolution of Russian Literature from the 10th to the 17th Centuries, 1973; A Great Heritage: The Classical Works of Old Russian Literature, 1975; The World of Laughter in Ancient Russia, 1975; The 'Laughing World' of Old Russia, 1976; Russische Literatur and Europaische Kaltur des 10-17 Jahrhunderts, 1977; The Slovo and the Culture of the Time, 1977; The Poetics of Ancient Russian Literature, 1978; numerous others. Recipient State Prize, 1952, 69. Mem. Bulgarian Acad. Scis. (hon.), Hungarian Acad. Scis., Serbian Acad. Scis. and Arts, Austrian Acad. Scis. (corr. fgn. mem.), Brit. Acad. Home: 34 Prospekt Shvernika Apt 16, 194021 Leningrad USSR Office: USSR Acad of Scis, 14 Leninsky Prospekt, Moscow V-71 USSR *

LILES, PAUL B., real estate and securities executive; b. Bronx, N.Y., Dec 26, 1941; s. Henry and Lillian L.; B.B.A., CUNY, 1970; m. Paula Margolies Feb. 23, 1964. Investment officer N.Y. Life Ins. Co., N.Y.C., 1970-80; pres Radnor Realty Services and Radnor Securities Corp., N.Y.C., 1980—; instr. Real Estate Inst., N.Y.U., Nat. Council Econ. Devel. Mem. Am. Arbitration Assn. (nat. real estate council), Nat. Assn. Securities Dealers, Am. Inst. Real Estate Appraisers, Am. Soc. Appraisers, Soc. Real Estate Appraisers, Nat. Assn. Rev. Appraisers, Bldg. Owners and Mgrs. Assn. Am., Real Estate Bd. N.Y., Soc. Real Property Adminstrs., Urban Land Inst., Real Estate Syndications and Securities Inst., Internat. Assn. Fin. Planning, Sigma Alpha. Office: Radnor Group 100 E 42d St New York NY 10017

LILJA, HANS AKE, airline executive; b. Stockholm, June 30, 1940; s. Hans and Maria (Johansson) L.; m. Gunilla (Gestblom) Lilja, Mar. 18, 1967; children: Karin, Erik. MS in Electronics, Royal Inst. Tech., Stockholm, 1966; BBA, U. Stockholm, 1974. Systems analyst EDP Scandinavian Airlines, Stockholm, 1966-68, EDP researcher, 1968-70, EPD systems planner, 1970-72, mgr. EDP systems planning, 1972-74, mgr. scheduling, 1974-78, dir. traffic planning, 1978-81, dir. cent. planning, 1981-86, dir. prodn. mgmt., 1986—. Served to capt. Swedish Army. Mem. Assn. European Airlines (exec. chmn. 1981—), KSSU Group (mgmt. mem. 1982—). Office: Scandinavian Airlines, Sto Mosk Frosundaviks alle 1, Solna, 16187 Stockholm Sweden

LILJEGREN, JAN RAGNAR GUSTAF, circulation auditing company executive; b. Gothenburg, Sweden, July 31, 1929; s. Ragnar Gustaf Oscar and May Gunvor Ann-Margret (Petré) L.; m. Harriet Thyra Wahlén, Apr. 25, 1965; children: Harriet Mikaela, Harriet Camilla, Carl Jonas; 1 child by previous marriage, Per Johan Gustaf. BS, Stockholm Sch. Econs., 1972; LLB, Stockholm U., 1974. Mgr. Nyman & Schultz Travel Bur., Stockholm, 1956-62; sales mgr. AB Nyman & Schultz, Stockholm, 1962-64; gen. sales mgr. Vingresor AB, Gothenburg, Sweden, 1964-66, dir., 1965; mng. dir., dir. AB Finnlines Ltd., Stockholm, 1967-75; mng. dir. Tidningsstatistik AB (Swedish Audit Bur. of Circulations), Solna, Sweden, 1976-80, dir., 1978-80, fin. exec., 1981—; fin. exec. TS Forvaltn AB, Solna, 1986—; mng. dir. Reklamstatistik AB (Advt. Stats. Ltd.), 1976-80, dir. 1976—; chmn. Lingmerths Travel Bur., Eksjo, 1981-85, SAM Bus Tour Operators AB, Stockholm, 1982-84, Flygresebyran AB, Stockholm, 1984-85, Air Travel Sweden AB, Stockholm, 1984-85, Alandia Cruise Line GmbH, Lubeck, Fed. Republic of Germany, 1986—; dir. Nordic Incoming Service AB, Kumla, Sweden, 1982-84, Bus. Travel Info. Ltd., Stockholm, 1985—; exec. Scan-Concepts Stockholm HB, 1986—. Author: Turistens Uppslagsbok, 1963. Mem. Stockholm Mktg. Assn. (dir. 1976-79), Stockholm Skalclub. Home: Mantalsvagen 8, S 17543 Jarfalla Sweden Office: Virebergsvagen 20, S 17121 Solna Sweden

LILLEY, GEOFFREY MICHAEL, aeronautical engineer, educator; b. Isleworth, Middlesex, Eng., Nov. 16, 1919; s. Emily L.; grad. Acton Tech. Coll., 1939, Battersea Poly., 1941, Northampton Poly., 1942; M.Sc. in Engring., Imperial Coll., 1944; m. Leslie Marion Wheeler, Dec. 18, 1948; children—Grete Dorothea, Elisabeth Meta, Michael Moreland. Trainee engr. various cos., Eng., 1936-40; draftsman, research engr., drawing office and wind tunnel dept. Vickers Armstrongs, Weybridge, 1940-46; lectr. Coll. Aeronautics, Cranfield, 1946-51, sr. lectr., 1951-56, dep. head aerodynamics, 1956-61, prof. exptl. fluid mechanics, 1961-63; prof. aeros. and astronautics U. Southampton (Eng.), 1963-83, prof. emeritus, 1983—; cons. Rolls Royce, 1967-84; mem. Noise Adv. Council, 1970-81; mem. Com. Aero. Research Council, 1957-81; vis. prof. Stanford U., 1977-78. Decorated Order Brit. Empire. Fellow Royal Aero. Soc. (Gold medal 1983), Inst. Math. and Applications, Royal Soc. Arts; mem. Inst. Mech. Engrs., AIAA (aeroacoustics award 1984). Mem. Ch. of England. Patentee in field. Home: Highbury Pine Walk, Chilworth, Southampton S01 7HQ England Office: Dept Aeronautics & Astronautics, Univ Southampton, Southampton S09 5NH England

LILLEY, JAMES RODERICK, ambassador, consultant; b. Tsingtao, China, Jan. 15, 1928; s. Frank Walder and Inez (Bush) L.; m. Sally Booth, May 1, 1954; children: Douglas, Michael, Jeffrey. BA, Yale U., 1951; MA, George Washington U., 1972. Fgn. affairs officer U.S. State Dept., various East Asian posts, 1958-75; dep. asst. sec. of state U.S. State Dept., Washington, 1985-86; nat. intelligence officer CIA, Washington, 1975-78; sr. East Asian specialist Nat. Security Council, Washington, 1981; dir. Am. Inst. in Taiwan, Taipei, 1982-84; ambassador U.S. Embassy, Seoul, Korea, 1986—; cons. Hunt/Sedco Oil Co., Dallas, 1979-81, United Techs., Hartford, Ct., 1979-80, Otis Elevator, Farmington, Ct., 1984-85, Westinghouse, Balt., 1984. Served to 1st lt. USAFR, 1951-54. Recipient Disting. Intelligence medal, CIA, 1979. Republican. Club: Met. (Washington). Home and Office: American Embassy San Francisco CA 96301

LILLIE, JOHN MITCHELL, retail executive; b. Chgo., Feb. 2, 1937; s. Walter Theodore and Mary Ann (Hatch) L.; m. Daryl Lee Harvey, Aug. 23, 1987; children: Alissa Ann, Theodore Perry. B.S., Stanford U., 1959, M.S., M.B.A., 1962-64. Various positions including dir. systems devel., also asst. to pres. Boise Cascade Corp., 1964-68; v.p., chief financial officer Arcata Nat. Corp., Menlo Park, Calif., 1968-70; exec. v.p., chief operating officer Arcata Nat. Corp., 1970-72; pres., chief exec. officer Leslie Salt Co., Newark, Calif., 1972-79; exec. v.p. Lucky Stores Inc., Dublin, Calif., 1979-81, pres., 1981-86, chmn., chief exec. officer, 1986—, also dir. Mem. Beta Theta Pi, Tau Beta Pi. Office: Lucky Stores Inc 6300 Clark Ave Dublin CA 94568

LILLIE, RICHARD HORACE, investor, real estate developer, retired surgeon; b. Milw., Feb. 3, 1918; s. Osville Richard and Sylvia Grace (Faber) L.; B.S., Haverford Coll., 1939; M.D., Harvard U., 1943; M.S. in Surgery, U. Mich., 1950; m. Jane Louise Zwicky, Sept. 24, 1949; children—Richard Horace, Diane Louise. Intern, U. Mich. Hosp., Ann Arbor, 1943-44, resident, 1946-50; chief of surgery, Milw. Hosp., 1968-80; practice medicine specializing in surgery, Milw., 1951-81; clin. prof. emeritus Med. Coll. Wis.; pres. Lillie 18-94 Corp.; trustee Northwestern Mut. Life Ins. Co.; dir. The Lynde and Harry Bradley Found.; investor, real estate developer, 1981—. Bd. dirs. emeritus Goodwill Industries. Served with M.C. AUS, 1944-46. Mem. Am. Bd. Surgery, A.C.S., Central Surg. Assn., AMA, Wis. Surg. Soc. Episcopalian. Clubs: Univ. of Milw., Milw. Yacht, Town. Contbr. articles to surg. jours. Home: 6500 N Lake Dr Milwaukee WI 53217

LILLIENSTEIN, MAXWELL JULIUS, lawyer; b. Bklyn., Dec. 18, 1927; s. Benjamin and Lillian (Camporeale) L.; m. Janet Newman, June 23, 1951; children: Steven, Robert, Carol. B. Social Scis. cum laude, CCNY, 1949; J.D., Columbia U., 1952. Bar: N.Y. 1952. Partner Friedberg, Blue & Rich, N.Y.C., 1958-63; ptnr. Rich, Lillienstein, Krinsly, Dorman & Hochhauser, N.Y.C., 1963—; mng. ptnr. Maxwell Assocs., 1982-87; gen. counsel Am. Booksellers Assn.; Pres. Maxwell Fund, 1967-72; dir. numerous corps.; investment adviser; lit. agt. 5 authors. Contbr. numerous articles to mags. and newspapers. Pres. Ardsley (N.Y.) Democratic Club, Westchester County, 1966-67, mem. exec. bd., 1966-70, Westchester County Dem. committeeman; trustee Village of Ardsley, 1968-71, village atty., 1971-79; Chmn. Ardsley (N.Y.) Library Com., 1967-68; co-founder Ardsley Pub. Library, 1970; mem. Ardsley Narcotics Guidance Council, 1971-78. Served with AC AUS, 1946-47. Home: 7 Rest Ave Ardsley NY 10502 Office: Rich Lillienstein et al 99 Park Ave New York NY 10016

LILLY, THOMAS GERALD, lawyer; b. Belzoni, Miss., Sept. 17, 1933; s. Sale Trice and Margaret Evelyn (Butt) L.; m. Constance Ray Holland, Dec. 29, 1962; children: Thomas Gerald Jr., William Holland, Carolyn Ray. BBA, Tulane U., 1955; LLB, U. Miss., 1960, JD, 1968. Bar: Miss. 1960. Asso. firm Stovall & Price, Corinth, Miss., 1960-62; asst. U.S. atty. No. Dist. Miss., Oxford, 1962-66; asso. firm Wise Carter Child & Caraway (and predecessor), Jackson, Miss., 1966-67; partner Wise Carter Child & Caraway (and predecessor), 1967—. Served with USNR, 1955-58; rear adm. Res. Decorated Legion of Merit, Navy Commendation medal. Mem. Fed. Bar Assn. (2d v.p. 1977-78, pres.-elect 1978-79, pres. 1979-80), Am. Bar Assn., Hinds County (Miss.) Bar Assn., Miss. State Bar, Miss. Bar Found., Res. Officers Assn., Naval Res. Assn., Naval Order of U.S., Navy Supply Corps Assn., Navy League, Mil. Order World Wars, Omicron Delta Kappa, Phi Delta Phi. Methodist. Club: Nat. Lawyers (Washington). Office: 600 Heritage Bldg PO Box 651 Jackson MS 39205

LIM, GOH TONG, company chairman, managing director; b. Ann Koai, Republic of China, Feb. 28, 1918; came to Malayasia, 1938; s. Sek Chuan and Ban (Goh) L.; m. Lee Kim Hua, Sept. 28, 1944; children: Siew Lay, Siew Lian, Siew Kim, Tee Keong, Kok Thay, Chee Wah. Carpenter Kuala Lumpur, Malayasia; contractor Kien Huat Berhad, Kuala Lumpur, Malayasia; businessman Kuala Lumpur, Malayasia; dir. Genting Berhad, Kuala Lumpur, Malayasia, 1968-79, chmn., mng. dir.; 1979—; bd. dirs. Indsl. & Comml. Bank Ltd., Singapore, 1979—, The Comml. Bank of Hong Kong Ltd., 1979—; mng. dir. Kien Huat Berhad, Malaysia, 1951—. Recipient Malaysian Entrepreneur award Asian Inst. Mgmt., 1985. Buddhist. Club: Royal Selangor Golf, Kuala Lumpur.

LIM, HENG HUAT, physician; b. Kuala Lumpur, Malaysia, Nov. 19, 1950; s. Kuan Hoo Lim and Kim Hing Ong. MB, BChir, U. Malaya, 1975, MPH, 1980; diploma in indsl. health, England, 1981; AM (hon.), Acad. of Med., Malaysia, 1985. cert. Malaysian Med. Council, Gen Med. Council of Britain. House physician and surgeon Ministry of Health Gen. Hosp., Ipoh, Malaysia, 1975-76; med. officer Ministry of Health Gen. Hosp., Kelang, Malaysia, 1976-77; med. health officer Ulu Langat Health Dist., Selangor, 1977-78; lectr. U. Malaya, Malaysia, 1978-80, lectr. in occupational med., 1981-84; research scholar U. Bristol, England, 1980-81; dir., cons., physician Mediviron Cons., Malaysia, 1984—; cons. Ministry of Sci., Tech., and Environ., Ministry of Labor; med. advisor. contbr. numerous articles to internat. jours. Mem. edn. com. Asian Assn. on Occupational Health. Recipient Franklin-Adams scholarship, U. Bristol, 1981. Fellow Australian Coll. Occupational Med.; mem. Faculty Community Med. (assoc.), U.K., Royal Coll. Physicians, Malaysian Med. Assn., British Med. Assn. Home: 29 Jalan 21/5, Sea Park, Petaling Jaya, Selangor 46300, Malaysia Office: Mediviron Cons, 257-2 Jalan Tun, Sambanthan, Kuala Lumpur 50470, Malaysia

LIM, MANUEL QUINTOS, JR., agribusiness executive; b. Manila, Dec. 19, 1930; s. Manuel Moran and Emilia Tempongko (Quintos) L.; m. Maria Socorro Tablante Gomez, Nov. 11, 1953; children—Sabina Emilia, Manuel Martin. B.A., Ateneo de Manila, 1951; M.B.A., 1966; B.S. in Mech. Engring., U. Philippines, 1953. Registered profl. engr. Power plant supt. Atlas Consol. Mgmt. and Devel., Toledo, Cebu, 1953-59; exec. v.p. Econ. Devel. Found., Makati, Philippines, 1964-67, TDR, Inc., Luzon, Mindanao, Philippines, 1967-72; pres. Blue Bar Coconut Philippines, Luzon, 1970-72; exec. v.p. Luzon Stevedoring Corp., Philippines, 1975-77; pres. JVA Mgmt. Corp., Luzon, Davao, Philippines, 1975—; dep. minister Ministry of Agr., Philippines, 1980-83; farming systems cons. U.S. AID-assisted Rainfed Resources Project at Ministry of Agriculture, 1984-86; assoc. exec. trustee in Asset Privatization Trust, 1987—. Mem. Mgmt. Assn. of Philippines, Philippine Assn. Mech. and Elec. Engrs., Quezon City C. of C. and Industry (dir., founder 1961-62), Ateneo Alumni Assn. (pres. Quezon City 1968). Club: Quezon City Sports. Lodge: Rotary. Office: JVA Mgmt Corp, State Cond Salcedo St, Legaspi Village, Makati, Metro Manila 3116, Philippines

LIM, OOI-KONG, hotel executive; b. Kuala Lumpur, Malaysia, Mar. 24, 1950; s. Lim Foo-Yong and Chu Yin-Mooi. Degree, Lewis Hotel/Motel Sch., N.Y.C., 1972. Exec. dir., gen. mgr. Hotel Merlin Inc., Hong Kong, 1975—; bd. dirs. Maple Ltd., Singapore, Banguan Sdn. Bhd., Kuala Lumpur, Lim Foo Yong Sendirian Berhad, Kuala Lumpur, Chulan Realty Sdn. Bhd., Kuala Lumpur; pres. Hotel Merlin Inc., San Francisco. Decorated knight His Royal Highness Sultan Kelantan, 1988. Recipient Seri Mahkota award H.R.H. Sultan of Kelantan, 1982, Jaksa Perdamai award His Royal Highness, Sultan of Kelantan, 1985. Mem. Malaysian Assn., Am. Hotel and Motel Assn. Club: Royal Selangor Golf. Home: 38 Cloudview Rd, Evelyn Towers, Apt G-26, Hong Kong Hong Kong Office: Hotel Merlin Ltd, 5/D, Trust Tower, 68, Johnston Rd, Hong Kong Hong Kong

LIM, PHILLIP KIAH THIOW, constrn. co. exec.; b. Singapore, Feb. 28, 1948; s. Moh Chuan and Moh Heok (Heng) L.; student bldg. sci. Coll. Estate Mgmt., London. With Frank & Vargeson, Chartered Quantity Surveyors, Brunei, East Malaysia, 1971-74; partner Sabah Quantity Surveyors (East Malaysia), 1974-79; exec. dir. Syarikat Setia Menanti Sdn. Bhd., Sabah, 1980—; mng. dir. Jaya Kerja Mgmt. Cons. Sdn. Bhd., 1980-87; v.p. S.S.M., Inc., Rosemead, Calif., 1987— . Fellow Inst. Dirs.; mem. Am. Inst. Mgmt. (exec. council), chartered Inst. Bldg., Am. Mgmt. Assn. Internat., Inc. Assn. Architects and Surveyors. Clubs: Sabah Golf and Country, Yacht, Flying, Recreation. Office: PO Box 1759 Rosemead CA 91770-0988

LIM, PIN, university executive; b. Penang, Malaysia, Jan. 12, 1936; m. Shirley Loo-Lim, Mar. 21, 1964; children—Jui, Jiun, Hsuen. M.B. B.Chir., U. Cambridge, 1963, M.A., 1964, M.D., 1970. Housemanship, Addenbrooke's Hosp., Cambridge, Eng., 1964; Commonwealth med. fellow dept. medicine Royal Infirmary, Edinburg, U.K., 1970; sr. lectr. in medicine U. Singapore, 1971-73, assoc. prof. medicine, 1974-77; prof. and head dept. medicine, Nat. Univ. Singapore, 1978-81, dep. vice-chancellor, 1979-81, vice-chancellor, 1981—; chmn. Applied Research Corp., Singapore, 1982; dir. Neptune Orient Lines, Singapore, 1981; overseas advisor Royal Coll. Physicians of London. Bd. dirs. Nat. Univ. Hosp., 1985; mem. Com. on Nat. Computerisation, 1985, Nat. Productivity Council, 1981. Contbr. writings to profl. jours. in field U.S., Brit., Australia. Queen's scholar, 1957; Eisenhower exchange fellow, 1982; recipient Pub. Adminstrn. Medal Republic of Singapore, 1984; named Officer l'Ordre des Palmes Academiques, 1988. Fellow Royal Coll. Physicians, Royal Australasian Coll. Physicians, ACP, Coll. Gen. Practitioners Singapore (hon.); mem. Inst. East Asian Philosophies (bd. govs.), Inst. Policy Studies (bd. govs.). Club: Singapore Island Country. Office: Nat U Singapore, Kent Ridge, Singapore 0511, Singapore

LIM, POH K., engineer; b. Tokai, Kedan, Malaysia, Sept. 17, 1950; arrived in Singapore, 1974; s. Y.C. Lim and C.G. Ong; m. L.T. Lim; children: Darrell, Joyce. B in Tech., IIT, Madras, 1974. Product engr. TI Singapore, 1974-77, mgr. engring., 1977-82, mgr. quality research assurance, 1982-83, mgr. ops., 1983—. Fellow Inst. Electronics Radio Engrs. (chmn. 1986—); mem. Inst. Engrs. Malaysia, Brit. Inst. Mgmt. Home: 731 Bedok Reservoir Rd, #03-5102, Singapore 1647, Singapore

LIM, SHUN PING, cardiologist; b. Singapore, Jan. 12, 1947; came to U.S., 1980; s. Tay Boh and Si Moi (Foo) L.; m. Christine Sock Kian Ng; 1 child, Corinne Xian-li. MBBS with honors, Monash U., Clayton, Australia, 1970, PhD, 1981; M in Medicine, Nat. U. Singapore, 1975; M, Royal Australasian Coll. Physicians, 1975. Research scholar Australian Nat. Health and Med. Research Council, Canberra, 1978-79; fellow in cardiology Michael Reese Hosp., Chgo., 1980-82; chief noninvasive cardiovascular imaging Cin. V.A.M.C., 1982-86; asst. prof. U. Cin., 1982-86; cardiologist Quain and Ramstad Clinic, Bismarck, N.D., 1986-88; clin. asst. prof. U. N.D., Bismarck, 1986—; pvt. practice cardiovascular diseases 1988—. Contbr. articles to profl. jours.; catheter tip polarographic lactic acid and lactate sensor. Fellow Royal Australian Coll. Physicians, Am. Coll. Angiology; mem. AAAS, Am. Coll. Physicians, Am. Fedn. Clin. Research, Am. Heart Assn. (grantee 1984-85), Ohio Med. Assn., N.Y. Acad. Scis. (life), Sixth Dist. Med. Soc., N.D. Med. Assn., Am. Soc. Echocardiography, Am. Inst. Ultrasound in Medicine, Am. Diabetes Assn. (councils on complications and exercise). Methodist. Office: 225 N 7th St Suite C Bismarck ND 58501

LIMA-FILHO, FRANCISCO PAULA, banker; b. Andradina, Brazil, Dec. 4, 1941; s. Francisco Paula and Carmen (Barbaro) Lima; m. Suely Daher Lima, Oct. 3, 1978; children—Bruna, Gustavo; children by previous marriage—Francisco, Aleksandra. Acct., Colegio Alianca, Sao Paulo, 1972; postgrad. in Bus. Adminstrn. and Econs., Internat. div. Sophia U., Japan, 1976. Exec. v.p. Oliveira Lima S/A., Capinas, Brazil, 1961-68; br. mgr. Banespa Bank (Banco do Estado de Sao Paulo S/A), Tokyo, 1973-76, Asuncion, Paraguay, 1977, Sao Paulo, 1978-80, directory advisor, 1984—; internat. dir. Bergamo Co. Ind., Guarulhos, Brazil, 1980-83; internat. cons. Inducon Brasil S/A., Sao Paulo, 1973; article writer Fin. and Money Mag., Sao Paulo, 1971—; research/lectr. Japan Found., 1976—, ICT-Labor Cultural Inst., 1984—. Contbr. articles to profl. jours. Mem. CRC Acctg. Council, Yomiuri Soc. Clubs: Delphi, Banespa E.C., Assn. Computing Machinery. Lodge: Rotary. Avocations: microcomputing; joinery; camping. Home: Rua Pamplona 391 Apto 24, 01405 Sao Paulo Brazil Office: Banco do Estado de Sao Paulo SA, Rua Dr Falcao 56-9th, 01007 Sao Paulo Brazil

LIMBACHER, JAMES LOUIS, film historian, educator; b. St. Marys, Ohio, Nov. 30, 1926; s. Fritz J. and Edith (Smith) L.; B.A., Bowling Green State U., 1949, M.A., 1954; M.S. in Edn., Ind. U., 1955; M.S. in L.S., Wayne State U., 1972. Audio-visual librarian Dearborn (Mich.) Dept. Libraries, 1955-83; instr. history and appreciation motion picture Univ. Center for Adult Edn., Detroit, 1965-72, Marygrove Coll., 1966-67, Wayne State U., 1973-82. Recipient Mich. Librarian of Yr. award, 1974. Mem. Am. Fedn. Film Socs. (nat. pres. 1962-65), ALA, Ednl. Film Library Assn. (nat. pres. 1966-70), Soc. Cinema Studies, Alpha Tau Omega, Theta Alpha Phi, Omicron Delta Kappa, Beta Phi Mu. Author: Four Aspects of the Film, 1969; A Reference Guide to Audiovisual Information, 1972; Film Music: From Violins to Video, 1973; The Song List, 1973; Sexuality in World Cinema, 1982. Editor: Using Films, 1967, Feature films, annually 1968—; Haven't I Seen You Somewhere Before, 1979, Keeping Score, 1981; monthly columnist Previews, 1963-77; weekly columnist to Dearborn Press, 1956-73; host TV series: Vista, 1955; Shadows on the Wall, 1974; The Screening Room, 1978; Talking Pictures, 1984-85; Movie Memories, 1987-88; Movietime U S.A., 1988—. Home: 21800 Morley Ave Dearborn MI 48124-2234

LIMHAISEN, MOHAMMED ABDULRAHAM, banker; b. Al Sulfi, Saudi Arabia, Dec. 29, 1949; s. Abdulrahman Abdul Mohsin; m. Modhi Nasir Abdulrahman Al Nowaiser, June 14, 1978; children: Sarah Mohammed, Abdulrahman Mohammed, Majed Abdulrahman. BS, Washington State U., 1973, BS in Chemistry, 1974; MBA, NW Mo. State U. Credit officer Chase Manhattan Bank, 1976-77; loan officer, project mgr. Saudi Indsl Devel. Fund, Saudi Arabia, 1977-788, controller gen., 1980; asst. gen mgr. United Saudi Comml. Bank, Riyadh, Saudi Arabia, 1983-86, corp. sec., 1983—, dep. gen. mgr., 1986—; chmn. bd. dirs. Riyadh Internat. Med. Co.; bd. dirs. Saudi So. Dairy Co., Riyadh, Saudi Shares Registration Co., Riyadh. Mem. Am. Mgmt. Assn., Arab Bankers Assn., Minninger Found. Club: Equestrian (Riyadh). Home: PO Box 56013, Riyadh 11476, Saudi Arabia Office: PO Box 3533, Riyadh 11481, Saudi Arabia

LIMOGES, SERGE, information service company executive; b. Amos, Que., Can., Jan. 13, 1946; s. Jacques and Yvette (Dorion) L.; m. Georgette Tanguay, May. 27, 1967; children: Caroline, Jacques, Geneviève. B in Comml. Scis., U. Montreal, 1969. Dir. Que. region Texaco Can. Inc., Montreal, 1969-79; sr. v.p., gen. mgr. Fed. des P. Desjardins Abitibi, Amos, 1979-84; chief exec. officer Visa Desjardins, Montreal, 1984-86; sr. v.p. mktg. and systems La Confédération des caisses populaires et d'économie Desjardins du Que., Montreal, 1986-87, sr. v.p. info. mgmt. and networks, 1987—. Mem. Can. Bank Card Assn. (exec. com., treas. 1987—, pres. 1988—), Can. Payments Assn., Corp. Profl. des Adminstrs. agrées du Que. Office: CCPEDQ, 1, Complexe Desjardins, 40th Fl, Montreal, PQ Canada H5B 1B2

LIMPERT, JOHN H., JR., not-for-profit executive; b. Bklyn., May 14, 1933; s. John H. and Sophia (Douropoulos) L.; A.B., Harvard U., 1955, postgrad., 1955-56; m. Michelle Van der Leur, Jan. 26, 1963; children—Alexandra Michelle, John Harold III. Public relations mgr. Frankfort Distillers Co. div. Seagram, N.Y.C., 1959-63; account exec. McCann-Erickson, Inc., N.Y.C., 1963-65, account dir., 1965-68; v.p. Ted Bates & Co., Inc., N.Y.C., 1968-71; mgr. lectrs. and speakers Keedick Lecture Bur., Inc., N.Y.C., 1971-73; dir. membership and devel. Mus. Modern Art, N.Y.C., 1973-83, dir. devel., 1983-86; v.p. for devel. and mktg. The N.Y. Bot. Garden, 1986-88; v.p. devel. Lincoln Ctr. for the Performing Arts Inc., 1988—; mem. adv. com. The Cultural Assistance Center, Inc.; trustee Children's Aid Soc., 1966-74, Festival Orch. and Chorus, 1967-69, Schola Cantorum, 1963-65; bd. dirs. Assoc. Harvard Alumni, 1967-69, 73-74. Served with U.S. Army, 1956-58. Cert. fund raising exec. Mem. Nat. Soc. Fund Raising Execs. (dir. chpt.). Home: 470 West End Ave New York NY 10024 Office: Lincoln Ctr for the Performing Arts Inc 140 W 65th St New York NY 10023

LIN, ALICE LEE LAN, physicist, researcher, educator; b. Shanghai, China, Oct. 28, 1937; came to U.S., 1960, naturalized, 1974; d. Yee and Tsing Tsing (Wang) L.; m. A. Marcus, Dec. 19, 1962 (div. Feb. 1972); 1 child, Peter A. Lin-Marcus. AB in Physics, U. Calif.-Berkeley, 1963; MA in Physics, George Washington U., 1974. Research asst. in radiation damage Cavendish Lab., Cambridge U., Eng., 1965-66; statis. asst. dept. math. U. Calif.-Berkeley, 1962-63; info. analysis specialist Nat. Acad. Scis., Washington, 1970-71; teaching fellow, research asst. George Washington U., Catholic U. Am., Washington, 1971-75; physicist NASA/Goddard Space Flight Ctr., Greenbelt, Md., 1975-80, Army Materials Tech. Lab., Watertown, Mass., 1980—. Contbr. articles to profl. jours. Mencius Ednl. Found. grantee, 1959-60. Mem. N.Y. Acad. Scis., AAAS, Am. Phys. Soc., Am. Ceramics Soc., Am. Acoustical Soc., Am. Men and Women of Sci., Optical Soc. Am. Democrat. Avocations: rare stamp and coin collecting, art collectibles, home computers, opera, ballet. Home: 28 Hallett Hill Rd Weston MA 02193 Office: Army Materials Tech Lab Mail Stop MRS Bldg 39 Watertown MA 02172

LIN, CHIEN-CHANG, chemist; b. Hsinchu, Taiwan, Republic of China, Feb. 28, 1937; s. Fu-lo and Pao (Chi) L.; m. Jing Jan, Aug. 19, 1967; children—Kelly M., Arthur M., Eunice M. B.S. in Chem. Enging., Tunghai U., Taiwan, Republic of China, 1959; Ph.D. in Chemistry, U. N.Mex., 1968. Research asst. Tsinghua U., Taiwan, Republic of China, 1961-63; postdoctoral research assoc. Washington U., St. Louis, 1967-70; tech. leader Gen. Electric Co., San Jose, Calif., 1971—; vis. prof. Tsinghua U., Taiwan, 1980. Mem. Am. Chem. Soc., Sigma Xi. Current work: Nuclear power reactor chemistry; nuclear and radiochemistry; radiochemical analysis; radiological technology; water treatment. Subspecialties: Nuclear chemistry; Physical chemistry. Home: 4683 Northdale Dr Fremont CA 94536

LIN, CHIN-CHU, physician, educator, researcher; b. Taichung, Republic of China, Oct. 24, 1935; came to U.S., 1969; s. Kung Yen and Nung (Chiang) L.; m. Sue S. Hsu; children: Jim, John, Juliet. BS, Nat. Taiwan U., 1956, MD, 1961. Diplomate Am. Bd. Ob-Gyn., Am. Bd. Maternal-Fetal Medicine (bd. examiner 1986—). Research fellow SUNY Downstate Med. Ctr., N.Y.C., 1969-71; resident in ob-gyn Columbia U., N.Y.C., 1972-74; fellow in maternal-fetal medicine Albert Einstein Med. Coll., 1974-76; lectr., staff Nat. Taiwan U. Hosp., Taipei, 1966-69, 1971-72; staff, asst. prof. U. Chgo., 1976-80, assoc. prof., 1980-87, prof., 1987—; maternal-child health adv. com. Dept. of Health, Chgo., 1985—; frequent keynote speaker numerous internat. confs. Editor-in-Chief: Taiwan Tribune Medical Issues, 1986—, author: Intrauterine Growth Retardation, 1984; contbr. over 60 articles to profl. jours., chpts. to books; reviewer for Jour. Obstetrics and Gynecology, Jour. Perinatal Medicine. Chmn. Taiwanese United Fund, 1984-85. Disting. Scholar Lectr. award Formosa Med. Assn., 1981, Keynote Speaker award Asia-Oceania Congress Perinatology, 1986. Mem. Am. Coll. Ob-Gyn (jour. reviewer 1982—, Purdue Frederick award 1978), Assn. Profs. Ob-Gyn, N.Am. Taiwanese Profs. Assn., N.Am. Taiwanese Med. Assn. (chmn. ednl. com. 1984-86), Cen. Assn. Ob-Gyn., Soc. Perinatal Obstetricians, Internat. Soc. Study of Hypertension in Pregnancy. Home: 18 S Stough Hinsdale IL 60521 Office: U Chgo Dept Ob-Gyn 5841 S Maryland Ave Chicago IL 60637

LIN, CHUAN-YU, cardiologist; b. Anhsi Hsien, Fukien, Republic of China, Oct. 11, 1934; parents: Chih-Jen and Hsiu-Hua (Fu) L.; m. Hsiu-Mei Su, Nov. 24, 1962; children: Lin Chung-Kuang, Lin Pei-Yi, Lin Yi-Yi, Lin Chun-Yu. BS, Nat. Def. Med. Ctr., Taipei, Republic of China, 1961. Resident in internal medicine 1st Army Gen. Hosp., Taipei, 1962-66; chief resident Triservice Gen. Hosp., Taipei, 1966-67; cardio-vascular specialist Govt. Employees Ctr. Clinic, Taipei, 1967—; vis. doctor Triservice Gen. Hosp., Taipei, 1967-71; cardiologist Taipei Mcpl. Jen-Ai Hosp., 1971-74, Taipei Country Hosp., 1971-79, Chung-Hwa Hosp., Taipei, 1979-85; cardiovascular sect. chief Chung-Sun Hosp., Taipei, 1985—; cons. internal medicine Triservice Hosp., 1986—. Home and Office: 125 Sect I, Kee-lung Rd, Taipei Republic of China

LIN, CHUN CHIA, research physicist, educator; b. Canton, China, Mar. 7, 1930; s. Yue Hang Lam and Kin Ng. B.S., U. Calif.-Berkeley, 1951; M.A., 1952; Ph.D., Harvard U., 1955. Asst. prof. physics U. Okla., Norman, 1955-59; assoc. prof. physics, 1959-63, prof. physics, 1963-68, U. Wis., Madison, 1968—; cons., univ. retainee Tex. Instruments Inc., 1960-68; cons. Sandia Labs., 1976-81; sec. Gaseous Electronics Conf., 1972-73. Contbr.: sci. research articles to publs. including Jour. Chemical Physics, Phys. Rev. Sloan Found. fellow, 1962-66; research grantee NSF and Air Force Office Sci. Research. Fellow Am. Phys. Soc. (sec. div. electron and atomic physics 1974-77). Subspecialties: Atomic and molecular physics; Condensed matter physics. Current work: Atomic and molecular collision processes; radiation of atoms and molecules excited by electron impact and laser irradiation; electronic energy band theory of crystalline solids, impurity atoms in solids, amorphous solids. Home: 1652 Monroe St Apt C Madison WI 53711 Office: U Wis Dept Physics Madison WI 53706

LIN, CHUNG-SHENG, internist, cardiologist, educator; b. Taichung, Republic China, Apr. 20, 1947; s. Hsi-Jin and Tuan-Yueh (Shih) L.; m. Su-Mei Hsu, July 19, 1975; children: Chin-Jong, Chih-Ming, Chih-Wen. MD, Chung-Shan Med. and Dental Coll., Taichung, 1971. Intern 803d Army Gen. Hosp., Taichung, 1970-71; registrar Chung-Shan Med. and Dental Coll. Hosp., Taichung, 1972-76, attending physician, 1976-80, dir. ICU, 1980-81, chief dept. internal medicine, 1982—, chief cardiology div., 1982—, assoc. prof. medicine, 1983—; cons. cardiologist Yu-Ming Hosp., Tsau-Tung, Republic China, 1984—. Contbr. articles to med. jours. Recipient disting. award Taiwan Med. Promoted Found., 1984. Fellow Republic China Soc. Cardiology; mem. Formosan Med. Assn., Soc. Ultrasound in Medicine Republic China. Home: 6th Floor 85-19 Ning-Han St, Taichung 40711, Republic of China Office: Chung Shan Med and Dental Coll, 23 sec 1 Taichung Kang Rd, Taichung 40334, Republic of China

LIN, EDWARD DANIEL, anesthesiologist; b. Apr. 19, 1953; s. Henry and Ruth Lin. BS magna cum laude, SUNY, Fredonia, 1973; DO, U. Osteopathic Medicine and Health Scis., Des Moines, 1980. Intern. in gen. medicine Millard Fillmore Hosp., Buffalo, 1980-81, emergency physician, 1981-82; resident in anesthesiology Yale-New Haven Med. Ctr., 1982-84; attending anesthesiologist Doctors Hosp., Massillon, Ohio, 1984—; dep. coroner Stark County, Ohio, 1984—; asst. prof. anesthesiology Ohio U. Coll. Osteopathic Medicine, Athens, 1984—; guest lectr. on spinal opiates and pain therapy nat. profl. meetings. Inventor Urethral Catheter Preventing Ascending Urinary Tract Infections,1980; patentee in field. Fellow (Woodburn) Roswell Park Meml. Inst., Buffalo, N.Y., 1974-76. Mem. Am. Soc. Anesthesiologists, Internat. Anesthesia Research Soc., Ohio Soc. Anesthesiologists, Am. Osteopathic Assn., Ohio State Med. Assn., Ohio Ostepathic Assn., Stark County Med. Soc. Home: 556 Roxbury Ave NW Massillon OH 44646 Office: Doctors Hosp 400 Austin Ave NW Massillon OH 44646

LIN, JAMES CHIH-I, electrical and biomedical engineer, educator; b. Seoul, Korea, Dec. 29, 1942; m. Mei Fei, Mar. 21, 1970; children—Janet, Theodore, Erik. B.S., U. Wash., 1966, M.S., 1968, Ph.D., 1971. Asst. prof. U. Wash., Seattle, 1971-74; prof. Wayne State U., Detroit, 1974-80; prof. U. Ill.-Chgo., 1980—, head dept. bioengring., 1980—, dir. robotics and automation lab., 1982—; vis. prof. in Beijing, Rome, Shan Dong, Taiwan Univs.; cons. Battelle Meml. Inst., Columbus, Ohio, 1973-75, SRI Internat., Palo Alto, Calif., 1978-79, Arthur D. Little, Inc., Cambridge, Mass., 1980-83, Ga. Tech. Research Inst., Atlanta, 1984-86, Walter Reed Army Inst. Research, 1973, 87, 88, Naval Aerospace Med. Research Labs., Pensacola, 1982-83, U.S. Corp., San Francisco, 1985-87; program chmn. Frontiers of Engring. and Computing Conf., Chgo., 1985; chmn., convener URSI Joint Symposium Electromagnetic Wakes in Biol. Systems, Tel-Aviv, 1987. Author: Microwave Auditory Effects and Applications, 1978, Biological Effects and Health Implications of Radiofrequency Radiation, 1987; also numerous papers. Panelist NSF Presdl. Young Investigator award com., Washington, 1984, mem. NIH diagnostic radiology, 1981-85, chmn. spl. study sect., 1986-88. Recipient IEEE Transaction Best Paper award, 1975; Nat. Research Services award, 1982. Fellow IEEE (bd. dirs., assoc. and guest editor transactions on biomed. engring; guest editor transactions on microwave theory and techniques); mem. Biomed. Engring. Soc. (sr.), Robotics Internat., Am. Soc. Engring. Edn., Nat. Soc. Profl. Engrs., Bioelectromagnetics Soc. (charter), Com. on Man and Radiation (vice chmn.), Sigma Xi, Phi Tau Phi (v.p.), Tau Beta Pi. Office: U Ill Chgo Dept Bioengring Box 4348 Chicago IL 60680

LIN, JAMES SHIH CHIEH, business executive; b. Ping Tung, Taiwan, Republic of China, July 2, 1938; s. Bi Fong Lin and Hai Tsu Yuen; m. Bi Chai Lin, Feb. 5, 1966; children: Men Li, I Lin, Mei Chun. BA, Chen Kung U., Tainan, Republic of China, 1961. Tchr. English Tainan Home Econs. Coll., 1963-68; pres. Victors Enterprise Co., Ltd., Tainan, 1969—. Home and Office: 243 Nan Men Rd, Tainan Republic of China

LIN, JEN-KUN, biochemistry educator; b. Chia-Yi, Taiwan, Republic of China, Dec. 4, 1935; parents: You-Chuen and Sha (Ho) Chen; m. Shoei-Yn Lin-Shiau, Nov. 2, 1962; children: Jung-Shin, Cheng-Yen, Tsu-Wei. BS in Pharmacy, Nat. Taiwan U., 1958, MS in Biochemistry, 1961; PhD in Oncology, U. Wis., Madison, 1968. Mem. faculty Nat. Taiwan U., Taipei, Republic of China, 1962—; prof. biochemistry Nat. Taiwan U., 1973—; research assoc. U. Wis.-Madison, 1968-69, vis. prof., Forgaty Internat. fellow, 1975-76; vis. scientist Lab. Molecular Oncology, Nat. Cancer Inst.-NIH, Frederick, Md., 1984; dir. students Coll. Medicine, Nat. Taiwan U., 1979-83. Editor Sci. Monthly, 1970—, proceedings Nat. Sci. Council, Republic of China, 1980—; co-editor Molecular Biology Neoplasia, 1985. Recipient Acad. award Chung-Shan Sci. and Art Found., Taipei, 1982, outstanding Professorship award Ministry Edn., Taipei, 1983-85, Outstanding Investigator award Nat. Sci. Council, Taipei, 1985-87, 88—, Acad. award Ministry Edn. Medicine, 1987. Mem. Formosan Med. Assn. (outstanding thesis award 1963, 72), Chinese Biomed. Soc., Chinese Oncol. Soc., Am. Assn. Cancer Research, Sigma Xi. Buddhist. Club: Taita Tennis (Taipei). Office: Nat Taiwan U, Inst Biochemistry Coll Medicine, Number 1 Se-t 1, Jen ai Rd, Taipei 100, Republic of China

LIN, JU-CHUI (RAY), polymer scientist, patent agent, consultant; b. Taoyuan, Republic of China, Apr. 25, 1947; came to U.S., 1974; s. Pai-Liang and Mai (Wang) L.; m. Jing-Fang Wang, Dec. 24, 1975; children: Amy Monica, Tom Albert, Audrey Alice. B.S. in Chemistry, Nat. Taiwan Normal U., 1972; M.S. in Chemistry, Southwest Tex. State U., 1977; Ph.D. in Macromolecular Sci., Case Western Res. U., 1985. Tchr. Taipei Gimmei Jr. High Sch., Taiwan, 1971-73; lab. instr. Nat. Central U., Chungli, Taiwan, 1973-74; cons. Polytronics Inc., Cleve., 1983-85; chemist Sohio Research Ctr., Warrensville Heights, Ohio, 1983, DPJ Research Ctr., SCM Corp., Strongsville, Ohio, 1984-86; sr. scientist Spectrum Control Research Ctr., Erie, Pa., 1986—. Author youth sci. books Youth Ency., 1970; also papers in field. Patentee in field of conductive polymers, electrical active polymers, resins and coatings, elastomers, encapsulations for electronics, potting, ceramics. Mem. Am. Chem. Soc., Soc. Plastics Engring., Engring. Am. Phys. Soc., Am. Ceramics Soc. Avocation: ceramic works. Office: Spectrum Control Inc 2185 W 8th St Erie PA 16505

LIN, OTTO CHUI CHAU, materials scientist, educator; b. Swatow, China, Aug. 8, 1938; s. Wei-min and Yen-Ching (Chang) L.; m. Ada Ma, Sept. 7, 1963; children—Ann, Gene, Dean. B.S., Nat. Taiwan U., 1960; M.A., Columbia U., 1963, Ph.D., 1967. Research chemist E.I. duPont, Wilmington, 1967-69, sr. research chemist, 1969-71, research assoc., supr., 1971-78, 79-83; dean engring., prof. Nat. Tsing-Hua U., Hsinchu, Taiwan, 1978-79; dir. materials research lab. Indsl. Tech. Research Inst., Hsinchu, Taiwan, 1983—, v.p., 1985—; dir. materials sci. ctr. Nat. Tsing Hua U., 1984—. Patentee in polymers; contbr. numerous articles to profl. jours. Mem. Am. Chem. Soc., Am. Inst. Physics, Chinese Soc. Materials Sci (bd. dirs. 1984—, pres. 1986—). Roman Catholic.

LIN, SHAOW BURN, polymer scientist; b. Taipei, Republic of China, Mar. 20, 1953; came to U.S. 1979, naturalized, 1984; s. Chen-Ming and Yu-Hsein (Yeh-Wang) L.; m. Feng Yin, Jan. 14, 1979; children—Karen Y., Alan G. BS, Cheng Kung U., Republic of China, 1975, MS, 1979; PhD, Case Western Res. U., 1982. Teaching asst. Cheng Kung U., 1977-79; research asst. Case Western Res. U., Cleve., 1979-82; research assoc. U. Wis., Madison, 1982-83; staff researcher Syntex Ophthalmics, Inc., Phoenix, 1983-85; research assoc. PPG Industries, Inc., Pitts., 1985—. Patentee polymer hydrogels and transparent functional coatings. Rotary Found. fellow, 1979. Mem. Am. Chem. Soc., Am. Phys. Soc., Soc. Plastics Engrs. Current work: Synthesis and modification of polymer hydrogels, siloxane copolymers and urethane photoresists, structure-property-morphology of polyurethane copolymers and blends; subspecialties: Polymers (materials science), Polymer chemistry.

LIN, TUNG YEN, civil engineer, educator; b. Foochow, China, Nov. 14, 1911; came to U.S., 1946, naturalized, 1951; s. Ting Chang and Feng Yi (Kuo) L.; m. Margaret Kao, July 20, 1941; children: Paul, Verna. BSCE, Chiaotung U., Tangshan, Republic of China, 1931; MS, U. Calif., Berkeley, 1933; LLD, Chinese U. Hong Kong, 1972, Golden Gate U., San Francisco, 1982, Tongji U., Shanghai, 1987, Chiaotung U., Taiwan, 1987. Chief bridge engr., chief design engr. Chinese Govt. Rys., 1933-46; asst., then asso. prof. U. Calif., 1946-55, prof., 1955-76, chmn. div. structural engring., 1960-63, dir. structural lab., 1960-63; chmn. bd. T.Y. Lin Internat., 1953—, hon. chmn. bd., 1987—; pres. Inter-Continental Peace Bridge, Inc., 1968—; cons. to State of Calif., Def. Dept., also to industry; chmn. World Conf. Prestressed Concrete, 1957, Western Conf. Prestressed Concrete Bldgs., 1960. Author: Design of Prestressed Concrete Structures, 1955, rev. edit., 1963, 3d edit. (with N.H. Burns), 1981, (with B. Bresler, Jack Scalzi) Design of Steel Structures, rev. edit, 1968, (with S.D. Statesbury) Structural Concepts and Systems, 1981; contbr. articles to profl. jours. Recipient Berkeley citation award, 1976, NRC Quarter Century award, 1977, AIA Honor award, 1984, Pres.'s Nat. Medal of Sci., 1986, Merit award Am. Cons. Engrs. Council, 1987; named Outstanding Alumni of Yr., U. Calif. Engring. Alumni Assn., 1984, Hon. Prof., Chiaotung U., 1982, Hon. Prof., Tongji U., 1984, Hon. Prof., Shanghai Chiaotung U., 1985; U. Calif. at Berkeley fellow. Mem. ASCE (hon., life, Wellington award, Howard medal), Nat. Acad. Engring., Academia Sinica, Internat. Fedn. Prestressing (Freyssinet medal), Am. Concrete Inst. (hon.), Prestressed Concrete Inst. (medal of honor). Home: 8701 Don Carol Dr El Cerrito CA 94530 Office: 315 Bay St San Francisco CA 94133

LIN, WILLIAM WEN-RONG, economist; b. Pintung, Taiwan, Sept. 5, 1942; came to U.S., 1967; naturalized, 1976; s. Ming-Lay and Shyr-Mey (Chow) L.; m. Kimy Kuei-mei Juan, Oct. 5, 1964; children—Susan, George, Roger. B.S., Chung-Hsing U., Taichung, Taiwan, 1964; M.S., U. Calif.-Davis, 1969, Ph.D., 1971. Economist Oak Ridge Nat. Labs., Tenn., 1974-76; agrl. economist U.S. Dept. Agriculture, Washington, 1976-80, sect. head Econ. Research Service, 1982—; economist U.S. Dept. Energy, Washington, 1980-81, U.S. Dept. Interior, 1981-82; cons. in field. Contbr. articles to profl. jours. Mem. Taiwanese Am. Assn., 1976-86; legis. affairs com. Saratoga Community Assn., Springfield, Va., 1983; mem. Asian Am. Fedn., 1984. U. Calif. fellow, 1967-68, Disting. scholar, 1969-71; Merit award U.S. Dept. Agr., 1979, 85. Mem. Am. Agrl. Econ. Assn. (productivity com. 1978-80, lectr. 1977), Am. Econs. Assn., Western Agrl. Econ. Assn. (lectr. 1979), Southern Agrl. Econ. Assn. Home: 7771 Tangier Dr Springfield VA 22153 Office: USDA Econ Research Service 1301 New York Ave NW Room 1034 Washington DC 20005

LIN, WUU-LONG, economist; b. Taiwan, Apr. 28, 1939; came to U.S., 1966, naturalized, 1977; s. Yeu-Chung and Lu-Jing (Lu) L.; B.S., Nat. Taiwan U., 1965; M.S. (Ford Found. fellow 1966), Kans. State U., 1968; Ph.D. (Univ. fellow 1968-72), Stanford U., 1972; m. Ai-Ai Anna Kuo, Dec. 26, 1970; children—Joel, Pansy. Tchr., Taipei Chuang-San Sch., 1958-61; research asso. Kans. State U., 1968, Harvard U., 1970; vis. economist Chinese-Am. Joint Commn. Rural Reconstrn., Taipei, 1971; research economist, vis. scholar Stanford U., 1972-75; econometrician FAO, Rome, 1974-77; economist UN, N.Y.C., 1978—; lectr. econ. info. systems and population and devel. UN Mission to China, 1983, 85, macroecons. at Peking U., 1987; cons. in field. Author: Planning and Control of Public Current Expenditure: Lessons of Country Experience, 1987. Served as officer Chinese Army, 1965. Recipient 1st pl. stats. award Republic of China, 1962; grantee NSF, 1971-72. Mem. Am. Econ. Assn., Am. Agrl. Econs. Assn., Stanford U. Alumni Assn. (life), Phi Kappa Phi. Democrat. Author papers, reports in global devel. and country planning. Home: 61 Old Knollwood Rd White Plains NY 10607 Office: UN Devel and Adminstrn div New York NY 10017

LINARDOS, NICOLAS GERASSIMOS, business executive; b. Athens, Greece, Sept. 14, 1960; s. Gerassimos and Magda (Matsakas) L. Diploma, Ecole Européenne des Affaires, Paris, 1983. Mng. dir. N. Linardos S.A. (Auto Parts Distribrs.), Athens, 1983—. Mem. Hellenic Mgmt. Assn., Young Businessmen's Assn. Office: 46 Constantinoupoleos Ave, 118-54 Athens Greece

LINCHITZ, RICHARD MICHAEL, physician, psychiatrist; b. Bklyn., Mar. 29, 1947; B.A. cum laude in Psychology, Cornell U., 1967, M.D., 1973; student L.I. Univ., 1967-68, U. Lausanne Med. Sch., 1968-71; m. Rita A. Colao, Sept. 22, 1973; children—Elise Ann, Michael Benjamin, Jonathan Adam. Intern, Moffit Hosp., San Francisco, 1973-74; resident in psychiatry Langley Porter Neuropsychiat. Inst., San Francisco, 1974-77; practice medicine specializing in psychiatry and treatment of chronic pain conditions, Roslyn, N.Y., 1977—; med. dir. Roslyn Mental Health Ctr. (N.Y.), 1978—, Pain Alleviation Center, Roslyn, 1978—. Recipient letter of commendation White House, 1977; Nathan Seligman award Cornell U. Med. Coll., 1973; Nat. Psychiat. Endowment Fund award Langley Porter Neuropsychiat. Inst., 1977; Langley Porter Youth Service award, 1977. Mem. Am. Psychiat. Assn., Acad. Pain Research, Am. Pain Soc., Nassau Psychiat. Soc., Am. Acad. of Pain Medicine, Alpha Omega Alpha. Author: Life Without Pain, 1987. Office: 55 Bryant Ave Roslyn NY 11576

LINCOLN, FRANKLIN BENJAMIN, JR., lawyer; b. Bklyn., Jan. 18, 1908; s. Franklin Benjamin and Anna (Ellensberg) L.; m. Helen C. Benz, Oct. 8, 1938; children: Carol Concors, Franklin Benjamin III. A.B., Colgate U., 1931, LL.D. (hon.), 1960; J.D., Columbia, 1934. Bar: N.Y. bar 1934, D.C. bar 1960, U.S. Supreme Ct. bar 1944. With Sullivan & Cromwell, N.Y.C., 1934-41, Lundgren, Lincoln & McDaniel, N.Y.C., 1941-59; prin. analyst Hdqrs. Army Service Forces, Washington, 1943; civilian counsel to fiscal dir. Dept. Navy, 1944-45; asst. sec. def. 1959-61; pres. Monroe Internat., Inc., 1961-64; v.p. Litton Industries, Inc., 1961-64; partner Seward & Kissel, 1964-66; sr. partner Mudge, Rose, Guthrie & Alexander, from 1966, now of counsel; v.p., dir. Cypress Communications Corp., 1965-69; dir., chmn. exec. com. Shelter Resources Corp., 1968-70; dir. Pacific Tin Consol. Corp., 1969—, Itel Corp., 1970-83, Barnes Engring. Co., 1958-59, 61-62; Advisory bd. Nat. Council for Gifted; Pres. Nixon's rep. in 1968-69 Transition; mem. Pres.' Fgn. Intelligence Advisory Bd., 1969-73. Author: Presidential Transition, 1968-1969. Trustee Colgate U., 1967-75, chmn. bd., 1975-79; bd. dirs. World Bd. of Trade, 1973-75; bd. dirs., chmn. Fed. Home Loan Bank Bd. N.Y., 1972-78. Served to lt. USNR, 1943-44. Recipient Disting. Pub. Service medal Def. Dept., 1961; Colgate U. Alumni award for disting. service, 1977. Mem. Phi Beta Kappa, Delta Upsilon, Delta Sigma Rho, Phi Delta Phi. Republican. Christian Scientist. Home: 22 Roland Dr Short Hills NJ 07078 Office: 180 Maiden Ln New York NY 10038

LINCOLN, KENDALL T., engineering company financial executive; b. Adrian, Mo., Aug. 23, 1932; s. Howard Thomas and Frances Eddith (Timmons) L.; B.S. in Bus. Adminstrn., U. Mo., 1954; m. Patricia Lee Gratz, Apr. 6, 1957 (dec.); 1 dau., Debra Lee. Auditor U.S. Army Audit Agy., Denver, 1954-55; accountant firm Peat, Marwick, Mitchell & Co., Kansas City, Mo., 1957-63; controller firm Howard, Needles, Tammen & Bergendoff, Kansas City, Mo., until 1974, finance dir., 1974-76, assoc., dir. finance, 1976—; cons. Engr., Kansas City, 1963—. Served with AUS, 1955-57. C.P.A., Mo., Kans. Mem. Am. Inst. C.P.A.s, Mo. Soc. C.P.A.s, Nat. Assn. Accountants, Financial Execs. Inst., Profl. Services Mgmt. Assn., Beta Gamma Sigma. Home: 6324 Dearborn Dr Mission KS 66202 Office: 9200 Ward Pkwy Kansas City MO 64114

LIND, BRUCE ELVIN, land developer; b. Twin Falls, Idaho, June 25, 1941; s. Wyland Herman and Helen Eileen (Bailey) L.; B.S., Utah State U., 1967, B.S. in Bus. Edn., 1968, M.S. in Mktg., 1969; m. Patricia Zohner; children—Billie Jean, Bonita, Ben, Katy, Tyler, Tara, Corbin, Jess. Product mgr., wholesaler Boise Cascade Corp. (Idaho), 1968-70; asst. to nat. sales mgr. Trus-Joist Corp., Boise, 1970-71; founder, pres. A.M.R. Corp., Idaho Falls, Idaho, 1971—, chmn. bd., 1972—. Mem. Delta Phi Kappa. Club: Lions. Office: A M R Corp 244 Broadway Idaho Falls ID 83402

LIND, JAMES PETER, computer science consultant; b. Chgo., June 8, 1932; s. James and Mabel Antoinette (Nelson) L.; B.A. (Nat. Def. Transp. scholar), U. Minn., 1954, M.A.P.A., 1965. Mgmt. analyst Bur. Employment Security, Dept. Labor, Washington, 1965-66; dean of men U. Bridgeport (Conn.), 1966-68; sr. budget analyst Montgomery County (Md.), Rockville, 1968-72; dir. planning Office of Gov. S.C., Columbia, 1972-73; sr. cons. Northrop Services, Arlington, Va., 1973-75; v.p.-fin. Ability Devel. Services, Washington, 1975-76, dir., 1975—; sr. program analyst Social Rehab. Services, HEW, Washington, 1976-77; dept. mgr. Computer Scis. Corp., Falls Church, Va., 1977—; bd. dirs. Mid-Atlantic Capital Corp., Human Achievement and Outreach Inst. Contbr. articles to adminstrn. jours. Ward officer Democratic Farmer Labor Party, Mpls., 1959-65; bd. dirs. Human Outreach and Achievement Inst. Served to 1st lt. U.S. Army, 1955-58. Mem. Am. Soc. Pub. Adminstrs., Internat. City Mgmt. Assn., Internat. Platform Assn., World Future Soc., Am. Inst. Planners, Friendly Applications (bd. dirs.), IFGE (bd. dirs.). Democrat. Presbyterian. Home: Apt 1416 5375 Duke St Alexandria VA 22304 Office: 6565 Arlington Blvd Falls Church VA 22046

LIND, MAURICE DAVID, research physicist; b. Jamestown, N.Y., July 25, 1934; s. Paul William Frederic and Florence Rosemond (Hedstrom) L.; m. Carol Norma Dickson, Apr. 21, 1962; 1 child, Diana Nadine. BS, Otterbein Coll., 1957; PhD, Cornell U., 1962. Postdoctoral fellow Cornell U., Ithaca, N.Y., 1962-63; research scientist Union Oil Co., Brea, Calif., 1963-66, Rockwell Internat., Thousand Oaks, Calif., 1966—; vis. prof. applied physics Tech. U. Denmark, Lyngby, 1985. Contbr. articles to profl. jours. Recipient Pub. Service award NASA, 1976. Mem. Am. Phys. Soc., Am. Crystallographic Assn., Am. Assn. Crystal Growth, Sigma Xi. Home: 1690 Stoddard Ave Thousand Oaks CA 91360 Office: Rockwell Internat 1049 Camino Dos Rios Thousand Oaks CA 91360

LINDBECK, ASSAR, economist; b. Umea, Sweden, Jan. 26, 1930; s. Karl and Eugenia (Sundelin) L.; Ph.D. in Econs., U. Stockholm, 1963; m. Dorothy Nordlund, Dec. 28, 1953; children—Dan, Maria. Asso. prof. econs. U. Stockholm, 1962-63; with Swedish Treasury Dept., 1953-54; researcher in U.S., 1957-58; asst. prof. U. Mich., 1958; vis. prof. Columbia U., 1968-69, U. Calif., Berkeley, summer 1969, Nat. U. Australia, Canberra, 1970, Yale U., 1976, Stanford U., 1977, Simon Fraser U., Vancouver, B.C., 1981; prof. econs. Stockholm Sch. Econs., 1964-71; prof. internat. econs. dir. Internat. Econs., Stockholm, 1971—; chmn. Nobel Prize Com. Econs.; expert cons. in field OECD, UN orgns., World Bank, others. Fellow Econometric Soc.; hon. mem. Am. Econ. Assn. Author: A Study in Monetary Analysis; Swedish Economic Policy; Economics of the Agricultural Sector; The Political Economy of the New Left; Inflation—Global, International and National Aspects. Home: 50 Ostermalmsgat, 11426 Stockholm Sweden Office: Universitetsv, 10691 Stockholm Sweden

LINDBERG, BERTIL CHARLES, management consultant; educator; b. Helsingborg, Sweden, Jan. 26, 1927; came to U.S., 1966; s. Uno Ernst Fredrik and Elsa Maria (Bokelund) L.; m. Mary Frances Friedman, Oct. 12, 1979; 1 child, Erik; children by previous marriage—Cornelia, Jacqueline. M.S. in Elec. Engring., Royal Inst. Tech., Stockholm, 1951; M.B.A., Stockholm Sch. Econs., 1953; postgrad. Columbia U., 1965-66. Businessman, Sweden, 1952-59, Italy, 1959-63; European mgr. Puregas Equipment Corp., Copiague, N.Y., 1961-66; sr. cons. Mentor Internat., San Francisco, 1966-71, Darling & Alsobrook, Los Angeles, 1973-75; mgmt. cons., Los Angeles, 1975-79, N.Y.C., 1979—; lectr. bus. mgmt. Northrop U., Inglewood, Calif., 1973-76, Calif. State Poly. U., Pomona, 1975-76; adj. asst. prof. York Coll., CUNY, Jamaica, N.Y., 1982-83; adj. assoc. prof. NYU, 1984-85. Author: (with others) Power Supply-A Technology, Systems Design and Market Assessment, 1973, Electronic Packaging: Connectors and Terminals, Backplanes and Sockets, Printed Circuits, and Integrated Circuit Packages, 1974, International Transfer of International Technology by U.S. Firms and Their Implications for the U.S. Economy, 1976, Trends in Microlithography, 1979; The U.S. Semiconductor Products and Test Equipment Markets, 1979; Digital Class 5 Switches, 1979; Remote Monitoring, Alarm and Control Systems Markets, 1980, 85; The Bell System Market for Transmission Products, 1980; (with others) Electronic Capital Equipment Markets & Technologies-Printed Wiring Fabrication, Assembly & Test, 1981; Non-Impact Printers, 1981; The Market and Future for Multiplexers and Concentrators, 1981; Data, Text and Voice Encryption Equipment, 1981; Teletext and Videotex, Markets and Technology, 1983; U.S. Communications Networks, 1983; Electronic Mail, 1984; Teleconferencing, 1984; Graphics and Documents Communications, 1984; Broadband Data Transport Facilities Provided by Local Telephone Companies, 1984; Fourth Generation PBX's, 1985; Telecommunications Test Equipment, 1985; Signal Processing Opportunities, 1985; Peripherals for the ISDN D-Channel, 1986; Nuerocomputing: The Technology, The Players, The Potential, 1987; contbr. articles to profl. jours. Bd. govs. Am.-Swedish Hist. Found., Phila., 1970-85; bd. dirs., v.p. Swedish Am. C. of C. for Western U.S., San Francisco, 1971-73. Mem. IEEE (sr.), IEEE Computer Soc. (sr., chmn. N.Y. chpt. 1987-88), Am. Mktg. Assn. Home: 3 Hanover Sq New York NY 10004

LINDBERG, FRANCIS LAURENCE, JR., management consultant; b. Jacksonville, Fla., Mar. 13, 1948; s. Francis Laurence and Mildred Hortense (Parrish) L.; m. Anne Louise Stearns, Dec. 29, 1972 (div.); 1 child, Kristen Anne; m. Alexis Jean Parker, Nov. 12, 1983. Student Eckerd Coll., 1965-66; BA, Jacksonville U., 1969; MBA, U. North Fla., 1976. CPA, Ga. Actuarial asst. Gulf Life Ins. Co., Jacksonville, 1967-73; asst. actuary Am. Heritage Life, Jacksonville, 1973-77; asst. sec.-treas., prin. acctg. officer Atlantic Am. Corp., Atlanta, 1977-84; assoc. v.p. fin. Security Benefit Group, Topeka, 1985-86; exec. v.p., chief fin. officer Am. Way Group of Cos., Southfield, Mich., 1986-87; prin. The Lindberg Group, Atlantaand Southfield, 1987—; treas., bd. dirs., bd. advisors Good News Communications, Inc. Mem. Nat. Assn. Accts. (Membership Achievement award 1983), Am. Inst. CPA's, Ga. Soc. CPA's, Acctng. Research Assn. Republican. Episcopalian. Office: The Lindberg Co 1264 Weatherstone Dr Bldg 13 Atlanta GA 30324

LINDBERG, HELGE, airline company executive; b. London, Sept. 17, 1926; arrived in Norway, 1936; s. Carl Andreas and Sigrid Kristine (Bay) L.; m. Kerstin Hildegard Sjunnesson, Oct. 23, 1970; children by previous marriage: Sigrid Kristine, Carl Andreas. Grad., Treiders Handelsskole, Oslo, 1944. With Scandinavian Airlines System, 1946—; dist. mgr. Scandinavian Airlines System, Arabian Gulf, 1958; asst. regional mgr. Scandinavian Airlines System, Middle East, 1959-60; traffic sales mgr., dep. mng. dir. Scanair Charter Co. subs. Scandinavian Airlines System, Copenhagen, 1961-68; div. mgr. Scanair Charter Co. subs. Scandinavian Airlines System, Finland, Eastern Europe, 1969-72; v.p. industry assn. affairs Scanair Charter Co. subs. Scandinavian Airlines System, Stockholm, 1973-75, v.p. passenger mktg., 1976-78, exec. v.p. comml., 1979-83, chief operating officer, 1983-86; dep. pres. Scandinavian Airlines System Group, Oslo, Stockholm, 1986—; chmn. Scandinavian Air Tour Prodn., Stockholm, 1976-79; bd. dirs. Nymann & Schultz Travel Agy., Stockholm, 1976-81, Widerøe's Airline, Oslo, Diners Nordic A/S; mem. traffic com. Internat. Air Traffic Assn., Geneva, 1973-74, chmn. 1975-76. Bd. dirs. World Wildlife Fund, 1986—. Mem. Assn. European Airlines (chmn. comml. and air polit. com. 1981-83), Scandinavian Multi Access System for Travel Agts. (chmn. 1983-85). Home: Lappstigen 3, 162 40 Vallingby Sweden Office: Scandinavian Airlines System, 161 87 Stockholm Sweden

LINDEGAARD, MOGENS CHRISTENSEN, airline executive; b. Copenhagen, Denmark, Feb. 21, 1942; s. Johan C. and Else (Sorensen) L.; m. Ulla Bente Pedersen, Apr. 15, 1971; 1 child, Peter. Grad., Copenhagen Sch. Commerce, 1963. Traffic officer Scandinavian Airlines, Copenhagen, 1960-64; dist. mgr. Scandinavian Airlines, Seoul, Republic of Korea, 1977-79; cargo officer Lufthansa Airlines, Copenhagen, 1964-66; sta. mgr. Internord Aviation Co., Copenhagen, 1966-68; tng. officer East African Airlines, Nairobi, Kenya, 1969-71; mgmt. advisor Air Tanzania Corp., Daressalaam, 1980-85; cargo sales mgr. Scandinavian Airlines, Copenhagen, 1985—; tutor, lectr. Sch. of Transp., Copenhagen, 1986—. Author: International Transport, 1976. Served with Danish Air Force, 1963. Mem. Chaine de Rotisseurs (chevalier), Inst. Transport, Jaycees. Lodge: Rotary. Home: Tinggards Hegnet 17, Tune, 4000 Roskilde Denmark Office: Scandinavian Airlines, Engvej 139 Cphafsk, 2770 Kastrup Denmark

LINDELL, ANDREA REGINA, college dean, nurse; b. Warren, Pa., Aug., 21, 1943; d. Andrew D. and Irene M. (Fabry) Lefik; m. Warner E. Lindell, May 7, 1966; children—Jennifer I., Jason M. B.S., Villa Maria Coll., 1970; M.S.N. Catholic U., 1975, D.N.Sc., 1975; diploma R.N., St. Vincent's Hosp., Erie, Pa. Instr. St. Vincent Hosp. Sch. Nursing, 1964-66; dir. Rouse Hosp., Youngsville, Pa., 1966-69; supr. Vis. Nurses Assn., Warren, Pa., 1969-70; dir. grad. program Cath. U., Washington, 1975-77; chmn., assoc. dean U. N.H., Durham, 1977-81; dean, prof. Oakland U., Rochester, Mich., 1981—; cons. Moorehead U., Ky., 1983. Editor; Jour. Profl. Nursing, 1985; contbr. articles to profl. jours. Mem. sch. bd. Strafford Sch. Dist., N.H., 1977-80; Gov.'s Blue Ribbon Commn. Direct Health Policies, Concord, N.H., 1979-81; vice chmn. New England Commn. Higher Edn. in Nursing, 1977-81; mem. Mich. Assn. Colls. Nursing, 1981—. Named Outstanding Young Woman Am., 1980. Mem. Nat. League Nursing, Am. Assn. Colls. Nursing, Sigma Theta Tau. Democrat. Roman Catholic. Avocations: water skiing; roller skating; reading; fishing; camping; Office: Oakland U 428 O Dowd Hall Rochester MI 48309

LINDEMANN, BERNHARD JOHANNES, English language educator; b. Mülheim-Ruhr, Fed. Republic Germany, Mar. 12, 1949; s. Karl and Mechtilde (Conrads) L.; m. Roswitha Mayer, June 7, 1974. Cert., Ruhr U., 1974, Dr phil, 1976. Asst. in English dept. Ruhr U., Bochum, Fed. Republic Germany, 1976-79, lectr., 1979—. Author: Experimental Film as Meta-Film, 1977; contbr. articles to profl. jours. Office: Ruhr U Dept English, Universitatstrasse 150, D-4630 Bochum Federal Republic of Germany

LINDEMANN, WILLI, mathematical crystallography educator; b. Kassel, Germany, Jan. 15, 1921; s. Friedrich and Luise (Voigt) L.; m. Anna-Luise Koeberle, Mar. 20, 1944. Dr.phil.nat., U. Erlangen, Fed. Republic Germany, 1951, Dr. habil., 1959. Lectr. U. Erlangen, 1960-66; assoc. prof. U. Wuerzburg, Fed. Republic Germany, 1966-71, full prof. math. crystallography, 1971—. Patentee mikroskopmanipulator. Mem. N.Y. Acad. Scis., Am. Math. Soc., Gesellschaft fü r Angewandte Mathematik und Mechanik, Deutsche Bunsengesellschaft fü r physikallische Chemie, Arbeitsgemeinschaft Kristallographie. Home: Pfisterstrasse 3, Bamberg Federal Republic of Germany Office: U Wuerzburg, Kristallstrukturlehre, Am Hubland, D-8700 Wuerzburg Federal Republic of Germany

LINDENBAUM, S(EYMOUR) J(OSEPH), physicist; b. N.Y.C., Feb. 3, 1925; s. Morris and Anne L.; m. Leda Isaacs, June 29, 1958. A.B., Princeton U., 1945; M.A., Columbia U., 1949, Ph.D., 1951. With Brookhaven Nat. Lab., Upton, N.Y., 1951—; sr. physicist Brookhaven Nat. Lab., 1963—, group leader high energy physics research group, 1954—; vis. prof. U. Rochester, 1958-59; Mark W. Zemansky chair in physics CCNY, 1970—; cons. Centre de Etudes Nucleaire de Saclay, France, 1957, CERN, Geneva, 1962; dep. for sci. affairs ERDA, 1976-77. Author: Particle Interaction Physics at High Energies, 1973. Contbr. articles to profl. jours. Fellow Am. Phys. Soc.; mem. N.Y. Acad. Scis., AAAS. Office: Dept Physics Brookhaven Nat Lab Upton NY 11973

LINDENMUTH, RICHARD ALAN, telecommunications company executive; b. Phila., Dec. 28, 1944; s. Ralph Lester and Evelyn Josephine (Zimmerman) Dedel L.; m. Christine Louise Ulmer, Sept. 7, 1968 (div.); children—Michael, Carol Anne. B.A. in Internat. Affairs, U. Colo., 1970; M.B.A., Wharton Sch., U. Pa., 1971. Gen. mgr. North and West Africa Singer, Beirut, Lebanon, 1972-77; dir. internat. ops. Bendix Corp., Southfield, Mich., 1978-80; pres. Lexar Bus. Communications, Inc., Woodland Hills, Calif., 1980-82; v.p., gen. mgr. Imaging Systems div. Burroughs Corp., Danbury, Conn., 1982-83; pres. Bus. and Consumer Communications div. ITT, Raleigh, N.C., 1983-86; pres., chief exec. officer Robinson Nugent Inc., New Albany, Ind., 1986—. Mem. nat. adv. bd. Ctr. Study Presidency, N.Y.C., 1982—; bd. dirs. Internat. Trade, Raleigh, 1983—; cons. on middle east U.S. Govt., 1982-83. Served with USN, 1962-66. Republican. Presbyterian. Club: Capital City (Raleigh). Avocations: flying; sailing; travel; tennis.

LINDER, GORDON FORREST, accountant; b. Washington, Dec. 8, 1937; s. Forrest Edward and Gretchen Alma L.; B.S., Am. U., 1969, M.B.A., 1972; m. Peggy Ann Walker, Apr. 8, 1960; children—Shirley Jean, Janet Gretchen, Ronald Gordon, Stacy Kim, Joyce Peggy. Treas., controller Scope Electronics, Reston, Va., 1968-77; pres. Gordon F. Linder, P.A., Bowie, Md., 1977—; assoc. prof. acctg., dept. chmn. Prince George's Community Coll., Largo, Md., 1981—. C.P.A., Md. Mem. Am. Inst. C.P.A.s, Md. Assn. C.P.A.s. Office: 14300 Gallant Fox Ln Bowie MD 20715

LINDGREN, DONALD, minister; b. Lynn, Mass., May 28, 1930; s. Raymond and Effie Marshal (MacLeod) L. B.A., Yankton Coll, 1953; B.Th., Yankton Coll. Theology, 1954; Th.M., Eden Theol. Sem., 1961; postgrad., Edinburgh U. (Scotland), 1962-64. Ordained to ministry United Church of Christ, 1954. Minister Congl. Ch., Genoa, Nebr., 1953-56, Sauk Centre, Minn., 1956-60; interim minister Colonial Ch. Edina, Minn., 1960-61; asst. minister Ch. Highlands, White Plains, N.Y., 1961-62; minister Musselburgh Congl., Scotland, 1968—; hon. minister Congl. Ch., Genoa, Nebr.; hon. chaplain 297 Musselburgh Squadron, Air Tng. Corps. Author: Designs for Christian Living, 1962. Author: Musselburgh in Old Picture Postcards, 1987; contbr. articles to newspapers. Lodges: Rotary, Masons. Home: 8 The Grove, Musselburgh, Midlothian EH21 7HD, Scotland

LINDHARD, JENS, physicist, educator; b. Tystofte, Denmark, Feb. 26, 1922; s. Erik and Agnes (Nielsen) L. Mag.scient., U. Copenhagen, 1945. Staff Niels Bohr Inst., Copenhagen, 1945-56; prof. theoretical physics U. Aarhus (Denmark), 1956—. Recipient Rigmor & Carl Holst Knudsens Videnskabspris, 1965, H. C. Orsted madeljen, 1974, Filtenborgs Aereslegat, 1978. Mem. Royal Danish Acad. Scis. and Letters (pres. 1982—), Danish Acad. Tech. Scis., Hollandsche Maatschappij der Weutenschappen. Office: Univ Aarhus, Dept Physics, DK-8000 Aarhus C Denmark also: Royal Danish Acad of Sci & Letters, Hans Christian Andersen Blvd 35, DK-1553 Copenhagen V Denmark

LINDHOLM, RICHARD WADSWORTH, finance educator; b. Mankato, Minn., June 11, 1913; s. Theodore E. and Elizabeth S. (Swanson) L.; m. Mary M. Trunko, Sept. 11, 1948; 1 son, Richard Theodore. B.A., Gustavus Adolphus Coll., 1935; M.A., U. Minn., 1938; Ph.D., U. Tex., 1942. Tchr. Souris (N.D.) Jr. High Sch., 1935, Worthington (Minn.) High Sch., 1938-39; mem. Minn. Income Study, 1939-40; instr. Coll. St. Thomas, 1940-41, U. Tex., 1941- 42; asst. prof. Tex. A&M Coll., 1942, Ohio State U., 1946-48; assoc. prof. Mich. State U., 1948-50, prof., 1950-58; dean Coll. Bus. Adminstrn., U. Oreg., 1958-71; founder, dean Coll. Bus. Adminstrn., U. Oreg. (Grad. Sch. Mgmt. and Bus.), 1967-71, prof. finance, 1971-79; dean, prof. fin. emeritus 1979—; Fiscal economist Fed. Res. Bd., 1950-51, 64-65; econ. cons. 1st Nat. Bank of Oreg., 1961-69; mem. Mich. Employment Com., 1954; sr. tax adviser, cons. econ. devel. ICA, Saigon, Viet-Nam, 1955-57; bus. tax cons. Mich. Legislature tax study, 1958; coordinator econ. adv. group in, Korea, 1959-61; nat. com. Taxation, Resources and Econ. Devel.; tax com. to increase exports Dept. Commerce, 1965—; tax adviser Australian Govt., 1969, Gov. of Oreg., 1970-71; Cons. U.S. Dept. State, 1972-75, Dept. Planning, Istanbul, Turkey, 1974, U.S. Com. Ways and Means, 1975, 79; tax adviser, Philippines, 1977, 80, Taiwan, 1983. Author: The Corporate Franchise as the Basis of Taxation, 1944, Taxation in Ohio, 1946, Public Finance of Air Transportation, 1948, Introduction to Fiscal Policy, 2d edit, 1955, (with others) Public Finance and Fiscal Policy, 2d edit, 1958, Money and Banking, 3d edit, 1969, Money and Finance, 1951, Taxation of the Trucking Industry, 1951, Principles of Money and Banking, 1954, Money and Banking and Economic Development in Free Viet-Nam, 1957, Our American Economy, 1958, 4th edit., 1970, The Tax Systems of Michigan with Recommendations, 1958, Economic Development Policy, 1964, A Description and Analysis of Oregon's Fiscal System, 1971; Editor, contbr.: Viet-Nam: The First Five Years, 1959, Property Taxation U.S.A, 1967, Property Taxation and the Finance of Education, 1974, A Business Approach to Taxation, 1966, Business Taxation Notes, 1967, Taxation of Timber Resources, 1973, New Tax Directions for the United States, 1975, Value Added Tax, 1976, Property Tax Reform, 1977, Money Management and Institutions, 1978, Finance and Management of State and Local Government, 1979, The Economics of VAT, 1980, Land Value Taxation, 1981, A New Federal Tax System, 1984, Examination of Basic Weaknesses of Income as Major Federal Tax Base, 1985; contbr. articles to profl. jours. Chmn. Chinju-Eugene Sister City Com., 1961; Mem. Oreg. Econ. Adv. Com., 1966—. Served from pvt. to capt. AUS, 1942-45, ETO. Decorated 5 battle stars.; Fulbright lectr. Pakistan, 1952; Lincoln Inst. Land Policy grantee, 1976, 77; Lincoln Found. scholar, 1977. Mem. Am. Econ. Assn., Western Econ. Assn., Nat. Tax Assn. (dir. 1967-70), Western Tax Assn., Asia Soc., Pi Beta Delta, Beta Gamma Sigma (distinguished scholar 1975-76), Pi Gamma Mu. Home: 2520 Fairmount Blvd Eugene OR 97403

LINDNER, MICHAEL WALTER, manufacturing company executive; b. Leipzig, Fed. Republic Germany, May 23, 1949; s. Walter and Annemarie (Schmidt) L.; m. Daniela Simone Diemer, Feb. 10, 1956; children: Nicolas Walter, Vanessa Anna-Marie. Dip. Betriebswirt, Fachhoschschule fur Wirtschaft, Fed. Republic Germany, 1974. Head market research dept. Wander GmbH, Frankfurt, Fed. Republic Germany, 1974-76; regional sales force mgr. Wander-Sandoz, Nurenberg, Fed. Republic Germany, 1976-78; pres. Borlind GmbH, Calw-Altburg, Fed. Republic Germany, 1978—. Lodge: Rotary. Office: Borlind GmbH, Lindenstr 15, D-7260 Calw-Altburg Federal Republic of Germany

LINDO, ARTHUR JESURUN, housewares and cosmetics merchant, airline executive; b. Panama, Panama, Dec. 17, 1928; s. Otto Jesurun and Eulalie (Delgado) L. AA, Menlo Coll., Calif., 1948; BS, U. So. Calif., 1950. Mng. dir. Lindo & Maduro, S.A., Panama City, 1954—. Jewish. Club: SKAL of Panama (founder 1955, treas. 1955-61, 63—, Pres. N.Am. area com., 1981). Office: Lindo & Maduro SA, Calle 29E 1-21, Panama 5, Panama

LINDON, JEROME, publishing company executive; b. Paris, France, June 9, 1925; s. Raymond and Therese (Baur) L.; student Lycée Pasteur a Neuilly/Seine, 1936-39; Baccalauréat Lycée Mignet á Aix-en-Provence, 1942; m. Marié Rosenfeld Annette, July 1, 1947; children—Irène, André , Mathieu. Prés., dir.-gen. Editions de Minuit, Paris, 1948—. Office: Editions de Minuit, 7 rue Bernard Palissy, Paris 6e France

LINDON, JOHN ARNOLD, psychiatrist, psychoanalyst; b. Chgo., Mar. 11, 1924; s. Albert and Rose L.; m. Ruth N. Blumenson, May 22, 1953 (dec. 1971); children: Julia Helen, Mark Lincoln; m. Marilyn Becker, June 4, 1973. M.D., U. Louisville, 1948; Ph.D., So. Calif. Psychoanalytic Inst., 1977. Diplomate: Am. Bd. Psychiatry and Neurology, Nat. Bd. Med. Examiners. Intern Cedars of Lebanon Hosp., Los Angeles, 1948-49; resident Brentwood Neuropsychiat. Center, 1949-52; psychonalytic tng. Inst. Psychoanalytic Medicine So. Calif. (now So. Calif. Psychoanalytic Inst.), 1950-55, both Los Angeles; mem. faculty Inst. Psychoanalytic Medicine So. Calif. (now So. Calif. Psychoanalytic Inst.), 1958—; pvt. practice psychiatry and psychoanalysis Beverly Hills, Los Angeles, 1951—; instr. Coll. Med. Evangelists, 1952-53; asst. clin. prof. psychiatry U. So. Calif., 1960-68; asso. clin. prof. psychiatry Med. Sch. U. Calif. at Los Angeles, 1968—; also asso. vis. psychiatrist hosp. and clinics UCLA; cons. Calif. Dept. Mental Hygiene, Los Angeles, 1957-72, Calif. Dept. Correction, 1962-74; sr. cons. Met. State Hosp., Norwalk, Calif., 1957-72; pres. Psychiat. Research Found., 1958—. Author numerous books, also articles profl. jours.; Editor-in-chief: Psychoanalytic Forum, 1965—; contbg. editor: Ann. Survey of Psychoanalysis, 1959—. Served with AUS, 1942-46. Fellow Am. Psychiat. Assn.; mem. AAAS, Am. Psychoanalytic Assn., So. Calif. Psychoanalytic Soc. (past v.p.), Internat. Psychoanalytic Assn. (clin. essay prize 1957), Am., Calif., Los Angeles County med. assns., UCLA Med. Soc., Fedn. Am. Scientists, Am. Soc. for Adolescent Psychiatry, So. Calif. Psychoanalytic Inst. (supervising and tng. analyst, also trustee 1960-63, 68-74, 1988—, sec.-treas. 1971-74, chmn. 1978-80, pres. 1978-80), So. Calif. Psychiat. Soc. (bd. dirs. Grad. Ctr. for Child Devel. and Therapy, 1988—). Office: 10921 Wilshire Blvd Los Angeles CA 90024

LINDOP, CLIVE ARTHUR, education educator; b. Fenton, Eng., Apr. 22, 1942; arrived in Australia, 1952; s. Arthur James and may (Wood) L.; m. Margaret Elizabeth Curtis, Aug. 8, 1973; children: Agnes, Rowena, Clare. BSc, Adelaide U., 1963, diploma in edn., 1964; MA in Edn., Simon Fraser U., 1972. Tchr. sci. Edn. Dept. South Australia, 1965-68, Neutral Hills Sch., Alta., Can., 1968-69; grad. asst. Simon Fraser U., B.C., Can., 1970-71; lectr. in edn. Maria Grey Coll. Edn., London, 1971-72, U. Nariobi, Kenya, 1972-74, Warrnambool (Australia) Inst. Advanced Edn., 1978—; tutor in edn. U. Western. Australia, 1975-78; mem biology curriculum com. South Australia Dept. Edn., 1966-68; external examiner faculty edn. U. Uganda, 1972-73; cons. faculty edn. U. Melbourne, australia, 1976-77, Warrnambool Edn. Ctr., 1986—. Contbr. articles to ednl. jours. Councillor Subiaco Council, Perth, Australia, 1976-77; exec. Victoria Acad. Staff Assn., 1980—; sec. Alansford Sch. Bd., Warrnambool, 1983-85; dir. Warrnambool Sheltered Workshop, 1985-87; treas. Wangboom Progress Assn., Victoria, 1986—. Mem. Australian Assn. Research in Edn., australian Coll. Edn., South Pacific Assn. Tchr. Edn., Philosophy of Edn. Soc., Philisophy of Edn. Soc. in Australia, Australian Inst. Philosophy for Children (mem. exec. com. 1986—). Clubs: Warrnambool City, Wangoom Sports. Office: Warrnambool Inst Advanced Edn, Warrnamool 3280, Australia

LINDOW, LESTER WILLIAM, former telecasters organization executive; b. Milw., Apr. 11, 1913; B.A. in Journalism, U. Wis., 1934; m. Baroness Andree de Verdor, Dec. 7, 1946; 1 dau., Suzanne Helene Lindow Gordon. Assoc. editor Advt. Almanac, Hearst Newspapers, N.Y.C., 1934-35; comml. dept. sta. WCAE, Pitts., 1935-36, nat. sales mgr., 1936-38, comml. mgr., asst. to the gen. mgr., 1938-40; sec., gen. mgr. WFBM, Inc., Indpls., 1940-42; gen. mgr. stas. WRNY and WRNY-FM, Rochester, N.Y., 1946-47; sec., gen. mgr. Trebit Corp. operators sta. WFDF, Flint, 1947-60, sec., dir., 1948-60, v.p., 1954-60; sec.-treas. Landsmore Corp., 1952-57, v.p., 1954-57; mem. exec. com. NBC Radio Affiliates, 1955-57, chmn. exec. com., 1956-57; exec. dir. Assn. Maximum Service Telecasters, Inc., 1957-77, pres., 1977-78; v.p., dir. Grelin Broadcasting, Inc., sta. WWRI, West Warwick, R.I., 1957-69, Radio Buffalo, Inc., sta. WWOL and WWOL-FM, Buffalo, 1959-62. Treas., dir. ARC, 1953-56, Palm Beach County chpt., 1981—; nat. fund vice chmn. for Mich., 1956-57, bd. dirs. Palm Beach County chpt.; dir. Flint YMCA, 1956-57; bd. dirs., mem. exec. com. Radio Free Europe/Radio Liberty, Inc., Washington. Mem. Palm Beach Civic Assn.; Served from 1st lt. to lt. col. AUS, 1942-46; apptd. to Gen. Staff Corps, War Dept., 1946-47; col. U.S. Army Res. (ret.) 1964. Mem. Mich. Assn. Broadcasters, Mich. A.P. Broadcasters' Assn. (dir.), Res. Officers' Assn., Nat. Assn. Radio and TV Broadcasters (dir. AM radio com.), Radio Advt. Bur. (Mich. chmn.), Asso. Press Radio Programming Com. N.Y.C., Assn. Profl. Broadcasting Edn. (dir.), Asso. Press Radio and TV Assn. (v.p., dir.), TV Allocations Study Orgn. (alt. dir.), Ret. Officers Assn., English Speaking Union, Union U. Wis. Alumni Assn., Nat. Broadcasters Club Washington (bd. govs. 1959-61, pres. 1964-65, chmn. 1965-66), Internat. Radio and TV Soc., Radio-TV Pioneers, Soc. of Four Arts, Alpha Chi Rho, Scabbard and Blade, Iron Cross, White Spades, Sigma Delta Chi. Clubs: Flint Golf, Rotary (pres.) (Flint); Broadcast Pioneers, Radio Execs. (N.Y.C.); Internat., Congressional Country (Washington), Elks; Beach, Pundits (Palm Beach, Fla.), circumnavigators. Home: Apt 406/7 3475 S Ocean Blvd Palm Beach FL 33480

LINDQUIST, EVAN, artist, educator; b. Salina, Kans., May 23, 1936; s. E.L. and Linnette Rosalie (Shogren) L.; B.S.E., Emporia State U., 1958; M.F.A., U. Iowa, 1963; m. Sharon Frances Huenergardt, June 8, 1958; children—Eric, Carl. One man shows: Mo. Arts Council, 1973-75, Albrecht Art Mus., St. Joseph, Mo., 1975, S.E. Mo. State U., 1977, Sandzen Gallery, Lindsborg, Kans., 1978, Galerie V. Kunstverlag Wolfbrum, Vienna, 1979, Poplar Bluff, Mo., 1987; group shows include: Benjamin Galleries, Chgo., 1976, City of Venice, 1977, Boston Printmakers, 1971-87, Visual Arts Center of Alaska, Anchorage, 1979, Western Carolina U., 1980, Pa. State U., 1980, Kans. State U., 1980, U. N.D., 1981, Ariz. State U., 1981, Barcelona, Cadaques, Girona, Tulsa, 1982, Jay Gallery, N.Y.C., 1983, Artists Books, E.Ger., 1984, U. Tenn.-Knoxville, 1985, Memphis State U., 1985, Ark. Arts Ctr., 1983-83, Miss. State U., 1986, Hunterdon Art Ctr., Clinton, N.J., 1986-87, Washington, 1988; represented in permanent collections: Albertina, Vienna, Art Inst. Chgo., Nelson-Atkins, Kansas City, Phoenix Art Mus., Uffizi Gallery, Florence, Municipal Gallery, Dublin, San Francisco Art Mus., Whitney Mus. Am. Art, N.Y.C., St. Louis Art Mus., Museo Espanol del Arte Contemporaneo, Madrid, others; staff artist Emporia State U., 1958-60; prof. Ark. State U., 1963—, pres.'s fellow, 1981-82, 84-85. Mem. Soc. Am. Gr., Coll. Art Assn. Am., MidAm. Coll. Art Assn., Visual Artists and Galleries Assn. Office: Box 2782 State University AR 72467

LINDQUIST, HANS GEORG, linguist; b. Simrishman, Sweden, Oct. 14, 1951; s. Sven Georg Lindquist and Anna Kerstin (Olsson) Nilsson; m. Agneta Maria Elisabeth Jonasson, Apr. 14, 1976; children: Mattias, Maja. Grad., Lund U., Sweden, 1975; MA, UCLA, 1984. Research asst. English dept. Lund U., Sweden, 1981-83; teaching assoc. linguistics dept. UCLA, Los Angeles, 1984; asst. lectr. English dept. Lund U., Sweden, 1985-86; pub. mgr. humanities Studentlitteratur, Lund, Sweden, 1987—. Editor: (dictionary) Amerikanskt Slanglexikon, 1979, Bonniers Engelsk-Svenska Ordbok, 1987; translator: (short stories) Pegasen från Prärien, 1983; author: (novel) Neuromancer, 1987; contbr. articles to profl. jours. Grantee British Council, London, 1978-79; grantee Swedish-Am. Found. Mem. Dictionary Soc. of Am., European Assn. Lexicography, Linguistic Soc. Am., Linguistic Assn. Can. and U.S., Swedish Assn. Applied Linguistics (treas. 1986—). Office: Studenflitteratur, Box 141, S-22100 Lund Sweden

LINDQVIST, LARS PETER, mathematician, educator; b. Hangö, Finland, Mar. 8, 1951; s. Sven Lars and Sylvia Margareta (Blomqvist) L.; m. Julia Ruth Donner, May 9, 1987. MS, U. Helsinki, 1974, PhD, 1980. Asst. Helsinki U. of Tech., Helsingfors, Finland, 1974-77, spl. tchr., 1977-87, lectr., 1987—; docent U. Helsinki, Helsingfors, Finland, 1984—; vis. prof. Luleå (Sweden) Tech. U., 1986, U. Mich., Ann Arbor, 1987-88. Contbr. articles to sci. and math. jours. Grantee Magnus Ehrnrooth Soc., 1978, Svenska Vetenshapliga Central Rådet i Finland, 1980. Mem. Finnish Math. Soc. Lutheran. Office: Helsinki Univ Tech, Helsinki, Nyland 02150, Finland

LINDROS, JOHN EDWARD, lawyer; b. Elizabeth, N.J., June 26, 1949; s. Edward John and Edna Frances (Fitzsimmons) L.; m. Marie Anne Sztukowski, Dec. 11, 1971; children—John Randolph, Victoria Marie, Brian Michael. B.A., St. Josephs U., 1971; J.D., Rutgers U., 1975. Bar: Del. 1976, U.S. Dist. Ct. Del. 1977, U.S. Tax Ct. 1979, Pa. 1982. Atty. Williams, Gordon & Martin, Wilmington, Del., 1975-80, Murdoch & Walsh, Wilmington, 1980-81; tax counsel Atlantic Richfield Co., Phila., 1981-85, mgr. European taxes, Eton, Berks., Eng., 1985-88, asst. tax officer Los Angeles div., 1988—; instr. bus. law U. Del., Newark, 1977. Contbr. articles to profl. jours. Founder, 1st pres., officer Piermont Woods Civic Assn., Newark, 1977-80; chmn. Tasis Eng. Sch. Parents Council, 1986-87. Mem. ABA, Del. Bar Assn. Republican. Roman Catholic. Clubs: Wentworth (Va. Water, Eng.), Silvermere Golf (Cobham, Eng.), Univeristy (Los Angeles). Home: 31927 Kingspark Ct Westlake Village CA 91361 Office: Atlantic Richfield Co 515 S Flower ST Los Angeles CA 90071

LINDSAY, DELROY FITZHERBERT, association executive, economist; b. Duckenfield, St. Thomas, Jamaica, May 5, 1951; s. Douglas O'Neil Lindsay and Kerlena (Brown) Biggs; m. Patricia Elizabeth Walker, July 20, 1974. BS in Econs. and Adminstrn. with honors, U. London, 1976, MA in Econs., 1979. Securities exec. Midland Bank Ltd., London, 1971-73; 1st sec. for politics and econs. Jamaican Fgn. Service, London, 1976-81; desk officer for Middle East Ministry Fgn. Affairs, Kingston, Jamaica, 1981-82; dir. research and planning Ministry Industry and Commerce, Kingston, 1982-84; mng. dir. Pamaco Ltd., Kingston, 1984; dir. econs. Pvt. Sector Orgn. Jamaica, Kingston, 1984-86, dep. exec. dir., 1986, acting exec. dir., 1986-87, exec. dir., 1987—. Author: Policy Framework for Economic Development in Jamaica, 1985; columnist for fin. paper; broadcaster on fin., polit. and econ. issues. Club: Liguanea (Kingston). Office: Pvt Sector Orgn Jamaica, 39 Hope Rd, Kingston 10 Jamaica

LINDSAY, PAMELA JANINE, human resources specialist, social psychological researcher; b. Philipsburg, Pa., Mar. 26, 1954; d. Ronald N. and Sandra J. (Lindsay) Thomas; m. Alan Chickinsky, Oct. 1979. BA in Labor Relations, Pa. State U.-University Park, 1978; AS in Bus Adminstrn., Pa. State U.-Altoona, 1974; ALM in Social Psychology, Harvard U., 1987, postgrad. research, 1987—. Employee relations asst. P.P.G. Industries, Tipton, Pa., 1976-77; indsl. relations mgr. Smith/Eggo Foods, Pottstown, Pa., 1978-80; human resources cons. Scott Paper Co., Winslow, Maine, 1980; personnel rep. NEC Am., Fairfax, Va., 1980-81; labor relations cons., 1980-81; human resources specialist Data Gen. Corp., Westborough, Mass., 1981-82; mgr. human resources, NEC Electronics, Natick, Mass., 1983-86; dir. human resources Exeter Cos., Cambridge, Mass., 1986-87; organizational cons., 1987; dir. research and assessment services, PsychoMETRICS, Lexington, Mass., 1987—. Mem. Am. Assn. Counseling and Devel., Am. Soc. Personnel Adminstrn., Am. Soc. Tng. and Devel., Am. Mgmt. Assn., Am. Psychol. Assn., Am. Psychiat. Assn., AERA, NCME, NCDA, MCDA, MBACD, AHED, AMECD, NECA. Republican. Home: 96 Hancock St Lexington MA 02173

LINDSAY, ROGER ALEXANDER, management executive; b. Dundee, Tayside, Scotland, Feb. 18, 1941; s. Archibald Carswell Lindsay and Edith (Paterson) Bisset. Student, The Morgan Acad., Dundee; marticulated in law, Queen's Coll., Scotland. Asst. acct., office mgr. Andrew G. Kidd Ltd., Dundee, 1964, Associated British Foods Ltd., London, 1966; sec., treas. Wittington Investments Ltd., Toronto, Can., 1971; exec. v.p. Wittington Investments Ltd., 1981. Fellow British Inst. Mgmt., Inst. Dirs.; mem. Inst. Chartered Accts. Scotland, Soc. of Antiquaries of Scotland. Clubs: The Nat. (Toronto), Royal Can. Yacht (Toronto); Coral Beach (Bermuda). Office: Wittington Investments Ltd, 22 St Clair Ave East, Toronto, ON Canada M4T 2S3

LINDSELL, HAROLD, clergyman, educator, editor; b. N.Y.C., Dec. 22, 1913; s. Leonard Anthony and Ella Briggs (Harris) L.; B.S., Wheaton Coll., 1938; M.A., U. Calif., 1939, Ph.D., N.Y. U., 1942; D.D., Fuller Theol. Sem., 1964; m. Marion Joanne Bolinder, June 12, 1943; children—Judith Ann (Mrs. William C. Wood), Joanne (Mrs. Robert Webber), Nancy J. (Mrs. Daniel Sharp), John H. Prof. history, missions, registrar Columbia Bible Coll., 1942-44; ordained to ministry Baptist Ch., 1944; prof. missions, asso. prof. ch. history No. Bapt. Theol. Sem., 1944-47, prof., 1947-51, registrar, 1947-50, dean, 1950-51; dean faculty, prof. missions Fuller Theol. Sem., 1951-61, v.p., prof. missions, 1961-64; assoc. editor Christianity Today, 1964-67, editor, pub., 1968-78; prof. Bible, Wheaton (Ill.) Coll., 1967-68; dir. M.A. program Simon Greenleaf Sch. Law, 1984—. Mem. exec. com. Internat. Congress on World Evangelization. Trustee emeritus Westmont Coll., Wheaton Coll.; chmn. Gordon Conwell Theol. Sem., Outreach, Christianity Today. Mem. Tournament Roses, Nat. Assn. Bible Instrs., Am. Hist. Assn., Am. Soc. Ch. History, Nat., Greater Washington (pres. 1966-67) assns. evangelicals, NEA, Am. Acad. Polit. and Social Scis., Evang. Theol. Soc. (pres. 1970-71), Pi Gamma Mu, Pi Kappa Delta, Alpha Gamma Omega. Republican. Clubs: Nat. Press, Cosmos (Washington). Author: Abundantly Above, 1944; The Thing Appointed, 1949; A Christian Philosophy of Missions, 1949; Park Street Prophet, 1951; (with C.J. Woodbridge) Handbook of Christian Truth, 1953; Missionary Principles and Practice, 1955; The Morning Altar, 1956; Daily Bible Readings from the Revised Standard Version, 1957; Christianity and the Cults, 1963; Harper Study Bible (rev. standard version), 1964; When You Pray, 1969; The World, The Flesh and The Devil, 1974; The Battle for the Bible, 1976; God's Incomparable Word, 1978; The Bible in the Balance, 1979; The Lindsell Study Bible in the Living Bible, 1980; The Gathering Storm, 1980; Free Enterprise: a Judeo-Christian Defense; The Holy Spirit in the Latter Days, 1983; Armageddon Spectre, 1984, The People's Study Bible in KJV and Living Bible, 1986, The New Paganism, 1987; also articles. Editor: The Church's Worldwide Mission, 1966, Harper Study Bible (New Am. Standard Version), 1985. Home: 5395 A Paseo del Lago Laguna Hills CA 92653

LINDSEY, DOTTYE JEAN, educator; b. Temple Hill, Ky., Nov. 4, 1929; d. Jesse D. and Ethel Ellen (Bailey) Nuckols; B.S., Western Ky. U., 1953, M.A., 1959; m. Willard W. Lindsey, June 14, 1952 (div.). Owner, Bonanza Restaurant, Charleston, W.Va., 1965; tchr. remedial reading Alice Waller Elem. Sch., Louisville, 1967-75, tchr., 1953-67, 1975—, contact person for remedial reading, 1968—; profl. model Cosmo/Casablancas Modeling Agy., Louisville, 1984—. Bn. sponsor ROTC Western Ky. U., 1950; local precinct capt., 1987—; election officer, 1984—. Named Miss Ky., 1951. Mem. NEA, Ky. Edn. Assn., Jefferson County Tchrs. Assn., various polit. action coms., Internat. Reading Assn., Am. Childhood Edn. Assn., Met. Louisville Women's Polit. Caucus (treas. 1980—). Democrat. Baptist. Office: 7410 LaGrange Rd Suite 104 Louisville KY 40222

LINDSKOG, MARJORIE OTILDA, educator; b. Rochester, Minn., Oct. 13, 1937; d. Miles Emery and Otilda Elvina (Hagre) L. BA, Colo. Coll., 1959, MA in Teaching, 1972. Field advisor/camp dir. Columbine council Girl Scouts U.S., Pueblo, Colo., 1959-65; staff mem. Wyo. Girl Scout Camp, Casper, 1966, dir., 1967; tchr. Sch. Dist. 60, Pueblo, 1966—; asst. dir. camp Pacific Peaks Girl Scouts U.S., Olympia, Wash., 1968, dir., 1969; instr. Jr. Gt. Books Program, 1981—; chmn. credit com. Pueblo Tchr.'s Credit Union. Author: (series of math. lessons) Bronco Mathmania, 1987, 88; area co-chair Channel 8 Pub. TV Auction, Pueblo, 1983-87; contbr. articles to profl. jours. Bd. dirs. Columbine Girl Scout Council, 1983-85, Dist. #60 Blood Bank, 1985—; mem. Pueblo Greenway and Nature Ctr., 1981—. Recipient Thanks badge Girl Scouts U.S. Mem. Colo. Archeol. Soc., Assn. for Supervision and Curriculum Devel., Colo. Assn. for Gifted and Talented, Nat. Council for Tchrs. Math., Intertel, Mensa, Phi Delta Kappa (editor newsletter), Alpha Phi. Lutheran. Club: Pueblo Country. Lodge: Sons of Norway. Home: 2810 7th Ave Pueblo CO 81003 Office: Sunset Park Sch 110 Univ Circle Pueblo CO 81005

LINDSTROM, RAIMO MATTI, electronic company executive; b. Helsinki, Finland, Feb. 14, 1943; came to Sweden, 1949; s. Mattias Edvard and Alina (Tamminen) L.; m. Anita Marianne Akerstrom, Dec. 1, 1973; children—Mattias, Lena. Engr., Tekniska Gymnasiet, Gothenburg, Sweden, 1964. Mng. dir., chmn. Sound Elektronikservice AB, Gothenburg, Sweden, 1965—; chmn. Punos Electronic, Gothenburg, 1978—; dir. Elektro Punos, Helsinki, 1982—, Stig Starke, Vaxjo, Sweden, 1984—. Patentee loom electronics, 1979. Office: Sound Elektronik Service AB, Knipplagatan 6, S041474 Gothenburg Sweden

LINDVALL, ERIK TORGNY, mathematics educator, researcher; b. Goteborg, Sweden, Mar. 17, 1945; s. Erik and Elsa (Johansson) L. BS, U. Göteborg, 1967, PhD, 1973, Docent Competence, 1979. Research asst. U. Göteborg, 1973-82, lectr. math., 1982—; vis. researcher Stanford U., U. Wis., U. Copenhagen, U. Cambridge, 1975—. Contbr. articles on probability theory to math. jours. Mem. Sweden-Am. Found grantee, 1979, Swedish Nat. Sci. Found. grantee, 1982—. Mem. Inst. Math. Stats., Bernoulli Soc. Lutheran. Office: U Göteborg, Dept Math, 412 96 Göteborg Sweden

LINELL, PER FOLKE, communications educator; b. Malmo, Sweden, May 15, 1944; s. Folke S. and Astrid E. (Gamstedt) L.; m. Siv. B. Carlsson, Sept. 14, 1968; children: Mats H., Tomas O. BA, Uppsala (Sweden) U., 1965, PhD in Linguistics, 1974. Lectr. in linguistics U. Uppsala, Sweden, 1967-74, asst. prof., 1974-80; researcher in psycholinguistics Swedish Research Council for Humanities and Social Scis., 1980-81; prof. communication studies U. Linkoping, Sweden, 1981—. Author: Psychological Reality in Phonology, 1979, Languages of Man, 1978, and others; over 40 published sci. articles. Mem. Linguistic Soc. Am., Nordic Assn. Linguists, Soc. Linguistica Europeae. Home: Lovsbergsvagen 26, S 58269 Linkoping Sweden Office: Univ Linkoping, Dept Communication Studies, S 58183 Linkoping Sweden

LING, ROBERT F., statistics educator, consultant; b. Hong Kong, Apr. 21, 1939; U.S., 1957, naturalized, 1968. B.A., Berea (Ky.) Coll., 1961; M.A., U. Tenn., 1963; M.Phil., Yale U., 1968, Ph.D., 1970. Asst. prof. stats. U. Chgo., 1970-75; assoc. prof. math. scis. Clemson (S.C.) U., 1975-77, prof., 1977—; vis. prof. Vanderbilt U., Nashville, 1982, U Chgo., 1983; vis. lectr. Com. of Pres. of Statis. Socs., 1984-86. Co-author: Exploring Statistics with IDA, 1979; IDA: A User's Guide to the Interactive Data Analysis and Forecasting System, 1982; Conversational Statistics with IDA, An Introduction to Data Analysis and Regression, 1982; assoc. editor: Am. Statis. Assn, 1977-85; mem. editorial bd.; Jour. of Classification, 1983—. Office of Naval Research grantee, 1973-82. Fellow Am. Statis. Assn. (Frank Wilcoxon prize best practical application paper 1984); mem. Internat. Assn. for Statis. Computing, Mensa. Research on applied stats. and data analysis, cluster analysis and classification; numerical approximations of statis. distbns. statistical computing. Home: 103 Brookhaven Dr Clemson SC 29631-1907 Office: Clemson U Dept Math Scis Clemson SC 29631

LING, SUILIN, management consultant; b. Shanghai, China, Oct. 13, 1930; s. Chunchen and Maisan (Dunn) L.; came to U.S., 1949, naturalized, 1963; B.S., U. Mich., 1952; Ph.D., Columbia U., 1961; m. Avril Marjorie Kathleen Button, Apr. 4, 1964; children—Christopher Charles, Charmian Avril. Mech. engr. Ebasco Services, Inc., 1953-54; with research div. Foster Wheeler Corp., 1954-64; mgmt. cons. The Emerson Cons., Inc., 1964-65; sr. economist Communications Satellite Corp., 1965-67; chief economist Northrop-Page Communication Engrs., Inc., 1967-70; founder-dir., chief economist Teleconsult, Inc., Washington, 1970-82; founder, pres. Communications Devel. Corp., 1982-87, chmn. bd. dirs., 1987—; lectr. econs. Bernard M. Baruch Sch. Bus. and Pub. Adminstrn., CCNY. Mem. Am. Mgmt. Assn., Am. Econ. Assn., Am. Soc. M.E., Am. Acad. Polit. and Social Sci. Author: Economies of Scale in the Steam-Electric Power Generating Industry, 1964. Home: 2735 Unicorn Ln NW Washington DC 20015 Office: 2828 Pennsylvania Ave NW Washington DC 20007

LINGHAM, MARCELLA ERMA, community health center administrator; b. Phila., Jan. 15, 1942; d. Harry Boyd and Gladys Marcella Lawson; student Temple U., 1960-62; B.S. in edn., Cheyney State Coll., 1965; M.Ed., Temple U., 1970; Ed.D., Rutgers U., 1980. Tchr., Sch. Dist. Phila., 1965-70; curriculum devel. specialist, reading specialist RCA Service Co., Cherry Hill, N.J., 1970-72; project dir., curriculum developer, ednl. cons. Research for Better Schs., Inc., Phila., 1972-79; asst. prof. Rutgers U. Newark Coll. Arts and Scis., 1980-83; exec. dir. Primary Community Health Ctr. of Mantua, Inc., 1983-84; project dir. Mantua Community Devel. Corp., 1984-85; learning specialist Rutgers U. Coll. Nursing, 1985-86; exec. dir. 2501 Primary Community Health Care Ctr., Inc., 1986—. Vice chairperson bd. dirs. 2501 Health Care Corp., Phila., 1980-83, bd. dirs. Black Family Services. Mem. Am. Ednl. Research Assn., Internat. Reading Assn., AAUW, Am. Pub. Health Assn., Assn. Supervision and Curriculum Devel. Democrat. Baptist. Home: 2708 S 86 St Philadelphia PA 19153 Office: 2501 Primary Community Health Care Ctr Inc 2501 W Lehigh Ave Philadelphia PA 19132

LINI, WALTER HADYE, prime minister Republic of Vanuatu, clergyman; b. Pentecost, 1942. Ed. Solomon Islands, N.Z. Ordained deacon Anglican Ch., 1968, priest, 1970. Dep. chief minister, also minister social services New Hebrides (now Vanuatu), 1979, chief minister, also minister justice, 1979-80; prime minister Vanuatu, 1980—. Pres., Vanuaaku Pati (formerly Nat. Party). Address: Office of Prime Minister, PO Box 110, Port Vila Vanuatu *

LINK, HERBERT FERDINAND OTTO, manufacturing company executive; b. Bangkok, Thailand, Aug. 5, 1910; s. Adolf Heinrich Albert and Erna Helen Charlotte (Krito) L.; m. Alma Catharine Sturm, Aug. 26, 1939. Certificate, U. Hamburg, Ger., 1930-31, U. Munich, 1931-32. Clk., B. Grimm & Co., Hamburg, Ger., 1931-32; clk. B. Grimm & Co., ROP., Bangkok, Siam, 1932-39, mgr. Bangkok, Thailand, 1939-49, mng. ptnr., 1949—. Mem. Siam Soc., Bangkok, 1933—; observer for Ger. ECAFE-Subcom., Bangkok, 1950-53; dir. Siri-Wattana Cheshire, Bangkok, 1964—. Decorated Crown Order IV Class, H.M. The King of Thailand, 1960, Elephant Order IV Class, 1963; Merit Order I Class, Fed. Republic of Germany, 1964, Merit Grand Cross, 1975. Mem. German Bus. Group in Thailand (founder/chmn. 1959-62), Bd. of Trade, German-Thai C. of C., Siam Soc. Lutheran. Clubs: Rotary (pres. 1971-72), Royal Bangkok Sports, " DER" . Home: 25 Chitlom Ln, Bangkok 10500, Thailand Office: 1634/4 Phetburi Rd, Bangkok 10310, Thailand

LINK, MAE MILLS (MRS. S. GORDDEN LINK), space medicine historian and consultant; b. Corbin, Ky., May 14, 1915; d. William Speed and Florence (Estes) Mills; m. S. Gordden Link, Jan. 11, 1936. B.S., George Peabody Coll. for Tchrs., Vanderbilt U., 1936; M.A., Vanderbilt U., 1937; Ph.D., Am. U., 1951; grad., Air War Coll., 1965. Instr. social sci. Oglethorpe U., 1938-39; instr. English Drury Coll., 1940-41; asso. dir. edn. Ga. Warm Springs Found., 1941-42; mil. historian Hdqrs. Army Air Forces, 1943-45, Office Mil. History, Dept. of Army, 1945-51; spl. asst. to surgeon gen., sr. med. historian U.S. Air Force, Washington, 1951-62; cons. in documentation and space medicine historian NASA, Washington, 1962-64; coordinator documentation, life scis. historian NASA, 1964-70; research asso. Ohio State U. Found., 1970-72; Mem. exec. com. Orgn. for Advancement Coll. Teaching; mem. nat. adv. bd. Am. Security Council. Author: Medical Support of the Army Air Forces in World War II, 1955, Annual Reports of the U.S. Air Force Medical Service, 1949-62, Space Medicine in Project Mercury, 1965; (with others) USA/USSR Joint Publ. Foundations of Space Biology and Medicine, 1976; Editor: U.S. Air Force Med. Service Digest, 1957-62; Contbr. to profl. jours.; Collier's Ency., Ency. Brit.; Contbr. to.; Funk and Wagnall's New Ency. Recipient Meritorious Service award U.S. Air Force, 1955, Ann. Outstanding Performance awards, 1956-62, Outstanding Alumna award Sue Bennett Coll., 1977. Fellow Am. Med. Writers Assn. (past pres. Middle Atlantic region); mem. Aerospace Med. Assn., Air Force Hist. Found. (charter), Internat. Congress History Medicine, Societe

International d'Histoire de la Medecine, Planetary Soc. (charter). Republican. Episcopalian. Clubs: Garden of Va.; Army-Navy (Washington).

LINNENBERG, CLEM CHARLES, JR., economist; b. Houston, May 20, 1912; s. Clem Charles and Maggie (White) L.; student So. Meth. U., 1930; B.A., M.A., U. Tex., 1933; Ph.D., Yale U., 1941; postgrad. Am. U., 1954; m. Marianne Sakmann, Aug. 15, 1942. Economist, Dept. Labor, 1934-35, Social Security Bd., 1936, antitrust div. Dept. Justice, 1938-39, Bur. Budget, 1939-51; program planning officer Office Sec. Commerce, 1951-53; chief econ. analysis sect. Office Internat. Trade, Dept. Commerce, 1953; transp. economist Gen. Services Adminstrn., 1953-54, Dept. Agr., 1954-59; chief div. statistics and studies Office Vocational Rehab., Dept. Health Edn. and Welfare, 1959-62; economist USPHS, 1962-69; ind. cons. in econs. and statistics, 1969—. Lectr. in transp. Georgetown U., 1956-57. Mem. Am. Pub. Health Assn., Phi Beta Kappa, Pi Sigma Alpha, Sigma Delta Pi. Democrat. Methodist. Author: Twixt Chaos and Conformism, 1950; The Agricultural Exemptions in Interstate Trucking: Mend Them or End Them?, 1960; Economics in Program Planning for Health, 1966; Organizing and Staffing for the Program Planning Function, 1967; other monographs. Home and Office: 4000 Cathedral Ave NW Apt 806-B Washington DC 20016

LINO, MANUEL AUGUSTO BRAGA, mechanical industry executive; b. Gaviao, Vila Nova Famalicao, Portugal, May 15, 1935; s. Laurindo Ferreira and Araci Braga L.; div.; children—Susana Maria Ferreira Braga Lino, Manuel Augusto Ferreira Braga Lino. Ph.D. in Engring., Faculty of Engring., Oporto, 1962. Cert. mech. engr. Exec., Ferreira Lino & Irmao Lda., Ermesinde, 1962—; mem. techno-pedagogical commn. Centro de Formaç ã o Profissional de Indú stria de Fundiç ã o. invited tchr. Faculty of Engring., Oporto, 1971-80. Mcpl. dep., Valongo, 1976-79. Mem. Order of Engrs., Assn. dos Antigos Alunos do Dept. de Engenharia Mecanica (pres. bd. 1982-84); Associaç ã o dos Indú striais Metalú rgicos (pres. gen. meeting 1983-86), AIMMN (pres. bd. dirs. 1986—, pres. Mcpl. Assembly 1985—). Home: Rua da Bela 30, 4445 Ermesinde Portugal Office: Ferreira Lino & Irmao Lda, Rua da Bela 30, 4445 Ermesinde Portugal

LINOWES, DAVID FRANCIS, political economy and public policy educator; b. N.J., Mar. 16, 1917; m. Dorothy Lee Wolf, Mar. 24, 1946; children: Joanne Linowes Alinsky, Richard Gary, Susan Linowes Allen, Jonathan Scott. B.S. (with honors), U. Ill., 1941. Founder, ptnr. Leopold & Linowes, Washington, 1946-62; cons. sr. ptnr. Leopold & Linowes, 1962-82; nat. founding ptnr. Laventhol & Horwath, 1965-76; chmn. bd, chief exec. officer Mickleberry Corp., 1970-73; dir. Horn & Hardart Co., 1971-77, Piper Aircraft, 1972-77, Saturday Rev./World Mag., Inc., 1972-77, Chris Craft Industries, Inc., 1958—, Work in Am. Inst., Inc.; cons. DATA Internat. Assistance Corps., 1962-68, U.S. Dept. State, UN, Sec. HEW, Dept. Interior; chmn. Fed. Privacy Protection Commn., Washington, 1975-77, U.S. Commn. Fair Market Value Policy for Fed. Coal Leasing, 1983-84, Pres.'s Commn. on Fiscal Accountability of Nation's Energy Resources, 1981-82; chmn. Pres.' Commn. on Privatization, 1987-88; mem. Council on Fgn. Relations; cons. panel GAO; adj. prof. mgmt. NYU, 1965-73; Disting. Arthur Young Prof. U. Ill., 1973-74, Harold Boeschenstein prof. polit. economy and pub. policy, 1976—; emeritus chmn. internat. adv. com. Tel Aviv U.; headed U.S. State Dept. Mission to Turkey, 1967, to India, 1970, to Pakistan, 1968, to Greece, 1971; U.S. rep. on privacy to Orgn. Econ. Devel. Intergovtl. Bur. for Informatics, 1977-81, cons., N.Y.C., 1977-81. Author: Managing Growth Through Acquisition, Strategies for Survival, Corporate Conscience; commn. report Personal Privacy in an Information Society, Fiscal Accountability of Nation's Energy Resources, The Privacy Crisis in Our Time, contbr. articles to profl. jours. Trustee Boy's Club Greater Washington, 1955-62, Am. Inst. Found., 1962-68; assoc. YM-YWHA's Greater N.Y., 1970-76; chmn. Charities Adv. Com. of D.C., 1958-62; emeritus bd. dirs. Religion in Am. Life, Inc.; former chmn. U.S. People for UN; chmn. citizens com. Combat Charity Rackets, 1953-58. Served to 1st lt. Signal Corps, AUS, 1942-46. Recipient 1970 Human Relations award Am. Jewish Com.; U.S. Pub. Service award, 1982. Mem. Am. Inst. C.P.A.s (v.p. 1962-63), U. Ill. Found. (emeritus bd. dirs.), Phi Kappa Phi (nat. bd. dirs.), Beta Gamma Sigma. Clubs: Cosmos, Federal City (Washington); Harmonie (N.Y.C.); Council on Fgn. Relations (N.Y.C.). Home: 9 Wayside Ln Scarsdale NY 10583 also: 803 Fairway Dr Champaign IL 61820 Office: U Ill 308 Lincoln Hall Urbana IL 61801

LINOWITZ, SOL MYRON, lawyer, diplomat; b. Trenton, N.J., Dec. 7, 1913; s. Joseph and Rose (Oglenskye) L.; m. Evelyn Zimmerman, Sept. 3, 1939; children: Anne, June, Jan, Ronni. AB, Hamilton Coll., 1935; JD, Cornell U., 1938; LLD (hon.), Allegheny Coll., Amherst Coll., Bucknell U., Babson Inst., Colgate U., Curry Coll., Dartmouth Coll., Elmira Coll., Georgetown U., Hamilton Coll., Ithaca Coll., Oberlin Coll., St. John Fisher Coll., St. Lawrence U., Jewish Theol. Sem., Washington U., St. Louis, U. Miami, Marietta Coll., Muskingum Coll., Notre Dame U., U. Pacific, U. Pa., Rutgers U., Pratt Inst., Rider Coll., Roosevelt U., Chapman Coll., U. Mich., Govs. State U., U. Mo., Syracuse U., Brandeis U.; LHD, Am. U., Yeshiva U., Marietta Coll., U. Judaism, Wooster Coll.; PhD (hon.), U. Haifa. Bar: N.Y. 1938. Asst. gen. counsel OPA, Washington, 1942-44; ptnr. Sutherland, Linowitz & Williams, 1946-58, Harris, Beach, Keating, Wilcox & Linowitz, Rochester, N.Y., 1958-66; chmn. Nat. Urban Coalition, 1970—; chmn. bd. dirs., chmn. exec. com., gen. counsel Xerox Corp., 1958-66; chmn. bd. dirs. Xerox Internat., 1966; sr. ptnr. Coudert Bros., 1969—; ambassador to OAS, 1966-69; trustee Mut. Life Ins. Co. N.Y.; co-negotiator Panama Canal treaties, 1977-78; spl. Middle East negotiator for Pres. Carter, 1979-81; chmn. Am. Acad. of Diplomacy, 1984—; co-chmn. Inter-Am. Dialogue, 1981—; pres. Fed. City Council, 1974-78; chmn. Pres.'s Commn. World Hunger, 1978-79; bd. dirs., co-founder Internat. Exec. Service Corps; chmn. State Dept. Adv. Com. on Internat. Orgns., 1963-66. Author: (memoir) The Making of a Public Man, 1985, This Troubled Urban World, contbr. articles to profl. jours. Trustee Hamilton Coll., Cornell U., Johns Hopkins U., Am. Assembly. Served to lt. USNR, 1944-46. Fellow Am. Acad. Arts and Scis.; mem. Am. Assn. for UN (pres. N.Y. State), Rochester Assn. for UN (pres. 1952), Rochester C. of C. (pres. 1958), ABA, N.Y. Bar Assn., Rochester Bar Assn. (v.p. 1949-50), Am. Assn. UN (bd. dirs.), Council on Fgn. Relations, Order of Coif, Phi Beta Kappa, Phi Kappa Phi. Office: Coudert Bros 1627 I St NW Washington DC 20006

LINVILLE, THOMAS MERRIAM, engineer; b. Washington, Mar. 3, 1904; s. Thomas and Clara (Merriam) L.; m. Eleanor Priest, Nov. 25, 1939; children—Eleanor, Thomas Priest, Edward Dwight. E.E., U. Va., 1926; grad. advanced mgmt. program, Harvard U., 1950; mod. engring. program, U. Calif. at Los Angeles, 1960. Various govt. positions 1918-26; with Gen. Electric Co., 1926-66; beginning with Gen. Electric Co. (Advanced Engring. Program), to 1931, successively at corp. level chmn. rotating machines product com., chmn. rotating machines devel. com., staff asst. to mgr. engring., 1926-51, mgr. engring. edn., mgmt. consultation div., 1926-51, mgr. exec. devel., mgr. research operation, mgr. research application and info., 1951-66; chief exec. Linville Co. (Engrs., Research & Devel.), 1966—; mem. USN tech. missions, Pearl Harbor, 1942, Europe, 1945; mem. NRC, 1960-68. Author books (Linville Books) and papers on elec. machine design and application. Chmn. Schenectady City Planning Commn., 1951; pres. N.Y. State Citizens Com. for Pub. Schs., 1952-53; mem. Gov.'s Council Advancement Research and Devel. N.Y. State, 1960—; pres. Schenectady Mus., 1964-69; chmn. Community Chest, 1964, Devel. Council for Sci., Rensselaer Poly. Inst., 1960-67; vis. com. Norwich U., 1970—, Clarkson Inst. Tech., 1959-65; pres. Mohawk-Hudson council ETV-WMHT Channel 17, 1966-70; bd. dirs. Sunnyview Hosp.; pres. Schenectady Indsl. Devel. Corp., 1967-69. Served to lt. USNR, 1940-42. Recipient Charles A. Coffin award, IEEE Centennial medal, USN Certificate of Commendation; Schenectady Profl. Engrs. Soc. Engr.-of-Year award, 1960. Fellow ASME, AAAS, IEEE (dir. 1953-57, Centennial medal 1984); mem. Nat. Soc. Profl. Engrs. (pres. 1966-67), N.Y. State Soc. Profl. Engrs. (pres. 1954-55), Am. Soc. Engring. Edn., Engrs. Joint Council (dir. 1954-59), N.Y. Acad. Scis., Schenectady C. of C. (past dir., v.p.), Raven Soc., Tau Beta Pi (eminent mem., nat. pres. 1974-76), Theta Tau, Delta Upsilon. Unitarian (pres. 1940-45). Clubs: Rotary, Mohawk, Mohawk Golf. Address: 1147 Wendell Ave Schenectady NY 12308

LINZ, ANTHONY JAMES, osteopathic physician, consultant; b. Sandusky, Ohio, June 16, 1948; s. Anthony Joseph and Margaret Jane (Ballah) Linz; m. Kathleen Ann Kovach, Aug. 18, 1973; children—Anthony Scott, Sara Elizabeth. B.S., Bowling Green State U., 1971; D.O., U. Ostep Med. and Health Scis., 1974. Diplomate Nat. Bd. Osteo. Examiners; bd. cert., diplomate Am. Osteo. Bd. Internal Medicine, Internal Medicine and Med. Diseases of Chest. Intern, Brentwood Hosp., Cleve., 1974-75, resident in internal medicine, 1975-78; subsplty. fellow in pulmonary diseases Riverside Meth. Hosp., Columbus, Ohio, 1978-80; med. dir. pulmonary services Sandusky Meml. Hosp., 1980-85; med. dir. cardio-pulmonary services, Firelands Community Hosp., 1985—; also cons. pulmonary diseases and internal medicine, active staff sect. internal medicine, chmn. dept. medicine, head div. pulmonary medicine; cons. staff dept. medicine Good Samaritan Hosp., 1982-85; also sect. internal medicine specializing pulmonary diseases; cons. pulmonary and internal medicine Providence Hosp., Sandusky, Willard Area Hosp.; clin. prof. internal medicine Ohio U. Coll. Osteo. Medicine; clin. asst. prof. med. Med. Coll. of Ohio at Toledo; adj. assoc. prof. applied scis. Bowling Green State U.; mem. respiratory therapy adv. bd. Firelands Campus, Bowling Green State U., 1983—; med. dir. Respiratory Therapy program., Bowling Green State U.; 39 Contbr. article on early detection lung cancer to profl. jour. Water safety instr. ARC; med. dir. Camp Superkid Asthma Camp; bd. trustees Stein Hospice. Fellow Am. Coll. Chest Physicians, Am. Coll. Osteo. Internists; mem. Am. Osteo. Assn., Ohio Osteo. Assn. (past. pres., past v.p., past. sec.-treas. 5th dist. acad.), Am. Coll. Osteo. Internists, Am. Heart Assn., Am. Thoracic Soc., Ohio Thoracic Soc., Am. Lung Assn. (pres., 1st v.p., med. adv. bd. chmn., exec. bd. dirs., bd. dirs. Ohio's So. Shore sect. 1984—), Nat. Assn. Med. Dirs. Respiratory Care, Ohio Soc. Respiratory Therapy (med. adviser/dir.), Soc. Crit. Care Medicine, Found. Crit. Care (mem. founder's circle), Alpha Epsilon Delta, Beta Beta Beta, Pi Kappa Alpha, Atlas Med. Fraternity. Roman Catholic.

LINZ, VINCENT ARTHUR, periodontist, television producer; b. Cin., July 20, 1953; s. Vincent Harold Linz and Virginia Zettel. BS magna cum laude, U. Cin., 1974; DDS, Ohio State U., 1977, MS, 1979. Diplomate Am. Bd. Periodontology; cert. laser surgeon, tissue integrated prosthesis surgeon. Pvt. practice periodontics Cin., 1979—; producer Big Bang Productions, Cin., 1983—; cons. Music Video Productions, Cins., 1985—, U. Cin., 1986—. Producer, dir. (video art) Sloppy Seconds, 1984 (Philo award 1984), Raw Meat, 1985 (Philo award 1985). Recipient first place award Warner/Amex Cable TV, Cin., 1985. Mem. ADA, Am. Bd. Periodontology, Am. Acad. Periodontology, Midwest Soc. Periodontology, Ohio Acad. Periodontists, Western Hills Dental Study Club. Roman Catholic. Home: 5615 Wynnburne Ave Cincinnati OH 45238 Office: 4966 Glenway Cincinnati OH 45238

LIONBERGER, ERLE TALBOT LUND, Republican committeewomen; b. St. Louis, Apr. 29, 1933; d. Joel Y. and Erle (Harsh) Lund; m. John S. Lionberger, Jr., June 23, 1956; children: Erle Talbot, Louise Shepley. Student Mary Inst., 1951; AB, Vassar Coll., 1955. Republican committeewoman Hadley Twp., St. Louis County, 1965—; mem. St. Louis County Rep. Central Com., 1965—; mem. Rep. State Com., 1968-78, 84—; del. Rep. Nat. Conv., 1972, 76, 80, 84, alt. del., 1968; Mo. rep. Rep. Nat. Platform Com., 1988; Mo. chmn. Women for Reagan-Bush, 1984. Bd. dirs. Landmarks Assn. St. Louis, Inc., 1973-76, counselor, 1982—, coordinator Historic Preservation Pilgrimage, 1974; bd. dirs. Friends of Winston Churchill Meml., 1975-76, Save Grant's White Haven, Inc., 1985—; mem. women's exec. bd. Mo. Bot. Garden, 1977-80; mem. St. Louis County Hist. Bldg. Commn., 1976—, Capitol Complex Commn. on Fine Arts, 1983—; chmn. Mo. 7th Senatorial Dist. Com., 1978-84; chmn. Mo. Adv. Council on Hist. Preservation, 1982—; Mo. rep. Lewis and Clark Nat. Hist. Trail Adv. Council, 1984—; bd. dirs. Mo. Heritage Trust, 1982—, Mo. Parks Assn., 1982—Mem. Jr. League St. Louis, Mo. Fedn. Republican Women (bd. dirs. 1980-84), Nat. Soc. Colonial Dames Am. (Mo. bd. dirs. 1976-80, hist. properties chmn. 1975-81, pub. chmn. 1987—), St. Louis Christmas Carols Assn. (area co-chmn. 1979-85). Address: 21 Dartford St Saint Louis MO 63105

LIOTTI, GIOVANNI ANTONIO, psychotherapist; b. Tripoli, Libya, Mar. 27, 1945; s. Nicola and Maria Anna (Aleotti) L.; m. Patrizia Salinari (div. 1983); 1 child, Laura; m. Sandra DeBiase; 1 child, Luca. BS in Medicine, U. La Sapienza, Rome, 1969, MD in Psychiatry, 1973. Researcher U. La Sapienza, Rome, 1974-85. Author: (with others) Cognitive Processes and Emotional Disorders, 1983; contbr. articles to profl. jours. Research grantee Ministry Edn. Govt. of Italy, 1972. Fellow Italian Assn. Behavioral and Cognitive Therapies (dir. tng. programs 1973—); mem. Italian Assn. Med. Psychotherapy, Italian Assn. Psychiatry, Italian Assn. Pyschology. Roman Catholic. Office: Centro Di Psicoterapia Cognitiva, Via Degli Scipioni 245, 00192 Rome Italy

LIPCON, CHARLES R., lawyer; b. N.Y.C., Mar. 20, 1946; s. Harry H. and Rose Lipcon; m. Irmgard Adels, Dec. 1, 1974; children—Lauren, Claudia. B.A., U. Miami, 1968, J.D., 1971. Bar: Fla. 1971, U.S. Dist. Ct. (so. dist.) Fla. 1971, U.S. Ct. Appeals (5th cir.) 1972, U.S. Supreme Ct. 1976, U.S. Ct. Appeals (D.C. cir.) 1980, U.S. Dist. Ct. (so. dist.) Tex. 1982. Sole practice, Miami, Fla., 1971—; lectr. U. Miami Sch. Law. Author: Help for the Auto Accident Victim. Named Commodore of High Seas, Internat. Seaman's Union. Mem. Fla. Bar Assn., Am. Trial Lawyers Assn., ABA, Fla. Trial Lawyers, Dade County Bar Assn., Dade County Trial Lawyers. Club: Rotary (Key Biscayne). Contbr. articles to profl. jours. Office: 2 S Biscayne Blvd Suite 2480 Miami FL 33131

LIPE, LINDA BON, lawyer; b. Clarksdale, Miss., Jan. 10, 1948; s. William Ray and Gwendolyn (Strickland) Lipe; m. Larry L. Gleghorn, Feb. 15, 1983 (div. Feb. 1988). BBA in Accountancy, U. Miss., 1970, JD, 1971. Bar: Miss. 1971, Ark. 1976, U.S. Dist. Ct. (no. dist.) Miss. 1971, U.S. Dist. Ct. (ea. dist.) Ark. 1976, U.S. Ct. Appeals (8th cir.) 1985. Sr. tax acct. Arthur Young & Co., San Jose, Calif., 1971-74, A.M. Pullen & Co., Knoxville, Tenn., 1975; legal counsel to gov. State of Ark., Little Rock, 1975-79; dep. pros. atty. 6th Jud. Dist. Ark., Little Rock, 1979-80; chief counsel Ark. Public Service Commn., Little Rock, 1980-83; asst. U.S. atty. Eastern Dist. Ark., Dept. Justice, Little Rock, 1983—. Mem. ADA, Miss. State Bar, Ark. State Bar Assn. Episcopalian. Office: US Atty's Office 600 W Capitol PO Box 1229 Little Rock AR 72203

LI PENG, government official of People's Republic of China, electrical engineer; b. Chengdu, Sichuan Province, People's Republic of China, Oct. 1928; s. Li Shouxun and Zhao Juntao; m. Zhu Lin, 1958; 3 children. Attended Yan'an Inst. Natural Scis., Moscow Power Inst., 1948. Dep. dir., chief engr. Fengman Hydro-elec. Power Plant; dep. chief engr., head disdatcher's office Northeast Power Bur.; head Beijing Telecommunication Adminstrn.; joined Chinese Communist Party, 1945, mem. 12th Cen. Com., 1982—, mem. Politburo, 1985—, Secretariat of Cen. Com., 1985-87, mem. Standing Com., 1987—; vice-minister Electric Power Industry, People's Republic of China, 1979-81, minister Electric Power Industry, 1981-82; vice-minister Water Conservancy and Electric Power, 1982-83; vice chmn. State Council, 1983-87, acting premier, 1987-88, premier, 1988—; minister in charge of State Edn. Commn.; head Leading Group for Devel. Rural Energy, 1984, Leading Group for Electronics Industry, 1984—, State Nuclear Power Leading Group, 1985—; chmn. Environ. Protection Com., 1984; minister State Econ. Commn., 1985; minister in charge of State Restructuring of Econ. System Comm., 1988—. Pres. Wu Yuzhang Found. Office: care State Council, Office of Vice Premier, Beijing People's Republic of China *

LIPKIN, MARTIN, physician, scientist; b. N.Y.C., Apr. 30, 1926; s. Samuel S. and Celia (Greenfield) L.; m. Joan Schulein, Feb. 16, 1958; children—Richard Martin, Steven Monroe. A.B., NYU, 1946, M.D., 1950. Diplomate: Nat. Bd. Med. Examiners. Fellow Cornell U. Med. Coll., 1952; practice medicine specializing in internal medicine, gastroenterology and neoplastic diseases N.Y.C.; mem. staff N.Y. Hosp., Meml. Hosp. for Cancer and Allied Diseases; assoc. prof. medicine Cornell U. Med. Coll., N.Y.C., 1963-78; prof. medicine Cornell U. Med. Coll., 1978—, prof. Grad. Sch. Med. Scis., 1978—; attending physician and head Lab. of Gastrointestinal Cancer Research, Meml. Sloan Kettering Cancer Center; mem. Meml. Sloan-Kettering Cancer Ctr., 1985—; vis. physician Rockefeller U. Hosp., 1981—; hon. lectr. Israeli Med. Assn. and Gastroenterology Soc., 1982; mem. bd. sci. consultants Inst. for Familial Mgmt. and Control, 1979—. Mem. editorial bd. Cell and Tissue Kinetics, Cancer Research, Cancer Letters; editor: Gastrointestinal Tract Cancer, 1978, Inhibition of Tumor Induction and Development, 1981, Gastrointestinal Cancer: Endogenous Factors, 1981; contbr. articles to Cancer Research, other profl. jours. Served as officer USN, 1953-55. Recipient NIH career devel. award, 1962-71; Albert F.R. Andresen ann. award and lectureship N.Y. State Med. Soc., 1971—. Fellow A.C.P., A.C.G.; mem. Med. Soc. State of N.Y. (assoc. chmn. sci. program com. 1977—, vice chmn. sci. program com. 1985-87), Digestive Diseases Soc. (founding), Internat. Soc. Investigative Gastroenterology (founding), Am. Soc. Clin. Investigation, Am. Physiol. Soc., Am. Assn. Cancer Research, Am. Gastroenterol. Assn., Am. Coll. Gasterenterology, Soc. for Exptl. Biology and Medicine, Harvey Soc. Office: 1275 York Ave New York NY 10021

LIPKIN, MARY CASTLEMAN DAVIS (MRS. ARTHUR BENNETT LIPKIN), retired psychiatric social worker; b. Germantown, Pa., Mar. 4, 1907; d. Henry L. and Willie (Webb) Davis; student grad. sch. social work U. Wash., 1946-48; m. William F. Cavenaugh, Nov. 8, 1930 (div.); children—Molly C. (Mrs. Gary Oberbillig), William A.; m. 2d, Arthur Bennett Lipkin, Sept. 15, 1961 (dec. June 1974). Nursery sch. tchr. Miquon (Pa.) Sch., 1940-45; caseworker Family Soc. Seattle, 1948-49, Jewish Family and Child Service, Seattle, 1951-56; psychiat. social worker Stockton (Calif.) State Hosp., 1957-58; supr. social service Mental Health Research Inst., Fort Steilacoom, Wash., 1958-59; engaged in pvt. practice, Bellevue, Wash., 1959-61. Former mem. Phila. Com. on City Policy. Former diplomate and bd. mem. Conf. Advancement of Pvt. Practice in Social Work. Mem. Acad. Cert. Social Workers, Nat. Assn. Social Workers, Linus Paul Inst. Sci. and Medicine, Menninger Found., Union Concerned Scientists, Physicians for Social Responsibility, Center for Sci. in Pub. Interest, Jr. League, Seattle Art Mus., Asian Art Council, Wing Luke Mus., Bellevue Art Mus., Pacific Sci. Center, Western Wash. Solar Energy Assn., Nature Conservancy, Wilderness Soc., Sierra Club, Common Cause, ACLU, Pa. Acad. Fine Arts. Clubs: Cosmopolitan, Cricket (Phila.); Women's University (Seattle); Nassau (Princeton, N.J.), Friday Harbor Yacht (Washington). Home: 10022 Meydenbauer Way SE #202 Bellevue WA 98004

LIPMAN, IRA ACKERMAN, security service company executive; b. Little Rock, Nov. 15, 1940; s. Mark and Belle (Ackerman) L.; m. Barbara Ellen Kelly Couch, July 5, 1970; children: Gustave K., Joshua S, M Benjamin. Student, Ohio Wesleyan U., 1958-60; LL.D. (hon.), John Marshall U., Atlanta, 1970. Salesman, exec. Mark Lipman Service Inc., Memphis, 1960-63; v.p. Guardsmark, Inc., Memphis, 1963-66; pres. Guardsmark, Inc., 1966—, chief exec. officer, 1968—, chmn. bd., 1968—; bd. dirs. Nat. Council Crime and Delinquency, 1975, chmn., mem. exec. com., 1986—, chmn. fin. com., treas., 1978-79, vice chmn., 1982-86—; bd. dirs. Greater Memphis Council Crime and Delinquency, 1976-78, vice chmn. bd. nat. council, 1982-86, chmn. exec. com., 1986—; entrepreneurial fellow Memphis State U., 1976; mem. environ. security com., pvt. security adv. council Law Enforcement Assistance Adminstrn., 1975-76; mem. planning com. 2d Nat. Law Enforcement Explorer Conf., 1980—. Author: How to Protect Yourself From Crime, 1975, 2d edit., 1981; contbr. numerous articles to profl. jours., mags. and newspapers. Bd. dirs. Memphis Jewish Community Center, 1974, Memphis Shelby County unit Am. Cancer Soc., 1980-81, Memphis Orchestral Soc., 1980-81, Memphis Jewish Fedn., 1974-83; chmn. Shelby County com. U.S. Savs. Bonds, 1976; mem. president's council Memphis State U., 1975—, mem. visual arts council, 1980-82; Memphis met. chmn. Nat. Alliance Businessmen, 1970-71; mem. task force Reform Jewish Outreach, Union Am. Hebrew Congregations, 1979-83; mem. young leadership cabinet United Jewish Appeal, 1973-78, mem. S.E. regional campaign cabinet, 1980; exec. bd. Chickasaw council Boy Scouts Am., 1978-81; bd. dirs., exec. com. Tenn. Ind. Coll. Fund, 1979; trustee Memphis Acad. Arts, 1977-81, 1980-83; mem. president's club Christian Bros. Coll., 1979; bd. dirs. Future Memphis, 1980-83, 83-86; nat. trustee NCCJ, 1980—, exec. com., 1981—, nat. co-chmn., 1985—, bd. dirs. Memphis chpt., 1980-85, life bd. dirs. Memphis chpt. 1985—; group II chmn. for 1982 campaign United Way Greater Memphis, 1981; trustee Memphis Brooks Mus. Art, 1980-83, Yeshiva U., Simon Wiesenthal Ctr., 1982—, chmn. campaign com., 1983—; bd. dirs. Nat. Alliance against Violence, 1983-85, United Way of Greater Memphis, 1984-85, gen. campaign chmn., 1985-86; founder, bd. overseers B'nai B'rith, 1980—; bd. dirs. Tenn. Gov.'s Jobs for High Sch. Grads. Program, 1980-83, v.p., 1983-84, pres., 1984-85, chmn. exec. com., 1984-85; vol. United Way Am. Second Century Initiative Vol. Involvemnet com. and chmn. task force on critical mkts., 1987; nat. Jewish co-chmn. NCCJ, 1985-88, nat. chmn., 1988—; bd. trustees Ohio Wesleyan U., 1988—. Recipient Humanitarian of Yr. award NCCJ, 1985, Outstanding Community Sales award Sales and Mktg. Execs. Memphis, 1987, Jr. Achievement Master Free Enterprise award, 1987; one of 10 cited as Best Corp. Chief Exec. of Achievement, Gallagher Pres.'s Report, 1974. Mem. Internat. Assn. Chiefs Police, Am. Soc. Criminology, Internat. Soc. Criminology, Am. Soc. Indsl. Security (cert. protection profl.). Republican. Clubs: 100, B'nai B'rith, Ridgeway Country, Racquet, Summit, Delta, Economic bd. dirs. 1980-85, v.p. 1983-84, pres. 1984-85, chmn. exec. com. 1984-85), Petroleum (Memphis); International (Washington). Office: 10 Rockefeller Plaza New York NY 10020

LIPMAN, RICHARD PAUL, pediatrician; b. Cambridge, Mass., Aug. 1, 1935; s. Hyman Zelig and Betty (Likovsky) L.; m. Mary Alice Wilcox, Aug. 25, 1963; children—Gregory, Susan. A.B. magna cum laude, Harvard U., 1957; M.D. cum laude, Tufts U., 1961. Diplomate Am. Bd. Pediatrics. Intern, Boston Floating Hosp., 1961-62, jr. resident, 1962-63, sr. resident, 1963-64, chief resident, 1964; research fellow infectious disease Med. Sch. U. N.C., Chapel Hill, 1967-69; practice pediatrics, Peabody and Lynn, Mass., 1969—; mem. staff North Shore Children's Hosp., Salem, Mass., asso. chief of staff, 1974-76, pres., chief of staff, 1976-79, chief of medicine, 1979-83, trustee, 1980-84, corporator, 1985—; mem. staff Tufts-New Eng. Med. Center, Boston, Boston Children's Hosp. Med. Center, Lynn Hosp., Salem Hosp. Clin. instr. pediatrics Tufts U. Sch. Medicine, Boston, 1969-74, asst. clin. prof., 1974-78, asso. clin. prof., 1978—. Contbr. articles to profl. jours. Served to capt. M.C., AUS, 1964-66. Fellow Am. Acad. Pediatrics; mem. Am. Soc. Microbiology, New Eng. Pediatric Soc., Mass. Med. Soc., AMA, Tufts Alumni Assn., Nat. Assn. Watch and Clock Collectors. Office: 1 Roosevelt Ave West Peabody MA 01960 also: 225 Boston St Lynn MA 01904

LIPNER, JULIUS JOSEPH, comparative religion educator; b. Patna, India, Aug. 11, 1946; arrived in Eng., 1971.; s. Vojtech and Sylvia Teresa (Coutts) L.; m. Anindita Neogy, Feb. 20, 1971; children: Tanya, Julius. BA and Lic. in Philosophy summa cum laude, Pontifical Athenaeum, Pune, India, 1969; PhD, Kings Coll. U. London, 1974. Lectr. dept. Theology U. Birmingham (Eng.), 1973-74; lectr. comparative study of religion U. Cambridge (Eng.), 1975—; fellow St. Edmund's Coll., 1976—; lectr. 1981. Author: The Face of Truth, 1986, A Net Cast Wide, 1987; Purity, Abortion and Euthanasia (with others), 1988; contbr. articles and revs. to learned jours. Mem. Brit. Assn. History of Religions, Catholic Theol. Assn. Gt. Britain (founding mem.), Soc. for Study of Theology, Cambridge Theol. Soc. Roman Catholic. Office: Divinity Sch U Cambridge, St Johns St, Cambridge CB2 1TW, England

LIPNIK, MORRIS JACOB, physician; b. Detroit, Aug. 27, 1922; s. Louis and Lillian (Portney) L.; m. Lois Russine Wertheimer, Dec. 8, 1946; children—Susan, Carol. B.A., Wayne State U., 1943, M.D., 1946. Diplomate Am. Bd. Dermatology. Intern, Detroit Receiving Hosp., 1946-47; resident Johns Hopkins Hosp., Balt., 1947-48, Hosp. of U. Pa., 1949-51; practice medicine specializing in dermatology, Southfield, Mich., 1953—; mem. staff Sinai Hosp., Detroit, 1954-60, Cottage Hosp., Grosse Pointe, Mich., 1957-60, St. John Hosp. Detroit, 1954-60, Mt. Carmel Hosp., Detroit, 1966—; spl. lectr. U. Detroit Dental Sch., 1958-63; adj. clin. prof. dermatology Marygrove Coll., Detroit, 1979—. Contbr. articles to med. jours. Mem. Founders' Soc. Detroit Inst. Arts, 1962; pres. Center Theatre, Detroit, 1963; patron Detroit Symphony Orch., 1978, Mich. Opera Theatre, Detroit, 1980, Detroit Community Music Sch., 1981, 82, 83. Served to capt. AUS, 1947-49. Mem. Mich. Dermatol. Soc., AMA, Am. Acad. Dermatology, Phi Delta Epsilon. Clubs: Renaissance (Detroit), Fairlane (Dearborn). Office: MJ Lipnik PC 17000 W 8 Mile Rd Suite 226 Southfield MI 48075 also: 29829 Telegraph Rd Southfield MO 48034 also: Bloomfield Hills MI 48013-6349

LIPP, NORMA, insurance company executive; b. Ottawa, Ont., Can., Dec. 7, 1938; d. Isadore and Mary (Magalnick) Klaman; m. Lawrence D. Meno, Feb. 1, 1964 (div. 1969); m. Jules Lipp; children—Michael, Traci, A.J. B.A., Mansfield Finishing Sch., 1959; grad. Sch. Design, Miami, Fla., 1978. Asst., Dept. Nat. Revenue, Ottawa, Ont., 1956-58; supr. info. services Can. Broadcast Corp., Ottawa, 1961-63; mgr., comptroller Metr Petroleum Co., Miami, Fla., 1968-69; asst. to pres. Gabor & Co., Inc., Miami, 1969-82; treas., dir. Fin. Planning Assocs., Miami, 1982—; chmn., dir. Fin. Planning Realty, Miami, 1985—. Assoc. Com. to Elect the Pres., Miami, 1984; assoc. mem. Rep. Nat. Com., Miami, 1984. Club: Westview Country (Miami); Williams Island Club. Home: 20251 NE 25th Ave Miami FL 33180 Office: Fin Planning Assocs 15105 NW 77 Ave Miami Lakes FL 33014

LIPPE, PHILIPP MARIA, neurosurgeon, educator; b. Vienna, Austria, May 17, 1929; s. Philipp and Maria (Goth) L.; came to U.S., 1938, naturalized, 1945; m. Gail B. Busch, 1977; children by previous marriage—Patricia Ann Marie, Philip Eric Andrew, Laura Lynne Elizabeth, Kenneth Anthony Ernst. Student Loyola U., Chgo., 1947-50; B.S. in Medicine, U. Ill. Coll. Medicine, 1952, M.D. with high honors, 1954. Rotating intern St. Francis Hosp., Evanston, Ill., 1954-55; asst. resident gen. surgery VA Hosp., Hines, Ill., 1955, 58-59; asst. resident neurology and neurol. surgery Neuropsychiat. Inst., U. Ill. Research and Ednl. Hosps., Chgo., 1959-60, chief resident, 1962-63, resident neuropathology, 1962, postgrad. trainee in electroencephalography, 1963; resident neurology and neurol. surgery Presbyn.-St. Luke's Hosp., Chgo., 1960-61; practice medicine, specializing in neurol. surgery, San Jose, Calif., 1963—; instr. neurology and neurol. surgery U. Ill., 1962-63; clin. instr. surgery and neurosurgery Stanford U., 1965-69, clin. asst. prof., 1969-74, clin. assoc. prof., 1974—; staff cons. in neurosurgery O'Connor Hosp., Santa Clara Valley Med. Center, San Jose Hosp., Good Samaritan Hosp., Los Gatos Community Hosp., El Camino Hosp. (all San Jose area); founder, exec. dir. Bay Area Pain Rehab. Center, San Jose, 1979—; clin. adviser to Joint Commn. on Accreditation of Hosps.; mem. dist. med. quality rev. com. Calif. Bd. Med. Quality Assurance, 1976—, chmn., 1976-77. Served to capt. USAF, 1956-58. Diplomate Am. Bd. Neurol. Surgery, Nat. Bd. Med. Examiners. Fellow ACS; mem. AMA (Ho. of Dels. 1981—), Calif. Med. Assn. (Ho. of Dels. 1976-80, sci. bd., council 1979-87, sec. 1981-87), Santa Clara County Med. Soc. (council 1974-81, pres. 1978-79), Chgo. Med. Soc., Congress Neurol. Surgeons, Calif. Assn. Neurol. Surgeons (dir. 1974-82, v.p. 1975-76, pres. 1977-79), San Jose Surg. Soc., Am. Assn. Neurol. Surgeons (dir. 1983-86, 87—), Western Neurol. Soc., San Francisco Neurol. Soc., Santa Clara Valley Profl. Standards Rev. Orgn. (dir., v.p., dir. quality assurance 1975-83), Fedn. Western Socs. Neurol. Sci., Internat. Assn. for Study Pain, Am. Pain Soc. (founding mem.), Am. Acad. Pain Medicine (sec. 1983-86, pres. 1987—), Alpha Omega Alpha, Phi Kappa Phi. Contbr. articles to profl. jours. Pioneered med. application centrifugal force using flight simulator. Office: 2100 Forest Ave Suite 106 San Jose CA 95128

LIPPE, RICHARD ALLEN, lawyer; b. Bklyn., July 24, 1938; s. Al A. and Thelma (Spaeth) L.; m. Gail C. Lippe, June 20, 1965; children: Wendy, David. BA, Tufts U., 1960; LLB, U. Pa., 1964. Bar: N.Y. 1965, U.S. Dist. Ct. (ea. and so. dists. N.Y.) 1965, U.S. Supreme Ct. 1975. Dept. county atty. Nassau County, N.Y., 1965-68; ptnr. Lippe, Ruskin, Schlissel & Moscou, Nassau County, 1968-79; ptnr. Meltzer, Lippe & Goldstein, Mineola, N.Y., 1979—; village atty. Inc. Village of Great Neck Plaza, N.Y., 1972—; gen. counsel The Wainrite Group, Inc., 1981—, Poly Ventures, Ltd. Partnership; gen. counsel, dir. New Generation Foods, Inc., Coinmach Industries Co., 1983—; bd. dirs. L.I. Venture Capital Group; counsel Manhasset-Great Neck Econ. Opportunity Council, 1965-68; gen. ptnr. Contemporary Art Consortium; pres. Contemporary Art Pub. Consortium. Sec., Nassau Law Services Com., Inc., 1966—; dir. Nassau County Legal Aid Soc., 1978-81; bd. dirs. Waldemar Med. Research Found., 1966-68. Mem. ABA, N.Y. Bar Assn., Nassau County Bar Assn., Fed. Bar Council. Jewish. Contbr. articles to profl. jours. Home: 1 Ipswich Ave Great Neck NY 11021 Office: 190 Willis Ave Mineola NY 11501

LIPPER, KENNETH, investment banker; b. N.Y.C., June 19, 1941; s. George and Sally (Hollander) L.; m. Evelyn Rebecca Gruss, June 12, 1966; children: Joanna Helene, Daniella, Tamara, Julie. BA, Columbia U., 1962; JD, Harvard U., 1965; LLM, NYU, 1966; postgrad., Faculté de Droit et Economique, Paris, 1967. Bar: N.Y. 1965. Assoc. Fried, Frank, Harris, Shriver & Jacobson, N.Y.C., 1967-68; dir. industry policy Office Fgn. Direct Investment, Washington, 1968-69; assoc. ptnr. Lehman Bros., N.Y.C., 1969-75; mng. dir., ptnr. Salomon Bros., N.Y.C., 1976-82; dep. mayor City of N.Y., 1983-85; chmn. Lipper & Co., 1986—; adj. prof. internat. affairs Sch. Internat. and Pub. Affairs, Columbia U., N.Y.C., 1976-83, 87—; Donaldson Disting. Vis. fellow in mcpl. affairs Yale U., 1987—; bd. dirs. Neutrogena Corp., Fiat. Author: Wall Street, 1987 and chief tech. advisor movie, 1987; co-producer mus. rev. Sing Hallelujah, 1987. Trustee Sch. Orgn. and Mgmt., Yale U., 1983—, Archaeol. Inst. Am., 1986—, Ctr. for Nat. Policy, 1987—, Am. Council on Germany, 1982—. Recipient medal of distinction City of N.Y., 1985; Ford Found. fellow, 1966-67. Mem. Council Fgn. Relations, Econ. Club N.Y., Phi Beta Kappa. Clubs: Century, University (N.Y.C.). Office: Lipper & Co 375 Park Ave New York NY 10022

LIPPES, RICHARD JAMES, lawyer; b. Buffalo, Mar. 18, 1944; s. Thomas and Ruth (Landsman) L.; m. Sharon Richmond, June 4, 1972; children: Amity, Joshua, Kevin. BA, U. Mich., 1966; JD cum laude, SUNY-Buffalo, 1970. Bar: N.Y. 1970, U.S. Dist. Ct. Md. 1970, U.S. Ct. Appeals (4th cir.) 1970, U.S. Ct. Appeals (2d cir.) 1971, U.S. Dist. Ct. (we. dist.) N.Y. 1971, U.S. Dist. Ct. (no. and so. dists.) N.Y. Clk. to presiding judge U.S. Ct. Appeals, Balt., 1970; exec. dir. Center for Justice Through Law, Buffalo, 1971; sole practice, Buffalo, 1971-77; ptnr. Moriarity, Allen, Lippes & Hoffman, Buffalo, 1977-79, Allen, Lippes & Shonn, Buffalo, 1979—; lectr. SUNY-Buffalo, 1978, 79; contbr. numerous articles to profl. jours. Chmn. Atlantic chpt. Sierra Club, 1980-83; chmn. Buffalo chpt. Am. Jewish Com., 1986-88; chmn. lawyers com. Niagara Frontier chpt. N.Y. Civil Liberties Union, 1971, chpt. chairperson, 1972-74; chmn. City of Buffalo Environ. Mgmt. Commn., 1987-88; bd. dirs. Empire State Ballet, also gen. counsel; chmn. City of Buffalo Task Force, 1986-87; various others. Recipient Am. Jurisprudence award, 1968; Urban and Environ. Law fellow, 1969. Mem. ABA, N.Y. State Bar Assn., Erie County Bar Assn. (chmn. pub. interest law com., chmn. prepaid legal services com.). Democrat

LIPPITT, ELIZABETH CHARLOTTE, writer; b. San Francisco; d. Sidney Grant and Stella Lippitt; student Mills Coll., U. Calif.-Berkeley. Writer, performer own satirical monologues; contbr. articles to 85 newspapers including N.Y. Post, Los Angeles Examiner, Orlando Sentinel, Phoenix Republic, also advt. Recipient Congress of Freedom award, 1959, 71-73, 77, 78; writer on nat. and polit. affairs for 85 newspapers including Muncie Star, St. Louis Globe-Democrat, Washington Times, Utah Ind., Jackson News. Mem. Commn. for Free China, Conservative Caucus. Mem. Nat. Assn. R.R. Passengers, Nat. Trust for Hist. Preservation, Am. Security Council, Internat. Platform Assn., Am. Conservative Union, Nat. Antivivisection Soc., High Frontier, For Our Children, Childhelp U.S.A., Free Afghanistan Com., Humane Soc. U.S., Young Ams. for Freedom, 8 antivivisection orgns. Clubs: Metropolitan, Olympic, Commonwealth. Pop singer, recorder song album Songs From the Heart. Home: 2414 Pacific Ave San Francisco CA 94115

LIPPMAN, ALFRED JULIAN, retired real estate executive; b. Newark, May 7, 1900; s. Lewis Isaac and Henrietta (Meyer) L.; m. Rosa Maria Muniz, 1982. With L. Bamberger & Co. Dept. Store, Newark, 1912-22; buyer Symons Dry Goods Co., Butte, Mont., 1922-26; asst. mdse. mgr. Stix, Baer & Fuller Co., St. Louis, 1926-28; mdse. mgr. Union Co., Columbus, Ohio, 1928; supr. N.J. br. offices Eisele & King, mems. N.Y. Stock Exchange, 1928-38; owner real estate bus. 1928-38; salesman, broker Feist & Feist, Newark, 1938-41; ptnr. real estate firm John E. Sloane & Sons, Newark, 1941-45; owner, pres. successor firm Alfred J. Lippmann Inc., 1945-80; pres. Fereday & Meyer Co. Inc. Contractors, Newark, 1938-80; exec. dir. Latin Am. Devel. and Ops. Co. V.p. Aerovias Latino Americanos, S.A. of Mexico, 1951-52; N.J. rep. to 3 presdl. inaugurations in Mexico; mem. N.J. Planning Bd., 1936-43; chmn. Sea Bright (N.J.) State Park Commn., 1938; mem. Mcpl. Sanitation Commn., 1952; vice chmn. solid wastes tech. com. N.J. Dept. Health; dir. Children to Children Orgn.; dir. extension course on solid wastes disposal Rutgers U., 1962-71. Served with USN, World War I, USCGR, World War II. Decorated Order of Aztec Eagle (Mexico), 1952, L'Ordre Internacional du Bien Public Comandeur, comdr. Order Holy Cross Jerusalem; named outstanding citizen of N.J. by K.P., 1955, Man of Yr., Acapulco, Mexico, 1971; recipient Disting. Achievement award Advt. Club N.Y., 1964, diploma and Gold medal for extraordinary contbn. Mexican Nat. Tourist Council, 1967, Gold medallion Port Authority N.J. and N.Y., 1975; named Outstanding Citizen of N.J. by K.P., 1955, Man of Yr., Acapulco, Mex., 1971, hon. consul Mex., 1957-77, hon. consul gen. Mex., 1977-78, Consul of Yr., Consular Corps. Coll., 1970, to Hon. Order Ky. Cols. Mem. Am. Legion (life), Soc. Solid Waste Technicians (pres.), Circus Saints and Sinners (nat. v.p.), Nat. Sweepstakes Regatta of Red Bank, N.J. (past rear commodore), Mexican Acad. Internat. Law, Mexican C. of C. of U.S. (pres. 1962-78, chmn. bd. 1978—), N.J. World Trade Com., Consular Corps Coll. Republican. Jewish. Clubs: Old Red Bank Yacht (N.J.) (past commodore); Rio Chumpan Yacht (Mex.) (commodore). Lodges: Masons, Elks. Home: 2100 S Ocean Ln Fort Lauderdale FL 33316

LIPSCHULTZ, M. RICHARD, accountant; b. Chgo., July 5, 1913; s. Morris David and Minnie (Moskowitz) L.; student Northwestern U., 1930-35; J.D., De Paul U., 1948; m. Evelyn Smolin, May 16, 1945 (dec. 1963); m. Phyllis Siegel, July 11, 1965; children—Howard Elliott, Carl Alvin, Saul Martin. Admitted to Ill. bar, 1948; auditor State of Ill., Chgo., 1938-41; conferee IRS, Chgo., 1941-49; tax acct. A.I. Grade & Co., C.P.A.s, Chgo., 1949-50; sr. ptnr. Lipschultz Bros., Levin and Gray and predecessor firms, C.P.A.s, Chgo., 1950-82; fin. v.p., dir. Miller Asso. Industries, Inc., Skokie, 1973-74; dir. Miller Builders, Inc.; dir., chmn. exec. com. Portable Electric Tools, Inc., Geneva, Ill., 1963-67; mem. exec. com. Midland Screw Corp., Chgo., 1958-66; faculty John Marshall Law Sch., 1951-64. Bd. dirs.; pres. bd. dirs. Lipschultz Bros. Family Found. Served with USAAF, 1943-46. C.P.A., Ill. Mem. Ill. Soc. C.P.A.s, Am. Inst. C.P.A.s, ABA, Fed., Chgo., Ill. bar assns., Decalogue Soc. Lawyers, Am. Legion, Nu Beta-Epsilon. Mem. B'nai B'rith. Clubs: Standard (Chgo.); Ravinia Green Country (Deerfield, Ill.). Contbr. articles to profl. jours. Home: 1671 E Mission Hills Rd Northbrook IL 60062

LIPSCOMB, ANNA ROSE FEENY, hotel executive; b. Greensboro, N.C., Oct. 29, 1945; d. Nathan and Matilda (Carotenuto) L. B.A. in English and French summa cum laude, Queens Coll., 1977. Reservations agt. Am. Airlines, St. Louis, 1968-69, ticket agt., 1969-71; coll. rep. CBS, Holt Rinehart Winston, Providence, 1977-79, sr. acquisitions editor Dryden Press, Chgo., 1979-81; owner, mgr. Taos Inn, N.Mex., 1981—; bd. dirs. N.Mex. Hotel and Motel Assn., 1986—. Editor: Intermediate Accounting, 1980; Business Law, 1981. Contbr. articles to profl. jours. Bd. dirs., 1st v.p. Taos Arts Assn., 1982-85; founder, bd. dirs. Taos Spring Arts Celebration, 1983—; founder, dir. Meet-the-Artist Series, 1983—; bd. dirs. and co-founder Spring Arts N.Mex., 1986; founding mem. Assn. Hist. Hotels, Boulder, 1983—; organizer Internat. Symposium on Arts, 1985; bd. dirs. Arts in Taos, 1983, Taoschool, Inc., 1985—. Recipient Outstanding English Student of Yr. award Queens Coll., 1977; named Single Outstanding Contributor to the Arts in Taos, 1986. Mem. Millicent Rogers Mus. Assn., Taos Lodgers and Restaurant Assn., Taos County C. of C. (1st v.p., bd. dirs. 1988-89). Internat. Platform Assn., Phi Beta Kappa. Democrat. Home: Talpa Route Taos NM 87571 Office: Taos Inn PO Drawer N Taos NM 87571

LIPSCOMB, WILLIAM NUNN, JR., physical chemist, educator; b. Cleve., Dec. 9, 1919; s. William Nunn and Edna Patterson (Porter) L.; m. Mary Adele Sargent, May 20, 1944; children: Dorothy Jean, James Sargent; m. Jean Craig Evans, 1983. BS, U. Ky., 1941, DSc (hon.), 1963; PhD, Calif. Inst. Tech., 1946; DrHC, U. Munich, 1976; DSc (hon.), L.I. U., 1977, Rutgers U., 1979, Gustavus Adolphus Coll., 1980, Marietta Coll., 1981. Phys. chemist OSRD, 1942-46; with U. Minn., 1946-59, successively asst. prof., asso. prof. and acting chief phys. chemistry div., prof. and chief phys. chemistry div., 1954-59; prof. chemistry Harvard U., Cambridge, Mass., 1959-71, Abbott and James Lawrence prof., 1971—, chmn. dept. chemistry, 1962-65; mem. U.S. Nat. Com. for Crystallography, 1954-59, 60-63, 65-67; chmn. program com. 4th Internat. Congress of Crystallography, Montreal, 1957; mem. sci. adv. bd. Robert A. Welch Found.; mem. research adv. bd. Mich. Molecular Biol. Inst.; mem. adv. com. Inst. for Amorphous Studies; bd. dirs. Dow Chem. Co. Author: The Boron Hydrides, 1963, (with G.R. Eaton) NMR Studies of Boron Hydrides and Related Compounds, 1969; assoc. editor: (with G.R. Eaton) Jour. Chemical Physics, 1955-57; contbr. articles to profl. jours.; clarinetist, mem.: Amateur Chamber Music Players. Guggenheim fellow Oxford U., Eng., 1954-55; Guggenheim fellow Cambridge U., Eng., 1972-73; NSF sr. postdoctoral fellow, 1965-66; Overseas fellow Churchill Coll., Cambridge, Eng., 1966, 73; Robert Welch Found. lectr., 1966, 71; Howard U. distinguished lecture series, 1966; George Fisher Baker lectr. Cornell U., 1969; centenary lectr. Chem. Soc., London, 1972; lectr. Weizmann Inst., Rehovoth, Israel, 1974; Evans award lectr. Ohio State U., 1974; Gilbert Newton Lewis Meml. lectr. U. Calif., Berkeley, 1974; also lectureships Mich. State U., 1975, U. Iowa, 1975, Ill. Inst. Tech., 1976, numerous others; also speaker confs.; Recipient Harrison Howe award in Chemistry, 1958; Distinguished Alumni Centennial award U. Ky., 1965; Distinguished Service in advancement inorganic chemistry Am. Chem. Soc., 1968; George Ledlie prize Harvard, 1971; Nobel prize in chemistry, 1976; Disting. Alumni award Calif. Inst. Tech., 1977; sr. U.S. scientist award Alexander von Humboldt-Stiftung, 1979; award lecture Internat. Acad. Quantum Molecular Sci., 1980. Fellow Am. Acad. Arts and Scis., Am. Phys. Soc.; mem. Am. Chem. Soc. (Peter Debye award phys. chemistry 1973, chmn. Minn. sect. 1949-50), Am. Crystallographic Assn. (pres. 1955), Nat. Acad. Sci., Netherlands Acad. Arts and Scis. (fgn.), Math. Assn. Bioinorganic Scientists (hon.), Academie Europeenne des Sciences, des Arts et des Lettres, Royal Soc. Chemistry (hon.), Phi Beta Kappa, Sigma Xi, Alpha Chi Sigma, Phi Lambda Upsilon, Sigma Pi Sigma, Phi Mu Epsilon. Office: Harvard U Dept Chemistry Cambridge MA 02138 *

LIPSMAN, RICHARD MARC, lawyer, educator; b. Bklyn., Aug. 17, 1946; s. Abraham W. and Ruth (Weinstein) L.; m. Geri A. Russo, 1980; children: Eric, Dara Briana. BBA, City Coll. of City of N.Y., 1968; JD, St. John's Univ., Jamaica, N.Y., 1972; LLM in Taxation, Boston U., 1976. Bar: N.Y. 1973, Mass. 1975, U.S. Dist. Ct. (ea. and so. dists.) N.Y. 1977, U.S. Supreme Ct. 1978, U.S. Tax Ct. 1979; CPA, N.Y., Mass. Tax atty. Arthur Young & Co., N.Y.C., 1972-74; assoc. Gilman, McLaughlin & Hanrahan, Boston, 1974-76, Lefrak, Fischer & Meyerson, N.Y.C., 1976-77; ptnr. Tarnow, Landsman & Lipsman, N.Y.C., 1978; sole practice N.Y.C., 1979—; faculty Baruch Coll. CUNY, 1984-86, curriculum specialist Research Found. CUNY, 1977-78; faculty Pratt Inst., Bklyn., 1974, Queensboro Coll., Bayside, N.Y., 1978-80. Author, producer book/cassette program, Learning Income Taxes, 1978. Mem. ABA, N.Y. State Bar Assn., Assn. of the Bar of the City of N.Y., Am. Inst. CPA's, N.Y. State Soc. CPA's. Jewish. Office: 777 3d Ave New York NY 10017

LIPSTEIN, MICHAEL, real estate and construction company executive; b. Bklyn., June 8, 1936; s. Phillip and Grace (Gleichanhaus) L.; student Boston U., 1954-55; A.A., Pratt Inst., 1957; student Bernard Baruch Grad. Sch. Bus. Adminstrn., CCNY, 1959, Practising Law Inst., 1959; m. Judith Anne Paulson, June 3, 1973; children—Keith, Evan, Hillary. Partner various real estate cos., N.Y.C., 1955-80; prin. Michael Lipstein Constrn. Co., N.Y.C., 1966—. Mem. various com. Fedn. Jewish Philanthropies and Fedn. Served with U.S. Army, 1955-56. Mem. Young Mens Real Estate Assn., Real Estate Bd. N.Y., B'nai B'rith Real Estate Assn. Home: 48 Potters Ln Kings Point NY 11024 Office: 136 E 56th St New York NY 10022

LIPTON, LESTER, ophthalmologist, entrepreneur; b. N.Y.C., Mar. 14, 1936; s. George and Rita (Steinbaum) L.; B.A., N.Y.U., 1959; M.D., Chgo. Med. Sch., 1964; m. Harriet Arfa, June 25, 1960; children—Sherri, Brandi, Shawn. Research fellow Chgo. Med. Sch., 1959-60; intern Brookdale Hosp. Ctr., Bklyn., 1964-65; resident Harlem Eye and Ear Hosp., N.Y.C., 1965-68; asso. attending Polyclinic, French hosps., N.Y.C., 1968-75; asst. attending physician, ophthalmologist, surg. instr. St. Clare's Hosp., N.Y.C., 1975—; attending ophthalmologist Cabrini Med. Ctr., N.Y.C., 1982—; founder Lipton Eye Clinic, N.Y.C., 1981—; v.p. Van Arfa Realty, N.Y.C. Mem. U.S. Congl. Adv. Bd. Served with AUS, 1956-58. Named Internat. Amigo, OAS. Mem. N.Y. Med. Soc., Am. Assn. Individual Investors, Bronx High Sch. Sci. Alumni Assn., United Shareholders Assn., Internat. Platform Assn. Republican. Mem. Quaker Fellowship. Club: Vanderbilt U. Cabinet. Home: Interlaken Estates Lakeville CT 06039 also: 1199 Park Ave New York NY 10128 Office: 51 E 90th St New York NY 10028

LIS, ANTHONY STANLEY, business administration educator; b. Easthampton, Mass., Aug. 11, 1918; s. Anthony Stanley and Anna Barbara (Kaczmarczyk) L.; m. Jane Ann Mikus, June 25, 1951 (dec.); children: Anthony, Judith A., Sandra J.; m. Sophie A. Pobieglo, June 24, 1983. B.S., Mass. State Coll., Salem, 1950; M.S., Okla. State U., 1951; Ph.D., U. Minn., 1961. Asst. prof. Okla. State U., Stillwater, 1951-55; assoc. prof. U. Tulsa, 1956-62; mem. faculty U. Okla., Norman, 1962—, prof. bus. adminstrn., 1967-86, prof. emeritus, 1986—; vis. prof. Central Sch. Planning/Stats., Warsaw, Poland, 1984; del. II Congress Scholars of Polish Descent, Warsaw, 1979; cons. to numerous bus. and govtl. agys. Served with U.S. Army, 1937-40, 1942-46. Decorated Bronze Star; recipient Superior Profl. and Univ. Service award U. Okla., 1981; Summer fellow Found. Econ. Edn., 1954. Mem. Am. Bus. Communication Assn., Polish Am. Hist. Assn., Am. Assn. Advancement Slavic Studies, Adminstrv. Mgmt. Soc., Southwestern Social Sci. Assn., Delta Pi Epsilon, Beta Gamma Sigma, Delta Sigma Pi. Roman Catholic. Lodge: Lions. Home: 1827 Peter Pan Norman OK 73072 Office: U Okla Coll Bus Adminstrn Norman OK 73019

LISANKE, ROBERT JOHN, chemical engineer, consultant; b. N.Y.C., June 7, 1932; s. Clement Joseph and Anne Mary (Campbell) Liszanckie; m. Patricia Ann Traum, Nov. 16, 1957; children: Robert John, Joseph, Michael, Jeanne. BS, Fordham U., 1954; MS, U. Notre Dame, 1956; postgrad., Fairleigh Dickinson U., 1962-63, Pa. State U., 1969, Syracuse U., 1972-73, U. Calif., 1977. Teaching fellow U. Notre Dame, Ind., 1954, research asst., 1954-56, 1954-56; research chemist silicones div. Union Carbide Corp., Sistersville, W.Va., 1956-59, Hooker Chem. Corp., Niagara Falls, N.Y., 1959-60; with fuels devel. group Mobile Oil Corp., Paulsboro, N.J., 1960-66; process chemist video display equipment op. Gen. Electric Co., Syracuse, N.Y., 1966-73; sr. materials engr. Pratt & Whitney Aircraft div. United Techs. Corp., West Palm Beach, Fla., 1974-83; sr. design engr. Morton Thiokol Corp., Brigham City, Utah, 1983-86; cons. Orange State Cons., Inc., Palm Beach Gardens, Fla., 1986—. Patentee in field. Regional dir. Bayberry Community Assn., 1972-74; mem. nat. adv. bd. Am. Security Council. Mem. Am. Chem. Soc., ASTM, AIAA, ASME, Soc. Advancement of Material and Process Engring., IEEE, Am. Def. Preparedness Assn. Republican. Roman Catholic. Club: U.S. Chess Fedn. Mailing Address: PO Drawer 31028 Palm Beach Gardens FL 33410-7028

LISCH, HOWARD, accountant, tax lawyer; b. N.Y.C., Dec. 30, 1950; s. Simon and Edith (Sachs) L.; m. Audrey Robin Ginsberg, 1973; children—Sari Victoria, Melissa Dawn, Jeremy Harold. B.S., NYU, 1972; J.D., Bklyn. Law Sch., 1975. CPA, Conn., N.J., N.Y. Tax acct. Arthur Andersen & Co., N.Y.C., 1975-77; tax supr. Coopers & Lybrand, Stamford, Conn., 1977-79; internat. tax mgr. Pitney Bowes, Stamford, 1979-80; tax mgr. Deloitte, Haskins & Sells, N.Y.C., 1980-82; chief fin. officer Campus Entertainment Network, N.Y.C., 1982-83, Black Tie Network, N.Y.C., 1982-83; tax mgr. Schachter & Co., White Plains, N.Y., dir. tax services Sobel & Co., Roseland, N.J., 1983-85; tax mgr. Rosenberg, Leffler & Zach, N.Y.C., 1985-86; pvt. practice acctg., N.Y.C., 1986—. Active Freehold Twp. Transp. Bd. Mem. Am. Arbitration Assn. (arbitrator), ABA, Am. Inst. CPA's, N.J. Soc. CPA's, N.Y. Soc. CPA's. Republican. Jewish. Address: 11 Nathan Hale Dr Freehold Township NJ 07728 Office: 305 Broadway Suite 601 New York NY 10007

LISHER, JOHN LEONARD, lawyer; b. Indpls., Sept. 19, 1950; s. Leonard Boyd and Mary Jane (Rafferty) L.; m. Mary Katherine Sturmon, Aug. 17, 1974. B.A. with honors in History, Ind. U., 1975, J.D., 1975. Bar: Ind. 1975. Dep. atty. gen. State of Ind., Indpls., 1975-78; asst. corp. counsel City of Indpls., 1978-81; assoc. Osborn & Hiner, Indpls., 1981-86; ptnr. Osborn, Hiner & Lisher, 1986—. Vol. Mayflower Classic, Indpls., 1981—; asst. vol. coordinator Marion County Rep. Com., Indpls., 1979-80; vol. com. to re-elect Theodore Sendak, Indpls., 1976—, Don Bogard for Atty. Gen., Indpls., 1980, Steve Goldsmith for Prosecutor, Indpls., 1979, 83, Sheila Suess for Congress, Indpls., 1980. Recipient Outstanding Young Man of Am. award Jaycees, 1979, 85, Indpls. Jaycees, 1980. Mem. ABA, Ind. Bar Assn., Indpls. Bar Assn. (membership com.), Assn. Trial Lawyers Am., Ind. U. Alumni Assn., Hoosier Alumni Assn. (charter, founder, pres.), Ind. Trial Lawyers Assn., Ind. Def. Lawyers Assn., Ind. U. Coll. Arts and Scis. (bd. dirs. 1983—, pres. 1986-87), Wabash Valley Alumni Assn. (charter), Founders Club, Presidents Club, Phi Beta Kappa, Eta Sigma Phi, Phi Eta Sigma, Delta Xi Alumni Assn. (charter, v.p., sec., Delta Xi chpt. Outstanding Alumnus award 1975, 76, 79, 83), Delta Xi Housing Corp. (pres.), Pi Kappa Alpha (midwest regional pres. 1977-86, parliamentarian nat. conv. 1982, del. convs. 1978-80, 82, 84, 86, trustee Meml. Found. 1986—). Presbyterian. Avocations: reading; golf; jogging; Roman coin collecting. Home: 5725 Huntersglen Rd Indianapolis IN 46226 Office: Osborn Hiner & Lisher 8330 Woodfield Crossing Blvd Suite 380 Indianapolis IN 46240

LISK, FRANKLYN ATHANASIUS, economist, researcher; b. Rotifunk, Southern Province, Sierra Leone, Mar. 3, 1946; s. Fatruba Archibald and Rosa Rovina (Zizer) L.; m. Muriel Janet Davies, Apr. 26, 1975; children—Lynette Yoko, Francis Atiya, Lorraine Yema. B.A., U. Durham, 1968; M.Sc., Queen's U., 1970; Ph.D., U. Birmingham, 1974. Tutorial asst. U. Birmingham (U.K.), 1970-72; vis. research fellow U. Sierra Leone, Freetown, 1972; lectr. econs. Birmingham (U.K.) Poly./Aston U., Birmingham, 1972-74; research economist ILO, Geneva, Switzerland, 1974-79, sr. research economist, 1979-85, regional adviser employment policies and manpower planning Caribbean office, Port-of-Spain, Trinidad, 1986—; adviser Ministry of Planning Kenya, Nairobi, 1979-83; Internat. Labour Office rep. on exec. bd. UN Research Inst. for Social Devel., Geneva, 1980-83; editorial adviser Longmans Pub. Co., U.K., 1976—. Co-author, editor: Basic Needs Planning in Kenya, 1979; Popular Participation Planning for Basic Needs, 1985; contbr. articles in field to profl. jours. Sec., African Students Assn., Belfast, U.K., 1969-70. English Speaking Union of the Commonwealth travelling fellow, 1971. Mem. Royal Econ. Soc., African Studies Assn., Trade Policy Research Centre, Royal African Soc., Devel. Studies Assn. Anglican. Home: 40 Chemin de la Dauphine, 1291 Commugny Switzerland Office: ILO Caribbean Office, 11 St Clair Ave, PO Box 1201, Port-of-Spain Trinidad

LISKA, IVAN, ballet dancer; b. Prague, Czechoslovakia. Student Ballet Sch. Nat. Theater, Prague, Conservatory, Prague. Former dancer Deutsche Operam Rhein, Dusseldorf; dancer Munich State Opera, 1974-77, soloist, 1975-77; prin. dancer Hamburg Ballet, 1977—; guest with ballet cos. in Berlin, Munich, Stuttgart, Geneva, Oslo, Rome, Tokyo, London and Vienna, John Neumeier (artistic dir. Hamburg Ballet) created for him such roles as Lysander (A Midsummer Night's Dream), Orlando (As You Like It), leading parts in Saint Matthew Passion, Don Quixote, Streichquintett C-Dur von Franz Schubert; other important roles in repertoire include Oberon (A Midsummer Night's Dream), Prince Desire, Catalabutte and Blue Bird (The Sleeping Beauty), Gunther (Nutcracker), Armand and Gaston (The Lady of the Camellias), Angel (Legend of Joseph), Romeo, Petrucchio and Lucentio (The Taming of the Shrew by Cranko), Onegin, Tristan, Albrecht (Giselle), Ivan (Firebird), The Moor (Moor's Pavane by Jose Limon) and leading roles in Vaslav, Bach Suite-2, Mozart 338 and John Neumeier's Mahler Ballets. Office: care Press Relations, Ballet Hamburgischen Staatsoper, Gr Theaterstrasse 34, D-2000 Hamburg 36 Federal Republic of Germany

LISKI, ERKKI PELLERVO, researcher, educator; b. Hameenlinna, Finland, Mar. 12, 1947; s. Matti and Senja Emilia (Nousianinen) L.; m. Leena Marjatta Linnokari, Mar. 1, 1980; children—Antti Mikael, Anni Maarit, Eero Kristian. M.S., U. Tampere (Finland), 1971, Ph. Lic., 1973, Ph.D., 1979. Asst. in stats. U. Tampere, 1977-79, sr. asst., 1979-80, lectr. stats., 1981, acting prof., 1982-83; sr. researcher Acad. Finland, Tampere, 1983-86; fellow in research Humboldt, 1986-87. Author: (with S. Puntanen) Basic Course in Statistics, 1976, Regression Analysis, 1976, Linear Models, 1977; On Reduced Risk Estimation in Linear Models, 1979. Mem. Am. Statis. Assn., Bernoulli Soc. Math. Stats., Biometric Soc., Statis. Soc. Finland. Office: U Tampere, PO Box 607, SF-33101 Tampere 10 Finland

LISS, HERBERT MYRON, newspaper publisher, communications company executive; b. Mpls., Mar. 23, 1931; s. Joseph Milton and Libby Diane (Kramer) L.; m. Barbara Lipson, Sept. 19, 1954; children: Lori-Ellen, Kenneth Allen, Michael David. BS in Econs., U. Pa., 1952. With mktg. mgmt. Procter & Gamble Co., Cin., 1954-63, Procter & Gamble Internat., various countries, 1963-74; gen. mgr. Procter & Gamble Comml. Co., San Juan, Puerto Rico, 1974-78; v.p., mgr. internat. ops. InterAm. Orange Crush Co. subs. Procter & Gamble Co., Cin., 1981-84; pres. River Cities (Ohio) Communications Inc, 1985—; pub. The Downtowner Newspaper, Cin., 1985—. Bd. dirs. Charter Com., Cin., 1958-63, Promotion & Mktg. Assn. U.S., 1978-81, Jr. Achievement, Cin., 1980—, Downtown Council, Cin., 1985—. Served to 1st lt. U.S. Army, 1952-54, Korea. Clubs: Manila Yacht, Manila Polo; Equitación De Somos Aguas (Madrid). Home: 8564 Wyoming Club Dr Cincinnati OH 45215 Office: The Downtowner Newspaper 128 E 6th St Cincinnati OH 45202

LISTE, HARTMUT, language professional, researcher; b. Aug. 20, 1947. Diplom-Philologe, Humboldt U. Berlin, 1971, PhD, 1975. Scientific asst., language educator Humboldt-U. Berlin, German Democratic Republic, 1974—. Author: Taschenlehrbuch Tschechisch, 1980, 2nd edit. 1983, 3rd edit. 1985, 4th edit. 1987, Taschenwörterbuch Tschechisch-Deutsch, 1986, 2nd edit. 1987. Mem. Union Interpreters in Fedn. of Newspapermen, Philately sect. of Union of Culture, Trade Union Sci., Soc. German-Soviet Friendship. Home: Willi-Bredel-Str 26, 1071 Berlin German Democratic Republic

LITEWKA, ALBERT BERNARD, communications and publishing company executive; b. N.Y.C., Feb. 5, 1942; s. Joel and Leah L. B.A. summa cum laude, UCLA, 1964; postgrad., U. Calif., Berkeley, 1964-65. Mgr. purchasing McGraw-Hill Book Co., N.Y.C., 1965-67; pres. Mktg. Innovations, Inc., N.Y.C., 1967-69; v.p. Westinghouse Leisure Time Industries, N.Y.C., 1972-75; exec. v.p. mktg. The Baker & Taylor Co. (W.R. Grace & Co.), N.Y.C., 1975-77; pres. Pix of Am. (W. R. Grace & Co.), N.Y.C., 1978; v.p. consumer services group W.R. Grace & Co., N.Y.C., 1977-79; pres. Macmillan Gen. Books div., N.Y.C., 1980-82; sr. v.p. Macmillan Pub. Co., Inc., 1980-82; pres. Warner Software, Inc., 1982-85; chmn., pres., chief exec. officer Jacobs & Gerber, Inc., Los Angeles and N.Y.C., 1986—. Internat. Ladies Garment Workers Union Nat. scholar, 1959-64, U. Calif. Regents scholar, 1959-64; Woodrow Wilson Nat. Grad. fellow, 1964-65; recipient 1st prize Acad. Am. Poets, 1964. Mem. Authors Guild, Authors League Am. Home: 562 West End Ave New York NY 10024 Office: Jacobs & Gerber Inc 36 E 20th St New York NY 10010 also: 731 N Fairfax Ave Los Angeles CA 90046

LI TIEYING, government official; b. 1936; s. Li Weihan. Grad. in solid physics, Charles U., Czechoslovakia, 1961. Technician, chief engr., dep. dir. 3 research insts., Shenyang, until 1978; sec. Shenyang Municipality Communist Party, 1981-85; alt. mem Chinese Communist Party Cen. Com., 1982; sec. Liaoning Province Communist Party, 1983-85; minister of electronics industry 1985-88; mem. 12th Cen. Com. Chinese Communist Party, 1985; minister state restructuring of econ. system commn. until 1988, minister state edn. commn., 1988—; state councilor State Council, 1988—. Elected a labor hero, 1978. Office: Ministry State Edn, Beijing Peoples Republic of China *

LITLE, PATRICK ALAN, psychologist, educator; b. Pomona, Calif., Nov. 14, 1946; s. Ralph and Doris Elizabeth (Little) L. m. Patricia J. Litle, Oct. 18, 1986; children: Lauren, Philip. MusB, U. Redlands, 1968; MA, Calif. State U., Long Beach, 1982; PhD, U. Del., 1986. Cert. tchr., Va., Calif. Band dir. Chesapeake Public Schs., Va., 1973-75; music therapy intern Lanterman State Hosp., Pomona, Calif., 1977; music therapist Coll. Hosp., Cerritos, Calif., 1977-78; instr. psychology U. Del., 1980—; clin. psychology intern Perry Point VA Med. Center, Md., 1981-82, health scis. specialist, 1984-86; clin. psychology intern Los Angeles VA Outpatient Clinic, 1982-83; psychology technician Coatesville VA Med. Ctr., 1983-84, clin. psychologist, 1986—. Contbr. 200 articles to profl. jours. Served with USN, 1969-72. Mem. Am. Psychol. Assn., Nat. Assn. Music Therapy (registered music therapist), Psychomusicology Soc., Phi Kappa Phi. Home: 4 Forest Creek Dr Hockessin DE 19707 Office: Psychology Service Coatesville VA Med Ctr Coatesville PA 19320

LITMAN, ROBERT BARRY, physician, author, television commentator; b. Phila., Nov. 17, 1947; s. Benjamin Norman and Bette Etta (Saunders) L.; m. Niki Thomas, Apr. 21, 1985; children: Riva Belle, Nadya Beth, Caila Tess. BS, Yale U., 1967, MD, 1970, MS in Chemistry, 1972, MPhil in Anatomy, 1972, postgrad. (Life Ins. Med. Research Fund fellow) Yale U. Coll. Hosp., U. London, 1969-70; Am. Cancer Soc. postdoctoral research fellow Yale U., 1970-73; resident in gen. surgery Bryn Mawr (Pa.) Hosp., 1973-74; USPHS fellow Yale U. Sch. Medicine, 1974-75; practice medicine and surgery, Ogdensburg, N.Y., 1977—; mem. med. staff, chmn. program and edn. com. A. Barton Hepburn Hosp.; Commentator Family Medicine Sta. WWNY-TV and WTNY-Radio. Diplomate Am. Bd. Family Practice. Fellow Am. Coll. Allergy and Immunology, Am. Acad. Family Physicians; mem. AMA (Physicians Recognition award 1970—), N.Y. State, St. Lawrence County med. assns., Joint Council Allergy and Immunology, Nat. Assn. Physician Broadcasters (charter), Book and Snake Soc., Gibbs Soc. of Yale U. (founder), Sigma Xi, Nu Sigma Nu, Alpha Chi Sigma. Author: Wynnefield and Limer, 1983; contbr. articles to numerous sci. publs. Home: 604 Crescent Ogdensburg NY 13669 Office: 124 King St Ogdensburg NY 13669

LITSIOS, SUSAN CLARKE, artist; b. Phila., Jan. 20, 1937; d. Ernest Barlow Clarke and Enid Vivienne (Kendig) Meyer; m. Socrates Litsios, June 9, 1957; children: Kenneth, Steve, Melissa, James, Rebecca, Valerie. Diploma in art, Cooper Union, 1957. Represented by Galerie L'Entr'Acte, Lausanne, Switzerland, 1980—, Mickelson Gallery, Washington, 1980—; exhibited in group shows U.S.A., Zimbabwe, Korea; one-woman shows include Centre Genevois De La Gravure Contemporaine, Geneva, 1978, Galerie L'Entr'Acte, 1980, 84; illustrator, editor, printer: Seven Limericks, Seven Woodcuts, 1980, The Pocket Print Collection, 1981; editor: (with T. Bourquin) CH, 1980, Le Cirque, 1983. Home and Office: Rue Des Scies, 1446 Baulmes Vaud Switzerland

LITTELL, FRANKLIN HAMLIN, educator; b. Syracuse, N.Y., June 20, 1917; s. Clair F. and Lena Augusta (Hamlin) L.; m. Harriet Davidson Lewis, June 15, 1939 (dec. 1978); children: Jennith, Karen, Miriam, Stephen; m. 2d Marcia S. Sachs, 1980. BA, Cornell Coll., 1937, DD, 1953; BD, Union Theol. Sem., 1940; PhD, Yale U., 1946; Dr. Theology, U. Marburg, 1957; LittD (hon.), Thiel Coll., 1968; DHL (hon.), Widener Coll., 1969, Hebrew Union Coll., 1975, Gratz Coll., 1977. Dir. Lane Hall, U. Mich., 1944-49; chief protestant adviser to U.S. High Commr., other service in Germany, 1949-51, 53-58; prof. Chgo. Theol. Sem., 1962-69; prof. religion Temple U., 1969-86; pres. Hamlin Inst. Studies in Religious Liberty Persecution; chief exec. officer Phila. Inst. Study World Religions, 1987—; Walker-Ames prof. U. Wash., 1976; adj. prof. Inst. Contemporary Jewry, Hebrew U., Israel, 1973—; Berman vis. prof., 1986; guest prof. numerous univs.; major addresses at Biennial Conv. of Union Am. Hebrew Congregations, Annual Conf. of Presidents of Major Jewish Orgns., Deutscher Evangelischer Kirchentag, Triennial Conv. of Nat. Council Chs.; also over 400 addresses on univ. campuses, in chs. and synagogues internationally. Author over 24 books including The Anabaptist View of the Church: an Introduction to Sectarian Protestantism (Brewer award Am. Soc. Ch. History), 1952, rev. edit., 1958, 64, From State Church to Pluralism, 1962, rev., 1970; (with Hubert Locke) The German Church Struggle and the Holocaust, 1974; The Crucifixion of the Jews, 1975, 86, The Macmillan Atlas History of Christianity, 1976, Religious Liberty in the Crossfire of Creeds, 1978, Reflections on the Holocaust, 1980; (with Marcia Sachs Littell) A Pilgrim's Interfaith Guide to the Holy Land, 1981; editor or assoc. editor numerous jours. including Jour. Ecumenical Studies, The Mennonite Quarterly Review, A Jour. of Ch. and State and Holocaust Genocide Studies; author weekly syndicated columns Lest We Forget and Proclaim Liberty!; also over 300 major articles or chpts. of books in field of modern religious history. cons. NCCJ, 1958-83; vice chmn. Ctr. for Reformation Research, 1964-77; nat. chmn. Inst. for Am. Democracy, 1966-69, sr. scholar, 1969-76; pres. Christians Concerned for Israel, 1971-78, Nat. Leadership Conf. for Israel, 1978-84, pres. emeritus 1985—; founder, chmn. ecumenical com. Deutscher Evangelischer Kirchentag, 1953-58; co-founder, cons. Assn. Coordination Univ. Religious Affairs, 1959—; mem. U.S. Holocaust Meml. Council, 1979; founder, hon. chmn. Anne Frank Inst., Phila., 1975—; exec. com. mem. Notre Dame Colloquium, 1961-68; named observer to Vatican II. Decorated Grosse Verdienstkreuz (Fed. Republic Germany); recipient Jabotinsky medal, Israel. Mem. European Assn. Evang. Acads. (co-founder), Phi Beta Kappa, Phi Beta Kappa Assocs. Clubs: Locust, Yale, George Town. Home: PO Box 172 Merion PA 19066 Office: Temple U Dept Religion Philadelphia PA 19122

LITTELL, KATHERINE MATHER, fine arts dealer, writer; b. Seattle, June 5, 1936; d. Norman M. and Katherine M. (Maher) Littell. B.A. Magna cum laude in English, Radcliffe Coll., 1958; postgrad. (German Exchange Service scholar) U. Munich, 1958-59; M.A. in German Lit., Harvard U., 1961; Ph.D. in Germanic Langs. and Lit., Columbia U., 1972. Instr. German, SUNY-New Paltz, 1965-66; instr. German lang. and lit. Tchrs. Coll., Columbia U., N.Y.C., 1966-69; instr. German and humanities SUNY-Stonybrook, 1968-69; asst. prof. Edinboro (Pa.) State Coll., 1969-70, assoc. prof., 1970-72, prof. methods of fgn. lang. teaching, German lit., 1972-76; asst. prof. dept. modern langs. Bucknell U., Lewisburg, Pa., 1976-78, research assoc., 1976-82; propr. Fine Arts Research Assoc., 1982—; lectr. Santa Rosa Jr. Coll., Yuba City Community Coll.; cons. bilingual edn. Central Susquehanna Intermediate Unit, 1972-76, dir. Bilingual Program. Author: Jeremiah Gotthelf's Die Kaserel in der Vehfeude, A Didactic Satire, 1977, Chris Jorgensen, California Pioneer Artist; contbr. articles to profl. jours., newspapers, mags. Nat. Inst. Edn. grantee, 1973; Bucknell U. Grantee, 1975; Pro Helvetia grantee, 1978, grantee Ministry Edn., People's Republic of China. Mem. Robert G. Sproul Assocs. U. Calif.-Berkeley, Harvard Club San Francisco, M.H. DeYoung Mus. Soc. Republican. Lutheran. Clubs: Sulgrave, Harvard Radcliffe of N.Y. Home: 20124 Forest Vista Dr Twain Harte CA 95383

LITTLE, CHARLES EDWARD, mathematics educator, university administrator; b. Kansas City, Kans., Apr. 18, 1926; s. Clarence A. and Anna Lu (Brown) L.; m. Janet R. Thompson, June 18, 1947; children: Steven, Jennifer, Timothy. AB, U. Kans.-Lawrence, 1948; MS, Ft. Hays Kans. State U., 1955; Ed.D., U. No. Colo., 1964. Tchr., adminstr. Burdett pub. schs., Kans., 1951-61; instr. math. U. No. Colo., Greeley, 1961-64; asst. prof. math. No. Ariz. U., Flagstaff, 1964-65, assoc. prof., 1965-68, prof., 1968—, chmn. dept. math., 1967-70, dean Coll. Arts and Sci., 1974-84; mem. adv. com. Ariz. State Bd. Edn. math., 1986-87, com. on essential skills for math., 1987; dir. Math Tchr. Retng. Program, 1987-88; adv. commn. textbook, math selection Ariz. State Bd Edn. Author: Mathematics for Liberal Arts, 1965, Programmed Instruction, 1967, Basic Concepts of Mathematics, 1967. Bd. dirs. Flagstaff Federated Ch., 1967; bd. dirs. Univ. Heights Corp., Flagstaff, 1969—, pres., 1969-76; mem. Flagstaff City Council, 1974-78. Mem. Math. Assn. Am., Nat. Council Tchrs. Math., Phi Kappa Phi, Phi Delta Kappa, Kappa Mu Epsilon, Lambda Sigma Tau. Office: No Ariz U Flagstaff AZ 86011

LITTLE, ELBERT LUTHER, JR., dendrologist, botanist; b. Fort Smith, Ark., Oct. 15, 1907; s. Elbert L. and Josephine (Conner) L.; m. Ruby Rema Rice, Aug. 14, 1943; children: Gordon Rice, Melvin Weaver, Alice Conner. B.A., U. Okla., 1927, B.S., 1932; M.S., Ph.D., U. Chgo., 1929; postgrad., U. Mich., 1927, Utah State U., 1928. Botanist Okla. Div. Forestry, 1930, 77-78; asst. prof. biology Southwestern Okla. State U., 1930-33; from asst. to asso. forest ecologist Forest Service, U.S. Dept. Agr., Tucson, 1934-42; dendrologist Forest Service, U.S. Dept. Agr., Washington, 1942-67; chief dendrologist 1967-76, cons., 1986—; botanist Fgn. Econ. Adminstrn., Bogotá, Colombia, 1943-45; prodn. specialist U.S. Comml. Co., Mexico, 1945; prof. dendrology Universidad de Los Andes, Mérida, Venezuela, 1953-54, 60; botanist U. Md., Guyana, 1955; cons. UN Mission, Costa Rica, 1964-65, 67, Ecuador, 1965, 75, Nicaragua, 1971; cons. Peace Corps, Paraguay, 1984; vis. prof. biology Va. Poly. Inst. State U., 1966-67; prof. U. D.C., 1979; mem. Internat. Commn. for Nomenclature of Cultivated Plants, 1956-76; collaborator U.S. Nat. Mus. Natural History, Smithsonian Instn., 1965-76, research assoc., 1976—. Author: Common Trees of Puerto Rico, Arboles Comunes de Esmeraldas, Ecuador, Atlas of United States Trees, Alaska Trees and Shrubs, Checklist of United States Trees, Forest Trees of Oklahoma, Audubon Society Field Guide to North American Trees, Common Fuelwood Crops; also tech. articles. Recipient Superior Service award U.S. Dept. Agr., 1960, Distinguished Service award, 1973. Fellow Soc. Am. Foresters (Barrington Moore award 1986), AAAS, Washington Acad. Scis., Okla. Acad. Sci., Explorers Club; mem. Am. Inst. Biol. Scis. (gov. bd. 1956-60), Am. Forestry Assn. (Disting. Service award 1981), Bot. Soc. Am., Internat., Am. socs. plant taxonomists, Ecol. Soc. Am., Phi Beta Kappa, Sigma Xi, Phi Sigma, Beta Beta Beta. Home: 924 20th St S Arlington VA 22202 Office: Smithsonian Instn Dept Botany Washington DC 20560

LITTLE, FREED SEBASTIAN, petroleum equipment mfg. co. exec.; b. Ft. Smith, Ark., May 4, 1926; s. Jess Edward and Floy Kimbrough (Witt) L.; B.A., U. Ark., 1950; m. Jana V. Jones, Dec. 9, 1951 (div.); 1 son, Mark McKenna. With Gilbarco Inc., Houston, 1964—, central area mgr., Chgo., 1969-73, Western regional mgr., Houston, 1974-85, Western/Pacific regional mgr., 1986—. Patron, Houston Mus. Fine Arts. Served with USAAF, 1945-46. Mem. Am. Petroleum Inst., Petroleum Equipment Inst., Am. Mgmt. Assn., Sigma Alpha Epsilon. Presbyterian. Clubs: Houston City, Memorial Drive Country. Office: 2909 Hillcroft Suite 210 Houston TX 77057 Home: 10121 Valley Forge Houston TX 77042

LITTLE, GRAHAM, language educator; b. Sydney, Australia, Feb. 4, 1930. BA with honors, U. Sydney, 1951; MEd with honors, U. New South Wales, Australia, 1975. Tchr. New South Wales Dept. Edn., 1952-66, insp. schs., 1968-75; vis. lectr. Commonwealth Inst., London, 1967; prin. lectr. edn. Canberra (Australia) Coll. Advanced Edn., 1976-86; cons. on edn. Sydney, 1987—; cons. Schs. Commn., Canberra, 1975, 85, Edn. Dept., Tasmania, Australia, 1977—, Victoria, Australia, 1978-79, 85; hon. vis. lectr. U. Ill., U. London, 1978-79; lectr. Mgmt. and Policy Studies Centre, Canberra, 1987—. Author: Approach to Literature, 1966; contbr. articles to profl. jours.; producer (documentary) The Gift of Speech, 1987. Mem. English Tchrs.' Assn. New South Wales (hon. life). Home and Office: 282 Sydenham Rd, 2204 Marrickville New South Wales, Australia

LITTLE, MELVYN, biochemist; b. Manchester, Eng., Jan. 6, 1945; s. Kenneth and Irene (Wolstencroft) L.; m. Sibylle Alwine Maria Gadow, Mar. 16, 1973; children: Christine Patricia, Bodo Kenneth. BS in Chem. with honors, U. Coll. North Wales, Bangor, 1966, PhD in Biochemistry, 1970; postdoctoral study, Habilitation, U. Heidelberg, Fed. Republic Germany, 1985. Research assoc. Max Planck Inst. for Cell Biology, Wilhelmshaven, Fed. Republic Germany, 1970-75; with German Cancer Research Ctr., Heidelberg, 1975—; instr. biochemistry U. Heidelberg, 1986—; research biochemist Palmer Sta. Antartica, 1987. Editor Mitosis: Facts and Questions, 1977; contbr. numerous articles to profl. jours. NATO grantee, 1979, German Research Community grantee, 1985. Mem. German Soc. for Cell Biology, German Soc. for Biol. Chemistry. Home: Fritz von Briesen St 10, 6903 Neckargemünd Dilsberg Federal Republic of Germany Office: German Cancer Research Ctr, Inst Cell & Tumor Biol, 69 Heidelberg Federal Republic of Germany

LITTLE, R. DONALD, architect; b. Gastonia, N.C., Mar. 18, 1937; s. Coy Marshall and Stella May (Pruett) L.; B.A., U. Md., 1972; B.Arch., Catholic U. Am., 1980, M.Arch., 1981; m. Jacqueline Beatrice Mandel, June 10, 1967; children by previous marriage—Tina June Whitman, Diana Dawn Little, Laura Marie Van Meel. Blood bank and med. technologist Dr. Oscar B. Hunter Meml. Lab., Washington, 1961-66; biol. lab. technologist Navl. Med. Research Inst., Bethesda, Md., 1966-68; blood bank and med. technologist, supr. Central Lab., Doctor's Hosp., Washington, 1959-79; jr. architect VVKR Inc., University Park, Md.; supr. architect; br. head design div. Naval Surface Weapons Center, Silver Spring, Md., 1981-87; supr. architect, chief facility engrng.br. Agrl. Research Service, USDA, 1987—. Served with USN, 1956-61. Mem. Am. Assn. Blood Banks, Am. Soc. Med. Technologists. Home: 13417 Rich Lynn Ct Highland MD 20777 Office: USDA-Agrl Research Service Facility Engrng Br Bldg 426 BARC-E Beltsville MD 20705

LITTLE, RICHARD ALLEN, mathematics and computer science educator; b. Coshocton, Ohio, Jan. 12, 1939; s. Charles M. and Elsie Leanna (Smith) L.; m. Gail Louann Koons, June 12, 1960; children: Eric, J. Alice, Stephanie. BS in Math. cum laude, Wittenberg U., 1960; MA in Edn., Johns Hopkins U., 1961; EdM in Math., Harvard U., 1965; PhD in Math. Edn., Kent State U., 1971. Tchr. Culver Acad., Ind., 1961-65; instr., curriculum cons. Harvard U., Cambridge, Mass. and Aiyetoro, Nigeria, 1965-67; from instr. to assoc. prof. Kent State U., Canton, Ohio, 1967-75; from assoc. prof. to prof. Baldwin-Wallace Coll., Berea, Ohio, 1975—; cons. in field; vis. prof. math. Ohio State U., Columbus, 1987-88; lectr. various colls. and univs.; pres. Cleve. Collaborative on Math. Edn., 1986-87. Contbr. articles to profl. jours. Bd. dirs. Canton Symphony Orch., 1973-75; Catechism tchr. St. Paul Luth. Ch., Berea, 1976-84, lector, 1980—; bd. deacons Holy Cross Luth. Ch., Canton, 1968-74, chmn., 1971-74. Mem. Nat. Council Tchrs. Math. (mem. profl. devel. and status adv. com. 1987—), Ohio Council Tchrs. Math. (pres. 1974-76, v.p. 1970-73, sec. 1982-84, dir. state math. contest, 1983—), Greater Cleve. Council Tchrs. Math. (bd. dirs. 1979-82), Greater Canton Council Tchrs. Math. (pres. 1969-70), Math. Assn. Am. (pres. Ohio sect. 1983-84, editor 1978-83). Avocations: jogging, tennis, handball. Home: 20201 Lorain Ave #411 Fairview Park OH 44126 Office: Baldwin-Wallace Coll Math and Computer Sci Dept Berea OH 44017

LITTLEFIELD, ROY EVERETT, III, assn. exec., legal educator; b. Nashua, N.H., Dec. 6, 1952; s. Roy Everett and Mary Ann (Prestipino) L.; 1 child, Leah Marie. B.A., Dickinson Coll., 1975; M.A., Catholic U. Am., 1976, Ph.D., 1979. Aide, U.S. Senator Thomas McIntyre, Democrat, N.H., 1975-78, Nordy Hoffman, U.S. Senate Sergeant-at-arms, 1979; dir. govt. relations Nat. Tire Dealers and Retreaders Assn., Washington, 1979-84; exec. dir. Service Sta. and Automotive Repair Assn., 1984—; cons. Am. Retreaders Assn., 1984—; mem. faculty Catholic U. Am., Washington, 1979—. Mem. Nat. Democratic Club, 1978—. Mem. Am. Soc. Legal History, Am. Retail Fedn., Small Bus. Legis. Council, Md. Hwy. Users Fedn. (pres.), Md. Soc. Assn. Execs. (bd. dirs., pres.), Nat. Capitol Area Transp. Fedn. (v.p.), N.H. Hist. Soc., C. of C., Phi Alpha Theta. Roman Catholic. Club: KC (Milford, N.H.). Author: William Randolph Hearst: His Role in American Progressivism, 1980; The Economic Recovery Act, 1982; The Surface Transportation Assistance Act; 1984; contbr. numerous articles to legal jours. Home: 15900 Pinecroft Ln Bowie MD 20716 Office: 9420 Annapolis Rd Suite 307 Lanham MD 20706

LITTLEJOHNS, RICHARD, language professional; b. Rosyth, Scotland, Feb. 3, 1943; s. Albert Edward Littlejohns and Mary Beatrice Norsworthy; m. Norma Mavis Daniels, Sept. 3, 1966; children: Julie, Adrian. B of Literature, U. Oxford, Eng., 1964, B Literature, 1969; PhD, U. Birmingham, Eng., 1986. Lang. asst. U. Münster, Fed. Republic of Germany, 1965-66; lectr. U. St. Andrews, Scotland, 1967-72, U. Birmingham, Eng., 1972—; examiner, awarder U. Oxford Delegacy of Local Examinations, 1974—. Author: Wackenroder-Studien, 1987; contbr. articles to acad. jours. Gov. various Birmingham schs., 1977—. Recipient Oskar Seidlin prize German Eichendorff Soc., 1988. Office: U Birmingham Dept German, PO Box 363, Birmingham B15 2TT, England

LITVAK, KING JAIME, archaeologist; b. Mexico D.F., Mex., Dec. 10, 1933; s. Abraham and Eugenia (King) L.; m. Elena Kaninski, 1954 (div. 1968); m. Carmen Aguilera, 1972 (div.); 1 dau., Noemi. Licenciatura, Escuela Nacional de Antropología, Mex., 1962; M.A., U. Mex., 1963, Ph.D., 1971. Researcher Inst. Nacional de Antropología, Méx., 1962-66, head computer ctr. Mus., 1966-68; researcher U. Mex., 1968-73, head anthrop. sect., 1973, dir. inst. anthrop. research, 1973-85, exec. bd., 1983—, mem. council, dir. gen. academic projects, 1985-86; chmn. dept. anthropology U. Ams., Puebla, 1986-88; mellon prof. humanities Tulane U., New Orleans, 1988; dir. bd. Inst. Nacional Indigenista, Mexico, 1975—; chmn. U. Ams., Anthrop, 1986—. Author: Cihuatlán y Tepecoacuilco, 1971; Arqueología y Derecho en México, 1978, Secuencia Cultural del Valle de México, 1982; Ancient Mexico; Todas las Piedras tienen; Una Introduccion A La Arqueologia; El Valle de Xochicalco, 1970; adv. editor: Editorial Alhambra, 1982—. Recipient mención honorífica Escuela Nacional de Antropología, 1963, U. México, 1970; Fray Bernardino de Sahagún Mexican Nat. Ward for Anthropology, 1970. Fellow Mexican Anthrop. Soc. (sec. 1971-76, 82-83), Soc. Archaeol. Sci., Am. Archaeol. Assn., Am. Archaeology Soc; mem. Sci. Research Acad. Mex. (Nat. Researcher award 1984). Office: Inst de Investig Antropoligicas, Ciudad Universitaria, 04510 Mexico City Mexico

LITWIN, BURTON LAWRENCE, music company executive, theatrical producer; b. N.Y.C., Jan. 1, 1931; s. Samuel G. and Eleanore (Kos) L.; m. Dorothy Beth Lefkowitz, Nov. 18, 1956; children: Richard Seth, Robert Aron, Kenneth David. BA, Washington and Lee U., 1951; LLB, NYU, 1953. Bar: N.Y. 1954, U.S. Dist. Ct. (so. dist.) N.Y. 1958, U.S. Ct. Appeals (2d cir.). Assoc. Wilzin and Halperin, N.Y.C., 1956-64; ptnr. DaSilva and Litwin, N.Y.C., 1964-65; sole practice, N.Y.C., 1965-67; v.p., dir. bus. affairs Belwin-Mills Pub. Corp., N.Y.C., 1967-74, v.p., gen. mgr., counsel, 1975-86; pres., chief exec. officer Newcal Properties and Prodns., Ltd., Newcal Music Co., Dobbs Ferry, N.Y., 1986—; bd. dirs. Nat. Teaching Aids, Inc., Garden City Park, N.Y. Producer (theatrical works) Sophisticated Ladies, N.Y.C., Tokyo, Paris, 1980—, Poppy, London, 1982-83, Stardust, N.Y.C., 1986—. Pres. Temple Beth Abraham, Tarrytown, N.Y., 1982-83; bd. dirs. Creative Arts Rehab. Ctr., N.Y.C., 1983-84. Served to sgt. U.S. Army, 1953-55. Recipient Tony award nomination League of N.Y. Theatres, 1982; ann. Image award NAACP, 1982, Outer Critics Circle award, 1987. Mem. N.Y. State Bar Assn., ABA, Copyright Soc. USA, ASCAP (bd. appeals 1981-83, adv. com. 1985—), League of Am. Theatres and Producers. Club: Friars. Lodge: B'nai B'rith. Avocations: photography, traveling, tennis. Home and Office: Newcal Properties and Prodns 12 Crescent Ln Dobbs Ferry NY 10522

LITZENBERGER, LEONARD NELSON, research physicist; b. East Macungie, Pa., Oct. 15, 1945; s. Nelson George and Cora Maggie (Hausman) L.; m. Anne Fabiola Ward, Oct. 19, 1974; 1 child, Julie Beth. B.S. in Engrng. Physics with highest honors, Lehigh U., 1967; S.M. in Physics, MIT, 1969, Ph.D. in Physics, 1971. Prin. research scientist Avco Research Lab., Inc., Mass., 1971—. Contbr. articles to profl. jours. Patentee in field of laser isotope separation. Mem. Am. Phys. Soc., Sigma Xi, Phi Beta Kappa, Tau Beta Pi. Current work: excimer laser research and development. Office: Avco Research Lab Inc 2385 Revere Beach Pkwy Everett MA 02149

LITZENBOERGER, WOLFGANG, software engineering executive, industrial consultant; b. Hannover, West Germany, June 10, 1935; s. Ernst Joachim and Martha Emma (Althoff) L.; m. Ingeborg Meinhold, May 26, 1940; children: Dominique, Wolf-Rene, Nathalie. Ed., U. Bari (Italy), 1959-60, U. Sorbonne, Paris, 1961, U. Barcelona, Spain, 1962, U. Bologna, Italy, 1963, Pacific Western U., Los Angeles, 1982-83. Gen. mgr. Pisani and Rickertsen, Istanbul, 1956-59; pres., ptnr. INHA Internat. AG, Mauren, Switzerland, 1963-73; mng. dir., owner IDC Indsl. Devel. Cons. GmbH, Duesseldorf, Fed. Republic of Germany, 1972—; owner, mng. dir. PDC Planning and Devel. Cons. GmbH, Duesseldorf, 1981-85; mng. dir., shareholder Indsl. Informatics GmbH, Freiburg, Fed. Republic of Germany, 1985—. Contbr. articles to profl. jours. Fellow Inst. of Dirs. (London); mem. Institut fuer interdisziplinare Denkschulung und Publikationen e.V. (v.p. 1984—). Home: 34 Am Adels, D 4030 Ratingen 6 Federal Republic of Germany Office: 2i Indsl Informatics GmbH, 20e Haierweg, Freiburg Federal Republic of Germany

LIU, CHING-TONG, research physiologist; b. Kiangsu, China, Oct. 19, 1931; s. Lien Yi and Su Ju (Ku) L.; m. In-May Hsin, Feb. 28, 1970; children—Rex, Grace, Jeannette, Christine. B.S., Nat. Taiwan U., 1956; M.S., U. Tenn., Memphis, 1959, Ph.D., 1963. Assoc. research biologist Sterling-Winthrop Research Inst., Renssalaer, N.Y., 1965-66; asst. prof. physiology Baylor Coll. Medicine, Houston, 1966-73, adj. prof., 1979—; research physiologist, chief dept. clin. and exptl. physiology U.S. Army Med. Research Inst. Infectious Diseases, Ft. Detrick, Md., 1973—; adviser postdoctoral research assocs. NRC, Washington. Contbr. numerous articles to profl. jours. Recipient Outstanding Performance award U.S. Army, 1976-77, Superior Performance award, 1980-81, Exceptional Performance rating, 1982-84, Merit Performance award, 1984-87. Mem. Soc. Exptl. Biology and Medicine, Am. Physiol. Soc., Am. Soc. Pharmacology and Exptl. Therapeutics, Am. Soc. Nephrology. Home: 7915 W 7th St Frederick MD 21701 Office: Fort Detrick USAMRIID Disease Assessment Div Frederick MD 21701-5011

LIU ENBO, dancer, academic administrator; b. Tangshan, Hopei, Peoples Republic China, Jan. 6, 1931; d. Zean and Guifan (Wu) L.; m. Lijuan Liu, Jan. 22, 1963; children: Ding, Yan. Diploma, Peking Acad., 1951, Cen. Acad. Dramatic Arts, Beijing, 1952, Tng. Ctr. for Tchrs. Dance, 1954. Asst. Cen. Acad. Dramatic Arts, Beijing, 1952-53; tchr. Beijing Sch. Dances, 1954-55; research worker, editor Chinese Dancers Assn., Beijing, 1955-73; assoc. researcher Inst. Dance Research, Beijing, 1973—; dir. reference room Chinese Acad. Arts, 1973—. Co-author: Art of Chinese Dances, 1981, An Introduction to the Folk Dances of Hans, 1981, 86, Beijing Traditional

Custom and Dance, 1986; asst. editor-in-chief Complete Collection of Chinese Folk Dances, 1986—; co-editor: Dictionary of Chinese Dances, 1987—. Recipient award China Youth Daily, 1956. Mem. Chinese Dancers Assn., Inst. Dunhuang and Tulufan Research, Folk Arts Soc. of Chong Wen Dist. Beijing (advisor in arts), Chinese Folklore Soc. Home: No 9 Ent 2 Bldg 15 Block 10, Heping St, Beijing Peoples Republic of China Office: Chinese Acad of Arts, Qian Hai Xi Jie 17, Beijing Peoples Republic of China

LIU, HAI-SOU, painter, calligrapher, poet; b. Changchow, China, Mar. 16, 1896; s. K.F. Liu and Hoong Shu-Yih; m. Hsia J-Chiao; children—Liu Fou-T'Tun, Liu Pao, Liu Ling, Liu Ying-Lun, Liu Qiu, Liu Hung, Liu Tsan. Founder, dir. Acad. of Shanghai of Arts, China, 1912-52; pres. East China Acad. Arts, 1953-58; pres. and chief examiner of Kiansou Provincial Exhbn., 1924; pres., 1st class prof. Nanking Acad. Arts, 1979—; gen. rep. for organizing famous modern Chinese Painting exhbns. in Germany, Sino-German Joint Conf., Berlin, 1931; lectr. China Inst., Frankfurt, Germany, 1934; guest lectr. various European cities including Berlin and Dü sseldorf, Germany, Amsterdam, Netherlands, Geneva, London, Prague, Czechosolovakia; one-man shows of paintings include Tokyo, 1927, 84, Prussian Mus., Berlin, 1934, China Inst., Frankfort, Ger., 1931, Klinmann Gallery, Paris, 1931, Bruet Gallery, 1935, New Burlington Gallery, London, 1935; numerous group shows including exhbns. Switzerland, 1929, Egypt, 1929, Belgium, 1930, Italy, 1930, Germany, 1934, New Britain Gallery, London, 1935, Salon des Tuileries, Paris, 1930, Salon'd'Autaume, Paris, 1931, Klinmann Gallery, Paris, 1931, various exhbns. in Jakarta, 1939, Singapore, 1940, Shanghai, 1957, 80, 82, Peking, 1979, 82, Nanking, 1979, Hong Kong, 1977, 81; represented in permanent collections: Klinmann Gallery, Bruet Gallery, East Mus., Berlin, Asahi Kinbun Gallery, Tokyo. Recipient Silver Cup award Emperor of Japan, 1927, Prize of Honour, Internat. Exposition Centinary Nat. Independence, Belgium, 1930; diploma of merit, Italy U. Arts, Italy, 1981, 82; Gold medal artistic merit Internat. Parliament for Safety and Peace, U.S.A., 1982; recognized as Le Maitre de la Renaissance Chinoise, 1931. Mem. Internat. Arts Assn., Accademia Italia delle Arti (life), Nat. Joint Men of Letters and Artists Assn. (commr.). Author: (books on history of painting) including: Later Stage Impressionists and Shih-Tao, 1928; Shih-Tao and his View-points on Arts, 1934; On the Six Principles about Chinese Paintings, 1931; Theory of Paintings, 1931; On Modern Paintings, 1936; A General Statement on Sources of Chinese Traditional Painting, 1936; editor Fine Arts monthly, 1918, Arts Weekly, 1924. Home: 512 Fushing Rd, Central Shanghai Peoples Republic of China

LIU, HAN-SHOU, space scientist, researcher; b. Hunan, China, Mar. 9, 1930; came to U.S., 1960, naturalized, 1972; s. Yu-Tin and Chun-Chen (Yeng) L.; m. Sun-Ling Yang Liu, May 2, 1957; children—Michael Fu-Yen, Peter Fu-Tze. Ph.D., Cornell U., 1963. Research asst. Cornell U., 1962-63; research assoc. Nat. Acad. Sci., Washington, 1963-65; scientist NASA Goddard Space Flight Center, Greenbelt, Md., 1965—; Pres. Mei-Hwa Chinese Sch., 1980-81. Contbr. articles to profl. jours. Fellow AAAS; mem. Am. Astron. Soc., Am. Geophys. Union, Planetary Soc., AIAA. Home: 2301 Laurelwood Terr Silver Spring MD 20904 Office: NASA Goddard Space Flight Ctr Code 621 Greenbelt MD 20771

LIU, KATHERINE CHANG, artist, art educator; b. Kiang-si, Peoples Republic of China; came to U.S., 1963; d. Ming-fan and Ying (Yuan) Chang; m. Yet-zen Liu; children: Alan S., Laura Y. MS, U. Calif., Berkeley, 1965. lectr. N.J. Watercolor Soc., Pitts. Watercolor Soc., Oreg. Watercolor Soc., Tex. Watercolor Soc., Ohio Watercolor Soc., Ariz. Watercolor Assn., Rocky Mountain Watercolor Workshop, U. Va. extension, Longwood. Coll., Va. One-man shows include Harrison Mus., Utah State U., Riverside (Calif.) Art Mus., Ventura (Calif.) Coll., Roanoke (Va.) Mus. Fine Arts, Fla. A&M U., Louis Newman Galleries, Los Angeles, Lung-Men Gallery, Taipei, Republic of China; sole juror Watercolor State Open Competitions, N.J., Oreg., Pa. 1988; Western Fedn. Exhibition, Houston, 1986, San Diego Internat. Watercolor Exhbn., 1986, Ohio Watercolor Soc., 1986. Recipient Rex Brandt award San Diego Watercolor Internat., 1985, Purchase Selection award Watercolor USA and Springfield (Mo.) Art Mus., 1981, Gold Medal, 1986, Mary Lou Fitzgerald Meml. award Allied Arts Am. Nat. Arts Club, N.Y.C., 1987; NEA grantee, 1979-80. Mem. Nat. Watercolor Soc. (life, chmn. jury 1985, pres. 1983, Top award 1984, cash awards 1979, 87.), Watercolor USA Honor Soc., Nat. Soc. Painters in Casein and Acrylic (2d award 1985), Rocky Mountain Nat. Watermedia Soc. (juror 1984, awardee 1978, 80, 86), West Coast Watercolor Soc.

LIU, KUANG-CHI, government agency official; b. Peking, Peoples Republic of China, June 2, 1933; s. Hsi-Lin and Ying (Pai) L.; m. Chung-Rei Hsiang; children Wei-Li, I-Li. BS, Chinese Naval Acad., Tsoying, Taiwan, Peoples Republic of China, 1954; MSEE, Nat. Chiao Tung U., Hsingchu, Taiwan, 1965. Instr. electronics and math. Naval Acad. and Rates Tng. Ctr. Chinese Navy, Taipei, 1958-63; design engr. TDC Civ. Chu Assn., Mass., 1966-68; design team leader TRR reactor project Inst. Nuclear Energy Research, 1970-72; dir. div. instrumentation, dept. electronics Chun-Shan Inst. Sci. and Tech., Taoyuan, Peoples Republic of China, 1968-69, dir. div. nuclear instrumentation, 1972-76, dep. dir., 1976-84, dir., 1984-87; sec. gen. Atomic Energy Council, Exec. Yuan, Taipei, 1987—. Served to capt. Peoples Republic of China Navy, 1954-65, Taipei. Mem. Nondestructive Testing Soc. (chmn. Taipei chpt. 1987—), Nuclear Energy Soc. (standing dir. Taipei chpt. 1985—), Am. Nuclear Soc. (sec. Taiwan chpt., chmn. Taipei chpt. 1988—). Home: 7 Fl 23 Lane 40, Yu Min I Rd, Pei Tou Dist Taipei Taiwan, Peoples Republic China 10772 Office: Atomic Energy Council, 67 Lane 144, Keelung Rd Sec 4, Taipei Taiwan, Peoples Republic China 10772

LIU, MING-WOOD, Chinese philosophy educator; b. Kuang-chou, Kuangtung, Peoples Republic of China, Dec. 14, 1947; arrived in Hong Kong, 1950; parents Yue-wah and Kwai-chu (Yue) L. BA, U. Hong Kong, 1969, M in Philosophy, 1974; PhD, UCLA, 1979. Lectr. U. Hong Kong, 1979—; vis. scholar Harvard-Yenching Inst., Cambridge, Mass., 1985-86. Author: The Teaching of Chia-hsiang Chi-tsang, 1985; contbr. articles to jours. Mem. Internat. Assn. Buddhist Studies. Office: U Hong Kong, Chinese Dept, Pokfulam Rd, Hong Kong Hong Kong

LIU, PETER PI, cardiologist, researcher; b. Taipei, Taiwan, Republic of China, Oct. 12, 1953; arrived in Canada, 1966; s. Ping-Jen and Ping-Lin Liu. MD, U. Toronto, Can., 1978. Intern then resident Toronto Gen. Hosp., 1978-80; fellow in cardiology Sunnybrook and Toronto Gen. Hosps., 1980-83; fellow in nuclear cardiology Mass. Gen. Hosp., Boston, 1983-85; asst. prof. medicine Toronto Gen. Hosp. U. Toronto, 1985, co-dir. nuclear cardiology, 1986, asst. prof. radiology, dir. cardiovascular research, 1987—; cardiology cons., U. MR Utilization Com., Toronto 1986; mem. publ. com. NIH Myocarditis Trial, Bethesda, Md., 1986. Contbr. articles to profl. jours. Cardiology cons. Heart to Heart program, Heart Found., Toronto, 1985. Grantee Heart Foundation, 1986-87, U. Toronto, 1985; IODE Scholar, 1984. Fellow Am. Coll. Cardiology, Clin. Radiology Consults, Am. Heart Assn., Am. Fedn. Clin. Research, Royal Coll. Physicians, Mass. Med. Soc., Soc. Magnetic Resonance in Medicine. Office: Toronto Gen Hosp, 200 Elizabeth St, GW 1-512, Toronto, ON Canada M5G 2C4

LIU, PING YUAN, chemist, researcher; b. Hwai-an, China, May 12, 1931; came to U.S., 1959, naturalized, 1973; s. Soo-noon and Chee (Hang) L.; m. Lily Tehyu Chen; children—Henry Heng, Ingrid Ying. B.S., Nat. Taiwan U., 1955; M.S., Case Western Res. U., 1962, Ph.D., 1966. Research chemist Monsanto, Bloomfield, Conn., 1972-74, Amoco Chem. Corp., Naperville, Ill., 1974-77; advanced devel. chemist Gen. Electric Co., Mt. Vernon, Ind., 1977—. Translator: Chemical Plant Design with Fiber Reinforced Plastics, 1970. Numerous U.S. and fgn. patents. Sloan fellow, 1966-68; Tech. Innovation award Gen. Electric Engring Materials Group, 1980. Fellow Soc. Plastics Engrs.; mem. Am. Chem. Soc., Soc. Rheology. Club: Toastmasters (Mt. Vernon) (pres. 1986-87). Avocation: bridge. Office: Gen Electric Co Hwy 69 South Mount Vernon IN 47620

LIU, SHOU-PEN, government official, senior specialist; b. Hsin-Pu, Hsin-Chu, Taiwan, Republic of China, Feb. 8, 1938; s. King-Sun Liu and Shih-Mei Pong; m. Hsio-Hsiang Chuan, July 3, 1966; children—Chia-Shih, Pai-Ho, Wen-Shih. B.S., Taiwan Normal U., 1965. Geologist Chinese Petroleum Corp., Miao-Li, 1966-69; mining engr. Dept. of Mines, Ministry of Econ. Affairs, Taipei, Taiwan, Republic of China, 1969-81, sr. specialist, 1981—. Author: Rock Mechanics and Roof Control, 1983, Mine Safety Management and Loss Control, 1983. Fellow Mine Ventilation Soc. South Africa, Chinese Inst. Mining and Metall. Engrs.; mem. Chinese Inst. Engrs., Standard Soc. China, Sino-Am. Tech. Corp. Assn. Buddhist. Avocations: photography; stamp collecting; gardening. Office: Ministry of Econ Affairs, Dept of Mines, 15 Fo-chow St, Taipei 19722, Republic of China

LIU, TS'UN-YAN, Chinese educator; b. Peking, Republic of China, Aug. 11, 1917; s. Tsung-chuan and Yu-shu (Huang) L.; m. S.Y. Chiang; children: Frank T.P., Selina N.C. Fung. BA, Peking U., 1939; BA with hons., London U., 1954, PhD, 1957, D. Lit., 1969; D. Lit. (hon.), Yeungnam U., Republic of Korea, 1972; D. Letters (hon.), Hong Kong. U., 1988. Chmn. Chinese Panel U. Hong Kong, 1952-59; lectr. in charg, Northcote Coll. Edn., Hong Kong, 1959-62; chmn. Chinese subcom. post-sec. colls. joint establishment bd. Hong Kong, 1961-62; sr. lectr. Chinese and Australian Nat. U., Canberra, Australia, 1962-65, reader in Chinese, 1965-66, prof., head dept. Chinese, 1966-82, dean faculty of Asian studies, 1970-72, 73-74, prof. emeritus in Chinese, 1983—, univ. fellow, 1983-85. Author: Buddhist and Taoist Influences on Chinese Novels, 1962, Chinese Popular Fiction in Two London Libraries, 1968, Selected Papers from the Hall of Harmonious Wind, 1976, New Excursions from the Hall of Harmonious Wind, 1983. Fellow Royal Asiatic Soc., 1957, Australian Acad. Humanities, 1969, Nippon Dokyo Gakkai, Tokyo, 1969. Fellow Oriental Soc. Australia. Office: China Ctr Faculty Asian Studies, Australian Nat U, Canberra 2601, Australia

LIU, WILLIAM HUILIN, economist, educator; b. Shanghai, China, July 24, 1934; arrived in Eng., 1963; s. Shun Ch'iao and Feng Yun (Tai) L.; m. Helen Tuanh, Sept. 11, 1965; children: Janet, Cynthia, Sonia, Richard. MPhil, reading (Eng.) U., 1967; PhD, Edinburgh (Scotland) U., 1970, The China Acad., Republic China, 1971; postgrad. cert. in edn., Exeter (Eng.) U., 1964. Head dept. English Tenom Secondary Sch., North Borneo, 1961-62; head Chinese studies Edinburgh U., 1966-81, dir. East Asia studies, 1981—; vis. prof. USSR Acad. Scis., Moscow, 1982, 84. Author: Marxian Economics and a Post-Mao Model, 1988; contbr. articles on econs., politics, law and edn. to profl. jours. Standing mem. Standing conf. Nat. and Univ. Libraries, London, 1966—. Research grantee Endinburgh U., 1981. Mem. European Assn. Sinological Librarians, Brit. Assn. Chinese Studies. Home: 15 Redhall Crescent, Edinburgh EH14 2HU, Scotland Office: Edinburgh U, George Sq, Edinburgh EH8 9LJ, Scotland

LIU, YUNG YUAN, materials/energy research engineer; b. Taipei, Taiwan, Mar. 20, 1950; came to U.S., 1973, naturalized, 1982; s. Kan C. and Mon W. (Chou) L.; m. Teresa L. Ngai, Jan. 4, 1975; children—Sharon H.Y., Alvin H.L. B.S., Nat. Tsing-Hua U., Taiwan, 1971; M.S., MIT, 1976, Sc.D., 1978. Staff engr. Entropy Ltd., Lincoln, Mass., 1977-78; asst. nuclear engr. Argonne (Ill.) Nat. Lab., 1978-81, nuclear engr., prin. investigator, theorist, 1981—; mem. life code com. U.S. Dept. Energy, 1978-81, mem. fuel performance evaluation task force, 1978-81, task mgr. office of fusion energy blanket design studies, 1982-84; cons. Los Alamos Nat. Lab., 1982. Contbr. articles to profl. jours.; editor-in-chief: Free Chinese Monthly, Cambridge, Mass., 1973-75. Mem. Am. Nuclear Soc., Am. Soc. Metals, Materials Research Soc., AAAS. Baptist. Home: 333 Hampton Pl Hinsdale IL 60521 Office: Argonne Nat Lab Materials and Components Tech 9700 S Cass Ave Argonne IL 60439

LIVIJN, CLAES-OLOF EINAR, financial executive; b. Stockholm, Mar. 28, 1923; s. Claes Gustaf and Ellen (Ekendahl) L.; m. Sonja Flodin, May 2, 1962; children—Katarina, Rikard, Mikael, Henrik. Handelsbanken, Stockholm, 1950-62; pres. Svenska Finans AB, Stockholm, 1963-84, vice-chmn. bd., 1984-85; chmn. Factors Chain Internat., Amsterdam, 1971-72, Internat. Fin. and Leasing Assn., U.K., 1968; vice-chmn. Assn. Swedish Fin. Houses, Stockholm, 1976-78, chmn., 1978-80; chmn. Finax Finans Service AB, 1985, Paravan AB, 1985—; vice-chmn. Barkman & Co. AB 1986; bd. dir. Elcon Finans A/S, Norway, 1985—. Author, editor: Studies in Financial History, 1968-79. Mem. Par Bricole. Consul Gen. Royal Kingdom of Nepal. Home: Karlavagen 97, S-115 22 Stockholm Sweden Office: Loxia Trading AB, Eriksbergsgatan 1A, 114 30 Stockholm Sweden

LIVINGSTON, JOHNSTON R., manufacturing executive; b. Foochow, China, Dec. 18, 1923; s. Henry Walter V and Alice (Moorehead) L.; m. Caroline Johnson, Aug. 17, 1946 (dec.); children: Henry, Ann, Jane, David; m. Patricia Karolchuck, Sept. 4, 1965. B.S. with honors in Engring., Yale U., 1947; M.B.A. with distinction (Baker scholar), Harvard U., 1949. With Mpls.-Honeywell Regulator Co., 1949-55; with Whirlpool Corp., 1956-66, v.p., until 1966; v.p. Redman Industries, Dallas, 1966-67; dir. Constrn. Tech., Inc., Dallas, 1967—; chmn. bd., pres. Constrn. Tech., Inc., Denver, 1974—; chmn. bd. Enmark Corp., Denver, 1979—; pres. Marcor Housing Systems, Inc., Denver, 1971-74; dir. 1st Colo. Bank & Trust, Denver, Beco Corp., Denver. Former mem. industry adv. com. Nat. Housing Center; dir., past pres. Nat. Home Improvement Council; chmn. bd., pres. Denver Symphony Assn., 1977—; chmn. bd. Rocky Mountain Region Internat. Inst. Edn.; trustee BonGils-Stanton Found., 1980—. Served with USAAF, 1943-46. Mem. Chevaliers du Tastevin, Sigma Xi, Tau Beta Pi. Clubs: Denver Country. Home: 869 Vine St Denver CO 80206 Office: 5070 Oakland St Denver CO 80239

LIVINGSTONE, DAVID NOEL, Geographer; b. Banbridge, Northern Ireland, Mar. 15, 1953; s. Robert and Winifred (Turkington) L.; m. Frances Allyson Haugh, July 26, 1977; children: Emma Allyson, Justin David. BA, Queen's U., Belfast, Northern Ireland, 1975, Ph.D., 1982. Research fellow Queen's U., Belfast, Northern Ireland, 1982-84, research officer, curator maps, 1984-88, sr. research officer, 1988—. Author: Nathaniel Southgate Shaler and the Culture of American Science, 1987, Darwin's Forgotten Defenders, 1987; contbr. articles to profl. jours. Mem. religious adv. panel BBC, Northern Ireland, 1986-88. Mem. History of Sci. Soc., Brit. Soc. History Sci., Inst. Brit. Geographers, Royal Irish Acad.'s Nat. Com. for History and Philosophy of Sci. Presbyterian. Home: 91 Castlemore Ave, BT69RH Belfast Northern Ireland Office: Dept Geography, Queens Univ, BT71NN Belfast Northern Ireland

LIVINGSTONE, RODNEY SIMON, German language educator; b. London, Feb. 26, 1934; s. David Livingstone and Muriel (Harris) Ogus; m. Angela Mary Hobbs, Aug. 30, 1959 (div. 1970); children: Sonia Mary, Benjamin Simon; m. Anna Krystyna Dziedzic, Aug. 30, 1972; 1 child, Judith Hannah. BA, Trinity Hall, Cambridge, Eng., 1956; postgrad., Münster U., Fed. Republic Germany, 1956-57; MA, Trinity Hall, Cambridge, Eng., 1960. Lectr. Adelaide U., S. Australia, Australia, 1960-62, Monash U., Melbourne, Australia, 1963-6; from lectr. to sr. lectr. Southampton (Eng.) U., 1966—; vis. prof. Frankfurt U., Fed. Republic Germany, 1979. Editor: Lukács, Essays on Realism, 1981; translator: Karl Marx, Herr Vogt, 1980, Lukács, History and Class Consciousness, 1971; contbr. articles to profl. jours. Mem. Leo Baeck Inst. (mem. com.). Jewish. Home: 86 Highfield Ln, Southampton, Hampshire SO2 1RJ, England Office: Southampton U, German Dept, Highfield, Southampton SO9 5NH, England

LI XIANNIAN, government official People's Republic of China; b. 1909, Huangan, Hubei; m. Lin Jiamei; 3 daus., 1 son. Joined Chinese Communist Party, 1927; polit. commissar 30th Army, 4th Front Red Army, 1935; Comdr. 5th Column, New 4th Army, 1938, Cen. China Mil. Region, 1944; mem. 7th Cen. Com., Chinese Communist Party, 1945; chmn. Provincial Govt. of Hubei, 1949; Comdr. polit. commissar Hubei Mil. Dist., People's Liberation Army, 1949; mayor Wuhan, 1952-54; vice premier State Council, 1954-80; mem. Nat. Def. Council, 1954; dep. 1st Nat. People's Congress, Hubei Province, 1954, 5th Nat. People's Congress, 1978; appointed army gen., 1954; minister of fin., 1957-75; mem. Politburo, 8th Congress, Chinese Communist Party, 1956, mem. secretariat of Cen. Com., 1958-66; dir. Fin. Econ. Affairs Com. Bur., State Council, 1959; vice chmn. State Planning Comm., 1962-72; mem. Politburo and Cen. Com., 9th Congress, Chinese Communist Party, 1969, 10th Cen. Com. Congress, 1973, vice chmn. Cen. Com., 11th Congress, 1977-82, mem. Standing Com., 1977; vice chmn. State Fin. Econ. Commn., 1979-81; del. head 6th Congress Workers' Party of North Korea, 1980; mem. Presidium 12th Congress, 1982; pres. People's Republic of China, 1983-88; chmn. 7th nat. com. Chinese People's Polit. Consultative Conf., 1988—. Chmn. Cen. Patriotic Health Campaign Com., 1978-83. Decorated Star Socialist Republic Romania, 1984. Avocation: jogging. Address: Chinese People's Polit Cons Conf, Beijing People's Republic of China *

LJOLJE, KRUNOSLAV, theoretical physicist; b. Jajce, Yugoslavia, July 29, 1928; s. Ilija and Ana (Benes) L.; B.Sc., U. Zagreb, 1951, Ph.D. in Physics, 1954; m. Zrinka Juric, Nov. 16, 1974; children—Marijana, Marije. Mem. faculty U. Sarajevo, 1951—, prof. theoretical physics, 1967—, dean Faculty Sci., 1981-84; research asst. prof. U. Ill., Urbana, 1960-62; head commn. sci. work Assn. Socs. Mathematicians, Physicists and Astronomers Yugoslavia, 1975-81. Served with Yugoslavian Army, 1954-55. Recipient July 27 award Bosna and Hercegovina, 1975, award Veselin Maslesa, 1986. Mem. Acad. Scis. and Arts Bosna and Hercegovina, Soc. Mathematicians, Physicists and Astronomers Bosna and Hercegovina. Roman Catholic. Author papers in field. Home: 2A R Jankovic, 71000 Sarajevo Yugoslavia Office: 43 V Putnika, 71000 Sarajevo Yugoslavia

LJUNGSTRÖM, GÖRAN, association executive; b. Stockholm, Apr. 11, 1933; s. Thord G.L. and Ewa-Maja (Holmer) L.; m. Barbro Margareta Bredberg; children: Fredrik, Anna Maria. Student, Officers Acad., 1955; LLB, U. Stockholm, 1958. Negotiation officer Swedish Employers Confedn., Stockholm, 1959-62; chief negotiations Swedish Motortrade Employers Assn., Stockholm, 1962-70, mng. dir., 1970—; mng. dir. Employers Assn. Swedish Petroleum Industry, Stockholm, 1980—; mem. Joint Indsl. Tng. Council; exec. com. Council Indsl. Salaried Staff Tng.; chmn. Vocat. Tng. and Working Environment Council of Transport Trades, Health and Safety Services of Transport Trades, Vocat. Tng. Bd. Swedish Motor Trade. Comdr.-in-chief Motor Repair Service for Swedish Total Def. Club: Sällskapet. Home: Slottsvagen 74, 183 52 Taby Sweden Office: Employers Assn Swedish, Petroleum Industry, Blasieholmsgatan 4A, 111 48 Stockholm Sweden

LLANOS, JOSEPH KALALANG, physician; b. Manila, Philippines, Sept. 16, 1952; s. Dominador Torres and Lilia Lebrilla (Kalalang) L.; m. Maria Socorro Zarate Cruz, Mar. 14, 1987. BS, U. Santo Tomas, Manila, 1972, MD, benemeritus (hon.), 1976. Rural health practice physician Ministry of Health, Zamboanga, Philippines, 1976; intern U. Philippines Gen. Hosp., Manila, 1976-77; head infirmarian, med. cons. Soc. of Divine Word, Tagaytay, Philippines, 1977-79; resident trainee I U. Philippines Gen. Hosp., Manila, 1978; med. dir. St. Camillus Polyclinic, Makati, Philippines, 1980-85, Pasig, Philippines, 1986—; house doctor Franciscan Missionary of Mary, Religious of Good Sheperd, Order of Agustinian Recollect Sisters, St. Agustine Maj. Sem., Mission Soc. of Philippines, Tagaytay, 1977-78; instr. in sociology and human sexuality Divine Word Sem., Tagaytay, 1978-79; med. examiner Atlanta Vinyl Corp., Wel-Best Corp., Marblecraft Inc., Philcan Indsl. Corp., Arcometals, Hansson Paper Philippines Corp., Pasig, 1986—. Head med. services Love The Sick, Makati and Pasig, 1981—. Order of St. Camillus grantee, 1985; recipient Humanitarian award Caloocan Jaycees, 1986. Mem. Philippine Med. Assn., U. Santo Tomas Med. Alumnae Assn. Roman Catholic. Home: 23 Production St, GSIS Project 8, Quezon City Philippines Office: St Camillus Polyclinic, 116 E Amang Rodriguez Ave, Bo Santolan, Pasig Philippines

LLAU, PIERRE, economics educator, researcher; b. Toulouse, Haute-Garonne, France, Nov. 21, 1934; s. Albert and Rose (Saura) L.; m. Anne-Marie Mathieu, July 15, 1959; children—Pascal, Philippe, Christophe. Ed. Faculté Droit-Economie, Toulouse, France, 1954, Superieur, Paris, 1959. Cert. economist, France. Prof. econs. U. Grenoble, France, 1962-70, U. Paris X Nanterre, 1970—; cons. mem. Nat. Taxation Council, Paris, 1982-84. Author: The Determination of Interest Rates (recipient Lescure prize 1962), 1962; Economics of Finance, 1975; Taxation and Economic Choices, 1978. Cons., Commissariat Gen. du Plan, Paris, 1980, 83; Economics of Finance, 1985. Served to sgt. French Army, 1960-62. Mem. Conseil Superieur des Universites, Groupe d' Experts Council National du Credit, Preparation Marché, CEE. Roman Catholic. Home: 3 Ave de la Tranquillité, 7800 Versailles Yvelines France Office: Univ Paris X Nanterre, 200 Ave Republique, 92001 Nanterre Cedex France

LLAURADO, JOSEP G., nuclear medicine physician, scientist; b. Barcelona (Catalonia), Spain, Feb. 6, 1927; s. José and Rosa (Llaurado) Garcia; m. Deirdre Mooney, Nov. 9, 1966; children—Raymund, Wilfred, Mireya; m. Catherine D. Entwistle, June 28, 1958 (dec.); children—Thadd, Oleg, Montserrat. B.S., B.A., Balmes Inst., Barcelona, 1944; M.D., Barcelona U., 1950; Ph.D. in Pharmacology, 1960; M.Sc. Biomed. Engring., Drexel U., 1963. Diplomate: Am. Bd. Nuclear Medicine. Resident Royal Postgrad. Sch. Medicine, Hammersmith Hosp., London, 1952-54; fellow M.D. Anderson Hosp. and Tumor Inst., Houston, 1957-58, U. Utah Med. Coll., Salt Lake City, 1958-59; asst. prof. U. Otago Dunedin, N.Z., 1954-57; sr. endocrinologist Pfizer Med. Research Lab., Groton, Conn., 1959-60; assoc. prof. U. Pa., 1963-67; prof. Med. Coll. Wis., Milw., 1970-82, Marquette U., 1967-82; clin. dir. nuclear medicine service VA Med. Ctr., Milw., 1977-82; chief nuclear medicine service VA Hosp., Loma Linda, Calif., 1983—; prof. dept. radiation scis. Loma Linda U. Sch. Medicine, 1983—; U.S. rep. symposium on dynamic studies with radioisotypes in clin. medicine and research IAEA, Rotterdam, 1970, Knoxville, 1974. Editor: Internat. Jour. Biomed. Computing. Contbr. numerous articles to profl. jours. Merit badge counselor Boy Scouts Am., 1972—; pres. Hales Corners (Wis.) Hist. Soc., 1981-83. Recipient Commendation cert. Boy Scouts Am., 1980. Fellow Am. Coll. Nutrition; mem. Soc. Nuclear Medicine (computer and acad. councils), IEEE (sr.), IEEE in Medicine and Biology Soc. (nat. adminstrv. Com. 1986—), Biomed. Engring. Soc. (charter), Am. Physiol. Soc., Am. Soc. Pharmacology and Exptl. Therapeutics, Soc. Math. Biology (founding), Endocrine Soc., Royal Soc. Health, Sociedad Catalana de Biologi a. Roman Catholic. Office: VA Hosp 115 Loma Linda CA 92357

LLEWELLYN, BETTY HALFF, archivist; b. Midland, Tex., June 12, 1911; d. Henry Mayer and Rose (Wechsler) Barnet; m. Martin Zinn, Jr., Nov. 12, 1935 (div. 1947); children: Martin III, Henry Harold, Mary Elizabeth Zinn Stewart; m. 2d, George W. Llewellyn, Nov. 9, 1948 (div. 1966). B.A., So. Meth. U., 1934; grad. Gemological Inst. Am., Santa Monica, Calif., 1968. Dir., New Theater, Dallas, 1936-40; exec. dir. McCord Theater Collection, Dallas, 1968—; ptnr. Halff Interests, Dallas, 1934—; pub. Walnut Hill Pub., Dallas, 1983—; contbr. to numerous schs. and museums, 1978—. Author: (with A.C. Greene) I Can't Forget, 1984. Officer, Lake Charles (La.) LWV, 1946-47; bd. dirs. Lake Charles ARC, 1941-45. Recipient James Smithson Bronze medal Smithsonian Instn., 1978, James Smithson Silver medal, 1980. Mem. So. Meth. U. Alumni Assn., Circus Fans Am., Circus Hist. Assn., Clowns of Am., Mineral. Assn. Dallas, Lone Star Showmans Club, James Smithson Soc., Dallas Gem and Mineral Soc., B'nai B'rith Women, Zeta Phi Eta. Jewish. Club: Pleasant Oaks Gem & Mineral (Tex.).

LLEWELLYN, FREDERICK EATON, mortuary executive; b. Mexico, Mo., Mar. 28, 1917; s. Frederick William and Mabel (Eaton) L.; BS, Calif. Inst. Tech., 1938; MBA (Baker scholar), Harvard, 1942; LLD, Pepperdine U., 1976; m. Jane Althouse, Aug. 15, 1940; children: Richard, John, Ann Marie. Asst. gen. mgr., dir. Forest Lawn Life Ins. Co., Glendale, Calif., 1940-41, pres., 1959-61; asst. to gen. mgr. Forest Lawn Meml. Park, Glendale, 1941-42, exec. v.p., 1946-66, gen. mgr., 1966—; pres. Forest Lawn Found., 1961—, Forest Lawn Co., 1967—; chmn. bd. Am. Security & Fidelity Corp., Founders Financial Corp., Glendale, 1971—, Upstairs Galleries Inc., 1974—, Met. Computer Center, 1973-81, Calif. Citrus Corp., 1971-80, Forest Lawn Mortgage Corp., 1974-81; dir. Calif. Fed. Savs. & Loan, IT Corp. Recon Political; chmn. Trust Services Am., Inc., 1983—. Mem. Found. for the 21st Century, 1986—, Orthopaedic Hosp., 1976—, chmn., 1983—; chmn. Glendale Meml. Hosp., 1980, trustee, 1982-85; pres. So. Calif. Visitors Council, 1976-77; chmn. Council of Regents, Meml. Ct. of Honor. Mem. Mayor's Ad Hoc Energy Com., Los Angeles, 1973-74, Los Angeles County Reorgn. Commn., 1978; bd. dirs. Los Angeles County Heart Assn., 1957; trustee U. Redlands, 1966-77, chmn. bd., 1969-72; mem. Univ. Bd., Pepperdine Coll., 1966—, chmn., 1976-79, bd. regents, mem. exec. bd., 1977—; bd. dirs. Pasadena Found. Med. Research, 1967-72, So. Calif. Bldg. Funds, 1975—, Met. YMCA Los Angeles, 1975—; trustee San Gabriel Valley council Boy Scouts Am., 1968-74; trustee Calif. Mus. Sci. and Industry, 1977—, pres., 1983-85, chmn., 1986; bd. govs. Dept. Mus. Natural History, Los Angeles County, 1968-72; mem. Los Angeles County Energy Commn., 1974-80; chmn. Mayor's Ad Hoc Water Crisis Commn., 1977—. Served with USNR, 1942-45. Decorated knight Order of Merit (Italy). Mem. Nat. Assn. Cemeteries (pres. 1956-57), Los Angeles Area C. of C. (dir. 1969-70, bd. chmn. 1974, pres. 1973), Calif. C. of C. (dir. 1977—), Newcomen Soc., Tau Beta Pi. Clubs: California, San Marino, Lincoln, One Hundred,

Twilight, Walnut Elephant. Lodge: Order of St. Hubertus. Contbr. articles to profl. jours. Home: 1521 Virginia Rd San Marino CA 91108 Office: 1712 S Glendale Ave Glendale CA 91205

LLIBOUTRY, LOUIS ANTONIN, geoscience educator; b. Madrid, Spain, Feb. 19, 1922; s. Jacques and Jeanne (Macabies) L.; m. Claude A. Micanel, Apr. 5, 1954; children—Emmanuel, Olivier. Licencees Sci. Phys., Ecole Normale Superieure, Paris, 1943, Doctorate, U. Grenoble, 1950. Asst., U. Grenoble, 1945-51; assoc. prof. U. de Chile, 1951-56; maitre de conferences U. Grenoble, 1956-61, prof., 1961—; dir., Lab. Glaciology CNRS, Grenoble, 1959-83; cons. Electroperu, 1967-69, UNESCO, 1970; mem. Nat. Com. Univs. Geophysics France, 1969-73, 76-79. Author: Nieves y glaciares de Chile, 1956; Physique de base, 1959, 2d edit., 1963; Traité de Glaciologie, Vol. 1, 1964, Vol. 2, 1965; Tectonophysique et Geodynamique, 1982; Very Slow Flow of Solids, 1987; contbr. articles to profl. jours. Decorated commandeur des Palmes Academiques Ministere de l'Education Nat. France, 1977; recipient sports gold medal Republica Argentina, 1952, prizes Acad. Sci., 1966, 84, French Influence prize in math. and physics, 1985. Mem. Internat. Glaciol. Soc. (hon.), Club Andino Bariloche (hon.), Nat. Assn. Study Snow and Avalanches (v.p. 1971—), European Geophys. Soc. (pres. 1976-78), Internat. Union Geodesy and Geophysics (pres. Internat. Commn. Snow and Ice 1983-87). Home: 3 ave de la Foy, 38700 Corenc France Office: Laboratoire de Glaciologie, BP 96, 38042 St-Martin d'Heres cedex France

LLOYD, ARLEEN MARTIN, business educator, account executive, marketing consultant; b. N.Y.C., May 18, 1957; d. David Paul and Ligia (Zeledon-Masis) L.; m. Leonardo Napoles. A.A., Miami Dade Community Coll., 1976; B.B.A., Fla. Internat. U., 1979, M.A. in Internat. Bus., 1983. Cert. tchr., Fla. Sales mgr. Jordan Marsh, Miami, Fla., 1979-80, asst. dir. selling services, 1980-81, asst. buyer, 1981-82; tchr. Miami Springs Sr. High Sch. (Fla.), 1981—; v.p. sales Expediter, Inc., Miami, 1983; bus. instr. Internat. Fine Arts Coll., Miami 1983—; pvt. practice mktg. cons., Miami, 1983-84; account exec. Avanti, Miami, 1984-86; dir. mktg. Paul Mitchell Systems , 1986-88; pres., owner Abstract Sugar, 1988—. Recipient fund raising award United Way Dade County, 1979. Mem. Dade County Tchrs. Assn., Nat. Assn. Female Execs., Bus. and Profl. Womens Assn., Nat. Assn. Women Bus. Owners, Internat. Platform Assn., Delta Epsilon Chi (advisor 1983). Republican. Roman Catholic. Home and Office: 73 Ludlum Dr Miami Springs FL 33166

LLOYD, DAVID BRUCE, investment manager; b. Guernsey, U.K., June 19, 1941; s. Alec Ivor and Joan Alison (Currie) L.; m. Susan Mary Oakley, June 6, 1970 (div. 1974). London U. degree in Chem. Engring., Battersea Coll. Advanced Tech., London, 1964; Diploma in Internat. Affairs, City Lit. Inst., London, 1968; M. Bus. Studies, London Bus. Sch., 1968. Chem. Engr. Brit. Petroleum, London, 1964-68; investment analyst Hoare & Co., London, 1968-70, Commonwealth Devel. Fin. Co., London, 1970-78; fin. mgr. Bank Credit and Commerce Internat., S.A., London, 1978-83; investment mgr. new ventures Imperial Chem. Industries Agrl. div., Billingham, Eng., 1984-86; dir. Anglo Internat. Hotels, Nigerian Indsl. Devel. Bank, Nigerian Sugar, Guma Valley Water Co., Flour Mills Fiji, R.C. Baxter, S.B. Captital Corp. for C.D.F.C. Editor Bus. Grad. Mag., 1978-82; writer Banking World, London, 1983—, Asian Finance, Hong Kong, 1977-84; contbr. articles to profl. jours. Mem. Bus. Grad. Assn. (chmn. 1985-86), Inst. Chem. Engrs., British Inst. Mgmt. (council mem. 1982—, chmn. audit com. 1986—), Strategic Planning Soc. (council mem. 1983—, editorial bd. of long range planning). Home: 48 Aberdare Gardens, London NW6 3QA, England

LLOYD, LEONA LORETTA, lawyer; b. Detroit, Aug. 6, 1949; d. Leon Thomas and Naomi Mattie (Chisolm) L. BS, Wayne State U., 1971, JD, 1979. Bar: Mich. 1982, U.S. Dist. Ct. (ea. dist.), U.S. Ct. Appeals, U.S. Supreme Ct. Speech, English tchr. Detroit Bd. Edn., 1971-75; instr. criminal justice Wayne State U., Detroit, 1981; sr. ptnr. Lloyd and Lloyd, Detroit, 1982—. Wayne State U. scholar, 1970, 75; recipient Kizzy Image award, 1985, Nat. Coalition of 100 Black Women Achievement award, 1986, Community Service award Wayne County exec. William Lucas, 1986, cert. merit U. Detroit Black Law Students Assn., 1986, Minority Bus. of Yr. award Wayne State U. Assn. Black Bus. Students, 1986, Fred Hampton Image award, 1984; named to Black Women Hall of Fame. Mem. ABA, Wolverine Bar Assn., Mary McLeod Bethune Assn. Office: Lloyd & Lloyd 600 Renaissance Ctr Suite 1400 Detroit MI 48243

LLOYD, ROBERT ANDREW, opera singer; b. Southend-on-Sea, England, Mar. 2, 1940; m. Sandra Watkins; 4 children. Grad., Keble Coll., Oxford, Eng., 1962, London Opera Ctr. Schoolmaster London Pub. Schs., 1962-63; lectr. internat. affairs Bramshall Police Coll., 1966-68; prin. bass Sadlers Wells, London Coliseum, 1969-72, Royal Opera House, Convent Garden, London, 1972—. Debut at Fernando in Fidelio, London U. Opera; records for EMI, Decca, Philips, Telare, Erato; film of Parsifal; frequent radio talks and TV presenter. Address: Harrison/Parrot Ltd 12, Penzance Pl, London W11 4PA, England

LLOYD, SIMON RODERICK, advertising executive; b. Surrey, Eng., Mar. 25, 1947; s. Desmond C.F. and Ambrosine Wallace (Barr) L.; m. Susan Margaret Cuthbert, Apr. 28, 1972; children: Rebecca, Andrew. Grad., Wellington Coll., Berkshire, Eng., 1966. Trainee George Trollope and Sons, London, 1967-68; media exec. Garland Compton Ltd., London, 1968-74; media dir. Foote Cone and Belding, London, 1974-81, vice chmn., 1981-86, mng. dir., 1986-87; dir. Foot Cone and Belding Europe, London, 1987—. Contbr. articles to profl. jours. Mem. Inst. Practitioners in Advt., U.K. Media Circle (chmn. 1985, 86, 87), Internat. Advt. Assn. Clubs: M.C.C., Royal London, Yacht.

LLOYD, THOMAS GRANT, architect; b. St. Louis, Jan. 16, 1933; s. Robert E. and Virginia A. (Battles) L.; B. Arch., Washington U., St. Louis, 1956; m. Marilyn M. Worseldine, June 12, 1971; children—Mark, Matthew, Maude, Michael, Megan. Vice pres. Winkler Thompson & Lloyd, Inc., St. Louis, 1958-69; exec. v.p. Barrier Industries, Ltd., St. Louis, 1969-76; pres., dir. Grant & Asso., Inc., St. Louis, 1973—; sr. policy analyst Arthur D. Little, Inc., Washington, 1975-79; pres. Grant & Assocs., Inc., Washington, 1979—; dir. Worseldine Graphic Design. Served with AUS, 1956-58. Mem. AIA, Am. Mgmt. Assn., Am. Mktg. Assn., Assn. Travel Mktg. Execs., Travel and Tourism Research Assn., Am. Soc. Pub. Adminstrn., AAAS, Acad. Polit. Sci., World Future Soc. Home and Office: 3040 Cambridge Pl Washington DC 20007

LLOYD-JONES, DAVID MATHIAS, musician; b. London, Nov. 19, 1934; s. Sir. Vincent Lloyd-Jones; student Westminster Sch. Magdalen Coll., Oxford, Eng.; 1955-59; m. Anne Carolyn Whitehead, 1964, 3 children. Chorus master New Opera Co., 1961-64; conductor Bath Festival, 1966, City of London Festival, 1966, Wexford Festival, 1967-70, Scottish Opera, 1968, Welsh Nat. Opera, 1968, Sadler's Wells Opera Co. (now English Nat. Opera), 1969—, Royal Opera, Covent Garden, 1971; music dir. Opera North, 1977—; conductor TV operas Eugene Onegin, The Flying Dutchman, Hansel and Gretel; appeared with British symphony orch. Edited original score Boris Godunov; translated several Russian operas; contbr. to numerous publications. Home: 94 Whitelands House, Cheltenham Terr, London SW3 4RA England Office: Opera North, Leeds Grand Theatre, Leeds LS1 6NZ England *

LLOYD-JONES, PETER HUGH JEFFERD, educator; b. St. Peter Port, Jersey, U.K., Sept. 21, 1922; s. William and Norah Leila (Jefferd) Lloyd-J.; M.A., Oxford U., 1948; D.H.L. (hon.), U. Chgo., 1970, D.Phil. (hon.), U. Tel Aviv, 1984; m. Frances E. Hedley, 1953 (div. 1981); children—Edmund Stephen, Ralph Alexander, Antonia; m. 2d Mary R. Lefkowitz, 1982 Fellow, Jesus Coll., Cambridge U., 1948-54, fellow and E.P. Warren praelector in classics Corpus Christi Coll., 1954-60; Regius prof. Greek, Oxford U., 1960-89; vis. prof. Yale U., 1964, 67, U. Chgo., 1972, Harvard U., 1976; Sather prof. U. Calif., Berkeley, 1969. Served in Brit. Army, 1942-45. Fellow Brit. Acad.; hon. fgn. mem. Am. Acad. Arts and Scis., Acad. Athens, Rheinisch Westfälische Akademie, Accademia dei Archeologia, Lettere e Belle Arti, Naples. Author: The Justice of Zeus, 1971; Blood for the Ghosts: Classical Survivals, 1982; (with P.J. Parsons) Supplementum Hellenisticum, 1983; (with N.G. Wilson) Sophorh's Fabulae, 1989; (with N.G. Wilson) Sophorlea, 1989; others. Translator Oresteia (Aeschylus), 1970. Home: Christ Church, Oxford OX1 1DP England Other: 15 West Riding Wellesley MA 02181

LLOYD WEBBER, ANDREW, composer; b. London, Mar. 22, 1948; s. William Southcombe and Jean Hermoine (Johnstone) Lloyd W.; m. Sarah Jane Tudor Hugill, July 24, 1971 (div. 1983); children: Imogen, Nicholas.; m. Sarah Brightman, Mar. 1984. Ed., Magdalen Coll., Oxford U., Royal Coll. Music. Composer: musicals Joseph and The Amazing Technicolor Dreamcoat, 1967, Jesus Christ Superstar, 1970, Jeeves, 1975, Evita, 1976, Cats, 1981, Song & Dance, 1982, Starlight Express, 1984,"Orchestral-Choral Works" Requiem, 1985, Variations, 1985 (Evita Suite 1978), The Phantom of the Opera, 1986; also record album Variations, 1978; producer plays: Daisy Pulls It Off, 1983, The Hired Man, 1984, Lend Me a Tenor, 1986. Recipient 3 Tony awards, 1980, 2 in 1983, 1 in 1988, Drama Desk award, 1971, 80, 83, Grammy award, 1984, 86, Triple Play award ASCAP, 1988. Office: 20 Greek St, London W1V 5LF, England

LLUIS-PUEBLA, EMILIO, mathematician; b. Mexico City, Sept. 16, 1952; s. Emilio R. and Marta (Puebla) Lluis; m. Martha Gómez, Dec. 19, 1975; children: Emilio Mauricio, Alexis Leonardo. BA, U. Nat. Autónoma de Mexico, 1975, MS, 1977; PhD, U. of Western Ont., Can., 1980. Researcher Inst. Math. U. Nat. Autónoma de Mexico, Mexico City, 1980-83; prof. faculty of sci. 1983—. Author: Homological Algebra, Cohomology of Groups and Algebraic K-theory, 1987; contbr. articles to profl. jours. Recipient scholarship Univ. Nat. Autónoma de Mexico, 1974, Can. Council, 1977, Social Scis. and Humanities Research Council Can., 1978; grantee Sec. Pub. Edn., 1984—. Mem. Am. Math. Soc., Soc. Math. Mexico, Inst. Mexicano de Ciencias y Humanidades. Home: Vitrales 30, 16050 Mexico City Mexico Office: Facultad de Ciencias UNAM, Circuito Exterior Cd Uni, 04510 Mexico City Mexico

LO, CHI NING, educator; b. Hong Kong, Aug. 7, 1958. MS with distinction, London Sch. Econs. U. London, 1983. Asst. lectr. Hang Seng Sch. Commerce, Hong Kong, 1984-85; lectr. City Poly. Hong Kong, 1985—. Fellow Royal Statis. Soc.; mem. Math. Assn. Am., Inst. Math. and its Applications, Inst. Statisticians. Office: City Poly Hong Kong, 700 Nathan Rd, Mongkok Hong Kong

LO, LIBO, mathematics educator, editor; b. Tokyo, Sept. 9, 1936; s. Kelin Lo and Saiyin Ning; m. Yunqin Wang, June 6, 1947; children: Nancy, Susan. BS, Beijing Normal U., 1956, MS, 1958, 80; PhD, U. Mich., 1984. Asst. prof. U. Miss., Oxford, 1984-86; prof. Beijing Normal U., 1986—. Contbr. articles to profl. jours. Rep. to 7th people's congress Peoples Republic of China. Recipient Nat. Prize of Sci. and Tech., Govt. of China, Beijing, 1986. Mem. Am. Math. Soc. Home: Beijing Normal U, Dept Math, Beijing Peoples Republic of China

LO, VICTOR TANG SEONG, restaurant executive; b. Mayshien, Kwung Tung, People's Republic of China, Jan. 19, 1915; s. Chin Hing and Yee Mui Lo; m. Anita Kiu Ying, Dec. 17, 1949; children: Linda, Anita, Pauline, Sunny. Student, King's Coll., Hong Kong, 1935-37. Instr. Far East Flying Tng. Sch., Hong Kong, 1948-49; sales rep. China Internat. Motors, Hong Kong, 1949-50; factory mgr. Hong Kong Soya Bean Products Co. Ltd. Aberdeen, Hong Kong, 1950-62; gen. mgr. Hong Kong Soya Bean Products Kwun Tong, Hong Kong, 1962-69; chmn. Wellos Enterprise Ltd., Hong Kong, 1969-86, Café De Coral Group Ltd., Hong Kong, 1986—. Club: Hong Kong Country, The Chines (Hong Kong). Office: Café De Coral Group Ltd, 801-806 South Tower, World Fin C, Hong Kong Hong Kong

LOADER, PETER JOHN, psychiatrist; b. London, Dec. 22, 1946; s. Herbert Clendon Court and Florence Winifred Mary (Hookings) L.; m. Eva Barbro Eskilson, Feb. 4, 1973; children: Joseph, Sarah. MBBS, U. London, 1970, MRC in Psychology, 1976. Sr. house officer U. London Hosp., 1973-74, St. Mary's Hosp., London, 1974-75; registrar Hosp. for Sick Children, London, 1975-78, sr. registrar, 1978-81, research fellow, 1981—; cons. Hornsey Rise Child Guidance Unit, London, 1984—; hon. sr. lectr. Med. Sch., U. Coll. and Middlesex Hosp. Med. Sch., London, 1984—; vis. tchr. Tavistock Clinic, London, 1985—. Contbr. articles to profl. jours. Mem. Brit. Med. Assn., Assn. Child Psychologists and Psychiatrists, Inst. Family Therapy (mem. tchr. and research com.), Assn. Family Therapy. Office: Hornsey Rise Child Guidance Unit, Hornsey Rise, London N19 4DF, England

LOASBY, BRIAN JOHN, economist, educator, researcher; b. Kettering, Northamptonshire, Eng., Aug. 2, 1930; s. Frederick Thomas and Mabel Phyllis (Burrett) L.; m. Judith Ann Robinson, Sept. 7, 1957; children: Caroline Ann, Sarah Janet. BA, U. Cambridge, Eng., 1952, MLitt, 1957. Asst. in polit. economy U. Aberdeen, Scotland, 1955-58; Bournville research fellow U. Birmingham, Eng., 1958-61; tutor in mgmt. studies U. Bristol, Eng., 1961-67; mgmt. fellow Arthur D. Little, Inc., Cambridge, Mass., 1965-66; lectr. U. Stirling, Scotland, 1967-68, sr. lectr., 1968-71, prof. mgmt. econs., 1971-84, prof. emeritus, 1984—. Author: Choice, Complexity and Ignorance, 1976. Mem. Royal Econ. Soc. (council 1981-86), Scottish Econ. Soc. (council 1981-86), Scottish Econ. Soc. (pres. 1987—), Am. Econ. Assn., Brit. Inst. Mgmt. Office: U Stirling, Stirling FK9 4LA, Scotland

LOBACHEV, VLADIMIR KONSTANTINOVICH, ambassador; b. Moscow, Aug. 8, 1925; m. Ludmila Lobachev. Grad., Moscow State Inst. of Internat. Relations, 1949, High Diplomatic Sch., 1960. Ofcl. Ministry of Fgn. Affairs, Moscow, 1949-52, 57-60, 63-65, 69-72, 79-82; attaché, 3d, 2d sec. Embassy of USSR, Washington, 1952-57; 1st sec. Embassy of USSR, Hanoi, N. Vietnam, 1960-63; gen. consul Gen. Consulate of USSR, Bombay, 1965-69; dir. UN Dept. Confs. and Gen. Services, Geneva, 1972-79; ambassador Embassy of USSR, Brazzaville, People's Republic of Congo, 1982—. Decorated Sign of Honor Order medal, Order of People's Friendship Presidium of Supreme Soviet of USSR. Office: Embassy of USSR, BP 2132, Brazzaville People's Republic of Congo

LOBASHEV, VLADIMIR MIKHAILOVICH, physicist; b. Leningrad, USSR, July 29, 1934; s. Mikhail Yephimovich and Nina Vladimirovna (Yevropeitseva) L. BS in Physics, State U., Leningrad, 1957; MS, Radium Inst. of the Acad. Scis., Leningrad, 1963; DSc, A.F. Ioffe Physico-Tech. Inst., Leningrad, 1968. Engr., researcher A.F. Ioffe Physico-Tech. Inst., Leningrad, 1957-70; head of lab. Leningrad Inst. Nuclear Physics, 1970—; head div. Inst. Nuclear Research USSR Acad. Scis., Moscow, 1972—. Contbr. numerous articles to profl. jours. Recipient Lenin Prize, 1974. Mem. Communist Party. Office: USSR Acad of Scis, Inst of Nuclear Research, 60th Anniversary October, Revolution Prospect, 117312 Moscow USSR

LOBEL, IRVING, clothing mfg. co. exec.; b. Bklyn., Jan. 18, 1917; s. Benjamin and Jennie (Gross) L.; B.S. in Econs., U. Pa., 1937; m. Selma Agar, Jan. 23, 1943; children—Bonnie, Douglas, Robert. Partner, Lo-Bel Co., N.Y.C., 1937—. Bd. dirs. Cannon Points Coop., 1985—; mem. U. Pa. Ann. Giving Com.; mem. U. Pa. Anniversary com., treas. bd. cooperatives. Served with U.S. Army, 1942-46. Mem. Infants and Childrens Wear Assn. (dir.), Mu Sigma, Sigma Alpha Mu. Democrat. Jewish. Club: Inwood Country. Home: 45 Sutton Pl S New York NY 10022

LOBEL, MARTIN, lawyer; b. Cambridge, Mass., June 19, 1941; s. I. Alan and Dorothy W. Lobel; m. Geralyn Krupp, Mar. 15, 1981; children: Devra Sarah, Rachel Melissa, Hannah Krupp. AB, Boston U., 1962, JD, 1965; LLM, Harvard U., 1966. Bar: Mass. 1965, D.C. 1968, U.S. Supreme Ct. 1968. Ptnr. Lobel & Lobel, Boston, 1965-66; asst. prof. law U. Okla., Norman, 1967; Congressional fellow, Washington, 1968; legis. asst. to Senator William Proxmire, 1968-72; ptnr. Lobel, Novins, Lamont & Flug, Washington, 1972—; lectr. Law Sch. Am. U., Washington, 1972—; resellers referee, U.S. Dist. Ct., Wichita. Chmn. tax notes/tax analysts. Mem. ABA (chmn. subcom. improving land records), Mass. Bar Assn., D.C. Bar Assn. (chmn. consumer affairs com. 1976-77, chmn. steering com. on antitrust and consumer affairs sect.), Order of Coif. Contbr. articles to legal jours. Home: 4525 31st St NW Washington DC 20008 Office: Lobel Novins Lamont & Flug 1275 K St NW #770 Washington DC 20005

LOBENIUS, NILS MAGNUS, marketing executive; b. Västeras, Sweden, Mar. 13, 1938; s. Lars Uno and Britta Mariana (Gesteby) L; m. Inga Carin Nilsson, June 21, 1962; children: Jonas, Anna, Maria. Studentexamen, Högre Allm Läroverket, Falun, Sweden, 1958; officer, Flygkadettskolan, Uppsala, Sweden, 1962; ekonom, Vuxenskolan, Norköping, Sweden, 1975. Airline capt. Scandinavian Air Service, 1965—; flight instr. SAS, 1970-76; chief Airforce Civil Flying Sch., 1979-80; mgr. pub. relations Cumulus Invest AB, Stockholm, 1984—; dep. man dir. Avamark AB, Stockholm, 1985—. Editor: golf mag. Peg-and Putt, 1975-84, Golfa i Sigtuna, 1984-88, Sigtunada och nu; contbr. articles to profl. jours. Chmn. Home and Sch., Sigtuna, 1974-78, dist. golf union. Served to capt. Swedish Air Force, 1958-65. Mem. Conservative party. Lutheran. Club: Friluftsfrämjandet (Sigtuna). Lodges: Rotary, Masons. Home: Uppsalavägen 2, S-193 00 Sigtuna Sweden Office: Avamark Ab, Drottningholmsvagen 31, 112 42 Stockholm Sweden

LOBER, PAUL HALLAM, pathology educator; b. Mpls., Sept. 25, 1919; s. Harold A. and Minnie (Toraason) L.; 1 son, Patrick B. B.S., U. Minn., 1942, M.D., 1944, Ph.D. in Pathology, 1951. Intern, resident Hennepin County Gen. Hosp., 1944-46; fellow dept. pathology U. Minn., Mpls., 1948-51; faculty Med. Sch., 1951—, prof. pathology, 1963-86, emeritus prof., 1986—; surg. pathologist Univ. Hosps., Mpls., 1951-74, Abbott-Northwestern Hosp., Mpls., 1974—. Served to capt. AUS, 1946-48. Fellow Coll. Am. Pathologists; mem. AMA, Am. Soc. Clin. Pathologists, Internat. Acad. Pathology, Am. Assn. Pathologists, Am. Soc. Cytology, N.Y. Acad. Scis., Alpha Omega Alpha. Home: 1525 W 28th St Minneapolis MN 55408 Office: Pathology Dept Abbott-Northwestern Hosp 800 E 28th St Minneapolis MN 55407

LOBERG, THOMAS JOHN, accountant; b. St. Paul, Mar. 14, 1955; s. Robert John and Rose Kathryn (Ginnaty) L.; m. Carolyn Ann Woodruff, June 30, 1979; B.S. in Acctg., U. Minn., 1976. C.P.A., Minn. Sr. auditor Arthur Andersen Co., St. Paul, 1977-79; mgr. audit Borowicz, Holmgren, Burnsville, Minn., 1980-81, audit ptnr. Borowicz, Holmgren, Loberg Co., 1981-83; ptnr., audit practice dir., pres. Bergren, Holmgren Loberg Ltd., 1983—, now chmn., also vice chmn. bd. dirs.; adviser Jr. Achievement of St. Paul, 1977-81. Mem. Am. Inst. CPA's, Minn. Soc. CPA's, Alpha Kappa Psi (alumni chpt. v.p., 1983-84, pres. 1984-85). Republican. Roman Catholic. Club: Mendakota Country (West St. Paul). Lodge: Elks (exalted ruler 1983-84, trustee 1984-86). Office: Bergren Holmgren & Loberg Ltd 501 E Hwy 13 Burnsville MN 55337-2877

LOBITZ, WALTER CHARLES, JR., physician, educator; b. Cin., Dec. 13, 1911; s. Walter Charles and Elsa (Spangenberg) L.; m. Caroline Elizabeth Rockwell, July 11, 1942; children: Walter Charles III, John Rockwell, Susan Hastings. Student, Brown U., 1930-31; B.Sc., U. Cin., 1939, M.B., 1940, M.D., 1941; M.Sc., U. Minn., 1945; M.A. (hon.), Dartmouth, 1958; LL.D., Hokkaido U., 1976. Diplomate Am. Bd. Dermatology (bd. dirs. 1955-64, pres. 1962). Intern Cin. Gen. Hosp., 1940, resident medicine, 1941; fellow Mayo Found., 1942-45; 1st asst. Mayo Clinic, 1945-47; chmn. sect. dermatology Hitchcock Clinic, Hanover, N.H., 1947-59; bd. dirs. Hitchcock Clinic, 1955; faculty Dartmouth Med. Sch., 1947-59, prof. dermatology, 1957-59; prof. dermatology, head div. U. Oreg. Med. Sch., 1959-69, chmn. dept., 1969-77; prof. U. Oreg. Health Scis. Ctr., until 1980, emeritus prof., 1980—; area cons. VA, 1949-59; mem. commn. cutaneous diseases Armed Forces Epidemiologic Bd., 1955-75; cons., mem. gen. med. study sect. USPHS, 1961-65; mem. grant rev. com. United Health Found., 1964-65; cons. dermatology tng. grants com. Nat. Inst. Arthritis and Metabolic Diseases, 1966-70; cons. VA Hosp., U. Oreg. Med. Sch., 1959—; civilian cons. to surg. gen. USAF, 1969-79; U.S. Air Force-Nat. cons. to Surgeon Gen., 1970-80; Dohi Meml. lectr. Japanese Dermatol. Assn., 1964; lectr. U. Copenhagen, Denmark, 1969, 74. Author numerous articles in field.; Co-editor: The Epidermis; editorial bd.: Jour. Investigative Dermatology, 1958-61, Excerpta of Medicine, 1961-78, Clinics in Dermatology, 1982; mem. editorial bd.: Archives Dermatology, 1960-77, chief editor, 1963-68. Trustee Dermatology Found., Med. Research Found. Oreg., 1972, exec. com., 1977-80, v.p., 1975-76, pres., 1977-78; music adv. com. Oreg. Symphony Orch., 1970-73; mem. Oreg. Ballet Council, 1974; bd. govs. Hitchcock Hosp., 1955; trustee Hitchcock Found., 1958-59, exec. com., 1958-59. Recipient Outstanding Achievement award U. Minn., 1964. Fellow ACP, Am. Acad. Dermatology (hon.); bd. dirs. 1958-61, 66-69, pres. 1969, gold medal 1985, Master in Dermatology 1987), Phila. Coll. Physicians (hon.); mem. AMA, Am. Dermatol. Assn. (bd. dirs. 1962-67, pres. 1972, hon. 1982), Soc. Investigative Dermatology (hon.); v.p. 1952, bd. dirs. 1953-58, pres. 1957, N.H., Multnomah County, Oreg., med. socs., N.Y. Acad. Scis., AAAS, Pacific N.W. Dermatol. Assn. (pres. 1971), Pacific Dermatol. Assn., Israeli Dermatol. Assn. (hon. mem.), Northwest Soc. Clin. Research, Oreg. Dermatol. Soc. (pres. 1969), Portland Acad. Medicine, Am. Fedn. Clin. Research, Pacific Interurban Clin. Club (councillor 1971), Internat. Soc. Tropical Dermatology, Assn. Univ. Profs. Dermatology (founder, bd. dirs. 1961-66, pres. 1965-66), Sigma Xi, Pi Kappa Epsilon, Alpha Omega Alpha; hon. mem. Soc. Venezolana de Dermatologia and Leprologia, French Soc. Dermatology, Brit. Assn. Dermatology, Assn. parala Investigacion Dermatologica (Venezuela), Soc. Dermatol. Danicae, Italian, Japan, Hokkaido, Sapporo derm. socs. Presbyn. Home: 2211 SW 1st Ave Portland OR 97201

LOBL, HERBERT MAX, lawyer; b. Vienna, Austria, Jan. 10, 1932; s. Walter Leo and Minnie (Neumann) L.; m. Dorothy Fullerton Hubbard, Sept. 12, 1960; children—Peter Walter, Michelle Alexandra. A.B. magna cum laude, Harvard U., 1953, LL.B., 1959; Fulbright scholar U. Bonn., Germany, 1954. Bar: N.Y. 1960, U.S. Tax Ct. 1963, French Conseil Juridique 1973. Assoc. Davis, Polk & Wardwell, N.Y.C., 1959-60; assoc. counsel to Gov. Nelson Rockefeller, Albany, N.Y., 1960-62; assoc. Davis, Polk & Wardwell, New York and Paris, 1963-69, ptnr., Paris, 1969—; dir. CII-Honeywell Bull, Paris, 1976-81, Alcatel USA Corp., 1985-87; supervisory bd. mem. CII-HB Internationale, Amsterdam, Holland, 1977-82. Gov. Am. Hosp. Paris, 1988—; trustee Am. Library, Paris, 1969-81. Served to 1st lt. USAF, 1954-56, Berlin. Mem. Internat. Fiscal Assn., Am. C. of C., Internat. Assn. Lawyers, Am. Soc. Internat. Law, N.Y. State Bar Assn., Assn. Bar City of N.Y. Club: Travellers (Paris); University, Harvard (N.Y.). Home: 242 Rue de Rivoli, Paris France also: Davis Polk & Wardwell 1 Chase Manhattan Plaza New York NY 10005

LOBO, ANTONIO ATAIDE, physician; b. Goa, India, Nov. 30, 1925; came to Portugal, 1951, naturalized, 1951; s. Antonio Faustino and Ana Elisa (Ataide) L.; m. Angela Matilde Pais, Feb. 14, 1958; 1 child, Francisco. Lic. medico-surg., Nova Goa Med. Coll., India, 1950; diploma Tropical Medicine Inst., Lisbon, 1952; diploma pub. health Superior Inst. Hygiene, Lisbon, 1962; M.D., U. Lisbon, 1962. Vol. civil hosps., Lisbon, 1952-56; chief med. officer Sao Salvador Health Dept., Angola, 1957-61; gen. surgeon Central Hosp. Health Dept., Praia, Cape Verde Islands, 1963-64, Lourenzo, Marques, 1965-67; chief surgeon Govt. Central Hosp., Macao, China, 1967-73; med. clinics asst. Regional Health Adminstrn., Lisbon, 1976—; gen. practice medicine Bank's Syndicate, Lisbon, 1983—. Author articles in field. Del. Portuguese Red Cross, 1961, 66; hon. dir. Anti-Cancer Clinic, Macao, 1970. Named Disting. Citizen, Mayor of Tarrafal, Cape Verde Islands, 1964. Fellow Portuguese Coll. Specialists in Gen. Surgery; mem. Lisbon Med. Council, Portuguese Soc. Cancerology, Portuguese Soc. Geriatrics. Roman Catholic. Lodge: Rotary (Lisbon). Avocation: reading. Home: Rua Manuel Ferreira, Andrade 14-4 E, Lisbon 1500, Portugal

LOBO, VICTOR MANUEL MATOS, electrochemist; b. Coimbra, Portugal, Feb. 18, 1940; s. Feliciano Martins and Maria Pereira (Matos) L.; M.A. in Chemistry and Physics, U. Coimbra, 1963; Ph.D. (NATO grantee 1966-70), Cambridge (Eng.) U., 1971; m. Maria Teresa H. Almeida e Sousa, Feb. 8, 1964; children—Victor, Paulo, Jorge. Mem. faculty U. Coimbra, from 1963, prof. electrochemistry, from 1975. Am. Field Service scholar, 1957; Gulbenkian Found. grantee, 1970-71; Deutscher Akademischer Austauschdienst grantee, 1978; Australian Nat. U. grantee, 1980-81; SERC grantee, 1985. Mem. Chem. Soc. London, German Chem. Soc., Portuguese Chem. Soc. (pres. gen. assembly), Porto Elec. Soc. (v.p. gen. assn.), IUPAC Commn. Electrochemistry (titular). Roman Catholic. Author: Electrolyte Solutions: Literature Data on Thermodynamic and Transport Properties, 1975; also other books and papers. Home: 184 Rua Malheiros, 3000 Coimbra Portugal Office: Univ Coimbra, Dept Chemistry, 3000 Coimbra Portugal

LOBOZ-GRUDZIEN, KRYSTYNA, cardiologist; b. Wroclaw, Poland, May 7, 1946; d. Piotr and Maria Loboz; m. Marek Grudzien, Dec. 29, 1973. MD, U. Wroclaw, 1969. Jr. asst. Dept. Cardiology T. Marciniak

Hosp., Wroclaw, 1969-77, asst. lectr., 1977-85, asst. prof. cardiology, 1985—. Contbr. articles to profl. jours. Mem. Polish Cardiology Soc., Cardiac Doppler Soc., Noninvasive Cardiology Soc. Home: Wroclaw 51 138, Zaleskiego 12 2, Poland Office: T Marciniak Hosp, Dept Cardiology, Traugutta 116, Wroclaw Poland 50-420

LOCASCIO, JAMES EDWARD, dentist; b. Detroit, July 25, 1955; s. Salvatore Antonio and Mary Louise (Barduca) L.; m. Mary Agnes Hall, June 24, 1977; children: James Edward, Michael Anthony, Gina Louise. BA, Wayne State U., 1977; DDS, U. Detroit, 1981. Gen. practice dentistry Joy Road Dental Ctr., Detroit, 1981-82, W.P. Scales and Assocs., Detroit, 1982-86, Pontiac Family Dental Ctr., Waterford, Mich., 1986—. Mem. Rep. Presdl. Task Force, Washington, 1984—, Rep. Senatorial Club, Washington, 1984—, Conservative Caucus, Washington, 1982—. Mem. ADA, Mich. Dental Soc., Detroit Dist. Dental Soc., Chgo. Dental Soc. Roman Catholic. Home: 1651 Brentwood Wixom MI 48096

LOCH, JOHN ROBERT, educational administrator; b. Sharon, Pa., Aug. 25, 1940; s. Robert Addison and Mary Virginia (Beck) L.; student Waynesburg Coll., 1958; AB, Grove City Coll., 1962; postgrad Pitts. Theol. Sem., 1962; MEd, U. Pitts., 1966, PhD, 1972; cert. Harvard U., 1984. Asst. to dean men U. Pitts., 1963-64, dir. student union, 1964-70, dir. student affairs research, 1970-71, dir. suburban ednl. services Sch. Gen. Studies, 1971-75; dir. continuing edn. and pub. service Youngstown (Ohio) State U., 1975-82, dir. continuing edn./edn. outreach, 1982—, assoc. mem. grad. faculty, 1980—; research assoc. Pres's Commn. on Campus Unrest, 1970. Trustee, Mahoning Shenango Health Edn. Network, 1976—, Career Devel. Ctr. for Women, 1978-80; trustee Youngstown Area Arts Council, 1980-85, pres., 1981-83; bd. dirs. Protestant Family Services, 1981-83; trustee Mahoning County RSVP, 1983—, chmn. evaluation com., 1983-84, chmn. personnel com., 1984-85, chmn. bd. trustees, 1986-87; coordinator fund raising Nat. Unity Campagn, Mahoning County, 1980; state chmn. Young Rep. Coll. Council Pa., 1960. Mem. Adult Edn. Assn. USA, Am. Assn. Higher Edn., Nat. U. Continuing Edn. Assn., Ohio Council Higher Continuing Edn. (pres. 1979-80), Ohio Continuing Higher Edn. Assn. (co-chmn. constn. com. 1982, v.p. state univs. 1984-85, pres.-elect 1985-86, pres. 1986-87), Omicron Delta Kappa, Kappa Kappa Psi, Phi Kappa Phi (pres. 1980-81), Alpha Phi Omega, Alpha Sigma Lambda, Phi Delta Kappa. Presbyterian. Clubs: Kiwanis (dir. 1981-82), Youngstown Traffic (hon. life). Home: 242 Upland Ave Youngstown OH 44504 Office: Youngstown State U Youngstown OH 44555

LOCHHEAD, IAN JAMES, art history educator; b. Ashburton, Canterbury, New Zealand, Nov. 6, 1950; s. John Kilpatrick and Anne ELizabeth (Callander) L.; m. Lynnette Elsie Taylor, Apr. 3, 1976; children: Elizabeth Sarah, James Alexander. BA, U. Auckland, New Zealand, 1972, MA, 1975; PhD, Bryn Mawr Coll., 1981. Lectr. U. Canterbury, Christchurch, New Zealand, 1981-85, sr. lectr., 1986—. Author: The Spectator and the Landscape, 1982; contbr. articles to profl. jours. Chester Dale fellow Nat. Gallery Art, Washington, 1978-79, Whiting Found. fellow, N.Y.C., 1979-80. Mem. New Zealand Hist. Places Trust (mem. Canterbury regional com.). Home: 7 Stratford St, Christchurch 1, Canterbury New Zealand Office: U Canterbury, Sch Fine Arts, Private Bag, Christchurch New Zealand

LOCHIANO, STEPHEN ANTHONY, controller; b. Liberal, Kans., Mar. 2, 1949; s. Rocco LoChiano and Margie Louise (Pitts) LoChiano Wooden; m. Ellen Jane Walker, Aug. 28, 1971; children—Anthony Paul, Ryan Michael, Eric Stephen. B.S. in Bus. Adminstrn., U. Nebr., Lincoln, 1975; postgrad. U. Nebr., Omaha, 1980—. Office mgr. trainee Roberts Dairy, Omaha, 1976-78; controller Security Internat., Omaha, 1978, Jubilee Mfg. Co., Omaha, 1978-80, Omaha Box Co., 1983-85; controller Plastr Glas, Inc., Omaha, 1985-87; plant acct. Weyerhaeuser Co., Omaha, 1980-83. Served as sgt. U.S. Army, 1973-75. Mem. Nat. Assn. Accts. (controllers council 1984—), Nat. Assn. Credit Mgrs., Internat. Soc. Wang Users, Toastmasters (dist. treas. 1980-81). Republican. Lutheran. Club: Park Ave. Health (Omaha). Avocations: camping, computer programming. Home: 10205 R St Omaha NE 68127 Office: Profl Administrative Services Inc 9290 W Dodge #205 Omaha NE 68114

LOCK, THOMAS GRAHAM, metals and chemical company executive; b. Cardiff, Wales, Oct. 19, 1931; m. Janice Olive Baker Jones, 1954; children: Sian, Sara. BSc in Metallurgy, U. Coll. of South Wales and Monmouthshire, 1953; postgrad., Coll. of Advanced Tech., Aston, Eng.; BS in Bus., Harvard U. Chartered engr. With Lucas Industries Ltd., 1959-61; prodn. mgr. Lucas Electrical, 1961-66; dir. Lucas Girling Ltd., Koblenz, Fed. Republic Germany, 1966-73; mng. dir. overseas service Lucas Girling Ltd., 1973-79; mng. dir. indusl. div. Amalgamated Metal Corp. PLC, London, 1979-83, chief exec. officer, 1983—, also bd. dirs.; bd. dirs. Lucas World Service Ltd., Lucas Industries Inc., Birmingham, Mich. and other overseas subs.; non-exec. dir. Marshals Universal plc, Evode Group plc. Served as lt. Royal Navy, 1956-79. Named Freeman City of London. Fellow Inst. Metallurgists; mem. Brit. Inst. Mgmt. (companion). Lodge: Gold and Silver Wyre Drawers (liveryman). Home: The Cottage, Fulmer Way, Gerrands Cross SL9 8AJ, England Office: Amalgamated Metal Corp plc, Adelaide House, London Bridge, London EC4R 9DT, England

LOCKHART, JAMES BICKNELL, III, insurance brokerage firm executive; b. White Plains, N.Y., May 13, 1946; s. James Bicknell Jr. and Mary Ann (Riegel) L.; m. Carolyn Strahan Zoephel, June 17, 1972; children: James Bicknell IV, Grace Strahan. BA, Yale U., 1968; MBA, Harvard U., 1974. Asst. treas. Gulf Oil(E.H.), London, 1979-80; fin. dir. Gulf Oil Belgium, Brussels, 1980-81; sr. mgr. Gulf Oil Corp., Pitts., 1982-83, asst. treas., 1982-83; v.p., treas. Alexander and Alexander Services, N.Y.C., 1983—. Contbr. articles to profl. jours. Treas. Reps. Abroad, London, 1978-80. Served to lt. USN, 1969-72. Fellow Assn. Corp. Treas. (England); mem. Nat. Assn. Corp. Treas. Office: Alexander and Alexander Services 1211 Ave of the Americas New York NY 10030

LOCKHART, MADGE CLEMENTS, educator; b. Soddy, Tenn., May 22, 1920; d. James Arlie and Ollie (Sparks) Clements; m. Andre J. Lockhart, Apr. 24, 1942 (div. 1973); children: Jacqueline, Andrew, Janice, Jill. Student, East Tenn. U., 1938-39; BS, U. Tenn., Chattanooga and Knoxville, 1955, MEd, 1962. Elem. tchr. Tenn. and Ga., 1947-60, Brainerd High Sch., Chattanooga, 1960-64, Cleveland (Tenn.) City Schs., 1966-88; owner, operator Lockhart's Learning Ctr., Inc., Cleveland and Chattanooga, 1975—; co-founder, pres. Hermes, Inc., 1973-79; co-founder Dawn Ctr., Hamilton County, Tenn., 1974; apptd. mem. Tenn. Gov.'s Acad. for Writers. AuthAor poetry, short stories and fiction; contbr. articles to profl. jours. and newspapers. Pres. Cleveland Assn. Retarded Citizens, 1970, state v.p., 1976; pres. Cherokee Easter Seal Soc., 1973-76, Cleveland Creative Arts Guild, 1980; bd. dirs. Tenn. Easter Seal Soc., 1974-77, 80-83; chair Bradley County Internat. Yr. of Child. Recipient Service to Mankind award Sertoma, 1978, Gov.'s award for service to handicapped, 1979; mental health home named in her honor, Tenn., 1987. Mem. NEA (life), Tenn. Edn. Assn., Am. Assn. Rehab. Therapy, Cleveland Edn. Assn. (Service to Humanity award 1987). Mem. Ch. of Christ. Clubs: Byliners, Fantastiks. Home: 3007 Oakland Dr Cleveland TN 37312

LOCKHART, RON, producer, composer; b. Pitts., Apr. 6, 1946; s. Irwin and Lillian (Hoffman) L.; student Emerson Coll., 1967-68. Mus. asst. to Mitch Leigh of Music Makers, N.Y.C., 1968; producer Columbia Record Club (div. CBS), N.Y.C., 1968-73; composer, producer (freelance) radio and TV, N.Y.C., 1968-73; pres., creative dir. Ron Lockhart Inc., N.Y.C., 1973-86; v.p. Osman-Lockhart Properties, 1986—; pres. The Lockhart Orgn. Inc., 1986—; lectr. NYU, 1985-88. Producer, Suffolk Air Fair, N.Y., 1977; v.p. 200 Edgewater Assocs. Mem. Nat. Assn. Rec. Arts & Scis., Nat. Assn. TV Arts and Scis. (awards com.), Am. Soc. Composers and Pubs. Home and office: 95 Horatio St New York NY 10014

LOCKHART, THOMAS PAUL, chemist; b. Washington, Feb. 6, 1954; s. Luther Bynum and Betty Jane (Brodman) L.; m. Francesca de Ferra. BS in Chemistry, Duke U., 1976; PhD in Chemistry, Calif. Inst. Tech., 1981. Staff scientist Gen. Electric, Schenactady, N.Y., 1980-83; assoc. nat. research council Nat. Bur. Standards, Gaitersburg, Md., 1983-85; staff scientist Du-Pont Cen. Research Group, Wilmington, Del., 1985-86; cons., group leader Eniricerche, San Donato Milanese, Italy, 1987—. Contbr. articles to profl. jours. Patentee in field. Recipient Dushman award Gen. Electric, 1983. Mem. Am. Chem. Soc. Office: Eniricerche, via Mauritana 26, 20097 San Donato Milanese Italy

LOCKWOOD, FRANK JAMES, manufacturing company executive; b. San Bernadino, Calif., Oct. 30, 1931; s. John Ellis and Sarah Grace (Roberts) L.; children from previous marraige: Fay, Frank, Hedy, Jonnie, George, Katherine, Bill, Dena; m. 2d. Crystal Marie Miller, 1986. Student, Southeast City Coll., Chgo., 1955, Ill. Inst. Tech., 1963-64, Bogan Jr. Coll., Chgo., 1966. Foreman Hupp Aviation, Chgo., 1951-60; dept. head UARCO, Inc., Chgo., 1960-68; pres. XACT Machine & Engring., Chgo., 1968—; chmn. bd., pres., bd. dirs. Lockwood Engring., Inc., Chgo.; Ill. Nat. Corp., Chgo., and cons. engr., Chgo. Patentee printing equipment, beverage cans, gasoline pump dispenser "Super Pin", bus. forms equipment. Participant Forest Land Mgmt. Program; mem. Ill. Ambassadors, Mt. Vernon Econ. Devel. Commn.; commr. Econ. Develop. Commn., Mt. Vernon, Ill., 1985. Served with USN, 1948-50. Named Chgo. Ridge Father of the Yr., 1964. Mem. Ill. Divers' Assn. (pres. 1961-62), Ill. Ambassadors. Lodge: Masons (32 degree), Shriners (past master 2). Home: Rt 1 Texico IL 62889 Office: 7011 W Archer Ave Chicago IL 60638

LOCKWOOD, MOLLY ANN, communications company executive; b. London, Sept. 19, 1936; d. Warren Sewell and Ann Frances (Gleason) L.; B.S., Pa. State U., 1958. With exec. tng. program Lord & Taylor, N.Y.C., 1958-60; assoc. merchandising editor House & Garden Mag., N.Y.C., 1960-65; advt. dir. Status Mag., N.Y.C., 1965-70; merchandising dir. Holiday Mag., N.Y.C., 1970; account mgr. Ladies' Home Journal Mag., N.Y.C., 1970-72; adv. dir. Girl Talk Mag., N.Y.C., 1972-74; mktg. dir./asso. pub. East/West Network Mag., N.Y.C., 1974-77; pres., chief exec. officer ptnr. Catalyst Communications, Inc., N.Y.C., 1977—, Catalyst Pub. Inc., pres., 1987—; sec. bd. 244 Madison Realty Corp., 1984—; mktg. and sales dir. Mus. Mag., 1979-83. Mem. Advt. Women N.Y., Kappa Kappa Gamma Alumnae Assn. Club: Liberty. Home: 1133 Park Ave New York NY 10128 Office: Catalyst Communications Inc 244 Madison Ave New York NY 10016

LODGAARD, SVERRE, researcher; b. Trö ndelag, Norway, Apr. 6, 1945; s. Emil Andreas and Ingeborg (Morseth) L.; m. Ingrid Eide, July 9, 1969; 1 son, Christian Eide. Magister, U. Oslo, 1971. Research fellow Norwegian Endowment for Sci. and Humanities, 1972-73; univ. scholar U. Oslo, 1973-77; dir. research Internat. Peace Research Inst., Oslo, 1974-76, researcher, 1977-80; researcher Stockholm Internat. Peace Research Inst., 1980-86, dir. Internat. Peace Research, 1987—. Author: Nuclear Disengagement in Europe, 1983, No First Use, 1984, Overcoming Threats to Europe, 1987; contbr. articles to profl. jours. Mem. Norwegian Govt.'s Adv. Council on Arms Control and Disarmament, 1972—; chmn. Norwegian Pugwash Com., 1980—. Lutheran. Home: Sarpsborggate 16D, 0468 Oslo 444 Norway Office: Internat Peace Research Inst, Fuglehauggt 11, 0260 Oslo 2 Norway

LODGE, TOM, political science educator; b. Manchester, Lancashire, Eng., Aug. 19, 1951; arrived in Republic of South Africa, 1978.; s. Roy and Vera (Kotasova) L.; m. Carla Grootenboer, June 26, 1979; children: Kim, Guy. BA, Univ. York, Yorkshire, Eng., 1974, B in Philosophy, 1975, D in Philosophy, 1985. Research fellow Ctr. for So. African Studies U. York, 1975-77; lectr. dept. polit. studies U. of the Witwatersrand, Johannesburg, Republic of South Africa, 1978-85, sr. lectr., 1985—. Author: Black Politics in South Africa Since 1945, 1983; editor: Resistance and Ideology in Settler Societies, 1986; contbr. articles to profl. jours. Home: 93 7th St, Parkhurst 2193, Johannesburg 2193, Republic of South Africa Office: U of the Witwatersrand, 1 Jan Smuts Ave, Johannnesburg 2050, Republic of South Africa

LODWICK, GWILYM SAVAGE, radiologist, educator; b. Mystic, Iowa, Aug. 30, 1917; s. Gwylim S. and Lucy A. (Fuller) L.; m. Maria Antonia De Brito Barata; children by previous marriage: Gwilym Savage III, Philip Galligan, Malcolm Kerr, Terry Ann. Student, Drake U., 1934-35; B.S., State U. Iowa, 1942, M.D., 1943. Resident pathology State U. Iowa, 1947-48, resident radiology, 1948-50; fellow, sr. fellow radiologic and orthopedic pathology Armed Forces Inst. Pathology, 1951; asst., then asso. prof. State U. Iowa Med. Sch., 1951-56; prof. radiology, chmn. dept. U. Mo. at Columbia Med. Sch., 1956-78, research prof. radiology, 1978—, interim chmn. dept. radiology, 1980-81, chmn. dept. radiology, 1981-83, prof. bioengring., 1969-83, acting dean, 1959, assoc. dean, 1959-64; assoc. radiologist Mass. Gen. Hosp., 1983-88, radiologist, 1988—; vis. prof. dept. radiology Harvard Med. Sch., 1983—; cons. in field; vis. prof. Keio U. Sch. Medicine, Tokyo, 1974; chmn. sci. program com. Internat. Conf. on Med. Info., Amsterdam, 1983; trustee Am. Registry Radiologic Technologists, 1961-69, pres., 1964-65, 68-69; mem. radiology tng. com. Nat. Inst. Gen. Med. Scis., NIH, 1966-70; com. radiology Nat. Acad. Scis.-NRC, 1970-75; chmn. com. computers Am. Coll. Radiology, 1965, Internat. Commn. Radiol. Edn. and Info., 1969—; cons. to health care tech. div. Nat. Ctr. for Health Services, Research and Devel., 1971—; dir. Mid-Am. Bone Tumor Diagnostic Ctr. and Registry, 1971-83; adv. com. mem. NIH Biomed. Image Processing Grant Jet Propulsion Lab., 1969-73; nat. chmn. MUMPS Users Group, 1973-75; mem. radiation study sect. div. research grants NIH, 1976-79, mem. study sect. on diagnostic radiology and nuclear medicine div. research grants, 1979-82, chmn. study sect. on diagnostic radiology div. research grants, 1980-82; mem. bd. sci. counselors Nat. Library of Medicine, 1985, chmn. 1987—; dir. radiology Spaulding Rehab. Hosp., 1986—. Adv. editorial bd. Radiology, 1965-86, cons. to editor, 1986—; adv. editorial bd. Current/Clin. Practice, 1972—; mem. editorial bd.: Jour. Med. Systems, 1976—, Radiol. Sci. Update div. Biomedia, Inc, 1975—; mem. cons. editorial bd.: Skeletal Radiology, 1977—, Contemporary Diagnostic Radiology, 1978-80. Served to maj. AUS, 1943-46. Decorated Sakari Mustakallio medal Finland; named Most Disting. Alumnus in Radiology, State U. Ia. Centennial, 1970; recipient Sigma Xi Research award U. Mo., Columbia, 1972, Gold medal XIII Internat. Conf. Radiology, Madrid, 1973. Fellow AMA (radiology rev. bd. council med. edn., council rep. on residency rev. com. for radiology 1969-74), Am. Coll. Radiology (co-chmn. ACR-NEMA standardization com. 1983—); mem. Am. Coll. Med. Informatics (founding), Nat. Acad. Practice, European Soc. Radiology (European steering com. on computers), Radiol. Soc. N.Am. (3d v.p. 1974-75, chmn. ad hoc com. representing assoc. scis. 1979—, chmn. assoc. scis. com. 1981-87), Assn. Univ. Radiologists, Mo. Radiol. Soc. (1st pres. 1961-62), Salutis Unitas, Alpha Omega Alpha; hon. mem. Portuguese Soc. Radiology and Nuclear Medicine, Tex. Radiol. Soc., Ind. Roentgen Soc., Phila. Roentgen Ray Soc., Finnish Radiol. Soc. (hon.). Clubs: Harvard of Boston, Cosmos. Home: One Devonshire Pl Apt 2713 Boston MA 02109

LOEB, FRANCES LEHMAN, civic leader; b. N.Y.C., Sept. 25, 1906; d. Arthur and Adele (Lewisohn) Lehman; student Vassar Coll., 1924-26; L.H.D. (hon.), NYU, 1977; m. John L. Loeb, Nov. 18, 1926; children—Judith Loeb Chiara, John L., Ann Loeb Bronfman, Arthur Lehman, Deborah Loeb Brice. N.Y.C. commr. for UN and Consular Corps, 1966-78. Exec. com. Population Crisis Com., Washington; life mem. bd. Children of Bellevue, Inc., 1974—; bd. dirs. Bellevue Assn., Internat. Presch., Inc., N.Y. Landmarks Conservancy; chmn. bd. East Side Internat. Community Center, Inc.; mem. UN Devel. Corp., 1972—; mem. Women's Nat. Republican Club; life trustee Collegiate Sch. for Boys, N.Y.C.; trustee Cornell U., 1979-88, trustee emeritus, 1988—, trustee Vassar Coll., 1988—; bd. overseers Cornell U. Med. Coll., 1983-88 (life mem. 1988—), Inst. Internat. Edn. (life). Mem. UN Assn. (dir.). Clubs: Cosmopolitan, Vassar, Women's City (N.Y.C.). Home: 730 Park Ave New York NY 10021 also: Anderson Hill Rd Purchase NY 10577 other: Lyford Cay, New Providence The Bahamas

LOEBER, DIETRICH ANDRÉ, law educator; b. Riga, Latvia, Jan. 4, 1923; s. August J. and Emilie E. (Mentzendorff) L.; m. Anita B. Hasselblatt, Apr. 7, 1955; children: Tatjana, Silvia, Alexis, John. Diploma, The Hague (Netherlands) Acad. Internat. Law, 1951; MA, Columbia U., 1953; Dr. iuris, U. Marburg, Fed. Republic Germany, 1951; exchange scholar, Moscow State U., 1961. Sr. research fellow Max-Planck Inst., Hamburg, 1958-66; prof. law U. Kiel, Fed. Republic Germany, 1966—; vis. prof. UCLA, 1970, 74, Stanford U., 1971, 73, Adelaide U., 1977, Columbia U., 1980-81, 83; research assoc., Harvard Law Sch., 1963-64. Author: books Urheberrecht der UdSSR, 1966, 2d edit. 1981, Der hoheitlich gestaltete Vertrag, 1969, Diktierte Option, 1972, 2d edit. 1974; compiler East-West Trade, 4 vols., 1976-77. Mem. Assn. des Auditeurs de l'Academie de Droit Internat. de La Haye (life), Am. Assn. for the Advancement of Slavic Studies, Assn. for the Advancement of Baltic Studies. Mem. Evang. Reformed Ch. Home: Gehlenkamp 14, D-2000 Hamburg 56 Federal Republic of Germany Office U Kiel, D-2300 Kiel 1 Federal Republic of Germany

LOEBNER, EGON EZRIEL, physicist; b. Plzen, Czechoslovakia, Feb. 24, 1924; s. Emil and Josephine (Koeser) L.; came to U.S., 1947, naturalized, 1952; BA in Physics, U. Buffalo, 1950, PhD in Physics, 1955; m. Sonya S. Sajovics, June 18, 1950; children: Gary Emil, Benny Joseph, Mindy Sue. Draftsman, Danek & Co., Bolevec, Czechoslavakia, 1941-42, asst. to chief engr. Terezin Waterworks, 1942-44; sr. engr. Sylvania Electric Products, Inc., Buffalo and Boston, 1952-55; mem. tech. staff RCA Labs., Princeton, N.J., 1955-61; mgr., research specialist H.P. Assos., Palo Alto, Calif., 1961-65; dept. head, research adviser Hewlett-Packard Labs., 1965-74, lab. assoc., 1976-77, mgr. data base mgmt. systems dept., 1977-80, mgr. cognitive interface dept., 1980-85, counselor sci. and tech. 1985—; counselor sci. and technol. affairs U.S. embassy, Moscow, 1974-76; lectr. Stanford U., part-time 1968-74; lectr. U. Calif. at Santa Cruz, 1972-74. Mem. N.J. Commn. on Radiation Protection, 1960-62; mem. lay adv. com. on math. Unified Palo Alto Sch. Dist., 1964-66. Bd. dirs. Jewish Center, Princeton, 1957-59. Mem. Am. Phys. Soc., IEEE, Semiotic Soc. Am., Am. Assn. Artificial Intelligence, Am. Optical Soc., NSPE, Calif. Soc. Profl. Engrs., AAAS, Sigma Xi, Assn. for Computing Machinery, Cognitive Sci. Soc., N.Y. Acad. Scis., Calif. Acad. Scis., Soc. Hist. Tech., Hist. Sci. Soc., Sigma Alpha Mu. Democrat. Jewish. Club: Palo Alto Hills Golf and Country, Commonwealth. Research in physics, chemistry, electronics, metalurgy, psychology, biophysics, cybernetics, math., sci. policy linguistics data processing, constitutional law, hist. tech. and hist. sci. Patentee in optoelectronics. Home: 2934 Alexis Dr Palo Alto CA 94304 Office: Hewlett Packard Labs 1501 Page Mill Rd Palo Alto CA 94304

LOEFFEL, BRUCE, software company executive, consultant; b. Bklyn., Aug. 13, 1943; s. Samuel and Loretta (Bleiweiss) L.; m. Gail Wildman, Dec. 3, 1966; children—Alisa, Joshua. B.B.A., Pace U., 1966; M.B.A., St. John's U., 1971. Certified data processor. Mgr. fin. systems Gibbs & Hill Inc., N.Y.C., 1973-76; mgr. sales/tech. support Mgmt. Sci. Am. Inc., Fort Lee, N.J., 1976-81; dir. mktg. Info. Scis., Inc., Montvale, N.J., 1981-82; dir. bus. devel. Cullinet Software, Inc., Westwood, Mass., 1982-85; v.p. mktg. Online/Data Base Software Inc., Pearl River, N.Y., 1985—; cons. Online/Data Base Specialists, New City, N.Y., 1982-85. Served with U.S. Army, 1966-71. Mem. Inst. Cert. of Computer Profls. Democrat. Jewish. Avocations: sports; electronics. Home: 350 Phillips Hill Rd New City NY 10956 Office: Online Database Software Inc 1 Blue Hill Plaza Pearl River NY 10965

LOEFFLER, WILLIAM ROBERT, quality productivity specialist, engineering educator; b. Cleve., Aug. 31, 1949; s. Harry T. and Frances R. (Pearson) L.; m. Beth Ann Manderfield, Dec. 1978; children—Lindsay Brooke, Kelly Lynn, Robert Jason. B.A., Wittenberg U., 1971; M.A., SUNY-Stony Brook, 1972; Ed. Specialist, U. Toledo, 1979; Ph.D., U. Mich., 1984. Dir. alternate learning ctr. Lucas County Schs., Toledo, 1977-79; dir. chem. and metall. services Toledo Testing Lab., 1979-82; pres. Chem. Resources, Lambertville, Mich., 1982-83; v.p. Benchmark Techs., Toledo, 1983-86; pres. Loeffler Group, Inc., 1986—; pres. Tech. Soc. Toledo, 1985-86; conf. chmn. Am. Soc. Quality Control. Deming Conf., Toledo, 1984; mem. Nat. Task Force ALARA Atomic Indsl. Forum, Washington; congl. sci. counselor PACCOS, Ohio; Ford Motor Co. prof. Statis. quality studies Eastern Mich. U., 1986. Editor Jour. Toledo Tech. Topics 1982—; asst. editor Jour. English Quarterly, 1976-77. Contbr. articles to profl. jours. Vice chmn. Pvt. Industry Council, Monroe County, Mich., 1983, 84; chmn. Bus.-Industry-Edn. Day Toledo C. of C., 1984; trustee Bedford Pub. Schs., Mich., 1982-85; chmn. Robotics Internat., 1985. Fellow SUNY-Stony Brook 1975-76, Cambridge U. 1976-77. Recipient Harvard Book award 1967. Mem. Am. Chem. Soc. (chmn. Toledo chapt. 1984), Am. Soc. Non-Destructive Testing, Phi Delta Kappa, Phi Kappa Phi. Methodist. Club: U. Mich. (Toledo). Lodge: Rotary. Office: Loeffler Group Inc 3018S Republic Blvd Suite 302 Toledo OH 43615

LOELLGEN, HERBERT HANS, cardiologist; b. Bonn, Fed. Republic Germany, Jan. 5, 1943; s. Artur and Maria (Decker) L.; m. Inge Horres, Apr. 28, 1944; children: Ruth, Deborah, Noëmi, Eva. MD, Rheinische Friedrich Wilhelms U. Bonn, 1968; PhD, U. Mainz, 1979. Asst. prof. U. Mainz, Fed. Republic Germany, 1970-72, 77-78, Hosp. Bethanien, Moers, Fed. Republic Germany, 1973-76; vice-head dept. cardiology U. Freiburg, Fed. Republic Germany, 1978-82; head dept. med., cardiology Hosp. Limburg, Fed. Republic Germany, 1983-85, Mcpl. Hosp. Remscheid, Fed. Republic Germany, 1986—. Author: Ergometrie, 1983, Kardiopulmonale Funktionsdiagnostik, 1983, EKG-Beurteilung, 1986; (with G. Meuret) Reanimation, 1988; editor: Herz-Rhythmusstörungen, 1983, Progress in Ergometry, 1984. Chmn. working group ergometry UNESCO; mem. Med. Bd. German Astronauts. Mem. Assn. Sports Medicine (pres. 1986—), several internat. and nat. med. socs. Roman Catholic. Home: Bermesgasse 32B, D-5630 Remscheid Federal Republic of Germany Office: Mcpl Hosp, Burger Str 211, D-5630 Remscheid Federal Republic of Germany

LOERTSCHER, ALFRED, editor; b. La Chaux de Fonds, Switzerland, Dec. 27, 1915; s. Auguste and Julia (Godat) L.; student U. Neuchatel, 1934-37; m. Odette Luginbuhl, July 7, 1958; 1 son, Patrick; children by previous marriage—Denis Gerald, Brigitte Meyer. Prof. linguistics Leipzig, 1937-38, Neuchâtel, 1938; editor, then chief editor L'Express, Neuchâtel, 1939-45; chief editor Curieux mag. weekly, Geneva, 1945-51; chief editor, mgr. monthly rev. Trente Jours, Lausanne, 1954-86. Co-founder, gen. mgr. Editions Avanti, Neuchâtel, 1952-80. Recipient Silver-Gild medal Soc. Acad. Arts, Scis., Letteres, Paris, 1987. Home: 18 Ave des Toises, 1005 Lausanne Switzerland also: La Renardière, 1837 Château d'Oex Switzerland Office: 23 rue du Pré-du-Marche, 1004 Lausanne Switzerland

LOESCH, KATHARINE TAYLOR (MRS. JOHN GEORGE LOESCH), educator; b. Berkeley, Calif., Apr. 13, 1922; d. Paul Schuster and Katharine (Whiteside) Taylor; student Swarthmore Coll., 1939-41, U. Wash., 1942; B.A., Columbia U., 1944, M.A., 1949; grad. Neighborhood Playhouse Sch. of Theatre, 1946; postgrad. Ind. U., 1953; Ph.D., Northwestern U., 1961; m. John George Loesch, Aug. 28, 1948; 1 son, William Ross. Instr. speech Wellesley (Mass.) Coll., 1949-52, Loyola U., Chgo., 1956; asst. prof. English and speech Roosevelt U., Chgo., 1957, 62-65; assoc. prof. communication and theatre U. Ill. at Chgo., 1968—; assoc. prof. emerita speech in communication and theater, U. Ill., Chgo., 1987—. Active ERA, Ill., 1975-76. Am. Philos. Soc. grantee, 1970; U. Ill., Chgo., grantee, 1970. Mem. Am. Soc. Aesthetics, Linguistics Soc. Am., Speech Communication Assn. (Golden Anniversary prize award 1969, chmn. interpretation div. 1979-80), MLA, Honorable Soc. Cymmrodorion, Pi Beta Phi. Episcopalian. Contbr. writings to profl. publs. Office: U Ill Dept Communication and Theatre PO Box 4348 MC/132 Chicago IL 60680

LOESCHE, PETER HANSJOERG, political science educator; b. Berlin, Feb. 13, 1939; s. Bruno Waldemar and Dorothea (Ludwig) L.; m. Christel Stüber, Mar. 31, 1969; children: Daniel, Nina-Suzanne. PhD, Free U., Berlin, 1966, D. Hab, 1973. Research asst. Free U., Berlin, 1963-66, asst. prof., 1966-69; Kennedy fellow Harvard U., Cambridge, Mass., 1969-71; prof. U. Hamburg, Fed. Republic Germany, 1971-72, U. Goettingen, Fed. Republic Germany, 1973—. Author: American Politics, 1977, Anarchism, 1977, Party Financing, 1984, Party System in Germany, 1986. bd. dirs. Bundeszentrale für Politische Bildung, Bonn, Fed. Republic Germany. Mem. Am. Polit. Sci. Assn., Am. Hist. Assn., German Polit. Sci. Assn. (v.p. 1973-75), Indsl. and Labor Relations Research Assn., Hist. Commn. Berlin. Office: U Goettingen, Platz der Göttinger, Sieben 3, 3400 Goettingen Federal Republic of Germany

LOEVINGER, LEE, lawyer; b. St. Paul, Apr. 24, 1913; s. Gustavus and Millie (Strouse) L.; m. Ruth Howe, Mar. 4, 1950; children: Barbara L., Eric H., Peter H. BA summa cum laude, U. Minn., 1933, JD, 1936. Bar: Minn. 1936, Mo. 1937, D.C. 1966, U.S. Supreme Ct., 1941. Assoc. Watson, Ess, Groner, Barnett & Whittaker, Kansas City, Mo., 1936-37; atty., regional atty. NLRB, 1937-41; with antitrust div. Dept. Justice, 1941-46; ptnr. Larson, Loevinger, Lindquist & Fraser, Mpls., 1946-60; assoc. justice Minn. Supreme Ct., 1960-61; asst. U.S. atty. gen. charge antitrust div. Dept. Justice,

1961-63; commr. FCC, 1963-68; ptnr. Hogan & Hartson, Washington, 1968-85; of counsel Hogan & Hartson, 1986—; v.p., dir. Craig-Hallum Corp., Mpls., 1968-73; dir. Petrolite Corp., St. Louis., 1978-83; U.S. rep. com. on restrictive bus. practices Orgn. for Econ. Cooperation and Devel., 1961-64; spl. asst. to U.S. atty. gen., 1963-64; spl. counsel com. small bus. U.S. Senate, 1951-52; lectr. U. Minn., 1953-60; vis. prof. jurisprudence U. Minn. (Law Sch.), 1961; professorial lectr. Am. U., 1968-70; chmn. Minn. Atomic Devel. Problems Com., 1957-59; mem. Adminstrv. Conf. U.S., 1972-74; del. White House Conf. on Inflation, 1974; U.S. del. UNESCO Conf. on Mass Media, 1975, Internat. Telecommunications Conf. on Radio Frequencies, 1964, 66. Author: The Law of Free Enterprise, 1949, An Introduction to Legal Logic, 1952, Defending Antitrust Lawsuits, 1977; author first article to use term-Jurimetrics, 1949; contbr. articles to profl. jours.; editor, contbr.: Basic Data on Atomic Devel. Problems in Minnesota, 1958; adv. bd. Antitrust Bulletin, Jurimetrics Jour. Served to lt. comdr. USNR, 1942-45. Recipient Outstanding Achievement award U. Minn., 1968; Freedoms Found. award, 1977, 84. Mem. ABA (del. of sci. and tech. sect. to Ho. of Dels. 1974-80, del. to joint conf. with AAAS 1974-76, liaison 1984—, chmn. sci. and tech. sect. 1982-83, council 1986—, standing com. on nat. conf. groups), Minn. Bar Assn., Hennepin County Bar Assn., D.C. Bar Assn., FCC Bar Assn., AAAS, Broadcast Pioneers, U.S. C. of C. (antitrust council), Phi Beta Kappa, Sigma Xi, Delta Sigma Rho, Sigma Delta Chi, Phi Delta Gamma, Tau Kappa Alpha, Alpha Epsilon Rho. Clubs: Cosmos, City Club (Washington). Home: 5669 Bent Branch Rd Bethesda MD 20816 Office: Hogan and Hartson 555 13th St NW Washington DC 20004

LOEWENSTEIN, GEORGE WOLFGANG, retired physician, UN consultant; b. Fed. Republic of Germany, Apr. 18, 1890; s. Julius Max and Augusta Victoria (Klettschoff) L.; m. Johanna Sabath, Nov. 27, 1923; children: Peter F. Lansing (dec.) and Ruth Edith Gallagher (twins). Student, Royal William Coll., Fed. Republic of Germany, 1909, Friedrich William U., Fed. Republican of Germany, 1919, London Sch. Tropical Hygiene and Medicine, 1939. Dir. pub. health Berlin Neubabelsberg, 1920-22, dir. pub. health and welfare City of Borliu, Germany, 1923-33; pvt. practice medicine, Berlin, 1933-38, Chgo., 1940-46, Chebeague and Dark Harbor, Maine, 1947-58; instr. Berlin Acad. Prevention of Infant Mortality, Postgrad. Acad. Physicians; permanent cons., v.p., rep. Internat. Abolitionists Fedn. at ECOSOC, UN, 1947-82; med. cons. German Gen. Consulate, 1963; lectr. Morton Plant Hosp., Clearwater, Fla., also Clearwater campus St. Petersburg Jr. Coll.; guest prof. U. Bremen, Berlin, 1981-82. Co-author: Public Health Between the Time of Imperium and National Socialism, The Destruction of Public Health Reforms of the First German Republic, 1985, others; contbr. 300 articles to med. jours. and revs. to books. Served with German Army, 1914-18. Decorated Cross Merit I Class (Germany), 1965; recipient Commendation awards Pres. of U.S., 1945, 70, 65 Year Gold Service Pin, AMA and ARC, 1985, Service to Mankind award Sertoma, 1972-73, Sport award Pres. Carter, 1977, Musicologist award Richey Symphony, 1979, Reconciliation award Germany-U.S.A., 1983, Friendship award Fed. Republic of Germany, U.S.A., 1985, Teaching award Morton Plant Hosp., 1988, others. Fellow Am. Acad. Family Physicians (charter, life, 40-Yr. Service award 1986), AAAS, Am. Coll. Sport Medicine (emeritus, charter, life), Am. Pub. Health Assn. (life, 40-Yr. Service award 1984), Brit. Soc. (emeritus); mem. World Med. Assn. (life), German Assn. History of Medicine (life), Acad. Mental Retardation (charter, life), Am. Pub. Health Assn. (life, 40 Yr. Service award), Fla. Health Assn. (life), Brit. Pub. Health Assn. (life), AMA (hon.), Am. Assn. Mil. Surgeons (life), Acad. Preventive Medicine (life), Steuben Soc., Richey Symphony Soc. (charter, Musicologist 1979), World Peace Through World Law Ctr. Clubs: City (Chgo. chmn. hygiene sect. 1944-46). Lodges: Rotary (Harris fellow 1980), Masons (32 deg.), Shriners (comdr., life v.p.). Home: 2470 Rhodesian Dr #34 Clearwater FL 33515

LOEWINGER, KENNETH JEFFERY, lawyer; b. Washington, Sept. 22, 1945; s. Myron Arthur and Lenore (Kopf) L.; m. Margaret Irene Krol, May 5, 1978. BA, Georgetown U., 1967, JD, 1971. Bar: U.S. Dist. Ct. D.C. 1971, U.S. Ct. Mil. Appeals 1972, U.S. Ct. Appeals (D.C. cir.) 1972, U.S. Supreme Ct. 1979. Law clk. to presiding judge D.C. Superior Ct., Washington, 1971-72, D.C. Ct. Appeals, Washington, 1972-74; sr. ptnr. Loewinger, Brand & Kappstatter, Washington, 1975—; pres. N.Am. Title and Escrow Co., Inc., Nat. Trading Sales Corp.; com. mem. D.C. Superior Ct., 1976—; mem. adv. com. U.S. Bankruptcy Ct., 1985-86. Author: Loewinger on Landlord and Tenant, 1986. Commr. Housing Prodn. Com., D.C., 1986-87. Mem. ABA, D.C. Bar Assn., Supreme Ct. Hist. Soc. Office: Loewinger Brand & Kappstatter 471 H St NW Washington DC 20001

LOFTUS, JOHN PATRICK, diplomat; b. Phila., Sept. 15, 1943; s. John Joseph and Ann (O'Donnell) L.; m. Saiyud Kunyot, July 9, 1950; 1 child, Rachanee. BA in Classical Langs., La Salle U., Phila., 1967. Vol. U.S. Peace Corps, Gwalior, India, 1967; mil. info. specialist USAF, Phoenix, 1968-70; editor USAF, Nakorn Rajchasima, Thailand, 1970-71; asst. mng. editor The Key West (Fla.) Citizen, 1972-73; editor bus. publs. The Bangkok Post, 1973-77; dir. PRESKO Pub. Relations Group, Bangkok, 1977-80; info. officer UN, Bangkok, 1980—; corr. ABC News, N.Y.C., 1976-80, Asian Bus. & Industry mag., Hong Kong, 1974-80, Asiaweek mag., Hong Kong, 1976-79. Editor: Portrait of Bangkok, 1982, Agropesticides, 1983, The Secret of Borobudur, 1984; author: China's Agricultural Banking System, 1985; copy editor Thai Jour. of Internal Medicine and Asian Pacific Jour. of Allergy and Immunology, 1981-86. Mem. Pan-Pacific Pub. Relations Orgn. Club: Chaine des Rotisseurs (Paris) (chevalier 1984—). Home: 220-94 Soi Sahavaree, Pradipat Rd, Bangkok 10400, Thailand Office: UN ESCAP, Rajdamnern Nok Ave, Bangkok 10200, Thailand

LOFTUS, THOMAS DANIEL, lawyer; b. Seattle, Nov. 8, 1930; s. Glendon Francis and Martha Helen (Wall) L. B.A., U. Wash., 1952, J.D., 1957. Bar: Wash. 1958, U.S. Ct. Appeals (9th cir.) 1958, U.S. Dist. Ct. Wash. 1958, U.S. Ct. Mil. Appeals, U.S. Supreme Ct. Trial atty. Northwestern Mut. Ins. Co., Seattle, 1958-62; sr. trial atty. Unigard Security Ins. Co., Seattle, 1962-68, asst. gen. counsel, 1969-83, govt. relations counsel, 1983—; mem. Wash. Commn. on Jud. Conduct (formerly Jud. Qualifications Commn.), 1982—, vice-chmn., 1987-88; judge pro tem Seattle Mcpl. Ct., 1973-81. Sec., treas. Seattle Opera Assn., 1980—; pres., bd. dirs. Vis. Nurse Services, 1979-88; pres., v.p. Salvation Army Adult Rehab. Ctr., 1979-86; vice chmn. Young Republican Nat. Fedn., 1963-65; pres. Young Reps. King County, 1962-63; bd. dirs. Seattle Seafair, Inc., 1975; bd. dirs., gen. counsel Wash. Ins. Council, 1984-86, sec., 1986—; bd. dirs. Arson Alarm Found. Served to 1st lt. U.S. Army, 1952-54, to col. Res., 1954-83. Fellow Am. Bar Found.; mem. Am. Arbitration Assn. (nat. panel arbitrators 1965—), Wash. Bar Assn. (gov. 1981-84), Seattle King County Bar Assn. (sec., trustee 1977-82), ABA (ho. of dels. 1984—), Internat. Assn. Ins. Counsel, Def. Research Inst., Am. Judicature Soc., Res. Officers Assn., Wash. Ins. Council (v.p., sec., gen. counsel, bd. dirs. 1984—), U. Wash. Alumni Assn., Phi Delta Phi, Theta Delta Chi. Republican. Presbyterian. Clubs: Coll. of Seattle, Wash. Athletic. Lodges: Masons, Scottish Rite, Shriners. Home: 3515 Magnolia Blvd West Seattle WA 98199 Office: 1215 4th Ave 18th Floor Seattle WA 98161

LOGAN, DAVID SAMUEL, investment banker; b. Chgo., Jan. 10, 1918; s. Morris and Gertrude (Irving) L.; m. Reva Frumkin, Jan. 24, 1943; children: Daniel Joel, Richard Elliot, Jonathan Charles. BA, U. Chgo., 1939, JD, 1941. Bar: Ill., 1941, U.S. Supreme Ct., 1950. Lawyer Bd. of Econ. Warfare, Washington, 1942-46; mng. ptnr. Associated Hotels, Chgo., 1947-55, Mercury Investments, Chgo., 1955—. Chmn. Artists-in-Residence, Lit., Budget, Ill. Arts Council, Chgo., 1982—; exec. com. Nat. Archives Council, Chgo., 1975-80, Ill. State Arts Council, Chgo., 1977—. Recipient Civil Govt. award U. Chgo. Mem. Ill. State Bar Assn., Chgo. Bar Assn. Jewish. Clubs: Arts, Carlton, Caxton. Home: 209 E Lake Shore Dr Chicago IL 60611 Office: Mercury Investments 919 N Michigan Ave Suite 3301 Chicago IL 60611

LOGAN, GRACE ELEANOR MILLER (MRS. HENRY WHITTINGTON LOGAN), educator; b. Valencia, Pa., June 22, 1908; d. Alvah John and Lillian (Gibson) Miller; B.S., Temple U., 1930, M.S., 1931; postgrad., 1955-56; m. Henry Whittington Logan, Mar. 16, 1940; 1 son, Henry Whittington III. English instr. Temple U., 1930-33; asst. prof. to dept. head Moravian Coll., Bethlehem, Pa., 1933-42; assoc. prof. edn. and philosophy Widener U., Chester, Pa., 1956-67, prof. English, 1967-85, prof. emeritus, adj. prof. 1985—; dir. Coll. Reading Services, 1958-85; dir. Fed. Office of Edn. Equal Opportunities Tng. Br. Insts., 1965—; bd. dirs. 1683 Caleb Pusey House, Upland, Pa., dir. bd. of friends, 1986—; cons., lectr. in biblical studies, 1985—; only woman on faculty any mil. coll. U.S. for 8 yrs. Elder, Presbyn. Ch.; mem. adv. bd. Pa. Inst. Tech. Mem. AAUP, Delaware County Hist. Soc. (dir.), Nat. Council Tchrs. English, Coll. English Assn., Coll. Reading Assn., Internat. Reading Assn., Pa. Council of Tchrs., Am. Acad. Religion, Questers Potpourri, Kappa Delta Epsilon, Pi Delta Epsilon. Home: 201 Sykes Ln Wallingford PA 19086 Office: Widener Univ Chester PA 19013

LOGAN, HAROLD ROY, industrial executive; b. Rogers, Ark., Aug. 4, 1921; s. John Hubert and Mary Alice (Hoover) L.; m. Freda Townsend, Aug. 17, 1941 (dec. June 1984), children: Harold, Mary Betts; m. Tolita I. Christensen, Jan. 1985. BS, Okla. State U., 1942. Budget dir. Dept. Def., Washington, 1955-60; sr. v.p., dir. Grace Line, Inc., N.Y.C., 1960-67, pres., chief exec. officer, 1967-68, chmn. bd., 1968-70; exec. v.p., dir. W.R. Grace & Co., N.Y.C., 1968-81, vice chmn., dir., 1981-86; chmn. Comstock Resources Inc.; dir. Chelsea Industries, Inc., Energy Fund Inc., IC Industries, Inc., Pnuemo-Abex Corp., Ill. Cen. Gulf R.R., Cowstech Pesaures, Inc. Served to lt. comdr. USNR, 1942-46. Republican. Congregationalist. Clubs: Links, N.Y. Yacht, Harvard (N.Y.C.); Army-Navy, Kenwood Country, Metropolitan (Washington); Aspetuck Valley Country (Weston, Conn.); Yacht and Country (Stuart, Fla.); Winged Foot Golf (Manaroneck, N.Y.). Home: 3172 SE Fairway W Stuart FL 33497

LOGAN, LEE ROBERT, orthodontist; b. Los Angeles, June 24, 1923; s. Melvin Duncan and Margaret (Seltzer) L.; B.S., UCLA; 1952; D.D.S., Northwestern U., 1956, M.S., 1961; m. Maxine Nadler, June 20, 1975; children—Fritz, Dean, Scott, Gigi, Chad, Casey. Gen. practice dentistry, Reseda, Calif., 1958-59; practice dentistry specializing in orthodontics, Northridge, Calif., 1961—; pres. Lee R. Logan D.D.S. Profl. Corp.; mem. staff Northridge Hosp., Tarzana Hosp.; owner Maxine's Talent Agy.Served to lt. USNR, 1956-58. Diplomate Am. Bd. Orthodontics. Named (with wife) Couple of Yr. Austic Children Assn., 1986; recipient Nat. Philanthropy award, 1987. Fellow Internat. Acad. Nutrition; mem. Am., San Fernando Valley dental assns., Am. Assn. Orthodontists, Pacific Coast Soc. Orthodontists (dir., pres. so. sect. 1974-75, chmn. membership 1981-83), Found. Orthodontic Research (charter mem.), Calif. Soc. Orthodontists (chmn. peer rev. 1982-87), G.U. Black Soc. (charter mem.), Angle Soc. Orthodontists (pres. 1986-87, bd. dirs. 1982-87, nat. pres. 1985-87), Xi Psi Phi. Club: U.S.C. Century. Contbr. articles to profl. jours. Home: 4830 Encino Ave Encino CA 91316 Office: 18250 Roscoe Blvd Northridge CA 91324

LOGAN, WILLIAM STEWART, university dean; b. Melbourne, Australia, Jan. 19, 1942; s. William Eric and Norma (Thurlow) L.; m. Denise Coral, May 17, 1965; children: Katrina Ellen, Anna Kristen. BA with honors, U. Melbourne, 1963, diploma in Edn., 1964, MA, 1967; PhD, Monash U., 1980. Tutor U. Melbourne, 1965-67, lectr., 1971-73; tchr. Heaton Sch., Newcastle, Eng., 1968, Long Close Sch., London, 1969-70; prin. lectr. Footscray Inst. Tech., Victoria, Australia, 1974-87; dean Victoria Coll., Toorak, Australia, 1987—; cons. UNESCO, Paris, 1986. Author: A Question of Size, 1975, The Gentrification of Inner Melbourne, 1985, (with others) Australia's Urban Network, 1975; contbr. articles to profl. jours. Chmn. Urban Conservation Com., Nat. Trust of Australia, Melbourne, 1981—. Mem. Royal Australian Planning Inst., Australian Inst. Geographers, Council for the Hist. Environment. Office: Victoria Coll Arts Faculty, Glenferrie Rd, Toorak Victoria 3144, Australia

LOGORECI, ANTON, freelance journalist; b. Shkoder, Albania, July 19, 1910; s. Peter and Marie (Toska) L.; m. Doreen Clements, Jan. 1, 1952; 1 child, Philip. BS in Econs., London Sch. Econs., 1940. Journalist, contbg. author various periodicals and newspapers Albania, 1927-37; broadcaster, scriptwriter BBC, London, 1940-74; freelance journalist London, 1974—. Author: The Albanians, 1977; contbr. articles to London Times Literary Supplement, Contemporary Rev., Index on Censorship (London), Problems of Communism (Washington), Current History (Phila.). Home: 18 Disraeli Gardens, London SW15 2QB, England

LOH, CHOW KHUAN, engineering contractor; b. Taiping, Perak, Malaysia, Dec. 15, 1932; s. Thow Yoong Loh and Quee Chow (Lee) L.; m. Koay Lim, Oct. 14, 1964; children—Ching Fook, Ching Soo, Ching Lin. B.Sc. in Engring., U. London, 1962. Jr. design engr. Ove Arup and Ptnrs., London, 1960-63; asst. design engr. Steen Sehested and Ptnrs., Singapore, 1964-66; sect. engr. Sir William Halcrow and Ptnrs., Alor Star, Kedah, Malaysia, 1966-69; civil engr. Coode and Ptnrs., Port Klang, Selangor, 1969-72; exec. engr. Pub. Works Dept., Parit Buntar, Perak, 1972-77; exec. dir. Loh Thow Yoong Sdn, Bhd., Taiping, Perak, 1977-86, mng. dir., 1986—. Vice pres. N. Perak Kayin Assn., 1983-85, pres., 1986-87, 88—. Mem. Instn. Civil Engrs. London, Instn. Engrs. Malaysia. Club: New (Taiping). Home: 234 Jalan Taman Kerjasama, Taiping, Perak Malaysia Office: Loh Thow Yoong Sdn, Bhd, 204 Jalan Kuarantin Lama, Taiping, Perak Malaysia

LOHANI, PRAKASH CHANCRA, minister of housing and physical planning of Nepal; b. Apr. 21, 1944; s. Bed Prakash L.; m. Mridula, 1971; 2 children. B.Com., Tribhubam U., Kathmandu, Nepal; M.B.A. in Fin., Ind. U.; Ph.D., UCLA. Mem. Nat. Legislature, Kingdom of Nepal, Kathmandu, 1971-75, 81, Nat. Devel. Council, Kathmandu; fin. minister His Majesty's Govt. of Nepal, from 1983, now minister of housing and phys. planning; vis. prof. CEDA. Author books and monographs, also articles in nat. and internat. profl. jours. Fulbright scholar, U.S.A., 1962-64. Home: Prakash Kunj, Gyaneswar, Kathmandu Nepal Office: Ministry of Housing, Kathmandu Nepal *

LOISANCE, DANIEL YVES, cardiologist; b. Rennes, France, Apr. 13, 1945; s. Yves R. and Renée (Allain) L.; m. Elizabeth Forgeois, Mar. 4, 1967; children: Charlotte, William. MD, U. Paris, France, 1971. Intern Pub. Assistance, Paris, 1967-71; research assoc. Yale U., New Haven, 1971-72; head of clin. Henri Mondor's Hosp., Créteil, 1972-81, surgeon, 1981—; prof. U. Paris, 1981—; dir. Surg. Research CNRS, Créteil, 1981—; Gov. ESAO, Geneva, 1981-86. Contbr. articles to profl. jours. Mem. European Soc. Surg. Research (delegate), Congress Artificial Organs (pres. 1986). Served as lt. French Army, 1967-68. Home: 14 rue St Gothard, 75014 Paris France Office: Henri Mondor Hosp, 94000 Creteil France

LOK, SILMOND RAY, pharmaceutical executive; b. Columbus, Ohio, Dec. 14, 1948; s. Fee and Oilene (Yee) L.; m. Thresa Carlene Dale, Aug. 27, 1978. BS in Pharmacy, Ohio State U., 1973; MBA, Capital U., 1982. Registered pharmacist. Pharmacist, Federated Stores, Columbus, Ohio, 1975-82; pharm. salesman Ives Labs., Columbus, 1982, Squibb, Columbus, 1982-85; dir. pharmacy services Wendt-Bristol Co., 1985—. Mem. Grove City Civic Assn. Served to 1st lt. USAF, 1973-75. Mem. Cen. Ohio Acad. Pharmacy, Sigma Phi Epsilon, Kappa Psi (grand regent grad. chpt. 1973-75). Avocation: Kenpo karate (black belt, 1st degree). Home: 2591 McDonald Ct Grove City OH 43123

LOKHAUG, KARIN ELISE, operations administrator; b. Oslo, Dec. 18, 1943; d. Thomas Kaurin and Ruth (Larsen) Holmgrunn; m. Knut O. Lokhaug, July 6, 1963; 1 dau., Elizabeth. B.A., Bank Acad., Oslo, 1971. Asst., Christiania Bank, Oslo, 1962-70, mgr., 1970-73; mgr. Bergen Bank, Oslo, 1973-78; asst. v.p. Kjobmands Banken, Oslo, 1978-79; asst. v.p. Christiania Bank, Sandvika, Baerum, 1979-82; sr. v.p., Oslo, 1982-85; comptroller UNICEF, N.Y.C., 1985-87, dep. dir. ops., 1987—; dir. Store Norske, Spitsbergen Kulkompani, Longyearbyen, Svalbard, 1982-85, ETCI, Bruxelles, Belgium, 1983-85, Handverks-og Smaindustrifondet, Oslo, 1983-85; pres. Berum, Handelstands Forening, 1982-84. Mem. city council group Conservative party, Oslo, 1984. Mem. Bankokonounsk Forening, Polyteknisk Forening. Office: UNICEF 3 UN Plaza New York NY 10017

LOLLAR, ROBERT MILLER, industrial management executive; b. Lebanon, Ohio, May 17, 1915; s. Harry David and Ruby (Miller) L.; Chem E., U. Cin., 1937, M.S., 1938, Ph.D., 1940; m. Dorothy Marie Williams, Jan. 1, 1941; children—Janet Ruth (Mrs. David Schwarz), Katherine Louise (Mrs. James Punteney, Jr.). Cereal analyst Kroger Food Found., Cin., 1935-37; devel. chemist Rit Product div. Corn Products, Indpls., 1937-39, 40-41; asso. prof. U. Cin., 1941-59; tech. dir. Armour & Co., Chgo., 1959-73; mgmt. and tech. cons., pres. Lollar and Assocs., 1973—; tech. dir. Leather Industries Am., Cin., 1975-86, cons., 1986—. Dir. OSRD, 1942-45. Recipient Alsop award Am. Leather Chemists Assn., 1954, Fraser Muir Moffat medal Leather Industries Am., 1986. Mem. Am. Leather Chemists Assn. (pres., editor-in-chief), Inst. Food Technologists, Am. Chem. Soc. (nat. councillor), Am. Soc. Quality Control, World Mariculture Soc., Sigma Xi, Tau Beta Pi, Alpha Chi Sigma. Address: 5960 Donjoy Dr Cincinnati OH 45242

LOLLI, DON R(AY), lawyer; b. Macon, Mo., Aug. 9, 1949; s. Tony and Erma Naomi (Gerlich) L.; m. Deborah Jo Mrosek, May 29, 1976; children: Christina Terese, Joanna Elyse, Anthony Justin. BA in Econs., U. Mo., 1971, JD, 1974. Bar: Mo. 1974, U.S. Dist. Ct. (we. dist.) Mo. 1974, U.S. Ct. Appeals (8th cir.) 1976, U.S. Ct. Appeals (10th cir.) 1979, U.S. Supreme Ct. 1979, U.S. Tax Ct. 1981. Assoc. Beckett & Steinkamp, Kansas City, Mo., 1974-79, ptnr., 1980—; lectr. continuing legal edn. seminar U. Mo. Sch. Law, Kansas City, 1984. Mem. ABA, Mo. Bar Assn., Kansas City Bar Assn., Lawyers Assn. Kansas City, U. Mo. Alumni Assn., Beta Theta Pi Alumni, Phi Delta Phi (pres. Tiedman Inn 1973-74, Merit cert. 1974). Roman Catholic. Club: Kansas City (Mo.). Home: 633 W 62d St Kansas City MO 64113 Office: Beckett & Steinkamp PO Box 13425 Kansas City MO 64199

LOLLOBRIGIDA, GINA, actress; b. Sibiaco, Italy, July 4, 1927; d. Giovanni and Giuseppina Mercuri; m. Milko Skofic, 1949; 1 son. Ed. Liceo Artistico, Rome. Film debut in Pagliacci, 1947; since appeared in numerous films, including: Campane a Martello, 1948; Cuori senza Frontiere, 1949; Achtung, banditi!, 1951; Enrico Caruso, 1951; Fanfan la Tulipe, 1951; Altri Tempi, 1952; The Wayward Wife, 1952; Les belles de la nuit, 1952, Pane, amore e fantasia, 1953; La Provinciale, 1953; Pane, amore e gelosia, La Romana, 1954; Il Grande Gioco, 1954; La Donna più Bella del Mondo, 1955; Trapeze, 1956; Notre Dame de Paris, 1956; Solomon and Sheba, 1959; Never So Few, 1960; Go Naked in the World, 1961; She Got What She Asked For, 1963; Woman of Straw, 1964; Le Bambole, 1965; Hotel Paradiso, 1966; Buona Sera Mrs. Campbell, 1968; King, Queen, Knave, 1972. Author, photographer: Italia Mia, 1974, The Philippines. Address: Via Appia Antica 223, I-00178 Rome Italy *

LOMAS, BERNARD TAGG, college chancellor; b. Mackinaw City, Mich., Aug. 14, 1924; s. Percy L. and Eva (Tagg) L.; m. Barbara Jean West, June 21, 1947; children: Paul Neil, David Mark. AB, Albion Coll., 1946, DD, 1965; BD, Oberlin Grad. Sch. Theology, 1948; MDiv., Vanderbilt U., 1967; LLD, Adrian U., 1983. Ordained minister Meth. Ch., 1948. Minister William St. Meth. Ch., Delaware, Ohio, 1950-54; counsellor to students Ohio Wesleyan U., 1950-54; sr. minister Trinity Meth. Ch., Portsmouth, Ohio, 1954-60; sr. minister heading staff of five ministers Epworth-Euclid Ch., Univ. Circle, Cleve., 1960-70; pres. Albion (Mich.) Coll., 1970-83, chancellor, 1983—; dir. City Bank & Trust Co., Albion and Jackson; cons. Am. Enterprise Inst., Washington, 1980-81. Author: Litanies for a Space Age, 1968, Worship Aids for a Space Age, 1969, Space Age Family Discussions, 1969, Roots and Wings for a Space Age, 1969, Look What They've Done To The Twenty-Third Psalm, 1970. Organizer, head Citizens Com. for Law Enforcement, Portsmouth, 1957-58; founding mem. pres. Christian Residences Found.; bd. dirs. Goodwill Industries Cleve.; trustee St. Lukes Hosp., Cleve.; bd. govs. Greater Mich. Found.; bd. dirs. Christian Children's Fund.; counselor Heritage Found., Washington, 1984—. Mem. Internat. Platform Assn. Clubs: Detroit Athletic, Economic (Detroit); City, Union (Cleve.) Lodges: Masons, Shriners, Rotary.

LOMAX, RICHARD EARL, land surveyor, state government official; b. Gratiot County, Mich., Jan. 25, 1936; s. Earl Bell and Lola Pearl (Sabin) L.; m. Linnie S. Sharp, Sept. 1957 (div.); children: Richard L., Rhonda L., Brian A., Robert E., John R.; m. Doye Juanita Rogers Pullano, Aug. 25, 1973. Student Chgo. Tech. Coll., 1954-55, Mich. State U., 1955-59, Lansing Community Coll., 1979-80. Registered land surveyor, Mich. Draftsman Dept. of Hwys., State of Mich., Lansing, 1954-61, plat examiner Dept. Auditor Gen., 1961-66, supr. plat sect. Dept. Treasury, 1966-70, mgr. subdiv. control Dept. Treasury, 1970-81, adminstr. subdiv. control and county zoning Dept. Commerce, 1981—; prin. Richard Lomax, Surveyor, Charlotte, Mich., 1973-76; mem. Ingham County Remonumentation and Survey Bd., Mich., 1977-81. Co-editor: Mich. Surveyor mag., 1983-85, editor, 1986—. Chmn. Charlotte City Planning Commn., 1976—, chmn. 1979—; Tri County Regional Planning Commn., Lansing, 1979—, chmn. 1988. Fellow Mich. Soc. Registered Land Surveyors (dir. 1976—, pres. 1985-86), Am. Congress on Survey and Mapping (chmn. Gt. Lakes council of affiliates 1982-84); rep. Mich. bd. of govs. Nat. Soc. Profl. Surveyors. Republican. Home: 243 S Sheldon St Charlotte MI 48813

LOMBARD, HERBERT WILLIAM, JR., lawyer; b. Eugene, Oreg., June 26, 1930; s. Herbert W. and Verna D. (Skade) L.; m. Rita Guard, July 10, 1980; children: Kurtis, Karen, Kristi, Erin, Tina. B.S. in Econs., U. Oreg., 1952, LL.B., 1957. Bar: Oreg. 1957, U.S. Dist. Ct. Oreg. 1957, U.S. Supreme Ct. 1975. Ptnr. Lombard, Lombard, Williams & Ackley, Cottage Grove, Oreg., 1957-69; gen. counsel Bohemia, Inc., Eugene, 1969-73; ptnr. Sahlstrom & Lombard, Eugene, 1973-77; ptnr. Lombard, Gardner, Honsowetz, Brewer & Schons, Eugene, 1977—. Served to 1st lt. USAF, 1952-54. Mem. ABA, Lane County Bar Assn. (past pres.), Oreg. State Bar (bd. govs., 1970-73), Oreg. Trial Lawyers Assn., Assn. Trial Lawyers Am., Oreg. Law Sch. Alumni Assn. (past pres.), Cottage Grove C. of C. (past dir., v.p.), Eugene Area C. of C. (past dir.). Republican. Clubs: Rotary Internat., Lions, Elks, Masons. Address: 1612 Russet Dr Eugene OR 97440 Office: Lombard Gardner Honsowetz Brewer & Schons 725 Country Club Rd PO Box 10332 Eugene OR 97440

LOMBARD, JACQUES-LOUIS, research engineer; b. Bellegarde, France, Aug. 4, 1950; s. Gilbert Pierre and Angeline Therese (Stragiotti) L. Master, Instn., Saclay, France, 1975; PhD, U. Aix-Marseille, 1978. Research engr. Centre d'etude sur l' Evaluation de la Protection dans le domaine Nucleaire, Fontenay, France, 1977—; cons. Internat. Atomic Energy Agy., Vienna, Austria, 1984, Internat. Commn. Radiol. Protection, 1985; lectr. Institut Nat. des Scis. et Techniques Nucleaires, Saclay, 1980, Commn. European Communities/Joint Research Ctr., Ispra, Italy, 1985. Home: 1 Allee des Rives de Bagatelle, 92250 Suresnes France Office: CEPN, PO Box 48, 92260 Fontenay France

LOMBARDI, DAVID ENNIS, JR., lawyer, lectr.; b. San Francisco, Mar. 5, 1940; s. David E. and Ruth Harriet (Harrison) L.; m. Suzanne C. Woodbury, June 20, 1970; children—Sara Ennis, Eric David. B.A., U. Calif.-Berkeley, 1962; postgrad. U. Florence (Italy), 1964; J.D., Yale U., 1966. Bar: Calif. 1966. John Woodman Ayer fellow at law U. Calif.-Berkeley, 1963; assoc. Brobeck, Phleger & Harrison, San Francisco, 1967-73; adj. prof. bus. law U. Md., NATO Hdqrs., Belgium and Italy, 1974-75; sr. atty. Crown Zellerbach Corp., San Francisco, 1975-76; sr. ptnr. Lombardi & Lombardi, San Francisco, 1976-83; sr. ptnr. Steinhart & Falconer, San Francisco, 1983—; lectr. bus. litigation Golden Gate U. Sch. Law 1979; dir. various bus. corps., mem. chancellor's com. for univ. affairs U. Calif. 1962-63; mem. alumni adv. com. U. Calif., 1968-69; trustee, Head Royce Sch., 1983-86, San Dominco Sch., 1986—; trustee Kentfield Schs. Found., 1985—. Mem. ABA, Calif. Bar Assn. (prin. referee Calif. State Bar Ct. 1977-86), San Francisco Bar Assn., Am. Soc. Internat. Law, Yale U. Law Sch. Alumni Assn. (v.p. No. Calif. 1982-84). Clubs: Pacific-Union (San Francisco), Olympic (San Francisco), Priory (Kentfield, Calif.). Home: 30 Hanken Dr Kentfield CA 94904 Office: 333 Market St 32d Floor San Francisco CA 94105

LOMBARDI, LUCA, composer, educator; b. Rome, Dec. 24, 1945; s. Franco and Jole (Tagliacozzo) L.; m. Irene Siebert, Sept., 1971; 1 child, Filippo. Degree in composition, Conservatorio G. Rossini, Pesaro, Italy, 1970; D in Lit., U. Rome, 1975. Prof. composition Conservatorio G. Rossini, 1973-78, Conservatorio G. Verdi, Milan, 1978—; artistic co-dir. Cantiere Internat. D'Arte, Montepulciano, Italy, 1983-86. Composer more than 40 compositions published; author: Conversazioni con Petrassi, 1980; co-author: Instrumentation in der Musik des XX, 1985; editor: Musica Della Rivoluzione (H. Eisler), 1978, Con Brecht (H. Eisler), 1978; co-editor: Musik im Übergang, 1977; mem. editorial bd. Musica/Realta, 1978. Office: Conservatorio G Verdi, Via Conservatorio 12, Milano 20122, Italy

LOMBARDO, DAVID ALBERT, writer, aviation consultant and educator; b. Chgo., Jan. 31, 1947; s. Ignace Palmeri and Diane Marion (Balducci) L. BS, U. Ill., 1974, MEd, 1977. Tchr. York Community High Sch.,

Elmhurst, Ill., 1974-75; instr. Coll. Edn., U. Ill., Urbana, 1975-77, asst. dir. career devel. and placement, 1977-79; with Accelerated Ground Schs., Urbana, 1978-81, dir. nat. flight inst. refresher clinics; pres. Flying Illini, Inc., Savoy, Ill., 1972-80; curriculum devel. cons. LEAP, 1975-79, CFI Programs, 1979-82; dir. program devel. Airmanship, Inc., Rockford, Ill., 1981-82; gen. aviation cons. Lombardo & Assocs., 1981-82, tech. writer, gen. aviation cons., 1982—; asst. prof. profl. aviation La. Tech. U., Ruston, 1982-85; instr. Flight Safety Internat., 1980-81; dir. tng. Frasca Internat., 1985—; chief instr. Greater St. Louis Flight Instrs. Assn., 1980-81; accident prevention counselor FAA, 1980—. Author: Aircraft Systems: Understanding Your Airplane, 1988 contbg. editor Pvt. Pilot Mag., 1984—; contbr. articles to profl. jours. Bd. dirs. Ruston community Theater, 1983-85; founder, bd. dirs. Hill Country Arts Council, 1983-85. Served with AUS, 1966-69, Vietnam. Decorated Vietnamese Gallantry Cross; recipient Flying Col. award Delta Air Lines, 1978, Ark. Traveler award Gov. of Ark., 1978, Flight Inst. Proficiency award Phases I, II, III, IV, FAA, 1980, Plaque of Appreciation, Greater St. Louis Flight Instrs. Assn., 1981, Excellence award La. Tech. U., 1984. Recipient Teaching Excellence award La. Tech U., 1984, numerous other awards for contbns. to field. Mem. Aircraft Owners and Pilot's Assn., Univ. Aviation Assn. (pubs. com. 1985—, chmn. simulation com., 1987—), Aviation Space Writers, Assn. of Aviation Psychologists, Human Factors Soc., Alpha Eta Rho (advisor 1983-85), Chi Gamma Iota, Phi Delta Kappa. Republican. Roman Catholic. Home: PO Box 6028 Champaign IL 61821-8028 Office: Frasca Internat 606 S Neil St Champaign IL 61820

LOMBARDO, MICHAEL JOHN, state assistant attorney general, educator; b. Willimantic, Conn., Mar. 25, 1927; s. Frank Paul and Mary Margaret (Longo) L.; children: Nancy C., Claire M. BS, U. Conn., 1951, MS, 1961, JD, 1973.Bar: Conn. 1974, U.S. Dist. Ct. Conn. 1975, U.S. Supreme Ct. 1979, U.S. Ct. Appeals (2d cir.) 1980. Div. controller Jones & Laughlin Steel Corp., Willimantic, 1956-67; adminstrv. officer health ctr. U. Conn., Hartford, 1968-69; dir. adminstrv. services South Central Community Coll., New Haven, 1969-70; asst. dir. adminstrn. Norwich (Conn.) Hosp., 1970-77; asst. atty. gen. State of Conn., Hartford, 1977—; adj. asst. prof. U. Hartford, 1961-70; adj. prof. bus. Old Dominion U., 1973-81; adj. lectr. in law and bus. Ea. Conn. State U., 1973—. Vol. Windham Ctr. (Conn.) Fire Dept. Served to sgt. U.S. Army, 1945-46, to 1st lt. USAF, 1951-53, ret. 1987, to col. USAFR 1953-87. Mem. The Retired Officers Assn., Conn. Bar Assn., Windham County Bar Assn., Mensa Internat., Am. Legion, VFW. Lodge: Lions (bd. dirs. Willimantic chpt. 1960-64). Home: 35 Oakwood Dr Windham CT 06280 Office: 30 Trinity St Hartford CT 06106

LOMNICKI, TADEUSZ JAN, actor, stage manager, educator; b. Podhajce, Poland, July 18, 1927; s. Marian and Jadwiga (Kleinberger) L.; children: Jacek, Piotr; m. Maria Krystyna Bojarska, Feb. 29, 1984. Qualified actor Stary Teatr: Studio Teatralne, Cracow, Poland, 1947; cert. stage mgr. Panstwowa Wyzsza Szkola Teatralna, Warsaw, 1977. Actor, Stary Teatr, Cracow, 1945, Teatr Wyspianskiego, Katowice, 1946-47; actor, stage mgr. Teatr Wspolczesny and Teatr Narodowy, Warsaw, 1949-73; actor, stage mgr., dir. Teatr na Woli, Warsaw, 1975-81; actor, stage mgr. Teatr Polski, Warsaw, 1981-84, Teatr Studio, Warsaw, 1984—, Transform Theater, West Berlin, 1986—; rector Panstwowa Wyzsza Szkola Teatralna, Warsaw, 1969-81. Appeared in films including Generation, 1955, Eroica, 1958, Pan Wolodyjowski, 1969, Man of Marble, 1976, Hands Up, 1981, The Devils; stage roles include Our Town, 1957, Music Hall, 1958, Macbeth, Arturo Ui, 1962, Zoo Story, 1962, Play Strindberg, 1970, Lear, 1974, Bed-Bug, Amadeus, 1981, Affabulazione, 1984, Architruc, Krapp's Last Tape, 1985, Endgame, 1986, Operetta, 1987, I, Feuerbach, 1988; author plays including: Noah and His Menagerie, 1948; (book) Theatrical Meetings; also essays. Mem. Polish Workers United Party, 1951-81, mem. central com., 1973-81. Recipient State prize, Warsaw, 1955, 68, 78; Minister of Culture's award, 1963, 73; Golden prize for Best Male Actor, Internat. Film Festival, Moscow, 1969; Golden Mask for Best Polish Actor, Jour. Express readers' poll, Warsaw, 1970, Solidarity Cultural prize. Roman Catholic. Address: Piwna 21/23 M 2, 00-625 Warsaw Poland

LOMNITZ, CLAUDIO WALTER, anthropology educator; b. Santiago, Chile, June 2, 1957; arrived in Mex., 1968; s. Cinna and Larissa (Adler) L.; m. Elena Climent, Oct. 24, 1982; children: Enrique, Elisa. Lic., U. Met. Mexico City, 1978; MA, Stanford U., 1980, PhD, 1987. Dir. research Mexico City Ministry Edn., 1982-83; assoc. prof. anthropology U. Autonoma Met., Mexico City, 1983-85; assoc. prof. Coll. Mex., Mexico City, 1986—; acad. coordinator Ctr. Study Sociology, 1987—; assoc. prof. N.Y. U., 1988—. Author: Evolucion de una sociedad rural, 1982; contbr. articles to profl. publs. Mem. Am. Anthrop. Assn., Coll. Anthropology and Ethnology. Jewish. Office: Coll Mexico, Camino al Ajusco 20, 01000 Mexico City Mexico

LOMNITZ-ADLER, JORGE SIMON, physicist, researcher; b. Tel Aviv, Mar. 23, 1954; s. Cinna and Larissa (Adler) Lomnitz; m. Gale Lynn, June 28, 1962; children: Michael, Jason. MSc, Nat. Poly Inst., Mexico City, 1975; DPhil, U. Oxford, 1978. Research assoc. U. Ill., Urbana, 1978-80; researcher inst. physics U. Nacional Autonoma Mex., 1981—. Contbr. articles to sci. jours. Mem. Soc. Mexicana Fisica. Home: Iglesia 2 Torre D-504, Colonia Tizapan de San Angel, 01090 Mexico City Mexico Office: U Nacional Autonoma Mexico, Inst Physics, Apartado Postal 20-364, 01000 Mexico City Mexico

LONDON, CHARLOTTE ISABELLA, reading specialist; b. Guyana, S.Am., June 11, 1946; came to U.S., 1966, naturalized, 1980; d. Samuel Alphonso and Diana Dallett (Daniels) Edwards; m. David Timothy London, May 26, 1968 (div. May 1983); children: David Tshombe, Douglas Tshaka. BS, Fort Hays State U., 1971; MS, Pa. State U., 1974, PhD, 1977. Elem. sch. tch., Guyana, 1962-66, secondary sch. tchr., 1971-72; instr. lang. arts Pa. State U., University Park, 1973-74; reading specialist/ednl. cons. N.Y.C. Community Coll., 1975; dir. skills acquisition and devel. center Stockton (N.J.) State Coll., 1975-77; reading specialist Pleasantville (N.J.) Public Schs., 1977—; ind. specialist United Nations Devel. Programme , Guyana, 1988—; v.p. Atlantic County PTA, 1980-82; del. N.J. Gov.'s Conf. Future Edn. N.J., 1981. Sec. Atlantic County Minority Polit. Women's Caucus. Mem. Internat. Reading Assn., Nat. Council Tchrs. English, Assn. Supervision and Curriculum Devel., NEA, N.J. Ednl. Assn., AAUW, Pi Lambda Theta, Phi Delta Kappa (sec.). Mem. African Methodist Episcopal Ch. Home: 1419 Cedar Dr Mays Landing NJ 08330 Office: Pleasantville Pub Schs W Decatur Ave Pleasantville NJ 08232

LONDON, RAY WILLIAM, clinical, consulting and medical psychologist, researcher; b. Burley, Idaho, May 29, 1943; s. Loo Richard and Maycelle Jerry (Moore) L. A.S., Weber State Coll., 1965, B.Sc., 1967; M.S.W., U. So. Calif., 1973, Ph.D., 1976, Exec. MBA, 1987-88. Diplomate: Am. Bd. Psychol. Hypnosis (dir. 1984—), Am. Acad. Behavioral Medicine, Am. Bd. Psychotherapy, Am. Bd. Med. Psychotherapy, Internat. Acad. Medicine and Psychology., Am. Bd. Profl. Neuropsychology, Am. Bd. Family Psychology, Clin. Soc. Work; cert. Am. Assn. Sex Therapists, Soc. Med. Hypnosis. Congl. asst. U.S. Ho. of Reps., 1964-65; research assoc. Bus. Advs., Inc., Ogden, Utah, 1965-67; dir. counseling and consultation services Meaning Found., Riverside, Calif., 1966-69; mental health and mental retardation liaison San Bernardino County (Calif.) Social Services, 1968-72; clin. trainee VA Outpatient Clinic, Los Angeles, 1971-72, Children's Hosp., 1972-73, clin. fellow, 1973-74; clin. trainee Reiss Davis Child Study Ctr., Los Angeles, 1973-74, Los Angeles County-U. So. Calif. Med. Center, 1973; psychotherapist Benjamin Rush Neuropsychiat. Ctr., Orange, Calif., 1973-75; clin. psychology postdoctoral intern Orange County (Calif.) Mental Health, 1976-77; postdoctoral fellow U. Calif.-Irvine-Calif. Coll. Medicine, 1978; clin. psychologist Orange Police Dept., 1974-80; pvt. practice consultation and assessment, Santa Ana, Calif., 1974—; cons. to public schs., agys., hosps., bus., nationally and internationally, 1973—; pres. bd. govs. Human Factor Programs, Ltd., 1976—; pres. Internat. Bd. Medicine and Psychology, 1980—; chief exec. officer Human Studies Ctr., 1987—, London Assocs. Internat., Organizational Behavior-Crisis-Devel. Cons., 1987—; research affil. Ctr. for Crisis Mgmt. U. So. Calif. Grad. Sch. Bus. Adminstrn., 1988—; mem. faculty UCLA, U. So. Calif., Calif. State U., U. Calif., Irvine, Calif. Coll. Medicine, Internat. Cong. of Hypnosis and Psychosomatic Medicine, Soc. Clin. and Exptl. Hypnosis, Internat. Coll.; research assoc. Nat. Commn. for Protection of Human Subjects of Biomed. and Behavioral Research, 1976; fellow Inst. for Social Scientists on Neurobiology and Mental Illness, 1978. Editor: Internat. Bull. Medicine and Psychology, 1980, A.B.C.D. Report, 1988 behavioral medicine Australian Jour., 1980, adv. editor Internat. Jour. Clin. and Exptl. Hypnosis, 1981; cons. editor Internat. Jour. Psychosomatics, 1984; Experimentelle und Klinische Hypnose, 1987, cons. Am. Jour. Forensic Psychology, 1986; pub.: London Behavioral Medicine Assessment, 1982; producer: TV series Being Human, 1980; contbg. author World Book Ency. and books; contbr. articles to profl. jours. Recipient Congl. recognition U.S. Ho. of Reps., 1978; named scholar laureate Erickson Advanced Inst., 1980. Fellow Internat. Acad. Medicine and Psychology (dir. 1981—), Soc. Clin. Social Work (dir. 1979-80), Royal Soc. Health, Am. Coll. Forensic Psychology, Soc. Clin and Experimental Hypnosis (bd. dirs. 1985—, treas. 1987—); mem. Acad. Mgmt., Acad. Psychosomatic Medicine, Am. Psychol. Assn., Am. Group Psychotherapy Assn., Am. Orthopsychiat. Assn., Assn. Profl. Cons., Internat. Soc. Hypnosis, N.Y. Acad. Sci., Soc. Behavioral Medicine, Internat. Psychosomatic Inst., Australian Coll. Pvt. Clin. Psychologists, Australian Psychol. Soc., Phi Delta Kappa, Delta Sigma Rho, Tau Kappa Alpha, Pi Rho Phi, Lambda Iota Tau. Club: Toastmasters. Home and Office: 1125 E 17th St Suite E-209 Santa Ana CA 92701

LONE, HARRY EDWIN, waterproofing company executive, vehicle leasing company executive; b. Council Bluffs, Iowa, Oct. 20, 1923; s. Harry Edwin and Lula (Wakefield) L.; m. Wanda Lu Selindh, Mar. 16, 1946; children—Stanley Craig, Allen Eugene, Gregory Lynn, Janet Elaine Lone Davis. Student Princeton U., 1945, DePauw Coll., Greencastle, Ind., 1945-46, Purdue U., Lafayette, Ind., 1946. Motor machinist apprentice Rock Island R.R., Des Moines, 1946-47; bakery sales Continental Bakery, Des Moines, 1947-49; dairy route sales A&E Dairy, Des Moines, 1949-52; route supr. Hilan Dairy, Ames, Iowa, 1953-60; route sales mgr. Borden Co., Marshalltown, Iowa, 1960-63; ter. mgr. Gen. Foods Corp., White Plains, N.Y., 1963-78; pres., chief exec. officer Central States Waterproofing, St. Louis, 1978—; pres. Gold Key Enterprises, Maryland Heights, Mo., 1982—, Lone Advt., Maryland Heights, 1982—. Mem. nat. and state elections com. Mo. Republican Com., 1983; mem. Rep. Nat. Com., Washington, 1983; mem. Rep. Senatorial Com., Washington, 1983. Recipient Pres.' Medal of Merit, Republican Presdl. Task Force, 1982. Mem. Nat. Assn. for Remodeling Industry, Nat. Fedn. Ind. Bus., Nat. Assn. Waterproofing, Homebuilders Assn. Kansas City. Club: U.S. Senatorial. Lodges: Eagles, Toastmasters. Home: 14864 Grassmere Ct Chesterfield MO 63017 Office: Cen States Waterproofing Mo Inc 13738 Rider Trail N Earth City MO 63045

LONERGAN, THOMAS FRANCIS, III, criminal justice consultant; b. Bklyn., July 28, 1941; s. Thomas Francis and Katherine Josephine (Roth) L.; B.A., Calif. State U., Long Beach, 1966, M.A., 1973; M.P.A., Pepperdine U., 1976; postgrad. U. So. Calif.; m. Irene L. Kaucher, Dec. 14, 1963; 1 son, Thomas F. Dep. sheriff Los Angeles County Sheriff's Dept., 1963-68; U.S. Govt. program analyst, 1968—; fgn. service officer USIA, Lima, Peru, 1970-71; dep. sheriff to lt. Los Angeles Sheriff's Office, 1971-76, aide lt. to div. chief, 1976-79; dir. Criminal Justice Cons., Downey, Calif., 1977—; cons. Public Adminstrv. Service, Chgo., 1972-75, Nat. Sheriff's Assn., 1978, 79; cons. Nat. Inst. Corrections, Washington, 1977—, coordinator jail ctr., 1981—; tchr. N. Calif. Regional Criminal Justice Acad., 1977-79; lectr. Nat. Corrections Acad., 1983—; spl. master, U.S. Dist. Ct. (no. dist.) Ohio, 1984-85, Santa Clara Superior Ct. (Calif.), 1983—, U.S. Dist. Ct. Ga., Atlanta, 1986—, U. S. Dist. Ct. (no. dist.) Calif., 1984—, U.S. Dist. Ct. (no. dist.) Idaho, 1986—; also ct. expert. Mem. Air Force Assn., U.S. Naval Inst., U.S. Strategic Inst., Nat. Jail Assn., Nat. Jail Mgrs. Assn., Nat. Sheriff's Assn., Am. Polit. Sci. Assn., Zeta Beta Tau. Democrat. Roman Catholic. Author: California-Past, Present & Future, 1968; Training-A Corrections Perspective, 1979; AIMS-Correctional Officer; Liability-A Correctional Perspective; Liability Law for Probation Administrators; Liability Reporter; Probation Liability Reporter; Study Guides.

LONG, ALFRED B., former oil co. exec., cons.; b. Galveston, Tex., Aug. 4, 1909; s. Jessie A. and Ada (Beckwith) L.; student S. Park Jr. Coll., 1928-29, Lamar State Coll. Tech., 1947-56, U. Tex., 1941; m. Sylvia V. Thomas, Oct. 29, 1932; 1 dau., Kathleen Sylvia (Mrs. E.A. Pearson, II). With Sun Oil Co., Beaumont, Tex., 1931-69, driller geophys. dept., surveyor engring. dept., engr. operating dept., engr. prodn. lab., 1931-59, regional supr., 1960-69, cons., 1969—. Mem. Jefferson County Program Planning Com., 1964; mem. tech. adv. group Oil Well Drilling Inst., Lamar U., Beaumont. Mem. Soc. Petroleum Engrs., Am. Petroleum Inst., Am. Assn. Petroleum Geologists, IEEE, Houston Geol. Soc., Gulf Coast Engring. and Sci. Soc. (treas. 1962-65), U.S. Power Squadron, Soc. Wireless Pioneers. Inventor various oil well devices. Office: PO Box 7266 Beaumont TX 77706

LONG, BERNARD ROBERT, electronics executive; b. Paris, Jan. 23, 1929; s. Bernard Eugene and Marie Jeanne (Bailleul) L.; B., Ecole des Hautes Etudes Commerciales, Paris, 1950; lic. en droit, Paris U., 1950; M.B.A. with high distinction, Harvard U., 1953; m. Simone Charlotte Lenoir, Jan. 24, 1957; children—Jean-Pierre, Jean-Christophe, Laurent. Asst. sales mgr. Le Pyrex, 1953-55; sales and devel. mgr. Sovirel, 1955-64; mng. dir. Sovcor Electronique, 1964-73; gen. mgr. Corning Electronics Europe, 1973-74; chmn. bd. Gedis, 1974-84; chmn. Reela S.A., 1975-77; cons., 1978-80; mng. dir. Jaeger Regulation S.A., France, 1980-85; mng. ptnr. Internat. Growth Cons., 1980—; mng. dir. Corocor S.A., 1986—. Mem. parish council Roman Catholic Ch. Served to ensign French Navy, 1950-51. Decorated chevalier Ordre National du Merite. Clubs: Automobile, French Naval Res., HBS of Paris. Home: 81 rue des Vallees, 91800 Brunoy France Office: 202 rue de Rivoli, 75001 Paris France

LONG, CHARLES FARRELL, insurance company executive; b. Charlottesville, Va., Nov. 19, 1933; s. Cicel Early and Ruth Elizabeth (Shifflett) L.; m. Ann Tilley, May 28, 1960; children—C. Farrell, Linda. C.L.U., The Am. Coll., 1972; also chartered fin. analyst. Founder, pres. Casualty Underwriters Inc., Charlottesville, 1959-72; founder, pres. Group Underwriters Inc., Charlottesville, 1959—; trustee P.A.I. Ins. Trust. Mem. Assay Commn. of U.S., 1975. Bd. dirs. Heart Assn.; mem. U. Va. Student Aid Found. Served with USN, 1954-58. Mem. Central Va. Estate Planning Council, Am. Soc. C.L.U.s, Central Va. C.L.U.s Assn. (dir.), Va. Press Assn., Va. Assn. Life Underwriters, Million Dollar Round Table. Club: Farmington Country. Creator Queen's medal for Queen Elizabeth, 1976. Home: 1400 W Leigh Dr Charlottesville VA 22901 Office: Madison Park Charlottesville VA 22901

LONG, ERNESTINE MARTHA JOULLIAN, educator; b. St. Louis, Nov. 14, 1906; d. Ernest Cameron and Alice (Joullian) Long; A.B., U. Wis., 1927; M.S., U. Chgo., 1932; Ph.D., St. Louis U., 1976; postgrad. Washington U., St. Louis, 1932-68, Eastman Sch. Music, 1956, (NSF fellow) So. Ill. U., 1969-70. Tchr. scis. pub. schs. Normandy dist., St. Louis, 1927-66, Red Bud, Ill., 1966-70, St. Louis, 1970-75; coordinator continuing edn. U. Mo., St. Louis, 1976-79; ednl. cons. Area IV, St. Louis Pub. Schs.; dir. Project Think, Mo. and Ill., 1976-88. Recipient Community Service award St. Louis Newspaper Guild, 1978-79. Mem. AAAS, Am. Physics Tchrs. Assn., Am. Personnel and Guidance Assn. (treas. St. Louis br. 1954), Am. Chem. Soc., Cen. Assn. Sch. Sci. Math. Tchrs. (chmn. chemistry sect.), Am. Soc. for Microbiology, LWV, St. Louis Symphony Soc. (women's div., docent), Am. Guild Organists, NEA, Nat. Sci. Tchrs. Assn. Home: 245 N Price Rd Ladue MO 63124

LONG, FRANK LESLIE, economist, educator; b. Linden, Demerara, Guyana, Jan. 5, 1945; s. Edwin and Irma (McGowan) L.; m. Zemenay Lakew, Sept. 9, 1981; 1 child, Fasiledes. MBA, U. P.R., 1971; postgrad. diploma, The Hague, 1972, M of Social Sci., 1974; MS, Oxford U., 1975; PhD, U. Basel, 1977; postdoctoral study Oxford U., Yale U. Economist, UN Conf. Trade and Devel., Geneva, 1975-77; vis. fellow Queen Elizabeth House, Oxford U., Eng., 1977-79, 81-82; dir. tech. policy Nat. Sci. Council Guyana, 1979-81; advisor Govt. of Guyana, 1979-81; vis. fellow Yale U., New Haven, Conn., 1982—, dir. Tech. and Devel. Project, 1982-83, Grad. Sch. for Social Scis., U. Guyana, 1985—; sr. advisor Internat. Ctr. for Pub. Enterprises, Yugoslavia, 1982; spl. advisor to sec. gen. African, Caribbean and Pacific Group of States, Secretariat, Brussels, 1983—; professorial fellow Inst. Devel. Studies, 1985—; spl. adviser to pres. Guyana, 1985—; mem. Internat. Expert Group on Pub. Enterprises, Internat. Expert Group on Small Enterprises and Indsl. Devel., OECD-UNIDO; cons. in field. Author: Ragnar Frisch, Planning Studies, 1972, Restrictive Business Practices, 1981, Economic Development in the Caribbean, 1983, Employment Effects of Multinational Enterprises in Export Processing Zones in the Caribbean, 1986; editor: The Political Economy of ACP-EEC, 1979; mem. editorial bd. Pub. Enterprises; contbr. numerous articles to profl. jours. Mem. Royal Econ. Soc., Soc. for Caribbean Studies, Wolfson Coll. (sr.). Clubs: Oxford Soc., Oxford Union, Oxford and Cambridge Univ. (Eng.). Home: 16 Dowding St, Georgetown, Kitty Guyana Office: Yale U Latin American Studies PO Box 1881 New Haven CT 06520

LONG, GERALD H., tobacco company executive; b. Mineola, N.Y., 1928. Grad., Adelphi U., 1952; postgrad., NYU, 1962. With R.J. Reynolds Tobacco Co., Winston-Salem, N.C., 1969—, exec. v.p., mem. exec. com., 1979-81, pres., chief operating officer, 1981-84; chmn., chief exec. officer R.J. Reynolds Tobacco USA, Winston-Salem, N.C., 1984—, also dir.; bd. dirs. RJR/Nabisco. Office: RJR Nabisco Inc PO Box 105642 Atlanta GA 30348 *

LONG, GILLES, academic administrator; b. Clair, N.B., Can., Feb. 27, 1940; s. Liguori and Léonie (Cyr) L.; m. Alda Lizotte, July 20, 1963; children: Guylaine, François, Daniel. BA, U. Saint-Louis, Edmunston, N.B., 1960; BEd, U. Saint-Jospeh, Moncton, N.B., 1961; M in Psychology, U. Moncton, 1968; cert., Ecole Internat. Bordeaux, France, 1979. Prof. U. Saint-Louis, 1961-66; guidance counsellor Coll. Saint-Louis, 1968-71, asst. dean studies, 1971-72; sec. gen. Coll. Saint-Louis-Maillet, Edmundston, 1972-79, U. Moncton, 1979—. Campaign dir. ARC, Madawaska County, N.B., 1974. Mem. Assn. Registrars Univs. and Colls. Can., Assn. Collegiate Registrars and Admissions Officers, Can. Soc. Study Higher Edn., Assn. des secrétaires généraux des établissements univs. Roman Catholic. Office: U de Moncton, Taillon Bldg, Moncton, NB Canada E1A 3E9

LONG, LINDA ANN, public affairs and government relations consultant; b. Durham, N.C., Feb. 8, 1952; d. Grover Cleveland and Ellen (Parnell) L. BA, U. Del., 1974; JD, Widener U., 1979. Lobbyist, Legis. Services, Inc., Dover, Del., 1977-79; campaign staff Connally for Pres., Arlington, Va., 1979-80; exec. dir. Reagan-Bush Com. Del., Wilmington, 1980; spl. asst. for legis. affairs Gov. Pierre S. duPont IV, Dover, Del., 1981; regional rep. pub. affairs Gulf Oil Corp., Phila., 1981-83; dir. GULFPAC, area dir. pub. affairs, Gulf Oil Corp., Pitts., 1983-85; pres. Long Cons. Inc., 1985—; comml. space transp. adv. com. U.S. Dept. Transp., 1988—; bd. dirs., exec. com. Air and Space Heritage Council, 1987—; loaned exec. pub. affairs dept. NASA, 1984-85. Mem. Rep. Bus. Council Del., 1982-83; cons., asst. to chmn. Rep. Nat. Com., 1986—; mem. Gov.'s Commn. Status of Women Speakers Bur., 1981-83; mem. Wright Meml. Dinner Com., 1985. Mem. Am. Petroleum Inst. (com. pub. relations 1981-84), U.S. Dept. Transp. Comml. Space Transp. adv. com., 1988—. Baptist. Club: Capitol Hill. Office: Long Cons Inc 1156 15th St NW Suite 550 Washington DC 20003

LONG, MARY COLE, retired English language educator, author; b. Dallas, Oct. 1, 1922; d. Ernest E. and Sadie Flynn (Boone) Farrow; B.A., Baylor U., 1944; M.A., 1965; m. William Bowman Long, June 3, 1944; children—William Farrow, Daryl Elizabeth, Robert John, Linda Sue. Instr. English. Mary Hardin-Baylor U., Belton, Tex., 1965-72, asst. prof. English, 1972-83; v.p. Bearttollow Pubs. Pres., Leon Heights PTA, 1956, City Council PTA, 1957. Author: Stranger in a Strange Land, 1986. Mem. Central Tex. Poetry Soc. (pres. 1972-77), Poetry Soc. Tex. Home: 415 Downing St Belton TX 76513

LONG, MARY LOUISE, retired government official; b. Macon, Ga., Aug. 25, 1922; d. Willie and Sarah (Sparks) Tyson; A.B., Morris Brown Coll., Atlanta, 1946; m. Samuel F. Long, Apr. 14, 1962. Supervisory procurement clk. Dept. Def., N.Y., 1954-62, purchasing agt. Phila. Procurement Dist., 1962-64, Army Electronic Command, Phila., 1964-66, Med. Directorate, Def. Personnel Support Center, Phila., 1966-75, contracting officer, 1975-80, sect. chief/contracting officer, 1980-83. Active NAACP, YMCA; established Mary Louise Tyson Long Scholarship Fund, Morris Brown Coll., 1986. Named Alumnus of Yr. Morris Brown Coll., 1987. Mem. Beta Omicron, Iota Phi Lambda. Congregationalist. Home: 617 E Mount Airy Ave Philadelphia PA 19119

LONG, NGO VAN, economics educator, researcher; b. Nov. 28, 1948; m. Kim Chau Pham-Thi, 1970; children: Chi, Bach. B of Econs., Latrob U., Melbourne, Australia, 1972; PhD in Econs., Australian Nat. U., Canberra, 1975. Lectr. in econs. Australian Nat. U., 1975-78, sr. lectr., 1979-82, reader in econs., 1983-85, prof., 1987—; research assoc. Harvard U., Cambridge, Mass., 1978, CORE, U. Louvain, Louvain-la-Neuve, Belgium, 1983; vis. prof. Mannheim (Fed. Republic Germany) U., 1982, Carleton U., Ottawa, Can., 1986; vis. fellow Kobe (Japan) U., 1986. Author: Exhaustible Resources, 1980, Essays in Resource Economics, 1984, Optimal Control Theory, 1987; contbr. articles to profl. jours. Recipient Univ. medal Latrobe U., 1972, Crawford prize Australian Nat. U., 1976; Fulbright fellow Australian-Am. Found., 1978, Von Humboldt Found. fellow, 1982. Mem. Australian Econs. Soc., Am. Econs. Assn., Econometrics Soc., European Econs. Soc. Office: Australian Nat U, Acton St 2601, Canberra ACT, Australia

LONG, ROLAND JOHN, secondary school principal; b. Chgo., Nov. 15, 1921; s. John and Lillian Catherine (Sigmund) L.; m. Valerie Ann Zawila, Nov. 13, 1954; children: Ronald J., Thomas E. BS, Ill. State Normal U., 1949, MA, Northwestern U., 1951; EdD, Ill. State U., 1972. Instr. of social sci. Ball State U., Muncie, Ind., 1951; comdt. Morgan Park Mil. Acad., Chgo., 1952-54; tchr. history Hyde Park and Amundsen high schs., Chgo., 1955-62; prin. Hubbard Elementary Sch., Chgo., 1962; founder, prin. Hubbard High Sch., Chgo., 1963-85; prin. Chgo. High Sch. for Met. Studies, 1985—; mem. doctoral adv. com. of Ill. State U., 1973-75; panelist Gen. Assembly State of Ill. Sponsored Conf. Ednl. Reform. Author: Dr. Long's Old-Fashioned Basic Report Card and Parent Helper, 1977. Mem. Chgo. Police Dist. 8 steering com., 1974-77; bd. dirs. West Communities YMCA, Chgo., Greater Lawn Mental Health Ctr., Chgo.; mem. Accademia Italia, 1983. Served to 1st lt., inf., U.S. Army, ETO. Decorated Silver Star, Purple Heart, Bronze Star; Ford Found. fellow, 1973; recipient Sch. Mgmt. citation Ill. Gen. Assembly, 1972, Medal of Honor Am. Biog. Inst., 1988. Fellow (hon.) Harry S. Truman Library Inst.,; mem. Ill. Assn. for Supervision and Curriculum Devel., Nat. Assn. of Secondary Sch. Prins., Am. Legion, Phi Delta Kappa (Educator of Yr. aw ard 1980), Pi Gamma Mu, Kappa Delta Pi. Club: Elks. Home: 6701 N Ionia Ave Chicago IL 60646 Office: 4950 N Avers Ave Chicago IL 60625

LONGAIR, MALCOLM SIM, astronomer, educator; b. May 18, 1941; s. James Sim and Lily (Malcolm) L.; m. Deborah Janet Howard, 1975; 2 children. B.Sc. in Electronic Physics, Queen's Coll., Dundee, U. St. Andrews, 1963; M.A., Cavendish Lab., U. Cambridge, Ph.D., 1967; LL.D. (hon.), U. Dundee, 1982. Research fellow Royal Commn. for Exhbn. of 1951, 1966-68; Royal Soc. exchange fellow to USSR, 1968-69; research fellow Clare Hall, Cambridge U., 1967-71, ofcl. fellow, 1971-80, univ. demonstrator in physics Cambridge U., 1970-75, univ. lectr. in physics, 1975-80; astronomer royal for Scotland, 1980—; Regius prof. astronomy U. Edinburgh (Scotland), 1980—; dir. Royal Obs., Edinburgh, 1980—; vis. prof. radio astronomy Calif. Inst. Tech., 1972; vis. prof. astronomy Inst. Advanced Study, Princeton, N.J., 1978; chmn. A II com. astronomy Space and Radio Bd. SRC, 1979-80; mem. Space Telescope Adv. Panel, 1977—; mem. com. European Space Agy. Astronomy Working Group, 1975-78, European Space Agy. Space Telescope Working Group, 1977—; NASA Space Telescope Sci. working Group, 1977—. Author: (with J. E. Gunn and M. J. Rees) Observational Cosmology, 1978; High Energy Astrophysics: an Informal Introduction, 1980; Theoretical Concepts in Physics, 1984; author numerous papers, pub. mainly in Monthly Notices of Royal Acad. Scis.; editor: Confrontation of Cosmological Theories with Observational Data, 1974; (with J. Einaso) The Large-Scale Structure of the Universe, 1978; (with J. Warner) The Scientific Uses of the Space Telescope, 1980; (with H.A. Bruck and G. Coyne) Astrophysical Cosmology, 1982. Recipient Britannica award, 1986. Office: care Royal Obs, Blackford Hill, Edinburgh EH9 3HJ, Scotland

LONGBINE, ROBERT FRANK, forest products company executive; b. Rochester, N.Y., Sept. 13, 1924; s. Edward C. and Loretta (Rudig) L.; m. Geraldine Haag, Aug. 30, 1946; children: Linda, Laurie, Karen, Ellen. BS in Mech. Engring., Rensselaer Poly. Inst., 1946. Mill supt. Westvaco, Covington, Va., 1956-63; asst. ops. mgr. Champion Internat. Corp., Pasadena, Tex., 1963-65; ops. mgr. Champion Internat. Corp., Canton, N.C., 1965-67; v.p. paper div. Champion Internat. Corp., Hamilton, Ohio, 1974-80; pres., chief operating officer Champion Internat. Corp., Stamford, Conn., 1980—. Trustee Rensselaer Poly. Inst.; dir. VF Corp. Served with USNR, 1943-46, 52-53. Office: Champion Internat Corp 1 Champion Plaza Stamford CT 06921 *

LONGEWAY, PAUL ALLEN, physical chemist; b. Washington, Jan. 31, 1947; s. Leroy I. and Mary C. (Stein) L. B.A., Messiah Coll., 1968; M.S., Shippensburg U., 1979; Ph.D., Pa. State U., 1982. High sch. chemistry tchr., 1969-76; mem. tech. staff David Sarnoff Research Ctr., Princeton, N.J., 1981—. Contbr. articles to profl. jours. Patentee in field. Karate instr. Nat. Am. TaeKwonDo Assn., 1984—. Mem. IEEE, Am. Chem. Soc., Mensa. Democrat. Lodge: Masons. Current work: Vapo phase epitaxial growth of III-V compounds for use in semiconductors; chemistry of silanes; deposition of amorphous Si:H; plasma kinetics; semiconductor properties of III-V materials. Subspecialties: Solid state chemistry; Physical chemistry.

LONGHOFER, RONALD STEPHEN, lawyer; b. Junction City, Kans., Aug. 30, 1946; s. Oscar William and Anna Mathilda (Krause) L.; m. Martha Ellen Dennis, July 9, 1981; children: Adam, Nathan, Stefanie. B.Music, U. Mich., 1968; J.D., 1975. Bar: Mich. 1975, U.S. Dist. Ct. (ea. dist.) Mich., U.S. Ct. Appeals (6th cir.), U.S. Supreme Ct. Law clk. to judge U.S. Dist. Ct. (ea. dist.) Mich., Detroit, 1975-76; ptnr. firm Honigman, Miller, Schwartz & Cohn, Detroit, 1976—. Editor Mich. Law Rev., 1974-75. Served with U.S. Army, 1968-72. Mem. ABA, Detroit Bar Assn., Fed. Bar Assn., Order of Coif, Phi Beta Kappa, Phi Kappa Phi, Pi Kappa Lambda. Clubs: Detroit Econ., U. Mich. Pres's. Home: 3901 Six Mile Rd S Lyon MI 48178 Office: Honigman Miller Schwartz & Cohn 2290 1st National Bldg Detroit MI 48226

LONGLEY, BERNIQUE, painter, sculptor; b. Moline, Ill., Sept. 27, 1923; d. Eli James and Effie Marie (Coen) Wilderson; 1 child, Bernique Maria Glidden. Grad., Art Inst. Chgo., 1945. One-woman shows, Mus. N.Mex., 1947, 50, 52, Appleman Gallery, Denver, 1950, VanDieman-Lillienfield Galleries, N.Y.C., 1953, Knopp-Hunter Gallery, Santa Fe, 1954, 57, 58, Gallery Five, Santa Fe, 1964, 65, Coll. Santa Fe, 1967, Sanger-Harris, Dallas, 1968, Lars Laine Gallery, Palm Springs, Calif., 1969, Canyon Rd. Gallery, Santa Fe, 1972, Summer Gallery, Santa Fe, 1973, 74, 75, 76, Cushing Galleries, Dallas, 1977, Gov.'s Gallery, N.Mex. State Capitol, 1978, Santa Fe East, Austin, Tex., 1979, Santa Fe East Gallery, 1985, 86, 88, Leslie Levy Gallery, 1985-86; group shows include, Denver Art Mus., 1948, N.Mex. Highlands U., 1957, Lars Laine Gallery, 1961, 63, Santa Fe Festival of Arts, 1977, 78, 79, 80, Leslie Levy Gallery, Scottsdale, Ariz., 1985-86, Santa Fe East, 1985-86, Invitational Mask Exhbn., Bank of Santa Fe, 1987, many others, retrospective exhbn., Santa Fe East Gallery, 1982; represented in permanent collections, Mus. N.Mex., Fine Arts Center, Colorado Springs, Coll. Santa Fe, Coll. of Oprah Winfrey, 1987, other pvt. collections.; subject of book Bernique Longley-A Retrospective, 1982. Bryan Lathrop Fgn. Travelling fellow, 1945. Mem. Art Inst. Chgo. Alumni Assn., Artists Equity Assn. Home and. Home and Studio: 427 Camino del Monte Sol Santa Fe NM 87501

LONGLEY, DAVID ANTHONY, historian; b. London, Mar. 15, 1938; s. Harold Henry and Patricia Elisabeth (Condry) L.; m. Helen Celia Brief, Oct. 24, 1964 (div. Apr. 1984); children: Sean, Adam; m. Jean Dorothy MacNicoll, Aug. 30, 1985; stepchildren: Nicholas, Simon. BA, Magdalen Coll., Oxford, Eng., 1961; grad., Inst. Edn. U. London, 1962; PhD, U. Birmingham, Eng., 1978; MA (hon.), Magdalen Coll., Oxford, Eng., 1976. Lectr. Brixton Coll., London, 1967-69; teaching fellow history U. Birmingham, Eng., 1972-73; Brit. Council scholar U. Moscow, 1973-74; lectr. history King's Coll. U. Aberdeen, Scotland, 1974—; co-founder, chmn. Study Group on Russian Revolution, 1975-82. Contbr. numerous articles on Soviet Studies to scholarly jours. Served to lt. Brit. Army, 1956-58. Fellow Royal Hist. Soc. Anglican. Home: Culdrain House, Gartly AB5 4PY, Scotland Office: Univ of Aberdeen, Dept History, Aberdeen AB9 2UB, Scotland

LONGLEY, JAMES WILDON, mathematician, researcher; b. San Saba, Tex., Oct. 29, 1913; s. Leon and Emily Armenti (Patton) L.; m. Catherine C. Cook, 1936 (div. 1946); 1 child, Roger Wayne; m. Phoebe E. Romberger, 1949 (div. 1960). BA, Tex. Agrl. and Mech. U., 1936, MS, 1937; MA, Harvard U., 1946, PhD, 1947. Economist, numerical analyst Bur. Labor Stats., U.S. Dept. Labor, Washington, 1955-83; researcher in applied math. and stats., 1983—. Author: Least Squares Computations Using Orthogonalization Methods, 1984, also book in pure and applied math.; contbr. articles to profl. jours. Mem. Assn. for Computing Machinery, Am. Statis. Assn., Am. Math. Soc., Math. Assn. Am., Am. Soc. Quality Control, Soc. Indsl. and Applied Math., N.Y. Acad. Scis., Biometric Soc., AAAS. Republican. Methodist. Developer of Longley Problem used to measure accuracy of LS Programs. Home: 8200 Cedar St Silver Spring MD 20910

LONGOBARDI, GIUSEPPE, language educator; b. Rome, Aug. 20, 1955; s. Pompeo and Amelia (Turbacci) L.; m. Alessandra Giorgi, Mar. 23, 1985. Grad., U. Pisa, 1978; diploma, Sch. Normale Superiore, 1978. Postdoctoral fellow Sch. Normale Superiore, Pisa, Italy, 1979-81, asst. prof., 1981-87; assoc. prof. U. Venice, Italy, 1987—. Contbr. articles to profl. publs. Home: Via San Marino 21, 00198 Rome Italy Office: Seminario di Linguistica, Ca' Garzoni-Moro, S Marco 3417, 30124 Venice Italy

LONGOBARDI, PATRIZIA G., mathematics educator; b. Naples, Italy, Jan. 1, 1954; d. Ugo and Maria Rosaria (Capuozzo) L. Degree in math., U. Naples, Italy, 1976. Scholar Consiglio Nazionale delle Ricerche, Naples, 1976-82; researcher U. Naples, 1982-87, assoc. prof., 1987—. Mem. Unione Math. Italiana, Am. Math. Soc., London Math. Soc. Office: U Naples Dept Math, Via Mezzocannone 8, 80134 Naples Italy

LONGRIGG, PAUL, electrical research engineer, consultant; b. Eng., Apr. 27, 1927; came to U.S., 1966, naturalized, 1983; s. Sidney and Mabel Alice (Sibson) L.; m. Mary-Anne Holdar, Nov., 1966; B.Sc. with honors, U. Wales, 1950, Lanchester Tech. U., Eng., 1958. Chartered profl. engr., Eng. Radar design engr. Hawker-Siddeley Dynamics, Stevenage, Eng., Woomera, South Australia, 1958-66; sr. mfg. research engr. L.T.V. Aerospace Corp., Warren, Mich., 1967-69; research and devel. scientist Forney Engring. Co., Dallas, 1969-74; chief engr. Crompton-Ark. Mills, Morrilton, 1974-76; meteorologist N.Z. Meteorol. Service, Wellington, 1976-79; sr. research engr. Solar Energy Research Inst., Golden, Colo., 1980—; pres. Modus Tech. Cons. Inc., Dallas, Golden, Colo., 1973-85. Inventor coal combustion detection and laser systems. Tchr. Jr. Achievement, Warren, 1970, Adopt A Sch. Program, Denver, 1983; active Boy Scouts of Great Brit. Served to lt. Brit. Royal Navy, 1943-53. ETO, Korea. Recipient Energy Conservation award Brit. Petroleum, 1979. Fellow Brit. Interplanetary Soc.; sr. mem. IEEE (chmn. subcom. 1980-85, del. to Peoples Republic of China, 1983). Mem. Ch. of Eng. Club: Am. AX POW (Denver); Prestatyn Conservative Club.

LØNNING, PER, bishop; b. Bergen, Norway, Feb. 24, 1928; s. Per and Anna (Strømø) L.; m. Ingunn b.Bartz-Johannessen, Aug. 5, 1929; children: Per Eystein, Jan Tore, Ingunn Margrete, Dag Audun. Candidate theology, Free Theol. Faculty, Oslo, 1949; ThD, U. Oslo, Norway, 1955, PhD, 1959; LittD (hon.), St. Olaf Coll., Northfield, Minn., 1986. Asst. pastor Lilleborg Luth. Ch., Oslo, 1951-53; lectr. Oslo Tchr.'s Tng. Coll., 1954-64; dean Bergen Cathedral, Norway, 1964-69; bishop of Borg Fredikstad, Norway, 1969-75, resigned as bishop, 1975; prof. history Christian Thought U. Oslo, Denmark, 1976; research prof. Inst. Ecumenical Research, Strasbourg, France, 1981-87; bishop of Bergen Norway, 1987—; chmn. Norwegian Pastors' Assn., 1962-64; vis. prof. U. Aarhus, Denmark, 1976. Author: The Dilemma of Contemporary Theology, Off the Beaten Path, Pathways of the Passion, and 30 other books on theology, philosophy, and religious devotion, 1954—. Active Norwegian Parliament, Oslo, 1957-65; mem. Sch. Bd. Oslo, 1960-64; mem. Nat. Broadcasting Council, 1968-77. Recipient Pax Christi award St. John's U., Collegeville, Minn., 1975. Mem. Royal Norwegian Soc. Scis., Norwegian Acad. Scis. and Humanities. Home: Landaastien 78, N-5030 Bergen Norway

LONNQUIST, BIRGER, banker; b. Malmo, Sweden, Apr. 16, 1924; s. Carl and Elsa (Zimmer) L.; degree in social scis. U. Lund, 1949; m. Else Juhl, 1949; children—Birgitta, Lars. With Fgn. Exchange Control Office, 1949-50; mem. stats. and credit market depts. Central Bank Sweden, 1950-56; sec. to bd. SwedBank, 1956-60, dep. mng. dir., 1960-71, mng. dir., 1971-84, group chief exec. SwedBank Group, Stockholm, 1977—; dir. various cos. Decorated knight Royal Order Vasa; recipient Royal Medal. Home: 2 Solrosvagen, 181 61 Lidingo Sweden Office: 8 Brunkebergstorg, 105 34 Stockholm Sweden

LOO, RANDY S. W., marketing executive; b. Johor, Malaysia, Feb. 24, 1951. Grad. high sch., Johor. Advt. clk. New Straits Times, Kuala Lumpur, Malaysia, 1970-73; sales rep. Plessey Malaysia, Kuala Lumpur, 1973-75; tech. mktg. exec. Microdata Corp., Kuala Lumpur, 1975—. Mem. Inst. Reprographic Tech. (AMIRT award 1980), Soc. Photographic Scientists and Engrs., Internat. Micrographic Congress (Citation of Honor 1980), Jaycees Kuala Lumpur (founding pres. west region 1973, chmn. long-range planning com. 1987-88, internat. senator 1980), Mensa. Office: Microdata Corp, 21 Jalan Hujan Emas Lapan, Taman Overseas Union, Kuala Lumpur 58200, Malaysia

LOOMIS, HOWARD KREY, banker; b. Omaha, Apr. 9, 1927; s. Arthur L. and Genevieve (Krey) L.; AB, Cornell U., 1949, MBA, 1950; m. Florence Porter, Apr. 24, 1954; children—Arthur L. II, Frederick S., Howard Krey, John Porter. Mgmt. trainee Hallmark Cards, Inc., Kansas City, Mo., 1953-56; sec., controller, dir. Mine Service Co., Inc., Ft. Smith, Ark., 1956-59; controller, dir. Electra Mfg. Co., Independence, Kans., 1959-63; v.p., dir. The Peoples Bank, Pratt, Kans., 1963-65, pres., 1966—; pres., dir. Gt. Plains Leasing, Inc., Pratt, 1966-80, Central States Inc., Pratt, 1970-76, Krey Co. Ltd., Pratt, 1978—; dir. Garland Coal & Mining Co., Ft. Smith, All Ins., Inc., Pratt, Kans. Devel. Credit Corp., Topeka, Fed. Res. Bank of Kansas City. Past pres. Pratt County United Fund; bd. dirs., past chmn. Cannonball Trail chpt. ARC; past pres. Kanza council Boy Scouts Am. Served with AUS, 1950-52. Mem. Kans. (past transp. chmn., v.p., dir.), Pratt Area (past pres., dir.) chambers commerce, Financial Execs. Inst., Kans. Bankers Assn. (past dir.), Sigma Delta Chi, Chi Psi. Republican. Presbyterian. Club: Park Hills Country (past pres.). Lodges: Elks, Rotary. Home: 502 Welton St Pratt KS 67124 Office: The Peoples Bank 222 S Main St Pratt KS 67124

LOOMIS, JACQUELINE CHALMERS, photographer; b. Hong Kong, Mar. 9, 1930 (parents Am. citizens); d. Earl John and Jennie Bell (Sherwood) Chalmers; m. Charles Judson Williams III, Dec. 2, 1950 (div. Aug. 1973); children: Charles Judson IV, John C., David F., Robert W.; m. Henry Loomis, Jan. 19, 1974; stepchildren: Henry S., Mary Loomis Hankinson, Lucy F., Gordon M. Student, U. Oreg., 1948-50, Nat. Geog. Soc., 1978-79, Winona Sch. Profl. Photography, 1979, Sch. Photo Journalism, U. Mo., 1979. Pres. J. Sherwood Chalmers Photographer, Jacksonville, Fla., 1979—; pres. Windward Corp., Washington, 1984—. Contbr. photos to Nat. Geog. books and mag., Fortune mag., Ducks Unltd., Living Bird Quar., Orvis News, Frontiers Internat., others, also calendars; one-woman show Woodbury-Blair Mansion, Washington, 1980; rep. in pub. and pvt. collections. Trustee Sta.-WJCT-TV, Jacksonville, Fla., 1965-73, mem. exec. com., chmn., 1965-66; co-chmn. Arts Festival, Jacksonville, 1970, chmn., 1971; bd. dirs., mem. exec. com. Nat. Friends Pub. Broadcasting, N.Y.C., 1970-73; bd. dirs. Washington Opera, 1976—, Pub. Broadcasting Service, Washington, 1972-73, Planned Parenthood of North Fla., 1968-70; bd. dirs. Jacksonville Art Mus., 1968-70, treas., 1968; bd. dirs. Jacksonville Symphony Assn., 1988—. Recipient Cultural Arts award Jacksonville Council Arts, 1971, award Easton Waterfowl Festival, 1982, 1st and 2d prizes, 1984. Mem. Profl. Photographers Am. (Merit award 1982), Photog. Soc. Am., Am. Soc. Picture Profls., Jr. League Jacksonville Inc. Republican. Presbyterian. Clubs: Fla. Yacht (Jacksonville); Amelia Island Plantation (Fla.); Ctr. Harbour Yacht (Brooklin, Maine). Avocations: travel, golf, sailing, skiing, riding. Home and Office: 4141 Ortega Blvd Jacksonville FL 32210

LOOMIS, JOHN NORMAN, psychiatrist; b. Dallas, Aug. 9, 1933; s. Glenn LaVerne and Maria Jeanette (Doyle) L.; B.A., Rice U., 1954; M.D., Cornell U., 1958. Intern Meth. Hosp., Bklyn., 1958-59; resident Westchester div. N.Y. Hosp., White Plains, N.Y., 1959-62; practice medicine specializing in psychiatry, N.Y.C., 1962-78; asst. attending staff N.Y. Hosp., 1972-80; asst. prof. Cornell U. Med. Coll., 1972-80; dir. Loomis Internat. Inc., oil field service co., Houston, 1964—, v.p., 1970-75, chmn. bd., 1975—. Bd. dirs. Madison Square Boys' and Girls' Club, N.Y.C., 1965—, The Hudson Rev., N.Y.C., 1983—. Mem. Am. Psychiat. Assn., N.Y. Acad. Scis., Phi Beta Kappa. Clubs: Knickerbocker (N.Y.C.); St. Anthony (San Antonio). Office: PO Box 6408 Pasadena TX 77502

LOONEY, RALPH EDWIN, newspaper editor; b. Lexington, Ky., June 22, 1924; s. Arville Zone and Connie Elizabeth (Boyd) L.; m. Clarabel Richards, Dec. 7, 1944. B.A., U. Ky., 1948. Successively proof reader, photographer, chief photographer, sports writer, reporter Lexington Leader, 1943-52; reporter Albuquerque Tribune, 1953-54; reporter, copy editor, chief copy editor St. Louis Globe-Democrat, 1955-56; city editor Albuquerque Tribune, 1956-68, asst. mng. editor, 1968-73, editor, 1973-80; editor Rocky Mountain News, Denver, 1980—. Author: Haunted Highways, the Ghost Towns of New Mexico, 1969; contbr.: articles to mags. including Nat. Observer; others, photographs to mags. Founder, mem. N.Mex. Motion Picture Commn., 1967-76; v.p., dir. Albuquerque C. of C., 1971-75; bd. dirs. Albuquerque Indsl. Devel. Service, 1971-80; bd. advisors Lovelace Med. Center, Albuquerque, 1976-80; bd. advs. UPI, 1983-86; bd. dirs. Newspaper Features Council, 1984—; mem. exec. council St. Joseph Hosp., 1986—. Recipient N.Mex. medal of Merit, 1968, Robert F. Kennedy Journalism award, 1970, George Washington Honor Medal Freedoms Found., 1969, 19 E.H. Shaffer awards for editorial writing, reporting and photography N.Mex. Press Assn., 1965-80. Mem. N.Mex. Press Assn. (state pres. 1976), Colo. Press Assn. (bd. dirs. 1982-85), Sigma Delta Chi (N.Mex. pres. 1960). Methodist. Office: Rocky Mountain News 400 W Colfax St Denver CO 80204

LOONEY, WILLIAM FRANCIS, JR., lawyer; b. Boston, Sept. 20, 1931; s. William Francis Sr. and Ursula Mary (Ryan) L.; m. Constance Mary O'Callaghan, Dec. 28, 1957; children: Willam F. III, Thomas M., Karen D., Martha A. AB, Harvard U., JD. Bar: Mass. 1958, D.C. 1972, U.S. Supreme Ct. 1972, U.S. Dist. Ct. (ea. dist.) Mich. 1986. Law clk. to presiding justice Mass. Supreme Jud. Ct., 1958-59; assoc. Goodwin, Procter & Hoar, Boston, 1959-63; chief civil div. U.S. Attys. Office, 1964-65; ptnr. Looney & Grossman, Boston, 1965—; asst. U.S. atty. U.S. Dist. Ct. Mass., 1962-65; spl. hearing officer U.S. Dept. of Justice, 1965-68. Mem. Zoning Bd. of Appeals, Dedham, Mass., 1971-74; bd. dirs. Boston Latin Sch. Found., 1981-85, pres. 1981-84, chmn. bd. dirs. 1984-86; dir. USCG Found., 1987—. Served to capt. U.S. Army, 1953-55. Fellow Am. Coll. Trial Lawyers; mem. ABA (Ho. of Dels.), Mass. Bar Assn. (co-chair standing com. lawyers' responsibility for pub. service 1987—), Boston Bar Assn. (chmn. litigation sect. 1980-82, v.p. 1982-84, pres. 1984-85, council mem. 1985—), Nat. Assn. Bar Pres.'s, Boston Latin Sch. Assn. (v.p. 1978-80, pres. 1980-82, life trustee 1982—; Man of Yr. 1985). Democrat. Roman Catholic. Clubs: Harvard, Union (Boston). Home: 43 Coronation Dr Dedham MA 02026 Office: 101 Arch St 9th Floor Boston MA 02110-1112

LOOPER, DONALD RAY, lawyer; b. Ft. Worth, Sept. 4, 1952; s. Rudolph Winnard and Margie Lee (Nix) L.; m. Marcia Lynn Graves, May 8, 1976; children: Scott Aaron, Cory Michael, Jonathan Reed. BBA with honors, U. Tex., Austin, 1974, M in Profl. Acctg., 1976; JD cum laude, U. Houston, 1979. Bar: Colo. 1979, Tex. 1981. Assoc. Cohen, Brame, Smith & Krendl, Denver, 1979-81; assoc. dir. Reynolds, Allen & Cook, Houston, 1981-85, head tax sect., 1984-85; dir. Looper, Reed, Ewing & McGraw, Houston, 1985—; lectr. Houston Soc. CPA's, 1984; acquisition negotiations in Europe, Asia U.S., and OPEC Countries., 1987-88. Coach nationally ranked Women's Softball Team 1st Bapt. Ch., Houston, 1981—. Named one of Outstanding Young Men Am., 1980, 84. Mem. ABA, Tex. Bar Assn. (speaker seminars 1983-85, divorce tax com. 1985-86, lectr. tax sect. 1983-86), Houston Bar Assn. (tax sect. council 1985—), Phi Delta Phi (Internat. Grad. of Yr. 1979, province pres. 1984-86), Am. Softball Assn. (winner Nat. Championship 1981). Republican. Baptist. Home: 11264 Memorial Dr Houston TX 77024 Office: Looper Reed Ewing & McGraw 9 Greenway Plaza 1717 Houston TX 77046

LOOS, AUGUST WALTER, JR., cable and chain company executive; b. Pomfret, Conn., Mar. 14, 1928; s. August Walter and Edith (Peterson) L.; B.A., Brown U., 1954; m. Joan C. Timmons, Sept. 14, 1961; children—William T., John P. Sales engr. Danielson Mfg. Co. (Conn.), 1954-58; v.p. sales Sanlo Mfg. Co., Michigan City, Ind., 1958-59; sales mgr. W.S. Shamban Co., Inc., Fort Wayne, Ind., 1959-61; chmn. bd. Loos & Co., Inc., Pomfret, Conn., Fiberoptics Tech., Inc., Cableware Tech., Inc., Hamlet Hill Vineyards, Steelplast Can. Inc., Granby, Que. Served with USAAF, 1945-48. Mem. Soc. Plastic Engrs. Lodges: Masons, Lions. Patentee plastic coated chain, mech. cables. Home: Elsinore Pomfret CT 06258 Other: 2375 Lantern Ln Port Royal Naples FL 33940 Office: Cable Rd Pomfret CT 06258 Other: 900 Industrial Blvd Naples FL 33942

LOOTSMA, FREERK AUKE, mathematics educator; b. Franekeradeel, The Netherlands, Jan. 21, 1936; s. Auke Freerk and Elbertha (Timmerman) L.; m. Hendrika Beerekamp, Sept. 5, 1961; children: Johanna, Auke, Rutger. MSc, State U., Utrecht, The Netherlands, 1961; PhD, U. Tech., Eindhoven, The Netherlands, 1970. Scientist Philips Research Lab., Eindhoven, 1962-72, Mullard Research Lab., Horley, Eng., 1970-71; scientist, automation dept. Philips Info. Systems, Eindhoven, 1972-74; sr. prof. math. Delft (The Netherlands) U. Tech., 1974—; cons. on energy. Author: (novel) The Bach Project, 1983; editor: Proc. Numerical Methods Nonlinear Optimization, 1972; contbr. 40 articles to sci. jours. Regent Computer Ctr. Dutch Ref. Ch., Delft, 1976-86. Served to 2d lt. Netherlands Navy, 1961-62. Mem. Math. Programming Soc. (treas. 1975-81), Brit. Computer Soc. Home: Doorniksestraat 8 25 7XL, The Hague The Netherlands Office: Delft U Tech, Julianalaan, 132 262 BL Delft The Netherlands

LOPEZ, REMI, architect, educator; b. Paris, Mar. 21, 1939; s. Raymond and Simonne (Pillet) L.; m. Claire Le Roy, May 2, 1964; children—Caroline, Cedric, Charlotte, Julie. Architect's diploma with distinction Ecole Des Beaux-Arts, Paris, 1966. Collaborator architect's office, London, 1961, Hamburg, W.Ger., 1962, Raymond Lopez Architecture Office, Paris, 1962-66; sr. ptnr. Remi Lopez et Associes-Architects and Planners, Paris, 1966—; prof. design health facilities Ecole Nationale de la Sante Publique, Rennes, France, 1981—. Architect numerous housing devels., ednl. and cultural facilities, hosps., office bldgs., refurbishings, France, shopping center, Odienne, Ivory Coast, 1972, Amiri hosp., Kuwait, 1981, pilot indsl. and tech. inst., Jeddah, Saudi Arabia, 1980, postal centers, Riyadh, Jeddah and Dammam, Saudi Arabia, 1982, color TV center, Jeddah. Decorated chevalier Ordre National du Merite, chevalier Ordre Arts et Lettres (France). Mem. Academie d'Architecture, Cercle d'etudes architecturales, Regional Council Order Architects (treas. 1978-82, v.p. 1982-84, pres. 1984-86), Nat. Council Order Architects (pres. 1986—), Nat. Geog. Soc. (life). Club: Cercle St.-Germain (Paris). Office: Remi Lopez et Associés, 242 Blvd Raspail, 75014 Paris France

LOPEZ, ROSALIE MERCEDES, personnel executive; b. Tucson, Sept. 6, 1954; d. Manuel Rodriguez and Geraldine (Bender) Lopez; m. Myron Paul Boots, Feb. 1, 1975; children: Seth Clayton Paul Boots, Vanessa Catherine. AS, No. Ariz. U., 1979; BSBA, U. No. Colo., 1980; MBA, North Tex. State U., 1982. Mgr. office Lockhart Exploration Co., Casper, Wyo., 1979-80; personnel rep. Continental Telephone, Dallas, 1980-83; mgr. field personnel Hewlett-Packard Co., San Antonio and Houston, 1983-85; mgr. regional human resources MCI Telecommunications, Houston, 1985-86; founder, dir. Resource and Evaluation Ctr. for Career Strategies, Houston, 1986—, Hispanas Adelante, Houston, 1986. Mem. Rep. Nat. Hispanic Assembly of Harris County, Houston, sec., 1985, vice-chair, 1986; apptd. state sec. Rep. Nat. Hispanic Assembly of Tex.; Houston core group leader Hispanic Women's Network of Tex., founding mem., 1987. Mem. Am. Soc. Personnel Adminstrn. (nat. EEO com. 1980-85). Office: 2302 Fannin Suite 202 Houston TX 77002

LOPEZ CONTRERAS, CARLOS, Honduran government official, lawyer; b. Marcala, La Paz, Honduras, Jan. 31, 1942; s. Enrique Lopez Arellano and Auristele Contreras; m. Armida Maria Villela, Jan. 7, 1969; children: Armida Maria, Carlos Miguel. Law degree, U. Honduras, Tegucigalpa, 1969. Bar: Honduras. Ambassador to Nicaragua Honduras, 1970-71, ambassador to Malta, 1972-76, ambassador to Great Britain and Ireland, 1973-76, dep. minister fgn. affairs, 1979-80, adviser to minister fgn. affairs, 1982-86, minister fgn. affairs, 1986—. Author: Peace Negotiations, My Point of View, 1984. Roman Catholic. Lodge: Rotary. Home: Colonia Tepeyac, PO Box N 1104, Tegucigalpa Francisco Morazan, Honduras Office: Ministry Fgn Affairs, Avenida La Paz, Tegucigalpa Honduras

LOPEZ TRUJILLO, ALFONSO CARDINAL, archbishop of Medellin; b. Villahermosa, Colombia, Nov. 8, 1935. Ordained priest Roman Catholic Ch., 1960. Instr. maj. sem., Colombia; pastoral coordinator Internat. Eucharistic Congress, Bogota, Colombia, 1968; vicar gen. of Bogota, 1970-72; consecrated bishop of Boseta, 1971; aux. bishop of Bogota, 1971-72; sec.-gen. CELAM, 1972-78, pres., 1979-83; organizer 1979 Puebla Conf.; apptd. coadjutor archbishop of Medellin (Colombia), from 1978; archbishop of Medellin, 1979; elevated to Sacred Coll. of Cardinals, 1983; pres. Bishop's Conf. Mem. Social Communications Commn. Latin Am. Address: Arzobispado, Calle 57, 49-44, Medellin Colombia *

LOPREATO, JOSEPH, sociology educator, author; b. Stefanaconi, Italy, July 13, 1928; s. Frank and Marianna (Pavone) L.; m. Carolyn H. Prestopino, July 18, 1954 (div. 1971); children: Gregory F., Marisa S.; m. Sally A. Cook, Aug. 24, 1972 (div. 1978). B.A. in Sociology, U. Conn., 1956; Ph.D. in Sociology, Yale U., 1960. Asst. prof. sociology U. Mass., Amherst, 1960-62; vis. lectr. U. Rome, 1962-64; assoc. prof. U. Conn., Storrs, 1964-66; prof. sociology U. Tex., Austin, 1968—; chmn. dept. sociology U. Tex., 1969-72; vis. prof. U. Catania, Italy, 1974, U. Calabria, Italy, 1980; mem. steering com. Council European Studies, Columbia U., 1977-80; chmn. sociology com. Council for Internat. Exchange of Scholars, 1977-79; mem. Internat. Com. Mezzogiorno, 1986—; Calabria Internat. Com., 1988—. Author: Vilfredo Pareto, 1965, Peasants No More, 1967, Italian Americans, 1970, Class, Conflict and Mobility, 1972, Social Stratification, 1974, The Sociology of Vilfredo Pareto, 1975, La Stratificazione Sociale Negli Stati Uniti, 1977, Human Nature and Biocultural Evolution, 1984. Mem. Nat. Italian-Am. Com. for U.S.A. Bicentennial; mem. exec. com. Congress Italian Politics, 1977-80. Served to cpl. U.S. Army, 1952-54. Fulbright faculty research fellow, 1962-64, 73-74; Social Sci. Research Council faculty research fellow, 1963-64; NSF faculty research fellow, 1965-68. Mem. Internat. Sociol. Assn., Am. Sociol. Assn., Am. Biol. Assn., European Sociobiolog. Soc., Southwestern Sociol. Assn., So. Sociol. Soc. Roman Catholic. Office: Univ of Tex Dept Sociology Austin TX 78712

LORCH, EDGAR R., mathematician, educator; b. Switzerland, July 22, 1907; s. Henry John and Marthe (Racine) L.; m. Elise B., July 31, 1937 (div. 1955); children: Edwin Duncan, Madeleine Louise, Ingrid Jacqueline; m. Maristella de Panizza Bové, Mar. 25, 1956; children: Lavinia Edgarda, Donatella Livia. B.A. summa cum laude, Columbia U., 1928, Ph.D., 1933. Instr. math. Columbia U., 1935-41, asst. prof., 1941-44, assoc. prof., 1944-48, prof., 1948-74, Adrain prof., 1974—, chmn. dept. math., 1968-72, co-chmn. univ. seminar Computers, Man and Society, 1982—; chmn. dept. Barnard Coll., 1948-63, chmn. com. on instrn., 1961; vis. prof. Carnegie Inst. Tech., 1949, U. Rome, 1953-54, 82, U. Florence, 1953-54, 75, Coll. de France, 1958, Stanford U., 1963, Middle East Tech. U., Ankara, 1965; vis. lectr., France, Germany, Scandinavia, Switzerland, Italy; univ. lectr. Fordham U., 1966-72; mem. secondary sch. Matte. Curriculum Improvement Study, 1966-72; counselor Scientifique du President Lycée, Francais de N.Y., 1977-88; exec. com. Ctr. Internat. Scholarly Exchange. Author: Spectral Theory, 1962, Precalculus, 1973, Analisis Funcional, 1977; editor: University Texts in Math. Sciences, La Qualità, Seminari Interdisciplinari di Venezia, 1974; mem. editorial bd.: Indiana Math. Jour, 1966-74; contbr. articles to math. jours. Sci. adviser Gen. Staff, U.S. Army, 1948. NRC fellow Harvard, 1933-34; Cutting Travel fellow Europe, 1934-35; research mathematician NDRC, 1944-45; Fulbright lectr. Italy, 1953-54; Fulbright lectr. France, 1958; Fulbright lectr. Colombia, 1977. Mem. Am. Math. Soc. (council 1952-55, chmn. com. on nominations 1958, mem. editorial bd. 1945-50), Math. Assn. Am. (vis. mathematician 1961-63), Societé Mathématique de France, Oesterreichische Mathematische Gesellschaft, Unione Matematica Italiana, Zürcher Gespräche, Sierra Club, Wilderness Soc., Catskill Center, Environ. Def. Fund, Nature Conservancy, Friends of Riverside Park (v.p. 1982-84), Phi Beta Kappa, Sigma Xi. Home: 445 Riverside Dr New York NY 10027

LORD, HAROLD WILBUR, electrical engineer and electronics consultant; b. Eureka, Calif., Aug. 20, 1905; s. Charles Wilbur and Rossina Camilla

(Hansen) L.; B.S., Calif. Inst. Tech., 1926; m. Doris Shirley Huff, July 25, 1928; children—Joann Shirley (Mrs. Carl Cook Disbrow), Alan Wilbur, Nancy Louise (Mrs. Leslie Crandall), Harold Wayne. With Gen. Electric Co., Schenectady, 1926-66, electronics engr., 1960-66; pvt. cons. engr., Mill Valley, Calif., 1966—. Coffin Found. award Gen. Electric Co., 1933. Fellow IEEE (life, tech. v.p. 1962, Centennial medal 1984, IEEE Magnetics Soc. 1984 Achievement award). Contbr. articles to profl. jours. Patentee in field. Home and Office: 336 Corte Madera Ave Mill Valley CA 94941

LORD, JACK, actor, director, producer; b. N.Y.C., Dec. 30, 1930; s. William Lawrence and Ellen Josephine (O'Brien) Ryan; m. Marie de Narde, Apr. 1, 1952. BS in Fine Arts, NYU, 1954. pres. Lord and Lady Enterprises, Inc., 1968—. Works exhibited in galleries, museums including Corcoran Gallery, Nat. Acad. Design, Whitney Mus., Bklyn. Mus., Met. Mus. Art, N.Y.C., Library of Congress, Brit. Mus., London, Bibliotheque Nationale, Paris, Mus. Modern Art, N.Y.C., Met. Mus. Art, Brit. Mus., Bklyn. Mus., Bibliotheque Nationale, Paris, Fogg Mus., Harvard U., Santa Barbara (Calif.) Mus. Art, John and Mable Ringling Mus. Art, Sarasota, Fla., Grunwald Graphic Arts Found., UCLA, Brooks Meml. Art Gallery, Memphis, Cin. Art Mus., Atkins Mus. Art, Kansas City, Mo., Fine Arts Gallery, San Diego, Colby Coll. Art Mus., Waterville, Maine, Ga. Mus. Art, U. Ga., Atlanta, DePauw U. Art Mus., Greencastle, Ind., Chouinard Art Inst., Los Angeles, Free Library Phila., Columbia U., N.Y.C., Lycoming Coll., Williamsport, Pa., Rutgers U., New Brunswick, N.J., U. Maine, Orono; represented in permanent collections, Dartmouth Coll., Hanover, N.H., Colgate U. Library, Hamilton, N.Y., Simmons Coll., Boston, Kalamazoo Inst. Arts, U. N.C., Chapel Hill, Evansville (Ind.) Mus. Arts, Massillon (Ohio) Mus., Hebrew Union Coll., Cin., N.Y.C., Los Angeles, Jerusalem, Flint (Mich.) Inst. Arts, Lehigh U. Coll. Arts, Bethlehem, Pa., Birmingham (Ala.) Mus. Art, Case Western Res. U., Cleve., Coll. of Wooster (Ohio), Calif. Inst. Arts; Broadway appearances include Traveling Lady, Cat on a Hot Tin Roof, Flame-Out, The Illegitimist, (TV shows) Stoney Burke (star); producer, star of 280 hours in 12 yrs. of series Hawaii Five-O; creator (TV series) The Hunter; creator, dir., producer: (TV film) M Station: Hawaii, 1980; writer (original screenplay) Melissa, 1968; dir. episodes Hawaii Five-O; appeared in feature films The Court Marshall of Billy Mitchell, Williamsburg, The Story of a Patriot, Tip on a Dead Jockey, God's Little Acre, Man of the West, The Hangman, Walk Like a Dragon, Dr. No, Ride to Hangman's Tree, Doomsday Flight; leading TV roles include Omnibus, Playhouse 90, Goodyear Playhouse, Studio One, U.S. Steel Hour, Have Gun Will Travel, Untouchables, Naked City, Rawhide, Bonanza, Americans, Route 66, Gunsmoke, Stagecoach West, Dr. Kildare, Greatest Show on Earth, Combat, Chrysler Theater, 12 O'Clock High, Loner, Laredo, FBI, Invaders, Fugitive, Virginian, The Man from UNCLE, High Chaparral, Ironside, Alcoa Theatre, Loretta Young Show, The Millionaire, Checkmate, Climax, Kraft, Philco, Danger, Suspense, The Web, You Are There, Lineup, Grand Hotel, Kraft Suspense Theatre. Served as 2d officer U.S. Merchant Marines. Recipient St. Gauden's Artist award, 1948, Fame award, 1963, Spl. Law Enforcement award, Am. Legion, 1973, Adminstr.'s award VA, 1980, Legend in His Own Time award State of Hawaii, 1980; named to Cowboy Hall of Fame, 1963. Mem. Dirs. Guild Am., Screen Actors Guild.

LORD, JACQUELINE WARD, accountant, photographer, artist; b. Andalusia, Ala., May 16, 1936; d. Marron J. and Minnie V. (Owen) Ward; m. Curtis Gaynor, Nov. 23, 1968. Student U. Ala., 1966, Auburn U., 1977, Huntingdon Coll., 1980, Troy State U., 1980; B.A. in Bus. Adminstrn., Dallas Bapt. U., 1985. News photographer corr. Andalusia (Ala.) Star-News, 1954-59, Sta. WSFA-TV, Montgomery, Ala., 1954-60; acct., bus. mgr. Reihardt Motors, Inc., Montgomery, 1962-69; office mgr., acct. Cen. Ala. Supply, Montgomery, 1969-71; acct. Chambers Constrn. Co., Montgomery, 1972-75; pres. Foxy Lady Apparel, Inc., Montgomery, 1973-76; acct. Rushton, Stakely, Johnston & Garrett, attys., Montgomery, 1975-81; acctg. supr. Arthur Andersen & Co., Dallas, 1981-82; staff acct. Burgess Co., C.P.A.s, Dallas, 1983; owner Lord & Assocs. Acctg. Service, Dallas, 1983—; tax acct. John Hasse, C.P.A., Dallas, 1984-86; Dallas Bapt. Assn., 1986—. Vol. election law commr. Sec. of State of Ala. Don Siegelman, Montgomery, 1979-80; mem. Montgomery Art Guild, 1964-65, Ala. Art League, 1964-65, Montgomery Little Theatre, 1963-65, Montgomery Choral Soc., 1965. Recipient Outstanding Achievement Bus. Mgmt. award Am. Motors, 1968. Mem. Am. Soc. Women Accts. (pres. Montgomery chpt. 1976-77, area day chmn. 1978, del. ann. meeting 1975-78). Home: 5209 Meadowside Dr Garland TX 75043

LORD, JAMES GREGORY, marketing and fundraising consultant; b. Cleve., Aug. 23, 1947; s. James Nelson and Esther Lord; student U. Md., Far East Campus, 1966-68, Cleve. State U., 1968-72; m. Wendy Franklin, July 10, 1977. TV news producer Far East Network, Tokyo, 1965-68; wire editor News-Herald, Willoughby, Ohio, 1968-69; pub. relations assoc. United Way, Cleve., 1969-70; free-lance pub. relations person, Cleve., 1970-72; dir. pub. relations Ketchum, Inc., Pitts., 1972-77; cons. mktg., devel. philanthropic instns., Cleve., 1977—; chief devel. officer Cleve. Mus. Art, 1984-85; lectr. Served with USN, 1964-68, Japan. Author: Philanthropy and Marketing, 7th edit., 1981; The Raising of Money, 1983 (nat. bestseller); Communicating with Donors, 1984; Building Your Case, 1984; The Campaign Manuals, 1985; The Development Consultant, 1985, Guide for the Professional, 2d edit., 1986, The Perfect Development Officer, 1986, others; contbr. numerous articles on philanthropy, mktg. and quality of life in Am. cities to various publs.; developed one-man photography exhbns., 15 worldwide sites, 1968-72. Home: 28050 S Woodland Rd Pepper Pike OH 44124 Office: care of Third Sector Press 2000 Euclid Ave PO Box 18044 Cleveland OH 44118

LORD, PRISCILLA SAWYER (MRS. PHILIP HOSMER LORD), author; b. Woburn, Mass.; d. Frank Hayward and Emelyn (Strang) Sawyer; m. Philip Hosmer Lord, Feb. 10, 1938; children—Beverly, Roberta (Mrs. William H. Moore, Jr.). A.B., Boston U., 1933. Readers' adviser Woburn Public Library, 1933-38; story teller Book Reviewer, 1933—. Bd. dirs. Mass. Soc. Univ. Edn. for Women, 1965—; active Girl Scouts U.S.A.; vol. chmn. scholarship com., past v.p. Marblehead Hosp. Aid Assn.; ednl. chmn. Possum Long Nature Center, Stuart, Fla. Mem. Herb Soc. Am. (nat. bd., chmn. New Eng. unit, historian), Mass. Descs. of Mayflower, Nat. Soc. Colonial Dames Am., Alpha Gamma Delta. Clubs: Marblehead Garden (past pres.), Winter Garden (past pres.). Author: (with Daniel J. Foley) Easter Garland, 1963, The Folk Arts and Crafts of New England, 1965, The Eagle, 1968, Easter The World Over, 1970; (with Virginia Clegg Gamage) Marblehead: The Spirit of '76 Lives Here, 1971, The Lure of Marblehead, 1973; Marblehead Neck Wildlife Sanctuary: Self-Guiding Trail Guide, 1979; Footnotes on Footwear, 1986; co-author: A Basket of Herbs, 1983; editor: A Few Unsung Colonial and Pioneer Women, 1982, The History of the Herb Society of America, 1983, Under the Golden Cod, 1984, Footnotes on Footwear, 1986; contbr. articles to periodicals. Home: 42 Dennett Rd Marblehead Neck MA 01945

LORD, WILLIAM JACKSON, JR., educator; b. Milam, Tex., May 10, 1926; s. William Jackson and Ida Clara (Neal) L.; m. Shirley Ruth Loveless, June 12, 1948 (dec. Sept. 1985); children: Michal Anne, William David, Mark Gregory. B.B.A., U. Tex., 1950, M.B.A., 1953; Ph.D. (Authors League grantee, Gulf Oil Co. grantee), U. Ill., 1961. Instr. W. Tex. State U., 1951-54; instr. to assoc. prof. U. Ill., 1954-64; prof. U. Tex., Austin, 1964—, Tex. Commerce Bancshares Centennial prof. bus. communication, 1982—; chmn. dept. mgmt. sci. and info. systems U. Tex., 1974-80; John R. Emens Disting. prof. Ball State U., Muncie, Ind., 1977-78; cons. communications Franklin Life Ins. Co., Springfield, Ill., 1958-64, Austin Nat. Bank, 1971-74. Author: Functional Business Communication, 1968, 2d edit., 1974, 3d edit., 1983, Spanish edit., 1973, How Authors Make a Living, 1962; editorial assoc.: Social Sci. Quar, 1965-79; editorial assoc.: Jour. Bus. Communication, 1965-79. Served with AUS, 1944-46. Decorated Bronze Star (3).; Recipient teaching excellence awards Student Assn., 1965, 66, 70, Jack G. Taylor award Coll. Bus. Adminstrn., 1984-85. Fellow Am. Bus. Communication Assn.; mem. Assn. Bus. Communication (pres. 1974), S.W. Fedn. Adminstrv. Disciplines, Council Communication Socs., Delta Sigma Pi (life), Phi Kappa Phi, Pi Kappa Alpha. Baptist. Home: 3500 Hillbrook Dr Austin TX 78731

LORD, WINSTON, diplomat; b. N.Y.C., Aug. 14, 1937; s. Oswald Bates and Mary (Pillsbury) L.; m. Bette Bao, May 4, 1963; children: Elizabeth Pillsbury, Winston Bao. B.A., Yale U., 1959; M.A., Fletcher Sch. Law and Diplomacy, Tufts U. in cooperation with Harvard U., 1960; LL.D. (hon.), Williams Coll., 1979. Mem. staff congl. relations, polit.-mil. and econ. affairs U.S. Dept. State, Washington, 1962-64, Geneva, 1965-67; mem. staff internat. security affairs U.S. Dept. Def., Washington, 1967-69; mem. staff NSC, White House, Washington, 1969-73; also spl. asst. to asst. to pres. for nat. security affairs NSC, White House, 1970-73; dir. policy planning staff U.S. Dept. State, Washington, 1973-77; pres. Council on Fgn. Relations, N.Y.C., 1977-85; U.S. ambassador to People's Republic of China Beijing, 1985—. Bd. dirs. Atlantic Council of U.S., Center for Inter-Am. Relations, Americas Soc., Internat. Rescue Com.; bd. govs. Atlantic Inst. for Internat. Affairs; bd. advisors Fletcher Sch. Law and Diplomacy, Am. Ditchley Found.; mem. Trilateral Commn., Asia Soc. Served with AUS, 1961. Home: 740 Park Ave New York NY 10021 Office: US Embassy, Beijing Peoples Republic of China *

LOREN, PAMELA, international telecommunications company executive; b. Paris, Jan. 11, 1944; d. Theodore and Mattie (Ephron) L.; BS in Sociology, Columbia U., 1964; MS in Sociology, U. Madrid, 1968, MS in Langs., 1970; m. Morton P. Levy, June 2, 1963; children—Cristopher Aram, Stirling Brett, Cristina Sahula. Pres., Pamela Loren, Ltd., N.Y.C., 1969-74, Loren Communications Internat., Ltd., N.Y.C., 1972-74; chmn. bd. Loren Communications Internat., Caracas, Venezuela, London, Milan, Italy and N.Y.C., 1974—; exec. v.p. Cinnamon World Trade Corp., 1974—; dir. Panda Internat. Export Corp., Durable Housing Internat., Loren Group, Danbury, Conn., Crespi, Rosann & Potti; speaker on interdependence of medicine and communications. Bd. dirs. Burden Ctr. for Aging. Recipient Humanitarian award Community Service Soc., 1972, Burden Ctr. for Aging, 1977, Soc. Order Helpers, 1978, 82, 86, 88, Otty award, 1986; named Young Woman of Achievement YWCA, 1983, Woman of Vision, Caracas, 1986, Woman of the Future, Madrid, 1988. Mem. Am. Arbitration Assn., Am. Mgmt. Assn., Soc. Latin-Am. Bus. Owners, N.Y. Assn. Women Bus. Owners, Women's Econ. Round Table, Am. Soc. Prevention Cruelty to Animals (media adv. bd.). Club: Columbia University. Author: The Generation In-Between, 1977; Looking Ahead to Thirty-Five, 1978, Slowing Down in the Fast Lane, 1987, When Having It All Isn't Enough, 1988. Home: 1125 Park Ave New York NY 10028 Office: Loren Communications Internat 155 E 55th St New York NY 10022

LOREN, SOPHIA, actress; b. Rome, Italy, Sept. 20, 1934; d. Riccardo Scicolone and Romilda Villani; m. Carlo Ponti, Sept. 17, 1967; children: Carlo Ponti, Edoardo. Student, Scuole Magistrali Superiori. First appearance in Aida, 1951; leading role in Italian motion pictures including The Gold of Naples, 1954, Woman of the River, 1954, Too Bad She's Bad, Luck of Being a Woman, 1955; actress in U.S. motion pictures including Pride and Passion, 1955, Boy on a Dolphin, Legend of Lost, 1956, Desire Under the Elms, 1957, Houseboat, 1958, That Kind of Woman, 1958, Black Orchid, 1959, The Key, Heller with a Gun, Yesterday, Today, Tomorrow, 1963, Marriage Italian Style, Judith, 1965, Arabesque, 1966, The Countess from Hong Kong, 1965, Happily Ever After, The Verdict, Olympia, 1959, It Started in Naples, 1960, The Millionaires, 1961, Two Women, 1962, Boccacio 70, 1962, Condemned of Altona, El Cid, The Fall of Roman Empire, 1962, Five Miles to Midnight, 1963, Madame, 1963, More Than a Miracle, 1967, Ghosts-Italian Style, 1969, Sunflower, 1970, The Priests Wife, 1971, Man of La Mancha, 1972, Lady Liberty, 1972, White Sister, 1973, The Cassandra Crossing, 1977, A Special Day, 1977, Brass Target, 1978, Firepower, 1979; TV film appearances include Sophia Loren: Her Own Story, 1980, Aurora, 1985, Courage, 1986, The Fortunate Pilgrims, 1987. Recipient award for best film performances Festival of Venice, 1958; recipient Oscar for best film performance, Japan, 1958, Acad. award for Best Actress, 1962, N.Y. Film Critics Award, 1961, Gold Palm, Cannes Film Festival, 1961, named best fgn. actress Com. of Film Francais, and 6 Golden Donatello in Italy, 6 Victoires in France, 8 Bambi in Germany, Nastro D'Argento in Italy, Best Actress award Moscow Film Festival. *

LORENCEAU, BERNARD JEAN, plastic surgeon; b. Boulogne, France, July 7, 1947; s. Bernard Sven and Monique (Rust) L.; m. Dominique Sebilleau, June 25, 1970; children: Pauline, Elise, Camille. MD, Janson de Sailly, Paris, 1978. Intern in medicine Hosp. Orleans, France, 1970-71; intern Hosp. Paris, 1973-78, resident, 1978-81; chief plastic surgery unit Hosp. Pontoise, France, 1981—; asst. chief Microsurgery Research Lab., St. Louis, France, 1976-85; expert in plastic surgery Wur D'appel, 1982-87. Contbr. articles to profl. publs. Mem. French Plastic and Reconstructive Surgery Soc., French Coll. Plastic Surgeons. Roman Catholic. Home: 24 Rue Lalo, 75116 Paris France Office: 6 Rue Carnot, 95300 Pontoise France

LORENTZEN, ERLING SVEN, industrial company executive; b. Oslo, Jan. 28, 1923; s. Oivind and Ragna (Nielsen) L.; m. Princess Ragnhild, May 15, 1953; children: Haakon, Ingeborg Lorentzen Ribeiro, Ragnhild Alexandra. MBA, Harvard U., 1948. Pres., mng. dir. Companhia Brasileira de Gás (now Supergasbras), Rio De Janeiro, 1953-72; pres. Lorentzen Empreendimentos, S.A., Rio De Janeiro, 1972; pres., chmn. bd. Aracruz Celulose S.A., Rio de Janeiro, 1972-87, 1972—; mem. adv. bd. Mesbla, S.A., Rio De Janeiro, Unibanco, São Paulo, Brazil; mem. internat. adv. bd. BSN Danone, Evian, France; former mem. RJR Nabisco Inc. Internat. Adv. Council, Atlanta. Bd. dirs. Acão Comunitária Do Brasil, Rio De Janeiro. Recipient St. Olav award with Oak Leaf (Norway), Medal with Star (Norway), King Haakon Meml. Cruzeiro Do Sul-Com. (Brazil). Mem. Royal Swedish Acad. Engring. Scis. Office: Lorentzen Empreendimentos SA, Av Augusto Severo 8-7o And, Lapa, Rio De Janeiro Brazil

LORENZ, KONRAD ZACHARIAS, zoologist; b. Vienna, Austria, Nov. 7, 1903; s. Adolf and Emma (Lecher) L.; student medicine, N.Y.C., Vienna, M.D., 1928; Ph.D. in Zoology, Vienna, 1933; Ph.D. (hon.), U. Leeds, Eng., 1962; M.D. (hon.), U. Basel, 1966, Yale U., 1967; Sc.D. (hon.), U. Oxford, 1968, Loyola U., Chgo., 1970, Durham, 1972, U. Birmingham, 1974, Vet. U., Vienna, 1980; m. Margarethe Gebhardt, June 24, 1927; children—Thomas, Dagmar, Agnes Lorenz von Cranach. Asst. 2d, Anat. Inst., Vienna, 1928-35; lectr. comparative anatomy, psychology U. Vienna, 1937-38, asst. prof., 1938-40; prof. psychology, head dept. U. Konigsberg (Germany), 1940-42; head Inst. Comparative Ethology, Altenberg, Austria, 1949-51; head research dept. comparative ethology Max-Planck Found., Buldern, Germany, 1951-54, vice dir. inst., 1954-61, Seewiesen, dir., 1961-73; dir. dept. for animal sociology Austrian Acad. Sci., 1973-82; dir. Konrad-Lorenz Inst. Austrian Acad. Sci., 1982—; lectr., U. Vienna; hon. prof. U. Munster, U. Munich; vis. prof. U. Colo., Denver. Recipient Golden medal Zool. Soc. N.Y., Preis der Stadt Wien, Goldene Wilhelm Bolsche Medaille, Osterreichisches Ehrenzeichen für Wissenschaft and Kunst, Ehrenmedaille der Bundeshauptstadt Wien in Gold, Prix Mondial Cino del Duca, Jean Delacour Medaille, Ordre Pour Le Mérite, Grosses Verdienstkreuz mit Stern der Bundesrepublik Deutschland, Nobel prize in physiology and medicine, 1973, Bayerischer Verdienstorden, Cervia Ambiente Naturschutzpreis, Ehrenmedaille d. Katholischen Univ. Mailand, Bayer. Maximiliansorden. Mem. Austrian Acad. Sci., Bavarian Acad. Sci., Nat. Acad. Scis. (fgn. assoc.), N.Y. Zool. Soc., Royal Soc., Am. Acad. Arts and Scis., numerous others. Author: On Agression, 1966, Evolution and Modification of Behavior, 1966, King Solomon's Ring, 1952, Man Meets Dog, 1954, Civilized Man's Eight Deadly Sins, 1973, Behind the Mirror, 1977, The Year of the Greylag Goose, 1980, The Foundations of Ethology, 1981, The Waning of Humaneness, 1987. Pioneer in modern ethology; formulated school of study based on concept that an animal's behavior is a product of adaptive evolution. Address: Osterreichische Acad, der Wissenschaften, Adolf-Lorenz-Gasse 2, A-3422 Altenberg Austria

LORENZ, RUEDIGER, neurosurgeon; b. Niederfischbach, Ger., Sept. 9, 1932; s. Johannes and Ena (Mueller) L.; Study of medicine University Bonn and Goettingen, 1951-1956; Dr. med. U. Goettingen, 1956; m. Gunde Hussmann, Feb. 13, 1959; children—Matthias, Mechthild. Medical training in internal medicine, general pathology, general surgery, obstetrics and gynaecology 1957-1959. Special training in general surgery 1959-1962, neurophysiology 1963, neurosurgery since 1963. Specialist in neurosurgery 1966. Habilitation for Neurosurgery U. Giessen 1971; prof. neurosurgery U. Giessen Faculty Medicine, 1973-80; prof. neurosurgery, head dept. Univ. Hosp., Frankfurt, 1980—; vis. clin. prof. Yonsei University, Med. Sch., Seoul, Korea, 1980. Mem. Med. Acad. Zaragoza (Spain), Med. Acad. Burma, Med. Acad. Argentina. Author articles in field, chpts. in books, monographs. Home: Lerchesbergring 86a, D-600 Frankfurt/Main 70 Federal Republic of Germany Office: Leiter der Abteilung fuer, Allgemeine Neurochirurgie, 2-16 Schleusenweg, D-6000 Frankfurt/Main 71 Federal Republic of Germany

LORIMER, ANDREW ROSS, cardiology consultant; b. Glasgow, Scotland, May 5, 1937; s. James and Catherine (Ross) L.; m. Fiona Marshall, June 20, 1962; children: Alan, Stuart, Michael. MB, BS, MD, U. Glasgow, 1960. Research fellow in medicine Vanderbilt U. Hosp., Nashville, 1961-63; lectr. cardiology U. Glasgow, 1965-72; cardiology cons. Royal Infirmary, Glasgow, 1972—. Contbr. articles to med. jours. Fellow Royal Coll. Physicians London, Royal Coll. Physicians Edinburgh, Royal Coll. Physicians Glasgow. Office: Royal Infirmary Dept Cardiology, Glasgow G4 OSF, Scotland

LORING, RICHARD WILLIAM, psychotherapist; b. Bronx, N.Y., May 26, 1928; s. William Maurice and Jeannette Edith (Bass) L.; B.A., DePauw U., 1952; M.A., Ind. U., 1954; Ph.D., Columbia Pacific U., 1982; m. Janet Teetor, Aug. 22, 1953; children—Steven, David, Lynne. Psychiat. social worker Richmond (Ind.) State Hosp., 1954-56; asst. dir. Tippecanoe County Mental Health Center, Lafayette, Ind., 1956-62; exec. dir. Venango County Mental Health Center, Oil City, Pa., 1962-71; adminstr. Mental Health/Mental Retardation Authorities, Oil City, 1970-71; dir. Venango Human Services Center, Franklin, Pa., 1971-75; clin. program dir., dir. consultation and edn. Erie County Mental Health Dept.; pvt. practice psychotherapy, Oil City, 1976—; mem. staff dept. psychiatry Oil City Hosp., sr. psychotherapist Vets. Adminstrn. Vietnam Vets. Outreach Program, 1986—; part-time prof. sociology DePauw U., 1956-62; part-time prof. psychology Pa. State U., 1968-69; field prof. U. Pitts., 1969-74; prof. sociology Clarion State Coll., part-time, 1972-73; part-time prof. mental health counseling Gannon Coll., 1975; spl. cons. Corps Chaplains, U.S. Army, 1971-75; mem. profl. adv. com. Crippled Children and Adults Com., 1971-75; mem. profl. adv. com. Clarion State Coll. Sch. Nursing, 1981—. Bd. dirs. Pa. Mental Health Assn., 1969-77, mem. exec. com., 1973-77; del., mem. task force on aging White House Conf. on Aging, 1971; del. Nat. Conf. on Mental Health, 1975; bd. dirs. Franklin Light Opera Co., 1970-74; chmn. project rev. com. Venango Regional Comprehensive Health Planning, 1973-75; chmn. Gt. Lakes Forum on Primary Prevention in Mental Health, 1976; chmn. N.W. Pa. Family Planning Council, 1974; mem. N.W. region steering com. Pub. Com. for Humanities in Pa., 1971-74. Served with AUS, World War II. Named Boss of Yr., Ft. Venango chpt. Nat. Secs. Assn., 1972. Mem. Psychiat. Outpatient Centers Am. (exec. sec. 1966-74), Am. Pub. Health Assn., Am. Coll. Clinic Adminstrs. Editor: Selected Papers of Psychiatric Outpatient Centers, 1967; Psychiatric Outpatient Centers and Low Income Populations, 1968. Home: 406 W 7th St Oil City PA 16301 Office: Glenview Profl Bldg 9 Glenview Ave Oil City PA 16301

LORMAN, WILLIAM RUDOLPH, civil engineer, retired naval officer; b. Cleve., Sept. 26, 1910; s. Rudolph Calman and Theresa Mary (Pollock) L.; m. Hulda Wanita Babel, May 2, 1936 (dec. May 1980); children: Jonathan, Timothy. BS, Case Western Res. U., 1933; MS, U. Colo., 1939, profl. degree CE, 1956. Asst. dep. engr. Cuyahoga County Engrs., Cleve., 1935-36; asst. engr. U.S. Bur. Reclamation, Denver and Redding, Calif., 1936-42; commd. lt. (j.g.) USN, 1942, advanced through grades to lt. comdr., 1948, ret., 1970; spl. projects officer USN, Vanuatu, 1943-44; helium officer USN, Moffett Field Air Station, Calif., 1944; flag staff officer USN fleet aircraft command, Alameda, Calif., 1945-46; civil engr. USN, San Francisco, 1946-48; materials research engr. USN, Solomons, Md., Port Hueneme, Calif., 1948-82; cons. USN liason DuBridge Oil Lease Panel, Los Angeles, 1969, Com. Status of Cement and Concrete Research in U.S., Washington, 1979-81. Contbr. over 80 articles to profl. jours. Fellow ASCE, Am. Concrete Inst.; mem. ASTM, The Ret. Officers Assn. (life, sec. Ventura County, Calif. chpt. 1983-87), Nat. Assn. Retired Fed. Employees (life), Sigma Xi. Republican. Home: 510 Ivywood Dr Oxnard CA 93030

LORNE, SIMON MICHAEL, lawyer; b. Hampton, Eng., Feb. 1, 1946; came to U.S., 1952, naturalized, 1961; s. Henry Thomas and Daphne Mary (Brough) L.; A.B. cum laude, Occidental Coll., 1967; J.D. magna cum laude, U. Mich., 1970; m. Patricia Ann Coady, Aug. 12, 1967; children—Christopher, Michele, Allison, Nathan James, Katrina. Admitted to Calif. bar, 1971; assoc. firm Munger, Tolles & Olson, Los Angeles, 1970-72, ptnr., 1972—; vis. assoc. prof. law U. Pa., 1977-78, acting dir. Ctr. Study of Fin. Instns., 1977-78; lectr. in law, corp. fin. U. So. Calif., 1986—. Author: Acquisitions and Mergers: Negotiated and Contested Transactions, 1985. Mem. Los Angeles Mayor's Com. on Internat. Trade Devel., 1979-81; bd. dirs., sec. Los Angeles Internat. Trade Devel. Corp., 1982-85; mem. adv. com. to U.S. Senator S.I. Hayakawa on Internat. Trade, 1979-82; bd. govs. Econ. Literacy Council Calif., 1981-88. Served with USMCR, 1967-68. Mem. Los Angeles Area C. of C. (exec. com., internat. commerce com., leadership mission to People's Republic of China, 1980), ABA, Los Angeles County Bar Assn. (exec. com. bus. and corps. law sect., chmn. 1984-85). Republican. Roman Catholic. Clubs: Jonathan; Stock Exchange; Lake Arrowhead Yacht. Office: Munger Tolles & Olson 355 S Grand Ave 35th Floor Los Angeles CA 90071

LOROCH, KIM JOSEPH, transportation company executive, consultant; b. Koscierzyna, Poland, June 8, 1923; came to U.S., 1950; s. Piotr and Marta (Schuetz) L.; m. Claudia Gorecka, Nov. 30, 1951 (div.); children—Eugene M., Albert I.; m. 2d, Nena Laczkowska, Oct. 11, 1962. B. Commerce, U. London, 1950; M.B.A., Baruch Sch., CCNY, 1965. Marine economist Bethlehem Steel, N.Y.C., 1954-59; shipbroker Maxwell Harris Co., N.Y.C., 1960-62; port analyst Port Authority N.Y. and N.J., 1962-69; dir. UN/FAO World Food Program, Rome, 1969-74; transport advisor UN World Food Conf., Rome, 1974; cons., Monte Carlo, Monaco, 1975—, Govt. Italy, Cagliari, 1974-75, Hamburg, Germany, 1978—, transport advisor UNCTAD, 1987—; Govt. Malta, Valletta, 1980-81; bus. mgr. Jour. Commerce, 1982-87; conf. speaker. Author: Vessel Voyage Data Analysis, 1966; contbr. articles to profl. jours. Served with Free Polish Merchant Marine, 1939-47. Decorated World War II decorations (5), 1945; Cullman fellow Port Authority of N.Y. and N.J., 1966-67. Mem. Chartered Inst. Transport. Roman Catholic. Home and Office: Loroch Cons, Lilienstrasse 32, D-2000 Hamburg 1 Federal Republic of Germany

LORSCHEIDER, ALOISIO CARDINAL, archbishop of Fortalezo; b. Linha Geraldo, Brazil, Oct. 8, 1924. Joined Franciscan Order, Roman Catholic Ch., 1942; ordained priest, 1948; prof. theology The Antonianum, Rome; dir. Franciscan Internat. House of Studies; consecrated bishop of Santo Angelo (Brazil), 1962; archbishop of Fortalezo (Brazil), 1973—; elevated to Sacred Coll. of Cardinals, 1976; pres. Latin Am. Bishops Conf., 1975; gen. sec. Brazilian Bishops Conf., 1968-71, pres., 1971-79. Address: Cardinal's Residence, CP 9, Fortalezo 60000 Est do Ceara, Brazil *

LORTIE, JOHN WILLIAM, solar research company executive; b. Chgo., July 11, 1920; s. William Arthur and Alice Marie (McNamee) L.; m. Mary Elaine Sullivan, Sept. 21, 1946; children: Colleen, Kevin, Timothy. Student, Ill. Inst. Tech., 1940-42, U. Ala., 1976. Radar technician Western Electric Co., Westchester, Ill., 1946-50; pres. William A. Lortie & Sons, Westchester, 1950-65, Monark Instant Homes, Ocean Springs, Miss., 1965-75; dir. research Energy Research Corp., Mobile, Ala., 1974-88; pres. Essential Solar Products, Mobile, 1980—; pres. Energy Internat., Inc., 1981-88; solar cons.; bd. dirs. Internat. Solar Acad., 1988—; head dept. solar tech. Carver State Tech. Coll., 1976-81. Served with U.S. Army, 1942-46. Mem. Ala. Acad. Scis., Ala. Solar Energy Assn. (state chmn.), Ala. Solar Industries Assn. (bd. dirs., pres.), Internat. Solar Energy Soc., Nat. Assn. Solar Contractors. Republican. Roman Catholic. Home: 4775 Bit Spur Rd Mobile AL 36608

LOSEE, JOHN FREDERICK, JR., manufacturing executive; b. Milw., Apr. 27, 1951; s. John Frderick and Helen (Francis) L.; m. Jane Agnes Trawicki, Aug. 25, 1973; children: Nicole Marie, John Michael. BSME, Marquette U., 1973, MS in Indsl. Engring., 1982. Registered profl. engr., Wis.; cert. numerical control mgr., Wis. Mfg. engr. OMC-Evinrude div. Outboard Marine Corp., Milw., 1975-78, mfg. engr. supr., 1978-80, mgr. tool engring., 1980-85, mgr. process and tool engring., 1985-86, dir. mfg. engring., 1986—. Mem. Numerical Control Soc., Soc. Mfg. Engrs., Computer and Automated Systems Assn. Republican. Episcopalian. Home: W264 N6565 Hillview Dr Sussex WI 53089 Office: OMC Evinrude Div Outboard Marine Corp 6101 N 64th St PO Box 663 Milwaukee WI 53201

LOSI, MAXIM JOHN, medical communications executive; b. Jersey City, Dec. 27, 1939; s. Maxim Fortune and Carrie (Rivoli) L.; AB, Princeton U., 1960; postgrad. Albert Einstein Coll. Medicine, N.Y. Med. Coll., 1960-62; PhD, N.Y.U., 1972; m. Mary Ann De Grandis, May 30, 1968; children—Christopher, Benjamin. Lectr. English, C.W. Post Coll. at L.I. U., Greenvale, N.Y., 1965-67; instr. English, Centenary Coll. for Women, Hackettstown, N.J., 1967-71, chmn. dept., 1970-71; med. abstractor/indexer Council for Tobacco Research, N.Y.C., 1972-73; freelance med. writer, 1973-74; sr. clin. info. scientist Squibb Inst. Med. Research, Princeton, N.J., 1974-77, project team leader, 1975-77; chief med. writer ICI Ams., Wilmington, Del., 1977-79; dir. biomed. communications Revlon Health Care Group, Tuckahoe, N.Y., 1979-86; pres. Max Losi Assocs., Trenton, N.J., 1986-87; dir. project mgmt., sci. documentation G.H. Besselaar Assocs., Princeton, N.J., 1987—; FDA cons. Microbiol. Assocs., Bethesda, Md., 1973; mgmt. cons. Robert S. First Assocs., N.Y.C., 1974; vis. lectr. med. writing techniques St. George U. Med. Sch., Grenada, W.I., 1977. Mem. Am. Med. Writers Assn. (nat. pres. 1987-88), Drug Info. Assn., Council of Biology Editors, Soc. Tech. Communication. Roman Catholic. Home: 1194 Parkside Ave Trenton NJ 08618

LOSONCZI, PAL, former president Hungarian People's Republic; b. Sept. 18, 1919. Former agrl. laborer; organizer, chmn. Red Star Coop. Farm, 1948; mem. Parliament, 1953—; minister agr. Hungary, 1960-67; pres. Hungarian People's Republic, 1967-87. Mem. cen. com. Hungarian Socialist Workers Party, Presidium Nat. Council Patriotic Peoples' Front. Chmn. Nat. Council Coop. Farms, 1965-67. Decorated Hero Socialist Labor, Order Hungarian People's Republic, 1954; Order of October Revolution (USSR), 1979; recipient Kossuth prize, 1956. Address: Presdl Council, Kossuth Lajos ter 1/3 1055, Budapest Hungary *

LOTEMPIO, JULIA MATILD, accountant; b. Budapest, Hungary, Oct. 14, 1934; came to U.S., 1958, naturalized 1962; d. Istvan and Irma (Sandor) Fejos; m. Anthony Joseph, Mar. 11, 1958. AAS in Lab. Tech. summa cum laude, Niagara County Community Coll., Sanborn, N.Y., 1967; BS in Tech. and Vocat. Edn. summa cum laude, SUNY, Buffalo, 1970; MEd in Guidance and Counseling, Niagara U., 1973, BBA in Acctg. summa cum laude, 1983. Sr. analyst, researcher Great Lakes Carbon Co., Niagara Falls, N.Y., 1967-71; tchr. sci. Niagara Falls Schools, 1973-75; tchr. sci. and English Starpoint Sch. System, Lockport, N.Y., 1975-77; instr. applied chem. Niagara County Community Coll., Sanborn, 1979; club adminstr., acct. Twinlo Racquetball, Inc., Niagara Falls, 1979-81; bus. cons. Twinlo Beverage, Inc., Niagara Falls, 1981-85; staff acct. J.D. Elliott & Co. PC, CPAs, Buffalo, 1986-87; acct. Lewiston, N.Y., 1988—; bd. dirs. Niagara Frontier Meth. Home Inc., Niagara Frontier Nursing Home Inc., The Blocher Homes Inc., Buffalo. Mem. faculty continuing edn. United Meth. Ch., Dickersonville, N.Y., 1985—; guest speaker, counselor, tchr. Beechwood Service Guild, Buffalo, 1987—; bd. dirs. Niagara Frontier Meth. Home, Inc., Getzville, N.Y., 1988—, Niagara Frontier Nursing Home Co., Inc., Getzville, 1988—, Blocher Homes, Inc., Williamsville, N.Y., 1988—. Mem. Nat. Assn. Accts., Nat. Assn. Female Execs., Nat. Fedn. Bus. and Profl. Women's Club, Internat. Platform Assn., Niagara U. Alumni Assn., SUNY Coll. at Buffalo Alumni Assn., Niagara County Community Coll. Alumni Assn. Home and Office: 1026 Ridge Rd Lewiston NY 14092

LOTON, BRIAN THORLEY, business executive; b. Perth, Australia, May 17, 1929; s. Ernest Thorley and Grace May (Smith) L.; m. Joan Kemelfield, Jan. 12, 1956; children—Andrew, Virginia, Carolyn, Warwick. B.Met.Eng., Melbourne U., 1953. Cadet, The Broken Hill Pty. Co., Ltd., Melbourne, 1954, gen. mgr. Newcastle Steelworks, 1970, exec. gen. mgr. Steel div., 1973, chief gen. mgr., 1977, mng. dir., 1982—, chief exec. officer, 1985—; vice chmn. Def. Industry Com., Canberra, 1976-88. Fellow Instn. Engrs. Australia (hon.); mem. Australian Mining Industry Council (pres. 1983-84), Australasian Inst. Mining and Metallurgy (pres. 1982). Club: Melbourne, Australian. Office: Broken Hill Proprietary Co Ltd, 140 William St, Melbourne 3001, Australia

LOTT, FELICITY ANN, opera singer; b. Cheltenham, Gloucestershire, Eng., May 8, 1947; d. John Albert and Whyla (Williams) L.; m. Robin Golding, 1973 (div. 1982); m. Gabriel Woolf, Jan. 19, 1984; 1 child, Emily. BA (hons.) in French, U. London Royal Holloway Coll., 1969; student, Royal Acad. of Music, London, 1969-73. Prin. roles with Glyndebourne Festival Opera, English Nat. Opera, Covent Garden, Scottish Opera, Welsh Opera; world-wide recitals. Fellow Royal Acad. Music; mem. The Songmakers' Almanac (founder). Office: Lies Askonas, 186 Drury Ln, London NC28 5RY, England

LOTZ, GEORGE MICHAEL, computer graphics executive; b. Balt., Aug. 28, 1928; s. Michael Henry and Mina Catherine (Fleck) L.; m. Anna Mae Carlson, July 21, 1951; 1 child, Georgeanna. Student Md. Inst. Art, 1956-58, Johns Hopkins U., 1957-58, Catonsville Community Coll., 1975, Essex Community Coll., 1976-78. Mech. draftsman, designer Sinclair Scott Canning House Machinery Co., Balt., 1943-50; illustrator, designer Communications div. Bendix Corp., Towson, Md., 1950-69, supr. graphic arts, photography, 1969-73, art dir., 1974-78, mgr. computer graphics dept., 1978—; art dir., pres. Glen Arm Graphic, 1963-74; advisor Md. State Dept. Art Edn., 1973-78, U. Md. Coll. Human Ecology, 1981—, Essex Community Coll. Computer Graphics, 1981—, Community Coll. Balt. Graphics, 1978—; mem. panel Nat. Endowment Arts. 1977-78; conf. chmn. Indsl. Graphics Internat. U. Md., 1974, adv. Coll. of Human Ecology & Art Design, 1981—; advisor graphic arts Community Coll. Balt., 1978—, Essex Community Coll., 1981—; guest speaker various local colls., 1973, 77, profl. groups, 1967-78. Judge, Jr. Miss Pagent, Reisterstown, Md., 1971, 72. Served with USNR, 1947-48. Recipient 38 nat. awards for art direction, graphics design including 1st pl. newsletter design Nat. Assn. Indsl. Artists. 1970; 1st pl. award Assoc. Printing Industries Am., 1976, 1st place award Soc. Tech. Communications, 1977; award of excellence Printing Industries Md., 1978, 79; 1st place in photography 1982 World's Fair Design. Competition. Mem. Indsl. Graphics Internat. (pres. 1975-77, exec. dir., 1980—, Award of Merit 13th ann. design competition for promotional photography, Vancouver, B.C., 1986), Council Communication Soc. (dir. 1984-85), Advt. Assn. Balt. (dir. 1971-78). Clubs: Bendix Emblem, Bendix Mgmt. (pres. 1982-83), Balt. Camera. Contbr. articles on graphic art and edn. to profl. jours. Home: 11212 Old Carriage Rd Glen Arm MD 21057 Office: Bendix Corp 1300 E Joppa Rd Baltimore MD 21204

LOTZ, JOHN JACOB, bldg. contractor; b. Phila., Aug. 19, 1922; s. William F. and Amelia (Albright) L.; B.S. in Civil Engring., Lehigh U., 1947; D.H.L., Combs Coll., 1970; m. Evelyn L. Buckley, Sept. 16, 1944; children—Joan Lotz Subotnick, Mary Lotz Dare. Pres., Lotz Designers, Engrs., Constructors, Horsham, Pa., dir. Frankford Trust Co. Past mem. Cheltenham Twp. Bd. Edn., Sch. Authority Abington Twp.; vice chmn. bd. trustees Spring Garden Coll.; past pres. Carpenters' Co. Phila. (Carpenters Hall); bd. dirs. YWCA, Pen Jer Del. Served with Combat Engrs. U.S. Army, World War II. Benjamin Franklin fellow Royal Soc. Arts, London, 1976; named Engr. of Yr., Delaware Valley Engring. Soc., 1977. Fellow ASCE, Soc. Am. Mil. Engrs. (past pres.); Mem. Gen. Bldg. Contractors Assn. Phila. (dir., past pres.), Montgomery County Indsl. Devel. Corp. (dir.), Nat. Assn. Indsl. and Office Parks (past pres., chmn. Edn. Found.), N.E. Mfrs. Assn. (past pres.), Mfrs. Assn. of Delaware Valley (dir.), Engrs. Club Phila. (George Washington Gold medal for Engring. Excellence 1983), Am. Concrete Inst., Northeastern Ind. Devel. Assn., Am. Indsl. Devel. Council, Indsl. Developers Research Council, Prudential Bus. Campus Assn. (past pres.), Soc. Indsl. Realtors, Council Urban Econ. Dirs., Urban Land Inst., Landmarks Soc. Phila. (dir.), Beta Theta Pi (past chpt. pres.). Clubs: Masons, Shriners (trustee), Kiwanis, Seaview Country, Mfrs. Country. Contbr. articles to profl. jours.; nat. lectr. on balanced econ. growth, environ. concerns and economic need, indsl. and office park devel. Home: 1846 Hemlock Circle Abington PA 19001 Office: 601 Dresher Horsham PA 19044

LOUBE, SAMUEL DENNIS, physician; b. Rumania, Aug. 26, 1921; came to U.S., 1922, naturalized, 1927; s. Harry and Rebecca (Pollack) L.; m. Emily Wallace, Apr. 14, 1976; children—Julian M., Jonathan B., Susan C., Karen E., Patricia A., Pamela B., Brian R. A.B., George Washington U., 1941, M.D. cum laude, 1943. Diplomate: Am. Bd. Internal Medicine. Intern, then resident in medicine Gallinger Municipal Hosp., Washington, 1943-46; physician USPHS, 1946-48; postdoctoral fellow NIH, 1948-50; research fellow in endocrinology Michael Reese Hosp., Chgo., 1948-49; research fellow in metabolism and endocrinology May Inst. Jewish Hosp., Cin., 1949-50; mem. faculty George Washington U. Med. Sch., 1950—, clin. prof. medicine, 1975—; practice medicine specializing in endocrinology and metabolic diseases, Washington, 1950—; mem. Washington Internal Medicine Group, 1965—; former chmn. sect. endocrinology Sibley Meml. Hosp. Contbr. articles to med. jours. Fellow A.C.P.; mem. Am. Diabetes Assn., Endocrine Soc., AMA, Am. Soc. Internal Medicine, Am. Fedn. Clin. Research, Diabetes Assn. D.C. (past pres.), Jacobi Med. Soc. (past pres.). Jewish. Office: 730 24th St NW Suite 7 Washington DC 20037

LOUBSER, EDUARD ANTONIE, diplomat; b. Cape Town, Cape, Republic South Africa, Dec. 26, 1935; s. Edward William and Alida Jacoba (Lombard) L.; m. Susanna Elizabeth Bezuidenhout, Jan. 19, 1962; children: Eloïse Adèle, Eduard Anton, Rupert Emile. BCom, U. Stellenbosch, Republic S. Africa, 1956; BA, U. S. Africa, Pretoria, 1971; BA honors, U. Pretoria, 1979, MA Internat. Politics, 1983. Cadet Dept. Fgn. Affairs, Pretoria, 1958, second sec. later first sec., 1965, counselor, 1976, chief of protocol, 1984; third sec. S. African Embassy, Paris, 1961; counselor S. African Embassy, Brussels, 1970; minister plenipotentiary S. African Embassy, Paris, 1980, chief of protocol, 1984; ambassador Republic S. Africa, Israel, 1986-88; consul gen. Republic S. Africa, Copenhagen, 1988—. Dutch Reformed Ch. Mem. Huguenot Soc. S. Africa, Simon van der Stel Found., Alliance Francaise Cape Town (com. mem. 1985-86). Lodge: Rotary. Clubs: Round Table (Paris, Pretoria). Office: Dept Fgn Affairs, Pvt Bag X 152, Pretoria 0001, Republic of South Africa

LOUCKS, VERNON REECE, JR., hospital supply company executive; b. Kenilworth, Ill., Oct. 24, 1934; s. Vernon Reece and Sue (Burton) L.; m. Linda Kay Olson, May 12, 1972; children: Charles, Greg, Suzy, David, Kristi, Eric. B.A. in History, Yale U., 1957; M.B.A., Harvard U., 1963. Sr. mgmt. cons. George Fry & Assos., Chgo., 1963-65; with Baxter Travenol Labs., Inc. (now Baxter Internat.), Deerfield, Ill., 1966—, exec. v.p., 1973-76, dir., 1975—, pres., chief exec. officer, 1976—, chief exec. officer, 1980—, chmn., 1987—; dir. Dun & Bradstreet Corp., Emerson Electric Co., Quaker Oats Co. Chmn. Met. Crusade of Mercy, 1977; bd. dirs. Lake Forest Hosp.; trustee Rush-Presbyn.-St. Lukes Med. Center; assoc. Northwestern U.; successor trustee Yale Corp.; John L. and Helen Kellogg Found.; chmn. Yale Devel. Bd. Served to 1st lt. USMC, 1957-60. Recipient Citizen Fellowship award Chgo. Inst. Medicine, 1982, Nat. Health Care award B'nai B'rith Youth Services, 1986; named 1983's Outstanding Exec. Officer in the healthcare industry Financial World; elected to Chgo.'s Bus. Hall of Fame, Jr. Achievement, 1987. Mem. Health Industry Mfrs. Assn. (chmn. 1983), Bus. Roundtable, Chgo. Com. of Chgo. Council on Fgn. Relations. Clubs: Chgo. Commonwealth, Commercial, Mid-America. Office: Baxter Internat Inc 1 Baxter Pkwy Deerfield IL 60015

LOUD, PATRICIA RUSSELL, literary agent, editor; b. Eugene, Oreg., Oct. 4, 1926; d. Thomas Osmonde Summers and Myrle Margaret (Lill) R.; m. William Carberry Loud, Mar. 1, 1950 (div. Sept. 1971); children: Alanson, Kevin, Grant, Delilah, Michele. BA, Leland Stanford Jr. U., 1948. V.p. in charge pub. relations Am. Essence Co., N.Y.C., 1974; asst. lit. agt. Ron Bernstein Agy., N.Y.C., 1975-81; lit. agt. Loud/Munro Agy., N.Y.C., 1981-85; freelance editor Bath, Eng., 1985—. Author: Pat Loud, A Woman's Story, 1973. Mem. Jr. League (Eugene). Home: 12 Lansdown Crescent, Bath BA1 5EX, England

LOUDON, AARNOUT ALEXANDER, corporate executive; b. The Hague, The Netherlands, Dec. 10, 1936; m. Talitha Adine Charlotte Boon, 1962; 2 children. Ed. U. Utrecht. With Bank Mees & Hope, 1964-69, head new issues dept., 1967-69; with AKZO Group, 1969—, dir. cen. staff dept. fin., 1971-72; fin. dir. Astral subs. AKZO Coatings, France, 1972-75; pres. AKZO Brazil, 1975-77; mng. dir. AKZO NV, 1977-78, dep. pres., 1978, pres., 1982—, also bd. dirs. Home: Kluizenaarsweg 6, 6881 Velp The Netherlands Office: Akzo NV, 6 Velperweg Box 186, 6800 Arnhem The Netherlands *

LOUGHLIN, JOHN PATRICK, university lecturer; b. Belfast, Northern Ireland, Sept. 9, 1948; s. John Patrick and Margaret (McLaughlin) L. BA with honors, Ulster (Northern Ireland) Poly. U., 1982; PhD, European U. Inst., Florence, Italy, 1987. Monk Trappist Order, Portglenone, Ireland, 1968-73; organizer United Farm Workers Am., Montreal, Que., Can., 1973-77; researcher European U. Inst., 1982-85; lectr. U. Ulster, 1985—; chair Faith and Politics Study Group, Newtownabbey, Northern Ireland, 1987—; dir. European Consortium Polit. Research Workshop, Amsterdam, Holland, 1987. Contbr. articles and book chpts. on French politics to profl. publs., articles on Irish politics to newspapers. Mem. Internat. Polit. Sci. Assn., Ireland Polit. Studies Assn., Assn. Univ. Tchrs., Brit. Assn. Irish Studies. Office: U Ulster, Dept Pub Adminstrn, BT37 0QB Newtownabbey Northern Ireland

LOUIS, LESLIE BERTRAM, pianist; b. Singapore, Aug. 13, 1948; s. Gnanapragasam Lawrence and Ellen Gladys Louis; student Royal Coll. Music, 1968-72, asso., 1971; student Trinity Coll. Music, London, 1972-74. Musician (piano, organ, accordian), cruises, restaurants and hotels, Walton-on-Thames, Eng., 1973—; asst. music dir. No. Ballet Co., Manchester, 1974-75; co. pianist Essen Ballet Co (Germany), 1982-83. Mem. Anglo Austrian Music Soc., Incorporated Soc. Musicians, Musicians Union, London Philharm. Choir, Internat. Songwriters Assn. Roman Catholic. Clubs: Badminton, Tennis. Address: 40 St Johns Rd, St Johns, Woking, Surrey GU21 1SA, England

LOUIS, PAUL ADOLPH, lawyer; b. Key West, Fla., Oct. 22, 1922; s. Louis and Rose Leah (Weinstein) L.; m. Nancy Ann Lapof, Dec. 28, 1971; children: Louis Benson, IV, Connor Cristina and Marshall Dore (twins). B.A., Va. Mil. Inst., Lexington, 1947; LL.B., U. Miami, Fla., 1950, J.D., 1967. Bar: Fla. 1950, U.S. Dist. Ct. (so. dist.) Fla. Asst. state atty. 1955-57; atty. Beverage Dept. Fla., 1957-60; spl. asst. atty. gen. State of Fla., 1970-71; partner firm Sinclair, Louis, Siegel, Heath, Nussbaum & Zavertnik (P.A.), Miami, 1960—; mem. Fed. Jud. Nominating Commn., 1977-80; mem. peer rev. com. U.S. Dist. Ct. for So. Dist. Fla., 1983—. Author: Defamation, How Far Can You Go, Trial and Tort Trends, 1969; contbr.: chpts. to Fla. Family Law, 1967, 72. Founder mem. Palm Springs Gen. Hosp. Scholarship Com., 1968; mem. Dade County Health Facilities Authority, 1979—. Served to maj. USAAF, 1943-45, ETO. Decorated Air medal with five oak leaf clusters, Bronze Star (7), Purple Heart. Mem. ABA, Fla. Bar (bd. cert. civil trial lawyer and marital and family law, bd. govs. 1970-74), Dade County Bar Assn. (dir. 1954-55, 66-69), Assn. Trial Lawyers Am., Am. Judicature Soc., Va. Mil. Inst. Alumni Assn. Democrat. Jewish. Club: Miami. Home: 4411 Palm Ln Miami FL 33137 Office: 1125 A I duPont Bldg 169 E Flagler St Miami FL 33131

LOURDUSAMY, SIMON CARDINAL, cardinal Roman Catholic Church; b. Kalleri, Pondicherry, India, Feb. 5, 1924. ordained 1951. Consecrated bishop Titular Ch. Sozusa, Libya, 1962; titular archbishop Philippi, 1964; archbishop Bangalore, 1968-71; proclaimed cardinal 1985; sec. Congregation for the Evangelization of Peoples, 1973-85; pres. Pontifical Missionary Work. Home: Palazzo Propaganda Fide, Piazza di Spagna 48, 00187 Rome Italy Office: Congregation for Ea Chs, Plazzo dei Convertendi, Via della Conciliazione 34, 00193 Rome Italy *

LOURIE, SYLVAIN, educational planning institute executive, education economist; b. Paris, Oct. 9, 1928; s. Michel and Sarah (Krynker) L.; m. Sofia Sjostrand, Dec. 26, 1956 (div.); 1 child, Sven-Michel; m. Dominique Louise Luccioni, Dec. 12, 1975; children—Lisa, Nina. BA, Lehigh U., 1947; MA, Columbia U., 1954; doctorate Paris Sorbonne U., 1956; research fellow Ecole Pratique des Hautes Etudes, 1960. Author: Education and Development in Central America, 1984, (with others) Partners in Development, 1969, Learning to Be, 1972; contbr. articles to profl. jours. Dir. div. edn., planning UNESCO, Paris, 1969-73, regional edn. advisor, Cen.Am., 1973-79, asst. dir. policy and planning, 1987; prof. econs. U. Aix-Marseille II, 1980; edn. advisor, Paris, 1981; dir. Internat. Inst. Edn. Planning, Paris, 1982-88; asst. dir. gen. studies and programming UNESCO, 1988—. Home: 2615 Rue Raymond Losserand, 75014 Paris France Office: UNESCO, Place de Fontenoy, 75007 Paris France

LOUTFY, ALY, economist, educator; b. Cairo, Oct. 6, 1935; s. Mahmoud L.; m. Eglal Mabrouk, 1966; 1 son. Ed. Ain Shams U., Louzan U. Joined staff Faculty of Commerce, Ain Shams U., 1957, prof. econs., chmn. dept. econs., 1980—; prof. High Inst. Co-op. and Adminstrv. Studies; prof. Inst. Arab Research and Studies, Cairo; dir. Bank of Commerce and Devel., Cairo; mem. Legis. Polit. Sci. and Econ. Assn., 1977, Delta Sugar Co., 1978, Bank of Commerce and Devel., 1980—; minister of fin. Govt. Egypt, 1978-80. Author: Economic Evolution; Economic Development; Economic Planning; Studies in Mathematical Economy and Econometrics; Financing Problems in Under-Developed Countries; Industrialization Problems in Under-Developed Countries; 25 research papers in econs. Recipient Ideal Prof. award Egyptian Univs., 1974, Gold Mercury Internat. award, 1979. Home: 29 Ahmed Heshmat St, Zamalek, Cairo Egypt Office: Ain Shams U, Kasr-El-Zaafaran, Abbasiya, Cairo Egypt *

LOUVARIS, KIMON MILTON, psychotherapist; b. Athens, Greece, May 15, 1915; s. Milton K. and Hellen John (Pappas) L.; m. Mary A. Petropoulos, June 15, 1947; children—Thomas, Annast, Milton, Katherine. B.Sc., La Salle U., Chgo., 1965; LL.B., U. Chgo., 1964. Pvt. practice psychotherapy, West Palm Beach, Fla., 1974-83, S.I., N.Y., 1983—; exec. dir. Panhellenic Soc. Inventors of Greece (U.S.A.), Merrick, N.Y., 1983—; chmn. Greek Am. Counselor Ctr. of Greece in U.S.A., Merrick, 1982—; counsellor, tchr. polit. systems. Author: Diesel Engines; Television and Radio Guide (in Greek and English). research in abnormal psychotherapy, mental illness. Served with U.S. Mcht. Marines, 1941-45. Decorated Order of St. John of Jerusalem. Mem. Nat. Psychol. Assn. Episcopalian. Home: 2053 Narwood Ave Merrick NY 11566 Office: 32 Fort Hill Circle Saint George Staten Island NY 10301

LOUX, JOSEPH ANTHONY, JR., clergyman; b. Albany, N.Y., Oct. 2, 1945; s. Joseph Anthony and Claire (Finkle) L.; m. Marjorie Anne Bronk, May 5, 1973; 1 child, Joseph Anthony III. A.A. cum laude, Jr. Coll. of Albany, 1965; B.A. in History and English, SUNY-Albany, 1967; M.Div. cum laude in Counseling, New Brunswick Theol. Sem., 1970; Doctorandus in de Godgeleerdheid in Ch. History, U. Leyden, Netherlands, 1972, Ph.D. in Philosophy, Roosevelt U., Belgium, 1985. Pastor, tchr. Helderberg Ref. Ch., Guilderland Center, N.Y., 1973-86, 2d Ref. Ch., Coxsackie, N.Y., 1986—; pres. Loux Music Pub. Co., 1984—; organized Guilderland Interfaith Council, 1973; retreat dir. Capital Dist. Ch. Women United, 1973; dir. Capital Area Council Chs., 1975-76; organizer, chmn. 350th Ann. Com. Synod of Albany, Ref. Ch. in Am., 1977-78, sec. Commn. on History, 1979-82, pres. Reverend Classis of Schenectady, 1982-83. Author: The Boels of Hilversum, 1970; Moderation vs. Dogma, 1972, Boels Complaint against Frelinghuisen, 1980; also articles in profl. jours. Organizer, chmn. Town of Guilderland Bicentennial com., 1975-76; founder, organizer Capital Dist. chpt. Am. Recorder Soc., 1976; founder mem. adj. faculty Schenectady County Community Coll., 1982-83, SUNY-Albany, 1983. Mem. Ref. Ch. Am. Hist. Soc. (organizer, founder Rensselaerswyck chpt. No. 1). Home: 2 Hawley Ln Box 34 Hannacroix NY 12087 Office: 2d Reformed Ch Washington Ave Coxsackie NY 12087

LOVATT, ARTHUR KINGSBURY, JR., manufacturing company executive; b. Ventura, Calif., Mar. 12, 1920; s. Arthur Kingsbury and Flora (Mercedes) L.; B.S., U. So. Calif., 1941; M.B.A., Queens U., 1943; m. Juanita Gray, Feb. 1, 1946; children—Sherry Lynn, Tim Arthur. Leaseman, Shell Oil Co., Los Angeles, 1946-51; dir. indsl. relations Willys-Overland Motors, Inc., Los Angeles, 1952-55; asst. to pres. and gen. mgr. Pastushin Aviation Corp., Los Angeles, 1955-57; pres. Lovatt Assos., Los Angeles, 1957-66; chemn. bd., pres., gen. mgr. Lovatt Tech. Corp., Santa Fe Springs, Calif., 1966—, also dir.; chmn. bd. Lovatt Sci. Corp., Santa Fe Springs, Metal Ore Processes, Inc., Santa Fe Springs; dir. Lovatt Industries, Inc., others. Mem. Calif. Republican State Central Com., 1964—; state adviser U.S. Congl. Adv. Bd.; chartered mem. Republican Pres. Task Force. Served with U.S. Army, 1943-45. Mem. Am. Legion (post comdr. 1946), AAAS, Nat. Space Inst., Am. Soc. Metals, Los Angeles C. of C., U. So. Calif. Alumni Assn. (life), Nat. Hist. Soc. (founding assoc.), N.Y. Acad. Scis., Internat. Oceanographic Found., Smithsonian Assos., Am. Ordnance Assn., Disabled Am. Vets., U.S. Senatorial Club, Nat. Rifle Assn. Club: Masons (past master, Shriner). Inventor, developer tech. processes. Office: Lovatt Tech Corp 10106 Romandel Ave Santa Fe Springs CA 90670

LOVE, JACK WAYNE, surgeon; b. Belleville, Ill., Sept. 20, 1930; s. Charles H. and Helen M. (Golden) L.; student Harvard, 1948-49, U.S. Mil. Acad., 1950-51, U. Ill., Chgo., 1951-52; MD cum laude, Yale U., 1958; D Philosphy (Rhodes scholar), Oxford U., Eng., 1956; m. Elizabeth J. Vogt, Nov. 19, 1960; children: Charles S., John W., Elizabeth P., Richard M., George F., Sarah L. Intern Barnes Hosp., St. Louis, 1959-60, resident in gen. surgery, 1960-61, fellow in thoracic surgery, 1961-63; resident in gen. surgery Walter Reed Gen. Hosp., Washington, 1963-65; practice medicine specializing in cardiovascular surgery; chief of thoracic surgery William Beaumont Gen. Hosp., El Paso, Tex., 1965-67, dir. intern tng., 1966-67; chief div. thoracic and cardiovascular surgery Balt. City Hosps., 1967-69; asso. prof. surgery Johns Hopkins U. Sch. Medicine, Balt., 1967-70; staff surgeon Johns Hopkins Hosp., 1967-70, Greater Balt. Med. Center, 1969-70; Union Meml. Hosp., 1969-70, Md. Gen. Hosp., 1969-70; cons. thoracic surgeon Good Samaritan Hosp., 1969-70, Mt. Wilson State Hosp., 1969-70, Santa Barbara (Calif.) Cottage Hosp., 1970—, Goleta (Calif.) Valley Community Hosp., 1970—, attending thoracic surgeon Harbor Gen. Hosp., Los Angeles, 1974—; assoc. clin. prof. surgery U. Calif., Los Angeles, 1974— . Served from capt. to maj. U.S. Army, 1963-67. Diplomate Am. Bd. Surgery, Am. Bd. Thoracic Surgery. Fellow ACS, Am. Coll. Cardiology, Am. Coll. Chest Physicians; mem. Soc. for Vascular Surgery, Internat. Cardiovascular Soc., Am. Assn. Thoracic Surgery, Soc. of Thoracic Surgeons, Western Thoracic Surg. Assn., Pacific Coast Surg. Assn., N.Y. Acad. Scis., Am. Trauma Soc., Am. Gastroent. Assn., Pan Pacifica Surg. Assn., Soc. Internat. Chirurgie, Sigma Xi, Alpha Omega Alpha. Republican. Roman Catholic. Contbr. numerous articles to med. jours.; editorial bd. Jour. AMA, 1973-77; patentee blood oxygenator, prosthetic heart valve. Home: 785 Carosam Rd Santa Barbara CA 93110 Office: Santa Barbara Med Found Clinic Santa Barbara CA 93110

LOVE, JEFFREY BENTON, lawyer; b. Houston, Oct. 4, 1949; s. Benton Fooshee and Margaret (McKean) L.; m. Katherine Brownlee, Dec. 30, 1972; children—Benton Fooshee III, Elizabeth Houston. B.A., Vanderbilt U., 1971; J.D., U. Tex., 1976. Bar: Tex. 1976. Assoc. Liddell, Sapp, Zivley Hill & LaBoon, Houston, 1976-81, ptnr., 1982—; dir. Tex. Commerce Bank-River Oaks Nat. Assn., Kinark Corp., 1985-88; hon. consul gen. Sweden in Tex., 1983—. Pres. Sunrisers Houston Breakfast Assn., Houston, 1979; dir. exec. com. Houston Grand Opera Assn., Houston, 1979—; dir., chmn. Children's Fund, Inc., Houston, 1981-82; bd. dirs. Tex. Bus. Hall of Fame Found., 1985—, chmn. bd. dirs., 1987; bd. dirs. March of Dimes, Houston, 1986; adv. dir. Eileen McMillin Blood Ctr., Meth. Hosp.; bd. govs., exec. com., sec. The Forum Club, 1987—; bd. dirs., exec. com. Nat. Conf. Christians and Jews, Inc., 1987—; mem. devel. council Tex. Children's Hosp., 1987—; mem. adv. bd. Covenant House Tex., 1988—; mem. fund-raising com. Houston READ Commn.-Campaign for Literacy, 1988—. Recipient Outstanding Young Texas Ex award U. Tex. Ex Students Assn., 1988, 5 Outstanding Young Houstonian awards Houston Jr. C. of C., 1988, 5 Outstanding Young Texan awards Tex. Jaycees, 1988; named one of Outstanding Young Men in Am., U.S. Jaycees, 1980, 81. Mem. ABA, Houston C. of C., Houston Bar Assn., Tex. Bar Assn., Swedish Am. Trade Assn. (bd. dirs. 1983—), U. Tex. Law Alumni Assn. (bd. dirs. 1981—, pres. 1986-87), Phi Delta Theta Alumni Assn. Presbyterian. Clubs: River Oaks, Allegro, Houston. Home: 2038 Timberlane Houston TX 77027 Office: Liddell Sapp Zivley Hill & LaBoon 3400 Texas Commerce Tower Houston TX 77002-3095

LOVE, JOSEPH WILLIAM, JR., retired oil company executive, real estate broker; b. Tulsa, Mar. 31, 1928; s. Joseph William and Eva Elizabeth (Henderson) L. Student Okla. State U., 1945-47; B.S., U. Tulsa, 1949; postgrad. U. Houston, 1957-60. Lic. real estate broker, Tex. Various mgmt. positions Union Tex. Petroleum Corp., 1956-84; cons. in field. Served to capt., USAF, 1951-55. Decorated Air Medal. Mem. Nat. Assn. Bus. Economists, Aircraft Owners and Pilots Assn., Sigma Phi Epsilon. Methodist. Club: Waterwood Nat. Country. Home: 4022 Norfolk Houston TX 77027

LOVE, MICHAEL, design company executive, facilities management consultant; b. Summit, N.J., May 21, 1925; d. Michael and Ethel (Sears) Slifer; m. Edwin P. Love (div.); children—Pamela, Michele. Student Traphagen Sch. Design, 1943-45, U. Miami (Fla.), 1946, Pratt Inst., 1949-50, Parsons Sch. Design, 1980-82. Pres. Quadric Inc., N.Y.C., 1970-78, 82—; v.p. design and constrn. Bankers Trust, N.Y.C., 1978-82; dir. Crestview of Am., Scotch Plains, N.J., 1980—. Lamp designer Am. Soc. Interior Designers; editor articles on interior design Home Mag. Mem. Met. Mus. Art., N.Y.C. Mem. Chief Exec. Officers Club, Am. Soc. Interior Designers (dir.), Constrn. Specifications Inst., Assn. Real Estate Women, Internat. Facilities Mgmt. Assn., Art Deco Soc. N.Y. (pres. 1984—), Profl. Women in Constrn. Club: City (N.Y.C.). Home: 215 E 24th St New York NY 10010 Office: Quadric Inc 686 Lexington Ave New York NY 10022

LOVE, WALTER BENNETT, JR., lawyer; b. Monroe, N.C., Nov. 14, 1921; s. Walter B. and Pearl (Hamilton) L.; m. Elizabeth Cannon, Dec. 28, 1951; children: Elizabeth Sheldon Love Sturges, Walter Bennett III, Linda Louise. BS in Commerce, U. N.C., 1942, JD, 1949; Indsl. Coll. Armed Services, 1972. Bar: N.C. 1949, Fed. bar 1949. Ptnr. Love and Love, Monroe, N.C., 1949-52; sr. ptnr. Love and Milliken, attys. for City of Monroe, 1958—; dir. and counsel Heritage Fed. Sav. and Loan Assn. of Monroe, N.C. Bd. dirs. Nat. Bd. Am. Cancer Soc., 1969-82, pres. N.C. div., 1984, chmn. bd., 1985; past chmn. bd. trustees Cen. United Meth. Ch., 1977-86, lay leader, 1986—; trustee United Meth. Found. for Western N.C. Conf., 1988—; past sec. bd. trustees, Ellen Fitzgeral Hosp. and Union Mem. Hosp. Served to col. USAF and USAFR, WWII and Korea. Decorated with Disting. Unit citation, Victory Medal. Mem. ABA, N.C. Bar Assn., 29th Jud. Dist. Bar Assn. (past pres.), Union County Bar Assn. (past pres.). Democrat. Methodist. Clubs: Rolling Hills Country, Tower, Lions (past pres. and zone chmn. Monroe). Home: 217 Ridgewood Dr Monroe NC 28110 Office: 108 E Jefferson St Monroe NC 28110

LOVEDAY, ANTHONY JOSEPH, librarian; b. Manchester, Eng., Nov. 20, 1925; s. George Edward and Mary (Cullinan) L. MA in English with honors, Cambridge (Eng.) U., 1946; diploma, Univ. Coll. London, 1950. Asst. librarian Univ. Coll. London, 1950-57, U. Malaya, Singapore, 1957-59, U. London Library, 1960-62; dep. librarian Makerere U., Kampala, Uganda, 1962-65; librarian U. Zambia, Lusaka, Zambia, 1965-72; sec. Standing Conf. Nat. and Univ. Libraries, London, 1972—; cons. U. Malawi, Zomba, 1979. Mem. Internat. Fedn. Library Assns. (chmn. div. gen. research libraries 1982-86, mem. profl. bd. 1985-88), Zambia Library Assn. (hon. life mem., chmn. 1967-69). Club: Athenaeum (London). Office: Standing Conf Nat, and Univ Libraries, London NW1 2HA, England

LOVEJOY, THOMAS EUGENE, biologist, association executive, conservationist; b. N.Y.C., Aug. 22, 1941; s. Thomas Eugene and Audrey Helen (Paige) L.; B.S. (scholar), Yale U., 1964, Ph.D. in Biology, 1971; m. Charlotte Seymour, 1966 (div. 1978); children—Elizabeth Paige and Katherine Seymour (twins), Anne Williams. Research assoc. in biology U. Pa., 1971-74; exec. asst. to sci. dir. Acad. Natural Scis., Phila., 1972-73, asst. to v.p. for resources and planning, 1972-73; program dir. World Wildlife Fund-U.S., Washington, 1973-78, v.p. for sci., 1978-85, exec. v.p., 1985-87; asst. sec. external affairs Smithsonian Inst., Washington, 1987— ; bd. dirs. Manhattan Life Ins. Co., N.Y.C., chmn. 1986—; research assoc. in ornithology Acad. Natural Scis., 1971—; chmn., bd. dirs. Wildlife Preservation Trust Internat., 1974—; treas. Internat. Council for Bird Preservation—Pan Am. Sect., 1973-84; sci. fellow N.Y. Zool. Soc., 1978—; mem. adv. bd. Environ. Assessment Council, 1980—; vis. lectr. on tropical ecology Yale U. Sch. Forestry and Environ. Studies, 1982; dir Manhattan Life Corp., 1975-86, chmn. 1986; chmn. exec. com., 1982-86 ; mem. Smithsonian Council, 1982-87; trustee Millbrook Sch., N.Y., 1971—, Rocky Mountain Biol. Lab., 1984—, Acad. Natural Scis. Phila., 1987—; mem. U.S.-Brazil panel White House Office of Sci. and Tech., Washington, 1986-87; chmn. U.S. Man and Biosphere Com., 1987—; sec. J. Paul Getty Wildlife Conservation prize, Washington, 1974-87, jury mem. 1988— ; mem. adv. & tech. bd. Fundacion Neotropica and de Parques Nacional, Costa Rica, 1987—; mem. White House Sci. Council, exec. office Pres., 1988—; dir. N.Y. Rainforest Alliance, 1988—; mem. sci. council, FPCN (Conservation Found., Peru), 1988—; mem. adv. bd. Am. Soc. Protection Nature Israel, 1988—; co-prin. investigator World Wildlife Fund/INPA, North Manaus, Brazil, 1979—; bd. govs. N.Y. Botanical Garden, N.Y.C., 1986—; dir. Ctr. for Plant Conservation, 1987—. Grantee Nat. Geog. Soc., NIH, NSF, Mellon Found., Rockefeller Found.; recipient Ibero-Am. award II Ibero Am. Ornithological Congress, 1983, Cert. of Merit, Goeldi Mus., 1985; named comdr. Order of Merit of Mato Grosso, 1987, commdr. Order of Rio Branco, Brazil, 1988. Fellow N.Y. Zool. Soc., AAAS (wildlife panel 1981), Linnean Soc. London; mem. Am. Inst. Biol. Scis., Am. Ornithologists Union (elective), Ecol. Soc. Am., Brit. Ecol. Soc., Brit. Ornithologists Union, Cooper Ornithol. Soc., Soc. Study of Evolution, Internat. Union for Conservation of Nature (species survival commn.). Clubs: Century, Cosmos, Knickerbocker, New Haven Lawn. Co-author: Nearctic Avian Migrants in the Neotropics, 1983; co-editor: Key Environments: Amazonia, 1985, Conservation of Tropical Forest Birds, 1985; contbr. articles, chpts. to profl. publs. Home: 8526 Georgetown Pike McLean VA 22102 Office: Smithsonian Inst Washington DC 20560

LOVELL, ALAN LEONARD, lottery company executive; b. Melbourne, Australia, Aug. 13, 1920; s. Leonard Victor and Clarice (Edna) L.; m. Elizabeth Mansfield, Dec. 23, 1943; 1 dau., Nadine Elizabeth. Student Melbourne U., 1945-47. Mgr. Comml. Bank of Australia Ltd., New South Wales, 1958-60; mgr. Tattersall-George Adams, Melbourne, 1961-73; exec. dir. Melbourne C. of C., 1973-77; mng. dir. Lotto Mgmt. Services Ptdy., Ltd., Sydney, Australia, 1979—, Australian Soccer Pools Pty., Ltd., 1977-79. Served with Royal Australia Air Force, 1941-43. Fellow Inst. Dirs., Australian Mgmt. Inst., Australian Mktg. Inst. Anglican. Club: Lodge of Commerce. Home: Unit 30, 15-23 Sutherland St, Cremorne 2090, Australia

LOVELL, SIR (ALFRED CHARLES) BERNARD, educator, astronomer; b. Oldland Common. Gloucestershire, Eng., Aug. 31, 1913; s. Gilbert and Emily Laura (Adams) L.; student U. Bristol; LL.D. (hon.), univs. Edinburgh, 1961, Calgary, 1966; D.Sc. (hon.), univs. Leicester, 1961, Leeds, 1966, Bath, 1967, London, 1967, Bristol, 1970; D.Univ., U. Stirling, 1974, U. Surrey, 1975; m. Mary Joyce Chesterman, Sept. 14, 1937. Asst. lectr. physics U. Manchester, 1936-39, with telecommunications research establishment, 1939-45. lectr., sr. lectr., reader physics, 1945-51, prof. radio-astronomy, dir. Nuffield Radio Astronomy Labs., Jodrell Bank, 1951-81; Reith lectr. Brit. Broadcasting System. 1958. Decorated officer Order Brit. Empire, 1946; Comdr.'s Order of Merit (Poland); recipient Duddell medal Phys. Soc., 1954; Royal medal Royal Soc., 1960, Daniel and Florence Guggenheim Internat. Astronautics award, 1961; Order du Merite pour la Recherche et l'Invention, 1962; Churchill gold medal Soc. Engrs., 1964; Benjamin Franklin medal Royal Soc. Arts, 1980. Hon. fellow Instn. Elec. Engrs., Royal Swedish Acad., Inst. Physics; fellow Royal Soc.; mem. Am. Acad. Arts and Scis. (hon. fgn.), Royal Astron. Soc. (pres. 1970-71; Gold medal 1981), N.Y. Acad. Scis. (hon. life). Author: Science and Civilization, 1939; World Power Resources and Social Development, 1945; Radio Astronomy, 1952; Meteor Astronomy, 1954; The Exploration of Space by Radio, 1957; The Individual and the Universe (The Reith Lectures), 1958; The Exploration of Outer Space, 1962; Discovering the Universe, 1963; Our Present Knowledge of the Universe, 1967; editor: (with T. Morgerison) The Explosion of Science: The Physical Universe, 1967; The Story of Jodrell Bank, 1968; The Origins and International Economics of Space Exploration, 1973; Out of the Zenith: Jodrell Bank 1957-70, 1973; Man's Relation to the Universe, 1975; P.M.S. Blackett—a Biographical Memoir, 1976; In the Center of Immensities, 1978; Emerging Cosmology, 1980; The Jodrell Bank Telescopes, 1984, Voice of the Universe, 1987. Contbr. articles to phys. and astron. jours. Home: Quinta Swettenham nr Congleton, Cheshire England Office: Nuffield Radio Astronomy Labs, Jodrell Bank, Macclesfield, Cheshire England also: care Royal Soc, 6 Carlton House Terr, London SW1Y 5AG, England

LOVELL, EMILY KALLED, journalist; b. Grand Rapids, Mich., Feb. 25, 1920; d. Abdo Rham and Louise (Claussen) Kalled; student Grand Rapids Jr. Coll., 1937-39; B.A., Mich. State U., 1944; M.A., U. Ariz., 1971; m. Robert Edmund Lovell, July 4, 1947. Copywriter, asst. traffic mgr. Sta. WOOD, Grand Rapids, 1944-46; traffic mgr. KOPO, Tucson, 1946-47; reporter, city editor Alamogordo (N.Mex.) News, 1948-51; Alamogordo corr., feature writer Internat. News Service, Denver, 1950-54; Alamogordo corr., feature writer El Paso Herald-Post, 1954-65; Alamogordo news dir., feature writer Tularosa (N.Mex.) Basin Times, 1957-59; co-founder, editor, pub. Otero County Star, Alamogordo, 1961-65; newscaster KALG, Alamogordo, 1964-65; free lance feature writer Denver Post, N.Mex. Mag., 1949-69; corr. Electronics News, N.Y.C., 1959-63, 65-69; Sierra Vista (Ariz.) corr. Ariz. Republic, 1966; free lance editor N.Mex. Pioneer Interviews, 1967-69; asst. dir. English skills program Ariz. State U., 1976; free-lance editor, writer, 1977—; part-time tchr., lectr. U. Pacific, 1981-86; part-time interpreter Calif., 1983—, Interpreters Unlimited, Oakland, 1985—; sec., dir. Star Pub. Co., Inc., 1961-64, pres., 1964-65. 3d v.p., publicity chmn. Otero County Community Concert Assn., 1950-65; mem. Alamogordo Zoning Commn., 1955-57; mem. founding com. Alamogordo Central Youth Activities Com., 1957; vice chmn. Otero County chpt. Nat. Found. Infantile Paralysis, 1958-61; charter mem. N.M. Citizens Council for Traffic Safety, 1959-61; pres. Sierra Vista Hosp. Aux., 1966; pub. relations chmn. Ft. Huachuca chpt. ARC, 1966. Mem. nat. bd. Hospitalized Vets. Writing Project, 1972—. Recipient 1st Pl. awards N.Mex. Press Assn., 1961, 62. Pub. Interest award Nat. Safety Council, 1962. 1st Pl. award Nat. Fedn. Press Women, 1960, 62; named Woman of Year Alamogordo, 1960. Editor of Week Pubs. Aux., 1962, adm. N.Mex. Navy, 1962, col. a.d.c. Staff Gov. N.Mex., 1963, Woman of Yr., Ariz. Press Women, 1973. Mem. N.Mex. (past sec.), Ariz. (past pres.) press women, N.Mex. Fedn. Womens Clubs (past dist. pub. relations chmn.), N.Mex. Hist. Soc. (life), N.Mex. Fedn. Bus. and Profl. Womens Clubs (past pres.), Pan Am. Round Table Alamogordo, Theta Sigma Phi (past nat. 3d v.p.), Phi Kappa Phi. Democrat. Moslem. Author: A Personalized History of Otero County, New Mexico, 1963; Weekend Away, 1964; Lebanese Cooking, Streamlined, 1972; A Reference Handbook for Arabic Grammar, 1974, 77; contbg. author: The Muslim Community in North America, 1983. Home: PO Box 7152 Stockton CA 95207

LOVELL, FRANCIS JOSEPH, III, investment company executive; b. Boston, Mar. 21, 1949; s. Frank J. and Patricia Anna (Donnellan) L.; B.B.A., Nichols Coll., 1971. With Brown Bros. Harriman & Co., Boston, 1971, asst. mgr., 1984—. Mem. New Eng. Historic General. Soc. Republican. Home: 25 Pomfret St West Roxbury MA 02132 Office: 40 Water St Boston MA 02109

LOVELY, THOMAS DIXON, savings and loan executive; b. N.Y.C., Apr. 2, 1930; s. Thomas John and Margaret Mary (Browne) L.; A.B., Adelphi U., 1954, M.A., 1956, M.B.A., 1958; m. Erna Susan Fritz, June 16, 1956; children—Thomas John Hall, Richard Robert. Treas., Pepsi Cola Bottling Co., Garden City, N.Y., 1957-60; assoc. prof. mgmt. and communications CUNY, 1958-77; dist. adminstr. Lido Beach (N.Y.) Pub. Schs., 1971-80; chmn. bd., pres. Fidelity Fed. Savs. and Loan Assn., Floral Park, N.Y., 1980-82, chmn. bd., pres. Fidelity N.Y., 1982—; v.p., dir. N.Y. Enterprise Co. Vice chmn. bd. trustees Adelphi U., 1967—, chmn. bd. govs. Univ. Sch. Banking and Money Mgmt., 1975—; trustee Nassau County (N.Y.) Med. Center, 1982—. Exec. v.p., treas. Nassau County Council Boy Scouts Am., 1986—; regional chmn. campaign U.S. Treasury Savs. Bonds Sales, Long Island, 1987—. Mem. SAR, L.I. Insured Savs. Group (v.p.). Clubs: Pinehurst Country (N.C.), Cherry Valley Country (Garden City). Home: 52 Locust St Garden City NY 11530 Office: Fidelity NY Fed Savs Bank 1000 Franklin Ave Garden City NY 11530

LOVENBACH, THIERRY JACQUES, chemical company executive; b. Boulogne S/Seine, France, Aug. 19, 1946; s. Jan and Juliette Myriam (Philippson) L.; m. Cecelene Cover, Nov. 10, 1974. Baccalaureat Maths, Lycee Janson, 1964; B.B.A., Ecole Supè rieure de Commerce, 1969; M.B.A., Harvard Grad. Sch., 1971. Asst. gen. mgr. Rhone Poulenc Agrl. Div., New Brunswick, N.J., 1976-78; dir. chemicals div. Rhone Poulenc Inc., New Brunswick, 1978-79; chmn. bd. Lautier (Rhone Poulenc Group), Grasse, France, 1979-81; dir. mktg. Rhone Poulenc Specialites Chimiques, Paris, 1981; chmn. bd., chief exec. officer Prolabo (Rhone Poulenc Group), Paris, 1982—. Mem. Assn. Fabricants Labo (v.p., bd. dirs. 1982-87), Assn. Pour Le Salon Du Laboratoire (v.p. 1983-87), CIFL (v.p., bd. dirs. 1982—). Club: Racing Club de France (Paris), Anglo-Belgian (London). Avocations: scuba diving; sailing; riding. Home: 1 Square du Roule, 75008 Paris France Office: Prolabo, 12 rue Pelee, 75011 Paris France

LOVENTHAL, MILTON, librarian, writer, playwright, lyricist; b. Jan. 19, 1923; m. Jennifer McDowell, July 2, 1973. BA, U. Calif., Berkeley, 1950, MLS, 1958; MA in Sociology, San Jose State U., 1969. Researcher Hoover Instn., Stanford, Calif., 1952-53; librarian San Diego Pub. Library, 1957-59; librarian, bibliographer San Jose (Calif.) State U., 1959—; tchr. writing workshops, poetry readings, 1969-73; co-producer lit. and culture radio show Sta. KALX, Berkeley, 1971-72. Author: Books on the USSR 1917-57, 1957, Black Politics, 1971, A Bibliography of Material Relating to the Chicano, 1971, Autobiographies of Women 1946-70, 1972, Blacks in America, 1972, The Survivors, 1972, Contemporary Women Poets an Anthology, 1977, Ronnie Goose Rhymes for Grown-Ups, 1984; co-author: (Off-Off-Broadway plays) The Estrogen Party To End War, 1986, Mack the Knife: Your Friendly Dentist, 1986, Betsy & Phyllis, 1986, The Oatmeal Party Comes to Order, 1986; co-writer: (musical comedy) Russia's Secret Plot to Take Back Alaska, 1987. Recipient Bill Casey award in Letters, 1980; grantee San Jose State U., 1962-63, 84. Mem. ALA, Assn. Calif. State Profs., Calif. Alumni Assn., Calif. Assn. Research Librarians, Calif. Theatre Council. Office: PO Box 5602 San Jose CA 95150

LOVESTED, GARY EARL, safety engineer; b. Moline, Ill., Apr. 24, 1936; s. Earl Ivan and Bernice Estelle (Gould) L.; B.A. in Bus. Adminstrn., Augustana Coll., 1968; m. Coleen Adair Clark, June 27, 1964; 1 son, Brandon Gary. Occupational safety rep. Deere & Co., Moline, Ill., 1968-77, occupational safety specialist, 1979—; v.p. loss control Alliance of Am. Insurers, Chgo., 1977-79; instr. indsl. engring. program St. Ambrose Coll.; dir. Devco Research & Mktg., Inc.; bd. dirs. Internat. Loss Control Mgmt. Coll. Chmn. city adv. safety com. City of Moline, 1972-73. Served with USNR, 1955-59. Recipient regional award Hartford Nat. Loss Prevention Competition, 1980; hon. Ky. Col.; cert. safety profl. and hazard control mgr. Mem. Am. Soc. Safety Engrs. (past pres. Quad City chpt.), Human Factors Soc., Nat. Safety Council (Cameron award), Indsl. Safety Assn. Quad Cities (past pres.). Republican. Clubs: Valley Sports Car, Masons. Home: 2100 3 St B East Moline IL 61244 Office: Deere and Co John Deere Rd Moline IL 61265

LOVETT, JAMES EVERETT, nuclear scientist; b. Phila., June 6, 1930; s. Everett Allen and Pauline (Gaither) L.; m. Ruth Marie Glenn, June 18, 1955. BS in Chemistry, U. Kans., 1952; student, Oak Ridge Sch. Reactor Tech., Tenn., 1962-63. Chemist, staff scientist U.S. Atomic Energy Commn., Washington, 1954-65; mgr. nuclear materials control, Nuclear Materials & Equipment Corp., Apollo, Pa., 1966-72; sr. scientist Internat. Atomic Energy Agy., Vienna, Austria, 1972—. Author: Nuclear Materials Accountability, Management, Safeguards, 1974. Active Wiener Singverein Symphony Chorus, 1972—. Fellow Inst. Nuclear Materials Mgmt. (exec. com. 1966-73, chmn. exec. com. 1969-72). Home: Wipplingerstrasse 29-6, A-1010 Vienna Austria Office: Internat Atomic Energy Agy, PO Box 200, A-1400 Vienna Austria

LOVVORN, ROBERT HENRY, insurance company executive; b. Columbia, S.C., Mar. 9, 1916; s. William Barnes and Helen (Cannon) L.; student Am. Coll. Life Underwriters, 1947-52; m. Ellen Childs Seabrook, June 11, 1938; children—Robert Henry, Mary (Mrs. Allen Robinson). Acting mgr. Vol. State Life Ins. Co., 1943, asst. mgr., 1946-48; mgr. Atlantic Life Ins. Co., 1948-54; pres. Calhoun Life Ins. Co., Columbia, S.C., 1954-70; v.p., dir. Appalachian Nat. Life Ins. Co., Columbia, 1970—; pres. Credit Life Services, Inc., 1983—; dir. Appalachian Nat. Corp., So. Bank & Trust, Guardian Fidelity Corp., S.C. Mental Retardation Found. Mem. at large Nat. Social Welfare Assembly, 1950-73; chmn. S.C. Mental Retardation Commn., 2d Congl. Dist., 1968—, Univ. Assos. U. S.C., 1970—. Past pres. Jr. C. of C., Better Bus. Bur., S.C. Mental Health Assn. Decorated Order of Palmetta, Gov. of S.C. Recipient Vol. Recognition award U.S. Dept. Health and Human Services. Served with USNR, 1944-46. Mem. Columbia C. of C., Com. of 100, Sales Execs. Club (past pres.), S.C. Bankers Assn., S.C. Ind. Bankers Assn., S.C. Credit Ins. Assn. (chmn. 1982—), S.C. Assn. Life Ins. Cos. (past pres.). Clubs: Forest Lake Country, Tarantella, Palmetto, Columbia Ball, Cotillion, Sertoma Internat. (life), Quadrille. Home: 4120 Linwood Rd Columbia SC 29205 Office: 5219 Trenholm Rd Columbia SC 29260

LOVY, ANDREW, osteopathic physician, psychiatrist; b. Budapest, Hungary, Mar. 15, 1935; came to U.S., 1939; s. Joseph and Elza (Kepecs) L.; m. Madeline Rotenberg, Aug. 16, 1959; children: Daniel, Jordan, Howard, Jonathan, Elliot, Richard, Mickey. Student Wayne State U., 1956; BS, Ill. Coll. Optometry, 1957, OD, 1958. DO, Chgo. Coll. Osteopathy, 1962. Intern, Mt. Clemens (Mich.) Hosp., 1962-63; resident VA Hosp., Augusta, Ga., 1971-74; practice medicine specializing in psychiatry, Detroit, 1982; prof. psychiatry, chmn. dept. psychiatry Chgo. Coll. Osteo. Medicine, 1981-82; dir. psychiat. tng. program Mich. Osteo. Med. Ctr., Detroit, 1982-86 ; adj. prof. psychiatry W.Va. Coll. Osteo. Medicine, 1984; clin. prof. psychiatry N.Y. Coll. Osteo. Medicine, 1984; med. dir. Eastwood Clinics, 1987. Served with M.C., U.S. Army, 1966-68; Vietnam. Decorated Air medal, Bronze Star with oak leaf cluster, Purple Heart, Army Commendation medal. Fellow Am. Coll. Neuropsychiatry; mem. Am. Osteo. Assn., Am. Heart Assn. (mem. stroke com. 1987—), Am. Psychiat. Assn., Am. Osteo. Acad. Sports Medicine, Assn. Acad. Psychiatrists, Assn. Clin. Hypnosis, Am. Osteo. Coll. Neuropsychiatry (pres.-elect 1982-83, pres. 1983-84), Am. Med. Joggers Assn. Author: Vietnam Diary, 1971. Office: 14600 Farmington Rd Livonia MI 48154

LOW, ANTHONY, English language educator; b. San Francisco, May 31, 1935; s. Emerson and Clio (Caroli) L.; m. Pauline Iselin Mills, Dec. 28, 1961; children: Louise, Christopher, Georgianna, Elizabeth, Peter, Catherine, Nicholas, Alexandra, Michael, Frances, Jessica, Edward. A.B., Harvard U., 1957, M.A., 1959, Ph.D., 1965. Mem. faculty Seattle U., 1965-68; mem. faculty NYU, N.Y.C., 1968—; prof. English lit. NYU, 1978—; vis. scholar Jesus Coll., Cambridge, Eng., 1974-75. Author: Augustine Baker, 1970, The Blaze of Noon, 1974, Love's Architecture, 1978, The Georgic Revolution, 1985; editor: Urbane Milton, 1984. Mem. Milton Soc., Donne Soc., MLA, Renaissance Soc., Modern Humanities Research Assn., Phi Beta Kappa. Club: Tarratine. Home: 7 Christopher Rd Ridgefield CT 06877 Office: NYU Dept English 19 University Pl New York NY 10003

LOW, BIN TICK, dermato-venereologist; b. Kuala Lumpur, Malaysia, Mar. 5, 1942; s. Koon Hong and Chean (Goh) L.; m. Regina Kim Mooi Lee, Feb. 27, 1966; children: Julia, Gary, Jacqueline. MBBS, U. Singapore, 1968; diploma in venereology, cert. in aviation medicine, London Inst. Aviation Medicine, 1974; diploma in dermatology, U. London, 1976. Lic. Royal Coll. Gen. Practitioners, Royal Coll. Physicians. Med. officer, acting registrar Gen. Hosp., Kuala Lumpur, 1968-71; with Kuala Lumpur Clinic, 1971-72; sr. house officer London Hosp., 1973-74; cons. venereology Kuala Lumpur Spl. Clinic, 1976-86; cons. dermato-venereologist Kuala Lumpur Skin Clinic, 1986—; cons. Chinese Maternity Hosp., Kuala Lumpur, 1980—; sec. gen. S.E. Asian and Western Pacific Br. Internat. Union Against Veneral Disease and Treponemation, WHO; bd. dirs. Medic Alert Found. Malaysia, 1981—; dep. comdr.-in-chief St. John Ambulance, Malaysia. Named Officer Order St. John, 1979, Ahli Mangku Negara, Malaysia, 1983. Fellow Am. Acad. Dermatology; mem. Royal Coll. Gen. Practice, Royal Coll. Physicians, Royal Coll. Gen. Practice Australia, Malaysian Coll. Gen. Practitioners, Acad. Medicine Malayia, Malaysian Med. Assn., Brit. Med. Assn., Nat. Heart Found. Malaysia, Malaysian Sports Medicine Assn., Dermatol. Soc. Malaysia, Singapore Med. Alumni (chmn. cen. br.), Malaysian Chinese Assn. Home: 20 Lorong Hujan Dua, Taman Oug, Kuala Lumpur 58200, Malaysia Office: Kuala Lumpur Skin Clinic, 88 Jalan Bukit Bintang 2d Floor, Kuala Lumpur 55100, Malaysia

LOW, EMMET FRANCIS, JR., mathematics educator; b. Peoria, Ill., June 10, 1922; s. Charles Walter and Nettie Alys (Baker) Davis; m. Lana Carmen Wiles, Nov. 23, 1974. B.S. cum laude, Stetson U., 1948; M.S., U. Fla., 1950, Ph.D., 1953. Instr. physics U. Fla., 1950-54; aero. research scientist NACA, Langley Field, Va., 1954-55; asst. prof. math. U. Miami, Coral Gables, Fla., 1955-60; assoc. prof. U. Miami, 1960-67, prof., 1967-72, chmn. dept. math., 1961-66; acting dean U. Miami (Coll. Arts and Scis.), 1966-67, assoc. dean, 1967-68, assoc. dean faculties, 1968-72; prof. math. Clinch Valley Coll., U. Va., 1972—, dean, 1972-86, chmn. dept. math. scis., 1986—; vis. research scientist Courant Inst. Math. Scis., NYU, 1959-60. Contbr. articles to profl. jours. Served with USAAF, 1942-46. Mem. Am. Math. Soc., Math. Assn. Am., Soc. Indsl. and Applied Math., Nat. Council Tchrs. of Math., Southwest Va. Council Tchrs. of Math., AAUP, AAAS, Sigma Xi, Delta Theta Mu, Phi Delta Kappa, Phi Kappa Phi. Clubs: Univ. Yacht (Miami, Fla.); Kiwanis. Office: PO Box 3417 Wise VA 24293

LOW, JAMES PATTERSON, professional association executive; b. Hartford, Conn., July 25, 1927; s. Marshall and Margaret (Fleming) L.; m. Patricia Marian Siegman, Oct. 20, 1956; children—Lisa Patricia Low Lawson, Lori Patterson. B.A., U. Md., 1953; M.B.A., Fla. Atlantic U., 1972; LL.D., Northwood Inst., 1974. Mgr. Pulaski County (Va.) Indsl. Devel. Corp. and C. of C., 1953-55; mgr. Assn. dept. U.S. C. of C., Washington, 1958-66; pres. Am. Soc. Assn. Execs., 1966-82; chmn., chief exec. officer Dynamics, Inc., Washington, 1982-87; chief exec. officer, exec. v.p. Assn. for Fgn. Investors in U.S. Real Estate, 1987—. Bd. dirs. U. Md. Found. Served with USMCR, 1945-46; to capt. U.S. Army, 1951-54. Named Assn. Exec. of Yr. Assn. Trends mag., 1980; decorated Bronze Star. Mem. Am. Historic and Cultural Soc. (bd. dirs.), Am. Soc. Assn. Execs., Sigma Nu. Clubs: Congressional Country (Bethesda, Md.); Metropolitan (Washington).

LOW, JOHN HENRY, banker; b. N.Y.C., Apr. 5, 1954; s. Henry John and Vaike M.L.; B. Sci. Engring., Princeton U., 1976; M.B.A., Wharton Sch. U. Pa., 1985. Mgmt. trainee Mellon Bank, Pitts., 1976-78, credit analyst, Frankfurt, W. Ger., 1978-80, internat. rep., N.Y.C., 1980, Asst. internat. officer, 1980-81, internat. officer, 1981-82, asst. v.p., 1982-85, v.p., 1986—. Mem. AIAA, IEEE, Aircraft Owners and Pilots Assn. Clubs: Univ., Princeton (N.Y.C.); Rolling Rock; Harvard-Yale-Princeton (Pitts.). Home: 64 E 86th St New York NY 10028 Office: Mellon Bank Mellon Fin Ctr 551 Madison Ave New York NY 10022

LOW, WALTER CHENEY, neurophysiology educator, scientist; Madera, Calif., May 11, 1950; s. George Chen and Linda Quan (Gong) L.; m. Margaret Mary Schwarz, June 4, 1983. B.S. with honors, U. Calif.-Santa Barbara, 1972; M.S., U. Mich., 1974, Ph.D., 1979. Postdoctoral fellow U. Cambridge, Eng., 1979-80, U. Vt., Burlington, 1980-83; asst. prof. neurophysiology Ind. U. Sch. Med., Indpls., 1983—; dir. grad. program in physiology and biophysics, Sch. Medicine Ind. U., 1985—. Contbr. numerous publs. to profl. jours. on brain research. Recipient Individual Nat. Research Service award Nat. Heart, Lung and Blood Inst., 1981-83, Nat. Inst. Neurol., Communicative Disorders and Stroke, 1979, Bank of Am. Lab. Scis. award, 1968; grantee NIH, 1984, 85, 87, Am. Heart Assn., 1987; Rackham U. Mich., 1976-78; internat. programs travel Ind. U., 1984; AGAN research fellow Am. Heart Assn., 1980-81; Rotary scholar, 1968-69. Mem. Soc. for Neurosci. (pres. Indpls. chpt. 1985-87), AAAS, Internat. Brain Research Orgn., Calif. Scholastic Fedn. (life), N.Y. Acad Sci., Sigma Xi. Avocations: tennis, cross-country skiing, sailing. Home: 4565 Broadway Indianapolis IN 46205 Office: Ind U Sch Medicine Dept Physiology and Biophysics Indianapolis IN 46223

LOWE, BARBARA LEWIS, telecommunications and healthcare company executive; b. Balt., Aug. 19, 1946; d. Warren Ashby and Averal Lois (Marchant) Lewis; m. Todd H. Lowe, Jan. 30, 1983. BS, U. Ala.-Tuscaloosa, 1969; MBA, U. Ala.-Birmingham, 1978. Various mgmt. positions Bell System, Birmingham, Ala., N.Y.C., 1969-82; dir. planning, adminstrv. asst. Allnet Communications Services, Chgo., exec. dir., customer service, residential sales, 1982-83, exec. dir. engring., 1983-85, asst. v.p., Chgo., 1985, v.p. adminstrn., 1985-86; v.p., Personal Monitoring Technologies, Rochester, N.Y., 1986-87; v.p. sales and mktg. Indsl. Products Co., Langhorn, Pa., 1988—. Avocations: backgammon, student pilot, skiing. Home: 77 Oak Knoll Berwyn PA 19312

LOWE, CHARLES RICHARD, public utility executive, accountant; b. Champaign, Ill., Dec. 8, 1946; s. Richard Morgan and Mary Letitia (Smith) L.; m. Martha Elizabeth Coblentz, June 17, 1967; children—Leah, Richard, Brenner. B.S., So. Ill. U., 1971. C.P.A., Ill. Sr. acct. Touche Ross & Co., St. Louis, 1971-74; ptnr. in charge Charles R. Lowe, C.P.A., St. Elmo, 1974-84;

sec., treas., gen. mgr. Monarch Gas Co., 1974-83, pres. 1983-85, chmn. bd. dirs., 1985—; sec., treas., dir. Rainbow Farms, Inc., St. Elmo, 1983—; dir. Land No. 820, Inc., St. Elmo, 1980—; co-founder Ill. Small Utility Assn., Salem, Ill., 1980—. Mem. adminstrv. bd. St. Elmo 1st United Meth. Ch., 1978—. Recipient Outstanding Young Men of Am. award U.S. Jaycees, 1982, Loaned Exec. award St. Louis United Fund, 1972. Mem. Am. Gas Assn., Am. Inst. C.P.A.s, Ill. Inst. C.P.A.s, Ill. Gas Rate Engrs., Soc. Advancement of Mgmt. (pres. 1969-71, honor 1971), Altamont C. of C. (indsl. com. 1975-83), Jr. C. of C. Lodge: Lions (St. Elmo) (pres. 1979-81). Avocations: golfing; hunting; chess; fishing; boating. Home: 103 N Walnut St Elmo IL 62458 Office: Monarch Gas Co 408 N Main St St Elmo IL 62458

LOWE, ETHEL BLACK, artist; b. Kiowa County, Okla., Jan. 30, 1904; d. Benjamin Alonzo and Harriet Ann (Heaton) Black; B.A., Central State U., Okla., 1926; M.A., U. Tulsa, 1937; postgrad. U. Okla., U. Colo., Columbia, U. Hawaii; m. William Glenn Lowe, June 5, 1939 (dec. 1942). Tchr. pub. schs., Okla., 1922-39, N.Y., 1942-49, 50-68, ret.; teaching prin. Dragon Sch., Sasebo, Kyushu, Japan, 1949-50; works exhibited 1945—; exhibits include Nat. Assn. Women Artists, 1953, 55, 71, 75, 77, Terry Nat. Art Exhibit, 1952, Provincetown Art Assn., 1952-53, Nassau Community Coll., 1971. Reproductions of works in newspapers, mags. Mem. N.Y. State Ret. Tchrs. Assn., Nat. Assn. Women Artists, Am. Watercolor Soc., Nat. Ret. Tchrs. Assn., Delta Kappa Gamma. Home: 48-50 44th St Woodside NY 11377

LOWE, JOHN CHRISTOPHER BURPEE, classicist, educator; b. Toronto, Ont., Can., Nov. 16, 1930; came to Eng., 1939; s. John and Ruth Maud (Burpee) L.; m. Anne Celia Rosemary Elizabeth Goodbody, July 5, 1958; children: Antony John, Philip Edward, Timothy Mark. MA, U. Oxford, Eng., 1953, BLitt, 1961. Craven fellow U. Oxford, 1955-57; lectr. classics The Queen's Coll., Oxford, 1957-60, St. Edmund Hall, Oxford, 1958-60; lectr. Latin Bedford Coll., London, 1960-82; vis. assoc. prof. classics U. Calif., Berkeley, 1984. Rev. editor: Jour. Hellenic Studies, 1974-87; contbr. articles to profl. jours. Mem. Soc. for Promotion Hellenic and Roman Studies (hon. librarian). Mem. Ch. of Eng. Home: 47 Corringham Rd, London NW11 7BS, England Office: U London Inst Classical Studies, 31-34 Gordon Square, London WC1H 0PP, England

LOWE, MICHAEL CRAIG, pharmacologist; b. Colfax, Wash., July 24, 1942; s. Judson Nathaniel and Joyce Leland (Johnson) L.; B.S. in Zoology, Wash. State U., 1964; M.S. in Pharmacology (USPHS fellow), U. Wash., 1968, Ph.D. in Pharmacology (USPHS fellow), 1970; m. Constance Rita Birr, Sept. 1, 1961; children—Laurie Lynne, Jamison Anne, Todd Michael Johnson, Robert Michael Judson. Asst. prof. U. Wash., Seattle, 1973-78; Cancer expert Lab. of Toxicology, Nat. Cancer Inst., NIH, Bethesda, Md., 1978-83, acting chief toxicology Nat. Cancer Inst., 1980-82; health scientist adminstr. Nat. Heart, Lung and Blood Inst., NIH, Bethesda, 1983-85; v.p. toxicology ICF-Clement, Washington, 1985-88; prin. Weinberg Cons. Group, Washington, 1988—; cons. toxicology FDA. V.p., citizens adv. council Lake Washington Sch. Dist., Kirkland, Wash., 1975-76; coach Montgomery Soccer, Inc., Bethesda, 1979-81; team rep. Montgomery County Swim League, Bethesda, 1981-84, rules chmn., bd. dirs., 1985—. NIH grantee, 1975-78; Nat. Merit Scholar, 1960; Pharm. Mfrs. Assn. Found. Pharmacology and Morphology fellow, 1971-73. Mem. AAAS, Electron Microscopy Soc. Am., Western Pharmacology Soc., Am. Soc. Pharm. and Exptl. Therapeutics, Catecholamine Club. Democrat. Conglist. Researcher cardiovascular pharmacology, toxicology of antineoplastic agts, environmental risk assessment. Home: 8904 Liberty Ln Potomac MD 20854 Office: Weinberg Cons Group 2828 Pennsylvania Ave NW Suite 305 Washington DC 20007

LOWE, RICHARD GERALD, JR., computer programmer manager; b. Travis AFB, Calif., Nov. 8, 1960; d. Richard Gerald and Valerie Jean (Hoeffer) L. Student, San Bernardino Valley Coll., 1978-80. Tech. specialist Software Techniques Inc., Los Alamitos, Calif., 1980-82, sr. tech. specialist, 1982-84, mgr. tech. services, 1984-85; mgr. cons. services Software Techniques Inc., Cypress, Calif., 1985-86; sr. programmer BIF Accutel, Camarillo, Calif., 1986-87; systems analyst BIF Accutel, Camarillo, 1987-88; mgr. project Beck Computer Systems, Long Beach, Calif., 1986—. Contbr. articles to profl. jours. Mem. Assn. Computing Machinery, Digital Equipment Corp. Users Group. Office: Beck Computer Systems 5372 Long Beach Blvd Long Beach CA 90805

LOWE, ROBERT CHARLES, lawyer; b. New Orleans, July 3, 1949; s. Carl Randall and Antonia (Morgan) L.; m. Theresa Louise Acree, Feb. 4, 1978. 1 child, Nicholas Stafford. B.A., U. New Orleans, 1971; J.D., La. State U., 1975. Bar: La. 1975, U.S. Dist. Ct. (ea. dist.) La. 1975, U.S. Ct. Appeals (5th cir.) 1980, U.S. Dist. Ct. (we. dist.) La. 1978, U.S. Supreme Ct. 1982. Assoc. Sessions, Fishman, Rosenson, Boisfontaine, and Nathan, New Orleans, 1975-80, ptnr., 1980-87; ptnr. Lowe, Stein, Hoffman, and Allweiss, 1987—. Author: Louisiana Divorce, 1984. Contbr. articles to profl. jours. Mem. La. Law Rev., 1974-75. Mem. ABA, La. State Bar Assn. (chmn. family law sect. 1984-85), La. Assn. Def. Counsel, New Orleans Bar Assn., Order of Coif, Phi Kappa Phi. Republican. Home: 9421 Roslyn Dr River Ridge LA 70123 Office: Lowe Stein Hoffman and Allweiss 650 Poydras St Suite 2450 New Orleans LA 70130

LOWENTHAL, F. JULIO, automobile dealer; b. N.Y.C., Sept. 30, 1927; arrived in Guatemala, 1929; s. Julio and Elvira (Foncea) L.; m. Alicia Arceyuz, Sept. 30, 1951; children: Marialys, Enrique, Julio (dec.), Maryan. BArch, U. Calif., Berkeley, 1951. Pvt. practice architecture San Diego, 1951-57; franchised automobile dealer Guatemala City, Guatemala, 1957—; pres., gen. mgr. dealership Guatemala City, 1972—, dealer Komatsu, Clark, Ingersoll-Rand products, 1975—; Hon. Consul-Gen. Republic South Africa from Guatemala 1985—; pres. Guatemalan Light and Power Co., 1975; bd. dirs. CICA Fin., Banco Internacional, Guatemala. Pres. bd. trustees Francisco Marroquin U., 1978, bd. dirs., 1970—; asst. mayor Guatemala City, 1969-71; state councillor, 1970-74. Decorated Order of Good Hope (Republic South Africa), 1979, Order St. Fortunat (Austria) 1988. Mem. Caribbean and Cen. Am. GM Dealers Assn. (pres. 1971-72), Guatemala Mgmt. Assn., Guatemala C. of C. (pres. 1969-70). Roman Catholic. Club: Country of Guatemala. Lodge: Rotary. Office: 30-57 10 Ave, Guatemala City 5, Guatemala

LOWERY, LEE LEON, JR., civil engineer; b. Corpus Christi, Tex., Dec. 26, 1938; s. Lee Leon and Blanche (Dietrich) L.; children: Kelli Lane, Christianne Lindsey. B.S. in Civil Enging, Tex. A&M U., 1960, M.E., 1961, Ph.D., 1965. Prof. dept. civil enging. Tex. A&M U., 1960; research engr. Tex. A&M Research Found., 1962—; pres. Pile Dynamics Found. Enging., Inc., Bryan, Tex., 1962—; pres. Tex. Measurements, Inc., College Station, 1965—; pres. Interface Enging. Assos., Inc., College Station, 1969—; dir. Braver Corp. Bd. dirs. Deep Found. Inst. Recipient Faculty Disting. Achievement award Tex. A&M U., 1979; NDEA fellow, 1960-63. Mem. ASCE, Nat. Soc. Profl. Engrs., Tex. Soc. Profl. Engrs., Am. Soc. Stress Analysis, Soc. Marine Tech., Am. Soc. Enging. Edn., Prestressed Concrete Inst., Sigma Xi, Phi Kappa Phi, Tau Beta Pi. Baptist. Home: 2905 S College St Bryan TX 77801 Office: Tex A&M U Dept Civil Enging College Station TX 77843

LOWERY, WILLIAM HERBERT, lawyer; b. Toledo, June 8, 1925; s. Kenneth Alden and Drusilla (Pfanner) L.; m. Carolyn Broadwell, June 27, 1947; children: Kenneth Latham, Marcia Mitchell. Ph.B., U. Chgo., 1947; J.D., U. Mich., 1950. Bar: Pa. 1951, U.S. Supreme Ct. 1955. Assoc. Dechert Price & Rhoads, Phila., 1950-58, ptnr., 1958—, mng. ptnr., 1970-72; policy com. counsel S.S. Huebner Found. Ins. Edn., Phila., 1970—. Author: Insurance Litigation Problems, 1972, Insurance Litigation Disputes, 1977. Pres. Stafford Civic Assn., 1958; chmn. Tredyffrin Twp. Zoning Bd., Chester County, Pa., 1959-75; bd. dirs., pres. Paoli Meml. Hosp., Pa., 1964—. Served to 2d lt. USAF, 1943-46. Mem. ABA (chmn. life ins. com. 1984-85, chmn. Nat. Conf. Lawyers and Life Ins. Cos. 1984—), Jud. Conf. 3d Cir. Ct. Appeals. Clubs: Waynesborough Country (Paoli); Urban (Phila.); Naples Bath and Tennis (Fla.). Home: 5 Etienne Arbordeau Devon PA 19333 Office: Dechert Price & Rhoads 3400 Ctr Sq W 1500 Market St Philadelphia PA 19102

LOWINGER, DANIEL, financial analyst, controller; b. Bratislava, Czechoslovakia, Jan. 6, 1935; s. Kalman and Elizabeth (Kohn) L.; m. Rachel Lowinger, June 30, 1957; children: Ofer Kalman, Amir Yacob, Orit Revital. BSc, London U., 1968; MBA, Tel Aviv U., 1977. Head fin. dept. The Weizman Inst. Sci., Rehovot, Israel, 1961—; comptroller Dept. Statistics Israel Govt., 1958-61. Lodge: Rotary. Home: PO Box 1243, Rehovot Israel Office: The Weizman Inst Sci, PO Box 26, Rehovot Israel

LOWN, DAVID JOLLEY, architect; b. Shreveport, La., Apr. 16, 1948; s. Franklin David, Jr. and Lona Marceia (Jolley) L.; m. Patricia Alice Kidwell, July 29, 1972; children—Todd Kidwell, Marisa Josephine. B.Arch., Tex. Tech. U., 1971; M.Arch., U. Wash., 1984; student Coll. of William and Mary, 1967, Seattle Community Coll., 1976. Registered architect, Wash. Designer R.D. Anderson & Ptnrs., Seattle, 1973-74; project mgr. The Richardson Assocs., Seattle, 1974-78; prin. David J. Lown, Seattle, 1978-80, 87—; project architect T.R.A. Architects, Engrs., Seattle, 1980-86; assoc. Roger Williams Architects AIA, Seattle, 1986-87; also dir. Design architect: Metro Transit Shelters, 1974 (Seattle chpt. AIA Honor award 1976, U.S. Dept. Transp. and Nat. Endowment Arts commendation for design excellence 1981), Trident Support Base B.O.Q. (AIA and Naval Facilities Enging. command 1st Honor award, 1980, Sec. Def. Merit award 1980), U. Wash. Biology Facility, 1977, Wash. State U. Wegner Hall, 1977-78. Advisor Explorer Scouts, Boy Scouts. Am., 1982-83, mem. Seattle Art Mus., 1978-80, Henry Gallery Assn., U. Wash., 1977—. Served as 1st lt. USAF, 1971-73. James Dewitt Meml. scholar, Tex. Soc. Architects, 1970. Mem. AIA (com. chmn. 1981-83). Home: PO Box 10457 Bainbridge Island WA 98110 Office: PO Box 10457 Bainbridge Island WA 98110

LOWNDES, JOHN FOY, lawyer; b. Medford, Mass., Jan. 1, 1931; s. Charles L. B. and Dorothy (Foy) L.; m. Rita Davies, Aug. 18, 1983; children: Elizabeth Anne, Amy Scott, John Patrick, Joseph Edward. BA, Duke U., 1953, LLB, 1958. Bar: Fla. 1958. Sole practice, Daytona Beach, Fla., 1958, Orlando, Fla., 1959-69; sr. ptnr., chmn. bd. dirs. Lowndes, Drosdick, Doster, Kantor & Reed, P.A., Orlando, 1969—; mem. adv. bd. Atlantic Nat. Bank Fla., 1982-86, Coll. Bus. Adminstrn. U. Cen. Fla., chmn. bd. visitors; bd. dirs. First Union Nat. Bank Fla. Trustee Orlando Mus. Art, 1986—; bd. visitors Duke U. Served to capt. USMC, 1953-55. Mem. So. Fed. Tax Inst. (founding trustee). Republican. Clubs: Orlando Country, Citrus, Univ. (Orlando). Home: 715 Via Bella Winter Park FL 32789 Office: Lowndes Drosdick et al 215 N Eola Ave Dr Orlando FL 32802

LOWREY, RICHARD WILLIAM, architect; b. Phila., June 11, 1938; s. Charles William and Ethel May (Straley) L.; divorced; children—Jodi, Erika. B.Arch., Pa. State U., 1962. Registered architect Mass., Pa. Project mgr. Nolen, Swinburne & Assocs., Phila., 1962-64, project architect, 1968-69; project architect Harold E. Wagoner, FAIA, Phila., 1964-68; constrn. mgr. Cape Lands Realty & Bldg. Corp., Brewster, Mass., 1969-70; v.p. David M. Crawley Assocs., Inc., Plymouth, Mass., 1970-75; owner Lowrey Assocs., Architects, 1975-84; pres. Architects Lowrey & Blanchard, Inc., 1984-88, owner Richard W. Lowrey, R.A., 1988—. Mem. Plymouth Hist. Dist. Commn., 1979—; trustee Old Colony Natural History Soc., 1979—; corp. mem. Plymouth Pub. Library, 1984—, Old Colony Club, 1986—. Congregationalist. Lodge: Masons, Kiwanis (disting. past pres. Plymouth chpt. 1980-81). Avocations: music; photography; reading; racquetball; darts.

LOWRY, BETTY, writer; b. Hollywood, Calif., July 24, 1927; d. Hans and Emily Paula (Doerges) Trishman; A.B., U. Calif. at Berkeley, 1948; M.A., Boston Coll., 1977; m. Ritchie P. Lowry, Sept. 5, 1948; children—Peter Ritchie, Robin Emily. Copy chief account exec. Abbott Kimball Co., San Francisco, 1948-50; dir. young homemaker div. Jackson's Furniture Co., Oakland, Calif., 1950-52; columnist Family Travel, N.Y.C., 1968-73; free lance writer, especially travel essays, 1946—; columnist Only Collect for Good Money, Montpelier, Vt., 1982—. Mem. Nat. League Am. Pen Women (chpt. pres. 1970-72, Mass. pres. 1982-84), New Eng. Poetry Club, Women In Communications, Poetry Soc. Am. Democrat. Home: 79 Moore Rd Wayland MA 01778

LOWRY, CHARLES WESLEY, clergyman, lecturer; b. Checotah, Okla., Mar. 31, 1905; s. Charles Wesley and Sue (Price) L.; m. Edith Clark, June 14, 1930; children: Harriet Richards Lowry King, Charles Wesley, Atherton Clark, James Meredith Price, m. Kate Rowe Holland, Jan. 11, 1960. B.A., Washington and Lee U., 1926, D.D., 1959; M.A., Harvard, 1927; B.D., Episcopal Theol. Sch., 1930; D.Phil., Oxford (Eng.) U., 1933. Ordained deacon Episcopal Ch., 1930, priest, 1931; traveling fellow Episc. Theol. Sch., 1930-32; Episc. chaplain U. Calif., 1933-34; prof. systematic theology Va. Theol. Sem., 1934-43; rector All Saints' Ch., Chevy Chase, Md., 1943-53; lectr. theology Seabury Western Theol. Sem., 1947, Phila. Div. Sch. (Bohlen lectr.), 1947, 49-50, Gen. Theol. Sem., 1951-52; chmn. Bd. Examining Chaplains, Diocese of Washington, 1945-53, sec., standing com., 1945-51; ofcl. del. from U.S. Internat. Conv. on Peace and Christian Civilization, Florence, Italy, 1952; chmn., exec. dir. Found. for Religious Action in Social and Civil Order, 1953-59, pres., 1960—, project research dir. on morals revolution, 1973-75; cons. FCDA, 1953-55; cons. Air War Coll., 1953, lectr., 1953-54; lectr. Naval War Coll., 1955, Nat. War Coll., 1957, 59-61, Command and Staff Coll., 1961-62, Indsl. Coll. Armed Forces, 1963, Inst. Lifetime Learning, 1964-66, Campbell Coll. Sch. Law, 1979, 80; also lectr. various seminars; lectr. philosophy and polit. sci. Sandhills Community Coll., 1967-69, 71; spl. lectr. Oxford (Eng.) Poly. Coll., 1974; spl. lectr. Washington and Lee U., 1977, baccalaureate preacher, 1984; dir. Nat. Conf. on Spiritual Founds. Am. Democracy, Washington, 1954-55, 57, 59; minister The Village Chapel, Pinehurst, N.C., 1966-73; mem. faculty Wallace O'Neal Day Sch., Southern Pines, N.C., 1976—; columnist Pinehurst Outlook, 1977-78, Moore County News, 1978-79, The Pilot, 1979—; priest assoc. Emmanuel Epis. Ch., Southern Pines, 1981—. Author: (with others) Anglican Evangelicalism, 1943, Ency. of Religion, 1945, The Trinity and Christian Devotion, 1946, Christianity and Materialism (Hale Sermon), 1948, (with others) Lenten Counsellors, 1951, The Anglican Pulpit To-Day, 1953, Communism and Christ, rev. edit, 1962 (Brit. edit. 1954), Conflicting Faiths, 1953, The Ideology of Freedom vs. The Ideology of Communism, 1958, To Pray or Not to Pray, rev. edit, 1968, The Kingdom of Influence, 1969, William Temple: An Archbishop for All Seasons, 1982; Editor: Blessings of Liberty, 1956—, The First Theologians, 1986; Contbr. articles to profl. pubjs. Chmn. Nat. Jefferson Davis Hall of Fame Co., 1960, 64-65; Candidate for U.S. Congress 10th Dist. Va., 1962; mem. N.C. Bicentennial Constn. Conv., 1985—. Recipient George Washington medal Freedoms Found., 1955, 59, 61, 68, other award, 1953, 81. Mem. Am. Peace Soc. (past pres.), Am. Polit. Sci. Assn., Internat. Platform Assn., Am. Theol. Soc. (treas. 1955-70, 72, past v.p.), Cum Laude Soc. (pres. O'Neal chpt.), World Conf. Faith and Order, Phi Beta Kappa, Omicron Delta Kappa, Delta Sigma Rho, Sigma Upsilon. Clubs: Achilles (Oxford and Cambridge); Rotary (dist. gov. 1970-71), Chevy Chase, Pinehurst Country, Nat. Press. Address: Box 1829 Pinehurst NC 28374

LOWRY, EDWARD FRANCIS, JR., lawyer; b. Los Angeles, Aug. 13, 1930; s. Edward Francis and Mary Anita (Woodcock) L.; m. Patricia Ann Palmer, Feb. 16, 1963; children—Edward Palmer, Rachael Louise. Student, Ohio State U., 1948-50; A.B., Stanford, 1952, J.D., 1954. Bar: Ariz. bar 1955, U.S. Supreme Ct. bar 1969, D.C. bar 1970. Camp dir. Quarter Circle V Bar Ranch, 1954; tchr. Orme Sch., Mayer, Ariz., 1954-56; trust rep. Valley Nat. Bank Ariz., 1958-60; practice in Phoenix, 1960—; assoc. atty. Cunningham, Carson & Messinger, 1960-64; partner Carson, Messinger, Elliott, Laughlin & Ragan, 1964-69, 70-80, Gray, Plant, Mooty, Mooty & Bennett, 1981-84, Eaton, Lazarus, Dodge & Lowry Ltd., 1985-86; gen. counsel Bus. Realty Ariz., 1986—; sole practice Scottsdale, Ariz., 1986-88; ptnr. Lowry & Froeb, 1988—; asst. legislative counsel Dept. Interior, Washington, 1969-70; Mem. Ariz. Commn. Uniform Laws, 1972—, chmn., 1976—; judge pro tem Ariz. State Ct. Appeals, 1986. Chmn. Council of Stanford Law Socs., 1968; vice chmn. bd. trustees Orme Sch., 1972-74, treas., 1981-83; bd. trustees Heard Mus., 1965—, pres., 1974-75; bd. visitors Stanford Sch. Law; magistrate Town of Paradise Valley, Ariz., 1976-83; juvenile ct. referee Maricopa County, 1978-83. Served to capt. USAF, 1956-58. Fellow Ariz. Bar Found. (founder); mem. ABA, Maricopa County, D.C. bar assns., State Bar Ariz. (chmn. com. on uniform laws 1979-85), Stanford Law Soc. Ariz. (past pres.), Scottsdale Bar Assn., Ariz. State U. Law Soc. (dir.), Nat. Conf. Commrs. Uniform State Laws, Delta Sigma Rho, Alpha Tau Omega, Phi Delta Phi. Home: 7600 N Moonlight Ln Paradise Valley AZ 85253 Office: Lowry & Broeb 6900 E Camelback Rd Suite 1040 Scottsdale AZ 85251

LOWRY, JAMES DAVID, banker; b. Wichita, Kans., May 24, 1942; s. Frederick Brennan and Mary (Mullendore) L.; m. Adeline Louise Newbold; children: Anne Harrison, Blythe Brennan, Terrell Brennan, James Sargent. B.S., Okla. State U., 1965; LL.B., U. Okla., 1968. Bar: Pa. bar 1968. Mem. Liebert, Harvey, Bectle & Short, Phila., 1968-69; counsel Systems Capital Corp., Phila., 1969-71; v.p., counsel Provident Nat. Bank, 1971-73; sr. v.p., sec., dir. ops. Provident Nat. Corp., Phila., 1973-76; exec. v.p., chief adminstrv. officer Provident Nat. Corp., 1976-78; also dir. subs.; v.p.-fin., gen. mgr. Petroleum Heat and Power Co., Phila., 1978-80; chmn., pres., chief exec. Bancshares of N.J., 1981-83, No. Nat. Corp.; chmn., pres. The Bank of N.J.; chmn. The Trustees' Pvt. Bank, 1981-84; pres., chief exec. officer Equibank, Equimark, 1984-85; mng. dir. Lowry Bittel, Perrot & Co., 1985—; chmn. Hopper Soliday Corp., 1986—. Served with U.S. Army, 1960-62. Mem. Am., Pa., Phila. bar assns. Clubs: Racquet, Corinthian Yacht, Rittenhouse (Phila.); Mill Dam (Wayne, Pa.); Bar Harbor Yacht (Maine). Home: Evergreen 111 Old Gulph Rd Wynnewood PA 19096 Office: 1600 Market St Philadelphia PA 19103

LOWTHER, FRANK EUGENE, research physicist; b. Orrville, Ohio, Feb. 3, 1929; s. John Finger and Mary Elizabeth (Mackey) L.; m. Elizabeth E. Koons, Apr. 21, 1951; children—Cynthia E., Victoria J., James A., Frank Eugene. Grad. Ohio State U., Columbus, 1952. Scientist missile systems div. Raytheon Corp., Boston, 1952-57, Gen. Electric Co., Syracuse, N.Y., and Daytona Beach, Fla., 1957-62; mgr. ozone research and devel. W.R. Grace Co., Curtis Bay, Md., 1972-75; sr. engring. assoc. Linde div. Union Carbide Corp., Tonawanda, N.Y., 1975-79; chief scientist, Purification Sci. Inc., 1979-81; chief scientist, Atlantic Richfield-Energy Conversion and Materials Lab, 1981-83; prin. scientist Atlantic Richfield-Corp. Tech., 1983-85, sci. adv., 1985-88, research adv., 1988—. Recipient Inventor of Yr. award Patent Law Assn. and Tech. Socs. Council, 1976. Assoc. fellow AIAA; mem. IEEE (sr.). Club: Masons. Patentee in field of ozone tech., plasma generators, solid state power devices, internal combustion engines, electro-desorption, thermoelectrics, virus and bacteria disinfection systems. Home: 2928 Clear Spring Plano TX 75075-7602 Office: 2300 W Plano Pkwy Plano TX 75075

LOYN, HENRY ROYSTON, historian, educator; b. Cardiff, Wales, June 16, 1922; s. Henry George and Violet Monica (Thomas) L.; m. Patricia Beatrice Haskew, Mar. 22, 1926; children: Richard Henry, John Andrew, Christopher Edward. BA in English, Univ. Coll. Cardiff, 1944, BA in History, 1945, DLitt, 1968. Asst. lectr., lectr. Univ. Coll. Cardiff, 1966, reader, prof., 1966-77; prof. Westfield Coll., U. London, 1977-86, prof. emeritus, 1986—, vice prin., 1980-86, acting. prin., 1985-86, dean students union, 1968-70, 75-76. Author: Anglo-Saxon England and the Norman Conquest, 1962, Norman Conquest, 1965, etc.; contbr. articles to profl. jours. Mem. Hist. Assn. (pres. 1976-79), Soc. for Med. Archaeology (pres. 1983-86), Soc. Antiquaries of London, (v.p. 1982-86), Royal Hist. Soc. (v.p. 1983-86), Brit. Acad. (council 1983-85). Club: Athenaeum. Home: 25 Cunningham Hill Rd, Saint Albans AL1 5BX, England

LOZADA, SALVADOR MARIA, lawyer, educator; b. Buenos Aires, Jan. 7, 1932; s. Eduardo Lozada Chaves and Marta (Hechart) de Lozada; m. Maria Helena Garcia Hamilton, May 11, 1954; children: Juan Cruz, Maria Helena, Ezequiel, Guillermo, Martin. JD, U. Cordoba, 1954, PhD, 1965. Cert. lawyer, Pub. Coll. Lawyers, Buenos Aires1955. Dist. atty. Judicial Power, Buenos Aires, 1959-63; judge Buenos Aires, 1963-74; pres. Latin-Am. Assn. Constitutional Law, Buenos Aires, 1972—; founder, 1st. v.p. Internat. Assn. constitutional Law, Buenos Aires, 1981—; prof. law Buenos Aires U., 1962-76; sec. gen. Latin-Am. Orgn. Catholic Univs., 1967-76. Author: Institution of Public Law, 1966, Constitutional Law, 1972, Multinational Enterprises, 1973. Recipient Gral Moscony award Argentine Inst. Econ. Devel., 1972, Scalabrini Ortiz award Buenos Aires U. Pub. House, 1974. Mem. Argentine League Human Rights (co-pres. 1981—), Inst. of Constitutional Law (dep. dir.). Home: Ave Santa Fe 2108 4A, 1123 Buenos Aires Argentina

LOZANO, JOSE JAVIER, industrial engineer; b. Madrid, Nov. 21, 1955; s. Pedro Lozano and Julia Rojo; m. Maribel Sanchez, 1987. Degree in indsl. engring., Poly. U., Madrid, 1979; student, Davidson Coll., 1979-80. Engr. trainee Rade Koncar Elektroporcelan, Novi Sad, Yugoslavia, 1979; system engr. Etime, S.A., Madrid, 1981-82; mgr. process control Crisa, Madrid, 1982-85; sales support engr. Esso Espanola, S.A. div. Exxon, Madrid, 1985; project mgr. Intelligent Decision Systems, S.A., Madrid, 1986, indsl. div. mgr., 1986—. Recipient Trainee Engrs. Exchange Program award Internat. Assn. Exchange of Students for Tech. Experience, 1979. Mem. Tech. Mktg. Soc. Am., Assn. Espanola Para el Control de Calidad. Roman Catholic. Home: Lopez de Hoyos 60, 28002 Madrid Spain Office: Intelligent Decision Systems SA, Paseo Castellana 93 4th Floor, 28046 Madrid Spain

LOZANO, OLEGARIO, educational administrator; b. Soria, Spain, Mar. 26, 1946; s. Jesus Lozano and Claudia Cuadra; m. Maria Perez, Mar. 10, 1974; children: Olegario Jose, Jesus. Student in tourism mgmt., Escuela de Turismo, Madrid, 1976, Student in real estate adminstrn., Coll. Nat. Adminstrn., Las Palmas, Spain, 1978; Cert. mktg., Inst. Mktg., Eng., 1978; Diploma in mktg., Inst. Nat. Empleo, Spain, 1979; Postgrad., Pacific State U., 1987. Accts. clk. Brit. European Airways, Madrid, 1965-70; sales rep. Brit. Airways, Malaga, Spain, 1970-74; dist. officer Brit. Airways, Almeria, Spain, 1974-77, Canaries, Las Palmas, 1977-84; dir. ptnr. English Ctr. Coll. Langs., Almeria, 1984—; with Inst. Andaluz Estudios Empresariales, Almeria, 1985—. Mem. Inst. Mktg. (assoc.), Asempal Employers Assn., Almeria C. of C. Home: Rafael Alberti 11-70 B, Almeria 04004, Spain Office: Viajar Ahora, Jose Artes de Arcos 34, Almeria 04004, Spain

LOZIER, CYNTHIA WOOLEY, physician; b. Mobile, Ala., Sept. 10, 1948; d. Samuel Oliphant and Mary Emma (Chambers) Wooley; m. Phillip Blocker, Feb. 18, 1966 (div. June 1972); m. Mark Davis Lozier, Dec. 15, 1978; children—Darren, Nancy, Joshua. B.S. in Chemistry, U. South Ala., 1974, M.D., 1979. Intern in surgery U. South Ala., Mobile, 1979-80; physician, med. dir. Mostellar Med. Clinic, Bayou La Batre, Ala., 1980-83; practice gen. medicine, Mobile, 1983—; assoc. dir. Famlicare Med. Ctr., Jan. to June, 1986; med. dir. Downtowner Med. Ctr., 1987-88, North Mobile Med. Clinic, Eight Mile, Ala., 1988—; mem. staff Knollwood Park Hosp., Springhill Meml. Hosp., Mobile Infirmary, Doctors Hosp., Providence Hosp., Mobile Community Hosp., U. South Ala. Med. Ctr.; mem. staff dept. community medicine U. Ala.-Birmingham; med. dir. Grandbay Nursing Home, Midsouth Home Health Assn., 1983-87. Served with USPHS, 1980-83. Recipient Commd. Officer award USPHS, 1982, Outstanding Career Woman award, 1984. Mem. AMA, Med. Assn. State Ala., Mobile County Med. Soc., So. Med. Assn., Am. Med. Women's Assn., Mobile C. of C. Roman Catholic. Club: Zonta.

LU, CHIH-YUAN, electronics engineer, physicist; b. Canton, China, Aug. 13, 1950; came to U.S., 1972; s. Shan-Tung and You-Chen (Tang) L.; m. Fen-Fen Chang, Apr. 3, 1978; children—Jim Kuan-Chi, Charlin Chia-Ning. B.S., Nat. Taiwan U., 1972; M.A., Columbia U., 1974, M.Ph., 1975, Ph.D., 1977. Assoc. prof. Nat. Chiao-Tung U., Hsin-Chu, Taiwan, 1978-81, prof., 1981-83; research mem. energy com. Republic of China, Taipei, Taiwan, 1979-83; adv. research mem. Sci. and Tech. Adv. Group, Taipei, 1981-83; assoc. prof. N.C. State U., Raleigh, 1983-84; mem. tech. staff AT&T Bell Labs., Allentown, Pa., 1984—. Contbr. articles to profl. jours. Pres., editor Sci. Monthly Mag., 1978-83. J.C. Pfister fellow. Mem. IEEE (sr.), Electron Device Soc. (sr.), Am. Phys. Soc. (life), Electrochem. Soc., Phys. Soc. of Republic of China (life; exec. bd. dirs. 1981-84), Chinese Inst. Engrs. (life). Home: 5371 Andrea Dr Wescosville PA 18106 Office: AT&T Bell Labs 555 Union Blvd Allentown PA 18103

LU, HONGWEN, mathematics educator; b. Zhejiang, Peoples Republic of China, Oct. 22, 1939; s. Yongchang and Luyu (Wu) L.; m. Guangheng Ji, 1974; children: Qiaoyang, Qiaoying. BS, Wuhan U., Peoples Republic China, 1962; PhD, Acad. Sinica Inst. Math., Beijing, Peoples Republic of China, 1966. Tchr. U. Sci. and Tech. China, 1966-78, lectr., 1978-79, prof. math., 1981—; vis. scholar U. Calif., Berkeley, 1980-81; vis. prof. MPI for Math., Bonn, Fed. Republic Germany, 1981, IHES, France, 1986; advisor PhD candidate State Council Peoples Republic of China, 1986; reviewer Math. Rev., USA, 1981—, Founds. for Edn. Ministry, Peoples Republic

China, 1985—; bd. dirs. research group U. Sci. and Tech. of China Dept. Math., 1987—. Author: Study for Number Theory, 1979 (Sci. prize Acad. Sinica 1980); contbr. articles to profl. jours., 1964—. Grantee Founds. Acad. Sinica, 1984-86, Founds. Edn., Ministry of China, 1985—, NSF of China, 1987—. Mem. Am. Math. Soc., Acad. Com. U. Sci. and Tech. China, Math. Soc. Peoples Republic China. Office: U Sci and Tech of China, Dept Math, Hefei, Anhui Peoples Republic of China

LU, KAU U., mathematics educator; b. Canton, China, July 10, 1939; came to U.S., 1963; s. Shuk-to and Shon (Haung) L.; m. Huey Mei Lee, Sept. 12, 1968; 1 dau., Pamela. B.S. E.E., Nat. Taiwan U., 1961; Ph.D. in Math, Calif. Inst. Tech., 1968. Asst. prof. Calif. State U.-Long Beach, 1968-75, assoc. prof., 1975-79, prof. math., 1979—; cons. Tridea Electronics, El Monte, Calif., 1969-70; research assoc. U. Calif.-Berkeley, 1981. Contbr. articles to profl. publs. Mem. Am. Math. Soc., Pacific Astronomy Soc., Soc. for Indsl. and Applied Math. Democrat. Research on applied math., math. analysis, astronomy, astrophysics, solar physics, analytic number theory. Office: Calif State Univ Dept Math Long Beach CA 90840

LU, MILTON MING-DEH, plastic surgeon; b. Chengtu, China, Nov. 12, 1919; s. Yow-Cheng and Su-Cheng (Cheng) L.; D.D.S., W. China Union U., 1943, M.D., 1951; M.S., U. Rochester (N.Y.), 1952; m. Hiltrud Marie M. Reineke, Dec. 27, 1963; children—Barbara Ann, Winfred, Rita Doreen, Oliver. Came to U.S., 1946, naturalized, 1955. Resident Strong Meml. Hosp., Rochester, N.Y., 1947-51; fellow in plastic surgery, St. Louis, 1952-56; asst., instr. Strong Meml. Hosp.-Sch. Medicine and Dentistry U. Rochester, 1946-50; asst. plastic surgeon Barnes Hosp.-Washington U., 1952-56; gen. surgeon VA Hosp., Lebanon, Pa., 1956-58; plastic surgeon St. Joseph's Hosp., Lancaster, Pa., Lancaster Gen. Hosp.; cons. Good Samaritan Hosp., Lebanon, Pa. Served to maj. Med. Unit, Chinese Army, 1945. Fellow Internat. Coll. Dentists, Royal Coll. Health, A.C.S; mem. Robert Ivy Soc. Plastic Surgeons AMA, Pa., Lancaster County med. socs., Am. Trauma Soc. (founder mem.), Am. Burn Assn. Mem. Soc. of Friends. Contbr. articles to profl. jours. Home: 2114 Oregon Pike Lancaster PA 17601 Office: 614 N Duke St Lancaster PA 17602

LU, ZENGBIAO, publishing executive; b. Ningbo, Zhejiang, China, Sept. 19, 1930; s. Minshen and Chuijing Lu; married; 1 child, Lin. BA, Tsinghau U., Beijing, 1953. Registered architect. Asst. dept. architecture Tsinghau U., 1954-55, lectr., prof. architecture, 1957—; designer Beijing Inst. Archtl. Design, 1956-57; chief editor World Architecture mag., Beijing, 1980—; cons. World Architecture Review mag. Shenzhen, People's Repub. China, 1985—. Author: Planning and Design of LIbrary Building, 1979; contbr. articles to profl. jours.; mem. editorial bd. Architects mag., 1979—. Names Dist. Scholar Com. Scholarly Communication wtih P.R. of china, 1984. Mem. Chinese Inst. Architects, Beijing Inst. Architects (mem. com. archtl. theory and history).

LUAN, WEN GUI, mathematics educator; b. Taixing, Jiangsu, People's Republic of China, Sept. 20, 1936; s. Shu Zhai Luan and Bao (Ying) Dai; m. Yu Lan Yang, Oct. 10, 1961; 1 child, Yu Hong. BS, Jilin U., Changchun. Asst. U. Sci. Tech. China, Beijing, 1961-64; asst. engr. Beijing Geol. Inst. Ministry Metall. Industry, 1965-74; asst. prof. Computing Ctr., Acad. Sinica, Beijing, 1975-85, assoc. prof., 1986—; reviewer Math. Reviews, Ann Arbor, Mich., 1984—. Contbr. articles to profl. jours. Mem. Beijing Math. Soc., Beijing Computing Math. Soc., Chinese Geophysical Soc. , Am. Math. Soc. Office: Computing Ctr Acad Sinica, Shongguancun, Beijing 2719, People's Republic of China

LUBACHIVSKY, MYROSLAV IVAN CARDINAL, Ukranian Rite archbishop; b. Dolyna, West Ukraine, June 24, 1914; came to U.S., 1947, naturalized, 1952; s. Eustahi and Anna (Oliynik) L. Student, Theol. Acad. Lvov; Grad., Faculty of Theology, U. Innsbruk, 1939, S.T.D., 1942; M. in Biblical Studies, Papal Biblical Inst., 1943; M.Phil., Gregorian U., Rome, 1945; student in medicine U. Rome, before 1947. Ordained: Priest, Catholic Ch. of the Ukranian Rite, 1938. Began pastoral career in U.S., 1947, apptd. archbishop of Ukranian-rite archeparchy of Phila., 1979; coadjutor archbishop of Lvov of the Ukranians, 1980; archbishop of Lvov and major archbishop of Ukranians, 1984, cardinal, 1985; titular ch., St. Sofia. Office: Ukrainian Cath Ch, The Vatican Vatican City *

LÜBBE, WILLEM JOHANNES, engineer; b. Orange Free State, Republic South Africa, Sept. 18, 1947; s. Johann Joachim and Maria Smit (Cilliers) L.; m. Isabelle Murray Van Wijk, June 24, 1972; children: Johann, Jeanne. BSc, U. Stellenbosch, 1968, BSc in Engring., 1972; MBL, U. South Africa, 1984. Lic. profl. engr. Student engr. ESCOM, Johannesburg, Republic South Africa, 1973-74, asst. supt., 1975-76; supt. Duvha Power Sta., 1977-83; site mgr. Kendal Power Sta., Republic South Africa, 1984, regional comml. mgr., 1985, mgr. power sta., 1986—. Mem. South African Council for Profl. Engrs., South African Acad. for Arts and Scis (assoc.). Mem. Nationalist Party. Dutch Reformed Ch. in South Africa. Home: PO Box 2229, Witbank 1035, Republic of South Africa Office: Pvt Bag X501, Khuthala 2232, Republic of South Africa

LUBBERS, RUUD (RUDOLPHUS FRANCISCUS MARIE), prime minister of Netherlands; b. Rotterdam, May 7, 1939; m., 3 children. Ed. Canisius Coll., Nijmegen, Netherlands, U. Rotterdam. Sec. to mng. bd. Lubbers Constrn. Workshops and Machinefabriek Hollandia BV, 1963-65, co-dir., 1965; chmn. Young Christian Employers Assn., then Cath. Assn. Metalwork Employers; mem. council Fedn. Mech. and Elec. Engring. Industries. Mem. Parliament of Netherlands, also leader of Christian Democratic Alliance; minister econ. affairs, 1973-77, prime minister Kingdom of Netherlands, 1982—. Address: Office of Prime Minister, PO Box 20001, The Hague The Netherlands

LUBBOCK, JAMES EDWARD, writer, photographer, publicity cons.; b. St. Louis, Sept. 12, 1924; s. Winans Fowler and Hildegard Beauregard (Whittemore) L.; B.A. in English, U. Mo., 1949; m. Charlotte Frances Ferguson, Aug. 24, 1947; children—Daniel Lawrason (dec.), Brian Wade, Kathleen Harper. Asst. editor St. Louis County Observer, 1949-51; staff writer St. Louis Globe-Democrat, 1951-53, state editor, 1954-56; mng. editor Food Merchandising mag., 1956-57; free-lance indsl. writer-photographer, cons., St. Louis, 1958—; pres. James E. Lubbock, Inc., 1981—.Served with Signal Corps, U.S. Army, 1943-46. Mem. Soc. Profl. Journalists, Sigma Delta Chi, St. Louis Press Club, ACLU, Common Cause. Democrat. Home and Office: 10734 Clearwater Dr Saint Louis MO 63123

LUBECK, MARVIN JAY, physician; b. Cleve., Mar. 20, 1929; s. Charles D. and Lillian (Jay) L.; A.B., U. Mich., 1951, M.D., 1955, M.S., 1959; m. Arlene Sue Bitman, Dec. 28, 1955; children—David Mark, Daniel Jay, Robert Charles. Intern, U. Mich. Med. Center, 1955-56, resident ophthalmology, 1956-58, jr. clin. instr. ophthalmology, 1958-59; practice medicine, specializing in ophthalmology, Denver, 1961—; mem. staff Rose, Children's, Mercy, St. Luke's hosps.; asso. clin. prof. U. Colo. Med. Center; cons. ophthalmologist State of Colo. Served with U.S. Army, 1959-61. Diplomate Am. Bd. Opthalmology. Fellow ACS; mem. Am. Acad. Ophthalmology, Denver Med. Soc., Colo. Ophthalmol. Soc., Am. Intraocular Lens Implant Soc. Home: 590 S Harrison Ln Denver CO 80209 Office: 3865 Cherry Creek N Dr Denver CO 80209

LUBIN, STANLEY, lawyer; b. Bklyn., May 7, 1941; children: David Christopher, Jessica Nicole; m. Barbara Ann Perpich. AB, U. Mich., 1963, JD with honors, 1966. Bar: D.C. 1967, Mich. 1968, U.S. Ct. Appeals (D.C. cir.) 1967, U.S. Ct. Appeals (6th cir.) 1968, U.S. Supreme Ct. 1970, Ariz. 1972, U.S. Ct. Appeals (9th cir.) 1976. Atty. NLRB, Washington, 1966-68; asst. gen. counsel UAW, Detroit, 1968-72; assoc. Harrison, Myers & Singer, Phoenix, 1972-74, McKendree & Tountas, Phoenix, 1975; ptnr. McKendree & Lubin, Phoenix and Denver, 1975-84; shareholder Treon, Warnicke & Roush, P.A., 1984-86; sole practice, Phoenix, 1986—; mem. Ariz. Employment Security Adv. Council, 1975-77. Active ACLU, dir. Ariz. chpt. 1974-81; mem. Ariz. State Cen. Com. Democratic Party, 1973-78, 84—; vice-chmn. Ariz. State Dem. Party, 1986—, mem. state exec. com., 1986—, Ariz. Dem. Council, 1987—, Thomas Jefferson Forum, 1987—, chmn., 1988—. Mem. ABA, State Bar Ariz., Maricopa County Bar Assn., Indsl. Relations Research Assn., Ariz. Indsl. Relations Assn. (exec. bd. 1973—, pres. 1979-80, 84). Club: University. Co-author: Union Fines and Union Discipline Under the National Labor Relations Act, 1971. Home: 719 E Orangewood Ave Phoenix AZ 85020 Office: 2700 N Central Ave Suite 975 Phoenix AZ 85004

LUBINIECKI, ANTHONY STANLEY, microbiologist; b. Greensburg, Pa., Oct. 4, 1946; s. Stanley Anthony and Helen Marie L.; m. Robin Lea Brudowsky, June 8, 1968; 1 child, Gregory. BS, Carnegie-Mellon U., 1968; ScD in Microbiology, U. Pitts., 1972. Research asst. U. Pitts., 1971-72, asst. research prof., 1972-74; prin. scientist Meloy Labs., Inc., Springfield, Va., 1974-78, mng. dir., 1979-80; tech. dir. biol. products Flow Labs., Inc., McLean, Va., 1980-82; mgr. cell culture ops. Genentech Inc., South San Francisco, 1982-83, dir. cell culture research and devel., 1983—; v.p. biopharmaceutical mfg. and devel. Smith Kline & French Labs., King of Prussia, Pa., 1988—. Contbr. articles to profl. jours. Mem. Reston Community Assn., 1976—. NIAID/NIH grantee, 1973-74, 74-82, others. Mem. Am. Soc. Microbiology, AAAS, Pharm. Mfrs. Assn. (biol. sect., chmn. process tech. com.), Am. Assn. Immunologists, N.Y. Acad. Scis., European Soc. Animal Cell Tech., Soc. Exptl. Biology and Medicine, Parenteral Drug Assn. Roman Catholic. Office: Smith Kline & French Labs 709 Swedeland Rduno Blvd King of Prussia PA 19406

LUBRECHT, HEINZ D., publishing company executive, antiquarian book expert, appraiser; b. Reutlingen, Fed. Republic Germany, Dec. 2, 1908; came to U.S., 1928, naturalized, 1935; s. Adolf Carl and Amelia Sophie (Grueninger) L.; m. Anne M. Ficke, Oct. 2, 1937; children—Peter Thomas, Charles Frederick. Student pub. schs., Stuttgart, Fed. Republic Germany. Vice pres. Hafner Pub. Co., N.Y.C., 1928-69; v.p., editor Macmillan Pub. Co., N.Y.C., 1969-74; pres. Lubrecht & Cramer, Ltd., Monticello, N.Y., 1974—. Co-author: Early American Botanical Works, 1967. Mem. N.Y. Bot. Garden, Old Book Table, N.Am. Mycological Assn., Antiquarian Booksellers Assn. Republican. Lutheran. Home: RD 1 Box 244 Forestburgh NY 12777 Office: Lubrecht & Cramer Ltd RD 1 Box 244 Forestburgh NY 12777

LUCAN, MATEJ, Czechoslovakian government official; b. Gotovany, Czechoslovakia, Jan. 11, 1928. Ed. Comenius U., Bratislava, Czechoslovakia. Head dept. Marxism-Leninism, Comenius U., 1952-53; head dept., central com. Communist Party Slovakia, 1951-52, 53-56, mem. central com., 1958-68, 69-71; mem. presidium Slovak Nat. Council, 1963-68, commr. for edn. and culture, 1963-67, commr. for edn., 1967-68; minister edn. Slovak Socialist Republic, 1969-70; premanent rep. to Internat. Office for Edn., 1964-68; dep. premier Czechoslovakia, 1970—; mem. Ho. of Nations, Czechoslovak Fed. Assembly, 1970—; mem. central com. Communist Party Czechoslovakia, 1970—; chmn. State Com. for Culture, Sci. and Health Regulations with Fgn. Countries, 1971—, Govt. Population Commn., 1971—; dep. chmn. Govt. Com. for Sci. and Tech., 1971—; chmn. Govt. Com. for Phys. Edn. and Sport, 1981—, Com. for Klement Gottwald state prize, 1981—. Decorated Order of Labor, Order Victorious February. Address: Presidium of Czechoslovakia, Office of Deputy Premier, Prague 1 Czechoslovakia *

LUCAS, AUBREY KEITH, university president; b. State Line, Miss., July 12, 1934; s. Keith Caldwell and Audelle Margaret (Robertson) L.; m. Ella Frances Ginn, Dec. 19, 1955; children: Margaret Frances, Keith Godbold (dec.), Martha Carol, Alan Douglas, Mark Christopher. B.S., U. So. Miss., 1955, M.A., 1956; Ph.D., Fla. State U., 1966. Asst. dir. reading clinic U. So. Miss., Hattiesburg, 1955-56; dir. admissions U. So. Miss., 1957-61, registrar, 1963-69; dean U. So. Miss. (Grad. Sch.), 1969-71; instr. Hinds Jr. Coll., Raymond, Miss., 1956-57; pres. Delta State U., Cleveland, Miss., 1971-75, U. So. Miss., 1975—. Author: The Mississippi Legislature and Mississippi Public Higher Education, 1890-1960; contbg. author: A History of Mississippi, 1973. Bd. dirs. United Way, Pine Burr Area council Boy Scouts Am., So. Regional Edn. Bd., Miss. Assn. Colls., 1979-80; Bd. dirs. Miss. Arts Commn., 1977-87, chmn., 1983-85; campaign chmn. Forrest Lamar United Way, 1979; state chmn. Am. Cancer Soc., 1978; mem. Commn. on Nat. Devel. in Postsecondary Edn., 97th Congress; pres. Miss. Econ. Council, 1982-83. Mem. Hattiesburg C. of C., Miss. Forestry Assn., Newcomen Soc. N.Am., Am. Assn. State Colls. and Univs. (bd. dirs. 1982-86, chmn. 1984-85), Am. Council Edn. (bd. dirs. 1984-86), Miss. Inst. Arts and Letters, Sigma Phi Epsilon, Omicron Delta Kappa, Phi Kappa Phi, Pi Gamma Mu, Pi Tau Chi, Kappa Delta Pi, Phi Delta Kappa, Kappa Pi. Methodist (conf. lay leader 1980-88, adminstrv. bd.). Club: Red Red Rose. Lodge: Kiwanis. Office: U So Miss Office of Pres Hattiesburg MS 39406-5001

LUCAS, BARBARA DOREEN, data processing educator; b. Columbus, Ohio, Aug. 14, 1949; d. Bernard Arthur and Louella (Call) Downs; m. David Eberst Lucas, June 23, 1970 (div.); 1 child, Doreen Bethany. BS in Edn., Ohio U., 1970, postgrad., 1970—; MA, Ohio State U., 1984; JD, Capital U., 1987. Cert. edn., Ohio. Info. systems assoc. Western Electric Co., Columbus, 1970-74; systems programmer, analyst Xerox Corp., Columbus, 1974-75; safety systems analyst State Ohio Hwy. Dept., Columbus, 1975-77; sr. systems analyst State Ohio Dept. Taxation, Columbus, 1977-79; sr. data processing instr. SouthWestern City Schs., Grove City, Ohio, 1979—; lectr. Ohio State U., Columbus, 1974—; instr. Eastland Vocat. Sch., Groveport, Ohio, 1979—, Paul C. Hayes Tech. Sch., Grove City, 1979—. Mem. civilian rev. bd. SSS; vol. Girl Scouts U.S. Mem. Bus. and Profl. Women's Club (sec. Grove City chpt.), Assn. for Computing Machinery, Ohio Edn. Assn. (advisor, mem. sch. curriculum com.), S.W. Edn. Assn., Ohio Vocat. Assn., Nat. Assn. for Female Execs., Ohio State U. Alumni Assn., Ohio Assn. for Adult Edn., Nat. Women's Hall of Fame, Inc. Contbr. articles to profl. jours. Home: 5515 Ebright Rd Groveport OH 43125 Office: 4436 Haughn Rd Grove City OH 43123

LUCAS, BERT A., pastor, social services administator, consultant; b. Hammond, Ind., Mar. 26, 1933; s. John William and Norma (Gladys) Graham; m. Nanci Dai Hindman, Sept. 10, 1960; children: Bradley Scott, Traci Dai. BA, Wheaton Coll., 1956; BD, No. Bapt. Theol. Sem., 1960, ThM, 1965; MSW, U. Mich., 1971; ThD, Ea. Bapt. Theol. Sem., 1988. Licensed social worker, Ohio; ordained clergyman Am. Baptist Conv. Chaplain Miami Children's Ctr., Maumee, Ohio, 1967-83; assoc. pastor First Bapt. Ch., La Porte, Ind., 1959-62; pastor Maumee Bapt. Ch., 1963-67; adminstrv. social work supr. Lucas County (Ohio) Children Services, 1967—; pastor Holland (Ohio) United Meth. Ch., 1979—; adj. prof. Bowling Green (Ohio) State U., 1972-79; family life cons. New Horizon's Acad., Holland, 1984-86, co-dir. family services 1985-86; cons. parenting, marriage enrichment, Toledo, 1986—. Rep. precinct capt., Toledo, 1984. Bert A. Lucas Day proclaimed City of Holland, 1984. Mem. Am. Assn. Counseling and Devel., Am. Assn. Marriage and Family Therapy (assoc.), Assn. for Couples in Marriage Enrichment, Hist. Preservations of Am. (Community Leader and Noteworthy Ams. award 1976-77), Council Family Relations.

LUCAS, DALE ALFRED, petroleum marketing agent; b. Melfort, Sask., Can., Oct. 6, 1937; s. Howard Henry Joseph and Ruby Viola (Svare) L.; m. Marlene Ann Anderson, Sept. 8, 1962; children: Sandra Patrice, Nancy Jane, Geoffrey Lorne. BSChemE, U. Alta., Edmonton, Can., 1961, BA in Econs., 1976. Engr. Syncrude Can., Edmonton, 1961-68; minister's asst. Dept. Energy Govt. Can., Ottawa, Ont., 1968-69; 1st sec. Embassy of Can., Washington, 1969-73; mgr. B.P. Alaska, N.Y.C., 1973-77; pres. B.P. Pipelines, San Francisco, 1977-80; v.p. B.P. Can. Exploration, Calgary, Alta., 1980-84; chmn. Alta. Petroleum Mktg. Commn., Calgary, 1984—; Chmn. petroleum mktg. agy. Clubs: Univ. (San Francisco); Bow Valley (Calgary). Office: Alta Petroleum Mktg Commn, 1900 250 6th Ave SW, Calgary, AB Canada T2P 3H7

LUCAS, DARRELL BLAINE, educator; b. Greene, Iowa, Sept. 26, 1902; s. Leonard and Ursula (Whitten) L.; B.S., Iowa State U., 1922, M.S., 1923; Ph.D., N.Y. U., 1928; m. Dorothy Carl, Dec. 24, 1924; 1 dau., Ann Harriet Lucas Eustace. Asst. agrl. engr. Rutgers U., 1923-24, instr., 1924-27, asst. prof., 1927-29; asso. prof. psychology Iowa State U., 1929-30; asso. prof. mktg., N.Y. U., 1930-42, prof., 1942—, chmn. dept. marketing, 1950-61, 65-68, chmn. marketing Area Grad. Sch. Bus. Adminstrn., 1964-68, joint chmn. marketing Schools Bus., 1965-68, tech. dir. Advt. Research Found., 1944-59; research counsel Batten, Barton, Durstine & Osborn, 1943-68, A.C. Nielsen Co., 1959-64; co-inventor (with J. B. Davidson) of automatic plow; originator controlled recognition method for measuring mag. advt. audiences, first applied in surveys of Colliers', Life and Sat. Eve. Post, 1941. Mem. Life mag. com. continuing study mag. audiences, 1938-41; mem. joint com. measurement pub. opinion, attitudes and consumer wants NRC-Social Sci. Research Council, 1945-54; dir. Psychological Corp., 1944-47; mem. bd. Ednl. Film Inst., N.Y. U., 1939-42; pres. Market Research Council N.Y., 1943-44; advt. research cons., 1932—. Designated Leader in Mktg., Jour. of Mktg., 1971; elected to Hall of Fame in Mktg. Research, 1979; licensed psychologist, N.Y. State. Fellow Am. Psychol. Assn.; mem. Am. Mktg. Assn., Beta Theta Pi, Delta Sigma Pi, Tau Beta Pi, Phi Kappa Phi, Gamma Sigma Delta, Phi Delta Kappa, Alpha Delta Sigma. Ind. Republican. Presbyterian. Club: Dutch Treat (N.Y.C.). Lodge: Masons. Author: Psychology for Advertisers (with C.E. Benson), 1930; Psychology of Selling, 1940; Advertising Psychology and Research (with S. H. Britt), 1950; Measuring Advertising Effectiveness (with S.H. Britt), also Spanish, Italian, German, Dutch and Japanese transl. 1963. Contbg. author: Dartnell Handbook on Marketing, 1981. Contbr. articles to jours. on engring., advt. psychology, advt. research. Home: 20 Sunset Park Upper Montclair NJ 07043

LUCAS, DONALD LEO, entrepreneur; b. Upland, Calif., Mar. 18, 1930; s. Leo J. and Mary G. (Schwamm) L.; B.A., Stanford U., 1951, M.B.A., 1953; m. Lygia de Soto Harrison, July 15, 1961; children—Nancy Maria, Alexandra Maria, Donald Alexander. Assoc. corp. fin. dept. Smith, Barney & Co., N.Y.C., 1956-59; gen., ltd. partner Draper, Gaither & Anderson, Palo Alto, Calif., 1959-66; pvt. investor, Menlo Park, Calif., 1966—; chmn. bd. Oracle Corp., Inc., Belmont, Calif.; bd. dirs. HBO & Co., Atlanta, ICOT Corp., Mountain View, Liconix, Mountain View, Robinton Products, Inc., Sunnyvale, Calif., Kahler Corp., Cadence Design Systems, Santa Clara, Calif., Tri-Data Corp., Inc. Mem. bd. regents Bellarmine Coll. Prep., 1977—; regent emeritus U. Santa Clara, 1980—. Served to 1st lt., AUS, 1953-55. Mem. Am. Council for Capital Formation, Stanford U. Alumni Assn., Stanford Grad. Sch. Bus. Alumni Assn., Zeta Psi. Clubs: Commonwealth (San Francisco); Stanford Buck; Vintage (Indian Wells, Calif.); Menlo Country (Woodside, Calif.); Menlo Circus (Atherton, Calif.); Jackson Hole Golf. Home: 224 Park Ln Atherton CA 94025 Office: 3000 Sand Hill Rd #3 Menlo Park CA 94025

LUCAS, GEORGES, publisher, consultant; b. Rennes, France, Aug. 29, 1915; s. Rene and Madeleine (Bazin) L.; m. Evelyne Torres, May 7, 1941; 1 son, Yannick. Baccalaureat, U. Rennes (France), Licence en Droit. With B.N.C.I. (bank), Algeria and Tunisia, 1941-43; dep. adminstr. Groupe Bertrand, Lisbon, Portugal, 1948-75; pres. D.I.F.E.L., Rio Sao Paulo, Brazil, 1950-77; v.p., adminstr., dir.-gen. Banque Franco-Portuguese d'Outre Mer, Paris, 1965-72; adminstr. Editions Robert Laffont, Paris, 1967-78, dir. gen., 1975-78; pres., dir. gen. Librairie Larousse, Paris, 1978-85, now counselor. Served to capt. French Army. Decorated Legion D'Honneur, Croix De Guerre. Mem. Union Internat. Editeurs (dir. com., life). Roman Catholic. Clubs: Yacht & Golf (Estoril, Portugal); Inter Allié (Paris). Office: Librairie Larousse, 15/17 Rue Montparnasse, 75298 Paris France *

LUCAS, GEORGETTA MARIE SNELL, retired educator, artist; b. Harmony, Ind., July 25, 1920; d. Ernest Clermont and Sarah Ann (McIntyre) Snell; m. Joseph William Lucas, Jan. 29, 1943; children—Carleen Anita Lucas Underwood-Scrougham, Thomas Joseph, Joetta Jeanne Lucas Allgood. BS, Ind. State U., 1942; MS in Edn., Butler U., 1964; postgrad. Herron Sch. of Art, Indpls., 1961-65, Ind. U., Indpls. and Bloomington, 1960, 61, 62, 65. Music, art tchr. Jasonville City Schs., Ind., 1942-43, Van Buren High Sch., Brazil, Ind., 1943-46, Plainfield City Schs., Ind., 1946-52, Met. Sch. Dist. Wayne Twp., Indpls., 1952-56, 1959-68; art tchr. Met. Sch. Dist. Perry Twp., Indpls., 1968-81; chmn. of artists Internat. Platform Assn., 1987; Ind. State U. art chmn. for Nat. League of Am. PEN Women, 1984-88. Illustrator: (book) Why So Sad, Little Rag Doll, 1963; artist (painting) Ethereal Season, 1966, (lithograph) Bird of Time, 1965-66: represented in permanent collections Ind. State U., Ind.-Purdue U.-Indlps.; lectr. Art Educators Assn. Ind., Ind. U.-Bloomington, 1976, Internat. Platform Assn., Washington, 1975, 77, 78, 82, 84 (Recipient Silver award 1978, appointed gov. 1983—). Named Best of Show, Nat. League Am. Pen Women State Show, 1983. Mem. Nat. Assn. Women Artist, Ind. Artist-Craftsmen, Inc. (pres. 1979-85, 87—), Ind. Fedn. Art Clubs (pres. 1986-87), Hoosier Salon, NEA, Art Edn. Assn. Ind., Nat. League Am. Pen Women (state art chmn. 1984—), Fine Art for State Ind. (Internat. Women's Yr. fine art chmn. 1977), Internat. Platform Assn. (bd. dirs. 1983—, chmn. art com. 1987—), Cen. Ind. Artists (hon.), Alpha Delta Kappa (Ind. state chmn. of art 1973-77, pres. 1972-74). Republican. Methodist. Lodge: Eastern Star. Avocations: genealogy, travel, numismatics. Home and Office: 9702 W Washington St Indianapolis IN 46231

LUCAS, JAMES RAYMOND, manufacturing executive, management consultant; b. St. Louis, Mar. 9, 1950; s. James Earl and Anna LaVerne (Ryan) L.; m. Pamela Kay Petersen, June 10, 1972; children: Laura Christine, Peter Barrett, David Christopher, Bethany Gayle. BS in Engring. Mgmt., U. Mo., Rolla, 1972. Registered profl. engr., Mo., Kans. Product analyst The Lee Co., Westwood, Kans., 1971-73; mgr. planning Black & Veatch, Kansas City, Mo., 1973-79; dir. constrn. Hallmark Cards, Kansas City, Mo., 1979-81; project mgr. The Pritchard Corp., Kansas City, Mo., 1981-83; freelance author Overland Park, Kans., 1983—; gen. mgr., pres., chief exec. officer EPIC Mfg., Kansas City, Mo., 1984-86; dir. CWI Bus. Systems, North Kansas City, Mo., 1986—; pres. Luman Cons., Prairie Village, Kans., 1983—; bd. dirs. Emergency Systems Services and Computer Workshop, Inc.; ops. mgr. PSM, Inc., 1987—. Author: Weeping In Ramah, 1985. Spokesman Mother and Unborn Baby Care, Overland Park, 1985—; elder Ch. of Living Faith in Jesus, 1985—. Mem. Soc. Mfg. Engrs. (sr.), Bible Sci. Assn., Creation Sci. Assn. Mem. Bible Believing Christian Ch. Home: 7303 Rosewood Prairie Village KS 66208 Office: Luman Cons PO Box 2566 Shawnee Mission KS 66201

LUCAS, PERCY HYLTON CRAIG, conservation consultant; b. Christchurch, Canterbury, N.Z., June 9, 1925; s. Percy Charles and Ethel Lena (Craig) L.; m. Kura Joyce Pitcher, Nov. 20, 1948; children—Murray Hylton, Marian Joy. Student pub. schs., Christchurch. Dir. nat. parks Dept. Lands and Survey, Wellington, N.Z., 1969-75, asst. dir.-gen., 1975-78, dep. dir.-gen., 1978-82, dir. gen., 1982-86; vice chmn. Internat. Commn. on Nat. Parks, 1975-86; regional councillor Internat. Union for Conservation of Nature, 1978-84, dep. chmn., 1986—; cons. UNESCO, Nepal, 1980, China, 1987, UN, Indonesia, 1983. Author: To the Glory of God, 1965; The Blue and Gold, 1965; Conserving New Zealand's Heritage, 1970. Lyricist, Saultalk, 1974. Councillor, Borough Council, Tawa, 1971-83. Winston Churchill fellow, 1969. Mem. N.Z. Inst. Parks and Recreation Adminstrn. (assoc.), Internat. Fedn. Parks and Recreation Adminstrn. (assoc.). Baptist. Avocations: photography; nature; cricket; soccer. Home and Office: 1/268 Main Rd, Tawa, Wellington 6203, New Zealand

LUCAS, PETER WILLIAM, physical anthropologist, researcher in oral biology; b. Stamford, Lincolnshire, Eng., May 21, 1952; arrived in Singapore, 1983; s. John Thorpe and Monica (Usher) L.; m. Maria Atilia Gutierrez Hernandez, Nov. 11, 1978; children: Katherine, Diana. BS in Anthropology with honors, U. Coll. London U., 1976; PhD in Phys. Anthropology, U. London, 1980. Tng. fellow Med. Research Council, London, 1980-83; lectr. Anatomy Dept. Nat. U., Singapore, 1983—; Contbr. articles to profl. jours. Recipient Daryll Forde award for anthropology U. Coll. London, 1976. Mem. Internat. Assn. Dental Research, Internat. Primatolological Soc., Am. Assn. Phys. Anthropologist. Liberal. Anglican. Club: Faculty. Office: Nat U Singapore Anatomy Dept, 10 Kent Ridge Crescent, 0511 Singapore Singapore

LUCAS-BACHERT, URSULA ERNA MARARETE, public relations executive; b. Lübeck, Fed. Republic Germany, Mar. 23, 1938; d. Fritz A. and Susel (Schweikert) Bachert; m. Bernd Lucas, Oct. 4, 1942 (div. Apr. 1975); m. Horst G. Slesina, July 29, 1982. Diploma volkswirt, Rupprecht-Karl U., Heidelberg, 1965; student, U. of Econs., Mannheim, Fed. Republic Germany. Editor Bibliographic Inst., Mannheim, Fed. Republic Germany, 1965; sci. co-worker German Fedn. Work Study Practitioners, Darmstadt, Fed. Republic Germany, 1966-69; journalist A.P., Frankfurt, Fed. Republic Germany, 1970-72; pvt. practice pub. relations Frankfurt, 1972—. Contbr. articles to profl. jours. Mem. German Journalists Assn., German Pub. Relations Soc., Pub. Relations Agys. Assn. Club: Golf (Frankfurt). Office: Siesmayerstrasse 10, 6000 Frankfurt Federal Republic of Germany

LUCE, JOHN VICTOR, classicist, educator; b. Dublin, Ireland, May 21, 1920; s. Arthur Aston and Lilian Mary (Thompson) L.; m. Marjorie Lyndall Miles, June 21, 1948; children: Christina, Jane, Alice. BA with honors, Trinity Coll., Dublin, 1942, MA, 1945; MA, Oxford (Eng.) U., 1945; LittD, Trinity Coll., 1978. Jr. lectr. Trinity Coll., Dublin, 1942-45, fellow in classics, 1948—, assoc. prof., 1972-84, prof., 1984—, vice provost, 1987—; lectr. in Greek Glasgow (Scotland) U., 1946-48; vis. prof. Trinity Coll., Hartford, 1961-62, U. Mich., 1969, U. Ind., 1975; pub. orator Dublin U., 1972—; guest lectr. SWan Hellenic Cruises, various locations, 1964—. Author: Lost Atlantis, 1969, The End of Atlantis, 1969, Homer and the Heroic Age, 1975; co-author: Quest for Am., 1971, Quest for Ulysses, 1974; contbr. articles to scholarly jours. Bd. govs. Dublin High Sch., 1972—. Mem. Royal Irish Acad. Mem. Ch. Ireland. Office: Trinity Coll, Dept Classical Studies, Dublin 2 Ireland

LUCHS, FRED EMIL, clergyman, lecturer; b. Ridgeway, Pa., Apr. 2, 1904; s. Simon and Margaretha (Ruef) L.; m. Evelyn Mae Coulter, Aug. 8, 1933; children: Lewis Richard, Mark William, Michael Charles, Margaret Jane. BD, U. Chgo., 1931; DD, Franklin and Marshall Coll., 1952. Served as pastor throughout the U.S 1931-73; assoc. editor 20th Century Quarterly, 1945-55; established 1st co-ed youth camp in U.S., 1932; exchange preacher to Eng. and Am. Chs. in Berlin and Paris, 1939; interim pastor St. John's Evang. Protestant Ch., Columbus, Ohio, 1973; chaplain aboard 14 trips worldwide; mem. Gen. Motors speakers, 1960-72. Author: Lenten Tryst, 1947, If I Had Never Been Born, 1987, Christmas Letters: 1945-87, 1987; writer weekly prayers Christian Century; works trans. into several langs. Nat. Sermon contest winner, 1949; named One of Ten Best Speakers in Am. Internat. Speakers Network, One of Ten Outstanding Presbyn. Preachers in U.S., 1952; Honorary Alumnus award Ohio U., 1985. Home: 93 Wonder Hills Dr Athens OH 45701

LUCHSINGER, MATTHISA HARRO, textile consultant; b. Glarus, Switzerland, July 14, 1928; m. Margaret Slater, Feb. 2, 1931; children: Catrina Martha, Marianne Louise. Grad. high sch., Switzerland. Sales engr. various cos. Africa and Europe, 1951-70; mgr. Scanhold AG, Kuesnacht, Switzerland, 1970-76; sales dir. Saladin AG, Sirnach, 1976-81; bd. dirs. M.H. Luchsinger Cons., Henau, Switzerland, 1981—. Mem. Chamber of Econ. Relations, People's Republic China-Switzerland Textile Inst. Manchester. Lodge: Flumen Luminus Reunion and Fellowship. Office: M H Luchsinger Cons, PO Box 21, CH-9247 Henau Switzerland

LUCHTERHAND, RALPH EDWARD, financial planner; b. Portland, Oreg., Feb. 9, 1952; s. Otto Charles II and Evelyn Alice (Isaac) L.; m. JoAnn Denise Adams, Aug. 13, 1983; children: Anne Michelle, Eric Alexander. B.S., Portland State U., 1974, MBA, 1986. Registered profl. engr., Oreg., Wash.; gen. securities broker NYSE/NASD. Mech. engr. Hyster Co., Portland, 1971-75, service engr., 1975-76; project engr. Lumber Systems Inc., Portland, 1976-79; prin. engr. Moore Internat., Portland, 1979-81, chief product engr., 1981-83; project engr. Irvington-Moore, Portland, 1983, chief engr., 1983-86; ind. cons. engr., 1986; engring. program mgr. Precision Castparts Corp., Portland, 1986-87; reg. rep./personal fin. planner IDS Fin. Services, Clackamas, Oreg., 1987—. Treas. Village Bapt. Ch., Beaverton, Oreg., 1988—. Mem. ASME (pres. student chpt. 1973-74). Republican. Home: 3000 NW 178th Ave Portland OR 97229 Office: IDS Fin Services Inc 8800 SE Sunnyside Rd Suite 300 Clackamas OR 97015

LUCICH, PETER HENRY, anthropologist, educator; b. Bridgetown, Australia, July 25, 1939; s. Stephen Peter Lucich and Ilse (Pokorny) Lucich; m. Tuanchai Seng Chem, Dec. 5, 1968; children—Tom, Milovan. B.Sc. with honors, U. Western Australia, Perth, 1960, M.Sc., 1968. Research asst. dept. anthropology U. Western Australia, 1967; lectr. in sociology U. New Eng., Armidale, New South Wales, Australia, 1969—. Author: The Development of Omaha Kinship Terminologies in Three Australian Aboriginal Tribes of the Kimberley Division, W.A., 1968; Genealogical Symmetry, 1987; Compiler: Children's Stories from the Worora, 1969. Contbr. revs. to profl. jours. 1964-83. Mem. Australian Anthrop. Soc., U. New Eng. Tchr.'s Assn. Home: 72 Jeffery St, Armidale, New South Wales 2350, Australia Office: U New Eng, Dept Sociology, Armidale, New South Wales 2350, Australia

LUCIDO, NAOMI HERNANDEZ, gastroenterologist; b. San Pablo, Laguna, Philippines, June 29, 1934; d. Roman Marvive and Ynes (Abas) Hernandez; m. Jose M. Lucido, June 23, 1972 (dec Oct. 1986); 1 child, Lavinia Marie. Diplomate Am. Bd. Gastroenterology. Rotating intern Evang. Deaconess Hosp., Milw., 1961-62; resident in internal medicine St. Joseph's Hosp., Chgo., 1962-64, Mercy Hosp., Chgo., 1964-65; fellow in gastroenterology St. Mary's Hosp., Montreal, Que., Can., 1965-67; research fellow in gastroenterology Hotel Dieu Hosp., Kingston, Ont., Can., 1967-68; cons. in gastroenterology San Pablo Doctors Hosp., Community Hosp., San Pablo City, Philippines, 1970—. Mem. ALAKBAY, San Pablo City, 1986—; dir. Puericulture Ctr., San Pablo City, 1986—. Fellow Philippines Soc. of Gastroenterology; assoc. fellow Philippine Coll. of Physicians; mem. Philippine Diabetes Assn., San Pablo City Med. Assn., Philippine Women's Med. Assn. Roman Catholic. Home and Office: 10 G Aquino, 4000 San Pablo Laguna Philippines

LUCK, MICHAEL FREDERICK, health care administrator; b. Burlington, Vt., Mar. 26, 1947; s. William Henry and Mary Agnes (Leddy) L.; BS, Johnson State Coll., 1970; MA, So. Ill. U., 1972, PhD, 1974; m. Barbara Colby Wilson, June 24, 1978; children: Sean Michael, Holly Marie, Johnathan Thomas Wilson. Teaching asst. and field investigator dept. anthropology and Coll. Edn., So. Ill. U., Carbondale, 1970-72, spl. asst. to pres. and exec. v.p., 1972-74, asst. dir. devel. So. Ill. U. Found., 1974; asst. dir. devel. M.I.T., Cambridge, 1974-75, acting dir. devel., 1975, dir. devel., 1975-78; pres. Rutgers U. Found., New Brunswick, N.J., 1978-80; co-adj. prof. dept. Am. studies Douglass Coll., Rutgers U. and Grad. Sch. of Edn., 1979-80; v.p. devel. and pub. affairs Wayne State U., Detroit, 1980-85; v.p. pub. affairs and devel. Healtheast, Inc., Allentown, Pa., 1985—, v.p. devel., Healtheast, Inc.; mem. Lehigh County Indsl. Devel. Authority. Exec. dir. Jackson County YMCA Debt Retirement Campaign, Carbondale, 1973-74; bd. dirs. Pa. Stage Co., exec. com., v.p. major ind. gifts and endowment com.; mem. Lehigh Valley Visitors and Conv. Bur.; mem. profl. div. Lehigh County United Way, mem. endowment com.; co-founder, dir. 4-H Devel. Fund, 1978. Served to capt., N.G., 1966-78. Wenner Gren Anthrop. Found. grantee, 1972, Grad.-Leadership Detroit III, 1982. Mem. Nat. Soc. Fund-Raising Execs. (exec. com.), Council for Advancement and Support Edn., Am. Hosp. Assn., Hosp. Assn. Pa., Nat. Assn. for Hosp. Devel., Lehigh County C. of C.Lodge: Rotary. Author: Selected Bibliography in Higher Education, 1973, aslo co-editor; Community College Development: Alternative Fund-Raising Strategies, 1978; contbr. articles on edn. adminstrn., anthropology and devel. to profl. jours. Home: RD 1 Box 134 Zionsville PA 18092 Office: Healtheast Trust Fund 50 College Dr Allentown PA 18104

LUCKIE, ROBERT ERVIN, JR., advertising executive; b. Clanton, Ala., May 3, 1917; s. Robert Ervin and Eliza (Goodwyn) L.; m. Lois Katherine Drolet, May 15, 1942; children: Katherine (Mrs. Andrew J. Shackelford), Robert Ervin III, Anne Claire, Thomas George. A.B., Birmingham-So. Coll., 1940. Reporter-columnist Birmingham News, Ala., 1940-41; organizer Luckie & Forney, Inc. (and predecessor), Birmingham, 1953; since chmn. prin. owner Luckie & Forney, Inc. (and predecessor); dir. South Trust Bank of Ala.; pres. Nat Advt. Agy. Network, 1960. Chmn. for Ala. Radio Free Europe, 1964; co-chmn. Jefferson County United Appeal, 1968; pres. Met. Devel. Bd., 1976; bd. dirs. Blue Cross/Blue Shield, of Ala., Ala. Motorist's Assn. Served to lt. comdr. USNR, 1942-45. Recipient Disting. Alumni award Birmingham-So. Coll., 1968, Silver medal award Advt. Fedn. Am. and Printer's Ink, 1964. Mem. Birmingham-So. Coll. Alumni Assn. (pres. 1966), Omicron Delta Kappa, Kappa Alpha. Methodist. Clubs: Kiwanis (past pres.), Birmingham Country (pres. 1975), Relay House (past pres.), Downtown, The Club (Birmingham) (pres. 1980-81). Home: 3238 Country Club Rd Birmingham AL 35213 Office: Luckie & Forney Inc 600 Luckie Dr Suite 200 Birmingham AL 35223

LUCKING, PETER STEPHEN, industrial engineering consultant; b. Kalamazoo, Oct. 11, 1945; s. Henry William, Sr., and Mary (Lynn) L.; m. Marilyn Barbara Jensen, Dec. 18, 1971. B.A., Western Mich. U., 1968; B.S. in Indsl. Engring., 1973. Indsl. engr. Motorola, Phoenix, 1974, Revlon, Inc., Phoenix, 1974-75; indsl. engr. Hooker Chem. and Plastics Co., Niagara Falls, N.Y., 1975-76, sr. corp. indsl. engr., 1976-77; indsl. engr. Carborundum Co., Niagara Falls, 1977-78; cons. H.B. Maynard and Co., Pitts., 1978-85; mgr. indsl. engring. Carrier, Tyler, Tex., 1985-88; cons. H.B. Maynard and Co., Pitts., 1988—. Advisor, Jr. Achievement, Niagara Falls, 1977. Served with U.S. Army, 1969-70, Vietnam. Mem. Inst. Indsl. Engrs. (sr. mem., region v.p. 1983-85), Inst. Indsl. Engrs. (pres. Niagara Frontier chpt. 1977-78). Democrat. Roman Catholic. Home: 816 Elmridge Dr Tyler TX 75703 Office: HB Maynard and Co Inc 235 Alpha Dr Pittsburgh PA 15238

LUDER, OWEN (HAROLD), architect; b. London, Aug. 7, 1928; s. Edward Charles and Ellen Clara (Mason) L.; m. Rose Dorothy Broadstock, Jan. 27, 1951; children—Jaqueline, Kathryn, Sara, Judith, Peter (dec.). Student in architecture Regent St. Poly, London, Brixton Sch. Bldg., London, 1946-51. Chartered architect. Architect asst., various offices, London, 1945-56; prin. Owen Luder Architect, London, 1956-63; sr. ptnr. Owen Luder Partnership, London, 1963-78, chmn., mng. dir., 1978-87; ind. cons., 1988—; dir Owen Holdings Ltd., London; cons. on environ. design of Vale of Belvior Coalfields, Nat. Coal Bd. Eng., 1975-87; cons. on redevel. of Shildon and Swindon Works. Author: A Housing Strategy for the 1980s (Housing and Town Planning Assn. Jubilee medal 1981), 1981; contbr. numerous articles to nat. archtl., constrn. publs., 1963—, pub. mag. Pres. Norwood Soc., London, 1981—. Served with Royal Arty., 1946-48. Fellow Royal Inst. Brit. Architects (council 1967—, hon. treas. 1975-78, pres. 1981-83, various awards including Bronze medal for Architecture 1963). Conservative. Mem. Ch. of England. Club: Savage (London). Office: Owen Luder Consultancy, 418 Premier House, 10 Greycoat Pl, London SW1 England

LÜDERITZ, BERNDT, cardiologist; b. Braunschweig, Fed. Republic Germany, Mar. 26, 1940; s. Bernhard and Theda (Winter) L.; m. Hedwig Muschol, Nov. 29, 1969; children: Florian, Martin, Stephan. MD, U. Heidelberg, Fed. Republic Germany, 1965. Cert. Med. State Bd., Munich, 1965. Intern U. Munich, 1965-67; resident U. Munich and Göttingen, 1967-74; asst. prof. cardiology U. Göttingen, Fed. Republic Germany, 1972-79; assoc. prof. cardiology U. Munich, 1979-83; prof. chmn. dept. medicine, cardiology U. Bonn, Fed. Republic Germany, 1983—; chmn. German Working Group on Cardiac Pacing, 1983-88. Editor: (book) Cardiac Pacing, 1976; co-editor: (book) Myocardial Failure, 1977; mem. editorial bd. PACE, 1981, Intervention Cardiol., 1988. Fellow Am. Coll. Cardiology, Am. Heart Assn.; mem. German Cardiac Soc. (exec. bd. 1984-88, Arthur Weber prize 1980), N.Am. Soc. Pacing and Electrophysiology. Lutheran. Home: 10 Erich-Böger, D-5300 Bonn Federal Republic of Germany Office: U Bonn Dept Medicine and Cardiology, 25 Sigmund Freud, D-5300 Bonn Federal Republic of Germany

LUDIN, ROGER LOUIS, physics educator; b. Jersey City, June 13, 1944; s. Fredric E. and Gwendolyn C. (Rogers) L.; m. Diane E. Wilson, Aug. 26, 1966; children: Stephen L., Joyce E. BS in Physics, Brown U., 1966; MS in Physics, Worcester Polytech. Inst., 1968, PhD in Physics, 1969. Postdoctoral fellow Worcester (Mass.) Polytech. Inst., 1969-70; prof. Burlington County Coll., Pemberton, N.J., 1970-85; lectr. Calif. Poly. State U., San Luis Obispo, 1984—. Author lab. manuals for introductory physics; author computer assisted instrn. for gen. physics. Active Medford Lakes (N.J.) Bd. Edn., 1976-84, pres. 1978-84; bd. dirs. Medford Lakes Athletic Assn., 1974-84; soccer coach Morro Bay (Calif.) High Sch., 1985—. Named Tchr. of Yr. Burlington County Coll., 1982, 83. Mem. Am. Assn. Physics Tchrs. (sec., treas. N.J. Jersey sect. 1976-84, named Outstanding Contbr. to Physics Edn., 1984, editor So. Calif. sect. 1985-87, v.p. 1987—), Am. Phys. Soc., AAAS, Sigma Xi. Lodge: Lions. Home: 2691 Koa Ave Morro Bay CA 93442 Office: Calif Poly State U Physics Dept San Luis Obispo CA 93407

LUDWIG, CHRISTA, mezzo-soprano; b. Berlin; d. Anton and Eugenie (Besalla) L.; m. Walter Berry, Sept. 29, 1957 (div. 1970); 1 son, Wolfgang; m. Paul-Emile Deiber, Mar. 3, 1972. Ed. German schs. Appeared at Staedtische Buehnen, Frankfurt, W.Ger., 1946-52, Landestheater, Darmstadt, W. Ger., 1952-54, Hannover, W.Ger., 1954-55, Vienna (Austria) State Opera, 1955—, Avery Fisher Hall, N.Y.C., 1978, appearances in, U.S., 1958—, including Met. Opera, N.Y.C., 1959, 66-71, 73-74, Carnegie Hall, N.Y.C., 1959, 69, 70, 71, 74, Lyric Opera, Chgo., 1959-60, 70-71, 73-74, Philharmonic Hall, N.Y.C., 1968, 69, 72, 74, guest artist, London, Buenos Aires, Munich, Berlin, Tokyo, Salzburg Festival, Athens Festival, Saratoga Festival, Hunter Coll., Met. Mus., Scala Milano, Expo 67, Montreal, and others, rec. artist. (Named Kammersaengerin, Govt. of Austria 1962, recipient Mozart medal, Mahler medal, Hugo Wolf medal, Silver Rose, Vienna Philharm., Golden Ring, Vienna Staatsoper.). Recipient Commdr. Des Arts et Des Lettres (France, Goldenes Ehren Zeichen Stadt Salzburg, Goldene Ehrennadel Stadt Wien (Austria). Office: Heidrun Artmueller, Goethegasse, 1010 Vienna Austria also: care Colbert Artists Mgmt 111 W 57th St New York NY 10019

LUDWIG, DAVID WILLARD, corporate professional; b. Wilkinsburg, Pa., June 17, 1926; s. Harold Louis and Frances (Willard) L.; m. Kathryn Leanna Scofield, Sept. 2, 1950; children: David Willard Jr., Thomas Arthur, Scott Edward. BS in Ceramic Engring., Pa. State U., 1951. Cert. fin. planner. Shift supr. Harbinson Walker, Clearfield, Pa., 1951-52; tech. devel. PPG Industries, Pitts., 1952-60, tech. sales engr., 1960-64, sales mgr., 1964-69, gen. mgr., 1969-72; exec. v.p., chief fin. officer MART Inc., Huntsville, Ala., 1972-74; pres. Tenn. Valley Industries, Inc., Huntsville, Ala, 1974—. Editor Gt. Am. Outdoors mag., 1983—. Served with U.S. Army, 1943-46. Mem. Inst. Cert. Fin. Planners, Internat. Assn. Fin. Planners, Estate Planning Council. Republican. Methodist. Lodges: Rotary, Masons. Home: 712 Corlett Dr SE Huntsville AL 35802 Office: Tenn Valley Industries Inc 2707 Artie St Suite 4 300 Exec Pkwy S Huntsville AL 35805

LUDWIG, EDMUND VINCENT, judge; b. Phila., May 20, 1928; s. Henry and Ruth (Viner) L.; m. Sara Marie Webster, Nov. 1, 1982; children from previous marriage: Edmund Jr., John, Sarah, David. AB, Harvard U., 1949, LLB, 1952. Assoc. Duane, Morris & Hecksher, Phila., 1956-59; ptnr. Barnes, Biester & Ludwig, Doylestown, Pa., 1959-68; judge Common Pleas Ct., Bucks County, Pa., 1968-85, U.S. Dist. Ct. (ea. dist.), Phila., 1985—; mem. faculty Pa. Coll. of the Judiciary, 1974-85; presenter Villanova (Pa.) U. Law Sch., 1975-80, lectr., 1984—; vis. lectr. Temple Law Sch., 1977-80; clin. assoc. prof. Hahnemann U., Phila., 1977-85; mem. Pa. Juvenile Ct. Judge's Commn., 1978-85; chmn. Pa. Chief Justice's Ednl. Com., 1984-85; pres. Pa. Conf. State Trial Judges, 1981-82. Chmn. Children and Youth Adv. Com., Bucks County, 1978-83; mem. Pa. Adv. Com. on Mental Health and Mental Retardation, 1980-85; founder, bd. dirs. Today, Inc., Newtown, Pa., 1971-85, Probation Vols., Bucks County, 1971-81; mem. Pa. Joint Council on Criminal Justice, Inc., 1979-80; mem. Joint Family Law Council Pa., 1979-85; vice chmn. Human Services Council Bucks County, 1979-81; mem. Com. to Study Unified Jud. System Pa., 1980-82, Pa. Legislative Task Force on Mental Health Laws, 1986-87. Recipient Disting. Service award Bucks County Corrections Assn., 1978, Spl. Service award Big Bros., 1979, Humanitarian award United Way Bucks County, 1980, Founder's award Vol. Services, 1982, Spl. award Bucks County Juvenile Ct., 1985. Mem. ABA, Pa. Bar Assn., Fed. Bar Assn. (hon.). Club: Harvard (N.Y.C. and Phila.) (v.p. 1979-80), Phila. Office: 12614 US Courthouse Independence Mall West 601 Market St Philadelphia PA 19106

LUDWIG, KLAUS-DIETER, linguist; b. Waldheim, Germany, Sept. 22, 1937; married; 2 children. Diploma, U. Leipzig, German Dem. Republic, 1961; PhD, U. Leipzig, 1973. With Cen. Inst. for Linguistics, Acad. Scis., Berlin, German Dem. Republic. Author: Zum Verhältnis von Sprache und Wertung, 1976; co-author: Wörterbuch der deutschen Gegenwartssprache, 1961-77, Synonymwörterbuch, 1st edit., 1973, 11th edit., 1987, Wörterbuch der Sprachschwierigkeiten, 1st edit., 1984, 2d edit., 1986; contbr. articles to profl. jours. Office: Zentralinst Sprachwissenschaft, Prenzlauer Promenade 149-152, 1100 Berlin German Democratic Republic

LUDWIG, MARIO, international trade consultant; b. Berne, Switzerland, June 6, 1923; s. Fritz and Lydia (Meichtry) L.; m. Monique de May, Aug. 21, 1953; children: Patrick Beat, Viviane Marguerite. JD, U. Berne, 1948; LLM, Yale U., 1949. Jr. exec. Esso Standard Oil, N.Y.C., Zurich,, Switzerland, 1950-53; bd. dirs. Internat. Textile Mfrs. Fedn., Manchester, Zurich, 1953-70; exec. v.p. Doctor Rudolf Farner Agencies, Zurich, 1970-71; exec. dir. Swiss Office for Trade Promotion, Zurich, Lausanne, 1971-86; cons. Internat. Trade Ctr., Geneva, Switzerland, 1986—. Author and contbr. numerous books and articles on subjects of internat. trade policy and cultural history. Mem. Yale Law Sch. Assn., Am. Assn. Polit. and Social Sci., Internat. Advt. Assn. Freisinnig Democrat. Club: des habits Rouges. Home: Grundwiesstrasse 29, 8700 Kuesnacht Switzerland

LUDWIG, ROLF MARTIN, internist; b. Bautzen, Germany, June 3, 1924; came to U.S., 1953; s. Martin Max and Doris (Metz) L.; m. Shirley Jean Ray, Oct. 26, 1956 (div. June 1983); 1 child, Mark Stephen. M.D., Eberhard Karls U. Tuebingen, Germany, 1953. Intern, Mary's Help Hosp., San Francisco, 1953-54, then resident in internal medicine; resident in internal medicine Franklin Hosp., San Francisco, Huntington Meml. Hosp., Pasadena, Calif., Wadsworth VA Gen. Hosp., Los Angeles, 1959-60. Internist, Kaiser/Permanente, Fontana, Calif., 1960-63, 73-87; practice medicine specializing in internal medicine, Yucaipa, Calif., 1963-72; retired, 1987. Served to capt. M.C., U.S. Army, 1956-59. Mem. Am. Soc. Internal Medicine, Calif. Soc. Internal Medicine, Inland Soc. Internal Medicine. Republican. Lutheran. Home: 11711 Holmes St Yucaipa CA 92399

LUDWIG, WILLIAM ORLAND, sugar company executive, lawyer; b. Pontiac, Mich., Jan. 9, 1931; s. Austin Lewis and Nina C. (Wixon) L.; m. Maureen Condon, July 6, 1957; children—John, James, Kathryn, Andrew, Amy, Stephen. A.B., Alma Coll., 1952; J.D., Salmon P. Chase Coll. Law, 1964; LL.M. in Taxation, Boston U., 1972. Bar: Ohio 1964; C.P.A., Utah; cert. mgmt. accountant. Various fin. mgmt. positions Procter & Gamble Co., Cin., 1956-68; div. controller Polaroid Corp., Cambridge, Mass., 1968-72; controller The Kingsford Co. subs. Clorox Co., Oakland, Calif., 1972-78; v.p. fin. Amalgamated Sugar Co., Ogden, Utah, 1978-82; sr. v.p. fin., chief fin. officer Holly Sugar Corp., Colorado Springs, Colo., 1982—; lectr. law Chase Coll., 1965. Served to 1st lt. U.S. Army, 1952-56. Mem. Fin. Execs. Inst., Assn. U.S. Army, Nat. Assn. Accts., U. of Ams. Found., Inst. Cert. Mgmt. Accts. Republican. Methodist. Lodges: Masons, Shriners. Office: PO Box 1052 Colorado Springs CO 80901

LUEDECKE, WILLIAM HENRY, engineer; b. Pittsburg, Tex., Apr. 5, 1918; s. Henry Herman and Lula May (Abernathy) L.; B.S., U. Tex., 1940; m. Mary Anne Copeland, June 3, 1939; children—William Henry, John Copeland. Mech. engr. Columbian Gasoline Corp., Monroe, La., 1940-41; supr. shipbldg., mech. engr. USN, Orange, Tex., 1941-42; gen. supr. factory mgrs. N. Am. Aviation Co., Dallas, 1944-46; mech. engr., charge Chrysler Airtemp. div. Chrysler Corp., Los Angeles, 1946-50; owner Luedecke Engring. Co., Austin, Tex., 1950—, also Luedecke Investment Co.; chmn. bd. dirs. Mut. Savs. Instn., Austin; dir. City Nat. Bank, Austin, 1st Tex. Fin. Corp., Dallas. Bd. dirs. Travis County Heart Fund, Austin YMCA. Named Man of Year, Tex. Barbed Wire Collectors Assn.; registered profl. engr., Tex. Mem. Am. Soc. Heating, Refrigerating and Air Conditioning Engrs. (dir., pres. Austin chpt.), Tex., Nat. socs. profl. engrs., C. of C., Econ. Devel. Council, Better Bus. Bur., Nat. Fedn. Ind. Bus. (nat. adv. council). Lutheran. Clubs: Rotary, Austin, Westwood Country (treas., dir.). Home: 3403 Foothills Pkwy Austin TX 78731 Office: 1007 W 34th St Austin TX 78705

LUELLEN, CHARLES J., oil company executive; b. Greenville, S.C., Oct. 18, 1929; s. John B. and Dorothy C. (Bell) L.; m. Jo S. Riddle, July 11, 1953; children: Margaret A., Nancy J. B.S., Ind. U., 1952. Sales rep. Ashland Oil, Inc., Ky., 1952-70, v.p. sales, 1970-72, group v.p. sales, 1972-80, pres., chief operating officer, 1986—, also dir.; pres. Ashland Petroleum Co., 1980-86; bd. dirs., budget adv. com. Am. Petroleum Inst., Washington, 1982—, Asphalt Inst., Washington, 1974-76; mem. energy and natural resources com. U.S. C. of C., Washington, 1987—; mem. 25 Yr. Club, Washington. Bd. dirs. Kings Daus., Hosp., Ashland, 1981—, Ashland area YMCA, 1980—, Nat. Chamber Found., Washington, 1987; trustee Centre Coll., Danville, Ky., Joint Council on Econ. Edn., N.Y.C. Mem. Ind. Univ. Fellows, U.S. C. of C. (mem. energy & natural resources com.), Beta Gamma Sigma. Club: Bellefonte Country (Ashland); Pendennis (Louisville). Home: 4400 Oak Hollow Dr Ashland KY 41101 Office: Ashland Oil Inc PO Box 391 Ashland KY 41114

LUETHY, HANS ARMIN, art institution administrator, author; b. Zurich, Switzerland, Apr. 30, 1932; S. Fritz and Elizabeth (Heubes) L.; m. Mascha Strobel, Mar. 17, 1962; children: Cilly, Gregor, Florian. PhD, U. Zurich, 1963. Dir. Swiss Inst. Art Research, Zurich, 1963—. Author: Albert Anker, 1981, Giovanni Segantini, 1983, Swiss Painting 20th Centrury, 1985; contbr. articles to profl. jours. Pres. Johanna Spyri Found., Zurich, 1979—; bd. dirs. Swiss Acad. Human Scis., 1986—. Getty Trust scholar, 1985-86. Mem. Com. Internat. History of Art. Club: Zurich Limmat. Lodge: Lions. Office: Swiss Inst Art Research, Waldmannstrasse 6/8, Zurich Switzerland 8024

LUFI, DUBI, psychology educator; b. Sarid, Israel, Aug. 24, 1948; s. Arie and Braha (Spector) L.; m. Orna Horesh, June 6, 1954; children: Dekel, Saar. BS in Psychology cum laude, Wash. State U., 1975, PhD in Counseling Psychology, 1979; MS in Psychology, U. Idaho, 1977. Clin. psychologist Child and Family Clinic, Kiryat-Tivon, Israel, 1980—, Beit Levinstien Rehab. Hosp., Rannana, Israel, 1981-82; lectr. U. Haifa, Israel, 1981-83; intern psychology Rambam Med. Ctr., Haifa, 1984-85; intern child psychology Child Devel. Clinic, Haifa, 1985-86; Head coaching staff Emek Israel Sch. of Gymnastics, Kibbutz Yifat, 1983—. Contbr. articles to profl. jours. Mem. Israeli Psychol. Assn., Am. Psychol. Assn., Gymnastics Fedn. (mem. tech. com. 1984—87). Home: Kibbutz Yifat, Yifat 30069, Israel Office: Child and Family Clinic-Oranim, Kiryat-Tivon 36000, Israel

LUFT, AUDREY ELAINE, temporary employment service executive; b. Eckville, Alberta, Can., Jan. 2, 1947; d. Adolf Herman and Helen (Mottl) Rohe; m. Hans-Bernd Luft, 1970; children: Bernie, Danny. Student, U. Alberta. Sec. Manpower Temporary Service, Vancouver, 1967, Great W. Life Ins., Toronto, Ont., 1967-68, R.L. Crain Ltd., Edmonton, Alberta, 1968-70; personnel cons. Girl Friday/Slate Personnel, Edmonton, 1970-76; mgr. Competitive Edge Employment Services (formerly Right Hand Employment Service), Edmonton, 1976-82; gen. mgr. Manpower Temporary Service, Edmonton, 1982—; regional mgr. Manpower Temporary Service, Edmonton and Calgary, 1988; instr. Grant MacEwan Community Coll., Edmonton, 1982-87. vol. Aldermanic Campaign, Edmonton, 1979, Liberal Party, Edmonton, 1980, Mayoralty Campaign, Edmonton, 1983, Progressive Conservative Party, Edmonton, 1986. Recipient Bill Coke award Fedn. Temporary Help Services, 1984. Mem. Edmonton Personnel Assn. (legislative com. 1986-87), No. Alberta Inst. Tech. (adv. bd.), Edmonton Exec. Assn. (bd. dirs., pres. 1986-87), Fedn. Temporary Help Services (past pres., regional v.p., founding mem. Edmonton chpt.). Lutheran. Club: Zonta Internat. (Edmonton). Home: 104 Windermere Crescent, Edmonton, AB Canada T6H 4N7

LUFTGLASS, MURRAY ARNOLD, manufacturing company executive; b. Bklyn., Jan. 2, 1931; s. Harry and Pauline (Yaged) L.; children by previous marriage: Paula Jean, Bryan Keith, Robert Andrew, Richard Eric; m. Christine L. Novick, May 29, 1988. BS, Ill. Inst. Tech., 1952; MS, U. So. Calif., 1959; MBA, U. Conn., 1972.With Shell Chem. Co., Torrance, Calif., 1955-60, N.Y.C., 1960-61, Wallingford, Conn., 1961-64, Torrance, 1964-66, N.Y.C., 1966-69; asst. gen. mgr. Westchester Plastics div. Ametek, Inc., Mamaroneck, N.Y., 1969-75; dir. corp. devel. Ametek, Inc., N.Y.C., 1975-76, v.p., 1976-83, sr. v.p. corp. devel., 1984—; instr. survey modern plastics Soc. Plastics Industry, Los Angeles. Bd. dirs. Sunny Hill Children's Center. Served to lt. (j.g.) USN, 1952-55. Mem. NAM, Soc. Plastics Industry, Assn. Corp. Growth, Soc. Plastics Engrs., Tau Beta Pi, Beta Gamma Sigma, Phi Lambda Upsilon. Club: University (N.Y.C.). Contbr. articles to profl. jours., publs. Patentee in field. Home: PO Box 552 Hoboken NJ 07030 Office: Ametek Inc 410 Park Ave New York NY 10022

LUGAR, RICHARD GREEN, U.S. senator; b. Indpls., Apr. 4, 1932; s. Marvin L. and Bertha (Green) L.; m. Charlene Smeltzer, Sept. 8, 1956; children: Mark, Robert, John, David. B.A., Denison U., 1954; B.A., M.A. (Rhodes scholar), Oxford (Eng.) U., 1956. Mayor Indpls., 1968-75; vis. prof. polit. sci. U. Indpls., 1976; mem. U.S. Senate, 1977—, chmn. com. fgn. relations, 1985-86; chmn. Nat. Rep. Senatorial Com., 1983-84; Treas. Lugar Stock Farm, Inc.; mem. Indpls. Sch. Bd., 1964-67, v.p., 1965-66; vice chmn. Adv. Commn. on Intergovtl. Relations, 1969-75; pres. Nat. League of Cities, 1970-71; mem. Nat. Commn. Standards and Goals of Criminal Justice System, 1971-73; Del., mem. resolutions com. Republican Nat. Conv., 1968, del., mem. resolutions com., Keynote speaker, 1972, del., speaker, 1980.

Trustee Denison U.; trustee U. Inpls. Served to lt. (j.g.) USNR, 1957-60. Pembroke Coll., Oxford U. hon. fellow. Mem. Blue Key, Phi Beta Kappa, Omicron Delta Kappa, Pi Delta Epsilon, Pi Sigma Alpha, Beta Theta Pi. Methodist. Club: Rotary. Office: 306 Hart Senate Bldg Washington DC 20510

LÜHR (SCHENK), ROSEMARIE, educator; b. Fürth, Bayern, Fed. Republic of Germany, Mar. 23, 1946; d. Schenk Franz and Margarete Schenk (Erdel) L.; m. Joachim Lühr, Aug. 16, 1974. D, U., Fed. Republic of Germany, 1977; cert. in teaching, U. Regensburg, Fed. Republic of Germany, 1984. Privatdozentin U. Regensburg, Regensburg, 1984. Author: Studien zur Sprache des Hildebrandliedes, 1982, Neuhochdeutsch, 1986, Expressivität und Lautgesetz im Germanischen, 1988. Home: Friedrich Ebert Str 32, 84 Regensburg Bavaria Federal Republic of Germany Office: U of Regensburg, Universitätsstr 31, Regensburg Federal Republic of Germany

LUHRMANN, TANIA MARIE, social anthropologist; b. Dayton, Ohio, Feb. 24, 1959; arrived in Eng., 1981.; d. George William and Winifred Myrtle (Bruce) L. BA, Harvard U., 1981; MPhil, Cambridge U., 1982, PhD, 1986. Research fellow Christ's Coll. U. Cambridge, 1985—. Author: Persuasions of the Witche's Craft, 1988; contbr. articles to jours. Recipient Partington prize, Soc. History of Alchemy and Chemistry, 1984. Mem. Am. Anthrop. Assn. (Stirling prize 1986), Royal Anthrop. Inst. Home and Office: Christs Coll, Cambridge CB2 3BU, England

LUHRS, HENRY RIC, toy manufacturing company executive; b. Chambersburg, Pa., Mar. 22, 1931; s. Henry E. and Pearl (Beistle) L.; m. Grace Barnhart, June 12, 1973; children by previous marriage—Stephen Frederick, Christine Michelle, TerriAnn, Patricia Denise. B.A., Gettysburg Coll., 1953. With The Beistle Co., Shippensburg, Pa., 1948-53, 1959—; pres., gen. mgr. Beistle Co., 1962—, chmn. bd., 1978—; dir. First Nat. Bank of Shippensburg, 1964-80, Commonwealth Nat. Bank, 1980—, Commonwealth Nat. Fin. Corp., 1981—, Capital Tech. Corp., 1984—, Fla. Atlantic U. Found., 1988—; dir., vice chmn. CompuPix Tech. Inc., 1984—, pres., 1986—; gemologist, 1977—; pres. South Lac Devel. Co., 1986—; owner Luhrs Gem Testing Lab., 1977—, Luhrs Jewelry, 1976—, Allied Leasing Co., Shippensburg, 1968; pres. South Lac Devel. Co., 1986—. Pres. Shippensburg Public Library, 1964-66, 1970-72, 76-78, bd. dirs., 1963-82; pres. Community Chest, 1965, dir., 1963-72; pres. Shippensburg Area Devel. Corp., 1966-72; bd. dirs., trustee Carlisle (Pa.) Hosp., 1967-71, Chambersburg Hosp., 1969-75; mem. consumer advisor council Capital Blue Cross, 1976-78. Served to capt. USAF, 1953-59. Mem. Shippensburg Hist. Soc. (dir. 1968), Nat. Sojourners, SAR (life), Shippensburg C. of C. (pres. 1965, dir. 1964-65), Toy Mfrs. Assn. (dir. 1969-71), Nat. Small Businessmen's Assn., Nat. Rifle Assn. (life), Shippensburg Fish and Game Assn. (pres. 1963), Am. Legion. Lutheran. Clubs: Cumberland Valley Indsl. Mgmt, York of Printing House Craftsmen. Lodges: Masons (32 deg.), Shriners, Elks, Tall Cedars of Lebanon. Office: 14-18 E Orange St Shippensburg PA 17257

LUI, JIMMY WING YIU, personnel executive, electrical engineer; b. Hong Kong, Dec. 9, 1946; s. Man-Chiu and Anna Sing-Kwan (Chan) L.; m. Vendy Kay San Wong, Nov. 15, 1971; children: Vincent Wing Tsung, Jane Wing Chi. BS, U. Hong Kong, 1967; MBA, Chinese U. of Hong Kong, 1980. Registered profl. engr., Calif. Asst. engr. China Light and Power Co., Ltd., Hong Kong, 1967-69, telemetry engr., 1969-71, line communication engr., 1971-79, tech. services engr., 1979-83, west regional mgr., 1983-85, personnel mgr., 1985—; edn. officer Hong Kong Tech. Coll., Hong Kong, 1971. Contbr. articles to profl. jours. Fellow Hong Kong Inst. Engrs., Inst. Elect. Engrs., Inst. Engrs. Australia; mem. IEEE (sr.), Inst. Electronic and Radio Engrs. Office: China Light and Power Co Ltd, 147 Argyle St, Kowloon Hong Kong

LUIG, KLAUS FRIEDRICH, lawyer, educator; b. Krefeld, Fed. Republic of Germany, Sept. 9, 1935; s. Kae and Clara (Plückhahn) L.; m. Hildegard Mennicken, Aug. 26, 1966; children: Eva, Sibylle, Judith. JD, U. Göttingen, Fed. Republic of Germany, 1963. Wiss. referent Max Planck Inst. for European Legal History, Frankfurt, 1965-79; privat docent U. Frankfurt, Fed. Republic of Germany, 1978; prof. law U. Passau, Fed. Republic of Germany, 1979-84; prof. U. Cologne, Fed. Republic of Germany, 1984—, dir. Inst. for Neure Privatrechts geschichte, 1984—. Editor: (jour.) Zeitschrift für Historische Forschung, 1973—. Roman Catholic. Home: Wilhelm Backhaustrasse 9, 5 Cologne Federal Republic of Germany Office: U Cologne, Albertus Magnus Platz, 5 Cologne Federal Republic of Germany

LUK, HONG YU, mechanical engineer, consultant; b. Shanghai, Republic of China, Apr. 28, 1938; s. Jun Ren and Shuk Kam (Ching) L.; m. Jing-Zhi Hua, June 6, 1966; children—Lu Chun Jia, Lu Chun Jie. B.Sc., Jiao Tong U., Shanghai, 1961. Technician Shanghai Wen Jiao Jixie Chang, 1961-81, engr., 1981-87; cons. Shanghai Dahua Decoration & Engring. Co., Ltd., 1984-85; engr. China Nat. Packaging & Devel. Centre for Light Industry, 1987—, Package Sci. Research Inst. Ministry of Light Industry, 1987—. Fellow Shanghai Packaging Tech. Assn.; mem. Computer Workers Assn. Shanghai Adminstrn. Mech. & Elec. Industry. Roman Catholic. Office: China Nat Packaging &, Devel Centre, 441/8 Beijing West Rd, Shanghai Peoples Republic of China

LUKÁCS, LÁSZLÓ ISTVÁN, cardiovascular surgeon, educator; b. Budapest, Hungary, May 10, 1945; s. Géza and Mária (Szabó) L.; m. Rozália Mészáros, Nov. 17, 1970; 1 child, Zsófia. MD, Semmelweis Med. U., Budapest, 1970. Postgrad. fellow Inst. Traumatology, Budapest, 1970-74; resident Postgrad. Med. Sch., Budapest, 1974-80; asst. prof. Hungarian Inst. Cardiology, Budapest, 1980—. Mem. Hungarian Soc. Surgeons, Hungarian Soc. Cardiology, European Soc. for Cardiovascular Surgery. Roman Catholic. Home: Lipto u 5, 1124 Budapest Hungary Office: Hungarian Inst Cardiology, Haman K u 29, 1450 Budapest Hungary

LUKAS, ELSA VICTORIA, radiobiologist, radiobiochemist; b. Baden nr. Vienna, Austria, Feb. 28, 1927; d. Johann and Victoria (Hauer) L.; Degree for High Sch. Tchrs., U. Vienna, 1952, Ph.D., 1955; DSc in Physics, Biology and Physiology (hon.) Marquis Giuseppe Scicluna Internat. U., 1987. Researcher, Max Planck Inst. Biophysics, Frankfurt/Main, Federal Republic Germany, 1959-64, Path. Inst. Justus Liebig U., Giessen, Fed. Republic Germany, 1961-64, Oak Ridge Nat. Lab., U. Radiation Biology, U. Tenn., Knoxville, 1964-67; high sch. tchr., country insp. schs., Vienna, 1967—; research. Author numerous publs. on biochem. effects of ionizing radiation in living cells, especially in their nucleic acids. Recipient Dr. J. Kowarschick award, 1957, Dr. Karl Luick award 1957, Theodor Kö rner prize 1960, Alexander von Humboldt award, 1961, Vibert Douglas award Internat. Fedn. Univ. Women, 1962; named hon. citizen State of Tenn., 1965; Fulbright Hays scholar, 1964. Mem. Biophys. Soc., Radiation Research Soc., Soc. German Scientists and Physicians, Austrian Biochem. Soc., Am. Inst. Biol. Scis., Soc. Parapsychology, German Bot. Soc., Soc. German Biologists, Gregor Mendel Soc., Soc. Austrian Chemists, Univ. Assn. Alma Mater Rudolphina. Roman Catholic. Home: 60 Elisabethstrasse, Baden bei Vienna 2500, Austria

LUKAS, GAZE ELMER, accountant; b. Austria, Hungary, Nov. 9, 1907; s. Victor and Theresa (Dinzenberger) L.; came to U.S., 1909, naturalized, 1920; B.S. in Accountancy with honors, U. Ill., 1930, M.S., 1933, J.D. first in class, 1956; m. Frances Adelaide Lyman, Nov. 25, 1932 (dec.); 1 son, Victor Thomas; m. Adelaide W. Bosselman, Jan. 7, 1987; Instr. U. Ill., Urbana, 1930-35, asst. prof., 1954-55, asso. prof., 1955-56, prof., 1956-69, prof. emeritus, 1969—; dir. fin. U.S. Farm Security Adminstrn., Washington, 1935-42; chief accountant UNRRA, Washington, 1945-46; chief of renegotiation Quartermaster Gen.'s Office, Fgn. Service, State Dept., Rome, New Delhi, 1947-54; partner Paul M. Green & Assos., Bus. Edn. Cons., Champaign, Ill., 1955-68; Elmer Fox vis. prof. accounting Wichita (Kans.) State U., 1970-71; vis. prof. accounting Fla. Tech. U., Orlando, 1968-70, Fla. Atlantic U., Boca Raton, 1971-72; comptroller Palm Beach Atlantic Coll., West Palm Beach, Fla., 1979-81, cons., 1981-85. Mem. County Audit Adv. Bd. of Ill., 1962-68, chmn., 1964-66, recipient pub. service award, 1968. Served to maj. AUS, 1942-45; ETO. Decorated Bronze Star; recipient Meritorious Civilian Service award Q.M. Gen., 1947, Americanism medal Nat. Soc. DAR, 1986. C.P.A., Ill. Mem. Am. Inst. C.P.A.'s, Ill. C.P.A. Soc. (life), Appraisers Assn. Am., Order of Coif, Beta Gamma Sigma, Beta Alpha Psi, Pi Kappa Phi, Phi Eta Sigma, Sigma Alpha Epsilon, Phi Delta Phi, Alpha Kappa Psi. Contbr. articles to profl. jours. Address: 719 Lori Dr #19-210 Palm Springs FL 33461

LUKE, CHU-YEN, food educator, electrical engineer; b. Chung Leo, China, July 18, 1938; came to U.S., 1948; s. Gene Soon and Sin Hong (Chin) Look; m. Pansy Wong Luke, Aug. 17, 1963; children—Ala, Asa. E.E., Ill. Inst. Tech., Chgo., 1969. Lab. engr. Skil Corp., Chgo., 1965-69; lab. mgr. No. Electric Co., Chgo., 1969-76; food educator Oriental Food Market and Cooking Sch., Chgo., 1976—; cons. Oriental Cookbook, 1977. Served with U.S. Army, 1961. Home: 2500 W Jarvis Ave Chicago IL 60645 Office: Oriental Food Market and Cooking Sch 2801 W Howard St Chicago IL 60645

LUKE, FREDERIC DAVEY, language professional, educator; b. Clevedon, Somerset, Eng., July 13, 1921; s. Thomas Davy and Jane Thompson (Pattison) L. MA, Oxford U., Eng., 1944, D Phil, 1947. Lectr. German Manchester U., Eng., 1947-59; lectr., tutor German Oxford U., Christ Ch., 1959-88; vis. lectr. various U.S. univs., 1967—. Translator numerous books; contbr. articles to profl. jours. Rockefeller Found. scholar Villa Serbelloni, Bellagio, Italy, 1985. Mem. Conservative party. Mem. Orthodox ch. Office: Christ Church, Oxford Oxfordshire OX1 1DP, England

LUKE, WARREN K.K., investment company executive; b. Honolulu, May 22, 1944; s. Kan Jung and Beatrice (Lum) L.; B.S. in Bus. Adminstrn., Babson Inst. Bus. Adminstrn., 1966; M.B.A., Harvard U., 1970; m. Carolyn Ching, 1970; children—Kevin James, Catherine, Bryan, Joanne. Pres., dir. Indsl. Investors, Inc., Honolulu, 1970—; vice chmn.Hawaii Nat. Bank, Honolulu, 1972—; v.p., dir. Bancard Assn. Hawaii Inc., 1976—; treas., dir. Computer Systems Internat. Inc.; v.p., sec., dir. KJL, Inc., Honolulu, 1974—; pres. Loyalty Devel. Co., Ltd., Honolulu, 1970—, Hawaii Nat. Bancshares, Inc., 1987—; pres., dir. Mgmt. Resources Cons., Inc., Honolulu, 1973—; dir. Loyalty Enterprises, Ltd., Honolulu, Loyalty Ins. Co., Ltd., Honolulu, Barclay Corp., Honolulu. First vice chmn. Hawaii State chpt. ARC, 1973-77, bd. dirs. 1972—, chpt. chmn., 1977-78, mem. Pacific div. adv. council, 1976-80, chmn. Western field office adv. council, 1979-80, nat. bd. govs., 1983—; treas., exec. com. mem. Community Scholarship Program, Honolulu, 1974-85; mem. Gov.'s Task Force Jobs for Vets., 1975-76; trustee Honolulu Jr. Acad., 1979-85, Hawaiian Meml. Park Cemetery Assn., Honolulu, 1975-85, Univ. of Hawaii Found., 1986—; bd. dirs. Hawaii Theatre Ctr., 1988—; mem. deans adv. council U. Hawaii Coll. Bus. Adminstrn., 1975—. Mem. Navy League U.S. (treas. Honolulu council 1974-76, dir. 1973-76, adv. com. 1977—), Chinese C. of C. (dir. 1980—, pres. 1985-86), Robert Morris Assocs., The Deputies, Western Ind. Bankers Assn. (pres. 1986—). Office: 84 N King St Honolulu HI 96817

LUKENS, ALAN WOOD, foreign service officer; b. Phila., Feb. 12, 1924; s. Edward Clark and Frances (Day) L.; m. Susan Atkinson, Dec. 29, 1962; children: Lewis Alan, Susan Atkinson, Frances Day, Timothy Eric. A.B., Princeton U., 1948; postgrad., Sorbonne, Paris, 1948, U. Madrid, 1948, Georgetown U., 1951. Tchr., St. Albans Sch., Washington, 1950-51; joined U.S. Fgn. Service, 1951; vice consul Ankara, Turkey, 1952, Istanbul, Turkey, 1953; pub. affairs officer Martinique, 1954-56; with news div. State Dept., 1956-57; U.S. del. 12th UN Gen. Assembly, 1957; mem. internat. staff NATO, Paris, 1958-60; consul Brazzaville, 1960; U.S. rep. to Independence of Congo, Brazzaville, Chad, Gabon, Central African Republic, 1961; charge d'affaires Am. embassy, Bangui, Central African Republic, 1961, Paris, 1961-63, Rabat, Morocco, 1963-65; chief personnel Bur. African Affairs, State Dept., 1965-67; dep. chief mission, counselor embassy Dakar, 1967-70, Nairobi, 1970-72; chief jr. officer div. personnel State Dept., 1973-75; dir. Office Iberian Affairs, 1974-75; counselor, dep. chief mission Am. Embassy, Copenhagen, 1975-78; with Bur. African Affairs, Dept. State, Washington, 1978-79; consul gen. Cape Town, South Africa, 1979-82; dir. office analysis for Western Europe, Bur. Intelligence and Research, Dept. State, Washington, 1982-84; A.E.& P. People's Republic of Congo, 1984-87; cons. Dept. of State. Served with AUS, 1943-46. Recipient Commendable Service award State Dept., 1961. Episcopalian. Clubs: Princeton (N.Y.C.) (Nairobi) (pres. Paris 1971-72); Explorers (N.Y.C.); Muthaiga Country (Nairobi); Royal Cape Yacht, Royal Cape Golf, Chevy Chase, Royal Danish Yacht; Rungsted Golf (Copenhagen). Office: 18 Grafton St Chevy Chase MD 20815

LUKMAN, RILWANU, government official; b. Zaria City, Nigeria, Dec. 20, 1937; s. Mallam Salihu and Malama Ramatu L.; m. Amina Abdullahi; children: Ramatu, Ahmed, Salihu. Student, Barewa Coll., Zaria, 1952-57, Nigerian Coll. Arts, Sci. and Technology, Zaria, 1957-59; degree in Mining Engring., Royal Sch. Mines, London, 1962; postgrad., U. Mining and Metallurgy, Leoben, Austria, McGill U., Can. With mines div. Fed. Ministry Mines and Power, Nigeria, from 1962; gen. mgr., chief exec. Nigerian Mining Corp., from 1974; former chief exec. Cement Co. of Northern Nigeria, Sokoto; minister of mines, power and steel Nigeria, 1984-85, 85-86; oil minister Petroleum Ministry, Nigeria, 1986; pres. Orgn. Petroleum Exporting Countries, 1986—. Fellow Nigerian Mining and Geoscis. Soc. (past pres.), Inst. Mining and Metallurgy (overseas mem. council for Nigeria); mem. Assn. Geoscientists for Internat. Devel. (v.p.), Soc. of Mining Engrs. of AIME. Address: Ministry of Petroleum Resources, Lagos Nigeria *

LUK'YANENKO, VLADIMIR MATVEYEVICH, Soviet government official; b. 1927. Mem. Communist Party Soviet Union, 1963—; with M. V. Frunze machinebuilding factory; minister Ministry Chem. Machinebuilding Industry, Moscow, 1986—. Address: Ministry Chem Machinebuilding, Industry, Moscow USSR *

LUMADUE, DONALD DEAN, hobby and crafts executive; b. El Reno, Okla., Sept. 30, 1938; s. Harry Basil and Muriel Ellen (Craven) L.; m. Joyce Anne Hayes, June 28, 1958; children: Dawnia, Donald, Robert, Ronald. Student USCG Acad., 1956-57. Lab. technician Charles Pfizer & Co., Groton, Conn., 1957-60; indsl. engr. Sonoco Products, Mystic, Conn., 1960-67; partner Joydon's, New London, Conn., 1958—, House of Leisure, New London, 1965—; Hobby Crafts, New London, 1968—; pres. NEI, Inc., New London, 1968-83. Mem. New Eng. Hobby Industry Assn. (pres. 1973-74, 86—, bd. dirs. 1983—), Hobby Industry Assn. Am. (chmn. Wholesaler bd. 1976-78, 82-88, Pres.'s award 1986), Nat. Assn. Wholesalers (trustee 1976—), Mgmt. Club S.E. Conn. (pres. 1961-62, 77-78). Office: 78-88 Captain's Walk New London CT 06320

LUMB, RICHARD DARRELL, law professor, legal consultant; b. Melbourne, Victoria, Australia, May 1, 1934; s. Ely Richard Lumb and Eileen (Thomson) McNamara; m. Moira Agnes Monahan, Jan. 30, 1960; Stephen R., Joanne M., Brendan T. LLB, U. Melbourne, 1955, LLM, 1956; PhD, U. Oxford, 1958. Research asst., tutor in law U. Melbourne, 1955-56; lectr. in law U. Queensland, Brisbane, 1958-72, sr. lectr. in law, 1963-66, reader in law, 1967-80, head of dept., 1974-75, 84-85, prof. of law, 1980—; assoc. to high ct. justice High Ct. of Australia, Sydney, New South Wales, 1960; cons. Queensland Govt., Brisbane, 1973-74, Northern Territory Govt., Darwin, 1978-82; vis. fellow Australian Nat. U., 1977. Author: The Constitutions of the Australian States, 4th edit., 1977, The Constitution of Australia Annotated, 4th edit., 1986, The Law of the Sea and Australian Off-Shore Areas, 2d edit., 1978, Australian Constitutionalism, 1983. Patron Australian Family Assn., Brisbane, 1982—. Home: 31 Euree St, Kenmore, 4069 Brisbane, Queensland Australia Office: U Queensland, St Lucia, 4067 Brisbane, Queensland Australia

LUMENTA, REYN ALTIN JOHANNES, transportation executive; b. Surabaya, East Java, Indonesia, Feb. 26, 1933; s. Max Reinier Waworuntu and Dien Aleida (Tenda) L.; m. Rebecca Vermeulen (div. 1964); children: Altin, Johan; m. Erica Colleen Wondal; children: Ronald, Alice, Joan, Rita. Engr. Garuda Indonesia, Jakarta, 1957-59, chief quality control, 1959-69, chief prodn., 1969-71, mgr. aircraft maintenance, 1071-75, corp. sec., 1975-79, pres., 1984—; pres. Merpati Nusantara Airlines, Jakarta, 1979-84, bd. dirs., 1984—. Mem. Golkar, Jakarta. Mem. Pacific Area Travel Assn. (chmn. Indonesian chpt. 1985—). Office: Garuda Indonesia, Jalan Medan Merdeka, Selatan 13, Jakarta Indonesia 10110

LUMINGKEWAS, STEFANUS BUANG, mechanical engineer; b. Semarang, Indonesia, Dec. 19, 1937; s. Henry Budiono and Molly (Kamini) Budiono Suliando; m. Wulan Maramis Lumingkewas, Oct. 1, 1965; children—Ingrid, Maudy Pingkan. M.S. in Mech. Engring., Inst. Tech. Bandung (Indonesia), 1962. Mgr. P.T. Gruno Nasional, Surabaya, Indonesia, 1963-78, mng. dir., 1978-82; pres. P.T. Encoxim, Surabaya, 1982—. Lodge: Rotary (pres. 1988—). Avocations: swimming; reading; body building. Home: Trunojoyo 62, Surabaya 60264, Indonesia Office: PT Encoxim, KBPM Duryat 20, Surabaya 60262, Indonesia

LUNA, DENNIS R., lawyer; b. Los Angeles, Aug. 21, 1946; B.S. in Petroleum Engring., U. So. Calif., 1968, M.S. in Petroleum Engring., 1969, M.B.A., 1971; J.D., Harvard U., 1974. Bar: Calif. 1974; Assoc. firm McCutchen, Black, Verleger & Shea, Los Angeles, 1974-81, partner, 1981—. Commr. Bd. Recreation and Parks, City of Los Angeles, 1984—; alt. commr., Los Angeles Meml. Coliseum Commn., 1987—. Contbr. articles to legal jours. Registered profl. petroleum engr., Calif. Mem. Soc. Petroleum Engrs., ABA (sect. of corp., banking and business law, sect. natural resources law), State Bar of Calif. Office: 600 Wilshire Blvd Los Angeles CA 90017

LUNA, MANUEL FERNANDEZ, machines tool manufacturing company executive; b. Ubeda, Jaen, Spain, May 13, 1935; s. Fernandez Pedro and Leticia (Luna) F.; m. Ana Maria Rodriguez, Nov. 28, 1967; children: Ana-Irene, Juan Manuel, Victoria, Pablo, Leticia. Bachelor Degree, Instituto Cervantes, Puertollano, Spain, 1953; Indsl. Engring. Degree, Esc. Tech. Sch., Madrid, 1963; Dr. Indsl. Engring., U. Madrid, 1972. Project engr. Westinghouse SA, Cordoba, Spain, 1964-66; mfg. mgr. Westinghouse SA, 1966-67, div. mgr., 1967-69; sr. cons. H.B. Maynard and Co., Inc., Madrid, 1970-72; plant mgr. Am. Air Filter S.A., Vitoria, Spain, 1972-77; gen. mgr. Peddinghaus Española, S.A., Vitoria, 1977-80, Madrid, 1980—. Mem. Colegio Oficial Engring. Industriales. Roman Catholic. Club: Real Automovil. Home: Paseo Rebeco 32, San Sebastian de los Reyes, Madrid Spain Office: Peddinghaus Espanola SA, Estebanez Calderon 50, 657 01 42 Madrid 91 Spain

LUNA, PATRICIA ADELE, food manufacturing company executive; b. Charleston, S.C., July 22, 1956; d. Benjamin Curtis and Clara Elizabeth (McCrory) L. BS in History, Auburn U., 1978, MEd in History, 1980; MA in Adminstrn., U. Ala., 1981, EdS in Adminstrn., 1984, PhD, ABD in Adminstrn., 1986. Cert. tchr., Ga., Ala. History tchr. Harris County Middle Sch., Ga., 1978-79, head dept., 1979-81; residence hall dir. univ. housing U. Ala., 1981-83, asst. dir. residence life, 1983-85; intern Cornell U., Ithaca, N.Y., 1983; dir. of mktg. Golden Flake Snack Foods, Inc., Birmingham, Ala., 1985—; cons., lectr. in field. Author: Specialization: A Learning Module, 1979, Grantsmanship, 1981, Alcohol Awareness Programs, 1984; University Programming, 1984; Marketing Residential Life, 1985; The History of Golden Flakes Snack Foods, 1986; Golden Flake Snack Foods, Inc., A Case Study, 1987. Fundraiser, U. Ala. Alumni Scholarship Fund, Tuscaloosa, 1983, Am. Diabetes Assn., Tuscaloosa, 1984, Urban Ministries, Birmingham, 1985-88; fundraiser com. chmn. Spl. Olympics, Tuscaloosa, 1985, Am. Cinema Soc. (fundraiser 1988); chmn. Greene County Relief Project, 1982-88; bd. dirs. Cerebral Palsy Found., Tuscaloosa, 1985-86; lay rector and com. chmn. Kairos Prison Ministry, Tutwiler State Prison, Ala., 1986—; lobbyist and mem. task force Justice Fellowship, 1988—; Rep. com. chmn. Recipient Dir. of Yr. award U. Ala., 1982, 83; Skeets Simonis award for Outstanding Contbns., U. Ala., 1984, nat. award Joint Council on Econ. Edn., 1979, research award NSF, 1979; named to Hon. Order Ky. Cols. Commonwealth of Ky., 1985—, Rep. Senatorial Inner Circle, 1986; Mem. Sales and Mktg. Execs. (chmn. com. 1985-86), Leadership Ala. (pres. 1982-83, disting. leadership award 1987, commemorative medal of honor 1988), Am. Mktg. Assn., Assn. Coll. and Univ. Housing Officers (com. chmn. 1983-85), Nat. Assn. Student Personnel Officers, Snack Food Assn. (mem. mktg. com. and conf. presenter), Commerce Exec. Soc., Omega Rho Sigma (pres. 1983-84), Omicron Delta Kappa, Phi Delta Kappa, Kappa Delta Pi, Phi Alpha Theta. Republican. Methodist. Clubs: Emmaus (chmn. com. 1985-88); Sailing (Tuscaloosa). Avocations: skiing, racquetball, community work, public speaking. Home: 11 Vestavia Hills Northport AL 35476 Office: Golden Flake Snack Foods Inc 110 6th St S Birmingham AL 35201

LUND, BERT OSCAR, JR., publisher; b. Stillwater, Minn., Nov. 8, 1920; s. Bert O. and Mary O. (Vordal) L.; m. Katherine Kingsley, July 31, 1943; children—Katherine Lund Cohen, Julie Lund Everett, Bert Oscar. B.B.A., U. Minn., 1942; postgrad., Harvard U., 1943. Advt. salesman Webb Co., St. Paul, 1946-54; advt. mgr. Webb Co., 1954-61; pub. Farmer Mag., 1961—, v.p. pub., 1963—, also dir.; v.p. pub. Pub. Cons., 1985—; dir. Audit Bur. Circulations, Gt. No. Ins. Co.; pres. Midwest unit Farm Papers, Inc., 1971; dir. Gt. No. Ins. Co., 1980—. Vice pres. Indianhead Council, Boy Scouts Am., 1974, Minn. Agrl. Soc., 1981; chmn. ops. com. St. Paul Civic Center Authority, 1972; bd. dirs. Minn. Council on Econ. Edn., 1969, Cath. Digest, 1980; chmn., trustee Dunwoody Inst., 1980, Hill Reference Library, 1984. Served to lt. USNR, 1943-46. Mem. Agrl. Pubs. Assn. (past pres., dir.), State Farm Mag. Bur. (past pres., dir.), Advt. Club Minn (past pres.), U. Minn. Alumni Assn. (treas.), Sigma Alpha Epsilon. Republican. Episcopalian. Clubs: Minnesota, Minn. Press, St. Paul Athletic, Hole-in-Wall Golf, Somerset Country. Home: 2151 Upper St Dennis Rd Saint Paul MN 55116 Office: 46 E 4th St Suite 1104 Saint Paul MN 55116

LUND, HANS BRUNO, business development adviser; b. Copenhagen, Apr. 21, 1933; s. Bruno Ave Fischer and Esther Sophie (Thronsen) L.; m. Ursula Theresia Thiemann, Aug. 17, 1957; children: Christian Bruno, Anne-Birthe Lund Christensen, Susanne. Diplom Wirtschaftsingenieur (FH), Munich, 1957; diplom in Indsl. Orgn., Copenhagen, 1959; tekn. dr., U. Lund, Sweden, 1976. With Brdr. S. & B. Lund, Copenhagen, 1957-79, plant engr., 1957-59, prodn. mgr., 1959-60, chief exec. research and devel., 1960-69, chmn. bd. dirs., 1969-79; ind. cons. various pvt. corps. and govtl. agys., Copenhagen, 1965—; pres., chief exec. off. DCF and Dansk Arabinfabrik, Copenhagen, 1979-84; chief advisor research and edn. Fedn. Danish Industries, Copenhagen, 1984-86, bus. devel. cons., 1986—; researcher and cons. in product devel. theory, systems analysis and devel., orgn. and communication devel., human resources devel., artificial intelligence, computer-aided mgmt. Editor: Planlaegning og Styring af Undervisning, 1971; author: The Maximum Value Method (MVM) in Chemical Product Development, 1965, Maksimal Vardi Metoden, 1976; Organisation, 1981, Produktudvikling, 1986, others; contbr. numerous articles to mgmt. jours. Served with Royal Danish Life Guards, 1952-54. Mem. Verein Deutscher Ingenieure, Danish Mgmt. Assn., Verein der Wirtschaftsingenieure, Soc. Chem. Industry, SCI Paper and Textile Chems. Group, SCI Plastics and Polymer Group, Skandinavisk Förening för Värdeanlys, Pedagogical Soc., VDI-Gesellschaft Entwicklung Konstruktion Vertrieb, SCI Colloid and Surface Chemistry Group, SCI Mgmt. Group, Danish Soc. Chem, Civil, Elec. and Mech. Engrs., DIF Chem. Engrs. Group, others. Conservative. Roman Catholic. Clubs: Copenhagen Golf, others. Home: Egebaekvej 213, DK-2850 Naerum Denmark

LUNDBAK, ASGER NIELSEN, geophysicist; b. Gilleleje, Denmark, Sept. 7, 1914; s. Laurits and Christie (Feilberg) N.; m. Gunhild Uldall Jensen, June 5, 1953; children—Henrik, Karen. M.Sc. in Physics, U. Copenhagen, 1940. Oceanographer, Skalling Lab., Esbjerg, Denmark, 1938-42; tchr. sr. schs., Copenhagen, 1942-45; head Geomagnetic Obs., Godhavn/Greenland, 1945-46; research asst. Meteorology Inst., Copenhagen, 1946-54, sr. geophysicist, 1954-81, ret. 1982; head Geomagnetic Obs., Rude Skov, Denmark, 1956-81; founder, head Space Obs., Rude Skov, 1962-81; freelance broadcaster Danmarks Radio, 1958—. Author: Atomet og Universet, 1949; Bogen om Maanen, 1969; contbr. articles to profl. jours. Mem. Danish Space Soc. (pres. 1961-63), Spacewarn, European Assn. Exploration Geophysicists, Am. Geophys. Union. Home: Stigaardsvej 3, DK-2900 Hellerup Denmark

LUNDE, ASBJORN RUDOLPH, lawyer; b. S.I., N.Y., July 17, 1927; s. Karl and Elisa (Andenes) L.; A.B., Columbia U., 1947, LL.B., 1949. Admitted to N.Y. bar, 1949, since practiced in N.Y.C.; with firm Kramer, Marx, Greenlee & Backus, and predecessors, 1950-68, mem., 1958-68; individual practice law, 1968—; dir. numerous cos. Bd. dirs., v.p. Orchestra da Camera, Inc., 1964—; bd. dirs. Sara Roby Found., 1971—, The Drawing Soc., 1977—. Mem. Am., N.Y. State bar assns., Assn. Bar City N.Y., Met.

Opera Club. Home: 525 W 238th St Riverdale NY 10463 Office: La Branche Rd RD 1 Hillsdale NY 12529

LUNDEBERG, MATS, information systems educator; b. Stockholm, June 4, 1943; s. Jan and Birgit (Bysjo) L.; m. Agneta Brun, June 3, 1967; children—Magnus, Anna, Mikael. M.Sc., Royal Inst. Tech., Stockholm, 1965, Ph.D., 1970, D.B.A., 1976; M.B.A., Stockholm Sch. Econs., 1966. Asst. tchr. Royal Inst. Tech., 1965-67, asst. prof., 1967-72, assoc. prof., 1972-81; dir. Inst. for Devel. of Activities in Orgns., Stockholm, 1981—; prof. bus. info. processing Stockholm Sch. Econs., 1986—; seminar leader, lectr. on info. systems, Europe, U.S.A., Can., 1970—. Author: Informations Systems Development-A Systematic Approach, 1981, several books in Swedish; contbr. articles to profl. jours. Mem. Internat. Fedn. for Info. Processing (tech. com. on info. systems, Swedish nat. rep. 1975—), Swedish Soc. for Info. Processing. Office: Inst Devel Activities in Orgns, Stureplan 6 IV, S-11435 Stockholm Sweden

LUNDEBERG, STEFFAN CARL ARTHUR, bus. exec.; b. Malmo, Sweden, Aug. 13, 1924; s. Nils Arthur and Margit Carolina (Gemzell) L.; degree in Bus. Adminstrn., Stockholm U., 1945; m. Ursula Klapp, May 9, 1969; children—Melanie Rose, Marc Christian. Sales mgr. Electrolux Ltd., Johannesburg, S.Africa, 1951-54; mng. dir. Electrolux N.V., The Hague, Netherlands, 1954-59, Electrolux Gmbh, Hamburg, 1959—, Vienna, 1968—. Decorated Order Vasa 1st class (Sweden). Mem. Swedish C. of C. Dusseldorf (v.p. 1976—), Fedn. Europeenne de Vente et Service a Domicile (dir.). Clubs: Anglo-German, Ubersee, Swedish (past pres.), Hamburger Golf (Hamburg, W.Ger.). Lutheran. Home: 26 Eichenallee, D-2000 Hamburg 52 Federal Republic of Germany Office: 163 Max Brauer Allee 163, D-2000 Hamburg 50 Federal Republic of Germany

LUNDEEN, ROBERT WEST, chemical company executive; b. Astoria, Oreg., June 25, 1921; s. Arthur Robert and Margaret Florence (West) L.; m. Betty Charles Anderson, Dec. 26, 1942; children: John Walter, Peter Bruce, Nancy Patricia. B.S., Oreg. State U., 1942; postgrad., Inst. Meteorology, U. Chgo., 1942-43. With Dow Chem. Co., 1946-87; dir. bus. devel. Dow Chem. Internat., Midland, Mich., 1963-66; pres. Dow Chem. Pacific, Hong Kong, 1966-77, Dow Chem. Latin Am., from 1978; exec. v.p. Dow Chem. Co., 1978-82, chmn. bd., 1982-87, dir., 1973-87; chmn. Tektronix Inc., Beaverton, Oreg., 1987—. Chmn. City Planning Commn., Concord, Calif., 1960-61; trustee Kettering Found., Dayton, Ohio, Monterey Inst. Internat. Studies, Calif., Oreg. State U. Found., Corvallis, Orcas Island Library Dist., 1987—. Served with U.S. Army, 1942-46. Decorated Bronze Star. Mem. Am. Inst. Chem. Engrs., Am. Chem. Soc. Republican. Clubs: Hong Kong, Royal Hong Kong Yacht; Orcas Tennis, Orcas Island Yacht. Office: Tektronix Inc PO Box 500 Beaverton OR 97077 *

LUNDESTAD, GEIR, historian, educator; b. Sulitjelma, Nordland, Norway, Jan. 17, 1945; s. Bjarne and Anny Elvine (Nilsen-Nygaard) L.; m. Aase Synnøve Liland, July 29, 1967; children: Erik, Helge. MA, U. Oslo, 1970; PhD, U. Tromsø, 1976. Asst. prof. history U. Tromsø, Norway, 1974-79, prof., 1979—; vis. scholar Ctr. for Internat. Affairs Harvard U., Cambridge, Mass., 1983; v.p. U. Tromsø, 1981-83; TV, radio commentator Norwegian Broadcasting. Author: The American Non-Policy Towards Eastern Europe 1943-47, 1976, America, Scandinavia and the Cold War, 1980, East, West, North, South, 1987; contbr. articles to profl. jours. Chmn. council Norwegian Inst. Internat. Affairs, Oslo, 1977—; Active Norwegian Arms Control and Disarmament Adv. Council. Mem. Soc. for Historians Am. Fgn. Relations, Nordic Assn. for Am. Studies. Mem. Labor Party. Lutheran. Home: Mellomveien 67, Tromsø 9000, Norway Office: U Tromsø, PO Box 1040, Tromsø 9001, Norway

LUNDGREEN-NIELSEN, KAY, historian, educator; b. Hillerød, Denmark, June 12, 1940; s. Otto Nielsen and Edith (Mortensen) Lundgreen-Nielsen; m. Dorte Andersen, July 20, 1985. Cand mag, U. Copenhagen, Denmark, 1967; Dr phil, U. Odense, Denmark, 1979. Researcher U. Copenhagen, 1968-74; asst. prof. contemporary history U. Odense, Denmark, 1974—. Author: The Polish Problem at the Paris Peace Conference; A Study of the Policies of the Great Posers and the Poles 1918-1919, 1979; contbr. articles to profl. jours. Served as sgt. Denmark Air Force, 1958-60. Recipient Damian Wandycz Prize Pilsudski Inst., N.Y., 1979. Home: HP Simonsens Alle 153, 5250 Odense Denmark Office: Odense Universitet, Campusvej 55, 5230 Odense Denmark

LUNDGREN, ANDERS, association executive; b. Malmoe, Sweden, May 17, 1956; s. Torsten and Ebba (Olsson) L.; m. Itte Knutz, Apr. 4, 1985; children: Anna, Rasmrs. MBA, Stockholm Sch Econs., 1979; grad. Internat. Tchrs. Program, Manchester Bus. Coll., 1981; PhD, Stockholm Sch Econs., 1986. Controller Sveriges Radio, Stockholm, 1977-79; researcher, then lectr. Stockholm Sch. Econs., 1979-85; program dir. Swedish Inst. Mgmt., Stockholm, 1985—; investigator dept. memory Swedish Inst. Mgmt., 1986—. Author: The Work of Boards of Directors, 1985, Actions and Systems, 1986; contbr. articles to profl. jours. Office: Swedish Inst Mgmt, Sverågen 65, 11383 Stockholm Sweden

LUNDGREN, JAMES REINHOLD, civil engineer, transportation association executive; b. Vancouver, B.C., Jan. 11, 1945; came to U.S., 1968; s. Nels Reinhold and Agnes May (Fulton) L.; m. Angela Andrian Plaza, Nov. 24, 1973; children: Steven, Douglas, Mary. BS, U. B.C., 1968; MS, U. Ill., 1970. Registered profl. engr., Que. Project engr., sr. project engr. Can. Nat. Rys., Montreal, 1971-76; mgr. FAST project Assn. Am. R.R.s, Pueblo, Colo., 1976-77, mgr. track research div., Chgo., 1977-78, dir. research, test ops., Pueblo, 1978-82, exec. dir. transp. test ctr., 1982-83, asst. v.p. research, test dept. transp. test ctr., 1983—. Contbr. articles to profl. jours.; editor, Technical Proceedings FAST Engineering Conference, 1981. Recipient scholarship Union Carbide Can., Ltd., Vancouver, 1963; Lafarge Cement Can., Ltd., U. B.C. 1967; Golder, Brauner Assocs., 1967; Nat. Research Council Canada, 1968. Mem. ASME, Am. Ry. Engring. Assn., Roadmasters and Maintenance of Way Assn., Car Dept. Officers Assn., Ry. Fuel and Operating Officers Assn., Pueblo C. of C. (hon. dir. 1982—). Presbyterian. Home: 1138 Bluestem Pueblo CO 81001 Office: Assn Am Railroads Transp Test Ctr PO Box 11130 Pueblo CO 81001

LUNDH, LARS GUNNAR F., banker; b. Uppsala, Sweden, July 2, 1933; s. Herbert T. and Brita (Bring) L.; m. Doris M. Burvall, Apr. 16, 1960; 1 child, Fredrik. LLB, Uppsala U., 1956; BSc in Econs., Stocholm Sch. Econs., 1962. Bank lawyer Uplands Banken, Uppsala, 1960-65, asst. to chief exec., 1965-67, gen. mgr. internat., 1967-70, dep. chief exec., 1970-73, pres., chief exec., 1973-85; dep. chief exec. Nord Banken, Stockholm, 1985—; bd. dirs. Stockholm Stock Exchange, Arduthnot Latham Bank, London. Lodge: Rotary. Office: Nordbanken, Regering S G 38, S10387 Stockholm Sweden

LUNDQUIST, VIOLET ELVIRA, agency administrator; b. Bristol, Conn., Jan. 28, 1912; d. Otto Nimrod and Mabel Elvira (Lindeen) Ebb; diploma music Augustana Coll., Rock Island, Ill., 1932; postgrad. mgmt. systems U. Mo., 1969; m. Vernon Arthur Lundquist, May 14, 1935; children—Karen Ebb, Jane Christine. Tchr. music, public schs., Olds, Iowa, 1932-35; editor Warsaw (Mo.) Times, 1935-45, Anthon (Iowa) Herald, 1945-57; field dir. Iowa Heart Assn., Des Moines, 1957-66; exec. dir. S.E. Iowa Community Action Program, Burlington, 1966-74; adminstrn. dir. S.E. Ariz. Govts. Orgn. Community Services, Bisbee, Ariz., 1975-77; statewide advocate developmentally disabled adults, 1977—; adminstr. Arizona City Med. Ctr., part-time, 1979-80; adminstr. Dist. V Council on Devel. Disabilities, 1980-87. Bd. dirs. Cen. Ariz. Health Systems Agy., 1979—, chmn., 1986—; chmn. Arizona City Home and Property Owners Assn., 1979-82; bd. dirs. Ariz. State Health Planning Council, 1986—; mem. Ariz. Statewide Health Coordinating Council, 1986—, Ariz. Dist. V Human Rights Com., 1986—; pres. Pinal County Assn. for Retarded Citizens, 1987—, v.p., vice chmn. state assn. Recipient Carol Lane award Nat. Safety Council, 1956, 1st place award Nat. Fedn. Press Women, 1952, 53, 55, 57; USPHS scholar, Columbia U., summers 1963, 64; cert. vocat. rehab. adminstr. Mem. Nat. Soc. Community Action Program Dirs. (dir. 1966-75), Ariz. Fedn. Press Women. Lutheran. Clubs: Zonta (area dir. 1984-86), Women of Moose. Home and Office: 609 W Cochise St PO Box 2265 Arizona City AZ 85223

LUNDSTEN, S. R. HENRIK, petroleum company executive, lawyer; b. Helsinki, Finland, May 5, 1934; s. K. Ragnar and Leena S. (Ahlroth); m. Ritva T. Oksanen, Nov. 1, 1966. LLM, Helsinki U., 1956. Dist. atty. Helsinki, 1956-60; asst. dept. head Assn. Finnish Cities, Helsinki, 1961-71; pres. Finnish Petroleum Fedn., Helsinki, 1971—; with Govt. Commn. on Hwy Code Renewal, 1967-68, com. Transport Dangerous Goods, 1975—; permanent advisor Nat. Energy Council, 1979—. Author: Finnish Road Safety Manual, 36 edits., 1966—. Bd. dirs. Helsinki Port Authority, 1977—; v.p., trustee bd. Ekokem Oy, 1986—. Decorated Knight French Star Legion, Knight 1st Class Finnish Order White Rose. Fellow Inst. Petroleum; mem. Permanent Council World Petroleum Congresses, Nat. Com. World Petroleum Congresses (sec. 1972—), Coordinating European Council for Devel. Performance Test for Engine Fuels and Lubricants (pres. 1987—), Finnish Automobile Assn. Home: Luoteisvayla 16 D, SF 00200 Helsinki Finland Office: Finnish Petroleum Fedn, Fabianinkatu 8, SF 00131 Helsinki Finland

LUNDSTRÖM, JARL OLOF, executive; b. Helsinki, Finland, Apr. 27, 1933; s. Jarl Albin and Siska (Tallroth) L.; children: Pekka, Mark, Otto. Student, U. Munich, Fed. Republic Germany, 1955, Oakland (Calif.) Jr. Coll., 1957-58; MBA, U. Helsinki, 1960. Export mgr. Cinderella, Helsinki, 1958-68; dir. Leipom Hilden, Helsinki, 1958-74, Finnhotels, Helsinki, 1974-77; mng. dir. Karl König, Helsinki, 1977-87, ADLON, Helsinki, 1984-86; sec. gen. ISBC-1988, Helsinki, 1987—; chmn. Finnish Bakers Assn., Helsinki, 1974-82, Finnish Entrepreneurs Assn., Helsinki, 1982-84. Pres. local Rotary, 1973; v.p. JCI-Finland, 1965. Home: Runebergink 60 B 33, 26 Helsinki Finland

LUNS, JOSEPH MARIE ANTOINE HUBERT, former secretary-general of NATO; b. Rotterdam, Netherlands, Aug. 28, 1911; s. Hubert and Henriette (Louvrier) L.; ed. London Sch. Econs., Deutsches Institut für Auslander, Berlin U.; D.C.L. (hon.), Univs. of Oxford, Canterbury, Dublin and Harvard; m. Baroness Elisabeth Cornelia van Heemstra, Jan. 10, 1938; children—Hubert, Cornelia. Entered Fgn. Service, 1938, attaché, 1938, 2nd sec. of Embassy, 1943, 1st sec., 1945, counselor, 1949; with Ministry for Fgn. Affairs, 1938-40; Legation, Berne, 1940-41, Lisbon, 1941-43, Netherlands Ministry for Fgn. Affairs, London, 1943-44, Embassy, London, 1944-49, permanent del. to UNO, 1949-52, minister Fgn. Affairs, 1952-71, sec.-gen. of NATO, Brussels, Belgium, 1971-85. Decorated knight grand cross Order of Netherlands Lion, officer Order of Orange of Nassau, Netherlands Royal Silver Wedding medal, knight Sovereign Order of Malta, officer, Companion of Honor, Mil. Order of Christ (Portugal), knight, Order of Leopold of Belgium, comdr. Order of Prakyat Trishaki Patti of Nepal, grand cross of following orders: St. Olav (Norway), So. Cross (Brazil), Merit (Italy), Georgios I (Greece), Leopold I (Belgium), Dannebrog (Denmark), Legion of Honour (France), Menelik II (Ethiopia), Ploar Star (Sweden), White Elephant (Thailand), Oak Crown (Luxembourg), Merit (Austria), Boyacá (Colombia), Civil and Mil. Merits of Adolf of Nassau (Luxembourg), Merit for Spl. Services (Peru), Star of Africa (Liberia), Manuel Amador Guerrero (Panamá), Vasa (Sweden), St. Michael and St. George (U.K.), Pius (Holy See), Ruben Darío (Nicaragua), Isabel la Católica (Spain), Carlos Manuel de Céspedes (Cuba), Cuarte Sánchez y Mella (Dominican Republic), Homayou (Iran), Francisco Morazán (Honduras), Sun (Peru), Sardara Aala (Afghanistan), Merit (Germany), Liberator (Argentina), Office of l'Instruction Publique (France), Order of Crown of Thailand, Aztec Ealge (Mexico), Order of Merit Bernardo O'Higgins (Chile), Order of Merit (Ecuador), Order of the Falcon (Iceland), Order of the Liberator of Venezuela, Order of Merit of Tunisia, Order of Gorkha Dashina Bahu of Nepal, Nat. Order of Republic of Senegal, knight Order of Valour (Federal Republic Cameroun) Ataturk International Peace Prize, 1986; hon. fellow London Sch. Econs.; recipient Charlemagne prize City of Aachen, 1967. Address: Sec Gen NATO 1110, Brussels Belgium *

LUNZ, RAIMUND GEORG, advertising executive; b. Würzburg, Fed. Republic of Germany, Oct. 22, 1936; s. Pankraz and Elisabeth (Fisher) L.; m. Elisabeth Sinner; 1 child, Alexandra. Student, Advert Tech. Sch., Hamburg. Copywriter J.W. Thompson, Frankfurt, Fed. Republic of Germany, 1960-63, creative group, 1973-78, account rep., 1978-80, account dir., 1980-85; mng. dir. J. Walter Thompson Deltakos, Frankfurt, 1985—; copy chief LPE, Düsseldorf, Fed. Republic of Germany, 1964-68; creative dir. LPE/Leo Burnett, Düsseldorf, 1979-72. Home: Hammarskjoldring 112, 6000 Frankfurt Federal Republic of Germany Office: JW Thompson Deltakos, Bockenheimer Landstr 104, 6000 Frankfurt Federal Republic of Germany

LUO, REN-CHYUAN, engineering educator, researcher; b. Taoyuan, Republic of China, Sept. 8, 1949; came to U.S., 1982, naturalized, 1984; s. Chi-Hsin and I-Mei (Tsao) L.; m. Lan-Chien Hsueh, Sept. 5, 1976; children—Alice Luo. B.S., Feng-Chia U., Republic of China, 1973, M.S., 1975; M.S., Technische U., Berlin, 1980, Ph.D., 1982. Registered profl. engr., Berlin. Chief engr. Taichung Machinery Co., Republic of China, 1974-76; sci. research fellow Fraunhofer Inst., IPA, Berlin, 1977-80, Technische U., Berlin, 1980-82; project leader U. R.I., Kingston, 1982-83; asst. prof. elec. engring. U. Ill.-Chgo., 1983-84, assoc. prof. N.C. State U., Raleigh, 1984—. Contbr. numerous articles to sci. jours. Recipient China-Germany Tech. Cooperative Research award Bundesministerium fü r Forschungs und Tech., 1976; research grantee Deutsche Forschungs Gemeinschaft, 1980; research scholar award NSF, 1984-86; research grantee DOD, NASA. Mem. Chinese Soc. Engrs., Verein Deutsche Inginieure, Robotics Internat. Soc. Mfg. Engrs., IEEE. Subspecialties: Robotics; Sensory processes; Computer vision. Home: 224 Jansmith Ln Raleigh NC 27615 Office: Dept Electrical and Computer Engring NC State U PO Box 7911 Raleigh NC 27695

LUO, ZHAOHUA, mathematician; b. Changsha, Hunan, People's Republic of China, Dec. 28, 1950; s. Jiguang Luo and Zhongying Li. Student, Northeastern Normal U., Changchun, People's Republic of China, 1974-77; MA, Wayne State U., Detroit, 1981; PhD, Brandeis U., Waltham, Mass., 1985. Asst. researcher Inst. Systems Sci., Acad. Sinica, Beijing, 1985-88; assoc. researcher Inst. Systems Sci., Acad. Sinica, Beijing, People's Republic of China, 1988—. Mem. Am. Math. Soc. Home: Bldg 10 #508, Jian Wai Yong An Nan Li, Beijing People's Republic of China Office: Inst Systems Sci, Acad Sinica, 100080 Beijing People's Republic of China

LUPBERGER, EDWIN ADOLPH, utility executive; b. Atlanta, June 5, 1936; s. Adolph and Esma L.; m. Kathryn Corr Carstarphen, Apr. 24, 1965; children—David Todd, Edward Townsend. A.B. in Econs, Davidson (N.C.) Coll., 1958; M.B.A., Emory U., 1963. Asst. v.p. Southern Co. Services, Inc., Atlanta, 1963-69; v.p., treas. Gulf Power Co., Pensacola, Fla., 1969-77; sr. v.p. fin. Indpls. Power & Light Co., 1977-79; sr. v.p., chief fin. officer Middle South Utilities, Inc., New Orleans, 1979-85, chmn., pres., 1985—. Served as ensign USN, 1960. Mem. Edison Electric Inst., Southeastern Electric Exchange (exec. com.). Presbyterian. Clubs: Univ., World Trade Ctr., Board Room (N.Y.C.), Metropolitan.

LUPERT, LESLIE ALLAN, lawyer; b. Syracuse, N.Y., May 24, 1946; s. Reuben and Miriam (Kaufman) L.; m. Roberta Gail Fellner, May 19, 1968; children: Jocelyn, Rachel, Susannah. BA, U. Buffalo, 1967; JD, Columbia U., 1971. Bar: N.Y. 1971. Ptnr. Orans Elsen & Lupert, N.Y.C., 1971—. Contbr. articles to profl. jours. Mem. ABA, N.Y. State Bar Assn., N.Y.C. Bar Assn. (com. fed. legislation 1977-80, profl. and jud. ethics com. 1983-86, com. on fed. cts. 1986—), Phi Beta Kappa. Club: Columbia Univ. (N.Y.C.). Office: Orans Elsen & Lupert 1 Rockefeller Plaza New York NY 10020

LUPO, CARMINE, marketing professional; b. Auletta, Campania, Italy, Nov. 24, 1956; came to France, 1958; Degree in Chem. Engring., Inst. National Superieur de Chimie de Rouen (France), 1979; Degree in Mgmt., Inst. of Adminstrn. for Enterprise, Paris, 1981. Sales engr. Soc. d'Exploitation de Produits Pour l'Industrie Chimique, Paris, 1981-86; mktg. researcher Compagnie Française de Produits Industriels, Gennevilliers, France, 1986—. Contbr. articles to profl. jours. Roman Catholic. Home: 29 Rue de Verdun, 78110 Le Vesinet France Office: CFPI, 28 Bd Camelinat, 92233 Gennevilliers France

LUPO, SAMUEL ELDRED, diplomat; b. Walnut Creek, Colo., Sept. 26, 1933; m.; three children. BA, UCLA, 1961. Mgmt. intern VA, 1961-63, personnel officer, 1963-64, computer systems analyst, 1964-66; personnel officer U.S. Embassy, Manila, 1966-68, La Paz, Bolivia, 1969-71; spl. asst. to Asst. Sec. State for Adminstrn. U.S. Govt., 1972-73; adminstrn. officer U.S. Embassy, Dublin, Ireland, 1973-75, Lima, Peru, 1976-77, Brasilia, Brazil, 1977-79; exec. dir. Bur. Inter.-Am. Affairs, Dept. State U.S. Govt., 1979-81; consul gen. U.S. Govt., Rio de Janeiro, Brazil, 1981-85; dep. asst. sec. personnel, Dept. State U.S. Govt., 1985-87, U.S. Ambassador to Guinea, 1987—. Served with USAF, 1951-55. Office: US Ambassador to Guinea care Dept of State Washington DC 20520 *

LUPPI, MICHAEL DENNIS, lawyer; b. Medford, Mass., Aug. 12, 1946; s. Armand Lazarus and Violet (Queques) L. B.A., UCLA, 1968, J.D., 1972. Bar: Calif. 1973, U.S. Dist. Ct. (cen. dist.) Calif. 1973, U.S. Ct. Appeals (9th cir.) 1978, U.S. Supreme Ct. 1976. Sole practice, Los Angeles, 1973-75; assoc. Myers and D'Angelo, Los Angeles, 1975-78; assoc. Pilot & Spar, Los Angeles, 1979-81; sole practice, Glendale, Calif., 1981—. Mem. Los Angeles County Bar Assn., ABA, Glendale Bar Assn. Democrat. Roman Catholic. Club: Los Angeles Turf (Arcadia, Calif.). Address: 352 Amherst Dr Burbank CA 91506

LUPU, RADU, pianist; b. Galati, Romania, Nov. 30, 1945; s. Meir and Ana (Gabor) L. Attended, Conservatoire, Moscow, USSR, 1961-69. London debut, 1969, Berlin, 1971, U.S. debut with, Cleve. Orch. in, N.Y.C., appearances with worldwide maj. orchs., including, Berlin Philharmonic, Israel Philharmonic, Orch de Paris, Concertgebouw, N.Y. Philharmonic, Phila., Chgo. Symphony Orch., Cleve., rec. artist, Decca Records.; recs. include: Beethoven cycle with Israel Philharmonic and Zubin Mehta. Recipient 1st prize Van Cliburn Internat. Piano Competition, 1966; Enescu Competition, 1967; Leeds Internat. Piano Competition, 1969.

LUQMANI, MUSHTAQ, marketing and international business educator, consultant; b. Karachi, Pakistan, Nov. 5, 1944; came to U.S., 1967; s. Arif A. and Badar (Beg) Lukmani; m. Zahida M. Luqmani, Mar. 15, 1973. B.S. with honors, U. Karachi, 1966; B.S. in Chem. Engring., Ind. Inst. Tech., 1969; M.B.A., Mich. State U., 1971, Ph.D. in Mktg. and Internat. Bus., 1978. Ptnr., Hotel Properties, Karachi, 1963-66; mktg. mgr. Al-Afia Resorts, Karachi, 1972-73; teaching asst. Mich. State U., East Lansing, 1973-76; assoc. prof. mktg. Western Mich. U., Kalamazoo, 1977—. Mem. Am. Mktg. Assn. (pres. West Mich. chpt. 1983-84), Acad. Mktg. Sci., Acad. Internat. Bus., West Mich. World Trade Club, Beta Gamma Sigma. Lodge: Lions (Kalamazoo). Contbr. articles to profl. jours. Home: 7600 Orchard Hill Kalamazoo MI 49002 Office: Western Mich U 230 N Hall Kalamazoo MI 49008

LURIA, SALVADOR EDWARD, biologist; b. Turin, Italy, Aug. 13, 1912; came to U.S., 1940, naturalized, 1947; s. David and Ester (Sacerdote) L.; m. Zella Hurwitz, Apr. 18, 1945; 1 son, Daniel. M.D., U. Turin, 1935. Research fellow Curie Lab., Inst. of Radium, Paris, 1938-40; research asst. surg. bacteriology Columbia U., 1940-42; successively instr., asst. prof., assoc. prof. bacteriology Ind. U., 1943-50; prof. bacteriology U. Ill., 1950-59; prof. microbiology M.I.T., 1959-64, Sedgwick prof. biology, 1964—, Inst. prof., 1970—, dir. center cancer research, 1972—; non-resident fellow Salk Inst. Biol. Studies, 1965—; lectr. biophysics U. Colo., 1950; Jesup lectr. zoology Columbia U., 1950; Nieuwland lectr. biology U. Notre Dame, 1959; Dyer lectr. NIH, 1963; with OSRD, Carnegie Instn., Washington, 1945-46. Asso. editor: Jour. Bacteriology, 1950-55; editor: Virology, 1955—; sect. editor: Biol. Abstracts, 1958-62; editorial bd.: Exptl. Cell Research Jour, 1948—; adv. bd.: Jour. Molecular Biology, 1958-64; hon. editorial adv. bd.: Jour. Photochemistry and Photobiology, 1961—. Guggenheim fellow Vanderbilt U. and Princeton U., 1942-43; Guggenheim fellow Pasteur Inst., Paris, 1963-64; Co-recipient Nobel prize for medicine, 1969. Mem. Am. Philos. Soc., Am. Soc. Microbiology (pres. 1967-68), Nat. Acad. Scis., Am. Acad. Arts and Scis., AAAS, Soc. Gen. Microbiology, Genetics Soc. Am., AAUP, Sigma Xi. Office: MIT Dept Biology Room E17-113 Cambridge MA 02139 *

LURIX, PAUL LESLIE, JR., chemist; b. Bridgeport, Conn., Apr. 6, 1949; s. Paul Leslie and Shirley Laurel (Ludwig) L.; m. Cynthia Ann Owens, May 30, 1970; children—Paul Christopher, Alexander Tristan, Einar Gabrielson. B.A., Drew U., 1971; M.S., Purdue U., 1973; postgrad., 1973—. Tech. dir. Analysts, Inc., Linden, N.J., 1976-77; chief chemist Caleb Brett USA, Inc., Linden, 1977-80; v.p. Tex. Labs., Inc., Houston, 1980-82; pres. Lurix Corp., Fulshear, Tex., 1982—; cons. LanData, Inc., Houston, 1980—, Nat. Cellulose Corp., Houston, 1981—, Met. Transit Authority, Houston, 1981—, Phillips 66, Houston, 1986—; dir. research and devel. Stockbridge Software, Inc., Houston, 1986—; v.p. Diesel King Corp., Houston, 1980-82. Contbr. article to profl. jour. Patentee distillate fuel additives. Fellow Am. Inst. Chemists; mem. Am. Chem. Soc., ASTM, AAAS, Soc. Applied Spectroscopy, N.Y. Acad. Sci., Phi Kappa Phi, Phi Lambda Upsilon, Sigma Pi Sigma. Republican. Methodist. Lodge: Kiwanis (pres., 1970-71). Current work: Infrared spectroscopy; data base programming for science and industrial applications. Subspecialties: Infrared spectroscopy; Information systems, storage, and retrieval (computer science). Avocations: tennis, golf, piano. Home: 32602 Hepple White Dr Fulshear TX 77441

LURVEY, IRA HAROLD, lawyer; b. Chgo., Apr. 6, 1935; s. Louis and Faye (Grey) L.; m. Barbara Ann Sirvint, June 24, 1962; children: Nathana, Lawrence, Jennifer, Jonathan, David, Robert. BS, U. Ill., 1956; MS, Northwestern U., 1961; JD, U. Calif., Berkeley, 1965. Bar: Calif. 1965, Nev. 1966, U.S. Dist. Ct. (cen. dist.) Calif. 1966, U.S. Tax Ct. 1966, U.S. Ct. Appeals (9th cir.) 1966, U.S. Supreme Ct. 1975. Law clk. to presiding justice Nev. Supreme Ct., Carson City, 1965-66; from assoc. to ptnr. Shea & Gould and predecessor firm Pacht, Ross, Warne, Bernhard & Sears, Inc., Los Angeles, 1966-84; founding ptnr. Lurvey & Shapiro, Los Angeles, 1984—; lectr. legal edn. programs; mem. Chief Justice's Commns. on Ct. Reform. Editor Community Property Jour., 1979—; contbr. articles to profl. jours. Former chmn. Los Angeles Jr. Arts Ctr.; past pres. Cheviot Hills Homeowners Assn.; exec. v.p., counsel gen. studies com. Hillel Acad. Sch., Beverly Hills, Calif., 1977—. Served with U.S. Army, 1957-58. Fellow Am. Acad. Matrimonial Lawyers, Internat. Acad. Matrimonial Lawyers; mem. ABA (governing council 1986—, chmn. support com., chmn. continuing legal edn., policy and issues com., family law sect., vice chmn. com. arbitration and mediation, bd. editors mag.), Calif. Bar Assn. (editor jour. 1982-85, chmn. family law sect. 1986-87, specialization adv. bd. family law), Los Angeles County Bar Assn. (chmn. family law sect.), Beverly Hills Bar Assn. (chmn. family law sect. 1982-83). Home: 2729 Motor Ave Los Angeles CA 90064 Office: Lurvey & Shapiro 2121 Avenue of the Stars Suite 1550 Los Angeles CA 90067

LUSCOMB, ROBERT CHARLES, JR., automotive executive; b. Lansing, Mich., Apr. 29, 1936; s. Robert Charles and Gertrude Ann Luscomb; m. Karen Marie; children: Mark C., Roberta D., Philip Z., James D., David C. Kipp. BS in Mech. Engring., Gen. Motors Inst., 1958; SM in Mgmt., MIT, 1970. Registered profl. engr., Mich. Supt. press plants Oldsmobile div. Gen. Motors Corp., Lansing, 1970-73, dir. prodn. engring., 1973-76, mgr. mfg. plants Cadillac div., 1976-84, mgr. mfg. engring, 1984—. Active Boy Scouts Am., 1945—. Sloan fellow, 1970. Mem. Soc. Automotive Engrs., Soc. Mfg. Engrs. Office: Gen Motors Corp Cadillac Motor Car Div 2860 Clark St Detroit MI 48232

LUSCOMBE, DAVID EDWARD, historian; b. London, July 22, 1938; s. Edward Dominic and Nora (Cowell) L.; m. Megan Philips, Aug. 20, 1960; children: Nicholas, Mark, Philip, Amanda. BA, Cambridge U., Eng., 1959, MA, 1962, PhD, 1964, LittD, 1987. Fellow King's Coll. Cambridge U., Eng., 1962-64, Churchill Coll., Cambridge, Eng., 1964-72; prof. Medieval History U. Sheffield, Eng., 1972—, dean faculty of arts, 1985-87. Author: The School of Peter Abelard, 1969, Peter Abelard's Ethics, 1971; editor: Church and Government in the Middle Ages, 1976; adv. editor Cambridge Studies in Medieval Life and Thought, 1983—; contbr. articles to profl. jours. European vis. fellow Leverhulme Trust, Paris, 1973. Fellow Brit. Acad., Royal Hist. Soc. (council mem. 1981-85), Soc. Antiquaries; mem. Internat. Soc. for Study Medieval Philosophy (mem. bur. 1982-87, v.p. 1987—). Roman Catholic. Home: 4 Caxton Rd, Sheffield S10 3DE, England

LÜSEBRINK, HANS-JÜRGEN, language educator; b. Lüdenscheid, Fed. Republic Germany, Apr. 22, 1952; s. Hans and Käthe (Belz) L.; m. Claire Ratelle, May 26, 1979; 1 child, Natalia. LittD, U. Bayreuth, Fed. Republic

Germany, 1981; D in History, U. Paris, 1984. Asst. prof. history U. Bayreuth, 1979-81, assoc. prof., 1982-88; prof. U. Passau, Fed. Republic Germany, 1988—. Author: Kriminalität und Literatur, 1983, Histoires de Cartouche, 1984; co-author, editor: Feindbild und Faszination, 1984, Geschichte beider Iudien, 1988; mem. editorial bd. Mentalities/Mentalitiés, 1985—, Dix-Huitième Siècle, 1986—, Komparatistische Hefte, 1980—, Literarische Kanonbildung in der Romania, 1987. Home: Am Wimhof 85, 8390 Passau Federal Republic of Germany

LUSINCHI, JAIME, president of Venezuela, pediatrician; b. Clarines, Venezuela, May 27, 1924. M.D., Central U., Caracas, Venezuela, 1947. Mem., founder Accion Democratica party, 1941—, mem. nat. exec. com., 1958—, sec.-gen., 1980-83, party leader, 1980—; jailed because of polit. activities, 1952; in exile, Argentina, Chile, N.Y.C., 1952-58; dep. Ho. of Deps. Venezuela, 1958-84, senator, from 1979; pres. Venezuela, 1984—. Mem. Am. Acad. Pediatrics. Address: Office of the President, Palacio de Miraflores, Caracas Venezuela *

LUSK, GLENNA RAE KNIGHT (MRS. EDWIN BRUCE LUSK), librarian; b. Franklinton, La., Aug. 16, 1935; d. Otis Harvey and Lou Zelle (Bahm) Knight; B.S., La. State U., 1956, M.S., 1963; m. John Earle Uhler, Jr., May 26, 1956; children—Anne Knight, Camille Allana; m. 2d, Edwin Bruce Lusk, Nov. 28, 1970. Asst. librarian Iberville Parish Library, Plaquemine, La., 1956-57, 1962-68; tchr. Iberville Parish Pub. Schs., Plaquemine, 1957-59, Plaquemines Parish Pub. Schs., Buras, La., 1959-61; dir. Iberville Parish Library, Plaquemine, 1969—; chmn. La. State Bd. Library Examiners, 1979—. Mem. Iberville Parish Econ. Devel. Council, Plaquemine, 1970-71; sec. Iberville Parish Bicentennial Commn., 1973—; mem. La. Bicentennial Commn., 1974. Named Outstanding Young Woman Plaquemine, La. Jr. C. of C., 1970. Mem. La. (sect. chmn. 1967-68), Riverland (sec. 1973-74) libraries assns., Capital Area Libraries (chmn. com. 1972-74). Democrat. Episcopalian. Author: (with John E. Uhler, Jr.) Cajun Country Cookin' 1966; Rochester Clarke Bibliography of Louisiana Cookery, 1966; Royal Recipes from the Cajun Country, 1969; Iberville Parish, 1970. Home: 206 Pecan Tree Ln Plaquemine LA 70764 Office: 1501 J Gerald Berret Blvd Plaquemine LA 70764

LUSSING, FRANK ANTON, trading co. exec.; b. Losser, Netherlands, Nov. 14, 1922; s. Frans Bertus and Francisca Maria (Haverkort) L.; student various tech. colls.; divorced; children—Frank, Lisbeth, Judith, Stephen, Sylvia, Karen. Group prodn. mgr. Bata Best Co., 1940-62; gen. mgr. Bata Belgium, 1962-65; indsl. mgr. Erdal Group, Netherlands, 1965-72; mng. dir. Wayne Rubber Group, South Africa, 1972-74; propr. Frank Lussing Agys. S/A, 1974—, leather hand made footwear and products Vicci Leathers, Durban, South Africa, 1976-80; propr. Mariners Rest, Durban, 1983—; cons. in field. Served with RAF, World War II. Mem. Durban C. of C., Dutch Bus. Club South Africa. Roman Catholic. Clubs: Vereniging Nederland, Dutch South Africa Bus. (vice chmn. 1974—). Home: PO Box 37-339, 4067 Overport Republic of South Africa

LUSTGARTEN, STEWART J., dental marketing executive; b. N.Y.C., Jan. 4, 1943; s. Samuel H. and Kate (Motelson) L.; m. Susan Figa, Aug. 14, 1969; children: Jennifer, Shelby, Jillian. Student U. Miami, Fla., 1960-63. Asst. v.p. Columbia Dentoform Corp., N.Y.C., 1964-77; dir. bio-materials div. Parkell Inc., Farmingdale, N.Y., 1977; v.p. Healthco Internat., Inc., Boston, 1977-86; chief exec. officer Lustgarten Multi-Tech Internat. Inc., Framingham, Mass., 1986—; v.p., bd. dirs. Roeko U.S.A., Inc., Framingham, 1987—; cons. Roeko GmbH, Ulm, Fed. Republic Germany, 1987—, Adiesse Founitures Dental, Florence, Italy, 1986—, P.S.P. Dental Ltd, Belv. Kent, England, 1986, Macrochem Corp., Woburn, Mass., 1987—, Warner Lambert Corp., Morristown, N.J., 1972-74, Primary Med. Communications, Inc., N.Y.C., 1971-74, Denar Corp., Anaheim, Calif., 1977-78, dept. dental materials Coll. Dentistry, NYU, 1974-77, dept. dental materials N.J. Coll. Dentistry, Newark, 1974-77 and numerous other cos.; bd. dirs. Dental Mfrs. Am., Phila., 1974-77. Patentee dental materials and methods. Served with USNR, 1964-70. Recipient cert. of appreciation Mass. Dental Assts. Assn., 1983, 84. Mem. Am. Assn. Dental Schs., Am. Assn. for Dental Research, Acad. Operative Dentistry. Avocations: boating; dancing; music, writing. Home: 73 Dalton Rd Holliston MA 01746 Office: 1661 Worcester Rd Framingham MA 01701

LUSTIG, ARNOST, writer, screenwriter, educator; b. Prague, Czechoslovakia, Dec. 21, 1926; came to U.S., 1970; s. Emil Lustig and Terezie Löwy; m. Vera Weislitz, July 24, 1949; children—Josef, Eva. M.A., Coll. Polit. and Social Sci., Prague, 1951, Ing., 1954; D Hebrew Letters (hon.), Spertus Coll. Judaica, 1986. Arab-Iraeli corr. Radio Prague, 1948-49; corr., Czechoslovak Radio, 1950-68; screenwriter Barrandov Film Studies, Prague, 1960-68; writer Kibutz Hachotrim, Israel, 1968-69; screenwriter Jadran Film Studio, Zagreb, 1969-70; mem. internat. writers program U. Iowa, Iowa City, 1970-71, vis. lectr. English, 1971-72; vis. prof. English, Drake U., Des Moines, 1972-73; prof. lit. and film Am. U., Washington, 1973—; head Czechosolovak film del. San Sebastian Film Festival, 1968; mem. jury Karlovy Vary Internat. Film Festival, 1968, Internat. Neustad Prize, 1981; lectr. in field. Author: Night and Hope, 1958; Diamonds of the Night, 1958; Street of Lost Brothers, 1959; (stories) Dita Saxova, 1962; (novel) My Acquaintance Vili Feld, 1962; A Prayer for Katarina Horovitzova, 1964; Nobody Will Be Humiliated, 1964; Bitter Smell of Almonds, 1968; Darling, 1969, The Unloved (From the Diary of a Seventeen Year Old), 1979, Indecent Dreams, 1988, also others; (screenplays) Transport from Paradise, 1963, Diamonds of the Night, 1964, Dita Saxova, 1968, A Bit to Eat, 1960; (TV scripts) The Blue Day, 1960, A Prayer for Katerina Horovitzova, 1965 (with Ernest Pendrell) Terezin, 1965, Stolen Childhood, 1966, (text for symphonic poem) Night and Hope, 1961, (text for cantata) The Beadl from Prague, 1984, Precious Legacy, 1984; (commentary to documentary) The Triumph of Memory, 1988; corr. lit. mags., 1950-58; editor Mlady svet mag., 1958-60. Recipient 1st prize Mlada fronta Publishing House, 1962; 1st prize Monte Carlo Film Festival, 1966; 1st prize Czechoslovak Radio Corp., 1966, 67; Klement Gottwald State prize, 1967; San Sebastian Film Festival 2d prize, 1968; B'nai B'rith prize, 1974; Nat. Jewish Book award, 1980, Nat. Book award, 1986, Emmy award, 1986, also others. Mem. Authors Guild, Authors League Am., PEN, Film Club (Prague). Home: 4000 Tunlaw Rd NW Apt 825 Washington DC 20007 Office: Am University Dept Literature Washington DC 20016

LUSTIG, HARRY, physicist, educator, administrator; b. Vienna, Austria, Sept. 23, 1925; came to U.S., 1939, naturalized, 1944; s. Hans and Hedwig (Faltitschek) L.; m. Judith Louise Hirshfield, Sept. 20, 1953 (dec. July 1975); children: Valerie Jean (dec.), Lawrence John, Nicholas Daniel (dec.); m. Rosalind Wells, Feb. 23, 1980. B.S., CCNY, 1948; M.S. (fellow), U. Ill., 1949, Ph.D., 1953. Teaching asst. U. Ill., 1949-51, research asst., 1951-53; mem. faculty CCNY, 1953—, prof. physics, 1967-86, resident prof., 1986—, chmn. dept., 1965-70, exec. officer physics doctoral program, 1968-71, assoc. dean for sci., 1972-75, dean Coll. Liberal Arts and Sci., 1973-82, dean of sci. Coll. Liberal Arts and Sci., 1975-82, provost, vice pres. acad. affairs, 1982-85; prin. scientist Nuclear Devel. Corp. Am., 1955-60; vis. research asst. prof. U. Ill., 1959-60; Fulbright prof. Univ. Coll., Dublin, Ireland, 1964-65; vis. scholar Stanford, summer 1963; vis. prof. U. Colo., summer 1966, U. Wash., summer 1967, 69; sec. Univs. Com. on Problems of War and Peace of Greater N.Y., 1962-64, chmn., 1965-67; sr. officer UNESCO, 1970-72, cons., 1972-75, 79; cons. U.S. Internat. Communications Agy, 1978, U. S.D., 1980, U. South Fla., 1981, N.J. State Dept. Higher Edn., 1983, 85, 87, U. Mass., 1983, 84; mem. U.S. liason com. for Internat. Union of Pure and Applied Physics, 1986—. Contbr. articles to profl. jours. Served with AUS, 1944-46. Fellow N.Y. Acad. Scis. (chmn. edni. adv. com. 1982-84, bd. govs. 1982-84, v.p. 1984); mem. Am. Phys. Soc. (treas. 1985—), Am. Assn. Physics Tchrs., Am. Inst. Physics (gov. bd. 1985—), Am. Inst. Sci. and Tech. (bd. trustees 1986-88), Inst. for Schs. of Future (bd. trustees 1984—, chmn. 1984-87), CCNY Alumni Assn. (Townsend Harris medal 1985), Phi Beta Kappa, Sigma Xi (pres. CCNY 1963-64). Home: 54 Riverside Dr New York NY 10024

LUSTIGER, JEAN-MARIE CARDINAL, archbishop of Paris; b. Paris, Sept. 17, 1926; s. Charles and Gisèle Lustiger. Ed. U. Paris, Sorbonne and Carmelite Sem., Inst. Catholique de Paris. Ordained priest Roman Catholic Ch., 1954. Chaplain to students Sorbonne, 1954-69; dir. Centre Richelieu, 1959-69; pastor Sainte-Jeanne-de-Chantal parish, Paris, 1969-79; consecrated bishop, 1979; bishop of Orléans, 1979-81; archbishop of Paris, 1981—; elevated to cardinal, 1983. Author: Sermons d'un curé de Paris, 1978; Pain de vie, Peuple de Dieu, 1981; Osez croire/Osez vivre, 1985; Premiers pas dans la prière, 1986, Six sermons aux élus de la Nation, 1987, Le Choix de Dieu, 1987. Home: Maison diocésaine, 8, rue de la Ville-l'Evêque, 75384 Paris Cedex 08 France

LUSTMAN, MARCEL HUBERT, ophthalmologist; b. Paris, Aug. 26, 1931; s. Avram and Anna (Zissu) L.; m. Jacqueline Frankel, July 8, 1958; children: Francis, Caroline. Lic. in Physics and Chemistry, U. Paris, 1949, MD, 1959. Cert. in Ophthalmology, 1961. Externe des hopitaux Assistance Publique, Paris, 1951-57, interne, 1957-58, attaché des hopitaux, 1958-84; pvt. practice ophthalmology Paris, 1961—. Contbr. articles to profl. jours. Served with Mil. Health Service of France, 1954-57, Algeria. Mem. French Ophthal. Soc. Club: Stade Francais (St. Cloud). Home: 36 rue des Sablons, 75116 Paris France Office: 36 rue des Sablons, 75116 Paris France

LUTALI, A. P., governor; b. Aunu'u, American Samoa, Dec. 24, 1919; married. Governor AS, 1985—. Office: Office of the Gov Pago Pago AS 96799 *

LUTCHMEENARAIDOO, SEETANAH, deputy prime minister and minister of finance; b. Mauritius, Mauritius, May 24, 1944; m. Suzanne Poli, Apr. 10th, 1971; 3 sons. Degree in Mgmt., diploma in Mktg., Ecole Superieure de Commerce, France. Economist Ministry Commerce and Industry, Mauritius, Mauritius, 1973-80; stand mgr. various internat. trade fairs, Mauritius, 1980-81; mgr., industl. mgmt. cons. INTRACORP, Mauritius, 1981-83; minister finance Govt. of Mauritius, 1983—, dep. prime minister, 1986—; gov. Internat. Monetary Fund, 1983—, African Devel. Bank and Fund, 1983—; nat. authorizing officer European Devel. Fund. Recipient Médaille de l'Université de Paris-Dauphine, 1987. Office: Ministry of Finance, Govt House, Port Louis Mauritius

LUTER, JOHN, newsman, educator; b. Knoxville, Tenn., Jan. 17, 1919; s. John Thomas and Bertha Mae (Carver) L.; m. Mary Hickey, 1948 (dec.); 1 dau., Linda; m. Yvonne Spiegelberg, 1966 (div. 1971); m. Nan Hoyt Lawrence, 1974. B.A., St. Mary's U., Tex., 1939; postgrad. Coll. Law, St. Mary's U., 1939-42; fellow Time Inc, Sch. Advanced Internat. Studies, Washington, 1945. Reporter San Antonio Light, 1939-42, Washington Star, 1942-44; corr. Time mag., 1944-45; war corr. Time mag., Pacific, 1945; fgn. corr. Time and Life mags., Southeast Asia, 1945-46, Japan, 1946-47, Israel, 1948-49, Italy, 1949-54; asst. editor internat. edit. Life mag., 1954-56; reporter, writer CBS News, 1957-58; asso. editor Newsweek mag., 1958-61; radio news commentator stas. WQXR and QXR-FM Network, 1960-61; coordinator advanced internat. reporting program Columbia Grad. Sch. Journalism, 1961-72; dir. Maria Moors Cabot Prize Program, 1961-74; mem. profl. staff Bank St. Coll. Edn., 1973-74; prof., dir. journalism U. Hawaii, Honolulu, from 1974, now prof. and chmn. journalism dept. Adv. editor: Columbia Journalism Rev., 1961-72. Chmn. internat. relations com. N.Y.C. Protestant Council, 1968-71; chmn. adv. screening com. communications Sr. Fulbright Program, 1970-73; trustee Overseas Press Club Found., 1962-72, chmn., 1964-65; bd. dirs. UN Assn. N.Y., 1973-74; chmn. Honolulu Community Media Council, 1982-84. Mem. Assn. Edn. Journalism and Mass Communications, Assn. Schs. Journalism and Mass Communications, Honolulu Com. Fgn. Relations, Pacific and Asian Affairs Council, Sigma Delta Chi (mem. chpt. exec. council 1966-69), Japan Am. Soc. Clubs: Overseas Press (pres. N.Y.C. 1960-62), Honolulu Press, Outrigger Canoe. Home: 2442 Halekoa Dr Honolulu HI 96821 Office: U Hawaii 208 Crawford Hall 2550 Campus Rd Honolulu HI 96822

LUTHEY, GRAYDON DEAN, JR., lawyer, educator; b. Topeka, Sept. 18, 1955; s. Graydon Dean Sr. and S. Anne (Murphy) L.; m. Deborah Denise McCullough, May 26, 1979; children: Sarah Elizabeth, Katherine Alexandra. BA in Letters with highest honors, U. Okla., 1976, JD, 1979; Diploma in Theology, Oxford (Eng.) U., 1976. Bar: Okla. 1979, U.S. Ct. Appeals (10th cir.) 1979, U.S. Dist. Ct. (no., we. and ea. dists.) Okla. 1980, U.S. Supreme Ct. 1982. Assoc. Jones, Givens, Gotcher, Bogan & Hilborne, Tulsa, 1979-84, ptnr., 1984—, also bd. dirs.; adj. assoc. prof. U. Tulsa, 1985-87, adj. prof., 1987—. Chancellor Diocese of Okla., 1985—. Nat. Merit scholar U. Okla., 1973; vis. research fellow Keble Coll., 1975. Mem. ABA, Okla. Bar Assn. (continuing legal edn. com.), Tulsa County Bar Assn. (bd. dirs. 1983—), Phi Beta Kappa, Omicron Delta Kappa. Clubs: Tulsa, Oaks Country (Tulsa). Office: Jones Givens Gotcher et al 3800 First Nat Tower Tulsa OK 74103

LUTHY, J. WILLIAM, retired chemical company executive; b. Staefa, Switzerland, Jan. 31, 1919; came to U.S., 1947, naturalized, 1954; s. Jakob and Anna (Amsler) L.; dipl. chem. eng. Swiss Fed. Inst. Tech., 1944, Sc.D., 1947; m. Margaret M. Marko, Mar. 13, 1948; children—Madeleine, Peter, Susan. With Sandoz, Inc., 1948-84, applications dir. chem. div., N.Y.C., 1951-59, tech. mgr. dyes div., 1959-84, exec. v.p. Sandoz, Inc., 1964-84, pres. colors and chems. div., 1968-84, also dir. Mem. Am., Swiss chem. socs., Columbia Grad. Sch. Bus. Exec. Assn. Republican. Home: 643 Mountain Rd Kinnelon NJ 07405

LUTIN, DAVID LOUIS, real estate development and finance consultant; b. East Hartford, Conn., Apr. 18, 1919; s. Solomon and Esther (Newman) L.; A.B., Ohio No. U., 1946; M.B.A., Syracuse U., 1949; m. Dorothy Marmor, Dec. 3, 1944; children—Gary, Marnie (Mrs. George Wittig). Housing economist and field rep. HHFA, Washington, 1950-57; dir. urban renewal City of Brookline, Mass., 1957-58; cons. on urban renewal and housing Com. for Econ. Devel., N.Y.C., 1958-59; propr. David L. Lutin Assocs., real estate devel. and fin. cons., Rye, N.Y., 1959-73, Phoenix, 75—; v.p. real estate and mortgages Am. Bank and Trust Co., N.Y.C., 1973-75. Research assoc. Albert Farwell Bemis Found., M.I.T., 1951-52. Served to capt. AUS, 1942-46. Decorated Purple Heart. Mem. Am. Econ. Assn., Nat. Planning Assn., Mortgage Bankers Assn., Urban Land Inst., Am. Planning Assn., Am. Statis. Assn., Nat. Assn. Home Builders. Contbr. articles and reports on econs., housing and urban devel. to profl. jours. Home and Office: 11419 N Century Ln Scottsdale AZ 85254

LUTOSLAWSKI, WITOLD, composer; b. Warsaw, Poland, Jan. 25, 1913; s. Jozef and Maria (Olszewska) L.; degree in piano State Conservatory Music, Warsaw, 1936, degree in composition, 1937; hon. doctorate Cleve. Inst. Music, 1971, Northwestern U., 1972, Warsaw U., 1973, Lancaster U., 1975, U. Glasgow, 1977, Copernicus U., 1980, Durham U., Jagiellonian U. Cracow, Baldwin-Wallace Coll., Cambridge U., 1987, Royal No. Coll. Manchester, 1987, Belfast U., 1987; m. Maria-Danuta Dygat, Sept. 24, 1946. Composer, 1922—; first public performance orch. piece, 1933, performances, Europe, Am., Asia, Australia, Africa; tchr. composition Berkshire Music Center, Tanglewood, Mass., 1962, Dartington, Devon, Eng., 1963, 64, Swedish Royal Acad. Music, 1965, Aarhus, Denmark, 1968; condr. orchs. and Choris, 1963—; mem. program com. Warsaw Autumn Festival, 1956-74. Recipient Warsaw Prize, 1948, State Music Prize, 1952, 55, 64, Minister Culture Prize, 1962, 1st prize Internat. Music Council and Gesellschaft der Musikfreunde, Vienna, 1963, Serge Koussevitzky Internat. Rec. award, 1964, Leonie Sonning Music prize, 1967, Gottfried-von-Herder prize, 1967, Maurice Ravel prize, 1971, Sibelius de Wihuri prize, 1973, E. von Siemen's prize, 1983, Solidarity prize, 1984, Grawemeyer award for musical composition U. Louisville, 1985, gold medal Royal Philharm. Soc., 1985, Queen Sofia of Spain prize, 1985, Internat. Critics award, 1986, GRAMMY award, Jurzykowski Found. prize, N.Y., 1988, also others. Mem. Polish Composers' Union (hon. mem., recipient prize 1959, 73), Assn. Profl. Cokmposers (hon. London), Royal Swedish Acad. Music, Freie Akad. der Künste, Hamburg, Akademie der Künste, Berlin, Deutsche Akademie der Künste zu Berlin, Bayerische Akademie der Schönen Künste, Munich, Am. Acad. Arts and Letters, Nat. Inst. Arts and Letters, Royal Acad. Music (London), Acad. des Beaux Arts (Paris), Acad. Européenne des Sciences, des Arts, et des Lettres, Acad. Royale de Belgique, Acad. Nazionale de Santa Cecilia (hon. Rome), Internat. Soc. Contemporary Music (hon.), Konzert hausgesellschaft Vienna (hon.). Composer symphonic works, vocal music, string quartet. Home: 39 Smiala, 01-523 Warsaw Poland

LUTVAK, MARK ALLEN, computer company marketing executive; b. Chgo., Feb. 9, 1939; s. Joseph Issac and Jeanette Nettie (Pollock) L.; B.S. in Elec. Engring., U. Mich., 1962; M.B.A., Wayne State U., Detroit, 1969; m. Gayle Helene Rotofsky, May 24, 1964; children—Jeffrey, Eric. Sales rep. IBM Corp., 1962-64; successively sales rep., product mktg. mgr., corp. product mgr. Burroughs Corp., Detroit, 1964-76; mgr. product mktg. Memorex Corp., Santa Clara, Calif., 1976-80, product program gen. mgr., 1980-81; dir. product mktg. Personal Computer div. Atari, Inc., Sunnyvale, Calif., 1981-83; dir. mktg., v.p. Durango Systems, San Jose, Calif., 1983-85; dir. mktg. ITTQUME Corp., San Jose, 1985-87; v.p. Optimem, Mountain View, Calif., 1987—; prof. Applied Mgmt. Center, Wayne State U., 1967-72, Walsh U., Troy, Mich., 1974-76, West Valley Coll., Saratoga, Calif., 1977-78. Trustee, pres. brotherhood Temple Emanuel, San Jose, Calif., 1979-80. Mem. IEEE, Soc. Applied Math., Alpha Epsilon Pi. Home: 1364 Box Canyon Rd San Jose CA 95120

LUTWAK, ERWIN, mathematician, educator; b. Chernovtsy, USSR, Feb. 9, 1946; came to U.S., 1956, naturalized, 1961; s. Herman and Anna (Halpern) L.; m. Nancy Ruth Selwyn, Mar. 7, 1968. BS, Poly. Inst. N.Y., Bklyn., 1968, MS, 1972; PhD, 1974. Instr. math. Poly. Inst. N.Y., Bklyn., 1975-77, asst. prof., 1977-81, assoc. prof., 1981-86, prof. 1986—. Mem. editorial bd.: Ency. of Math. and its Applications; co-editor: N.Y. Acad. Sci. publ., 1985; contbr. articles to sci. jours. Named Disting. Prof. of Yr., Student Govt., Poly. Univ., Bklyn., 1980. Mem. Am. Math. Soc., London Math. Soc., Math. Assn. Am., N.Y. Acad. Scis.(chmn. math. sect. 1988—), Sigma Xi. Home: 1623 11C 3d Ave New York NY 10128 Office: Poly U 333 Jay St Brooklyn NY 11201

LUTZ, CARL FREDERICK, inn keeper; b. Bklyn., Mar. 20, 1917; s. Frederick and Emily (Hirtreiter) L. B.A., Duke U., 1938. With R.H. Macys, N.Y.C., 1940-69; innkeeper, owner Logan Inn, New Hope, Pa., 1969—. Author play: The Princess and the Unicorn, 1965; designer sets and costumes Henry Street Playhouse, 1961-66. Mayor, New Hope, 1977-81. Bd. dirs Hist. Soc. New Hope, 1970-74. Mem. New Hope C. of C. (pres., 1975-77). Home: 16 Stoney Hill Rd PO Box 179 New Hope PA 18938

LUTZ, EDWARD OSCAR, accountant, educator; b. Bklyn., July 31, 1919; s. A. George and Selema (Holtzmann) L.; m. Alice M. Lessem, Jan. 3, 1944; children—Terry Jane Lutz Goldring, Richard Henry, William Weitzmann. B.S., Columbia U., 1940; postgrad. Golden Gate Law Sch., San Francisco, 1943-45. C.P.A., N.Y. Founding ptnr. Lutz and Carr, C.P.A.s, N.Y.C., 1949-69; instr. dept. econs. Bklyn. Coll., 1948-57, asst. prof., 1958-65, assoc. prof., 1965-69, prof., 1970—, dir. acctg. programs, 1981-84, chmn. dept. econs., 1984-88; exec. dir. Musical Arena Theatres Assn., N.Y.C., 1954-69; vis. prof. Yale U., 1970, New Sch. Social Research, 1963-64; founder, dir. Performing Arts Mgmt. Inst., N.Y.C., 1958-69; exec. dir. Ray Moore Found., Dennis, Mass., 1984-88; comptroller Universal Motors Co. of N.Am.; bd. dirs. Indian Motors Co. Co-author: Accounting Practice Manual, 1962; Attorney's Handbook-Accounting, 1965, 6th edit., 1988; Ency. of Auditing, 1971. Contbr. articles to profl. jours. Treas., bd. dirs. N.Y. ACLU, Bklyn., 1963-79; chmn. grievances Profl. Staff Congress, Bklyn., 1966-79. Served to 1st lt. U.S. Army, 1942-46. Named Outstanding Tchr. Grad. Students Bklyn. Coll., 1981. Mem. Am. Inst. C.P.A.s, N.Y. State Soc. C.P.A.s, Am. Acctg. Assn., AAUP, Nat. Assn. Accts. Jewish. Home: B2109 1655 Flatbush Ave Brooklyn NY 11210 Office: Dept Econs Brooklyn Coll Brooklyn NY 11210

LUTZ, JOHN SHAFROTH, lawyer, investment company general counsel; b. San Francisco, Sept. 10, 1943; s. Frederick Henry and Helena Morrison (Shafroth) L.; m. Elizabeth Boschen, Dec. 14, 1968; children—John Shafroth, Victoria. B.A., Brown U., 1965; J.D., U. Denver, 1971. Bar: Colo. 1971, U.S. Dist. Ct. Colo. 1971, U.S. Ct. Appeals (2d cir.) 1975, D.C. 1976, U.S. Supreme Ct. 1976, U.S. Dist. Ct. (so. dist.) N.Y. 1977, U.S. Tax Ct. 1977, U.S. Ct. Appeals (10th cir.) 1979, N.Y. 1984. Trial atty. Denver regional office U.S. SEC, 1971-74; spl. atty. organized crime, racketeering sect. U.S. Dept. Justice, So. Dist. N.Y., 1974-77; atty. Kelly, Stansfield and O'Donnell, Denver, 1977-78; gen. counsel Boettcher & Co., Denver, 1978-87; spl. counsel Kelly, Stansfield and O'Donnel, Denver, 1987—; allied mem. N.Y. Stock Exchange, 1978-87. Bd. dirs. Cherry Creek Improvement Assn., 1980-84, Spalding Rehab. Hosp., 1986—. Served to lt. (j.g.), USN, 1965-67. Mem. ABA, Colo. Bar Assn., Denver Bar Assn., Am. Law Inst., Securities Industry Assn. (state regulations com. 1982-86), Nat. Assn. Securities Dealers, Inc. (nat. arbitration com.), St. Nicholas Soc. N.Y.C. Republican. Episcopalian. Clubs: Denver Law, Denver Country, Denver Tennis, Denver Athletic, Rocky Mountain Brown (founder, past pres.); Racquet and Tennis (N.Y.C.). Home: 144 Race St Denver CO 80206 Office: Kelly Stansfield & O'Donnell 550 15th St Denver CO 80202

LUTZ, JOHN THOMAS, author; b. Dallas, Sept. 11, 1939; s. John Peter and Esther Jane (Gundelfinger) L.; m. Barbara Jean Bradley, Mar. 15, 1958; children—Steven, Jennifer, Wendy. Student Meramec Community Coll., 1965. Mem. Mystery Writers Am. (Scroll 1981, Edgar award 1986), Private-Eye Writers Am. (Shamus award 1982). Democrat. Author: The Truth of the Matter, 1971; Buyer Beware, 1976; Bonegrinder, 1977; Lazarus Man, 1979; Jericho Man, 1980; The Shadow Man, 1981; (with Steven Greene) Exiled, 1982; (with Bill Pronzini) The Eye, 1984; Nightlines, 1984; The Right to Sing the Blues, 1986; Tropical Heat, 1986; Ride the Lightning, 1987, Scorcher, 1987; Dancers Debt, 1988; contbr. short stories and articles to mystery and private-eye mags. Home and Office: 880 Providence Ave Webster Groves MO 63119

LUTZKER, EDYTHE, historian, writer; b. Berlin, Germany, June 25, 1904; d. Solomon and Sophia (Katz) Levine m. Philip Lutzker, June 14, 1924; children—Michael Arnold, Arthur Samuel, Paul William B.A., City Coll. N.Y., 1954; M.A., Columbia U., 1959. Bookkeeper, sec., exec. for bus. cos., N.Y.C., 1922-49; research asst. to Prof. Edward Rosen, City Coll. N.Y., 1951-54; author: Women Gain a Place in Medicine, 1969; Edith Pechey-Phipson M.D., Story of England's and India's Foremost Pioneering Woman Doctor, 1973, The Touchstone, A Biography of Waldemar Mordecai Haffkine. Pres. Child Care Center Parents Assn., 1943-51. Grantee Am. Philos. Soc., 1964, 65, Nat. Library of Medicine, 1966, 68-71, 72-74. Fellow Royal Soc. Medicine; mem. Am. Assn. History of Medicine, Am. Soc. for Microbiology, Soc. Internat. History Medicine, History of Sci. Soc., Am. Hist. Assn., Jewish Acad. Arts and Scis., Fawcett Soc. Democrat. Contbr. articles profl. publs., lectr. profl. orgns. Founder, v.p. Waldermar M. Haffkine Internat. Meml. Com. Home and Office: 201 W 89th St New York NY 10024

LUVISETTO, MARIA LUISA, computer scientist, high energy physics researcher; b. Asmara, Ethiopia, Jan. 10, 1941; d. Giannina Luvisetto; m. Ugolini Luvisetto, July 24, 1965. D. Physics, Inst. G. Marconi, Rome, 1963. From level 5 to level 2 computer scientist Nat. Inst. Nuclear Physics, Bologna, Italy, 1963-83, class 1 computer scientist, 1983—. Contbr. articles to profl. publs. Developer software, hardware. Mem. Am. Math. Soc. Office: Centro Nazionale Analisi, Fotogrammi-INFN, via Mazzini 2, 40 138 Bologna Italy

LUZZATI, MICHELE, medieval history professor; b. Turin, Piedmont, Italy, Mar. 21, 1939; s. Emilio and Clelia (Diena) L.; m. Francesca Maria Laganà, July 11, 1963; children: Tommaso, Chiara. Laurea in lettere, U. degli Studi Pisa (Italy), 1962; diploma in lettere, Sch. Normale Superiore, Pisa, 1962. Cert. Libera Docenza. Researcher U. Degli Studi, Pisa, 1963-64; lectr. U. degli Studi, Pisa, 1971-83; tchr. various schs., Pisa, 1965-68; researcher Inst. Storico Italiano per il Medioevo, Rome, 1969-70; asst. Sch. Normale Superiore, Pisa, 1970-83, assoc. prof., 1983-85; researcher Monumenta Germaniae Historica, Munich, Fed. Republic Germany, 1977-78; dir. d'etudes Ecole Hautes Etudes En S.S., Paris, 1983; prof. U. degli Studi, Sassari, Italy, 1985—. Author: Giovanni Villani, 1971, Una Guerra di Popolo, 1973, La Casa dell' Ebreo, 1985; editor (book) Storia di Piero Vaglienti, 1982. Fellow Assn. Italiana per lo Studio del Giudaismo; mem. Soc. Storica Pisana (sec. 1972-75, 78—). Home: Via Giunta Pisano 22, I-56100 Pisa Toscana Italy Office: U degli Studi Sassari, Dipartimento di Storia, 07100 Sassari Italy

LUZZATTO, EDGAR, lawyer; b. Milan, Italy, Nov. 25, 1914; s. Enrico and Maria (Norsa) L.; m. Mirella Del Monte, Apr. 4, 1948; children—Diana, Ariel, Kfir, Marco, Rossana. Dr. Chem. Engring., Polytechnic, Milan, 1935; Dr.Law, U. Milan, 1957. Patent agt. David Moscovitz, Atty., N.Y.C., 1946-48; sole practice, Milan, 1949-75, Ashkelon, Israel, 1976-81; sr. ptnr. Luzzatto & Luzzatto, Beer-Sheva, Israel, 1982—; lectr. Polytechnic, Milan, 1958-62; mem. Italian delegation to Lisbon Conf. for revision of Paris Conv., 1958. Author: Il Consulente Tecnico, 1954; Teoria e Tecnica Brevetti, 1960; The Industrial Property Factor in Industrial Research, 1978. Contbr. articles to profl. jours. Served with U.S. Army, 1941-46. Mem. Internat. Assn. for Protection Indsl. Property, Internat. Fedn. Indsl. Property Attys. Office: Mercaz Ha'Negev Bldg Suite 27, Metzada Rd PO Box 5352, Beer-Sheva 84 548, Israel

LWOFF, ANDRE MICHEL, microbiologist, virologist; b. Ainy-le-Chateau, France, May 8, 1902; s. Salomon and Marie (Siminovitch) L.; Licence es Scis. Naturelles, Paris, 1921, Dr. Med., 1927, Dr. Scis. Naturelles, 1932; hon. doctorates U. Chgo., Oxford U., 1959; m. Marguerite Bourdaleix, Dec. 5, 1925. Became fellow Pasteur Inst., Paris, 1921, asst., 1925, head lab., 1929, head dept. microbiol. physiology, 1938; prof. microbiology Faculty Scis., Sorbonne, Paris, 1959-68; head Cancer Research Inst., Villejeuf, 1968-72. Pres., French Family Planning Movement, 1970—. Recipient Nobel prize (with François Jacob and Jacques Monod) in medicine and physiology, 1965. Fellow Royal Soc. (fgn.); mem. N.Y. Acad. Scis., Nat. Acad. Scis., Academie des Sciences, 1976. Author: Problems of Morphogenesis in Ciliates: the Kinetosomes in Development, Reproduction and Evolution, 1950; Biological Order, 1962; also articles. Research on nature and fuction of growth factors, physiology of viruses; induction and repression of enzymes; explained phenomenon of lysogenic bacteria; demonstrated existence latent bacterial virus; condr. studies on protozoa nutrition; identified vitamins as microbial growth factors, demonstrated that vitamins function as co-enzymes. Home: 69 avenue de Suffren, 75007 Paris France Office: Inst Pasteur, 25 rue du Dr Roux, F-75024 Paris France *

LYASHKO, ALEKSANDR PAVLOVICH, Soviet state official; b. Ukraine, Nov. 30, 1915. Grad. Donetsk Indsl. Inst., 1947. Worked as mechanic and tchr., 1934-41; joined Communist Party Soviet Union, 1942; engr., dep. dept. head, dep. dir. and party sec., machine mfg. plant, 1945-52; 1st sec. Kramatorsk City Com. Ukrainian Communist Party, 1952-54, 1st sec. Donetsk Oblast Dist. Com., 1960-63; mem. draft bills commn., 1958-66; chmn. commn. communications and transport Soviet of Union, USSR Supreme Soviet, 1966-69; mem. Cen. Com. Ukrainian Communist Party, 1960—, sec., 1963-66, mem. Presidium and Politburo, 1963—, 2d sec., 1966-69, Politburo chmn. for industry, 1963-64; mem. Cen. Com. Communist Party Soviet Union, 1961—; chmn. presidium Supreme Soviet Ukrainian Soviet Socialist Republic, 1969-72, chmn. Council of Ministers, 1972-87; dep. chmn. presidium USSR Supreme Soviet, 1969-72. Served with Soviet Army, 1941-45. Decorated Order of Lenin. Address: Ukranian Communist Party, Ukrainian SSR, Kiev Ukrainian SSR USSR *

LYCOUDIS, MICHAEL DIONISIOS, film and television director; b. Athens, Greece, Dec. 10, 1953; s. Dionisios and Areti (Theodoratos) L. BA in Econs., ASOEE (Athens Grad. Sch. Econs. and Bus. Sci.), 1977; BA in Mass Media, Stavracos Coll., 1980; postgrad., Athens U., 1987—. TV and film dir. ERT (Hellenic Radio-TV), Athens, 1984—; researcher of econs. of mass media. Served as sgt. Greek Air Force, 1982-84. Recipient Drama Festival award, Greece, 1981, Dir.'s award EEC, Paris, 1982. Mem. Greek Dir.'s Soc., Econ. Chamber Greece. Home: Zisimopoulou 111-113, 175 61 Athens Greece Office: Hellenic Radio Tv, Mesogion 432, 153 42 Athens Greece

LYDIC, FRANK AYLSWORTH, retired riverman, poet; b. Farnam, Nebr., Jan. 22, 1909; s. Robert Johnston and Lula Ethel (Aylsworth) L.; B.F.A., Kearney (Nebr.) State Coll., 1931; m. Florence Faye Meadows, July 2, 1934 (dec. 1984); children—Marcelle, Bernice Joy (dec.), Robert Norman; m. Nellie Snyder Yost, Aug. 30, 1984. Tchr. schs., Calif., 1931-56; riverman various vessels Mississippi River, from 1961; now ret.; del. Nat. Maritime Union Conv., 1966, 69, 72, 76, named union poet laureate, nat. conv., 1980. Served in U.S. Mcht. Marine, 1943-48, 56-61. Mem. Western Writers Am. (asso.), Nebr. Writers Guild, Nebr. Poets Assn. (asso.), Ill. State Poetry Soc. (pres. 1983—), Chgo. Poets and Patrons, Little Big Horn Assos. Democrat. Author: Desert Lure, 1971, 3d edit., 1984; Rhymes of a Riverman, 1973; When My Stretch on the River is Done, 1974; Nebraska! Oh Nebraska, 1975; San Francisco Revisited, 1976; At the Little Bighorn, 1976; The Far West's Race with Death, 1979; Rhymed Lines from the River, 1980; Comanche! Oh Comanche!, 1982; Custer Controversies, 1983; In Praise of Texas Jack, 1984, The Bones of Sitting Bull, 1986, He Saved the Buffalo, 1987. Home: 1505 W D St North Platte NE 69101

LYELL, EDWARD HARVEY, business educator; b. San Francisco, Nov. 11, 1944; s. Aubrey Sheridan and Ila Mae (Franklin) L.; B.A., San Francisco State U., 1968, M.B.A., 1970; D. Bus. Adminstrn., U. Colo., 1977; 1 son, Kelly; stepchildren—Erin, Heather Creagh. Asst. dean research San Francisco State U., 1968-70, part-time faculty mem., 1969-70; part-time faculty mem. U. Colo., 1970-76, 78, Community Coll., Denver, 1973-74, Met. State U., 1977; dir. policy analysis Colo. Commn. on Higher Edn., 1973-76; asst. prof. Grad. Sch. Pub. Affairs, asso. dir. info. sci./genetic resources U. Colo., Boulder, 1978-79; asst. prof. bus. and econs. Colo. Coll., Colorado Springs, 1979-81; asso. prof. bus. Met. State Coll., Denver, 1981—; pres. Colo. Planning and Mgmt. Systems, Inc., Boulder. Scoutmaster Boy Scouts Am., 1977-84; guide White Water River, 1974—; del. Boulder County Democratic Conv., 1976-86, Colo. Dem. Conv., 1976-86; mem. issues com. Colo. Dem. Com., 1981—; mem. Colo. Gov.'s Sci. and Tech. Adv. Council, 1980-85; statewide candidate Colo. Bd. Edn., 1982, 88. Mem. AAAS, Am. Assn. Higher Edn., Am. Econ. Assn., Am. Ednl. Research Assn., Am. Mktg. Assn., Assn. Instnl. Research, Inst. Mgmt. Sci., Acad. Ind. Scholars, World Future Soc. Quaker. Author: Education Evaluation and Assessment System for You, 1972; contbr. articles to profl. jours. Office: Met State Coll Bus Sch Mgmt Dept 1006 11th St Denver CO 80204

LYKOUDIS, MARIA-ZOE, archaeologist, educator; b. Athens Attica, Greece, Nov. 18, 1927; d. Nicholas George and Helene (Emmanuel) Komis; m. Paul S. Lykoudis, Nov. 26, 1953 (div. 1984) 1 son, Michael N.; Diploma in French Lit., Inst. Francais, Athens, 1949; BA in Classics and Archaeology, U. Athens, 1950; MA in Archaeology, Bryn Mawr Coll., 1951; postgrad., Am. Sch. Classical Studies, Athens, 1951-52, Radcliffe Coll., 1953-54. Lectr. Office of Greek Tourism, Athens, 1952-53; vol. tchr. Purdue U. and various other schs., 1964-84; instr. Lafayette (Ind.) Mus. Art, 1982-84; researcher roots of Greek cooking and alimentation Lafayette, 1982-85, Athens, 1985—. Contbr. articles to textbooks and jours., short stories for children to various mags. Vol. Democratic Party, Lafayette, 1964-84. Fulbright travel grantee, 1950; scholar Bryn Mawr Coll., 1950, Greek State Found., 1953-54. Mem. Am. Archaeol. Inst. Greek Orthodox. Home and Office: Aristippou 50, 10676 Athens Greece

LYMAN, DAVID, lawyer; b. Washington, Sept. 25, 1936; s. Albert Moses and Freda (Ring) L.; m. Nancy Wilson Ternent, Feb. 7, 1965 (div. May 1974); 1 child, Jessica Kim; m. Yubol Pumsathit, Nov. 10, 1979. B.S. in Elec. Engring., Duke U., 1958; cert. U.S. Naval Submarine Sch., 1960; J.D., U. Calif.-San Francisco, 1965; postgrad. in fgn. and comparative law Columbia U., 1974. Bar: Calif. 1966; registered elec. engr., Thailand. Assoc. Fitzsimmons & Petris, Oakland, Calif., 1965-66; Lempres & Seyranian, Oakland, 1966-67; assoc. ptnr. Tilleke & Gibbins, R.O.P., Advocates and Solicitor, Bangkok, 1967-84, ptnr., 1984—; dir. Goodyear (Thailand) Ltd., Bangkok, Data Gen. (Thailand) Ltd., Ciba Geigy (Thailand) Ltd., Rena Ware Thailand Ltd., FMC (Thailand) Ltd., Nat. Semicondr. (Bangkok) Ltd., SSCI Systems (Thailand) Ltd., Triumph Internat. (Thailand) Ltd.; founding mem. Prime Minister Thailand's Fgn. Investment Adv. Council, 1975. Contbr. articles to profl. publs. Chmn. King Bhumiphol Rama IX Park U.S. Geodesic Dome Pavillion Com., 1987—. Served with U.S. Navy; lt. comdr. Res. Recipient U.S. Naval Inst. prize, 1958, Am. Jurisprudence prize, 1965, U.S. Dept. Commerce cert., 1987; Paul Harris fellow, 1987. Mem. Am. C. of C. in Thailand (bd. govs. 1973—, v.p. 1974, 83-85, pres. 1975, 86), Am. C. of C. (vice chmn. Asia Pacific council 1975-77, 85-86, bd. dirs. 1975-86), Thai Bd. Trade (bd. dirs. 1975, 86), Fgn. Chambers Commerce Working Group (sec. Bangkok 1982-85), ABA, Calif. Bar Assn., World Peace Through Law, Asian Patent Attys. Assn., Internat. Bar Assn., Thailand Trademark Assn., World Econ. Forum, U.S. Naval Inst. (life), 999 Wildlife Trust, Wildlife Fund Thailand, Chaine Des Rotisseurs (charge de mission), Jewish Assn. Thailand, Nat. Trust (U.K.), Tau Epsilon Phi, Phi Alpha Delta. Republican. Jewish. Clubs: Royal Bangkok Sports, Heritage (founder gov. 1985), Mariner's Fgn. Corrs. of Thailand. Lodge: Rotary (sec., v.p. Bangkok 1982, 84), Community Services of Bangkok (founder, v.p., bd. dirs. 1985—). Avocations: scuba diving, swimming. Home: 5/2 Soi Chidlom, Off Ploenchit Rd, Bangkok 10500, Thailand Office: Tilleke and Gibbons ROP, 64/1 Soi Ton Son Ploenchit Rd, Bangkok 10500, Thailand

LYMAN, GARY HERBERT, cell biologist, cancer researcher, educator; b. Buffalo, Feb. 24, 1946; s. Leonard Samuel and Beatrice Louise L.; m. Carolyn Gertrude Zalewski, Nov. 21, 1979; children by previous marriage—Stephen Leonard, Christopher Henry, Robert Dean. B.A., SUNY-Buffalo, 1968, M.D., 1972; M.P.H., Harvard U., 1982. Diplomate: Am. Bd. Internal Medicine (med. oncology, hematology). Resident in medicine U. N.C.-Chapel Hill, 1972-74; fellow in oncology Roswell Park Meml. Inst., Buffalo, 1974-77; research instr. medicine SUNY Med. Sch.-Buffalo, 1974-77; mem. faculty U. South Fla. Coll. Medicine, Tampa, 1977—, assoc. prof. medicine, 1980-86, prof. medicine, 1986—, dir. div. med. oncology, 1979—, chief medicine H. Lee Moffitt Cancer Ctr. and Research Inst. Co-author: Cancer Chemotherapy Therapeutics Agents: Handbook of Clinical Data, 2d edit., 1982; Contbr. articles to profl. jours., chpts. to books. Spl. fellow Leukemia Soc. Am., 1976-77; postdoctoral fellow biostats. Harvard U., 1981-82; spl. clin. fellow Roswell Park Meml. Inst., Buffalo, 1975-76. Fellow ACP, Am. Coll. Preventive Medicine, Am. Coll. Clin. Pharm.; mem. Physicians for Social Responsibility. Subspecialties: Oncology; Epidemiology. Current work: Cancer clinical trials, biostatistics, epidemiology, clinical decision analysis. Office: 12902 Magnolia Dr Tampa FL 33612

LYMAN, HOWARD B(URBECK), psychologist; b. Athol, Mass., Feb. 12, 1920; s. Stanley B(urbeck) and Ruth Mary (Gray) L.; A.B., Brown U., 1942; M.A., U. Minn., 1948; Ph.D., U. Ky., 1951; m. Patricia Malone Taylor, May 4, 1966; children—David S., Nancy M., D. Jane Lyman Paraskevopoulos; stepchildren—Richard P. Taylor, Martha C. Kitsinis, Robert M. Taylor, David P. Taylor. Acting dir. student personnel E. Tex. State Tchrs. Coll., Commerce, 1948-49; counselor, research asst. univ. personnel office U. Ky., Lexington, 1949-51; research psychologist tests and measurements U.S. Naval Exam. Center, Norfolk, Va. and Gt. Lakes, Ill., 1951-52; asst. prof. psychology U. Cin., 1952-62, asso. prof., 1962-85 , prof. emeritus, 1986—; dir. Acad. Edn. and Research in Profl. Psychology Ohio 1975-84. Served with AUS, 1942-46. Licensed psychologist, Ohio. Fellow Am. Psychol. Assn.; mem. Ohio Psychol. Assn. (dir. 1960-84 , Distinguished Service award 1974), Midwestern, Cin. psychol. assns., Assn. Measurement and Evaluation in Guidance, Nat. Council Measurement in Edn., Cheiron Soc., Psi Chi. Author: Single Again, 1971; Test Scores and What They Mean, 4th edit., 1985; editor Ohio Psychologist, 1967-79. Home: 3422 Whitfield Ave Cincinnati OH 45220

LYMAN, PRINCETON NATHAN, foreign service officer; b. San Francisco, Nov. 20, 1935; s. Arthur and Gertrude (Kramer) L.; m. Helen Carolyn Ermann, July 7, 1957; children: Cindy, Sheri, Lori. B.A., U. Calif.-Berkeley, 1957; M.A., Harvard U., 1959, Ph.D., 1961. Program officer U.S. Aid Mission, Seoul, Korea, 1964-67; research assoc. Harvard U., Cambridge, Mass., 1967-68; dir. civic participation div. AID, Washington, 1968-71, equal employment counselor, 1969-71, dir. devel. resources for Africa, 1971-76; dir. U.S. Aid Mission, Addis Ababa, Ethiopia, 1976-78; dep. asst. sec. Africa Bur. U.S. Dept. State, Washington, 1981-86; Ambassador to Nigeria 1986—; professorial lectr. Johns Hopkins U., Washington, 1980-86. Contbr. articles and book chpts. to profl. pubs. Recipient AID Meritorious Honor award, 1966; recipient Superior Honor award, 1970, 86. Mem. Am. Fgn. Service Assn. (v.p. 1969-70, bd. dirs.). *

LYMAN, RICHARD WALL, foundation executive, historian; b. Phila., Oct. 18, 1923; s. Charles M. and Aglae (Wall) L.; m. Elizabeth D. Schauffler, Aug. 20, 1947; children: Jennifer P., Holly Lyman Antolini, Christopher M., Timothy R. B.A., Swarthmore Coll., 1947, LL.D., 1974; M.A., Harvard U., 1948, Ph.D., 1954, LL.D., 1980; LL.D., Washington U., St. Louis, 1971, Mills Coll., 1972, Yale U., 1975; L.H.D., U. Rochester, 1975. Teaching fellow, tutor Harvard U., 1949-51; instr. Swarthmore Coll., 1952-53; instr., then asst. prof. Washington U., St. Louis, 1953-58; mem. faculty Stanford U., 1958—, prof. history, 1962-80, 88—, Sterling prof., 1980—, assoc. dean Sch Humanities and Scis., 1964-66, v.p., provost, 1967-70, pres., 1970-80, pres. emeritus, 1980—, dir. Inst. Internat. Studies, 1988—; pres. Rockefeller Found., 1980-88; spl. corr. The Economist, London, 1953-66; bd. dirs. Council on Founds., 1982 , Independent Sector, 1980—, chair, 1983-86; Nat. Com. on U.S.-China Relations, 1986—; dir. IBM, Chase Manhattan Bank. Author: The First Labour Government, 1957; editor: (with Lewis W. Spitz) Major Crises in Western Civilization, 1965; mem. editorial bd. Jour. Modern History, 1958-61. Mem. Nat. Council on Humanities, 1976-82, vice chmn., 1980-82; chmn. Commn. on Humanities, 1978-80; trustee Rockefeller Found., 1976—, Carnegie Found. Advancement of Teaching, 1976-82; bd. dirs. Nat. Assn. Ind. Colls. and Univs., 1976-77; chmn. Assn. Am. Univs., 1978-79. Served with USAAF, 1943-46. Decorated officier Legion of Honor; Fulbright fellow London Sch. Econs., 1951-52, hon. fellow, 1978—; Guggenheim fellow, 1959-60. Fellow Royal Hist. Soc.; mem. Am. Acad. Arts and Scis., Am. Hist. Assn., Council on Fgn. Relations, Conf. Brit. Studies, Phi Beta Kappa. Office: Rockefeller Found 1133 Ave of the Americas New York NY 10036

LYMPANY, MOURA, concert pianist; b. Saltash, Cornwall, Eng., Aug. 18, 1916; d. John and Beatrice Johnstone; educated in Belgium, Austria, Eng.; pvt. studies with Mathilde Verne; m. Colin Defries, 1944 (div. 1950); m. 2d, Bennett Korn, 1951 (div. 1961); 1 son, dec. First performance, Harrogate, Eng., 1929; has played in U.S., Can., S. Am., Australia, N.Z., India and most European countries including USSR; recs. for Decca, HMV. Recipient 2d prize Ysaye Internat. Piano Competition, 1938; decorated Comdr. Order of the Crown, Belgium, 1980, Comdr. Order Brit. Empire, Fellow Royal Acad. Music. Address: care Ibbs & Tillett, 450/452 Edgware Rd, London W2 England *

LYNCH, DELL MARIE RYAN, civic worker, writer, artist; b. Scranton, Pa.; d. Cornelius James and Alice Wall (Burke) Ryan; BA, Manhattanville Coll., 1922; m. James Merriman Lynch, Apr. 6, 1926 (dec. Feb. 1982); 1 child, Nathaniel Merriman. Exhibited in group shows Pala Art Show, Showcase of Arts, Bank Am. Exhibit, Fireside Restaurant Exhibit, Country Squire Exhibit; one-woman show Woman's Club, 1979; publicity chmn. Santa Barbara County Med. Aux., 1947-48; co-chmn. Garden sect. Palomar Meml. Hosp. Aux., 1958-61; bd. mem. Friends of Leonell Strong Cancer Found., 1969-70; v.p. Yole Dames, 1928-29, Friends of Pala Indian Mission Sch., 1967-72, Friends of Escondido Library, 1972-73; chmn. Showcase of Arts Gallery, 1967-68; project chmn. Exceptional Girl Scouts U.S.A., 1957-58. Recipient award for over 20 yrs. vol. service Palomar Meml. Hosp., 1981; hon. mention state poetry award Women's Club, 1980. Mem. Felicita Found. (life), Escondido Hist. Soc. (life), Palomar Meml. Hosp. Aux. (life), Friends of Escondido Library (life), Escondido Art Assn. (life), Chaparral Poets, AAUW (life; area rep. for cultural interests 1964-65, courtesy chmn. 1968-77, cultural interests chmn. 1977-78, creative writing chmn. 1978-81, cert. of appreciation 1977-78). Clubs: Woman's (chmn. creative writing 1977-81, creative writing chmn. 1977-81, , cert. of appreciation 1977-78, 1st place poetry, writing contest 1978, 1st, 2d, 3d places poetry, 1979, 3 1st place awards for poetry, 2d place for prose 1980, 1st place and 2d place for poetry 1981), Escondido Garden (therapy co-chmn., Cert. Appreciation, 1986). Author (poetry) Bright Orbits, 1974, Have A Nice Day, 1980, Challenge, 1984; contbr. poems to poetry anthologies and jours. AAUW Ednl. Found. grad. student fellowship named in her honor, 1977. Home: 810 Omar Dr Escondido CA 92025

LYNCH, JOHN BROWN, plastic surgeon, educator; b. Akron, Ohio, Feb. 5, 1929; s. John A. and Eloise L.; student Vanderbilt U., 1946-49; M.D., U. Tenn., 1952; m. Jean Crane, July 2, 1950; children—John Brown, Margaret Frances Lynch Callihan. Rotating intern John Gaston Hosp., Memphis, Tenn., 1953-54; resident in gen. surgery U. Tex. Med. Br., Galveston, 1956-59, resident in plastic surgery, 1959-62, instr., 1962, asst. prof. surgery, 1962-67, asso. prof., 1967-72, prof., 1972-73; prof., plastic surgery, chmn. dept. plastic surgery Vanderbilt U. Med. Center, 1973—. Served as capt. USAF, 1954-56. Diplomate Am. Bd. Plastic Surgery (chmn.). Fellow ACS; mem. Singleton Surg. Soc. (pres. 1982-83), AMA, Am. Soc. Plastic and Reconstructive Surgeons (pres. 1983-84), Am. Assn. Plastic Surgeons, Plastic Surgery Research Council, Am. Cleft Palate Assn., Am. Burn Assn., Soc. Head and Neck Surgeons, Internat. Burn Assn., Pan Am. Med. Assn., Am. Cancer Soc. (pres. Galveston County, Tex., Chpt. 1968), So. Med. Assn. (pres.-elect 1983-84), Tenn. med. Assn., Nashville Acad. Medicine, Tenn. Soc. Plastic Surgeons, Southeastern Soc. Plastic Surgeons, Southeastern Surg. Soc., H. William Scott, Jr. Soc., Nashville Surg. Soc., Am. Soc. Maxillofacial Surgeons, So. Surg. Assn., Am. Surg. Assn., Sigma Xi. Contbr. numerous articles to med. publs.; editor: (with S.R. Lewis) Symposium on the Treatment of Burns, 1973. Home: 2312 Valley Brook Rd Nashville TN 37215 Office: Vanderbilt Hosp Room S-2221 Nashville TN 37232

LYNCH, PATRICIA GATES, ambassador; b. Newark, N.J., Apr. 20, 1926; d. William Charles and Mary Frances (McNamee) Lawrence; m. Mahlon Eugene Gates, Dec. 19, 1942 (div. 1972); children: Pamela Townley Gates Sprague, Lawrence Alan; m. William Dennis Lynch. Student, Dartmouth Inst., 1975. Broadcaster Sta. WFAX-Radio, Falls Ch., Va., 1958-68; pub. TV host Sta. WETA, Washington, 1967-68; broadcaster NBC-Radio, Europe, Iran, USSR, 1960-61; internat. broadcaster, producer Voice of Am., Washington, 1962-69; staff asst. to First Lady The White House, Washington, 1969-70; host Breakfast Show, Morning show, 1970-86; U.S. ambassador to Madagascar and the Comoros 1986—; worldwide lectr., 196-86; adv. com. Ind. Fed. Savs. and Loan Assn., Washington, 1970-86. Author stories on Am. for English teaching dept. Radio Sweden, 1967-68, others on internat. broadcasting. Chairperson internat. service com. Washington chpt. ARC, 1979-68. Grantee USIA, 1983; recipient Pub. Service award U.S. Army, 1960. Mem. Council Am. Ambassadors, Am. Women in Radio and TV (pres. 1966-67), Am. News Women's Club. Republican. Episcopalian. Clubs: Sulgrave (Washington). Office: care Dept State Antananarivo Madagascar Washington DC 20520-2040

LYNCH, PAUL VINCENT, safety engineer; b. Bklyn., Apr. 11, 1932; s. John Andrew and Mary Catherine L.; BA, St. Anselm's Coll., Manchester, N.H., 1954; postgrad. Fordham U. Law Sch., 1958-59, U. N.H., 1969-71; m. Muriel Dubuc, Jan. 25, 1956; children: David, Marianne. Reg. profl. engr. in safety engring. Corp. ins. specialist Allied Chem. Corp., 1959-66; asst. to dir. risk mgmt. Am. Metal Climax, Inc., N.Y.C., 1966-68; lectr. risk mgmt., adminstr. safety U. N.H., Durham, 1969-71; asso. prof. safety N.H. Vocat.-Tech. Coll., 1971-75; pres. Lynch Assocs., Inc., cons., Pittsfield, N.H., 1972-75; regional safety officer GSA, 1976-79; safety mgr. for Calif., U.S. Bur. Land Mgmt., Sacramento, 1979-86, chief safety mgmt., Washington, 1986—; v.p. N.H. Safety Council, 1972-74; instr. safety mgmt. Am. River Coll., Sacramento, 1975-76. Active, Boy Scouts Am., 1962—, dist. vice chmn. Nat. Capitol Area council, 1987—, membership chmn., mem. exec. bd. Golden Empire Council, 1978-86, dist. chmn., 1984-85. Served with U.S. Army, 1955-57. Recipient Silver Beaver award Boy Scouts Am., 1977. Mem. Am. Soc. Safety Engrs. (pres. Sacramento chpt. 1981-82; regional v.p.; nat. long range planning com.; chmn. legis. affairs com., adminstr. pub. sector div., named div. Safety Profl. of Yr. 1986, Sacramento chpt. Safety Profl. Yr. 1986), Am. Indsl. Hygiene Assn., Vets of Safety (pres. Sacramento chpt. 1984-85). Lodge: Rotary (sec. Pittsfield club 1970-73). Author, editor govt. publs.

LYNCH, PETER JOHN, dermatologist; b. Mpls., Oct. 22, 1936; s. Francis Watson and Viola Adeline (White) L.; m. Barbara Ann Lanzi, Jan. 18, 1964; children: Deborah, Timothy. Student, St. Thomas Coll., 1954-57; B.S., U. Minn., 1958, M.D., 1961. Intern U. Mich. Med. Center, 1961-62, resident in dermatology, 1962-65; clin. instr. U. Minn., 1965; chief dermatology and venereal disease Martin Army Hosp., Columbus, Ga., 1966-68; asst. prof. to asso. prof. dermatology U. Mich. Med. Center, 1968-73; asso. prof. to prof. dermatology U. Ariz., Tucson, 1973-86; chief sect. dermatology U. Ariz., 1973-86, asso. head dept. internal medicine, 1977-86; prof., head dermatology U. Minn. Med. Ctr., Mpls., 1986—. Author: (with S. Epstein) Burckhardt's Atlas and Manual of Dermatology and Venereology, 1977, Dermatology for the House Officer, 1982, 2d edit., 1987. Served with AUS, 1966-68. Decorated Army Commendation Medal; recipient Disting. Service award for faculty U. Mich., 1970, Disting. Faculty award U. Ariz., 1981. Mem. Am. Acad. Dermatology (dir. 1974-78), Assn. Profs. Dermatology (dir. 1976-80), Internat. Soc. Study of Vulvar Disease (dir. 1976-79, pres. 1983), Soc. Investigative Dermatology, Am. Soc. Dermatopathology, Am. Venereal Disease Assn., Am. Bd. Dermatology (bd. dirs. 1984—), Gougerot Soc. (Bronze medal award), Alpha Omega Alpha. Democrat. Roman Catholic. Home: 863 Osceola St Saint Paul MN 55105 Office: U Minn Med Ctr 420 Delaware St Box 98 Minneapolis MN 55455

LYNCH, WALTER KENNETH, textile engineering educator; b. Lincoln County, N.C., Apr. 17, 1929; s. Walter R. and Eva (Kiser) L.; m. Martha Anne Jeffreys, Aug. 18, 1951; children—Carol, Kaye. B.S., N.C. State U., 1959, M.S., 1966; Ph.D., U. Leeds (Eng.), 1971. Head dept. Superior Yarn Mills, Mount Holly, Inc., 1952-56; textile engr. Union Carbide Corp., South Charleston, W.Va., 1959-62; instr., asst. prof., assoc. prof. N.C. State U., Raleigh, 1964-75; prof., head dept. textile engring. Auburn (Ala.) U., 1975—; vis. lectr. U. Leeds 1969-71. Burlington Industries scholar, 1957-59. Mem. Rayon Acetate Council (chmn. bd. dirs.), Nat. Council Textile Edn. (pres.), Textile Quality Control Assn., Assn. Textile Technologists, Am. Assn. Textile Chemists and Colorists, Acad. Mgmt. Methodist. Club: Saugahatchee Country. Lodge: Lions (sec.). Office: Textile Engring Dept Auburn Univ Auburn AL 36849

LYNE, STEPHEN RICHARD, diplomat; b. Fall River, Mass., May 20, 1935; s. Horace James and Anne (Bromley) L.; m. Mary duBignon Henry, June 20, 1959; children: Deborah Elizabeth, Richard James. BA, Amherst Coll., 1958; MA, Stanford U., 1960, PhD, 1965. Fgn. service officer Washington, Gabon, New Zealand, Vietnam and Cambodia, 1961-74; Am. Polit. Sci. Assn. Congl. intern U.S. Congress, Washington, 1974-75; dep. chief mission U.S. Embassy, Algiers, Algeria, 1975-77; sr. seminar Dept. State, Washington, 1977-78, office dir., 1978-80; dep. chief mission U.S. Embassy, Canberra, Australia, 1980-84, Beirut, Lebanon, 1984-85; adj. prof. Boston U., 1985-86; ambassador U.S. Embassy, Accra, Ghana, 1986—. Recipient Pres.'s Meritorious Honor award, 1986. Episcopalian. Office: US Ambassador to Ghana care US State Dept Washington DC 20520

LYNETT, LAWRENCE WILSON, electronics company executive; b. N.Y.C., Sept. 11, 1921; s. James Degge and Lillian (Lonquist) L.; 1 dau., Michele. B.B.A., Manhattan Coll., 1943. With IBM Corp., 1946—, mgr. adminstrv. research, 1966—; assoc. adminstrv. mgmt. Simmons Coll., 1966—; Mem. Nat. Adv. Com. for Bus. Edn. Curriculum Devel., 1973—. Chmn. editorial bd.: Impact, 1977—; mem. editorial bd. Adminstrv. Mgmt. Mag., 1983—. Chmn. bd. trustees AMS Research Found. Served to lt. USNR, World War II, PTO. Decorated Navy Commendation ribbon; Presdl. Commendation for devel. adminstrv. mgmt. program for U.S. Govt. Mgrs., 1966. Mem. Adminstrv. Mgmt. Soc. (internat. pres. 1966-67, dir. 1980-83, Diamond Mgmt. key 1963, Internat. Mgmt. award 1967, Internat. Ambassador award 1985, Silver medal for mgmt. achievements and outstanding service, 1988), Office Execs. Assn. N.Y. (pres. 1960-61, Leadership award 1961), Am. Mgmt. Assn. (v.p. gen. services div., dir. 1975-87). Home: Putnam Green Greenwich CT 06830 Office: IBM Corp Old Orchard Rd Armonk NY 10504

LYNFORD, JEFFREY HAYDEN, investment banker; b. N.Y.C., Oct. 7, 1947; s. Franklyn Jerome and Ruth (Kahn) L.; m. Carol Lynford, Sept. 2, 1974; children: Victoria, Andrew. BA, SUNY, Buffalo, 1969; M in Pub. Affairs, Princeton U., 1971; JD, Fordham U., 1975. Bar: N.Y. V.p. Internat. Paper Realty, N.Y.C., 1974-77; assoc. White, Weld & Co., Inc., N.Y.C., 1977-78; mng. dir. A.G. Becker Paribas, N.Y.C., 1978-84; ptnr. Bear Stearns, N.Y.C., 1984-86; chmn. bd. Wellsford Group, Inc., 1986—; mem. investment com. Calif. Fed. Syndications, Inc., Los Angeles, 1984—; bd. dirs. Keaau Macadamia Corp., Honolulu, 1983—; chmn. Quality Hill Redevel. Corp., Kansas City, 1985—; trustee Lynford Family Charitable Trust, N.Y.C., 1985. Trustee Nat. Trust for Hist. Preservation, 1987; bd. dirs. Alan Guttmacher Inst., N.Y.C., 1987—. Mem. ABA, N.Y. Bar Assn. Democrat. Club: Princeton (N.Y.C.).

LYNG, RICHARD EDMUND, secretary of agriculture; b. San Francisco, June 29, 1918; s. Edmund John and Sarah Cecilia (McGrath) L.; m. Bethyl Ball, June 25, 1944; children: Jeanette (Mrs. Gary Robinson), Marilyn (Mrs. Daniel O'Connell). Ph.B. cum laude, U. Notre Dame, 1940. With Ed J. Lyng Co., Modesto, Calif., 1945-66; pres. Ed J. Lyng Co., 1949-66; dir.

Calif. Dept. Agr., 1967-69; asst. sec. Dept. Agr., Washington, 1969-73; dep. sec. Dept. Agr., 1981-85; vice chmn. Commodity Credit Corp., 1981-85; pres. Lyng & Lesher, Inc., Washington, 1985-86; Sec. of Agr. Dept. Agr., Washington, 1986—; pres. Am. Meat Inst., Washington, 1973-79; pvt. cons., 1980; dir. Commodity Credit Corp., 1969-73, Nat. Livestock and Meat Bd., 1973-76, Tri-Valley Growers, 1975-81; bd. govs. Refrigeration Research Found., 1974-77, Chgo. Merc. Exchange; chmn. food industry trade adv. com. Commerce Dept.; chmn. U.S. Child Nutrition Adv. Com., 1971-73; mem. animal health com. Nat. Acad. Sci. Chmn. Stanislaus County (Calif.) Republican Central Com., 1961-62; dir. agr. div. Pres. Ford Com., 1976; co-dir. farm and food div. Reagan-Bush Campaign, 1980; trustee Farm Found. Served with AUS, 1941-45. Roman Catholic. Clubs: Washington Golf and Country, Capitol Hill. Lodge: Rotary. Office: Dept Agr Office of the Sec 14th & Independence Ave SW Washington DC 20250

LYNN, JAMES T., insurance company executive, lawyer; b. Cleve., Feb. 27, 1927. B.A., Western Res. U., 1948; LL.B., Harvard U., 1951. Bar: Ohio 1951, D.C. 1977. Gen. counsel U.S. Dept. Commerce, 1969-71; under sec. U.S. Dept. State, 1971-73; sec. HUD, 1973-75; dir. Office Mgmt. and Budget, 1975-77; asst. Pres. U.S., 1975-77; with Jones, Day, Reavis & Pogue, 1951-69, 77-84, ptnr., 1960-79, mng. ptnr., 1979-84; with Aetna Life & Casualty Co., Hartford, Conn., 1984—, vice chmn., 1984-85, chmn., 1985—, chief exec. officer, from 1985, now also pres., also bd. dirs. Case editor Harvard Law Rev., 1950-51. Served with USNR, 1945-46. Mem. Phi Beta Kappa. Office: Aetna Casualty & Surety Co 151 Farmington Ave Hartford CT 06156 *

LYNN, JOHN WARREN, retail company executive; b. Bklyn., Mar. 4, 1921; s. Thomas Robert and Olga (Clemens) L.; m. Adele Grant, Feb. 5, 1944; children: Suzanne Lynn Falkenbush, Dianne Lynn Nofi, Robert, Thomas. Student, Syracuse U., 1939-41. Vice pres. Mid-Altantic region F.W. Woolworth Co., N.Y.C., 1965-67; v.p. Northeastern region F.W. Woolworth Co., 1968, corp. v.p. sales and advt., 1969, v.p. merchandising, 1970-74, sr. v.p. merchandising, 1975-76, exec. v.p., 1977-78, pres. Woolworth/Woolco div., 1978-79, sr. exec. v.p., 1979-80, vice chmn. bd., 1980-82, chmn. bd., 1982-87, dir., 1970—, also chmn. exec. com.; dir. Borden Inc., F.W. Woolworth Co. Ltd., Can., Woolworth Mexicana S.A. de C.V. Served with USAAF, World War II. Decorated Purple Heart; decorated Air medal with 8 oak leaf clusters. Mem. Newcomen Soc. Clubs: Boca Raton Hotel, Boca West. Office: FW Woolworth Co Woolworth Bldg 233 Broadway New York NY 10007 *

LYNN, THEODORE STANLEY, lawyer; b. N.Y.C., Aug. 2, 1937; s. Irving and Sydell (Gorlie) L.; m. Linda Isabel Freeman, July 21, 1968; children—Jessica, Douglas. AB, Columbia U., 1958; LLB, Harvard U., 1961; LLM, NYU, 1962; SJD, George Washington U., 1972. Law clerk U.S. Tax Ct., Washington, 1962-64; teaching fellow in law George Washington U., Washington, 1963-64; assoc. Webster & Sheffield, N.Y.C., 1964-68, ptnr., mgmt. com. mem., 1969—; cons. Adminstrv. Conf. U.S., Washington, 1974-75; founding counsel Pension Real Estate Assn., Washington, 1981-84. Author: Real Estate Limited Partnerships, 2d edit., 1985, Real Estate Investment Trusts, 1987; contbr. articles to profl. jours. Sec., Manhattan Sch. of Dance, N.Y.C., 1974—; spl. asst. Mayor John V. Lindsay, N.Y.C. 1966-69; trustee Birch Wathen Sch., N.Y.C., 1976—; dir. Plaza 400 Owners Corp., Manhattan Community Bd. #6, N.Y.C., 1977—, Dungannon Found. Conn., 1986. Mem. Fed. Bar Council, Assn. Bar City N.Y., ABA, N.Y. State Bar Assn. Clubs: Met., Univ., Can., Town Tennis, Harvard. Office: Webster & Sheffield 237 Park Ave New York NY 10017

LYNN, WILLIAM MAX, financial administrator; b. Fox, Okla., July 20, 1927; s. Warren A. and Mary (Johnston) L.; B.S., UCLA, 1952; m. Elinor Jane Treiber, Feb. 28, 1953; children—Kevin Edward-Holmes, Daniel Warren, Nancy Edith, Colleen Erin. Mem. publicity dept. Metro-Goldwyn-Mayer Studios, Culver City, Calif., 1952-53; dir. bus. and finance United Ch. of Religious Sci., Los Angeles, 1953-82, asst. chief exec. officer, 1982-85, dir. devel., 1985-87; exec. dir. Sci. of Mind Found., 1987—; lectr., cons. ch. adminstrn. Served with AUS, 1945-48. Mem. Am. Mgmt. Assn., Am. Soc. for Tng. and Devel., Conf. Bd., Nat. Assn. Ch. Bus. Adminstrs., Town Hall, Newcomen Soc. Am., Acacia. Republican. Club: City (San Marino). Lodge: Rotary. Mem. United Ch. Religious Sci. Home: 2100 El Molino Ave San Marino CA 91108 Office: Sci Mind Found 3251 W 6th St Los Angeles CA 90020

LYON, JAMES BURROUGHS, lawyer; b. N.Y.C., May 11, 1930; s. Francis Murray and Edith May (Strong) L. BA, Amherst Coll., 1952; LLB, Yale U., 1955. Bar: Conn. 1955, U.S. Tax Ct. 1970. Asst. football coach Yale U., 1953-55; assoc. Murtha, Cullina, Richter and Pinney (and predecessor), Hartford, Conn., 1956-61, ptnr., 1961—; mem. adv. com., lectr. and session leader NYU Inst. on Fed. Taxation, 1973-86. Chmn. 13th Conf. Charitable Orgns. NYU on Fed. Taxation, 1982, chmn. adv. com. Hartford Downtown Council, 1986—; trustee Kingswood-Oxford Sch., West Hartford, Conn., 1961—, chmn. bd. trustees, 1975-78; trustee Old Sturbridge Village, Mass., 1974—, vice chmn. bd. trustees, 1988—, Ella Burr McManus Trust, Hartford, 1980—, Howard and Bush Found., Hartford, 1987—, Hartford YMCA, 1985—, Conn. River Mus. at Steamboat Dock, Essex, 1985—; trustee Wadsworth Atheneum, Hartford, 1968—, pres., 1981-84; trustee Howard and Bush Found., Hartford, 1987—; corporator Inst. of Living, 1981—, Mt. Sinai Hosp., Hartford, 1972—, Hartford Hosp., 1975—, St. Francis Hosp., Hartford, 1976, Hartford Art Sch., 1979—, Hartford Pub. Library, 1979—. Recipient Eminent Service medal Amherst Coll., 1967, Nathan Hale award Yale Club Hartford, 1983, Disting. Am. award No. Conn. chpt. Nat. Football Found. Hall of Fame, 1983. Fellow Am. Coll. Tax Counsel, Am. Bar Found.; mem. ABA (tax sect. exempt orgn. com., chmn. com. mus.'s and other cultural instns. 1987—), Conn. Bar Assn. (lectr. continuing legal edn. programs 1963—), Hartford County Bar Assn., Assn. Bar City N.Y., Conn. Bar Found. (bd. dirs. 1975-86), Am. Law Inst., Phi Beta Kappa (assocs.). Republican. Roman Catholic. Clubs: Hartford, Hartford Golf, Univ. (pres. 1976-78), Tennis (Hartford); Yale, Union (N.Y.C.); Limestone Trout (East Canaan, Conn.); Univ. (Washington); Dauntless (Essex, Conn.); Mariner Sands (Stuart, Fla.). Office: City Place 185 Asylum St City Pl Hartford CT 06103

LYON, PHILIP K(IRKLAND), lawyer; b. Warren, Ark., Jan. 19, 1944; s. Leroy and Maxine (Campbell) L.; m. Jayne Carol Jack, Aug. 12, 1982; children by previous marriage—Bradford F., Lucinda H., Suzette P., John P., Martin K., Meredith P.; J.D. with honors, U. Ark., 1967. Bar: Ark. 1967, U.S. Supreme Ct. 1970. Sr. ptnr., dir. ops. House, Wallace, Nelson & Jewell, P.A., Little Rock, 1967-86; pres. Jack, Lyon & Jones, P.A, Little Rock, 1986—. Instr. bus. law, labor law, govt. bus. and collective bargaining U. Ark., Little Rock, 1969-72, lectr. practice skills and labor law, U. Ark. Law Sch., 1979-80. Co-author: Schlei and Grossman Employment Discrimination Law, 2d edit., 1982. Bd. dirs. Ark. Law Rev., 1978—, Southwestern Legal Found., 1978—. Mem. Ark. State C. of C. (bd. dirs. 1984-88), Greater Little Rock C. of C. (chmn. community affairs com. 1982-84, minority bus. affairs 1985), ABA (select com. for liason with office of fed. contract compliance programs 1982—, select com. liason with EEOC 1984—, select com. immigration law), Ark. Bar Assn. (chmn. labor law com. 1977-78, chmn. labor law sect. 1978-79), Pulaski County Bar Assn., Assn. Trial Lawyers Am., Ark. Trial Lawyers Assn., Am. Soc. Personnel Adminstrn. Clubs: Little Rock Racquet, Capitol. Home: 17 Heritage Park Circle North Little Rock AR 72116 Office: Jack Lyon & Jones PA 3400 TCBY Tower Capitol at Broadway Little Rock AR 72201

LYON-COOK, JONNETTA SUE, business executive, administrative management consultant, author, lecturer; b. Custer, Ky., Apr. 28, 1935; d. Sparrel K. and Ava (Lockard) Lyon; student Blackburn Coll., 1953-57, U. West Fla., 1970-72; B.S., U. Md., 1975; Calif. State U., Northridge, 1978, U. So. Calif., 1979; M.B.A., Calif., Luth. Coll., 1979; M.Accountancy, U. Denver, 1982, Ind. U., 1983; m. Larry Lester Cook, Nov. 16, 1957 (div. Dec. 1982); children—Larry Lee, Vicki Sue. Asst. to foundry div. supt. Nat. Steel & Shipbldg., San Diego, 1966-69; adminstrv. asst. faculty fin. and acctg. U. West Fla., Pensacola, 1969-72; Okinawa br. adminstrv. mgr. Price Waterhouse & Co., 1972-75; corp. acct. Trust Co. of West, Los Angeles, 1975-76; controller Nuclear Medico Services, Inc., Van Nuys, Calif., 1976-79; officer Am. Nucleonics Corp., Westlake Village, Calif., 1980-81; partner Cooks' R.I.T.Y., Klamath, Calif., 1979-81; dir. fiscal services South Central Community Mental Health Center, Bloomington, Ind., 1982-83; owner, mgr. New Life Enterprises, Sebring, Fla., 1983-87; regional sales mgr. Mktg. Mgmt. Corp. Am., St. Petersburg Fla., 1983-85; founding dir. BASIC Internat. Ministries Inc., 1986—; pres., chief exec. officer, Whatever It Takes, Inc., 1987—; practice adminstr., Drs. Murray and Graham, Altamonte Springs, Fla. fin. cons.; presenter seminars on money mgmt., retirement investments. Committeewoman, Fla. Gulf Coast council Boy Scouts Am., 1970-72; mem. Orlando Christian Ctr.; active Reagan and Robertson presdl. campaigns; active local polit. campaigns. Cert. adminstrv. mgr.; CPA.Mem. Mensa, Assn. M.B.A. Execs., Adminstrv. Mgmt. Soc. (sec. Los Angeles area chpt. 1979-80, com. of 500 1987—), Nat. Assn. Female Execs., Am. Mgmt. Assn., Soc. Advancement Mgmt., Women's Network So. Calif., Christian Businesswomen's Network (founder), Internat. Platform Assn., Am. Inst. CPA's, Fla. Inst. CPA's, Med. Office Mgrs. Assn. Republican. Home and Office: 2816 Plaza Terrace Dr Orlando FL 32803-2616

LYONS, J. ROLLAND, civil engineer; b. Cedar Rapids, Iowa, Apr. 27, 1909; s. Neen T. and Goldie N. (Hill) L.; B.S., U. Iowa, 1933; m. Mary Jane Doht, June 10, 1924; children—Marlene Lyons Sparks, Sharon Lyons Hutson, Lynn Lyons Panichi. Jr. hwy. engr. Works Projects Adminstrn. field engr. Dept. Transp., State Ill., Peoria, 1930-31, civil engr. I-IV Central Office, Springfield, 1934-53, civil engr. V, 1953-66, municipal sect. chief, civil engr. VI, 1966-72. Civil Def. radio officer Springfield and Sangamon County (Ill.) Civil Def. Agy., 1952—. Recipient Meritorious Service award, Am. Assn. State Hwy. Ofcls., 1968; 25 Yr. Career Service award, State Ill., 1966; Certificate Appreciation, Ill. Municipal League, 1971. Registered profl. engr., Ill.; registered land surveyor, Ill. Mem. Ill. Assn. State Hwy. Engrs., State Ill. Employees Assn., Am. Pub. Works Assn., Am. Assn. State Hwy. Ofcls., Amateur Trapshooters Assn. Clubs: K.C., Sangamon Valley Radio; Lakewood Golf and Country. Address: 3642 Lancaster Rd Springfield IL 62703

LYONS, JERRY LEE, mechanical engineer, engineering research executive; b. St. Louis, Apr. 2, 1939; s. Ferd H. and Edna T. L. Diploma in Mech. Engring., Okla. Inst. Tech., 1964; M.S.M.E., Southwest U., 1983, Ph.D. in Engring. Mgmt., 1984. Registered profl. engr., Calif. Project engr. Harris Mfg. Co., St. Louis, 1965-70, Essex Cryogenics Industries, St. Louis, 1970-73; mgr. engring. research Chemetron Corp., St. Louis, 1973-77; cons. fluid controls Wis. U., 1977—; pres. Yankee Ingenuity, Inc., St. Louis, 1973—; v.p., gen. mgr. engring. research and devel. Essex Fluid Controls div. Essex Industries, Inc., St. Louis, 1977—; pres. Lyons Pub. Co., St. Louis, 1983—; chmn. exec. bd. continuing engring. edn. in St. Louis for Mo., Univ. in Columbia, 1980-81; chmn. bd. Intertech., Inc., Houston, 1986-87; cons. fluid power dept. Bradley U., Peoria, 1977-84, U. Wis. Author: Home Study Series Course on Actuators and Accessories, 1977, The Valve Designers Handbook, 1983, The Lyons' Encyclopedia of Valves, 1975, The Designers Handbook of Pressure Sensing Devices, 1980, Special Process Applications, 1980, , Lyons Valve Designers Handbook, 1983; contbr. articles to profl. jours. Served with USAF, 1957-62. Named Businessman of Week (KEZK radio), Eminent Churchill fellow Winston Churchill Wisdom Soc. Fellow ASME; Mem. Soc. Mfg. Engrs. (chmn. Mo. registration com. 1975—, chmn. St. Louis chpt. 1979-80, internat. dir. 1982-84, 85-87, Engr. of Yr. 1984, internat. award of merit 1985), Nat. Soc. Profl. Engrs., Mo. Soc. Profl. Engrs., St. Louis Soc. Mfg. Engrs. (chmn. profl. devel., registration and cert. com. 1975-79), Instrument Soc. Am. (mem. control valve stability com. 1978-84), Computer and Automated Systems Assn. (1st chmn. St. Louis chpt. 1980-81), St. Louis Engrs. Club (award of merit 1977, Wisdom award of Honor 1987, mem. Wisdom Hall of Fame 1987), Am. Security Council (committeeman 1976—), Nat. Fluid Power Assn. (mem. com. on pressure ratings 1975-77), Am. Legion. Lutheran. Office: 7700 Gravois Ave Saint Louis MO 63123

LYONS, JOHN MATTHEW, telecommunications executive, broadcasting executive; b. N.Y.C., Nov. 5, 1948; s. Matthew Joseph and Anna (Coroneos) L.; m. Cynthia C. Hotaling, Apr. 23, 1988. BSEE, Roosevelt U., Chgo., 1970, MSEE, 1976; BSE, Century U., Los Angeles, 1981, MBA in Engring. Mgmt., 1982; PhD in Communications, Loyola U., Chgo., 1979; PhD in Broadcasting (hon.), Sicluna U. Found., 1987. Cert. Profl. Engr., 1987—. Engr., producer Sta. WRFM-Radio, N.Y.C., 1965-69; sr. facilities planning and project engr. Sta. WWRL-Radio, N.Y.C., 1969-76; sr. facilities planning, project engr. Sta. WWRL/WRVR-Radio, N.Y.C., 1976-78; asst. chief engr. Sta. WOR-Radio, Inc., N.Y.C., 1978-80; chief engr. Sta. WRKS-FM, N.Y.C., 1980—; pres. Lyon Records, N.Y., 1971—, Short Lines Co., N.Y., 1980—; chmn. master antenna com. Empire State Bldg., N.Y., 1980—; bd. dirs. The Document Ctr., N.Y.; cons. broadcasting and telecommunications. Producer: (radio broadcast) The Cuban Missile Crisis, 1962 (Peabody award 1963); exec. producer: (broadcast series) Radio: The First 50 Years, 1970, Sta. WOR-Radio 60th Anniversary Program, 1982 (Armstrong award 1983, Internat. Radio Festival award 1983), Sta. WOR-Radio 65th Anniversary Program, 1987; chmn. media curriculumcom. Westchester Community Coll., N.Y., 1987—; v.p. U.S. Amateur Ballroom Dancers Assn., 1987—. Served with USAF, 1967-70. Sr. fellow Soc. Broadcast Engrs. (cert., bd. dirs. 1974-78); mem. Nat. Assn. Radio and Telecommunications Engrs. (cert.), Broadcast Music, Inc., Audio Engring. Soc., IEEE, Internat. Radio and TV Soc., VA Hosp. Radio and TV Guild (v.p. 1976-82, 84—, pres. 1982-84, chmn. exec. com. 1984—, Bennie award 1981), Broadcast Pioneers, Am. Soc. Composers, Authors, and Pubs., BMI, U.S. Amateur Ballroom Dancers Assn. (regional v.p. 1987—). Named to Knights of Malta, 1986. Avocation: competitive ballroom dancing, photography. Home: 305 E 86th St New York NY 10028 Office: Sta WRKS 1440 Broadway New York NY 10018

LYONS, JONATHON EDWARD, financial executive; b. Leeds, Yorkshire, Eng., May 1, 1951; s. Jack and Roslyn Marion (Rosenbaum) L.; m. Miriam Djanogly, Dec. 30, 1975; children—Jacob Simon, Simon Henry, Deborah Sophie. Ed. Carmell Coll., nr. Oxford, Eng. Exec. sales Alexandre Ltd., Leeds, Eng., 1968-71; chief exec. John David Ltd., London, 1971—, H. Allen Smith Ltd., London, 1983—; dir. Britimpex Ltd., Can., 1972—; ptnr. Internat. Investments, London, 1978—; fin. cons. Lyons Internat. Investments, London, 1978—; dir. J.L.C. Ltd. (formerly J. Lyons-Chamberlayne Ltd.). Mem. Conservative Indsl. Fund, London, 1978—; mng. dir. J.E. London Properties, Ltd., 1987; mem. Fedn. Jewish Relief Orgns., London, 1977—; joint chmn. Hyde Park com. Central Brit. Fund, London, 1975-80; com. mem. Royal Coll. Music, London. Mem. Inst. Dirs., Bentley Owners Club, Insignia Club (hon.). Conservative. Jewish. Clubs: Carlton, Marks (London). Avocations: art, music, writer sports, classic postwar cars. Home: 35 Loudoun Rd, St Johns Wood, London NW8 0NE, England Office: John David Ltd, 186 Earls Ct Rd, London SW3, England

LYONS, JOSEPH NORMAN, insurance executive; b. Boston, Sept. 5, 1901; s. George Alfred and Alice Antoinette (Sheehan) L.; m. Helen Mary O'Karski, June 27, 1942; children—Joseph Norman, Christie Ann, Mary Candace. Grad., Boston Latin Sch., 1917. With John Paulding Meade Co. (ins.), Boston, 1917-34; founder, pres. Cushing, Lyons, Inc., Boston, 1934—; founder Am. Ednl. Ins. Fund, 1960—; organizer Pilgram Ins. Co., 1960. Trustee Mass. Regional Arthritis and Rheumatism Found.; mem. Fides com. Boston Coll.; trustee Ins. Library Assn. Boston. Mem. Mass. Brokers Assn. (past dir.). Club: Arundel Beach. Home: 11 Beechcroft Rd Newton MA 02158 Office: 89 Broad St Boston MA 02110

LYONS, M. ARNOLD, lawyer, educator; b. Mpls., June 3, 1911; s. Simon Harry and Sarah (Schoenberger) Labovitz; m. Vera Nissenson Dec. 22, 1935; children: David, Barbara, Lisa. BA, U. Minn., 1932, JD, 1934. Bar: Minn. 1934, U.S. Dist. Ct. Minn. 1935, U.S. Ct. Appeals (8th cir.) 1938, U.S. Tax Ct. 1941, U.S. Supreme Ct. 1948. Ptnr. Robins, Zelle, Larson & Kaplan and predecessor firm Robins, Davis & Lyons, Mpls., 1938—; prof. law U. Minn., Mpls., 1974-76, Hamline U., St. Paul, 1975-85. Co-author: Stein on Probate, 1986. Mem. ABA, Minn. Bar Assn., Hennepin County Bar Assn, Am. Judicature Soc., Am. Arbitration Assn. (nat. panel). Lodges: Masons, Shriners.

LYONS, RICHARD CHAPMAN, urologist; b. Corry, Pa., Nov. 23, 1919; s. Arch C. and Araline (Drought) L.; m. Norma Lydia Wright, Dec. 25, 1945; children—Dorothy A., John C., Sanford D., Timothy R., Valerie A. Grad. U. Pa., 1940; M.D., U. Pitts., 1944. Diplomate Am. Bd. Urology. Intern, St. Elizabeth Hosp., Washington, 1945; resident, Mayo Clinic, Rochester, Minn., 1945-46, 48-50; civilian physician U.S. Army, 1946-47; chmn. dept. urology, Hamot Med. Ctr., Erie, Pa., 1955-68, practitioner, surgeon, 1950—, founder, head urology residency program, 1955-68; mem. med. staffs St. Vincent Health Ctr., Erie, 1951—; mem. Pa. State Bd. Med. Edn. and Licensure, 1971—, chmn., 1976-78, 81—; dir. NW Pa. Corp., Oil City, Mellon-North, Erie. Trustee Gannon U. Named Disting. Pennsylvanian, Gannon U., 1981. Fellow ACS (gov. 1975-81); mem. AMA, Pa. Med. Soc., Erie County Med. Soc., Pa. Urologic Assn. (pres. 1974), Urol. Assn. Pa., Mayo Clinic Alumni Assn., Mayo Urol. Alumni Assn. (pres. 1976). Republican. Roman Catholic. Clubs: Erie, Kahkwa, Erie Yacht, University (Pitts.). Home: 52 Royal Palm Dr Fort Lauderdale FL 33301

LYSAUGHT, JEROME PAUL, educator; b. Kansas City, Kans., Mar. 4, 1930; s. Michael Clarence and Minnie Hazel (Hill) L.; A.B., U. Kans., 1954, M.A., 1954; Ed.D., U. Rochester, 1964; D.Litt. (hon.), D'Youville Coll., 1982; m. Dolores Marie Gergick, June 6, 1953; children—Jan Marie, Paula Marie, Clare Marie, Eileen Marie. Indsl. relations specialist Eastman Kodak Co., Rochester, N.Y., 1954-62; mem. faculty U. Rochester, 1963—, assoc. prof., 1966-69, prof. edn./preventive medicine, 1969—; dir. Nat. Commn. for Study of Nursing and Nursing Edn., 1967-73; dir. Comprenetics, Inc.; cons. in field. Chmn. adv. bd. Community Coll. of Air Force, 1973-84; trustee D'Youville Coll., 1980—; trustee Phi Kappa Theta Found., 1969-74; pres. Collegiate Assn. for Devel. Ednl. Adminstrn., 1977-81. Served with USMC, 1948-49, 50-52. Recipient Outstanding Long Term Contbn. award Nat. Soc. for Programmed Instrn., 1968; Am. Jour. Nursing Book of the Yr. in Nursing selections, 1974, 80; Univ. Mentor award U. Rochester, 1982; Am. Dental Hygiene Assn. Manuscript of Yr. award, 1979; Meritorious Civilian Service medal U.S. Air Force, 1984. Mem. Am. Acad. Polit. and Social Sci., Am. Assn. Higher Edn., Irish Am. Cultural Inst., Assn. Am. Med. Colls., Am. Ednl. Research Assn., Health Sci. Communications Assn., Phi Beta Kappa, Phi Kappa Theta, Phi Delta Kappa (Disting. research award 1986), Pi Sigma Alpha, Pi Gamma Mu, Omicron Delta Kappa, Pi Kappa Delta, Pi Lambda Theta, Kappa Phi Kappa, Kappa Delta Pi, Sigma Phi Omega, Rho Chi Sigma, Sigma Theta Tau (nat. hon. mem.). Democrat. Roman Catholic. Clubs: Quill, Meliora, Ancient Order of Hibernians in Am., Pachacamac. Author: A Guide to Programmed Instruction, 1963; An Abstract for Action, 1970; Action in Nursing, 1974; others; mem. editorial and rev. bds.; contbr. articles to profl. jours. Home: 17 Bretton Woods Dr Rochester NY 14618 Office: 405 Lattimore Hall U Rochester Rochester NY 14627

LYSOHORSKY, ONDRA (ERWIN GOY), poet, linguist, translator, educator; b. Frydek, Austria-Silesia, July 6, 1905; s. Jozef and Alojzyja (Palik) G.; student German U. Prague (Czechoslovakia), 1924-28, Ph.D., 1928; student U. Paris, 1926, U. Rome, 1930; D. hon. causa, Free U. Asia, 1972; D.Litt. (hon.), World U., 1979; m. Maria Bezdek, Oct. 3, 1931 (dec. July 6, 1974). Tchr. grammar schs., Kremnica, Bratislava, Trnava, Ostrava, 1930-39; lectr. high sch. fgn. langs. Moscow, Tashkent, and Mil. High Sch. Red Army, Moscow, 1940-46, head chair Czech lang.; tchr. kindergarten nurses Czechoslovakia, then Comml. Sch.; prof. Grammar Sch.; librarian; chmn. Western langs. U. Bratislava, 1956-61; works include: The Singing Fist, 1934, The Voice of the Soil, 1935, Selected Poems, 1936, 37, Song About the Mother, 1942, My Country, 1942, Songs of the Sun and the Earth, 1945, Poems, 1946, The Lachian Rivers Too Flow into Sea, 1958; Through the Furrow to the Universe, 1960, Poems, 1960, Thanksgiving, 1961, Selected Poems, 1962, Century, Be You My Yardstick, 1962, But Life is Stronger, 1963, The Unique Cup, 1964 Day of Life, 1971, Selected Poems, 1971, 73, In the Eye of the Storm, 1976, I Ripen in My Time, 1978, Karel Klimsa, 1984, Lachian Poetry, 1988; translations into 70 langs. including English by W. H. Auden, Christopher Fry, David Gill, Russian by Boris Pasternak, Marina Cvetajeva, French by Pierre Garnier,; also criticisms of Goethe, Verlaine, Rilke, Otokar Brezina; contbr. to numerous jours. and anthologies, France, Eng., Greece, Norway, Switzerland, W. Ger., E. Ger., USSR, U.S., Can., Australia, India, Philippines, Republic of China and other countries; translator of poetry from and into German and Lachian lang. Candidate Nobel prize for lit., 1970; hon. officer Eastern Europe, United Poets Laureate Internat. (UPLI), 1970; named poet laureate World Acad. Arts and Cluture, 1981. Fellow Societas Polyglottica Universalis (Amsterdam) (hon.), I.B.A. (hon.) (life); mem. World Poetry Soc., Assn. des Amis de Romain Rolland, Assn. Franç aise des Amis d'Albert Schweitzer, Goethe Gesellschaft, Internat. Poetry Soc., also many other hon. memberships. Home: Mytna 21, PO Box 812 99 810 00, Bratislava Czechoslovakia

LYTLE, MICHAEL ALLEN, university official, consultant; b. Salina, Kans., Oct. 22, 1946; s. Milton Earl and Geraldine Faye (Young) L.; m. Bjorg Lindqvist, Mar. 12, 1984; 1 child, Eric Alexander. BA, Ind. U., 1973; grad. cert. Sam Houston State U., Huntsville, Tex., 1977; MEd, Tex. A&M U., 1978; postgrad. Nat. Def. U., 1988. Substitute high sch. tchr., Butler County, Kans., 1969; instr. criminal justice Cleveland State Community Coll., Tenn., 1974-77; adj. instr. criminal justice U. Tenn., Chattanooga, 1975-76; teaching asst. Tex. A&M U., 1977-80, intern adminstrv. asst. Office Vice Chancellor Legal Affairs and Gen. Counsel, Tex. A&M U. System 1980, staff asso. Office Chancellor, 1980-81, asst. to chancellor, 1981-83, asst. dir. govt. relations, 1983-84, spl. asst. to Chancellor for fed. relations, 1984-87; dir. research devel. and spl. asst. to v.p. for research and grad. studies, Syracuse U., 1987; exec. dir. for Govt. Relations, 1987—; sr. research assoc. Tech. and Info. Policy Program Maxwell Sch. Citizenship and Pub. Affairs Syracuse U., 1987—; rep. Council on Fed. Relations, Assn. of Am. Univs.; instl. rep. Research Univs. Network; exec. dir. Tex. Com. for Employer Support of the Guard and Res., 1982-86, N.Y. com., 1987—. Mem. editorial bd. Jour. Tech. Transfer, 1987—. Mem. militarily critical techs. adv. com. U.S. Internat. Trade Adminstrn.; bd. advisers Ctr. Internat. Bus. Studies Tex. A&M U., 1986-87; edn. com. Business Council fo N.Y.; Res. asst. army attache to Republic of Ireland, 1985-88; mem. exec. com. N.E. Parallel Architectures Ctr. Contbr. articles to profl. jours. Served with USAR, 1970-72, Vietnam. Decorated Bronze Star, Army Commendation medal with 2d oak leaf cluster, Meritorous Service medal, Tham Muu Boi Tinh medal; Inter-Univ. Seminar Armed Forces and Soc. fellow, 1979; assoc. Ctr. NATO Studies, Kent State U. Mem. AAAS, N.Y. Acad. Scis., Tech. Transfer Soc., Nat. Assn. State Univs. and Land-Grant Colls. (vet. affairs and nat. service com.). Am. Council Young Polit. Leaders, Policy Studies Orgn., Council on European Studies, Am. Soc. for Pub. Adminstrn., U.S. Global Strategy Council, Atlantic Council U.S. (councilor), Res. Officers Assn., Am. Def. Preparedness Assn., Phi Delta Kappa. Republican. Episcopalian. Club: Army and Navy.

LYTTELTON, HUMPHREY RICHARD ADEANE, musician, bandleader, writer; b. Eton, Bucks, Eng., May 23, 1921; s. George William L.; m. Patricia Mary Braithwaite, 1948 (dissolved 1952); 1 dau.; m. 2d, Elizabeth Jill Richardson, 1952; 3 children. Ed. Eton Coll.; self-taught in music. With Camberwell Art Sch., 1947-48; cartoonist Daily Mail, 1949-53; formed his own band, 1948; leader Humphrey Lyttelton's Band, 1953—; free-lance journalist, 1953—; numerous recs., TV appearances; recent jazz festival appearances: Bracknell, Zurich, Camden, Montreux, Newcastle, Warsaw; Compère BBC Jazz programes: Jazz Scene, Jazz Club, others; author: I Play as I Please, 1954; Second Chorus, 1958; Take it from the Top, 1975; The Best of Jazz: Basin Street to Harlem, 1978; Humphrey Lyttelton's Jazz and Big Band Quiz, 1979; The Best of Jazz II, 1983; contbr. to Melody Maker, 1954—, Reynolds News, 1955-62, Sunday Citizen, 1962-67, Harper's & Queen's, Punch. Served with Grenadier Guards, 1941-46. Home: Alyn Close, Barnet Rd, Arkley, Herts England Office: BBC Light Music Dept, Broadcasting House, Portland Pl, London W1A 4WW England *

LYYTINEN, KALLE TUHANI, computer science educator; b. Helsinki, Aug. 19, 1953; s. Veli Kaarlo and Raili Annikki (Lehto) L.; m. Pirjo-Riitta Taipale, Apr. 9, 1974; children: Joonas, Juho, Markus. BA, U. Jyväskylä (Finland), 1976, MA, 1977, Licenciate in Econs., 1981, PhD, 1986. Asst. U. Jyväskylä, 1977-80, assoc. prof. computer sci., 1982-83, assoc. prof., 1987, prof., 1987—; researcher U. Stockholm, 1981-82; prin. researcher Acad. Finland, Jyväskylä, 1983-85; assoc. prof. U. Turku, Finland, 1986; vis. researcher London Sch Econs., 1986; cons. TT-Innovation, Helsinki, 1987. Contbr. articles to profl. jours. Served to 2d lt. inf. Finnish Army, 1972-73. Mem. Internat. Fedn. Info. Processing (tech. com. 8, 1985—, sec. working group on info. systems and orgns. 1987—). Home: Saratie 4as5, 40250 Jyväskylä Finland Office: U Jyväskylä, Dept Computer Sci Seminaarink 15, 40100 Jyväskylä Finland

MA, TSU SHENG, chemist, educator; b. Canton, China, Oct. 15, 1911; came to U.S., 1934, naturalized 1956; s. Shao-ching and Sze (Mai) M.; m. Gioh-Fang Dju, Aug. 27, 1942; children—Chopo, Mei-Mei Hewitt. B.S., Tsinghua U., Peking, 1931; Ph.D., U. Chgo., 1938. Mem. faculty U. Chgo., 1938-46; prof. Peking U., 1946-49; sr. lectr. U. Otago (N.Z.), 1949-51; mem. faculty NYU, 1951-54; mem. faculty CUNY, 1954—, prof. chemistry, 1958—, prof. emeritus, 1980—; vis. prof. Tsinghua U., 1947, Lingnan U., 1949, NYU, 1954-60, Taiwan U., 1961, Chiangmei U., 1968, Singapore U., 1975; specialist Bur. Ednl. and Cultural Affairs State Dept., 1964. Fulbright lectr., 1961-62, 68-69; recipient Benedetti-Pichler award in microchemistry, 1976. Fellow N.Y. Acad. Sci., AAAS, Royal Soc. Chemistry, Am. Inst. Chemists; mem. Am. Chem. Soc., Soc. Applied Spectroscopy, Am. Microchem. Soc., Sigma Xi. Author: Small-Scale Experiments in Chemistry, 1962; Organic Functional Group Analysis, 1964; Microscale Manipulations in Chemistry, 1976; Organic Functional Group Analysis by Gas Chromatography, 1976; Quantitative Analysis of Organic Mixtures, 1979; Modern Organic Elemental Analysis, 1979; Organic Analysis Using Ion-Selective Electrodes, 1982; Trace Element Determination in Organic Materials, 1988; editor: Mikrochimica Acta, 1965—; contbr. articles to profl. jours., chpts. to books. Home: 7 Banbury Ln Chapel Hill NC 27514 Office: CUNY Dept Chemistry Brooklyn NY 11210

MAAG, PETER, orchestra conductor; b. St. Gallen, Switzerland, May 10, 1919; s. Otto and Nelly (Mayer) M.; m. Marica Franchi, May 26, 1980; 1 dau, Constance; 1 son by previous marriage, George. Student theology and philosophy U. Zurich, U. Geneva; studied piano with Cortot, conducting with Ansermet. Asst. to Furtwangler, 1949-52; condr., Dusseldorf, W.Ger., 1952-54; music dir., Bonn, 1954-59; chief condr. Vienna Volksoper, 1964-67; artistic adviser Opera Parma (Italy), 1968-72, Teatro Regio Torino, 1974-76; chief condr. Berne Symphony, Switzerland, 1984—; free-lance condr. throughout world, including Met. Opera, N.Y.C., Vienna Opera, Berlin, Hamburg, Venice, Covent Garden, London, London Symphony and Philharm., festivals in Zurich, Salzburg, Aix, Glyndebourne, also others; mem. faculty Acad. Siena, Juilliard Sch. Music, N.Y.C. Author new editions of Paer, Myslivecek, Offenbach one-act operas. Recipient Verdi medal, Parma, 1970, Toscanini baton, Parma, 1971, Premio Biancamano, Rome, 1979, Grand Pres du Disque, Paris, 1980. Clubs: Mozart (Vienna), Aurora (N.Y.). Office: ICM Artists Ltd 40 W 57th St New York NY 10010

MAAZEL, LORIN, conductor, violinist; b. Paris, Mar. 6, 1930; s. Lincoln and Marie (Varencove) M.; m. Miriam Sandbank, 1952 (div. 1969); m. Israela Margalit, Sept. 29, 1969 (div.); children: Ilann Sean, Fiona; m. Dietlinde Turban June 7, 1986. Mus. D. (hon.), U. Pitts., 1968; H.H.D., Beaver Coll., 1973. Debut as conductor, 1953; condr. festivals in Edinburgh, Scotland), Bayreuth, Fed. Republic Germany, Salzburg, Austria, 1960-70; world tours include Japan, Far East, Asia, Europe, Latin Am., Australia, USSR; artistic dir. Deutsche Oper, Berlin, 1965-71; mus. dir. Radio Symphony Orch., Berlin, 1965-75; music dir., Cleve. Orch., 1972-82, condr. emeritus, 1982—; prin. guest condr., New Philharmonia Orch., London, from 1976, Radio France, Paris, Pitts. Symphony Orch., 1977—; mgr., artistic dir. Vienna State Opera, 1982-84; recording of Cleve. Orch., Vienna Philharmonic for London Records, Deutsche Grammophon, Berliner Philharmonie, Angel Records, New Philharmonia, CBS. Office: Pitts Symphony Orch 600 Penn Ave Pittsburgh PA 15222 *

MABBETT, IAN WILLIAM, Asian history and religion educator; b. London, Apr. 27, 1939; s. Frank wilfred and Phyllis May (Mack) M.; m. Jacqueline Diana June Towns; children: Anna-Marie Lonsdale, Birgitta Rosalie. BA, Oxford U., 1960, MA, DPhil in Oriental Studies, 1963. Asst. lectr. Thanet Tech. Coll., Ramsgate, Kent, Eng., 1963-64; lectr. Monash U., Melbourne, Australia, 1965-70, sr. lectr., 1971-83, reader, 1984—. Author: Short History of India, 1968, revised edit., 1983, Modern China, 1985, Kings and Emperors of Asia, 1985, contbr. articles to learned jours. Mem. Australian Soc. Authors, Fedn. Australian Writers. Anglican. Office: Monash U, Clayton, Victoria 3168, Australia

MABEE, GWYNNE, corporation executive; b. Little Rock, Apr. 19, 1924; d. John and Doris (Nichols) Rouse; children: Dorinda Cheryl Marlborough, Ronald C., Debra Lynn Witt. BA, U. Houston, 1944. CPA, Tex. Sec.-treas. Igloo Corp., Houston, 1958-65; gen. mgr. Modern Dynamics, Houston, 1969-71; pres. Yschek, Inc., Houston, 1975-80; cons. dir. Jacqueline Stallone, Ltd., Las Vegas, Nev., 1983—; pres. Score Sales & Mfg., Inc., Salt Lake City, 1984-87, ret.; dir. Jacqueline Stallone, Ltd., Score Sales & Mfg., Inc., Salt Lake City, Record Systems, Inc., Las Vegas. Named one of Top 50 Business Women, Harvard Bus. Rev., 1962. Mem. Am. Inst. CPA's, Nat. Data Processing Mgrs. Assn., St. Rose de Lima Soc. Republican. Presbyterian. Avocations: painting, writing, reading, dancing.

MABILEAU, ALBERT, political scientist, educator; b. Paris, Sept. 12, 1927; s. Georges and Madeleine (Gross) M.; m. Janine Cheltiel, Dec. 23, 1953; 1 child, Bernard. Diploma, Inst. d'Etudes Politiques, Paris, 1947; PhD, U. Paris faculte de droit, Paris, 1951. Prof. Faculte de Droit, Saigon, Vietnam, 1952-54; prof. faculte droit and inst. d'etudes politiques U. Bordeaux, France, 1954—; bd. dirs. Ctr. d'Etude Recherche sur la vie locale. Author: Le Parti Liberal Britannique, 1951; author, editor: La Personnalisation du Pouvoir, 1964, Les Citoyens et la Politique Locale, 1988. Recipient Ordre de Legion d'Honneur, 1975, Ordre du Mérite, 1987, Pres. of the Republic. Mem. Com. Nat. Ctr. Nat. Recherche Scientifique, French Assn. Polit. Sci. (v.p. 1983—). Home: 38 Blvd President Wilson, 33000 Bordeaux France Office: Inst d'Etudes Politiques, Domaine U, 33405 CEDEX Talence France

MABOMBA, RODRICK SAMSON, library director; b. Blantyre, Malawi, Sept. 25, 1948; s. Simeon Samson and Flonnie (Kalonga) M.; m. Catherine Kanthambi; children: Samson, Joseph, Martha, Angela. Assoc. Library Assn., Coll. Librarianship, Wales, U.K., 1970; MLib, U. Wales, 1985. Asst. librarian U. Malawi Libraries, Zomba, 1971-75; chief librarian British Council Libraries, Blantyre, 1975-78; dir. Malawi Nat. Library Service, Lilongwe, 1978—. Contbr. articles to profl. pubs. Fellow U.K. Library Assn.; mem. Malawi Library Assn. Home: Box 50 MBAME, Blantyre Malawi Office: Nat Library Service, Box 30314, Lilongwe 3 Malawi

MABON, CAROLINE BILLARD, physician; b. Quimper, Finistère, France, Jan. 7, 1951; d. Guy and Suzanne (Le Mao) Billard; m. Eric Mabon, Sept. 30, 1977; children: Pauline, Clémence, Camille. MD, U. Bretagne Occidentale, France, 1978. Resident Hosp. A. Morvan, Brest, 1976-78; gen. practice in medicine Quemeneven, Brittany, France, 1979—. Roman Catholic. Home and Office: Kerheol, 29136 Quemeneven, Brittany France

MABRY, NELLOISE JOHNSON, former educator; b. Valdosta, Ga., Sept. 8, 1921; d. Hansford Duncan and Maudelle (Williams) Johnson; student Bethel Woman's Coll., 1938-39, Wesleyan Conservatory, 1941; A.B., Mercer U., 1943, M.Ed., 1949; m. William Herbert Mabry, Mar. 5, 1942 (div. Nov. 1947); 1 son, William Herbert. Tchr., Cynthia H. Weir Elem. Sch., Macon, Ga., 1950-80. Mem. NEA, Ga., Bibb edn. assns., Ga. Assn. for Childhood Edn. (state pres. 1964-66), Delta Kappa Gamma (chpt. scrapbook chmn. 1966-68, chpt. program chmn. 1974-76, chpt. chmn. personal growth and services 1980-82, chpt. social chmn. 1982-84, 2d v.p. chpt. 1984-86, state dir. 3d dist. 1985-87, chpt. mem. chmn. 1986-88, 1st v.p. chpt. 1988—), Alpha Delta Pi, Alpha Psi Omega. Republican. Baptist. Club: Macon Woman's (chmn. 1986—, edn. chmn. 1986-88). Home: 1575 Adams St Macon GA 31204

MACARIO, ALBERTO JUAN LORENZO, physician; b. Naschel, Argentina, Dec. 1, 1935; came to U.S., 1974, naturalized, 1980; s. Alberto Carlos and Maria Elena (Giraudi) M.; M.D., Nat. U. Buenos Aires, 1961; m. Everly Conway, Mar. 16, 1963; children—Alex, Everly. Intern, Ramos Mejia Hosp., Buenos Aires, 1958-60, resident 1960; resident Rivadavia Hosp., Buenos Aires, 1961-62, physician-hematologist, 1962-64; fellow NRC Argentina, Buenos Aires, 1964-69; head dept. radioactive isotopes Inst. Hematological Investigations, Nat. Acad. Medicine Argentina, Buenos Aires, 1967-69; Eleanor Roosevelt fellow Internat. Union Against Cancer, Dept. Tumorbiology, Karolinska Inst., Stockholm, 1969-71; mem. sci. staff Lab. Cell Biology, NRC Italy, Rome, 1971-73; head Lab. Immunology, Internat. Agy. Research on Cancer, WHO, Lyons, France, 1973-74; research scientist Brown U., Providence, 1974-76, Div. Labs. and Research, N.Y. State Dept. Health, Albany, 1976-79; chief hematology Clin. Lab. Center, N.Y. State Dept. Health, Albany, 1979-81, dir. clin. and exptl. immunology sect. Lab. Medicine Inst., 1981-83; research physician, 1981—; Wadsworth Ctr. for Labs. and Research N.Y. State Dept. of Health; prof. Sch. Pub. Health Scis., SUNY-N.Y. State Dept. Health, 1985—. Recipient Diploma de Honor prize Nat. U. Buenos Aires, 1961, Bernardino Rivadavia prize Nat. Acad. Medicine Argentina, 1967, Ciencia e Investigation prize Argentinian Soc. Advancement Sci., 1967; Ford Found.-Nat. Acad. Scis. travel fellow, 1968, Eleanor Roosevelt fellow, 1969. Mem. Scandinavian Soc. Immunology, Italian Assn. Immunologists, French Soc. Immunology, Am. Assn. Immunologists, Am. Soc. Microbiology, Am. Assn. Pathologists. Contbr. articles to profl. jours., chpts. to sci. books. Editor multivol. treatise Monoclonal Antibodies Against Bacteria. Office: NY State Dept Health Wadsworth Ctr Labs Research Albany NY 12201

MACARTNEY, NIGEL SEYMOUR, librarian; b. Manchester, Eng., July 7, 1947; s. Donald William and Joyce (Worthington) MaC.; m. Yolande Jacqueline Alexander; 1 child, Ewan A. BA in History with honors, Cambridge U., 1968, MA with honors, 1971; diploma in Library Sci., U. London, 1970; Cert. Edn., U. Leeds, 1977. Trainee librarian Leeds (Eng.) City Libraries, 1968-70, asst. librarian, 1970-72; librarian Hertfordshire Coll. Agriculture, St. Albans, Eng., 1972-77; sr. tutor librarian Hatfield Poly., Eng., 1978-79, 82—; dep. librarian Hatfield Polytech., ., Eng., 1979-82; project head CIMTECH, Hatfield, 1982—. Mem. Library Assn. (adv. com. for Brit. library bibliography service 1984—, adv. com. for Brit. library document supply ctr. 1985—). Home: 6 Lakeside Pl, London Colney, Saint Albans, Hertfordshire England AL2 1PZ Office: Hatfield Polytech, College Ln, Hatfield AL1 9AD, England

MACARY, PIERRE HENRI, civil engineer; b. Arbois, France, Apr. 11, 1943; s. Arsene Fernand Pierre and Suzanne (Maire) M. Ingenieur Civil de l'Aeronautique, Ecole Nat. Superieure de l'Aeronautique, 1967; M.B.A., Columbia U., 1972. Engr. United Air Lines, San Francisco, 1967-68; spl. asst. Mfrs. Hanover Banque Nordique, Paris, 1974; mgmt. cons. Ceplam, Paris, 1975-77; marketer Diebold France, Paris, 1977-80; free-lance mgmt. cons., Paris, 1980—. Served to sub.-lt. French Air Force, 1968-70. Mem. Cercle de l'Opinion, Ligue Europeenne de Cooperation Econ. Club: Domont Golf.

MACAULAY, HUGH L., retail company executive; b. Toronto, Jan. 31, 1925; s. Leopold and Hazel Charlton (Haight) M.; m. Dorothy Jean Taylor, Sept. 11, 1946; children—Barbara, Robert James, Andrew Taylor. B.A. in Journalism, U. Western Ont., 1948. With Pub. & Indsl. Relations Ltd., 1948-52; with Ford Motor Co., 1952-54, Lawrence Motors Ltd., 1954-55; owner York Mills Pontiac Ltd. and York Mills Leasing Ltd., 1955-70; vice chmn. Ont. Hydro, Toronto, 1979, chmn., 1979-83; chmn. Can. Tire Corp. Ltd., Toronto, 1984—, chief exec. officer, 1985-87, also dir. Mem., chmn. bd. Ryerson Poly. Inst., 1964-71; bd. govs. York U.; mem. Commn. on Post-Secondary Edn., 1969-71; chmn. Commn. on Orgn. of Progressive Conservative Party, 1971-76. Served with Royal Can. Naval Vol. Res., 1943-45. Clubs: Rosedale Golf, John's Island (Vero Beach, Fla.), Albany, Bent Pine Golf. Office: Can Tire Corp Ltd, 2180 Yonge St, Box 770 Station K, Toronto, ON Canada M4P 2V8

MACBAIN, JOHN HOWARD, marketing executive; b. Niagara Falls, Can., Feb. 13, 1958; s. Arthur Alister and Rachel Viola (Kennedy) M.; m. Loise Blouin; 1 child, Alexandra. BA, McGill U., Montreal, Quebec, 1980; degree in law, Oxford U., 1982; MBA, Harvard U., 1984. Exec. asst. to v.p. Can. Gen. Electric, Toronto, 1982; mgmt. cons. The Boston Cons. Group, Paris, 1983; mktg. dir. Power Fin. Corp., Montreal, 1984-87; owner, pres., chief exec. officer Auto Mag Inc., Montreal, 1987. Editorial bd. dir. McGill News, Montreal, 1985. Sec. Jr. Assocs. Montreal Mus. Fine Arts, 1984-86; chmn., bd. dirs. Montreal Youth Enterprise Ctr., 1986. Rhodes scholar, Quebec & Wadham, 1980; valedictorian Oxford U., 1980. Clubs: Univ. (Montreal), Hillside Tennis (Montreal). Home: 604 Clarke Ave, Montreal, PQ Canada H3Y 3E4 Office: Auto Mag Inc, 130 de Liege East, Montreal, PQ Canada H2P 1J1

MACBETH, HUGH JAMES, data processing and telecommunications executive; b. N.Y.C., Jan. 19, 1947; s. John Brown and Josephine Earl (Olsen) Macb. BA, Hiram Coll., 1968. Gen. mgr. 9-20 Inc., Great Barrington, Mass., 1971-73; acct. Chem. Constrn. Corp., N.Y.C., 1973-75; owner, gen. mgr. The Fairfield Inn, Great Barrington, 1975-78; v.p. Am. Agy. Data Systems, Merritt Island, Fla., 1978-80; pres. Advanced Info. Mgmt., Cocoa Beach, Fla., 1980-81; mgr. info. systems and telecommunications Greater Orlando (Fla.) Aviation Authority, 1981—; pres. Exec. Info. Services, Cocoa Beach, 1985—. Columnist: Orlando Bus. Jour., 1984—. Mem. U.S. working party to UN Jt. Commn. on Electronic Document Interchange. Mem. Airport Ops. Internat. (chmn. info. systems sub-commn. 1985-86, chmn. internat. airport ops. computer fair, 1988), Am. Assn. Airport Execs. (chmn. computer com.). Republican. Episcopalian. Home: 2815 S Atlantic Ave 102 Cocoa Beach FL 32931 Office: Greater Orlando Aviation Auth Orlando Internat Airport Orlando FL 32812

MAC CALLUM, ROBERT ALEXANDER, diplomat, government official, consultant; b. Pitts., Aug. 24, 1943; s. Samuel Wayne and Dorothy Louise (Smith) Mac C.; m. Alice Reiko Sugihara, July 11, 1970; children: Margaret R., Elizabeth S. AB, Wabash Coll., 1965; MS, MIT, 1971. Dep. dir. Mutual Def. Assistance Office, Tokyo, 1978-80; dir. Asia/Pacific CPT Corp., Mpls., 1980-82; first sec., consul U.S. Embassy, Manila, Philippines, 1982-83; counselor U.S. Mission to the UN, N.Y.C., 1983-85; exec. dir. Bur. of Intelligence and Research, Washington, 1985-87; counselor U.S. Embassy, Manila, 1987—. Mem. Am. Mgmt. Assn., Am. Fgn. Service Assn., Japan Soc., Greater Wabash Found., Phi Beta Kappa, Beta Theta Pi. Episcopalian. Clubs: Okura Internat. Office: American Embassy Manila APO San Francisco CA 96528

MACCAULEY, HUGH BOURNONVILLE, banker; b. Mt. Vernon, N.Y., Mar. 12, 1922; s. Morris Baker and Alma (Gardiner) MacC.; m. Rachael Gleaton, Aug. 320, 1943 (div. May 1980); m. Felice Cooper, Dec. 2, 1980. Student, Rutgers U., 1939-41, Tex. Christian U., 1948-50, U. Omaha, 1957-59. Commd. 2d lt. U.S. Army, 1942; advanced through grades to col. U.S. Army, USAF, Washington, 1943-73; v.p. Great Am. Securities, San Bernardino, Calif., 1979—; chmn. bd. Desert Community Bank, Victorville, Calif., 1980—. bd. dirs. Air Force Village West, 1986; chmn. bd. Gen. and Mrs. Curtis E. Lemay Found., 1987—. Decorated Air medal, Legion of Merit. Mem. Dadaelian Soc. Republican. Presbyterian. Lodge: Rotary. Home: 1630 Monroe St Riverside CA 92504 Office: Great Am Securities Inc 334 W 3d Suite 201 San Bernardino CA 92401

MACCHI, EUGENE EDWARD, package company executive; b. Kearney, N.J., July 20, 1926; s. Louis Robert and Teresa D. (Maher) M.; student Army spl. tng. program, Carnegie Inst. Tech., 1943-44; student Swarthmore Coll., 1945-47; BA, Kalamazoo Coll., 1948; m. Josephine M. Towle, May 5, 1951; children—Eugene E., Michael S., Mary Jo, Karen M., Robert C., Thomas J., Charles J.; m. 2d, Constance A. Dill, June 28, 1981; children—Robin, Rhys, Rhett, Ryan, Rourke, Rowan. Sales supr. Wyandotte Chems. Corp., 1948-54; mgr. Eastern div., Hankins Container div. MacMillan Bloedell, Union, N.J., 1954-62; pres., chmn. bd. Continental Packaging Corp., Kenilworth, N.J., New Castle, Pa., Macon, Ga., 1962-75, also dir.; pres., chmn. bd. Ind. Corrugated Container Corp. Am., Paterson, N.J., 1975—. Commr. NW Bergen County Sewer Authority, 1966-69, 75-80, chmn., 1967-69, 76-80. Served with USAAF, World War II. Mem. Assn. Eastern Corrugated Box Mfrs. (pres. 1973-75), Fibre Box Assn., Assn. Ind. Corrugated Converters (pres. 1975-77), C. of C., Young Pres. Orgn., Phi Sigma Kappa. Contbr. articles to trade mags. Home: 63 Arbor Dr Ho-Ho-Kus NJ 07423 Office: 55 Jersey ST Paterson NJ 07501

MACCHIA, ANTHONY FRANCIS, economist, management consultant; b. N.Y.C., Dec. 21, 1952; s. Frank and Stella M.; m. Irene Leung, Sept. 11, 1982. BA in Econs., SUNY-Stony Brook, 1973, B Engring., 1973; PhD, U. Pa., 1979. Economist, Office of Sec., Dept. Interior, Washington, 1976; instr. Wharton Sch.-Fels Ctr., U. Pa., Phila., 1977-78; sr. economist, antitrust div. Dept. Justice, Washington, 1979-81; mem. Atty. Gen.'s AT&T Relief Task Force, Washington, 1980-81; sr. assoc. Mgmt. Analysis Ctr., Washington, 1981-83; pres. Macchia & Co., Phila., 1983—; chief cons. mergers, acquisitions and bus. disputes Japanese and U.S. cos. Author: The Hospital and the Industrial Organization of the Hospital Market, 1979, The Challenges of a New Era: Competitive Strategy, Value Creation and Securitization, 1987, The Securitization of Real Estate: Strategies for Investment Banking, 1987; mem. bd. contbg. editors The Real Estate Fin. Jour., 1987—. Wharton-Fels fellow U. Pa., 1973-77; recipient U.S. Atty. Gen.'s Spl. Achievement award Dept. Justice, 1980. Fellow Tau Beta Pi; mem. Am. Econ. Assn., Am. Fin. Assn., Omicron Delta Epsilon. Roman Catholic. Home: 1945 Panama St Philadelphia PA 19103 Office: Macchia & Co 1411 Walnut St Suite 200 Philadelphia PA 19102

MACCOY, DOUGLAS MAIDLOW, veterinary surgeon; b. Washington, Aug. 15, 1947; s. Edgar Milton and Charlotte (Maidlow) MacC. B.S. in Animal Scis., Purdue U., 1969; D.V.M. magna cum laude, U. Ga., 1973. Diplomate Am. Coll. Vet. Surgeons. Intern, N.Y. State Coll. Vet. Medicine, Cornell U., Ithaca, N.Y., 1973-74, surg. resident, 1974-76, asst. prof. surgery, 1976-82; dir. avian rehab. project Coll. Vet. Medicine, U. Ill., Urbana, 1982—, asst. prof. surgery, 1982—. Mem. AVMA, Am. Animal Hosp. Assn., Assn. Avian Veterinarians, Vet. Cancer Soc., Am. Assn. Vet. Med. Records Adminstrn., Am. Assn. Vet Clinicians, Am. Motorcyclist Assn., Nat. Riflemans Assn., Raptor Research Found., Sigma Xi, Omega Tau Sigma, Phi Zeta. Home and Office: 1008 W Hazelwood Dr Urbana IL 61801

MACCRIMMON, KENNETH ROBERT, educator; b. Hamilton, Ont., Can., Dec. 28, 1937; s. Archibald Robert and Dorothy Anna (Williams) MacC.; m. Marilyn L. Turner, Feb. 3, 1962; children: Karyn, Keith, Brian. B.S., UCLA, 1959, M.B.A., 1960, Ph.D., 1965. Asst. prof. bus. adminstrn. Carnegie-Mellon U., 1964-68, asso. prof., 1968-70; prof. bus. adminstrn. U. B.C. (Can.), Vancouver, 1970-81; E.D. MacPhee prof. mgmt., 1981—, asst. dean grad. studies, 1978-79; J.L. Kellogg Disting. Prof. strategy and decision Northwestern U., Chgo., 1980-82; cons. to industry and govt.; vis. prof. econs. and psychology U. Calif., Santa Barbara, 1985; vis. prof. mgmt. Shanghai Jiao Tong U., China, 1985; Social Scis. and Humanities Research Council sabbatical leave fellow, 1975-76, 83-84; mem. adv. panel Nat. Sci. Found., 1988—. Co-author: Taking Risks, 1986. Contbr. articles on mgmt., econs, and psychology to acad. and profl. publs.; editorial bd.: Jour. Enterprise Mgmt, 1978—, Jour. Risk and Uncertainty, 1987—. Social Scis. and Humanities research grantee, 1972-88. Mem. Econometric Soc., Am. Econ. Assn., Public Choice Soc., Ops. Research Soc., Instl. Mgmt. Scis., Can. Assn. Univ. Tchrs. Office: Faculty of Commerce U BC, Vancouver, BC Canada V6T 1Y8

MACCUTCHEON, EDWARD MACKIE, naval architect, marine engineer; b. Bridgeport, Conn., Nov. 12, 1915; s. Edward Mackie and Laura (Stout) MacC.; BS, Webb Inst. Naval Arch., N.Y.C., 1937; postgrad. U. Md., 1948-49; M in Engring. Adminstrn., George Washington U., 1958; m. Jean Loeffler, June 20, 1942; children: Barbara Jean MacCutcheon Smith, Maryann MacCutcheon Lucero. With N.Y. Shipbldg. Co., Camden, N.J., 1937-38, U.S. Coast Guard, Washington, 1938-48, David Taylor Model Basin, Dept. Navy, 1948-49, Bur. Ships, 1949-55, Office of Naval Research, Washington, 1955-57; tech. dir. Naval Civil Engring. Lab., Port Hueneme, Calif., 1957-62; chief research and devel. Maritime Adminstrn., Dept. Commerce, Washington, 1962-66; dir. systems devel., Nat. Ocean Survey, NOAA, Rockville, Md., 1966-72; cons. engr., Bethesda, Md., 1973—. Served to lt. comdr. USCGR, 1943-46. Registered profl. engr., Md., D.C. Fellow Soc. Naval Architects and Marine Engrs., Marine Tech. Soc. ; mem. Am. Soc. Naval Engrs. (council), Fed. Exec. and Profl. Assn. (past nat. pres.), Accreditation Bd. for Engring. Tech. (engring. accreditation commn.). Address: 6405 Earlham Dr Bethesda MD 20817

MACDONALD, DONALD MICHAEL, dermatologist, educator; b. Wexford, Ireland, Feb. 9, 1944; came to U.K., 1946; s. Donald Francis and Patricia Mary (Daly) MacD.; m. Lesley Margaret Capper, July 1970; children—Alasdair Donald James, Christopher Michael Leslie. M.A., Cambridge U., 1966, M.B., 1969, B.Chir., 1969. Sr. registrar Inst. Dermatology, U. London, 1975-77, sr. lectr., 1985—; cons. dermatologist Guy's Hosp., London, 1977—, dir. Lab. of Applied Dermatopathology, 1977—; lectr. Guy's Hosp. Med. Sch., U. London, 1978—; examiner diploma of dermatology U. London, 1980—, med. doctorate degree, 1984—. Editor: Immunodermatology, 1984; contbr. numerous articles to profl. jours.; asst. editor Jour. Clin. and Exptl. Dermatology; mem. editorial bd. Am. Jour. Dermatopathology, Dermatologica. Wellcome European travelling fellow, 1977-78. Fellow Royal Coll. Physicians; mem. Soc. for Cutaneous Ultrastructure Research (sec. 1983-86, pres. 1986-88), European Soc. Dermatol. Research (bd. dirs. 1986—), Am. Acad. Dermatology, Am. Soc. Dermatopathology, Internat. Soc. Dermatopathology, Brit. Assn. Dermatologists, Brit. Soc. Investigative Dermatology, Brit. Soc. Dermatopathology, Royal Soc. Medicine (sec. sect. dermatology 1981-83), Societe Francaise de Dermatologie (hon.), Austrian Dermatology Soc., Korean Dermatol. Soc. (hon.), Phillipines Dermatol. Soc. (hon.). Roman Catholic. Avocations: travel; skiing; waterskiing; motorcars; antique furniture. Home: 75 Copers Cope Rd, Beckenham, Kent BR3 1NR, England Office: Guy's Hosp, London SE1 9RT, England

MACDONALD, FLORA ISABEL, Canadian government official; b. North Sydney, N.S., Can., June 3, 1926; d. George Frederick and Mary Isabel (Royle) MacD. Attended Empire Bus. Coll.; grad., Nat. Def. Coll., 1972; D.H.L. (hon.), Mt. St. Vincent U., 1979. Formerly in various secretarial positions; with Progressive Conservative Party Hdqrs., Ottawa, Ont., Can., 1956-65, exec. dir., 1960-65; adminstrv. officer, tutor dept. polit. studies Queen's U., 1966-72; also adv. Student Vocat. Bur.; mem. Can. Parliament for Kingston and the Islands, Ont., 1972—; Progressive Conservative spokesman for Indian affairs and no. devel. Can. Parliament, 1972; for housing and urban devel. 1974; chmn. Progressive Conservative Caucus Com. on Fed.-Provincial Relations, 1976; sec. of state for external affairs 1979-80, for external affairs and nat. def., 1980, minister employment and immigration, 1984-86, minister of communications, 1986—; V.p. Kingston and Islands Progressive Conservative Assn., 1962-72; nat. sec. Progressive Conservative Assn. of Can., 1966-69; exec. dir. Com. for Ind. Can., 1971; pres. Elizabeth Fry Soc. of Kingston, 1968-70. Mem. Can. Inst. Fgn. Affairs (dir. 1969-73), Can. Polit. Sci. Assn. (dir. 1972-75), Can. Inst. Internat. Affairs, Can. Civil Liberties Assn. Mem. United Ch. of Canada. Office: Minister of Communications, House of Commons, Ottawa, ON Canada K1A 0A6 *

MACDONALD, IAN GRANT, mathematician, educator; b. Brentford, Middlesex, Eng., Oct. 11, 1928; s. Douglas Grant and Irene Alice (Stokes) M.; m. Margaretha Maria Lodewijk Van Goethem, July 31, 1954; Alexander Grant, Christopher John, Catherine Ann, Helen Susan, Nicola Mary. BA, Cambridge (Eng.) U., 1952, MA, 1957; MA, Oxford U., 1963. Asst. prin. Ministry Supply, London, 1952-57, prin., 1957; asst. lectr. U. Manchester, Eng., 1957-60, Fielden prof. math., 1972-77; lectr. U. Exeter, Eng., 1960-63; fellow, tutor math. Oxford U., 1963-72; prof. math. U. London, 1977—. Author: Symmetric Functions and Hall Polynomials, 1979; (with M.F. Atiyah) Introduction to Commutative Algebra, 1969; contbr. articles to math. jours. Chmn. math. com. Sci. and Engring. Research Council, 1979-82. Served with Brit. army, 1947-49. Fellow Royal Soc. London; mem. London Math. Soc., Am. Math. Soc., Math. Assn. Am. Office: Queen Mary Coll Sch Math Scis, Mile End Rd, London E1 4NS, England

MACDONALD, JAMES CRAIG, language educator, writer; b. Fort Erie, Ont., Can., Feb. 19, 1948; s. Lloyd Francis and Mabel Evelyn (Wale) MacD.; B.A., Waterloo Luth. U., Ont., 1970; M.A., U. Toronto, Can., 1975. Prof. Humber Coll., Rexdale, Ont., Can., 1976-81, program coordinator, 1981-84, sr. program coordinator, 1984—, chmn. 1986—; cons. Ont. Heads of English, 1981—, Toronto High Sch. Bd., 1982—, Holt Rinehart & Winston, Prentice-Hall, Addison-Wesley, Research Pub., Toronto, 1981—. Contbr. articles to profl. jours. Fellow U. Toronto, 1973-75. Mem. MLA, Soc. Tech. Communication, Am. Med. Writers Assn., Writers Devel. Trust. Home: 390 Huron St Apt 2, Toronto, ON Canada M5S 2G6 Office: Humber Coll Dept Humanities, 205 Humber College Blvd, Etobicoke, ON Canada M9Z 1N6

MACDONALD, JEROME EDWARD, consultant school psychologist; b. Newark, Aug. 16, 1925; s. Jerome A. and Olvinia Regina (McKenna) MacD.; B.S., Niagara U., 1947, M.A. (grad. fellow), 1950; M.A. in Ednl. Psychology (experienced tchr. fellow), also profl. diploma in sch. psychology

Jersey City State Coll., 1970; postgrad. Fordham U., 1950-55; m. Nan Elizabeth Kennington, June 2, 1951; children—Jerome C., Mary Jane, Charles, Blanche (Mrs. Carroll Kohler), Ruth, Gregory, Paul, Robert, Carol. Asst. prof. philosophy Seton Hall U., South Orange, N.J., 1948-55, lectr. in philosophy, edn. 1955-61; tchr. English, Newark pub. schs., 1955-60, guidance counselor, 1960-62, chmn. dept., 1963-69, psychologist, 1969-71; psychologist Metuchen (N.J.) pub. schs., 1971-86; vis. tchr. NDEA Reading Inst., Bowling Green (Ohio) U., 1966-67; extern psychologist N.J. Diagnostic Center, Menlo Park, 1969; consulting psychologist Dept. Health and Social Services, Province of Prince Edward Island, 1987—. Troop treas. Boy Scouts Am., 1967-69. Served with inf., AUS, 1943-46. Decorated Bronze Star medal. Mem. Nat. Assn. Sch. Psychologists, Internat. Reading Assn., NEA, Am., N.J. psychol. assns., N.J. Assn. Sch. Psychologists, Middlesex County Sch. Psychologists Assn. (pres. 1976-77, 81-82), Psychol. Assn. Prince Edward Island, N.J. Catholic Tchrs. Guild (pres. 1966), VFW, Am. Legion, DAV, Holy Name Soc., Can. Legion, Mensa, Phi Delta Kappa. Roman Catholic. Clubs: Lions. Editor: (with Eli Levinson) The English Curriculum in Secondary Schools: Ninth Grade, 1964. Home: 1 MacDonald Rd, North Rustico, PE Canada C0A 1X0

MACDONALD, KAREN CRANE, occupational therapist, geriatric counselor; b. Denville, N.J., Feb. 24, 1955; d. Robert William and Jeanette Wilcox (Crane) M. B.S., Quinnipiac Coll., 1977; M.S., U. Bridgeport, 1982; postgrad. NYU, 1983—. Cert. occupational therapist; instr. NYU, 1985-88, Quinnipiac Coll., 1986—. occupational therapist, coordinator of special care unit Jewish Home for the Elderly, Fairfield, Conn., 1987—, N.Y. Inst., N.Y.C., 1984-86; pvt. practice, Fairfield County, Conn., 1977-88; lectr., cons. in field. Contbr. articles to profl. jours. Youth leader, deacon Union Meml. Ch., Stamford, Conn., 1980—. Teaching fellow NYU, 1983-86. Mem. World Fedn. Occupational Therapy, Am. Occupational Therapy Assn. (scholar 1985, council edn.), Conn. Occupational Therapy Assn. (gerontology liaison 1980-83). Avocations: photography; poetry writing; painting. Home: 56 Pepperbush Ln Fairfield CT 06430 Office: Jewish Home for Elderly 175 Jefferson St Fairfield CT 06430

MACDONALD, R. FULTON, venture developer, business educator; b. Monmouth County, N.J., Dec. 24, 1940; s. James Fleming Smith Macdonald and Jane Macfarlane Barnes Abbott; m. Carol Jean Archer, Mar. 29, 1963 (div. Jan. 1982); 1 child, Paige Brubaker Smith. A.B., U. Pa., 1963; M.B.A., 1969; Sr. mktg. mgmt. cert. Stanford U., 1979. Systems mgr., mcht. John Wanamaker, Inc., Phila., 1969-74; prin. Booz, Allen & Hamilton, N.Y.C., 1974-79; pres. Irwill Industries, N.Y.C., 1979-82; pres. Internat. Bus. Devel. Corp., N.Y.C., 1982—; chmn. IBEX Mktg. Corp., N.Y.C., 1988—; pres. Simfer Operational Internat., Inc., N.Y.C., 1984; vice chmn. Neusteter Co., Denver, 1984-85; dir. Fragrances Selective, Inc., 1985-87; mng. dir. Stuyvesant Group Internat., Dutch Am. Bus. Advisors, N.Y.C. and Amsterdam, 1987—; chmn. IBEX Mktg. Corp., N.Y.C., 1988—; adj. prof. Grad. Bus. Sch., Columbia U., N.Y.C., 1984-85. Designer Manpower Mgmt. Concepts computer system, 1972—; contbr. articles to bus. publs. Served to capt. inf. U.S. Army, 1963-67, Fed. Republic Germany, Vietnam. Decorated Bronze Star. Mem. Ripon Soc., Inst. Mgmt. Consultants, Global Econ. Action Inst., Soc. Mayflower Descendants, Soc. Coll. Alumni U. Pa. (pres. 1973-74). Republican. Christian Scientist. Avocation: squash. Home: Trump Tower 721 Fifth Ave New York NY 10022 Office: Internat Bus Devel Corp 237 Park Ave 21st Floor New York NY 10017

MACDONALD, RICHARD ANNIS, physician, educator; b. Manistee, Mich., July 23, 1928; s. Robert R. and Julia (Graczyk) MacD.; m. Jean Marie McLaughlin, June 7, 1954; children: Linda Anne, Richard Annis, Marie Aran. A.B., Albion Coll., 1951; M.D., Boston U., 1954. Intern Boston City Hosp., 1954-55, resident in pathology, 1955-59; mem. faculty Harvard Med. Sch., 1958-65, instr., 1959-60, asst. prof., 1962-65; prof. pathology Sch. Medicine U. Colo., 1966-69, Boston U. Med. Sch., 1969-70; prof. pathology, chmn. dept. pathology U. Mass. Med. Sch., Worcester, 1970-73; prof. pathology Boston U. Sch. Medicine, 1973-85, U. South Fla., 1985—; chief pathology service Norwood (Mass.) Hosp., 1973-83; assoc. chief staff research and edn. Denver VA Hosp., 1968-69; chief lab. service 1968-69, Boston VA Hosp., 1969-70, VA Hosp., Bay Pines, Fla., 1985—; Mem. study sec. NIH, 1967-69; mem. evaluation com. on research and edn. VA, 1966-68. Author: Hemochromatosis and Hemosiderosis, 1964, Computers in Pathology; also articles. Served with USNR, 1943-45. Mem. AMA, Am. Soc. Exptl. Pathology, Internat. Acad. Pathology, Mass. Med. Soc., New Eng. Soc. Pathology, Soc. Computers in Medicine, Mass. Soc. Pathology (treas. 1979-81, exec. com. 1977-85, pres. 1981-83), Phi Beta Kappa. Home: PO Box 516 Bay Pines FL 33504 Office: VA Hosp Seminole Blvd Bay Pines FL 33504 Other: 551 Sandy Hook Rd Saint Petersburgh FL 33706

MAC DONALD, ROBERT WILLIAM, life insurance company executive, author, lecturer; b. Rochester, N.Y., Feb. 11, 1943; s. Robert Ruben and Rosemary (McPhee) MacD.; m. Patricia K. Crean, Feb. 17, 1968; children: Ryan, Brandy, Piper, Colin, Braden, Robert. Student, Loyola U., Los Angeles, 1961-65; JD, Western State Coll. Law, Anaheim, Calif., 1975. CLU, 1976. Agt. New Eng. Life Ins. Co., Los Angeles, 1965-70; regional agy. mgr. Jefferson Standard Life Ins. Co., Los Angeles, 1970-75; v.p. mktg. devel. State Mut. Life Ins. Co., Worcester, Mass., 1976-77; sr. v.p., dir. mktg., then exec. v.p. ITT Life Ins. Corp., Mpls., 1977-79, exec. v.p., 1979-80, pres., chief exec. officer, 1980-87; chmn., chief exec. officer Life USA Holding Co., 1987—, Universal Security Assurance Life, 1987—. Author: Save The Agents, Control Your Future, Cheat To Win, 1986; contbr. articles to profl jours. bd. dirs. Mpls. council Girl Scouts U.S., 1982—. Served with USNG, 1965-71. Mem. Nat. Assn. Ind. Investors (bd. dirs.), Interfin. Assn. (bd. dirs.). Republican. Roman Catholic. Club: Wayzata Country (Minn.). Office: Life USA Holding Co 300 S County Rd 18 Minneapolis MN 55426

MACDONOGH, STEPHEN JOHN, publisher; b. Dublin, Ireland, Sept. 3, 1949; s. Jack Albert Middleton and Barbara Kathleen (Sullivan) McD. BA, York U., 1971. Chmn. Irish Writers' Co-operative, Dublin, 1977-81; editorial dir. Brandon Book Pubs. Ltd., Dingle, Kerry, Ireland, 1982—. Author: York Poems, 1972, My Tribe, 1982, Green and Gold, 1983, Visitors' Guide to Dingle, 1985. Mem. CLE (pres. 1987—). Office: Brandon Book Pubs Ltd, Cooleen, Dingle Kerry Ireland

MACDOUGALL, (GEORGE) DONALD (ALASTAIR), economist; b. Glasgow, Scotland, Oct. 26, 1912; s. Daniel Douglas and Beatrice Amy (Miller) MacD.; M.A. (George Webb Medley jr. and sr. scholarships in polit. economy), Balliol Coll., Oxford U., 1936; LL.D. (hon.), U. Strathclye, 1968; Litt.D. (hon.), U. Leeds, 1971; D.Sc. (hon.), U. Aston, Birmingham, 1979; m. Bridget Christabel Bartrum, 1937 (dissolved 1977); children—John Douglas, Mary Jean; m. 2d, Laura Margaret Hall, 1977. Asst. lectr., then lectr. econs. U. Leeds, 1936-39; with statis. br. Office First Lord Admiralty, 1939-40, Office Prime Minister, 1940-45; offcl. fellow Wadham Coll., Oxford U., 1945-50, domestic bursar, 1946-48, hon. fellow, 1964—, faculty fellow Nuffield Coll., 1947-50, professorial fellow, 1950-52, ofcl. fellow, 1952-64, first bursar, 1958-64, hon. fellow, 1967—, univ. Nuffield reader internat. econs., 1950-52; econ. dir. Orgn. European Econ. Cooperation, Paris, 1948-49; chief adv. statis. br. Office Prime Minister, 1951-53; vis. prof. Australian Nat. U., Canberra, 1959, M.I.T. Center Internat. Studies, New Delhi, 1961; econ. dir. Nat. Econ. Devel. Office, 1962-64; mem. Turnover Tax Com., 1963-64; dir. gen. Dept. Econ. Affairs, 1964-68; head govt. econ. service, chief econ. adv. Treasury, 1969-73; chief econ. adv. Confedn. Brit. Industry, 1973-84. Decorated knight, 1953, officer Order Brit. Empire, 1942, comdr., 1945. Fellow Brit. Acad.; mem. Council Royal Econ. Soc. (pres. 1972-74), Nat. Inst. Econ. and Social Research (chmn. exec. com. 1974-87), Soc. Strategic and Long-Range Planning (pres. 1977-85), Soc. Bus. Economists (v.p. 1978—). Club: Reform (London). Author: The World Dollar Problem, 1957; The Dollar Problem: A Reappraisal, 1960; Studies in Political Economy, 2 vols., 1975; Don and Mandarin: Memoirs of an Economist, 1987; co-author: Measures for International Economic Stability, 1951; The Fiscal System of Venezuela, 1959; chmn. EEC Report of Study Group on Role of Public Finance in European Intgration, 1977; contbr. articles to profl. publs.

MACDOUGALL, HARTLAND MOLSON, trust company executive; b. Montreal, Que., Can., Jan. 28, 1931; s. Hartland Campbell and Dorothy (Molson) MacD.; m. Eve Gordon, Oct. 29, 1954; children: Cynthia, Wendy, Keith, Willa, Tania. Ed., LeRosey, Switzerland, 1947-48, McGill U., 1949-53, Advanced Mgmt. Program, Harvard U., 1976. With Bank Montreal, various locations, 1953-84; sr. v.p. Alta. div. Bank Montreal, 1968-69, sr. v.p. Ont. div., 1969-70; exec. v.p. Bank Montreal, Toronto, 1970-73, Montreal, 1973-74; exec. v.p., gen. mgr. central ops. Bank Montreal, 1975-76, exec. v.p., gen. mgr. corp. banking, 1976-81; vice chmn. Bank Montreal (Ont. div.), 1981-84, also dir., 1974-84; chmn., dir. Royal Trustco Ltd., Toronto, 1984—; also chmn., dir. The Royal Trust Co. (subs.), Montreal; dep. chmn. Trilon Fin. Corp., Lonvest Corp., London Life Ins. Co.; bd. dirs. Paccar Can. Ltd., Royal LePage Ltd. Founding chmn. Heritage Can.; gov., past chmn. Council Can. Unity; pres. Duke of Edinburgh Awards in Can.; mem. adv. council Faculty of Commerce, U. B.C.; gov. Olympic Trust; trustee Lester B. Pearson Coll. of Pacific; bd. dirs. Can. Soc. for Weismann Inst., Empire Club Found., St. Michaels Hosp.; senator Stratford Shakespearean Found. Awarded Order of Can., 1981. Clubs: Vancouver, Vancouver Lawn Tennis and Badminton; Ranchmen's, Calgary Petroleum (Calgary, Alta.); St. James, Montreal Indoor Tennis, Mt. Royal, Montreal Racket, York, Badminton and Racket, Queen's, Toronto, Caledon Riding and Hunt, Caledon Ski. Office: Royal Trustco Ltd, PO Box 7500, Station A, Toronto, ON Canada M5W 1P9 *

MACDOUGALL, WILLIAM RODERICK, lawyer, county official; b. Nevada City, Calif., May 14, 1914; s. William Stewart and Ethel Martha (Hutchison) McDougall; m. Carol Bernie Keane, May 1, 1937; children—Marcia MacDougall Williams, James Stewart. A.A., Sacramento City Coll., 1930-32; student U. Calif.-Berkeley, 1933-34; J.D., U. of Pacific, 1941. Bar: Calif. 1941, U.S. Dist. Ct. (no. dist.) Calif. 1941, U.S. Supreme Ct. 1950. Library page Calif. State Library, Sacramento, 1932-33; sr. auditor Office of Controller, State of Calif., Sacramento, 1934-37; chief bur. of collections Calif. Social Welfare Dept., Sacramento, 1937-42; gen. counsel County Suprs. Assn. Calif., Sacramento, 1946-70; exec. dir. U.S. Intergovt. Relations Commn., Washington, 1970-75; planning commr. County of Orange, Santa Ana, Calif., 1976-84; chief counsel Calif. Alcoholic Beverage Control Appeals Bd., 1984—; exec. dir. Calif. County Govt. Edn. Found., 1965-69; chmn. home rule com. Nat. Assn. Counties, 1963-67. Mem. Fed. Public Assistance Adv. Council, 1959-60, Gov.'s Commn. on Met. Problems, Calif., 1960; pres. Laguna Beach Sch. of Art (Calif.), 1983-84. Mem. Am. Planning Assn., Nat. Assn. County and Pros. Attys. (hon.), Calif. County Planning Commrs. Assn. (dir. 1981-84). Republican. Presbyterian. Office: 1001 6th St #401 Sacramento CA 95814-3324

MACE, DAVID M., banker; b. 1938. B.A., Amherst Coll., 1960; LL.B., U. Va., 1964. Assoc. Cadivalader, Wickersham & Taft, 1964-65; sec. Irving Bank Corp., 1967; with Irving Trust Co., N.Y.C., 1966—, resident counsel, 1966-70, v.p. loan adminstrn., 1970-71, v.p. internat. ops., 1971-74, v.p., mgr., Tokyo branch, 1974-79, sr. v.p. internat. corp. banking, 1979-80, exec. v.p. internat. banking group, 1980-82, sr. exec. v.p. internat. banking activities, 1982-84, pres., 1984—, dir. Office: Irving Trust Co One Wall St New York NY 10005 *

MACE, SHARON ELIZABETH, physician; b. Syracuse, N.Y., Oct. 30, 1949; d. James Henry and Leona Helen (Bednarski) M.; B.S., Syracuse U., 1971; M.D., SUNY, 1975. Intern and resident in pediatrics Case-Western Res. U. Hosps., Cleve., 1975-77, fellow in cardiology, 1977-79, instr. dept. emergency medicine, 1980—; research assoc. div. investigative medicine Mt. Sinai Med. Center, Cleve., 1979-80, staff physician depts. emergency medicine and investigative medicine, 1980-86, coordinator emergency medicine residency program; asst. dir. dept. emergency medicine Mt. Sinai Med. Ctr.; dir. emergency dept. Saratoga Hosp., Saratoga Springs, N.Y., 1986-88; dir. emergency dept. St. Mary's Hosp., Rochester, N.Y., 1988—; former instr. Case Western Res. U. Sch. Medicine; helicopter flight physician; lectr. Lakeland Community Coll.; instr. Advanced Cardiac Life Support. Contbr. articles to med. jours. Mem. Am. Coll. Emergency Physicians (edn. com., dir. Ohio chpt., bd. dirs. N.Y. chpt.), Soc. Tchrs. Emergency Medicine, Univ. Assn. for Emergency Medicine. Congregationalist. Home: 68 Waterview Circle Rochester NY 14626 Office: St Mary's Hosp 89 Genesee St Rochester NY 14625

MACEDA, JAIME M., chemist; b. Pagsanjan, Laguna, Philippines, Mar. 12, 1943; came to U.S., 1968; s. Vicente Fernandez and Julieta (Maceda) M.; m. Remedios Belmonte Paat, Oct. 19, 1974; 1 child, Therese Marie-Juliet. B.S. in Chemistry, Mapua Inst. Tech., Manila, 1965. Quality control supr. Mercury Drug Co., Manila, 1965-68; quality control chemist Consol. Distilled Products, Chgo., 1968-70; supr. chemistry Rosner-Hixon Lab., Chgo., 1970-78; chief chemist Rosner-Runyon Lab., Chgo., 1978-86; div. mgr. Aqualab Inc., Chgo., 1986—; judge Chgo. Pub. Schs. Sci. Fair, 1971—. Mem. Assn. Vitamin Chemists, Am. Chem. Soc. Roman Catholic. Office: Aqualab Inc 222 S Morgan St Chicago IL 60607

MACER, DAN JOHNSTONE, hospital administrator; b. Evansville, Ind., May 25, 1917; s. Clarence Guy and Ann (Johnstone) M.; m. Eugenia Loretta Andrews, June 1, 1943; children: Eugenia Ann, Dan James. B.S., Northwestern U., 1939, M.S. in Hosp. Adminstrn. with distinction, 1959. Chief hosp. ops. VA br. office, St. Paul, 1947-50; asst. mgr. VA hosps., Ft. Wayne, Ind., 1951, Kerrville, Tex., 1952, Augusta, Ga., 1952-56; mgr. VA Hosp., Sunmount, N.Y., 1956-58; dir. Va Research Hosp., Chgo., 1958-62; mem. hosp. adminstrn. faculty Northwestern U., 1959-61; dir. VA Hosps., Pitts., 1962-67; asst. vice chancellor health professions U. Pitts., 1968-71; prof. med. and hosp. adminstrn. U. Pitts. Grad. Sch. Pub. Health, 1962-71; prof. Coll. Health and Coll. Medicine, U. Okla., 1971—; dir. VA Hosps. and Clinics, Oklahoma City, 1971-76, VA Med. Dist. 20 (Okla.-Ark.), 1971-76; lectr. George Washington U., 1961-71; v.p. Hosp. Casualty Co., Oklahoma City, 1978—; pres. Dan J. Macer & Assos., Inc.; cons. to health field; cons. nat. health profl. assns., indsl. corps., archtl. corps, health planners; cons. Health Services and Mental Health Adminstrn., HEW, 1968. Mem. editorial bd.: Nursing and Health Care, 1980—; author articles in field. Coordinator civil def. and disaster planning all hosps., Chgo. nr. North Side, 1961; chmn. welfare and planning council Savannah River Community Chest, Augusta, 1954-56; chmn. group 17 fed. sect., govt. div. United Fund Allegheny County, 1964-65; mem. Fed. Interagy. Bd. Dirs., 1964-68; sec. U. Pitts. Health Center, 1969-71; chmn. health com. Health and Welfare Assn. Allegheny County, 1970-71; chmn. devel. com. Northwestern U. Alumni Program in Hosp. Adminstrn.; chmn. adv. com. Regional Med. Program Western Pa., 1966-71; mem. steering com. Comprehensive Health Planning Western Pa.; dir. Am. States Regional Conf., 1971; vice chmn. procedures com., mem.-at-large exec. com. Okla. Regional Med. Program, 1971-78; mem. Gov's Adv. Com. Comprehensive Health Planning, 1971-80, Gov's Com. Employment of Handicapped, 1972, Pres.'s Com. Employment of Handicapped, 1962; chmn. VA chief med. dir.'s com. for evaluation and reorgn. VA health care delivery services, 1974-76; chmn. planning com. for constrn. New Children's Meml. Hosp., 1974-78; chmn. Gov.'s Ad Hoc Com on Fed.-State Planning, 1973-78; mem. Gov.'s Health Scis. Center planning and adv. com., 1973-78, State Health Planning Council, 1973-78; chmn. Okla. Health Goals and Planning Priorities Com., 1973—; bd. dirs. Comprehensive Health Planning Agy., Western Pa.; bd. dirs. Health Services Corp., 1969-71, Okla. affiliate Am. Heart Assn., 1980—; trustee Okla. Council Health Careers and Manpower, 1976-80; Examiner Am. Coll. Hosp. Adminstrs. Served maj. Med. Adminstrv. Corps AUS, 1941-46. Decorated Bronze Star, Purple Heart; recipient citations VFW, 1959, citations Am. Legion, 1956, 58, citations DAV, 1964, citations Okla. Regional Med. Program, 1976, citations Okla. Gov.'s Office Health Planning, 1976, Laura G. Jackson award in recognition exceptional service in field of hosp. adminstrn., 1971, Disting. Service award Coll. Pub. Health U. Okla., 1987, Disting. Dedicated Service award Okla. Hosp. Assn., 1987; Established Leadership programs in his honor. Fellow Am. Pub. Health Assn., Am. Coll. Health Care Execs. (life); mem. Am. Hosp. Assn. (life, mem. council med. edn. 1976-79), Hosp. Assn. Pa. (vice chmn. med. relations 1965-66, chmn. rehab. com. 1965-66, vice chmn. council on profl. practices, dir.), Hosp. Council Western Pa., Assn. Am. Med. Colls. (exec. com. council teaching hosps.), Oklahoma City C. of C. (vice chmn. research and edn. div. 1975-80), Northwestern U. Alumni Assn. (pres. Acacia chpt. 1961, hosp. adminstrn. chpt. 1962). Clubs: Kiwanian. (Chgo.); University (Pitts.); Twin Hills Golf and Country. Home and Office: Dan J Macer & Assocs Inc 2925 Pelham Dr Oklahoma City OK 73120

MACER-STORY, EUGENIA ANN, writer, artist; b. Mpls., Jan. 20, 1945; d. Dan Johnstone and Eugenia Loretta (Andrews) Macer; divorced; 1 child, Ezra Arthur Story. BS in Speech, Northwestern U., 1965; MFA, Columbia U., 1968. Writing instr. Polyarts, Boston, 1970-72; theater instr. Joy of Movement, Boston, 1972-75; artistic dir. Magik Mirror, Salem, Mass., 1975-76; artistic dir. Magick Mirror Communications, Woodstock, N.Y., 1977—. Author: Congratulations: The UFO Reality, 1978, Angels of Time, 1982, Project Midas, 1986; (plays) Fetching the Tree, Archeological Politics, Strange Inquiries, others; philosophy writer; contbr. articles to profl. jours.; author poetry in Woodstock Times, Manhattan Poetry Rev., others; feature writer, editorial cons. Body, Mind, Spirit mag. Shubert fellow, 1968. Mem. Dramatists Guild, AAAS, N.Y. Acad. Sci., U.S. Psychotronics Assn., Center for UFO Studies. Democrat. Avocations: swimming, outdoor activities, hiking. Office: Magick Mirror Communications Box 854 Woodstock NY 12498

MACFADYEN, ALEXANDER HUGH, corporate financial executive; b. Tarrytown, N.Y., Oct. 6, 1931; s. Andrew Aird and Joan (Fraser) MacF.; m. Constance De Michelle, Apr. 29, 1961; children: Hugh, Alison. BBA, Iona Coll., 1959. Auditor Touche Ross and Co., N.Y.C., 1959-63; asst. controller Westrex div. Litton Inds., New Rochelle, N.Y., 1964-68; treas. Litton Ednl. Publs., Inc., N.Y.C., 1969-71, v.p. fin., 1972-75; v.p., controller Litton Inds. Pub. Group, Oradell, N.J., 1975-81; v.p. fin. NFL Properties, Inc., N.Y.C., 1982—. Served to staff sgt. USAF, 1951-55. Mem. Nat. Assn. Accts., Mag. Pubs. Assn., Controllers Council, The Bus. Planning Bd. Republican. Clubs: Pascack Valley Radio Control Flying (pres. 1984-87), Rockland Radio Control Flying. Home: 12 Edgebrook Ln Monsey NY 10952 Office: NFL Properties Inc 410 Park Ave New York NY 10022

MAC FADYEN, BRUCE VISCHER, JR., physician and surgeon; b. Phila., Nov. 4, 1942; s. Bruce V. and Renee S. (Smith) MacF.; B.S., Wheaton Coll., 1964; M.D., Hahnemann Med. Coll., 1968; m. Rosemary Mortensen, June 18, 1965; children—Sharon Ruth, Deborah Renee, Bruce Vischer, Christina Elizabeth. Intern, Hosp. of U. Pa., 1968-69, asst. resident gen. surgery, 1969-72, Hermann Hosp., Houston, 1972-73, chief resident surgery, 1973-74; research fellow Harrison dept. surg. research U. Pa. Sch. Medicine, Phila., 1971-72; practice medicine specializing in surgery, Phila., 1968-72, Houston, 1972—; asst. instr. surgery U. Pa., Phila., 1969-72; instr. surgery U. Tex. Med. Sch., Houston, 1973-74, asst. prof. surgery, 1974-77, asso. prof. surgery, 1977—; mem. staff Hermann, Meml. S.W., Diagnostic, Park Plaza hosps., Houston. Diplomate Am. Bd. Surgery. Fellow ACS; mem. Assn. Acad. Surgery, Am. Soc. Parenteral and Enteral Nutrition, Soc. Surgery of Alimentary Tract, Internat. Soc. Parenteral Nutrition, Soc. Surg. Oncology, Am. Cancer Soc. (dir. 1976-80), Harris County Med. Soc., AMA, Tex. Med. Assn., Christian Med. Soc., Tex. Surg. Soc., Ravdin-Rhoads Surg. Soc., Am. Soc. Laser Medicine and Surgery, Collegium Internat. Chirurgiae. Baptist. Contbr. numerous articles on nutrition, surgery and oncology to med. jours. Home: 303 Glenchester Houston TX 77079 Office: 6431 Fannin St Houston TX 77030

MACFARLANE, JUDY ANNE, librarian; b. Montreal, Que, Can, Feb. 20, 1955; d. George Yates and Catherine Lorna (Boyd) Hamilton; m. Peter Edward Campbell, Sept. 19, 1981; 1 child, Brendan Ian George. BA, McGill U., 1977, MLS, 1980. Reference librarian Cote St. Luc Pub. Library, Montreal, Que., Can., 1978-80, Govt. Documents dept. McGill U., Montreal, 1979-80; librarian Montreal West High Sch., 1980; mgr. info. resources Peat Marwick, Montreal, 1980—; prin. J.A. Macfarlane & Assocs., Montreal, 1987—. Contbr. to book Internat. Guide to Security Exchanges, 1987. Mem. Spl. Libraries Assn. (past pres., mem. profl. devel. com. Ea. Can. chpt., 1987—), Canadian Tax Found., Assn. de Planification Fiscale et Financière. Mem. Liberal party. Club: Southwest One (Pointe-Claire, Que., Can.). Home: 124 Hastings Ave, Pointe Claire Can H9R 3P5 Office: Peat Marwick, 1155 Dorchester Blvd W, Suite 2000, Montreal Can H3B 2J9

MACGEACHY, ROBIN WILLIAM, manufacturing company executive; b. Lennoxtown, Scotland, July 2, 1964; s. Robert Blackwood and Clementina (Henderson) MacG. Student, Gordonstoun Coll., Elgin, Scotland, 1983. Salesman Jun-Air, A/S, Aalborg, Denmark, 1983-84; mktg. mgr. Jun-Air (U.K.) Ltd., Glasgow, Scotland, 1984-85, mng. dir., 1987—; mktg. mgr. Jun-Air, Inc., Racine, Wis., 1985-86; tutor, tchr. Leadership Trust Mgmt. Sch., Ross on Wye, Eng., 1987—; bd. dirs. Complete Protection Ltd., Glasgow. Mem. Conservative Party. Club: Western (Glasgow). Home: 3 Boclair Crescent, Bearsden, Glasgow G61 2AG, Scotland Office: Jun-Air (UK) Ltd, Bridge St, Linwood Paisley PA3 3DG, Scotland

MAC GOWAN, MARY EUGENIA, lawyer; b. Turlock, Calif., Aug. 4, 1928; d. William Ray and Mary Bolling (Gilbert) Kern; m. Gordon Scott Millar, Jan. 2, 1970; 1 dau., Heather Mary. A.B., U. Calif., Berkeley, 1950; J.D., U. Calif., San Francisco, 1953. Bar: Calif. bar. Research atty. Supreme Ct. Calif., 1954, Calif. Ct. Appeals, 1955; partner firm MacGowan & MacGowan, Calif., 1956-68; individual practice law San Francisco, 1968—. Bd. dirs. San Francisco Speech and Hearing Center, San Francisco Legal Aid Soc., J.A.C.K.I.E. Mem. Am., Calif., San Francisco bar assns., Queen's Bench. Clubs: San Francisco Lawyers, Forest Hill Garden. Office: The Monadnock Suite 400 685 Market St San Francisco CA 94105

MACGREGOR, ROBERT NEIL, museum director, art historian; b. Glasgow, Scotland, June 16, 1946; s. Alexander Rankin and Anna Fulton (Neil) MacG. MA, Oxford U., 1967; LLB, Edinburgh U., Scotland, 1970; MA, Courtland Inst. Art, London, 1975. Advocate Faculty of Advocates, Edinburgh, Scotland, 1972—; lectr. U. Reading, England, 1976-81; editor The Burlington Mag., London, 1981-86; dir. The Nat. Gallery, London, 1987—. Office: The Nat Gallery, Trafalgar Sq, London WC2 5DN, England

MACHARSKI, FRANCISZEK CARDINAL, archbishop of Cracow; b. Cracow, Poland, May 20, 1927. D.Theology. Ordained priest Roman Cath. Ch., 1950; engaged in pastoral work, 1950-56; theol. studies, Fribourg, Switzerland, 1956-60; tchr. pastoral theology Faculty Theology, Cracow, 1963; rector Archdiocesan Sem., Cracow, 1970; archbishop of Cracow, 1979—; elevated to Sacred Coll. of Cardinals , 1979; titular ch., St. John at the Latin Gate; mem. Congregation of Clergy, 1979, Congregation of Cath. Edn., 1981, Congregation for Bishops, 1983, council for pub. affairs, 1984; v.p. Polish Bishops Conf., 1979; vice chair Sci. Council Polish Episcopate, 1981, Episcopate Com. for Gen. Ministry, 1979; chair Episcopate Com. for Laity, 1981, mem. Episcopate Com. for Cath. Sci., 1983, Episcopate Com. for Emigration Ministry, 1988. Address: ul Franciszkanska 3, 31-004 Krakow Poland

MACHEMEHL, JERRY LEE, civil engineer, educator; b. Bryan, Tex., Jan. 8, 1938; s. Louis Arnold and Martha Lillian (Anderson) M.; BS in Archtl. Constrn., Tex. A&M U., 1970, BSCE, 1962, MS in Hydraulic Engring., 1968, Ph.D. in Civil Engring., 1970; diploma U.S. Army Command and Gen. Staff Coll., 1977; m. Pat Curry, Dec. 26, 1959; children—Terri, David, Traci. Civil engr. U.S. Army Engr. Dist., Little Rock, 1964, hydraulic engr., 1965; engring. research assoc. coastal and ocean engring. div., dept. civil engring. Tex. A&M U., College Station, 1967-68, instr., 1969-70; research engr. Wilson Industries, Houston, Tex., 1969-70; asst. prof. civil engring. N.C. State U., Raleigh, 1970-76, assoc. prof. civil engring., 1976-78, assoc. prof. marine sci. and engring., 1978-80; sr. staff civil engr. ARCO Oil & Gas Co., Dallas, 1980-87; assoc. prof. ocean and civil engring. dept. civil engring. Tex. A&M U., College Station, 1987—; cons. ocean and coastal engring., 1970—. Served with USAR, 1962—. U.S. Army C.E. fellow, 1968-69; W.G. Mills Meml. fellow, 1969; registered profl. engr., Tex., N.C., Alaska. Fellow ASCE; mem. Tau Beta Pi, Chi Epsilon, Sigma Xi, Phi Delta Kappa, Tau Sigma Delta, Phi Kappa Phi. Baptist. Contbr. numerous articles on Arctic, coastal and marine engring. to profl. jours.; research in hydrodynamics and coastal processes. Office: Tex A&M U Ocean Engring Program Dept Civil Engring Wisenbaker Engring Research Ctr College Station TX 77843

MACHOVER, CARL, computer graphics cons.; b. Bklyn., Mar. 26, 1927; s. John Herman and Rose (Alter) M.; BEE, Rensselaer Poly. Inst., 1951; postgrad. NYU, 1953-56; m. Wilma Doris Simon, June 18, 1950; children: Tod, Julie, Linda. Mgr. applied engring. Norden div. United A/C Corp., 1951-59; mgr. sales Skiatron Electronics & TV, N.Y.C., 1959-60; v.p. mktg., dir. Info. Displays, Inc., Mount Kisco, N.Y., 1960-73, v.p., gen. mgr., 1973-76; pres. Machover Assocs. Corp., White Plains, N.Y., 1976—; adj. prof. Rensselaer Poly. Inst. Mem. adv. bd. Pratt Center for Computer Graphics in

Design. Served with USNR, 1945-46. Recipient Frank Oppenheimer award Am. Soc. for Engring. Edn., 1971, Orthagonal award N.C. State U., 1988; named to Computer Graphics Hall of Fame Fine Arts Mus. of L.I., Hempstead, N.Y., 1988. Fellow Soc. for Info. Display (pres. 1968-70); mem. IEEE, Assn. for Computing Machinery, Am. Inst. Design and Drafting, Nat. Soc. Profl. Engrs., Nat. Computer Graphics Assn. (dir., pres.-elect 1988), Computer Graphics Pioneer, Sigma Xi, Tau Beta Pi, Eta Kappa Nu. Author: Gyro Primer, 1957; Basics of Gyroscopes, 1958; mem. editorial bd. IEEE Computer Graphics and Applications, Computers and Graphics, Spectrum, S. Klein Newsletter on Computer Graphics; co-editor CAD/CAM Handbook, 1980, Computer Graphics Rev.; contbr. articles to profl. jours. Home: 152 Longview Ave White Plains NY 10605 Office: 199 Main St White Plains NY 10601

MACHT, STUART MARTIN, defense contractor executive; b. Balt., June 18, 1930; s. Louis Ephraim and Nettie (Harris) M.; m. Ann Custis Boyd, Nov. 12, 1951; children: Steven Craig, Linda Lee, Andrew Parks. BSME, Duke U., 1951. Registered profl. engr. Md. Exptl. test engr. Pratt & Whitney Aircraft, East Hartford, Conn., 1951-52; mech. engr. Indsl. Research Lab., Balt., 1952; v.p., treas., controller AAI Corp., Balt., 1953—; mem. Balt. County Fin. Adv. Group, 1987-88. Author numerous tech. handbooks for company design use, 1956-79. Bd. gov's. Goodwill Industries, Balt., 1986, bd. dirs., 1988—; pres. Montview Community Assn., 1987-88; mem. fin. adv. group Balt. County Govt., 1987-88. Mem. Am. Def. Preparedness Assn., Am. Mgmt. Assn., ASME, Balt. County C. of C. (sr. v.p., bd. dirs. 1984-85, pres. 1986), Towson State U. Industry Luncheon Club (chmn. bd. dirs. 1985-88), Pi Mu Epsilon, Tau Beta Pi, Pi Tau Sigma, Phi Beta Kappa. Office: AAI Corp PO Box 126 Hunt Valley MD 21030-0126

MACHTIGER, HARRIET GORDON, psychoanalyst; b. N.Y.C., July 27, 1927; d. Michael J. and Miriam D. (Rand) Gordon; B.A., Bklyn. Coll., 1947; dipl. with distinction, U. London, 1966, Ph.D., 1974; m. Sidney Machtiger, Feb. 7, 1948; children—Avram Coleman, Marcia Gordon, Bennett Rand. Tchr., Phila. Public Schs., 1962-64; ednl. therapist Child Guidance Tng. Center, London, 1966-68; ednl. therapist Sch. Psychol. Service, Inner London Edn. Authority, 1968-70; therapist Paddington Day Hosp., London, 1970-71, London Centre for Psychotherapy, 1971-74, Staunton Clinic, U. Pitts., 1974-78; pvt. practice psychoanalysis, Pitts., 1976—; pres. C.G. Jung Center, Pitts., 1976-81; cons. in field. Mem. SW Pitts. Community Mental Health, 1976-78. Recipient award for Disting. Contributions to Advancement in Edn., Pa. Dept. Edn., 1962; Social Sci. Research Council award, 1973; cert. psychologist, Pa. Fellow Am. Orthopsychiat. Assn.; mem. Inter-Regional Soc. Jungian Analysts. (dir. Pitts. program 1975-85), Am. Acad. Psychotherapists, Am. Psychol. Assn., N.Y. Assn. Analytical Psychologists, Internat. Assn. Group Psychotherapists, Pa. Psychol. Assn., Brit. Psychol. Soc., Brit. Assn. Psychotherapists, Assn. Child Psychology and Child Psychiatry, Western Pa. Group Psychotherapy Assn., Nat. Assn. for Advancement Psychoanalysis, NOW. Home: 207 Tennyson Ave Pittsburgh PA 15213 Office: 110 The Fairfax 4614 5th Ave Pittsburgh PA 15213

MACHULAK, EDWARD LEON, real estate, mining and financial corporation executive; b. Milw., July 14, 1926; s. Frank and Mary (Sokolowski) M.; B.S. in Accounting, U., Wis., 1949; student spl. courses various univs.; m. Sylvia Mary Jablonski, Sept. 2, 1950; children—Edward A., John E., Lauren A., Christine M., Paul E. Chmn. bd., pres., Commerce Group Corp., Milw., 1962—, San Luis Estates, Inc., 1973—, Homespan Realty Co., Inc., 1974—, Universal Developers, Inc., 1972—, Picadilly Advt. Agy., Inc., 1974—; chmn. bd., chief exec. officer, Gen. Lumber & Supply Co., Inc., 1952—; bd. dirs., v.p., San Sebastian Gold Mines, Inc., 1969-73, chmn. bd., pres., 1973—; bd. dirs. sec., LandPak, Inc., 1985—; bd. dirs. Edjo Ltd., 1974—, sec., 1976—; ptnr., Weem Assocs., 1974—. Mem. Nat. Adv. Council U.S. SBA, 1972-74, co-chmn. 1973, 74. Recipient Recognition award U.S. SBA, 1975. Mem. Nat. Assn. Small Bus. Investment Co's (nat. chmn. legis. com. 1968-73, bd. govs. 1970-74, exec. com. 1971-74, sec. 1972-74, Disting. Service award to Am. Small Bus. 1970), Midwest Regional Assn. Small Bus. Investment Cos. (bd. dirs. 1968-74, v.p. 1970-71, pres. 1971-72, Outstanding Services award 1972), State of Wis. Council on Small Bus. Investment (chmn. 1973-74), Wis. Bd. Realtors (various coms. 1955—), Milw. Bd. Realtors (various coms. 1955—). Pres.' Council Marmion Mil. Acad., Aurora, Ill., 1966-79, lay life trustee, 1972, fin. advisor 1967-71, chmn. spl. fund raising com. 1966-67, planning com. 1972-79, chmn. adv. bd. Jesuit Retreat House, Oshkosh, Wis., 1966-68; chmn., bd. dirs. Spencerian Coll. of Bus., 1973-74; chmn. St. John Cathedral Symphony Concert Com., Milw., 1978; sustaining mem. Met. Mus. Art, 1974—. Served with AUS, 1945-46. Recognized bus. leader in Congl. Record, 1976; named Hon. Life Mem., Mid-Continental Railway, 1963. Clubs: Milw. Athletic, Tripoli Golf (Milw.); Met., Canadian (N.Y.C.). Lodge: KC (4th degree 1971—). Home: 903 W Green Tree Rd River Hills WI 53217 Office: 6001 N 91st St Milwaukee WI 53217

MACHUNGO, MARIO DA GRACA, government official. Prime minister Mozambique, 1986—. Address: Office of Prime Minister, Maputo Mozambique *

MACICA, JOSEPH MILES, industrial manufacturing company official; b. Baroda, Mich., Oct. 2, 1936; s. Joseph Miraslav and Helen Antonia (Cesnak) M. Student Western Mich. U., 1959-60, Bates Coll., Lewiston, Maine, 1963; B.S.B.A. in Indsl. Mgmt., U. Fla., 1965. European tour condr. Olson Travel Orgn., Chgo., 1965-66; asst. to pres. Basic C Corp., Bridgman, Mich., 1967-68; mgr. telecontrol hydraulics div. Bendix, St. Joseph, Mich., 1968-74, product coordinator engine controls div., Newport News, Va., 1974-76, planner, 1976-80, supr. prodn. control, 1980-81; sr. planner, supr. prodn. control Bendix Electronic Controls div. Allied Automotive, Newport News, 1981-84, planner internat. trade zone ops., 1985—. Pres. bd. dirs. Sonoma Woods Condo, Newport News, 1978—. Served with U.S. Army, 1955-57. Mem. Phi Kappa Phi, Beta Gamma Sigma. Club: Twin City Camera (St. Joseph) (pres. 1972-73); Keel (Newport News, Va.). Home: 1441 Ventura Way Newport News VA 23602 Office: Bendix Electronic Controls div Allied Automotive 615 Bland Blvd Newport News VA 23602

MACK, ALAN WAYNE, interior designer; b. Cleve., Oct. 30, 1947; s. Edmund B. and Florence I. (Oleska) M. BS in Interior Design, Case Western Res. U., 1969. Designer interior design dept. Halle's, Cleve., 1969, 71-73; designer Nahan Co., New Orleans, 1973-75, Hemenway's Contract Design, New Orleans, 1975-76; ptnr. Hewlett-Mack Design Assocs., New Orleans, 1976-86; assoc. dir. interior design Hansen Lind Meyer, Inc., 1986—; adv. com. interior design dept. Delgado Jr. Coll., New Orleans; mktg./merchandising adv. council St. Mary's Dominican Coll., New Orleans. Served with U.S. Army, 1969-71. Co-author audiovisual presentation Nat. Home Improvement Council Conf., 1981. Mem. ASID (profl. mem., presdl. citation, 1980, treas. La. dist. chpt. 1984), Found. for Interior Design Edn. Research (standards com., 1972-76, bd. visitors 1977-80, accreditation com., 1981). Home: 9 Parsons Ave Iowa City IA 52240

MACK, BRENDA LEE, sociologist, public relations consulting company executive; b. Peoria, Ill., Mar. 24; d. William James and Virginia Julia (Pickett) Palmer; A.A., Los Angeles City Coll.; B.A. in Sociology, Calif. State U., Los Angeles, 1980; m. Rozene Mack, Jan. 13 (div.); 1 child, Kevin Anthony. Ct. clk. City of Blythe, Calif.; partner Mack Trucking Co., Blythe; ombudsman, sec. bus facilities So. Calif. Rapid Transit Dist., Los Angeles, 1974-81; owner Brenda Mack Enterprises, Los Angeles, 1981—; lectr., writer, radio and TV personality; co-originator advt. concept View/Door Project; pub. News from the United States newsletter through U.S. and Europe. Past bd. dirs. Narcotic Symposium, Los Angeles. Served with U.S. WAC. Mem. Women For, Calif. State U. Los Angeles Alumni. Home: 8749 Cattaraugus Ave Los Angeles CA 90034 Office: Brenda Mack Enterprises PO Box 5942 Los Angeles CA 90055

MACK, JOHN OSCAR, lawyer; b. Columbus, Ohio, May 10, 1932; s. Eugene Henry and Eunice A. (Genthner) M.; m. Cristina Ann Iannone, Nov. 19, 1967; children—John Whitney, Elizabeth Ann, Andrew Laughlin. B.S. in Econs., U. Pa., 1954, LL.B. cum laude, 1961. Bar: Calif. 1962, U.S. Dist. Ct. (no. dist.) Calif. 1962, U.S. Supreme Ct. 1979, U.S. Ct. Appeals (9th cir.) 1981. Assoc. firm Pillsbury, Madison & Sutro, San Francisco, 1961-63; asst. v.p., sec. Bank of Calif. (N.A.), San Francisco, 1963-75, v.p., sec., 1972-75, BanCal Tri State Corp., 1972-75; practice law, San Francisco, 1976—; sr. mng. ptnr. firm Mack, Hazlewood, Franecke & Tinney, San Francisco, 1978—; gen. ptnr. Red Hills Investment Co., 1979—. Bd. dirs. Lone Mountain Children's Ctr., 1973—, pres., 1977-85. Served to lt. USNR, 1954-58. Republican. Home: 2963 23d Ave San Francisco CA 94132 Office: Mack Hazlewood et al 221 Pine St Suite 600 San Francisco CA 94104

MACKAY, ALEXANDER RUSSELL, retired physician; b. Bottineau, N.D., Oct. 8, 1911; s. Alexander Russell and Eleanor (Watson) M.; B.S., Northwestern U., 1932, M.D., 1936; M.S. in Surgery, U. Minn., 1940; m. Marjorie Andres, July 16, 1941; children—Andrea, Alexander Russell. Intern, Med. Center, Jersey City, 1935-37; fellow in surgery Mayo Clinic, Rochester, Minn. 1937-41; practiced medicine specializing in gen. surgery, Spokane, Wash., 1941-82, now ret.; former staff Deaconess, Sacred Heart hosps., Spokane. Served from lt. to capt., M.C., AUS, 1942-45. Diplomate Am. Bd. Surgery. Fellow ACS; mem. Spokane Surg. Soc., North Pacific Surg. Assn., Alpha Omega Alpha, Phi Delta Theta, Nu Sigma Nu, Phi Beta Kappa. Home: E 540 Rockwood Blvd Spokane WA 99202

MACKAY, CLAYTON ANGUS, veterinarian, consultant; b. Calgary, Alta., Can., Aug. 15, 1944; s. Duncan Campbell and Beatrice Jane (Finlay) MacK.; m. Mary Lynn Enns, June 29, 1968; children: David, Michael. DVM, Ont. Vet. Coll., Guelph, Can., 1970. Staff vet. MacKay Animal Clinic, Whitby, Ont., Can., 1970-72, ptnr., owner, hosp. dir., 1972-87; cons. Delta Soc., Renton, Wash., 1984-87; mem. animal welfare com. Am. Vet. Med. Assn., Chgo., 1987—; bd. dirs. Whitby br. Ont. Humane Soc., 1970-83, pres., 1978. Group chmn. Oshawa-Whitby United Way, 1976-87; vet. advisor Pickering-Ajax-Whitby Animal Control, 1976-87. Mem. Can. Vet. Med. Assn., Soc. Ont. Vets (bd. dirs. 1983-87, pres. 1986), Ont. Vet. Assn. (bd. dirs. 1976-81, pres. 1980), Durham Reigon Vet. Assn., Am. Animal Hosp. Assn. (area dir. 1981-87), Am. Assn. Animal Behavior, Toronto Acad. Vet. Medicine (bd. dirs. 1972-74), Am. Vet. Med. Assn. (assoc.). Mem. United Ch. Home: 6 Fernway Cresc, Whitby, ON Canada L1N 7G7 Office: MacKay Animal Clinic, 421 Dundas St E, Whitby, ON Canada L1N 2J2

MACKENZIE, ALEXANDER GRAHAM, librarian; b. Glasgow, Scotland, Dec. 4, 1928; s. Thomas Dingwall and Catherine (Herbert) M.; m. Elizabeth Astrid MacKinven, Dec. 23, 1950; children: Alasdair Duncan, Elizabeth Sandra. MA, Glasgow U., 1950. Keeper sci. books Durham U. Library, 1952-60; dep. librarian Nottingham U. Library, 1960-61, Brotherton Library, Leeds, Eng., 1961-63; librarian Lancaster (Eng.) U., 1963-76, dir. library research unit, 1968-76; librarian St. Andrews (Scotland) U., 1976—; cons. in field. Mem. editorial bd. Jour. Documentation, 1964—; contbr. articles to profl. jours. Mem. Conf. Nat. and Univ. Libraries (hon. treas. standing conf. 1980—), Brit. Library Assn. (assoc.). Office: St Andrews U Library, North St, Saint Andrews KY16 9TR, Scotland

MACKENZIE, JOHN MACDONALD, historian; b. Manchester, Eng., Oct. 2, 1943; s. Alexander and Hannah (Whitby) MacK. MA, U. Glasgow, Scotland, 1964; PhD, U. B.C., Can., 1969. Sr. lectr. U. Lancaster, 1968—; vis. lectr. U. Zimbabwe, Harare, 1973-74; prin. County Coll. Lancaster, 1976-81; vis. lectr. U. Liverpool, 1976-77. Author: Propaganda and Empire, 1984, The Empire of Nature, 1988; co-author: The Railway Station: A Social History, 1986; editor: Imperialism and Popular Culture, 1986. Gov. Morecambe and Heysham High Schs., 1981—, Lancaster and Morecambe Coll. of Further Edn., 1985—; gov., chmn. Great Wood Sch., 1981—. Recipient Research awards Dame Lillian Penson Fund, Leverhulme Found., U. Zimbabwe. Fellow Royal Hist. Soc., Royal African Soc. Club: Royal Commonwealth Soc. (London). Home: 249 Heysham Rd, Morecambe LA3 1 NP, England Office: U Lancaster, Bailrigg, Lancaster LA1 4YG, England

MACKENZIE, KENNETH VICTOR, physicist; b. Brandon, Man., Can., Aug. 29, 1911; came to U.S., 1923, naturalized, 1939; s. William Franklin and Allie Esther (Stinson) M.; m. Catherine Jane Oleson Morales, Oct. 18, 1968; children by previous marriage: Dorothy Kay Mighell, Robert Bruce, Kenneth Donald, Jessie Jean Gerlach. Student, Willamette U., 1930-33, DSc (hon.), 1983; BS in Math., Physics, U. Wash., 1934, MS in Physics, 1936. Registered profl. engr., Oreg., Wash. Physicist Oreg. State Hwy. Dept., 1936-41; head physicist Puget Sound Magnetic Survey Range USN, Kingston, Wash., 1941-44; assoc. physicist applied physics lab. U. Wash., Seattle, 1944-46; group leader, deep and shallow water propagation Navy Electronics Lab., San Diego, 1946-51, sec. head scattering and oceanography, 1951-55, head shallow water acoustical process sect., 1955-61, chief scientist deep submergence program, 1962-67; sr. physicist acoustic propagation div. Undersea Surveillance and Ocean Sci. Dept. Naval Undersea Ctr. (formerly Navy Electronics Lab.), San Diego, 1967-73; exchange scientist Her Majesty's Underwater Weapons Establishment, Eng., 1961-62; sr. staff scientist, primary adviser sci. and engring. directorate staff U.S. Naval Oceanographic Office, Washington, 1973-76; sr. staff physicist environ. research requirements office Naval Ocean Research and Devel. Activity, Bay St. Louis, Miss., 1976-79; pres. Mackenzie Marine Sci. Cons., San Diego, 1979—; lectr. Oceanology Inst., Qingdao, Shipbuilding Engring. Inst., Harbin, Peking U., Beijing, Nanjing U., 35 others, 1983—; hon. committeeman Internat. Ocean Devel. Conf., Tokyo, 1971—; speaker Joint Oceanographic Assembly IUGG, Edinburgh, Scotland, 1976, Acad. Sci., Beijing, Fifth Def. Agy, Tokyo, 1980; cons. allied govts. and def. industry. Contbr. 175 papers to profl. publs., chpts to books. Recipient Cert. Exceptional Service, Bur. Ordnance, 1945, Cert. Merit, Office Sci. Research, 1945, Navy Electronics Lab. award, 1960, Commendation Navy Unit, 1963, Alumni Citation, Willamette U., 1969, Superior Achievement award Inst. Navigation, 1971, Meritorious Civilian Service award USN, 1979. Fellow Acoustical Soc. Am., Explorers Club, Marine Tech. Soc. (co-founder); mem. Am. Geophys. Union, Am. Phys. Soc., Inst. Navigation (nat. marine chmn. 1965-66, Western regional councilor 1966-68, 73-75), Instrument Soc. Am. (nat. dir. marine scis. div. 1968-70), Navy League, U.S.-China Peoples Friendship Assn., Sigma Xi. Office: PO Box 80715 Midway Sta San Diego CA 92138

MAC KENZIE, MALCOLM ROBERT, personnel management consultant; b. Revere, Mass., Oct. 12, 1924; s. Malcolm John and Helen Margaret (Pelrine) MacK.; m. Chieko Yoshida, Nov. 4, 1954; 1 child, Kenneth Andrew. BA, Tufts U., 1945; Japanese Lang. cert. Sophia U., Tokyo, 1951; Advanced Mgmt. Program U. Hawaii, 1966. Dep. civilian personnel dir. U.S. Army, Camp Zama, Japan, 1959-63, civilian personnel dir., Fort Shafter, Honolulu, 1963-65, chief employee mgmt. U.S. Army Pacific Hdqrs., 1965-69, civilian personnel dir. electronics command, Fort Monmouth, N.J., 1969-76; command civilian personnel mgr. Naval Edn. and Tng., Naval Air Sta, Pensacola, Fla., 1976-81; personnel mgmt. cons., Gulf Breeze, Fla., 1981—. Mem. Human Rights Advocacy Com., Dist. I, Pensacola, 1982-84; asst. dist. dir. Fla. Spl. Olympics, Pensacola, 1982-86; bd. dirs. Pensacola Penwheels, Employ the Handicapped, Pensacola, 1983—; pres. Pensacola Spl. Steppers retarded dancers, 1983; mem. Fla. Gov.'s Com. on Employment of Handicapped, 1983; co-chmn. com. for handicapable dancers United Square Dancers Am., 1984—; active Handicapped Boy Scouts, Gulf Breeze; pres. Assn. Retarded Citizens-Escambia, Pensacola, 1985-87, Fla. State Assn. for Retarded Citizens, 1987—. Served with USNR, 1943-45, PTO. Recipient Commemorative medallion Tokyo Met. Govt., 1963, cert. Appreciation, Chief of Staff, Ground Office, Defense Agy., Japan, 1963, dir. fgn. affairs. Kanagawa Prefecture, Japan, 1963, dir. fgn. affairs, Saitama Prefecture, Japan, 1963. Mem. Internat. Personnel Mgmt. Assn. (pres. far east chpt. 1960-63, Honolulu chpt. 1964-65, N.J. chpt. 1973-74), Am. Soc. Pub. Adminstrn., Fed. Personnel Council Pacific (chmn. 1965-66), Fed. Personnel Council N.J. (chmn. 1972-73), Gulf State Fed. Personnel Council (vice-chmn. 1980-81), Indsl. Relations Research Assn., Am. Soc. Tng. and Devel., Fla. Pub. Personnel Assn., Eastern Regional Orgn. for Pub. Adminstrn., Am. Arbitration Assn. (mem. comml. and trade panels). Democrat. Roman Catholic. Lodges: KC, Civitan, Elks (treas. 1976-78). Avocations: bowling; golf. Home and Office: 2652 Venetian Way PO Box 280 Gulf Breeze FL 32561

MAC KENZIE, NORMAN HUGH, educator, writer; b. Salisbury, Rhodesia, Mar. 8, 1915; s. Thomas Hugh and Ruth Blanche (Huskisson) MacK.; m. Rita Mavis Hofmann, Aug. 14, 1948; children: Catherine, Ronald. B.A., Rhodes U., South Africa, 1934, M.A., 1935, Diploma in Edn., 1936; Ph.D. (Union scholar), U. London, 1940. Lectr. in English Rhodes U., South Africa, 1937, U. Hong Kong, 1940-41, U. Melbourne, Australia, 1946-48; sr. lectr.-in-charge U. Natal, Durban, 1949-55; prof., head English dept. U. Coll., Rhodesia, 1955-65; dean Faculty Arts and Edn. U. Coll., 1957-60, 63-64; prof., head English dept. Laurentian U., Ont., Can., 1965-66; prof. English Queen's U., Kingston, Ont., 1966-80; emeritus prof. Queen's U., 1980—, dir. grad. studies in English, 1967-73, chmn. council grad. studies, 1971-73, chmn. editorial bd. Yeats Studies, 1972-74; Exec. Central Africa Drama League, 1959-65; mem. exec. com. Can. Irish Studies, 1968-73. Author: South African Travel Literature in the 17th Century, 1955, The Outlook for English in Central Africa, 1960, Hopkins, 1968, A Reader's Guide to G.M. Hopkins, 1981; editor: (with W.H. Gardner) The Poems of Gerard Manley Hopkins, 1967, rev. edit., 1970; Poems by Hopkins, 1974, U. Natal Gazette, 1954-55; contbr.: chpts. to Testing the English Proficiency of Foreign Students, 1961, English Studies Today-Third Series, 1963, Sphere History of English Literature, Vol. VI, 1970, rev. edit., 1987, Readings of the Wreck of the Deutschland, 1976, Festschrift for E.R. Seary, 1975, British and American Literature 1880-1920, 1976, Myth and Reality in Irish Literature, 1977; articles to Internat. Rev. Edn., Bull. Inst. Hist. Research, Times Lit. Supplement, Modern Lang. Quar., Queen's Quar., others. Served with Hong Kong Vol. Def. Corps, 1940-45; prisoner of war, China and Japan 1941-45. Brit. Council scholar, 1954; Killam sr. fellow, 1979-81. Fellow Royal Soc. Can.; mem. English Assn. Rhodesia (pres. 1957-65), So. Rhodesia Drama Assn. (vice chmn. 1957-65), Hopkins Soc. (pres. 1972-75), Yeats Soc. (life), MLA (life), Internat. Hopkins Assn. (bd. scholars 1979—), Internat. Assn. for Study Anglo-Irish Lit. Home: 416 Windward Pl, Kingston, ON Canada K7M 4E4

MAC KENZIE, ROLAND REDUS, realty executive; b. Washington, Mar. 13, 1907; s. Albert Redus and Mary J. (Hummer) MacK.; grad. Brown U., 1929; m. Louise Parker Fownes, May 11, 1940; children—Clark Fownes, Margot Fownes. Rep. U.S. Walker Cup Golf Team, 1926, 28-30; with Dupont Laundry, Washington, 1930-32; pres., dir. Shamrock Properties, Inc., Balt., 1938—, pres. Shamrock Realty Co., Greentree Realty Co., Townson, Md., Scottish Devel. Corp. Presbyn. Clubs: Country of N.C., Pinehurst Country (Pinehurst, N.C.); Gulf Stream Golf, St. Andrews, Little (Del Ray Beach); Elkridge-Greenspring (Balt.). Home: 3210 Polo Dr Gulf Stream FL 33444 also: McCaskill Rd Pinehurst NC 28374 also: Mac Kenzie Bldg Southern Pines NC 28387

MACKENZIE, SCOTT JAMES, manufacturing company executive; b. Bklyn., Mar. 11, 1937; arrived in Can., 1980; s. Albert James and Elizabeth Marie (Storck) Mack.; m. Inza Carol Areskog, Aug. 27, 1960; children: Kenneth James, Adriene Carol. BS in Marine Engring., SUNY, Ft. Schuyler, 1958; MS in Mech. Engring., Columbia U., 1961. Registered profl. engr., Pa., Calif. Nuclear project engr. Foster Wheeler Corp., N.Y.C., 1960-64; chief indsl. engr. Foster Wheeler Energy Corp., Mountaintop, Pa., 1964-68, mgr. prodn. control, 1968-70; project dir. Livingston, N.J., 1972-73, asst. mgr. quality assurance, 1975-80; mgr. heat exchange engring. Gulf Gen. Atomics, San Diego, 1970-72; plant supt. Nuclear Power Products Co., Panama City, Fla., 1973-75; quality assurance mgr. Foster Wheeler Ltd., St. Catharines, Ont., Can., 1980-83, v.p. projects, 1983—; instr. Pa. State U., Hazelton, 1967-69; mem. quality assurance com. Am. Boiler Mfg. Assn., Washington, 1978-82; chmn., bd. dirs. Chapleau Cogeneration, Ltd., Ont. Pres. bd. deacons Presbyn. Ch., Wilkes-Barre, Pa., 1966-68, elder, 1969; committeeman Bergan County Dems., Palisades Park, N.J., 1961. Mem. ASME. Office: Foster Wheeler Ltd, PO Box 3007, Saint Catharines, ON Canada L2R 7B7 Home: 18 Parkhill Rd Forthill ON

MACKERRAS, (ALAN) CHARLES (MAC LAURIN), conductor; b. Schnectady, N.Y. (parents Australian citizens), Nov. 17, 1925; s. Alan Patrick and Catherine M.; m. Helena Judith Wilkins, 1947; 2 daus. Student with Vaclav Talich, Prague Acad. Music, 1947-48. Prin. oboist Sydney Symphony Orch., Australia, 1943-46; staff condr. English Nat. Opera (formerly Sadler's Wells Opera), London, 1949-53, musical dir., 1970-77; prin. condr. BBC Concert Orch., 1954-56; freelance condr. with most Brit. and many continental orchs., concert tours USSR, S. Africa, N. Am., Australia, 1957-66, U.S. coast-to-coast, 1983; prin. condr. Hamburg State Opera, 1966-69; chief guest condr. BBC Symphony Orch., 1976-79; chief condr. Sydney Symphony Orch., Australian Broadcasting Commn., 1982-85; mus. dir. Welsh Nat. Opera, 1987—; appearances many internat. festivals and opera houses; frequent radio and TV broadcasts; many comml. recordings, notably Handel series for DGG and Janacek operas for Decca. Published ballet arrangements Pineapple Poll (Sullivan), Lady and the Fool (Verdi), reconstrn. Sullivan's lost Cello Concerto. Contbr. articles to Opera Mag., Music and Musicians, other jours. Recipient Evening Standard award for opera 1977, Janacek medal, 1978, Gramophone Record of Yr. award, 1978, 80, 83, 84; Grammy award for best opera recording, 1981; prix Fondation Jacques Ibert, 1983; Record of Yr. award Stereo Rev., 1983; decorated comdr. Order Brit. Empire, 1974; created Knight, 1979; Brit. Council scholar, 1947-48. Fellow Royal Coll. of Music. Office: co ICM Artists Ltd 8899 Beverly Blvd Los Angeles CA 90048

MACKESY, PIERS GERALD, historian, educator; b. Aberdeen, Scotland, July 15, 1924; s. Pierse Joseph and Leonora Dorothy (Cook) M.; previous marriage Sarah Katharine Davies; children: William, Catherine, Serena; m. Patricia Amy Gore. Ma with honors, Oxford U., 1950, D in Philosophy, 1953, DLitt, 1978. Research fellow Oxford U., 1950-53; Harkness fellow HarvardU., Cambridge, Mass., 1953-54; fellow Oxford U., 1954-87, emeritus fellow, 1988—; vis. prof. Calif. Inst. Tech., 1966; vis. fellow Inst. for Advanced Studies Princeton U., 1961-62. Author: The War in the Mediterranean, 1803-10, 1957, The War for America, 1775-83, 1964, Statesmen at War, 1798-99, 1974, The Coward of Minden, 1979, War Without Victory: The Downfall of Pitt, 1799-1802, 1984. Mem. council Nat. Army Mus., London, 1983—. Served to lt. Brit. Army, 1943-47, ETO. Fellow Royal Hist. Soc., Brit. Acad.; mem. Soc. for Army Hist. Research (mem. exec. council 1985—), Inst. for Early Am. History (mem. exec. council 1970-73). Home: The Dowerhouse Cottage, Heythrop, Chipping Norton OX7 5TL, England

MACKIE, PETER FEARING, banker; b. Englewood, N.J., May 19, 1941; s. John Milton and Ruth Anewalt (Gomery) M.; B.A., Trinity Coll., 1964; m. Catherine Bodin Foster, Dec. 30, 1983; children—Tyler Godding, Prescott Milton, Elisabeth Turlay, Stewart Andrews, Thomas Ives. With Bankers Trust Co., N.Y.C., 1964—, asst. v.p., 1972-79, v.p., 1979-85, pres. Bankers Trust Co. of Fla. N.A., 1985—, bus. mgr. Rockefeller Ctr. office, 1983-85; mem. investment com. Bankers Trust AG, Zurich, Switzerland, 1972-75; mem. trust and investment com. Bankers Trust Co., London, 1972-75. Mem. asso. vestry Christ the Redeemer Episcopal Ch., Pelham Manor, N.Y., 1970-72, 1976-77, jr. warden, 1977-80, sr. warden, 1980-81, vestryman, 1981-84; bd. dirs. Pelham Day Care Center, 1976-81, pres., 1978-81; bd. dirs. United Way of Pelham, 1977-84, residential chmn., 1978, coach Pelham Youth Soccer League, 1978-81; mem. allocations com. United Way of Westchester, 1982-85; chmn., founding bd. dirs. Young Audiences Palm Beach County Inc., 1986—; bd. dirs. Cancer Care Inc., 1981-88 ,Nat. Cancer Care Found., 1981-88 , asst. treas., 1984-85. Served with U.S. Army, 1967. Republican. Clubs: Men's (dir. 1975-78, pres. 1977-78), N.Y. Athletic, Lake Paupac (Greentown, Pa.); Palm Beach Yacht, Beach (Palm Beach), Atlantis Golf. Home: 220 N Country Club Dr Atlantis FL 33462 Office: 505 South Flagler Dr West Palm Beach FL 33401

MACKINNON, KENNETH MACALPIN, sociologist, educator; b. London, Aug. 26, 1933; s. Harry Simpson and Elizabeth Clara (Walters) MacK.; m. Rosalie Dorothy Butler, May 7, 1955; children: Niall Lachlann, Morag Anne. BS in Econs., U. London, 1954, MA in Edn., 1971, PhD, 1975. Tchr. Essex (Eng.) Secondary Schs., 1956-59; lectr. Essex Tech. Colls., 1965-66; mayor County-Borough of Southend-on-Sea, Essex, Eng., 1965-66; head of dept. social studies Barking Coll. Tech., London, 1966-76; sr. lectr., prin. lectr. in sociology Hatfield Poly., Hertfordshire, Eng., 1976-83, reader in sociology of lang., 1983—; course tutor Open U., England, 1971-75; organizing tutor Wansfell Adult Coll., Essex, 1976—; summer sch. prof., U. Coll. Cape Breton, Sydney, Nova Scotia, 1975; cons. An Comunn Gàidhealach, Scotland, 1978-85; presenter of acad. papers to various internat. acad. confs. Author: The Lion's Tongue, 1974, Language, Education and Social Processes in a Gaelic Community, 1977. Councillor County Borough of Southend-on-Sea, Essex, 1958-66, alderman 1964-70, mayor 1965-66; chmn. town planning, spokesperson on Gaelic affairs, Scottish Green Party, Highland Region, 1987—. Served with Brit. Royal Arty., 1954-56. Social Sci. Research Council grantee, 1976; recipient research award Econ. and Social Research Council, 1985. Mem. Folklore Soc., Univs. Forum on Langs. of Scotland, Brit. Sociol. Assn. Methodist. Clubs: Hoy at Anchor Folk Song, Benfleet Hoymen Morris and Sword Dance. Home: Ivy Cottage, Ryefield by Conon Bridge, The Black Isle, Ross-Shire Scotland IV7 8HX Office: Hatfield Polytech, Sch Bus and Social Scis, Hertford Campus, Balls Park, Hertford, Hertfordshire England SG13 8QF

MACKINTOSH, FREDERICK ROY, oncologist; b. Miami, Fla., Oct. 4, 1943; s. John Harris and Mary Carlotta (King) MacK.; m. Judith Jane Parnell, Oct. 2, 1961 (div. Aug. 1977); children: Lisa Lynn, Wendy Sue; m. Claudia Lizanne Flournoy, Jan. 7, 1984. BS, MIT, 1964, PhD, 1968; MD, U. Miami, 1976. Intern then resident in gen. medicine Stanford (Calif.) U., 1976-78, fellow in oncology, 1978-81; asst. prof. med. U. Nev., Reno, 1981-85, assoc. prof., 1985—. Contbr. articles to profl. jours. Fellow ACP; mem. Am. Soc. Clin. Oncology, Am. Cancer Soc. (pres. Nev. div. 1985, pres. 1987—), No. Nev. Cancer Council (bd. dirs. 1981—), No. Calif. Cancer Program (bd. dirs. alt. 1983-87, bd. dirs. 1987—). Office: Nev Med Group 781 Mill St Reno NV 89502

MACKINTOSH, NICHOLAS JOHN, psychology educator; b. London, July 9, 1935; s. Ian and Daphne (Cochrane) M.; m. Janet Ann Scott, July 16, 1960 (div.); children: Alasdair, Lucy; m. Bundy Wilson, Sept. 23, 1978; children: Duncan, Douglas. BA, Oxford U., 1960, MA, 1963, PhD, 1964. Research assoc. Oxford (Eng.) U., 1964-65, lectr., 1965-67; research prof. psychology Dalhousie U., Halifax, N.S., 1967-73; prof. psychology U. Sussex, Eng., 1973-81, Cambridge (Eng.) U., 1981—. Fellow Royal Soc.; mem. Brit. Experimental Psychology Soc. Home: King's Coll, King's Parade, Cambridge England CB2 1ST Office: Cambridge U, Dept Experimental Psychology, Downing St, Cambridge England CB2 3EB

MACKO, GEORGE STANLEY, hospital administrator; b. Chgo., June 10, 1944; s. Stanley George and Marion (Falborski) M.; m. Donna Lee Gammaitoni, June 29, 1968; children: Steven, Susan, Cynthia, David. BS, St. Louis U., 1968, M in Hosp. Adminstrn., 1970. Hosp. resident St. Joseph Hosp., Omaha, 1969-70; chief exec. officer St. Francis Hosp., Blue Island, Ill., 1970-80; pres. Coordinated Services, Wichita, Kans., 1980-82; chief exec. officer St. Mary's Regional Health Ctr., Roswell, N. Mex., 1982—; adj. prof. St. Mary of the Plains Coll.; instr. Eastern N. Mex. U., Roswell; bd. mem., treas., sec. N.M. Hosp. Assn. Author: (with others) Money Makers, 1982. Bd. dirs. N. Mex. Emergency Med. Services Council; bd. dirs. N. Mex. Health Systems Agency; mem. community Improvement Commn. Spring River Found., Cath. Health Assn. Com. on Multi-Hosp. Orgns.; crusade chmn. Am. Cancer Soc., Roswell, 1984-85; bd. dirs. Roswell YMCA; asst. scoutmaster Boy Scouts Am., Roswell; mem. City of Roswell Beautification and Improvement Commn., Roswell Community Improvement Commn.; chmn. Assumption Parish Ch. Fund Drive. Served as cap. N.M. Nat. Guard. Named an Outstanding Young Man of Am., Ill. Jaycees, 1975. Fellow Am. Coll. Hosp. Adminstrs. (N.Mex. Regent), Am. Acad. Med. Adminstrs.; mem. Am. Health Care Assn., Am. Hosp. Assn. (personal), Am. Registry of Radiologic Tech., Hosp. Fin. Mgmt. Assn. (advanced), N.Mex. Hosp. Assn. (legis., joint unemployment compensation, pub. relations, planning and org. coms.), Hosp. Equipment Loan Council (treas. 1986), Roswell C. of C. Lodge: Rotary. Home: 3003 Diamond A Dr Roswell NM 88201 Office: St Marys Regional Health Ctr PO Box 1938 Roswell NM 88201

MACLACHLAN, JAMES MORRILL, management educator; b. Geneva, Ill., Mar. 21, 1934; s. John Andrew and Gladys (Morrill) MacL.; m. Sally Gerig, Oct. 21, 1978; children—Sheila, Carolyn, Laura. B.S., Carnegie Inst. Tech., 1956; M.B.A., Harvard U., 1971; Ph.D., U. Calif.-Berkeley, 1975. Pubr. The Tri-Town News, Sidney, N.Y., 1958-69; asst. prof. NYU, N.Y.C., 1975-79; assoc. prof. Columbia U., N.Y.C., 1980. Rensselaer Poly. Inst., Troy, N.Y., 1981—; pres. Timely Decisions, Inc., Delmar, N.Y., 1978—. Biblical Films, Inc., Delmar, 1981—. Author: Response latency: New Measure of Advertising, 1977. Served with U.S. Army, 1956-58. Mem. Soc. Motion Picture and TV Editors. Club: Harvard. Home: 310 Elm Ave S Delmar NY 12054 Office: Rensselaer Poly Inst Lally Mgmt Bldg Troy NY 12181

MAC LAREN, DAVID SERGEANT, pollution control manufacturing corporation executive; b. Cleve., Jan. 4, 1931; s. Albert Sergeant and Theadora Beidler (Potter) MacL.; children: Alison, Catherine, Carolyn. AB in Econs., Miami U., Oxford, Ohio, 1955. Chmn. bd., pres., Jet, Inc., Cleve., 1961—; founder, chmn. bd., pres. Air Injector Corp., Cleve., 1958-78; founder, pres., chmn. bd. Fluid Equipment, Inc., Cleve., 1962-72, T&M Co., Cleve., 1963-71, Alison Realty Co., Cleve., 1965—; chmn. bd., pres. Sergeant Realty, Inc., 1979-86; mem. tech. com. Nat. Sanitation Found., Ann Arbor, Mich., 1967—. Patentee in field. Mem. Rep. State Cen. Com., 1968-72; bd. dirs. Cleve. State U. Found., 1986—. Served with arty. AUS, 1955-58. Fellow Royal Soc. Health (London); mem. Nat. Environ. Health Assn., Am. Pub. Health Assn., Nat. Water Pollution Control Fedn., Cen. Taekwondo Assn. (2d Dan), Jiu-Jitsu/Karati Black Belt Fedn. (black belt instr.), Mercedes Benz Club N.Am. (pres. 1968), H.B. Leadership Soc. (sch. headmaster soc., devel. com. 1976-78), SAR, Soc. Mayflower Descendants, Delta Kappa Epsilon (nat. bd. dirs. N.Y.C. chpt. 1974-86, bd. dirs. Kappa chpt. 1969—). Clubs: Mentor Harbor Yachting, The Country Club, Cotillion Soc. (Cleve.); Union League, Yale, Deke (N.Y.C.). Home: West Hill Dr Gates Mills OH 44040 Office: Jet Inc 750 Alpha Dr Cleveland OH 44143

MACLAY, IAN KENNETH, orchestral managing director; b. London, May 7, 1950; s. William Ferguson and Joan Mabel (Clarson) M.; m. Lisa Mary Niblett, Apr. 28, 1979; children: Fiona Jane, Graham Philip. Grad. high sch., London. Concert mgr. Royal Philharm. Orch., London, 1970-77, mng. dir., 1982—; planning mgr. Royal Festival Hall, London, 1978-82. Home: Carisbrooke, Carew Rd, Northwood, Middlessex HA6 3WA, England Office: Royal Philharmonic Orch, 16 Clerkenwell Green, London EC1R OPD England

MACLEAN, GUY ROBERTSON, emeritus university president; b. Sydney, N.S., Can., Dec. 21, 1929; s. Charles Whitmore and Mary Malinda (Nicholson) MacL.; m. Mary Judith Hunter, June 29, 1963; children—Colin Hunter, Mary Jocelyn. B.A., Dalhousie U., 1951, M.A., 1953; B.A. (Rhodes scholar), Oxford U., 1955, M.A., 1959; Ph.D., Duke, 1958. Asst. prof. Dalhousie U., Halifax, N.S., 1957-61; asso. prof. Dalhousie U., 1961-65, prof., 1965—, dean of residence, 1961-63, acting chmn. dept. history, 1963-64; asst. dean Dalhousie U. (Faculty Grad. Studies), 1965-66, dean, 1966-69; dean Dalhousie U. (Faculty Arts and Sci.), 1969-75, v.p. academic, 1974-80; pres. Mount Allison U., 1980-86, pres. emeritus, 1986—; dean of men Kings Coll., 1957-61; lectr. U. Alta., 1963, N.S. Tech. Coll., 1965-66. Editor: introduction The Life and Times of A.T. Galt, 1966; Contbr. articles to profl. jours. Mem. Rhodes Scholarship Com., N.S.; mem. Maritime Provinces Higher Edn. Commn., Social Scis. and Humanities Research Council Can., 1978—; bd. dirs. Donner Canadian Found., Toronto; bd. govs. Coll. of Cape Breton; chmn. bd. dirs. Opera East. Served as 2d lt. Canadian Army, 1949-51. Recipient Centennial medal, 1967, Jubilee medal, 1978; Can. Council fellow, 1968-69. Mem. Canadian Hist. Assn. (exec. council 1967-68), Canadian Inst. Internat. Affairs (pres. Halifax 1965), Canadian Rhodes Scholar Assn., Nova Scotia Soccer Assn. (pres. 1976-78). Mem. United Ch. of Can. Club: Waegwoltic. Home: Mount Allison Univ, Sackville, NB Canada E0A 3C0

MACLENNAN, BERYCE W., psychologist; b. Aberdeen, Scotland, Mar. 14, 1920; came to U.S., 1949, naturalized, 1965; d. William and Beatrice (MaCrae) Mellis; m. John Duncan MacLennan, Nov. 29, 1944. B.Sc. with honors, London Sch. Econs., 1947; Ph.D., London U., 1960. Group psychotherapist, youth specialist cons. N.Y.C. and Washington, 1949-63; dir. Center for Prevention Juvenile Delinquency and New Careers, Washington, 1963-66; sect. chief NIMH, Mental Health Study Center, Adelphi, Md., 1967-70; chief NIMH, Mental Health Study Center, 1971-74; regional adminstr. Mass. Dept. Mental Health, Springfield, 1974-75; sr. mental health adv. GAO, Washington, 1976—; clin. prof. George Washington U., 1970—; mem. tech. adv. com. Prince George's County Mental Health Assn., 1968-85. Fellow Am. Psychol. Assn., Am. Orthopsychiat. Assn., Am. Group Psychotherapy Assn. Democrat. Club: So. Md. Sailing. Office: NIH Bldg 31 2B 11 Bethesda MD 20892

MACLEOD, ANTHONY MICHAEL, diversified utility company executive; b. Manila, Dec. 30, 1947; s. Anthony Macaulay and Dorothy (Amend) M.; m. Carol Jeanne Silvani, Aug. 5, 1972; children: Ryan Elissa, Anthony Matthew, Colin Macaulay. A.B. magna cum laude, U. Notre Dame, 1969; J.D., U. Va., 1972. Law clk. Supreme Ct. Conn., Hartford, 1972-73; assoc. atty. Hirschberg, Pettengill, Strong & Nagle (now Whitman & Ransom), Greenwich, Conn., 1973-76; div. counsel The Flintkote Co., Stamford, Conn., 1977-80, sec., chief counsel, 1980-82, v.p., sec., chief counsel, 1982-84; v.p., gen. counsel The Hydraulic Co., Bridgeport, Conn., 1984-86, sr. v.p. law and adminstrn., 1986—, sec., 1988—; bd. dirs. Stamford Water Co., Bridgeport Econ. Devel. Corp.; team dir. Mgmt. Decision Lab. NYU Grad. Sch. Bus. Adminstrn., Purchase, NY, 1983-84; law program chmn Conn. Career Opportunities Program, Greenwich, 1975-76. Chmn. exploring com. Greenwich council Boy Scouts Am., 1975-79, mem. exec. bd., 1975-81; mem. S.W. Area Commerce and Industry Assn. Conn., 1982-84, Greenwich Flood and Erosion Control Bd., 1987—, chmn., 1988—; rep. Greenwich Town Meeting, 1984-85; bd. dirs. Youth Shelter, 1984-86, Conn. Forest and Park Assn., 1988—; bd. regents Fairfield Coll. Prep. Sch., 1985—; bd. trustees Whitby Sch., 1986—. Mem ABA, Conn. Bar Assn. (exec. com. young lawyers sect. 1974-75), Conn. Supreme Ct. Law Clks. Assn., Am. Corp. Counsel Assn., Westchester Fairfield Corp Counsel Assn. Clubs: Notre Dame Alumni (Fairfield County, Conn.) (dir. 1982—); Greenwich Country. Home: 124 Old Stone Bridge Rd Greenwich CT 06807 Office: The Hydraulic Co 835 Main St Bridgeport CT 06601

MACLEOD, (J.M.) JACK, oil company executive; b. Beddeck, N.S., Can., 1931; m. Beverley Ann Thurston; children: Heather, Carol, Sandra. Alan. B in Engring., Tech. U. N.S., Halifax, 1954, D in Engring. (hon.), 1982. Petroleum engr. Shell Can. Ltd., Calgary, Alta., 1954-69, mgr. dept. prodn., 1969-71, gen. mgr. frontier div., exploration and prodn., 1971-72, gen. mgr. prodn., 1972-73; gen. mgr. supply & logistics Shell Can. Ltd., Toronto, Ont., 1973-75; v.p. corp. planning and pub. affairs Shell Can. Ltd., Calgary, 1975-77, v.p. exploration and prodn., sr. v.p. resources, 1977-82, exec. v.p., 1982-83, pres., chief exec. officer, 1985—, also bd. dirs.; coordinator natural gas Shell Internat. Petroleum Co., London, 1983-85; bd. dirs. C.D. Howe Inst. Bd. dirs. Calgary Philharmonic Soc., The Council for Can. Unity, The Council for Bus. and the Arts in Can. Mem. Assn. Profl. Engrs. Geologists and Geophysicists Alta., Can. Inst. Mining and Metallurgy, Bus. Council on Nat. Issues. Clubs: Calgary Petroleum, Calgary Golf and Country, Mississauga Golf and Country. Office: Shell Can Ltd, 400 4th Ave SW, Calgary, AB Canada T2P 0J4

MACLEOD, JOHN AMEND, lawyer; b. Manila, June 5, 1942; s. Anthony Macaulay and Dorothy Lillian (Amend) M.; children—Kerry, Jack. B.B.A., U. Notre Dame, 1963, J.D., 1969. Bar: D.C. 1969, U.S. Supreme Ct. 1980. Assoc., Jones, Day, Reavis & Pogue, D.C., 1969-73; ptnr., 1974-79; ptnr. Crowell & Moring, Washington, 1979—, mem. mgmt. com., 1979-82, 83-86, chmn., 1984-85. Trustee, mem. exec. com. Eastern Mineral Law Found.; bd. dirs. St. Francis Ctr. Served to lt. U.S. Army, 1963-65. Mem. ABA, D.C. Bar Assn., Notre Dame Law Assn. (dir., exec. bd.). Club: Metropolitan (Washington). Editor-in-chief Notre Dame Law Rev., 1968-69. Contbr. articles to profl. jours. Home: 1733 Que St NW Washington DC 20009

MACLEOD, JOHN GRAEME, industrial engineer; b. Hastings, Eng., Feb. 20, 1930; came to U.S., 1972; s. Hugh Graeme and Hilda Norris (St. John) M.; children: Christopher, Robert, Neil; m. Margarette Cagle, Jan. 1, 1984. HNC Mech. Engring., Loughborough Coll., Eng., 1950, ONC Elec. Engring., 1951; HNC Indsl. Adminstrn., Watford Coll., Eng., 1955. Registered profl. engr., Can. Apprentice, draftsman, engr. Various Cos., Eng. and Can., 1946-67; chief engr. Rockwell Can., Montreal, 1967-72; mgr. plug valve devel. Rockwell Internat., Pitts., 1972-78; mgr. engring. Ecolaire Valve Co., Allentown, Pa., 1978-81; project mgr. new products SII McEvoy, Houston, 1981-83; mgr. research, devel. and engring. ITT Hoffman, Indpls., 1983-87; chmn. pipeline valves CSA, Toronto, 1968-78, chmn. gas valves, 1968-80, chmn. oilfield valves, 1970-76; mem. adv. com. on gen. purpose valves, 1969-72. Patentee in field. Mem. Order Engrs. Que., Soc. Am. Value Engrs., Am. Soc. for Quality Control, Soc. Mfg. Engrs., Nat. Model Railroad Assn., Mensa. Home and Office: PO Box 268 Big Sandy TX 75755

MACMILLAN, ALEXANDER ROSS, banker; b. Tain, Scotland, Mar. 25, 1922; s. Donald and Johanna (Ross) M.; student Tain Royal Acad.; m. Ursula Miriam Grayson, June 17, 1961; children—Alexandra Miriam, David Ross, Niall Ross. With Clydesdale Bank Ltd., various locations, 1938-82, supt. brs., Glasgow, 1965-67, gen. mgr.'s asst., 1967-68, asst. gen. mgr., 1968-71, gen. mgr., 1971-73, chief gen. mgr., 1973-82, also dir.; bd. dirs. Edinburgh Fin. Trust PLC, Wilsons Garage (Argyll) Ltd., Wilsons Fuels Ltd., New Generation Housing Soc. Ltd., Castle Wynd Housing Soc. Ltd., Highland-North Sea Ltd., Highland Deephaven Ltd., Radio Clyde PLC, Scottish Devel. Fin. Ltd., Kelvin Tech. Devels. Ltd. Served with RAF, 1942-45. Mentioned in dispatches; freeman Royal Burgh of Tain. Fellow Inst. Bankers Scotland (past pres.); mem. Nat. House-Building Council Scotland, Ct. of U. Glasgow. Mem. Ch. of Scotland. Clubs: Glasgow Golf, Oil (Glasgow). Address: 16 Ledcameroch Rd, Bearsden, Glasgow G61 4AB Scotland

MACMILLAN, KENNETH, choreographer, ballet director; b. Dumfermline, Scotland, Dec. 11, 1929; s. William and Edith (Shreeve) Mc.M. Dance tng. received at Sadler's Wells Sch., London; Dr. (hon.), U. Edinburgh, 1976; m. Deborah Williams, Mar. 22, 1974; 1 dau., Charlotte. Founding mem., dancer Sadler's Wells Theatre Ballet, London, from 1946; dancer, then choreographer Sadler's Wells Ballet, 1952-66; dir. Deutsche Oper Ballet, Berlin, 1966-69; resident choreographer, dir. The Royal Ballet, London, 1970-77, prin. choreographer, 1977—; artistic assoc. Am. Ballet Theatre, N.Y.C., 1984—. Ballets choreographed include: Somnambulism, 1953, Laiderette, Dances Concertantes, Noctambules, 1956, The Burrow, 1958, Le Baiser de la Fee, 1960, The Invitation, 1960, The Rite of Spring, 1962, Romeo and Juliet, 1965, Das Lied von der Erde, 1965, Anastasia, Manon, 1974, Elite Syncopations, Requiem, 1976, My Brother, My Sisters, 1978, Mayerling, 1978, La Fin du Jour, Gloria, Isadora, 1981, The Wild Boy, 1981, Quartet, 1982, Orpheus, 1982, Valley of the Shadows, 1982, Different Drummer, Solitaire, Agon, and others. Knighted (Eng.) 1983; recipient Evening Standard Ballet award, 1979. Office: Royal Opera House, Covent Garden, London WC2, England *

MACNAMARA, JOHN, steel company executive; b. Hamilton, Ont., Can., Mar. 22, 1925; s. John E. MacN.; m. Mary Jane Anne Walsh, Oct. 15, 1949; children: John Alexander, Dean Stafford, Peter MacEvery, Stephen Walsh. B.Sc., McMaster U., Hamilton, 1947, M.Sc., 1949, Ph.D., 1951. With Algoma Steel Corp. Ltd., Sault Ste Marie, Ont., 1951—, v.p, works mgr. steelworks div., 1971-73, v.p., 1973, exec. v.p., 1973-76, pres., 1976-81, chief operating officer, 1976-81, chmn., chief exec. officer, 1976-88, chmn. bd., 1988—; dir. Cannelton Industries, Charleston, W. Va., Redpath Industries, Toronto. Home: 6 Summit Ave, Sault Sainte Marie, ON Canada P6B 2S1 Office: The Algoma Steel Corp Ltd, 503 Queen St East, Sault Sainte Marie, ON Canada P6A 5P2

MACNAUGHTON, ANGUS ATHOLE, finance company executive; b. Montreal, Que., Can., July 15, 1931; s. Athole Austin and Emily Kidder (MacLean) MacN.; children—Gillian Heather, Angus Andrew. Student, Lakefield Coll. Sch., 1941-47, McGill U., 1949-54. Auditor Coopers & Lybrand, Montreal, 1949-55; acct. Genstar Ltd., Montreal, 1955; asst. treas. Genstar Ltd., 1956-61, treas., 1961-64, v.p., 1964-70, exec. v.p., 1970-73, pres., 1973-76, vice chmn., chief exec. officer, 1976-81, chmn. or pres., chief exec. officer, 1981-86; pres. Genstar Investment Corp., 1987—; dir. Can. Pacific Ltd., Sun Life Assurance Co. Can. Ltd., Am. Barrick Resources Corp., Varian Assocs. Inc.; past pres. Montreal chpt. Tax Exec. Inst. Bd. govs. Lakefield Coll. Sch.; sr. mem. Conf. Bd. N.Y. Clubs: Pacific Union, World Trade (San Francisco), Mount Royal, Toronto. Office: Genstar Investment Corp 801 Montgomery St Suite 500 San Francisco CA 94133

MACNEAL, EDWARD ARTHUR, economic consultant; b. Winona Lake, Ind., Apr. 19, 1925; s. Kenneth Forsyth and Marguerite Josephine (Giroud) MacN.; student Harvard, 1943; B.A., U. Chgo., 1948, M.A., 1951; m. Priscilla Creed Perry, Dec. 27, 1952; children—Catherine Wright, Madeleine Creed. Exec. sec. Internat. Soc. Gen. Semantics, Chgo., 1947-51; staff cons. James C. Buckley, Inc., N.Y.C., 1951-55; market researcher Socony Mobil Oil Co., N.Y.C., 1955-58; research dir. O.E. McIntyre, Inc., N.Y.C., 1958-61; econ. cons., N.Y., 1956-66, Wayne, Pa., 1966—; adv. local govt. agys. Served with AUS, 1943-46; ETO. Mem. Am. Statis. Assn., Am. Econ. Assn., Internat. Soc. Gen. Semantics (dir.), Inst. Gen. Semantics (dir.), Am. Sociol. Assn., Am. Assn. Airport Execs., Travel Research Assn., Travel Research Forum. Clubs: Nat. Aviation; Harvard (Phila.); Wings. Author: The Semantics of Air Passenger Transportation, 1981, MacNeal's Master Atlas of Decision Making, 1988. Home: 348 Louella Ave Wayne PA 19087 Office: PO Box 249 Wayne PA 19087

MACOBOY, (KENNETH) STIRLING, editor, writer; b. Melbourne, Victoria, Australia, Jan. 4, 1927; s. Keith Esmond and Emily Earl (Stirling) M. Student, Scotch Coll., Melbourne, Australia. Radio writer, producer J. Walter Thompson Co., Sydney, Australia, 1946-51; editor TV script N.Y.C., 1952-54; dir. creative services Sydney, 1954-58; dir. TV prodns. George Patterson Pty., Ltd., Sydney, 1959-76; editor garden sect. Better Homes and Gardens mag., Sydney, 1978—; cons. gardens Advertiser Mags., Sydney, 1976—; broadcaster various networks, Australia, Eng., 1976—; free-lance author, photographer on horticultural subjects, 1976—. Author, photographer What Flower is That?, 1969, Joy of Flowers, 1977, What Tree is That?, 1978, Color dictionary of Camellias, 1982, and 17 others; contbr. numerous articles to mags. Mem. tree planting com. North Sydney Mcpl. Council, 1981-83. Served with Royal Australian Air Force, 1945. Recipient Logie award TV Week Mag., 1968, Penguin award Savage Club, 1964. Fellow Royal Horticultural Soc., Irish Geneal. Soc.; mem. Internat. Camellia Soc., Am. Camellia Soc. Liberal. Home and Office: 87 Undercliff St, Neutral Bay, New South Wales 2089, Australia

MACON, IRENE ELIZABETH, designer, consultant; b. East St. Louis, Ill., May 11, 1935; d. David and Thelma (Eastlen) Dunn; m. Robert Teco Macon, Feb. 12, 1954; children—Leland Sean, Walter Edwin, Gary Keith, Jill Renee Macon Martin, Robin Jeffrey, Lamont. Student Forest Park Coll., Washington U., St. Louis, 1970, Bailey Tech. Coll., 1975, Lindenwood Coll., 1981. Office mgr. Cardinal Glennon Hosp., St. Louis, 1965-72; interior designer J.C. Penney Co., Jennings, Mo., 1972-73; entrepreneur Irene Designs Unltd., St. Louis, 1974—; vol. liaison Pub. Sch. System, St. Louis, 1980-82; cons. in field. Inventor venetian blinds for autos, 1981, T-blouse and diaper wrap, 1986; author 26th Word newsletter, 1986. Committeewoman Republican party, St. Louis, 1984; vice chair 4th Senatorial Dist. of Mo., 1984, vol. St. Louis Assn. Community Orgns., 1983; instr. first aid Bi-State chpt. ARC, St. Louis, 1984; block capt. Operation Brightside, St. Louis, 1984; co-chair Status and Role of Women, Union Meml. United Meth. Ch., 1986—. Named one of Top Ladies of Distinction, St. Louis, 1983. Mem. Am. Soc. Interior Designers (assoc.), NAACP, Nat. Mus. Women in the Arts (charter), Internat. Platform Assn., Nat. Council Negro Women (1st v.p. 1984), Invention Assn. of St. Louis (subcom. head 1985), Coalition of 100 Black Women, St. Louis Assn. Fashion Designers. Methodist. Club: Presidents, (Washington). Avocations: reading; designing personal wardrobe; modeling; horseback riding; boating. Home and Office: 5469 Maple St Saint Louis MO 63112

MACOTELA, ENRIQUE, architect; b. Mexico City, Mar. 18, 1941; s. Elias and Luz Maria (Perez) M.; m. Herminia Dosal, Oct. 19, 1967 (div. 1972); 1 child, Enrique Macotela. Degree in architecture, U. Iberoamericana, Mexico City, 1965. Chief archtl. designer Estructuras, Construcciones Y Acabados, S.A., Mexico City, 1966-69, gen. dir., 1970-74; gen. dir. Enrique Macotela Y Asociados, S.A., Mexico City, 1974—, Immobiliaria "Q", S.A. de C.V., Mexico City, 1974—, Sexto Set, S.A.De C.V., Mexico City, 1975—, Astro "Q", S.A.De C.V., Mexico City, 1979—; prof. projects Sch. Architecture U.N.A.M., Mexico City, 1965, prof. prefabrication Sch. Architecture U.I.A., Mexico City, 1966. Author: Mi Primer Circulo, 1973, Variaciones S/Mismo Tema, 1975, 20 Diseños de Pref. Y Arq., 1979, Remembranzas, 1987. Named God Father of Generation Civil Engrs., Ceneti, Mexico City, 1972; sch. named in his honor, Zacatepeque, Guatemala, 1975. Mem. Colegio de Arquitectos de Mexico. Office: Enrique Macotela Y Asociados SA, Jose Maria Pereda 605, 11000 Mexico City Mexico

MACPHAIL, IAN SHAW, conservationist; b. Aberdeen, Scotland, Mar. 11, 1922; s. Robert Shaw and Edith (Hadden) MacP.; m. Armorel Davie (div. 1950); 1 child, Diana; m. Michal Hambourg, June 19, 1950; 1 child, Robert. Diploma in graphic design, Grays Sch. Art, Aberdeen, 1943. Asst. music controller Entertainment-Nat. Services Assn., London, 1944-46; asst. music dir. Arts Council Great Britain, London, 1946-52; dir. publicity Dexion Ltd., London, 1952-58; dir. Greenway Printers, London, 1958-60; pub. relations cons. Brewers Soc. Eng., London, 1960-61; gen. dir. World Wildlife Fund, London, 1961-67; chief info. officer Arthur Guiness Ltd., London, 1967-69; communications cons. London, 1969-74; European coordinator Internat. Fund for Animal Welfare, London, 1974—. Author: You and the Orchestra--A Guide, 1949; co-author: Bird Life of Europe, 1974. Named comdr. Order of Sun, Peruvian Pres., Lima, 1985, Order of Golden Ark, Prince Bernard of Netherlands, Amsterdam, 1986. Fellow Inst. Pub. Relations. Clubs: Savile, Wig and Pen (London). Home and Office: 35 Boundary Rd, London NW8 0JE, England

MACPHERSON, IAN RICHARD, language professional; b. Aberdeen, Scotland, Jan. 4, 1934; s. George and Violet Alice (Warwick) M.; m. Sheila Constance Turner; children: David John, Peter Jeremy. MA in Modern Langs., Aberdeen U., Scotland, 1956; PhD, Manchester U., Eng., 1960. Lectr. U. Wales, 1960-64, U. Durham, Eng., 1964-72; vis. prof. U. Wis., Madison, 1970-71; sr. lectr. U. Durham, Eng., 1972-75, reader, 1975-80, prof., 1980—, chmn. Spanish and Italian dept., 1984—; bd. dirs. Brit.-Spanish Mixed Commn., 1986—; Hispanic editor Durham Modern Langs. Series, 1978—; mem. editorial bd. Bull. of Hispanic Studies, Liverpool, 1986—; adv. bd. Sem. of Hispanic Studies, Madison, Wis., 1985—. Author: (with R.B. Tate) Juan Manuel, Libro de los Estados, 1974; (with Alan Deyermond) The Age of the Catholic Monarchs, 1988; Spanish Phonology, 1975; editor: Juan Manuel Studies, 1977, The Manueline Succession, 1979, Juan Manuel: A Selection, 1980; translator: (with Jacqueline Minett) Federico García Lorca, Yerma, 1987. Decorated Comendador de la Orden de Isabel la Católica King of Spain. Mem. Assn. Hispanists of Gt. Britain and Ireland (pres. 1986-88), Asociacion Internacional de Hispanistas, Asociacion Hispánica de Literatura Medieval. Office: Sch Modern European Langs, Elvet Riverside New Elvet, Durham DH1 3JT, England

MACPHERSON, STEWART, social science educator; b. Dagenham, Essex, Eng., Apr. 12, 1945; s. William and Peggy (Woolgar) MacP.; m. Andrea Clare Lucy, July 26, 1967; children: Catie Anna, James Michael. BA, Keele U., 1970; M.Phil., York U., Eng., 1972; PhD, U. Nottingham, Eng., 1980. Lectr., Makerere U., Kampala, Uganda, 1972-73, U. Papua New Guinea, Port Moresby, 1977-79, U. Nottingham, 1973-88; prof. anthropology, sociology, U. Papua New Guinea, 1988—; cons. WHO, Geneva, 1981—; adviser Brit. Council, London, 1974, 82, 85; examiner U. West Indies, Kingston, 1985—. Author: Social Policy in the Third World, 1982, Comparative Social Policy and the Third World, 1987, 500 Million Children, Child Welfare in the Third World, 1987; editor: Approaches to Welfare, 1983, Public Issues, Private Pain, 1988. Mem. Social Policy Assn., Internat. Sociol. Assn. Avocations: diving, long distance running. Office: U Papua New Guinea, Dept Anthropology Sociology, Box 320, Port Moresby Papua New Guinea

MACQUARRIE, JOHN, divinity educator; b. Renfrew, Scotland, June 27, 1919; s. John and Robina (McInnes) M.; m. Jenny Fallow Welsh, Jan. 17, 1949; children—John Michael, Catherine Elizabeth, Alan Denis. M.A., U. Glasgow, 1940, Ph.D., 1954, D.Litt., 1964; D.D., U. Oxford, Eng., 1981; S.T.D. (hon.), U. of South, Tenn., 1967, Gen. Theol. Sem., N.Y., 1968; D.D. (hon.), U. Glasgow, 1969. Ordained priest, 1965. Lectr., U. Glasgow, Scotland, 1953-62; prof. systematic theology Union Theol. Sem., N.Y.C., 1962-70; Lady Margaret prof. div. U. Oxford, Eng., 1970-84; pres. Inst. Religion and Theology of Gt. Britain and Ireland, 1982-85. Author: Principles of Christian Theology, 1966; Existentialism, 1972; In Search of Humanity, 1982; In Search of Deity, 1984. Pres., Caledonian Soc. Oxford, 1982-84. Served to capt. Brit. Army, 1945-48. Territorial Decoration, Brit. Army, 1962. Fellow Brit. Acad. Address: 206 Headley Way, Oxford, Oxford OX3 7TA, England

MACRAE, DONALD RICHARD, metallurgist, research scientist; b. Poughkeepsie, N.Y., July 14, 1934; s. Farquhar and Eliza Jessie (Urguhart) MacR.; 1 child, Alley-Cade. B.S. in Chem. Engring., Syracuse U., 1956; M.S. in Engring., Princeton U., 1958; Ph.D., Royal Inst. Tech., Stockholm, 1961.

Research engr. Royal Inst. Tech., Stockhom, 1962-66; research engr. Bethlehem Steel Corp., Pa., 1967-68, research supr., 1969-81, sr. scientist, 1982—. Author: Electric Arc Furnace Dust Recycle, Recovery and Disposal, 1985. Editor: Plasma Technology and Application to Metallurgy, 1984. Editor Plasma Chemistry and Plasma Processing periodical. Inventor of method of reducing ores. Contbr. articles in field of plasma metall. processes to profl. jours. Mem. Am. Inst. Metall. Engrs., Am. Ceramic Soc. Home: 418 High St Bethlehem PA 18016 Office: Bethlehem Steel Corp Research Dept Tech Group Bethlehem PA 18016

MACRÍ, MARLO UGO RICCARDO, physicist; b. Catania, Italy, Oct. 28, 1944; s. Arcangelo and Clelia (Licciardello) M.; m. Adela Robla, Feb. 9, 1974; children: Alessandra, Irene. Degree in physics, U. Genoa, Italy, 1970. Asst. prof. physics U. Genoa, 1971, fellow, 1973-75; researcher Inst. Nat. Fisica Nuclear, Genoa, 1979—; fellow European Ctr. for Nuclear Research, Geneva, 1975-79; research assoc. C.E.R.N., Geneva, 1979—; group leader Inst. Nat. Fisica Nuclear, 1977-81, 83—. Office: CERN, 1202 Geneva Switzerland

MACROE-WIEGAND, VIOLA LUCILLE, psychiatrist, psychoanalyst; b. Indiana, Pa., May 17, 1920; d. Joseph Cyprian and Lucy E. (Colson) Macro; BA, St. Joseph's Coll. for Women, 1941; MA, Columbia U., 1942, PhD, 1958; MD, U. Hamburg (Germany), 1962; m. Thomas F. Gordon, Nov. 23, 1977. Instr. and chief psychologist Manhattan Eye and Ear Hosp., N.Y.U. Med. Sch., N.Y.C., 1952-58; lectr. dept. psychiatry SUNY, Bklyn., 1962-63; psychiat. fellow Creedmore State Hosp., Queens, N.Y. 1962-63; intern U. Hamburg, 1962-63; resident St. George's Hosp., Hamburg, 1963-64; research fellow in neurology Mt. Sinai Hosp., 1963-64; resident in psychiatry P.R. Inst. of Psychiatry, 1976-79; practice internal medicine and psychiatry, San Juan, P.R., 1974—; psychologist geriatrics Little Sisters of Poor Hosp., Bklyn., 1965-67; mem. staff dept. neurology Kingsbrook Med. Ctr., Bklyn., 1967-68; asst. prof. psychology Kingsborough Community Coll., N.Y., 1966-67, CCNY, summer, 1968; mem. staff psychiatry Rio Piedras State Hosp., San Juan, 1974-82, P.R. Inst. of Psychiatry, San Juan, 1976-82: psychiatrist dept. mental health Knud Hansen Meml. Hosp., St. Thomas, V.I., 1978-82; fellow L.I. Inst. Psychoanalysis, Nassau County Med. Clinic, East Meadow, L.I., 1982—; neurol. and psychol. research dir., adminstr. Humboldt Med. Arts Bldg., 1988—. Fellow Am. Assn. Mental Deficiency; mem. Am. Psychol. Assn., Ea. Psychol. Assn., N.Y. State Psychol. Assn., AMA, Am. Psychiat. Assn., P.R. Med. Assn., Associación Hermandad en las Carreteras de P.R. (v.p. 1975—), Pi Lambda Theta, Kappa Delta Pi. Roman Catholic. Contbr. articles on physiol. psychology to profl. jours.; research in visual and auditory perception. Home: 185 Clinton Ave Brooklyn NY 11205 Office: Think Thin Inc 109 Jackson St Brooklyn NY 11211

MACRURY, KING, management counselor; b. Manchester, N.H., Oct. 14, 1915; s. Colin H. and Lauretta C. (Shea) MacR.; 1 son, Colin C. A.B., Rollins Coll., 1938; postgrad., St. Anselms Coll., L.I. Coll. Medicine, Princeton. Asst. personnel dir. Lily-Tulip Cup Corp., 1939; asst. dir. market research Ward Baking Co., 1940-41; staff mem. Nat. Indsl. Conf. Bd., 1941-43; cons. indsl. relations and orgn. planning McKinsey & Co., 1946-48; internal cons. Oxford Paper Co., 1949-50; installer, dir. indsl. relations Champion Internation Co., 1950-51; pvt. practice mgmt. counselor 1951—; lectr. Indsl. Edn. Inst., 1962-68, Mgmt. Center, Cambridge, 1968-71, Dun & Bradstreet, 1979—; extension div. U. N.H., 1968—; extension program U. Maine, 1978—; also U. Bridgeport, extension program U. Conn.; coordinator mgmt. edn. extension div. U. Conn., 1964-68, Philippine Council Mgmt., 1969—, Econ. Devel. Found. Philippines, 1969—, Am. Metal Stamping Assn., 1969—; condr. mgmt. seminars for Asian Assn. Mgmt. Orgns. C.I.O.S., 1972; Mem. Indsl. Devel. Commn. Andover, 1957-58; manpower com. U.S. Dept. Labor Bus. Adv. Council, 1958-61. Author: Developing Your People Potential; Contbr. numerous articles in field to profl. jours. Served to lt. USNR, 1943-46. Mem. N.H. Dental Soc. (hon.). Office: Box 215 Rye NH 03870

MACUMBER, JOHN PAUL, insurance company executive; b. Macon, Mo., Jan. 21, 1940; s. Rolland Deardorf and Althea Villa (Cason) M.; B.A., Central Meth. Coll., Fayette, Mo., 1962; Asso. in Risk Mgmt., Ins. Inst. Am., 1978; m. Marilyn Sue Ashe, Nov. 10, 1962; children—Leanne, Cheryl. Casualty underwriter U.S. Fidelity & Guaranty Co., St. Louis, 1962-66; automobile underwriter Am. Indemnity Co., Galveston, Tex., 1966-69; auto casualty underwriter St. Paul Cos., New Orleans, 1969-73; sr. comml. casualty underwriter Chubb/Pacific Indemnity, Portland, Oreg., 1973-75; casualty underwriter Interstate Nat. Corp., Los Angeles, 1975-76, underwriting supr., 1976-78, v.p., br. mgr., Mpls., 1978-82, also v.p. subs. Chgo. Ins. Co.; umbrella/spl. risk supr. Guaranty Nat. Ins. Co., Englewood, Colo., 1982-85; br. mgr. Burns & Wilcox, Ltd.-West, Salt Lake City, 1985—. Served with USAF, 1962-68. Nat. Methodist scholar, 1958. Mem. Minn. Assn. Spl. Risk Underwriters, Ins. Assn. Utah, Profl. Ins. Agts. Utah, Ind. Ins. Agts. Utah, Surplus Line Assn. Utah, Nat. Assn. Profl. Surplus Lines Offices. Republican. Mem. Unity Ch. (sec. bd. dirs. 1979). Lodges: Optimists (charter pres. 1968) (Friendswood, Tex.); Kiwanis (charter pres. 1979) (Bloomington, Minn.). Clubs: Insurance, Blue Goose (Mpls.); Salt Lake City. Home: 9683 S Buttonwood Dr Sandy UT 84092 Office: 455 E South Temple Suite 101 Salt Lake City UT 84111

MAC WHINNIE, JOHN VINCENT, artist; b. Rockville Centre, N.Y., Apr. 22, 1945; s. Milton Joseph and Inez Genevieve (LaFlamme) Mac W.; m. Virginia Gail Gettling, June, 1985; 1 child, Milton John. B.A. magna cum laude, Southampton Coll., 1972. Artist, painter Water Mill, N.Y. Exhibited in group shows: Met. Mus. Art, 1979, Guggenheim Mus., 1979, Lehigh U., 1979, Bklyn. Mus., 1981, Am. Acad. and Inst. Arts and Letters, 1981, New Orleans Mus. Contemporary Art, Guild Hall, Easthampton, N.Y.; one-man shows include: Marlborough Gallery, N.Y., Andre Emmerich Gallery, N.Y.; represented in permanent collections: Guggenheim Mus., Bklyn. Mus., Phillips Collection, Walker Art Ctr., Parrish Art Mus., Guild Hall, numerous others. Recipient First prize in painting Parrish Art Mus., 1971, Excellence in Painting award Heckscher Mus., 1974. Avocations: motorcycling; gardening, antique collecting. Home and Studio: Deerfield Rd Water Mill NY 11976

MADAN, SHARAD YESHWANT, architect; b. Bombay, Feb. 12, 1929; s. Yeshwant Atmaram and Sonabai Yeshwant (Dhulekar) M. Grad., Sir J.J. Sch. Architecture, Bombay, 1954. Archtl. asst. G.B. Mhatre & Assocs., Chartered Architect, Bombay, 1953-54; asst. architect Gunton & Gunton, Chartered Architect, London, 1954-57; ptnr. Bajpai, Madan, Palki, Razdan, Chartered Architects, Bombay, 1957-75; prin. S.Y. Madan, Architects, Bombay, 1975—. Fellow Indian Inst. Architects; mem. Royal Inst. Brit. Architects (assoc.). Club: Royal Bombay Yacht. Home: 225 Khetwadi Main Rd, Bombay Maharashtra 4000 004, India Office: SY Madan Architects, Calcot House, 8 Tamarind Ln, Bombay 400 023, India

MADDEN, IAN BERESFORD, lawyer, researcher; b. Auckland, N.Z., Feb. 27, 1931; s. Charles Beresford and Elsie Madge (Masefield) M. B.A., U. N.Z., Auckland U. Coll., 1954, M.A., 1956; LL.B., U. Otago, Dunedin, N.Z., 1969. Bar: Supreme Ct. Dunedin, 1971. Staff mem. Alfred Buckland & Sons Ltd. and successors, Auckland and Dunedin, 1949-56, 68-73; tchr. Otahuhu Coll., Auckland, 1956-57; legal officer State Advances Corp., Auckland, 1958-66; staff mem. Earl, Kent, Massey, Auckland, 1967-68, Dyer & Dowd, Auckland, 1973-74, Peak, Longland & Co., Auckland, 1975; property mgr., Auckland, 1975—. Author: Riverhead, The Kaipara Gateway, 1966; Antique Fair and Exhibition Handbook, 1965. Contbr. articles on history, genealogy, heraldry, antiques and architecture to jours. and texts. Found. mem. Mus. of Transport and Tech., Auckland, 1960—. Mem. Soc. Genealogists (London, life mem.), Soc. Genealogists (Australia, life mem.), Soc. N.Z. Genealogists (life mem., mem. Auckland br. com.), Heraldry Soc. (found. mem.), N.Z. Founders Soc., Auckland Hist. Soc. (v.p. 1962-65, pres. 1966, life mem. 1988, mem. 1963-88), Nat. Historic Places Trust, Auckland Inst. and Mus., Royal Soc. N.Z (life mem.). Mem. National Party. Mem. Ch. of Eng. Home and office: Rosslea, 15 Belvedere St, Epsom, Auckland 3 New Zealand

MADDEN, LLOYD WILLIS, petroleum geologist; b. Lewis, Kans., Aug. 27, 1918; s. Oscar Thomas and Grace (Schuffelburger) M.; m. Shirley A. Bergstrom, Sept. 10, 1950; children: Deborah Kay, Steven Douglas, Kim Ashley, Victoria Angela. Geol. Engr. Colo. Sch. Mines, 1941; student in physics U. Chgo.; M.S. in Physics, UCLA, 1942. Geologists, Shell Oil Co., San Antonio, 1946-47, Corpus Christi, Tex., 1947-49, Wichita Falls, Tex., 1949-52; mgr. McElroy Ranch Co., Midland, Tex., 1952-65; dist. geologist Mobil Oil Corp., Midland, 1965-76; cons. Resources Investment Corp., Denver, 1976-82, Internat. Oil and Gas Corp., Houston, Vinson Exploration Co., Midland, 1983—. Served to maj. USAAF, 1940-46. Mem. Am. Assn. Petroleum Geologists, Tau Beta Pi. Republican. Methodist. Lodge: Masons. Home: 1804 N H St Midland TX 79705 Office: Cons Geologist 300 Western United Life Bldg Midland TX 79701

MADDEN, PAUL R., lawyer; b. St. Paul, Nov. 13, 1926; s. Ray Joseph and Margaret (Meyer) M.; student St. Thomas Coll., 1944; A.B., U. Minn., 1948; J.D., Georgetown U., 1951; m. Rosemary R. Sorel, Aug. 7, 1974; children—Margaret Jane, William, James Patrick, Derek R. Sorel, Lisa T. Sorel. Admitted to Ariz., Minn., D.C. bars; asso. firm Hamilton & Hamilton, Washington, 1951-55; legal asst. to commr. S.C., Washington, 1955-56; asso. Lewis and Roca, Phoenix, 1957-59, partner, 1959—; counsel to The Indsl Devel. Authority of City of Phoenix; asso. gen. counsel Blood Systems, Inc., Scottsdale, Ariz. Sec. Minn. Fedn. Coll. Rep. Clubs, 1947-48; chmn. 4th dist. Minn. Young Rep. Club, 1948; nat. co-chmn. Youth for Eisenhower, 1951-52; mem. Ariz. Rep. Com., 1960-62; bd. dirs., past. pres. Ariz. Club, Phoenix, Mesa Airlines, Farmington, N.Mex.; bd. dirs., past chmn. Found. for Sr. Living, Phoenix; bd. dirs., vice chmn., Cen. Ariz. chpt. ARC; past bd. dirs., past pres. Jr. Achievement Cen. Ariz., Inc.; bd. dirs. Camelback Hosps., Inc., Scottsdale. Served with USNR, 1946-48. Mem. Am., Ariz., Maricopa County, Fed. Bar Assns., Internat. Assn. Ins. Counsel, Fedn. Ins. Counsel, Nat. Health Lawyers Assn., Am. Soc. Hosp. Attys., Nat. Assn. Bond Lawyers, Ariz. Assn. for Indsl. Devel., East Valley Partnership, Phi Delta Phi. Clubs: The Barristers (Washington), Arizona. Home: 3732 E Pierson St Phoenix AZ 85018 Office: 100 W Washington Phoenix AZ 85003

MADDOCKS, MORAG, clinical psychologist; b. Whitehaven, Eng., Apr. 4, 1947; s. John Melvin and Enid (Woodnorth) M.; m. William Martin Maddocks, May 21, 1976; children: Tom, Fiona. BA in Psychology, Manchester U., 1968; MSc in Clin. Psychology, Newcastle U., 1970. Probation psychologist Prudhoe & Monkton Hosp., Northumberland, Eng., 1968-70; clin. psychologist St. Francis Hosp., Sussex, Eng., 1970-72; sr. psychologist Sheffield Health Authority, Eng., 1972-82, prin. psychologist, 1982—; sec. Trent Region Psychology Adv. Com., 1985-87; cons. Homestart, Sheffield, 1985—. Contbr. articles to profl. jours. Chmn. Sheffield Nat. Childbirth Trust, 1981. Social Sci. Research Council grantee, 1975. Mem. Brit. Psychol. Soc., Brit. Assn. Behavioral Psychology. Office: Psychology Dept, Whiteley Wood Clinic, Woofindin Rd, Sheffield England

MADDOX, CHARLES J., JR., lawyer; b. Cameron, Tex., Oct. 8, 1949; s. Charles J. and Mary Jo (Fikes) M.; m. Sandra Peppin, Apr. 29, 1984; children: Elizabeth Asleigh, Kathryn Austin. Student Tex. A&M U., 1968-70; BBA, U. Tex., 1972, JD, 1976. Bar: Tex. 1977, U.S. Dist. Ct. (no., so., ea. and we. dists.) Tex. 1980, U.S. Ct. Appeal (5th and 11th cirs.) 1981, U.S. Supreme Ct. 1982. Staff auditor Walgreen Co., Chgo. and Houston, 1973; asst. atty. gen. State of Tex., Austin, 1977-80; sr. and mng. ptnr. firm Maddox, Perrin & Kirkendall, Houston, 1981—. Sponsor Rep. fund, Washington, 1983—; sustaining mem. Rep. Nat. Com., Washington, 1984—. NSF scholar 1965, Newhause scholar 1968. Mem. Tex. Bar Assn., Houston Bar Assn., Sigma Iota Epsilon, Alpha Kappa Psi (life mem., treas. 1971-72). Republican. Presbyterian. Clubs: Quail Valley Country (Missouri City, Tex.), Plaza, Govs. (Houston). Office: Maddox Perrin & Kirkendall 5100 Republic Bank Ctr Houston TX 77002

MADDOX, YVONNE TARLTON, medical communications company executive; b. Lubbock, Tex.; m. George Allman, Nov. 2, 1974. B.A., Okla. State U. Pres., World Health Info. Services, Inc., N.Y.C., 1970-83; v.p. Health Edn. Technologies, Inc. div. Batton, Barton, Durstine & Osborn, Inc., N.Y.C., 1984-86; pres. Internat. Communications in Medicine, Inc., N.Y.C., 1986—; v.p. S.E.R.A.D., Inc., San Francisco, 1988—. Mem. Pharm. Advt. Council, Am. Women in Radio and TV (past dir.). Home: 245 E 50th St New York NY 10022

MADELAINE, RICHARD ELTON RAYMOND, college educator; b. Sutton, Surrey, Eng., Aug. 26, 1947; came to Australia, 1951; s. Vernon Frederick and Doris Evelyn (Nicholls) M.; m. Louise Moira Miller, Dec. 11, 1976; 1 child, Claire. BA with hons., U. Adelaide, 1969; PhD, U. London, 1973. Lectr. U. New South Wales, Australia, 1973-82, sr. lectr., 1982—. Contbr. articles to ednl. jours. Hon. treas. Malone Soc., Australasian Univs. Lang. and Lit. Assn. Anglican. Avocations: 18th century British paintings and drawings, Chinese and Japanese Literati paintings. Office: Sch of English, U of New South Wales, PO Box 1, Kensington NSW 2033, Australia

MADER, JON TERRY, physician; b. Madison, Wis., Mar. 21, 1944; s. John Henry and Louise E. (Hancock) M.; B.A., Wabash Coll., 1966; M.D., Ind. U., 1970; m. Joan Eileen Piper, Nov. 29, 1969; children—Travis Jon, Amy Eileen, Bret Mark. Intern, U. Tex. Med. Br., Galveston, 1970-71, resident in internal medicine, 1971-73, fellow in infectious disease, 1973-74, 76-77, instr., 1977-78, asst. prof. dept. internal medicine, 1978-82, assoc. prof. internal medicine div. infectious diseases, 1982—; mem. med. staff, 1977—; chief hyperbaric medicine, div. marine medicine Marine Biomed. Inst., Galveston, 1979—; trainee in hyperbaric oxygenation therapy NASA Manned Spacecraft Center, Houston, 1973; bd. advisors Ocean Corp., Houston; med. advisor, dir. Nautilus Corp., Houston. Served with M.C., USN, 1974-76. Diplomate Am. Bd. Internal Medicine; cert. Am. Bd. Infectious Diseases; recipient numerous fellowships and grants. Fellow Am. Bd. Internal Medicine; mem. Am. Soc. Microbiology, Undersea Med. Soc. (exec. comm.), Am. Fedn. Clin. Research, Can. Infectious Disease Soc., Infectious Disease Soc. Am., ACP. Episcopalian. Contbr. articles to profl. jours. Home: 1015 Church St Galveston TX 11550 Office: U Tex Med Br Dept Internal Medicine Galveston TX 77550

MADGETT, JOHN PATRICK, III, business executive; b. Hastings, Nebr., Dec. 12, 1940; s. John Patrick, Jr. and Marian Ellen (Dominy) M.; m. Jean Belli, June 15, 1966 (div. 1979); children—Kimberly, John Patrick, Robyn, David. B.A. in Math. and Physics, Carleton Coll., 1962; B.S.E.E., Columbia U., 1963; M.B.A., Stanford U., 1965. Case writer Harvard Bus. Sch., Cambridge, Mass., 1965; indsl. economist Stanford Research Inst., Palo Alto, Calif., 1965; fin. analyst Kaiser Aluminum & Chem. Corp., Oakland, Calif., 1965-68; pres., dir. Ajax Towing Co., Mpls., 1968-77, United Dock Service, Rochester, Ky., 1968-77, Ener-Tran, Inc., Mpls., 1975-81, United Barge Co., Mpls., 1968-77, Wellspring Energy Corp., Mpls., 1977—, Wellspring Fin. Corp., Mpls., 1980—; pres., dir. Wellspring Offshore Services Corp., New Orleans, 1980—; pres., chief exec. officer, dir. Wellspring Corp., Mpls., 1980—; chmn., dir. Wellspring Properties, 1984—; chmn. Wellspring Andrena Ltd., 1984—; chmn., dir. Trend Sci., Inc., Mpls., Tecnetics Industries Inc., St. Paul, Minn.; cons. German Pub. Utility Industry, Joint Engring. Council U.S.A. and Europe, N.Y.C., 1962. Co-author: World of Science and Technology, 1975. Trustee, Breck Sch., Mpls., 1978-81; active vol. mgmt. Mpls. United Way, 1968-76, fund raising Campus Crusade for Christ International, San Bernardino, Calif., 1978-88. Mem. Nat. Feed & Grain Dealers Assn., Water Transprt Assn., Young Pres. Orgn. (treas. 1973-80), Propellar Club. Republican. Episcopalian. Clubs: Marsh Lake, Five Fifty-Five, Minneapolis, Minikahda. Office: Wellspring Corp 4530 IDS Center 80 S 8th St Minneapolis MN 55402

MADHAVAN, ANANTANARAYANA, ambassador; b. India, 1933; married. MA in Econs. and Politics, U. Madras, 1954; postgrad., Cambridge U., 1957-58. With Indian Fgn. Service, 1956—; served in Burma, Switzerland, Peoples Republic of China, U.K., Hong Kong, USSR; with Ministry of External Affairs, New Delhi, India, 1965-68, 81; ambassador to Japan Tokyo, 1985—. Harvard U. Centre for Internat. Affairs fellow, 1980-81. Office: Embassy of India, Tokyo Japan

MADISON, T. JEROME, business executive; b. N.Y.C., June 2, 1940; s. Theodore H. and Eleanor E. (Leonard) M.; m. Marsha A. Heeb, Sept. 26, 1964; children: Jill, Kim, Ryan. BS, U. Pa., 1962; MBA, Monmouth Coll., 1975. CPA, N.J. Mgr., Peat, Marwick, Mitchell & Co., Newark and Trenton, N.J., 1970-75; mgr. Abbott Labs., North Chicago, Ill., 1976; chief internal auditor Rorer Group, Inc., Fort Washington, Pa., 1977-78, corp. controller, 1979-82; v.p. fin. Cytogen Corp., Princeton, N.J., 1982-86; pres., dir. Outwater & Wells Ventures, Inc., 1981-85, Atlantic Capital Resources Group, Inc., 1985—, Founders Court Investors Inc., Princeton, N.J., 1986—; chmn., chief exec. officer Pilling Co., 1986—; chmn. Capital Controls Corp, 1987—; dir., chmn. fin. com. Carrier Found. Served with USN, 1962-66. Mem. Delaware Valley Venture Group, Fin. Execs. Inst., Am. Inst. CPA's. Lodge: Rotary. Office: Founders Ct Investors Inc 92 Nassau St Princeton NJ 08542

MADLE, ROBERT ALBERT, author; b. Phila., June 2, 1920; s. Vincent Robert and Mary Virginia (Kidwell) M.; B.S., Drexel U., 1951, M.B.A., 1953; m. Billie Franklin Lindsay, Nov. 7, 1943; children: Robert, Richard, Jane, Mary Anne. Asst. to sales mgr. Masland Duraleather, Phila., 1951-53; asst. to dir. indsl. relations Chadbourne Hosiery, Charlotte, N.C., 1953-54; personnel and credit mgr. Shaw Mfg. Co., Charlotte, 1954-56; personnel research specialist U.S. Army, Washington, D.C., 1956-59, research psychologist, program mgr. U.S. Navy, Washington, 1959-80. Served with U.S. Army, 1942-46. Guest of honor World Sci. Fiction Conv., Miami, 1977, U. Md. Sci. Fiction Conv., 1982. Mem. Sci. Fiction Writers Am., Washington Sci. Fiction Assn., First Fandom (pres. 1959-82). Contbr. articles to sci. fiction and sports mags.; specialist in field of sci. fiction and fantasy lit.; condr. search service rare books in field of sci. fiction and fantasy lit. Home and Office: 4406 Bestor Dr Rockville MD 20853

MADOLE, DONALD WILSON, lawyer; b. Elkhart, Kans., July 14, 1932; Student Kans. State Tchrs. Coll., 1950-51; B.S., U. Denver, 1959, J.D., 1959. Bar: Colo. 1960, U.S. Dist. Ct. Colo. 1960, U.S. Ct. Appeals (10th cir.) 1960, D.C. 1971, U.S. Supreme Ct. 1972, U.S. Ct. Appeals (1st cir.) 1976, U.S. Ct. Appeals (5th cir.) 1977, U.S. Ct. Appeals (6th cir.) 1982, U.S. Ct. Appeals (7th and 9th cirs.) 1975, U.S. Ct. Appeals (11th cir.) 1981. Vice pres. Mountain Aviation Corp., Denver, 1958-59; trial atty. FAA, Washington, 1960-62; sr. warranty adminstr. Am. Airlines, Tulsa, 1962-63; chief hearing and reports div., atty. adviser CAB, Washington, 1963-66; ptnr. Speiser, Krause & Madole, Washington, 1966—; pres. Aerial Application Corp., Burlingame, Calif., 1968-69; v.p., dir. Environ. Power Ltd., Pitts., 1972—; dir. Unitrade Ltd., Washington, Bus. Ins. Mgmt. Inc., Bethesda, Md., Entertainment Capitol Corp., N.Y.C.; gen. counsel Nat. Aviation Club, 1978-80, Internat. Soc. Air Safety Investigators, 1977; mem. blue ribbon panel on airworthiness Nat. Acad. Sci., 1980; adviser U.S. Govt. del. Internat. Civil Aviation Orgn., 1965; U.S. Govt. rep. Aircraft Inquiry, Montreal, P.Q., Can., 1964. Author: Textbook of Aviation Statutes and Regulations, 1963; International Aspects of Aircraft Accidents, 1963; CAB, Aircraft Accident Investigation, 1964. Mem. chancellor's soc. U. Denver, 1982—. Served to comdr. USNR, 1953-57. Recipient Outstanding Performance award FAA, 1961; Meritorious Achievement award Am. Airlines, 1962; Outstanding Performance awards CAB, 1963-65; Fed. Govt. Outstanding Pub. Service award Jump-Meml. Found., 1966. Fellow Internat. Trial Lawyers; mem. ABA, Colo. Bar Assn., Fed. Bar Assn., D.C. Bar Assn., Assn. Trial Lawyers Am., Lawyer-Pilots Assn., Phi Delta Phi, Phi Mu Alpha. Clubs: Congl. Country, Nat. Aviation, Nat. Press. Home: 2800 Jenifer St NW Washington DC 20015 Office: 1216 16th St NW Washington DC 20036

MADRIGAL-NIETO, RODRIGO, minister of foreign affairs of Costa Rica, lawyer; b. San Jose, Costa Rica, Mar. 14, 1924. D. in Law, U. Costa Rica, 1947, postgrad. in Econs. and Fin. Dir., Costa Rican Social Security Found., 1947-56; del. to Internat. Conf. of Labor, Uruguay, 1949, Switzerland, 1955; pres. Chamber of Industries, Costa Rica, 1954-61, del. to UN, 1954, del. to Central Am. Conf. for Ministers of Econ. Affairs, 1958, pres. Central Am. Chamber of Industries, 1960-61, dir. newspaper La Republica, 1968-78; mem. council to the pres. Inter.-Am. Devel. Bank, 1968-70; dep. Legis. Assembly, Costa Rica, 1978-82, pres., 1978-79, pres. spl. commn. to U.S. for econ. assistance to Central Am., 1983—; Minister of Fgn. Affairs, Costa Rica, 1986—; pres. and dir. numerous Costa Rican industries. Gen. sec. Inter-Am. Soc. of Press, 1969-70, 2d v.p., 1970-71, first v.p., 1971-72, pres., 1972. Office: Ministry of Fgn Affairs, San Jose Costa Rica *

MADSEN, JAN BIRGER LOVGREN, airport restaurant executive; b. Glostrup, Denmark, May 5, 1944; s. Poul Lovgren and Anna Elmelund (Olsen) M.; m. Kirsten Dyrum, Oct. 17, 1975; children: Anja Dyrum, Ulla Dyrum. Cert., Ltoftegaard Studk., 1969; MS in Sociology, U. Copenhagen, 1979. Apprentice Restaurant 7 Nations, Copenhagen, 1961-65; head chef Danish Masonic Lodge, Copenhagen, 1968-77; prodn. mgr. SAS Service Ptnr., Copenhagen, 1979-82; cons. Mercuri Urval, Copenhagen, 1982-83; prodn. mgr., adminstrv. mgr. SAS Service Ptnr., Riyadh, 1983-86; mng. dir. SAS Service Ptnr., Dublin, Ireland, 1986—. Home: Ramore Thormanby Rd, Howth, Dublin 13 Ireland Office: Dublin Airport Restaurants Ltd, Terminal Bldg, Dublin Airport Ireland

MADSEN, LINDA GAIL, controller; b. Cleburne, Tex., Dec. 7, 1942; d. Raymond Woodrow and Georgialee (Stephens) Madsen. Student Tex. Lutheran Coll., 1961-62, El Camino Coll., 1964-69. Jr. accountant Inglewood Wholesale Electric Co. (Calif.), 1962-66; office mgr. Christensen Orthopedic Co., Redondo Beach, Calif., 1966-71, Dryterior Inc., Lawndale, Calif., 1971-72; controller, corp. officer Patraco Inc., Gardena, Calif., 1973-74; chief fin. officer, dir. Head Shampoo, Inc., Carson, Calif., 1974-80; controller Cloverleaf Group Inc., Los Angeles, 1980-87; office adminstr. Iskowitz & Koo CPA's, Los Angeles, 1987—. Mem. Christian Bus. and Profl. Women's Council (treas. 1978-82), Nat. Assn. Female Execs., Nat. Notary Assn. Democrat. Lutheran. Home: 3724 Spencer St Apt 319 Torrance CA 90503 Office: Iskowitz & Koo 1801 Century Park E Suite 1000 Los Angeles CA 90067

MADSEN, RUD FRIK, sugar company executive; b. Helsingor, Denmark, Apr. 24, 1930; s. Janus Frederik and Asta (Pedersen) M.; m. Gerda Andersen, May 4, 1957; children—Lisbet, Jens Peter. M.Sc., Tech. U. Copenhagen, 1953, dr.techn., 1978. Engr., Danish Sugar Corp., Nakskov, Denmark, 1953-65, head research, 1965-78, dir. research, Copenhagen, 1978—; dir. Filmtec, Inc., Mpls., 1980-85, Pasilac, Inc., Mpls., 1983-85, Pasilac Therm A/S, Kolding, Denmark, 1980-86, Hojbygard Papirfabrik, Denmark, 1980-88; dir. Grenaa Papirfabrik, 1988—. Commn. Sci. des Membranes, France, 1987—; hon. prof. U. Lund, Sweden, 1985; mem. EEC Sci. Commn. for Tech., 1985—; v.p. I.C.U.M.S.A., 1986—. Author: Hyperfiltration and Ultrafiltration in Plate and Frame Systems, 1977; (with Masters and Wiegand) Membrane Filtration, Evaporation and Spray Drying in the Dairy and Cheese Industry, 1984; contbr. articles in field to profl. jours.; patentee decanter centrifuges, membrane systems, sugar machinery. Mem. Acad. Tech. Sci. Denmark, Indsl. Research Com. Denmark. Lutheran. Home: 38 Strandpromenaden, 4900 Nakskov Denmark Office: De Danske Sukkerfabrikker, 5 Langebrogade, 1001 Copenhagen Denmark

MADUAKOR, OBIAJURU, educator; b. Isulo, Anambra, Nigeria, July 5, 1942; s. Albert Enemo Maduakor and Angelina Afubekwe Okeke; m. Chijioke Obiageli Nwankwo, July 12, 1969; children: Ifeanyi, Chukwuka, Chinedu. BA with honors in English, U. Ibadan (Nigeria), 1965; MA in English, U. Leeds (England), 1972; PhD in English, U. Ottawa (Canada), 1977. Lectr. U. Gabon, Libreville, 1971-72; instr. U. Ottawa, 1972-77; asst. prof. U. Ife (Nigeria), 1978-81; assoc. prof. U. Nigeria, Nsukka, 1984-86, prof., 1987—; chief moderator prose fiction Joint Admissions and Matriculation Bd., Lagos, Nigeria, 1982—. Author: Wole Soyinka: An Introduction to His Writing, 1987; contbr. articles to profl. jours. Mem. African Lit. Assn., Literary Soc. Nigeria. Office: Univ Nigeria Dept English, Nsukka, Anambra State Nigeria Home: Godway House, Isulo Orumba LGA, Anambra State Nigeria

MADUKA, CHIDI THOMAS, literary lecturer; b. Neni, Anambra, Njikoka, Nigeria, Mar. 4, 1940; s. Daniel Ofobuike and Appolonia Uzo (Obiora) M.; m. Ngozi Patricia Ibeme, May 16, 1975; children: Chukwuma, Chinwe, Chinenye. BA in French, U. Laval, Quebec, Can., 1968, MA in French, 1970; PhD in Comparative Literature, U. Iowa, 1976. Teaching fellow French dept. U. Iowa, Iowa City, 1970-74; instr. French dept. U. Moncton, New Brunswick, Can., 1973; asst. prof. dept. English U. Utah, Salt Lake City, 1974-77; lectr. comparative literature U. Port Harcourt(Nigeria), 1977-80; dept. head, program coordinator U. Port Harcourt (Nigeria), 1983-85, sr. lectr. comparative literature, 1980—. Mem. African Lit. Assn. Am., Linguistic Assn. Nigeria, African and Comparative Lit. Nigeria, Literary Soc. Nigeria (fin. sec., treas. 1984—). Office: U Port Harcourt, Comparative Literature Programme, Port Harcourt Nigeria

MADURO, OTTO, philosophy and sociology of religion educator; b. Caracas, Venezuela, Apr. 14, 1945; s. Josè Manuel and Celia (Lang) M.; m. Nancy Noguera. Grad. in Philosophy, U. Central de Venezuela, 1968; Cath. U. Louvain (Belgium), 1973, Ph.D. magna cum laude in Philosophy of Religion, 1977, M.A. magna cum laude in Sociology of Religion, 1978. Instr. U. de los Andes, Estado Mérida, Venezuela, 1969-71, asst., 1971-75, aggregate, 1975-81, assoc. prof. philosophy and sociology of religion, 1981-86; invited lectr. U. Notre Dame, Ind., 1982; vis. prof. Maryknoll Sch. Theology, 1982, 85, 86, 87—; cons. for various Cath. religious orders including Jesuits, Maryknoll, Dominicans. Author: Marxismo Religion, 1977; Revelación y Revolución, 1970; Religion y Lucha de Clases, 1979, English edit., German edit., Portugese edit. Sec. edn. Christian Dem. Youth, Venezuela, 1965-67; mem. nat. council Christian Left Party, Venezuela, 1967-69. Recipient essay prize Nat. Council on Cultural Affairs, Venezuela, 1977-78. Mem. Internat. Sociol. Assn. (research com. on sociology of religion), Internat. Conf. on Sociology of Religion, Internat. Cath. Movement of Intellectuals-Pax Romana, Association Française de Sociologie Religieuse (Paris), Soc. for Sci. Study Religion (U.S.), Assn. for Sociology of Religion (U.S.). Roman Catholic. Office: Maryknoll Sch Theology Maryknoll NY 10545

MAEDER, JEAN-BERNARD, marketing consulting company executive; b. Neuchatel, Switzerland, June 9, 1949; s. Jean-William and Suzanne-Marie (Selier) M.; m. Nicole Fabine, Sept. 18, 1980; children: Camille-Cecile, Basile-Victor. BS, Gymnase Cantanal, Neuchatel, 1970; M. Econs., U. Neuchatel, 1974. Lic. economist. Mktg. services gen. mgr. SSIM, Biel, Switzerland, 1976-79, adviser to chief exec, officer, 1978-80; v.p. mktg. Omega Watches, Biel, 1979-81; mng. dir. Creative Mktg. Cons., Neuchatel, 1981—. Author: Structure Industrielles de la Suisse, 1974. Mem. European Soc. for Opinion and Market Research. Office: Creative Marketing Cons, Rue du Bassin 14, CH-2000 Neuchatel Switzerland

MAEKAWA, KAZUKO, college librarian; b. Osaka, Japan, Aug. 12, 1946; s. Kazuo and Kikuko (Shibuya) M. BA, Keio U., Tokyo, 1975. Librarian Ohtani Women's Jr. Coll., Tondabayashi-city, Japan, 1967—, chief librarian, 1973—. Author: Essays in Honour of the Seventieth Anniversary of Professor Shigeru Tachibana's Birthday; contbr. articles to profl. jours. Recipient Shimizu Fukuichi Meml. prize Assn. Pvt. Jr. Colls. Japan, 1975. Mem. Japan Library Assn. (advisor 1983-87), Nippon Assn. Librarianship. Home: 4-4-15 Tanabe Higashisumiyoshi-ku, 546 Osaka Japan Office: Ohtani Womens Jr Coll, 942-1 Nishigori Oaza, 584 Tondabayashi Japan

MAEKAWA, TAIJIRO, manufacturing executive; b. Tokyo, Jan. 5, 1925; s. Eijiro and Tei Maekawa; children: Yasuaki, Yasuhisa, Yasunori. BA, Tokyo Comml. Coll., 1948. Sr. mng. dir. Maekawa Co. Ltd., Tokyo, 1948-57, Anmin Mfg. Co. Ltd., Tokyo, 1957—, Nishikawa Bed Co. Ltd., Tokyo, 1968—, Nishikawa Sangyo Co. Ltd., Tokyo, 1977—, Japan Research Lab. of Sleep Sci., Tokyo, 1984—; chmn. Nishikawa Corp. Assn., 1965—. Mem. Japan Sleep Research Soc., Japan Textile Soc., Japan Textile Machinery Soc., Japan Down Products Corp. Assn. (vice chmn. 1978—), Internat. Feather Bur., Japan Bedding Products Corp. Assn. (bd. dirs.). Club: Nippon Country. Home: 1-24-15 Kichijoji Kitamachi, Musashino, Tokyo 180, Japan Office: Nishikawa Sabgyo Co Ltd, 8-8 Nihonbashi-Tomizawacho, Tokyo 103, Japan

MAEKAWA, ZYUN-ITI, acoustical engineering educator; b. Osaka, Japan, Nov. 2, 1925; s. Tsunehachi and Tori (Nishio) M.; m. Keiko Nakamura, Mar. 23, 1955; children: Masato, Arito, Kazuto, Muneto. B in Engring., Kyoto U., Japan, 1948, D in Engring., 1962. Asst. prof. Kyoto U., 1950-52; lectr. Kobe U., Japan, 1952-53, assoc. prof., 1953-63, prof., 1963—; advisor Ken'on Engring. Co. Ltd., Kobe, 1973—; mem. Internat. Commn. on Aconstics, 1984—. Author: Noise Reduction by Screens, 1968, Acoustics 1974, 1975, Auditorium Acoustics, 1975; editor: Internat. Jour. Applied Acoustics, 1987. Fellow Acoustical Soc. Am.; mem. Archtl. Inst. Japan (awardee 1964), Acoustical Soc. Japan (v.p. 1977-79, Sato medal 1963), Inst. Noise Control Engring. Japan (v.p. 1978-80, 82-84), Inst. Noise Control Engring. USA (corres. mem.). Home: Takanodai 3-15-7, Suita, Osaka 565, Japan Office: Kobe U Faculty Engring, Rokko Nada, Kobe 657, Japan

MAENHOUT, LAURENT-ANDRE, marketing executive; b. Knocke, Belgium, Nov. 13, 1943; s. Ciriel-Camiel and Alice (Moyaert) M.; m. Viviane Gryson, July 8, 1967; children: Vincent, Caroline. Student, Ecole d'Ergologie, Brussels, 1968-69, Ipamn, Nivelles, 1962-67; MBA, Boston U., 1977. Trainee Ateliers Constrns. Electriques de Charleroi, Belgium, 1962-63; tech.-comml. supr. Semal A Ets, Brussels, 1964-66; mgr., devel. supr. Caterpillar Belgium, Gosselies, 1966-70; zone mgr. Unispar S.A., Charleroi, 1970-72, Elf Belgique SA, Brussels, 1972-74; export mgr. Ansul Fire Protection SA, Brussels, 1974-78; salaried cons. Hay Assocs. Belgium, Brussels, 1978-81; prof. European U., Brussels, 1985—; mng. cons. M-Mktg., Braine L'Alleud, Belgium, 1981—. Mem. C. of C. Brussels, Boston U. Alumni Assn. (pres. 1980-83). Home and Office: Chee Bara 152, 1420 Braine L'Alleud Belgium

MAES, MARC JOZEF, language educator; b. Dendermonde, Oost-Vlaanderen, Belgium, July 26, 1949; s. Frans Desideer and Elvire (Van Der Meirssche) M.; m. Michelle Francou, Jan. 10, 1981; 1 child, Anais. Grad., State U. Ghent, 1971. Cert. secondary tchr. Tchr. state schs., Dendermonde, Belgium, 1971-81, Brussels, 1981-87; pedagogical cooperator Ministry Edn., Brussels, 1985-86; tchr. English, Dutch and German Royal Athenaeum, Brussels, 1986—. Contbr. article to profl. jours. on lit. and didactics. Socialist. Home: Dekensstraat 10, B 1040 Brussels Brabant, Belgium Office: Royal Athenaeum, Moutstraat 24, B 1000 Brussels Brabant, Belgium

MAESEN, WILLIAM AUGUST, educational administrator; b. Albertson, N.Y., May 18, 1939; s. August and Wilhelmina (Gaska) M.; B.A., Oklahoma City U., 1961, B.S. in Bus., 1961; M.A., Ind. State U., 1968; Ph.D., U. Ill., Chgo., 1979, postgrad., 1982-83; postgrad. Mich. State U., 1980-81, John Marshall Law Sch., 1984, Seabury-Western Theol. Sem., 1984-85; m. Sherry Lee Jaeger, Aug. 13, 1971 (div. Jan. 1985); children—Ryan and Betsy (twins), Steven. Instr. sociology Aquinas Coll., Grand Rapids, Mich., 1967-70; asso. prof. behavioral sci. Coll. St. Francis, Joliet, Ill., 1970-78; lectr. U. Ill., Chgo., 1974-78; asso. prof. M.S.W. program Grand Valley State Coll., Allendale, Mich., 1978-82; field instr. Jane Addams Sch. Social Work, 1982-83, Loyola U. Sch. of Social Work, 1987—; pres. Chgo. Inst. for Advanced Studies, 1982—; intake coordinator, examiner Ill. State Psychiat. Inst., 1984—; adminstr. Chgo. div. Phila. Sch. Psychoanalysis, 1983-85; city editor Denni Hlasatel, 1984—; dir. residential treatment Cathedral Shelter of Chgo., 1982-83. Chmn., Christian social relations dept. Episcopal Diocese Western Mich., 1979-80, mem. Bishops Council, 1979-80; postulant for Holy Orders, Episc. Diocese of Chgo., chmn. bd. RSVP program Catholic Charities, Diocese of Joliet, 1974—(exec. bd. 1988—). Served with USAFR, 1962-68. Mem. Nat. Assn. Social Workers,Clin. Sociology Assn. (exec. bd.), Community Devel. Soc., ABA, Beta Gamma, Alpha Kappa Delta. Founding Editor: Clin. Sociology Rev., 1980-81; contbr. articles to profl. jours. Home: PO Box 4380 Chicago IL 60680

MAESTRONE, FRANK EUSEBIO, diplomat; b. Springfield, Mass., Dec. 20, 1922; s. John Battista and Margaret Carlotta (Villanova) M.; B.A., Yale U., 1943; grad. Naval War Coll., 1963; m. Jo Colwell, Jan. 20, 1951; children—Mark, Anne. Joined U.S. Fgn Service, 1948; assigned Vienna and Salzburg, Austria, 1948, 54, Hamburg, Germany, 1949, Khorramshahr, Iran, 1960, NATO, Paris, 1963, Brussels, 1968; dep. asst. sec. gen. NATO, Brussels, 1968-71; counselor of embassy for polit. affairs, Manila, 1971-73; Dept. State adviser to pres. Naval War Coll., 1973; minister-counselor, Cairo, 1974; ambassador to State of Kuwait, 1976—; diplomat-in-residence U. Calif., San Diego, 1979; spl. rep. Pres., dir. U.S. Sinai Support Mission, 1980; exec. dir. World Affairs Council San Diego, 1984-86; adj. prof. int. relations U.S. Internat. U., San Diego, 1986—; mem. bd. dirs. World Affairs Council, San Diego. Served with AUS, 1943-46. Named chevalier du Merite Agricole (France). Mem. Inst. Strategic Studies. Office: USIU 10455 Pomerado Rd San Diego CA 92131

MAFTEI, DENIS SORIN NICULAE, environmental control engineer; b. Bucharest, Romania, Aug. 22, 1948; came to Can., 1977, naturalized, 1980; s. Constantin M. and Denisa Silvia (Ionescu) M.; m. Andrea Alexandra Nitescu, Oct. 6, 1973; children—Mark, Micaela. M.A.Sc. in Chem. Engring., Poly. Inst., Bucharest, 1972; M.Engring. in Environ. Control, U. Toronto, Ont., Can., 1984. Registered profl. engr., Toronto. Environ. control engr. Ministry of Chem. Industry, Bucharest, 1972-77; corp. environ. Control engr. ESB-INCO Electroenergy, Toronto, 1977-82; sr. source assessment engr. Ministry of Environment, Toronto, 1982—; cons. Denco Services, Toronto, 1982—. Contbr. articles to profl. publs. Patentee in field. Recipient several chemistry and chem. engring. awards. Mem. Assn. Profl. Engrs. Ont., Can. Assn. Profl. Engrs., Air Pollution Control Assn. Mem. Christian Orthodox Ch. Club: Epcot (Toronto) Home: 90 Edgewood Ave, Unit 116, Toronto, ON Canada M4L 3H1 Office: Ministry of Environment, 880 Bay St 4th Floor, Toronto, ON Canada M5S 1Z8

MAGAIA, DANIEL TOMÉ, diplomat; b. Maputo, Mozambique, Jan. 10, 1925; s. Tomé Ferreira Dick Magaia and Martha Pitta Tembe; married, 1951; children: Fulgencio Odilia, Crescêngio, Eunice. Grad. high sch., Maputo. Salesman J. Salvado & Costa y Branco, Ltd., Maputo, 1948-62; journalist Voz Africana and Diario, Maputo, 1962-65; propagandist CODUL, Maputo, 1966-74; with pub. relations Ministry of Labour, Maputo, 1974-76; head dept. fgn. exchange Ministry of Fin., Maputo, 1976-80; ambassador to Swaziland, Mbabane, 1980—. Comisser Frelimo Party, Maputo, 1974. Recipient Vet. of liberation struggle award Frelimo Party, 1981. Office: Embassy, Republic of Mozambique, Highland View PO Box 1212, Ubabane Swaziland

MAGALA, SLAWOMIR JAN, sociology and philosophy educator; b. Kielce, Poland, Sept. 28, 1950; s. Stanislaw and Stanislawa (Adzierejko) M.; m. Joanna Ramlau, Oct. 12, 1974; children: Jacek, Magdalena. MA, A. Mickiewicz U., Poznan, Poland, 1973, PhD, 1976. Asst. prof. Wroclaw U., Poland, 1975; adj. prof., researcher Polish Acad. of Scis., Poznan and Warsaw, 1977-85; assoc. prof. sociology and philosophy Erasmus U., Rotterdam, The Netherlands, 1985—. Author: Simmel, 1980, Future of Philosophy, 1981, Modern Philosophical Doctrines, 1984, Photography in Modern Culture, 1985, Polish Student Theatre as an Element of Counter Culture, 1987. Chmn. Poznan Polish Acad. Scis. br. Solidarity, 1981—. A. von Humboldt Stiftung Research fellow, 1981, 85. Mem. Polish Philos. Soc., Polish Translators' Assn. Roman Catholic. Home: Marseillehof 6, 3067WH Rotterdam The Netherlands Office: Erasmus U, F1-23 Bedrijfskunde PO Box 1738, 3000DR Rotterdam The Netherlands

MAGALLANES, DEBORAH JEAN, business consulting company executive; b. Gary, Ind., May 22, 1951; d. Ray Daniel and Courtney Ann (Manders) M.; m. Gary Allen DeBardi, 1975. Student pub. schs., Crown Point, Ind. Adminstrv. asst. Fasfax Corp., Nashua, N.H., 1971-75; mgr. adminstrn. Advanced Tech. Labs., Bellevue, Wash., 1975, part-time, 1975-77; sales asst. VMC Corp., Woodinville, Wash., 1975-76; cons. personnel Bus. Men's Clearing House, Bellevue, 1976-79; salesperson, gen. mgr. Cypress Steel, Inc., Bellevue, 1979, part-time, 1979-80; pres. Magallanes, Inc., Bellevue, 1979—; cons., project mgr. in field. Author: (with others) Guide to Better Relationships Through Dealmaking, 1985. Mem. Up With People, 1969—, Seattle-King County Conv. and Visitors Bur.; bd. dirs. Friends of Youth, Renton, Wash., 1984—, v.p., 1986—; vol. Save the Elephants Campaign, Seattle, 1984—; bd. dirs. Bellevue Leaders, pres., 1982—. Mem. Women's Bus. Exchange (bd. dirs. 1981-85, Networker of Yr. 1983), MIT Alumni Assn. (hon. nat. officer 1984). Club: Briefcase Brigade (Bellevue), Hetty Green Partnership (pres. 1987—). Lodge: Soroptimists (bd. dirs. 1986, 88). Avocations: investments, canoeing, fishing, drill team. Office: 405 114th Ave SE #300 Bellevue WA 98004

MAGARINOS D., VICTOR, artist; b. Lanus, Buenos Aires, Argentina, Sept. 1, 1924; s. Jose Magarinos D. and Antonia Maria Sanchez; m. Hilda Mans. Student, Escuela Nat. des Artes Visuales. One-man exhbns. include Galeria Juan Cristóbal 1950, Inst. Arte Moderno 1950-51; other exbhns. include Mus. Modern Art 1963, El Nuevo Arte Argentino, Walker Art Ctr., Mpls., A Decade of Latin-Am. Art Guggenheim Mus. 1965-66, Mus. Modern Art, N.Y.C., Mus. Nat. Bellas Artes, Mus. Arte Moderno, Buenos Aires, Ctr. Art and Communication, Argentina, Premio d'Italia 1986, Mus. Arte Moderno, Brussels, 1986. Pres. Argentine com. Internat. Assn. Plastic Arts, UNESCO, 1958. Served with Argentine Armed Forces, 1945. Recipient Premio Milano Inst. d'Arte Contemporanea de Milano, 1988, Premio Centauro de Oro Instituido por el Consejo Artistico del Premio Cuatrienal de la Academia de Italia, 1988. Mem. Acad. Arti Laboro Perme (Gold medal). Address: Los Talleres, Estaf No 5, CP 7167 Pinamar Argentina

MAGAT, ROMULO DELIZO, physician, consultant; b. Urdaneta, Philippines, Oct. 29, 1940; s. Rufino Ferreras and Severina Marzan (Delizo) M.; m. Pacita Peralta, June 6, 1971; children: Rodney P., Sherry Anne, Richard P. AA, U. Santo Tomas, Manila, 1958, MD, 1965. Gen. practice medicine Urdaneta, 1968—; med. examiner Philamlife Ins. Co., Urdaneta, 1969—; instr. midwifery Urdaneta Community Coll., 1973-75, 78-87, acting prin. nursing, 1976-77; pediatric cons. Urdaneta Doctor's Hosp., 1975-79; med. dir. St. Jude Med. Children's Clin., Urdaneta, 1978—; med. examiner Insular Life Ins. Co., Urdaneta, 1980—; pediatric cons. Urdaneta Sacred Heart Hosp., 1980—; br. physician Philippine Nat. Bank, Urdaneta, 1987; med. examiner Philamlife Ins. Co., Urdaneta, 1969—, Insular Life Ins. Co., Urdaneta, 1980—; instr. midwifery Urdaneta Community Coll., 1973-75, 78-87, prin. nursing, 1976-77; cons. pediatrics Urdaneta Doctor's Hosp., 1975-79, Urdaneta Sacred Heart Hosp., 1980—; med. dir. St. Jude Med. Children's Clin., Urdaneta, 1978—. Mem. anti-graft bd. Urdaneta Mcpl. Govt., 1987—. Recipient Pontifical award Holy Sacrament Internat. Ch., 1982, Kaunlaran award Far East Social and Civic Orgn., 1983, Giliw and Hivas award Loyola Life Plan, 1984-87. Mem. Philippine Med. Assn. (life), Philippine Hosp. Assn. (v.p. 1987-88), Pangasinan Med. Soc., Philippine Acad. Family Physicians, Philippine Maternal and Child Health Assn. Lodge: Rotary (pres. Urdaneta club 1982-83, dist. rep. 1985-86, area coordinator polio fund drive 1987-88, Leadership award 1983, Gov.'s award 1986). Home: Dona Pepang Subdivision, Urdaneta Pangasinan 0737, Philippines Office: St Jude Med Childrens Clin, Alexander St, Urdaneta Pangasinan 0737, Philippines

MAGAZINE, ALAN HARRISON, association executive, consultant; b. Cambridge, Mass., May 16, 1944; s. Arnold Lloyd and Ruth Magazine; m. June Ann O'Donohue, June 20, 1971 (div. Feb. 1984); children—Sarah Elizabeth, David Michael; m. Cynthia Louise Cordiner, Aug. 30, 1984. B.A., Monmouth Coll., 1966; M.P.A., Kent State U., 1968; Ph.D., U.Md., 1976. Sr. cons. Real Estate Research Corp., Washington, 1969-72; exec. dir. Nat. Ctr. for Pub. Service Internships, Washington, 1972-75; nat. policy coordinator Internat. City Mgmt. Assn., Washington, 1973-76; dep. asst. dir. U.S. Commn. on Fed. Paperwork, Washington, 1976-78; dir. office of intergovernmental relations EPA, Washington, 1978-81; dir. Business-Higher Edn. Forum, Washington, 1981-86, pres. council on competitiveness, 1986—; ptnr. MB Assocs., cons., Washington, 1984—; adv. com. Congl Tech. Policy Task Force, 1986—; adv. bd. George Mason U. Ctr. Conflict Resolution, 1986—, Brookings Inst. Ctr. Econ. Progress and Employment, 1986—; bd. dirs. Congl. Econ. Leadership Inst., 1986—. Author: Environmental Management in Local Government, 1977. Bd. dirs. Met. Washington Council of Govts., 1972-79; mem. Fairfax County Bd. Suprs., Va., 1972-79; chmn. No. Val. Transp. Commn., Arlington, 1974-75; mem. No. Va. Planning Dist. Commn., Fairfax, 1976-79. Served with USAFR, 1968-71. Ford Found. fellow, 1970-71. Mem. Soc. for Research Adminstrs., Am. Soc. for Pub. Adminstrn., Am. Enterprise Inst. Democrat. Jewish. Avocation: reading. Home: 1302 Chancel Pl Alexandria VA 22314 Office: Council on Competitiveness 1331 Pennsylvania Ave Suite 900 Washington DC 22004

MAGEE, BRYAN, writer, broadcaster; b. London, Apr. 12, 1930; s. Frederick and Sheila (Lynch) M.; m. Ingrid Söderlund, 1954 (dec. 1986); 1 child, Gunnela. MA, Oxford U., 1956; postgrad., Yale U., 1955-56. Ind. writer, critic, broadcaster 1956—; hon. sr. research fellow history of ideas King's Coll., U. London, 1984—; M.P., 1974-83; presenter numerous TV and radio programs. Author 15 books, including Modern British Philosophy, 1971, Men of Ideas, 1978, The Philosophy of Schopenhauer, 1983, The Great Philosophers, 1987 (books transl. into 15 langs.). Recipient silver medal Royal TV Soc., 1978. Mem. Critics Circle Gt. Britain (Pres. 1983-84). Clubs: Garrick, Brook's, Beefsteak, Savile (London). Home: 12 Falkland House, Marloes Rd, London W8 5LF, England

MAGGARD, WOODROW WILSON, JR., management consultant; b. Quincy, Ill., Feb. 5, 1947; s. Woodrow Wilson and Claire Lorene (Lyons) M.; B.A., Brigham Young U., 1971; M.P.A., Consortium of Calif. State U., 1978; m. Linda Margaret Davis, Dec. 30, 1967; children—Jared Isaac, Erin Leigh-Taylor, Solveig Kirsten, Christian Heinrich, Anica May, Kayla Margaret. Div. mgr. Sears, Roebuck & Co., Provo, Utah and Ventura, Calif., 1967-74; adminstrv. officer County of Ventura (Calif.), 1974-78; founding partner Maggard, Maughan, Gress and Assos., Ventura, 1976-83; founder Intermountain Property Services, Ventura, 1974—; v.p. econ./bus. devel. Dineh Coops., Inc., Chinle, Navaho Nation, Ariz., 1978-80; dir. econ. devel. City of Scottsdale (Ariz.), 1980-81; exec. dir., chief exec. officer Fairbanks Devel. Authority (Alaska), 1981-87; co-founder Pacific Rim Inst., 1984—; founder Maggard & Maggard, Fairbanks, 1983—. Instr. real estate econs./appraisal Oxnard (Calif.) Coll., 1975-78; instr. bus. Utah Tech. Coll., Provo, 1978. Active Boy Scouts Am.; high priest Ch. of Latter-Day Saints. Recipient Dixwell Pierce award, 1975, Alaska Environ. Enhancement award, 1983; cert. rev. appraiser; registered mortgage underwriter. Mem. Am. Soc. Public Adminstrn., Internat. Right-of-Way Assn. (internat. property mgmt. com.), Nat. Assn. Rev. Appraisers and Mortgage Underwriters (sr.), Nat. Council on Urban Econ. Devel., Urban Land Inst., Acad. Polit. Sci., United Indian Planners., Phi Alpha Theta. Democrat. Club: Rotary. Contbr. articles to profl. jours. Home: 1003 Woodall Rd Altamonte Springs FL 32714 Office: 955 W Lancaster Rd Suite 219 Orlando FL 32809

MAGINN, ROBERT ALLEN, JR., management consultant company executive, investment and import-export company executive; b. Kearney, N.J., Oct. 31, 1956; s. Robert Allen, Sr. and Valerie Audrey (Jarusik) M.; m. Stacy Beverly Vladimer, July 4, 1987. Student Mich. State U., 1975-77; BBA summa cum laude, U. Dayton, 1979; ALM in Govt., Harvard U., 1981, MBA with distinction in Bus. Adminstrn., 1983. Corp. acct. Dayton Walther, Dayton, Ohio, 1977-79; audit, tax acct. Arthur Andersen & Co., Boston, 1979-80; instr., researcher Harvard Bus. Sch., Boston, 1980-81, mgmt. cons. Bain & Co., Boston, 1983-87, Tokyo, 1987—; dir. Midwestern Consol. Enterprises, Waynesville, Ohio, Internat. Trade & Commerce Corp., Boston. Contbr. articles to profl. publs. Sustaining mem. Rep. Nat. Com., Washington, 1980—; supporting mem. Calcutta Mission of Mercy, Tacoma, 1975—. Mem. Harvard Bus. Sch. Fund (chief fund agt. 1983—), Assn. MBA Execs., Am. C. of C. (Japan). Episcopalian. Clubs: Harvard, Harvard Bus. Sch., Tokyo Am. Avocations: tennis, skiing, traveling.

MAGNES, G(ERALD) DONALD, dentist; b. Chgo., Sept. 27, 1933; s. Herman S. and Fae (Ray) M.; m. Loretta Bass, Aug. 5, 1956; children—Scott A., Craig N. B.S., U. Ill., 1956, D.D.S., 1958. Individual practice dentistry, Chgo., 1958—. Cons., Warner-Chilcott Labs., Morris Plains, N.J., 1964—; instr. U. Ill. Coll. Dentistry. Recipient certificate recognition Am. Dental Assn., 1967; award winning exhibit Nat. Am. Dental Assn., 1967; donor sci. exhibit U. Ill. Med. Sch., 1968. Contbr. articles to profl. jours. Fellow Royal Soc. Health, Ill. State Dental Soc.; mem. Am. Dental Assn., Chgo. Dental Soc., Am. Cancer Soc. (speaker 1969-70), Internat. Assn. Dental Research, Am. Assn. Dental Research, U. Ill. Alumni Assn., Alpha Omega. Home: 4625 W Grove St Skokie IL 60076 Office: 2601 W Peterson Ave Chicago IL 60659

MAGNHAGEN, BENGT ÅKE, corporate executive; b. Osby, Sweden, Sept. 21, 1937; s. Ivar Anders and Siri Tyra (Friis) M.; m. Margitha Karin Sterning, Oct. 6, 1962; children: My, Camilla. MSEE, Chalmers U., Gothenburg, Sweden, 1965; D in. Tech., Linköping U., Sweden, 1977. Devel. engrs. Saab-Scania, Linköping, 1965-69, mgr. hardware devel., 1970-74, mgr. CAE system devel., 1975-82; pres. Digsim Systems, Linköping, 1982—. Author 4 books. Served to capt. Swedish mil. 1961-62. Mem. Internat. Fedn. Info. Processing. Lodges: Rotary, Odd Fellows. Office: Digsim Systems, PO Box 10 004, 580 10 Linkoping Sweden

MAGNO, CARLO RICARDO, telecommunications company executive, management consultant, educator; b. Iloilo, Panay, Philippines, Aug. 25, 1935; s. Segundino Sobrepena and Fredesvinda Francisco (Hernandez) M.; m. Felicisima Porcincula San Diego, Aug. 25, 1959; children—Carlo R. Jr., Excelsis, Mona Liza, Catherine Bernadette. B.S. in Commerce, Jose Rizal Coll., 1959; diploma in Bus. Adminstrn., Waterloo Luth. U., 1968; diploma in Indsl. Relations, U. Philippines, 1983, M. in Indsl. Relations, 1984; Ph.D. in Commerce, U. Santo Tomas, 1987. Sec. to gen. mgr. G.A. Machineries, Inc., Manila, 1957-59, head ins. div., 1959-60; office mgr. Facilities, Inc., Manila, 1960-61; with G.A. Machineries, Inc., Valenzuela, 1961-68, field ops. asst. to v.p., 1961-64, office services mgr., 1965-68, personnel mgr., 1964-68; traffic ops. mgr. Philippines Long Distance Telephone Co., Manila, 1968-73, inter-co. relations mgr., Makati, 1973-79, sr. mgr. human resources mgmt., 1979-80, asst. v.p., 1980-87, v.p. manpower adminstrn., 1987—; pres. Metro Manila Savs. Coop. Bank, Quezon City, 1981-85, PLDT Employees Service Coop, Inc., Makati, 1978—; chmn. Coop Ins. System of Philippines, Quezon City; vice chmn. MACE Ins. Agy., Inc., Manila, 1982—; mem. Philippine Productivity Team to Taiwan, 1986. Author handbooks. Pres. Araneta for Senator Movement, Valenzuela, 1965, GAMI Coop. Credit Union, Valenzuela, 1966-67, Our Lady of Grace PTA, Caloocan, Philippines, 1970-72, St. Pauls Coll. Parents Aux., Quezon City, 1972-73; chmn. council elders Our Lady of Fatima Pastoral Council, Valenzuela, 1978-85. Served as lt. col. Philippines Army Res., 1971-85. Recipient Meritorious Services award Dept. Edn. and Culture Manila, 1975; Presdl. award Enterprise Sports Assn. Philippines Manila, 1975; honor award Armed Forces Communications and Electronics Assn., Manila, 1976; Presdl. award Philippine Electronics and Telecommunication Fedn., 1978. Fellow Philippine Soc. Fellows In Personnel Mgmt. (mem. accreditation council 1984-86); mem. Personnel Mgmt. Assn. Philippines (bd. dirs. 1967, 73, 83), Jose Rizal Coll. Alumni Assn., U. Philippines Indsl. Relations Alumni Assn., Philippine Council Mgmt. (pres. 1986), ASEAN Coop. Orgn. (Philippian del. 1987, counsellor 1988—). Clubs: Pvt. Car Owners Assn. Philippines (v.p. 1971-75), Enterprise Sports Assn. Philippines (Manila); Valenzuela Golfers Assn.; Matabungcay Beach (Batangas); Odyssey (Baguio). Lodge: K.C. Avocations: sports; travel; reading; gardening. Home: Legion of Mary, Valenzuela, Metro Manila Philippines Office: Philippines Long Distance Tel, PO Box 952 Makati, Metro Manila Philippines

MAGNO, VITO, editor, journalist; b. San Vito, Brindisi, Italia, May 31, 1946; s. Francesco and Lavinia (Epifani), M. Diploma in communicazioni sociali, Antoniano, Roma, 1973, lic. in teologia, 1075; vaticanista, Citta 'del Vaticano, 1984. Redattore rogate PP. Rogazionisti, Roma, 1973-87, sacerdote, 1974, direztore rogate, 1980—; collaboratore Radio Vaticana, Osservatore Romano, Avvenire, Roma, 1973—. Author: Come Lui, 1978; editrice rogate (film) Prete Preche, Signore Manda Me, Realizzarsi in Cristo, 1987. Mem. Ordine Giornalisti Del Lazio, Sierra Club. Office: Libreria Editrice Rogate, Via dei Rogazionisti 8, I-00182 Rome Italy

MAGNUSON, ROGER JAMES, lawyer; b. St. Paul, Jan. 25, 1945; s. Roy Gustaf and Ruth Lily (Edlund) M.; m. Elizabeth Cunningham Shaw, Sept. 11, 1982; children—James Roger, Peter Cunningham, Mary Kerstin. B.A., Stanford U., 1967; J.D., Harvard U., 1971; B.C.L., Oxford U., 1972. Bar: Minn. 1973, U.S. Dist. Ct. Minn. 1973, U.S. Ct. Appeals (8th, 9th, 10th cirs.) 1974, U.S. Supreme Ct. 1978. Chief pub. defender Hennepin County Pub. Defender's Office, Mpls., 1973; ptnr. Dorsey & Whitney, Mpls., 1972—. Author: Shareholder Litigation, 1981, Are Gay Rights Right. Contbr. articles to profl. jours. Elder, Straitgate Ch., Mpls., 1980—. Mem. ABA, Christian Legal Soc. Republican. Home: 625 Park Ave Mahtomedi MN 55115 Office: Dorsey & Whitney Suite 2200 1st Bank Pl E Minneapolis MN 55402

MAGNUSSON, MAGNUS, writer, broadcaster; b. Iceland, Oct. 12, 1929; s. Sigursteinn Magnusson and Ingibjorg Sigurdardottir; M.A. with honors, Jesus Coll., Oxford (Eng.) U., 1951; Doctor honoris causa, Edinburgh (Scotland) U., 1978; D.Univ., York (Eng.) U., 1981; m. Mamie Baird, June 30, 1954; children—Sally, Margaret, Anna, Siggy (dec.), Jon. Asst. editor Scottish Daily Express, Glasgow, 1953-61, The Scotsman, Edinburgh, 1961-68; freelance writer and broadcaster, 1968—; presenter of many TV programs, including Chronicle, Mastermind, Tonight, BC: The Archaeology of the Bible Lands, Living Legends, Vikings!; Pebble Mill at One. Trustee Nat. Mus. Scotland, 1985—. Author: Introducing Archaeology, 1972; Viking Expansion Westwards, 1973; The Clacken and the Slate, 1974; Viking Hammer of the North, 1976; BC: The Archaeology of the Bible Lands, 1977;

Landlord or Tenant--A View of Irish History, 1978; Iceland, 1979; Vikings!, 1980; Magnus on the Move, 1980; Treasures of Scotland, 1981; Lindisfarne: The Cradle Island, 1984; Iceland Saga, 1987; translator various books. Chmn., Ancient Monuments Bd. for Scotland, 1981—. Decorated knight comdr. Order Icelandic Falcon, Queen's Silver Jubilee medal (Eng.). Fellow Soc. Antiquaries Scotland, Royal Soc. Edinburgh. Editor Bodley Head Archaeologies, 1970-80, Popular Archaeology, 1979-80. Home and Office: Blairskaith House, Balmore-Torrance, Glasgow G64 4AX Scotland

MAGNUSSON, MAGNUS, chemical company executive; b. Reykjavik, Iceland, Feb. 22, 1954; s. Magnus Bjarnason and Susanna Kristjansdottir; m. E. Kristrun Gudbergsdottir, Aug. 28, 1976; children: M.B. Magnusson, J.G. Magnusdottir. Diploma in mech. engring., Tech. Coll., Reykjavik, 1974; BSc in Mech. Engring., Leeds U., Eng., 1978, MSc in Material Sci., 1979. First mech. engr. Isal Aluminium Ltd., Hafnafjördur, Iceland, 1974-77; chief engr. Stálsmidjan Shipbuilders, Reykjavik, 1978; scientist Tech. Inst. Iceland, 1979-82; tech. dir. Icelandic Metals Ltd., Reydarfjördur, Iceland, 1982-85; mng. dir. Reykjanes Geo-Chems. Ltd., Keflavik, Iceland, 1985—; bd. dirs. Investment Found. Hávöxtunarfelagid, Reykjavik, Odin Derma a/s, Oslo, Norway, Sagasalt Ltd., Gardabae, Iceland; adv. bd. Tech. Inst. Iceland. Inventor Aluminum Pumice Composite, 1979; author: Tube making of Polymers, 1979. Mem. Icelandic Engring. Soc., Icelandic Mgmt. Soc., Project Mgmt. Soc. Iceland. Club: Icelandic Squash. Home: Kopavogsbraut 18, K-200 200 Kopavogur Iceland Office: Reykjanes Geo-Chems Ltd, PO Box 194, 230 Keflavik Iceland

MAGNUSSON, STAFFAN M. E., biochemist; b. Stockholm, June 29, 1933; s. J. Henning and Ingrid C. (Lenander) M.; m. K. Birgitta Jorpes, June 15, 1957; children: Johan, Lisa, Nils, Kristina. Degrees, Karolinska Inst., Stockholm, 1952, med. lic., 1957, MD, 1965, D in Med. Chem., 1965. Various teaching and research positions in chemistry dept. Karolinska Inst., Stockholm, 1953-65; vis. scientist dept. health div. research N.Y. State, Albany, 1965-66; staff mem. M.R.C. Lab. of Molecular Biology, Cambridge, Eng., 1967-70; dept. head Molecular Biology U. Aarhus (Denmark), 1970—. Contbr. articles to profl. jours. Recipient Keilin medal Biochem. Soc., 1976, Novo prize, 1984. Mem. Am. Chem. Soc., Swedish Biochem. Soc., Danish Biochem. Soc. (bd. dirs.), Royal Danish Acad. Scis. and Letters, Am. Soc. Biochemistry and Molecular Biology, (hon.), Danish Cancer Soc. (sci. fund. com.). Home: Sosvinget 50, DK-8250 EGA Aarhus Denmark Office: Aarhus Univ, Dept Molecular Biology, C F Moller's Allé, DK-8000 Aarhus Denmark

MAGOWAN, PETER ALDEN, grocery chain executive; b. N.Y.C., Apr. 5, 1942; s. Robert Anderson and Doris (Merrill) M.; m. Jill Tarlau (div. July 1982; children—Kimberley, Margot, Hilary; m. Deborah Johnston, Aug. 14, 1982. B.A., Stanford U.; M.A., Oxford U., Eng.; postgrad., Johns Hopkins U. Store mgr. Safeway Stores, Inc., Washington, 1968-70; dist. mgr. Safeway Stores, Inc., Houston, 1970-71; retail ops. mgr. Safeway Stores, Inc., Phoenix, 1971-72; div. mgr. Safeway Stores, Inc., Tulsa, 1973-76; mgr. internat. div. Safeway Stores, Inc., Toronto, Ont., Can., 1976-78; mgr. western region Safeway Stores, Inc., San Francisco, 1978-79; chmn. bd., chief exec. officer Safeway Stores, Inc., Oakland, Calif., 1980—; bd. dirs. Pacific Gas and Electric, Chrysler Corp. Mem. U.S. C. of C., Food Mktg. Inst. (bd. dirs.), Bus. Roundtable. Office: Safeway Stores Inc 201 4th St Oakland CA 94660

MAGRATH, C. PETER, university president; b. N.Y.C., Apr. 23, 1933; s. Laurence Wilfrid and Guilia Maria (Dentice) M.; m. Deborah C. Magrath, 1988; children: Valerie Ruth, Monette Fay. BA summa cum laude, U. N.H., 1955; PhD, Cornell U., 1962. Mem. faculty Brown U., Providence, 1961-68, prof. polit. sci., 1967-68, assoc. dean grad. sch., 1965-66; dean Coll. Arts and Scis. U. Nebr., Lincoln, 1968-69, dean faculties Coll. Arts and Scis., 1969-72, interim chancellor univ., 1971-72, prof. polit. sci., 1968-72, vice chancellor for acad. affairs, 1972; pres. SUNY, Binghamton, 1972-74, prof. polit. sci., 1972-74; pres. U. Minn., Mpls., 1974-84, U. Mo., Columbia, 1985—. Author: The Triumph of Character, 1963, Yazoo: Law and Politics in the New Republic, The Case of Fletcher v. Peck, 1966, Constitutionalism and Politics: Conflict and Consensus, 1968, Issues and Perspectives in American Government, 1971, (with others) The American Democracy, 2d edit., 1973, (with Robert L. Egbert) Strengthening Teacher Education, 1987; contbr. articles to profl. jours. Served with AUS, 1955-57. Mem. Nat. Assn. State Univs. and Land Grant Colls. (chmn. 1984-85), Assn. Am. Univs. (chmn. 1985-86), Phi Beta Kappa, Phi Kappa Phi, Pi Gamma Mu, Pi Sigma Alpha, Kappa Tau Alpha. Office: U of Mo Cen Adminstrn Cen Office Univ Hall Columbia MO 65211

MAGUIRE, BASSETT, botanist; b. Alabama City, Ala., Aug. 4, 1904; s. Charles T. and Rose (Bassett) M.; m. Ruth Richards, 1926; children: Bassett, Grace (Mrs. Daniel N. MacLemore, Jr.); m. Celia Kramer, Mar. 25, 1951. B.S., U. Ga., 1926; grad. student, U. Pitts., 1926; Ph.D., Cornell U., 1938. High sch. tchr. sci. and biology Athens, Ga., 1926-27; instr. botany U. Ga., 1927-29, Cornell U., 1929-31, 37-38; prof. Utah State U., 1931-43; curator, head curator N.Y. Bot. Garden, 1943—, Nathaniel Lord Britton distinguished sr. curator, 1961—, asst. dir., 1968-69, dir. botany, 1969-71, 73-75, dir. emeritus, sr. scientist, mem. bd. mgrs., 1971—; dir. botany Jardin Botánico Nacional, Santo Domingo, Dominican Republic; exec. dir. Orgn. for Flora Neotropica, 1964-75; aquatic botanist N.Y. State Conservation Dept., 1930-31, U.S. Bur. Fisheries, 1932, 34; ecologist, spl. agt. U.S. Conservation Service, Dept. Agr., 1934-35; adj. prof. botany Columbia, N.Y.C., 1961—, CUNY; non-resident prof. Utah State U.; Del. UNESCO, 1947, 64, FAO, 1961; dir. sci. N.Y. Bot. Garden, 1974—; also mem. corp.; founder, exec. dir. Orgn. for Flora Neotropica, 1964-76; cons. Eli Lilly, Warner-Lambert, Tex. Instrument, Nat. Bulk Carriers. Mem. editorial bd. Flora of Ecuador, Moscosoa, Santo Domingo; author articles, treatises on Western Am. botany, Neotropics vegetation and geography. Mem. corp. N.Y. Bot. Garden; trustee Mary Cary Arboretum. Recipient Sarah Gildersleeve Fife Meml. award, 1952; David Livingstone centenary medal Am. Geog. Soc., 1965; grantee NSF; grantee Am. Philos. Soc.; grantee Guggenheim Found.; grantee Explorers Club. Corr. mem. Royal Netherlands Bot. Soc. (hon.); hon. fellow Assn. for Tropical Biology (founder; pres. 1964-65); mem. Orgn. Tropical Studies (founder), Torrey Bot. Club (pres. 1963-64), N.Y. Acad. Scis., Sociedad Venezolana de Ciencias Naturales (hon.), Torrey Bot. Club (pres. 1963-64), AAAS, Bot. Soc. Am., Internat. Soc. Plant Taxonomy, Am. Soc. Plant Taxonomists, Orgn. Flora Neotropica (commn.), Soc. Bot. Dominicana (hon.), Am. Geog. Soc. (hon.), Newcomen Soc. (life), Academia de Ciencias de la Républica Dominicana (founder, mem. biology com.). El Patronato Jardín Botánico Nacional (Santo Domingo, Dominican Republic). Home: 120-24 Dreiser Loop Bronx NY 10475 also: Quinta Najayo, San Cristobal Dominican Republic Office: NY Bot Garden Bronx New York NY 10458

MAGUIRE, CHARLOTTE EDWARDS, physician; b. Richmond, Ind., Sept. 1, 1918; d. Joel Blaine and Lydia (Betscher) Edwards; m. Raymer Francis Maguire, Sept. 1, 1948 (dec.); children—Barbara, Thomas Clair II. Student, Stetson U., 1936-38, U. Wichita, 1938-39; B.S., Memphis Tchrs. Coll., 1940; M.D., U. Ark., 1944. Intern and resident Orange Meml. Hosp., Orlando, Fla., 1944-46; resident Bellevue Hosp. and Med. Ctr., NYU, N.Y.C., 1954, 55; instr. nurses Orange Meml. Hosp., 1947-57, staff mem., 1946-68; staff mem. Fla. Santarium and Hosp., Orlando, 1946-56, Holiday House and Hosp., Orlando, 1950-62; mem. courtesy and cons. staff West Orange Meml. Hosp., Winter Garden, Fla., 1952-67; active staff, chief dept. pediatrics Mercy Hosp., Orlando, 1965-68; med. dir. med. services and basic care Fla. Dept. Health and Rehab. Services, 1975-84; med. exec. dir., med. services div. worker's compensation Fla. Dept. Labor, Tallahassee, 1984-87; chief of staff physicians and dentists Central Fla. div. Children's Home Soc. of Fla., 1947-56; dir. Orlando Child Health Clinic 1949-58; engaged in pvt. practice medicine Orlando, 1946-68; asst. regional dir. HEW, 1970-72; pediatric cons. Fla. Crippled Children's Commn., 1952-70, dir., 1968-70; med. dir. Office Med. Services and Basic Care, sr. physician Office of Asst. Sec. Ops., Fla. Dept. Health and Rehab. Services; clin. prof. dept. pediatrics U. Fla. Coll. Medicine, Gainesville, 1980-87; mem. Fla. Drug Utilization Rev/. 1983-87; real estate salesperson, Investors Realty, 1982—. Mem. profl. adv. com. Fla. Center for Clin. Services at U. Fla., 1952-60; del. to Mid-century White House Conf. on Children and Youth, 1950; U.S. del from Nat. Soc. for Crippled Children to World Congress for Welfare of Cripples, Inc., London, 1957; pres of corp. Eccleston-Callahan Hosp. for Colored Crippled Children, 1956-58; sec. Fla. chpt. Nat. Doctor's Com. for Improved Med. Services, 1951-52; med. adv. com. Gateway Sch. for Mentally Retarded, 1959-62; bd. dirs. Forest Park Sch. for Spl. Edn. Crippled Children, 1949-54, mem. med. adv. com., 1955-68, chmn., 1957-68; mem. Fla. Adv. Council for Mentally Retarded, 1965-70; dir. central Fla. poison control Orange Meml. Hosp.; mem. orgn. com., chmn. com. for admissions and selection policies Camp Challenge; participant 12th session Fed. Exec. Inst., 1971; del. White House Conf. on Aging, 1980. Mem. Nat. Rehab. Assn., Am. Congress Phys. Medicine and Rehab., Fla. Soc. Crippled Children and Adults, Central Fla. Soc. Crippled Children and Adults (dir. 1949-58, pres. 1956-57), Am. Assn. Cleft Palate, Fla. Soc. Crippled Children (trustee 1951-57, v.p. 1956-57, profl. adv. com. 1957-68), Mental Health Assn. Orange County (charter mem.; pres. 1949-50, dir. 1947-52, chmn. exec. com. 1950-52, dir. 1963-65), Fla. Orange County Heart Assn., AMA, Am. Med. Women's Assn., Am. Acad. Med. Dirs., Fla. Med. Assn. (chmn. com. on mental retardation), Orange County Med. Assn., Fla. Pediatric Soc. (pres. 1952-53), Fla. Cleft Palate Assn. (counselor-at-large, sec.). Club: Governors. Home: 2013 E Randolph Circle Tallahassee FL 32312

MAGUIRE, JACK RUSSELL, writer, columnist; b. Denison, Tex., Apr. 10, 1920; s. Jeff Edward and Elizabeth (Russell) M.; student No. Tex. State Coll., 1940-41; BJ, U. Tex., Austin, 1944; m. Ann Roddy Smith, Aug. 16, 1986; children from previous marriage: Jack Russell, Kevin Maguire. Reporter AP, Austin, 1943-44; pub. relations rep. M.-K.-T. R.R., St. Louis, 1945-50, T. & P. Ry., Dallas, 1950-51; dir. pub. relations Tex. Ins. Adv. Assn., Austin, 1950-56; exec. dir. U. Tex. Ex-Students Assn., 1956-76; exec. dir. U. Tex. Inst. Texan Cultures, San Antonio, 1976-83; pub. relations cons., Austin, 1950-76. Trustee Ednl. Projects for Edn., Inc., Washington, S.W. Research Inst.; mem. Tex. Sesquicentennial Commn. Recipient Master Publicist award San Antonio Advt. Fedn., 1979. Author: Talk of Texas, 1973, Texas: Amazing, but True, 1982, (with others) The Governors Who Lived the Mansion, 1984, Texas and Texans, 1987, The Capitol Story: The Statehouse in Texas, 1988; editor: A President's Country; columnist Talk of Texas, Texas Yesterday; contbr. articles to profl. jours. Mem. Am. Ry. Mag. Editors Assn., Pub. Relations Soc. Am., Am. Soc. Assn. Execs., Philos. Soc. Tex., Sigma Delta Chi. Presbyterian. Clubs: Torch, Headliner, Argyle. Lodge: Rotary. Address: PO Box 1097 Fredericksburg TX 78624

MAHAFFAY, WILLIAM EDWARD, mechanical engineer. s. James W. and Ida (Hyink) M.; m. Carolyn Dahlquist, Oct. 15, 1935; 1 son, John W. B.S., Northwestern U., 1933. Registered engr., Ind. Various positions Internat. Harvester Co., 1935-42; plant engr. Internat. Harvester Co. (Refrigeration div.), 1942-45, chief engr. advanced engring sect., 1945-51; exec. engr. Whirlpool Corp., St. Joseph, Mich., 1951-53; dir. engring. and research Whirlpool Corp., 1953-56, v.p. engring. and research, 1956-65, group v.p., 1965-70; dir. Robbins Myers, Dayton, Ohio, 1970—, Ranco Inc., Columbus, Ohio, 1970—; engring. cons.; adj. prof. U. Mich., 1970—; vis. prof. Purdue., 1970; Life regent Northwestern U.; tech. adv. com. Purdue U. Mem. ASHRAE, ASME, Acacia, Northwestern U. Alumni Assn., Instrument Soc. Am., Sigma Xi, Tau Beta Pi, Pi Tau Sigma. Clubs: Union League (Chgo.); Paradise Valley Country (Scottsdale). Home: 86 Colonia Miramonte Scottsdale AZ 85253

MAHAFFEY, JOAN, nurse, association executive; b. Richmond, Utah, Feb. 7, 1926; d. Joseph Perry and Annie Marie (Christofferson) Peart; R.N., Meth. Hosp., Los Angeles, 1950; B.S. in Health Sci., Calif. State U., Northridge, 1971, M.P.H., 1976; m. J.B. Mahaffey, June 5, 1949 (div. Jan. 1967). Hosp. and office nurse, Calif., 1951-72; mem. staff Calif. Nurses Assn., 1972-81, regional dir. epicenter region 3, Van Nuys, 1981-83, pres. region 3, 1983-85; dir. registry Epicenter Region Nurses Profl. Registry Inc., 1974—; cons., speaker in field. Mem. Am. Nurses Assn., Valley Nursing Edn. Council. Democrat. Mormon. Clubs: Soroptimist, San Fernando Emblem 37. Home: 6620 Glade Ave Canoga Park CA 91303 Office: Epicenter Region Nurses Profl Registry Inc 7 Van Nuys Blvd Suite O Van Nuys CA 91405

MA HAIDE, government official, physician; b. Buffalo, 1910; arrived in People's Republic China, 1933; naturalized, 1949.; Grad. medicine. Physician Communist base, No. Shaanxi Province, People's Republic China, 1936; joined Chinese Red Army; advisor Ministry of Pub. Health, 1950—; mem. 5th Chinese People's Polit. Consultative Conf., 1979; mem. standing com. 6th Chinese People's Polit. Consultative Conf., 1983; hon. dir.-in-chief Welfare Fund for Handicapped, 1984. *

MAHAKKANUKRAUH, CHANINTR SIAM, orthopedics educator; b. Patoomthani, Thailand, Jan. 18, 1936; s. Sakool and Naiyana (Sae Jeng) Mingmolee; m. Mallika Chanasuk; children: Chanika, Ajanee, Busakorn, Jatuporn. MD, Mahidol (Siriraj) U., Bangkok, 1962; cert. in orthopedic surgery, U. Pa., 1967, cert. in hand surgery, 1971; cert. in orthopedic pathology, Temple U., 1967. Diplomate Am. Bd. Orthopedic Surgery. Intern Faculty Medicine Chiegmai (Thailand) U., 1962-63, resident surgery, 1963-65, instr. in orthopedics, 1965-66, asst. prof. in othopedics, 1974; chmn. dept. orthopedics Faculty of Medicine Khon Kaen (Thailand) U., 1974-86, dep. dean for planning, 1984, acting dean, 1985, cons., 1986—; chief of orthopedics Srinagarind Hosp., Khon Kaen, 1974—. Mem. Internat. Assn. Med. Assistance to Travellers, Khon Kaen, 1986. Fellow ACS; mem. Thai Orthopedic Assn., Western Pacific Othopedic Assn., Internat. League Against Rheumatism, Royal Coll. Surgeons of Thailand. Buddhism. Home: 123/462 Friendship Hwy, Khon Kaen 40002, Thailand Office: Srinagarind Hosp, 123 Friendship Hwy, Khon Kaen 40002, Thailand

MAHALINGAM, PADMANABHAN, engineer, consultant; b. Chidambaram, Tamil Nadu, India, Mar. 1, 1954; s. Padmanabhan and Neela (Muthuswamy) M.; m. Latha Ranganathan, Aug. 24, 1984; children: Jahnavi, Lakshmi. BS in Engring., Thiagarajar Coll. Engring., Madurai, Tamil Nadu, 1975; MBA, Ill. State U., Normal, 1982. Cons., promoter Surge o Therm Apparatus, Madras, India, 1975-76; assoc. designer Nat. Inst. Design, Ahmedabad, India, 1976-80; dir., lectr., cons. Ill. State U., 1980-84; mgr. planning and bus. devel. Hindustan Motors Ltd., Madras, 1984-87; mng. assoc. P Mahalingham, Designers, Madras, 1984—; chmn., chief exec. officer Teleconnectors Ltd., Madras, 1987—; cons. in field. Contbr. articles to periodicals. Charter v.p. Hindu Soc. Cen. Ill., Bloomington, 1982; founding coordinator The Pub. Adminstrn. Help Tank, Madras, 1987—. Mem. Mensa.

MAHAN, D. DULANY, JR., lawyer, real estate developer; b. Hannibal, Mo., Dec. 22, 1914; s. D. Dulany and Sarah (Marshall) M.; m. Eleanor F. Bethea, Sept. 14, 1948 (div. 1953). AB, U. Mo., Columbia; J.D., Harvard U., 1940. Assoc., Office of George M. Clark, N.Y.C., 1940-42; asst. atty. FTC, Washington, 1948-51; assoc. Adams & James, N.Y.C., 1951-68; assoc. Kurnick & Hackman, N.Y.C., 1968—; ptnr. Tall Pines Estates Devel., Jacksonville, Fla., 1971—; atty., prin. Magnolia Grove Real Estate Devel., Dunedin, Fla., 1976—. Served with U.S. Army, 1942-46. Mem. ABA, Internat. Bar Assn., World Assn. Lawyers, N.Y. Bar Assn., Fed. Bar Assn. Republican. Clubs: Harvard (N.Y.C.); Nat. Lawyers (Washington). Home: 98 Ralph Ave White Plains NY 10606 Office: 660 Madison Ave New York NY 10021

MAHATHIR BIN MOHAMAD, prime minister of Malaysia; b. Alor Setar, Kedah, Malaysia, Dec. 20, 1925; MBBS, U. Malaya, Singapore, 1947; m. Siti Hasmah, 1956; 3 sons, 2 daus. Med. officer, Alor Star, Langkawi and Perlis, Malaysia, 1953-57; practice medicine, 1957—; M.P. for Kota Setar Selatan, 1964-69, for Kubang Pasu, 1974; apptd. senator, 1973; chmn. FIMA (Food Industry of Malaysia), 1973; minister of Edn., 1974-76; dep. prime minister, 1976-81; minister of Trade and Industry, 1977-81; prime minister, 1981—, minister of def. until 1986, min. of home affairs, 1986—, now with minister of justice; mem. supreme council United Malay Nat. Orgn., 1965-69, v.p., 1975, dep. pres., 1978; del. to UN, 1965; chmn. 1st Higher Edn. Council, 1968; mem. Higher Edn. Adv. Council, 1972; chmn. Univ. Kebangsaan Council, 1974. Former chmn. Kedah Anti Tb Assn., chmn. Kedah Child Welfare Council. Author: The Malay Dilemma, 1969. Office: Office of the Prime Minister, Jalan Dato Onn, Kuala Lumpur Malaysia *

MAHBUBANI, KISHORE, Singapore ambassador; b. Singapore, Oct. 24, 1948; s. Mohandas and Janki (Devki) M.; m. Anne King Markey, Mar. 30, 1985. B.A. with honors in Philosophy, U. Singapore, 1971; M.A. in Polit. Philosophy, Dalhousie U., Can., 1976. Adminstrv. officer Ministry Fgn. Affairs, Singapore, 1971-73; charge d'affaires Singapore embassy, Phnom Penh, Kampuchea, 1973-74; counsellor Singapore High Commn., Kuala Lumpur, 1976-70; dep. dir. Ministry Fgn. Affairs, 1980-82; dep. chief mission Singapore embassy, Washington, 1982-84; permanent rep. Singapore Permanent Mission to UN, N.Y.C., 1984—. Contbr. articles to profl. jours. Avocations: tennis; reading. Office: Singapore Mission to UN Two United Nations Plaza 25th Floor New York NY 10017

MAHDI, SADIQ AL, Sudanese government official; b. 1936; s. Siddik El M. Ed., Comboni Coll., Khartoum, Sudan, St. John's Coll., Oxford, Eng. Leader Umma Mahdist Party, 1961—; prime minister Sudan, Khartoum, 1966-67, 86—, minister def., from 1986; mem. com. Sudanese Socialist Union, 1978-79; mem. Nat. Assembly, 1986—. Author: Problems of the South Sudan. Led mediation mission in U.S. hostages in Iran Crisis, 1980. Vis. fellow St. Anthony's Coll., Oxford, 1983. Address: Office of the Prime Minister, Khartoum Sudan *

MAHER, FRAN, advertising agency executive; b. Chgo., June 22, 1938; d. Edward Stephan and Virginia Rose (Harrington) M.; m. Anthony Peter Petrella, Sept. 17, 1957; children: Roland, Louis, Marcus. Student (univ. scholar) U. Minn., 1956-57; student Spectrum Inst., 1968-71; BA summa cum laude, Kean Coll. N.J., 1979. Office mgr. Lead Supplies, Inc., Mpls., 1957-59; freelance artist and writer, Warren, N.J., 1968-72; prin. Visuals, Warren, N.J., 1974-79; pres. Fran Maher, Inc., Stirling, N.J., 1980—; dir. Parent Edn. Advocacy Tng. Center, Alexandria, Va., 1979-85. Officer Friends of Weigand Farm, Milton, N.J., 1977-80, Somerset County Assn. for Retarded Citizens, 1982—, pres., bd. dirs. 1987—; founding mem. Flintlock Boys' Club. Recipient N.J. Art Dirs. Show award, 1978, 1st place award in graphics Watchung Art Center, 1980. Mem. Art Dirs. Club N.J., Am. Women's Econ. Devel. Corp., Advt. Agy. Network Internat., Internat. Platform Assn. Office: 1390 Valley Rd Stirling NJ 07980

MAHER, FRANK ALOYSIUS, research and development executive, psychologist; b. Jamaica, N.Y., Mar. 31, 1941; s. Frank A. and Gertrude F. (Peterson) M.; m. Barbara A. Eggers, Aug. 14, 1965 (div. 1978); children: B. Kelly, F. Scott, Erin K.; m. Karen S. Adcock, June 28, 1980. BA, U. Dayton, 1966, MS, 1971. Licensed psychologist, Ohio. Research psychologist Ritchie Inc., Dayton, Ohio, 1965-68, Bunker Ramo, Dayton, 1968-70; lectr., research assoc. Wright State U., Dayton, 1970-71; research psychologist USAF, Wright Patterson AFB, Ohio, 1971-84; dir. Perceptronics, Inc., Dayton, 1984-87; research and devel. exec. Unisys, Dayton, 1987—; counseling psychologist Eastway Mental Health Ctr., Dayton, 1974-75, Good Samaritan Mental Health Ctr., Dayton, 1979. Conbtg. author: Perceptions in Information Sciences; editor: Developmental Learning Handbook. Bd. dirs. Miami Valley Mental Health Assn., Dayton, 1974-77, Greene Mental Health Assn., Xenia, Ohio, 1977. Roman Catholic. Home: 7881 Stanley Mill Centerville OH 45459 Office: Unisys 4140 Linden Ave Suite 200 Dayton OH 45432

MAHER, WILLIAM JAMES, entertainment industry executive; b. Chgo., Feb. 23, 1937; s. Alexander E. and Merle G. M.; B.B.A., Marquette U., 1961. Merchandising exec. Montgomery Ward & Co., Inc., Chgo., 1962-68; mgmt. cons. Cresap, McCormack & Paget, N.Y.C., 1968-69; v.p., treas. Solar Prodns., Inc., Hollywood, Calif., 1969-72; v.p., sec., treas. Creative Mgmt. Assocs., Los Angeles, 1972-74; v.p., dir. Josephson Internat., Inc., Los Angeles, 1974-83; pres. Tipperary Prodns., Inc., Beverly Hills, Calif., 1983—. Office: Tipperary Prodns Inc 1930 N Beverly Dr Beverly Hills CA 90210

MAHESHWARI, BHANWAR LAL, business association director; b. Ajmer, Rajasthan, India, Mar. 5, 1934; s. Harsukhlal and Gyarasi Devi Maheshwari; m. Sandra Barber; children: Sunita, Vijai. BA, Agra U., 1956, MA, 1958; MA, Rajasthan U., Jaipur, 1960; PhD, U. Pa., 1966. Lectr. Rajasthan U., Jaipur, 1958-63; asst. prof. Columbus (Ga.) Coll., 1965-66; sr. faculty mem. Adminstrv. Staff Coll. India, Hyderabad, 1967-80; dir. Cen. for Orgn. Devel., Hyderabad, 1980—; cons. Andra Pradesh Indsl. Devel. Corp., Hyderabad, 1968, Bharat Electronics Ltd., Bangalore, 1984—, Bharat Bijlee Ltd., Bombay, 1974—, Blue Star Ltd., Bombay, 1977-80, Equatorial Trust Corp., London, 1985—, Export Import Bank India, Bombay, 1982-84, Govt. Gujarat, Ahemedabad, 1977-81, Hindustan Copper, Calcutta, 1973-78, Hindustan Zinc Ltd., Udaipur, 1977-79, various other cos.; chmn. adv. com. on second survey research in mgmt. Indian Council Social Sci. Research, New Delhi, 1979-84; mem. bd. mgmt. Khorakiwala Found., Bombay, 1985—; chmn. bd. dirs. Hitech Print Systems Ltd., Hyderabad; bd. dirs. Bank Madura, Madras. Author: Management by Objectives, 1980, Decision Styles, 1980; editor: Centre-State Relations, 1973, Quality Circles, 1987; editor Adminstrv. Staff Coll. India Jour. Mgmt., 1972-80. Mem. syndicate Katatiya U., Warangal, 1976-78. Fulbright fellow, 1963; fellow Ford Found., 1970. Mem. Indian Inst. Pub. Adminstrn. (life), Indian Inst. Mgmt. (life), Am. Study Research Cen., Indian Soc. for Tng. and Devel. Hindu. Clubs: Secunderabad; Kodaikanal Golf. Home: Suvima Rd 12, Banjara Hills, Hyderabad 500 034, India Office: Cen for Orgn Devel, Nageena Rd 3, Banjara Hills, Hyderabad 500 034, India

MAHEU, JEAN, museum president, French government official; b. Paris, Jan. 24, 1931; s. Rene and Ines (Allafort du Verger) M.; m. Isabelle Viennot; children—Emmanuel, Anne, Sophie, Pascale, Jean-Philippe, Delphine. Ed. Institut d'Etudes Politiques, Ecole Nationale d'Administration, 1956-58. Mission charge Secretariat Gen. of Presidency of the Republic, 1962-67; referendary counsellor Audit Office France, 1964—, head counsellor, 1985—; dir. youth and socioednl. activities Office of Sec. State of Youth, Sports and Leisure, Paris, 1967-74; dir. music, lyric art and dance Ministry of Culture and Communication, 1974-79; pres. Centre National d'Art et de Culture Georges Pompidou, Paris, 1983—. Author: (poetry) Les nus et les trembles, 1984. Decorated chevalier Legion d'Honneur; comdr. Ordre des Arts et des Lettres; officier l'Ordre National du Merite, Ordre du Merite de la Republique Federale d'Allemagne, Grand Insignie d'Argent Republique d'Autriche, Ordre de Soleil Levant, Japon. Office: Cour des Comptes, 13 rue Cambon, 75001 Paris France also: Centre Nat d'Art et Culture, 75191 Paris 4, France

MAHFOOD, STEPHEN M., state agency director; b. Evansville, Ind., Feb. 12, 1949; s. George Mahfood and Bonnie (Short) Morse; m. Bernadette Scarani, Oct. 16, 1976; children: Nadia Joan, Leila Emma. BS, Rutgers U., 1971. Planning cons. Area V Health Services Adminstrn., Poplar Bluff, Mo., 1976-77; planner Mo. State Health Planning & Devel. Agy., Jefferson City, Mo., 1977-78, chief of planning, 1978-80, dir., 1980-82; gen. mgr. Chimney Rock (N.C.) Co., 1982-84; dir. Mo. Environ. Improvement & Energy Resources Authority, Jefferson City, 1984—; tchr. courses related to environ. and mgmt. agy. topics. Vol. YMCA, Beirut, Lebanon, 1974; bd. dirs. Jefferson City Montessori Sch. (pres.), 1980, Council of Pollution Control Fin. Agys., Internat. Reuse Alliance; appointed Nat. Govs. Assn. Hazardous Minimization Assurance Adv. Group; appointed Cingressman Anthony's House Ways and Means Task Force on Pub. Fin. Recipient Disting. Service award Mo. Div. of Health and Mo. Dept. Social Services, Achievement award Mo. Waste Control Coalition, 1986. Mem. Am. Soc. for Pub. Adminstrn., Am. Mgmt. Assn., Am. Planning Assn., Nat. Assn. Environ. Profl., Am. Pub. Health Assn. Home: 1416 Herron Dr Jefferson City MO 65191 Office: Mo Environ Improvement & Energy Resources Authority PO Box 744 Jefferson City MO 65101

MAHLER, HALFDAN THEODOR, physician, health organization executive; b. Vivild, Denmark, Apr. 21, 1923; s. Magnus and Benedicte (Suadicani) M.; m. Ebba Fischer-Simonsen, Aug. 31, 1957; children: Per Bo, Finn. MD, U. Copenhagen, 1948, postgrad. degree in pub. health; LLD (hon.), U. Nottingham, (Eng.), 1975; MD (hon.), Karolinska Inst., Stockholm, 1977; Docteur de l'Universite des Sciences Sociales de Toulouse, France, 1977; DPH (hon.), Seoul Nat. U., 1979; ScD (hon.), U. Lagos, Nigeria, 1979; MD (hon.), Warsaw Med. Acad., 1980; LHD, U. Nacional Federico Villareal, Lima, Peru, 1980; MD (hon.), Charles U., Prague, 1982, Mahidol U., Bangkok, Thailand, 1982; LHD (hon.), U. Gand, Belgium, 1983, Univ. Nacional Autonoma de Nicaragua, 1983; Dr. Honoris Causa, The Semmelweis U. of Medicine, Budapest, Hungary, 1987. Specialized tng. in T, active field of internat. pub. health work; planning officer mass Tb campaign Ecuador, 1950-51; sr. officer nat. Tb program WHO, India, 1951-61; chief Tb unit, Hdqrs., WHO, Geneva, 1962-69, sec. to expert adv. panel on Tb, 1962-69, dir. project systems analysis, 1969-70, asst. dir.-gen. div. health services and div. family health, 1970-73, dir.-gen., 1973-88. Contbr. articles on epidemiology and control of Tb, polit., social, econ, and technol. priorities in health sector, application of systems analysis to health care problems to profl. jours. Decorated comdr. de l'Ordre Nat. du Mali, 1982, Grand Officer de l'Ordre du Merite de la Rep. du Senegal, 1982, comdr. 1st class Order White Rose (Finland); recipient Jana Evangelisty Purkyne medal (Presdl. award) Prague, 1974, Comenius U. gold medal Bratislava, 1974, Carlo Forlanini gold medal Federazione Italiana contro la Tubercolosi et le Malattie Polmonari Sociali Rome, 1975, Ernest Carlsens Found. Prize Copenhagen, 1980, Georg Barfred-Pedersen prize Copenhagen, 1982, Hagedorn medal and prize Denmark, 1986; hon. prof. U. Nacional Mayor de San Marcos, Lima, Peru, U. Chile Faculty of Medicine, Beijing Med. Coll., Rep. of China, Shanghai Med. U. Fellow Royal Coll. Physicians (London), Faculty Community Medicine of Royal Colls. Physicians U.K. (hon.), Indian Soc. for Malaria and other Communicable Diseases (hon.), Royal Soc. Medicine (London) (hon.), London Sch. Hygiene and Tropical Medicine (hon.); mem. Med. Assn. Argentina (hon.), Latin Am. Med. Assn. (hon.), Italian Soc. Tropical Medicine (hon.), Belgium Soc. Tropical Medicine (assoc.), Societe medicale de Geneve (hon.), Union internationale contre la Tuberculose (hon.), Societe francaise d'Hygiene, de Medecine sociale et de Genie sanitaire (hon.), Uganda Med. Assn. (hon. life), Coll. Physicians and Surgeons, Bangladesh Royal Coll. Gen. Practitioners (ad eundem), List of Honour of the Internat. Dental Fedn. Home: 12 Chemin du Pont-Ceard, CH 1290 Versoix Switzerland Office: Dir Gen World Health Orgn, 20 Ave Appia, 1211 Geneva 27, Switzerland

MAHMOOD ISKANDAR IBNI SULTAN ISMAIL, King of Malaysia; b. Johore Baru, Malaysia, Apr. 8, 1932; s. Sultan Ismail Ibni Sultan Al-Marhum Ibrahim; married; 10 children. Ed. English Coll., Johore Baru, also ed. Australia and Eng. With Johore Civil Service, from 1959; apptd. Raja Madu, 1966; Sultan of Johore, 1981-84; King of Malaysia (paramount ruler), 1984—. Office: care Embassy of Malaysia Press Info Office 2401 Massachusetts Ave NW Washington DC 20008

MAHMUD, IBNI AL-MARHUM TUANKU SULTAN ISMAIL NASIRUDDIN, Sultan of Trengganu; b. Kuala Trengganu, Malayasia, Apr. 29, 1930; s. Tuanku Ismail Nisruddin Shah; m. Tengku Bariah, Mar. 22, 1951. Ed., Eng., 1949-50. Named Yang Di Pertuan Muda of Trengganu, 1950-79, regent, 1954, 65, sultan, 1979—. Hon. maj. Royal Malay Army, 1958; lt. col. Malaysian Wataniah Army, 1968. Office: care Press Attache Malaysian Embassy 2401 Massachusetts Ave Washington DC 20008 *

MAHONEY, FRANCIS XAVIER, personnel consultant, executive; b. Boston, Oct. 1, 1931; s. Francis Dennis and Miriam Virginia (McCarthy) M.; B.S., Boston Coll., 1953; M.Ed., U. Vt., 1964, M.S., 1966; Ed.D., U. Houston, 1973; postgrad. U.S. Army Command and Gen. Staff Coll., Indsl. Coll. of Armed Forces, 1975; m. Alice Catherine Duffy, June 13, 1953; children—Francis Xavier, Stephen Patrick, Alice Jean. Commd. 2d lt. U.S. Army, 1953; advanced through grades to maj., 1964; instr., aide-de-camp Arty. Sch., Ft. Sill, Okla., 1957-61; ops. officer, Korea, 1961-62; asst. prof. mil. sci. U. Vt., Burlington, 1962-66; resigned, 1966; mgmt. trainer Humble Oil (now Exxon Co. USA), Houston, 1966-69, head dept. indsl. relations Baton Rouge refinery, 1969-71, hdqrs. personnel devel. advisor, Houston, 1971-78, personnel advisor med. activities, Houston, 1980-82, hdqrs. personnel devel. cons., Houston, 1982-83; v.p. mgmt. tng. systems Inst. Mgmt. Improvement and Thoughtware, Inc., Coconut Grove Fla., 1983-85; pres. F.X. Mahoney Assoc., 1985—; exec. dir., founder Ctr. Instl. Effectiveness, 1988—;mktg. dir. (on loan from Exxon USA) Higher Edn. Mgmt. Inst., 1978-80; spl. cons. Am. Council on Edn., 1978-81; cons. Inst. for Mgmt. Improvement in Nonprofit Orgns., 1980-83; adj. prof. mgmt. Houston Bapt. U. Grad. Sch.; adj. prof. edn. U. Houston Grad. Sch. Served to col. USAR, 1966-83 (comdt. USAR Sch., Houston, 1979—). Consulting editor: Computers in Personnel Adminstrn., 1985—; contbr. editor: Personnel, 1984—. Cert. U.S. Army Research and Devel. Specialist. Decorated Legion of Merit, Meritorious Service medal. Mem. Am. Soc. Tng. and Devel. (recipient Torch Award, 1977), Am. Mgmt. Assn., Am. Psych. Assn., Soc. Indsl. Orgnl. Psychs., Cert. Cons. Internat. (charter mem.), Orgn. Devel. Network, Exec. Service Coprs-Houston, Res. Officers Assn., U. Houston Alumni (dir., exec. com.). Author numerous monographs, articles, ednl. programs; contbr. articles in field to profl. jours. Home: 14754 Riverforest Dr Houston TX 77079 Office: 15119 Memorial Dr Suite 212 Houston TX 77079

MAHONEY, LOUIS EMMET, JR., physician, public health administrator; b. Santa Monica, Calif., Mar. 9, 1939; s. Louis Emmett and Ruth Elizabeth (Miller) M.; B.A., U. Calif. at Los Angeles, 1960, M.D., 1964, M.P.H., 1967, Dr. P.H., 1970; m. Antoinette Diana Scott, June 26, 1965; children: Vivien, Gillian. Intern Los Angeles County Gen. Hosp., 1964-65; chief med. officer Peace Corps, Kuala Lumpur, Malaya, 1965-67; resident physician U. Calif. at Los Angeles, 1968-70; dir. immunization project, Los Angeles County, 1970-75; chief non-communicable disease epidemiology, Los Angeles County, 1973-75; city health officer Long Beach (Calif.), 1975; dir. pub. health, San Bernardino County, Calif., 1975-83; med. dir., capt. USPHS, 1983—; assoc. dir. med. response Nat. Disaster Med. System, 1984—; asst. prof. preventive and social medicine, UCLA Sch. Medicine and Public Health, 1970-77, assoc. prof. epidemiology, 1977-84; adj. asso. prof. biomed. sci. U. Calif., Riverside, 1980-83; cons. WHO, 1974—, USPHS, 1971—; mem. Calif. Emergency Med. Service Commn., 1981-83; bd. dirs. Inland Counties Emergency Med. Authority, 1976-83; chmn., 1980-83; dir. Calif. Conf. Local Health Officers, 1976-83. Mem. Am. Soc. Tropical Medicine and Hygiene, Am. Pub. Health Assn., Royal Soc. Medicine, Calif. Med. Assn., Calif. Pub. Health Assn. (gov. council 1975-77), World Assn. Emergencies and Disaster Medicine (Club of Mainz), Malaysian Soc. Parasitology and Tropical Medicine. Am. Statis. Assn., Assn. Mil. Surgeons of U.S., U.S. Naval Inst., Res. Officers Assn. of U.S., Muintir Mathúna, Ireland (bd. dirs. 1985—, v.p. 1988—), UCLA Pub. Health Alumni Assn. (v.p. 1974). Democrat. Roman Catholic. Contbr. articles to med. jours. Office: 10638 Weymouth St #1 Bethesda MD 20814

MAHONEY, PATRICIA ANN NORDSTROM, personal services company executive; b. Hastings, Minn., Apr. 13, 1939; d. Harold Edward and Mary Patricia (Ahern) Nordstrom; m. Edward J. Mahoney, 1962 (div. 1987); children: Patrick Sean, Erin Mary. BS cum laude, U. Minn., 1961. Tchr., head curriculum com. Hopkins (Minn.) Sr. High Sch., 1961-64; mgr. Bridal Services, Inc., Mpls., 1969-73; buyer, gen. mgr. Anderson's Wedding World Stores, Mpls., 1973-77; dir. fashion div. Nat. Bridal Service, Richmond, Va., 1975—, also bd. dirs.; mktg. and tng. specialist Minn. Dept. Edn., 1977-80; edn. cons. Mpls. Star & Tribune Newspapers, 1981-83, mgr. edn. services, 1983-85, single copy sales mgr., 1985—. Mem. Phi Beta Kappa. Home: 5604 Colfax Ave S Minneapolis MN 55419

MAHONEY, RICHARD JOHN, manufacturing company executive; b. Springfield, Mass., Jan. 30, 1934; m. Barbara Marsden Barnett, Jan. 26, 1956; 3 children. B.S. in Chemistry, U. Mass., 1955, LL.D., 1983. Product devel. specialist Monsanto Co., 1962; market mgr. new products Monsanto Co., St. Louis, 1965-67; plastic products and resins div; market mgr. bonding products, div. sales dir. Kenilworth, N.J., 1967-71; sales dir. Agrl. div. Monsanto Co., St. Louis, 1971-74, dir. internat. ops., 1974-75, gen. mgr. overseas div., 1975; corp. v.p., mng. dir. Monsanto Agrl. Products Co., 1975-76; group v.p., mng. dir. Monsanto Plastics & Resins Co., 1976-77, exec. v.p., 1977-80, pres., 1980, chief operating officer, 1981, bd. dirs., 1979—; pres., chief exec. officer Monsanto Co., St. Louis, 1983-86; chmn., chief exec. officer Monsanto Co., 1986—; dir. Centerre Bancorp., Met. Life Ins. Co., G.D. Searle & Co., Fisher Controls Internat. Bd. dirs. U.S.-USSR Trade and Econ. Council, Council Aid to Edn., trustee Washington U., St. Louis; adv. bd. St. John's Mercy Med. Ctr.; bd. mgrs. Central Inst. Deaf. Recipient Frederick S. Troy Alumni Achievement award U. Mass., Amherst, 1981; hon. fellowship Exeter Coll., Oxford, 1986. Mem. Chem. Mfrs. Assn., Soc. Chem. Industry, Bus. Council, Bus. Round Table. Clubs: Log Cabin, St. Louis, Bellerive Country. Office: Monsanto Co 800 N Lindbergh Blvd Saint Louis MO 63167

MAHONEY, THOMAS HENRY DONALD, historian, educator, government official; b. Cambridge, Mass., Nov. 4, 1913; s. Thomas Henry, Jr. and Frances (Lucy) M.; m. Phyllis Norton, July 14, 1951; children: Thomas Henry IV, Linda, David, Peter, Philip. A.B., Boston Coll., 1936, A.M., 1937; Ph.D., George Washington U., 1944; M.P.A., Harvard U., 1967. Instr. Gonzaga Sch., Washington, 1937-39, Dunbarton Coll., Washington, 1938-39; instr., then asst. prof. history Boston Coll., 1939-44; asst. prof. history Holy Cross Coll., 1944-46; vis. lectr. history and govt. Smith Coll., 1944-45, Wellesley Coll., 1947-48; mem. faculty Mass. Inst. Tech., 1945—, prof. history, 1961—, chmn. sect. history, 1963-65, 73-79; vis. prof. U. So. Calif., summer 1950; Lowell lectr., Boston, 1957; Carnegie fellow Harvard Law Sch., 1965-66; sec. elder affairs Commonwealth of Mass., 1979-83; head Mass. del. White House Conf. on Aging, 1981; mem. ethnic com. U.S. Dept. Edn., 1979-83; chmn. UN NGO Com. on Aging, N.Y., 1967—; corporator, trustee Cambridgeport Savs. Bank; participant, panelist, cons. numerous internat. confs. on gerontology. Author: Edmund Burke and Ireland, 1960; co-author: Readings in International Order, 1951, China, Japan and the Powers, 2d edit, 1960, The U.S. in World History, 3d edit, 1963, Edmund Burke: The Enlightenment and the Modern World, 1967, 1776, 1977; Editor: Burke's Reflections, 1955, Selected Writings and Speeches of Edmund Burke on America, 1964. Mem. Cambridge Sch. Com., 1948-54; mem. Mass. Fulbright Com., 1953-74, chmn., 1966-74; observer Vatican City Consistories, 1956, 73, 85; bd. dirs. Mass. Civic League, 1967—; state rep. Mass. Gen. Ct., 1971-78, chmn. energy com., 1977-78, chmn. ethics com., 1977-78; Trustee Cambridge Library, 1948-54, Mass. State Library, 1952-61; bd. dirs. Internat. Student Fedn.; mem. Cambridge City Council, 1964-72; mem. community adv. council Jr. League Boston, 1982-86; advisor Congressman Claude Pepper's Internat. Com. on Issues and Questions of Aging, 1985—; UN rep. InterParliamentary Conf., Ottawa, 1985, Congress Latin Am. Socs. Gerontology and Geriatrics, Lima, Peru, 1984, UN NGO Forum on Aging, 1985—, chmn. 1986-87; N.Y. and Washington rep. Centre Internat. de Gerontologie Sociale, Paris, 1985—, bd. dirs., 1986—; cons. on aging to Congressman Claude Pepper, 1985—; keynote speaker on aging Inter-Parl. Union, Bangkok, 1987. Recipient Humanitarian of Yr. award Mass. Psychol. Soc., 1983; Am. Council of Learned Socs. fellow, 1938; Guggenheim fellow, 1961-62. Fellow Royal Hist. Soc.; mem. Am. Hist. Assn., Am. Cath. Hist. Assn. (pres. 1957), Mass. Hist. Assn., Cath. Commn. Cultural and Intellectual Affairs, Conf. Brit. Studies, Nat. Conf. State Legislators (sci. and tech. com., intergovtl. relations com. 1973-78, mem. del. Peoples Republic of China 1976, 78). Home: 130 Mt Auburn Ave Apt 410 Cambridge MA 02138

MAI, AMALIA ISABEL, editor; b. Corozal Dist., Belize, May 11, 1960; d. Jose and Rosenda (Carillo) M. Diploma, Coll. Journalism, London, 1981. News editor Radio Belize, Belize City, 1981-84; editor Disweek, Belize City, 1984-85, Belize Times, Belize City, 1985-87; stringer AFP, Belize City, 1987. Active Hosp. Aux., Belize City. Mem. Media Alliance Belize. Mem. People's United Party. Roman Catholic. Office: The Belize Times, 3 Queen St, Belize City Belize

MAI, CHAO CHEN, engineer; b. Kwangchow, Canton, China, Feb. 26, 1936; came to U.S. 1962, naturalized 1973; m. Shao Shen Yam; children—Glenn, Kenneth. M.S.E.E., Oreg. State U., 1964; Ph.D. in E.E., Utah State U., 1967. Project engr. Sylvania Electric Co., Woburn, Mass., 1967-70; mgr. research and devel. Mostek Corp., Carrollton, Tex., 1970-76, v.p. research and devel., 1976-84; founder v.p. engring. Dallas Semiconductor Corp., 1984—. Patentee Silicon gate combined with depletion load process, 1974; method for making a semicondr. device, 1985. MOSFET Fabrication Process, 1984. Mem. IEEE, Electrochem. Soc. Current work: Advanced processing technology in integrated circuits. Subspecialties: Integrated circuits; Microchip technology (engineering).

MAIDEN, ROBERT MITCHELL, banker; b. Montrose, Tayside, Scotland, Sept. 15, 1933; s. Harry and Georgina (Robertson) M.; m. Margaret Nicolson, Apr. 12, 1958. Grad. sec. sch., Tayside. Various positions The Royal Bank of Scotland, 1950-74; supt. of brs. The Royal Bank of Scotland, London, 1974-76, treas., 1976-77; chief acct. The Royal Bank of Scotland, Edinburgh, Scotland, 1977-81, gen. mgr. of fin., 1981-82, exec. dir., 1982-86, mng. dir., 1986—. Bd. dirs. Edinburgh Jr. C. of C., 1965-67, Edinburgh C. of C., 1983-85. Fellow Inst. of Bankers in Scotland (v.p. 1986), Brit. Inst. of Mgmt. Mem. Ch. of Scotland. Club: New (Edinburgh). Office: Royal Bank of Scotland, 42 Saint Andrew Sq, Edinburgh Scotland EH2 2YE

MAIDIN, ZAINUDDIN, editor-in-chief; b. Alor Star, Kedah, Malaysia, June 29, 1939; m. Zaiton Zainal Abidin; children: Zairani, Zakinah, Zairin, Zaidan. Diploma, Berlin Inst. Journalismn, 1969. Staff reporter Utusan Melayu (Malaysia) Berhad, Kuala Lumpur, 1961-62, chief reporter, 1963-71, news editor, 1971-75, editor, 1976-82, group chief editor, 1983—; fgn. rep. Utusan Melayu (Malaysia) Berhad, London, 1975-76. Office: Utusan Malaysia, 46 M Lima, off Jalan Chan Sow Lin, Kuala Lumpur Malaysia

MAIDMAN, RICHARD HARVEY MORTIMER, lawyer; b. N.Y.C., Nov. 17, 1933; s. William and Ada (Seegle) M.; m. Lynne Rochelle Lateiner, Apr. 3, 1960 (div. Sept. 1987); children—Patrick, Mitchel, Dagny. B.A., Williams Coll., 1955; J.D., Yale U., 1959; postgrad. N.Y. U. Grad. Sch. Bus., 1957, Grad. Sch. Law, 1960, 77. Bar: N.Y. 1961, Fla. bar, 1961, U.S. Dist. Ct. 1962, 79, U.S. Ct. Appeals 1966, U.S. Supreme Ct., 1978. Assoc. Saxe, Bacon & O'Shea, N.Y.C., 1962-64; ptnr. Weiner, Maidman & Goldman, N.Y.C., 1964-67; sole practice, N.Y.C., and Fla., 1968—; dir. Microbiol. Scis., Inc.; Nat. Over-the-Counter List, Providence, 1971—, sec., 1971—; pres. MBS Equities, Inc., Fashion Wear Realty Co., Inc., N.Y.C., 1975—; mng. gen. ptnr. Richard and David Maidman, N.Y.C., 1972—, Barcelona Hotel Ltd., Miami Beach, Fla., 1975-84; legis. counsel Theodore R. Kupferman, 17th Congl. Dist. N.Y., 1966-68; of counsel Shwal, Thompson & Bloch, N.Y.C. and Geneva, 1976—; receiver Halloren House Hotel, N.Y.C., 1981. Contbr. articles to profl. jours. Mem. ABA, N.Y. State Bar Assn., Fla. Bar Assn., Assn. Bar City N.Y., Bankruptcy Lawyers Assn. N.Y.C. Home: Steamboat Landing Sands Point NY 11050 also: 1726 M St Washington DC 20036

MAIER, GERALD JAMES, natural gas transmission and petroleum company executive; b. Regina, Sask., Can., Sept. 22, 1928; s. John Joseph and Mary (Passler) M. Student, Notre Dame Coll. (Wilcox), U. Man., U. Alta., U. Western Ont. With petroleum and mining industries Can., U.S., Australia, U.K.; responsible for petroleum ops. Africa, United Arab Emirates, S.E. Asia; pres., chief exec. officer TransCan. Pipelines, Toronto, 1985—, also bd. dirs.; bd. dirs. Bell Can. Enterprises Inc., Bank of N.S., TransAlta Utilities Corp., Du Pont Can. Inc., Great Lakes Gas Transmission Co., TransQué. & Maritimes Pipeline Inc., Foothills Pipe Lines (Sask.) Ltd; past pres. Assn. Profl. Engrs., Geologists and Geophysicists of Alta.; now vice chmn. Can. Nat. Com. for World Petroleum Congresses; bd. govs. Bus. Council on Nat. Issues, Can. Com. for World Energy Conf. Recipient Past Pres.'s Meml. medal Can. Inst. Mining and Metallurgy, 1971; hon. lt. col. of King's Own Calgary Regiment. Mem. Am. Gas Assn. (bd. govs.), Can. Petroleum Assn. (bd. govs.). Office: TransCan Pipelines Ltd, PO Box 54, Commerce Ct W, Toronto, ON Canada M5L 1C2

MAILLARD, GASTON-FRANCOIS, plastic surgeon, educator; b. Fribourg, Switzerland, July 28, 1939; s. Arthur Jean and Gertrude Erni M.; m. Catherine Brignon, Sept. 28, 1978; children—Sophie, Veronique. B., Coll. Fribourg, Switzerland, 1960; M.D., U. Lausanne, Switzerland, 1967, Plastic Surgeon, 1974, Privat Docent (hon.), 1977. Resident Hopitaux de Paris, 1969-72; sr. resident U. Hospital, Zurich, 1973; co-chief surgeon Leprosy Hosp., Mashad, Iran, 1974; chief resident U. Hosp., Lausanne, 1975-77; clin. fellow U. Miami, Fla., 1977. Author: Plastic Surgery of the Orbit, 1976; Plastic Surgery of the Orbito-Palpebral Region, 1978; Surgery of the Breast, 1984. Mem. Swiss Soc. Senology (pres. 1984—), French and Swiss Soc. Plastic, Reconstructive and Aesthetic Surgery, French and Swiss Soc. Hand Surgery. Office: Avenue de la Dole 17, CH-1005 Lausanne Switzerland

MAILLON, MICHEL, business executive; b. Rive de Gier, France, Jan. 31, 1942; s. Etienne and Dorival M.; m. Anne Marie, 1968; children: Muriel, Antoine, Juliette. Diploma in Engring., Bus. Inst., Nancy, France, 1967. Bus. mgr. Mil S Sa, Lyon and Paris, France, 1970; pres. Mil S Sa, Barcelona, Spain, 1983. Mem. Lyon C. of C. (consul del.). Lodge: Rotary. Home: Le Prieure Ecully, 69130 Rhone France Office: Mil S Sa, 17-25 Ave P Santy, F69371 Lyon, Cedex 08 France

MAIMAN, THEODORE HAROLD, physicist; b. Los Angeles, July 11, 1927. B.S. in Engring. Physics, U. Colo., 1949; M.S. in Elec. Engring., Stanford U., 1951, Ph.D. in Physics, 1955. Sect. head Hughes Research Labs., 1955-61; pres., founder Korad Corp., Santa Monica, Calif., 1961-68, Maiman Assocs., Los Angeles, 1968—; v.p., founder Laser Video Corp., Los Angeles, 1972-75; v.p. advanced tech. and new ventures TRW Inc. Electronics and Def. Sector, Los Angeles, 1975-83; dir. Plesscor Optronics Inc. Author papers in field. Adv. bd. Indsl. Research mag. Served with USNR, 1945-46. Recipient award Fannie and John Hertz Found., 1966; Ballantine award Franklin Inst., 1962; award for devel. laser Aerospace Elec. Soc.-Am. Astron. Soc., 1965, Light award Braille Inst., 1982, Wolf prize in physics, 1984; named Alumni of Century U. Colo., 1976; inducted into U.S. Nat. Inventors Hall of Fame, 1984; named Laureate Japan Prize (electro-optics), 1987. Fellow Soc. Motion Picture and TV Engrs., Am. Phys. Soc. (Oliver E. Buckley prize 1966), Optical Soc. Am. (R.W. Wood prize 1976), Soc. Photog. and Instrumentation Engrs.; mem. Nat. Acad. Engrs., Nat. Acad. Scis., IEEE, Soc. Info. Display, Sigma Xi, Sigma Pi Sigma, Sigma Tau, Pi Mu Epsilon.

MAIN, ROBERT GAIL, communications and training consultant, television and film producer, educator, former army officer; b. Bucklin, Mo., Sept. 30, 1932; s. Raymond M. and Inez L. (Olinger) M.; m. Anita Sue Thoroughman, Jan. 31, 1955; children: Robert Bruce, David Keith, Leslie Lorraine. BS magna cum laude, U. Mo., 1954; grad. with honors, Army Command and Gen. Staff Coll., 1967; MA magna cum laude in Communications, Stanford U., 1968; PhD, U. Md., 1978. Commd. 2d lt. U.S. Army, 1954, advanced through grades to lt. col., 1968; various command and staff assignments field arty., 1954-64; sr. instr. and div. chief Pershing missile div. U.S. Army Arty. and Missile Sch., Ft. Sill, Okla., 1964-66; mem. faculty U.S. Army Command and Gen. Staff Coll., 1968-70; chief speechwriting and info. materials div. U.S. Army Info. Office, 1971, chief broadcast and film div., 1972-73; dir. def. audiovisual activities Office of Info. for Armed Forces, 1973-76, ret., 1976; prof., grad. adv. Coll. Communications, Calif. State U., Chico, 1976-87; pres. Grant & Main, Inc., corp. communications and tng. cons. Author: Rogues, Saints and Ordinary People, 1988; contbr. articles on audiovisual communications to profl. publs.; producer: Walking Wounded, TV documentary, 1983; producer army info. films, army radio series, 1972-73; creating family heritage videos. Decorated Legion of Merit, Meritorious Service medal, Commendation medal with oak leaf cluster, combat Inf. Badge; Vietnamese Cross of Gallantry; recipient Freedom Found. awards, 1972, 73, 74; Bronze medal Atlanta Film Festival, 1972; Best of Show award Balt. Film Festival, 1973; Creativity award Chgo. Indsl. Film Festival, 1973; Cine gold award Internat. Film Producers Assn., 1974; named an Outstanding Prof. Calif State U., 1987-88. Mem. Assn. for Ednl. Communications Tech., Am. Soc. of Curriculum Developers, Nat. Assn. Ednl. Broadcasters, Phi Eta Sigma, Alpha Zeta, Phi Delta Gamma, Omicron Delta Kappa, Alpha Gamma Rho. Mem. Christian Ch.

MAIN, ROGER PAUL, marketing professional; b. St. Louis, Aug. 6, 1939; came to Fed. Republic Germany, 1969; s. George Henry and Lillie Mae (Poleos) M.; m. Brigitte Ursula Sanzenbacher, June 13, 1963 (div. Apr. 1979); children: Rebecca, Phillip; m. Galina Viktorovna Kungurova, Aug. 16, 1979. Student, Washington U., 1957; BS in Physics, St. Louis U., 1961; postgrad. in physics, UCLA, 1966-68. Aerospace technologist NASA/GSFC, Greenbelt, Md., 1961-63; research scientist Philco-Ford Research Labs, Newport Beach, Calif., 1963-65, Heliodyne Corp., Van Nuys, Calif., 1965-70; product mgr. Tekelec-Airtronic GmbH, Stuttgart, Fed. Republic Germany, 1969-70; gen. mgr. Spex Industries GmbH, Stuttgart, 1971-74; sales mgr. Spectra-Physics GmbH, Stuttgart, 1974-81; service mgr. Coherent GmbH, Neu-Isenburg, Fed. Republic Germany, 1981; sr. cons. R.P. Main Cons., Darmstadt, Fed. Republic Germany, 1982—; cons. numerous European firms, 1982—; adv. bd. Laser Innovation GmbH, Stuttgart, 1984-87; dir., prin. cons. ELBA Assocs. SA, Geneva, Switzerland, 1985—. Author: Director of European Suppliers of Military Laser Hardware, 1984, Beam Weaponry, 1986, Lasers at Work, 1987; editor-in-chief, 1988: Optical Engring. Reports, European Edition; contbg. editor: Lasers and Optronics, Fiberoptic Product News; cons. to pub.: Laser Magazin; contbr. articles to: Lasers and Optics Internat., Sensor Review. Recipient Danforth Found. scholarship, 1957, Woodrow Wilson Found. fellowship, 1961. Mem. Am. Physics Soc., N.Y. Acad. Scis., Soc. Photo-Optical Instrumentation Egrs. Home: Julius-Reiber-Strasse 16, D-6100 Darmstadt 1 Federal Republic of Germany Office: Hindenburgstrasse 1, D-6100 Darmstadt 1 Federal Republic of Germany

MAING, I. YOUNG, food company executive; b. Seoul, Republic of Korea, July 9, 1942; came to U.S., 1968, naturalized, 1968; s. Kwang Ho Maing and In Sun Lee; m. Jeanne Lee, Aug. 12, 1968; children: Michelle, Juhn-Michael. BS, Seoul Nat. U., 1967; MS, U. Ga., 1970; PhD, U. Wis., 1972. Sr. food technologist Armour Foods, Oak Brook, Ill., 1974-75; project leader Gen. Foods, Tarrytown, N.Y., 1975-77, group leader, 1977-79, sr. research specialist, 1980-82; exec. mgr. Gen. Foods Internat., Honolulu, 1982—; also bd. dirs. Gen. Foods Internat., Seoul; dir. USDA, Washington, 1980-82; exec. dir. Korea Indsl. Research Inst., Seoul, 1982—, strategy and policy com. Gen. Foods, Korea, 1985—; invited scientist German Research Inst., Kulmbech, 1972-74. Inventor in field. Mem. Rep. Presdl. Task Force, Washington, 1984, Statue of Liberty Ellis Island Found., N.Y.C., 1984. Grantee Internat. Child Health Found., N.Y.C., 1969; FDA fellow U. Ga., Athens, 1967. Mem. Am. Cereal Chemists Soc., Inst. Food Technologists (counselor 1984—), Am. Chem. Soc., Korean-Am. Food Scientists Assn. (chmn. 1978). Home: 52 Village Walk Wilton CT 06897 Office: Gen Foods Worldwide 250 North St White Plains NY 10625

MAINGUY, JEAN-PIERRE, computer manufacturing company executive; b. Paris, Aug. 29, 1948; s. Pierre and Jacqueline (Constant) M.; m. Denise Maurice, July 5, 1974; children: Emmanuelle, Marie-Madeleine, Pierre. PhD in Math., U. Paris, 1978. Research asst. U. Paris, 1977-78; mem. European mktg. staff Hewlett-Packard Germany, Boeblingen, 1979-81, mgr. tng. European div., 1981-85, mgr. sect. research and devel., 1985-88, gen. mgr. mfg. systems ops., 1988—. Served as lt. French Navy, 1974-75. Mem. Soc. Mech. Engrs. (sr.), IEEE, German-French Assn. Roman Catholic. Home: Autenriethstrasse 21, 7400 Tubingen Federal Republic of Germany Office: Hewlett-Packard GmbH, Herrenbergerstrasse 130, 7031 Boeblingen Federal Republic of Germany

MAIORIELLO, RICHARD PATRICK, otolaryngologist; b. Phila., Mar. 17, 1936; s. Gesumino Theodore and Angelina (Del Rossi) M.; A.B., U. Pa., 1960; M.D., Jefferson Med. Coll., 1964; M.S., Thomas Jefferson U., 1972; m. Susan Hemenway, Mar. 6, 1979; children—Gabriel, Angela, Richard. Commd. 2d lt., U.S. Air Force, 1963, advanced through grades to col., 1977; ret., 1979; intern Keesler Hosp., 1965-67; chief flight medicine USAF Base, Bitburg, W. Ger., 1965-68; resident in otolaryngology Thomas Jefferson Hosp., Phila., 1968-71, 72-73; fellow in physiology Thomas Jefferson U., 1971-72; dir. med. edn. Andrews AFB, 1974-78; assoc. prof. uniformed services Univ. Health Scis., 1978-79; assoc. prof. Northeastern Ohio U. of Medicine, 1983—; mem. staff Aultman Hosp., 1979—; assoc. staff Timken Mercy Med. Ctr., 1981—; cons. otolaryngology to Surgeon Gen., 1977—; pres. Mid-Ohio Dressage Assn. Served with USNR, 1954-58. Decorated Air Force Commendation medal; diplomate Nat. Bd. Med. Examiners, Am. Bd. Otolaryngology. Fellow ACS, Am. Soc. Head and Neck Surgery; mem. Am. Acad. Otolaryngology, Am. Acad. Facial Plastic and Reconstructive Surgery, Am. Assn. Cosmetic Surgery, Vail Cosmetic Surg. Soc., Hanoverian Soc. (exec. v.p.). Republican. Roman Catholic. Club: Centurion. Office: 1445 Harrison St NW Canton OH 44708

MAISONROUGE, JACQUES GASTON, former business machines company executive, French government official; b. Cachan, France, Sept. 20, 1929; s. Paul and Suzanne (Cazas) M.; Engr., Ecole Centrale de Paris, 1948; Dr. Honoris Causa, Poly. Faculty of Madrid, 1980; m. Francoise Feron, Mar. 30, 1948; children—Christine Maisonrouge Bertagna, Florence Maisonrouge McAuliffe, Sylvie Maisonrouge Gillespie, Francois, Anne-Sophie. With IBM, 1948—, engr. IBM France, 1948-56, mgr. product planning IBM Europe, Paris, 1956-58, regional mgr., 1958-59, asst. gen. mgr., 1959-62, v.p. IBM World Trade Corp., N.Y.C., 1962-64, pres. IBM Europe, Paris, 1964-67; pres. IBM World Trade Corp. and v.p. IBM Corp., N.Y.C., 1967-72, sr. v.p. IBM, 1972-84, chief exec. officer IBM World Trade Corp., 1973-74, chmn., chief exec. officer IBM World Trade Europe/Middle East/Africa Corp., 1974-81, chmn. bd. IBM World Trade Corp., 1976-84, mem. corp. office and corp. mgmt. com., 1981-84, mem. corp. mgmt. bd. and bus. ops. com., 1983-86, dir. IBM Corp., 1983-86; dir.-gen. and sr. civil servant

Ind. Ministry, 1986—; dir. Air Liquide, Moet Hennessy, Philip Morris Inc. Chmn. bd. trustees Ecole Centrale, 1976—. Decorated officier Legion d'Honneur; comdr. Order of Merit. (France). Fellow Internat. Acad. Mgmt.; mem. Soc. French Scientists. Club: Automobile de France. Office: care Ministry of Industry, 101 rue de Grenelle, Paris 75700, France *

MAISTER, DAVID HILTON, consultant; b. London, July 21, 1947; came to U.S., 1973; s. Alfred and Bertha (Spanglett) M. B in Soc. Sci., U. Birmingham, Eng., 1968; MSc, London Sch. Econs., 1971; DBA, Harvard U., 1976. Asst. prof. U. B. C., Can., 1976-78; assoc. prof. Harvard Bus. Sch., Mass., 1979-85; pres. Maister Assocs., Boston, 1985—; cons. to profl. service firms. Author: The Owner Operator, 1975, The Motor Carrier Industry, 1977, The Domestic Airline Industry, 1977, Management of Owner Operator Fleets, 1979, Cases in Operations Management, 2 vols., 1982, Professional Service Firm Management, 1987, Success Strategies for the Design Professions, 1987. Home: 90 Commonwealth Ave Boston MA 02116 Office: Maister Assocs 545 Boylston Boston MA 02116

MAITLAND, GUY EDISON CLAY, lawyer; b. London, Dec. 28, 1942 (mother Am. citizen); s. Paul and Virginia Francesca (Carver) M. B.A., Columbia U., 1964; J.D., N.Y. Law Sch., 1968. Bar: N.Y. 1969, U.S. Dist. Ct. (so. and ea. dists.) N.Y. 1969, U.S. Ct. Appeals (2d, D.C. cirs.) 1969. Assoc., Burlingham, Underwood & Lord, N.Y.C., 1969-74; admiralty counsel Union Carbide Corp., N.Y.C., 1974-76; exec. v.p., gen. counsel, dir. Liberian Services, Inc., N.Y.C. and Reston, Va., 1976—; del. UN Conf. on Trade and Devel., Manila, 1979, Belgrade, 1983; participant London Conf. on Limitation of Maritime Liability, 1976; mem. legal com. Internat. Maritime Orgn. (UN), London, 1980—; del. UN Conf. on Law of the Sea, 1976-82, London UN Maritime Law Conf., 1984; co-founder The Admiralty-Fin. Forum, N.Y.C., 1986. Author articles on maritime law, U.S. shipping policy. Sec. N.Y. Rep. County Com., 1976-87, vice chmn., 1988—; co-chmn. Citizens for Reagan, N.Y. State, 1979-80; mem. N.Y.C. Mayor's Port Devel. Council, 1983—. Named Outstanding Young Man of Am., U.S. Jaycees, 1975; hon. del Rep. Nat. Convention, Dallas, 1984. Mem. Assn. Bar City N.Y. (chmn. admiralty com. 1982-85), Maritime Law Assn. U.S. (chmn. com. on intergovernmental orgns. 1987—), Maritime Assn. Port of N.Y. (dir. 1984-87), ABA, D.C. Bar Assn., Phi Delta Phi. Republican. Episcopalian. Clubs: Capitol Hill, University (Washington); Princeton, Down Town Assn. (N.Y.C.). Office: Office of Gen Counsel Liberian Services Inc 551 Fifth Ave New York NY 10176

MAITLAND-SMITH, GEOFFREY, financial services company, accountant; b. Feb. 27, 1933; s. Philip John and Kathleen (Goff) M-S. Student, U. London. Chartered acct. Ptnr. Thornton Baker and Co., 1960-70; dir. Sears Holdings plc, 1971—, dep. chmn., 1978-85, joint chmn., 1984; chief exec. Sears plc, 1978—, chmn., 1985—; chmn. Brit. Shoe Corp. Ltd., 1984—, Butler Shoe Corp. (USA), 1984—, Lewis's Investment Trust Ltd., 1985—, Selfridges Ltd., 1985—, Garrard and Co. Ltd., 1985—, Mappin and Webb Ltd., 1985—, Malltee plc, 1986—; bd. dirs. Asprey and Co. plc, 1980—, Cen. Ind. TV plc, Courtaulds plc, Imperial Group plc, Midland Bank plc. Mem. council University Coll. Sch. Mem. Inst. of Mktg. (pres. 1987), Worshipful Co. of Gardeners (liveryman). Club: Cripplegate Ward. Office: 40 Duke St, London W1A 2HP, England *

MAJ, STANISLAW JOZEF, hematologist, researcher; b. Staszow, Poland, Jan. 28, 1932; s. Jozef and Anna (Zielinska) M.; m. Aleksandra Berlowicz, July 28, 1958 (div. 1971); 1 son, Tomasz; m. Barbara Maria Drzewiecka, May 8, 1973; children—Malgorzata, Marta, Grzegorz, Robert. Diplomate in medicine Med. Acad., Warsaw, 1957, M.D., 1965, D.S., 1973. Research asst. Inst. Hematology, Warsaw, 1957-64, asst. prof. hematology, 1965-73, assoc. prof., 1974-85, prof., 1986—; head dept., 1977—; consulting hematologist Med. Coop., Warsaw, 1970—, Central Railway Hosp., Warsaw, 1978—. Author: Normal Values and Interpretation of Laboratory Test in Internal Medicine, 1971, 77, 81; Use of 'Polfa' Drugs in Treatment of Blood Diseases, 1984; editor: Progress in Hematology, 1979, 83, 88; editor-in-chief Jour. Acta Haematologica Polonica; contbr. numerous articles to profl. jours. Recipient Outstanding Health Service Worker award Ministry of Health Poland, 1966, Medal XL Yrs. of Polish People's Republic, 1974, Gold Cross of Merits, 1976. Mem. Polish Med. Assn., Polish Soc. Hematologists and Transfusiologists, Internat. Soc. Hematology. Roman Catholic. Home: Korotynskiego 19/22, 02123 Warsaw Poland Office: Inst Hematology, Chocimska 5, 00-957 Warsaw Poland

MAJALI, ABDUL WAHHAB, former deputy prime minister and minister of education of Hashemite Kingdom of Jordan; b. Karak, Jordan, 1924; married. B.A. in Law, Damascus U., 1945; postgrad. in commerce and developing industries Toledo U., 1954. Under-sec. Econs. Ministry, Jordan, 1959, minister, 1962; minister of interior, 1965-66; minister of edn., 1966-67; minister of state for prime ministry affairs, 1967, 70; minister fin., 1967; mem. Upper House Parliament, 1970—; mem. Nat. Consultative Council; dep. prime minister, minister of edn., 1985-88. Office: Upper House Parliament, Amman Jordan *

MAJEKODUNMI, MOSES ADEKOYEJO, obstetrician, gynecologist; b. Abeokuta, Nigeria, Aug. 17, 1916; s. James Bernard and Alice Oladunni (Soetan) M.; m. Nora C. MacLaughlin, 1943 (div. 1963); children—Olufemi Adetokunbo, Terrance Adekoyejo, Sylvia Folashade Akinyemi, Desmond Olumuyiwa, Oladapo Olugboyega, Koforowola Adedamola, Adefolake Iyabo, Modupe Adeyooly Adebisi; m. Katsina Saratu Atta, July 22, 1964. Student St. Gregory's Coll., Nigeria, 1931-34; M.B., Ch.B., B.A.O., Trinity Coll., Dublin, Ireland, 1941; M.A., M.D., 1942, M.A.O., 1949, LL.D., T.C.D., 1964; D.Sc., U. Lagos, Nigeria, 1974, F.R.C.P.I., 1955, F.M.C.O.G., F.W.A.C.S., F.R.C.O.G., 1983. House physician Nat. Children's Hosp., Dublin, 1941-43; med. officer, Nigeria, 1943-49; specialist obstetrician Govt. Maternity Hosp., Lagos, 1949-60; cons. obstetrician Massey State Maternity Hosp., Gen. Hosp., Creek Hosp., Lagos, 1949-60; sr. specialist obstetrician Nigerian Fed. Govt. Med. Services, 1949-60; Minister of State for Army, 1960; Fed. Minister Health, 1961-66; adminstr. Western Nigeria, 1962; med. dir., chmn. bd. govs. St. Nicholas Hosp., Lagos, 1967—; pres. 16th World Health Assembly, 1963; Internat. v.p. 3rd World Conf. Med. Edn., New Delhi, 1966; chmn. bd. dirs. Lion Bldgs. Ltd.; dir. Abbott Labs. Nigeria, Swiss Nigeria Chem. Co., Johnson & Johnson Ltd., Nigeria; senator, leader senate 1960-66. Contbr. articles to profl. jours. Trustee J.K. Randle Meml. Hall, Lagos; bd. govs. St. Gregory's Coll., Lagos; comdr. Fed. Republic Nigeria, 1982. Decorated Companion Order St. Michael, St. George, 1963. Mem. Soc. Ob-Gyn. Nigeria (pres. 1968-72). Clubs: Lagos Island, Met., Lagos Polo. Lodges: Scotia, Hope. Home: 3 Kingsway, Ikoyi, Lagos Nigeria Office: 57 Campbell St, Lagos Nigeria *

MAJETE, CLAYTON AARON, sociology educator; b. Woodland, N.C., Apr. 19, 1941; s. Barnabus and Doreather (Jefferson) M.; 1 child from previous marriage—Lisa. BA, Morgan State U., 1965; MA, NYU, 1967, PhD, 1984. Lectr., Nassau Community Coll., L.I., N.Y., 1967-69; lectr. Baruch Coll. CUNY, N.Y.C., 1970-84, prof. sociology and anthropology, 1984—. Mem. Gov. Harry Hughes' internal staff for 1986 Gubernatorial campaign; researcher for N.Y. Times and WCBS-TV and published on front page of N.Y. Times a study on Race Relations in N.Y.C., 1985; exec. dir. Bedford Stuyvesant Community Corp., Bklyn., on leave, 1977-78; cons. Okla. U. Med. Sch., Norman. Assoc. editor Jour. Intergroup Relations; contbr. articles to black studies jours. Commr., Boy Scouts Am., Bklyn., 1980-83. NIMH fellow, Johns Hopkins Med. Sch., 1969; fellow Wharton Sch. U. Pa., 1981. Mem. Morgan State U. Alumni Assn. (chmn. scholarship and recruitment com.), Inst. Urban Affairs (chmn. bd. dirs.), AAUP, Am. Sociol. Assn., NAACP. Democrat. Home: 9061 Queen Maria Ct Columbia MD 21045 Office: CUNY Baruch Coll 17 Lexington Ave New York NY 10010

MAJEWSKI, FRANK WALTER, insurance company executive; b. Warsaw, Poland, Jan. 4, 1922; s. Walter and Josephine (Michalski) M.; came to U.S., 1922, naturalized, 1940; B.B.A., St. John's U., 1947; m. Kathleen Curley, Aug. 13, 1949; children—Raymond, Kenneth. Sr. auditor, Jos. Fraggatt & Co., N.Y.C., 1947-51; audit mgr. Allstate Ins. Co., Newark, 1951-53, CIT Fin. Corp., N.Y.C., 1951-65, also treas. subs. Patriot Life Ins. Co., N. Am. Accident & Health Ins. Cos.; sr. cons. Frank Lang Assos., N.Y.C., 1965-67; founder, pres. A & M. Mgmt., Cranford, N.J., 1967—, also Auten Majewski, Monley & Assos., Cranford; co-founder, v.p. R.M. Donaldson Assos., 1967—, also dir.; pres., founder Phillips, Majewski and Assocs., 1981—. Active Boy Scouts Am.; pres. Colonial Gardens Civic Assn., 1960-64. Served with U.S. Army, 1943-46. Republican. Roman Catholic. Clubs: St. Vincent DePaul Soc., K.C. Home: 14 Denman Dr Fords NJ 08863 Office: 35 Walnut Ave Clark NJ 07066

MAJUNKE, WERNER HANS, pharmaceutical company executive; b. Grosskrotzenburg, Hessen, Fed. Republic Germany, Feb. 1, 1948; s. Karl and Gertrud (Hoffman) M.; m. Doris Bergmann, Dec. 18, 1981; children: Judith, Markus, Julia. Dr. rerum naturalium, Goethe U., Frankfurt, Fed. Republic Germany, 1978; postgrad., Inst. Organic Chemistry, Frankfurt, 1978. Product mgr. Boehringer Mannheim GmbH, Mannheim, Baden-Württemberg, Fed. Republic Germany, 1978-83, regional mgr., 1983-84, product mgr. Fed. Republic Germany, 1984-86, regional sales mgr., 1986—. Co-author: Analytiker Taschenbuch, 1985; contbr. articles to profl. jours. Chmn. parliamentary group Christian Dem. Union, Hettenleidelheim, 1984. Served with German Army, 1967-68. Roman Catholic. Home: Waldstrasse 12, Carlsberg, 6719 Rhineland-Palatinate Federal Republic of Germany Office: Boehringer Mannheim GmbH, Westendstrasse 195, 8000 Munich Federal Republic of Germany

MAK, YAT CHEONG, physician; b. Hong Kong, People's Republic of China, May 14, 1941; d. Kwong Shau Mak and Woon Ling Chien. BS, MB, U. Hong Kong, 1966. Med. officer Tung Wah Hosp., Hong Kong, 1967-68, U. Health Service U. Hong Kong, Hong Kong, 1968-69, Kwong Wah Hosp., Hong Kong, 1969-71; med. officer Hong Kong & Kowloon Wharf & Godown Co. div. The Star Ferry Co., Hong Kong, 1971-74, gen. practitioner, 1974—. Mem. Tantrism Ch. Home: #7 Seymour Rd, Block C 11-F, Hong Kong Hong Kong Office: 22 Man Tai St G-F, Hunghom, Hong Kong Hong Kong

MAKADOK, STANLEY, management consultant; b. N.Y.C., Mar. 30, 1941; s. Jack and Pauline (Speciner) M.; BME, CCNY, 1962; MS in Mgmt. Sci., Rutgers U., 1964; m. Lorraine Edith Dubin, Aug. 24, 1963; 1 son, Richard. Bus. systems analyst Westinghouse Electric Corp., Balt., 1964-65; project engr., corp. cons. Am. Cyanamid Corp., Pearl River, N.Y., Wayne, N.J., 1965-68; v.p., bus. devel. and planning Pepsico Inc. and affiliates, Purchase, N.Y., Miami, Fla., 1968-75; mgr. fin. and planning cons. Coopers & Lybrand, N.Y.C., 1975-77; pres. Century Mgmt. Cons., Inc., N.Y.C., Ridgewood, N.J., 1977—. Contbr. articles to profl. jours. Office: Century Mgmt Cons Inc 4 Wilsey Sq Suite 9 Ridgewood NJ 07450

MAKAREM, ESSAM FAIZ, manufacturing company executive; b. Lagos, Nigeria, Aug. 20, 1936; s. Faiz Mahmoud and Jamal Mohammed Makarem; Diploma in English and Arabic, Nat. Coll., Aley Lebanon, 1953; BS in Bus. Adminstrn. U. Beverly HIlls, 1987; m. Ghada Mahmoud Aawar, Oct. 5, 1969; children—Hitaf, Wael, Nader, Joumana, May, Ussama. Dir., gen. mgr. Faiz Moukarim & Sons Ltd., Kano, Nigeria, 1954—, also dir.; mng. dir. Moukarim Metalwood Factory Ltd., Kano, Ikeja, Katsina and Jos Nigeria, 1959—; dir. Borno Engring. and Steel Mfrs. Ltd., Nigeria Gas Industries Ltd., Moukarim Bros. Ltd.; Mgmt. and Fin. Internat. Ltd., Beirut, United Devel. Corp. (Holding), Beirut. Pres. Nat. Council Nigeria, World Lebanese Cultural Union, 1972-73, v.p. world council, 1976-83; sec. gen. Druse Found. for Soc. Welfare, Beirut, 1983—, Kamal Jumblatt Soc. Found., Beirut, 1981—. Mem. C. of C. and Industry of Kano, Assn. Steel Tube Mfrs. (chmn. 1979-80), Assn. Foam Mfrs. Druse Moslem. Lodges: Rotary (pres. local club 1971-72), Kano Lebanon (pres. 1973-76) (Kano); Masons, Odd Fellows. Office: Plot M Awosika Ave, PO Box 160, Ikeja, Lagos Nigeria

MAKAROVA, NATALIA, ballerina; b. Leningrad, Russia, Nov. 21, 1940; m. Edward Karkar, 1976; 1 child, Andrei Michel. Grad., Vaganova Ballet Sch., Leningrad Choreographic Sch., 1959. assoc. artist London Festival Ballet, 1985—. Formerly ballerina with Leningrad Kirov Ballet, performed at Royal Opera House, Covent Garden, London, 1961; toured U.S., 1961, 64; roles include Giselle, Swan Lake, Les Sylphides, Sleeping Beauty, Cinderella, Raymonda, La Bayadere, Onegin (London Evening Standard award 1985), others; joined Am. Ballet Theatre, 1970; guest appearances in U.S. and Europe, 1972—; presented Makarova & Co., 1980 (one season); staged full-length prodn. of La Bayadere for Am. Ballet Theatre, 1980; appeared in Broadway prodn. On Your Toes, 1983 (Tony award 1984, Oliver award), appeared in TV and film prodns. Makarova: Class of her Own, Channel 4, 1984, Natasha Special, BBC, 1985, (4-part documentary) Ballerina, BBC, 1987; author: A Dance Autobiography, 1979. Recipient Gold medal 2d Internat. Ballet Competition, Varna, Bulgaria 1965. Office: care Herbert Breslin Inc 119 W 57th St New York NY 10019 also: Am Ballet Theatre 888 7th Ave New York NY 10019 *

MAKASIAR, GARY SANTOS, energy industrial executive, consultant; b. Manila, Nov. 15, 1947; s. Felix Valencia and Teofista (Flores) Santos M.; children: Mary Anne, Janice Gayle, Gyron Julius, Gavyn James. BA in Math., Ateneo U., Quelon City, Philippines, 1967; M in Econs., U. Philippines, Quezon City, 1970; M in Pub. Adminstrn., Harvard U., 1976; MBA, Ateneo Grad. Sch. Bus., Makati, Philippines, 1978. Applied registered rep. Bache & Co., Inc., Makati, Philippines, 1969-70; asst. to chmn. Philippine Nat. Bank, Manila, 1970; cons. on econ. devel. office chmn. Nat. Econ. Council, Manila, 1970-72; assoc. dir. devel. mgmt. staff Exec. Office Pres., Manila, 1972-76; v.p. Philippine Nat. Oil Co., Makati, 1976-87; exec. dir. Policy Reserach Ctr. for Energy, Telecommunications, Transp. and Related Pub. Utility Services, Philippines, 1987—; dir. planning Ministry Energy, Makati, 1977-86, policy research Energy Devel. Bd., Makati, 1976-77, strategic research Tech. Resource Ctr. Found., Makati, 1986-87; cons. energy Asian Devel. Bank, Pasay City, Philippines, 1986-87; exec. dir. Power Devel. Council, Makati, 1976-79. Editor various govt. publs. Bd. dirs., treas. Philippine Soc. Youth Sci. Clubs, Paranaque, Philippines, 1984-87. Mem. Internat. Assn. Energy Econmists, Internat. Inst. Valuers, Philippine Econ. Soc. (bd. dirs. 1985-86). Home: 4553 Cattleya St, Sun Valley Subdiv, Paranque, Met Manila Philippines Office: Policy Research Ctr for Energy, Telecommunications Transp and, Related Pub Utility Service, Makati Philippines

MAKDISI, GEORGE, language educator; b. Detroit, May 15, 1920; s. Abraham George and Sophie (Chater) M.; m. Margaret Anderson Gray, June 7, 1948 (dec.); children: John, Catherine, Thomas, Theresa, Anne, Jeanne; m. Nicole Renée Guillemette, Jan. 5, 1979. BA, U. Mich., 1947; MA, Georgetown U., 1950; LittD, U. Paris, 1964; MA (hon.), Harvard U., 1961, U. Pa., 1973. From asst. prof. to assoc prof. Near Eastern Studies U. Mich., Ann Arbor, 1953-59; mem. faculty Harvard U., Cambridge, Mass., 1959-73, prof. Arabic, 1964-73; prof. Arabic and Islamic Studies U. Pa., Phila., 1973—, chmn. dept. Oriental Studies, 1975-78; dir. Summer Inst. in Basic Disciplines in Medieval Studies, 1976, 79; dir. Ctr. for Study of Byzantium, Islam, and the Latin West, 1979—; chaire d'etat Coll. de France, U. Paris, 1969; vis. prof. U. Paris Sorbonne, 1978-79; dir. studies Hautes Etudes, 1981-82. Author: Kitab at-Tauwabin: Le Livre des Pénitents d'Ibn Qudáma, 1961, Ibn Qudáma's Censure of Speculative Theology, 1962, Ibn Aqil et la Resurgence del'Islam Traditionaliste au XIe Siecle, 1963, Arabic and Islamic Studies in Honor of Hamilton A.R. Gibb, 1965, Le Livre de la Dialectique d'Ibn Aqil, 1967, Notebooks of Ibn Aqil, 1971, The Scholastic Method in Medieval Education, 1974, L'Islam Hanbalisant, 1975, Medieval Education in Islam and the West, 1977, The Rise of Colleges, 1981, La Notion d'Autorité au Moyen Age: Islam, Byzance, Occident, 1982, Prédication et Propagande au Moyen Age: Islam, Byzance, Occident, 1983, La Notion de Liberte au Moyen Age: Islam, Byzance, Occident, 1985, The Juridical Theology of Shafici: Origins and Significance, 1984, The Guilds of Law in Medieval Legal Histroy: An Inquiry into the Origins of the Inns of Court, 1984, The Diary in Islamic Historiography: Some Notes, 1986. Served with U.S. Army, 1942-45. Guggenheim fellow, 1957-58, 67-68, Fulbright-Hays fellow, 1967. Mem. Social Sci. Research Council (Inter-Univ. Lang. Com.), Am. Assn. Tchrs. Arabic (founding, past chmn.), Nat. Undergrad. Program for Overseas Study of Arabic (adv. council 1965), Am. Inst. Islamic Studies (chmn. bd. dirs. 1967-68), Inst. Internat. Edn. (nat. screening com. 1967), Am. Oriental Soc. (pres. 1987-88), Medieval Acad. Am., Mid. East Inst., Mid. East Studies Assn. (pres. 1976-77), Royal Asiatic Soc., Am. Soc. Legal History, Assn. Espanola de Orientalistas, Am. Council Learned Socs., French Oriental Soc. (hon.). Home: 751 Farnum Rd Media PA 19063 Office: U Pa Williams Hall Philadelphia PA 19104

MAKHULU, WALTER PAUL KHOTSO, archbishop; b. Johannesburg, Republic of South Africa, July 2, 1935; s. Paul M.; m. Rosemary Makhulu, 1966; 1 child. Student, Coll. of the Resurrection, Birmingham, Republic of South Africa, St. Andrews Coll., Birmingham, Republic of South Africa. Area sec. Ea. Africa and African refugees Commn. on Inter-Ch. Aid Refugee and World Service, World Council of Chs., 1975-79; bishop Botswana, 1979—; archbishop Cen. Africa, 1980—; pres. All Africa Conf. of Chs., 1981-86, World Council of Chs., 1983; hon. curate Holy Trinity, Geneva. Named Offcier l'Ordre des Palmes Academiques, 1981. Home: PO Box 769, Gaborone Botswana Office: World Council of Chs, 150 Rt de Ferney PO Box 66, 1211 Geneva 20 Switzerland

MAKHZOUMI, ZIAD, management consultant; b. Beirut, Jan. 20, 1955; s. Mustapha and Aicha (Zeidan) M.; m. Zeina Takieddine; children: Hala, Tarek. BS in Engring., U. Manchester, 1978, MBA, 1981. Assoc. Booz Allen & Hamilton Co., N.Y.C., 1981-85; dir. Future Mgmt. Services, London, 1985—, Olliff & Ptnrs. PLC, London, 1987—, Intercapital Group SA, Switzerland, 1987—. Contbr. Am.-Arab Affairs Council, Washington, 1987. Moslem. Office: Future Mgmt Services Ltd, 116 Gloucester Pl, London W1H 3BD, England

MAKI, FUMIHIKO, architect, educator; b. Tokyo, Sept. 6, 1928; m. Misao, 1960; 2 children. Ed. U. Tokyo, Cranbrook Sch. Art, Mich. and Harvard U.; M.Arch.; Washington U. (hon.). Assoc. prof. Washington U., St. Louis, 1956-62, Harvard U., 1962-66; lectr. dept. urban engring. U. Tokyo, 1964—, prof. architecture, 1979—; prin. ptnr. Maki and Assocs., 1964—; mem. Trilateral Commn., 1975—; vis. prof. U. Calif.-Berkeley, 1970, UCLA, 1977, Colombia U., 1977, Tech. U. Vienna, 1978. Maj. works include: Toyoda Meml. Hall, Nagoya U., 1960; Rissho U. Campus, 1966; Nat. Aquarium, Okinawa, 1975; Tsukuba U. Complex, 1976; Hillside Terr. Housing Complex, 1978; The Royal Danish Embassy in Tokyo, 1979; author: Investigations in Collective Form, 1964; Movement Systems in the City, 1965; Metabolism, 1960. Recipient awards, including: Gold medal Japan Inst. Architects, 1964, 1st prize Low Cost Housing Internat. Competition, Lima, Peru, 1969, Art award Mainichi Press, 1969. Fellow AIA (hon.); mem. Japan Inst. Architecture.

MAKINDE, JONATHAN BABATUNDE, state agency offical, accountant; b. Ilesa, Oyo, Nigeria, Apr. 21, 1941; s. Amos Adeleke and Felicia Olaitan (Ogedengbe) M.; m. Kate Ndidi Anene, May 24, 1973; children: Enny, Folokae, Dupe, Tunde, Dare, Muyiwa. ACCS, Corp. Secs. London, 1969. Head dept. accounts and commerce Western Coll. Commerce, Lagos, Nigeria, 1970-73; head accounts dept. Renascent High Sch., Ibadan, Oyo, 1973-78; head fin. dept. Indsl. Tng. Fund, Ilorin, Kwara, Nigeria, 1978—; course coordinator Bus. Study Group, Ibadan, 1974-80. Censor's offcl. no. zone Govt. Nigeria, 1975. Mem. Nigerian Inst. (assoc.), Inst. Credit Mgmt. (assoc.), Assn. Bus. Execs. (assoc.). Office: Indsl Tng Fund Box 655, 219 Ibrahim Taiwo Rd, Ilorin Nigeria

MAKINIEMI-AALTO, ELISSA, architect; b. Kemi, Finland, Nov. 22, 1922; d. Johan August and Aino Maria (Kemppainen) Makiniemi; m. Hugo Alvar Henrik Aalto, Oct. 4, 1952 (dec. May 1976). Grad. architect Tech. U. Helsinki, 1949. Architect, Alvar Aalto Architects Ltd., Helsinki, 1949-58, ptnr., 1958—; dir. Artek, Helsinki, 1971—. Decorated comdr.'s cross Order of Dannebrog (Denmark), 1973; knight 1st class Order of White Rose (Finland), 1982. Hon. fellow AIA. Lutheran. Office: Alvar Aalto Architects Ltd, Tiilimaki 20, SF-00330 Helsinki Finland

MAKINS, JAMES EDWARD, dental educator, educational adminstrator, dentist; b. Galveston, Tex., Feb. 22, 1923; s. James and Hazel Alberta (Morton) M.; m. Jane Hopkins, Mar. 4, 1943; children—James E. Jr., Michael William, Patrick Clarence, Scott Roger. D.D.S., U. Tex.-Houston, 1945; postdoctoral, SUNY-Buffalo, 1948-49. Lic. dentist, Tex. Practice dentistry specializing in orthodontics, Lubbock, Tex., 1949-77; dir. clinics Dallas City Dental Health Program, 1977-78; dir. continuing edn. Baylor Coll. Dentistry, Dallas, 1978—. Author: (book chpt.) Handbook of Texas, 1986. Chmn. profl. div. United Fund, Lubbock, 1958; pres. Tex. State Bd. Dental Examiners, Austin, Tex., 1968; instl. chmn. United Way, Dallas, 1983. Served to lt. comdr., USNR, 1945-47. Recipient Community Service award W. Tex. C. of C., Abilene, 1968, Clinic award Dallas County Dental Soc., 1981. Fellow Am. Coll. Dentists, Internat. Coll. Dentists; mem. Tex. Dental Assn. (v.p. 1954, Goodfellow 1973), West Tex. Dental Assn. (pres. 1955), Am. Assn. Dental Examiners, Omicron Kappa Upsilon. Club: Park City. Methodist. Lodge: Rotary. Avocation: dental history. Home: PO Box 12689 Dallas TX 75225 Office: Baylor Coll Dentistry 3302 Gaston Ave Dallas TX 75246

MAKIOS, VASILIOS, electronics educator; b. Kavala, Greece, Dec. 31, 1938; s. Thrassivoulos and Sophia M. Dipl.Ing., Tech. U. Munich, 1962; Dr. Ing., Max Planck Inst. for Plasmaphysics and Tech. U. Munich, 1966. Profl. engr., Ger., Ont., Greece. Research assoc. Max Planck Inst., Munich, 1962-67; asst. prof. dept. electronics Carleton U., Ottawa, Ont., 1967-70, assoc. prof., 1970-73, prof., 1973-77; prof. and head Electromagnetics lab. U. Patras, Greece, 1975—; cons. in field; dean engring. U. Patras, 1980-82; hon. adj. prof. Carleton U., 1977—. Contbr. articles to profl. jours. Patentee in field. Recipient Silver medal German Elec. Engring. Soc., 1984; numerous grants for research in Can., Greece and European community. Mem. IEEE, German Phys. Soc., German Inst. Elec. Engrs., Can. Assn. Physicists, Greek Tech. Chamber. Greek Orthodox. Avocations: classical music; swimming; skiing. Home: 2 Lefkosias Str, 26441 Patras Greece Office: Lab Electromagnetics, Univ Patras, Patras Greece

MAKITA, TERUHIKO, architect; b. Nagano, Japan, Mar. 21, 1944; s. Sojiro Taguchi and Takako (Makita) M.; m. Momoyo Momose, Feb. 22, 1973; children: Mikihiko, Masahiko. BArch, Nihon U., Tokyo, 1966. Registered architect. Jr. architect Ishimoto Architects and Planners, Tokyo, 1966-71; sr. architect RMJM & Ptnrs., Welwyn Garden City, Eng., 1971-80; mgr. bldg. design Kumagai-Gumi, Tokyo, 1980—; chmn. energy com. Bldg. Contractors Soc., Tokyo, 1982; project mgr. Japan Project Industry Council, Tokyo, 1983. Founder Makita Scholarship Found., Tokyo, 1987. Recipient Energy Conservation prize Inst. Bldg. Energy Conservation, Tokyo, 1983. Mem. Archtl. Inst. Japan. Club: Nanso Golf (Chiba); Tokyo Riding. Home: 20 Kikui-cho, Shinjuku-ku, 162 Tokyo Japan Office: Kumagai-Gumi, 17 Tsukudo-cho, Shinjuku-ku, 162 Tokyo Japan

MAKÓ, CSABA, sociology professor, researcher; b. Gödöllő, Pest, Hungary, Apr. 26, 1945; s. András and Aranka (Tóth) M.; m. Hedvig Makó, Feb. 11, 1968; children: András, Eszter. PhD, Eötvös Lóránd U., Budapest, 1973, Great Doctors' title in Sociology, 1983. Chmn. bd. sociology orgnl. div. Inst. Sociology Hungarian Acad. Scis., Budapest, 1983—; prof. Dept. Sociology Econs. Karl Marx U., Budapest, 1985—; vis. prf. U. Montreal (Can.), autumn 1981, spring 1982. Author: Workers Behaviour and the Socialist Enterprise, 1972, Work, Technology and Work Organization, 1982. Mem. steering com. Nat. Council of Mgmt. Ministry of Culture, Budapest, 1984—. Scholar Social Sci. Council, 1981-82, Japanese Soc. Promotion of Sci., 1986; fellow Eisenhower Exchange Feloowship, 1987. Home: Varoskuti ut 20/A, 1125 Budapest Hungary Office: Inst Sociology HAS, Uri utca 49, 1250 Budapest Hungary

MAKO, WILLIAM LAWRENCE, real estate developer; b. Cleve., June 16, 1958; s. Lawrence M. and Margret E. (Borchard) M. BA in Bus., Wittenberg U., 1981. V.p. Conmak, Inc., Conneaut, Ohio, 1981-82; pres. Le Bears' Inc., Moreland Hills, Ohio, 1982-83; mgr. Wendy's Old-Fashioned Hamburgers, Bozeman, Mont., 1984; exec. v.p. Great Lakes Properties Corp., Conneaut, 1984-88; v.p. Conneaut Harbor Devel. Co., Ohio, 1988—. Mem. Am. Resort and Residential Devel. Assn., Safari Club Internat., N. Am. Hunting Club. Republican. Roman Catholic. Home: 711 Bunker Hill Rd Apt 10 Ashtabula OH 44004 Office: Great Lakes Resort 6231 Weaver Rd Conneaut OH 44030

MAKRIS, ANDREAS, composer; b. Salonica, Greece, Mar. 7, 1930; came to U.S., 1950, naturalized, 1962; s. Christos and Kallitza (Andreou) M.; m. Margaret Lubbe, June 12, 1959; children: Christos, Myron. Grad. with highest honors, Nat. Conservatory, Salonica, 1950; Exchange Student Program grantee, Phillips U., Enid, Okla., 1950; postgrad., Kansas City

(Mo.) Conservatory/Mannes Coll. Music, 1956, Aspen Music Festival, Fontainbleau (France) Sch.; pupil of, Nadia Boulanger. adv. to Maestro Rostropovich for new music, 1979—. Compositions premiered and performed in, U.S., Europe, Can., S.Am., Japan; composer-in-residence, Nat. Symphony Orch., 1979—; prin. works include Scherzo for Violins, 1966, Aegean Festival, 1967, Efthymia, 1972, Sirens, 1976, Chromatokinesis, 1978, Anamnesis, 1970, Viola Concerto, 1970, Concerto for Strings, 1966, In Memory, 1979, Fanfare Alexander, 1980, Variations and Song for orch, 1979, Mediterranean Holiday, 1974, Five Miniatures, 1972, Concertino for Trombone, 1970, Fantasy and Dance for saxaphone, 1974, Fourth of July March, 1982, Violin Concerto, 1983, Nature-Life Symphonic Poem, 1983, Caprice "Tonatonal", 1986, Intrigues for solo clarinet and wind ensemble, 1987, Concertante for violin, cello, clarinet F. Horn Percussion and Orchestra, 1988; also works for violin, string quartets, voice quintets, duets and arrangements of, Paganini and Bach. Recipient citation Greek Govt., 1980; grantee Nat. Endowment Arts, 1967; grantee Martha Baird Rockefeller Fund, 1970; grantee Damrosh Found., 1958. Mem. ASCAP (award 1980). Greek Orthodox. Home: 11204 Oak Leaf Dr Silver Spring MD 20901 Office: Nat Symphony Orch Kennedy Ctr Washington DC 20566

MAKSYMIUK, JERZY, conductor; b. Poland. Former prin. condr. Polish Radio Nat. Symphony Orch.; now music dir. Polish Chamber Warsaw; also prin. condr. BBC Scottish Symphony Orch., 1983—; guest conducting appearances include: Calgary Philharm., Nat. Arts Centre Orch. of Ottawa, English Chamber Orch., Scottish Chamber Orch., Birmingham Symphony Orch., others; has toured Europe, U.S., Australia with Polish Chamber Orch. Address: care Polish Chamber Orch, Nowogrodzka 49, 00-695 Warsaw Poland also: care Harold Shaw 1900 Broadway 2d floor New York NY 10023 *

MALABARBA, FRANK JOSEPH, computer specialist, consultant; b. Chelsea, Mass., Mar. 20, 1947; s. Louis F. and Cathrine (Frye) M.; m. Stalle Mae Sharum, Aug. 8, 1970; children: Scott, Janet, Karen. BSBA, Lowell Tech. Inst., 1968; cert. in computer systems Am. U., 1955. Computer specialist Naval Ordnance Sta., Indian Head, Md., 1968-78; mgr. automatic data processing tech. transfer program Naval Data Automation Command, Washington, 1978-85; dir. info. resources mgmt. Pacific Missile Test Ctr., Point Mugu, Calif., 1985—; part time instr. Charles County Community Coll., LaPlata, Md., 1984; guest lectr. CIA, 1982-84; speaker in field. Contbr. articles to profl. jours. Adult leader Nat. Capital area Boy Scouts Am., LaPlata, 1984, Ventura County Council, Camarillo, Calif., 1985-87. Recipient Spl. Achievement award USN, 1982. Mem. Computer Soc. of IEEE (dep. chmn. compcon 1984, chmn. trends and applications conf. 1983, vice chmn. Washington chpt. 1983-84), Nat. Micrographics Assn. (disting. service citation 1980, chmn. publs. com. 1980-81). Republican. Office: Pacific Missile Test Ctr Code 0301 Point Mugu CA 93042

MALACH, HERBERT JOHN, lawyer; b. N.Y.C., Aug. 3, 1922; s. James J. and Therese (Lederer) M.; A.B., Iona Coll., 1951; J.D., Columbia U., 1955; m. Patricia Sweeny, Sept. 12, 1953 (dec. 1972); children: Therese, Herbert John, Helen. Bar: N.Y. 1957, D.C. 1958, U.S. Dist. Ct. (ea. and so. dists.) N.Y. 1958, U.S. Ct. Appeals (2d cir.) 1960, U.S. Supreme Ct. 1961, U.S. Dist. Ct. (no. and we. dists.) N.Y. 1988, U.S. Ct. Appeals (Fed. cir.) 1988, U.S. Tax Ct. 1988. Practiced in N.Y.C., 1957-72, New Rochelle, N.Y., 1960—; lectr. bus. law Iona Coll., New Rochelle, 1957-59, asst. to pres. for community services, 1959-62. Vice chmn., exec. dir. Iona Coll. Westchester County Law Enforcement Inst.; spl. counsel N.Y. State Temporary Commn. on Child Welfare; mem. Westchester County Youth Adv. Council, 1969-73; mem. Law Enforcement Planning. Agy., New Rochelle, 1968-69; adv. counsel Westchester Police Youth Officers Assn.; mem. Westchester County Child Abuse Task Force; mem. New Rochelle Narcotics Guidance Council, 1972-75; adv. council New Rochelle Salvation Army, 1976-79; legal adviser East-End Civic Assn.; law guardian Westchester County Family Ct.; referee New Rochelle City Ct.; arbitrator Civil Ct., Bronx; arbitrator Supreme and County Ct., Westchester. Bd. dirs. Art Inst., Iona Coll., mem. adv. bd. radio activities, adv. bd. criminal justice Iona Coll., bd. dirs. Westchester County Youth Shelter. Served with AUS, 1942-46. Recipient Patrick B. Doyle award for outstanding service, 1969, William B. Cornelia Founders award, 1976 (both Iona Coll.). Hon. dep. sheriff Westchester County. Mem. Am. (family law sect.), N.Y. State (com. family law, com. family ct.), Bronx County (com. family ct.), Westchester County, New Rochelle Bar assns., Am. Judicature Soc., N.Y. County Lawyers Assn. (family ct. com.), Criminal Cts. Bar Assn. Westchester County, Am. Fedn. Police, Internat. Narcotic Enforcement Officers Assn., Internat. Acad. Criminology, Am. Acad. Polit. and Social Sci., Am. Profl. Soc. on Abuse of Children, Law Guardians Assn. Westchester County (pres.), Am. Psychology-Law Soc., Internat., N.Y. State, Bergen County chiefs of police, Nat. Assn. Council for Children, Nat. Sheriffs Assn., Am. Soc. Internat. Law, Iona Coll. Alumni Assn., Inc. (pres., chmn. bd. dirs. 1958-60, 62-64, 72-74, 74-76, dir. 1954-58, 68-72, 76-86, v.p. 1966-68). Address: 105 Harding Dr New Rochelle NY 10801

MALACH, MONTE, physician; b. Jersey City, Aug. 15, 1926; s. Charles and Yetta (Pascher) M.; m. Ann Elaine Glazer, June 15, 1952; children: Barbara Sandra, Cathie Tara, Matthew David. B.A., U. Mich., 1949, M.D., 1949. Diplomate: Am. Bd. Internal Medicine, Nat. Bd. Med. Examiners. Intern Beth Israel Hosp., Boston, 1949-50; resident Beth Israel Hosp., 1950-51, chief resident, 1951-52; chief resident Kings County Hosp., Bklyn., 1954-55; practice medicine specializing in internal medicine and cardiology Bklyn., 1955—; dir. coronary care unit Bklyn. Hosp., 1965—; pres. profl. staff Bklyn. Hosp., 1966-69, chmn. med. bd., 1971-72; attending staff Caledonian Hosp., pres. profl. staff, 1984-85; pres. profl. staff Bklyn. Hosp.-Caledonian Hosp., 1987—, chmn. med. bd., 1985; cons. Kings County Hosp.; teaching fellow Tufts Med. Sch., 1951-52; instr. medicine Downstate Med. Center, Bklyn., 1955-59, clin. asst. prof. medicine, 1959-68, clin. asso. prof., 1969-76, clin. prof., 1976—; bd. dirs. Bay St. Landing One Owners Corp., 1985—. Kings County committeeman Democratic Party, 1964, 65. Served with USNR, 1944-46, to 1st lt. M.C. U.S. Army, 1952-54. Recipient 1st Prize for Crisis Mgmt. Habitat Mag., 1987. Fellow Am. Coll. Chest Physicians, ACP, Am. Coll. Cardiology; mem. N.Y. Heart Assn., AMA (chmn. sect. council for internal medicine 1980), Am. Soc. Internal Medicine (trustee 1975-79, sec.-treas. 1979—, pres. elect 1981, pres. 1982-83), N.Y. State Soc. Internal Medicine (pres. 1973-74, dir. 1966—, chmn. Bklyn. chpt., v.p. 1971, award of merit 1978), Bklyn. Soc. Internal Medicine (mem. council 1965, pres. 1969-72), Med. Soc. State of N.Y. (chmn. sect. internal medicine 1976), Federated Council for Internal Medicine (chmn. 1979-80), Med. Soc. County Kings (censor 1985—). Address: 55 Rugby Rd Brooklyn NY 11226

MALACHOWSKI, CARLA, investment company executive; b. Southington, Conn., Nov. 26, 1953; d. Carl Raymond and Jeanette Ann (Zoni) Malachowski; m. Frank J. Csencsits, Mar. 20, 1982 (div. 1986); AA, Endicott Jr. Coll., 1973; BA in History, Newton Coll./Boston Coll., 1975. Admissions rep. Katharine Gibbs Sch., Boston, 1977-79, cons., 1981; mgr. sales tng. and devel. Katharine Gibbs Sch. subs. Macmillan Inc., N.Y.C., 1979-81; mgr. mgmt. info. systems Fidelity Investments, Boston, 1982-85, dir. market mgmt., 1985-86, asst. v.p. 1986-88, v.p., 1988—; speaker, panelist profl. assn. Mem. Am. Soc. Tng. and Devel., Nat. Assn. Securities Dealers. Office: Fidelity Investments 82 Devonshire St L12A Boston MA 02109

MALAGON-LONDOÑO, GUSTAVO, orthopedic educator; b. Bogotá, Columbia, July 20, 1930; s. Elías F. and Amelia (Londoño) M.; m. Marina Baquero, Apr. 18, 1959; children: Gustavo, Roberto, Marcela, Claudia. MD, Univ. Javeriana, Bogotá, 1956. Specialist orthopedy and traumatology Hosp. Militar, Bogotá, 1959-64, head emergency div., 1964, head continuous edn., 1965, vice dir., 1975-77; mgr. CORPAL Ministry of Health Colombia, Bogotá, 1969-70; dean, founder Militar Dept. Medicine, Bogotá, 1978-86; pres. Colombian Assn. Med. Schs., Bogotá, 1982-86; prof. Militar U., Bogotá, 1987—; cons. Panamanian Health Orgn., Washington, 1980—, Academia Nacional de Medicina, Bogotá, 1986—, Colombian Assn. Med. Schs., 1986—, Militar Hosp., 1986—. Author: Study to Create Militar School of Medicine, 1977, Community Education, 1985, Attention to Locomotion System Primary Level, 1987. Mem. Ptnrs. of Ams., Miami-Bogotá, 1972—; pres. Assn. Friends of Medical Schs., Bogotá, 1985—. Recipient Jorge Bejarano medal Ministry of Health, 1970, Cross of Boyacá, Republic of Colombia, 1982, Rio Branco Order, Pres. Brazil, 1982, Nat. Acad. Medicine medal, 1986, various others from Govtl. orgns. Mem. Nat. Acad. Medicine (Medal 1986), Am. Acad.Orthopedy, World Acad. Orthopedy, Colombian Soc. Orthopedy, Latin Am. Soc. Orthopedy, Am. Assn. Military Surgeons. Mem. Conservative Party. Roman Catholic. Clubs: Los Lagartos, Militar, Fundación (Bogotá) (trustee 1972—). Home: Calle 108 No 19A-14, Bogata Colombia Office: ASCOFAME, Calle 45A #9-77, 60 piso, Bogota Colombia

MALAN, MAGNUS ANDRE DE MERINDOL, South African minister of defense; b. Pretoria, South Africa, Jan. 30, 1930; student U. Pretoria; m. Margietha Johanna Van der Walt, Feb. 2, 1962; 2 sons, 1 dau. Commd. South African Army, advanced through grades to gen.; comdg. officer S.W. Africa Command, 1966-68; assigned to South African Mil. Acad., 1968-72; comdr. Western Province, 1972-73; chief of Army Staff, 1973; chief of Army, 1973-76; chief of South African Def. Force, 1976-80; minister of def., 1980—; mem. for. Modderfontein constituancy South African Parliament, 1981—. Decorated Star of South Africa, Southern Cross; recipient Pro Patria medal, 1977. Office: Ministry of Def, Private Bag X414, Pretoria 0001 Republic of South Africa *

MALANY, LE GRAND LYNN, lawyer, engineer; b. Chgo., May 14, 1941; s. LeGrand Franklin and Marion (Jaynes) M.; m. Barbara Bumgarner, June 26, 1965; children: LeGrand Karl, Siobhan, Carleen. BS in Engring. Physics, U. Ill., 1964, JD, 1970. Bar: Ill. 1970, U.S. Dist. Ct. (cen. dist.) Ill. 1970, Ill. Supreme Ct., 1970, U.S. Dist. Ct. (so. dist.) Ill. 1974, U.S. Dist. Ct. (no. dist.) Ill. 1981, U.S. Ct. Appeals (7th cir.) 1972, U.S. Supreme Ct. 1975, U.S. Ct. Mil. Appeals 1971; registered profl. engr., Ill.; lic. real estate broker. Asst. astronomer Adler Planetarium, Chgo., 1960-63; research asst. Portland Cement Research Assn., Skokie, Ill., 1964; instr. dept. gen. engring. U. Ill., 1965-70, instr. Office Instrn. Resources, 1967-68, instr. Hwy Traffic Safety Ctr., 1968-69; lectr. Police Tng. Inst., Urbana, Ill., 1969-70; project dir. driver control program U.S. Dept. Transp., 1971-73, project dir., author driver license examiner tng. curriculum, 1973; assoc. drivers license adminstr. State of Ill., Springfield, 1973-74, asst. auditor gen., 1977-83, asst. atty. gen., dir. policy, planning and tech. State of Ill., 1983-85, chief internal auditor office of atty. gen., 1985-86, spl. asst. atty. gen., 1986—, spl. asst. auditor gen. and gen. counsel office of auditor gen., 1986—, gen. counsel state comptroller Cusas II project, 1986—; ptnr. Kabumoto, Lappe and Malany, Springfield, 1986—; pres. Microgeneral Ltd., 1983—, Mgmt. Control Systems, Inc., 1986; chmn. bd. Flowers LaGrand Ltd., 1985—; expert U.S. Fed. Energy Adminstrn., 1974; counsel juvenile div. Circuit Ct., Sangamon County, Ill., 1973-75; chief counsel Ill. Dept. Motor Vehicles, Springfield, 1974. Trustee Meret Center, Inc., 1973-75; Dem. candidate for States Atty., Sangamon County, Ill., 1980. Recipient Midwest Intergovtl. Audit Forum Recognition award, 1981. Mem. ABA, Am. Phys. Soc., Nat., Soc. Profl. Engrs., Ill. Socs. Profl. Engrs., Ill. Farm Bur., Ill. Christmas Tree Growers Assn., Ill. Foster Parents Assn. Lodge: Rotary (Springfield chpt. sec. 1983—, pres. 1986-87). Developer statewide motorcycle driver licensing program. Home: 600 S Rosehill St Springfield IL 62704 Office: 524 S 2d St Springfield IL 62706

MALATESTA, STANLEY ALAN, real estate and mortgage banker; b. Wapakoneta, Ohio, Aug. 26, 1948; s. Leo J. Jr. and Ellen (Kelly) M.; m. Catherine Anne Gardner, June 15, 1974; children: Matthew, Sarah, Ryan. Student, St. Joseph Coll., Ind., 1966-68; BBA, Ohio State U., 1974. With W. Lyman Case & Co. subs. Nat. City Corp., Columbus, Ohio, 1974—, ptnr., 1980-83, v.p., 1983—; sec. Conquest Corp.; co-owner, Congard, Inc., Columbus, Ctl.; instr. fin. Ohio State U. Bd. dirs., pres. Children's Hosp. Devel. Bd. of Columbus. Served with USAF, 1968-72. Mem. Columbus Mortgage Bankers Assn. (past pres., bd. dirs.) Nat. Assn. Indsl. and Office Parks (past pres., bd. dirs. Cen. Ohio chpt., v.p. Ohio chpt. 1985-86), Ohio Mortgage Bankers Assn. (past bd. dirs.), Ohio Assn. Realtors, Columbus Bd. Realtors. Republican. Roman Catholic. Clubs: Athletic of Columbus; Scioto Country (Upper Arlington, Ohio). Home: 2667 Sandover Rd Upper Arlington OH 43220 Office: 55 Nationwide Blvd Suite 200 Columbus OH 43215

MALAURIE, JEAN LEONARD, anthropo/geographer; b. Mainz, Ger., Dec. 22, 1922; s. Albert and Isabelle (Regnault) M.; m. Monique Laporte, Dec. 27, 1951; children—Guillaume, Eleonore. Dr. es lettres, U. Paris. Attaché, then research fellow Nat. Ctr. Sci. Research, 1948-56, mem. nat. com. geography, 1955-67, 80—; prof. Arctic geomorphology and anthropo/geography Ecole des Hautes Etudes, Sorbonne, 1957-79, 82—; founder, 1957, since dir. Ctr. Arctic Studies, Nat. Sci. Ctr. Research, dir. Arctic research, 1979—; pres. Fond Francaise d'Etudes Nordiques, 1957-75, Société Arctique Francaise, 1981—, Inter-Nord, Internat. Jour. Arctic Studies, 1963—; chmn. Polar geography commn. Com. Nat. Geography, 1974—; chmn. 12 Arctic internat. congresses, chmn. dels. internat. meetings. Founder-dir. anthrop. serie: Terre Humaine, 1955; author: The Hoggar, 1953, The Last Kings of Thule, 1955 (transl. into 16 langs.), Thèmes de recherches geomorphologiques dan le N.O. du Groenland, 1968, Les Civilisations Esquimaudes: Essai d'Anthropo/Geography, 1975; 9 films. Contbr. 200 articles to profl. jours. Recipient Polar medal Soc. Geographie, 1953, 71, award Ordre Merite 1982 Acad. des Scis., 1967, Acad. Francaise, 1968, LÈgion d'Honneur, 1987. Mem. Academie de Rouen.

MALAVAUD, ANDRE PIERRE, intensive care physician; b. Blida, Algiers, France, Jan. 10, 1928; s. Fernand Francois and Renée Suzanne (Pelage) M.; m. Madeleine Laure Francais, Dec. 29, 1952; children: René-Pierre, Jean-Christian, Pierre-André, Jacques-Louis. MD, Algiers U., 1957, cert. anesthesiology, 1959. Houseman Civilian Hosp., Oran, Algeria, France, 1953-57, resident in anesthesiology, 1957-60, fellow in anesthesiology, 1960-62; fellow in anesthesiology Civilian Hosp., Tolone, France, 1962-72, chief anesthesiologist, 1972-73; intensive care chief Gen. Hosp., Tolone, France, 1973—; clinic teaching asst. Marseilles (France) Med. U., 1977-79, clinic teaching dir. 1979-81; clinic teaching asst.eNice (France) Med. U., 1977-79, clinic teaching dir. 1979-81. Editor: Rein et Anesthesie Reanimation, 1969, Maladie Thrombo-Embolique Post-Operative, 1973; contbr. multiple articles and papers on anesthesiology and intensive care to profl. jours. Founder France-USA Assn., Tolone, 1967. Mem. Societé Francaise d' Anesthesis-Réanimation, Societé Française d' Anesthesis-Réanimation Adminstrv., World Fedn. Anesthesiologist Societies (French delegate), Assn. des Medecins Catholiques. Roman Catholic. Home: Ave Bellegarde, 83100 Tolone France Office: Cen Hospitalier Gen, Rue Colonel Picot, 83056 Tolone France

MALCOLM, JOHN GRANT, government official; b. Missoula, Mont., Apr. 15, 1941; s. Grant and June (Smith) M.; m. Sharon Lee McDonald, 1960; children: Lynn Conrad Linda Kim. BA with honors, U. Md., 1970, MBA, 1971. Sales rep. Olivetti Corp., Washington, 1971-72; mgmt. analyst USPHS, Washington, 1972-78; chief, Mgmt. Systems Div. Nat. Hwy. Traffic Safety Adminstrn., U.S. Dept. Transp., 1978-79; printing officer Dept. HHS, Washington, 1979—; v.p. Mgmt. Factors Orgn., McLean, Va.; pres. Puffin Projects, Silver Spring, Md.; lectr. U. Md., 1975—. Bd. dirs. World Nature Assn., King Realty. Served with U.S. Army, 1960-68. Def. Dept. fellow, 1970-71. Mem. Am. Mktg. Assn., Am. Mgmt. Assn., World Future Soc., Am. Ornithology Union, Md. Ornithol. Assn. (bd. dirs.) Episcopalian. Office: US HHS 200 Independence Ave SW Room 514G Washington DC 20201

MALCOLMSON, RICHARD DONALD, business executive; b. Colac, Victoria, Australia, Feb. 24, 1926; s. Arthur Richard and Rose Gillies (Miller) M.; m. Dorothy Anne Parker, June 28, 1967; children—Sophie Elizabeth, Charles Richard. B.S. with honors in Physics, U. Melbourne, 1946; B.S. ad eundum gradum, U. Queensland, 1950. Asst. lectr. physics, U. Queensland, Brisbane, Australia, 1948-50; various positions in explosives, textiles, personnel, ICI Australia Ltd., Melbourne, 1951-77, gen. mgr. Nobel Group, 1978-79, exec. dir., 1980-86; chmn. ICI Fiji Ltd., 1982-85, ICI Papua New Guinea P/L, 1982-85; dir. Incitec Ltd., Brisbane, 1982-86, chmn., 1984-86; dir. Lloyds Bank NZA Ltd., Beneficial Fin. Group, Woodmason's Ltd.; dep. chmn. Spencer Stuart & Assocs., 1986—. Pres. Internat. Social Service, Melbourne, 1959-66; chmn. Victorian Com. for World Refugee Yr., 1959-60; chmn. appeal Nat. Gallery and Cultural Centre, 1960-61; pres. Nat. Gallery Soc. Victoria, 1962-63; exec. com. Australian Conservation Found., 1965-73; mem. bd. studies Victoria Inst. Colls., 1969-74; exec. council of trustees World Wildlife Fund Australia, 1978-88, pres., 1984-88; mem. Land Conservation Council Victoria, 1986—. Decorated mem. Order Brit. Empire. Fellow Australian Inst. Mgmt. (councillor 1978—, pres. Victoria div. 1981-83, dep. nat. pres. 1984-85, pres. 1986-88); mem. Inst. Personnel Mgmt. Australia, Inst. Physics U.K., Australian Inst. Physics. Clubs: Melbourne, Royal Melbourne Golf. Home: 21 Hill St, Toorak, Victoria 3142, Australia

MALEC OLOVSON, ELZBIETA TERESA, plastic surgeon; b. Krakow, Poland, July 8, 1932; went to Sweden, 1958; d. Franciszek and Flora (Sobierajski) Malec; m. Thore Gudmar Olovson, 1966. Grad. Med. Acad., Krakow, 1955; grad. Karolinska Inst., Stockholm, 1963, Specialist in Plastic Surgery, 1971, Ph.D., 1978. Asst. Inst. Anatomy, Krakow, 1953-58; resident Surg. Clin., City Hosp., Krakow, 1955-58; vol. asst. Karolinska Hosp., St. Göran's Hosp., Stockholm, 1958-59; resident plastic surgeon Betania Hosp., Stockholm, 1959-63, Ersta Sjukhus, Stockholm, 1963-68; resident Plastic Surg. Clinic, Karolinska Hosp., 1968—. Contbr. articles on plastic surgery and malignant melanoma epidemiology to profl. jours. Mem. Swedish Assn. Plastic Surgons, Internat. Confederation for Plastic and Reconstructive Surgery, Scandinavian Assn. Plastic Surgeons, Swedish Soc. Medicine, Royal Soc. Medicine (affiliate). Club: Zonta (Stockholm) (v.p. 1978-80). Home: Lilla Erstagatan 4, 116-35 Stockholm Sweden Office: Karolinska Hosp Univ Hosp, Plastic Surgery Clinic, 104-01 Stockholm Sweden also: Brahegatan 52, 114 37 Stockholm Sweden

MALEK, GUSTAVO, science association administrator; b. Buenos Aires, Argentina, Mar. 29, 1929; s. Agustin and Ester (Szana) M.; m. Esther Mercedes Perramón, Mar. 8, 1956; children: Alejandro, Marcelo, Patricio, Carolina, Andrés. D of Chemistry, U. Nacional del Sur, Bahia Blanca, Argentina, 1955. Assoc. prof., then prof. ind. chemistry U. Nacional del Sur, Bahía Blanca, 1955-70, gen. acad. sec., 1968-70, rector, 1970-71; minister Govt. of Argentina Dept. of Culture and Edn., Buenos Aires, 1971-73; internat. coordinator UN Devel. Program/UNESCO Projects, Bogotá, Colombia, 1973-76; dir. Regional Office for Sci. and Tech. in Latin Am. and Caribbean UNESCO, Montevideo, Uruguay, 1976—. Contbr. articles to profl. jours. Recipient awards from Govt. Brazil, Govt. Italy and Govt. Venezuela, 1971, 73, Golden medal Argentina Assn. Textile Chemistry, 1968, Golden medal Orgn. de los Estados IberoAmericanos, 1987. Office: UNESCO Office Sci/Tech in Latin, Am/Caribbean Blvd Artigas 1320, Montevideo Uruguay

MALEK, MARLENE ANNE, nurse, foundation executive; b. Oakland, Calif., June 22, 1939; d. William Alexander and Yolanda Katherine (Stella) McArthur; m. Frederic Vincent Malek, Aug. 5, 1961; children: Frederic William, Michelle Ann. AA, Armstrong U., 1959; AS in Nursing, Marymount U., 1979; cert. in hospice tng., Arlington, Va., 1980. Dir. Psychiat. Inst. Found., Washington, 1982—; women's bd. Am. Heart Assn., 1973—, bd. treas., 1983—, chmn. ann. luncheon, 1988. Bd. dirs. Nat. Fed. Rep. Women, Washington, 1972-74, Marymount U. Va., Arlington, 1974— ; chmn. Eisenhower Meml. Found., Washington, 1972-74; cons. hospitality Presdl. Inaugural Com., Washington, 1984; mem. adv. bd. Second Genesis Drug Rehab. Program, Bethesda, Md., 1983—, chmn. Second Genesis Benefit, 1968, 84-85; founding mem. Arena Stage Guild, Washington; bd. dirs. Nat. Mus. Women in Arts, 1987, Claude Moore Colonial Farm, 1986. Episcopalian. Avocations: skiing, collecting antiques, painting, running.

MALEK, NICOLAS GEORGE, electrical, instrumentation and control company executive; b. Tripoli, Lebanon, Aug. 2, 1947; came to U.S., 1966; s. George Antoine and Yvonne (Abboud) M.; m. Marian S. Moses, July 17, 1971; children—Nicole B., George N., Sean N. B.S. in Elec. Engring., La. State U., 1970, M.S., 1972. Registered profl. engr., La. Elec. and instrumentation engr. Barnard & Burk, Baton Rouge, La., 1969-73; sect. head engring. and instrumentation C.F. Bean, New Orleans, 1973-75; asst. mgr. Bean/Volker, Jubail, Saudi Arabia, 1975-78; mgr. engring. Bean Dredging, New Orleans, 1978-79; mgr. elec., instrumentation and controls div. Walk, Haydel & Assocs., New Orleans, 1979—. Mem. Instrumenta Soc. Am. (sr.), IEEE (sr.), La. Engring. Soc., Friends of Zoo, YMCA, Nat. Law Enforcement Assn., Tau Beta Pi, Eta Kappa Nu, Phi Kappa Phi. Republican. Greek Orthodox. Home: 2101 Butternut Ave Metairie LA 70001 Office: Walk Haydel & Assocs 600 Carondelet St New Orleans LA 70130

MALEKZADEH, REZA, gastroenterologist, educator; b. Kazerun, Iran, Jan. 15, 1952; parents: Javad and Soghra; m. Azam Malekzadeh; children: Fatemeh, Zinab. MD, Shiraz U., Iran. Diplomate Bd. Internal Medicine, Bd. Gastroenterology. Resident Shiraz U., 1979-82, asst. prof. dept. medicine, 1982—, vice chancellor, 1982-83, chancellor, 1983-87. Contbr. articles to profl. jours. Mem. Iranian Med. Orgn., Iranian Bd. Internal Medicine. Home: Motthari St, Kocheh Nemazee Shiraz Iran Office: Shiraz U Med Sch, Dept Medicine Hosp No 9, Shiraz Iran

MALERBA, LUIGI, author; b. Berceto, Parma, Italy, Nov. 11, 1927; s. Pietro and Maria Olari; m. Anna Lapenna, 1962; 2 children. Ed. Liceo Classico Romagnosi di Parma and Faculty Law, U. Parma. Dir. rev. Sequenze, 1948-51; advt. mgr. rev. Discoteca, 1956-60, editor, 1960-65. Author: La scoperta dell' alfabeto, 1963, Il Serpente (premio Selezione Campiello), 1966, Salto mortale (Premio Sila, French prix Medicis for best non-French novel), 1968; (with Tonino Guerra, illustrations by Adriano Zannino) Storie dell'Anno Mille, 1969-71; Il Protagonista, 1973, Le rose Imperiali, 1974, Mozziconi, 1975, Storiette, 1977, Le parole abbandonate, 1977, Pinocchio con gli stivali, 1977, Il pataffio, 1978, C'era una vola la cittá di Luni, 1978, La storia e la gloria, 1979, Dopo il pescecane, 1979, Le galline pensierose, 1980, Diario di un sognatore, 1981, Storiette tascabili, 1984, Cina Cina, 1985, Il pianeta azzurro, 1986 (Premio Mondello 1987), Testa d'argento, 1988; TV film: Ai poeti non si spara (Internat. TV Festival of Monte Carlo Golden Nymph award, 1966).

MALERCZYK, VITUS GERHARD, mathematician, biometrician; b. Wiesbaden, Fed. Republic of Germany, Oct. 17, 1940; s. Wilhelm Josef and Dorothea Maria (Nieslon) M.; m. Katharina Kosfeld; children: Claudius, Cornelius, Corinna, Clarissa. Diploma, U. Kiel, Federal Republic Germany, 1966. Systems analyst Computer Ctr. U. Kiel, 1966-68; head computer ops. Children's Hosp., U. Kiel Med. Sch., 1968-79; sr. biometrician in clin. research Hoechst A.G., Frankfurt, Federal Republic Germany, 1979—; cons. Biologica, Hofheim, Federal Republic Germany, 1976—. Contbr. articles to sci. jours. Mem. Mathematicians in Pharm. Industry, Paul Ehrlich Soc. Home: Rheingaustrasse 41, D6238 Hofheim Federal Republic of Germany

MALETTKE, KLAUS LUDWIG GUSTAV, modern history educator; b. Rastenburg, Prussia, Germany, May 30, 1936; s. Karl and Margarete (Baecker) M.; m. Waltraut E. Suthoff-Gross, July 23, 1965; 1 dau., Nicole Mariette. B.A., Castrop-Rauxel, 1956; Brevet de Langue Francaise, U. Dijon (France), 1958; Ph.D., Philipps-U. Marburg, Hessen, 1965. Asst., Free U. Berlin, 1965-69, asst. prof., 1969-71, prof., 1971-80; prof. Philipps-U. Marburg, Hessen, Fed. Republic Germany, 1980—. Author: Opposition to Louis XIV, 1976; Jean-Baptiste Colbert, 1977; editor: Venality of Offices, 1980; Social and Political Conflicts in France during the Ancient Regime, 1982; Nationalsocialism in Power, 1984; contbr. articles on French modern history to profl. jours. Mem. Soc. Constitutional History, Sci. Soc. Berlin, Hist. Commn. Berlin, Hist. Commn. Hessen, German Inst. History in Paris (mem. council bd. 1984). Home: Pappelweg 28, Marburg/Lahn, D-3550 Marburg, Hessen Federal Republic of Germany Office: Philipps U Fachbereich Geschichtswissenschaften, Wilhelm-Roepke-Str 6C, Marburg/Lahn, D-3550 Marburg, Hessen Federal Republic of Germany

MALEY, CHARLES DAVID, lawyer; b. Highland Park, Ill., Aug. 18, 1924; s. Lyle West and Irene (Davis) M.; A.B., State U. Iowa, 1948; J.D., De Paul U., 1952; m. Mildred J. Tobin, Apr. 27, 1957; 1 dau., Annabel Irene. Bar: Ill. 1952, U.S. Cir. Ct. (7th cir.) Ill., U.S. Supreme Ct. 1956. Assoc. firm Friedlund, Levin & Friedlund, Chgo., 1952-58; pvt. practice law, Chgo., 1958-68, Lake Bluff, Ill., 1966-72, Lake Forest, Ill., 1972-83; mem. firm Ori, Tepper, Fox & Maley, Waukegan, Ill., 1983—; pub. adminstr. Lake County, 1971-74. Asst. dist. commr. Boy Scouts Am., 1963-65; trustee Lake County Mus. Assn., 1978-79, Lake Forest-Lake Bluff Hist. Soc., 1979-81; bd. dirs. Petite Ballet, 1975-80. Mem. Lake County Republican Central Com., 1967-72, 76-88, Rep. State Com., 1971-74; bd. govs. Lake County Rep. Fedn., 1980-83. Served with AUS, 1943-46. Decorated Purple Heart with oak leaf cluster, Bronze Star. Mem. ABA, Chgo., Lake County bar assns., SAR, Am. Legion (post comdr. 1967-68, 74-81, service officer 1968-69, adj. 1982-84, chaplain 1984-86), Am. Arbitration Assn. (mem. panel 1965-67), Phi Gamma Delta, Phi Alpha Delta. Republican. Presbyterian. Clubs: Capitol

Hill (Washington); Tower (Chgo.). Home: 241 W Washington St Lake Bluff IL 60044 Office: 301 W Washington St Suite 100 Waukegan IL 60085

MALHERBE, BERNARD, surgeon; b. Rethel, France, Apr. 9, 1930; s. Maurice Eugene and Marguerite Elise (Drapier) M.; m. Camille Redon, May 10, 1952; children—Chantal, Philippe, Magali. MD, U. Paris, 1962. Intern, Paris Hosp.; resident in surgery various hosps.; clinic chief Hosp. Pitie-Salpetaient, Paris, 1962; mem. med. faculty U. Paris, 1962—; surgeon Clinic Leonardo da Vinci, Paris, 1970—; pres. Coll. Med. L'Hospitalisation Privee. Served to lt. French Air Force, 1956-58. Roman Catholic. Lodge: Lions. Home: 12 rue Felicien David, 75016 Paris France Office: Clinique Leonard da Vinci, Ave Parmentier 95, 75011 Paris France

MALHOTRA, IQBAL CHAND, management consultant; b. Bombay, May 6, 1956; s. Romesh Chand and Sarla (Bhagat) M. BA with honors in Econs., Shriram Coll. Commerce, 1976; BA, Queen's Coll., Cambridge, Eng., 1979, MA, 1983. Researcher Mr. P.N. Handa, fin. advisor, New Delhi, India, 1976-77; with Arthur Andersen & Co. div. MCS, London, 1979-80; cons. advisor Comml. Cable Co., Ltd., London, 1980; cons. A.F. Ferguson & Co. div. MS, New Delhi, 1980-82; dir. Amalgamated Cons. Unit, New Delhi, 1982—; advisor The Sudan Nat. Oil Co., Khartoum, Sudan, 1985, Societe Marocaine des Industrialisation d'Petrole, Rabat, Morocco, 1987; cons. Internat. Labour Orgn., New Delhi, 1987—. Author: Stockton International Business Report-India, 1985; editor: Stockton International Business Reports on Asia, 1985. Election agt. Janata Party, New Delhi, 1977. Wrenbury scholar Cambridge U., 1979; Found. scholar Queen's Coll., 1979. Hindu. Clubs: Willingdon (Bombay); Delhi Gymkhana (Delhi). Office: Amalgamated Cons Unit, Malhotra Bldg, F-46 Connaught Pl, New Delhi 110011, India

MALHOTRA, MAHARAJ KRISHEN, psychologist, educator; b. Mirpur, India, Nov. 2, 1926; arrived in Fed. Republic Germany, 1952; s. Harkishen Lal and Kaushalaya Rani (Kapur) M.; m. Donja Elisabeth Ludenia, Dec. 30, 1958; children: Ralph, Armin. MA in Psychology, Panjab (India) U., 1948, MA in Philosophy, 1950; PhD, Berlin Free U., 1955. Postdoctoral research scholar Berlin Free U., 1956-60; head fgn. dept. Donors Assn. for German Sci., Essen, 1960-67; asst. Essen Med. Coll., 1967-69; lectr. psychology Ruhr U. Edn., Dortmund/Duisburg, 1969-72; prof. psychology Wuppertal (Fed. Republic Germany) Bergian U., 1972—. Editor: The Scientific and Academic World, 1962, Scientific and Academic Life in the Federal Republic of Germany, 1963; contbr. articles to profl. jours. Mem. German Psychol. Soc. Home: Daimlerstrasse 10, D-4300 Essen 1 Federal Republic of Germany Office: Wuppertal Bergain U, Gaussstrasse 20 S 12 07, D-5600 Wuppertal 1 Federal Republic of Germany

MALIETOA TANUMAFILI, II, head of state Independent State of Western Samoa; b. Jan. 4, 1913; ed. Wesley Coll., Pukehohe, New Zealand; married; 5 children. Adv., Samoan Govt., 1940; mem. New Zealand del. to UN, 1958; former mem. Council of State; joint head of state of Western Samoa, 1962-63, sole head of state, 1963—; fautua of Maliena. Decorated comdr. Order Brit. Empire. *

MALIK, ABDUL KARIM, medical officer; b. Jammu, Kashmir, Pakistan, Feb. 17, 1909; s. Mohammad Ramzan and Roshan Ara Begum Malik; m. Ahmad Bibi, 1929; children: Imtinan Elahi, Farrukh Shaheen. BSc, U. Punjab, Pakistan, 1932, Lic. state med. faculty, 1936; diploma in X-ray and Electrotheraphy, G.T. Hosp., Bombay, 1939. With X-ray dept. S.G.S. Hosp., Jammu, 1943-47; with T.B. Hosp., Sialkot, Pakistan, 1950-53; health officer Municipality of Sialkot, 1953-54; chief med. officer Jammu Meml. Hosp., Sialkot, 1954—. Author: Allopathy, Patent Medicines, Message of Health, An Ideal Physician, Astronomy, The March of Life, The Conquest of Nature, Search for Reality, others; chief editor Urdu Monthly, 1972. V.p. Pakistan Peoples Party, Sialkot City. Recipient Citation, WHO, Cert. Appreciation local Pakistani govt. authorities. Mem. Pakistan Med. Assn. Lodge: Masons (master Wahab lodge). Home: 9 Civil Lines, Pak-Pura, Sialkot Punjab Pakistan

MALIK, JAVAID MAHMOOD, industrial engineer; b. Lahore, Punjab, Pakistan, July 27, 1949; arrived in Saudi Arabia, 1980.; s. Abdul Rahman and Manzoor (Fatima) M.; m. Shamaila Javaid, Apr. 5, 1975; children: Faisal, Yasir, Mahwash, Fahd, Shuaib. BS, Punjab U., 1969, M of Adminstrv Sci, 1973. Ops. and mgmt. analysis U. Punjab, Lahore, 1973-74; area sales mgr. 7-Up Bottling Co., Ltd., Lahore, 1974-75; ops. and mgmt. officer, indsl. engring. officer Pakistan Internat. Airlines, Karachi, 1975-80; indsl. engr. Saudi Arabian Airlines, Jeddah, 1980—. Mem. Am. Inst. Indsl. Engrs. (sr.). Home: SE 4-11 A Saudia City, Jeddah 21231, Saudi Arabia

MALIK, ROBERT KEVIN, financial services company official; b. New York City, Dec. 8, 1942; s. Robert and Sylvia Malik; m. Georgette Cullen, Sept. 10, 1966; children: Robert, Lisa. BBA, Hofstra U., 1971; MS in Computer Sci., Pratt Inst., 1982; postgrad. in exec. mgmt., Pa. State U., 1987. Analyst Allied Chemical Corp., N.Y.C., 1966-69; cons. Mobil Oil Corp., N.Y.C., 1969-73; dir. W.R. Grace & Co., N.Y.C., 1973-76; v.p. data processing Md. Nat. Bank, Balt., 1976-78; mgr. Touche Ross & Co., Washington, 1978-83; dir. group ins. systems Cigna Corp., Hartford, Conn., 1980-83, asst. v.p. systems, 1983-85; v.p. corp. fin. and investment groups systems div. Travelers Corp., Hartford, 1985-87; v.p. corp. tech. The Travelers Cos., Hartford, 1987-88, v.p. corp. tech. and agy. mktg. group property and casualty group, 1988—; tchr. computer sci U. Hartford, 1982, exec. mgmt. program Pa. State U.; mem. MIT Enterprise Forum. Chmn. United Way Campaign, 1983-84. Republican. Roman Catholic. Home: 38 Copplestone Avon CT 06001 Office: Travelers Corp Corp Fin and Investment Groups Systems Div Hartford CT 06152

MALIN, HOWARD GERALD, podiatrist; b. Providence, Dec. 2, 1941; s. Leon Nathan and Rena Rose (Shapiro) M. A.B., U. R.I., 1964; M.A., Brigham Young U., 1969; B.Sc., Calif. Coll. Podiatric Medicine, 1969, D.P.M., 1972; M.Sc., Pepperdine U., 1978; postgrad. in classic, U. So. Calif., 1983—. Diplomate: diplomate Am. Bd. Podiatric Orthopedics. Extern in podiatry VA Med. Ctr., Wadsworth, Kans., 1971-72, Marine Corps Res. Dept., San Diego, 1972; resident in podiatric medicine and surgery N.Y. Coll. Podiatric-Medicine, N.Y.C., 1972-73; resident in podiatric surgery, instr. in podiatric surgery N.Y. Coll. Podiatric Medicine, N.Y.C., 1973-74; pvt. practitioner in podiatric medicine and surgery Bklyn., 1974-77; mem. staff Prospect Hosp., Bronx, N.Y., 1974-77; chief podiatry service, mem. staff David Grant U.S. Air Force Med. Ctr., Travis AFB, Calif., 1977-80; chief podiatric sect., mem. staff VA Med. Ctr., Martinsburg, W.Va., 1980—; cons. podiatric sports medicine David Grant USAF Med. Ctr., Travis AFB, Calif., 1977-80; instr. ednl. devel. program VA Med. Ctr., Martinsburg, W.Va., 1981—; clin. prof. med. sci. Alderson-Broaddus Coll; clin. assoc. prof. U. Osteopathic Medicine and Health Scis. Editorial rev. bd.: Archives Podiatric Medicine and Foot Surgery, 1978-80, Jour. Current Podiatric Medicine. Served to capt. USAF, 1977-80. Fellow Am. Coll. Foot Orthopedics, Am. Soc. Podiatric Medicine, Am. Soc. Podiatric Dermatology, Am. Assn. Hosp. Podiatrists; mem. Am. Acad. Podiatric Sports Medicine (assoc.), Assn. Mil. Surgeons U.S. (life), Phi Kappa Theta, Phi Kappa Psi. Lodge: Masons. Office: care VA Med Ctr Dept Podiatry Martinsburg WV 25401

MALIN, IRVING, English educator, literary critic; b. N.Y.C., Mar. 18, 1934; s. Morris and Bertha (Silverman) M.; m. Ruth Lief, Dec. 18, 1955; 1 child, Mark. B.A., Queens Coll., 1955; Ph.D., Stanford U., 1958. Acting instr. English Stanford U., 1955-58; instr. English Ind. U., 1958-60; instr. English Coll. City N.Y., 1960-63, asst. prof., 1964-68, asso. prof. English, 1969-72, prof., 1972—; cons. Jewish Publ. Soc., 1964, Am. Quar., 1964, Nat. Endowment for Humanities, 1972, 79, 80, B'nai B'rith, 1974-75, Yaddo, 1975-77, Jewish Book Council, 1976, 79, PEN, 1978-82, Princeton U. Press, 1979, Fairleigh Dickinson Press, 1980, Wayne State U. Press, 1980, Internat. Council Exchange of Scholars, 1980-81, NEH, 1981, 82, Duke U. Press, 1981, Jewish Daily Forward, 1981, U. Pitts. Press, 1981, Papers on Lang. and Lit., 1981, U. Ga. Press, 1983, Edward Lewis Wallant award, 1985—, MacArthur Found., 1986, So. Ill., 1988. Author: William Faulkner: An Interpretation, 1957, New American Gothic, 1962, Jews and Americans, 1965, Saul Bellow's Fiction, 1969, Nathanael West's Novels, 1972, Isaac Bashevis Singer, 1972; Co-editor: Breakthrough: A Treasury of Contemporary American Jewish Literature, 1964, William Styron's The Confessions of Nat Turner: A Critical Handbook, 1970, The Achievement of William Styron, 1975; Editor: Psychoanalysis and American Fiction, 1965, Saul Bellow and the Critics, 1967, Truman Capote's In Cold Blood: A Critical Handbook, 1968, Critical Views of Isaac Bashevis Singer, 1969, Contemporary American-Jewish Literature: Critical Essays, 1973, Conrad Aiken's Prose, 1982; adv. editor: Studies in American Jewish Literature, 1982, Saul Bellow Newsletter, 20th Century Literature; reviewer: Newsday, Rev. Contemporary Fiction, Hollins Critic; co-editor Paul Bowles, 1986, Spl. Issue of 20th Century Lit. fellow Yaddo, 1963; fellow Nat. Found. for Jewish Culture, 1963-64; fellow Huntington Library, 1978. Mem. MLA, Am. Studies Assn., Am. Jewish Hist. Soc., Melville Soc., PEN (cons. 1978-79), Authors League Am., Soc. for Study So. Lit., AAUP, Poe Studies Assn., English Inst., Nathaniel Hawthorne Soc., N.Y. Acad. Scis., AAAS, Poetry Soc. Am., Popular Culture Assn., Nat. Book Critics Circle, Sherwood Anderson Soc., Internat. Assn. Univ. Profs. English, Kafka Soc., English-Speaking Union, Multi-Ethnic Lit. U.S. Soc., Hastings Center, Am. Jewish Congress, Phi Beta Kappa. Jewish. Home: 96-13 68th Ave Forest Hills NY 11375 Office: Coll City NY New York NY 10031

MALJERS, FLORIS ANTON, manufacturing company executive; b. Aug. 12, 1933; s. A.C.J. Maljers and L.M. Maljers-Kole; m. J.H. Maljers-de-Jongh, 1958; 2 sons. Student, U. Amsterdam. With Unilever, 1959—; mng. dir. Unilever-Columbia, 1965-67, Unilever-Turkey, 1967-70; chmn. Unilever NV; also vice-chmn. Unilever plc, 1984—; chmn. Van den Bergh and Jurgens, Netherlands, 1970-74; co-ordinator mgmt. group edible fats and dairy, Unilever, 1974; mem. Unilever's spl. com. 1982—. Office: 34 Cadogan Pl, London SW1, England *

MALLAMS, JOHN THOMAS, physician, educator; b. Ashland, Pa., Aug. 29, 1923; s. Raymond E. and Elizabeth (Bevan) M.; student Lafayette Coll., 1941-43; M.D., Temple U., 1946; m. Ruth Carolyn Smith, June 21, 1945; children—David John, John Harry, Faith Ann. Intern USN Hosp., Phila., 1946-47, resident radiology, 1946-47; fellow radiology Robert Packer Hosp. and Guthrie Clinic, 1950-51; Am. Cancer Soc. fellow clin. radiation therapy Frances Delafield Hosp., Columbia Presbyn. Med. Center, 1951-52; practice medicine, specializing in radiology, Houston, 1952-54, Dallas, 1954-68; asst. prof. radiology Coll. Medicine, Baylor U., Houston, 1952-54, dir. Irradiation Therapy and Tumor Clinics, Baylor Med. Center, Dallas, 1954-66, dir. Sammons Research div., 1954-68, prof. radiotherapy Baylor Coll. Dentistry, 1966-68; prof. radiology Southwestern Med. Sch. U. Tex., Dallas, 1966-68; prof. clin. radiology Yale U. Med. Sch. New Haven, 1968-70; prof., Coll. Medicine and Dentistry N.J., N.J. Med. Sch., 1970-85, emeritus prof., 1985—, chmn. dept. radiology, 1970-82, asso. dean patient services, 1971-72; disting. cons. radiology oncology Baylor U. Health Scis. Ctr., Dallas, 1986—; scientific dir. Mary C. Crowley Research Found., Baylor Research Found., Dallas; attending radiotherapist Yale U.-New Haven Med. Center, 1968-70. Served with USNR, 1942-50. Fellow Am. Coll. Radiology; mem. Tex. Radiol. Soc. (past pres.). Am. Radium Soc., Am. Club Therapeutic Radiologists, Am. Roentgen Ray Soc., Radiol. Soc. N.Am., Am. Assn. Cancer Research. Radiation Research Soc., Am. Cancer Soc. (past pres. Dallas County unit), Essex County Med. Soc., Phi Beta Pi. Methodist. Clubs: Masons (32 deg.), Shriners. Contbr. articles profl. jours. Home: B503 1860 N Atlantic Ave Cocoa Beach FL 32931

MALLARAPU, MUNIDRISHNA REDDY, demographer; b. Tirupati, India, Jan. 1, 1952; s. Ranga Reddy Mallarapu; m. Nagamani Mallarapu, Feb. 29, 1980; 2 children. MA in Sociology, S.V. U., Tirupati, 1976, diploma in Population Studies, 1977, M. of Philosophy in Population Studies, 1980, PhD in Social Anthropology, 1986. Prin. investigator Population Research Ctr. Andhra U., Visakhapatnamu, India, 1983—; advisor on population edn., 1983—. Contbr. articles to profl. jours. Mem. Indian Assn. For the Study of Population. Office: Andhra U, Population Research Ctr, Visakhapatnamu 530 003, India

MALLARY, RAYMOND DEWITT, lawyer; b. Lenox, Mass., Oct. 5, 1898; s. R. DeWitt and Lucy (Walker) M.; m. Gertrude Slater Robinson, Sept. 15, 1923; children: R. DeWitt, Richard Walker. A.B., Dartmouth Coll.,, 1921; J.D., Harvard U., 1924. Bar: Mass. 1924, Vt. 1953. Partner Wooden, Small & Mallary, 1924-31, Mallary & Gilbert, 1931-51; pvt. practice, counsel to Richardson, Dibble & Atkinson, Springfield, Mass., 1951-56, Bulkley, Richardson, Godfrey & Burbank, 1956-64, Wilson, Keyser and Otterman, Chelsea and Bradford, Vt., 1961-63, Otterman & Allen, Bradford, Vt., 1965-70; dir., mem. exec. com. Mass. Mut. Life Ins. Co., 1944-73, Cen. Vt. Pub. Service Corp, 1959-80; ptnr. Mallary Farm; dir. mem. audit com. Vt. Electric Power Co., 1973-84; numerous other directorships. Chmn. bd. selectmen Town of Fairlee, Vt., 1953-57, moderator, 1972-76, mem. planning bd., 1983—; chmn. Orange County Tax Appeal Bd., 1964-65; Vt. mem. New Eng. Govs. Com. on Pub. Transp., 1955—; dir. Conn. River Watershed Council, Inc., 1977; trustee emeritus Am. Internat. Coll., Hitchcock Found.; trustee Eastern States Expn., 1942—, chmn. exec. com. 1943-53, pres. 1953-58, chmn. bd. 1958-68, hon. chmn. bq. 1968—, dir. chmn. Vt. trustees, 1975—; past bd. dirs. Springfield Family Welfare Assn.; chmn. Springfield Bd. Pub. Welfare, 1931-34; numerous other directorships. Served with U.S. Army, 1918, capt. Res. ret. Recipient citations for outstanding service North Atlantic region Future Farmers Am., 1963, U. Conn. Coll. Agrl. Extension Service, 4-H 1965; achievement award Internat. Assn. Fairs and Expns., 1960; co-recipient Master Breeder's award Vt. Holstein-Friesian Assn., 1979. Mem. New Eng. Fellowship Agrl. Adventurers, Holstein-Friesian Assn. Am. (dir., mem. exec. com. 1957-64, pres., mem. exec. com. 1967-69), ABA, Vt. Bar Assn., Hampden County Bar Assn., Orange County Bar Assn., New Eng. States Holstein Friesian Assn. (pres. 1943-46, dir. 1946-49), Purebred Dairy Cattle Assn. Am. (past pres. and dir.), Am. Legion, Psi Upsilon. Club: Dartmouth (past pres. Hanover area); Exchange (past pres. Springfield).). Home: Mallary Farm Bradford VT 05033 Office: Bradford VT 05033

MALLATT, MARK EDWARD, dental researcher and educator, consulting clinical examiner; b. Gary, Ind., July 6, 1950; s. Russell Clayton and Marjorie May (Hoagl) M.; m. Kathleen Ann Quill, Aug. 21, 1976. B.S., Ind. U., 1972, D.D.S., 1975. Clin. research assoc. Oral Health Research Inst., Indpls., 1975-77, assoc. dir. clin. research, 1978—; instr. Ind. U. Sch. Dentistry, 1977-78, asst. prof. preventive dentistry, 1978-87, assoc. prof., 1987—; cons. clin. examiner for pvt. industry, Ind., Ohio, Tex., Can., 1977—. Pvt. industry grantee, 1977—. Mem. Am. Assn. Dental Research (v.p. Ind. sect. 1981-82, pres. sect. 1982-83), Am. Assn. Dental Schs., ADA, Ind. Dental Assn., Psi Omega (Achievement award 1974), Omicron Kappa Upsilon (faculty mem. Theta Theta chpt.). Republican. Research on assessing the efficacy and safety of oral health products and procedures relative to dental caries, gingivitis, plaque, calculus, pellicle, and oral soft tissue pathology. Home: 1753 Esther Ct Plainfield IN 46168 Office: Oral Health Research Inst 415 Lansing St Indianapolis IN 46202

MALLE, LOUIS, film director; b. Thumeries, France, Oct. 30, 1932; s. Pierre and Francoise (Beghin) M.; m. Anne-Marie Deschodt (div.); 1 son; m. Candice Bergen, Sept. 27, 1980; 1 child, Chloe. Student Inst. d'Etudes Politiques, Paris, 1951-53, Inst. des Hautes Etudes Cinematographiques, Paris, 1953-54; Asst. to Jacques Cousteau, 1953-55; co-producer The Silent World, 1955; tech. collaborator with Robert Bresson for Un condamne a mort s'est echappe; dir. films Ascenseur pour l'echafaud, 1957 (Prix Louis-Delluc 1958), Les Amants, 1958 (Spl. Jury prize Venice Film Festival 1968), Zazie dans le metro, 1960, Vie Privee, 1962, Le Feu Follet (Spl. Jury prize Venice Film Festival 1963), Viva Maria, 1965, La Voleur, 1966, William Wilson, 1967, Le Souffle au Coeur, 1971, Lacomb Lucien, 1973, Black Moon, 1975, Pretty Baby, 1978, Atlantic City, 1980, My Dinner with Andre, 1980, Crackers, 1984, Alamo Bay, 1985, Au Revoir Les Enfants, 1987; also TV short subjects India, 1970. *

MALLERY, RICHARD, lawyer; b. Akron, Ohio, June 7, 1937; s. William Harrison and Elizabeth Mae (Whitmer) M.; m. Frances Ann Kohfeldt, June 7, 1964; children: Kathleen Ann, Craig Taylor, David Whitmer, Patricia Lynn. B.A., DePauw U., 1959; M.A. (Woodrow Wilson fellow 1959), Cornell U., 1960; J.D., Stanford U., 1963. Bar: Ariz. 1964. Law clk. to chief justice Ariz. Supreme Ct., 1963-64; mng. sr. ptnr. Snell & Wilmer, Phoenix, 1964—; spl. counsel to appropriations com. Ariz. Ho. of Reps., 1967-68; lectr. law U. Ariz., 1969-71; gen. counsel, dir., mem. exec. com. Southwest Savs. & Loan Assn., 1972-76; lectr. real estate trans. Ariz. State U., 1976-79; vice chmn., dir., mem. exec. com. Sunbelt Holdings, S.A., 1981—. Chmn. exec. com. bd. visitors Law Sch., Stanford U., 1987—; mem. Internat. Steering Com., vice-chmn. of U.S. sect. Pacific Basin Econ. Council, 1988—; v.p., bd. dirs. Combined Met. Phoenix Arts Assn., 1967-76, chmn. adv. bd., 1976-79; pres., bd. dirs. men's arts council Phoenix Art Mus., 1968-70; chmn. charter govt. com. City of Phoenix, 1973, chmn. environ. quality commn., 1971-73; mem. Ariz. Council on Humanities and Pub. Policy, 1977-78; bd. dirs., chmn. exec. com. Ariz. Tomorrow, Inc., 1977—; founding pres. Herberger Theater Ctr. of City of Phoenix 1983—; mem. San Francisco regional panel Pres.'s Commn. on White House Fellows, 1975-79; trustee Heard Mus. Indian Art and Anthropology, 1971-78, Phoenix Country Day Sch., 1972-76, DePauw U., 1978-85, Hudson Inst., 1979—, Nat. Symphony, 1981-85, Ariz. Parklands Found., 1984—. Am. Field Service Internat. scholar Germany, 1954; Fulbright scholar Eng., 1960. Mem. Am., Ariz., Maricopa County bar assns., Ariz. Acad., Council Fgn. Relations, Sigma Chi. Democrat. Methodist. Clubs: Paradise Valley Country, University, Arizona, Plaza. Home: 2201 E Georgia Ave Phoenix AZ 85016 Office: 3100 Valley Center Phoenix AZ 85073

MALLET, MICHEL MARIE-JOSEPH, ophthalmologist; b. Bayonne, France, Dec. 12, 1934; s. Jacques Alfred and Marguerite Jeanne (Barbeau) M.; divorced. MD, U. Paris, 1961. Intern, then resident in opthalmology Hosp. Saint-Louis, Paris, 1959-64; practice medicine specializing in opthalmology Levallois Perret, France, 1964—. Served to lt. Medical Service French mil., 1962-63. Roman Catholic. Home: 65 Rue du Rocher, 75008 Paris France

MÄLLINEN, TEUVO SAKARI, editor-in-chief; b. Sievi, Finland, Sept. 16, 1940; s. Aate Sakari and Eeva Amalia (Hytinkoski) M.; m. Riitta Kyllikki Mäkelä, July 12, 1964; 1 child, Jarno Sakari. M in Social Scis., U. Helsinki, 1962. Editorial writer Helsingin Sanomat, Helsinki, 1968-74; editorial writer, chief polit. news dept. Kaleva newspaper, Oulu, Finland, 1974-77, editor-in-chief, 1977—. Editor: Kaleva 1899-1979.

MALLORY, V(IRGIL) STANDISH, geologist, educator; b. Englewood, N.J., July 14, 1919; s. Virgil Sampson and Sarah Lauris (Baum) M.; m. Miriam Elizabeth Rowan, Feb. 3, 1946; children—Charles Standish, Stefan Douglas, Peter Sommers, Ingrid Lauris. A.B., Oberlin Coll., 1943; M.A., U. Calif. at Berkeley, 1948, Ph.D. (Standard Oil of Calif. fellow in paleontology), 1952. Preparator U. Calif. Museum Paleontology, Berkeley, 1946-48; curator foraminifera U. Calif. Museum Paleontology, 1948-50, cons., 1951; lectr. paleontology U. Calif. at Berkeley, 1951; asst. prof. geology U. Wash., 1952-59, asso. prof., 1959-62; prof., chmn. div. geology and paleontology, curator of paleontology Burke Meml. Wash. State Mus., 1962-84, prof. emeritus, mus. curator, 1984—; Cons. in petroleum geology and mus. curation; mem. Gov. Wash. Commn. on Petroleum Regulations, 1956-57; mem. NSF Paris Basin Field Inst., Paris, Belgium and Luxembourg, 1964; co-dir. NSF Inst. Secondary Sch. Tchrs., Western Wash. State Coll., summers 1963, 65. Author: Lower Tertiary Biostratigraphy of California Coast Ranges, 1959, Lower Tertiary Foraminifera From Media Agua Creek Drainage Area, Kern County, California, 1970, Biostratigraphy—A Major Basis of Paleontologic Correlation, 1970; contbg. author: Lincoln Library Essential Knowledge, 1965, Ency. Brit., 15th edit, 1974; Editor paleontology: Quaternary Research Jour, 1970-77; Contbr. articles to profl. jours. Served with AUS, 1944-46, PTO. Am. Assn. Petroleum Geologists Revolving Fund grantee, 1957; U. Wash. Agnes Anderson Fund grantee, 1963. Fellow AAAS (council 1964—), Geologic Soc. Am.; mem. Am. Assn. Petroleum Geologists (sect. council 1964-84, com. on stratigraphic correlations 1979-85), Paleontologic Soc. (chmn. sect. 1956-58), Geol. Soc. Am., Soc. Econ. Paleontology and Mineralogy, Paleontol. Research Soc., Paleontogogische Gesellschaft, Geologische Gesellschaft, Internat. Paleontological Union, N.W. Sci. Soc., Am. Assn. Museums, Mineral Mus. (adv. council 1974-87), Sigma Xi, Theta Tau. Home: 5209 Pullman Ave NE Seattle WA 98105 Office: Burke Meml Wash State Mus DB10 U Wash Seattle WA 98195

MALLOY, EDWARD ALOYSIUS, priest, university administrator, educator; b. Washington, May 3, 1941; s. Edward Aloysius and Elizabeth (Clark) M. BA, U. Notre Dame, 1963, MA, 1967, ThM, 1969; PhD, Vanderbilt U., 1975. Ordained priest Roman Cath. Ch., 1970. Instr. theology Aquinas Jr. Coll., Nashville, 1972-73; teaching asst. U. Notre Dame, Ind., 1969-70, instr., 1974-75, asst. prof., 1975-81, assoc. prof., 1981—, assoc. provost, 1982-87, pres.-elect, 1987, pres., 1987—. Author: Homosexuality and the Christian Way of Life, 1981, The Ethics of Law Enforcement and Criminal Punishment, 1982; contbr. articles to profl. jours. Mem. Ind. Organ Transplantation Task Force, 1986; bd. regents U. Portland, Oreg., 1985; lectr. Zoning and the Right to Equal Protection Ind. chpt. Council for Humanities and South Bend League of Women Voters, 1976; cons. Cath. Bishops of Ind. legis. on defining the moment of death and the right to die, 1976-77; mem. Instl. Rev. Com. of Meml. Hosp., South Bend, 1981—; mem. Instl. Rev. Bd. St. Joseph Med. Ctr., 1983—. Mem. Cath. Theol. Soc. Am., Soc. Christian Ethics, Bus. and Higher Edn. Forum. Home: U Notre Dame 141 Sorin Hall Notre Dame IN 46556 Office: U Notre Dame Office of Pres Notre Dame IN 46556

MALLOY, JOHNN EDWARD, radio and television educator, author; b. Superior, Wis., Jan. 1, 1940; s. Robert Francis and Celestine Marie (Evenson) M. BS, U. Wis., LaCrosse, 1962; MS, Winona (Minn.) State U., 1967; MS in Edn., Chgo. State U., 1970; EdS, Ea. Ill. U., 1977; ArtsD, U. No. Colo., 1982. Cert. K-14 tchr., Ill., Wis., Colo. Tchr. speech and English Merrill (Wis.) Pub. Schs., 1962-65; tchr. radio and TV Harvey (Ill.) Sch. Dist., 1965—; instr. speech and theatre Thornton Community Coll., South Holland, Ill., 1968-70, 75-77, 85; media lectr. Chgo. State U., 1970-72; supr. media lab. U. No. Colo., Greeley, 1980-82. Author: Communication in the High School: Speaking and Listening, 1972, Instructional Guides to Media Communication, 1982; producer TV mag. series Getting Around, 1981—. Active in CAP, Chgo., 1965—. Recipient degree of distinction Nat. Forensic League, Ripon, Wis., 1982, Silver Medalist Canon USA Photo Contest, 1985; Cert. of Recognition in CBS TV Worth Teaching Program, 1987. Mem. NEA, Ill. Speech and Theatre Assn., Ill. Edn. Assn., Faculty Assn. Dist. 205, Speech Communication Assn., Air Force Assn. Lutheran. Home: PO Box 487 Park Forest IL 60466 Office: Thornton Twp High Sch TV Studio 151st & Broadway Harvey IL 60426

MALLOY, MICHAEL PATRICK, lawyer, educator, author, consultant; b. Haddon Heights, N.J., Sept. 23, 1951; s. Francis Edward and Marie Grace (Nardi) M.; m. Mary McGinty, May 11, 1972; 1 child, Elizabeth McGinty. BA magna cum laude (scholar), Georgetown U., 1973, PhD, 1983; JD (scholar), U. Pa., 1976. Bar: N.J. 1976. Research asso. Inst. Internat. Law and Econ. Devel., Washington, 1976-77; atty. advisor Office Fgn. Assets Control, Dept. Treasury, Washington, 1977-80, Office of Comptroller of Currency, Washington, 1981; spl. counsel SEC, Washington, 1981-82; asst. prof. N.Y. Law Sch., N.Y.C., 1982-83; spl. asst. Office of Gen. Counsel, U.S. Dept. Treasury, Washington, 1985; assoc. prof. Seton Hall U. Sch. Law, Newark, 1983-86, prof., assoc. dean, 1986-87; prof. law Fordham U., N.Y.C., 1987—; law lectr. Morin Ctr. Banking Law Studies Boston U. Sch. Law, 1986—; cons. banking and pvt. internat. law matters. Recipient Spl. Achievement award Dept. Treasury, 1982. Mem. Am. Soc. Internat. Law (exec. council), Hegel Soc. Am., L'Association des Auditeurs et Anciens Auditeurs de l'Academie de Droit International de la Haye, Phi Beta Kappa. Author: Corporate Law of Banks (2 vols.), 1987; contbr. articles, revs. and comments to profl. jours. Office: Fordham U Sch Law 140 W 62d St New York NY 10023

MALLUCHE, HARTMUT HORST, nephrologist, educator; b. Breslau, Germany, Jan. 1, 1943; came to U.S., 1975, naturalized, 1985; s. Harald E. and Renate (Muenzberg) M.; m. Gisela Gleich, Dec. 19, 1975; children—Nadine, Danielle, Tiffany. Abitur, Albertus Magnus Coll., Koenigstein, Germany, 1963; postgrad. Phillips U., Marburg/Lahn, Fed. Republic of Germany, 1963-65, U. Innsbruck, Austria, 1965-66, U. Vienna, Austria, 1966; M.D., J. W. Goethe U., Frankfurt, Fed. Republic of Germany, 1969. Diplomate German Bd. Internal Medicine. Intern, County Hosp., Aichach, Fed. Republic of Germany, 1969-70; resident in internal medicine and fellow in nephrology Ctr. Internal Medicine, Univ. Hosp., Frankfurt am. Main, 1970-75, asst. prof. medicine U. So. Calif., Los Angeles, 1975-78, assoc. prof., 1978-81; prof., dir. Div. Nephrology, Bone and Mineral Metabolism U. Ky. Med. Ctr., Lexington, 1981—; cons. NIH; grant reviewer NYU, Kidney Found. Can. Contbr. articles to profl. jours. and books. Grantee NIH, 1982,

84, 86, Shriner's Hosp. for Crippled Children, Lexington, 1982, 83, 87. Fellow ACP; mem. Am. Soc. Nephrology, Am. Soc. Clin. Investment, Am. Soc. Bone and Mineral Research, Am. Soc. Physiol. Endocrinology, European Dialysis and Transplantation Assn., Am. Fedn. Clin. Research, Internat. Soc. Nephrology, AAAS.

MALM, RITA P., securities executive; b. May 8, 1932; d. George Peter and Helen Marie (Woodward) Pellegrini; student Packard Jr. Coll., 1950-52, N.Y. Inst. Fin., 1954, Wagner Coll., 1955; m. Robert J. Malm, Apr. 19, 1969. Sales asst. Dean Witter & Co., N.Y.C., 1959-63, asst. v.p., compliance dir., 1969-74; v.p., dir. Securities Ind. Assocs., N.Y.C., 1969-72; chief exec. officer Muriel Siebert & Co., Inc., N.Y.C., 1981-83; pres. Madison-Chapin Assocs., N.Y.C., 1984—; art mktg. cons. Mem. Women's Bond Club N.Y. (dir., v.p., program chmn., pres. 1980-82). Office: 3 Hanover Sq New York NY 10004

MALMQUIST, LARS ERIC, advertising agency executive; b. Stockholm, Jan. 9, 1930; s. Nils Erik and Signe Maria (Eilertz) M.; MBA, Stockholm Bus. High Sch., 1957; PhD, Kensington U., 1987; m. Marianne Dickman, Oct. 20, 1958; children—Ann Elisabeth, Eva Madelaine. Pres., Publimondial Sweden, Stockholm, 1972—, also dir., v.p. Problemlosarna Advt. Agy., Stockholm, 1979—, also dir. Home: 110 Sandviksvagen, S-16240 Vallingby Sweden Office: 34 Tegnergatan, PO Box 45092, S-10430 Stockholm Sweden

MALMSTRÖM, BO GUNNAR, biochemist, educator; b. Stockholm, Sweden, May 11, 1927; s. Edgar Teodor and Ida Konstantia (Bergström) M.; B.S., Muhlenberg Coll., Allentown, Pa., 1948; Ph.D., U. Minn., 1951; D.Sc., Uppsala U., 1956; D.Sc. (hon.), U. Utrecht, 1986; m. Betty Hallberg, July 7, 1951; children—Barbro, Jan. Research fellow in physiol. chemistry U. Minn., Mpls., 1950-51; research fellow in biochemistry U. Uppsala (Sweden), 1952-56, asst. prof., 1956-60, research asst. prof., 1960-63; biochemistry, dept. head U. Göteborg (Sweden), 1963-82; vis. prof. biochemistry U. So. Calif., 1963; vis. Miller prof. dept. biochemistry U. Calif., Berkeley, 1973-74; vis. prof. dept. organic chemistry U. Utrecht (Holland), 1978; Sherman Fairchild Disting. scholar Calif. Inst. Tech., 1980-81; chmn. Nobel Prize Award Com. for Chemistry. Recipient King Oscar II Jubilee prize Uppsala U., 1962; Celsius medal Uppsala Acad. Sci. and Letters, 1972; Bror Holmberg medal, 1985; USPHS grantee, 1960-72; grantee Swedish Natural Sci. Research Council, 1958—. Mem. Swedish Chem. Soc. (Norblad-Ekstrand medal 1972), Swedish Phys. Soc., Swedish Biochem. Soc., Gothenburg Acad. Scis., Royal Swedish Acad. Scis., Am. Soc. Biol. Chemists (hon.). Editor procs. profl. conf., 1967, various jours.; adv. bd. European Jour. Biochemistry, 1967-71; editorial bds. Chemica Scripta, 1971—, FEBS Letters, 1973-82; bd. advs. Jour. Inorganic Biochemistry, 1979—; contbr. research articles to profl. publs. Home: Bergsbogatan 13, S-421 79 Västra Frölunda Sweden Office: Dept Biochemistry & Biophysics, Chalmers U Tech, S-412 96 Göteborg Sweden

MALMSTRÖM, SUNE KARL GUSTAF, hotel executive; b. Stockholm, Sweden, Apr. 13, 1929; s. Sune J. and Lisa (Bergsten) M.; m. Helina Talmet, Mar. 31, 1953. MBA, Stockholms Handelshögskola, 1954. Mgr., owner Grängesbergsbolaget, Stockholm, 1959-62; mng. dir. Hotell Diplomat AB, Stockholm, 1963—. Office: Hotell Diplomat AB, Box 14059, S-104 40 Stockholm Sweden

MALONE, RUTH MOORE, author; b. Clarendon, Ark.; d. John Burton and Bessie (Branch) Moore; grad. Ward Belmont Coll., Nashville; student U. Ark.; m. Charles Edmund Malone; children—Margaret (Mrs. Hubert de Marcy). Bess (Mrs. Dick Lankford). Free lance writer Am. Home, Good Housekeeping, Parents, Sunday mags., Memphis Comml. Appeal, Shreveport (La.) Times, Ark. Democrat, Ark. Gazette, 1944-65; weekly syndicated feature writer Palmer Media Group, South Ark. newspapers, 1959-65; asso. editor Ark. State Mag., 1961-62; food editor Holiday Inn mag., 1962-75; mem. editorial bd. Curtis Pub. Co., Indpls.; food envoy Holiday Inn Worldwide System, Little Rock, 1962—. Mem. Ark. Fedn. Womens Clubs (dist. pres. 1960-61), Nat. League Am. Pen Women (br. pres. 1966-68), Ark. Press Women, Nat. Fedn. Press Women, Confrérie des Chevaliers du Tastevin, Pi Beta Phi (alumni pres. 1964-65). Author-editor: Where to Eat in the Ozarks-How It's Cooked, 1961, 62, 64; Swiss Holiday Recipes, 1965-69; Holiday Inn Cookbook and Travel Guide, 1962-66, 1968-70; Holiday Inn International Cook Book, 1970, 1972—; Dogpatch Cook Book, 1975, 77, 79, 86—; Ozark Folk Center Cookbook, 1975, 77, 79, 86—. Home: 22 Sunset Dr Little Rock AR 72207

MALONE, WILLIAM GRADY, lawyer; b. Minden, La., Feb. 19, 1915; s. William Gordon and Minnie Lucie (Hortman) M.; m. Marion Rowe Whitfield, Sept. 26, 1943; children—William Grady, Gordon Whitfield, Marion Elizabeth, Helen Ann, Margaret Catherine. B.S., La. State U., 1941; J.D., George Washington U., 1952. Bar: Va. 1952, U.S. Supreme Ct. 1971. Statis. analyst Dept. Agr., Baton Rouge, 1941; investigator VA, Washington, 1946-59; legal officer, dep., gen. counsel, asst. gen. counsel 1959-79; individual practice law Arlington, Va., 1979—. Editor: Fed. Bar News, 1972-73. Pres. Aurora Hills Civic Assn., 1948-49; spl. asst. to treas. Com. of 100, 1979-81, chmn., 1982-83; pres. Children's Theater, 1968-69; trustee St. George's Episcopal Ch., 1979—; chmn. Arlington County Fair Assn., 1979-83. Served to lt. col. AUS, 1941-46, ETO. Decorated Legion of Merit; recipient Disting. Service award, 1979, 3 Superior Performance awards, 1952-72, Outstanding Alumni award George Washington Law Sch., 1978. Mem. Fed. Bar Assn. (pres. D.C. chpt. 1970-71, nat. pres. 1978-79), Va. Bar Assn., Arlington County Bar Assn., Nat. Lawyers Club (dir.). Clubs: Arlington Host Lions, Ft. Myer Officers. Home: 224 N Jackson St Arlington VA 22201 Office: 2060 N 14th St Suite 310 Arlington VA 22201

MALONEY, CLEMENT GARLAND, international marketing consultant; b. Hot Springs, Ark., July 4, 1917; B.A. in Bus. Adminstrn., Northwestern U., 1940; m. Monique Pearl Nguyen; 1 son, Thomas C. Dep. dir. Chgo. unit War Assets Adminstrn., 1946-48; chief major procurement USAF, Washington, 1948-51; chief aircraft div. office Asst. Sec. Def., Washington, 1951-53, program adminstr., Paris, France, 1953-55; spl. asst. for financial control air force resources to asst. sec. Air Force, 1955-58; spl. asst. to pres. Hoffman Electronics, Los Angeles, 1958-59; spl. asst. to pres. for domestic and internat. mktg. Gen. Dynamics-Electronics div. Gen. Dynamics Corp., N.Y., 1959-61; v.p. charge domestic and internat. mktg. Kollsman Instrument Corp., Elmhurst, N.Y., 1961-64; cons. to U.S. sec. def., 1964-66, 67-69; internat. mktg. cons. Philco Corp. div. Ford Motor Co., 1966-67; internat. mktg. cons. to sec. Def., 1967-69; spl. asst. to pres. Control Data Corp., 1969-72; fin. mgmt. and mktg. cons., 1972—; commr. Armed Services Commn., Long Beach, Calif. Mem. adv. bd. Salvation Army. Served to col. USAAF, World War II, Korea, Vietnam; col. Calif. State Mil. Res. Recipient Exceptional Civilian Service award USAF. Mem. Air Force Assn., Am. Def. Preparedness Assn., Mil. Order World Wars, Am. Mgmt. Assn., Mil. Order of Carabao, Res. Officers Assn. Home: Galaxy Towers 2999 E Ocean Blvd Apt 2040 Long Beach CA 90803

MALONEY, JOHN CLEMENT, marketing consultant; b. Laurel, Nebr., Aug. 19, 1929; s. Clement Mathew and Annette (McCabe) M.; B.A., U. Nebr., 1951; M.S., Purdue U., 1953, Ph.D., 1954; m. Maybelle Margaret Reinsch, Aug., 1950; children—Connie (Mrs. Leland Robinson), Sheila, Barbara, Jane, Lynn. Mgr. personnel testing Mpls. Honeywell Co., 1954-55; dir. market research Omar, Inc., Omaha, 1955-58; mgr. research and devel. Leo Burnett Co., Chgo., 1958-66; research dir. Urban Journalism Center, assoc. prof. advtg. and journalism Northwestern U., 1966-72; v.p. research Arthur Meyerhoff Assocs., Inc., Chgo., 1972-78; pres. John C. Maloney & Assos., Inc., Chgo., 1978—. Cons. various ednl. and research founds., corps., govt. agys. Ford Found. grantee, 1968-69. Mem. Am. Psychol. Assn. (dir. consumer psychology div. 1964-65), AAUP (pres. Northwestern U. chpt. 1970), Am. Mktg. Assn., AAAS. Contbr. articles to profl. jours. Home: 147 Plumtree Rd Deerfield IL 60015 Office: 345 N Canal St Suite 1102 Chicago IL 60606

MALONEY, LEONARD JOHN, county administrator; b. Phila., June 24, 1941; s. John J. and Anne (Hettel) M.; B.A., Xavier U., 1963; m. Frances H. Suder, Oct. 26, 1963; children—Matthew, Tracey Ann. Claim supr. Employers Ins. of Wausau, Phila. and Pitts., 1965-71; div. claims mgr. Argonaut Ins. Co., Phila., 1971-78; sr. v.p. claims Vaughan Ins. Group, Phila., 1978-80; ins. cons., Broomall, Pa., 1980-81; dir. personnel, dir. risk mgmt. County of Delaware, Media, Pa., 1981—, now also asst. dir. county co. Pres., Babe Ruth Baseball, 1979-81; commr. Hilltop Baseball, 1977-78; active Boy Scouts Am., 1975-76; pres. Hilltop Civic Assn., 1975, Bryn Mawr Hills Civic Assn., 1980; bd. dirs. Vassar Assn.; asst. ward leader Havertown (Pa.), 1977-78. Served with USMCR, 1962-68. Recipient various awards. Mem. Internat. Personnel Mgmt. Assn., Risk Mgmt. Assn., Del-Chester Claim Assn., Lower Bucks Claim Assn., Pa. Def. Inst., Phila. Claim Mgrs. Council. Home: 4012 State Rd Drexel Hill PA 19026

MALONEY, LUCILLE TINKER, civic worker; b. Twin Falls, Idaho, Mar. 13, 1920; d. Edward Milo and Lillian (Schaefer) Tinker; tchr.'s cert. Idaho State U., 1940; student U. Wash., 1941; m. Frank E. Maloney, Feb. 20, 1943 (dec.); children—Frank E., JoAnn Maloney Smallwood, Elizabeth Maloney Hurst. Pres., U. Fla. Women's Club, 1960-61, Gainesville Women's Club, 1974-75, Friends of Five Sta. WUFT-TV, Public Broadcasting, 1976-77; chmn., organizer Gainesville Spring Pilgrimage, 1976; founder, pres. Thomas Center Assos., 1978-80; v.p. U. Fla. Art Gallery Guild, 1981, pres., 1982-84; mem. Fla. Gov.'s Challenge Program Com., 1981; trustee Fla. House, Washington; patron, organizer, trustee Hippodrome State Theatre; chmn. Santa Fe Regional Library Bd., 1980-81; pres. Gainesville Women's Forum, 1984-85; mem. Exec. Commn. Fla. for Statue of Liberty-Ellis Island Centennial; trustee Displaced Homemakers, Santa Fe Community Coll.; bd. dirs. Friends of Payne's Prairie, Inc. Recipient Fla. Leadership pin Gov. LeRoy Collins, 1961; Disting. Service award Women in Communication, Inc., 1975, Appreciation plaque Sta. WUFT-TV, 1977, Community Service award Gainesville Sun, 1979, Appreciation cert. Rotary Club Gainesville, 1980, Paul Harris fellowship Rotary Club, 1986, Gainesville Area Woman of Distinction award Santa Fe Community Coll., 1987, Outstanding Service award Jr. League, 1980, Bicentennial plaque Alachua County Bicentennial Com., 1976. Mem. Friends of Library, Fla. State Mus. Assocs. (pres. 1985-87), Friends of Music, Hist. Gainesville, Inc., Found. for Promotion Music, Civic Chorus, Fla. Trust for Hist. Preservation, Fla. League Conservation Voters (bd. dirs. 1983—), Gainesville C. of C. (pub. affairs com. 1983-84), Altrusa Internat., Internat. Platform Assn., Fla. Women's Network. Clubs: Gainesville Garden, Heritage (bd. govs.), Designer, Christmas Wreath So. Living mag., 1982. Home: 1823 N W 10th Ave Gainesville FL 32605

MALOOF, FARAHE PAUL, lawyer; b. Boston, Feb. 10, 1950; s. Farahe and Emily Suzanna (Puchy) M.; m. Brigitte Lucienne DeLugré. BS, Georgetown U., 1975, JD, 1978. Bar: Washington 1978, Va. 1981. Assoc. Corcoran & Rowe, Washington, 1978-81; sole practice Washington, 1982, 86—; ptnr. Berliner & Maloney, Washington, 1983-85; spl. counsel Advocacia Oliveira Ribeiro, Sao Paulo, Brazil, 1985-86; lectr. Am. U., Washington, 1984-85, Internat. Law Inst., Washington, 1986-87. Served to cpl. USMC, 1968-70, Vietnam. Mem. ABA, Va. Bar Assn., D.C. Bar Assn., Georgetown U. Alumni Assn. (co-chmn. 1983-84). Republican. Roman Catholic. Home: 1506 Dewberry Court McClean VA 22101 Office: Maloof & Assocs 1450 G St NW Suite 1200 Washington DC 20005-2088

MALOOLEY, DAVID JOSEPH, electronics and computer technology educator; b. Terre Haute, Ind., Aug. 20, 1951; s. Edward Joseph and Vula (Starn) M. B.S., Ind. State U., 1975; M.S., Ind. U., 1981, doctoral candidate. Supr., Zenith Radio Corp., Paris, Ill., 1978-79; assoc. prof. electronics and computer tech. Ind. State U., Terre Haute, 1979—; cons. in field. Served to 1st lt. U.S. Army, 1975-78. Mem. Soc. Mfg. Engrs., Nat. Assn. Indsl. Tech., Am. Vocat. Assn., Instrument Soc. Am. (sr.), Phi Delta Kappa, Pi Lambda Theta, Epsilon Pi Tau. Democrat. Christian. Home: Rural Rt 52 Box 594D Terre Haute IN 47805 Office: Ind State U Terre Haute IN 47809

MALOTT, ALAN MARC, lawyer; b. Bklyn., Jan. 18, 1953; s. Irving and Diana (Goldenberg) M.; m. Linda Ellen McNeil, Aug. 23, 1981; 1 child, Brian Joel. BS in Criminal Justice, Ariz. State U., 1976; JD, U. N.Mex., 1979. Bar: N.M. 1979, U.S. Ct. Appeals (10th cir.) 1980. Assoc. Shaffer Law Firm, Albuquerque, 1979-81, Harold B. Albert, P.A., Albuquerque, 1981; sole practice, Albuquerque, 1981-88; founder Malott, Barudin & dunn, 1988; legal counsel N.Mex. Chiropractic Assn., 1983—. Contbr. articles to profl. jours. Mem. N.Mex. Workmen's Compensation Rules Com., 1986—. Recipient Criminal Procedure plaque Bancroft-Whitney Pubs., 1978, Equity Practice plaque, 1978. Mem. Ct. Practice Inst. (diplomate), Assn. Trial Lawyers Am., Huning Highlands Hist. Assn. Democrat. Jewish. Office: 300 Central Ave SW Suite 1000 East Albuquerque NM 87102

MALPAS, HENRI AUGUSTIN, manufacturing company executive; b. Manage, Hainaut, Belgium, Aug. 14, 1924; s. Augustin J. and Leonie R. (Staquet) M.; m. Jeannine A. Fromont, Aug. 16, 1949; children—Liliane, Annie. Grad. Elec. and Mech. Engr., Faculte Polytechnique, Mons, Belgium, 1948. Engrng. mgr. Ateliers de & a, Familleureux, Belgium, 1948-52; tech. mgr. TRC, Houdeng Aimeries, Belgium, 1952-65; mgr. Basse-Sambre, Moustiers/Sambre, Belgium, 1965-67; plant mgr. Clark Automotive Europe, Brugge, Belgium, 1968-78, gen. mgr., 1979—, mng. dir. and gen. mgr. Clark Equipment Belgium, Brugge. Decorated Officer in the Order of Leopold. Mem. Fabrimetal, Ste Royale Ingenieurs and Industriels, Ste des Ingenieurs and Scientifiques de France, Vlaams Ekonomisch Verbond. Club: Brugse Hanze (Brugge). Home: Vogelzanglaan 17, De Haan, B8420 West Vlaanderen Belgium Office: Clark Equipment Belgium N V, Ten Briele 3 Brugge, B-8200 West Vlaanderen Belgium

MALPHURS, ROGER EDWARD, insurance company executive; b. Lake Worth, Fla., Dec. 15, 1933; s. Cecil Edward and Muriel Thelma (Ward) M.; m. Carolyn Sue Calapp, Feb. 2, 1963; children: Steven, Brian, Darren, Regina, Victoria. BS, U. Utah, 1961. Cert. med. technologist. Supr. spl. chemistry Cen. Pathology Lab., Santa Rosa, Calif., 1968-73; mgr. lab. Community Hosp., Santa Rosa, 1973-76; supr. chem., staff asst. Meml. Hosp., Santa Rosa, 1976-85; pres., chief exec. officer R.E. Malphurs Co., Sunnyvale, Calif., 1972—; owner, developer REMCO Mktg. Assocs., Santa Rosa, 1970-72, Better Bus. Forms and Typeset, Santa Rosa, 1977-81. Author: A New, Simple Way to Win at Blackjack, 1972. Served as squadron commdr. CAP USAF Aux., 1982-84. Mem. Am. Chiropractic Assn., Calif. Chiropractic Assn. Republican. Club: Optomists Internat. (Santa Rosa)(youth awards chmn. 1969-74).

MALSKY, STANLEY JOSEPH, physicist; b. N.Y.C., July 15, 1925; s. Joseph and Nellie (Karpinski) M.; m. Gloria E. Gagliardi, Oct. 15, 1965; 1 son, Mark A. B.S., NYU, 1949, M.A., 1950, M.S., 1953, Ph.D., 1963. Nuclear physicist Dept. Def., 1950-54; chief physicist VA, 1954-73; from instr. to asst. prof. physics NYU, 1960-64; adj. asso. prof., then prof. radiol. sci. Manhattan Coll., Bronx, N.Y., 1960-74; non-resident research collaborator med. div. Brookhaven Nat. Labs., Upton, N.Y., 1964-69; research prof. radiology NYU Sch. Medicine, N.Y.C., 1975-77; pres. Radiol. Physics Assn., White Plains, N.Y., 1965—, Therapy Physics Services, 1980—, Sigmasel Dosimetry, 1986—; bd. trustees Doggs Ferry Hosp., N.Y. Contbr. chpts. to books. Served with U.S. Army, 1945-46. Recipient James Picker Found. award, 1963-67; Founder's Day award NYU, 1964; Leadership award Manhattan Coll., 1969; AEC grantee, Bureau of Radiological Health grantee, Nat. Cancer Inst. grantee. Fellow Am. Public Health Assn., AAAS, Royal Soc. Health; charter mem. Am. Assn. Physicists in Medicine, Health Physics Soc., Sigma Xi, Sigma Pi Sigma, Phi Delta Kappa. Roman Catholic. Address: 119 Lansdowne Westport CT 06880

MALT, HAROLD LEWIS, urban designer and planner, educator, author, consultant; b. Pitts., Apr. 11, 1918; s. Isadore and Florence (Horance) M.; m. Carol Nora, Sept. 3, 1976; children: Bruce Elliot, Ilene Susan. B of Indsl. Design, Carnegie-Mellon U., 1940; M of Environ. Design, Syracuse U., 1964. With various archtl. firms Chgo., N.Y.C., 1940-42; mem. faculty design and engr. dept. SUNY, Buffalo, 1947-51; pres. Malt and Ness, Inc., Buffalo, 1951-63, Harold Lewis Malt Assocs., Inc., Washington, Miami, Albany, Ga., 1964—, Ctr. for Design Planning, Washington, Miami, 1974—; prof. architecture and planning U. Miami, Coral Gables, 1972—, dept. chmn., 1975-76; cons. Westinghouse co., Gen. Dynamics, Gen. Electric, def. agys., also U.S. Army, USN, USAF, 1951-63; nat. cons. to cities, HUD, Dept. Transp., Dept. Interior, Dept. Justice, urban agys., developers, 1964—. Author: Furnishing the City, 1970, Streetscape Equipment Sourcebook, 1979, 81; contbr. numerous articles to profl. jours.. Served as pilot USAAC, 1942-45. Recipient nat. prizes for designs. Mem. Am. Inst. Cert. Planners, Am. Soc. Landscape Architects, Am. Soc. Interior Designers, Sigma Chi. Home: 1208 N McKinley St Albany GA 31701 Office: U Miami Sch Architecture Coral Gables FL 33124 also: HLMA PO Box 8484 Coral Gables FL 33124

MALTBY, JOHN NEWCOMBE, oil company executive; b. Esher, Surrey, Eng., July 10, 1928; s. Paul Copeland and Winifred (Paterson) M.; m. Sylvia Harris, July 28, 1956; children—Caroline Jane, William John, Sophia Louise. M.A., Clare Coll., U. Cambridge, 1951. Exec. Royal Dutch-Shell, 1951-69; mng. dir. Panocean Shipping, 1969-79; dir. Burmah Oil plc (U.K.), Swindon, Wiltshire, Eng., 1980-83, chmn., 1983—; non-exec. dir. DRG PLC, Harrisons and Crosfield PLC, U.K. Atomic Energy Authority. Served to 2d lt. Brit. Army, 1946-48. Comdr. Order of Brit. Empire. Mem. Brit. Inst. Mgmt. (companion). Mem. Ch. of England. Club: Naval and Mil. (London). Avocations: sailing; history; gardening. Office: Burmah Oil plc, Pipers Way Burman House, Swindon, Wiltshire SN3 1RE, England

MALULA, JOSEPH CARDINAL, archbishop of Kinshasa; d. Kinshasa, Zaire, Dec. 12, 1917. Ordained priest Roman Cath. Ch., 1946; titular bishop of Attanaso, also aux. bishop of Kinshana, 1959; archbishop of Kinshasa, 1964—; elevated to Sacred Coll. Cardinals, 1969; titular ch. Ss. Protomartyrs (Via Aurelia Antica); mem. Congregation Evangelization of Peoples. Address: Archeveche, BP 1700, Kinshasa 1 Democratic Republic of the Congo *

MALURA, OSWALD, painter; b. Boleslau, Fed. Republic Germany, Oct. 9, 1906; s. Thomas and Anna (Kaschny) M.; m. Frieda Anken Brand, Nov. 20, 1942; 1 son. Student, Munich Acad. Art, 1926-30. Scholar Munich Acad. Art in India, 1930-33; lectr., then prof. painting and drawing State Sch. Munich, 1933-38; free-lance painter Munich, 1938-42, owner various art galleries, 1948-51, 57-67; lectr. in Argentina 1951-55, free-lance painter, 1966—. One-man shows include Munich, 1957, Festival des Arts Plastiques Sur la Cote d'azur, France, 1963-66; author: As A Painter Through India, 1949; also articles. Served with German Army, 1942-45. Mem. HausderKunst München. Roman Catholic. Home: Hohenzollern Strasse 16, 8 Munich 40 Federal Republic of Germany

MÁLYUSZ, KÁROLY, mathematician; b. Budapest, Hungary, Apr. 21, 1939; s. Elemér and Edith (Császár) M. MA, Eötvös U., Hungary, 1962; PhD, Moscow State U., 1977. Researcher Math. Inst. of Hungarian Acad. Sci., Budapest, 1962-65, 68-72, Inst. Computer Sci. and Automation, Budapest, 1973-74, Statis. Office, Inst. Appl. Computer Sci., Budapest, 1975-79, Statis. Office, Computer Service for State Adminstrn., Budapest, 1979-80; mathematician, actuary Ins. Enterprize of the State, Budapest, 1984—. Contbr. articles on math. to profl. jours. Mem. J. Bolyai Math. Soc. Home: Batthyány 26, H-1015 Budapest Hungary Office: Állami Biztositó, Üllői út 1, H-1813 Budapest Hungary

MALZEKE, HARRY FRANCIS, oil and gas co. exec.; b. Trainor, Pa., July 10, 1929; s. Harry F. and Regina C. (Flanagan) M.; B.Sc., Washington and Lee U., 1954; J.D., George Washington U., 1958; m. Ernestine Marie Secrest, June 4, 1955; children—Karen Lynne, Harry Francis, Michael Philip. Admitted to D.C. bar, 1959, also U.S. Supreme Ct.; legal specialist corp. mergers, liquidations, acquisitions nat. office IRS, Washington, 1959-65; asso. firm McClure & Trotter, Washington, 1965-69; corp. tax specialist Ernst & Whinney, Cleve., 1969-71; prin. The Malzeke Co., Cleve., 1971-75; pres., owner Atoka Gas & Oil Inc., Abilene, Tex. and Cleve., 1975—. Served with USAF, 1951-52. Mem. John Marshall Inn, Phi Delta Phi. Republican. Roman Catholic. Club: Canterbury Golf.

MAMAT, FRANK TRUSTICK, lawyer; b. Syracuse, N.Y., Sept. 4, 1949; s. Harvey Sanford and Annette (Trustick) M.; m. Kathy Lou Winters, June 23, 1975; children—Jonathan Adam, Steven Kenneth. B.A., U. Rochester, 1971; J.D., Syracuse U., 1974. Bar: D.C. 1976, Fla. 1977, Mich. 1984, U.S. Dist. Ct. (no. dist.) Ind. 1984, U.S. Dist. Ct. (ea. dist.) Mich. 1983, U.S. Ct. Appeals (D.C. cir.) 1976, U.S. Dist. Ct. (D.C. cir.) 1976, U.S. Ct. Appeals (6th cir.) 1983, U.S. Supreme Ct. 1979. Atty., NLRB, Washington, 1975-79; assoc. Proskauer, Rose, Goetz & Mendelsohn, Washington, N.Y.C., and Los Angeles, 1979-83; assoc. Fishman Group, Bloomfield Hills, Mich., 1983-85, ptnr., 1985-87, ptnr. Honigman, Miller, Schwartz and Cohn, 1987— . Gen. counsel Rep. Com. of Oakland County, 1987—, bd. dirs. 300 Club, Mich., 1984—; Rep. Nat. Com., Nat. Rep. Senatorial Com., Presdl. Task Force; City dir. West Bloomfield, 1985-87; pres. West Bloomfield Rep. Club, 1985-87; fin. com. Rep. Com. of Oakland County, 1985—; vice. chmn. lawyers for Reagan-Bush, 1984; v.p. Fruehauf Farms, West Bloomfield, Mich., 1985—; bd. dirs. B'nai B'rith Barristers Unit, Detroit, 1983—, pres. 1985-87; mem. staff Exec. Office of Pres. Of U.S. Inquiries/Comments, Washington, 1981-83. Mem. ABA, Oakland County Bar Assn., D.C. Bar Assn., Fed. Bar Assn., Detroit Bar Assn., Fla. Bar Assn. (Labor com. 1977—), Founders Soc. (Detroit Inst. of Art). Club: Econ. of Detroit. Lodge: B'nai Brith (v.p. 1982-83, pres. 1985—, trustee Detroit council, 1987—). Office: Honigman Miller et al 2290 First National Bldg Detroit MI 48226

MAMBA, GEORGE MBIKWAKHE, Swaziland government official; b. July 5, 1932; s. Ndabazebelungu Mamba and Gertrude Mthwalose Thwala; m. Sophie Sidzandra Sibande, 1960; 3 sons, 2 daughters. Ed., Morija Tchr. Tng. Coll., Cambridge Inst. Edn., Nairobi U., Kenya. Head tchr. Makhonza Mission Sch., 1956-60; tchr. Kwaluseni Cen. Sch., 1961-65; head tchr. Enkamheni Cen. Sch., 1966-67; inspector schs. Manzini Dist., 1969-70; welfare and aftercare officer Prison Dept., 1971-72; counsellor Swaziland High Commn., Nairobi, 1972-77; high commr. in U.K. 1978-88; minister fgn. affairs Swaziland, Mbabane, 1988—. Author: Children's Play, 1966. Address: Ministry Fgn Affairs, Mbabane Swaziland *

MAMMONE, RICHARD JAMES, engineering educator; b. N.Y.C., Sept. 3, 1953; s. Americo Anth and Helen (Kowalski) M.; m. Valerie Altman, June 29, 1981; children—Robert, Jason. B.E., CCNY, 1975, M.E., 1977; Ph.D., CUNY, 1981. Computer systems analyst Picatinny Arsenal, Dover., N.J., 1975-77; research fellow CCNY, 1977-81; asst. prof. Manhattan Coll., Riverdale, N.Y., 1981-82; assoc. prof. engrng. Rutgers U., Piscataway, N.J., 1981—; co-founder Computed Anatonomy Inc., N.Y.C., 1982; cons. in field. Co-Author Image Recovery: Theory and Applications, Acad. Press Pubs., 1987; contbr. articles to profl. jours.; patentee in field. Assoc. Whitaker Found. grantee, 1982; Internat. Tel. & Tel. grantee, 1984; CAIP Research Ctr. grantee, 1985; Henry Rutgers fellow, 1985-87; U.S. Nat. Security Agy. grantee, 1986—; USAF grantee, 1986—; Temeplex grantee, 1986—. Mem. IEEE (sr., editor Communications Jour. 1983—), N.Y. Acad. Scis.. Office: Rutgers U Dept Elec Engring Piscataway NJ 08854

MAMULA, BRANKO, Yugoslavian government official; b. Slavonsko Polje, Croatia, 1921; grad. Coll. of Yugoslav People's Army; married; 2 sons. Mem. Yugoslav Communist Party, 1942—; commd. officer Yugoslav Navy, advanced through grades to adm.; polit. commissar of Fleet and Maritime Zone; head operative dept. of Navy Command; asst. naval comdr., then comdr. Naval Region, head naval adminstrn.; asst. fed. sec. for nat. def.; comdr. Naval Sector; chief of staff of Yugoslav People's Army, from 1979; fed. sec. for Nat. Def., 1982-88; mem. central com. Yugoslav League of Communists. Author: Navies in Large and Small Seas; also articles. Office: Federal Secretariat for, National Defense, Belgrade Yugoslavia *

MANALIS, MELVYN SAMUEL, research physicist, educator; b. Los Angeles, Oct. 16, 1939; s. Barney M. and Kathryn (Swiler) M.; m. Marilyn Jean White, June 21, 1965; children—Andrew, Scott, Jeremy. B.A. in Math, Calif. State U.-Northridge, 1961; M.S. in Physics, U. N.H., 1964, Ph.D., U. Calif.-Santa Barbara, 1970. Instr. dept. physics Colby Coll., Waterville, Maine, 1963-64; scientists Jet Propulsion Lab., Calif. Inst. Tech., Pasadena, 1965; research scientist II U. Colo., Boulder, 1966; physicist Nat. Bur. Standards, Washington, 1967; scientist The Te Co., Santa Barbara, Calif., 1970-72; research physicist U. Calif.-Santa Barbara, 1972-79, lectr., 1975, adj. lectr. environ. studies, 1975—, research physicist, 1975—; invited wind resource scientist, China. Contbr. articles on physics to profl. jours. Cons. Santa Barbara County Bd. Suprs. Gen. Motors fellow, 1967-68; U. Calif. Sea grantee, 1977-78, 1978-79. Mem. Am. Inst. Physicists, Am. Assn. Physics Tchrs., Sigma Xi. Club: Friends of the Earth. Office: Dept Environ Studies U Calif Santa Barbara CA 93106

MANASSAH, JAMAL TEWFEK, electrical engineering and physics educator, consultant; b. Haifa, Palestine, Feb. 23, 1945; s. Tewfek George and Alia Nasrallah (Kardoush) M.; m. Azza Tarek H.I. Mikdadi, Mar. 16, 1979; children—Tala, Nigh. B.Sc., Am. U. Beirut, Lebanon, 1966; M.A., Columbia U., 1968, Ph.D., 1970. Mem. Inst. Advanced Study, Princeton, N.J., 1970-72, 74-79; asst. prof. Am. U. Beirut, 1972-75; chief sci. adviser Kuwait Inst. Sci. Research, 1976-81; chief operating officer Kuwait Found., 1979-81; prof. dept. elec. engring. City Coll. CUNY, N.Y.C., 1981—; cons. Columbia Radiation Labs., N.Y.C., 1970-73, Ford Found., N.Y.C., 1973-79, NSF, Washington, 1978-83; chmn. Internat. Symposium Series, Kuwait, 1979-81; dir. Technopro, N.Y.C., 1982-86; mng. dir. Khayatt and Co., Inc., N.Y.C., 1982—; mem. organizing com. Chem. Research Applied to World Needs II, Internat. Union Pure and Applied Chemistry, 1980-83; mem. Welfare Assn., Geneva, 1984—. Editor: Alternate Energy Sources (2 vols.), 1981; (with others) Advances in Food Producing Systems for Arid and Simiarid Lands (2 vols.), 1981; Innovations in Telecommunication (2 vols.), 1982. Author monographs in theoretical physics, photonics engring. and techno-econs. Commr. Lebanese Boy Scouts Assn., Beirut, 1972-75; adviser internat. program NSF, 1979-83. Columbia U. faculty fellow, 1966-68; Pfister fellow, 1968-70; grantee NSF, 1982-87; recipient CUNY Recognition Scroll, 1985, ABI Key award, 1987. Mem. Optical Soc. Am., AAAS, N.Y. Acad. Sci., Assn. Mems. of Inst. for Advanced Study., Internat. Platform Assn. Christian Orthodox. Club: Princeton (N.Y.C.). Office: CUNY Dept Elec Engring Convent Ave at 140th St New York NY 10031

MANASSERO, HENRI J. P., hotel executive; b. Carcassonne, France, July 2, 1932; s. Jean and Paule (Guiraud) M.; m. Moya Corrigan, June 7, 1962. Degree in Hotel Adminstrn., French Hotel Sch., 1950. Mgr., Carlton Hotel, Cannes, France, Park Hotel, Bremen, Ger., Midland Hotel, Manchester, Eng.; gen. mgr. Royal Hibernian Hotel, Dublin, 1963-69; dir. food and beverage Trust Houses Forte Internat., 1970-72; asst. mng. dir. Trust Houses Forte Internat., London, 1973-79; v.p., gen. mgr. Pierre Hotel, N.Y.C., 1979-85; pres. Exclusive Hotels div. Trust Houses Forte Hotels Inc., 1986—; pres. Ashling Cons.; guest lectr. confs., India, Ireland, U.S. Contbr. articles on food and beverage to European trade mags. Bd. dirs. Am. French Found., Inc. Decorated Chevalier French Order of Merit, 1985. Mem. Irish Hotels and Restaurants Mgrs. Assn. (pres. 1969), Hotel and Catering Inst. Brit., Wine and Food Soc. N.Y. Hotel Assn. (dir.). Clubs: Westchester Country (Rye); Paris-Am; Doubles (N.Y.C.). Address: PO Box 660 Lakeville CT 06039

MANCHEE, KATHERYN HAIT DORFLINGER, historian, lecturer; b. Bklyn., Sept. 21, 1904; d. James Merritt and Belle (Silvey) Hait; student Parsons Sch. Art, 1923, Newark Sch. Art, 1924, Western Res. U., 1941-43; m. William F. Dorflinger, Apr. 1927 (dec. 1944); 1 dau., June (Mrs. John Alexander Hardy, Jr.); m. Arthur Leavens Manchee, Sept. 21, 1957; stepchildren—Mrs. R.W. Bachelder, Mrs. M.D. Brown, Mrs. Harry Wortman. Instr., lectr. Cleve. Mus. Art, 1941-44; lectr., historian Steuben Glass, N.Y.C., 1946-48; dir. advt. and publicity Midhurst Importing Corp., N.Y.C., 1952-54; dir. pub. relations and product promotion Fostoria Glass Co., N.Y.C., 1954-58. Mem. Jr. League Morristown (N.J.), 1930-39, 45-54, Jr. League Cleve., 1939-44; vice chmn. jr. council Cleve. Mus. Art, 1943-44; vol. Cleve. Orch. Woman's Com., 1942-44, ARC drives, Cleve., 1939-44; leader Girl Scouts U.S.A., Cleve., 1934-35. Fellow Met. Mus. Art (life); mem. Nat. Home Fashions League, Am. Women in Radio and TV, Nat. Soc. Colonial Dames, China Inst. Am., Asia Soc., Fgn. Policy Assn., English Speaking Union, Soc. Woman Geographers, Clubwomen's League Patriotic Services, Mus. Natural History, Newark Mus., Corning Mus. Glass, Drama League N.Y., Naples Council World Affairs, Naples Art Assn., Southwest Heritage, Friends Art Museums (membership chmn.). Presbyterian. Clubs: Colony (N.Y.C.); Garden of Onteora. Contbr. articles profl. publs. Home: Lions Gate 2919 Gulf Shores Blvd N Naples FL 33940

MANCHESTER, WILLIAM, writer; b. Attleboro, Mass., Apr. 1, 1922; s. William Raymond and Sallie Elizabeth (Thompson) M.; m. Julia Brown Marshall, Mar. 27, 1948; children: John Kennerly, Julie Thompson, Laurie. BA, U. Mass., 1946; AM, U. Mo., 1947; LHD (hon.), U. Mass., 1965, U. New Haven, 1979; LittD (hon.), Skidmore Coll., 1987, U. Richmond, 1988. Reporter Daily Oklahoman, 1945-46; reporter, fgn. corr., war corr. Balt. Sun, 1947-55; mng. editor Wesleyan U. Publs., 1955-64; fellow Wesleyan U. Ctr. for Advanced Studies, Middletown, Conn., 1959-60; writer-in-residence Wesleyan U., Middletown, 1975—, adj. prof. history, 1979—. Author: Disturber of the Peace, 1951, The City of Anger, 1953, Shadow of the Monsoon, 1956, Beard the Lion, 1958, A Rockefeller Family Portrait, 1959, The Long Gainer, 1961, Portrait of a President, 1962, The Death of a President, 1967 (Book-of-the-Month Club selection), The Arms of Krupp, 1968 (Lit. Guild selection), The Glory and the Dream, 1974 (Lit. Guild selection), Controversy and Other Essays in Journalism, 1976, American Caesar: Douglas MacArthur, 1880-1964, 1978 (Book-of-Month Club selection), Goodbye, Darkness, 1980 (Book-of-the-Month Club selection), The Last Lion: Visions of Glory, 1983 (Book-of-the-Month Club selection), One Brief Shining Moment, 1983 (Book-of-the-Month Club selection), Tha Last Lion: Alone, 1988 (Book-of-the-Month Club selection); contbr. to Ency. Brit., various publs. Pres. bd. trustees Friends of U. Mass. Library, 1970-71, trustee, 1970-74. Served as sgt. USMC, 1942-45, PTO. Decorated Purple Heart; recipient Dag Hammarskjöld prize Association Internationale Correspondents Diplomatiques, Rome, 1967, citation for best book on fgn. affairs Overseas Press Club, 1968, U. Mo. Honor award for disting. service in journalism, 1969, Conn. Book award, 1975, Pres.'s Cabinet award U. Detroit, 1981, Frederick S. Troy medal U. Mass., 1981, McConnaughy award Wesleyan U., 1981, Disting. Pub. Service award Conn. Bar Assn., 1985, Lincoln Literary award Union League Club N.Y., 1983, Blenheim award Internat. Churchill Soc., 1986, Washington Irving award, 1988; Guggenheim fellow, 1959-60. Mem. PEN, Soc. Am. Historians, Am. Hist. Assn., Authors Guild. Democrat. Episcopalian. Clubs: Williams, Century. Office: Box 329 Wesleyan Sta Middletown CT 06457

MANCINELLI, JACOB EMIL, corporate executive, consultant; b. Smock, Pa., Oct. 1, 1919; s. Joseph and Claudia (Di Russo) M.; BA, Harvard U., 1948; m. Sumiko Ogura; children: Teresa Ann, Kathryn Jean, Robin. With fin. dept. Gen. Electric Co. and G.E. C.C., Louisville, 1948-62; sr. v.p. U.S. Leasing Corp., San Francisco, 1962-69; sec., dir. Silver State Leasing Corp.; v.p., dir. Air Lease Corp., Barrel Leasing Corp., Cargo Vans Ltd., Comml. Pacific Corp., Fleet Leasing Corp., San Francisco, 1962-69; pres., dir. Compass Fin. Corp. (formerly Whittaker Leasing Corp.), Burlingame, Calif., 1969-73; pres., dir. TRE Fin. Corp., San Mateo, Calif., 1973-74; chmn. bd., pres. Dome Fin. Corp., Burlingame, 1974—; chmn. bd. Highridge, Inc., Redwood City, Calif., 1974-81; owner The Dome Co., Dome Realty, San Mateo, Calif., 1980—; instr. U. Calif. Extension. Pres., Foster City (Calif.) Home Improvement Assn., 1964-66; mem. Foster City Park and Recreation Commn., 1968—; chmn. Foster City Com. for Better Govt., 1973—; chmn. bd. United Assn. Union City, 1986-87; exec. bd. San Mateo council Boy Scouts Am.; bd. dirs. Foster City Community Assn., 1972—, pres., 1973—; chmn. bd. United Assn. Union City, 1986—. Served as officer USAF, 1939-54. Decorated Air medal with 2 clusters, Presdl. citation. Mem. Nat. Comml. Fin. Conf. (dir. 1967—), Greater San Francisco (mcpl. legis. com. 1967-69), Foster City (dir. 1972) C. of C., Internat. Platform Assn., Res. Officers Assn. Roman Catholic (council 1972—). Clubs: Commonwealth of Calif., Marina Point Tennis (pres.), Arnhem 1944 Vets. Author: Love Thoughts and Other Things, 1980. Home: 4927 Antioch Loop Union City CA 94587 Office: PO Box 381 Union City CA 94587

MANDAL, MANAS KUMAR, psychologist; b. Burdwan, India, Nov. 1, 1956; s. Chitta Ranjan and Shanti Rani Mandal; m. Sanjukta, Feb. 17, 1984. BA with honors, Scottish Ch., Calcutta, India, 1977; MA with honors, Calcutta U., 1979, PhD, 1984. Lectr. Banaras Hindu U., Varanasi, India, 1983—. Contbr. articles to profl. jours. Nat. scholarship Calcutta U., 1977; recipient Gold medal Calcutta U., 1980, Career award, 1988; Fulbright fellow, 1986. Mem. Indian Sci. Congress (life mem., Young Scientist 1986). Home: 46/9 SN Banerjee Rd, Calcutta 700014, India Office: Banaras Hindu Univ, Dept Psychology, Varanasi 221005, India

MANDEL, BENJAMIN JORGE, dentist, consultant; b. Mexico City, May 13, 1944; s. Maurice and Victoria (Eskenazi) M.; m. Olga Sherr, Dec. 27, 1970; children—Joshua, Jonathan. B.S. in Chemistry, U. Calif.-Berkeley, 1966; M.S. in Chemistry, C.I.E.A.-I.P.N., Mexico City, 1969; D.D.S., NYU, 1975. Research asst. C.I.E.A.-I.P.N., 1967-69; research assoc. U. Wis.-Madison, 1970-71, Hoffman La Roche, Nutley, N.J., 1971-72; gen. practice resident VA Hosp., Martinez, Calif., 1975-76; gen. practice dentistry, San Jose, Calif., 1976—; cons. Mission Convalescent Home, San Jose, 1976, Child Health and Disability Prevention Program, San Jose, 1978-80; speaker in field; lectr. health-related topics, Tahiti, 1986, Jamaica, 1987. Author: Dentistry for the 21st Century. Vol. Kron Health Fair, San Jose, 1977; TV guest People and Progress Show, 1985. Recipient appreciation award Mexican Ctr. for Research and Oral Rehab., 1984; Herman Muehlstein scholar, 1974. Mem. ADA, Calif. Dental Assn. (lectr. annual meetings 1984—, presenter ann. meeting 1986), Santa Clara County Dental Soc. (hosp. and dental health com. 1978-81), Am. Soc. Clin. Hypnosis, Western Soc. Periodontology (bd. dirs. 1982—), Am. Acad. Gnathological Orthopedics, Santa Clara Periodontics Study Club (founder, chmn. 1980—), Internat. Platfrom Assn., Alpha Omega. Republican. Office: 74 Harold Ave San Jose CA 95117

MANDEL, ERNEST, educator; b. Apr. 5, 1923. Cert., Ecole Pratique des Hautes Etudes, Paris, 1967; PhD, Free U., Berlin, 1972. Prof. Vrije U., Brussels, 1970—. Author: Marxist Economic Theory, 1962, Late Capitalism, 1972, The Long Waves of Capitalist Development, 1979, Revolutionary Marxism Today, 1979, The Second Slump, 1982, Delightful Murder, 1985, The Meaning of the Second World War, 1987, After Peterstroika, 1988. Home: 127 Rue Jos Impens, 1030 Brussels Belgium

MANDEL, KARYL LYNN, accountant; b. Chgo., Dec. 14, 1935; d. Isador J. and Eve (Gellar) Karzen; m. Fredric H. Mandel, Sept. 29, 1956; children: David Scott, Douglas Jay, Jennifer Ann. Student, U. Mich., 1954-56, Roosevelt U., 1956-57; AA summa cum laude, Oakton Community Coll., 1979. CPA, Ill. Pres., nat. bd. mem. Women's Am. Orgn. for Rehab. through Tng., 1961-77; pres. Excel Transp. Service Co., Elk Grove, Ill., 1958-78; tax mgr. Chunowitz, Teitelbaum & Baerson, CPA's, Elk Grove, Ill., 1958-78; tax mgr. Chunowitz, Teitelbaum & Baerson, CPA's, Northbrook, Ill., 1981-83, tax ptnr., 1984—; sec-treas. Lednam, Inc.; mem. acctg. curriculum adv. bd. Oakton Community Coll., Des Plaines, Ill., 1987—. Contbg. author: Ill. CPA's News Jour. Recipient State of Israel Solidarity award, 1976. Mem. Am. Inst. CPA's, Am. Soc. Women CPA's, Women's Am. ORT, Ill. CPA Soc. (vice chmn. estate and gift tax com. 1985-87, chmn. estate and gift tax com., 1987—, mem. legis. contact com. 1981-82, pres. North Shore chpt., award for Excellence in Acctg. Edn.), Chgo. Soc. Women CPA's, Chgo. Estate Planning Council, Nat. Assn. Women Bus. Owners. Office: 401 Huehl Rd Northbrook IL 60062

MANDEL, MICHEL, university professor in physical chemistry; b. Antwerp, Belgium, Jan. 24, 1926; arrived in The Netherlands, 1958; s. Henri and Rose (Mateles) M.; m. Sophia A. Peters, Feb. 5, 1938; children: Caroline, Daniel H. Licencié Sc. Chimiques, Univ. Libre, Brussels, 1949, PhD, 1955; PhD (hon.), U. Uppsala, Sweden, 1985. adj. prof. physical chemistry Univ. Libre, 1961—. Instr. Univ. Libre, 1949-58; lector, reader Leiden (The Netherlands) U., 1958-61, prof. phys. chemistry, 1961—. Prin, editor internat. sci. jour. Biophysical Chemistry; mem. adv. bd. series Advances in Chemical Physics; contbr. articles to profl. jours. Mem. Soc. Royale Chimique de Belgique, Koninklijke Nederlandse Chemische Vereniging, Royal Soc. Chemistry. Home: Boerhaavelaan 47, 2334 EE Leiden The Netherlands Office: Leiden U Gorlaeus Labs, PO Box 9502, 2300 RA Leiden The Netherlands

MANDEL, NEWTON W., lawyer; b. Bklyn., Aug. 27, 1926; s. Nathan and Rose (Tenenbaum) M.; m. Ellen Tannenbaum, Nov. 27, 1954; children: Sherry, Harlan. BS, N.C. State U., Raleigh, 1948; JD, N.Y. Law Sch., 1951. Bar: N.Y. 1951, U.S. Dist. Ct. (ea. and so. dists.) N.Y. 1951, U.S. Ct. Appeals (2d cir.) 1953. Ptnr. Mandel & Beck, 1951-58, Mandel & Blum, 1958-64; v.p., gen. counsel 1st Republic Corp. Am., N.Y.C., 1964-69; v.p., counsel G & W Realty Corp., Madison Sq. Garden Corp., 1969-72; sr. atty. Dreyer & Traub, 1973-78; prin. Zimton Group, real estate developers, 1978—; of counsel Lefrak, Fischer & Myerson, 1981-84; ptnr. Certilman, Haft, Lebow, Balin, Buckley & Kremer, 1984-87; of counsel Reavis & McGrath, N.Y.C., 1987—. Bd. govs. Long Island U. CW Post Ctr. for Real Estate and Community Devel.; trustee Cen. Synagogue, N.Y.C. Served with USNR. Mem. ABA (chmn. syndications com., real property div., tax sect., corp. sect.), N.Y. State Bar Assn. (real property sect., tax sect.), LIU Real Estate Inst. Clubs: Knickerbocker Yacht (Port Washington, N.Y.); Yacht Racing Assn. L.I. Sound. Lodge: B'nai Brith. Office: 345 Park Ave New York NY 10154

MANDELA, NELSON ROLIHLAHIA, South African politician and lawyer; b. 1918, Transkei; m. Winnie Mandela. Ed. U. Coll. of Fort Hare, U. Witwatersrand. LLD (hon.), Nat. U. Lesotho, 1979, CCNY, 1983; DLitt (hon.) Calcutta U., 1986. Legal practice, Johannesburg, 1952; nat. organizer African Nat. Congress (A.N.C.); on trial for treason 1956-61 (acquitted 1961); arrested 1962, sentenced to five years' imprisonment Nov. 1962; on trial for further charges Nov. 1963-June 1964, sentenced to life imprisonment June 1964. Author: No Easy Walk to Freedom, 1965. Recipient Jawaharlal Nehru award, India, 1979, Bruno Kreisky prize for Human Rights, 1981, Freedom of City of Glasgow, 1981, Simon Bolivar Internat. prize UNESCO, 1983, Third World prize, 1986; named Hon. Citizen of Rome, 1983. *

MANDELA, NOMZAMO WINNIE, cultural organization member; b. Bizana, Pondoland, Transkei, 1934; d. Columbus Masikzela; m. Nelson Mandela, 1958. Chmn. bd. Orlando br. ANC, 1960; social worker Child Welfare Soc., 1962; med. social worker Baragwanath Hosp.; founder Black Parents Assn., 1976; mem. Nat. Exec. African Nat. Congress Women's League. First social worker in Republic of South Africa; banned under Suppression Communism Act 1962-75; twice charged for contravening banning order 1967; detained under Sec. 6 Terrorism Act 1969 and held in solitary confinement for 17 mos.; acquitted 1970; banned and placed under house arrest 1970; charged a number of times for breaking banning orders and received suspended sentence for communicating with another banned person 1971; detained under preventive detention clause of Internal Security Act., 1976; banished to Phatakahle, Brandfort, Orange Free State, 1977; subsequently served with banning orders, 1982-83; banning orders under rev., 1986. Recipient Third World prize, 1985. Mem. Nat. Exec. Fedn. of Republic of South Africa. Address: Internat Com Apartheid Racism, Colonialism So Africa, PO Box 38, London N1 9PR, England also: Soweto, Transvaal Republic of South Africa *

MANDELBAUM, MOSHE Y., banker; b. Jerusalem, Mar. 3, 1933; s. Yehiel Mandelbaum; m. Sara Salomon, 1957; children—Yehiel, Shmuel, Abigail. B.A. in Econ. Stats., Hebrew U., Jerusalem, 1956, M.A. in Econ. Internat. Relations, 1959; M.A. in Econs., Vanderbilt U., 1961, Ph.D., 1968. Dir. gen. Ministry of Industry and Commerce, Jerusalem, 1974-78; vice chmn. Indsl. Devel. Bank, Tel Aviv, 1978-81; dep. gov. Bank of Israel, Jerusalem, 1981-82, gov., 1982-86; sr. lectr. Bar Ilan U., Ramat-Gan, Israel. Author numerous articles on econ. subjects. Jewish. Home: 18 Harav Berlin St, Jerusalem Israel Office: Bank of Israel, Bank of Israel Bldg PO Box 780, Jerusalem 91007, Israel

MANDELKER, GERSHON, finance educator; b. Dubno, Poland, Dec. 12; came to U.S., 1968, naturalized, 1982; s. Isaac and Pearl M.; m. Ester Stock, Jan. 14, 1964; children: Eiran, Sigal. BA, Hebrew U., Jerusalem, 1965; MBA, U. Chgo., 1971, PhD, 1973. Lectr. fin. U. Chgo., 1972-73; asst. prof. indsl. adminstrn. Carnegie-Mellon U., 1973-77; prof. bus. fin. U. Pitts., 1977—; fin. and investment cons.; speaker in field. Assoc. editor: Jour. Fin. Research, Fin. Rev. jour., Fin. Mgmt. jour.; contbr. articles to profl. jours. Mem. Am. Fin. Assn., Am. Econ. Assn., Fin. Mgmt. Assn., Western Fin. Assn., Ea. Fin. Assn. (v.p.). Home: 1323 Murdoch Rd Pittsburgh PA 15217 Office: Grad Sch Bus U Pitts Pittsburgh PA 15260

MANDERS, KARL LEE, neurological surgeon; b. Rochester, N.Y., Jan. 21, 1927; s. David Bert and Frances Edna (Cohan) Mendelson; m. Ann Laprell, July 28, 1969; children—Karlanna, Maidena; children by previous marriage—Karl, Kerry, Kristine. Student, Cornell U., 1946; M.D., U. Buffalo, 1950. Diplomate Am. Bd. Neurol. Surgery, Am. Bd. Clin. Biofeedback, Nat. Bd. Med. Examiners. Intern U. Va. Hosp., Charlottesville, 1950-51, resident in neurol. surgery, 1951-52; resident in neurol. surgery Henry Ford Hosp., Detroit, 1954-56; practice medicine specializing in neurol. surgery Indpls., 1956—; med. dir. Community Hosp. Rehab. Ctr. for Pain, 1973—; med. dir. Head Injury and Coma Arousal Ctr., Community Hosp. North Profl. Bldg., Indpls.; chief hosp. med. and surg. neurology Community Hosp., 1983; coroner Marion County, Ind., 1977; pres. Neurosurgical Assocs. Ind., Hyperbanic Oxygen Assocs. Ind. Served with USN, 1952-54, Korea. Recipient cert. achievement Dept. Army, 1969. Fellow ACS, Internat. Coll Surgeons, Am. Acad. Neurology; mem. AMA, Am. Assn. Neurol. Surgery, Congress Neurol. Surgery, Internat. Assn. Study of Pain, Am. Assn. Study of Headache, N.Y. Acad. Sci., Am. Coll. Angiology, Am. Soc. Contemporary Medicine and Surgery, Am. Holistic Med. Assn. (a founder), Undersea Med. Soc., Am. Acad. Forensic Sci., Am. Assn. Biofeedback Clinicians, Soc. Cryosurgery, Pan Pacific Surg. Assn., Biofeedback Soc. Am., Acad. Psychosomatic Medicine, Pan Am. Med. Assn., Internat. Back Pain Soc., North Am. Spine Soc., Am. Soc. Stereotaxic and Functional Neurosurgery, Soc. for Computerized Tomography and Neuroimaging, Ind. Coroners Assn. (pres. 1979), Royal Soc. Medicine, Am. Pain Soc., Midwest Pain Soc. (pres. 1988), Cen. Neurol. Soc., Interurban Neurosurg. Soc., Internat. Soc. Aquatic Medicine, James A. Gibson Anat. Soc., Am. Bd. Med. Psychotherapists (mem. profl. adv. council). Clubs: Brendonwood Country, Highland Country. Home: 5845 Highfall St Indianapolis IN 46226 Office: 5506 E 16th St Indianapolis IN 46218

MANDL, GEORGE THOMAS, paper mill executive; b. Prague, Czechoslovakia, Aug. 8, 1923; emigrated to U.K., 1949, to Switzerland, 1974; s. D. Gottfried and Hanna (Ascher) M. Student U. Prague, 1945-47. Chmn., Thomas & Green Holdings Ltd., Wooburn Green, High Wycombe, Buckinghamshire, Eng., 1971—, Papierfabrik Netstal AG (Switzerland), 1974, G. T. Mandl & Co. A/S, Otterup, Odense, Denmark, 1968—; dep. chmn. Linthesa Holding AG, Netstal, Switzerland, 1983—, Linthkraft AG, Netstal, 1982—; dir. Indupa NV Zaventem Belgium, 1983. Author: 300 Years Papierfabrik Netstal, 1979; 300 Years in Paper, 1985. Ct. mem. Worshipful Co. Stationers and Newspaper Makers, City of London, 1982. Served with Allied Forces, 1941-45. Recipient Gold medal Paper Industry, 1981. Mem. Brit. Paper and Board Industry Fedn. (council 1963-73, 84—). Club: City Livery (London). Office: Papierfabrik Netstal AG, CH-8754 Netstal Switzerland

MANDLER, GEORGE, psychologist; b. Vienna, Austria, June 11, 1924; came to U.S., 1940, naturalized, 1943; s. Richard and Hede (Goldschmied) M.; m. Jean Matter, Jan. 19, 1957; children: Peter Clark, Michael Allen. B.A., NYU, 1949; M.S., Yale U., 1950, Ph.D., 1953; postgrad., U. Basel, Switzerland, 1947-48. Asst. prof. Harvard U., 1953-57, lectr., 1957-60; prof. U. Toronto, Ont., Can., 1960-65; prof. psychology, dir. Ctr. Human Info. Processing U. Calif.-San Diego, 1965—, chmn. dept. psychology, 1965-70; hon. research fellow Univ. Coll. London. Author: books the most recent being Mind and Emotion, 1975, (German edit.), 1980, Mind and Body, 1984, (Japanese edit.), 1987, Cognitive Psychology, 1985; contbr. articles and revs. to profl. jours.; editor: Psychol. Rev., 1970-76. Served with U.S. Army, 1943-46. Fellow Ctr. for Advanced Study in Behavioral Scis., 1959-60; vis. fellow Oxford U., Eng., 1971-72, 78; Guggenheim fellow, 1971-72; hon. research fellow Univ. Coll., London U., 1977-78, 82—. Fellow AAAS; Am. Assn. Advancement Psychology (1974-82); Psychonomic Soc. (governing bd., chmn. 1983), Am. Psychol. Assn. (pres. div. exptl. psychology 1978-79, pres. div. gen psychology 1982-83, mem. council reps. 1978-82, William James prize 1986), Internat. Union Psychol. Scis. (U.S. com. 1985—), Soc. Exptl. Psychologists, Fedn. Behavioral Psychol. and Cognitive Scis. (pres. 1981), AAUP. Home: 1406 La Jolla Knoll La Jolla CA 92037 Office: U Calif San Diego Dept Psychology La Jolla CA 92093 also: 3 Perrins Ln, London NW3 1QY, England

MANDLIKOVA, HANA, professional tennis player; b. Prague, Czechoslovakia, Feb. 19, 1962. Winner New South Wales Open, 1979, South Australian Open, 1979, 80, Australian Open, 1979, 80, 87, Toyota Classics, 1979, Darrison's Classics, Atlanta, 1980, Volvo Cup, 1980, 81, U.S. Open, 1985, Virginia Slims of Calif., 1985, Women's Tennis Classic, 1987, Va. Slims of Washington, 1987. Address: care US Tennis Assn 51 E 42d St New York NY 10017 *

MANEATIS, GEORGE A., utility company executive; b. 1926. BS in Elec. Engring., Stanford U., 1949, MS in Elec. Engring., 1950. With Gen. Elec. Co., 1950-53; with Pacific Gas & Elec. Co., San Francisco, 1953—, v.p., 1979-81, sr. v.p., 1981-82, exec. v.p., 1982-86, pres., 1986—, also dir. Office: Pacific Gas & Electric Co 77 Beale St San Francisco CA 94106 *

MANELI, MIECZYSLAW, political science, law educator; b. Poland, 1924; children: Elizabeth, Lester. MA in Econs., Law, Warsaw U., 1949, PhD in Law, 1953. Prof. law, chmn. Inst. Polit.-Juridical Doctrines Warsaw U., 1954-68, vice dean, 1956-62, dean, 1963-64; polit. adv. to pres. Indonesia Govt., 1964; with polit. sci. dept. Queens Coll., Flushing, N.Y., 1968—; co-founder, editor-in-chief Politics and Morality, 1986—. Author: The Activity of a Socialist State, 1957, The Functions of the State, 1963, Art of Politics, 1967, Machiavelli, a Monograph, 1968, Foundations, 1968, History of Political and Juricical Ideas, 1968, War of the Vanquished, 1971, Juridical Positivism and Human Rights, 1981, Freedom and Tolerance, 1984; columnist Law and Life, 1957-68. Co-chmn. European Juridical Commn. to Prosecute Nazi Jurists, 1958-68. Served with Polish Underground, WWII; imprisoned Majdanek and Auschwitz concentration camps. Office: Queens Coll CUNY Polit Sci Dept Flushing NY 11367

MANFORD, BARBARA ANN, contralto; b. St. Augustine, Fla., Nov. 13, 1929; d. William Floyd and Margaret (Kemper) Manford; Mus.B. in Voice, Fla. State U., 1951, Mus.M., 1970; studied with L. Palazzini, A. Strano, Japelli, E. Nikolaidi, E. Joseph. Appearances in Europe, performing major roles in 12 leading opera houses, 1951-68, with condrs. including Alfred Strano, Felice Cilario, Robert Shaw, Arnold Gamson, Guiseppe Patané, Ottavio Ziino, also numerous concerts and recitals in Paris and throughout Italy and Belgium; performed in world premiere Fugitives (C. Floyd), Fla. State U., Tallahassee, 1950; chosen by Gian Carlo Menotti for leading role in world premiere The Leper, Fla. State U., 1970; numerous radio, TV, and concert appearances, U.S., 1968—; artist-in-residence, asso. prof. voice Ball State U., Muncie, Ind., 1970—; numerous recs. Semi-finalist vocal contest, Parma, Italy, 1964; winner contest, Lonigo, Italy, 1965. Mem. Nat. Assn. Tchrs. Singing, Chgo. Artists Assn., Am. Tchrs. Nat. Assn., Sigma Alpha Iota, Pi Kappa Lambda. Christian Scientist. Home: 104 Colonial Crest Apts Muncie IN 47304 Office: Ball State Univ Muncie IN 47306

MANFREDA, MICHAEL JOSEPH, lawyer, cons.; b. New Haven, Dec. 28, 1951; s. Joseph Michael and Margaret Mary (Dunn) M. B.A. in History, Coll. of Holy Cross, 1974; J.D., Suffolk U., 1977. Bar: Mass. 1977, U.S. dist. ct. Mass. 1978, U.S. Ct. Appeals (1st cir.) 1978, Conn. 1980, U.S. Supreme Ct. 1982. Substitute tchr. Wallingford (Conn.) Pub. Schs., 1974-77; prosecutor Boston Juvenile Ct., 1976-77; law clk. to dist. atty., Boston, 1977; asst. dist. atty. Suffolk County, Boston 1977-79; prin. Michael J. Manfreda & Assocs., Boston and Wallingford, Conn., 1979—; cons. and lectr. in field; dir. Cele-Nav Industries, Inc. Ward coordinator Democratic campaign, 1978, coordinator, 1980, active other campaigns, 1978—. Recipient Am. Jurisprudence award, 1976. Mem. ABA, Mass. Bar Assn., Conn. Bar Assn., Boston Bar Assn., New Haven County Bar Assn., Tolland County Bar Assn., Internat. Platform Assn. Roman Catholic. Office: 101 Tremont St Boston MA 02108

MANGAN, EDMUND LAWRENCE, technical and business consultant, business executive; b. Los Angeles, Dec. 20, 1938; s. Francis A. and Edith D. (Perry) M.; m. Suzanne Marie Yelle, Feb. 2, 1960; children—Alan, Michele, Meredith, Maureen. BS in Engring., U.S. Naval Acad, 1960; MBA, Lehigh U., 1975. With Bethlehem Steel Corp. (Pa.), 1964-82, spl. engr. gen. mgr.'s staff, 1978-79, asst. div. supt. Saucon Mills, 1979-80, supt. dept. tech., 1980-82; ind. tech. and bus. cons., 1983—; v.p. engring. and mktg. SI Handling Systems, Easton, Pa., 1983-86; sr. industry exec. World Bank, Washington, 1986—. Served as ensign U.S. Navy, 1960. Mem. IEEE, Assn. Iron and Steel Engrs. (Kelly award 1973). Contbr. articles on indsl. measurement and control to profl. jours.; patentee indsl. measurement and control equipment.

MANGER, WILLIAM MUIR, physician; b. Greenwich, Conn., Aug. 13, 1920; s. Julius and Lilian (Weissinger) M.; B.S., Yale U., 1944; M.D., Columbia U., 1946; Ph.D., Mayo Found., U. Minn., 1958; m. Lynn Seymour Sheppard, May 30, 1964; children—William Muir, Jr., Lilian Wade, Stewart

Sheppard, Charles Seymour. Intern, Presbyn. Hosp., N.Y.C., 1946-47, resident, 1949-50; fellow internal medicine Mayo Found., 1950-57; asst. physician Presbyn. Hosp., 1957—; dir. Manger Research Found., 1961-77; clin. asst. vis. physician Columbia div. Bellevue Hosp., 1964-68; asst. attending NYU Bellevue Hosp. 1969-77; asso. attending, 1977-83, attending, 1983— ; instr. medicine Columbia U. Coll. Phys. and Surg., 1957-66, asso. medicine, 1966-70, lectr., 1981—; asst. attending physician Presbyn. Hosp., 1966—; asst. clin. prof. medicine N.Y.U. Med. Center, 1968-75, assoc. clin. prof. medicine, 1975-83, prof. clin. medicine, 1983—; mem. Internat. Med. Council on Drug Use, 1977—; mem. devel. com. Mayo Clinic, 1981-87; vice chmn. bd. Manger Hotels, Inc., 1957-73. Bd. govs. St. Albans Sch., Washington, 1958-64, 67-73, 83—, chmn., 1967-69; trustee Found. Research in Medicine and Biology, 1971-77, Buckley Sch., 1975-85, Found. for Advancement Internat. Research in Microbiology, 1977—, Thyroid Found., 1980-85; trustee Found. for Depression and Manic Depression, 1978—, pres., 1980—. Served as lt. (j.g.) M.C., USNR, 1947-49. Recipient Meritorious Research award Mayo Found. Alumni, 1955. Diplomate Nat. Bd. Med. Examiners, Am. Bd. Internal Medicine. Fellow ACP, Acad. Psychosomatic Medicine, Am. Geriatric Soc., N.Y. Acad. Medicine (admission com. 1976-78, edn. com. 1979—), Am. Coll. Cardiology, Am. Coll. Clin. Pharmacology, Royal Soc. Health, Am. Inst. Chemists; trustee Nat. Hypertension Assn. (chmn. 1977—), AMA, N.Y. State, N.Y. County med. socs., Am. Heart Assn. (fellow council on circulation and council for high blood pressure research), Inter-Am. Soc. Hypertension, Internat. Soc. Hypertension, Am. Thoracic Soc., N.Y. Acad. Sci., AAAS, Am. Physiol. Soc., Am. Chem. Soc., Am. Soc. Pharmacology and Exptl. Therapeutics, Am. Soc. for Clin. Pharmacology and Therapeutics, Clin. Autonomic Research Soc., Med. Strollers, N.Y.C., Endocrine Soc., Pan Am. Med. Assn., Harvey Soc., Soc. Exptl. Biology and Medicine, Research Discussion Group (founding mem., sec.-treas. 1958-80), Am. Fedn. Clin. Research, Am. Soc. Nephrology, Royal Soc. Medicine (affiliate), Fellows Assn. Mayo Found. (v.p., pres. 1953), Mayo Alumni Assn. (v.p. 1981-82, exec. com. 1981—, pres. elect 1982-85, pres. 1985-87), Catecholamine Club (a founder, (sec.-treas. 1967-80, pres. 1981-82), Doctors Mayo Soc., Albert Gallatin Assos., New Eng. Soc., S.R. (chmn. admissions com. 1959-67, bd. mgrs. 1959-67, 69-70), Soc. Colonial Wars, Sigma Xi, Nu Sigma Nu, Phi Delta Theta. Presbyterian (elder 1968-71, trustee 1962-72, 80-84, deacon 1959-61). Clubs: Explorers, Meadow (L.I., N.Y.); University, Yale, N.Y. Athletic (N.Y.C.); Southampton Bathing Corp. Co-author: Chemical Quantitation of Epinephrine and Norepinephrine in Plasma, 1959; co-author: Pheochromocytoma, 1977; author: Catecholamines in Normal and Abnormal Cardiac Function; editor, contbr. Hormones and Hypertension, 1966; editor: Am. Lecture Series in Endocrinology, 1962-75; contbr. articles to profl. and lay jours. Office: 324 E 30th St New York NY 10016 also: 400 E 34th St New York NY 10016

MANGES, JAMES H., investment banker; b. N.Y.C., Oct. 8, 1927; s. Horace S. and Natalie (Bloch) M.; m. Joan Brownell, Oct., 1969 (div.); m. Mary Seymour, Mar. 28, 1974; children: Alison, James H. Jr. Grad., Phillips Exeter Acad., 1945; BA, Yale U., 1950; MBA, Harvard U., 1953. With Kuhn, Loeb & Co., N.Y.C., 1954-77, ptnr., 1967-77; mng. dir. Lehman Bros., Kuhn Loeb Inc., N.Y.C., 1977-84, Shearson Lehman Bros., N.Y.C., 1984—. Trustee The Episcopal Sch., 1978—, St. Bernard's Sch., 1985—, Phillips Exeter Acad., 1984—. Served with CIC, AUS, 1946-48. Clubs: Bond, Yale (N.Y.C.); City Midday, Century Country (Purchase, N.Y.). Home: 875 Park Ave New York NY 10021 Office: Shearson Lehman Hutton Inc World Fin Ctr Am Express Tower New York NY 10285

MANGLANI, CHATRU, accountant; b. Bambay, Maharashtra, India, Dec. 11, 1948; s. Kanayo Lachiram and Rukmani Kanayo (Tourani) M.; m. Jyoti Chatru Mahbubani, Aug. 3, 1972; children: Sharmila, Manju, Deepak. Assoc. chartered acct., 1971, fellow chartered acct., 1979. Audit mgr. Thornton Baker & Co., Manchester, Eng., 1972-74; sr. tax asst. corp. tax div. Price Waterhouse & Co., Manchester, 1974-76; exec. Hispano Gina SA., Tenerife, Spain, 1976—. treas. Brit. Yeoward Sch., Puerto De La Cruz, Tenerife, 1983-85, 87. Fellow Inst. Chartered Accts. Eng. Wales. Club: India (treas. 1979).

MANGLAPUS, RAUL S., Philippine government official; b. Manila, Oct. 20, 1918; m. Pacita Arguelles La O. BA summa cum laude, Ateneo de Manila, 1939, LLB, 1946; postgrad., Georgetown U., 1948. Undersec. fgn. affairs Philippines, 1954-57, sec. fgn. affairs, 1957, 87—, senator, 1961-67, 87—; sec.-gen. founding conf. SEATO, 1954—; vice-chmn. Philippine delagation Asian-African Conf., Bandung, Indonesia, 1955; del. Philippine Constitutional Conv., 1970-72. Address: Sec Fgn Affairs, Ministry Fgn Affairs, Manila Philippines *

MANGOPE, LUCAS MANYANE, tribal chief and politican of Bophuthatswana, South Africa; b. Motswedi, Zeerust, Dec. 27, 1927; s. Manyane and Semakaleng Mangope; m. Leah Tsholegelo, 1950; 4 sons, 3 daus. Ed. St. Peter's Coll., Bethel Coll. Worked in Dept. Bantu Adminstrn. and Devel., taught at Motswedi; succeeded his father as chief of Bahurutshe-Boo-Manyane, Sept. 1959; vice-chmn. Tswana Territorial Authority, 1961-68, chief councillor, 1968-72; chief minister of Bophuthatswana, South Africa, 1972-77, pres. of Republic of Bophuthatswana, 1977—. Office: Office of Pres, Pvt Bag X2005, Murikeng Bophuthatswana, Republic of South Africa *

MANGWENDE, WITNESS, minister information, posts, and telecommunications Republic of Zimbabwe; b. Charter, Zimbabwe, Oct. 15, 1946; student U. Rhodesia; B.A. in Internat. Relations, Southampton (Eng.) U.; Ph.D. in Internat. Relations, London Sch. Econs.; married. Pres., Zimbabwe Student's Union; chief rep. ZANU (Zimbabwe African Nat. Union), Mozambique, from 1979; minister of fgn. affairs Govt. of Zimbabwe, until 1988, minister info., posts and telecommunications., 1988—. Office: Ministry of Info, Harare Zimbabwe *

MANHOLD, JOHN HENRY, medical dentistry educator author, consultant; b. Rochester, N.Y., Aug. 20, 1919; s. John Henry and Helen Martha (Shulz) M.; m. Beverly Schecter, 1953 (div. 1969) 1 child (dec.); m. Enriqueta Andino, Mar. 20, 1971. B.A., U. Rochester, 1940; D.M.D., Harvard U., 1944; M.A., Washington U., 1956. Instr. Tufts U. Coll. Medicine, Boston, 1948-50; asst. prof., chmn. gen. and oral pathology Washington U. Coll. Dentistry, St. Louis, 1954-56; from asst. prof. to prof., chmn. dept. gen. and oral pathology Seton Hall Coll. Medicine and Dentistry (now called U. Medicine and Dentistry N.J.), Newark, 1956-87; med. dir., Woog Internat., 1987—; cons. Johnson & Johnson, New Brunswick, N.J., 1960-70, Richardson-Vicks, Shelton, Conn., 1981-87, Los Produits Associes, Geneva, Switzerland, 1965-87. Author: Introductory Psychosomatic Dentistry, 1956; Outline of Pathology, 1960; Clinical Oral Diagnosis, 1965; Tissue Respiration and Oxigenating Agents, 1977; Practical Dental Management: Patients and Practice, 1984; (with others) Handbook of Pathology, 1987. Editor: Illustrated Dental Terminology: A Lexicon for the Dental Profession, 1985. Editor Clinical Preventive Dentistry jour., 1979—. World wide lectr. Contbr. numerous articles to profl. jours. Named to Sr. Soc. Harvard Sch. Dental Medicine, 1984; recipient Pres. award Alumni Assn. U. Medicine and Dentistry N.J., 1980, Letter of Appreciation Asara Mihara former minister Japan, 1980, Cert. Achievement U. Md., 1965; fellow Internat. Coll. Dentists, 1965. Mem. Acad. Psychosomatic Medicine (pres. 1977-78, sec. 1975-76, treas. 1970-75), Am. Soc. Clin. Pathologists, Am. Psychol. Assn., Internat. Assn. Dental Research, Sigma Xi. Clubs: Pass-A-Grille Yacht. Home and Office: PO Box 9159 Treasure Island FL 33740

MANIBUSAN, ROY CRUZ, school administrator, educator; b. Agana, Guam, July 17, 1939; s. Jesus Leon Guerrero and Engracia Garcia (Cruz) M.; m. Zenaida Lopez Galura; children—Adrian, Jessica, Rowena. B.A. in Sociology, U. Guam, 1969; M.A. in Couseling and Psychology, Ball State U., 1973; postgrad. U. Ark., 1973-74; EdS U. Nev.-Las Vegas. Cert. edn. adminstrn., counselor. Served as enlisted man U.S. Air Force, 1958-69, commd. 2d lt., 1969, advanced through grades to capt., 72; ret., 1980; prin. St. Christopher Sch., North Las Vegas, Nev., 1979-86; adj. instr. psychology, sociology and counseling Nicholls State U., Thibodaus, La., Park Coll., St. Louis, Clark County Community Coll., Las Vegas, 1975—. Pres., founder Maranatha Acad., Inc., North Las Vegas, Nev., 1987—; trustee Nev. Assn. Latin Ams., 1985—. Mem. Nat. Assn. Elem. Sch. Prins., Nat. Cath. Edn. Assn., Assn. Supervision and Curriculum Devel., Assn Private and Parochial Schs. Nev. (charter, trustee), AAUP. Republican. Roman Catholic. Club: K.C.

MANIGAT, LESLIE F., former president of Haiti; b. Port-Au-Prince, Haiti, Aug. 16, 1930; s. Francois and Haydee (Augustin) M.; m. Mirlande Hyppolite, 1970. Grad., U. Paris, 1949. With Ministry Fgn. Affairs, Haiti, 1953-60; prof., co-founder ctr. secondary studies U. Haiti, 1953-63, prof. law, 1953-57; prof. internat. relations U. Simon Bolivar, Caracas, Venezuela, 1978-86; acad. assessor Inst. Higher Studies Nat. Def., Caracas, 1983-84; former pres. Republic Haiti, 1988; now polit. sci. prof. Wilson Ctr., Washington. Office: Woodrow Wilson Internat Ctr for Scholars Smithsonian Instn Bldg Washington DC 20560 *

MANIGLIER, BERNARD, computer company executive; b. Scionzier, France, May 6, 1943; s. Louis and Marie (Blanchet) M.; m. Marie-Josee Bruel, Dec. 27, 1969; children—Berangere, Fabrice. Ingenieur, Ecole Catholique D'Arts et Metiers, Lyon, France, 1964; M.S.E.E., Stanford U., 1965, M.B.A., 1970. Devel. engr. IBM Corp., La Gaude, France, 1966-68; salesman, then sales mgr., subs. gen. mgr. CEGI-Tymshare, Paris, Brussels and Amsterdam, 1970-81; gen. mgr. Osborne Micro-Portable Co., Paris, 1982-84, Compaq Computer France, Paris, 1984—. Fulbright fellow, 1964, French Govt. fellow, 1964. Mem. Stanford Bus. Club (exec. com. 1970—), Internat. Bus. Club (pres. Stanford chpt. 1969-70). Avocations: skiing; tennis; sailing. Home: 17 Avenue d'Italie, 75013 Paris France Office: Compaq Computer France, 5 Ave de Norvege, BP 245-91944 Les Ulis Cedex France

MANIJAK, WILLIAM, history and government educator; b. Holyoke, Mass., July 4, 1913; s. Stanley and Catherine (Padlo) M.; m. Phyllis Mae Hatch, Aug. 13, 1949; children: William Stafford, Catherine Anne. BA in English cum laude, Am. Internat. Coll., 1949; MA in Journalism, U. Wis., 1952, postgrad., 1952-59; PhD, Ball State U., 1975. Copy chief Kulzick Advt. Agy., Madison, Wis., 1952-55; continuity dir. Sta. WISC, Madison, 1956-57; pub. relations, editor Gardner Baking Co., Madison, 1957-58; editor Am. Press, Madison, 1958; asst. coordinator internat. tchr. devel. program U. Wis., Madison, 1959; dir. pub. relations, inst. history, chmn. div. social scis., sec. lay bd. trustees St. Francis Coll., Ft. Wayne, Ind., 1959-66, chmn. dept. social studies, 1960-78, v.p. coll. relations, 1966-71, prof. emeritus history and govt., 1978—, coll. athletic rep., 1966-72; book reviewer, guest columnist Ft. Wayne News-Sentinel; resource person, lectr. Negro history Sta. WANE-TV, Ft. Wayne, 1977; mem. council, exec. com., chmn. Interdisciplinary Approach to Classroom Teaching; lectr. in field. Contbr. articles to profl jours. V.P. Community Betterment Assn., Ft. Wayne, 1966; mem. mayor's subcom. on neighborhoods, Ft. Wayne, 1970; coordinator 4th Congl. Dist. History Day, 1978. Served with USAAF, 1940-45. Recipient honors competition Am. Coll. Pub. Relations Assn., 1960; U.S. Dept. Edn. grantee, 1982. Mem. Am. Hist. Assn., Assn. Am. Historians, Ind. Hist. Soc., Ind. Acad. Social Scis., Polish-Am. Hist. Assn., Polish-Am. Mus., Kosciuszko Found., Ft. Wayne-Allen County Hist. Soc., Ft. Wayne-Allen County C. of C. (edn. and state policies coms. 1962-70), Polish Inst. Arts and Scis. Am., Acad. Polit. Sci., Civil War Round Table, Profl. Writers Club, Sigma Delta Chi. Democrat. Roman Catholic. Lodges: KC, Elks.

MANILI, PIER LUIGI, chemical executive, consultant; b. Rome, Jan. 31, 1945; s. Sante and Bernardina (Volpe) M.; m. Maria Grazia Antonioli, Apr. 12, 1980; children: Daniela, Francesca, Claudia. Diploma in elec. engring., Enrico Fermi, Rome, 1966; MA in Physics, Kent State U., 1971; D in Physics, Rome U., 1973. Sales engr. Varian Assocs., Rome, 1973-76, area mgr., 1977-79; area sales mgr. Varian Assocs., Milan, 1980-81; chief exec. officer Gammatom SPA, Como, Italy, 1981—; cons. John Cabot Internat. Coll., Rome, 1973-80. Contbr. articles to profl. jours. Served to lt. Italian Air Force, 1966-69. Fullbright scholar, 1972; NATO grantee, 1971, 72. Mem. Italian Assn. Non-Destructive Testing, Italian Assn. Qualified Experts. Roman Catholic. Lodge: Lions. Office: Gammatom SPA, Via 24 Maggio 14, 22070 Guanzate, Como Italy

MANILLA, (JACK) JOHN ALLAN, office furniture company executive; b. Sharon, Pa., July 17, 1941; s. Vito John and Helen Elizabeth (Papai) M.; B.S., Youngstown State U., 1966; postgrad. Duquesne U., 1967-68; M.S. in Mgmt., Aquinas Coll., 1984; m. Paula Gale Jurko, 1960; children—Jacqueline Lee, John Paul, Paul Allan, Bradley James. V.p. Yankee Lake Amusement Co., Yankee Lake Village, Ohio, 1961-66, 70-71; sr. staff asst. Elevator Co., Westinghouse Electric Corp., Pitts., 1966-68, salesman I, 1968-70, salesman II, Union, N.J., 1971, Miami, Fla., 1971-72, dist. mgr., Indpls., 1973-77, regional mgr. archtl. and furniture systems div., Grand Rapids, Mich., 1977-79, nat. field sales mgr., 1979-81; mgr. strategic programs Herman Miller, Inc., Zeeland, Mich., 1981, group mktg. mgr., 1981, dir. mktg., 1981-84, dir. corp. distbn. resources, 1984; dir. sales and mktg. Gen. Office Equipment Co., Inc., Saddle Brook, N.J., 1984-86, v.p. sales and mktg., 1987—; elevator and office environment cons. architects, engrs., bldg. owners and facilities mgrs., contractors. Chief, YMCA Indian Guides, Allison Park, Pa., 1970; asst. scoutmaster Boy Scouts Am., Dania, Fla., 1971-72; asst. to Boys Scouts Am., Ind. Sch. for Blind, Indpls., 1973; jr. high sch. prin., instr. Christian Doctrine, St. Ursula Ch., Allison Park, 1968-70, St. Sabastion Ch., Masury, Ohio, 1970-71; pres. bd. edn. Our Lady of Mt. Carmel Sch., Carmel, Ind., 1973-76; mem. Carmel Dad's Club, 1973-74; pres. Princeton Estates Homeowners Assn., 1982; co-chmn. capital endowment campaign-continuing edn. div. Aquinas Coll., 1982, mem. master's program scholarship fund com., 1983-84; active Grand Rapids Bishop's Service Appeal, 1982, Grand Rapids Arts Council, 1980; mem. fin. and bldg. fund cons. St. Mary Magdalen Ch., 1984—; exec. com. Kentwood High Sch. Acad. Boosters, Mich., 1984. Recipient First in Performance award Westinghouse Electric Corp., 1972, 120 Club Honor Roll, 1968, 69, 70, 71, 72. Mem. Bldg. Owners and Mgrs. Assn., Constrn. Specification Inst., Assn. Gen. Contractors Ind., Am. Water Ski Assn., Mich. Water Ski Assn., West Mich. Water Ski Assn., Lake Mohawk Ski Hawks (trustee, v.p., chief tow boat driver), N.J. State Water Ski Fedn. (v.p., asst. chair), Cornerstone Playhouse (lighting director), Clubs: Rotary, Indpls. Athletic; Yankee Lake (Ohio) Water Ski (pres.); Renaissance (Detroit). Office: Gen Office Equipment Co Inc 94 Wagon Wheel Rd Sparta NJ 07871

MANLEY, MICHAEL NORMAN, government official; b. St. Andrew, Jamaica, Dec. 10, 1924; s. Norman Washington and Edna (Swithenbank) M.; m. Barbara Ann Lewars, June 25, 1966 (dec.); children: Rachael, Sarah, Joseph; m. Beverly Anderson, June 11, 1972; children: Natasha, David. BSc in Econs. with honors, London U., 1949; LLD (hon.), Morehouse Coll., 1973; student, Jamaica Coll., Kingston, 1935-43. Freelance journalist BBC, London, 1949-51; assoc. editor Pub. Opinion Kingston, 1951-52; staff mem., organizer Nat. Workers Union, Kingston, 1952—; elected mem. People's Nat. Party, Kingston, 1952; mem. Jamaican senate Kingston, 1962-67; v.p. People's Nat. Party, Kingston, 1967, mem. parliament Central Kingston, 1967, pres., 1969—; prime minister Govt. of Jamaica, Kingston, 1972-80, opposition leader, 1980—; vis. lectr. Columbia U., 1984; v.p. Socialist Internat., 1979; chmn. socialist Internat. Econ. Commn., 1983; mem. Caribbean Labour Congress, Sugar Industry Labour Welfare Bd., Sci. Research Council, Pensions Authority, Labour Adv. Council. Author: The Politics of Change, 1974, A Voice at the Workplace, 1976, The Search for Solutions, 1977, Jamaica: Struggle in the Periphery, 1982. Served with RAF, 1943-45. Decorated Order of Liberator (Venezuela), Order Mexican Eagle, Order José Martí (Cuba); recipient Jaliot Curie Peace prize, UN anti-apartheid award. Mem. Machado Employees Union (pres.), Caribbean Bauxite and Mineworkers Fedn. (pres. 1964-72), Jamaica Clerical Workers Assn. Methodist. Office: People's National Party, 89 Old Hope Rd, Kingston Jamaica *

MANLY, WILLIAM DONALD, metallurgist; b. Malta, Ohio, Jan. 13, 1923; s. Edward James and Thelma (Campbell) M.; m. Jane Wilden, Feb. 9, 1949; children—Hugh, Ann, Marc, David. Student, Antioch Coll., 1941-42; B.S., U. Notre Dame, 1947, M.S., 1949; postgrad., U. Tenn., 1950-55. Metallurgist Oak Ridge Nat. Lab., 1949-60, mgr. gas cooled reactor program, 1960-64; mgr. materials research Union Carbide Corp., N.Y.C., 1964-65; gen. mgr. Union Carbide Corp. (Stellite div.), N.Y.C., 1967-69; v.p. Union Carbide Corp. (Stellite div.), Kokomo, Ind., 1969-70; sr. v.p. Cabot Corp., Boston, 1970-83; exec. v.p. Cabot Corp., 1983-86; ret. 1986; also dir. chmn. adv. com. for reactor safety AEC, 1964-65. Served with USMC, 1943-46. Recipient Honor award U. Notre Dame, 1974. Fellow Am. Soc. Metals (pres. 1972-73), AIME, Am. Nuclear Soc. (Merit award 1966); mem. Nat. Acad. Engring., Nat. Assn. Corrosion Engrs., Metall. Soc. Presbyterian. Clubs: Cosmos, Masons. Home: Route 1 Box 197A Kingston TN 37763 Office: Cabot Corp 125 High St Boston MA 02110

MANN, ANGELA BIGGS, educational administrator; b. Atlanta, Apr. 4, 1951; d. Homer Daniel and Jewel (McCoy) Biggs; m. Justin S. Mann, Sept. 21, 1971; children—Justina, Alexis, Rahman. Degree in psychology and edn. Fisk U., 1968-72; postgrad. U. Minn., 1984—. Dir. edn. U. Islam, Nashville, 1973-75; math. instr. U.L. St. Acad., St. Paul, 1975; edn. coordinator Head Start, St. Paul, 1976; dir. child care Phyllis Wheatley Sch., Mpls., 1978-79; pub. relations mgr. Town Square, St. Paul, 1980-82; dir. Head Start, Ramsey Action Program, St. Paul, 1983—; resource access rep. Portage Project, Wis., 1984—. Bd. dirs. Minn. Assn. for Edn. Young Children, St. Paul, 1988—; rules rev. mem. Dept. Human Services State Child Care Rules Rev., St. Paul, 1985—; chmn. arts enrichment St. Anthony Park Sch. Assn., St. Paul, 1984-85; mem. youth allocations com. United Way, 1987—, youth day planning com. C. of C. Leadership, 1986-87; mem. St. Paul Pub. Schs. Early Childhood Family Edn. Adv. Council. Recipient Outstanding Service award Child Care Council, 1977. Mem. Nat. Assn. Edn. Young Children, Resources for Child Caring (v.p. 1977), Nat. Head Start Assn., Minn. Head Start Dirs. Assn. (v.p. 1986—), Nat. Black Child Devel. Inst. C. of C. (child care task force 1986-87), Nat. Assn. Female Execs., Fisk U. Alumni Assn. (sec. 1981—), Delta Sigma Theta (fin. sec. 1987-88). Democrat. Baptist. Home: 1291 Thomas Ave Saint Paul MN 55104 Office: Ramsey Action Program Head Start 586 Fuller Ave Saint Paul MN 55103

MANN, ARTHUR, historian, educator, writer; b. Bklyn., Jan. 3, 1922; s. Karl and Mary (Koch) Finkelman; m. Sylvia Blut, Nov. 6, 1943; children: Carol Ruth, Emily Betsy. B.A. summa cum laude, Bklyn. Coll., 1944; M.A., Harvard U., 1947, Ph.D., 1952. Tutor, Bklyn. Coll., 1946; from instr. to asst. prof. MIT, 1948-55; from asst. prof. to prof. Smith Coll., 1955-66; prof. Am. history U. Chgo., 1966—, Preston and Sterling Morton prof. Am. history, 1971; vis. prof. Columbia U., U. Mass., Williams Coll., U. Mich., U. Wyo., Harvard U., Salzburg (Austria) Seminar Am. Studies. Author: Yankee Reformers in the Urban Age, 1954, Growth and Achievement, Temple Israel, 1854-1954, 1954, La Guardia, A Fighter Against His Times, 1882-1933, 1959, The Progressive Era, 1963, rev. edit., 1975, La Guardia Comes to Power, 1933, 1965, Immigrants in American Life, 1968, rev. edit., 1974, (with Harris and Warner) History and the Role of the City in American Life, 1972, The One and the Many: Reflections on the American Identity, 1979; editor: series The University of Chicago Press Documents in American History; adv. editor Am. History, U. Chgo. Press; mem. editorial bd.: Ethnicity; editorial cons.: Social Service Rev. U.S. Dept. State lectr., Venezuela, 1970, USIA lectr., Fiji, Indonesia, Malaysia, N.Z., Singapore, 1974, Portugal, Germany, Yugoslavia, Romania, 1976, Hong Kong, Japan, 1979. Served with AUS, 1943-46. Recipient Alumni award of merit Bklyn. Coll., 1968, Outstanding Scholarship award LaGuardia Archives, 1987; Fellow Am. Council Learned Socs., 1962-63; Fulbright-Hays sr. scholar Australia, 1974. Mem. Am. Hist. Assn., Orgn. Am. Historians, Soc. Am. Historians. Home: 4919 S Woodlawn Ave Chicago IL 60615

MANN, BILLY JOE, JR., computer services executive; b. Dayton, Ohio, Oct. 1, 1960; s. Billy Joe and June Elizabeth (Mossbarger) M. Student, Ohio State U., 1981-86. Data entry supr. Cole, Layer & Trumble, Dayton, 1978-79; programmer, analyst Automated Systems, Inc., Dayton, 1979-81; dir. computer services Mgmt. Foresight, Inc., Columbus, 1981—; cons. Buckeye Employee Benefits Services, Inc., Columbus, 1984-86. Mem. Am. Mgmt. Assn., Data Processing Mgmt. Assn., N. Coast Datapoint Users Group, Columbus Computer Soc. Republican. Home: 7749 Amberfalls Ct Dublin OH 43017 Office: Mgmt Foresight Inc 1670 Fishinger Rd Columbus OH 43221

MANN, CHARLES KELLOGG, economist; b. Los Angeles, Oct. 22, 1934; s. Stuart Nelson and Margaret (Webster) M.; B.A., Williams Coll., 1956; M.P.A. (fellow Nat. Inst. Public Affairs 1967), Harvard U., 1968, Ph.D. (Littauer fellow 1968-70, Dissertation award Am. Agrl. Econs. Assn. 1972), 1971; m. Susanne Gates Johnson, Jan. 28, 1967; children—Charles Griffith, Caitlin Lee. Staff adminstr. packaging products Aluminum Co. Am., 1960-62; budget examiner internat. div. Bur. Budget, 1964-67; chief econ. analysis staff AID, Turkey, 1971-74; economist field staff, then rep. in Turkey, Rockefeller Found., 1974-78, asso. dir. agrl. and social scis., 1978-85; research assoc. Harvard U. Inst. for Internat. Devel., Cambridge, Mass., 1985—; vis. prof. Middle East Tech. U., Ankara, Turkey, 1974-78. Mem. Fulbright Commn. for Turkey, 1977-78. Served as officer USNR, 1957-60. Recipient Disting. Service award Dept. Agr., 1972. Mem. Am. Econ. Assn., Am. Agrl. Econs. Assn., Internat. Assn. Agrl. Economists. Author: Tobacco: The Ants and The Elephants, 1975; editor: Food Policy: Frameworks for Analysis and Action, 1986, Co-editor, contbr. Micrpcomputers in Public Policy Applications for Developing Countries, 1986, 87; (Videotape) The Food Policy Forum, 1983; (audiotape) The Powersharing Series, 1985, 87; also articles. Office: 1 Eliot St Cambridge MA 02138

MANN, GORDON TYLER, food products company executive, energy management company executive; b. Apex, N.C., Oct. 7, 1936; s. Winfred Bright and Grace (Mason) M. Student Wake Forest U., 1954-56; A.B.A., Cameron Coll., Lawton, Okla., 1972; Assoc. in Mgmt., U. Okla., 1974. Supr. FAA, Houston, 1962-76, dir. air traffic controllers, Austin, Tex., 1968-69; owner retail store, Austin, 1964-74, Simpson-Mann Oil Producers, San Angelo, Tex., from 1974; owner, exec. Simpson-Mann, Inc., San Angelo, pres., dir., from 1982; ptnr., exec. v.p. Pecan and Gourmet Co., 1986—; sec., treas. Western Energy Mgmt. Co., Inc., San Angelo. Bd. dirs. Downtown San Angelo, 1983—; pres. San Angelo Found., 1983—; mem. President's Club, Washington. Mem. bldg. com. San Angelo Fine Arts Mus., 1983, bd. dirs., 1984—. Served with USAF, 1957-61. Recipient Spl. Achievement award FAA, 1971; named Boss of Yr., Desk and Derrick Club, San Angelo, 1978. Mem. Ind. Petroleum Assn. Am., Tex. Ind. Producers and Royalty Owners, Permian Basin Petroleum Assn. (bd. dirs. 1978-79), San Angelo Geol. Soc., Tex. Pecan Growers Assn., Pecan Shellers Assn., West Geol. Soc. (bd. dirs. 1979), San Angelo Assn. Republican. Episcopalian. Office: Adobe Pl 133 W Concho Ave San Angelo TX 76903

MANN, KAREN, consultant, educator; b. Kansas City, Mo., Oct. 9, 1942; d. Charles and Letha (Anderson) M. BA, U. Calif.-Santa Barbara, 1964; MPA, Golden Gate U., 1975, PhD, 1988. Cert. lay minister Order of Buddhist Contemplatives. Tchr. Sisters of Immaculate Heart, Los Angeles, 1964-68; group counselor San Francisco and Marin County Probation Depts., parole agt. Calif. Dept. Corrections, Sacramento and San Francisco, 1970-86; researcher and cons. Non-profit Orgnl. Devel., 1986—, Computer Applications for Persons with Disabilities, 1986—; adj. faculty Grad. Theol. Union, Berkeley, 1984—. Co-author: Prison Overcrowding, 1979; Community Corrections: A Plan for California, 1980. Active Buddhists Concerned for Animals, San Francisco, 1983—, Fellowship of Reconciliation, N.Y., 1970—; co-founder Network Ctr. for Study of Ministry, San Francisco, 1982; pres. San Francisco Network Ministries, 1980-82; mem. Disabled Children's Computer Resource Group, 1988—, Springwater Ctr. for Meditative Inquiry and Retreats, 1986—. Office: PO Box 377 Lagunitas CA 94938

MANN, MICHAEL MARTIN, electronics company executive; b. N.Y.C., Nov. 28, 1939; s. Herbert and Rosalind (Kaplan) M.; m. Mariel Joy Steinberg, Apr. 25, 1965. BSEE, Calif. Inst. Tech., 1960, MSEE, 1961; PhD in Elec. Engring. and Physics, U. So. Calif., 1969; MBA, UCLA, 1984. Mgr. high power laser programs office Northrop Corp., Hawthorne, Calif., 1969-76; mgr. high energy laser systems lab. Hughes Aircraft Co., El Segundo, Calif., 1976-78; mgr. E-0 control systems labs. Hughes Aircraft Co., El Segundo, 1978-83, asst. to v.p., space & strategic, 1983-84; exec. v.p. Helionetics Inc., Irvine, Calif., 1984-85, pres., chief exec. officer, 1985-86, also bd. dirs.; ptnr. Mann Kavanaugh Chernove, 1986—; sr. cons. Arthur D. Little, Inc., 1987—; mem. Army Sci. Bd., Dept. Army, Washington, 1986—; cons. Office of Sec. of Army, Washington, 1986—, Inst. of Def. Analysis, Washington, 1978—; bd. dirs. Squire-Whitehouse Corp., San Diego, Safeguard Health Enterprises, Inc., 1987—, Am. Video Communications, Inc., 1987—, Meck Industries, Inc., 1987—, Micro-Frame, Inc., 1988—; chmn. bd. HLX Laser, Inc., 1984-86; research assoc., mem. extension teaching staff U. So. Calif., Los Angeles, 1964-70. Contbr. over 50 tech. articles; 12 patents. Adv. com. to Engring Sch., Calif. State U., Long Beach, 1985—; chmn. polit. affairs Am. Electronics Assn., Orange County Council, 1986—, mem. exec. com. , 1986—; adv. com. several Calif. congressmen, 1985—; mem. dean's council UCLA Grad. Sch. Mgmt., 1984-85; bd. dirs. Archimodes Circle U. So. Calif., 1983-85, Ctr. for Innovation and Entrepreneurship, 1986—, Caltech/MIT Venture Forum, 1987—. Hicks fellow in Indsl. Relations, Calif. Inst. Tech., 1961, Hewlett Packard fellow.' Mem. So. Calif. Tech. Execs. Network, IEEE (sr.), Orange County CEO's Roundtable, Am. Defense Preparedness Assn., Security Affairs Support Assn., Internat. Platform Assn. Republican. Club: King Harbor Yacht (Redondo Beach, Calif.). Home and Office: 4248 Via Alondra Palos Verdes Estates CA 90274

MANN, MONROE YALE, lawyer; b. N.Y.C.; m. Carolyn Hensas, Jan. 31, 1972; children—Emily, Monroe, Hilary. B.A., Bklyn. Coll., 1943; J.D., St. John's U., 1949; M.A., Bklyn. Coll., 1952; M.A., NYU, 1979, Ph.D., 1976. Bar: N.Y. 1949, D.C. 1962, U.S. Dist. Ct. (so. dist.) N.Y., U.S. Dist. Ct. (ea. dist.) N.Y., U.S. Dist. Ct. Conn., U.S. Ct. Appeals (2d cir.) 1962, U.S. Supreme Ct. 1958. Spl. asst. dist. atty. Westchester County (N.Y.); police prosecutor, then corp. counsel Port Chester, N.Y., 1957-59; sole practice, Port Chester, N.Y., 1952—; adj. prof. econs. Westchester Community Coll., 1976-77; adj. prof. criminal justice L.I. U., 1976—; adj. assoc. prof. pub. adminstrn. NYU, 1976—; law guardian Family Ct.; atty. Port Chester-Rye Town Police Assn., 1973—; atty. Tri-County Fedn. Police, 1978-80; disaster coordinator Fed. Emergency Mgmt. Agy., 1983—. Served with USAAF, World War II. Mem. Port Chester-Rye Bar Assn. (past treas., pres. 1984—), ABA, N.Y. State Bar Assn., Westchester County Bar Assn., N.Y. County Lawyers Assn., D.C. Bar Assn., Jewish War Vets. (past comdr.), Am. Radio Relay League (legal counsel), Am. Legion (judge adv.), DAV, Mil. Order World Wars, Res. Officers Assn., Air Force Assn., Am. Soc. Pub. Adminstrn., Nat. Def. Exec. Res. Clubs: Rolls Royce Owners (past pres., legal counsel), Ghost. Office: Monroe Mann Law Firm 316 Westchester Ave Port Chester NY 10573

MANN, PHILIP ROY, lawyer; b. N.Y.C., Jan. 31, 1948; s. Elias and Gertrude Esther (Levbarg) M. AB, Cornell U., 1968; JD, NYU, 1971, LLM, 1975. Bar: N.Y. 1972, U.S. Dist. Ct. (so. and ea. dists.) N.Y. 1983, U.S. Ct. Appeals (2nd cir.) 1973, U.S. Dist. Ct. (no. dist.) N.Y. 1974, U.S. Ct. Mil. Appeals 1974, U.S. Supreme Ct. 1975, D.C. 1976, U.S. Dist. Ct. (we. dist.) N.Y. 1976, U.S. Tax Ct. 1976, U.S. Ct. Appeals (D.C. cir.) 1978, Conn. 1983, U.S. Dist. Ct. D.C. 1983, U.S. Ct. Claims 1983, U.S. Ct. Appeals (3rd and fed. cirs.) 1983. Assoc. Levin & Weintraub, N.Y.C., 1971-74; assoc. Shea & Gould, N.Y.C., 1974-79, ptnr., 1979-84; sole practice N.Y.C., 1984—. Served to maj. USAR 1969—. Mem. ABA, Fed. Bar Assn. Democrat. Jewish. Clubs: City Mid-Day, World Trade Ctr. (N.Y.C.). Home: 250 E 87th St Apt 26H New York NY 10128 Office: 250 E 87th St New York NY 10128

MANN, ROLAND, editor; b. Boston, June 24, 1926; s. Roland William and Florence Chapman (DeWolf) M.; m. Ingrid P.A.G. Ziska, Aug. 17, 1947; children: Elisabeth M., William R. Z., Christopher F. BA, U. Maine, 1951; MA, NYU, 1962. Editor Am. Mgmt. Assn., N.Y.C., 1952-57; mng. editor Dun's Revs. (Dun & Bradstreet), N.Y.C., 1957-62; fin. editor Med. Econs., Oradell, N.J., 1962-63; dir. editorial services McKinsey & Co., N.Y.C., 1963-79; dir. publs. McKinsey & Co., London, 1979-87; cons. in field. Author: Careers in Business Management, 1965; editor: The Arts of Top Management, 1971; editor The McKinsey Quar., 1964-87. Served with inf., U.S. Army, 1944-46, ETO. Fulbright scholar U. Mysore, India, 1951. Club: Reform (London). Home and Office: 15 York Close, Kings Langley, Herts WD4 9HX, England

MANN, SANTA SINGH, diversified company executive; b. Ganganager, India, June 28, 1933; s. Dalip Singh and Kartar Kaur (Sahota) M.; came to U.S., 1956, naturalized, 1968; B.S. in Elec. Engring., U. Ariz., 1968; M.S., in Math., U. Calif. at San Diego, 1963; m. Balbir Kaur Sandhu, July 8, 1951; children—Sohan, Babu, Sahib, Prem Eileen Beatrice. Mgr., Transdata Inc., San Diego; sr. staff engr. Hoffman El Corp., Los Angeles; exec. v.p. Electro Technology, Inc., San Diego; cons. Arvin Industries & Rohr Corp.; ind. bus. exec., Hayward, Calif., 1966—. Bd. dir. MPS Corp., San Diego. Pres. Internat. Sikh Forum. Gen. sec. Indo-Am. Farmers Friendship, Inc., 1974—; sec. Central Singh Sabha Com. Inc., 1974—; pres. Alameda County Consumer Action, 1972—. Mem. Nat., Calif., So. Alameda County, Yuba County, Sutter County bds. realtors. Home: 2103 S King Rd San Jose CA 95122 Office: 436 E San Fernando St San Jose CA 95112

MANN, WARD PALMER, artist; b. Detroit, Oct. 3, 1921; s. Lloyd Leo and Ruth E. (Yoder) M.; m. Joan Marie Butler, Aug. 7, 1943; children: Robert W., Craig R., Kim L. B.S. in Mech. Engring., U. Mich., 1949; M.B.A., 1962. Mgr. quality assurance Holley Carburetor, Detroit, 1940-58; mgr. quality analysis Vickers Inc., Detroit, 1958-62; mgr. reliability engring. Xerox Corp., Webster, N.Y., 1962-81; artist, Webster, 1963—. Pres. Joe Berg Sci. Found., Detroit, 1961; chmn. Sea Scouts Boy Scouts Am., Webster, 1966-68. Served to 1st lt. USA Air Corps, 1942-45. Recipient Internat. Soc. Artists award, 1979; Anco Found. award, 1979; Gold medal for painting, 1980; Coast Guard Artist award U.S. Coast Guard, 1983. Mem. Rochester Art Club (pres. 1972-74), Artists Fellowship Inc., Rocky Neck Art Colony, (pres. 1982-83), Genesse Group Artists (pres. 1975—), Salmagundi Club (Salmagundi award 1979, 84, 85, 86, 87, 88, A. Sharpe award 1978), Am. Artist Profl. League, Hudson Valley Art Assn. (Spradling prize 1983, 84), Rockport Art Assn. (painting award 1983, 84, 88), Acad. Artists Assn. (Painting award 1988). Republican. Club: Rotary Internat. (sgt.-at-arms 1983-84). Home: 163 Stony Point Trail Webster NY 14580 Office: 77 Rocky Neck Ave Gloucester MA 01930

MANNAN, ABDUL, economist, educator, consultant, Islamic economist; b. Seraj Ganj, Bangladesh, Jan. 10, 1938; s. Khadem and Regia Ali; m. Nargis Mannan, Mar. 19, 1964; children—Reshmi, Ghalib. M.A. in Econs., Rajshahi U., Bangladesh, 1960; M.A. in Econs., Mich. State U., 1972, Ph.D., 1973, Cert. in Devel., 1972; cert. in fin. and budgeting Nat. Inst. Pub. Adminstrn.-Pakistan, Bangladesh, 1963-64. Prof. econs. Seraj Ganj Coll., Rajshahi U., Bangladesh, 1960-63; magistrate, collector Govt. of Bangladesh, 1963-64; asst. fin. advisor Govt. of Pakistan, Islamabad, 1964-67, asst. chief Fed. Planning Commn., 1968-71; sr. research assoc. Mich. State U., East Lansing, 1970-73; sr. lectr. econs. and bus. studies Papua New Guinea U. Tech., Lae, 1974-77; research prof. Internat. Ctr. Islamic Econs., King ABdulaziz U., Jeddah, Saudi Arabia, 1978-84; sr. economist, highest profl. level Islamic Research and Tng. Inst., Islamic Devel. Bank, Jeddah, 1984—, cons. Islamic Devel. Bank, 1979-83; cons. Asian Devel. Bank, 1983; vis. prof. Muslim Inst., London, 1980-81; vis. scholar Contemporary Ctr. for Arab Studies, Georgetown U., Washington, 1982; hon. chmn. proposed Islami Ummah Bank ltd., Bangladesh, 1987—. Author: An Introduction to Applied Economics, 1963; Economic Problems and Planning in Pakistan, 1968, 4th edit. 1970; Islamic Economics: Theory and Practice, 1970; Trends and Issues in the Economics of Non-formal Education, 1974; The Economic Aspects of Non-formal Education, 1975; The Making of Islamic Economic Society, 1984; The Frontiers of Islamic Economics, 1984. Contbr. articles to profl. jours. Gen. sec. Govt. Econs. and Statis. Assn., Class I, Islamabad, Pakistan, 1968-70; v.p., editor Seraj Ganj Students' Assn. Coll. Jour., 1956-57; founder Bangladesh Social Peace Found., 1984. Recipient Acad. award Pakistan Writers Guild, 1970. Assoc. fellow Papua New Guinea Inst. Mgmt.; mem. Am. Econ. Assn., Econ. Soc. Australia and N.Z., Am. Ednl. Studies Assn. Muslim. Home: Shohid Ganj, Saraj Ganj Bangladesh Office: Islamic Research and Tng Inst, Islamic Devel Bank, Box 5925, Jeddah 21432 Saudi Arabia

MANNDORFF, HANS, museum director, professor; b. Hinterbrühl, Austria, Apr. 26, 1928; s. Max and Albertine (Mannlicher) M.; m. Gertrude Graf, Sept. 28, 1955 (div.); children: Wolfgang, Rudolf; m. Elisabeth Bauer, Mar. 10, 1984; 1 child, Hemma. PhD, U. Vienna, Austria, 1953; postgrad., Sch. Oriental and African Studies, London, 1955-56, 59. Anthrop. researcher UNESCO, India, 1953-54, 56-57; head Southern Asia Dept. Mus. Ethnology, Vienna, 1950—, dir., 1976—; field researcher UN Asia Found., Northern Thailand, 1961-62, 63-65; researcher Mus. Ethnology Vienna in India, 1973-75, 80, 82; docent U. Vienna, 1965, prof., 1971—. Author of numerous books, handbooks; contbr. articles to sci. jours. Decorated officer Order Southern Cross (Brazil), Cross of Honor, Decoration of Honor for Merit (Austria). Mem. Nat. Assn. Ethnology, Anthropology and Prehistory, Internat. Assn. Ethnology, Anthropology and Prehistory. Home: Johannesstrasse 3, A-2371 Hinterbrühl Austria Office: Mus of Ethnology, Neue Hofburg, A-1014 Vienna Austria

MANNING, CHRISTOPHER ASHLEY, venture capital executive; b. Los Angeles, June 26, 1945; s. Ashley and Vivian LaVerne (Wagner) M.; m. Cathy Ann Nichols, July 30, 1977. BS, San Diego State U., 1967; MBA, Northwestern U., 1971; PhD, UCLA, 1983. Corp. loan officer Security Pacific Nat. Bank, Los Angeles, 1971-75; v.p. fin. Solitude Ski Resort, Bravo Ski Corp., Salt Lake City, 1975-78; pres. Sequoia Spa Co., Los Angeles, 1976-79; pres. Manning and Co., Los Angeles, 1971-86, Manning's Little Red Piano Shop, Los Angeles, 1971-86; instr. corp. fin. Pepperdine U., Los Angeles, 1979-83; instr. corp. fin. and real estate Long Beach State U. (Calif.), 1983-86; assoc. prof. fin. Loyola Marymount U., Los Angeles, 1986—. Served to 1st lt. U.S. Army, 1967-70. Decorated Bronze Star medal. Mem. Beta Gamma Sigma. Republican. Episcopalian. Home: 14 Crest Rd W Rolling Hills CA 90274 Office: 29438 Quailwood Dr Rancho Palos Verdes CA 90274

MANNING, MARGUERITE, university dean, clergywoman; b. Phoenix; d. Walter Jerald and Elizabeth (Smith) Manning; A.B., Scarritt Coll., 1942; M.A., Boston, 1943; M.Div., Union Theol. Sem., 1957; M.A., Columbia Tchrs. Coll., 1966, Ed.D., 1975. Ordained to ministry Congregationalist Ch.; dir. student activities U. Tenn., 1943-46; ednl. asst. Riverside Ch., N.Y.C., 1947-55; parish worker East Harlem Protestant Parish, 1955-57; minister East Congl. Ch. and Waits River Meth. Ch., Vt., 1958-61; tchr. English and phys. edn. Baghdad (Iraq) High Sch., 1961-62; adminstrv. asst. dept. guidance and student personnel adminstrn. Columbia Tchrs. Coll., 1962-66; research asso. Bank St. Coll. Edn., N.Y.C., 1966-68; with Bur. Research, N.Y.C. Bd. Edn., 1968-69; sec. personnel United Bd. Christian Higher Edn. in Asia, 1969-71; dean student affairs Rutgers U., Newark, 1971—. Active Red Feather drive; social worker ARC, Camp Shanks, N.Y., World War II; moderator Grafton-Orange Assn. Congl. Chs.; mem. minister's assn. Vt. Congl. Conf., 1958; pres. Women of Grace Ch., Newark; bd. dirs. YWCA. Mem. Nat. Assn. Women Deans and Counselors, Am. Assn. Ednl. Research, Am. Personnel and Guidance Assn., NEA, Am. Assn. Higher Edn., Am. Assn. U. Adminstrs., Bus. and Profl. Women's Club, Pi Lambda Theta (pres. Alpha Epsilon chpt. 1966-68, treas., 1969-72, chmn. nat. nominating com. 1966-67), Kappa Delta Pi, Phi Delta Kappa. Home: 351 Broad St Apt 1009 Newark NJ 07104

MANNING, TIMOTHY CARDINAL, former archbishop; b. Cork, Ireland, Nov. 15, 1909; came to U.S., 1928, naturalized, 1944; s. Cornelius and Margaret (Cronin) M. Student, St. Patrick's Sem., Menlo Park, Calif., 1928-34; D.C.L., Gregorian U., Rome, 1938. Ordained priest Roman Catholic Ch., 1934; asst. pastor Immaculate Conception Ch., Los Angeles, 1934-35; consecrated bishop 1946; appt. titular bishop of Lesvi and chancellor Roman Catholic Archdiocese of Los Angeles, 1946-67; first bishop of Fresno 1967-69, titular archbishop of Capri and coadjutor archbishop of Los Angeles, 1969-70, archbishop of Los Angeles, 1970-85, created cardinal, 1973-85. Office: 1531 W 9th St Los Angeles CA 90015 *

MANNING, WALTER SCOTT, accountant, former educator, consultant; b. nr. Yoakum, Tex.; B.B.A., Tex. Coll. Arts and Industries, 1932; M.B.A., U. Tex., 1940; m. Eleanor Mary Jones, Aug. 27, 1937; children—Sharon Frances, Walter Scott, Robert Kenneth. Asst. to bus. mgr. Tex. Coll. Arts and Industries, Kingsville, 1932; tchr. Sinton (Tex.) High Sch., 1933-37, Robstown (Tex.) High Sch., 1937-41; prof. Tex. A&M U., College Station, 1941-77; cons. C.P.A. C.P.A., Tex. Walter Manning Outstanding Jr. and Outstanding Sr. awards at Coll. Bus. Adminstrn., Tex. A&M U. named in his honor. Mem. AAUP, Am. Acctg. Assn., Am. Inst. C.P.A.s, Tex. Soc. C.P.A.s, College Station C. of C. (past pres.), Tex. Assn. Univ. Instrs. Acctg. (pres. 1963-64), Knights York Cross of Honor, Alpha Chi, Beta Gamma Sigma, Beta Alpha Psi. Democrat. Presbyterian (elder). Clubs: Masons, (32 deg.), Shriners, K.T., Kiwanis (past pres., past lt. gov. div. IX Tex. Okla. dist.). Home: 405 Walton Dr E College Station TX 77840

MANNING, WINTON HOWARD, psychologist, educational administrator; b. St. Louis, Feb. 9, 1930; s. Winton Harry and Jane (Swanson) M.; m. Nancy Mercedes Groves, Aug. 1, 1959; children—Cecelia Groves, Winton H. A.B. with honors, William Jewell Coll., Mo., 1947; Ph.D. in Psychology, Washington U., St. Louis, 1959. Instr. psychology William Jewell Coll., Liberty, Mo., 1954-55, asst. prof., acting head dept. psychology, 1955-56; research psychologist Washington U., St. Louis, 1956-58, research asso., 1958-59, vis. lectr., summer, 1961, 62; asst. prof. psychology Tex. Christian U., Fort Worth, 1959-61, asso. prof., 1961-64, prof., 1964-65, asso. dir. univ. honors program, 1962-65; asso. dir. research Coll. Entrance Examination Bd., N.Y.C., 1965-66, dir. program devel., 1966-68, exec. dir. research and devel., 1968-69; dir. developmental research div. Ednl. Testing Service, Princeton, N.J., 1969-70, v.p., 1970-77, sr. v.p. devel. and research, 1977-83, sr. scholar, 1983—; pres. Ednl. Devel. Service, Princeton, 1983—; pres. Jacques Molle Inc., 1987—; vis. fellow Princeton U., 1982-83. Trustee, Nat. Chicano Council on Higher Edn., 1977—, Assn. for Advancement of Handicapped People, 1975-78, N.J. Arts Festival, 1980—; vice-chair Found. for Books to China, 1980—; chair bd. trustees Princeton Day Sch., 1981—; chair Affordable Housing Bd. of Princeton Borough, 1987—; sr. warden All Saints Episcopal Ch., 1987—; adv. council U. Okla. Ctr. for Research on Minority Edn., 1987—, Ind. Sch. Chmn. Assn., 1987—; cons. Carnegie Found. for Advancement of Teaching., 1987—, Coll. Bd., 1988—; special cons. Commn. on Admission to Grad. Mgmt. Edn., 1987—. Recipient Alumni Achievement citation William Jewell Coll., 1970. Mem. Am. Psychol. Assn., Eastern Psychol. Assn. (recipient Pendragon prize, 1987), Am. Assn. for Higher Edn., Psychometric Soc., Am. Ednl. Research Assn., Nat. Council on Measurement in Edn. (mem. com. on legal issues in measurement 1977-79), N.Y. Acad. Scis. Phi Beta Kappa. Clubs: Nassau (Princeton); Pendragon (Cork); Bucks Harbor Yacht. Author: The Pursuit of Fairness in Admissions to Higher Education, 1977; Student Manual for Essentials of Psychology, 1960. Contbr. articles on ednl. measurement and psychology of learning to profl. publs. Patentee in field. Home: 12 Morven Pl Princeton NJ 08540 Office: Educational Testing Service Princeton NJ 08541

MANNIX, CHARLES RAYMOND, lawyer, law educator; b. Elizabeth, N.J., Aug. 2, 1950; s. Charles Raymond and Helen Joan (French) M.; m. Sherry Anne Stetson, May 6, 1979. B.A., Duquesne U., 1972, M.A., 1976, J.D., 1976. Bar: Iowa 1976, U.S. Ct. Claims 1976, U.S. Tax Ct. 1976, U.S. Ct. Mil. Appeals 1976, U.S. Ct. Internat. Trade 1976, U.S. Ct. Appeals (4th and 5th cirs.) 1977, U.S. Ct. Appeals (D.C. cir.) 1977, U.S. Dist. Ct. Va. 1980, U.S. Supreme Ct. 1980, Va. 1980, D.C. 1980, U.S. Ct. Appeals (D.C. cir.) 1980, U.S. Ct. Appeals (fed. cir.) 1982, Commd. 2d lt. U.S. Air Force, 1973, advanced through grades to maj., 1982; intern UN Office of Legal Affairs, N.Y.C., 1975; various legal assignments; law clk. McCrady, Kreimer, Ravick, Bonistalli, Pitts., 1973-76; lectr. bus. law, crim. law, internat. law and philosophy, 1976-80, St. Leo Coll. Fla., City Coll. Chgo.; lectr. USAF Med. Law Cons. Program, 1981-83; adj. faculty Georgetown U., Washington, 1984—, bd. advisors paralegal program; asst. prof. Health Law U. Md. Grad. Sch., asst. prof. clin. jurisprudence uniformed services. Decorated Meritorious Service medal, Air Force Commendation medal with Oak Leaf clusters. Mem. ABA, Assn. Trial Lawyers Am., D.C. Bar Assn., Va. State Bar Assn., Am. Judicature Soc., Fed. Bar Assn., Am. Soc. Internat. Law, Inter-Am. Bar Assn., Internat. Bar Assn., Am. Soc. Law and Medicine, Am. Arbitration Assn. (arbitrator). Home: 10205 Walker Lake Dr Great Falls VA 22066 Office: U Health Scis Office Gen Counsel Uniformed Services Jones Bridge Rd Bethesda MD 20815

MANOLESCU, NICOLAE MANOLACHE, veterinary science researcher; b. Romania, July 21, 1936; s. Manolache and Olga (Budachievici) M.; grad. in Vet. Surgery, Vet. Acad. Bucharest, 1966, D.Sc., 1969; m. Ioana Badescu, Mar. 1, 1973; children—Manuela, Bogdan. Vet. surgeon, Agrl. Sta., Rusetu, Romania, 1966-67; asst. to prof. Vet. Acad., Bucharest, Romania, 1967-69; chief lab. morphopathology and electronic microscopy Pasteur Inst. for Vet. Research and Biol. Production, Bucharest, 1969-87; sci. researcher Oncol. Inst. Bucharest, 1987—; prof. morphopathology Timiscara Vet. Acad., 1987—. Author 200 sci. papers and 10 books in field including: Normal and Pathological Cytology of Animals, 1980; Leukemic Cells, Comparative Cytopathology, 1981; Comparative Histology in SEM, 1982; Hematologic Guide for Animals in Industrial Breeding, 1978; The Ultrastructure of Some Sanguine Cells in SEM, 1979; Comparative Black/White and Colours Images for Electronic Microscopy, 1984; Comparative Hematologie, 1985; Comparative General Histopathology in SEM, 1985. Mem. Comparative Pathology Soc. (sec. 1980—), Romanian Acad. (Ion Ionescu Dela Brad prize). Home: 6 Hristo Botev, 70335 Bucharest Romania Office: 333 Giulesti, 77826 Bucharest Romania

MANOUX, DOMINIQUE, oncologist; b. Paris, Jan. 6, 1950; s. Marc and Eliane (Bernard) M.; m. Annie Ceresa, Mar. 22, 1972; children: Julie, Charlotte. MD, U. Paris, 1974, specialist degree in Oncology, 1978. Cert. in radiation and med. oncology. Sr. oncologist Clinique du Sud, Thiais, France, 1979—; cons. oncologist Necker Hosp., Paris, 1981—. Author: (with others) Decisions in Oncology, 1986. Mem. Radiation Soc., French Pvt. Oncology Soc. Office: Oncology Ctr, 112 Ave du General de Gaulle, 94320 Thiais France

MANSBERGER, ARLIE ROLAND, JR., surgeon; b. Pitts., Oct. 13, 1922; s. Arlie Rol and Mayme (Smith) M.; m. Anna Ellen Piel, July 27, 1946; children—Ellen Lynn, John Arlie, Leigh Ann. B.A., Western Md. Coll., 1943, D.Sc. (hon.), 1974; M.D., U. Md., 1947, D.Sc. (hon.), 1978. Diplomate: Am. Bd. Surgery (dir., vice chmn.). Intern U. Md. Hosp., 1947-49, resident in surgery, 1947-54; chief wound shock br. biophysics div. Army Chem. Center, 1954-56; instr. surgery U. Md., 1956-59, asst. prof., 1959-61, asso. prof., 1961-69, prof. surgery, 1969-73; clin. dir. shock-trauma unit 1962-73; prof. surgery, chmn. dept. Med. Coll. Ga., Augusta, 1973—; cons. surgeon Dwight David Eisenhower Army Med. Center, VA Hosp. Editor: Essence of General Surgery, 1975; chmn. editorial bd.: Bull. U. Md. 1971-73; editor-in-chief: The Am. Surgeon, 1973—; surg. editor: Resident and Staff Physician, 1979—; contbr. articles to profl. jours., chpts. to books. Trustee Western Md. Coll., 1971—, Med. Research Found. Ga., 1973—. Served to col. U.S. Army, 1943-46, 54-56. Recipient Man of Yr. award U. Md., 1970, 72, Golden Apple teaching award U. Md., 1968, 72, Disting. Faculty award Med. Coll. Ga., 1979. Fellow A.C.S. (gov.); mem. Am. Surg. Assn., Soc. Univ. Surgeons, So. Surg. Assn., Soc. Internationale de Chirurgie, Am. Assn. Surgery of Trauma, Southeastern Surg. Congress, Soc. Surgery of Alimentary Tract, AMA, Soc. Consultants to Armed Forces, Med. Assn. Ga. (editorial bd. 1987—), Am. Bd. Family Practice (bd. dirs. 1987—), 29th Div. Assn., Alpha Omega Alpha. Episcopalian. Home: 3128 Walton Way Augusta GA 30909 Office: Dept Surgery Med Coll Ga Augusta GA 30912

MANSFIELD, KAREN LEE, lawyer; b. Chgo., Mar. 17, 1942; d. Ralph and Hilda (Blum) Mansfield; 1 child, Nicole Rafaela. BA in Polit. Sci., Roosevelt U., 1963; JD, DePaul U., 1971; student U. Chgo., 1959-60. Bar: Ill. 1972, U.S. Dist. Ct. (no. dist.) Ill. 1972. Legis. intern Ill. State Senate, Springfield, 1966-67; tchr. Chgo. Pub. Schs., 1967-70; atty. CNA Ins., Chgo., 1971-73; law clk. Ill. Apellate Ct., Chgo., 1973-75; sr. trial atty. U.S. Dept. Labor, Chgo., 1975—. Contbr. articles to profl. jours. Vol. Big Sister, 1975-81; bd. dirs. Altgeld Nursery Sch., 1963-66, Ill. div. UN Assn., 1966-72, Hull House Jane Addams Ctr., 1977-82, Broadway Children's Ctr., 1986—; research asst. Citizens for Gov. Otto Kerner, Chgo., 1964; com. mem. Ill. Commn. on Status of Women, Chgo., 1964-70; del. Nat. Conf. on Status of Women, 1968; candidate for del. Ill. Constl. Conv., 1969. Mem. Chgo. Council Lawyers, Women's Bar Assn. Ill., Lawyer Pilots Bar Assn., Fed. Bar Assn. Unitarian. Clubs: Friends of Gamelan (performer), 99's Internat. Orgn. Women Pilots (legis. chmn. Chgo. area chpt. 1983-86, legis. chmn. North Cen. sect. 1986-88, legis. award 1983, 85). Home: 204 S Taylor Ave Oak Park IL 60302 Office: US Dept Labor Office Solicitor 230 S Dearborn 8th Floor Chicago IL 60604

MANSFIELD, MICHAEL JOSEPH, ambassador, former U.S. senator; b. N.Y.C., Mar. 16, 1903; s. Patrick and Josephine (O'Brien) M.; m. Maureen Hayes, Sept. 13, 1932; 1 dau., Anne Mansfield Marris. Student, Mont. Sch. Mines, 1927-28; A.B., U. Mont., 1933, A.M., 1934; student, U. Calif., 1936, 37. Seaman U.S. Navy, 1918-19; with U.S. Army, 1919-20, U.S. Marines, 1920-22; miner and mining engr. 1922-1931; prof. history and polit. sci. U. Mont., 1933-42; mem. 78th-82d Congresses from 1st Dist. Mont., 1943-53; U.S. Senator from Mont. 1953-77, asst. majority leader, 1957-61, majority leader, 1961-77; mem. Com. on Fgn. Relations, Appropriations Com.; chmn. Dem. Conf., Policy Com., Steering Com.; ambassador to Japan Tokyo, 1977—; Presdl. rep. in, China, 1944; U.S. del. IX Inter-Am. Conf., Colombia, 1948, 6th UN Assembly, Paris, 1951-52, Southeast Asia Conf., Manila, 1954, 13th UN Gen. Assembly, 1958; Presdl. assignment, West Berlin, Southeast Asia, Vietnam, 1962, Europe, Southeast Asia, 1965, 69, visited People's Republic of China on invitation of Premier Chou-En-lai, 1972, on invitation of Govt. of People's Republic of China, 1974, 76, 77, 78. Recipient Nelson Rockefeller Pub. Service award, 1988. Home: Missoula MT 59801 Office: APO San Francisco CA 96503 also: Am Embassy, Akasaka 1-10-5, Minato-ku, Tokyo 107, Japan *

MANSHARDT, CLIFFORD, sociologist; b. Albany, Oreg., Mar. 6, 1897; s. George A. and Ina (Green) M.; m. Agnes Helene Lloyd, May 16, 1925 (dec.); children—Thomas Brewster, Michael Clifford. Student, Bradley Poly. Inst., Peoria, Ill., 1914-15; Ph.B., U. Chgo., 1918, A.M., 1921, Ph.D., 1924; B.D., Chgo. Theol. Sem., 1922, D.D., 1932; student, Union Theol. Sem., 1922-23. Asst. gen. sec. Religious Edn. Assn., 1924-25; dir. Nagpada Neighborhood House, Bombay, India, 1925-41, Sir Dorabji Tata Trust, Bombay, 1932-41; founder, dir. Tata Inst. Social Scis., Bombay, 1936-41; vis. prof., Alden Tuthill lectr. Chgo. Theol. Sem., 1932, lectr., 1942-43; vis. prof., spl. Earl lectr. Pacific Sch. Religion, 1941; dir. Bethlehem Community Center, Chgo., 1942-51; U.S. fgn. service officer, 1951-63; cultural affairs officer, attaché Am. embassy, New Delhi, India, 1951-55, dep. pub. affairs officer, attaché, 1955-58, pub. affairs officer, sec., information counselor, Karachi, Pakistan, 1958-63. Author: The Social Settlement as an Educational Factor in India, 1931, Christianity in a Changing India, 1933, The Hindu-Muslim Problem in India, 1936, The Delinquent Child, 1939, Freedom Without Violence, 1946, The Terrible Meek-An Appreciation of Mohandas K. Gandhi, 1948, The Mahatma and the Missionary, 1949, Pioneering on Social Frontiers in India, 1967; Editor: Religious Edn, 1924-25; founder, editor: Indian Jour. Social Work, 1936-41; Contbr. articles periodicals and profl. jours. Served in U.S. Army, 1918-19. Mem. United Ch. of Christ. Address: 1745 N Gramercy Pl Hollywood CA 90028

MANSHARDT, THOMAS BREWSTER, concert pianist, music educator; b. Wai, India, Mar. 23, 1927; s. Clifford George and Agnes Helene (Lloyd) M.; B.Mus., Oberlin Coll., 1953; tutored by Alfred Cortot, Lausanne, Switzerland, 1957-62. Debuts include Vienna, 1954; London, 1955; Bonn, Germany, 1956; Los Angeles, 1964; N.Y.C., 1965; concert tours include Germany, Austria, India, Pakistan, U.S., Canada; numerous radio and TV appearances; prof. music U. Regina, Sask., Can., 1966—. Served with AUS, 1945-46. Home: 1830 College Ave Apt 1301, Regina, SK Canada S4P 1C2 Office: U Regina, Dept Music, Regina, SK Canada S4S 0A2

MANSUKHANI, THAKUR VISHINDAS, consultant; b. Karachi, Sind, India, Jan. 8, 1934; s. Vishindas Udharam and Hasi Bai (Advani) m.; m. Sheela Parmanand, May 20, 1960; children: Vineet, Arul. BS in Engring., Coll. Engring., Poona, India, 1954. Cert. engr. Mgr. HMT Ltd., Bangalore, India, 1955-61; gen. mgr. HMT Ltd., Pinjore, India, 1961-70, Kalamassery, India, 1970-74; executive dir. HMT Ltd., Kalamassery, 1974-76, Pinjore, India, 1976-78; chmn. mng. dir. Bharat Heavy Plate and Vessels Ltd., Vishkapatnam, India, 1978-81, HMT Ltd., Bangalore, 1981-86; chief exec. T.V. Mansukhani and Co., Bangalore, 1986—; dir. Gabriel India Ltd., Bombay, 1987—, Mysore Kirloskar Ltd., Harihar, India,1987—. Contbr. articles to profl. jours. Trustee PMT trust, Bangalore, 1981—. Fellow Inst. Prodn. Engrs., Indian Inst. Prodn. Engring. Club: Bangalore Golf. Home and Office: T V Mansukhani and Co, 92 V Block Koramangala, Bangalore, Karnataka 560034, India

MANTILLA, NECTARIO RUBÉN, banker; b. Guayaquil, Guayas, Ecuador, July 26, 1940; s. Nectario and Juanita (Zambrano) M.; m. Helen Mantilla, Sept. 8, 1965; 1 child, Xavier. BS, NYU, 1971, MBA, 1972; postgrad., Stanford U., 1981. Mktg. asst. Hallmark Cards, Inc., N.Y.C., 1966-72; account mgr. Citibank N.A., Guayaquil, Ecuador, 1973-75, br. mgr., 1976-78, corp. bank head, v.p., 1979-82; exec. v.p. Banco Continental, Guayaquil, 1983-86; pres., founder Interleasing S.A., Guayaquil, 1987—, Interconsult SA, Guayaquil, 1988—; prof. Guayaquil U., 1974-75; participant, guest speaker numerous bank and mgmt. seminars, 1984—; cons. Jouvin Group, 1983-84, Massuh Group, 1983-86. Author: Financial Structure and the Cost of Capital, 1972, Account Management: A Dynamic Marketing Approach, 1981, Micro/Macroeconomic Analysis of the Sugar Industry, 1975, Risk Analysis in the Extension of Credit, 1985, Ecuador's

Economic Survey, 1986, How to Invest In Ecuador, 1988. Served with U.S. Army, 1960-62. Recipient Western Hemisphere award Citibank, 1978, Exec. award Stanford U., 1981. Mem. Ecuadorian-Am. C. of C., V. Rocafuerte High Sch. Alumni Assn. (pres. 1981-82). Roman Catholic. Clubs: Union, Country. Home: PO Box 10383, Guayaquil Ecuador

MANTON, ANTHONY, computer company executive; b. London, Nov. 20, 1946; s. Alfred Harris and Rose (Bobrofsky) M.; m. Nicola Suzanne Portnoi, Oct. 27, 1977; children: Adam, Richard, James. Sales dir. Eurocalc Ltd., London, 1975-80; product support mgr. Rank Xerox, London, 1980-83; product mgr. Casio Electronics Co. Ltd., London, 1983—. Office: Casio Electronics Co Ltd, Unit 6 1000 N Circular Rd, London NW2 7JD, England

MANUEL, ROBERT, dramatist, theater director; b. Paris, Sept. 9, 1916; s. Alexandre and Alice (Kahn) M.; m. Leonne Mail, Oct. 30, 1944; children—Catherine, Christine; m. Claudine Coster, Oct. 30, 1963; children: Jean-Baptiste, Marie-Silvia. Baccalaureat, Lycee Carnot, Paris; 2 first prizes Nat. Conservatory Dramatic Arts, 1933-36. Mem. Comédie-Française, France, 1936-63, hon. mem., 1963—; prof. Nat. Conservatory Dramatic Arts and Conservatoire de la rue Blanche, France, 1956—; artistic dir. Theatre Marigny, Paris, 1965—; creator of Festivals du Theatre au mer (Mermoz-Paquet), 1977—; treas. Syndicat nat. des metteurs-en-scene d'ouvrages dramatiques, lyriques, ou choreagraphiques, 1966—. Plays produced or interpreted: Les Trois Valses, Man of La Mancha, 1968, L'amour Masque, 1970, La Mamma, Les Cloches de Corneville, Mam'zelle Nitouche, Les Precieuses ridicules, On se Saurait Penser à tout, Mariage Force, Bidule, Les Croulant se Portent bien, La Greve des amoureux, Gigi, Que les hommes sont chers, O.S.S. 117, La Grande Duchesse de Gerolstein, Une Femme qui ne cache rien, J'y suis, j'y reste, Pauline Borghese, Les Noces de Jeanette, Le Marchand de soleil; films include: Orage, La valse de Paris, Police judiciare, Croquemitouffle, Le Gorille vous salue bien, La Vie à deux, La Bourgeois gentilhomme, Certains l'aiment froide, Recours de grace, Candide, Mis Shunway jette un Sort, La Tulipe noire, Une Souris chez les hommes, Les Femmes d'abord, Cent briques et des tuiles, Chasse à la mafia, L'Opera de quat'sous, Judith Therpauve; TV programs: L'Enfant du 17e, Les Auteurs gais, Mademoiselle Moliere, 1964, Donogoo, 1971, Maitre Bolbec et son mari, 1973, La Purée, 1973, L'Or et la Fleur, 1974, Inspecteur Grey, 1976, Le Tresor hollandias, 1976, La Rabouilleuse, 1976, Colinette, 1977, Comme Chien et chat, 1980, Lysistrata, 1973, Ta Bouche, L'Avocar du Diable, 1978; author: Quallais je faire dans cette galere?, Merci Moliere, Le Juste Milieu, others. Mayor of Roqyubrunne-sur Argens (France), 1971-74. Served with French Army. Decorated officier Légion d'honneur, 1956; comdr. Ordre Nat. du Mérite, 1969; médaille d'or des Arts et Lettres; officier des Palmes Académiques; médaille d'or des Arts, Scis. et Lettres, others. Club: Rotary. Office: Theatre Marigny, Carre Marigny, Paris 8e France *

MANVILLE, STEWART ROEBLING, archivist; b. White Plains, N.Y., Jan. 15, 1927; s. Leo and Margaret (Roebling) M.; B.S., Columbia U., 1962; m. Ella V. Grainger, Jan. 19, 1972 (dec.). Various office positions, N.Y.C., 1947-51, 56-58; asst. stage dir. several European opera houses, 1951-55; editor Jas. T. White & Co., N.Y.C., 1959-63; archivist, curator Percy Grainger Library, White Plains, N.Y., 1963—. Mem. CAP. Mem. Hist. House Assn. Am., Nat. Trust Hist. Preservation, Victorian Soc. in Am. (past dir. N.Y. chpt.), Société des Antiquaires de Picardie, Soc. Archtl. Historians, Westchester County Hist. Soc., Titanic Hist. Soc., White Plains Battle Monument Com., Appalachian Trail Conf., Westchester Trails Assn. (past dir.). Quaker. Author: The Manville/Manvel Families in America; contbr. articles and revs. on music to mags. and newspapers. Office: 7 Cromwell Pl White Plains NY 10601

MANZO, SALVATORE EDWARD, university administrator; b. Bklyn., Oct. 23, 1917; s. Salvatore and Mary (Sireci) M.; B.S., U.S. Mil. Acad., 1939; m. Flournoy Davis, Mar. 11, 1960; children—Janeen, John, Joanne, Molly. Commd. 2d lt. USAF, 1939, advanced through grades to col., 1944, ret., 1962; v.p. C.H. Leavell & Co., El Paso, 1962-65; exec. dir. Met. Airlines Com., N.Y.C., 1965-67; dir. aviation City of Houston, 1967-69; pres. Trans-East Air Inc., Bangor, Maine, 1969-70; aviation mgmt. cons., Bangor, 1970-72, Sao Paulo, Brazil, 1972-74; exec. asst. to pres. Hidroservice, Sao Paulo, 1974-77; assoc. Charter Fin. Group, Inc., Houston, 1977-79; dir. exec. devel. Jesse H. Jones Grad. Sch. Adminstrn., Rice U., Houston, 1979-85, asst. dean for exec. devel., 1985—; pres., bd. dirs. Manzo Devel. Co., 1969—, 1st Tex. Venture Capital Corp., 1983—; dir. Headlines U.S.A., Houston, 1987—. Pres. El Paso Indsl. Devel. Corp., 1965; vestryman Christ Ch. Cathedral, Houston, 1979-81. Decorated Silver Star, Legion of Merit, D.F.C. (2), Soldier's medal, Air medal (5), Commendation medal (2); Croix de Guerre with palm (France); recipient Entrepreneur of Yr. award Arthur Young and Venture Mag., 1988. Mem. Houston C. of C., El Paso C. of C. (pres. 1965). Republican. Episcopalian. Author: (with Edward E. Williams) Business Planning for the Entrepreneur: How to Write and Execute a Business Plan, 1983. Home: 1111 Hermann Dr 16-C Houston TX 77004 Office: Rice U PO Box 1892 Houston TX 77251

MAO, YU-YAN, child psychologist; b. Beijing, People's Republic China, June 1, 1926; d. Yi-sheng Mao and Chuan-hui Dai; m. Shi-chuan Lu, Oct. 11, 1952; children: Xi-jing, Xi-chun. BA, Jing-ling U., Nanjing, People's Republic China, 1950. Lic. psychologist. Research asst. Inst. Psychology Chinese Acad. Scis., Beijing, 1951-60, asst. research fellow, 1960-79, assoc. research fellow, 1979-86, research fellow, 1986—; vis. scholar Cornell U., Ithaca, N.Y., 1981; mem. acad. com. Inst. Psychology, 1985—. Author: (with others) Human Intelligence, 1983 (1st prize 1983). Contbr. articles to psychology jours. Mem. exec. com. All-China Women's Fedn., Beijing, 1983—; dir. Child Mental Health Com., Chinese United Com. for the Handicapped, 1986—. Mem. Chinese Psychol. Soc. (v.p. Beijing br., 1982—), Chinese Mental Health Soc. (dir. 1985—, v.p. 1987—), Rehib. Assn. Office: Chinese Acad Scis Inst Psych, Zhong Guan Chun, Beijing People's Republic of China

MAOATE, TEREPAI, government official; b. Rarotonga, Cook Islands, Sept. 1, 1934; s. Mataina (Peckham) Maoate; m. Marito Kau Mapu; children: Mii, Terepai, Teariki, Tereinga, Bob, Peckham. Diploma in medicine and surgery, Fiji Sch. Medicine, Suva, 1954; diploma in obstetrics, Auckland (New Zealand) U., 1973; MPH, Amsterdam U., 1976. Med. officer Govt. Cook Islands, 1954-75, dir. hosp. and clin. services, 1975-81, minister of health and agr., 1983, 1984-85, mem. parliament, 1983-84, dep. prime minister, minister conservation, agr., health, stats., planning and econ. devel., 1985-88; pvt. practice med. practitioner Cook Islands, 1981-83; cons. gen. surgery Ministry of Health, Rarotonga, 1983-87. Mem. parliament Ngatangiia Constituency, 1983—. Mem. Commonwealth Parliamentary Assn., Cook Islands Med. and Dental Assn. Mem. Cook Islands Party for Coalition. Mem. Christian Ch. Lodge: Rotary. Home: Ngatangiia, Rarotonga Cook Islands Office: Ministry Agr, Avarua, Rarotonga Cook Islands

MAOUAD, JOSEPH, cardiologist; b. Chiah, Lebanon, Sept. 16, 1939; arrived in France, 1960; s. Samir and Eugénie (Ghossein) M.; m. Isabelle Soucadaux, Dec. 2, 1965 (div. 1972); m. Helge Eilentrop, May 17, 1972; 1 child, Dunya. MD, Faculty of Medicine, Paris, 1967; cardiology specialist, 1968. Diplomate French Bd. Cardiology. Externe, assistance Publique de Paris, 1963-68; attaché Paris, 1968—, cons., 1980—; co-chief catheterization and interventional cardiology Am. Hosp. Paris, 1984—; pvt. practice specializing in cardiology cons. Paris, 1969—. Contbr. articles to profl. jours. Fellow Royal Soc. Medicine London, Am. Coll. Cardiology; mem. Soc. French Cardiology, San Francisco Heart Inst. (cons.). Home: 31 B rue Campagne Premiere, 75014 Paris France Office: Am Hosp Paris, 63 BD Victor Hugo, 92200 Neuilly-sur-Seine France

MAPA, DOMINGO ONGPIN, II, management information; b. Manila, Oct. 26, 1962; s. Domingo Ledesma Mapa and Lirio Melevo Ongpin; m. Cherisse Codina Gonzalez, Mar. 30, 1987. BS in Mgmt., Ateneo U., Manila, 1983; postgrad., Inst. Advanced Computer Tech., Manila, 1984, Arthur Andersen Ctr. Profl. Edn., St. Charles, Ill., 1986-87, IBM Edn. Ctr., Manila, 1987. Tech. staff I Sycip, Gorres, Velayo & Co. (mem. firm SGV Group and Arthur Andersen, S.C.), Manila, 1984-85, tech. staff II, 1985-87, tech. staff III, 1987-88, mgr., 1988—; project cons. Bd. Investments, Manila, Tech. Transfer Bd., Manila, Asian Devel. Bank, Manila, Arthur Andersen & Co., Chgo., IBM, N.Y.C., Philippine Airlines, Manila. Co-author: SGV Special Report on Local Area Networks, 1985. Roman Catholic. Home: 5022 P Burgos St Apt 12-C, Makati, Manila Philippines Office: SGV Development Ctr, 105 De La Rosa St, Makati, Manila Philippines

MAPP, ALF JOHNSON, JR., writer, historian; b. Portsmouth, Va., Feb. 17, 1925; s. Alf Johnson and Lorraine (Carney) M.; m. Hartley Lockhart, Mar. 28, 1953; 1 son, Alf Johnson III; m. Ramona Hartley Hamby, Aug. 1, 1971. A.A., Coll. William and Mary, 1945, A.B. summa cum laude, 1961. Editorial writer Portsmouth Star, 1945-46, asso. editor, 1946-48, editorial chief, 1948-54; news editor, editorial writer Virginian-Pilot, Norfolk, 1954-58; free-lance writer 1958—; lectr. Old Dominion U., 1961-62, instr., 1962-67, asst. prof. English and history, 1967-73, asso prof. English, journalism, creative writing, history, 1973-79, prof., 1979-82, eminent prof., 1982—; profl. lectr., 1948—; lectr. Brookings Inst., 1984—. Host: TV series Jamestown to Yorktown, 1975-77; Author: The Virginia Experiment, 1957, 3d edit., 1987, Frock Coats and Epaulets, 1963, 3d edit., 1987, America Creates Its Own Literature, 1965, Just One Man, 1968, The Golden Dragon: Alfred the Great and His Times, 1974, 75, 80, Thomas Jefferson: A Strange Case of Mistaken Identity, 1987 (one of 40 best books of 1987); co-author: Chesapeake Bay in the American Revolution, 1981; co-author Portsmouth: A Pictorial History, 1988; The Nature of Constitutionalism, 1988; also film and TV scripts.; Co-editor: Place Names of Early Portsmouth, 1973, 74; nonfiction editor: New Va. Rev., 1984-85; contbr. articles to N.Y. Times; other newspapers, mags. also Worldmark Ency. Mem. Portsmouth-Norfolk County Savs. Bond Com., 1948-51, Va. Com. on Library Devel., 1949-50; mem. publs. com. 350th Anniversary of Rep. Govt. in the Western World, 1966-69, War of Independence Commn., 1967-83; mem. editorial bd. Jamestown Found., 1967—; chmn. Portsmouth Revolutionary Bicentennial Com., 1968-81; chmn. awards jury Baruch award United Daus. Confederacy-Columbia U., 1976, mem., 1980; chmn. Portsmouth Mus. and Fine Arts Commn., 1983-85, Southeastern Va. Anglo-Am. Friendship Day, 1976, Bicentennial Commemoration of Cornwallis' Embarkation for Yorktown, 1981, World Premiere of Mary Rose Marine Archeol. Exhibit, 1985; mem. grant rev. com. Va. Commn. for the Arts, 1986-87; bd. dirs. Portsmouth Pub. Library, 1948-58, v.p., 1954-56; bd. dirs. Va. Symphony, 1986-87, trustee, 1987—; mem. taxes and mandates com. City of Portsmouth, 1982—; mem. adv. com. City Mgr. of Norfolk, 1988—; bd. dirs. Portsmouth Area Community Chest, 1948-52, Va. YMCA Youth and Govt. Found., 1950-52; mem. All-Am. cities com. for award-winning city Nat. League Municipalities, 1976. Named Portsmouth Young Man of Year, 1951; recipient honor medal Freedoms Found., 1951, Disting. Research award Old Dominion U., 1987, Great Citizen award Hampton Roads, 1987, Notable Citizen award Portsmouth, Va., 1987; English award Old Dominion Coll., 1961; Troubadour, Great Tchr. award, 1969; Outstanding Am. Educator award, 1972, 74; Nat. Bicentennial medal Am. Revolution Bicentennial Adminstrn., 1976; medal Comité Français du Bicentenaire de l'Independence des Etats-Unis, France, 1976; (with Ramona Mapp) Nat. Family Service award Family Found. Am., 1980; Laureate award Commonwealth of Va., 1981; Disting. Alumnus award Old Dominion U., 1982; Liberty Bell award Portsmouth Bar Assn., 1985; Old Dominion U. Triennial Phi Kappa Phi Scholar award, 1986; Portsmouth Downtown Merchants award, 1984, 85. Mem. Am. Hist. Assn., Va. Hist. Soc., Portsmouth Hist. Soc. (historiographer 1975-82, v.p. 1982-84, pres. 1985), Norfolk Hist. Soc. (dir. 1965-72), No. Neck Hist. Soc., Hist. Socs. Eastern Va. (dir. 1971—), SAR, Am. Assn. U. Profs., Authors Guild, Va. Library Assn. (legislative com. 1950-51), Poetry Soc. Va. (pres. 1974-75, adv. com. 1976—), Va. Writers Club, Assn. Preservation of Va. Antiquities, Order of Cape Henry (dir. 1970—, nat. pres. 1975-76), Jamestowne Soc. (chief historian 1975-77, internat. sec. state 1978-79), English Speaking Union (dir. 1976-77), Modern Lang. Assn., Phi Theta Kappa, Delta Phi Omega (chpt. pres. 1961), Phi Kappa Phi. Home: Willow Oaks 2901 Tanbark Ln Portsmouth VA 23703 Office: Old Dominion U Norfolk VA 23508

MAPUA, EDMUND ONG, chemical company executive; b. Manila, Feb. 12, 1937; s. Tianchu C. and Purita O. Mapua; m. Rose Uy, May 6, 1962; children—Rose Carolyn, Roland, Winston, Edmund Newton, Irene. B.S. in Textile Chemistry, Lowell Technol. Inst., 1959, M.S. in Textile Chemistry, 1960. Asst. chief chemist Textile Aniline & Chem. Co., Lawrence, Mass., 1960-61; resident mgr. Nyanza Color & Chem. Co., Manila, 1961-65; pres. Eastman Chem. Industries, Inc., Manila, 1965—; pres. DFE Chem. Corp., Manila, 1980—, dir., 1972—; gen. mgr. Polystyrene Mfg. Co. Inc., Valenzuela, 1972—, Peroxide Philippines Corp., Valenzuela, 1971—; dir. Bataan Pulp & Paper Mills, Inc., Manila. Recipient cert. of appreciation Ateneo de Manila U., 1976. Mem. Am. Chem. Soc., Am. Assn. Textile Chemists and Colorists, Philippine Textile Dye and Chem. Suppliers Assn. (dir., sec.), Chem. Industries Assn. of Philippines, Jaycee Internat. (senator 1978). Clubs: Wack-Wack, Manila Polo (Manila). Lodges: Manila 761, Rotary of Manila. Home: 1 Hibiscus St, Barangay Marina, Quezon City Philippines Office: Eastman Chem Industries Inc, 14 Ilang-Ilang St, Quezon City Philippines

MARA, RATU SIR KAMISESE KAPAIWAI TUIMACILAI, prime minister of Fiji; b. May 13, 1920; Ratu Ratu Tui Nayau and Adi Lusiana Qolikoro; student Otago (N.Z.) Med. Coll.; M.A., Wadham Coll., Oxford (Eng.) U.; postgrad. London Sch. Econs., 1961-62; LL.D. (hon.), U. Guam, 1969, U. Otago, 1972, U. New Delhi, 1975, Tokai (Japan) U., 1980, U. Papua (New Guinea), 1982; D.Polit. Sci. (hon.), U. Yonsei (Korea), 1978; D.Univ. (hon.), U.S. Pacific, 1980; m. Adi Lady Lala; 8 children. Joined Colonial Service U.K., 1950; dist. officer, acting dep. sec. Fijian affairs, div. commr., 1951-61; mem. Legis. Council, 1953—; mem. Exec. Council Fiji, 1959-61, mem. for natural resources, 1964-66; 1st chief minister Govt. of Fiji, 1967-70; prime minister Fiji, 1970-87, reinstated after mil. coup, 1987—, also minister of fgn affairs, home affairs, nat. youth service and army service. Pres. Alliance Party, Fijian Assn. Created knight, 1969, mem. Privy Council, 1973; decorated grand master Order Nat. Lion Senegal; grand Kwanghwa Order Diplomatic Service Merit (Republic Korea); hon. fellow Wadham Coll., 1971. Office: Ministry of Fgn Affairs, Battery Rd, Suva Fiji *

MARABLE, SIMEON-DAVID, artist; b. Phila., May 10, 1948; s. Daniel Berry and Marsima (Maddela); B.A. in Art and English, Lea Coll., Minn., 1970; postgrad. Tyler Sch. Art, Phila.; m. Pamela Joyce Sorenson, June 1, 1969; children—Simeon-David dePaul, Daniel-Dale Christopher, Jason-Andrew Bartley, Jo Anna Lee, Benjamin Arthur Kurtis. Tchr. 7th and 8th grade art Pennsbury (Pa.) Sch. System, 1970-88; tchr. 9th and 10th grade art Charles H. Boehm High Sch., Pennsbury, 1988—; tchr. Neshaminy Adult Edn., 1972-82; resident artist Middletown Hist. Assn., 1976, Three Arches Corp., 1975, also treas.; sculptures represented in Albert Lea (Minn.) Library; painting in chapel Ft. Dix, N.J.; portraits of Mr. Mike Schmidt, 1986, Mr. Lee Elia, 1986; creator Phila. City of Champs logo. Mgr. Boys Soccer League, Boys Little League, Middletown Twp.; mem. Presdl. Task Force. Served with USAR, 1970. Creator children's ednl. programs Falls Township 300th, Pennsylvania Statehood. Named Artist of Year, Albert Lea Lions Club, 1970. Mem. Buck County Art Educators (pres. 1973-74), Levittown Artists Assn., Nat. Soc. Arts and Lit., Internat. Platform Assn. Roman Catholic. Home: 18 Spindletree Rd Levittown PA 19056 Office: 600 S Olds Blvd Fairless Hills PA 19053

MARACAS, DIMITRI VAGIANOS, financial company official, market and environment researcher; b. Cairo, Feb. 14, 1958; arrived in Greece, 1975; s. Vagianos M. and Magdalini D. (Papadimitriou) M.; m. Loren V. Purvis, Sept. 11, 1987. Abitur, German Sch., Athens, Greece and Beirut, 1977; BBA, Am. Coll. Athens, 1981; MBA, Century U., Calif., 1983. Sales rep. Egyptair, Athens, 1978-83; sales mgr. Marriott Hotel, Athens, 1984-85; sales mgr. for traveler's checks in Greece and Cyprus Am. Express Internat., Athens, 1985-88; fraud prevention specialist card products Am. Express Germany, Frankfurt, Fed. Republic Germany, 1988—. Served with Greek Navy, 1981-83. Greek Orthodox. Home: 27 Theobald-Christ Str, 6000 Frankfurt Federal Republic of Germany Office: Am Express, 46 Mainzer Landstrasse, 6000 Frankfurt Federal Republic of Germany

MARACLE, DAVID EARL, electrical engineer; b. Everett, Mass., Mar. 18, 1948; s. Lorne Hilton and Ida Lillian (Davis) M.; B.S.E.E., Lowell Tech. Inst., 1969, M.S.E.E., 1974; m. Linda Elaine Griffin, June 21, 1969; children—Tabitha, Matthew, Timothy. Design engr. Tactical Ground Def. Systems, Raytheon Corp., 1969-71, design engr. Bedford Labs. (Mass.), 1971-75, lead engr., 1975-78, sect. mgr. fire control hardware Tactical Ground Def. Systems, 1978-81, sect. mgr., project engr. for product improvement, 1981-84; tech. dir. Hawk Ground Support Equipment, 1985, radar programs mgr., 1986—, project engring. mgr., 1986—; cons., ptnr. Wheeler & Maracle, Topsfield, Mass., 1974-84. Contbr. articles to profl. publs. Mem. IEEE. Republican. Mem. Protestant Assemblies of God Ch. Home: 4 Apollo Circle Andover MA 01810 Office: Hartwell Rd Bedford MA 01730

MARADADU, BALACHANDAR VEDAPURI, hotel executive; b. Marudadu, Madras, India, Sept. 2, 1950; s. Vedapuri Venkatramayya and Saraswati Vedapurt (Muthukrishnaya) M.; m. Rani Balachandar; children: Sarayu, Narmada. Diploma in Hotel Mgmt., Inst. Hotel Mgmt., Tamilnadu, 1967; postgrad. diploma in Tchr. Tng., Inst. Hotel Mgmt., Bombay, 1976; diploma in Tchr. Tng., Ith Salzburg, Austria, 1977; cert. in hotel adminstrn., Cornell U., Madras; cert. in French, Cen. Inst. English and Fgn. Langs., 1974; diploma in mgmt., Indira Gandhi Open U., New Delhi, 1988; postgrad. in sociology, Mysore (India) U., 1988—. Mgr. Facor/Seaview Hotel, Andhra Pradesh, India, 1967-72; lectr. Inst. Hotel Mgmt. Hyd, Andhra Pradesh, 1972-79; head dept. mgmt. Inst. Hotel Mgmt. Madras, Tamilnadu, 1979-80; prin. Inst. Hotel Mgmt. Bangalore, Karnataka, India, 1980—; mem. Hotels Restaurants Classification Com., Karnataka region, Delhi; mem. Govt. Karnataka Hotel and Restaurant Classification Com., Bangalore; mem. syllabus com. Bharathiar U., Tamlinadu, 1987—. Author: Front Office Operations, 1975; co-author: Hotel Management, 1988. Mem. Dakshni State Cultural Com. SAARC Festival, Bangalore, 1986; mem. Indian Red Cross Soc., Bangalore; mem. vocat. guidance cells State Edn. Bds., Bangalore; hon. program dir. competency based curriculum on catering restaurant mgmt. Nat. Council Ednl. Research and Tng., Ministry of Edn., New Delhi, 1987—. Fulbright fellow, 1987; recipient Belfield Smith award Ihmctan, Bombay, 1975, ITH, Govt. Austria and India, 1977. Mem. Assn. Food Scientists and Technolgists (sec. 1983-84), Fedn. Hotels and Restaurants India, Karnataka Pradesh Hoteliers and Restaurants Assn., Indian Soc. Tng. and Devel., Indian Soc. Bakers, Karnataka C. of C. (tourism and pub. relations com.). Club: Century (Bangalore) (catering com. 1984-85). Lodges: Lions (mem. vocat. guidance cell), Rotary (mem. vocat. guidance cell). Office: Inst Hotel Mgmt, SJP Campus, Seshadri Rd, Bangalore, Karnataka 560 001, India

MARAINI, DACIA, writer; b. Florence, Italy, Nov. 13, 1936. Free-lance writer Rome. Author: (novels) La vacanza, 1962, English edit., 1966, French edit., 1967, L'eta' del malessere, 1963, 11 other edits., Memorie di una ladra, 1967, Femme en Guerre, 1977, Donna in guerra, 1978, Lettere a Marina, 1981, English edit., 1987, Il treno per Helsinky, 1984, 2d edit., 1987, Isolina, 1985, (short stories) Mio marito, 1968, Mi marido, 1975, Wintershlaf, 1985, (poems) Crudelta' all' aria aperta, 1968, Donne mie, 1974, Mangiami pure, 1979, Dimenticato di dimenticare, 1982, Devour me too, 1987, (essays) Cent' anniddi poesia giapponese, 1968, E tu chi eri, 1973, Fare teatro, 1974, Storia di piera, 1980, Histoire de Piera, 1983, La Bionda, la bruna e l' asino, 1987. Recipient Formentor prix, 1963, Sain Vincent premio, 1974, Riccione premio, 1977, 79, Villadeste premio, 1981, Aghof award, 1982, Agrigento premio, 1983, Telemone premio, 1984, Fregene premio, 1985, Efebo d'Oro, 1985, Citta' Di Rapallo premio, 1986. Home and Office: Via Beccaria 18, 00196 Rome Italy

MARANGOS, AKIS, management and shipping company executive; b. Kyrenia, Cyprus, Aug. 18, 1940; came to Greece, 1974; s. Charalambos and Nina (Vrachas) D.; children—Charalambos, Maria-Theresa, Sofia-Katherina. Grad., Ecole Hoteliere, Lausanne, Switzerland, LaSalle U.-Chgo., 1966. Dir. mktg. Astir S.A., Athens, 1974-76; prof. K.A.T.E. Higher Edn. Ctr., Athens, 1974-76; gen. mgr. Itas Ges MbH, Vienna, 1976-77; v.p. ISTS-Intercontinental, Munich and Athens, 1977-80; chief exec. EOMA Corp., Athens, 1980—; cons. A. Marangos Assocs. Ltd., Athens, 1974—. Contbr. articles to profl. jours. Fellow Hotel Catering and Instl. Mgmt. Assn.; mem. Brit. Inst. Mgmt. London, Inst. Mktg. London, Ancien Eleve Ecole Hoteliere. Office: Marangos Assoc Ltd, PO Box 30351, 100 33 Athens Greece also: EOMA Corp, 9 Amerikis St, 10672 Athens Greece

MARANZANA, ENRICO GIUSEPPE, manufacturing company executive; b. Genova, Italy, Sept. 11, 1928; s. Giuseppe Giacomo and Angela (Vigo) M.; m. Silvia Marabelli, Oct. 16, 1961. Degree in electromech. engring., U. Genova, 1953; degree in econs., Bocconi U., Milan, 1957; postgrad., Engring. Research Inst. Stanford U., 1960-61. With Edison Group (now Montedison Group), Milan, 1954-74, dir. group purchasing dept., 1961-72, controller, 1972-74; gen. mgr. SOIMI Group, Milan, 1974-78, mng. dir., 1978—. Contbr. articles to mfg. jours.

MARASCO, LOUIS JOSEPH, real estate executive; b. Jersey City, July 24, 1946; s. Joseph and Maria Josephine (Parisi) M.; B.A., U. Pitts., 1968; postgrad. Hofstra U., 1973; m. Rosemary Lee D'Acunto, July 31, 1971; children—Michelle Marie, Louis Joseph. Personnel adminstr. 1st Nat. City Bank, N.Y.C., 1968-70; adminstr. real estate investment trust Chase Manhattan Bank., N.Y.C., 1970-72; pres. Ramlaw Bldg. Corp., Island Park, N.Y., 1972—; v.p. Walmer Realty, Island Park, 1976—; sr. v.p. Litelco Communications Inc.; dir. Trailer Realty Inc. Lic. real estate broker, N.Y. Mem. Nat. Assn. Real Estate Brokers, L.I. Bd. Realtors, L.I. Builders Assn., N.Y. Realtors Assn., Internat. Platform Assn. Clubs: Masons. Home: 225 Merrifield Ave Oceanside NY 11572 Office: 221 Atlantic Ave Oceanside NY 11572

MAŘATKA, TOMÁS PAVEL, cardiologist; b. Prague, Bohemia, Czechoslovakia, May 26, 1944; s. Zdeněk and Elvira (Kohoutová) M.; m. Stanislava Strejcková, Mar. 10, 1973; children: Vit, Tomás, Barbora. MD, Charles U., Prague, 1968. Intern in medicine Inst. Nat. Health, Kolin, Czechoslovakia, 1969-80; cons. cardiology Hosp., Kolin, 1980—, also chief ICU. Mem. Soc. Czechoslovak Physicians, Soc. Czech Cardiologists. Office: Nemocnice, 280 20 Kolin II Czechoslovakia

MARBURGER, JOHN HARMEN, III, university president, physics educator; b. S.I., N.Y., Feb. 8, 1941; s. John H., Jr. and Virginia A. (Smith) M.; m. Carol Preston Godfrey, June 12, 1965; children: John Harmen, Alexander Godfrey. B.A. in Physics magna cum laude, Princeton U., 1962; Ph.D. in Applied Physics (NASA trainee), Stanford U., 1967. Physicist Goddard Space Flight Center, NASA, 1962-63; asst. prof. physics and elec. engring. U. So. Calif., Los Angeles, 1966-69, assoc. prof., 1969-75, prof., 1975-80, chmn. physics dept., 1972-75, interim dean Coll. Letters, Arts and Scis., 1976-77, dean Coll. Letters, Arts and Scis., 1977-80; prof. physics and elec. engring., pres. SUNY, Stony Brook, 1980—; cons. laser fusion program Lawrence Livermore Labs., 1972-75; chmn. N.Y. State fact finding panel on Shoreham Nuclear Power Facility, 1983; chmn. council of pres.'s Universities Research Assn., 1986; bd. dirs. N.Y. State Edn. and Research Network, Inc., 1986—. Contbr. articles to tech. publs. Bd. dirs. Mus. at Stony Brook, 1980—, L.I. Assn., Inc., 1983—, Action Com. for L.I., 1980-83, L.I. Forum for Tech., Inc., 1980—; bd. trustees Princeton U., 1985—; chmn. N.Y. State Energy Office Rev. Commn., 1980-81, Suffolk County (N.Y.) Task Force on Priorities in Fin., 1980-81. Recipient Shuichi Kusaka Meml. Prize Princeton U., 1962. Mem. Assn. of Colls and Univs. State of N.Y. (v.p. 1986-87), Coleman Chamber Music Assn. (bd. dirs. 1969-80). Office: SUNY Stony Brook NY 11794

MARC, JEAN, marine organization executive; b. Perpignan, France, Jan. 19, 1930; came to Eng., 1982; s. Jean and Jeanne (Ribeill) M.; m. Genevieve Louise Jeanne Payan, Aug. 20, 1959; children: Xavier, Simon, Claire. Adminstr. des Affaires Maritimes, Affaires Maritime, St. Servan, France, 1962. Tchr., Affaires Maritimes Sch., Bordeaux, France, 1968-72; head ships safety bur. Ministry Transport, Paris, 1972-80; head navigation div. Ministry of the Sea, Paris, 1980-82; maritime counsellor French Embassy, London, 1982—; head various French delegations Internat. Maritime Orgn., London, 1974-82, permanent rep. of France, 1982—. Served to lt. French Navy, 1951-52. Recipient Merite award French Govt., 1982, Legion d 'Honneur, Merite Maritime award French Govt., 1984; named to Royal Victorian Order, Her Majesty Queen Elizabeth II, 1984. Mem. Nautical Inst. London. Roman Catholic. Avocations: reading, drawing. Office: French Embassy Maritime Counsellor, 2 Queens Gate, London SW7 5EH, England

MARCATANTE, JOHN JOSEPH, educational administrator; b. N.Y.C., Mar. 3, 1930; s. Joseph and Matilda Clara (Grasso) M.; student NYU, 1948-50; A.B., Bklyn. Coll., 1955; M.S. in Edn., Hunter Coll., 1958. Tchr. English secondary schs., N.Y.C., 1955-72; asst. prin. Astoria Intermediate Sch., N.Y.C., 1967—; instr. Hunter Coll., 1963; lectr. in edn. Grad. Sch., Queens Coll., N.Y.C., 1965-67. Cons., Anglo-Am. Seminar on Teaching English, Dartmouth Coll., 1966, Anglo-Am. Seminar on Teaching the Disadvantaged, West Midlands Coll., Great Britain, 1968. Mem. Nat. Council Tchrs. English, N.Y.C. Tchrs. English, Council Supervisory Assns., Cath. Tchrs. Assn., Columbia Assn. N.Y.C., Poetry Soc. Am. Author: Identification and Image Stories, 1964, American Folklore and Legends, 1967, (with others) Macmillan Gateway English Series, 1969, Tales from World Epics, 1988; also numerous articles in profl. jours., poetry; editor: Fourteenth Yearbook N.Y. Society for Experimental Study for Education, 1970. Home: 52 Daffodil Ln Wantagh NY 11793 Office: 31-51 21st St Long Island City NY 11106

MARCEAU, MARCEL, pantomimist, actor, director, painter, poet; b. Strasbourg, France, Mar. 22, 1923; s. Charles and Anne (Werzberg) Mangel. Student, Sch. Dramatic Art, Sarah Bernhardt Theatre, Paris, 1946; D (hon.), Linfield Coll., Princeton U., U. Ann Arbor. Dir. artistique Ecole De Mimodrame de Paris Marcel Marceau. Performer role of Arlequin, pantomime Baptiste; Praxitele and the Golden Fish, Sarah Bernhardt Theatre; creator character Bip, 1947; performer Maggio Musicale in Florence and Edinburgh festivals; organizer, Pantomime Co., Paris; producer: The Overcoat, The Three Wigs, 14th of July, The Pawn Shop, Pierrot de Montmartre,Paris qui rit Paris qui pleure, Don Juan; performer extensive tours U.S., S.Am., Africa, Australia, China, Japan, South East Asia, Russia, Europe, 1950—; performer worldwide TV shows; appeared in motion pictures: Barbarella, 1967, Shanks, 1974, Silent Movie, 1976; appeared as Scrooge in TV film A Christmas Carol, 1973; author, illustrator: The Story of Bip, Pimporello; lithographer The 7 Deadly Sins, The Third Eye. Decorated officier Legion d'Honneur; comdr. Order Arts and Letters; Officer of Merit (France); recipient Emmy awards, 1956, 68, Medaille Vermeil de la ville de Paris, 1978. Mem. Acad. Fine Arts Berlin, Acad. Fine Arts Munich. Address: care Ronald A Wilford Columbia Artist Mgmt Inc 119 W 57th St New York NY 10019 also: Ecole de Mimodrame de Paris, 17 Rue Rene Boulanger, 75010 Paris France

MARCEL, GEORGES ANTHONY, physician, laboratory executive; b. Watlington, U.K., Dec. 11, 1940; immigrated to France, 1947; s. Georges and Rosa (Newman) M.; m. Corinne Warniez, June 11, 1977; 1 dau. by previous marriage, Florence. Baccalaureat, Lycée Janson de Sailly, Paris, 1958; M.D., U. Paris, 1967; Insead, Fontainebleau, France, 1980. Intern, St. Anne's Hosp., Paris, 1962, Lariboisiere Hosp., Paris, 1963, Pitie Hosp., Paris, 1964; resident R. Poincare Hosp., 1965-66, St. Louis Hosp., Paris, 1967-68; chief Intensive Care Clinic, Henri Mondor Hosp., Paris, 1969-74; asst. med. mgr. Hoechst, Paris, 1974-75, mktg. mgr., 1975-76, devel. mgr., 1976-80, asst. gen. mgr., 1980-83; gen. mgr. Roussel, Paris, 1983-86; dir. health devel., mem. Comite' de Direction Generale of Roussel-uclaf, 1986—; founder French Group for Study of Red Cell Filterability. Editor: Medecine Actuelle, 1970, Clinical Haemorheology, 1982; contbr. numerous articles to med. jours. Decorated knight Nat. Order of Merit (France). Fellow Royal Soc. Medicine; mem. Internal Soc. Haemostasis and Thrombosis, Internat. Soc. Biorheology. Home: 30 rue des Ecoles, 75005 Paris France Office: Roussel-Uclaf, 35 Bld des Invalides, 75007 Paris France

MARCELLI, MIROSLAV, philosopher; b. Zilina, Slovakia, Czechoslovakia, Sept. 9, 1947; s. Ján and Ida (Majercíková) Marcelliová; m. Mária Lacová, Mar. 23, 1951; children: Martin, Jana. PhD, Comenius U., Bratislava, Czechoslovakia, 1976. Asst Comenius U., 1971-84, reader in history, philosophy, 1984—; populazier French contemporary philosophy Slovak Lit. Fund, Bratislava, 1978—. cons. editor Pravda pub. house, Bratislava, 1975; translator, editor sci. jours. Fellow Slovak Philosphical Soc. Mem. Communist Party Czechoslovakia. Home: Botevova 2, 851 01 Bratislava Czechoslovakia Office: Comenius U, Gondova 2, 801 00 Bratislava Czechoslovakia

MARCELLO, AMEDEO ALFRED, newspaper editor; b. Providence, Apr. 19, 1904; s. Luigi and Teresa (Villani) M.; m. Elsie Ann Lynum, June 2, 1930. Student, Byrant-Stratton Coll., 1919-20, Am. Press Inst., Columbia, 1948. Reporter Providence News, 1923; state editor, city editor, drama editor, news editor News-Tribune, Providence, 1925-37; pub. weekly West Warwick (R.I.) News, 1937-38; reporter Worcester (Mass.) Telegram, 1938, asst. city editor, 1938-49, city editor, 1949-66, exec. news editor, 1966-71; founder OSIA News (nat. publ.); Sons of Italy, 1946, dir., 1946-63, nat. pub. relations chmn., 1957-63; mem. adv. council N.E. Fed. Savs. Author: Ready for Retirement?, 1972, Blueprint for Retirement, 1973. Mem. Pres.'s Com. Employment Handicapped, 1950—; mem. Mass. Gov.'s Com. for Refugees, 1954-58; chmn. bd. communications Worcester Catholic Diocese.; Sec., bd. dirs. Central Mass. chpt. Nat. Safety Council; bd. dirs. St. Vincent Hosp. Research Found., Worcester Hist. Soc.; incorporator St. Vincent Hosp.; nat. exec. sec. Sons of Italy Found., 1957-63. Recipient Pall Malls Big Story award, 1953, citation for work with Com. Employment Handicapped, 1957, Star of Solidarity Italian Republic, 1957, Order of Merit Italian Republic, 1966. Mem. Sigma Delta Chi.

MARCELO, MARINA SALEM, physician; b. Indang, Cavite, Philippines, Mar. 5, 1939; U.S. citizen by naturalization; d. Mauro Cabal Slaem and Regina Gener Pulido; m. Percival N. Marcelo, June 16, 1966; children: Svetlana Jean, Percival II, Millicent Grace. MD, Manila Central U., Caloocan City, 1964. Medical extern Laguna Provincial Hosp., Santa Cruz, Laguna, Philippines, 1965-66, adjunct resident, 1966; gen. practice medicine Santa Cruz, 1966—. Contbr. poetry and narrative to jours. Mem. Immaculate Conception Parish, Santa Cruz. Mem. Philippine Med. Assn. (life), Philippine Med. Women's Assn. (life), Laguna Med. Soc. (life), World Ecologists. Roman Catholic. Home and Office: 270 Elbo St, 4009 Santa Cruz, Laguna Philippines

MARCH, JACQUELINE FRONT, chemist; b. Wheeling, W.Va. B.S., Case Western Res. U., 1937, M.A., 1939; Wyeth fellow med. research U. Chgo., 1940-42; postgrad. U. Pitts., 1945, Ohio State U., 1967, Wright State U., 1970-76; m. A. W. Marcovich, Oct. 7, 1945 (dec. 1969); children—Wayne Front, Gail Ann March Cohen. Diplomate Am. Bd. Radiology. Chemist, Mt. Sinai Hosp., Cleve., 1934-40; med. research chemist U. Chgo., 1940-42; research analyst Koppers Co., also info. scientist Union Carbide Corp., Mellon Inst., Pitts., 1942-45; propr. March. Med. Research Lab., etiology of diabetes, Dayton, Ohio, 1950-70; guest scientist Kettering Found., Yellow Springs, Ohio, 1953; Dayton Found. fellow Miami Valley Hosp. Research Inst., 1956. mem. chemistry faculty U. Dayton, 1959-69, Research Inst. U. Dayton, 1968-79, info. scientist Research Inst., 1968-79; prin. investigator Air Force Wright Aero. Labs., Wright-Patterson AFB Tech. Info. Center, 1970-79; chem. info. specialist, div. tech. services Nat. Inst. Occupational Safety and Health, HHS, Cin., 1979—; propr. JFM Cons., 1980—; designer info. systems, speaker in field. Recipient Recognition cert. U. Dayton, 1980. Mem. Am. Soc. Info. Sci. (treas. South Ohio 1973-75), Am. Chem. Soc. (pres. Dayton 1977), Soc. Advancement Materials and Process Engring. (pres. Midwest chpt. 1977-78), Affiliated Tech. Socs. (Outstanding Scientist and Engr. award 1978), Am. Congress Govtl. Indsl. Hygienists (rev. com. toxic chemicals 1983—), AAUP (exec. bd.), Sigma Xi (treas. Dayton 1976-79, Conrad P. Straub lectr. 1982, pres. Cin. Fed. Environ. chpt. 1986-87, del. nat. meeting 1987—). Contbr. articles to profl. publs. Home: 154 Stillmeadow Dr Cincinnati OH 45245 Office: 4676 Columbia Pkwy Cincinnati OH 45226

MARCHAC, DANIEL ALEXANDER, plastic surgeon; b. Boulogne Billancourt, France, Dec. 3, 1936; s. Gregoire and Elga Valentine (de Spengler) M.; m. Delphine Dupont, Dec. 12, 1964 (div. 1975); children: Valentine, Gregoire; m. Nina Mitz, Oct. 10, 1979; children: Alexander, Nathalie. M.D., Med. Faculty, Paris, 1966. Diplomate French Bd. Plastic Surgery. Resident, Hôpital Paris, 1963-67; fellow under Dr. Millard, Miami, and Dr. Converse, N.Y.C., 1967-68; chef de clinique Dr. Dufourmentel, Paris, 1968-70; cons. plastic surgery Hôpital Paris, 1970—; teaching fellow French Coll. Plastic Surgeons, 1978—; dir. Craniofacial Team Hôpital Enfants-Malades, Paris. Author: Craniofacial Surgery for Craniosynostosis, 1982; Surgical Treatment Baso Cell of the Face, 1986, Craniofacial Surgery, 1987. Mem. French Soc. Plastic Surgeons (treas. 1978), Am. Soc. Plastic Surgeons, European Soc. Craniofacial Surgery (gen. sec. 1984), Internat. Soc. Craniomaxillofacial Surgery (founding mem.), Internat. Craniofacial Club. Club: Automobile de France. Avocations: primitive art; sailing. Home: 130 rue de la Pompe, 75116 Paris France

MARCHAIS, GEORGES, French political leader; b. La Hoquette, June 7, 1920; s. Rene and Germaine (Boscher) M.; m. Paulette Noetinger, 1941 (div.); 3 children; m. Liliane Garcia; 1 child. Former metal worker; sec. Metal-workers Union, Issy-le-Moulineaux, 1946, Union des syndicats de travailleurs de la metallurgie de la Seine, 1953-56; mem. French Communist Party, 1947—, mem. Central Com., 1956, Polit. Bur., 1959, sec. Central Com., 1961, dep. sec.-gen., 1970, sec.-gen., 1972—; dep. for Val-de-Marne, Nat. Assembly, 1973, 78; mem. European Parliament, 1979—. Author: Qu'est-ce que le parti communiste français?, 1970; Le défi démocratique, 1973; La politique du parti communiste français, 1974; Parlons franchement, 1977; Reponses, 1977; L'espoir au present, 1980; co-author: Les communistes et les paysans, 1972. Address: Parti Communiste Français, 2 place du Colonel Fabien, 75019 Paris France *

MARCHAIS, PIERRE JULIEN, psychiatrist; b. Paris, Apr. 21, 1924; s. Julien and Emilienne M.; m. Bernadette Somma, Sept. 23, 1954; children: Dominique, Christine, Bénédicte, Thomas. MD, Faculté de Médecine, Paris, 1952. Resident Psychiat. Hosp., Seine, France, 1949-51; resident Cen. Nat. d'Orientation des Prisons, Fresnes, France, 1950-52, asst., 1952-65; resident Foch Hosp., Suresnes, France, 1950-52, asst., 1952-60, dept. head, 1960-70; head dr. Psychiat. Service, 1970—; v.p. Com. d'Etude des Termes Médicaux Français, Paris, 1980. Author: Psychopathologie en Pratique Medicale, 1964, Les Processus Névrotiques, 1968, Psychiatrie et Méthodologie, 1970, Glossaire de Psychiatrie, 1970, Introduction á la Psychiatrie Théorique, 1971, Psychiatrie de Synthése, 1973, Métapsychiatrie, 1974, Magie et Mythe en Psychiatrie, 1977, Les Processus Psychopathologiques de l'Adulte, 1981, Les Mouvances Psychopathologiques, 1983, Permanence et Relativité du Trouble Mental, 1986, Le Phénoméne moral, 1988; contbr. 200 articles to sci. jours. Recipient Prix Ritti Nat. Acad. Medicine, 1972, Prix Bordin French Acad., 1973. Mem. Soc. Argentine Psycho-Pharmacology (hon.), Internat. Coll. Psychosomatic Medicine (bd. dirs.), Can. Psychiat. Assn., Soc. Psychopharmacology, Soc. Médico-Psychologique (pres. 1982), Soc. Moreau de Tours (pres. 1966), Soc. Médico-Psychologique (sec. gen., 1983—). Roman Catholic. Home: Lacepede 33, 75005 Paris France Office: Hosp Foch, 40 rue Worth, 92151 Suresnes France

MARCHAL, GUY PAUL, historian; b. Basel, Switzerland, Sept. 29, 1938; s. Paul and Erica (Weiss) M., m. Monika Stoecklin, Jan. 15, 1966; children: Eric, Mi Hwa. Doctorate, Basel U., 1970. Sci. asst. Helvetia Sacra, Basel, 1967-72; teaching asst. Historisches Seminar, Basel, 1972-78, prof., 1978—; hist. cons. Chancery of Canton Lucerne (Switzerland), 1982-86; mem. Commn. New History of Canton Baselland, 1987—. Author and editor: Weltliche Kollegiatiatstifte, Helvetia Sacra II/2, 1977; author: Die frommen Schweden in Schwyz, 1976, Sempach 1386, Von den Anfängen d.Kantons Luzern, 1986; co-author: Geschichte der Schweiz und der Schweizer, 1982, 2d edit. 1986, Handbuch der Europäischen Geschichte 2, 1987. Mem. Allgemeine Geschichtsforschende Gesellschaft der Schweiz, Historisch-Antiquarische Gesellschaft d.Kantons Basel, Historische Gesellschaft d.Kantons Luzern. Roman Catholic. Home: Gotthardstrasse 104, CH-4054 Basel Switzerland Office: Historisches Seminar, Hirschgässlein 21, CH-4051 Basel Switzerland

MARCHAND, JEAN-JACQUES, educator; b. Yverdon-les-Bains, Vaud, Switzerland, Aug. 25, 1944; s. Maurice and Rita (Redi) M. MA, U. Lausanne, Switzerland, 1968, PhD, 1976. Asst. prof. U. Lausanne, 1969-73, assoc. prof., 1973-83, prof., 1983—; assoc. prof. U. Neuchâtel, Switzerland, 1980-85. Editor, author: N. Machiavelli. I primi scritti politici (1491-1512), 1975, E. Rod et les écrivains it., 1980; contbr. articles in field. Mem. Associazione Internazionale per gli Studi di Lingua e Letteratura Italiana, Collegium romanicum (sec. 1977-80), Soc. Acad. Vaudoise (Univ. award 1975), Deputazione Storia Patria per Toscana (fgn. mem.), Assn. Suisse Lit. Gén. et Comparée (com. 1983-87), Cent. Studi: Europa delle Corti. Home: Rue Léon Michaud 1, CH-1400 Yverdon-les-Bains Vaud Switzerland Office: U Lausanne Faculté Lettres, BFSH2, CH-1015 Lausanne Switzerland

MARCHAND, MARC EDOUARD LOUIS JOSEPH, architect; b. Winksele, Belgium, Oct. 6, 1933; s. Jacques Marchand and Isabelle Walckiers; m. Gobbe Marie-Louise, Sept. 24, 1960; children: Isabelle, Bruno, Charlotte, Sophie. Degree in architecture, Inst. Superieur Architecture St. Luc, Brussels, 1959; degree in town planning, Inst. Superieur & Internat. D'Urbanisme Appliqué, Brussels, 1960. Practice architecture specializing in housing, factories, warehouses, decoration, offices Brussels, 1964—; mem. Conseil de L'Ordre des Architectes, 1982-83; sec. Conseil d'Appel de L'Ordre des Architectes a Liege, 1982-83. Contbr. articles to nat. and internat. profl. jours. Recipient Silver Medal awards Habitation Space Internat. S.N.C. Milano, Italy, 1980, 81. Mem. Union Profl. Architectes St. Luc (councillor 1972—), Fedn. des Soc. d'Architectes en Belgique (councillor 1977-82), Centre Scientifique et Technique de la Construction (concillor 1980—, sec. architects services 1986-87). Office: Marc Marchand & Associes, Av Chantemerle 11, B-1180 Brussels Belgium

MARCHER, FLEMMING, business executive; b. Copenhagen, July 8, 1937; s. Johannes and Gunver (Schroll) M.; m. Nina Marianne, Nov. 19, 1963; children: Klaus, Nanett, Susanne. Asst. rep. The East Asiatic Co., Ltd., Copenhagen, 1954-60; rep. The East Asiatic Co., Ltd., Osaka, Japan, 1960-65; with import and indsl. depts. The East Asiatic Co., Ltd., Copenhagen, 1965-67; rep. The East Asiatic Co., Ltd., Osaka, Japan, 1960-65; gen. mgr. The East Asiatic Co., Ltd., Copenhagen, 1980—; mktg. mgr. Neckelmann Ltd., Hammarsdale, Republic of South Africa, 1967-71; gen. mgr. Flamingo Knitting Mills, Hammarsdale, 1971-73, Dumex Pharms., Ltd., Ikeja, Nigeria, 1973-75; dep. mng. dir. R.T. Briscoe, Ltd., Lagos, Nigeria, 1975-77; mng. dir. R.T. Briscoe, Ltd., Lagos, 1977-79; gen mgr. The East Asiatic Co., Ltd., Copenhagen, 1980—; chmn. CompuDan, EAC Data Innovation Corp.; dir. Erik Levison, R.T. Briscoe, Ltd. Mem. Nigerian Inst. of Mgmt. Home: 9 Bispekrogen, 2830 Virum Denmark Office: East Asiatic Co Ltd, 2 Holbergsgade, 1059 Copenhagen Denmark

MARCHESE, NICOLA GERARDO, lawyer, educator; b. San Nicola da Crissa, Italy, Sept. 2, 1922; s. Gregorio and Giovannarosa (Galati) M.; m. Sara Signarello, Sept. 12, 1955; children: Giovanna, Caterina. JD, Università di Messina, Italy, 1953. Lawyer Azienda Comunale Elettricità ed Acqua del Comune, Rome, 1962—; cons. civil ct., Rome, 1977—; prof. water pollution law U. Perugia. Author: I Servizi Pubbli Nello Spazio Regionale, 1978, Il Volto Sconosciuto dei Bronzi de Riasce, 1981, Calabria Dimenticata, 1982, La Civiltá della Magna Grecia, 1985. Recipient Gold medal Internat. Assn. Brutium. Mem. Nat. Acad. for History Medicine. Mem. Democratic Christian Party. Roman Catholic. Home: Via dei Giuochi Istmici 43, 00194 Rome Italy

MARCHMAN, DENNIS LEROY, accountant; b. White Plains, Ga., Feb. 20, 1915; s. Clarence Moore and Lillie Mae (Darnell) M. Student Oglethrope U., 1934, Southern Brothers Law Sch., 1936-37. With Miami (Fla.) Herald, 1936-38; bookkeeper Vultee Aircraft Co., Miami, 1941-42; acct. C.F. Wheeler Builder, Miami, 1946-49; controller Hardy Houses, Laurel, Md., 1949-50; v.p. Tec-Bilt Homes, Miami, 1950-55, Carl G. Fisher Corp., Nassau, Bahamas, 1955-57; controller Brook Gas Co., Miami, Fla., 1957-67; controller Auto-Marine Engrs., Inc., Miami, 1967—; v.p., dir. Aviation Marine and Auto Supply, Inc., 1975—. Served with USNR, 1942-45. Democrat. Baptist. Home: 5330 SW 62d Ave Miami FL 33155

MARCHUK, GURIY IVANOVICH, academic association executive; b. Orenburg, Ukraine, USSR, June 8, 1925; s. Ivan Petrovich and Elizaveta Marchuk; m. Olga Nikolaevna Belyaeva, Feb. 23, 150; children: Alexander, Andrey, Nikolay. MS, Leningrad (USSR) State U., 1949; PhD, Inst. Geophysics, USSR Acad. Sci., Moscow, 1952; DSc, Phys. Inst. Power Engring., Obninsk, USSR, 1957; DSc honoris causa, Karlov U., Czechoslovakia, 1978, Toulouse (France) U., Dresden (German Dem. Republic) Tech. U., 1978. Jr. research worker Inst. Geophysics USSR Acad. Sci., Moscow, 1952-53; dir. Computing Ctr. Siberian br. USSR Acad. Sci., Novosibirsk, 1964-79; mem. div. oceanology atmosphere physics and geography USSR Acad. Sci., 1968—; v.p. Siberian br. USSR Acad. Sci., Novosibirsk, 1969-75, pres. Siberian br., 1975-80; pres. USSR Acad. Sci., Moscow, 1986—, dir. dept. computational math.; head lab. Phys. Inst. Power Engring., Obninsk, 1954-62; dep. dir. Inst. Math., Novosibirsk, 1962-63. Mem. cen. com. Communist Party, Moscow; dep. prime minister, pres. USSR State Com. on Sci. and Tech., 1980-86. Recipient Lenin prize Lenin Prize Com., 1961, USSR Prize of the State Lenin Prize Com., 1979. Mem. Acad. Finland (fgn. mem.), Indian Nat. Sci. Acad., Bulgarian Acad. Sci. (fgn. mem.), Czechoslovakian Acad. Sci. (gold medal 1981). Office: USSR Acad Scis, Leninsky Prospekt, 14, Moscow V-71 USSR

MARCINOWICZ, LESZEK ANDRZEJ, personnel manager; b. Lancaster, Eng., May 7, 1950; s. Stefan and Halina Anna (Plachta) M.; m. Christine Lesley Newell, Jan. 21, 1978; children: Adam Leszek, Hannah Louise. MA, Cambridge (Eng.) U., 1972. Grad. trainee Turner and Newall PLC, Manchester, Eng., 1972-73; officer employee relations Ferodo Ltd. (subs. Turner and Newall), Chapel-En-Le-Frith, Eng., 1973-75, mgr. employee relations, 1975-78, chief mgr. personnel, 1979-81; mktg. exec. Botb/British Food Export Council, London, 1981-83; chief mgr. personnel Canning Town Glass, Yorkshire, Eng., 1983-85; mgr. personnel Parker Hannifin Corp., Watford, Eng., 1985—. Roman Catholic. Home: 28 Cassiobury Dr, Watford WD1 3AB, England Office: Parker Hannifin Corp., 69/71 Clarendon Rd, Watford WD1 1DQ, England

MARCO, GUY ANTHONY, librarian; b. N.Y.C., Oct. 4, 1927; s. Gaetano Mongelluzzo and Evelyn Capobianco; m. Karen Csontos, July 23, 1949; 1 son, Howard William. Student, DePaul U., 1947-50; B.Mus., Am. Conservatory Music, Chgo., 1951; M.A. in Music, U. Chgo., 1952, M.L.S., 1955, Ph.D. in Musicology, 1956. Librarian, instr. musicology Chgo. Mus. Coll., 1953-54; asst. classics library U. Chgo., 1954; asst. librarian, instr. music Wright Jr. Coll., Chgo., 1954-56; librarian, instr. music Amundsen Jr. Coll., Chgo., 1957-60; asso. prof. library sci., chmn. dept. Kent State U., 1960-66; prof., dean Kent State U. (Sch. Library Sci.), 1966-77; chief gen. reference and bibliography div. Library of Congress, Washington, 1977-78; dir. for N.Am., Library Devel. Cons.'s, London, 1979-81; prof., dir. div. library sci. San Jose State U., 1981-83; exec. dir. Global Research Services, Washington, 1984-85; chief library activities U.S. Army, Ft. Dix, N.J., 1985—; vis. lectr. library sci. U. Wis., summer 1955; reference librarian Chgo. Tchrs. Coll., summer 1957; vis. prof. library sci. N.Y. State Coll. Tchrs., Albany, summer 1956, 58; guest lectr. library sci. U. Denver, summer 1959; vis. prof. U. Okla., summer 1960, Coll. Librarianship, Wales, summer 1974, 76, 77, U. Md., summer 1978. Author: The Earliest Music Printers of Continental Europe, 1962, An Appraisal of Favorability in Current Book Reviewing, 1959, (with Claude Palisca) The Art of Counterpoint, 1968, Information on Music, Vol. I, 1975, Vol. II, 1977, Vol. III, 1984, Opera: A Research and Information Guide, 1984; also articles, book reviews. Served with AUS, 1946-47. Mem. ALA, Music Library Assn., Am. Musicol. Soc., Internat. Fedn. Library Assns. Home: 117 N 15th St Philadelphia PA 19102 Office: Library Bldg 6501 Fort Dix NJ 08640

MARCONI, DIEGO, philosopher, educator; b. Turin, Italy, June 10, 1947; s. Ruggero and Vera (Gay) M.; m. Elisabetta Benenati, Oct. 19, 1970 (Separated 1987); 1 child, Sara. Laurea in Philosophy, U. Turin, 1969; PhD in Philosophy, U. Pitts., 1979. Researcher Agnelli Found., Turin, 1970-72; fellow dept. philosophy U. Turin, 1969-73, asst. prof. dept. philosophy, 1973-77, prof. incaricato dept. philosophy, 1977-82, assoc. prof. coll. letters, 1982—; cons. Olivetti SPA, Ivrea, Italy, 1982-84. Author: Il Mito del linguaggio Scientifico, 1971, Dizionari e Enciclopedie, 1982, L'eredità di Wittgenstein, 1987; editor: La Formalizzazione della d., 1979; editorial bd. L'Indice, Rivista di Linguistica, Jour. Non-Classical Logic; contbr. articles to profl. jours. Nat. v.p. GI, 1967-69; city chmn. MPL, Turin, 1971-72. Harkness fellow Commonwealth Fund, 1974; sr. fellow Ctr. for Philosophy Sci., 1983, NATO-CNR, 1987. Mem. Soc. Italiana di Logica e Filosofia Della Sci., Soc. Italiana di Linguistica, Lab. Artificial Intelligence. Home: Via Santa Giulia 47, 10124 Turin Italy Office: U Torino, Via S Ottavio 20, 10124 Turin Italy

MARCONNET, ROGER ANDRE CHARLES, physician; b. Bannes, Lorraine, France, Apr. 6, 1931; s. Eugene Alexandre and Charlotte Marie (Petitot) M.; m. Ginette Genevieve Petit, Mar. 12, 1960; children: Sophie, Aurélie, Arnaud. MD, Faculty of Medicine, Nancy, France, 1962; degree in sculpture, Sch. Fine Arts, Nancy, France, 1960. Extern Hosp. Nancy, 1953-58; gen. practice medicine Beaune, France, 1962—. Author: Beaune Historic Town, 1968; executed several sculptures located at Beaune, Calais, Talmont. Pres. The Friends of Hist. Town Beaune, 1964. Served to col. French Army. Roman Catholic. Office: 6 Place Monge, 21200 Beaune France

MARCOS-MARIN, FRANCISCO, linguist; b. Madrid, June 20, 1946; s. Francisco Marcos and Carmen Marin; m. Maria Soledad Salazar, July 16, 1969; children: Sol, Carmen, Francisco, Elvira. BA, U. Granada, Spain, 1963; MA, U. Madrid, 1968, PhD, 1969. Asst. prof. U. Autónoma de Madrid, 1968-69, U. Montreal, Que., Can., 1969-71, U. Autónoma de Madrid, 1971-75; assoc. prof. U. Saragossa, 1975-76; prof. U. Valladolid, 1976-81, U. Autónoma de Madrid, 1981—; spl. collaborator Real Academia Española, Madrid, 1971-74; chmn. dept. Romance Philology U. Valladolid, Spain, 1976-81; cons. UNESCO, Beijing, People's Republic of China, 1981; group dir. EUROTRA European Community, Madrid, 1987—. Author: Curso de Gramatica, 1980; editor: Libro de Alexandre, 1987; author 14 books, 1971-87; contbr. articles to profl. jours. Decorated Knight Order Alfonso X (Spain); recipient Spl. MA award Govt. of Spain, 1968. Mem. Am. Assn. Tchrs. Spanish and Portuguese, Asociación Internacional de Hispanistas, Asociación Marroqui de Literatura Comparada, Societas Linguistica Europaea, Asociación de Historia de la Lengua Española. Roman Catholic. Club: Real Madrid. Office: Universidad Autónoma, Ap 46348, 28080 Madrid Spain

MARCOULLIS, GEORGE PANAYIOTIS, hematologist-oncologist, medical educator, biochemical science researcher; b. Limassol, Cyprus, Apr. 4, 1949; s. Panayiotis Stylianou and Aggeliki (Joannou) M.; m. Erato Kozakou, Aug. 20, 1970; 1 son, Panos. M.D., Athens U., 1974; Ph.D., Helsinki U., 1978. Med. licensure, Finland, Greece, Del., N.Y.; diplomate Am. Bd. Internal Medicine. Jr. researcher Athens U., 1971-73; biomed. researcher Minerva Inst., Helsinki, 1973-77; mem. staff Maria Hosp., Helsinki, 1976-77; asst. prof. medicine N.Y. Med. Coll., 1977-79; vis. asst. prof. U. Nancy (France) Faculty of Scis., 1979-80; vis. assoc. prof. Nancy Med. Sch., 1981-82; assoc. prof. medicine SUNY-Downstate Med. Ctr., Bklyn., 1980-83; med. resident Washington VA Hosp., 1983; chief med. resident Mt. Vernon Hosp., N.Y., 1983-84; fellow in hematology-oncology N.Y. Med. Coll., 1984-86, assoc. prof., 1984—; fellow in hematology-oncology Albert Einstein Coll. Medicine, Bronx, N.Y., 1986-87; dir. sect. hematology-oncology Med. Ctr., Lewes, Del., 1987—. Author: (with others) Contemporary Issues in Clinical Nutrition, 1983, Progress in Gastroenterology, Vol. IV, 1983; contbr. articles to profl. jours. Recipient medal award Nancy U., 1980; grantee Athens U., 1971-74, WHO, 1975-77, INSERM, 1977-79, VA, 1982; co-grantee NIH, 1979-82. Mem. ACP, N.Y. Acad. Scis., Am. Fedn. Clin. Research, Soc. for Exptl. Biology and Medicine. Research on use of protein chemistry techniques to delineate the structure and role of membrane receptors and transport proteins in cellular recognition, in hormone, drug and nutrient metabolism, and in receptor-related diseases. Home: 453 E 14th St Apt 11C New York NY 10009 Office: Med Ctr P O Box D224 Lewes DE 19958

MARCOVITZ, LEONARD EDWARD, retail executive; b. Bismarck, N.D., Sept. 6, 1934; s. Jacob and Frieda M. Asst. mgr. Greengard's Clothing, Mandan, N.D., 1955-58; mgr. K-G Men's Stores, Inc., Bismarck, 1958-61, Billings, Mont., 1961-69; v.p. store ops. K-G Men's Stores, Inc., 1969-73; pres. Leonard's Men's Stores, Yakima, Wash. and Billings, Mont., 1973-77; chief exec. officer K-G Retail div. Chromalloy Am. Corp., Englewood, Colo., 1977-81; pres. DeMarcos Men's Clothing, Casper, Wyo., 1982—, Idaho Falls, Idaho, 1984—, Billings, Mont., 1986—. Mem. Menswear Retailers Am. (past dir.). Club: Elks. Home: PO Box 23344 Billings MT 59104

MARCUS, DONALD HOWARD, advertising agency executive; b. Cleve., May 16, 1916; s. Joseph and Sarah (Schmitman) M.; m. Helen Olen Weiss, Feb. 12, 1959; children: Laurel Kathy Marcus Heifetz, Carol Susan, James Randall (dec.), Jonathan Anthony. Student, Fenn Coll., 1934-35. Mem. publicity dept. Warner Bros. Pictures, Cleve., 1935-37; mem. advt. dept. RKO Pictures, Cleve., 1937-40; mem. sales dept. Monogram Pictures, Cleve., 1940-42; pres. Marcus Advt. Inc., Cleve., 1946-85, chmn., 1986—; ptnr.

North Coast Cable, Cleve., 1985—. Guarantor N.E. Ohio Opera Assn., 1965—; mem. Ohio Democratic exec. com., 1969-70, del. nat. conv., 1968; vice-chmn. communication div. Jewish Welfare Fund Appeal Cleve., 1969-70, chmn., 1971-72; trustee Jewish Community Fedn., 1973-74, Cleve. Israel Bond Com., 1964-73; trustee Cleve. Jewish News, 1974—, v.p., 1983-85; trustee no. Ohio regional office Anti Defamation League of B'nai B'rith, 1986—; bd. dirs. Cuyahoga County unit Am. Cancer Soc., 1979—, Ohio Soc. to Prevent Blindness, 1981, Cleve. State U. Devel. Found., 1987—. Served to 1st lt. USAAF, 1942-46. Mem. Nat. Acad. TV Arts and Scis., Ohio Commodores, Brandeis U. Club, Cleve. Advt. Club, Cleve. Growth Assn., Mensa. Jewish (trustee temple). Clubs: Beechmont Country (pres. 1973-74), Union, Commerce (Cleve.). Home: 22449 Shelburne Rd Shaker Heights OH 44122 Office: Marcus Advt Inc 25700 Science Park Dr Beachwood OH 44122

MARCUS, JOSEPH, child psychiatrist; b. Cleve., Feb. 27, 1928; s. William and Sarah (Marcus) Schwartz; m. Furmanovitz, Oct. 3, 1951; children: Oren, Alon. B.Sc., Western Res. U., 1963; M.D., Hebrew U., 1958. Intern Tel Hashomer Govt. Hosp., Israel, 1956-57; resident in psychiatry and child psychiatry Ministry of Health, Govt. of Israel, 1958-61; acting head dept. child psychiatry Ness Ziona Rehab. Ctr., 1961-62; sr. psychiatrist Lasker dept. child psychiatry Hadassah U. Hosp., 1962-64; research asso. Israel Inst. Applied Social Research, 1966-69; practice medicine specializing in psychiatry Jerusalem, 1966-72; assoc. dir. devel. neuropsychiatry Jerusalem Infant and Child Devel. Ctr., 1969-70; dept. head Eytanim Hosp., 1970-72; cons. child psychiatrist for Jerusalem Ministry of Health, 1970-72; dir. dept. child psychiatry and devel. Jerusalem Mental Health Ctr., 1972-75; prof. child psychiatry, dir. unit for research in child psychiatry and devel. U. Chgo., 1975-85, prof. emeritus, co-dir. unit for research in child psychiatry and devel., 1986—; vis. research psychiatrist UCLA Dept. Psychiatry, 1987—. Chief editor: Early Child Devel. and Care, 1972-76; mem. editorial bd.: Israel Annals of Psychiatry and Related Disciplines, 1965-70, Internat. Yearbook of Child Psychiatry and Allied Professions, 1968-74; contbr. articles to med. jours. Mem. Am. Acad. Child Psychiatry (com. on research, com. on psychiat. aspects of infancy), Soc. Research in Child Devel., Internat. Assn. Child Psychiatry and Allied Professions (asst. gen. sec. 1966-74), European Union Paedopsychiatry (hon.), World, Israel psychiat. assns., Internat. Coll. Psychosomatic Medicine, Israel Center Psychobiology. Home: 910 Chelham Way Santa Barbara CA 93108 Office: 5841 S Maryland Box 411 Chicago IL 60637

MARCUS, STANLEY, retail merchant, lecturer, marketing consultant, miniature book publisher; b. Dallas, Apr. 20, 1905; s. Herbert and Minnie (Lichtenstein) M.; m. Mary Cantrell, Nov. 7, 1932 (dec.); children: Jerrie (Mrs. Frederick M. Smith, II), Richard and Wendy (Mrs. Henry Raymont) (twins); m. Linda Cumber, Mar. 30, 1979. Student, Amherst Coll., 1921; BA, Harvard U., 1925, postgrad. in bus., 1926; HHD (hon.), So. Meth. U., Dallas, 1965; LittD (hon.), North Tex. State U., 1983; LLD, Pratt Inst., 1986. With Neiman-Marcus, Dallas,, 1926-75; sec. treas., dir. Neiman-Marcus, 1928, mdse. mgr. sportswear shop, 1928, mdse. mgr. all apparel divs., 1929, exec. v.p., 1935-50, pres., 1950-72, chmn. bd., 1972-75, chmn. exec. com., 1975-77, chmn. emeritus, 1977—; with Stanley Marcus Consultancy Services; owner, operator Somesuch Press, Inc.; past corp. exec. v.p., hon. dir. Carter Hawley Hale Stores, Inc., Los Angeles; dir. Jack Lenor Larsen Inc. Author: Minding the Store, 1974, Quest for the Best, 1979, His and Hers, 1982; contbr. numerous articles to mags. Mem. exec. com. Ctr. for the Book, Library of Congress; former co-chmn. Dallas br. Interracial Council for Bus. Opportunity; founding mem. Bus. Com. for Arts; past mem. exec. com. Nat. Council Arts and Edn.; past regional v.p. Nat. Jewish Hosp., Denver; bd. govs. Common Cause, 1976-79; past bd. dirs. Dallas Council World Affairs, Grad. Research Ctr. of S.W., Tex. Law Enforcement Found., Am. Council to Improve Our Neighborhoods, Ctr. Study Dem. Instns.; former bd. govs. USO; bd. dirs., past pres. Dallas Symphony Soc.; past pres., past bd. dirs. Dallas Citizens' Council; bd. dirs. emeritus North Tex. Commn.; trustee Tex. Research Found., Com. Econ. Devel., Pub. TV Found. North Tex., Am. Craft Council, Eisenhower Exchange Fellowships, Urban Inst.; mem. bd. publs., trustee So. Meth. U., also past chmn. library advancement program; past mem. Tex. Fine Arts Commn.; past pres. Dallas Art Assn.; former overseer Harvard U., mem. vis. com. univ. of resources, 1978-79; chmn. Tex. Com. Selection Rhodes Scholarship, 1975; past trustee, chmn. exec. com. Hockaday Sch. Girls, Dallas; mem. retail adv. group U. Tex., Arlington; mem. wage and hour millinery com. War Prodn. Bd., 1940; mem. 1st adv. council Hahn Ctr. for Entrepreneurship, Ariz. State U.; mem. community adv. bd. Transplant Resources and Services Ctr., U. Tex. Health Sci. Ctr. at Dallas; hon. chmn. Regents' Circle, Mus. N.Mex.; apptd. mem. Tex. World Trade Council, 1986; chmn. Dallas Transp. Think Tank, 1987—; bd. dirs. Sch. Am. Research, Santa Fe. Decorated chevalier Legion of Honor, officier Legion of Honor, comdr. Nat. Order Merit France, Star of Solidarity, Commendatore del Merito della Republica Italiana, Italy, Hon. Order of Brit. Empire, chevalier Order of Leopold II Belgium, Royal Order of Dannebrog Danish Govt., Great Cross of Austria; recipient Tobe award for disting. service to Am. retailing, 1945, N.Y. Fashion Designers award, 1958, Ambassador award for achievement, London, 1962, 1st Milw. medallion, 1968, Gold medal Nat. Retail Mchts. Assn., 1961, B.A.M.B.I. Flying Colors award, 1978; named Headliner of Yr., Dallas Press Club, 1958, to Tex. Bus. Hall of Fame, 1984; Library of Fashion established in his honor So. Meth. U., 1976. Fellow AIA (hon.; George Harrell Foster award Dallas chpt. 1986); mem. Nat. Urban League (trustee), Council on Fgn. Relations (past bd. dirs.), Eta Mu Pi (hon.). Clubs: Harvard (N.Y.C. and Dallas); City, Dallas. Home: 1 Nonesuch Rd Dallas TX 75214 Office: 1st Republic Bank Ctr 4800 Tower II Dallas TX 75201

MARCUS, STEPHEN CECIL, printing co. exec.; b. Phila., Mar. 8, 1932; s. Jerome Milton and Helen Gertrude (Jacobs) M.; B.S., Drexel U., 1957; m. Seena Hymowitz, Nov. 2, 1958; children—Nancy Joy, Julie Bea; m. Lois Simon, Oct. 7, 1984. Jr. partner Liess-Marcus Co., Inc., Phila., 1957-59; v.p. sales Mid-City Press, Inc., Phila., 1959-70; pres., chief exec. officer, founder Mars Graphic Services, Inc., Westville, N.J., 1970-86, chmn. 1986—; mem. Phila. Mgmt. Negotiating Com., Jr. Execs./Graphic Arts, Phila. br. Trustee, Friends' Central Sch., 1977-80; trustee/co-founder Beth Tovin Synagogue, Phila., 1972—; active Am. Cancer Soc., Phila. Big Bros. Served with U.S. Army, 1953-55. Recipient Annual award Exchange Club N.J., 1981; awards Big Bros. Am., Am. Cancer Soc., Am. Arbitration Assn. Mem. Am. Arbitration Assn., Nat. Direct Mail Mktg. Assn., Graphic Arts Tech. Found., South Jersey Graphic Arts Assn., Graphic Arts Assn. of Del. Valley (bd. dirs. 1988), Tau Kappa Epsilon. Republican. Jewish. Clubs: Radnor Valley Country (Villanova, Pa.); Poor Richard (Phila.). Home: 644 Robinson Ln Haverford PA 19041 Office: 1012 Edgewater Ave Westville NJ 08093

MARCUSS, ROSEMARY DALY, economist; b. Stamford, Conn., Aug. 27, 1945; d. Eugene Lawrence and Margaret Mary (Murphy) Daly; B.A. in Econs. cum laude, Newton (Mass.) Coll., 1967; M.S., U. Md., 1973, Ph.D., 1979; m. Stanley J. Marcuss, July 6, 1968; children—Elena Daly, Aidan Stanley. Jr. staff economist President's Council of Econ. Advisers, 1968-70; economist, asst. to pres. Am. Fedn. State, County and Mcpl. Employees, Washington, 1973; economist, mgmt. cons. Data Resources, Inc., Washington, 1974-78; dep. asst. dir. tax analysis Congressional Budget Office, Washington, 1980-83, asst. dir. tax analysis, 1983—. NSF fellow, 1970-73. Mem. Am. Econ. Assn., Nat. Tax Assn., Tax Inst. Am., So. Econ. Assn., Soc. Govt. Economists, Nat. Economists Club, Washington Women Economists. Home: 4616 29th Pl NW Washington DC 20008 Office: Congressional Budget Office House Annex 2 Washington DC 20515

MARCUSSEN, HENRIK, physician; b. Copenhagen, Denmark, Jan. 17, 1938; s. Freddy and Gerda (Skaalum) M.; m. Marianne E. Witt-hansen, Apr. 11, 1964; children: Anders, Torben Eskild. MD, Copenhagen U., 1964, Internist, 1974, Cert. in gastroenterology, 1976. Resident Gentofte County Hosp., Copenhagen, 1964-69; resident Rigshospitalet, Copenhagen, 1970-72, 1st registrar G-I, 1970-72; 1st registrar G-I dept. B Bispebjerg Hosp., Copenhagen, 1975-79; chief physician Ringsted Hosp., 1979—; cons. Amnesty Internat., Denmark, 1980—, Rehab. Ctr. for Torture Victims, Denmark, 1983—. Contbr. articles to profl. jours. Home: Falkoner Allé 36, 2000 Fredericksberg Denmark Office: Ringsted Hosp, Bøllingsvej, 4100 Ringsted Denmark

MARCZ, ROLAND PAUL, interior designer; b. Zurich, Switzerland, June 4, 1954; arrived in Hong Kong, 1977.; s. Jacob and Irma (Zimmerman) M.; m. Annie C.P. Ching, Nov. 6, 1982. Bus. Adminstrn., KV Sch., St. Gallen, Switzerland, 1973. Ins. inspector Continental Ins. Co., Zurich, Switzerland, 1974-77; bd. dirs. Ianmclean Design, Hong Kong, 1977-80; owner, bd. dirs. Monsoon Antiques, Hong Kong, 1980-86, Oriental Gallery, Hong Kong, 1986—, C.P. Ching Fine Oriental Art, Hong Kong, 1985—, Roland Marcz Design Assocs., Hong Kong, 1980—. Home: 58 Conduit Rd, Apt 102, Hong Kong Hong Kong Office: Roland Marcz Design Assocs, 30 Hollywood Rd, Hong Kong Hong Kong

MARDER, WILLIAM ZEV, mechanical engineer; b. Phila., Nov. 4, 1947; s. Isadore Myron and Nancy Annette (Segall) M.; B.S. in Mech. Engring., U. Pa., 1970, B.A., 1970; m. Mona Marlene Kaufman, June 28, 1970. Div. mgr. Kulicke and Soffa Industries, Horsham, Pa., 1972-74; pres. Zevco Enterprises, Inc., Penllyn, Pa., 1974—; sr. devel. engr. Air Shields, Inc., Hatboro, Pa., 1977-78; mem. tech. staff RCA, Princeton, N.J., 1978-81; v.p. engring. Kulicke Design, Inc., Ivyland, Pa., 1981-83; tech. mgr., cons. PA Tech., Hightstown, N.J., 1984—. Patentee self-priming centrifugal pump, knife sharpener, apparatus for handling deformable components supported in a matrix, numerically controlled method of machining cams and other parts. Home and office: 147 S Main St Pennington NJ 08534

MARDIGIAN, EDWARD STEPHAN, machine tool company executive; b. Stambul, Turkey, Oct. 25, 1909; s. Stephan and Agavine (Hagopian) M.; came to U.S., 1914, naturalized, 1929; student Wayne U., 1932-34; m. Helen Alexander, June 5, 1938; children—Marilyn, Edward, Robert. Asst. tool engr. Briggs Mfg. Co., Detroit, 1935-37, chief tool engr., Eng., 1937-45, chief project engr., 1945; owner, operator Mardigian Corp., Warren, Mich., 1948-69, Marco Corp., Warren, 1954, bought Buckeye Aluminum Co., Wooster, Ohio, 1956, Mardigian Car Corp., Warren, 1966—; pres. Hercules Machine Tool & Die Co., Warren, 1973—; chmn. bd. Central States Mfg. Co., Warren, 1973—. Pres. Armenian Gen. Benevolent Union Am., 1972—; chmn. Chief Exec. Orgn., Warren, 1974, Chief Exec. Orgn. Internat. Decorated medal St. Gregory by Vasken 1st Supreme Patriarch of All Armenians, 1966; named Man of Year Diocese Armenian Ch. N.Am., 1977. Home: 1525 Tottenham Rd Birmingham MI 48009 Office: Hercules Machine Tool & Die Co 13920 Address: E Ten Mile Rd Warren MI 48089

MAREE, ANDREW MORGAN, III, business management and investment advisor; b. Detroit, Mar. 9, 1927; s. Andrew Morgan, Jr., and Elizabeth Lathrop (Cady) M.; B.A., Claremont Men's Coll., 1950; M.B.A., U. Chgo., 1951; J.D., Whittier Coll., 1982; m. Wendy Patricia Haymes, Dec. 20, 1980; children: Samantha, Andrew Morgan, IV. Trust analyst Hanover Bank & Trust Co., N.Y.C., 1951-52; pres. A. Morgan Maree, Jr., & Assocs. Inc., Los Angeles, 1952-86, chmn. bd., 1987—; dir. Carson Estate Co. Served with USNR, 1944-46. Mem. Acad. Motion Picture Arts and Scis., The Players, Am. Film Inst. Office: PO Box 960 Lake Arrowhead CA 92352

MARELLA, PHILIP DANIEL, broadcasting company executive; b. Italy, Sept. 9, 1929; came to U.S., 1930; s. T. Joseph and Julia (Santolina) M.; m. Lucinda Minor, Dec. 30, 1955; children: Philip Daniel, Laura Ann, William Scott. B.S., Calif. State Coll., 1955; M.S., Syracuse U., 1956. Account exec. WGR-TV, Buffalo, 1956-57; account exec., sales mgr. WIIC-TV, Pitts., 1957-66; gen. mgr. WCHS-TV, Charleston, W.Va., 1966-68; v.p. radio and television Rollins, Inc., Atlanta, 1968-70; pres. WAVY-TV, Inc., Tidewater, Va., 1970—; v.p. ops. Lin Broadcasting, Inc., N.Y.C.; also dir.; pres., owner WMGC-TV, Binghamton, N.Y., 1978—; chief exec. officer, pres. Pinnacle Broadcasting Co., 1987—; chief exec. officer Pinnacle Broadcasting Co., 1987. Bd. dirs. Salvation Army, 1966-68; bd. dirs., v.p. United Fund; bd. dirs. Portsmouth chpt. ARC, Tidewater Regional Health and Planning Commn.; bd. dirs., v.p. Binghamton Symphony. Served with USMC, 1948-49, 50-52. Mem. Nat. Assn. Broadcasters (v.p.), Va. Assn. Broadcasters, Variety Club Pitts., Radio and TV Club, Portsmouth C. of C. (pres. elect), Norfolk C. of C., Newport News C. of C. Clubs: Cavalier Golf and Yacht (Virginia Beach, Va.); N.Y. Athletic. Home: 2073 Cheshire Rd Binghamton NY 13903 Office: Executive Plaza Suite 719 150 W 51st St New York NY 10019

MARENBON, JOHN ALEXANDER, university educator; b. London, Aug. 26, 1955; s. Arthur and Zena (Jacobs) M.; m. Sheila Margaret Mary Lawlor, July 1, 1981. BA, U. Cambridge, Eng., 1975, MA, PhD, 1979. Teaching fellow Trinity College, Cambridge, 1979—. Author: From the Circle of Alcuin, 1981, Early Medieval Philosophy, 1983, Later Medieval Philosophy, 1987, (pamphlet) English our English, 1987; contbr. articles to profl. jours. Research fellow Trinity Coll., 1978. Mem. Conservative Party. Roman Catholic. Office: U Cambridge, Trinity College, Cambridge CB2 1TQ, England

MARETTE, JACQUES CLAUDE, mortuary equipment manufacturing executive; b. Stouen, France, Sept. 10, 1928; s. Raymond Louis and Marie (Abit) M.; m. Josette Fick, Feb. 12, 1950; children—Michelle, Francis, Marie Claude. Student Lycee Concorcet. Mgr. Hygeco, Stouen, France, 1955-58, mng. dir., 1958—; mng. dir., chmn. Colson Heubes, France, 1979—; chmn. Lear of London, U.K., 1978—. Author: La Thanatoraxie, 1963. Mem. Institut Francais de Thanatopraxie (pres. 1963), Internat. Fedn. Thanatologists (gen. sec. 1970) 1st v.p. 1984). Roman Catholic. Lodge: Rotary. Avocation: golf. Home: 14th Ave No 62, Lamorlaye, 60260 Picardie France

MARGARET ROSE, PRINCESS, princess, countess of Snowdon; b. Glamis Castle, Scotland, Aug. 21, 1930; d. King George VI of Eng. and Queen Elizabeth; D.Mus., U. London, 1957; LL.D., U. Keele, 1962, U. Cambridge; m. Anthony Charles Robert Armstrong-Jones, 1st Earl Snowdon, May 6, 1960 (div. 1978); children: David Albert Charles (Viscount Linley), Lady Sarah Frances Elizabeth. Pres., Dr. Barnardo's Dockland Settlements, Friends of the Elderly, Invalid Children's Aid Assn. (chmn. of the council), also Royal Ballet, National Society for the Prevention Cruelty to Children, Sadler's Wells Found., Scottish Children's League, Sunshine Homes, Victoria League, Horder Centres for Arthritics, English Folk Dance and Song Soc.; joint pres. of Lowland Brigade Club; chancellor of the U. of Keele; mast of bench Lincoln's Inn; patron of Brit. Sailors Soc. Guild, English Harbour Repair Fund (patron-in-chief), Queen Alexandra's Royal Army Nursing Corps Assn., Bristol Royal Workshops for the Blind, Friends of St. John's, also the patron of the Friends of Southwark Cathedral, Light Inf. Club, Guild St. Margaret's Chapel (Edinburgh Castle); migraine trust Nat. Pony Soc., Princess Margaret Rose Hosp. (Edinburgh), Services Cinema Corp., Barrister's Benevolent Assn. Mary Hare Grammer Sch. for the Deaf, Suffolk Regimental Assn., West Indies Olympic Assn., also Scottish Assn. Youth Clubs, Scottish Community Drama Assn., Union Girls Schs. for Social Service, Zebra trust U. London pres. St. John Ambulance Brigade; dep. col.-in-chief Royal Anglian Regt.; col.-in-chief Queen Alexandra's Royal Army Nursing Corps, Highland Fusiliers Can., 15/19 Slash 19 King's Royal Hussars, Princess Louise Fusiliers, Royal Highland Fusiliers, Women's Royal Australian Army Corps.; pres. Girl Guides Assn.; freewoman Haberdashers' Co.; freeman City London. Decorated Grand Cross of Royal Victorian Order, Order Crown India, Dame Grand Cross Order of St. John of Jerusalem, Order of Crown, Lion and spears Toro Kingdom, Grand Cross Order of Lion (Netherlands); Order Brilliant Star of Zanzibar 1st class, grand cross Order of Crown of Belgium, Grand Cross 1st class Order of Merit (Republic of Germany); Order of Precious Crown 1st class (Japan). Hon. fellow Royal Soc. London (life); fellow Royal Coll. Surgeons Eng., Royal College Obstetricians and Gynecologists; hon. mem. Automobile Assn., Order of Inst. Brit. Architects. Royal Soc. Medicine, Zool. Road, Royal Automobile Club; life mem. Brit. Legion (women's sect.); hon. mem., patron Grand Antiquity Assn. of Glasgow. *

MARGARETTEN, MICHAEL ELLIOT, pediatric optometrist; b. Bklyn., May 27, 1937; s. Elias Joseph and Frances Pearl (Kuhn) M.; m. Ellen Pliner Lapin, June 6, 1961; children—Mark, Jeffrey. Student U. Rochester, 1959; B.S., Pa. Coll. Optometry, 1960, O.D., 1961. Diplomate in optometric medicine. Resident developmental vision Yale U., Gesell Inst. Child Devel., 1962; pvt. practice pediatric optometry, N.Y.C., 1961-71, North Miami Beach, Fla., 1971—; adj. prof. Pa. Coll. Optometry, 1978—, preceptor, 1978—; instr. Miami Dade Community Coll., 1971-75; adj. prof. So. Coll. of Optometry, 1986—; Fla. state dir. Coll. Optometrists in Vision Devel., 1979—; bd. dirs. Optometric Center S. Fla., 1975—; Fla. state assoc. dir. Optometric Extension Program, 1973-77; mem. profl. adv. bd. Banyan Sch., Clin. Facility for Children with Learning Disabilities, Hollywood, Fla., 1980—; preceptor Optometric Extension Program Found., Inc., 1978—. Served with USCG, 1961-69. Recipient State of Fla., Dade County Sch. award, 1974; Dade County Pub. Sch. Bd. Disting. award, 1975; Dade County Pub. Sch. Disting. award, 1975, 76, 77; Dade County Optometric Assn. Disting. award 1975, Coll. Optometrists in Vision Devel. Disting. award, 1976. Diplomate Nat. Bd. Examiners in Optometry. Fellow Am. Acad. Optometry, Coll. Optometrists in Vision Devel., Nat. Soc. Optometrists in Vision Devel., N.Y. Acad. Optometry, Am. Coll. Optometric Physicians; mem. Am. Pub. Health Assn., Dade County Optometric Assn. (pres. 1981-82), Am. Health Plan Referring Com., Am. Optometric Assn., Optometric Extension Program Found., Inc. (clin. assoc.), Broader Opportunities for Learning Disabilities, So. Council Optometrists, N.Y. Acad. Scis., Fla. Optometric Assn. Home: 20300 W Country Club Dr North Miami Beach FL 33180 Office: 951 NE 167th St North Miami Beach FL 33162

MARGARITOFF, DIMITRI ANDREJ, business executive; b. Berlin, Germany, Sept. 12, 1947; s. Peter and Tamara (Holl) M.; m. Karen Andrea Hollihan, Aug. 2, 1985; 1 child, Peter Andrej. MEE, Swiss Fed. Inst. Tech., Zürich, 1973; MBA, U. Rochester, 1975. Mktg. engr. Edmac Assocs., Rochester, N.Y., 1975-76; mktg. mgr. Hawesko GmbH, Hamburg, Fed. Republic Germany, 1977-80, pres., 1981—, co-owner, 1987—; bd. dirs., co-owner CWD GmbH, Hamburg, 1986—; bd. dirs. Chateaux & Domaines GmbH, Hamburg. Home: Weetenkamp 1, 2000 Hamburg 52 Federal Republic of Germany Office: Hawesko GmbH, Hamburger Str 14, 2082 Tornesch/Hamburg Federal Republic of Germany

MARGAT, JEAN FRANCOIS, geologist; b. Paris, Nov. 11, 1924; s. Yves and Elisa (Felix) M.; m. Pierrette Deroche, Oct. 1950; children: Claire, Anne-Lise. MS, U. Paris, 1946; grad., Ecole Nat. Sup. Geologie, Nancy, France, 1947. Project mgr. Hudrogeol. Studies Ctr., Geol. Survey Morocco, Rabat, 1947-60; dep.-mgr. water resources div. Nat. Office Irrigations, Rabat, 1960-61; chief hydrogeol. dept. Bur. Research Geol. Minerals, Paris and Orleans, France, 1961-71; dep.-mgr. Nat. Geol. Survey Bur. Research Geol. Minerals, Orleans, 1971-75, mgr. Applied Geology Agy., 1975-77, hydrogeologist, 1977—; mem. water sci. com. Ministry of Environment, Paris, 1979—; mem. Nat. Com. Water, Paris, 1980—. Author: Dictionary of Hydrogeology, 1977, Groundwater in France, 1980, Water Economics, 1983, National Water Account, 1986. Recipient H. Milon award French Hydrotech. Soc., 1961. Mem. Geol. Soc. France (L. Barrabe award 1961), Internat. Assn. Hydrogeologists, Internat. Assn. Hydrogeol. Scis. (mem. nat. French com. 1981—). Home: 403 Rue de Gare, 45590 Saint Cyr en Val France Office: Bur Research Geol Minerals, Ave de Concyr BP 6009, 45060 Orleans, Cedex France

MARGER, EDWIN, lawyer; b. N.Y.C., Mar. 18, 1928; s. William and Fannie (Cohen) M.; m. Kaye Sanderson, Oct. 1, 1951; children: Shari Ann, Diane Elaine, Sandy Ben; m. L. Suzanne Smyth, July 5, 1968; 1 child, George Phinney; m. Mary Susan Hamel, May 4, 1987; 1 child, Charleston Faye. BA, U. Miami, 1951, JD, 1953. Bar: Fla. 1953, Ga. 1971, D.C. 1978. Sole practice, Miami Beach, Fla., 1953-67, Atlanta, 1971—; spl. asst. atty. gen. Fla., 1960-61; of counsel Richard Burns, Miami, 1967—. Tchr. Nat. Inst. Trial Advocacy. Mem. Miami Beach Social Service Commn., 1957; chmn. Fulton County Aviation Adv. Com., 1980—; trustee Forensic Scis. Found., 1984-88, v.p., 1986-88; lt. col., a.d.c. Gov. Ga., 1971-74, 80-84; col., a.d.c. Gov. La., 1977-87; Khan Bahador and mem. exiled King of Afghanistan Privy Council and Kham Bahador, 1980—. Served with USAAF, 1946-47. Fellow Am. Acad. Forensic Scis. (chmn. jurisprudence sect. 1977-78, sec. 1976-77, exec. com. 1983-86); mem. ABA, Fla. Bar Assn. (aerospace com. 1971-83, bd. govs. 1983-87), State Bar Ga. (chmn. sect. environ. law 1974-75, aviation law sect. 1978), Ga. Trial Lawyers Assn., Nat. Assn. Criminal Def. Lawyers, Ga. Assn. Criminal Def. Lawyers, Assn. Trial Lawyers Am., Am. Judicature Soc., Am. Arbitration Assn. (comml. panel 1978—), Inter-Am. Bar Assn. (sr.), World Assn. Lawyers (founding), Advocates Club, Lawyer-Pilots Bar Assn. (founding; v.p. 1959-62), Def. Research Inst., VFW. Contbr. articles to legal jours. Office: 6666 Powers Ferry Rd Atlanta GA 30339

MARGOLIN, ABRAHAM EUGENE, lawyer; b. St. Joseph, Mo., Oct. 16, 1907; s. Jacob and Rebecca (Cohn) M.; LL.B., J.D., Washington U., St. Louis, 1929; m. Florence Solow, Feb. 1, 1931; children—Robert J., Judith (Mrs. Goodman), James S. Admitted to Mo. bar, 1929, since practiced in Kansas City; sr. partner firm Margolin & Kirwan, 1949—; dir. United Mo. Mortgage Co., Tension Envelope Corp. Mem. nat. exec. council Am. Jewish Com., mem. nat. council Am. Jewish Joint Distbn. Com., 1970; v.p. Jewish Fedn. and Council Greater Kansas City, 1968—; mem. Pres.'s Council, also fellow, Brandeis U., Waltham, Mass., 1970—; mem. council of fellows Nelson Gallery Found. Chmn. bd. dirs., chmn. bd. trustees Menorah Med. Center, Kansas City; bd. dirs. Met. Health Planning Council Kansas City, Truman Med. Center, Kansas City, Mo.; bd. dirs., pres. central governing bd. Children's Mercy Hosp. Kansas City, Mo.; trustee City Trusts of Kansas City (Mo.), B'nai B'rith Found. Recipient Brotherhood citation NCCJ, 1978; Guardian of the Menorah award, 1975, Disting. Alumnus award Washington U. Law Sch., 1987; named Man of Year, Jewish Theol. Sem. Am., 1980. Mem. Am. Bar Assn., Mo. Bar Assn., Lawyers' Assn. Kansas City, Supreme Ct. Hist. Soc., Order Coif, Delta Sigma Rho, Pi Lambda Phi. Jewish (life dir. congregation). Clubs: B'nai B'rith, Oakwood Country (Kansas City, Mo.); Nat. Lawyers (Washington). Home: 1201 W 57th St Kansas City MO 64113 Office: 1000 United Missouri Bank Bldg 928 Grand Ave Kansas City MO 64106

MARGOLIS, FRED SHELDON, pediatric dentist, educator; b. Lorain, Ohio, Mar. 31, 1947; s. Benjamin Barnett and Zelma (Bordo) M.; m. Susan Kreiter, Sept. 12, 1971; children—David S., Adam R. BS, Ohio State U., 1969, DDS, 1973; cert. pediatric dentistry U. Ill.-Chgo., 1976. Dental intern Mt. Sinai Hosp., Chgo., 1973-74; practice dentistry North Suburban Dental Assocs., Skokie, Ill., 1974-84; practice dentistry, Arlington Heights, Ill., 1979—; chief of dentistry Northwest Community Hosp., Arlington Heights; asst. prof. pediatric dentistry Loyola U. Dental Sch., Maywood, Ill., 1982-83, guest lectr. pediatric dentistry, 1983-87; dental cons. Delta Dental Plan, Chgo., 1983—; staff dentist Glenkirk Schs., Glenview, Ill., 1984—; pres. Smile Makers Seminars, 1984—. Contbr. articles to profl. publs. Cubmaster N.E. Ill. council Boy Scouts Am., 1984, 87—, Den Leader, 1986-87. Mem. Am. Dental Assn., Am. Acad. Pediatric Dentistry, Ill. State Dental Soc., Am. Soc. Dentistry for Children, Chgo. Dental Soc. (v.p. North Side br. 1987—), Alpha Omega. Jewish. Lodge: B'nai B'rith. Avocations: photography, golf, piano, tennis. Office: 3325 N Arlington Heights Rd Suite 500-B Arlington Heights IL 60004

MARGOLIS, GERALD JOSEPH, psychiatrist, psychoanalyst; b. Bronx, N.Y., May 7, 1935; s. Max and Sophie (Siegel) M.; A.B., U. Rochester, 1957; M.D., U. Chgo., 1960; postgrad. Inst. Phila. Assn. Psychoanalysis, 1972; m. June Edelman Greenspan, July 13, 1976; children—David J., Peter S., Steven J. Intern, psychiat. resident, Upstate Med. Center, SUNY, Syracuse, 1960-64, instr. psychiatry, 1966-67; from instr. to clin. prof. psychiatry Med. Sch., U. Pa., Phila., 1967—; practice medicine specializing in psychiatry and psychoanalysis, Cherry Hill, N.J.; tng. and supervising analyst Inst. of Phila. Assn. for Psychoanalysis. Served with M.C., USAF, 1964-66. Diplomate Am. Bd. Psychiatry and Neurology. Mem. Am. Psychoanalytic Assn. (cert.), Am. Psychiat. Assn., AMA, Phila. Assn. for Psychoanalysis (tng. and supervising analyst), Phi Beta Kappa. Club: B'nai B'rith. Contbr. articles to profl. publs. Home: 103 Sussex Dr Cinnaminson NJ 08077 Office: 1 Cherry Hill Suite 930 Cherry Hill NJ 08002

MARGRETHE, HER MAJESTY (MARGRETHE ALEXANDRINE PORHILDUR INGRID), II, Queen of Denmark; b. Copenhagen, Apr. 16, 1940; d. King Frederik IX and Queen Ingrid; baccalaureate U. Copenhagen, U. Aarhus; diploma prehistoric archaeology, Cambridge U., 1961, LL.D. (h.c.), 1975; student Sorbonne, Paris; student London Sch. Econs., hon. fellow, 1975; LL.D. (h.c.), U. London, 1980; m. Count Henri de Laborde de Monpezat (now Prince Henrik of Denmark), June 10, 1967; children: Crown Prince Frederik André Henrik Christian, Prince Joachim Holger Waldemar Christian. Succeeded to throne of Denmark in Jan., 1972 on death of King Frederik IX. Mem. com. Union Internat. des Scis. préhistoriques et protohistoriques. Decorated Order Elephant; decorated Knight of Garter.

Royal hon. mem. Soc. Antiquaries London. Address: Amalienborg, 1257 Copenhagen K Denmark *

MARGULIES, MARTIN B., lawyer, educator; b. N.Y.C., Oct. 6, 1940; s. Max N. and Mae (Cohen) M.; m. Beth Ellen Zeldes, July 26, 1981. A.B., Columbia Coll., 1961; LL.B., Harvard U., 1964; LL.M., NYU, 1966. Bar: N.D. 1968, N.Y. 1974, Mass. 1977, U.S. Dist. Ct. Mass. 1977, Conn. 1984, U.S. Ct. Appeals (2d cir.) 1984. Asst. prof. law U. N.D., Grand Forks, 1966-69; editor-in-chief Columbia Coll. Today, Columbia U., N.Y.C., 1969-71; assoc. editor Parade Mag., N.Y.C., 1971-72; assoc. prof. law Western New Eng. Law Sch., Springfield, Mass., 1973-76; Bernard Hersher prof. law U. Bridgeport, Conn., 1977—. Author: The Early Life of Sean O'Casey, 1970. Contbr. articles to profl. jours. Cooperating atty. Conn. Civil Liberties Union, Hartford, 1979—, bd. dirs., 1982—; bd. dirs. Conn. Attys. for Progressive Legislation, New Haven, 1982—; bd. dirs. ACLU, 1987—, chmn. bd. dirs. Fairfield County Civil Liberties Union, 1982—, Hampden County Civil Liberties Union, 1976-78; bd. dirs. Civil Liberties Union Mass., Boston, 1975-78, Greater Springfield Urban League, 1976-78, Conn. Civil Liberties Union, 1982—, ACLU, 1987—. Recipient Media award N.Y. State Bar Assn., 1972; Gavel award ABA, 1973. Mem. Mass. Bar Assn., N.Y. State Bar Assn. Jewish. Home: 79 High Rock Rd Sandy Hook CT 06482 Office: Univ Bridgeport Law Sch 303 University Ave Bridgeport CT 06601

MARGUTTI, VICTOR MARIO, physician; b. Oakland, Calif., May 22, 1906; s. Louis Henry and Estelle (Rodust) M.; m. Mary Belle Dibble, Nov. 25, 1933; children: Marilyn (Mrs. William Gary Pickens), Laura, Elizabeth. A.B., U. Calif.-Berkeley, 1931; D.O., Coll. Osteo. Physicians and Surgeons, Los Angeles, 1945; M.D., Calif. Coll. Medicine, 1962. Diplomate: Am. Bd. Homeotherapeutics. Practice osteopathy Elsinore, Calif., 1946-48, Pasadena, Calif., 1948-55; Practice osteopathy San Diego, 1955—, practice medicine, specializing in internal medicine, especially homeotherapeutics and psychosomatic medicine, 1962—; med. dir. Operation Sama han Clinic, National City, Calif., 1977-84. Author: Acupuncture Biodynamic Energies and Homeopathy, A Therapeutic Etude; Contbr. articles to profl. jours. Fellow Royal Soc. Health (London), Am. Inst. Homeopathy (pres. 1972-73), Calif. Homeopathic Soc. (pres. 1973-74, 76-77). Office: 1508 W Lewis St San Diego CA 92103

MARI, REGINALD R., JR., civil engineer; b. Springfield, Ill., June 18, 1931; s. Reginald and Rose (Colantino) M. BS, U. Ill., 1955. Registered profl. engr., Ill. Foreman pipe mill Youngstown Sheet & Tube Co., Indiana Harbor, Ind., 1955-57; field supr. constrn. elevated hwys., sewers, sts., tunnels, dock walls and airport facilities City of Chgo., 1957-76, head constrn. subsect. airport programs Bur. Engring., 1976—. Mem. ASCE, Ill. Soc. Profl. Engrs., Mid Am. Commodity Exchange. Home: 5241 NE River Rd Chicago IL 60656 Office: City of Chgo Bur Engring 320 N Clark St Chicago IL 60610

MARIAM, MENGISTU HAILE See **MENGISTU HAILE MARIAM**

MARIANI, GIUSEPPE MARIO, film producer; b. Rome, Jan. 15, 1926; s. Cesare and Lucia (Angius) M.; m. Maria Grazia Minetti, Oct. 11, 1958; children: Valerio, Flavia. Sci. diploma, Liceo Scientifico Cavour, Rome. Freelance dir. Rome, 1952-57; dir. Paneuropa, Rome, 1958-60; dir., gen. mgr. Film IRIS, Rome, 1960-69; mgr. Filmakers, Rome, 1969-73; gen. mgr. TVM (S.R.L-Produzioni Cinematografiche e Televisive), Rome, 1973-86, TVM and TVMA, Rome, 1986—. Served as 2d lt. arty. Italian Army, 1962-63. Club: Parioli (Rome). Office: TVM, Via Tommaso Salvini 25, 00197 Rome Italy

MARIEL, photographer, former fabrication company executive; b. Pasadena, Calif., Aug. 5, 1938; d. Oscar Branche and Mary Lincoln (Hicks) Jackson; 1 adopted child, William Nathan Turner; m. Donald E. Coombes, June 13, 1957 (div. June 1972); children: William Cullen, Anna Maria, Joel Howard; 1 child by previous marriage, Scott Craig Goodwin. Co-incorporator Mineral Harvesters Inc., Salem, Oreg., 1966-71, Ariz. Custom Mfg. Inc., Phoenix, 1971-81, bus. mgr., pres., 1972-81; pres. Ariz. Custom Steel, Phoenix, 1976-81, Eagle Erectors, Phoenix, 1979-81; owner, photographer, writer Lazarus Enterprises, Portland, Oreg., 1981—; former co-owner WCS Constrn., Inc. Freelance photographer and writer. Asst. dist. coordinator Oreg. Rep. Party, 1964. Mem. Nat. Assn. Women Bus. Owners, Nat. Assn. Female Execs., Ariz. Network Profl. Women, Women Emerging, Internat. Platform Assn., Tolsum Farm Homeowners Assn., Ariz. Steel Fabricators Assn. (past pres.), Mensa. Mem. Reorganized Ch. Jesus Christ of Latter-day Saints. Club: Intertel. Home: PO Box 69325 Portland OR 97201

MARIN, EMILIO, archaeologist; b. Split, Croatia, Yugoslavia, Feb. 6, 1951; s. Ante and Nevis (Orlandini) M.; m. Hajdi Vidic, June 9, 1984. MA, U. Zagreb, Yugoslavia, 1977. Asst. keeper Archaeol. Mus., Split, Yugoslavia, 1973-79, sr. keeper, 1980-85, prin. keeper, 1986-87, dir., 1988—; external researcher Centre A. Merlin-CNRS, Paris, 1980—; asst. prof. Inst. Art & Archaeology, U. Sorbonne, Paris, 1981-83; co-dir. Yugoslavian-French archaeol. project for researching early Christian artifacts, Split, Paris, Rome, 1983—; vis. fellow All Souls Coll., Oxford, Eng., 1985. Author: Muzej Imaginacije, 1982; editor: Don Frane Bulic, 1984, Disputationes Salonitanae III, 1986, Po Rusevinama Stare Salone, 1986. Grantee Govt. of France, 1980-81, 86, Brit. Council, 1983, 85, Govt. of Bulgaria, 1987, U. Split, 1987—. Mem. Yugoslav Archaeol. Soc., Yugoslav Soc. for Ancient Studies, French Soc. for Classical Archaeology, Croatian Archaeol. Soc., Croatian Soc. for Classical Philology. Home: Istarska 18, 58000 Split Croatia, Yugoslavia Office: Arheoloski Muzej, Zrinsko-Frankopanska 25, 58000 Split Croatia, Yugoslavia

MARIN, LOUIS AIMÉ, educator; b. La Tronche, Isère, France, May 22, 1931; s. Marin Augustin and Milhaud Fernande; m. Françoise M. Stoullig; children: Anne, Frederique, Judith. Licence in philosophie, U. Paris Sorbonne, 1952, agrégation in philosophie, 1953, LittD (hon.), 1973. Cultural counselor Office of the Ambassador of France, Turquie, 1961-64; dir. Inst. Français, London, 1964-67; prof. U. Nanterre, Paris, 1967-70, U. Calif., San Diego, 1970-74; prof. Johns Hopkins U., Balt., 1974-77, vis. prof., 1985—; prof. estude des systèmes de représentation aux XVIè et XVIIème siècles Ecole Hautes Etudes Sci. Sociales, Paris, 1977—. Author: Utopiques, 1973, Critique du Discours, 1975, Détruire la peinture, 1977, La récit est un piège, 1978, La voix excommuniée, 1981, Portrait du Roi, 1981, La Parole Mangée, 1982. Office: Ecole Hautes Etudes Sci Sociales, 54 Blvd Raspail, 75006 Paris France

MARINHO, ROBERTO, communication executive; b. Rio de Janeiro, Dec. 3, 1904; s. Irineu Marinho Coelho De Barros and Francisca (Pisani) Barros.; m. Stell Goulart (div. 1971); children: Roberto Irineu, Paulo Roberto (dec.), João Roberto, José Roberto; m. Ruth Albuquerque. Grad. in humanities, Aldridge Sch., Rio de Janeiro; D honoris causa, Fed. U. Brasília, Brazil, Fed. U. State Rio Grande do Norte, Brazil, Gama Filho U., Rio de Janeiro, Fed. U. State of Ceará, Brazil, U. Uberlândia, Minas Gerais, Brazil. Dir., editor in chief O Globo newspaper, Rio de Janeiro, 1925—; pres. Globo Radio System, Rio de Janeiro; pres., gen. dir. Globo TV Network, Rio de Janeiro. Brazilian del. to UN, 1952; pres. Roberto Marinho Found.; mem. Helen Kellogg Inst. for Internat. Studies, U. Notre Dame, Ind. Served with Brazilian Nat. Service. Decorated Govts. of Argentina, Austria, Belgium, Chile, Republic of China, Spain, France, Italy, Mexico, Poland, Portugal, Vatican City, Venezuela; recipient Maria Moors Cabot Gold medal Columbia U., Emmy Internat. prize Internat. Council Nat. Acad. Arts and Scis.; named Man of Yr. Brazilian Am. C. of C. Mem. Inst. Cooperación Ibero Americana, Nat. Merit Order (pres., chancellor merit book permanent commn. 1960-67). Office: Globo TV Network Brazil, Rua Lopes Quintas, 303, 22460 Rio de Janeiro Brazil

MARINO, JOSEPH JOHN, refractory co. exec.; b. Stamford, Conn., Sept. 12, 1937; s. Frederick and Lucy (Sansone) M.; B.S. in Mech. Engring., U. Conn., 1961; m. Mary Fedele, May 25, 1957; children—Laura, Jayne. With Dorr-Oliver, Inc., Stamford, 1961-69; chief engr. Quigley Co. subs. Pfizer, Inc., N.Y.C., 1969-78, dir. tech. ops., 1978—. Mem. ASME (undergrad. award, Old Guard prize 1961), Am. Ceramic Soc. Patentee in field. Home: 61 Scarlet Oak Dr Wilton CT 06897 Office: 235 E 42d St New York NY 10017

MARION, DOUGLAS WELCH, magazine editor; b. Des Moines, May 9, 1944; s. Francis Orville and Alice Virginia (Welch) M.; m. Patricia Fisher, Sept. 2, 1967; children—Douglas Welch, Anne Welch. B.A., Parsons Coll., 1970; postgrad., Fresno State U., 1970. Staff editor Argus Publs., Los Angeles, 1976—, editor Super Chevy Mag., 1979—; cons. in field. Contbr. articles to profl. jours. Named Man of Yr., Classic Chevy Club, Dearborn, Mich., 1981. Republican. Office: Super Chevy Mag 12100 Wilshire Blvd Suite 250 Los Angeles CA 90025

MARION, JEAN ALBERT, mathematician, educator; b. Montelimar, Drome, France, Aug. 25, 1936; s. Roméo Joseph and Alix Augusta (Dupre) M.; m. Edith Alberte Lillamand, Mar. 3, 1962; children—Sylvie Alix, Ludmilla Eliette. Agregation and Doctorate in Math., U. Aix-Marseille II. Tchr. math. Lyceum, Aubagne, France, 1967-74; lectr. U. Marseille-Luminy, France, 1974—; educator in math. Institut de Recherche sur L'enseignement des Mathematiques, Marseille, 1972—; cons. Ecole d'Architecture, Marseille, 1983—. Author: Géométrie I, 1984; also articles in profl. jours. Editor Colloque inter-I.R.E.M. Géométria-Journees S.M.F., 1985. Served with French Army Engrs., 1961-63, Algeria. Decorated knight-compagnion Palmes Academiques (France). Mem. Société Mathématiques de France, Am. Math. Soc. Avocations: speleology; piano. Office: Dept Math Faculté Scis Luminy, 70 Route Léon Lachamp, 13288 Marseille France

MARION, PATRICE JULES JEAN, physician; b. Solesmes, France, Aug. 16, 1949; s. Jules Jean and Fernande (Alexandre) M.; m. Marie-Claire Gillette Nayna, Apr. 17, 1971 (dec. Nov. 1987); children: Laurence, Emmanuel. MD, U. Lille (France), 1976; Degree in Tropical Medicine, U. Marseille (France), 1978. Asst. in hematology and immunology Hosp. Complex of Abidjan (Ivory Coast), 1977-78; gen. practice medicine, Abidjan, 1978, Dunkerque, France, 1979-84; practice homeopathic medicine and acupuncture Dunkerque, 1984—. Fellow Orgn. for Study and Devel. Acupuncture; mem. Homoeopathia European. Office: 166 Rue de Gembloux, 59240 Dunkerque France

MARION, YVES LOUIS, French government official, university administrator; b. Paris, Sept. 27, 1923; s. Marcel Louis and Yvonne Anne (Perichon) M.; m. Colette Adrienne Prevot, Aug. 31, 1948; children—Jacques, Herve. Baccalaureat, Lycee Hoche, Versailles, France, 1943; Licence, Faculte De Droit Et De Sci. Econs., Paris, 1961, Maitrise, 1962. Master Lycee Pierre Curie, Goussainville Val d'oise, France, 1946-48; master Lycee Le Rebours, Paris, 1958-78, 1st sec. of adminstrn. council, 1978—; adminstr. French Senate, Paris, 1948-77, dir., 1977—, chief security dept., 1981-83, dir. gen., 1984—. Author: La Correspondance Commerciale, 1960, Expression Francaise Professionnelle, 1970; contbr. articles to profl. jours. Mayor dep. Marell-Marly-Yuelines, France, 1959—. Decorated chevalier Legion D'Honneur, Order Nat. Du Merite (France); Order of Leopold (Belgium). Roman Catholic. Office: Senat, Palais du Luxembourg, 75291 Paris France

MARITZ, PIETER, mathematics educator, researcher; b. Postmasburg, Cape Province, Republic of South Africa, July 23, 1943; s. Erasmus Jacobus and Ivy Gertrude (Hauptfleisch) M.; m. Annemarie Kruger, July 6, 1968; children—Erasmus Jacobus, Erich Leo. B.Sc., U. Orange Free State, Bloemfontein, Republic of South Africa, 1964, B.Sc. with honors, 1965, M.Sc., 1966; Dr. Wis. Nat., State U. Leiden, The Netherlands, 1975. Lectr. Rhodes U., Grahamstown, Republic of South Africa, 1967-72; research State U. Leiden, 1972-75; sr. lectr. U. Stellenbosch, Republic of South Africa, 1975-83, 85—, asst. prof., 1987—; vis. prof. Kans. U., Lawrence, 1984. Author: Integration of Set-Valued Functions, 1975; Elementere Analise, 1985; also articles, 1966—. Active Rapportryer Service Orgn., Stellenbosch, 1976—; group leader Voortrekker Youth Movement, Stellenbosch, 1977, 82; sec. ward com. National Party, Grahamstown, 1969-72. Served with South African Navy, 1961. South African Sci. Council overseas study grantee State U. Leiden, 1972-75, Kans. U., 1984; Dutch Minsitery Edn. stipendee, 1972-75. Mem. South African Math. Soc. (treas. 1987—), Am. Math. Soc. Mem. Reformed Ch. Avocations: philately; squash; jogging. Home: 8 Schoongezicht St, Stellenbosch, Cape Province 7600, Republic of South Africa Office: U Stellenbosch Dept Math, Stellenbosch, Cape Province 7600, Republic of South Africa

MARJAI, JÓZSEF, Hungarian government official; b. Budapest, Hungary, Dec. 18, 1923; s. József Marjai and Erzóbet Bihary; 4 sons. Ambassador to Switzerland, Czechoslovakia and Yugoslavia, dep. fgn. minister Hungary, 1970; sec. state Hungary, Budapest, 1973, ambassador to Moscow, 1976; mem. cen. com. Hungarian Socialist Workers' Party, 1976; dep. prime minister Hungary, Budapest, 1978—. Address: Dep Prime Minister's Office, Budapest V, Kossuth Lajos ter 1 Hungary *

MARK, HANS MICHAEL, university official, physicist, engineer; b. Mannheim, Germany, June 17, 1929; came to U.S., 1940, naturalized, 1945; s. Herman Francis and Maria (Schramek) M.; m. Marion G. Thorpe, Jan. 28, 1951; children: Jane H., James P. A.B. in Physics, U. Calif. at Berkeley, 1951; Ph.D., MIT, 1954; Sc.D. (hon.), Fla. Inst. Tech., 1978; D. Eng. (hon.), Poly. Inst. N.Y., 1982. Research assoc. MIT, 1954-55, asst. prof., 1958-60; research physicist Lawrence Radiation Lab., U. Calif. at Livermore, 1955-58, 60-69, exptl. physics div. leader, 1960-64; assoc. prof. nuclear engring. U. Calif. at Berkeley, 1960-66, prof., 1966-69, chmn. dept. nuclear engring., 1964-69; lectr. dept. applied sci. U. Calif. at Davis, 1969-73; cons. prof. engring. Stanford, 1973-84; dir. NASA-Ames Research Center, 1969-77; undersec. Air Force, Washington, 1977-79; sec. Air Force, 1979-81; dep. adminstr. NASA, Washington, 1981-84; chancellor U. Tex. System, Austin, 1984—; mem. Pres.'s Adv. Group Sci. and Tech., 1975-76; trustee MITRE Corp. Author: (with N.T. Olson) Experiments in Modern Physics, 1966 (with E. Teller and J.S. Foster, Jr.) Power and Security, 1976, (with A. Levine) The Management of Research Institutions, 1983, The Space Station-A Personal Journey, 1987; also numerous articles.; Editor: (with S. Fernbach) Properties of Matter Under Unusual Conditions, 1969. Recipient Distinguished Service medal NASA, 1972, 77, Exceptional Sci. Achievement award, 1984; Exceptional Civilian Service award U.S. Air Force, 1979; Disting. Public Service medal Dept. Def., 1981. Fellow Am. Phys. Soc., AIAA; mem. Nat. Acad. Engring., Am. Nuclear Soc., Am. Geophys. Union, Council on Fgn. Relations. Office: U Tex System Office of Chancellor 601 Colorado St Austin TX 78701

MARK, HENRY ALLEN, lawyer; b. Bklyn., May 16, 1909; s. Henry Adam and Mary Clyde (McCarroll) M.; m. Isobel Ross Arnold, June 26, 1940; BA, Williams Coll., 1932; JD, Cornell U., 1935. Bars: N.Y. 1936, Conn. 1981, U.S. Dist. Ct. (so. dist.) N.Y. 1943. Assoc. firm Allin & Tucker, N.Y.C., 1935-40; mng. atty. Indemnity Ins. Co. of N.Am., N.Y.C., 1940-43; assoc. firm Mudge, Stern, Williams & Tucker, N.Y.C., 1943-50, Cadwalder, Wickersham & Taft, N.Y.C., 1950-53; ptnr. Cadwalader, Wickersham & Taft, 1953-74, of counsel, 1974—; lectr. Practicing Law Inst., N.Y.C., 1955-68. Mem. adv. com. zoning Village of Garden City (N.Y.), 1952-54, planning commn., 1957-59, zoning bd. appeals, 1959-61, trustee, 1961-65, mayor, 1965-67; chmn. planning commn. Town of Washington (Conn.), 1980-84. Mem. ABA, N.Y. Bar Assn., Assn. Bar City of N.Y., Conn. Bar Assn., Litchfield County Bar Assn., Cornell Law Assn. (pres. 1971-73), St. Andrew's Soc., Phi Beta Kappa. Republican. Congregationalist. Lodge: Masons. Address: 10 Millay Ct Litchfield CT 06759

MARK, RACHEL, gynecologist; b. Quetta, Baluchistan, Pakistan, Dec. 29, 1936; d. Lazarus and Grace Motilal; m. Wilbert Jean Mark, Oct. 23, 1963; children: Wilma Sheba, Abraham Joshua, Haroon Johnathan. B in Medicine and B in Surgery, Dow Med. Coll., Karachi, Pakistan, 1969; cert. in occupational health, U. London, 1981. Asst. lady med. officer Govt. Pakistan, Quetta, 1961-63, Mastung, 1963-64, Gulistan, 1965-66; lady med. officer Tb Sanatorium, Govt. Pakistan, Quetta, 1968-70; lady med. officer Pakistan Indsl. Devel. Corp., Quetta, 1970-73, sr. lady med. officer, 1974-76; sr. lady med. officer Pakistan Mineral Devel. Corp., Quetta, 1976—; cons. physician Command and Staff Coll., Quetta, 1977-78, St. Joseph's Convent Sch., Quetta, 1977-78, Muslim Comml. Bank, Quetta; hon. cons. physician So. Sui Gas Co., Quetta. Recipient Silver Jubilee medal Merck, Sharp & Dome, 1987; scholar Internat. Labour Orgn. Mem. Pakistan Med. and Dental Assn. (v.p. Quetta). Home: 9-14/168 Gilani Rd, Quetta, Baluchistan Pakistan

MARK, REUBEN, consumer products company executive; b. Jersey City, N.J., Jan. 21, 1939; s. Edward and Libbie (Berman) M.; m. Arlene Slobzian, Jan. 10, 1964; children: Lisa, Peter, Stephen. AB, Middlebury Coll., 1960; MBA, Harvard U., 1963. With Colgate-Palmolive Co., N.Y.C., 1963—; pres., gen. mgr. Venezuela, 1972-73, Can., 1973-74; v.p., gen. mgr. Far East div. 1974-75, v.p., gen. mgr. household products div., 1975-79, group v.p. domestic ops., 1979-81, exec. v.p., 1981-83, chief operating officer, 1983-84, pres., 1983—, chief exec. officer, 1984—, chmn. bd., 1986—; lectr. Sch. Bus. Adminstrn., U. Conn., 1977. Served with U.S. Army, 1961. Mem. Soap and Detergent Assn. (bd. dirs.), Grocery Mfrs. Am. (dir.), Nat. Exec. Service Corp. Office: Colgate-Palmolive Co 300 Park Ave New York NY 10022 *

MARKANDAN, PAUL S., consulting company executive, investment banker; b. Malaya, Malaysia, Apr. 9, 1927; s. M. and G. (Sinnathamby) Sinnathamby; Sr. Cert., St. George's Instn., Cambridge, 1947; student Raffles Coll., 1949; postgrad. Syracuse U., 1960; m. ; 1 son, Steven Patrick. Exec., Southeast Sawmills Ltd., Malaysia, 1950-52; staff writer Singapore Standard, 1952-54; editor Fefs Ltd., Singapore, 1954-58, dir., 1958-64; head dept. Imperial Chem. Industries, Malaysia also Singapore, 1965-70; chmn. MPRC Asia, Kuala Lumpur, Malaysia, 1970—; chmn. MPRC Asia Inc. U.S.A.; dir. Lesong Tin Mines; chmn. MPRC Trading Sdn. Bhd., Malaysia; sr. cons. numerous cos. and banks. Author numerous bus. books. Chmn., Kuala Lumpur Social Interaction Group, 1974-78; hon. sec. Study Group Movement, Brit. Council, Singapore, 1954-58. Am. Council for Edn. fellow, 1960. Mem. Sales Mktg. Execs. Internat., Am. Mgmt. Assn. Internat., Am. Entrepreneurs Assn., Inst. Public Relations. Roman Catholic. Clubs: Royal Selangor, K.K.B. Country and Golf. Office: T/X MA 30188, Kuala Lumpur Malaysia

MARKARIAN, NOUBAR, textile company executive; b. Larnaca, Cyprus, Dec. 15, 1922; s. Paul and Gulenia (Torikian) M.; came to U.S., 1938; student Coll. S. Murat, Sevres, France, 1935-38; B.S., Sch. Engring., Columbia, 1944; m. Judith Armistead Isley, Feb. 23, 1946; children—Judy, Beverly, Linda, Nancy, Amy, Richard. Partner, v.p. Mark Knitting Mills, Bergenfield, N.J., 1945—; v.p. Valette Undergarments, Inc., Fajardo, P.R., 1958-61; sec.-treas. Johnson Corp., Bergenfield, 1961—. Vice chmn. bd. dirs. No. Valley chpt. ARC; v.p. bd. trustees Dwight Sch., Englewood, N.J. Mem. Internat. House Assn. Episcopalian. Clubs: Bay Head (N.J.) Yacht; Englewood (N.J.) Field; Rotary (pres. Bergenfield 1962-63), Columbia Alumni of Bergen County (pres. 1957-58); Columbia of N.Y.; Mantoloking (N.J.) Yacht. Home: 71 Franklin St Englewood NJ 07631 Office: 26 Palisade Ave Bergenfield NJ 07621

MARKE, JULIUS JAY, educator, law librarian; b. N.Y.C., Jan. 12, 1913; s. Isidore and Anna (Taylor) M.; m. Sylvia Bolotin, Dec. 15, 1946; 1 dau., Elisa Hope. B.S., CCNY, 1934; LL.B., NYU, 1937; B.S. in L.S., Columbia U., 1942. Bar: N.Y. 1938. Reference asst. N.Y. Pub. Library, 1937-42; pvt. practice N.Y.C., 1939-41; prof. law, law librarian NYU, 1949-83, prof. law emeritus, 1983—, interim dean of libraries, 1975-77; prof., dir. law library St. John's U. Sch. Law, 1983—; lectr. Columbia Sch. Library Service, 1962-78, adj. prof., 1978-85; Cons. Orientation Program Am. Law, 1965-68, Found. Overseas Law Libraries Am. Law, 1968-79 ; cons. copyright Ford Found.; cons. to law libraries, others. Author: Vignettes of Legal History, 1965, 2d Series, 1977, Copyright and Intellectual Property, 1967, (with R. Sloane) Legal Research and Law Library Management, 1982, supplement, 1986; editor: Modern Legal Forms, 1953, The Holmes Reader, 1955, The Docket Series, 1955—, Bender's Legal Business Forms, 4 vols, 1962; compiler, editor: A Catalogue of the Law Collection at NYU with Selected Annotations, 1953, Dean's List of Recommended Reading for Pre-Law and Law Students, 1958, 2d edit., 1984; co-editor, contbr.: Internat. Seminar on Constl. Rev, 1963, Coordinated Law Research, 1977; editor: Holmes Reader, rev. edit, 1964; co-editor: Commerical Law Information Sources, 1971; chmn. editorial bd.: Oceana Group, 1977—; chmn. editorial adv. bd.: Index to Legal Periodicals, 1978—. Contbr. articles to profl. jours. Mem. publs. council N.Y. U., 1964-80. Served to sgt. AUS, 1943-45. Decorated Bronze Star. Mem. Am. Assn. Law Libraries (pres. 1962-63, Disting. Service award 1986), Am. Bar Assn., Assn. Am. Law Schs., Council of Nat. Library Assns. (exec. bd., v.p. 1959, 60), Law Library Assn. Greater N.Y. (pres. 1949, 50, chmn. joint com. on library edn. 1950-52, 60-61), NYU Law Alumni Assn. (Judge Edward Weinfeld award 1987), Columbia Sch. Library Service Alumni Assn. (pres. 1973-75), Order of Coif (pres. NYU Law Sch. br. 1970-83), Phi Delta Phi, Field Inn 1966—). Club: N.Y. University Faculty (pres. 1965-66). Home: 4 Peter Cooper Rd #8F New York NY 10010

MARKER, JAMSHEED, diplomat; b. Hyderabad, India, Nov. 24, 1922; d. Kekobad and Mahran (Pestonji) M.; m. Arnaz Minwalla, July 12, 1980; children by previous marriage—Niloufer, Ferdza. B.A. with honors, Forman Christian Coll., Lahore, 1942. Dir. shipping co., Karachi, Pakistan, 1947-65; ambassador of Pakistan to Ghana, Guinea and Mali, 1965-67, Romania and Bulgaria, 1967-69, Russia and Finland, 1969-72, France and Iceland, Paris, 1982-86, U.S.A. and Jamaica, Washington, 1986—. Served to lt. Indian Navy, 1943-46. Recipient Madarski Konik (Bulgaria), 1969; Stiara-E-Quaid-E-Azam (Pakistan), 1970, Officer du Grand Ordre Du Merit (France), 1986. Clubs: Royal Naval, Cercle de l'Union Interallié. Office: Ambassador of Pakistan 2315 Massachusetts Ave NW Washington DC 20008

MARKER, LEONARD K., composer; b. Vienna, Austria; s. Joseph and Erna (Stamm) Kuhmarker; student harmony and counterpoint with Hans Gal; pvt. pupil composition Alban Berg, Vienna, 1930-34; student Acad. Music, Vienna; m. Gertrude Osterer, Oct. 28, 1943; 1 son, James Steven. Came to U.S., 1942, naturalized, 1945. Mem. faculty Hunter Coll., N.Y.C.; composer symphony music, motion picture scores; musicals for stage: Tilted Hat, Max Reinhardt prodn., Ministry is Insulted and Why Do You Lie, Cherie? (7,000 performances in Europe, S.Am.); Twenty-Four Beautiful Hours; The Ant Hill; music for Bobino (play); music for various Erwin Piscator prodns.; also new arrangements of various operas including Wozzeck, Rosenkavalier, Love of Three Oranges. Mem. Broadcast Music Inc.; hon. mem. Alban Berg Soc. Co-author: (with Olin Downes) Ten Operatic Masterpieces; contbr. articles to N.Y. Times, Opera News, Musical Am., others. Address: 150 Claremont Ave New York NY 10027

MARKER, MARC LINTHACUM, lawyer, leasing company executive; b. Los Angeles, July 19, 1941; s. Clifford Harry and Voris (Linthacum) M.; m. Sandra Yocom, Aug. 29, 1965; children—Victor, Gwendolyn. B.A. in Econs. and Geography, U. Calif.-Riverside, 1964; J.D., U. So. Calif., 1967. Asst. v.p., asst. sec. Security Pacific Nat. Bank, Los Angeles, 1970-73; sr. v.p., chief counsel, sec. Security Pacific Leasing Corp., San Francisco, 1973—; pres. Security Pacific Leasing Services Corp., San Francisco, 1977-85, dir., 1977—; bd. dirs., sec. Voris, Inc., 1973-86; bd. dirs. Refiners Petroleum Corp., 1977-81, Security Pacific Leasing Singapore Ptc Ltd., 1983-85; lectr. in field. Served to comdr. USCGR. Mem. ABA, Calif. Bar Assn., D.C. Bar Assn., San Francisco Bar Assn., Am. Assn. Equipment Lessors. Republican. Lutheran. Club: University (Los Angeles). Office: Security Pacific Leasing Corp 4 Embarcadero Ctr #1200 San Francisco CA 94111

MARKERT, KURT ENGELBERT, anti-trust administrator, law educator; b. Sennfeld, Bavaria, Fed. Republic of Germany, June 22, 1933; s. August and Maria (Volk) M.; m. Birgit Kuckartz, July 18, 1980. Diploma econs., U. Würzburg, Fed. Republic of Germany, 1957; M in Comparative Jurisprudence, NYU, 1959; JD, U. Würzburg, Fed. Republic of Germany, 1961; prof. of law (hon.), Free U., West Berlin, 1975. Adminstr. Fed. Cartel Office, West Berlin, 1962—; cons. UNCTAD, Geneva, 1969-72. Author: Immenga/Mestmaecker, GWB, 1981; editor: Handbuch des Wettbewerbs, 1981. Mem. adv. council Consumer Testing Found., West Berlin 1971-84. Mem. Social Democrat Party Germany. Roman Catholic. Home: Jlmenauer Str 2A, 1000 Berlin 33 Federal Republic of Germany Office: Fed Cartel Office, Mehringdamm 129, 1000 Berlin 61 Federal Republic of Germany

MARKEWICH, MAURICE ELISH (REESE), psychiatrist, musician; b. Bklyn., Aug. 6, 1936; s. Arthur and May (Elish) M.; A.B., Cornell U., 1958; M.S. in Social Work, Columbia U., 1960; M.D., N.Y. Med. Coll., 1970; certificate Center for Modern Psychoanalytic Studies, 1976; m. Linda Lawner, June 19, 1960; children—Jennifer Beth, Melissa Ann. Social worker Jewish Family Service, N.Y.C., 1961-64; resident Beth Israel Med. Center, N.Y.C., 1970-73; practice medicine specializing in psychiatry, N.Y.C., 1973—; mem. staff Beth Israel Med. Center; jazz musician, 1954—; pianist, flutist Reese Markewich Quintet, 1955-60; various appearances N.Y. State. Served with U.S. Army, 1960-61. Cert. social worker, N.Y.; lic. physician, N.Y. Mem. Am. Psychiat. Assn., Med. Soc. County N.Y., Club: Masons. Author music books: Inside Outside, 1967; The Definitive Bibliography of Harmonically Sophisticated Tonal Music, 1970; The New Expanded Bibliography of Jazz Compositions Based on the Chord Progressions of Standard Tunes, 1974; Jazz Publicity II, 1974. Home: Bacon Hill Town of Mount Pleasant Pleasantville NY 10570 Office: 207 E 16th St New York NY 10003

MARKHAM, CHARLES BUCHANAN, lawyer; b. Durham, N.C., Sept. 15, 1926; s. Charles Blackwell and Sadie Helen (Hackney) M. A.B., Duke U., Durham, N.C., 1945; postgrad., U. N.C. Law Sch., Chapel Hill, 1945-46; LL.B., George Washington U., Washington, 1951. Bar: D.C. 1951, N.Y. 1961, N.C. 1980, U.S. Ct. Appeals (2d cir.) 1962, U.S. Ct. Appeals (D.C. cir.) 1955, U.S. Supreme Ct. 1964. Reporter Durham Sun, N.C., 1945; asst. state editor, editorial writer Charlotte News, N.C., 1947-48; dir. publicity and research Young Democratic Clubs Am., Washington, 1948-49, exec. sec., 1949-50; polit. analyst Dem. Senatorial Campaign Com., Washington, 1950-51; spl. atty. IRS, Washington and N.Y.C., 1952-60; assoc. Battle, Fowler, Stokes and Kheel, N.Y.C., 1960-65; dir. research U.S. Equal Employment Opportunity Commn., Washington, 1965-68; dep. asst. sec. U.S. Dept. Housing and Urban Devel., Washington, 1969-72; asst. dean Rutgers U. Law Sch., Newark, 1974-76; assoc. prof. law N.C. Central U., Durham, 1976-81, prof. law, 1981-83; mayor City of Durham, N.C., 1981-85; ptnr. Markham and Wickham, Durham, 1984-86; Trustee Hist. Preservation Soc. Durham, 1982-86; bd. dirs. Stagville Ctr., 1984-86; mem. Gov's Crime Commn., Raleigh, 1985; dep. commr. N.C. Indsl. Commn., Raleigh, 1986—. Editor: Jobs, Men and Machines: The Problems of Automation, 1964. Mem. ABA, Durham County Bar Assn., Greater Durham C. of C. (bd. dirs. 1982-86), Phi Beta Kappa, Omicron Delta Kappa, Phi Delta Theta. Republican. Episcopalian. Club: Chapel Hill Country. Home: 204 N Dillard St Durham NC 27701 Office: NC Indsl Commn Dobbs Bldg Raleigh NC 27611

MARKHAM, JAMES MORRIS, journalist; b. Washington, Mar. 7, 1943; s. James Morris and Mary Paul (Rix) M.; m. Stephanie Reed; children: Katherine Rix, Samuel Reed. BA, Princeton U., 1965; Rhodes scholar, Oxford U., Eng., 1965-67. Stringer Time Mag., New Delhi, 1966-67; reporter AP, New Delhi, 1968-69, Lagos, Nigeria, 1969-70; reporter N.Y. Times, 1971-73; bur. chief N.Y. Times, Saigon, Vietnam, 1973-75, Beirut, 1975-76, Madrid, 1976-82, Bonn, Fed. Republic Germany, 1982-87, Paris, 1987—. Office: Bureau Chief, NY Times, 3 Rue Scribe, 75009 Paris France

MARKHAM, JESSE WILLIAM, economist; b. Richmond, Va., Apr. 21, 1916; s. John James and Edith (Luttrell) M.; A.B., U. Richmond, 1941; postgrad. Johns Hopkins U., 1941-42, U.S. Fgn. Service Sch., 1945; M.A., Harvard U., 1947, Ph.D., 1949; m. Penelope Jane Anton, Oct. 15, 1944; children—Elizabeth Anton Markham McLean, John James, Jesse William. Accountant, E.I. duPont de Nemours Co., Richmond, 1935-38; teaching fellow Harvard U., 1946-48; asst. prof. Vanderbilt U., 1948-52, asso. prof., 1952-53; chief economist FTC, Washington, 1953-55; asso. prof. Princeton U., 1955-57, prof. econs., 1957-68; prof. Harvard Grad. Sch. Bus. Adminstrn., 1968-72, Charles Edward Wilson prof., 1972-82, prof. emeritus, 1982—; vis. prof. Columbia U., 1958; prof. Harvard U. Extension Service, 1984—; Ford Found. vis. prof. Harvard Grad. Sch. Bus. Adminstrn., 1965-66; research prof. Law and Econs. Ctr., Emory U., 1982-84; research staff, mem. bd. editors Patent Trademark Copyright Research Inst., George Washington U., 1955-70; econs. editor Houghton Mifflin Co., 1961-71; U.S. del. commn. experts on bus. practices European Productivity Agy., OEEC, 1956, 57, 58, 59, 61; vis. prof. Harvard U., 1961-62; dir. Ford Found. Seminar Region II, 1961; adv. com. mktg. to sec. commerce, 1967-71; mem. Am. Bar Assn. Commn. to study FTC, 1969. Active Boy Scouts Am.; chmn. Harvard Parents Com. Served as lt. USNR, World War II. Ford Found. research prof., 1958-59. Mem. Am., So. econ. assns., U.S. C. of C. (econ. policy com.), Phi Beta Kappa. Episcopalian. Club: Harvard (N.Y.C.). Author: Competition in the Rayon Industry, 1952; The Fertilizer Industry: Study of an Imperfect Market, 1958; The American Economy, 1963; (with Charles Fiero and Howard Piquet) The European Common Market: Friend or Competitor, 1964; (with Gustav Papanek) Industrial Organization and Economic Development, 1970; Conglomerate Enterprise and Public Policy, 1973 (with Paul Teplitz) Baseball Economics and Public Policy, 1981; sect. on oligopoly Internat. Ency. Social Scis.; contbr. articles to econ. jours. Home: 663 Martin Point Rd Friendship ME 04547 Office: Harvard U Grad Sch Bus Adminstrn Aldrich 135-D Boston MA 02163

MARKIEWICZ, WLADYSLAW, sociologist, educator; b. Ostrow Wielkopolski, Poland, Jan. 2, 1920; s. Jozef and Bronislawa M.; m. Ludgarda Trzybinska, 1949; 2 children. Ed. Poznan U. Doctor Poznan U. (Poland), 1959-61, docent, 1961-66, assoc. prof., 1966-72, prof., 1972—, dir. Inst. Sociology, 1969-72; head dept. sociology of labor and organ. Warsaw U. (Poland), 1972-76. Author: Przeobrazenia swiadomosci narodowej reemigrantow polskich z Francji, 1960; Spoleczenstoiw i socjologia w Niem Hieckiej Republice Federalnej, 1966; Sociology in People's Poland, 1970; Propedeutyka nauki o spoleczenswtie, 1971; Socjologia a sluzba spoleczna, 1972; Polskie Kryzysy, 1983, Spraw polskich splatanie, 1986; contbr. numerous articles to profl. pubs.; editor-in-chief Studia Socjologiczne; editor-in-chief Polish Western Affairs. Active mem. youth orgns., 1947-50; mem. Commn. for investigation into social conflicts PZPR Central Com., 1981-83; mem. Voivodship Nat. Council, Poznan, 1949-54; vice dir. Western Inst. Poznan, 1962-64, dir., 1965-71; vice chmn. Polish Com., UNESCO. Decorated Gold Cross of Merit, knight's and officer's cross Order Polonia Restituta, medals of 10th, 30th and 40th Anniversaries of People's Poland, Order Banner of Labor (1st and 2d class); recipient Gold award Polish Tchrs. Assn. Mem. Polish Sociol. Soc. (pres. 1968-72), Polish Acad. Scis. (corr. 1971-76, ordinary mem. 1976—, mem. presidium 1981—), Polish Acad. Scis. (dept. social scis. sec. 1972-83, v.p. 1984—), Pugwash Confs. (Polish com.).

MARKLAND, BJÖRN WALTER, professional society administrator; b. Stockholm, Aug. 2, 1943; s. Walter and Göta (Norén) M.; m. Marika Sjögren, Apr. 15, 1972. Grad., Stockholm Sch. Econs., 1967. Authorized pub. acct. Acct. Bohlins Revisionsbyrå subs. Deloitte Haskins & Sells, Stockholm, 1967-81, dep. sr. ptnr., 1981-85; pres. Swedish Inst. Authorized Pub. Accts. (F.A.R.), Stockholm, 1982-84, sec. gen., 1985—; del. the Nordic countries Fedn. Experts Comptables Européens, Brussels, 1987—. Contbr. articles to profl. jours. Mem. Ch. of Sweden. Office: FAR Swedish Inst Authorized Pub Accts, Norrtullsgatan 6, Box 6417, S-11382 Stockholm Sweden

MARKLE, CHERI VIRGINIA CUMMINS, nurse; b. N.Y.C., Nov. 22, 1936; d. Brainard Lyle and Mildred (Schwab) Cummins; m. John Markle, Aug. 26, 1961 (dec. 1962); 1 child, Kellianne. RN, Ind. State U., 1959; BS in Rehab. Edn., Wright State U., 1975; BSN, Capital U., 1987; postgrad. in Nursing Adminstrn., Wright State U., 1987—. Coordinator Dayton (Ohio) Children's Psychiat. Hosp., 1962-75; dir. nursing Stillwater Health Ctr., Dayton, 1975-76; sr. supr. VA, Dayton, 1977-85, alcohol rehab. nurse coordinator, 1985-86; dir. nursing Odd Fellows, Springfield, Ohio, 1987—; rehab. cons., Fairborn, Ohio, 1976—. rehab. cons., Fairborn, Ohio, 1976—; newspaper columnist Golden Times, Clark County. Served to 1st lt., USAF, 1959-61. Mem. Am. Nurses Assn. (cert. adminstrn. 1983, cert. gerontology 1984), Ohio Nurses Assn., Dist. 10 Nurses Assn., Nurse Mgrs. Assembly, Gerontological Nurse Assembly, Nat. Assn. Female Execs., Rehab. Soc., Wright State U. Alumni Assn., Am. Legion, Alpha Sigma Alpha, Sigma Theta Tau. Democrat. Roman Catholic. Home: 539 South St Fairborn OH 45324 Office: Odd Fellows 404 E McCreight Ave Springfield OH 45503

MARKLE, GEORGE BUSHAR, IV, surgeon; b. Hazleton, Pa., Oct. 29, 1921; s. Alvan and Gladys (Jones) M.; m. Mildred Donna Umstead, July 3, 1944; children: Donna Markle Partee, Melanie Jones Markle, George Bushar, Christian. B.S., Yale U., 1943; M.D., U. Pa., 1946. Diplomate Am. Bd. Surgery. Intern Geisinger Med. Ctr., Danville, Pa., 1946-47, resident, 1947-49; surg. fellow Mayo Clinic, Rochester, Minn., 1949-52; chief surgery U.S. Army Hosp., Ft. Monroe, Va., 1952-54; practice gen. surgery Carlsbad, N.Mex., 1954—; surg. staff Carlsbad Regional Med. Ctr., 1954-77, Guadalupe Med. Ctr., 1977—; panelist Voice of Am. Author: Ill Health and Other Foolishness, 1966, How to Stay Healthy All Your Life, 1968, The Teka Stone, 1983; Contbr. articles to profl. jours.; newspaper columnist, radio health series. Served with M.C. U.S. Army, 1952-54. Recipient Distinguished Service award Jr. C. of C., 1956. Fellow Internat. Coll. Surgeons (regent), Southwestern Surg. Congress, Priestley Surg. Soc., Western Surg. Assn.; mem. Eddy County Med. Soc., Ogden Surg. Soc. Republican. Presbyterian. Lodge: Kiwanis. Home: 1003 N Shore Dr Carlsbad NM 88220 Office: 911 N Canal St Carlsbad NM 88220

MARKMAN, SHERMAN, mortgage-banker, venture capital investor; b. Denver, Aug. 21, 1920; s. Abe and Julia (Rosen) M.; student So. Meth. U., 1962-64; children—Michael, Joan, Lori Ann. Vice pres. Lester's, Inc., Oklahoma City, 1940-59; exec. v.p. Besco Enterprises, San Francisco, 1960-61; sr. v.p. Zale Corp., Dallas, 1962-69; pres. Designcraft Industries, N.Y.C., 1969-75, chief exec. officer, 1969-75; pres. Tex. Internat. Export Co., Dallas, 1975—, CAC Fin. Group (Tex.), Dallas, 1982—; dir. Pipelife Service Corp., Coverage Cons., N.Y.C., Transworld Ins. Intermediaries, Ltd.; charter mem. N.Y. Ins. Exchange; guest lectr. fin. risk confs., 1982—. Mem. Dallas Council World Affairs, 1962—. Served with USMCR, 1942-45; PTO. Mem. Young Men's Philanthropic League N.Y. NCCJ. Clubs: Press, Columbian, Lancers, City (Dallas); India Temple (Oklahoma City); Los Angeles Athletic. Office: Premier Place 5910 North Central Expwy Suite 1000 Dallas TX 75206

MARKO, VICTOR SPERO, architect; b. Toronto, Ont., Can., Sept. 28, 1936; s. Spero Vassel and Sophia (Dimitri) M.; m. Elizabeth Anne Stewart, Aug. 26, 1960; children—Jennifer, Jeffrey, Jodie. B.Arch., Case Western Res. U., Cleve., 1964; Dipl. Arch. Tech., Ryerson Poltech., Toronto, 1957. Design architect, Mies Van Der Rohe, Chgo., 1964-66; project architect Victor Prus Architects, Montreal, Que., Can., 1966-67; vice chmn. NORR Airport Planners, Toronto, 1967-82; program mgr. Can. Dept. External Affairs, Ottawa, Ont., 1982—; tech. mgr. NORR Cons. Asia, Singapore, 1977-82. Coauthor: Guide for Passenger Terminal Facilities, 1970. Charles Schweinforth travelling fellow, 1983. Mem. Royal Architects Inst. Can., Can. Inst. Planners, Epsilon Delta Rho. Avocations: gardening; bicycling; hiking. Office: Dept External Affairs, 125 Sussex Dr, Ottawa, ON Canada

MARKOE, M. ALLEN, leasing company executive; b. St. Paul, Feb. 23, 1927; s. Julius and Bernice (Jacobson) M.; student Drake, 1947-48; B.S. U. Wis., 1950; m. Joan B. Lewensohn, Aug. 7, 1949; children—Guy Leigh, Sara Lynne, Robin Dawn. Owner, Diversified Bus., Milw., 1950-54; dir. mgmt. adv. services Profit Counselors, Inc., Chgo., N.Y.C., 1954-60; pres. Pacific Am. Leasing Corp., Phoenix, 1961-80; ret., 1980; founder, pres. Markoe Fin. Group, Markoe Leasing; pres. AM Leasing Ltd., Phoenix; chmn., chief operating officer Shillelagh Ventures, Chartered Pub. Co., Phoenix. Served with AUS, 1945-46. Mem. Am. Indsl. Devel. Council, Ariz. Assn. Mfrs., Soc. for Advancement Mgmt., N.Am. Soc. Sci. Mgmt., Assn. Equipment Lessors, Western Assn. Lessors, Phoenix C. of C., Am. Legion, Frat. Order Police (assoc.). Republican. Jewish. Clubs: Ariz. Aikido Kai, Lions. Home: 7050 N Wilder Rd Phoenix AZ 85021 Office: 5815 N Black Canyon Hwy Phoenix AZ 85015

MARKOVITS, ANDREI STEVEN, political science educator; b. Timisoara, Rumania, Oct. 6, 1948; came to U.S., 1960, naturalized, 1971; s. Ludwig and Ida (Ritter) M.; B.A. (N.Y. State scholar, univ. pres.'s fellow), Columbia U., 1969, M.B.A., 1971, M.A., 1973, M.Phil., 1974, Ph.D., 1976. Mem. faculty N.Y.U., 1974, John Jay Coll. Criminal Justice, CUNY, 1974, Columbia U., 1975; research assoc. Inst. Advanced Studies, Vienna, Austria, 1973-74, Wirtschafts und Sozialwissenschaftliches Inst., German Trade U. Fedn., Duesseldorf, W.Ger., 1979, Internat. Inst. Comparative Social Research, Sci. Center Berlin, 1980; asst. prof. govt. Wesleyan U., Middletown, Conn., 1977-83; assoc. prof. polit. sci. Boston U., 1983—; vis. prof. Tel Aviv U., fall 1986, Osnabrück U., 1987; research assoc. Center for European Studies, Harvard U., 1975—. B'nai B'rith Found. fellow, 1976-77; Kalmus Found. fellow, 1976-77; Ford Found. fellow, 1979; Hans Boeckler Found. fellow, 1982. Mem. Am. Polit. Sci. Assn., Internat. Polit. Sci. Assn., AAUP. Author, editor books and papers in field. Home: 287 Harvard St Cambridge MA 02139 Office: Boston U 232 Bay State Rd Boston MA 02215 also: Harvard U Ctr for European Studies Cambridge MA 02138

MARKS, ALBERT AUBREY, JR., brokerage house executive; b. Phila., Dec. 19, 1912; s. Albert A. and Edythe (Lilian) M.; grad. Harrisburg (Pa.) Acad., 1928; student Williams Coll., 1928-30; B.S., U. Pa., 1932; m. Mary Kay Bryan; children—Albert Aubrey, Christina M., Robert B. Br. office mgr. Newburger & Co., Phila., 1934-42, gen. ptnr. Newburger & Co., Atlantic City, N.J., 1946—, Advest Co.; pres. Atlantic Co. N.J.; dir. Guarantee Bank & Trust Co., Atlantic City, Anchor Savs. and Loan Assn.; allied mem. Am., N.Y., Phila., Balt. stock exchanges. Vice pres. N.J. Mid-Atlantic Farm Show, 1952-54; dir. Atlantic City Conv. Bur., 1951-54, treas., 1962; pres. Miss Am. Pageant, 1962-64, chmn. bd., 1966; chmn. Boardwalk Adv. Commn.; mem. Bd. Edn., Margate, N.Y.; vice chmn. Com. Adult Edn. So. N.J.; pres. Atlantic County Community Chest and Welfare Council, 1953; gen. campaign chmn. Community Chest, 1956; former pres. 4-Club Council; mem. exec. council Boy Scouts Am., Atlantic County; trustee So. N.J. Devel. Council, 1951-54; mem. N.J. Legis. Study Commn., Securities Adv. Com. N.J. State, Conflict Interest Com. Gov. Betty Bacharach Home Afflicted Children; chmn. Com. of 50, Atlantic City, 1972—, Atlantic County Improvement Authority, 1975; pres. Atlantic City Med. Ctr. Found., 1986—. Served from 2d lt. to lt. col. USAAF, 1942-46. Named Citizen of Year, Atlantic City, 1953; Citizen of Decade, Elks, 1972. Mem. Investment Bankers Assn., Security Traders Assn., Nat. Assn. Security Dealers, Assn. Stock Exchange Firms, Atlantic City (pres. 1952-53), So. N.J. (chmn. devel. council 1951-54) C.'s of C., Atlantic City Centennial Assn. (v.p. 1953-54), Mil. Order World Wars (companion), Res. officers Assn., Air Force Assn., Newcomen Soc., Pa. Soc., Newcomen Soc. Roman Catholic. Clubs: Masons, Kiwanis (pres. 1954), Press, Haddon Hall Racquet, Osborne Beach; Williams, Marco Polo (N.Y.C.). Home: 1 N Osborne Ave Margate NJ 08402 Office: 20 S Tennessee Ave Atlantic City NJ 08401

MARKS, ARTHUR, prosthodontist, educator; b. N.Y.C., June 5, 1920; s. Louis and Elizabeth (Levine) M.; AB, NYU, 1942, DDS, 1944; m. Ruth Flamberg, July 18, 1948; children: Pauline, Deborah, Frances. Practice dentistry, N.Y.C., 1947—; assoc. vis. oral surgeon Sydenham Hosp., N.Y.C., 1947-75; mem. speakers bur. N.Y. Oral Hygiene Com.; dental rep. interprofl. socs. adv. com. on Medicaid to commr. health N.Y.C.; asst. clin. prof. removable prosthodontics, asst. clin. prof. dept. family practice NYU Coll. Dentistry, 1981-87, assoc. clin. prof. prosthodontics and occlusion, comprehensive care and practice adminstrn., 1987—. Hon. asst. chmn. Democratic State Conv., N.Y., 1966; mem. New Rochelle Dem. City Com.; mem. New Rochelle Columbus Day Com., 1981, 82. Served with Dental Corps, AUS, 1944-47. Recipient N.Y. U. Alumni Meritorious Service award, 1976. Fellow Am. Coll. Dentists, Acad. Gen. Practice, Am. Endodontic Soc., Internat. Coll. Dentists; mem. Am. Acad. Prosthodontics, ADA, Am. Soc. Advancement Gen. Anesthesia in Dentistry, Am. Soc. Childrens Dentistry, Am. Dental Soc. Anaesthesiology, N.Y. Inst. Clin. Oral Pathology, Alumni Assn. N.Y. U. Dental Sch. (dir. 1961—, chmn. installation dinner 1963-64, 65, 67, chmn. constl. by-laws com. 1964-66, sec. 1968-69, pres. elect 1970-71, pres. 1971-72), Alumni Fedn. N.Y. U. (past pres., dir.), N.Y. Hort. Soc., Am. Acad. Polit. and Social Sci., Eastern Dental Soc. (pres. 1978), First Dist. Dental Soc. (dir., chmn. govt. funded health care com.), Empire Dental Polit. Action Com. (sec. 1976-77), Sydenham Hosp. Dental Clin. Soc. (pres. 1971-72), Grand St. Boys Assn., Assn. Mil. Surgeons, Thomas Paine Hist. Soc. Democrat. Club: N.Y. University College of Dentistry Century (organizing com. N.Y.C., dir. 1961-66). Home: 85 Hilary Circle New Rochelle NY 10804 Office: 601 W 139th St New York NY 10031

MARKS, DOROTHY LIND, mathematics tutor; b. N.Y.C., Apr. 30, 1900; d. Alfred Daniel and Martha (Herzog) Lind; m. Norman Lincoln Marks, May 29, 1923 (dec. 1959); 1 son, Alfred Lind (dec. 1980). B.A., Barnard Coll., 1921. Substitute tchr. N.Y. high schs., 1921-28; math tutor The Brearley Sch., N.Y.C., 1953-62, The Marlborough Sch., Los Angeles, 1973—, pvt. and pub. secondary schs., Los Angeles, 1973—, NYU, 1965-72; chmn. math dept. The Lenox Sch., N.Y.C., 1960-70. Bd. dirs. women's orgn. Temple Rodeph Sholem, N.Y.C., 1925-50, fin. sec., 1925-47. Mem. Phi Beta Kappa (recipient Kohn Math. Prize 1921, sec.-treas. Barnard chpt. 1925-50, chartermem. alumnae in N.Y.). Republican. Jewish. Avocations: reading, music, theatre, concerts, ballet.

MARKS, GERALD, surgeon; b. Bklyn., Apr. 14, 1925; s. Maurice and Lee (Leib) M.; m. Barbara Ann Hendershot, Nov. 25, 1950; children: Richard M., James M., John H. Grad., Villanova U., 1945; M.D., Jefferson Med. Coll., 1949. Diplomate: Am. Bd. Surgery, Am. Bd. Colon and Rectal Surgery (examiner). Intern Jefferson Med. Coll. Hosp., Phila., 1949-51, resident in surgery, 1952-57, resident in proctology, 1953-54; asst. dir. Tumor Clinic Jefferson Med. Coll. Hosp., 1959-68; practice medicine specializing in gen. and colorectal surgery Phila., 1957—; asst. chief surgery Phila. Gen. Hosp., 1957-70, chief Proctology Clinic, 1968-70, coordinator student surg. edn. Jefferson Surg. Service, 1960-70; asst. attending physician in surgery Thomas Jefferson U. Hosp., 1957—, sec. med. staff, 1974-77, dir. Comprehensive Rectal Cancer Ctr., Colorectal Surgery Residency Program, exec. dir. Colorectal Surgical Found., co-dir. Colorectal Cancer Genetics Ctr.; dir. div. internat. surg. edn. and practice Ctr. for Research in Med. Edn. and Health Care; instr. surgery Jefferson Med. Coll., 1958-67, assoc. in clin. surgery, 1967-68, clin. assoc. prof. surgery, 1974-78, prof., 1978—; chief sect. colorectal surgery, cons. in colon-rectal surgery Pa. Hosp.; cons. in colon-rectal surgery VA Hosp., Coatesville, Pa., 1959—, San Juan, P.R., 1968—, Wilmington, Del., 1977—; cons in colon-rectal surgery USN Regional Med. Ctr., Phila., 1977—; adj. prof. surgery U. Pa. Sch. Medicine. Sr. editor (jour.) Surg. Endoscopy, Ultrasound and Interventional Techniques; assoc. editor (jour.) Diseases of the Colon and Rectum, 1977—; cons. editor Pa. Medicine; editorial cons. Jour. AMA, New Eng. Jour. Medicine; contbr. articles to profl. jours.; developed colonoscopic colon teaching model. Served with USN, 1943-46; served to capt. M.C. USAF, 1951-52. Mem. ACS (rep. to bd. govs. 1983, council Met. Phila. chpt.), AMA, Pa. Soc. Colon and Rectal Surgery (pres. 1981-82), Am. Soc. Colon and Rectal Surgery, Am. Soc. Clin. Oncology, Internat. Soc. Univ. Colon and Rectal Surgeons, Coll. Physicians Phila., Royal Soc. Medicine (affiliate), Ea. Surg. Soc., Phila. Acad. Surgery (mem. council), Pa. Med. Soc., Phila. County Med. Soc. (bd. dirs., v.p., chmn. publs. com., pub. affairs com., v.p. 1986—), Soc. Surgery Alimentary Tract, Am. Soc. Gastrointestinal Endoscopy, Italian Soc. Gastrointestinal Endoscopy (hon.), Soc. Am. Gastrointestinal Endoscopic Surgeons (founder, pres. 1980, bd. govs.), Ileostomy Rehab. Assn. (med. advisor 1973—), Italian Soc. Surgery (hon.), Northeastern Soc. Colon and Rectal Surgeons (past pres.), Jefferson Vol. Faculty Assn. (pres. 1973-74), Alpha Omega Alpha. Home: 45 Fairview Rd Narberth PA 19072 Office: 1100 Walnut St Suite 700 Philadelphia PA 19107

MARKS, JAMES JOHN, restaurateur, developer; b. Chgo., Aug. 23, 1911; s. Nicholas John and Stella (Giani) M.; B.S., U. Mich., 1935; m. Christine Constance Tampary, Nov. 11, 1939; children—Lianna Sandra, James John. Forestry technician U.S. Forestry Service, Ava, Mo., 1934; forest supr. Mich. Conservation Dept., Lansing, 1934-35; cons. forester, Ann Arbor, Mich., 1936-37; owner Martine's Restaurant, Pensacola, Fla., 1942—, Martine's Ice Cream Co., Pensacola, 1942—; pres. Esquire House, Warrington, Fla., 1934—, Martine's, Pensacola, 1947—, Marwood Motors, Pensacola, 1955—, Ky. Fried Chicken, Biloxi and Gulfport, Miss., 1964—, Ky. Fried Chicken, Mobile, Ala., 1964—, New Orleans, 1967—, Col. Sanders Ky. Fried Chicken Corp., 1970—; sec.-treas. Circle Sanitation, Pensacola, 1959—. Mem. adv. bd. Fla. Hotel and Restaurant Commn., 1961-62; mem. bd. Fla. Hospitality Edn. Program, 1962-63; chmn., pres. Fla. Tourism Council, 1962-63; mem. Fla. Council of 100, 1963—, mem. exec. com.; mem. council advisors U. W.Fla., 1975—; advisor to council advisors Univ. System Fla.; mem. Baptist Hosp. Health Care Found., 1975—, vice chmn. exec. com., 1976—; elector Presdl. Electoral Coll., 1984—; owner, mgr. Bellview Shopping Ctr., N. Palafox Plaza Shopping Ctr. Served to comdr. USNR, 1937-45. Named Outstanding Fla. Restaurateur, 1964. Mem. Am. Restaurants Hall of Fame, 1961. Mem. Nat., Fla. (pres. 1961-62) restaurant assns., Sales Execs. Club. Mem. Hellenic Christian Orthodox Ch. (v.p. parish council 1976). Rotarian (past local pres., Paul Harris fellow). Clubs: Toastmasters; Mobile Country; Pensacola Country. Home: 4002 Marlane Dr Pensacola FL 32506 Office: 4101 Mobile Hwy Pensacola FL 32506

MARKS, LILLIAN SHAPIRO, educator; b. Bklyn., Mar. 16, 1907; d. Hayman and Celia (Merowitz) Shapiro; B.S., N.Y. U., 1928; m. Joseph Marks, Feb. 21, 1932; children—Daniel, Sheila Blake, Jonathan. High sch. tchr., N.Y.C., 1929-30; tchr. Evalina de Rothschild Sch., Jerusalem, Palestine, 1930-31; social worker United Jewish Aid, Bklyn., 1931-32; tchr. Richmond Hill High Sch., 1932-40, Andrew Jackson High Sch., Cambria Heights, N.Y., 1940-71; mem. faculty New Sch. Social Research, N.Y.C., 1977-87 ; staff Vassar Summer Inst., 1946. Mem. Am. Fedn. Tchrs., English-Speaking Union, Inst. Ret. Profls. Democrat. Am. editor: Teeline, A System of Fast Writing, 1970; author: College Teeline, 1977; College Teeline Self-Taught, 1983; Touch Typing Made Simple, 1985. Home and Office: 117-16 Park Lane S Kew Gardens NY 11418

MARKS, PAUL ALAN, oncologist, cell biologist; b. N.Y.C., Aug. 16, 1926; s. Robert R. and Sarah (Bohorad) M.; m. Joan Harriet Rosen, Nov. 28, 1953; children: Andrew Robert, Elizabeth Susan, Matthew Stuart. A.B. with gen. honors, Columbia U., 1945, M.D., 1949; D. Biol. Sci. (hon.), U. Urbino, Italy, 1982; PhD (hon.), Hebrew U., Jerusalem, Israel, 1987. Fellow Columbia Coll. Physicians and Surgeons, 1952-53, assoc., 1955-56, mem. faculty, 1956—, dir. hematology tng., 1961-74, prof. medicine, 1967-82, dean faculty of medicine, v.p. med. affairs, 1970-73, dir. Comprehensive Cancer Ctr., 1972-80, v.p. health scis., 1973-80, prof. human genetics and devel., 1969-82, Frode Jensen prof. medicine, 1974-80; prof. medicine and genetics Cornell U. Coll. Medicine, N.Y.C., 1981—; attending physician Presbyn. Hosp., N.Y.C., 1967-82; pres., chief exec. officer Meml. Sloan-Kettering Cancer Center, 1980—; attending physician Meml. Hosp. for Cancer and Allied Diseases, 1980—; mem. Sloan-Kettering Inst. for Cancer Research, 1980—; adj. prof. Rockefeller U., 1980—; vis. prof. Coll. de France, Paris, 1988; vis. physician Rockefeller U. Hosp., 1980—; instr. Sch. Medicine, George Washington U., 1954-55; cons. VA Hosp., N.Y.C., 1962-66; assoc. investigator Nat. Inst. Arthritis and Metabolic Diseases, NIH, Bethesda, Md., 1953-55; mem. adv. panel hematology tng. grants program NIH, 1969-73, chmn. hematology tng. grants program, 1971-73; vis. scientist Lab. Cellular Biochemistry, Pasteur Inst., 1961-62; vis. prof. Chemica Biologica, U. Genoa, Italy, 1963; mem. adv. panel on developmental biology NSF, 1964-67; mem. Delos Conf., Athens, Greece, 1971, 72; mem. founding com. Radiation Effects Research Found., Japan, 1975; mem. Pres.'s Biomed. Research Panel, 1975-76, Pres.'s Cancer Panel, 1976-79, Pres.'s Commn. on Accident at Three Mile Island, 1979; chmn. exec. com. div. med. scis. Nat. Acad. Scis.-NRC, 1973-76; ad hoc adviser White House Conf. on Aging, 1981; council div. cancer treatment Nat. Cancer Inst., 1980-83; adviser Leopold Schepp Found.; dir. Pfizer, Inc., Life Techs., Inc., Dreyfus Mut. Funds. Editor: Monographs in Human Biology, 1963; Contbr. over 300 articles to profl. jours.; mem. editorial bd.: Blood, 1964-71, assoc. editor, 1976-77, editor-in-chief, 1978-82; editor-in-chief Jour. Clin. Investigation, 1967-72. Trustee St. Luke's Hosp., 1970-80, Roosevelt Hosp., 1970-80, Presbyn. Hosp., 1972-80; mem. jury Albert Lasker Awards, 1974-82; bd. dirs. Pub. Health Research Inst., N.Y.C., 1971-74; bd. govs. Weizmann Inst., 1976—; bd. dirs. Revson Found., 1976—; bd. sci. counselors, div. cancer treatment Nat. Cancer Inst., 1980-83; mem. council div. biol. scis. and Pritzker Sch. Medicine, U. Chgo.; mem. tech. bd. Milbank Meml. Fund, 1978-85 ; trustee Metpath Inst. Med. Edn., 1977-79. Recipient Charles Janeway prize Columbia, 1949, Joseph Mather Smith prize, 1959, Stevens Triennial prize, 1960, Swiss-Am. Found. award in med. research, 1965, Columbia U. Coll. Physicians and Surgeons Disting. Service medal, 1980; Found. for Promotion of Cancer Research, Japan Medal, 1984; Commonwealth Fund fellow, 1961-62, Ayrey fellow postgrad. med. sch. U. London, 1985, Centenary Medal, Institut Pasteur, 1987. Fellow Am. Acad. Arts and Scis., AAAS; mem. Inst. Medicine (mem. council 1973-76), Nat. Acad. Scis. (chmn. sect. med. genetics, hematology and oncology 1980-83, chmn. Acad. Forum Adv. Com. 1980-81, mem. council 1984-87), Red Cell Club (past chmn.), Am. Fedn. Clin. Research (past councillor Eastern dist.), Am. Soc. Clin. Investigation (pres. 1972-73), Am. Soc. Biol. Chemists, Am. Soc. Human Genetics (past mem. program com.), Am. Assn. Cancer Research, ACP, Am. Soc. Cell Biology, Am. Soc. Hematology (pres.-elect 1983, pres. 1984), Assn. Am. Physicians, Enzyme Club, Harvey Soc. (pres. 1973-74), Internat. Soc. Developmental Biologists, Interurban Clin. Club, Soc. for Study Devel. and Growth,. Home: Beach Hill Rd Bridgewater CT 06752 Office: Meml Sloan-Kettering Cancer Ctr 1275 York Ave New York NY 10021

MARKS, RICHARD SAMUEL, lawyer, real estate development executive; b. Milw., May 8, 1937; s. Lewis and Ruth Francis (Brindis) M.; m. Julia F. Newman, Aug. 7, 1962; children: Joseph, Richard, Steven. B.A., U. Wis., 1960, D. Jud. Sci., 1963. Bar: Wis. 1963; cert. property mgr. Prin. Hillmark Corp., Madison, Wis., 1960—, chief exec. officer, 1979—, chmn. bd., 1979—; trustee State Wis. Bond Bd., Madison, 1975-76; chmn. State Wis. Investment Bd., Madison, 1976-78. Chmn. State Wis. Small Cities Israel Bonds., Madison, 1975-76; bd. dirs. Metro YMCA, Madison, 1974-76, Madison Jewish Fedn., 1974-77, Atlanta Civic Opera Assn., 1983, 20th Century Art Assn. of High Mus., 1983. Mem. Young Pres.'s Orgn., World Bus. Council. Clubs: Masons, Shriners, Elks. Home: 6040 Winterthur Dr Atlanta GA 30328 Office: 1820 The Exchange #550 Atlanta GA 30339

MARKUN, FRANK O., food services executive; b. Des Moines, Oct. 22, 1947; s. Frank Oliver and Grace Ellen (Marshall) M.; m. Milagros Macuja, Dec. 29, 1971; children—Michael Allen, Jeffrey Patrick. B.S., Iowa State U., 1969; M.B.A., Eastern Mich. U., 1974. Registered dietitian; disting. health care foodservice adminstr. Dietitian II, South Quadrangle, U. Mich., Ann Arbor, 1969-71, food service supr. II Bursley Hall, 1971-77, food service mgr. II, Residential Coll., 1977-80, West Quadrangle Complex, 1980-81; dir. food services Cabell Huntington Hosp. (W.Va.), 1981—. Contbr. articles to profl. jours. Recipient various prizes for recipes; Statler Found. scholar, 1965; Mem. Am. Dietetic Assn., W.Va. Dietetic Assn. (pres. 1984-85; Outstanding W.Va. dietitian 1983-84), W.Va.-Ohio-Ky. Dist. Dietetic Assn. (chmn. council on practice 1981, pres. 1982-83, chmn. nominating com. 1984-85, adv. com. 1985-88), Am. Soc. Hosp. Food Service Adminstrs. (pres. W.Va. chpt. 1985-86, nat. nominating com. 1988—). Republican. Roman Catholic. Home: 54 Twin View Ln RR 4 Huntington WV 25704 Office: Cabell Huntington Hosp 1340 Hal Greer Blvd Huntington WV 25701

MARKUS, GYORGY, philosopher, educator; b. Budapest, Hungary, Apr. 13, 1934; arrived in Australia, 1978.; s. Nandor and Friderica (Roth) M.; m. Maria Renata Otto, July 9, 1956; children: Gyorgy Jr., Andras. Grad. in Philosophy, Lomonosow U., Moscow, 1957. Lectr. to sr. lectr. philosophy Eotvos U., Budapest, 1957-65; research fellow Inst. Philosophy, Budapest, 1958-73; vis. prof. Inst. Philosophy Freie U., Berlin, 1977-78; reader Dept. Gen. Philosophy, U. Sydney, Australia, 1978—. Author: Marxism and Anthropology, 1978, (with others) Lukacs Revalued, 1983, (with others) Dictatorship Over Needs, 1983, Language and Production, 1986; contbr. articles to profl. jours. Ford Found. post-doctoral fellow, 1957-58. Home: 55 Abercrombie St, Chippendale, New South Wales 2008, Australia Office: U Sydney, Dept Gen Philosophy, Sydney, New South Wales 2006, Australia

MARKUS, MANFRED WILHELM, English language and literature educator; b. Hagen, Westphalia, Fed. Republic Germany, Feb. 15, 1941; arrived in Austria, 1981; s. Erich and Lilly (Heckeler) M.; m. Ingrid Müller, Apr. 19, 1968; children: Dirk, Ronald. Grad., U. Göttingen, Fed. Republic Germany, 1967; PhD, U. Regensburg, Fed. Republic Germany, 1970, habilitation, 1980. Asst. prof. U. Regensburg, 1968-81; ordinary prof. U. Innsbruck, Austria, 1981—, dir. Dept. English, 1985—; vis. prof. U. Mass., Amherst, 1974-75. Author: Moderne Erzählperspektive in den Werken des Gawain-Autors, 1977, Tempus und Aspekt, 1977, Point of View im Erzähltext; editor 2 books; contbr. articles to profl. jours. Mem. Anglistenverband, Mediävistenverband, Soc. Linguistica Europea. Home: Knappenweg 9, A-6020 Innsbruck Austria Office: U Innsbruck, Innrain 52, A-6020 Innsbruck Austria

MARKWARDT, JOHN JAMES, lawyer; b. Phila., Jan. 12, 1950; s. John Frederick and Rita Mary (Lafferty) M.; m. Joann Marie Olivo, Aug. 16, 1969; 1 child, Kelly Ann. Student, Rutgers U., 1968-71; JD cum laude, Albany Law Sch., 1974. Bar: N.Y. 1975, U.S. Dist. Ct. (no. dist.) N.Y. 1975, N.J. 1976, U.S. Dist. Ct. N.J. 1976, Pa. 1977, U.S. Supreme Ct. 1978, U.S. Dist. Ct. (ea. dist.) Pa. 1978, U.S. Ct. Appeals (3d cir.) 1981, Fla. 1984. Staff atty. N.Y. State Law Revision Commn., Albany, 1974-75; assoc. Richard M. Meyers, Albany, 1975-76; sole practice Blackwood, N.J., 1976-82; ptnr. Horn, Kaplan, Goldberg, Gorny & Daniels, Atlantic City, 1982—; legis. aide N.J. State Senate, Trenton, 1976. Mem. Gloucester Twp. Council, Camden County, N.J., 1979-81; mem. Gloucester Twp. Rent Control Bd., 1979-81, solicitor, 1977; mem. Gloucester Twp. Planning Bd., 1980. Recipient Forneron Career award Highland Regional High Sch., 1981. Mem. N.J. State Bar Assn., Atlantic County Bar Assn. Roman Catholic. Home: 850 2nd St Ocean City NJ 08226 Office: Horn Kaplan Goldberg Gorny & Daniels 1300 Atlantic Ave Atlantic City NJ 08401

MARKWARDT, L(ORRAINE) J(OSEPH), consulting engineer; b. Lansing, Iowa, Nov. 26, 1889; s. Joseph F. and Louisa (Besch) M.; B.S., U. Wis., 1912, C.E., 1922; m. Lula May Starks, June 21, 1917 (dec. 1974). Asst. city engr., Madison, Wis., 1912; instr. drawing, descriptive geometry, engring. coll. U. Wis., 1915-17; research engr. U.S. Forest Products Lab., Madison, 1912-14, asst. chief div. timber mechanics, 1917-39, chief, 1939-43, asst. dir., 1943-59, cons. engr., 1959—. Del. timber research conf. Internat. Union Forest Research Orgns., Princes Risborough, Eng., 1937, 39; U.S. del. internat. confs. mech. wood tech. FAO, UN, Geneva, Switzerland, 1948, 49, Igls, Austria, 1951, Paris, France, 1954, Madrid, , 1958; chmn. program com. Forest Products sect. 5th World Forestry Congress, 1958-59; mem. subcom. wood and plastics for aircraft NACA, 1944-47, aircraft structural materials, 1947-49. Dep. mem. materials com. Resources and Devel. Bd., Dept. Def., 1952-53; mem. materials adv. bd. and bldg. research adv. bd. Nat. Acad. Scis., NRC, 1954-59. Recipient hon. citation for engring. achievement U. Wis., 1950, Superior Service award USDA 1957; Hitchcock award for outstanding research accomplishments in wood industry Hitchcock Pub. Co. and Forest Products Research Soc., 1963; Friend of Edn. award Allamakee Sch. Dist., 1982; Disting. Contbr. to Wood Engring. and Research award U.S. Forest Service, 1985; Hist. Preservation award State Hist. Soc. Wis., 1985; ann. L.J. Markwardt Wood Engring. Research award established by ASTM and Forest Products Research Soc., 1970; awards given in his name to sr. boy and girl for outstanding merit Kee High Sch., Lansing, 1982—. Mem. ASTM (Edgar Marburg lectr. award 1943, Walter C. Voss award 1965, dir. 1944-54, v.p. 1948-50, pres. 1950-51, chmn. com. wood 1948-64; hon.), Am. Standards Assn. (chmn. sect. com. methods testing wood, 1922—, sect. com. safety code constrn., care, use of ladders 1950—, mem. constrn. standards bd., 1943—, sect. com. specifications wood poles, 1946—), Am. Wood Preservers Assn., Am. Ry. Engring. Assn. (com. wood bridges and trestles since 1944), ASCE, Nat. Soc. Profl. Engrs., Soc. Am. Foresters, AAAS, Forest Products Research Soc., Internat. Wood Research Soc. (v.p.), Am. Inst. Timber Constrn. (chmn. tech. rev. bd. 1960-75, profl. life mem.), Sigma Xi, Tau Beta Pi, Chi Epsilon. Presbyn. Mason, Rotarian (pres. Madison 1950-51). Club: Black Hawk Country (Madison). Author: Descriptive Geometry (with Millar and Maclin), 1919, also subsequent revisions; The Mosquito Bomber, 1986; The Blackhawk Country Club and its Historic Indian Heritage, 1976; sect. on Blackhawk Indian Mounds, Nat. Registry of Historic Places, 1979;The Mosquito Bomber, 1986; sects. on timber several engring. handbooks; govt. bulls., tech., sci. papers. Address: 12 Lathrop St Madison WI 53705

MARKWELL, DICK R(OBERT), retired chemist; b. Muskogee, Okla., Feb. 20, 1925; s. Alex J. and May (Albright) M.; m. Virginia Ann Gass, Aug. 28, 1949; children—Steven R., Scot L., Eric R., Cheryl F. B.S., Wichita State U., 1948, M.S., 1950; Ph.D., U. Wis., 1956. Commd. 2d lt. U.S. Army, 1951, ret. lt. col., 1967, with Office Chief Research and Devel.; asso. prof. chemistry San Antonio Coll., 1967-74; chemist Corpus Christi Dept. Health, 1975-77; supr. chemistry sect. lab. div. San Antonio Met. Health Dist., 1977-87. Served with USMC, 1942-45. Mem. Am. Chem. Soc. Home: PO Box 8274 San Antonio TX 78208

MARLAND, ALKIS JOSEPH, leasing company executive, computer science educator, financial planner; b. Athens, Greece, Mar. 8, 1943; came to U.S., 1961, naturalized, 1974; s. Basil and Maria (Pervanides) Mouradoglou; m. Anita Louise Malone, Dec. 19, 1970; children: Andrea, Alyssa. BS, Southwestern U., Tex., 1963; MA, U. Tex., Austin, 1967; MS in Engring. Adminstrn., So. Meth. U., 1971. Cert. data processing; chartered fin. cons.; cert. fin. planner. With Sun Co., Richardson, Tex., 1968-71, Phila., 1971-76, mgr. planning and acquisitions Sun Info. Services subs. Sun Co., Dallas, 1976-78, v.p. Helios Capital Corp. subs. Sun Co., Radnor, Pa., 1978-83; pres. ALKAN Leasing Corp., Wayne, Pa., 1983—; prof. dept. computer sci. and bus. adminstrn. Eastern Coll., St. Davids, Pa., 1985-87; prof. math. Villanova (Pa.) U., 1987—. Bd. dirs. Radnor Twp. Sch. Dist., 1987—. Mem. Assn. Computing Machinery, IEEE, Internat. Assn. Fin. Planners, Am. Soc. CLU & ChFC, Am. Assn. Equipment Lessors, Inst. Cert. Fin. Planners, Fin. Analysts Phila., Phila. Fin. Assn., World Affairs Council Phila. Republican. Lodges: Rotary (Wayne), Masons. Home: 736 Brooke Rd Wayne PA 19087 Office: PO Box 153 Radnor PA 19087

MARLAND, DAVID, research manager; b. Oldham, Eng., Nov. 12, 1944; s. Harry and Marry Ann (Rogers) M.; m. Judith Sylvia Bowden, June 4, 1945; children: Louise Anne, Gareth Andre. BSc. with Honors, U. Coll. North Wales, 1966; design engr., Ferranti Ltd., Manchester, Eng., 1966-70. Engr. Cern., Geneva, 1970-79; design mgr. Systime Ltd., Leeds, Eng., 1979-84; mgr. research and devel. Tunstall Telecom Ltd., Whitley Bridge, Eng., 1985—. Office: Tunstall Telecom Ltd, Whitley Lodge, Whitley Bridge DN14 0JT, England

MARLAS, JAMES CONSTANTINE, holding company executive; b. Chgo., Aug. 22, 1937; s. Constantine J. and Helen (Cotsirilos) M.; m. Kendra S. Graham, 1968 (div. 1971); m. Glenn Close, 1984 (div. 1987). A.B. cum laude, Harvard U., 1959; M.A. in Jurisprudence, Oxford (Eng.) U., 1961; J.D., U. Chgo., 1963. Bar: Ill. 1963, N.Y. 1966. Assoc. firm Baker & McKenzie, London and N.Y.C., 1963-66; exec. v.p. South East Commodity Corp., N.Y.C., 1967-68; chmn. bd. Union Capital Corp., N.Y.C., 1968—; vice chmn. bd. Mickelberry's Food Products Co., N.Y.C., 1970-71; pres., dir. Mickelberry Corp., N.Y.C., 1972—; chief exec. officer Mickelberry Corp., 1973—, chmn. bd., 1984—; chmn. bd., chief exec. officer Newcourt Industries, Inc., 1976—; chmn. bd. Bowmar Instrument Corp., 1976-83, chmn. exec. com., 1983—; dir. mem. Empire Blue Cross and Blue Shield Greater N.Y. Co-editor: Univ. Chgo. Law Rev, 1962-63; Contbr. articles to profl. jours. Bd. dirs. N.Y.C. Opera, Commanderie de Bordeaux. Mem. Am. Fgn. Law Assn., Young Pres.'s Orgn. Clubs: Boodle's (London); Racquet and Tennis (N.Y.C.). Office: Mickelberry Corp 405 Park Ave New York NY 10022

MARLER, KERRY FRANCIS, management consulting executive; b. Baton Rouge, Mar. 6, 1948; s. Derrille Edgar and Lynn Joyce (Webre) M.; m. Peggy Elizabeth Duchamp, Mar. 25, 1970; children: Sean Patrick, Chad Michael. BS, U. Southwestern La., 1970; MBA, U. New Orleans, 1979. CPA, La. Exec. v.p., chief operating officer Enertech, Inc., Belle Chase, La., 1979-82; pres., chief exec. officer, dir. Apache Marine Cleaning & Coating, Inc., Morgan City, La., 1980-82; v.p. Dolphin Workboats, Inc., Morgan City, 1983-84; chmn., pres., chief exec. officer Coral Marine Services, Inc., Morgan City, 1984-85; chmn., pres., chief exec. officer Kerry F. Marler & Assocs., Inc., Kenner, La., 1982—, also bd. dirs.; exec. v.p., chief operating officer Assix Internat., Inc., Tampa, 1988—. Instr. ARC, New Orleans, 1981—, adv. com. 1984, chmn. publicity com., 1984; instr. underwater activities YMCA, Atlanta, 1981—. Fellow Middle East Soc. Associated Accts.; mem. Am. Inst. CPA's, La. Soc. CPA's, Internat. Arabian Horse Assn. Republican. Roman Catholic. Club: Petroleum (Morgan City). Home: 143 Bunting Ln Land O' Lakes FL 34639 Office: 505 E Jackson St Suite 220 Tampa FL 33602

MARLETT, DE OTIS LORING, retired management consultant; b. Indpls., Apr. 19, 1911; s. Peter Loring and Edna Grace (Lombard) M.; m. Ruth Irene Pillar, Apr. 10, 1932 (dec. Feb. 1969); children: De Otis Neal, Marilynn Ruth; m. Marie Manning Ostrander, May 1, 1970 (dec. Apr. 1982); m. Peggie P. Whittlesey, Jan. 15, 1983. B.A., M.A., U. Wis., 1934; postgrad., Northwestern U., (part time), 1934-39, Harvard U.; postgrad. (Littauer fellow in econs. and govt.), 1946-47. C.P.A., Wis., 1935. Staff mem. Ill. Commerce Commn., 1934-39; lectr. in econs. and pub. utilities Northwestern U., (part time), 1936-39; staff mem. Bonneville Power Adminstrn., U.S. Dept. Interior, 1939-45, asst. adminstr., 1945-52; acting adminstr. Def. Electric Power Adminstrn., 1950-51; asst. to v.p., gen. mgr. Dicalite and Perlite divs. Gt. Lakes Carbon Corp., 1952-53, v.p., also gen. mgr. Dicalite, Perlite, Mining and Minerals divs., 1953-62, v.p. property investment dept., 1962-81; pres., chief exec. officer Great Lakes Properties, Inc., 1981-83, ret., 1983—; pres., dir. Rancho Palos Verdes Corp., G.L.C. Bldg. Corp., Del Amo Energy Co., Torrance Energy Co., Calif. Phosphate Corp. Contbr. articles and reports on public utility regulation, operation and mgmt. to profl. jours. Past bd. dirs. United Cerebral Palsy Assn. Los Angeles County; bd. dirs., past co-chmn. So. Calif. region NCCJ, mem. nat. trustee, mem. nat. exec. bd., nat. protestant co-chmn., 1987; past mem. Orthopaedic Hosp. Adv. Council; past trustee City of Hope; past pres., dir. Los Angeles area council, past chmn. relationships com., past pres. Sunshine area, pres. Western region Boy Scouts Am., 1978-81, nat. exec. bd., 1978—, past mem. nat. exec. com., past chmn. properties com., chmn. logistics for world jamboree delegation to Australia, 1987-88; past trustee Nat. Scouting Mus.; mem. internat. com. Baden Powell fellow World Scouting Found., 1984; past mem. Western Govs. Mining Adv. Council, Calif. State Mining Bd.; bd. govs. Western div. Am. Mining Congress, chmn., 1962-63; incorporator, past pres., bd. dirs. Torrance Meml. Hosp. Med. Center Health Care Found.; region III dir., mem. corp. adminstrn. and fin. com., Los Angeles United Way. Recipient Disting. Service medal U.S. Dept. Interior, 1952; named knight Order of Crown Belgium; commd. Ky. Col.; recipient Silver Beaver, Silver Antelope, Silver Buffalo awards Boy Scouts Am., 1984. Mem. Fin. Execs. Inst., Los Angeles World Affairs Council, Wis. Alumni Assn., Perlit Inst. (past pres., dir.), AIME, Am. Inst. CPA's, Los Angeles C. of C. (past dir., chmn. mining com.), Mining Assn. So. Calif. (past pres., dir.), Calif. Mine Operators Assn. (past dir.), Bldg. Industry Assn. So. Calif., Town Hall, Phi Kappa Phi, Beta Gamma Sigma, Phi Beta Kappa, Beta Alpha Psi, Lambda Alpha Internat. Democrat. Clubs: Calif., Portuguese Bend (past pres.). Lodge: Rotary. Home: 32759 Seagate Dr Apt 104 Rancho Palos Verdes CA 90274

MARLOW, AUDREY SWANSON, artist, designer; b. N.Y.C., Mar. 3, 1929; d. Sven and Rita (Porter) Swanson; student (scholarships) Art Students League, 1950-55; spl. courses SUNY (Stony Brook), L'Alliance Française m. Roy Marlow, Nov. 30, 1968. With Cohn-Hall-Marx Textile Studio, 1961-65, R.S. Assos. Textile Studio, 1965-73; freelance designer, illustrator Prince Matchabelli, Lester Harrison Agy., J. Walter Thompson Agy., 1957-78; portrait and fine artist, Wading River, N.Y., 1973—; instr. Phoenix Sch. Design (N.Y.C.); exhibits include: Nat. Arts Club, NAD, Parish Art Mus., South Hampton, N.Y., Guild Hall, East Hampton, N.Y., Portraits Inc., Lincoln Ctr., Chung-Cheng Art Gallery, St. John's U., Mystic (Conn.) Art Assn., Harbour Gallery, St. Thomas, V.I. Trustee, Middle Island Public Library, 1972-76. Recipient John W. Alexander medal, 1976, award Council on Arts, 1978, award of excellence Cork Gallery, Lincoln Center, 1982; Grumbacher Bronze medal, 1983; Grumbacher Silver medal 1986; Best in Show award N.Y. Arts Council, 1986. Mem. Pastel Soc. Am. (award 1977, 80), Am. Artists Profl. League (2 1st prize awards), Hudson Valley Art Assn. (award), Knickerbocker Artists (2 awards), Catharine Lorillard Wolfe Art Club (award 1982), Salmagundi Club (5 awards), Nat. League Am. Pen Women (Gold award, Gold medal of Honor). Works represented at N.Y. U., pvt. collections; one-woman show Salmagundi Club, 1982. Home: 76 Northside Rd Wading River NY 11792

MARLOW, DAVID ZACHARY, lawyer; b. N.Y.C., Sept. 21, 1943; m. Ann; children—Marc Stephen, Ian Michael. B.A., L.I. U., 1965; J.D., Bklyn. Law Sch., 1968. Bar: N.Y. 1969, U.S. Dist. Cts. (no., so., ea. and we. dists.) N.Y. 1972, U.S. Tax. Ct. 1972, U.S. Ct. Appeals (2d cir.) 1972, U.S. Supreme Ct. 1972. Tax atty. Prentice Hall, Inc., Englewood Cliffs, N.J., 1970-71; counsel Am. Internat. Group Inc., N.Y.C., 1971-76; gen. counsel Midland Ins. Group Cos., N.Y.C., 1976-79; sr. ptnr. Bennet, Ayervais & Bertrand, P.C., N.Y.C., 1979—; adj. asst. prof. Coll. of Ins., N.Y.C.; arbitrator Am. Arbitration Assn., N.Y. Ins. Exchange. Mem. N.Y. State Bar Assn., ABA, Fedn. Ins. Counsel, Phi Delta Phi. Office: Bennet Ayervais & Bertrand PC 30 Vesey St Suite 1200 New York NY 10007

MARLOW, ROBERT ALLEN, family physician; b. Brighton, Colo., Mar. 13, 1948; s. Herbert Allen and Ima Jean (Campbell) M.; B.A. in Math. and Gen. Studies cum laude, U. Colo., 1970, M.D. magna cum laude, 1974; m. Iva Loraine Warren, Aug. 14, 1971; children—Courtney Paige, Kimberly Nicole. Intern, U. Colo. Med. Center, Denver, 1974-75, resident in family practice, 1974-77, asst. prof. family medicine and preventive medicine, 1977-78; practice medicine specializing in family practice, Sterling, Colo., 1978-84; partner N.E. Colo. Family Medicine Assos., P.C., 1978-84; asst. clin. prof. family medicine and preventive medicine U. Colo. Health Scis. Ctr., 1978-84; asst. dir. family practice residency program Scottsdale Meml. Hosp. Recipient Joseph and Regina Glaser Med. Student Research award U. Colo. Med. Sch., 1974; Boetteher Found. scholar, 1966-70. Fellow Am. Acad. Family Physicians; mem. Ariz. Acad. Family Physicians, Ariz. Med. Soc., Christian Med. Soc. Phi Beta Kappa, Alpha Omega Alpha. Republican. Baptist. Home: 1976 E Manhatton Dr Tempe AZ 85282 Office: Scottsdale Meml Hosp Family Practice Ctr 7301 E 4th St Suite 22 Scottsdale AZ 85251

MARMET, GOTTLIEB JOHN, lawyer; b. Chgo., Mar. 24, 1946; s. Gottlieb John and Margaret Ann (Saylor) M.; m. Jane Marie Borkowski, Sept. 12, 1970; children: Gottlieb John, Philip Stanley, Thomas Jacob. BS with distinction in Acctg., San Diego State U., 1967; JD, Northwestern U., 1970. Bar: Ill. 1970, U.S. Dist. Ct. (no. dist.) Ill. 1970, U.S. Tax Ct. 1981; CPA, Calif., Ill., Minn. Tax acct. Touche Ross & Co., Chgo., 1970-75; assoc. atty. Howington, Elworth, Osswald & Hough, Chgo., 1975-79; tax mgr. Peat, Marwick, Mitchell & Co., Mpls., 1979-81; assoc. Shefsky, Saitlin & Froelich, Ltd., Chgo., 1981-83; prin. G. John Marmet, Glenview, Ill., 1983—; lectr. corp. law William Rainey Harper Coll., Arlington Heights, Ill., 1984; instr. Ill. Soc. CPA's, 1976, 77, Minn. Soc. CPA's, 1980. Active Northeast Ill. Council Boy Scouts Am., 1984—, dist. chmn. Skokie Valley, 1988. Recipient Hon. Mention, Chgo. Bar Assn. Art Show, 1972. Mem. ABA (fed. tax com.) Ill. Bar Assn., Chgo. Bar Assn., Am. Inst. Cert. Pub. Accts., Beta Gamma Sigma, Beta Alpha Psi, Phi Alpha Delta. Lodge: Rotary (Service Above Self award 1985-86, community service dir. 1988—). Author: Farm Corporations and Their Income Tax Treatment, 1970, 1974; contbr. articles to jours., publs. Office: 950 Milwaukee Ave Suite 318 Glenview IL 60025

MARMO, EMILIO, pharmacologist; b. Anzio, Italy, Jan. 11, 1933; s. Achille and Giovanna (Ziccardi) M.; m. Gerta Osswald; children: Giovanna, Andrea, Caterina. Degree in medicine with honors, 1957. Cert. univ. tchr. in pharmacology, 1963, univ. tchr. in Chemotherapy, 1966. Prof. U. Naples, 1965-75, full prof., 1975—, head clin. pharmacology services, 1978, head Sch. of Specialization in Pharmacology the 1st Faculty Medicine, 1980, head Inst. Pharmacology and Toxicology 1st Faculty Medicine, 1981, coordinator Doctorate of Research in Pharmacology, Toxicology and Chemotherapy 2d, 3d, 4th cycle, 1985—. Office: U Naples Inst Pharmacology & Toxicology, Via S Andrea delle Dame 8, 80138 Naples Italy

MARMON, DENNIS CARL, accountant, auditor; b. Kew Gardens, N.Y., Dec. 20, 1949; s. Carmine Alphose and Marie (Tersigni) M.; m. Phyllis Theresa Marmon, May 24, 1981; 1 child, Karla Denise Marmon; student SUNY, Farmingdale, 1968-70; A.A.S. cum laude, Nassau Community Coll., 1971; B.B.A., Adelphi U., 1973. Acct., Electronic Systems div. Gen. Instruments Corp., Hicksville, N.Y., 1973-75, Exxon Internat., Exxon Corp., N.Y.C., 1975-76; acct./auditor N.Y. State Dept. Taxation and Fin., Mineola, 1976-85. Mem. Inst. Mgmt. Acctg. (profl.), Assn. Spl. Tax Auditors N.Y. State. Republican. Roman Catholic. Club: Rockville Centre Advanced Intermediates Tennis League (N.Y.); Beverly Hills. Lodge: Lions. Home and Office: 3288 N Maidencane Dr Beverly Hills FL 32665

MARON, MILFORD ALVIN, judge; b. Chgo., Jan. 21, 1926; s. Martin and Anna (Newman) M.; BA cum laude, U. So. Calif., 1949, MA, 1953, LLB, 1954, LLM, 1958; m. Esther Kass, Dec. 24, 1966; childrenchildren: Steven, Dean, Melissa, Adam. Bar: Calif. 1955. Dep. commr. corps. Calif. Div. Corps., Los Angeles, 1955-57; trial counsel SEC, Los Angeles, 1957-61, Calif. Div. Labor Law Enforcement, 1961-63; adminstrv. law judge Calif. Office Adminstrv. Hearings, Los Angeles, 1963-88, adminstrv. law judge supvr., 1988—. Served with AUS, 1944-46. Mem. Bar Assn. Calif. Democrat. Jewish. Office: Calif Office Adminstrv Hearings 314 W 1st St Los Angeles CA 90012

MARONDE, ROBERT FRANCIS, internist, clinical pharmacologist, educator; b. Monterey Park, Calif., Jan. 13, 1920; s. John August and Emma Florence (Palmer) M.; m. Yolanda Cerda, Apr. 15, 1970; children—Robert George, Donna F. Maronde Varnau, James Augustus, Craig DeWald. B.A., U. So. Calif., 1941, M.D., 1944. Diplomate: Am. Bd. Internal Medicine. Intern Los Angeles County-U. So. Calif. Med. Center, 1943-44, resident, 1944-45, 47-48; asst. prof. physiology U. So. Calif., Los Angeles, 1948-49; asst. clin. prof. medicine U. So. Calif., 1949-60, asso. clin. prof. medicine, 1960-65, asso. prof. medicine and pharmacology, 1965-67, prof., 1968—; cons. FDA, 1973. Served to lt. (j.g.) USNR, 1945-47. Fellow ACP; mem. Am. Soc. Clin. Pharmacology and Therapeutics, Alpha Omega Alpha. Home: 785 Ridgecrest St Monterey Park CA 91754 Office: U So Calif 2025 Zonal Ave Los Angeles CA 90033

MAROUF, TAHA MUHYIDDIN, Iraqi government official; b. Sulaimaniyah, Iraq, 1924; s. Muhyiddin and Fatima M. Ed., Coll. Law U. Baghdad, Iraq. Practiced la; with Iraqi Diplomatic Service, 1949; minister state Iraq, Baghdad, 1968-70, minister works and housing, 1968, ambassador to Italy, non-resident ambassador to Malta and Albania, 1970-74, v.p., 1974—. Address: Office Vice Pres Republic, Nat Assembly Bldg, Baghdad Iraq *

MARPLE, WESLEY WOOLEY, JR., finance educator; b. Trenton, N.J., Feb. 22, 1932; s. Wesley W. and Mildred (Brubaker) M.; m. Betty Louise Nitchie, Sept. 28, 1957; children—Caroline L., Edward W., Douglas A. AB, Princeton U., 1954; MBA, Harvard U., 1956, DBA, 1967. Adminstrv. asst. to dean Harvard U. Grad. Sch. Bus., Boston, 1956-59, asst. dean, 1959-62; assoc. prof. fin. Northeastern U., Boston, 1966-70, prof. fin., 1970—; vis. prof. bus. adminstrn. Harvard U., 1980-81; trustee Eastern Utilities Assocs., Boston, 1976—; trustee various Scudder Funds, Boston, 1982—; cons. IBM, 1974—, Arthur D. Little Inc., 1964—. Contbr. articles in fin. mgmt. Mem. Commonwealth of Mass. Fin. Adv. Bd., Boston, 1977—, chmn., 1987—; treas. First Parish in Weston (Mass.), 1983—. Served to capt. U.S. Army, 1957. Mem. Fin. Execs. Inst., Fin. Mgmt. Assn., Am. Fin. Assn. Unitarian. Clubs: Harvard, Weston Golf. Office: Northeastern U 413 Hayden Hall Boston MA 02115

MARQUARDT, DONALD WESLEY, statistician, researcher; b. N.Y.C., Mar. 13, 1929; s. Kurt C. and Amelia P. (Moller) M; m. Margaret E. Rittershaus, Sept. 13, 1952; children—Paul E. (dec.), Joan N. A.B., Columbia U., 1950; M.A., U. Del., 1956. Research engr./mathematician E.I. du Pont de Nemours & Co., Inc., Wilmington, Del., 1953-57, research project engr./sr. mathematician, 1957-64, cons. supr., 1964-72, cons. mgr. engring. dept., 1972—; mem. NRC eval. panel for applied math. for Nat. Bur. Standards, 1981-84; mem. Am. Nat. Standards Inst. com. on quality assurance, vice chmn., 1983, chmn., 1984, dir.-at-large, 1985—; rep. to Internat. Standards Orgn. tech. coms. on statis. methods and quality assurance, chmn. coordinating groups; adj. prof. U. Del., 1983—. Mem. editorial bd. Communications in Stats.; assoc. editor: Jour. Bus. and Econ. Stats., 1982-85; contbr. articles to profl. jours. Served with U.S. Army, 1951-52. Fellow Am. Statis. Assn. (pres. 1986), AAAS, Am. Soc. for Quality Control (Youden prize 1974, Shewell prize 1984, Shewhart Medalist 1986); mem. Assn. for Computing Machinery, Soc. for Indsl. and Applied Math., Am. Inst. Chem. Engrs., Sigma Xi. Presbyterian. Research on quality mgmt. systems tech., non-linear estimation, analysis of unequally-spaced time series. Home: 1415 Athens Rd Wilmington DE 19803 Office: EI du Pont de Nemours & Co Inc Engring Dept Wilmington DE 19898

MARQUARDT, JOHN E., business consultant; b. Bridgeport, Conn., 1929. BA in Journalism, U. Ga., 1952. Radio news editor 1952-62; then county and state legislator State of N.Y., 1962-70; head Dept. of Commerce State of N.Y., Tokyo, 1973-85; dir. Internat. Execs. Assn., N.Y.C., 1970-73; owner Japan-Am. Coop. Services, Ltd., Tokyo, 1985—; internat. liaison Nippon Steel Corp., Tokyo, 1987—. Served with U.S. Army, 1946-48, Japan. Office: Nippon Steel Corp, 6-3 Ote-Machi 2-chome, Chiyoda-ku, Tokyo 100 Japan *

MARQUES, JOSÉ FERREIRA, psychology educator; b. Lisbon, Portugal, Dec. 23, 1936; s. José Marques and Carmelina Borba Costa; m. Olga Maria Henzler, July 25, 1965; children—Jose Frederico, Tomas, Luis. M.A., U. Lisbon, 1959, Ph.D., 1970. Asst. faculty arts U. Lisbon, 1959-60, 63-69, aux. prof., 1970-72, extraordinary prof., 1972-78, prof., 1979-80, prof. psychology Faculty Psychology and Edn., 1981—, pres. bd. dirs., 1981—. Author: Estudos Sobre a WISC, 1969; Guidance and the School Curriculum, 1978; editor: Guidance in 1975 and Its Perspectives on the Near Future, 1976-77; contbr. sci. articles to profl. jours. Mem. Portuguese Psychol. Soc. (pres. 1982-84), Internat. Assn. Ednl. and Vocat. Guidance (bd. dirs. 1979-83, 83-87), Internat. Assn. Applied Psychology (exec. com. 1982-90), Assn. Psychologie Scientifique de Langue Française (exec. com. 1981—). Home: Rua S Felix 37 R/C D, 1200 Lisbon Portugal Office: Faculty of Psychology and Edn, Rua Pinheiro Chagas 17-1, 1000 Lisbon Portugal

MARQUES, WALTER WALDEMAR PEGO, bank executive; b. Cartaxo, Ribatejo, Portugal, May 24, 1936; s. Augusto Rossini and Aida (Pego) M.; m. Cassilda Viana, Sept. 3, 1961; children: Walter Augusto, Pedro Alexandre, Marina Sofia. Licenciatura, I.S.C.E.F., Lisbon, Portugal, 1959. Economist Banco Fomento Nacional, Lisbon, 1959-61; research and mng. cons. CUF, Lisbon, 1961-69; sec. state for econ. and fin. Angola Govt., Luanda, 1970-74; dir. Banco de Portugal, Lisbon, 1974-83, vice gov., 1983—; sec. state for trade Govt. Portugal, Lisbon, 1981, sec. state for treasury, 1981-83; asst. prof. I.S.C.D.F., 1960-69; prof. U. Cath., Lisbon, 1979-81; bd. dirs. Inst. Superior Gestao. Lisbon, 1983-88; cons. Assn. Comercial Lisbon, 1959-60, Govt. Mozambique, Lourenco Marques, 1966; mem. monetary com. EEC Countries for Portugal, 1986-88. Author: Problems of Economics Angola, 1965, Problems of Statistics, 1967, Problems of Econometrics, 1968, Monetary Policy, 1987; contbr. articles on fin. and economy to profl. jours. V.p. Partido Social Democrats, Lisbon, 1983-86. Recipient Honor award Govt. USA, 1982, Honor award Inst. Defesa Nacional, Lisbon, 1984. Fellow Sociedade de Geografia; mem. Asociacao A. Defesa Nacional (chmn. 1985-86). Roman Catholic. Club: Les Ambassadeurs (London). Home: Predios Campave Lote E 6 D, Miraflores, 1495 Lisbon Portugal Office: Banco de Portugal, R do Comercio, Lisbon 148, Portugal

MARQUESS, LAWRENCE WADE, lawyer; b. Bloomington, Ind., Mar. 2, 1950; s. Earl Lawrence and Mary Louise (Coberly) M.; m. Barbara Ann Bailey, June 17, 1978; children: Alexander Lawrence, Michael Wade. B.S. in Elec. Engring., Purdue U., 1973; J.D., W.Va. U., 1977. Bar: W.Va. 1977, U.S. Dist. Ct. (so. dist.) W.Va. 1977, Tex. 1977, U.S. Dist. Ct. (no. dist.) Tex. 1977, Colo. 1980, U.S. Dist. Ct. Colo. 1980, U.S. Ct. Appeals (10th cir.) 1980, U.S. Supreme Ct. 1984, U.S. Dist. Ct. (no. dist.) Ohio 1988. Assoc. Johnson, Bromberg, Leeds & Riggs, Dallas, 1977-79; assoc. Bradley, Campbell & Carney, Golden, Colo., 1979-82, ptnr., 1983-84; assoc. Stettner, Miller & Cohn P.C., Denver, 1984-85, ptnr., 1985-87; of counsel Nelson & Harding, Denver, 1987—. Mem. faculty Am. Law Inst.-ABA Advanced Labor and Employment Law Course, 1986, 87. Mem. ABA (labor and litigation sects.), Colo. Bar Assn. (program com., labor law com.), Denver Bar Assn. (program com., labor law com.), 1st Jud. Dist. Bar Assn. Sierra Club, Nat. Ry. Hist. Soc., ACLU. Democrat. Methodist. Home: 2293 Yellowstone St Golden CO 80401 Office: Nelson & Harding 717 17th St Suite 2600 Denver CO 80202-3357

MARQUET, JEAN FERNAND EDOUARD, physician, educator; b. Berchem, Belgium, Feb. 18, 1928; s. Fernand and Maria (Froidbise) M.; M.D., Catholic U. Louvain (Belgium), 1954, postgrad. in otorhinolaryngology, 1958; m. Viviane Leclef, Apr. 7, 1956; children—Olivier, Pierre, Therese, Frederic. Intern, U. Hosp. Louvain, 1952-54, resident, 1954-57; practice medicine specializing in ear, nose and throat, Antwerp, Belgium, 1957—; chief dept. microsurgery Bunge Inst., Antwerp, 1959-79; chief ear, nose and throat service Med. Inst. St. Augustinus, Wilrijk, Belgium, 1961—; prof., chmn. dept. otorhinolaryngology U. Antwerp, 1972—. Served with mil. health service, 1956-57. Recipient Dr. Joshi award, 1976, Joseph Toynbee Meml. lectr., 1980; George Coates Meml. lectr., 1974. Mem. Internat. Fedn. Otological Soc. (gen. sec. 1981), Hungarian Soc. ORL. Roman Catholic. Developer concept of human transplantation tissue in middle ear surgery artificial bionic ear "Laura", 1987. Home: 91/12 Fruithoflaan, 2600 Berchem Belgium Office: 1 Universiteitsplein, 2610 Wilrijk Belgium

MARQUET, JEAN-FRANCOIS, educator; b. Tours, France, Jan. 27, 1938; s. Daniel and Yvonne (Lageon) M.; m. Danièle Dano, Sept. 9, 1964; children Olivier, Bèrengère, Maxence. Agrégation Philosophy, École Normale Supérieure, St. Cloud, France, 1960; Doctorate, U. Paris, 1971. Researcher Found. Thiers, Paris, 1963-64, Ctr. Nat. Recherche Sci., Paris, 1963-68; prof. history modern philosophy U. Tours, 1968-85; prof. U. Paris-Sorbonne, 1985—. Author: Liberté et Existence, 1973; translator Contribution à L'Histoire de la Philosophie Moderne, 1983; contbr. articles to profl. jours. Decorated Palmes Académiques, 1979. Mem. Conseil Supérieur des Univs., Com. Nat. Recherche Sci. Roman Catholic. Home: 33 Ter Rue Traversière, 37000 Tours France Office: U Paris Sorbonne, 1 Rue Victor Cousin, 75230 Paris Cedex 05, France

MARQUIS, WILLIAM OSCAR, lawyer; b. Fort Wayne, Ind., Feb. 26, 1944; s. William Oscar Marquis and Lenor Mae (Gaffney) Marquis; m. Mary Frances Funderburk, May 11, 1976; children—Lenor, Kathryn, Timothy Patrick, Daniel, Ann. BS, U. Wis.-Madison, 1973; JD, South Tex. Coll. Law, 1977. Bar: Wis. 1979, U.S Dist. Ct. (we. dist.) Wis. 1979, U.S. Dist. Ct. (ea. dist.) Wis. 1982, U.S. Tax Ct. 1983, U.S. Ct. Appeals (7th cir. 1985). With Wis. Dept. Vet. Affairs, Madison, 1977-79; corp. counsel Barron County, Wis., 1979-80; assoc. Riley, Bruns & Riley, Madison, 1980-81; assoc. Jastroch & LaBarge, S.C., Waukesha, Wis., 1981-84; ptnr. Groh, Hackbart, Marquis & Luchini, 1984—. Served to sgt. USAF, 1966-70. Mem. Assn. Trial Lawyers Am., Wis. Trial Lawyers Assn., Waukesha Bar, Milw. Bar, ABA, Wis. Bar, Nat. Assn. Criminal Defense Attys., Wis. Assn. Criminal Defense Attys. Office: 6525 W Bluemound Milwaukee WI 53213

MARR, CARMEL CARRINGTON, state ofcl.; b. Bklyn.; d. William Preston and Gertrude Clementine (Lewis) Carrington; B.A., Hunter Coll., 1945; J.D., Columbia U., 1948; m. Warren Marr, II, Apr. 11, 1948; children—Charles Carrington, Warren Quincy. Admitted to N.Y. State bar, 1948; law asst. firm Dyer & Stevens, N.Y.C., 1948-49; practiced in N.Y.C., 1949-53; adviser legal affairs U.S. mission to UN, N.Y.C., 1953-67, sr. legal officer Office Legal Affairs, UN Secretariat, 1967-68; mem. N.Y. State Human Rights Appeal Bd., 1968-71; mem. N.Y. State Pub. Service Commn., 1971-86; cons. Gas Research Inst., 1987—; lectr. N.Y. Police Acad., 1963-67. Contbr. articles to profl. jours. Mem. N.Y. Gov.'s Com. Edn. and Employment of Women, 1963-64; mem. Nat. Gen. Services Pub. Adv. Council, 1969-71; mem., former chmn. adv. council Gas Research Inst.; mem., chmn. tech. pipeline safety standards com. Dept. Transp., 1979-85; former mem. task force Fed. Energy Regulatory Commn. and EPA to examine PCBs in gas supply system; past chmn. gas com. Nat. Assn. Regulatory Utility Commrs.; past pres. Great Lakes Conf. Pub. Utilities Commrs., mem. exec. com.; mem. UN Devel. Corp., 1969-72; chmn. bd. dirs. Amistad Research Center, New Orleans; bd. dirs. Bklyn. Soc. Prevention Cruelty to Children, Helen Keller Services for Blind, Nat. Arts Stblzn. Fund, Prospect Park Alliance, bd. visitors N.Y. State Sch. Girls, Hudson, 1964-71; mem. exec. bd. Plays for Living, N.Y.C., 1968-75; pres. bd. dirs. Billie Holiday Theatre, 1972-80; mem. nat. adv. council Hampshire Coll. Mem. ABA, Bklyn. Bar Assn., Nat. Assn. Women Lawyers, UN Assn. U.S.A. (nat. council), Phi Beta Kappa, Alpha Chi Alpha. Alpha Kappa Alpha. Republican. Home and Office: 333 New York Ave Brooklyn NY 11213

MARR, WARREN QUINCY, II, former editor; b. Pitts., July 31, 1916; s. Warren Quincy and Cecelia Antoinette (McGee) M.; student Wilberforce U., 1934-37, N.Y. Sch. Interior Decoration, 1948-49, New Sch. for Social Research, 1962-63; m. Carmel Dolores Carrington, Apr. 11, 1948; children—Charles Carrington, Warren Quincy III. Linotype operator St. Louis Argus, 1938-39; with The Plaindealer, Kansas City, Kans., 1939-42, asst. editor, 1941-42; impressario Warren Marr, II, Presents, N.Y.C., 1943-48; decorator James Lassiter & Sons, Madison, N.J., 1948-52; pres. Dilworth-Leslie Sponsors, 1949-66; propr. House of Marr, Inc., Bklyn., 1952-56; plant mgr. Nisonger Corp., New Rochelle, N.Y., 1956-60; sec. Am. Missionary Assn. Coll. Centennials, N.Y.C., 1961-68; pub. relations asst. NAACP, N.Y.C., 1968-74, editor The Crisis mag., 1974-81. Founder, dir. Amistad Awards, 1962—; co-founder Amistad Research Center, Tulane U., 1966; founder, vol. exec. dir. Friends of Amistad, 1971—; pres. art com. Tougaloo Coll., Jackson, Miss., 1966-67, York Coll., N.Y.C., 1984; chmn. bd. dirs. Waltann Sch. Creative Arts, 1963-70; mem. Art Commn. of N.Y.C., 1981—; bd. dirs. Bklyn. Arts and Culture Assn., Community Council of Medgar Evers Coll., Internat. Art of Jazz, Access. Recipient various awards; named hon. citizen of New Orleans, 1979; awarded key to City of Cin., 1983. Editor: (with Maybelle Ward) Minorities and the American Dream: A Bicentennial Perspective, 1976; (with Harry Ploski) The Negro Almanac, 1976; contbr. articles to various jours.

MARRA, FRANK S., manufacturing company executive; b. Clarksburg, W.Va., Nov. 23, 1927; s. Frank and Sarah (Mancina) M.; m. Phyllis Marra, Nov. 10, 1951; children: Lynn, Sarah, Terri Marie, Lisa Ann. B.S.M.E., Lawrence Inst. Tech., 1949; DSc, Ferris State Coll., 1986. Exec. v.p., gen. mgr. DME Co. div. VSI Corp., Madison Heights, Mich., 1963-65, pres., 1965-81; exec. v.p. VSI Corp., Madison Heights, Mich., 1981-82; pres. VSI Corp., Madison Heights, 1982-84; sr. v.p. Fairchild Industres, Germantown, Md., 1982-84; pres. Marra Internat. Assocs., Bloomfield Hills, Mich., 1984—. Contbr. articles to profl. jours. Trustee Mich. Opera Theatre, 1983; mem. Founders Soc., Detroit Inst. Arts, 1970—. Served with U.S. Navy, 1944-45, 50-51. Mem. Soc. Plastics Engrs. (Disting., v.p. 1955-60 cert. of merit, chmn. credentials com. 1965—). Roman Catholic. Office: Marra Internat Assocs 431 W Long Lake Rd Bloomfield Hills MI 48013

MARRA, P(ETER) GERALD, manufacturers representative distributor firm executive; b. Cranbrook, B.C., Can., June 29, 1940; came to U.S., 1964, naturalized, 1973; s. John and Angela Rose Marra; B.Sc., U. B.C., 1963, postgrad., 1963-64; divorced; children: Amber Eileen, Anne-Marie Geraldine. Computer engr. Canadair Ltd., Montreal, Que., 1962-63; research engr. Boeing Corp., Seattle, 1964-68; hardware specialist Computer Sci. Corp., Toronto, Ont., Can., 1969; pres., gen. mgr. D.I.S.C., Seattle, 1970-74; sales mgr. Hayes Tech. Co., Seattle, 1975; owner, pres. Marra & Assocs., Bellevue, Wash., 1976—; cons. small bus., 1970—. Republican party platform chmn. King County, 1976-78, legis. dist. chmn., 1978; pres., dir. fundraising for U. B.C., Friends of U. B.C., 1975—; asst. chmn. archery com. Wash. State Sportsmen's Council, 1980, chmn., 1981-83, chmn. big game com. 1981-83; mem. Mt. Rainier Wildlife Com., 1981—. IBM scholar, 1964. Mem. Can. Soc. of Northwest (exec. com. 1985—), U. B.C. Alumni (pres. Seattle, Pacific N.W. chpt. 1974—). Club: Cedar River Bowman Archery. Home: 1739 172d Pl NE Bellevue WA 98008

MARRIAGE, GEORGE DAVID, flour milling executive; b. Chelmsford, Eng., Aug. 26, 1951; s. Sampson David and Pearl Dorothy Marriage; m. Helen Veronica Jarratt. BSc in Engring., Warwick U., Coventry, Eng., 1973; MSc in Bus., London Bus. Sch., 1978; postgrad. in bus., Chgo. U., 1978. Engr. Metal Box Co. Ltd., London, 1973-76; with Davy Internat., Loughborough, Eng., 1978-80; dir. W. & H. Marriage and Sons. Ltd., Chelmsford, 1980—. Office: W & H Marriage and Sons Ltd, Chelmer Mills, Chelmsford CM1 1PN, England

MARRINER, SIR NEVILLE, orchestra conductor; b. Lincoln, Eng., Apr. 15, 1924; s. Herbert Henry and Ethel May (Roberts) M.; m. Diana Margaret Corbutt, May 10, 1949 (div. 1957); m. Elizabeth Sims, Dec. 20, 1957; children—Susan Frances, Andrew Stephen. Ed., Royal Coll. Music, Paris Conservatory. Prof. Eton Coll., 1947, Royal Coll. Music, 1952. Violinist, Martin String Quartet, 1946-53, Virtuoso String Trio, 1950, Jacobean Ensemble, 1952, London Philharmonia, 1952-56, London Symphony Orch., from 1956, condr., Los Angeles Chamber Orch., 1969-77, music dir., Minn. Orch., 1979-86, guest condr., Berlin Philharm., N.Y. Philharm. Orch., Orchestre de Paris, Cleve. Orch., Concertgebouw Orch., others; dir., South Bank Festival of Music, 1975-78, Meadow Brook Festival, Detroit, 1979-84; music dir. Stuttgart Radio Symphony Orch., 1986—. Bd. dirs., founder Acad. of St. Martin-in-the Fields, 1959—. Recipient Grand Prix du Disque, Edison award, Mozart Gemeinde prize, Tagore prize, others. Office: care Harold Holt Ltd, 31 Sinclair Rd, London W14 0NS, England Address: care Acad St Martin in Fields, 109 Boundary Rd, London NW8 0RG, England *

MARS, FRANÇOIS, gastroenterology; b. Bayonne, France, May 13, 1953; s. Jacques and Miren (Gorostidi) M.; m. Nicole Lemaitre, Aug. 27, 1977; children: Laurent, Benoit, Pierre. MD, U. Bordeaux, France, 1977. Diplomate Bd. Hepatology and Gastroenterology. Resident Hosp. Gen., Bayonne, 1977-80, Univ. Hosp., Bordeaux, France, 1981-83; practice medicine specializing in gastroenterology Lormont, Gironde, France, 1984—. Author: Internal Microbiology, 1982. Served to capt. French Navy, 1980-81. Roman Catholic. Home and Office: 132 bis rue des Gravieres, 33310 Lormont, Gironde France

MARS, HENRI-CLAUDE, physician; b. Constantine, Algeria, France, Aug. 13, 1925; s. Emile-Emmanuel and Germaine (Josserand) M.; m. Simone Jacquenot, April 22, 1950 (div. 1977); children: Nicole, Jean-Philippe, Michel; m. Michele Boitel, July 13, 1978; children: Marie-Francoise, Marie-Hélène. MD, Faculty of Medicine-Algiers, Algeria, 1953. Cmmd. French armed forces, 1944, advanced through grades to lt. col., resigned, 1971; officer French Air Force, Morocco, Algeria, 1944-46; lt. col. medical branch, Tunisia, Sahara, Algeria, 1948-71; asst. prof. Lycée Duveyrier, Blida, Algeria, 1947-48; physician Civilian Med. Orgn., France, 1971—. Author: Mars Genealogy, 1984; contbr. articles to profl. jours. Decorated Chevalier Legion of Honour (France), 1968.

MARSAN, JEAN-CLAUDE, architect, university dean; b. St-Eustache, Que., Can., Oct. 7, 1938; s. Aimé and Gertrude (Bolduc) M.; children: Jean-Sébastien, Marc-Aurèle. B.A., U. Montreal, 1960, B.Arch., 1965; M.Sc. in Urban Planning, U. Edinburgh, 1968, Ph.D. in Urban Planning, 1975. Assoc. prof. Sch. Architecture, U. Montreal, 1975-84, dir., 1975-79; research prof. Institut québécois de recherche sur la culture, 1980-82; prof. Sch. Architecture, U. Montreal, 1984—, dean Faculté de L'Aménagement, 1985—; pres. Com. to Study the Future of Olympic Installations, Montreal, 1977. Author: Montréal en évolution, 1974, Montréal une esquisse du futur, 1983. Contbr. articles to profl. jours. and newspapers, chpts. to books. Founding mem. Save Montreal, 1973-78, Mcpl. Action Group, 1978; pres. Heritage Montreal, 1983—; bd. dirs. Mus. Fine Arts Montreal, 1975-87, v.p., 1978-87. Mem. Ordre des Architectes du Que. (Prix Paul-Henri Lapointe 1984, 85, 87), Royal Soc. Can. Office: U Montreal, Faculté de l'Aménagement, PO Box 6128 Station A, Montreal, PQ Canada H3C 3J7

MARSH, COLIN JAMES, education educator; b. Denmark, West Australia, Australia, Sept. 3, 1939; s. Leonard William and Ethel Joyce (Redman) M.; m. Glenys Elizabeth Catherall, Aug. 24, 1963; children: Ross David, Jenny Suzanne, Alison Julie. BA, U. West Australia, Perth, 1961, Diploma in Edn., 1962, MA, 1971; PhD, Ohio State U., 1973. Elem. tchr. Edn. Dept. West Australia, 1958-59, secondary tchr., 1960-68; lectr. Graylands (West Australia) Tchrs. Coll., 1969-71, sr. lectr., 1974; teaching assoc. Ohio State U., Columbus, 1972-73; assoc. prof. Murdoch U., Perth, 1975-81, 86—, dean Sch. Edn., 1982-85. Author: Curriculum Practices, 1975, 2d edit., 1986, Curriculum Issues, 1984, 2d edit., 1987; editor jour. Curriculum Perspectives, 1979; contbr. articles to profl. jours. Sr. traveling fellow Assn. Commonwealth Univs., 1985. Mem. Australian Curriculum Studies Assn. (pres. 1983-85), South Pacific Assn. Tchr. Educators (exec. 1978-82), Am. Ednl. Research Assn. Home: 37 Dilkara Way, City Beach, Western Australia 6015, Australia Office: Murdoch U Sch Edn, Perth, Western Australia 6150, Australia

MARSH, IAN, political science educator, consultant; b. Sydney, Australia; s. Malcolm Howard and Grace (Reeves) M.; m. Lorine Lightfoot. BA, U. Newcastle, 1968; MPA, Harvard U., 1978, AM, 1985, PhD, 1985. Personal asst. Australian Minister for Def., 1969-72; cons. McKinsey & Co., Australia, 1972-74; research dir. Liberal Party of Australia, Canberra, 1974-77; sr. lectr. Australian Grad. Sch. Mmgt., Kensington, 1983—; project dir. strategic issues forum Com. for Econ. Devel., Australia, 1985—. Author: Policy Making in a Three Party System, 1986, An Australian Think Tank, 1979; editor: Australia Con Compete, 1987. Mem. Am. Polit. Sci. Assn., Australian Polit. Studies Assn. Home: 21 Glenview St, 2021 Paddington Australia Office: Australian Grad Sch Mgmt, PO Box 1, 2033 Kensington Australia

MARSH, JOSEPH VIRGIL, commercial real estate and investment broker; b. Winston-Salem, N.C., Apr. 28, 1952; s. Gilliam Hughes and Dovie Elizabeth (Watson) M.; student Surrey Community Coll., 1970-72; Coop. Engring. Program, U.S. Govt. Schs., Md., S.C., Washington, 1972-74; grad. N.Y. Inst. Fin., 1978. With Joint Armed Services Tech. Liaison, Washington, 1974-75; cons. U.S. Govt., 1975-76; corr., cons. individuals, bus. on tech. matters, Ararat, N.C., 1977—; registered adviser SEC, 1981—. Mem. U.S. Presdl. Task Force, 1981—. Comml. real estate broker, N.C. Mem. Internat. Entrepreneurs Assn., VFW (hon.), Armed Forces Assn., Ind. Consultants Assn., Internat. Assn. Sci. Devel., Council Civilian Tech. Advisers. Republican. Address: PO Box 12 R 1 NC 2019/2026 Ararat NC 27007-0012

MARSH, ROBERT HARRY, chemical company executive; b. Camden, N.J., Sept. 6, 1946; s. Harry Louis and Margaret Charlotte (Starke) M.; B.A., B.S. in Mech. Engring., Rutgers U., 1969; M.B.A. in Mgmt. and Fin., Temple U., 1980; m. Margaret Sammartino, Mar. 21, 1970. From mech. engr. to mech. specialist and project engr. Rohm & Haas Engring., Bristol, Pa., 1969-76; from staff engr. to sr. engring. specialist Hercules, Inc., Wilmington, Del., 1976-80, sr. fin. analyst for corp. strategic planning, 1980-81, sr. bus. analyst bus. group, 1982-83; mgr. bus. analysis Himont, Inc., 1983-86, dir. strategy and planning, 1988, dir., bus. mgmt., 1988—. Active Haddonfield civic affairs. Mem. ASME (nat. power com. 1977—, vice chmn. awards com. 1980, membership chmn. 1982), Nat. Soc. Profl. Engrs., Am. Bus. Mgmt. (bd. dirs. 1988—), Beta Gamma Sigma, Engrs. Club Phila. Club: Hercules Country. Contbr. articles to profl. jours. Home: 433 Maple Ave Haddonfield NJ 08033 Office: 3 Little Falls Wilmington DE 19899

MARSHALL, BARRY JAMES, gastroenterologist; b. Kalgoorlie, Western Australia, Australia, Sept. 30, 1951; came to U.S., 1986; s. Robert William and Marjory Jean (Donald) M.; m. Adrienne Joyce Feldman, Dec. 27, 1972; children: Luke, Bronwyn, Caroline, Jessica. MBBS, U. Western Australia, Perth, 1974, postgrad., 1986. Intern Sir Charles Gairdner Hosp., Western Australia, 1975-76, resident, 1976-77, med. registrar, 1977-78; med. registrar Royal Perth Hosp., Western Australia, 1979-82; med. registrar Fremantle Hosp., Western Australia, 1983-84, microbiology register, 1984; research scientist Royal Perth Hosp., Western Australia, 1985-86; research fellow U. Va. Sch. Med., Charlottesville, 1986-87, asst. prof. medicine, 1988—; cons. Procter and Gamble Co., Cin., 1984—, Delta West Perth, 1985—; bd. dirs. JARM Pty. Ltd., Perth, 1987—. Inventor Clotest (rapid urease test), 1985, Carbon-14 Urea Breath Test, 1985. Named one of Outstanding West Australians, Perth Jaycees, 1985; research grantee Australian Nat. Health and Med. Research Council, 1985-86. Fellow Royal Australian Coll. Physicians, Am. Coll. Gastroenterolgy; mem. Australian Med. Assn., Australian Gastroent. Soc. Office: U Va Med Ctr Dept Internal Medicine Box 145 Charlottesville VA 22908

MARSHALL, CEDRIC RUSSELL, minister for foreign affairs and disarmament and arms control; b. Nelson, New Zealand, Feb. 15, 1936; s. Cedric Thomas and Gladys Margaret (Hopley) M.; children: Philip, Timothy, Susannah; m. Barbara May Watson, Jan. 14, 1961. Student, Nelson Coll., New Zealand, Christchurch Tchrs. Coll., 1953-54, Trinity Theological Coll., Auckland, New Zealand, 1958-60; diploma in Teaching, Canterbury U., Christchurch, New Zealand, 1963, Canterbury U., New Zealand, 1964. Ordained to ministry Meth. Ch., 1963. Tchr. Nelson Edn. Bd., 1955-56; tchr. Reefton, New Zealand, Murchison, New Zealand; Meth. minister Spreydon, Christchurch, New Zealand, 1960-66, Masterton, New Zealand, 1967-71; tchr. Wanganui High Sch., New Zealand, 1972; member Wairarapa Labour Electorate Com., Wanganui, 1969-71; M.P. Parliament, New Zealand, 1972—, M.P., Labour edn. spokesman, 1975-84; Chief Opposition Whip Parliament, 1978-79; member Labour Party Exec., 1977-78; minister edn. Govt. New Zealand, 1984-87, minister environ., 1984-86, minister conservation, 1986-87, minister foreign affairs, disarmament and arms control, 1987—. Mem. Wanganui City Council, 1983-84, Wanganui Regional Devel. Council, 1973—. Office: Unity Centre, 1 Bell St, Wanganui New Zealand

MARSHALL, COLIN, SIR, airline executive; b. Edgware, Middlesex, Eng., Nov. 16, 1933; s. Edward Leslie and Florence Mary Marshall; m. Janet Winifred Cracknell, May 10, 1958; 1 child. Student, U. Coll. Sch., Hampstead, Eng., 1946-51. Mgmt. trainee Hertz Corp., Chgo. and Toronto, Ont., Can., 1958-59; gen. mgr. Hertz Corp., Chgo. and Toronto, Mex. City, 1959-60; asst. to pres. Hertz Corp., Chgo. and Toronto, N.Y.C., 1960; gen. mgr. U.K. div. Hertz Corp., Chgo. and Toronto, London, 1961-62; gen. mgr. U.K. The Netherlands and Belgium div., 1962-64; regional mgr., v.p. Avis Co., London, 1964-66; gen. mgr. Europe and Middle East div. Avis Co., 1966-69, v.p. gen. mgr. Internat. div., 1969-71; exec. v.p., chief operating officer Avis Co., N.Y.C., 1971-75; pres., chief operating officer Avis Co., 1975-76, pres., chief exec. officer, 1976-79; exec. v.p., sector exec. Norton Simon Inc., N.Y.C., 1979-81; dir. dep. chief exec. Sears Holdings Plc, London, 1981-83; chief exec. officer Brit. Airways, London, 1983—; bd. dirs. Brit. Airways, 1983—, Brit. Tourist Authority, S. Bank Bd. Awarded Knight Bachelor, Her Majesty the Queen, 1987. Club: Queens. Office: Brit Airways PLC, Box 10 Heathrow Airport, London, Middlesex TW6 2JA, England

MARSHALL, DAVID, orthodontist; b. Syracuse, N.Y., Feb. 4, 1914; s. Moses and Fanny (Bagelman) Salutsky; B.S., Syracuse U., 1932-35; D.D.S., U. Md., 1938-42; postgrad. Columbia, 1943-45, Tufts Coll., Northwestern U.; m. Rita Stein, June 20, 1944 (dec.); children—Robert Andrew, Howard Randy, Douglas S. (dec.), Susan Beth, Robin (dec.); m. Marjorie Kaufman, Sept. 7, 1973. Practice dentistry specializing in orthodontics, Syracuse, mem. staff St. Joseph's Hosp., Crouse-Irving Hosp., University Hosp., Meml. Hosp.; mem. cons. School Speech, Syracuse U.; orthodontic cons. N.Y. State Health Dept.; lectr. in field, producer sci. exbns., Anat. Mus. Recipient Hektoen medal AMA, 1970. Diplomate Am. Bd. Orthodontists. Mem. Royal Soc. Medicine, ADA, N.Y. Dental Soc., Syracuse Dental Soc., 5th Dist. Dental Soc., Syracuse C. of C., Northeastern (qualifying com.), Am. orthodontists socs., Pierre Fauchard Acad. Contbg. author textbooks dentistry and orthodontics; contbr. articles to dental publs. Home: 5231 Brockway Ln Fayetteville NY 13066 Office: 1124 E Genesee St Syracuse NY 13210

MARSHALL, GEORGE NICHOLS, clergyman, author; b. Bozeman, Mont., July 4, 1920; s. James Wallace and Grace (Nichols) M.; m. Barbara Ambrose, June 14, 1946 (div. 1966); 1 child, Charles Hopkinson. A.B., Tufts U., 1940, S.T.B., 1941, A.M., 1943; M.A., Columbia U., 1942; Th.M., Harvard U., 1946; Ph.D., Walden U., 1976; D.D., Meadville/Lombard Theol. Sch., 1976. Ordained to ministry Unitarian Ch., 1941. Pastor, Natick, Mass., 1941-43, Plymouth, Mass., 1946-52, Niagara Falls, N.Y., 1952-60; pastor Ch. of Larger Fellowship, Boston, 1960-85, minister emeritus, 1985—. Author: Church of the Pilgrim Fathers, 1950; Unitarian Universalism as a Way of Life, 1966 (revised as Challenge of A Liberal Faith, 1979, 3d edit., 1988); An Understanding of Albert Schweitzer, 1966; (with David Poling) Schweitzer, A Biography, 1970; Facing Death and Grief, 1981; (biography) Buddha, The Quest for Serenity, 1978; co-author Encounters with Eternity, 1986; Introduction to Hibakusha, 1986. Assoc. dir. dept. extension Unitarian-Universalist Assn., 1960-70; treas. Unitarian Ministers Assn., 1954-56; chmn. Unitarian Commn. Ch. and Returning Servicemen, 1944-46; sec. Commn. Unitarian Universalist Union, 1949-53, Council Liberal Chs., 1953-55; pres. Niagara Falls Religious Fellowship, 1950-52. Bd. dirs. N.Y. chpt. Americans for Democratic Action, 1955-56; pres. Niagara County Planned Parenthood Assn., 1953-59, mem. N.Y. State bd., 1955-59; chmn. Unitarian Universalist Commn. Scouting; mem. Nat. council Boy Scouts Am., 1960-70; del. White House Conf. Against Discrimination, 1958; program chmn. Albert Schweitzer Fellowship, N.Y.C., 1972—. Served to capt. USAAF, 1943-46. Recipient Freedom House award of merit, 1949. Mem. African Study Assn. (pres. 1966-67), Albert Schweitzer World Confedn. (sec.), Am. Friends of Albert Schweitzer. Home: 718 Craigville Beach Rd West Hyannisport MA 02672

MARSHALL, GRAYSON WILLIAM, JR., biomaterials scientist, educator; b. Balt., Feb. 12, 1943; s. Grayson William and Muriel Marie M.; B.S. in Metall. Engring., Va. Poly. Inst., 1965; Ph.D. in Materials Sci., Northwestern U., 1972, D.D.S., 1986; m. Sally Jean Rimkus, July 4, 1970; children—Grayson W. III, Jonathan Charles. Research asso., design and devel. center Northwestern U., Evanston, Ill., 1972-73, NIH fellow, 1973, instr. Dental and Med. schs., Chgo., 1973-74, asst. prof. Dental Sch., 1974-78, asso. prof. Dental Sch. and Grad. Sch., 1978-87; prof. restorative dentistry U. Calif., San Francisco, 1987—, chief biomaterials sect., 1988—; cons. Greenmark, Inc. Vis. fellow U. Melbourne (Australia), 1981. Recipient Spl. dental research award Nat. Inst. Dental Research, 1975. Fellow AAAS, Acad. Dental Materials (exec. sec. 1983-85, chmn. credentials 1984—, bd.

dirs. 1985—, mem. editorial bd. Scanning Microscopy 1987—); mem. Am. Assn. Dental Schs. (sect. officer 1981-83), Soc. Biomaterials, Internat. Assn. Dental Research (Chgo. sect. officer 1978-80), Am. Coll. Sports Med., Am. Soc. Metals, Electron Microscopy Soc. Am., AIME, Midwest Biolaser Inst. (trustee), Navy League U.S., N.Y. Acad. Scis., ADA, Acad. Gen. Dentistry, Calif. Acad. Scis., U.S. Naval Inst., Inst. Nav., U.S. Power Squadrons, Alpha Sigma Mu, Sigma Xi, Sigma Gamma Epsilon, Omicron Kappa Upsilon. Contbr. articles to profl. jours. Office: U Calif Dept Restorative Dentistry San Francisco CA 94143-0758

MARSHALL, J. HOWARD, II, lawyer; b. Phila., Jan. 24, 1905; s. S. Furman and Annabelle (Thompson) M.; m. Eleanor Pierce, June 20, 1931; children: J. Howard III, Pierce; m. Bettye M. Bohanan, Dec. 10, 1961. AB, Haverford Coll., 1926, LLD, 1985; JD magna cum laude, Yale U., 1931. Instr. and asst. cruise dir. Floating Univ., 1926-27, cruise dir., 1928-29; asst. dean, asst. prof. law Yale U., 1931-33; mem. Petroleum Adminstrv. Bd., U.S. Dept. Interior, 1933-35; spl. asst. to U.S. atty. gen. and asst. solicitor Dept. Interior, 1933-35; spl. counsel Standard Oil Co. Calif., 1935-37; partner Pillsbury, Madison & Sutro, San Francisco, 1938-44; chief counsel Petroleum Adminstrn. for War, 1941-44, asst. dep. adminstr., 1943-44; gen. counsel U.S. del. to Allied Commn. on Reparations, 1945; mem. firm Meyers, Marshall & Meyers (Attys.), Washington.; Mem. Mil. Petroleum Adv. Bd. to joint chiefs staff, 1944-50, 54-59; pres., dir. Ashland Oil & Refining Co. (and subs. corps.), 1944-51; v.p., dir. Signal Oil & Gas Co., 1952-59, exec. v.p., dir., 1959-60, also subs. and affiliated corps.; pres., dir. Union Texas Natural Gas Corp., 1961-62; dir. Allied Chem. Corp., 1962-68; pres. Union Tex. Petroleum div., exec v.p. Allied Chem. Corp., 1965-67; dir. Tex. Commerce Bank Nat. Assn., Houston; dir., mem. exec. com. M-K-T R.R.; dir. Koch Industries, Inc., Wichita; chmn., dir. Petroleum Corp.; chmn. exec. com., dir. Coastal Corp.; dir. Presidio Oil Co., 1987; cons. sec. interior petroleum def. program, 1950-52. Author (with N.L. Meyers); series monographs Yale Law Jour., 1931, 33. Vice-pres., bd. mgrs. Haverford Coll. Mem. 25 Year Club, Am. Petroleum Inst. (v.p., dir.), Nat. Petroleum Council, Soc. Petroleum Engrs., Am., Calif., Ky. bar assns., AIME, Order of Coif, Beta Rho Sigma. Mem. Soc. of Friends. Clubs: Bohemian (San Francisco), Pacific-Union (San Francisco); 29 (N.Y.C.); River Oaks Country (Houston). Home: 11100 Meadowick Houston TX 70024 Office: PO Box 42808-L Houston TX 77042

MARSHALL, L. B., medical technologist; b. Chgo., Feb. 10; s. Gillman and Ethel (Robinson) M.; BS, U. Puget Sound; postgrad. San Francisco State U., City Coll. San Francisco; medical technologist; m. Esther Wood, Sept. 28, 1961; 1 dau., Lelani. Pres., Med. Offices Health Services Group Inc., San Francisco, 1964—. Served with U.S. Army, 1947-53. Decorated Bronze Star, Med. Combat Badge. Recipient certificate of appreciation Pres. Nixon, 1973, Urban League, 1973, Calif. Dept. Human Resources, 1973. Mem. Am., Calif. Assns. Med. Technologists, Calif. State Sheriff's Assn. (assoc.), Black Am. Polit. Assn. Calif., NAACP (life). Club: Oyster Point Yacht; Press, Commonwealth (San Francisco).

MARSHALL, LINDA RAE, cosmetic company executive; b. Provo, Utah, Aug. 1, 1940; d. Arvid O. and Tola V. (Broderick) Newman; children—James, John. Student Brigham Young U., 1958-59, U. Utah, 1960-61. Buyer, Boston Store, 1961-62; sec. Milw. Gas & Light Co., 1962-64; mktg. rep. Elysee Cosmetics, Madison, Wis., 1971-75, pres., 1975-87; v.p., Dionne, Inc., 1987—, ptnr.; Pres. Falk Sch. PTA, Madison. Mem. Aestheticians Internat. Assn. (adv. bd.), Cosmetic, Toiletry and Fragrance Assn. (exec. com., bd. dirs., chmn. voluntary program, chmn. small cosmetic com., membership com. task force). Club: Dental Wives. Author: Discover the Other Woman in You; monthly beauty columnist Beauty Fashion Mag.; contbg. author Cosmetic Industry Sci. and Regulatory Found., 1984. Address: Box 4084 Madison WI 53711

MARSHALL, MAUREEN GRETA, management company executive; b. Yorkshire, Eng., Aug. 14, 1921; d. George Cyril and Greta Beatrice (Hall) Stevenson; came to U.S., 1952; B.A. with distinction, U. Calif. at Berkeley, 1969, M.A., 1970; m. Sherwood Barnett Marshall, Nov. 1, 1952; 1 dau., Virginia Maureen Marshall Lang. Vice pres. Alameda (Calif.) Convalescent Hosp., 1968-70, Sonoma (Calif.) Convalescent Hosp., 1970-74; gen. ptnr. Valley View Lodge, Walnut Creek, Calif., 1974-82; exec. v.p. SAV Service Corp., Walnut Creek, 1975—; pres. Tri-County Supply Inc., Walnut Creek, 1978—; v.p. Kristina Odysseys, Ltd., Del., 1979. Served with Canadian Women's Army Corps, World War II. Mem. San Francisco Women's Artists (pres. 1977-79), Phi Beta Kappa. Episcopalian. Paintings exhibited at Calif. Inst. Art, Mus. Modern Art, San Francisco, Worth Ryder Gallery, San Francisco, U. Calif. at Berkeley, San Francisco Art Commn. Gallery, St. Mary's Coll., Moraga, Calif., Internat. Ctr. for Contemporary Art, Paris, 1983, Percy Basse Gallery, London, 1985, also at juried shows. Office: care Seiler & Co 120 Montgomery St Suite 2250 San Francisco CA 94104

MARSHALL, PHYLLIS ELLINWOOD, mental health system executive, consultant; b. Kansas City, Mo., Dec. 20, 1929; d. Herbert Dwight and Mildred (Gillham) Ellinwood; m. John D. Reich, July 1, 1950 (div. 1964); children—Martha Reich Millican, Michael David, Donald Martin; m. C. Randolph Marshall, Nov. 27, 1969. B.A., Washington U., St. Louis, 1951, M.S.W., 1969. Adult program dir. St. Louis YWCA, 1962-64, dir. decentralized programs, 1964-67; alcoholism caseworker Malcolm Bliss Mental Health Ctr., St. Louis, 1968; exec. dir. Cobb County YWCA, Ga., 1969-72; dir. Coastal Area Community Mental Health Ctr., Brunswick, Ga., 1973-77; dir. Mental Health Services, Ga. Dept. Human Resources, Atlanta, 1977-84; exec. dir. Integrated Mental Health, Inc., Rochester, N.Y., 1984—; cons. NIMH, Washington, 1979-84, So. Regional Ednl. Bd., Atlanta, 1979-84, N.Y. State Office Mental Health, Albany, 1980-84; co-chair Metro Atlanta Deinstitutionalization Task Force, 1983-85; bd. dirs. Children Have All Rights, Legal, Ednl. and Emotional, Menninger Found. project, Atlanta, 1983-84; mem. council Fingerlakes Health Systems Agy., Rochester, 1985. Contbg. author: Perspectives in Mental Health, 1980, New Directions for Mental Health Services, 1988. Contbr. articles to profl. publs. Bd. dirs. Human Resources Credit Union, Atlanta, 1982-84. Recipient Boss of Yr. award Brunswick Jaycees, 1977, Good Friend award Brunswick Mental Health Assn., 1977, Community Mental Health award Atlanta U., 1980. Mem. AAUW (chpt. pres. 1978), Assn. Mental Health Adminstrs., Ga. Assn. Community Mental Health Ctrs. (pres. 1975-77), Rochester Women's Network. Club: Midtown Tennis (Rochester). Avocations: ocean sailing; music; tennis. Office: Integrated Mental Health Inc Monroe Sq 259 Monroe Ave Rochester NY 14607

MARSHALL, RICHARD TREEGER, lawyer; b. N.Y.C., May 17, 1925; s. Edward and Sydney (Treeger) M.; m. Dorothy M. Goodman, June 4, 1950; children—Abigail Ruth Marshall Bergerson, Daniel Brooks; m. 2d, Sylvia J. Kelley, June 10, 1979. B.S., Cornell U., 1948; J.D., Yale U., 1951. Bar: Tex. 1952, U.S. Ct. Appeals (5th cir.) 1966, U.S. Ct. Appeals (10th cir.) 1980, U.S. Supreme Ct., 1959. Sole practice, El Paso, Tex., 1952-59, 61-79; assoc. Fryer & Milstead, El Paso, 1952; sr. ptnr. Marshall & Wendorf, El Paso, 1959-61; sr. ptnr. Marshall & Volk, El Paso, 1979-81; sr. atty. Richard T. Marshall & Assocs., P.C., El Paso, 1981-85; sr. ptnr. Marshall, Thomas & Winters, El Paso, 1985-87, sr. atty. Marshall & Winters, 1987—; instr. ins. law C.L.U. tng. course Am. Coll.; officer, dir. Advance Funding, Inc., El Paso. Mem. ABA, State Bar Tex., El Paso Bar Assn., El Paso Trial Lawyers Assn. (pres. 1965-66), Tex. Trial Lawyers Assn., Assn. Trial Lawyers Am. (sec. personal injury law sect. 1967-68, nat. sec. 1969-70, sec.-treas. environ. law sect. 1970-71, vice chmn. family law litigation sect. 1971-72); Roscoe Pound-Am. Trial Lawyers Found. (Commn. on Profl. Responsibility 1979-82), Am. Arbitration Assn. (nat. panel arbitrators). Editor: El Paso Trial Lawyers Rev., 1973-80; contbr. articles to legal jours. Office: 6070 Gateway E Suite 103 El Paso TX 79905

MARSHALL, ROBERT CHARLES, research scientist; b. Brisbane, Queensland, Australia, Oct. 5, 1945; s. Raymond Alexander and Dorothy Mabel (Enever) M.; m. Wendy Olive Moore, Jan. 10, 1970; children: Scott Robert, Brenton Charles, Michelle Wendy. BSc, U. Queensland, 1966, BSc with honors, 1967, PhD, 1971. Research assoc., chemistry dept. Ind. U., Bloomington, 1971-73; research scientist, sr. prin. research scientist CSIRO, Div. Wool Technology, Melbourne, Victoria, Australia, 1973—, leader wool and fibrous proteins program, 1981—. Contbr. over 65 articles to profl. jours. Recipient Edward Taylor Meml. award U. Queensland, 1965, University medal, 1967, CSR Chems. prize, 1968, Philip Allen award, 1982; Fulbright-Hays exchange scholar Australian-Am. Edn. Found., 1971-73; Alexander von Humboldt research fellow, Fed. Republic Germany, 1982-83. Mem. Australian Biochem. Soc., Australian Soc. Cosmetic Chemists (Lester Conrad Meml. award 1987). Mem. Anglican Ch. Home: 5 Kiama Close, 3094 Montmorency Australia Office: CSIRO Div Wool Technology, 343 Royal Parade, 3052 Parkville Australia

MARSHALL, SALLY JEAN, biomaterials scientist; b. Racine, Wis., Jan. 8, 1949; d. Charles and Adele Ruth Rimkus; B.S. with distinction in sci. engring., Northwestern U., 1970, Ph.D. in Materials Sci. and Engring., 1975; m. Grayson William Marshall, Jr., July 4, 1970; children—Grayson William III, Jonathan Charles. Instr. biol. materials Northwestern U., Chgo., 1974-75, asst. prof., 1975-80, assoc. prof., 1980-86, prof., 1986-87, prof. restorative dentistry U. Calif., San Francisco, 1987—, vice chair research, 1988—; varsity swimming coach Northwestern U., Evanston, Ill., 1970-81; vis. fellow U. Melbourne (Australia), 1981. Recipient spl. dental research award Nat. Inst. Dental Research, 1977. Fellow Acad. Dental Materials (treas. 1983-85, v.p. 1985-87, pres. 1987—, bd. dirs. 1983—); mem. Am. Soc. Metals, AIME, Assn. Women in Sci., Am. Swimming Coaches Assn., Ill. Swimming Assn. (Women's Collegiate Coach of Year 1978-79), Internat. Assn. Dental Research, Am. Assn. Dental Research (1st place research award Chgo. sect.), N.Y. Acad. Scis., Am. Coll. Sports Medicine, Soc. Biomaterials, Sigma Xi, Tau Beta Pi, Omicron Kappa Upsilon. Contbr. articles to sci. jours. Home: 45 Wiltshire Ave Larkspur CA 94939 Office: U Calif Restorative Dentistry 707 Parnassus Ave Box 758 San Francisco CA 94143-0758

MARŠIK, FRANTIŠEK, physicist, researcher; b. Humpolec, South Bohemia, Czechoslovakia, Oct. 17, 1942; s. František and Anna (Loskot) M.; m. Šarka Zamek, Sept. 17, 1967; children: Marketa, Martin. MSc, Faculty of Tech. Nuclear Physics, Prague, Czechoslovakia, 1967; PhD, Inst. Thermomechanics Czechoslovak Acad. Scis., Prague, 1974. Asst. research worker Inst. Thermomechanics Czechoslovak Acad. Scis., 1972-74, sr. research worker, 1974-79, prin. research worker, 1980—; cons. Czechoslovak Radio, Prague, 1977-78, Inst. Communication Tech., Prague, 1985—. Co-author: Biothermodynamics, 1982; contbr. articles to profl. jours. Acad. Scis. USSR fellow, Minsk, 1971, Ministère l'Education Nat. Culture Française fellow, Univ. Libre Brussels, 1981, Solvay Inst. Internat. Physique Chimie, Univ. Libre Brussels. Fellow: Committee Biomechanics, Bd. Defence PhD Degree; mem. Czechoslovak Soc. Mechanics. Office: Inst Thermomechanics, Dolejskova 5, 18200 Prague Czechoslovakia

MARSTON, ALFRED J., economist, business executive; b. Silesia, Poland, July 22, 1924; s. Alovsius and Martha (Von Stackberg) M.; Ph.D., U. Paris, 1950; postgrad. Ecole des Sci. Politiques, 1945-47; m. Vilma Mercaldi, Nov. 30, 1956. Analyst, Internat. Public Opinion Research, N.Y.C., supr. European research operation, 1951-52; analyst, research supr. UNGRAN, N.Y.C., 1953-55; econ. analyst terminals Port of N.Y. Authority, 1956-60, asst. transp. economist, 1961-62, economist, 1962-79; v.p., econ. and bus. cons. Inversion, Inc., N.Y.C., 1980—; dir., pres. Chatham Towers Inc., N.Y.C. Pres., Manhattan Downtown Community Council; mem. steering com. Health Systems Agy. N.Y.C.; dir. Elisabeth Blackwell Found.; trustee, chmn. adv. bd. N.Y. Infirmary-Beekman Downtown Hosp.; mem. N.Y.C. Local Planning Bd.; pres., dir. POMOC, Inc., N.Y.C. Served with French Army, 1943-45. Mem. Am. Econ. Assn., Am. Statis. Assn., Nat. Acad. Scis. (transp. research bd.), Polish Inst. Arts and Scis., URISA (chmn. internat. sig. com.). Author: The French Legion of Haiti, 1952; contbr. to publs. in transp. field, articles to profl. jours. Home: Indian Neck Ln Peconic NY 11958 Office: 170 Park Row New York NY 10038

MARSTON, MICHAEL, urban economic consultant; b. Oakland, Calif., Dec. 4, 1936; s. Lester Woodbury and Josephine (Janovic) M.; B.A., U. Calif. at Berkeley, 1959; postgrad. London Sch. Econs., 1961-63; m. Alexandra Lynn Geyer, Apr. 30, 1966. Vice pres. Larry Smith & Co., San Francisco, 1969-72, exec. v.p. urban econ. div., 1969-72; chmn. bd. Keyser Marston Assocs., Inc., San Francisco, 1973-87; gen. partner The Sequoia Partnership, 1979—; pres. Marston Vineyards and Winery, 1982—, Marston Assocs., Inc., 1982—. Chmn., San Francisco Waterfront Com., 1969-86; chmn. fin. com., bd. dirs., mem. exec. com., treas. San Francisco Planning and Urban Research Assn., 1976-87; trustee Cathedral Sch. for Boys, 1981-82, Marin Country Day Sch., 1984—, St. Luke's Sch., 1986—; pres. Presidio Heights Assn. of Neighbors, 1983-84; v.p., bd. dirs., mem. exec. com. People for Open Space, 1972-87, chmn. adv. com., 1988 ; mem. Gov.'s Issue Analysis Com. and Speakers Bur., 1966; mem. speakers bur. Am. embassy, London, 1961-63; v.p., bd. dirs. Democratic Forum, 1968-72; v.p., trustee Youth for Service. Served to lt. USNR. Mem. Urban Land Inst., Order of Golden Bear, Lambda Alpha. Clubs: Bohemian, Pacific Union. Home: 3375 Jackson St San Francisco CA 94118 Office: 55 Pacific Ave Mall San Francisco CA 94111

MARTEL, JOHN SHELDON, lawyer, author; b. Stockton, Calif., Jan. 1, 1931; s. Henry T. and Alice L. M.; children: John Sheldon, Melissa Ann. B.S., U. Calif.-Berkeley, 1956, J.D., 1959. Bar: Calif. Dep. dist. atty. Alameda County, 1960-61; assoc. trial atty. firm Bronson, Bronson & McKinnon, San Francisco, 1961-64; ptnr. firm Farella, Braun & Martel, San Francisco, 1964—; now sr. trial ptnr. Farella, Braun & Martel, 1948—; also profl. musician. Author, editor legal publs.; composer-writer popular songs; author (novel), Partners, 1988. Served as pilot USAF, 1951-54. Winner Am. Song Festival awards, 1978-80, 82. Fellow Am. Coll. Trial Lawyers (state chmn. 1985-87); mem. ABA (dist. chmn. contrn. litigation com. 1975-80), Calif. State Bar, San Francisco Bar Assn. (chmn. com. bus. litigation 1976), Am. Fedn. Musicians, Phi Delta Phi, Kappa Sigma. Office: Farella Braun & Martel 235 Montgomery St Russ Bldg Suite 3100 San Francisco CA 94104

MARTENS, CLAUS OTTO, electronic data processing consultant; b. Berlin, Germany, Nov. 17, 1941; s. Claudius Martens and Kaethe (Otto) Martens Schneider; m. Annelie Heins, July 2, 1965; children—Robert, Jan-Henning, Hendrik. Dipl.Ing., Phys. Tech. IH, Wedel, Germany, 1967. System engr. Telefunken, Hamburg, Germany, 1967-68; sales engr. ERA, Aachen, Germany, 1968-69, Siemens, Hamburg, 1969-70; regional sales mgr. Generalautomation, Hamburg, 1970; gen. mgr. Geveke Gmbh, Dusseldorf, Germany, 1971-74; pres. Digitronic GmbH, Hamburg, 1975—; cons. EDP. Patentee in field. Lodge: Rotary. Office: Digitronic GmbH, Am Kamp 17, 2081 Holm Federal Republic of Germany

MARTENS, JOHN DALE, telecommunications company executive; b. Wayne, Nebr., Nov. 12, 1943; s. Leonard William and Irma Bertha (Von Seggern) M.; m. Laura Elizabeth Price, Dec. 28, 1966. BSBA, U. Colo., 1966; MS, Thurderbird Grad. Sch. Internat. Mgmt., 1972; postgrad. Queen Mary Coll., U. London, 1976. Analyst overseas ops. Ford Motor Co., Dearborn, Mich., 1972-73; internat. mktg. ofcl. Agrico Chem. Co., Tulsa, 1973-76; tech. and comml. devel. ofcl. Resource Scis. Co., Tulsa, 1976-78, planning and corp. devel. ofcl., 1978-80; chief exec. officer, pres., treas., dir. Sterling Oil of Okla., Inc., Tulsa, 1980-82; dir. strategic devel. MCI Communications Corp., Washington, 1983-84, v.p. corp. devel., 1984-86; v.p. mktg. So. New Eng. Telecommunications Co. Inc., New Haven, 1986. Served to capt. USAF, 1967-70. Episcopalian. Clubs: So. Hills Country (Tulsa); Quinnipiack (New Haven), New Haven Country. Office: So New Eng Telecommunications Co Inc 195 Church St 10th Floor New Haven CT 06510

MARTENS, ROY MICHAEL, lease finance representative; b. Des Moines, Feb. 7, 1950; s. Roy Edwin and Maxine Hayworth M. BA, Luther Coll., 1972; MBA, U. Minn., 1978. Auditor Honeywell, Mpls., 1972-75; supr. Northwest SW, Mpls., 1975-78; fin. analyst Amhoist, St. Paul, 1979-81; sr. fin. analyst Farm Credit Services, St. Paul, 1981-88; lease finance rep. Dataserv, Eden Prairie, Minn., 1988—. Mem. Twin City Cash Mgmt. Assn., Epsilon Delta Omicron. Republican. Lutheran. Club: Wayzata Yacht (measurer 1985, sec. 1988). Home: 2511 Chesnutt Ave W Minneapolis MN 55405

MARTENS, WILFRIED, prime minister of Belgium; b. Sleidinge, Belgium, Apr. 19, 1936; D.Laws, Cath. U. Louvain, Lic. Notary Sci., B.Thomistic Philosophy; m. Lieve Verschroeven; children: Chris, Ann. Barrister, Ct. of Appeal Gent; adv. to Office Prime Minister, 1965-68; charge de mission to Office Minister Community Affairs, from 1968; mem. exec. com. Flemish Nat. Movement; pres. juniors Christian Social Party, 1967, pres. party, 1972; mem. Chamber of Deps. from Gent-Eekolo Dist., 1974—; a leader European Union Christian Democrats; co-founder European People's Party; prime minister of Belgium, 1979—. Roman Catholic. *

MARTENS, WOLFGANG WILHELM, educator; b. Templin, Germany, Jan. 12, 1924; s. Wilhelm Ferdinand and Sophie (Schrimpff) M.; m. Helga Nina Seemann, July 22, 1953; children: Brigitte, Corona, Andrea. Dr. Phil., U. Cologne, Fed. Republic Germany, 1952; Dr. Habil., Free U. Berlin, 1968. Asst. German dept. U. Cologne, Fed. Republic Germany, 1957-58; wissenschaftlicher rat. German dept. Free U. Berlin, 1958-68; full prof., dir. German dept. U. Munster, Fed. Republic Germany, 1968-72; full prof., head German dept. U. Vienna, Austria, 1972-79; prof. German dept. U. Munich, 1979—, also dir. Author: Bildund Motiv im Weltschmerz, 1957, Die Botschaft der Tugend, 1968, Lyrik Kommerziell, 1975; editor 12 German texts; contbr. 60 articles to profl. jours. Mem. Austrian Acad. Sci. (corr.), Internat. Lessing Soc. (hon.), Lessing Akademie Wolfenbuttel (mem. senate), Germanistische Kommission of Deutsche Forschungsgemeinschaft. Home: Nockstr 15, Murnau Federal Republic of Germany Office: Inst Deutsche Phieologie, Schellingstr 3, D-8000 Munich Federal Republic of Germany

MÅRTENSSON, BENGT KRISTER, engineer, researcher; b. Lund, Sweden, Sept. 6, 1956; s. Hugo Valdemar and Astrid Elisabet (Ekelin) M. MSc, Lund Inst. Tech., 1982, Licensiate, 1985; postgrad., Harvard U., 1983-84; PhD, Lund Inst. Technology, Sweden, 1986. Lectr. Lund Inst. Tech., 1986-87; postdoctal fellow U. Waterloo, Ont., Can., 1987; researcher U. Bremen, Fed. Republic of Germany, 1987—. Fulbright scholar, 1983-84, Sweden-Am. Found. scholar, 1983-84. Mem. Soc. Indsl. and Applied Math. Home: Riddarg 33, S-290 34 Fjalkinge Sweden Office: U Bremen, Postfach 330440, 2800 Bremen Federal Republic of Germany

MARTI, MANUEL, architect; b. Havana, Cuba, Aug. 6, 1940; came to U.S., 1967; s. Manuel Antonio and Olga (Munoz) M.; m. Patricia Damm, Apr. 15, 1967 (div. Dec. 1973); children—Patricia, Manuel Alberto, Michelle; m. Patricia A. Stillman, Aug. 25, 1978. BArch., Nat. U. of Mex., 1966, M in Archaeology, 1967. Registered architect, Ariz., Fla., Wis. Designer, Barry Sugerman Architects, Miami, Fla., 1967-73; project mgr. Potter, Lawson, & Pawlowsky, Madison, Wis., 1973-81; project mgr., assoc. Anderson DeBartolo Pan, Inc., Tucson, 1981—. Author: Space Operational Analysis, 1981; No Place to Hide, 1984. Recipient Medal of Merit, Nat. U. Mex. Mem. AIA, World Future Soc., Ariz. Soc. Architects. Democrat. Home: 6121 N Camino Padre Isidoro Tucson AZ 85718 Office: Anderson DeBartolo Pan Inc 2480 N Arcadia Ave Tucson AZ 85712

MARTIKAINEN, A(UNE) HELEN, retired health education specialist; b. Harrison, Maine, May 11, 1916; d. Sylvester and Emma (Heikkinen) M.; A.B., Bates Coll., 1939, D.Sc. (hon.), 1957; M.P.H., Yale, 1941; D.Sc., Harvard U., 1964, Smith Coll., 1969. Health edn. sec. Hartford Tb and Public Health Assn., 1941-42; cons. USPHS, 1942-49; chief health edn. WHO, Geneva, 1949-74; chair Internat. Relations N.C. div. AAUW, 1986—. Trustee, Bridgton Acad., North Bridgton, Maine; mem program adv. bd., also membership com. U.S. Assn. Club of Rome; citizen councillor Atlantic Council U.S.A., 1987—; mem. N.C. Citizens Council Pub. Health, N.C. Women's Forum, 1984—; N.C. Center of Laws Affecting Women, Inc.; mem. adv. bd. Sch. Pub. Health, U. N.C., Chapel Hill; cons. Commn. on Women's Issues of Episcopal Diocese of N.C., N.C. Women's Resource Ctr., 1987—; bd. dirs. Orange and Durham Counties chpt. U.N. Assn.; citizen councillor Atlantic Council U.S.A., 1987—; bd. dirs., membership com U.N.A. Orange and Durham County, N.C. Recipient Delta Omega award Yale; Nat. Adminstrv. award Am. Acad. Phys. Edn.; Bates Key award; Internat. Service award, France, 1953; Prentiss medal, 1956; spl. medal, certificate for internat. health edn. service Nat. Acad. Medicine for France, 1959; profl. award Soc. Public Health Educators, 1963. Fellow Am. Public Health Assn. (chmn. health edn. sect., Excellence award 1969); mem. AAUW (rep. to N.C. Council Social Legis.), U.S. Soc. Pub. Health Educators, Internat. Union Health Edn. (Parisot medal, tech. adviser), Acad. Phys. Edn. (asso.), Phi Beta Kappa. Episcopalian. Home: PO Box 3059 Chapel Hill NC 27514

MARTIN, ALBERT V. J., communications specialist, editor, consultant; b. Lyon, France, Nov. 24, 1920; s. Albert and Marthe (Duchamp) M.; m. Jacqueline Forlini, Oct. 3, 1960; children: Patricia, Olivier. Doctor of Scis., U. Paris, 1956, Doctor of Human Biology, 1973, MD, 1970. Spec. in medical electronics and Tropical Medicine 1981-82; head info. div. European Space Agy., Noordwijk, Netherlands, 1959-80; head info. Internat. Livestock Ctr. for Africa, Addis Ababa, Ethiopia, 1980-82; cons. WHO, Geneva, 1983—; cons., editor Internat. Service for Nat. Agrl. Research, The Hague, Netherlands, 1982—. Author 15 books and numerous articles; 15 patents. Recipient Medaille du Merite et de l'Invention. Fellow Inst. Electronic and Radio Engrs. (retired). Roman Catholic. Home: Ave Van Ostadelaan 5, 2343EL Oegstgeest Holland Office: Isnar Oranjebuitensingel, 6, Den Haag Holland

MARTIN, ARCHER JOHN PORTER, retired chemistry educator; b. London, Mar. 1, 1910; s. William Archer Porter and Lilian Kate (Brown) M.; m. Judith Bagenal, Jan. 9, 1943; 5 children. Student, Peterhouse, Cambridge, Eng., 1929-32, MA, 1936; PhD, DSc, Leeds U., 1968; LLD (hon.), U. Glasgow, Scotland, 1973; laurea honoris causa, U. Urbino, Italy, 1985. Chemist Nutritional Lab., Cambridge, 1933-38, Wool Industries Research Assn., Leeds, 1938-46; research dept. Boots Pure Drug Co., Nottingham, Eng., 1946-48; staff Med. Research Council, 1948-52; head phys. chemistry div. Nat. Inst. Med. Research, Mill Hill, 1952-56; chem. cons. 1956-59; dir. Abbotsbury (Eng.) Labs. Ltd., 1959-73; profl. fellow U. Sussex, Eng., 1973-77; Robert A. Welch prof. chemistry U. Houston, 1974-78; guest prof. Ecole Polytechnique Fed. de Lausanne, Switzerland, 1980-85; cons. Wellcome Research Labs., Beckenham, Eng., 1970-73; Extraordinary prof. Tech. U., Eindhoven, The Netherlands, 1965-74. Decorated comdr. Brit. Empire; Order of Rising Sun Japan; recipient Berzelius Gold medal Swedish Med. Soc., 1951, Nobel prize chemistry (with R.L.M. Synge) for invention of partition chromatography, 1952, John Scott award, 1958, John Price Wetherill medal, 1959, Franklin Inst. medal, 1959, Koltoff medal Acad. Pharm. Sci., 1969, Callendar medal Inst. Measurement & Control, 1971, Fritz-Pregl medal Austrian Chemical Soc., 1985. Fellow Royal Soc.; mem. (Leverhulme medal 1964). Club: Chemist's (N.Y.C.) (hon.). Home: 47 Roseford Rd, Cambridge CB4 2HA, England Office: Univ of Houston Chemistry Dept Houston TX 77004

MARTIN, ARTHUR LEE, JR., lawyer; b. Montgomery, Ala., Jan. 13, 1949; s. Arthur Lee and Blanche (Bush) M.; m. Mary Lynne Ortmeyer, Sept. 29, 1973; children—Elizabeth Leah, Rachel Blanche. B.A. cum laude, Vanderbilt U., 1971; J.D. U. Chgo., 1974. Bar: U.S. Dist. Ct. (no. dist.) Ill. 1972, U.S. Ct. Appeals (7th cir.) 1972, Ill. 1975, Ala. 1979, U.S. Dist. Ct. (no. dist.) Ala. 1979, U.S. Ct. Appeals (5th cir.) 1979. Law clk. to Sr. judge U.S. Ct. Appeals (5th cir.), Montgomery, 1974-75; assoc. D'Ancona & Pflaum, Chgo., 1975-78; ptnr. Haskell, Slaughter & Young, Birmingham, Ala., 1978—. Trustee Arlington Hist. Mus., Birmingham, 1980—; dir. Birmingham Housing Devel. Corp., Ala., 1981—. Mem. Nat. Assn. Bond Lawyers, ABA, Ala. State Bar, Birmingham Bar Assn., Phi Delta Phi. Democrat. Congregationalist. Clubs: Relay House, Downtown Democratic. Home: 4501 10th Ave S Birmingham AL 35222 Office: Haskell Slaughter & Young 800 1st Nat-So Nat Bldg Birmingham AL 35223

MARTIN, BOYD ARCHER, emeritus political science educator; b. Cottonwood, Idaho, Mar. 3, 1911; s. Archer Olmstead and Norah Claudine (Imbler) M.; m. Grace Charlotte Swingler, Dec. 29, 1933; children: Michael Archer, William Archer. Student, U. Idaho, 1929-30, 35-36, B.S., 1936; student, Pasadena Jr. Coll., 1931-32, U. Calif. at Los Angeles, summer 1934; A.M., Stanford, 1937, Ph.D., 1943. Research asst. Stanford U., 1936-37, teaching asst., 1937-38; instr. polit. sci. U. Idaho, 1938-39; acting instr. polit. sci. Stanford U., 1939-40; John M. Switzer fellow, summer 1939-40; chief personnel officer Walter Butler Constrn. Co., Farragut Naval Tng. Center, summer 1942; instr. polit. sci. U. Idaho, 1940-43, asst. prof. polit. sci., 1943-44, asso. prof. polit. sci., 1944-47; prof., head dept. social sci., asst. dean U. Idaho (Coll. Letters and Sci.), 1947-55, dean, 1955-70, Borah Distinguished prof. polit. sci., 1970-73, prof., dean emeritus, 1973—; Vis. prof. Stanford U., summer 1946, spring 1952, U. Calif., 1962-63; affiliate Center for Study Higher Edn., Berkeley, 1962-63; mem. steering com. N.W. Conf. on Higher

Edn., 1960-67, pres. conf., 1966-67; mem. bd. Am. Assn. of Partners of Alliance for Progress; chmn. Idaho Adv. Council on Higher Edn.; del. Gt. Plains UNESCO Conf., Denver, 1947; chmn. bd. William E. Borah Found. on Causes of War and Conditions of Peace, 1947-55; mem. Commn. to Study Orgn. Peace; dir. Bur. Pub. Affair Research, 1959-73, dir. emeritus, 1973—; dir. Inst. Human Behavior, 1970—. Author: The Direct Primary in Idaho, 1947, (with others) Introduction to Political Science, 1950, (with other) Western Politics, 1968, Politics in the American West, 1969, (with Sydney Duncombe) Recent Elections in Idaho (1964-70), 1972, Idaho Voting Trends: Party Realignment and Percentage of Voters for Candidates, Parties and Elections, 1890-1974, 1975, In Search of Peace: Starting From October 19, 1980, 1980, Why the Democrats Lost in 1980, 1980, On Understanding the Soviet Union, 1987; editor: The Responsibilities of Colleges and Universities, 1967; contbr. to: Ency. Britannica, 1974; also articles. Mem. Am. Polit. Sci. Assn. (exec. council 1952-53), Nat. Municipal League, Am. Soc. Pub. Adminstrn., Fgn. Policy Assn., UN Assn., AAUP, Western Polit. Sci. Assn. (pres. 1950), Phi Beta Kappa, Pi Gamma Mu, Kappa Delta Pi, Pi Sigma Alpha. Home: 516 Eisenhower Moscow ID 83843

MARTIN, CHIPPA, counseling psychologist; b. Bronx, N.Y., Sept. 6, 1942; d. Murray and Rose (Kaplan) Riback; B.A., Queens Coll., 1964; M.A., Goddard Coll., 1978; children—Tara, Beth. Tchr., Manhasset (N.Y.) High Sch., 1964-65; tchr., humanities cons. Millbrook (N.Y.) High Sch., 1972-74; certifier Cambridge (Mass.) Govt. Housing, 1975-77; dir., counselor Aradia Counseling, Boston, 1978—; ptnr. real estate investment co., 1982—. Vice-pres., League Preservation of Hudson Valley, 1972. Lic. social worker, Mass.; nat. cert. counselor art. Mem. Nat. Assn. Social Workers, Am. Personnel and Guidance Assn., Assn. Specialists in Group Work, Assn. Women in Psychology, Boston Visual Artists' Union, Cape Cod Art Assn., Falmouth Artists' Guild, Provincetown Art Assn. Recipient numerous art awards at one-woman and group exhbns.; work included in pvt. collections. Home: 251 Mill St Newtonville MA 02668

MARTIN, CLAUDE RAYMOND, JR., marketing consultant, educator; b. Harrisburg, Pa., May 11, 1932; s. Claude R. and Marie Teresa (Stapf) M.; m. Marie Frances Culkin, Nov. 16, 1957; children: Elizabeth Ann, David Jude, Nancy Marie, William Jude, Patrick Jude, Cecelia Marie. B.S., U. Scranton, 1954, M.B.A, 1963; Ph.D., Columbia U., 1969. Newsman Sta. WILK-TV, Wilkes-Barre, Pa., 1953-55; news dir. Sta. WNEP-TV, Scranton, Pa., 1955-60; dir. systems Blue Cross & Blue Shield Ins., Wilkes-Barre, 1960-63; lectr. mktg. St. Francis Coll., Bklyn., 1964, U. Mich., Ann Arbor, 1965-68; asst. prof. U. Mich., 1968-73, asso. prof., 1973-77, prof., 1977-80, Isadore and Leon Winkelman prof. retail mktg., 1980—, chmn. mktg. dept., 1986—; dir. Perry Drug Stores; cons. mktg., 1966—; spl. cons. on research changes in U.S. currency Fed. Reserve System, 1978—. Contbr. articles on mktg. analysis, consumer research to profl. publs. Served with USNR, 1955-57. Mem. Acad. Mktg. Sci., Am. Mktg. Assn., S.W. Mktg. Assn., Bank Mktg. Assn., Assn. Consumer Research, Am. Collegiate Retailing Assn., Am. Acad. Advt. Roman Catholic. Home: 1116 Aberdeen Dr Ann Arbor MI 48104

MARTIN, CLYDE VERNE, psychiatrist; b. Coffeyville, Kans., Apr. 7, 1933; s. Howard Verne and Elfrieda Louise (Moehn) M.; m. Barbara Jean McNeilly, June 24, 1956; children—Kent Clyde, Kristin Claire, Kerry Constance, Kyle Curtis. Student Coffeyville Coll., 1951-52; A.B., U. Kans., 1955; M.D., 1958; M.A., Webster Coll., St. Louis, 1977; J.D., Thomas Jefferson Coll. Law, Los Angeles, 1985. Diplomate Am. Bd. Psychiatry and Neurology. Intern, Lewis Gale Hosp., Roanoke, Va., 1958-59; resident in psychiatry U. Kans. Med. Ctr., Kansas City, 1959-62, Fresno br. U. Calif.-San Francisco, 1978; staff psychiatrist Neurol. Hosp., Kansas City, 1962; practice medicine specializing in psychiatry, Kansas City, Mo., 1964-84; founder, med. dir., pres. bd. dirs. Mid-Continent Psychiat. Hosp., Olathe, Kans., 1972-84; adj. prof. psychology Baker U., Baldwin City, Kans., 1969-84; staff psychiatrist Atascadero State Hosp., Calif., 1984-85; clin. prof. psychiatry U. Calif., San Francisco, 1985—; chief psychiatrist Calif. Med. Facility, Vacaville, 1985-87; pres., editor Corrective and Social Psychiatry, Olathe, 1970-84, Atascadero, 1984-85, Fairfield, 1985—. Contbr. articles to profl. jours. Bd. dirs. Meth. Youthville, Newton, Kans. 1965-75, Spofford Home, Kansas City, 1974-78. Served to capt. USAF, 1962-64, col. USAFR. Fellow Royal Soc. Health, Am. Assn. Mental Health Profls. in Corrections, World Assn. Social Psychiatry, Am. Orthopsychiat. Assn.; mem. AMA, Am. Psychiat. Assn., Assn. for Advancement Psychotherapy, Am. Assn. Sex Educators, Counselors and Therapists (cert.), Assn. Mental Health Adminstrs. (cert.), N.Y. Acad. Sci., Phi Beta Pi, Pi Kappa Alpha. Methodist (del. Kans. East Conf. 1972-80, bd. global ministries 1974-80). Clubs: Carriage; Kansas City. Lodge: Mason. Office: PO Box 3365 Fairfield CA 94533

MARTIN, ESMOND BRADLEY, geographer; b. N.Y.C., Apr. 17, 1941; s. Esmond Bradley and Edwina (Atwell) M.; B.S., U. Ariz., 1964, M.A., 1966; Ph.D., U. Liverpool, 1970; m. Chryssee MacCasler Perry, Oct. 22, 1966. Research asso. U. Nairobi, 1967-83, U. Dar es Salaam, 1974-75, Dept. Edn., Zanzibar, 1975-76; cons. World Wildlife Fund and IUCN, 1978—; researcher Ministry of Info. and Culture, Sultanate of Oman, 1978. Mem. Lamu Soc. (mem. council 1973—), Kenya Mus. Soc. (founding mem., chmn. publs. com. 1971—), Royal Geograph. Soc., Explorers' Club, Inst. Brit. Geographers, Assn. Am. Geographers, Am. Geog. Soc., African Studies Assn., Royal African Soc., Geog. Assn. U.K., U.K. African Studies Assn. Club: Muthaiga. Author: The History of Malindi, 1973; Cargoes of the East: The Ports, Trade and Culture of The Arabian Seas and Western Indian Ocean, 1978; Zanzibar: Tradition and Revolution, 1978; Run, Rhino, Run, 1982; Rhino Exploitation, 1983; The Japanese Ivory Industry, 1985; editor: African Perspectives, 1981—. Office: PO Box 15510, Mbagathi, Nairobi Kenya

MARTIN, FRED KENNETH, JR., solar energy and real estate executive; b. Fresno, Calif., Nov. 21, 1942; s. Fred K. and Emma B. (Balmer) M.; m. Maria Armanno, June 5, 1976; children: Kenneth, Mario. AA, Fresno City Coll., 1964; Sec. of the Navy nomination to US Naval Acad., 1965; student, U. Santa Clara, 1986. With Travelers Corp., San Jose Calif. and Hartford, Conn., 1967-72, regional sales dir. L.H. & F.S., prodn. mgr., 1972-75; with Fafco Inc., Menlo Park, Calif., 1976—, nat. comml. sales mgr., 1971-78, gen. mgr., Bay Area Distbn. Co., 1978; pres., Fafco Solar Systems, 1979-83; dir., v.p. Solar Energy Sales, Inc.; pres., chmn. bd. Martin & Mickle Ins. and Fin. Corp., 1983-85; mgmt. cons., 1985-86; exec. v.p. Century 21 Bonus Realty, 1986—, also bd. dirs.; pub. Bonus News Inc., 1986—; mem. Century 21 Brokers Council and Advt. Com.; solar energy advisor Pacific Gas & Utility Co., U.S. Congressman Pete McCloskey, Calif. Solar Energy Commn., 1983-84. Contbg. author articles to profl. jours. Served with USMCR, 1960-68. Mem. Calif. Solar Energy Soc. (state bd. dirs.), Calif. Solar Energy Industries Assn., Calif. Insulation Contractors Assn. (div., chmn. govtl. affairs, chmn. polit. action com.), Internat. Solar Energy Soc., Nat. Assn. Realtors, Calif. Assn. Realtors, San Jose Real Estate Bd., Los Gatos-Saratoga Real Estate Bd. Republican. Lutheran.

MARTIN, FREDERICK, securities dealer, broker; b. Indpls., Mar. 24, 1908; s. William Nelson and Ida Martin; A.B., Butler U., 1928; postgrad. Harvard Law Sch., 1929; M.B.A., Harvard U., 1931; m. Eleanor Lauderdale Rankin, Feb. 14, 1942; children—Frederick, Melissa, Laurel. Round-the-world seaman S.S. Isthmian, 1932; acct. Cooney Mining Co., Silver City, N.Mex., 1933; security analyst Thomson & McKinnon, N.Y.C., 1934-39, Nat. Investors, 1940-41, Sterling Grace & Co., 1945-48, Joseph Faroll & Co., 1948-50; treas. Standard Cable Corp., Okla., 1951-52; exec. v.p. Dorsett Labs., 1952-58; owner Fred Martin & Co., Norman, Okla., 1959-68, La Jolla, Calif., 1969—; chmn. Naturizer Inc., Norman, 1958-59; pres. Investment Securities Assn., Oklahoma City, 1966; mem. N.Y. Soc. Security Analysts, 1946-61; spl. instr. bus. fin. Okla. U., 1958, 68; mem. U.S. Senatorial Bus. Adv. Bd., 1982. Sec., Park Bd. Norman, 1955-57, Bd. Adjustment Norman, 1958-60; mem. La Jolla Town Council, 1973. Served to lt. comdr. USNR, 1942-45. Recipient award San Diego Union Review, 1980. Mem. Stock & Bond Club, Nat. Assn. Securities Dealers, Securities Investor Protection Corp. Club: La Jolla Beach and Tennis. Contbr. articles, book reviews to profl. jours. Home and Office: 5551 Warbler Way La Jolla CA 92037

MARTIN, HAROLD EUGENE, publishing executive, consultant; b. Cullman, Ala., Oct. 4, 1923; s. Rufus John and Emma (Meadows) M.; m. Jean Elizabeth Wilson, Nov. 25, 1945; children: Brian, Anita. B.A. in History with honors, Howard Coll., Birmingham, Ala., 1954; M.A. in Journalism, Syracuse U., 1956. Asst. gen. mgr. Birmingham News Newhouse Newspapers, 1960-63, asst. prodn. mgr. St. Louis Globe-Democrat, 1958-60, asst. bus. mgr. Syracuse Herald Jour., 1957-58; pub. Montgomery Advertiser and Ala. Jour., Ala., 1963-70; pres. Multimedia Newspapers, editor and pub. Montgomery Advertiser and Ala. Jour. Multimedia, Inc., 1970-78, v.p., mem. mgmt. bd., 1973-78, also corp. dir.; exec. v.p., chief exec. officer So. Baptist Radio and TV Commn., Ft. Worth, 1979; pres. Jefferson Pilot Publs., Inc., Beaumont, Tex., 1980-85; pres., pub. Beaumont Enterprise, 1981-85; owner, pub. Herald Citizen daily newspaper, Cookeville, Tenn., 1970-78, News-Observer, Crossett, Ark., 1970-78; co-owner, pub Baxter Bull., Mountain Home, Ark., 1970-78; dir. Jefferson Pilot Corp.; Disting. vis. Prof. Sch. Journalism, U. Fla., 1979-80; mem. faculty Samford U., 1961; juror Pulitzer Prize, 1971-72. Contbr. articles to newspapers. Bd. dirs. Billy Graham Evangelistic Assn., Mpls. Recipient awards for articles; recipient citation Howard Coll, 1965, award of Outstanding Merit Ala. Dental Assn., 1966, Community Service award AP Assn., 1969, 72, 73, Pulitzer prize, 1970, First Place Newswriting award AP, 1971, Newswriting award for Best Stories of Yr. by Ala. Reporters AP, 1974, 75, Canon award, 1972, Ann. award for outstanding contbn. to health care Ala. State Nurses's Assn., 1973, News award Ala. State Nurses' Assn., 1976, Ala. Bapt. Communications award Ala. Bapt. State Conv., 1975; named Alumnus of Yr. Samford U., 1970. Mem. Am. Soc. Newspaper Editors, Am. Newspaper Pubs. Assn., So. Newspaper Pubs. Assn.. (editorial com.), Alumni Assn. Samford u. (pres. 1967), Sigma Delta Chi (Green Eye Shade citation for Reporting 1969). Baptist. Home: 4958 Overton Woods Ct Fort Worth TX 76109

MARTIN, HELEN ELIZABETH, teacher; b. West Chester, Pa., Feb. 19, 1945; d. Thomas Edwin and Elizabeth Temple (Walker) M.; B.A., The King's Coll., Briarcliff Manor, N.Y., 1967; M.Ed., West Chester U., 1970; postgrad. Goethe Inst., Freiberg, Fed. Republic Germany, 1979, Oxford U., 1979. Tchr. math. and sci. Unionville (Pa.) High Sch., 1967—; mem. Carnegie Forum on Edn. and the Economy. Mem. Pa. Republican State Com., Rep. Com. of Chester County, 1987—. Named Alumna of the Yr. The King's Coll., 1987. Fellow Am. Sci. Affiliation; mem. AAAS, Nat. Bd. Profl. Teaching Standards, Nat. Sci. Tchrs. Assn., Nat. Council Tchrs. Math., History Sci. Soc., So. Chester County Rep. Women's Council, Red Clay Valley Assn., Brandywine Valley Assn. Clubs: Delaware Camera, Women's Rep. of Chester County, Nat. Sci. Tchrs. Assn. (internat. lectr. 1987), Assn. for Sci. Edn. in U.K. (internat. lectr. 1987). Home: 329 Lambortown Rd West Grove PA 19390 Office: Unionville High Sch Unionville PA 19375

MARTIN, IAN GEORGE, food products company executive; b. Melbourne, Victoria, Australia, Dec. 4, 1927; s. Cecil George Thomas and Frances Gertrude (Usher) M.; m. Patricia Anne Torney; children: Prudence Anne, David Cameron, Jonathan Ian. Diploma in export, U. Melbourne, 1958. Asst. acct. Trotting Control Bd., Melbourne, 1948-50; freight clk. Wilh Wilhelmsen Agy., Melbourne, 1950-52; with Kraft Foods Ltd., Melbourne, 1952—, export mgr., 1973-81, export dir., 1981—; v.p. Kraft Asia Pacific, Melbourne, 1986—; mng. dir. Kraft Middle East, London, 1988—. Decorated Order of Australia, 1985. Mem. Australian Inst. Export, Australian Mfrs. Export Council. Club: Melbourne Cricket. Home: 165 Gipps St, East Melbourne 3802, Australia Office: Kraft Mid East, 77 S Audely St, London England

MARTIN, JAMES GRUBBS, governor of North Carolina; b. Savannah, Ga., Dec. 11, 1935; s. Arthur Morrison and Mary Julia (Grubbs) M.; m. Dorothy Ann McAulay, June 1, 1957; children: James Grubbs, Emily Wood, Arthur Benson. BS, Davidson Coll., 1957; PhD, Princeton U., 1960. Assoc. prof. chemistry Davidson (N.C.) Coll., 1960-72; mem. 93d to 98th Congresses from N.C., 1973-85; gov. State of N.C., 1985—; mem. Mecklenburg (N.C.) Bd. County Commrs., 1966-72, chmn., 1967-68, 70-71; founder, 1st chmn. Centralina Council Govts., Charlotte, N.C., 1968-70; v.p. Nat. Assn. Regional Councils, 1970-72; pres. N.C. Assn. County Commrs., 1970-71; mem. exec. com. Nat. Rep. Congressional Com.; del. Rep. Nat. Conv., 1968. Danforth fellow, 1957-60. Mem. Beta Theta Pi (v.p., trustee 1966-69, pres. 1975-78). Presbyterian (deacon). Clubs: Masons (32 deg.), Shriners. Office: Office of the Gov 116 W Jones St Raleigh NC 27611 *

MARTIN, JAMES NICOLAS, linguist, educator; b. Detroit, Nov. 15, 1939; s. Hugh and Bernice Martin. BA in Econs., Wayne State U., 1961; MA in Linguistics, UCLA, 1969. Personnel analyst State of Calif., Los Angeles, 1964-65; researcher Chancellor's Office, Calif. State Colls. and Univs., 1965-67, U. Wroclaw, Poland, 1970-71; lectr. Adam Mickiewicz U., Poznan, Poland, 1971-72, Freie U. Berlin, 1972-77, U. Münster, Fed. Republic Germany, 1977-80; adminstrn. lectr. Coll. of Bus., Münster, 1980—; lectr. Econs. Inst., Boulder, Colo., 1977; cons. USIA, Washington, 1970-78, Polish Govt., 1970-72, Yugoslav Govt., 1977, Münster C. of C., 1983-87. Contbr. articles to profl. jours. V.p. Deutsch-Amerikanische Gesellschaft, Münster, 1983-87. Fulbright prof., Poland, 1970-72; various acad. awards; N.Am. championship in rowing, 1960. Mem. Internat. Assn. Tchrs. English as Second Lang. Club: Bogenschutzen (Münster) (v.p.). Office: Fach Hochschule Münster, Corrensstrasse 25, 4400 Münster Federal Republic of Germany

MARTÍN, JOSÉ GINORIS, nuclear and solar energy engineer, educator; b. Havana, Cuba, Feb. 4, 1941; came to U.S., 1961, naturalized, 1967; s. José and María Ginoris; m. Dagma Faria Neto, Sept. 2, 1976, B.S. with honors in Nuclear Engring., Miss. State U., 1964; M.S., U. Wis., 1966, Ph.D., 1971. OAS prof. Instituto Politécnico Nacional del Méx., 1971, prof., 1972-75; vis. prof. Instituto Militar de Engenharia, Rio de Janeiro, Brazil, 1973; mem. faculty U. Lowell (Mass.), 1975—, prof. dept. energy engring., 1980—; chief evaluator Internat. Energy Agy. Small Solar Power Systems, Spain, 1983-85; cons. in field; vis. prof. U. Mex., Ariz. State U. Coll. Architecture; instr. Internat. Solar Sch., Igls, Austria, 1985; Prof. alternative energy, Urbino, Italy, 1985. Contbr. articles to profl. jours.; co-editor: Procs. Internat. Workshop on Distributed Solar Collectors, 1983. Mem. U.S. del. Internat. Energy Agy. Solar Project; bd. dirs. UNITAS, Lowell; mem. Talented and Gifted Magnet Program Com.; councilor Master Adv. Bd. for Bilingual Programs. Fellow Wis. Alumni Research Found., 1974-75; U.S. AEC fellow, 1975-78; NSF grantee, 1979-80; prin. investigator NRC, 1976-80. Fellow Am. Soc. Engring. Edn.; mem. Am. Nuclear Soc., Sociedad Mexicana de Física, Sigma Xi, Tau Beta Pi, Phi Kappa Phi. Home: 85 Mansur St Lowell MA 01852 Office: U Lowell Energy Ctr 1 University Ave Lowell MA 01854

MARTIN, JOSEPH, JR., lawyer, diplomat; b. San Francisco, May 21, 1915; m. Ellen Chamberlain Martin, July 5, 1946; children: Luther Greene, Ellen Myers. AB, Yale U., 1936, LLB, 1939. Assoc. Cadwalader, Wickersham & Taft, N.Y.C., 1939-41; ptnr. Wallace, Garrison, Norton & Ray, San Francisco, 1946-55, Pettit & Martin, San Francisco, 1955-70, 73—; gen. counsel FTC, Washington, 1970-71; ambassador, U.S. rep. Disarmament Conf., Geneva, 1971-76; mem. Pres.'s Adv. Com. for Arms Control and Disarmament, 1974-78; bd. dirs. Arcata Corp., Allstar Inns, Astec Industries, Inc. Pres. Pub. Utilities Commn., San Francisco, 1956-60; Rep. nat. committeeman for Calif., 1960-64; treas. Rep. Party Calif., 1956-58; bd. dirs. Patrons of Art and Music, Calif. Palace of Legion of Honor, 1958-70, pres., 1963-68; bd. dirs. Arms Control Assn., 1977—; pres. Friends of Legal Assistance to Elderly, 1983—. Served to lt. comdr. USNR, 1941-46. Recipient Ofcl. commendation for Outstanding Service as Gen. Counsel FTC, 1973, Distinguished Honor award U.S. ACDA, 1973, Lifetime Achievement award Legal Assistance to the Elderly, 1981. Fellow Am. Bar Found. Clubs: Burlingame Country, Pacific Union. Home: 2580 Broadway San Francisco CA 94115 Office: Pettit & Martin 101 California St San Francisco CA 94111

MARTIN, JOSEPH E., management consultant; b. Kelvington, Sask., Can., Jan. 13, 1937; s. George Herbert and Margaret J.S. (Einarsson) M.; m. Sally Ann Dagg, Nov. 9, 1938; children: Michelle, Jon, Michael, Meredith. BA with honors, U. Man., Can., 1959; postgrad., Harvard U., 1982-83. Cert. mgmt. cons. Investment analyst Monarch Life Co., Winnipeg, Man., 1959-61; exec. asst. to Premier Provincial Govt. Man., Winnipeg, 1961-66; cons. Touche Ross Mgmt. Cons., Winnipeg, 1966-68, sr. cons., 1968-72, ptnr., 1972-78, ptnr.-in-charge, 1978—; chmn. Touche Ross Internat. Mgmt. Cons., Winnipeg, 1983. Contbr. articles to profl. jours. Pres. Man. Young Conservatives, 1959-61; mem. adv. council Can. Mus. of Civilization, Ottawa, 1985—. Fellow Inst. Cert. Mgmt. Cons. of Ont. (pres. 1981-82); Man. Hist. Soc. (pres. 1967-68), Can. Assn. Mgmt. Cons. Mem. Conservative Party. Mem. Anglican Ch. Clubs: Albany, Cricket (Cambridge). Office: Touche Ross Mgmt Cons, PO Box 12, 100 King St W, Toronto, ON Canada M5X 1B3

MARTIN, JUDITH CAROL MORAN, lawyer; b. Ann Arbor, Mich., Feb. 10, 1943; d. D. Lawrence and Donna E. (Webb) Moran; children: Laura C., Paul M., A. Lindsay; m. Daniel B. Ventres Jr., Dec. 27, 1984. BA, U. Mich., 1963; postgrad., Universite de Jean Moulin, Institut du Droit, Lyon, France, 1982; JD, U. Minn., 1982; cert., Am. Coll., 1986. Bar: Minn. 1982; CLU, chartered fin. analyst. Tax supr., dir. fin. planning, asst. nat. dir. Coopers & Lybrand, Mpls., 1981-84; dir. fin. planning Investors Diversified Services subs. Am. Express, Mpls. and N.Y.C., 1984-85; sr. tax mgr., dir. fin. planning KPMG Peat Marwick Main & Co., Mpls., 1985—. Author contg. edn. materials on taxation and income and estate planning. Mem. Mpls. C. of C. campaign, Downtown Council Coms., Mpls., 1982-84, Metro Tax Planning Group, 1984-86, Mpl. Estate Planning Council, 1985—; class chmn. fundraising campaign U. Minn. Law Sch., Mpls., 1985; usher Christ Presbyn. Ch., Edina, Minn., 1983—; mem. adv. council on planned giving ARC. Mem. ABA (task force on legal fin. planning), Minn. Bar Assn., Hennepin County Bar Assn., Minn. Soc. CPA's (instr. continuing legal edn. 1983-84, continuing profl. edn. 1986, individual trust and estate provisions 1986 tax reform act 1983-86), Am. Assn. Independent Investors (speaker), Am. Soc. CLU's, Minn. Soc. CLU's (spl. interest groups), Minn. Women Lawyers, Lex Alumnae, U. Mich. Alumni Assn., U. Minn. Alumni Assn. (council govs. 1988—), Minn. World Trade Assn., Internat. Assn. Fin. Planners, Twin Cities Assn. Fin. Planners, U. Minn. Alumni Club (council govs.), Kappa Kappa Gamma. Clubs: Interlachen, Athletic, Lafayette (Mpls.). Home: 1355 Vine Place Orono MN 55364 Office: KPMG Peat Marwick Main & Co IDS Tower Suite 1700 Minneapolis MN 55402

MARTIN, KATHLEEN ANNE, information management consultant; b. Rochester, N.Y., Aug. 19, 1942; d. Edwin Wilkins and Hilda Ellen (Hartell) Martin; B.A., Marygrove Coll., Detroit, 1964; M.A. in L.S. (Josenhans scholar 1965), U. Mich., 1965; advanced online tng. cert. Nat. Library Medicine, 1979; m. Oliver Kalman Peterdy, Oct. 15, 1971 (div. 1981); children—Elizabeth, Matthew. Librarian, Detroit Public Library, 1964-66; bibliographer, then asst. tech. services librarian Edward G. Miner Med. Library, U. Rochester, 1969-72; librarian lab. indsl. medicine Eastman Kodak Co., Rochester, 1966-69, librarian health, safety and human factors lab., 1972-78, tech. info. analyst, 1978-84, health and environment lab., 1978-86; pres. Info Edge, Inc., 1987—. Mem. AAUW (treas. Rochester br. 1979-80), Spl. Libraries Assn., Med. Library Assn., Nat. Assn. Female Execs. Home and Office: 4 Belmont Rd Rochester NY 14612

MARTIN, LAURA BELLE, real estate and farm land manager, retired teacher; b. Jackson County, Minn., Nov. 3, 1915; d. Eugene Wellington and Mary Christina (Hanson) M. BS, Mankato State U., 1968. Tchr. rural schs., Renville County, Minn., 1937-41, 45-50, Wabasso (Minn.) Pub. Sch., 1963-81; pres. Renville Farms and Feed Lots, 1982—. Pres., Wabasso Minn. Edn. Assn., 1974-75, publicity chmn., 1968-74; sec. Hist. Renville Preservation Com., 1978-86, Town and Country Boosters, Renville, 1982-83, publicity chmn., 1988—; pub. chmn. Renville Mus., 1978—. Mem. Genealogy Soc. Renville County, Am. Legion Aux. Democrat. Lutheran. Home and Office: Box 567 Renville MN 56284

MARTIN, LUCY Z., public relations executive; b. Alton, Ill., July 8, 1941. BA, Northwestern U., 1963. Adminstrv. asst., copywriter Batz-Hodgson-Neuwoehner, Inc., St. Louis, 1963-64; news reporter, Midwest fashion editor Fairchild Publs., St. Louis, 1964-66; account exec. Milici Advt. Agy., Honolulu, 1967; publs. dir. Barnes Med. Ctr., St. Louis, 1968-69; communications cons. Fleishman-Hillard, St. Louis, 1970-74, Portland, Oreg., 1974-86; pres.and chief exec. officer Lucy Z. Martin & Assocs., Inc., Portland, 1987—. Chmn. women's adv. com. Reed Coll., Portland, 1977-79; mem. Oreg. Commn. for Women, 1984-87; bd. dirs. Ronald McDonald House Oreg., 1986, Oreg. Sch. Arts & Crafts, 1988-90. Recipient MacEachern Citation Acad. Hosp. Pub. Relations, 1978, Rosey awards Portland Advt. Fedn., 1979, Achievement award Soc. Tech. Communications, 1982, Disting. Tech. Communication award, 1982, Exceptional Achievement award Council for Advancement and Support Edn., 1983, Monsoon award Internat. Graphics, Inc., 1984; named Woman of Achievement Daily Jour. Commerce, 1980. Mem. Pub. Relations Soc. Am. (pres. Columbia River chpt. 1984, chmn. bd. 1980-84, Oreg. del. 1984-86, judicial panel N. Pacific dist 1985-86, exec. bd. health care sect. 1986-87, mem. Counselors Acad., Spotlight awards 1985, 86, 87), Portland Pub. Relations Roundtable (chmn. 1985, bd. dirs. 1983-85), Assn. Western Hosps. (editorial adv. bd. 1984-85), Best of West awards 1978, 80, 83, 87), Oreg. Hosp. Pub. Relations Orgn. (pres. 1981, chmn. bd. 1982), Acad. Health Service Mktg., Am. Hosp. Assn., Am. Mktg. Assn., Am. Soc. Hosp. Mktg. & Pub. Relations, Healthcare Communicators Oreg., Internat. Assn. Bus. Communicators (18 awards 1981-87), Oreg. Assn. Hosps. Oreg. Press Women, Nat. and Oreg. Soc. Healthcare Planning & Mktg., Women in Communications (Matrix award 1977). Office: 4380 SW Macadam Ave Suite 285 The River Forum Bldg Portland OR 97201-6408

MARTIN, MICHAEL JOHN CHARLES, educator, consultant; b. Wellingborough, Northamptonshire, Eng., June 8, 1931; s. Alfred Ernest and Catherine Eliza (Rowell) M.; m. Cynthia Pauline, Sept. 1964; children: David Charles, Kathryn Julia. BSc with honors, Nottingham U., 1954; PhD, Sheffield U., 1959. Sci. officer Royal Naval Sci. Service, Portland, Dorset, U.K., 1954-55; research demonstrator in physics Sheffield U., 1955-58; sr. physicist Philips Research Labs., Redhill, Surrey, U.K., 1958-60; O.R. cons. Brit. Coal, London, 1961-64; sr. lectr. Mgmt. Ctr., Bradford U., Eng., 1964-73; vis. prof. systems engring. Iowa State U., Ames, 1970-71; vis. prof. bus. adminstrn. U. Ill., Urbana, 1971-72; prof. bus. St. Mary's U., Halifax, Can., 1973-76; prof. technol. mgmt. Dalhousie U., Halifax, 1976—. Author: Managing Technological Innovation & Entrepreneurship, 1984, 3 other books, numerous chpts. and articles. Served with mil., 1950-51. Recipient miscellaneous research grants. Office: Dalhousie U Sch Bus, 6152 Coburg Rd, Halifax, NS Canada B3H 1Z5

MARTIN, MICHAEL TOWNSEND, racing horse stable executive, sports marketing consultant; b. N.Y.C., Nov. 21, 1941; s. Townsend Bradley and Irene (Redmond) M.; m. Jennifer Johnston, Nov. 7, 1964 (div. Jan. 1977); children: Ryan Bradley, Christopher Townsend; m. Jean Kathleen Meyer, Mar. 1, 1980. Grad. The Choate Sch., 1960; student Rutgers U., 1961-62. Asst. gen. mgr. N.Y. Jets Football Club, N.Y.C., 1968-74; v.p. NAMANCO Prodns., N.Y.C., 1975-76; v.p., gen. mgr. Cosmos Soccer Club, N.Y.C., 1976-77; exec. asst. Warner Communications, N.Y.C., 1978-84; owner, operator Martin Racing Stable, N.Y.C., 1983—; chmn., chief exec. officer Hydro-Train Systems Inc., 1987—; ptnr. Halstead Property Co., 1987—; bd. advisors N.Y. Zool. Soc., N.Y.C., 1984—, N.Y. Aquarium, Coney Island, 1983—, Bklyn. Sports Found., 1987—. Bd. dirs. Old Westbury Gardens, Westbury, N.Y., 1983—, Phipps Houses, 1986—; trustee The Pennington Sch.; trustee, pres. Alumni and Parents Assn. Choate Rosemary Hall Sch.; bd. dirs. Ptnrs. for Youth, Inc., Los Angeles, 1983—, Very Spl. Arts, 1982—, Served to E-4 USN, 1963-67. Mem. Athletics Congress (life, cert. official 1984—), U.S. Tennis Assn. (life, N.Y.C.), Internat. Oceanographic Found. (Miami life mem.), Eastern N.Y. Thoroughbred Breeders Assn. (bd. dirs. 1987—), Fla. Thoroughbred Breeders Assn. Republican. Episcopalian. Clubs: N.Y. Athletic; Quogue Field (N.Y.). Avocations: major collection Inuit (Eskimo) art; marathon running. Home: 131 E 69 St Apt 11-A New York NY 10021 Office: 575 Madison Ave Suite 1006 New York NY 10022

MARTIN, PAUL, transportation executive; b. Windsor, Ont., Can., Aug. 28, 1938; s. Paul Joseph and Eleanor (Adams) M.; m. Sheila Ann Cowan, Sept. 11, 1965; children—Paul William James, Robert James Edward, David Patrick Anthony. BA in Philosophy and History, U. Toronto, Can., 1962, LLB, 1965, LL.B., 1965. Bar: Ont. 1966. Exec. asst. to pres. Power Corp. Can. Ltd., 1966-69, v.p., 1969-71; v.p. spl. projects Consol.-Bathurst Ltd., 1971-73; v.p. planning and devel. Power Corp., Can., 1973-74; pres. Can. S.S. Lines Ltd., Montreal, 1974-80, chief exec. officer, 1976-80; pres., chief exec. officer CSL Group Inc., 1980—, also dir.; chmn. bd., chief exec. officer, Can. Steamship Lines Inc.; bd. dirs. Redpath Industries Ltd., Fednav Ltd., Imasco Ltd., C.B. Pak Inc., Mfrs. Life Ins. Co., Can. Shipbuilding and

Engring. Ltd. Mem. C.D. Howe Inst. Policy Analysis Com., Brit. N.Am. Com.; bd. dirs. Can. Council Christians and Jews, Can. Com. Lloyd's Register Shipping, North-South Inst., Can. Council Native Bus.; bd. govs. Concordia U., vice chmn. Mem. Can. Shipowners Assn. (chmn.), Gt. Lakes Waterways Assn. (bd. dirs.), Can. Shipbuilding and Ship Repairing Assn., Chartered Inst. Transport, Amnesty Internat. Clubs: University, Mt. Bruno Country, Mt. Royal. Office: CSL Group Inc, 759 Victoria Sq, Montreal, PQ Canada H2Y 2K3

MARTIN, PAUL E(DWARD), lawyer; b. Atchison, Kans., Feb. 5, 1928; s. Harres C. and Thelma F. (Wilson) M.; m. Betty Lou Crawford, Aug. 28, 1954; children—Cherry G., Paul A., Marylou. B.B.A., Baylor U., 1955, LL.B., 1956; LL.M., Harvard U., 1957. Bar: Tex. 1956, Pa. 1958. Assoc. Ballard, Spahr, Andrews & Ingersoll, Phila., 1957-58; ptnr. Fulbright & Jaworski, Houston, 1959-77; sr. ptnr. Hrdlicka, White, Johnson Williams & Martin, 1977—; instr. in estate planning U. Houston. Exec. com. Met. Houston March of Dimes, 1980-82 ; chmn. deacons West Meml. Baptist Ch., 1979-80; trustee Baylor U., 1970—, Meml. Hosp. System, 1980—, Fgn. Mission Bd., So. Bapt. Conv.; pres. Baylor U. Devel. Council, 1973-74. Served to lt. comdr. USN, 1947-53. Fellow Am. Coll. Probate Council; mem. ABA (sect. real property, probate and trust law and sect. taxation), State Bar Tex., Houston Bar Assn., Houston Estate and Fin. Forum (pres. 1965-66), Houston Bus. and Estate Planning Council, Phi Delta Phi. Republican. Club: Houston. Co-author: How to Live and Die with Texas Probate. Office: 1400 Citicorp Ctr 1200 Smith St Houston TX 77002

MARTIN, PETER SCOTT, banker; b. Napier, Hawkes Bay, New Zealand, Dec. 11, 1936; s. Archibald Laurenson and Helen Brenda (Tylee) M.; m. Joan Lorraine Milne, Oct. 24, 1959; children: Michelle Ann, Jacqueline Lee, Brett Andrew Scott. Grad. advanced mgmt. program, Harvard U., 1980. Examiner Inland Revenue Dept., Auckland, New Zealand, 1955-64; sec., mgr. Fiji Devel. Co., Suva, 1964-68; controller New Zealand Steel Ltd., Auckland, 1968-74; gen. mgr. Feltex Internat. Ltd., Auckland, 1974-84; mng. dir. Countrywide Banking Corp. Ltd., Auckland, 1984—; chmn. bd. dirs. Temple St. Investments Ltd., Auckland. Fellow New Zealand Soc. Accts. (chartered, cost and mgmt. acct.). Club: Auckland. Lodge: Rotary. Office: Countrywide Banking Corp Ltd, PO Box 5445, Mairangi Bay, Auckland New Zealand

MARTIN, R. KEITH, educator, university dean; b. Seattle, Sept. 5, 1933; s. Jerome Milton and Winifred (Gifford) M.; m. Carolyn Joanne Carosella, June 15, 1957; children—Jefferson, Sean, Jennifer, Katherine. A.B., Whitman Coll., 1955; M.B.A. with high honors, CCNY, 1965; Ph.D., U. Wash., 1973. Registered profl. engr.; cert. data processing, cert. systems profl. Div. mgr. Campus Merchandising Bur., Inc., N.Y.C., 1955-56; sales rep IBM, Seattle, 1956, Service Bur. Corp. subs. IBM, N.Y.C., 1957-58; mgr. mgmt. adv. services Price Waterhouse & Co., N.Y.C., 1959-65, Seattle, 1965-67; dir. mgmt. systems dept. U. Wash., 1967-71, lectr. dept. acctg. Sch. Bus. Adminstrn, 1971-73; asst. prof. dept. accountancy Baruch Coll., CUNY, 1973-76, assoc. prof., 1977-79; prof. acctg. and info. systems Fairfield U., 1979—, assoc. dean Sch. Bus., 1980-82, dean, 1982—; v.p. Eastalco Systems, 1971-72; faculty fin. div. Am. Mgmt. Assn., 1963-64; part-time lectr. Bellevue Community Coll., 1967-69, Shoreline Community Coll., 1968-72, Seattle U., 1971-72. Co-author: Management Control of Electronic Data Processing, 1965. Author: Management Information Systems in Higher Education: Case Studies at Three Universities, 1973, Effective Business Communications, 1976, 79, Systems Development and Computer Concepts, 1977. Assoc. editor: Industry Guides for Accountants and Auditors, 2 vols., 1980. Mem. editorial rev. bd. Dickenson Pub. Co., 1974-75, Prentice-Hall, Inc., 1977-78, 87-88, Reston Pub. Co., 1977-78, Jour. Acctg. Edn., 1981-83. Author monographs and articles. Mem. Citizens' Legis. Rev. Com., 1968-69; mem. City of Seattle EDP Adv. Com., 1968-71, chmn., 1968-69; vice chmn. subcom. Citizens Adv. Com. Licensing and Consumer Affairs, 1970-73; chmn. indsl. engring. adv. com. Shoreline Community Coll., 1968-72; mem. mgmt. info. systems data element task force Western Interstate Commn. Higher Edn., 1968-70, adv. council, 1969-71; mem. com. for non-partisan nomination and election of Bronxville Sch. Bd. Trustees, 1976-78, chmn., 1977, chmn. mgmt. policies and procedures com., 1981-82, mem. fin. com., chmn. audit subcom., 1985-86; cons. to Urban Acad., City N.Y., 1974-78; chmn., pres. Loft Film and Theatre Ctr., Inc., 1977-78, mem. adv. bd., 1982-83; v.p. Normandy Homeowners Assn., 1978-80, pres., 1983; sec.-treas. governing mem., mem. of policy com. The Com. on Developing American Capitalism, 1982—; bd. dirs. Intelligent Communications Network, 1982-86, chmn. audit com., 1983-86, mem. compensation com., 1982-86; trustee Conn. Joint Council Econ. Edn., 1982—; trustee Ctr. Fin. Studies, 1983—, vice chmn. audit com., 1983—, mem. exec. com., 1985—; cons. examiner and mem. com. bus. Charter Oak Coll., 1984—, co-chmn., 1987—, com. on degrees, 1987—; bd. advisers Econ. Club of Conn., Nat. Assn. Economists, 1985-86; mem. Am. Assembly of Collegiate Schs. of Bus. Task Force on Faculty Renewal, 1985-87; adv. bd. So. Conn. Bus. Jour., 1987-88; bd. edn. Village of Bronxville, 1987—; acad. policy and standards com. Inst. for Fin. Planning, 1987—; exec. com. Deans of Jesuit Schs. of Bus., 1987—, sec.-treas., 1988—. Recipient cert. of appreciation Am. Mgmt. Assn., 1966, cert. of merit for disting. service to Mgmt. Scis., 1969, for disting. service to info. systems profession, 1973; Merit award Assn. Systems Mgmt., 1971, Achievement award, 1972; cert. for service City of Seattle, 1973; named Outstanding Young Man Am., 1970, One of 300 Outstanding Alumni, Whitman Coll., 1979; Kellogg fellow, 1971-72, Price Waterhouse faculty fellow, 1976. Mem. Am. Inst. Indsl. Engrs. (dir. Seattle chpt. 1967-70, chmn. regional conf. 1969), Nat. Assn. Accts. (assoc. dir. N.Y. chpt. 1963-64, 75-85 Seattle chpt. 1967-70), Assn. Systems Mgmt. (sec. 1968-69, v.p. 1969-70, pres. Pacific N.W. chpt. 1970-71), Data Processing Mgmt. Assn., Assn. Computing Machinery, Soc. Cert. Data Processors, NSPE, N.Y. Soc. Profl. Engrs., Soc. Mgmt. Info. Systems, AAUP, Am. Acctg. Assn., Phi Delta Theta (province pres. 1986-87), Mu Gamma Tau, Phi Delta Kappa, Beta Alpha Psi. Club: Bronxville Field. Home: 2 Normandy Rd Bronxville NY 10708

MARTIN, RANDOLPH B., international development administrator; b. Decatur, Ill., Apr. 19, 1955; s. R. Leslie and MaryEllen (Tucker) M. BA Applied Behavioral Sci. magna cum laude, George Williams Coll., 1976; MA in Polit. Sci., New Sch. for Social Research, N.Y.C., 1984. Social worker Village of Downers Grove, Ill., 1974-75; rural devel. H.O.M.E. Coop., Vista, Orland, Maine, 1975; devel. worker Truk (Micronesia) Govt., YMCA, 1976; world services worker YMCA, Cairo, 1978-81; field adminstr. Internat. Rescue Com., Eau, Sudan, 1985; ops. mgr. Internat. Rescue Com., Gedaref, Sudan, 1985-86; country dir. Internat. Rescue Com., Khartoum, Soudan, 1986—; chmn. Volag Coordinating com., Showak, Sudan, 1985-86. Chmn. President St. Tenants Assn., Bklyn., 1982-85. Mem. Common Cause, Amnesty Internat. Home: 1686 W Sunset Decatur IL 62522 Office: Internat Rescue Com, PO Box 8269, Khartoum Sudan

MARTIN, RAYMOND BRUCE, plumbing equipment manufacturing company executive; b. N.Y.C., Oct. 23, 1934; s. Raymond M. and Margaret (Lennon) M.; m. Suzanne Ruth Longpre, Sept. 3, 1960; 1 son, Christopher Haines. A.B., Villanova U., 1956. With Corning Glass Works (N.Y.), 1956-68, nat. plumbing sales mgr., 1966-68; v.p. mktg. Briggs Mfg. Co., Warren, Mich., 1968-69, v.p., gen. mgr. plumbing fixture div., 1969-72; pres., chief exec. officer Water Control Internat. Inc., Troy, Mich., 1972—; dir. Internat. Tech. Corp., Cash Control Products Inc. Served with AUS, 1957-58. Mem. Am. Soc. Plumbing Engrs., Plumbing Mfrs. Inst. (chmn. HUD Task Group 1981-82, chmn. communications com. 1983-86), Am. Nat. Standards Inst., Am. Soc. Sanitary Engrs., ASME (panel 19), Republican. Roman Catholic (trustee 1982-86). Clubs: Orchard Lake Country, L'Arbre Croche. Patentee in field. Office: 2820-224 W Maple Rd Troy MI 48084

MARTIN, RICHARD BLAZO, chemist; b. Winchendon, Mass., July 1, 1917; s. William Butler and Elizabeth (Ela) M.; A.B., Clark U., 1939, M.A., 1940, Ph.D., 1949; m. Dorothy Mae Holway, Sept. 20, 1941; children—Lawrence Sanborn, Richard Holway, Janet Lois, Jean Leslie. Instr. chemistry Clark U., Worcester, Mass., 1946-49, asst. prof., 1949-53; chemist research br., research and devel. div. AEC, Oak Ridge Ops., 1953-56, chief research br., 1956-59, dep. dir. research and devel. div., 1959-66, dep. dir. lab. and univ. div., 1966-72, asst. br. chief waste mgmt. br., research and tech. support div., 1972-73, phys. scientist classification and tech. support br., research and tech. support div., 1973-77; cons. Dept. Energy, 1978-82, Los Alamos Tech. Assocs., Inc., 1981-83, Martin Marietta Energy Systems Inc., 1984—. Pack com. chmn. Great Smoky Mountain council Boy Scouts Am., 1964; pres. Cedar Hill PTA, 1963-64, mem. Oak Ridge PTA Council, 1963-64. Served to lt. comdr. USNR, 1941-46; capt. Res. ret., 1968. Mem. Am. Chem. Soc. (treas. Central Mass. sect. 1952-53), Res. Officers Assn. (pres. chpt. 1971-72, sec.-treas. 1973-74, historian 1977-78, Navy v.p. Tenn. dept. 1977-78), Mil. Order World Wars, Ret. Officers Assn., Am. Nuclear Soc., N.Y. Acad. Scis., AAAS, Naval Res. Assn., Navy League, Sigma Xi, Lambda Chi Alpha. Republican. Clubs: Nat. Campers and Hikers Assn. (pres. 1966-67, 80-82, v.p. 1984-86, 87—) (Oak Ridge); Smoky Mountain Coachmen (v.p. 1972-74) (Knoxville). Home: 117 Meadow Rd Oak Ridge TN 37830

MARTIN, RICHARD DOUGLAS, nuclear engineer, consultant; b. Englewood, N.J., May 17, 1959; s. Douglas Harry and Christine (Jacob) M.; m. JoAnne Diodato, Nov. 21, 1981. B.S. in Nuclear Engring., Pa. State U., 1981; postgrad. Poly. Inst. N.Y., White Plains, 1984. Cert. sr. reactor operator. Staff nuclear engr. Gen. Physics, Linfield, Pa., 1981-83; tng. coordinator PSE&G, Salem, N.J., 1983; tech. dir. LOM-TECH, Inc., Elmsford, N.Y., 1983-85; v.p., dir. CDS Techs., Inc., Allentown, Pa., 1985-87; pres. Douglas Martin & Assocs. Inc., Allentown, 1987—. Delegate 1988 Gov.'s Conference on Small Bus., Pa. Co-author: Mitigating Core Damage, 1982; Basic Chemistry Principles, 1986. Contbr. articles to profl. publs. Mem. alumni admissions bd. Pa. State U., 1983. Mem. Am. Nuclear Soc. (John and Muriel Landis award 1980), Am. Assn. Radon Scientists and Technologists (reg., nat. dir.), IEEE, AAAS, Allentown/Lehigh County C. of C. (chmn. environ. com., v.p. small council). Republican. Presbyterian. Current work: Nuclear power plant operations in the area of emergency condition evaluation and response, operations support, and training. Cons. on indoor radon remedial techniques. Operator gamma spectroscopy lab. Subspecialties: Plasma engineering; Information systems, storage, and retrieval (computer science). Office: Douglas Martin & Assocs Inc 520 Chestnut St Emmaus PA 18049

MARTIN, ROBERT RICHARD, managing director; b. Hempstead, N.Y., Mar. 4, 1947; s. John H. and Winifred (Schnieder) M.; m. Pamela A. Sutphen, Aug. 26, 1967; children: Tricia A., Colette S. BA, L.I. U., 1968; MBA, NYU, 1974. Fin. analyst Colgate Palmolive, N.Y.C., 1973-74, sr. product mgr., 1974-76; gen. mgr. Colgate Palmolive, Ivory Coast, 1976-80; asst. to exec. v.p. Colgate Palmolive, N.Y.C., 1980-82; gen. mgr. Colgate Palmolive, Panama, 1982-86, Thailand, 1987—. Founder Internat. Sch. Ivory Coast, 1976, Internat. Sch. Panama, 1982, Ivory Coast, 1979. Recipient Oral Care achievement award Panama Dental Assn., 1986, Country Contribution award Panama Govt., 1986. Mem. Am. C. of C. (Ivory Coast 1979, bd. dirs. Panama 1985, v.p., officer bd. govs. 1987—). Home: GPO Box 571, Bangkok 10500, Thailand Office: Colgate Palmolive Co, GPO Box 571, Bangkok Thailand

MARTIN, ROGER LLOYD, management executive; b. Kitchener, Ont., Can., Aug. 4, 1956; s. Lloyd Milton and Delphine Elvera (Horst) M.; m. Nancy Lorraine Lang, Sept. 24, 1983; children: Robert Lloyd, Jennifer Frances. BA in Econs., Harvard U., 1979, MBA, 1981. Prin. Can. Cons. Group, Toronto, Ont., Can., 1981-85; mng. dir., chief exec. officer Monitor Co. Can. Ltd., Toronto, 1986—; mem. editorial bd. Can. Competition Policy Record, Ottawa, Ont., 1986—; bd. dirs. Hamilton Group Ltd., Mississauga, Ont., 1986—. Contbr. antitrust and internat. trade articles to profl. jours. Clubs: Royal Can. Yacht (Toronto), Osler Bluffs Ski (Collingwood). Home: 70 Glenview Ave, Toronto, ON Canada M4R 1P8 Office: Monitor Co, 150 Bloor St W, Suite 710, Toronto, ON Canada M5S 2X9

MARTIN, RONALD, bank executive; b. Doncaster, Yorks, Eng., July 11, 1929; s. Albert and Elizabeth (Hudson) M.; m. Stella Bottomley, May 24, 1952 (div. June 1986): children: Theo, Bobette, Pollyanna. Grad., Royal Mil. Acad., Sandhurst, Eng. Commd. 2d lt. Corp of Royal Engrs. British Army, 1950, advanced through grades to maj., ret., 1968; mgr. Exporters Refinance Corp., London, 1968-72, Balfour, Williamson, London, 1972-78; mng. dir. Swaziland Bus. Devel. and Comml. Tng. Services, Ltd., Mbabane, 1978—; exec. dir. African Bus. Corp., Mbabane, 1986—; ptnr., cons. Contra Assocs., Mbabane, 1984—. Mem. Royal Swaziland Soc. of Sci. and Tech. (sec. 1980—). Anglican. Club: Army & Navy (London). Home: PO Box 344, Mbabane Swaziland Office: Swaziland Bus Devel &, Commercial Tng Services Ltd, PO Box 344, Mbabane Swaziland

MARTIN, ROSE, government law information specialist; b. Pozsony, Hungary, Aug. 25, 1928; came to U.S., 1949, naturalized, 1954; d. Ferenc and Zsuzsanna (Nehai Szabo) Kocsis; m. Donald L. Martin, Aug. 23, 1961; 1 child, Virginia Kim. Student Seton Hall U., 1960-61; B.B.A., Kensington U., Glendale, Calif., 1968-69; cert. Cath. U. Am. 1981, George Washington U., 1982. Documents librarian Seton Hall U., South Orange, N.J., 1958-61; mem. office staff Dept. Def., Washington, 1962-63, Dept. Agr., Washington, 1963-67; info. specialist-law Office Adminstrv. Law Judges, Dept. Labor, Washington, 1976—. Active Republican Club, Great Falls, Va., 1986—. Recipient Meritorious award Dept. Agr., 1966, Outstanding award Dept. Labor, 1977. Mem. Am. Assn. Law Libraries, Gt. Falls Woman's Club. Roman Catholic. Club: River Bend Golf and Country (Great Falls). Avocations: travel; tennis; reading; swimming; cooking. Home: PO Box 513 The Plains VA 22171

MARTIN, WAYNE MALLOTT, lawyer, real estate company executive; b. Chgo., Jan. 9, 1950; s. Mallott Caldwell and Helen (Honkisz) M.; m. Josephine Ann Giordano, Mar. 18, 1978; 1 child, Bradley. BA, Drake U., 1972; JD, De Paul U., 1977. Bar: Ill. 1978. Loan officer Clyde Savs. & Loan Assn., Chgo., 1972-75, Am. Nat. Bank, Chgo., 1976-77; sales dir., atty. financing Inland Real Estate Corp., Chgo., Oak Brook, then Palatine, Ill., 1977-83; pres. Inland Property Sales, Inc., Palatine, 1983-84, Oak Brook, Ill., 1984-86; Dome Investments, Inc., Northbrook, Ill., 1986-87; Bramar Mortgage Corp., 1988—; Quest Mortgage Co., Rolling Meadows, Ill., 1986—. Mem. ABA, Ill. Bar Assn., Chgo. Bar Assn., Nat. Bd. Realtors, Ill. Bd. Realtors, Chgo. Bd. Realtors (bd. dirs. 1986—, trustee action com. 1986—, fin. com. 1986—, chmn. orientation com. 1987-88), Chicagoland Assn. Real Estate Bds. (chmn. 1987-88), Westside Bd. Realtors (bd. dirs. 1983-84, pres. 1984—), Interboard Real Estate Affairs Council (chmn. 1987-88). Home: 1618 RFD Picardy Ct Long Grove IL 60047 Office: Bramar Mortgage Corp 2701 Algonquin Rd Suite 202 Rolling Meadows IL 60008

MARTIN, WILFRED SAMUEL, management consultant; b. Adamsville, Pa., June 11, 1910; s. Albert W. and Elizabeth (Porter) M.; B.S., Iowa State U., 1930; M.S., U. Cin., 1938; m. Elizabeth Myers, July 9, 1938; children—Peter, Judith (Mrs. Peter Kleinman), Nancy (Mrs. Richard Foss), Paula (Mrs. Dale Birdsell). Chem. engr. process devel. dept. Procter & Gamble Co., Cin., 1930-50, mgr. drug products mfg., 1950-51, asso. dir. chem. div., 1952-53, dir. product devel., soap products div., 1953-63, mgr. mfg. and products devel. Food Products div., 1963-71, sr. dir. research and devel., 1971-75; mgmt. cons., 1975—. Mem. Wyoming (Ohio) Bd. Edn., 1961-69, pres., 1965-68. Bd. dirs. Indsl. Research Inst., 1964-68, v.p., 1968-69, pres., 1970-71; chmn. trustee Ohio Presbyn. Homes, Columbus, Ohio, 1959-69, 73-77; vice chmn. bd. trustees Pikeville (Ky.) Coll., 1973-76, 80-86, trustee emeritus, 1986—, chmn. bd. trustees, 1976-78, 83-84, mem., 1980-84. Adv. council Clarkson Coll., Potsdam, N.Y., 1975-81. Fellow AAAS, Am. Inst. of Chemists; mem. Am. Chem. Soc., Am. Inst. Chem. Engrs., Soc. Chem. Industry, Am. Oil Chemist Soc., Engring. Soc. Cin. (dir. 1972-75), N.Y. Acad. Scis., Am. Mgmt. Assn. (research devel. council 1974-81), Soc. Research Adminstrs. Club: Wyoming Golf (Cin.). Home: 504 Hickory Hill Ln Cincinnati OH 45215

MARTIN, WILLIAM RAYMOND, financial planner; b. Phila., Oct. 16, 1939; s. Clyde Davis and Mary Anna (Coates) M.; m. Michaela Smink, Sept. 8, 1962 (div. 1969); 1 child, James; m. Margaret Scouten, Oct. 16, 1970 (div. 1983); children: Mary Frances, Susanna; m. Joan Friedman Kennedy, Jan. 29, 1988. BSME, Lehigh U., 1960; MBA, U. Pa., 1973. Mem. engring. staff Pa. R.R., 1960-65; asst. gen. mgr. Excelsior Truck Leasing, Phila., 1965-71; sr. analyst Assn. Am. R.R.s, Washington, 1973-76, mgr. engring. econ., 1976-78; mgr. fin. analysis So. Ry., Washington, 1978-83; dir. fin. planning Norfolk So. Corp., Va., 1984—. Contbr. articles to profl. jours. Bd. dirs. The Williams Sch., Norfolk, 1988—. Mem. Soc. Automotive Engrs., ASME. Home: 2605 Ridley Pl Virginia Beach VA 23454 Office: Norfolk So Corp Three Commercial Pl Norfolk VA 23510

MARTINA, DON, former prime minister Netherlands Antilles. Former fin. officer Govt. of Curacao, Netherlands Antilles, head govt. social affairs; M.P. Netherlands Antilles, 1979—, prime minister, 1979-84, 85-88, former minister gen. affairs; founder, leader New Antilles Movement, 1979. Address: Office of Prime Minister, Willemstad Netherlands Antilles *

MARTIN DE BARTOLOMÉ, HELEN ELIZABETH DAWN, radio station director; b. York, England, Jan. 10, 1924; d. Alfred Ernest and Katharine Helen (Graham) Irvine; m. Stephen Martin de Bartolomé, Sept. 13, 1947; children: Helen, Charles, John. BA, Oxford U., Eng., 1948; MA, Oxford U., 1964. Lectr. Manchester U., Eng., 1947-48, 1951-52; dir. Radio Hallam, Sheffield, Eng., 1974—. vol. charity work, 1952—. Anglican. Home: 16 Dalewood Dr, Sheffield S8 0EA, England Office: Radio Hallam, PO Box 194, Sheffield S1 16P, England

MARTIN DEL CAMPO, DIEGO RAMIRO, chemical executive; b. Guadalajara, Jalisco, Mex., Dec. 6, 1929; s. Ramon R. and Maria Guadalupe (Fernandez del Valle) Martin del C.; B.Chem.Engring., McGill U., Montreal, Que., Can., 1951; M.Econs. and Adminstrn., U. Autonoma Guadaljara, 1975; m. Giomar von Knobloch, Mar. 3, 1973; children—Diego, Rosalia, Francisco, Juan Valente, Giomar, Carmen. Engr., Resinera Uruapan, S.A., Uruapan, 1951-55, Michoacana de Occidente, Mexico City, 1955-59; with Resinera del Tigre, S. de R.L. de C.V., Guadaljara, 1959-85, pres., chmn. bd., 1977—; with Newport Mexicana, S.A. de C.V., Guadalajara, 1965—, pres., chmn. bd., 1977—; with Nuodex Mexicana, S.A. de C.V. Mexico City, 1974—, pres., chmn. bd., 1974—; pres., chmn. bd. Concord N.V. Curazao, 1979—, Victory Internat. Investment Corp., Panama, 1982—; chmn. bd. Hotel Victoria, S.A. Decorated Orden de la Lealtad, 1974. Mem. Am. Inst. Chem. Engrs., Mex. Inst. Chem. Engrs., Camara Industrias Derivadas de la Silvicultura (dir. 1971-76), Union Nacional Resineros (dir., del.), Assn. Jalisciense Titulares de Aprovechamientos Forestales (dir. from 1960). Roman Catholic. Clubs: Industrial (Mexico City); Guadalajara Country. Home: 130 Calderonde la Barca, Guadalajara, Jalisco Mexico also: Taine 731, Mexico City Mexico Office: 2560 Calle, 26 Z Ind Guadaljara, Jalisco Mexico Other: Galileo 20, Piso 2, Mexico City Mexico

MARTINEAU, JEAN-CHARLES, architect; b. Montcerf, Que., Can., Sept. 30, 1934; s. Leonard and Jeanne (Mathieu) M.; m. Huguette Tetrault, Aug. 29, 1959; children—Liliane, Philippe. BArch., McGill U., Montreal, Que., 1959, postgrad., 1961. Prin. J.C. Martineau, Architect, Montreal, 1960-67, Bisson, Hebert & Martineau, Montreal, 1967-68; asst. dir. Montreal U., 1968-73; dir. architecture Hydro-Quebec, Montreal, 1973—; pres. profl. inspection com. Order of Architects, Montreal, 1975—. Recipient Best Use of Concrete award Am. Concrete Inst. 1982, Excellence in Architecture award Order of Architects, 1981. Mem. Ordre des Architectes du Que, Royal Archtl. Inst. Can., Can. Elec. Assn. Clubs: Yacht (Longdevil); Am. Orchid Soc., Montreal Orchid Soc. Montreal. Avocations: skiing, jogging, sailing, horticulture in glass-house with solar heat. Office: Hydro-Quebec, 1001 de maisonneuve East, Montreal, PQ Canada H2L 4S7

MARTINET, GILLES HENRI, French ambassador; b. Paris, Aug. 8, 1916; s. Henri and Colette M.; m. Iole Liliana Buozzi, July 7, 1938; children—Michele Krivine, Laure Meuro. Diplome études supérieur d'histoire, Sorbonne, U. Paris, 1938. Chief editor France Press, Paris, 1944-49; dir. L'Observateur, Paris, 1950-64; nat. sec. PSU and Socialist Party of France, Paris, 1960-79; mem. European Parliament, Strasbourg, France, 1979-81; ambassador of France to Italy, Rome, 1981-85. Author 7 books. Decorated Légion d'Honneur; médaille de la Résistance; comdr. Order Arts and Lettres; comdr. Ordre National du Merite; grand cross Order of Merite of the Italian Republic. Office: Ministiere Affaires Etranger, Paris France

MARTINET, HANNE, French language educator; b. Copenhagen, Mar. 3, 1929; d. André Martinet and Karen Mikkelsen-Sørensen; m. Frans Lichtenberg (div. 1972); children: Ivan, Martin. MA, U. Copenhagen, 1974. Teaching asst. U. Copenhagen, 1973-78, U. Odense, Denmark, 1974; teaching asst. Copenhagen Sch. Econs. and Bus., 1974-75, jr. lectr. French, 1975-79, sr. lectr., 1979—. Co-author: Grammaire fonctionnelle du français, 1979; mem. editorial bd. Sprint, 1978—; contbr. articles to profl. jours.; translator drama, films, novel. Mem. Linguistic Circle Copenhagen (sec./treas. 1981—), Assn. Danish Authors (exec. com. 1984—).

MARTINEZ, BETTY ELNORA, chemical company executive; b. Oklahoma City, Jan. 7, 1947; d. Jim and Jewell Frances Smith; B.S., Oklahoma City U., 1974, M.B.A., 1975; divorced. Pvt. booking agt. and bus. mgr. local rock and roll bands, Okla., Colo., 1960-67; with Kerr McGee Corp., Oklahoma City, 1965-81, acct., 1974-76, solvent sales rep., from 1975, assoc. sales rep. until 1981; petrochems. sales rep. No. Petrochem. Co., Ramsey, N.J., 1981-85; Southern area sales rep. AC Polyethylene Allied/Signal Corp., Morristown, N.J., 1985—. Del. Okla. Democratic Conv., 1972; vol. Grady Hosp., Atlanta, Ga. Rape Crisis Ctr. Mem. M.B.A. Club Oklahoma City U. (pres. 1975), ACLU, Soc. Plastic Engrs. (bd. dirs. 1987-88), Toastmasters (adminstrv. v.p., 1988). Home and Office: PO Box 70426 Marietta GA 30007

MARTINEZ, JOSÉ ULISES, accountant; b. El Banco, Colombia, Sept. 2, 1922; s. Ramon Arturo Martinez and Maria del Carmen Pedriques; m. Clara Ines Lara, Dec. 30, 1950 (div. July 1965); children: Patricia, Fernando, Ernesto, Rodrigo, Adriana; m. Maria Helena Abadia Puentes, July 15, 1970. Grad. in acctg., Nat. Faculty Econ. Sci., Bogota, Colombia, 1952; postgrad., London Sch. Econs., 1957; D in Comml. Sci., London Inst. Applied Research, 1973. CPA, cert. internal auditor. Gen. auditor Coltejer Co., Medellin, Colombia, 1958-61; controller Aliadas-McKesson Co., Medellin, 1962-64; mng. ptnr. Coopers & Lybrand, Bogota, 1965-72; rep. Horwath & Horwath, Bogota, 1973-77; gen. auditor Banco Santander, Bogota, 1977-84; mng. ptnr. José Ulises Martinez & Co. CPA's (affiliate Ernst & Whinney), Bogota, 1984—. Author: Contabilidad Hotelera, 1981; editor Ejecutivo Financiero, 1978-84. Mem. Inst. Internal Auditors (cert.), Colombia Assn. Bank Auditors (pres. 1978—), Soc. Econ. Amigos del Pais, Biblioteca Pensamiento Liberal, Assn. Civica Baranquillera, Soc. of London Sch. Econs. Liberal. Roman Catholic. Club: Ejecutivos (Bogota). Home: Apartado Aero, 8805 Bogota Colombia Office: Cra 10 28-49, Floor 22, Bogota Colombia

MARTÍNEZ, LUÍS OSVALDO, radiologist, educator; b. Havana, Cuba, Nov. 27, 1927; came to U.S., 1962, naturalized, 1967; s. Osvaldo and Felicita (Farinas) M.; m. Norma Rodriguez, Nov. 20, 1955; children: María Elena, Luis Osvaldo, Alberto Luis. MD, U. Havana, 1954. Intern Calixto García Hosp., Havana, 1954-55; resident in radiology Jackson Meml. Hosp., Miami, Fla., 1963-65, fellow in cardiovascular radiology, 1965-67; instr. radiology U. Miami, 1965-68, asst. prof., 1968, clin. asst. prof., 1968-70, assoc. prof., 1970-76, prof., 1976—; assoc. dir. dept. radiology Mt. Sinai Med. Ctr., Miami Beach, Fla., 1969—, chief div. diagnostic radiology, 1970—, dir. residency program in diagnostic radiology; dir. Spanish Radiology Seminar. Reviewer Am. Jour. Radiology, Radium Therapy and Nuclear Medicine, 1978; editor Revista Interamericana de Radiologia, 1975; contbr. articles to profl. jours. Former pres. League Against Cancer. Mem. Internat. Soc. Lymphology, Interam. Coll. Radiology (pres.), Internat. Coll. Surgeons, Internat. Coll. Angiology, Internat. Soc. Radiology, Interam. Coll. Radiology (Gold medal 1975, pres. editor Jour.), Cuban Med. Assn. in Exile, Am. Coll. Chest Physicians (assoc.), AAUP, AMA, Radiol. Soc. N. Am., Am. Coll. Radiology, Am. Roentgen Ray Soc., Am. Assn. Fgn. Med. Grads., Am. Profl. Practice Assn., Am. Thoracic Soc., Pan Am. Med. Assn., Am. Assn. Univ. Radiologists, Brit. Inst. Radiology, Am. Heart Assn. (mem. council cardiovascular radiology), Faculty Radiologists, Soc. Gastrointestinal Radiologists, Am. Geriatrics Soc., Am. Coll. Angiology, Royal Coll. Radiologists, Am. Soc. Therapeutic Radiologists, Assn. Hosp. Med. Edn., Am. Coll. Med. Imaging, Interasma, So. Med. Assn., N.Y. Acad. Scis., Fla. Thoracic Soc., Fla. Radiol. Soc., Dade County Med. Assn., Greater Miami Radiol. Soc., Cuban Radiol. Soc. (sec.), Can. Assn. Radiologists, Soc. Thoracic Radiologists (founding mem.); hon. mem. numerous med. socs. of Mex., Cen. and S.Am. Roman Catholic. Office: 4300 Alton Rd Miami Beach FL 33140

MARTINEZ, ROBERT, governor of Fla.; b. Tampa, Fla., Dec. 25, 1934; s. Serafin and Ida (Carreno) M. B.S., U. Tampa, 1957; M.A., U. Ill., 1964. Tchr., Hillsborough County, 1957-62, 63-66; pres., Cafe Sevilla Spanish Restaurant, 1975-83; mayor of Tampa, 1979-86; gov. Fla., 1987—; mem. Pres.'s Adv. Com. on Intergovtl. Relations. Office: Office of Gov The Capitol Tallahassee FL 32301-8047 *

MARTINEZ, VICTOR HIPOLITO, vice president of Argentina; b. Corboda, Argentina, Nov. 21, 1924. Grad. law and Social Scis., U. Cordoba. Prof. agrarian law and mining U. Cordoba; pvt. practice law, Cordoba; v.p. Republic of Argentina, 1983—. Mem. Nat. Acad. Law, Fedn. Lawyers, Nat. Inst. Agrarian Law, Commn. Natural Resources. Author: La tutela en el derecho civil argentino, Derechos reales in mineria, La segunda republica. Union Civica Radical (v.p.). *

MARTÍNEZ DOMÍNGUEZ, GUILLERMO, economist, financial executive; Monterrey, N.L., Mex., Jan. 8, 1923; s. Alfonso and Rafaela Martínez Domínguez; degree in Econs., Nat. Faculty of Econs., Mexico City, 1947; m. Mina Benavides, July 1, 1953; children—Rosa Laura, Ana Silvia, Paula Daniela. Prices dir. Mexico, 1947-48; dir. small commerce Nat. Bank, Mexico City, 1952-55; chief budgetary control and ofcl. mayor Fed. Power Commn., Mexico City, 1955-59, dir. gen., 1964-70; counselor Mexican Coffee Inst. and tech. coordinator Sugar Industry Planning Fund, 1960-64; dir. gen. Nacional Financiera S.A., Mexico City, 1970-74; dir. equity investment Interam. Devel. Bank, Washington, 1978-80; tchr. Nat. Sch. Econs., 1948-64; counselor Petróleos Mexicanos, 1964-74, Teléfonos de México, others; bus./fin. counselor, Mexico City, 1970-74. Pres., Liga de Economistas Revolucionarios, 1952-54. Recipient Nat. Prize Journalism, Assn. Mexicana de Periodistas, 1953; others. Mem. Colegio Nacional de Economistas (pres. 1954-56), Am. Econs. Assn. Author: Los Braceros, 1946; Mexican Social Security Financial Crisis, 1947; Attempts for Price Control in Mexico, 1951; Mexican Electric Industrial Integration, 1971; 50 Years of Mexican Development Bank, 1980. Home: Cerrada de Presa Escolta 24, 10200 Mexico City Mexico Office: Soria 6 esq Eje, Central Lazaro, Cardenas Mexico

MARTINEZ-GÓMEZ, LUIS, philosopher, educator; b. Cañizar, Spain, Feb. 9, 1911; s. Hermenegildo and Luisa (Gómez) Martínez. Degree, U. Comillas, Spain. Dr. philosophy Granada-Oña-Marneffe, Belgium, 1930-33; dr. theology Entre-os-Rios, Portugal, 1936-40; dr. philosophy Oña, Burgos, Spain, 1941-44; docent philosophy Chamartín, Alcalá U. Comillas, Madrid, 1944-88, prof. emeritus, 1980—. Author: Philosophica: Alfilo de la Historia, 1987. Author: Philosophica: Al Filo de la Historia, 1987. Office: Univ Comillas, Filosofia Dept, Madrid Spain

MARTINEZ-MAURICA, JAVIER, educator; b. Bilbao, Basque, Spain, July 4, 1952; s. Segundo Martinez and Purificación Maurica; m. Pilar Fernandez-Ferreiros, Dec. 17, 1977; children: Iñigo, Borja. B in Math., U. Bilbao, 1974, PhD, 1977. Teaching asst. U. Bilbao, 1974-76; research asst. U. Santander, Spain, 1976-77, asst. prof., 1977-79, assoc. prof., 1979-87, full prof., 1988—; full prof. U. Oviedo, Spain, 1987; chmn. Teoria Funciones dept. U. Santander, 1985-87. Contbr. articles to profl. jours. Mem. Am. Math. Soc., Real Sociedad Matematica Española. Home: General Davila 34-A 10 D, 39005 Santander, Cantabria Spain Office: U Santander, Ave Los Castros, 39071 Santander, Cantabria Spain

MARTINEZ-MENDIETA, MARCOS, diplomat; b. Lambare, Paraguay, Apr. 25, 1940; came to U.S., 1984; s. Blas Martinez Valenzuela and Adela Concepcion (Mendieta) Mendieta de Martinez; m. Francoise Charles de la Brousse, July 10, 1973; children—Federico Xavier, Roberto Stephane. B.A. in Philosophy, Nat. U. Paraguay, 1960; D. Internat. Relations, El Colegio de Mex., 1966. Career diplomat Ministry Fgn. Relations, 1960—; ambassador to Japan, 1977-83; ambassador to U.S., 1984—. Decorated grand officer Orden de Mayo (Argentina); comdr. Orden Nacional do Cruceiro do Sul. (Brazil); Order of Rising Sun (Japan). Mem. Kodokan Inst. Japan, Paraguay Internat. Law Inst., Am. Mgmt. Assn. Roman Catholic. Office: Embassy of Paraguay 2400 Massachusetts Ave NW Washington DC 20008

MARTIN GARCIA, MIGUEL ANGEL, economist, business strategies consultant; b. Madrid, May 25, 1947; s. Angel Martin and Carmen Garcia; m. Dolores Lola Bonet, Aug. 16, 1972; children: Aranzazu, Maria, Rodrigo, Rocio, Almudena. Licence, Central U., Madrid, 1971; PDG, Inst. de Estudios Superiores de Empreso, 1985. Sr. auditor Arthur Andersen & Co., Madrid, 1971-75; controller Cutler Hammer Co., Madrid, 1975-77; plant ops. mgr. San Miguel Breweries, Malaga, Spain, 1977-87; pres. Marhold S.A., Madrid, 1984—; v.p. Qualidist S.A., Madrid, 1987—; cons. mgr. Mayam Cons., Madrid, 1984—; bd. dirs. C.E.M., Malaga, 1983-88. Contbr. articles on bus. strategies to profl. pubs. Recipient Silver medal Malaga C. of C., 1987. Mem. Strategic Mgmt. Soc., Long Range Planning Inst., Assn. Espanola Planificacion. Clubs: Ateneo (Malaga); Am. Musica (Marbella, Spain). Home: Dr Esquerdo 114, 28007 Madrid Spain Office: Marhold SA, Juan Hurtado de Mendoza 11, 28030 Madrid Spain

MARTINI, CARLO MARIA CARDINAL, archbishop of Milan; b. Turin, Italy, Feb. 15, 1927. Joined Soc. of Jesus, Roman Cath. Ch., 1944, ordained priest, 1952; biblical scholar; sem. prof., Chieri, Italy, 1958-61; prof., rector Pontifical Biblical Inst., 1969-78; rector Pontifical Gregorian U., 1978-79; archbishop of Milan, 1980; elevated to Sacred Coll. of Cardinals, 1983. Author: theological, biblical and spiritual works. Mem. Council for Pub. Affairs of the Ch. Address: Palazzo Arcivescovile, Piazza Fontana 2, 20122 Milan Italy

MARTINI, ROBERT FRANK, aircraft company executive; b. Somerville, Mass., Mar. 21, 1928; s. Robert C. and Phyllis (Ferri) M.; student Northeastern U., 1949-52; B.S., Stanford U., 1954; cert. bus. mgmt. UCLA, 1966; M.B.A., Loyola Marymount U., 1978; m. Mary Jane Conner, June 25, 1955; 1 son, James Robert. Staff engr. Instrumentation Lab., M.I.T., Cambridge, 1955-57; group leader Lockheed Missile and Space Co., Sunnyvale, Calif., 1957-61; labs. mgr. Hughes Aircraft Co., Culver City, Calif., 1961—. Mgmt. adv. Jr. Achievement program, Culver City, 1967. Served with USN, 1946-48. Mem. IEEE, Assn. Computing Machinery, Am. Mgmt. Assn., Loyola Marymount U. M.B.A. Alumni Assn. (dir. 1981-83). Republican. Roman Catholic. Club: Hughes Management. Home: 7886 Truxton Ave Los Angeles CA 90045 Office: PO Box 92426 Los Angeles CA 90009

MARTINO, ROCCO LEONARD, management consultant; b. Toronto, Ont., Can., June 25, 1929; s. Domenic and Josephine (DiGiulio) M.; BSc, U. Toronto, 1951, MA, 1952; PhD, Inst. Aerospace Studies, 1955; m. Barbara L. D'lorio, Sept. 2, 1961; children: Peter Domenic, Joseph Alfred, Paul Gerard, John Francis. Dir., Univac Computing Service Center, Toronto, 1956-59; pres. Mauchly Assos. Can. Ltd., Toronto, 1959-62, v.p. Mauchly Assos., Inc., Ft. Washington, Pa., 1959-61; mgr. advanced systems Olin Mathieson Chem. Corp., N.Y.C., 1962-64; dir. advanced computer systems Booz, Allen & Hamilton, N.Y.C., 1964-65; pres., chmn. bd. Info. Industries, Inc. and subs.'s, Wayne, Pa., 1965-70; chmn. bd., chief exec. officer XRT, Inc., Malvern, Pa., 1970—; chmn. bd. MBF Computer Ctr. for Handicapped Children; mem. bd. St. Joseph's U., Phila., Gregorian U. Found., N.Y.; mem. exec. com. Gregorian U., N.Y. and Rome, 1987—, pontifical circle; asso. prof. math. U. Waterloo, 1959-62, prof. engring., dir. Inst. Systems and Mgmt. Engring., 1964-65; adj. asso. prof. N.Y. U., 1963-64, adj. prof. math., 1964-65, 66; lectr. on computers mgmt.; chmn. Gov. Ill. Task Force, 1970-71, Ill. Bd. Higher Edn. Task Force, 1971-72, Computer-Use Task Force FCC, 1972-73, Computer-Use Planning Task Force U.S. Postal Service, 1973-74. Trustee Gregorian Found., N.Y.C. and Rome, 1984—; bd. govs. St. Joseph's U. Sch. Bus., 1983—. Mem. Assn. Computing Machinery, Ops. Research Soc. Am., Porfl. Engrs. Ont., Computing Soc. Can. Clubs: K.C., Lions, Overbrook Golf and Country, Yacht of Sea Isle City (commodore 1973-74, trustee 1975-86, chmn. 1983-86), Commodores; S. Jerry Yacht Racing (commodore 1979-81, sec. 1981-83, officer 1983—). Lodges: Papal Knight, Equestrian Order Holy Sepulchre (knight 1986), Order of Malta. Author books, most recent being: Resources Management, 1968; Dynamic Costing, 1968; Project Management, 1968; Information Management: The Dynamics of MIS, 1968; MIS-Management Information Systems, 1969; Decision Patterns, 1969; Methodology of MIS, 1969; Personnel Information Systems, 1969; Integrated Manufacturing Systems, 1972; APG-Virtual Application Systems, 1981; contbr. numerous articles on mgmt., computers and planning in profl. publs.; designer, developer Application Program Generator computer system, 1974-75; developer cash mgmt. and on-line internat. trading systems, 1984. Home: 512 Watch Hill Rd Villanova PA 19085 Office: 989 Old Eagle Sch Rd Suite 806 Wayne PA 19087

MARTINS, ANTONIO GENTIL, pediatric and plastic surgeon; b. Lisbon, Portugal, July 10, 1930; s. António Augusto da Silva and Maria Madalena Gentil; m. Maria Guilhermina Ivens Ferraz Jardim; children: António Vasco, Inês Maria, Luis Carlos, Teresa Maria, Ana Maria, Rita Maria, Sofia Maria, Joao Manuel. MD, Faculdade de Medicina, Lisbon, 1953; degree in Pedagogical Scis., Faculdade de Letras, Lisbon, 1954. Diplomate in Pediatric and Plastic Surgery. Intern Hospitais Cívis de Lisbon, 1954-56; scholar Brit. Council, London, 1956-57; registrar Alder Hey Hosp., Liverpool, 1958-59; pediatric surgeon Hosp. D.Estefânia, Lisboa, 1965; founder and head pediatric dept. Inst. Português Oncologia de Francisco Gentil, Lisboa, 1960-85, cons. pediatric surgery, 1986-88; prof. pediatric surgery Faculdade de Ciências Médicas, Lisbon, 1986-88; dir. pediatric surgery Hosp. D.Estefânia, Lisbon, 1987-88. Editor: Proc.Luso-Brasilian Met. Ped Surg, 1970, Proc Luso-Spanish Met. Ped Surg, 1971, (jour.) Revista da Ordem dos Médicos, 1980-86. Cons. WHO, Prague, Czechoslovakia, 1977; mem. working group Council of Europe, Italy, 1981-82. Recipient Diploma of Honor Cuban Med. Assn. in Exile, Miami, 1983, Keys to City of Miami and Dade County, Fla., 1983; named Grande Official da Ordem do Infante D. Renrique, Pres. Republic of Portugal, 1984. Mem. CPCEE, CIO, UEMS, Med. Students Assn. (pres. 1952), Ordem dos Medicos (pres. 1978-86), World Med. Assn. (pres. 1981-83), Portuguese Soc. Plastic Surgery (pres. 1968-74), Portuguese Soc. Pediatric Surgeons (pres. 1975-84), World Fedn. Assn. Pediatric Surgeons (council mem. 1983—), Internat. Soc. Pediatric Oncology (sci. com. mem. 1982-84); hon. mem. Brasilian Soc. Pediatric Surgeons, Spanish Soc. Pediatric Surgeons, Greek Soc. Pediatric Surgeons. Roman Catholic. Club: Internat. Futebal, Lisbon. Home: Rua D Francisco Manuel de Melo 1 3, 1000 Lisbon Portugal Office: Ordem dos Medicos, Av Almirante Reis 242 2 Esq, 1000 Lisbon Portugal

MARTINS, HEITOR MIRANDA, foreign language educator; b. Belo Horizonte, Brazil, July 22, 1933; came to U.S., 1960; s. Joaquim Pedro and Emilia (Miranda) M.; m. Teresomja Alves Pereira, Nov. 1, 1958 (div. 1977); children—Luzia Pereira, Emilia Pereira; m. Marlene Andrade, Jan. 11, 1984. A.B., U. Federal de Minas Gerais, 1959; Ph.D., U. Federal de Minas Gerais, 1962. Instr. U. N.M., Albuquerque, 1960-62; asst. prof. Tulane U., New Orleans, 1962-66; assoc. prof. Tulane U., 1966-68; prof. dept. Spanish and Portuguese Ind. U., Bloomington, 1968—; chmn. dept. Ind. U., 1972-76; vis. prof. U. Tex., Austin, 1963, Stanford U. 1968. Author: poetry Sirgo nos Cabelos, 1961; essay Manuel de Galhegos, 1964; essays Oswald de Andrade e Outros, 1973; critical anthology Neoclassicismo, 1982; Essays Do Barroco a Guimarães Rosa, 1983; editor: essays Luso-Brazilian Literary Studies. Social Sci. Research Council grantee, 1965; Fulbright-Hays Commn. grantee, 1966; Ford Found. grantee, 1970, 71. Mem. MLA, Renaissance Soc. Am., Am. Comparative Lit. Assn., Am. Assn. for 18th Century Studies. Home: 223 S Jordan Ave Bloomington IN 47401 Office: Indiana U Dept Spanish and Portuguese Bloomington IN 47405

MARTIN SANCHEZ, JUAN ANTONIO, plant breeder; b. Berganciano, Salamanca, Spain, Feb. 21, 1940; s. Julian Martin Rodriquez and Maria Bernarda Sanchez Delgado; Agrl. Engr. Superior, High Tech. Sch. Agrl. Engrs., Madrid, 1964; Dr. Agrl. Engr., 1982. Prof., Lab. Genetics and Plant Breeding, High Tech. Sch. Agrl. Engrs., Madrid, 1965-70; mgr. research in plant breeding MAHISSA, Maices Hibridos y Semillas, CIBA Geigy, Borjas Blancas, Spain, 1970-83; tchr. genetics and plant breeding Tech. Sch. Agr. of Poly. U. Barcelona, Lerida, Spain, 1975-78; prof. Tech. Sch. Agr. Engrs., Lerida, 1977—, dir. Tech. Sch. Agr. and High Tech. Sch. Agrl. Engrs. Lerida, 1978-84. Decorated comdr. Order Civil Merit in Agr. Mem. Nat. Assn. Agrl. Engrs., Spanish Assn. Genetics, Genetics Soc. Am., Eucarpia. Roman Catholic. Developer 6 varieties of wheat, 3 of Triticale. Office: Escuela Tecnica Superior de Ingenieros, Agronomos, Departmento de Genetica, Alcade Ravira Roure, 177 Lerida Spain

MARTIN-VALLAS, BRUNO, corporate director; b. Paris, Mar. 3, 1948; s. Georges and Marie Thérèse (Clement) M.-V.; m. Parsa Nairé, July 3, 1982; children: Alice, Antoine. B in engring., Paris Poly. U., 1968; MBA, European Inst. Bus. Adminstrn., Fontainebleau, France, 1972. Engr. Esso, France and Eng., 1972-76; prof. Chamber de Commerce et Industrie, France, 1976-84; dir. cons. Motiv, France, 1984-86; bd. dirs. Sunseil, France, 1987—, iDRH Cons. Co., Houilles, France, 1988—. Served to lt. French Marines, 1971. Home: 4 rue de la Mission Marchand, 78800 Houilles France Office: ESCP, 79 av. de la Republique, 75543 Paris France

MARTLAND, THOMAS RODOLPHE, philosophy educator; b. Port Chester, N.Y., May 29, 1926; s. Thomas Rodolphe and Anne Elizabeth (Newbury) M.; BS magna cum laude, Fordham U., 1951; MA, Columbia U., 1955, PhD, 1959; m. Agatha Murphy, Apr. 3, 1952; children: David Allen, Luke Thomas. Asst. prof. Lafayette Coll., Easton, Pa., 1959-65; assoc. prof. So. Ill. U., Carbondale, 1965-66; assoc. prof. philosophy SUNY-Albany, 1966-84, prof., 1984—, dir. religious studies program, 1980-87; Jeannette K. Watson vis. prof. of religion, Syracuse U., 1987—; Served to lt. (s.g.) USN, 1944-47, 51-53. Faculty Exchange Guest scholar 1976-77, research fellow, 1967, 68, 71, 87; Jones Fund award Lafayette Coll., 1962-63. Mem. Am. Philos. Assn., Am. Soc. Aesthetics (steering com. 1985-88), Internat. Assn. Philosophy and Lit. (exec. com. 1976-81). Author: Religion as Art: An Interpretation, 1981; The Metaphysics of William James and John Dewey, 1969; editorial bd. Jour. Comparative Lit. & Aesthetics, 1982—; guest editor Annals of Scholarship, 1982. Home: 216 Lancaster St Albany NY 12210 Office: SUNY/Albany Dept Philosophy Albany NY 12222

MARTON, EVA HEINRICH, opera singer; b. Hungary, June 18, 1943; m. Zoltan Marton; children: Zoltan, Diana. Student, Liszt Acad.; studied under, Gerald Mortier and Laszlo Halasz. Debut Budapest Opera, 1968, performed with, 1968-72; performed with Frankfurt Opera, 1972-77, Maggio Musicale Fiorentino, Vienna State Opera, La Scalatate Opera, Milan, Met. Opera, N.Y.C., Lyric Opera, Chgo., San Francisco Opera, Bayreuth Opera, Teatro Colon, Buenos Aires, Rome Opera, others. Roles include Eva in Die Meistersinger, Venus and Elizabeth in Tannhauser, Tosca, Leonora in Il Trovatore, Chrysothemis in Electra, Empress in Die Frau ohne Schatten, Senta in Fliegender Hollander, Lady MacBeth, also others; featured on albums of Puccini Arias and Wagner Arias; mem. Hungarian Nat. Volleyball Team. Office: care Edgar Vincent Cynthia Robbins Assn 124 E 40th St Suite 304 New York NY 10018 *

MARTONI, CHARLES J., educational administrator; b. Pitts., Aug. 24, 1936; s. John and Virginia (Caputo) M. A.A., Community Coll. Allen County, 1969; B.S., California State Coll. (Pa.), 1971, M.A., 1977; M.S., Duquesne U., 1976, M.Ed., 1972; Ph.D., U. Pitts., 1988. Cert. counselor, nat. and Pa. Asst. dir. fin. aid Boyce Campus Community Coll. Allen County, Monroeville, Pa., 1971-73, dir. fin. aid, 1973-76, dir. fin. aid and counseling, 1976-80, dean of students, 1980—; mem. exec. bd. Tri-State Conf. on Steel. Mayor Swissvale, Pa., 1984; bd. dirs. East Communities YMCA, Penn Hills, 1984, Southwestern Girl Scouts U.S.A., Pitts., 1984. Served with U.S. Army, 1958-60. John Hart scholar, 1970; named Outstanding Alumnus, Boyce Campus, Community Coll. Allen County, 1978. Mem. Pa. Personnel and Guidance Assn., Pa. Mayors Assn., Nat. Assn. Student Personnel Adminstrs., Am. Assn. Counseling and Devel., Nat. Cert. Counselors. Democrat. Roman Catholic. Home: 7114 Church St Swissvale PA 15218 Office: City Hall Swissvale PA 15218

MARTORELL, CÉSAR DUCH, paper company executive; b. Barcelona, Spain, Oct. 3, 1950; s. César Duch Plana and Pilar Martorell Paris; m. Maria Parera Torns, July 25, 1976; children: Salvi, Cesar, Ivette. Degree in Econs., Cen. U., Barcelona, 1974, Degree in Law, 1980. Researcher Macrometrica, Barcelona, 1973-75, research mgr., 1975-76, mktg. mgr., 1976-77; study and adminstrn. mgr. Inpacsa, Barcelona, 1977-80, div. mgr., 1980-84, export mgr., 1984—; lectr. advt. and mktg. research Univ. Bus. Coll., Sabadell, Spain, 1982—; coordinator internat. mgmt. Esmai, Barcelona, 1984—. Author: Trading Companies, 1988, Advertising Media, 1986, International Marketing, 1988, ESMAI, Techniques of Market Research, 1987. Mem. European Mktg. Assn., Barcelona Advt. Assn., Barcelona Mktg. Club (sec. bd. dirs. 1986., merit award 1986, adv. Spanish Fedn. of Mktg. 1988). Home: Carlos III, 62 60 4a, 08028 Barcelona Spain Office: Impacsa Plaza, Urquinaona 430, 08010 Barcelona Spain

MARTORI, JOSEPH PETER, lawyer; b. N.Y.C., Aug. 19, 1941; s. Joseph and Teresa Susan (Fezza) M.; m. Julia Ann D'Orlando, Mar. 7, 1964 (div. Mar. 1978); children: Joseph Peter, Christina Ann; m. Terres Edith Wolff, Dec. 23, 1980; 1 child, Arianne Terres. BS summa cum laude, NYU, 1964, MBA, 1968; JD cum laude U. Notre Dame, 1967; Bar: D.C. 1968, U.S. Dist. Ct. D.C. 1968, U.S. Dist. Ct. Ariz. 1968, U.S. Ct. Appeals (9th cir.) 1969, U.S. Supreme Ct. 1977. Assoc. Sullivan & Cromwell, N.Y.C., 1967-68, Snell & Wilmer, Phoenix, 1968-69; pres. Goldmar Inc., Phoenix, 1969-71; ptnr. Martori, Meyer, Hendricks & Victor, P.A., Phoenix, 1971-85; ptnr. Brown & Bain, P.A., Phoenix, 1985—; bd. dirs. Met. Bank, Phoenix, Internat. Leisure Enterprises, Phoenix. Author: Street Fights, 1987; also articles, 1966-70. Bd. dirs. Men's Arts Council, Phoenix, 1972—; trustee Boys' Clubs Met. Phoenix, 1974—. Mem. ABA, State Bar Ariz., Maricopa County Bar Assn., Lawyers Com. for Civil Rights Under Law (trustee 1976—). Republican. Roman Catholic. Clubs: Phoenix Country, Plaza (founding bd. govs. 1979—) (Phoenix). Office: Brown & Bain PA 222 N Central Ave Phoenix AZ 85001

MARTOSUWIGNYO, SUWARSO, engineering consultant; b. Solo, Indonesia, Dec. 28, 1928; s. Raden and Nyonya M.; m. Chairyah, June 20, 1969; children—Mirwan, Marwin. M.S., Tech. U., Bandung, Indonesia, 1955; Ph.D., Tech. U., Munich, Fed. Republic Germany, 1967. Engr. Philips, Eindhoven, Holland, 1955-56; systems engr. Siemens Ag, Munich, 1956-58; dir. Panatraco Ltd., Jakarta, Indonesia, 1958-70; pres. Pansystems, Jakarta, 1970—; cons. Telecommunications Adminstrn., Jakarta, 1975—, Internat. Telecommunication Union, Geneva, 1980-85. Contbr. articles to profl. jours. Fellow Asia Electronics Union; mem. IEEE, Indonesian/German C. of C. (v.p. 1970-72). Club: Indonesian Petroleum (Jakarta). Avocation: golf. Home: Jalan Selat Bangka No 1 Kemang, Jakarta Indonesia Office: Pansystems, Menara Duta Bldg Kuningan, Jakarta Indonesia

MARTUCCI, GLORIA MARTHA, educator, former insurance agent; b. Bronx, N.Y., Dec. 19, 1934; d. Thomas Angelo and Martha Marie (De Marco) M.; BA, Fla. State U., 1960; MS, SUNY at New Paltz, 1973; cert. of mgmt. Mercy Coll., Yorktown Heights, N.Y., 1979. Tchr. French and history, Bunnell, Fla., 1960-62, Dept. of Army, Okinawa, 1962-63, U.S. Air Force, Itazuke, Japan, 1963-64; tchr. langs. Yorktown Jr. High Sch., Yorktown Heights, N.Y., 1965; tchr. French and bus. Mahopac (N.Y.) Sr. High Sch., 1966-78, Mahopac Jr. High Sch., 1979-85; ins. agt. Mut. of Omaha, Poughkeepsie, N.Y., 1985-87; educator, Tucson, 1988—. Pinellas County (Fla.) teaching scholar, 1958-60. Mem. Am. Assn. Tchrs. French, N.Y. State Assn. Fgn. Lang. Tchrs., Nat. Bus. Edn. Assn., Bus. Tchrs. Assn. N.Y. Republican. Roman Catholic. Club: Single Profls. Westchester (2d v.p. 1978-79). Home: 4381 E Orchard Dr Tucson AZ 85712 Office: Mutual of Omaha 205 South Ave Poughkeepsie NY 12601

MARTUSCELLI, EUGENIO GERARDO, physician; b. Rome, Feb. 27, 1952; s. Luigi and Amelia (Pistolese) M. MD, Rome U., 1976; cert. cardiology, Bari U., Italy, 1979. Diplomate Italian Bd. Cardiology. Staff mem., researcher Rome U., 1980—; speaker in field. Contbr. articles to profl. jours. Grantee, Consiglio Nationale delle Ricerche, 1979-80, 84. Mem. Italian Soc. Cardiology. Home: V Cola Di Rienzo 212, 00192 Rome Italy

MARTY, FRANCOIS CARDINAL, former archbishop of Paris; b. Pachins, France, May 18, 1904. Ordained priest Roman Cath. Ch., 1930; bishop of St.-Flour, 1952; titular archbishop of Emesa, also coadjutor archbishop of Rheims, 1959; archbishop of Rheims, 1960-68, of Paris, 1968—; elevated to Sacred Coll. of Cardinals, 1969; titular ch. St. Louis of France; ret. as archbishop, 1981; ordinary for Eastern Rite Catholics in France without ordinaries of their own rites; mem. Congregation Oriental Chs., Congregation Clergy, Sacraments and Divine Worship, Commn. Revision of Code of Canon Law. Address: 30 rue Barbet-de-Jouy, Paris 75 France *

MARTY, RAYMOND, physician; b. Bklyn., Oct. 26, 1929; s. Harry Kenneth and Pearl (Bailin) M.; B.A., UCLA, 1952; M.D., U. Lausanne (Switzerland), 1959; m. Carole M. Perry, Jan. 25, 1960. Intern, Hosp. Good Samaritan, Los Angeles, 1960-61; resident in diagnostic radiology Albert Einstein Sch. Medicine, Bronx, N.Y., 1962; fellow radiation therapy Stanford Med. Sch., 1962-63; dir. out patient clinic St. Joseph's Hosp., San Francisco, 1963-65; fellow Tumor Inst., Seattle, 1965-66, mem. staff, 1966—, dir nuclear medicine/ultrasound, 1967—; assoc. clin. prof. nuclear medicine tech. Seattle U. Med. Sch., 1972—; asst. clin. prof. nuclear medicine U. Wash. Med. Sch., Seattle, 1974—. Mem. AMA, Am. Coll. Radiology, Radiol. Soc. N.Am., Am. Coll. Nuclear Physicians, Soc. Nuclear Medicine, N.Y. Acad. Scis., Fedn. Am. Scientists, AAAS. Clubs: Seattle Yacht, The Lakes (Bellevue, Wash.); La Chaine des Rotisseurs; Lahaina Yacht (Maui, Hawaii). Contbr. articles to profl. jours. Home: 4607 103rd Ln NE Kirkland WA 98033 Office: 1229 Madison St Suite 1150 Seattle WA 98104

MARTY, ROBERT FRANCOIS, semiotics/mathematics educator; b. Perpignan, France, May 22, 1936; s. Marcel and Rosa Adela (Ibars) M.; m. Claude Jeannette Bruzy, July 27, 1957; children—Yves, Florence, Julie. Lic. de Mathematiques, U. Montpellier, 1960, diplome d'Etudes Superieures, 1961, Doctorat d'Etat es Scis., 1969, Doctorat d'Etat es Lettres, 1987. Asst. math. U. Perpignan, 1961-65, maitre-asst., 1965-69, prof. semiotics, math., 1969—. Author: L'Algèbre des Signes, Benjamin B.V. ed.; contbr. articles to profl. jours. Mem. Town Council of Perpignan, 1983. Mem. Research Group Semiotics Perpignan (bd. dirs.), Assn. Española de Semiotica, Internat. Assn. for Semiotics Studies., French Assn. Semiotics (sec.). Home: 16 rue Petite la Real, F-66000 Perpignan France Office: U Perpignan, Ave de Villeneuve, F-66025 Perpignan France

MARUYA, SAIICHI, novelist; b. Yamagata, Japan, Aug. 27, 1925; parents: Kumajiro and Sen M.; m. Ayako Nemura, Oct. 1954; 1 child, Ryo. Degree in English lit., U. Tokyo, 1950. Assoc. prof. Kokugakuin U., Japan, 1953-65; lectr. U. Tokyo, 1965-67. Author: (novel) Toshi No Nokori, 1968 (Akutagawa prize 1968), (novel) Singular Rebellion, 1972 (Tanizaki prize 1972), (criticism) Chushingura To Wa Nanika, 1984 (Noma Lit. prize 1985). Mem. Japan Writer's Assn. Home: 2-10-45-401 Mita Meguroku, 153 Tokyo Japan

MARUYAMA, KOSHI, pathologist, educator; b. Sapporo, Hokkaido, Japan, Feb. 19, 1932; s. Kotaro and Eiko (Nakamura) M.; m. Rumy Misawa, May 6, 1961; children: Nariyuki, Narihiro, Yumie. MD, U. Hokkaido Sch. Medicine, 1957, PhD, 1962. Diplomate Japanese Bd. Pathology. Staff pathologist Nat. Inst. Leprosy Research, Tokyo, 1962-65, Nat. Cancer Ctr. Research Inst., Tokyo, 1965-67; assoc. prof., assoc. virologist U. Tex. M.D. Anderson Hosp. and Tumor Inst., Houston, 1967-75; dir. dept. pathology Chiba Cancer Ctr. Research Inst., Japan, 1975—. Contbr. articles to profl. jours. Assoc. editor: Japanese Jour. Cancer Clinic, 1978—, The Cancer Bull., 1978—, The Year Book of Cancer, 1978. Trustee Tex. Gulf Coast chpt. Leukemia Soc. Am., Houston, 1973-75. Leukemia Soc. Am. scholar, 1968. Fellow N.Y. Acad. Sci., Japanese Pathol. Soc., Japanese Cancer Assn., Japan Soc. Reticuloendothelial System; mem. Am. Assn. Cancer Research, AAAS, Am. Soc. Microbiology, Am. Assn. Pathologists, Japan Assn. Hosp. Pathologists, Internat. Assn. Comparative Research on Leukemia and Related Diseases, Internat. Soc. Preventive Oncology. Office: Chiba Cancer Ctr Research Inst, Dept Pathology 666-2 Nitona-cho, Chiba 280, Japan

MARVAN, MILAN, physicist; b. Kolín, Czechoslovakia, July 29, 1932; s. Viktor and Otilie (Seidler) Marvanová; m. Věra Derka, Dec. 1, 1962; children: Mira, Ivo. Grad. in physics, Faculty Math. and Physics, Prague, Czechoslovakia, 1957, PhD, 1969. Lectr. theoretical physics Faculty of Math. and Physics, 1957-75, lectr. polymer physics, 1975—; vis. prof. U. Moscow, 1963, Czechoslovakian Acad. Scis., Prague, 1964-65, U. Riga, USSR, 1975. Author: Negative Absolute Temperatures, 1966; contbr. articles to profl. jours. Mem. Union of Czechoslovakian Mathematicians and Physicists.

MARVIN, DAVID EDWARD SHREVE, lawyer; b. Lansing, Mich., Jan. 6, 1950; s. George Charles Marvin and Shirley Mae (Martin) Schaible; m. Mary Anne Kennedy, Sept. 16, 1972; 1 child, John. BS cum laude, Mich. State U.,

1972; JD cum laude, Wayne State U., 1976. Bar: Mich. 1976, U.S. Dist. Ct. (ea. dist.) Mich. 1976, U.S. Dist. Ct. (we. dist.) Mich. 1978, U.S. Ct. Appeals (7th cir.) 1977, U.S. Ct. Appeals (6th cir.) 1979, U.S. Supreme Ct. 1979, U.S. Ct. Appeals (D.C. cir.) 1982. Asst. mgr. Alta Supply Co., Lansing, 1972-73; research asst. Wayne State U., Detroit, fall 1975; jud. intern. U.S. Dist. Ct., Detroit, summer, 1975; ptnr. Fraser Trebilcock Davis & Foster, P.C., Lansing, 1976—. Exec. editor: Wayne Law Rev., 1975-76; contbr. articles to law jours. Commr. Mich. Solar Resource Adv. Panel, Lansing, 1978-81, Mich. Commn. Profl. & Occupational Licensure, 1981-83; chmn. Ingham County Energy Commn., Mason, Mich., 1978-80 (state bar rep. assembly 1985—); treas. Lansing Lawyer Referral Service, 1981; state del. Nat. Solar Congress, Washington, 1978; hearing officer City of East Lansing, 1985; Tri-County Council of Bar Leaders (chmn. 1986—). Named Outstanding Young Man Am., 1984, The Outstanding Young Lawyer in Mich., 1985-86; Wm. D. Traitel scholar, 1975. Mem. ABA, State Bar Mich. (com. chmn., sect. council 1982—), Ingham County Bar Assn. (pres. 1985-86), Pro Bono Lawyers Service (pres. 1982-83), Lansing Regional C. of C. (v.p. 1987), Phi Alpha Delta, Phi Eta Sigma, Theta Delta Chi (pres. 1972). Republican. Clubs: Downtown Coaches (bd. dirs., pres. 1987), Mich. State U. Pres.'s. Home: 1959 Groton Way East Lansing MI 48823 Office: Fraser Trebilcock Davis & Foster PC Michigan Nat Tower 10th Floor Lansing MI 48933

MARVIN, JOHN GEORGE, clergyman, church organization executive; b. Summit, N.J., May 8, 1912; s. George and Caroline (Whitman) M.; B.S., Davidson Coll., 1933; Th.B., Princeton Theol. Sem., 1936; D.D., Coll. of Emporia, 1964; LL.D., Tarkio Coll., 1964; m. Elizabeth Anne Wheater, June 30, 1944; children—Caroline Wheater Dorney, Elizabeth Anne West, Martha Jane Hobbs, Frances Alice Heidel. Ordained to ministry Presbyterian Ch., 1936; pastor, Windsor, N.Y., 1936-37, Montrose, Pa., 1937-44, Lewistown, Pa., 1944-52, Denton, Tex., 1952-61; presbytery exec. Greater Kansas City, Mo., 1961-65; pastor 1st Presbyn. Ch., Bartlesville, Okla., 1965-69; sr. minister Chevy Chase Presbyn. Ch., Washington, 1969-77, pastor emeritus, 1978—; interim sr. minister Catonsville Ch., Balt., 1978, 3d Ch., Rochester, N.Y., 1978-79, 1st Ch., Ft. Worth, 1979-80, Gaithersburg, Md., 1980-81, Westfield, N.J., 1981-82, Ch. of Palms, Sarasota, Fla., 1982-83, Bethel Ch., Balt., 1983-84, Pine Shores Ch., Sarasota, Fla., 1984, Interfaith Chapel, Silver Spring, Md., 1984-87; mem. exec. com. Pa. Council Chs., 1949-52, Tex. Council Chs., 1953-61; mem. exec. com., long range chmn. Greater Kansas City Council Chs., 1962-65; chmn. campus Christian Life Tex. Synod, 1958-61; chmn. nat. mission Pa. Synod, 1949-52; sec. nomination com. Gen. Assembly U.P. Ch., 1955-58, chmn. com. on baptized children, 1969-70, mem. com. of nine on synod bounderies, 1970-72; bd. dirs. Midwest Christian Counseling Ctr., Kansas City, Mo., 1963-69, Presbyn. Homes of Okla., Inc., 1966-69; mem. jud. commn. Synod of Okla.-Ark., 1966-69; mem. strategy com. Bd. Nat. Missions, 1968-70, British-Am. Preaching Exchange, preaching missions to Alask and Mexico; leader and lectr. on religious heritage tours in Europe, Mid. East, Egypt, Caribbean and Orient, 1972-84. Bd. dirs. Tarkio Coll., 1961-67, Westminster Found., Pa. State U., 1945-52, North Tex. State U., 1952-61; mem. ministerial relations com. Nat. Capital Union Presbytery, 1973-78; bd. visitors Warren Wilson Coll. Mem. Beta Theta Pi. Republican. Club: Rotary. Contbr. articles to religious publs. Home: 14500 Elmhan Ct Silver Spring MD 20906

MARWAH, JOE, pharmacologist, educator; b. Uganda, May 27, 1952; came to U.S., 1978, naturalized, 1984; s. Suraj Prakash and Kamla Rani (Kapur) M.; m. Carmen Kim Fonkalsrud, Dec. 20, 1978. B.Sc. with honours, U. London, 1974; Ph.D., U. Alta. Sch. Medicine, 1978. Instr. U. Colo. Health Scis. Ctr., Denver, 1978-80; research scientist Yale U. Sch. Medicine, New Haven, 1980-81; asst. prof. pharmacology and life scis. Ind. U. Sch. Medicine, Terre Haute, 1981-83, assoc. prof., 1983-85; prof. U. Medicine and Dentistry N.J., Camden, 1985—. Contbr. articles to sci. jours. Mem. Soc. for Neurosci., AAAS, Am. Soc. Pharmacology and Exptl. Therapeutics, Am. Physiol. Soc., Soc. Biol. Psychiatry (A.E. Bennet award 1981), N.Y. Acad. Scis., Pharm. Soc. Can., Sigma Xi. Research on neurotransmitters, neuroreceptors, hormones, electrophysiology, monoamines, central nervous system. Office: 10312 Castlehedge Terr Silver Spring MD 20892

MARX, WILL, banker; b. Cologne, Germany, Aug. 28, 1919; s. Paul and Maria (Klagges) M.; m. Anne-Gret Zapp, Dec. 2, 1942; children—Peter, Eveline, Regine, Gabriele, Christoph. Mgr. Commerzbank AG, Dusseldorf, 1948-57, gen. mgr., Hamburg/Frankfurt, 1957-69; partner Sal. Oppenheim Jr. & Cie., Cologne and Frankfurt, 1969—; chmn. Köln Düsseldorfer Rheinschiffahrt AG, Köln; dir. Strabag Bau-AG, Thyssen Industrie AG, Essen, other cos. Mem. German Bankers Assn. (bd. dirs.). Office: 20 Bockenheimer Landstrasse, D-6000 Frankfurt am Main Federal Republic of Germany

MARX, WOLFGANG, psychology educator; b. Weidenau, Fed. Republic Germany, June 20, 1943; s. Johann Friedrich and Maria (Andersen) M.; m. Erika Stimpfl, May 15, 1970; 1 child, Julia. Diploma in Psychology, U. Munich, 1968, PhD, 1972, Dr. Philosophy Habilitation, 1978. Prof. U. Munich, 1980—, editor univ. publs., 1985—. Editor: Verbales Gedächtnis und Informationsverarbeitung, 1988; co-editor: Semantische Dimensionen, 1984. Office: U Munich, Geschwister Scholl Pl 1, D-8000 Munich Federal Republic of Germany

MAS, YVES, diplomat; b. Tablat, Algeria, Oct. 1, 1923; s. Leopold and Alice (Bourdier) M.; 1 child, Olivier-Philippe. Diploma in Polit. Sci., U. Paris, 1946. Adminstr. Residence Gen. de France, Morocco, 1947-56; sec. French Embassy, various locations, 1956-64, counsellor, 1964-79; consul gen. Gen. Consulat, Hamburg, Fed. Republic of Germany, 1979-83; ambassador French Embassy, Reykjavik, Iceland, 1985—; del. to Conf. on Security in Europe, Madrid, 1982-83. Recipient Legion d'Honneur, 1969, Mérite Nationale, 1975. Home: 9 rue Sade, 06600 Antibes France Office: Embassy of France, PO Box 1750, 101 Reykjavik Iceland

MASAMI, ONUKI, electronics educator; b. Kobe, Japan, Feb. 11, 1926; s. Jitsuji and Teru Onuki; m. Kazuko Shimada, May 24, 1957; 1 child, Masao. BS, Osaka U., 1949. Asst. Osaka City U., 1950-61, lectr., 1961; group leader Matsushita Research Inst., Tokyo, 1961-71, dir., 1971-75, supr., 1975-79; cons. bd. Matsushita Elec. Indsl. Co., Osaka, 1978-82; prof. electronics Kumanoto U., Japan, 1982—; mem. com. Nihon Gakujitsu Shinkokai, Tokyo, 1983—. Co-author: Crystal Technology Handbook, 1971. Mem. Japan Applied Physics Soc., Physical Soc. Japan, Inst. Electronics Information and Communication Engrs., Inst. Elec. Engrs. Japan, Kumamoto City C. of C. and Industry (expert 1986—). Home: Ohe 2-6-35, 862 Kumamoto Japan Office: Kumamoto U Faculty Engring, Kurokami 2-39-1, 860 Kumamoto Japan

MASANOFF, MICHAEL DAVID, lawyer; b. Jersey City, N.J., May 5, 1951; s. Abraham and Rose (Markowitz) M.; m. Faye Ann Sander, Aug. 7, 1977. BA, Am. Internat. Coll., 1972; JD, Hofstra U., 1977. Bar: N.J. 1977, Pa. 1977, U.S. Dist. Ct. N.J. 1977, U.S. Dist. Ct. (ea. dist.) Pa. 1977, U.S. Tax Ct. 1979. Law clk. SEC, N.Y.C., 1976, Community Legal Asst. Corp., Hempstead, N.Y., 1977; research asst. Tax Analysts & Advocates, Washington, 1976; ptnr. Brener Wallack & Hill, Princeton, N.J., 1977—; sec. Svecia Antigua U.S.A., Inc.; gen. counsel Cabot Med. Corp., 1983—. Research editor Tax Notes, 1976. Trustee, pres. Village Homeowners Assn., Lawrenceville, N.J., 1980-81. Hofstra Law fellow, 1977; Hofstra Moot Ct. Honor, 1975; Shalan Found. Tax fellow, 1976. Mem. Princeton Bar Assn., Mercer County Bar Assn., N.J. State Bar, ABA. Home: 99 Poe Rd Princeton NJ 08540 Office: Brener Wallack & Hill 210 Carnegie Ctr Princeton NJ 08543-5226

MASCHWITZ, EDUARDO ENRIQUE, finance company executive; b. Buenos Aires, June 2, 1957; s. Eduardo Alberto Maschwitz and Alicia Maria Pasman; m. Constancia Maria Miguens, Nov. 6, 1981; children: Constancia, Eduardo Martin, Martin. Lic. en administración de empresas, U. Catolico Argentina, Buenos Aires, 1981. Fin. analyst Exprinter S.A., Buenos Aires, 1981-82, dealer, 1982-84, fin. mgr., 1984—. Mem. Union de Centro Democratico. Roman Catholic. Club: Jockey (Buenos Aires). Office: Juan Jose Diaz 630, 1642 San Isidro Argentina also: Exprinter SA, San Martin 170, 1004 Buenos Aires Argentina

MASCIE-TAYLOR, CHRISTOPHER GUY NICHOLAS, biology educator; b. Llandrindod, Wales, June 2, 1949; s. Henry Hugo and Madeline (Wilding) Mascie-T.; m. Margaret Foster, Dec. 30, 1972; 1 child, Sarah-Louise Phillippa Margaret. BS, U. Surrey, Eng., 1971; MA, U. Cambridge, Eng., 1974, PhD, 1977. Asst. prof. U. Cambridge, 1974-79, prof. epidomiology and human biology, 1979—; prof. Overseas Devel. Adminstrn., 1988—; cons. USAID, 1985—. Churchill Coll. fellow, 1980—. Fellow Human Biology Council; mem. Genetics Soc. Office: U Cambridge, Dept Biol Anthropology, Cambridge CB2 3DZ, England

MASEK, BARRY MICHAEL, accountant; b. Beatrice, Nebr., Nov. 18, 1955; s. Charles Joseph and Patricia Anne (Hynek) M.; m. Mary Ellen McNamara, Nov. 27, 1981; children: Katherine Marie, Caroline Christine. BS in Acctg., U. Nebr., 1979. CPA, Nebr., Ill. Staff asst. Arthur Andersen & Co., Chgo., 1979-81, sr. acct., 1981-84, mgr. acctg. and auditing, 1984—. Mem. Am. Inst. CPA's, Nebr. State Soc. CPA's, Ill. State Soc. CPA's. Roman Catholic. Home: 815 S Home Ave Park Ridge IL 60068 Office: Arthur Andersen & Co 33 W Monroe St Chicago IL 60603

MASENS, LIANA YVONNE, industrial developement specialist; b. Paris, Aug. 28, 1938; d. Vilis and Stase (Luksaite) M. BS, Columbia U., 1956; PhB, U. Madrid, Spain, 1958; diplome Pour Les Professors De Francais A L'etranger, Sorbonne, Paris, 1960; postgrad., Webster Coll., Vienna, Austria, 1983. Indsl. devel. officer UN Indsl. Devel. Orgn., Vienna, 1967—; sec. UN Indsl. Devel. Orgn., Paris, 1977, tech. sec., Beiging, China, 1980. Contbr. articles to profl. jours. Mem. Pi Phi (life). Republican. Roman Catholic. Home: Walfischgasse 10527, 1010 Vienna Austria Office: UN Indsl Devel Orgn, Vienna International Ctr, 1022 Vienna Austria

MASHIMA, SABURO, medical association administrator; b. Utsunomiya, Japan, Jan. 1, 1932; s. Tenji Tokita and Kuniko (Mashima) M.; m. Isaoko Sasaki, Jan 26, 1962 (dec. May 1967); 1 child, Yumiko; m. Michiko Izumi, June 1, 1969; children: Jun, Kei, Yu. MD, U. Tokyo, 1962. Research assoc. U. Vermont, Burlington, 1965-68; asst. prof. U. Tokyo, 1976-83; med. dir. Zenkyoren, Tokyo, 1983—; assoc. prof. Showa U., Yokohama, Japan, 1986—. Author: Electrocardiography, 1973; contbr. articles to profl. jours. Mem. Japanese Circulation Soc., Japanese Soc. Electrocardiology. Home: Nakazato 3-970-14, 204 Kiyose, Tokyo Japan Office: Zenkyoren, Hirakawa Cho 2-7-9, 102 Tokyo Japan

MASI, JANE VIRGINIA, marketing and sales consultant; b. N.Y.C., June 6, 1947; d. Vincent Joseph and Virginia Marie (Beddow) Masi; m. Charles Walter Friedman, Feb. 14, 1976. BA in Communications and Psychology, Mercy Coll., N.Y., 1969; MA, New Sch. Social Research, 1979, now PhD candidate. Asst. sales mgr. Chevron Chem., N.Y.C., 1969-71; writer, 1973-75; ptnr. Masi-D'Angelo Constrn. and Devel. Assocs., N.Y.C., 1979-83; pres., founder Beddow Mills Inc., N.Y.C., 1982-85, Beddow Mfg. Ind., 1983-85; co-pres. TRS Mktg. Inc., N.Y.C., 1985—; founder Energy Works, 1985; founder, dir. TRS Inc. Profl. Suite, 1986—. Author 38 novellas. N.Y. Regents scholar, 1965-69. Mem., Trans-Species Unltd., Soc. Ethical Treatment of Animals. Avocations: woodworking, carpentry, advocating animal rights, design psychology. Office: TRS Mktg Inc 7 E 30th St New York NY 10016

MASIRE, QUETT, president of Botswana; b. Kanye, July 23, 1925; ed. Tiger Kloof (South Africa); m. Gladys Olebile; 6 children. Tchr.; journalist; a founder, sec.-gen. Bechuanaland Democratic Party, 1962—; dep. prime minister, 1965-66, minister of finance, 1966-78, minister devel. planning, 1967-78; v.p. Botswana, 1966-80, pres., 1980—. Recipient Master Farmer certificate Dept. Agr., 1957. Address: State House, Private Bag 001, Gaborone Botswana *

MASIRONI, ROBERTO, scientist, program administrator; b. Rome, Sept. 19, 1931; came to Switzerland, 1967; s. Mario and Renata (Ferrucci) M.; m. Liliana Di Marco, Aug. 25, 1958; children—Fulvio, Paola. Ph.D. in Biology, U. Rome, 1954, Ph.D. in Pharmacy, 1956. Research asst. Nat. Nuclear Energy Commn., Rome, 1957-63; postdoctoral fellow Nat. Research Council, Ottawa, Ont., Can., 1958-60; vis. investigator Acad. Scis., Moscow, 1961-62, Oak Ridge Nat. Lab., 1963-64; research assoc. Emory U., Atlanta, 1964-67; scientist WHO, Geneva, 1967—, mgr. tobacco or health program, 1983—; vis. investigator USDA, Beltsville, Md., 1976; vis. prof. U. Waterloo, Ont., Can., 1979-80. Co-author: Fundamentals of Exercise Testing, 1971; Habitual Physical Activity and Health, 1978; Physical Activity in Diseases Prevention, 1983; contbr. numerous articles to profl. jours. Named hon. citizen of Tenn., Gov. of Tenn., 1963; recipient recognition for acad. activities Chinese Acad. Med. Scis., Beijing, 1982. Fellow Am. Coll. Nutrition; mem. (hon.) Union Antitabaquica Argentina. Roman Catholic. Club: UN Sailing (Geneva Lake). Office: WHO, Ave Appia, 1211 Geneva 27 Switzerland

MASLOWSKI, PIOTR, biochemist; b. Warsaw, Poland, June 10, 1919; s. Hilary and Albina Szymonowicz M.; m. Halina Gunin, Oct. 26, 1945; children: Lech, Ewa. MSc, A. Mickiewicz U., Poznań, Poland, 1950, PhD, 1959; DR, N. Copernicus U., Toruń, Poland, 1965. Asst. prof., head of biochemistry dept. Agrl. U., Olsztyn, Poland, 1960-69; prof., head of biochemistry dept. N. Copernicua U., Torun, 1970—. Author: Research Experiences in Chemistry, 1954, Organic Chemistry, 1955; contbr. Jours. Progress of Biochemistry, Biochemistry, Acta, Phytochemistry. Mem. Polish Biochem. Soc., Polish Acad. Scis., Polish Soc. Chemistry, Sci. Soc. Toruń. Roman Catholic. Home: Kraszewskiego 20/2, 87-100 Torun Poland Office: N Copernicus U Dept Biochemistry, Gasgarina 7, 87-100 Torun Poland

MASLYUKOV, YURIY DMITRIEVICH, Soviet government official; b. Leninabad, Tadzhik, USSR, Sept. 30, 1937. Ed., Leningrad Inst. Math. Mem. Commnunist Party Soviet Union, 1966—; chief engr. Izhevsk machine-bldg. plant, USSR, 1970-74; head adminstrn. USSR Ministry Def. Industry, 1974-82; head chair USSR Gosplan, 1982-85; dep. to Council Nationalities, USSR Supreme Soviet, 1984—; dep. chair, chair mil-indsl. com. USSR Council Ministers, from 1985, 1st dep. chmn., 1988—; mem. Cen. Com. Communist Party Soviet Union, 1986—. Decorated Order of Oct. Revolution, Order of the Red Banner Badge of Honour. Address: Cen Com CPSU, Staraya pl 4, Moscow USSR *

MASOL, VITALY ANDREEVICH, Soviet government offical; b. Ukraine, USSR, Nov. 14, 1928; married; 1 son. Grad., Kiev Poly. Inst., USSR. Foreman, shop mgr., dep. chief engr., dir. works, dir. gen. Indsl. Combine Kramatorsk, USSR, 1951-72; 1st dep. chmn. State Planning Com., Kiev, Ukranian Soviet Socialist Republic, USSR, chmn., 1972-87; dep. chmn. Council Ministers, Kiev, 1972-87, chmn., 1987—. Mem. Communist Party Soviet Union, 1956—, mem. cen. auditing commn., 1986; chmn. planning and budgetary commn. Soviet Union USSR Supreme Soviet, 1983-87. Decorated Order of Lenin (twice), Order of Oct. Revolution, Order Red Banner Labour, Order Badge Honour, other medals. Office: Council of Ministers, Kiev Ukranian SSR, USSR *

MASON, AIMEE HUNNICUTT ROMBERGER, retired educator; b. Atlanta, Nov. 3, 1918; d. Edwin William and Aimee Greenleaf (Hunnicutt) Romberger; m. Samuel Venable Mason, Aug. 16, 1941; children: Olivia Elizabeth (Mrs. Mason Butcher), Christopher Leeds. BA, Conn. Coll., 1940; postgrad. Emory U., 1946-48; MA, U. Fla., 1979, PhD, 1980; MA, Stetson U., 1968. Jr. exec., merchandising G. Fox & Co., Hartford, Conn., 1940-41; air traffic controller CAA, Atlanta, 1942; ptnr. Coronado Concrete Products, New Smyrna Beach, Fla., 1953-81; adj. faculty Valencia Jr. Coll., Orlando, Fla., 1969; instr. philosophy and humanities Seminole Community Coll., Sanford, from 1969, now ret. Area cons. ARC, 1947-50; del. Nat. Red Cross, Washington, 1949; founding mem. St. Joseph Hosp. Aux., Atlanta, 1950-53; v.p., treas. New Smyrna Beach PTA 1955-60. Bd. dirs. Atlanta Symphony Orch., Fla. Symphony Orch., 1954-59. Served to lt. USCGR, 1943-46. Recipient award in graphics Nat. Assn. Women Artists, 1939, 41, Golden Hatter award Stetson U., 1973, 74. Mem. Am. Philos. Assn., AAUP, AAUW (founding mem. New Smyrna Beach, exec. bd. 1984-85, chmn. scholarship com. 1984-87, coll./univ. liaison, 1987—), Fla. Philos. Assn. (exec. council 1978-79), Collegium Phenomenologicum, Soc. Existential and Phenomenological Philosophy, Soc. Phenomenology in Human Scis., Merleau-Ponty Circle, Fla. Assn. Community Colls., DAV. Home: 2103 Ocean Dr New Smyrna Beach FL 32069

MASON, DEAN TOWLE, cardiologist; b. Berkeley, Calif., Sept. 20, 1932; s. Ira Jenckes and Florence Mabel (Towle) M.; m. Maureen O'Brien, June 22, 1957; children: Kathleen, Alison. B.A. in Chemistry, Duke U., 1954, M.D., 1958. Diplomate: Nat. Bd. Med. Examiners, Am. Bd. Internal Medicine (cardiovascular diseases). Intern, then resident in medicine Johns Hopkins Hosp., 1958-61; clin. asso. cardiology br., sr. asst. surgeon USPHS, Nat. Heart Inst., NIH, 1961-63, asst. sect. dir. cardiovascular diagnosis, attending physician, sr. investigator cardiology br., 1963-68; prof. medicine, prof. physiology, chief cardiovascular medicine U. Calif. Med. Sch., Davis-Sacramento Med. Center, 1968-82; dir. cardiac ctr. Cedars Med. Ctr., Miami, Fla., 1982-83; physician-in chief Western Heart Inst., San Francisco, 1983—; chmn. dept. cardiovascular medicine St. Mary's Med. Ctr., San Francisco, 1986—; co-chmn. cardiovascular-renal drugs U.S. Pharmacopeia Com. Revision, 1970-75; mem. life scis. com. NASA; med. research rev. bd. VA, NIH; vis. prof. numerous univs., cons. in field; mem. Am. Cardiovascular Splty. Certification Bd., 1972-78. Author: Cardiovascular Management, 1974, Congestive Heart Failure, 1976, Advances in Heart Disease, Vol. 1, 1977, Vol. 2, 1978, Vol. 3, 1980, Cardiovascular Emergencies, 1978, Principles of Noninvasive Cardiac Imaging, 1980, Myocardial Revascularization, 1981, Cardiology, 1981, 82, 83, 84, 85, 86, 87, 88, Clinical Nuclear Cardiology, 1981, Love Your Heart, 1982; also numerous articles.; assoc. editor: Clin. Cardiol. Jour; editor-in-chief: Am. Heart Jour; mem. editorial bds. sci. jours. Recipient Research award Am. Therapeutic Soc., 1965; Theodore and Susan B. Cummings Humanitarian award State Dept.-Am. Coll. Cardiology, 1972, 73, 75, 78; Skylab Achievement award NASA, 1974; U. Calif. Faculty Research award, 1978; named Outstanding Prof. U. Calif. Med. Sch., Davis, 1972. Fellow Am. Coll. Cardiology (pres. 1977-78), A.C.P., Am. Heart Assn., Am. Coll. Chest Physicians, Royal Soc. Medicine; mem. Am. Soc. Clin. Investigation, Am. Physiol. Soc., Am. Soc. Pharmacology and Exptl. Therapeutics (Exptl. Therapeutics award 1973), Am. Fedn. Clin. Research, N.Y. Acad. Scis., Am. Assn. U. Cardiologists, Am. Soc. Clin. Pharmacology and Therapeutics, Western Assn. Physicians, AAUP, Western Soc. Clin. Research (past pres.), Phi Beta Kappa, Alpha Omega Alpha. Republican. Methodist. Club: El Marcero Country. Home: 3015 Country Club Dr El Macero CA 95618 Office: Western Heart Inst St Mary's Med Ctr 450 Stanyan St San Francisco CA 94117

MASON, ELLSWORTH GOODWIN, librarian; b. Waterbury, Conn., Aug. 25, 1917; s. Frederick William and Kathryn Loretta (Watkins) M.; m. Rose Ellen Maloy, May 13, 1951 (div. Oct. 1961); children: Kay Iris, Joyce Iris; m. Joan Lou Shinew, Aug. 16, 1964; 1 son, Sean David. B.A., Yale U., 1938, M.A., 1942, Ph.D., 1948; L.H.D., Hofstra U., 1973. Reference asst. Yale Library, 1938-42; export license officer Bd. Econ. Warfare, 1942-43; instr. English Williams Coll., 1948-50; humanities div. Marlboro (Vt.) Coll., 1951-52; serials librarian U. Wyo. Library, 1952-54; reference librarian Colo. Coll. Library, Colorado Springs, 1954-58; librarian, lectr. English Colo. Coll. Library, 1958-63; prof., dir. library services Hofstra U., Hempstead, N.Y., 1963-72; prof., dir. U. Colo. Libraries, Boulder, 1972-76; pres. Mason Assos., Ltd., 1977—; research asso. U. Calif.-Berkeley, 1965; vis. lectr. Colo. Coll., 1965, Syracuse U., 1965-68, Elmira Coll., 1966, Columbia U., 1966-68, U. Ill., 1972, Lincoln U., 1969, U. B.C. (Can.), 1969, U. Toronto, 1970, U. Tulsa, 1971, 76, Rutgers U., 1971, Colgate U., 1972, Simmons Coll., 1972, U. Oreg., 1973, Hofstra U., 1974, U. N.C., 1976, U. Ala., 1976, Ball State U., 1977, U. Lethbridge, Can., 1977, U. Ariz., 1981, Victoria U. (N.Z.), 1983, U. Canterbury (N.Z.), 1983, Hofstra U., 1974, 85; vis. prof. U. Ill., Urbana, summer 1968; v.p., pres.-elect Bibliog. Center Research, Rocky Mountain Region, 1961-63; exec. bd. Hist. Soc. Pikes Peak Region, 1960; chmn. Colo. Council Library Devel., 1962-63, Conf. on U. Library Standards, Boston, 1967; planning com. L.I. Library Resources Council, 1967-68, trustee, 1970-72, chmn. personnel com., 1970-72; dir. workshop on surveys Can. Assn. Coll. and Univ. Libraries, 1968; mem. jury Colo. Gov.'s award, 1982; chancellor's council U. Tex., 1982—; lectr. Conf. on Acad. Library Bldgs., Drexel Inst. Tech., 1966; library bldg. cons. 135 ednl. instnl. libraries. (Recipient design award N.Y. State Assn. Architects-AIA 1974, Progressive Architecture award 1974); Editor: (with Stanislaus Joyce) The Early Joyce, 1955, Xerox U.M. edit., 1964, (with Richard Ellmann) The Critical Writings of James Joyce, 1959, Critical Commentary on A Portrait of the Artist as a Young Man, 1966; translator: Recollections of James Joyce (S. Joyce), 1951, Essais de J. Joyce, 1966, Escritos Criticos de James Joyce, 1973, 75, James Joyce's Ulysses and Vico's Cycle, 1973, Kritische Schriften v. James Joyce, 1975, Mason on Library Buildings, 1980; editor: Colorado College Studies, 1959-62; editor and compiler: Focus on Robert Graves, 1972—; editor: The Booklover's Bounty, 1977—; editorial bd.: Serial Slants, 1937-39, The Serials Librarian, 1977—, Choice, 1962-65, Coll. & Research Libraries, 1969-72. Served with USNR, 1943-46. Harry Bailly speaker's award Assn. Colls. of Midwest, 1975; Council on Library Resources fellow, 1969-70; grantee Am. Council Learned Socs.; grantee Council Library Resources; grantee Edn. Facil. Labs.; grantee Hofstra U.; grantee U. Colo. Mem. ALA (councillor-at-large 1961-65), Colo. Library Assn. (pres. So. dist. 1960-61), Bibliog. Soc. Am., Library Assn. (London), N.Z. Library Assn., MLA, Pvt. Libraries Assn., Alcuin Soc., Conf. Editors Learned Jours., Colo. Book Collectors (founder, pres. 1975—), Inst. Vico Studies, James Joyce Found. (chmn., sect. on translation from Joyce, 2d Internat. James Joyce Symposium, Dublin 1969), Alpha Sigma Lamda, Sigma Kappa Alpha (pres. 1969-70). Clubs: Caxton, Archons of Colophon; Ghost Town (Colorado Springs). Home: 3137 N Cleveland Rd Lexington KY 40516 also: 39 Discovery Dr, Whitby New Zealand

MASON, FRANKLIN HARRELL, education consultant, musician; b. Dallas, Tex., Dec. 3, 1929; s. Harrell C. and Hazel (Wager) M.; B.A., N. Tex. State U., 1952, M.A., 1957; postgrad. Stephen F. Austin State U., summer, 1972; Litterarum D. (hon.), Sussex Coll. Tech., 1973; pvt. study in harpsichord, 1956; master classes in organ, 1949-71. Instr. in French, Spanish, Latin, Greek and English, Tyler (Tex.) public schs., 1956-74, chmn. div. fgn. langs., 1971-74; profl. church organist, 1946—; numerous organ recitals, Tex., Ga. and Ark., 1955—; asst. organist First Presbyterian Ch., Tyler, 1968—; organist Tex. Fedn. Bus. and Profl. Women's Clubs, 1959; cons. in edn. and langs., since 19—. Served with U.S. Army, 1954-56. Recipient Amicii Latina award, 1969, Hawthorne award, 1972; Tyler Citizen Service award, 1982; various awards in religious service, 1947-68. Mem. Am. Guild of Organists (del. to southwest regional conv. 1963, historian, exec. council East Tex. chpt. 1980—), Nat. Council Tchrs. of English (del. to nat. conv. 1966), Organ Hist. Soc., Tex. Fgn. Lang. Assn., Tex. State Tchrs. Assn., East Tex. Latin Assn., Am. Mensa Soc., Am. Legion, Tyler Citizens League, Pi Delta Phi, Phi Eta Sigma, Sigma Delta Pi. Democrat. Presbyterian. Author: Curriculum Guide for Foreign Languages, 1964; Plot and Characterization in the Episodios Nacionales of Benito Perez Galdos, 1957; Historical Pipe Organs of Eastern Texas, 1981; contbr. articles to lit., mus. jours. and Ency. Am. Theater Organ, 1985. Address: 505 Sunnyside Dr Tyler TX 75702

MASON, GEORGE ROBERT, surgeon, educator; b. Rochester, N.Y., June 10, 1932; s. George Mitchell and Marjorie Louise (Hooper) M.; m. Grace Louise Bransfield, Feb. 4, 1956; children—Douglas Richard, Marcia Jean, David William. B.A., Oberlin Coll., 1955; M.D. with honors, U. Chgo., 1957; Ph.D. in Physiology (Giannini fellow 1966-67), Stanford U., 1968. Diplomate: Am. Bd. Surgery (examiner 1977-80, dir. 1980-86), Bd. Thoracic Surgery. Tchg. asst. pathology U. Chgo., 1954-56; rotating intern U. Chgo. Clinics, 1957-58; tchg. asst. surgery, NIH postdoctoral fellow, USPHS fellow surgery Stanford U., 1960-62; from asst. resident in surgery to sr. and chief resident in surgery Stanford U. Hosps., 1962-66; mem. faculty Stanford Med. Sch., 1965-71, asso. prof., 1970-71; prof., chmn. dept. surgery U. Md. Med. Sch., Balt., 1971-80; also prof. physiology; prof., chmn. dept. surgery U. Calif., Irvine, 1980—; mem. review com. for surgery, 1981-87. Contbr. to profl. jours., med. textbooks. Served to capt. M.C. USAF, 1958-60. Recipient Markle scholarship in acad. medicine, 1968-74. Mem. Am. Assn. Thoracic Surgery, AAUP, Am. Coll. Chest Physicians, A.C.S., AMA, Am. Physiol. Soc., Am. Gastroent. Assn., Pacific Coast Surg. Assn., Assn. Acad. Surgery, Balt. Acad. Surgery, Los Angeles Surg. Soc., Halsted Soc., Chesapeake Vascular Soc., Soc. Internat. de Chirurgie, Soc. Clin. Surgery, Soc. Surgery Alimentary Tract, Soc. U. Surgeons, Sigma Xi, Alpha Omega Alpha. Home: 18712 Via Torino Irvine CA 92715 Office: Dept Surgery U Calif Irvine CA 92717

MASON, KENNETH M., photographic mfg. co. exec.; b. Rochester, N.Y., Sept. 21, 1917; s. Marcenus C. and Matilda (Starke) M.; B.A., Washington and Jefferson Coll., 1938; student U. Rochester; m. Janice Lyle Kurtz, Apr.

24, 1982; children by previous marriage—Kenneth M., John L., Richard K., Thomas S., Stephen W. Engr., Eastman Kodak Co., Rochester, 1946-50, regional mgr., Chgo., 1951-64, regional mgr. East Coast div., N.Y.C., 1965-70, regional mgr. West Coast div., Hollywood, Calif., 1970-74, mgr. product programs, Rochester, 1974, asst. vice-pres., gen. mgr., 1974-78, vice-pres., gen. mgr. motion picture and audiovisual markets div., 1978-83, ret.Bd. dirs. Will Rogers Hosp. and Inst.; bd. dirs. Univ. Film and Video Found., Allied Film and Video Lab.; pres. bd. trustees Washington and Jefferson Coll. Served with USNR, 1943-46. Mem. Soc. Motion Picture and TV Engrs., (hon. mem., past pres.), British Kinematograph Sound and TV Soc. (hon. fellow), Acad. Motion Picture Arts and Scis., Am. Soc. Cinematographers, Univ. Film and Video Assn. Republican. Congregationalist. Clubs: Oak Hill Country; Greenwich Country. Home: 14 New England Dr Rochester NY 14618

MASON, PETER IAN, lawyer; b. Bellfonte, Pa., Mar. 20, 1952; s. Robert Stanley and Abelle (Dinkowitz) M.; m. Margaret Ellen Bremner, July 9, 1983; 1 child, Henry Graham. AB Bard Coll., 1973; JD cum laude, Boston U., 1976. Bar: Ill. 1976, U.S. Dist. Ct. (no. dist.) Ill. 1976, N.Y. 1981. Assoc. Rooks, Pitts, Fullagar and Poust, Chgo., 1976-80, 81-83, Shearman & Sterling, N.Y.C., 1980; mng. ptnr. Freeborn & Peters, Chgo., 1983—; dir. U.S. Robotics, Inc., Chgo., 1983—; gen. counsel Graphisphere Corp., Bradley Printing Co., Brown-Sexton Specialty Corp., Lavelle Industries Inc. Mem. ABA, Ill. State Bar Assn., Chgo. Bar Assn., Ill. Oil and Gas Assn. Republican. Episcopalian. Clubs: The Attic, Union League of Chgo. Office: Freeborn & Peters 11 S LaSalle St Chicago IL 60603

MASON, RAYMOND K., diversified manufacturing company executive; b. Jacksonville, Fla., 1927. Grad., U. N.C., 1949. Chmn. bd. dirs. The Charter Co., Jacksonville, 1982—, pres., chief exec. officer, 1982-84, also bd. dirs.; chmn. bd. dirs. Charter Mortgage Co., Beach Fed. Savs. & Loan Assn.; bd. dirs. Fla. First Nat. Bank, Jacksonville. Office: The Charter Co 1 Charter Plaza Box 2017 Jacksonville FL 32202 *

MASRI, TAHER NASHAT, minister of foreign affairs Hashemite Kingdom of Jordan; b. Nablus, Jordan, 1942; married; 2 children. B.B.A. in Commerce, North Tex. State U., 1965. Dep. chief dept. fin. Central Bank of Jordan, 1965-73; mem. Lower House Parliament, 1973—; minister of state for occupied territory affairs, 1973, chief exec. office for occupied terr. affairs, 1973-74; ambassador to Spain, 1975-78, to France, 1978-83; rep. UNESCO, 1978-83; ambassador to U.K., 1983-84; minister fgn. affairs, 1984—. Decorated French Order of Merit, German Order of merit, Brit. GBE, French Legion of Honor, Spanish Civil Merit, Jordanian Al-Kawkab Star. Office: Ministry Fgn Affairs, PO Box 1577, Amman Jordan *

MASSAAD, KHATER, industrial engineer, consultant; b. Remaich, Lebanon, June 17, 1953; s. Abdallah and Saada (Habib) M.; m. Zeina Alam, Aug. 19, 1984; 1 child, Ariane. Degree in Engring., Lausanne Poly. U., 1978, PhD in Geophysics, 1984. Projects engr. Geoconsult, The Hague, The Netherlands, 1979-81; projects mgr. Geoconsult, Fujairah, United Arab Emirates, 1981-82; mng. dir. Emirates Ceramic Factory, Fujairah, 1983—, Fujairah Rockwool Factory, Fujairah, 1983—, Fujairah Marble and Tiles, Fujairah, 1983—; indsl. cons. Fujairah Govt., 1982—. Author: Management in Gulf Industries, 1987. Mem. Devel. Com. Fujairah, 1987—. Office: Geoconsult, PO Box 751, Fujairah United Arab Emirates

MASSENGALE, JOHN EDWARD, 3D, lawyer; b. Kansas City, Mo., Nov. 18, 1921; s. John Edward, Jr. and Frances (Haig) M.; m. Jean Mitchell Montague, Dec. 8, 1942; children: Sarah Choate Massengale Gregg, John Edward IV, Thomas Haig. A.B., Harvard U., 1942, LL.B., 1948. Bar: N.Y. 1949, D.C. 1971. Practice law N.Y.C., 1948—; partner firm Paul, Weiss, Rifkind, Wharton & Garrison, 1958—; bd. dirs. Wellington Industries, Inc. Rep. town meeting, Darien, Conn., 1955-61, 63-70; mem. Zoning Bd. Appeals, 1985-86, Darien Planning and Zoning Commn., 1986—. Served to lt. USNR, 1942-45. Mem. Assn. Bar City N.Y., N.Y. State Bar Assn., ABA. Club: Noroton Yacht. Home: Goodwives River Rd Noroton CT 06820 Office: 1285 Ave of the Americas New York NY 10019

MASSENGILL, ELLEN WEBB, librarian; b. Littlefield, Tex., Mar. 6, 1932; d. Lester L. and Bessie (Webb) M.; BS, Tex. Tech U., 1953, MS, 1959; MLS, North Tex. State U., 1969. Homemaking tchr., Floyd, N.M., 1953-55, Crane, Tex., 1955-56, Seminole, Tex., 1956-68, Littlefield, Tex., 1971-73; librarian Odessa (Tex.) High Sch., 1969-71, Littlefield Jr. High Sch., 1973-82, Littlefield Ind. Sch. Dist., 1982-83, Littlefield High Sch. and Jr. High Sch., 1983-84, Littlefield High Sch., 1984—; dist., area, state adv. bd. mem. Future Homemakers Am., N.Mex., Tex., 1954-68, adv. mem. nat. exec. council, 1954-55; adv. Young Homemakers Tex., 1958-73; co-leader Girl Scouts U.S.A., 1948-49; del. Nat. Citizenship Council, 1954. Recipient Home Econs. Scholarship award Borden Co., 1953, Panhellenic award Lubbock (Tex.) Panhellenic Soc., 1953; Forum award Tex. Tech. U., 1953. Mem. AAUW (reporter, historian, sec., parliamentarian 1956-68), Sch. Library and Info. Sci. Assn., NEA, Am. Home Econs. Assn., Am. Vocat. Assn., PTA, Tex. State Tchrs. Assn. (life), ALA, Tex. Library Assn. (life; sec. dist. 9), Tex. Classroom Tchrs. Assn., Vocat. Homemaking Tchrs. Assn. Tex., Tex. Home Econs. Assn., Lamb County Tchrs. Assn. (treas.), Littlefield Classroom Tchrs. Assn. (treas.), Phi Kappa Phi, Phi Upsilon Omicron, Alpha Lambda Delta, Alpha Chi, Alpha Lambda Sigma, Beta Phi Mu, Delta Kappa Gamma (sec., charter mem. Iota Eta chpt., 2d v.p. 1987—). Democrat. Baptist. Home: 510 E 6th St Littlefield TX 79339 Office: 1100 W 10th St Littlefield TX 79339

MASSET, ROYAL ANDREW, political lobbyist, consultant; b. Bklyn., Oct. 20, 1945; s. George Rowe and Aimee (Toner) M. A.B. cum laude, Princeton U., 1967; M.Div., Episcopal Theol. Sem. of Southwest, 1976; postgrad. U. Tex., 1973-76. Bar: Tex. 1977. Exec. dir. Austin Citizens League, 1976—, Tex. Taxpayers League, Austin, 1978-79; researcher, cons. Republican Party of Tex., Austin, 1980-85; polit. dir. Republican Party of Tex., 1985—; counsel Tex. Senate Com. on Intergovernmental Relations, Austin, 1983; exec. dir. Tex. Conservative Coalition, 1985. Contbr. articles to profl. jours. Mem. Austin Charter Revision Com., 1975-77; campaign mgr. Tom Pauken for Congress, Dallas, 1980; founder, atty. Citizens for Honest Electric Rates, Austin, 1983—; trustee Austin Community Edn. Consortium, Austin, 1981-83; bd. dirs. Citizens for Better Schs., Austin, 1978-79; various civic bds. and commns., 1975—. Named Disting. Citizen, City of Austin, 1977; named one of 1980s Most Interesting People in Austin, Austin Homes & Garden, 1980. Mem. Travis County Young Lawyers Assn., Travis County Bar Assn., Tex. Bar Assn., Austin Citizens League (v.p. 1975-76). Mormon. Office: Republican Party Tex 211 E 7th St #620 Austin TX 78701

MASSEVITCH, ALLA GENRIKHOVNA, astronomer; b. Tbilissi, Georgia, USSR, Oct. 9, 1918; d. Caesar Henrik and Natalie (Zhgenti) M.; m. Joseph Friedlander, 1942; 1 child, Natalie. Diploma in Astrophysics, Moscow U., 1942, D of Theoretical Astrophysics, 1942-45. Prof. astrophysics Moscow U., 1948-70; prof. satellite geodesy Moscow Tech. U. Geodesy and Cartography, 1970-76; v.p. and chief scientist Astronomical Council of the USSR Acad. Scis., 1952—; mem. steering com. Internat. Halley's Comet Watch, 1983-87; dep. sec.-gen. UNISPACE '82 (2d conf. of UN on Peaceful Use of Outer Space), N.Y.C., 1982; chmn. COSPAR Tracking and Telemetering of Satellites, USSR, 1961-70. Editorial bd. Astrophysics Jour., 1984—; co-editor Astrophysics and Space Science, 1985—; author: Physics and Evolution of Stars, 3 vols., 1972, 81, 88, Observations of Satellites for Geodesy, 1979; contbr. numerous articles in field to sci. jours. V.p. USSR Peace Com., USSR-U.S. Friendship Soc. Named Honorary Scientist Emeritus USSR, 1978; recipient Prize Galabert, 1961, USSR State Prize, 1975, several decorations and medals USSR, Bulgaria, Mongolian Peoples Republic, German Dem. Republic since 1961. Fellow Brit. Royal Astronomical Soc., Indian Acad. Scis., Austrian Acad. Scis. (corr.); mem. Internat. Acad. Astronautics (v.p. Internat. Astron. Union commn. on extraterrestrial astronomy 1964-67, pres. commn. on internal structure of stars 1967-70, pres. com. for space sci. 1983-86). Home: 1 Vosstania Sq, Apt 403, 123242 Moscow USSR Office: Astronomical Council, USSR Acad of Scis, 48 Pjatnitskaya St, 109017 Moscow USSR

MASSEY, DONALD WAYNE, microfilm consultant; b. Durham, N.C., Mar. 7, 1938; s. Gordon Davis and Lucille Alma (Gregory) M.; student U. Hawaii, 1959, U. Ky., 1965, U. Va., 1970, Piedmont Community Coll., 1982; m. Violet Sue McIlvain, Nov. 2, 1958; children—Kimberly Shan (dec.), Leon Dale, Donn Krichele. Head microfilm sect. Ky. Hist. Soc., Frankfort, 1961; dir. microfilm center U. Ky., Lexington, 1962-67; dir. photog. services and graphics U. Va., Charlottesville, 1967-73; pres. Micrographics II, Charlottesville, Va. & Charleston, S.C., 1973—; pub. Micropublishing Series, 18th Century Sources for Study English Lit. and Culture; instr. U. Va. Sch. Continuing Edn., 1971-72, Central Va. Piedmont Community Coll., 1976; cons. Microform Systems and Copying Centers; owner Massland Farm, Shadwell, Va.; basketball coach Rock Hill Acad., 1975-77. Author: Episcopal Churches in the Diocese of Virginia, 1988. Pres., Rock Hill Acad. Aux., 1975-76; pres. bd. Workshop V for handicapped, Charlottesville, Va., 1972-73; mem. Emmanuel Episc. Ch., Greenwood, Va. Served with USMCR, 1957-60. Named Ky. Col.; recipient Key award Workshop V. Mem. Am., Va. library assns., Soc. Reprodn. Engrs., Nat. (library relations com. 1973-—), Va. (Pioneer award 1973, pres. 1971-72, v.p. 1973-74, program chmn. ann. conf. 1974), Ky. (Outstanding award 1967, pres. 1964-67) microfilm assns., Assn. for Info. and Image Mgmt., Thoroughbred Owners and Breeders Assn., Am. Rose Soc., Thomas Jefferson Rose Soc. (charter), Nat. Rifle Assn. Contbg. editor Va. Librarian, 1970-71, Micro-News Va. Microfilm Assn., 1970-71, Plant & Print Jour., 1983-85; contbr. articles to profl. publs. Home: Rt 2 Box 44 Keswick VA 22947 Office: PO Box 191 Keswick VA 22947

MASSEY, THOMAS BENJAMIN, academic administrator; b. Charlotte, N.C., Sept. 5, 1926; s. William Everard and Sarah (Corley) M.; m. Bylee Hunnicutt Massey, July 10, 1968; children: Pamela Ann, Caroline Forest. A.B., Duke U., 1948; M.S., N.C. State U., 1953; Ph.D., Cambridge U., 1968. Lic. psychologist, Ga. Assoc. dean students Ga. Inst. Tech., Atlanta, 1950-58; lectr. London div. U. Md., College Park, 1960-66, asst. dir. London div., 1966-69, dir. Toyko div., 1969-71, dir. Heidelberg (Fed. Republic of Germany) div., 1971-76, vice chancellor, 1976-78, chancellor, 1978—; bd. dirs. Internat. Univ. Consortium for Telecommunications in Learning, 1983—. Served with USN, 1943-46. Mem. Am. Assn. Adult and Continuing Edn., Soc. Research in Higher Edn., Nat. Univ. Continuing Edn. Assn., Am. Psychol. Assn., Am. Assn. Higher Edn., Internat. Confs. on Improving Univ. Teaching (chmn., editor Proceedings 1975—). Office: U Md Univ Coll University Blvd at Adelphi Rd College Park MD 20742-1600

MASSEY, WILLIAM JAMES, III, manufacturing company executive; b. Muncie, Ind., Aug. 5, 1942; s. William James Jr. and Ruth Edna (Readnour) M.; m. Sharon Ann Allen, Sept. 6, 1965 (div. July 1984); children: William James IV, Thomas Allen; m. Carmen Cepeda, Aug. 7, 1987. BS, Mich. Tech. U., Houghton, 1964; MBA, Harvard U., Cambridge, Mass., 1966. Regional prodn. dir. Goodyear Internat., Akron, Ohio, 1980-83; prodn. dir. Goodyear Mex., Mexico City, 1984—. Office: Goodyear, Apdo Pos 1028 CP, 06000 Mexico City Mexico

MASSICK, JAMES WILLIAM, heavy equipment manufacturing company executive; b. Seattle, Jan. 19, 1932; s. Peter James and Annetta Jean (Dormier) M.; m. Joyce Allair Puckey, Apr. 7, 1973; children—Scott, Christopher, Kit, Timothy, Nina, Sally, John, Jill. BS, U. Wash., 1954; MBA, U. Calif. at Los Angeles, 1966. Constrn. engr. Kaiser Engrs., Oakland, Calif., 1957-60; project mgr. Ralph M. Parsons Co., Los Angeles, 1960-65; engring. mgr. Weyerhauser Co., Tacoma, 1965-68; ops. mgr. Western Gear Corp., Everett, Wash., 1968-70; pres. Truckweld Equipment Co., Seattle, 1970—; dir. Truckweld Corp., Truckweld Utilities, Inc., Puget Sound Lease Co., Pacific N.W. Utility & Supply Co. Served to capt. USNR, 1950, 54-57. Decorated Navy Cross, Silver Star, Legion of Merit, Purple Heart. Mem. ASCE, Soc. Am. Mil. Engrs., Seattle C. of C., Mcpl. League. Theta Delta Chi. Episcopalian. Club: Overlake Golf and Country. Patentee in field. Home: 8815 SE 54th ST Mercer Island WA 98040

MASSIE, ROBERT JOSEPH, publishing company executive; b. N.Y.C., Mar. 19, 1949; s. Franklin Joseph and Genevieve Helen (Savarese) M.; m. Barbara Ellen Batchelder, Apr. 16, 1982; children—David Chance, Caroline Courtenay, Laura Brett. B.A., Yale U., 1970; M.B.A., Columbia U., 1974, J.D., 1974; Diploma, U. d'Aix en Provence, France, 1969. Bar: D.C. 1974. Assoc. Covington & Burling, Washington, 1975-79; mgmt. cons. McKinsey & Co., N.Y.C., 1979-82; v.p. Harlequin Enterprises, Toronto, Ont., Can., 1982-84, exec. v.p. overseas div., 1984—; chmn. bd. dirs. Harlequin Mondadori, Milan, Italy, 1985—; dir. Harlequin Hachette, Paris, Cora Verlag, Hamburg, Fed. Republic Germany, Mills & Boon, Sydney, Australia, Harlenik Ltd., Athens, Greece. Contbr. articles to law jours. Harlan Fiske Stone scholar, 1974. Mem. Bd. Trade Toronto. Club: Yale (N.Y.C.). Home: 23 Eastbourne Ave, Toronto, ON Canada M5P 2E8 Office: Harlequin Enterprises, 225 Duncan Mill Rd, Don Mills, ON Canada M3B 3K9

MASSIGNON, DANIEL, physicist, educator; b. Paris, Apr. 9, 1919; s. Louis and Marcelle (Dansaert-Testelin) M.; D.Sc., U. Paris, 1955; m. Nicole Deney, Apr. 24, 1970; 1 child, Bérengère. With Nat. Center for Sci. Research, Paris, 1945-56; dep. head phys. chemistry dept. Commissariat l'Énergie Atomique, Paris, 1956-70, head chem. physics dept., 1969—; mem. faculty statis. mechanics U. Paris, 1956-75. Decorated officer Legion of Honor; recipient Prix La Caze, French Acad. of Sci., 1976, also Prix Doistau-Blutel, 1980. Mem. French Phys. Soc., French Chem. Soc., Am. Phys. Soc., European Phys. Soc., Am. Inst. Chem. Engrs. Roman Catholic. Author: Mécanique Statistique des Fluides, 1957; Cours de Mécanique Statistique, 1961; Uranium Enrichment by Gaseous Diffusion, 1979, Russian transl., 1983. Patentee in field. Home: 6 rue de la Source, 75016 Paris France Office: CEN, Saclay PB 2, Gif sur Yvette France

MASSIMO, LUISA MARIA ELENA, pediatrician; b. Genova, Italy, Dec. 22, 1928; d. Diodato F. and Ada G.M. (Nicola) Massimo. MD cum laude, U. Genova, 1953, spec. in pediatrics cum laude, 1955, PhD in Pediatrics, 1962, in Child Health, 1965. Asst., U. Genova, 1955-65, asst. prof. pediatrics, 1965-72, faculty Sch. Specialization in Pediatrics, Hematology, Oncology, 1972—; dir. dept. pediatric hematology and oncology Inst., G. Gaslini Children's Hosp., Genova, 1972—. Contbr. articles to profl. jours. Supt. social services County of Genova, 1985; pres. Nat. Sci. Cancer Inst. Genova, 1986. Recipient prize Accademia Nazionale dei Lincei, 1971; Centre Internat. de l'Enfance fellow for pediatric oncology, 1959, Basel, Switzerland, 1960. Mem. Internat. Soc. Pediatric Oncology, European Soc. Pediatric Hematology and Immunology, Société Suisse de Pediatrie, Associazione Ital. di Ematologia e Oncologia Pediatrica, N.Y. Acad. Scis., Internat. Coll. Pediatrics, Collegio Ematologi Clinici Italiani, Società Italiana di Pediatria. Roman Catholic. Lodge: Soroptimist. Home: 8 Viale Brigata Bisagno, 16129 Genoa Italy Office: 39 via 5 Maggio, Quarto, 16148 Genoa Italy

MASSING, OTWIN PETER, political scientist, sociologist; b. Namborn, W.Ger., May 3, 1934; s. Otto Joh and Berta (Veit) M.; m. Gisela Schmitt, 1960; children—Anja, Erik. Diplom-Soz., U. Frankfurt, 1962, Phd, 1964. Sci. asst. Inst. for Polit. Sci., Frankfurt, 1962-67; scholarship Deutsche Forschungsgemeinschaft, Bonn, 1968-79; dir., prof. polit. sci. SOWI, Munich, 1970-74; prof. U. Hannover, 1975—. Author: Fortschritt und Gegenrevolution, 1966; Anagogische Modelle, 1967; Adorno und die Folgen, 1970; Politische Soziologie, 1974; Reform im Widerspruch, 1976; Verflixte Verhältnisse, 1987. Mem. Deutsche Vereinigung für Politische Wissenschaft, Redaktionsrat Politische Vierteljahresschrift, Goerresgesellschaft, Vereinigung für Parlamentsfragen, Deutsche Gesellschaft für Soziologie, Deutsche Gesellschaft für Friedens-und Konfliktforschung. Social-Democrat. Roman Catholic. Home: Moltkeplatz 6, 3000 Hannover 1 Federal Republic of Germany Office: Univ Hannover, Hanomagstr 8, 3000 Hannover Federal Republic of Germany

MASSLER, HOWARD ARNOLD, lawyer, corporate executive; b. Newark, July 22, 1946; s. Abraham I. and Sylvia (Botwin) M.; m. Randee Elyce Karch, July 1, 1977; children: Justin Scott, Jeremy Ross. BA, U. Pa., 1969; JD, Rutgers U., 1973; LLM in Taxation, NYU, 1977. Bar: N.J. 1974, U.S. Dist. Ct. N.J. 1974, D.C. 1975, U.S. Ct. Appeals (D.C. cir.) 1975, N.Y. 1977, U.S. Dist. Ct. (we. dist.) N.Y. 1977, U.S. Tax Ct. 1977. Counsel house banking, currency and housing com. U.S. Ho. Reps., Washington, 1974-76; tax atty. Lipsitz, Green, Fahringer, Roll, Schuller & James, N.Y.C. and Buffalo, 1977-79; sole practice Mountainside, N.J., 1979—; pres. Bestway Products Inc., A.A. Records Inc., Servor Corp., 1979-85; pres., chief exec. officer, chmn. bd. Bestway Group Inc., Dover, Del., 1985—; of counsel Sonageri, Pearce, Siegel & Wille, Chgo. and Hackensack, N.J.; arbitrator U.S. Dist. Ct. N.J., 1985—; adj. prof. tax law Seton Hall U., South Orange, N.J., 1984-85, 88, N.J. Inst. for Continuing Legal Edn., 1986; lectr. N.J. Inst. for Continuing Legal Edn., 1986—; assoc. dir. United Jersey Bank/Franklin State Bank, 1987—; del. adv. com. on indsl. trade and econ. devel. U.S./China Joint Sessions, Beijing, People's Republic of China, 1988. Author: QDROs (Tax and Drafting Considerations), 1986, 2nd. ed., 1987; contbr. West's Legal Forms, Vol. 7., 2d ed., 1987,Domestic Relations with Tax Analysis; tax author: Matthew Bender, NYCP-Matrimonial Actions and Equitable Distribution Actions, 1988, Matthew Bender, Alimony, Child Support & Counsel Feeds, 1988, Matthew Bender, Valuation & Distribution of Marital Property, 1988, How to Make Legal Fees Tax Deductible, 1988; contbg. editor Pensions and Ins. Problems, 1984—, Taxation, 1984—, Fair$hare, 1984—, Law & Bus., Inc., 1984—; staff contbr., N.J. Law Jour., 1986—; contbr. articles to profl. jours. Bd. dirs., legal counsel western N.Y. chpt. Nat. Handicapped Sports and Recreation Assn., 1977-79; counsel Union County, N.J., 1984-85; candidate Springfield (N.J.) Twp. Commn., 1986. Mem. ABA, N.J. Bar Assn. (vice chmn. taxation comm. family law section 1987—), N.Y. Bar Assn. (taxation com., subcom. on criminal and civil penalties), D.C. Bar Assn., Erie County Bar Assn. (sec. taxation com. 1977-79, continuing edn. lectr. taxation 1977—), Essex County Bar Assn. (tax com. 1981—), Union County Bar Assn. (chmn. tax com. 1984—). Republican. Lodge: Kiwanis. Office: 1125 Globe Ave Mountainside NJ 07092

MASSON, ANDRE EMILE, optics company executive; b. Paris, Jan. 27, 1921; s. Andre Adophe and Francoise Juliette (Leguay) M.; m. Genevieve Rose Boyer, Oct. 25, 1941; children: Jacqueline, Helene, Bernard, Catherine, Francoise, Jacques. Grad., Physique U. Paris, 1946; Ingenie Jr.-Docteur, Ecole Superieure d'Optique, Paris, 1948. Engr. Optique et Precaion de Levalloid, 1948-52; dir. engring. Ets P. Angenieux, Saint-Heand, France, 1952—. Patentee surg. lighting apparatus. Decorated Medal Research and Invention, Chevalier Ordre du Merite, French Govt., 1984. Mem. Internat. Soc. Optical Engring., Soc. Photo-Optical Instrumentation Engrs., Optical Soc. France. Roman Catholic. Club: Alpin Francais. Home: 27 BD Ravel de Malval, 42570 Saint Heand France Office: ETS P Angenieux, 42570 Saint Heand France

MASSOT, FEDERICO CHRISTIAN, editor, publisher; b. Manila, Dec. 28, 1949; s. Federico Ezequiel and Diana (Julio) M. Lic. in Sociology, U. Buenos Aires; MS, Columbia. Contbg. editor El Burgués, Buenos Aires, 1971-74; books rev. editor La Nueva Provincia, Buenos Aires, 1972-74, asst. editor, asst. pub., 1974-80, editor, 1980-87, editor, assoc. pub., 1987—; chief exec. officer L.U. 2 Radio Bahia Blanca, L.U. 80 TV Canal 9 Telenueva, Cable Total, La Imprenta S.R.L. Contbr. articles to profl. jours. Mem. adv. com. Argentine Council Fgn. Relations; bd. dirs. Foundl Advancement Sci. Edn. and Culture, Ezequiel Martinez Estrada Found., Bahía Blanca Hist. Soc. Mem. Argentine Pubs. Assn. (exec. com., bd. dirs., F.A. Rizzuto award 1972), Inter-Am. Press Assn. (advisor tech. ctr., exec. com., vice chmn. fin. com., v.p. scholarship fund), Soc. Argentine Bibliophiles (bd. dirs.), Sigma Delta Chi. Roman Catholic. Clubs: Old Georgian, Círculo de Armas, Jockey, Francés (Buenos Aires); Argentino, de Golf Palihue (Bahía Blanca). Home: Sarmiento 54, Bahía Blanca, 8000 Buenos Aires Argentina Office: La Nueva Provincia, Sarmiento 54/64 Bahía Blanca, 8000 Buenos Aires Argentina

MASSURA, EILEEN KATHLEEN, nursing educator, family therapist; b. Chgo., July 25, 1925; d. John William and Loretta (Feil) Stratemeier; m. Edmund Karamanski, July 24, 1948 (dec.); children: John, Kathleen; m. Alfred Massura, Aug. 30, 1963; children: Michael, Kathryn, Mark. BS in Nursing, DePaul U., 1963; MS in Nursing, St. Xavier Coll., 1971. RN; cert. family therapist. Dir. nurses Franklin Blvd. Hosp., Chgo., 1958-62; adminstr. Mich. Ave Hosp., Chgo., 1962-64; instr. St. Xavier Coll., Chgo., 1972-74, Joliet (Ill.) Jr. Coll., 1972-81; family therapist Oak Lawn (Ill.) Family Service, 1978—; prof. nursing Govs. State U., University Park, Ill., 1981—; family therapist McCarthy & Assocs., Oak Lawn, 1982—; preceptor to grads. St. Xavier Coll., 1980—, Govs. State U., 1980—; co-leader Clin. Study Med./Surgical Nursing, Moscow, 1984; presenter Am. Nursing Rev., Ala., Fla., Va., Pa., Tex., Md., 1985-86. Leader Campfire Girls, Oak Lawn, 1964-74; co-leader Orient/Am. Med./ Surg. Nursing, 1987; mem. Marist Women's Bd., Chgo., 1978-82, Bro. Rice Women's Bd., Chgo., 1969-72; Luth. Family Service Bd. Day Care for Srs., 1988-89. Grantee HEW, 1969-71; named Disting. Nurse Alumnae, St. Xavier Coll., 1985; named Nursing Prof. of Yr., Govs. State U., 1983. Mem. Am. Nurses Assn. (nominating com. 1982—), Ill. Nurses Assn. (program com. 1980-84), Am. Assn. Marital and Family Therapists, Sigma Theta Tau (v.p. 1971-75). Roman Catholic. Lodge: Cath. Order Foresters. Office: 5660 W 95th St Oak Lawn IL 60453

MAST, FREDERICK WILLIAM, construction company executive; b. Quincy, Ill., Jan. 3, 1910; s. Christian Charles and Jessie Minnie (Pape) M.; B.S., U. Ill., 1933; m. Kathryn Mary Boekenhoff, Sept. 15, 1932 (dec. Jan. 17, 1975); children—Robert Frederick, Janet (Mrs. James Austin Jones), Susan (Mrs. Edward Hoskins Wilson), Linda (Mrs. William Frederick Bohlen), Teresa Ann (Mrs. Charles Edward Connell); m. 2d, Elaine Ellen Thies Driver, Feb. 14, 1976. Hwy. engr. Adams County (Ill.) Hwy. Dept., Quincy, 1929-33; jr. engr. Ill. Div. Hwys. Rd. Office, Springfield, 1933-35, asst. hwys. architect, 1935-39; estimator Jens Olesen & Sons Constrn. Co., Waterloo, Iowa, 1939-41, v.p., 1941-54, exec. v.p., 1954-65, pres., 1965-76, chmn. bd., 1970-80; owner Frederick W. Mast & Assos., Waterloo, 1946-60; pres. Broadway Bldg. Co., 1951—, Kimball Shopping Center, Inc., 1964-78; dir. First Fed. Savs. Bank of Waterloo, 1957-78, Nat. Bank of Waterloo, 1958-79. Mem. Council Constrn. Employers, Washington, 1968-72, chmn., 1969; ofcl. U.S. del. to Soviet Union under U.S./USSR Exchanges Agreement, 1968-69; del. 8th and 9th sessions bldg., civil engring. and public works com. ILO, Geneva, 1971, 77; sr. builder specialist Tech. for the Am. Home Exhibit USIA, USSR, 1975; mem. Nat. Def. Exec. Res., assigned to Fed. Emergency Mgmt. Agy., 1969—. Mem. Iowa Bldg. Code Council, Des Moines, 1947-50; mem. Bd. Zoning Adjustment, Waterloo, 1947-59; mem. City Plan and Zoning Commn., Waterloo, 1955-78; chmn. Community Devel. Bd., City of Waterloo, 1959-70; fin. chmn. Black Hawk County Republican Central Com., 1958-60; chmn. Waterloo-Cedar Falls Symphony Orch. endowment fund dr., 1977-79, St. Francis Health Care Found., 1980-86; chmn. bd. dirs. St. Francis Hosp., 1976-78; chmn. contractors adv. com. Iowa Coll. Found., 1972-73. Served to col., C.E., AUS, 1941-46. Decorated Legion of Merit; recipient Disting. Service award Waterloo C. of C., 1962; Ky. Col. Registered architect, Ill., Iowa. Mem. Asso. Gen. Contractors Am. (dir. 1956—, mem. exec. com. 1959-62, 66-72, nat. pres. 1968, SIR award Nev. chpt. 1970), Master Builders Iowa (pres. 1952, hon. mem. 1981), Am. Inst. Constructors, Contractors Mut. Assn. Washington (dir. 1971-83, chmn. exec. com. 1971-73), Iowa Engring. Soc., Nat. Soc. Profl. Engrs., Soc. Am. Mil. Engrs., Waterloo Tech. Soc., Amvets, Am. Legion, Phi Eta Sigma, Sigma Phi Epsilon, Tau Beta Pi, Tau Nu Tau, Theta Tau. Roman Catholic. Clubs: Sunnyside Country. Lodges: Elks, Kiwanis. Home: 3309 F Inverness Rd Waterloo IA 50701-4629 Office: PO Box 575 Waterloo IA 50704-0575 also: 321 W 18th St Waterloo IA 50702

MASTBAUM, WILLIAM EDWARD, container manufacturing company executive; b. Dayton, Ohio, Feb. 28, 1923; s. Herman J. and Dorothy (Thurman) M.; student U. Ill., 1946-48; B.S.C., Ohio U., 1949; M.B.A., Harvard U., 1951; m. Carole S. Baloun, Mar. 1, 1986; children—Shelley Mastbaum Weathered, Thomas L. With Container Corp. Am., 1951-82, sr. v.p. employee relations, Chgo., 1977-79, group v.p. for Timber, Pulp Paperbd. Mills and Container div., 1979-80, group v.p. for Domestic Fabricating—Composite Cans, Plastics, Folding Cartons, Corrugated Shipping Containers & Doerfer and staff depts. communication and market research, 1980-82, also dir.; cons., 1982-84; chmn., dir. Belkin Packaging of Am., 1984—; dir. Hawthorne Bank of Wheaton, Belkin, Inc. Bd. dirs., mem. exec. com. Jr. Achievement Greater Chgo., 1975-82. Served to lt. s.g. AC, USN, 1942-46. Mem. Paperbd. Packaging Council (chmn.), Boxboard Research & Devel. Assn (trustee). Roman Catholic. Clubs: Harvard Bus. Sch. of Chgo., Univ. of Chgo. Office: 15 Spinning Wheel Rd Suite 116 Hinsdale IL 60521

MASTERS, GEORGE WINDSOR, JR., electrical engineer; b. Annapolis, Md., Mar. 11, 1930; s. George Windsor and Ruby Lena (Jess) M.; m. Barbara Lyons Wilson, Feb. 27, 1950; children: Barbara Anne, George Windsor III. BS in Physics, MIT, 1952, MS, 1954; PhD in Elec. Engring.,

U. Fla., 1966. Staff engr. MIT Instrumentation Lab., Cambridge, 1952-55; chief engr. Dynamic Instrument Co., Cambridge, 1955-58; sect. head Electro-Mech. Research, Inc., Sarasota, Fla., 1958-62; sect. head The Aerospace Corp., El Segundo, Calif., 1962-72, sr. staff, 1972-75; chief engr. Airborne Systems br. USN Test Pilot Sch., 1975—, established airborne systems curriculum, 1975. Contbr. articles to profl. jours.; inventor in field. MIT grantee, 1953-54; Aerospace corp. fellow, 1965-66; recipient Spl. Achievement award USN Test Pilot Sch., 1979. Mem. IEEE, AIAA, Am. Def. Preparedness Assn., Internat. Test and Evaluation Assn., Kappa Sigma. Republican. Episcopalian. Lodge: Elks. Home: Joy Chapel Rd RR 4 Box 213 Hollywood MD 20636 Office: USN Test Pilot Sch Naval Air Test Ctr Patuxent River MD 20670

MASTRAN, JOHN LEO, management consultant; b. Peekskill, N.Y., Mar. 29, 1920; s. John and Mary (Costella) M.; B.S. in Commerce, U. Va., 1942; Indsl. Adminstr., Harvard U., 1943; m. Carol Ann Righter, Oct. 7, 1950; children—Mary Isabel Mastran Paterson, Elizabeth Righter Mastran Small. Orgn. planning adviser RCA, Camden, N.J., 1943-49, asst. to v.p. and to gen. plant mgr. RCA Electron Tube div., Harrison, N.J., 1949-53, mgr. orgn. planning and mgmt. devel., Camden, 1953-67, dir. orgn. planning and mgmt. devel., 1967-71, dir. orgn. planning, 1971-80, staff v.p. orgn. planning, 1980-87, ind. mgmt. cons. Orgn. planning adviser 3d Internat. Conf. Mfrs. of NAM, 1956; chmn. adv. council on orgn. planning Nat. Indsl. Conf. Bd.; mgmt. course guest speaker Am. Mgmt. Assn. Mem. Orgn. Devel. Council (chmn., pres.), Contact Teleministries USA, Inc. (nat. bd. dirs.), Harvard Bus. Sch. Assn., Beta Gamma Sigma, Alpha Kappa Psi. Clubs: Netherland Luncheon, Harvard (N.Y.C.); Moorestown Field (pres.). Home: 508 Stanwick Rd Moorestown NJ 08057

MASTROIANNI, MARCELLO, actor; b. Fontana Liri, Italy, Sept. 28, 1924; s. Ottone and Ida (Irolle) M.; ed. U. Rome; m. Flora Carabella, 1950; 1 child, Barbara. Cashier, Eagle Lion Films, Rome, 1944; debut U. Rome stage prodn. Angelica, 1948; appeared in films including: Una Domenica d'Agosto, 1949, Le Notti Bianche, 1957, I Soliti Ignoti, 1958, Beli' Antonio, 1960, La Dolce Vita, 1960, La Notte, 1961, A Very Private Affair, 1961, Divorce—Italian Style, 1961, 8 1/2, 1963, Family Diary, 1963, Yesterday, Today and Tomorrow, 1964, Fantasmi a Roma, 1964, Casanova 70, 1965, Marriage—Italian Style, 1965, The Organizer, 1965, The 10th Victim, 1965, Ciao Rudy, 1966, Lo Straniera, 1967, Viaggio di G. Mastorna, 1967, Shout Louder, I Don't Understand, L'Etranger, 1967, The Man with the Balloons, 1968, Diamonds for Breakfast, 1968, Leo the Last, 1970, The Priest's Wife, 1970, Drama of Jealousy, (prize for best actor Cannes 1970), 1970, Sunflower, 1970, The Pizza Triangle, 1970, What?, 1972, La Grande Bouffe, 1973, Salut L'Artiste, 1973, Massacre in Rome, 1973, Touche Pas la Femme Blanche, 1974, Allonsanfan, 1975, Gangster Doll, 1975, Down the Ancient Stairs, 1975, The Sunday Woman, 1976, A Special Day, 1977, Bye Bye Monkey, 1978, Stay as You Are, 1979, La Cite des Femmes, 1979, Blood Feud, 1981, The New World, 1981, Gabriella, 1982, Nuit de Varennes, 1983, Allonsanfan, 1985, Macasoni, 1985, Ginger and Fred, 1986, Dark Eyes (best actor Cannes Film Fest.), 1987; Recipient Silver Ribbon, Italian film critics, 1958, 61. *

MASUD, KHAWAJA DAUD, civil engineer; b. Quetta, Baluchistan, Pakistan, Oct. 13, 1946; s. Khawaja and Riffat Masud; m. Rubina Daud, Jan. 23, 1977; children: Khawaja Saud, Khawaja Omer. Student in Pre-Engring., Govt. Coll., Quetta, 1964; BSc in Civil Engring., West Pakistan U., 1968; MS in Civil Engring. Structures, Poly. Bklyn. Inst., 1975. Asst. engr. Communications & Works Dept., Quetta, 1968-73; structural engr. Green Hut & Taffel, N.Y.C., 1973-76; gen. mgr. Baluchistan Devel. Authority, Quetta, 1976-80; project mgr. Nat. Constrn. Co., Lahore, Pakistan, 1980-82; chief engr. Oil & Gas Devel. Corp., Islamabad, Pakistan, 1982-83; engring. rep. Dallah Establishment, Riyadh, Saudi Arabia, 1983-85; mng. dir. Mohandisin-e-Masud Baluchistan Ltd., Quetta, Pakistan, 1985—; research dir. Low Cost Constrn. in Houses. Mem. ASCE, Pakistan Engring. Counsil, Inst. Engring. Pakistan, Pakistan Engring. Congress, Internat. Housing Soc. Am. Clubs: Gymkhana, Quetta. Home: Faiz Mohhamad Rd 3-7/2, Quetta Pakistan Office: 7-B Jinnah Town, Quetta, Baluchistan Pakistan

MASUDA, GOHTA, physician, educator; b. Tokyo, Japan, Nov. 21, 1940; s. Ryota and Chiyo (Ikeuchi) M.; m. Mitsuko Taguchi, May 14, 1983. M.D., Keio U., 1966, Ph.D., 1977. Intern, Keio Univ. Hosp., Tokyo, 1966-67; instr. Keio U., Tokyo, 1967-74, 76-78; asst. prof. Kitasato Med. Coll., Kanagawa-Ken, Japan, 1974-76; chief dept. infectious diseases Tokyo Met. Komagome Hosp., 1978—; asst. prof. Toho U., Tokyo, 1985—, Keio U., 1986—. Contbr. articles to profl. jours. Mem. Japanese Assn. for Infectious Diseases, Japan Soc. Chemotherapy, Am. Soc. Microbiology, Brit. Soc. for Antimicrobial Chemotherapy, N.Y. Acad. Scis. Buddhist. Home: 1-14-12-305 Komagome, Toshima-ku, 170 Tokyo Japan Office: Dept Infectious Diseases, Tokyo Met Kogamome Hosp, 3-18-22 Honkomagome, Bunkyo-ku 113 Tokyo Japan

MASUDA, YUJI, economist, educator; b. Choshi, Chiba, Japan, July 3, 1938; s. Takeshi and Tsune M.; m. Michiko, Mar. 15, 1972; children: Yoko, Hiroshi, Yasushi. B in Western History, Waseda U., Tokyo, 1963, M in Econs., 1967; B in Econs., Tokyo U., 1965. Sr. economist Japan Soc. for the Promotion of Machine Industry, Econ. Research Inst., Tokyo, 1967—; prof. Osaka City U. Econ. Research Inst., 1983—. Tokyo Keizai U. Inst. Econs. and Bus. Administrn., 1987— . Author: Aerospace Industry, 1979, Advanced Technology Industry, 1980, New Stream of Technological Innovation, 1983, New Age of Information Technology, 1981, New Age of Info-Communication, 1985, Approaches to Knowledge-Intensive Society, 1985, Information Economics, 1987, Manufacturing-System in Information Society, 1988, Strategic Choice of Japan in the 1990's, 1988. Mem. Econ. Policy Soc. Japan, Peace Study Soc. Japan. Home: 2-15-31-905 Takanawa, Minato-ku, Tokyo 108, Japan Office: Tokyo Keizai U, Inst Econs Bus Adm, 1-7 Minamicho, Kokubunji-City, Tokyo 185, Japan

MATALAMAKI, MARGARET MARIE, educator, consultant; b. Hampton, Iowa, May 10, 1921; d. Byron Jacob and Vera Margaret (Wheaton) Myers; m. William Matalamaki, Sept. 11, 1942 (dec. 1978); children—Judith Marie Gerlinger-Thiem, William Micheal. A.A., Itasca Community Coll., 1941; student U. Minn., 1941-42, 72. High sch. instr. Sch. Dist. 1, Bigfork, Minn., 1942-45, U. Minn. Sch. Agr., Grand Rapids, Minn., 1955-58; high sch. substitute Sch. Dist. 318, Grand Rapids, 1967-69; vocat. instr. Itasca Community Coll., Grand Rapids, 1970-78. bd. dirs. Blandin Found., Grand Rapids, trustee, 1981—, v.p., 1985-87, chmn. 1988—; bd. dirs. Christus Home, Grand Rapids; cons. to Keewatin Community Devel. Corp., Grand Rapids, 1985; mem. consumer adv. bd. Land of Lakes Inc., St. Paul, 1984-87, chmn. 1986-87; pres. Kooch-Itasca Action Council, Grand Rapids, 1981-84; adv. council mem. Women's Econ. Devel. Corp., Mpls., 1984-87; bd. dirs. Itasca Meml. Hosp., 1975-85, Itasca County Nursing Home, 1975-85, No. Itasca Nursing Home, 1982-85, Itasca County Social Services, 1975-85; county commr. Itasca County, 1981-85; legis. coordinator Luth. Ch. Am., 1983-86, staff, advocacy coordinator Minn. Synod, 1983-86; mem. adv. council Inst. Agr., Forestry and Home Econ. U. Minn., 1981—; 4-H club leader, Esko, Minn., 1945-49, Grand Rapids, Minn., 1949-63; home extension leader, Esko, 1945-49, Grand Rapids, 1949-63; county fair judge No. Minn., 1950-84; bd. dirs. United Way Grand Rapids, 1980-84; mem. Grand Rapids Citizen's League, 1980—, Minn. Women for Agr., 1982—, Joint Religious Legis. Coalition, Mpls., 1977-78, U. Minn. Nat. Alumni bd. dirs., 1987—, U. Minn. 4H Found. bd. dirs., 1987—, U. Minn. North Cen., Research Station Found./Fund, 1987— ; bd. dirs. Luth. Social Serives Minn., 1986—, vice chair, mem. adv. bd. Luth. Social Services North Eastern Minn., 1986-87 ; mem. Minn. Child Abuse Team, 1986-87; pres. Luth. Ch. Women, 1959-62, Luth. Ch. Women Synodical Bd., 1972-76, dist. chmn., 1964-65; com. mem. Commn. for a New Luth. Ch., 1985, chmn. transition team, 1986-87 , mem. exec. com. Synod Council, 1976-79; trustee Gustavus Adolphus Coll. Bd., 1988—. Recipient Good Govt. award Grand Rapids Jr. C. of C., 1977, Good Neighbor award WCCO Radio, 1976. Mem. Grand Rapids C. of C. (life). Mem. LWV. Club: PEO (pres., sec. 1964—). Avocations: cross country skiing, canoing, traveling. Home and Office: 5734 Sunny Beach Rd Grand Rapids MN 55744

MATALKA, ISSA MICHAEL, mechanical engineer; b. Amman, Jordan, Dec. 27, 1958; s. Michael Dick Matalka and Kamelah (Metri) Karadsheh; m. Basma Faiq Karadsheh, July 6, 1980; 1 child, Reem. ME, Oxford U., 1980; engr., Matalka and Musa Co., 1985—. Mech. engr. Queen Alia Internat. Airport, Amman, 1980-81; chief engr., maintenance dept. mgr. Housing Bank Commercial Ctr., Amman, 1981-85. Mem. Friends of Polics Soc. Mem. Humanitarian Forum, Arab Thought Forum, Royal Soc. for Nature Conservation, Hussein Soc. for Handicapped (letter of appreciation 1986), Amal Soc. for Mentally Retarded. Lodge: Rotary (Phila.). Home: Shmaisani near UN Bldg., Amman 538, Jordan Office: Matalka and Muse Co, Al-Sayegh Comml Ctr 6th Floor, Abdali, Amman 538, Jordan

MATAXIS, THEODORE CHRISTOPHER, consultant, lecturer, writer, retired army officer; b. Seattle, Aug. 17, 1917; s. Chris P. and Edla (Osterdahl) M.; m. Helma Mary Jensen, Aug. 27, 1940; children: Shirley Jeanne (Mrs. J. L. Slack), Theodore Christopher, Kaye Louise (Mrs. Vernon P. Isaacs, Jr.). B.A., U. Wash., 1940; student, Def. Services Staff Coll., India, 1950-51, Army War Coll., 1957-58; M.A. in Internat. Relations, George Washington U., 1965. Commd. 2d lt. U.S. Army, 1940, advanced through grades to brig. gen., 1967; inf. bn. comdr. Europe, World War II; regt. comdr. Korea, 1952-53; mem. Gov. Harriman's Presdl. Mission to Establish Mil. Aid Program India, 1962; mil. asst., speech writer for chmn. Joint Chiefs of Staff 1962-64; sr. adviser II Vietnamese Army Corps, Pleiku, 1964-65; dep. comdr. 1st Brigade, 101st Airborne Div. 1966, asst. div. comdr. 82d Airborne Div., 1967; chief army sect. Army Mission/MAAG Iran, 1968-70; asst., acting div. comdr. Americal Div. Vietnam, 1970; chief mil. equipment delivery team Cambodia, 1971-72; ret. 1972; edn1. and systems mgmt. cons. Republic of Singapore, 1972-74; asst. supt., comdt. cadets Valley Forge Mil. Acad., Wayne, Pa., 1975-83; dir. AZED Assocs., Ltd., Southern Pines, N.C., 1983—. Author: (with Seymour Goldberg) Nuclear Tactics, 1958, (chpt.) International Affairs in South West Asia, 1984; also numerous mil. and hist. articles. Mem. adv. council Com. for Free Afghanistan; mem. Com. for Free Cambodia. Decorated D.S.M., Silver Star, D.F.C., Bronze Star with 3 oak leaf clusters with V, Commendation medal with 3 oak leaf clusters and V, Joint Services Commendation medal, Purple Heart with oak leaf cluster, Legion of Merit with 2 oak leaf clusters, Air medal with V and 30 oak leaf clusters, Combat Inf. Badge with 2 stars (U.S.); Nat. Order 5th class; Distinguished Service Order; 4 Gallantry crosses; Honor medal 1st class; Air medal Vietnam; Def. medal Order of Republic Cambodia; Chapel of Four Chaplains-Legion of Honor. Mem. Oral History Assn., Am. Mil. History Inst., U.S. Commn. on Mil. History, Mil. Order World Wars (life), Am. Council for Study Islamic Socs. (bd. dirs.), Am. Legion, VFW, Airborne Assn. (life), 70th Div. Assn., Assn. U.S. Army, Nat. Rifle Assn. (endowment mem.), 82d Airborne Div. Assn. (life), 101st Airborne Div. Assn. (life), Am. Security Council (speakers bur.), Ends of the Earth, Scabbard and Blade (adv. council nat. soc.). Clubs: Elks (Southern Pines), Army Navy (Washington); Tanglin (Singapore). Office: AZED Assocs Ltd PO Box 1643 Southern Pines NC 28387

MATEK, ORD, psychotherapist, educator; b. Kamenetzpadolsk, USSR, May 10, 1922; came to U.S., 1923; s. Samson and Sonia (Torgow) M.; m. Betsy Stein, July 11, 1948; children: Beth Matek Weinstein, Deborah Matek Schwartz, Joel, Michael. BS, Roosevelt U., 1949; MA, U. Chgo., 1951. Caseworker Jewish Children's Bur. of Chgo., 1951-56; adminstr. Eisenberg unit Marks Nathan Hall, Chgo., 1956-69; pvt. practice psychotherapy, Chgo., 1959—; assoc. prof. Jane Addams Coll. Social Work, U. Ill., Chgo., 1969—; cons. to social work agys., psychiat. facilities, schs.; adj. faculty Ill. Sch. Profl. Psychology. Author: The Bible Through Stamps, 1974; founding editor: Jour. Residential Group Care and Treatment; cons. editor: Jour. Social Work and Human Sexuality. Served with U.S. Army, 1943-46. Fellow Internat. Council Sex Educators and Parenthood; mem. Nat. Assn. Social Workers, Acad. Cert. Social Workers, Am. Assn. Children's Residential Ctrs., Nat. Assn. Temple Educators (Curriculum award 1965), Am. Assn. Sex Educators, Counselors and Therapists. Jewish. Home: 9000 Ewing St Evanston IL 60203 Office: U Ill Box 4348 Chicago IL 60680 also: 67 Old Orchard Skokie IL 60077

MATHE, PIERRE HENRI, nephrologist; b. Paris, June 18, 1917; s. Marcel and Gisclon Mathe; m. Simone Legrand, July 12, 1939; children: Annie, Jacques, Monique, Daniel. MD, Ecole Sante Nauhle, Bordeaux, France, 1952. Prof. ecole Annexe de Medecine Navale, Rochefort, France, 1950-56; dir. Ecole Sante Nauhle, 1956-60; chief of medicine Ctr. of Reanimation Hopital, Toulon, France, 1961-69, Ctr. de Hemodialyse, Lagarde, Toulon, 1969-85. Responsible for establishing first Hemodialysis Ctr. for chronic patients in region and first ICU in French Navy. Served to col. French mil. Recipient Legion d Honneur Chevalier award, 1962, Ordre Nat. du Herite award, 1969. Mem. European Dialysis and Transplantation, Internat. Soc. Nephrology. Home: Chemin Vial 157, 83130 Lagarde France

MATHENY, CHARLES WOODBURN, JR., retired army officer, retired civil engineer, former city offcial; b. Sarasota, Fla., Aug. 7, 1914; s. Charles Woodburn Sr. and Virginia (Yates) M.; m. Jeanne Felkel, July 12, 1942; children: Virginia Ann, Nancy Carolina, Charles Woodburn III. BSCE, U. Fla., 1936; grad., Army Command and Gen. Staff Coll., 1944. Sanitary engr. Ga. State Dept. Health, 1937-39; civil engr. Fla. East Coast Ry., 1939-41; commd. 2d lt. F.A., USAR, 1936, 2d lt. U.S. Army, 1942, advanced through grades to col., 1955; arty. bn. comdr., Fed. Republic of Germany, 1945-47; gen. staff Dept. Army, 1948-51; qualified army aviator, 1952, aviation officer 25th Inf. Div., Korea, 1952-53; sr. aviation adviser Korean Army, 1954; dep. commdt., dir. combat devel. Army Aviation Sch., 1954-55; dep. dir. research dept. tactics Arty. Sch., 1955-57; aviation officer 7th U.S. Army, Germany, 1957-58; Munich sub area comdr. So. Area Command, Europe, 1959, qualified sr. army aviator, 1959, dep. chief staff for info. So. Area Command, 1960; Mich. sector comdr. VI Army Corps, 1961-62; ret., 1962; asst. dir. Tampa (Fla.), Dept. Pub. Works 1963-77, asst. to dir., 1977-81, ret., 1981. Initiator tact. use of helicopters in Army, 1949, warrant officer aviator program, combat units equipped with helicopter mobility, 1st state legis. to establish profl. sch. civil engring. for state of Fla. Mem. troop com. Boy Scouts Am., 1965-73; active various community and ch. activities; patron Tampa Art Mus., 1965-83, Tampa Community Concert Series, 1979-82; bd. dirs. Tampa YMCA, 1967-71, Fla. Easter Seal Soc., 1978, Easter Seal Soc. Hillsborough County, 1971-84, hon. bd. dirs. 1984—, treas., 1973-76, pres., 1977. Decorated Bronze Star with oak leaf cluster, Air medal with three oak leaf clusters; named to U. Fla. Student Hall of Fame, 1936. Mem. ASCE (pres. West Coach br., dir. Fla. sect. 1973, Engr. of Yr. award West Coast br. Fla. sect. 1979, life mem. 1980), Am. Soc. Profl. Engrs. (sr.), Fla. Engring. Soc., Am. Pub. Works Assn. (pres. West Coast br. Fla. chpt. 1972, exec. com. Fla. chpt. 1972-77, v.p. 1977, pres. 1978), Ret. Officers Assn., Army Aviation Assn., SAR, Fla. Blue Key, Alpha Tau Omega. Episcopalian. Lodge: Kiwanis. Home: 4802 Beachway Dr Tampa FL 33609

MATHENY, TOM HARRELL, lawyer; b. Houston; s. Whitman and Lorene (Harrell) M. BA, Southeastern La. U., 1954; JD, Tulane U., 1957; LLD (hon.), Centenary Coll., 1979, DePauw U. Bar: La. 1957. Ptnr. firm Pittman & Matheny, Hammond, La., 1957—; trust counsel, chmn. bd. 1st Guaranty Bank, Hammond; v.p. Edwards & Assocs., So. Brick Supply, Inc.; faculty Southeastern La. U., 5 yrs., Holy Cross Coll., New Orleans, 3 yrs.; lectr. Union Theol. Sem., Law Sci. Acad.; mem. com. on conciliation and mediation of disputes World Peace through Law Ctr. Chmn. advancement com. Boy Scouts Am., Hammond, 1960-64, mem. dist. council, 1957-66, mem. exec. bd. Istrouma council, 1966—, adv. com. to dist. area council; pres. Tangipahoa Parish Mental Health Assn.; mem. La. Mental Health Advocacy Service; co-chmn. La. Mental Health Advocacy Bd.; sec. Chep Morrison Scholarship Found.; mem. men's com. Japan Internat. Christian U. Found; chmn. speakers com., mem. com. on community action and crime prevention, La. Commn. on Law Enforcement and Adminstrn. Criminal Justice; campaign mgr. for Dem. gov. La., 1959-60, 63-64; bd. dirs. La. Moral and Civic Found., Tangipahoa Parish ARC, 1957-67, Hammond United Givers Fund, 1957-68, La. Council Chs., Southeastern Devel. Found., La. Mental Health Assn.; bd. dirs. Wesley Found., La. State U., 1965-68, 70—, chmn. bd.; trustee Centenary Coll., 1964-70, Scarritt Coll., 1975-81; hon. trustee John F. Kennedy Coll.; hon. sec. U.S. com. Audenshaw Found.; pres. jud. council United Meth. Ch., 1976—, trustee La. annual conf., pres. bd. trustees, 1984—, del. world conf. in London, 1966, Denver, 1971, Dublin, 1976, Hawaii, 1981, del. to gen. confs., 1968, 70, 72. Recipient Man of Yr. award Hammond, 1961, 64, also La. Jaycees, 1964, Layman of Yr. award La. Ann. Conf. United Meth. Ch., 1966, 73, Disting. Alumnus award Southeastern La. U., 1981, W.L. "Bill" May Outstanding Christian Bus. award La. Moral and Civic Found., 1986. Fellow Harry S. Truman Library Inst (hon.); mem. ABA (com. on probate), La. Bar Assn. (past gen. chmn. com. on legal aid, com. prison reform), 21st Jud. Dist. Bar Assn. (past sec.-treas., v.p. 1967-68, 71), Comml. Law League Am. (past mem. com. on ethics), La. Alumni Council (pres. 1963-65), Acad. Religion and Mental Health, La. Assn. Claimant Compensation Attys., Southeastern La. U. Alumni Assn. (dir., pres. 1961-62, dir. spl. fund 1959-62, dir. Tongipahoa chpt.), Tulane Sch. Law Alumni Assn., Assn. Trial Lawyers Am., Am. Judicature Soc., Law-Sci. Inst., World Peace Through Law Acad., Acad. Polit. Sci., Am. Acad. Polit. and Social Sci., Internat. Acad. Law and Sci., Common Cause, Internat. Platform Assn., UN Assn., La. Hist. Assn., Friends of Cabildo, Gideons Internat., Nat. Assn. Conf. Lay Leaders of United Meth. Ch. (pres. 1966-82), Assn. Conf. Lay Leaders South Central Jurisdiction (pres.), Hammond Assn. Commerce (dir. 1960-65), Intern Soc. Barristers, Intern Assn. Valuers, La. Mental Health Assn. (pres.-elect), Phi Delta Phi, Phi Alpha Delta. Democrat. Methodist. Lodges: Masons, Scottish Rite (33 degree), Demolay (dist. dep. to supreme council 1964—, Legion of Honor), Kiwanis (v.p., dir., Layman of Yr. award for La., Miss. and West Tenn. 1972), Rotary. Home: PO Box 221 Hammond LA 70404 Office: 401 E Thomas St PO Box 1598 Hammond LA 70401

MATHER, KENNETH, geneticist, educator; b. June 22, 1911; s. R.W. Mather; B.Sc., U. Manchester, 1931; m. Mona Rhodes, 1937; 1 son. Ministry Agr. and Fisheries Research scholar, 1931-34; lectr. Galton Lab., Univ. Coll., London, 1934-47; Rockefeller research fellow, Calif. Inst. Tech. and Harvard U., 1937-38; head genetics dept. John Innes Hort. Instn., 1938-48; prof. genetics U. Birmingham, 1945-65, hon. prof., 1971-84, prof. emeritus, 1984—; vice chancellor U. Southampton, 1965-71, now emeritus prof. Mem. Agrl. Research Council, 1949-54, 55-60, 69-79, Sci. Research Council, 1965-69; mem. Genetic Manipulation Adv. Group, 1976-78. Mem. Wessex Regional Hosp. Bd., 1968-71. Created knight, 1979. Fellow Royal Soc. Author: The Measurement of Linkage in Heredity, 1938; Statistical Analysis in Biology, 1943; Biometrical Genetics, 1950, 2d edit., 1971, 3d edit., 1982; Human Diversity, 1964; The Elements of Biometry, 1967; Genetical Structure of Populations, 1973, others; contbr. articles to profl. jours. Home: The White House, 296 Bristol Rd Edgbaston, Brimingham B5 7SN England Office: Dept Genetics, U Birmingham, Birmingham B15 2TT, England *

MATHER, ROBERT JAMES, non-profit rehabilitation facility executive, consultant; b. Manhattan, Kans., May 7, 1940; s. James Warren and Evelyn (Ezell) M.; m. Janet Hadley, June 19, 1965; children: Stacia Lynn, Kristin Ann. BS, Kent (Ohio) State U., 1965, MEd, 1968. Cert. rehab. counselor, Ohio. Grahic arts specialist Design and Devel., Independence, Ohio, 1967-68; supr., counselor Vocat. Guidance and Rehab. Services, Cleve., 1968, edn1. dir., 1968-70, assoc. exec. dir., 1970-78; pres., chief operating officer Progress Industries, Newton, Iowa, 1978—; cons. adminstrv. program Commn. on Accreditation of Rehab. Facilities, Tucson, 1967—; pres. Progress Industries Found., Newton, 1979—. Author: Projects with Industry, 1978. Served with USCG, 1959-67. Named Profl. of Yr., Iowa Assn. for Retarded Citizens, 1985. Mem. Nat. Assn. Fund Raising Execs., Iowa Assn. Rehab. and Residential Facilities, Nat. Rehab. Assn. (pres. Ohio chpt. 1978, Spl. Citation award 1985, cons. editor Jour. 1985—). Democrat. Methodist. Lodge: Rotary. Home: 1304 W 15th St Pl S Newton IA 50208 Office: Progress Industries 1017 E 7th St N Box 366 Newton IA 50208

MATHESON, LINDA, clinical social worker; b. Martna, Estonia, Dec. 29, 1918; came to U.S., 1962, naturalized, 1969; d. Endrek and Leena Endrekson; Diploma, Inst. for Social Scis., Tallinn, Estonia, 1944; M.S., Columbia U., 1966, Diplomate Clin. Social Work; m. Charles McLaren Matheson, Feb. 5, 1955. Social work officer UN Rehab. and Resettlement Assn., Germany, 1946-48; social worker Victorian Mental Hygiene, Australia, 1955-62; research assoc., social work project dir. Arthritis Midway Ho., N.Y.C., 1966-68; researcher Columbia Presbyn. Med. Center, N.Y.C., 1971-75, now social worker; field instr. Columbia U. Sch. Social Work, 1977-79. Family Found. fellow, 1966; NIMH grantee, 1969-72. Mem. Nat. Assn. Social Workers, Am. Security Council, Nat. Wildlife Fedn., Center for Study of Presidency, Smithsonian Assn., English Speaking Union, Alliance Francaise, Columbia U. Alumni Assn., Internat. Platform Assn., Nat. Trust Historic Preservation, Met. Mus. of N.Y. Lutheran. Home: 30-95 29th St Astoria NY 11102

MATHESON, WILLIAM LYON, lawyer, utility company executive; b. Coeburn, Va., Dec. 5, 1924; s. Julius Daniel and Ruth Steele Lyon M.; m. Katrina B. Hickox; children: Katherine, William Lyon, Alline, Thornton; m. Marjorie H. Anderson, Nov. 26, 1977. Student, Emory U., 1946-47; A.B., Mercer U., 1944; LL.B., U. Va., 1950. Bar: N.Y. 1951. Assoc. firm Patterson, Belknap & Webb, N.Y.C., 1950-57; assoc. Wertheim & Co. (investments), N.Y.C., 1957-58; partner Webster & Sheffield, N.Y.C., 1959-65; individual practice law N.Y.C., 1965—; chmn. bd. Mich. Energy Resources Co., Monroe, 1959—. Bd. dirs. Madison Sq. Boys' Club, N.Y.C., 1958-76, assoc. mem. bd. dirs., 1977—; trustee Police Athletic League, N.Y.C., 1962—. Served to lt. (j.g.) USN, 1942-46. Mem. Assn. Bar City N.Y., Am. Gas Assn. Democrat. Clubs: Links (N.Y.C.); Piping Rock (Locust Valley, N.Y.); Meadow Brook (Jericho, N.Y.); Nat. Golf Links (Southampton, N.Y.); Seminole Golf (North Palm Beach, Fla.), Island (Hobe Sound, Fla.). Home: 430 South Beach Rd Hobe Sound FL 33455 also: Sunset Hill Heather Ln Mill Neck NY 11765 Office: 277 Park Ave New York NY 10172

MATHEWS, IAN RICHARD, newspaper editor; b. Mitcham, Surrey, Eng., Jan. 29, 1933; came to Australia, 1960; s. George James and Dorothy (Williams) M.; m. Joyce Morris, Mar. 30, 1957; children—Deborah, Paul. Grad. Sir Joseph Williamson's Math. Sch., Rochester, Kent, Eng., 1949. Local govt. clk. Guy's Hosp., London, 1949; writer Royal Fleet Aux., 1945-55, Kent & Sussex Courier Group Newspapers, Tunbridge, Wells, Kent, Eng., 1955-59, Express & Echo, Exeter, Eng., 1959-60; sub-editor News Ltd.-Adelaide, South Australia, Australia, 1960-63; from chief sub-editor to asst. editor Canberra Times, Australia, 1963-72, editor, 1972-85, editor-in-chief, 1985—. Mem. Nat. Consultative Com. on Peace and Disarmament, Canberra, 1985—, Nat. Health and Med. Research Com., Royal Australasian Coll. Physicians Social Issues Com. Mem. Ch. of England. Clubs: Commonwealth (Canberra), Nat. Press. Avocations: reading; travel; writing, medieval history. Office: Canberra Times, 18 Mort St, Canberra 2601, Australia

MATHEWS, LOUISE ROBISON, real estate broker; b. Tecumseh, Okla., Sept. 22, 1917; d. Clarence and Irene (Buzzard) Robison; student E. Central State Coll., 1935, 38, Okla. Bapt U., 1936-37; m. William F. Mathews (dec.); 1 son, William F. Law sec. firm Robison-McKinnis, Shawnee, Okla., 1932-36; with Greene's Women's Specialty Shop, Shawnee, 1944-47; v.p. Streets Women's and Children's Splty. Shops, Oklahoma City, 1947-79; broker Assoc. Stewart-Van Cleef Realtors, 1979-86; chmn. Oklahoma City Fashion Week, 1973-75. Pres. Oklahoma County Council for Mentally Retarded Children, 1953-55, 1969-71: parent-observer White House Conf. Mental Retardation, 1963; chmn. 1st Ladies Okla. Gown Collection; Gov.'s Task Force Mental Retardation; mem. Okla. Mental Health Planning Com., 1963-65; hon. curator First Ladies Okla. Gown Collection. Mem. Okla. Retail Mchts. Assn. (dir. 1971-85), Oklahoma City Regional Fashion Group (dir., pres. 1969-70), Nat. Assn. Realtors, Okla. Hist. Soc., Okla. Assn. Mentally Retarded (past pres.), Nat. Assn. for Mentally Retarded Citizens (bd. dirs. 1958-60), Better Bus. Bur., DAR, Oklahoma City Retailers Assn. Democrat. Presbyn. Club: Altrusa, Women's Econ., Greens County. Home: 2700 NW Grand Blvd Oklahoma City OK 73116

MATHEWS, RUSSELL LLOYD, economist, educator, consultant; b. Geelong, Victoria, Australia, Jan. 5, 1921; s. Percival Samuel and Rose Florabell (Goslin) M.; m. Joan Marie Tingate, Dec. 13, 1947; children: Susan Joan, Peter Lawrence. B of Commerce with honors, U. Melbourne, 1949. Asst. to vice-chancellor, adminstrv. officer Australian Nat. U., Canberra, 1949-53; reader, prof. commerce U. Adelaide, 1953-64, UCLA, Ohio State U., 1966-71; prof. acctg. and pub. fin. Australian Nat. U., Canberra, 1965-77, dir. ctr. for research on fed. fin. relations, 1972-86; prof. emeritus Australian Nat. U., 1986—; mem. Commn. of Inquiry into Land Tenures Australian Govt., 1973-76, chmn. com. inquiry into inflation, taxation, 1974-75; chmn. Adv. Council Inter-Government Relations Australian Govt., 1977-79; adviser taxation and fiscal federalism matters to governments of Fiji Tonga, Cook Island, Papua, New Guinea, Cyprus. Author: Inflation and Company Finance, 1958, Militia Battalion at War, 1961, Accounting for Economists, 1962, Public Investment in Australia, 1967, The Accounting Framework,

1971, 79, 87, Federal Finance, 1972, Fiscal Equalisation in Education, 1983. Served to capt. inf. Australian Army, 1941-45. Grantee Carnegie Corp., 1959; named to Comdr. Order of British Empire Australian Govt., 1978, Officer Order of Australia, 1987. Fellow Acad. Social Scis. in Australia; mem. Commonwealth Grants Commn. Club: Commonwealth (Canberra), Royal Canberra Golf; Royal Automobile Club Victoria (Melbourne). Home: 22 Cobby St, 2601 Canberra Australia

MATHEWSON, HUGH SPALDING, physician, educator; b. Washington, Sept. 20, 1921; s. Walter Eldridge and Jennie Lind (Jones) M.; m. Dorothy Ann Gordon, 1943 (div. 1952); 1 child, Jane Mathewson Holcombe; m. Hazel M. Jones, 1953 (div. 1978); children: Geoffrey K., Brian E., Catherine E., Jennifer A.; m. Judith Ann Mahoney, 1979. Student, Washburn U., 1938-39; A.B., U. Kans., 1942, M.D., 1944. Intern Wesley Hosp., Wichita, Kans., 1944-45; resident anesthesiology U. Kans. Med. Center, Kansas City, 1946-48; practice medicine, specializing in anesthesiology Kansas City, Mo., 1948-69; chief anesthesiologist St. Luke's Hosp., Kansas City, 1953-69; med. dir., sect. respiratory therapy U. Kans. Med. Center, 1969—, asso. prof., 1969-75, prof., 1975—; examiner schs. respiratory therapy 1975—; oral examiner Nat. Bd. Respiratory Therapy; mem. Council Nurse Anesthesia Practice, 1974-78. Author: Structural Forms of Anesthetic Compounds, 1961, Respiratory Therapy in Critical Care, 1976, Pharmacology for Respiratory Therapists, 1977; contbr. articles to profl. publs.; editorial bd.: Anesthesia Staff News, 1975-84; assoc. editor: Respiratory Care, 1980—. Trustee Kansas City Mus. Served to lt. comdr. USNR, 1956. Recipient Bird Lit. prize Am. Assn. Respiratory Therapists, 1976. Mem. Mo. Soc. Anesthesiologists (pres. 1963), Kans. Soc. Anesthesiologists (pres. 1974-77), Kans. Med. Soc. (council), Phi Beta Kappa, Sigma Xi. Office: Kans Med Center 39th and Rainbow Sts Kansas City KS 66103

MATHIAS, MARGARET GROSSMAN, manufacturing company executive, leasing company executive; b. Detroit, June 26, 1928; d. D. Ray and Lila May (Skinner) Grossman; m. Robert D. Mathias, Oct. 1, 1955 (div. Feb. 1982); children: Deborah, Robert, Lesley, Jennifer, Mary. BA, Mt. Holyoke Coll., 1949; cert., Am. Acad. Art, 1951. Artist and co-mgr. Mary Chase Marionettes, N.Y.C., 1951-54; exec. v.p. L & J Press Corp., Elkhart, Ind., 1970—, also bd. dirs., sec., chmn. bd., 1985—; exec. v.p. Star Five Corp., Elkhart, 1978-85, pres., treas., chmn. bd., 1985—; chmn. MAGCo Inc., Elkhart, 1986—. Mem. fin. com. United Fund, Elkhart, 1960-64, parents adv. bd. Furman U., Greenville, S.C., 1978-83, art adv. com. Mount Holyoke Coll., South Hadley, Mass., 1982—; pres. Tri Kappa Service Orgn., Elkhart, 1965-66; trustee Stanley Clark Sch., South Bend, Ind., 1977—. Mem. Elkhart C. of C. Republican. Clubs: Elcona Country (Elkhart), Woman's Athletic (Chgo.), Thursday (Elkhart) (pres. 1976).

MATHIAS, WILLIAM JAMES, composer, educator; b. Whitland, Dyfed, Wales, Nov. 1, 1934; s. James Hughes and Marian (Evans) M.; m. Margaret Yvonne Collins, 1959; 1 dau. Ed. Univ. Coll. Wales; D.Mus., Royal Acad. Music, 1966. Lectr., Univ. Coll. North Wales, 1959-68, prof. music, head dept., 1970—; sr. lectr. U. Edinburgh (Scotland), 1968-69; mem. Welsh Arts Council, 1974-81; bd. govs. Nat. Mus. Wales, 1973-78; mem. music adv. com. Brit. Council, 1974-83, mem. Welsh adv. com. 1979—; mem. Central Music Adv. Com., BBC, 1979-86; artistic dir. North Wales Music Festival, 1972—. Composer orchestral pieces: Symphony, 1969, Piano Concerto No. 2, 1964, Piano Concerto No. 3, 1970, Harp Concerto, 1973, Clarinet Concerto, 1976, Celtic Dances, 1974, Divertimento for Strings, 1961, Serenade, 1963, Preluda Aria and Finale, 1966, Vistas, 1977, Laudi, 1978, Helios, 1978, Requiescat, 1978, Vivat Regina (for brass band), 1978, Dance Variations, 1979, Investiture Anniversary Fanfare, 1979, Reflections on a Theme by Tomkins, 1981; Chamber Music: Violin Sonata, 1963, Piano Sonata No. 1, 1965, String Quartet No. 1, 1970, String Quartet No. 2, 1981, Wind Quintet, 1976, Zodiac Trio, 1977, Clarinet Sonatina, 1978, Concertino, 1977; Choral and Vocal: Wassail Carol, 1965, Three Medieval Lyrics, 1966, Ave Rex, 1970, A Babe is Born, 1971, A Vision of Time and Eternity (for contralto and piano), 1974, Ceremony after a Fire Raid, 1975, This Worlde's Joie (for solo, chorus and orchestra), 1975, Elegy for a Prince (for baritone and orch.), 1976, The Fields of Praise (for tenor and piano), 1977, A Royal Garland, 1978, A May Magnificent, 1980, Shakespeare Songs, 1980, Songs of William Blake (for mezzo and orch.), 1980, Rex Gloriae, 1982, Te Deum (for soli, chorus and orch.), 1982; organ: Variations in a Hymn Tune, 1963, Partita, 1963, Postlude, 1964, Processional, 1965, Chorale, 1967, Toccata Giocosa, 1968, Jubilate, 1975, Fantasy, 1978, Canzonetta, 1978, Antiphonies, 1982, Organ Concerto, 1984, Berceuse, 1985, Recessional, 1986, A Mathias Organ Album, 1986, Fanfare for Organ, 1987; Anthems and Ch. Music: O Sing unto the Lord, 1965, Make a Joyful Noise, 1965, Festival Te Deum, 1965, Communion Service in C, 1968, Psalm 150, 1969, Lift up your heads, 1970, O Salutaris Hostia, 1972, Gloria, 1972, Magnificat and Nunc Dimittis, 1973, Missa Brevia, 1974, Communion Service (Series III), 1976, Arise, shine, 1978, Let the People Praise Thee, O God (for marriage of Prince and Princess of Wales), 1981, Praise ye the Lord, 1982, All Wisdom is from the Lord, 1982, Except the Lord Build the House, 1983, A Grace, 1983, Jubilate Deo, 1983, O How Amiable, 1983, Tantum Ergo, 1984, Let Us Now Praise Famous Men, 1984, Alleluia! Christ is Risen, 1984, Missa Aedis Christi-in Memoriam William Walton, 1984, Salve Regina, 1986, O Clap Your Hands, 1986, Let All the World in Every Corner Sing, 1987, Rejoice in the Lord, 1987, I Will Lift Up Mine Eyes unto the Hills, 1987, Cantate Domino, 1987, Thus Saith God the Lord-An Orkney Anthem, 1987, O Lord our Lord, 1987, As Truly as God is our Father, 1987; Opera: (libretto by Iris Murdoc) The Servants, 1980. Recipient Arnold Bax Soc. prize, 1968. Address: Anglesey, Y Graigwen, Cadnant Rd, Menai Bridge, Gwynedd LL59 5NG Wales *

MATHIESEN, MATTHIAS A., Icelandic government official; b. Hafnarfjordur, Iceland, Aug. 6, 1931; m. Sigrun Th. Mathiesen, Apr. 10, 1956; children: Arni Matthias, Halldóra, Thorgils Ottar. Grad. Reykjavik Coll., 1951; grad. in Law, U. Iceland, 1957. Bar: Supreme Ct. Iceland 1967. Dir., Hafnarfjordur Savs. Bank, 1958-67, chmn. bd., 1967-83, 86—; practice law, Hafnarfjordur, 1967-74, mem. Althing, Iceland, 1959—, speaker Lower House, 1970-71, minister of fin., 1974-78, minister of commerce, banking and Nordic affairs, 1983-85, minister of fgn. affairs, 1986-87, minister of communications and Nordic affairs, 1987—; dir. Nat. Bank of Iceland, 1961-74, 80-83, dep. chmn. bd., 1966-72; Icelandic del. to World Bank Group, 1974-78, 83-85; del. North Atlantic Assembly, 1963-69, chmn. Icelandic del., 1964-69, pres. assembly, 1967-68; Icelandic del. to Nordic Council, 1965—, chmn. Icelandic del. and mem. council bd., 1971-72, 73-74, 80-82, pres. council, 1970-71, 80-81. Chmn. Hafnarfjordur Youth Assn. of Independence Party of Iceland, 1952-55; chmn. Hafnarfjordur bd. reps. of Independence Party, 1962-66, mem. party cen. com., 1965—. Office: Ministry of Communications, Reykjavik Iceland

MATHIESON, IAN DOUGLAS, property company director; b. London, Oct. 1, 1942; s. Robert James and Violet Lilian (Jones) M.; m. Lesley Glass, Aug. 19, 1967; children: Mark James, John Robert. BSc, Coll. Estate Mgmt., London, 1965; diploma in Town Planning, Univ. Coll., London, 1968. Surveyor Greater London Council, 1965-68, Fuller Horsey Sons & Castle, London, 1968-73; dep. property investment mgr. Comml. Union Properties Ltd., London, 1973-74, property investment mgr., 1974-80, dir., 1980-83, dep. mng. dir., 1983, mng. dir., 1984—; mem. PAG, Wycombe Dist. Health Authority, 1983—. Fellow Royal Instn. Chartered Surveyors; mem. Inc. Soc. Valuers and Auctioneers. Clubs: Royal Overseas League, Royal Automobile. Office: Comml Union Properties Ltd, 80-82 Pall Mall, London SW1 5HF, England

MATHIEU, GEORGES VICTOR ADOLPHE, artist; b. Boulogne, Jan. 27, 1921; s. Adolphe Mathieu d'Escaudoeuvres and Madeleine Dupre d'Ausque. Ed. Facultés de droit et des lettres, Lille, France. Tchr. English; mgr. pub. relations U.S. Lines. Exhbns.: Paris, 1950, N.Y.C., 1952, Japan, 1957, Scandinavia, 1958, Eng., Spain, Italy, Switzerland, Ger., Austria and S.Am., 1959, Middle East, 1961-62, Can., 1963, Musée Municipal d'Art Moderne, Paris, 1963, Galerie Charpentier, Paris, 1965, Musée Nat. d'Art Moderne, Paris, 1967, Musée de la Manufacture Nat. des Gobelins, 1969, Antibes, 1976, Ostend, 1977, Grand Palais, Paris, 1978, Wildenstien Gallery, N.Y.C., Dominion Gallery, Montreal, Que., Can., 1979, Musée de la Poste, Paris, 1980, Palais des Papes, Avignon, 1985; works include: Hommage à la Mort, 1950, Hommage au Marechal de Turenne, 1952, Les Capetiens Partout, 1954, La Victoire de Denain, 1963, Hommage à Jean Cocteau, 1963, Paris, Capitale des Arts, 1965, Hommages aux Freres Boisseree, 1967, Hommages à Condillac, 1968, La prise de Berg op Zoom, 1969, Election de Charles Quint, 1971, Matta-Salums, 1978, La Liberation de Paris, 1980, La liberation d'Orleans par Jeanne d'Arc, 1982, Le Massacre des 269, 1985; designed gardens and bldgs. for B.C. transformer factory, Fontenay-le-comte, 1966; 16 posters for Air France; tapestries; 18 medals for Paris Mint, 1971, new 10 F coin, 1974; creater Tachism; author: Audela du Tachisme; Le privilege d'Etre; De la Revolté à Rénaissance; La Réponse de l'Abstraction lyrique; L'Abstraction Prophetique. Mem. Acad. Fine Arts.

MATHIEU, JEAN-PIERRE ADOLPHE, finance company executive; b. Liege, Belgium, Sept. 27, 1934; s. Lucien Pierre and Eugenie Marie (Lux) M.; m. Anny Burton; children: Riquier, Nadine, Sylviane, Stephane. Degree in electro-mech. engring., U. Liege, 1957, degree in aero. engring., 1958; M. of Aero. Scis., Ecole Nat. Supérieure de l'Aero., Paris, 1963. With U. Liege Internal Combustion Lab., 1957-62; cons. Brouhon, 1960-62; research at ENSA and UCLA for ESA, NATO, Paris and Los Angeles, 1962-64; devel. engr. Phillips Electronics Co., Brussels, 1964-65; design engr. Sabca, Brussels, 1965-70, mgr. program, 1970-75, promoter, mktg. and product mgr., 1975-84, thermal engring. and mktg. cons., 1984-86; research and devel. exec. TCA Fin. Co., Tervueren, Belgium, 1987—. Contbr. numerous articles to profl. jours. Served with the Belgium Air Force, 1958-59. Recipient Applied Mechanics award Belgium Royal Soc. Indsl. Engrs., 1963, others; U. Liege research fellow, 1961-62, NATO and ESA fellow, 1963-64. Office: TCA Fin Co, 1 Ave Hanssens, 1980 Tervueren Belgium

MATHIEU, PHILIPPE, computer science educator; b. Ottignies, Belgium, Dec. 16, 1952; s. Roger and Odette (Magtelinck) M.; m. Tove Mogensen, Jan. 24, 1986; 1 child, Fejda. BA in Math., U. Louvain, 1974; PhD, DSc, U. Paris, 1980. Asst. prof. U. Louvain, Belgium, 1974-76; prof. math. Scuola Normale Superiore, Italy, 1977-79, U. Lille, France, 1980-83; vis. prof. computer sci. Inria, France, 1984-85; research fellow Swedish Inst. Computer Sci., Sweden, 1986—; cons. on artifical intelligence E.E.C. Esprit project, Belgium, 1984-87, Philips & MBLE Associated, Belgium, 1985-87. Contbr. articles to profl. jours. Recipient Medal of the Belgium Govt., 1970. Mem. Am. Math. Soc., Am. Assn. Artifical Intelligence, Norwegian Math. Soc., Belgian Assn. Artifical Intelligence. Office: Swedish Inst Computer Sci, PO Box 1263, S-164 28 Kista Sweden

MATHIEU-HARRIS, MICHELE SUZANNE, association executive; b. Chgo., Mar. 24, 1950; d. Joseph Edward Mathieu and Mary Ellen (Knapp) Fisher; m. Robert Steven Harris, May 1, 1988. Student DePaul U., 1971, 74-76, Regents Coll., Albany, N.Y., 1987—. Broadcast coordinator Grey-North Advt., Chgo., 1967-71; head drama dept. Patricia Stevens Coll., Chgo., 1972; instr. beginning acting Ted Liss Sch. of Performing Arts, Chgo., 1973-75; project coordinator grants and contracts Am. Dietetic Assn., Chgo., 1974-81, adminstr. govt. affairs, 1981-86, mgr. licensure communications, 1986—; grant proposal cons. various performance arts, Chgo., 1978—. Editor Legis. Newsletter, 1981-86; contbg. editor Nutrition Forum, 1986, Courier, 1987—; contbr. articles to profl. jours., mags., newspapers. Treas. Am. Dietetic Assn. polit. action com., Washington, 1981-86; adv. bd. Rejoice Repertory Theatre Company, Inc., Chgo. Ill. Arts Council grantee, 1981. Mem. Nat. Assn. Female Execs. Roman Catholic. Avocations: reading, jazzercise. Office: Am Dietetic Assn 216 W Jackson Blvd Chicago IL 60606

MATHIJSEN, PETRUS SERVATIUS, head European food processors industries; b. Tilburg, Netherlabds, Mar. 7, 1924; s. Francois and Irma Emilie (Brouwers) M.; m. Beverly June Olson, Mar. 1, 1954; children: Claire, Benedicte, Stephanie, Valerie, Olivia, Daphne. BA in Lit. and Philosophy, Faculté St. Louis, Brussels, 1944; MA, Leiden U., Netherlands, 1951; LLB, Lieden U., 1957; MA in Econs., U. Minn., 1952. Attache Ct. of Justice ECSC, Luxembourg, 1952-58; legal advisor EEC, Brussels, 1958-68; dir. competition European Commn., Brussels, 1968-77; dir. gen. regional policy EEC, Brussels, 1977-86; prof. law U. Nijmegen, Netherlands, 1968-86, U. Brussels, 1986—; del. gen. Fedn. European Food Industries, Brussels, 1986—. Author: Le Droit de la CECA, 1957, Guide to European Community Law, 1972, 4th edit., 1985; contbr. articles to profl. jours. Served to capt. Army of Netherlands, 1944-48. Christian Democrat. Roman Catholic. Club: Royal Golf. Home: Ave Blucher 190, 1180 Brussels Belgium Office: CIAA, Rue Joseph II 40, 1040 Brussels Belgium

MATHIS, FRANZ, historian, educator; b. Hohenems, Vorarlberg, Austria, Nov. 27, 1946; s. Rudolf and Anna (Amann) M.; m. Ursula Berek, Apr. 23, 1973; 1 child, Claudia. BA, U. Innsbruck, 1971, MA, 1973, PhD, 1979. Asst. prof. U. Innsbruck, Austria, 1973-79; asst. prof. history U. Innsbruck, 1979—. Author: Tyrol in 1703, 1975, Austrian Cities in the 17th Century, 1978, Big Business in Austria, 1987; editor: Zwanowetz-Festschrift, 1984; contbr. articles to profl. jours. Mem. Gesellschaft fuer Sozial und Wirtschaftsgeschichte, Gesellschaft fuer Unternehmensgeschichte, Oesterreichisches Lateinamerika Inst., Austrian Asst. For Am.Studies, Inst. fuer Oesterreichkunde. Home: Kranewitterstrasse 51, A-6020 Innsbruck Austria Office: Univ Innsbruck, Innrain 52, A-6020 Innsbruck Austria

MATHIS, JACK DAVID, advertising executive; b. La Porte, Ind. Nov. 27, 1931; s. George Anthony and Bernice (Bennethum) M.; student U. Mo., 1950-52; B.S., Fla. State U., 1955; m. Phyllis Dene Hoffman, Dec. 24, 1971; children—Kane Cameron, Jana Dene. With Benton & Bowles, Inc., 1955-56; owner Jack Mathis Advt., 1956—; cons. films, including That's Action!, 1977, Great Movie Stunts: Raiders of the Lost Ark, 1981, The Making of Raiders of the Lost Ark, 1981, An American Legend: The Lone Ranger, 1981; Heroes and Sidekicks: Indiana Jones and the Temple of Doom, 1984. Mem. U.S. Olympic Basketball Com. Recipient citation Mktg. Research Council N.Y. Mem. Alpha Delta Sigma. Author: Valley of the Cliffhangers. Office: Box 738 Libertyville IL 60048

MATHIS, JAMES FORREST, retired petroleum company executive; b. Dallas, Sept. 28, 1925; s. Forrest and Martha (Godbold) M.; m. Frances Ellisor, Sept. 4, 1948; children: Alan Forrest, Lisa Lynn. BS in Chem. Engring., Tex. A&M U., 1946; MS, U. Wis., 1951, PhD, 1953. Research engr. Humble Oil & Refining Co., Baytown, Tex., 1946-49, 53-61, mgr. research and devel., 1961-63, mgr. Splty. products planning, 1963-65; v.p. Exxon Research & Engring. Co., Linden, N.J., 1966-68; sr. v.p., dir. Imperial Oil Ltd., Toronto, Ont., Can., 1968-71; v.p. tech. Exxon Chem. Co., Florham Park, N.J., 1971-80; v.p. sci. and tech. Exxon Corp., N.Y.C., 1980-84; ret., 1984; cons. Arthur D. Little, Inc., 1984—. Bd. dirs. Chem. Industry Inst. Toxicology, 1975-83, treas., 1977-80, chmn., 1980-83; trustee Wis. Alumni Research Found., 1984—; bd. chem. sci. and tech. of Nat. Research Council, 1987—. Served with AC, USNR, 1944-45. Fellow Am. Inst. Chem. Engrs. (interim exec. dir., sec., 1987-88, chmn. N.J. State Commn. on Sci. and Tech. 1988—); mem. Am. Chem. Soc., AAAS, Sigma Xi, Phi Lambda Upsilon, Tau Beta Pi. Presbyterian. Home: 96 Colt Rd Summit NJ 07901 Office: Box 3 Summit NJ 07901

MATHISEN, HAROLD CLIFFORD, investment analyst; b. East Orange, N.J., Apr. 1, 1924; s. Harold and Ottilie Christine (Nordland) M.; A.B., Princeton U., 1943; M.B.A., Harvard U., 1948; m. Dora Elizabeth Bachtel, Sept. 14, 1946; children—Margaret Bennett, Harold, Elizabeth Mathisen Andersen, Barbara. Asst. to controller Kaiser Frazer Corp., Willow Run, Mich., 1948-52; investment analyst Smith Barney & Co., N.Y.C., 1952-61; pres. Alliance Found., N.Y.C., 1961—; treas. AGF Mgmt. Co., N.Y.C., 1969-85; asst. treas., investment mgr. Christian and Missionary Alliance, Nyack, 1978-80; pres. Alliance Growth Fund, N.Y.C., 1968-78; asst. treas. N.Y. Internat. Bible Soc., N.Y.C., 1980-82; portfolio mgr. Legg Mason Wood Walker, Inc., N.Y.C., 1967-78, 82—. Trustee, treas. McAuley Water St. Mission, N.Y.C., 1967—. Served as lt. USNR, 1944-46. Mem. N.Y. Soc. Securities Analysts, Inst. Chartered Fin. Analysts, Phi Beta Kappa, Sigma Xi. Home: 11 Stanley Oval Westfield NJ 07090 Office: 63 Wall St New York NY 10005

MATHISEN, RHODA SHARON, communications consultant; b. Portland, Oreg., June 25, 1942; d. Daniel and Mildred Elizabeth Annette (Peterson) Hager; m. James Albert Mathisen, July 17, 1964 (div. 1977). B.A. in Edn., Music, Bible Coll., Mich., 1964. Community Relations officer Gary-Wheaton Bank, Wheaton, Ill., 1971-75; br. mgr. Stivers Temporary Personnel, Chgo., 1975-79; v.p. sales Exec. Technique, Chgo., 1980-83; prin. Mathisen Assocs., Downers Grove, Ill., 1983—; presenter seminars; featured speaker Women in Mgmt. Oak Brook Chpt., 1988.; cons. Haggai Inst., Atlanta; adv. mem. Nat. Bd. Success Group, 1986. Pres. chancel choir Christ Ch. of Oak Brook, 1985-87. Mem. Bus. and Profl. Women (charter mem. Woodfield chpt.), Execs. Club Oak Brook, Internat. Platform Assn., Nat. Assn. Female Execs., Sales & Mktg. Execs. Chgo., Chgo. Council Fgn. Relations, Chgo. Assn. Commerce and Industry (named Ambassador of Month N.W. suburban chpt. 1979), Oak Brook Assn. Commerce and Industry (mem. membership com.), Women Entrepreneurs of DuPage County (membership chmn., featured speaker Jan. 1988), Art Inst. Chgo., Internat. Platform Assn. Republican. Office: Mathisen Assocs Box 9208 Downers Grove IL 60515

MATHIVHA, MATSHAYA EDWARD RAZWIMISANI, language and literature educator; b. Sibasa, Republic South Africa, Dec. 24, 1921; s. Gedzula Muswadzi and Mavhungu Mukona Mathivha; m. Tshihume Mathivha, Apr. 9, 1949; children: Tendani, Hamandishe, Gedzula, Lufuno, Tshimbiluni, Khakhu, Marubini. BA with honors, U. South Africa, 1961, MA, 1966, DLitt, 1972; EdD (hon.), Internat. Univ. Found., 1987. Asst. prof. U. of the North, Sovenga, Republic South Africa, 1961-70, prof. Venda languages, literature, 1970—, chmn. dept., 1966—, vice-prin., 1984—; bd. dirs. Mankweng Devel. Co. Ltd., African Devel. and Holding Co. Ltd. Author: The Toneme Patterns of the Venda Noun, 1966, Survey of Literary Achievement in Venda, 1972, The Balemba/Basena, 1972. Pres. Lemba Cultural Assn., 1981—. Mem. Black Acad. Staff Assn., D.E.T. South Africa (chmn. edn. council 1986—). Home: PO Box 137, Sovenga 0727, Republic of South Africa Office: U of the North, Private Bag 1106, Sovenga 0727, Republic of South Africa

MATHUR, ASHOK, telecommunications engineer, educator, researcher; b. Gorakhpur, Uttar Pradesh, India; came to U.S., 1979; s. Raj Swarup and Savitri Mathur; m. Jayanti Srivastava, May 31, 1978; children: Menka, Puja. BS, U. Agra, India, 1963, MS, 1965; PhD, U. Southampton, Hampshire, Eng., 1974. Cert. telecommunications engr., Calif., tchr., Calif. Lectr. upper atmospheric physics Kanpur, India, 1965-68; doctoral researcher U. Southampton, 1968-73; postdoctoral research fellow U. Poitiers, Vienne, France, 1973-74; assoc. prof., research supr U. Kanpur, 1974-79; mem. tech. staff telecommunications sci. and engring. div. Jet Propulsion Lab. Calif. Inst. Tech., Pasadena, 1979—. Contbr. numerous publs. to profl. jours.; mem. editorial bd. Acta Ciencia Indica Jour., 1975-78. Recipient 5-Year Service award Jet Propulsion Lab. Calif. Inst. Tech., 1984, Cert. of Merit for Disting. Services Internat. Biog. Centre, Cambridge, England, 1988. Mem. IEEE, AIAA (vice chmn. pub. policy San Gabriel Valley, sec. Los Angeles 1987—), The European Phys. Soc., Calif. Inst. Tech. Mgmt. Club., Armed Forces Communications and Electronics Assn. Republican. Hindu. Home: 1923-B Huntington Dr Duarte CA 91010 Office: Calif Inst Tech Jet Propulsion Lab 4800 Oak Grove Dr MS 126-322 Pasadena CA 91109

MATHUR, DEEPAK, aviation company executive; b. Lucknow, Uttar Predesh, India, Sept. 16, 1942; arrived in France, 1967, naturalized, 1983; s. Brij Raj Bahadur and Rajeshwari (Saksena) M.; m. Kiran Seth, June 11, 1968; children—Nivedita, Savita. B.Sc., U. Lucknow, India, 1962; B.Tech. (Hons.), Loughborough U. Tech., Eng., 1967. Registered aero. engr. Systems engr. Avions Marcel Dassault Breguet Aviation, Velizy, France, 1968-71, Biarritz, France, 1971-79, coordinator Indian Jaguar project, Biarritz, 1979-85, mgr. indsl. automation, Biarritz, 1985—. Organizer exhbns. on India, dance performances, France. Assoc. Royal Aero. Soc. London. Lodge: Rotary Bayonne-Biarritz. Avocations: organization of cultural activities for company and city. Office: Avions Marcel Dassault, Breguet Aviation BP 208, 64200 Biarritz France

MATHUR, PREM BEHARI, research administrator; b. Allahabad, India, Oct. 29, 1928; s. Atal Behari Lal and Shyama Devi M.; m. Sarojini Mathur, May 20, 1956; children: Piyush Kumar, Rajeev Kumar, Deepti, Amit Kumar. BSc, Allahabad (India) U., 1951, MSc, 1954, PhD, 1956. Asst. prof. Birla Coll., Pilani, India, 1957-58; sr. scientific officer Cen. electrochem. Research Inst., Karaikudi, India, 1958-66, asst. dir., 1966-85, dep. dir., 1985—; sec. research adv. council Cen. Electrochem. Research Inst., Karikudi, 1985—, mem. exec. com., 1985—; adv., com. for battery and chems. Bur. of Indian Standards, New Delhi, 1985—. Contbr. articles to profl. jours.; patentee in field. Recipient Nat. award India, 1969, Internat. award Baypren Internat., Fed. Repub. Germany, 1969. Fellow Indian Chem. Soc. (life), Indian Nat. Acad. Scis. (life), Soc. Advancement of Electrochem. Sci and Technology (founder). Home: 105 Alanganj, Allahabad 211002, India Office: Electrochem Research Inst, Karaikudi 623006, India

MATIN, ABDUL, microbiology educator, consultant; b. Delhi, India, May 8, 1941; came to U.S., 1964, naturalized, 1983; s. Mohammed and Zohra (Begum) Said; m. Mimi Keyhan, June 21, 1968. BS, U. Karachi, Pakistan, 1960, MS, 1962; PhD, UCLA, 1969. Lectr. St. Joseph's Coll., Karachi, 1962-64; research assoc. UCLA, 1964-71; sci. officer U. Groningen, Kerklaan, The Netherlands, 1971-75; from asst. to assoc. prof. microbiology Stanford U., Calif., 1975—; cons. Engenics, 1982-84, Monsanto, 1984—; chmn. Stanford Recombinant DNA panel; convener of microbiological workshop and confs. Mem. editorial bd. Jour. of Bacteriology; guest mem. editorial bd. Ann. Rev. Microbiol., Rev. of NSF and other Grants; contbr. numerous publs. to sci. jours. Fellow Fulbright Found., 1964, NSF, 1981—, Ctr. for Biotech. Research, 1981-85, EPA, 1981-84, U.N. Tokten, 1987. Mem. AAAS, AAUP, Am. Soc. Microbiology, Soc. Gen. Microbiology, Soc. Indsl. Microbiology, Biophys. Soc. Home: 690 Coronado Ave Stanford CA 94305 Office: Stanford U Microbiology and Immunology Fairchild Sci Bldg Stanford CA 94305

MATIN, M. A., government official; b. Bangladesh, Dec. 1, 1937. Grad., Dhaka (Bangladesh) Med. Coll. With Royal Eye Hosp. King's Coll. Hosp. and St. Alban's City Hosp., Eng., 1964-67; assoc. prof. ophthalmology Inst. Postgrad. Medicine and Research, Dhaka, 1967-72, prof. then head of dept., 1972—; M.P., minister civil aviation and tourism People's Republic Bangladesh, 1979, minister for youth devel., 1981, minister for home affairs, 1981-82, minister for commerce, 1984, minister for works, 1985, dep. prime minister, minister for home affairs, 1986—, minister health and population control, 1988—; cons. Diabetic Assn. Bangladesh, Dhaka Shishu (Children's) Hosp., Combined Mil. Hosp., 1976—. Contbr. articles to over 21 publs. Recipient Internat. award Asian Pacific Acad. Ophthalmology, 1981. Fellow Royal Coll. Surgeons; mem. Ophthalmol. Soc. Bangladesh (past sec.-gen., pres.), Bangladesh Med. Research Council (vice-chmn.), Bangladesh Nat. Soc. for Blind (sec.-gen.), Bangladesh Med. Services Assn. (pres.). Lodges: Rotary, Lion. Office: Ministry of Home Affairs, Bangladesh Secretariat, Dhaka Bangladesh *

MATLICK, DAYTON HARRIS, magazine publisher; b. Haviland, Kans., Nov. 14, 1934; s. John Orville and Helen (Dayton) M.; m. Mary Patricia Castle, Dec. 8, 1968; children: Scott Dayton, Gregory Trent, Leslie Ann, Peter Scott, Joseph Paul, Heather Lynn. BA, U. Ky., 1957; MA, Mich. State U., 1977. Field editor Ky. Farmer, Tenn. Farmer, Ind. Farmer mags., Louisville, 1959-60; assoc. editor Ky. Farmer, Tenn. Farmer mags., 1960-61; editor Tenn. Farmer, Nasville, 1961-62; mng. editor Mich. Farmer, Lansing, 1962-66, editor, 1966-76; v.p., editorial dir. Harvest Pub. Co., Cleve., 1976-78, sr. v.p. editorial, prodn. and circulation, 1978-81; group pub., gen. mgr. Specialized Agrl. Publs., Inc., Raleigh, N.C., 1980-81, chief exec. officer, 1982—, pres., 1983—; pub. Tobacco Reporter, Flue Cured Tobacco Farmer, Peanut Farmer mags., 1982—; pub., editor Rice Jour., 1986—; lectr. journalism Mich. State U., 1970-73; active Mich. Health Council, 1966-77, Mich. Rural Safety Council, 1966-77, Mich. Pork Council, 1968-75; mem. poultry adv. com. Mich. State U., 1967-69, dairy adv. council, 1969-75. Assoc. chmn. Nat. Amateur Athletic Union Tae Kwon Do Jr. Olympics subcom., 1977-80. Served with AUS, 1957-59. Recipient Hon. State Future Farmers Am. degree, 1968, Animal Agr. award Am. Feed Mfrs. Assn., 1965, Editors Soil Mgmt. award Nat. Plant Food Inst., 1969, Oscar award in Agr. Dekalb Agresearch, Inc., 1969, Soil Conservation Merit cert. Mich. chpt. Soil Conservation Soc. Am., 1969, Editors Profl. Improvement award Chgo. Bd. Trade, 1971, Mich. 4-H citation, 1973, 4th deg. Black Belt Tae Kwon Do, 1975. Mem. Am. Agrl. Editors Assn., Agrl. Criculation Mgrs. Assn., Am. Mgmt. Assn., Mich. Agrl. Conf. (bd. dirs.), Am. Soc. Bus. Press Editors, Mich. Kang Duk Won Assn. (pres. 1970-73, adviser 1973-80), Am. Midwest Tae Kwon Do-Karate Fedn. (pres. 1973-75, adviser 1975-80), Raleigh C. of C., N.C. Agribus. Council, Sigma Delta Chi. Home: 6210 Dixon Dr Raleigh

NC 27609 Office: Specialized Agrl Publs Inc 3000 Highwoods Blvd Suite 300 Raleigh NC 27625

MATLINS, STUART M., management consultant; b. N.Y.C., July 25, 1940; s. Louis Karl and Lillian (Keit) M.; student London Sch. Econs., 1958-59; B.S., U. Wis., 1960; A.M., Princeton U., 1962, postgrad., 1962-63; m. Andrea Cines, June 20, 1960 (div.); children—Seth, Andrew; m. 2d, Antoinette Leonard, Oct. 9, 1977. Internat. economist Bur. Internat. Commerce, U.S. Dept. Commerce, Washington, 1963-66; cons. Booz Allen & Hamilton, Inc., N.Y.C., 1966-67, asst. to pres. internat./adminstrv. dir., 1967-70, v.p. internat. ops., 1970-71, v.p./mng. officer, instl. and pub. mgmt. div., 1971-74; pres. Stuart Matlins Assocs., Inc., mgmt. cons., South Woodstock, Vt., 1974—; chmn. bd., dir. LongHill Ptnrs., Inc.; dir. Johnson, Smith & Knisely, Inc., Comprehensive Addiction Programs, Inc., The Fur Vault, Inc., Gemstone Press. Bd. dirs. Health Edn. Found.; mem. Woodstock Town Fin. Com. Woodrow Wilson fellow, 1960-61; Herbert O. Peet fellow, 1961-62; Phillip A. Rollins fellow, 1962-63. Club: Princeton (N.Y.C.). Home: High Riding South Woodstock VT 05071 Office: PO Box 276 South Woodstock VT 05071

MATLOCK, CLIFFORD CHARLES, retired foreign service officer; b. Whittier, Cal., Nov. 6, 1909; s. William Holl and Clara Louisa (Wallace) M.; m. Nina Stolypin, Nov. 6, 1934 (dec. Dec. 1969); m. Elisabeth Thompson Scobey, May 3, 1971. A.B., Stanford U., 1932; A.M., Harvard U., 1940, certificate pub. adminstrn. (Littauer fellow), 1940. Economist USDA, 1938-41, U.S. Treasury, 1941-42; economist, adminstr. Bd. Econ. Warfare, Fgn. Econ. Adminstrn., 1942-45; econ., polit. officer Dept. State, 1946-62; polit. adviser European coordinating com. Dept. State, London, 1949-50; polit. officer U.S. delegation North Atlantic Council, London, 1950-52; polit. officer, then dir. plans and policy staff Office U.S. spl. rep. in Europe, Paris, 1952-53; spl. asst. Am. ambassador, Tehran, 1955-57; spl. asst. econ. affairs asst. sec. state for Far Eastern affairs, also alternate to Dep. Asst. Sec., 1959-62, ret.; acting dep. asst. Sec. of State, 1959; spl. asst. for polit. and econ. affairs to asst. adminstr. East Asia AID, Dept. of State, 1962-68, dir. East Asia tech. adv. staff, 1966-68, cons. Bur. for East Asia, 1968-71; coordinator interdisciplinary Devel. Cycles Research Project, 1971-76, prin., 1977-84; U.S. del. Econ. Commn. for Asia and Far East (UN), Tokyo, Japan, 1962; U.S. del. to devel. assistance com. Orgn. for Economic Cooperation and Devel., Paris, France, 1962; Member U.S. delegation Colombo Plan Consultative Com., Seattle, 1958, London, 1964; Member Development Assistance Group, Orgn. Econ. Coop. and Development, Washington, 1960; U.S. alternate rep. UN Econ. Commn. for Asia and Far East, Bangkok, 1960; adviser, mem. U.S. del. bds. govs. Internat. Monetary Fund, Internat. Bank for Reconstrn. and Devel., Tokyo, Japan, 1964; exec. com. SE Asia Devel. Adv. Group, 1965-70. Author: Man and Cosmos: A Theory of Endeavor Rhythms, 1977. Recipient Superior Honor award AID, 1968. Mem. Fgn. Service Assn., Diplomatic and Consular Officers Ret., Phi Beta Kappa. Clubs: Metropolitan (Washington), Harvard (Washington); Harvard of Western N.C. Home: Route 1 Box 388 Lowry Rd Balsam Heights Waynesville NC 28786

MATLOCK, JACK FOUST, JR., government official; b. Greensboro, N.C., Oct. 1, 1929; s. Jack Foust and Nellie (McSwain) M.; m. Rebecca Burrum, Sept. 2, 1949; children: James, Hugh, Nell, David, Joseph. A.B. summa cum laude, Duke U., 1950; M.A., Columbia U., 1952; cert., Russian Inst., 1952. Instr. Dartmouth, 1953-56; fgn. service officer Dept. State, 1956—; assigned Washington, 1956-58, Am. Embassy, Vienna, Austria, 1958-60; Am. consul. gen. Munich, Germany, 1960-61; assigned Am. Embassy, Moscow, 1961-63, Accra, Ghana, 1963-66; assigned Am. Consulate, Zanzibar, 1967-69, Am. Embassy, Dar es Salaam, Tanzania, 1969-70, Sr. Seminar in Fgn. Policy, Dept. State, 1970-71; country dir. for USSR State Dept., 1971-74; minister-counselor, dep. chief mission Am. Embassy, Moscow, 1974-78; diplomat-in-residence Vanderbilt U., Nashville, 1978-79; dep. dir. Fgn. Service Inst., Washington, 1979-80; chargé d'affaires ad interim Am. Embassy, Moscow, 1981; ambassador to Czecholslovakia 1981-83; spl. asst. to pres., sr. dir. European and Soviet Affairs Nat. Security Council, 1983-87; U.S. ambassador to the Soviet Union Moscow, 1987—. Compiler, editor: Index to J.V. Stalin's Works, 2d edit, 1971. Home: 2913 P St NW Washington DC 20007 Office: Ambassador to Soviet Union care US Dept State Washington DC 20520 *

MATLOFF, GREGORY LEE, consulting environmental, space and computer scientist; b. N.Y.C., Mar. 2, 1945; s. Simon and Eudice (Strom) M.; B.A., Queens Coll. CUNY, 1965; M.S., N.Y.U., 1969, Ph.D., 1976. Engr., Kollsman Inst. Corp., Elmhurst, N.Y., 1965-67, Grumman Aerospace Co., Bethpage, N.Y., 1967-69; research engr. United Aircraft Research Co., East Hartford, Conn., 1969-70; research assoc. Wesleyan U., Middletown, Conn., 1970-71; asst. editor Am. Inst. Physics, N.Y.C., 1971-72; research asst. N.Y.U., 1972-75, postdoctoral research scientist, 1975-77; cons. staff scientist Systems and Applied Sci. Corp., Riverdale, Md., 1978-81; cons. environ. scientist, Bklyn., 1980—; mem. faculty Pratt Inst., 1980-82, adminstr., 1983-85; mem. faculty N.Y.C. Tech. Coll., 1979-82, Baruch Coll. CUNY, 1986—. Dir. Astronomy program N.Y.C. Dept. Parks and Recreation, 1987—. NSF grantee, 1975. Fellow Brit. Interplanetary Soc.; mem. Am. Meteorol. Soc., Am. Optical Soc., N.Y. Acad. Scis., AAAS, Sigma Xi. Lodge: K.M. Contbr. articles to profl. jours. Home: 419 Greene Ave Brooklyn NY 11216

MATOS, CRUZ ALFONSO, UN official; b. N.Y.C., Mar. 6, 1929; s. José and Gertrudes (Manzanares) M.; B.Engring. Sci., Oxford U., 1957, M.Engring. Sci., 1958; m. Aurelia Santos, Dec. 13, 1963; children—Miguel, Veronica, Monica, Angélica. Pres., Fischer & Porter de P.R., 1964-69; asst. sec. Dept. Public Works, Govt. of P.R., 1969-70, exec. dir. Environ. Quality Bd., 1970-72, sec. Dept. Natural Resources, cabinet mem., 1972-74; dir. Inst. Marine Affairs, Trinidad and Tobago, 1975-79; officer-in-charge UN devel. programs, Trinidad & Tobago, Barbados, Surinam and Dutch West Indies, 1978-80, chief tech. adviser UN Deep Sea Minerals Exploration of the South Pacific, Suva, Fiji, 1980—, also dir. CCOP/SOPAC; mem. adv. panel UN Environ. Program, Caribbean Program; mem. U.S. Commn. Man in the Biosphere Program; research asso. Island Resources Found.; mem. various adv. panels and overseas mission U.S. Nat. Acad. Scis. Trustee, Conservation Found., bd. dirs., World Wildlife Fund-U.S.A.; mem. tech. adv. panel Mission Industrial de P.R. Served with U.S. Army, 1952-54. Recipient Caribbean conservation award, 1971; various awards Caribbean countries and Thailand. Contbr. articles to sci. jours. and mags. Office: care United Nations, Private Mail Bag, Suva Fiji

MATSA, LOULA ZACHAROULA, social services adminstr.; b. Piraeus, Greece, Apr. 16, 1935; came to U.S., 1952, naturalized 1962; d. Eleftherios Georgiou and Ourania E. (Fraguiskopoulou) Papoulias; student Pierce Coll., Athens, Greece, 1948-52; B.A., Rockford Coll., 1953; M.A., U. Chgo., 1955; m. Ilco S. Matsa, Nov. 27, 1953; 1 son, Aristotle Ricky. Marital counselor Family Soc. Cambridge, Mass., 1955-56; chief unit II, social service Queen's (N.Y.) Children's Psychiat. Center, 1961-74; dir. social services, supr.-coordinator family care program Hudson River Psychiat. Center, Poughkeepsie, N.Y., 1974—; field instr. Adelphi, Albany and Fordham univs., 1969—. Fulbright Exchange student, 1952-53; Talcott scholar, 1953-55. Mem. Internat. Platform Assn., Internat. Council on Social Welfare, Nat. Assn. Social Workers, Assn. Cert. Social Workers, Civil Service Employees Assn., Pierce Coll. Alumni Assn. Democrat. Greek Orthodox. Contbr. articles to profl. jours.; instrumental in state policy changes in treatment and court representation of emtionally disturbed and mentally ill. Home: 81-11 45th Ave Elmhurst NY 11373 Office: Hudson River Psychiat Ctr Br B Poughkeepsie NY 12601

MATSESHE, JOHN WANYAMA, gastroenterologist; b. Kakamega, Kenya, June 5, 1941; s. James K. and Anyachi S. (Nyikuli) M.; came to U.S., 1970; M.D., Makerere U., Kampala, Uganda, 1969; m. Rebecca Z. Wazome, Mar. 14, 1970; children—Lily, Carolyn, Lynn, Andrew. Intern, Stamford (Conn.) Hosp., 1971-72; resident in medicine Northwestern U. Hosps., 1972-74; fellow in gastroenterology Mayo Clinic, Rochester, Minn., 1974-77, cons. in medicine and gastroenterology, 1977-78; instr. medicine Mayo Med. Sch., 1976-78, asst. prof., 1978; practice medicine specializing in gastroenterology, Libertyville, Ill., 1978—; asst. prof., Chgo. Med. Sch., U. of Health Scis., 1981; cons. Condell Meml. Hosp., St. Therese Hosp., Waukegan, VA Hosp., North Chicago. Diplomate Am. Bd. Internal Medicine (gastroenterology; recognized for advanced achievement 1988). Mem. AMA, A.C.P., Am. Gastroent. Assn., Am. Soc. Gastrointestinal Endoscopy, Sigma Xi. Address: 890 Garfield St No 210 Libertyville IL 60048

MATSSON, LEIF, physicist; b. Mariestad, Sweden, June 23, 1940; s. Mats Artur Torulf and Olga Margareta (Johansson) Pettersson; Phil.Kand., Gothenbourg (Sweden) U., 1964, Phil.Dr., 1971, Docent, 1975; m. Barbro Elise Longum, Apr. 6, 1974; children—Janna Elise, Susanna Margareta, Pauline Ann-Marie. Research asst. and lectr. Gothenbourg U., 1964-74; Nordita fellow, Copenhagen, 1974-75, CERN fellow, Geneva, 1975-77, CERN travelling fellow Steklov Math. Inst., Leningrad, USSR, 1977-78; mng. dir. Medic Herb AB, Goteborg, 1979—. Mem. Swedish, European phys. socs. Contbr. articles to profl. jours. Home: Kopparasvagen 58, 42700 Billdal Sweden Office: Medic Herb AB, Box 30060, S-40043 Goteborg Sweden

MATSUDA, EIICHI, civil engineer; b. Matsumoto, Nagano, Japan, Sept. 28, 1948; s. Takao and Kayo (Makinoshima) M.; m. Hiroko Matsuishi, Dec. 17, 1978; children: Izumi, Takuya, Shohei. B of Engring., Tokyo U., 1971, M of Engring., 1973. Staff Corvac Co., Tokyo, 1973-78, chief sect., 1978-87, mgr. offshore engring., 1987—. Author: Recent Developments in Offshore Structures, 1985, Steel Design Manual, 1987, Safety in Offshore Structures, 1988. Mem. Japan Soc. Civil Engrs. (commr. 1985-87), Japan Soc. Mech. Engrs. Home: 4-29-6 Hijirigaoka, Tama Tokyo 206, Japan Office: Corvac Co, Taiso Blvd 1-26-12, Shinjuku Tokyo 160, Japan

MATSUDA, ISAO, electronics executive; b. Kobe, Hyōgo, Japan, Oct. 19, 1926; s. Jūkichi and Chiga Matsuda; m. Kazuko Ōta, Apr. 5, 1958; children: Hiroshi, Yōko Akiyama. Degree in Electric Tech., Kyōto Imperial U., 1948; D (hon.), Kyōto Imperial U., 1962. Registered profl. engr. Mgr. engring. dept. Kōbe, 1963-66; deputy gen. mgr. Peripheral Equipment Div., Kawasaki, 1974-78; mng. dir. Fuji Electrochem. Co. Ltd., Tokyō, 1978-84, exec. v.p., 1984—; cons. Matsushita Densō Co. Ltd., Tokyō, 1973-78. bd. dirs. Japan Electronic Material Assn., Tokyō, 1983, Japan Battery Assn., Tokyō, 1984. Home: 2-8-21 Higiri-gama Kōnanku, Yokohama 233, Japan Office: Fuji Electrochem Co Ltd, 5-36-11 Shinbashi Minatoku, Tokyo 105, Japan

MATSUDA, MASAYUKI MORRIS, manufacturing executive; b. Ashiya, Hyogo, Japan, July 27, 1933; s. Shigeji Matsuda and Toku Nakata; m. Taeko Iwahashi, May 25, 1969; children: Atsunobu, Shio. B of politics, Keio U., Tokyo, 1962. Sales rep. NGK Insulators, Ltd., Sydney, Australia, 1967-68; dep. gen. mgr. Porcelain Enamelled Products Div. NGK Insulators, Ltd., Tokyo, 1981—; sales mgr. NGK Insulators Am., Ltd., N.Y.C., U.S., 1971-74; pres. Towa Sangyo Co. Ltd., Tokyo, 1984—; bd. dirs. NGK Wall Sales Co. Ltd., Tokyo, 1984—. Rep. Graduates' Assn. Seijyo Ednl. Inst., Tokyo, 1986. Home: 3-10-31 Seijyo, Setagaya, 157 Tokyo Japan Office: NGK Insulators Ltd, 1-5-1 Marunouchi, 100 Chiyoda-ku, Tokyo Japan

MATSUDA, YASUHIRO, computer scientist; b. Ako, Hyogo, Japan, Jan. 29, 1947; s. Eiichi and Kiyoko M.; m. Eiko Miura, Sept. 19, 1981. B.S., Osaka U., Suita, Osaka, Japan, 1969, M.Engring., 1971, D.Engring., 1980; M.S., Yale U., 1982. Systems engr. IBM Japan Ltd., Osaka, 1971-80, adv. researcher, Tokyo, 1983-85, mgr. research group, 1985-87; prof., Shinshu U., Nagano, 1987—; postdoctoral assoc. Yale U., New Haven, 1981-82; lectr., author corr. course Japan Daily Indsl. Newspaper Co., Ltd., Tokyo, 1977—; spl. lectr. Kyoto U., 1976. Recipient Ann. award for best paper Textile Machinery Soc. Japan, 1975; IBM Japan Ltd. grantee, 1980-82. Mem. Japan Soc. Mech. Engrs., Inst. Electronics and Communication Engrs. Japan, Japan Info. Processing Soc. Home: N 201, 53 Wakasato, 380 Nagano Japan Office: Dept Mech Engring, Shinshu Univ, 500 Wakasato, 380 Nagano Japan

MATSUDAIRA, KAZUAKI, banker; b. Tokyo, Apr. 1, 1927; came to U.S., 1963; d. Chokichi and Fumiko (Tanahashi) Nakashige; B.A. in Polit. Sci. and Econs., Waseda U., Tokyo, 1951; m. Renko Matsudaira, Apr. 25, 1961. With fgn. exchange dept. Sumitomo Bank, Ltd., Tokyo, 1951-54, asst. mgr. fgn. dept., 1958-63; with acctg. dept. Sumitomo Bank Calif., San Francisco, 1954-58; with internat. div. Crocker Nat. Bank, San Francisco, 1963-86, internat. banking officer, 1971-74, asst. v.p., 1974-77, v.p. internat. div., 1977-86; v.p. Sumitomo Bank of Calif., San Francisco, 1987—. Mem. Japanese C. of C. No. Calif., Japan Soc. No. Calif. Buddhist. Clubs: Calif. Golf. Home: 302 27th Ave San Francisco CA 94121 Office: 300 California St San Francisco CA 94104

MATSUI, YOSHIHIKO, business executive; b. Osaka, Japan, Nov. 9, 1921; s. Kaichi and Tomo (Tachibana) M.; Toshiko Takechi, Mar. 28, 1950; 1 child, Eri. Student, Osaka Coll. Fgn. Lang., 1939-41; B. in Econs., Kobe U., 1949. Mng. dir. Kogyo Rubber Co., Ltd., Osaka, 1962-68; exec. v.p. Towa Denki Co., Ltd., Tokyo, 1968-76; pres. Towa Kagaku Co. Ltd., Kobe, Japan, 1976—. Buddhist. Home: 3-12-11 Mikageyamate Higashinadaku, Kobe 658, Japan Office: Towa Kagaku Co Ltd, 2-2-8 Kaguracho Nagataku, Kobe 653, Japan

MATSUI, YOSHIRO, bank executive; b. Fukuoka Prefecture, Japan, Mar. 27, 1936; s. Yoheiji and Hana (Sano) M.; m. Takako Tanaka, Feb. 19, 1963; children: Akinori, Toshinori, Shigeki. B. of Liberal Arts and Scis., Tokyo U., 1959. Gen. mgr. bus. planning dept. Sumitomo Bus. Cons. Co. Ltd., Tokyo, 1977-79; mgr. Tokyo Br. Grindlays Bank Ltd., 1979-81; joint gen. mgr. merchant banking dept. Sumitomo Bank Ltd., Tokyo, 1981-87, joint gen. mgr. internat. fin. dept., 1987—. Mem. Liberal Dem. Party. Buddhist. Home: 14-11 Koenjiminami 3-chome, Suginami-ku, Tokyo 166, Japan Office: The Sumitomo Bank Ltd, 3-2 Marunouchi 1-chrome, Chiyoda-ku, Tokyo 100, Japan

MATSUKAWA, MICHIYA, securities company executive; b. Aizu-wakamatsu, Fukushima, Japan, Dec. 22, 1924; s. Tomiyasu and Koh Matsukawa; m. Ryoko Sakakibara, June 12, 1931; children: Makiko Watanabe, Kikuko Murofushi. BA in Polit. Sci., Tokyo Imperial U., 1947; MA in Economics, U. Ill., 1951. Various positions held throughout Japan Ministry of Fin., 1947-73, dir. gen. internat. fin. bur., 1973-74, dep. vice minister fin., 1974-75, dir. gen. fin. bur., 1975-76, vice minister fin. internat. affairs, 1976-78, spl. advisor to Minister Fin., 1978-80; advisor Tohmatsu Aoki and Sanwa, Tokyo, 1982—; chmn. inst. Nikko Research Ctr. Ltd., Tokyo, 1982—; chmn. bd. dirs. Nikko Internat. Capital Mgmt. Co. Ltd., Tokyo; bd. dirs. Nippon Investors Service Inc., Tokyo; sr. advisor to pres. Nikko Securities Co. Ltd., Tokyo, 1980—; mem. adv. bd. Morgan Stanley Co. Inc., N.Y.C., 1986; dir. Fedn. Economic Orgns., Tokyo, Japan Inst. Fgn. Affairs; mem. U.N. investment com. U.N. Pension Fund, N.Y.C., U.N. U., N.Y.C. Trustee Soc. Internat. Cultural Exchange; mng. dir. Eisaku Sato Meml. Found. Cooperation with U.N. U. Served with Japanese Navy, 1944-45. Mem. Japan Securities and Economics Club (counsellor). Clubs: Tokyo, Keidanren. Office: Nikko Securities Co Ltd, 3 3 1 Marunouchi, Chiyoda ku, Tokyo 100, Japan

MATSUMOTO, HIDEO, architect; b. Hyogo, Japan, Mar. 11, 1952; s. Masao and Misako (Morishita) M.; m. Yayoi Nakasuji, May 1, 1981; 1 child, Naoki. BArch, Tokyo U., 1976. Staff mem. Kuraray, Osaka, Japan, 1976-78; asst. architect S. Urabe Architect & Assoc., Osaka, 1978-80; chief architect Ouchi & Tateishi Architects, Kyoto, Japan, 1980-83; asst. project mgr. Internat. Engring. Service, Bagdad, Iraq, 1984-85; chief planner Chiyoda Engring. Cons., Tokyo, 1985—. Home: 4-3-7-402 Nagayama, Tama, Tokyo 206, Japan Office: Chiyoda Engring Cons, 3-3-7 Iidabashi Chiyoda, Tokyo 102, Japan

MATSUMOTO, SEIYA, electronics company executive; b. Feb. 27, 1929; m. Mie Matsumoto. Grad., Chuo U., Japan, 1951. Pres. Pioneer Electronic Corp., Tokyo. Home: 32-15 Okamoto 2-chome, Setagaya-ku, Tokyo Japan Office: Pioneer Electronic Corp, 4-1 Meguro 1-chome, Meguro-ku, Tokyo Japan *

MATSUMOTO, YUKIMICHI, machine manufacturing company executive; b. Kuwana, Mie, Japan, June 21, 1937; s. Tadanobu and Ayako (Ishikura) M.; m. Keiko Sano. BD om Engring.d, Knobe U., Japan, 1961. Engr. Okuma Iron Works Co., Nagoya, Aichi, Japan, Fuji Tekko Co., Neyagawa, Osaka, Japan, 1964-72; dir. Fuji Tekko Co., Neyagawa, Osaka, 1972-83, pres., 1984—. Patentee in field. Home: 4-18-2 Chime Kuzuha, Misaki Hirakatashi, Osaka 573 Japan Office: Fuji Tekko Co, 5-51-5 Hoshida Kita, Katanoshi Osaka 576 Japan

MATSUMURA, AKIRA, engineering educator; b. Tokyo, Nov. 18, 1929; s. John Yutaka and Koh (Morita) M.; m. Takako Utashiro, Dec. 18, 1960; children: Hinako, Ichiro. B of Engring., Tokyo Inst. Tech., 1954, M of Engring., 1956. Tech. official Ministry of Constrn., Tokyo, 1956-61; research fellow Tokyo Inst. Tech., 1961-68; lectr. engring. Kanagawa U., Yokohama, Japan, 1967-68, assoc. prof., 1968—. Author: (with others) Special Reinforced Concrete, 1972, Tests on Masonry Building, 1985; author: Shear Strength of Masonry Walls, 1987. Mem. Archtl. Inst. Japan (vice chmn. wall structures com. 1975—), Japan Concrete Inst., Am. Concrete Inst., Masonry Soc. Office: Kanagawa U, 3-27-1 Rokkakubashi, Kanagawa-Ku, Yokohama 221, Japan

MATSUMURA, VERA YOSHI, pianist; b. Oakland, Calif.; d. Naojiro and Aguri Tanaka; B.A. in Piano Pedagogy, Coll. of Holy Names, Oakland, 1938; pvt. studies with F. Moss, M. Shapiro, L. Kreutzer, P. Jarrett; m. Jiro Matsumura, Aug. 8, 1942; 1 son, Kenneth N. Staff mem., pianist Radio Sta. KROW, Oakland, 1938-39; numerous concert performances in Far East (Japan, Thailand), 1940—; numerous teaching appointments, 1940—; dir. Internat. Music Council, Berkeley, Calif., 1969—. Named to Hall of Fame, Piano Guild, 1968. Mem. Music Tchrs. Nat. Assn., Music Tchrs. Assn. Calif., Internat. Platform Assn., Alpha Phi Mu. Methodist. Home: 2 Claremont Crescent Berkeley CA 94705

MATSUNAGA, FUMIO, architectural educator; b. Shizuoka, Japan, Jan. 1, 1921; s. Heitaro and Kaya Oda; m. Fumiko Matsunaga, Nov. 11, 1948; children: Yoko, Takako. Degree, Kogakushi U., Japan. Lic. architect, Japan. Architect Fukuoka Prefecture, Japan, 1946-47; asst. lectr., then lectr. Kyoto (Japan) U., 1948-51; structural engr. Constrn. Ministry Pub. Bldg., Kyushu, 1952-73; asst. prof. Nishinihon Inst. Tech., Fukuoka, 1973—; extraordinary lectr. Seinan Tanki Daigaku, Kukira, 1956-63, Towa U., Fukuoka, 1960-62, Kinki U., Iizuka, 1963-67. Contbr. articles to archtl. publs. Served to tech. lt. Japanese Air Force, 1944-45. Mem. Archtl. Inst. Japan (trustee 1981), Internat. Assn. Bridge and Structural Engring. Home: Sakurazaka 2, chome 5-34 Ku, Fukuoka, Kyushu 810, Japan Office: Nishinihon Inst Tech, Obase Kanda Machi Miyako gun, Fukuoka ken Kyushu 800 Japan

MATSUNAGA, SPARK MASAYUKI, U.S. senator; b. Kauai, Hawaii, Oct. 8, 1916; s. Kingoro and Chiyono (Fukushima) M.; m. Helene Hatsumi Tokunaga, Aug. 6, 1948; children: Karen (Mrs. Hardman), Keene, Diane, Merle, Matthew. Ed.B. with honors, U. Hawaii, 1941; J.D., Harvard U., 1951; LL.D. (hon.), Soochow U., 1973, St. John's U., 1977, Eastern Ill. U., 1978, U. Md., 1979; H.L.D., Lincoln U., 1979. Bar: Hawaii 1952. Vets. counsellor U.S. Dept. Interior, 1945-47; chief priority claimants div. War Assets Adminstrn., 1947-48; asst. pub. pros. City and County of Honolulu, 1952-54; practice of law Honolulu, 1954-62; mem. Hawaii Ho. of Reps., 1954-59, majority leader, 1959; mem. U.S. Ho. Reps. 88th-94th Congresses; mem. Rules, Aging, Steering and Policy coms., dep. majority whip; U.S. senator from Hawaii, 1976—; mem. Fin., Energy and Natural Resources, Vets.' Affairs coms., chief dep. whip.; Mem. Hawaii statehood delegations to Congress, 1950, 54, Pacific War Meml. Commn., 1959-62; adv. com. Honolulu Redevel. Agy., 1953-54. Author: Rulemakers of The House, 1976. Chmn. bd. Kaimuki YMCA; pres. Naturalization Encouragement Assn. Honolulu.; Bd. dirs. World Brotherhood. Soc. Crippled Children and Adults, Honolulu Council Social Agys. Served from 2d lt. to capt., inf. AUS, 1941-45; ret. lt. col. JAGC 1969. Decorated Bronze Star with valor clasp, Purple Heart with oak leaf cluster. Mem. Am., Hawaii bar assns., D.A.V., V.F.W., Japan-Am. Soc., U. Hawaii Alumni Assn. Democrat. Episcopalian. Clubs: Lions (Honolulu), 100 (Honolulu). Office: 109 Hart Senate Office Bldg Washington DC 20510 *

MATSUO, AKIRA, accounting company executive; b. Himeji, Hyogo, Japan, Feb. 3, 1948; s. Kiyoshi and Tomiko (Fujimoto) M.; m. Makiko Yanagawa, Apr. 3, 1982; children: Manabu, Minoru. BBA, Kobe U., Japan, 1971. CPA, Japan, N.Y. Mem. staff Coopers & Lybrand, Tokyo, 1972-81, mgr., 1981-84; ptnr. Chou Audit Corp. div. Coopers & Lybrand, Tokyo, 1984—; lectr. Nihon U., Japan, GAO, Tokyo. Author: Information Systems Auditing for Management, 1987; editor: Information Systems Auditing, 1984. Mem. Japan Inst. CPAs (chmn. info. systems com., 1985—), Am. Inst. CPAs, EDP Auditors Assn. (asst. v.p., 1987—), Japan Soc. Systems Audit (standing dir. 1987—), Internat. Fedn. Accts. (tech. advisor, 1985—, speaker World Congress Accts, 1987). Home: 3-1-18-305, Eda Higashi Midoriku, Yokohama 227, Japan Office: Chuo Audit Corp, Kasumigaseki Bldg Box 50, 100 Tokyo Japan

MATSUO, HIROSHI, internist, educator; b. Fukuoka, Japan, June 8, 1934; s. Yoshiro and Masa (Koga) M.; m. Emi Watanabe, Dec. 2, 1966; children: Satomi, Mika. MD, U. Tokyo, 1960, PhD, 1968. Intern, then resident St. Louis City Hosp., 1961-63; clin. fellow 2d dept. internal medicine Faculty Medicine, U. Tokyo, 1963-71, research fellow, 1972-83, asst. prof. internal medicine, 1984; prof. Saitama (Japan) Med. Ctr.-Saitama Med. Sch., 1985—. Mem. editorial bd. Japan Heart Jour., 1988—; contbr. articles to profl. jours. Referee med. jours. Japan Heart Found., 1971—. Grantee Japan Ministry Edn., 1984, 87, Japan Ministry Pub. Welfare, 1984. Mem. Japan Soc. Electrocardiology, Japan Soc. Cardiac Pacing (exec. editor, auditor 1986—), Japan Circulation Soc., Japan Soc. Med. Engring., Japan Soc. Internal Medicine. Home: 3-9-11 Ikejiri Setagaya-ku, 154 Tokyo Japan Office: Saitama Med Sch, 1981 Tsujido Kamoda Kawagoe, Saitama 350, Japan

MATSUO, TAIICHIRO, business executive; b. June 7, 1910; m. Yuki Matsuo. Grad., U. Tokyo, 1934. With Ministry of Internat. Trade and Industry, 1956; advisor Marubeni Corp., Tokyo, 1960, v.p., 1966, pres., 1975, now chmn.; chmn. Nihon Peru Oil Kabushiki Kaisha. Mem. C. of C. and Industry, Fedn. Econ. Orgn. (trustee). Home: 32-14 Akatsutumi 1-chome, Setagaya-ku, Tokyo 156 Japan Office: Marubeni Corp, 4-2 Ohtemachi 1-chome, Chiyoda-ku, Tokyo 100-91 Japan *

MATSUSHIMA, ITSURO, cosmetics company executive; b. Udagun, Nara, Japan, Mar. 9, 1935; s. Yoshiaki and Mieko (Yoshida) M.; m. Toshiko Masuda, Sept. 23, 1959; children: Masakazu, Hiroki. Degree in econs., Ritsumeikan U., Kyoto, Japan, 1957. Mgr. sales Daito Kagakukogyo Co. Ltd., Osaka, Japan, 1957-70, dir. sales, 1971-73, exec., 1974-76; pres. Kallen Co., Ltd, Osaka, 1976—. Buddhist. Home: Shigisanhigashi Sangocho 636, Ikoma, Nara Japan Office: Kallen Co Ltd, 3-10 Abikohigashi 2-Chome, Sumiyoshi-ku Osaka 558, Japan

MATSUSHITA, MASAHARU, electronics company executive; b. Tokyo, Sept. 17, 1912; s. Eiji and Shizuko Hirata; m. Sachiko Matsushita; 3 children. Ed. Tokyo Imperial U. With Mitsui Bank, 1935-40, Matsushita Electric Indsl. Co., Ltd., 1940—, auditor, 1944-47, dir., mem. bd., 1947-49, exec. v.p., 1949-61, pres., 1961-77, chmn. bd., 1977—; dir. Matsushita Electronics Corp., chmn., 1972-85, dir. 1985—; auditor Matsushita Real Estate Co., Ltd., 1952-67, dir., 1968—; dir. Matsushita Communication Indsl. Co., Ltd., 1958-70, chmn., 1970-86, dir. 1986-87; dir. Matsushita Seiko Co. Ltd., 1956-87, Kyushu Matsushita Electric Co. Ltd., 1955-87, Matsushita Electric Corp. Am., 1959-74, Mausushita Refrigeration Co., 1961-87; pres. Electronics Industries Assn. of Japan, 1968-70; rep. dir. Kansai Com. for Econ. Devel., 1962—, dir., 1975—. Recipient Blue Ribbon medal, 1972; Ordem de Rio Branco , 1984, Ordem do Mérito Indsl. na classe Ofl. (Brazil), 1984; Decorated Comdr. Order of Orange-Nassau (Netherlands), 1975; Comdr. Order De La Cournne (Belgium), 1981; Comdr's. Cross Order of Merit (Fed. Republic Germany), 1986. Mem. Osaka C. of C. (mem. standing com.), Kansai Econ. Fedn. (standing dir.).ng dir.). Office: Matsushita Electric Corp of Am One Panasonic Way Secaucus NJ 07094

MATSUSHITA, SHIGENORI, systems engineer; b. Tokyo, Mar. 11, 1936; s. Naoji and Umeko (Kikuchi) M.; m. Sumie Onuki, Sept. 21, 1964; children: Koshi, Aiki. BS, U. Tokyo, 1959, PhD in Engring., 1974; MS, U. Ill., 1963. Design engr. Toshiba Corp., Komukai Works, Kawasaki, Japan, 1959-67; sr. mgr. devel. Ome Works, Tokyo, 1970-76, sr. mgr. planning, hdqrs., 1976-78, sr. mgr. prodn. control, 1979-80, sr. mgr. office automation, 1980-81, dep. exec. tech., 1981-82, gen. mgr. planning, 1983, group exec. tech., 1984—; bd.

dirs. Toshiba Computer Engring. Corp., Computervision Japan Corp. Patentee in field. Mem. Info. Processing Soc. Japan, Inst. Electronics, Info. and Communication Engrs. of Japan. Home: 1-9-7 Nan Yodai Hachioji, 192-03 Tokyo Japan Office: Toshiba Corp, Toshiba Bldg 34D, 1-1-1 Shibaura Minato-ku, 105 Tokyo Japan

MATSUURA, TAKANORI, business administration educator; b. Hokkaido, Japan, July 5, 1940; s. Sueji and Miyoshi Matsuura; m. Kazuko Hashimoto, Oct. 25, 1943; 1 child, Masa. JD, Chuou U., 1963. Mem. editorial staff Mgmt. Today, Diamond, Inc., Tokyo, 1967-71, asst. to pres., 1971-73; researcher Inst. Social Engring., Tokyo, 1975-82; caster NHK ETV Culture Series, Tokyo, 1978-82; assoc. prof. Chubu Inst. Tech., Kasugai, Japan, 1982-84, assoc. prof. Coll. Bus. Adminstrn., 1984—; part time lectr. faculty bus. adminstrn. Meiji U., Tokyo, 1981—. Author: Recruiting--Company and Undergraduate on the Job Market in Japan, 1978, The Research of Japanese Corporation and Management Climate, 1983, The New Research of Japanese Corporation and Management Climate, 1987. Mem. Acad. Assn. Orgnl. Sci. Home: 1-7-14 Takaban, Meguro-ku Tokyo 152, Japan Office: Coll Bus Adminstrn and Info Sci, Chubu U, 1-7-14 Takaban, Meguro-ku Tokyo 152, Japan

MATTEI, JANET AKYUZ, astronomer, consultant; b. Bodrum, Turkey, Jan. 2, 1943; d. Baruh and Polise (Isbir) Akyuz; m. Michael Mattei, Dec. 17, 1972. B.A., Brandeis U., 1965; Yuksek Lisans-Astron., Ege U., Izmir, Turkey, 1970, D.Astronomy, 1982; M.S. in Astronomy, U. Va., 1972. Tchr. physics, astronomy and phys. sci. Ameri Collegiate Inst., Izmir, 1967-69; teaching asst. astronomy Ege U., Izmir, 1969-70; research asst. astronomy Maria Mitchell Obs., Nantucket, Mass., summer 1969; asst. to dir. Am. Assn. Variable Star Observers, Cambridge, Mass., 1972-73, dir., 1973—; also cons., lectr.; prin. investigator NASA, 1979-80, 85-86, NSF, 1979-83, Research Corp., Tucson, 1981. Contbr. articles to profl. publs. Mem. Internat. Astron. Union (prin. investigator 1985-86), Am. Astron. Soc. (prin. investigator 1983-84), Astron. Soc. Pacific. Office: Am Assn Variable Star Observers 25 Birch St Cambridge MA 02138

MATTER, MICHAEL CARL, pharmacist; b. Williamsport, Pa., Sept. 25, 1945; s. Paul H. and Mary L. (Gladewitz) M.; B.Sc. in Pharmacy, Temple U., 1968; M.B.A., Ohio U., 1984; m. Pamela Sue Gault, Feb. 9, 1974; children: Drew Michael-Paul, Graham Sang-Joon, Abby Hee-Jung, Alex Hee-Sung. Resident in hosp. pharmacy Bethesda Hosp., Zanesville, Ohio, 1968-69, spl. project pharmacist, 1969; dir. pharmacy services Med. Center Hosp., Chillicothe, Ohio, 1970-87; div. dir. support services Med. Ctr. Hosp., 1987—; evening instr. pharmacology Hocking Tech. Coll., Chillicothe, 1977-82. Mem. Am. Soc. Hosp. Pharmacists (preceptor; residency in hosp. pharmacy 1977-87), Ohio Soc. Hosp. Pharmacists (treas. 1979-85), Central Ohio Soc. Hosp. Pharmacists, Nat. Order Symposiarchs (past pres. Zeta chpt.). Home: 204 Vine St Chillicothe OH 45601 Office: Med Center Hosp 272 Hospital Rd Chillicothe OH 45601

MATTERN, DOUGLAS JAMES, electronics reliability engineer; b. Creede, Colo., May 19, 1933; s. John A. and Ethel (Franklin) M.; student San Jose (Calif.) City Coll., San Jose State U., 1956-58; m. Noemi E. Del Cippo, May 4, 1963. Reliability engr. Intersil, Sunnyvale, Calif., 1973-80; sr. engr. Data Gen. Corp., Sunnyvale, 1981-87; staff engr. Apple Computer, 1987—. Contbr. 35 articles to profl. jours. Sec. Gen. World Citizens Assembly, San Francisco, 1975—; dir. World Citizens Internat. Registry, U.S. Ctr., San Francisco, 1976—, World Citizen Diplomats, Palo Alto, Fla., 1988—; del. Peoples Congress, Paris, 1980—; editor World Citizen Newspaper, 1973—. Served with USN, 1951-55. Mem. Electron Microbean Analysis Soc., Union of Concerned Scientists Promoting Enduring Peace. Home: 2671 Southcourt St Palo Alto CA 94306 Office: PO Box 51867 Palo Alto CA 94303

MATTESON, ROBERT ELIOT, college administrator, government official; b. St. Paul, Sept. 13, 1914; s. Charles Dickerman and Adelaide Gridley (Hickcox) M.; m. Jane Elizabeth Paetzold, June 21, 1940; children: Adelaide (Mrs. David Elliott Donnelley), Robert Eliot, Fredric L., Sumner W., Elizabeth C. B.A., Carleton Coll., Northfield, Minn., 1937; intern, Nat. Inst. Pub. Affairs, 1937-38; M.A., Harvard U., 1940; student, Nat. War Coll., 1964-65. Instr. polit. sci. Carleton Coll., 1940-42; dir. Stassen research staff, Republican presdl. nomination, 1946-48; asst. to pres. U. Pa., 1948-52; asst. dir. Fgn. Operation Adminstrn., Washington, 1953-55; dir. White House Disarmament Staff, 1955-58; asst. to Sherman Adams, White House, 1958; mem. bd. nat. estimates CIA, 1959-62; dir. policy planning staff U.S. Disarmament Adminstrn., 1961; dir. research council, dir. program planning staff, sr. adviser ACDA, 1962-67; dep. CORDS, II Corps, Vietnam, 1967-68; dir. Office Internat. Tng., AID, Washington, 1968-71, Fgn. Affairs Exec. Seminar, Dept. State, 1971-72, Sigurd Olson Environmental Inst. Northland Coll., Ashland, Wis., 1972-74; Mem. planning bd. Nat. Security Council, 1955-58; dep. dir. U.S. Disarmament delegation, London, 1956-57; adviser to U.S. delegation Fgn. Ministers Conf., Geneva, 1957, Summit Meeting and Geneva 10 Nation Disarmament Talks, Paris, 1960, 18 Nation Disarmament Talks, 1962, Geneva; mem. adv. bd. Wis. Environ. Edn. Council, 1972-76; mem. Wis. Wild Resources Adv. Council, 1974-78, Wis. Snowmobile Council, 1974-76; chmn. Pres.'s Adv. Com. on Quetico-Superior, 1976-78; bd. dirs. Duluth-Superior Area Ednl. TV, 1977-81, Environ. Learning Center Minn., 1977-79, Minn. Sci. Mus., St. Paul, 1972—, Minn. Hist. Soc., 1981—. Trustee Northland Coll., 1974-75; chmn. bd. Glenview Found., 1981—. Served with 80th Inf. Div., 3d Army AUS, 1943-46, ETO. Decorated Combat Infantry badge, Silver Star for capture of Nazi Gestapo chief SS Gen. Kaltenbrunner; Littauer fellow, 1938-40. Mem. Assn. Governing Bds. Am. Colls. and Univs. (bd. mentor 1976—), Minn. Environ. Balance Assn., Internat. Inst. Strategic Studies. Clubs: Harvard of Minn; Explorers (N.Y.C.); Mill Reef (Antigua). Lodge: Lions. Home: Cable WI 54821

MATTHAI, DIEGO, architect, artist; b. Mexico City, Mar. 19, 1942; s. Horst and Margot (Springer) M.; m. Regina Esquivel-Obregon, Oct. 31, 1968 (div. 1973); 1 child, Cecil; m. Veronica Longoria, Sept. 19, 1974 (div. 1979); 1 child, Veronica; m. Beatriz Calles, Mar. 25, 1984. Architect (hon. degree), , Universidad Iberoamericana, Mexico City, 1965. Draftsman Jaime Herrasti Architect, Mexico City, 1962-69; prin. Diego Matthai Architect, Mexico City, 1968-72; ptnr. Matthai Arquitectos, Mexico City, 1972-77; pres. Matthai S.A., Mexico City, 1977—; ptnr. K.M.R. Designs, N.Y.C., 1984—; prof. basic design Escuela Nacional de Arquitectura, Universidad Nacional Autonoma de Mexico, Mexico City, 1972-80. One-man shows: Galeria Espace, Mexico City, 1970, Galeria I'Tatti, Mexico City, 1971, Palacio de Ballas Artes, Mexico City, 1973, W. Hunter Gallery, Beverly Hills, Calif., 1973, Ex-Convento del Carmen, Bellas Artes, Guadalajara, 1974, Galeria G.D.A., Mexico City, 1974, Galeria Pecanins, Mexico City, 1975, Galeria Edan, Acapulco, 1976, Galeria Mer Kup, Mexico City, 1976, Unicorne D'or Ltd., N.Y.C., 1979, Galeria El Nueve, Mexico City, 1980, Galeria Misrachi, Mexico City, 1981, 83, Foxworth Gallery, N.Y.C., 1985, Mexico's Gen. Consulate, N.Y.C., 1988; exhibited in numerous group shows, Mexico, U.S.; prin. works include various archtl. designs, design for line of furniture. Contbr. articles to various publs. Central Sch. Art and Design scholar, London, 1970. Mem. Colegio de Arquitectos de-Mexico, Sociedad Mexicana de Arquitectos, Artistas Independientes. Ind. study architecture, design and art in Europe, North and Central Am., 1966—; subject of numerous profl. publs.; subject of films, TV films. Avocations: writing; reading; traveling. Office: Matthai SA, Ave Parque Mexico 65, 06100 Mexico City Mexico

MATTHEI AUBEL, FERNANDO, military officer, government official; b. Osorno, Chile, June 11, 1925; m. Elda Fornet Fernández, 1951; 5 children. Student, German Colls., Osorno and Santiago, Air Force Sch. Commd. 2d lt. Chilean Air Force, 1948, advanced through grades to col., 1972, squadron comdr., 1960; adjutant to comdr. in chief, mem. personal staff 1961; group comdr. Chilean Air Force, 1966; sub-dir. Air Force Acad., 1967; group comdr. Air Force Group #7, 1968; air force attaché Chilean Embassies, U.K. and Sweden, 1971; head of mission London, 1972; dir. Air Force Acad., 1974; dir. ops., gen. staff Air Force, 1974; minister of public health 1976-78; comdr. in chief Air Force, 1978—; mem. mil. junta 1978—. Recipient numerous mil. decorations. Address: Oficina del Presidente, Santiago Chile *

MATTHEW, DAVID CHARLES CAMERON, information resources executive; b. Kans. City, Mo., Nov. 21, 1944; s. David Charles Cameron and Jewell (Cameron) M.; B.A. (Nat. Merit scholar), Columbia U., 1966, M.A., 1967, Ph.D., 1974; m. Marie Louise Nickerson, July 26, 1968; children—Elizabeth Constance Adams, Sayre Cameron Adams. Adminstrv. asst. Morningside Heights, Inc., N.Y.C., 1965-69; lectr. Bronx (N.Y.) Community Coll., 1968-70; instr. N.Y. Inst. Tech., 1970-71, City Coll. N.Y., 1971-74; editor Sagarin Press, N.Y.C., 1975; devel., mktg. cons. Model Decisions Corp., Breton Assos., Corporate Reporting Services, Rainhill Group Inc., N.Y.C., 1975—; program dir. Penton Pub. Co., N.Y.C., 1976-79; mgr. program devel. and adminstrn. Center for Mgmt. Devel., Am. Mgmt. Assns., N.Y.C., 1979-82; v.p., dir. Internat. Tech. and Comml. Services, Inc., 1978-82; editor Squash News, 1978-82; pres., chief exec. officer ITCS Software, 1982-84; mgr. strategic devel. Xerox Info. Resources Group, 1984-85; mng. dirs. Cameron Investment Advisors, 1985—. Volunteer promotional work state, local, fed. election campaigns, State of N.Y., 1966-68. Recipient Outstanding Sci. Student award A.T. & T.; writing award Nat. Inst. Arts and Humanities; Bausch & Lomb Sci. medal. scholar. Mem. IEEE Computing Group, Am. Soc. Tng. and Devel. (conf. dir. nat. productivity rev. 1980—), Assn. Computing Machinery, Nat. Trust for Hist. Preservation, Communications Industry Soc. Democrat. Club: Columbia. Author numerous mag. and newspapers articles, manuals, brochures. Home: 425 Riverside Dr New York NY 10025 Office: 1 Pickwick Plaza Greenwich CT 06830

MATTHEW, HENRY COLIN GRAY, historian, educator, editor; b. Inverness, Scotland, Jan. 15, 1941; s. Henry Johnston Scott and Joyce Mary (McKendrick) M.; m. Sue Ann Curry, Dec. 16, 1970; children: David H.C., Lucy E., Oliver J.G. BA, Oxford (Eng.) U., 1963, DPhil, 1970; PhD, Oxford U. Edn. officer Tanzania, 1963-66; lectr. Gladstone studies Christ Ch., Oxford, 1970—; fellow, tutor modern history St. Hugh's Coll., Oxford, 1978—; editor Gladstone Diaries, 1972—. Author: The Liberal Imperialists, 1973, The Gladstone Diaries, vols. 3-9, 1974-86, Gladstone 1809-1874, 1986; contbr. articles to profl. jours. Literary dir. Royal Hist. Soc., 1985—. Office: St Hugh's Coll, Oxford OX2 6LE, England

MATTHEW, LYN, art marketing consultant and educator; b. Long Beach, Calif., Dec. 15, 1936; d. Harold G. and Beatrice (Hunt) M.; m. Wayne Thomas Castleberry, Aug. 12, 1961 (div. Jan. 1976); children—Melanie, Cheryl, Nicole, Matthew. BS, U. Calif.-Davis, 1958; MA, Ariz. State U., 1979. Pres., Davlyn Cons. Found., Scottsdale, Ariz., 1979-82; cons., vis. prof. The Art Bus., Scottsdale, 1982—; vis. prof. Maricopa Community Coll., Phoenix, 1979—, Ariz. State U., Tempe, 1980-83; cons. Women's Caucus for Art, Phoenix, 1983—. Bd. dirs. Rossom House and Heritage Square Found., Phoenix, 1987-88. Author: The Business Aspects of Art, Book I, 1979, Book II, 1979; Marketing Strategies for the Creative Artist, 1985. Mem. Women Image Now (Achievement and Contbn. in Visual Arts award 1983), Women in Higher Edn., Nat. Women's Caucus for Art (v.p. 1981-83), Ariz. Women's Caucus for Art (pres. 1980-82, hon. advisor 1986-87), Vocat. Edn. Assn. (sec. 1978-80), Ariz. Visionary Artists (treas. 1987—), Ariz. Acad. Performing Arts (v.p. bd. dirs. 1987—, pres. 1988—).

MATTHEWS, DORIS BOOZER, education educator; b. Lexington, S.C., Aug. 18, 1932; d. Otto Raymond and Ruth (Sox) Boozer; B.S., Newberry Coll., 1952; M.Ed., U. S.C., 1955, advanced cert., 1971, Ph.D., 1972; m. Charles L. Matthews, Aug. 20, 1952; children—Shirley Ruth, Charles Ray, Sylvia Ann. Tchr., Brennen Sch., Columbia, S.C., 1952-64; supr. counseling S.C. State Employment Service, Columbia, 1964-66; counseling supr. and basic edn. specialist S.C. Com. for Tech. Edn., Columbia, 1966-68; instr. elem. edn. U. S.C., Columbia, 1968-72; asst. prof. Coll. of S.C. State Coll., Orangeburg, 1972-75, asso. prof., 1975-79, prof., 1979-86, disting. prof. 1986—; profl. lectr. Chmn., Columbians Youth Com., 1968-72, treas., 1966-72; chmn. Cayce Neighborhood Center, 1967-70. Mem. S.C. Edn. Assn., Assn. Supervision and Curriculum Devel., Employment Counselors Assn., Am., S.C. (pres. 1976-77) vocat. guidance assns., Am., S.C. personnel and guidance assns., S.C. Assn. Tchrs. and Educators (pres.-elect), AAUP (pres. chpt. 1976-79, pres. S.C. conf. 1981-83), Assn. Tchr. Educators, Assn. for Individually Guided Edn., Am. Vocat. Assn., Am. Humanistic Edn. and Devel., Internat. Stress and Tension Control Soc., Delta Kappa Gamma, Phi Delta Kappa (v.p. local chpt. 1978-79, pres. 1979-81). Lutheran (pres. ch. women 1971-74). Clubs: Cayce Womens (pres. 1965-67), Fashion Rose Garden (pres. 1962-64). Contbr. numerous articles to profl. jours. Home: 101 Deliesseline Rd Cayce SC 29033 Office: SC State Coll Orangeburg SC 29117

MATTHEWS, GARY LYNN, foreign service officer; b. Springfield, Mo., Jan. 24, 1938; s. Delbert Lee and Maurine (Cochran) M.; m. Virginia Webster, Feb. 28, 1967; children—Catherine, Andrew, Sarah. B.A., Drury Coll., Springfield, Mo., 1960; M.A., Okla. State U., 1961; M. Internat. Affairs, Columbia U., 1969. Commd. fgn. service officer Dept. State, 1961; rotational officer Am. embassy, Bonn, Fed. Republic Germany, 1962-64; ops. ctr. watch officer Dept. State, Washington, 1964-65; Polish lang. trainee Washington, 1965-66; consular officer Am. embassy, Warsaw, Poland, 1966-67; polit. and econ. officer Am. consulate, Poznan, Poland, 1967-68; internat. relations officer Office Soviet Union Affairs, Dept. State, Washington, 1969-71; asst. province adviser Quang Nam, Vietnam, 1971-72; dep. and sr. province adviser Thua Thien and Hue, Vietnam, 1972-73; dep. consul gen., polit.-econ. officer Am. Consulate Gen., Leningrad, USSR, 1973-76; dir. internat. bus. devel. State Govt. Mo. and Office of Gov., 1976-77; officer-in-charge multilateral polit. relations Office Soviet Union Affairs, Dept. State, Washington, 1977-80; spl. asst. to sec. of state's spl. adviser on Soviet affairs Dept. State, Washington, 1980-81, exec. asst. to undersec. of state for polit. affairs, 1981-82, exec. asst. to dep. sec. of state, 1982; mem. Exec. Seminar in Nat. and Internat. Affairs, Washington, 1982-83; sr. dep. asst. sec. of state for human rights and humanitarian affairs Dept. State, Washington, 1983-85; ambassador to Republic of Malta Valletta, 1985-87; spl. coordinator Soviet Union and Eastern Europe U.S. Dept. State, Washington, 1987—. Served with U.S. Army, 1955-58. Decorated Cross of Gallantry with bronze star (Vietnam); recipient Superior Honor award Dept. State, 1980. Mem. Am. Fgn. Service Assn. Home: 1204 Raymond Ave McLean VA 22101 Office: Special Coordinator M/SC Dept of State 1204 Raymond Ave McLean VA 22101

MATTHEWS, LESLIE SCOTT, orthopedic surgeon, educator; b. Balt., Sept. 18, 1951; s. Warren Gamelial and Jane (Black) M.; m. Julie Ann Nolan, June 13, 1981; children: Jonathan Nolan, James Nathan. B.A. in Natural Sci. Johns Hopkins U., 1973; M.D., Baylor U., 1976. Intern Johns Hopkins Hosp., Balt., 1976-77, resident in surgery, 1976-78, resident in orthopedics, 1978-81, asst. prof. orthopedic surgery, 1981—; asst. chief orthopedic surgery Union Meml. Hosp., Balt., 1981—; cons. Loch Raven VA Hosp., Balt., 1981—, Bethesda (Md.) Naval Hosp. Trustee St. Paul's Sch. Boys, Brooklandville, Md., 1982. Recipient C. Markland Kelly award Johns Hopkins U., 1972, 73, Barton Cup, 1973. Fellow ACS, Am. Acad. Orthopedic Surgeons; mem. Johns Hopkins Med. and Surg. Soc., Arthroscopy Assn. N.Am., Am. Soc. Sports Medicine. Episcopalian. Research on arthroscopic surg. techniques, particulary involving shoulder joint. Home: 101 Cotswold Rd Baltimore MD 21210 Office: Union Meml Hosp 201 E University Pkwy Baltimore MD 21218

MATTHEWS, ROBERT CHARLES OLIVER, economist, educator; b. Edinburgh, Scotland, June 16, 1927; s. Oliver Harwood and Ida (Finlay) M.; m. Joyce Lloyds, 1948; 1 child. M.A., Corpus Christi Coll. and Nuffield Coll., Oxford U.; D.Litt. (hon.), Warwick U., 1981. Asst. univ. lectr., then lectr. Cambridge U. (Eng.), 1949-65, master of Clare Coll., 1975—, prof. polit. economy, 1980—; Drummond prof. polit. economy All Souls Coll., Oxford U. (Eng.), 1965-75; chmn. Social Sci. Research Council, 1972-75. Author: A Study in Trade Cycle History, 1954; The Trade Cycle, 1958; (with F.H. Hahn) Economic Growth: A Survey, 1964; (with C.H. Feinstein, J. Odling-Smee) British Economic Growth 1856-1973, 1982; contbr. articles to profl. jours.; editor: Economic Growth: Trends and Factors, 1981. Fellow St. John's Coll., Cambridge U., 1950-65, All Souls Coll., Oxford U., 1965-75; hon. fellow Corpus Christi Coll., Oxford U. Office: Cambridge U, Clare Coll Master's Lodge, Cambridge CB2 1TL, England

MATTHEWS, WILBUR LEE, lawyer; b. Big Spring, Tex., Jan. 20, 1903; s. Robert D. and Sallie (Bourland) M.; m. Mary LeNoir Kenney, June 22, 1932 (dec. Oct. 1972); children: Wilbur Lee, John Kenney; m. Helen P. Davis, May 28, 1976. LL.B. with highest honors, U. Tex., 1926. Bar: Tex. 1926. Since practiced in San Antonio; with Matthews & Branscomb (and predecessors firms), 1926—, partner, 1930—. Contbr. articles to legal publs.; author: San Antonio Lawyer, 1983. Mayor City of Terrell Hills, 1939-41; mem. Tex. Finance Adv. Commn., 1960; trustee, chmn. San Antonio Med. Found. Fellow Am. Coll. Trial Lawyers; mem. Am. Law Inst., Am. Judicature Soc., ABA. Clubs: San Antonio Country, Argyle, San Antonio. Home: 200 Patterson Ave #806 San Antonio TX 78209 Office: One Alamo Ctr 106 S Saint Mary's St San Antonio TX 78205

MATTHEWS, WILLIAM JOHN, small business owner; b. Croswell, Mich., Jan. 1, 1919; s. Silas Oliphant and Lois O. (Arnot) M.; divorced; children: Lois, Carol, James, John, Robert. B of Music, U. Calif., Santa Barbara, 1941; student, Florence Conservatory, Italy, 1945. Owner, operator Wm. J. Matthews Piano Studio, Long Beach, Calif., 1946—. Author: Matthews Modern Music Methods for Piano and Organ (6 vol.), 1965—. Served to sgt. Signal Corps, U.S. Army, 1942-46. Republican.

MATTHIES, MARY CONSTANCE T., lawyer; b. Baton Rouge, Mar. 22, 1948; d. Allen Douglas and Mazie (Poche) Tillman. B.S., Okla. State U., 1969; J.D., U. Tulsa, 1972. Bar: Okla. 1973, U.S. Ct. Appeals (10th cir.) 1974, U.S. Ct. Appeals (8th and D.C. cirs.) 1975, U.S. Supreme Ct. 1976. Assoc., ptnr. Kothe, Nichols & Wolfe, Inc., Tulsa, 1972-78; pres. sr. prin. Matthies Law Firm, P.C., Tulsa, 1978—; guest lectr. U. Tulsa Coll. Law, U. Okla. Sch. Law, Oral Roberts U. Sch. Law. Mem. Women's Task Force, Tulsa Community Relations Commn., 1972-73; Recipient Tom Brett Criminal Law award, 1971; Am. Jurisprudence awards, 1971. Mem. ABA (mem. spl. subcom. for liaison with EEOC, 1974—, spl. subcom. for liaison with OFCCP, 1979—, mgmt. co-chmn. equal employment law subcoms. on nat. origin discrimination 1974-75, class actions and remedies 1975-80), Okla. Bar Assn. (council mem. labor law sect. 1974-80, chmn. 1978-79), Women's Law Caucus, Phi Delta Phi. Presbyterian. Contbr. articles on law to profl. jours.; mem. staff Tulsa Law Jour., 1971-72. Office: Reunion Ctr Suite 300 Tulsa OK 74103

MATTHIEU, FRANS, microbiologist; b. Aalst, Belgium, May 2, 1931; s. Benoit and Gabrielle (Lemaitre) M.; m. Therese Desaeger, July 28, 1978; children—Wolfgang, Igor, Johan. M.D., U. Liège, 1956; Dr. in Biochemistry, U. Ghent, 1958. Dir., Lab. Dr. Matthieu, Aalst, Belgium, 1960-82, Hosp. Lab., Aalst, 1964—. Dir. blood transfusion ctr. Red Cross, Aalst, 1960—. Author: Bloodtranfusion, 1964. Served to maj. Belgian Army, 1958-78. Mem. Soc. de Biologie Clinique. Roman Catholic. Lodges: Kiwanis. Home: Ninoofse Steenweg 109, 9440 Erembodegem Belgium

MATTILA, AARNE ILMARI, ceramics company executive; b. Oripää, Finland, Oct. 4, 1937; s. Kalle Juho and Maire Mirjam (Lehtinen) M.; m. Arja Onerva Voutilainen, June 10, 1967; children: Kristiina T., Klaus T., Karol, Kiril. PhD, U. Helsinki, Finland, 1969. Mng. dir. Oppikoulunopettajien Keskusjärjestö, Helsinki, 1966-70; personnel mgr. Säästöpankkien-Keskus- Osake-Pankki, Helsinki, 1970-73, Oy Wärtsilä AB, Helsinki, 1973-81; dir. personnel Oy Arabia AB, Helsinki, 1981—. Author: Työmarkkinasuhteiden Murros Suomessa, 1969; contbr. articles to newspapers and mags. Lutheran. Home: Ruonasalmentie 18 C, 00830 Helsinki Finland

MATTILA, SAKARI MARTTI, computer information scientist, consultant; b. Tampere, Finland, Sept. 14, 1949; s. Niilo J. and Edit M.; m. Hilkka K. Hanhenoja, May 23, 1973; 1 child, Esko Sakari Johannes. BS, U. Helsinki, 1975, MS, 1978. Systems analyst Population Registration Ctr., Helsinki, 1974-76; coordinator Finnish Data Products Assn., Helsinki, 1976-78; sr. scientist Tech. Research Ctr. of Finland, Espoo, 1979—; cons. in field of informatics. Author: (in Finnish) Software Industry in Finland, 1983, Research Aimed at Advancing Software Industry, 1984; editor: Nokia Compus, 1982, Collected References to Finnish EDP-Research, 1979; mem. editorial bd. Valokynä mag.; contbr. articles to profl. jours. Served with Finnish Army, 1978-79. Mem. Finnish Data Processing Assn. (mem. bd. reps. for membership 1981-83, pub. relations bd.), Helsinki Data Processing Assn. (bd. dirs.), Assn. Computing Machinery, IEEE, Assn. Computational Linguistics. Home: Laajalahdentie 26B25, SF-00330 Helsinki 33 Finland Office: Tech Research Ctr, Lehtisaarentie 2A/ATK, SF-00340 Helsinki 34 Finland

MATTOCK, JOHN NICHOLAS, Arabic studies educator; b. Horsham, Sussex, Eng., Jan. 6, 1938; s. Gilbert Arthur James and Margaret Kathleen (Gale) M. BA, Pembroke Coll., Cambridge, Eng., 1961, MA, 1964, PhD, 1968. Lectr. U. Glasgow, Scotland, 1965-76, sr. lectr., 1976-87; prof. arabic and islamic studies U. Glasgow, 1987—; organizer Arabic Poetry Symposium, 1981—; com. mem. Sch. Abbasid Studies, 1983—; United Kingdom rep. European Union Arabists and Islamists, 1986—. Editor Jour. Arabic Literature, 1970—; contbr. articles to periodicals. Fellow Brit. Soc. Middle Ea. Studies. Clubs: New Golf (St. Andrews). Office: The University, Glasgow G12 8QQ, Scotland

MATTON, GUIDO EMILE, plastic surgeon, educator; b. Etterbeek, Belgium, May 24, 1930; s. Gerard Gustaaf and Alice Jeanne (Van Langenhove) M.; m. Maria Theresia Van Leuven. MD, State U. of Gent (Belgium), 1955. Diplomate Am. Bd. of Plastic Surgery. Resident surgery St. Joseph Hosp., Mechelen, Belgium, 1956-57; fellow surgery Duke U. Hosp., Durham, N.C., 1957-58, resident plastic surgery, 1958-61, instr. plastic surgery, 1961-62; lectr. plastic surgery U. Hosp., Gent, 1962-69, prof. plastic, maxillofacial surgery, 1970—; plastic surgeon Holy Family Hosp., Gent, 1962—. Contbr. articles to profl. jours. Perrin C. Galpin fellow Belgian-Am. Ednl. Found., 1957-59. Fellow ACS; mem. Am. Soc. Plastic Surgeons (corr.), British Assoc. Plastic Surgeons (assoc.), Belgian Soc. Plastic Surgeons (pres. 1971-76), Dutch Soc. Plastic Surgery (hon.), Societe Francaise De Chirurgie Plastique. Home: P de Smet de Naeyerplein 5, 9000 Gent Belgium Office: Univ Hosp, De Pintelaan 185, 9000 Gent Belgium

MATTOON, HENRY AMASA, JR., advertising and marketing consultant, writer; b. Waterbury, Conn., Jan. 14, 1914; s. Henry A. and Sarah Currie (Hallock) M.; m. Dorothy Ann Teeter, June 20, 1936; children: Ann Brooks Wofford, David Scott, Sara Halsey, Judith Scott. B.S., Yale U., 1935. Mail boy, then copywriter, copy supr. Compton Advt. Inc., N.Y.C., 1935-44; v.p., creative dir. Compton Advt. Inc., 1944-50; v.p., chmn. plans bd. Ruthrauff & Ryan, Inc., 1950-52; v.p., creative dir. Dancer-Fitzgerald-Sample, Inc., 1952-54; pres., dir. Reach, Yates & Mattoon, Inc., 1954-56; chmn. marketing plans bd. McCann-Erickson, Inc., 1956-57, v.p., assoc. creative dir., 1957-62; v.p., gen. mgr. McCann-Erickson, Inc., Los Angeles, 1962-65; sr. v.p. and mgr. McCann-Erickson, Inc., Houston, 1965-68; v.p., dir. advt., pub. relations and sales promotion Yardley of London, Inc., 1968-69; partner Walter Weintz & Co., Inc., Stamford, Conn., 1969-70; prin. Otto Man Assos., 1967—; pres. Hamandot Co., 1976—; exec. v.p. Mktg. Lab, Inc., Danbury, Conn., 1986—; also bd. dirs. Mktg. Lab, Inc. Mem. Chi Phi. Clubs: Yale (N.Y.C.); Aspetuck Valley Country (Weston, Conn.). Home and Office: 11 October Dr Weston CT 06883

MATTSON, WALTER EDWARD, publishing company executive; b. Erie, Pa., June 6, 1932; s. Walter Edward and Florence Evelyn (Anderson) M.; m. Geraldine Anne Horsman, Oct. 10, 1953; children: Stephen, William, Carol. B.S., U. Maine, 1955; A.S., Northeastern U., 1959, hon. doctorate, 1980; postgrad., Harvard U. Advanced Mgmt. Program, 1973. Printer various cos. 1948-53; advt. mgr. Anderson Newspapers Co., Oakmont, Pa., 1954; asst. prodn. mgr. Boston Herald Traveler, 1955-58; cons. Chas. T. Main Co., Boston, 1959; with N.Y. Times Co., N.Y.C., 1960—, sr. v.p., 1972-74, exec. v.p., 1974-79, pres., 1979—, chief operating officer. Bd. dirs. nat. council Northeastern U. Served with USMC, 1951. Named Distinguished Alumni Northeastern U., 1974. Mem. ANPA (vice chmn. prodn. mgmt. com.). Office: The NY Times Co 229 W 43rd St New York NY 10036 *

MATUSZEWSKI, STANLEY, priest; b. Morris Run, Pa., May 4, 1915; s. Andrew and Mary (Czekalski) M.; grad. St. Andrew's Prep. Sem., Rochester, N.Y.; student La Salette Coll., Hartford, Conn., Scholastic Sem., Altamont, N.Y. Ordained priest Roman Catholic Ch., 1942; disciplinarian, prof. classics, La Salette Sem., Olivet, 1942-46, dir., 1948—; superior Midwest province LaSalette Fathers; founding editor Our Lady's Digest, 1946—; exec. bd. Nat. Catholic Decency in Reading Program; faculty adv. Midwest Conf. of Internat. Relations Clubs sponsored 1944 in Chgo. by Carnegie Endowment for Internat. Peace. Trustee Nat. Shrine of Immaculate Conception, Washington. Honored by Rochester, N.Y. Centennial Com. 1934 as Monroe County (N.Y.) orator. Mem. Mariological Soc. Am. (1954 award), Missionaries of Our Lady of La Salette, Catholic Press Assn., Canon Law Soc., Catholic Broadcasters' Assn., Religious Edn. Assn., Polish-Hungarian World Fedn. (trustee). K.C. Author: Rochester Centennial Oration; Youth Marches On. Home: Box 777 Twin Lakes WI 53181

MATZDORFF, JAMES ARTHUR, investment banker; b. Kansas City, Mo., Jan. 3, 1956; s. Ralph G. and Sophia (Barash) M. BS, U. So. Calif., 1978; MBA, Loyola U., Los Angeles, 1980. Comml. loan officer Bank of Am., Los Angeles, 1976-78; mng. ptnr. James A. Matzdorff & Co., Beverly Hills, Calif., 1978—. Mem. Rep. Nat. Com., 1980-88. Mem. Am. Fin. Assn., Phi Delta Theta. Republican. Office: 9903 Santa Monica Blvd Suite 374 Beverly Hills CA 90212

MATZEL, KLAUS HELLMUTH, linguist, educator; b. Borsdorf, Germany, Oct. 11, 1923; s. Hellmuth Paul and Margaretha (Werner) M.; m. Renate Sigrid Langer, Aug. 10, 1956; children: Katharina, Klaus. Abitur, Oberschule, Hamburg, 1946; PhD, Free U., Berlin, 1956; postgrad., Staatsexamen U., Berlin, 1957; Habilitation, U. Wurzburg, Fed. Republic Germany, 1968. Lectr. U. Ceylon, Sri Lanka, 1959-61; asst. prof. U. Wurzburg, Fed. Republic of Germany, 1961-68, prof., 1975-76; prof. linguistics U. Regensburg, Fed. Republic of Germany, 1968-75, 76—. Author: Die Ahd Isidor-Sippe, 1970, Einführung in die Singhalesische Sprache, 3d edit., 1987; contbr. articles on history of German lang. to profl. publs. Hon. fellow Sri Lanka Sahitiya Mandalaya, 1969. Home: Carl Thiel Strasse 12, 8400 Regensburg Federal Republic of Germany Office: U Regensburg, UniversitätsStrasse 31, 8400 Regensburg Federal Republic of Germany

MATZIORINIS, KENNETH, economist; b. N.Y.C., May 4, 1954; s. Neocles N. and Penelope (Gregoratos) M.; m. Catherine Marina Astrakianakis, July 27, 1985. B.A., McGill U., 1976, M.A., 1979, Ph.D., 1985. Asst. economist Nat. Bank Greece (Can.), Montreal, 1978-81; lectr. econs. McGill U., Montreal, 1977—; prof. econs. John Abbott Coll., Montreal, 1981—; pres. Canbek Econ. Cons., Inc., Montreal, 1983—. Econs. adviser to bd. dirs. Internat. Orgn. Psychophysiology, 1982—; bd. dirs. Can. Inst. Study Pub. Enterprise, 1980—. Author: Introduction to Macro Economics: An Applied Approach, 1988; editor: Vital Graphs of Canadian Economy, 1984; contbr. articles to profl. jours. Vice pres. Westmount Liberal Riding Assn., Montreal, 1975-77; bd. govs. McGill U., 1978-81; bd. govs. John Abbott Coll., 1988—; chmn. bd. dirs. Community Service Ctr. St. Louis, Montreal, 1978-80. Mem. Am. Econ. Assn., Can. Econ. Assn., Can. Assn. Bus. Economists, Internat. Orgn. Psychophysiology, Assn. Evolutonary Econo. Greek Orthodox. Club: Graduate (Montreal). Home: 619 67th Ave, Laval, PQ Canada H7V 3N9

MAU, WILLIAM KOON-HEE, financier; b. Honolulu, Apr. 25, 1913; s. Wah Hop and Mau (Ho Shee) M.; m. Jean Lau, Oct. 17, 1936; children—Milton, Cynthia, Lynette, Leighton, Letitia. Ed. pub. schs., Hawaii; LL.D., Pacific U., 1969. Chmn. bd., chief exec. officer Am. Security Bank, Honolulu, 1958-69; pres. Tropical Enterprises, Ltd. and Ambassador Hotel of Waikiki, Honolulu, Top of Waikiki Revolving Restaurant, Honolulu, 1955—; owner, developer Waikiki Bus. Plaza, Waikiki Shopping Plaza, Aloha Motors Properties; pres. Empress Ltd., Hong Kong, 1962-70, Aloha Motors, Inc. Vice chmn. Hawaii Bd. Land Natural Resources, 1959-63; Bd. dirs. Chinese Cultural Found., Hawaii, 1960—, Aloha United Fund, 1966—, Am. Nat. Red Cross, 1965—; past mem. exec. bd. Boy Scouts Am.; trustee Kauikeolani Children's Hosp., 1959-61. Recipient Golden Plate award Am. Acad. Achievement Bd. Govs., 1969; Wisdom Hall of Fame award of honor, 1969; named Bus. Man of Year Hawaii Bus. and Industry mag., 1966. Mem. Am., Hawaii bank assns., Newcomen Soc. N.Am., Am. Bd. Arbitration, Downtown Improvement Assn., United Chinese Soc., Tsung Tsin Assn., Hawaii Visitors Bur., Hawaii Islanders, Hawaii Pub. Links Golf Assn., Chinese C. of C. (dir., auditor 1959-62). Home: 3938 Monterey Pl Honolulu HI 96816 Office: Waikiki Bus Plaza 2270 Kalakaua Ave Honolulu HI 96815

MAUCERI, JOHN FRANCIS, conductor, educator, producer; b. N.Y.C., Sept. 12, 1945; s. Gene B. and Mary Elizabeth (Marino) M.; m. Betty Ann Weiss, June 15, 1968; children—Benjamin Robert. B.A., Yale U., 1967, M.Phil., 1971. Mus. dir. Yale Symphony Orch., New Haven, Conn., 1968-74; assoc. prof. Yale U., New Haven, Conn., 1974-84; mus. dir. Wash. Opera, Washington, 1979-82; music dir. orchs. Kennedy Ctr, Washington, 1979—, Am. Symphony Orch, N.Y.C., 1985-87; music dir. Scottish Opera, 1987—, Leonard Bernstein Festival, London Symphony Orch., 1986; conductor Am. Nat. Tour Boston Pops Orch., 1987; cons. mus. theater Kennedy Ctr. for Performing Arts, Washington, 1982—. Co-producer mus. play: On Your Toes, 1983; musical supr. Song and Dance, Broadway, 1985; music dir. PBS-TV Gala of Stars, 1987. Recipient Antoinette Perry award League of N.Y. Theatres & Producers, 1983, Drama Desk award, 1983, Outer Critics Circle award, 1983, Arts award Yale U., 1985; Grammy award for recording of Candide, 1987. Mem. Charles Ives Soc. (bd. dirs. 1986—), Am. Inst. for Verdi Studies (adv. bd. 1986—), Nat. Inst. for Music Theater (trustee 1986—). Office: care CAMI 165 W 57th St New York NY 10019

MAUCK, ELWYN ARTHUR, educator, administrator; b. Toledo, Iowa, May 5, 1910; s. Garfield Arthur and Elsie Caroline (Buck) M.; m. Mary Frank Helms, June 4, 1948. A.B., Cornell Coll., Iowa, 1932, LL.D., 1973; A.M. (Roberts fellow 1932-36), Columbia U., 1933, Ph.D., 1937. Staff mem. Inst. Pub. Adminstrn., N.Y.C., 1935, Inst. Pub. Adminstrn. (N.Y. Commn. for Rev. of Tax Laws), 1935-37; asst. prof. polit. sci. U. N.C., 1937-45, asso. prof., 1945-47; on leave 1942-47; chief reports and awards div. Office Civilian Def., Washington, 1942-45; teaching staff Dept. Agr. Grad. Sch., Washington; vis. prof. pub. adminstrn. U. P.R., Rio Piedras, 1945-46; chief orgn. and methods div. War Assets Adminstrn. (Nashville region), 1946-47; prof. govt. and politics U. Md., 1947-49; dir. Md. Fiscal Research Bur., Balt., 1948-53; lectr. McCoy Coll., Johns Hopkins U., 1949-53; vis. lectr. Goucher Coll., 1951, 52; pub. adminstrn. adviser Inst. Inter-Am. affairs, 1953-57; chief pub. and bus. adminstrn. div. USOM, Brazil, 1954-57; prof. pub. adminstrn. N.Y. U. in Ankara, Turkey, 1958-59; prof. U. Minn. Project in Seoul, Korea, 1959-62; prof. pub. adminstrn. U. Pitts., 1962-75, prof. emeritus, 1975—; chief party U. Mich. Project in Taipei, Taiwan, 1963-64, U. Pitts. Project in Zaria, Nigeria, 1965-67; dean Faculty of Adminstrn., Ahmadu Bello U., Nigeria, 1967; coordinator of GSPIA Doctoral Study, 1968-73; dir. GSPIA Nigeria program, 1968-73; mem. Md. Commn. on Pub. Welfare, 1948; exec. sec. Md. Joint Legis. Com. to Study State Mental Hosps., 1949, 51; cons. Md. Tax Survey Commn., 1949-51; staff dir. Md. Commn. on Adminstrv. Orgn. of State, 1951-53. Author: Financial Control in the Suburban Areas of N.Y. State, 1937; contbg. author: Public Administration in Puerto Rico, 1948, Outside Readings in American Government, 1949, County Government Across the Nation, 1951; editor: County and Twp. Sect., Nat. Municipal Rev, 1940-53; contbr. numerous articles to profl. mags., other publs. Vol. info. specialist Smithsonian Instn., Washington, 1976—; vol. tax cons. for elderly, 1986—. Mem. Am. Polit. Sci. Assn. (sec. D.C. home rule com. Washington chpt. 1947-48, exec. council 1948-50), Am. Soc. Pub. Adminstrn. (charter mem., pres. Md. chpt. 1949-50), Phi Beta Kappa, Pi Sigma Alpha (nat. sec., treas. 1949-52, nat. pres. 1952-54), Tau Kappa Alpha. Address: Route 1 Box 155-U Indian Head MD 20640

MAUDLIN, LLOYD ZELL, physicist; b. Miles City, Mont., Feb. 20, 1924; s. Lloyd Zell and Effie Lenora (Vick) M.; m. Lauralee Rose Williams, June 26, 1946; children—Craig, Lynn, Alicia, Dawn. B.A. in Physics, U. Calif. at Los Angeles, 1949; M.S. in Physics, U. So. Calif., 1952. Physicist, U.S. Naval Ordnance Test Sta., Pasadena, Calif., 1951-68; physicist Naval Ocean Systems Center, San Diego, 1968-82, electronics scientist, 1953-59, sr. physicist, 1960-82, head simulation and computer sci. dept., 1977-81; pres. Lloyd Z. Maudlin and Assocs., 1981—; group v.p. advanced sci. ctr. Integrated Systems Analysts Inc., Chula Vista, Calif., 1981—. Exec. v.p. JIL Systems, Inc., Arlington, Va., 1988—. Pres. Gifted Children's Assn., Los Angeles, 1968-70; trustee Los Angeles City Missionary Soc., United Methodist Ch., 1961-73. Served in USAAF, 1943-46. Recipient U.S. Govt. Meritorious Civilian Service award, 1953. Mem. IEEE (pres. oceanic engring. soc.), Computer Soc., Soc. for Computer Simulation, Am. Ordnance Assn., N.Y. Acad. Sci., AAAS. Republican. Patentee in field. Home: 5461 Toyon Rd San Diego CA 92115 Office: 70 Bay Blvd Chula Vista CA 92010

MAULÉON, SVEN VILHELM, management consultant; b. Lund, Sweden, Sept. 19, 1947; s. Yngue and Anna Greta M.; m. Elisabeth Arvidsson; children: Christina, Jennifer, Helena. MBA, Gothenburg Sch. Bus. Adminstrn., Sweden, 1971. Product mgr. Rank Xerox AB, Stockholm, 1971-73; corp. planning mgr. Rank Xerox AB, London, 1973-75; mktg. mgr. Rank Xerox AB, Stockholm, 1975-77, Wicander AB, Gothenburg, 1977-85, Uponor AB, Bora, Sweden, 1977-85; mgmt. cons. INDEVO AB, Hovas, Sweden, 1985—; bd. dirs. Scand Cons., Gothenburg. Contbr. articles to profl. jours. Bd. dirs. health dept. City of Gothenburg, 1981-86. Mem. Svenska Marknadsledargruppen, Svenska Civilekonom föreningen. Mem. Conservative Party. Home: Erik Dahlbergsg 6A, 41126 Gothenburg Sweden Office: INDEVO, Box 1035, 43080 Hovas Sweden

MAUND, DAVID JOHN, aerospace executive; b. Cheadle, Cheshire, Eng., Dec. 12, 1936; arrived in Australia, 1983; s. Harry and Mabel (Gleave) M.; m. Wendy Anne Bower; children: Susan, Timothy. BS in Physics, U. London, 1959; MS in Math., U. Ala., 1966. Aero. engr. A.V. Roe Co., Ltd., Woodford, Eng., 1959-61; research engr. Boeing Comml. Airplane Co., Seattle, 1961-83; sales dir. Boeing Internat. Corp., Sydney, Australia, 1983—. Patentee automatic flight control design. Mem. Royal Aero. Soc. Clubs: Australian Golf, Am. Nat. Office: Boeing Internat Corp, 60 Margaret St, 2000 Sydney Australia

MAUNG MAUNG, Burmese government official; b. Jan. 11, 1925. Law student, London and Netherlands. Past instr. Yale U.; former chief justice Supreme Ct., Burma, atty. gen., until 1988; pres. Burma, 1988; chmn. Burma Socialist Programme Party, 1988. Served with Burmese Independence Army, World War II. Address: Office of Pres, Rangoon Burma *

MAUNG MAUNG KHA, former prime minister of Burma, b. Nov. 2, 1917. Formerly mng. dir. Heavy Industry Corp.; minister of labour Socialist Republic of the Union of Burma, 1973-74, minister of industry, 1973-75, minister of mines, 1975-77, prime minister, 1977-88; mem. cen. exec. com. Burma Socialist Programme Party; mem. State Council, 1977—. Office: Office of the Prime Minister, Rangoon Burma *

MAUREL, RAYMOND ADRIEN AUGUSTIN, chemist, educator; b. Quins, France, Apr. 25, 1928; s. Emile and Marthe (Alary) M.; m. Adrienne Rudelle, July 30, 1951; children—François, Jean, Philippe, Michel. Agregation Physique, Ecole Normale Superieure, Paris, 1953; Ph.D., Lille U., 1959. Lectr. in chemistry Ecole Normale Supérieure 1954-57; asst. prof. Lille U., 1957-66; prof. chemistry U. Poitiers, 1966—; sci. dir. Nat. Center Sci. Research, Paris, 1977-84; dir. Inst. Catalysis, Lyon-Villeurbanne, 1984—; sci. adv. Elf Aquitaine; mem. sci. bd. Inst. Francais Petrole, Gaz de France, adminstrv. bd. Pechiney. Author papers on heterogeneous catalysis. Decorated officer Palmes Academiques, chevalier Legion of Honor, officier Ordre National du Merite. Mem. French Chem. Soc., Am. Chem. Soc. Home: 38 Ave de Bordeaux, 86130 Jaunay Clan France Office: IRC 2, Ave Albert Einstein, 69626 Villeurbanne-Cedex France

MAURER, CLAUDE EMILE, oil and gas mining executive; b. Chatillon sur/Seine, Cote d'or, France, Dec. 21, 1924; s. Robert and Yvonne (Chanonat) M.; Gladys May Espinosa, Sept. 7, 1966; children: Victor, Valerie, Yves. Degree engring., Ecole Nat. Arte e Métiers, Paris, 1945. Research engr. Soc. Nat. De Constrn. Aeronautique Du Nord, Paris, 1945-46; field engr. Schlumberger Overseas S.A., Indonesia, 1947-50; research engr. Ste. Prospection Electrique, Paris, 1950-56; field ops. supr. Schlumberger Surenco, Venezuela, Peru, Brazil and Argentina, 1956-62; mgr. field ops. Schlumberger Surenco, Caracas, Venezuela, 1962-64; pres., chief exec. officer Minar SAPS, Buenos Aires, Argentina, 1966—; pres., chief exec. officer Precimeca, Buenos Aires, 1974—, Maurer Tools Inc., Houston, 1979—, WYC, Inc., Houston, 1981—. Served to lt. French Navy, 1946-47. Mem. Soc. Petroleum Engrs., Inst. Argentino Petróleo. Roman Catholic. Clubs: River Plate (Capital Federal) Tiro Federal Argentina. Office: Minar SAPS, Maipu 267 piso 20, 1084 Buenos Aires Argentina

MAURER, JOSE CLEMENTE CARDINAL, German ecclesiastic; b. Puttlingen, Trier, Mar. 13, 1900. Ordained priest, 1925. Titular Bishop of Cea, 1950-51; Archbishop of Scure, Bolivia, 1951-83; elevated to Sacred Coll. of Cardinals, 1967; entitled SS. Redentore e S. Alfonso in via Merulana. Address: Arzobispado, Casilla 205, Sucre Bolivia *

MAURER, ROBERT (STANLEY), osteopath; b. Bklyn., Feb. 10, 1933; s. Gustav and Hilda Maurer; A.B. in Chemistry, U. Pa., 1953; D.O., Phila. Coll. Osteo. Medicine, 1962; m. Beverly Greenberg, Sept. 4, 1960; children—Ellen Jo, David, Andrew. Intern, Phila. Coll. Osteo. Medicine, 1962-63; gen. practice osteo. medicine, Iselin, N.J., 1963-75, Avenel, N.J., 1975-85; mem. med. staff Meml. Gen. Hosp., Union, N.J.; mem. med. staff JFK Med. Center, Edison, N.J., utilization rev. coordinator, 1985-88; dir. Med. Inter-Ins. Exchange N.J.; police and fire surgeon City Iselin; clin. asst. prof. N.J. Sch. Osteo. Medicine; clin. assoc. prof. Rutgers Med. Sch.; dir. alumni affairs UMDNJ Sch. Osteo. Medicine, 1986-88. Mem. N.J. State Gov.'s Task Force on Med. Malpractice, 1985-88; chmn. legis. com. N.J. State Med. Underwriters; candidate for N.J. State Senate, 1983, for N.J. State Assembly, 1987; dir. Osteopathic Mut. Ins. Trust, 1987-88, chmn. claims com. Served as lt. USNR, 1953-58; Korea. Fellow Am. Osteo. Coll. Rheumatology, Am. Coll. Gen. Practice; mem. N.J. Council Ambulatory Physicians (v.p. 1977-80), N.J. Assn. Osteo. Physicians and Surgeons (pres. 1976-77), Middlesex County Osteo. Soc. (pres. 1973-74), Am. Osteopathic Assn. Bur. Ins., N.J. Osteo. Edn. Found. (pres. 1984-88), Physicians Review Orgn. (bd. dirs. N.J. 1987-88), Phila. Coll. Osteo. Medicine Alumni Assn. (pres. 1981), VFW.

MAURIAC, CLAUDE, author; b. Apr. 25, 1914; s. Francois M.; m. Marie-Claude Mante, 1951; 3 children. D.Iur. Sec. to Gen. de Gaulle, 1944-49; film critic Figaro Litteraire. Author weekly lit. column La Vie des Lettres, Le Figaro; contbr. to L'Express, 1972—; Adminstrv. Soc. Figaro-Edition, 1972—; non-fiction: Aimer Galzac; Malraux ou le mal du heros; André Breton (prix Sainte-Beuve 1949); Marcel Proust par lui-meme; Conversation avec André Gide; Hommes et idées d'aujourd'hui; La litterature contemporaine; Un autre de Gaulle 1944-54, 1971; novels: Toutes les femmes sont fatales, 1957; Le diner en ville (prix medicis 1959), 1959; La Marquise sortit a cinq heures, 1951; L'agrandissement, 1963; L'oubli, 1966; plays: La conversation, 1964; Une amitie contrariee, 1970; Ici, maintenant, 1971; Une certaine rage, 1977; l'Eternité parfois, 1978; memoirs: Le temps immobile, vol. I, 1974, Les espaces imaginaires, vol. II, 1975, Et comme l'esperance est violente, vol. III, 1976, La terrasse de Malagar, vol. IV, 1977, Aimer de Gaulle, vol. V, 1978, Le Rire des peres dans les yeux des enfants, vol. VI, 1981; novels include Le Boudha s'est mis a trembler, 1979; Un coeur tout neuf, 1980; Radio Nuit, 1982, Zabé, 1984. Address: 24 quai de Bethune, 75004 Paris France *

MAURIZIO, BORGONOVO, sales executive; b. Milan, Oct. 1, 1953; m. Ciarmoli Rita Maurizio, Feb. 12, 1974; 1 child, Andrea Lupo. With sales dept. Italguns Ravizza Spa, Trezzano, Italy, 1971-75, Dalmine Spa, Milan, 1975-84, Redaelli Tecna Spa, Colognor, Italy, 1984—. Office: Redaelli Tecna SPa, via Pasubio 35, 20037 Paderno Dugnano Italy

MAURSTAD, TORALV, actor, director, theater manager; b. 1926. Ed., Royal Acad. Dramatic Arts, London. Mgr. Oslo Nye Teater, 1967-78, Nationaltheatret, Oslo, 1978-85. Appeared in plays, including: Peer Gynt, 1954, 85; A Midsummer Night's Dream, 1958; Hamlet, 1964; Arturo Ui, 1965; Brand, 1966; Cabaret, 1968; A Moon for the Misbegotten, 1976; films including: Song of Norway, After Rubicon, 1987; TV series: Last Place on Earth, 1984; dir. plays, including: Amadeus, 1980; Much Ado About Nothing, 1981; Hamlet, 1983. Office: Nationaltheatret, Stortingagt 15, Oslo 1 Norway

MAUSEL, PAUL WARNER, geography educator; b. Mpls., Jan. 2, 1936; s. Paul George and Esther Victoria (Sundstrom) M.; m. Jean Frances Kias, July 2, 1966; children: Paul Brandon, Catherine Suzanne, Justin Thomas. B.A. in Chemistry and Geography, U. Minn., 1958, M.A. in Geography, 1961; Ph.D., U. N.C., 1966. Asst. prof. geography Eastern Ill. U., Charleston, 1965-70, assoc. prof., 1970-71; assoc. prof. geography Ind. State U., Terre Haute, 1971-75, prof., 1975—, dir. Remote Sensing Lab., 1975—; research geographer Lab. Applications of Remote Sensing Purdue U., West Lafayette, Ind., 1972-73; soils geographer cons. U. Mo. at Columbia, summer 1974; lectr. in field. Contbr. articles to profl. jours., Chpts. to textbooks. NSF fellow, 1978; recipient research award Ind. State U., 1983. Mem. Assn. Am. Geographers, Soil Sci. Soc. Am., Am. Soc. Photogrammetry and Remote Sensing, Sigma Xi. Home: Rural Route 32 Box 85 Terre Haute IN 47803

MAVRINAC, ALBERT ANTHONY, educator; b. Pitts., Nov. 24, 1922; s. Anthony and Mary Theresa (Kvaternik) M.; A.B., U. Pitts., 1943; M.A., 1950; student Columbia, summer 1948; Ph.D., Harvard U., 1955; A.M., Colby Coll., 1960; Fulbright scholar, Inst. Superieur de Philosophie, U. Louvain (Belgium), 1950-51; Carnegie fellow law and polit. sci., Harvard Law Sch., 1961-62; m. Marilyn Parks Sweeney, July 3, 1954; children—Georgia Ireland, Susan Edwards Mullens, Sarah Clay, Emily Gregor, Anthony John. Labor relations specialist Office Mil. Govt., Hesse, Germany, 1946-48; lectr. polit. sci. U. Pitts., 1948-50; instr. Wellesley Coll., 1953; teaching fellow Harvard, 1953-55, instr., 1955-57, lectr., 1958, Allston Burr sr. tutor, 1956-58; Fulbright prof. univs Rennes and Montpellier (France), 1958-59; prof. govt. Colby Coll., Waterville, Maine, 1958-78, Charles A. Dana prof. govt., 1978—, chmn. dept. history and govt., 1958-79, chmn. dept. govt., 1979-82, acting dean students, 1970-71; nat. preceptor Grad. Program Public Adminstrn., Nova U., 1973—; fellow Duke, summer 1960; asso. dir. Insts. Communism and Am. Constitutionalism Am. U., summer 1963; project specialist Ford Found. and Inst. Pub. Adminstrn. for Egyptian Adminstrn., also adviser Govt. UAR, 1965-67; spl. asst. for legislation to gov. Maine, 1968-69; faculty fellow NASA, 1969; chief party Inst. Pub. Adminstrn. Adv. Group to Nat. Inst. Adminstrn., Vietnam, 1971-72; chmn. Nat. Fulbright-Hays Scholarship Screening Com. for France, 1976; Nat. Endowment for Humanities fellow Princeton U., summer 1977; lectr., cons. in field. Com. chmn. Gov. Maine Task Force Govt. Reorgn., 1967-68; founding mem. No. Kennebec Valley Community Action Com., 1965; mem. Maine Council Humanities and Pub. Policy, 1975-79; mem. U.S. del. to Madrid meeting European Security and Coop., 1980-82; active numerous Democratic campaigns in Maine, also nat. campaigns. chmn. Maine for Muskie, 1970. Served to 1st lt. AUS, 1943-46; ETO. Decorated Bronze Star, Combat Inf. badge; recipient Toppan prize Harvard, 1955. Mem. Am., New Eng. (past pres.) polit. sci. assns., Am. Soc. Polit. and Legal Philosophy, Am. Soc. Pub. Adminstrn. Roman Catholic. Author monographs, articles. Home: 47 Winter St Waterville ME 04901

MAWN, PAUL EVERETT, petroleum company executive, consultant; b. Woburn, Mass., Dec. 12, 1941; s. Everett James and Anastatia (McAvoy) M.; m. June Ellen Carroll, Aug. 1, 1964; children: Paul Everett, Christopher Alan, Elizabeth Carroll. AB in Geology, Harvard U., 1963; MBA, Rutgers U., 1970. Mgr. ops. Exxon Corp., Houston, 1965-73; sr. cons. Arthur D. Little, Cambridge, Mass., 1973-78; mgr. corp. planning Amerada Hess, N.Y.C., 1978-82; exec. v.p. Transmar, Boston, 1982-84; dir. petroleum Charles River Assocs., Boston, 1984-88; prin. Temple Barkder and Sloane, Lexington, Mass. Trumpet player Concord (Mass.) Band, 1974—. Served to lt. (j.g.) USN, 1963-65, capt. USNR, 1965—. Mem. Naval Res. Assn. Republican. Roman Catholic. Clubs: Harvard U. (N.Y.C.), Wardroom (Boston); Harvard U. of Boston; Nashawtuc Country. Avocations: music, jogging, tennis. Home: 11 Munnings Dr Sudbury MA 01776 Office: Temple Barker & Sloane Inc 33 Hayden Ave Lexington MA 02173

MAWYER, C. EDWARD, JR., retail company executive; b. Washington, Nov. 2, 1945; s. Clarence Edward and Doris Marie (Lytton) M. Sales mgr. wholesale div. Thom McAn Shoe Co., Worcester, Mass., 1967-74; dir. mktg. Wohl Shoe Co., N.Y.C., 1975; pres., chief exec. officer Mawyer Enterprises, Inc., Houston, 1976—; chmn. Mawyer Corp., Houston, 1981—; dir. Tex. Commerce Bank. Mem. Republican Nat. Com.; life mem. Two/Ten Nat. Found.; mem. Citizen's Adv. Bd. Sugarland, Tex. Mem. Nat. Shoe Retailers Assn. (bd. dirs.). Clubs: Sweetwater Country. Home: 206 Lombardy St Sugar Land TX 77478 Home: Mahogany Run Saint Thomas VI 00801 Office: 12852 Park One Dr Sugar Land TX 77478

MAXWELL, CHESTER ARTHUR, broadcasting executive; b. San Antonio, Mar. 29, 1930; s. Chester A. and Clara A. (Olle) M.; m. Carolyn King, Aug. 7, 1969; children by previous marriage: Sheryl Ann Mann, Karen Kay Maxwell Cervantes. Student, Trinity U., San Antonio, 1948-51; postgrad., U. Dallas, 1977-79. With advt. dept. Joskes of Tex. (dept. store), San Antonio, 1952-56; account exec., sales mgr. Sta. KBAT, San Antonio, 1956-63; account exec. Sta. KILT, Houston, 1964-68; asst. gen. mgr. Sta. KBOX/KMEZ, Dallas, 1969-71; v.p., gen. mgr. Sta. KBOX/KMEZ, 1972-86; founder, operator Sta. KEMM, Greenville, Tex., 1980-83; founder, pres. Metro Broadcast Monitor, Inc., 1987—; instr. Tex. Assn. Broadcasters Student Clinic, Howard Payne U., Abilene, Tex., 1962. Pres. Greater Dallas chpt. Muscular Dystrophy Assn., 1971-73; vice chmn., trustee North Tex. Multiple Sclerosis Soc., 1973-85 (Hope Chest award 1979); bd. dirs. Better Bus. Bur. Greater Dallas, 1983-87; v.p. Dallas/Ft. Worth Refugee Inter agy., 19834-87. Served with USMC, 1946-48. Named one of Dallas Men of Yr., Women's Equity Action League, 1975, 76; 1980 honoree Dallas Women's Ctr. Mem. Dallas Advt. League, Assn. Broadcast Execs. Tex. (sec. 1971, pres. 1974), Mensa. Club: Las Colinas Country (Dallas). Office: 5815 Grass Hill Dr San Antonio TX 78238-2327

MAXWELL, DAVID OGDEN, federal mortgage association executive; b. Phila., May 16, 1930; s. David Farrow and Emily Ogden (Nelson) M.; m. Joan Clark Paddock, Dec. 14, 1968. BA, Yale U., 1952; LLB, Harvard U., 1955. Bar: Pa. 1955, D.C. 1955. Assoc. Obermayer, Rebmann, Maxwell & Hippel, Phila., 1959-67, ptnr., 1963-67; ins. commr. State of Pa., 1967-69, adminstrn. and budget sec., 1969-70; gen. counsel HUD, Washington, 1970-73; pres., chief exec. officer Ticor Mortgage Ins. Co., 1973-81; chmn. bd., chief exec. officer Fed. Nat. Mortgage Assn., Washington, 1981—; bd. dirs. Kaufman and Broad, Inc.; trustee The Urban Inst., The Enterprise Found. Bd. dirs. Alliance to Save Energy. Served with USNR, 1955-59. Mem. ABA, Am. Bar Found. Home: 3525 Springland Ln NW Washington DC 20008 Office: Fed Nat Mortgage Assn 3900 Wisconsin Ave NW Washington DC 20016 *

MAXWELL, FLORENCE HINSHAW (MRS. JOHN WILLIAMSON MAXWELL), civic worker; Nora, Ind., July 14, 1914; d. Asa Benton and Gertrude (Randall) Hinshaw; B.A. cum laude, Butler U., 1935; m. John Williamson Maxwell, June 5, 1936; children—Marilyn, William Douglas. Coordinate, bd. dirs. Sight Conservation and Aid to Blind, 1962-73, nat. chmn., 1969-73; active various fund drives; chmn. jamboree, hostess coms. North Central High Sch., 1959, 64; Girl Scouts U.S.A., 1937-38, 54-56; mus. chmn. Sr. Girl Scout Regional Council, 1956-57; scorekeeper Little League, 1955-57; bd. dirs. Nora Sch. Parents' Club, 1958-59, Eastwood Jr. High Sch. Triangle Club, 1959-62, Ind. State Symphony Soc. Women's Com., 1965-67, 76-79, Symphoguide chmn., 1976-79; vision screening Indpls. innercity pub. sch. kindergartens, pre-schs., 1962-69, also Headstart, 1967—; asst. Glaucoma screening clinics Gen. Hosp., Glendale Shopping Center, City County Bldg., Am. Legion Nat. Hdqrs., Ind. Health Assn. Conf., 1962-73; chmn. sight conservation and aid to blind Nat. Delta Gamma Found., Indpls., Columbus, Ohio, 1969-73; mem. telethon team Butler U. Fund, 1964; symphoguide hostess Internat. Conf. on Cities, 1971, Nat. League of Cities, 1972; mem. health adv. com. Headstart, 1976—, health adv., social services com., 1987, sec., 1980—, assessment team of compliance steering com., 1978-79, 84, 85, 86, 87; initiated vision screening and eye safety edn. Jameson Camp, 1987; founder People of Vision Aux., 1981, bd. dirs., 1981—. Recipient Cable award Delta Gamma, 1969, Outstanding Alumna award, 1973, scholarship honoree, 1981; stellar award, 1986; appreciation award Headstart, 1983; Key to City of Indpls., 1972, those Spl. People award Women in Communication, 1980. Mem. Nat., Ind. (dir. 1962—, exec. com. 1971, sec. 1971-83, v.p. 1983-86, life hon. v.p. 1983—, vol. rep. to nat. 3-yr. program planning conf. Houston 1985, Internal Analysis Services Task Force for Strategic Plan, 1987, acting cast of Save the Sights of Ind. video film, 1988, Sight Saving Award 1974) socs. to prevent blindness, Delta Gamma (chpt. golden anniversary celebration decade and communication chmn. 1975, treas. Alpha Tau house corp. 1975-78, nat. chmn. Parent Club Study Com. 1976-77; Service Recognition award 1977, Shield award 1981, Stellar award 1986). Republican. Home: 1502 E 80th St Indianapolis IN 46240

MAXWELL, KATHERINE GANT, school psychologist, educational consultant; b. El Paso, Tex., Nov. 27, 1931; d. Leslie and Lillian (Beard) Gant;

B.S., Abilene Christian U., 1955; M.S., Miss. State U., 1967, Ph.D., 1974; m. Fowden Gene Maxwell, July 14, 1955; children—Steve, Becky Harvey, Randy. Teaching asst. Miss. State U., Starkville, 1969-72, practicum in sch. psychology, 1973-74; adminstr. psychol. tests Starkville Pub. Schs., 1974-75; sch. psychologist Dixie & Gilchrist (Fla.) County Schs., 1977-79; instr. continuing edn. dept. U. LaVerne (Calif.), 1979-80; sch. psychologist Bryan (Tex.) Ind. Sch. Dist., 1979-80; owner, dir. Reading Improvement Center, College Station, Tex., 1979-80, Assn. Interpersonal Devel., Inc., 1982—; sch. psychologist, ednl. diagnostician Temple (Tex.) Ind. Sch. Dist., 1980-81; sch. psychologist Franklin (Tex.) Ind. Sch. Dist., 1981-82; ednl. cons., College Station, Tex., 1982—; treas. Humana Sunshine Hosp. Aux., 1987-88; newsletter editor Friends Assn. of Symphony Orch., 1987-88, corr. sec., 1988—. Author: What Makes Bosses Tick, 1986. Cub Scout leader Boy Scouts Am., Starkville, 1960; Brownie leader Girl Scouts U.S.A., Starkville, 1961-64; pres. Starkville Overstreet PTA, 1962; sec. Starkville Civic League, 1962-65; vol. Crestview Retirement Home and Brazos Food Bank; active Mental Health Assn. Alachua County (Fla.), 1976-77; treas. Citizens Com. for Mental Health in Bryan, 1979-80, Humana Sunshine Hosp. Aux., treas., 1986-88; editor newsletter Friends Assn. Symphony Orch., 1987-88, corresponding sec., 1988-89; sec.-treas. Am. Cancer Soc. Brazos Valley, 1988—; vol. Crestview Retirement Home, Brazos Food Bank. Mem. Nat. Assn. Female Execs., Mid-South Ednl. Research Assn., Miss. Psychol. Assn., AAAS, Am. Psychol. Assn., Tex. Psychol. Assn., Brazos Valley Psychol. Assn., Council for Exceptional Children, AAUW (women's com. 1984—), Bryan-College Station C. of C. (OPAS gala program chmn. 1988), Bus. and Profl. Women's Club (Bryan/College Station br. newsletter editor, award com. mem.), Opera and Performing Arts Soc. (College Station/Bryan OPAS Gala Program chmn. 1988—, yearbook chmn. 1988—, sponsor 1987-89), Arts Council Brazos Valley, Nat. Edn. Honor Soc., LWV, Am. Pen Women (assoc.), Phi Delta Kappa. Clubs: Sorosis (sec. 1962-65, beginning bridge chmn. 1987-88), Tex. A&M Faculty Wives (beginning bridge chmn. 1987-88, sec. 1987-88), Tex. A&M Newcomers, Altrusa, Extension Service (1st v.p. 1984, sec. 1987-88, pres. 1988—), Exec. Wives, Campus Study (pres. 1988—), Book Rev., Brazos Beautiful (sponsor), Tex. A&M U. Social (pres. fine arts sect. 1988—, 3d v.p. 1988—). Clubs: TAMU Social (v.p. 1988-89), Fine Arts (pres. 1988-89). Address: Redmond Terr Sta PO Box 10027 College Station TX 77840

MAXWELL, RICHARD ANTHONY, retail executive; b. N.Y.C., Apr. 1, 1933; s. Arthur William and Mary Ellen (Winestock) M.; m. Jacqueline Ann Creamer, Oct. 27, 1962. Student NYU, 1957-58, Acad. Advanced Traffic, 1959. Import ops. mgr. Associated Merchandising Corp., N.Y.C., 1950-52, 56-65; v.p. Associated Dry Goods Corp., N.Y.C., 1965-86, sr. v.p. mktg., 1980-82, exec. v.p. mktg., 1982-86; pres. A.D.G. Export Mktg., Florence, Italy, 1982-86; pres. Assoc. Dry Goods Ltd., Hong Kong, 1983-86; pres. Inter Textyle Corp., 1987—; mem. industry sector adv. com. Dept. Commerce, 1984—. Mem. shippers adv. com. Nat. Maritime Council. Served with USAF, 1952-56. Recipient Silver medal for contbns. to trade expansion Republic of China, 1980; appt. to rank of comdr. in Order of Merit in recognition of improvement of trade between Italy and U.S., Republic of Italy, 1985. Mem. Am. Assn. Exporters and Importers (past pres., dir.), Shippers Conf. Greater N.Y. (past pres., dir.), Nat. Retail Mchts. Assn. (vice chmn. fgn. trade com.), Nat. Com. Internat. Trade Documentation (past vice chmn. gen. bus. com.), Transp. Assn. Am., Italy-Am. C. of C. (past pres., dir.), Am. Soc. of Italian Legion of Merit (dir.). Home: 47 Hardenburgh Ave Demarest NJ 07627 Office: 990 Avenue of the Americas New York NY 10018

MAXWELL, (IAN) ROBERT, publisher, film producer; b. Selo Slatina, Czechoslovakia, June 10, 1923; naturalized, 1945; s. Michael and Ann (Hoch) M.; m. Elisabeth Meynard, Mar. 15, 1945; children: Anne, Philip, Christine, Isabel, Ian, Kevin, Ghislaine. Self-educated; hon. doctorate, Moscow U., 1983; D.Sc. (hon.), Poly Inst. N.Y., 1985. Head press and publs. div. German sect. British Fgn. Office, 1945-47; founder, chmn., pub. Pergamon Press Ltd., Oxford, Eng., 1949—, also dir.; chmn. bd., pres. Pergamon Press Inc., N.Y.C., 1950—; chmn. Brit. Cable Services Ltd., 1984—, Mirrorvision, 1985—; chmn., chief exec. officer Maxwell Communication Corp. plc (formerly BPCC Ltd.), 1981—; chmn. United Oxford Football Club, plc, 1982-87, Derby County Football Club, 1987—, SelecTV plc, 1982, Mirror Group Newspapers Ltd., 1986; dir. Central Ind. TV plc, Hollis plc, The Solicitors' Law Stationery Soc. PLC, 1985—; chmn. MTV Europe 1987—; dir. TFL, 1987—, Agence Centrale de Presse, 1987—, Maxwell Media, Paris, 1987—; chmn. Gt. Britain-Sasakawa Found., 1985—; pres. European Satellite TV Broadcasting Consortium, 1986—. Co-producer films: Mozart's Don Giovanni, Salzburg Festival, Bolshoi Ballet, 1957, Swan Lake, 1968; producer children's TV series DODO the Kid from Outer Space, 1968; author: Public Sector Purchasing, 1968; Editor: Progress in Nuclear Energy: The Economics of Nuclear Power, 1963; Gen. editor: Leaders of the World series, 1980—, The Econs. of Nuclear Power, 1965, Pub. Sector Purchasing, 1968; co-author: Man Aive, 1968. Labour mem. Parliament for Buckingham, 1964-70; Chmn. Labour Fund Raising Found., 1960-69; chmn. labour working party on sci., govt. and industry, 1963-64; treas. Round House Trust Ltd., 1965-83; chmn. Commonwealth Games (Scotland 1986), Ltd., 1966; chmn. Nat. Aids Trust fundraising group, 1987—. Kennedy fellow Harvard, 1971. Mem. Newspaper Pubs. Assn. (council 1984—), Human Factors Soc., Fabian Soc. Gt. Brit., Internat. Acad. Astronautics (hon.), Club of Rome. Office: Maxwell House Fairview House Elmsford NY 10523

MAXWELL, WILLIAM STIRLING, retired lawyer; b. Chgo., May 2, 1922; s. W. Stirling and Ethel (Bowes) Maxwell Reineke. A.B. with distinction, U. Mich., 1947, postgrad., 1946-49, J.D., 1949. Bar: Ill. 1949, U.S. Ct. Mil. Appeals 1951, U.S. Supreme Ct. 1951. Assoc. Sidley & Austin, Chgo., 1949-60, 61, ptnr., 1962-84; now ret; sr. legis. counsel U.S. Treasury, Washington, 1960-61; dir. Santa Catalina Island Co., Avalon, Calif., 1974—. Trustee Mid-North Animal Shelter Found., Chgo., 1971—. Mem. Order of Coif, Phi Beta Kappa. Republican. Episcopalian. Clubs: Law, Legal (Chgo.). Home: PO Box 1776 Brookings OR 97415

MAXWELL-BROGDON, FLORENCE MORENCY, school administrator; b. Spring Park, Minn., Nov. 11, 1929; d. William Frederick and Florence Ruth (LaBrie) Maxwell; m. John Carl Brogdon, Mar. 13, 1957; children—Carole Alexandra, Cecily Ann, Daphne Diana. B.A., Calif. State U.-Los Angeles, 1955; M.S., U. So. Calif., 1957; postgrad. Columbia Pacific U., San Rafael, Calif., 1982-86. Cert. tchr., Calif. Dir. Rodeo Sch., Los Angeles, 1961-64; lectr. Media Features, Culver City, Calif., 1964—; dir. La Playa Sch., Culver City, 1968-75; founding dir. Venture Sch., Culver City, 1974—, also chmn. bd.; bd. dirs., v.p. Parent Coop. Preschools, Baie d'Urfe Quebec, Calif., 1964—. Author: Let Me Tell You, 1973; Wet 'n Squishy; 1973; Balancing Act, 1977; (as Morency Maxwell) Framed in Silver, 1985; (column) What Parents Want to Know, 1961—. Editor: Calif. Preschooler, 1961-74. Contbr. articles to profl. jours. Treas. Democrat Congl. Primary, Culver City, 1972. Mem. Calif. Council Parent Schs. (bd. dirs. 1961-74), Parent Coop. Preschools Internat. (advisor 1975—), Mystery Writers of Am. (affiliate), Internat. Platform Assn. Libertarian. Home: 10814 Molony Rd Culver City CA 90230 Office: Venture Sch 5333 S Sepulveda Blvd Culver City CA 90230

MAY, BRIAN ALBERT, academic administrator, agricultural engineering educator; b. Eastry, Eng., June 2, 1936; s. Albert Robert and Eileen (Ladd) M.; m. Brenda Ann Smith, Aug. 2, 1961; children: Christopher, Timothy, Jeremy. BSME, Aston (Eng.) U., 1962. Chartered engr., Eng. Design engr. Massey-Ferguson Co., 1962-63; lectr., then sr. lectr. Silsoe Coll. (formerly Nat. Coll. Agrl. Engring.), Bedford, Eng., 1963-72, head dept. agrl. engring., 1972-75, prof., 1975—, head Coll., 1976—, dean faculty, 1976-87; chmn. Brit. Agrl. Edn. and Tng. Service, 1984—; dir. Brit. Agrl. Export Council, 1985-88; mem. Brit. Council Agrl. and Vet. Adv. Com., 1985—. Author: Power on the Land, 1975; editor: Agrl. Engr. mag., 1970-75. Fellow Royal Agrl. Socs. U.K., Royal Agrl. Soc. Eng. (mem. council 1985—), Instn. Agrl. Engring. (pres. 1984-86), Am. Soc. Agrl. Engring., Instn. Mech. Engrs., Soc. for Research in Agrl. Engring. (bd. dirs. 1978—). Mem. Ch. of England. Club: Farmers (London). Office: Silsoe Coll, Bedford MK45 4DT, England

MAY, ERNEST MAX, charitable organization official; b. Newark, July 24, 1913; s. Otto Bernard and Eugenie (Morgenstern) M.; m. Harriet Elizabeth Dewey, Oct. 12, 1940; children: Ernest Dewey, James Northrup, Susan Elizabeth. B.A., Princeton, 1934, M.A., 1935; Ph.D. in Organic Chemistry, U. Chgo., 1938. With Otto B. May, Inc., Newark, 1938-73; successively chemist, gen. mgr. Otto B. May, Inc., 1938-52, pres., 1952-73; trustee Youth Consultation Service Diocese of Newark, 1952-59, 61-66, 68—, pres. Youth Consultation Service, 1971-75; dir. Cone Mills Corp., 1960-73, mem. exec. com., 1968-71; Tech. adviser to spl. rep. trade negotiations, 1964-67. Councilman, Summit, N.J., 1963—70; Mem. Summit Environ. Com., 1971-75, chmn., 1974; pres. Family Service Assn. Summit, 1959-61, Mental Health Assn. Summit, 1954, Summit Council Chs. Christ, 1962-63; mem. exec. com. Christ Hosp., Jersey City, 1971—, v.p., chmn., 1974—; Trustee, organizer Summer Organic Chemistry Inst., Choate Sch., Wallingford, Conn.; mem. Union County Mental Health Bd., 1973-76; bd. dirs. N.J. Mental Health Assn., 1974—; trustee Montclair (N.J.) State Coll., 1975-85, vice-chmn., 1976-80, chmn., 1980-83; adviser applied prof. psychology Rutgers U., 1976—; mem. Nat. Commn. on Nursing, 1980-83; adviser dept. music Princeton U.; trustee Assn. for Children in N.J., 1975—, Citizen's Com. on Biomed. Ethics in N.J., 1984—. Fellow Am. Inst. Chemists; mem. Am., Swiss, German chem. socs., Synthetic Organic Chem. Mfrs. Assn. (bd. govs. 1952-54, 63-70, v.p. 1966-68, chmn. internat. comml. relations com. 1968-73, hon. mem.), Vol. Trustees Not-For-Profit Hosps. (trustee 1986—), Sigma Xi. Republican. Episcopalian (vestry 1950-60). Clubs: Metropolitan Opera (N.Y.), Chemists (N.Y.); Beacon Hill (Summit, N.J.); Essex (Newark); Nassau (Princeton). Home: 57 Colt Rd Summit NJ 07901 also: State Rd Chilmark MA 02535

MAY, JAMES, industrial designer; b. Heilbronn, Germany, Feb. 27, 1921; s. Henry and Thekla (Saenger-Mai) M.; 1 dau., Vicki Barbara Anderson; came to U.S., 1936, naturalized, 1942. Vice-pres. Perspectives Inc., N.Y.C., 1948-49; dir. Inspire Industrial Design Workshop, N.Y.C., 1950-58; pres. James May Orgn. Inc., N.Y.C., 1959-81; pres. Vienna Workshop Ltd., 1981—, also dir. Exhibited Austrian Inst., N.Y.C., 1982, Mus. Applied Art, Vienna, 1984, Fashion Inst. Technology, N.Y.C., 1984, Bienale di Venezia, 1984, Williams Coll. Mus. Art, 1985, Mus. Modern Art, N.Y.C., 1986; represented in permanent collections: World Bank, Washington, Library of Congress, Washington, Met. Mus. Art, N.Y.C., Art Inst. Chgo., Research Libraries, N.Y. Public Library, N.Y.C., Germanisches Nat. Mus., Nürnberg, UNICEF, UN Children's Fund; guest lectr. art and design Kidderminster Coll., Worcester, Eng., Stellenbosch U. Cape of Good Hope Republic South Africa; guest speaker carpet symposium Durban, Republic South Africa, also Frankfurt (Fed. Republic Germany) Internat. Trade Fair. Mem. N.Y.C. Mayor's Adv. Council for Interior Furnishings and Design Industry, 1979—. Served to capt., Signal Corps, U.S. Army, 1942-46. Recipient Silver medal of Vienna, 1986. Author: Carpet Printing, 1973; The Vienna Workshop in America, 1982; Vienna Workshop/USA, 1983. Office: Vienna Workshop Ltd 137 E 36th St New York NY 10016

MAY, JOHN RALPH, journalist, editor; b. Worthing, W Sussex, England, Apr. 29, 1950; s. Ralph Whistler and Grace Kathleen (Shipton); m. Tanya Seton; children: Alex, Louis. Co-founder Clanose Pubs., London, 1972-81; freelance journalist 1974—; editorial dir. Greenpeace Books, Lewes, Eng., 1986—. Co-author: An Index of Possibilites, 1974, Worlds within Worlds, 1977, Curious Facts, 1980, Weird and Wonderful Wildlife, 1982, The Book of Beasts, 1982; author: Curious Facts 2, 1984, The Greenpeace Book of Antartica, 1988; contbr. over 300 articles to newspapers, mags., and jours.

MAY, PHYLLIS JEAN, businesswoman; b. Flint, Mich., May 31, 1932; d. Bert A. and Alice C. (Rushton) Irvine; m. John May, Apr. 24, 1971. Grad. Dorsey Sch. Bus., 1957; cert. Internat. Corr. Schs., 1959, Nat. Tax Inst., 1978; MBA, Mich. U., 1970. Notary pub.; registered real estate agt. Office mgr. Comml. Constrn. Co., Flint, 1962-68; bus. mgr. new and used car dealership, Flint, 1968-70; controller 6 corps., Flint, 1970-75; fiscal dir. Rubicon Odyssey Inc., Detroit, 1976—; acad. cons. acctg. Detroit Inst. Commerce, 1980-81; pres. small bus. specializing in adminstrv. cons. and acctg., 1982—; supr. mobile service sta., upholstery and home improvement businesses; owner retail bus. Pieces and Things. Pres. PTA Westwood Heights Schs., 1972; vol. Fedn. of Blind, 1974-76, Probate Ct., 1974-76; mem. citizens adv. bd. Northville Regional Psychiat. Hosp., 1988. Recipient Meritorious Service award Genesee County for Youth, 1976, Excellent Performance and High Achievement award Odyssey Inc., 1981. Mem. Am. Bus. Women's Assn. (treas. 1981, rec. sec. 1982, v.p. 1982-83, Woman of Yr. 1982), Nat. Assn. Profl. Female Execs. (bd. dirs.), Internat. Platform Assn., Pi Omicron (officer 1984-85). Baptist. Home: 12050 Barlow St Detroit MI 48205 Office: Rubicon Odyssey Inc 7441 Brush St Detroit MI 48202

MAY, RANDOLPH JOSEPH, lawyer; b. Wilmington, N.C., Aug. 11, 1946; s. Aaron and Norma (Eisen) M.; m. Laurie Eisenberg, Mar. 28, 1971; children—Joshua, Brooke. A.B., Duke U., 1968, J.D., 1971. Bar: D.C. 1973: U.S. Dist. Ct. D.C. 1973, U.S. Ct. Appeals (D.C. cir.) 1973, U.S. Supreme Ct. 1980. Law clk. U.S. Ct. Appeals (D.C. cir.), Washington, 1972-73; assoc. Steptoe and Johnson, Washington, 1973-78; assoc. gen. counsel FCC, Washington, 1978-81; ptnr. McKenna, Wilkinson & Kittner, Washington, 1981-86, Bishop, Cook, Purcell & Reynolds, Washington, 1986—. Pres. Chancellor Farms Civic Assn., Springfield, Va., 1975, Voluntary Action Ctr., Fairfax, Va., 1976. Named Outstanding Sr. Exec. FCC, 1980. Mem. ABA, D.C. Bar Assn., Fed. Bar Assn. (communications com. 1979-81), Fed. Communications Bar Assn. (jud. rev. com. 1981-83). Jewish. Home: 10701 Stapleford Hall Dr Potomac MD 20854 Office: Bishop Cook Purcell & Reynolds 1400 L St NW Washington DC 20005

MAY, TIMOTHY JAMES, lawyer; b. Denver, Aug. 3, 1932; s. Thomas Henry and Helen Frances (O'Connor) M.; m. Monica Anita Gross, Aug. 24, 1957; children: Stephanie Jean, Maureen, Cynthia Marie, Timothy James, Anthony C. B.A., Cath. U. Am., 1954; LL.B., Georgetown U., 1957, LL.M., 1960. Bar: D.C. 1957. With firm Covington & Burling, Washington, 1958-61; cons. Exec. Office President Kennedy, 1961-62; acting chief counsel subcom. stock piling U.S. Senate, 1962-63; mng. dir. Fed. Maritime Commn., 1963-66; gen. counsel Post Office Dept., Washington, 1966-69; mng. ptnr. Patton, Boggs & Blow, Washington, 1969—; gen. counsel New Process Co., Parcel Post Assn., Mail Order Assn. Am., Nat. Assn. Postal Suprs.; Lectr. English lit. Catholic U. Am., 1955-57; Mem. Nat. Finance Council Dem. Nat. Com. Mem. bd. regents Cath. U. Am. Recipient Presdl. award for economy achievement, 1964; Jump Meml. Found. Meritorious award, 1965, 66, 67; Arthur Flemming award, 1965; Postmaster Gen.'s Benjamin Franklin award, 1969; named Young Lawyer of the Year Fed. Bar Assn., 1967. Mem. Blue Key, Bar Assn. of D.C. (bd. dirs.), Legal Aid Soc. (trustee). Clubs: Metropolitan (Washington), Congressional Country (Washington); Indian Creek Country (Bal Harbour, Fla.). Home: 3828 52d St NW Washington DC 20016 Office: Patton Bogg Blow et al 2550 M St NW Washington DC 20037

MAYAUX, DANIEL HENRY, physician; b. Savonnieres, Meuse, France, Nov. 15, 1931; d. Eugene and Simone (Martinot) M.; m. Janine-Marié Martet, July 19, 1955; children: Luke, John, Mary-Peter, Francis. MD, U. Nancy, France, 1957. Practicing medicine specializing in gen. practice Montsous-Vaudrey, France, 1960—. Served as lt. French mil. forces, 1958-59, Algeria. Decorated Cross Mil. Valor with bronze star (France), medal of Algeria. Roman Catholic. Address: 8 Pointelin St, 39380 Mont-Sous-Vaudrey France

MAYE, RICHARD BOYKIN, clergyman; b. Uniontown, Ala., Oct. 25, 1933; s. Johnny and Frances (May) Boykin; B.A., Sangamon State U., Springfield, Ill., 1972, M.A., 1972, PhD, Internat. Theol. Sem., Van Nuys, Calif.; m. Rose Owens, June 24, 1978; children—Darryl Kermit, Byron Keith, Larry Lewis-Maye. Juvenile parole agt. Ill. Dept. Corrections, Chgo., 1967-70, adminstrv. asst., Springfield, 1970-72; lectr. polit. sci. Ill. State U., Normal, 1973-77; ordained to ministry Baptist Ch., 1960; pastor Pleasant Grove Bapt. Ch., Springfield, 1970—; mem. faculty Chgo. Bapt. Inst., 1968-70. Mem. Springfield Civil Service Commn., 1979—; mem. sch. integration commn., Springfield, 1977-79; bd. dirs. Morgan-Washington Home Girls, Springfield, 1977, Lincoln Library, Springfield, 1975-76, Springfield Area Arts Council; mem. grad. council So. Ill. U., 1975-76; mem. citizen's adv. com. Ill. Dept. Children and Family Services, Springfield, 1980-81, now chairperson com.; chmn. bd. dirs. Access to Housing, Springfield, 1981-83; sec., bd. dirs One Ch., One Child; bd. dirs. United Way, Sangamon County, Ill. Served with AUS, 1954-56. Grad. fellow U. Iowa, 1977-78, 79-80; grad. dean fellow So. Ill. U., 1975-76; recipient Citizen of Year award Springfield NAACP, 1976, Public Service award U.S. Dist. Ct., Springfield, 1978. Mem. Nat. Polit. Sci. Assn., Greater Springfield Interfaith Assn. (v.p.).

MAYER, AUGUSTIN CARDINAL, cardinal Roman Catholic Church; b. May 23, 1911. ordained 1935. Consecrated bishop Titular See Satrianum, 1972; then archbisho, proclaimed cardinal, 1985; prefect Congregation for Sacrements and Divine Worship. Address: Citta del Vaticano, Rome Italy *

MAYER, DIETER HEINZJORG, mathematical physicist; b. Freising, Federal Republic Germany, Sept. 22, 1943; s. Joseph and Rosalia (Abel) M.; m. Christiane Marie Guilbert, Oct. 1, 1977; 1 child, Francois-Claude. Diploma in Physics, U. Munich, 1969, Dr.rer.nat., 1972. Research fellow U. Munich, 1968-72; asst. prof. Aachen Inst. Tech., 1972-74; applied prof. Aachen Inst. Tech., 1985; vis. prof. I.H.E.S., Bures sur Yvette, France, 1975-76, 84, 85, Stephan Banach Inst., Warsaw, 1986, U. Warwick, Coventry, England, 1987; postdoctoral fellow Simen Fraser U., Vancouver, B.C., Can., 1976; vis. prof. U. Giessen, U. Essen, U. Heidelberg, U. Stuttgart, 1980-88; Heisenberg fellow Aachen Inst. Tech., 1981—. Author: The Ruelle-Araki Transfer Operator in Classical Statist. Mechanics, 1980. Contbr. articles to profl. jours. Heisenberg fellow, Deutsche Forschungs Gemeinschaft, Bonn, 1981. Mem. N.Y. Acad. Scis., Am. Math. Soc., German Phys. Soc., Assn. Math. Physicists. Home: Stolbergerstr 142, D-5100 Aachen 5100 Office: RWTH Aachen Theoretical Physics, Sommerfeldstr, D-5100 Aachen Federal Republic of Germany

MAYER, FREDERICK MILLER, retired business executive; b. Youngstown, Ohio, Oct. 8, 1898; s. Rev. Frederick and Carrie Ann (Miller) M.; m. Mildred Katherine Rickard, Nov. 25, 1926; children: Frederick Rickard, Elizabeth Ann (Mrs. Boeckman). B.A., Heidelberg Coll., Tiffin, Ohio, 1920, LL.D., 1948; J.D., Harvard U., 1924. Bar: Ohio 1924. Practice in Akron, 1924-26, Youngstown, 1926-32; treas. Continental Supply Co., Dallas, 1932-33; v.p. Continental Supply Co., 1933-45, dir., 1933-55, pres., 1945-56; pres. Continental-Emsco Co. div. Youngstown Sheet and Tube Co., 1957-64; v.p. Youngstown Sheet and Tube Co., 1956-64, mem. exec. com., 1964-69, dir., 1958-69; pres., dir. Continental-Emsco Co., Ltd., Continental-Emsco Co. Compania Anonima, Venezuela, 1956-64, Continental-Emsco Co. de Mexico S.A. de C.V., 1962-64; pres. Fibercast Co. div. Youngstown Sheet and Tube Co., 1960-64; chmn. Continental-Emsco Co. (Gt. Britain), Ltd., Eng., 1957-64; mem. Nat. Petroleum Council, 1961-62; industry advisor U.S. Dept. Commerce. Co-chmn. war fin. com. State of Tex., 1942-46; trustee Dallas Found. for Arts, Heidelberg Coll.; past mem. Dallas Transit Bd., Dallas Park Bd.; hon. trustee Dallas Mus. Fine Art, pres., 1959-61, chmn. bd., 1966-68. Mem. Am. Petroleum Inst. (past dir.), Mid-Continent Oil and Gas Assn., Petroleum Equipment Suppliers Assn. (hon. dir., past pres.), Ind. Petroleum Assn., Acacia, Huguenot Soc. Ohio, S.A.R., Pi Kappa Delta. Republican. Conglist. Clubs: Idlewild, Brook Hollow, Dallas Petroleum, Dallas Hunting and Fishing, Dallas (Dallas). Home: 3131 Maple Ave Apt 14H Dallas TX 75201

MAYER, JEAN, university president, scientist; b. Paris, France, Feb. 19, 1920; s. André and Jeanne Eugénie (Veille) M.; m. Elizabeth Van Huysen, Mar. 16, 1942; children: Andre, Laura, John-Paul, Theodore, Pierre. B.Litt. summa cum laude, U. Paris, 1937, B.Sc. magna cum laude, 1938, M.Sc., 1939; Ph.D. in Physiol. Chemistry (Rockefeller Found. fellow), Yale U., 1948; Dr.-ès-Sc. in Physiology summa cum laude, Sorbonne, 1960; hon. degrees; A.M., Harvard U., 1965; M.D., J.E. Purkyne Coll. Medicine, Prague, Czechoslovakia, 1968; D.Sc., Wittenberg U., 1975, Mass. State Coll. at Framingham, 1976, Worcester Poly. Inst., 1977, Ball State U., 1981, Med. Coll. Pa., 1982, U. Medicine and Dentistry N.J., 1983, Tokai U., Tokyo, 1985; D.B.A., Johnson and Wales Coll., 1976; L.H.D., Northeastern U., 1976, U. Lowell, 1988, Worcester Poly. Inst., 1977, Western New Eng. Coll., 1977, Starr King Sch. for Ministry, 1977; LL.D., Curry Coll., 1978. Fellow Ecole Normale Superieure, Paris, 1939-40, Rockefeller Found. Yale U., New Haven, Conn., 1946-48; nutrition officer FAO, UN, 1948-49; from asst. prof. to prof. nutrition Harvard U., 1950-76, lectr. history pub. health, 1961-76; mem. Center for Population Studies, 1968-72, 75-77, co-dir., 1975-76; master Dudley House, 1973-76; hon. asso., former master Population Studies (Dudley House), 1976—; pres. Tufts U., Medford, Mass., 1976—; Spl. cons. to Pres. U.S., 1969-70; chmn. White House Conf. on Food, Nutrition and Health, 1969; chmn. nutrition div. White House Conf. on Aging, 1971—; mem. Pres.'s Consumer Adv. Council, 1970-77; mem., vice chmn. President's Commn. on World Food Problems, 1978-80; gen. coordinator U.S. Senate Nat. Nutrition Policy Study, 1974; mem. FAO-WHO Adv. Mission to Ghana, 1959, to Ivory Coast and West Africa, 1960; mem. UNICEF mission to, Nigeria-Biafra, 1969, FAO-WHO Joint Expert Com. on Nutrition, 1961—; mem. protein adv. group UN, 1973-75; dir. Priorities on Child Nutrition UNICEF, 1973-75; bd. dirs. Monsanto Co., 1970-88, Nat. Intergroup, 1980—, Sta. WGBH, 1976—, Lycée Français N.Y.C., 1984—, Oppenheimer Fin. Corp., 1987—. Nat. Steel. Adv. bd. Sargent Coll. Boston U., 1955-72; mem. subcom. on med. services U.S. Olympic Com., 1966-70; mem. child health adv. com. Hood Found., 1964-69, chmn., 1968-69; mem. bd. inquiry on hunger in U.S., Citizens' Crusade against Poverty, 1967; chmn. Nat. Council on Hunger and Malnutrition in U.S., 1968-69; mem. food and nutrition bd. Nat. Acad. Scis., 1973-76. Author: Overweight: Causes, Cost, Control, 1968, Human Nutrition, 1972, A Diet for Living, 1975, Food and Nutrition in Health and Disease, 1977; Editor: (with others) Food and Nutrition in Health and Disease, 1972, U.S. Nutrition Policies in the Seventies, 1973, (with W. Aykloyd) Nutrition Terminology, 1973, Health, 1974, World Nutrition: A U.S. View, 1978, Food and Nutrition in a Changing World (with J. Dwyer), 1979, also numerous sci. articles.; Asso. editor: Nutrition Revs, 1951-54; nutrition editor: Postgrad. Medicine, 1959-71; editorial bd.: Jour. Applied Physiology, 1960-65, Family Health, 1969—, Postgrad. Medicine, 1976—; cons. editor: Environ. Research, 1967—, Jour. Nutrition Edn, 1968-70, Geriatrics Digest, 1968—; Syndicated columnist. Bd. dirs. Action for Boston Community Devel., 1964-70; bd. dirs. Am. Kor-Asian Found., 1976-83, French-Am. Found., 1976—, World Affairs Council, 1976—; bd. overseers Shady Hill Sch., Cambridge, Mass., 1965-68; mem. New Eng. Bd. Higher Edn., 1978—. Served to capt. French Army, 1940-45. Decorated Croix de Guerre with two palms, Gold Star and Bronze Star, knight Legion of Honor, Resistance medal, numerous others; recipient Gold medal City of Paris, 1936, Calvert Smith prize Harvard Alumni Assn., 1961, Alvarenga prize Coll. Physicians Phila., 1968, Atwater prize Agrl. Research Adminstrn., 1971; Presdl. citation AAHPER, 1972; Bradford Washburn prize Boston Mus. Sci., 1975; Golden Door award Internat. Inst., 1975; Poiley Gold medal N.Y. Acad. Sci., 1975; Pub. Edn. award Greater Boston chpt. Am. Heart Assn., 1976; gold medal Franklin Inst., 1978; Lemuel Shattuck medal Mass. Public Health Assn., 1980; numerous lectureships including 1st Charles Francis Adams lecture Tufts U., 1983, 15th McDougall Meml. lectr. FAO, UN, 1987. Fellow Am. Acad. Arts and Scis. (mem. council 1970-73), AAAS; fgn. mem. French Academie des Sciences; mem. Am. Inst. Nutrition (mem. council 1972-75), Am. Physiol. Soc. (editorial bd. 1960-66), Soc. for Nutrition Edn. (pres. 1974-75), Am. Soc. for Clin. Nutrition, Am. Pub. Health Assn. (chmn. food and nutrition sect. 1972-73), Phi Beta Kappa, Delta Omega, Sigma Xi, Beta Beta Beta. Unitarian (chmn. bd. trustees 1st parish, Sudbury, Mass., moderator 1959-66, vestryman 1970-74, sr. warden King's Chapel, Boston 1974-83). Clubs: Harvard (Boston), Somerset (Boston); Annisquam Yacht (Gloucester, Mass.); University (N.Y.C.). Office: Tufts U Medford MA 02155

MAYER, MICHAEL S., historian, educator; b. Balt., Aug. 27, 1952; s. Maurice Victor and Ruth Jane (Sobeloff) M.; m. Susan Elizabeth Bonar, May 20, 1984. BA magna cum laude, Duke U., 1974, MA, 1975; MA, Princeton U., 1977, PhD, 1984. Asst. instr., lectr. Princeton (N.J.) U., 1979-81; asst. prof. St. Vincent Coll., Latrobe, Pa., 1982-83; vis. asst. prof. U. Ala., Tuscaloosa, 1983-84; lectr. history U. Auckland, New Zealand, 1984—; vis. asst. prof. U. Ill., Urbana-Champaign, 1986-87. Author: Simon E. Sobeloff, 1980; contbr. articles to hist. jours. Mem. Am. Hist. Assn., Orgn. Am. Historians, So. Hist. Assn., Australian and New Zealand Am. Studies Assn., New Zealand Assn. Univ. Tchrs. Jewish. Office: U Ill 810 S Wright St Urbana IL 61801

MAYER, PETER EDUARD, consulting company executive; b. Munich, Dec. 13, 1945; s. Edward L. and Charlotte M. (Buck) M. MS in Engring., Tech. U. Munich, 1972; MBA, Inst. Européen d'Adminstrn. des Affaires, Fontainebleau, France, 1973; PhD in Tech., Tech. U. Innsbruck, Austria, 1987. Research asst. I.N.S.E.A.D., 1973-74; cons. Donhauser & Ptnr.,

Munich, 1974-75, sr. ptnr., 1976-78; pres. Prof. Burkhardt GMBH & Co., Munich, 1979—; bd. dirs. EGB, Munich; lectr. Augsburg Tech. Coll., also in field. Contbr. articles to profl. jours. Served with the West German armed forces, 1965-67. Mem. Inst. European d'Adminstrn. des Affaires Alumni Orgn., Verein Beratender Ing., Gesellschaft Fuer Project Mgmt., Dabei. Home: Wurzerstr 11, D-8000 Munich 22 Federal Republic of Germany Office: Prof Burkhardt GMBH & Co, Schwanthalerstr 73, D-8000 Munich Federal Republic of Germany

MAYER, WILLIAM EMILIO, investment banker; b. N.Y.C., May 7, 1940; s. Emilio and Marie Mayer; m. Katherine Mayer, May 16, 1964; children: Kristen Elizabeth, William Franz. BS, U. Md., 1966, MBA, 1967. Mng. dir., mem. exec. com., chmn. mgmt. com. First Boston Corp., N.Y.C., 1967—; bd. dirs. First Boston Inc., N.Y.C., Modular Computer Systems, Ft. Lauderdale, Fla. Bd. dirs. U. Md. Found., College Park, 1984—; trustee Cancer Research Inst. Served to 1st lt. USAF, 1961-65. Mem. Bond Club N.Y., Investment Assn. of N.Y. Clubs: Manhasset Bay (N.Y.); Univ. (N.Y.C.); Mashomack Fish & Game. Home: 172 Long Neck Point Darien CT 06820 Office: The First Boston Corp Park Ave Plaza New York NY 10055

MAYER, YANNICK MADELEINE, furnishing fabrics company executive; b. Fontenay, France, Feb. 14, 1954; d. Jacques and Gisèle (Gauttier) Thibault; m. Bertrand Mayer, Dec. 15, 1982; children: Maxime, Etienne. Student, European Bus. Sch., 1978. Asst. to dir. Preiss, Paris, 1978-80; asst. to dir. Romanex de Boussac, Paris, 1980-82, area export mgr., 1982-87, export mgr., 1987—. Home: 6 Rue Raspail, 92300 LeVallois France Office: Romanex de Boussac, 131 Rue du Bac, 75007 Paris France

MAYER-KOENIG, WOLFGANG, industrial director, author, educator; b. Vienna, Austria, Mar. 28, 1946; s. Ernst and Hertha (Koenig) Mayer. Sec. of Fed. Chancellor Austria, 1971-77; indsl. dir., mem. bd. Porr Co., 1978—; chmn. Austrian Meetings of Execs., 1974-77; founder Literarische Situation, Austrian U. Cultural Center, 1968-70; lectr. univs., France, Italy, U.S., Austria, 1978-82; mem. bd. Austrian Inst. Research Conflict; pres. Mozart Co.; mem. bd. Karl Renner Inst.; v.p. Pro Austria Nostra; exec. dir. Transportbeton KG; mem. adv.bd. PORR-Internat. AG; coordinator Internat. Meeting on Future Sci. and Tech.; coordinator negotiations between Austria and Arab States, 1975; chmn. Munich-Brenner-Verona railway line consortium; 1st v.p. internat. consortium "Asse Munich-Verone": co.-author Austrian Civil Service Law; author: Sichtbare Pavillons, 1969; Stichmarken, 1970; Psychologie und Literatursprache, 1975; Texte und Zeichnungen, 1975; Language-Politics-Aggression, 1977; Italienreisen Goethes, 1978; Robert Musils Möglichkeitsstil, 1979; In den Armen unseres Waerters, 1980; Vorlaeufige Versagung, 1985, Chagrin non dechiffre, 1986, Colloqui nella Stanza, 1986, The Corselet of the Mighty, 1986; also articles. Decorated Austrian Cross of Honor for Sci. and Arts, 1976; officer Egypt Order of Merit, 1979; Ordre des Arts et des Lettres de la Republique Francaise; Cross of Honor of Lower Austria, 1981; comdr. Order of St. Agatha, Republic of San Marino, 1982; Golden Medal of Merit, Internat. ARC, 1982; Papal Lateran Cross 1st class; Cross of Merit 1st class Abbas ducalis of Lilienfeld; Cross of Merit of Greek-Orthodox Papal-Patriarch of Alexandria, Egypt numerous others; recipient Theodor Körner prize, 1974. Mem. Accademia Tiberina, Akademie Burckhardt St. Gallen, Accademia Cosentina, Accademia d'Europa. Mem. Social Democratic Party. Roman Catholic. Home: 41 Hernalser Guertel, A-1170 Vienna Austria Office: 12 Rennweg, 1031 Vienna Austria

MAYER-KUCKUK, THEO, German nuclear physicist; b. Rastatt, May 10, 1927; m. Marianne Meyer, 1965; 2 children. Grad. U. Heidelberg. Research fellow Max Planck Institut fur Kernphysik, Heidelberg, 1953-59, sci. mem., 1964; research fellow Calif. Inst. Tech., Pasadena, 1960-61; dozent U. Heidelberg, 1962, Tech. U. Munich, 1963; prof. physics U. Bonn, 1965—, dir. Inst. Nuclear and Radiation Physics, 1965—; v.p. Internat. Union Pure and Applied Physics, 1984—. Author: Kernphysik, 4th edit., 1984, Atomphysik, 1977, 3d edit., 1985; contbr. articles to profl. jours. Mem. Acad. of Scis. of Nordrhein-Westfalen. Address: Inst fur Strahlen-und Kernphysik, Univ Bonn, Nussallee 14-16, D-5300 Bonn Federal Republic of Germany

MAYERSAK, JEROME STEPHEN, urologist; b. Superior, Wis., July 4, 1938; s. Joseph Walter and Libby Jean (Conroy) M.; B.A., Johns Hopkins, 1960; M.D., George Washington U., 1964; m. Priscilla M. Kurtzweil, Mar. 27, 1976; children: Kathlyne Mary, Priscilla Kathlyne, Tzena Lynne. Intern dept. surgery George Washington U. Hosp., Washington, 1964-65, resident in urology, 1966, chief resident, 1968; resident in surgery D.C. Gen. Hosp., 1965-66, resident in urology, 1966-67, sr. resident, 1967; resident in urology George Washington U. Sch. Medicine, 1966-69; sr. resident VA Hosp., 1968, chief resident, Washington, 1969; practice medicine specializing in urology, Wisconsin Rapids, Wis., 1969-71, Merrill, Wis., 1971—; urologist Med. Arts Group, Wisconsin Rapids, 1969-71; mem. staff Taylor County Meml. Hosp., Medford, Wis., 1970—, Good Samaritan Health Ctr. (formerly Holy Cross Hosp.), Merrill, Wis., 1971—, Tri-County Meml. Hosp., Whitehall, Wis., 1971—, Wausau Hosp. Ctr., Wis., 1985—; mem. cons. staff Riverview Hosp., Wisconsin Rapids, 1969-73, Sacred Heart Hosp., Tomahawk, Wis., 1971—, Wild Rose (Wis.) Community Meml. Hosp., 1970—, Neillsville (Wis.) Meml. Hosp., 1969-73; jr. cons. to St. Elizabeth's Hosp., Washington, 1968-69; clin. staff priveleges U. Minn. Hosps. and Clinic, dept. urology, Minneapolis; urologist J.S. Mayersak Service Corp., Merrill, 1971—; cons. urologist Langlade County Meml. Hosp., Antigo, Wis., Eagle River (Wis.) Hosp., Park Falls (Wis.) Hosp. Chmn. adv. airport com. to Airport Commn., Merrill, Wis., 1970-75; bd. dirs. Tri-County Meml. Hosp.; mem. peer review com. N. Cen. Health Protection Plan. Fellow William Beaumont Hon. Research Soc., St. George Cancer Soc., Internat. Coll. Surgeons; mem. AMA, State Med. Soc. Wis., Am. Assn. Physicians and Surgeons, Am., Internat. socs. nephrology, Minn. Urology Soc. (charter), Twin Cities Urol. Socs., Endourol. Soc., Flying Physicians Assn., Wis., Lincoln County (pres. 1974-78, 87), Aerospace med. socs., Am. Soc. Microbiology, A.C.S., Am. Coll. Utilization Rev. Physicians, Va. Acad. Scis., Pan Am. Med. Assn., Renal Physicians Assn., Royal Soc. London, Asociación Médica Panamericana, Sociedad Ecuatoriana de Urología (hon.), Am. Fertility Soc., Internat. Platform Assn., AAAS, Mensa, Soc. Profl. Pilots (charter), Sigma Xi, Nu Sigma Nu. Lodges: Elks, Moose. Home and Office: 717 Tee Lane Dr Merrill WI 54452

MAYES, S. HUBERT, JR., lawyer; b. Little Rock, Sept. 6, 1931; J.D., U. Ark., 1954. Bar: Ark. 1954. Asst. sec. Ark. State Senate, 1953; atty. Ark. State Revenue Dept., 1954-55; dep. pros. atty. 6th Jud. Dist., Ark., 1957-58; spl. asst. atty. gen. State of Ark., 1963; practice law, Little Rock. Fellow Ark. Bar Found., Am. Coll. Trial Lawyers; mem. ABA, Ark. Bar Assn., Pulaski County Bar Assn., Def. Research Inst., Assn. Trial Lawyers Am., Ark. Trial Lawyers Assn. Home: 2021 Beechwood St Little Rock AR 72207 Office: Laser Sharp & Mayes PA One Spring St Little Rock AR 72201

MAYFIELD, RONALD KEITH, endocrinologist; b. Morgantown, W.Va., July 15, 1950; s. Albert Keith and Mary Kathleen (Lemley) M.; m. Karen Elizabeth Gaspar, Dec. 27, 1970; children—Douglas Keith, Cortnie Anne. M.D., W.Va. U., 1975. Diplomate Am. Bd. Internal Medicine, Am. Bd. Endocrinology and Metabolism. Intern in internal medicine W.Va. U. Sch. Medicine, Charleston Area Med. Ctr., 1975-76, resident, 1976-78; fellow in endocrinology-metabolism and nutrition Med. U. S.C., Charleston, 1978-80, instr. medicine, 1980-81, asst. prof., 1981-86, asst. prof. lab. medicine, 1983-86, assoc. prof. medicine, pathology and lab. medicine, 1986—; staff physician, 1980—; cons. in endocrinology Med. U. Hosp., Charleston VA Med. Ctr., Charleston Meml. Hosp.; dir. specialized diagnostic and therapeutic unit VA Med. Ctr., 1984—. Bd. govs. scholar W.Va. U. Sch. Medicine, 1971-75; Mosby scholar W.Va. U. Sch. Medicine, 1972; Spl. Emphasis Research Career award NIH, 1980-85. Fellow ACP; mem. Am. Diabetes Assn. (research-rev. com. 1986—outstanding profl. service award S.C. affiliate 1983, bd. dirs. S.C. affiliate 1981-88), AAAS, Am. Fedn. Clin. Research, N.Y. Acad. Scis., Alpha Epsilon Delta. Democrat. Contbr. articles to profl. jours. Home: 1534 Candlewood Dr Mount Pleasant SC 29464 Office: Med Univ SC 171 Ashley Ave Charleston SC 29425

MAY-LEVIN, FRANCOISE, oncologist; b. Nancy, France, May 5, 1929; d. Adrien and Germaine (Picard) May. MD, U. Medicine, Paris, 1960. Research assoc. Hosp. Special Surgery, N.Y.C., 1960-62, N.J. Hosp., Jersey City, 1962-65; sr. med. instr. N.J. Coll. Medicine, Jersey City, 1963-65; chief of dept. med. oncology Inst. Gustave-Roussy, Villejuif, France, 1965—. Contbr. articles to profl. jours. Mem. European Soc. Med. Oncology, European Soc. Internal Medicine. Home: 49 Rue D'Alleray, 75015 Paris France Office: Inst Gustave-Roussy, Rue Camille Desmoulins, 94805 Villejuif France

MAYNARD, CLEMENT T., deputy prime minister, minister of foreign affairs and tourism of The Bahamas; m. Zoe Cumberatch; 5 children. Senator, Bahamas govt., 1967—, govt. leader, minister without portfolio, 1967—, minister of works, 1968-69, minister of tourism, 1969-79, 1984—, minister of labour and home affairs, 1979-84, M.P., Yellow Elder, 1979, 82, minister of fng. affairs, 1984—, dep. prime minister, 1987—. Mem. Progressive Liberal Party, 1954—. Address: Ministry Fgn Affairs and Tourism, Nassau The Bahamas *

MAYNARD, JOHN RALPH, lawyer; b. Seattle, Mar. 5, 1942; s. John R. and Frances Jane (Mitchell) Maynard Kendryk; m. Mary Ann Mascagno, May 1, 1945; children: Bryce James, Pamela Ann. BA, U. Wash., 1964; JD, Calif. Western U., San Diego, 1972; LLM, Harvard U., 1973. Bar: Calif. 1972, Wis. 1973. Assoc. firm Whyte & Hirschboeck, Milw., 1973-78, firm Minahan & Peterson, Milw., 1979—. Bd. dirs. Am. Heart Assn. of Wis., Milw., 1979-82. Mem. Wis. Adv. Council to U.S. SBA, 1987—. Served to lt. USN, 1964-69. Mem. ABA. Republican. Clubs: University (Milw.); Harvard (Wis.). Home: 6110 N Bay Ridge Ave Milwaukee WI 53217 Office: Minahan & Peterson SC 411 E Wisconsin Ave Milwaukee WI 53202

MAYNARD, LUTHER DEVERE, insurance company executive; b. Bridgetown, Barbados, Nov. 18, 1937; s. Martin Luther and Mabel Finlayson (Vaughan) M.; m. Yvonne Brinhilda Lewis, May 20, 1967; children: Kevin Devere, Astrid Yvette. BA, U. Man., Winnipeg, 1964, MA, 1965. Long grade clk. Acct. Gen.'s Office, Bridgetown, 1956-59; tchr. Portage La Prairie (Man.) Sch. div. #24, 1965-66; adult edn. instr., adminstr. Spl. Programs dept. Edn., Winnipeg, 1966-67; manpower counsellor, cons. Dept. Manpower and Immigration, Toronto, 1967-74; sr. project officer, dist. mgr. Employment Devel. br. Employment and Immigration Commn., Toronto, 1974-80; corp. sec. Ins. Corp. Barbados, Bridgetown, 1981—, Sedgwick Group Mgmt. Services (Barbados) Ltd., Bridgetown, 1985; manpower counsellor, cons. Youth Employment Service, Toronto, 1971-74; pres. York Condominium Corp. #125, Toronto, 1978-80; bd. dirs. Lynch's Secondary Sch. Ltd., Bridgetown, Barbados. Chmn. fund raising com. Combermere Sch. Parent Tchr. Assn., St. Michael, Barbados, 1984, 2d v.p., 1986—. Mem. Ins. Inst. Barbados (exec. council 1986—), Internat. Ins. Soc. Inc., Risk and Ins. Mgmt. Soc. Inc. Anglican. Office: Ins Co Barbados, Roebuck St, Bridgetown Barbados

MAYNARD, REID NORRIS, American literature educator; b. Oakley, Tenn., Dec. 31, 1924; s. Finis Connel and Eula Pearl (Smith) M.; m. Barbara Ann Kehoe, Apr. 1, 1961 (div. Feb. 1973). B.A., U. Calif.-Berkeley, 1953; M.A., San Francisco State U., 1960; Ph.D., U. Calif.-Davis, 1970. Instr. English, La. State U., Baton Rouge, 1960-62, Mills Coll., Oakland, Calif., 1962-63, Mont. State U., Bozeman, 1963-64, U. Colo., Boulder, 1964-66; teaching assoc. U. Calif.-Davis, 1966-70, lectr., 1972-76; assoc. prof. U. Toulouse (France), 1970-72; prof. U. Lille (France), 1976-77, U. Düsseldorf (W.Ger.), 1979-83; prof., head dept. English, U. Zululand, S.Africa, 1984—. Contbr. articles on Am. lit., poems, short stories to Am., French, German lit. jours., 1961—. Served with U.S. Army, 1943-48; ETO. Mem. MLA, German Assn. Am. Studies, English Acad. So. Africa.

MAYO, CLYDE CALVIN, organizational psychologist; b. Robstown, Tex., Feb. 2, 1940; s. Clyde Culberson and Velma (Oxford) M.; m. Jeanne Lynn McCain, Aug. 24, 1963; children—Brady Scott, Amber Camille. B.A., Rice U., 1961; B.S., U. Houston, 1964, Ph.D., 1972; M.S., Trinity U., 1966. Lic. psychologist, Tex. Mgmt. engr. LWFW, Inc., Houston, 1966-72, sr. cons., 1972-78, prin., 1978-81; ptnr. Mayo, Thompson, Bigby, Houston, 1981-83, founder Mgmt. and Personnel Systems, Houston, 1983—; counselor Interface Counseling Ctr., Houston, 1976-79; dir. Mental Health HMO Group, 1985-87; instr. St. Thomas U., Houston, 1979—, U. Houston Downtown Sch., 1972, U. Houston-Clear Lake, 1983—, U. Houston-Central Campus, 1984—; dir. mgmt. devel. insts. U. Houston Woodlands and West Houston, 1986—. Author: Bi/Polar Inventory of Strengths, 1978, LWFW Annual Survey of Manufacturers, 1966-1981. Coach, mgr. Meyerland Little League, 1974-78, So. Belles Softball, 1979-80, S.W. Colt Baseball, 1982-83; bd. dirs. Friends of Fondren Library of Rice U., 1988—. Mem. Houston C. of C., Houston Psychol. Assn. (membership dir. 1978, sec. 1984), Houston Area Quality Circle Soc., Tex. Psychol. Assn., Am. Psychol. Assn., Bus. Execs. for Nat. Security, Houston Area Indsl. Orgnl. Psychologists. Baptist. Club: Meyerland (bd. dirs. 1988—). Home: 8723 Ferris St Houston TX 77096 Office: Mgmt and Personnel Systems 4545 Bissonnet Bellaire TX 77401

MAYO, LOUIS ALLEN, corporation executive; b. Durham, N.C., Nov. 27, 1928; s. Louis Allen and Amy Earl (Overton) M.; student Calif. State Poly. Coll., 1948-50; B.A. in Criminology, Calif. State Coll., Fresno, 1952; M.A. in Public Adminstrn., Am. U., 1960, Ph.D. in Public Adminstrn., 1983; postgrad. U. So. Calif., 1960-62; m. Emma Jean Minshew, Oct. 31, 1953 (div.); children—Louis Allen III, Robert Lawrence, Carolyn Jean; m. 2d, Myrna Ann Smith, Feb. 16, 1980. Spl. agt. U.S. Secret Service, Treasury Dept., Los Angeles, 1956-58, 60-63, White House, Washington, 1958-60, 63-66; program mgr. law enforcement Office Law Enforcement Assistance, Justice Dept., 1967-68; acting chief Research Center, research program mgr. Nat. Inst. Law Enforcement and Criminal Justice, 1968-74; dir. tng. and testing div. Nat. Inst. Justice, 1975-87; pres. Murphy, Mayo & Assocs., Fairfax, Va., 1987—; lectr. criminology Armed Forces Inst. Tech., 1954-55; professorial lectr. Am. U., 1974-82. Served from 2d lt. to 1st lt. USAF, 1952-56. Mem. Internat. Assn. Chiefs of Police, Am. Soc. Public Adminstrn. (nat. chmn. sect. on criminal justice adminstrn. 1975-76), Am. Probation and Parole Assn., Acad. Criminal Justice Scis., Police Exec. Research Forum, Police Mgmt. Assn., Pi Sigma Alpha. Methodist.

MAYOCK, ROBERT LEE, internist; b. Wilkes-Barre, Pa., Jan. 19, 1917; s. John F. and Mathilde M.; m. Constance M. Peruzzi, July 2, 1949; children: Robert Lee, Stephen Philip, Holly Peruzzi. B.S., Bucknell U., 1938; M.D., U. Pa., 1942. Diplomate: Am. Bd. Internal Medicine. Intern Hosp. U. Pa., Phila., 1943-44; resident Hosp. U. Pa., 1944-45, chief med. resident, 1945-46, attending physician, 1946—; chief pulmonary disease sect. Phila. Gen. Hosp., 1959-72, sr. cons. pulmonary disease sect., 1972—; asst. prof. clin. medicine U. Pa., 1949-59, assoc. prof., 1959-70, prof. medicine, 1970-87, prof. emeritus, 1987—; mem. med. adv. com. for Tb Commonwealth of Pa., 1965-74, mem. med. adv. com. on chronic respiratory disease, 1974—, chmn. adv. com., 1981—; cons. Subsplty Bd. Pulmonary Disease Am. Bd. Internal Medicine, 1971-76; nat. bd dirs. Am. Lung Assn., 1983—, local bd. dirs. 1961—, local pres. 1966-69, dir. at large 1983—. Contbr. articles in field to med. jours. Served to capt. U.S. Army, 1952-54. Fellow ACP, Am. Coll. Chest Physicians (regent 1972-79); mem. Pa. Med. Soc., Phila. County Med. Soc., Physiology Soc. Phila., Laennec Soc. Phila. (pres. 1963-64), Am. Thoracic Soc., N.Y. Acad. Scis., AMA, Am. Fedn. Clin. Research, Am. Heart Assn., Pa. Lung Assn. (dir. 1976-86), Sigma Xi, Alpha Omega Alpha. Clubs: Merion Cricket, Swiftwater Reserve. Home: 244 Gypsy Ln Wynnewood PA 19096 Office: U Pa Ravdin Bldg 3d Floor Suite 1 Philadelphia PA 19104

MAYOR ZAROGOZA, FEDERICO, university official, politician; b. Barcelona, Spain, Jan. 27, 1934; s. Federico Mayor and Juana Zaragoza; m. Maria Angeles Menéndez, 1956; 3 children. Studetn, Madrid U. Prof. biochemistry Faculty Pharmacy Granada (Spain) U., 1963, rector, 1968-72; rector Autonomous U., Madrid; chair Higher Council of Sci. Investigations; under-sec. Ministry for Edn. and Sci. Govt. of Spain, 1974, minister for edn. and sci., 1981-82; mem. Cortes for Granada, 1977-78; chair Adv. Com. Sci. and Tech. Investigations, 1977; dep. dir.-gen. UNESCO, 1978-81, dir., 1987—; pres. Com. for Study of Spl. Set of Rules for the Four Catalan Provinces, 1976. Contbr. articles to profl. jours. Mem. Royal Acad. of Pharmacy, European Acad. of Arts, Scis. and Humanities, Internat. Brain Research Orgn., (mem. policy bd., interaction council), Club of Rome. Office: UNESCO, 7 place de Fontenay, 75700 Paris France *

MAYS, WILLIAM GAY, II, lawyer, real estate developer; b. Washington, Mo., Apr. 8, 1947; s. Frank G. and Geneva Pauline (Brookhart) M.; m. Judith Ann Kriete, Oct. 5, 1974; 1 son, Daniel Brookhart. A.B., U. Mo., 1969, J.D., 1972. Bar: Mo. 1972, U.S. Dist. Ct. (we. dist.) Mo. 1972. Legis. researcher State of Mo., 1972; pub. defender 13th Jud. Cir. Mo., 1973-77; ptnr. Holt, Mays & Brady, Columbia, 1977—; ptnr. and gen. counsel comml. real estate devel. firm. Mem. Jud. Planning Commn., Mo., 1977. Served to capt. USAFR, 1969-82. Named Outstanding Young Man of Am., 1974. Mem. Mo. Bar Assn., Boone and Callaway County Bar Assn., Mo. Trial Lawyers Assn., Mo. Pub. Defender Assn. (pres. 1976-77), Beta Theta Pi. Republican. Club: Masons. Office: The Mays Bldg 200 E Walnut Columbia MO 65203

MAYSTADT, PHILIPPE, government official; b. Mar. 14, 1948; married; 3 children. LLB, Cath. U., Louvain, Belgium; MA in Pub. Adminstrn. Asst. prof. Cath. U. of Louvain, 1973; counselor minister of Walloon Affairs Govt. of Belgium, 1974; mem. Ho. of Reps. Dist. of Charleroi, Belgium, 1977; jr. minister of regional economy and planning Walloon Region, 1979-80; minister pub. service and sci. policy 1981-85, minister of econ. affairs, 1985-88, vice prime minister, 1986-88, minister of fin., 1988—. Co-author book The Intervention of Pub. Authorities in the Econ. Life, 1973 (recipient spl. prize Belgian Lawyers Assn.). Office: Ministry of Fin, Brussels Belgium *

MAYUR, RASHMI, urban planner, director; b. Bombay. MA, Bombay U., 1954; PhD, NYU. Dir. Urban Devel. Inst., Bombay, 1976-86; pres. Global Futures Network, Bombay, 1986—. Editor: Optimistic Outlooks, 1982, Bombay 2000 AD, 1986. Recipient Sci. and Tech. award Internat. Jaycees, Bombay, 1979, Indo-Japanese Assn. award, Bombay, 1987.

MAZANKOWSKI, DONALD FRANK, Canadian government official; b. Viking, Alta., Can., July 27, 1935; s. Frank and Dora (Lonowski) M.; m. Lorraine Poleschuk, Sept. 6, 1958; children: Gregory, Roger, Donald. Student, pub. schs. Mem. Progressive Conservative House of Commons, 1968—, chmn. com. transp., 1972-74, mem. com. govt. ops., 1976-77, mem. com. trans. and communication, 1977-79; minister of transp. Can. Govt., 1979-80, 84-86; minister responsible for Can. Wheat Bd., 1979-80; dep. prime minister, pres. Queen's Privy Council, govt. leader in House of Commons, pres. Treasury Bd. 1986—; apptd. minister responsible for Privatization and Regulatory Affairs. Trustee Vegreville Sch. Bd., 1963-68; mem. Vegreville and Dist. Credit Union; regional dir. Alta. Progressive Conservative Assn., 1962, No. v.p., 1963, No. chmn. orgn., 1964; pres. Vegreville Progressive Conservative Assn., 1963-68. Mem. Commonwealth Parliamentary Assn., Interparliamentary Union, Can. NATO Parliamenty Assn., Can. World Federalist Parliamentary Assn., Vegreville C. of C., Royal Can. Legion (hon.), Alta. Fish and Game Assn., Indian Assn. Alta. Roman Catholic. Club: Vegreville Rotary (past dir.). Lodge: KC. Office: House of Commons, Ottawa, ON Canada K1A 0A6

MAZARAKIS, MICHAEL GERASSIMOS, physicist, researcher; b. Volos, Greece, Apr. 25, 1947; came to U.S., 1966, naturalized, 1980; s. Gerassimos Nikolaos and Anthie Gerassimos (Kappatos) M. B.S. in Physics, U. Athens, Greece, 1960; M.S. in Physics, U. Sorbonne, Paris, 1963, Ph.D. in Physics, 1965; Ph.D. in Physics, U. Pa., 1971; cert. in mgmt., MIT, 1976. Mem. faculty Rutgers U., New Brunswick, N.J., 1971-74; v.p. and dir. exptl. program Fusion Energy Corp., Princeton, N.J., 1974-77, also exec. v.p., 1975-77; research physicist Argonne Nat. Lab., U. Chgo., 1978-81; research physicist Sandia Nat. Lab. Div. 1272, Albuquerque, 1981—. Contbr. articles to profl. jours. Patentee in field. Bd. dirs. Orthodox Ch., Albuquerque, 1981-83; Served to maj. Greek Army, 1960-62. Recipient award Italian. Govt., 1956, Greek Govt., 1956-60, French Govt., 1962-65; Yale U. grantee, 1966. Mem. Am. Phys. Soc., IEEE, Alliance Francaise, N. Mex. Mountain Club, N.Y. Acad. Sci., Sigma Xi. Current work: Particle beam physics, accelerator research and development, inertial fusion, pulse power technology, plasma physics. Subspecialty: Nuclear fusion, particle beam physics.

MAZDA, FRED RUSTOM, furniture rental and sales company executive; b. Poona, India, Mar. 7, 1928; came to U.S., 1949; s. Rustom Fraidoon and Gool Banoo (Irani) M.; m. Concetta Theresa Mallace, Sept. 12, 1953; children—Russell Fred, Kenneth Fred, Sheila Estelle. B.Commerce, U. Poona, 1949; M.B.A., U. Pa., 1951. Head buyer John Wanamaker Dept. Store, Phila., 1975-77, sr. head buyer, 1977-80, divisional mdse. mgr., v.p., 1980; pres., chief exec. officer Nationwide Furniture Rentals and Sales, Inc., Phila., 1981—, chmn., 1981—; cons. Tech. Services, Phila., 1983—. Active Republican Nat. Com., 1981—; life mem. Rep. Presdl. Task Force. Zoroastrian. Mem. Am. Security Council (nat. adv. bd.). Club: U.S. Senatorial. Avocations: golf, travel, tennis, swimming, photography. Home: 409 Atwater Rd Broomall PA 19008 Office: Nationwide Furniture Rental and Sales Inc 2440 E Venango St Philadelphia PA 19134

MAZEL, JOSEPH LUCAS, corporate publications executive; b. Paterson, N.J., Oct. 1, 1939; s. Joseph Anthony and Anne (Kidon) M.; children—Joseph William, Jeanne Eileen. B.M.E., Newark Coll. Engring., 1960. Mech. engr. Austin Co., Roselle, N.J., 1960-61; engr. Western Electric Co., Newark, Atlanta, 1961-62; asst. asso., sr. editor Factory mag. McGraw-Hill Publs. Co., N.Y.C., 1962-71, editor-in-chief, sr. editor 33 Metal Producing mag., 1971-85, chmn. editorial bd., 1980-82; pub. relations account supr. Hammond Farrell Inc., N.Y.C., 1985-87; mgr. publs. Siemens Corp. Research and Support, Inc., Iselin, N.J., 1987—; guest lectr. Writers Conf., N.J. Inst. Tech., 1972-83; mem. editorial adv. com. Tech. and Soc. publ., 1981-85. Mem. N.G., 1963-69. Recipient Apolloneer award Gen. Electric Co., 1966; Jesse H. Neal cert. of merit, 1977, 79, 83; Jesse H. Neal Editorial Achievement award, 1979; named to Alumni Achievement Honor Roll, N.J. Inst. Tech., 1979, Wise Old Owl award U.S. Steel Corp. Mem. Soc. Profl. Journalists, Sigma Delta Chi. Lodge: KC (grand knight 1967-68, trustee); Pitts. Press; Deadline. Home: 40-22 Tierney Place Fair Lawn NJ 07410

MAZE-SENCIER, ROBERT ALFRED, business executive; b. Paris, Oct. 15, 1930; s. Jacques and Henriette Pinot (de Villechenon) M.-S.; m. Marie-Joseph Minier, Oct. 15, 1966; children: Emmanuel, Clémence. Degree in Advanced Mgmt. Program, Harvard U., 1970. Chief orgn. Kodak Pathe, 1961; dir. comml., Africa Librairie Hachette, 1962-69; pres., dir. Soc. Applied Research, 1972-77; exec. v.p. Christian Dior, S.A., Paris, 1981-82; dir. Moet-Hennessy, Paris, 1982—; pres., dir. RoC, S.A., Colombes, France, 1985—. Office: Moet-Hennessy, 30 Ave Hoche, Paris France

MAZLEN, ROGER GEOFFREY, physician, clinical pharmacologist and nutritionist; b. Bklyn., Nov. 23, 1937; s. Henry Gershwin and Ann Kurland (Shapero) M.; m. Sandra Phyllis Kuritzky, Aug. 7, 1960; children—James Edward, Vivien Gayle. B.S. in Biology, Rensselaer Poly. Inst., 1959; M.D., State U. N.Y., Bklyn., 1963. Intern, Maimonides Med. Center, Bklyn., 1963-64; resident in medicine, 1964-65; research asso. NIH, Bethesda, Md., 1965-67; resident in med. ophthalmology Mt. Sinai Med. Center, N.Y.C., 1967-69; asso. med. dir. Pfizer Inc., N.Y.C., 1970-71; asst. dir. clin. research Ayerst Labs., N.Y.C., 1971-75; asso. dir. clin. research Schering Corp., Bloomfield, N.J., 1975-78; adj. asso. prof. biology Rensselaer Poly. Inst.; adj. asst. prof. medicine N.Y. Med. Coll.; sr. clin. asst. prof. Mt. Sinai Sch. Medicine; med. dir. Clearview Nursing Home, Whitestone, N.Y.; med. cons. Profl. Children's Sch.; cons. in clin. nutrition and metabolism South Oaks Hosp. Bd. dirs. Bayside Hills Civic Assn., 1970-80; adv. mem. bd. dirs. U.S.A., Inc., 1970-72; founder, chmn. Queens County (N.Y.) Common Cause, 1972-75, vice chmn. N.Y. State, 1974-75; chmn. hyperalimentation com. Astoria Gen. Hosp., N.Y.; cons. in clin. nutrition and metabolism South Oaks Hosp. Served with USPHS, 1965-67. Fellow Am. Coll. Nutrition (sec.-treas.; chmn. council on nutrition and cardiovascular disease 1976-85); mem. Am. Soc. Clin. Pharmacology and Therapeutics, Am. Soc. Parenteral and Enteral Nutrition, Am. Soc. Internal Medicine, Queens County Med. Soc. (pub. health com.), N.Y. State Soc. Internal Medicine, Clin. Soc. N.Y. Diabetes, N.Y. Cardiol. Soc., Soc. Biol. Therapy. Republican. Club: Williams (N.Y.C.). Author: A New Manifesto for Middle America, 1972; (with others) Nutrition and Health Care; contbr. chpt. to Quick Reference to Clinical Nutrition. Office: 775 Park Ave Suite 155 Huntington NY 11743

MAZO, MARK ELLIOTT, lawyer; b. Phila., Jan. 12, 1950; s. Earl and Rita (Vane) M.; m. Fern Rosalyn Litman, Aug. 19, 1973; children: Samantha Lauren, Dana Suzanne, Ross Elliott, Courtney Litman. AB, Princeton U., 1971; JD, Harvard Law Sch., 1974. Bar: D.C. 1975, U.S. Dist. Ct. D.C.

1975, U.S. Claims Ct. 1975, U.S. Ct. Appeals (D.C. cir.) 1976, U.S. Supreme Ct. 1979. Assoc. Jones, Day, Revis & Pogue, Washington, 1974-79; Crowell & Moring, Washington, 1979-81; ptnr. 1981—. Contbr. articles to profl. jours. White House intern Exec. Office of Pres., Washington, 1972. Served to capt. USAR, 1971-79. Mem. Harvard Law Sch. Assn., ABA, D.C. Bar Assn., Phi Beta Kappa. Republican. Clubs: University (Washington); Columbia Country., Princeton, (N.Y.C.); Colonial. Home: 3719 Cardiff Rd Chevy Chase MD 20815 Office: Crowell & Moring 1001 Pennsylvania Ave NW Washington DC 20004-2505

MAZRUI, ALI AL'AMIN, political science educator, researcher; b. Mombasa, Kenya, Feb. 24, 1933; came to U.S., 1960; s. Al'Amin Ali and Safia (Suleiman) M.; m. Molly Vickerman, 1962 (div. 1982); children—Jamal, Al'Amin, Kim Abubakar. B.A. with distinction, U. Manchester, Eng., 1960; M.A., Columbia U., 1961; D.Phil., Oxford U., 1966. Lectr. Makerere U., Kampala, Uganda, 1963-65, prof. polit. sci., head dept. polit. sci., 1965-73; dean Faculty Social Scis., Makerere U., Kampala, Uganda, 1967-69; prof. polit. sci. U. Mich., Ann Arbor, 1974—; prof. Ctr. Afroam. and African Studies, U. Mich., Ann Arbor, 1974—; Andrew D. White prof.-at-large Cornell U., Ithaca, 1986—; research prof. polit. sci. U. Jos, Nigeria, 1981-86; Reith lectr. BBC, London, 1979; vis. prof. various univs. including U. London, U. Chgo., Oxford U., U. Pa., Ohio State U., Manchester U., Harvard U., Nairobi U., UCLA, Northwestern U., U. Singapore, Colgate Coll., U. Australia, Stanford U., U. Cairo, Sussex U., U. Leeds, 1965—; mem. Banks Council of African Advisers, World Bank, Washington, 1988—. Author: Towards A Pax Africana, 1967; The Trial of Christopher Okigbo, 1971; A World Federation of Cultures, 1976; Africa's International Relations, 1977, Political Values and the Educated Class, 1978; The African Condition, 1980; (with Michael Tidy) Nationalism and New States in Africa, 1984; author, narrator, presenter BBC, London, 1981-86, The Africans: A Triple Heritage, 1986; editor series: UNESCO General History of Africa, 1973—; editorial bd. various profl. jours., 1963—; contbr. articles to profl. publs. Fellow Ctr for Advanced Study in Behavioral Scis., Palo Alto, Calif., 1972-73; sr. fellow Hoover Instn. on War, Revolution and Peace, Stanford, Calif., 1973-74, Mich. Soc. Fellows, 1978-82; Ghana Acad. Arts and Scis. hon. fellow, 1985. Fellow Ghana Acad. Arts and Scis. (hon.), Internat. Assn. Middle Eastern Studies; mem. African Studies Assn. (exec. bd. 1975—, pres. 1978-79), Internat. Congress African Studies (v.p. 1978-85), Internat. Polit. Sci. Assn. (v.p. 1970-73), World Order Models Project (dir. African sect. 1968-83), Royal African Soc., Royal Commonwealth Soc. Clubs: United Kenya (Nairobi); Athenaeum (London). Office: U Mich Ctr Afro-Am & African Studies 550 E University Ann Arbor MI 48109-1092

MAZUR, MARGIE ELLA HANDLEY MEREDITH, reading educator; b. Tulsa, Mar. 27, 1941; d. Joyce Samuel and MaryPaul (Ellsworth) Handley; m. Don Leroy Mazur, Aug. 31, 1962 (div. Nov. 1974); children: Susan Diane, Michael. BA in Art, U. Tulsa, 1962, M of Teaching Arts in Spl. Edn., 1967; postgrad., Calif. State U., Los Angeles, UCLA, Purdue U., Calumet, Ind., San Jose State U. Accredited tchr., reading specialist, adminstr., Calif. Classroom tchr. Tulsa Pub. Schs., 1963-65; fellow, clinician, diagnostician, instr. Mabee Reading Clinic, U. Tulsa, 1965-67; instr. So. Meth. U. Reading Clinic, Dallas, fall 1969; classroom tchr. Los Angeles Unified Sch. Dist., 1975-76; reading specialist Sierramont Middle Sch., Berryessa Union Sch. Dist., San Jose, Calif., 1976—; pvt. tutor, San Jose, 1976—; owner, operator Eastside Learning Ctr. and Reading Clinic, San Jose, 1978-82. Cons., activist in women's and children's rights in child-support enforcement; chmn. child-support enforcement task force San Jose-South Bay chpt. NOW, 1984-85; mem. child support div. rev. ad-hoc. com. Santa Clara County Bd. Suprs. Entrance Exam. scholar U. Tulsa, 1959; John Mabee grad. fellow, 1966; recipient 1st place Bronze award Am. Waltz, Palo Alto, Ca., 1987; named Woman of Achievement, Santa Clara County, 1987. Mem. Santa Clara County Reading Council, Calif. Reading Assn., Internat. Reading Assn., Women Leaders in Edn., Lantern Hon. Soc., Scroll Hon. Soc., Mortar Bd., Alpha Delta Kappa, Kappa Alpha Theta (chpt. pres. 1961-62). Mem. Baháí Faith Ch. Avocations: ballroom dancing, skiing, sailing, reading, sewing. Home: PO Box 32744 San Jose CA 95152 Office: Sierramont Mid Sch 3155 Kimlee Dr San Jose CA 95132

MAZUR, PETER, cell physiologist, cryobiologist; b. N.Y.C., March 3, 1928; s. Paul M. and Adolphia (Kaske) M.; m. Drusilla Stevens, May 28, 1953 (dec. May 1982); 1 child, Timothy Stevens; m. Sara Jo Bolling, June 16, 1984. A.B. magna cum laude, Harvard U., 1949, Ph.D., 1953. NSF postdoctoral fellow, Princeton U., N.J., 1957-59; research staff biology div. Oak Ridge Nat. Lab., 1959—, group leader theoretical and applied cryobiology, 1966—, sci. dir. biophysics and cell physiology, biology div., 1974-75, corporate fellow, 1985; mem. vis. com. biology Harvard U. Bd. Overseers 1972-77; prof. U. Tenn.; mem. Space Sci. Bd. of Nat. Acad., 1975-77. Contbr. articles to prof. jours. Served to capt. USAF, 1953-57. Recipient Author of Yr. award Martin-Marietta Energy Systems, 1985; Lalor fellow Harvard U., 1952, John Harvard fellow, 1951. Sigma Xi Nat. lectr., 1980. Fellow AAAS; mem. Soc. for Cyrobiology (pres. 1973-74, bd. govs., 1979—), Phi Beta Kappa. Club: Cosmos (Washington). Current work: Cryobiology mechanisms of freezing injury in living cells and tissues. Subspecialties: Cell biology; Biophysics (biology). Home: 125 Westlook Circle Oak Ridge TN 37830 Office: Oak Ridge Nat Lab Biology Div P O Box Y Oak Ridge TN 37831

MAZUR-BAKER, DEBORAH JOAN, educator; b. Highland Park, Mich., Apr. 22, 1958; d. Frank J. and Joan A. (Cader) Mazur; m. Michael J. Baker, Sept. 20, 1986. B.S., Western Mich. U., 1981. Spl. edn. resource room tchr. Capac Community Schs., Mich., 1981-82; supr. group home Blue Water Developmental Housing, Port Huron, Mich., 1982-83; unit adminstr. group home Luth. Social Services of Mich., Detroit, 1983-85; mgr. sales Fin. Services of Am., Inc., Madison Heights, Mich., 1985-86; clinician, case mgr. Ditty, Lynch, and Assocs., Birmingham, Mich., 1986-87; spl. edn. tchr. Pontiac Sch. Dist., 1987—. Mem. Council Exceptional Children, Am. Behavioral Assn., Western Mich. U. Alumni Assn. (bd. dirs.).

MAZZIA, VALENTINO DON BOSCO, physician, educator, lawyer; b. N.Y.C., Feb. 17, 1922; s. Alexander Lloret and Francesca (D'Alessandro) M.; m. Rosana Sgarlata, Sept. 2, 1974; children: Lisa Mitchell, Donald Mitchell, Christopher Mitchell. B.S. cum laude, CCNY, 1943; M.D., NYU, 1950; postgrad., U. So. Calif. Sch. Law, 1973-74; J.D., U. Denver, 1978. Bar: Colo. 1978, U.S. Dist. Ct. Colo. 1978, Calif. 1979, U.S. Dist. Ct. (So. dist.) Calif. 1979, U.S. Supreme Ct. 1982, Ala. 1984, U.S. Dist. Ct. Ala. 1984, N.Y. 1987; diplomate: Am. Bd. Anesthesiology., Am. Bd. Law in Medicine. Intern Kings County Hosp., Bklyn., 1950-52; resident N.Y. Hosp., N.Y.C., 1952-54; asst. prof. Cornell U. Med. Coll., N.Y.C., 1952-61; prof. anesthesiology, chmn. dept. Coll. Medicine NYU, N.Y.C., 1961-72, prof. anesthesiology, chmn. dept. Postgrad. Med. Sch., 1961-72, prof. anesthesiology Coll. Dentistry, 1962-72; dir., attending anesthesiologist Univ. Hosp., N.Y.C., 1961-72; vis.-in-charge, dir. anesthesia service Bellevue Hosp. Center, N.Y.C., 1961-72; cons. N.Y. VA Hosp., Manhattan State Hosp., 1961-72; dir. anesthesiology Los Angeles County/Martin Luther King Jr. Gen. Hosp., 1971-73; chief anesthesiology Kern County Gen. Hosp., Bakersfield, Calif., 1973; practice medicine specializing in anesthesiology Bakersfield, Los Angeles; sole practice Las Vegas; staff 35 hosps. 1973-75; prof. anesthesiology U. Colo. Health Scis. Center and Dental Sch., Denver, 1976-83; clin. prof. U. Colo. Health Scis. Center and Dental Sch., 1984—; clin. dir. operating room for anesthesiology Univ. Hosp., 1976-82; vis. prof., chmn. anesthesiology Charles R. Drew Post Grad. Med. Sch., Los Angeles, 1971-73; vis. prof. anesthesiology UCLA, 1972; asst. med. examiner, cons. forensic anesthesiology Office of Chief Med. Examiner, N.Y.C., 1962-73; dep. coroner, asst. med. examiner County Coroner's Office, Los Angeles, 1973-82; of counsel Cunningham Bounds Yance Crowder & Brown, Mobile, Ala., Kenneth L. Knapp P.C., Newport Beach, Calif. Co-author: Practical Anethesiology, 1962—; also articles. Served with USAAF, 1943-45; med. dir. USPHS Res. Fellow Am. Coll. Anesthesiology, N.Y. Acad. Medicine, Am. Coll. Chest Physicians, Am. Osteo. Coll. Anesthesiologists, Am. Coll. Legal Medicine; mem. Am. Soc. Anesthesiologists, Harvey Soc., Assn. Trial Lawyers Am., Ala. Trial Lawyers Assn., Phi Beta Kappa, Sigma Xi, Alpha Omega Alpha. Club: New York Athletic (life). Office: 1000 Venetian Way Penthouse 2201 Miami FL 33139-1001

MAZZITELLI, GUIDO, lawyer; b. Gaeta, Latina, Italy, Sept. 7, 1919; arrived in Savona, 1955.; s. Oscar and Emma M.; m. Rosanna Bruno; children: Emma, Fausto. Jurisprudence, Univ., Genoa. Dir. Cesarano Armatore, Imperia, Italy, 1951-55, Gabriele Zunini Armatore, Savona, Italy, 1955-70, Unione s.n.c., Savona, 1963-65, Ligure Marittima Internazionale, Genoa, Italy, 1964-69, Navigazione Alga SpA., Genoa, 1965-72; dir., pres. Ligure Sarda di Navigazione Ltd., Cagliari, Italy, 1969-80, Freccero e Scotti Ltd., Savona, 1979; dir. Fintransport Internat. Ltd., Milano, Italy, 1981. Author: Parghelia, 1976, Trucioli di Storia Vol.1, 1977, vol.2, 1978, Due Calabresi nel XVIII secolo, 1985. Pres. Associazione degli Spedizionieri ed Agenti Marittimi del Porto di Savona, 1981; dir. Cassa di Risparimo Savona, 1983, Port Aythority, Savona, 1987. Mem. Confitarma, Federagenti (dir. 1981), Sezione Marittimo-Portuale C. of C. (pres. 1981). Roman Catholic. Club: Skal (Savona,Italy). Lodge: Lions. Office: Freccero & Scotti SpA, Via Chiodo 18/R, 17100 Savona Italy

MBAH, BRIAN CHIBUIKE, synthetic and yarn manufacturing company administrator; b. Obohia Okike, Imo, Ikwuano, Nigeria, May 5, 1956; s. Abraham and Aforinwa (Ezekwu) M.; m. Catherine Chinyere, July 3, 1984; children: Uloma Ihuoma L., Osinachi Mc Wisdom. Student Inst. Chartered Secs. and Adminstrs. London. Exec. sec. Stokvis Nigeria Ltd., Kano, Nigeria, 1976-78; adminstrv. asst. Universal Spinners Ltd., Kano, 1978—. Author: Gods Never Lie, 1985. Fin. dir. Obohia Devel. Union, Kano State, vice chmn. Assoc. mem. Inst. Export London; mem. Nigerian Inst. Mgmt., Nigerian Inst. Personnel Mgmt. Avocations: reading; motor race. Home: Independence Rd, Kano Nigeria 2471 Office: Universal Spinners Ltd, PO Box 2471, Kano Nigeria

MBAYE, SALIOU, archivist; b. Louga, Senegal, Sept. 27, 1946; s. Amadou and Magotte (Thiam) M.; m. Camara Fetou, Oct. 1974; children: Marieme, Amadou, Ousmane, Ibrahima, Aminata. Grad. in History, U. Paris, 1972, grad. in Linguistics, 1973. Asst. dir. Archives of Senegal, 1970-72, dir., 1972—. Contbr. articles to profl. jours. Mem. Conseil Internat. des Archives. Home: 3 rue Kleber, Dakar Senegal Office: Archives de Senegal, Immeuble Administratif, Dakar Senegal

MBELE, JOSEPH LEODGAR, literature educator, folklorist; b. Litembo, Ruvuma, Tanzania, Aug. 17, 1951; s. Leodgar Jinga and Josefa (Komba) M.; m. Heribertha Ndunguru, Dec. 28, 1977; children: Bernadetha, Assumpta. BA, U. Dares Salaam, Tanzania, 1976, MA, 1978; MA, U. Wis.-Madison, 1982, PhD, 1986. Tutorial asst. U. Dares Salaam, Tanzania, lectr., 1981-86, sr. lectr. lit., 1986—; vis. scholar U. Burundi, 1980. Editor: (book) Viewpoints: Essays on Literature and Drama, 1980; translator folktales; contbr. articles to profl. jours. Pres. African Students Union, U. Wis., Madison, 1982-84. Recipient Vice-Chancellor's prize U. Dares Salaam, 1973-74, East African Acad. award, 1975-76, Brit. Inst. in Ea. Africa research award, 1988; Fulbright scholar, 1980-85; Dean's fellow U. Wis., 1984-85; Pitt-Rivers Mus. (Oxford U.) research grant, 1988. Mem. Tanzania Translators Assn., Tanzania Writers Assn., African Lit. Assn. Roman Catholic. Home: PO Box 35041, Dares Salaam Tanzania Office: Univ Dares Salaam, PO Box 35041, Dares Salaam Tanzania

MBILINYI, MICHAEL SIMON, economics educator, diplomat; b. Mahanje-Songe, Tanzania, July 20, 1934; s. Michael and Epiphania (Mbangule) Ngonyani Mhelema; m. Marjorie Jane Power, 1967; children: Nnali, Anina, Lyungai. BSc, Cornell U., 1965; MA, Stanford U., 1966; PhD, Dates Salaam (Tanznia) u., 1974. Exec. Shell/BP East Africa Ltd., Tanzania, 1956-61; chief economist Nat. Bank Commerce, Dates Salaam, 1969-70; tutor Agrl. Tng. Inst., Ukiriguru, Mwanza, Tanzania, 1966-67; sr. research fellow U. East Africa, Dates Salaam, 1967-70; prof., dir. Econ. Research Bur. Tanzania U. Dates Salaam, 1970-75; chief econ. advisor Pres J. K. Nyerere, Tanzania, 1975-83; prin. sec. Ministry Agriculture and Livestock Devel., Tanzania, 1983-85; ambassador Govt. United Republic Tanzania, Brussels, 1985—. Author: Agricultural Research for Rural Development, The Economics of Peasant Coffee Production: The Case of Tanzania, 1968; contbr. articles to profl. jours. Mem. East African Legis. Assembly, 1970-77. Mem. Internat. Agrl. Econs. Assn. (country rep. 1967-83), Tanzania Agrl. Econs. Assn. Tanu/CCM. Roman Catholic. Home: Ave Wellington 150, 1190 Brussels Belgium

M'BOW, AMADOU-MAHTAR, former director general UNESCO; b. Dakar, Senegal, Mar. 20, 1921; s. Fara-N'Diaye and N'Gone (Casset) M'B.; Licencées lettres, U. Paris; hon. doctorates numerous univs., including: U. Buenos Aires (Argentina), 1974, U. Granada (Spain), 1975, U. West Indies, 1975, Open U., Belfast, No. Ireland, 1976, U. Nairobi (Kenya), 1976, U. Philippines, 1977, U. Malaya, 1977, U. Venice (Italy), 1977, U. Uppsala (Sweden), 1977, U. Moscow, 1977, U. Paris, Sorbonne, 1977, U. Andes, Bogota, Colombia, 1978, State U. Haiti, 1978, U. Khartoum (Sudan), 1978, U. Sri Lanka, 1978, Charles U., Prague, Czechoslovakia, 1979, Que. U. (Can.), 1979, Nat. U. Zaire, 1980, U. Madras (India), 1980, Nat. U. Ivory Coast, 1980, U. Ankara (Turkey), 1981, U. Ghent (Belgium), 1982, State U. Kiev (USSR), 1982, Quaid-i-Azam U. (Pakistan), 1983, Aix-Marseille U. (France), 1983, Beijing U. (China), 1983, Chulalongkorn U. (Thailand), 1983, Sokoto U. (Nigeria), 1984; m. Raymonde Sylvain, July 27, 1951; children: Fara-Edy, Awa-Martha, Marie-Amy. Prof., Coll. de Rosso, Mauritania, 1951-53; dir. Service Fundamental Edn., Senegal, 1953-57; minister edn. and culture Senegal, 1957-58; prof. Lycée Faidherbe, St. Louis, Senegal, 1958-64, Ecole Normale Supérieure, Dakar, 1964-66; minister of edn., 1966-68, of culture, youth and sport, 1968-70; asst. dir. gen. edn. UNESCO, 1970-74, dir. gen., 1974-87; hon. prof. Ind. U. Santo Domingo, 1978, Ecole normale supérieure, Dakar, 1979, Nat. Ind. U. Mex., 1979. Decorated Order of Stara Planina (Bulgaria); grand cross Order of Liberator, Order of Andres Bello, Order of Francisco Miranda (Venezuela); Nat. Order of Merit (Ecuador); Order of the Sun (Peru); Order of Merit (Dominican Republic); Nat. Order of Lion (Senegal); Order of Alphonso the Wise (Spain); Nat. Order of So. Cross (Brazil); numerous others; recipient Man and His World Peace prize, Can., 1978; freeman cities of Lima and Cuzco (Peru), Quito and Guayaquil (Ecuador), Sofia (Bulgaria), Kotor (Yugoslavia), Ouro Preto (Brazil), Seoul (Korea), Olinda (Brazil), Tashkent (USSR); hon. mayor Commune of Valdivia (Colombia). Mem. Royal Acad. Fine Arts San Telmo (Spain) (hon.), Acad. Athens (fgn.), Acad. of Kingdom of Morocco, Academie des Sciences d'Outre-Mer (France), Soc. senegalaise des prefesseurs d'histoire et géographie (hon. chmn.). Office: UNESCO, 7 place de Fontenoy, 75700 Paris France *

MC ABEE, THOMAS ALLEN, psychologist; b. Spartanburg, S.C., Mar. 31, 1949; s. Thomas Walker and Doris Lee (Gillespie) McA.; student Ga. Inst. Tech., 1967-69; B.A., Furman U., 1971; M.A., U. S.C., 1975, Ph.D., 1979. Clin. counselor Adolescent Inpatient Service, William S. Hall Psychiat. Inst., Columbia, S.C., 1971-73; counselor children's therapeutic camp Columbia Area Mental Health Center, 1974; co-dir. community problems survey Eau Claire Community Project, Columbia, 1975; asst. aging services planner Central Midlands Regional Planning Council, Columbia, 1976; instr. U. S.C., 1976; NSF intern S.C. State Legislature, 1978; research dir. S.C. Legis. Gov.'s Com. on Mental Health and Mental Retardation, Columbia, 1979-80; co-dir. TV project "Feelings Just Are," Columbia Area Mental Health Center, 1980—, cons., 1977-79; cons. S.C. Protection and Advocacy System for Handicapped Citizens, 1980, 81, S.C. Dept. Mental Health, 1981; psychologist, S.C. Dept. Mental Retardation, 1982—; mem. deinstitutionalization task force S.C. Developmental Disabilities Council, 1979-80; mem. subcom. State Commr.'s Ad Hoc Com. to Study and Develop Work/Lodge System for S.C., S.C. Dept. Mental Health, 1979-80; mem. Media Task Force of Gov.'s Adv. Com. on Early Childhood Devel. and Edn., 1980-81; chmn. primary prevention public media com. S.C. Dept. Mental Health, 1979-81. Recipient Palmetto Pictures Photography award, 1977; NIMH fellow, 1976-77. Mem. ACLU (bd. dir. S.C. chpt. 1979-83), Am. Assn. Mental Retardation, Low Country Assn. Sch. Psychologists, Am. Psychol. Assn. (mem. community psychology div.). Home: 9989 Dorchester Rd Waters Edge #2H Summerville SC 24485 Office: Jamison Rd Ladson SC 29456

MCADAMS, HERBERT HALL, II, banker; b. Jonesboro, Ark., June 6, 1915; s. Herbert Hall I and Stella (Patrick) McA.; children by previous marriage: Judith (Mrs. Walter A. DeRoeck), Sandra (Mrs. Robert C. Connor), Herbert Hall III, Penny (Mrs. Tim Hodges); m. Shelia Wallace, Nov. 27, 1970; 1 child, Nicole Patrick. BS, Northwestern U., Evanston, Ill., 1937; postgrad., Harvard U., 1937-38, Loyola U., Chgo., 1938-39; JD with honors, U. Ark., 1940; LLD (hon.), Ark. State U., 1984. Bar: Ark. 1940, U.S. Dist. Ct. Ark., U.S. Supreme Ct. 1944, U.S. Ct. Appeals (8th cir.) 1944, U.S. Ct. Claims 1944,. Chmn. bd., chief exec. officer Citizens Bank, Jonesboro, 1958—, Union Nat. Bank, Little Rock, 1970—, Citizens Bancshares Corp., 1979—, Union Ark. Corp., 1980—; McAdams-Frierson chair bank mgmt. Ark. State U., 1987; bd. dirs. 1st Ark. Devel. Fin. Corp. Pres. Jonesboro Sch. Dist., 1948-50, Bapt. Med. Ctr. System Real Estate Corp., 1977—; state chmn. Citizen's Com. on Edn., 1950; mem. Ark. Indsl. Devel. Commn., 1965-73, chmn., 1967-72; trustee Ark. Children's Hosp., 1972-75, Bapt. Med. Ctr.System, 1975-77, Bapt. Found., 1975; bd. govs. Ark. State Fair and Livestock Show Assn.; mem. Bapt. Med. Ctr. System Corp., Fifty for Future; chmn. bd. govs. Ark. State U. Found.; bd. visitors U. Ark., Little Rock, 1978-82; bd. dirs. Nat. Children's Eye Care Found., 1987—, numerous others. Served with USNR, World War II. Decorated Purple Heart; recipient William F. Rector Meml. award Fifty for the Future, 1987. Mem. ABA (uniform state laws com. 1961-66, mem. tax sect. 1954—), Ark. Bar Assn., Am., Ark. bankers assns., Ark. Council Econ. Edn., Craighead (Ark.) County Bar Assn. (past. pres.), Pulaski (Ark.) County Bar Assn., Met. C. of C. (dir.), Sales and Marketing Execs. (Top Mgmt. Honoree 1972), Sigma Nu. Bapt. Clubs: Country of Little Rock, Little Rock, Pleasant Valley Country (Little Rock); Capital. Lodge: Rotary. Home: 47 Edgehill Little Rock AR 72207 Office: Union National Bank Little Rock AR also: Citizens Bank Bldg Jonesboro AR 72401

MC AFEE, CARRIE R. HAMPTON (MRS. JOSHUA O. MC AFEE), principal; b. Galveston, Tex., Dec. 30, 1932; d. Tom and Daisy (Charlton) Hampton; B.A., Tex. So. U., 1952, M.A., 1963; postgrad. Lincoln U., 1958, Columbia, 1960, U. Calif.-Berkeley, 1964; m. Joshua O. Mc Afee, July 31, 1964; children—Rhonda Maria, Roy Bernard. Tchr., Houston Ind. Sch. Dist., 1953-65, counselor, 1965-68, vice prin., 1968-74, prin., 1974—. Counselor, Neighborhood Youth Corps, 1969—; vol. nurses aid ARC, 1964—; active YWCA; bd. dirs. San Jacinto Lung Assn., 1977—; Tex. bd. dirs. Am. Lung Assn., 1984—, Evan E. Worthing Scholarship (sec. bd.). Recipient Outstanding Alumni award Tex. So. U., 1975, Profl. award Houston League of Nat. Assn. Bus. and Profl. Women, 1976, 86, Gov.'s Yellow Rose of Tex. award, 1976, award of merit Alpha Phi Alpha, 1984, 86, Nat. Coalition 100 Women Ednl. Leadership award, 1986, Mayor's Proclamation Community Service award, 1986; Forward Times Newspaper Woman of Year award; Brentwood Dolphins Community Service award, 1986. Mem. Am. Assn. Sex Edn. and Counselors, Assn. Supervision and Curriculum Devel., Tex. Tchrs. Assn., Tex. Houston assns. supervision and curriculum devel., Houston Sch. Adminstrs. Assn., Am. Bridge Assn. (dir.), Am. Contract Bridge League, Nat., Tex. (adv. bd. dirs. 1976—, Distinguished Service award 1977) assns. secondary sch. prins., Nat. Assn. Female Execs., Zeta Phi Beta, Alpha Phi Alpha. Roman Catholic. Club: City Wide (life). Home: 3618 S MacGregor Way Houston TX 77021 Office: 13719 White Heather St Houston TX 77045

MCAFEE, WILLIAM GAGE, lawyer; b. N.Y.C., Mar. 23, 1943; came to Hong Kong, 1976; s. Horace J. and Kathryn (Gage) McA.; m. Linda June 3, 1978; children—Zachary, Dallas, Matthew. A.B., Harvard U., 1965; J.D., Columbia U., 1968. Legal adviser AID, Dept. State, Saigon, Vietnam, 1969-71; adj. prof. Saigon U. Faculty Law, 1970-71; assoc. Davis Polk Wardwell, N.Y.C., 1971-73; ptnr. Coudert Bros., Singapore, Hong Kong, 1973—; advisor consultative com. for the basic law of Hong Kong; pres. AmCham, 1984-86, chmn. govt. relations com., trustee Charitable Found.; mem. Hong Kong C. of C., chmn.'s com., chamber council, gen. com., legal com., chmn. corp. contbn. program; campaign com. Community Chest of Hong Kong; sec. Law Assn. for Asia and the Western Pacific energy section. Editor Energy Law and Policy in Asia and the Western Pacific, 1985, Introduction to the Energy Laws of Asia, 1984; contbg. editor Oil & Gas Law & Taxation Rev.; hon. cons. Econ. & Law Rev.; adv. com. China Oil mag.; advisor Asian Devel. Bank; assoc. Urban Land Inst.; comml. panel arbitrators Am. Arbitration Assn. Mem. Internat. Inst. Strategic Studies, Bar Supreme Ct. U.S., D.C. Bar Assn., N.Y. Bar Assn., Chartered Inst. Arbitrators (legal panel Hong Kong br.). Episcopalian. Clubs: Procellian (Cambridge); Harvard (N.Y.C., Hong Kong); Pacific (bd. govs.), Fgn. Correspondents', Hong Kong People's Assn. Home: Severn Villa, 3 Severn Rd The Peak, Hong Kong Hong Kong Office: 31/F Alexandra House, 20 Chater Rd Central, Hong Kong Hong Kong

MC ALESTER, ARCIE LEE, JR., geologist, educator; b. Dallas, Feb. 3, 1933; s. Arcie Lee and Alverta (Funderburk) McA.; m. Virginia Wallace Savage; children: Kirstie Martine, Archibald Keven. B.A., B.B.A., So. Methodist U., 1954; M.S., Yale U., 1957, Ph.D., 1960. Mem. faculty Yale U., 1959-74, prof. geology, 1966-74; curator invertebrate paleontology Peabody Mus., 1966-74; prof. geol. scis. So. Meth. U., Dallas, 1974—; dean Sch. Humanities and Scis. So. Meth. U., 1974-77. Author: The History of Life, 1977, The Earth, 1973, History of the Earth, 1980, Physical Geology, 1984, (with V.S. McAlester) A Field Guide to American Houses, 1984, Discover Travel Guides, 1988—; also articles.; assoc. editor Am. Scientist, 1970-74. Served to 1st lt. USAF, 1954-56. Guggenheim fellow Glasgow U., Scotland, 1965. Mem. Geol. Soc. Am., Paleontol. Soc., Am. Assn. Petroleum Geologists, AAAS. Clubs: Yale (N.Y.C.); Dallas Country. Office: So Meth U Dept Geol Scis Dallas TX 75275

MCALESTER, VIRGINIA SAVAGE, historic preservationist; b. Dallas, May 13, 1943; d. Wallace Hamilton and Dorothy Minnie (Harris) Savage; m. Clement McCarty Talkington, Nov. 25, 1965 (div. 1976); children—Clement McCarty Jr., Amy Virginia; m. A. Lee McAlester, July 11, 1977. B.A., Harvard U., 1965. Founding mem. Historic Preservation League, Dallas, 1972—, pres., 1975-76; founder, trustee, pres. Friends of Fair Park, Dallas, 1984-86; bd. dirs. Ctr. for Hist. Resources, Tex. A&M U., 1986—. Author: The Making of an Historic District, 1974, A Field Guide to American Houses, 1984 (Nat. Trust Honor award 1986), Discover Dallas-Fort Worth, 1988. Founding mem. 500, Inc., Dallas, 1965; bd. dirs. Dallas Central Bus. Dist. Assn., 1976-78, mem. Jr. League, Dallas; pres. Friend of Fair Park, 1984-86. Recipient Janus award Historic Preservation League, 1980, 84, Humanities award Dallas Hist. Soc., 1984, Honor award San Antonio Conservation Soc., 1984, John Neely Bryan award Dallas County Hist. Commn., 1986. Mem. Nat. Trust for Hist. Preservation (bd. advisor 1974-83, Honor award 1986), Soc. Archtl. Historians, Tex. Soc. Architects (hon. 1987). Episcopalian. Clubs: Dallas Country, Harvard (Dallas) (pres. 1987—). Office: 240 Boll St Dallas TX 75204

MCALLISTER, JAMES ADDAMS, electrical, computer and ocean engineering educator, retired naval officer, archaeology photographer; b. Covington, Va., Dec. 16, 1915; s. Hugh Maffit and Evaline (Long) McA.; m. Bernice Jacklyn Lyons, June 26, 1942; children—Bruce Hugh, John Milton. B.S. in Engring., U.S. Naval Acad., 1939; M.S. in Physics, UCLA, 1949. Commd. ensign U.S. Navy, 1939, advanced through grades to capt., 1958; officer of the deck USS Md., Pearl Harbor, 1941; rep. U.S. Navy Electronic Labs., Am. Mgmt. Assn. Conf., N.Y., 1958; asst. dir. Ship Electronic div. Navy Dept., Washington, 1952-54; electronic and radiol. safety officer San Francisco Naval Shipyard, 1954-56; asst. dir. Navy Electronics Lab., San Diego, 1956-59; asst. dir. Supreme Allied Command Atlantic Antisubmarine Warfare Research Ctr., La Spezia, Italy, 1959-61; dir. underseas research and devel. Navy Dept., Washington, 1962; ret., 1962; asst. prof. physics Calif. Western U., San Diego, 1962-64; assoc. prof. elec., computer and ocean engring. Calif. State Poly. U., Pomona, 1964—, assoc. dean engring., 1967-69; crew photographer archeol. excavation crews, Cucamonga, Temecula, Calico, Calif., Korea, Italy, Turkey and other Asian, Middle East and European sites; lectr., cons. in field; protocol chmn. Internat. Starboat Races, San Diego, 1958; dir. ocean engring. and electronics engring. exhibits Los Angeles County Fair, 1977. Contbr. articles to profl. jours. Co-inventor Gunnery Star-Shell Computer WW II. Recipient Letter of Appreciation Calif. State Legis., 1958, Letter of Commendation, Am. Soc. Engring. Edn., 1971; Letter of Appreciation Lord Louis Mountbatten, First Sea Lord Great Britain, 1958. Mem. IEEE, Am. Soc. Engring. Edn., Acoustical Soc. Am., Am. Inst. Physics, U.S. Naval Acad. Alumni Assn., Ret. Officers Assn., Calif. Poly. U. Alumni Assn. (hon.), NEA, Calif. Tchrs. Assn., Calif. State Employees Assn., Archaeol. Survey Assn. Clubs: Long Beach Navy Yacht (Calif.); Naval Officers Yacht (La Spezia); San Diego Yacht. Office: Calif State Poly Univ 3801 W Temple Ave Pomona CA 91768

MC ALLISTER, JOSEPH CHARLES, civil engineer; b. Mariners Harbor, S.I., N.Y., Aug. 25, 1928; s. Harry Eli and Blanche Edythe (Bergen) McA; Civil Engr., CCNY, 1953; postgrad. Columbia, 1956-57; m. Anne Bargiuk, June 29, 1957; children—Rosanne, Joseph, Michael. Laborer, Brighton

Marine Shipyard, S. I., 1944; carpenter Brewer Dry Dock Co., S.I., 1945; constrn. supt. Raymond Concrete Pile Co., 1953-55; soils and found. design engr. U.S. Army C.E., N.Y. dist., 1955-57, chief paving sect., 1957-62, chief fallout shelter updating sect., 1962-63, constrn. engr., 1963-68, asst. area engr. So. N.J. area, Wrightstown, 1968-71, chief office engr. sect. Secaucus Area, Jersey City, 1971-73, civil engr. N. Atlantic Div., N.Y.C., 1973-85. Pres. Solutions to All U.S. and World Problems Found., Inc. Served with AUS, 1946-49. Recipient Sustained Superior Performance award C.E., 1963, Suggestion awards, 1969; Achievement award Civic Congress S.I., 1973. Registered profl. engr., Vt. Mem. Rosicrucian Order. Democrat. Author: (with Robert F. McAllister) Solutions to all United States and World Problems, Book 1, 1970, Book 2, 1976. Home and Office: 125 Shirley Ave Staten Island NY 10312

MCALPINE, STUART GEMMELL, physician; b. Glasgow, Scotland, Mar. 6, 1927; s. George and Elizabeth Harvey (Gemmell) McA.; m. Cynthia Joan McPherson, Mar. 31, 1954; children—Lawrence George, Howard McPherson, Carole Matheson Gemmell. M.B., CH.B., Glasgow U., 1949, M.D., 1959. Sr. registrar Royal Infirmary Dumfries, Scotland, 1957-59; sr. registrar, asst. cardiologist Royal Infirmary Glasgow, 1959-63; cons. physician Royal Alexandra Infirmary, Paisley, Scotland, 1963—; examiner in medicine U. Glasgow, 1983—. Contbr. med. papers to profl. lit. Mem. Argyll and Clyde Health Bd., Paisley, 1983—. Served to capt. Royal Army Med. Corps, 1950-52. Fellow Royal Coll. Physicians and Surgeons Glasgow (med. examiner 1964—), Royal Coll. Physicians (London); mem. Brit. Med. Assn., Royal Medico-Chirurgical Soc. Glasgow (pres. 1986-87, v.p. 1985-86), Scottish Soc. of Physicians (pres. 1987-88). Mem. Ch. of Scotland. Club: Royal Scottish Automobile (Glasgow). Avocations: golf, fishing, motor cars. Home: Windyknowe, 168 Southbrae Dr, Glasgow G13 1TY, Scotland Office: Royal Alexandra Hosp, Paisley PA2 9PN, Scotland

MCAMIS, EDWIN EARL, lawyer; b. Cape Girardeau, Mo., Aug. 8, 1934; s. Zenas Earl and Anna Louise (Miller) McA.; m. Malin Eklof, May 31, 1959 (div. 1979); 1 child, Andrew Bruce. A.B., Harvard U., 1956, LL.B., 1959. Bar: N.Y. 1960, U.S. Dist. Ct. N.Y., U.S. Supreme Ct. 1965, U.S. Ct. Appeals (2d, 3d and D.C. cirs.). Assoc. law firm Webster, Sheffield & Chrystie, N.Y.C., 1959-61, Regan Goldfarb Powell & Quinn, N.Y.C., 1962-65; assoc. law firm Lovejoy, Wasson, Lundgren & Ashton, N.Y.C., 1965-69, ptnr., 1969-77; ptnr. Skadden, Arps, Slate, Meagher & Flom, N.Y.C., 1977—; adj. prof. law Fordham U., 1984-85, Benjamin N. Cardozo Sch. Law, N.Y.C., 1985—. Bd. dirs. Aston Magna Found. for Music, Inc., 1982—. Served with U.S. Army, 1961-62. Mem. ABA, Assn. Bar City N.Y., Selden Soc. Club: Univ. (N.Y.C.). Office: Skadden Arps Slate Meagher & Flom 919 3d Ave New York NY 10022

MC ANALLY, DON, editor, publisher; b. Sewell, N.J., Oct. 27, 1913; s. James C. and Ina (MacLeod) McA.; grad. high sch.; m. Edith P. McKinney, Dec. 11, 1934; 1 dau., Shirley M. English. Reporter, Woodbury (N.J.) Daily Times, 1932-45; editor Owens-Ill. Co. publs. in N.J. and Ohio, 1945-47; asst. advt. mgr. Libbey-Owens-Ford Glass Co., also Libbey-Owens-Ford Glass Fibers Co., Toledo, 1947-59; editor Pacific Oil Marketer, Los Angeles, 1960-66; editor-publisher O&A Marketing News, La Canada, Calif., 1966—, The Automotive Booster of Calif., 1974—, Calif. Sr. Citizen News, La Canada, 1977-84, Calif. Calif. Businesswoman, 1978; Good Neighbor award Toledo, 1948; award Western Oil Industry, 1971; Man of Yr. award Pacific Oil Conf., 1977, Diamond Pin award Pacific Oil Conf., 1986; awards Douglas Oil Co., 1978, Automotive Affiliated Reps., 1979, So. Calif. Petroleum Industry Golf and Tennis Tournament, 1984, Intermountain Oil Marketers Assn., 1985, Silver Card award Pacific Automotive Show, 1988. Mem. Calif. Ind. Oil Marketers Assn., Am. Petroleum Inst. (basin chpt.), Automotive Hall of Fame (v.p. So. Calif. chpt. 1984), OX5 Aviation Pioneers, Nat. Speakers Assn., Internat. Platform Assn., Petroleum Writers of Am. Clubs: Lions, Masquers, Gabby, Silver Dollar, Roorag (Los Angeles), Greater Los Angeles Press, Hollywood Press. Home: 4409 Indiana Ave La Canada CA 91011 Office: PO Box 765 La Canada CA 91011

MCAULEY, VAN ALFON, aerospace mathematician; b. Travelers Rest., S.C., Aug. 28, 1926; s. Stephen Floyd and Emily Floree (Cox) McA. B.A., U. N.C., Chapel Hill, 1951; postgrad. U. Ala.-Huntsville, 1956-57, 60-63. Mathematician Army Ballistic Missile Agy., Huntsville, Ala., 1956-59; physicist NASA, Marshall Center, Huntsville, 1960-61, research mathematician, 1962-70, mathematician, 1970-81. Contbr. articles to profl. jours. Served with U.S. Army, 1944-46. Recipient Apollo achievement award NASA, 1969, cost savs. award, 1973, Skylab achievement award, 1974, Outstanding Performance award, 1976. Mem. Am. Math. Soc., Soc. Indsl. and Applied Math., AAAS, N.Y. Acad. Scis., Phi Beta Kappa. Research on documentation of methods devised for the numerical solution of heat flow equations involving both elliptic and parabolic partial differential equations. Patentee in field, of control system invention. Home: 3529 Rosedale Dr Huntsville AL 35810

MCAULIFFE, DENNIS PHILIP, retired army officer, government official; b. N.Y.C., Apr. 8, 1922; s. Michael and Mary (Ryan) McA.; m. Kathleen Bolton, June 2, 1946; children: Carolyn McAuliffe Shoemaker, Dennis Philip, Kathleen Ann. BS, U.S. Mil. Acad., 1944; MSEE, U. Pa., 1950. Commd. 2d lt. U.S. Army, 1944, advanced through grades to lt. gen., 1975; asst. comdr. I Corps Arty., Korea, 1964-65; with Army Gen. Staff, Washington, 1959-63, 65-66; mem., exec. to chmn. Joint Chiefs Staff, Washington, 1966-69; asst. div. comdr. 1st Inf. Div., Vietnam, 1969; sr. adviser III Corps and Mil. Region 3, Vietnam, 1970; chief policy Supreme Hdqrs. Allied Powers Europe, Belgium, 1971-73; dep. comdg. gen. U.S. Army Combined Arms Ctr., 1973-74; dir. European region Office Sec. Def., 1974-75; comdr.-in-chief So. Command, 1975-79; adminstr. Panama Canal Commn., 1979—. Chmn. bd. mgmt. YMCA, Balboa, Panama. Decorated DSM (Army and Defense), Legion of Merit with 2 oak leaf clusters, DFC with oak leaf cluster, Bronze Star with oak leaf cluster, Republic of Vietnam Gallantry Honor medal, Dominican Republic Honor medal; recipient Disting. Civilian Service award Sec. of Army, 1985. Mem. Assn. Grads. U.S. Mil. Acad., Assn. U.S. Army, Nat. War Coll. Alumni Assn., Sons of Xavier, SHAPE Officers Assn., Soc. 1st Div., Soc. 89th Div. World War II. Office: Panama Canal Commn APO Miami FL 34011 also: Panama Canal Commn, Balboa Heights, Panama City Panama

MCAVANEY, KEVIN LAWRENCE, mathematician, educator; b. Adelaide, Australia, Sept. 22, 1946; s. Reginald Lawrence and Ivy Gwen (Reynolds) McA.; m. Evelyn Joyce Hooper, May 6, 1972; children: Christopher, Nicholas, Katherine. BSc with honors, U. Adelaide, 1969; MSc, U. Melbourne, Australia, 1974, PhD, 1984. Asst. lectr. Gordon Inst. Tech., Geelong, Victoria, Australia, 1970-72, lectr., 1973-76; lectr. Deakin U., Geelong, 1977-86, sr. lectr., 1987—; vis. asst. prof. Simon Fraser U., Vancouver, B.C., Can., 1985-86; bd. dirs. 8th Australian Conf. on Combinatorial Math., Geelong, 1980, 31st Ann. Meeting of Australian Math. Soc., 1987. Editor: Combinatorial Mathematics, 1981; contbr. articles to profl. jours. Coordinator Geelong Community Radio, 1978-82; pres. Bellaire Primary Sch. Council, Geelong, 1982-85, 1st City of South Barwon Scout/Cub Group, Geelong, 1986—; sec. St. Luke's Highton Pre-Sch., Geelong, 1979-86; editor parish news Highton-Barrabool Hills Uniting Ch., Geelong, 1983-85. Mem. Australian Math. Soc. (council mem. 1986—), Am. Math. Soc., Combinatorial Math. Soc. Australasia (pres. 1980). Office: Deakin U, Geelong, Victoria 3217, Australia

MCBEATH, GERALD ALAN, political science educator, researcher; b. Mpls., Sept. 13, 1942; s. Gordon Stanley and Astrid Elvira (Hjelmeir) McB.; m. Jenifer Huang, June 7, 1970; children—Bowen, Rowena. B.A., U. Chgo., 1963, M.A., 1964; Ph.D., U. Calif.-Berkeley, 1970. Vis. asst. prof. polit. sci. Rutgers Coll., New Brunswick, N.J., 1970-72; asst. prof. John Jay Coll., CUNY, N.Y.C., 1972-74, 75-76; assoc. prof. Nat. Chengchi U., Mucha, Taipei, Taiwan, 1974-75; prof. U. Alaska, Fairbanks, 1976—; cons. Inst. Social and Econ. Research, Anchorage, 1976-77; contract researcher Alaska Dept. Natural Resources, Alaska Dept. Edn., Nat. Inst. Edn., others; staff dir. task force on internat. trade policy Rep. Conf., U.S. Senate. Sr. author: Dynamics of Alaska Native Self-Government, 1980; author monograph: North Slope Borough Government and Policymaking, 1981; jr. author: Alaska's Urban and Rural Governments, 1984; sr. editor Alaska State Government and Politics, 1987; editor: Alaska's Rural Development, 1982. Mem. bd. edn. Fairbanks North Star Borough, 1986—. Named Outstanding Faculty Mem., Assn. Students U. Alaska, Fairbanks, 1979, Alumni Assn. U. Alaska, Fairbanks, 1981; grantee Nat. Inst. Edn., 1980-83, Alaska Council on Sci. and Tech., 1982-84, Spencer Found., 1987-88. Mem. Asian Studies on Pacific Coast (program chmn. 1983, bd. dirs. 1982-83), Assn. Asian Studies, Western Polit. Sci. Assn., Am. Polit. Sci. Assn., Am. Soc. Pub. Adminstrn., Fairbanks N. Star Borough Bd. Edn. Democrat. Home: 1777 Red Fox Dr Fairbanks AK 99709 Office: U Alaska Dept Polit Sci Fairbanks AK 99775

MCBRIDE, KENNETH EUGENE, lawyer, abstract company executive; b. Abilene, Tex., June 8, 1948; s. W. Eugene and I. Jean (Wright) McB.; m. Peggy Ann Waller, Aug. 7, 1969 (div. 1980); m. Katrina Lynne Small, June 1, 1985; 1 child, Katherine Jean. B.A., Central State U., 1971; J.D., Oklahoma City U., 1974. Bar: Okla. 1974. Assoc. Linn, Helms & Kirk, Oklahoma City, 1974-76; city atty. City of Edmond, Okla., 1976-77; v.p., gen. counsel Am. First Land Title Ins., Oklahoma City, 1977-81; pres. Am.-First Abstract Co., Norman, Okla., 1981—; pres. Okla. Land Title Assn., 1987-88. Bd. dirs. Norman Bd. Adjustment, 1982-85, Leadership Okla. Inc. Mem. ABA, Okla. Bar Assn., Cleveland County Bar Assn., Norman C. of C. (bd. dirs.), Norman Bd. Realtors. Democrat. Presbyterian. Avocation: sailing. Office: Am-First Abstract Co 111 E Comanche Norman OK 73069

MC BRIDE, RAYMOND ANDREW, physician, educator; b. Houston, Dec. 27, 1927; s. Raymond Andrew and Rita (Mullane) McB.; m. Isabelle Shepherd Davis, May 10, 1958 (div. 1978); children—James Bradley, Elizabeth Conway, Christopher Ramsey, Andrew Gore. B.S., Tulane U., 1952, M.D., 1956. Diplomate: Am. Bd. Pathology. Surg. intern Jefferson Davis Hosp., Baylor U. Coll. Medicine, Houston, 1956-57; asst. in pathology Peter Bent Brigham Hosp., Boston, 1957-60; sr. resident pathologist Peter Bent Brigham Hosp., 1960-61; resident pathologist Free Hosp. for Women, Brookline, Mass., 1959; asst. resident pathologist Children's Hosp. Med. Center, Boston, 1960; teaching fellow pathology Harvard Med. Sch., Boston, 1958-61; research trainee Nat. Heart Inst., NIH, HEW, 1958-61; spl. postdoctoral fellow Nat. Cancer Inst., HEW, McIndoe Meml. Research unit Blond Labs., East Grimstead, Sussex, Eng., 1961-63; asst. attending pathologist Presbyn. Hosp., N.Y.C., 1963-65; asst. prof. pathology Coll. Physicians and Surgeons, Columbia U., 1963-65; research asso. Mt. Sinai Hosp., N.Y.C., 1965-68; assoc. prof. surgery and immunogenetics Mt. Sinai Sch. Medicine, N.Y.C., 1965-68; career scientist Health Research Council City N.Y., 1967-73; attending pathologist Flower and Fifth Ave. Hosps., N.Y.C., 1966-78, Met. Hosp. Center, N.Y.C., 1968-78; prof. pathology N.Y. Med. Coll., 1968-78, Baylor Coll. Medicine, Houston, 1978—; attending pathologist Harris County Hosp. Dist., Ben Taub Gen. Hosp., Houston, 1978—; chief pathology service Harris County Hosp. Dist., 1988—; assoc. staff Meth. Hosp., Houston, 1978-81, active staff, 1981—; vis. grad. faculty Tex. A & M U., College Station, 1979—; clin. prof. pathology U. Tex. Grad. Sch. Biomed. Scis., Galveston, 1982—, U. Tex. Med. Br., Galveston, 1982—; exec. dean N.Y. Med. Coll., Valhalla, 1973-75; exec. dir., chief operating officer, bd. dirs. Westchester Med. Center Devel. Bd., Valhalla, 1974-76. Contbr. articles to profl. jours.; editorial bd. Jour. Immunogenetics, Exptl. and Clin. Immunogenetics. Bd. dirs. Westchester Artificial Kidney Found., Inc., 1974-78, Westchester Med. Center Library, 1974-78, Westchester div. Am. Cancer Soc., 1973-78; trustee Tuxedo Park (N.Y.) Sch., 1975-78, Tuxedo Library, 1976-78; co-chmn. Westchester Burn Center Task Force, 1975-76. Grantee Health Research Council, N.Y.C., 1963-73; Grantee Am. Cancer Soc., 1971-72; Grantee NIH, USPHS, 1964—; Grantee NSF, 1965-68. Fellow Royal Soc. Medicine; mem. Transplantation Soc., Am. Soc. Exptl. Pathology, Reticuloendothelial Soc., AAAS, Am. Assn. Pathologists and Bacteriologists, Am. Assn. Immunologists, AAUP, AMA, Tex. Med. Assn., Harris County Med. Soc., Tex. Soc. Pathologists, Coll. Am. Pathologists, Am. Assn. Clin. Pathologists, Houston Acad. Medicine, Houston Soc. Clin. Pathologists, Assn. Am. Med. Colls., Fedn. Am. Scientists, Am., N.Y. cancer socs., Soc. Health and Human Values, Am. Acad. Med. Ethics, Alpha Omega Alpha. Republican. Roman Catholic. Club: Tuxedo (Tuxedo Park, N.Y.). Home: 12431 Woodthorpe Ln Houston TX 77024 Office: Baylor Coll Medicine Dept Pathology Tex Med Ctr One Baylor Plaza Houston TX 77030

MCBRIDE, WILLIAM GRIFFITH, research gynecologist; b. Sydney, Australia, May 25, 1927; s. John and Myrine (Griffith) McB.; m. Patricia Mary Glover, Feb. 16, 1959; children: Louise, Catherine, John R., David W. MBBS, U. Sydney, 1950; MD, 1961. Resident med. officer St. George Hosp., 1950, Launceston Hosp., 1950, Women's Hosp., Sydney, 1952-53; med. supt. Women's Hosp., 1955-57, gynecologist, 1958-82, founder, dir. Found. 41, birth defects research, Sydney, 1972—; cons. ob-gyn Royal Hosp. for Women, WHO study com. safety oral contraceptives, 1971—; mem. expert com. EPA. examiner in Ob-Gyn, U. Sydney, U. New South Wales; dir. Barrington Pastoral Co. Pty. Ltd. Bd. dirs. Australian Opera, 1979—, Women's Hosp. of Sydney, 1973-79. Recipient Gold medal Brit. Petroleum/Inst. de la Vie for discovering teratological effects of thalidomide, 1971; decorated comdr. Order British Empire, Order Australia. Fellow Royal Coll. Ob-Gyn, Royal Soc. Medicine, Senate U. of Sydney, Royal Australian Coll. Obstetricians and Gynecologists, Royal Soc. Medicine; mem. Teratology Soc., Reproductive Biology Soc., Endocrine Soc., Australian Med. Assn. (pres. Ob-Gyn sect. 1966-76), Soc. Risk Analysis, Am. Coll. Toxicology, Royal Agrl. Soc. New South Wales (council), N.Y. Acad. Sci., Royal Soc. Medicine. Clubs: Union, Australian Jockey, Royal Sydney, Palm Beach Surf. Contbr. numerous articles to books, profl. jours. Home: 123 Queen St, Sydney 2025, Australia Office: Foundation 41, 365 Crown St, Sydney 2010, Australia

MC BRYDE, FELIX WEBSTER, geographer, ecologist, consultant; b. Lynchburg, Va., Apr. 23, 1908; s. John McLaren and Flora O'N. (Webster) McB.; B.A., Tulane U., 1930, LL.D. (hon.), 1967; Ph.D., U. Calif., Berkeley, 1940; postgrad. (research fellow) U. Colo., 1930-31, Clark U., 1931-32; m. Frances Van Winkle, July 23, 1934; children—Richard Webster, Sarah Elva, John McLaren. Geographer-photographer 4th Tulane Expdn. across Cen. Am. Maya Area, 1927-28; geology teaching asst. Tulane U., 1929-30. Utah-Smithsonian Uinta Ute Expdn., No. Utah, 1931; field fellow Clark U.-Carnegie Inst., Washington, Guatemala, 1932; research fellow Middle Am. Research Inst., Tulane U., 1932-33; teaching asst. geography U. Calif., Berkeley, 1933-35, 37; predoctoral field fellow social sci. Social Sci. Research Council N.Y., Guatemala and El Salvador, 1935-36; instr. geography Ohio State U., 1937-42, UCLA, 1940; field fellow NRC, Washington, also Berkeley, Guatemala, Mexico, 1940-41; expert cons., sr. geographer M.I., War Dept., Washington, 1942-45; lectr. geography Western Res. U., summer 1944; dir. Peruvian office Inst. Social Anthropology, Smithsonian Instn., Washington, Lima, 1945-47; spl. rep. Inst. Andean Research, Lima, 1947-48; lectr. Fgn. Service Inst., Dept. State, 1949-53; prof. geography U. Md., 1948-59, cons. prof., 1959-63; geog. cons. internat. statistics U.S. Bur. Census, Washington and Latin Am., 1948-56; chief U.S. Census Mission, tech. advisor 1st Nat. Census of Ecuador, Quito, 1949-51; dir. regional planning Gordon A. Friesen Assos., Inc., Washington and San Jose, Costa Rica nat. master hosp. plan, 1956-58; survey dir. Greater Southeast Hosp., Washington, 1957-58; pres. F.W. McBryde Assocs., Inc., Washington and Guatemala, 1958-64, Inter-Am. Inst. Modern Langs., Guatemala, 1962-66; Latin Am. cons. Inst. Modern Langs., Washington, 1962-66; chief phys. and cultural geography br., natural resources div. Inter-Am. Geodetic Survey, U.S. Army, Fort Clayton, C.Z., 1964-65; field dir. Bioenvironmental Program, Atlantic-Pacific Interoceanic Sea-Level Canal Studies in Panama and Colombia (AEC contract), Battelle Meml. Inst., Columbus, Ohio, 1965-70, field dir. Andean ecology project, S.Am., 1967-69, dir. project devel. program, Central Am. and Mex., 1968-69; cons. in ecology, 1970—; founder-dir. McBryde Center for Human Ecology, 1969—; cons. in human ecology and Latin Am., Transemantics, Inc., Washington, 1970—; with UN Devel. Program, ecologist (tourism), expert Jamaica, W.I., 1971; hydrology ecologist, expert Parana River Nav. Improvement Project, Argentina, 1972; ecol. cons. Battelle Meml. Inst., Panama and Brazil, 1972; U.S. Bur. Census geography adviser to Govt. of Honduras on cartography for 1973 population census, 1972; Battelle cons., procedural analysis in internat. project devel., 1972; ecologist World Bank environ. impact analysis Bayano River Hydroelectric Project, one-man mission to Panama; Battelle cons., ecologist, prin. investigator and field coordinator, environ. impact study Darien Gap Hwy., Panama-Colombia for U.S. Dept. Transp., 1973; cons. Enviro Plan; expert ecologist (biology) Engr. Agy. Resources Inventories, C.E., U.S. Army, Washington, 1974; dir. recruitment, dir. internat. bus. intelligence, 1975-80, dir. Geog. Research div. Transemantics, Inc., Washington, 1975—; cons. geographer Census Office, Govt. of Honduras, 1981; cons. ecologist UN Tech. Cooperation and Devel., Cerro Colorado Copper Mine, Panama, 1981. Mem. nat. adv. bd. Am. Security Council; state advisor U.S. Congl. Adv. Bd., Am. Security Council Found.; charter founder Ronald Reagan Republican Ctr., Washington, 1988, Pres., founder Trust Rep. Nat. Com., 1988. Fellow Explorers Club (life); mem. Am. Anthrop. Assn., AAAS, Am. Congress on Surveying and Mapping, Am. Ethnol. Soc., Am. Geog. Soc., Assn. Am. Geographers (formerly Am. Soc. for Profl. Geographers founding pres., sec., treas., editor publs. 1943-44), Am. Hort. Soc., Am. Geophys. Union (life), Am. Inst. Biol. Scis., Conf. Latin Americanist Geographers, Arctic Inst. of N.Am., Assn. Tropical Biology, Chesapeake Bay Found., Citizens for Ocean Law, Am. Soc. Photogrammetry and Remote Sensing, Ecuadorian Inst. Anthropology and Geography (founder dir. 1950-52, hon. dir. 1952—), Inter-Am. Council (organizing sec. 1953-59, pres. 1959-62), Internat. Soc. for Tropical Ecology, Jefferson Edn. Found., N.Y. Acad. Scis., Washington Acad. (adv. bd. 1981—), Lima Geog. Soc., Oceanography Soc. (charter mem.), Ohio Acad. Sci., Soc. Am. Archeology, Soc. Am. Mil. Engrs., Soc. Econ. Botany, Soc. for Med. Anthropology, Marine Tech. Soc., N.Am. Cartographic Info. Soc., Guatemalan Soc. History and Geography, Internat. Oceanographic Found., Oceanic Soc., Nature Conservancy Internat. Program, Mexican Soc. Geography and Statistics, Potomac Glen Assn. (dir.), U.S. Naval Inst., World Wildlife Fund, Nat. Wildlife Fedn. (world assoc.), Phi Beta Kappa, Sigma Nu, others. Episcopalian. Author: Solola, 1933; Cultural and Historical Geography of Southwest Guatemala, 1947, Spanish edit., 1969; (with P. Thomas) Equal-Area Projections for World Statistical Maps, 1949; founding editor Profl. Geographer; contbr. numerous articles to profl. jours.; patentee equal-area world map series; new world map projections. Home: 10100 Falls Rd Potomac MD 20854

MCBURNEY, GEORGE WILLIAM, lawyer; b. Ames, Iowa, Feb. 17, 1926; s. James William and Elfie Hazel (Jones) McB.; m. Georgianna Edwards, Aug. 28, 1949; children: Hollis Lynn, Jana Lee, John Edwards. B.A., State U. Iowa, 1950, J.D. with distinction, 1953. Bar: Iowa 1953, Ill. 1954, Calif. 1985. With Sidley & Austin and predecessor, Chgo., 1953—, ptnr., 1964—; resident ptnr. Singapore, 1982-84. Editor-in-chief: Iowa Law Rev., 1952-53. Mem. Chgo. Crime Commn., 1966-84; trustee Old People's Home of City of Chgo., 1968-83, sec., 1967-69, exec. v.p., 1969-74, pres., 1974-82, hon. life trustee, 1983—; hon. life trustee Georgian, Evanston, Ill., trustee, counsel, 1976-82, v.p., 1980-82. Served with inf. AUS, 1944-46. Fellow Am. Coll. Trial Lawyers, Am. Bar Found.; mem. ABA, State Bar of Calif., Los Angeles County Bar Assn., Am. Judicature Soc., Bar Assn. 7th Fed. Circuit, Am. Arbitration Assn. (panel), Assn. Bus. Trial Lawyers, The Ctr. for Internat. Comml. Arbitration Los Angeles (bd. dirs., v.p.), Nat. Coll. Edn. (bd. assocs. 1967-84), U.S. C. of C. (govt. and regulatory affairs com. of council on antitrust policy 1980-82), Phi Kappa Psi, Omicron Delta Kappa, Delta Sigma Rho, Phi Delta Phi. Republican. Presbyterian. Clubs: Union League, Mid-Day, Law (life), Legal (Chgo.); American, Cricket, Town (Singapore); Marina City (Marina del Rey, Calif.). Home: Malibu Pacifica 13 3601 Vista Pacifica Malibu CA 90265 Office: Sidley & Austin 2049 Century Park E 35th Floor Los Angeles CA 90067

MCCABE, FRANCIS JOSEPH, manufacturing company executive; b. Phila., May 2, 1936; s. Felix and Josephine (Murtha) McC.; m. Florence McCabe; children: Alison, Diane. Student, Drexel Inst. Exec. v.p., dir. Air Balance Inc., Phila., 1962-65; cons. Ruskin Mfg. Co, Kansas City, Mo., 1965; v.p. engring. M&T Engring. Co., Chgo., 1966-67; pres. Prodn. Tool Corp. div. Inductotherm Corp., Rancolas, N.J., 1967-68, Prefco Products Inc., PHL Inc. & Levr/Air Inc., Buckingham, Pa., 1968—; gen. ptnr. McDemco, McGadeke (research and devel. ventures). Contbr. articles to on fire protection to profl. jours.; holder numerous patentsin field. Served with USN, 1958-64. Mem. ASHRAE (best jour. paper 1986), Nat. Fire Protection Assn., Air. Movement and Control Assn., Smoke Control Assn. (treas., dir.), Doylestown C. of C., Buckingham Bus. Assn. Republican. Roman Catholic. Home: 239 Hastings Ct Doylestown PA 18901 Office: PO Box 425 Buckingham PA 18912

MCCABE, JAMES J., lawyer; b. Phila., May 8, 1929; A.B., LaSalle Coll., 1951; J.D., Temple U., 1955. Bar: Pa. and fed. cts., 1956, U.S. Supreme Ct. 1971. Assoc., Duane, Morris & Heckscher, Phila., 1955-64, ptnr. 1964—; chmn. litigation dept., 1984—; lectr. med. and ins. law, trial technique Practising Law Inst., N.Y. Law Jour. Seminars, Defense Research Inst.; adj. prof. family medicine Thomas Jefferson U. Sch. Medicine, Phila. Trustee Phila. Bar Found., 1979-81; past pres. St. Thomas More Soc.; vol. in Miss. Lawyers' Com. for Civil Rights, 1968. Fellow Am. Coll. Trial Lawyers, Am. Bd. Profl. Liability Attys.; mem. ABA, Pa. Bar Assn., Phila. Bar Assn., Am. Bd. Trial Advocates (pres. Pa. chpt.), Am. Coll. Legal Medicine, Assn. Ins. Attys., Assn. Defense Counsel Phila. (past pres.), Internat. Assn. Ins. Counsel, Defense Research Inst. (Pa. chmn. 1973-77, v.p. Atlantic region 1977-80, dir. 1980-83). Office: Duane Morris Et Al 1 Franklin Plaza Philadelphia PA 19102

MCCABE, JOHN LEE, teacher; b. Fond du Lac, Wis., Mar. 26, 1923; s. Arthur Lee and Florence Gertrude (Molleson) McC.; m. M. Leora Harvey, Mar. 17, 1946; 1 child, Steven Lee. Student, Western Mich. U., 1941-42, U. Colo., 1946-47; Community Coll. Aurora, 1984-85. Designer project assignments, Denver, 1947-50; archtl. engr. The Austin Co., Denver, 1950-52; resident engr. Peter Kiewit Sons Co., Portsmouth, Ohio, 1953; dist. mgr. Hugh J. Baker Co., Evansville, Ind., 1953-56; engr. Lauren Burt Inc., Denver, 1956-58; project mgr. Denver Steel Products Co., Commerce City, Colo., 1958-66; pres. corp. McCabe and Co., Aurora, Colo., 1966-75; master tchr. high sch. Sch. Dist. 50, Westminster, Colo., 1975-83; tchr. Aurora pub. schs., 1983—. Author: Word Problems Simplified, 1986, Everyday Algebra, Everyday Geometry, 1987, Everyday Mathematics-A Study Guide , 1988. Served with USAAF, 1943-46; PTO. Mem. Colo. Soc. Engrs. (life). Roman Catholic. Club: Nat. Writers'. Lodge: Optimists. Home: 750 S Clinton St Denver CO 80231 Office: Aurora Pub Schs 500 Buckley Rd Aurora CO 80011

MCCAFFERTY, JAMES ARTHUR, sociologist; b. Columbus, Ohio, Jan. 1, 1926; s. James A. and Marjorie Agatha (Gilchrist) McC.; m. Jane Roush, June 13, 1948 (dec. Oct. 1984); children: Lucinda Jane Martin, James Stanley Thomas, Bridget Anne Roush Green; m. Carolyn Ring Bradley, Nov. 7, 1987. Social research analyst Ohio State Dept. Public Welfare, 1948-51; criminologist U.S. Bur. Prisons, Washington, 1951-63; asst. chief div. info. systems Adminstrv. Office of U.S. Cts., Washington, 1963-77, chief statis. analysis and reports div., 1977-86, ret.; vis. lectr. American U., 1959, 62-64; adj. instr. Fordham U., 1978—. Editor: Capital Punishment, 1972; contbr. articles on criminology to profl. jours. Pres. Potomac area council Camp Fire Girls of U.S., 1966-67; v.p. Prince George's County (Md.) Council of PTAs, 1964-65; chmn. Prince George's County Youth Commn., 1970-72; mem. Hypoglycemia Assn., Inc. Served with USAAF, 1944-46. Mem. Am. Sociol. Assn., Am. Correctional Assn. (life), Assn. Correctional Research and Info. Mgmt., Am. Statis. Assn., Prince George's County Geneal. Soc. (past pres.), Md. State PTA (life), Judicature Soc., Am. Soc. of Criminology, Nat. Council on Crime and Delinquency, Md. State Beekeepers Assn., AAUP, SAR (bd. mgrs. Md. chpt.), DAV (life), Sons of Union Vets. Civil War. Presbyterian. Home: 613 Rosier Rd Fort Washington MD 20744

MCCAIN, JOHN SIDNEY, III, senator from Arizona; b. Panama Canal Zone, Aug. 29, 1936; s. John Sidney and Roberta (Wright) McC.; m. Cindy Hensley, May 17, 1980; children: Douglas, Andrew, Sidney, Meghan, Jack. Grad. U.S. Naval Acad., 1958; grad., Nat. War Coll., 1973. Commd. ensign U.S. Navy, 1958, capt., 1977; prisoner of war Vietnam, 1967-73; dir. Navy Senate Liaison Office, Washington, 1977-81; mem. 98th-99th Congress from 1st Ariz. Dist.; U.S. senator from Ariz. 1987—. Bd. dirs. Community Assistance League, Phoenix, 1981-82. Decorated Legion of Merit; decorated Silver Star, Bronze Star, Purple Heart, D.F.C., Vietnamese Legion of Honor. Mem. Soc. of the Cin., Am. Legion, VFW. Republican. Episcopalian. Office: US Senate 111 Russell Senate Office Bldg Washington DC 20510 •

MCCALL, CANDACE SMITH, medical supply company executive; b. Grand Rapids, Mich., Sept. 3, 1947; d. Gerald Robert Smith and Helen (Swanson) Saylor; m. Herbert A. M. McCall, June 25, 1967; 1 child, Brian Eric. B.A., Mary Washington Coll. U. Va., 1972; M.S. in Adminstrn., George Washington U., 1981; postgrad. Georgetown U., 1988. Exec. Garfinckel, Brooks Bros. Miller & Rhoads, 1975-78; exec. May Dept. Stores, Washington, 1978-81; owner Potomac Profl. Pharmacy Inc., Woodbridge,

Va., 1981-88, Fairfax Profl. Pharmacy Inc., Annandale, Va., 1981-87, Potomac Med. Supply, Inc., Vienna, Va., 1984-88, Medi-Spec, Inc., Vienna, 1984-87. Bd. dirs. Hunter Mill Country Day Sch., 1983-88, chmn. bd. dirs., 1987-88. Mem. ABA, LWV, Assn. Trial Lawyers Am., Amnesty Internat., Soc. Cybernetique. Republican. Presbyterian. also: Potomac Pharmacies Inc 1936-B Opitz Blvd Woodbridge VA 22191

MCCALL, CLYDE SAMUEL, JR., petroleum engineer; b. Memphis, May 29, 1931; s. Clyde Samuel and Marguerite (Rogers) McC.; m. Dodie McDonald, July 21, 1962; children: Clyde Samuel III, Amy Woolsey McDonald. BS in Commerce, Washington and Lee U., 1953; BS in Petroleum Engring., U. Tex.-Austin, 1959. Registered profl. engr., Tex. Engr. to sr. petroleum engr. Amoco Prodn. Co., Andrews and Midland, Tex., 1959-69; cons. petroleum engr., Midland, Tex., 1969-73; petroleum engr. James A. Lewis Engring., Dallas, 1973-81, exec. v.p. 1974-76, pres., 1977-81; exec. v.p. McCord-Lewis Energy Services, Dallas, 1981-83; petroleum cons., pres. Cenesia Petroleum Corp., 1983—. Served with U.S. Army, 1954-56. Mem. Soc. Petroleum Engrs., Ind. Petroleum Assn. Am., Tex. Mid-Continent Oil and Gas Assn., Soc. Ind. Profl. Earth Scientists, Dallas Mus. Fine Arts, Kappa Alpha Order. Republican. Presbyterian. Clubs: Steeplechase, Dallas Petroleum, Energy of Dallas, Brook Hollow Golf, Confriere des Chevalier du Tastavin. Address: Two Energy Sq Suite 435 4849 Greenville Ave Dallas TX 75206

MC CALL, DANIEL THOMPSON, JR., retired state justice; b. Butler, Ala., Mar. 12, 1909; s. Daniel Thompson and Caroline Winston (Bush) McC.; m. Mary Edna Montgomery, Apr. 3, 1937; children: Mary Winston McCall Laseter, Daniel Thompson III, Nancy McCall Poynor. A.B., U. Ala., 1931, LL.B., 1933, LL.D. (hon.), 1981. Bar: Ala. 1933, U.S. Supreme Ct. Practice law Mobile, 1933-60; ptnr. Johnston, McCall & Johnston, 1943-60; circuit judge Mobile County, 1960-69; assoc. justice Supreme Ct. Ala., 1969-75; dir. Title Ins. Co., 1959-69; pres. Jr. Bar Ala., 1937. Mem. Mobile County Bd. Sch. Commrs., 1950-56, 58-60; trustee Julius T. Wright Sch. Girls, 1953-63; adv. council U. Ala. Med. Ctr.; mem. com. U. Ala. Hosps.; dir. U. Ala. Law Sch. Found., Ala. bar commrs., 1957-60; trustee U. Ala., 1965-79, nat. alumni pres., 1963, pres. Mobile chpt., 1961. Served to lt. USNR, World War II. Recipient Dean's award U. Ala. Law Sch., 1974, Julius T. Wright Sch. Disting. Service award, 1979, U.M.S. Preparator Sch. Outstanding Alumnus award, 1980. Mem. ABA, Ala. Bar Assn. (grievance com. 1954-57), Mobile Bar Assn. (pres. 1953), Am. Judicature Soc., Farrah Law Soc. (charter), Cumberland Law Sch. Order Jurisprudence, Inst. Jud. Adminstrn., Nat. Trust Hist. Preservation, Navy League U.S. (pres. Mobile 1963-65), Am. Legion, Ala. Hist. Soc., Res. Officers Assn. U.S., Mil. Order World Wars, 40 and 8, St. Andrew's Soc. Mid-South, Omicron Delta Kappa, Phi Delta Phi, Sigma Nu. Democrat. Episcopalian. Clubs: Athelstan (pres. 1967-69); University (Tuscaloosa). Home: 2253 Ashland Pl Mobile AL 36607

MCCALL-SMITH, ALEXANDER, writer; b. Zimbabwe, Aug. 24, 1948; m. Elizabeth Parry, Sept. 4, 1982; children: Lucy Ishbel, Emily Rose. LLB, U. Edinburgh, Scotland, 1971, PhD, 1979. Author 10 books, including The White Hippo, 1980, The Perfect Hamburger, 1982, Film Boy, 1987 (translated into Japanese and German); writer short stories and broadcast plays for BBC. Office: care Murray Pollinger Lit Agy, 4 Garrick St, London WC2E 9BH, England

MCCAMMOND, DONALD BARR, toxic waste and energy information foundation executive, public relations executive, consultant; b. Boston, Dec. 21, 1915; s. John and Henrietta (Barr) McC.; m. Nancy Deane Day, May 11, 1957; children—John Day, Donald, Jr., Sara Deane. LL.B., Northeastern U., 1937. Bar: Mass. Reporter Christian Science Monitor, Boston, 1936-47; eastern region pub. relations mgr. Monsanto Corp., Boston, 1947-54; dir. advertising and pub. relations Dewey & Almy, Cambridge, Mass., 1954-55; exec. asst. legis. and pub. affairs Dept. Defense, Washington, 1955; v.p. Reynolds Metals Co., Richmond, Va., 1956-68, Am. Can. Co., N.Y.C., 1968-70, Va. Electric & Power, 1970-80; exec. v.p. Am. Energy Week, Inc., Washington, 1980-85; sr. cons. Clean Sites, Inc., Alexandria, Va., 1985—. Contbr. articles to profl. jours. Chmn., Gov.'s Conf. on State, County and Mcpl. Relations, Mass., 1952-54; mem. Richmond Civil War Centennial Commn., 1960-65; pres. Hist. Richmond Found., 1972. Va. Council on Econ. Edn., Richmond, 1972; chmn. Patrick Henry 250th Anniversary Commn., 1985-86, Richmond Bicentennial Commn., 1976-80; trustee St. Paul's Coll., Lawrenceville, Va., 1970-78; mem. council of dirs. Richmond U.; trustee Va. Children's Home Soc., 1960—, pres., 1979-80. Served to capt. USAF, 1942-45. Named Businessman of Yr., Va. Council on Econ. Edn., 1974; One of 40 World Pub. Relations Leaders, 1984. Mem. Pub. Relations Soc. of Am. (pres. 1970, recipient Gold Anvil award 1983), New Eng. Pub. Relations Soc. of Am. (founder 1952, pres. 1954), Old Dominion Pub. Relations Soc. Am. (founder and pres. 1961, recipient Thomas Jefferson award 1980), Internat. Pub. Relations Assn. Republican. Christian Scientist. Clubs: Country of Va., Commonwealth (Richmond); Prouts Neck Country, Prouts Neck Yacht (Maine); Sky (N.Y.C.). Home: Five Virginia Ave Richmond VA 23226 Office: Clean Sites Inc 1199 N Fairfax St Alexandria VA 22314

MC CANDLESS, ANNA LOOMIS, club woman; b. Aspinwall, Pa., July 21, 1897; d. George Wilberforce and Estella (Loomis) McC.; B.S., Carnegie-Mellon U., 1919. Pres., Vis. Nurses Assn. of Allegheny County, 1955-57; mem. vis. com. Margaret Morrison Carnegie Coll., 1962-66; v.p. Alumni Fedn. Carnegie Inst. Tech., 1963-66. Trustee Carnegie-Mellon U., 1966—. Mem. AAUW. Clubs: Coll., Univ., Twentieth Century (pres. 1956-58) (Pitts.); Appalachian Mountain. Home: Park Plaza Apts Craig St Pittsburgh PA 15213

MCCANN, DEAN MERTON, lawyer, pharmaceutical company executive; b. Ontario, Calif., Mar. 13, 1927; s. James Arthur and Alma Anis (Hawes) McC.; m. Carol Joan Geissler, Mar. 23, 1957. AA, Chaffey Coll., 1948; BS in Pharmacy, U. So. Calif., 1951; JD, U. Calif., San Francisco, 1954; LLM, NYU, 1955. Bar: Calif. 1955; lic. pharmacist, Calif. Pharmacist San Francisco and Ontario, 1951-54; sole practice Los Angeles, 1955-60; ptnr. MacBeth, Ford & Brady, Los Angeles, 1960-65, McCann & Berger, Los Angeles, 1965-68; v.p., sec. and gen. counsel Allergan Pharms., Inc., Irvine, Calif., 1968-78; sr. v.p., sec., gen. counsel Allergan, Inc., Irvine, 1978—; instr. pharmacy law U. So. Calif., Los Angeles, 1956-68; exec. v.p. Pharm. Wholesaler Assn., Los Angeles, 1956-68. Mem., past. chmn. bd. counsellors Sch. Pharmacy U. So. Calif., Los Angeles, 1975—, mem., past chmn. QSAD centurion, 1963—. Served with USNR, 1945-46. Fellow Food and Drug Law Inst., 1954-55. Mem. ABA, Calif. Bar Assn., Orange County Bar Assn., Am. Pharm. Assn., Calif. Pharm. Assn., Orange County Pharm. Assn., U. So. Calif. Alumni Assn. (past pres.), Phi Delta Chi. Republican. Clubs: Balboa Bay (Newport Beach, Calif.); Skull and Dagger (Los Angeles). Home: 21 Rockingham Dr Newport Beach CA 92660 Office: Allergan Inc 2525 Dupont Dr Irvine CA 92715

MCCANN, JOAN CELIA, school administrator; b. Malden, Mass., Jan. 23, 1936; d. Vincent Jacob and Helen Lorraine (Pontone) Celia; A.B. cum laude, Tufts U., 1957; M.A., U. Mich., 1968; Ed.D., Fordham U. 1986; m. William J. McCann, Aug. 23, 1958; children—Susan, Peter. Tchr. 1st grade Gleason Sch., Medford, Mass., 1957-58, Hutchinson Sch., Pelham, N.Y., 1958-61; tchr. 1st grade Siwanoy Sch., Pelham, 1968-69, reading cons., 1969-71, prin., 1971-75; prin. Fox Meadow Sch., Scarsdale, N.Y., 1975—; mem. adminstrv. adv. com. internship St. John's U., 1973—. Mem. Pelham Bicentennial Com., 1974—, sch. cons. Between the Lines publ., 1975; mem. adv. bd. Scarsdale Hist. Soc., 1975—; chmn. Pelham Bicentennial Ball, 1976; adv. com. Westchester County Office of Aging; adv. bd. Prins. Forum at Fordham U. Recipient award in appreciation for cooperation Pelham Manor Fire Dept., 1974; IDEA fellow Charles Kettering Found., 1976, 77. Mem. Internat. Reading Assn., N.Y. State Adminstrs. Assn., Nat. Assn. Elementary Sch. Prins., Nat. Congress Parents and Tchrs. (life), Am. Assn. sch. Adminstrs., Beatrix Potter Soc., Jean Piaget Soc., Jackson Coll. Alumnae Assn., U. Mich. Alumni Assn., Fordham Sch. Edn. Alumni Bd. (rec. sec.), Phi Delta Kappa, Chi Omega. Club: Internat. Garden. Home: 242 Eastland Ave Pelham NY 10803 Office: Fox Meadow Sch Brewster Rd Scarsdale NY 10583

MCCANN, JOHN FRANCIS, financial services company executive; b. South Orange, N.J., Nov. 30, 1937; s. Frank Charles and Dorothy Marie (Devaney) McC.; m. Mary Ellen Howland, Aug. 4, 1962; children—Sean Francis, Maureen Ellen, Darragh Siobain, Kevin Patrick. Student, LaSalle Mil. Acad., 1951-55, U. Notre Dame, 1955-57, Niagara U., 1959-61, N.J. Nat. Guard, 1959-67, The Wharton Sch., 1984-86. Vice-pres., sales mgr. Imco Container Co., N.Y.C., 1962-68; vice-pres., sales mgr. Eastman Dillon, Union Securities Co., N.Y.C., 1968-72; sr. v.p., sales mgr. Faulkner, Dawkins & Sullivan, N.Y.C., 1972-75; sr. v.p., br. mgr. Faulkner, Dawkins & Sullivan, Chatham, N.J., 1975-77; sr. v.p. Shearson Loeb Rhoades, Chatham, N.J., 1977-83; exec. v.p. Shearson Am. Express, N.Y.C., 1983-84; exec. v.p., dir. Shearson Lehman Bros., N.Y.C., 1984—. Fund raiser Riverview Hosp. Found., Red Bank, N.J., 1983; regional dir. Am. Express Found., N.Y.C., 1985—. Served to 2d lt. N.J. N.G., 1959-67. Mem. N.Y. Stock Exchange, Securities Industry Assn. Republican. Roman Catholic. Clubs: Navesink Country, Monmouth Beach Bath and Tennis, Beacon Hill. Home: 135 Bingham Ave Rumson NJ 07760 Office: Shearson Lehman Bros 151 Bodman Pl Red Bank NJ 07701

MCCANN, JOSEPH LEO, lawyer, government official; b. Phila., Aug. 27, 1948; s. Joseph John and Christina Mary (Kirwan) McC.; m. Aida Laico Kabigting, Dec. 6, 1986. B.A., St. Charles Sem., Phila., 1970, postgrad. in theology, 1970-71; M.A., Temple U., 1975, J.D., 1977. Bar: Pa. 1977, U.S. Dist. Ct. (ea. dist.) Pa. 1977, U.S. Dist. Ct. (mid. dist.) Pa. 1978, U.S. Ct. Appeals (3d cir.) 1978, D.C. 1986, U.S. Supreme Ct. 1986, Md. 1987. Law clk. to chief justice Pa. Supreme Ct., Phila., 1977-78; dep. atty. gen. Pa. Dept. Justice, Harrisburg, 1978-80; atty. U.S. GAO, Washington, 1980—. Mem. ABA, Pa. Bar Assn., Phila. Bar Assn., D.C. Bar Assn., Md. Bar Assn. Roman Catholic. Home: 204 Bookham Ln Gaithersburg MD 20877 Office: Office Gen Counsel US GAO 441 G St NW Washington DC 20548

MCCANN, OWEN CARDINAL, archbishop; b. Woodstock, South Africa, June 26, 1907. PhD, Urbanianum; BCom, Cape Town, DLitt (hon.); DHL (hon.) Portland, Maine. Ordained priest Roman Catholic Ch., 1935, titular bishop of Stettorio and vicar apostolic of Cape Town (South Africa), 1950; 1st archbishop of Cape Town, 1951-84, archbishop emeritus, 1984—; cardinal, 1965; titular ch. St. Praxedes. Office: Cathedral Pl, 12 Bouquet St, Cape Town 8001 Republic of South Africa

MCCARTHY, FREDERICK WILLIAM, investment banker; b. Boston, Nov. 25, 1941; s. Frederick William and Josephine Leona (Pannier) McC.; children: Daniel Arthur, Frederick William III, Kathryn Elizabeth. BA magna cum laude, Harvard U., 1963, MBA with high distinction, 1967. Mgmt. cons. Booz Allen & Hamilton Inc., Chgo., 1967-70; 1st v.p. investment banking Shearson, Hammill & Co. Inc., N.Y.C., 1970-72, Chgo., 1972-74; mng. dir., bd. dir. Drexel Burnham Lambert Inc., Boston, 1974—; bd. dirs. Avery, Inc., Am. Capital Corp., Banner Industries, Inc., Copelco Lease Receivables Corp., Seminole Kraft Corp., The Westwood Group Inc. Served to 1st lt. U.S. Army, 1963-65. Home: 65 East India Row Unit 28C Boston MA 02110 Office: Drexel Burnham Lambert Inc 1 Federal St Boston MA 02110

MC CARTHY, JOSEPH MICHAEL, historian; b. Lynn, Mass., Oct. 2, 1940; s. Joseph Donald and Johanna (Downing) Mc C.; A.B., St. John's Sem., 1961, postgrad., 1961-63; A.M., Boston Coll., 1968, Ph.D., 1972; m. Kathleen Frances Wright, July 30, 1966; children—Joanna, Kristen, Erika, Joseph Michael. Tchr., Bishop Fenwick High Sch., Peabody, Mass., 1964-67; asst. dir. student fin. aid Boston Coll., 1967-69, 70-71; asst. dir. Inst. Human Scis., Chestnut Hill, Mass., 1969-70; lectr. in edn. Boston Coll., 1971-73; prof. edn. grad. program coordinator, dir. leadership programs Suffolk U., 1973—; adj. lectr. Merrimack Coll., 1975, Boston U., 1973; gen. editor Garland Bibliographies in Contemporary Edn., 1979—. Recipient Ahearn scholarship, 1959-61, fellowship, 1961-63. Mem. Assn. Ancient Historians, Am. Assn. Higher Edn., Am., Cath. Hist. Assns., Soc. for Medieval and Renaissance Philosophy, Medieval Acad. Am., Phi Alpha Theta, Phi Delta Kappa. Author: An International List of Articles on the History of Education, Published in Non-Educational Serials, 1965-74, 1977; Guinea-Bissau and Cape Verde Islands: A Comprehensive Bibliography, 1977; Humanistic Emphases in the Educational Thought of Vincent of Beauvais, 1976; Pierre Teilhard de Chardin, 1981; Training School Administrators: The Principal, 1984; Training School Administrators: The Supervisor, 1984; assoc. editor The Urban and Social Change Rev., 1969-72; asst. editor occasional papers series The Bureaucrat, Inc., 1974-76. Home: 344 West St Box 1193 Duxbury MA 02331-1193 Office: Suffolk U Beacon Hill Boston MA 02114

MCCARTHY, VINCENT PAUL, lawyer; b. Boston, Sept. 25, 1940; s. John Patrick and Marion Priscilla (Buckley) McC.; children: Vincent, Sybil, Hope. AB, Boston Coll., 1962; JD, Harvard U., 1965. Bar: Mass. 1965. Ptnr. Hale and Dorr, Boston, 1965—, sr. ptnr., 1976—. Bd. dirs., sec. Pine St. Inn, Inc., Robert F. Kennedy Action Corps, Inc., Boston Alcohol Detoxification Project, Inc., Mass. Housing Partnership; mem. Gov.'s Adv. Council on Alcoholism, Gov.'s Adv. Commn. Homeless; trustee, sec. Franklin Sq. House; chmn. Boston Ctr. for Arts; bd. dirs., sec. Charlesbank Apts.; bd. dirs. Fund for Homeless, Fund for Boston Neighborhood. Mem. ABA (Pro Bono Publico award 1987), Mass. Bar Assn., Boston Bar Assn.

MCCARTHY, WILLIAM JOSEPH, lawyer, financial service executive; b. Bklyn., Feb. 13, 1923; s. William Joseph and Louise Ann (Malonson) M.; m. Carol E. Martin, Jan. 22, 1949 (dec. Jan. 1987); children—Christian, Mark, Margaret, Kelley, Mary. B.S., Georgetown U., 1944, LL.B., 1947; M.B.A., N.Y.U., 1965. Bar: D.C. 1947, U.S. Ct. Appeals (2d cir.) 1948, N.Y. 1947. Assoc., Hill, Rivkins & Middleton, 1947-49, Sullivan, Donovan, Heenehan & Hanrahan, 1949-52, Hawkins, Delafield & Wood, 1952-56; dep. U.S. mem. Validation Bd. for German Dollar Bond, 1956-60; mcpl. analyst Shearson, Hammill & Co., N.Y.C., 1960-62, sr. analyst, 1962-68, v.p., 1970, dir. new issue service, 1962-72; mcpl. bond research div., Moody's Investors Services, Inc., N.Y.C. 1972-75; v.p., mgr. mcpl. research Blyth, Eastman, Dillon & Co., NYC, 1975-80; v.p., mgr. mcpl. div. Fitch Investors Service, Inc., N.Y.C., 1980—. Active North East Yonkers Taxpayers Assn. (pres. 1970-71), Mohegan Heights Homeowners Assn. Mem. Soc. Mcpl. Analysts (pres. 1983), Assn. for Mcpl. Leasing and Fin. (dir. 1982-83), N.Y. Mcpl. Analysts (chmn. 1967-68), The Money Marketeers, Mun. Forum of N.Y., Met. Econ. Assn. Republican. Roman Catholic. Club: Mcpl. Bond (N.Y.C.). Lodge: K.C. Home: 36 Shawnee Ave Yonkers NY 10710 Office: 5 Hanover Sq New York NY 10004

MC CARTIN, THOMAS RONALD, marketing, communications and newspaper publishing executive; b. Jersey City, June 15, 1934; s. James A. and Margaret V. (Kelly) McC.; m. Ann Daley, Feb. 8, 1958; children: Margaret McCartin Harris, Maureen McCartin Schwartz, Michele, Michael, Matthew. Student, Glendale Jr. Coll., 1955-56, UCLA, 1959. Asst. dir. advt. Los Angeles Times, 1959-73; v.p. sales Washington Post, 1973-76; exec. v.p. Dallas Times Herald, 1975-80, pres., 1980-81, pub. and chief operating officer, 1981-83; founder, pres., chief exec. officer Times Mirror Nat. Mktg., 1983-85; sr. ptnr. Criswell Devel. Co., 1985-87; pres., chief exec. officer McCartin Co., 1986—; guest exec. lectr. Baylor U. Sch. Bus. Trustee Marymount Coll., 1970-73; mem. exec. com. Ctr. Mktg. and Design, North Tex. State U., 1976-83; chmn. council Coll. Communication, U. Tex., mem. adv. bd. sch. mgmt.; bd. dirs. McCartin Scholarship; mem. Mayor's Com. on Internat. Devel.; mem. adv. bd. sch. Middle East studies Brandeis U.; chmn. bd. dirs. U. Tex. Grad. Sch. Mgmt., Dallas Cultural Com.; mem. internat. bd. dirs. Up with People; bd. dirs., chmn. mktg. Dallas Ballet; bd. dirs. United Way, Dallas North Tex. Commn., Afro Am. Cultural and Art Mus., Folkloric Dallas, Internat. Irish Cultural Inst., Dallas County Hist. Soc., St. Paul Hosp. Found., Dallas, Dallas Found., Baylor Hosp. Found, Dallas, Childrens' Hosp. Found., Dallas Communications Council, Dallas Salvation Army, Dallas Citizen Council, NCCJ, Nat. Mus. of Communication, Dallas Hist. Soc., Theatre Ctr.; mem. cultural com. internat. devel. bd. City of Dallas, Goals for Dallas; mem. Dallas Mus. Fine Arts; vice chmn. TACA; bd. dirs., bd. govs. Dallas Symphony Orch.; mem. Tex. Bus. Com. for Arts; pres. Palos Verdes Peninsula (Calif.) City Council, 1971-73. Served with USN, 1951-55. Decorated Knight of Malta; recipient cert. and key of appreciation City of Los Angeles, 1973, The First Proclamation City of Rancho Palos Verdes, 1974; Obelisk award for arts City of Dallas, 1981; Father of the Yr., City of Dallas, 1983. Mem. Met. Sunday Newspapers (bd. dirs.), Newspaper Advt. Bur., Am. Assn. Newspaper Reps. (v.p. (1964-65), Tex. Pubs. Assn., Navy League (bd. dirs. Dallas/Ft. Worth chpt.). Roman Catholic. Clubs: Congl. Country, Nat. Press (Washington); Dallas, Dallas Press, Royal Oaks, Trinity River Yacht (commodore) (Dallas); Stone Horse Harbor Yacht (Harwichport, Mass.). Home: 3616 Centenary Dr Dallas TX 75225 Office: 240 Expressway Tower Dallas TX 75206

MCCARTNEY, (JAMES) PAUL, musician; b. Liverpool, Eng., June 18, 1942; s. James and Mary Patricia (Mohin) McC.; m. Linda Eastman, Mar. 12, 1969; 4 children. Hon., Univ. Sussex, Brighton, 1988. With, John Lennon and George Harrison in groups Quarrymen, Moondogs, Silver Beatles, 1956-62, also with Ringo Starr in group The Beatles, 1962-70, solo performer and with group, Wings, 1970—; film appearances include: A Hard Day's Night, 1964, Help!, 1965, Let It Be, 1970, Give My Regards to Broad Street, 1984; TV appearances include Magical Mystery Tour, 1967, James Paul McCartney, 1973, Wings Over the World, 1979; producer animated film The Oriental Nightfish, 1978; composer numerous songs including (with John Lennon) Please Please Me, I Want To Hold Your Hand, All My Loving, Can't Buy Me Love, I Saw Her Standing There, Love Me Do, Yesterday, Michelle, She's a Woman, Here, There and Everywhere, Good Day Sunshine, Penny Lane, She's Leaving Home, Fool on the Hill, Back in the USSR, Martha My Dear, Blackbird, Helter Skelter, Hey Jude, Let It Be, The Long and Winding Road, Get Back, (solo) Maybe I'm Amazed, My Love, Live and Let Die, Band on the Run, Silly Love Songs, Another Day, No More Lonely Nights, With a Little Luck; rec. artist: (albums with The Beatles) Meet the Beatles, Introducing the Beatles, Hard Day's Night, Help!, Rubber Soul, Revolver, Sgt. Pepper's Lonely Hearts Club Band, Magical Mystery Tour, The Beatles, Yellow Submarine, Abbey Road, Hey J de, Let It Be; solo albums include McCartney, 1970, Ram, 1971, Red Rose Speedway, 1973, Band on the Run, 1973, Venus and Mars, 1975, Wings Over America, 1975, Wings at the Speed of Sound, 1976, London Town, 1978, Wings Greatest, 1978, Back to the Egg, 1979, McCartney II, 1980, Tug of War, 1982, Press to Play, 1986, All The Best, 1987. decorated Order of Brit. Empire, 1965; Acad. award (with Beatles) for Best Original Song Score, Let It Be, 1970; 5 Grammy awards with Beatles, 2 solo, 1 with Wings.; named to Rock and Roll Hall of Fame, 1988. Office: care MPL Communications Ltd, 1 Soho Sq, London W1V 6BQ, England also: Columbia Records 51 W 52d St New York NY 10019 *

MC CARTNEY, RALPH FARNHAM, lawyer, district judge; b. Charles City, Iowa, Dec. 11, 1924; s. Ralph C. and Helen (Farnham) McC.; J.D., U. Mich., 1950; B. Sci., Iowa State U., 1972; m. Rhoda Mae Huxsol, June 30, 1950; children—Ralph, Julia, David. Bar: Iowa 1950. Mem. firm Miller, Heuber & Miller, Des Moines, 1950-52, Frye & McCartney, Charles City, 1952-73, McCartney & Erb, Charles City, 1973-78; judge Dist. Ct. Iowa, Charles City, 1978—; chief judge 2d. Judicial Dist.; mem. jud. coordinating com. Iowa Supreme Ct. Chmn., Iowa Republican Conv., 1972, 74; chmn. Supreme Ct. Adv. Com. on Adminstrn. of Clks. Offices; mem. Iowa Ho. of Reps., 1967-70, majority floor leader, 1969-70; mem. Iowa Senate, 1973-74. Bd. regents U. Iowa, Iowa State U., U. No. Iowa, Iowa Sch. for Deaf, Iowa Braille and Sight Saving Sch. Served with AUS, 1942-45. Mem. ABA, Iowa Bar Assn., Iowa Judges Assn. Home: RFD 1 Charles City IA 50616 Office: Ct Chambers Courthouse Charles City IA 50616

MC CARTNEY, ROBERT CHARLES, lawyer; b. Pitts., May 3, 1934; s. Nathaniel Hugh and Esther Mary (Smith) McC.; m. Janet Carolyn Moore, June 16, 1956; children: Ronald K., Sharon S., Carole J. A.B., Princeton U., 1956; J.D. (Princeton fellow), Harvard U., 1959. Bar: D.C. 1959, Pa. 1960. Asso. firm Eckert, Seamans, Cherin & Mellott, Pitts., 1959-64; partner Eckert, Seamans, Cherin & Mellott, 1965—; sec., gen. counsel Ryan Homes, Inc.; asst. sec., gen. counsel Washington Trotting Assn., Inc., Mountain Laurel Racing, Inc.; sec., gen. counsel Edn. Mgmt., Inc.; bd. dirs. United Methodist Found. of Western Pa., 1972—, v.p., 1981-85, chmn., 1985-86. Solicitor North Pitts. Community Devel. Corp., 1968-76, alt. dir., 1968-80; mem. McCandless Twp. Govt. Study Commn., 1973-74; solicitor, asst. sec. McCandless Indsl. Devel. Authority, 1972—; mem. exec. com. Princeton U. Alumni Council, 1966-70, 76-85, vice chmn., 1981-83, chmn., 1983-85; trustee Otterbein Coll., 1975-83; corp. bd. North Hills Passavant Hosp., 1976—; chmn. conf.-wide endowment program United Meth. Conf. Western Pa., 1985-87; mem. long-range planning com. Civic Light Opera Assn., 1984—, dir., 1986—, v.p., 1987—. Mem. ABA, Pa. Bar Assn., Allegheny County Bar Assn., Princeton U. Alumni Assn. of W.Pa. (pres. 1976-78), Golden Triangle YMCA. Republican. Clubs: Harvard-Yale-Princeton, Allegheny, Duquesne (Pitts.); Princeton (N.Y.C.); Rolling Rock (Ligonier, Pa.). Home: 9843 Woodland Rd N Pittsburgh PA 15237 Office: US Steel Bldg 600 Grant St 42nd Floor Pittsburgh PA 15219

MCCARTY, CHESTER EARL, lawyer, retired air force officer; b. Pendleton, Oreg., Dec. 31, 1905; s. Albert Guy and Nancy Elizabeth (Odom) McC.; m. Julia Caroline Gromoff, July 17, 1926. J.D., Northwestern Coll. of Law, Portland, Oreg., 1929; student, George Washington U., 1952. Bar: Oreg. 1928. Since practiced in Portland; sr. mem. McCarty, Swindells & Nelson and predecessor firms, 1929-77; of counsel Gleason & Scarborough, 1977—; legal adviser to Gov. of Oreg., 1931-33; spl. asst. atty. gen. Oreg., 1931-36; chmn. Republican Central Com., Multnomah County, Oreg., 1934-36; elected state senator (declined to serve due to mil. service) 1943; advanced through grades to col. A.C. U.S. Army, 1942-46; commr. Port of Portland (Oreg.), 1950-54; brig. gen. USAF, 1948-52; mem. Res. Forces Policy Bd., 1948-50, maj. gen., 1953; comdr. 305th Air Div. Very Heavy Bombardment, 1948-50, 403d Troop Carrier Wing, 1951-52, 315th Air Div. (combat cargo), also Korean Airlift, 1952-54; Airlift ans Sr. Air Force mem. O'Daniel mission to Indo-China during French occupation, 1952-54 comdr. 18th Air Force, 1954-57; comdr. 12th Air Force, 1957-59, 14th Air Force, 1959-60; asst. chief staff Reserve Forces, USAF, 1960-63; chief staff U.S. Air Forces in Europe, 1963-66, ret. as maj. gen.; former mem. Jud. Conf. 4th and 9th U.S. Circuits. Trustee Lewis and Clark Coll., Air Force Hist. Soc., Northwestern Sch. Law, 1969-87, now life trustee; bd. dirs. Oreg. Trail chpt. ARC, 1966-79. Decorated D.S.M., Legion of Merit with oak leaf cluster, D.F.C., Distinguished Marksman's Medal, Bronze Star, Air Medal with 4 oak leaf clusters; hon. mem. 82d Airborne Div. U.S. Army; hon. pilot French, Thailand and Chinese Air Forces; French Fgn. Legion (hon.); Order of Cloud and Banner China; comdr. Quissam Alouite Cherifien Morocco, Nicham-Iftikhar Tunis; Order of Crown Thailand; Order of Taiguk; Presdl. Citation Korea; Citation and medal for distinguished acts Kingdom of Greece; hon. comdr. of mil. div. Most Execllent Order Brit. Empire. Mem. Air Res. Assn. (nat. pres. 1947-48), ABA, Fed. Bar Assn. (Oreg. pres. 1977-78), Oreg. State Bar, Res. Officers Assn. (life), Nat. Rifle Assn. (life), Air Force Assn. (life), Izaak Walton League Am. (life), Lang Syne Soc. (pres. 1971), Explorers Club, Am. Rod and Gun Clubs of Europe (hon. v.p.), Mil. Order World Wars (life), Am. Legion (life), VFW (life), DAV (life), Order Daedalians (life), Delta Theta Phi (life). Presbyterian. Clubs: Rotary, Arlington, Waverley Country, University (hon. life mem.), Multnomah Athletic (Portland); El Dorado Country (Indian Wells, Calif.); Ends of Earth, OX5 Aviation Pioneers; Prince Albert (Brussels, Belgium). Lodges: Scottish Rite (33 deg.), Royal Order Scotland, Shriners, Jesters. Home: 2323 SW Park Pl Portland OR 97205 Office: 710 SW 3d Ave Portland OR 97204

MCCARTY, DEBORAH HUSCH, insurance company executive; b. Washington, Aug 4, 1960; d. Jakob and Ingrid (Fischer) Husch; m. Gregory D. McCarty, Aug. 15, 1987. B.S. in Mktg., U. Md., 1982. Food and beverage mgr. Washington Boat Lines, 1982-84; dist. rep. Aid Assn. for Lutherans, Appleton, Wis., 1984—. Mem. Nat. Assn. Life Underwriters, Women's Life Underwriters Conf., D.C. Life Underwriters Assn., Nat. Assn. Fraternal Ins. Counselors (Pres.'s award 1987), Nat. Assn. Female Execs., Million Dollar Round Table. Republican. Lutheran. Avocations: aerobics; running; reading; hiking; camping. Home: 6301 Sandy St Laurel MD 20707 Office: Aid Assn for Luths 6301 Sandy St Laurel MD 20707

MCCAUGHRIN, WENDY BORDOFF, educator; b. Windsor, Ont., Can., Nov. 23, 1944; d. Jack and Tillie (Starker) Bordoff; B.A., Wayne State U., 1967; B.A. with honors, U. Windsor, 1974; M.A., Merrill Palmer Inst., 1977; M.S., U. Ill., 1981, PhD, 1988; m. Scott James McCaughrin, July 1, 1972. Guidance counselor, instr. high sch., Chatham, Ont., 1967-70; reading therapist, instr., Windsor, Ont., 1971-77; reading and lang. therapist The Reading Group Program, Urbana, Ill., 1980-81; researcher computer-assisted instrn. for head-injured patients, Mercy Hosp., Urbana, 1984-85; ednl. cons. Learning Abilities Program, Mercy Hosp., Urbana, 1981-87, Christie Clinic, Champaign, 1987—; researcher transition of handicapped youth from tng. programs to competitive employment, U. Ill., 1986-87; ednl. researcher, Transition Inst. U. Ill., Urbana, 1987—. Mem. Cousteau Soc., Am. Speech-

Lang.-Hearing Assn., Orton Soc., Internat. Reading Assn., Kappa Delta Pi. Jewish. Author reading and writing tests. Home: 36 Hillside Ln Briar Cliff Mahomet IL 61853 Office: U Ill 110 Edu Bldg Urbana IL 61801

MCCAULEY, CLEYBURN LYCURGUS, lawyer; b. Houston, Feb. 8, 1929; s. Reese Stephens and Elizabeth Ann (Burleson) McC.; m. Elizabeth Kelton McKoy, June 7, 1950; children—Stephens Francis, Lillian Elizabeth, Cleyburn, Lucy Annette. B.S., U.S. Mil. Acad., 1950; M.S. in Engring. Econ., Statistical Quality Control and Indsl. Engring., Stanford U., 1959; J.D., Coll. William and Mary, 1970. Bar: D.C. 1971, Va. 1970, Tex. 1970, U.S. Ct. Claims 1971, U.S. Tax Ct. 1971, U.S. Supreme Ct. 1973. Commd. 2d lt. U.S. Air Force, 1950, advanced through grades to lt. col., 1971; ret., 1971; sole practice, Washington, 1975—. Mem. Fed. Bar Assn., Va. Bar Assn., Tex. Bar Assn., D.C. Bar Assn., IEEE, AIAA, Am. Soc. Quality Control, Phi Alpha Delta. Office: 1900 S Eads St Suite 1007 Crystal House 1 Arlington VA 22202

MCCAULEY, RAYNOR, pastor; b. Johannesburg, Republic of South Africa, Oct. 1, 1949; s. James and Doreen Priscilla (Miller) McC.; m. Lyndie Trehair, Mar. 13, 1976; 1 child, Joshua. Student, Rhema Bible Tng. Centre, Tulsa, 1978. Profl. body-builder, owner health studios Republic of South Africa, 1958-76; pastor, evangelist Rhema Ministries of South Africa, Randburg, 1979—. Author: Our God Reigns, 1985. Office: Rhema Ministries of South Africa, Hans Schoeman Dr, 2125 Randburg Republic of South Africa

MCCAULEY, RICHARD GRAY, real estate developer, lawyer; b. Balt., June 17, 1940. B.A. cum laude, Williams Coll., 1962; LL.B., U. Va., 1965. Bar: Md. 1969, U.S. Supreme Ct. 1969. Assoc. Piper & Marbury, Balt., 1965-69; asst. atty. gen. State of Md., 1969-71; sr. v.p., gen. counsel, sec. Rouse Co. and subs., Columbia, Md., 1971—; chmn. bd. Md. Deposit Ins. Fund Corp., 1985-86; gen. counsel Howard Research and Devel. Corp., Columbia, 1972—; lectr. Am. Law Inst.; bd. dirs. First Atlanta Bank N.Am., 1986—. Bd. dirs. Columbia Park and Recreation Assn., 1972—, chmn. exec. com., 1972-78, chmn. bd., 1978-83; trustee The Columbia Found., 1984—, pres., 1987—; trustee Howard Community Coll. Ednl. Found., 1982-88,vice chair, 1985-88. Mem. Md. Bar Assn., Am. Bar Assn., Balt. City Bar Assn., Am. Judicature Soc., Urban Land Inst., Am. Corporate Counsel Assn. Office: Rouse Co 10275 Little Patuxent Pkwy Columbia MD 21044

MCCHESNEY, KATHRYN MARIE, educator; b. Curwensville, Pa., Jan. 14, 1936; d. Orland William and Lillian Irene (Morrison) Spencer; B.A., U. Akron, 1962; M.L.S., Kent State U., 1965, postgrad., 1971-84; m. Thomas David McChesney, June 12, 1954; 1 son, Eric Spencer. Tchr. English, Springfield Local High Sch., Akron, Ohio, 1962-63, librarian, 1963-64, head librarian, 1965-68; asst. to dean, instr. Kent (Ohio) State U. Sch. Library Sci., 1968-69, asst. dean, 1969-77, asst. prof., 1969—. Rep. Uniontown Community Council, 1964-66. Mem. Am., Ohio (chmn. Library Edn. Roundtable 1971-72, exec. council Div. VI Library Edn. 1972-73) library assns., AAUP, Am., Ohio assns. sch. librarians, Beta Phi Mu, Phi Sigma Alpha, Phi Alpha Theta, Sigma Phi Epsilon. Club: Uniontown Jr. Womans (pres. 1965-66). Co-author: The Library in Society, 1984. Contbr. articles, book revs. to profl. periodicals. Home: 3611 Edison St NW Uniontown OH 44685 Office: Kent State U Kent OH 44242

MCCHRISTIAN, JOSEPH ALEXANDER, international business executive; b. Chgo., Oct. 12, 1914; s. Robert Lee and Lillian (Alexander) McC.; B.S. in Mil. Sci., U.S. Mil. Acad., 1939; grad. Command and Gen. Staff Coll., 1942, Armed Forces Staff Coll., 1951, Army War Coll., 1955, Army Lang. Sch., 1956; m. Dempsie Catherine Van Fleet, Sept. 26, 1940; children—Joseph Alexander, Anne, Lillian. Enlisted U.S. Army, 1933, commd. 2d lt., 1939, advanced through grades to maj. gen., 1961; various assignments 1933-44; successively armored inf. bn. comdr., asst. chief staff plans and ops., chief staff 10th Armored Div., ETO, 1944-45; asst. chief staff intelligence Hdqrs. 3d U.S. Army, Germany, 1945-47; dep. dir. intelligence U.S. Forces, Austria, 1947-48; comdg. officer 2d Bn., 3d Inf., Ft. McNair, D.C., 1948-49; spl. asst. to chief JUSMAG, Greece, 1949-50; S3 dept. tactics U.S. Mil. Acad., 1951-53, comdg. officer 1st Regt., U.S. Corp Cadets, 1953-54; U.S. Army attache, Greece, 1956-60; comdg. officer 1st Armored Regt. (tng.), also comdg. officer U.S. Army Tng. Center, Armor, Ft. Knox, Ky., 1960-61; chief Western div. Office Asst. Chief Staff-Intelligence, Dept. Army, 1962-63; asst. chief staff intelligence Hdqrs. U.S. Army Pacific, 1963-65; chief Army, Navy, Air Force and Marine Corps Intelligence, Hdgrs. U.S. Mil. Assistance Command, Vietnam, 1965-67; comdg. gen. 2d Armored Div., also III Corps, Ft. Hood, Tex., 1967-68; asst. chief of staff for intelligence Dept. Army, 1968-71; v.p. Overseas Basic Industries, Fla., 1972-74; v.p., gen. mgr. Société des Eaux, Athens, Greece, 1972-74; v.p. Ulen Mgmt. Co., Fla., 1972-75, Van Fleet Estates, Inc., Fla., 1970-77. Commr., Town of Jupiter Island (Fla.), 1975-83. Decorated D.S.M. with oak leaf cluster, Silver Star, Legion of Merit, Bronze Star with 3 oak leaf clusters, Air medal, Commendation ribbon, Combat Inf. badge; Croix de Guerre with gold star and bronze star (France); comdr. Royal Order King George 1st, also Distinguished Service medal (Greece); Nat. Order 5th class and Distinguished Service Order 1st class (Republic Vietnam); Mil. Merit medal, Chung Mu (Korea). Mem. Mil. Order World Wars, Alumni Assn. U.S. Mil. Acad. Clubs: Army and Navy (Washington); Hobe Sound Yacht, The Island (Hobe Sound, Fla.); Ends of the Earth. Home: 366 S Beach Rd Hobe Sound FL 33455

MCCLAFFERTY, JOHN JOSEPH, clergyman; b. N.Y.C., Apr. 9, 1906; s. John and Margaret (Moran) McC. A.B., Cathedral Coll., 1927; grad., St. Joseph's Sem., 1930; A.M., Catholic U., 1932; diploma, N.Y. Sch. Social Work, 1936; LL.D., Loyola U., Los Angeles, 1947. Cert. social worker, N.Y. State. Ordained priest Roman Catholic Ch., 1930, apptd. papal chamberlain, 1943; apptd. Domestic Prelate, 1953, Protonotary Apostolic, 1965; asst. dir. div. social action Catholic Charities, N.Y.C., 1936-41; dir. div. social research Catholic Charities, 1941-47; Dean Nat. Cath. Sch. of Social Service, Catholic U. Am., 1947-55, asst. to rector for univ. devel., 1955-63; pastor St. Peter's Ch., S.I., 1963-66, St. Francis de Sales Ch., N.Y.C., 1966-81; pastor emeritus St. Francis de Sales Ch., 1981—; chaplain Carmel Richmond Nursing Home, S.I., N.Y., 1982—; Exec. sec. Nat. Legion Decency, 1936-47; mem. bd. consultors Ch. of the Air CBS, 1940-47; bd. advisors Radio Chapel MBS, 1941-47; bd. dirs. Casita Maria Settlement, 1941-47; com. discrimination N.Y. State War Council, 1942-44; Am. del. to Pan-Am. Congress, Caracas, Venezuela, 1948; del. 3d Congress of Inter-Am. Cath. Social Action Confederation, Rio de Janeiro, Brazil, 1948; Mem. Point Four Mission to Colombia, S.A., 1951. Editor: Cath. U. of Am. Bull, 1956-63. Mem. nat. exec. fact-finding coms. Mid-Century White House Conf. on Children and Youth, 1950; Del. White House Conf. Children and Youth, 1960. Served as capt. (chaplain) 5th regiment of N.Y. Guard, 1941-43; col. (chaplain) Hdgrs. N.Y. Guard, 1943-49. Fellow Royal Soc. Health; mem. Nat. Assn. Social Workers, Acad. Cert. Social Workers. Home: 88 Old Town Rd Staten Island NY 10304

MCCLAIN, WILLIAM ANDREW, lawyer; b. Sanford, N.C., Jan. 11, 1913; s. Frank and Blanche (Leslie) McC.; m. Roberta White, Nov. 11, 1944. A.B., Wittenberg U., 1934; J.D., U. Mich., 1937; LL.D. (hon.), Wilberforce U., 1963, U. Cin., 1971; L.H.D., Wittenberg U., 1972. Bar: Ohio 1938, U.S. Dist. Ct. (so. dist.) Ohio 1940, U.S. Ct. Appeals (6th cir.) 1946, U.S. Supreme Ct. 1946. Mem. Berry, McClain & White, 1937-58; dep. solicitor, City of Cin., 1957-63, city solicitor, 1963-72; mem. Keating, Muething & Klekamp, Cin., 1972-73; gen. counsel Cin. Br., SBA, 1973-75; judge Hamilton County Common Pleas Ct., 1975-76; judge Mcpl. Ct., 1976-80; of counsel Manley, Barke & Fischer, Cin., 1980—; adj. prof. U. Cin., 1963-72, Salmon P. Chase Law Sch., 1965-72. Exec. com. ARC, Cin., 1978—; bd. dirs. NCCJ, 1975—. Served to 1st lt. JAGC, U.S. Army, 1943-46. Decorated Army Commendation award; recipient Nat. Layman award, A.M.E. Ch., 1963; Alumni award Wittenberg U., 1966; Nat. Inst. Mcpl. Law Officers award, 1971. Fellow Am. Bar Found.; mem. Am. Judicature Soc., World Peace Through Law Ctr., Cin. Bar Assn., Ohio Bar Assn., ABA, Fed. Bar assn., Nat. Bar Assn., Alpha Phi Alpha, Sigma Pi Phi. Republican. Methodist. Clubs: Bankers, Friendly Sons of St. Patrick Lodge: Masons (33 deg.). Address: 2101 Grandin Rd Apt 904 Cincinnati OH 45208

MCCLANAHAN, BETTY COLLEEN, publishing company executive; b. Altoona, Iowa, Jan. 19, 1924; d. Ezra Guy and Minnie (Hersbergen) Plummer; m. Willard Dale McClanahan, Oct. 7, 1944; children—Bonnie Sue McClanahan Hosler, Nancy Jo McClanahan Miller, Sarah Jane McClanahan Valenti. Student Altoona, Iowa schs. With Denniston & Partridge Lumber Co., Altoona, 1942-46; farm bookkeeper, Bondurant, Iowa, 1944—; owner, mgr. Hiawatha Book Co., Bondurant, 1980—; mem. Farmers Elevator Co.; rep. Ramsey Meml. Home Guild, 1978-84; mem. steering com. Spiritual Frontiers Fellowship, Des Moines, 1978—. Adaptor psalms to music. Mem. Builders of the Adytum, Theosphical Soc., Assn. Research and Enlightenment, Huna Assoc. Mem. Ch. of the Brethren. Avocations: stamp collecting, astrology, I Ching, Tarot, esoteric philosophies, piano. Home: 420 SE Grant Ankeny IA 50021 Office: Hiawatha Book Co 7567 NE 102 Ave Bondurant IA 50035

MC CLANAHAN, RUE (EDDI-RUE MC CLANAHAN), actress; b. Healdton, Okla.; d. William Edwin and Dreda Rheua-Nell (Medaris) McC.; 1 child, Mark Thomas Bish. B.A. cum laude, U. Tulsa, 1956. Actress: Erie (Pa.) Playhouse, 1957-58; theatrical, film and TV appearances, Los Angeles, 1959-64, N.Y.C., 1964-73; mem. cast: (TV series) Maude, 1973-78, Apple Pie, 1978, Mama's Family, 1982-84, Golden Girls, 1985— (Emmy award for best actress in a comedy show 1987); appeared on Broadway: Jimmy Shine, 1968-69, Sticks and Bones, 1972, California Suite, 1977. Recipient Obie award for leading off-Broadway role in Who's Happy Now, 1970; Emmy award Best Actress in a comedy, 1987; named Woman of Yr., Pasadena Playhouse, 1986; Spl. scholar Pasadena (Calif.) Playhouse, 1959, Phi Beta Gamma scholar, 1955. Mem. Actors Studio, Actors Equity Assn., AFTRA, Screen Actors Guild. Office: Internat Creative Mgmt 8899 Beverly Blvd Los Angeles CA 90048

MCCLARY, JAMES DALY, retired contractor; b. Boise, Idaho, July 19, 1917; s. Neil Hamacker and Myrtle (Daly) McC.; m. Mary Jane Munger, Feb. 2, 1939; children—Pamela, John. Student, Boise Jr. Coll., 1934-36, A.A., 1957; A.B., Stanford, 1938; LL.D., Gonzaga U., 1976. Laborer to supt. Morrison-Knudsen Co., Inc., Boise, 1932-42, project mgr., asst. dist. mgr., 1942- 47; gen. mgr. Mexican subs. Morrison-Knudsen Co., Inc., 1947-51, asst. to gen. mgr., 1951-53, asst. gen. mgr., 1953-60, dir., 1955-78, v.p., 1956-60, exec. v.p., 1960-72, chmn. bd., 1972-78; mem., vice chmn. Idaho Permanent Bldg. Fund Adv. Council, 1961-64, chmn., 1964-71. Treas. Idaho Republican Central Com., 1964-70; Presdl. elector, 1968; Trustee Boise Jr. Coll., 1960-83, vice chmn., 1967-73, chmn., 1973-83; bd. dirs. Boise State U. Found., Inc., 1964—, pres., 1970-81; bd. dirs., pres. AGC Edn. and Research Found., 1974—; elector Hall of Fame for Great Ams., 1976—; trustee St. Alphonsus Regional Med. Center, 1976-82, vice chmn., 1981-82. Recipient George Washington medal of honor Freedoms Found., Valley Forge, Pa., 1977; decorated Chevalier and Legion of Honor, Order of DeMolay; named Disting. Alumnus of Yr. Boise State U. Alumni Assn., 1971, Ky. Col. Fellow ASCE, Am. Inst. Constructors; mem. Internat. Road Fedn. (dir. 1972-78, vice chmn. 1977-78), Soc. Am. Mil. Engrs., Asso. Gen. Contractors Am. (dir. 1958—, exec. com. 1961-78, pres. 1972), Cons. Constructors Council Am., Newcomen Soc., Conf. Bd. (sr. mem.), Idaho Assn. Commerce and Industry (dir., chmn. 1974-77), The Moles (hon., mem. award 1978). Episcopalian. Clubs: Elk, Hillcrest Country (dir. 1965-67, 69, pres. 1967), Arid (exec. com. 1966); Ariz. Country (Phoenix); University (Mexico City); Stanford (Boise); Capitol Hill, International (Washington). Home: 4903 Roberts Rd Boise ID 83705

MCCLAUGHERTY, JOE L., lawyer, educator; b. Luling, Tex., June 1, 1951; s. Frank Lee and Elease (Terrell) McC.; m. Katherine Morrison Witte, Feb. 24, 1980. B.B.A. with honors, U. Tex., 1973, J.D. with honors, 1976. Bar: Tex. 1976, N.Mex. 1976, U.S. Dist. Ct. N.Mex. 1976, U.S. Ct. Appeals (10th cir.) 1976, U.S. Supreme Ct. 1979. Assoc. firm Rodey, Dickason, Sloan, Akin & Robb, P.A., Albuquerque, 1976-81, ptnr., dir., 1981-87, resident ptnr., Santa Fe, 1983-87, mng. ptnr., 1985-87, ptnr. Kemp, Smith, Duncan & Hammond, P.C., 1987—, resident ptnr., Santa Fe, 1987—, mng. ptnr., 1987—; adj. prof. law U. N.Mex., Albuquerque, 1983—; faculty Nat. Inst. Trial Advocacy, so. regional, So. Meth. U. Law Sch., 1983—, Rocky Mt. regional, U. Denver Law Sch., 1986—, nat. session U. Colo. Law Sch., 1987— ; faculty Hastings Ctr. for Trial and Appellate Advocacy, 1985—; bd. dirs. MCM Corp., Raleigh, N.C., Brit.-Am. Ins. Co., Ltd., Nassau, The Bahamas, 1985—. Mem. N.Mex. Bar Assn. (bd. dirs. trial practice sect. 1976-85, chairperson 1983-84, dir. young lawyers div. 1978-80), N.Mex. Assn. Def. Lawyers (pres. 1982-83, bd. dirs. 1982-85). Office: Kemp Smith Duncan & Hammond PC PO Box 8680 Santa Fe NM 87504

MCCLEAN, CELEITA A., aerospace marketing executive; b. Huntington, W.Va., Dec. 14, 1956; d. Raymond Ray and Sylvia May (Kinser) Breakiron. BS in Art and Edn. cum laude, W.Va. State Coll., 1980; MS in Aviation Mgmt. cum laude, Embry-Riddle Aero. U., 1985; grad. numerous aviation and mgmt. courses, U.S. Army. Lic. comml. pilot. Counselor, tutor W.Va. State Coll., Institute, 1975-80; mgr. army program GE Aerospace, Washington, 1984—. Serving as co. comdr. USAR, 1987—. Recipient Sikorsky Aircraft Rescue award U.S. Army; numerous other ribbons and badges. Mem. Assn. U.S. Army, Assn. U.S. Res., Marine Corp. Aviation Assn., Army Aviation Assn. Am., Am. Defense Preparedness Assn., Naval Helicopter Soc., Am. Helicopter Soc., Nat. Assn. Female Execs., Whirly Girls, Alpha Kappa Mu. Home: PO Box 216 South Point OH 45680 Office: GE Aerospace 1331 Pennsylvania Ave NW Washington DC 20004

MCCLEAN, RICHARD ARTHUR FRANCIS, communications company executive; b. London, Dec. 5, 1937; s. Donald Stuart and Marjory Cathleen (Franks) McC.; m. Janna Doresa, Aug. 29, 1959; children: Lucinda, Paul, Philippa. Student, Marlborough Coll. Advt. rep. Financial Times, London, 1955-75, advt. dir., 1975-77, mktg. dir., 1979-81, mktg. dir. Europe, 1981-83, dep. chief exec., 1983—, also bd. dirs. Served to lt. Welsh Guards, Eng. Anglican. Clubs: Garrick (London); Royal St. George's (Sandwich, Eng.). Office: The Financial Times Ltd, Bracken House 10 Cannon St, London EC4PB, England

MCCLEARY, BENJAMIN WARD, investment banker; b. Washington, July 9, 1944; s. George William and Nancy (Grim) McC.; m. Deirdre Stillman Marsters, May 6, 1967 (div. 1977); children: Benjamin, Katherine; m. Jean Luce Muchmore, Oct. 15, 1983. AB, Princeton U., 1966. Trainee Chem. Bank, N.Y.C., 1969-70, asst. sec., 1970-72, asst. v.p., 1972-74, v.p., 1974-81; sr. v.p. Lehman Bros. Kuhn Loeb, N.Y.C., 1981-84; mng. dir. Shearson Lehman Bros., Inc. (formerly Lehman Bros. Kuhn Loeb), N.Y.C., 1984-87; exec. dir. Shearson Lehman Hutton Internat., London, 1987—. Served with USN, 1966-69. Episcopalian. Club: Dunes (Naragansett, R.I.). Office: Shearson Lehman Bros Internat Inc, 1 Broadgate, London EC3 7HA, England

MCCLEARY, PAUL FREDERICK, voluntary agency executive; b. Bradley, Ill., May 2, 1930; s. Hal C. and Pearl (Aeicher) McC.; A.B., Olivet Nazarene U., Kankakee, Ill., 1952; M.Div., Garrett-Evang. Sem., Evanston, Ill., 1956; M.A., Northwestern U., 1972; D.D., MacMurray Coll., Jacksonville, Ill., 1970; m. Rachel Timm, Jan. 26, 1951; children—Leslie Ann, Rachel Mary, John Wesley, Timothy Paul. Ordained to ministry United Methodist Ch., 1956; missionary in Bolivia, 1957-68; exec. sec. structure study commn. United Meth. Ch., 1969-72, asst. gen. sec. to Latin Am., 1972-75; exec. dir. Ch. World Service, N.Y.C., 1975-84; assoc. gen. sec. for research Gen. Council on Ministries, United Meth. Ch., 1984-87; exec. v.p. Save the Children, Westport, Conn., 1987-88; exec. dir. Christian Children's Fund Inc., 1988—; mem. exec. com., bd. dir. Overseas Devel. Council; mem. adv. com. on economic matters World Council Chs.; mem. com. on African Devel. Strategies; mem. Com. on Dialogue and Devel., Nat. Leadership Commn. on Health Care, Bretton Woods Com. Mem. Am. Soc. Missiology, Hastings Center, AAAS, Acad. Polit. Sci., N.Y. Acad. Scis., Latin Am. Studies Assn., Alpha Kappa Lambda. Democrat. Club: Masons. Author: Global Justice and World Hunger, 1978; co-author: Quality of Life in a Global Society, 1978; contbr. articles to mags. Office: Save The Children 54 Wilton Rd Westport CT 06880

MCCLEERY, WINSTON THEODORE, computer consulting company executive; b. Mobile, Ala., Sept. 6, 1935; s. Robert Alton and Theadora K. (Kiebel) McC.; B.S., Springhill Coll., 1958; postgrad. U. Ala., 1955-57; m. Sandra Thoss, Dec. 28, 1958; children—Winston T., Sandra. Logic design engr. Autonetics N.Am. Aviation, Anaheim, Calif., 1960-63; dir. info. systems Litton Industries, Los Angeles, 1963-69; founder Winston T. McCleery, 1970, owner, 1970—; pres. Mgmt. Resources, Inc., Mobile, 1979—. Served with U.S. Army, 1958-60. Mem. Data Processing Mgmt. Assn., Assn. Computer Machinery, Am. Mgmt. Assn., Ind. Computer Cons.'s Assn. Club: Optimist (pres. 1972). Home: 5213 Janekyn Dr Mobile AL 36609 Office: 4920 Cottage Hill Rd Mobile AL 36609

MCCLELLAN, ROBERT EDWARD, civil engineer; b. Atlanta, Feb. 27, 1922; s. Robert Edward and Maria Elizabeth (Ameln) McC.; m. Mary Margaret Billetter, Oct. 21, 1944; children: Kathleen Mary, Mary Elizabeth, Patricia Maura, Eileen Mary, Robert Edward III, Mary Margaret, Thomas Francis. BCE, U. So. Calif., 1947, MSCE, 1956, PhD in Engring., 1970. Registered profl. civil and structural engr., Calif. Gen. supr. design Rocketdyne, Canoga Park, Calif., 1959-62; mem. tech. staff The Aerospace Corp., El Segundo, Calif., 1962-69, mgr. strategic studies, 1980-85; chief tech. staff The Ralph M. Parsons Co., Pasadena, Calif., 1969-80; v.p. research and devel. Apollo Systems Tech., Canyon Country, Calif., 1985—, also bd. dirs. Served to lt. (j.g.) USN, 1943-46, PTO. Recipient Outstanding Civil Engring. Grad. award U. So. Calif., 1977. Mem. AIAA, Am. Def. Preparedness Assn., Structural Engrs. Assn. So. Calif., Am. Soc. Indsl. Security, AAAS, Internat. Platform Assn., N.Y. Acad. Scis., Tau Beta Pi, Sigma Xi, Chi Epsilon. Republican. Roman Catholic. Club: Los Angeles Athletic. Office: PO Box 6186 Woodland Hills CA 91365

MCCLELLAN, ROGER ORVILLE, toxicologist; b. Tracy, Minn., Jan. 5, 1937; s. Orville and Gladys (Paulson) McC.; m. Kathleen Mary Dunagan, June 23, 1962; children—Eric John, Elizabeth Christine, Katherine Ruth. D.V.M. with highest honors, Wash. State U., 1960; M.Mgmt., U. N.Mex., 1980. diplomate Am. Bd. Vet. Toxicology, cert. Am. Bd. Toxicology. From biol. scientist to sr. scientist Gen. Electric Co., Richland, Wash., 1957-64; sr. scientist biology dept. Pacific N.W. Labs., Richland, Wash., 1965; scientist med. research br. div. biology and medicine AEC, Washington, 1965-66; asst. dir. research, dir. fission product inhalation program Lovelace Found. Med. Edn. and Research, Albuquerque, 1966-73; v.p., dir. research adminstrn., dir. Lovelace Inhalation Toxicology Research Inst., Albuquerque, 1973-76, pres., dir., 1976-88; chmn. bd. dirs. Lovelace Biomedical and Environ. Research Inst., Albuquerque, 1988—; pres. Chem. Industry Inst. Toxicologyand Research, Triangle Park, N.C., 1988—; mem. research com. Health Effects Inst., 1981—; bd. dirs. Toxicology Lab. Accreditation Bd., 1982—, treas., 1984—; adj. prof. Wash. State U., 1980—, U. Ark., 1970—; clin. assoc. U. N.Mex., 1971—, adj. prof. toxicology, 1985—; mem. dose assessment adv. group U.S. Dept. Energy, 1980-87, mem. health and environ. research adv. com., 1984-85; mem. exec. com. sci. adv. bd. EPA, 1974—, mem. environ. health com., 1980-83, chmn., 1982-83, chmn. radionuclide emissions rev. com., 1984-85, chmn. Clean Air Sci. Adv. Com., 1987—; mem. com. on toxicology Nat. Acad. Sci.-NRC, 1979-87, chmn., 1980-87, ad hoc mem. bd. environ. studies and toxicology, 1980-87; mem. Dept. Labor adv. com. , 1988; bd. dirs. Lovelance Anderson Endowment Found.; pres. Am. Bd. Vet. Toxicology, 1970-73; mem. adv. counciFl Ctr. for Risk Mgmt., Resources for the Future, 1987—; council mem. Nat. Council for Radiation Protection, 1970—. Contbr. articles to profl. jours. Editorial bd. Jour. Toxicology and Environ. Health, 1980—, assoc. editor, 1982—; editorial bd. Fundamental and Applied Toxicology, 1984—, assoc. editor, 1987—; editorial bd. Toxicology and Indsl. Health, 1984—; editor CRC Critical Revs. in Toxicology, 1987—; assoc. editor Inhalation Toxicology Jour., 1987—. Recipient Herbert E. Stokinger award Am. Conf. Govtl. Indsl. Hygienists, 1985, Alumni Achievement award Wash. State U., 1987, Disting. Assoc. award Dept. Energy, 1987. Fellow AAAS, Am. Acad. Vet. and Comparative Toxicology; mem. Radiation Research Soc. (sec.-treas. 1982-84, chmn. fin. com. 1979-82), Health Physics Soc. (chmn. program com. 1972, Elda E. Anderson award 1974), Soc. Toxicology (v.p.-elect to pres. 1987-90; inhalation specialty sect. v.p. to pres. 1983-86; bd. publs. 1983-86, chmn. 1983-85), Am. Assn. Aerosol Research (bd. dirs. 1982—, treas. 1986—), Soc. Risk Analysis, Am. Vet. Med. Assn., Gesellschaft fur Aerosolforschung, Sigma Xi, Phi Kappa Phi, Phi Zeta. Republican. Lutheran. Home: 1111 Cuatro Cerros SE Albuquerque NM 87123 Office: Lovelace Inhalation Toxicology Research Inst PO Box 5890 Albuquerque NM 87185

MCCLELLAND, JAMES RAY, lawyer; b. Eunice, La., June 21, 1946; s. Rufus Ray and Homer Florene (Nunn) McC.; m. Sandra Faye Tate, Feb. 6, 1971; children—Joseph Ray, Jeffrey Ross. B.S., La. State U., 1969, M.B.A., 1971, J.D., 1975. Bar: La. 1975, U.S. Ct. Appeals (5th cir.) 1976, U.S. Dist. Ct. (ea. dist.) La. 1976, U.S. Dist. Ct. (we. dist.) La. 1976. Assoc. Aycock, Horne, Caldwell, Coleman & Duncan, Franklin, La., 1975-78, ptnr., 1978—; dir. Bayou Bouillon Corp., Cotten Land Corp. Mem. exec. com. Democratic Party, St. Mary Parish, 1980—; del. La. Dem. Party, 1982, 84. Mem. La. State Bar Assn. (ho. of dels. 1982—, law reform com. 1984—), St. Mary Parish Bar Assn. (pres. 1978-79), Order of Coif. Club: Rotary (pres. 1981-82). Home: PO Box 268 Franklin LA 70538 Office: PO Box 592 Franklin LA 70538

MC CLELLAND, JOHN PETER, winery executive; b. N.Y.C., Aug. 17, 1933; s. Harold Stanley and Helen Lucille (Gardner) McC.; m. Ann Carolyn Campbell, Aug. 27, 1954; children: John, Kristen. Student, UCLA, 1951-53. With Almadén Vineyards, Inc., San Jose, Calif., 1958-83; v.p. sales, then v.p. mktg. Almadén Vineyards, Inc., 1970-76, pres., 1976-83; chmn. bd., chief exec. officer Geyser Peak Winery, 1983—. Served with AUS, 1954-56. Mem. Wine Inst. (chmn. public relations com. 1977—, exec. com. 1979—, chmn. 1986-87), Sonoma County Wine Bd., Internat. Wine and Food Soc., Supreme Knight of the Vine, Chaine Des Rotisseurs. Republican. Presbyterian.

MC CLELLAND, ROBERT NELSON, surgeon, educator; b. Gilmer, Tex., Nov. 20, 1929; s. Robert Hilton and Verna Louise (Nelson) McC.; m. Connie Logan, May 5, 1958; children: Robert Christopher, Alison, Julie. B.A., U. Tex., Austin, 1952; M.D., U. Tex., Galveston, 1954. Diplomate Am. Bd. Surgery. Rotating intern U. Kans. Med. center, 1954-55; resident in gen. surgery Parkland Hosp., Dallas, 1957-59, 60-62; instr. surgery Southwestern Med. Sch., U. Tex., Dallas, 1962-63; asst. prof. Southwestern Med. Sch., U. Tex., 1963-67, asso. prof., 1967-71, prof., 1971—, Alvin Baldwin prof. surgery, 1977—; examiner Nat. Bd. Med. Examiners. Editor Audio Jour. Rev. Gen. Surgery, 1971-82, Selected Readings in Gen. Surgery, 1974—; contbr. numerous articles to profl. jours., chpts. to books. Served to capt. M.C. USAF, 1955-57. Fellow A.C.S.; mem. Dallas County Med. Soc., AMA, Tex. Med. Assn., Western Surg. Assn., Soc. Surgery of Alimentary Tract, Am. Gastroent. Assn., Southwestern Surg. Soc., Am. Surg. Assn., So. Surg. Assn., Phi Beta Kappa, Alpha Omega Alpha. Republican. Lutheran. Home: 3601 Potomac St Dallas TX 75205 Office: 5323 Harry Hines Blvd Dallas TX 75235

MCCLEMENTS, ROBERT, JR., oil company executive; b. Phila., Dec. 1, 1928; s. Robert and Emma (Connor) McC.; m. Barbara Joan Rose, Dec. 20, 1952; children: Kathleen, Mary Anne. B.C.E., Drexel U., 1952; Advanced Mgmt. Program, Harvard U., 1977. Project engr. Foster-Wheeler Co., Livingston, N.J., 1952-54; project mgr. Catalytic Construction Co., Phila., 1956-65; plant mgr., v.p. Sun-Great Can. Oil, Ft. McMurray, Alta., Can., 1965-71; dir., materials mgr. Sun Co., Phila., 1971-72, dir. engring., 1972-74; v.p. energy ventures Sun Co., Dallas, 1974-75, pres. Sunoco Energy Devel. Co., 1975-77; exec. v.p. Sun Co., Radnor, Pa., 1977-81, pres., 1981-86, chief exec. officer, 1985—; chmn. bd. Sun Co., Radnor, 1987—; dir. First Pa. Corp., Phila., chmn., 1987—. Bd. trustees, Drexel U., Thomas Jefferson U., Grove City Coll.; pres. adv. council, Ea. Coll.; mem. Assoc. United Ways, Pa., N.J., Greater Phila. First Corp., Pennsylvanians for Effective Govt., Phila. Orch., LISC Phila. policy Bd. Served with U.S. Army, 1954-56. Mem. Am. Petroleum Inst. (bd. dirs.), Am. Productivity Ctr., Greater Phila. C. of C., Nat. Indsl. Adv. Council, Pa. Bus. Roundtable, Urban Affairs Partnership. Clubs: Union League (Phila.); Aronimink Golf (Newtown Square, Pa.). Home: 773 Sugartown Rd Malvern PA 19355 Office: Sun Co Inc 100 Matsonford Rd Radnor PA 19087

MCCLINTOCK, BARBARA, geneticist, educator; b. June 16, 1902. Ph.D. in Botany, Cornell U., 1927; D.Sc. (hon.), U. Rochester, U. Mo., Smith Coll., Williams Coll., Western Coll. for Women. Instr. botany Cornell U., Ithaca, N.Y., 1927-31, research assoc., 1934-36, Andrew D. White prof.-at-large, 1965—; asst. prof. U. Mo., 1936-41; mem. staff Carnegie Instn. of Washington, Cold Spring Harbor, N.Y., 1941-47, Disting. Service mem.,

1967—; cons. agrl. sci. program Rockefeller Found., 1962-69. NRC fellow, 1931-33; Guggenheim Found. fellow, 1933-34; recipient Achievement award AAUW, 1947; Nat. medal of Sci., 1970; MacArthur Found. prize; Rosentiel award, 1978; Nobel prize, 1983. Mem. Nat. Acad. Scis. (Kimber genetics award 1967), Am. Philos. Soc., Am. Acad. Arts and Scis., Genetics Soc. Am. (pres. 1945), Bot. Soc. Am. (award of merit 1957), AAAS, Am. Inst. Biol. Sci., Am. Soc. Naturalists. Office: Carnegie Instn of Washington Cold Spring Harbor Lab Cold Spring Harbor NY 11724 *

MCCLINTOCK, SHIRLEY SPRAGUE, govt. ofcl.; b. Flushing, N.Y., Jan. 3, 1928; d. George Wilkie and Mary Dorothea (O'Rourke) Sprague; student Cornell U., 1949-51; m. John William McClintock, Sept. 22, 1951; children—Barton, Charles, Scott. Personnel adminstr. Gen. Motors Co., 1952-54, analyst, overseas ops., N.Y.C., 1965-68; mem. U.S. Govt. Transition Com., 1968-69; housing adminstr. HUD, N.Y.C., 1969-79, 82—, Buffalo, 1979-82. . Bd. dirs. Soc. Prevention Cruelty to Children Mass., 1962-64; sec. LWV, N.Y.C., 1960-62. Recipient Cert. Superior Service, HUD, 1975. Mem. Cornell Club Greater Buffalo (pres. 1981—), Cornell U. Alumni Assn. Club: Cornell (N.Y.C.). Home: 541 E 20th St New York NY 10010 Office: 26 Federal Plaza New York NY 10278

MC CLOSKEY, BERTRAM PAYNE, public health physician; b. Melbourne, Australia, Feb. 6, 1923; s. Henry and Edith May (Payne) McC.; B.S., M.B., Melbourne U., 1945, M.D., 1951; D.P.H., Sydney U., 1953; m. Dorothy Jean Barber, June 1, 1949; children—Jenny Colleen, Michael John, David Sherwin. Resident med. officer, Royal Melbourne Hosp., Royal Children's Hosp., Melbourne, 1945-47; practice medicine specializing in paediatrics, Melbourne, 1947-48; med. supr. poliomyelitis Dept. Health, Melbourne, 1948-57, dir. child health medicine, 1957-61, asst. chief health officer, child health, 1961-66, public health, 1966-71, dep. chief health officer, 1972-75, chief health officer, chmn. Commn. Public Health, 1975-78, dir. public health, 1978-86, cons., 1986— ; mem. Nat. Health and Med. Research Council, 1975-78, Australian Inst. Human Relations Found., 1968-81, chmn., 1969-72; chmn. Standing Com. on Pre-school Child Devel., 1975-78, Victorian Food Standards Com., 1975-86; mem. faculty of medicine U. Melbourne, 1975-78; cons. WHO, Republic of Singapore, 1971; mem. planning div. Adminstrn. Appeals Tribunal, 1987—. Mem. Nat. Fitness Council, 1957-78, Victorian Consultative Com. on Social Devel., 1974-82, State Council on Spl. Edn., 1976-82, State Recreation Council, 1978-82; life gov. Burwood Boys' Home, 1962—; hon. life mem. Children's Welfare Assn., Victorian Family Council; vis. prof. Sch. Public Health, U. Calif., Berkeley, 1979; mem. World Health Fellowship, 1963-64. Fellow Royal Australasian Coll. Physicians, Royal Australian Coll. Med. Adminstrs.; mem. Australian Med. Assn. (Prize, 1952), Australian Coll. Pediatrics, Inst. Health Edn. U.K., Australian Soc. Infectious Disease Found. Clubs: Melbourne Cricket, Univ. High Sch. No. 517, Goodwill 80, Bd. Benevolence, United Grand Lodge of Victoria, 1977—. Editor: (with F. W. Clements) Child Health: Its Origins and Promotion, (Edward Arnold London), 1964; contbr. articles to profl. med. publs. Home: 32 Nevis St, Camberwell, Victoria 3124, Australia

MCCLOUD, PEGGY, painting contracting company executive; b. Ft. Worth, Apr. 27, 1954; d. Leland Webb and Carolyn (Schmitz) McC. B.A. in Psychology, U. Calif.-Davis, 1975; M.A. in Psychology, Humboldt State U., 1985. Plant mgr. S&W, Buena Park, Calif., 1978-82; prodn. control mgr. Inter-Am., Costa Mesa, Calif., 1982-83; owner, operator Jill of all Trades, Los Angeles, 1983—; speaker women's conf. Mem. Women in Mgmt., Women in Bus., Nat. Assn. Women Bus. Owners. Democrat. Home: 1354 N Benton Way Los Angeles CA 90026

MCCLUNG, CHRISTINA JUNE, training company executive; b. Newark, N.J., Jan. 19, 1948; d. Frederick and Maria (Dallinger) Palensar; m. Kenneth Austin McClung, Mar. 21, 1975. B.A., Kean Coll., 1970; M.A. in Edn., Seton Hall U., 1973; Ed.D. in Instructional Tech., U. So. Calif., 1976. Tchr. Chatham Twp. (N.J.) pub. schs., 1970-74; instructional designer Tratec Co., Los Angeles, 1976-79; asst. prof. Lehman Coll., Bronx, N.Y., 1977-79; ind. cons., 1978-80; v.p., bd. dirs. Instructional Design Group, Morristown N.J., 1980—; gen. ptnr. MGM Investments, 1985—. Mem. Nat. Soc. Performance Instrn. (v.p. programs N.J. chpt.), Phi Delta Kappa. Author 5 book series Computers for Professionals, 1983. Office: Instructional Design Group 144 Speedwell Ave Morristown NJ 07960

MCCLUNG, JOHN ROBINSON, JR., advertising company executive; b. Sewanee, Tenn., Sept. 14, 1914; s. John Robinson and Mary Merle (McCall) McC.; m. Edith Logue, Feb. 3, 1944; children: John T., Bonnie McClung Chappa, Marilyn Michele McClung Rositas. BS in Bus. and Journalism, Kans. State U., 1937. Reporter Manhattan (Kans.) Mercury, 1934-36; advt. staff, editor Aetna Life and Casualty Co., Hartford, Conn., 1938-41; account exec., assoc. mgr. Kirschner and Co., San Francisco and Palo Alto, Calif., 1947-65; v.p. Art Blum Agy., San Francisco, 1966; founder, chmn., pres. McClung Advt. Agy., Inc., Palo Alto, 1967—; former mem. San Francisco Advt. Club, 1947-62. Editor Ins. Adjuster mag., 1963-65, others. Served to capt. Signal Corps, U.S. Army, 1941-45, PTO. Mem. Adcrafters Club (pres. 1954), Peninsula Advt. Club (bd. dirs. 1971-74), Beta Theta Pi (Calif. dist. chief 1954-63, pres. internat. conv. 1965, editor mag. 1977—), Sigma Delta Chi. Republican. Methodist. Club: Palo (Palo Alto). Office: McClung Advt Agy Inc PO Box 60699 Palo Alto CA 94306

MCCLUNG, MERLE STEVEN, lawyer; b. Clara City, Minn., June 30, 1943. BA, Harvard U., 1965, JD, 1972; AB, MA, Oxford U., Eng., 1967. Bar: Mass. 1973. Instr. Miles Coll., Birmingham, Ala., 1969-70; staff atty. Harvard Ctr. Law & Edn., Cambridge, Mass., 1972-79; dir. law and edn. ctr. Edn. Commn. States, Denver, 1979-81; gen. counsel Pendleton Land & Exploration, Inc., Denver, 1981—; legal cons. Conn. Dept. Edn., Hartford, 1974-77, Calif. Dept. Edn., Sacramento, 1978-81. Contbr. articles to profl. jours. Rhodes scholar Oxford U., Eng., 1965. Mem. ABA, Mass. Bar Assn., Phi Beta Kappa. Home: 6048 S Locust Circle Englewood CO 80111 Office: Pendleton Land and Exploration Inc 8085 S Chester St Englewood CO 80112

MCCLURE, BROOKS, management consultant; b. N.Y.C., Mar. 8, 1919; s. Walter Harsha and Angelica (Mendoza) McC.; m. Olga Beatrice Gallik, Oct. 15, 1949; 1 dau., Karen. A.B. summa cum laude, U. Md.; distinguished grad., U.S. Naval War Coll. N.Y. corr. Western Press Ltd., Australia, 1939-42; copy editor Washington Eve. Star, 1946-51; joined U.S. Fgn. Service, 1951; information officer, attache embassy Copenhagen, 1951-53; press Attache embassy Vienna, 1953-55; information officer, attache embassy Cairo, 1956-57, Seoul, 1957-60, Bonn, 1960-63; policy officer Europe USIA, 1963-66; pub. affairs officer 1st sec. embassy, Copenhagen, 1967-72; spl. asst. policy plans and nat. security council affairs, internat. security affairs Dept. Def., 1972-76; internat. security adviser USIA, 1976-77; program coordinator Crisis Assessment Staff, Dept. Commerce, 1977-78; dir. ops. Internat. Mgmt. Analysis and Resources Corp., 1978-81, v.p., 1982—; various spl. assignments, Europe, Asia, Africa; lectr. FBI Acad., Fgn. Service Inst., Inter-Am. Def. Coll., Army War Coll., Navy War Coll. Contbg. author: Modern Guerrilla Warfare, 1962, Dynamics of Terrorism, 1977, International Terrorism in Contemporary World, 1978, Corporate Vulnerability and How to Assess it: Political Terrorism and Business, 1979, Business and the Middle East, 1981, Political Terrorism and Energy, 1981; Contbr. articles profl. jours.; author report to Senate Judiciary Com. on internat. terroism and hostage def. measures; testifier on internat. security, hostage behavior, def. of Alaska pipeline, FBI charter U.S. Senate, 1975-79. Served with AUS, 1942-46. Mem. Am. Fgn. Service Assn., Assn. Polit. Risk Analysts, Am. Polit. Sci. Assn., Acad. Polit. Sci., Royal United Services Inst. (London), Phi Kappa Phi, Alpha Sigma Lambda. Clubs: Nat. Press., Dacor. Home: 6204 Rockhurst Rd Bethesda MD 20817 Office: IMAR Corp Box 34528 Bethesda MD 20817

MCCLURE, CHARLES RICHARD, marketing executive; b. Dayton, Ohio, June 3, 1947; s. Richard Allison and Mary Lois McC.; m. Patricia Ann Stridsberg, Apr. 4, 1969; children: Lisa Marie, Richard Ryan. BA, Ohio State U., 1970. Asst. dir. pub. relations Ohio State U., Columbus, 1970-73; communications dir. Columbus Devel. Dept., 1973-75; account exec. Paul Werth Assos., 1975-78; account exec., pub. relations mgr. Howard Swink Advt., 1978-82; v.p. Shelly Berman Communicators, 1982-87; sr. v.p. Brucken/Goettler Advt., Columbus, 1987-88; sr. cons. McClure Consumer Research, 1988—; mem. mktg. faculty Ohio State U., 1979—. Served to 1st lt. Army N.G., 1969-73. Mem. Am. Mktg. Assn., Pub. Relations Soc. Am., Columbus Advt. Fedn., Ohio Press Club. Episcopalian. Clubs: Athletic, Ohio State U. Faculty.

MC CLURE, JAMES A., senator; b. Payette, Idaho, Dec. 27, 1924; s. W. R. and Marie McC.; m. Louise Miller; children: Marilyn, Kenneth, David. J.D., U. Idaho, 1950; J.D. hon. doctorate, 1981; DL (hon.), Coll. Idaho, 1986. Mem. Idaho State Senate, 1961-66; asst. majority leader 1965-66; city atty. City of Payette (Idaho); pros. atty. Payette County; Mem. 90th-92d Congresses from 1st Idaho Dist., 1967-73; U.S. Senator from Idaho 1973—; Energy and Natural Resources Com.; mem. Com. on Rules and Adminstrn., Com. on Appropriations; subcom. on Interior and related agys.; mem. subcoms. on agrl., def., energy/water devel. Trustee Kennedy Center; bd. govs. Council for Nat. Policy. Mem. Phi Alpha Delta. Methodist (trustee). Clubs: Elks, Masons, Kiwanis. Office: 309 Hart Senate Bldg Washington DC 20510 *

MCCLUSKEY, EDWARD JOSEPH, engineering educator; b. N.Y.C., Oct. 16, 1929; s. Edward Joseph and Rose (Slavin) McC.; m. Lois Thornhill, Feb. 14, 1981; children by previous marriage—Edward Robert, Rosemary, Therese, Joseph, Kevin, David. A.B. in Math. and Physics, Bowdoin Coll., Brunswick, Maine, 1953, B.S., M.S. in Elec. Engring., 1953; Sc.D., MIT, 1956. With Bell Telephone Labs., Whippany, N.J., 1955-59; asso. prof. elec. engring. Princeton, 1959-63, prof., 1963-66, dir. Computer Center, 1961-66; prof. elec. engring. and computer sci. Stanford (Calif.) U., 1967—, dir. Digital Systems Lab., 1969-78; dir. Center for Reliable Computing, 1976— ; tech. advisor VLSI Systems Design, 1987—. Author: A Survey of Switching Circuit Theory, 1962; Introduction to the Theory of Switching Circuits, 1965; Design of Digital Computers, 1975; Logic Design Principles with Emphasis on Testable Semicustom Circuits, 1986. Editor: Prentice-Hall Computer Engineering Series, 1988—; assoc. editor: IRE Transactions on Computers, 1959-65, ACM Jour., 1963-69; editorial bd. IEEE Design & Test, 1984-86; assoc. editor, IEEE Trans. Computer Assisted Design, 1986-87. Patentee in field. Fellow IEEE (pres. computer soc. 1970-71, Centennial medal 1984, Computer Soc. Tech. Achievement award 1984), AAAS, Am. Fedn. Info. Processing Socs. (dir., exec. com.), Internat. Fedn. Info. Processing (charter), Japan Soc. Promotion of Sci. Office: Computer Systems Lab Ctr Reliable Computing Stanford CA 94305-4055

MCCOLL, GREGORY DUNCAN, economics educator; b. Nanango, Queensland, Australia, Feb. 23, 1931; s. Herbert Reginald and Ada Mildred (Brondell) McC.; m. Gertrude Faye Richmond; children: Marianne, Annabelle. BSc in Econs., London Sch. Econs., 1960, MSc, 1962; PhD, U. London, 1974. Lectr., sr. lectr. in econs. U. New South Wales, Sydney, Australia, 1967-74, assoc. prof. econs., 1974—, head dept. econs., 1983-87, dir. ctr. for applied econ. research, 1988—; cons. econs. Secretariat G.A.T.T., Geneva, Switzerland, 1974, Comalco Ltd., Melbourne, Victoria, 1981-83; cons. evaluation Australian Devel. Bur., Canberra, 1977-81; chmn. Com. of Inquiry into Gas and Elec. Tariffs, Perth, 1984-85. Author: Australian Balance of Payments, 1965, Economics of Electricity Supply in Australia, 1976; editor: Overseas Trade and Investment, 1972; contbr. articles to profl. jours. Econ. advisor Fraser Island Environ. Inquiry, 1975-76, Ranger Uranium Environ. Inquiry, 1976-77; leader of study Great Barrier Reef Marine Park Authority, 1981-82; mem. Nat. Energy Research Demonstration and Devel. Council, Canberra, 1985—. Mem. Royal Econ. Soc., Econ. Soc. Australia, Am. Econ. Assn., Internat. Assn. Energy Economists. Club: University of New South Wales. Sr. Home: 29 Acacia St, Collaroy Plateau, New South Wales 2098, Australia Office: Univ New South Wales, PO Box 1, Kensington, New South Wales 2033, Australia

MCCOLLOUGH, MICHAEL LEON, astronomy educator; b. Sylva, N.C., Nov. 3, 1953; s. Stribling Mancell and Vivian Hazel (Bradley) McC. B.S., Auburn U., 1975, M.S., 1981; Ph.D. candidate, Ind. U. Lab. instr. Auburn (Ala.) U., 1974-75, grad. asst., 1975-77, lab. technician, 1977-78; assoc. instr. Ind. U., Bloomington, 1978-86; vis. asst. prof. U. Okla., Norman, 1987—; vis. lectr. Okla. State U., Stillwater, 1986-87. Mem. Am. Astron. Soc., N.Y. Acad. Scis., AAAS, Royal Astron. Soc., Astron. Soc. Pacific, Am. Phys. Soc., Optical Soc. Am., Am. Assn. Physics Tchrs., Soc. Physics Students, Sigma Xi (assoc.), Sigma Pi Sigma. Baptist. Home: PO Box 2516 Norman OK 73070 Office: U Okla Dept Physics and Astronomy Norman OK 73019

MCCOLLUM, JAMES FOUNTAIN, lawyer; b. Reidsville, N.C., Mar. 24, 1946; s. James F. and Dell (Frazier) McC.; m. Susan Shasek, Apr. 26, 1969; children—Audra Lynn, Amy Elizabeth. B.S., Fla. Atlantic U., 1968; J.D., Fla. State U., 1972. Bar: U.S. Ct. Appeals (5th cir.) 1973, Fla. 1972, U.S. Ct. Appeals (11th cir.) 1982. Assoc., Kennedy & McCollum, 1972-73, James F. McCollum, P.A., 1973-77, McCollum & Oberhausen, P.A., 1977-80, McCollum & Rhoades, Sebring, Fla., 1980-86, McCollum & Waite, P.A., 1986—; pres. Highlands Devel. Concepts, Inc., Sebring, 1982—; sec. Focus Broadcast Communications, Inc., Sebring, 1982-87; mng. ptnr. Highlands Investment Service. Treas., Highlands County chpt. ARC, 1973-76; vestryman St. Agnes Episcopal Ch., 1973-83, chancellor, 1978—; mem. Com. 100 of Highlands County, 1975-83, bd. dirs., 1985-87, chmn. Highlands County High Speed Rail Task Force; chmn. bd., treas. Central Fla. Racing Assn., 1976-78; chmn. Leadership Sebring; life mem., past pres. Highlands Little Theatre, Inc. (most valuable player award, 1986); bd. dirs. Sebring Airport Authority, 1988—, Palms of Sebring Nursing Home, 1988—, Palms Estate Mobile Home Park. Recipient citation ARC, 1974; Presdl. award of appreciation Fla. Jaycees, 1980-81, 82, 85; named Jaycee of Year, Sebring Jaycees, 1981; Outstanding Local Chpt. Pres., U.S. Jaycees, 1977; Greater Sebring C. of C. most valuable dir. award, 1985-86, 1986-87; Outstanding Service award Highlands Council of 100, 1988. Mem. ABA, Am. Trial Lawyers Assn., Commercial Law League Am., Am. Arbitration Assn. (comml. arbitration panel), Fla. Bar (Fla. Bar Jour. com.), Highlands County Bar Assn. (past chmn. legal aid com.), Greater Sebring C. of C. (bd. dirs. 1982—, pres. 1986-87), Fla. Jaycees (life mem. internat. senate 1977—). Republican. Episcopalian. Club: Lions (dir. 1972-73, Disting. award 1984). Office: 129 S Commerce St Sebring FL 33870

MC COLPIN, CARROLL WARREN, corp. exec., ret. air force officer; b. Buffalo, Nov. 15, 1914; s. Joseph Warren and Doris (McCarthy) McC.; grad. Armed Forces Staff Coll., 1950, Air War Coll., 1955; B.A., Golden Gate U., 1969; m. Mary Joan Martin, Mar. 4, 1943; children—Mary Patricia, Carol Warren. Pilot and squadron leader RAF, 1940-42, trans. to USAAF, 1942, advanced through grades to maj. gen. USAF, 1965; comdr. 336th Fighter Squadron 4th Fighter Group, Eng., 1942; Hdqrs. USAAF, Washington, 1943; ops. officer 423d Fighter Group, Deridder AFB, La., 1943; comdr. 407th Fighter Group, Lakeland, Fla., 1943-44, 404th Fighter Group, Eng., France and Belgium, 1944-45; dir. combat ops. 29th Tactical Air Command, Belgium, 1945; comdr. 3d Fighter Command Gunnery Sch., Pinellas, Fla., 1945-46; comdr. 355th and 52d Fighter Group, Germany, 1946-47, 31st Fighter Group, Turner AFB, Ga., 1947-50; dir. ops. and tng. Hdqrs. Air Def. Command, Colorado Springs, Colo., 1950-52; dep. for ops. Hdqrs. Eastern Air Def. Force, Stewart AFB, Newburgh, N.Y., 1952-54; comdr. 64th Air Div., Nfld., Can., 1955-58; dir. ops. Hdqrs. NORAD/CONAD, Ent. AFB, Colo., 1961-62; comdr. San Francisco Air Def. Sector, Beale AFB, Calif., 1962-63, Portland Air Def. Sector, Adair AFB, Oreg., 1963-64; comdr. 28th Air Div., Hamilton AFB, Calif., 1964-65, 4th Air Force, Hamilton AFB, 1966-68; now pres. Brit. Bancorp., Commonwealth Ins. Group, Inc.; chmn. bd. dirs. Brit. Indemnity Group Inc. Decorated Legion of Merit with 3 oak leaf clusters, D.F.C., D.S.M., Air medal with 16 oak leaf clusters; D.F.C. (Eng.); Croix de Guerre with palm, Fourragère (France and Belgium). Mem. Fighter Aces Assn., Air Force Assn., Order Daedalians, Nat. Rifle Assn., Eagle Squadron Assn. Lodge: Rotary. Home: 205 Country Club Dr Novato CA 94947

MCCOMB, JOHN PAUL, lawyer; b. Bellevue, Pa., Oct. 7, 1922; s. John Paul and Kathryn Elizabeth (McKinnon) M.; m. Anne Nutting Mercur, Nov. 8, 1944; children—Sarah, Stewart, David, Richard. B.A., Princeton U., 1944; J.D., Harvard U., 1948. Bar: Pa. 1949, U.S. Supreme Ct. 1980. Assoc. Griggs, Moreland, Blair & Douglass, 1949-53; ptnr. McComb & Wolfe, 1953-58; sec., counsel J.H. Hillman & Sons, 1958-63; ptnr. Buchanan Ingersoll and predecessor firm Moorhead & Knox, 1963—; trustee Hosp. Assn. Pa., 1983—; chmn., trustee Shadyside Hosp.; sec., bd. dirs. Action, Housing Inc. Served to capt. USMCR, 1944-46, 1951-52. Mem. ABA, Pa. Bar Assn., Allegheny County Bar Assn., Am. Judicature Soc. Republican. Presbyterian. Clubs: HYP, Duquesne, Pitts. Golf. Home: 530C Guyasuta Rd Pittsburgh PA 15215 Office: 57th Floor 600 Grant St Pittsburgh PA 15219

MCCOMBS, ROLLIN KOENIG, radiation oncologist; b. Denver, Aug. 17, 1919; s. Curtis and Emma Elizabeth (Koenig) McC.; m. Judy Louise Bacon, Sept. 20, 1952; children: David, Daniel, Susan, Kathleen, Michael. BA in Chemistry, U. Colo., 1941, MA in Physics, 1944; MD, Stanford U., 1954. Diplomate Am. Bd. Radiology, Am. Bd. Nuclear Medicine. Research fellow, assoc. physician Donner Lab. Med. Physics, Berkeley, Calif., 1954-57; resident VA Hosp., Long Beach, Calif., 1957-67, staff; dir. radiation oncology Long Beach Community Hosp., 1967-86; instr. physics U. Colo., Boulder, 1942-48; asst. clin. prof. radiology U. So. Calif. Sch. Medicine, Los Angeles, 1978-84, assoc. clin. prof. radiology, 1984-88. Contbr. articles to profl. jours. Recipient Chmn's. award U. So. Calif. Sch. Medicine, 1983. Mem. AMA, Am. Coll. Radiology, Soc. Nuclear Medicine, Brit. Inst. Radiology, Am. Assn. Physicists in Medicine, Am. Soc. Therapeutic Radiology and Oncology, Sigma Xi, Phi Beta Kappa. Democrat. Presbyterian. Home: 1802 Tulane Ave Long Beach CA 90815

MC COMBS, SHERWIN, oil and gas co. exec.; b. Sterling, Ill., Jan. 27, 1934; s. C. Vernon and Helen (Jennings) McC.; grad. Palmer Chiropractic Coll., 1956-60; m. Rita J. Page, Feb. 8, 1957; children—Kim, Kelly, Jeff, Terry. Owner McCombs Chiropractic Clinic, Sterling, Ill., 1960—, McCombs Petroleum Prodns., Sterling, 1966—; v.p., dir. Coyote Oil & Gas Corp., Casper Wyo., 1968-75, exec. v.p., dir., 1975—; v.p., dir. Coyote Assos., Inc., Ankeny, Iowa, 1970-72; pres., dir. Coyote Oil & Gas Programs, Inc., Ankeny, 1970-72; with McCombs-Conrad & Barrett Oil & Gas Properties, Sterling, Ill., 1972-82. Served with USNR, 1952-54. Mem. Internat., Prairie, Whiteside County chiropractic assns., Internat. Chiropractic Honor Soc. Home: 1808 Thome Dr Sterling IL 61081 Office: 507 W 3d St Sterling IL 61081

MCCOMSEY, ROBERT RONALD, investment company and pension fund executive; b. Lancaster, Pa., Oct. 13, 1944; s. Robert Marvin and Fern Louisa (Dunwoody) McC.; m. Susan Kay Wing, Dec. 23, 1972; children: Michelle Tiffany, Douglas Ryan. BS in Ceramic Engring., Alfred U., 1966; MBA, U. Chgo., 1972. Sr. engr. electronic components div. RCA Corp., Harrison, N.J., 1966-68; sr. tech. mktg. specialist electronic components div. RCA Corp., Chgo., 1968-71; fin. dir. electronic components div. RCA Corp., N.Y.C., 1971-72; pension cons. A.G. Becker & Co., N.Y.C., 1972-74, asst. v.p., 1974-75, v.p., sr. pension cons., 1975-77; exec. v.p. pension mgmt. Neuberger & Berman, N.Y.C., 1977-82, gen. ptnr., 1980—, chief operating officer, pension mgmt., 1982—. Patron Viennese Opera Ball, N.Y.C., 1975—; trustee Alfred U., Alfred, N.Y., 1980—, mem. exec. com., chmn. investment com.; trustee The Hackley Sch., Tarrytown, N.Y., 1982—, mem. exec. com., chmn. investment com.; trustee Briarcliff Manor-Scarborough (N.Y.) Hist. Soc., 1983—; trustee U.S. Mil. Acad., West Point, 1984—, Fifth Ave. Presbyn. Ch., N.Y.C., 1985—; co-chmn. hist. bldgs. and renovations com. U.S. Mil. Acad., West Point, 1985—. Named Cost Reduction Systems Engr. of Yr. RCA Corp., Harrison, N.J., 1968. Mem. Army Athletic Assn. (comdr. in chief A-Club). Republican. Clubs: University (N.Y.C.); Sleepy Hollow (Scarborough). Home: Linden Circle Scarborough-on-Hudson NY 10510 Office: Neuberger & Berman 522 Fifth Ave New York NY 10036

MC CONAGHA, GLENN LOWERY, advancement associate and chancellor emeritus; b. New Concord, Ohio, June 2, 1910; s. David Hawthorne and Lida (Taylor) McC.; m. Pearl Esther Hook, Apr. 8, 1939. A.B., Muskingum Coll., 1932; A.M., Ohio State U., 1934, Ph.D., 1941; D.H.L. (hon.), Blackburn U., 1988; student, U. Pitts., 1936-37. Instr. social studies Alquippa (Pa.) High Sch., 1934-38; asst. prof. edn. Muskingum Coll., summers 1935-38; instr. edn. Ohio State U., Columbus, 1939-40; asst. dir. field service 1941-42; pre-induction classification officer U.S. Army, Huntington, W. Va., 1943; exec. officer U.S. Armed Forces Inst., Madison, Wis., 1944-45; (commd. U.S. Army 1947), comdt., 1945-49, ednl. dir., 1949-50, civilian dir., 1950-53; exec. v.p. Muskingum Coll., 1953-62, pres., 1962-64; dean Blackburn Coll., Carlinville, Ill., 1964-65; pres. Blackburn Coll., 1965-74, chancellor, 1974-77, spl. cons., 1977-79, advancement assoc., chancellor emeritus, 1979—. Author: Blackburn College 1837-1987: An Anecdotal and Analytical History of the Private College; also articles in profl. jours.; contbr. to: Bull. of Nat. Assn. Secondary Sch. Prins; Author: monthly publ. Train of Thought, 1965-72. Former trustee Lincoln Acad. Ill.; former mem. Presbyn. Coll. Union, pres., 1972-73. Decorated Army Commendation ribbon Presdl. Unit Citation.; Hon. mem. Brit. Royal Edn. Corp. Mem. Am. Council Assn., Higher Edn. Assn., Asso. Colls. Ill., Mil. Order World Wars, Am. Ednl. Research Assn., NEA, AAUP, Phi Gamma Mu, Alpha Phi Gamma, Phi Delta Kappa. Club: Mason. Home: 10 Taggart Dr Carlinville IL 62626

MCCONNAUGHEY, JAMES WALTER, telecommunications consultant; b. Washington, May 8, 1951; s. William Eugene and Eunice (Ensor) McC.; m. Rosemarie Fuchs, June 23, 1984. BS with high honors in Econs., U. Md., 1973; MA in Econs., George Washington U., 1979. Industry economist FCC Common Carrier Bur., Washington, 1973-80, sr. economist, 1981-83; sr. assoc. Bolter and Nilsson, Bethesda, Md., 1983; mgr. research studies div. Bethesda Research Inst., 1984—. Author: (with others) Telecommunication Policy for the 1980's: The Transition to Competition, 1984, Telecommunications and the Economics of Public Utility Regulation, 1988. Campaign worker, contbr. nat. and local elections; coach No. Va. Boys' Clubs, Bowie (Md.) Boy's Club; mem. Neighborhood Open Space Com.; worker, contbr. numerous environ. and consumer orgns. Mem. Am. Econ. Assn., Pub. Utilities Group of Am. Econ. Assn., Eastern Econ. Assn., So. Econ. Assn., Soc. Govt. Economists, Indsl. Orgn. Soc., Phi Eta Sigma, Omicron Delta Epsilon, Beta Gamma Sigma, Phi Kappa Phi. Avocations: hiking; reading.

MCCONNELL, ANITA, science historian, former museum curator; b. London, Jan. 22, 1936; d. Giuseppe and Lottie Airoldi; m. Dennis McConnell, Feb. 22, 1964 (div. 1973). Diploma in Archaeology, Inst. Archaeology, London, 1968; BSc, U. Coll., London, 1971; PHD, U. Leicester, 1978. Curator Sci. Mus., London, 1964-87; free-lance sci. historian London, 1987—; ptnr. Nimbus Books, London, 1980—; owner Patrick Marney Barometers, London, 1986—; hon. research fellow Royal Instn. Ctr. for History Sci. and Tech., London, 1987—; vis. acad. Imperial Coll Sci. and Tech. U. London, 1987—. Author, co-author numerous books; contbr. articles to profl. jours. Fellow Royal Geog. Soc. Royal Meterol. Soc.; mem. Hakluyt Soc. (com. 1987). Home: 46 Defoe House, Barbican, London EC2 Y8DN, England

MCCONNELL, DAVID KELSO, lawyer; b. N.Y.C., July 12, 1932; s. David and Caroline Hanna (Kelso) McC.; m. Alice Schmitt, Dec. 26, 1953; children—Elissa Anne, Kathleen Anne, David Willet. B.C.E., CCNY, 1954; LL.B., Yale U., 1962. Bar: Conn. 1962, Pa. 1975, N.Y., 1986, U.S. dist. Ct. Conn. 1963, U.S. Dist. Ct. (ea. dist.) Pa. 1971, U.S. Ct. Appeals. (2d cir.) 1964, U.S. Ct. Appeals. (3d cir.) 1966, U.S. Sup. Ct. 1970, N.Y. 1985. Asst. counsel N.Y.N.H. & H. R.R., New Haven, 1962-65, counsel., 1966-68; asst. atty. gen. U.S. Virgin Islands, 1965-66; asst. gen. atty. Pa. Central Transp. Co., New Haven, 1969-70, asst. gen. counsel, Phila, 1970-71, sr. reorganization atty., 1971, adminstrv. officer and spl. counsel to trustees, 1971-76, gen. atty., 1977-78; asst. to chmn, chief exec. officer The Penn Central Corp., N.Y.C., 1979-80, corp. sec., 1980-82; v.p., gen. counsel Gen. Cable Co., Greenwich, Conn., 1982-85; sole practice Stamford, Conn., 1985-86; of counsel McCarthy, Fingar, Donovan, Drazen & Smith, White Plains, N.Y. and Greenwich, Conn., 1985—. councilman Town of Pelham, N.Y., 1986—. Trustee, deacon Huguenot Meml. Ch., Pelham N.Y. Served with U.S. Navy, 1954-59, USNR, 1959-79. Mem. ABA, Conn. Bar Assn., Assn. of Bar City of N.Y. Clubs: Yale Phila., Corinthians, St. Andrews Soc. N.Y. (bd. mgrs. 1986—, chmn. bd. mgrs. 1988). Home: 29 Storer Ave Pelham NY 10803 Office: 11 Martine Ave 12th Floor White Plains NY 10606

MCCONNELL, JAMES GUY, lawyer; b. Hinsdale, Ill., Sept. 24, 1947; s. William F. and Virginia (Brown) McC.; m. Debra Drue Wax, May 30, 1976; children: Colin, Nicholas, Joanna. BS in Journalism, Iowa State U., 1969; JD, Northwestern U., 1973. Bar: Ill. 1973, U.S. Dist. Ct. (no. dist.) Ill. 1973, U.S. Ct. Appeals (7th cir.) 1973, U.S. Supreme Ct. 1977. Assoc. Rooks, Pitts & Poust, Chgo., 1973-80, ptnr., 1980-85; ptnr. Bell, Boyd & Lloyd, Chgo., 1985—; adj. prof. Kent Coll. Law Ill. Inst. Tech., Chgo., 1978—. Author: Comparative Negligence Defense Tactics, 1985; contbg.

editor jour. Hazardous Waste & Toxic Torts Law & Strategy. Mem. dist. 102 Sch. Bd., LaGrange Park. Ill., 1975-76. Mem. ABA, Ill. Bar Assn., Chgo. Bar Assn., Soc. Trial Lawyers. Clubs: Legal of Chgo., Law of Chgo. Office: Bell Boyd & Lloyd Three First Nat Plaza Chicago IL 60602

MCCOOL, RICHARD BUNCH, real estate developer; b. Kokomo, Ind., Jan. 2, 1925; s. James Victor and Margaret (Bunch) M.C.; m. Victoria R. Middleton, Dec. 23, 1977; children: Kathryn, Suzanne, Rick; 1 stepchild, April. AB in Govt., Ind. U., 1950. Chmn., chief exec. officer Holida Corp., Indianapolis, 1950-70, Great Lakes Homes, Indpls., 1970-77, Am. Investment, Indpls., 1971—; bd. dirs. Am. Investment Group, Indpls., Investor Fin. Services, Indpls.; dir., gen. ptnr. Manor Group, Ind., Ky., 1977—; cons. Wickes Corp., 1970-77. Author: Real Estate Investments, 1981; contbr. articles to mags., newspaper column on contract bridge, 1966-74. Pres., chmn. various civic orgns., 1960-77; permanent mem. Nat. Rep. Senate Com., 1984. Recipient Geisenbier award Kokomo Jaycees, 1960; named to the Hon. Order Ky. Col. Served to capt., U.S. Army, 1943-46, PTO. Mem. Am. Contract Bridge League (life master 1972), No. Ind. Bridge Assn. (pres. 1974), Pvt. Pilot Assn. (pres. 1969), Nat. Contractors Assn. (founding pres. 1970, Contractor of Yr. 1974), Apt. Assns., Cert. Mgmt. Group (pres. 1980), Ind. U. Alumni Club, Sigma Nu. Congregationalist. Clubs: Columbia, Skyline (Indpls.). Lodges: Masons, Shriners. Office: 14904 Greyhound Ct Carmel IN 46032

MC CORD, GUYTE PIERCE, JR., retired judge; b. Tallahassee, Sept. 23, 1914; s. Guyte Pierce and Jean (Patterson) McC.; student Davidson Coll., 1933-34; B.A., J.D., U. Fla., 1940; m. Laura Elizabeth Mack, Dec. 16, 1939; children—Florence Elizabeth, Guyte Pierce III, Edward LeRoy. Admitted to Fla. bar, 1940; practiced in Tallahassee, 1940-60; dep. commr. Fla. Insl. Commn., 1946-47; pros. atty. Leon County, 1947-48; asst. gen. counsel Fla. Public Service Commn., 1949-60; judge 2d Jud. Circuit Fla., Tallahassee, 1960-74; judge Ct. Appeal 1st Dist. Fla., 1974-83, chief judge, 1977-79; mem. Fla. Senate Pres.'s Council on Criminal Justice 1972; mem. appellate ct. rules com. Fla. Supreme Ct., 1977-78, mem. appellate ct. structure commn. 1978-79. Pres., Murat House Assn., Inc., 1967-69; bd. dirs. Fla. Heritage Found., 1969-70, mem. exec. com., 1965-69; mem. Andrew Jackson staff of Springtime Tallahassee, 1973-74, 84-86, Andrew Jackson, 1987. Served to comdr. USNR, 1942-46, 52-53. Mem. Ret. Officers Assn., ABA, Fla. Bar, Tallahassee Bar Assn., Fla. Conf. Circuit Judges (sec.-treas. 1970, chmn. 1972), Phi Delta Phi, Sigma Alpha Epsilon. Presbyterian (elder 1960—, ch. trustee 1981-86). Club: Kiwanis (dir. 1958-59). Home: 502 S Ride St Tallahassee FL 32303 Office: PO Box 4121 Tallahassee FL 32315

MC CORD, JAMES ILEY, chancellor; b. Rusk, Tex., Nov. 24, 1919; s. Marshal Edward and Jimmie Oleta (Decherd) McC.; m. Hazel Thompson, Aug. 29, 1939; children—Vincent, Alison McCord Zimmerman, Marcia McCord Verville. B.A., Austin Coll., 1938, D.D., 1949; student, Union Theol. Sem., 1938-39; B.D., Austin Presbyn. Theol. Sem., 1942; M.A., U. Tex., 1942; student, Harvard, 1942-43, U. Edinburgh, 1950-51; Th.D., U. Geneva, 1958; S.T.D., Knox Coll., Toronto, Can., 1958; D.D., Princeton, 1960, Victoria U., Toronto, 1963, Westminster Coll., New Wilmington, Pa., 1969, U. Edinburgh, 1970, Presbyn. Coll., U. Montreal, 1975, Hamilton Coll., 1981; LL.D., Maryville Coll., 1959, Lafayette Coll., 1962, Tusculum Coll., 1964, Bloomfield Coll., 1966; Litt.D., Davidson Coll., 1959, Washington and Jefferson Coll., 1970, Rider Coll., 1977, Keimyung U., Taegu, Korea, 1979; L.H.D., Ursinus Coll., 1962; Th.D., Debrecen (Hungary) Ref. Theol. Faculty, 1967, United Protestant Theol. Coll., Cluj, Romania, 1974; LL.D., Park Coll., 1969; D.D., Davis and Elkins Coll., 1983, Taiwan Theol. Coll. & Sem., 1986, Alma (Mich.) Coll., 1986, Muskingum (Ohio) Coll., 1987, Yale U., 1987, Muskingum Coll., Ohio, 1987, Yale U., 1987. Instr. U. Tex., 1940-42; adj. prof. Austin Presbyn. Theol. Sem., 1944-45, dean, prof. systematic theology, 1945-59; pres. Princeton Theol. Sem., 1959-83; chancellor Center Theol. Inquiry, Princeton, 1983—; Vis. prof. Presbyn. Theol. Sem. of South, Campinas, Brazil, 1956; chmn. North Am. Area Council World Alliance Ref. Chs., 1958-60, N. Am. sec. alliance, 1959-77, also chmn. theol. dept., 1956-70; past chmn. faith and order com., past chmn. nat. faith and order colloquium Nat. Council Chs.; former mem. commn. faith and order World Council of Chs.; chmn. council theol. edn. U.P. Ch., 1964-67, chmn. council theol. sems., 1978-81, chmn. consultation on ch. union, 1961-63; past chmn. commn. on accrediting Assn. Theol. Schs. U.S. and Can.; pres. World Alliance Ref. Chs., 1977-82; pres. United Bd. for Christian Higher Edn. in Asia, 1983-86, chmn., 1986—; vice-chmn. Christian Ministry in Nat. Parks, 1987—. Vice chmn. Christian Ministry in the Nat. Parks, 1987—. Mem. Assn. Theol. Schs. in U.S. and Can. (pres. 1978-80). Home: 10 Ober Rd Princeton NJ 08540 Office: 50 Stockton St Princeton NJ 08540

MC CORMACK, EDWARD JOSEPH, JR., lawyer; b. Boston, Aug. 29, 1923; s. Edward J. and Mary T. (Coffey) McC.; m. Emily Rupils, Oct. 19, 1946; children—Edward Joseph III, John W. Student, Colby Coll., 1941-42; B.S., U.S. Naval Acad., 1946; JD cum laude, Boston U., 1952. Bar: Mass. 1952. Atty. Gen. Commonwealth of Mass., 1958-63. Mem. city council, Boston, 1953-58, pres., 1956; Chmn. Com. for Boston; trustee New Eng. Sch. Law., Boston Pvt. Industry Council, Boston Access Cable Commn. Served with USN, 1946-49. Club: 100 of Mass. (dir.). Home: 20 Rowes Wharf PH 9 Boston MA 02110 Office: 265 Franklin St Boston MA 02110

MCCORMACK, LOWELL RAY, oil producer, document examiner, graphoanalyst, lecturer; b. Ladonia, Tex., Oct. 26, 1925; d. Lowell and Orianna (McDonnold) Coney; m. Paul Ha. McCormack, June 4, 1948; children: Sharron Ann, Lowell Henry. Student Rutherford Met. Coll., Dallas, 1962, U. Tex., Arlington and Dallas, Eastfield Coll., Dallas; M. Graphoanalyst, Internat. Graphoanalysis Soc. Bookkeeper, Jot-Em-Down Gin Corp., Pecan Gap, Tex., 1947, Shedd-Bartush Foods, Dallas, 1948-52; acct., credit mgr. J. P. Ashcraft Co., Inc., Dallas, 1956-65; v.p., sec.-treas. Safari Oil Corp., Dallas, 1954—; pres. Scorpio Oil Corp., 1987—; chief fin. officer, v.p., sec.-treas. Dallas Title Co., 1965-83; instr. graphoanalysis Cooke County Coll., 1988; acctg. cons. to atty.; bd. dirs. First Nat. Bank, Cooper, Tex., 1986-87, Butterfield Stage, Gainesville, Tex.; lectr. in field. Leader troop Girl Scouts USA, 1955-65; founder Yarn Spinners, Gainesville, 1988. Columnist Cooke County Leader, 1988—. Mem. North Tex. Oil and Gas Assn., Internat. Graphoanalysis Soc. (life, v.p. Tex. chpt. 1978, pres. 1979, named Graphoanalyst of Yr. 1987, keynote address speaker, 1987, author weekly column Cooke County Leader, 1988—), Internat. Platform Assn. Baptist. Clubs: Zonta (co-chmn. fin. com. 1982, dir., 2d v.p. 1983-84), Soroptimist, Toastmistress (pres. 1981, com. chmn. for internat. conv. 1984) (Dallas), Kiwanis (one of first women mems. Gainesville chpt., 1988). Home: 631 S Lindsay Gainesville TX 76240

MCCORMACK, MARJORIE GUTH, communications educator, public relations consultant; b. Jersey City, Dec. 27, 1934; d. Joseph Leo and Vera Marie (Clossey) Guth; m. Kevin T. McCormack, Nov. 11, 1961. B.A., St. Peter's Coll., 1974; postgrad. Jersey City State Coll., 1983—. Editor, AT&T, N.Y.C., 1952-60, librarian, 1960-67; librarian St. Peter's Coll., Jersey City, 1967-71; pub. relations mgr. Blue Cross of N.J., Newark, 1971-81; instr. history, econs. St. Aloysius High Sch., Jersey City, 1981-82; pub. relations cons. Creative Pub. Relations Assocs., Jersey City, 1981—; adj. instr. communications St. Peter's Coll., 1982—; copy editor Glens Falls, (N.Y.) Post-Star, 1986. Bd. mgrs. Am. Cancer Soc., Jersey City, 1978-79; mem., sec. parish council St. Aloysius Ch., 1981-85; mem. Jersey City Tenants Orgn., 1981—, Rent Leveling Bd. Jersey City, 1983-86. Mem. AAUP, Nat. Assn. Female Execs. (pub. relations chmn. 1980-82), Jersey City Bus. and Profl. Women's Assn. (legis. chmn. 1975-77, Nat. Program award 1976, State Press award 1982), Hudson County Women's Network. Avocations: music, theater, gourmet cooking. Office: St Peter's Coll 2641 Kennedy Blvd Jersey City NJ 07306

MCCORMICK, RALPH EUGENE, accounting company executive; b. Nashville, May 11, 1948; s. Mildred Marie (Wells) McC.; A.S., King's Coll., 1972, acctg. cert., 1971; m. Eugenia Keitt, Aug. 24, 1974; children: Darby Eugenia, Caroline Keitt. Acct., Mercy Hosp., Charlotte, N.C., 1972-73; pres. MCAS, Inc., 1988—; dir. H. Clinton Co. Inc.; acct. W. A. Buening & Co., Inc., Charlotte, 1973-75, controller, 1975-77, treas., from 1977-86, now v.p. fin. and adminstrn., also dir. Served with U.S. Army, 1966-69. Mem. Nat. Assn. Accts., Am. Mgmt. Assn., Am. Soc. Personnel Adminstrn. Home: PO Box 33802 Charlotte NC 28233-3802 Office: MCAS Inc 516 Fenton Pl Charlotte NC 28207

MCCORMICK, WILLIAM EDWARD, business executive, consultant; b. Potters Mills, Pa., Feb. 9, 1912; s. George H. and Nellie (Mingle) McC.; m. Goldie Stover, June 6, 1935; children: John F. (dec.), Kirk W. B.S., Pa. State U., 1933, M.S., 1934. Tchr., Centre Hall (Pa.) High Sch., 1934-37; chemist Willson Products, Inc., Reading, Pa., 1937-43; indsl. hygienist Ga. Dept. Pub. Health, Atlanta, 1946; mgr. indsl. hygiene and toxicology B.F. Goodrich Co., Akron, Ohio, 1946-70; mgr. environ. control B.F. Goodrich Co., 1970-73; mng. dir. Am. Indsl. Hygiene Assn., Akron, 1973-83; exec. sec. Soc. Toxicology, 1976-83; chmn., treas. Envirotox Mgmt., Inc., 1983—; mem. exec. com. rubber sect. Nat. Safety Council, 1955-73; gen. chmn., 1971-72; mem. environ. health com. Chlorine Inst., 1968-73; mem. food, drug and cosmetic chems. com. Mfg. Chemists Assn., 1960-73, chmn., 1967-69, also mem. occupational health com., 1965-73; mem. adv. com. on heat stress U.S. Dept. Labor, 1973; mem. Nat. Adv. Com. Occupational Safety and Health, 1983-85; pres. Am. Indsl. Hygiene Found., 1984, trustee, 1982—. Contbr. articles to profl. jours. Served to capt. USPHS, 1943-46. Mem. Am. Chem. Soc., Soc. Toxicology, AAAS, Am. Indsl. Hygiene Assn. (pres. 1964), Indsl. Hygiene Roundtable, Am. Acad. Indsl. Hygiene. Republican. Episcopalian. Lodges: Masons (33 deg.) Shriner. Home: 419 Dorchester Rd Akron OH 44320 Office: 149 N Prospect St Ravenna OH 44266

MC CORMICK, WILLIAM MARTIN, broadcast executive; b. Hackensack, N.J., Dec. 15, 1921; s. John and Delia Theresa (Murphy) McC.; m. Joan Theresa Dowling, June 29, 1957; children: Jean Marie, Patricia, Joan, William Martin. Student, NYU, 1939-43, B.S., 1946; student, Harvard U., 1943-45. Account exec. Sta. WOR, N.Y.C., 1946-54; asst. sales mgr. Sta. WOR, 1955, dir. sales, 1956-59, v.p., dir. sales, 1959-60; pres., gen. mgr. Sta. WNAC-AM and FM and WNAC-TV, Boston, 1960-64; v.p., gen. mgr. Sta. WNAC-TV, 1964-69; area v.p. New Eng. WNAC-TV, 1970-72; pres. McCormick Communications, 1972-85, McCormick Broadcasting Corp., 1986—; trustee Charlestown Savs. Bank., 1968-83. Bd. dirs. Catholic TV Ctr., 1970-83, ARC, 1970—; pres. execs. club Greater Boston C. of C., 1965-66, bd. dirs., 1966-68; bd. dirs. Better Bus. Bur., 1966-70. Served with USN, 1941-46. Recipient award Greater Boston C. of C., 1962, citation of merit NCCJ, 1974. Mem. Nat. Assn. Broadcasters, Nat. Radio Broadcasters Assn., New Eng. Broadcasters Assn. Roman Catholic. Clubs: Weston Golf; Oyster Harbors (Osterville, Mass.); John's Island (Vero Beach, Fla.); Wianno (Mass.).

MCCOWEN, ALEC, actor; b. Tunbridge Wells, May 26, 1925; s. Duncan and Mary (Walkden) McC. Ed. Skinners Sch., Tunbridge Wells, and Royal Acad. Dramatic Art. Appeared as Touchstone, Ford, Richard II, Mercutio, Malvolio, Oberon at Old Vic Theatre, 1959-60; appeared with R—S—C—as Fool in King Lear, 1964, in Hadrian VII, 1968, The Philanthropist, 1970, The Misanthrope, 1972, as Dr. Dysart in Equus, 1972, as Henry Higgins in Pygmalion, 1974, as Ben in The Family Dance, 1976; appeared with Prospect Co. as Antony in Antony and Cleopatra, 1977, in solo performance of St. Mark's Gospel, 1978, 81, as Frank in Tishoo, 1979, as Malvolio in Twelfth Night (TV), 1980, of Kipling, 1984, as Reilly in The Cocktail Party, 1986, as Nicolai in Fathers and Sons, 1987, as Vladimir in Waiting for Godot, 1987; appeared with Nat. Theatre as Crocker-Harris in The Browning Version, Arthur in Harlequinade, Capt. Corcoran in H.M.S. Pinafore, 1981, Adolf Hitler in The Portage to San Cristobal of AH, 1982; films: Frenzy, 1971, Travels with my Aunt, 1973, Stevie, 1978, Personal Services, Cry Freedom, 1987; TV: Private Lives, 1976. Author: Young Gemini, 1979; Double Bill, 1980; Personal Mark, 1984. Named Best Actor, Evening Standard (now New Standard), 1968, 73, 82, Variety Club Stage Actor, 1970. Office: care Jeremy Conway, 109 Jermyn St, London SW1 Y6HB, England

MC COWN, GEORGE EDWIN, venture banking company executive; b. Portland, Oreg., July 1, 1935; s. Floyd Conly and Ada Elizabeth (Stephens) McC.; m. Karen Stone, Mar. 22, 1986; children: Taryn, Daniel, David; stepchildren: Bryan, Norman, Mark, Amy. BS, Stanford U., 1957; MBA, Harvard U., 1962. Asst. to the pres. through sr. v.p. Boise (Idaho) Cascade, 1963-80; chmn. Sequoia Corp., Boise, 1981-83; founder/mng. gen. ptnr. McCown De Leeuw & Co., Menlo Park, Calif. 1983—; chmn. bd. Western Lumber Co. Inc., BMC West Corp., MDV Holdings; vice chmn. Coast Gas Industries; mem. World Bus. Acad., World Bus. Forum. Trustee, chmn. com. on fin. and adminstrn. and subcom. on investment policy and evaluation Stanford U.; bd. dirs. New Childrens Hosp. Stanford; trustee Pacific Crest Outward Sch.; chmn. bd. govs. Wyo. Centennial Mt. Everest Expdn.; mem., past chmn. policy adv. bd. Harvard-MIT Joint Ctr. for Housing Studies. Served to capt. USAF, 1957-60. Republican. Avocations: organizing adventure travel treks. Home: 250 Greer Rd Woodsideo CA 94062 Office: McCown De Leeuw & Co 3000 Sand Hill Rd 3-290 Menlo Park CA 94025

MC COY, FREDERICK JOHN, plastic surgeon; b. McPherson, Kans., Jan. 17, 1916; s. Merle D. and Mae (Tennis) McC.; m. Mary Bock, May 17, 1972; children: Judith, Frederick John, Patricia, Melissa, Steven. B.S., U. Kans., 1938, M.D., 1942. Diplomate: Am. Bd. Plastic Surgery (dir. 1973-79, chmn. 1979). Intern Lucas County Hosp., Toledo, 1942-43; resident in plastic surgery U. Tex. Med. Sch., Galveston, 1946; preceptorship in surgery Grand Rapids, Mich., 1947-50; practice medicine specializing in plastic and reconstructive surgery Kansas City, Mo., 1950—; staff St. Mary's Hosp., 1950—, St. Joseph's Hosp., 1950—, N. Kansas City Meml. Hosp., 1955—; mem. staff, chief plastic surgery Kansas City Gen. Hosp. and Med. Center, 1952-72, Children's Mercy Hosp., 1954—, Research Hosp., 1950—, St. Luke's Hosp., 1951—, Baptist Hosp., 1958—, Menorah Hosp., 1950—; chief div. plastic surgery Truman Med. Ctr., 1972—; chmn. maxillo-facial surgery U. Kansas City Sch. Dentistry, 1950-57; assoc. prof. surgery U. Mo. Med. Sch., Kansas City, 1964-69; clin. prof. surgery U. Mo. Med. Sch., 1969—. Contbr. articles to, profl. jours.; editor: Year Book of Plastic and Reconstructive Surgery, 1971—. Bd. govs. Kansas City Mus., 1959—, pres., 1973-74. Served to maj. M.C. U.S. Army, 1943-46. Mem. Am. Soc. Plastic and Reconstructive Surgeons (sec. 1969-73, dir. 1973-76, pres. 1976, chmn. bd. 1977), Pan Pacific Surg. Soc., Singleton Surg. Soc. (v.p. 1965), Am. Assn. Plastic Surgeons (founding mem. Plastic Surgery Research Council), Am. Internat. Soc. Aesthetic Plastic Surgery, Am. Soc. Aesthetic Plastic Surgery, Jackson County Med. Soc. (pres. 1964-65), Kansas City Southwest Clin. Soc. (pres. 1971), Mo. Med. Assn. (v.p. 1975), AMA, A.C.S. (pres. Mo. chpt. 1973), Internat. Coll. Surgeons (v.p. 1969), Royal Soc. Medicine, Kansas City C. of C., Explorer's Club, Conservation Fedn. Mo., Natural Sci. Soc. (founder, chmn. 1973), Citizens Assn. Kansas City, Phi Delta Theta, Nu Sigma Nu. Republican. Mem. Christian Ch. Clubs: Mission Hills Country, Boone and Crocket. Home: 5814 Mission Dr Shawnee Mission KS 66208 Office: 4177 Broadway Kansas City MO 64111

MC COY, LARRY DEAN, government official; b. Greeley, Colo., June 20, 1938; s. Dean H. and Josephine Ann (Sorenson) McC.; B.A., Calif. State U. at San Diego, 1964; M.P.A., Am. U., 1969; m. Eddymarie Navarrete, Aug. 24, 1963; 1 son, Kevin. Engring. aide Gen. Dynamics-Convair Corp., San Diego, 1958-61, master scheduling analyst, 1961-62, engring. adminstrv. asst., 1962-64; mgmt. technician Library of Congress, Washington, 1964-65, adminstrv. officer Reference Dept., 1965-68, mgmt. analyst Copyright Office, 1968-71; asst. chief Office Adminstrv. Services, GAO, Washington, 1971-72, asst. to dir. Office Fed. Elections, 1972-74, supr. mgmt. analyst Fin. and Gen. Mgmt. div., 1974-75; dep. asst. staff dir. Fed. Election Commn., Washington, 1975—. Recipient Comptroller Gen.'s Honor award Comptroller Gen. U.S., 1974; certified Inst. Certified Records Mgrs. Office: 999 E St NW Washington DC 20463

MC COY, LOIS CLARK, county official, magazine editor; b. New Haven, Oct. 1, 1920; d. William Patrick and Lois Rosilla (Dailey) Clark; m. Herbert Irving McCoy, Oct. 17, 1943; children: Whitney, Kevin, Marianne, Tori, Debra, Sally, Daniel. BS, Skidmore Coll., 1942; student Nat. Search and Rescue Sch., 1974. Asst. buyer R.H. Macy & Co., N.Y.C., 1942-44, assoc. buyer, 1944-48; instr. Mountain Medicine & Survival, U. Calif. at San Diego, 1973-74; cons. editor Search & Rescue Mag., 1975, Rescue mag., 1988—; coordinator San Diego Mountain Rescue Team, La Jolla, Calif., 1973-75; exec. sec. Nat. Assn. for Search and Rescue, Inc., Nashville and La Jolla, 1975-80, comptroller, 1980-82; disaster officer San Diego County, 1980-86, Santa Barbara County, 1986—; editor-in-chief Response! mag., 1982-86; cons. law enforcement div.; Calif. Office Emergency Services, 1976-77; pres. San Diego Com. for Los Angeles Philharmonic Orch., 1957-58. Bd. dirs. Search and Rescue of the Californias, 1976-77, Nat. Assn. for Search and Rescue, Inc., 1980-87, pres., 1985-87, bd. trustees, 1987—; mem. Gov.'s Task Force on Earthquakes, 1981-82; chmn. Earthquake Preparedness Task Force, Seismic Safety Commn., 1982-85. Recipient Hal Foss award for outstanding service to search and rescue, 1982, Nasar Service award, 1985. Mem. Am. Astronautical Soc., AIAA, IEEE, Am. Soc. Indsl. Security, Nat. Assn. for Search and Rescue (Service award 1985), Council for Survival Edn., Mountain Rescue Assn., Nat. Jeep Search and Rescue Assn., San Diego Mountain Rescue Team, San Diego Amateur Radio Club, Sierra Club. Episcopalian. Author: Search and Rescue Glossary, 1974; contbr. to profl. jours. Office: PO Box 91648 Santa Barbara CA 93190

MCCOY, TRAVIS WALTON, III, corporate executive, political researcher; b. Little Rock, Jan. 14, 1943; s. Travis Walton, Jr. and Evelyn Lois (Greene) McC. B.A., U. Ark., 1968. Pres. Bovine Scatologists Inc., Washington, 1980—; exec. dir. Inst. for Fed. Policy Rev. Justice of the Peace, Pulaski County, Ark., 1966-70. Served with U.S. Army, 1962-65. Republican. Unitarian. Avocations: flying; swimming; hunting; duplicate bridge. Home: 1301 15th St NW #120 Washington DC 20005 Office: Bovine Scatologists Inc PO Box 65107 Washington DC 20035

MCCOY, WILLIAM EDWARD, III, electronics engineer; b. Oakland, Calif., Jan. 9, 1939; s. William Edward and Mary Venable (Tuckerman) McC. AA with honors, Umpqua Community Coll., 1974; BS in Gen. Sci., BS in Math. with high scholastic honors, Oreg. State U., 1977, BS in Computer Sci., 1980; MS in Computer Sci., Calif. State U., Chico, 1982; postgrad., UCLA, 1984-85, Oreg. State U., 1988—. Logic designer, research asst. Hughes Aircraft Co., Culver City, Calif., 1962-64, asst. data processing analyst, 1964-65; programmer Bulter Publs., Hawthorne, Calif., 1966-67; data processing, systems analyst Atlantic Richfield Co., Los Angeles, 1968-69, Autographics, Monterey Park, Calif., 1969-71; electronics engr. Naval Weapons Ctr., China Lake, Calif., 1980-81; engr. EDP applications SP Communications, Burlingame, Calif., 1981-83; engr. GTE Sprint Communications Corp., 1983-84; mem. tech. staff Rockwell Internat., Lakewood, Calif., 1984-86; engring. specialist Applied Techs. div. Litton, San Jose, Calif., 1986-87; sr. engr. Computer Tech. Assocs., 1987; research asst. Oreg. State U., Corvallis, 1988—; cons. computer tech., 1971. Pres. Indian Wells Valley Pro-Life Com., 1981. Served with USAF, 1956-60. Mem. AAAS, AIAA, IEEE (chmn. membership devel. China Lake sect. 1981), Am. Assn. Artificial Intelligence, Assn. Computing Machinery, Soc. Computer Simulation, Soc. Automotive Engrs., Am. Inst. Industrial Engrs., Profl. Software Programmers Assn. (chmn. cert. com. 1983-84, product reviewer 1984-86), Calif. Assn. Physically Handicapped (life, parliamentarian Ridgecrest chpt. 1981), Buena Park Jaycees (treas. 1964), Hawthorne Jaycees (state dir. 1966), Southside Jayees (v.p. 1968), DAV, Assn. Old Crows, NAACP (1981-82), Oreg. State U. Grad. and Profl. Students Assn. (pres. 1988—), Phi Kappa Phi (life). Clubs: Toastmasters (China Lake) (treas. 1980, sec. 1981); Applied Orators (pres. 1986-87, asst. area gov. 1987, area gov. 1983-84, named able toastmaster 1983). Lodges: K.C. (chancellor Ridgecrest council 1980-81, dep. grand knight 1981), Masons (sr. steward Corvallis#14, life mem. San Jose #10). Home: 1833 NW Tyler Corvallis OR 97330-5513

MCCRARY, EUGENIA (CAMPBELL) LESTER, civic worker, writer; b. Annapolis, Md., Mar. 23, 1929; d. John Campbell and Eugenia (Potts) Lester; A.B. cum laude, Radcliffe Coll., 1950; M.A., Johns Hopkins U., 1952; postgrad. Harvard U., spring 1953, Pa. State U., 1953-54, Drew U., 1957-58, Inst. Study of USSR, Munich, W.Ger., 1964; m. John Campbell Howard, July 15, 1955 (dec. Sept. 1965); m. 2d, Dennis Daughtry McCrary, June 28, 1969; 1 son, Dennis Campbell. Grad. asst. dept. Romance langs. Pa. State U., 1953-54; tchr. dept. math. The Brearley Sch., N.Y.C., 1954-57; dir. Sch. Langs., Inc., Summit, N.J., 1958-69, trustee, 1960-69. Dist. dir. Eastern Pa. and N.J. auditions Met. Opera Nat. Council, N.Y.C., 1960-66, dist. dir. publicity, 1966-67, nat. vice chmn. publicity, 1967-71, nat. chmn. public relations, 1972-75, hon. nat. chmn. public relations, 1976—; bd. govs., chmn. Van Cortlandt Mansion Mus., 1985—. Co-author: (with Allegra Branson) Frontiers Aflame, 1987. Mem. Nat. Soc. Colonial Dames Am. (bd. mgrs. N.Y.), Met. Opera Nat. Council, Soc. Mayflower Desc. (bd. dirs. N.Y. soc., chmn. house com.), Soc. Daus. of Holland Dames (bd. dirs., 3d directress gen.), Vestry L'Eglise Saint-Esprit, Huguenot Soc. Am. (governing council). Republican. Episcopalian. Club: Colony. Home: 24 Central Park S New York NY 10019

MC CRAVEN, CARL CLARKE, health services administrator; b. Des Moines, May 27, 1926; s. Marcus Henry and Buena Vista (Rollins) McC.; B.S. in Elec. Engring., Howard U., 1950; M.S. in Health Services Adminstrn., Calif. State U.-Northridge, 1976; m. Eva Louise Stewart, Mar. 18, 1978; 1 son, Carl B. Radiation physicist Nat. Bur. Standards, 1951-55; research engr. Lockheed Calif. Co., 1955-63; mem. tech. staff TRW Systems, 1963-72; assoc. adminstr. Pacoima Meml. Hosp., Lake View Terrace, Calif., 1972-74; pres. and chief exec. officer Hillview Mental Health Ctr., Inc., Lake View Terrace, 1974—; asst. prof. Calif. State U., Northridge, 1976-78. Regent Casa Loma Coll.; bd. dirs. San Fernando Valley Girl Scout Council, Pledgerville Sr. Citizens Villa, ARC; treas. San Fernando Valley Mental Health Assn. Recipient citation Calif. Senate, 1971, 88, Calif. Assembly, 1971, 88, City of Los Angeles, 1971, 78, 88, County of Los Angeles, 1988. Fellow Assn. Mental Health Adminstrs.; mem. Am. Public Health Assn., Am. Mgmt. Assn., Nat. Assn. Health Services Execs., NAACP (pres. so. area Calif. conf. 1967-71, nat. dir. 1970-76), Sigma Pi Phi. Lodge: North San Fernando Valley Rotary (pres.). Home: 17233 Chatsworth St Granada Hills CA 91344

MCCRAVEN, EVA STEWART MAPES, health service adminstr.; b. Los Angeles, Sept. 26, 1936; d. Paul Melvin and Wilma Zech (Ziegler) Stewart; B.S. magna cum laude, Calif. State U., Northridge, 1974, M.S., Cambridge Grad. Sch. Psychology, 1987; postgrad.; m. Carl Clarke McCraven, Mar. 18, 1978; children—David Anthony, Lawrence James, Maria Lynn Mapes. Dir. spl. projects Pacoima Meml. Hosp., 1969-71, dir. health edn., 1971-74; asst. exec. dir. Hillview Community Mental Health Center, Lakeview Terrace, Calif., 1974—; past dir. dept. consultation and edn. Hillview Ctr., developer, mgr. long-term residential program, 1986—; program mgr. Crisis Residential Program. Former pres. San Fernando Valley Coordinating Council Area Assn., Sunland-Tujunga Coordinating Council; bd. dirs. N.E. Valley Health Corp., 1970-73, Golden State Community Mental Health Ctr., 1970-73. Fellow Assn. Mental Health Adminstrs.; mem. Am. Pub. Health Assn., Women in Health Adminstrn., Health Services Adminstrn. Alumni Assn. (former v.p.), Bus. and Profl. Women (v.p.), LWV. Office: Hillview Community Mental Health Ctr 11500 Eldridge Ave Lake View Terrace CA 91342

MCCRAW, RONALD KENT, psychologist; b. Houston, Dec. 6, 1947; s. Leon Frank and Lorna Mae (Bailey) McC. B.A., U. Tex., 1970; M.A., U. Tex. Med. Br., Galveston, 1972; Ph.D., U. South Fla., 1981; diploma Squadron Officers Sch., Air U., 1982-83, Air Command and Staff Coll., 1985-86, Tex. Coll. Osteo. Medicine, 1986—. Diplomate Am. Acad. Behavioral Med.; lic. psychologist, Tex.; cert. instr. ARC. Research asst. div. child and adolescent psychiatry U. Tex. Med. Br., 1972-74; grad. asst. div. neuropsychology Fla. Mental Health Inst., Tampa, 1975-76; resident in clin. psychology U. Tex. Health Scis. Ctr., San Antonio, 1977-78; psychometrician Hillsborough Community Mental Health Ctr., Tampa, Fla., 1978-79; clin. psychologist U.S. Air Force Hosp., Chanute AFB, Ill., 1982-86; pvt. practice clin. psychology, 1987—. Film and book reviewer for AAAS Sci. Books and Films, 1977—, Birth, 1983—, Jour. Nurse-Midwifery, 1985—; editorial bd. Birth Psychology Bull., 1984—, Health Care of Women Internat., 1984—; abstractor Psychosomatics, 1985-87; contbr. articles to sci. jours. Coach Baytown Girls Softball Assn. (Tex.), 1980-82, Rantoul Ponytail Softball League (Ill.), 1983-85, Men's Varsity Softball Team, Chanute AFB, Ill., 1983-84, U.S. Slo-Pitch Softball Assn. State and Div. Qualifying Team, 1984. Served to capt. USAF, 1982-86, USAFR, 1987—. Decorated Commedation medal, 1986. Fellow Am. Orthopsychiat. Assn. (program subcom. 1974-76); mem. Am. Psychol. Assn., AAAS, Am. Acad. Behavioral Medicine, Assn. for Birth Psychology, Internat. Childbirth Edn. Assn. (alt. hour rev. subcom. 1985—), Acad. Psychosomatic Medicine, Soc. Behavioral Medicine, Soc. for Personality Assessment, U. Tex. Ex-Students Assn. (life), N.Y. Acad. Scis., Am. Soc. Clin. Hypnosis, Tex. Osteo. Med. Assn. (student), Am. Osteo. Assn. (student), Am. Bd. Med. Psychotherapists (clin. assoc.), Sigma Xi, Psi

Chi, Omicron Delta Kappa, Nu Sigma Nu, Phi Beta Pi-Theta Kappa Psi, Sigma Sigma Phi. Methodist. Lodges: Order DeMolay (chevalier), Masons. Home: 250 University Dr #12 Fort Worth TX 76107 Office: 1701 River Run Suite 310 Fort Worth TX 76107

MC CRAY, EVELINA WILLIAMS, librarian, researcher; b. Plaquemine, La., Sept. 1, 1932; d. Turner and Gertrude (Gordon) Williams II; m. John Samuel McCray, Apr. 7, 1955; 1 dau., Johnetta McCray Russ. BA, So. U., Baton Rouge, 1954; MS in Library Sci., La. State U., 1962. Librarian, Iberville High Sch., Plaquemine, 1954-70, Plaquemine Jr. High, 1970-75; proofreader short stories, poems Associated Writers Guild, Atlanta, 1982-86; library cons. Evaluation Capitol High Sch., 1964, Iberville Parish Educators Workshop, 1980, Tchrs. Core/Iberville Parish, 1980-81. Contbr. poetry New Am. Poetry Anthology, 1988, The Golden Treasury of Great Poems, 1988. Vol. service Allen J. Nadler Library, Plaquemine, 1980-82; librarian Local Day Care Ctr., Plaquemine, 1978-79; appointee La. Retired Tchrs.' Com. on Info. and Protective Services, 1988—. Recipient Golden Poet award World Poetry, 1988. Mem. ALA, La. Library Assn., Nat. Ret. Tchrs. Assn., La Ret. Tchrs. Assn. (cons. ann. workshops 1986—, state appointee to informative and protective services com. 1988—), Iberville Ret. Tchrs. Assn. (info. and protective services dir. 1981—). Democrat. Baptist. Home: PO Box Q Plaquemine LA 70765

MCCREA, WILLIAM HUNTER, theoretical astronomer; b. Dublin, Ireland, Dec. 13, 1904; s. Robert Hunter and Margaret (Hutton) McC.; m. Marian Nichol Core Webster, July 28, 1933; children: Isabella, Sheila, Roderick. PhD, Cambridge (Eng.) U., 1929, MA, 1931, ScD, 1958; ScD (hon.), Nat. U. Ireland, 1954, Queen's U. Belfast, No. Ireland, 1970, Nat. U. Cordoba, Argentina, 1971, Dublin U., 1972, U. Sussex, Eng., 1979. Lectr. in math. Edinburgh (Scotland) U., 1930-32; reader London U., 1932-36, prof., 1944-46; prof. Queen's U., 1936-44; prof. astronomy Sussex U., Brighton, Eng., 1966-72, prof. emeritus, 1972—; vis. prof. univs. in U.S., Can., Mex., Argentina, Egypt, Turkey, New Zealand, Belgium, USSR. Author: Relativity Physics, 1935, Analytical Geometry of Three Dimensions, 1942, Physics of the Sun and Stars, 1950, Royal Greenwich Observatory, 1985. Named Knight Bachelor; Bye-fellow Gonville and Caius Coll., Cambridge U., 1952-53. Fellow Royal Soc., Royal Astron. Soc. (pres. 1961-63, Gold medal 1976) Royal Soc. Edinburgh (Keith prize 1939-41); mem. Royal Irish Acad. Anglican. Club: Athenaeum (London). Home: 87 Houndean Rise Lewes, Sussex BN7 1EJ, England

MCCREE, PAUL WILLIAM, JR., systems design and engineering company executive; b. St. Louis, Oct. 27, 1926; s. Paul William and Hazel Elfrieda (Wilson) McC.; m. Carolyn Williams, Sept. 7, 1955; children—Brian, Paula, Ross. B.S. in Biochem. Scis., Harvard U., 1950. Mem. tech. staff System Devel. Corp., Santa Monica, Calif., 1956-62, Mitre Corp., Bedford, Mass., 1966-67; prin. engr., equipment div. Raytheon Co., Sudbury, Mass., 1963-66, 67-72; mem. tech. staff MIT Lincoln Labs., Lexington, 1972-76; mgr. Aerospace Systems div. Input Output, Waltham, Mass., 1976-79, tech. dir., 1979-80; mem. tech. staff Mitre Corp., Bedford, Mass., 1980-82; founder, pres. BPR Co., profl. cons. services (sci., engring. and bus. applications of computers), 1981—; sr. mem. tech. staff, mgr. subsystem design and devel. dept. GTE Strategic Systems Div., 1982-84; tech. dir. HH Aerospace and Design Co. Inc., Bedford, 1984-86; prin. engr., mem. tech. staff Raytheon Equipment div. Software Systems Lab., Sudbury, 1986-87; v.p. HH Aerospace and Design Co. Inc., Bedford, 1987—. Served with U.S. Army, 1944. Recipient Black Achiever award Greater Boston YMCA, 1977. Mem. AAAS, Am. Mgmt. Assn., Urban League, NAACP, N.Y. Acad. Scis. Democrat. Club: Harvard (Boston); Harvard Faculty (Cambridge). Home: 173 Goodman's Hill Rd PO Box #77 Sudbury MA 01776

MCCREERY, WILLIAM GESTAL, lawyer; b. Bklyn., July 12, 1932; s. William and Consuelo (Gestal) McC.; m. Gay Palutis, June 25, 1960; children—Bill, Sean, Tara, Jack. B.S., Villanova U., 1954; J.D., St. John's U., 1959; LL.M., NYU, 1969. Bar: N.Y. 1959. Atty. NLRB, N.Y.C., 1959-64; atty. Pfizer Inc., N.Y.C., 1964-70, corp. counsel, 1970-75, asst. gen. counsel, asst. sec., 1975—. Founder, trustee Scarsdale (N.Y.) Hist. Soc., 1973—; village trustee Scarsdale, 1985—. Served to lt. USN, 1954-56. Mem. ABA, N.Y. State Bar Assn. Club: Town (Scarsdale) (pres. 1982-83).

MC CRORY, ELLANN, radiologist; b. Butler Springs, Ala., Mar. 22, 1936; d. William Bryant and Eva Estelle (Stabler) McCrory. BS, U. Ala., 1956; MD, Med. Coll. Ala., 1960. Rotating intern Univ. Hosp., Birmingham, Ala., 1960-61; resident Bapt. Meml. Hosp., Memphis, 1961-64; instr. radiology U. Fla., 1964-65; pvt. practice radiology, Fort Payne, Ala., 1965—; chief of med. staff DeKalb County Hosp., 1977; speaker in field. Trustee, pres. Landmarks Inc., 1978-79. Recipient Bausch and Lomb Sci. award, 1953. Mem. Am. Coll. Radiology, Radiol. Soc. N.A., AMA, Am. Med. Women's Assn., So. Radiol. Assn., Am. Roentgen Ray Soc., Am. Assn. Women Radiologists (treas. 1987—), Mid-South Med. Assn., Med. Assn. Ala. (v.p. 1986-87, bd. census 1988—), DeKalb County Med. Soc. (pres. 1977), So. Med. Assn., Ala. Radiol. Soc., Fort Payne C. of C. (bd. dirs., pres. 1979-80) Ala. Hist. Soc., U. Ala. Alumni Assn. (pres. elect DeKalb County chpt. 1977, nat. dist. v.p.), Phi Beta Kappa, Alpha Lambda Delta. Methodist. Home: 1408 Alabama Ave SW Fort Payne AL 35967 Office: 309 Medical Center Dr PO Box 1298 Fort Payne AL 35967

MCCRORY, JOHN PAUL, manufacturing company executive; b. Anderson, Ind., Nov. 23, 1923; s. Ralph and Lola Ethel (Ashby) McC.; m. Rosemary Atkinson, June 29, 1946; children—Linda Sue McCrory Coleson, Michael David, James Lee. Guest student Northwestern U., Harvard U., Ind. U., FBI Acad. From clk. to staff capt. Ind. State Police, Indpls., 1942-62; factory rep. Best Lock Corp., 1962-72, v.p. mktg., Indpls., 1972—, also v.p. Best Locking Systems, Denver, Los Angeles, N.Y.C., Blsystems, Portland, Oreg., Blystems, Pitts. Inventor in field. Mem. Va. dist. bd. Wesleyan Ch., 1970-72, local bd., Rockville, Md., 1970-72, gen. bd., 1970-72; mem. local bd. Ch. of Nazarene, Indpls., 1982; trustee Owosso Coll., Mich., 1956-58. Served with USAAF, 1943-45, PTO. Named Boss of Yr., Indpls. chpt. Am. Bus. Women's Assn., 1960; hon. citizen of Tenn., 1958; Sagamore of Wabash, State of Ind., 1956. Mem. FBI Nat. Acad. Grads., Harvard Assn. Police Sci., Am. Soc. Indsl. Security, Pioneers Ind. State Police. Republican. Club: Brookshire Golf (Carmel, Ind.). Office: Best Lock Corp PO Box 50444 Indianapolis IN 46250

MCCRUDDEN, JOHN CHRISTOPHER, legal educator; b. Belfast, No. Ireland, Jan. 29, 1952; s. Gerard and Lillian Theodora (Dolan) McC. LLB, Queen's U., Belfast, 1974; LLM, Yale U., 1975; MA, Oxford U., Eng., 1980, PhD, 1981. Jr. research fellow Balliol Coll., Oxford, 1977-80; fellow, tutor in law Lincoln Coll., Oxford, 1980—; lectr. Oxford U., 1980—. Author: Regulation and Public Law, 1987; editor: Law in Context series, 1977—, Women, Equality and European Law, 1988. Mem. Standing Adv. Commn. on Human Rights, Belfast, 1985—, Commn. of European Communities Expert Network on Equality Directives, Brussels, 1986—. Harkness fellow Commonwealth Fund, 1974-76. Club: Yale (N.Y.C.). Office: Lincoln Coll, Turl St, Oxford OX1 3DR, England

MCCRUM, MICHAEL WILLIAM, educator; b. Gosport, Hampshire, England, May 23, 1924; s. Cecil Robert and Ivy Hilda (Nicholson) McCrum; m. Christine Mary McCrum, Sept. 6, 1952; 4 children. Student, Corpus Christi Coll., Cambridge, 1946-48, M.A., 1948. Asst. master Rugby Sch., Warwickshire, 1948-50; tutor Corpus Christi Coll., 1950-62, master, 1980—; head master Tonbridge Sch., Kent, 1962-70, Eton Coll., Berkshire, 1970-80; vice-chancellor Cambridge U., 1987. Joint author Select Documents of the Principates of the Flavian Emperors A.D. 68-96, 1961. Served to sub-lt., RNVR, 1943-45. Mem. Ch. of Eng. Clubs: Athenaeum, United Oxford and Cambridge, East India and Public Schools, Hawks. Address: The Masters Lodge, Corpus Christi Coll, Cambridge CB2 1RH England •

MCCUEN, JOHN FRANCIS, JR., auto parts manufacturing executive, lawyer; b. N.Y.C., Mar. 11, 1944; s. John Francis and Elizabeth Agnes (Corbett) McC.; children: Sarah, Mary, John. A.B., U. Notre Dame, 1966; J.D., U. Detroit, 1969. Bar: Mich. 1970, Fla. 1970, Ohio 1978. Legal counsel Kelsey-Hayes Co., Romulus, Mich., 1970-77; corp. counsel Sheller-Globe Corp., Toledo, 1977-79; v.p., gen. counsel Sheller-Globe Corp., 1979-86, sec., 1982-87, sr. v.p. gen. counsel, 1986—. Trustee Kidney Found. N.W. Ohio, 1979-88, pres., 1984-86. Mem. Am. Bar Assn., Ohio Bar Assn., Fla. State Bar. Clubs: Toledo, Inverness, Catawba Island. Home: 2745 Westowne Ct Toledo OH 43615 Office: Sheller Globe Corp 1505 Jefferson Ave Toledo OH 43697

MCCUEN, JOHN JOACHIM, defense contractor executive; b. Washington, Mar. 30, 1926; s. Joseph Raymond and Josephine (Joachim) McC.; m. Gloria Joyce Seidel, June 16, 1949; children: John Joachim Jr., Les Seidel. BS, U.S. Mil. Acad., 1948; M of Internatl. Affairs, Columbia U., 1961; grad., U.S. Army War Coll., 1968. Commd. 2d. lt. U.S. Army, 1948, advanced through grades to col.; dir. internal def. and devel. U.S. Army War Coll., Carlisle, Pa., 1969-72; chief U.S. Def. Liaison Group, Jakarta, Indonesia, 1972-74; chief field survey office U.S. Army Tng. and Doctrine Command, Ft. Monroe, Va., 1974-76; ret. U.S. Army, 1976; mgr. tng. Chrysler Def., Center Line, Mich., 1977-82; mgr. modification ctr. Land Systems div. Gen. Dynamics, Sterling Heights, Mich., 1982-83; mgr. field ops. Land Systems div. Gen. Dynamics, Warren, Mich., 1983—; ptnr. East West Connection, Birmingham, Mich.; armor advisor 3d Royal Thai Army, Utaradit, 1957-58; U.S. rep. users' com. NATO Missile Firing Installation Crete, Paris, 1964-66; advisor Vietnamese Nat. Def. Coll., Saigon, 1968-69; speaker on terrorism and counter insurgency. Author: The Art of Counter Revolutionary War-The Strategy of Counter Insurgency, 1966, Circulo Militar, 1967. Pres. Troy (Mich.) Community Concert Assn., 1985—; v.p. Mich. Oriental Art Soc., Birmingham, 1985—; mem. exec. bd., chmn. bldg. com. Granderview Assn. Sr. Housing and Nursing, Milford, Mich., 1984—. Mem. Soc. Logistics Engrs., Nat. Mgmt. Assn., Assn. U.S. Army. Republican. Home: 32863 Balmoral Birmingham MI 48009 Office: Gen Dynamics Land Systems Div PO Box 527 Warren MI 48090

MCCULLAGH, GRANT GIBSON, architect; b. Cleve., Apr. 18, 1951; s. Robert Ernest and Barbara Louise (Grant) McC.; m. Suzanne Dewar Folds, Sept. 13, 1975; children: Charles Weston Folds, Grant Gibson Jr. BArch, U. Ill., 1973; MArch, U. Pa., 1975; MBA, U. Chgo., 1979. Registered architect, Ill. Project designer Perkins & Will, Chgo., 1975-77; dir. mktg. The Austin Co., Chgo., 1977-83, asst. dist. mgr., 1983-84, dist. mgr., 1984-88, v.p., 1987-88; chmn., chief exec. officer McClier Corp., Chgo., 1988—. Contbr. articles to various indsl. publs. Mem. AIA, Chgo. Architecture Found. (exec. com., trustee, v.p. 1986-87, pres. 1988—), Chgo. Archtl. Found. Aux. Bd. (exec. v.p. 1983-86). Republican. Episcopalian. Clubs: Economics, Chicago, Casino, University; Indian Hill Country. Home: 43 Locust Rd Winnetka IL 60093 Office: McClier Corp 401 E Illinois St Chicago IL 60611

MCCULLOUGH, HENRY FREDERICK, aircraft company executive; b. Vancouver, B.C., Can., Sept. 18, 1926 (parents Am. citizens); s. John Andrew and Beatrice Victoria (Warburton) McC.; m. Constance Agnes Van Nes, Feb. 27, 1951; children—Linda, Katherine, Cynthia, John, Pamela, Lucille. Grad., Sch. Mgmt., UCLA. Cert. quality engr., Am. Soc. Quality Control, 1966. Aircraft specialist Boeing of Can., Vancouver, 1943-45; quality control preflight insp. Boeing Co., Seattle, 1945-49, 53—, quality control chief 707-727 system test, 1955-68, quality control mgr. 747 program, from 1968, now ret. Pres., commr. King County Water Dist. #107, 1965; past pres. and bd. dirs. Wash. State Assn. Water/Wastewater dists., chmn. legis. and membership coms.; charter mem. Presdl. Task Force, 1982-86, trustee, 1986; mem. Presdl. Commn., 1986; vol. crime prevention unit precinct III King County Police. Served with USAF, 1949-53. Decorated Air medal; recipient Silver Beaver award Boy Scouts Am., 1978; Golden Acorn, PTA, 1977; cert. Nat. Ct. of Honor for Life Saving, 1974, Recognition award for Vol. Service Water Pollution Abatement in King County. Fellow Am. Soc. Quality Control; mem. Am. Water Works Assn., Water Pollution Control Fedn., Boeing Mgmt. Assn. (life), Nat. Rifle Assn. (life). Republican. Episcopalian. Clubs: Meydenbauer Bay Yacht, Newport Hills Community (past pres., dir.), Renton Fishing and Game. Home: 6808 128th Ave SE Bellevue WA 98006

MC CULLOUGH, JOHN PHILLIP, management consultant, educator; b. Lincoln, Ill., Feb. 2, 1945; s. Phillip and Lucile Ethel (Ornellas) McC.; B.S., Ill. State U., 1967, M.S., 1968; Ph.D., U. N.D., 1971; m. Barbara Elaine Carley, Nov. 29, 1968; children—Carley Jo, Ryan Phillip. Adminstrv. mgr. McCullough Ins. Agy., Atlanta, Ill., 1963-68; ops. supr. Stetson China Co., Lincoln, 1967; asst. mgr. Brandtville Service, Inc., Bloomington, Ill., 1968; instr. in bus. Ill. Cen. Coll., 1968-69; research asst. U. N.D., Grand Forks, 1969-71; assoc. prof. mgmt. West Liberty State Coll., 1971-74, prof., 1974—, chmn. dept. mgmt., 1974-82, dir. Sch. Bus., 1982-86, dean Sch. Bus., 1986—, dir. Small Bus. Inst., 1978—; mgmt. cons., Triadelphia, W.Va., 1971—; instr. Am. Inst. Banking, 1971—; lectr. W.Va. U., 1971—; adj. prof. Wheeling Coll., 1972—, U. Steubenville, 1982—; lectr. Ohio U., 1982—; profl. asso. Inst. Mgmt. and Human Behavior, 1975—; v.p. West Liberty State Coll. Fed. Credit Union, 1976—; rep. W.Va. Bd. Regents Adv. Council of Faculty. Team leader Wheeling div. Am. Cancer Soc.; coordinator Upper Ohio Valley United Fund, 1972-74; instr. AFL-CIO Community Services Program, Wheeling; project dir. Ctr. for Edn. and Research with Industry; bd. dirs. Ohio Valley Indsl. and Bus. Devel. Corp., Labor Mgmt. Inst. Recipient Service award Bank Adminstrn. Inst., 1974, United Fund, 1973; Acad. Achievement award Harris-Casals Found., 1971. Mem. Soc. Humanistic Mgmt. (nat. chmn.), Orgn. Planning Mgmt. Assn. (exec. com.), Spl. Interest Group for Cert. Bus. Educators (nat. dir.), Soc. Advancement Mgmt. (chpt. adv.), Acad. Mgmt., Adminstrv. Mgmt. Soc. (cert.), Am. Soc. Personnel Adminstrn. (cert.), Nat. Bus. Honor Soc. (Excellence in Teaching award 1976, dir. 1974—), Alpha Kappa Psi (Dist. Service award 1973, Civic award 1977, chpt. adv. 1971—), Delta Mu Delta, Delta Pi Epsilon, Delta Tau Kappa, Phi Gamma Nu, Phi Theta Pi, Pi Gamma Mu, Pi Omega Pi, Omicron Delta Epsilon. Author: (with Howard Fryette) Primer in Supervisory Management, 1973; contbr. articles to profl. jours. Home: 68 Elm Dr Triadelphia WV 26059

MCCURDY, LARRY WAYNE, automotive parts company executive; b. Commerce, Tex., July 1, 1935; s. Weldon Lee and Eula Bell (Quinn) McC.; m. Anna Jean Ogle, June 2, 1956; children: Michael, Kimberly, Laurie. B.B.A., Tex. A&M U., 1957. Jr. acct. Tenneco Inc., Houston, 1958-60; sr. acct. Tenneco Oil Co., Houston, 1960-64; acctg. supr. Tenneco Chems., Houston, 1964-69; div. controller Tenneco Chems., Saddle Brook, N.J., 1970-72; corp. controller Tenneco Chems., 1972-74, v.p., fin., 1974-78; sr. v.p. fin. Tenneco Automotive, Deerfield, Ill., 1978-80; pres. Walker Mfg. Co., Racine, Wis., 1980-81; exec. v.p. N.Am. ops. Tenneco Automotive, Deerfield, 1981-82; v.p. fin. Echlin Inc., Branford, Conn., 1983, pres. chief operating officer, 1983-85; pres., chief exec. officer Moog Automotive Inc., St. Louis, 1985—; dir. Mohasco Corp. Trustee Somerset County Coll., Somerville, N.J., 1974-78; former mem. bd. dirs. Jr. Achievement, Chgo. Served with USAR, 1958-66. Mem. Fin. Execs. Inst., Nat. Assn. Accts., Motor Equipment Mfgrs. Assn. (bd. dirs.). Office: Moog Automotive Inc 6565 Wells Ave Saint Louis MO 63133

MC CURDY, RICHARD CLARK, engineering consultant; b. Newton, Iowa, Jan. 2, 1909; s. Ralph Bruce and Florence (Clark) McC.; m. Harriet Edith Sutton, Sept. 11, 1933; children: Gregor, Richard, Carolyn, Robert. A.B., Stanford U., 1931, E.M., 1933. Engring. and prodn. Shell Oil Co., 1933-47; prodn. mgmt. Shell Caribbean Petroleum Co., 1947-50; gen. mgr. Shell Group Companies, Venezuela, 1950-53; pres. Shell Chem. Co., N.Y.C., 1953-65; dir. Shell Oil Co., mem. exec. com., 1959-69, pres., chief exec. officer, 1965-69; assoc. adminstr. orgn. and mgmt. NASA, Washington, 1970-73; cons. NASA, 1974-82. Trustee United Seamans Service, 1954-70, Stanford U., 1965-70; trustee Hood Coll., 1968-86, trustee emeritus, 1986—, hon. trustee, 1987—; trustee Rensselaer Poly. Inst., 1974-86, hon. trustee, 1986—. Recipient Disting. Service medal NASA, 1972. Mem. Mfg. Chemists Assn. (dir. 1955-65, chmn. bd. 1961-62, chmn. exec. com. 1964-65), Am. Inst. Mining, Metall. and Petroleum Engrs., Am. Phys. Soc., Am. Petroleum Inst., Beta Theta Pi. Clubs: N.Y. Yacht, Noroton (Conn.) Yacht (commodore); Tokeneke (Darien, Conn.); St. Francis Yacht, Pacific Union (San Francisco); Links (N.Y.C.); Cruising of Am. (commodore 1980-82). Home: Contentment Island Darien CT 06820

MCCURLEY, CARL MICHAEL, lawyer; b. Denton, Tex., July 15, 1946; s. Carl and Geneva McC.; m. Mary Jo Trice, June 5, 1983; 1 child, Melissa Renee. B.A., N. Tex. State U., 1968; J.D., So. Meth. U., 1972. Bar: Tex. 1972, U.S. Dist. Ct. (no. dist.) Tex. 1972, U.S. Dist. Ct. (ea. dist.) Tex. 1974, U.S. Supreme Ct. 1977. Ptnr. McGuire, Levy & McCurley, Irving, Tex., 1972-82, Koons, Rasor, Fuller & McCurley, Dallas, 1982—. Co-editor Family Law Practice Manuals, 1984; contbr. articles to profl. jours. Mem. Irving Bar Assn. (pres. 1976-77), Dallas Bar Assn. (sec.-treas. 1979), Tex. Trial Lawyers Assn., Am. Acad. Matrimonial Lawyers, Internat. Acad. Matrimonial Lawyers. Home: 915 Liberty Ct Dallas TX 75204 Office: Koons Rasor Fuller & McCurley 2311 Cedar Springs Rd #300 Dallas TX 75201

MCDADE, JAMES RUSSELL, management consultant; b. Dallas, Jan. 15, 1925; s. Marion W. and Jeannette (Reneau) McD.; m. Elaine Bushey, Sep. 10, 1955. BSEE, So. Meth. U., Dallas, 1947; MBA, Northwestern U., Evanston, Ill., 1950. Asst. to pres. Davidson Corp., Chgo., 1951-52; asst. to pres. Mergenthaler Linotype Co., Bklyn., 1952-53, comml. works mgr., 1953-56; chief indsl. engr. Tex. Instruments, Inc., Dallas, 1956-57, v.p., 1961-64; chmn. bd. McDade Properties Co., Aspen (Colo.), Denver, Dallas, 1964—; bd. dirs. Pitkin City Bank, Aspen; chmn. bd. dirs. Harley-Davidson Tex., Westec Security of Aspen, Aspen Security, Inc. Founding mem. Aspen Art Mus., 1980; mem. Ballet Aspen, 1980—; pres. club Aspen Valley Hosp., 1984—. Served to 1st lt. USAF, 1943-46. Mem. Rep. Senatorial Inner Circle, Am. Mgmt. Assn., Presidents Assn. Home and Office: 1000 Red Mountain Rd PO Box 9090 Aspen CO 81612

MC DANIEL, JAMES EDWIN, lawyer; b. Dexter, Mo., Nov. 22, 1931; s. William H. and Gertie M. (Woods) McD.; m. Mary Jane Crawford, Jan. 22, 1955; children: John William, Barbara Anne. AB, Washington U., St. Louis, 1957, JD, 1959. Bar: Mo. 1959. Assoc. firm Walther, Barnard, Cloyd & Timm, 1959-60; assoc. firm McDonald, Barnard, Wright & Timm, 1960-63, ptnr., 1963-65; ptnr. firm Barnard, Timm & McDaniel St. Louis, 1965-73; ptnr. firm Barnard & Baer, St. Louis, 1973-82; ptnr. Lashly, Baer & Hamel, St. Louis, 1982—; sec., bd. dirs. Hosp. TV, Inc.; pros. atty. City of Glendale, Mo., 1968—; bd. dirs. Airtherm Mfg. Co. Leader legal del. Chinese-Am. Comparative Law Study, 1988, People's Republic China, 1988. Served with USAF, 1951-55. Mem. ABA (ho. of dels. 1976-80, 84—, state del. 1986—, chmn. Lawyers Conf., Jud. Adminstrn. Div. 1985-86), The Mo. Bar (pres. 1981-82, bd. govs. 1974-83), Bar Assn. Met. St. Louis (pres. 1972), Internat. Assn. Ins. Counsel, Assn. Def. Counsel St. Louis (past pres.), Phi Delta Phi. Congregationalist. Home: 767 Elmwood Glendale MO 63122 Office: Lashly Baer & Hamel 714 Locust St Saint Louis MO 63101

MCDANIEL, MYRA ATWELL, former state official, lawyer; b. Phila., Dec. 13, 1932; d. Toronto Canada, Jr. and Eva Lucinda (Yores) Atwell; m. Reuben Roosevelt McDaniel Jr., Feb. 20, 1955; children—Diane Lorraine, Reuben Roosevelt III. BA, U. Pa., 1954; JD, U. Tex., 1975; LLD, Huston-Tillotson Coll., 1984, Jarvis Christian Coll., 1986. Bar: Tex. 1975, U.S. Dist. Ct. (we. dist.) Tex. 1977, U.S. Dist. Ct. (so. and no. dists.) Tex. 1978, U.S. Ct. Appeals (5th cir.) 1978, U.S. Supreme Ct. 1978, U.S. Dist. Ct. (ea. dist.) Tex. 1979. Asst atty. gen. State of Tex., Austin, 1975-81, chief taxation div., 1979-81, gen. counsel to gov., 1983-84, sec. of state, 1984-87; asst. gen. counsel Tex. R.R. Commn., Austin, 1981-82; gen. counsel Wilson Cos., San Antonio and Midland, Tex., 1982; assoc. Bickerstaff, Heath & Smiley, Austin, 1984, ptnr., 1987—; mem. asset mgmt. adv. com. State Treasury, Austin, 1984-86; mem. legal affairs com. Criminal Justice Policy Council, Austin, 1984-86; mem. legal affairs com. Inter-State Oil Compact, Oklahoma City, 1984-86; bd. dirs. Austin Cos. Group, 1983-86; lectr. in field. Contbr. articles to profl. jours., chpts. to books. Del. Tex. Conf. on Libraries and Info. Scis., Austin, 1978, White House Conf. on Libraries and Info. Scis., Washington, 1979; mem. Library Services and Constrn. Act Adv. Council, 1980-84, chmn., 1983-84; mem. long range plan task force Brackenridge Hosp., Austin, 1981; clk. vestry bd. St. James Episcopal Ch., Austin, 1981-83; bd. visitors U. Tex. Law Sch., 1983—, vice chmn., 1983-85; bd. dirs. Friends of Ronald McDonald House of Cen. Tex., Women's Advocacy, Inc., Capital Area Rehab. Ctr.; trustee Episcopal Found. Tex., 1986—, St. Edward's U., Austin, 1986—; chmn. div. United Way/Capital area campaign, 1986. Recipient Tribute to 28 Black Women award Concepts Unltd., 1983; Focus on women honoree Serwa Yetu chpt. Mt. Olive grand chpt. Order of Eastern Star, 1979, Woman of Yr. Longview Metro C. of C., 1985, Woman of Yr. Austin chpt. Internat. Tng. in Communication, 1985, Citizen of Yr. Epsilon Iona chpt. Omega Psi Phi. Mem. ABA, Am. Bar Found., Tex. Bar Found. (trustee 1986—), Travis County Bar Assn., Travis County Women Lawyers' Assn., Austin Black Lawyers Assn., State Bar Tex. (chmn. Profl. Efficiency and Econ. Research subcom. 1978-84), Golden Key Nat. Honor Soc., Omicron Delta Kappa, Delta Phi Alpha, Order Coif (hon. mem.). Democrat. Home: 3910 Knollwood Dr Austin TX 78731 Office: San Jacinto Ctr Suite 1800 98 San Jacinto Blvd Austin TX 78701

MC DERMAID, RICHARD, pharmaceutical consultant; b. Logan, Utah, Apr. 25, 1914; s. William Tait and Annie (Ellis) McD.; B.S., U. Idaho, 1938; M.B.A., Harvard U., 1955; m. Marion Christensen, Aug. 9, 1939; 1 son, Richard Allen. Commd. 2d lt. USAAF, 1944, advanced through grades to col., 1966; service in Ger., 1946-49, Spain, 1955-59, Italy, 1960-64; ret., 1968; chief fgn. insp. staff FDA, 1968-81; pres. Richmar Internat., Inc., McLean, Va., 1981—. Decorated Legion of Merit; recipient Commendable Service award FDA, 1977. Mem. Internat. Fedn. Pharmacy, Harvard U. Bus. Sch. Club. Republican. Mormon. Author papers in field. Home: 1706 Birch Rd McLean VA 22101

MCDERMIT, ROBERT EDWARD, health services executive, consultant, educator; b. Moose Jaw, Sask., Can., Nov. 16, 1932; a. John and Barbara (Melvin) McD.; m. Ruth Elsie Erickson, May 17, 1955; children: Dale Robert, Mary Lyn, Leslie Ann. BS in Pharmacy, U. Sask., Saskatoon, 1957; Pharma. chemist, Sask. Pharmaceutical Assn., Regina, 1957; Cert. Hosp. Orgn. Mgmt., Can. Hosp. Assn., 1965; Licentiate in Health Adminstrn., Inst. Health Service Adminstrs., London, 1976. Cert. health exec. Can. Coll. Health Service Execs., Ottawa, Can., 1984. Instr. pharmacy U. Sask. Coll. Pharmacy, Saskatoon, Can., 1957-58; pharmacy cons., N.W. Regional Hosp. Council North Battleford, Sask., Can., 1958-61; chief pharmacist Notre Dame Hosp., North Battlefield, Sask., Can., 1958-61; dir. pharmacy Regina Grey Nuns' Hosp., Sask., Can., 1961-63, adminstrv. asst., 1963-65, asst. gen. adminstr., 1965-67; adminstr. Wascana Hosp., Regina, Sask., Can., 1967-68; asst. exec. dir. S. Sask. Hosp. Centre, Regina, Sask., Can., 1968-69, adminstr. Wascana div., 1968-69; dir. edn. Sask. Hosp. Assn., Regina, Sask., Can., 1969-71; gen. mgr., v.p. Gordon A. Friesen Can., Ltd., Calgary, Alta., Can., 1971-74; chief, health care plan Dept. Social Devel., Govt. N.W. Ters., Yellowknife, N.W.T., Can., 1974-77; asst. dir. dept. health and social services Govt. N.W. Terrs., Yellowknife, N.W.T., Can., 1977-78; dir. Dept. Health, Yellowknife, N.W.T., Can., 1978-79; sr. asst. dep. minister Profl. and Instl. Services, Ministry Health, Govt. B.C., Victoria, Can., 1979-81; adminstr. U. B.C. Health Scis. Centre Hosp., Vancouver, 1981-82; pres. U. B.C. Health Scis. Centre Hosp., Vancouver, Can., 1983-87; exec. dir., chief exec. officer St. John Ambulance B.C., Vancouver, 1987—; pres. Futuristic Health Concepts, Richmond, B.C., 1987—; clin. lectr. U. B.C., Vancouver, 1981—; lectr. faculty health info. scis. U. Victoria, B.C., Can., 1982—. Contbr. articles to profl. jours. Bd. dirs. Regina Boys' Pipe Band, 1967-69, 70-71; mem. Vancouver Bd. Trade. Recipient Merck prize in Chemistry, Frank W. Horner Meml. prize in Pharmacology, Gold medal Sask. Pharm. Assn.; scholar F.J. Fear, Robert Martin, Can. Found. for Advancement Pharmacy, Burroughs Welcome. Fellow Am. Coll. Hosp. Adminstrs., Can. Coll. Health Service Execs., (cert.) Bd. and Coms.; mem. Can. Pub. Health Assn. (pres. N.W.T. br. 1975-76), B.C. Health Assn., Bd. and Coms., Sask. Hosp. Assn. (bd. dirs. 1967-69). Sask. Assn. Hosp. Adminstrs. (pres. 1966-68), Sask. Pharm. Assn., Can. Soc. Hosp. Pharmacists (pres. 1963-64, v.p. 1962-63). Club: Vancouver Can. Home: 6740 Dunsany Pl, Richmond, BC Canada V7C 4N8 Office: St John Ambulance BC, 6111 Cambie St, Vancouver, BC Canada V5Z 3B2

MC DERMOTT, EDWARD ALOYSIOUS, lawyer; b. Dubuque, Iowa, June 28, 1920; s. Edward L. and Sarah (Larkin) McD.; m. Naola Spellman, Sept. 1, 1945; children: Maureen, Edward Aloysious, Charles Joseph, Daniel John. B.A., Loras Coll., Dubuque, 1939; J.D., State U., Iowa, 1942; J.D. (hon.), Xavier U., 1962, Loras Coll., 1973. Bar: Iowa, D.C., Nebr. 1942. Mem. legal dept. Travelers Ins. Co., Omaha, 1942-43, Montgomery Ward & Co., Chgo., 1943-46; atty. firm O'Connor, Thomas & O'Connor, Dubuque, 1946-50; chief counsel sub-com. privileges and elections U.S. Senate, 1950-51; partner firm O'Connor, Thomas, McDermott & Wright, Dubuque, 1951-61; prof. bus. law and econs. Loras Coll., also Clarke Coll., Dubuque; dep. dir. Office Civil and Def. Moblzn., 1961-62; dep. dir. Office Emergency Planning, 1961-62, dir., 1962-65; partner firm Hogan & Hartson, Washington, 1965-88;

Mem. Nat. Security Council, 1962-65; U.S. rep. to sr. com., other coms. NATO, 1962-65; chmn. Pres.'s Exec. Stockpile Com., 1962-65; bd. advisers Indsl. Coll. Armed Forces, 1962-65; mem. Nat. Conf. Uniform Commrs. State Laws, 1959-64; chmn. Nat. CD Adv. Council, 1962-65; mem. Pres.'s Com. Employment Handicapped, 1962-65, Pres.'s Com. Manpower, 1963-65, Pres.'s Com. Econ. Impact Def. and Rearmament, 1963-65, Pres.'s Sr. Adv. Com. on Govt. Reorgn., 1978-79; chmn. Com. on Assumptions for Nonmil. Planning, 1963-65; mem. Fed. Reconstrn. and Devel. Commn. Alaska, 1964-65; mem. adv. com. Fed. Emergency Mgmt. Adminstrn., 1980-85. Del. Democratic Nat. Conv., 1952, 56, 60, 64; trustee, sec. Ford's Theatre, Christ Child Soc., Religious Educators Found., Loras Coll.; mem. fin. council Archdiocese of Washington; chmn. emeritus Lombardi Cancer Inst.; regent emeritus Coll. Notre Dame; trustee emeritus Colgate U.; mem. council Hosp. St. John and St. Elizabeth, London, Maynooth Coll., Ireland; regent emeritus U. Santa Clara, Calif; bd. advisers Lynchburg (Va.) Coll., Iowa Law Sch. Found., Up With People; bd. dirs. Mercedez-Benz of N.Am., 1985—. Decorated knight Holy Sepulchre; recipient Amvets Spl. Silver Helmet award, 1963. Fellow ABA; mem. Am. Irish Found. (v.p., dir.), Fed. Bar Assn., Iowa Bar Assn. (bd. govs. 1956-60), D.C. Bar Assn., Am. Judicature Soc., John Carroll Soc. (Pres. 1972), Friendly Sons St. Patrick (pres. 1978-79), Knights of Malta (pres. 1979-82). Democrat. Clubs: The City (bd. dirs.), 1925 F Street, Metropolitan, International (Washington). Home: 5400 Albermarle St Bethesda MD 20816 Office: Columbia Sq 555 13th St NW Washington DC 20004

MCDERMOTT, EDWARD WILLIAM, marketing professional; b. Manchester, Lancashire, Eng., May 12, 1933; 3 children. BA, Open U., 1986. Engr. Ferranti, Manchester, Eng., 1959-77; salesman, mktg. mgr. Ferranti Computer Systems, Ltd., Manchester, Eng., 1977-85; mktg. mgr. Ferranti Offshore Industries Group, Edinburgh, Eng., 1985—. Author: Offshore Electronics, 1978. Served with RAF, 1952-54. Office: Ferranti Offshore Group, Thornybank Dalkeith, Midlothian EH12 7AP, Scotland

MCDEVITT, RAY EDWARD, lawyer; b. San Francisco, Nov. 15, 1943; s. Edward Anthony and Margaret Ann (Peterson) McD.; m. Mary Rolfs, July 1, 1967; children—Jessica, Devon. B.A., Stanford U., 1966, J.D., 1969; Diploma in Law, Oxford U., 1973. Bar: Calif., 1970, U.S. Supreme Ct., 1975. Teaching fellow Stanford U., 1969; law clk. Calif. Supreme Ct., 1970; atty. EPA, 1973-75, assoc. gen. counsel, 1975-76; ptnr. Hanson, Bridgett, Marcus, Vlahos & Rudy, San Francisco, 1976—. Mem. Marin County Conservation League, Marin Arts Council. Recipient Silver medal for outstanding service EPA, 1976. Mem. ABA, Calif. Bar Assn., Order of Coif. Club: Olympic (San Francisco). Office: 333 Market St Suite 2300 San Francisco CA 94105

MCDONALD, GREGORY JOHN, consumer goods company executive; b. Columbus, Ohio, Aug. 22, 1950; s. William Henry and Betty (Johnson) McD.; m. Gloria Noemi Sousa, Apr. 3, 1982; children: Christina Marie, Dustin Andrew, Kimberly Anne. BA, Wittenberg U., 1972; M in Internat. Mgmt., Am. Grad. Sch. Internat. Mgmt., 1974. Asst. products mgr. Colgate Palmolive, N.Y.C., 1974-75, mktg. mgr., Mexico City, 1976-80, mktg. dir. Buenos Aires, 1983-86, gen. mgr., Madrid, 1987— . Mem. Am. C. of C. (bd. dirs. 1983—), Am. Cultural Council (pres.), Pi Sigma Alpha. Republican. Methodist. Office: Colgate Palmolive SAE, Conde de la Cimera 6, 28040 Madrid Spain

MCDONALD, HEMPROVA GHOSH, pathologist, researcher; b. Habigunj, India, Feb. 24, 1918; came to U.S., 1951, naturalized, 1962; d. Kunja Behari and Kusum Kamini (Ray) Guha; m. Hendley A. McDonald, June 11, 1960. M.D., M.B., Calcutta Med. Coll., India, 1941. Diplomate Am. Bd. Pathologic Anatomy. Fellow div. cancer research Washington U., St. Louis, 1951-52, resident in pathology, 1952-55, instr. surg. pathology, 1956-59; chief lab. services VA Hosp., McKinney, Tex., 1959-65; clin. asst. prof. U. Tex. Med. Sch., Dallas, 1960-68; dir. Diagnostic and Cell Research Inst., Waco, Tex., 1965—; cons. pathologist Hillcrest Bapt. Med. Ctr., Waco, 1966—, Providence Hosp., Waco, 1966—. Contbr. articles to profl. jours. Fellow Coll. Am. Pathologists, Am. Soc. Clin. Pathologists; mem. Indian Med. Assn., AMA, Am. Med. Women's Assn., Am. Assn. Cancer Research, AAAS. Home: 2713 N 43d St Waco TX 76710

MCDONALD, JANE FRANCES, insurance company executive; b. Winthrop, Mass., Dec. 19, 1940; d. William Francis and Isabelle Frances (Mythen) Moran; m. James Joseph McDonald, Aug. 21, 1965 (div. 1976); children—Maureen Lynn, Susan Jill, Kevin James. B.S. in Edn., Salem State Coll., Mass., 1962; Assoc. in Underwriting, Ins. Inst., Malvern, Pa., 1983. Tchr., East Hartford Sch. System, Conn., 1962-66; acct. Watkin Bros. Piano & Organ, Hartford, 1975-76; policy analyst Hartford Steam Boiler Insp. & Ins., 1976-80; supervising underwriter Am. Nuclear Insurers, Farmington, 1981—. Mem. Nat. Assn. Ins. Women (cert.), Am. Nuclear Soc., Nat. Assn. Female Execs., N.Y. Acad. Scis., Hartford Assn. Ins. Women (by-laws chmn. 1984-85), Hartford Women's Network. Democrat. Roman Catholic. Avocations: reading, handwriting analysis, travel, crewel embroidery. Home: 675 Graham Rd South Windsor CT 06074 Office: Am Nuclear Insurers 270 Farmington Ave Farmington CT 06032

MCDONALD, JOHN FRANCIS PATRICK, electrical engineering educator; b. Narberth, Pa., Jan. 14, 1942; s. Frank Patrick and Lulu Ann (Hegedus) McD.; m. Karen Marie Knapp, May 26, 1979. B.S.E.E., MIT, 1963; M.S. in Engring., Yale U., 1965, Ph.D., 1969. Instr. Yale U., New Haven, 1968-69, asst. prof., 1969-74; assoc. prof. Rensselaer Poly. Inst., Troy, N.Y., 1974-86, prof., 1986—; founder Rensselaer Ctr. for Integrated Electronics, 1980—. Contbr. articles to profl. publs. Patentee in field. Recipient numerous grants, 1974—. Mem. ACM, IEEE, Optical Soc., Acoustical Soc., Vacuum Soc. Office: Rensselaer Poly Inst Ctr for Integrated Electronics Troy NY 12065

MC DONALD, JOHN WARLICK, diplomat, global strategist; b. Coblenz, Germany, Feb. 18, 1922; s. John Warlick and Ethel Mae (Raynor) McD.; m. Barbara Jane Stewart, Oct. 23, 1943 (div.); children: Marilyn Ruth, James Stewart, Kathleen Ethel, Laura Ellen; m. Christel Meyer, Oct. 1970. A.B., U. Ill., 1943, J.D., 1946. Bar: Ill. 1946, U.S. Supreme Ct. 1951. With legal div. Office Mil Govt., Berlin, 1947; asst. dist. atty. U.S. Mil. Govt. Cts., Frankfort, Germany, 1947-50; with Allied High Commn., Bonn, Germany, 1950-52; U.S. mission to NATO and OEEC, Paris, 1952-54; fgn. affairs officer Dept. State, Washington, 1954-55; exec. sec. to dir. ICA, Washington, 1955-59; U.S. econ. coordinator for CENTO affairs Ankara, Turkey, 1959-63; chief econ. and comml. sect. Am. embassy, Cairo, 1963-66; student Nat. War Coll., Washington, 1966-67; dep. dir. office econ. and social affairs Bur. Internat. Orgn. Affairs, Dept. State, 1967-68, dir., 1968-71; coordinator UN Multilateral Devel. Programs, Dept. State, 1971-74, acting dep. asst. sec. econ. and social affairs, 1971, 73; dep. dir. gen. ILO, Geneva, 1974-78; pres. INTELSAT Conf. Privileges and Immunities, 1978; U.S. coordinator Tech. Coop. among Developing Countries, 1978; rep. UN Conf. with rank of ambassador, 1978—; sec. gen. 27th Colombo Plan Ministerial Meeting, 1978; U.S. coordinator UN Decade on Drinking Water and Sanitation, 1979; U.S. coordinator, ambassador Third World Conf. on Indsl. Devel., 1979, World Assembly on Aging, 1980-82; chmn. fed. inter-agy. com. Internat. Yr. of Disabled Persons, 1980-81; U.S. rep. Internat. Youth Yr., 1981-83; coordinator multilateral affairs Ctr. Study of Fgn. Affairs, 1983-87, lectr. in conflict resolution, multilateral diplomacy and art of negotiation; U.S. del., alt. del. and adv. numerous UN confs.; lectr. law George Washinton U., Washington, 1987—. Author: The North-South Dialogue and the UN, 1982, How to Be a Delegate, 1984; co-editor: International Negotiation, 1985, Perspectives on Negotiation, 1986, Conflict Resolution: Track Two Diplomacy, 1987, Military Base Negotiations, 1987, U.S.-Soviet Summitry, 1987; articles on aging, terrorism and water. Bd. dirs. Global Water, 1982, Touchstone Theatre, 1982—, Am. Impact Found., 1987—, World Com.-UN Decade of Disabled Persons, 1987—, Countdown 2001, 1987—, People-to-People Com. for Handicapped, 1987—. Recipient Superior Honor award, 1972, Presdl. Meritorious Service award, 1984; named Patriot of Yr., 1987. Mem. ABA, Am. Fgn. Service Assn., U.S. Assn. for the Club of Rome, Am. Assn. Internat. Aging. (dir. 1983—, chmn. 1983—), Soc. Internat. Devel., Soc. Profls. in Dispute Resolution, Consortium on Peace Research, Edn. and Devel., Delta Kappa Upsilon, Phi Delta Phi. Club: Cosmos (Washington).

MC DONALD, JOSEPH VALENTINE, neurosurgeon; b. N.Y.C., June 7, 1925; s. Benedict and Catherine Eleanor (Chadney) Mc D.; m. Carolyn Alice Patricia Petersen, Apr. 30, 1955; children—Judith Katherine, Elizabeth Ann, Catherine Eleanor, Joseph Bede, David Randolph. A.B., Coll. Holy Cross, 1945; M.D., U. Pitts., 1949. Intern St. Vincent's Hosp., N.Y.C., 1949-50; research fellow neuroanatomy Vanderbilt U., 1950-51; gen. surgery asst. resident Cushing VA Hosp., Boston, 1951-52; neurology extern Lenox Hill Hosp., 1952; asst. resident neurosurgery Johns Hopkins Hosp., 1953-55, resident neurosurgeon, 1955-56; practice medicine specializing in neurol. surgery Rochester, N.Y., 1956—; prof., chmn. div. neurosurgery U. Rochester Med. Sch.; neurosurgeon-in-chief Strong Meml. Hosp.; cons. neurosurgery to hosps. Mem. Soc. Neurol. Surgeons, A.C.S., Acad. Neurology, Am. Assn. Neurol. Surgeons, Congress Neurosurgeons. Home: 800 Allens Creek Rd Pittsford NY 14618 Office: Strong Meml Hosp Div Neurosurgery Rochester NY 14642

MCDONALD, PEGGY ANN STIMMEL, automobile company official; b. Darbyville, Ohio, Aug. 25, 1931; d. Wilbur Smith and Bernice Edna (Hott) Stimmel; missionary diploma with honor Moody Bible Inst., 1952; B.A. cum laude in Econs. (scholar), Ohio Wesleyan U., 1965; M.B.A. with distinction, Xavier U., 1977; m. George R. Stich, Mar. 7, 1953 (dec.); 1 son, Mark Stephen (dec.); m. Joseph F. McDonald, Jr., Feb. 1, 1986. . Missionary in S. Am., Evang. Alliance Mission, 1956-61; cost acct. Western Electric Co., 1965-66; acctg. mgr. Ohio Wesleyan U., 1966-73; fin. specialist NCR Corp., 1973-74, systems analyst, 1974-75, supr. inventory planning, 1975, mgr. material planning and purchasing control, 1976-78; materials mgr. U.S. Elec. Motors Co., 1978; with Gen. Motors Corp., 1978—, shift supt. materials, Lakewood, Ga., 1979-80, gen. ops. supr. material data base mgmt. Central Office, Warren, Mich., 1980, dir. material mgmt. Gen. Motors Truck and Bus. div., Balt., 1980-87; vis. lectr. Inst. Internat. Trade, Jiao Tong U., Shanghai, China, 1985, Inst. Econs. and Fgn. Trade, Tianjin, China, 1986-87; part time instr. Towson (Md.) State U., 1986-87. Mem. Am. Prodn. and Inventory Control Soc., Am. Soc. Women Accts., AAUW, Balt. Exec. Women's Network, Balt. Council on Fgn. Relations, Baptist. Home: 125 Arbutus Ave Baltimore MD 21228 Office: Gen Motors Truck and Bus 2122 Broening Hwy PO Box 148 Baltimore MD 21203

MC DONALD, ROBERT EMMETT, conglomerate executive; b. Red Wing, Minn., Apr. 29, 1915; s. Mitchell W. and Olivia (Carlson) McD.; m. Marion L. Wigley, Sept. 14, 1946; children: Patricia L., Barbara C. B.B.A., B.E.E., U. Minn., 1940; postgrad., U. Chgo., 1942. Employment interviewer Commonwealth Edison Co., Chgo., 1940-43; supr. accessory maintenance Northwest Airlines, St. Paul, 1946-51; dir. maintenance No. region Braniff Airways, Mpls., 1951-53; mgr. ops., then v.p., mgr. def. div. Univac, St. Paul, 1953-64; pres. Univac div. Sperry Rand Corp., Blue Bell, Pa., 1966-71; exec. v.p. parent co. Univac div. Sperry Rand Corp., 1966-72; pres., chief operating officer Sperry Rand Corp., N.Y.C., 1972-79; vice chmn. bd. Sperry Rand Corp., 1979-80; dir. CertainTeed Corp., Valley Forge, Pa., SKF Industries, Phila., 1979-85, Glenmede Corp., Phila.; mgmt. cons. Trustee U. Minn. Found., 1975-85. Served to lt. USNR, 1943-46. Mem. Tau Beta Pi, Eta Kappa Nu, Acacia. Clubs: Phila. Country, Union League (Phila.). Home: 1125 Robin Rd Gladwyne PA 19035 Office: PO Box 500 Blue Bell PA 19424

MCDONALD, SHELLY LOUISE, accountant; b. Hammond, Ind., Oct. 25, 1955; d. Nolan Eugene and Lois Louise (Nettles) McD. BS in Acctg., S.W. Mo. State U., 1977. Foundations acct. Koch Industries, Inc., Wichita, Kans., 1978-79; acct., receivables supr. Abko Properties, Inc., Wichita, Kans., 1979-80; acct. Phillips Petroleum Co., Bartlesville, Okla., 1980-81; acct. II Manila, 1981; staff acct. Bartlesville, 1981-83; sr. staff acct. Abidjan, Ivory Coast, 1983-86, chief acct., 1986-88, controller, 1988—. Office: Phillips Petroleum Co, 01 BP 3857, Abidjan 01 Ivory Coast

MCDONALD, W. R., employee benefits consultant, developer; b. Mt. Vernon, Ill., Nov. 1, 1929; s. Archie R. and Vernadean Pearl (Bailey) McD. BS, Ind. State U., 1953. Pres. Youth, Inc., Terre Haute, Ind., 1947; dist. mgr. New Eng. Life Ins. Co., Sacramento, 1958-62; v.p. Sutter Sq., Inc., Sacramento, 1960-62, Southland Trust Co., Tucson, 1963-65, Am. Equity Group, Inc., Indpls., 1966-68; sr. ptnr. Ins. Investors' Guidance Systems, Mt. Vernon, 1972—; pres. Interstate Investors & Growers Syndicate, Inc., Indpls., 1975—; mng. ptnr. Halia Crest Land Trust, Mt. Vernon, 1977-79; pres. Intermed. Self-Ins. Group, Mt. Vernon, 1979—; sr. gen. ptnr. Interstate Investors Golf and Garden Solar Lodges, 1980—, Investors Strategies Group, St. Louis, 1982-85, Internat. Benefits Adv. Group, St. Louis, 1984; mng. gen. ptnr. Sundowners' Retirement Resorts, 1986—; bd. dirs. South land Trust Life Ins. Co., Phoenix, 1964; cons. So. Ill. U., Carbondale, 1973, 84—; mktg. cons. Total Health Care, Inc., Centralia, Ill., 1986—. Chmn. United Crusade, Sacramento, 1960; chmn. bd. dirs. Salvation Army, Sacramento, 1961; bd. dirs. USO, 1962. Served with USAF, 1951-57. Recipient Outstanding Flight Officer Achievement cert. USAF, 1957; named Disting. Grad., Aviation Cadets, 1952, U.S. Rookie of Year, New Eng. Life Ins. Co., 1959. Mem. Mt. Vernon C. of C. Republican. Lodge: Civitan (Sacramento Internat. chpt. pres. 1961). Office: PO Box 946 Mount Vernon IL 62864 also: 11 S Meridian Suite 810 Indianapolis IN 46204

MCDONALD, YOLANDE ELIZABETH, computer company executive; b. Halifax, N.S., Can., May 11, 1956; d. Arthur Hatheway and Rosemary Lavina (Wallace) McD.; m. William Ernest Coldwell, Oct. 13, 1985. BS, Dalhousie U., Halifax, 1976, MBA, 1987. Programmer, analyst Algonquin Coll., Ont., Can., 1976-80, Data Logic Ltd., Can., 1980; gen. mgr. SHL Systemhouse Inc., Halifax, 1981—. Roman Catholic. Office: SHL Systemhouse Inc, 1660 Hollis St, Halifax, NS Canada B3J 1V7

MCDONELL, ROBERT MICHAEL, telecommunications company executive; b. Monticello, Iowa, Apr. 7, 1950; s. William Francis and Patricia Ann (Oswald) McD.; m. Mary Lynn Jacobson, Sept. 6, 1975; children: Molly, Seth. BA in Psychology, Loras Coll., 1972; MS in Psychology, Miss. State U., 1974; MBA, Nova U., 1983. Staff psychologist Famco, Inc., Dubuque, Iowa, 1974-76; juvenile probation officer Linn County Juvenile Probation, Cedar Rapids, Iowa, 1976-78; market research mgr. Norand Corp., Cedar Rapids, 1978-81, mgr. corporate communications, 1981-86; dir. corp. communications Teleconnect Co., 1986-87, v.p., 1987—; mem. adj. faculty Nova U., Ft. Lauderdale, Fla., 1983—. Mem. Nat. Mgmt. Assn. (Outstanding Service award 1981). Democrat. Roman Catholic. Club: Civitan. Home: 7405 Normandy Dr N E Cedar Rapids IA 52402 Office: Teleconnect Co 500 2d Ave SE Cedar Rapids IA 52401

MCDONNELL, JOHN FINNEY, aerospace and aircraft manufacturing executive; b. Mar. 18, 1938; s. James Smith and Mary Elizabeth (Finney) McD.; m. Anne Marbury, June 16, 1961. BS in Aero. Engring., Princeton U., 1960, MS in Aero. Engring., 1962; postgrad. in bus. adminstrn. Washington U., St. Louis, 1962-66. Strength engr. McDonnell Aircraft Co. (subs. McDonnell Douglas Corp.), St. Louis, 1962, corp. analyst, 1963-65, contract coordinator, adminstr., 1965-68; asst. to v.p. fin. Douglas Aircraft Co. (subs. McDonnell Douglas Corp.), 1968; v.p. McDonnell Douglas Fin. Corp. (subs. McDonnell Douglas Corp.), 1968-71; staff v.p. fiscal McDonnell Douglas Corp., 1971-75, corp. v.p. fin. and devel., 1975-77, corp. exec. v.p., 1977-80, pres., 1980—, mem. exec. com., 1975—, chmn. and chief exec. officer, 1988—, also bd. dirs. Mem. Com. Decent Unbiased Campaign Tactics; bd. commrs. St. Louis Sci. Ctr.; trustee KETC, Washington U. Office: McDonnell Douglas Corp PO Box 516 Saint Louis MO 63166 *

MCDONNELL, SANFORD NOYES, aircraft company executive; b. Litte Rock, Oct. 12, 1922; s. William Archie and Carolyn (Cherry) McD.; m. Priscilla Robb, Sept. 3, 1946; children: Robbin McDonnell MacVittie, William Randall. BA in Econs., Princeton U., 1945; BS in Mech. Engring., U. Colo., 1948; MS in Applied Mechanics, Washington U., St. Louis, 1954. With McDonnell Douglas Corp. (formerly McDonnell Aircraft Corp.), St. Louis, 1948—, v.p., 1959-66, pres. McDonnell Aircraft div., 1966-71, corp. exec. v.p., 1971, corp. pres., 1971—, chief exec. officer, 1972—, chmn., 1980-88, also bd. dirs.; bd. dirs. Centerre Bancorp., St. Louis, Squibb Corp. Active St. Louis United Way; mem. exec. bd. St. Louis and nat. councils Boy Scouts Am.; bd. dirs. Ethics Resource Ctr.; trustee, elder Presbyn. Ch. Fellow AIAA; mem. Navy League U.S. (life), Tau Beta Pi. Office: McDonnell Douglas Corp PO Box 516 Saint Louis MO 63166

MCDONNELL, VIRGINIA BLEECKER, writer; b. Short Hills, N.J.; d. J. Barclay and Helen Borden (Farley) Bleecker; m. John Henry McDonnell, Feb. 13, 1954; 1 child, Gordon. Grad., Russell Sage Coll., 1942. Co-dir. Gore Mountain Ski Sch., North Creek, N.Y., 1947-55; reporter, feature writer Macy Westchester Rockland Newspapers, Westchester County, N.Y., 1959-61, editor, 1961-63; freelance author 1963—. Assoc. scriptwriter: (TV series) The Guiding Light, 1977—, Search for Tomorrow, 1982, As the World Turns, 1984, Santa Barbara, 1986; author: Your Future in Nursing, 1963, Aerospace Nurse, 1966, The Irish Helped Build America, 1969, Careers in Hotel Management, 1971, Miscalculated Risk, 1972, Silent Partner, 1972, The Deep Six, 1973, The Long Shot, 1974, (as Virginia Barclay) Emergency, 1981, High Risk, 1981, Trauma, 1981, Crisis, 1982, Life Support, 1982, Double Face, 1982, 35 Hidden Fears, 1987, Private Practice, 1988, numerous short stories and articles. Recipient citation Leukemia Soc., 1959, citation City of Hope, 1959. Mem. Authors Guild, Authors League, Mystery Writers Am., Romance Writers Am., Writers Guild Am. East, Nat. Acad. TV Arts and Scis. Home: 18 8th St Shalimar FL 32579 Office: care Richard Curtis Assocs Inc 164 E 64th St New York NY 10021

MC DONOUGH, HENRY CARROLL, merger and acquisition consultant; b. Balt., Mar. 24, 1948; s. John Martin and Norton (Carroll) McD.; B.A., Princeton U., 1970; M.B.A., U. Va., 1978. Registered rep. C.T. Williams & Co., Balt., 1971-73; instl. securities analyst Alex. Brown & Sons, Balt., 1973-75; pres. McDonough & Co., Inc., Balt., 1978—; dir. corp. devel. Am. Radio-Telephone Service, Inc., Balt., 1982-84. Clubs: Maryland, Cap and Gown. Home: 14936 Carroll Rd Sparks MD 21152 Office: 108 E Read St Baltimore MD 21202

MCDONOUGH, JAMES FRANCIS, civil engineer, educator; b. Boston, June 7, 1939; s. John Joseph and Blanche Cecelia (Murphy) McD.; m. Kathryn Ann Hilvert, Mar. 9, 1985; children by previous marriage: John, James, Jennifer. BS in Civil Engring., Northeastern U., 1962, MS in Civil Engring., 1964; PhD, U. Cin., 1968, MBA, 1981. Registered profl. engr., Ohio. Project engr. Fay, Spofford & Thorndike, Boston, 1962; teaching asst. Northeastern U., 1962-64; teaching asst. U. Cin., 1965, instr. civil engring., 1965-68, asst. prof., 1968-74, assoc. prof., 1974-78, William Thoms prof. civil engring., chmn. dept. civil and environ. engring., 1978-86, assoc. dean acad. affairs, 1986—; vis. prof. faculty engring. Kabul U., Afghanistan, 1969-71; vis. prof. N.C. State U., 1971. Contbr. articles to profl. jours. Pres. Greenhills Winton Sports Assn., 1981-83, treas., 1977-81. Recipient Teaching Excellence award U. Cin., 1973-75; Dow Chem. Outstanding Young Faculty award Am. Soc. for Engring. Edn., 1975; Outstanding Engring. Educator award Am. Soc. Engring. Edn.-Western Electric, 1977; Profl. Accomplishment award Acad.-Tech. and Sci. Council Cin., 1979. Mem. Am. Soc. Engring. Edn. (v.p. 1984-86, chmn. sect. 1982-83), ASCE (zone sec. 1983, sect. pres. 1982), NSPE (chmn. Ohio state bd. registration for engrs. and surveyors 1987—), Ohio Soc. Profl. Engrs., Sigma Xi, Tau Beta Pi, Chi Epsilon, Beta Gamma Sigma. Roman Catholic. Home: 3308 Bishop St Cincinnati OH 45220 Office: U Cin Mail Location 18 Cincinnati OH 45221

MCDOUGALL, DONALD BLAKE, provincial government library official; b. Moose Jaw, Sask., Can., Mar. 6, 1938; s. Daniel Albert and Donela (McRae) McD.; m. Norma Rose Peacock, May 19, 1962. B.A., U. Sask., 1966, B.Ed., 1966; B.L.S., U. Toronto, 1969, M.L.S., U. Alta., 1983. Classroom tchr., Regina Bd. Edn., Sask., 1960-63, vice prin., 1963-68; chief librarian Stratford Pub. Library, Ont., Can., 1969-72; head pub. services Edmonton Pub. Library, Alta., Can., 1972-74; legislature librarian Province of Alta. , Edmonton, 1974-87; asst. dep. minister, legis. librarian Legis. Assembly Alta., 1987—. Editor microfilm: Alberta Scrapbook Hansard, 1906-1964, 1976, editor Book: A History of the Legislature Library, 1979, Princess Louise Carline Albertta, Govt. Sask. scholar, 1965; recipient Queen's Silver Jubilee medal Govt. Can., 1977. Mem. Alta. Govt. Libraries Council (chmn. 1975), Assn. Parliamentary Librarians in Can. (pres. 1980-82), Edmonton Library Assn., Hist. Soc. Alta. (v.p. Edmonton chpt.), Library Assn. Alta., Can. Library Assn., Can. Soc. for Info. Sci., Beta Phi Mu. Presbyterian. Clubs: Edmonton Jaguar Drivers; Brit. Jaguar Drivers, Edmonton Scottish Soc., U. Alta. Faculty. Home: 9939 115th St, Apt 1704, Edmonton, AB Canada T5K 1S6 Office: Legislature Library, 216 Legislature Bldg, Edmonton, AB Canada T5K 2B6

MC DOWALL, RODDY, actor; b. London, Sept. 28, 1928. Educated, St. Joseph's Sch., London. Actor, Twentieth Century Fox, 1940—; films include: Scavenger Hunt, Man Hunt, How Green Was My Valley, Confirm or Deny, Son of Fury, On the Sunny Side, The Pied Piper, My Friend Flicka, Lassie Come Home, White Cliffs of Dover, Macbeth, Act, Rocky, Kidnapped, Big Timber, Tuna Clipper, Black Midnight, Killer Shark, Steel Fist, The Subterraneans, Midnight Lace, Cleopatra, The Longest Day, The Greatest Story Ever Told, Shock Treatment, That Darn Cat, The Loved Ones, The Third Day, Daisy Clover, Bullwhip Griffin, Lord Love a Duck, The Defector, It, The Cool Ones, Planet of the Apes, Conquest of the Planet of the Apes, The Poseidon Adventure, Funny Lady, Charlie Chan and the Curse of the Dragon Queen, Evil Under the Sun, Fright Night, Class of 84, 1984, Dead of Winter, Overboard, 1987; debut as dir. in The Devil's Widow, 1971; Broadway appearances include: Misalliance, Mean Johnny Barrows, Escapade, Doctor's Dilemma, No Time for Sergeants, Good as Gold, Compulsion, Handful of Fire, Look after Lulu, The Fighting Cock, 1959-60, Camelot, 1960-61, The Astrakhan Coat, 1966; numerous TV appearances on Macmillan & Wife; regular on TV series Planet of the Apes, 1974, Bridges to Cross, 1986—; TV films include: Miracle on 34th Street, The Elevator, 1974, Hart to Hart, 1979, The Martian Chronicles, 1980, The Memory of Eva Ryker, 1980, Mae West, 1982, This Girl for Hire, 1983, The Zany Adventures of Robin Hood, 1984. Recipient Emmy award for Best Supporting Actor, 1960; Tony award for Best Supporting Actor. Office: Badgley McQueeney & Connor 9229 Sunset Blvd Suite 607 Los Angeles CA 90069 *

MCDOWELL, DONNA SCHULTZ, lawyer; b. Cin., Apr. 23, 1946; d. Robert Joseph and Harriet (Parronchi) Schultz; m. Dennis Lon McDowell, June 20, 1970; children—Dawn Megan, Donnelly Lon. B.A. with honors in English, Brandeis U., 1968; M.Ed., Am. U., 1972; C.A.S.E. with honors, Johns Hopkins U., 1979; J.D. with honors, U. Md., 1982. Bar: Md. 1982. Instr., Anne Arundel & Prince George's Community Coll., Severna Park and Largo, Md., 1977-78; coll. adminstr. Bowie State Coll. (Md.), 1978-79; assoc. Miller & Bortner, Lanham, Md., 1982-83; sole practice, Lanham, 1983-87; ednl. cons. Chmn. Housing Hearing Com., Bowie, 1981-83; trustee Unitarian-Universalist Ch., Silver Spring, Md., 1979-83; bd. dirs. New Ventures, Bowie, 1983, Second Mile (Runaway House), Hyattsville, Md., 1983. Recipient Am. Jurisprudence award U. Md., 1981. Mem. ABA, Assn. Trial Lawyers Am., Md. Trial Lawyers Assn., Prince George's Bar Assn. Democrat. Club: Soroptimist. Home and Office: 24308 Hipsley Mill Rd Gaithersburg MD 20879

MCDOWELL, JENNIFER, sociologist, composer, playwright; b. Albuquerque, May 19, 1936; d. Willard A. and Margaret Frances (Garrison) McD.; m. Milton Loventhal, July 2, 1973. BA, U. Calif., 1957, MLS, 1963; MA, San Diego State U., 1958; PhD, U. Oreg., 1973. Tchr. English Abraham Lincoln High Sch., San Jose, Calif., 1960-61; freelance editor Soviet field, Berkeley, Calif., 1961-63; research asst. sociology U. Oreg., Eugene, 1964-66; editor, pub. Merlin Papers, San Jose, 1969—, Merlin Press, San Jose, 1973—; research cons. sociology San Jose, 1973—; music pub. Lipstick and Toy Balloons Pub. Co., San Jose, 1978—; composer Paramount Pictures, 1982—; tchr. writing workshops; poetry readings, 1969-73; co-producer radio show lit. and culture Sta. KALX, Berkeley, 1971-72. Author: Black Politics: A Study and Annotated Bibliography of the Mississippi Freedom Democratic Party, 1971, Contemporary Women Poets: An Anthology of California Poets, 1977, Ronnie Goose Rhymes for Grown-ups, 1984; co-author (plays off-off Broadway) Betsy and Phyllis, 1986, Mack The Knife Your Friendly Dentist, 1986, The Estrogen Party To End War, 1986, The Oatmeal Party Comes to Order, 1986; contbr. poems, plays, essays, short stories, book revs. to lit. mags. and anthologies; researcher women's autobiog. writings, contemporary writings in poetry, Soviet studies, civil rights movement and George Orwell, 1962—; writer: (songs) Money Makes A Woman Free, 1976, 3 songs featured in Parade of Am. Music; co-creator: musical comedy Russia's Secret Plot to Take Back Alaska, 1988. Recipient 8 awards Am. Song Festival, 1976-79, Bill Casey award in Letters, 1980; AAUW doctoral fellow, 1971-73; grantee Calif. Arts Council, 1976-77. Mem. Am. Sociol. Assn., Soc. Sci. Study of Religion, Soc. Study of Religion under Communism, Poetry Orgn. for Women, Dramatists Guild, Phi Beta

Kappa, Sigma Alpha Iota, Beta Phi Mu, Kappa Kappa Gamma. Democrat. Office: care Merlin Press PO Box 5602 San Jose CA 95150

MCDOWELL, JOHN EDISON, dental surgeon; b. Kingston, Jamaica, Nov. 9, 1923; s. Alfred James and Iris Florence (Murray) McD.; m. Lilla Evangeline Haughton, Aug. 19, 1950; children: Dawn-Maria, Ian. Student, Heriot-Watt U., Edinburgh, Scotland, 1952-53; BDS in Dental Surgery, Edinburgh U., 1957. Med. lab. technician Govt. Bacteriological Lab., Kingston, Jamaica, 1947-52; intern Guys Hosp., London, 1957; asst. dental surgeon Harrow, Middlesex, Eng., 1957-58; dental surgeon Kingston Pub. Hosp., Jamaica, 1958-59; practice dentistry specializing in dental surgery Ocho Rids, Jamaica, 1959—; vis. dental surgeon Govt. Clinics, St. Ann, Jamaica, 1959—. Pres. St. Ann C. of C., Ocho Rios, 1969-70; area dir. St. John Ambulance Assn. N. Cen. Jamaica, Ocho Rios, 1975—; pres. Jamaica Family Planning Assn., St. Ann's Bay, 1983—; chmn. Jamaica Assn. Mentally Handicapped Children, St. Ann br., 1975-87; mem. dental council Govt. of Jamaica, 1982-85. Decorated Officer of Order of Distinction Govt. of Jamaica, 1982; recipient Spl. award Jamaica Tourist Bd., 1982. Mem. Jamaica Dental Assn. Presbyterian. Clubs: Jamaica (Kingston). Lodge: Kiwanis (pres. Ocho Rios chpt. 1968-69). Home: Danian Heights, PO Box 31, Ocho Rios Jamaica Office: Pineapple Pl, PO Box 31, Ocho Rios Jamaica

MCDUFFIE, DEBORAH JEANNE, composer; b. N.Y.C., Aug. 8, 1950; d. Thomas Elliott and Nan Ruth (Woods) McD.; B.A., Western Coll. Women; children—Kijana Babatu, Kemal. Music producer, composer McCann-Erickson Advt., Inc., N.Y.C., 1971-81; music dir. Mingo Group, 1981—; pres. Jana Prodns, Inc., Janée Music Co., Great Music Mgmt. Co., N.Y.C., 1977—; profl. singer, composer, arranger, producer. Recipient numerous advt. awards. Mem. ASCAP, Screen Actors Guild, AFTRA, Am. Fedn. Musicians, Nat. Acad. Rec. Arts and Scis., Nat. Assn. Female Execs. Vocal arranger: I'd Like to Teach the World to Sing, 1972; composer, producer Miller High Life campaigns, 1975—; album: I Am an Illusion, 1981, Damaris, 1984; composer Hooray for Love; producer We Shall Overcome by Roberta Flack, 1986, Simon Estes, Cindy Valentine, Al Green, Isley-Jasper-Isley, Agneta Baumann.

MCELHATTON, JAMES, chemist, consultant; b. Gzira, Malta, Aug. 12, 1947; s. Gerald Redmond and Doris (Azzopardi) McE.; m. Yvonne Fenech, Sept. 9, 1978. BS with honors, Royal U. Malta, 1967, MS, 1968; PhD, U. Glasgow, Scotland, 1976. Lectr. U. Valetta, Malta, 1971-73; tech. dir. Castille Leathers, Malta, 1977-82; con. chemist Attard, Malta, 1982—. Mem. Royal Soc. Chemistry, Inst. Analyst and Programmers (companion mem.). Home and Office: Villa Yvonne, Notary Zarb St, Attard Malta

MCELVEEN, JOSEPH JAMES, JR., public broadcasting executive; b. Sanford, Fla., Feb. 23, 1939; s. Joseph James Sr. and Genevieve (Stoll) McE.; m. Idris Baker, Aug. 14, 1965 (div. 1975); m. Mary Louise Young, Aug. 18, 1979; 1 child, Ryan Leighton. BA, Furman U., 1961; MA, U. S.C., 1968. Editor, pub. West Ashley News, Charleston, S.C., 1951-57; reporter, photographer Charleston Post, 1955-57; tchr. English and journalism St. Andrew's Parish High Sch., Charleston, 1961-65; dir. info. Columbia Coll., S.C., 1965-68; prof. journalism U. S.C., Columbia, 1968-79; with pub. affairs FCC, Washington, 1979-81; dir. pub. affairs adminstrn. Nat. Cable TV Assn., Washington, 1981-87 ; dir. internal communications Corp. for Pub. Broadcasting, Washington, 1987—; ombudsman, columnist Alexandria (Va.) Gazette, 1981—. Author: Introduction to Creative Writing, 1963, Modern Communications, 1964; contbr. chpt. to International Biography (Mencken), 1986. Mem. Orgn. of News Ombudsmen, Soc. Profl. Journalists, Mencken Soc. Democrat. Episcopalian. Avocations: photography, reading. Office: Corp for Pub Broadcasting 1111 16th St NW Washington DC 20036

MCELYEA, LOUANN, automated systems and artificial intelligence consultant; b. Poplar Bluff, Mo., Sept. 10, 1946; d. Arthur Eugene and Hazel Irene (Trosper) McE.; BS, Washington U., St. Louis, 1975; MBA, Lindenwood Coll., 1982. Dir. adminstrv. services Washington U., 1972-77; account exec. Bache, Halsey-Stuart Shields, Inc., St. Louis, 1977-78; project mgr. office systems dept. Mallinckrodt, Inc., St. Louis, 1978-80; pres., founder Info. Systems, Inc., St. Louis, 1980—. Mem. Alpha Sigma Lambda. Baptist. Home: 806 Bailey St Campbell MO 63933 Office: Info Systems Inc Campbell MO 63933

MC EMBER, ROBERT ROLAND, association executive, musician; b. Ludington, Mich., Feb. 26, 1919; s. Francis Roland and Lillian Laurentine (Hansen) McE.; B.A., John B. Stetson U., 1946, B.M., 1946, M.A., 1951; m. Elizabeth Anderson Futch, Dec. 15, 1942; children—Sharon Leigh, Elizabeth Anne. Critic tchr. Western Mich. U., 1950-55; asst. prof. Purdue U., 1955-63; asso. prof. U. Wis., 1964-67; mgr. flight tng. aids and tech. writing Am. Airlines, 1967-69; mgr. flight tng. program devel. Eastern Airlines, Miami, Fla., 1970—; guest lectr.; leader workshops and seminars on instrnl. tech.; mus. dir., condr. Ludington Civic Symphony Orch., 1948-50; condr. Central Wis. Symphony Orch., 1964-67. Served with USAAF, 1942-45; col. Res., 1945-72. Recipient cert. of appreciation U.S. Air Force, 1972. Mem. Nat. Acad. Rec. Arts and Scis., Nat. Soc. Scabbard and Blade, Mil. Order World Wars, Daedalian Soc., Am. Soc. Tng. and Devel., Internat. TV Assn. (pres. 1974-75, dir., chmn. bd. 1976-77), Res. Officers Assn. U.S., Audio Visual Mgmt. Assn., Am. Fedn. Musicians, Phi Delta Kappa. Republican Lutheran. Author: C-124 Aircraft Homestudy, 1970; (with others) Communication Security for AF Personnel, 1972, Principles and Practices of Occupational Safety and Health, 1975; editorial adv. bd. Am. Soc. Tng. and Devel. Jour., 1979-82; editor Flight Line (Flight Safety Found. Publs. award 1980), 1957-81; contbr. articles to ednl. jours.; composer: All-American Bands, 1958; several works for symphony orch. Home: 8310 SW 81st Terr Miami FL 33143 Office: Audio Visual Mgmt Assn 7907 NW 53d St Suite 346 Miami FL 33166

MC ENROE, JOHN PATRICK, JR., professional tennis player; b. Wiesbaden, Germany, Feb. 16, 1959; s. John Patrick and Katy McE.; m. Tatum O'Neal, Aug. 1, 1986; children: Kevin Jack, Sean. Grad., Trinity Sch., N.Y.C., 1977; student, Stanford U. Winner numerous U.S. jr. singles and doubles title; winner jr. titles French Mixed Doubles, 1977, French Jr. Singles, 1977, Italian Indoor Doubles, 1978; winner Nat. Coll. Athletic Assn. Intercollegiate U.S. Men's Singles title, 1978; turned professional 1978; played on victorious U.S. Davis Cup Team, 1978; winner Stockholm Open, 1978, Benson and Hedges Tournament, 1978, Grand Prix Masters singles and doubles, Wembley, 1978, Grand Prix Masters Tournament, N.Y.C., 1979, New Orleans Grand Prix, 1979, WCT Milan Internat., Italy, 1979, Stella Artois Tournament, London, 1979, U.S. Open Men's Singles Championship, 1979, 80, 81, 84, World Championship Tennis Championship, 1979, 83, Australian Indoor Singles Championship, 1980-82, U.S. Indoor Singles Championship, 1980-83, Wimbledon Singles, 1981, 83, 84, Tournament of Champions, 1981, 83, AT & T Challenge, 1987, Japan Open, 1988. Office: care John P McEnroe Sr Paul Weiss Rifkind et al 1285 Ave of the Americas New York NY 10019 *

MCEWEN, JOHN, clinical pharmacologist; b. Uddingston, Scotland, Apr. 11, 1943; s. John Aitken and Martha Watt (Wilson) McE.; m. Vernonica Rosemary Iverson, Dec. 31, 1966; children: Catherine Jane, Jonathan Roy. MB ChB, St. Andrews U., Scotland, 1966; PhD, U. Dundee, Scotland, 1975. Resident physician Maryfield Hosp., Dundee, 1966-67; resident surgeon Dundee Royal Infirmary, 1967; research asst. Dept. Pharmacology U. Dundee, 1967-69, lectr. Dept. Therapeutics, 1969-75; research fellow Vanderbilt U., Nashville, 1972-74; head clin. pharmacology Hoechst U.K., Milton Keynes, Eng., 1975-83; med. dir. Drug Devel. (Scotland) Ltd., Dundee, 1983—; hon. cons. Tayside Regional Bd., Dundee, 1983—; hon. sr. lectr. U. Dundee, 1983—. Contbr. articles to profl. jours. Fellow Royal Soc. Medicine; mem. British Pharmacol. Soc., Assn. for Study Med. Edn. Episcopalian. Home: 1 Osborne Pl, Dundee DD2 1BE, Scotland Office: Drug Devel (Scotland) Ltd, Ninewells Hosp Med Sch, Dundee DD1 954, Scotland

MCEWEN, ROBERT JOSEPH, economics educator; b. Boston, June 6, 1916; s. Robert John and Mary Ellen (Aherne) McE. A.B., Boston Coll., 1940; Lic. Ph., Weston Sch. Philosophy, 1941; A.M., Fordham U., 1943; S.T.L., Weston Sch. Theology, 1947; Ph.D., Boston Coll., 1957. Instr. mktg. Boston Coll., 1942-43, instr. econs., 1948-51, asst. prof. econs., 1952-56, assoc. prof., chmn. econs., 1957-67, prof., 1968—; vis. prof. Loyola U., Los Angeles, 1963; founder, 1st pres. Consumer Fedn., Washington, 1968-69. Contbr. articles to profl. jours. 1st chmn. Adv. Cons. Council to Atty. Gen., Mass., 1958, State Consumers Council, Mass., 1964—; chmn. Ford Motor-Consumer Appeals Bd., New England, 1981—. Recipient Consumer Tribune award Better Bus. Bur., 1973. Mem. Am. Council on Consumer Interests (pres. 1965-67), Assn. Mass. Consumers (pres. 1971-77), Conf. Cons. Orgns. (vice chmn. 1973-85, chmn. 1985—). Roman Catholic. Club: State (Boston). Avocations: golf; photography. Home: 140 Commonwealth Ave Newton MA 02167 Office: Boston Coll Dept Econs 140 Commonwealth Ave Chestnut Hill MA 02167

MCFADDEN, JAMES FREDERICK, JR., surgeon; b. St. Louis, Dec. 5, 1920; s. James Frederick and Olivia Genevieve (Imbs) McF.; m. Mary Cella Switzer, Sept. 15, 1956 (div. Sept. 1969); children: James Frederick, Kenneth Michael, John Switzer, Mary Cella, Joseph Robert. AB, St. Louis U., 1941, MD, 1944. Intern Boston City Hosp., 1944-45; ward surgeon neorsurg. and orthopedics McGuire Gen. Hosp., Richmond, Va., 1945; ward surgeon in internal medicine Regional Hosp., Fort Knox, Ky., 1946; ward surgeon plastic surgery Valley Forge Gen. Hosp., Phoenixville, Pa., 1946-47; intern St. Louis City Hosp., 1947-48; resident in surgery VA Hosp., St. Louis, 1948-52; clin. instr. surgery St. Louis U., 1952-62; gen. practice medicine specializing in surgery St. Louis, 1952—; mem. staff St. Mary's Hosp., 1952-77, St. John's Mercy Hosp., 1952-74, Desloge Hosp., 1952-62, Frisco RR Hosp., 1953-64, DePaul Hosp., 1954—, Christian Hosp., 1955-66, 83—. Mem. St. Louis Ambassadors, 1979-81. Served to capt. AUS, 1945-47. Named Eagle Scout Boy Scouts Am., 1935. Fellow ACS, Internat. Coll. Surgeons; mem. St. Louis Med Soc., Am. Soc. Clin. Hypnosis, Internat. Soc. Hypnosis, Royal Soc. Medicine (affiliate), Am. Assn. RR Surgeons, St. Louis U. Student Conclave, Alpha Sigma Nu. Roman Catholic. Home: 11963 Villa Dorado Dr Saint Louis MO 63146 Office: 11500 Olive Blvd Saint Louis MO 63141

MCFADDEN, PATRICK JOSEPH JAMES, architect; b. Camden, N.J., Nov. 7, 1952; s. James Michael and Bernice Katherine (Nettleton) McF.; m. Cheryl Madelyn Evans, Sept. 18, 1971; children—Dawn Marie, Aubrey Elizabeth, Marianne Patrice, Patrice Candice. B.S. in Architecture, Drexel U., 1979. Registered architect, Pa., Del., Md., N.H., N.Y., Draftsman Synergo Co., Phila., 1971-72; draftsman, designer Ballinger Co., Phila., 1972-73; designer, job capt. Abbott W. Thompson, Media, Pa., 1973-75, drafting tchr. St. James High Sch., Chester, Pa., 1975-76; designer, job capt. Paul Restall Assocs., Media, 1976-79; v.p., ptnr. Richardson Gauzza McFadden, Chester Heights, Pa., 1979-87; pres., owner McFadden Architects, Chester Heights, 1987—; guest juror dept. architecture Drexel U., 1981-82; cons./ architect Thomas J. Glessner, Ridley Park, Pa., 1973-87 ; cons. planning commn., Chester Heights, 1979-80, Archtl. Control Commn., Valleybrook Homeowners, Chester Heights, 1980. Designer logo Valleybrook Civic Assn., 1977, Valleybrook Homeowners (1st place award), 1983; logo design entries Phila. Phillies Baseball, 1982, also 1987 logo design, front cover design newsletter 4 Seasons Internat. Fan Club (1st place award), 1977, trademark logo design McFadden Architects, 1987. Bldg. ofcl. Borough of Chester Heights, 1978—; v.p. Valleybrook Civic Assn., 1977-78; mem. program bldg. com. St. Thomas Parish Devel., 1987-88. Alumni Assn. scholar Drexel U., 1977-79; Am. Inst. Drafting scholar, 1970; recipient archtl. design award Dept. Architecture, Drexel U., 1972-73. Mem. AIA, Nat. Council Archtl. Registration Bds. Democrat. Roman Catholic. Clubs: Hi-Hopes Golf (chmn. 1986-87), Wally Byam Caravan Internat. (pres. 1987-88). Home: 57 Bishops Dr Chester Heights PA 19017 Office: McFadden Architects 15 Smithbridge Rd Box 487 Chester Heights PA 19017

MCFARLAND, DONNA REYNE, illustrator, educator, consultant; b. Charleston, W.Va., Oct. 24, 1948; d. Clyde Freeman and Ruby June (Summerfield) Armstrong; m. Elmer Reace McFarland, Oct. 28, 1966; children—Kelli Reyne, Jay Reace, B.A. in Art cum laude, W.Va. State Coll., 1985, postgrad. Marshall Univ., 1986—. Art dir. Calvary Bapt. acad., Hurricane, W.Va., 1980-84; art judge State Accelerated Christian Edn. High Sch. Competition, Jacksons Mill, W.Va., 1981— (Internat. Competition judge, 1987); owner, tchr. art Donna McFarland Studio, Scott Depot, W.Va., 1983—; art cons. Brandywine, Hurricane, W.Va., 1985—. Illustrator Kanawha's Black Gold and the Miner's Rebellions (book by V.B Harris, 1987). Wonderful W.Va. Mag., 1983. Pres. Teays Village Homeowners Assn., Scott Depot, 1986. Fellow Allied Artists W.Va.; mem. W.Va. Artists and Craftsmen's Guild. Republican. Baptist. Avocations: reading; classical music; walking; cooking. Home and Studio: 2642 Putnam Ave Hurricane WV 25526

MC FARLAND, H. RICHARD, food company executive; b. Hoopeston, Ill., Aug. 19, 1930; s. Arthur Bryan and Jennie (Wilkey) McF.; m. Sarah Forney, Dec. 30, 1967. B.S., U. Ill., 1952. With Campbell Soup Co., Camden, N.J., 1957-67; mgr. purchasing Campbell Soup Co., 1961-67; dir. procurement Keebler Co., Elmhurst, Ill., 1967-69; v.p. purchasing and distbn. Ky. Fried Chicken Corp., Louisville, 1969-74; v.p. food services, sales and distbn. Ky. Fried Chicken Corp., 1974-75; pres., dir. Mid-Continent Carton Co., Louisville, 1974-75, KFC Mfg. Corp., Nashville, 1974-75; owner, pres., dir. McFarland Foods Corp., Indpls., 1975—; bd. dirs. Fountain Trust Co., Ind., Federated Foods Inc., Arlington Heights, Ill., Covington Service Corp., Ind., Spring Valley Foods, Inc., Empire, Ala., 1972-75; pres., dir. K.F.C. Advt. Inc., Ind., 1975-87; mem. K.F.C. Nat. Franchise Adv. Council, 1979-85; dir. Ky. Fried Chicken Nat. Purchasing Coop., 1981-85, chmn. ins. com., 1982-84; mem. K.F.C. Nat. Advt. Co-op, 1985—; chmn. process foods com. World's Poultry Congress, 1974, exec. com., 1988; dir. KFC Nat. Advt. Council, 1985—. Life pres. U. Ill. Sr. Class of '52; bd. dirs. Ind. Fedn. Children and Youth, 1983-84; chmn. campaign Ind. K.F.C. March of Dimes, 1978-87. Served to 1st lt. USAF, 1952-54, Korea. Recipient President's award Ky. Fried Chicken Corp., 1970, Award of Merit, U. Ill., 1988; hon. chief police Louisville, 1970. Mem. Ky. (dir. 1970-75), Restaurant Assn., Nat. Broiler Council (bd. dirs. 1971-74), Ind. Restaurant Assn., Am. Shorthorn Breeders Assn., Great Lakes K.F.C. Franchise Assn. (dir. 1975—, 1st v.p. 1978-79, pres. 1979-80), Delta Upsilon. Presbyn. Clubs: Main Line Ski (Phila.) (pres. 1964); Hillcrest Country. Home: 6361 Avalon Ln East Indianapolis IN 46220 Office: 6440 E 82d St Indianapolis IN 46250

MC FARLAND, TERRY LYNN, construction company executive; b. Knoxville, Tenn., July 8, 1947; s. Jacob E. and Virginia Kay (Allen) McF.; student Ind. U., 1969-70, Wickes U., 1977-79; m. Hazel C. Davis, Nov. 1, 1975; Prodn. control staff R.R. Donnelley & Sons, Warsaw, Ind., 1965-68; insp. Bendix Corp., South Bend, Ind., 1968-69; mgr. Wickes Bldgs. div. Wickes Corp., Argos, Inc., 1970-71, Crawfordsville, Ind., 1971-73, Macon, Ga., 1973-76, dist. mgr. Midwest, 1976-78, regional mgr., 1978-80; v.p., gen. mgr. Douglass Bldg. div. of Stanley Smith & Sons, Columbia, S.C., 1980-81; ter. mgr. Butler Mfg. Co., Kansas City, Mo., 1981-84, southeastern area mgr., 1984-87, dist. mgr., 1987—. Served with U.S. Army, 1966-68; Korea. Mem. Am. Legion, Nat. Geog. Soc., Nat. Rifle Assn. Democrat. Clubs: Moose, Masons (Scottish Rite), Shriners. Home: 741 Springdale Woods Dr Macon GA 31210 Office: 7400 E 13th St Kansas City MO 64126

MCFARLAND, VIOLET VIVIAN, author; b. Seattle, Feb. 26, 1908; d. Judson Loring and Annie (Conners) Sweet; M. J. Lamar Butler, 1944 (div. 1953); m. Glen W. McFarland, 1958 (div. 1965). B.A., Wash. State U., 1928; M.A., Columbia U., 1933. Tchr., Konawaena High Sch., Kealakekua, Hawaii, 1928-30, Am. Sch. in Japan, Tokyo, 1930-31; soc. editor Japan Times, Tokyo, 1930-31, Hong Kong Telegraph, 1940; edit. asst. U.S. Dept. Justice, Washington, 1934-43; real estate assoc. Long Beach Bd., Calif., 1961—. Author (as Violet Sweet Haven): Hong Kong for Weekend, 1939; Many Ports of Call, 1940; Gentlemen of Japan, 1944. Contbr. articles to profl. jours. Recipient numerous internat. lit. awards. Fellow Internat. Inst. Arts and Letters (life); mem. Nat. Press Club (life), Calif. Bd. Realtors, Delta Zeta. Avocations: travel; curator Oriental art and lit. Address: PO Box 872 Lake Elsinore CA 92330

MCFARLANE, ALEXANDER COWELL, psychiatrist, educator, consultant; b. Adelaide, Australia, May 27, 1952; s. John Preiss and Nancy Douglas (Robertson) McF.; m. Catherine Mary Houen, June 26, 1977; children: James Alexander, David Anthony. MB, BS with honors, U. Adelaide, 1976, diploma in Psychotherapy, 1983. Intern Royal Adelaide Hosp., 1976; trainee in psychiatry Flinders Med. Ctr., Adelaide, 1977-80, vis. specialist, 1981—; lectr. psychiatry Flinders U. of South Australia, Adelaide, 1980-85, sr. lectr., 1985—; vis. specialist Repatriation Gen. Hosp., Adelaide, 1981—; research assoc. U. Sydney, Australia, 1985—. Contbr. articles to profl. jours. State com. chmn. examinining mgmt. of psychological morbidity of disasters. Everard scholar U. Adelaide, 1975. Fellow Royal Australian and New Zealand Coll. Psychiatrists (chmn. crisis, disaster com. 1985—, social issues com. 1988—, examination rev. sub-com. 1988—, Jr. Organon Research award 1986); mem. Australian Soc. for Psychiat. Research. Club: Royal Adelaide Golf. Home: 4 Barretts Rd, Torrens Park 5062, Australia Office: Flinders U South Australia, Bedford Park 5042, Australia

MCFARLANE, HARRY WILLIAM, otorhinolaryngologist; b. Broughty Ferry, Scotland, July 21, 1929; s. Harry and Anne Cramond (Rew) McF.; m. Zlata Dzinovic, Jan. 4, 1960. M.B., Ch.B., St. Andrews U., Scotland, 1952. House surgeon Royal Infirmary, Huddersfield, England, 1952-53; casualty officer Royal Infirmary, Dundee, Scotland, 1953, house physician, 1953-54, sr. house officer in surgery, 1954, surg. registrar, 1959; demonstrator in anatomy, lectr. physiology U. St. Andrews, Scotland, 1956-59; surg. registrar Aberdeen Group of Hosps., Scotland, 1959-61; registrar in otorhinolaryngology Royal Infirmary, Aberdeen, 1961-63, sr. registrar in otorhinolaryngology, 1963-65; cons. otorhinolaryngologist, 1965—; cons. otorhinolaryngologist Derby Group of Hosps., Royal Sch. for Deaf, Derby, Midlands Asthma and Allergy Research Assn. Eng., Brit. Army; med. examiner war pensions Dept. Health and Social Security, Eng., 1970—, med. examiner indsl. deafness, 1974—. Served to maj. Med. Service, Royal Air Force, 1954-62, Royal Army M.C., 1979—. Fellow Internat. Coll. of Surgeons, Royal Coll. Surgeons Eng., Royal Coll. Surgeons Edinburgh, Soc. for Ear Nose and Throat Advances in Children (bd. dirs., rep. for Europe), Royal Soc. Medicine, Brit. Inst. Mgmt.; mem. Brit. Assn. Otolaryngologists, Midland Inst. Otolaryngology, Brit. Med. Assn., European Working Group in Pediatric Otolaryngology, Derby Med. Soc. (treas. 1968-72, auditor 1972-76), Aberdeen Medico-Chirurgical Soc., Regional Hosp. Cons. and Specialists Assn., Midlands Asthma and Allergy Research Assn. (chmn. ethical com., chmn. research com.), Midlands Visitor Group in Otolaryngology, Inst. of Dirs. London. Clubs: Royal Army Medical College, Millbank (London). Lodge: Rotary. Avocations: sailing; economics. Home: 110 Whitaker Rd, Derby DE3 6AP, England Office: Royal Infirmary, London Rd, Derby DE1 2QY, England

MCFATRIDGE, KEITH WILLIAM, JR., banker; b. Wichita Falls, Tex., Mar. 28, 1946; s. Keith William and Margaret (Daniel) McF.; m. Marilyn Sue McFatridge, June 16, 1979; children—Keith, Kyle, Eric, Michael, Jeffrey. B.B.A., So. Meth. U., 1968, M.B.A., 1969. Exec. v.p., chief operating officer U.S. Nat. Bank, Galveston, Tex., 1975—; credit dept. officer Citizens Nat. Bank, Austin, Tex., 1971-73; treas. Woods Tucker Leasing, Hattiesburg, Miss., 1973-75; dir., mem. exec. com. U.S. Nat. Bank, 1980—. Bd. dirs. Salvation Army, 1980-85, Tex. Coastal Higher Edn. Authority, 1982-86, Ronald McDonald House, 1985—, Boy Scouts Am., 1984—, Galveston Crimestoppers, Inc., 1981—. Named Family of the Yr., Boy Scouts Am., 1982; Admiral of Tex. Navy, 1983. Mem. Robert Morris Assn., Am. Bankers Assn., Tex. Bankers Assn., C. of C. (past dir.). Republican. Methodist. Clubs: Bob Smith Yacht, Galveston Artillery, Galveston Country. Home: PO Box 179 Market St Galveston TX 77553

MC FEATTERS, DALE STITT, artist, retired electric company executive; b. Avella, Pa., Aug. 20, 1911; s. James Dale and Alice Mabel (Stitt) McF.; m. Tirzah McHenry Bigham, Sept. 29, 1938; children: Dale Bigham, Ann Carol McFeatters Koepke, Susan Love. Student, Art Inst. Pitts., U. Pitts. Reporter, feature writer, news commentator, fin. editor Pitts. Press., 1931-45; with Westinghouse Electric Corp., Pitts., 1945—; dir. employee info., dir. info. services, v.p. Westinghouse Electric Corp., 1954-73. Creator: nationally syndicated cartoon Strictly Business. Republican. Episcopalian. Clubs: Duquesne (Pitts.), Chartiers Country (Pitts.); Rolling Rock (Ligonier, Pa.); Nat. Press (Washington). Lodge: Masons. Home: 1461 Navahoe Dr Pittsburgh PA 15228

MCGAURAN, JOHN CHARLES, diversified company executive; b. Traralgon, Victoria, Gippsland, Australia, May 27, 1924; s. John and Kathleen (MacCarthy) McG.; m. Mary Margaret Hourigan, Feb. 6, 1952; children—Alexa, John, Peter, Julian, Rachel, Daria. Student Xavier Coll., Kew, Australia. Mng. dir. McGauran Holdings Pty Ltd., McGauran Properties Pty Ltd., John McGauran Pty Ltd., McGauran Pastoral Co., McGauran Rathdowne, McGauran (Downtowner) Pty Ltd., McGauran (Altona) Pty Ltd., McGauran (Traralgon) Pty Ltd., McGauran Securities Pty Ltd.; chmn., owner Canberra (Australia) Internat. Hotel. Life gov. Cen. Gippsland Hosp., Traralgon, 1965—; v.p. Gippsland Inst. Advanced Edn., 1976-80. Fellow Xavier Coll. Found., Kew, 1979—. Roman Catholic. Clubs: Victoria Racing, Melbourne Cricket. Home and office: Hollydale, Traralgon, Gippsland, Victoria 3844, Australia

MCGAVIN, ROBERT J., bank executive; b. Aug. 21, 1942. BPE, U. B.C., Can., 1965; MSc, U. Wash., 1966; postgrad., U. Oslo, 1966; PhD, U. Wash., 1969; cert. sr. mgmt. devel., Northestern U., 1985. With Can. Fgn. Service, 1968-79; dir. communications Bank of Montreal, 1979-81; v.p. pub. affairs Toronto Dominion Bank, 1981—. Mem. governing council U. Toronto, chmn. planning and resource com., mem. exec. com.; bd. dirs. Can. Adv. Council on Status of Women; bd. dirs., mem. long range planning com. Nat. Ballet of Can.; treas. Toronto Arts Awards; bd. dirs. Can. Olympic Assn., Can. Club, Jr. Achievement Can., Toronto Hosp.; mem. pres. adv. bd. U. B.C., Toronto Ont. Olympic Council. Mem. Can. Inst. Chartered Accts. (pub. relations com.), Conf. Bd. Council Pub. Affairs Execs., Can. Inst. Internat. Affairs. Clubs: Toronto Lawn Tennis; University (Washington); Albany (Toronto); The Fitness Inst. Office: Toronto Dominion Bank, PO Box 1 Toronto Dominion Ctr, Toronto, ON Canada M5K 1A2

MCGAW, KENNETH ROY, furniture wholesale company executive; b. Parry Sound, Ont., Can., Aug. 25, 1926; s. Dalton Earnest and Grace (Crockford) McG. Student, Denison U., 1946-48; B.A., Western Res. U., 1949. With Bigelow Carpets, N.Y. and Ohio, 1949-53; representing Frederick Cooper Lamps, Inc., Chgo., 1953—; home furnishing salesman Gates Mills, Ohio, 1958-74, Fort Lauderdale, 1974-77, Dallas, 1978-79; pres. Ken McGaw, Inc., Dallas, 1979—; factory rep. for maj. furniture and furniture accessory mfrs. Bd. dirs. Big Bros. Cleve., 1963-65, Dallas Opera Co., 1981—; v.p. Nat. Council on Alcoholism, Cleve., 1972-74; chmn. fundraising drive Wholesale div. Dallas Industry for Dallas Opera, 1982-83; ruling elder 1st Presbyterian Ch., Dallas., 1981—. Served to 2d lt. U.S. Army, 1944-46. Mem. Greater Dallas Home Furnishings Assn. (bd. dirs. 1985—), S.W. Homefurnishings Assn., S.W. Roadrunners Assn., Internat. Homefurnish Reps. Assn. Lodge: Rotary. Home: 5909 Luther Ln The Shelton #1005 Dallas TX 75225 Office: Ken McGaw Inc 9010 Dallas World Trade Ctr PO Box 58495 Dallas TX 75258 also: 8360 E San Bernardo Ave Scottsdale AZ 85258

MC GAW, SIDNEY EDWIN, educational consultant; b. Toronto, Ont., Can., Sept. 21, 1908; s. Sidney Anson and May (Bigelow) McG.; student Fresno State Coll., 1928-31; B.S., U. Calif. at Berkeley, 1944, M.A., 1948, Ed.D., 1952; m. Clara E. Eca da Silva, June 15, 1931; children—Bruce A., Laurie A., Kathleen C. (Mrs. Richard Chylinski). Instr., counselor pub. schs., Oakland, Calif., 1941-47; asst. supr. trade and tech. tchr. tng. Calif. State Dept. Edn., 1947-50, regional supr., 1950-65; dean instrn. San Jose City Coll., 1965-74; ednl. cons., 1974—; lectr. U. Calif. at Berkeley, summers 1948-66; workshop lectr. U. Nev., summers 1955-56. Pres., Calif. League for Nursing, 1967-69; chmn. edn. and tng. commn. Redwood Region Conservation Council, 1953-65. Mem. Nat. League for Nursing (bd. dirs. 1967-69). Lodge: Rotary (Berkeley, bd. dirs. West San Jose chpt. 1969-70). Club: Commonwealth of Calif. (San Francisco). Home: 1023 Ordway St Albany CA 94706

MCGEE, DOROTHY HORTON, author, historian; b. West Point, N.Y., Nov. 30, 1913; d. Hugh Henry and Dorothy (Brown) McG.; ed. Sch. of St. Mary, 1920-21, Green Vale Sch., 1921-28, Brearley Sch., 1928-29, Fermata Sch., 1929-31. Asst. historian Inc. Village of Roslyn (N.Y.), 1950-58; historian Inc. Village of Matinecock, 1966—. Author: Skipper Sandra, 1950; Sally Townsend, Patriot, 1952; The Boarding School Mystery, 1953; Famous Signers of the Declaration, 1955; Alexander Hamilton—New Yorker, 1957; Herbert Hoover: Engineer, Humanitarian, Statesman, 1959, rev. edit., 1965; The Pearl Pendant Mystery, 1960; Framers of the Constitution, 1968; author booklets, articles hist. and sailing subjects. Chmn., Oyster Bay Am. Bicentennial Revolution Commn., 1971—; historian Town of Oyster Bay, 1982—; mem. Nassau County Am. Revolution Bicentennial Commn.; hon. dir. The Friends of Raynham Hall, Inc.; treas. Family Welfare Assn. Nassau County, Inc., 1956-58; dir. Family Service Assn. Nassau County, 1958-69. Recipient Cert. of award for outstanding contbn. children's lit. N.Y. State Assn. Elem. Sch. Prins., 1959; award Nat. Soc. Children of Am. Revolution, 1960; award N.Y. Assn. Supervision and Curriculum Devel., 1961; hist. award Town of Oyster Bay, 1963; Cert. Theodore Roosevelt Assn., 1976. Fellow Soc. Am. Historians; mem. Soc. Preservation L.I. Antiquities (hon. dir.), Nat. Trust Hist. Preservation, N.Y. Geneal. and Biol. Soc. (dir., trustee), Oyster Bay Hist. Soc. (pres. 1971-75, chmn. 1975-79, trustee), Theodore Roosevelt Assn. (trustee), Townsend Soc. Am. (trustee). Republican. Address: Box 142 Locust Valley NY 11560

MCGEE, MICHAEL JAY, fire marshal, educator; b. Ft. Worth, June 9, 1952; s. Cecil Carl and Helen Ruth (Peeples) McG.; m. Carol Lee Garbarino, Sept. 18, 1982; children: Megan Rose, John Michael. Student, U. Tex., 1970-73, Colo. Mountain Coll., 1977—, Western Oreg. State U., 1983—. Driver Massengale Co., Austin, Tex., 1970-73; gen. mgr. Sundae Palace, Austin, 1973-74; staff mem. Young Life, Colorado Springs, Colo., 1970-75; mgr. Broadmoor Mgmt. Co., Vail, Colo., 1974-76; technician Vail Cable Communications, 1976-77; fire marshal Vail Fire Dept., 1977—; instr. Colo. Mountain Coll., 1980—; dist. rep. Joint Council Fire Dist. Colo., 1983-85; co-chmn. Eagle County Hazardous Materials, 1984-85, mem. planning com., 1987—. ARC Eagle County chpt. chmn., 1980-83, disaster chmn., 1977-80; tng. officer Eagle Vol. Fire Dept., 1988—. Mem. Nat. Fire Protection Assn., Colo. State Fire Marshals Assn., Colo. State Fire Chiefs Assn., Internat. Platform Assn. Office: Vail Fire Dept 42 W Meadow Dr Vail CO 81657

MCGEHEE, WILLIAM KENNETH, JR., alarm company executive, export trading company executive; b. Ft. Smith, Ark., Dec. 20, 1942; s. William Kenneth and Virginia Anne (Creekmore) McG.; m. Janet Ann Kirby, Sept. 7, 1979; children: William Kenneth III, MacKenzie Julian. Student U. Ark., 1960-62. Mgr. Houston div. Hickory Springs Mfg. Co., 1966-70; founder, owner, Mundo Sales Co., Ft. Smith, Ark., 1971—; owner Spurling Fire & Burglar Alarm, Ft. Smith, Little Rock and Fayetteville, Ark., 1978—; cons. internat. trade. Co-founder Judge Isaac C. Parker Found., Ft. Smith, 1978; fin. dir., bd. dirs. Mt. Magazine council Girl Scouts U.S., 1978; pres. Westark Area council Boy Scouts Am., 1985-86, v.p. south cen. region, 1987-88, nat. council, 1987-88; mission pilot CAP, Ft. Smith, 1981—, squadron ops. officer, 1981-82; founder Life Flight, N.W. Ark., 1982; chmn. Ark. Nat. Fedn. Ind. Bus., 1988, Ark. Small Bus. Council; pres. Ft. Smith chpt. United Way, 1988. Recipient Silver Beaver award Boy Scouts Am., 1983. 1978. Mem. Ark. Exporters Roundtable (chmn.), Ft. Smith Home Builders Assn., Ft. Smith/Van Buren Advt. Fedn. (club pres. 1979-80, club bd. dirs. 1980-81), Westark Pilots Assn. (pres. Ft. Smith area 1983-84), Ark. Pilots Assn. (pres. 1984-85), U.S. Pilots Assn. (nat. sec. 1983-84), Ark. C. of C. (bd. dirs. 1985). Ft. Smith C. of C. (Northwest Ark. polit. action com. 1979-83, Ft. Smith Aviation com. 1983), Ark. C. of C. (chmn. internat. trade com. 1988), Quiet Birdmen. Episcopalian. Club: Fianna Hills Country. Lodge: Rotary (pres. Ft. Smith club 1977-78, bd. dirs. club 1978—, dist. gov.'s rep. 1980-81, Paul Harris fellow 1978, del. 1986 White Ho. Conf. small bus.). Holder 2 aviation world speed records. Office: PO Box 4445 Fort Smith AR 72914

MCGERVEY, PAUL JOHN, III, mgmt. cons.; b. Indpls., Apr. 12, 1947; s. Paul John and Ethel Mae (Shaw) McG.; B.S., U. Minn., 1972. Buyer, Daytons Dept. Stores, Mpls., 1970-72; cons. Internat. Mktg. Cons., Devonshire, Bermuda, 1972-74; internal cons. E. F. McDonald Cos., Dayton, Ohio, 1974-76; mgmt. cons., Chgo., 1976-81; v.p. ops. Travel Mgmt. Inc., Chgo., 1981-84; v.p. tech. IVI Travel Inc., Northbrook, Ill., 1984-88, exec. v.p. corporate travel cons., Oak Brook, Ill.; voice and data communication specialist. Served with 101st Airborne Div., U.S. Army, 1967-69; Vietnam. Decorated Bronze Star medal; lic. single and multi engine, land and sea comml. pilot and flight instr. Mem. Am. Mgmt. Assn., Assn. Systems Mgmt. Home: 71 E Division St Chicago IL 60610

MCGIBBON, EDMUND LEAVENWORTH, lawyer, rancher; b. Grand Rapids, Mich., May 27, 1908; s. William and Franc (Leavenworth) McG.; A.B., Dartmouth Coll., 1929; J.D., Northwestern U., 1933; m. Catherine Jean Klink, Aug. 29, 1941; children—William A., Catherine Jean, Bonnie Laurie. Bar: Ill. 1934. Since practiced in Chgo., assn. Robertson, Crowe & Spence, 1934-38; partner Robertson & McGibbon, 1947-53, Williston, McGibbon, Stastny & Borman, 1953-62, Williston, Mc Gibbon & Stastny, 1962-66, Williston & McGibbon, 1966-70, Williston, McGibbon & Kuehn, 1970—. Chmn. bd. Santa Rita Ranch, Inc., Green Valley, Ariz. Bd. govs. Scottish Old Peoples Home. Served from lt. to comdr. USN, 1940-45, comdg. officer destroyer escort; capt. USNR (ret.). Decorated Bronze Star, Legion of Merit. Mem. ABA, Ill., Chgo. bar assns., Nat. Rifle Assn. (life), Am. Nat. Cattlemen's Assn., Ariz. Cattle Growers Assn., Ill. St. Andrew Soc. (past pres.), Soc. Genealogists (London), Nat. Geneal. Soc., Phi Kappa Psi, Phi Alpha Delta. Republican. Episcopalian. Clubs: University, Chicago; Barrington Hills (Ill.) Country; Tucson (Ariz.) Country. Home: 764 Old Barn Rd Barrington IL 60010 also: Santa Rita Ranch PO Box 647 Green Valley AZ 85622 Office: 102 N Cook St Barrington IL 60010

MCGILL, JAMES THOMAS, insurance company executive; b. Chgo., May 25, 1940; s. Clarence F. and Gladys E. (Taylor) McG.; m. Barbara S. Selix, June 23, 1962; children—Denise, Mary Beth, Mark, Keith. B.S.C., DePaul U., 1962. C.P.A., Ill. Audit supr. Peat, Marwick, Mitchell & Co., Chgo., 1962-70; v.p., treas., chief fin. officer Interstate Nat. Corp., Chgo., 1970—, dir., 1979—. Mem. Am. Inst. C.P.A.s, Ill. Soc. C.P.A.S., Midlothian C. of C. Clubs: Economic, Mid-Am., Executive (Chgo.). Home: 14638 Parkside Dr Dolton IL 60419 Office: Interstate Nat Corp 55 E Monroe St Chicago IL 60603

MCGILL, ROSS KIM, marketing professional; b. Newcastle, Eng., Sept. 4, 1955; s. Geoffrey Edward and Joyce (Bulman) McG.; m. Kathryn Ann West, Aug. 19, 1976; children: Kirsty Victoria, Elizabeth Alexandria. BSc with honors, Cert. in Edn., U. Bath, Eng., 1978. Sr. chemist Cadbury Schweppes Ltd., Cambridge, Eng., 1978-80; promotions exec. Levi-Strauss Ltd., London, 1980-82; internat. promotion mgr. Budget Rent-A-Car Internat., Inc., Hemel Hempstead, Eng., 1982-87, mgr. U.K. mktg., 1987-88; mgr. U.K. mktg. Truline Bldg. Products Ltd., Chelmsford, Eng., 1988—; Cons. Roadshow Promotions, Saffron Walden, Eng., 1985—. Vice chmn. Local Assn. for Mentally Handicapped, Haverhill, Eng., 1977—. Mem. Brit. Inst Mgmt., Royal TV Soc., Mktg. Soc., Assn. Conf. Execs. Home: 15 Foxburrow Close, Haverill CB9 9JJ, England Office: Truline Bldg Products, Montrose House, Montrose Rd, Chelmsford CM2 6TX, England

MCGILL, SCOTT DOUGLAS, information services executive, consultant; b. Meadville, Pa., Sept. 24, 1946; s. Gaylord Arthur and Margaret Annetta (Kebert) McG.; m. Cathleen Ann Chaffin, Nov. 28, 1970; children—Kelly Meghan, Kerry Shannon. B.S. in Math., Allegheny Coll., 1968; B.S. in Meteorology and Oceanography, NYU, 1971; M.A. in Computer Systems Mgmt., U. Nebr., 1972; MBA in Info. Sysytems U. Colo., 1985. Systems analyst Sperry Univac Co., Washington, 1972-73, sr. systems analyst, Colorado Springs, Colo., 1973-75; mgr. programming and design City of Colorado Springs, 1975-76, dir. data processing, 1976-86; exec. dir. Info. Resources Mgmt. Med. U. S.C., Charleston, 1986-87; dir. adminstrv. info. services Mich. State U., 1987—; hon. faculty U. Colo.-Colorado Springs, 1975-85; sr. instr. Mgmt. Devel. Found., Colorado Springs, 1978; dir. Cibar Systems Inst. Inc., Colorado Springs; mem. higher edn. computer adv. com. S.C. Commn., 1986-87; mem. Electronic Computing Health Oriented, 1986-87; mem. exec. bd. Med. Supercomputer Consortium, 1986-87. Mem. exec. bd. dirs. Pikes Peak council Boy Scouts Am., 1979-86; chmn. adminstrv. bd. Calvary United Methodist Ch., Colorado Springs, 1980-83; bus. adv. council Computer Tng. for Severely Handicapped, Denver, 1981—; bd. dirs. Goodwill Industries Colorado Springs, 1982-86, MUSC Children's Fund, 1987—; mem. Colo. Commn. on Children and Their Families, Denver, 1983-86; trustee Pikes Peak Library Dist., Colorado Springs, 1983-86. Served to capt. USAF, 1968-72. Recipient Disting. Greater Colo. Service award Denver Fed. Exec. Bd., 1980. Mem. Am. Mgmt. Assn., Assn. Computing Machinery (chmn. Pikes Peak chpt. 1977-78), Assn. Inst. Certification Computer Profls. (charter), Am. Pub. Power Assn. (chmn. 1985), Assn. Systems Mgmt., Am. Soc. Pub. Adminstrn., Univac Users' Assn., Colo. Info. Mgmt. Council, (dir. 1981-82, Outstanding Contbns. to Data Processing in Local Govt. award 1978), Data Processing Mgmt. Assn. (pres. 1978, internat. dir. so. Colo. chpt. 1983-86, Chpt. Mem. of Yr 1977, 78, Individual Performance award 1978, Individual Silver Performance award 1981, Gold Individual Performance award, 1985), IEEE (assoc.), Rocky Mountain Assn. Local Govtl. Computer Users (chmn. 1981-82, Outstanding Data Processor of Yr. 1979), S.C. Assn. Data Processing Dirs. (exec. com. 1986-87), Higher Edn. Network Assn., Coll. and Univ. Machine Records Conf., S.C. Commn. on Higher Edn., Soc. Info. Mgmt. (chmn. Rocky Mountain chpt. 1983), Higher Edn. Network Assn., Electronic Computing Health Oriented, Delta Tau Delta. Republican. Methodist. Clubs: James Island Yacht, Ducks Unlimited, Rocky Mountain (bd. dirs. 1981), Winter Night, Tues. Afternoon Rest and Aspiration (Colorado Springs). Lodges: Elks, Masons.

MCGILL, STEPHEN KENNETH, electronics company executive, financial consultant; b. Atlanta, Feb. 13, 1949; s. Stephen Kenneth and Edris Carol (Sadenwater) McG.; m. Louann L. Childress, 1984. B. Aerospace Engr., Ga. Inst. Tech., 1971; M.B.A., U. Calif.-Berkeley, 1978. Sales engr. Allen Bradley Co., San Francisco, 1972-78, dist. mgr., Ft. Lauderdale, Fla., 1978-80; mgr. operations Wyle-EMG, El Segundo, Calif., 1980-81, San Diego, 1981-83; mgr. sales operations Schweber Electronics, Phoenix, 1983-84, gen. mgr., 1984-86, v.p. customer service devel., Westbury, N.Y., 1986-88, v.p. nat. sales, 1988—; founder-part owner Circuit Services Inc., Santa Clara, Calif., 1979-88, also dir. Mem. Sales and Mktg. Execs., IEEE. Republican. Lodge: Optimist. Home: 17 Elderwood Dr Saint James NY 11780 Office: Schweber Electronics Westbury NY 11590

MC GILLICUDDY, JOHN FRANCIS, banker; b. Harrison, N.Y., Dec. 30, 1930; s. Michael J. and Anna (Munro) McG.; m. Constance Burtis, Sept. 9, 1954; children: Michael Sean, Faith Burtis, Constance Erin Mc Gillicuddy Mills, Brian Munro, John Walsh. A.B., Princeton, 1952; LL.B., Harvard, 1955. With Mfrs. Hanover Trust Co. subs. Mfrs. Hanover Corp., N.Y.C., 1958—, v.p., 1962-66, sr. v.p., 1966-69, exec. v.p., asst. to chmn., 1969-70, vice chmn., dir., 1970, pres., 1971—, chmn., chief exec. officer, 1979—; dir. Kraft Inc., USX Corp., Continental Corp., Allegis Corp., Fed. Reserve Bankof N.Y. Bd. dirs. Nat. Multiple Sclerosis Soc., 1969—; trustee N.Y. Hosp., Princeton U., N.Y. Pub. Library. Served to lt. (j.g.) USNR, 1955-58. Mem. Assn. Res. City Bankers, Bus. Council, Bus. Roundtable. Roman Catholic. Clubs: Westchester Country (Rye, N.Y.); Blind Brook (Port Chester, N.Y.); Princeton (N.Y.C.). Office: Mfrs Hanover Corp 270 Park Ave New York NY 10017

MCGILLIS, KEVIN DONALD H., management consultant; b. Cornwall, Ont., Can., July 30, 1951; s. Stanley Joseph and Mary McGillis; m. Denise Marie Daigle, May 17, 1986. B in Mktg., Algonquin Coll., Ottawa, Ont., 1974. Budget adminstr. Agr. Can., Ottawa, Ont., 1974-75; mgr. property Vet. Affairs Can., Ottawa, 1975-76, mgr. forms, 1976-78; mgmt. cons. Can. Pension Commn., Ottawa, 1978-80; systems cons. Home Oil Ltd., Calgary, Alta., Can., 1980-81; mgr. bus. methods Alta. Wheat Pool, Calgary, 1981-84, mgr. adminstrn., 1984—. Organizer Progressive Conservative Party, Calgary, 1984. Mem. Bus. Info. Mgmt. Service (exec. v.p. 1984-87). Mem. Progressive Party. Roman Catholic. Club: Youth Soc. (pres. 1967-69). Home: 2613 5th Ave NW, Calgary, AB Canada T2N OT7

MCGINLEY, NANCY ELIZABETH, lawyer; b. Columbia, Mo., Feb. 29, 1952; d. Robert Joseph and Ruth Evangeline (Garnett) McG. BA with high honors, U. Tex., 1974, JD, 1977. Bar: Tex. 1977, U.S. Dist. Ct. (no. dist.) Tex. 1979. Law clk. U.S. Dist. Ct. (no. dist.) Tex., Fort Worth, 1977-79; assoc. Crumley, Murphy and Shrull, Fort Worth, 1979-81; staff atty. SEC, Fort Worth, 1981-87; br. chief SEC Los Angeles Regional Office, 1987—. Mem. editorial staff Urban Law Rev. Mem. Tarrant County Young Lawyers Assn., Women Lawyers of Tarrant County, Fort Worth Bus. and Profl. Women's Assn., Mortar Bd., Phi Beta Kappa, Phi Kappa Phi, Alpha Lambda Delta. Methodist. Home: 3121 Sondra Dr Apt 203E Fort Worth TX 76107

MCGINN, FRANCIS PETER, gastoenterological and endocrine surgeon, consultant; b. Liverpool, Eng., July 28, 1940; s. Ronald and Mary Isabella (Morton) McG.; m. Drusilla Patience Grafton, Sept. 11, 1965; children—Piers Russell, Dominic Stuart, Joanna Frances Mary, Ross Andrew. M.B., B.S., London U., 1963, D. Obst., Royal Coll. Ob-Gyn, 1965, M. Phil., 1970, M.S., 1975; FRCS, Royal Coll. Surgeons Eng. 1969. Lectr. physiology Kings Coll., London U., 1965-67; sr. house officer Bristol Royal Infirmary, 1967-70; registrar Frenchay Hosp., Bristol, 1970-72; lectr. surgery Profl. Surgical Unit, Southampton U., 1972-76; cons. surgeon Southampton U. Hosp., 1976—; surgical tutor Royal Coll. Surgeons, Southampton, 1983—. Mem. Surg. Research Soc., Assn. Surgeons of Gt. Britain and North Ireland. Presbyterian. Clubs: Royal Lymington Yacht, Royal Southampton Yacht. Avocations: sailing; tennis; cycling. Home: Monkswell House Palace Ln, Beaulieu, Hampshire SO42 7YG, England Office: Southampton Gen Hosp, Tremona Rd Southampton, Hampshire SO9 4XY, England

MC GINNESS, WILLIAM GEORGE, III, manufacturing company executive; b. Lock Haven, Pa., Apr. 9, 1948; s. William George and Ruby Jean (Cooper) McG., children—Heather Jean, Patrick Robert. B.Chemistry, Lock Haven State U., 1970. Prodn. mgr. Am. Color & Chem. Corp., Lock Haven, Pa., 1969-75; lab. mgr. Novamont/Montedison, Florence, Ky., 1976-79; prodn. mgr. Sun Chem., Cin., 1979-80; v.p. tech. services Natmar, Inc., Cin., 1980-83; pres., chief exec. officer Angstrom Techs., Florence, Ky., 1983—; dir. Natmar, Inc., Sperti Drug Products, Inc., Antex Corp. Mem. Am. Chem. Soc., Soc. Profl. Engrs., Am. Assn. Textile Chemists and Colorists, Soc. Mfg. Engrs., Machine Vision Assn., Robotics Internat., AAAS. Republican. Lutheran. Clubs: Bankers (Cin.); Chemists (N.Y.C.). Home: 2251 Clarkson Dr Union KY 41091 Office: Angstrom Techs Inc 20 Kenton Lands Rd Erlanger KY 41018

MC GINNIS, THOMAS CHARLES, JR., hardware wholesaling executive; b. Morehead City, N.C., Sept. 3, 1949; s. Thomas C. and Mary Y. (Klutz) McG.; m. Carol A. Strickland; 1 dau., Ashley Katharine. B.A., Wittenberg U., 1971; M.A., Fairleigh Dickinson U., 1977; cert. Nat. Tax Tng. Sch. Asst., Counseling and Psychotherapy Center, Fair Lawn, N.J., 1972-73, adminstr., 1974, adminstrv. v.p., 1975-76; pres. Profl. Adminstrv. Services Corp., Fair Lawn, 1977-86; pres. Toca Distributors Inc., T/A Outwater Hardware Corp., Totowa, N.J., 1986—. No. N.J. Coll. chmn. Nixon Campaign staff, 1971-72. Served as sgt. USAR, 1971-77. Mem. Biofeedback Research Soc., Nat. Council Family Relations. Presbyterian. Club: N.Y.C. Sea Gypsy's Inc. Lodges: Rotary Internat. (pres. local club 1983-84). Author: The Early Years of Marriage, 1973; researcher: Open Family Living, 1976, Open Family and Marriage, 1975, Dynamics of Human Sexuality, 1974, Key Elements in Small Corporate Management, 1985. Home: 6 Old English Ct Woodcliff Lake NJ 07675 Office: 11 West End Rd Totowa NJ 07512

MCGIVERIN, DONALD SCOTT, retail company executive; b. Calgary, Alta., Can., Apr. 4, 1924; s. Alfred Chester and Ella (Scott) McG.; m. Margaret-Ann Weld, Sept. 9, 1950 (dec. Nov. 1968); children—Mary Edith, Richard Weld (dec.). B.Comm., U. Man., 1945; M.B.A., Ohio State U., 1946. Mng. dir. retail stores Hudson's Bay Co., Winnipeg, Man., Can., 1969-72, pres., dir., 1972-85, gov., dir., 1982—; dir. Markborough Properties Ltd., Mfrs. Life Ins. Co., Mfrs. Capital Corp., DuPont Can. Ltd., Noranda Inc. Bd. govs. Wellesley Hosp. Mem. Phi Kappa Pi, Beta Gamma Sigma. Clubs: Lambton Golf and Country, Rosedale Golf, Granite, York, Toronto; LyFord Cay (Nassau, Bahamas); St. Charles Country (Winnipeg); Loxahatchee (Jupiter, Fla.); Mt. Royal (Montreal). Home: 44 Charles St W, Toronto, ON Canada M4Y 1R7 Office: Hudson's Bay Co, 401 Bay St, Toronto, ON Canada M5H 1Y4

MCGLOTHLIN, MICHAEL GORDON, lawyer; b. Richlands, Va., Oct. 31, 1951; s. Woodrow Wilson and Sally Ann (Cook) McG.; m. Sandra Lee Keen, Oct. 1, 1983; children: Michael Alexander, Robert Aaron. BA, U. Va., 1974; JD, Coll. William and Mary, 1976. Bar: Va. 1977, U.S. Dist. Ct. (we. dist.) Va. 1978. Ptnr. McGlothlin, McGlothlin, Grundy, Va., 1977-79; commonwealth atty. Buchanan County, Grundy, 1980-83; ptnr. McGlothlin & Wife, Grundy, 1984—; atty.for Buchanan County, 1984—; bd. dirs. Gt. Southwest Home Commn. Mem. adv. bd. Clinch Valley Coll. Mem. ABA, Va. State Bar Assn., Buchanan County Bar Assn. (pres. 1984), Phi Alpha Delta. Democrat. Presbyterian. Home and Office: PO Drawer 810 Grundy VA 24614

MCGOLDRICK, MICHAEL DONALD, nephrologist; b. Galway, Ireland, Apr. 8, 1942; came to U.S. 1966; s. Michael P. and Ita (Collins) McG.; m. Victoria Robb, Jan. 4, 1969; children: Lillemor Maire, Michael Colin, Kevin Gene, Meghan Victoria. Student, Castleknock Coll., Dublin, Ireland, 1955-60, Nat. U. Ireland, Galway, 1960-66. Nephrology fellowship Albany (N.Y.) Med. Ctr., 1967-68, internal medicine resident, 1968-70; nephrologist Royal Victoria Hosp., Montreal, Can., 1970-72, attending staff internal medicine, cons. nephrologist, 1972-78; cons. nephrologist Queen Elizabeth Hosp., Montreal, 1972-78, ICU physician, asst. chief of medicine, 1974-78; assoc. prof. medicine, head renal div., attending nephrologist Albany Med. Coll., 1978—, prof. medicine, 1985—; cons. nephrologist Meml. Hosp., Ellis Hosp., St. Peter's Hosp., Albany Med. Ctr. Hosp., 1984—; med. co-dir. dialysis unit Albany Med. Ctr. Hosp., 1978—; cons. N.Y. Dept. Edn. Foreign Medical Sch. Evaluation, Manila, Phillipines, 1983; vis. prof. St. George's Med. Sch., Grenada, 1980, 82, 87. Author: chapter in medical textbook, 1985; contbr. articles to profl. jours. Mem. N.Y. State Mus. Gala Com., 1987. Recipient Resident of the Yr. award Albany Med. Ctr. Hosp., 1969, Tchr. of Excellence award McGill U., 1974, Royal Victoria Hosp., Royal Victoria Hosp., 1977, Clin. Golden Apple award, Albany Med. Coll., 1981, 85; named Attending Physician of the Yr. Albany Med. Coll., 1981, 83. Mem. Am. Soc. Nephrology, Internat. Soc. Nephrology, Am. Fedn. Clin. Research., Med. Soc. of Albany COunty. Roman Catholic. Office: Albany Med Coll of Union Univ Room Hun104 Albany NY 12208

MCGOUGH, ALICE MARIE, chem. co. purchasing agt.; b. Tarentum, Pa., June 25, 1937; d. Edward Albert and Frances Amelia (Gross) Gase; BA magna cum laude, Carlow Coll., 1957; postgrad. U. Pitts., 1958-59; children: Mary Gase, Paul Aidan, Daniel John. Research asst. in biophysics U. Pitts., 1957-59; lab. technician GAF Corp., Wayne, N.J., 1973, chems. buyer, 1973-76; buyer organic chems. div. Am. Cyanamid Co., Bound Brook, N.J., 1976-78, purchasing agt. materials planning and procurement div., 1978-81, purchasing agt. chems. group, 1981—. mem. exec. bd. LWV of Wayne Twp., N.J., 1969-72; vol. Paterson (N.J.) Task Force, Day Care Ctr., 1972, Contact Teleministries, Morris and Passaic Counties, 1987—. Mem. Smithsonian Instn. Democrat. Roman Catholic. Club: Sierra. Office: One Cyanamid Plaza Wayne NJ 07470

MCGOVERAN, DAVID ORNAN, consulting firm executive, automation systems consultant; b. Pittsburg, Calif., Mar. 17, 1952; s. Lowell Benage and Tressie Jane (Sanders) M.; m. Mary Louise Rhodes, July 7, 1978; 1 dau., Lauren Rachel. Student Diablo Valley Coll., 1970-73; AB in Physics, U. Chgo., 1976; postgrad. Stanford U., 1978-79. Physics assoc. Stanford Research Inst., Menlo Park, Calif., 1976-79; electronics engring. instr. Profl. Engring. Inst., Belmont, Calif., 1978-79; prof. dept. chmn. computer sci. and bus. mgmt. Condie Coll., San Jose, Calif., 1979-80; sales support mgr. GCA Corp., Santa Clara, Calif., 1980-82; CAM system mgr. Synertek, Santa Cruz, Calif., 1982-83; pres. Alternative Technologies, Santa Cruz, Calif., 1976—; vis. scholar Stanford U., 1987-88. Author: Electronics Engineering Technicians Handbook, 1980; Night Moods, 1982. Editor: Contributions to Combinatorial Physics, 1984; Discrete Approaches to Natural Philosophy, 1985. Contbr. articles to jours. and books. Inventor cable connecting tool, slide tube, FASTTRACK semiconductor automation system, algorithmic prediction of catalytic behaviour, constructive differential topology. U. Chgo. Merit scholar, 1974, 75, AAUW scholar, 1970; Richards Meml. scholar, 1973; Supplementary Ednl. Opportunity grantee, 1974. Fellow Meninger Found., 1979; research assoc. Inst. Noetic Scis., 1976; mem. Calif. Scholarship Found., 1970; sec. Electronics Experimenters League, 1969-70. Mem. IEEE, Assn. Computing Machinery, Condie Coll. Profl. Assn., Inst. for Advancement Noetics (pres., chmn. bd. 1975-78), Alternative Natural Philosophy Assn. (sec., treas., dir. 1978—), N.Y. Acad. Scis., Data Processing Mgmt. Assn., U. Chgo. Alumni Schs. Assn., Assn. Humanistic Psychology, AAAS, Md. Neurol. Soc., Delta Rocket Soc. (founding pres. 1966). Office: Alternative Techs 150 Felker St Suite E Santa Cruz CA 95060

MCGOVERN, JOHN HUGH, urologist, educator; b. Bayonne, N.J., Dec. 18, 1924; s. Patrick and Mary (McGovern) McG.; m. Mary Alice Cavazos, Aug. 2, 1980; children by previous marriage: John Hugh, Robert, Ward, Raymond. BS, Columbia U., 1947; MD, SUNY, Bklyn., 1952. Lic. physician, N.Y.; diplomate Am. Bd. Urology. Rotating intern Bklyn. Hosp., 1952-53, asst. resident in surgery Bklyn. VA Hosp., 1953-54, in urology, N.Y. Hosp., 1954-56; exchange surg. registrar West London Hosp., Eng., 1956-57; resident in urol. surgery N.Y. Hosp., 1957-58, research asst. pediatric urology, 1958-59; asst. attending surgeon James Buchanan Brady Found., N.Y. Hosp., 1959-61, assoc. attending surgeon, 1961-66, attending surgeon, 1966—; asst. in surgery Cornell U. Med. Coll., 1957-59, asst. prof. clin. surgery, 1959-64, assoc. prof., 1964-72, prof., 1972—; attending staff in urology Lenox Hill Hosp., 1969—, in-charge urology, 1969-83; cons. urology Rockefeller Inst., St. Vincent's Hosp., Mercy Hosp., Phelps Meml. Hosp.; chmn. council on urology Nat. Kidney Found., 1982. Contbr. articles to profl. jours., chpts. to books. Served to lt. M.C., U.S. Army, 1942-45. Recipient Conatvoy mos medal Chile, 1975; named Huesped de Honor, Mimunicipalidad de Guayaquil (Ecuador), 1976; award in urology Kidney Found. N.Y., 1977, Sir Peter Freyer medal, Galway, Ireland, 1980. Fellow N.Y. Acad. Medicine (exec. com. urol. sect. 1968-72, chmn. 1972), ACS, Am. Acad. Pediatrics; mem. N.Y. State Med. Soc. (chmn. urol. sect. 1975), AMA, Med. Soc. County N.Y., Am. Urol. Assn. (pres.-elect 1988, pres. N.Y. sect. 1979-80, N.Y. rep. exec. com. 1982-87, socioecons. com. 1987, chmn. fiscal affairs rev. com. 1987), N.Y. State Urol. Soc. (exec. com. 1982—), Pan Pacific Surg. Assn., Am. Assn. Clin. Urologists (pres.-elect 1987, bd. dirs. 1984—, mem. interpersonal relations com. 1975—), Assn. Am. Physicians and Surgeons, Pan Am. Med. Assn. (diplomate 1981—), Société Internationale d'Urologie, Urol. Investigators Forum, Soc. Pediatric Urology (pres.-elect 1979-80, pres. 1980-81), Am. Trauma Soc., Kidney Found. (med. adv. bd. N.Y. sect., trustee, 1979) Société Internationale d'Urologie (exec. com. U.S. sect.); hon. mem. Sociedad Peruana de Urologia, Sociedad Guatemala de Urologi a, Sociedad Ecuadoriana de . Urologia, affiliate mem. Royal Coll. Surgeons (London). Home: 969 Park Ave New York NY 10028 Office: 53 E 70th St New York NY 10021

MCGOVERN, JOHN PHILLIP, physician, educator; b. Washington, June 2, 1921; s. Francis and Lottie (Brown) McG.; B.S., M.D., Duke U., 1945; postgrad., London and Paris, 1949; hon. degrees: Ricker Coll., Union Coll., Kent State U., U. Nebr., Ill. Coll. Podiatric Medicine, Lincoln Coll., Emerson Coll., Ball State U., Huston-Tillotson Coll., John F. Kennedy U., Limestone Coll., Southeastern U., Tex. Christian U., Georgetown U., William Penn Coll., Catawba Coll., Fla. State U., Lamar U., Alaska Pacific U., Houston Grad. Sch. Theology, Troy State U., Pan Am. U., Thomas Jefferson U.; m. Kathrine Dunbar Galbreath, 1961. Intern pediatrics Yale-New Haven Gen. Hosp., 1945-46; resident pediatrics Duke U. Hosp., 1948; chief resident Children's Hosp., 1949-50, chief out-patient dept., 1950-51; John and Mary R. Markle scholar med. sci., asst. prof. pediatrics George Washington U. Sch. Medicine, 1950-54; chief George Washington U. pediatric div. D.C. Gen. Hosp., 1951-54; asso. prof. pediatrics Tulane U., 1954-56; vis. physician Charity Hosp., New Orleans; practice medicine specializing in allergy/immunology, Houston, 1956—; chief of allergy service Tex. Children's Hosp., Houston, 1957-74; dir., cons. McGovern Allergy Clinic, 1986—; clin. prof. pediatrics (allergy), adj. prof. dept. of microbiology Baylor Coll. Medicine; prof., chmn. dept. history of medicine U. Tex. Grad. Sch. Biomed. Sci., 1970-81, prof. history and philosophy of biol. sci., 1981—, clin. prof. allergy, 1956-70, clin. prof. M.D. Anderson Hosp. and Tumor Inst., 1976—; fellow Green Coll. Oxford U.; disting. adj. prof. health and safety edn. Kent State U., 1972—; adj. prof. dept. environ. sci. Sch. Public Health, U. Tex., 1978—, clin. prof. Sch. Medicine, 1978; cons. USPHS, New Orleans, 1954-56; regional cons. Lackland AFB, San Antonio; regional cons. nat. med. adv. council Asthmatic Children's Found., 1963—, bd. dirs., 1967-79. Chmn. bd. dirs. Tex. Allergy Research Found.; pres., bd. dirs. John P. McGovern Found.; bd. dirs. Allergy Found. Am., 1962-74; bd. regents Nat. Library Medicine, 1970-74, cons., 1975—. Served to capt., M.C., AUS, 1946-48. Recipient numerous awards including Disting. Alumni award Duke U. Sch. Medicine, 1976, John P. McGovern award Tex. Sch. Health Assn., 1977, President's citation Pres. Reagan, 1985, Royal Medallion of the Polar Star Sweden, 1988, l'Ordre national du Merite France, 1988, Pres.'s Medal Health Sci. Ctr. U. Texas, Houston, 1988. Diplomate Nat. Bd. Med. Examiners, Am. Bd. Pediatrics, subsplty. pediatric allergy, Am. Bd. Allergy and Immunology. Fellow Am. Coll. Allergists (pres. 1968-69), Am. Acad. Allergy, Am. Acad. Pediatrics, Am. Coll. Chest Physicians (Tex. chpt. pres. 1966-67), Am. Assn. Study Headache (pres. 1963-64); mem. Am. Assn. Immunologists, Soc. Exptl. Biology and Medicine, Am. Med. Writers Assn., Assn. for Research on Nervous and Mental Diseases, Am. Assn. Hist. Medicine, AMA, So. Med. Assn. (life mem.), Tex. Pediatric Soc., Assn. Convalescent Homes and Hosps. for Asthmatic Children (pres. Tex. chpt. 1969-70), Duke U. Med. Alumni Assn. (pres. 1968-69), Am. Assn. Cert. Allergists (pres. 1972-73), Am. Osler Soc. (pres. 1973-74), Am. Sch. Health Assn., ACP, Sociedad de Alergia y Ciencias Afines (Mexico, hon.), La Sociedad Mexicana de Alergia e Inmunologia (hon.), Westchester (hon.), Canadian (hon.) allergy socs., Asociacion Argentina de Alergia e Inmunologia (hon.), Royal Coll. Physicians (London) (hon.), Phi Beta Kappa, Alpha Omega Alpha, Sigma Xi (mem. com. on membership-at-large, editor newsletter 1970-71, dir. 1972-73), Sigma Pi Sigma, Pi Kappa Alpha. Clubs: Cosmos, Army-Navy Country (Washington), Osler (London), Vintage (Calif.). Author: (with Mandel) Bibliography of Sarcoidosis (1876-1963), 1964; (with James Knight) Allergy and Human Emotions, 1967; (with Charles Roland) Wm. Osler: The Continuing Education, 1969; (with Gordon Stewart) Penicillin Allergy: Clinical and Immunological Aspects, 1970; (with Chester Burns) Humanism in Medicine, 1974;lenn Knotts) School Health Problems, 1975; (with Earl Nation and Charles Roland) An Annotated Checklist of Osleriana, 1976; (with Michael Smolensky and Alain Reinberg) Chronobiology in Allergy and Immunology, 1977; (with others) Recent Advances in the Chronobiology of Allergy and Immunology, 1980; editor; A Way of Life (Osler), 1969; Davison Memorial Addresses, 1976; (with E.F. Nation) Student and Chief: The Osler-Camac Correspondence, 1980; (with J. Arena) Davison of Duke - His Reminiscences, 1980; (with C. Roland and J. Barondess) The Persisting Osler, 1985; (with C. Roland) The Collected Essays of Sir William Osler, Vols. I, II, III, 1985; (with J. Vay Eys) The Doctor as a Person, 1988; assoc. editor Annals of Allergy, 1965-80; editorial bd. Psychosomatics, Headache, Internat. Corr. Soc. Allergists; assoc. editor Jour. Asthma Research; editor Am. Lecture Series in Allergy and Immunology; assoc. editor Jour. Sch. Health, 1977-80; editorial adv. bd. Chronic Disease Mgmt., 1967-74; editorial bd. Forum on Medicine, 1978-81, The Classics of Medicine Library, 1978—; editorial bd. Acad. Achievement, 1967-75, Geriatrics, 1974-78, numerous others. Office: 6969 Brompton St Houston TX 77025

MCGOWAN, HAROLD, real estate developer, investor, scientist, author; b. Weehawken, N.J., June 23, 1909; s. Sylvester and Grace (Kalbfleish) McG.; m. Anne Cecelia McTiernan, Jan. 15, 1938; children—Linda Anne, Harold Charles, Janice Marie. Ed., Bklyn. Poly. Inst., Pratt Inst., N.Y. U., Hubbard (Eng.) U.; D.Sc., Coll. Fla. Chmn. bd. Atomic Research, Inc.; pres. Harold McGowan Builders; owner, developer Central Islip Shopping Center, Central Islip Indsl. Center; developer, builder Brinsley Gardens, Rolling Green, Slater Park, Clover Green, Maple Acres, Wheeler Acres; owner-donor Little League Baseball Parks. Sculptures include: Bless Them; Victory, Eternity, Love and Hate, Triumph; author: Green Flight, The Thoughtron Theory of Life and Matter, Race with Death across the Sahara, The Incorrigibles, The Frigid Trap, The Shah's Swiss Secret, Another World for Christmas, The Spirit of Christmas in Words and Sculpture, The Making of a Universalist, The Journeyman, $800,000 for Love, Beyond the Visible, Shock after Shock, Christmas Stories, Short Stories, Born Again, You Are Forever, Black Shroud Over Bagdad. Hwy. commr., Suffolk County; chmn. Recreation & Parks-Islip. Recipient Winston Churchill Medal of Wisdom, Wisdom Hall of Fame, Beverly Hills, Calif. Mem. AAAS, IEEE, Explorers Club, Mensa Internat. Address: 28 2d Ave Central Islip NY 11722

MCGOWAN, PATRICK FRANCIS, lawyer; b. N.Y.C., July 23, 1940; s. Francis Patrick and Sonia Veronica (Koslow) M.; m. Patricia Neil, June 6, 1964; children: Susan Claire, Kathleen Anne. BA, Rice U., 1962; JD, U. Tex.-Austin, 1965. Bar: Tex. 1965, U.S. Supreme Ct. 1971. Briefing atty. Tex. Supreme Ct., Austin, Tex., 1965-66; ptnr. Strasburger & Price, Dallas, 1966—; dir. Tex Lex, Inc. Mem. ABA (forum com. on franchising, trademark and unfair competition com., patent, trademark and copyright law sect.), State Bar Tex. (intellectual property sect., com. continuing legal edn.), Dallas Bar Assn., Internat. AntiCounterfeiting Assn., Tex. Law Review Editors Assn., Phi Delta Phi. Office: 4300 First Republic Bank Plaza Dallas TX 75202

MC GOWAN, THOMAS FRANCIS, manufacturing company executive; b. Boston, May 19, 1931; s. Thomas Francis and Catherine Mary (Chisholm) McG.; B.S. in Bus. Adminstrn., Boston Coll., 1952; M.B.A., Boston Coll., 1965; m. Mary Lisbeth Dumphy, Apr. 8, 1961; children—Caren Ann, John Timothy. Subcontract mgr. Martin-Marietta Corp., Orlando, Fla., 1959-63; with Rockwell Internat., Los Angeles, 1963—, material mgr., 1975—; instr. Fullerton (Calif.) Coll., 1975—, Coast Community Coll., Costa Mesa, Calif., 1979—. Mem. purchasing mgmt. adv. com. Fullerton Coll., 1975-81, Coastline Community Coll., 1975-81. Served with USN, 1952-59. Cert. purchasing mgr. Mem. Purchasing Mgmt. Assn. (pres. 1973-74), Nat. Assn. Purchasing Mgmt. Republican. Home: 1997 N Greengrove St Orange CA 92665 Office: PO Box 92098 Los Angeles CA 90009

MC GRATH, EARL JAMES, educator; b. Buffalo, Nov. 16, 1902; s. John and Martha Carolyn (Schottin) McG.; m. Dorothy Ann Leemon, May 12, 1944. B.A., U. Buffalo, 1928, M.A., 1930; Ph.D., U. Chgo., 1936; Ph.D. hon. degrees 53 colls. and univs, 1949—. Mem. faculty U. Buffalo, 1928-45; dean Coll. Liberal Arts, State U. Iowa, 1945-48; prof. U. Chgo., 1948-49; U.S. commr. edn. Office of Edn., FSA, 1949-53; pres., chancellor U. Kansas City, 1953-56; exec. officer Inst. Higher Edn., also prof. higher edn. Tchrs. Coll., Columbia, 1956-68; chancellor Eisenhower Coll., Seneca Falls, 1966-68; dir. Higher Edn. Center, Temple U., 1968-73; sr. cons. Lilly Endowment, Indpls., 1973-76; prof. U. Ariz., 1974-80; chmn. univ. adv. council Western Internat. U., Phoenix, 1978—; Mem. Fulbright Bd. Fgn. Scholarships, 1949-52; Mem. and former mem. many profl. coms. and commns., local state, nat. and internat. in field of edn. Frequent mem. U.S. govtl. agys. and commns. on study ednl. systems. Author and co-author several books, numerous articles. Trustee Antioch Coll., 1958-61, Muskingum Coll., 1961-64, 68-77, St. Michael's Coll., 1966-75, Buckingham (Eng.) Coll., 1973-76, Warner Pacific Coll., 1972-78; v.p. bd. trustees Western Internat. U., 1980-88; mem. adv. bd. Truman Library. Served to lt. comdr. USNR, 1942-44. Decorated Knight Order St. John of Jerusalem. Mem. many profl. orgns. and assns. related to field of edn. Phi Beta Kappa, Delta Chi, Beta Sigma Pi, Phi Delta Kappa, Delta Phi Alpha, Sigma Xi, Iota Lambda Sigma, Omicron Delta Kappa. Clubs: Cosmos (Washington); Century Assn. (N.Y.C.); Old Pueblo (Tucson), Tucson Nat. Golf (Tucson). Home: 632 W Roller Coaster Rd Tucson AZ 85704

MCGRATH, EDWARD LEO, bank executive; b. N.Y.C., Apr. 5, 1947; s. Edward Phillip McGrath and Mary Margaret (Kiley) Dennehy. BS, Fordham U., 1969; MBA, Columbia U., 1974. Sr. fin. analyst Mellon Bank, Pitts., 1974-75; controller Mellon Bank, Tokyo, 1975-78, Hong Kong, 1978-80; dir. internat. fin. Mellon Bank, Pitts., 1980, mgr. internat. credit, 1980-82, internat. controller, 1982-85; rep. Mellon Bank, Mexico City, 1985—; mng. dir. Mellon Overseas Capital, N.V., The Netherlands, 1983—; mem. fin. com. ABC Hosp., Mex., 1987—, also bd. dirs., Francisca Friars Minor, Pitts., 1984-85. Author: The Maquiladora Industry in Nicaragua, 1974. State dir. N.Y. State Young Dems., Nassau County, 1969; mem. Dems. Abroad, Mex., 1985—, chmn. fund raising com. 1988—. Recipient Cert. Achievement U.S. Govt., 1975. Mem. Airplane Owners and Pilots Assn., Am. Fin. Assn., Am. C. of C. in Mex. (mem. vigilance com., chmn. econ. banking and fin. com., 1988—), Alpha Kappa Psi (Chi chpt. pledgement dir. 1970). Clubs: Club de Golf (Chapultepec, Mex.); Princeton (N.Y.C.); Fgn. Corrs., American (Hong Kong). Office: Mellon NA, Campos Eliseos 345, 9 Piso, 11560 Mexico City Mexico

MCGRATH, KEVIN CHARLES, distribution company executive; b. Wallingford, Conn., Nov. 22, 1955; s. George T. and Joan (McGill) McG.; m. Susan Amy Braisted, Sept. 9, 1978; children: Kevin Jr., Erin J. BA, U. Bridgeport, 1978. Sales rep. Fairfield City Real Estate, Trumbull, Conn., 1976-77; mktg. rep. Ted Miller Inc., Fairfield, Conn., 1977-79, 3M Corp., Orange, Conn., 1979-81; sales mgr. Locke Mfg. Inc., Bridgeport, 1981-83, v.p., 1983-84, pres., 1984-86; exec. v.p. James Galt Co., Inc., Wallingford, Conn., 1986—; bd. dirs. Outdoor Power Equipment Inc., Washington, 1984—. Bd. dirs., corporator Milford (Conn.) Hosp., 1984—; pres. Foxwood Condominiums Assn., Milford, 1979-82, Boston Ave. Indsl. Park, Bridgeport, 1985—; mem. Town of Trumbull Bd. of Tax., 1977-78. Recipient Sales Master award Gen. Motors Inc., Fairfield, 1978, 79, Century Club award 3M Corp., 1980. Mem. Conn. Mfg. Assn. Home: 24 Miles St Milford CT 06460 Office: James Galt Co 63 North Plains Hwy Wallingford CT 06497

MC GRATH, RICHARD WILLIAM, osteopathic physician; b. Hartford, Conn., Nov. 17, 1943; s. William Paul and Stephanie Gertrude (Romash) McG.; B.S., St. Ambrose Coll., 1965; D.Osteo. Medicine and Surgery, Coll. Osteo. Medicine and Surgery, Des Moines, 1971; m. Mariette VanLancker, June 24, 1967; children—Shaun, Megan, Kelley. Osteo. physician Weld County Gen. Hosp., Greeley, Colo., 1971-72, Granby (Colo.) Clinic, 1972-75, Timberline Med. Ctr., P.C., Granby, 1975—; pres. Timberline Med. Center, 1976—, Bighorn Properties Inc., 1978—, Thia of Am. Corp., 1980—; med. coordinator/dir. regional emergency systems Colo. State Health Dept., 1978-79; mem. Colo. Comprehensive Health Planning Agy., 1975-77; assoc. prof. clin. medicine Tex. Coll. Osteo. Medicine; med. advisor Grand County Ambulance System, 1977—; vice chief staff Kremmling Meml. Hosp.; bd. dirs. M&L Bus. Machine Co., Denver, Sun-Flo Internat., Inc., Silver Creek Devel. Co. and Ski Area. Mem. steering com. to develop Colo. Western Slope Health System Agy., 1975-76, bd. dirs., 1977—; bd. dirs. St. Anthony Hosp. Systems Emergency Rooms, 1984—; med. dir. Community Hosp. and Emergency Ctr., Granby; officer, police surgeon Grand Lake and Granby, 1977—; mem. parent adv. bd. Granby Sch. System, 1975-76; chmn. East Grand County Safety Council, 1974-76; dep. coroner Grand County, 1973-75; med. advisor Grand County Rescue Team, 1974-78. Recipient award Ohio State U. Coll. Medicine, 1977. Mem. AMA, ACS (com. on trauma), Am. Coll. Emergency Physicians, Western Slope Physicians Alliance Assn., Colo. State Emergency Med. Technicians (med. chmn. 1982-84), Colo. Union of Physicians (dir.), C. of C. of Granby, Grand Lake and Fraser Valley. Republican. Roman Catholic. Home: PO Box 706 Granby CO 80446 Office: PO Box 857 Granby CO 80446

MCGRATH, ROBERT EDWARD, dentist; b. Pottsville, Pa., June 27, 1947; s. Edward Joseph and Frances Virginia (Weaver) McG.; m. Cheryl Julia Scherkenbach, July 25, 1970; children: Edward Joseph, Erin Colleen, Molly Maureen. DDS, Marquette U., 1972. With Mid-Towne Dental Assn., Wisconsin Rapids, Wis., 1972-73, sec., 1973-78, pres., 1978—; mem. med. staff, surg. com. Riverview Hosp., 1972-86; cons. claims Delta Dental Ins., Stevens Point, Wis., 1978-84, Preway Inc., Wis. Rapids, 1984—; cons. advisor Blue Cross United of Wis., Milw., 1985—; regional dental dir. Wis. Dental Plan, Green Bay, 1985—. Bd. mem. Sch. Dist. Wisconsin Rapids, 1976-78, 81-86, pres. 1978-81, 86—; mem. at large Spl. Edn. Adv., Wisconsin Rapids, 1973-78. Named one of Outstanding Young Men of Am., U.S. Jaycees, 1980. Fellow Acad. Gen. Dentistry (membership com. 1985—); mem. ADA, Wis. Dental Assn. (access planning 1986—), Cen. Wis. Dental Assn., Marquette U. Alumnae Admission, U.S. Jaycees (state dir. Wisconsin Rapids chpt. 1976). Republican. Roman Catholic. Lodges: Rotary (bd. dirs. Wisconsin Rapids club 1985—), Elks. Home: 4711 Townline Rd Wisconsin Rapids WI 54494 Office: Mid Towne Dental Assocs 1730 7th St S PO Box 1178 Wisconsin Rapids WI 54494

MCGRATH, THOMAS AUGUSTINE, priest, psychologist, educator; b. Quincy, Mass., May 4, 1919; s. Thomas Martin and Anna (Cronin) McG.; B.A., Boston Coll., 1943, M.A., 1944; M.A., Cath. U. Am., 1948; Ph.D., Fordham U., 1960. Joined Soc. of Jesus, 1937; ordained priest Roman Catholic Ch., 1950; dir. psychol. services Fairfield (Conn.) U., 1957-68, chmn. dept., 1962-70, 73-76; prof. psychology, 1969—; cons. to industry. Lic. psychologist, Conn. Mem. Am. Psychol. Assn., Am. Mgmt. Assn. Office: Fairfield U Psychology Dept Fairfield CT 06430

MCGRATH, THOMAS J., lawyer, writer, film producer; b. N.Y.C., Oct. 8, 1932; m. Mary Lee McGrath, Aug. 4, 1956 (dec.); children: Maura Lee, J. Connell; m. Diahn Williams, Sept. 28, 1974; 1 dau., Courtney C. B.A., NYU, 1956, J.D., 1960. Bar: N.Y. 1960. Assoc. Milbank, Tweed, Hadley & McCloy, N.Y.C., 1960-69; ptnr. Simpson, Thacher & Bartlett, N.Y.C., 1970—; lectr., writer Practicing Law Inst., 1976—, Am. Law Inst. ABA, 1976-81. Author: Carryover Basis Under Tax Reform Act, 1977; contbg. author: Estate and Gift Tax After ERTA, 1982; producer: feature film Deadly Hero, 1977. Served with U.S. Army, 1952-54, Korea. Fellow Am. Coll. Probate Counsel; mem. N.Y. State Bar Assn., ABA, Assn. Bar City N.Y. Home: 988 Fifth Ave New York NY 10021 Office: Simpson Thacher & Bartlett 425 Lexington Ave New York NY 10017

MCGRAW, JOHN PATRICK, journalist, music critic, broadcaster; b. Omaha, Mar. 20, 1947; s. Mac and Margaret (Higgins) McG.; m. Connie Ann Vondy, Sept. 12, 1976 (div. 1986); children—Charla, Colin. B.S. in Journalism, U. Colo. Staff writer Denver Post, 1969—, music critic, 1974—; show host KLZ radio, Denver, 1987—; contbg. writer Compuserve Info. Service, Columbus, Ohio, 1984-85, Colo. Country Connection. Chmn. Students for Kennedy, Colo., 1960; mem. Morgan County Arts Council. Recipient Story of Yr. award AP, Colo., 1984; named to Colo. Country Music Hall of Fame, 1985; Country Music Disk Jockey of Yr., 1987, 88. Mem. Country Mus. Assn., Colo. Country Music Assn., Bluegrass Music Assn. Colo., NAACP, Sigma Delta Chi. Democrat. Roman Catholic. Clubs: Boulder Press; Denver Press (News Story of Yr. award 1984). Office: Denver Post Box 1709 Denver CO 80201

MCGRAW, LAVINIA MORGAN, retail company executive; b. Detroit, Feb. 26, 1924; d. Will Curtis and Margaret Coulter (Oliphant) McG. AB, Radcliffe Coll., 1945. Sales assoc. The May Corp., Washington, 1977—. Mem. Phi Beta Kappa. Avocation: hiking. Home: 2501 Calvert St NW Washington DC 20008

MC GREGOR, DOUGLAS HUGH, pathologist, educator; b. Temple, Tex., Aug. 28, 1939; s. Harleigh Heath and Joyce Ellen (Lambert) McG.; m. Mizuki Kitani, July 6, 1969; children: Michelle Sakuya, David Kenji. BA, Duke U., 1961, MD, 1966; postgrad. U. Edinburgh, Scotland, 1961-62. Diplomate: Am. Bd. Pathology. Intern and chief resident in pathology UCLA Med. Ctr., Los Angeles, 1966-68; surgeon and lt. comdr. Atomic Bomb Casualty Commn., Hiroshima, Japan, 1968-71; chief resident in pathology Queens Med. Ctr., Honolulu, 1971-73; asst. and assoc. prof. pathology U. Kans. Med. Ctr., Kansas City, 1973-82, prof., 1982—; dir. anat. pathology VA Med. Ctr., Kansas City, Mo., 1975—. Contbr. numerous articles to profl. jours., chpts. to books. Leader YMCA Indian Princess Program, Overland Park, Kans., 1977-79, Indian Guide Program, 1978-80, Cub Scouts Am., Overland Park, 1980-82, Boy Scouts Am., Leawood, Kans., 1982—. Served as lt. comdr. USPHS, 1968-71; Japan. Grantee Merck, Sharp and Dohme, 1980, NIH, 1980. Fellow Coll. Am. Pathologists, Am. Soc. Clin. Pathologists; mem. Am. Assn. Pathologists, Internat. Acad. Pathologists, Soc. Exptl. Biology and Medicine, N.Y. Acad. Scis., AAAS, Kansas City Soc. Pathologists (sec.-treas. 1982-83, pres. 1983-84). Club Leawood Country. Research in biology and pathology of parathyroid hormone secretion; platelet-leukocyte aggregation; ultrastructure and pathobiology of neoplasms; radiation carcinogenesis; morphogenesis of atherosclerosis. Home: 9400 Lee Blvd Leawood KS 66206 Office: VA Medical Ctr 4801 Linwood Blvd Kansas City MO 64128

MCGREW, DAVID ROLLIN, manufacturing company executive; b. Uhrichsville, Ohio, July 9, 1936; s. Carl George and Mildred Elizabeth (Hall) McG.; m. Marilyn Dawn Heidt, Aug. 18, 1957 (div. June 1981); children: Michelle, Sean, Kristen. BS, Kent State U., 1958; cert. mktg. research, Columbia U., 1972. Tchr., coach Chardon (Ohio) High Sch., 1958-65; indsl. salesman Mystik Tape div. Borden Co., Columbus, Ohio, 1965-67; sales mgr. Mystik Tape div. Borden Co., Los Angeles, 1967-70; dir. sales, mktg. Mystik Tape div. Borden Co., Chgo., 1970-73; gen. sales mgr. W.H. Brady Co., Milw., 1973-77; owner, pres., chief exec. officer GEM-MAC Industries, Plymouth, Wis., 1977—; gen. ptnr., dir. GEM-MAC Assocs. & Factory Supply, Plymouth, Wis., 1983—. Active Rep. Presdl. Task Force, Washington, 1985—; pres., founder Cedarburg (Wis.) High Sch. Booster Club, 1983. Served with Ohio N.G., 1959-65. Named Coach of Yr., Northeast Ohio High Sch. Athletic Assn., 1963, Tchr. of Yr., Chardon High Sch., 1964, Mgr. of Yr., Borden Co., Los Angeles, 1969. Mem. Northeast Wis. Indsl. Council, Pressure Sensitive Tape Council (vice chmn. market devel. com. 1972-73). Republican. Clubs: Kent State Varsity, Kent State Alumni and Booster. Office: GEM-MAC Industries Inc 2100 Sunset Dr Plymouth WI 53073

MCGUINNESS, RAYMOND, radar meteorologist; b. London, Mar. 4, 1960; s. John and Patricia (Dooley) McG. BS in Electronics, Essex U., Colchester, Eng., 1981, PhD in Electronics, 1984. Lectr. Essex U., Colchester, 1984-85, research fellow in radio meteorology, 1985—. Contbr. articles to profl. jours. Mem. Soc. for Protection of Unborn Children. Mem. IEE. Social Democrat. Roman Catholic. Club: Crusaders (Colchester). Home: 27 Poplars Close, Colchester Essex C07 8BH, England Office: Essex U, Wivenhoe Park, Colchester Essex C04 3SQ, England

MCGUIRE, DENNIS EDWARD, construction executive; b. Lynn, Mass., Sept. 12, 1950; s. Thomas and June (Shoals) McG.; m. Jacqueline Kay Donn, Apr. 5, 1986; 1 child, Dennis Edward McGuire Jr. Student, Miami Dade Jr. Coll., 1973-75. Racing dir. Wheeling (W.Va.) Downs, 1976-77; pres. Adobe Constrn., Miami Lakes, 1977—; pres. franchise systems Crackers Restaurant, Miami Lakes, 1983—. Mem. United Cerebral Palsy Assn., Miami, 1985, Dolphin Booster Club; presiding judge Flagler Kennel Club, Miami, 1974-75. Served with USN, 1969-73. Recipient Clifford E. Butler award Fla. Nurseryman Growers Assn.,1984. Mem. Hialeah and Miami Springs C. of C. Democrat. Roman Catholic. Home: 7300 N Oakmont Dr Miami FL 33015 Office: Adobe Constrn 6447 Miami Lakes Dr E Suite 105 Miami Lakes FL 33014

MCGUIRE, PETER JAMES, chemical company executive; b. Sydney, New South Wales, Australia, Nov. 1, 1947; s. William James and Mavis (Barnes) McG.; m. Elizabeth Jill Shepherd, Dec. 2, 1971; children: Jock William, Rory John, Angus James. BS in Engring., U. Western Australia, Perth, 1968; MBA, U. New South Wales, Sydney, 1972. Engr. Pub. Works Dept., Perth, 1968-69, Fraser Cons., Perth, 1969; credit/mktg. rep. Citinational/FNCS, Sydney, 1972-74; mng. dir. McGuire Chemicals, Perth, 1974—. Mem. Australian Chem. Mfrs. Assn. Office: McGuire Chemicals, 23 Prindiville Ave Wanneroo, Perth, Western Australia 6065, Australia

MCGUIRE, THOMAS PETER, show boat captain; b. N.Y.C., Apr. 27, 1945; s. Thomas Edward and Susan Rose (Cafarelli) McG. B.A., Calif. State U., 1979, postgrad., 1979-83. co. mgr. Vaudeville Driftwood Floating Theatre, 1963-75; Tchr., St. Philip's Sch., Pasadena, Calif., 1981-83; prod. Driftwood Floating Theatre, 1968-75; owner, capt. Driftwood ShowBoat, Kingston, N.Y., 1983—; guest lectr. Hayden Planetarium, N.Y.C., 1960-64. Contbr. articles to profl. jours. Served with USN, 1966-68. Mem. Am. Guild Variety Artists, Soc. Am. Magicians. Roman Catholic. Avocations: writing; ballooning; astronomy. Home: care Driftwood Showboat Rt 213 on the Rondout at Eddyville PO Box 1032 Kingston NY 12401 Office: Driftwood Showboat PO Box 1032 Kingston NY 12401

MCGUIRL, MARLENE DANA CALLIS, law librarian, educator; b. Hammond, Ind., Mar. 22, 1938; d. Daniel David and Helen Elizabeth (Baludis) Callis; m. James Franklin McGuirl, Apr. 24, 1965. A.B., Ind. U., 1959; J.D., DePaul U., 1963; M.A.L.S., Rosary Coll., 1965; LL.M., George Washington U., 1978, postgrad. Harvard U., 1985. Bar: Ill. 1963, Ind. 1964, D.C. 1972. Asst., DePaul Coll. of Law Library, 1961-62, asst. law librarian, 1962-65; ref. law librarian Boston Coll. Sch. Law, 1965-66; library dir. D.C. Bar Library, 1966-70; asst. chief Am.-Brit. Law div. Law Library of Library of Congress, Washington, 1970, chief Am.-Brit. Law div., 1970—; library cons. Nat. Clearinghouse on Poverty Law, OEO, Washington, 1967-69, Northwestern U. Nat. Inst. Edn. in Law and Poverty, 1969, D.C. Office of Corp. Counsel, 1969-70; instr. law librarianship Grad. Sch. of U.S. Dept. of Agr., 1968-72; lectr. legal lit. Cath. U., 1972; adj. asst. prof., 1973—; lectr. environ. law George Washington U., 1979—; judge Nat. and Internat. Law Moot Ct. Competition, 1976-78; pres. Hamburger Heaven, Inc., Palm Beach, Fla., 1981—, L'Image de Marlene Ltd., 1986—, Clinique de Beauté Inc., 1987—, Heads & Hands Inc., 1987—, Horizon Design & Mfg. Co., Inc., 1987—; dir. Stoneridge Farm Inc., Gt. Falls, Va., 1984—. Mem. Georgetown Citizens Assn.; trustee D.C. Law Students in Ct.; del. Ind. Democratic Conv., 1964. Recipient Meritorious Service award Library of Congress, 1974, letter of commendation Dir. of Personnel, 1976, cert. of appreciation, 1981-84. Mem. ABA (facilities law library Congress com. 1976—), Fed. Bar Assn. (chpt. council 1972-76), Ill. Bar Assn., Women's Bar Assn. (pres. 1972-73, exec. bd. 1973-77, Outstanding Contbn. to Human Rights award 1975), D.C. Bar Assn., Am. Bar Found., Nat. Assn. Women Lawyers, Internat. Assn. Law Libraries, (exec. bd. 1973-77), Law Librarians Soc. of Washington (pres. 1971-73), Exec. Women in Govt. Clubs: Nat. Lawyers, Zonta. Contbr. articles profl. jours. Home: 3416 P St NW Washington DC 20007 Office: Am Brit Law Div Library Congress Washington DC 20540

MCGURK, DAN LOCKWOOD, investor, corporate director; b. Eufala, Ala., June 30, 1926; s. Herbert Lockwood and Mary (Bray) McG.; m. Frances Brady, Dec. 17, 1949 (div. Feb. 1962); children: Christine, Herbert L. II, W.A. Patrick, Michael F.; m. Shirley Reece, Nov. 27, 1963; children: Scott R. Cain, Kelly McGurk, Stacey McGurk. Student Tex. A&M U., 1943-45; BS, U.S. Mil. Acad., 1949; BA, Oxford U., 1952, MA, 1955. Commd. 2d lt. U.S. Air Force, 1949, advanced through grades to capt., 1954; resigned, 1958; v.p. Scantlin Electronics, Santa Monica, Calif., 1962-64; from v.p. to exec. v.p. Sci. Data Systems, El Segundo, Calif., 1964-69; pres. Xerox Data Systems, El Segundo, 1969-70; Computer Industry Assocs., Encino, Calif., 1972-75; assoc. dir. Exec. Office Pres., Office Mgmt. and Budget, Washington, 1976-77; chmn. Protype Corp. Sun Valley, Calif., 1983-84; pvt. investor, Woodland Hills, Calif., 1984—, Newport Beach, Calif.; chmn. Southland Title Corp., 1985—; bd. dirs. Datum, Inc., Anaheim, Calif., Fla. Fed. Savs. and Loan, St. Petersburg, Milton Roy Co., Saint Petersburg, Bowmar Instruments, Acton, Mass., Newport Corp., Fountain Valley, Calif. Editor: America Security Policy, 1959. Trustee Los Angeles County Mus. Found., Episcopal Theol. Sem., Claremont, Calif.; mem. exec. com. United Way, Los Angeles, 1974-83; vice chmn. ARC, Los Angeles, 1981-83; sr. warden St. Nicholas Ch., Encino, 1971-73, 79-82. Named Vol. of Yr., United Way, Los Angeles, 1983; Rhode's scholar Oxford U., 1949. Republican. Episcopalian. Clubs: Army Navy (Washington); Los Angeles Yacht; Newport Harbor Yacht; California. Home: 114 Via Lido Nord Newport Beach CA 92663 Office: 3471 ViaLido Newport Beach CA 92663

MCGURK, HARRY, psychology educator; b. Glasgow, Scotland, Feb. 23, 1936; s. Harry and Katherine (Gallagher) McG.; 1 child, Rhona. Diploma in Social Work, U. Glasgow, 1961; BA, U. Strathclyde, Glasgow, 1969, Phd, 1971. Probation officer City of Edinburgh, Scotland, 1961-63; edn. mgr. Presbyn. Ch. Nigeria, Ohafia, 1963-64; lectr. U. Surrey, Eng., 1973-76, sr. lectr., 1976-86, prof., 1986—; sec. gen. Internat. Soc. for Study of Behavior Devel., 1976-81; vis. prof. U. Minn., Mpls., 1981, 82, 85. Author, editor, contbr. numerous articles to profl. jours. Fellow Brit. Psychol. Soc.; mem. Soc. Research in Child Devel., Internat. Jour. for Behavioral Devel. (editor 1984—). Office: U Surrey, Dept Psychology, Guildford, Surrey 902 5XH, England

MC HARGUE, CARL JACK, research laboratory administr.; b. Corbin, Ky., Jan. 30, 1926; s. John David and Virginia (Thomas) McH.; B.S. in Metall. Engring., U. Ky., 1949, M.S., 1951, Ph.D., 1953; m. Edith Trovillion, Aug. 28, 1948; children—Anne Odell McHargue Diegel, Carol Virginia, Margaret Katherine McHargue Behrendt; m. 2d, Betty Ford, Sept. 30, 1960. Instr., U. Ky., Lexington, 1949-53; with Oak Ridge Nat. Lab., 1953—, sect. head, 1960-80, program mgr. for materials scis., 1961—; prof. metall. engring. U. Tenn., Knoxville, 1963—. Served with AUS, 1944-46. Fellow Metall. Soc. AIME, Am. Soc. for Metals; mem. Am. Nuclear Soc., Materials Research Soc., Sigma Xi, Tau Beta Pi. Republican. Presbyterian. Contbr. numerous articles in field to profl. jours. Home: 11517 Nassau Dr Farragut TN 37922 Office: Oak Ridge Nat Lab PO Box X Oak Ridge TN 37831

MCHARRIS, WILLIAM CHARLES, chemistry and physics educator, author; b. Knoxville, Tenn., Sept. 12, 1937; s. Garrett Clifford and Margaret Alice (Zimmerman) McH.; m. Orilla Ann Spangler, Aug. 27, 1960; 1 child, Louise Alice. BA, Oberlin Coll., 1959; PhD, U. Calif., 1965. Summer trainee Oak Ridge Nat. Lab., 1957-59; research student Lawrence Berkeley Lab., Calif., 1959-65; cons. Argonne Nat. Lab., 1965—; asst. prof. Mich. State U., East Lansing, 1965-68, assoc. prof., 1968-70, prof. chemistry, physics, 1970—; vis. prof., scientist Lawrence Berkeley Lab., 1970-71, 81—. Author: Into the Atom, 1985, Aria in the Key of Death, 1987, The Sciences of Chemistry , 1988; contbr. sci. articles to profl. jours. and popular mags.; composer organ, orchestral and choral works. Alfred E. Sloan fellow, 1971-75. Mem. Am. Chem. Soc., Am. Phys. Soc., Sigma Xi (Jr. Sci. award 1972). Congregationalist. Avocation: music. Home: 512 Beech St East Lansing MI 48823 Office: Mich State Univ Dept of Chemistry East Lansing MI 48824

MCHENRY, BARNABAS, lawyer; b. Harrisburg, Pa., Oct. 30, 1929; s. William Cecil and Louise (Perkins) McH.; m. Marie Bannon Jones, Dec. 13, 1952; children: Thomas J.P., W.H. Davis, John W.H. A.B., Princeton U., 1952; LL.B., Columbia U., 1957. Bar: N.Y. 1957. Assoc. Lord, Day, & Lord, N.Y.C., 1957-62; gen. counsel The Reader's Digest Assn., Inc., N.Y.C., 1962-85; exec. dir. Wallace Funds, N.Y.C., 1985-86. Contbr. articles to profl. jours. Trustee Boscobel Restoration, Inc., 1964, Am. Conservation Assn., 1977 Supreme Ct. Hist. Soc., 1980, Am. Mus. Nat. Hist., 1981, Hudson River Found. for Sci. and Environ. Research, Inc., 1981, Am. Nat. Theater at Kennedy Ctr., 1984, Hist. Hudson Valley Inc., 1984, Saratoga Performing Arts Ctr., 1984, Nat. Wildlower Research Ctr., 1985, N.Y. City Ballet, 1985, Glimmerglass Opera Theater, 1986; mem. N.Y. State Commn. on Restoration of Capitol, 1979; Membre Corr. Acad. des Beaux-Arts, Inst. de France, 1980; vice chmn. The Pres.' Com. on Arts and Humanitites, 1982; chmn. Empire State Plaza Art Commn., 1984; regent Smithsonian Inst., 1985; chmn. Empire State Performing Arts Ctr. Corp., 1985; chmn. Com. for Preservation Treasury Bldg., 1986; trustee Glimmerglass Opera, 1986; commr. Palisades Interstate Park Commn., 1987. Home: 164 E 72d St New York NY 10021

MC HENRY, MARTIN CHRISTOPHER, physician; b. San Francisco, Feb. 9, 1932; s. Merl and Marcella (Bricca) McH.; student U. Santa Clara (Calif.), 1950-53; M.D., U. Cin., 1957; M.S. in Medicine, U. Minn., Mpls., 1966; m. Patricia Grace Hughes, Apr. 27, 1957; children—Michael, Christopher, Timothy, Mary Ann, Jeffrey, Paul, Kevin, William, Monica, Martin Christopher. Intern, Highland Alameda County (Calif.) Hosp., Oakland, 1957-58; resident, internal medicine fellow Mayo Clinic, Rochester, Minn., 1958-61, spl. appointee in infectious diseases, 1963-64; staff physician infectious diseases Henry Ford Hosp., Detroit, 1964-67; staff physician Cleve. Clinic, 1967-72, head dept. infectious diseases, 1972—. Asst. clin. prof. Case Western Res. U., 1970-77, assoc. clin. prof. medicine, 1977—; asso. vis. physician Cleve. Met. Gen. Hosp., 1970—; cons. VA Hosp., Cleve., 1973—. Chmn. manpower com. Swine Influenza Program, Cleve., 1976. Served with USNR, 1961-63. Named Distinguished Tchr. in Medicine Cleve. Clinic, 1972; recipient 1st ann. Bruce Hubbard Stewart award Cleve. Clinic Found. for Humanities in Medicine, 1985. Diplomate Am. Bd. Internal Medicine. Fellow Infectious Diseases Soc. Am., A.C.P., Am. Coll. Chest Physicians (chmn. com. cardiopulmonary infections 1975-77, 81-83); mem. Am. Soc. Clin. Pharmacology and Therapeutics (chmn. sect. infectious diseases and antimicrobial agts., 1970-77, 80-85, dir.), Am. Thoracic Soc., Am. Soc. Clin. Pathologists, Royal Soc. Medicine of Great Britain (asso.), Am. Fedn. Clin. Research, Am. Soc. Tropical Medicine and Hygiene, Am. Soc. Microbiology, N.Y. Acad. Scis. Contbr. numerous articles to profl. jours., also chpts. to books. Home: 2779 Belgrave Rd Pepper Pike OH 44124 Office: 9500 Euclid Ave Cleveland OH 44106

MC ILHANY, STERLING FISHER, publishing company executive; b. San Gabriel, Calif., Apr. 12, 1930; s. William Wallace and Julia (Fisher) M. B.F.A. with high honors, U. Tex., 1953; postgrad. UCLA, 1953-54, 55-57, Universita per Stranieri, Perugia, Italy, 1957, Accademia delle Belle Arti, Rome, 1957-58. Teaching asst., lectr. in art history UCLA, 1953-54, 55-57; art supr. Kamehameha Prep. Sch., Honolulu, 1954-55; instr. Honolulu Acad. Arts, 1955; assoc. editor Am. Artist mag., N.Y.C., 1958-61, editor, 1969-70; host Books and the Artist network series Sta. WRVR, N.Y.C., 1961-62; sr. editor Reinhold Book Corp., N.Y.C., 1962-69; pres. IFOTA Inc., Los Angeles, 1981—; instr. Sch. Visual Arts, N.Y.C., 1961-69. Fellow Christ Coll., Cambridge. Author: Banners and Hangings, 1966; Art as Design—Design as Art, 1970; Wood Inlay, 1972; Simbari, 1975; also articles. Recipient First award tour European art ctrs. Students Internat. Travel Assn., 1952; Rotary fellow Accademia delle Belle Arti, 1957-58. Fellow Internat. Inst. Community Service London; mem. Nat. Soc. Lit. and Arts, Human Resource USA. Roman Catholic. Address: 6376 Yucca St Los Angeles CA 90028

MCILROY, HARRY ALEXANDER (BARON DI NOVARA), merchant banker; b. Belfast, No. Ireland, May 17, 1940; s. Henry and Harriet (Cooke) McI.; m. Winifred McKeown, Sept. 6, 1971; children—Catherine Harriet, Nicholas Henry Christopher. Owner, founder, chmn. bd. dirs. Unico Group Ltd., 1979—; underwriter Lloyd's of London, 1979—; mem. Internat. Fin. Futures Exchange, Bermuda, 1980—. Freeman, City of London. Mem. Worshipful Co. Basketmakers (liveryman), Worshipful Co. Marketors. Clubs: Carlton, East India, City Livery (London). Home: PO Box 1465, Dublin 4 Ireland

MC ILVEEN, WALTER, mechanical engineer; b. Belfast, Ireland, Aug. 12, 1927; s. Walter and Amelia (Thompson) McI.; came to U.S., 1958, naturalized, 1963; M.E., Queens U., Belfast, 1948; H.V.A.C., Borough Polytechnic, London, 1951; m. Margaret Teresa Ruane, Apr. 17, 1949; children—Walter, Adrian, Peter, Anita, Alan. Mech. engr. Davidson & Co., Belfast, 1943-48; sr. contract engr. Keith Blachman Ltd., London, 1948-58; mech. engr. Fred S. Dubin Assos., Hartford, Conn., 1959-64; chief mech. engr. Koton & Donovan, W. Haven, Conn., 1964-66; prin., engr. Walter McIlveen Assos., Avon, Conn., 1966—. Mem. IEEE, Illuminating Engring. Soc., ASME, Hartford Engring. Club, Conn. Engrs. in Pvt. Practice, ASHRAE. Mem. Ch. of Ireland. Home: 3 Valley View Rd Weatogue CT 06089 Office: 195 W Main St Avon CT 06001

MCILWRAITH, CYRIL WAYNE, veterinary surgery educator; b. Oamaru, New Zealand, Dec. 12, 1947; came to U.S., 1975; s. Cyril Alfred and Kathleen Avaca (O'Grady) McI.; m. Nancy Lynn Goodman, June 22, 1984. DVM, Massey U., Palmerston North, New Zealand, 1970; MS, Purdue U., 1977, PhD, 1979. Diplomate Am. Coll. Vet. Surgeons. Resident in vet. surgery Purdue U., West Lafayette, Ind., 1975-77, instr., 1977-79; asst. prof. equine surgery Colo. State U., Ft. Collins, 1979-81, assoc. prof., 1981-86, prof., 1986—; cons. surgeon. equine vet. practices, 1981—. Author: (textbook) Techniques in Large Animal Surgery ,1982; Diagnostic and Surgical Arthroscopy in the Horse, 1984, Advanced Techniques in Equine Surgery, 1986; pioneered the technique of arthroscopic surgery in the horse. Recipient Colo. State U. Am. Assn. Equine Practitioners Faculty award for Teaching Equine Medicine and Surgery, 1982, Colo. State U. Alumni Outstanding Faculty award, 1983. Mem. AVMA, Royal Coll. Vet. Surgeons, Am. Assn. Vet. Surgeons, Colo. Vet. Med. Assn., Am. Assn. Equine Practitioners, Vet. Orthopedic Soc. Home: 108 Blueridge Ct Fort Collins CO 80524 Office: Colo State U Vet Teaching Hosp 300 W Drake Fort Collins CO 80523

MCINALLY, THOMAS, industrial relations specialist; b. Glasgow, Scotland, Nov. 11, 1942; s. Thomas and Jean (Gallaher) McI.; m. Judith Ann Hancock, Dec. 21 1963; children: Fiona Anne, Neil Thomas. BS, Glasgow U., 1966. Indsl. engr. Formica Ltd., Tynemouth, Eng., 1966-68; deputy indsl. engring. mgr. Sterling Drug, Newcastle, Eng., 1968-70; indsl. engring. mgr. Guardbridge Papers Ltd., St. Andrews, Scotland, 1970-76; personnel mgr. Goodyear Tyre & Rubber Co., Glasgow, 1976-79; personnel, indsl. engring. mgr. MSA (Britain) Ltd., Coatbridge, Scotland, 1979—. Club: RSCDS (West Dunbartonshire)(sec. 1983-85). Office: MSA Britain Ltd, East Shawhead, Coatbridge ML5 4TD, Scotland

MCINERNEY, JAMES EUGENE, JR., association executive; b. Springfield, Mass., Aug. 3, 1930; s. James Eugene and Rose Elizabeth (Adikes) McI.; m. Mary Catherine Hill, July 17, 1963; children: Anne Elizabeth, James Eugene, III. B.S., U.S. Mil. Acad., 1952; M.S. in Engring., Princeton U., 1960; postgrad., Royal Air Force Staff Coll., 1964; M.S. in Internat. Affairs, George Washington U., 1970. Commd. 2d lt. USAF, 1952, advanced through grades to maj. gen., 1976; fighter pilot Korea, Japan and Ger.; comdr. tactical fighter squadron Thailand, 1967; tactical fighter wing Ger., 1971; sr. U.S. adviser Turkish Air Force, 1973; dir. mil. assistance and sales Hdqrs. USAF, 1975-78; comdt. Indsl. Coll. Armed Forces, 1978-79; dir. programs Hdqrs. USAF, 1979-80, asst. dep. chief of staff for programs and evaluation, 1980; dir. legis. liaison McDonnell Douglas Corp., Washington, 1980-83, dir. internat. affairs, 1983-86; v.p. Am. League for Exports and Security Assistance, 1986—. Decorated Air Force Cross, D.S.M. (2), Silver Star (3), D.F.C. (7), Bronze Star, Meritorious Service medal (2), Air medal (18), Air Force Commendation medal; Vietnamese Crosses of Gallantry with palm and star; Republic of Korea Cheongsu medal. Mem. Air Force Assn. (citation of honor 1968). Roman Catholic. Home: 1031 Delf Dr McLean VA 22101

MCINNIS, EMMETT EMORY, JR., lawyer; b. McAlester, Okla., Sept. 12, 1920; s. Emmett Emory and Helen Franc (Kohler) M.; m. Howardine Muse McAteer, Nov. 5, 1949; children—Howard Emmett (dec.), Guy Bruce, Susan Muse. B.S. in History, Northwestern U., 1945; LL.B., Yale U., 1948. Bar: Wash. 1951, Seattle-King County 1951, U.S. Supreme Ct. 1958. Sole practice Seattle, 1951—; lectr. in trust and probate. Mem., Exchange Club, Seattle, pres., 1956; mem. Republican Nat. Com., 1981—; mem. Estate Planning Council, Seattle, 1954—, pres., 1973. Mem. Seattle Power Squadron (comdr. 1971), Northwestern U. Alumni Assn. Western Wash. (pres. 1965), Nat. Rifle Assn., Purple Key, Computer Groups, Delta Tau Delta. Republican. Presbyterian. (elder 1961—). Club: Wash. Athletic (Seattle). Home: 5515 NE Penrith Rd Seattle WA 98105

MCINTOSH, LOUISA AICHEL, interior design firm and art gallery executive; b. Atlanta, June 1, 1925; d. Siegfried Louis and Margaret Katura (Rosser) Aichel; m. Alexander Preston McIntosh, Sept. 2, 1947 (dec. Jan. 1966); children: Alexa Louis McIntosh Selph, Preston Stuckey, Peter Aichel, Patricia Amelia. BA, Agnes Scott Coll. Owner Louisa McIntosh Interiors, Atlanta, 1967—; owner, dir. McIntosh Gallery, Atlanta, 1982—; design cons. Fed. Res. Bank, Atlanta, 1975-78, Sci. Atlanta, 1976-80, English Lang. Sch., Atlanta, 1980-82, Nat. Bank of Ga., 1984-85, Lantel Co., 1985. Treas., life mem. Midtown Bus. Assn., Atlanta, 1978, pres., 1979; trustee Atlanta Pub. Library, vice chmn. bd., 1981-82; trustee Atlanta Fulton Pub. Library, chmn. bd., 1983-85. Mem. Inst. Bus. Design, Women Bus. Owners. Episcopalian. Home: 75 Inman Circle NE Atlanta GA 30309 Office: Louisa McIntosh Interiors 1421 Peachtree St NE Atlanta GA 30309

MCINTOSH, RHODINA COVINGTON, lawyer, international development analyst; b. Chicago Heghts, Ill., May 26, 1947; d. William George and Cora Jean (Cain) Covington; m. Gerald Alfred McIntosh, Dec. 14, 1970; children: Gary Allen, Garvey Anthony, Ayana Kai. BA cum laude, Mich. State U., 1969; JD, U. Detroit, 1978. Asst. to dir. equal opportunity program Mich. State U., East Lansing, 1969-70; law clk. Bell & Hudson, P.C., Detroit, 1977-79; main rapporteur 1st All-Africa Law Conf., U. Swaziland and Botswana, 1981, lectr., 1981-83; chief info. and tech. assistance Office Pvt. and Vol. Cooperation, U.S. AID, Washington, 1983-87, chief info. and program support, 1987-88; corp. counsel Automated Research Systems Ltd., Alexandria, Va., 1988—; founding bd. mem. Women's Justice Ctr., Detroit, 1975-77; coordinator women's leadership conf. Wayne State U., Detroit, 1979, participant confs. and workshops. Contbr. articles and documents to profl. publs. Rep. coordinator urban program, Lansing, Mich., 1979-81; chair fgn. relations subcom. Nat. Black Women's Polit. Caucus, Washington, 1984; bd. dirs. Mayor's Com. to Keep Detroit Beautiful, 1980, Detroit Urban League, 1981, Am. Opportunity Found., Washington, 1984—. Nat. Achievement scholar Ednl. Testing Service, Princeton, N.J., 1965, Martin Luther King Jr. Ctr. for Social Change scholar, Atlanta, 1976; recipient Detroit Edison award, 1980, New Repubs. award, Mich., 1981, Disting. Leadership award ABI, 1987. Mem. Nat. Assn. Female Execs., GOP Women's Network, Delta Sigma Theta. Roman Catholic.

MCINTOSH, WILLIAM ANDREW, otorhinolaryngologist; b. Pretoria, Transvaal, Republic of South Africa, Dec. 2, 1944; s. William Wallace Morrison and Jacoba (Burger) McI.; m. Denise Elizabeth Meyer, Feb. 8, 1972; 1 child, Candace Elizabeth. B in Medicine, M in Surgery, U. Pretoria, Republic of South Africa, 1967. Med. officer Inst. Aviation Medicine, Pretoria, Republic of South Africa, 1969; registrar otorhinolaryngology Johannesburg Hosp., Republic of South Africa, 1969-72, registrar neurosurgery, 1973; sr. surgeon Pietersburg Hosp., Transvaal, Republic of South Africa, 1973-76; head otolaryngology Baragwanath Hosp., Johannesburg, Republic of South Africa, 1977; prin. surgeon Johannesburg Hosp., 1977-86; prof., head otorhinolaryngology U. Witwatersrand, Johannesburg, 1986—; chief surgeon Johannesburg Group Teaching Hosps., 1986—; bd. dirs. Balmac Timbers and Hardware, Pretoria; bd. dirs., cons. Kos Health Care Mgmt. Consultancy, Johannesburg, 1987—; sec., founder South African Hearing Found., Johannesburg, 1986—. Contbr. articles to profl. jours. Served to col. Republic of South Africa Med. Service. Decorated Southern Cross medal South African Def. Force, 1986. Fellow Coll. Medicine South Africa, Royal Coll. Surgeons (Edinburgh), Royal Coll. Physicians and Surgeons (Glasgow chpt.), ACS; mem. Assn. Mil. Surgeons of U.S. (life), Am. Soc. Head and Neck Surgery, Soc. Head and Neck Surgeons, Am. Acad. Facial Plastic and Reconstructive Surgeons, South African Aerospace Med. Soc. (life), South African Soc. Otorhinolaryngology (exec. mem.) , South African Head and Neck Oncology Soc. (exec. mem.), South African Med. Informatics Group (founder), South African Assn. Med. Edn. (founder), Med. Assn. South Africa, Internat. Skull Base Soc. (founder), Lighthouse Club (hon. mem.). Office: Univ of Witwatersrand, York Rd Parktown, Johannesburg 2193, Republic of South Africa

MCINTYRE, DONALD CONROY, opera singer, baritone; b. Auckland, New Zealand, Oct. 22, 1934; s. George D. and Hermyn McI.; m. Jill Redington, 1961; 3 children. Student, Auckland Tchrs. Tng. Coll., Guildhall Sch. Music, London. Prin. bass Sadler's Wells Opera, London, 1960-67, Royal Opera House-Covent Garden, London, 1967—. Appeared at Bayreuth Festival, 1967-81, 87, 88; frequent internat. guest appearances maj. opera houses; roles include: Wotan and Wanderer (Der Ring), Dutchman (Der Fliegende Hollander), Telramund (Lohengrin), Barak (Die Frau ohne Schatten), Pizzaro (Fidelio), Golaud (Pelleas et Melisande), Kurwenal (Tristan and Isold), Gurnemanz, Klingsor and Amfortas (Parsifal), Heyst (Victory), Jochanaan (Salome), Macbeth, Scarpia (Tosca), the County/Marriage of Figaro), Nick Shadow (The Rake's Progress), Hans Sachs (Die Meistersinger), Dr. Schone (Woyzeck), Cardillac (Cardillac Hindemith), Kasper (Der Frieshutz) Rocco (Fidelio); recs. include Pelleas et Melisande, Oedipus Rex, Il Torvatore, Parsifal, The Ring Damnation of Faust, Messiah Beethoven's 9th. Decorated Order of Brit. Empire. Home: Foxhill Farm, Jackass Ln, Keston BRG 2AN, England Office: care of, Ingpen and Williams, 14 Kensington Ct, London W8, England

MCINTYRE, DOUGLAS CARMICHAEL, II, lawyer; b. Lumberton, N.C., Aug. 6, 1956; s. Douglas Carmichael and Thelma Riley (Hedgpeth) McI.; m. Lola Denise Strickland, June 26, 1982; children: Joshua Carmichael, Stephen Christopher. BA, U. N.C., 1978, JD, 1981. Bar: N.C. 1981, U.S. Dist. Ct. (ea. dist.) N.C. 1984, U.S. Dist. Ct. (mid. dist.) N.C. 1985., U.S. Ct. Appeals (4th cir.) 1987, U.S. Supreme Ct., 1987. Assoc. Law Office Bruce Huggins, Lumberton, 1981-82, McLean, Stacy, Henry & McLean, Lumberton, 1982-86; ptnr. Price & McIntyre P.A., Lumberton, 1987—; mem. law-focused edn. adv. com. N.C. Dept. Pub. Instrn., 1986-87. Del. Dem. Nat. Conv., N.Y.C., 1980, N.C. Dems., Raleigh, 1974—; pres. Robeson County Young Dems., Lumberton, 1982; sec., treas. 7th Congl. Dist. Young Dems., N.C., 1983, chmn., 1984; 2d vice chmn. 7th Congl. Dist. Dems. So. N.C., 1986—; mem. state adv. bd. North Carolinians Against Drug and Alcohol Abuse, Raleigh, 1984-85; chmn. Morehead Scholarship Selection Com., Robeson County, 1985—; deacon Presbyn. Ch.; active Boy Scouts Am., Lumberton, 1983; mem. N.C. Commn. on Children and Youth; mem. Young Life Lumberton com., 1987—; chmn. Robeson County U.S. Constn. Bicentennial com., 1986-87; mem. lawyers' adv. com. to N.C. Commn. on Bicentennial of U.S. Constn., 1986—; bd. dirs. Robeson County Group Home, Lumberton, 1984-87, Lumberton Econ. Advancement for Downtown, Inc., 1987—, pres. 1988; mem. N.C. Mus. of History Assocs., 1987—, Internat. Platform Assn., 1988—. Morehead Found. scholar, 1974-78; named one of Outstanding Young Men in Am., 1981, 84, 85; Outstanding Young Dem. Robeson County Young Dems., 1984-85; one of State's Outstanding Young Dems. Young Dems. N.C., 1984, 85; recipient Algernon Sydney Sullivan award U. N.C., 1978, Outstanding Young North Carolinian award N.C. Jaycees, 1988, Outstanding Young North Carolinians, N.C. Jaycees, 1988. Nat. Bicentennial Leadership award for Individual Achievement Council for Advancement of Citizenship and Ctr. for Civic Edn., Washington, 1987. Mem. ABA (exec. com. citizenship edn. com. 1985—, nat. community law week com. 1982-83), Internat. Platform Assn., N.C. Bar Assn. (chmn. youth edn. and constn. bicentennial com. 1986-87, youth edn. com., exec. council young lawyers div. 1986-87), Robeson County Bar Assn. (founder, chmn. citizenship edn. com. 1983—, law day com.), 16th Jud. Dist. Bar Assn., N.C. Acad. Trial Lawyers, N.C. Coll. Advocacy, Christian Legal Soc. (state adv. bd 1986—, state pres. 1987), Lumberton C. of C. (legis. affairs and edn. coms., membership drive), Order of Old Well, Phi Beta Kappa, Phi Eta Sigma. Home: 1701 N Chestnut St Lumberton NC 28358 Office: Price & McIntyre PA 102 Elizabethtown Rd Lumberton NC 28358

MCINTYRE, JOAN CAROL, computer software company executive, author; b. Portchester, N.Y., Mar. 1, 1939; d. John Henry and Molly Elizabeth (Gates) Daugherty; m. Stanley Donald McIntyre, Aug. 24, 1957 (div. Jan. 1986); children—Michael Stanley, David John, Sharon Lynne. Student Northwestern U., 1956-57, U. Ill., 1957-58. Assoc. editor Writer's Digest, Cin., 1966-68; instr. creative writing U. Ala.-Huntsville, 1975; editor Strode Pubs., Huntsville, 1974-75; paralegal Smith, Huckaby & Graves (now Bradley, Arant, Rose & White), Huntsville, 1976-82; exec. v.p. Micro Craft, Inc., Huntsville, 1982-85, pres., 1985—; also dir. and co-owner. Author 8 computer-operating mans. for law office software, 1978-85; co-author: Alabama and Federal Complaint Forms, 1979; Alabama and Federal Motion and Order Forms, 1980; also numerous articles, short stories, poems, 1955-84. Editor: Alabama Law for the Layman, 1975. Bd. dirs. Huntsville Lit. Soc., 1976-77. Hon. scholar Medill Sch. Journalism, Northwestern U., 1956. Republican. Methodist. Office: Micro Craft Inc 688 Discovery Dr Huntsville AL 35806

MCINTYRE, KAYE MARIE, nonprofit organization executive, consultant; b. Hartford, Conn., Oct. 13, 1950; d. Richard Arthur and Helen Marie (von Richter) Tillotson; m. Daniel Brian McIntyre, Feb. 21, 1969; (div. Dec. 1979). AS in Human Services, N.W. Conn. Community Coll., Winsted, 1983; BSBA, Charter Oak Coll., Hartford, 1985; postgrad. Wesleyan U., Middletown, Conn., 1987—. Counselor McCall House, Torrington, Conn., 1979-80; freelance photographer, Torrington, 1980—; exec. dir. Warner Theatre, Torrington, 1982-84; exec. dir. Elderly Health Screening Service, Inc., Waterbury, Conn., 1982—; cons. in field. Asst. coordinator Conn. Earth Action Group, Litchfield, 1971; regional coordinator Conn. Citizens Action Group, Litchfield County, Conn., 1971-72; pres. N.W. Conn. Assn. for the Arts, Inc., Torrington, 1981-84; bd. dirs. Torrington Trust for Historic Preservation, Inc., 1981—; 6th dist. coordinator Office of Protection and Advocacy for the Handicapped and Developmentally Disabled, Litchfield County, 1982; chairperson adult programming com. YWCA of Waterbury, 1985—; v.p. Thomaston Opera House Found., 1985—. Recipient citation Conn. Soc. Prevention of Blindness, 1984; citation Conn. Gen. Assembly, 1984, 86; Project Health award, U.S. Dept. HHS Adminstrn aging, 1986; Secs. Excellence award U.S. Dept. HHS Community Health Promotion Program, 1986. Mem. Nat. Assn. Female Execs., Am. League Hist. Theatres, Community Assocs. of Conn., Inc. (bd. dirs.), Am. Pub. Health Assn., Nat. Assn. Fundraising Execs., Am. Soc. on Aging, Gerontological Soc. Am., Nat. Council on Aging, Conn. Assn. Hist. Theatres (pres. 1984—), Internat. Platform Assn., Nat. Trust for Hist. Preservation. Republican. Taoist. Club: Mensa (Litchfield County coordinator). Avocations: photography, writing, hiking. Office: Elderly Health Screening Service Inc 24 Central Ave Waterbury CT 06702

MCINTYRE, ROBERT MALCOLM, utility company executive; b. Portland, Oreg., Dec. 18, 1923; married. B.A., UCLA, 1950. Gen. sales mgr. So. Counties Gas Co. Calif., 1952-70; with So. Calif. Gas Co. (subs. Pacific Lighting Corp.), Los Angeles, 1970-74, v.p., asst. to chmn., then sr. v.p., 1974-80, former pres., from 1980, now chmn., chief exec. officer, also dir. Office: So Calif Gas Co 810 S Flower St Los Angeles CA 90017

MCJUNKIN, JAMES D., business consultant; b. Asheville, N.C., Nov. 5, 1931; s. Ambrose Milton and Lillian M. (McJunkin) Ducker; BA in Social Sci., Western Carolina U., 1954; postgrad. U. Calif., 1963-65. With Nat. Can Corp., Chgo., 1961-65; dir. corp. indsl. relations Rollins, Inc., Atlanta, 1968-70; ptnr., prin. Ennis & McJunkin Partnership, Signal Hill, Calif., 1970—; mng. ptnr. Ennis & McJunkin /DEWCO, 1986—; bd. dirs., treas. Nat. Systmes Group, Inc., Signal Hill, Calif., 1987—. Served with AUS, 1954-56. Democrat. Quaker. Office: 1813 Redondo Ave Signal Hill CA 90804

MC KASSON, ROBERT EDWARD, JR., insurance sales executive; b. Los Angeles, Feb. 3, 1945; s. Robert E. and Verda C. (White) McK. A.A., Fullerton Coll., 1967. Salesman various life ins. cos., 1967—; pres., chmn. bd. Ind. Bankers Ins. Services, Newport Beach, Calif., 1977—. Recipient Gold medal ins. sales awards, 1976, 78; Bronze medal Investors Guaranty Life, 1979. Mem. 6 Million Dollar Forum. Club: 20-30. Featured in Nat. Underwriter, Aug. 1983. Avocation: horse breeding. Home and Office: 124-31st St Newport Beach CA 92663-3004

MC KAUGHAN, HOWARD PAUL, linguistics educator; b. Canoga Park, Calif., July 5, 1922; s. Paul and Edith (Barton) McK.; A.B., UCLA, 1945; M.Th., Dallas Theol. Sem., 1946; M.A., Cornell U., 1952, Ph.D., 1957; m. Barbara Jean Budroe, Dec. 25, 1943; children—Edith (Mrs. Daniel Skene Santoro), Charlotte (Mrs. Martin Douglas Barnhart), Patricia (Mrs. Stephen B. Pike), Barbara (Mrs. Ronald Chester Bell), Judith (Mrs. Frank L. Achilles III). Mem. linguistic research team Summer Inst. Linguistics, Mexico, 1946-52; asso. dir. Summer Inst. Linguistics, Philippines, also assoc. dir. summer sessions U. N.D., 1952-57, dir. Philippine br., 1957-61; research asst. prof. anthropology U. Wash., 1961-62; research assoc. prof., 1962-63; assoc. prof. linguistics U. Hawaii, 1963-64, prof. linguistics, 1964-88, prof. emeritus, 1988—, chmn. dept., 1963-66, dir. Pacific and Asian Linguistics Inst., 1964, 1966-69, assoc. dean grad. div., 1965-72, dean grad. div., dir. research, 1972-79, acting chancellor, 1979, interim vice chancellor acad. affairs, 1981-82, acting dir research, 1982-84, acting dean grad. div., 1982-83, dean, 1984-87, dir. research relations, 1987-88; lectr. linguistics U. Philippines, summers, 1954, 60; Fulbright vis. prof. Philippine Normal Coll.-Ateneo Consortium, Philippines, 1977; prin. Wycliffe Sch. Linguistics, summers 1953, 61; vis. prof. Australian Nat. U., Canberra, 1970; adj. prof. linguistics U. Okla., summers 1984, 85, 86. Sr. scholar East-West Center, Honolulu, 1964; NDEA Maranao-Philippines research grantee, 1963-65; Office of Edn. Hawaii English grantee, 1965-66; NSF Jeh Language of South Vietnam grantee, 1969-70, Maranao Linguistic Studies, 1971-72, numerous other research grants. Mem. linguistic socs. Am., Philippines, Western Assn. Grad. Schs. (pres. 1978), Hawaii, Linguistic Circle N.Y., Philippine Assn. Lang. Tchrs., Hawaii Govt. Employees Assn., Phi Beta Kappa, Phi Kappa Phi. Author (with B. McKaughan): Chatino Dictionary, 1951; (with J. Forster) Ilocano: An Intensive Language Course, 1952; The Inflection and Syntax of Maranao Verbs, 1959; (with B. Macaraya): A Maranao Dictionary, 1967. Editor: Pali Language Texts: Philippines, 21 vols., 1971; The Languages of the Eastern Family of the East New Guinea Highlands Stock, 1973. Contbr. articles, chpts. to books, sci. jours. Home: 420 S Hill Rd McMinnville OR 97128

MCKAY, DIXIE ANN, educational administrator; b. Toledo, Oreg., Nov. 25, 1946; d. Ralph Warren and Dixie June (Knudsen) Deming; m. James William McKay, June 14, 1969. B.S., Oreg. Coll. Edn., 1969; M.Edn., U. Guam, 1973; postgrad. UCLA, 1980-85. Tchr. Salem Pub. Schs., Oreg., 1968-71, Govt. Guam, Agana, 1971-78; tchr. Saudi Arabian Internat. Sch., Dhahran, 1978-79, asst. prin., 1979-81, prin., 1982-84, area supt., 1984—; mem. accreditation team Middle States Assn. Schs. and Colls., Phila., 1981-86. Contbr. articles to newspapers. Mem. Am. Assn. Sch. Adminstrs., Assn. Supervision and Curriculum Devel., Exec. Females Assn. Republican. Avocations: scuba diving; sailing; ham radio; sewing; travel. Home: Saudi Arabian Internat Schs Jubail, PO Box 10059, Madinat Al-Jubail Al-Sinaiyah, Jubail 31961, Saudi Arabia also: 1047 SE Holly Rd Toledo OH 97391

MCKAY, DONALD ARTHUR, mechanical contractor; b. Providence, June 10, 1931; s. Benjamin Arthur and Florence (Heeney) McK.; m. Janette Capellaro, Dec. 30, 1978; children by previous marriage: Susan Kelly, Barbara Albury, Laura Lower, Douglas. AB, Harvard U., 1952. Registered profl. engr., Mass. Sales engr. C.P. Blouin, Cambridge, Mass., 1955-60; contract mgr. to v.p. Limbach Co., Boston, 1960-68; exec. v.p. Tougher Heating & Plumbing Co., Albany, N.Y., 1968-74; chmn., chief exec. officer Tougher Industries, Albany, 1986—, pres., 1974-86; bd. dirs. Home and City Savs. Bank; v.p. Spunduct Inc. Pres. Fifty Group of Columbia County, 1972-74; mem. corp. gifts com. Albany Med. Ctr., 1978-84; chmn. 25th reunion fund raising com. of upstate N.Y., Harvard Class '52; mem. curriculum adv. bd. Hudson Valley Community Coll.; chmn. bd. trustees Meml. Hosp.

Served with USN, 1951-54. Mem. ASHRAE, Nat. Soc. Profl. Engrs., Mech. Contractors Assn. Am. (pres. capital dist. 1981-82, asst. treas., pres. elect), Mech. Contractors Assn. N.Y. State (v.p. 1981-82, pres. 1981-82), Aircraft Owners and Pilots Assn., Exptl. Aircraft Assn. Congregationalist. Clubs: Harvard (pres. N.E. N.Y. chpt. 1987—), Ft. Orange (Albany); Masons (Dorchester, Mass.); Wolferts Roost Country. Home: 6 Park Ridge Menands NY 12204 Office: Tougher Industries 175 Broadway PO Box 4067 Albany NY 12204

MCKAY, KENNETH LESLIE, retired university professor, researcher in ancient Greek; b. Sydney, Australia, Feb. 5, 1922; s. Herbert Leslie and Florrie (Evans) McK.; m. Margaret Lesley Short, Jan. 17, 1948; children: Graham Richard, Lesley Robyn Earp, Alison Margaret Hoare, Elspeth Anne Ferguson, Katherine Ruth Hainsworth, Fiona Jean Conacher, Bruce Duncan. BA, U. Sydney, 1948, U. Cambridge, 1950; MA, U. Cambridge, 1955. Lectr. in classics U. Coll., Ibadan, Nigeria, 1950-56, Victoria U., Wellington, New Zealand, 1956-61; exchange lectr. in classics U. Leicester (Eng.), 1983-84; sr. lectr. in classics The Australian Nat. U., Canberra, 1961-65, reader in classics, 1965-87, head dept. of classics, 1976-78, 87, retired, 1987; invited contbr. Kühner Sesqui Centenary Colloqium U. Amsterdam, The Netherlands, 1986. Author: Greek Grammar for Students, 1974, 77; contbr. articles to profl. jours. Served with Australian Army, World War II, 1942-45. Mem. Australian Soc. Classical Studies (hon. sec. 1966-70, pres. 1971-72, v.p. 1973-74), Tyndale Fellowship for Biblical Research. Anglican. Home and Office: 41 Rawson St, Deakin 2600, Australia

MCKAY, RENEE, artist; b. Montreal, Que., Can.; came to U.S., 1946, naturalized, 1954; d. Frederick Garvin and Mildred Gladys (Higgins) Smith; B.A., McGill U., 1941; m. Kenneth Gardiner McKay, July 25, 1941; children—Margaret Craig, Kenneth Gardiner. Tchr. art Peck Sch., Morristown, N.J., 1955-56; one woman shows: Pen and Brush Club, N.Y.C., 1957, Cosmopolitan Club, N.Y.C., 1958; group shows include: Weyhe Gallery, N.Y.C., 1978, Newark Mus., 1955, 59, Montclair (N.J.) Mus., 1955-58, Nat. Assn. Women Artists, Nat. Acad. Galleries, 1954-78, N.Y. World's Fair, 1964-65, Audubon Artists, N.Y.C., 1955-62, 74-79, N.Y. Soc. Women Artists, 1979-80, Provincetown (Mass.) Art Assn. and Mus., 1975-79; traveling shows in France, Belgium, Italy, Scotland, Can., Japan; represented in permanent collections: Slater Meml. Mus., Norwich, Conn., Norfolk (Va.) Mus., Butler Inst. Am. Art, Youngstown, Ohio, Lydia Drake Library, Pembroke, Mass., many pvt. collections. Recipient Jane Peterson prize in oils Nat. Assn. Women Artists, 1954, Famous Artists Sch. prize in watercolor, 1959, Grumbacher Artists Watercolor award, 1970; Solo award Pen and Brush, 1957; Sadie-Max Tesser award in watercolor Audubon Artists, 1975, Peterson prize in oils, 1980; Michael Engel prize Nat. Soc. Painters in Casein and Acrylic, 1983. Mem. Nat. Assn. Women Artists (2d v.p. 1969-70, adv. bd. 1974-76), Audubon Artists (pres. 1979, dir. oils 1986-88), Artist Equity (dir. 1977-79, v.p. 1979-81), N.Y. Soc. Women Artists, Pen and Brush, Nat. Soc. Painters in Casein and Acrylic M.J. Kaplan prize 1984, Nat. Arts Club, Provincetown Art Assn. and Mus. Club: Cosmopolitan. Address: 200 E 66 St New York NY 10021

MC KAY, SAMUEL LEROY, clergyman; b. nr. Charlotte, N.C., Oct. 15, 1913; s. Elmer Ranson and Arlena (Benfield) McK.; A.B. cum laude, Erskine Coll., 1937; B.D. cum laude, Erskine Theol. Sem., 1939; postgrad. U. Ga., 1941-42, Union Theol. Sem., 1957; m. Martha Elizabeth Caldwell, Apr. 29, 1939; children—Samuel LeRoy, Mary Louise, William Ranson. Ordained to ministry of Presbyn. Ch., 1940; pastor Prosperity Assoc. Ref. Ch., Fayetteville, Tenn., 1942-46, Bethel Assoc. Ref. Ch., Oak Hill, Ala., 1946-50, 1st Asso. Ref. Ch., Salisbury, N.C., 1950-53, 1st Ch. U.S., Dallas, N.C., 1953-60, First Ch., Kernersville, N.C., 1960-66, Cooleemee (N.C.) Presbyn. Ch., 1966-69, Broadway (N.C.) Presbyn. Ch., 1969-80, Cape Fear Presbyn. Ch., 1983—, Sardis Presbyn. Ch., 1984-86; stated clk. Gen. Synod Assoc. Ref. Presbyn. Ch., 1950-53; commr. Gen. Assembly Presbyn. Ch. U.S., 1960, 69; permanent clk. Winston-Salem Presbytery, 1961-69, chmn. leadership edn. com., 1962-66, chmn. Christian edn. com., 1967-68; chmn. nominations com. Fayetteville Presbytery, 1977-79; mem. hunger task force Fayetteville Presbytery, 1984-88, chmn. com. on Bangladesh, 1985-87; supr. chaplaincy program Davie County Hosp., 1968-69. Pres. Dallas PTA, 1955-56; bd. mgrs. Kernersville YMCA, 1962-66, chmn. membership com., 1963, treas., 1964, pres., 1965-66; bd. dirs. Winston-Salem-Forsyth County YMCA, 1965-66. Mem. Kernersville Area Ministers Assn. (pres. 1963-64), N.C. Poetry Soc. (dir. 1971—, chmn. poetry contests 1970-72, 83-88, editor ann. book Award-Winning Poems 1972—; pres. 1972-74), Clan MacKay Soc. N.Am. (pres. 1971-75, chaplain 1976—, council 1983—, honored guest, prin. speaker 1985 internat. gathering Glasgow, Scotland 1985, speaker at Clan Mackay Soc. Centenary Celebration, Edinburgh, Scotland, 1988). Lodge: Lions. Contbr. articles and sermons to periodicals and publs.

MCKEAN, JOHN ROBERT, accountant; b. Evanston, Ill., May 30, 1930; s. Cuthbert and Mary E. (Ford) McK.; m. Mary M. Costoglus, June 17, 1956; children—John R., Pamela, Jacqueline. B.S., U. San Francisco, 1951; M.B.A., Golden Gate U., 1976. C.P.A., Calif. Controller, Hwy. Transport Inc., San Francisco, 1948-56; acct. George Kasch, C.P.A., San Francisco, 1956-58; prin. John R. McKean, C.P.A., San Francisco, 1958-73, pres., 1973—. Pres.'s ambassador U. San Francisco; pres. parish council Greek Orthodox Ch. of the Ascension, 1963-67; pres. Hearing Limited, 1964-68; appointed to U.S. Postal Service Bd. Govs., 1983-87, chmn. bd. govs., 1984-86; bd. dirs. Bayview Fed. Savs. and Loan Assn. Recipient Outstanding Alumnus award Golden Gate U., 1980. Mem. Am. Inst. C.P.A.s, Calif. Soc. C.P.A.s, Nat. Assn. Accts. and Fin. Council, Am. Acctg. Assn., Acctg. Research Assn. Club: San Francisco Commercial. Author articles in field. Home: 1596 Daily Ct San Leandro CA 94577 Office: 1 California St Suite 1200 San Francisco CA 94111

MC KEE, ALLEN PAGE, investment executive; b. Los Angeles, July 26, 1941; s. Norman C. and Eleanor (Page) McK.; B.A. in Econs., U. Mich., 1964; M.B.A., U. Calif.-Berkeley, 1971. Area relations officer internat. div. Bank of Am., San Francisco, 1967-70; investment officer Bamerical Internat. Fin. Corp., San Francisco, 1971-73; v.p. and dir. internat. investments Union Bank, San Francisco, 1973-74; pres. Montgomery Assocs., Inc., San Francisco, 1975—, dir., 1977—; mng. dir. Fal N.V., 1979-87, Willhurst Co. N.V., 1980-86; dir. Hawaiian Plantations, Inc., 1981-83, Dynodata, Inc., 1983—, Analytical Products, Inc., 1984—, A.T. Hunn Co., Inc., 1985—. Served to lt. USN, 1964-67, Vietnam. Mem. World Affairs Council No. Calif., Western Assn. Venture Capitalists, Soc. Calif. Pioneers, Calif. Bus. Alumni Assn., Delta Kappa Epsilon. Republican. Club: Commonwealth of Calif. Home: 18 Chaucer Ct Mill Valley CA 94941 Office: 555 Montgomery St Suite 1215 PO Box 2230 San Francisco CA 94126

MCKEE, BILL EARL, mining company executive; b. Sidney, Mont., Dec. 28, 1916; s. Earl Linn and Frances Elizabeth (Michaels) McK.; m. Natalie Parks, Aug. 31, 1941; children: Jerome Storm, Maureen Katherine, Craig North. BS, U. Idaho, 1937. With U.S. Forest Service, 1937-40; sr. design and flight test engr. Boeing Co., 1941-46; sales engr. C.M. Lovsted and Co., Seattle, 1947-54; pres. Atlas Boiler and Equipment Co., Spokane, Washington, 1955-56; pvt. practice cons. and sales engring. Spokane, 1957-64; project engr. Hecla Mining Co., Wallace, Idaho, 1965-67, gen. supt., 1967-81; pres. M&M Engring., Inc., 1981—; prof. Metall. engring. U. Idaho, Moscow, 1981-87. Chmn. bd. South Fork Coeur D'Alne Sewer Dist., 1975-79. Recipient Viet Howard Meml. award, 1987; NASA fellow, 1983-84. Mem. Am. Inst. Mining, Metall. and Petroleum Engrs., Idaho, Am. N.W. Mining Assn., Exptl. Aircraft Assn., Idaho Safe Pilots, Aircraft Owners and Pilots Assn., Tau Beta Pi. Republican. Clubs: Spokane, Elks. Home and Office: Box 242 Wallace ID 83873

MC KEE, DONALD DARRELL, real estate broker; b. Highland, Ill., July 20, 1932; s. Earl Michael and Leta Evelyn (Dresch) McK.; grad. high sch.; m. Emma A. Becker, Aug. 28, 1956; children—Dale Michael, Gail Ann. Sales clk. C. Kinne & Co., Highland, 1952-63; salesman Lowenstein Agy., Inc., Highland, 1963-69; owner Don McKee Ins., 1970-77; owner Don McKee Realty, Highland, 1969-73; owner Century 21-McKee Realty, Highland; owner Key Antiques, Key Sales Co; sales mgr. All Seasons Resorts, Inc., Lake Carlyle, Ill. Tchr. real estate So. Ill. U., Edwardsville, 1974-81, Lewis and Clark Community Coll., Godfrey, Ill., Belleville (Ill.) Area Coll.; pres. Real Estate Inst., 1973-79; exec. officer Edwardsville-Collinsville Bd. Realtors, 1975-76; pres. So. Ill. Conf. Real Estate. Mem. So. Ill. Tourism Council, 1969-79; mem. adv. bd. Friends of Lovejoy Library, So. Ill. U.-Edwardsville. Mem. So. Ill. Independent Ins. Agts. (pres. 1974-75), Edwardsville-Collinsville Bd. Realtors (pres. 1974), Nat., Ill. (v.p. dist. 1977) assns. Realtors, Highland C. of C., Highland Hist. Soc. (dir.), Helvetia Sharpshooters Soc., St. Louis Art Mus., Ill. Real Estate Educators, Nat. Real Estate Educators. Club: Highland Country. Contbr. articles to profl. jours. Home: 1403 Pine St Highland IL 62249 Office: 825 Main St Highland IL 62249

MCKEE, EDITH MERRITT, geologist; b. Oak Park, Ill., Oct. 9, 1918; d. Eustis Ewart and Edith (Frame) McK.; B.S., Northwestern U., 1946. Geologist, U.S. Geol. Survey, 1943-45, Shell Oil Co., 1947-49, Arabian Am. Oil Co., 1949-54, Underground Gas Storage Co. Ill., 1956-58; ind. cons. geologist, Winnetka, Ill., 1958—; mem. environ. adv. com. Fed. Energy Adminstrn., 1974; mem. Nat. Adv. Com. Oceans and Atmosphere, 1975; speaker, cons. in field. Commr., Winnetka Park Bd., 1976-79. Fellow Marine Tech. Soc., Geol. Soc. Am.; mem. Am. Geol. Inst., Am. Inst. Profl. Geologists (cert., charter), Assn. Engring. Geologists, Ill. Geol. Soc., Am. Oceanic Orgn. Research on shore erosion, mapping of Gt. Lakes basins and deep ocean basins, global econ. devel. programs and mineral exploration. Address: PO Box 3 Good Hart MI 49737

MCKEE, FRANCIS JOHN, association executive, lawyer; b. Bklyn., Aug. 31, 1943; s. Francis Joseph and Catherine (Giles) McK.; m. Antoinette Mary Sancis; children: Lisa Ann, Francis Dominick, Michael Christopher, Thomas Joseph. AB, Stonehill Coll., 1965; JD, St. John's U., 1970. Bar: N.Y. 1971. Assoc. firm Samuel Weinberg, Esquire, Bklyn., 1970-71, firm Finch & Finch, Esquire, Long Island City, N.Y., 1971-72; staff atty. Med. Soc. of State of N.Y., Lake Success, 1972-77; exec. dir. Suffolk Physicians Rev. Orgn., East Islip, N.Y., 1977-81, N.Y. State Soc. Surgeons, Inc., New Hartford, 1981—, N.Y. State Soc. Orthopaedic Surgeons, Inc., New Hartford, 1981—, Upstate N.Y. chpt. ACS, Inc., New Hartford, 1981—, N.Y. State Ophthalmol. Soc., 1984—, N.Y. State Soc. Obstetricians and Gynecologists, 1985—; bd. dirs. Med Econs. Bur., New Hartford. Served with U.S. Army, 1966-68. Mem. Oneida County Bar Assn., N.Y. State Bar Assn., Am. Soc. Assn. Execs., Am. Assn. Med. Soc. Execs., Utica C. of C. (chmn. health subcom. 1982-84) Republican. Roman Catholic. Clubs: Engine Eleven, Nightstick (Utica). Home: 19 Mulberry St Clinton NY 13323 Office: 210 Clinton Rd New Hartford NY 13413

MC KEE, GEORGE MOFFITT, JR., civil engineer, consultant; b. Valparaiso, Nebr., Mar. 27, 1924; s. George Moffitt and Iva (Santrock) McK.; student Kans. State Coll. Agr. and Applied Sci., 1942-43, Bowling Green State U., 1943; B.S. in Civil Engring., U. Mich., 1947; m. Mary Lee Taylor, Aug. 11, 1945; children—Michael Craig, Thomas Lee, Mary Kathleen, Marsha Coleen, Charlotte Anne. Draftsman, Jackson Constrn. Co., Colby, Kans., 1945-46; asst. engr. Thomas County, Colby, 1946; engr. Sherman County, Goodland, Kans., 1947-51; salesman Oehlert Tractor & Equipment Co., Colby, 1951-52; owner, operator George M. McKee, Jr., cons. engrs., Colby, 1952-72; sr. v.p. engring. Contract Surety Consultants, Wichita, Kans., 1974—. Adv. rep. Kans. State U., Manhattan, 1957-62; mem. adv. com. N.W. Kans. Area Vocat. Tech. Sch., Goodland, 1967-71. Served with USMCR, 1942-45. Registered profl. civil engr., Kans., Okla., registered land Surveyor, Kans. Mem. Kans. Engring. Soc. (pres. N.W. profl. engrs. chpt. 1962-63, treas. cons. engrs. sect. 1961-63), Kansas County Engr's. Assn. (dist. v.p. 1950-51), Northwest Kans. Hwy. Ofcls. Assn. (sec. 1948-49), Nat. Soc. Profl. Engrs., Kans. State U. Alumni Assn. (pres. Thomas County 1956-57), Am. Legion (Goodland 1st vice comdr. 1948-49), Colby C. of C. (v.p. 1963-64), Goodland Jr. C. of C. (pres. 1951-52). Methodist (chmn. ofcl. bd. 1966-67). Mason (32 deg., Shriner); Order Eastern Star. Home: 34 Lakeview Circle Rt 1 Towanda KS 67144 Office: 6500 W Kellogg Wichita KS 67209

MC KEE, JOHN CAROTHERS, industrial psychologist; b. San Diego, Apr. 25, 1912; s. John Joseph and Margaret (Giesman) McK.; B.A., U. So. Calif., 1935, M.A., 1937; Ph.D., Tulane U., 1947; m. Gladys Irene Michel, Jan. 10, 1941 (dec. Feb. 1968); children—John Michael, Hillary Barbara; m. 2d, Sara Forman, June 25, 1968; one son, Evan. Gen. mgr. Hotel Royal, La Ceiba, Honduras, 1932-33; mgmt. cons. Douglas Aircraft Co., Long Beach, Calif., 1942-67, exec. adviser, dir. operations control, 1967—, also pres. mgmt. assn. Douglas Space Systems Center; exec. adviser fin. mgmt. McDonnell Douglas Astronautics, v.p. Santa Monica Health Spot Shoe Corp., 1949—; pres. McKee Mgmt. Center, Volumetrics, Inc., Mentron Corp.; exec. v.p. Consearch Inc.; pres. McKee Mgmt. Center, Stanton, Calif., Quantek Internat. Inc.; partner McKee & Wright and Assn., Stanton; v.p. Advion Corp.; lectr. Acad. of Justice, Riverside, Calif.; cons. Space Systems Center, Huntington Beach, Calif., 1964—; cons. Hanford, Orange, Cypress police depts. (all Calif.), Shanick Police Dept., Victoria, B.C., Can., 1988; dir. Consultron, Inc. Author: Law Enforcement Manager's Handbook. Pres. sports council YMCA; bd. dirs. Long Beach YMCA. Asso. dir. Mgmt. Center, Chapman Coll.; bd. dirs. McKee Wright La Verne Coll. Mgmt. Center, Cavaliers Fencing Schs., 1935—, Law Enforcement Mgmt. Center, Calif.; mgr. Stanton Bd. Trade, 1978—; Olympic fencing coach, 1984; pres. Ctr. for Strategic Planning, Orange County, Calif.; mem. fed. res. adv. bd. Recipient Personagraph Speaker of Yr. award Indsl Mgmt. Assn.; Outstanding Law Enforcement Work award Calif. Atty. Gen., 1984; named to Am. Police Hall of Fame, 1984; Charles R. Able citation for co. mgmt., Certificate of Merit, Amateur Fencers League Am.; Citizen of Yr. award Calif. Office Atty. Gen., 1984; resolution of thanks for work with police City of Hartford; Resolution of Excellence Hartford City Council; Calif. Gov.'s award for civilian service to law enforcement; named Cavalier Fencing Coach of Yr., 1982; named to Pub. Hall of Fame, 1985; Nat. Police Hall of Fame, 1985; cert. instr. Calif. Dept. Justice POST program. Mem. Internat. Platform Assn., Am. Statis. Assn. (past pres., mem. nat. council). Nat. Mgmt. Assn. (recipient Silver Knight of Mgmt., 1961, v.p. area council), Nat. Assn. Chiefs of Police, Internat. Assn. Chiefs Police, Calif. Assn. Police Tng. Officers, Fedn. Internationale D'Esgrime, (hon.) Canadian Mounted Police, Amateur Fencers League Am., AAAS, C. of C. (mem. research com. of Los Angeles), Inst. Mgmt. Scis., Am. Assn. Indsl. Editors, Internat. Council Indsl. Editors, So. Calif. Indsl. Editors Assn., Nat. Assn. Bus. Economists, Orange County Econ. Roundtable (Exec. of Year award, pres.), Am. Soc. Quality Control (chmn. criminal justice sect.), Calif. Adminstrn. Justice Educators, Calif. Assn. Peace Officers, Can. Northwest Mounted Police, Phi Beta Kappa. Author: Learning Curves, Quantity-Cost Curves, Estimating Engineering Costs, Systems Analysis, Cost and Budgeting Analysis and Statistics for Non-Mathematical Managers; Zero Base Budgeting; The Fencer's Work Book; Fiscal Management; The Police Chief's Financial Handbook. Home: 16509 Harbour Ln Huntington Beach CA 92649 Office: Law Enforcement Mgmt Ctr 10801 Dale St Suite J-1 Stanton CA 90680

MCKEE, RUSSELL ELLSWORTH, food products executive; b. Hendersonville, N.C., Dec. 24, 1932; s. O.D. and Anna Ruth (King) McK.; m. Sharon Sue Sisson, June 21, 1953; children: Debra, Badia Huggins, Malinda, Russell Jr. BA in Bus. and Econs.k., So. Missionary Coll., 1954; DLaws (hon.), Andrews U., 1987. Shipping/receiving clk. Jack's Cookie Co., Charlotte, N.C., 1949-50; service, mixer, receiving, shipping, truckdriver, office mgr., prodn. supt. McKee Baking Co., Chattanooga, 1951-54, v.p. prodn. and fin., 1954-62; exec. v.p., treas. McKee Baking Co., Collegedale, Tenn., 1962-71, pres., chief exec. officer, 1971—; bd. dirs. Pioneer Bank, Chattanooga. Bd. dirs. So. Coll. of Seventh day Adventists, Collegedale, 1971—, Andrews U., Berrien Springs, Mich., 1976—, Chattanooga Area Healthcare Coalition, 1986—. Recipient Pvt. Sector Initiative Commendation Pres. Ronald Reagan, Washington, 1986. Mem. Cookie and Snack Bakers Assn. (pres. 1984-85), Ind. Bakers Assn., Bus. and Profl. Assn., U.S. C. of C. (bd. dirs. 1988). Seventh Day Adventist. Office: McKee Baking Co PO Box 750 Collegedale TN 37315

MCKEE, TIMOTHY CARLTON, taxation educator; b. South Bend, Ind., Mar. 9, 1944; s. Glenn Richard and Laura Louise (Niven) McK.; m. Linda Sykes Mizelle, Oct. 13, 1984; children: Brandon Richard. BS in Bus. Econs., Ind. U., 1970, MBA in Fin., 1973, JD, 1979; LLM in Taxation, DePaul U., 1980. Bar: Ill. 1980, U.S. Dist. Ct. (no. dist.) Ill. 1980; CPA, Ill., Va. Procedures analyst Assocs. Corp., South Bend, Ind., 1969-71; asst. dir. fin. Ind. U., Bloomington, Ind., 1971-79; sr. tax mgr. Peat Marwick Mitchell & Co., Chgo., Norfolk, Va., 1979-84; corp. counsel K & K Toys, Norfolk, 1984; asst. prof. acctg. Old Dominion U., Norfolk, 1985—; computer coordinator, Peat, Marwick, Mitchell & Co., 1982-84; micro computer cons. Old Dominion U., 1985—. Contbr. articles to profl. jours. Mem. Friends of Music, Bloomington, 1978, Art Inst., Chgo., 1981; loaned exec. United Way, Chgo., 1981; telethon chmn. Va. Orch. Group, Norfolk, 1983. Mem. Am. Acctg. Assn., Am. Tax Assn., Hampton Roads Tax Forum, Inst. Internal Auditors, Beta Alpha Psi. Home: 412 Rio Dr Chesapeake VA 23320-8039 Office: Old Dominion U Hughes Hall 2065 Norfolk VA 23529-0229

MC KEEN, CHESTER M., JR., helicopter company executive; b. Shelby, Ohio, Mar. 18, 1923; s. Chester Mancil and Nettie Augusta (Fox) McK.; m. Alma Virginia Pierce, Mar. 1946; children: David Richard, Karin, Thomas Kevin. B.S. in Mil. Sci., U. Md., 1962; M.B.A., Babson Coll., Wellesley, Mass., 1962. Enlisted in U.S. Army, 1942, commd. 2d lt., 1943, advanced through grades to maj. gen., 1970; service in Pacific Islands, Ger., Vietnam; dir. procurement Army Material Command; also comdr. Tank/Automotive Command 1972-77, ret., 1977; dir. logistics Bell Helicopter Internat., 1977-79; v.p.-procurement Bell Helicopter Textron, Ft. Worth, 1979-82, v.p. materiel, 1982—. Decorated D.S.M., Legion of Merit (3), Commendation medal (3). Mem. Am. Mgmt. Assn., Am. Def. Preparedness Assn. (v.p. S.W. region), Assn. U.S. Army (pres. 4th region), Sigma Pi. Club: Ridglea Country (Ft. Worth) Lodges: Rotary, Masons (32 degree KCCH), Shriners. Home: 2310 Woodsong Trail Arlington TX 76016 Office: PO Box 482 Fort Worth TX 76101

MCKELDIN, WILLIAM EVANS, management consultant; b. Richmond, Va., Aug. 14, 1927; s. Robert A.W. and Mary E. (Burke) McK.; BS in Bus. Adminstrn., Temple U., 1951, postgrad., 1951-53; postgrad. U. Pitts., 1953-54; m. Phyllis Shellhase, Jan. 23, 1982; children by previous marriage: William Evans, Roberts E. Various employee relations and mgmt. positions with Westinghouse Corp., Pitts., 1950-62, Farrel Corp., Rochester, N.Y., 1963-66, Gen. Signal Corp., Norwalk, Conn. and Watertown, N.Y., 1966-71, Copperweld Steel Co., Warren, Ohio, 1971-75, Tenn. Forging Steel, Knoxville, 1975-77, Val Bradley Assocs., West Chester, Pa., 1977-79; pres. and owner McKeldin Assocs., West Chester, 1979—. Bd. dirs. United Fund, YMCA, ARC, Rochester Inst. Tech., Jefferson Community Coll., Kent State U. Served with USAAF, 1945-47. Mem. Inst. Mgmt. Cons., Am. Soc. Safety Engrs., Am. Soc. Personnel Adminstrn., C. of C. (dir.). Republican. Presbyterian. Clubs: Masons, Rotary. Contbr. articles to trade jours. Address: McKeldin Assocs 125 Willowbrook Ln West Chester PA 19382

MCKELL, CYRUS M., education administator, biologist; b. Payson, Utah, Mar. 19, 1926; s. Robert D. and Mary C. (Ellsworth) McK.; m. Betty Johsnon; children: Meredith Sue, Brian Marcus, John Cyrus. BS, U. Utah, 1949, MS, 1950; PhD, Oreg. State U., 1956; postgrad., U. Calif., Davis, 1957. Instr. botany Oreg. State U., Corvallis, 1955-56; research plant physiologist U. Calif. USDA-Agrl. Research Service, Davis, 1956-60; prof., dept. chmn. U. Calif., Riverside, 1960-69; prof. dept. head., dir. Utah State U., Logan, 1969-80; v.p. research NPI, Salt Lake City, 1980-88; dean Sch. of Natural Scis. Weber State Coll., Ogden, Utah, 1988—; cons. Ford Found. 1968-72, Rockefeller Found., 1964-70, U.N., 1978, Nat. Acad. Sci., 1980, USAID, 1972. Editor Grass Biology and Utilization, 1971, Useful Wildland Shrubs, 1972, Rehabilitation of Western Wildlife Habitat, 1978, Paradoxes of Western Energy Development, 1984, Resource Inventory and Baseline Study Methods for Developing Countries, 1983, Shrub Biology and Utilization, 1989; contbr. numerous articles to profl. jours. Chmn. Cache County Planning Commn., Logan, 1974-79; mem. Energy Conservation and Devel. Council, Salt Lake City, 1976-79; active Commn. of the Californias, Riverside, 1965-68. Served to 1st lt. USAF, 1951-53. Fulbright scholar Spain, 1967-68; World Travel grantee Rockefeller Found., 1964. Fellow AAAS (com. chmn. 1979—, sci. exchange to China grantee 1984-85, sci, panel U.S.-Chile 1987); mem. Am. Soc. Agronomy, Soc. Range Mgmt. (pres. Calif. sect. 1965, pres. Utah sect. 1982). Mormon. Home: 2248 E 4000 S Salt Lake City UT 84124 Office: Weber State Coll Sch of Natural Scis Ogden UT 84108

MCKELLEN, IAN MURRAY, actor; b. Burnley, Eng., May 25, 1939; s. Denis Murray and Margery (Sutcliffe) McK.; ed. St. Catharine's Coll., Cambridge, Eng. First stage appearance as Roper in A Man for All Seasons, Belgrade Theatre, Coventry, Eng., 1961; numerous other parts include title roles in Henry V, Luther, Ipswich, 1962-63, Aufidius in Coriolanus, Arthur Seaton in Saturday Night and Sunday Morning, title role in Sir Thomas More, Nottingham Playhouse, 1963-64; London debut as Godfrey in A Scent of Flowers, 1964, Claudio in Much Ado About Nothing, Andrew Cobham in Their Very Own and Golden City, 1966; title part in O'Flaherty, V.C. and Bonapart in The Man of Destiny, 1966, (Broadway debut) Leonidik in The Promise, London, 1966-67, Richard II, Edward II, Hamlet, Prospect Theatre Co., 1968-71; Capt. Plume in The Recruiting Officer; founder-mem. Actors' Co., Edinburgh Festival, 1972 and touring as Giovanni in Tis Pity She's A Whore, Page-Boy in Ruling the Roose, title role Wood Demon; debut with R.S.C. as Dr. Faustus, Edinburgh Festival, 1974; title role in The Marquis of Keith, Philip the Bastard in King John, 1974-75, Young Vic Colin in Ashes, 1975; Royal Shakespeare Co.: Burglar in Too True to be Good, Romeo, Macbeth, Leontes in The Winter's Tale, Face in The Alchemist, Bernick in Pillars of the Community, Langevin in Days of the Commune, 1976-78, Ivanov in Every Good Boy Deserves Favour, Toby Belch in Twelfth Night, Andrei in The Three Sisters, Max in Bent, 1979, Amadeus, N.Y.C., 1980; European tour of one-man show Acting Shakespeare, 1983, also Los Angeles, N.Y.C., 1984; assoc. dir. Nat. Theatre, London, 1984-86, plays include: Venice Preserved, Wild Honey, Coriolanus, Duchess of Malfi, The Cherry Orchard, others; dir. first prodn. The Prime of Miss Jean Brodie, Liverpool Playhouse, 1969, A Private Matter, 1973, The Clandestine Marriage, 1975; films include: Alfred the Great, 1969, The Promise, 1969, A Touch of Love, 1969, The Keep, 1982, Plenty, Zina, 1985; TV appearances include: David Copperfield, 1965, Ross, 1969, Richard II, Edward II and Hamlet, 1970, Hedda Gabler, 1974, Macbeth, Every Good Boy Deserves Favour, Dying Day, 1979, Acting Shakespeare, 1981, The Scarlet Pimpernel, 1982. Recipient Clarence Derwent award, 1964; Variety and Plays and Players awards, 1966; Actor of Year, Plays and Players, 1976; award Soc. of West End Theatres for Best Actor in Revival, 1977, for Best Comedy Performance, 1978, for Best Actor in a New Play, 1979, Tony Award for Best Actor, Drama Desk Award, Outer Critics' Circle Award, N.Y. Drama League Award, 1981; Performer of Yr. award Royal TV soc., 1983. Decorated comdr. Order Brit. Empire. Mem. Brit. Actors' Equity (council 1970-71). Address: care James Sharkey Assocs, 15 Golden Sq, London W1R 3AG England Other: care Fraser and Dunlop, 91 Regent St, London W1 England *

MCKENNA, ANDREW JAMES, paper distribution company and printing company executive, baseball club executive; b. Chgo., Sept. 17, 1929; s. Andrew James and Anita (Fruin) McK.; m. Mary Joan Pickett, June 20, 1953; children: Suzanne, Karen, Andrew, William, Joan, Kathleen, Margaret. B.S., U. Notre Dame, 1951; J.D., DePaul U., 1954. Bar: Ill. Pres., chief exec. officer Schwarz Paper Co., Morton Grove, Ill., 1964—; dir. Chgo. Nat. Leauge Ball Club Inc., Chgo. Bears.; dir. Dean Foods Co., Lake Shore Nat. Bank, Skyline Corp., Tribune Co., AON Corp.; chmn. bd. Group II Communications, Inc., Franklin, Wis. Vice chmn. bd. trustees U. Notre Dame ; trustee La Lumiere Sch.; bd. dirs. Cath. Charities of Chgo., Children's Meml. Med. Ctr. Chgo. Mem. Assn. Governing Bds. Univs. and Colls. (bd. dirs.). Clubs: Chgo, Comml, Econs, Chgo. Athletic Assn; Glen View (Golf, Ill.). Home: 60 Locust Rd Winnetka IL 60093 Office: Schwarz Paper Co 8338 N Austin Ave Morton Grove IL 60053

MCKENNA, BERNARD JAMES, financial sevices executive; b. N.Y.C., July 17, 1933; s. Bernard James and Josephine (Fitzgerald) McK.; m. Ann Jean Noe, Nov. 27, 1954; children: William C., Geralyn M., Paul G., Michael G. BBA in Fin., Hofstra U., 1962. Instr. Adelphi U., Long Island, N.Y., 1964-67; agt. Conn. Gen. Life Ins. Co., Garden City, N.Y., 1963-67, Granate EquipmentLeasing Co., Garden City, 1967-68; mktg. mgr. Greyhound Equipment, N.Y.C., 1968-70; sr. loan officer Ford Motor Credit Co., Dearborn, Mich., 1970-80; pres., chief exec. officer Sanwa Bus. Credit Co., Chgo., 1980—. Contbr. articles to profl. jours. Vice chmn. Am. Conservatory of Music, Chgo., 1985—; pres. N.Y. chpt. Cystic Fibrosis Found., 1966-69, Detroit chpt. 1973-75, Chgo. chpt. 1980-81, nat. trustee, Washington, 1976-82. Served with U.S. Army, 1954-56. Mem. Am. Assn. Equipment Lessors (chmn. 1984-87), Am. Mgmt. Assn. (pres.'s council 1984—), Chgo. Council Fgn. Relations, Japan Soc. of Chgo., Internat.

Platform Assn., Chgo. Econ. Club, Exec. Club Chgo., Kingsmill C. of C. Republican. Roman Catholic. Clubs: LaSalle, Met., Edgewood Valley. Home: 1621 Coachmans Rd Darien IL 60559 Office: Sawwa Bus Credit Corp 1 S Wacker Dr Chicago IL 60606

MCKENNA, FAY ANN, electrical manufacturing company executive; b. Bennington, Vt., Jan. 7, 1944; d. George Francis and Barbara Mae (Youngangel) Hoag; m. James Dennis McKenna, Sept. 3, 1963 (div. 1983); children: Russell (dec.), Laura, James, Sean, Michael. Student, Mercy Coll. Key punch operator N.Y. State Taxation and Fin. Dept., Albany, 1960-61; receptionist Trine Mfg./Square D Co., Bronx, 1972-76; clk. Square D Co., Bronx, 1976-78, exec. sec., 1978-79, personnel mgr., 1979-86; mgr. mktg. adminstrn. Trine Products Corp., 1986—. Mfg. Fund raiser YMCA, Bronx, 1979—; mem. Community Bd. #9, Bronx, 1984—; Recipient Service to Youth award YMCA, 1985. Mem. Adminstrv. Mgmt. Soc. Republican. Roman Catholic. Avocations: physical fitness, reading, interior decorating. Home: 4100-20 Hutchinson River Pkwy E Bronx NY 10475 Office: Trine Products Corp 1430 Ferris Pl Bronx NY 10461

MCKENNA, JOHN DENNIS, environmental testing engineer; b. N.Y.C., Apr. 1, 1940; s. Hubert Guy and Elizabeth Ann (Record) McK.; B.S. in Chem. Engring., Manhattan Coll., 1961; M.Chem.Engring., Newark Coll. Engring., 1968; M.B.A., Rider Coll., 1974; m. Christel Klages, Dec. 26, 1964; children—Marc, Michelle. Tech. asst. to pres. Eldib Engring. & Research Co., Newark, 1964-67; program mgr. Princeton Chem. Research, Inc. (N.J.), 1967-68; projects dir. Cottrell Environ. Systems, Bound Brook, N.J., 1968-72; v.p., then pres. Enviro-Systems & Research, Inc., Roanoke, Va., 1973-79; pres. ETS, Inc., Roanoke, 1979—. Mem. Air Pollution Control Assn., Am. Inst. Chem. Engrs. Roman Catholic. Contbr. chpts. to books, articles to profl. jours. Home: 4118 Chaparral Dr SW Roanoke VA 24018 Office: ETS Inc 3140 Chaparral Dr SW Suite C-103 Roanoke VA 24018

MC KENNEY, WALTER GIBBS, JR., lawyer, publishing company executive; b. Jacobsville, Md., Apr. 22, 1913; s. Walter Gibbs and Mary (Starkey) McK.; m. Florence Roberta Rea, July 17, 1939. Student, Dickinson Sem., 1935-37; Ph.B. Dickinson Coll., 1939; J.D., U. Va., 1942; LL.D., Dickinson Sch. Law, 1964; D.H.L., Lycoming Coll., 1984. Bar: Md. 1942. Practiced in Balt. 1942—; partner McKenney, Thomsen & Burke; partner, gen. mgr., editor Taxes & Estates Pub. Co., Balt., 1946—; chmn. trust com. Equitable Bank, N.A., Balt., 1970-84; dir. Equitable Bancorp., 1960-84; lectr. Southwestern Grad. Sch. Banking, 1966-76. Editor Taxes and Estates, 1946—, Minimizing Taxes, 1946-84, The Educator, 1965—, The Patron, 1968-84. Pres. Kelso Home for Girls; mem. bd. child care Balt. Conf. Meth. Ch., pres., 1961-64; pres. Balt. Estate Planning Council, 1963-64; trustee Goucher Coll., 1968-84, Dickinson Coll., Lycoming Coll., Wesley Theol. Sem., Loyola Coll. at Balt., 1975-83, Franklin Sq. Hosp., Franklin Square Found., Franklin Square Health System, Helix Health System. Served to lt. USNR, 1942-45. Mem. ABA, Md., Balt. bar assns. Republican. Methodist. Home: 102 Estes Rd Baltimore MD 21212 Office: Munsey Bldg Baltimore MD 21202

MCKENNEY, JERE WESLEY, geological engineering firm executive; b. Okmulgee, Okla., Feb. 14, 1929; s. Jere Claus and Juanita (Hunter) McK.; m. Anne Ross Stewart, May 4, 1957; children: Jere James, Robert Stewart. BS in Geol. Engring. U. Okla., 1951, MS in Geol. Engring, 1952. With Kerr-McGee Corp., Oklahoma City, 1953—, mgr. oil and gas exploration, 1968-69, v.p. oil and gas, 1969-74, v.p. exploration, 1974-77, vice chmn., 1977—, pres., 1983—, chief operating officer, 1988—; Mem. alumni adv. council Sch. Geology and Geophysics U. Okla. Served with U.S. Army, 1953-55. Mem. Am. Assn. Petroleum Geologists, Am. Petroleum Inst. (dir.), Ind. Petroleum Assn. Am. (dir.), Houston Geol. Soc., Oklahoma City Geol. Soc., Sigma Xi, Sigma Gamma Epsilon. Episcopalian. Clubs: Oklahoma City Golf and Country, Whitehall. Home: 2932 Cornwall Pl Oklahoma City OK 73120 Office: Kerr-McGee Corp PO Box 25861 Oklahoma City OK 73125 *

MCKENZIE, CLIF ALLEN, Indian tribe official, accountant; b. Lawton, Okla., Sept. 29, 1942; s. Robert Allen and Rubie (Paukei) Williams; m. Michele Ann Martin, Aug. 4, 1972; children—Kasey Roberta, Kristen Marti. B.S. in Acctg., U. Okla., 1965; M.B.A., Pa. State U., 1976. Fin. analyst United Tribes of Okla., Shawnee, 1973-75; credit officer Bur. Indian Affairs, Dept. Interior, Horton, Kans., 1975-77, liaison officer, Syracuse, N.Y., 1977-80, program analyst, Denver, 1980-81; tribal adminstr. Kiowa Tribe of Okla., Carnegie, 1981-82; chief exec. officer, tribal bus. mgr. Cheyenne and Arapaho Tribe of Okla., Concho, 1982-84; pres. Indian Devel. Corp., Oklahoma City, 1973—; contracting officer Bur. Indian Affairs, Anadarko, Okla., 1984—, agy. ops. officer, Concho, Okla.; police commr. City of Horton, 1976-77, city commr., 1976-77; dir. LECO, Inc., Tulsa. Recipient H.M. Hefner First Amendment award Playboy Found., 1985. Life mem. DAV, U. Okla. Alumni Assn.; mem. Kiowa Black Legging Soc., Nat. Assn. Accts., Am. Soc. Notaries (dir. govt. affairs 1975-80), Nat. Taxpayers Investigative Fund (Whistleblower award 1982). Republican. Served to capt. U.S. Army, 1959-68. Lodges: Elks, Moose. Home: 3708 Epperly Dr Del City OK 73115 Office: Indian Devel Corp PO Box 15613 Del City OK 73155

MC KENZIE, HILTON EUGENE, construction co. exec.; b. Berlin, Pa., Sept. 5, 1921; s. Enoch Joeseph and Nellie Savilla (Colefleish) McK.; M.S.C.E. and M.E., M.I.T., 1941; C.E. and B.S.C.E., Va. Poly. Inst., 1939; m. Dorothy Elyea, May 19, 1949; children—Carol, Deborah, Cynthia, Hilton. Sr. cons. Bank Bldg. Corp., St. Louis, 1950-72; sec.-treas. Fin. Bldg. Cons., Atlanta, 1972-75; pres., chmn. Fin. Structures Inc., Atlanta, 1975—; instr. Cornell U., Ithaca, N.Y., 1976. Served to lt. col. U.S. Army, 1940-45. Decorated Bronze Star, Silver Star, Purple Heart. Mem. Nat. Soc. Profl. Engrs., N.C. Soc. Engrs., Soc. Am. Mil. Engrs. Protestant. Club: Elks. Home: Rt 1 Mansfield GA 30255 Office: 2990 Brandywine Rd Atlanta GA 30341

MCKENZIE, JAMES FRANKLIN, lawyer; b. Mobile, Ala., May 3, 1948; s. Frank L. McKenzie and Mary K. (Crow) McKenzie O'Neal; m. Randy Jo Jones, June 25, 1977; children—Katherine J., J. Alistair. B.A. magna cum laude, U. W. Fla., 1970; J.D. with honors, U. Fla., 1973. Bar: Fla. 1973, U.S. Dist. Ct. (no. dist.) Fla. 1973, U.S. Ct. Appeals (5th cir.) 1975, U.S. Ct. Appeals (11th cir.) 1982, U.S. Supreme Ct. 1988. Lectr. bus. law U. Fla., Gainesville, 1972-73; assoc. Levin, Warfield et al, Pensacola, Fla., 1973-76; ptnr. Myrick & McKenzie, P.A., Pensacola, 1976-82, McKenzie & Assocs., P.A., Pensacola, 1982—. Contbr. chpts. to books, articles to profl. jours. Pres. NW Fla. Easter Seal Soc., Pensacola, 1975; bd. dirs. Five Flags Sertoma Club, 1977; fund devel. chmn. Fla. Lawyers Action Group, Tallahassee, 1977—. Recipient Am. Jurisprudence award U. Fla., 1971, 72, 73. Mem. Acad. Fla. Trial Lawyers (coll. diplomates), 1st Circuit Acad. Trial Lawyers (founding mem., pres. 1984), Fla. Bar Assn. (cert. in civil trial law), ABA, Am. Trial Lawyers Assn., Acad. Fla. Trial Lawyers (bd. dirs. 1986—, diplomate), Escambia-Santa Rosa Bar Assn., Pensacola C. of C., Order of Coif, Phi Kappa Phi, Omicron Delta Kappa, Phi Delta Phi. Republican. Presbyterian. Clubs: Pensacola Country, Executive. Home: 4546 Lassassier Pensacola FL 32504 Office: McKenzie & Assocs PA 127 S Alcaniz St Pensacola FL 32501

MCKEON, THOMAS JOSEPH, lawyer, broadcaster, detective; b. Indpls., Feb. 3, 1948; s. Thomas Michael and Mary Rose (Luzar) McK. B.A., Ind. U., 1970; J.D. cum laude, Ind. U.- Indpls., 1974. Bar: Ind. 1974, U.S. Dist. Ct. (so. dist.) Ind. 1974, U.S. Supreme Ct. 1979. Assoc. Nisenbaum & Brown, Indpls., 1974-76, Osborn & Hiner, Indpls., 1976-82; counsel Am. Family Ins., Indpls., 1982—; asst. counsel Radio Earth Internat. Inc., Radio Earth Curacao, Netherlands Antilles, 1985—. Author: Post Traumatic Stress Disorder: Real or Imagined, 1986, Repetition Strain As A Compensable Injury, 1987; contbr. articles to profl. jours. Mem. ABA, Assn. Trial Lawyers Am. (assoc.), Ind. Bar Assn., Ind. Def. Lawyers Assn. Inc., Ind. Trial Lawyers Assn., Indpls. Bar Assn., Def. Research & Trial Lawyers Assn., Am. Corp. Counsel Assn., Ind. Assn. Pvt. Detectives. Office: Am Family Ins Group 1625 N Post Rd Indianapolis IN 46219

MCKEOWN, MARY ELIZABETH, educational administrator; d. Raymond Edmund and Alice (Fitzgerald) McNamara; B.S., U. Chgo., 1946; M.S., DePaul U., 1953; m. James Edward McKeown, Aug. 6, 1955. Supr. high sch. dept. Am. Sch., 1948-68, prin., 1968—, trustee, 1975—, v.p., 1979—. Mem. Nat. Assn. Secondary Sch. Prins., Central States Assn. Sci. and Math Tchrs. Nat. Council Tchrs. Math., Assn. for Supervision and Curriculum Devel., Adult Edn. Assn., LWV. Author study guides for algebra, geometry and calculus. Home: 1469 N Sheridan Rd Kenosha WI 53140 Office: 850 E 58th Chicago IL 60637

MC KERNAN, JOHN RETTIE, JR., governor of Maine; b. Bangor, Maine, May 20, 1948; s. John Rettie and Barbara (Guild) McKernan; 1 son, Peter Alexander. B.S., Dartmouth Coll., 1970; J.D., U. So. Maine, 1974. Bar: Maine. Atty. Verrill & Dana, Portland, Maine, 1976-82, Sterns & Finnegan, Bangor, Maine, 1974-76; mem. 98th-99th Congresses from 1st Dist. Maine, 1983-87; gov. of State Maine Augusta, 1987—. Mem. Pres. Commn. on Presidential Scholars, 1981. Republican. Office: Office of Gov State House Sta 1 Augusta ME 04333

MCKIM, PAUL ARTHUR, petroleum company executive; b. Milford, Conn., Feb. 1, 1923; s. Arthur Wheatley and Helen Agnes (Brennan) McK.; m. Daisy Flora Brown, June 18, 1945; 1 dau., Meredith Ann. Student, Lamar Inst. Tech., 1940-42; B.S. in Chem. Engring, La. State U., 1943, M.S., 1947, Ph.D., 1949; grad. Advanced Mgmt. Program, Harvard, 1959; grad. Aspen Inst. Humanistic Studies Exec. Program, 1970. With Ethyl Corp., 1949-62, asst. gen. mgr. research and devel. operations, 1958-62; v.p., gen. mgr. research and devel. Atlantic Refining Co., Phila., 1962-66; v.p. Atlantic Richfield Co., 1966-78; v.p. comml. devel. Arco Chem. Co., 1966-69, v.p. nuclear operations and comml. devel., 1969-78; exec. v.p. Sinclair Koppers Co., 1973; pres. Arco Polymers, Inc., 1974-78; asst. to pres. Tex. Eastern Corp., 1978-80, v.p., 1980-84, sr. v.p., 1985-88; Chmn. US Organizing com. for 12th World Petroleum Congress, Houston, 1987. Past bd. mgrs. Spring Garden Inst., vice chmn., past bd. mgrs. Franklin Inst. Research Labs; past vice chmn. bd. mgrs. Phila. Coll. Art.; past vice chmn. World Affairs Council of Phila. Served to lt. (j.g.) USNR, 1944-46. Mem. Am. Inst. Chem. Engrs., Am. Petroleum Inst., Greater Phila. C. of C. (bd. dirs.), Alpha Chi Sigma, Omicron Delta Kappa, Tau Beta Pi, Phi Lambda Upsilon, Phi Kappa Phi, Delta Kappa Epsilon. Clubs: Union League, Merion (Pa.) Cricket, Merion Golf, Houston, Houston Ctr, Lakewood Yacht; Shreveport (La.) Country. Home: 5405 Holly Springs Houston TX 77056 Office: Tex Eastern Corp Box 2521 Houston TX 77252

MCKIM, SAMUEL JOHN, III, lawyer; b. Pitts., Dec. 31, 1938; s. Samuel John and Harriet Frieda (Roehl) McK.; children—David Hunt, Andrew John; m. Eugenia A. Leverich. A.A. with distinction, Port Huron Jr. Coll., 1959; B.A. with distinction, U. Mich., 1961, J.D. with distinction, 1964. Bar: Mich. 1965, U.S. Dist. Ct. (so. dist.) Mich. 1965, U.S. Ct. Appeals (6th cir.) 1969. Assoc., Miller, Canfield, Paddock and Stone, Detroit, Birmingham, Kalamazoo, Lansing, Monroe, Traverse City and Grand Rapids, Mich., Washington, Boca Raton, Fla., 1964-71, ptnr., 1971—, mng. ptnr., 1979-85, chmn., mng. ptnr., 1984-85; mem. tax council State Bar Mich., 1981-84, chmn. state and local tax coms. Real Property sect., 1982—. Trustee, past chmn. Goodwill Industries; mem. exec. bd. and asst. counsel Detroit Area Council Boy Scouts Am. Mem. ABA, Detroit Bar Assn., Oakland County Bar Assn., Barrister's Soc., Order of Coif, Phi Delta Phi. Presbyterian. Club: Ostego Ski. Assoc. editor Mich. Law Rev. Office: 1400 N Woodward Ave PO Box 2014 Bloomfield Hills MI 48303-2014

MCKINLEY, BRUNSON, diplomat; b. Miami, Fla., Feb. 8, 1943; s. Kenneth William and Lois Rebecca (Hiestand) McK.; m. Nancy Padlon, Sept. 11, 1971; children: Harley Joseph, Sarah Elizabeth. BA, U. Chgo., 1962; MA, Harvard U., 1964. Third sec. U.S. Embassy, Rome, 1971-72; spl. asst. U.S. Liaison Office, Peking, Republic of China, 1973-74; dep. prin. officer U.S. Consulate Gen., Danang, Republic of Vietnam, 1975; staff officer Dept. State, Washington, 1975-76, officer-in-charge Italian affairs, 1976-78; first sec. Am. Embassy, London, 1978-81; dep. polit. advisor U.S. Mission, Berlin, 1981-83; dep. exec. sec. Dept. State, Washington, 1983-86; U.S. ambassador Am. Embassy, Port-Au-Prince, Haiti, 1986—. Served to capt. U.S. Army, 1965-71, Vietnam. Decorated Bronze Star, Award for Valor. Home: 7064 31st St NW Washington DC 20015 Office: Embassy Port-Au-Prince Care US Dept of State Washington DC 20520

MC KINNEY, JAMES MORTON, chemist; b. Rochester, N.Y., Apr. 5, 1918; s. William Arthur and Esther Florence (Morton) McK.; B.A., Oberlin Coll., 1940; postgrad. U. Chgo., 1941. With Wis. Steel Co., Chgo., 1942; analytical chemist Am. Cyanamid Co., Bound Brook, N.Y., 1946—. Served with Signal Corps, U.S. Army, 1942-45. Address: 19 New Rd Kendall Park NJ 08824

MC KINNEY, LOLA UTTERBACK, hospital administrative assistant; b. Corpus Christi, Tex., Nov. 18, 1934; d. Clifford Rogers and LaJuana (Knowles) Utterback; A.A., El Centro Jr. Coll. Sec., Gt. A&P Tea Co., Dallas, 1953-62; exec. secretarial asst. Baylor U. Med. Center, Dallas, 1962-79; office mgr., exec. sec. to v.p. Hamilton Assocs., Inc., Dallas, 1979-84; adminstrv. asst. Meth. Hosps. of Dallas, 1984—; mem. adv. com. Exec. Secretarial Sch.; mem. secretarial careers adv. com. Richland Jr. Coll., 1972-80, El Centro Jr. Coll., 1981—; Mem. com. on adminstrn. Central Br., YWCA, Dallas, 1976-85, chmn., 1977. Mem. Nat. Secs. Assn. (Big D Chpt. Sec of Yr. 1972). Republican. Baptist. Office: PO Box 655999 Dallas TX 75265-5999

MC KINNEY, ROBERT MOODY, editor and publisher; b. Shattuck, Okla., Aug. 28, 1910; s. Edwin S. and Eva (Moody) McK.; married, 1943; 1 child, Robin; m. Marie-Louise de Montmollin, May 7, 1970. AB, U. Okla., 1932; LLD, U. N.Mex., 1964. Investment analyst Standard Stats. Co., Inc. (now Standard and Poor's Co.), 1932-34; ptnr. Young-Kolbe & Co., 1934-38, Robert R. Young & Co., 1938-42; exec. v.p., treas. Pathe Film Co., 1934-39, Allegheny Corp., 1936-42, Pittston Corp. and subs., 1936-42; v.p. Fremkir Corp., 1937-50, Allan Corp., 1937-50; exec. v.p., treas. Mo. Pacific R.R., 1938-42; ptnr. Scheffmeyer, McKinney & Co., 1945-50; editor, pub. Santa Fe New Mexican, 1949—; chmn. bd. The New Mexican, Inc., 1949—; chmn. Robert Moody Found.; pres. Convivio Press, 1986; chmn. N.Mex. Econ. Devel. Commn. and Water Resources Devel. Bd., 1949-51; asst. sec. U.S. Dept. Interior, 1951-52; chmn. panel to report to Congress on impact of peaceful uses of atomic energy, 1955-56; U.S. ambassador to Internat. Atomic Energy Agy., Vienna, 1957-58; U.S. rep. Internat. Conf. Peaceful Uses Atomic Energy, Geneva, 1958; U.S. ambassador to Switzerland, 1961-63; exec. officer Presdl. Task Force on Internat. Investments, 1963-64; chmn. bd. visitors U. Okla., 1968-72; U.S. rep. Internat. Centre Settlement Investment Disputes, Washington, 1967-74; chmn. Presdl. Commn. on Travel, 1968. Author: Hymn to Wreckage: A Picaresque Interpretation of History, 1947, The Scientific Foundation for European Integration, 1959, On Increasing Effectiveness of Western Science and Technology, 1959, The Red Challenge to Technological Renewal, 1960, Review of the International Atomic Policies and Programs of the United States, 1960, The Toad and the Water Witch, 1985, Variations on a Marxist Interpretation of Culture, 1986, The Bolshoi Ballet's Last Tour, 1986. Mem. adv. bd. dirs. N.Y. Hosp.-Cornell Med. Ctr. Served from lt. (j.g.) to lt. USNR, 1942-45. Recipient Disting. Service medal U.S. Dept. Treasury, 1968, Disting. Service medal U. Okla., 1972. Mem. Am. Soc. Newspaper Editors, Council Fgn. Relations, Am. Newspaper Pubs. Assn., Phi Beta Kappa, Phi Gamma Delta. Democrat. Episcopalian. Clubs: Chevy Chase (Md.); F Street, Metropolitan (Washington); University, Brook, Century, Links, Knickerbocker, River (N.Y.C.). Home: Wind Fields Rt 1 Box 64 Middleburg VA 22117 Office: PO Box 1705 Santa Fe NM 87501

MCKINNEY, VIRGINIA ELAINE ZUCCARO, educational administrator; b. San Francisco, Nov. 18, 1924; d. Salvadore John and Elaine Agnes (Shepard) Zuccaro; B.A., Calif. State U.-Los Angeles, 1968; M.A., Calif. State U., Northridge, 1969; Ph.D., Claremont Grad. Sch., 1983; children—Joe, Walter Clifton Official ct. reporter Los Angeles County Superior Cts., 1948-59; tchr. speech-reading, adult edn. Los Angeles Bd. Edn., 1966-71; lang., reading specialist Marlton Sch. for the Deaf, Los Angeles, 1971-79; founder, pres., dir. communication skills program Center for Communicative Devel., Inc., Los Angeles, 1969-; part-time lectr. spl. edn. Calif. State U., Los Angeles, 1971-; cons. for various univs. and programs for the hearing-impaired; mem. adv. com. for deaf Calif. Dept. Rehab., 1979—, Atty.'s Gen. Commn. on Disability, 1987—. Recipient Leadership award Nat. Leadership Tng. Program in Area of Deaf, Calif. State U., Northridge, 1974; NEA Project Life grantee, 1970, Gallaudet Coll. Center for Continuing Edn. grantee, 1974. Mem. Nat., Alexander Graham Bell assns. for deaf, Profl. Rehab. Workers with Adult Deaf, Am. Instrs. of Deaf, Nat. Registery Interpreters for Deaf, Am. Speech and Hearing Assn., Greater Los Angeles Council on Deafness (pres. 1970-71), Beverly-Hollywood (Calif.) Hearing Soc. (pres. 1967-68). Republican. Presbyterian. Developer, producer audiovisual media, including 22 films and 4 books, to aid in speechreading and auditory tng., 1963-68; participant research project with Project Life on devel. of communication skills for multiply-handicapped deaf adults, 1970; developer, pub. Toe-Hold Literacy Packet, 1973, Linguistics 36, interactive computer lang. devel. program, 1986. Home: 420 N Louise St Apt 22 Glendale CA 91206 Office: 2550 Beverly Blvd Los Angeles CA 90057

MCKINNON, BAIN LAUGHLIN, retired plastics molding executive; b. Lethbridge, Alta., Can., Sept. 30, 1908 (parents Am. citizens); s. John William and Winnifred Eunice (Bain) McK.; B.S. in Chem. Engring., Oreg. State Coll., 1932, M.Sc., 1933; postgrad. U. Mich., 1934; m. Gladys Muriel Thompson, Sept. 7, 1942. Plant chemist exptl. sodium sulfate plant, Sask., Can., 1935; chemist B.C. Pulp & Paper Co., Can., 1937-42; research chemist Puget Sound Pulp & Timber Co., Bellingham, Wash., 1942-47; mfg. chemist Paschall Labs., Seattle, 1947-50; owner, operator McKinnon, Bain & Co., Detroit, 1951-80, ret., 1980. Pioneer in automatic injection molding of plastics; patentee plastic spray device for treatment of asthma; research on ethyl alcohol. Home and Office: 26530 Davison St Redford MI 48239

MCKINNON, JOHN B., food products company executive; b. 1934. AB, Duke U., 1956; MBA, Harvard U., 1961. Controller Olga Co., 1963-66; pres. textile & yarn div. Duplan Corp., 1966-73; v.p. fin. & treas. Hanes Corp., 1973-77, exec. v.p., 1977-79; with Sara Lee Corp., Chgo., 1979—, sr. v.p., then exec. v.p., now pres., 1986—, also dir. Office: Sara Lee Corp 3 First National Plaza Chicago IL 60602 *

MCKINNON, ROBERT HAROLD, insurance company executive; b. Holtville, Calif., Apr. 4, 1927; s. Harold Arthur and Gladys Irene (Blanchar) McK.; m. Marian Lois Hayes, Dec. 18, 1948; children: Steven Robert, Laurie Ellen, David Martin. BS, Armstrong Coll., 1950, MBA, 1952. Regional sales mgr. Farmers Ins. Group, Austin, Tex., 1961-66, Aurora, Ill., 1966-68; dir. life sales Farmers New World Life, Los Angeles, 1968-75; v.p. mktg. Warner Ins. Group, Chgo., 1975-82; mem. Canners Exchange Boy Adv. Com., 1977-82; sr. v.p. mktg. The Rural Cos. Scoutmaster Boy Scouts Am., 1971-72. Served with U.S. Army, 1944-45. Fellow Life Underwriters Tng. Council; mem. Am. Soc. CLU's, Soc. CPCU's, Internat. Ins. Seminars. Club: Nakoma Golf (Madison, Wis.). Lodge: Rotary. Home: 402 Walnut Grove Dr Madison WI 53717

MCKINSTRY, GRENETTA, microbial geneticist; b. Birmingham, Ala., Oct. 10, 1947; d. Willie D. and Willie Gertrude McKinstry; A.B. cum laude, Biology, Stillman Coll., 1968; M.A. (NDEA fellow) in Microbiology, Ind. U., 1970; Ph.D., Ohio State U., 1979; 1 son, Robert L. Harris. Researcher, Eli Lilly Pharm. Co., Indpls., 1970-72; tech. asst. dept. microbiology Ohio State U., 1972-76, teaching asst., 1976-79; tutor European Molecular Biology Orgn., U. Erlangen-Nurnberg (W. Ger.), 1979; postdoctoral asso. Max Planck Inst. for Molecular Genetics, West Berlin, 1979, Ohio State U., 1979; microbial geneticist Abbott Labs., North Chicago, Ill., 1980-85; sr. microbial geneticist Oak Ridge Research Inst., 1985-87; sr. microbiologist PEER cons., 1987—. Recipient Presdl. award, 1982. Mem. Am. Soc. for Microbiology, Assn. for Women in Sci., AAAS, N.Y. Acad. Scis., Am. Phytopath. Soc., Sigma Xi. Baptist. Contbr. articles on microbial genetics to sci. publs. Office: 575 Oak Ridge Turnpike Oak Ridge TN 37830

MCKNIGHT, JOHN FREDERICK, agricultural engineer; b. Kindersley, Sask., Can., Aug. 18, 1949; s. Kenneth Richard and Dorothy I. (Francis) McK.; m. Marlene Jean Kohls, July 20, 1972. BS in Agrl. Engring., U. Sask., Sask., Can., 1974; MBA, U. Sask., Saskatoon, Can., 1978. Resident engr. Sask. Hwys., 1974-76; sales mgr. Internat. Harvester Can., Saskatoon, 1977-79; engr. Yellowhead Cons. Engrs., Saskatoon, 1979-80; project engr. Sask. Water Corp., Outlook, 1980. Mem. Assn. Profl. Engrs. Sask., Am. Assn. Agrl. Engrs. Home: 142 Haight Crescent, Saskatoon, SK Canada S7H 4V9

MC KNIGHT, LENORE RAVIN, child psychiatrist; b. Denver, May 15, 1943; d. Abe and Rose (Steed) Ravin; student Occidental Coll., 1961-63; B.A., U. Colo., 1965, postgrad. in medicine, 1965-67; M.D., U. Calif., San Francisco, 1969; m. Robert Lee McKnight, July 22, 1967; children—Richard Rex, Janet Rose. Cert. adult and child psychiatrist Am. Bd. Psychiatry. Intern pediatrics Children's Hosp., San Francisco, 1969-70; resident in gen. psychiatry Langley Porter Neuropsychiat. Inst., 1970-73, fellow child psychiatry, 1972-74; child psychiatrist Youth Guidance Center, San Francisco, 1974-74; pvt. practice medicine specializing in child psychiatry, Walnut Creek, Calif., 1974—; asst. clin. prof. Langley Porter Neuropsychiat. Inst., 1974—; asst. clin. prof. psychiatry U. Calif. San Francisco Med. Center. Diplomate Am. Bd. Psychiatry and Neurology. Internat. Insts. Edn. fellow U. Edinburgh, summer 1964; NIH grantee to study childhood nutrition, summer 1966. Mem. Am. Acad. Child Psychiatry, Am. Psychiat. Assn., Psychiat. Assn. No. Calif., Am. Med. Women's Assn., Internat., Diablo arabian horse assns. Breeder Arabian horses. Home: 3441 Echo Springs Rd Lafayette CA 94549 Office: 130 LaCasa Via Walnut Creek CA 94598

MCKNIGHT, MICHAEL LANCE, marketing and financial executive; b. Painesville, Ohio, Nov. 8, 1939; s. Clinton Blair and Marianne Virginia (Marvin) McK.; m. Deborah Sue Coggins, Jan 28, 1978; children: Ryan Michael, Drew Boynton, Courtney Blair. Student, Ohio U., 1959, Ohio State U., 1960-63; Grad. Instalment Lending Sch., Kent State U., 1975; Grad. Nat. Comml. Lending Sch., U. Okla., 1978. V.p. Ameritrust Co., Cleve., 1975-78; sales mgr. Grantham Inc., Fairport, Ohio, 1978-81, Penn Compression, Pitts., 1981-83; v.p., gen. mgr. Pvt. Safe Place, Beachwood, Ohio, 1983—; owner, operator Knight-Rydre Co., 1984—; tchr. Lake Erie Coll., Painesville, 1975-78, Cuyahoga Community Coll., 1987. Loaned exec. United Way, Painesville, 1975-77; bd. dirs. Meadowlawn Assn., Mentor, Ohio, 1984-86, Am. Cancer Soc., Painesville, 1976-78. Served with U.S. Army, 1963-66. Mem. Am. Soc. Indsl. Security, Data Processing Mgmt. Assn. (bd. dirs. 1985—), Assn. Records Mgrs. and Adminstrs., Security Practitioners Group, Assn. Contingency Planners, Ohio Contingency Planners Assn. Republican. Lodges: Rotary, Elks. Home: 7637 Crimson Ct Mentor OH 44060 Office: Pvt Safe Place 24025 Commerce Park Beachwood OH 44122

MCLAIN, WILLIAM ALLEN, lawyer; b. Chgo., Oct. 19, 1942; s. William Rex and Wilma L. (Raschka) McL.; m. Cynthia Lee Szatkowski, Sept. 3, 1966; children—William A., David M., Heather A. B.S., So. Ill. U., 1966; J.D., Loyola U., Chgo., 1971. Bar: Ill. 1971, U.S. Dist. Ct. (no. dist.) Ill. 1971, U.S. Ct. Appeals (7th cir.) 1971, Colo. 1975, U.S. Dist. Ct. Colo. 1975, U.S. Ct. Appeals (10th cir.) 1975. Law clk. U.S. Dist. Ct. (no. dist.) Ill., Chgo., 1971-72; assoc. Sidley & Austin, Chgo., 1972-75; ptnr. Welborn, Dufford, Brown & Tooley, Denver, 1975-86; pres. William A. McLain PC, 1986—, Interact, Inc., 1986—. Mem. Dist. 10 Legis. Vacancy Commn., Denver, 1984-86. Served with U.S. Army, 1966-68. Recipient Leadership and Scholastic Achievement award Loyola U. Alumni Assn., 1971. Mem. ABA, Colo. Bar Assn. (lobbyist 1983-85), Denver Bar Assn., Assn. Trial Lawyers Am., Colo. Assn. Commerce and Industry (legis. policy council 1983—), Colo. Mining Assn. (state and local affairs com. 1978—). Republican. Clubs: Denver Athletic, Roundup Riders of the Rockies. Lodges: Masons, Shriners, Scottish Rite, York Rite. Home: 8679 Doane Pl Denver CO 80231 Office: 1700 Broadway Suite 500 Denver CO 80290

MCLAUCHLIN, LON ROYCE, telephone company executive; b. Hutnsville, Tex., Dec. 9, 1934; s. Aubrey Royce and Ara Lee (Cockrell) McL.; m. Glenda Lou Porter, Sept. 6, 1955; children—Lon, Kevin, Kimberly. B.B.A., N. Tex. State U., 1957. Mgr., Southwestern Bell Telephone Co., Uvalde, Tex., 1958, Houston, 1959-68, dist. mgr., 1968-69, div. supr., Kansas City, Mo., 1969-72, div. mgr., Springfield, Mo., 1972-83, div. staff mgr., St. Louis, 1983—; dir. Centerre Bank, Springfield. Bd. dirs. Jr. Achievement, Springfield, 1972-83, Boy Scouts Am., 1974-78, St. John's Hosp., Springfield, 1975-80, Community Found., 1980-83, Better Bus. Bur., 1982-83; pres. Downtown Springfield Assn., 1982-83; pres., organizer Safety Council S.W. Mo., 1983. Named Boss of Yr., Am. Bus. Women's Assn. Springfield, 1973; recipient Caring award Springfield council Girl Scouts U.S.A., 1976. Mem.

Springfield Area C. of C. (pres. 1977). Republican. Methodist. Club: Twin Oaks Country (Springfield). Lodge: Rotary (Springfield). Avocations: golf; camping. Home: 370 Greentrails Dr S Chesterfield MO 63017 Office: Southwestern Bell One Bell Center Saint Louis MO 63101

MCLAUGHLIN, ALEXANDER CHARLES JOHN, oil company executive; b. N.Y.C., June 3, 1925; s. Alexander and Margaret (Percival) McL.; m. Joan Kosak, June 10, 1950; 1 child, Jena Hilary. BS, Va. Poly. Inst. and State U., 1946; postgrad. Columbia U., 1947-48. With Standard Vacuum Oil Co., N.Y.C., Shanghai, China, Manila, Saigon, Indochina, Hongkong, Yokohama, Japan, 1946-50; with Trans Arabian Pipeline Co., Turaif, Saudi Arabia, 1951; with Andean Nat. Corp., Cartagena, Colombia, 1952-54; civil engr., N.Y.C., 1954-55; chief project engr. mktg. Am. Oil Co., N.Y.C., chief engr. South, Atlanta, sr. head engr., Chgo., 1955-64; sr. process engr. mfg. and mktg. dept. Amoco Internat. Oil Co., Europe, S.Am., Asia, N.Y.C., Chgo., 1969-72; mgr. distbn. Singapore Petroleum Co., 1972-73; constrn. supr. Iran Pan Am. Oil Co., 1973, onshore/offshore supr., 1974-75; sr. staff engr. Amoco Internat. Oil Co., Chgo., 1975-78, Amoco Prodn. Co. Internat., Houston, 1978-85, inspection supr. offshore and overseas constrn. dept., 1985-86; cons. oil and gas industry, 1986—; bd. dirs. Cancun Medicorp. Vol. fireman Long Beach Fire Dept., 1955-63; tng. officer USCG Aux., 1962; Eagle scout, scoutmaster, troop com. mem. Nassau County N.Y. council Boy Scouts Am., 1946-49. Decorated Order White Cloud. Fellow ASCE; mem. NSPE, Nat. Assn. Corrosion Engrs., Internat. Platform Assn., Omicron Delta Kappa. Republican. Clubs: Pathfinders (London); Columbia Country (Shanghai); Singapore Swim, Singapore Petroleum, Singapore Am.; Tehran Am. Lodge: Moose. Home: 3106 Cedar Knolls Dr Kingwood TX 77339

MC LAUGHLIN, ANN, federal official; b. Newark, Nov. 16, 1941; d. Edward Joseph and Marie (Koellhoffer) Lauenstein; m. John Joseph McLaughlin, Aug. 23, 1975. B.A., Marymount Coll. Supr. network comml. schedule ABC, N.Y.C., 1963-66; dir. alumnae relations Marymount Coll., Tarrytown, N.Y., 1966-69; account exec. Myers-Infoplan Internat. Inc., N.Y.C., 1969-71; dir. communications Presdl. Election Com., Washington, 1971-72; asst. to chmn. and press sec. Presdl. Inaugural Com., Washington, 1972-73; dir. Office of Pub. Affairs, EPA, Washington, 1973-74; govt. relations and communications exec. Union Carbide Corp., N.Y.C. and Washington, 1974-77; pub. affairs, issues mgmt. counseling McLaughlin & Co., 1977-81; asst. sec. for pub. affairs Treasury Dept., Washington, 1981-84; under sec. Dept. of Interior, Washington, 1984-87; cons. Ctr. Strategic and Internat. Studies, Washington, 1987; Sec. of Labor Dept. of Labor, Washington, 1987—; mem. Am. Council on Capital Formation, 1976-78; mem. environ. edn. task force HEW, 1976-77; mem. Def. Adv. Com. of Women in the Services, 1973-74. Mem. Washington Woman's Forum. Republican. Roman Catholic. Clubs: City. Office: 200 Constitution Ave NW Room S-2018 Washington DC 20210

MC LAUGHLIN, DAVID THOMAS, academic administrator; b. Grand Rapids, Mich., Mar. 16, 1932; s. Wilfred P. and Arlene (Sunderlin) McL.; m. Judith Ann Landauer, Mar. 26, 1955; children: William, Wendy, Susan, C. Jay. B.A., Dartmouth Coll., 1954, M.B.A., 1955. With Champion Internat. Co., 1957-70; v.p., gen. mgr. Champion Internat. Co. (Champion packages div.), 1957-70; pres., chief exec. officer Toro Co., Bloomington, Minn., 1970-77; chmn., chief exec. officer Toro Co., Mpls., 1977-81; pres. Dartmouth Coll., Hanover, N.H., 1981-87; chmn. Aspen Inst., Washington, 1987-88; pres., chief exec. officer Aspen Inst., Queenstown, Md., 1988—; dir. Dayton Hudson Corp., Mpls., Westinghouse Electric Corp., Pitts., Chase Manhattan Bank, Chase Manhattan Corp., N.Y., Horizon Banks Inc., Concord, N.H., 1988—; mem. adv. bd. SRI Internat., Menlo Park, Calif. Served with USAF, 1955-57. Mem. Nat. C. of C. Episcopalian. Office: Aspen Inst PO Box 222 Queenstown MD 21658

MC LAUGHLIN, DOLPHY T., lawyer; b. Jamaica, W.I., July 10, 1922; s. Joseph P. and Caroline (Patterson) McL.; student Northwestern U., 1949-52; LL.B., Loyola U., 1955; m. Nora Belle Facey, Nov. 2, 1946; 1 son, Norman Anthony. Admitted to Ill. bar, 1956; mem. firm Brown, Brown, Greene & McLaughlin and predecessor firm, Chgo., 1956—; asst. gen. counsel Victory Mut. Life Ins. Co., Chgo., 1962-67; mem. civil service bd. Met. San. Dist. Greater Chgo., 1966-67, prin. asst. atty., 1967-73, head asst. atty., 1973—; consul of Jamaica, Chgo., 1969—. Pres., Am. West-Indian Assn., 1962-67. Decorated officer of Order of Distinction (Jamaica), 1983. Mem. ABA, Chgo., Cook County bar assns., Phi Alpha Delta. Episcopalian. Home: 5415 N Sheridan Rd Chicago IL 60640 Office: 100 E Erie St Chicago IL 60611

MCLAUGHLIN, GEOFFREY HAROLD, airline executive; b. Wangarata, Victoria, Australia, July 7, 1933; s. Harold and Doreen (Moore) McL.; children: Darren Geoffrey, Cameron John. Grad., Wangarata Tech. Coll. Sta. mgr. Avis Rent-A-Car, Australia, 1959-72; sales mgr. Ansett Airlines of Papua New Guinea, Port Moresby, 1972-73, Air Niugini, Port Moresby, 1973-76; with pub. security Govt. of Papua New Guinea, Port Moresby, 1976-78; mgr. Reids Travel Agy., Ipswich, Qld., Australia, 1978-80; editor Paradise Mag., 1980—; pub. relations mgr. Air Niugini, Port Moresby, 1980—; dir. Avis Nationwide Co. Ltd., Port Moresby, 1982—. Justice of the Peace Queensland, Australia, 1965; commr. of oaths, Papua New Guinea, 1986. Named mem. Order Brit. Empire Her Majesty Queen Elizabeth II, 1986.

MCLAUGHLIN, GLEN HENRY, association executive; b. Abilene, Tex., Feb. 3, 1914; s. John Henry and Clara Elizabeth (Priddy) McL.; B.A., Hardin-Simmons U., 1935, postgrad. 1938-39; student Central State U. Okla., 1933-34; postgrad. U. Tex., Austin, 1937-38; m. Mary Evelyn Ivy, Nov. 19, 1939; 1 dau., Suzanne McLaughlin Rowden. Tchr. sci. Lewisville (Tex.) High Sch., 1935-36, Gatesville (Tex.) High Sch., 1936-37; instr. dept. physics Hardin-Simmons U., 1937; bacteriologist Tex. State Health Dept., Austin, 1937-38; meteorologist U.S. Weather Bur., Abilene, Tex., 1938-39; instr. dept. chemistry, Hardin-Simmons U., summer, 1939; chemist, toxicologist and lab. supr. Tex. Dept. Public Safety, Austin, 1939-45, chief identification and criminal records and dir. labs., 1945-57, chief personnel and staff services, 1957-73, chief adminstrn., 1973-77; exec. sec. Tex. Police Assn., Austin, 1977—; lectr. in field. Chmn. Tex. Commn. on Law Enforcement Officers Standards and Edn., 1965-73; mem. Gov.'s com. for devel. of position classification plan for state govt., Tex., 1953-54; div. dir. United Fund, 1958-59. Recipient citation, Tex. State Legislature, 1948, Tex. Law Enforcement Found., 1956; named Tex. Public Employee of the Yr., 1971; named Public Adminstr. of the Yr. Austin Soc. Public Adminstrn., 1972; Wallace Beasley award for outstanding contribution to law enforcement edn. in Tex., 1976. Fellow Am. Acad. Forensic Sci.; mem. Internat. Assn. for Identification (pres. 1950), Internat. Assn. Automobile Theft (pres. 1961), Harvard Assos. in Police Sci., Internat. Assn. Chiefs of Police, Sheriff's Assn. Tex., Austin Soc. for Public Adminstrn., Tex. Police Assn., Tex. Public Employees Assn. (dir.). Baptist. Clubs: Country of Austin, Austin, Austin Knife and Fork (pres. 1973). Asso. editor Tex. Police Jour., 1960—; contbr. articles to profl. jours. Home: 4114 Shoal Creek Austin TX 78756 Office: PO Box 4247 Austin TX 78765

MCLAUGHLIN, JAMES DANIEL, architect; b. Spokane, Wash., Oct. 2, 1947; s. Robert Francis and Patricia (O'Connel) McL.; B.Arch., U. Idaho, 1971; m. Willa Kay Pace, Aug. 19, 1972; children—Jamie Marie, Robert James. Project architect Neil M. Wright, Architect, AIA, Sun Valley, Idaho, 1971-74, McMillan & Hayes, Architects, Sun Valley, 1974-75; now pres., prin. McLaughlin Architects Chartered, Sun Valley. Prin. works include Oakridge Apts., Moscow, Idaho (Excellence in Design award AIA), Walnut Ave. Mall, Ketchum, Idaho (Excellence in Design award AIA, 1987), McMahan Residence, Sun Valley (Excellence in Design award AIA, 1987). Chmn., Ketchum Planning and Zoning Commn., Ketchum Planning Commn., Ketchum Zoning Commn.; vice chmn. Sun Valley Planning and Zoning Commn. Served to 1st lt. U.S. Army. Registered architect, 8 states including Idaho. Mem. AIA , Nat. Council Archtl. Registration Bds., Nat. Home Builders Assn., Ketchum-Sun Valley C. of C. (dir.). Roman Catholic. Club: Rotary. Prin. archtl. works include James West Residence, First Fed. Savs., Fox Bldg. Rehab., Walnut Ave. Mall, First St. Office Bldg. Home: Lot #5 Red Cliffs Subdivision Box 6 Ketchum ID 83340 Office: McLaughlin Architects Chartered PO Box 479 Sun Valley ID 83353

MCLAUGHLIN, JOHN D., food manufacturing, home development executive, retired army officer; b. San Francisco, Dec. 24, 1917; s. John and Lottie (Bruhns) McL.; m. Elizabeth Susan Stumper, July 11, 1946; children: John D., William F., Susan C. Ed., George Washington U.; grad., Armed Forces Staff Coll., 1956, Nat. War Coll., 1959, Advanced Mgmt. Program, Harvard U., 1963; Ph.D. (hon.), Johnson and Wales Coll. Commd. 2d lt. U.S. Army, 1942, advanced through grades to lt. gen.; staff asst. Office Sec. of Def., 1960-61; exec. officer Def. Supply Agy., 1961-63; asst. commandant U.S. Army Q.M. Sch., 1963-65; chief of staff U.S. Army, VietNam, 1965-66; dir. supply U.S. Army Gen. Staff, 1966-67; asst. chief of staff for logistics Pacific Command (CINCPAC), 1967-69; comdg. gen. Quartermaster Center, comdt. U.S. Army Quartermaster Sch., Ft. Lee, Va., 1969-73; comdr. U.S. Theater Army Support Command, Europe, 1973-74; v.p. L.J. Minor Corp., Cleve., 1974-79; pres. L.J. Minor Corp., 1979-83, chmn., chief exec. officer, 1983-87; pres. L.J. Minor Internat., 1987—; bd. dirs. Sovran Bank, Petersburg, Va.; chmn. bd. TEC of Am., Inc. Mem. Tri-cities Adv. bd.; mem. exec. council Richmond Boy Scouts Am.; adv. bd. Ednl. Inst. of Am. Culinary Fedn.; trustee Culinary Inst. Am.; pres. U.S. Culinary Team Found.; v.p. Q.M. Meml. Found. Served with AUS, 1934-74. Decorated D.S.M. with oak leaf cluster, Legion of Merit with 4 oak leaf clusters, Bronze Star Medal with 2 oak leaf clusters, Air medal U.S., Distinguished Service Medal Greece; recipient Silver Plate award Internat. Food Service Mfrs. Assn., 1973, Silver Beaver award Boy Scouts Am., 1973. Mem. Quartermaster Assn. (pres. Washington chpt. 1969-70), Harvard Bus. Sch. Alumni Assn., Am. Culinary Fedn., Gold and Silver Plate Award Soc., Am. Acad. Chefs (hon. life), Am. Legion, VFW, Mil. Order World Wars, Honorable Order Golden Toque. Clubs: Kiwanis of Petersburg (past dir.), Harvard of Va. Petersburg Country, Army-Navy Country; Commonwealth (Richmond, Va.). Home: 10 Nomas Ln Richmond VA 23233 Office: 436 Bulkley Bldg Cleveland OH 44115 also: 3235 Boulevard Colonial Heights VA 23834

MCLAUGHLIN, MICHAEL ANGELO, mortgage consultant, author; b. Medford, Mass., Mar. 13, 1950; s. Bernard Thadeus and Rose Francis (Di Stasio) McL.; m. Karen Jean Parker, Nov. 19, 1972 (div. 1985); m. Claudia Chuber, June 29, 1985; 1 child, Camila. B.S. with honors, Northeastern U., 1975, M.P.A., 1978. Asst. juvenile supr. Dept. Youth Services, Boston, 1972-73; correction officer Dept. Correction, Billerica, Mass., 1974, Dept. Correction-MCI Walpole, Boston, 1974-80; facility mgr. 1st Security Services Corp., Boston, 1980-82; from sales mgr. to owner Solar Resources Internat., Danvers, Mass., 1982-84; acct. exec. New Eng. Rare Coin Galleries, Boston, 1985, Progressive Consumers Fed. Credit Union, 1985—; lectr. Northeastern U., Boston, 1981; pres. local chpt. Am. Fedn. State, County and Mcpl. Employess, Mass., 1977-79. Candidate, Com. to Elect Mike McLaughlin Sheriff, Middlesex County, Mass., 1980; mem. Spl. Legis. Conf. Com., Boston, 1979, Jt. Labor Mgmt. Com., Boston, 1978. Mem. Am. Correctional Assn., Am. Jail Assn., Master of Pub. Adminstrn. Assn. (activities com. 1982), Sigma Epsilon Rho. Roman Catholic. Avocations: sailing; skiing; pocket billiards; tennis; racquetball. Author: Screw: The Guard Who Reformed Walpole, 1988.

MCLAUGHLIN, ROBERT FRANCIS, retired lawyer; b. Mountain Home, Idaho, July 11, 1920; s. Daniel and Mary C. McLaughlin; m. Patty McLaughlin, June 5, 1946; children—James D., John Patrick, Michael R., Mary, Anne Crim. B.A., U. Idaho, 1948, LL.B., 1950, J.D., 1969. Bar: Idaho 1950, U.S. Supreme Ct. 1958, U.S. Ct. Appeals (9th cir.) 1970. Pros. atty. Elmore County, Idaho, 1950-60; pvt. practice, Mountain Home, 1960-84, ret., 1984; city atty. Glenns Ferry, Idaho, 1952-54, Mountain Home, 1962-66; atty. Idaho State Land Bd., 1967-68. Democratic nominee U.S. Senate, 1960; mem. Kennedy-Johnson Natural Resources Com., 1960; active Boy Scouts Am. Served with U.S. Army, 1941-46; pres. U. Idaho Parents Assn., 1971; chmn. com. Idaho Vet. for Johnson and Humphrey, 1964. Mem. Am. Judicature Soc., Idaho Pros. Atty. Assn. (pres. 1959-60), Internat. Platform Soc., Idaho Trial Lawyers Assn. (pres. 1968-70), U. Idaho Law Sch. Alumni Assn. (pres. 1962-64). Democrat. Roman Catholic. Author: Idaho Magistrate Manual, 1958. Home: 875 Galena Ct Mountain Home ID 83647

MCLAUGHLIN, WALTER JOSEPH, actuary; b. N.Y.C., Dec. 7, 1931; s. Walter Joseph Sr. and Margaret Mary (Lynch) M.; m. Helen Joan Knecht, Sept. 5, 1955; children—John, Philip, Clare (dec.), James, Michael. A.B. in Econs., Fordham U., 1953. Asst. actuary Met. Life Ins. Co., N.Y.C., 1958-66; cons. actuary Cons. Actuaries Internat., N.Y.C., 1966-68, Stone, Young & Co., 1968-70, Marsh & McLennon, N.Y.C., 1970-73; rev. actuary Buck Cons., Inc., N.Y.C., 1973—; instr. pensions Rockland Community Coll., Monsey, N.Y., 1979-80. Chmn. Rockland County Basketball Newsletter, 1975-87, Rockland Basketball All Star teams, 1975-87. Served to 1st lt. U.S. Army, 1954-56, Recipient Disting. Services to Youth award Rockland County High Sch. Basketball Coaches, 1982. Fellow Soc. Actuaries (enrolled actuary, chmn. pub. relations com. 1976-78, mem. joint exam. com. for enrollment of actuaries 1978-81), Conf. Actuaries in Pub. Practice; mem. Am. Acad. Actuaries, Am. Pension Conf., N.Y. Actuaries Club (panel moderator, pension com. 1980-83), Am. Arbitration Assn. (panel of arbitrators), Rockland County 2000 Com. Republican. Roman Catholic. Office: Buck Cons 500 Plaza Dr Harmon Meadow NJ 07096-1533

MC LAUGHLIN, WILLIAM GAYLORD, metal products manufacturing company executive; b. Marietta, Ohio, Sept. 28, 1936; s. William Russell and Edna Martha (Hiatt) McL.; children: Debora, Cynthia, Leslie, Teresa, Kristin, Jennifer. BS in Mech. Engring., U. Cin., 1959; MBA, Ball State U., 1967. Plant engr. Kroger Co., Marion, Ind., 1959-62; with Honeywell, Inc., Wabash, Ind., 1962-75, mgr. metal products ops., 1971-72, gen. mgr. ops., 1972-75; pres. MarkHon Industries Inc., Wabash, 1975—; mem. N. Cen. Ind. Pvt. Industry Council, 1983-84; mem. bus. adv. bd. Manchester Coll. Patentee design electronic relay rack cabinet. Pres. Wabash Assn. for Retarded Children, 1974-75; gen. chmn. United Fund Drive, 1971; mem. Wabash County Arts Council; pres. Wabash Valley Dance Theater; treas., Young Reps., Wabash, 1968-70; bd. dirs. Youth Service Bur., Sr. Citizens, Jr. Achievement; mem. ofcl. bd. Meth. ch., 1966-71; pres. Meth. men, 1975-77. Recipient Ind. Jefferson award for public service, 1981, Disting. Citizen award Wabash, 1981; named Outstanding Young Man of Year, Wabash Jr. C. of C., 1972. Mem. Indsl. C. of C. (pres. 1973-74), Wabash Area C. of C. (pres. 1976), Precision Metal Forming Assn. (chmn. Ind. dist. 1978, chmn. metal fabrication div.), Ind. Mfg. Assn. (bd. dirs.), Young Pres.'s Orgn. Club: Wabash Country (v.p. 1972-76). Lodges: Rotary (pres. Cincinnatus Soc. 1970-71, dist. youth exchange officer 1974-77, dist. gov. 1979-80), Masons. Home: 141 W Maple St Wabash IN 46992 Office: 200 Bond St Wabash IN 46992

MCLAUGHLIN, WILLIAM LOWNDES, physicist, researcher; b. Stony Point, Tenn., Mar. 30, 1928; s. John Calvin Brown and Fanny Dargen (McCaa) M.; m. Nancy Elizabeth Shepherd, Mar. 27, 1951; children—Peter Shepherd, David Wallace. B.S. summa cum laude, Hampden-Sydney Coll., 1949; M.S. in Physics, George Washington U., 1963. Physicist, Nat. Bur. Standards, Washington, 1951—, Gaithersburg, Md., 1973—; cons. Riso Nat. Lab., Roskilde, Denmark, 1975—, Boris Kidric Inst., Vinca, Belgrade Yugoslavia, 1976—, Internat. Atomic Energy Agy., Vienna, 1977—. Editor: Trends in Radiation Dosimetry, 1982; editor-in-chief Applied Radiation and Isotopes; editorial bd. Radiation Physics and Chemistry. Author: Dosimetry for Food Irradiation, 1977. Patentee in field. Served with U.S. Army, 1954-56. Recipient Silver medal for research U.S. Dept. of Commerce, 1969, Gold medal, 1979; Tech., Radiation Sci. and Tech. award, Am. Nuclear Soc., 1987, Transfer award Fed. Lab. Consortium, 1984; Applied Research award Nat. Bur. Standards, 1985, R&D 100 award, 1988; Rotary Internat. fellow, 1950-51. Mem. St. Andrews Soc., Rockbridge Hist. Soc., N.Y. Acad. Sci., Optical Soc. Am., Am. Phys. Soc., Soc. Photographic Sci. and Engring. (dir. 1964-67), Radiation Research Soc. Presbyterian. Club: Cosmos. Home: 3901 Albemarle St NW Washington DC 20016

MC LAURIN, FRANCIS WALLIN (FRANK), radio broadcasting executive; b. Sioux Falls, S.D., Sept. 24, 1923; s. Archibald A. and Clementine B. (Wallin) McL.; student Calif. Jr. Coll., 1941-42; m. Barbara Lee Jones, May 26, 1956; 1 dau., Barbara Lyn. Announcer sta. KGGM, Albuquerque, 1946; in prodn., sta. KFXM, San Bernardino, Calif., 1947-51; gen. mgr. sta. KWRN, Reno, 1951-52; account exec. KFMB TV, San Diego, 1953-54; gen. mgr. sta. KSRO, Santa Rosa, Calif., 1954—; dir., v.p. Finley Broadcasting Co. (now owns KSRO AM and KREO FM), Santa Rosa. Mem. broadcast adv. bd. UPI. Bd. dirs. Boy Scouts Am. Recipient Young Man of Yr. award, Santa Rosa Jr. C. of C., 1957; Calif. Broadcasters Disting. award, 1984. Mem. Calif. Broadcasters Assn. (dir., past chmn.), Nat. Assn. Broadcasters (dir.), Santa Rosa C. of C. (pres. 1960). Republican. Presbyterian. Rotarian (pres. 1966-67). Home: 1708 Pamela Dr Santa Rosa CA 95404 Office: Stas KSRO - KREO FM College Ave Santa Rosa CA 95403

MCLAURIN, IAN CHARTER, business executive; b. Blackheath, Eng., Mar. 30, 1937; s. Arthur George and Evelina Florence MacLaurin; m. Ann Margaret Collar, 1961; 3 children. Student, Malvern Coll., Worcs., Eng. With Tesco, 1959—, bd. dirs., 1970, dep. chmn., 1983-85, mng. dir., 1973-85, chmn., 1985—; chmn. Food Policy Group, Retail Consortium, 1980-84; mem. mgmt. com. Inst. Grocery Distbn.; non-exec. dir. Enterprise Oil plc, 1984—, Guinness plc, 1986—. Gov., mem. council, Malvern Coll.; mem. com. Met. County Council, 1986—. Served with RAF, 1956-58. Mem. Inst. of Dirs., Carmen's Co. (liveryman 1982—). Clubs: Royal Automobile, MCC, Lord's Taverners, XL, Band of Brothers. Office: Tesco plc, Tesco House, Delamere Rd, Cheshunt, Herts England *

MCLAURIN, RONALD DE, political analyst, consultant, author, research analyst; b. Oakland, Calif., Oct. 8, 1944; s. Lauchlin De and Marie Annette (Friedman) McL.; m. Joan Adcock, June 11, 1966; children—Leila, Cara. B.A., U. So. Calif., 1965; student, U. Tunis, Tunisia, 1964-65; A.M., Tufts U., 1966, M.A.L.D., 1967, Ph.D., 1973. Instr. Merrimack Coll., North Andover, Mass., 1966-67; mgmt. asst. Office Sec. Def., Washington, 1967-68; asst. for Africa Office Asst. Sec. Def. for Internat. Security Affairs, 1968-69; research scientist Am. Inst. Research, Washington, 1969-75; sr. assoc. Abbott Assocs., Inc., Springfield, Va., 1975—; sec.-treas. Abbott Assocs., Inc., 1985-86, pres., 1986—; internat. research assoc. Inha U., Korea, 1985—; fellow Ctr. Internat. Devel., U. Md., 1983—; ptnr. Aurora, Ltd., 1986-87; dir. Lau-Mar, Ltd., Honolulu, 1981-86, also chmn.; cons. Am. Insts. Research, 1975-76, Analytical Assessments Corp., 1977-79, Ctr. Advanced Internat. Studies, U. Miami, 1973, Ctr. Advanced Research, Inc., 1977-82, Ctr. Strategic and Internat. Studies, Georgetown U., 1981, 85, Middle East Assessments Group, 1982—, Allen Wayne, Ltd., 1986, Getty Oil Co., 1982, Office of Pres. Lebanon, 1984-85, Office Crown Prince Jordan, 1982—, Office U.S. Sec. Def., 1973, Lebanese Ministry of Defense, 1984-85, Bus. Council on Internat. Understanding, 1984—, BDM Corp., 1985—, Trans Devel. Corp., 1986, TRW, 1987—. Author: The Middle East in Soviet Policy, 1975, The Art and Science of Psychological Operations, 2 vols., 1976, Foreign Policy Making in the Middle East, 1977, The Political Role of Minority Groups in the Middle East, 1979, Beyond Camp David, 1981, Military Propaganda, 1982, Middle East Foreign Policy: Issues and Processes, 1982, Lebanon and the World in the 1980s, 1983, The Emergence of a New Lebanon: Fantasy or Reality?, 1984, Jordan: The Impact of Social Change on the Tribes, 1984, U.S. Security Defense Posture in the Pacific, 1987, Alliance Under Tension: Critical Issues in U.S.-Korean Relations, 1988, The Dilemma of Third World Defense Industries: Supplier Controls and Recipient Autonomy, 1988; contbr. articles to profl. jours. Mem. Internat. Studies Assn., Inter-Univ. Seminar Armed Forces and Soc., Middle East Inst., Fgn. Policy Research Inst. Psychol. Ops. Soc. Home: 8600 Powder Horn Rd Springfield VA 22152 Office: Abbott Assocs Inc PO Box 2124 Springfield VA 22152

MCLAY, JAMES KENNETH, political, business consultant; b. Auckland, New Zealand, Feb. 21, 1945; s. Robert and Joyce Evelyn (Dee) McL.; m. Marcy Farden, Dec. 17, 1983. LLB, U. Auckland, 1967. Barrister, solicitor, then barrister High Ct. New Zealand, Wellington, 1968—; mem. New Zealand Parliament, Wellington, 1975-87; atty. gen., minister justice New Zealand, Wellington, 1978-84, dep. prime minister, 1984; leader opposition New Zealand Parliament, 1984-86; ind. bus., polit. cons. Contbr. articles to profl. jours. Served to lt. New Zealand Territorial Force, 1967-70. Recipient Queen's Service Order for Pub. Service, Queen Elizabeth II, 1987. Mem. New Zealand Nat. Party. Anglican. Home and Office: 8885 Symonds St, Northcote Point, Auckland 1 New Zealand

MC LEAN, GEORGE LEONARD, technical publications editor; b. Camas, Wash., Apr. 18, 1922; s. George Clinton and Mary Margaret (Brantner) McL.; student psychology Reed Coll., 1951-55; grad. Edison Tech. Sch., 1957, Renton Vocat. Sch., 1967; B.A. in Journalism, Seattle U., 1970; m. Apr. 18, 1962 (div.); 1 son, George Henry. Planner research and devel. Boeing Co., Seattle, 1957-62; illustrator, art editor Milmanco Co., Renton, Wash., 1966, chief editor, 1967-68; instr. Journalism Seattle U., 1968; chief editor Volt Publ. Co., Bellevue, Wash., 1969; tech. editor Western Gear Corp., Everett, Wash., 1969-70; freelance writer, editor, Sacramento, Calif., 1970-72; tech. publs. editor, illustrator Dept. Def., Keyport, Wash., 1972-79, supervisory tech. publs. editor, 1979-87; free-lance editor, writer, photographer, 1987—. Mem. Naval Unersea Warfare Mus. Found. Served with USN, 1942-46; ETO; USNR, 1946-54. Decorated Air medal (6), others. Recipient Nat. Newspaper Snapshot award, 1965. Mem. Soc. Tech. Communication (sr.), Mensa (life), Soc. Wireless Pioneers, Am. Def. Preparedness Assn, Internat. Clover Poetry Assn. (life), Am. Legion, Am. Assn. Ret. Persons, Reed Coll. Alumni Assn. Seattle U. Alumni Assn., Nat. Divorce Reform Assn. Club: Eagles. Home: PO Box 333 Keyport WA 98345

MCLEAN, MARGARET STONER, researcher; b. Victoria, Tex., June 5, 1915; d. Thomas Royal and Mame Victoria (Stoner) Stoner; A.A., Victoria Jr. Coll., 1936; B.S., U. Tex., 1939; m. Malcolm Dallas McLean, Feb. 11, 1939; 1 son, John Robertson. Receptionist, postmaster San Jacinto Mus. History, Houston, 1939-41; microfilm camera operator Library of Congress, Washington, 1942; bibliog. researcher, 1947-53; tchr. elem. sch., Fayetteville, Ark., 1954-55; elem. tchr. Am. Sch., Tegucigalpa, Honduras, 1957-58; tchr. English, U.S. Binat. Center and Am. High Sch., Guayaquil, Ecuador, 1959-61; newspaper microfilm archivist Amon Carter Mus. Western Art, Ft. Worth, 1963-73; microfilm research specialist Spanish Tex. Microfilm Center, Presidio La Bahia, Goliad, Tex., 1973-74; researcher, editorial asst. Papers Concerning Robertson's Colony in Tex., Ft. Worth, 1975—; bibliog. researcher Jenkins Garrett Library, U. Tex., Arlington, 1981-82. Mem. chancellor's council U. Tex. System, 1984—. Clubs: U. Tex. at Arlington Woman's; Texas Christian U. Woman's (Ft. Worth). Contbr. articles to profl. jours. Address: 409 Baylor Dr Arlington TX 76010

MCLEAN, WILLIAM GEORGE, engineering education consultant; b. Scranton, Pa., Mar. 15, 1910; s. Michael and Matilda Marie (Geueke) McL.; B.S. in Elec. Engring., Lafayette Coll., 1932; M.S., Brown U., 1933. Head math. dept. West Scranton (Pa.) High Sch., 1934-37; asst. prof. mech. engring. Lafayette Coll., Easton, Pa., 1937-44; asst. to supr. spl. products div. Eastman Kodak Co., Rochester, N.Y., 1944-46; prof., head engring. sci. Lafayette Coll., 1946-75, dir. engring., 1962-75; cons. in field, 1950—; mem. Pa. Registration Bd. Profl. Engrs., 1981-87. Chmn. Hugh Moore Park Commn., 1969—; mem. Am. Nat. Metric Practice Group, 1974—. Fellow ASME (nat. v.p. 1953-55, 70-72; Codes and Standards medal 1977, Performance Test Codes medal 1984); mem. Nat. Soc. Profl. Engrs. (pres. Pa. 1965-66), Am. Soc. Engring. Edn., Sigma Xi, Phi Beta Kappa, Tau Beta Pi, Eta Kappa Nu, Pi Tau Sigma, Kappa Delta Rho. Democrat. Roman Catholic. Author: (with E.W. Nelson) Engineering Mechanics, 1952, 4th editn., 1988; (with C.L. Best) Engring. Mechanics, 1965. Home and Office: 333 5th Ave Scranton PA 18505

MCLEAN, WILLIAM RONALD, electrical engineer, consultant b. Bklyn., Mar. 26, 1921; s. Harold W. and Helena Winifred (Farrell) McL.; m. Cecile L. Mills, Aug. 17, 1946 (div.); m. 2d, Evelyn Hupfer, Nov. 29, 1968. BA, Bklyn. Coll., 1980, BS, 1981. Chief electrician U.S. Mcht. Marine, 1942-64; elect. designer, engr., 65-76; sr. elect. engr. Rosenblatt & Son, Inc., N.Y.C., 1976-86; cons., 1986—. Mem. Soc. Naval Architects and Marine Engineers, IEEE, Am. Soc. Naval Engrs. Home and Office: 45 Grace Ct Brooklyn NY 11201

MCLELLAN, ROBERT, electronics executive; b. Falkirk, Stirlingshire, Scotland, July 31, 1933; s. James and Janet McKerron (Murray) McL.; m. Rita Joan Spain, Ja. 16, 1960; children: Andrew James, Stuart Craig, Robert Bruce, Louise Tracy. BSc in Biochemistry with honors, U. Edinburg, Scotland, 1959; MA in Edn., U. Exeter, Eng., 1971; PhD in Edn., U. Ariz., Phoenix, 1984. Chartered chemist, clin. hypnotherapist. Lectr. sci. Royal Australian Air Force Sch. of Tech. Tng., Wagga Wagga, Australia, 1958-60, Kent Edn. Com., Kent, Eng., 1965-71; dir. ergonomics group Div. of Occupational Health, Sydney, Australia, 1960-65; divisional gen. mgr. Roche Products P/L, Sydney, 1971-77; dir. pub. relations New South Wales Soc. Crippled Children, Sydney, 1977-81; mgr. tng. and health, safety environment BP Coal (Australia), Sydney, 1981-88; chief exec. officer Australia Med.

Devices & Diagnostics Assn., Dural, 1988—; chmn. New South Wales Health and Safety Unit, Sydney, 1986—, Australian Safety Centre, Sydney, 1986—; loss control cons. BP Kwinana and BP Bulwer Island Refineries, Australia, 1985-88. Contbr. articles to profl. jours. Mem. Mus. Soc., Dural & Sydney, 1984—; pres. Returned Services League of Australia Hills Dist. Br., 1983-86, sr. v.p. Far Western Council, 1984-86. Served with British Army, 1953-54, Malaya. Maj. research grantee Nat. Energy Devel. Council, New South Wales, 1987; recipient Sword of Honour British Safety Council, 1985. Fellow British Chem. Soc.; mem. Royal Australian Chem. Inst. (assoc.) Australian Coll. Edn., Inst. Personnel Mgrs. of Australia. Mem. Liberal Party. Presbyterian. Club: Imperial Service (Sydney). Lodge: Thespian. Home: 3 Vineys Rd, 2158 Dural, New South Wales 2158, Australia Office: Australian Med Devices and Diagnostics Assn, 77 Berry St N, Sydney, New South Wales 2080, Australia

MCLEMORE, MICHAEL KERR, lawyer; b. Atlanta, May 19, 1949; s. Gilbert Carmichael Sr. and Jeannie (Gulley) M.; m. Colleen Owen, Aug. 19, 1972; children: Megan, Shannon. BA, Haverford Coll., 1971; JD, U. Ga., 1974. Bar: Fla. 1974, U.S. Dist. Ct. (mid. and so. dists.) Fla. 1974, U.S. Ct. Appeals (5th cir.) 1974, U.S. Ct. Appeals (11th cir.) 1981, U.S. Supreme Ct. 1984. From assoc. to ptnr. Kimbrell and Hamann P.A., Miami, Fla., 1974—. Pres. Haverford Soc. South Fla., Miami, 1978—; Fla. alumni admissions rep. coordinator, Haverford Coll., 1978—, alumni council, 1980—; lay leader 1st United Meth. Ch., South Miami, 1986—, lay del. Fla. Annual Conf., 1986—; dist. bd. Missions and Ch. Extension, 1986—; co-chairperson Miami dist. Work Area on Stewardship, 1987—, lay del. to ann. conf., 1986—. Served to 1st lt. USAR, 1976-78. Mem. ABA, Fla. Bar Assn. (aviation sect.), Dade County Def. Bar Assn., Nat. Transp. Safety Bd. Assn. Democrat. Methodist. Lodge: Kiwanis. Home: 9430 SW 181st St Miami FL 33157 Office: Kimbrell and Hamann PA 799 Brickell Plaza Miami FL 33131

MCLENDON, HINKLE, JR., civil engineer; b. Americus, Ga., Jan. 30, 1919; s. Hinkle and Willie Estelle (Van Riper) McL.; m. Doris Irene Rogers, Dec. 31, 1942; children—Carol Jean McLendon Porter, James Hinkle. B.S. in Civil Engring., The Citadel, 1940; grad. U.S. Army Command and Gen. Staff Coll., 1963. Registered profl. engr., S.C. Concrete insp. Harza Engring. Co., Santee-Cooper hydroelec. dam and lock, S.C., 1940-41; resident engr. Vannort Engrs., Inc., Charlotte and Boone, N.C., 1945-48; structural design engr. J.E. Sirrine Engrs., Inc., Greenville, S.C., 1948-49; structural design engr. Westvaco Corp., Charleston, S.C., 1949-53, chief design engr. and project engr., 1953-62, purchasing agt., 1962—. Instl. rep. Coastal Carolina council Boy Scouts Am., 1960-63; bd. dirs. John C. Calhoun Homes, Inc. Served to maj. U.S. Army, 1941-45; PTO, ETO; to lt. col. USAR, 1949-67. Mem. ASCE (past pres. Eastern S.C. sect.), Civil Engrs. Club Charleston (past pres.), Nat. Soc. Profl. Engrs. (sec.-treas.), Res. Officers Assn. (life), S.C. Hist. Soc., Ga. Hist. Soc., N.C. Hist. Soc., N.Y. Geneal. and Biog. Soc., S.C. Geneal. Soc., Scottish Soc. Charleston (bd. dirs.), Citadel Alumni Assn. Methodist (past chmn. bd. stewards and bd. trustees). Club: Brigadier. Lodge: Masons (32 degree). Home: 7 Yeamans Rd The Crescent Charleston SC 29407 Office: Westvaco Corp Virginia Ave Charleston SC 29411

MC LEOD, NORMAN WILLIAM, civil engineer; b. Nichol Twp., Ont., Can., Nov. 26, 1904; s. William and Elizabeth Helen (Ewen) McL.; m. Irene Marguerite Briggs, Feb. 10, 1931; children: Norman Barrie, Muriel Irene McLeod Hodgins, Ruth Marilyn McLeod Wyand, Murray Graeme, Susan Eileen McLeod Burs. B.Sc. in Chem. Engring, U. Alta., Can., 1930; M.Sc. in Chem. Engring, U Sask., Can., 1936; Sc.D. in Civil Engring, U. Mich., 1938; D.Eng. (hon.), U. Waterloo, 1980. In charge asphalt constrn. and maintenance Sask. Dept. Hwys., 1930-38; asphalt cons. responsible for asphalt mfg. and quality Imperial Oil Ltd., Toronto, Ont., 1938-69; v.p., asphalt cons. McAsphalt Engring. Services, Toronto, 1970—; internat. lectr. in field; adj. prof. civil engring. U. Waterloo, 1970—; mem. U.S. Hwy. Transp. Bd. Contbr. articles on soil engring., flexible pavement structural design, and design asphalt surfaces to profl. jours. Recipient Hwy. Research Bd. award, 1946, Disting. Alumnus citation U. Mich., 1953; R.F. Legget award Can. Geotech. Soc., 1972. Fellow Royal Soc. Can., AAAS, ASTM (award of merit 1980); mem. Ont. Assn. Profl. Engrs. (Engring. medal 1979), ASTM (Dudley medal 1952, D-4 Prevost Hubbard award 1978), Assn. Asphalt Paving Technologists (award 1952, hon.), Asphalt Emulsion Mfg. Assn. (Recognition of Achievement award 1985), Can. Tech. Asphalt Assn. (award 1983, 85), Sigma Xi. Mem. United Ch. Can. Home: 41 Glenrose Ave, Toronto, ON Canada M4T 1K3 Office: 8800 Sheppard Ave E West Hill, Toronto, ON Canada M1E 4R2

MCLEOD, WALTON JAMES, JR., lawyer; b. Lynchburg, S.C., Aug. 7, 1906; s. Walton James and Pauline (Mullins) McL.; m. Rhoda Lane Brown, Feb. 2, 1935; children: Walton James III, Peden Brown, William Mullins, Thomas Gordon III. BA, Wofford Coll., 1926, LLD, 1988; LLB, U. S.C., 1930. Bar: S.C. 1930, U.S. Dist. Ct., U.S. Ct. Appeals (4th cir.) 1937, U.S. Supreme Ct. 1936. Ptnr. Jeffries & McLeod, Walterboro, S.C., 1930-40, Jeffries, McLeod & Unger, Walterboro, 1940-54, Jeffries, McLeod, Unger & Fraser, Walterboro, 1954-76, McLeod, Fraser & Unger, Walterboro, 1976-85, McLeod, Fraser & Cone, Walterboro, 1985—; city atty. Walterboro; mem. vice chmn. S.C. Hwy Commn. 1946-50. Mem. nat. exec. com. Young Dems., 1938-42, S.C. Dem. exec. com., 1960-88; Dem. chmn. Colleton County, 1950-60; temporary chmn. state conv., 1976; trustee Walterboro pub. schs., 1936-46, Wofford Coll., 1954-66. Served to lt. comdr. USNR, 1942-46. Recipient Disting. Alumni award Wofford Coll., Durant Disting. Service award S.C. Bar Found.; fellow Am. Bar Found. Mem. Am. Legion (comdr. S.C. 1949-50, mem. nat. exec. com. 1951-52), ABA (ho. of dels. 1950-76, bd. govs. 1964-67, chmn. resolutions com. 1961-62), S.C. (pres. 1969-70), Colleton County Bar Assns. (pres. 1962), Jud. Conf. U.S. Ct. Appeals 4th cir., Am. Coll. Probate Counsel, Am. Law Inst., Am. Judicature Soc., Am. Coll. Trial Lawyers, U. S.C. Law Sch. Assn. (pres., Kappa Alpha, Phi Delta Phi. Methodist. Lodges: Masons, Shriners. Home: 109 Savage St Walterboro SC 29488 Office: 111 E Washington St Walterboro SC 29488

MCLIN, NATHANIEL, JR., educator; b. Chgo., June 19, 1928; s. Nathaniel and Anna (Polk) McL.; m. Lena Mae, July 18, 1952; children—Nathaniel Gerald, Beverly Jane. Student Wilson Jr. Coll., Chgo., 1946-50, Roosevelt U., 1950-52; M.A. Govs. State U.; postgrad. (fellow), Walden U., 1976. Technician, Michael Reese Hosp., 1951-52, U. Chgo. Goldblatt Clinic, 1952-53; bus driver Chgo. Transit Authority, 1953-64; pub. relations dir. Opera Theater of Chgo., 1959-60; mgr. McLin Opera Co., Chgo., 1960-71; salesman Watkins Products Co., 1964-65; tchr. Chgo. Com. on Urban Opportunity, 1965-71; soloist Park Dist. Opera Guild, Chgo., 1964-68; creator, developer All Souls Universalist Childrens Theatre and Opera Workshop, 1986; dir. Centarus II Prodn. Co. Active Beatrice Caffrey Found., Chgo.; soloist Trinity United Ch. Mens Chorus, Chgo., 1962-66; active fund raising campaign pub. relations YMCA, 1963-64; cultural coordinator, dir. Halsted Urban Progress ctr., Chgo., 1966-71; dir. Faces of Crime Symposium All Souls Ch., Chgo., also lay leader, 1980—. Served with U.S. Army, 1946-47. Recipient Wheelers Social Club citation for efforts in nations cultural devel., 1962; named one of Outstanding Civic Leaders Am., 1967. Lodge: Fraternal Order of Police (pres. lodge 83 1980-81). Author: Parole: The Ex-offender's Last Hope, 1983. Home and Office: 7630 S Hoyne St Chicago IL 60620

MCLINTOCK, CHARLES ALAN, accountant; b. Glasgow, Scotland, Great Britain, May 28, 1925; s. Charles Henry and Charlotte Alison (Allan) McL.; m. Sylvia Mary Foster Taylor, Oct. 1, 1955; children—Caroline McLintock Chartres, Michael, Rosemary, Jennifer. Student pub. sch., Rugby, Warwickshire, 1939-43. Chartered acct. Apprentice, Thomson McLintock & Co. (name changed to KMG Thomson McLintock), London, 1948-52, qualified asst., 1952-54, ptnr., 1954-82, sr. ptnr., 1982-87; dir. Woolwich Bldg Soc., London, 1970, chmn., 1983; chmn. Govett Strategic, Govett Oriental and Govett Atlantic investment trust groups, Ecclesiastical Ins. Office, Gloucester, 1981—; dir. Nat. Westminster Bank, London, M & G Group PLC, London. Chmn. gov. Rugby Sch., 1988—; mem. Clergy Orphan Corp., London, 1964-84, v.p., 1985—; mem. ct. U. London. Served to capt. Royal Arty., 1943-47; U.K., India, Middle East. Mem. Inst. Chartered Accts. Scotland, Chartered Bldg. Socs. Inst., Inst. Dirs., Inst. Chartered Accts. in Eng. and Wales, Met. Assn. Bldg. Socs. (v.p.). Mem. Ch. of Eng. Club: Army and Navy (London). Home: The Manor House, Westhall Hill, Fulbrook, near Burford, Oxford OX8 4BJ, England Office: 74 Finsbury Pavement, London EC2A 1JD, England

MCLOON, MARILYN FOGG, real estate executive; b. Norwood, Mass., Nov. 8, 1931; d. Lester Burton and Gertrude Emelia (Thompson) Fogg; m. Richard Fisher McLoon, May 23, 1953; children—Lauren, David, Amy Beth, Christopher, Wendy. Student Boston U., 1949-52. Tchr. br. New Eng. Cons., Hamilton, Mass., 1968-76; sales assoc. Baribeau Agy., Wiscasset, Maine, 1980-81, Peter Coe Realty, Damariscotta, Maine, 1981-83; broker, owner Marilyn McLoon Real Estate, Damariscotta, 1984—; pres. McLoon Comml. Property, Damariscotta, 1986—, Coastal Home Care Inc., Damariscotta, 1987—; real estate broker Community-Home Improvement Project, Damariscotta, 1985-86. Bd. dirs. Lina Fund, Damariscotta, Ctr. for the Arts, Damariscotta, The Ira C. Darling Ctr. for Oceanographic Research, Walpole, Maine. Mem. Lincoln County Realtors (pres. 1986—), Maine Assn. Realtors (2 coms., co-chmn. task force), Nat. Assn. Realtors, Realtor Nat. Mktg. Inst. (CRB designee), Lincoln County Bd. (Realtor of Yr. 1985), Tri-State Realtor Inst. (bd. dirs.). Democrat. Episcopalian. Club, Hospital League (Damariscotta). Avocations: chamber music; needlework; raising labrador retrievers. Office: Bus Rt Damariscotta ME 04543-1025 also: Main St Waldoboro ME 04570

MC LOUGHLIN, ELLEN VERONICA, editor; b. Utica, N.Y.; d. James Henry and Mary Frances (Riley) McL. Student, Utica Free Acad.; A.B., Smith Coll., 1915; postgrad., Radcliffe Coll., 1921-22; L.H.D. (hon.), Lincoln Coll., 1949. Asst. editor woman's page Country Gentleman, 1915-17; circulation promoter Crowell Pub. Co., 1922-24; asst. advt. mgr. Grolier Soc., 1924-34, advt. mgr., 1934-41, editorial dir., 1947-59, v.p., 1956- 64; mng. editor Book of Knowledge, Children's Ency., 1936-42; editor Book of Knowledge Annuals, 1940-53, Book of Knowledge, 1942-60, Story of Our Time, 1947-53, L'Encyclopédie de la Jeunesse, 1948-60, Le Livre de l'Année, 1950-61, La Science Pour Tous, 1960-64; pres. Cragsmoor Free Library Assn., 1965-69. Author: (with Lucile Rathbun, Anetia McLoughlin) The Murder of Doctor Casenova, 1934; contbr. verse to mags. Roman Catholic. Home: 118 Genesee St New Hartford NY 13413

MCLOUGHLIN, PATRICK AMBROSE, dental surgeon; b. Dublin, Ireland, Mar. 14, 1952; s. Michael Joseph and Maura (Hanley) Mcl.; m. Jacinta Maria Gannon, June 19, 1976; 1 child, Stephen Ambrose. B Dental Sci., U. Coll. Dublin, 1974; MBA, U. Coll. Cork, Ireland, 1986. Cert. in Adminstrn., Primary F.F.D. House surgeon Western Health Bd., Galway, Ireland, 1976-77, Midland Health Bd., Tullamore, Ireland, 1977-81; prin./ chief dental officer Mid-Western Health Bd., Limerick, Ireland, 1981—; mem. Dublin Denatl Hosp. Bd., 1982—, nat. spokesperson Salaried Dental Surgeons, 1982-88; chmn. spl. com. on illegal practice Dental Council, 1985—, health bd. rep. to Dental Council, 1985—. Sr. advisor to politicians and polit. parties. Fellow Council of Europe, Royal Acad. Medicine; mem. Irish Dental Assn. (nat. group sec. 1978-85, chief salary negotiator (1980-86), Internat. Assn. Dental Research. Roman Catholic. Club: Badminton (Castletroy, Ireland). Office: Midwestern Health Bd, Roytown TCE, Old Clare St, Limerick Munster Ireland

MCMAHAN, GARY LYNN, medical foundation executive; b. Kansas City, Mo., Mar. 2, 1948; s. Stanley Owen and Edith Evelena (Shannon) McM.; m. Kathy Sue Brockman, Mar. 28, 1970 (div. 1974); m. 2d, Mary Garold Hearn, Aug. 20, 1976; 1 dau., Terri Lee. B.A., U. Mo., 1970, M.P.A., 1973. Sr. program planner Bendix Corp., Kansas City, Mo., 1971-73; project adminstr. U. Mo., Kansas City, 1973-79; exec. v.p. Acad. Health Profls., 1979-80, Family Health Found. Am., 1980—. Bd. sec. AAFP-MDIS Inc., 1981—. Author: An Evaluation Profile: Summary of the Evaluation Activities of the Individual Area Health Education Centers, 1977. Mem. task force Mo. Govs. Task Force on Rural Health, Jefferson City, 1978; bd. dirs., treas. Jackson County Bd. Services for the Developmentally Disabled, Kansas City, 1981—, pres., 1985—; bd. dirs. Shepherd Ctr., Kansas City. Mem. Mid Am. Soc. Assn. Execs., Soc. Tchrs. Family Medicine, N.Am. Primary Care Research Group, Nat. Soc. Fund Raising Execs. Home: 805 Burning Tree Lee's Summit MO 64063 Office: Family Health Found Am 1740 W 92d St Kansas City MO 64114

MCMAHON, EDWARD JOSEPH, engineering company executive; b. Newark, Dec. 8, 1937; s. William Vincent and Madge Eileen (Tittel) McMahon; B.S. in Mech. Engring., N.J. Inst. Tech., 1961, postgrad., 1964; postgrad. U. Ala., 1966, George Washington U., 1967-69; m. Virginia Karen Payne, Oct. 5, 1976; 1 child, Heather Noelle. Engr., Weston Instruments, Newark, 1961-64; reliability analyst Apollo Support Dept., Gen. Electric, Cocoa Beach, Fla., 1964-66; mgr. reliability engring. Chrysler Aerospace Co., Huntsville, Ala., 1966-67; systems analyst Vitro Labs., Silver Spring, Md., 1967-68; mgr. maintainability engring. Amecom div. Litton Systems, College Park, Md., 1968-71, mgr. reliability and maintainability engring. Columbia Research Corp., Gaithersburg, Md., 1971-75; pres. Reliability Scis., Inc., Arlington, Va., 1975—, also chmn. bd.; chmn. bd. Design & Engring. Applications. Served with Army N.G., 1961. Registered profl. engr., Ala. Grantee DOD Samll Business Innvovative Research Program. Mem. IEEE. Roman Catholic. Co-author: Electrostatic Discharge Control: successful Methods for Microelectronics Design and Manufacturing, 1985; conducted major research in areas of electrostatic discharge. Also author of handbooks, manuals. Contbr. articles to profl. jours. Home: Rt 1 Box 16A Middleburg VA 22117 Office: PO Box 1841 Middleburg VA 22117

MCMAHON, JOHN A., business consultant; b. N.Y.C., Apr. 5, 1937; s. John and Elizabeth M. (Lall) McM.; B.E.E., Manhattan Coll., 1960; m. Carole I. Taber, Nov. 21, 1959; children—John C., Carole M., Regina M. Bus. systems mgr. C-E-I-R Inc., N.Y.C., 1958-64; exec. v.p. Alphanumeric Inc., N.Y.C., 1964-73; pres. Dyad Corp., Bronxville, N.Y., 1973—, Devoe Lighting Corp., 1979-88, bd. dirs. Harrison-Rye Corp., 1984—. Cert. in data processing Inst. for Cert. of Computer Profls. Club: Westchester Country. Patentee photog. medium scanner. Home and Office: 2 Beechmont Ave Bronxville NY 10708

MCMAHON, JOHN FRANCIS, former social welfare administrator, consultant, lecturer; b. Buffalo, Sept. 16, 1910; s. John Francis and Rose Belle (Hayes) McM.; m. Irene Rebecca Hibbs, June 17, 1930 (dec. Nov. 1976); 1 child, John Francis. Student, U. Louisville, 1929-32, Marquette U., 1937, U. Wis., Milw. Program supr. Vols. of Am., East St. Louis, Ill., 1933-34; exec. dir. Milw., 1934-48; nat. field sec. 1948-58, gen. and comdr.-in-chief, 1958-80, also pres. bd. dirs., 1958-80, pres., chief exec. officer numerous non-profit housing corps., 1970-80; mem. U.S. Dept. Labor adv. com. on sheltered workshops, 1950-78; pres. grand field council, nat. exec. bd. and nat. field bd. Nat. Soc. Vols. Am., 1958-80; mem. gen. com., exec. com., various commns. Dept. Social Work, Nat. Council Chs.; mem. Pres.'s Com. Employment of Handicapped, Nat. Council on the Aging; v.p. Council Nat. Orgns. Children and Youth, 1972-75, pres., 1975—; v.p. Religion in Am. Life. Fellow Gerontol. Soc., Am. Protestant Correctional Assn.; mem. Nat. Assn. Social Workers, Acad. Certified Social Workers, Internat. Conf. Social Work, Am. Correctional Assn. (dir.), Am. Correctional Chaplains Assn., Nat. Conf. Social Welfare, N.Y. State Welfare Conf., Ch. Conf. Social Work (v.p. 1950-53), Internat. Platform Assn., Newcomen Soc. N.Am. Baptist Clubs: Masons (Scottish Rite); Kiwanis Internat. (pres. N.Y.C. club 1959, lt. gov. 1961, gov. N.Y. dist. 1964, internat. chmn. vocat. guidance 1966, internat. trustee 1966-70, trustee internat. found. 1972-78). Office: 8204 Seaford Dr Pleasure Ridge Park KY 40258

MCMAHON, WILLIAM ROBERT, lawyer, judge; b. Rochester, N.Y., Jan. 12, 1944; s. John Emmett and Kathryn F. (Hayes) McM.; m. Diane Sue Ballreich, Aug. 3, 1968; children: Lisa Marie, Timothy. BS in Bus. Adminstrn., Tri-State U., 1967; JD, Toledo U., 1970. Bar: Ohio 1971, U.S. Dist. Ct. (no. dist.) Ohio 1972, U.S. Supreme Ct. 1975. With Seneca County (Ohio) Pros. Atty.'s Office, 1970-73, asst. prosecutor, 1971, spl. asst. prosecutor, 1971-73; sole practice, Tiffin, Ohio and Toledo, 1970-79; ptnr. McMahon & Kelbley, Tiffin, 1979-80; judge Fostoria (Ohio) mcpl. ct., 1980—; mem. rules adv. com. Ohio Supreme Ct., 1982—. Co-author (videotape edn. series) Your Rights on the Job, Ohio Dept. Edn., 1986. Bd. dirs. Tiffin U., 1975—, sec., 1978-80, vice chmn. bd., 1980—; founding pres. bd. trustees Sandusky Valley Domestic Violence Shelter Inc., 1982; bd. dirs., pres. adv. bd. Seneca County Domestic Violence Shelter, 1980-82; bd. dirs. Sandusky Valley Bd. Substance Abuse, 1973-75, Big Bros./Big Sisters Seneca County, 1980-81, Fostoria Literacy Council, 1987—; bd. dirs., chmn. allocation com. United Way Seneca County, 1973-75; trustee Ohio Ctr. Law-Related Edn., 1984—; pres. Seneca County Young Reps., 1973-75; formerly active various polit. campaigns including Pres. Nixon, Pres. Ford, Pres. Reagan. Fellow Ohio Bar Found.; mem. ABA (Public Service award-Second Place Judiciary Lawday U.S.A. 1983, Nat. Conf. Spl. Ct. Judges 1982—, Nat. Conf. Bar Pres. 1980—, coms. on edn. and law-related edn. 1983—), Ohio Bar Assn. (jud. adminstrn. and legal reform com. 1981—, chmn. 1981-85, com. on law-related edn. 1980—, vice chmn. 1984-85), Seneca County Bar Assn. (pres. 1980), (trustee, treas. 1983—, chmn. Bar Assn., Am. Judicature Soc., Am. Judges Assn., Ohio Jud. Conf. (exec. com. 1986—), Ohio Mcpl. Ct. Judges (exec. adv. bd. 1980-81, trustee 1983—), Ohio County and Mcpl. Judges Assn. (trustee 1983—, treas. 1983-84, chmn. jud. adminstrn. rev. com., 2d. v.p. 1985-86, 1st v.p. 1985-87, pres. 1987—), Tiffin Area C. of C. (dir. 1972-75), Toledo Old Newsboys Assn., Horatio Alger Soc., Internat. Platform Assn. Club: Exchange (Exchangite of Yr. 1984, dist. pres. 1985-86). Lodges: KC (4th, advocate 1976-80), Kiwanis. Co-author: Scripts and Teachers Guide-State v. Gold E. Locks and B.B. Wolf v. Curly Pig, 1984, (film series) Your Rights on the Job, 1986, Ohio Trial Judges Resource Manual, 1986. Office: Fostoria Mcpl Ct 213 S Main St Fostoria OH 44830-1126

MCMANAMAN, KENNETH CHARLES, lawyer, judge, educator, naval officer; b. Fairfield, Calif., Jan. 25, 1950; s. Charles James and Frances J. (Holys) McM.; m. Carol Ann Wilson, Apr. 15, 1972; children—Evan John, Kinsey Bridget, Kierin Rose. B.A. cum laude, S.E. Mo. State U., 1972; J.D., U. Mo.-Kansas City, 1974; grad. Naval Justice Sch., Newport, RI., 1975; M.S. in Bus. Mgmt. summa cum laude, Troy State U., Montgomery, Ala., 1978. Bar: Mo. 1975, U.S. Dist. Ct. (we. dist.) Mo. 1975, U.S. Dist. Ct. (ea. Dist.) Mo. 1978, Fla. 1976, U.S. Dist. Ct. (no., mid. dists.) Fla. 1976, U.S. Ct. Mil. Appeals 1977, U.S. Ct. Appeals (5th, 8th cirs.) 1977, U.S. Supreme Ct. 1978, Ill. 1987. Ptnr. firm O'Loughlin, O'Loughlin & McManaman, Cape Girardeau, Mo., 1978—; prof. bus. law Troy State U., Ala., 1976-78; prof. bus. law S.E. Mo. State U., Cape Girardeau, 1978-84; instr. law Mo. Dept. Pub. Safety, S.E. Mo. Regional Law Enforcement Tng. Acad., 1979—; instr. law Cape Girardeau Police Res., 1983—; mcpl. judge City of Jackson, Mo., 1980—; spl. mcpl. judge City of Cape Girardeau, 1981—. Mem. Cape Girardeau County Council on Child Abuse, 1980-81; membership dir. S.E. Mo. Scouting council Boy Scouts Am., 1980-82; mem. Cape Girardeau County Mental Health Assn., 1982—; active local and state Dem. Party, del. Nat. Dem. Conv., San Francisco, 1984, chmn. County Dem. Com., 1984-86; mem. 8th Congl. Dist. Dem. Com., 1984-86, 27th State Dem. Senatorial Com., 1984-86; bd. dirs. Areawide Task Force on Drug and Alcohol Abuse, 1984-87. Served to lt. JAGC, USN, 1975, lt. commdr. USNR, 1981—. Named One of Outstanding Young Men of Am. 1981, 82, 84, 85. Mem. ABA (Mo. del. for young lawyers div. 1982-83)., Mo. Bar Assn. (chmn. trial advocacy task force 1982, psychology and the law task force 1983), Mo. Bar (young lawyers sect. council, rep. dist. 13, 1980-85), Fla. Bar Assn., Kansas City Bar Assn., Assn. Trial Lawyers Am., Fed. Bar Assn., Nat. Coll. Dist. Attys., Cape Girardeau County Bar Assn. (founder, pres. young lawyers sect. 1981-82), Mo. Mcpl. and Assoc. Cir. Judges Assn., Naval Res. Assn. (v.p. Southeast Mo.-So. Ill. chpt. 1980-85), Southeast Mo. State U. Alumni Council, Sigma Chi (numerous awards), Sigma Tau Delta, Pi Delta Epsilon. Roman Catholic. Home: 1135 Shawnee Jackson MO 63755 Office: O'Loughlin O'Loughlin et al 1736 N Kingshighway Cape Girardeau MO 63701

MCMANUS, IAN CHRISTOPHER, psychology educator; b. London, Mar. 1, 1951; s. Robert Victor McManus and June Lingard. BA, Cambridge U., 1972, MA, 1976, PhD, 1979; MBChB, Birmingham (Eng.) U., 1975; MD, U. London, 1985. Sr. lectr. psychology Univ. Coll., St. Mary's Hosp. Med. Sch., London, 1979—. Office: Dept Psychiatry, St Mary's Hosp, Praed St, London W2 1NY, England

MCMASTER, BRIAN JOHN, artistic director; b. Hitchin, Eng., May 9, 1943; s. Brian John and Mary Leila (Hawkins) McM.; student Wellington Coll., 1955-60; LL.B., Bristol U., 1963. With internat. artists dept. EMI, 1968-73; controller opera planning English Nat. Opera, 1973-76; mng. dir. Welsh Nat. Opera, Cardiff, 1976—; artistic dir. Vancouver Opera (B.C., Can.), 1983—. Home: 1 Cowper Ct, Wordsworth Ave, Cardiff Wales Office: Welsh Nat Opera, John St, Cardiff CF1 4SP, Wales also: Vancouver Opera Assn, 1132 Hamilton St, Vancouver, BC Canada V6B 2S2

MCMICHAEL, JEANE CASEY, real estate corporation executive; b. Jeffersonville, Ind., May 7, 1938; d. Emmett Ward and Carrie Evelyn (Leonard) Casey; m. Norman Kenneth Wenzler, Sept. 12, 1956 (div. 1968); m. Wilburn Arnold McMichael, June 20, 1978. Student Ind. U. Extension Ctr., Bellermine Coll., 1972-73, Ind. U. S.E., 1973—, Kentuckiana Metroversity, 1981—; Grad. Realtors Inst., Ind. U., 1982. Lic. real estate salesman, broker, Ind.; real estate broker, Ky. Owner, pres. McMichael Real Estate, Inc., Jeffersonville, 1979—; mgr., broker Bass & Weisberg Realtors, Jeffersonville, Ind., 1984-86. Pres., Mr. and Mrs. class St. Mark's United Ch. of Christ; chmn. social com. Republican party Clark County (Ind.). Recipient cert. of appreciation Nat. Ctr. Citizen Involvement, 1983; award Contact Kentuckiana Teleministries, 1978. Mem. Nat. Assn. Realtors, Ind. Assn. Realtors (state dir.), Nat. Women's Council Realtors (pres. chpt., chmn. coms.; state rec. sec., 1984, state pres. 1985-86. Nat. Achievement award 1982, 83, 84; nat. gov. Ind. 1987; v.p. region III 1988, Ind. Honor Realtor award 1982—), Ky. Real Estate Exchange, So. Ind. Bd. Realtors (program chmn. 1986-87, bd. dirs., pres., 1988—, Realtor of Yr. 1985), Psi Iota Xi. Democrat. Club: Toastmasters (pres. Steamboat chpt.). Office: Bass & Weisberg Realtors 1713 E 10th St Jeffersonville IN 47130

MC MILLAN, EDWIN MATTISON, physicist, educator; b. Redondo Beach, Calif., Sept. 18, 1907; s. Edwin Harbaugh and Anna Marie (Mattison) McM.; m. Elsie Walford Blumer, June 7, 1941; children—Ann B., David M., Stephen W. B.S., Calif. Inst. Tech., 1928, M.S., 1929; Ph.D., Princeton U., 1932; D.Sc., Rensselaer Poly. Inst., 1961, Gustavus Adolphus Coll., 1963. Nat. research fellow U. Calif. at Berkeley, 1932-34, research asso., 1934-35, instr. in physics, 1935-36, asst. prof. physics, 1936-41, asso. prof., 1941-46, prof. physics, 1946-73, emeritus, 1973—; mem. staff Lawrence Radiation Lab., 1934—, asso. dir., 1954-58, dir., 1958-73; on leave for def. research at Mass. Inst. Tech. Radiation Lab., U.S. Navy Radio and Sound Lab., San Diego, and Los Alamos Sci. Lab., 1940-45; mem. gen. adv. com. AEC, 1954-58; mem. commn. high energy physics Internat. Union Pure and Applied Physics, 1960-67; mem. sci. policy com. Stanford Linear Accelerator Center, 1962-66; mem. physics adv. com. Nat. Accelerator Lab., 1967-69; chmn. 13th Internat. Conf. on High Energy Physics, 1966; guest prof. CERN, Geneva, 1974. Trustee Rand Corp., 1959-69; Bd. dirs. San Francisco Palace Arts and Scis. Found., 1968—; trustee Univs. Research Assn., 1969-74. Recipient Research Corp. Sci. award, 1951; (with Glenn T. Seaborg) Nobel prize in chemistry, 1951; (with Vladimir I. Veksler) Atoms for Peace award, 1963; Alumni Distinguished Service award Calif. Inst. Tech., 1966; Centennial citation U. Calif. at Berkeley, 1968; Faculty Research lectr. U. Calif. at Berkeley, 1955. Fellow Am. Acad. Arts and Scis., Am. Phys. Soc.; mem. Nat. Acad. Scis. (chmn. class I 1968-71), Am. Philos. Soc., Sigma Xi, Tau Beta Pi. Office: U Calif Lawrence Berkeley Lab Berkeley CA 94720

MCMILLAN, JAMES ALBERT, electronics engineer, educator; b. Lewellen, Nebr., Feb. 6, 1926; s. William H. and Mina H. (Taylor) McM.; B.S. in Elec. Engring., U. Wash., 1951; M.S. in Mgmt., Rensselaer Poly. Inst., 1965; m. Mary Virginia Garrett, Aug. 12, 1950; children—Michael, James, Yvette, Ramelle, Robert. Commd. 2d lt. U.S. Air Force, 1950, advanced through grades to lt. col., 1970; jet fighter pilot Columbus AFB, Miss., Webb AFB, Tex., 1951-52, Nellis AFB, Nev., 1953, McChord AFB, Wash., 1953-54; electronic maintenance supr. Lowry AFB, Colo., 1954, Forbes AFB, Kans., 1954-56, also in U.K., 1956-59; electronic engr., program dir. Wright-Patterson AFB, Ohio, 1959-64; facilities dir. Air Force Aero Propulsion Lab., Wright-Patterson AFB, 1965-70, ret., 1970; instr., div. chmn. Chesterfield-Marlboro Tech. Coll., S.C., 1971-75; instr., chmn. indsl. div., Maysville (Ky.) Community Coll., 1976—, asst. prof., 1977, assoc. prof., 1980, prof. 1986—; cons. mgmt. and electronic maintenance, 1970—. Served with U.S. Army, 1943-45. Mem. IEEE (sr.), Soc. Mfg. Engrs. (sr.), Nat. Rifle Assn. (life), Sigma Xi (life). Republican. Presbyterian (elder). Clubs: Rotary (pres.-elect) (Maysville, Ky.), Masons (32 deg.), Shriners.

Author: A Management Survey, 1965. Home: 6945 Scoffield Rd Ripley OH 45167

MCMILLAN, MICHAEL REID, orthopedic surgeon; b. Conway, S.C., Aug. 28, 1941; s. Hoyt and Sara Best (Sherwood) McM.; B.S., The Citadel, 1963; M.D., Duke U., 1967. Intern in medicine Balt. City Hosps., 1967-68; fellow in medicine Johns Hopkins Hosp., Balt., 1967-68; resident in orthopedic surgery Greenville (S.C.) Hosp. Systems and Greenville Shriners Hosp., 1971-75; practice medicine specializing in orthopedic surgery, Conway, S.C., 1975—; mem. staff Conway Hosp., 1975—, chief of orthopedics, 1975-82; bd. dirs. Burroughs Co., Snow Hill Co., Conway, S.C. Trustee Burroughs Found., Conway, 1979—. Served to lt. comdr. MC, USN, 1968-71; Vietnam. Diplomate Nat. Bd. Med. Examiners, Am. Bd. Orthopedic Surgery; lic. physician, S.C. Mem. AMA, So. Med. Assn., S.C. Med. Assn., S.C. Orthopedic Assn., Horry County Med. Soc., Assn. of Citadel Men, Stelling Soc. Baptist. Club: Horry County Citadel. Home and Office: 1400 9th Ave Conway SC 29526

MCMILLIN, ARNOLD BARRATT, language educator; b. Newcastle-upon-Tyne, Northumberland, Eng., June 21, 1941; s. Robin McMillin and Kathleen Mary (Edmundson) Dudek; m. Caroline Henrietta Louisa Synge-Hutchinson, Mar. 15, 1969; children: Penelope, Diana. BA in Russian, London U., 1963, PhD in Slavonic Philology, 1971. Lectr. in Russian Lang. and Lit. London U., 1965-76, prof. Russian, 1987—; Bowes prof. Russian Liverpool U., Eng., 1976-87. Author: The Vocabulary of the Byelorussian Language in the 19th Century, 1971, A History of Byelorussian Literature from its Origins to the Present Day, 1977; contbr. articles to profl. jours. Mem. Modern Humanities Research Assn. (com. mem., Slavonic editor 1978-87), Assn. Tchrs. Russian (v.p. 1976—), Brit. Univs. Assn. Slavists (pres. 1984-86), Internat. Com. Slavists (Brit. rep. 1978—). Mem. Soc. Friends. Clubs: Formby Cricket (Lancashire, Eng.). Office: Sch Slavonic and East European Studies, Senate House, Malet St, London WC1E 7HU, England

MCMULLAN, JAMES FRANKLIN, insurance consultant, financial planner; b. Atlanta, Feb. 24, 1928; s. Jesse James and Ruth G. (Thomason) McM.; m. Jo Anne Lovern, Sept. 13, 1951; children—Anne McMullan Lord, Martha Jane (dec.), Lynn McMullan Hart, Robert L., Beth Lovern. B.B.A., Emory U., 1949; M.S.F.S., Am. Coll., 1986. Pres., Strategically Managed Assets Corp., 1987—. Elder, Word of Life Fellowship; pres. bd. dirs. The Cornerstone, 1976—; bd. dirs. Am. Vision, 1983—. Recipient Nat. Mgmt. award for Agency Building, 1973, life mem., 1977, nat. quality award, 1957-87. Chartered fin. cons.; CLU; registered prin. NASD. Mem. Am. Soc. CLU's, Million Dollar Found Table, Atlanta Estate Planning Council, Internat. Assn. Fin. Planners (Ga. chpt.), Atlanta Life Underwriters Assn. Republican. Home: 2935 Duke of Gloucester East Point GA 30344 Office: SMAC 1 Premier Plaza 5605 Glenridge Dr Suite 250 Atlanta GA 30342

MCMULLEN, BARBARA ELIZABETH, data processing company executive, writer; b. Phila., Aug. 2, 1942; d. Walter Woodrow and Nellie Elizabeth (Rojewski) Ludman; m. John F. McMullen, May 12, 1978; stepchildren: Claire Ann, Luke John. BS in Math., Pa. State U., 1963; postgrad. Pratt Inst., 1971, N.Y. Sch. Interior Design, 1973; MPA in Pub. Fin., NYU, 1976. Supr. AT&T, Mt. Kisco, N.Y., 1963-65; sr. programmer Pan Am. World Airways, N.Y.C., 1965-67; analyst N.Y. Stock Exchange, N.Y.C., 1967-69; project leader Bache Halsey Stuart, N.Y.C., 1974-76; mgr. Morgan Stanley & Co., N.Y.C., 1976-78; pres. McMullen & McMullen, Inc., Jefferson Valley, N.Y., 1978—; mem. faculty NYU, 1980-82, New Sch. for Social Research, N.Y.C., 1981—. Author: (with John F. McMullen) Microcomputer Communications, 1982; contbg. editor Computers & Electronics, 1984-85, Computer Living, 1985—, Computer Shopper, 1985—; contbg. editor PC Clones mag., 1988—; contbr. chpt. to book, articles to profl. jours. Recipient Lepesqueur award N.Y.U., 1976. Bd. dirs. Osceola Heights Assn., Jefferson Valley, 1984. Mem. Big Apple Users Group (sec. and bd. dirs. 1981-84), Boston Computer Soc., Assn. for Computing Machinery, N.Y. Personal Computer Club (sec., bd. dirs. 1982—), N.Y. Amateur Computer Club, Westchester IBM Users Group, Pa. State U. Club of N.Y. Roman Catholic. Clubs: Downtown Athletic (N.Y.C.); Jefferson Valley Racquet (N.Y.). Avocations: pvt. pilot, painting, needlework, tropical fish breeding, amateur radio. Home: Perry St Jefferson Valley NY 10535 Office: McMullen & McMullen Inc McM Plaza Jefferson Valley NY 10535

MCMURRAY, CHRISTINE, demographer, consultant; b. London, Apr. 11, 1945; arrived in Australia, 1970; BA with hons., Victoria U., New Zealand, 1966, MA in Geography, 1969. Cert. tchr. Lectr. in geography Victoria U., Wellington, New Zealand, 1967-69; tutor geography Australian Nat. U., Canberra, 1970-81, sr. tutor in demography, 1982—; cons. S. Pacific Commn., Noumea, New Caledonia, 1984, 86, Nat. Ctr. for Devel. Studies, 1985—, Australian Devel. Assistance Bur., Canberra, 1986, Micro Computer Tng., Canberra, 1983—. Co-author: Demographic Literature, 1988; contbr. numerous articles to profl. jours. Mem. Australian Population Assn., Asian Studies Assn. of Australia, Micro Computer Users Assn. Home: PO Box 115 O'Connor, Canberra 2601, Australia Office: Nat Ctr for Devel. Australian Nat Univ, PO Box 4, Canberra ACT, 2601, Australia

MC MURTRY, JAMES GILMER, III, neurosurgeon; b. Houston, June 11, 1932; s. James Gilmer and Alberta Elizabeth (Matteson) McM.; student Rice U., Houston, 1950-53; M.D. cum laude, Baylor U., Houston, 1957. Intern, Hosp. U. Pa., Phila., 1957-58; resident gen. surgery Baylor U. Affiliated Hosps., Houston, 1958-59; asst. neurol. surgery Coll. Physicians and Surgeons, Columbia U., N.Y.C., 1959-60; asst. resident neurol. surgery and neurology Neurol. Inst. N.Y., Columbia Presbyn. Med. Center, N.Y.C., 1960-62, chief resident neurol. surgery, 1962-63; Nat. Inst. Neurol. Disease and Blindness spl. fellow neurol. surgery Coll. Physicians and Surgeons, Columbia U., N.Y.C., 1963-64, instr. neurol. surgery, 1963-65, assoc., 1965-68, asst. prof. clin. neurol. surgery, 1968-73, assoc. prof., 1973—; asst. attending neurol. surgeon Neurol. Inst. N.Y., N.Y.C., 1964-73, assoc. attending neurol. surgeon, 1973—; chief neurol. surgery clinic Vanderbilt Clinic, Columbia Presbyn. Med. Center, N.Y.C., 1964-68; attending-in-charge neurosurgery Lenox Hill Hosp., N.Y.C., 1970—; assoc. cons. neurol. surgery Englewood (N.J.) Hosp., 1964—; asst. cons. neurol. surgery Harlem Hosp., N.Y.C., 1964—; cons. neurol. surgery Bronx (N.Y.) VA Hosp., 1964-65; mem. NIH Parkinson Research Group, Columbia U., 1965—; mem. med. adv. bd. N.Y. State Athletic Commn. Jesse H. Jones scholar Baylor U. Coll. Medicine, 1953-57, Allen fellow dept. neurol. surgery Columbia U., 1964-65. Diplomate Am. Bd. Neurol. Surgery. Fellow A.C.S.; mem. Am. Assn. Neurol. Surgeons, AAUP, AAAS, AMA, European Congress Pediatric Neurosurgery, Am. Soc. Stereotaxic Surgeons, Pan Am. Med. Assn., N.Y. State Soc. Surgeons, N.Y. State Neurosurgery Soc., N.Y. Acad. Sci., N.Y. Neurosurg. Soc., Med. Soc. State N.Y., N.Y. County Med. Soc., Osler Soc., Baylor U. Coll. Medicine Alumni Assn., Med. Strollers, The Med. Soc. of London, The Harveian Soc., Alpha Omega Alpha. Presbyn. Clubs: The Union (N.Y.C.), The Met. Opera (N.Y.C.), The Norfolk Yacht and Country. Author: Medical Examination Review Book-Neurological Surgery, 1970, rev. edit., 1975; Neurological Surgery Case Histories, 1975; contbr. articles to profl. jours. Home: 1 Cobb Lane Tarrytown NY 10591 Office: 710 W 168th St New York NY 10032

MCNAIR, JOHN WILLIAM, JR., civil engineer; b. Asheville, N.C., June 17, 1926; s. John William and Annie (Woody) McN.; m. June Clemens Kratz; children—Jeffry, Marsha, Cathy. B.S. in Forestry, Pa. State U., 1950; B.S.C.E., Va. Poly. Inst. State U., 1955; postgrad. in engring. U. Va., 1957-58. Registered profl. engr., Va. and other states. Forester U.S. Forest Service, Flagstaff, Ariz., 1950, U.S. Gypsum Co., Buena Vista, VA., 1951; mem. engring. faculty U. Va., Charlottesville, 1955-58; prin. John McNair & Assocs., Waynesboro, VA., 1958—; owner Brucheum Group, Waynesboro, 1983—; with Va. Bd. Architects, Profl. Engrs. and Land Surveyors, 1969-79, v.p., 1977-78, pres., 1978-79. Author numerous engring. and land mgmt. study reports. Mem. Waynesboro City Council, 1968-72, vice mayor, 1970-72; chmn. Waynesboro INdsl. devel. Authority, 1984—. Served to capt. AUS, 1944-46, 51-53; France, Okinawa. Recipient Disting. Service cert. Va. Soc. Profl. Engrs., 1971. Fellow ASCE; mem. Acad. Environ. Engrs. (diplomate), Acad. Ind. Scholars. Republican. Presbyterian. Club: Rappahannock Yacht (Irvington, Va.). Lodge: Rotary (local bd. dirs.). Office: John McNair and Assocs Wayne Ave L B & B Bldg Waynesboro VA 22980

MC NALLEN, JAMES BERL, marketing executive; b. Heber Springs, Ark., Feb. 17, 1930; s. George Berl and Sally Lou (Brown) McN.; AB, Columbia, 1951; MBA, N.Y.U., 1960, PhD, 1975; m. Marianne Patricia Kakos, Mar. 4, 1952 (div. Dec. 18, 1981); children: James Lawrence, Marianne Victoria, Thomas Berl, John Kennedy. Mktg. asst. Am. Petroleum Inst., N.Y.C., 1954-67, coordinator products mktg. 1967-69, asst. dir., div. fin. and acctg., 1969-70; corp. mgr. mktg. research Atlantic Richfield Co., N.Y.C., 1970-71; lectr. bus. adminstrn. Sch. Bus. Adminstrn. U. Conn., Storrs, 1972-75, asst. prof., 1975-76; mktg. research specialist, market research and mktg. div. Office Customer Service Support, Fed. Supply Service, GSA, Washington, 1976-78, mgr. mktg. research Office of Requirements, 1978-82, mgr. forecasting and bus. analysis Office of Mgmt., 1982-84; Mem. U.S. del. U.S.-Saudi Arabian Joint Econ. Commn., Riyadh, 1984-88, mktg. specialist, tng. officer Cen. Supply Mgmt. Devel. Project, 1988—; spl. asst. Office of Customer Service and Mktg. GSA Fed. Supply Service, Washington, 1988—; pres. McNallen Investment Co., Arlington, Va.; dir. McNallen Enterprise, Big Spring, Tex.;lectr. mktg. Va. Poly. Inst., Reston, 1976-77, George Mason U., 1977-84, Georgetown U., 1978-80; adj. prof. mgmt. Univ. District Columbia, 1980-84. Mem. planning bd. Twp. of South Brunswick (N.J.), 1966-67; sec., vice chmn. Brunswick Mcpl. Utilities Authority, 1966-68; pres. South Brunswick Library Assn., 1965-69. Served to lt. (j.g.) USN, 1951-54, capt. USNR, 1976-87. Mem. Naval Res. Assn., (pres. Washington chpt. 1978-79, pres. 5th dist. 1979-81, mem. nat. exec. com. 1979-81), Naval Order U.S., Mil. Order World Wars, Res. Officers Assn. (exec. v.p. Washington D.C. Nat. Navy chpt. 1982-84), U.S. Naval Inst., Smithsonian Assocs., S. Brunswick Jaycees (pres. 1964-65, state v.p. N.J. State Jaycees, named Jr. Chamber Internat. Senator). Lodge: Ancient Order Hibernians. Recipient Gold medal Am. Mktg. Assn., 1960. Roman Catholic. Clubs: Army-Navy (Washington); NYU (N.Y.C.). Contbr. articles in field to profl. jours. Home: The Portals of Alexandria #1404 E 511 Four Mile Alexandria VA 22313

MCNAMARA, ANN DOWD, medical technologist; b. Detroit, Oct. 17, 1924; d. Frank Raymond and Frances Mae (Ayling) Sullivan; BS, Wayne State U., 1947; m. Thomas Stephen Dowd, Apr. 23, 1949 (dec. 1980); children—Cynthia Dowd Restuccia, Kevin Thomas Dowd; m. Robert Abbott McNamara, June 15, 1985. Med. technologist Woman's Hosp. (now Hutzel Hosp.), Detroit, 1946-52, St. James Clin. Lab., Detroit, 1960-62; supr. histopathology lab. Hutzel Hosp., Detroit, 1962-72, Mt. Carmel Mercy Hosp., 1972-87. Mem. Am. Soc. Clin. Pathologists, Am. Soc. Med. Technology, Mich. Soc. Med. Technology, Nat. Soc. Histotechnology, Mich. Soc. Histotechnologists, Wayne State U. Alumni Assn., Smithsonian Assos., Detroit Inst. Arts Founders Soc. Home: 29231 Oak Point Dr Farmington Hills MI 48331

MC NAMARA, JOHN J., educator; b. Rochelle, Ill., Dec. 6, 1909; s. John and Grace (Campbell) McN.; B.E., No. Ill. U.; M.A., U. Iowa; Ph.D., Purdue U.; m. Hazel D. Dionne, Aug. 11, 1936; children—John, Denise, Carole, Michael, Terrence, Kevin. Tchr., St. Albans Acad., Sycamore, Ill., 1932-34; faculty St. Viator Coll., Kankakee, Ill., 1934-37; asso. prof. U. Detroit, 1937-43; head tng. div. Republic Aviation Corp., 1943-45; pres. M & M Candy, Hackettstown, N.J., 1945-59; dir. M & M Mars (now Mars Inc.), McLean, Va., 1952-62; chmn. bd. Uncle Ben's Rice, Houston, 1959-62; corp. mktg. adv. Warner Lambert Pharm. Co., Morris Plains, N.J., 1966-67; prof. No. Ill. U., DeKalb, 1970-78; prof. dept. mktg. Calif. State Coll., Bakersfield, 1978-80. Calcot-Kennedy disting. prof., 1980—. Recipient Chick Evans award and service award No. Ill. U., 1971; inducted into NIU Football Hall of Fame, 1984. Mem. Am. Assn. Advt. Agys. Sigma Xi, Phi Delta Kappa. Club: Stockdale Country. Contbr. articles to profl. publs. Home: 508 Malibu Ct Bakersfield CA 93309 Office: 9001 Stockdale Hwy Bakersfield CA 93309

MC NAMARA, JOSEPH PATRICK, lawyer, chemical company executive; b. Indpls., Apr. 14, 1906; s. Frank E. and Mary (Doherty) McN.; J.D. with honors, U. Notre Dame, 1929; J.D., Ind. U., 1939; Fellow of Inst., Bridgeport Engring. Inst., 1977; m. Harriett Day, Aug. 30, 1935. Bar: Ind. 1929, U.S. Dist. Ct. 1929, U.S. Supreme Ct. 1936, Conn. 1950, U.S. Ct. Claims 1954. Assoc. firm Gates, Walsh & Hoffmann, Indpls., 1929-33; dep. atty. gen. Ind., 1933-42; sr. mem. firm McNamara & Quinn, Indpls., 1941-42; counsel Ind. State C. of C., 1941-42; with Bridgeport Brass Co. (Conn.), 1946-63, asst. sec., counsel, 1953-59, staff dir. indsl. relations, 1955-59, v.p., 1959-63; v.p. Nat. Distillers & Chem. Corp., 1962-71; partner firm Brennan, Daly & McNamara, Bridgeport, 1970-81; mem. firm Brennan, McNamara and Brennan, Bridgeport, 1970—; Paul Adelson lectr.; lectr. Loyola U. Bd. dirs. New Eng. Council; Conn. rep. Council of 13 Original States, trustee fund, 1979—; Conn. del. U.S. Constl. Council, 1981—; chmn. bd. trustees Bridgeport Engring. Inst., 1971—. Served to col., Judge Adv. Gen.'s Dept., AUS, 1942-46; col., 1954. Named Man of Yr., Notre Dame U., 1955; fellow St. Joseph's Coll., Rennsalaer, Ind. Mem. Am. Bar Assn., Notre Dame Law Assn., Notre Dame, Ind. U. alumni assns., Am. Det. Preparedness Assn., Judge Adv. Assn., Res. Officers Assn. U.S., U.S., Conn. (dir.) chambers commerce, Council of State Chambers Commerce, Order of World Wars (companion 1980—), Res. Officers Assn., Am. Legion. KC (4 deg.), Rotarian (dir. 1981, sec. 1984—; Paul Harris fellow 1983). Clubs: University, Algonquin (Bridgeport); Notre Dame of Southwestern Conn.; Union League (N.Y.C.); La Coquille (Palm Beach). Author: Principles of Management, also numerous booklets on mgmt., also others; contbr. articles to profl. publs. Home: 23 Carmel Ridge Trumbull CT 06611 Office: 600 Brooklawn Ave Bridgeport CT 06605

MCNAMARA, TOM, scientific consulting corporation executive; b. Battle Creek, Mich., May 23, 1944; s. George P. (stepfather) and Mildred E. Lunt; grad. in Chemistry, Boston U., 1966; M.B.A., Northeastern U., 1970; m. Ellen K. LaRue, Sept. 24, 1977; 1 child, George Lunt. With corp. planning dept. Reynolds Aluminum, Richmond, Va., 1970-72; sr. cons. Technomic Cons., Chgo., 1972-74; founder, pres. NUVENTURES Consultants, Inc., Chgo. and San Diego, 1975—; speaker trade convs. and confs. worldwide. Republican nominee Ill. Gen. Assembly, 1974, 76; mem. various coms. United Fund and Chgo. Assn. Commerce and Industry, 1975-79. Served to 1st lt. Ordnance Corps, U.S. Army, 1966-69. Recipient Presdl. Commendation for heroism, 1974, Chgo. Police Dept. Commendation, 1974. Mem. Acacia. Club: San Diego Tennis and Racquet. Contbr. articles to publs. Office: PO Box 2489 La Jolla CA 92038

MCNAUGHTON, NEIL, psychology educator; b. Stockport, Eng., Apr. 16, 1947; arrived in New Zealand, 1982; s. Alastair Gordon Hamish and Margaret Leslie Hunter (Paton) McN.; m. Julia Clare Mayo; 1 child, Euan. BA, Oxford (Eng.) U., 1970, MA, 1975; PhD, Southampton (Eng.) U., 1977. Research assoc. exptl. psychology dept. U. Oxford, 1973-78, 79-82; royal soc. commonwealth bursar psychology dept. U. B.C., Vancouver, Can., 1978-79; lectr. psychology U. Otago, Dunedin, New Zealand, 1982-84, sr. lectr., 1984—; treas. Australasian Winter Conf. Brain Research, New Zealand, 1982—; chmn. exptl. div. New Zealand Psychol. Soc., 1986—. Contbr. articles to profl. jours. Med. Research Council grantee, New Zealand, 1983, 86, various other research-related grants. Mem. Brain Research Assn. (sec. local chpt. 1971-73), Internat. Brain Research Orgn., European Neuroscience Assn., Australian Neuroscience Soc. Office: U Otago Dept Psychology, PO Box 56, Dunedin New Zealand

MC NEAL, HARLEY JOHN, lawyer; b. Birmingham, Ala.; s. John Harley and Alfretta (Frederick) McN.; m. Virginia Marie Hutzel, Feb. 8, 1936; children: Virginia Ann, Sandra Jean McNeal Highley. A.B., U. Mich., 1932, student Law Sch., 1934, student Med. Sch., 1936; LL.B., Western Res. U., 1936, LL.M., 1966; student, Case Sch. Applied Sci., 1938-39, student Med. Sch., 1940; student, U. Wis. Law Sch., 1935, Cleve. Coll., 1938. Bar: Ohio 1935. Mem. firm John H. McNeal and Harley J. McNeal, Cleve., 1935-45; partner Burgess, Fulton & Fullmer, Cleve., 1945-50, McNeal & Schick, Cleve., 1950-69; sr. partner McNeal & Schick, 1969—; lectr. Western Res. U. Med. Sch., also Dental Sch., 1945-62, Cleve. Marshall Law Sch., 1958-60, Western Res. U. Law Sch., 1958-62; mem. Nat. Bd. Trial Advocacy, 1979—. Author numerous articles profl. jours.; co-author: Personal Injury Litigation in Ohio; asso. editor: The Forum, 1965-69. Mem. council, Bay Village, Ohio, 1950-52; mem. center com. on law and environ. World Peace Through Law Center, Belgrade, Yugoslavia, 1971; mem. adminstrn. of justice adv. com. Greater Cleve. Asso. Found.; mem. com. for justice Greater Cleve. Growth Assn.; bd. dirs. Def. Research Inst.; Rep. Committeeman. Served to capt. JAGD, USAAF, 1942-45, ETO. Fellow Am. Coll. Trial Lawyers (chmn. com. procedures and preservation oral argument), Internat. Acad. Trial Lawyers, Am. Acad. Forensic Scis., Am., Ohio bar founds.; mem. Am. Bd. Profl. Attys. (trustee), Internat. Assn. Ins. Counsel (pres. 1966-67), Fedn. Ins. Counsel Assn., ABA (chmn. rules and procedure and trial technique coms. ins. sect., co-chmn. profl. liability com. litigation sect., mem. council litigation sect. 1978-81), Internat. Bar Assn., Fed. Bar Assn., Inter-Am. Bar Assn., Ohio Bar Assn. (chmn. individual rights and responsibilities com.), Cleve. Bar Assn. (chmn. modern jud. system com., trustee), Bar Assn. Greater Cleve. (pres. 1980-81), Cuyahoga County Bar Assn., World Peace Through Law (maritime com., chmn. litigation sect.), Am. Judicature Soc., Ohio Jud. Conf. (rules adv. com.), Maritime Law Assn. U.S., Nat. Assn. R.R. Trial Lawyers, Am. Soc. Internat. Law, U. Mich. Alumni Assn., Internat. Acad. Law and Sci., Phi Delta Phi, Sigma Alpha Epsilon, Druids. Presbyterian. Clubs: Westwood Country (Rocky River, Ohio); Union, Nisi Prius, Hermit (Cleve.). Lodge: Mason (Rocky River, Ohio) (32, K.T.). Home: 26828 W Lake Rd Bay Village OH 44140 Office: 10th Floor Illuminating Bldg Cleveland OH 44113

MC NEAL, JAMES HECTOR, JR., manufacturing company executive; b. Dover, Del., Nov. 22, 1927; s. James Hector and Elizabeth Vickers (Hodgson) McN.; m. Lucy Cooper Finn, June 16, 1951; children: James Hector, Edwin Howell, Sarah Elizabeth. BS, U. Del., 1951. With Budd Co., 1951—; v.p. mfg. services Budd Co., Troy, Mich., 1972-73; group v.p. automotive products Budd Co., 1973-74, pres., chief operating officer, 1974-81, pres., chief exec. officer, 1981-86, chmn., chief exec. officer, 1986—, also bd. dirs.; bd. dirs. Am. Natural Resources, Econ. Club Detroit, Grand Trunk Western R.R. Co., NBD Bancorp, United Found., YMCA-Detroit. 1st v.p. Detroit Area council Boy Scouts Am. Served with USNR, 1945-46. Mem. Soc. Automotive Engrs. Clubs: Bloomfield Hills Country, Oakland Hills Country, Detroit Athletic. Office: The Budd Co 3155 W Big Beaver Rd Troy MI 48084

MC NEAL, R(ALPH) RICHARD, insurance consultant; b. Oakville, Iowa, Aug. 19, 1925; s. Ralph Vincient and Zella Barr (Wright) McN.; student U. Minn., 1943, Coll. St. Thomas, 1943-44; B.C.S., Drake U., 1948; m. Ruth Lucille Morgan, Aug. 31, 1947; children—Michael, Deborah (Mrs. Richard D. Wood), Nancy (Mrs. Jack Burtch). Mktg. rep. Aetna Life & Casualty Co., St. Louis, 1948-54; operator Kennesaw Land & Ins. Co., Atlanta, 1954-59; operator W. Lyman Case & Co., Columbus, Ohio, 1959-64; pres. R. Richard McNeal Assos., Co., Columbus, 1964—. Served with USNR, 1943-45. Recipient Young Man of Yr. award, Jr. C. of C., Cobb County, Ohio, 1958; Salesman of Yr. award Upper Arlington Civic Assn., 1972. Mem. Soc. of Ins. Research, Nat. Assn. Ins. Agts., Profl. Ins. Agts. Assn., Am. Assn. Risk Analysts (trustee 1969-74), Am. Mgmt. Assn. Clubs: Columbus Exec., Ohio State U. Pres., Scioto Country, Athletic, Capitol (Columbus); Arlington (Upper Arlington, Ohio). Contbr. articles to profl. jours. Home: 2171 Pinebrook Rd Columbus OH 43220 Office: 1880 Mackenzie Dr Columbus OH 43220

MCNEELY, MARK WRIGHT, lawyer; b. Shelbyville, Ind., Mar. 26, 1947; s. Carl R. and Elizabeth J. (Orebaugh) McN.; children—Patrick, Mary. Student Wabash Coll., 1965-67; A.B., Franklin Coll., 1970; J.D., Ind. U., 1974. Bar: Ind. 1974. Dep. state pub. defender State of Ind., 1972, pub. defender Shelby Superior Ct., 1973-76, Shelby County Ct., 1976—; atty. Shelby County Dept. Pub. Welfare, 1976-84; ptnr. McNeely & Sanders, Shelbyville, Ind., 1976—; pres. Land Title & Abstract Co. Author: System Book for Family Law: Post Trial Enforcement of Decree, 1983, Indiana Dissolution of Marriage Laws, 1988. Mem. parrish council, 1982-85, pres. 1983-85. Served with U.S. Army. Fellow Ind. State Bar Assn. (family law sect.); mem. ABA (pres. family law sect.), Shelby County Bar Assn. (sec.-treas. 1985, pres. 1986), Ind. Pub. Defender Council (pres. 1983-84, sec. 1986-87). Democrat. Roman Catholic. Clubs: Lions, Elks. Home: Rural Rt #2 PO Box 408 Shelbyville IN 46176-9488 Office: McNeely & Sanders 611 S Harrison PO Box 457 Shelbyville IN 46176

MCNEES, JAMES LAFAYETTE, JR., lawyer; b. Dallas, Oct. 25, 1916; s. James Lafayette Sr. and Elsie Mae (Holbert) McN. Grad., U. Tex., Arlington, 1936; JD, Cumberland U., 1939; grad., U.S. Army Command and Gen. Staff Coll., 1960, Indsl. Coll. Armed Forces, 1969. Bar: Tex., U.S. Supreme Ct. Ptnr. McNees & McNees, Dallas, 1940—; dir. Trinity Valley Bldg. Ctr. Inc., Oilchem. Corp., A.P.C. Foods Inc. Mem. USO Council; former nat. v.p. Leukemia Soc. Am., also exec. com., nat. trustee; life trustee Cumberland U., Tenn.; precinct chmn. Dem. Party; mem. exec. com. Dallas County Dem.; mem. exec. com. Dems. for Responsible Govt.; mem. adminstrv. bd. Highland Park Meth. Ch., also past. pres. Men's Bible Class, lay speaker. Served with inf. AUS, World War II, ETO; col. res. ret. Decorated Bronze Star, Combat Inf. Badge. Mem. ABA, Tex. Bar Assn., Dallas Bar Assn., Internat. Assn. Dallas-Ft. Worth, Greenway Parks Homeowners Assn. (former pres.), Dallas C. of C., Am. Legion (formerly post comdr.), U. Tex. at Arlington Alumni Assn. (past pres.), Sigma Alpha Epsilon. Lodges: Mason (32nd degree), K.P. Clubs: Gaiete, Dervish, Calyx, Willow Bend Polo and Hunt. Home: 6615 Preston Rd Dallas TX 75209 Office: 701 Commerce St Suite 400 Dallas TX 75202-4518

MC NEIL, CLARID F., social worker, former educator; b. nr. Hillsboro, Ohio, Jan. 19, 1908; s. Charles F. and Mary Anne (Tannehill) McN.; A.B., Ohio State U., 1931, M.A., 1947; m. Frances C. Dugan, Aug. 7, 1937; children—Jean Ann McNeil Martin, Patricia Lynn. Asso. sec. Community Welfare Council, Omaha, 1932-33; sec. Douglas County Emergency Relief Com., 1933-34, dir. relief div. Douglas County Relief Adminstrn., 1934-35, adminstr., 1935-36; dir. Omaha Community Chest, exec. v.p. Community Welfare Council, 1936-44; dir. personnel Community Chests and Councils Am., Inc., N.Y.C., 1944-47; prof., dir. sch. social adminstrn. Ohio State U., 1947-54; exec. dir. Health and Welfare Council, Inc., Phila., 1954-66; exec. dir. Nat. Assembly for Social Policy and Devel., Inc., N.Y.C., 1966-73; cons. Nat. Center Vol. Action, 1973-74, bd. dirs., 1974-79; mem. so. div. com. Del. Hospice, Inc.; assoc. Anderson-Stokes, Rehoboth Beach, Del., 1976—; mem. 501(C)(3) Group, chmn., 1972-73. Recipient Centennial Achievement award Ohio State U., 1970, Centennial Distinguished Service award Coll. Adminstrv. Scis., 1970. Mem. Rehoboth Beach C. of C. (bd. dirs.), Sussex County Bd. Realtors (bd. dirs.). Author: Community Orgn. for Social Welfare, monograph, 1951, 1954; Principles of Community Orgn., 1960; The Dynamics of Health and Welfare Planning Structures and Processes, 1964; contbr. articles and papers to profl. publs. Home: 21 Sussex Dr Lewes DE 19958

MC NEILL, CARMEN MARY, bus. broker; b. Charles City, Iowa, July 16; d. Benjamin T. and Mary (Orvis) McN. M.B.A., U. Chgo., 1957. Sec.-treas., Old Rep. Life Ins. Co., 1943-62; cons., officer life cos., 1962-70; broker-finder, owner Am. Cons., Chgo., 1970—. Methodist. Home: 918 Argyle Ave Flossmoor IL 60422 Office: 30 N Michigan Ave Suite 1314 Chicago IL 60602

MCNEILL, FREDERICK WALLACE, lawyer, educator, writer, aviation consultant, former military and commercial pilot; b. Chgo., Jan. 4, 1932; s. James Joseph and Irene Gertrude (Stevenson) McN.; m. Judith Carol Austin, Feb. 9, 1957; children: Marjorie, Tamelyn, Kenneth, Patricia, Darcy, Sean, Meghan. BBA, U. Ariz., 1974, JD, 1977. Bar: Ariz. 1977, U.S. Dist. Ct. Ariz., 1977. Served to maj. USAF, 1949-73; ret., 1973; bus. mgr. Engring. & Research Assocs., Inc., Tucson, 1973-74; mng. ptnr. ERA Shopping Ctr., Tucson, 1973-75; chief pilot, spl. agt. Narcotics Strike Force, Ariz., 1975-77; dep. county atty. Pima County, Ariz., 1977-79; atty. Ariz. Drug Control Dist., 1977-79; ptnr. Rees & McNeill, Tucson, 1979-84; writer, 1984—; coordinator legal asst. studies program and adj. prof. Nova U.-Panama Ctr., Republic of Panama, 1987—; of counsel Carreira-Pitti P.C. Abogados, Panama, Republic of Panama, 1987—; lectr. air smuggling seminars, organized crime seminars, Ariz., 1977-79. Vice pres. Indian Ridge Homeowners Assn., 1980-82; bd. dirs. Tucson Boys Chorus Bldg. Fund Com., 1972-74. Decorated DFC, Air medal (5), Air Force Commendation medal (2). Mem. ABA, Ariz. Bar Assn., Pima County Bar Assn., Assn. Trial Lawyers Am., Ariz. Trial Lawyers Assn., Lawyer Pilots Bar Assn., Internat. Platform Assn., Ret. Officers Assn., Air Force Assn. Clubs: Order of Daedelians, Quiet Birdmen. Office: PSC Box 845 APO Miami FL 34002

MCNEILL, JOHN HENDERSON, government official, lawyer; b. Phila., Jan. 31, 1941; s. John Henderson and Cecilia Marie (Murphy) McN.; m. Helen Elizabeth Foley, June 18, 1966; children: John Henderson III, Bronwyn Jane Foley, Andrew Patrick Joseph. BA, U. Notre Dame, 1962; JD, Villanova U., 1965; LLM, London Sch. Econs., 1971, PhD, 1974; diploma Hague Acad. Internat. Law, 1973. Bar: Pa. 1966, U.S. Supreme Ct. 1970, D.C. 1981. Assoc. Sheer & Mazzocone, Phila., 1966; asst. defender Defender Assn. Phila., 1966-67; law clk. to Hon. Wm. W. Vogel, Judge, U.S. Ct. Common Pleas, Montgomery County, Pa., 1969-70; internat. relations officer ACDA, 1974-75, atty. adv., 1975-78, asst. gen. counsel, 1979-83; asst. gen. counsel (internat.) U.S. Dept. Def., 1983—; legal adv. U.S. del. SALT, 1977-79, Intermediate Range Nuclear Forces Negotiations with USSR, 1981-82, Strategic Arms Reduction Talks with USSR, 1983, Dept. Defense. rep. Maritime Boundary Talks with USSR, 1984—; cons. Amnesty Internat., London, 1971-73, IAEA, Vienna, 1976; lectr. U. Notre Dame London Centre Legal Studies, 1973-74; adj. prof. law Georgetown U., 1987—. Bd. dirs. Crusade D.C. div. Am. Cancer Soc., 1976-77, recipient Leadership Honor award Nat. Capital Area Combined Fed. Campaign, 1982; bd. consultors Villanova U. Law Sch., 1978—. Served to 2d lt. USAF, 1967-68. Career mem. U.S. Sr. Exec. Service, 1983—. Recipient Meritorious Honor award ACDA, 1979; awarded rank of meritorious exec., U.S. Pres., 1987; Centre Studies and Research in Internat Law and Internat. Relations, Hague Acad. Internat. Law scholar, 1974; London Sch. Econs. Internat. Law scholar, 1973. Mem. Am. Soc. Internat. Law. (exec. council 1986—, exec. com. 1988—), Internat. Inst. Strategic Studies, ABA, Fed. Bar Assn., Inter-Am. Bar Assn. Club: Cosmos. Contbr. articles to legal jours. including Am. Jour. Internat. Law. Office: Pentagon Rm 3E963 Washington DC 20301-1600

MCNEILL, ROBERT PATRICK, investment counselor; b. Chgo., Mar. 17, 1941; s. Donald Thomas and Katherine (Bennett) McN.; m. Martha Stephan, Sept. 12, 1964; children—Jennifer, Donald, Victoria, Stephan, Elizabeth. B.A. summa cum laude (valedictorian), U. Notre Dame, 1963; M.Letters, Oxford U., 1967. Chartered investment counselor. Assoc. Stein Roe & Farnham, Chgo., 1967-72, gen. ptnr., 1972-77, sr. ptnr., 1977-86, exec. v.p., 1986—; underwriting mem. Lloyds of London, 1980—; dir. Comml. Chgo. Corp.; vice chmn. bd. Hill Internat. Prodn. Co., Houston, 1982—; dir., adv. bd. Touche Remnant Investment Counselors, London, 1983—. Voting mem., sec Ill. Rhodes Scholarship Selection Com.; voting mem. Ill. rep. Great Lakes Dist. Rhodes Scholarship Selection Com.; bd. dirs. Kennedy Sch. for Retarded Children, Palos Park, Ill., 1972—, Winnetka United Way, Ill., 1984—, Division St. YMCA, Chgo., 1972—; assoc. Rush-Presbyterian-St. Lukes Med. Ctr., Chgo., 1975—. Rhodes scholar, 1963. Fellow Fin. Analysts Fedn.; mem. Chgo. Council on Fgn. Relations (bd. dirs., vice chmn. 1975—), Inst. European Studies (bd. govs., treas. 1981—), Investment Analysts Soc. Chgo. (chgo. com., com. on fgn. affairs, com. on internat. and domestic issues). Clubs: Sunset Ridge Country (Northfield, Ill.) (bd. dirs. 1983—); Chicago; Econ. of Chgo. Office: Stein Roe & Farnham 1 S Wacker Dr Chicago IL 60606

MCNEILL, THOMAS HUGH, neuroanatomist; b. Denver, Jan. 1, 1947; s. Virgil Hugh and Gloria (Tenopir) McN.; m. Florence McNeill, July 26, 1980. B.S., Colo. State U., 1971; M.S., Colo. State U., 1974; Ph.D., U. Rochester, 1980. USPHS trainee U. Rochester, 1975-79, NIH postdoctoral fellow, 1979-81, research assoc., 1979-81, asst. prof. neurology, 1981-87, assoc. prof. neurology, neurobiology and anatomy and oncology, 1987— . Contbr. articles to profl. jours. NIH postdoctoral fellow, 1979-81; young investigator award, 1982-85 Alzheimer's Disease and Related disorders Assn. grantee, 1982-83; United Cancer Council grantee, 1982-83; Nat. Inst. Aging grantee, 1982—, research career devel. award, 1985—; United Parkinson's Found. grantee, 1987-88, Am. Cancer Soc. grantee, 1987—. Mem. Soc. for Neurosci., Am. Aging Assn., Histochem. Soc., Brit. Brain Research Assn., European Brain and Behavioral Soc., Am. Assn. Anatomists, Am. Acad. Neurology, Nat. Inst. Neurol. Com. Research on neurobiology of neurotransmitter and neuropeptide systems in aging and degenerative diseases; immunocytochemistry, fluorescence histochemistry, senile dementia, aging, development, neurotoxicity of anticancer drugs, Parkinson's disease, Alzheimer's disease. Home: 15 Alleyn's Rise Fairport NY 14450 Office: U Rochester Dept Neurology Box 673 Rochester NY 14642

MCNULTY, BRENDA KWEE POEY-LING, investment management company executive; b. Hong Kong, May 4, 1949; came to U.S., 1967; d. John Hin-Lim and Clara Sau-Chun (Yeung) Kwee; m. Richard Walter McNulty, July 28, 1973; 1 child, Sean Kwee. BA, LeMoyne Coll., 1971; MBA, Syracuse U., 1973; postgrad., NYU, 1975. Staff auditor Arthur Young & Co., N.Y.C., 1973-74; mgr. pension reports and adminstrn. W.R. Grace & Co., N.Y.C., 1975-77, bus. devel. analyst, 1978-79, mgr. fin. projects, 1979-81, dir. fin. planning, 1981-83, portfolio mgr., 1983-84; asst. v.p., engagement mgr. Citibank, N.A., N.Y.C., 1985-86; rep. Warburg Asset Mgmt., Hong Kong, 1987—; prin. Mgmt. Analysis Ctr. Asia Ltd., Hong Kong, 1986—. Com. mem. 115 E 87th Co-oping Com., N.Y.C., 1985. Mem. Pi Gamma Mu. Democrat. Roman Catholic. Club: American (Hong Kong); The Royal Hong Kong Jockey; The Hong Kong Overseas Bankers. Home: 8E Headland Rd, Repulse Bay, Hong Kong Hong Kong Office: Warburg Asset Mgmt, 20/F Alexandra House, 16-20 Chater Rd, Central, Hong Kong Hong Kong

MCNULTY, MATTHEW FRANCIS, JR., hospital administration educator, university administrator, consultant; b. Elizabeth, N.J., Nov. 26, 1914; s. Matthew Francis and Abby Helen (Dwyer) McN.; m. Mary Nell Johnson, May 4, 1946; children—Matthew Francis, Mary Lauren. BS, St. Peter's Coll., 1938, DHL (hon.), 1978; postgrad., Rutgers U. Law Sch., 1939-41; MHA, Northwestern U., 1949; MPH, U. N.C., 1952; ScD (hon.), U. Ala., 1969, Georgetown U., 1986. Contract writer, mgmt. trainee Prudential Life Ins. Co. Am., N.J., 1938-41; dir. med. adminstrn. VA, 1946-49; project officer VA Hosp., Little Rock, Chgo. and Birmingham, Ala., 1949-54; adminstr. Jefferson-Hillman Hosp., Birmingham, 1954-63; founding gen. dir. U. Ala. Hosps. and Clinics, 1963-66; prof. hosp. adminstrn. U. Ala. Grad. Sch., 1954-69, vis. prof., 1969—, founding dir. grad. program hosp. adminstrn., 1964-66, prof. epidemiology and preventive medicine Sch. Medicine, 1964-69, founding dean Sch. Health Services Adminstrn., 1966-69; founding dir. Council Teaching Hosps. and assoc. dir. Assn. Am. Med. Colls., 1966-69; prof. community medicine and internat. health Georgetown U., 1969-86, v.p. med. ctr. affairs, 1969-72, exec. v.p., med. ctr. affairs, 1972-74; chancellor Georgetown U. Med. Ctr., 1974-86, ret. 1986—; chmn. acad. affiars com. bd. trustees Hahnemann U., Phila, 1987—; founding chmn. bd. Univ. Affiliated Health Plan, Inc., 1974-78; founding chmn. bd. trustees Georgetown U. Community Health Plan, Inc., 1972-80, W.K. Kellogg Found.; vis. prof. Cen. U. Venezuela, 1957; hosp. cons., 1953—; dir. Kaiser-Georgetown Community Health Plan, Inc., Kaiser Health Plans and Hosps.; mem. spl. med. adv. group VA, 1978—, Spl. Higher Edn. Com. on Dental Schs. Curriculum, 1978-79; preceptor hosp. adminstrn. Northwestern U., George Washington U., U. Iowa, U. Minn., 1953-66; mem. nat. adv. com. health research projects Ga. Inst. Tech., 1959-65, 73-85; nat. adv. com. health research projects U. Pitts., 1956-60; adv. com. W.K. Kellogg Found., 1960-65; vis. cons., lectr. Venezuelan Ministry Health and Social Welfare, 1967-69; dir. Blue Cross-Blue Shield Ala., 1960-61, 65-68; trustee, mem. exec. com. Blue Cross and Blue Shield Nat. Capital Area, 1973—. Bd. dirs. Greater Birmingham United Appeal, 1960-66; trustee Jefferson County Tb Sanatorium, 1958-64; mem. health services research study sect. NIH, 1963-67; cons. USPHS, 1959, 63; mem. White House Conf. on Health, 1965, on Medicare Implementation, 1966, others; trustee Nat. Council Internat. Health, 1975-86; pres. Nat. League Nursing, 1979-81; bd. dirs. Kaiser Found. Health Plans and Hosps., 1980-85. Served from pvt. to maj. USAAF, 1941-46. Recipient Disting. Alumnus award Northwestern U., 1973, Disting. Alumnus award U. N.C., John Benjamin Nichol award Med. Soc. D.C., D.C. Matthew F. McNulty, Jr. Unanimous Recognition Resolution of 1986. Fellow Am. Pub. Health Assn., Am. Coll. Healthcare Execs. (bd. regents and council of regents 1961-67; Disting. Health Sci. Exec. award 1976); mem Am. Hosp. Assn. (life, Disting. Service award 1984), Ala. Hosp. Assn. (past pres.), Nat. League for Nursing (past pres.), D.C. League Nursing (past dir.), Council Med. Adminstrn., Internat. Hosp. Fedn., Jefferson County Ala. Vis. Nursing Assn. (past pres.; Disting. Service award), Ala. Pub. Health Assn. (past chmn. med. care sect.), Southeastern Hosp. Conf. (past dir.), Birmingham Hosp. Council (past pres.), Hosp. Council Nat. Capital Area (pres. 1985—), Assn. Univ. Programs in Hosp. Adminstrn. (Disting. award 1971), Greater Birmingham Area C. of C. (Merit award), Washington Acad. of Medicine, Am. Assn. Med. Colls. (chmn. teaching hosp. council 1964-65; Disting. Service Mem.), Royal Soc. Health, Am. Systems Mgmt. Soc. (Disting. award), Orgn. Univ. Health Ctr. Adminstrs., AAAS, Santa Gertrudis Breeders Internat., Omicron Kappa Upsilon. Clubs: University (Ala.); Cosmos, City Tavern, Nat. Press (Washington). Lodge: Knight of Malta.

MCNUTT, RICHARD HUNT, manufacturing company executive; b. Princeton, N.J., Mar. 11, 1943; s. John and Dorothy Elizabeth (Hunt) McN. Student Delaware Valley Coll. Sci and Agr., 1965-68; vocat. edn. cert. Temple U., 1978-81. Diemaker, Custom Tool Co., 1964-67; toolmaker Penn Engring., 1967-69; machine shop mgr., research and devel. engr. Inertial Motors Corp., 1969-73; machinery design engr. Phila. Rivet Co., Doylestown, Pa.; 1973-76; research and devel. mgr. PHL, Inc., Doylestown, 1976-82; asst. chief engr. PHL Inc., Levv/Air Inc., Prefco Products Inc., Prefco Products Internat., 1982-85, chief engr., 1985-86, v.p. ops., 1986—; owner Sunrise Solar Heat Co.; cons., Pipersville, Pa., 1976—. Exec. v.p. Del. Water Study Citizens Group for Sound Resource Mgmt.; councillor Probational Vol. Services; founding bd. dirs. Del-Aware Unltd., Inc., Del-Art Inc., Ctr. for the Arts, Bucks County, Pa.; mem. Environ. Polit. Action Com.; founder AWARE, Montgomery County, 1985—, STAND, Bucks County, 1986—. Served with USMC, 1960-64. Mem. Soc. Mfg. Engrs., Bucks County Assn. Corrections and Rehab., VFW, Am. Legion, Cen. Bucks County C. of C., Bucks County Conservation Alliance. Republican. Episcopalian. Home: RD 1 5556 Stump Rd Pipersville PA 18947 Office: Prefco Products Inc 2823 Old Durham Rd Buckingham PA 18912

MCPHEE, ALEXANDER HECTOR, consulting engineer; b. Bklyn., Nov. 26, 1911; s. Alexander Hendry and Charlotte Elizabeth (Kraus) McP.; student Pratt Inst., 1928-34, Bklyn. Poly. Inst., 1935-41; m. Cynthia Rose Agar, July 26, 1947; 1 son, Alexander Hector. Asst. chief engr. Peter Clark Inc., 1934-37; engr. U.S.S. Yorktown & Enterprise Airplane Elevators, 1934-37; partner Howard V. Harding & Co., 1937-38; asst. chief engr. Lukenweld div. Lukens Steel Co., 1938-44; partner McPhee & Johnston, 1945-48; pvt. practice cons. engr., 1948—; v.p. Hepworth Machine Co., Inc., Port Washington, N.Y., 1953-57, pres., 1957-80, chmn. bd., 1962-80, also dir.; v.p. Olaf Soot Assocs., P.C., 1979-81; cons. Midlantic Engring., P.C., 1985—; designer 90-foot turntable for Aircraft Nuclear Propulsion Project, Idaho Falls, Idaho, 1953, 76-foot turntable for Jones Beach Marine Amphitheatre; engring. cons. mfr. movable auditorium ceiling Juilliard Sch. Music, 1967-69; mech. stage equipment John F. Kennedy Center for Performing Arts, 1968-71; gondola hoists and controls Nassau County Vets. Meml. Coliseum, 1972; mech. and elec. cons. Bronx Zoo Skyride, 1972-73; approved welding inspection agy. N.Y.C. Dept. Bldgs. Troop com. mem., Eagle Scout, Scoutmaster Boy Scouts Am.; mem. bd. appeals Village of Plandome Heights, N.Y. Registered profl. engr., N.Y., N.J., Pa., Conn., D.C., P.R., W.Va., also nat. engring. cert. Nat. Council Engring. Examiners. Mem. ASME (life), ASTM, Am. Def. Preparedness Assn., Nat. Soc. Profl. Engrs., Nassau County Grand Jurors Assn., Mac Fie Clan Soc. N.Am. (life), Pi Tau Sigma (hon.). Patentee flashwelding machine control, vertical conveyor, centrifugal machines, dry cask handling system, alert hangar door, others. Home and Office: 89 The Waterway Plandome Heights NY 11030

MC PHEETERS, EDWIN KEITH, architectural designer; b. Stillwater, Okla., Mar. 26, 1924; s. William Henry and Eva Winona (Mitchell) McP.; m. Patricia Ann Foster, Jan. 29, 1950 (div. 1981); children: Marc Foster, Kevin Mitchell, Michael Hunter; m. Mary Louise Marvin, July 21, 1984. B.Arch., Okla. State U., 1949; M.F.A., Princeton U., 1956. Instr. architecture U. Fla., 1949-51; asst. prof. Ala. Poly. Inst., Auburn U., 1951-54; fellow Princeton U., 1955, 81; from asst. prof. to prof. U. Ark., 1956-66; prof. Rensselaer Poly. Inst., 1966-69, dean, 1966-69; prof. Auburn U., 1969—; dean Auburn U. (Sch. of Architecture), 1969-88; mem. Ala. State Bd. Registration for Architects, 1978-87; profl. adviser South Central Bell Telephone Co., 1977-79, So. Co., 1979-81, Ala. Power Co., 1979-81, Okla. State U., 1983, Ala. Sch. Fine Arts, 1985-86. Served to 2d lt. USAAC, 1943-45. Fellow AIA (pres. Ala. council 1978, recipient Merit award 1976); mem. Assn. Collegiate Schs. of Architecture (dir. 1970-77), Blue Key, Kappa Sigma, Omicron Delta Kappa, Kappa Kappa Psi, Tau Sigma Delta. Office: 221 Kimberly Dr Auburn AL 36830

MCPHERSON, EUGENE VIRGIL, broadcasting executive; b. Columbus, Ohio, Aug. 29, 1927; s. Arthur Emerson and Emma (Scott) McP.; B.A., Ohio State U., 1950; m. Nancy Marie Clark, June 13, 1953; children—Lynne, Scott. Prodn. exec. WBNS-TV, Columbus, 1952-62; exec. producer documentary unit WLWT-TV, Cin., 1962-64; dir. news and spl. projects WLWT-TV, Cin., 1964-66; v.p. news and spl. projects AVCO Broadcasting Co., Cin., 1966-69, v.p. programming, 1969-73; v.p., gen. mgr. WLWI-TV, Indpls., 1973-75; now pres. McPherson Media, Inc.; owner, operator WVLN, WSEI-FM, 1976-87, WRBI, 1978-83, KCTE 1978-83, KGVE 1980-83, now pres. McPherson Prodns. Served with AUS, 1946-47. Recipient creative writer producer award Alfred P. Sloan, 1966; Chris award Columbus Film Festival, 1960, 61, 62, 64, 71; Nat. Assn. TV Execs. Program award, 1968; Ohio State award, 1960, 63, 64; Freedom's Found. award, 1963, Regional Emmy, 1977; Cine Golden Eagle award, 1982; Blue Ribbon, Am. Film Festival, 1985. Mem. Broadcast Pioneers, Ill. Broadcasters Assn. (pres.). Author: (with Bleum and Cox) Television in the Public Interest, 1961. Writer, producer, dir. films The Last Prom, 1963, Death Driver, 1968, Citizen, 1962, Birth by Appointment, 1960, Diagnostic Countdown, 1962, Veil of Shadows, 1961, Rails in Crisis, 1963, Palm Trees and Ice Bergs, 1977, Tinsel Town and the Big Apple, 1979, Goodbye Carnival Girl, 1980, Atomic Legs, 1981, The Edison Adventures, 1981, The Championship, 1982, Little Arliss, 1984; Umbrella Jack, 1984; Buddies, 1985; That Funny Fat Kid, 1985; Zerk the Jerk, 1985; My First Swedish Bombshell, 1985, Charlie's Christmas Secret, 1985, Just For Kicks, 1986, Nags, 1987, My Father, the Clown, 1987, Charlie's Christmas Project, 1987, Narc, 1987, Pee Wee's Ragtime Band, 1988. Office: 627 S Elliott St Olney IL 62450 Office: 2220 Gilbert Ave Cincinnati OH 45206

MC PHERSON, FRANK ALFRED, corporation executive; b. Stilwell, Okla., Apr. 29, 1933; s. Younce B. and Maurine Francis (Strauss) McP.; m. Nadine Wall, Sept. 10, 1955; 4 children. B.S., Okla. State U., 1957. With Kerr-McGee, 1957—; gen. mgr. Gulf Coast Oil and gas ops., Morgan City, La., 1969-73; pres. Kerr-McGee Coal, 1973-76, Kerr-McGee Nuclear, 1976-77; vice chmn. Kerr-McGee Corp., 1977-80, pres., 1980—, chmn., chief exec. officer, 1983—; adv. dir. Liberty Nat. Bank. Bd. dirs. Okla. chpt. Nature Conservancy, U.S. Olympic Com. for Okla., Appeals Rev. Bd. Greater Okla., Leadership Oklahoma City, Bapt. Med. Ctr. of Okla., Okla. State U. Found., United Way of Greater Oklahoma City; mem. Okla. Found. Excellence; mem. adv. council Southwestern Bapt. Theol. Sem.; mem. council on competitiveness Okla. Acad. for State Goals. Served to capt. USAF, 1957-60. Mem. Conf. Bd., Soc. Mining Engrs., Am. Mining Congress (dir., exec. com., adv. council), Am. Petroleum Inst. (dir.), Nat. Petroleum Council, 25-Yr. Club of Petroleum Industry Oklahoma City C. of C. (dir.). Republican. Baptist. Office: Kerr-McGee Corp PO Box 25861 Oklahoma City OK 73125 *

MCPHERSON, GAIL, advertising and real estate executive; b. Fort Worth; d. Garland and Daphne McP. Student U. Tex.-Austin; BA, MS, CUNY. Advt. sales exec. Harper's Bazaar mag., N.Y.C., 1974-76; sr. v.p., fashion mktg. dir. L'Officiel/USA mag., N.Y.C., 1976-80; fashion mgr. Town and Country mag., N.Y.C., 1980-82; v.p. advt. and mktg. Ultra mag., Tex. and N.Y.C., 1982-84; fragrance, jewelry and automotive mgr. M. Mag., N.Y.C., 1984-85; sr. real estate sales exec. Fredric M. Reed & Co., Inc., N.Y.C., 1985—. Sponsor Southampton Hosp. Benefit Com., N.Y.; mem. jr. com. Mannes Sch. Music, N.Y.C., Henry St. Settlement, N.Y.C. Mem. Fashion Group N.Y., Advt. Women N.Y., Real Estate Bd., U. Tex. Alumni Assn. of N.Y. (v.p.). Republican. Presbyterian. Clubs: Corviglia (St. Moritz, Switzerland), Doubles, El Morocco (mem. jr. com. 1976-77), Le Club (N.Y.C.). Home: 429 E 52d St New York NY 10022 Office: 405 Park Ave New York NY 10022

MCPHERSON, KLIM, community medicine educator; b. St. Helens, Lancashire, Eng., Sept. 17, 1941; s. Anthony John and Barbara (Robinson) Willcock; m. Ann Egelnick, May 18, 1968; children—Sam, Tess, Beth. B.A., Cambridge U., 1964, M.A., 1966; Ph.D., London Sch. Hygiene and Tropical Medicine, 1971. Research officer dept. med. statistics London Sch. Hygiene, 1966-69; sci. staff Med. Research Council, London, 1969-76; asst. prof. Harvard Med. Sch., Boston, 1973-74; univ. lectr. dept. community medicine Oxford U., 1976—; mem. council Royal Statis. Soc., London, 1980-84; mem. manpower com. Study of Surg. Service in U.S., 1973-74. Nuffield Coll. fellow, 1977—. Home: 12 Fyfield Rd, Oxford OX2 6QE, England Office: Dept Community Medicine, Gibson Labs Radcliffe Infirmary, Radcliffe Infirmary, Oxford OX2 6HE, England

MCQUARRIE, IRVINE GRAY, neuroscientist, neurosurgeon, educator, consultant; b. Ogden, Utah, June 27, 1939; s. Irwin Bruce and Ruby Loretta (Epperson) McQ.; m. Katharine Gamble Rogers, Mar. 11, 1967 (div.); children—Michael Gray, Mollie; m. Maryann Kaminski, Aug. 14, 1980; children—Morgan Elizabeth, Gray. B.S. in Biology, U. Utah, 1961; M.D., Cornell U., 1965, Ph.D., 1977. Diplomate Am. Bd. Neurol. Surgery. Intern, asst. surgeon, surgeon N.Y. Hosp., N.Y.C., 1965-71, 72-73; research fellow dept. physiology Cornell U. Med. Coll., N.Y.C., 1971-72, 74-76, asst. prof. depts. physiology and surgery, 1976-81; vis. asst. prof. dept. anatomy Case-Western Res. U., Cleve., 1979-81, asst. prof. neurosurgery, 1981-85, assoc. prof., 1985—, asst. prof. devel. genetics and anatomy, 1981-85, assoc. prof., 1985—, clin. investigator in neurol. surgery VA Med. Center, Cleve., 1981-84, med. investigator in neurol. surgery, 1984—; asst. neurosurgeon Univ. Hosps. of Cleve., 1981—; mem. adv. bd. VA office Regeneration Research Programs, 1986—. Contbr. articles to sci. jours. Served to comdr., M.C. UNSR, 1973-74. Recipient Andrew W. Mellon Tchr.-Scientist award, 1977-79; NIH fellow, 1971-72, 74-76; VA career devel. award and individual research grantee, 1981—; Paralyzed Vets. Am. grantee, 1979-82; NIH grantee, 1981—, Spinal Cord Soc. grantee, 1986—. Mem. N.Y. Acad. Scis., AAAS, Soc. for Neurosci., Am. Soc. for Cell Biology, Am. Assn. Anatomists, Congress Neurol. Surgeons, Am. Assn. Neurol. Surgeons. Democrat. Presbyterian. Research on mechanism of axonal regeneration in central nervous system; biochem. investigations on maintenance and replacement of nerve cell processes (called axons and dendrites) by complex intraneuronal transport mechanisms. Home: 13805 Shaker Blvd Cleveland OH 44120 Office: 2119 Abington Rd Cleveland OH 44106

MCQUIRE, NEIL LESLIE, clinical psychologist; b. Blackpool, England, Apr. 13, 1951; s. Leslie Eric and Florence Jean (Daker) McQ.; m. Anne Howard, Dec. 29, 1986; children: Nathan, Ryan, Alexander. BA in Psychology with honors, U. London, 1973; PhD in Psychology, U. Leeds, England, 1986. Cert. clinical psychologist. Basic psychologist Rochdale (Eng.) Health Authority, 1975-77, sr. psychologist, 1977-82, prin. clin. psychologist, 1982—. Contbr. articles to profl. jours. Mem. Brit. Psychol. Soc. Home: 137 Harewood Rd, Norden Rochdale, Lancashire OL11 5TN, England Office: Birch Hill Hosp, Dept Clinical Psychology, Rochdale Lancashire England

MCRAE, HAMILTON EUGENE, III, lawyer; b. Midland, Tex., Oct. 29, 1937; s. Hamilton Eugene and Adrian (Hagaman) McR.; m. Betty Hawkins, Aug. 27, 1960; children: Elizabeth Ann, Stephanie Adrian, Scott Hawkins. BSEE, U. Ariz., 1961; student, USAF Electronics Sch., 1961-62; postgrad., U. Redlands, Calif., 1962-63; JD with honors and distinction, U. Ariz., 1967. Bar: Ariz. 1967, U.S. Supreme Ct. 1979. Elec. engr. Salt River Project, Phoenix, 1961; assoc. Jennings, Strouss & Salmon, Phoenix, 1967-71, ptnr., 1971-85, chmn. real estate dept., 1980-85, mem. policy com., 1982-85, mem. fin. com., 1981-85, chmn. bus. devel. com., 1982-85; ptnr. and co-founder Stuckey & McRae, Phoenix, 1985—; co-founder, chmn. bd. Republic Cos., Phoenix, 1985—; magistrate Paradise Valley, Ariz., 1983-85; juvenile referee Superior Ct., 1983-85; pres., dir. Phoenix Realty & Trust Co., 1970—; officer Indsl. Devel. Corp. Maricopa County, 1972-86; instr. and lectr. in real estate; officer, bd. dirs. other corps. Contbr. articles to profl. jours. Elder Valley Presbyn. Ch., Scottsdale, Ariz., 1973-75, 82-85, corp. pres., 1974-75, 84-85, trustee, 1973-75, 82-85, chmn. exec. com., 1984; trustee Upward Found., Phoenix, 1977-80, Valley Presbyn. Found., 1982-83, Ariz. Acad., 1971—; trustee, mem. exec. com. Phi Gamma Delta Ednl. Found., Washington, 1974-84; trustee Phi Gamma Delta Internat., 1984-86; trustee, bd. dirs. Archon, 1986-87; founder, trustee McRae Found.; trustee, mem. exec. com. Ariz. Mus. Sci. and Tech., 1984—, 1st v.p., 1985-86, pres., 1986-88, chmn. bd. dirs., 1988—; Lambda Alpha Internat. Hon. Land Econs. Soc, 1988—; bd. dirs. Ariz. State U. Council for Design Excellence, 1988—; Crisis Nursery Office of the Chair, 1988—, Maricopa Community Colls. Found., 1988—, Phoenix Community Alliance, 1988—; vol. fund raiser YMCA, Salvation Army, others; mem. Taliesin Council, Frank Lloyd Wright Found., 1985—; mem. fin. com. Kyl for Congress, 1985 ; mem. bond com. City of Phoenix, 1987-88; bd. dirs. Food for Hungry (Internat. Relief), 1985—, exec. com., 1986—, chmn. bd. dirs. 1987—; mem. Ariz. State U. Council of 100, 1985—, investment com., 1985—. Served with USAF, 1961-64. Recipient various mil. awards. Mem. ABA, Ariz. Bar Assn., Maricopa County Bar Assn., AIME, Ariz. Acad., U. Ariz. Alumni Assn., Clan McRae Soc. N.Am., Tau Beta Pi. Republican. Clubs: Phoenix Exec., Phoenix Country, Ariz., Continental Country, U. Ariz. Pres.'s, Econ. of Phoenix (bd. dirs. 1987—); Jackson Hole Racquet (Wyo.). Home: 8101 N 47th St Paradise Valley AZ 85253 Office: Republic Cos 5500 N 24th St Phoenix AZ 85016

MCRAE, HAMISH MALCOLM DONALD, financial journalist, newspaper editor; b. Barnstaple, Devon, Eng., Oct. 20, 1943; s. Donald Barrngton and Barbara Ruth L. (Budd) McR.; m. Frances Anne Cairncross, Sept. 10, 1971; children: Isabella, Alexandra. BA with honours, Trinity Coll., Dublin, Ireland, 1966. Editorial asst. The Banker, London, 1966-69, asst. editor, 1969-71, dep. editor, 1971-72; editor Euromoney, London, 1972-74; fin. editor The Guardian, London and Manchester, Eng., 1975—. Author: Capital City-London as a Financial Centre, 1973, The Second Great Crash, 1975. Named fin. journalist of yr. Wincott Found., London, 1979; recipient award of spl. merit Amex Bank, London and N.Y.C., 1987. Home: 6 Canonbury Ln, London N1 2AP, England Office: The Guardian, 119 Farrington Rd, London EC 1, England

MCROBBIE, MICHAEL ALEXANDER, logician, researcher; b. Melbourne, Australia, Oct. 11, 1950; s. Alexander Hewitt and Joyce Victoria (Gair) McR.; m. Andrea Shirley Gibson, Dec. 22, 1973; 1 child, Josephine Elizabeth Joyce. B.A. with honors I, U. Queensland, 1974; Ph.D., Australian Nat. U., 1979, reader, exec. dir. Ctr. for Info. Scis. Research, 1987—. Research fellow La Trobe U., Melbourne, 1979-81, U. Melbourne, 1981-83, Australian Nat. U., Canberra, A.C.T., 1983-87, dep. coordinator ops. Automated Reasoning Project, 1985—. vis. pof. U. Kaiserlautern, Fed. Republic Germany, 1987. Co-author: Automated Theorem Proving in Non-Classical Logics, 1986. Co-editor: Environmental Philosophy, 1980. Contbr. articles to profl. jours. Grantee La Trobe U., 1979-81, U. Melbourne, 1981-83, Australian Nat. U., 1983—, Fulgright sr. fellow, 1988 . Mem. IEEE, Am. Math. Soc., Assn. for Automated Reasoning, Assn. for Symbolic Logic, Australasian Assn. for Logic (sec. 1975-76, 80-81, pres. 1982-84), Australasian Assn. of Philosophy, Assn. for Computing Machinery. Club: University House (Australian Nat. U.). Avocations: aesthetics; gardening; reading; cricket; philately. Office: Australian Nat U Automated, Reasoning Project RSSS GPO Box 4, Canberra 2601, Australia

MCSHANE, ROBERT IVAN OWEN, investment company executive; b. Thames, Auckland, New Zealand, Mar. 18, 1941; s. William James and Vera Ruth (Harding) McS.; m. Heather Margaret Taylor, Jan. 9, 1963 (div. June 1978); children: Clifton David, Simon James; m. Jennifer Margaret Parkinson, July 4, 1978. BArch, U. Auckland, 1963, Diploma in town planning, 1965; M in City Planning, U. Calif., Berkeley, 1969. Research officer Auckland City Council, 1965-67; pvt. practice cons. Auckland, 1970-78; mgr. technology Devel. Fin. Corp., Auckland, 1978-84; project mgr. Challenge Venture Capital, Auckland, 1985-86; mgr. venture capital Venturecorp Investments, Auckland, 1986-87, gen. mgr., 1987-88; mng. dir. Restech Venture Mgmt., Auckland, 1988—; Bd. dirs. Options Merchandising, Ltd., Auckland, Klasse-Fuzhou (People's Republic of China), Ltd., Laser Imaging Systems, Ltd., Hong Kong, Restech Internat., Auckland, 1986—. Contbr. monthly columns, articles and numerous essays to profl. pubs. Pres. Kare Kare Residents' Trust, 1978-80, Newmarket Bus. Assn., 1983-85; v.p. New Zealand Venture Capital Assn., Auckland, 1986-87; chmn. L.E.S. Technology Commercialization Com., Auckland, 1986-87; apptd. to Govt. com. of enquiry into establishment of casinos in New Zealand, 1988; apptd. techn. licensing cons. to Waikato Tech. Found., 1988. Harkness fellow Commonwealth Fund, 1968. Office: Restech Venture Mgmt Ltd, 52 Quay St 4th Fl, Auckland 1 New Zealand

MCVEY, WILLIAM MOZART, sculptor; b. Boston, July 12, 1905; s. Silas R. and Cornelia (Mozart) McV.; m. Leza Marie Sullivan, Mar. 31, 1932. Grad. Cleve. Sch. Art, 1928; student Rice Inst., 1923-25, Acadamie Colarossi and Acadamie Scandinave, Paris, 1929-31; pupil of Dispiau, Paris, 1929-31; Tchr. Cleve. Mus., 1932, Houston Mus., 1936-38, U. Tex., Austin, 1939-46, Ohio State U., Columbus, summer 1946, Cranbrook Art Acad., Bloomfield Hills, Mich., 1946-53; head sculpture dept. Cleve. Inst. Art, 1953-67; vis. sculptor Sch. Fine Arts, Ohio State U., Columbus, 1963-64. Represented in permanent collections IBM, Univ. Mus., Pomona, Calif., Wichita Art Mus., Cleve. Mus., Houston Mus., Syracuse Mus., Cranbrook Mus., Harvard Library, Smithsonian Inst., Yale Library, Nat. Cathedral, Washington, Ariana Mus., Geneva, others; publicly owned works include heroic reliefs and doors San Jacinto Monument, Tex., door FTC, Washington, doors and reliefs Tex. Meml. Mus., reliefs Lakeview Terrace Housing Project, Cleve., heroic grizzly Nat. Hist. Mus., figure Abercrombie Lab., Rice Inst., monument to Davy Crockett, Ozona, Tex., to James Bowie, Texarkana, Tex.; 9 foot bronze of Winston Churchill, British Embassy, Washington; St. Margaret of Scotland and Jan Hus at Washington Cathedral, St. Olga of Russia, Simon de Monfort, Stephen Langton, Sir Edward Coke, Churchill Bay of Nat. Cathedral heroic U.S. Shields Fed. Bldg., Cleve., Jennings Meml., Univ. Circle, Cleve., granite hippo (with Victor Gruen) Eastgate Shopping Ctr., Detroit, 5-ton whale Lincoln Ctr., Urbana, Ill., bronze hippo Cleve. Heights Children's Library, Bell Tower, Hiram Coll., Berry Monument bronze Cleve. Hopkins Airport, panels (with Eero Saarinen) Christ Lutheran Ch., Mpls., bronze of George Washington at Washington Sq., Cleve., head of Churchill, Chartwell, Eng., stainless steel and bronze B clef logo Blossom Music Ctr., numerous others; exhibited honor ct. Paris Grand Salon, 1930, Salon d'Automne, 1931. Chmn. Nat. screening com. Fulbright grants. Served to maj. USAF, World War II. Recipient numerous awards Nat. Sculpture Show, Ceramic Nat., Nat. Archtl. Ceramic, Mich. Acad. Sci. Arts and Letters, Internat. Cultural Exchange Ceramic Exhibit. Fellow Nat. Sculpture Soc.; mem. Coll. Art Assn., Am. Soc. Aesthetics, Internat. Platform Assn., NAD (assoc.). Papers in Archives Am. Art, Smithsonian Inst. Home and Office: 18 Pepper Ridge Rd Cleveland OH 44124

MCVICAR, DIARMID, physiotherapist, inventor; b. Dunoon, Scotland, Mar. 7, 1946; s. John and Jessie Mary (McDiarmid) McV.; m. Margaret Adele Lusty, Dec. 18, 1971 (div.). Diploma in Physiotherapy, Royal Infirmary Sch., Glasgow, Scotland, 1969. Physiotherapist Lake of Woods Hosp., Kenora, Ont., Can., 1969-72, Winnipeg (Man.) Jets, World Hockey Assn., 1972-74, St. Boniface Hosp., Winnipeg, 1974, Sports Injury Ctr., Winnipeg, 1975-79; physiotherapist, owner D. Scotty McVicar Physiotherapy, Winnipeg, 1979-84, Qualicum Physiotherapy, Qualicum Beach, B.C., Can., 1984—; mem. Sports Medicine Council Can., Ottawa, 1978-81. Inventor The Waverly Wedge (aid for back pain); contbr. articles to jours., books in field. Bd. dirs. Man. Lotteries Commn., Winnipeg, 1979-81, East Kildonan Parks and Recreation, Winnipeg, 1981-82, Winnipeg Ambulance Commn., 1982-83; candidate Provincial Legislature, Man., 1981. Recipient Queens badge The Boys Brigade, Scotland, 1963, Duke of Edinburgh's award The Boys Brigade, Scotland, 1963. Mem. Can. Physiotherapy Assn. (pres. Man. br. 1976-78, chmn. sports physiotherapy 1979-81, pres. Can. Assn. 1985-86). Progressive Conservative. Presbyterian. Clubs: Golf & Country (Kenora) (capt. 1970-71); Women's Field Hockey (Man.) (coach 1975-77); Parksville Wallyball (pres. 1986-87). Home: 461 Linden Pl PO Box 878, Qualicum Beach, BC Canada V0R 2T0 Office: Qualicum Physiotherapy, 114 W First Ave Box 878, Qualicum Beach, BC Canada V0R 2T0

MCWHERTER, NED RAY, governor of Tennessee; b. Palmersville, Tenn., Oct. 15, 1930; s. Harmon Ray and Lucille Golden (Smith) McW.; children—Linda Ramsey, Michael Ray. Chmn. bd. Vol. Distb. Co. Inc., Eagle Distbrs. Inc., Vol. Express Inc., Hillview Nursing Homes Inc., Weakley Gas & Oil Co., Weakley County Mcpl. Electric System; dir. Weakley County Bank, Peoples Bank, Fed. Savs. & Loan; mem. Tenn. Ho. of Reps., 1968-87, speaker, 1973-87; Gov. of Tenn. Nashville, 1987—. Bd. govs. Council State Govts.; exec. com. So. Legis. Conf.; chmn. So. Speakers' Conf. Democrat. Methodist. Lodges: Elks, Moose, Eagles, Masons, Shriners, Lions. Office: Office of Gov State Capitol Bldg Nashville TN 37219 also: 22 Bypass Dresden TN 38225 •

MCWHIRTER, BRUCE J., lawyer; b. Chgo., Sept. 11, 1931; s. Sydney William and Martha (Krucks) McW.; m. Judith Elizabeth Hallett, Apr. 14, 1960; children—Cameron, Andrew. B.A., Northwestern U., 1952; LL.B., Harvard U., 1955. Bar: D.C. 1955, Ill. 1955, U.S. Ct. Appeals (7th cir.) 1963, U.S. Dist. Ct. (no. dist.) Ill. 1958. Assoc. Lord, Bissell & Brock, Chgo., 1958-62; assoc., then ptnr. Ross & Hardies, Chgo., 1962—, now sr. ptnr. Editor: SEC Handbook, 1972—; contbr. articles to profl. publs. Served with U.S. Army, 1955-57, Japan. Mem. Harvard Law Soc. Ill. (bd. dirs. 1984), Phi Beta Kappa. Democrat. Home: 111 Sheridan Rd Winnetka IL 60093 Office: Ross & Hardies 150 N Michigan Ave Suite 2500 Chicago IL 60601

MCWHIRTER, DIANE BALTZELLE, lawyer; b. Miami Beach, Fla., Sept. 12, 1958; d. Conner and Mary Athria (Marney) Baltzelle; m. John McWhirter. BA in Philosophy, Duke U., 1979; JD, U. Fla., 1982; postgrad. in comparative law Magdalen Coll., Oxford, Eng., summer 1980. Bar: Fla. 1983, U.S. Dist. Ct. (mid. dist.) Fla. 1983, U.S. Ct. Appeals (11th cir.) 1984. Asst. pub. defender, Pub. Defender's Office, Lake City, Fla., 1983-84, Orlando, Fla., 1984-86; sole practice, Orlando, 1987-88, gen. counsel Fla. United Meth. Children's Home, Inc., Enterprise, Fla., 1988—, trustee, 1985-88; teaching fellow Holland Law Ctr., Gainesville, Fla., 1982; lectr. Pub. Defender Spring Conf., 1985. Editor family law, Legal Aid Handbook, 1981-82. Mem. Fla. Symphony League, Orlando, 1983-84, Columbia Assn. for Retarded Children, Lake City, 1984; mem. choir 1st United Presbyn. Ch., Lake City, 1984; Sunday sch. tchr. 1st United Meth. Ch., Orlando, 1983, 85, mem. choir, 1986—; trustee Fla. United Meth. Children's Home, 1985-87. Mem. ABA, Fla. Bar Assn. (evidence com. 1985-86), Orange County Bar Assn. (vice chmn. law and edn. com. 1986-87), Phi Delta Phi (clk. 1981-82, historian 1982, cert. of merit 1981, 82). Democrat. Home: 220 N Clark St Enterprise FL 32725 Office: 51 Main St Enterprise FL 32725

MCWHIRTER, NORRIS DEWAR, publisher, author, broadcaster; b. London, Aug. 12, 1925; s. William Allan and Margaret Moffat (Williamson) McW.; m. Carole Eckert, Dec. 28, 1957 (dec. 1987); children—Jane Margaret, Alasdair William. Student Marlborough Coll., 1939-43; B.A. in Econs., Trinity Coll., Oxford, 1948, M.A. in Contract Law, 1950. Founder and dir. McWhirter Twins Ltd., London, 1951—; athletics corr. The Star, 1951-64, The Observer, 1951-67; editor Athletics World, 1952-57; dir. Guinness Superlatives Ltd., London, 1954—; mng. commentator Olympic Games BBC, 1952-72; presenter BBC Record Breakers, London, 1972-87; editor Guinness Book of Records, London, 1954-86; founder, chmn. Redwood Press, Trowbridge, Wiltshire, England, 1966-72; dir. Gieves and Hawks, 1972—; chmn. William McWhirter & Sons, Glasgow, 1955-87. Publications include: Get To Your Marks, 1951; Guinness Book of World Records (editor and compiler 262 editions in 31 langs. to 1988) 1955—; Dunlop Books of Facts, 1964, 1966; Guinness Book of Answers, 1976-87; Ross, Story of a Shared Life, 1976. Parliamentary candidate Conservative Party, Orpington, Kent County, 1962-66; mem. Sports Council for England, 1970-74; co-founder, chmn. The Freedom Assn., London, 1975—. Served to sub.-lt. R.N.V.R., 1943-46. Recipient comdr. Order Brit. Empire; recipient Free Enterprise Spl. award Aims of Industry, London, 1983. Anglican. Clubs: Vincent's (Oxford); Caledonian (London). Office: Guinness Books 33, London Rd, Enfield England

MCWHIRTER, WILLIAM BUFORD, business consultant; b. Waco, Tex., Aug. 23, 1918; s. Buford and Katherine (McCollum) McW.; A.B.A., Glendale Jr. Coll., 1937; B.A. with honors, U. Calif. Berkeley, 1939; m. Catherine Eugenia Forbes, Sept. 21, 1956. Br. mgr. IBM Corp., San Francisco, 1949-56, dist. mgr. N.Y. area, 1956-57, gen. mgr. supplies div., 1957-59, pres. data systems div., White Plains, N.Y., 1959-62, IBM dir. orgn., 1962-64, pres. indsl. products div., 1964-65; cons. to IBM, other firms, 1966—; dir. Amdahl Corp., Sunnyvale, Calif., Itel Corp., San Francisco, MHC Corp., N.Y.C. Trustee, Mus. of No. Ariz. Mem. Phi Beta Kappa, Theta Xi. Clubs: San Francisco Sales Executives (pres. 1955-56); Siwanoy (Bronxville, N.Y.); Metropolitan (N.Y.C.); Army-Navy (Arlington, Va.); Phoenix Country; Desert Forest (Carefree, Ariz.); Pauma Valley (Calif.). Home: Carefree AZ 85377

MC WHITE, BENSON CARWILE, textile company executive; b. Abbeville, S.C., June 2, 1924; s. John Reed and Mary Harley (Carwile) McW.; BEE, Clemson U., 1947; m. Martha Ashley, Dec. 19, 1971; children: Mary Carla McWhite Carter, John Evans, Thomas Benson, William Loftis, Nancy Lu Silverman, John Lewis, Robert Neil, Nancy Lynn. Mgmt. trainee Abbeville Mills, Deering Milliken Corp., 1947-49, indsl. engr., 1949, cost acct., McCormick, S.C., 1950, group adminstrn. mgr., Johnston, S.C., 1950-52, group planning mgr., Pendleton, S.C., 1953-55, supt. Excelsior finishing plant, Pendleton, 1955; group planning mgr. Amerotron Corp., Clarksville, Va., 1956-57, Raeford, N.C., 1958; div. planning mgr. Pacific Mills div. Burlington Industries, Halifax, Va., 1959, mgr. Raeford worsted plant, 1960, v.p./group mgr. Raeford Worsted div., 1960-65, v.p./dir. planning Burlington Worsted div., 1965-70, dir. planning Gayley & Lord div., Gastonia, N.C., 1970-71; planning systems dir. Milliken & Co., Spartanburg, S.C., 1971-73, product planning mgr., 1973-76, market research analyst, 1977-86, trade relations specialist, 1987—; mem. mgmt./labor textile adv. com. U.S. Dept. Commerce; industry adv. com. for trade policy U.S. Dept. State, U.S. Trade Rep.; textile industry adv. bilateral and multilateral trade negotiations U.S. Govt. Served with Signal Corps, U.S. Army, 1943-46. Mem. IEEE, Am. Mgmt. Assn., Am. Prodn. and Inventory Control Soc., Nat. Assn. Cost Accts., Advanced Computer Planning Systems Group, So. Woolen and Worsted Mfrs. Assn. (past pres.). Methodist. Clubs: Keowee Key, Foxcroft Assn., Lions. Home: 30 Queen Ann Rd Greenville SC 29615 Office: PO Box 1926 Spartanburg SC 29304

MCWILLIAM, ROY, architect; b. Geelong, Victoria, Australia, Mar. 14, 1929; s. James Robert Mitchell and Martha Ann (Jones) McW.; m. Beverley Marie Dardel, Jan. 8, 1955; children: Stuart Mitchell, Hilary Elizabeth, Fraser, Fiona Ann. Diploma in architecture, Melbourne U., 1954. Architect, assoc. Buchan, Laird & Buchan Pty. Ltd., Melbourne, Australia, 1948-65, architect, dir., 1969-72; architect, assoc. Philp, Lighton, Floyd & Beattie, Hobart, Tasmania, Australia, 1965-68, Cheesman, Doley, Brabham & Neighbor, Sydney, Australia, 1968-69, Geoffrey Twibill & Assocs., Sydney, 1972; architect, dir., mgr. McWilliam Assocs. Pty. Ltd., Sydney, 1972—. Fellow Royal Australian Inst. Architects (bd. dirs. practice bd. 1986—), Royal Soc. Arts (life); mem. Royal Inst. Brit. Architects (assoc.), Assn. Cons. Architects (pres. 1986—). Mem. Liberal Party. Mem. Ch. of England. Home: 58 Pembroke St, Epping, New South Wales 2121, Australia Office: McWilliam Assocs Pty Ltd, 507 Kent St, Sydney, New South Wales 2000, Australia

MCWILLIAMS, HARRY KENNETH, advertising executive; b. Middlesboro, Ky., July 20, 1907; s. John William and Mattie S. (Bayliss) McW.; student U. Colo., 1927, numerous spl. courses Denver Sch. Tech., 1925-26; m. Rosa di Giulio, June 3, 1936 (dec. Jan. 1988); children: Rosanne, Harry Kahle, Sarah Jane Fuller (Mrs. Gijs Van Stavern). Sales mgr. Acme Films, N.Y.C., 1930-32; owner Advt. Flag Co., 1930-37; publicity mgr. numerous chains, including Harry E. Huffman theatres and Paramount Publix Theatres, N.Y.C., Toledo, Denver, Dallas, 1926-30; advt. and publicity dir. Cin. Summer Opera, 15 seasons, also publicity mgr. concert booker number leading personalities including violinist Rubinoff, and radio program, mgr. Benton and Bowles, Ted Bates, Inc., also advance agt. San Carlo Opera Co., Legitimate Theatre Corp., USO Camp Shows, 1937-45; dir. exploitation Columbia Pictures Corp., N.Y.C., 1945-53; dir. advt. and pub. relations Screen Gems, Inc., 1953-54; pres., sales mgr. Air Programs, Inc., 1954-55; asst. dir. advt. and pub. Ben-Hur at MGM, 1959; coordinator advt. and pub. King of Kings, 1960: dir. advt. and pub. Pepe at Columbia Pictures, 1960; dir. community relations U. Cin., 1961-62; pvt. pub. relations counsellor, N.Y.C., promotion, publicity co-ordinator 1959, 60, 61, Acad. Awards Telecast, Motion Picture Assn. Am., Inc.; asst. advt. and pub. dir. Magna Theatres Corp.; advt. exec. 20th Century Fox Film Corp.; asst. gen. mgr. The Original Amateur Hour; pres., gen. mgr. Original Amateur Hour de Mexico, S.A., pres., gen. mgr. Harry K. McWilliams Assos., Inc., 1964-75; owner, gen. mgr. Pyramid Press, 1966-75; pres., owner MCW Orgn., Inc., N.Y.C., 1975—; world-wide distbr. fine arts films; pub. relations cons. Nat. Assn. Theatre Owners. Bd. dirs. Carolina Theatre. Recipient Silver Anvil award Am. Pub. Relations Assn., 1960. Mem. Assn. Theatrical Press Agt. and Mgrs. (gov., exec. com. 1955), Asso. Motion Picture Advertisers, Inc. (pres. 1950-52; dir., dean, founder sch. Showmanship, 1952-54), Pub. Relations Soc. Am. Club: Century Travelers (silver card). Home: 2124 W Front St Burlington NC 27215

MCWRIGHT, CORNELIUS GLEN, biological sciences educator; b. Sebree, Ky., Aug. 3, 1929; s. Robert Earl and Lockie Mae (Sutton) McW.; m. Carolyn Marie Martin, June 9, 1957; children—Glen Martin, Marta Lee, Michael Robert. B.A., U. Evansville, 1952; M.S., George Washington U., 1965, Ph.D., 1970. Spl. agt. FBI, Washington, 1955-57, supervisory spl. agt., 1957-73, chief biol. scis. research, 1973-77, chief research, 1977-79; adj. asst. prof. biol. scis. George Washington U., Washington, 1969, adj. assoc. prof., 1970-75, adj. prof. biol. and forensic scis., 1975—; sr. fellow Ctr. for Strategic and Internat. Studies, Georgetown U., 1982-85; cons. in forensic medicine, police sci., counter-terrorism tech. Nat. Inst. Justice, Rand Corp., 1987—. Mem. editorial bd. Jour. Forensic Sci. Served with USMC, 1946-48; to lt., USN, 1952-54. Fellow Am. Acad. Forensic Scis.; mem. Am. Soc. Microbiology, AAAS, Sigma Xi. Episcopalian. Club: George Washington. Home: 7409 Estaban Pl Springfield VA 22151 Office: George Washington U Dept Forensic Scis Washington DC 20052

MEAD, DANA GEORGE, forest products company executive; b. Cresco, Iowa, Feb. 22, 1936; s. George Francis and Evelyn Grace (Derr) M.; m. Nancy L. Cooper, Apr. 12, 1958; children: Dana George, Mark Cooper. B.S. (Disting. Cadet), U.S. Mil. Acad., 1957; Ph.D., M.I.T., 1967. Commd. 2d lt. U.S. Army, 1957, advanced through grades to col., 1974; service in W. Ger. and Vietnam; staff asst. to Pres. Nixon, 1970-72; assoc. dir., then dep. dir. Domestic Council, White House, 1972-74; permanent prof. social sci. dept., dep. head U.S. Mil. Acad., 1974-78; ret. 1978; v.p. human resources Internat. Paper Co., N.Y.C., 1978-81, v.p., group exec., 1981-87; sr. v.p. Internat. Paper Co., Purchase, 1987—; chmn. Internat. Paper Can. Author articles on nat. security and domestic policy, business and manufacturing planning. Mem. President's Commn. on White House Fellowships. Decorated Legion of Merit with oak leaf cluster, Bronze Star with oak leaf cluster, Meritorious Service medal, Air medal with 3 oak leaf clusters, Army Commendation medal, Presdl. Service badge, Combat Inf. badge; Vietnam Cross Gallantry with palm; silver and bronze stars; White House fellow, 1970-71. Mem. Council Fgn. Relations, Fgn. Policy Assn., West Point (N.Y.) Soc. (pres.), White House Fellows Found. (dir. 1978—), White House Fellows Assn. and Found. (pres. 1981-82), Assn. Grads. West Point (trustee). Republican. Clubs: University, Metropolitan (N.Y.C.); Bass River (Mass.) Yacht, S. Yarmouth (Mass.) Tennis (dir.). Home: 27 Strickland Rd Cos Cob CT 06807 Office: Internat Paper Co 2 Manhattanville Rd Purchase NY 10577

MEAD, HYRUM ANDERSON, JR., business executive; b. Pueblo, Colo., Mar. 24, 1947; s. Hyrum A. and Opal E. (Jarrell) M.; m. G. Rosemary Dunn, Jan. 2, 1974; children: Hyrum Brandon, Heather Rose, Holly Mary. BS, Brigham Young U., 1971; MBA, Utah State U., 1973. Cert. in vocat. edn., Colo. Missionary, Japan, 1966-69; instr. Midwest Bus. Coll., Pueblo, 1973; account rep. IBM, Denver, 1974-80; v.p. sales and mktg. Electro Controls, Inc., Salt Lake City, 1980-84, chief operating officer, 1984-86, pres. 1986—; bus. cons., 1975—; speaker lighting industry. Co-author: The Life of James Anderson, 1973; also sales manuals. Dist. commr. Boy Scouts Am., 1983-84; neighborhood coordinator State Emergency Preparedness Program, 1983-84. Recipient Presdl. citation, 1980. Mem. Illuminating Engring. Soc. (speaker), Nat. Assn. Broadcasters, Am. Theatre Assn., U.S. Inst. Theatre Tech., Nat. Home Builders Assn. Republican. Mormon. Home: 232 S Constitution Way North Salt Lake UT 84054 Office: Electro Controls Inc 2975 S 300 W Salt Lake City UT 84115

MEAD, JUDE, clergyman, educator; b. Waltham, Mass., May 26, 1919; s. J. Edward and Teresa Florence (Lawless) M.; student Holy Cross Coll., 1936-38, St. Paul Monastery, 1938-39; B.A., Passionist Monastic Sem., 1946; M.A., St. Michael Monastery, 1962; LL.D. (hon.), Mt. St. Joseph Coll., 1966; S.T.D., Teresianum U., Rome, 1975. Ordained priest Roman Catholic Ch., 1946, joined Passionist Order, 1938; spiritual dir. St. Michael Monastery and Sem., 1947-51; asso. editor SIGN, 1951-52; mem. Passionist Mission Band, 1952-58; dir. St. Gabriel Retreat House, Boston, 1958-64; internat. preacher of retreats for clergy, religious and laity groups for Passionist Order, 1964—; prof. spiritual theology Immaculata Coll., 1976-87; lectr. in field; panelist Internat. Congress on Wisdom of Cross, Rome, 1975; mem. provincial adv. bd., Eastern Province Passionists. Recipient Papal Cross of Jerusalem (D'argent) (Vatican), Soteriological award Confraternity of the Passion, 1985. Mem. Cath. Bib. Assn. Gt. Britain, Inst. on Religious Life (adv. bd. 1987). Author books, including: Priestly Spirituality, 1975; St. Paul of the Cross: A Source/Work Book For Paulacrucian Studies, 1983; St. Gabriel, Passionist, Youthful Gospel Portrait, 1986; contbr. articles to profl. publs. Home and Office: Passionist Monastery 86-45 178th St Jamaica NY 11432

MEAD, STANTON WITTER, paper company executive; b. Rockford, Ill., Sept. 2, 1900; s. George W. and Ruth E. (Witter) M.; m. Dorothy E. Williams, Sept. 1, 1926 (dec); children: George W. II, Gilbert D., Mary M. Price; m. Elvira Jens Schulz, Oct. 1968 (dec.). A.B., Yale U., 1922. Pres. Consol. Papers, Inc., Wisconsin Rapids, Wis., 1950-66; now dir. Consol. Papers, Inc.; dir. Consol. Water Power Co., Wisconsin First Nat. Bank, Wisconsin Rapids. Home: 730 1st Ave S PO Box 7 Wisconsin Rapids WI 54494

MEAD, THOMAS FRANCIS, journalist, author; b. Sydney, Australia, May 4, 1918; s. Robert George and Lillian Margaret (Ryan) M.; m. Vaila Margaret Pender, Apr. 5, 1947; children—Elizabeth Vaila, Richard Thomas, Warwick Robert, David. Leaving cert. Marcellin Coll., 1935. Sub-editor Courier-Mail, Brisbane, 1947-49; chief editorial staff Daily Telegraph, Sydney, 1955-60; mng. editor Suburban Publs., Sydney, 1960-65, editorial dir., 1978-82; chmn. dirs. The Manly Daily, Sydney, 1974-82; mng. dir. Newspaper & Media Services, Sydney, 1982—; editorial cons. Eastern Suburbs Newspapers, Sydney, 1983—. Author: Man is Never Free, 1946; Killers of Eden, 1961; A Newspaper Style Guide, 1981, North Head Goes South, 1987, Manly Ferries of Sydney Harbour, 1988. Mem. New South Wales Parliament, seat of Hurstville, 1965-76; mem. New South Wales State Exec. Liberal Party of Australia, 1978-83; govt. rep. City of Sydney Eisteddfod, 1966-76; bd. govs. New South Wales State Conservatorium Music, Sydney, 1966-78. Mem. Australian Suburban Newspapers Assn. (nat. pres. 1978-79), Australian Nat. Com. C Commonwealth Press Union, Commonwealth Parliamentary Assn., Sydney Journalists. Roman Catholic. Address: 42/1 Addison Rd, 2095 Manly, New South Wales Australia

MEADE, JAMES EDWARD, economist; b. Dorset, Eng., June 23, 1907; s. Charles Hippisley and Kathleen (Cotton-Stapleton) M.; student Oriel Coll., Oxford U., 1926-30, Trinity Coll., Cambridge U., 1930-31; M.A., Oxford U.; M.A., Cambridge U.; Hon. Dr., U. Basel, U. Hull, U. Essex, U. Bath, U. Oxford; Hon. fellow London Sch. Econs.; m. Elizabeth Margaret Wilson, Mar. 14, 1933; children—Thomas Wilson, Charlotte Elizabeth Meade Lewis, Bridget Ariane Meade Dommen, Carol Margaret Meade Dasgupta. Fellow, lectr. econs. Hertford Coll., Oxford U., 1930-37; editor World Econ. Survey, League of Nations, Geneva, 1937-40; mem. econ. sect. Cabinet Secretariat, London, 1940-45, dir., 1945-47; prof. commerce London Sch. Econs., 1947-57; prof. polit. economy Cambridge U., 1957-69, sr. research fellow Christ's Coll., 1969-74; vis. prof. Australian Nat. U., 1956; chmn. Econ. Survey Mission to Mauritius, 1960; chmn. Com. on Structure and Reform of Direct Taxation, 1974-77; gov. Nat. Inst. Econ. and Social Research, 1947—, LSE, 1960-74, Malvern Coll., 1972—. Decorated companion Order of Bath; recipient Nobel prize in econs., 1977. Fellow Brit. Acad.; mem. Royal Econ. Soc. (past pres.), Brit. Assn. (past sect. pres.), Nat. Acad. Scis. (U.S.) (fgn. asso.), Eugenics Soc. (past mem. council), Am. Acad. Arts and Scis. (fgn. hon.). Author: The Rate of Interest in a Progressive State, 1933; Economic Analysis and Policy, 1936; Consumers Credits and Unemployment, 1937; League of Nations World Economic Surveys, 1938 and 1939; Economic Basis of a Durable Peace, 1940; Planning and the Price Mechanism, 1948; The Balance of Payments, 1951; Trade and Welfare, 1955; A Geometry of International Trade, 1952; Problems of Economic Union, 1953; The Theory of Customs Unions, 1955; Control of Inflation, 1958; Neo-Classical Theory of Economic Growth, 1960; Efficiency, Equality and the Ownership of Property, 1964; The Sationary Economy, 1965; The Theory of Indicative Planning, 1967; The Growing Economy, 1968; The Controlled Economy, 1971; The Theory of Economic Externalities, 1973; The Intelligent Radical's Guide to Economic Policy, 1975; The Just Economy, 1976; Stagflation, Vol. I: Wage-Fixing, 1982, Vol. II, Demand Management, 1983, Alternate Systems of Business Organization and of Workers' Renumeration, 1986. Office: Christ's Coll, Cambridge England

MEADER, JOHN DANIEL, judge; b. Ballston Spa, N.Y., Oct. 22, 1931; s. Jerome Clement and Doris Luella (Conner) M.; m. Joyce Margaret Cowin, Mar. 2, 1963; children—John Daniel, Julia Rae, Keith Alan. B.A., Yale U., 1954; J.D., Cornell U., 1962. Bar: N.Y. 1963, U.S. Dist. Ct. (no. dist.) N.Y. 1963, U.S. Ct. Appeals (2d cir.) 1966, U.S. Supreme Ct. 1967, U.S. Ct. Mil. Appeals 1973, Ohio 1978, U.S. Dist. Ct. (no. dist.) Ohio 1979, Fla. 1983. Sales engr. Albany Internat., Inc. (N.Y.), 1954-59; asst. track coach Cornell U., 1959-62; asst. sec., asst. to pres. Albany Internat., Inc., 1962-65; asst. atty. gen. state N.Y., Albany, 1965-68; ops. counsel, attesting sec. Gen. Electric Co., Schenectady, 1968-77; gen. counsel, asst. sec. SCM Corp., Glidden Div., Cleve., 1977-81; chmn. bd., pres. Applied Power Tech. Co., Fernandina Beach, Fla., 1981-84; pres. Applied Energy, Inc., Ballston Spa, N.Y., 1984-88; judge Worker's Compensation Bd. of N.Y., Albany, 1988—; dir. Saratoga Mut. Fire Ins. Co. Candidate, U.S. Ho. of Reps., 29th Dist. N.Y., 1964, N.Y. Supreme Ct., 1975, 87. Serve to col. JAGC, USAR, 1968—, dep. staff judge adv. 3d U.S. Army, 1984. Nat. AAU High Sch. Cross Country Champion, 1948; Nat. AAU High Sch. Indoor Track 1000 Yard Champion 1949; Nat. AAU Prep. Sch. Indoor Track 440 and 880 Yard Champion, 1950; Nat. AAU Prep. sch. Track and Field Indoor Championships Outstanding Performer award Melrose Games Assn., 1950; Heptagonal Track 880 Yard Champion 1954; recipient Gardner Mallett award for courage, inspiration and sportsmanship Yale U., 1954. Mem. ABA, N.Y. State Bar Assn., Fla. Bar. Republican. Presbyterian. Clubs: Amelia Island Plantation (Fernandina Beach); Cyprus Temple, Masons (Schenectady); Yale of Jacksonville (Fla.) (pres.). Author: Labor Law Manual, 1972; Contract Law Manual, 1974. Home: Round Lake Rd Ballston Lake NY 12019 Office: N Y S Workers Compensation Bd 100 Broadway Albany NY 12241

MEADERS, PAUL LE SOURD, lawyer; b. Amarillo, Tex., Feb. 1, 1930; s. Paul Le Sourd and Lorna Irene (Pumroy) M.; m. Patricia Rockefeller, Mar. 21, 1953 (dec.); m. 2d Jane W. Dickely, Apr. 2, 1966; children—Phyllis P., Paul Le Sourd III. B.A., U. Va., 1952; LL.B., U. Tex., 1957; LL.M., NYU, 1961. Atty. office chief counsel IRS, 1957-59; asst. U.S. atty. So. Dist. N.Y., 1951-61; assoc. Breed Abbott & Morgan, N.Y.C., 1961-63, Reid & Priest, N.Y.C., 1963-67; ptnr. Morris & McVeigh, N.Y.C., 1967-77, McKenzie, Meaders & Ives, N.Y.C., 1977—. Active Vet. Corps of Arty., N.Y.C. Served to 1st lt. U.S. Army, 1952-54. Mem. ABA, (estate tax com. tax sect.) N.Y. State Bar Assn., Tex. Bar Assn., Seldon Soc., Brit. Inst. Internat. and Comparative Law, Internat. Bar Assn., U. Va. Alumni Assn. (pres. N.Y.C. chpt. 1982-84). Episcopalian. Clubs: Metropolitan, Church, Bronxville Field; Carlton (London); Southampton Bath and Tennis. Office: Suite 3105 535 Fifth Ave New York NY 10017

MEADOR, CHARLES LAWRENCE, computer consultant, educator; b. Dallas, Oct. 7, 1946; s. Charles Leon and Dorothy Margaret (Brown), m. Diane E. Collins, May 18, 1985; M. B.S. with honors in Mech. Engring., U. Tex., Austin, 1970; M.S. in Mech. Engring., M.S. in Mgmt., MIT, 1972. Mem. engring. staff Union Carbide Corp., Houston, 1967-68; instr. Alfred P. Sloan Sch. Mgmt., MIT, 1972-75, asst. dir. Ctr. Info. Systems Research, 1976-78, lectr. Sch. Engring., co-dir. Macro-Engring. Research Group, 1978—; founder, pres. Decision Support Tech., Inc., 1978—; v.p., dir. Research and Planning Inc., 1980-84; co-founder, vice chmn., dir. Software Productivity Research, Inc., 1985-87; mem. scientists adv. com. Environ. Def. Fund; cons. to govt. and industry. Editor: How Big and Still Beautiful? Macro-Engineering Revisited, 1980, Macro-Engineering: The Rich Potential, 1981, Macro-Engineering and the Future: A Management Perspective, 1982; mem. editorial adv. bd. Computer Communication, 1979—; mem. editorial bd. Communicacion e Informatica, 1980—. Contbr. papers in field. Wilfred Lewis fellow, 1971; Draper Lab. fellow, 1974; NSF trainee, 1970. Mem. Computer Soc. of IEEE (vice chmn. Eastern Hemisphere and Latin Am. area com. 1977-83), Assn. Computing Machinery, Ops. Research Soc. Am., Sigma

Xi, Tau Beta Pi, Pi Tau Sigma. Home: 18 Coltsway Wayland MA 01778 Office: MIT Room 3-282 Cambridge MA 02139

MEADORS, ALLEN COATS, health administrator, educator; b. Van Buren, Ark., May 17, 1947; s. Hal Barron and Allene Coats (Means) M. AA, Saddleback Coll., 1981; BBA, U. Cen. Ark., 1969; MBA, U. No. Colo., 1974; M. in Pub. Administrn., U. Kans., 1975; MA in Psychology, Webster U., 1979; MA in Health Services Mgmt., So. Ill. U., 1980, PhD in Administrn., 1980. Assoc. administr. Forbes Hosp., Topeka, 1971-73; asst. dir. health services devel. Blue Cross Blue Shield of Kans., Topeka, 1973-76; asst. dir. Kansas City Health Dept. (Mo.), 1976-77; program dir., asst. prof. So. Ill. U., Carbondale, and Webster U., St. Louis, 1978-82; assoc. prof., dir. div. health adminstrn. U. Tex.-Galveston, 1982-84; exec. dir. N.W. Ark. Radiation Therapy Inst., Springdale, Ark., 1984-87; prof., chmn. dept. health adminstrn. U. Okla., Oklahoma City; mem. faculty Calif. State U., Long Beach, 1977-81; grad. faculty U. Ark. Sch. Bus. Adminstrn., Fayetteville, 1984-87; prof., chmn. dept. health adminstrn. U. Okla., 1987—; cons. Surgeon Gen. Office and Air Force System Command. Bd. dirs. Martin Luther King Hosp., Health Care Services Adv. Bd.; mem. Orange County Health Planning Agy. Served with Med. Service Corps, USAF, 1969-73. Fellow Am. Coll. Hosp. Adminstrs., Ark. Hosp. Assn., Soc. Radiation Oncology Adminstrs., mem. Am. Hosp. Assn., Am. Pub. Health Assn., Am. Soc. Law and Medicine, Am. Assn. Health Planners. Contbr. articles to profl. jours. Home: PO Box 773 Edmond OK 73083-0773 Office: U Okla Dept Health Administrn PO Box 26901 Oklahoma City OK 73190

MEADORS, HOWARD CLARENCE, JR., electrical engineer; b. Chgo., July 31, 1938; s. Howard Clarence and Eileen May (Baker) M.; S.B., M.I.T., 1960, S.M., 1962, E.E., 1964; Ph.D., Poly. Inst. NY., 1976; m. Phyllis Anne Rennebaum, July 18, 1964; children—Henry Charles, William Howard, Laura Phyllis, Pamela Susan. Mem. tech. staff Bell Telephone Labs., Inc., Holmdel, N.J., 1966-82; mem. tech. staff AT&T Info. Systems Labs., Holmdel, N.J., 1983-85, supr. product devel., 1985-86, supr. adv. data communications AT&T Bell Labs., 1988—; ednl. counselor MIT, 1973—, regional vice chmn., 1983—. Served with Signal Corps, U.S. Army, 1964-66. Decorated Army Commendation medal; recipient Doctor Support Program award Bell Telephone Labs., 1974, 75; Disting. Tech. Staff award for sustained achievement Bell Telephone Labs., 1982, (with other) Best Paper award Bell System Tech. Jour., 1982. Mem. IEEE (sr. mem. 1987), Sigma Xi, Eta Kappa Nu. Inventor in field. Office: AT&T Info Systems Labs 200 Laurel Ave Middletown NJ 07748

MEADOWS, JOHN FREDERICK, lawyer; b. Manila, Philippines, Mar. 7, 1926; s. Grover Cleveland and Millie M.; m. Karen Lee Morris, Nov. 17, 1962; children—Ian Joseph, Marie Irene. A.A., U. Mich., 1944; B.A. (Freshman Alumni Scholar, 1943), U. Calif., Berkeley, 1948, LL.B., Boalt Hall, 1951. Bar: Calif. 1952, U.S. Dist. Ct. (no. dist.) Calif 1952, U.S. Ct. Apls. (9th cir.) 1952, U.S. Sup. Ct. 1958. Assoc. Wallace, Garrison, Norton & Ray, San Francisco, 1952-56; atty. advisor Maritime Adminstrn., U.S. Dept. Commerce, Washington, 1956; trial atty. Admiralty and Shipping Sect., U.S. Dept. Justice, West Coast Office, San Francisco, 1956-64, atty. in charge, 1964-72; sr. resident ptnr. Acret & Perrochet, San Francisco, 1972-76; sr. ptnr. Meadows, Smith, Lenker and Davis, San Francisco, Long Beach, Calif., Seattle, 1976—; cons. maritime law, UN, lectr. seminar Taipei, Taiwan, 1968; Served to lt. M.I. AUS, 1944-46. Mem. ABA, Assn. Def. Counsel, Maritime Law Assn., San Francisco Bar Assn., Council Am. Master Mariners. Republican. Roman Catholic. Clubs: San Francisco Comml., Merchants Exchange. Assoc. editor Am. Maritime Cases; author: Preparing a Ship Collision Case for Trial; contbr. articles to legal pubs. Home: 205 The Uplands Berkeley CA 94705 Office: 425 California St Suite 1700 San Francisco CA 94104

MEANS, GEORGE ROBERT, organization executive; b. Bloomington, Ill., July 5, 1907; s. Arthur John and Alice (Johnson) M.; m. Martha Cowart, Aug. 5, 1950. B.Ed., Ill. State U., 1930; A.M., Clark U., 1932; H.H.D. (hon.), Rikkyo U., Tokyo, Ill. Wesleyan U., Ky. Wesleyan Coll. Cartographer, map editor 1932-35; with Rotary Internat., 1935—; beginning as conv. mgr., successively head Middle Asia office Rotary Internat., Bombay, India; asst. gen. sec. Rotary Internat., 1948-52, gen. sec., 1953-72; sec. Rotary Found., 1953-72; hon. dir. Washington Nat. Corp.; dir. Hertzberg-New Method, Inc., Ind. State Retirement Home Guaranty Fund. Author: Rotary's Return to Japan, also numerous articles. Mem. at large nat. council Boy Scouts Am. Served as comdr. USNR, 1942-46. Decorated Legion of Honor France; Chilean Order of Merit; Japanese Order of Rising Sun; Italian Order of Merit; recipient Disting. Service award Geog. Soc. Chgo., 1972; Paul Harris fellow The Rotary Found. Fellow Am. Geog. Soc.; mem. Evanston Hist. Soc., Gamma Theta Upsilon (founding mem.). Club: Rotary (Evanston, Bloomington, Ill., Sydney, Australia, Kyoto, Osaka and Tokyo, Japan, Seoul, Korea, Cape Town, South Africa, Ituzaingo, Saavedra, Argentina, Greenwood, Ind.). Home: 1067 Smock Dr Greenwood IN 46143

MEANS, JOHN BARKLEY, foreign language educator, association executive; b. Cin., Jan. 2, 1939; s. Walker Wilson and Rosetta May (Miller) M. BA, U. Ill., 1960, MA, 1963; PhD, U. Ill. at Urbana, 1968. U.S. Govt. research analyst on Latin Am. Washington, 1962-64; assoc. prof. Portuguese Temple U., Phila., 1972-82, prof., 1982—; co-chmn. dept. Spanish and Portuguese Temple U., 1971-75, dir. Center for Critical Langs., 1975—, assoc. dir. Inst. for Langs. and Internat. Studies, dir. fgn. lang. programs, 1987—; cons. on Brazilian-Portuguese and self-instructional fgn. lang. edn., 1968—; cons. on fgn. lang. curricula to numerous U.S. univs., govt. agys. and acad. orgns; exec. dir. Nat. Assn. Self-Instructional Lang. Programs, 1977—. Editor: Essays on Brazilian Literature, 1971; contbr. articles to profl. jours. Served to capt. U.S. Army, 1960-61. NDEA fellow, 1962, 64; grantee U.S. Dept. Edn., 1979, 80, 81, Japan Found., 1980, 82. Mem. MLA, Latin Am. Studies Assn., Nat. Council on Langs. and Internat. Studies (bd. dirs.), Middle Atlantic Council Latin Am. Studies, Am. Assn. Tchrs. Spanish and Portuguese, Joint Nat. Com. for Langs. (bd. dirs.), Nat. Assn. Self-Instructional Lang. Programs (editor Jour. 1978—), Am. Council Teaching Fgn. Langs., AAUP, Assn. Asian Studies, S.R., Pi Kappa Phi (chmn. nat. Future Policy com.), Phi Lambda Beta, Sigma Delta Pi. Presbyterian. Home: PO Box 565 Yardley PA 19067 Office: Temple Univ Inst for Langs and Internat Studies Philadelphia PA 19122

MEANTI, LUIGI, gas company executive; b. Milan, Italy, Aug. 14, 1928; s. Alfredo and Antonia (Cerri) M.; m. Giuliana Creazzo, Apr. 14, 1955; children—Mauro, Alberto. Ph.D. in Civil Engring., Poly. U., Milan, 1953. Asst. prof. Poly. U., Milan, 1954-57; mem. staff research and devel. dept. SNAM S.p.A., Milan, 1958-65, with gas planning dept., 1966-69, dep. gen. mgr., 1970-72, gen. mgr., 1973-80, v.p., mng. dir., 1980—; dir. Italgas, Torino, Italy, SNAM Internat. Ltd., St. Helier, Jersey, Transitgas A.G., Zurich, Switzerland, TENP GmbH, Essen, West Germany, T.M.P.C. Ltd., St. Helier. Mem. Internat. Gas Union (v.p.). Office: SNAM SpA, Corso Venezia 16, 20121 Milan Italy

MEARS, PATRICK EDWARD, lawyer; b. Flint, Mich., Oct. 3, 1951; s. Edward Patrick and Estelle Veronica (Mislik) M.; m. Geraldine O'Connor, July 18, 1981. BA, U. Mich., 1973, JD, 1976. Bar: N.Y. 1977, U.S. Dist. Ct. (so. and ea. dists.) N.Y. 1977, Mich. 1980, U.S. Dist. Ct. (we. and ea. dists.) Mich. 1980, U.S. Ct. Appeals (6th cir.) 1983. Assoc. firm Milbank, Tweed, Hadley & McCloy, N.Y.C., 1976-79, ptnr. Warner, Norcross & Judd, Grand Rapids, Mich., 1980—; adj. prof. Grand Valley State Coll., Allendale, Mich., 1981-84. Author: Michigan Collection Law, 1981, 2d edit., 1983, Basic Bankruptcy Law, 1986, Bankruptcy Law and Practice in Michigan, 1987; contbr. articles to profl jours. Mem. coordinator basketball tournament Mich. Spl. Olympics, Grand Rapids, 1983. Mem. ABA, Mich. State Bar Assn., Am. Bankruptcy Inst., Comml. Law League Am., Irish Heritage Soc. Club: Peninsular (Grand Rapids). Office: Warner Norcross and Judd 900 Old Kent Bldg Grand Rapids MI 49503

MEAU, FRANÇOIS MARIE LÉON, plastic surgeon; b. Beaufort, Savoie, France, Oct. 22, 1948; s. Andre Marie Joseph and Marie Therese Francoise (Viallet) M.; m. Isabelle Suzanne Anne Marie Giraut, Oct. 30, 1982; 1 child, Alexandre. MD, Faculty of Medicine, Paris, 1978. Intern Cochin Hosp., Paris, 1975-76; resident Beaujon Hosp., Paris, 1976-78; sub-chief medicine Hosp. of L'isle Adam, 1976-80, Hosp. de la Paix, Meru, 1980-85; chief medicine Hosp. de la Paix, 1985—; practice medicine specializing in plastic and aesthetic surgery Paris, 1981—; cons. surgery Med. Ctr., Paris, 1984-87. Author: Lateral Osteotomy in Rhinoplasty, 1978, Enterocystoplasty, 1975; contbr. articles to newspapers, profl. jours. Mem. Ear Nose Throat Soc., Plastic and Reconstructive Surgery Soc., Aesthetic Surgery Soc., Aesthetic Dermatology Soc., Maxillofacial Surgery Soc. Roman Catholic. Clubs: Automobile Med. of France, Golf Med. of France. Home and Office: 270 Raspail Blvd, 75014 Paris France

MEBIAME, LEON, prime minister Gabon Republic; b. Libreville, Gabon, Sept. 1, 1934; ed. Coll. Moderne, Libreville, Contrede Préparation aux Carrières Administratives, Brazzaville, Ecole Fédérale de Police, Ecole Nat. de Police, Lyon, France, Sûreté Nat. Française, Paris, 1960-61. Posted in Chad, 1957-59; police supt., 1960; dep. dir. Sûreté Nat., Gabon, 1962-63, dir., 1963-67; successively undersec. state for interior, minister of interior, minister of state in charge of labor, social affairs and Nat. Orgn. Gabonese Women, 1967; v.p. of govt., keeper of the seals, minister of justice, 1968; v.p. govt. in charge of coordination, 1968-75; pres. Consultative Council, 1972—; prime minister, 1975—; minister coordination, housing and town planning, 1975-76, minister of land registry, 1976-78, minister of coordination, agr., rural devel., waters and forests, 1978—. Decorated comdr. Etoile Equatoriale; grand officer Order nat. de Côte d'Ivoire, du Mérite Centrafricain; chevalier Etoile Noire du Bénin. Office: Office of Prime Minister, BP546, Libreville Gabon *

MECKSEPER, FRIEDRICH, painter, printmaker; b. Bremen, Ger., June 8, 1936; s. Gustav and Lily (Debatin) M.; m. Barbara Muller, Jan. 5, 1962; children—Julia, Josephine, Cornelius. Student, Acad. Fine Arts, Stuttgart, 1955-57, Berlin, 1957-59. Prof. art Summer Acad., Salzburg, Austria, 1977-79; 200 one man shows including: Tokyo Galerie, 1972, Galerie Cramer Genf, 1973, Fischer Fine Art, London, 1976, Gimpel & Weitzenhoffer, N.Y.C., 1976, Mus. Boymans van Beuningen, Rotterdam, 1977, Worthington Gallery, Chgo., 1980; exhibited in group shows, internat. print biennales; represented in permanent collections at Staatsgalerie Stuttgart, Victoria and Albert Mus., London, Mus. Modern Art, N.Y.C., Nat. Gallery of Victoria, Melbourne, Mus. Boymans van Beuningen. Recipient German Rome prize Villa Massimo, 1964; Prize, Internat. Print-Biennale, Tokyo, 1970, Norwegian Internat. Print-Biennale, 1982. Address: Landhausstrasse 13, 1000 Berlin 31 Federal Republic of Germany

MEDFORTH, MICHAEL JOHN, marketing director; b. Withernsea, North Humberside, Eng., July 13, 1941; s. Eric and Honorah (Dodds) M.; m. Mary Holtby, Sept. 26, 1964; children: Sally Anne, Richard John. BS in Pure Math. and Physics, Hull U., 1962. Quality control mgr. Smith & Nephew Plastics, Hull, 1962-65; packaging technologist Reckitt & Colman Household Products, Hull, 1965-71, marketing product mgr., 1971-79; mktg. dir. Recuitts Colours Ltd., Hull, 1980—; bd. dirs. Rechittis Colours Ltd, Hull, 1980—. Sch. gov. Humberside County Council, Hull, 1985—. Home: 8 Bermuda Ave, Skirlaugh Hull 5HG, England Office: Reckitt's Colours Ltd, Morley St, Hull HU8 8DN, England

MEDGYESSY, PETER, Hungarian government official; b. Budapest, Hungary, 1942. Ed., Karl Marx U. Polit. Economy. Mem. Hungarian Socialist Workers Party, 1965—; with Ministry Fin., 1965-87, minister, from 1987; dep. prime minister Hungary, Budapest, 1988—; mem. Inst. State Financing, 1973—; bd. mem. fin. sect. Hungarian Econ. Soc., 1982—. Address: Office Dep Prime Minister, Kossuth Lajos ter 1, Budapest V Hungary *

MEDINA, ERNESTO, financial executive; b. Manila, May 1, 1940; s. Honorato and Natividad Lauriaga M.; m. Zenaid Villafranca, Mar. 30, 1975; children: Michael Francis, Marian Clarissa. BSBA, U. of the East, Manila, 1962. CPA, Philippines. Auditor-in-charge Sycip, Gorres, Velayo and Co., Makati, Metro Manila, Philippines, 1963-67; internal auditro then plant gen. mgr. Pepsi-Cola Bottling Co of the Philippines, Inc., Makati, 1967-77; mgr. fin. and adminstrn. Sandvik Philippines, Inc., Makati, 1978-79; v.p. Pulse Group of Cos., Pasig, Metro Manila, 1979-82; asst. v.p. CPJ Corp., Makati, 1982-83; v.p. Electrolux Philippines, Inc., Makati, 1983-86, Electrolux Mktg., Inc., Makati, 1986—; treas., bd. dirs. Electrolux Indsl., Inc., Makati; bd. dirs. Electrolux Gen. Services, Inc., Makati. Mem. Fin. Execs. Inst. of Philippines, Philippine Inst. CPAs. Roman Catholic. Club: Green Valley Country (Pasig, Philippines). Lodge: Rotary (sec. local chpt. 1985, bd. dirs. 1986). Office: Electrolux Mktg Inc, Pasong Tamo Extension, Makati Metro Manila 1200, Philippines

MEDINA, JOSE COLLADO, economist, Islamic economic researcher; b. Malaga, Spain, Aug. 31, 1952; s. Jose Collado Bernal and Aurora Medina Perez; m. Ma. Teresa Becerra Crespo, July 3, 1976; children—Rocio, Alberto, Noemi, Javier. Grad. Econs. Faculty, Malaga, 1977. Chief acct., Bartolosi Travel, Torremolinos, Spain, 1978-79; head mktg. Audelec SA, Malaga, 1980-83; sales mgr. Instrumatic Esp., Malaga, 1983-85; head computer dept. Areservice, Malaga, 1985—; cons. Fostaca, Venezuela. Contbr. articles to profl. jours. Mem. Economist Coll. Malaga, Soc. Computer Technicians. Avocation: martial arts. Home: PO Box 2078, Malaga Spain Office: Areservice, Ctra Cadiz-Malaga km 170, Marabella, Malaga Spain

MEDINA FERRER, HUGO MARTÍN, minister of defense; b. Montevideo, Uruguay, June 10, 1929; m. Ercilia Angela Ceruti; children: Julián Roberto, Angela Maráa. Minister of def. Montevideo, Uruguay, 1987—. Recipient numerous medals and awards. Address: Ministry of Defense, Monte Video Uruguay *

MEDINA-MORA, RAUL MARITN DEL CAMPO, lawyer, educator; b. Mexico City, July 17, 1919; s. Francisco M. and Concepcion (Martin del Campo) M.; m. Luisa Conrey Icaza, June 2, 1949; children: Luisa, Elena, Raul, José, Eduardo, Maricruz, Antonio. Lic. in Law, Nat. U. Mex., 1949. Researcher Mex. Inst. Comparative Law, Mexico City, 1939-45; sec. to dir. gen. Petroleos Mexicanos, Mexico City, 1946-58; ptnr. Medina Mora and Assocs., Mexico City, 1959—; prof. Sch. of Law, Nat. U. Mex., Mexico City, 1950-58, Carlos Septien Garcia Sch. Journalism, Mexico City, 1981-85; bd. dirs. Inst. Polit. Studies, Mexico City, 1970-84, chmn., 1979-83. Chmn. Christian Family Movement, Mexico City, 1965-68. Mem. Mex. Bar Assn. (dir. 1985-87, pres. econ. law commn.). Roman Catholic. Office: Medina Mora and Assocs, Amores 1816, Col Del Valle, 03100 Mexico City Mexico

MEDVEDEV, ZHORES ALEXANDROVICH, biochemist, gerontologist; b. Tbilisi, USSR, Nov. 14, 1925; s. Alexandr Romanovich and Yulia Isaakovna (Reiman) M.; BSc, PhD, K.A. Timiriasev Agrl. Acad., Moscow, 1950; m. Margarita Busina, Oct. 5, 1951; children—Alexandr, Dmitry. Jr. research scientist, then sr. research scientist dept. agrochemistry and biochemistry Moscow Timiriasev Agrl. Acad., 1950-62; head lab. molecular radiobiology Research Inst. Med. Radiology, Obninsk, 1962-69; sr. research scientist All Union Research Inst. Farm Animals, Borovsk, 1970-72; sr. research scientist genetic div. Nat. Inst. Med. Research, London, 1973—. Served with Russian Army, 1943. Recipient Book award Moscow Naturalist Soc., 1966; G. Mendel medal Mendal Mus., Brno, Czechoslovakia, 1969; Research award Am. Aging Assn., 1984; René Schubert award Louise-Eylmann Stiflung. Fellow Am. Gerontol. Soc.; mem. Brit. Biochem. Soc., N.Y. Acad. Scis. Author: Protein Biosynthesis, 1966; The Rise and Fall of T.D. Lysenko, 1969; The Molecular-Genetic Mechanisms of Development, 1970; Medvedev Papers, 1971; Ten Years After Ivan Denisovich, 1973; Soviet Science, 1978; Nuclear Disaster in the Urals, 1979; Andropov, 1983; Gorbachev, 1986; Soviet Agriculture, 1987; co-author: Question of Madness, 1971; Khruschev: The Years in Power, 1976; In Search of Common Sense, 1982. Address: Div Genetics, Nat Inst Med Research, London NW7 1AA England

MEDZIHRADSKY, FEDOR, biochemist, educator; b. Kikinda, Yugoslavia, Feb. 4, 1932; came to U.S., 1966; s. Miklos and Melanie (Gettmann) M.; m. Mechthild Westmeyer, Sept. 13, 1967; children—Sofia, Oliver. M.S. in Chemistry, Technische Hochschule Munich, Fed. Republic Germany, 1961, Ph.D. in Biochemistry, 1965. Instr. biochemistry U. Munich, 1965-66; postdoctoral assoc. U. Wis.-Madison and Washington U., St. Louis, 1966-69; asst. prof. biochemistry U. Mich., Ann Arbor, 1969-73, assoc. prof. biochemistry, 1973-81, assoc. prof. pharmacology, 1975-81, prof. biochemistry and pharmacology, 1981—, supr. biochemistry lab., Upjohn Ctr. Clin. Pharmacology, 1969-76; dir. and co-dir. biochemistry core lab. Mich. Diabetes Research and Tng. Ctr., U. Mich. Med. Ctr. 1977—; vis. assoc. prof. Stanford U., 1975-76; vis. prof. U. Calif.-San Diego, 1983-84; invited lectr. nat. and internat. meetings. Contbr. articles to profl. jours. and books; mem. editorial bd. Drug Metabolism and Disposition. Recipient Kaiser Permanente award for excellence in teaching U. Mich., 1985. NIH postdoctoral fellow, 1966-69; recipient Nat. Research Service award, 1975-76. Mem. Am. Soc. Neurochemistry, Am. Soc. Biol. Chemists, Am. Soc. Pharmacology and Exptl. Therapeutics, AAAS, Soc. Biol. Chem. Germany. Research areas: neurochemistry, molecular pharmacology, membrane biochemistry.

MEEHAN, FRANCIS J., political science educator, ambassador; b. East Orange, N.J., Feb. 14, 1924. M.B., U. Glasgow, 1945; M.P.A., Harvard U., 1957. Adminstrv. asst. Econ. Coop. Adminstrn., 1948-51; fgn. service officer Frankfurt, Hamburg and NATO, 1951-56; intelligence research specialist Dept. State, Washington, 1957-59; polit. officer Moscow, 1959-61; econ. officer, polit. officer Berlin, 1961-66; dir. Ops. Center, Dept. State, 1966-67, dep. exec. sec., 1967-68; dep. chief of mission Budapest, 1968-72; counselor for polit. affairs Bonn, 1972-75; dep. chief of mission Vienna, 1975-77, Bonn, 1977-79; ambassador to Czechoslovakia, 1979-81, to Poland, 1981-83; research prof. diplomacy Inst. Study Diplomacy, Sch. Fgn. Service, Georgetown U., Washington, 1983-85; U.S. ambassador to East Germany, 1985—. Office: Econ/Comml Sta East Germany US Dept of State Washington DC 20520 also: Am Embassy, Neustaedtische, Kirchstrasse 4-5, 1080 Berlin German Democratic Republic *

MEEK, EDWARD STANLEY, pathologist, psychologist, educator; b. Bristol, Eng., Oct. 9, 1919; s. Alfred Edward and Ann Mary Margaret (James) M.; m. Eileen Birrell (dec.); children: Pamela Ann, Patricia Susan. M.B., Ch.B. cum laude, U. St. Andrews, Scotland, 1951, Ph.D., M.D., 1955. Intern U. St. Andrews Hosps. and Clinics, Dundee, 1951-52; resident in pathology U. Bristol (Eng.) Hosps. and Clinics, 1952-56; practice medicine specializing in pathology U. Bristol, 1956-70; pathologist to coroner City of Bristol; prof. microbiology U. Iowa, Iowa City, 1970-73; prof. pathology, prof. ophthalmology U. Iowa, 1973-81; dir. med. research Johnson and Johnson Cardiovascular, Inc., King of Prussia, Pa., 1981-87; cons. Johnson and Johnson Corp. Office Sci. and Tech., 1980-81; cons. VA Hosp., Iowa City, 1970-80; panel mem. NSF; cons. Travenol Labs., Costa Mesa, Calif., FCS Industries, Tempe, Ariz., W.L. Gore & Assocs., Flagstaff, Ariz., Therakos (Johnson and Johnson), West Chester, Pa., FCS Industries, Tempe, Ariz.; vis. scientist Columbia U. Gen. Med. Research Ctr., N.Y., 1982-87; med. dir. affairs Toltzis Communications, Glenside, Pa., 1987—. Author books and articles in field. Served with Brit. Army, 1940-46. Fellow Am. Acad. Microbiologists, Royal Coll. Pathologists, Coll. Am. Pathologists, Inst. Biologists, Sigma Xi; mem. AMA, AAAS, Am. Assn. Immunologists, Am. Soc. Microbiologists, Brit. Med. Assn., Path. Soc. Gt. Britain, N.Y. Acad. Scis., Am. Psychol. Assn., Brit. Psychol. Soc. Home: 251 W DeKalb #603-D King of Prussia PA 19406 Office: Therakos Inc Brandywine Business Ctr West Chester PA 19380

MEEK, HEDLEY JACK, building executive; b. Leamington, Warwickshire, Eng., May 8, 1925; s. Leonard and Muriel Irene (Wooldridge) M.; children—Shirley Anne Bush, Elizabeth Rosemary Watson, Andrew Leonard William. Student secondary schs., Eng. Wages clk. Charles R. Price, London, 1942-45; co. sec., gen. mgr. George Potton & Sons, Ltd., London, 1945-54; sales mgr. Nevill Long & Co. Ltd., London, 1954-61; chmn., mng. dir., sole owner Nevill Long Group, Southall, Middlesex, 1961—; dir. Fibre Bldg. Bd. Orgn. Ltd., 1983—. Pres. 628 Southall-Norwood Cadet div. St. John Ambulance, Western Div. Fellow Inst. Dirs., Brit. Inst. Mgmt., Suspended Ceilings Assn. (v.p. 1980-82), Fibre Bldg. Bd. Fedn. (chmn. 1976-78), Southall C. of C. (pres. 1971-72). Conservative. Mem. Free Ind. Evang. Ch. Home: Little Bekkons, 10 Westfield Rd, Beaconsfield, Buckinghamshire HP9 1EG England Office: Nevill Long Group, North Hyde Wharf, Hayes Rd Southall, Middlesex UB2 5NL, England

MEEK, MARCELLUS ROBERT, lawyer, business consultant; b. N.Y.C., Nov. 20, 1929; s. Marcellus W. and Lillian D. (Hilward-Younes) M.; children—Susan J., Marcellus W. II, Mary F., Adam M. Student U. Ill., 1948-51; J.D., DePaul U., 1954; LL.M. (James Nelson Raymond fellow), Northwestern U., 1955. Bar: Ill. 1955, U.S. Supreme Ct. 1971, U.S. Dist. Ct. (no. dist.) Ill. 1955, U.S. Ct. Appeals (7th cir.) 1955, U.S. Ct. Appeals (5th cir.) 1971. Ptnr. Baker & McKenzie, firm specializing in internat. law, Chgo., 1956-77; sole practice, Chgo., 1977—; cons. fed. tax, bus., related fields to former internat. law practice; lectr. internat. law Marquette U., Milw., 1959-65; instr., dir. internat. law dept. John Marshall Law Sch., Chgo., 1964-69. Founder, chmn. bd. dirs. Tucson Jazz Soc., 1979—. Recipient citation for work with law rev. DePaul Law Sch., 1954; hon. justice Chgo. chpt. Moot Ct. competition, 1955; Nathan Burkan Meml. first award, ASCAP, 1954; Cert. contbg. author recognition DePaul Law Rev., 1966; Cert. distinction DePaul U., 1980. Mem. Ill. Bar Assn., ABA, Am. Judicature Soc., Am. Fgn. Law Assn., Celtic Legal Soc. Chgo., Am. Soc. Internat. Law, Chgo. Natural History Mus., Chgo. Hist. Soc., Art Inst. Chgo., Artists Guild Chgo. Republican. Presbyterian. Clubs: Mountain Oyster, Racquet, MG T Registry, Rod and Gun, Gun, Le Group, Foothills Yacht, Jaguar of So. Ariz. (Tucson); Racquet (Chgo.), Pima (Ariz.) County Polo. Author: Antiques, the Law and Taxes, 1964; Cases and Materials--International Commercial Transactions, 1964; (with H.J. Stitt) International Transactions, Commentaries and Forms, 1967; International Commercial Agreements, 1977; contbr. articles to profl. jours. Home: 3020 E Weymouth St Tucson AZ 85716

MEEK, PAUL DERALD, oil and chemical company executive; b. McAllen, Tex., Aug. 15, 1930; s. William Van and Martha Mary (Sharp) M.; m. Betty Catherine Robertson, Apr. 18, 1954; children: Paula Marie Meek Burford, Kathy Diane Meek Hasemann, Carol Ann Meek Miller, Linda Rae. B.S. in Chem. Engring, U. Tex., Austin, 1953. Mem. tech. dept. Humble Oil & Refining Co., Baytown, Tex., 1953-55; with Cosden Oil & Chem. Co., 1955-76, pres., 1968-76; dir. Am. Petrofina, Inc., Dallas, 1968—, v.p. parent co., 1968-76, pres., chief operating officer, 1976-83, pres., chief exec. officer, 1983-86, chmn. bd., pres., chief exec. officer, 1984-86, chmn. bd., 1986—. Contbg. author: Advances in Petroleum Chemistry and Refining, 1957. Chmn. chem. engring. vis. com. U. Tex., 1975-76; adv. council Coll. Engring. Found., U. Tex., Austin, 1979—; co-chmn. indsl. div. United Way of Met. Dallas, 1981-82; mem. adv. council YWCA of Dallas, 1983-87; trustee Southwest Research Inst.; assoc. bd. visitors U. Tex. M.D. Adnerson Cancer Ctr., 1985—. Named Disting. Engring. Grad. U. Tex., Austin, 1969. Mem. Am. Petroleum Inst. (exec., budget, awards and nominations coms. of bd. dirs.), Dallas Wildcat Com. (chmn. exec. com. 1987-88). Office: Fina Oil & Chem Co PO Box 2159 8350 N Central Expressway Dallas TX 75221

MEEKS, WILLIAM HERMAN, III, lawyer; b. Ft. Lauderdale, Fla., Dec. 30, 1939; s. Walter Herman, Jr. and Elise Walker (McGuire) M.; m. Patricia Ann Rayburn, July 30, 1965; 1 son, William Herman IV; m. 2d, Miriam Andrea Bedsole, Dec. 28, 1971; 1 dau., Julie Marie. A.B., Princeton U., 1961; LL.B., U. Fla., 1964; LL.M., NYU, 1965. Bar: Fla. 1964, U.S. Dist. Ct. (so. dist.) Fla. 1965, U.S. Tax Ct. 1966, U.S. Ct. Appeals (11th cir.) 1981, U.S. Supreme Ct. 1985. Ptnr. McCune, Hiaasen, Crum, Ferris & Gardner, Ft. Lauderdale, 1964—; dir. Attys. Title Services, Inc., 1978-79, Attys. Title Services of Broward County, Inc., 1971—, chmn. 1976-77. Active Ft. Lauderdale Mus., 1976—. Mem. ABA, Fla. Bar Assn., Broward County Bar Assn., Attys. Title Ins. Fund, Ft. Lauderdale Hist. Soc., Phi Delta Phi. Democrat. Presbyterian. Clubs: Kiwanis, Lauderdale Yacht, Tower (Ft. Lauderdale). Office: McCune Hiassen et al PO Box 14636 1 E Broward Blvd Fort Lauderdale FL 33302

MEEM, JAMES LAWRENCE, JR., nuclear scientist; b. N.Y., Dec. 24, 1915; s. James Lawrence and Phyllis (Deaderick) M.; m. Buena Vista Speake, Sept. 5, 1940; children: James, John. B.S., Va. Mil. Inst., 1939; M.S., Ind. U., 1947, Ph.D., 1949. Aero. research sci. NACA, 1940-46; dir. bulk shielding reactor Oak Ridge Nat. Lab., 1950-53, in charge nuclear operation aircraft reactor expt., 1954-55; chief reactor sci. Alco Products, Inc., 1955-57; in charge startup and initial testing Army Package Power Reactor, 1957; prof. nuclear engring. U. Va., Charlottesville, 1957-81; dept. chmn., dir. reactor facility U. Va., 1957-77, prof. emeritus, 1981—; cons. U.S. Army Fgn. Sci. and Tech. Ctr., 1981—; vis. cons. nuclear fuel cycle programs Sandia Labs., Albuquerque, 1977-78; vis. staff mem. Los Alamos Sci. Lab.,

1967-68; mem. U.S.-Japan Seminar Optimization of Nuclear Engring. Edn., Tokai-mura, 1973. Author: Two Group Reactor Theory, 1964. Fellow Am. Nuclear Soc. (sec. reactor ops. div. 1966-68, vice chmn. 1968-70, chmn. 1970-71, Exceptional Service award 1980); mem. Am. Phys. Soc., Am. Soc. Engring. Edn., SAR. Home: Mount Airy RFD 12 Box 45 Charlottesville VA 22901

MEESE, CELIA EDWARDS, pharmaceutical and nutritional supplement company executive; b. San Diego, May 10, 1938; d. Roy Clifford Edwards and Bessie Lucille (Lang) Hill; m. Jed D. Meese, July 6, 1963; 1 son, Scott Edwards. Student U. Calif.-Sacramento, 1958-60; B.A., U. Wis., 1964; B.A. (hon.), U. Taiwan, 1965. Office mgr. Pacific Telephone, San Jose, Calif., 1965-72; pres. Vitaline Corp., Incline Village, Nev., 1972—; v.p. RenalChem, Inc., San Jose, Calif., 1982—, Formulations Tech., Inc., Oakdale, Calif., 1982—; dir. Spectra Diagnostics, San Jose. Bd. dirs. Sierra Council on Alcoholism, Kings Beach, Calif., 1980—. English-Chinese Exchange Council, Taipei, 1964-65; vol. Brandon House, San Jose, 1965—, Children's Home Soc., San Jose, 1965—; mem. steering com. U.S. Rep. Mineta, Calif., 1974. Mem. Pharm. Mfrs. Assn., Am. Soc. Bariatric Physicians, Mensa (proctor 1985). Home: PO Box 4772 Incline Village NV 89450 Office: Vitaline Corp PO Box 6757 Incline Village NV 89450

MEESE, EDWIN, III, lawyer, former attorney general; b. Oakland, Calif., 1931; s. Edwin and Leone M. Meese; m. Ursula Herrick, 1958; children: Michael James, Dana Lynne. BA, Yale U., 1953; J.D., U. Calif., Berkeley, 1958; LLD, Del. Law Sch., Widener U., U. San Diego, Valparaiso U., Calif. Luth. Coll. Dep. dist. atty. Alameda County, Calif., 1959-67; sec. of legal affairs Gov. Reagan Calif., Sacramento, 1967-69, exec. asst., chief staff, 1969-75; v.p. Rohr Industries, Chula Vista, Calif., 1975-76; sole pratice law 1976-80; dir. ctr. criminal justice policy and mgmt. U. Calif., San Diego, 1977-81; counselor to Pres. Reagan, Washington, 1981-85; U.S. atty. gen. Washington, 1985-88; prof. law U. San Diego, 1978-81. V.p. Lutheran Ch., El Cajon, Calif. Served with U.S. Army. Office: US Dept Justice 10th and Constitution Ave Washington DC 20530 *

MEESE, ERNEST HAROLD, thoracic and cardiovascular surgeon; b. Bradford, Pa., June 23, 1929; s. Ernest D. and Blanche (Raub) M.; m. Rockell D. Dombar, Aug. 30, 1985; children from previous marriage: Constance Ann, Roderick Bryan, Gregory James. BA, U. Buffalo, 1950, MD, 1954. Diplomate Am. Bd. Surgery, Am. Bd. Thoracic Surgery. Resident in gen. surgery Millard Fillmore Hosp., Buffalo, 1955-59; resident in thoracic surgery U.S. Naval Hosp., St. Albans L.I., N.Y., 1961-63; group practice thoracic and cardiovascular surgery, Cin., 1965-88; pvt. practice, Cin., 1988—; asst. clin. prof. surgery Cin. Med. Ctr., 1972—; head sect. thoracic and cardiovascular surgery St. Francis-St. George Hosp., Deaconess Hosp.; mem. staff Good Samaritan Hosp., Bethesda Hosp., Christ Hosp., Providence Hosp., Childrens Hosp., Epp Meml. Hosp., St. Luke Hosp., Cin. Contbr. articles to profl. jours. and textbooks. Pres. bd. dirs., chmn. service com. Cin.-Hamilton County unit Am. Cancer Soc., trustee, mem. exec. bd., chmn. service com.; sec. bd. trustees, exec. bd. Ohio div. Am. Cancer Soc.; trustee Southwestern Ohio chpt. Am. Heart Assn. Served to comdr. M.C., USN, 1959-65. Fellow A.C.S., Internat. Coll. Surgeons; mem. Soc. Thoracic Surgeons, Am. Coll. Chest Physicians, Am. Coll. Angiology, Cin. Surg. Soc., Am. Coll. Cardiology; mem. Gibson Anat. Hon. Soc., AMA, Am. Thoracic Soc., Assn. Mil. Surgeons U.S., Acad. Medicine Cin., Assn. Advancement Med. Instrumentation, N.Am. Soc. Pacing and Electrophysiology, Phi Beta Kappa, Phi Chi (treas. 1952-54). Clubs: Western Hills Country, Queen City, Mediclub (pres. 1983-85) (Cin.). Lodge: Masons. Home: 174 Pedretti Rd Cincinnati OH 45238 Office: 5049 Crookshank Cincinnati OH 45211

MEGGINSON, LEON CASSITY, educator; b. Thomasville, Ala., July 26, 1921; s. William A. and Emma Frances (Cassity) M.; student Samford U., 1938-40; B.S., Miss. Coll., 1947; M.B.A., La. State U., 1949, Ph.D., 1953; m. Joclaire Leslie, June 14, 1985; children—Gayle (Mrs. Thomas A. Ross III), William Leon, William Jay. Factory rep. Hershey Chocolate Co., Birmingham, Ala., 1940-42; instr. bus. La. State U., 1949-50, asst. prof., 1951-54, assoc. prof., 1954-60, prof., 1960-77, prof. emeritus, 1977—, asst. dean Coll. Bus., 1957-60; research prof. mgmt. U. South Ala., 1978-84; J.L. Bedsole prof. bus. Mobile (Ala.) Coll., 1984—; Fulbright research scholar, Spain, 1961-62; resident advisor Ford Found., Karachi, Pakistan, 1968-70; cons. in mgmt. devel. for cos. and tng. instns. Mem. La. Adv. Council for Employment Security, 1956-64, chmn., 1960-64; chmn. East Baton Rouge Parish Family Ct., 1958-60. Trustee, mem. personnel com. Baton Rouge Gen. Hosp., 1957-61, 75-77; pres. W.A. Megginson Edn. Found. Served with AC, AUS, 1942-45. Decorated Air medal with 4 oak leaf clusters; recipient Distinguished Faculty Service award La. State U. Alumni Found., 1971; Phi Kappa Phi scholar U.S. Ala., 1982. Accredited personnel diplomate Am. Soc. Personnel Adminstrn. Mem. Acad. Mgmt. (dir.), So. Mgmt. Assn. (pres. 1972-73), Southwestern Social Sci. Assn. (pres. 1962-63), So. Case Research Assn. (pres. 1971-75). Republican. Baptist. Author: Personnel, 1967, 5th edit., 1985; (Acad. Mgmt. Book award 1967); Human Resources, 1968; (with son Bill Megginson) Successful Small Business Management, 1975, 5th edit., 1988; The Complete Guide to Your Own Business, 1977; (with Kae Chung) Organizational Behavior, 1981; (with Donald Mosley and Paul Pietri) Management Concepts and Applications, 3rd edit., 1989; (with dau. Gayle M. Ross) Business, 1985. Home: 166 S Georgia Ave Mobile AL 36604

MEHALCHIN, JOHN JOSEPH, financial executive; b. Hazleton, Pa., Aug. 8, 1937; s. Charles and Susan (Korba) M.; divorced; 1 child, Martin. B.S. with honors, Temple U., 1964; M.B.A., U. Calif., Berkeley, 1965; Student U. Chgo., 1964; Supr. costs Winchester-Western, New Haven, Conn., 1965-67; mgmt. cons. Booz-Allen & Hamilton, N.Y.C., 1967-68; mgr. planning TWA, N.Y.C., 1968-70; 2d v.p. Smith, Barney, N.Y.C. and Paris, 1970-74; chief fin. officer, pres. leasing co. Storage Tech. Corp., Louisville, Colo., 1974-79; sr. v.p. Heizer Corp., 1979; pres., founder Highline Fin. Services, Inc. and subs., Boulder, Colo., 1979—. Served with AUS, 1958-61. U. Calif. fellow, Berkeley, 1964; U. Chgo. scholar, 1964. Mem. Fin. Execs. Inst., Am. Assn. Equipment Lessors, Beta Gamma Sigma, Omicron Delta Epsilon. Home and Office: Highline Fin Services Inc 1881 9th St Suite 320 Canyon Ctr Boulder CO 80302

MEHDI, MOHAMMAD TAKI, newspaper editor; b. Baghdad, Iraq, Jan. 6, 1928; s. Al Haj M. and Zahara (Moenni) M.; came to U.S., 1949; m. Beverlee Turner, June 20, 1953; children: Anisa, Janan, Laila. BA, U. Calif., Berkeley, 1953, MA, 1954, PhD, 1960. Teaching asst. U. Calif., 1958-60; dir. Arab Info. Ctr., San Francisco, 1960-63; founder, sec. gen. Action Com. on Am.-Arab Relations, 1964—; exec. editor Islam in America Newspaper, N.Y.C., 1969—. Adviser to Arab dels. to UN, 1963-64; lectr. Arab and Mid. East Affairs, 1960—; co-chmn. Arab-Black Dialogue, 1979—; sec.-gen. Arab People To Am. People, 1980-83; founder, sec.-gen. Nat. Council on Islamic Affairs, 1983—; mem. hostage release del., Lebanon, 1987; also producer Arab People to Am. People TV, 1982—. Recipient Book of Yr. award Soc. of Friends of Book in Beirut, 1963. Mem. Am. Polit. Sci. Assn., Am. Soc. for Legal and Polit. Philosophy. Author: Constitutionalism, Western and Middle Eastern, 1961, A Nation of Lions Chained, 1963, Peace in the Middle East, 1967, Kennedy and Sirhan: Why?, 1968; editor: Palestine and the Bible, 1970, Peace in Palestine, 1976, Terrorism: Why America is the Target!, 1987. Address: PO Box 416 New York NY 10017

MEHENDALE, TRIVIKRAM D., electronics corporation executive; b. Pune, Maharashtra, India, May 3, 1947; came to Can., 1976; s. Dhondo Anant and Annapurnabai Mehendale; m. Margaret Elaine Mehendale, Aug. 4, 1978; 1 child, Kristen. MS, Pune U., 1968; PhD, King's Coll., 1971. Researcher Am. Forces Network, Stuttgart, Fed. Republic of Germany, 1971-73; owner RAB GmbH, Stuttgart, Fed. Republic of Germany, 1973-76; sales mgr. Brant Electronics Co., Brantford, Ont., 1976-77; cons. M.G. Electronics, Brantford, Ont., 1977-79; pres., chief exec. officer Intrepid Electronics, Inc., Brantford, Ont., 1979—; chief exec. officer Intrepid Electronics, Inc., Brantford, 1979—. Bd. dirs. UNICEF Can., Toronto, 1983—. Lodge: Lions (pres. local chpt. 1980-81, chmn. local chpt. 1981-82). Home: 53 Lakeside Dr, Branford, ON Canada N3R 5J5 Office: Intrepid Electronics Inc, 66 Mohawk St, Box 1600, Branford, ON Canada N3T 5V7

MEHERA, SAROJ KUMAR, tea trading company executive, consultant; b. London, Mar. 27, 1928; s. Bhagabati Prasad and Lalita Rani Devi (Maharaj Kumari of Burdwan) M.; m. Savita Baldev, Dec. 12, 1956; children—Sanjeev, Tilak. B.S. with honors, Calcutta U., India, 1948. Asst. mgr. James Finlay & Co., Ltd., Calcutta, 1949-62, mgr., 1962-72, sr. mgr. (chief exec.), 1972-76; mng. dir. Tata-Finlay Ltd., Calcutta, 1976-79; pres. Tata Tea Ltd., Calcutta, 1979-85; mng. ptnr. Calland House, Calcutta, 1985—; dir. numerous cos. Mem. Bengal C. of C. and industry (pres. 1979-80), Indian Tea Assn. (chmn. 1971-72, 1982-83). Hon. consul in Calcutta for Finland, Norway. Clubs: Royal Calcutta Golf, Oriental , R&A Golf of St. Andrews, Tollygunge, Calcutta. Hindu. Office: Calland House Chitrakoot, 6th Floor, 230A Acharya JC Bose Rd, Calcutta 700 020 West Bengal, India

MEHLENBACHER, DOHN HARLOW, civil engineer; b. Huntington Park, Calif., Nov. 18, 1931; s. Virgil Claude and Helga (Sigfridson) M.; B.S. in Civil Engring., U. Ill., 1953; M.S. in City and Regional Planning Ill. Inst. Tech., 1961; M.B.A., U. Chgo., 1972; m. Nancy Mehlenbacher; children—Dohn Scott, Kimberly Ruth, Mark James, Matthew Lincoln. Structural engr., draftsman Swift & Co., Chgo., 1953-54, 56-57, DeLeuw-Cather Co., Chgo., 1957-59; project engr. Quaker Oats Co., Chgo., 1959-61, mgr. constrn., 1964-70, mgr. real property, 1970-71, mgr. engring. and maintenance, Los Angeles, 1961-64; chief facilities engr. Bell & Howell Co., Chgo., 1972-73; v.p. design Globe Engring. Co., Chgo., 1973-76; project mgr. I.C. Harbour Constrn. Co., Oak Brook, Ill., 1976-78; dir. estimating George A. Fuller Co., Chgo., 1978; pres. Food-Tech Co., Willowbrook, Ill., 1979-80; dir. phys. resources Ill. Inst. Tech., Chgo., 1980—. Served with USAF, 1954-56. Registered profl. engr. and structural engr., Ill. Mem. Nat. Soc. Profl. Engrs., Am. Mgmt. Assn., ASCE, Constrn. Specifications Inst., Am. Arbitration Assn. Office: IIT Center Chicago IL 60616

MEHREN, GEORGE LOUIS, business executive, government official, economist; b. Sacramento, July 6, 1913; s. Gale Thomas and Faye Laura (Swain) M.; m. Jean Dorothy McMurchy, June 26, 1938; children: Peter William, Elizabeth Jean; m. Ingeborg E. Hitchcock, 1968; 1 son, George Louis. Student, Coll. Pacific, 1937; A.A., Sacramento Jr. Coll., 1931; A.B. with honors, U. Calif., 1938, Ph.D., 1942. Research asso. Giannini Found. Agrl. Econs., Agrl. Expt. Sta., U. Calif., 1942, dir., 1957-62, instr. to asso. prof., 1946-51, prof. agrl. econs., 1951-71, prof. emeritus, 1971; chmn. dept. agrl. econs., chmn. dept. agrl. bus. Giannini Found. Agrl. Econs., Agrl. Expt. Sta., U. Calif., Berkeley, Davis and Los Angeles, 1957-62; exec., adv., coordinating coms. Wild Lands Research Center, Water Resources Center Giannini Found. Agrl. Econs., Agrl. Expt. Sta., U. Calif., 1957-62, chmn. statewide curriculum agrl. bus. mgmt., 1957-62, exec. coms. Sch. Bus. Adminstrn., Inst. Internat. Studies, Inst. Indsl. Relations, 1958-62, mem. Legislative Assembly, 1960-62; asst. sec. U.S. Dept. Agr., Washington, 1963-68; dir. sci. and edn. U.S. Dept. Agr., 1965-68; spl. U.S. ambassador (spl.) to Panama 1968; pres. Agribus. Council Inc., 1968-71; gen. mgr. Associated Milk Producers, Inc., 1972-76; exec. cons. 1976-78; v.p. Hitchcock GmbH, W.Ger., 1976—, San Antonio-Chgo. Investment, 1973—, Overseas Mktg., Inc., 1977—, Select Wines, Inc., 1982—, I. Mehren of Tex., Inc., 1978—, Mehren Hills, 1983—; mem. Fed. Council on Sci. and Tech., 1965-68, Fed. Interagy. Com. on Edn., 1966-68, Nat. Adv. Council on Extension and Continuing Edn., 1966-68, Pres.'s Com. on Consumer Interests, 1964-67; bd. dirs. Commodity Credit Corp., 1963-68; mem. adv. panel AEC, 1966-68; mem. adminstrv. com. Center for Specialization and Research in Agrl. Econs. and Stats., U. Naples, Portici, Italy, 1956-59; dir. food and restaurant div. OPS, Washington, 1951, acting dir. price ops., 1952, cons. to dir., 1952-53; cons. Mut. Security Agy., Fgn. Ops. Adminstrn., 1952-53; adviser Brit. minister agr. and fisheries and sec. of state for Scotland, London, 1952-53; cons. Ministry of Agr. Venezuela, Caracas, 1952-53, 70, Consejo de Bienestar Rural, Venezuela, 1953-54, OCDM, 1956-58, USOM to Korea, Republic of Korea, Seoul, U.S. Office Emergency Planning, AID, to govts., Pakistan, Iran, Mexico, Morocco, Indonesia, 1968-71; Egypt, 1968-78, Argentina, Greece, Turkey, India, Thailand, Philippines, 1979; adviser Ministry Agr. and Forestry for Italy, Rome, 1956; cons. div. econs. FAO, Rome, 1956-57; dean, vis. prof. Internat. Center for Tng. Agrl. Econs. and Statistics, Govt. Republic of Italy, U. of Rome, FAO, 1956; contract collaborator U.S. and Calif. depts. agr. for appraisal European promotion programs, 1962; mem. gen. editorial bd. Jour. Marketing, Am. Marketing Assn., 1952-55, mng. editor, 1955-57, editor-in-chief, 1957-58. Contbr. to profl. jours. Chmn. Calif. exec. com. U.S. Food for Peace Program, 1961. Served to lt. USNR, 1942-45. Fellow Internat. Biographic Assn.; mem. Western Agrl. Econs. Research Council, Am. Farm Econs. Assn., Am. Marketing Assn., Western Farm Econs. Assn., Alpha Zeta. Home: 406 Country Ln San Antonio TX 78209

MEHREN, LAWRENCE LINDSAY, investment company executive; b. Phoenix, May 26, 1944; s. Lawrence and Mary Teresa (Stelzer) M.; B.A., U. Ariz., 1966; M.A., U. Ariz., 1968; m. Lynn Athon McEvers, June 5, 1965; children—Lawrence Lindsay, John Eskridge. Bus. mgr. Rancho Santa Maria, Peoria, Ariz., 1968-69; traffic mgr. Glen-Mar Mfg. Co., Phoenix, 1969-70; account exec. Merrill Lynch, Pierce, Fenner and Smith, Inc., Phoenix, 1970-77, sr. account exec., 1977-78, asst. v.p., 1978-80, v.p., 1980-82; v.p. Harbor Equity Funds, Inc., 1982-84; sr. v.p. Harbor Fin. Group, Inc., Phoenix, 1984-87; pres. Charles and Pierce Asst. Mgmt., Inc., 1987—. Mem. Maricopa County Citizens Action Com., Charter Govt. Com.; chmn. Madison Citizens Adv. Com., 1973-74; bd. dirs. Planned Parenthood, 1972-75, Brophy Coll. Prep. Sch., 1981-87, Prescott Coll., 1984-85. Recipient award Ariz. Hist. Found., 1968. Mem. Phoenix Stock and Bond Club (dir. 1979-82), Ariz. Acad. Public Affairs, Phoenix C. of C., Internat. Wine and Food Soc., Phi Alpha Theta, Beta Theta Pi. Club: Valley Field Riding and Polo. Office: 3104 E Camelback Rd Suite 607 Phoenix AZ 85016

MEHTA, MEENAKSHI NITIN, pediatrics professor, consultant; b. Bombay, Nov. 8, 1937; d. Rasikchandra Narottamdas and Indumati Merchant; m. Nitin, Feb. 20, 1965; children: Saloni, Shreya, Karishma. MBBS, Topiwalla Nat. Med. Coll., Bombay, 1962; DCH, Topiwalla Nat. Med. Coll., 1964; MD in Pediatrics, Topiwalla Nat. Med. Coll., Bombay U., 1965. House physician pediatrics Lokmanya Tilak Mcpl. Gen. Hosp., Bombay, 1962-63; casualty med. officer Bai Yamunabai Lakshman Nair Hosp., Bombay, 1963, Lokmanya Tilak Mcpl. Gen. Hosp., Bombay, 1964; preventive and social medicine registrar Topiwalla Nat. Med. Coll. and Bai Yamunabai Nair Hosp., Bombay, 1964-65, preventive and social medicine tutor, 1965-66, pediatrics registrar, 1966-67; pediatrics tutor Seth Gowardhandas Sundardas Med. Coll. and King Edward Meml. Hosp., Bombay, 1967-69, pediatrics sr. registrar, 1969-70, pediatrics asst. prof., 1970-75, 1970-75; pediatrics prof. Lokmanya Tilak Mcpl. Med. Coll. and Lokmanya Tilak Mcpl. Gen. Hosp., Bombay, 1975—; exec. com. mem. Indian Acad. of Pediatrics, 1976, Bombay Haematology Group, 1978-87, Nutrtion Soc. of India, 1974-78; convener Bombay Chapt. Nutrition Soc. of India, 1978,86; mem. subcommittee Child Abuse and Neglect and Child Labour Indian Acad. of Pediatrics, 1986—. Contbr. over 100 articles to profl. jours.;contbr. chpt. to textbook; mem. editorial com. The Indian Practitioner, 1983—. Exec. com. mem. Yuvak Biradari-Maharashtra, 1980—, S. Bombay Giants Internat., 1983; v.p. Women's Assn. Worli, Bombay, 1982-85; active various internat. congresses on child abuse and neglect. Recipient Sr. Tchrs. in Child Health award WHO, 1972; named Sr. Heinz fellow 1979. Mem. Indian Acad. Pediatrics (life), Indian Soc. Haematology and Blood Transfusion (life). Hindu. Office: Lokmanya Tilak Mcpl Med Coll, Sion, Bombay 400 022 Maharashtra, India

MEHTA, RAJESH ROHITBHAI, textiles executive; b. Bombay, Jan. 24, 1961; s. Rohit C. and Asha R. M. B. Commerce, U. Gujarat, India, 1981; MBA, U. Pitts., 1984. Mng. dir. Ramprosad Investments and Traders Pvt. Ltd., Ahmedabad, India, 1981-82; mgmt. trainee Rustom Mills and Industries Ltd., Ahmedabad, 1982-83; dir. Rohit Mills Ltd., Ahmedabad, 1983-87, mng. dir., 1987—; chmn. R.M. Traders Ltd., Ramtil Processors Pvt. Ltd. Mem. Indian Cotton Mills Fedn., Fedn. Indian Chambers Commerce and Industry. Office: Rohit Mills Ltd, Khokhra Mehmedabad, Ahmedabad 380 008 Gujarat India

MEHTA, SHAHROKH MINOCHERE, indsl. co. fin. exec.; b. Karachi, Pakistan, Nov. 20, 1939; s. Minochere Naoroji and Sheroo Minochere (Sarkari) M.; B. Commerce, Govt. Coll. of Commerce and Econs., Karachi, 1961; m. Gool S. Khambatta, Dec. 17, 1964; children—Kershaw, Parastu. Area adminstr. Reading & Bates Offshore Drilling Co., Pakistan/Iran, 1963-71; group fin. mgr. Pars Toshiba Industries, Iran, 1971-76; controller fin. and adminstrn. Carrier Thermo Frig., Iran, 1976-79; asst. to v.p. fin Carrier Internat. Corp., Syracuse, N.Y., 1980-81, mgr. fin. and adminstrn., indsl. refrigeration div., 1982—. Cert. acct., Pakistan. Mem. Inst. Chartered Accts. (Pakistan), Brit. Inst. Mgmt. (asso.). Zoroastrian (Parsee). Home: 107 Rosewell Meadow DeWitt NY 13214 Office: PO Box 4806 Syracuse NY 13221

MEHTA, ZUBIN, conductor, musician; b. Bombay, India, Apr. 29, 1936; came to U.S., 1961; s. Mehli Nowrowji and Tehmina (Daruvala) M.; m. Nancy Diane Kovack; children: Zarina, Merwan. Student, St. Xavier's Coll., Bombay, 1951-53, State Acad. Music, Vienna, Austria, 1954-60; LL.D., Sir George Williams U., Montreal, 1965; D.Mus. (hon.), Occidental Coll.; hon. doctorate, Colgate U., Bklyn Coll., Westminster Choir Coll., Weizmann Inst. Sci. (Israel). Music dir., Montreal (Can.) Symphony Orch., 1961-67, Los Angeles Philharmonic Orch., 1962-78; mus. dir.: Israel Philharmonic, 1969—; Music dir., N.Y. Philharmonic, 1978—, guest condr., Met. Opera, Salzburg (Austria) Festival, Vienna Philharmonic, Berlin Philharmonic, La Scala, Milan, Italy, music dir., Maggio Musicale Florence, Italy, rec. artist for, Decca, CBS, RCA, New World Records, (recipient 1st prize Liverpool (Eng.) Condrs. Competition 1958). Decorated Padma Bhushan India, 1967, commendatore of Italy. Address: care NY Philharm Avery Fisher Hall Broadway & 65th St New York NY 10023 also: 19A Air St, London W1 England

MEIER, WILBUR LEROY, JR., educator, university system chancellor; b. Elgin, Tex., Jan. 3, 1939; s. Wilbur Leroy and Ruby (Hall) M.; m. Judy Lee Longbotham, Aug. 30, 1958; children: Melynn, Marla, Melissa. BS, U. Tex., 1962, MS, 1964, PhD, 1967. Planning engr. Tex. Water Devel. Bd., Austin, 1962-66; cons. Tex. Water Devel. Bd., 1967-72; research engr. U. Tex., Austin, 1966; asst. prof. indsl. engring. Tex. A&M U., College Station, 1967-68; asso. prof. Tex. A&M U., 1968-70, prof., 1970-73, asst. head dept. indsl. engring., 1972-73; prof., chmn. dept. indsl. engring. Iowa State U., Ames, 1973-74; prof., head sch. of indsl. engring. Purdue U., West Lafayette, Ind., 1974-81; dean Coll. Engring., Pa. State U., University Park, 1981-87; chancellor U. Houston System, 1987—; cons. Indsl. Research Inst., St. Louis, 1979, Environments for Tomorrow, Inc., Washington, 1970—, Water Resources Engrs., Inc., Walnut Creek, Calif., 1969-70, Computer Graphics, Inc., Bryan, Tex., 1969-70, Kaiser Engrs., Oakland, Calif., 1971, Tracor, Inc., Austin, 1966-68; cons. div. planning coordination Tex. Gov.'s Office, 1969; cons. Office of Tech. Assessment, 1982-86, Southeast Ctr. for Elec. Engring. Edn., 1978—; mem. rev. team Naval Research Adv. Com.; bd. dirs. C-COR Electronics Inc., State College, Pa., 1982-87, corp. sec., 1986-87; bd. dris. M-Bank Houston, 1987—. Editor: Marcel Dekker Pub. Co., 1978—; Contbr. articles to profl. jours. Named Outstanding Young Engr. of Year Tex. Soc. Profl. Engrs., 1966; USPHS fellow, 1966; recipient Bliss medal Soc. Am. Mil. Engrs., 1986, Am. Spirit award USAF, 1984. Fellow Am. Inst. Indsl. Engrs. (dir. ops. research div. 1975, pres. Ind. chpt. 1976, program chmn. 1973-75, editorial bd. Trans., publ. chmn., newsletter editor engring. economy div. 1972-73, v.p. region VIII 1977-79, exec. v.p. chpt. ops. 1981-83, pres. 1985-86), IEEE (pres. 1985-86); mem. Ops. Research Soc. Am., Inst. Mgmt. Scis. (v.p. S.W. chpt. 1971-72), ASCE (sec.-treas. Austin br. 1965-66, chmn. research com., tech. council water resources planning and mgmt. 1972-74), Ind. Soc. Profl. Engrs., Am. Soc. for Engring. Edn. (chmn. indsl. engring. div. 1978-83), Am. Assn. Engring. Socs. (bd. govs. 1984—), Am. Soc. for Engring. Edn. (pres. Tex. A&M U. chpt. 1971-72), Nat. Assn. State Univ. and Land Grant Colls. (mem. engring. legis. task force 1983—), Assn. Engring. Colls. Pa. (pres. 1985-86, treas. 1981-87), Air Force Assn. (advisor sci. and tech. com. 1984—), Nat. Soc. Profl. Engrs., Profl. Engrs. in Edn. (vice chmn. N.E. region 1985—, bd. govs. 1983-85), Sigma Xi, Tau Beta Pi, Alpha Pi Mu (asso. editor Cogwheel 1970-75, regional dir. 1976-77, exec. v.p. 1977-80, pres. 1980-82), Phi Kappa Phi, Chi Epsilon. Clubs: River Oaks Country, Petroleum, Houston, Forum (Houston) (bd. dirs.). Lodge: Rotary. Home: 1505 South Boulevard Houston TX 77006 Office: U Houston System Office of Chancellor 4600 Gulf Freeway Suite 500 Houston TX 77023

MEIER-RUGE, WILLIAM ALFRED, pathologist; b. Rudolstadt, Germany, July 28, 1920; s. Artur Robert and Herta (Kruger) M.-R.; M.D., U. Berlin, 1954; m. Jutta Ruge, May 28, 1955; children—Peer, Cora, Tilman, Anja. Clin. asst. Gen. Hosp., Potsdam-Babelsberg, 1954-56; research asst. Pathology Inst., U. Berlin, 1956-61; research assoc. Pathology Inst., U. Basel (Switzerland), 1963—, assoc. prof., 1965; head lab. exptl. pathology and histochemistry, dept. biology, med. research div. Sandoz Ltd., Basel, 1967-69, head dept. basic med. research, 1969-79, head gerontol. brain research, div. preclin. research, 1979-83; head lab. gerontol. brain research, dept. neuropathology Inst. Pathology, U. Basel, 1984—. Recipient Rudolf Virchow prize, 1960. Mem. German Soc. Pathology, Swiss Soc. Pathology, Royal Soc. Medicine (London), Royal Microscopical Soc., German Histochem. Soc., Gerontol. Soc., Swiss Gerontol. Soc., Ibro Swiss, N.Y. Acad. Sci. Author: Medikamentose Retinopathie, 1967; CNS-Aging and Its Neuropharmacology, 1979, Teaching and Training in Geriatric Medicine, 1987. Home: 12 Oberwilerstrasse, CH-4103 Bottmingen/BL Switzerland Office: 35 Lichtstrasse, CH-4002 Basel Switzerland

MEIERS, DAVID EVAN, service executive; b. Hartley, Iowa, Apr. 11, 1947; s. Glen and Ruth Lenore (Olson) M.; m. Vivian Fern Nelson, Nov. 25, 1965; children: Michelle, Nicholas. BA, U. N.D., 1969, MA, 1972. Cert. assn. exec., N.D. Tchr., coach Kerkhoven (Minn.) Pub. Schs., 1969-71; prin. Wolford (N.D.) Pub. Schs., 1971-73; bus. adminstr. Three Affiliated Tribes, Newtown, N.D., 1973-76; adminstrv. dir. N.D. Srs. United, Minot, 1976-77; exec. dir. N.D. Pub. Employees Assn., Bismarck, 1977-83; exec. v.p. N.D. Hospitality Assn., Bismarck, 1983—; v.p. Assembly Govtl. Employees, Washington, 1980-82; chmn. N.D. Travel and Trade Network, Bismarck, 1984-86; mem. Gov's. Hwy. Safety Com., Bismarck, 1985-87. Candidate for N.D. Commr. of Labor, 1982. Recipient Greeter Feature award, Bismarck C. of C., 1986. Mem. Internat. Assn. Restaurant Execs. (bd. dirs. 1983-84), Internat. Assn. Hotel Execs., N.D. Jaycees (pres. Newton 1975-76, Outstanding Young Men award 1981). Democrat. Lutheran. Lodges: Kiwanis, Elks, Lions. Home: 738 Augsburg Ave Bismarck ND 58501 Office: ND Hospitality Assn 315 E Broadway Bismarck ND 58501

MEIGS, JOHN WISTER, epidemiology educator, consultant; b. Phila., Jan. 10, 1915; s. Edward Browning and Margaret (Wister) M.; m. Camilla Riggs, Jul. 6, 1940; children—Anne, Patience, Jonathan, Margaret. B.A., Princeton U., 1936; M.D., Harvard U., 1940. Diplomate Am. Bd. Preventive Medicine, Am. Bd. Occupational Medicine, Am. Bd. Indsl. Hygiene Intern Pa. Hosp., Phila., 1940-42; asst. resident in medicine Mass. Gen. Hosp., Boston, 1942-43; med. officer Pan Am Airways, Seattle, 1943-44, U.S. Steel Corp., New Haven, 1953-68; clin. prof. epidemiology Yale U., New Haven, 1947—, dir. Cancer Epidemiology Unit, 1974-82; vis. physician Yale-New Haven Hosp., 1947—; cons. occupational medicine Surgeon Gen., U.S. Army, Washington, D.C., 1947-68; cons. occupational medicine, epidemiology Upjohn Co., North Haven, Conn., 1965—, Olin Corp., Stamford, Conn., 1980—. Contbr. 70 articles on occupational medicine and cancer epidemiology. Pres. Fort Hunter Found., Harrisburg, Pa., 1956-81; dir. New Haven Rehab. Ctr., 1951-79. Served to major U.S. Army M.C., 1944-47. Recipient Golden Hours award New Haven Easter Seal, 1979, C E A Winslow award Conn. Pub. Health Assn., 1980. Fellow Am. Acad. Occupational Medicine, Am. Pub. Health Assn.; mem. Am. Indsl. Hygiene Assn., Am. Occupational Medicine Assn. (pres. Conn. chpt. 1972-73), AMA. Clubs: New Haven Lawn, Graduate. Home: 575 Ridge Rd Hamden CT 06517 Office: Yale U Dept Epidemiology and Pub Health 60 College St New Haven CT 06510

MEIJLER, FRITS LOUIS, cardiologist, educator; b. Den Ham, The Netherlands, Apr. 29, 1925; m. Annemarie P. Schendstok, Apr. 4, 1953; children: Annejet P., Gerda, Theo Dirk. HBS-B, Almelo, Eindhoven, 1947; MD, U. Amsterdam, 1957. Tng. in internal medicine and cardiology U. Amsterdam, The Netherlands, 1957-62; mem. staff Wilhelmina Gashuis, Amsterdam, 1962-67; prof. cardiology State U. Utrecht, The Netherlands, 1968—; prof. cardiology Interuniv. Cardiology Inst., 1973—, chmn. sci. council, 1983—. Contbr. numerous articles to profl. publs. Served with Royal Dutch Army, 1947-49. Decorated service decoration, House Order of Orange, Order of Dutch Lion. Fellow Am. Coll. Cardiology, Am. Heart Assn.; mem. Dutch Cardiac Soc. (hon.), Royal Netherlands Acad. Scis., Royal Soc. Medicine, Brit. Cardiac Soc., Internat. Group Research in Cardiac Metabolism. Home: De Meijlpaal, Ravelijn 1, 4351 TB Veere The Netherlands Office: Interuniv Cardiology Inst Netherlands, PO Box 19258, 3500 CG Utrecht The Netherlands

MEIKLE, THOMAS HARRY, JR., neuroscientist, educator, foundation administrator; b. Troy, Pa., Mar. 24, 1929; s. Thomas H. and Elizabeth (MacMorran) M.; m. Jane T. Germer, Aug. 26, 1966 (div. 1983); children: David Andrew, Sarah Elizabeth; m. Jaqueline Winterkorn, Sept. 27, 1986. A.B., Cornell U., 1951, M.D., 1954. Intern Jefferson Hosp., Phila., 1954-55; clin. fellow Inst. Neurology, London, Eng., 1957-58; research fellow Inst. Neurol. Scis., U. Pa., Phila., 1958-61; instr., asst. prof., assoc. prof., prof. anatomy Cornell U. Med. Coll., N.Y.C., 1961-87, acting dean medicine, 1976-77, dep. dean, 1977-79, dean, provost, 1980-87; dean Cornell U. Grad. Sch. Medicine, 1969-76; v.p. Josiah Macy, Jr. Found., N.Y.C., 1980, pres., 1987—; career scientist Health Research Council, N.Y.C., 1969-71. Served to capt. M.C. AUS, 1955-57, Korea. Markle Found. scholar in acad. medicine, 1963-68. Mem. Am. Physiol. Soc., Soc. Neuroscis. Home and Office: Josiah Macy Jr Found 46 E 64th St New York NY 10021

MEILLAND, GEORGES GUSTAVE, physician; b. Geneva, June 7, 1921; s. Gustave Alfred and Delphine Jeanne (Voisin) M. Student Coll. Geneva, 1934-41, Ph.D., 1947, F.M.H. (specialist diploma in surgery), 1951; diploma London Sch. Tropical Medicine and Hygiene, 1959; Diploma in Hygiene and Pub. Health U. London, 1961. Med. officer hosps., Switzerland and Eng., 1947-59; med. supt. internat. com. Red Cross, 1950; med. officer WHO, 1959-80; pub. health cons., 1983—; dir. health UNRWA, 1980-82; European rep. Medic Alert, Geneva, 1983—, pres., 1983—. Contbr. articles to profl. jours. Mem. Geneva Med. Soc., Geneva Fine Arts Soc., Royal Soc. Tropical Medicine (London), Swiss Med. Assn., Assn. Tropical Medicine and Hygiene, WHO Med. Soc. Roman Catholic. Club: Swiss Student Soc. Avocations: music; fine arts; traveling. Home: 18A Ave du Bouchet, 1209 Geneva Switzerland Office: 3 rue Ami Lullin, CH 1207 Geneva Switzerland

MEINER, RUDOLF CHARLES, space systems engineer; b. St. Gall, Switzerland, June 5, 1935; came to Netherlands, 1964; s. Charles A. and Paula (Rejhon) M.; m. Johanna Catharina Maria Anke Crone, Apr. 29, 1971; children—Rebecca Pavlova, Larissa Charlotte. Diploma, ETH, Zurich, 1958; degree in Engring. Stanford U., 1961. Tech. coordinator Copers, Paris, 1962-63; test engr. NASA-GSFC, Md., 1963-64; test engr. ESTEC, Delft, Netherlands, 1964-66; chief engr. ESLAB, Noordwijkerhout, Netherlands, 1966-69; project scientist ESTEC, Noordwijk, 1969-72; head Spacelab systems and test engr. ESA-ESTEC-SL, Noordwijk, 1972-82, head long-term planning for Spacelab, 1982-84; mgr. Columbus Service Vehicle, 1984-86, head Columbus spl. projects, 1987—; cons. Cosmo Ctr. Found., Houten, Netherlands, 1980—; astronaut candidate ESA, Paris, 1977. Contbr. articles to profl. jours. Mem. Nat. Space Soc. (Washington), Swiss Soc. Solar Energy, Space Studies Inst., Sunset Energy Council, Swiss Soc. Space Tech. Lodge: Lions (pres. 1983-84). Home: Bentveldsduinweg 3A, 2111 AK Aerdenhout The Netherlands Office: ESA-ESTEC Keplerlaan 1, 2201 AZ Noordwijk The Netherlands

MEINERS, PHYLLIS HALL, fund development consultant; b. Boston, Nov. 8, 1940; d. Samuel Henry and Edith (Salvin) Bloom; divorced; 1 child, Hilary Cynthia. BA, U. Calif., Berkeley, 1962; postgrad., MIT, 1973-74, Rockhurst Coll., 1980-83. Dir. research Harbridge House, Boston, 1964-70; research assoc. MIT, Cambridge, Mass., 1970-73; program adminstr. U. Hawaii, Honolulu, 1974-79, Mo. div. Community Devel., Kansas City, 1980-82; pres. Corp. Resource Cons., Kansas City, Mo., 1982—. Mem. Nat. Assn. Neighborhood Councils, 49/63 Neighborhood Coalition, South Town Council, Kansas City, 1986—, Friends of Art, Kansas City, 1986—; staff coordinator Mayor Charles B. Wheeler campaign, Kansas City, 1979. Mem. Nat. Soc. Fund Raising Execs. (bd. dirs.), Nat. Assn. Neighborhood Councils, Brush Creek Trolley Barn Assn., Greater Kansas City C. of C., Greater Kansas City Council Philanthropy, Nat. Assn. Female Execs., Brookside Neighborhood Assn., Special Libraries Assn. Democrat. Jewish. Home: 5800 Grand Ave Kansas City MO 64113 Office: 6233 Harrison Kansas City MO 64110

MEINHARDT, HANS, manufacturing company executive; b. Margretenhann, Germany, May 14, 1931. Degree in Econs., Abitur Fulda, 1951; PhD, 1957. With Linde AG, Wiesbaden, Fed. Republic Germany, 1955—, head of orgn. dept. cen. adminstrn., bus. mgr., 1962-63; head of orgn. dept. cen. adminstrn., bus. mgr. Linde AG, Güldner, Aschaffenburg, Fed. Republic Germany, 1963-65; bus. dir. Linde AG, Güldner, Fed. Republic Germany, 1965-70, dep. mem. of exec. bd., 1970-71; full mem., then chmn. of exec. bd. Linde AG, Wiesbaden, 1971—; mem. supervising bd. Still GmbH, Hamburg, Neckermann Versand AG, Frankfurt, BMW AG, Munich, Bayerische Hypotheken- und Wechselbank AG, Munich, Markt- und Kühlhallen AG, Hamburg. Home: Richard-Wagner Str 61, D-6200 Wiesbaden Federal Republic of Germany Office: Linde AG, Postfach 4020, D-6200 Wiesbaden Federal Republic of Germany *

MEINIG, WALTER PAUL, bank executive; b. Davidson, Sask., Can., Aug. 25, 1932; m. Jessie Eddleston, May 21, 1956; children: Elaine, John, Dianne, Sandra. Gen. mgr. western and no. Ont. region The Bank of N.S., Toronto, 1976-77, v.p. Can. regions, 1977-79, sr. v.p. Can. regions, 1979, sr. v.p. Ont. div., 1979-83, sr. v.p. Investment and Corp. Banking, 1983—. Bd. dirs. Riverdale Hosp., Toronto, 1978—. Clubs: St. George's Golf and Country (Toronto), The Nat. (Toronto). Office: The Bank of NS, 44 King St W, Toronto, ON Canada M5H 1H1

MEINKE, PERRIE S., artist; b. Boonton, N.J., Jan. 9, 1959; d. James Peter and Jeanne (Clark) M. BA, Eckerd Coll., St. Petersburg, Fla., 1979; MA, Rosary Coll. of Fine Arts, Florence, Italy, 1985. Group shows include Villa Schifanoia, Florence, 1985, 81st Ann. Watercolor Exhibition, N.Y.C., 1981, Watercolor exhibit, Belleair, Fla., 1981, The Emerging Female Voice, 1980. Mem. Women's Caucus for Art.

MEIR, ISAAC ALBERT, architect; b. Salonica, Macedonia, Greece, Mar. 1, 1957; arrived in Israel, 1975; s. Albert and Aliki Irene (Vitsentzatou) M.; m. Orna Herta Lavie, Aug. 16, 1984; 1 child, Dekel. BArch, Technion-Israel Inst. Tech., Haifa, 1981, MS in Architecture and Town Planning, 1984. Registered architect, Israel. Asst. faculty of architecture and town planning Technion-Israel Inst. Tech., 1981-84, architect researcher J. Blaustein Inst. for Desert Research, Sede Boqer campus, 1986—; free lance architect, Haifa, 1981-86; workshop head European Architecture Students Assembly, Aarhus, Denmark, 1984. Author: (with Etzion & Faiman) Energy Aspects of Arid Zone Design,1988; author, co-author articles, monograph. Max Harris and Betty Kranzberg fellow, 1981; research grantee Meml. Fund for Jewish Culture, N.Y., 1986; recipient photography award Nanyang U., Singapore, 1980. Mem. Union of Grad. Engrs. Israel, Assn. Engrs. & Architects Israel, Israel Regional Sci. Assn., Vols. in Tech. Assistance. Jewish. Office: J Blaustein Inst Desert Research, Desert Architecture Unit, Sede Boqer Campus 84993, Israel

MEISNER, JOACHIM CARDINAL, bishop of Berlin; b. Breslau, Germany, Dec. 25, 1933; s. Walter and Hedwig Meisner. Ed. U. Erfurt, Pastoral Sem. at Neuzelle. Ordained priest Roman Catholic Ch., 1962. Chaplain St. Agidien, Heiligenstadt, 1963-66, St. Crucis, Erfurt, 1966; rector Diozesencaritas of Erfurt, 1966-76, suffragan bishop, 1975-80; bishop of Berlin, 1980—; pres. Berliner Bischofskonferenz, 1982—; elevated to cardinal, 1983. Author: Das Auditorium Coelicum am Dom zu Erfurt, 1960; Nachreformatorische katholische Frommigkeitsformen in Erfurt, 1971; Sein, wie Gott uns gemeint hat—Betrchtungen zu Maria, 1988; contbr. articles to mags. Address: Wundtstrasse 48-50, D-1000 Berlin 19 Federal Republic of Germany

MEISSNER, HANS GUNTHER, marketing educator, consultant; b. Dusseldorf, Fed. Republic of Germany, Sept. 24, 1929; s. Karl and Helene (Steltmann) M.; m. Bettina Granow; children: Ruth Christiane, Patrick Jan. Diploma, U. Cologne, Fed. Republic Germany, 1955; Doctorate, U. Cologne, 1958. Habilitation, 1965. Prof. U. Cologne, 1965-73; prof. mktg. U. Dortmund, Fed. Republic Germany, 1973—, dean, 1974-75, 83-85. Author: Aussenhandels-Marketing, 1984, Strategic International Marketing, 1987. Mem. German Advt. Research Assn. (pres. 1980-84), European Internat. Bus. Assn. (pres. 1976-77, 87-88), Am. Mktg. Assn., Schmalenbach Gesellschaft, Deutsche Werbewissenschaftliche Gesellschaft. Home: Holderlinstrasse 87/89, 40 Cologne Federal Republic of Germany Office: U Dortmund, PO Box 500 500, 50 Dortmund Federal Republic of Germany

MEISTER, FREDERICK WILLIAM, state official, lawyer; b. Waterbury, Conn., May 21, 1938; s. William Frederick and Marion Callender (Tracy) M.; m. Joanne Marie Babich, June 12, 1982. B.A., Swarthmore Coll., 1960; M.B.A., Harvard U., 1962; J.D., U. Pitts., 1975. Bar: Pa. 1975, D.C. 1980. Fin. analyst First Pa. Bank, Phila., 1966-67; asst. comptroller Am. Friends Service Com., Phila., 1967-72; program analyst HEW, Washington, 1976-77; project mgr., program analyst Health Care Financing Adminstrn., Balt., 1977-82; chief Bur. of Fiscal and Contract Mgmt., Ariz. Health Care Cost Containment System, Phoenix, 1982-84, chief policy, planning and research, 1984—. Founding chmn. troop com. Valley Forge council Boy Scouts Am., Media, Pa., 1966-68; bd. dirs., mem. bus. com. Fellowship House and Farm, Inc., Phila., 1968-72; county dir. U.S. Senate Primary Campaign for H. John Heinz, Montgomery County, Pa., 1976., mem. fin. com. Am. Friends Sevice Com., Balt., 1980-82; mem. contracts task force Ariz. Dept. Health Services, Phoenix, 1983-84. Served to lt. USNR, 1962-65. Recipient Bur. Dirs. citation Bur. Quality Control, Health Care Financing Adminstrn., 1982. Mem. ABA, Fed. Bar Assn., Am. Soc. Pub. Adminstrn. Republican. Mem. Soc. Friends. Club: Harvard Bus. Sch., Harvard of Phoenix, Phoenix City. Home: 1722 W Earll Dr Phoenix AZ 85015 Office: Ariz Health Care Cost Containment System 801 E Jefferson St Phoenix AZ 85034

MEJIA, LUIS GONZALO, engineer, consultant; b. Andes, Colombia, May 19, 1950; s. Augusto Mejia and Ligia Canas; C.E., Universidad Nacional, Medellin, Colombia, 1973; M.S., T.H. Karlsruhe (Ger.), 1977; m. Gloria Isabel Valencia, Nov. 22, 1974; children—Carlos Federico, Maria Isabel. Structural engr. Ingenieria y Construcciones, Medellin, 1971-75; con. engr., dir. Luis Gonzalo Mejia C. y Cia, Medellin, 1978—; prof. Universidad Nacional, 1973-82. Mem. Am. Concrete Inst., Verein Deutscher Ingenieure, Asociacion Colombiana de Ingenieria Sismica, Goethe Inst., Sociedad Ecologica Colombiana. Roman Catholic. Club: Amigos de Alemania. Contbr. articles in field. Office: Carrera 70A 51-31, AA 54173 Medellin Colombia

MEKOUAR, MOHAMED, aviation executive; b. Fes, Morocco, Apr. 23, 1937. D in Engring. Civil Aviation, Ecole Nat. de l'Aviation Civille, Paris, 1961. Chief civil aeronautics Ministry of Pub., Morocco, 1961-65; dir. civil aviation Ministry of Transports, Morocco, 1965-81, dir. gen. air adminstrn., 1981-84; chmn., pres. of bd. dirs. Royal Air Maroc, Morocco, 1984—. Named to Chevalier de L'Ordre Du Trone, Morocco, 1969; named Personality of Yr., France, 1986. Home: Hay El Hana, rue 38 villa 45, Casablanca Morocco Office: Royal Air Maroc, Aeroport de Casablanca-Anfa, Rabat Morocco

MELAMED, ARTHUR DOUGLAS, lawyer; b. Mpls., Dec. 3, 1945; s. Arthur Charles and Helen Beatrix (Rosenberg) M.: m. Carol Drescher Weisman, May 26, 1983; children: Kathryn Henrie, Elizabeth Allyn. B.A., Yale U., 1967; J.D., Harvard U., 1970. Bar: D.C. 1970, U.S. Ct. Appeals (9th cir.) 1971, U.S. Ct. Appeals (2d cir.) 1975, U.S. Ct. Appeals (D.C. cir.) 1978, U.S. Ct. Appeals (8th cir.) 1981, U.S. Supreme Ct. 1981, U.S. Ct. Appeals (fed. cir.) 1985, U.S. Ct. Internat. Trade 1985. Law clk. U.S. Ct. Appeals for 9th Circuit, 1970-71; assoc. Wilmer, Cutler & Pickering, Washington, 1971-77, ptnr., 1978—. Contbr. articles to profl. jours. Class agt. alumni fund Yale U. Mem. ABA, D.C. Bar Assn. Office: 2445 M St NW Washington DC 20037

MELAND, BERNARD EUGENE, theologian, educator; b. Chgo., June 28, 1899; s. Erick Bernhard and Elizabeth (Hansen) M.; m. Margaret Evans McClusky, Aug. 6, 1926 (dec.); children: Bernard Eugene (dec.), Richard Dennis. A.B., Park Coll., 1923, D.D., 1956; student, U. Ill., 1918, 23-24, McCormick Theol. Sem., 1924-25; B.D., U. Chgo., 1928; Ph.D., 1929; postgrad., U. Marburg, Germany, 1928-29. Ordained to ministry Presbyn. Ch., 1928; prof. religion and philosophy Central Coll., Fayette, Mo., 1929-36; asso. prof. religion, head dept. Pomona Coll., Claremont, Calif., 1936-43; prof. religion Pomona Coll., 1943-45, Clark lectr., 1947; prof. constructive theology U. Chgo., 1945-64; prof. emeritus U. Chgo. (Div. Sch.), 1964, vis. prof. theology, 1965-68, pastors inst. lectr., 1945; vis. prof. philosophy of religion Union Theol. Sem., N.Y.C., 1968-69; Hewitt vis. prof. humanities Ottawa U., Kans., 1971; Barrows lectr., Calcutta and Bangalore, India, Rangoon, Burma; vis. lectr. Serampore Coll., India, 1957-58; Burrows lectr. U. Calcutta, Poona, 1964-65. Author: Modern Man's Worship, 1934, (with H.N. Wieman) American Philosophies of Religion, 1936, Write Your Own Ten Commandments, 1938, The Church and Adult Education, 1939, Seeds of Redemption, 1947, America's Spiritual Culture, 1948, The Reawakening of Christian Faith, 1949, Higher Education and the Human Spirit, 1953, Faith and Culture, 1953, The Realities of Faith: The Revolution in Cultural Forms, 1962, The Secularization of Modern Cultures, 1966, Fallible Forms and Symbols, 1976; editor, contbr.: The Future of Empirical Theology, 1969; co-editor: Jour. Religion, 1946-64. Served with U.S. Army, 1918. Mem. Am. Theol. Soc. (v.p. 1951-52, pres. Midwest div. 1960-61). Home: 5842 Stony Island Ave Chicago IL 60637

MELANDRI, PIERRE CHRISTIAN, American civilization educator; b. Nice, France, June 15, 1946; s. Henri and Mireille (Noat) M.; m. Anne Catherine Thyss; children: Fabrice, Priscille. Master, Sorbonne U., 1968, doctorat D'Etat, 1977; PhD, U. Nice, 1972. Asst. prof. U. Paul Valéry, Montpellier, France, 1970-77; assoc. prof. U. Paul Valéry, Montpellier, 1977-79, Ecole Normale Supérieure, Paris, 1979-81; prof. Am. civilization U. Lille III, France, 1981—; mem. Commn. Publn. Des Documents Diplomatiques Français, 1984—. Author: Les Etats-Unis Face à l'Unification de l'Europe, 1980, Histoire des Etats-Unis depuis 1865, 1975, L'Alliance Atlantique, 1979, La Politique Extérieure des Etats-Unis de 1945 à Nos Jours, 1982; contbr. articles to profl. jours. Augustus Clifford Tower fellow Harvard U., 1969-70, ACLS scholar, 1974; Fulbright scholar French-Am. Co., 1978, guest scholar Wilson Ctr., 1983, 87. Mem. Assn. Française d'Etudes Américaines (v.p. 1984-87), Societe des Anglicistes de l'Enseignement Supérieur, Société Tocqueville, Soc. d'Histoire des Relations Internat. Contemporaines. Home: 16 Blvd Soult, 75012 Paris France Office: U Lille III, BP 149, 59653 Lille France

MELBY, ALAN KENNETH, linguist, educator; b. Murray, Utah, Mar. 25, 1948; s. Kenneth O. and Charlotte (Bryner) M.; B.S., Brigham Young U., 1973, M.A., 1974, Ph.D., 1976; m. Ulla-Britta L. Sandholm, Aug. 14, 1970; children—Eric, Roland, Irene, Philippe, Yvette, Vivianne. Assoc. prof. linguistics Brigham Young U., Provo, Utah, 1977—, chmn. translation research group; v.p. LinguaTech Internat., Inc. Mem. Linguistic Soc. Am., ACM, Assn. Computational Linguistics, Linguistic Assn. Can. and U.S., Acoustical Soc. Am., Am. Translators Assn. (accredited translator French to English). Republican. Mormon. Mem. editorial bd. (jour.) Computers and Translation; contbr. articles to profl. jours. Home: 1223 Aspen Ave Provo UT 84604 Office: Brigham Young U Linguistics Dept Provo UT 84602

MELCHER, ANDREW STEPHEN, insurance executive; b. Phila., July 20, 1949; s. Harold Porter and Joan (Decker) M.; m. Cynthia Gould, June 26, 1972; children: Adam, Chapin. BA, Wesleyan U., Middletown, Conn., 1972. With U.S. Peace Corps, Republic of Korea, 1972-73; asst. treas. Morgan Guaranty Trust, N.Y.C., 1973-79, Marsh & McLennan Cos., Inc., N.Y.C., 1979-83; fin. dir. C.T. Bowring & Co. Ltd. (Ins.), London, 1983-86; gen. mgr. C.T. Bowring Non-Marine Brokers Ltd., London, 1986-88; fin. dir. Eagle Star Ins. Co. Ltd., London, 1988—. Office: Eagle Star Ins Co Ltd, Saint Mary Axe House, Saint Mary Axe, London EC13, England

MELCHER, JOHN, U.S. senator; b. Sioux City, Iowa, Sept. 6, 1924; m. Ruth Klein, Dec. 1, 1945; children: Terry, Joan, Mary, Robert, John. Student, U. Minn., 1942-43; D.V.M., Iowa State U., 1950. Ptnr. Yellowstone Valley Vet. Clinic, Forsyth, Mont., operator cattle feed lot, 1953-55; alderman City of Forsyth, 1953-55; mayor City of Foryth, 1955-61; mem. Mont. Ho. of Reps. from Rosebud County, 1961-62, 69, Mont. Senate, 1963-67, 91st-94th congresses from 2d Mont. Dist., 1969-77; U.S. senator from Mont. 1977—; Former mem. Mont. Legis. Council. Democratic candidate for U.S. Ho. of Reps., 1966. Served with AUS, 1943-45, ETO. Decorated Purple Heart, Bronze Star, Combat Infantryman's Badge; recipient Disting. Service award Nat. Assn. Conservation Dists., 1985, Centennial medal U. Pa. Sch. Vet. Medicine, 1984. Democrat. Office: 730 Hart Senate Bldg Washington DC 20510

MELCHIORRI, PIERO, communications company executive; b. Rome, Italy, Apr. 26, 1939; came to U.S., 1953, naturalized, 1962; s. Giorgio Melchiorri and Eleonora (Castaldi) Orton. Student Dartmouth Coll., 1957-59, U. Cin., 1959-60. Dir. mktg. services Klemtner, N.Y.C., 1969-71, ZYMA, Milan, Italy, 1971-72; v.p., gen. mgr. PCP Co., Darien, Conn., 1972-75, HET Co., N.Y.C., 1975-81, Darome Act, Westport, Conn., 1981-82; pres. Logical Communications, Norwalk, Conn., 1982—; cons. Zweg Assocs., St. Louis, 1978-79. Contbr. articles to profl. jours. Mem. Am. Mktg. Assn., Am. Soc. Tng. and Devel., Pharm. Advt. Council. Democrat. Office: Logical Communications Inc 205 Liberty Sq East Norwalk CT 06855

MELDMAN, ROBERT EDWARD, lawyer; b. Milw., Aug. 5; s. Louis Leo and Lillian (Gollusch) M.; m. Sandra Jane Setlick, July 24, 1960; children—Saree Beth, Richard Samuel. B.S., U. Wis., 1959; LL.B., Marquette U., 1962; LL.M. in Taxation, NYU, 1963. Bar: Wis. 1962, U.S. Tax Ct. 1963, U.S. Supreme Ct. 1970, U.S. Ct. Claims 1971. Practice tax law Milw., 1963—; pres. Meldman, Case & Weine, Ltd., Milw., 1975-85; dir. Meldman & Weine div. Mulcahy & Wherry, S.C., Milw., 1985—; Adj. prof. taxation U. Wis., Milw., 1970—, mem. tax adv. council, 1978—; sec. Profl. Inst. Tax Study, Inc., 1978—. Author: (with Tom Mountin) text book Federal Taxation Practice & Procedure, 1983, 86; contbr. articles to legal jours. Recipient Adj. Taxation Faculty award UWM Tax Assn., 1987. Mem. ABA, Fed. Bar Assn. (pres. Milw. 1966-67), Milw. Bar Assn. (chmn. tax sect. 1970-71), Wis. State Bar (dir. tax sect. 1964-78, chmn. 1973-74), Marquette Law Alumni (dir. 1972-77), Phi Delta Phi, Tau Epsilon Rho (chancellor Milw. 1969-71, supreme nat. chancellor 1975-76). Jewish (trustee congregation 1972-77). Clubs: Milw. Athletic, Wisconsin. Lodge: B'nai B'rith (Ralph Harris meml. award Century Lodge, 1969-70, trustee). Home: 7455 N Skyline Ln Milwaukee WI 53217 Office: 815 E Mason St Milwaukee WI 53202-4080

MELDRUM, BRIAN STUART, research neuroscientist; b. Ipswich, Suffolk, Eng., Aug. 20, 1935; s. Frederick Stephen and Ada Mary (Singleton) M.; m. Mary Anne Fryer, Jan. 4, 1958 (div.); children—Julian, Judith, Andrew; m. Astrid Gronneberg Chapman, Aug. 14, 1981. B.A., Cambridge U., 1956, M.B.B.Ch., 1959; Ph.D., London U., 1964. Research asst. dept. physiology U. Coll., London, 1961-63; sci. staff mem. MRC Neuropsychiatry Unit, Carshalton, 1963-73; sr. lectr. dept. neurology Inst. Psychiatry, London, 1973-84; reader in exptl. neurology, London U., 1984-87; prof. experimental neurology, London U., 1988—. Editor: Recent Advances in Epilepsy, (1, 2, 3, 4) 1983-88. Contbr. articles to profl. jours. Recipient Michael prize Stiftung Michael, 1980-81; named William G. Lennox lectr. Am. Epilepsy Soc., 1980. Office: Inst Psychiatry, Dept Neurology, De Crespigny Park, London SE5 8AF England

MELÉNDEZ, NICHOLÁS EFRAIN, metal industry executive; b. Jalada, Veracruz, Mex., Sept. 10, 1932; s. Jose Dolores and Soledad (Lopez) M.; m. Rosa Maria Martin del Campo, May 29, 1970; children: Patricia, Efrain. Student, U. Mex., Mexico City, 1957. Prodn. mgr. Nacional de Cobre, Mexico City, 1957-70; plant mgr. Hidno Acero S.A., Tultitlan, Mex., 1970-79, Copresa, Cuatitlan, Mex., 1979-80; gen. mgr. Bujias Mexicana S.A. de C.U., Tlalnepamtla, Mex., 1980-83, Indsutria Electrica Automotric, Tlalnepamtla, Mex., 1983-86; pres., gen. mgr. DeVilbiss de Mex. S.A. de C.U., Tlalnepamtla, Mex., 1986—. Mem. Soc. Engrs., Soc. Mech. Engrs. Lodge: Lions Internat. (past pres. Maucalpan, Mex.). Home: Circuito Diplomaticos #33, 53100 Satelite, Maucalpan Mexico Office: Devilbissde Mex SA de CU, Via Dr Gustavo Baz #3990, 54110 Tlalnepantla Mexico

MELETINSKY, ELEAZAR M., humanities researcher; b. Kharkov, Ukraine, USSR, Oct. 22, 1918; s. Moses L. and Raisa I. (Margolis) M.; m. Irina Semenko, Aug. 18, 1957 (dec. May 1987); m. Helen Cumpan, June 4, 1988. BS in lit., Tashkent U., Moscow, 1945; D in Philology, Inst. World Lit., Moscow, 1966. Asst. prof. U. Tashkent, 1944-46; head dept. U. Petrozavodsk, USSR, 1946-55; researcher, sr. researcher, head dept., leading researcher Inst. World Lit. of Acad. Scis., Moscow, 1956—. Author: The Hero of the Tale of Magic, 1958, Origin of Heroic Epics, 1963, Edda and Early Forms of Epics, 1968, Poetics of Myth, 1976, Paleo-Siberian Mythological Epics, 1979, Medieval Romance, 1983, Historic Poetics of Epics, Romance and Novel, 1986; editor numerous books; contbr. over 200 articles to profl. jours. Served to lt. with USSR mil., 1941-43. Recipient Pitré prize internat. judges, Palermo, Italy, 1971. Fellow Internat. Soc. Folk Narrative Research; mem. Sci. Com. Semiotic Ctr. Urbino, Transls. in Folklore Studies Inst. for Study Human Issues (adv. bd.). Home: Udaltsova 12-36, 117415 Moscow USSR Office: Inst World Lit, Vorovskogo 25A, Moscow USSR

MELGAR, JULIO, retired mechanical engineer; b. Bklyn., July 4, 1922; s. Lorenzo and Maria (Lopez) M.; B.M.E., U. Detroit, 1952. Mech. engr. Chance Vought Aircraft, Dallas, 1952-53, Wyatt C. Hedrick Architects and Engrs., Dallas, 1953, Zumwalt & Vinther, Cons. Engrs., Dallas, 1953-54, Joe Hoppe, Inc., Dallas, 1954-55, A.J. Boynton & Co., Dallas, 1956-57, Wyatt Metal and Boiler Works, Dallas, 1958, Tinker AFB, Okla., 1958-60; mech. engr. FAA, Ft. Worth, 1960-85, ret., 1985. Mem. Metroplex Recreation Council, 1975—; mem. Tarrant County Mental Health and Mental Retardation, Ft. Worth Opera Guild, Dallas Opera Guild, Goodwill Industries; bd. dirs. Fort Worth Opera Assn., Tarrant County Humane Soc., Animal Protection Inst. Served with USMCR, 1943-45. Mem. Nat. Soc. Profl. Engrs., ASME, Am. Soc. Heating, Refrigerating and Air Conditioning Engrs., Profl. Soc. Protective Design, Fed. Bus. Assn., Amateur Athletic Union. Roman Catholic. Home: 6108 Menger Ave Dallas TX 75227

MELI, FRANCESCO GIOVANNI, literature educator; b. Brescia, Lombardy, Italy, Dec. 28, 1943; s. Angelo and Cleofe (Bertoldi) M.; m. Loraine Willis, Mar. 28, 1977; 1 child, Nicolas. Am. Lit. degree with honors, Istituto Univ. Lingue Moderne, Milan, 1973. Lectr. Istituto Univ. Lingue Moderne, Milan, 1975-81, asst. prof., 1983—; vis. scholar Columbia U., N.Y.C., 1976, 82. Contbr. literary criticisms (Thoreau, Steinbeck, Melville and others) to profl. jours.; translator: House Made of Dawn, by N.S. Momaday (Mondello Internat. Prize 1979); editor poetry collections, Am. Indian literature anthologies; freelance contbr. to pub. houses. Fulbright scholar, 1982. Mem. European Assn. for Am. Studies, Italian Assn. North Am. Studies (speaker confs. 1979-85). Home: 12 Corso Porta Ticinese, 20123 Milan Italy Office: Istituto Univ Lingue Moderne, 3 Piazza Volontari, 20145 Milan Italy

MELICH, MITCHELL, lawyer; b. Bingham Canyon, Utah, Feb. 1, 1912; s. Joseph and Mary (Kalembar) M.; m. Doris M. Snyder, June 3, 1935; children: Tanya (Mrs. Noel L. Silverman), Michael, Nancy, Robert A. LL.B., U. Utah, 1934. Bar: Utah bar 1934. Pvt. practice Moab, 1934-63, city atty., 1934-55; county atty. Grand County, 1940-42; sec., dir. Utex Exploration Co., Moab, 1953-62; pres., dir. Uranium Reduction Co., Moab, 1954-62; cons. to pres. Atlas Minerals, div. Atlas Corp., 1962-67; dir., treas. New Park Mining Co., 1962-65; partner firm Ray, Quinney & Nebeker, 1973—; solicitor Dept. Interior, Washington, 1969-73;. Mem. of Colorado River Com. of Utah, 1945-47; mem. Utah Water and Power Bd., 1947; chmn. Citizens Adv. Com. on Higher Edn., 1968; mem. nat. adv. council U. Utah, 1976—; Mem. Utah Senate, 1942-50, minority leader, 1949-50; mem. Utah Legislative Council, 1949-54; del. Republican Nat. Conv., 1952-72; mem. Rep. Nat. Com. for Utah, 1961-64; Rep. candidate for gov., 1964; cons. on staff Congressman Sherman P. Lloyd, Utah, 1967-68; Bd. dirs. St. Marks Hosp., 1973-88; bd. regents U. Utah, 1961-65, also mem. devel. fund com., mem. nat. adv. council, 1968-73, 76—; mem. Utah Statewide Health Coordinating Council, 1985. Recipient Distinguished Alumni award U. Utah, 1969. Mem. Am. Bar Assn., Utah State Bar, Utah Mining Assn. (pres. 1962-63), Kappa Sigma. Republican. Club: Alta Salt Lake Country (Salt Lake City). Lodges: Masons; Shriners. Home: 900 Donner Way Apt 708 Salt Lake City UT 84108 Office: 400 Deseret Bldg 79 S Main St Salt Lake City UT 84111

MELICHAR, ZDENEK JAN, architect; b. Prague, Czechoslovakia, Feb. 5, 1923; s. Balik Frantisek and Anna (Vondruska) M.; m. Radana Fiser, Apr. 30, 1955 (dec. Jan. 1964); 1 child, Marcela; m. Marie Cermin, Nov. 3, 1966; children: Klara, Lukas. BA, U. Prague, 1949, LittD, 1967, postgrad., 1976. Lectr. anatomy Charles Med. U., Prague, 1950-71; architect Fedn. Art Checoslovak, Prague, 1971—.

MELICHER, RONALD WILLIAM, finance educator; b. St. Louis, July 4, 1941; s. William and Lorraine Norma (Mohart) M.; m. Sharon Ann Schlarmann, Aug. 19, 1967; children: Michelle Joy, Thor William, Sean Richard. BSBA, Washington U., St. Louis, 1963; MBA, Washington U.,

1965, DBA, 1968. Asst. prof. fin. U. Colo., Boulder, 1969-71, assoc. prof., 1971-76, prof. fin., 1976—, chmn. fin. div., 1978-86; assoc. dir. space law, bus. and policy ctr. U. Colo., 1986-87; research cons. FPC, Washington, 1972-73; cons. NRC, Washington, 1975-76, GAO, Washington, 1981, Ariz. Corp. Commn., 1986-87, IBM Corp., 1985—. Co-author: Real Estate Finance, 2d edit., 1984, Finance, 7th edit., 1988, Financial Management, 5th edit., 1982; assoc. editor The Financial Review, 1988. Recipient NewsCtr. TV Teaching award, 1988, Boulder Faculty Assembly award, 1988, MBA/MS Assn. award, 1988; NSF grantee, 1974, NASA grantee, 1986, 87. Mem. Fin. Mgmt. Assn. (regional dir. 1975-77, assoc. editor 1975-80, v.p. meeting 1985, v.p. program 1987), Am. Fin. Assn., Western Fin. Assn. (bd. dirs. 1974-76), Fin. Execs. Inst., Midwest Fin. Assn. (bd. dirs. 1978-80), Alpha Kappa Psi, Beta Gamma Sigma. Presbyterian. Home: 5136 Forsythe Pl Boulder CO 80309 Office: U Colo Coll of Bus Campus Box 419 Boulder CO 80309

MELJON, ALINA, geodesist, cartographer; b. Warsaw, Poland, Dec. 9, 1931; d. Stanislaw and Eugenia (Janowska) Gladka; m. Jan Migda, Sept. 4, 1955 (div. 1961); m. Jan Janusz Meljon; Feb. 8, 1963; 1 child, Jolanta. Degree in Engring., Tech. U. Warsaw, 1955. Tech. editor Panstw. Przedsieb. Wydawn. Kartograf, Warsaw, 1955-68; chief tech, editorial dept. Panstwowe Zakl Kartograficzne, Warsaw, 1968-83, dir., 1983—. Editor Polish Cartographical Rev., 1983—. 1st sec. Polish United Workers' Party, Warsaw, 1978-83. Recipient Bachelor's Cross Poland Ministry Bdlg. and Constrn., 1986. Mem. Assn. Polish Geodesics, Polish Georgraphic Soc. Home: 21 Kazury St, 02 781 Warsaw Poland Office: Panstwowe Przedsiébiorstwo, Wydawnictw Kartograficznych im E Romera, 18 Solec St, 00-410 Warsaw Poland

MELL, GERTRUD MARIA, musician, sea captain. Ed, Sweden, Aug. 15, 1947; d. Torsten Georg and Iris Maria (Olofson) Mell. Student Music Conservatory, Lund, 1965-67; cert. ship's mechanic, ship's telephon operator, ship's engr. grad. sea officer mate Sea Officers High Sch., Goteborg, 1979, sea capt., 1981; student orch. conducting Music Conservatory Organist, music tchr., dir. choirs and orch., Ed, Bengtsfors and Töftedal, 1967-76; worker ships at sea, 1976-78; organist Göteborg, 1982—. Composer and pianist long playing record Mell, 1971; composer and singer single record Mermaid, 1977; composer 4 symphonies, 1 string quartet, chamber music, symphonic poems, organ-piano compositions; Älvsborgs Läns Landstings Kultur scholar, 1975. Mem. Kyrkomusikernas Riksförbund, Sveriges Tonsättares Internat. Musikbyrå. Home: Stromstadvagen 30, 66800 Ed Sweden Office: Sernhag Krokeg 9, 41318 Gothenburg Sweden

MELLERS, WILFRID HOWARD, musician, educator; b. Leamington, Warwickshire, Eng., Apr. 26, 1914; s. Percival Wilfrid and Hilda Maria (Lawrence) M.; m. Peggy Pauline Lewis, 1950 (dec. 1981); children: Judith, Olivia, Caroline, Sarah; m. Robin Stephanie Hildyard. BA, Cambridge (Eng.) U., 1936, MA, 1939, PhD, 1982; DMus, Birmingham U., 1960; DPhil, City U., London, 1982. Tutor in music Downing Coll., U. Cambridge, 1945-48; tutor in music extra mural dept. Birmingham (Eng.) U., 1948-60; Disting. Andrew Mellon prof. music U. Pitts., 1960-63; prof. music, head dept. music U. York, Eng., 1964-81, Wilfrid Mellers emeritus prof., 1981—; fellow Guildhall Sch. Music, Eng., 1982; advisor sundry pubs.; mem. music festival coms. Author: Francois Couperin and the French Classical Tradition, 1950, 2d. edit., 1987, Music in a New Found Land, 1964, 2d revised edit., 1988, Bach and the Dance of God, 1984, Beethoven and the Voice of God, 1986, 13 other books and 50 compositions. Named to Order of Brit. Empire, 1984. Office: U York, 17 Aldwark, York YO1 2BX, England

MELLOTT, ROBERT VERNON, advertising executive; b. Dixon, Ill., Jan. 1, 1928; s. Edwin Vernon and Frances Rhoda (Miller) M.; m. Sarah Carolyn Frink, June 11, 1960; children—Lynn Lorraine, Susan Michelle, David Robert. B.A., DePauw U., 1950; postgrad. Ind. U., 1950-51, Law Sch., 1959-61, M.A., 1983. TV producer, dir. Jefferson Standard Broadcasting Co., Charlotte, N.C., 1951-59; asst. dist. mgr. Gen. Motors Corp., Flint, Mich., Chgo., 1961-62; TV radio comml. supr. N.W. Ayer & Son, Chgo., 1962-65; TV radio producer FCB, Chgo., 1965-67, mgr. midwest prodn., 1967-69, mgr. comml. coordination, 1969-74, v.p., mgr. comml. services, Chgo., 1974—. Mem. media adv. com. Coll. of Dupage, Glen Ellyn, Ill., 1971-82; chmn. Cub Scout com., Wheaton, Ill., 1978-79; bd. dirs. Chgo. Unltd., 1969-71. Mem. Am. Assn. Advt. Agencies (broadcast adminstrn. policy com., broadcast talent union relations policy com.), World Communication Assn., Internat. Platform Assn., Phi Delta Phi, Alpha Tau Omega. Republican. Mem. Evangelical Christian Ch. Clubs: Chgo. Farmers, Chgo. Advt., Ind. U. Alumni. Home: 26 W 130 Tomahawk Dr Wheaton IL 60187 Office: FCB Ctr 101 E Erie St Chicago IL 60611-2897

MELNICK, BURTON ALAN, English educator; b. Woonsocket, R.I., Dec. 3, 1940; arrived in Switzerland, 1967; s. Arthur Sydney and Frances Irene (Diamond) M.; m. Mary Lee Corfman, June 18, 1983; 1 child, Jonathan Eli. BA, Harvard U., 1962; postgrad., Ctr. Dramatique Est, Strasbourg, France, 1962-63; MFA, Tulane U., France, 1967; postgrad., U. Lausanne, France, 1984—. English asst. Lycée Carnot, Paris, 1963-65; prof. English Am. Coll. Switzerland, Leysin, 1967-68; tchr. English Internat. Sch. Geneva, 1968—, head dept., 1977-79; prof. English Webster U. in Geneva, 1982—; examiner Interpreters Sch., U. Geneva, 1968-71, Internat. Baccalaureate Office, Geneva, 1971-72. Translator: Adolphe Appia, 1982; contbr. articles to profl. and lit. jours. Fulbright fellow, 1962-63, Woodrow Wilson nat. fellow, 1963. Mem. MLA, soc. Suisse Amis Mme de Charrière. Jewish. Clubs: Harvard of Switzerland, Diplomatic (Geneva). Home: 38 Chemin de Pont Ceard, 1290 Versoix Switzerland Office: Internat Sch of Geneva, 62 Route de Chene, 1208 Geneva Switzerland

MELOAN, TAYLOR WELLS, marketing educator; b. St. Louis, July 31, 1919; s. Taylor Wells and Edith (Graham) M.; m. Anna Geraldine Leukering, Dec. 17, 1944 (div. 1974); children: Michael David, Steven Lee; m. Jane Innes Bierlich, Jan. 30, 1975. B.S. cum laude, St. Louis U., 1949; M.B.A., Washington U., St. Louis, 1950; D.B.A., Ind. U., 1953. Advt. mgr. Herz Corp., St. Louis, 1941-42; sales promotion supr. Liggett & Myers Tobacco Co., St. Louis, 1942-43; asst. prof. mktg. U. Okla., Norman, 1953; from asst. prof. to assoc. prof. mktg. Ind. U., Bloomington, 1953-59; prof., chmn. dept. mktg. U. So. Calif., Los Angeles, 1959-69; dean Sch. Bus. Adminstrn. U. So. Calif., 1969-71, assoc. v.p. acad. adminstrn. and research, 1971-81, prof. mktg., 1959—; prof. bus. adminstrn. U. Karachi, Pakistan, 1962; vis. prof. mktg. Istituto Post U. Per Lo Studio Dell Organizzazione Aziendale, Turin, Italy, 1964; Disting. vis. prof. U. Witwatersrand, Johannesburg, 1978; editorial adviser bus. adminstrn. Houghton Mifflin Co., Boston, 1959-73; cons. to industry and govt., 1953—; bd. dirs. Council Better Bus. Burs., Inc., 1978-84, Nat. Advt. Rev. Bd., 1985—. Author: New Career Opportunities, 1978, Innovation Strategy and Management, 1979, Direct Marketing: Vehicle for Department Store Expansion, 1984, Preparing the Exporting Entrepreneur, 1986; co-author: Managerial Marketing, 1970, Internationalizing the Business Curriculum, 1968, Handbook of Modern Marketing, contbg. author, 1986; bd. editors: Jour. Mktg., 1965-72. Served with USNR, 1943-46. Mem. Newcomen Soc. N.Am., Am. Mktg. Assn. (pres. Los Angeles chpt. 1963-64), Order of Artus, Beta Gamma Sigma, Delta Pi Epsilon. Clubs: Calif. Yacht, University (Los Angeles). Lodge: Rotary. Home: 59 Lakefront Irvine CA 92714 Office: U So Calif Los Angeles CA 90089

MELOGRANI, PIERO, historian, educator; b. Rome, Nov. 15, 1930; s. Rafaello and Laura (Forges Davanzati) M.; m. Giula Vergombello, May 22, 1976. JD, U. Rome, 1954. Prof. contemporary history U. degali Studi, Perugia, Italy, 1971—. Author: Storia Politica della Grande Guerra, 1962, Gli Industriali e Mussolini, 1972, Saggio sui Potenti, 1977, Fascismo, Communismo e Rivoluzione Industriale, 1984, Il Mito della Rivoluzione Mondiale, 1985. Fellow Wilson Ctr., Washington, 1980. Home: Via Margutta 33, 00187 Rome Italy Office: U Perugia Via Pascoli, 06100 Perugia Italy

MELONI, PAOLO, navigation aids educator; b. Rome, Jan. 9, 1955; s. Antonio and Giorgia (Caruso) M. Physics degree, U. La Sapienza, Rome, 1982. Design and devel. dir. Aten Srl, Latina, Italy, 1978-83, now cons. engr., nav. aids educator Aeronautica Militare, Pratica di Mare, Italy, 1983—; cons. engr. Patentee sea sentinel, marine localizer beacon. Mem. IEEE, Assn. Electrotenica Italiana, Nat. Geog. Soc. Avocations: photographic reportages; writing novels; historical studies. Office: Aeroporto Pratica di Mare, Rome Italy

MELTON, JOHN LESTER, English educator; b. Walsenburg, Colo., Aug. 11, 1920; s. Harry W. and Elizabeth (Cahalan) M.; m. Virginia Anne Cadmus. B.A., U. Utah, 1948, M.A., 1949; Ph.D., Johns Hopkins U., 1955. Instr. Johns Hopkins U., Balt., 1950-55; from instr. to prof. John Carroll U., Cleve., 1955-68; assoc. prof. St. Cloud State U., Minn., 1968-69, prof. 1969-86, prof. emeritus, 1986—; cons. linguistics Western Res. U., Cleve., 1957-64. Author (TV series) Literature of the Am. Frontier, 1970. Editor: Semantic Code Dictionary, 1958. Contbr. articles to profl. jours. Mem. Home Rule Charter Commn., St. Cloud, 1970-79. Served to maj. U.S. Army, 1936-46. Mem. Internat. Arthurian Soc., Oreg. and Calif. Trails Assn., MLA, Coll. English Assn., Minn. Council Tchrs. English, Sierra Club, Phi Beta Kappa, Alpha Sigma Lambda, Lambda Iota Tau, Phi Kappa Phi. Avocations: camping, photography, travel. Home: 3040 Santa Fe Trail Saint Cloud MN 56301 Office: Saint Cloud State U Saint Cloud MN 56301

MELTON, RICHARD H., diplomat; b. Rockville, Md., Aug. 8, 1935; married; 3 children. BA, Cornell U., 1958; MA, U. Wis., 1971; student, Nat. War Coll., 1978-79. Joined Fgn. Service, 1961, internat. relations officer, 1971-73; spl. asst. Bur. Inter-Am. Affairs Dept. of State, 1973-75; polit. officer U.S. Embassy, Lisbon, Portugal, 1975-78, London, 1979-82; dep. chief of mission U.S. Embassy, Montevidio, Uruguay, 1982-85; dir. Office of Cen. Am. and Panamanian Affairs Dept. of State, 1985-87; ambassador to Nicaragua 1987—. Served with U.S. Army, 1958-61. Office: American Embassy, Km 4-1/2 Carretera Sur, Managua Nicaragua *

MELTZER, YALE LEON, economist, educator; b. N.Y.C., Nov. 3, 1931; s. Benjamin and Ada (Luria) M.; B.A., Columbia U., 1954, postgrad. Sch. Law, 1954-55; M.B.A., N.Y. U., 1966; m. Annette Schoenberg, Aug. 7, 1960; children—Benjamin Robert, Philippe David. Asst. to chief patent atty. Beaunit Mills, Inc., Elizabethton, Tenn., 1955-56, prodn. mgr., 1956-58, research chemist N.Y. Med. Coll., N.Y.C., 1958-59; research chemist H. Kohnstamm & Co., Inc., mfg. chemists, N.Y.C., 1959-66, mgr. comml. devel., market research, patents and trademarks, 1966-68; sr. security analyst Harris, Upham & Co., Inc., 1968-70; instr. dept. econs. N.Y. U., 1972-79; adj. asst. prof. dept. acctg., fin. and mgmt. Pace U., N.Y.C., 1974-80, adj. assoc. prof., 1980—; lectr. dept. polit. sci., econs. and philosophy Coll. S.I., CUNY, 1977-82, asst. prof. dept. polit. sci., econs. and philosophy, 1983—; lectr. bus., fin., econs., sci. and tech. Mem. AAAS, Am. Econ. Assn. Author: Soviet Chemical Industry, 1967; Chemical Trade with the Soviet Union and Eastern European Countries, 1967; Chemical Guide to GATT, The Kennedy Round and International Trade, 1968; Phthalocyanine Technology, 1970; Hormonal and Attractant Pesticide Technology, 1971; Urethane Foams: Technology and Applications, 1971; Water-Soluble Polymers: Technology and Applications, 1972; Encyclopedia of Enzyme Technology, 1973; Economics, 1974; Foamed Plastics; Recent Developments, 1976; Water-Soluble Resins and Polymers: Technology and Applications, 1976; Putting Money to Work: An Investment Primer, 1976; (with W.C.F. Hartley) Cash Management: Planning, Forecasting, and Control, 1979; Water-Soluble Polymers: Recent Developments, 1979; Putting Money to Work: An Investment Primer for the '80s, 1981, updated edit., 1984; Water-Soluble Polymers: Developments since 1978, 1981; Expanded Plastics and Related Products: Developments Since 1978, 1983. Contbr. articles to profl. publs. Translator, Russian and German tech. lit. Home: 141-10 82d Dr Jamaica NY 11435 Office: Coll SI Dept Polit Sci Econs Philosophy 130 Stuyvesant Pl Staten Island NY 10301

MELVIN, PETER ANTHONY PAUL, architect; b. Harrow, Middlesex, Eng., Sept. 19, 1933; s. Charles George Thomas and Elsie (Paul) m.; m. Muriel Faure, Apr. 23, 1960; children: Joanna Claire, Jeremy Paul, Stephen James. Diploma in architecture with distinction, The Poly. Sch. of Architecture, London, 1958. Chartered architect. Articled to chief architect Truman Hanbury Buxton and Co. Brewers, London, 1951-54; arcthl. asst. Ministry of Works, London, 1954-55, Frederick Gibberd and Ptnrs., Chartered Architects, London, 1955-56; assoc., then ptnr. Arthur Swift and Ptnrs., Chartered Architects and Planners, London, 1958-65; prin. Melvin Lansley and Mark, Chartered Architects, Berkhamsted, Hertfordshire, Eng., 1965—. Contbr. to numerous arcthl. designs, Eng.; contbr. articles to profl. jours. Vs. fellow Sch. of Architecture Natal (South AFrica) U., 1983. Fellow Royal Inst. Brit. Architects (v.p. 1982-83, 85-87), Royal Soc. of Arts. Anglican. Club: Arts (London). Office: Melvin Lansley and Mark, The Archway 105 High St, Berkhamsted Hp4 2DG, England

MELVIN, RUSSELL JOHNSTON, magazine publisher; b. New Castle, Pa., Nov. 16, 1925; s. Russell Conwell and Anna Katharine (Johnston) M.; m. Helen Margaret Connery, Aug. 6, 1949; children: Thomas Kirk, Meredith. B.A., U. Pa., 1949. Reporter Phila. Inquirer, 1949; copywriter, then asst. circulation mgr. Time mag., 1949-53; with Newsweek mag., 1953—, dir. Pacific edits., 1960-64, mng. dir. internat. edits., 1964-68; mng. editor internat. editorial service Newsweek mag. (Newsweek internat. edits.), 1969—; cons. internat. affairs and profl. edn. Mag. Pubs. Assn., 1986—; v.p. Newsweek, Inc., 1965-85; founding editor The Journal, Tokyo, 1963; founding dir. Newsweek Feature Service, 1968. Served with USNR, 1942-46. Mem. Internat. Advt. Assn. (chmn., chief exec. officer 1980-85, exec. dir. Chpts. Corp. 1985-86), , Internat. Fedn. Periodical Press (v.p.). Episcopalian. Clubs: Univ. (N.Y.C.); Chappaqua Tennis. Home: 153 Douglas Rd Chappaqua NY 10514 Office: care Mag Pubs Assn 575 Lexington Ave New York NY 10022

MEMDE, KAORU, illumination designer; b. Kita-ku, Japan, June 12, 1950; d. Shinasaku and Yukiko Tomizawa; m. Kazuko Mende, May 5, 1976. BA, Tokyo U. of Art, 1975, MA, 1977. Non-regular staff Nikken Sekkei, Tokyo, 1977-78; exec. dir. LD Yamagiwa Lab., Inc., Tokyo, 1978—, TL Yamagiwa La., Inc., Tokyo, 1980—; lectr. Tokai U., Kanagawa, 1985—, Tokyo U. Art, 1986—, Woman's Coll. Fine Arts, Tokyo, 1986—. Author: Akari no Hakubutushi, 1988, Light Light, 1988, Sicence of Lighting, 1988; author design mag. Architecture and Lighting, 1982. Mem. Illuminating Engring. Soc. N.Am. (Edwin F. Guth Meml. of Excellence award 1985, 87), Illuminating Engring. Inst. Japan, Archtl. Inst. Japan. Home: 1-3-1-608 Ecchujima, Koto-ku, Tokyo 135, Japan Office: TL Yamagiwa Lab Inc, 4-5-18 Higashinippori, Arakawa-ku, Tokyo 116, Japan

MÉNARD, JACQUES EDOUARD, historian; b. Montreal, Que., Can., Feb. 21, 1923; s. Leon Paul and Alice Marie (LaFrance) M.; B.A., lic. theology, U. Montreal, 1947, Dr. (hon.), 1978; Th.D. summa cum laude, U. Angelicum, Rome, 1948; lic. Bibl. scis. Bibl. Inst., Rome, 1950; diploma Ecole Pratique Hautes Etudes, Paris, 1960; D.Theology summa cum laude, U. Strasbourg, 1967; DEd (hon.) La Valette, Malta, 1988. Ordained priest Roman Cath. Ch., 1947; prof. N.T., U. Montreal Div. Sch., 1951-57; research worker Can. Council, 1957-61; research asst. Centre Nat. Recherche Sci., France, 1961-65; mem. Faculty Cath. Theology, U. Scis. Humaines, Strasbourg, France, 1965—, ordinary prof. history of religions, 1973—; dir. Can. project integral French edit. Nag Hammadi texts, 1973—; dir. Cahiers de la Bibliothèque Copte; co-editor Bibliothèque Copte de Hammadi, Quebec, 1977—; co-editor Nag Hammadi Studies, 1970—. Mem. Societas Novi Testamenti Studiorum, Internat. Assn. Coptic Studies (bd., founding pres., hon.). Author: Les Dons du Saint Esprit chez Monsieur Olier (Theologica), 1951, 2d edit., 1987, L'Evangile de Vérité, 1962, 2d edit., 1972, L'Evangile selon Philippe, 2d edit., 1967, 3d edit., 1987, Exégèse biblique et judaïsme, 1973, Le symbole, 1975, L'Evangile selon Thomas, 1975, Les textes de Nag Hammadi, 1975, La Lettre de Pierre à Philippe, 1977, L'Authentikos Logos, 1977; L'Epître à Rhèginos, 1983; Ecritures et traditions dans la littérature Copte, 1984; L'Exposé valentinien: Fragments du Baptême et de l'Eucharistie, 1985; Gnose et Manichéisme, 1986, Introduction à L'Histoire Des Religions, 1987, La Gnose De Philon D'Alexandrie, 1987, Le Chant de la Perle, 1988; also articles. Home: 10 rue Massenet, 67000 Strasbourg France Office: Faculty Cath Theology, Univ Scis Humaines, Palais Universitaire, 67084 Strasbourg France

MENDELSON, GEORGE, psychiatrist, consultant; b. Gdynia, Poland, July 3, 1946; arrived in Australia, 1959; s. Leon and Marysia (Goldbaum) M.; m. Danuta Wachenhauser, Aug. 8, 1970; children: Hannah, David. MBBS, U. Melbourne, 1970; MD, Monash U., Melbourne, 1986. Resident Alfred Hosp., Melbourne, 1971-72; registrar in psychiatry Prince Henry's Hosp., Melbourne, 1973-75, asst. psychiatrist, 1979—; cons. psychiatrist Pain Mgmt. Ctr. Royal So. Meml. Hosp., Melbourne, 1979—; hon. lectr. dept. psychol. medicine Monash U., Melbourne, 1979-86, hon. sr. lectr. 1986—. Author: Psychiatric Aspects of Personal Injury Claims, 1988; contbr. articles to profl. jours. Fellow Royal Australian Coll. and New Zealand Coll. Psychiatrists; mem. Australian Med. Assn., Internat. Assn. Study of Pain, Internat. Acad. Law Mental Health, Australian Neurosci. Soc., Australian Pain Soc. (pres. 1987—). Office: 7/30 Queens Rd, 3004 Melbourne Victoria Australia

MENDELSON, LEONARD (MELVIN), lawyer; b. Pitts., May 20, 1923; s. Jacob I. and Anna R. M.; m. Emily Solomon, Dec. 2, 1956; children: Ann, James R., Kathy S. AB, U. Mich., 1947; JD, Yale U., 1950. Bar: Pa. 1951, U.S. Supreme Ct. 1955. Mem., Hollinshead and Mendelson, Pitts., chmn. bd., 1974—; chmn. Lawyer-Realty Joint Com., Pitts., 1971-72. Mem. Pitts. Bd. Pub. Edn., 1975-76. Mem. ABA, Pa. Bar Assn., Allegheny County Bar Assn. Office: 230 Grant Bldg Pittsburgh PA 15219

MENDENHALL, CARROL CLAY, physician, surgeon; b. Missouri Valley, Iowa, July 26, 1916; s. Clay and Maude (Watts) M.; student U. So. Calif., 1942-44, Chapman Coll., 1946-47, Los Angeles City Coll., 1947-48; D.O., Coll. Osteo. Physicians and Surgeons, 1952; M.D., Calif. Coll. Medicine, 1962; m. Lucille Yvonne Bonvouloir, June 14, 1946 (div. July 1957); 1 son, Gregory Bruce; m. 2d, Barbara Marilyn Huggett-Davis, Sept. 28, 1974. Intern, Los Angeles County Osteo. Hosp., 1952-53; gen. practice medicine, 1953-82, specializing in weight control, Gardena, Calif., 1961-74, specializing in stress disorders and psychosomatic medicine, Ft. Worth, 1974-78, specializing in integral medicine and surgery, Santa Clara, Calif., 1978—; med. dir. Green's Pharms., Long Beach, Calif., 1956-64; v.p. Internat. Pharm. Mfg. Co., Inc., San Pedro, Calif., 1965-66; pres. Chemico of Gardena, Inc., 1964-69; staff Gardena Hosp.; active staff O'Connor Hosp., San Jose, Calif., 1979—; tchr., lectr. biofeedback, prevention and treatment of stress, creative thought; founder, dir. Eclectic Weight Control Workshop, 1971-74, Longevity Learning, Longevity Learning Seminars, 1980; past mem. adv. bd. dirs. Los Angeles Nat. Bank. Cadre med. dir. Gardena Civil Def., 1953-54, asst. to chief med. dir., 1954-60, chief med. and first aid services, 1960-64. Served as pharmacist's mate USNR, 1944-46. Fellow Royal Soc. Health, Am. Acad. Med. Preventics, Am. Acad. Homeopathic Medicine; mem. Calif. Med. Assn., Santa Clara County Med. Soc., Acupuncture Research Inst. (also alumni assn.), Los Aficionados de Los Angeles (pres. 1964-66), Am. Soc. Clin. Hypnosis. Flamenco Soc. No. Calif. (bd. dirs. 1986—). Republican. Address: 255 Crestview Dr Santa Clara CA 95050

MENDEZ, CELESTINO GALO, mathematics educator; b. Havana, Cuba, Oct. 16, 1944; s. Celestino Andres and Georgina (Fernandez) M.; came to U.S., 1962, naturalized, 1970; B.A., Benedictine Coll., 1965; M.A., U. Colo., 1968, Ph.D., 1974, M.B.A., 1979; m. Mary Ann Koplau, Aug. 21, 1971; children—Mark Michael, Matthew Maximilian. Asst. prof. math. scis. Met. State Coll., Denver, 1971-77, assoc. prof., 1977-82, prof., 1982—, chmn. dept. math. scis., 1980-82. Mem. advt. rev. bd. Met. Denver, 1973-79; parish outreach rep. S.E. deanery, Denver Cath. Community Services, 1976-78; mem. social ministries com. St. Thomas More Cath. Ch., Denver, 1976-78, vice chmn., 1977-78, mem. parish council, 1977-78; del. Adams County Republican Conv., 1972, 74, Colo. 4th Congl. Dist. Conv., 1974, Colo. Rep. Conv., 1982; alt. del. Colo. Rep. Conv., 1974, 76, 5th Congl. dist. conv., 1976; del. Douglas County Rep. Conv., 1976, 78, 80, 82, mem. rules com., 1978, 80, precinct committeeman Douglas County Rep. Com., 1976-78, mem. central com., 1976-78; bd. dirs. Rocky Mountain Better Bus. Bur., 1975-79, Rowley Downs Homeowners Assn., 1976-78; mem. exec. bd., v.p. Assoc. Faculties of State Inst. Higher Edn. in Colo., 1971-73; trustee Hispanic U. Am., 1975-78; councilman Town of Parker (Colo.), 1981-84, chmn. budget and fin. com. 1981-84; chmn. joint budget com. Town of Parker-Parker Water and Sanitation Dist. Bds., 1982-84. Recipient U. Colo. Grad. Sch. excellence in teaching award, 1965-67; Benedictine Coll. grantee, 1964-65. Mem. Math. Assn. Am., Am. Math. Soc., Nat. Council Tchrs. of Math., Colo. Council Tchrs. of Math., Colo. Internat. Edn. Assn., Asso. Faculties of State Insts. Higher Edn. in Colo. (v.p. 1971-73). Republican. Roman Catholic. Contbr. articles to profl. jours. and newspapers. Home: 11482 S Regency Pl Parker CO 80134 Office: 1006 11th St Denver CO 80204

MENDEZ, JOHN FRANK, horticulture company executive, accountant; b. Eureka, Nev., Sept. 12, 1942; s. John George and Neva June (Tognoni) M.; m. Edith Holmes Prentice, Jan. 29, 1966 (div. Dec. 1985); children: Damon, Derek. BA, Golden Gate U., 1968; MBA, Harvard U., 1970. CPA, Calif. V.p. Amfac Distbn., Burlingame, Calif., 1977-78; controller Amfac Electric Supply, Burlingame, 1979-80; asst. v.p. Amfac, Inc., San Francisco, 1980-82; pres. Amfac Garden Products, Burlingame, 1982-83; exec. v.p. Amfac Horticultural, Burlingame, 1983-84; pres. Tri-West, Inc., San Mateo, Calif., 1984—, also chmn. bd. dirs.; instr. Golden Gate U. MBA program, San Francisco, 1972-74. Commr. Am. Youth Soccer, Millbrae, Calif., 1981-85, Millbrae Youth Baseball, 1982. Served with U.S. Army, 1960-63. Mem. Am. Inst. CPA's, Calif. Soc. CPA's. Republican. Office: Tri-West Inc 1875 S Grant Ave Suite 520 San Mateo CA 94402

MENDEZ-EICHELMANN, FORTUNATO FRANCISCO, educational administrator, educator; b. Ciudad Valles, Mex., June 4, 1958; s. Fortunato Mendez-Jimenez and Elsa Lilia Eichelmann de Mendez. B.S., Monterrey Inst. Tech., Mex., 1980, Mencion Honorifica, 1980; M.B.A., Ind. U., 1983; cert. Am. U., Washington, 1981. Instr. (part-time) Monterrey Inst. Tech., 1979-81; investment analyst VISA Packaging Div., Monterrey, 1980-81; dir. Sch. of Bus. Adminstrn. Monterrey Inst. Tech., Tampico, Mex., 1984-87, dir. Sch. Engring. Monterrey Inst. of Tech., Tampico, 1984—, dir. Sci. Dept., 1987—, prof., 1984—; cons. Rayon Plant, CYDSA, Monterrey, Mex., 1980; systems analyst consumer electronics div. RCA, Bloomington, Ind., 1983. Mem. Monterrey Inst. Tech. Alumni Assn. in Tampico (sec. 1984-85), Ind. U. Alumni Assn., MBA Assn. Ind. U. Roman Catholic. Avocations: computer programming; karate; jogging. Home: Puebla 304, Col Guadalupe, 89120 Tampico Tamaulipas Mexico Office: Apdo Postal 58-Suc A, Cuidad Madero, 89120 Tamaulipas Mexico

MENDIS, D(EVAMITTA) ASOKA, physicist, educator; b. Colombo, Sri Lanka, Feb. 13, 1936; came to U.S., 1969; naturalized, 1980; s. Dixon Ashley and Leila Felicia (de Zoysa) M.; m. Janine Peters, May 30, 1975. B.Sc., U. Ceylon, 1960; Ph.D., U. Manchester, Eng., 1967, D.Sc., 1978. Lectr. U. Ceylon, Colombo, 1967-69; asst. research physicist U. Calif.-San Diego, 1969-75, assoc. research physicist, 1975-78, research physicist, 1978-86, prof., 1986—. Contbr. articles to profl. jours. Fellow Royal Astron. Soc. London; mem. Am. Astron. Soc., Am. Geophys. Union, Internat. Astron. Union, Com. Space Research, Internat. Acad. Astronautics. Current work: Solar system physics; cometary physics; physics of dusty plasmas; interstellar medium. Subspecialties: Solar physics; Cometary physics.

MENDOZA, GABINO ALBERTO, business management educator, consultant; b. Manila, Apr. 8, 1931; s. Gabino L. and Estela (Alberto) M.; m. Manolita Magsino, Sept. 20, 1956; children: Gabino Jr., Emmanuel, Jose Maria, Carlo, Juan Miguel, Maria Regina, Stela Maria, Sylvia Maria. BA, Ateneo Manila, 1953; MBA with distinction, Harvard U., 1966. Head tech., adminstrv. cons. Philippine Investment Mgmt. Cons. Inc., Makati, Philippines, 1956-64; asst. prof. Ateneo Grad. Sch. Bus., Makati, 1966-68; pres., dean, disting. prof. bus. mgmt. Asian Inst. Mgmt., Makati, 1968-86; chmn., founder S.E. Asian Grad. Sch. Bus.; mem. exec. com. Interman Steering Com., Geneva; cons. Asian Cons. Tng. Group Corp.; chmn. community bd. Exec. Suite Inc.; chmn. bd. dirs. Allied Metals Inc.; bd. dirs. Philippine Investment Mgmt. Cons. Inc., Manila. Columnist World Exec.'s Digest, 1965—. Fellow Internat. Acad. Mgmt., Eisenhower Fellowships Inc. Home: 52 Barcelona St, Merville Sub, Paranaque Metro Manila, Philippines Office: Asian Inst Mgmt, 123 Paseo de Roxas, Makati Manila Philippines

MENDOZA, HUGO RAFAEL, pediatrician, educator; b. La Vega, Dominican Republic, Aug. 7, 1930; s. Jorge and Lidia (Tapia) M.; M.D., U. Santo Domingo, 1955; m. Rosaleda Valdes, July 20, 1963; children—Hugo, Samuel, Juan, Lynette, Rosangela. Resident in pediatrics Santo Domingo (Dominican Republic) Children's Hosp., 1955-57, Elmhurst (N.Y.) City Hosp., 1960-62; fellow in child psy- endocrinology San Carlos Hosp., Madrid, Spain, 1957-58, in pediatrics Guy's Hosp., London, 1958; pediatrician in charge of neuropsychiatry service Santo Domingo Children Hosp.,

1962-68, dir. hosp., 1968-86; dir. Nat. Ctr. for Research on Mother and Child Health, 1986—; prof. pediatrics U. Santo Domingo, 1969—. Diplomate Am. Bd. Pediatrics, Dominican Bd. Pediatrics. Mem. Dominican Med. Assn., Dominican Pediatric Assn., Am. Acad. Pediatrics, Am. Acad. Scis., Dominican Acad. Scis. Roman Catholic. Club: Naco Sport. Author: Manual para Internos y Residentes en Pediatria, 1975, 76, 79; La Cara en el diagnóstico Pediatrico, 1976; Normas de Atencion Pediatrica, 1980, 3d rev. edit., 1986; contbr. numerous articles in field to profl. jours. Home: 3 El Vergel, Santo Domingo Dominican Republic Office: 30 Dr Delgado, Santo Domingo Dominican Republic

MENENDEZ DEL VALLE, EMILIO, ambassador; b. Madrid, June 20, 1945; m. Marisa Gonzalez Mostoles, Apr. 25, 1981; children: Irene, Alejandra. MA in Law, Madrid U., 1961; postgrad., Columbia U., 1973-75. Ambassador to Italy Rome. Socialist. Office: Embassy of Spain, Palazzo Borghese, Largo Fontanella Borghese 19, 00186 Rome Italy

MENEZES, CORNELIUS ANTONIUS, electrical engineer, educator; b. Poona, India, Aug. 22, 1938; came to U.S., 1972.; s. Cajetan Francisco and Muriel (D'Souza) M. BS with honors, Poona U., 1961, MS, 1962, PhD, 1966. Cert. profl. electrical engr. Research scientist Nat. Chem. Lab., Poona, 1966-72; research assoc. Stanford U., 1972-74; research assoc. Estudios Avanzados del I.P.N., Mexico City, 1976-79, prof., 1979—; co-dir. research program NSF-CONACYT, Stanford-CINVESTAV, 1979-86; vis. scholar Dept. Material Sci. Stanford U., 1980—; invited scientist INRS U. Quebec, Can., 1986-87. Contbr. numerous articles to profl. jours. Mem. IEEE, Jaycees (exec. mem. Poona 1971). Home: Moliere 340 Al, Col Polanco, 11560 Mexico City Mexico Office: Ctr Investigación y Estudios, Avanzados del IPN, Depto Fisica Apdo Postal 14-740, 07000 Mexico City Mexico

MENG, WANG, writer; b. Beijing, People's Republic of China, Oct. 15, 1934; s. Jindi and Min (Tong) W.; m. Ruifang Cui, Jan. 28, 1957; children: Shan, Shi, Yihuan. Ed., Ping Mine Schs. Sec. Communist Youth League, Beijing, 1949-62; tchr. Beijing Tchrs. Coll., 1961-63; farmer, free-lance editor, Xinjiang, 1963-78; writer, Writer's Assn. Beijing, 1978-83; editor-in-chief People's Lit. Monthly, Beijing, 1983-85; vice-chmn. China Writer's Assn., 1985—; minister of Culture People's Republic of China, 1986—. Author: Forever Youth, 1979, The Metamorphosis of Human Nature, Butterfly, The Canadian Moon, Selected Works of Wang Meng (1-4 vols.). Recipient Best Short Stories award Literary Works Awards Com., 1978, 80, 81; No. 1, No. 2 Best Novelettes awards, 1981-82; No. 3 All China Best Reportage awards, 1984-85; Prize for Lit. Italian Montello Internat. Fest. Vice chmn. China P.E.N. Ctr., 1982—. Mem. cen. com. Chinese Communist Party. Avocations: swimming, drinking. Office: Ministry of Culture, Shatan Beijie, Beijing People's Republic of China

MENGISTU HAILE MARIAM (MENGISTU HAILE MARIAM), head of state Ethiopia; b. 1937; ed. Holeta Mil. Acad.; m. Ubanchi Bishaw; 5 children. Commd. officer Ethiopian Army, advanced through grades to maj.; mem. Armed Forces Coordinating Com. (Derg), 1974—; took leading part in overthrow of Emperor Haile Sellassie, 1974; head Derg Exec. Com., 1974; 1st vice chmn. Provisional Mil. Adminstrv. Council, 1974-77, chmn., 1977—; pres. Council of Ministers, 1976—; sec. gen. Workers' Party Ethiopia, 1984—. Office: Office of Chmn Provisional Mil, Adminstrv Council, Addis Ababa Ethiopia *

MENON, MAMBILLIKALATHIL GOVIND KUMAR, physicist; b. Mangalore, Aug. 28, 1928; s. Kizhekepat Sankara and Mambillikalathil Narayaniamma M.; m. Indumati Patel, 1955; 2 children. Ed. Jaswant Coll., Jodhpur, India, Royal Inst. Sci., Bombay, India, U. Bristol (Eng.); M.Sc., Ph.D., D.Sc. (hon.), U. Jodhpur, U. Delhi, Sardar Patel, U. Roorkee, Banaras Hindu U., Jadavpur U., Sri. Venkateswara U., Allahabad U., Andhra U., Utkal U. and Aligarh Muslim U., Indian Inst. Tech., Madras, hon. D of Eng. Stevens Inst. Tech. Dir. Tata Inst. Fundamental Research, Bombay, 1966-75; chmn. Electronics Commn. and sec. to Govt. India Dept. Electronics, 1971-78; sci. adviser to Minister of Def., dir.-gen. Def. Research and Devel. Orgn., and sec. for def. research, 1974-78; dir.-gen. Council Sci. and Indsl. Research, 1978-81; sec. Dept. Environ., 1980-81; chmn. Commn. for Additional Sources Energy, 1981-82; chmn. sci. adv. com. to Indian Cabinet, 1982-85; sec. Dept. of Sci. and Tech., 1978-82; mem. Govt. Planning Commn., 1982—; scientific adv. to Prime Minister, 1986—. Recipient Sr. award Royal Commn. for Exhibition of 1851, 1953-55, Shanti Swarup Bhatnagar award for phys. Scis. Council Sci. and Indsl. Research, 1960, Repub. Day (nat.) awards Govt. India; Padma Shri, 1961; Padma Bhushan, 1968; Padma Vibhusham, 1985; Khaitan medal Royal Asiatic Soc., 1973, numerous other awards. Hon. fellow Nat. Acad. Scis. India, Inst. Electronics and Telecommunications Engring. India; mem. Am. Acad. Scis., Pontificial Acad. of Scis., USSR Acad. of Scis. (hon.), IEEE (hon.) Indian Union Pure and Applied Physics (chmn. cosmic ray commn. 1973-75, v.p. 1981-84), Indian Nat. Sci. Acad. (pres. 1981-82), Asia Electronics Union (pres. 1973-75), Indian Sci. Congress Assn. (pres. 1981-82). Office: Planning Commn Parliament St, Yojana Bhavan Room 125, New Delhi 110001 India Address: 81 Lodi Estate, New Delhi 110003 India

MENON, RAJAN GOPAL, oil company executive, management consultant; b. Ottapalam, Kerala, India, May 10, 1927; s. Mullasseri Gopal Menon and Sree Devi Amma; m. Ambaadi Shantha Rajan, June 6, 1960; children—Rita, Gita. D.Com., Bus. Mgmt., 1948; B.A., Kerala Varma Coll., 1950; Cert. in Statis. Quality Control, UN and Govt. India, 1952; cert. in systems analysis and Cobol programming. Chief acct. Rawal Rubber works Ltd., Bombay, India, 1952; cost and fin. acct. Solar Batteries & Flashlights Ltd., Bombay, 1952; paymaster Stanvac Refining Co. Ltd., Bombay, 1953-61; budget exec. Esso Standard Eastern Inc., Bombay, 1962-64; advisor econs. and mktg. strategies Exxon, India, 1965-76; chief acct. Nat. Contracting Co./Rezayat Co., Ltd., Alkhobar, Saudi Arabia, 1977—; gen. sec. founder Mgmt. Staff Assn., Bombay, 1970-73, v.p., 1974-75. Gen. sec. PTA, Bombay, 1973-76; sec., founder Co-op Housing Soc., Bombay, 1969-72. Mem. Assn. Cost and Works Accts Australia. Hindu. Club: Fine Arts Satkala Sangam (sec. 1975-76) (Bombay). Avocation: reading. Home: 1920 Ritz Apts Chembur, Bombay 400071, India

MENOTTI, GIAN CARLO, composer; b. Cadegliano, Italy, July 7, 1911; came to U.S., 1928; s. Alfonso and Ines (Pellini) M. Grad. in composition, Curtis Inst. Music, 1933, Mus.B. (hon.), 1945. Tchr. Curtis Inst. Music, 1941-45. Writer chamber music, songs and operas; composer: operas Amelia Goes to the Ball, 1936, The Old Maid and the Thief, The Island God, 1942; ballet Sebastian, 1943; opera The Telephone, 1947; orch. Concerto in A Minor for Piano and Orch, 1945; opera The Medium, 1946, The Consul, 1950; ballet Errand into the Maze, 1947; orch. Apocalypse, 1951; opera Amahl and the Night Visitors, 1951, The Saint of Bleecker Street; ballet The Unicorn, The Gorgon and The Manticore, 1956; opera Maria Golovin, 1958, The Last Savage, 1963; cantata The Death of the Bishop of Brindisi, 1963; TV opera Labyrinth, 1963; ch. opera Martin's Lie, 1964; song cycle Canti della Lontananza, 1967; opera Help, Help, the Globolinks, 1968; drama The Leper, 1970; symphonic piece Triplo Concerto atre, 1970; opera The Most Important Man in the World, 1971, Arrival, 1973, Tamu-Tamu, 1973, The Mad Woman, 1979; writer own libretti.; (Pulitzer prize for music 1954); Founder: Festival of Two Worlds, Spoleto, Italy, 1958; composer, artistic dir. Spoleto Festival USA, Charleston, S.C., 1988. Recipient Guggenheim award, 1946, 47, Pulitzer prize, 1950; N.Y. Drama Critics Circle award, 1954, Kennedy Ctr. award, 1984, N.Y.C. Mayor's Liberty award, 1986. Mem. ASCAP. Office: care Thea Dispeker Artists Rep 59 E 54th St New York NY 10022 *

MENSES, JAN, painter, draftsman, etcher, lithographer; b. Rotterdam, Netherlands, Apr. 28, 1933; emigrated to Can., 1960, naturalized, 1965; s. Jan and Elisabeth Wilhelmina (Schwarz) M.; m. Rachel Régine Kadoch, Dec. 7, 1958; children: Salomon, Hnina Sarah, Nechamah Elisabeth Halo. Student, Acad. Fine Arts, Rotterdam, Officers Acad. Royal Dutch Air Force, 1953-55. lectr. in fine arts Concordia U., Montreal, Que., 1973-76. One-man shows include Montreal Mus. Fine Arts, 1961, 65, 76, Isaacs Gallery, Toronto, Ont., Can., 1964, Delta Gallery, Rotterdam, 1965, Galerie Godard Lefort, Montreal, 1966, Gallery Moos, Toronto, 1967, Rotterdam Art Found., 1974, Galerie Mira Godard, Toronto, 1977, Montreal, 1978, Seasons Galleries, The Hague, 1980, U. B.C. Fine Arts Gallery, Vancouver, 1981, Galerie Don Stewart, Montreal, 1981, Mead Art Mus., Amherst, Mass., 1983, Agnes Etherington Art Mus., 1984, Blom and Dorn Gallery, N.Y.C., 1985, Marywood Coll. Mus., Scranton, Pa., 1985, Blom & Dorn Gallery, N.Y.C., 1986, 87, 88, Saraya-Wolfson Ctr., Safed, Israel, 1987, Mayanot Gallery, Jerusalem, 1987-88, Esperanza Gallery, Montreal, 1988; numerous group shows latest including, Montreal World Exhbn., 1967, Salon Internat. Art, Basle, Switzerland, 1972, 74, Canadian Nat. Exhbn., 1972, Centennial Exhbn., Royal Can. Acad., Toronto, 1980, Que. Biennale I, II, III, Montreal, 1977, 79, 81, Foire Internat. D'Art Contemporain Paris and Internat. Fair Koln Germany, 1986; represented in numerous permanent collections, including, Museo Ciani di Villa Caccia, Lugano, Switzerland, Museum Modern Art, N.Y.C., Phila. Mus. Art, Solomon R. Guggenheim Mus., N.Y.C., Yivo Inst., N.Y.C., Bklyn. Mus., Art Inst. Chgo., Cleve. Mus. Art, Detroit Inst. Arts, Yale U., U. Montreal, Queens U., Kingston, Mead Art Mus., Amherst Coll., Jonathan Edwards Coll., New Haven, Victoria & Albert Mus., London, Vatican Mus., Rome, Quebec Art Bank, Concordia U., Montreal, Haifa Mus. Modern Art, Hebrew U., Jerusalem, Govt. of Que., Yad Vashem Holocaust Meml., Jerusalem, Museum Boymans-van Beuningen, Rotterdam, Stedelijk Mus., Amsterdam, Rijksmuseum, Amsterdam, Nat. Gallery Can., Ottawa, Gallery Stratford, Montreal Mus. Fine Arts, Musée d'Art Contemporain, Montreal, Que. Provincial Mus., Art Bank of the Canada Council, Ottawa, Ariz. State Mus., Tucson, others; paintings include Klippoth Series, 1963-78, Kaddish Series, 1964-80, Hechaloth Series, 1973—, Tikkun Series, 1978—; mural for, Montreal Holocaust Meml. Center. Served with Royal Dutch Air Force Res., 1953-55. Recipient 5 1st prizes Nat. Art Exhbn., Quebec, Que., 1960-65; Grand prize Concours Artistiques de la Province de Que., 1965; prize X and XI Winnipeg (Man., Can.) Shows, 1966, 68; prize IX Internat. Exhbn. Drawings and Prints, Lugano, 1966; prize Ofcl. Centennial Art Competition, Toronto; 1st prize Hadassah, 1969, 71, 82; Recipient Imago award U. Montreal, 1971; award Reeves of Can., 1969; Tigert award Ont. Soc. Arts, 1970; Loomis and Toles award, 1972; J. I. Segal award J. I. Segal Fund Jewish Culture, 1975; Gold medal Accademia Italia Delle Arte, Italy, 1980; Gold medal Internat. Parliament U.S.A., 1982; Gran Premio delle Nazioni, Italy, 1983, European Banner of Arts with Gold medal, 1984, Oscar d' Italia, 1985, 1st prize III Que. Biennale, 1981, OSA award of merit, Toronto, 1981, 82; World Culture prize Italy, 1984; Golden Flame of World Parliament (U.S.A.) award, 1986; numerous others; Can. Council sr. arts fellow, 1969-70, 71-72, 81-82; grantee, 1966-67, 67-68; travel grantee, 1968, 73. Mem. Royal Canadian Acad. Arts, Société des Artistes en Arts Visuels du Qué., Accademia Italia Dêlle Arte e Del Lavoro., Accademia delle Nazioni, Maestro Accademico-Accademia Bedriacense, Italy, Jewish Am. Acad. Arts and Scis., L'Accademia D'Europa. Jewish. Office: care Blom & Dorn Gallery 164 Mercer St New York NY 10012

MENTING YOELL, PETER, lawyer; b. N.Y.C., Sept. 19, 1944; s. Roland Francis and Elizabeth (Woodcock) Yoell; m. Sandra Kathleen Gomez, May 31, 1969 (div. Mar. 1977); 1 child, Kirsten Margaret; m. Anna Carla Pillisio, Feb. 29, 1980; children: Michela Tay, Troy Peter, Claudia Robin Marie. BA in Polit. Sci., George Washington U., 1967, JD, 1972; LLM, Univ. Coll., London, 1974. Atty., advisor U.S. Environ. Protection Agy., Washington, 1972-73; sole practice Hamburg, Fed. Republic of Germany, 1974-80; gen. counsel Bomin Oil Co. Ltd., Bochum, Fed. Republic of Germany, 1980-82; sr. legal advisor Kuwait Petroleum Corp., 1982-85; gen. counsel Petrotrade, Inc., Geneva, 1985—. Mem. Reps. Abroad, Kuwait, 1983-85, U.S. Busimen's Council, Kuwait, 1985. Served with U.S. Army, 1968-69. Mem. Internat. Bar Assn., Washington Bar Assn. Roman Catholic. Clubs: New Tennis Sporting, Am. Internat. (Geneva). Office: Petrotrade Inc, care IMS Co Ltd, 5 Quai Dy Mont Blanc, 1211 Geneva Switzerland

MENTZ, PHILIP SHERWOOD, plastics company executive; b. New Orleans, May 19, 1930; s. Philip Sherwood and Juliette Jeromine (Shall) M.; m. Margaret Ann Moore, Feb. 16, 1952; children—Philip S., Anne V., Valerie J., Laura J. B.S. in Indsl. Engring., U. Ala., 1951; M.S. in Indsl. Engring., Purdue U., 1955; M.B.A., La. State U., 1962. Registered profl. engr., Ala., Calif. Cert. purchasing mgr. Engr. Sandia Corp., Albuquerque, 1951-53; engring. instr. Purdue U., Lafayette, Ind., 1953-55; tech. service engr. Ethyl Corp., Baton Rouge, 1955-63; mgr. indsl. engring. Kaiser Aluminum, Oakland, Calif., 1963-74; dir. purchasing United Fruit Co., N.Y.C., 1974-86; corp. purchasing mgr. Uniroyal Plastics Co., Mishawaka Ind., 1986—. Chmn. lay adv. bd. St. Agnes Roman Catholic Ch., Greenwich (Conn.), 1982-84. Mem. N.Y. Acad. Scis., Am. Inst. Chem. Engrs., Inst. Indsl. Engrs., Nat. Assn. Purchasing Mgmt. Republican. Club: Knollwood Country. Avocations: flying; model building. Home: 51167 Huntington Ln Granger IN 46530 Office: Uniroyal Plastics Co 312 N Hill St Mishawaka IN 46544

MENTZONI, DOUGLAS KARL LENNART, marketing professional; b. Lysekil, Sweden, Mar. 26, 1939; s. Thorstein and Ebba (Holmgren) M.; m. Gun Sällström; 1 child, Helene. Degree in machine engring., Högre Teknist Lèroverk, Norrköping, 1961; degree in fin., Hermods, Malmö, 1962. Tech. advisor SKF, Gothenburg, Sweden, 1962-67, internat. sales, 1970-75, internat. trader, 1981—; sales mgr. SKF, Stockholm, 1968-70; worldwide mktg. mgr. Couplings SA, Brussels, 1976-80. Served to lt. Swedish Air. Def. Home: Cedergatan 15, 421 74 Gothenburg Sweden Office: SKF, Hornsgatan 1, 415 50 Gothenburg Sweden

MENUHIN, YEHUDI, violinist; b. N.Y.C., Apr. 22, 1916; s. Moshe and Marutha M.; m. Nola Ruby Nicholas, May 26, 1938; children: Zamira, Krov; m. Diana Gould, Oct. 19, 1947; children: Gerard, Jeremy. Educated by pvt. tutors; studied music under, Sigmund Anker, Louis Persinger, San Francisco, Georges Enesco, Rumania and Paris, Adolph Busch, Switzerland; MusD (hon.), U. Oxford, 1962, Queen's U., Belfast, 1965, U. Leicester, 1965; LLD (hon.), U. St. Andrews, 1963, U. Liverpool, 1963, U. Sussex, 1966, U. Bath, 1969; LittD (hon.), U. Warwick, 1968; MusD (hon.), U. London, 1969, U. Cambridge, 1970. Established Yehudi Menuhin Sch. at Stoke D'Abernon, Eng.; pres. Internat. Music Council of UNESCO, Folkestone Menuhin Internat. Violin Competition. Completed his first round-the-world concert tour, 1935; appearing in 110 concert engagements; has toured in Latin Am., S.Am., Australia, South Africa and Pacific Islands; played 22 concerts during 12 day tour in Israel; filmed series of complete concert programs; opened Japan to world concert artists, 1951, concert tours in India, 1952, 54, also charity concerts various instns.; has own yearly summer festival in Gstaad, Switzerland, 1957—; debut as condr. symphony orch. in Am. with Am. Symphony Orch., Carnegie Hall, 1966, dir., Bath Festival, Eng., 1958-68, Bath Festival Orch. (now the Menuhin Festival Orch.); presented his first festival at Windsor, 1969; held over 500 concerts for armed forces, Red Cross, others; followed U.S. Army into, France and Belgium, first artist to play in liberated Paris, Brussels, Bucharest, Budapest and Antwerp, also first in Moscow after cessation of hostilities; author: The Violin: Six Lessons by Yehudi Menuhin, 1971, Theme and Variations, 1972, The Violin and Viola, 1976, The King, the Cut, and the Fiddle, 1983, Life Class, 1986; autobiography Unfinished Journey, 1977; co-author: autobiography The Music of Man, 1979. Decorated officer Legion of Honor; chevalier de L'Ordre des Arts et des Lettres France; Order of Leopold Belgium; Ordre de la Couronne Belgium; Order of Merit West German Republic; hon. knight comdr. Order Brit. Empire Gt. Britain; Royal Order Phoenix Greece; Recipient Jawaharlal Nehru award for Internat. Understanding India, 1968, Mendelssohn prize, 1986, 10 Grammy awards, Golden Viotti prize, 1987. Fellow World Acad. Art and Sci.; mem. and/or officer numerous U.S., fgn. orgns. Office: care Columbia Artists Mgmt Inc Cami Bldg 165 W 57th St New York NY 10019 Address: care Anglo Swiss Artists Mgmt, 4 and 5 Primrose Mews, Regents Park Rd, London NW1 8YL, England *

MENZIES, JEAN STORKE, retired newspaperwoman; b. Santa Barbara, Calif., Dec. 30, 1904; d. Thomas More and Elsie (Smith) Storke; B.A., Vassar Coll., 1927; M.A. in Physics, Stanford, 1931; m. Ernest F. Menzies, Oct. 20, 1937; children—Jean Storke (Mrs. Dennis Wayne Vaughan), Thomas More. Teaching asst. dept. physics Stanford, 1927-29; instr. of physics Vassar Coll., 1929-30; tchr. math., chemistry, gen. sci. Sarah Dix Hamlin Sch., San Francisco, 1931-34; sec. to Dr. Samuel T. Orton, N.Y.C., 1935-36; press reporter, spl. writer Santa Barbara News-Press, 1954-63. Vol. rec. sec. nat. YWCA, India, Burma and Ceylon, 1941-42; rec. sec., Calcutta YWCA, 1942-47, v.p., 1949-51; sec. Tri-County adv. council Children's Home Soc., Santa Barbara, 1952-54; founding dir., sec. corp. Santa Barbara Film Soc., Inc., 1960-66. Bd. dirs. Santa Barbara County chpt. Am. Assn. UN, 1954-59, Friends U. Calif. at Santa Barbara Library, 1970-74, Small Wilderness Area Preservation, 1971-79; sec. bd. trustees Crane Country Day Sch., 1955-57; trustee Mental Hygiene Clinic of Santa Barbara, 1956-60, U. Calif. Santa Barbara Found., 1974-80, Santa Barbara Mus. Natural History, 1977-81; adv. council Santa Barbara Citizens Adult Edn., 1958-62, v.p., 1960-62; bd. dirs. Internat. Social Sci. Inst., sec., 1963-68, mem. adv. bd., 1969; bd. dirs. Planned Parenthood Santa Barbara County, Inc., 1964-65, adv. council, 1966-67; trustee Santa Barbara Botanic Garden, 1967-81, hon. trustee, 1981—; trustee. Santa Barbara Trust for Historic Preservation, 1967-68, 72-77; mem. affiliates bd. dirs. U. Calif. at Santa Barbara, 1960-61, 67-70, 72-77; sec. Santa Barbara Mission Archive-Library, 1967—; mem. Santa Barbara Found., 1977-81. Mem. Santa Barbara Hist. Soc. (dir. 1957-62, founding mem. women's projects com. 1959-63, sec. 1961-62), Channel City Women's Forum (v.p. 1969-73, bd. dirs. 1973-87), Phi Beta Kappa, Sigma Xi. Club: Vassar of Santa Barbara and the Tri-Counties (1st v.p., founding com. 1956-57, 2d v.p. 1959-61, chmn. publicity com. 1961-73). Home: 2298 Featherhill Rd Santa Barbara CA 93108

MENZIES, THOMAS NEAL, art consultant, art critic; b. Long Beach, Calif., Mar. 1, 1945; s. Thomas Warren and Frances (Starks) M. BA, U. Calif., Irvine, 1972. Library dir. Parsons Sch. Design, Los Angeles, 1980-82; art coordinator Hirsch/Bedner & Assocs., Santa Monica, Calif., 1982-84; pres. Neal Menzies Contemporary Art Inc., Los Angeles, 1984—. Contbg. editor ARTWEEK mag., Oakland, Calif., 1979-83. Founder Mus. Contemporary Art, Los Angeles; docent Venice (Calif.) Art Walk. Mem. So. Calif. Art Writers Assn., Los Angeles Contemporary Exhibitions (friend), Los Angeles County Mus. Art.

MEOKO, CORNELIS, trading company executive; b. Makassar, Indonesia, Sept. 3, 1932; s. Landangi and Weniyeti (Palandouw) M.; B.A., Banking Acad. Jakarta (Indonesia), 1957; m. Ho Miu Chun, Mar. 10, 1968; children—Regina, Alexander. Officer, Bank Negara Indonesia, Banjarmasin, 1957-60, asst. mgr., Chirebon, 1960-62, mgr., Gorontalo, 1962-64, dep. gen. mgr. Hong Kong br., 1964-68; exec. dir. Tunas (H.K.) Ltd., Hong Kong, 1968—; gen. mgr. Tunas Tour and Travel. Christian. Clubs: Indonesian, Six Continents. Home: 20 Belleview Dr 2nd Floor, Repulse Bay Hong Kong Office: 802 Kai Tak Comml Bldg, 317 Des Voeux Rd Central, Hong Kong Hong Kong

MERA, KOICHI, economist, educator; b. Keijo, Japan, Oct. 13, 1933; s. Kazuomi and Ayaha Mera; B.S. in Engring., U. Tokyo, 1957, M.S., 1959; Ph.D., Harvard U., 1965; m. Masako Mitsunaga, Sept. 3, 1960; children—Yuhka, Yumi, Eiki. Instr. econs. Harvard U., Cambridge, Mass., 1965-67, asst. prof. econs., 1967-70; economist World Bank, Washington, 1969-72; sr. economist Internat. Devel. Center of Japan, Tokyo, 1972-75; prof. socio-econ. planning U. Tsukuba, Japan, 1975-83; regional devel. adv. World Bank, 1982-86; prof. commerce Tokyo Internat. U.; cons. World Bank, UN, Govt. of Japan; v.p. Applied REgional Sci. Conf., 1988. Recipient Nikkei Outstanding Econs. Lit. award, 1976. Mem. Internat. Inst. Applied Systems Analysis (mem. adv. com. 1975—), Regional Sci. Assn., Am. Econs. Assn., Econometric Soc., Japan City Planning Assn., Japan Assn. Theoretical Economists, Japan Planning Adminstrn. Assn. Author: Income Distribution and Regional Development, 1975, Solutions for the Tokyo Problem, 1988; contbr. articles to profl. jours.; bd. editors Internat. Regional Sci. Rev., 1980—, Transp., 1972—, Man, Environment, Space and Time, 1981—, Planning and Adminstrn., 1981—. Home: 11-4 Seijo 4-chome, Setagaya-ku, Tokyo 157 Japan

MERCADAL VALLES, JAVIER, chemical engineer; b. Barcelona, Spain, May 11, 1954; s. Miguel Mercadal Ibarz and McRosa (Vales Ferrer); m. Rosalind M. Greehy, Sept. 5, 1983; 1 child, Ana. Chem. engring., Polytech., Barcelona, 1977. Registered chem. engr. Prodn. supr. Sider S.A., Barcelona, 1979, process and maintenance mgr., 1980; engring. mgr. Reckitt & Coluran S.A., Bilbao, Spain, 1981-82, quality control mgr., 1983-84; factory mgr. Paniker S.A., Barcelona, 1985; asst. to gen. mgr. Plasticol Del Cinca, Barcelona, 1986; gen. mgr. Airopak S.A., Barcelona, 1987—. Club: Royal Maritime. Office: Airopak SA, Consejo De Ciento 355, 08009 Barcelona Spain

MERCADO, MEDWIN ARIANO, physician; b. San Pablo City, Philippines, May 29, 1949; s. Jose Lejarzo Mercado and Eufrosina (Biglete) Ariano; m. Julieta Munsayac Talens; children: Jose Alfonso, Mariclaire, Juan Paolo. BS in Gen. Scis., U. St. Tomas, Manila, 1969, MD, U. St. Tomas, 1973. Diplomate Philippine Specialty Bd. Family Medicine. Intern Makati (Philippines) Med. Ctr., 1973-74; gen. practice medicine San Pablo City, 1975—; Cons. physician Kaunlaran Industries, 1975-79, St. Joseph Sch., 1980—, St. Peter's Coll. Seminary, 1981—, Philippine Long Distance Telephone Co., 1985-87, Coca-Cola Bottlers Philippines, 1986—, Health Maintenance Inc. San Pablo br., 1984—, San Pablo Drs. Hosp., 1981—, Community Hosp., 1981—. Fellow Philippine Acad. Family Physicians (sec. 1981—, mem. bd. examiners 1986—); mem. San Pablo City Med. Soc. Roman Catholic. Lodges: KC, Kiwanis. Home and Office: 141 Colago Ave, San Pablo City Laguna 4000, The Philippines

MERCADO, PETER NELSON, real estate executive; b. Bklyn., Oct. 9, 1947; s. Roy and Gloria Mercado; m. Anne M. Harrell, Mar. 1, 1974; 1 child, Alexander Peter. AA, Atlantic County Coll., Blackwood, N.J., 1971; BA, Stockton State Coll., Pomona, N.J., 1973; M in Pub. Adminstrn., Cen. Mich. U., 1975; cert. pub. mgr., Rutgers U., 1985. Lic. real estate broker, 1986. Asst. to v.p. for campus programs Stockton State Coll., Pomona, 1975-77, dir. student devel. and services, 1977-81, dean of students, 1981-85, asst. to pres., 1986; pres. Mercado Realty, Pleasantville, N.J., 1986—; Cons., mem. accrediting team Commn. of Higher Edn., New England States Assn., Middle States Assn., mem. legis. and comml. coms. Atlantic City and County Bd. Realtors; chmn. grant evaluating teams HEW; real estate cons. Price Enterprises, 1986, Delta IIne, 1986, Decadon, 1987. Treas. Atlantic County Task Force on Alcohol Abuse, Atlantic City, 1983-84; pres. Absecon (N.J.) City Council, 1985-86; bd. dirs. Atlantic County United Way, Atlantic County ARC, 1987-88, Inst. Human Devel., 1987-88; mem. exec. bd. United Ways of N.J. Served to cpl. USMC, 1967-69, Vietnam. Decorated Bronze Star, Purple Heart (2), D.S.M.; recipient Spl. Innovative Projects award N.J. Dept. Edn. 1975, Outstanding Service to Higher Edn. and Community award Am. Biog. Inst., 1988; named one of Outstanding Young Men of Am., U.S. Jaycees, 1977, 78, 79. Mem. Nat. Assn. Realtors, So. N.J. Tech. Consortium, So. N.J. Devel. Council, Nat. Assn. Student Personnel Adminstrs., Am. Personnel and Guidance Assn., DAV, Am. Legion, VFW. Home: 228 N Shore Rd Absecon NJ 08201 Office: Mercado Realty 236 Doughty Rd RD #3 Pleasantville NJ 08232

MERCER, JAMES LEE, management consultant; b. Sayre, Okla., Nov. 7, 1936; s. Fred Elmo and Ora Lee (Davidson) M.; B.S., U. Nev., 1964 M.B.A., 1966; cert. in mcpl. adminstrn. U. N.C., 1971; postgrad. exec. devel program Cornell U., 1979; m. Karolyn Lois Prince, Nov. 16, 1962; chil dren—Tara Lee, James Lee. Methods and results supr. Pacific Tel. & Tel. Sacramento, 1965-66; prodn. control supr. Gen. Dynamics, Pomona, Calif. 1966-67; nuclear submarine project mgr. Litton Industries, Pascagoula Miss., 1967-70; asst. city mgr. City of Raleigh (N.C.), 1970-73; nat. program dir. Pub. Tech., Inc., Washington, 1973-76; gen. mgr. Battelle So. Ops., Atlanta, 1976-79; v.p. Korn/Ferry Internat., Atlanta, 1979-81; pres. James Mercer & Assos. Inc., mgmt. cons., Atlanta, 1981-86; chief, Indsl. Ext. Div., Ga. Inst. of Tech., Atlanta, 1981-83; dir. govtl. cons. service Coopers & Lybrand, 1983-84; regional v.p. Wolfe & Assocs., Inc., 1984-86; pres., chmn. Mercer/Slavin Inc., 1986—; ad hoc prof. N.C. State U., 1972-73; dir. Taratec Corp.; chmn. Raleigh Mayor's Civic Center Authority Study Commn., 1971; founding bd. dirs. Mordecai Sq. Hist. Soc.; lectr., pub. spkr. Served with USN, 1955-59. Mem. Internat. City Mgmt. Assn., Nat. Mcpl. League; Am. Soc. Public Adminstrn., Am. Inst. Indsl. Engrs. (past pres.'s award 1970, pres. chpt. 1969-70), Tech. Transfer Soc. (dir. 1978-87,treas. 1985-86), Ga. Indsl. Devel. Assn.; U. Nev. Alumni Assn. (exec. com. 1969-79); founding mem., trustee U. Nev. Found., 1980—; founding mem. Calif. Poly. State U., (adv. council Coll. Bus. Adminstrn.) San Luis Obispo, 1980—; founding mem. U. So. Calif. Master of Pub. Adminstrn. adv. bd., 1987—. Active Atlanta C. of C. Republican. Clubs: Rotary, Masons, Shriners, Atlanta Commerce. Author: Public Management Systems, 1978; Public Technology, 1981; Managing Urban Government Services, 1981; current work strategic planning for local govts.; contbr. over 200 articles to profl. jours. Home: 1119 Aurora Ct Dunwoody GA 30338 Office: 3374 Hardee Ave Atlanta GA 30341

MERCER, JOHN BOYD, shipping company executive; b. Melbourne, Australia, Feb. 18, 1939; arrived in Singapore, 1978; s. Leslie Boyd and Joan (Richardson) M.; m. Alicia Ranoschy, Dec. 2, 1963; children: Suzanne, Tina, David Boyd. B of Commerce, U. Melbourne, 1961; diploma, Harvard Bus. Sch., 1978. Chief acct. Conmix Property Ltd., Melbourne, 1961-63, Hall Ham Concrete Ltd., London, 1963-65; sr. cons. Touche Ross and Ptnrs., Melbourne, 1965-67; fin. mgr. Buchan Laird & Buchan Ltd., Melbourne, 1967-69; asst. fin. controller The Australian Estates Ltd., Melbourne, 1969-71; group fin. mgr. TNT Shipping and Devel. Ltd., Sydney, Australia, 1971-78; resident dir. TNT South East Asia, Singapore, 1978—, also bd. dirs.; taxation advisor Melbourne, 1961-69. Editor Tip-Off mag., 1960-63, Harvard Bus. Sch. Newsletter, 1982—. Pres. Victorian Intercollegiate Basketball Assn., Melbourne, 1967-73; chmn. Am. Sch. Bd., Singapore, 1984-86. Mem. Australian Soc. Accts. (assoc.). Clubs: Tanglin, Singapore Cricket. Home: 25 Claymore Rd, Apt #14-02, Singapore 0922, Singapore Office: TNT South East Asia, #18-06, Singapore 0106, Singapore

MERCER, RICHARD JAMES, lawyer; b. New London, Conn., Oct. 2, 1950; s. James Wilson and Marianne (Wieczorek) M.; m. Ann Holly Gutting, Oct. 9, 1970 (div. 1977); m. Harriet Allston Jopson, May 1, 1982; 1 child, James. BBA, Old Dominion U., 1972; JD, Coll. William and Mary, 1975; LLM in Taxation, Boston U., 1977, LLM in Banking, 1986. Assoc. Epstein & Epstein, Norfolk, Va., 1975, Bernard A. Kaplan, Boston, 1975-76; sole practice, 1976-78, 1979-80; ptnr. Shagory & Shagory, Boston, 1978-79, Alpert, Thurman & Mercer, Boston, 1980-82; assoc. counsel First Nat. Bank Boston, 1983-85, asst. v.p., assoc. counsel, 1985-86, sr. counsel, 1986—. Town coordinator George Bush Presdl. Campaign, Weston, 1980. Mem. ABA, Boston Bar Assn., Am. Arbitration Assn. (arbitrator 1978), Mass. Bar Assn., Va. Bar Assn. Republican. Episcopalian. Office: First Nat Bank Boston 100 Federal St Boston MA 02110

MERCER, ROBERT E., tire company executive; b. Elizabeth, N.J., 1924; married. Grad., Yale U., 1946. With Goodyear Tire & Rubber Co., Akron, Ohio, 1947—, asst. to pres., 1973-74, pres. Kelly-Springfield Tire Co. (subs.), 1974-76, corp. exec. v.p., pres. tire div., 1976-78, corp. pres., from 1978, chief operating officer, 1980-82, vice chmn., chief exec. officer, 1982-83, chmn., chief exec. officer, 1983—, also dir. Served with USN. Office: Goodyear Tire & Rubber Co 1144 E Market St Akron OH 44316

MERCHANT, ISMAIL NOORMOHAMED, film producer; b. Bombay, Dec. 25, 1936; arrived in U.S., 1958; s. Noormohamed and Hazrabi (Memon) Rehman. BA, St. Xavier's Coll., Bombay, 1958; MBA, NYU, 1960. V.p. Merchant Ivory Prodns. Inc., N.Y.C., 1962—. Producer: (films) Creation of Woman, 1960, The Householder, 1963, The Delhi Way, 1964, Shakespeare Wallah, 1965, The Guru, 1969, Bombay Talkie, 1970, Adventures of a Brown Man in Search of Civilization, 1971, Savages, 1972, Helen, Queen of the Nautch Girls, 1973, Mahatma and the Mad Boy, 1973, Autobiography of a Princess, 1975, The Wild Party, 1975, Sweet Sounds, 1976, Roseland, 1977, Hullabaloo Over Georgie and Bonnie's Pictures, 1978, The Europeans, 1979, The Five Forty-Eight, 1979, Jane Austen in Manhattan, 1980, Quartet, 1981, The Courtesans of Bombay, 1982, Heat and Dust, 1983, The Bostonians, 1984, A Room with a View, 1986, Maurice, 1987, The Perfect Murder, 1988, The Deceivers, 1988, Slaves of New York, 1988—; author: (books) Ismail Merchant's Indian Cuisine, 1986, The Making of the Deceivers, 1988. Home: 400 E 52d St New York NY 10022 Office: 250 W 57th St Suite 1913A New York NY 10019

MERCHANT, ROLAND SAMUEL, SR., hospital administrator, educator; b. N.Y.C., Apr. 18, 1929; s. Samuel and Eleta (McLvmont) M.; m. Audrey Bartley, June 6, 1970; children—Orelia Eleta, Roland Samuel, Huey Bartley. B.A., N.Y.U., 1957, M.A., 1960; M.S., Columbia U., 1963, M.S.H.A., 1974. Asst. statistician N.Y.C. Dept. Health, 1957-60, statistician, 1960-63; statistician N.Y. TB and Health Assn., N.Y.C., 1963-65; biostatistician, adminstrv. coordinator Inst. Surg. Studies, Montefiore Hosp., Bronx, N.Y., 1965-72; resident in adminstrn. Roosevelt Hosp., N.Y.C., 1973-74; dir. health and hosp. mgmt. Dept. Health, City of N.Y., 1974-76; from asst. adminstr. to adminstr. West Adams Community Hosp., Los Angeles, 1976; spl. asst. to assoc. v.p. for med. affairs Stanford U. Hosp., Calif., 1977-82, dir. office mgmt. and strategic planning, 1982-85, dir. mgmt. planning, 1986—; clin. assoc. prof. dept. family, community and preventive medicine Stanford U., 1986-88, dept. health research and policy Stanford U. Med. Sch., 1988—. Served with U.S. Army, 1951-53. USPHS fellow. Fellow Am. Coll. Healthcare Execs., Am. Pub. Health Assn.; mem. Am. Hosp. Assn., Nat. Assn. Health Services Execs., N.Y. Acad. Scis. Home: 953 Cheswick Dr San Jose CA 95121 Office: Stanford U Hosp Stanford CA 94305

MERCIER, CLAUDE PAUL, vascular surgeon, educator; b. Lyon, France, Nov. 7, 1932; s. Jean and Suzanne (de Bouillanne) M.; m. Christiane Thevenot, Mar. 30, 1964; children: Frederic, Vincent. MD, Faculté de Medicine, 1956. Intern hosps., Marseilles, 1956-63; chief of clinic Faculty of Medicine, Marseilles, 1963, prof. vascular surgery, 1970—, chmn., 1979—. Author: Deep Venous Thrombosis, 1973, Thoracic Outlet Syndrome, 1979. Pres. Med. Com. Hosps., Marseille, 1988. Recipient Ordre Nat. du Merite, 1974. Mem. Acad. de Chirurgie, Internat. Soc. Vascular Surgery, Internat. Soc. Surgery. Roman Catholic. Lodge: Rotary. Avocation: golf. Home: 12 rue de Comdt Rolland, 13008 Marseille France Office: Hopital de la Conception, Blvd Baille, 13005 Marseille France

MERCIER, JACQUES LOUIS, industrial and commercial promotion company executive; b. Paris, July 7, 1933; s. Georgi Henri and Helene Corneille (Ryckembeush) M.; m. Marie-Annick Therese Ravet, Sept. 14, 1984; 1 child, Marie Helene. Degree in Engring., Fed. Inst. Tech., Zurich, Switzerland, 1958; PhD, U. Wash., Seattle, 1965; D. es-Scis., U. Paris, 1973. Engr. Amman and Whitney, N.Y.C., 1959-61; assoc. research engr. Boeing Co., Seattle, 1961-63; teaching assoc. U. Wash., Seattle, 1963-65; asst. prof. engring. scis. U. Md., College Park, 1965-66; assoc. prof. U. Md., Rio de Janeiro, U. Brazil, 1966-68; prof. Catholic U., Rio de Janeiro, U. Brazil, 1968-73; dir. UP VI Ecole Nat. Sup. des Beaux Arts, Paris, U. Brazil, 1973-74; dir., founder Montemer Internat. (substituting MASA Internat.), Rio de Janeiro, U. Brazil, 1975—; French fgn. trade counsellor Montemer Internat. (substituting MASA Internat.), Paris, U. Brazil, 1982—; mem. Jury for Candidacy Professorship Cath. U., Rio de Janeiro, 1972-75; counsellor French Fgn. Trade Council, Paris, 1982—. Author: An Introduction to Tensor Calculus, 1971; contbr. articles to engring. publs. Decorated officer French Ordre Nat. du. Merite, recipient Santos Dumont Merit medal Ministry of Aero., Brasilia, 1984; medal Friend of Brazilian Navy, Ministry of Navy, 1985. Mem. French C. of C. (bd. dirs. 1985—), ASME, Council Engrs. and Architects of Rio de Janiero, Swiss Soc. Engrs. and Architects, Sigma Xi. Roman Catholic. Club: Cercle de l'Union Interalliee (Paris). Home: Ave Atlantica 270/1402, 22010 Rio de Janeiro Brazil Office: Montemer Internat, Ed Monteiro Aranha, Ld Nossa Senhora 163, 22211 Rio de Janeiro Brazil

MERCIER, JEAN ROBERT, physician; b. Oloron-Sainte-Marie, France, July 25, 1918; s. Marc Charles and Jeanne Maria (Claracq) M.; m. Louise Marquerite Peyrottes, June 6, 1942; children: Marc, Genevieve, Jean-Michel, Louis. PhD, Faculte Medecine, Paris, 1945. Intern, then resident Faculte Medecine, Paris, 1945-51, asst., 1952-60; head ear, nose and throat dept. Neuilly Hosp., France, 1960-84; expert clinicien French Govt., Paris, 1984—. Author: Encyclopedie Medico-Chirurgicale; patentee in field. Served to lt. med. service corps, French Mil., 1939-45;. Named Knight of the French Legion of Honor, 1966. Fellow Soc. D'Orl Hôpitaux Paris; mem. Soc. Francaise D'Orl. Roman Catholic. Club: Cercle Interallié (Paris), Polo (Paris). Lodge: Rotary. Home and Office: 7 Bis Rue Raynouard, 75016 Paris France

MERCOUN, DAWN DENISE, manufacturing company officer; b. Passaic, N.J., June 1, 1950; d. William S. and Irene F. (Micci) M. BS in Bus. Mgmt., Fairleigh Dickinson U., 1978. Personnel payroll coordinator Bentex Mills, Inc., East Rutherford, N.J., 1969-72; employment mgr. Inwood Knitting Mills, Clifton, N.J., 1972-75; gen. mgr. Consol. Advance, Inc., Passaic, 1975-76; v.p. human resources Gemini Industries, Inc., Clifton, 1976—. Mem. Am. Soc. for Personnel Adminstrn., Am. Compensation Assn., Internat. Found. Employee Benefits, Earthwatch Research Team. Republican. Episcopalian. Office: 215 Entin Rd Clifton NJ 07014

MERCOURI, MELINA (MARIA AMALIA), actress, Greek government official; b. Athens, Greece, Oct. 18, 1925; d. Stamatis and Irene M.; ed. Acad. Nat. Theatre Greece; m. Jules Dassin, 1966. Films include: Stella, 1955, He Who Must Die, 1956, The Gipsy and the Gentleman, 1955, Never on Sunday, 1960, Topkapi, 1963, Les Pianos Mécaniques, 1964, 10:30 P.M. Summer, 1966, Phaedra, 1962, Gaily, Gaily, 1969, Promise at Dawn, 1970, Once Is Not Enough, 1975, Earthquake, 1974, A Dream of Passion, 1978; stage appearances include: Ilya, Darling, Lysistrata, 1972, Mourning Becomes Electra, A Streetcar Named Desire, Helen or the Joy of Living, The Queen of Clubs, The Seven Year Itch, Sweet Bird of Youth; mem. Greek Parliament for Port of Piraeus, 1977—; minister of culture and scis., 1981—. Author: I Was Born Greek, 1971. Recipient Tregene prize, 1984. Address: Ministry of Culture and Scis, Athens Greece *

MERCURIO, ANTONIO MARCO, anthropologist, psychotherapist; b. Messina, Sicily, Italy, Nov. 8, 1930; s. Paolo and Maria (Urso) M.; m. Paola Sensini, Dec. 28, 1974. Doctor in Classical Literature, State U. Messina, 1958; Lic. in Philosophy, Jesuit Faculty of Messina, 1953; Doctor in Theology, Cath. U. Paris, 1964. Prof. theology Gregorian Pontifical U., Rome, 1969-70; founder, dir. Inst. Analytical Psychotherapy, Rome, 1970—; founder, pres. Associazione Psicoterapeuti Italiana, Rome, 1974-78; founder, rector Sophia U., Rome, 1978—; founder Sophia U., Geneva, 1980, Sophia U., Brussels, 1981, Sophia U., Paris, 1984, European Ctr. Research in Life as a Masterpiece of Art, 1986. sci. supr. several insts. psychotherapy, Italy, 1974—. Author: Amore e Persona, 1976, Teoria della Persona, 1978, Amore Libertà e Colpa, 1980, La vita come opera d'arte, 1988; inventor sophianalysis, method of existential psychotherapy, 1970; contbr. articles in field to profl. publs. Mem. European Assn. Humanistic Psychology (co-founder 1979), Acad. Psychoanalysis of Berlin, Sociedade de Psicanalise Intergral of São Paulo (hon.). Home: 22 Via Claudio Achillini, 00141 Rome Italy Office: 258 Via dei Prati Fiscali, 00141 Rome Italy

MERDINGER, SUSAN, marketing, sales executive; b. Boston, Oct. 5, 1943; d. J. George and Bertha (Lotten) Greenfield; m. Edward Franklin Merdinger, Dec. 21, 1963; children: Mindy Beth, Matthew Joseph. AA, Green Mountain Coll., 1963. Asst. dir. pub. relations Filene's, Boston, 1963; real estate sales, Marlboro, N.J., 1970-78; nat. dir. edn. Network of Homes, Babylon, N.Y., 1978-79; v.p. homefinding Employee Transfer Co., Chgo., 1979-81; dir. mktg. Merrill Lynch Realty, Stamford, Conn., 1981-83, asst. v.p. communications and promotional services, 1983-84, dir. mktg. services, 1984-86; founder, pub. mag. Fine Homes, 1982-87; v.p. Fine Homes Internat., 1986-87; v.p. mktg. services, 1987-88, v.p. internat. mktg., 1988—; lectr. in field. Pres., founder Hadassah, Marlboro, N.J., 1972-75, mem. nat. membership com., 1972-75. Office: Merrill Lynch Realty Assocs 10 Stamford Forum Stamford CT 06901

MEREDITH, SCOTT, authors' representative; b. N.Y.C., Nov. 24, 1923; s. Henry and Esta (Meredith); m. Helen Kovet, Apr. 22, 1944; children: Stephen Charles, Randy Beth Meredith Sheer. Educated privately; Litt.D., Mercy Coll., 1983. Writer numerous mag. stories; established Scott Meredith Lit. Agy., Inc., N.Y.C., 1940; pres. Scott Meredith Lit. Agy., Inc., 1942—. Author: Writing to Sell, rev. edits, 1960, 74, 86, Writing for the American Market, 1960, The Face of Comedy, 1961, George S. Kaufman and His Friends, 1974, The Science of Gaming, 1974, Louis B. Mayer and His Enemies, 1986; also stories, novelettes, serials and articles; editor: The Best of Wodehouse, 1949, The Best of Modern Humor, 1951, Bar One Roundup, 1951, The Week-End Book of Humor, 1952, Bar Two Roundup, 1952, The Murder of Mr. Malone, An Anthology of Craig Rice Stories, 1953, Bar Three Roundup, 1954, Bar Four Roundup, 1955, 2d series, 1956, Bar Five Roundup, 1956, (with Ken Murray) The Ken Murray Book of Humor, 1957, Bar Six Roundup, 1957, (with Henry Morgan) The Henry Morgan Book of Humor, 1958, The Best from Manhunt, 1958, The Bloodhound Anthology, 1960, The Fireside Treasury of Modern Humor, 1963, Best Western Stories, 1964, Best Western Stories For Young People, 1965, (with P.G. Wodehouse) The Best of Humor, 1965, A Carnival of Modern Humor, 1966, (with Margaret Truman) The Harry S. Truman Memoirs, 1988; contbr. articles on humor to Ency. Brit, 1954-59, articles on fiction writing to Oxford Ency, 1960-61; frequent guest TV, radio shows. Served with USAAF, World War II. Clubs: Three Oaks Tennis (N.Y.C.), Spectator (N.Y.C.), Rare Book Soc. (N.Y.C.). Home: Kings Point NY 11024 Office: 845 3d Ave New York NY 10022 also: 44 Great Russell St, London WC1 England

MERENI, JOSEPH IBEWUIKE, university lecturer; b. Okigwe, Imo, Nigeria, Oct. 31, 1940. Primary sch. tchr. Nigeria Elem. Schs., 1959-65; secondary sch. tchr. Nigeria High Schs., 1970-75; lectr. Tchr's. Coll., Nigeria; univ. lectr. U. Nigeria, 1980—; sr. lectr. Dept. Adult Edn. U. Nsukka, Nigeria, 1983-87. Editor acad. texts Foundations of Adult Education, Administration of Adult Education, 1987, Adult Education: Theory and Practice, 1988. Mem. Counseling Assn. of Nigeria, Nigerian Nat. Counsel Adult Edn. Roman Catholic. Clubs: Okigwe Town WELFARE (pub. relations officer 1982-86). Office: U Nigeria Dept Adult Edn, Nsukka Anambra, Nigeria

MERENSKI, PAUL, marketing educator; b. Greenwich, Conn., Oct. 13, 1939; m. Frances M. Schaffner, Aug. 31, 1963; children—Dara, Dawn. B.S. summa cum laude in Bus. Adminstrn., Wright State U., 1971, M.B.A., 1972; Ph.D., U. Cin., 1982. Stress analyst Titan Project Office, Am. Machine and Foundry Co., Stamford, Conn., 1960-62; instr. Wright State U., Dayton, Ohio, 1972-73; account exec. No. Securities Co., Dayton, 1973-74; dist. mgr. Church's Fried Chicken Inc., Dayton, 1974-76; assoc. prof. mktg. U. Dayton, 1976—; cons. in field. Contbr. numerous articles to profl. jours. Served as officer USAF, 1962-69. Mem. Am. Mktg. Assn., Assn. Consumer Research, Am. Acad. Advt., Acad. Mktg. Sci., Inst. Mgmt. Sci., Am. Inst. Decision Scis., Mensa, Mu Kappa Tau. Address: 341 Signal Fire Dr Centerville OH 45458

MERÉNYI, FERENC, museum director, educator; b. Budapest, Hungary, Feb. 25, 1923. Degree in Architecture, Tech. U., 1950. Asst. prof. to lectr. Inst. History and Theory Architecture Tech. U., Budapest, 1950-59, prof., 1974-77; dir. Hungarian Acad., Rome, 1959-65, 77-83, Nat. Intendence Hist. Monuments and Sites, Budapest, 1965-74, Mus. Fine Arts, Budapest, 1984—; prof. Tech. U., Budapest, 1984—. Contbr. articles to profl. jours. Fellow Assn. Hungarian Architects; mem. Hungarian Acad. Scis. (history and theory of architecture bd., history of art). Home: Bajza utca 47, H-1062 Budapest Hungary Office: Szepmuveszeti Muzeum, Dozsa Gyorgy ut 41, H-1146 Budapest Hungary

MEREY, DAISY, physician; b. Tangiers, Morocco, Feb. 1, 1949, came to U.S., 1961; d. Theodore and Lilly (Roth) Breuer; m. John Howard Merey, Dec. 26, 1967; children: DeAnne, Andrew. BA, Barnard Coll., 1964; PhD, NYU, 1971; MD, St. George's U., 1979. Resident Broward Gen. Med. Ctr., Ft. Lauderdale, Fla., 1979-80; practice medicine, West Palm Beach, Fla., 1981—; med. cons. Vis. Nurse Assn., 1981-83. Recipient Founder's Day award NYU, 1970. Fellow Am. Soc. Bariatric Physicians, Interam. Physicians Assn.; mem. AMA (Physicians Recognition award 1982, 86), Am. Bariatric Assn., Internat. Bariatric Assn., Internat. Acad. Bariatric Physicians (internat. pres.), Am. Soc. Clin. Nutrition (cert.), Am. Soc. Contemporary Medicine and Surgery, Exec. Women Palm Beaches. Office: 900 N Olive Ave West Palm Beach FL 33401

MERGEN, ARMAND, criminologist; b. Heffingen, Luxembourg, Jan. 29, 1919; s. Jean and Maria (Faber) M.; m. Eva B. Lodde, Dec. 1977. Student, U. Brussels, 1938-40; L.D., U. Innsbruck, 1942, U. Luxembourg, 1947; Habilitation, U. Mainz, Fed. Republic Germany, 1952. Atty. Luxembourg, 1946-58; prof. criminology U. Mainz, 1948—; dir. Inst. Social Def. Luxembourg, 1952-60. Author: Tat und Täter, 1971, Krankheit und Verbrechen, 1972, Verunsicherte Kriminologie, 1975, Die Kriminologie, 1978, Die BKA-Story, 1987, Tod in Genf, 1988, others; contbr. articles to profl. jours. Served with Resistance, 1942-45. Decorated Chevalier de l'Ordre de St. Agathe; Officer l'Ordre de Merite. Mem. Internat. Soc. Criminology, German Soc. Criminology (hon. pres. 1979—), Am. Soc. Criminology, Defense Sociale, Inst. Grand-Ducal, PEN. Address: Rue de Strassen 20, L-8156 Bridel Luxembourg

MERGLER, HARRY WINSTON, engineering educator; b. Chillicothe, Ohio, June 1, 1924; s. Harry Franklin and Letitia (Walburn) M.; m. Irmgard Erna Steudel, June 22, 1948; children—Myra A. L., Marcia B. E., Harry F. B.S., MIT, 1948; M.S., Case Inst. Tech., 1950, Ph.D., 1956. Aero. research scientist NACA, 1948-56; mem. faculty Case Inst. Tech., 1957—, prof. engring., 1962—, Leonard Case prof. engring., 1973—; dir. Digital Systems Lab., 1959—; vis. scientist, USSR, 1958; vis. prof. Norwegian Tech. U., 1962; cons. to industry, 1957—; editor Control Engring. mag., 1956—; pres. Digital/Gen. Corp., 1968-72; cons. Exploratory Research div. NSF. Author: Digital Systems Engineering, 1961, also articles, chpts. in books. Served with AUS, 1942-45. Recipient Gold medal for sci. achievement Case Inst. Tech., 1980. Fellow IEEE (Lamme medal 1978, bd. dirs. 1987-89); mem. Indsl. Electronic Soc. (pres. 1977-79), Cleve. Engring. Soc., N.Y. Acad. Scis., Nat. Acad. Engring., Sigma Xi, Tau Beta Pi, Theta Tau, Pi Delta Epsilon, Zeta Psi, Blue Key. Home: 1525 Queen Anne's Gate Westlake OH 44145

MERICKEL, MICHAEL GENE, chiropractic physician, educator; b. Wells, Minn., Apr. 9, 1952; s. Elmer Dale and Wilma Jean (Conquest) M.; m. Diane H. Steinke, June 27, 1976; children: Eric, Alexa. A in Nursing, Kettering Coll. Med. Arts, 1973; D of Chiropratic, Palmer Coll. Chiropractic, 1980. Diplomate Nat. Bd. Chiropractic Examiners; RN. RN Kettering (Ohio) Hosp., 1969-73, Walla Walla (Wash.) Hosp., 1973-75; pvt. practice chiropractic medicine Ashland, Ohio, 1981—; instr., counselor 5-Day Stop Smoking Clinic, Tri-County area, 1983—. Contbr. articles to profl. jours. Tchr. Hale Farm and Village, Bath, Ohio, 1983-86, research vol., 1983—; mem. Tri-County Regional Safety Council, Ashland, 1982—. Mem. Internat. Chiropractors Assn., Am. Chiropractic Assn., Ohio State Chiropractic Assn., Internat. Platform Assn. Office: Ashland Chiropractic Ctr 1188 Simanton Rd Ashland OH 44805

MERILAN, CHARLES PRESTON, dairy husbandry scientist; b. Lesterville, Mo., Jan. 14, 1926; s. Peter Samuel and Cleo Sarah (Harper) M.; m. Phyllis Pauline Laughlin, June 12, 1949; children—Michael Preston, Jean Elizabeth. B.S. in Agr, U. Mo., 1948, A.M., 1949, Ph.D., 1952. Mem. faculty U. Mo., Columbia, 1950—; prof. dairy husbandry U. Mo., 1959—, chmn. dept., 1961-62; asso. dir. Mo. Agrl. Expt. Sta., 1962-63, asso. investigator space sci. research center, 1964-74, exec. sec., dir. grad. studies physiology area, 1969-72, chmn. univ. patent and copyright com., 1963-80. Served with USMC, 1944-45. Decorated Purple Heart. Mem. AAAS, Am. Chem. Soc., Am. Dairy Sci. Assn., Am. Soc. Animal Sci, Soc. Cryobiology, Sigma Xi, Alpha Zeta, Gamma Sigma Delta, Phi Beta Pi. Home: 1509 Bouchelle Ave Columbia MO 65201 Office: U Missouri Columbia MO 65211

MERILO, MATI, research engineer, research administrator; b. Tallinn, Estonia, Jan. 23, 1944; came to U.S., 1977; s. Arkadi and Hermeline (Dampf) M.; m. Kathleen Lorraine Frail, Aug. 21, 1971; children—Erik Grant, Aleksander Evan, Kristi-Anne. B.Eng., McGill U., Montreal, Que., 1966; M.S., Case Inst. Tech., 1968, Ph.D., 1972. Research engr. Atomic Energy of Can. Ltd., Chalk River, Ont., 1971-77; project mgr. Electric Power Research Inst., Palo Alto, Calif., 1977—. Editor: Thermal-Hydraulics of Nuclear Reactors, 1983; editorial adv. bd. Heat and Tech. contbr. articles to profl. jours. Mem. ASME, Am. Nuclear Soc. Office: Electric Power Research Inst 3412 Hillview Ave Palo Alto CA 94303

MERINO CASTRO, JOSÉ TORIBIO, Chilean naval officer; b. Dec. 14, 1915; m. Gabriela Margarita Riofrio Bustos, 1952; 3 children. Ed., specialized as gunnery officer Naval Acad. Naval Service in Maipo, 1936, Rancagua, 1939; instr. Blanco Encalada, 1940; div. officer Almirante Latorre, 1943; asst. officer USS Raleigh, 1944; arty. officer Serrano, 1945; comdr. Corvette Papudo, 1952; staff coll. course, 1954; tech. adviser of armaments, 1955; comdr. Destroyer Williams, 1962, Riveros, 1963; vice chief of gen. staff, 1964; comdr. in chief of fleet, 1970-71, of First Naval Zone 1972-73, of Navy, 1973—; mem. Govt. Junta, 1973—. Decorated Armed Forces medal III, II, I, Grand Star of Merit, Cross for Naval Merit, Decoration of Pres. of Republic (Chile). Office: care Naval Hdqrs, Santiago Chile

MERIWETHER, CHARLES MINOR, retail and wholesale drug company executive; b. Memphis, Feb. 15, 1911; s. Charles Minor and Leslie Allen (Stevens) M.; m. Beverly Alston, June 7, 1939; children—Leslie Ann (Mrs. A.M. Shuler Jr.), Beverly (Mrs. Frank Lockridge, Jr.) (dec.), Charles Minor. Student, U. Tenn., 1932; LL.B., Cumberland U., 1933; J.D., Sanford U., 1969. Engaged in ins. law and ins. mgmt. Memphis, 1933-42; in retail and wholesale drug bus. Birmingham, Ala., 1944-58; dir. finance Ala., 1958-61; bd. dirs. Export-Import Bank Washington, 1961-66; pres. Dewberry Drug Co., Inc., Birmingham, 1966—. Pres. Ala. Ednl. Authority, 1958-61, Ala. Hwy. Authority, 1958-61; chmn. investment com. Tchr. Retirement Fund and Employees Retirement Fund, Ala., 1958-61; bd. dirs. Jefferson State Jr. Coll. Found., 1984—; adv. bd. Family Ct. Jefferson County, 1983—; bd. dirs. Ala. Trust Fund, 1985—; dir. Ala. Adjustment Bd., 1958-61; Chmn. dirs. Ala. chpt. Nat. Multiple Sclerosis Soc., 1958-59. Served with U.S. Mcht. Marine, 1942-43. Mem. Phi Gamma Delta. Methodist. Clubs: Nat. Press (Washington); Downtown (Birmingham), Relay House (Birmingham), Nat. Dem. (Washington). Lodge: Odd Fellow. Home: 4421 Corinth Dr Birmingham AL 35213 Office: City Fed Bldg Birmingham AL 35203

MERK, GERHARD ERNEST, economics educator; b. Mannheim, Federal Republic of Germany, May 8, 1931; m. Martha Jansen, Mar. 14, 1964; children: Irene Lioba, Judith Hildegard. Diploma, U. Heidelberg, 1955, Dr. rer. pol, 1957; diploma, U. Mannheim, 1957. Market researcher Fried, Krupp, Essen, Federal Republic of Germany, 1958-66; prof. Econs. U. Siegen, Federal Republic of Germany, 1966—. Author more than 20 books and 40 articles on econs.; also author 10 books poetry. Festschrift for Gerhard Merk, 1981. Mem. several sci. institutions and orgns. Home: 2 Albertus-Magnus-St, D-5900 Siegen 1 Federal Republic of Germany Office: U Siegen, D-5900 Siegen 21 Federal Republic of Germany

MERKLE, HANS L., manufacturing executive; b. Pforzheim, Germany, Jan. 1, 1913; s. Emil M. and Zeline (Kilgus) M.; m. Annemarie Schlerff. Student law and econs. Mem. exec. bd. Ullrich Gminder AG, Reutlingen, Fed. Republic Germany, 1949-58; mng. dir. Robert Bosch GmbH, 1958-63, chmn. exec. bd., 1963—; chmn. supervising bd. BASF AG, Continental Gummiwerke, Deutsche Bank AG; mem. supervising bd. Allianz Vers./AG, AKZO N.V., Arnheim, Otto Wolff AG, Royal Dutch Petroleum Co., Volkswagenwerk AG. Author: Inflation und öffentliche Finanzen, 1975. Mem. Max-Planck-Gesellschaft (mem. sci. council). Home: Feuerbacher Heide, D-7000 Stuttgart 1 Federal Republic of Germany *

MERKLE, LINDA L., legal administrator, corporate controller; b. Washington, Apr. 6, 1947; d. Robert Clifton, Shreeves II and Esther A. (Harrison) Cumming; lic. real estate, Prince Georges Community Coll., Largo, Md., 1972; children: Christina L., Regina L. Various secretarial positions, 1964-65, 67-72; real estate saleswoman, 1973-74; div. sec. Prince Georges Community Coll., 1974-75; real estate saleswoman Harvest Realty Inc., Clinton, Md., 1974-75; legal adminstr., property mgr., investment mgr. firm Tucker, Flyer, Sanger, Reider & Lewis P.C., Washington, 1975-84; legal adminstr. Anderson, Heibey, Nauheim & Blair, Washington, 1984-85; v.p. fin. and adminstrn. Barnes, Morris & Pardoe, Inc., Washington, 1985—; dir. Md. Corp.; pres. Lawtabs Inc. Del. Corp.; cons., speaker Mem. Assn. Legal Adminstrs. (chmn. new adminstrs. and gen. adminstrn. sect. 1984-85), ABA (assoc.). Home: 4100 N River St Arlington VA 22207 Office: 919 18th St NW Washington DC 20006

MERLADET, JOSE FELIX, European community official; b. Portugalete, Vizcaya, Spain, Apr. 27, 1957; s. Jose Manuel Merladet Ardanza and Maria Del Carmen Mazorra Gutierrez De Arce; m. Elena Urigüen, Dec. 27, 1986. Lic. En Derecho, U. Navarra, 1979; LLM, Harvard U., 1981; cert., Inst. D'Etudes Polit., Paris, 1982; diploma, Escuela Diplomatica, Madrid, 1985. Legal advisor Remolcadores Del Norte S.A., Bilbao, Spain, 1979-80; intern UN, N.Y.C., summer 1981; with law firm, Madrid, 1982-84; dean colegio Mayor Cesar Carlos, Madrid, 1984-85; chief advisor Basque Community Autonomous Govt., Bilbao, 1986; adminstr. Commn. of the European Communities, Brussels, 1986—. Author: (with J. M. De Areilza) La Palabras, 1974 (Planeta's Nat. prize of Essay 1986), short stories. Mem. Soc. Inter-Americana, Assn. Para la Integracion Europa, Assn. De Antiguos Alumnos De Estudios Y Rels Internacionales (del. Belgium, EEC), Assn. De Funcionarios Españoles en la Comunidad Europea (founding com.). Roman Catholic. Clubs: Harvard (Spain and Belgium) (bd. dirs. Spanish chpt. 1984-85); Sociedad Bilbaina. Home: Urquijo 3, Las Arenas Vizcaya Spain Office: Commn European Communities, 200 Rue De La Loi, 1049 Brussels Belgium

MERLINO, ANDRES, business, marketing consultant; b. Buenos Aires; came to Spain, 1973; s. Andres A. and Genny (Steimberg) M.; m. Beatriz Aguilo, July 18, 1970 (div. Sept. 1983); children: Flavia, Florencia, Dolores; m. Ana Sacanelles, Feb. 22, 1984; 1 child, Ana Genny. Diploma in Polit. Sci., Gallup Ctr., 1968; grad., Pub. Relations Inst., 1969; diploma in Mktg., Am. Mgmt. Assn., Buenos Aires, 1973; M of Mktg. (hon.), Renmark, Madrid, 1979. Freelance mktg., pub. relations cons. numerous firms including Pond's, Unilever, Kodak, Harrods, Lockheed, Buenos Aires and Madrid, 1969-81; with Canary Cons. Group, Las Palmas, Spain, 1981—; lectr. Pub. Relations Inst., Human Relations Inst., Bus. Mgmt. Schs., Argentina and Spain, 1967—. Contbr. articles to S.Am. and Spanish profl. jours., 1967—. Recipient Gold medal Oficina Informativa de Comercio Exterior, 1977, Caballero, Orden Del Buho, 1977. Mem. Centro De Relaciones Publicas Internacionales, Bolsa De Comercio. Club: De Dirigentes De Mktg. Home: Santa Clara 16, Tafira Alta, Las Palmas Canary Islands Spain Office: Canary Cons Group, Rafael Ramirez 5, Las Palmas Canary Islands Spain

MERLINO, ANTHONY FRANK, orthopedic surgeon; b. Providence, Jan. 21, 1930; s. Anthony Frank and C. Mildred (Campagna) M.; B.S., Providence Coll., 1951; M.S., U. Conn., 1952; M.D., Jefferson Med. Coll., 1956; m. Dolores Mary Aucello, Nov. 22, 1956; children—Christa Marianne, Paula Nicole. Intern, St. Joseph Hosp., Providence, 1956-57; resident orthopedic surgery VA Hosp., Phila., 1959-63; practice medicine specializing in orthopedic surgery, Phila., 1963-68, Providence, 1968—; attending orthopedic surgeon St. Joseph Hosp., Providence, pres. med. staff, 1974-75, trustee, 1973-76, med. staff/trustee joint conf. com. 1982; attending orthopedic surgeon Our Lady of Fatima Hosp., North Providence, R.I.; vis. orthopedic surgeon R.I. State Hosp., Howard, 1968-75; asst. orthopedic surgery Hahnemann Med. Coll., Phila., 1965-69; pediatric orthopedic surg. cons. Crippled Children's Program of R.I., 1968-86; cons. orthopedic surgeon Roger Williams Gen. Hosp., Providence, 1969—; v.p. R.I. Orthopedic Group, Inc., Providence, 1969-83; pres., 1983—; team physician hockey and basketball teams Providence Coll., 1968-87; mem. R.I. Gov.'s Med. Malpractice Commn., 1975-77, R.I. Bd. Examiners in Chiropractic, 1977-80; mem. study commn. R.I. Med. Rev. Bd., 1977—; mem. corp. Blue Cross/Shield R.I., 1976-87; physician-adv. R.I. Assn. Med. Assts., 1979-84; mem. R.I. Workers' Compensation Adv. Panel, 1978—; mem. adv. bd. Cath. Social Services, 1981-84; police surgeon Am. Law Enforcement Officers' Assn., 1980; cons. orthopedic surgery Am. Assn. Medicolegal Cons., 1980—; pres. Hindle Bldg. Assocs., 1983—. Mem. med. splty. adv. bd. Medical Malpractice Prevention, 1985—. Served to capt., M.C., USAF, 1957-59. Recipient Dr. William McDonnell award Providence Coll. Alumni Assn., 1981. Diplomate Am. Bd. Orthopedic Surgery. Fellow Am. Acad. Orthopedic Surgeons, ACS, (pres. R.I. chpt. 1982-84), Internat. Coll. Surgeons, Latin Am. Soc. Orthopedics and Traumatology; mem. Orthopaedic Research and Edn. Found. (life), Am. Coll. Legal Medicine, Am. Fracture Assn., Pan-Pacific Surg. Assn., New Eng., R.I. (sec.-treas. 1978-80, v.p. 1980-82, pres. 1982-84), Ea. Orthopedic Socs., Jefferson Orthopaedic Soc., AMA, R.I. Med. Soc. (commr. profl. relations 1976, ho. of dels. 1976-82, commr. internal affairs 1982), Providence Med. Assn., Am. Profl. Practice Assn., Am. Acad. Compensation Medicine, Am. Coll. Sports Medicine, Am. Orthopedic Soc. for Sports Medicine, Am. Med. Photography Assn., Internat. Soc. Orthopedics and Traumatology, Internat. Soc. Research in Orthopedics and Trauma, Am. Soc. Law and Medicine, Thomistic Inst. Drs. Guild, R.I. Hist. Soc., Big East Team Physicians Assn. Roman Catholic. Clubs: Boston Orthopedic, Mal Brown, The 100 of R.I., Inc. Contbr. articles to profl. publs. Home: 2 Countryside Dr North Providence RI 02904 Office: 655 Broad St Providence RI 02907

MERLO, PIER ANTONIO, air conditioning company executive; b. Piacenza D'Adige, Padova, Italy, July 12, 1935; s. Luigi-Antonio and Lucia (Sartori) M.; m. Marina Jolanda Vanzina; children: Francesco, Roberto. DEE, Poly. U. Milan, 1960. Engring. trainee Marconi Instruments, St. Albans, Italy, 1961; design engr. Martelli Aerotechnica, Milan, 1962-64; area mgr. Chrysler Airtemp, Dayton, Ohio, 1965-78; exec. v.p. Chrysler Airtemp Italy, Milan, 1976-78; mng. dir. OMR Airtemp Italy, Milan, 1978—; cons. Engring. EQ Services, Milan, 1984, Brightstar, London, 1986—; bd. dirs. Imaco. Milan. Mem. ASCAP, Profl. Engrs. Milan. Home: 3 Senato, 20121 Milan Italy Office: Imaco, 3 Via Pinamonte, da Vimercate, 20121 Milan Italy

MERLO-FLORES, LUIS A., transportation executive; b. Buenos Aires, Argentina, Sept. 30, 1931; s. Luis F. and and Gilda (Lopez) M.; children: Diana, Luis Pablo, Marita, Diego, Maria Elena. Degree, George Washington U., Washington; degree in civil engring., Buenos Aires U.; postgrad., Columbia U., N.Y.C. Internat. rep. Galion Iron Works, Ohio, 1960-63; dist. mgr. Allis Chalmers Overseas, Madrid, 1963-66, regional mgr., 1966-70; mktg. mgr. Allis Chalmers Overseas, Rome, 1970-79; gen. mgr. Allis Chalmers Fiat-Allis, Buenos Aires, 1974-76, Grove Internat., Brussels, 1976-79; v.p. mktg. Fiat Automobiles, Buenos Aires, 1979-80; v.p., gen. mgr. Mavico SA, Buenos Aires, 1980-83; gen. mgr. Perkins Argentina, Buenos Aires, 1983-84; pres., sr. ptnr. Decisiones Empresarias SRL, Buenos Aires, 1983—; cons., chief exec. officer Domecq Garcia Shipyard, Argentina, 1985—, Compania Hotelera, 1985—, Argentian Railroad, 1986—, SKF, 1986—, Grandes Motores Diesel S.A. Author: Argentina Totalitaria, 1983; contbr. articles to profl jours. Bd. dirs. Comunal Citizens orgn., San Isidro, Argentina, 1986—. Served with Argentian Navy, 1948-51. Mem. Am. Mgmt. Assn., Pres.'s Assn. Roman Catholic. Clubs: Jockey, Nautico San Isidro. Office: Decisiones Empresarias SRL, Tucuman 2103, Buenos Aires Argentina

MERON, NATHAN DAVID, photographer; b. Lille, France, Oct. 24, 1933; came to Israel, citizen, 1954; s. Joseph Herz and Fela (Szykman) Milstein; m. Ayala Grosset, Oct. 24, 1964; children—Tikva, Ygal, Nily, Nava. Student Hebrew U., 1973. Founder, mgr. Semoplast Jerusalem Ltd., 1971, Colorama Ltd. 1972, MIB Ltd., 1973—, Diarama Ltd., 1982—, Welcome Gift Shops, 1984— . Served with Israeli Army, 1955-58. Pub. audivisual sets Tour the Holy Land, 1975; Jesus, 1976; Beduins of Sinai, 1977; Israel Past and Present, 1978; Living Reefs of the Red Sea, 1979; Holocaust, 1986. Mem. Labour Party. Office: Ariel Hotel, 31 Hebron Rd, Jerusalem Israel Office: PO Box 18060, Jerusalem 91180, Israel

MEROW, JOHN EDWARD, lawyer; b. Little Valley, N.Y., Dec. 20, 1929; s. Luin George and Mildred Elizabeth (Stoll) M.; m. Mary Alyce Smith, June 19, 1957; 1 dau., Alison Rasmussen. Student, UCLA, 1947-48; B.S.E., U. Mich., 1952; J.D., Harvard U., 1958. Bar: N.Y. 1958, U.S. Supreme Ct. 1971. Assoc. Sullivan & Cromwell, N.Y.C., 1958-64, ptnr., 1965—, vice chmn., 1986-87, chmn., sr. ptnr., 1987—; dir. KaiserTech Ltd., Seligman Group mut. funds. Mem. adv. council Ctr. for Study Fin. Instns., U. Pa Law Sch., 1974-83; mem. adv. bd. N.Y. Hosp.-Cornell Med. Ctr., legal affairs com. The N.Y. Hosp.; bd. dirs., sec. Met. Opera Club; warden St. Thomas Ch., N.Y.C., 1971-78; trustee, v.p. Am. Friends of Australian Nat. Gallery Found., Inc.; trustee U.S. Council Internat. Bus.; bd. dirs. Mcpl. Art. Soc. N.Y. Served to lt. USN, 1952-55. Mem. ABA, N.Y. State Bar Assn., Assn. Bar City N.Y. (chmn. com. on securities regulation 1974-77), Am. Law Inst. (advisor project on corp. governance), Union Internationale des Avocats, Council on Fgn. Relations, Am. Australian Assn. (chmn. bd. dirs.), Internat. Bar Assn. Clubs: Links, Piping Rock, Down Town, Church, Chatham Beach and Tennis, The Calif. Home: 350 E 69th St New York NY 10021 also: 51 Fruitledge St Brookville NY 11545 Office: Sullivan & Cromwell 125 Broad St New York NY 10004

MERRICK, JOAV, pediatrician; b. Copenhagen, Sept. 26, 1950; s. Abraham and Yona (Michaelson) M.; m. Yael Robinson, July 1, 1974; children—Michal Talia, Efrat Miriam. M.D., U. Copenhagen, 1977. Rotating intern internal medicine and surgery Univ. Hosp., Rigshospitalet, Copenhagen, 1977-78, resident ambulatory, community and social pediatrics, 1979-81, sr. resident in pediatrics, 1983-84, attending physician, dir. sect. ambulatory, community and social pediatrics, dept. pediatrics, sr. lectr. in community pediatrics, 1984-86, research pediatrician, subsequently dir. Prospective Pediatric Research Unit, 1980-87; intern internal medicine Vestre Hosp., Copenhagen, 1978-79; resident pediatrics Roskilde County Hosp., Denmark, 1981-82; resident Hosp. for Sick Children, Fuglebakken, Denmark, 1982; cons. community pediatrician, dir. child protection team Copenhagen County Dept. Social Service, 1984—; attending physician in pediatrics, dir. ambulatory pediatrics dept. pediatrics Holbeck (Denmark) Cen. Hosp., 1986—; dir. Children's House and nat. Ctr. for Prevention of Child Abuse and Neglect, Copenhagen, 1987—. Author: (children's book) Children and the Emergency Room, 1980; Child Abuse and Neglect, 1984. Editor: Incest and Child Sexual Abuse, 1983; Child Health and Development. The Scandinavian Textbook on Social and Community Pediatrics, 1984; Children in Alcohol-and-Drug-Abusing Families, 1985; A Scandinavian Textbook on Child Abuse and Neglect, 1985. Mem. Danish Pediatric Soc., Internat. Soc. for Prevention Child Abuse and Neglect (exec. council 1984—, editorial bd. internat. jour. 1986—), Assn. for Child Psychology and Psychiatry, Community Pediatric Group, Israeli Assn. for Child Protection (bd. dirs. 1985—). Home: Tuborgvej 76B, DK-2900 Hellerup Denmark Office: Children's House, Holsteinsgade 26, DK-2100 Copenhagen O, Denmark

MERRIFIELD, ROBERT BRUCE, educator, biochemist; b. Ft. Worth, July 15, 1921; s. George E. and Lorene (Lucas) M.; m. Elizabeth Furlong, June 20, 1949; children: Nancy, James, Betsy, Cathy, Laurie, Sally. B.A., UCLA, 1943, Ph.D., 1949. Chemist Park Research Found., 1943-44; research asst. Med. Sch., UCLA, 1948-49; asst. Rockefeller Inst. for Med. Research, 1949-53, assoc., 1953-57; asst. prof. Rockefeller U., 1957-58, assoc. prof., 1958-66, prof., 1966—. Assoc. editor: Internat. Jour. Peptide and Protein Research; contbr. aritcles sci. jours. Recipient Lasker award biomed. research, 1969; Gairdner award, 1970; Intra-Sci. award, 1970; Nichols medal, 1973; Alan E. Pierce award Am. Peptide Symposium, 1979; Nobel prize in chemistry, 1984. Mem. Am. Chem. Soc. (award creative work synthetic organic chemistry 1972), Nat. Acad. Scis., Am. Soc. Biol. Chemists, Sigma Xi, Phi Lambda Upsilon, Alpha Chi Sigma. Office: Rockefeller U New York NY 10021

MERRIGAN, WILLIAM JOSEPH, lawyer; b. Conception Junction, Mo., Sept. 28, 1934; s. Patrick James and Irene Anna (McLaughlin) M.; m. Sandra Craig Bartolina, Oct. 22, 1977. B.S., Creighton U., 1956; LL.B., Georgetown U., 1961. Bar: Va. 1961, Mo. 1961. Legis. asst. Congressman W. R. Hull, Jr., U.S. Ho. of Reps., 1958-59; legal counsel, asst. sec. Civil Air Transport, Southern Air Transport and Air America, Inc., Taipei, Taiwan, 1962-74; legis. counsel Dept. Army, Washington, 1974—. Served with AC, USN. Mem. ABA, Mo. Bar Assn., Va. Bar Assn., Supreme Ct. Hist. Soc. Republican. Roman Catholic. Home: 4931 Old Dominion Dr Arlington VA 22207 Office: Hdqrs Mil Traffic Mgmt Command Washington DC 20315

MERRILL, AMBROSE POND, JR., physician, health services consultant; b. Provo, Utah, Dec. 14, 1909; s. Ambrose Pond and Lydia (Stephens) M.; m. Elizabeth Call, Apr. 7, 1931. A.B., Stanford, 1932, M.D., 1935; M.H.A. with distinction, Northwestern U., 1948. Intern San Francisco County Hosp., 1934-35; surg. house officer Stanford U. Hosps., 1935-36; gen. practice medicine and surgery 1936-40; surgeon San Francisco Emergency Hosp. Service, Dept. Pub. Health, 1936-38; asst. supt. San Francisco County Hosp., 1938-40; asst. dir. St. Luke's Hosp., Chgo., 1940-42; med. dir. St. Luke's Hosp., 1942-45; exec. dir. St. Barnabas Hosp., N.Y.C., 1945-67; asst. dir. bur. hosp. certification N.Y. State Dept. Health, 1967-68; pres. A.P. Merrill, M.D. & Assos. (Hosp. and Health Services Consultants), Delmar, N.Y., 1968—; asst. clin. prof. phys. medicine and rehab. N.Y. U., 1955-60; lectr. Sch. Hosp. Adminstrn., Columbia, 1946-53, preceptor, 1946-67; Pres. Middle Atlantic Hosp. Assembly, 1958-59, Hosp. Assn. N.Y. State, 1956-57, Greater N.Y. Hosp. Assn., 1953-54; mem. N.Y.C. Mayor's Adv. Com. for the Aged, 1955-60; del. Nat. Health Assembly, 1948, Nat. Conf. on Aging, 1950, Internat. Gerontological Congress, 1951, Nat. Conf. on Care of Long-Term Patient, 1954, White House Conf. on Aging, 1961; chmn. com. on chronic illness Welfare and Health Council of N.Y.C., 1949-55; chmn. med. adv. com. Fedn. of Protestant Welfare Agys., N.Y.C., 1956-59; mem. subcom. on aging and chronic illness Interdepartmental Health Council, N.Y.C., 1957-60. Contbr.: chpt. to Functional Planning of Gen. Hospitals, 1969; also articles to hosp. and med. jours. Bd. dirs. Bronx Bd. Trade, 1955-67; bd. mgrs. Bronx YMCA, 1955-67, Bronx div. Protestant Council N.Y.C., 1950-65; donor student loan fund Stanford U., 1965. Recipient Brotherhood award NCCJ, 1967; Modern Hosp. award and medal, 1945; numerous others. Fellow N.Y. Acad. Medicine, Am. Coll. Hosp. Adminstrs., Am. Coll. Preventive Medicine; mem. N.Y. State, Bronx County med. socs., Am. Hosp. Assn. (life), Am. Pub. Health Assn., AAAS, Am. Geriatric Soc., N.Y. Acad. Scis., Am. Assn. Health Care Consultants, Internat. Hosp. Fedn., World Med. Assn., AMA., Alpha Kappa Kappa. Republican. Mem. Ch. of Jesus Christ of Latter-day Saints (high council N.Y. stake 1961-67, Hudson River stake 1969-72). Club: University (N.Y.C.). Home: 73 Greenock Rd Delmar NY 12054

MERRILL, GEORGE VANDERNETH, lawyer; b. N.Y.C., July 2, 1947; s. James Edward and Claire (Leness) M.; m. Janice Anne Humes, May 11, 1985. AB, Harvard U., 1968, JD, 1972; MBA, Columbia U., 1973. Bar: N.Y. 1973, U.S. Dist. Ct. (so. and ea. dists.) N.Y. 1974, U.S. Ct. Appeals (2d cir.) 1974. Assoc., Cleary, Gottlieb, Steen & Hamilton, N.Y.C., 1974-77, Hawkins, Delafield & Wood, N.Y.C., 1977-79; v.p. Irving Trust Co., N.Y.C., 1980-82; v.p., gen. counsel Listowel Inc., N.Y.C., 1982-84, bd. dirs., exec. v.p., gen. counsel, 1984—, also bd. dirs. Pres. Arell Found., N.Y.C., 1985—, also bd. dirs.; pres. Northfield Charitable Corp., N.Y.C., 1986—; v.p., sec. Brougham Prodn. Co., N.Y.C., 1986—, Cabriolet Prodn. Co., N.Y.C., 1986—; v.p. Sci. Design and Engring. Co., Inc., N.Y.C., 1987—. Recipient Detur Award Harvard U., 1968. Mem. ABA, Am. Mgmt. Assn., Assn. of Bar of City of N.Y. Clubs: The Brook, Union, Down Town, Knickerbocker, Racquet and Tennis, Players , Pilgrims of U.S. (all N.Y.C.). Home: 50 Glenbrook Rd Stamford CT 06902 Office: Listowel Inc 2 Park Ave New York NY 10016

MERRILL, RICHARD THOMAS, publishing executive; b. Chgo., June 26, 1928; s. Thomas William and Mary Ann (Colvin) M.; m. Lisi Y. Snyder, June 7, 1952; children: T. William II, James R., Stephen J. B.A., U. Mo., 1950, B.J., 1951. With Commerce Clearing House, Chgo., 1953—; v.p. Commerce Clearing House, 1962-76, exec. v.p., 1976-79, pres., chief exec. officer, 1980—, also dir.; dir. CCH Australia, CCH Canadian Ltd., Nat. Quotation Bur., CT Corp. System, Computax, State Capitol Info. Service, Facts on File, Blvd. Bank, Chgo., Blvd. Bancorp. Inc., Washington Service Bur., Quail Hill, Inc., Editorial Fiscal y Laboral (S.A. de C.V.). Served to capt. USAF, 1951-53. Home: 5 Astor Ct Lake Forest IL 60045 Office: Commerce Clearing House Inc 2700 Lake Cook Rd Riverwoods IL 60015

MERRILL, ROBERT, baritone; b. Bklyn., June 4, 1919; s. Abraham and Lillian (Balaban) Miller; m. Marion Machno, May 30, 1954; children—David Robert, Lizanne. MusD (hon.), Gustavus Adolphus Coll., 1970. Ind. baritone N.Y.C. and on tour, 1945—. Baritone in concert, opera and on radio and TV; winner, Met. Auditions of the Air, 1945, debut in opera, 1945; operatic roles include Escamillo in Carmen, Germont in La Traviata, Valentine in Faust, Amonasro in Alda, Marcello in La Boheme, Don Carlo in La Forza del Destino, Sir Henry Ashton in Lucia de Lammermoor; sang in La Traviata condr. Arturo Toscanini over NBC network; singer with NBC, 1946—; opened Met. Opera season Rodrigo in Don Carlo, 1950; appeared in Toscanini's final opera performance and rec. as Renato in Un Ballo in Maschera; opened Met. season as Valentine in Faust, 1953, as Figaro in Barber of Seville, 1954, Rigoletto in Rigoletto; Barnaba in Giocanda, Scarpia in Tosca, Renato in Un Ballo in Maschera, Iago in Otello, Count di Luna in Il Trovatore, Tonio in Pagliacci, Gerard in Andrea Chenier, 1962, Sir Henry in Lucia, 1964, Valentine in Faust, 1965, Germont in La Traviata, 1966, Amonasro in Aida, 1969; also opened Met. Opera season, 1971; opened Royal Opera House-Covent Garden season as Germont in La Traviata, 1967, Met. Opera visit to Japan, Tokyo, 1975; appeared in concerts, London, Bournemouth, Geneva, Israel, 1975; rec. artist: RCA-Victor, Angel, London, Columbia labels; stage debut as Tevye in Fiddler on the Roof, 1970; author: (novel) The Divas, 1978, (autobiography) Once More From the Beginning, 1965, Between Acts, 1976. Mem. Nat. Council of the Arts, 1968-74. Recipient Music Ann. award for rec., Ah, Dite Alla Giovine, 1946, Best Opera Rec. award Nat. Acad. Rec. Arts and Scis., 1962, 64, Harriet Cohen Internat. Music award, 1961, Handel medal City N.Y., 1970, Medallion award Westchester Community Coll. Found., 1981; named Father of Yr. in Music, 1980. Mem. Opera Guild, AFTRA, AGVA, Actors Equity Assn., Screen Actors Guild, Am. Guild Mus. Artists. Club: Friars (monk 1968—). Office: care Robert Merrill Assocs Inc 79 Oxford Rd New Rochelle NY 10804

MERRILL, ROBERT EDWARD, special machinery manufacturing company executive; b. Columbus, Ohio, Oct. 21, 1933; s. Robert Ray and Myrna Ione (Rinehart) M.; student Ohio State U., 1954-56 M.B.A., Pepperdine U.; m. Donna Rae Bernstein, Mar. 19, 1967; children—Robert Edward, Aaron Jay, Jonathan Cyrus, Raquel Naomi. Pres., PSM Corp., San Jose, Calif., 1974—. Served with AUS, 1950-51; Korea. Mem. Soc. Mfg. Engrs., Am. Soc. Metals, Soc. of Plastics Industry. Patentee in pneumatic applications for indsl. press machinery. Home: 858 Fieldwood Ct San Jose CA 95120 Office: Box 5156 San Jose CA 95150

MERRILL, WILLIAM H., lawyer, corporate professional; b. Indpls., Apr. 11, 1942; s. William H. and Jane (Robinson) M.; m. Winifred Jane Baur, July 25, 1964; children: Michele Jane, Betsy Diane. BS, Butler U., 1965; JD, Ind. U., 1967. Bar: Ind. 1967. Trust officer Mchts. Nat. Bank, Indpls., 1965-69; gen. counsel Everett I. Brown Co., Indpls., 1969-85; v.p., gen. counsel Landeco, Inc., Indpls., 1970-85; pres. Bash Seed Co., Indpls., 1975—; gen. ptr. Meta Ptnrs., 1984—; pres. Meta Investment Co., 1988—, Meta Mgmt. Co., 1988—; bd. dirs. Alpha Flex Industries, Inc., Med. Facilities Devel. Mgmt., Inc.. Mem. Carmel (Ind.) City Plan Commn., 1975-85, pres. 1982-85. Mem. ABA, Ind. Bar Assn., Indpls. Bar Assn., Am. Judicature Soc. Club: Crooked Stick Golf, Columbia. Home: 3725 W 106th St Carmel IN 46032 Office: 3205 W 71st St Indianapolis IN 46268

MERRING, ROBERT ALAN, lawyer; b. Middletown, N.Y., Oct. 5, 1951; s. Merton Joseph and Mabel Ruth M. Student Ohio Wesleyan U., 1969-70; A.B. with distinction and dept. honors, Stanford U., 1973; J.D. with honors in Internat. and Fgn. Law, Columbia U., 1977. Bar: Calif. 1977, U.S. Dist. Ct. (cen. dist.) Calif. 1978, U.S. Dist. Ct. (so. and ea. dists.) Calif. 1980, U.S. Ct. Appeals (9th cir.) 1980, U.S. Dist. Ct. (no. dist.) Calif. 1983, U.S. Supreme Ct. 1987. Assoc. Pacht, Ross, Warne, Bernhard & Sears, Inc., Los Angeles, 1977-79, Donovan Leisure Newton & Irvine, Los Angeles, 1979-81, Cutler and Cutler, Los Angeles, 1983-88, Friedemann & Hart, Anaheim, 1988—; clin. prof. Loyola U. Law Sch., Los Angeles, 1981-82. Columbia U. Internat. fellow, 1975-76. Mem. ABA, Orange County Bar Assn., Los Angeles County Bar Assn., Assn. Bus. Trial Lawyers. Editor Columbia Jour. Transnat. Law, 1976-77. Home: 4119 Via Marina Marina del Rey CA 90292

MERRISON, ALEXANDER WALTER, bank director; b. London, Mar. 20, 1924; s. Henry Walter and Violet Henrietta (Mortimer) M.; B.Sc., King's Coll., U. London, 1944; Ph.D., U. Liverpool, 1957; LL.D. (hon.), U. Bristol, 1971; D.Sc. (hon.), U. Ulster, 1976, U. Bath, 1977; m. Beryl Glencora Le Marquand, 1948 (dec. 1968); children—Jonathan, Timothy; m. Maureen Michele Barry, 1970; children—Andria, Benedict. Researcher, Signals Research and Devel. Establishment, Christchurch and AERE, Harwell, 1944-51; Leverhulme fellow, lectr. elementary particle physics U. Liverpool, 1951-57; physicist European Orgn. Nuclear Research, 1957-60; prof. exptl. physics Liverpool U., 1960-69, also dir. Daresbury Nuclear Physics Lab., 1962-69; vice chancellor Bristol U., 1969-84; chmn. Com. of Inquiry into Design and Erection of Steel Box Girder Bridges, 1970-73; mem. Council Sci. Policy. 1967-72, Nuclear Power Adv. Bd., 1973-76; chmn. Royal Commn. Nat. Health Service, 1976-79, Adv. Bd. for Research Councils, 1972-73, 79-82; chmn. Bristol region Lloyds Bank, 1983—, also dir. Chmn. Com. Inquiry into Regulation of Med. Profession, 1972-75; vice chmn. S.W. Regional Health Authority, 1973-76; dep. lt. County of Avon, 1974; chmn. Bristol Old Vic Trust, 1971—, Western Provident Assn., 1984—. Created knight, 1976; recipient Charles Vernon Boys prize Inst. Physics, 1961. Fellow King's Coll., 1973. Fellow Royal Soc., Royal Soc. Arts. Club: Athenaeum (London). Address: The Manor, Hinton Blewitt, Temple Cloud, Bristol England Office: care Royal Soc, 6 Carlton House Terrace, London SW1Y 5AG England

MERRITT, JEAN, consulting firm executive; b. N.Y.C., Oct. 29, 1952; d. Harry and Ruth (Happel) Packman; m. Richard L. Kashinsky, Aug. 2, 1976 (div.); m. Richard L. Merritt, May 5, 1985; 1 child, Melissa Morgan. Grad. high sch., Bayside, N.Y. Corp. exec. Kaswol Corp., Richmond Hill, N.Y., 1973-85, Federated Cons. Service Inc., Bayside, N.Y., 1985—. Coach Queens Spl. Olympics, 1985. Mem. Mus. Modern Art, Greenpeace, Nat. Fedn. Wildlife, Ctr. for Environ. Edn., Defenders of Wildlife. Presbyterian. Avocations: flying; painting; interior design; gourmet cooking. Home: 162-21 Powels Cove Blvd Beechhurst NY 11357 Office: Federated Cons Service Inc 45-34 Bell Blvd Bayside NY 11361

MERRIWETHER, DUNCAN, retired manufacturing executive; b. Greenville, Ala., June 9, 1903; s. Jacob and Claudia (Robinson) M.; m. Asenath Kenyon, Feb. 9, 1929; children: Duncan Charles, Virginia Ann (Mrs. L.B. Disharoon), Julia Elizabeth (Mrs. Harris Arnold), Jacob Douglass. B.S., Columbia U., 1928, M.S., 1938. Asst. to mgr. indsl. dept. Peat, Marwick, Mitchell & Co., N.Y.C., 1928-33; various assignments Irving Trust Co., 1933-39; chief accountant Rohm & Haas Co., Phila., 1939-41; asst. treas. Rohm & Haas Co., 1941-43, treas., dir., mem. exec. com., 1943-48, exec. v.p., 1948, vice chmn., 1953-58, past dir., mem. exec. com.; founder Hampshire Nat. Bank, South Hadley, Mass., 1962. Dir. William Penn Found, 1943-70; trustee Mt. Holyoke Coll., 1958-68, chmn. emeritus, 1968—. Mem. Columbia U. Assos. (Distinguished Alumni Service medal 1949), Am. Inst. C.P.A.'s, Alpha Kappa Psi, Beta Gamma Sigma. Episcopalian. Clubs: Mason. (Phila.), Merion Cricket (Phila.), Rittenhouse (Phila.); Hideaway (Marco Island, Fla.), Marco Island Yacht. Home: Sunset House N Apt 611 Marco Island FL 33937

MERSEL, MARJORIE KATHRYN PEDERSEN (MRS. JULES MERSEL), lawyer; b. Manila, Utah, June 17, 1923; d. Leo Henry and Kathryn Anna (Reed) Pedersen; A.B., U. Calif., 1948; LL.B., U. San Francisco, 1948; m. Jules Mersel, Apr. 12, 1950; 1 son, Jonathan. Admitted to D.C. bar, 1952, Calif. bar, 1955; Marjorie Kathryn Pedersen Mersel, atty., Beverly Hills, Calif., 1961-71; staff counsel Dept. Real Estate State of Calif., Los Angeles, 1971—. Mem. Beverly Hills Bar Assn., Trial Lawyers Assn., So. Calif. Women Lawyers Assn. (treas. 1962-63), Beverly Hills C. of C., World Affairs Council. Club: Los Angeles Athletic. Home: 13007 Hartsook St Sherman Oaks CA 91403 Office: Dept Real Estate 107 S Broadway Los Angeles CA 90012

MERTA, JAN (BARON GRAF VON GRATZ), marine engineer; b. Stare Mesto, Czechoslovakia, Apr. 24, 1944; arrived in Can., 1968; s. Jan and Marie (Sebkova) M.; divorced; 1 child, Iveta. Diploma, Coll. Social Work, Prague, Czechoslovakia, 1964-68; BS, McGill U., Montreal, Que., Can., 1971; PhD in Psychology, U. Aberdeen, Scotland, 1978. Pres., pub. Jan's Pub. Co., Montreal, 1972-74; supr. diving, deep sea diver self employed, North Sea, Middle East, Africa, 1974-78; dir. research and devel. Wharton-Williams Ltd., Aberdeen, 1978-79, Oceaneering Inc., Houston, 1979-81; chief inspector diving. Govt. Can., Ottawa, Ont., 1981—. Co-author: Exploring The Human Aura, 1976. Chmn. com. for survival suits Can. Gen. Standards Bd., 1983. Decorated chevalier Ordre Royal de la Couronne de Boheme (France), Order of the Golden Fleece (Germany). Recipient Spl. Industry award Can. Assn. Diving Contrators. Named Grand Master L'Ancient Temple Pan Slavonic, 1984, Cpt. Sea Eagle Legion, 1985. Fellow Inst. Diagnostic Engrs., Inst. Petroleum; mem. Soc. Fire Protection Engrs., Brit. Psychol. Soc., Undersea Med. Soc. Roman Catholic. Home: 308 MacKay St, Ottawa, ON Canada K1M 2B8 Office: Can Oil and Gas Lands, Adminstrn, 355 River Rd, Ottawa, ON Canada K1L 0E4

MERTA, PAUL JAMES, cartoonist, photographer, engr., restauranteur, real estate developer; b. Bakersfield, Calif., July 16, 1939; s. Stanley Franklin and Mary Ann (Herman) M.; A.A., Bakersfield Jr. Coll., 1962; B.S. in Engring., San Jose State Coll., 1962. Cartoonist nat. mags., 1959—; civilian electronics engr. Air Force/Missiles, San Bernardino, Calif., 1962-65; electronics countermeasures engr., acquisition program mgr. Air Logistics Command, Sacramento, 1965—; TV film animator, producer, owner Merge Films, 1965—; photographer, owner The Photo Poster Factory, Sacramento, 1971—; owner restaurant La Rosa Blanca, Sacramento, 1980—; ptnr. Kolinski and Merta Hawaiian Estates, 1981—; polit. cartoonist Calif. Jour., 1958-59, Sacramento Union Newspaper, 1979—, Sacramento Legal Jour., 1979. Home: 4831 Myrtle Ave #8 Sacramento CA 95841 Office: 1005 12th St Sacramento CA 95814

MERTENS, HANS-JOCHEM, mathematics educator; b. Monchengladbach, Fed. Republic of Germany, Mar. 26, 1951; s. Heinrich Anton and Gertrud (Hamacher) M.; m. Brigitta Gellissen, Feb. 15, 1975; children: Judith, Almut, Ansgar. Diploma, U. Aachen, Fed. Republic of Germany, 1974, PhD, 1979. Researcher U. Aachen, 1974-75; tchr. Monchengladbach Dept. Edn., 1980-86; mem. faculty Gymnasium Rheindahlen, Fed. Republic of Germany, 1976—; educator new tchrs. Seminar Duisburg, Fed. Republic of Germany, 1986—. Author: Multiplikatoren Zwischen, 1976, Banach-Raumen, 1976; contbr. articles to profl. jours. Mem. Gesellschaft für Deutsche Sprache. Roman Catholic. Home: Max Reger St, 4050 MG Rheindahlen Federal Republic of Germany Office: Seminar Wrangelstrasse, 4100 Duisburg Federal Republic of Germany

MERTING, JOHN WEBSTER, lawyer; b. Pensacola, Fla., June 17, 1943; s. Fritz and Elizabeth (Webster) M.; m. Linda Claytor, Jan. 12, 1974; children—Courtney Kristin, Shannon Michelle. B.A. cum laude, Fla. State U., 1965; LL.B., U. Va., 1968, J.D., 1970. Bar: Fla. 1968, U.S. Dist. Ct. (no. dist.) Fla. 1969, U.S. Dist. Ct. (mid. dist.) Fla. 1984. Assoc. Merritt & Merting, Pensacola, Fla., 1968-70, Jones Latham, Liberis & Merting, Pensacola, 1970-75, Liberis & Merting, Pensacola, 1975-78; sole practice, Pensacola, 1978; ptnr. Merting & Davis, P.A., 1978-86 ; pres. Merting & Denison, P.A., 1986—; adj. prof. U. W. Fla., 1968-69. Legis. asst. Sen. John Spottswood, Fla., 1965. Served with Fla. N.G., 1968-74. Recipient Spl. Recognition award Pensacola Sports Assn., 1970-71. Mem. Fla. Bar Assn., Acad. Fla. Trial Lawyers (sustaining), Assn. Trial Lawyers Am. (sustaining), N.Y. Trial Lawyers Assn., ABA, Southeastern Admiralty Law Inst. (dir. 1985-87), Maritime Law Assn. of U.S., Escambia-Santa Bar Assn., Phi Beta Kappa, Phi Kappa Phi, Omicron Delta Kappa. Republican. Episcopalian. Clubs: Sertoma (pres. 1979-80, chmn. 1980-81), Pensacola Yacht, Order of Tristan, Krewe of Lafitte, Rebellaires (pres. 1987-88), Hildagos, Pensacola Ski (pres. 1981-82), Pensacola Sports Assn., Gold Key. Founding editor The Summation, 1974-77; editor-in-chief The Va. Law Weekly, 1967-68; patentee in field. Home: 258 Sabine Dr Pensacola Beach FL 32561 Office: 421 N Palafox St Pensacola FL 32501

MERWIN, JOHN DAVID, lawyer, former governor; b. Frederiksted, St. Croix, V.I., Sept. 26, 1921; s. Miles and Marguerite Louise (Fleming) M.; m. Ludmila D. Childs, Nov. 8, 1958. Student, U. Lausanne, Switzerland, 1938-39, U. P.R., 1939-40; B.Sc., Yale U., 1943; LL.B., George Washington U., 1948. Bar: Conn., V.I. 1949. Practice law St. Croix, V.I., 1949-50, 1953-57, 67—; gen. counsel, v.p. Robert L. Merwin & Co., Inc., 1953-57; senator-at-large V.I. Legislature, 1955-57; govt. sec. for V.I. 1957-58, gov. V.I., 1958-61; rep. Chase Manhattan Bank, Nassau, Bahamas, 1961-65; exec. v.p. Equity Pub. Corp. Orford, N.H., 1965-67. Chmn. V.I. Port Authority, 1972-75. Served from 2d lt. to capt. F.A. AUS, 1942-46, 50-53. Decorated Bronze Star; Croix de Guerre with silver star. Mem. Internat., Conn., N.H., V.I. bar assns., Phi Delta Phi. Clubs: Tennis of St. Croix (V.I.); Yale (N.Y.C.). Home: PO Box 297 Franconia NH 03580

MESEC, DONALD FRANCIS, psychiatrist, neurologist; b. Waukegan, Ill., Aug. 29, 1936; s. Joseph Mesec and Johanna (Setnicar) M.; m. Francesca Auditore, June 20, 1964; 1 child, Steven Francis. B.S. cum laude, U. Notre Dame, 1958; M.D., N.Y. Med. Coll., 1963. Diplomate Am. Bd. Psychiatry and Neurology. Resident in psychiatry and neurology N.Y. Med. Coll.-Manhattan State Hosp., N.Y.C., 1964-67; chief of service Manhattan Psychiat. Ctr., N.Y.C., 1970-76, dir. psychiat. research, 1974-75, dir. Meyer Manhattan Alcohol Rehab. Ctr., 1975; med. dir. Meyer Day Ctr., N.Y.C., 1976-77; staff psychiatrist Asheville VA Hosp., N.C., 1977-78; practice medicine specializing in psychiatry, Phoenix, 1978—; instr. clin. psychiatry Columbia U., N.Y.C., 1972-77; dir. psychiat. edn. St. Joseph's Hosp., Phoenix, 1982—, co-dir. pain program, 1982—, vice chmn. dept. psychiatry, 1984—, chmn. dept. psychiatry, 1987—. Served with USPHS, 1963-64. Mem. New York County Med. Soc., Ariz. Med. Assn., Maricopa County Med. Soc., Ariz. Psychiat. Soc., AMA, Am. Psychiat. Assn.,Am. Acad. Clin. Psychiatrists. Office: 222 W Thomas Rd Phoenix AZ 85013

MESERVE, WALTER JOSEPH, drama studies educator; b. Portland, Maine, Mar. 10, 1923; s. Walter Joseph and Bessie Adelia (Bailey) M.; m. Mollie Ann Lacey, June 18, 1981; children by previous marriage—Gayle Ellen, Peter Haynes, Jo Alison, David Bryan. Student, Portland Jr. Coll., 1941-42; A.B., Bates Coll., Lewiston, Maine, 1947; M.A., Boston U., 1948; Ph.D., U. Wash., Seattle, 1952. Instr. to prof. U. Kans., Lawrence, 1951-68; prof. dramatic lit. and theory Ind. U., Bloomington, 1968-88, assoc. dean research and grad. devel., 1980-83, dir. Inst. for Am. Theatre Studies, 1983-88; disting. prof. Grad. Ctr. SUNY, N.Y.C., 1988—; v.p. Feedback Services, N.Y.C., 1983—. Author: History of American Drama, 1965, Robert Sherwood, 1970, An Emerging Entertainment, 1977, Heralds of Promise, 1986; editor: Plays of WD Howells, 1960; editor-in-chief: Feedback Theatrebooks, 1985—. Served to cpl. AC, U.S. Army, 1943-46. Fellow NEH, 1974-75, 83-84, 88-89, Rockefeller Found., 1979, Guggenheim Found., 1984-85. Mem. Am. Soc. for Theatre Research (exec. com. 1980-83), Am. Studies Assn., Authors Guild, Dramatists Guild (assoc.). Club: Cosmos (Washington). Office: CUNY Grad Ctr PhD Program Theater 33 W 42nd St New York NY 10036 Also: Feedback Services 305 Madison Ave Suite 311 New York NY 10165

MESQUITA, FRANCISCO NETO, communications company executive; b. São Paulo, Brazil, July 6, 1955; s. José Vieira de Carualho and Thereza Izabel (Sampaio) M.; m. Monica Bobbio, Aug. 26, 1978; children: Rita, Vera, Francisco. BA, U. Mackenzie, São Paulo, 1977; MBA, Columbia U., 1980. Asst. dir. O Estado de São Paulo, Brazil, 1976-78, comml. dir., 1980-84; supt. dir. O Estado de São Paulo Group, Brazil, 1984—; bd. dirs. Papel de Imprensa, OESP Grática, Circulation Audit Bur. Mem. Sch. Mktg. and Advt. (bd. dirs.). Clubs: Harmonia; Paulistano. Office: S/A O Estado de São Paulo, Av Eng Caetano Alvares 55, 02598 São Paulo Brazil

MESSARI, MOHAMED-LARBI, journalist; b. Tetouan, Morocco, July 8, 1936; s. Ahmed Mohamed and Fatima (Memmouhi) M.; m. Touria Cherkaovi-Gasmi, 1963; children—Nizar, Mouna, Yasser. Ed., Radio Broadcasting Inst., Cairo, 1959. With radio broadcasting company, Rabat, Morocco, 1959-63; journalist Al-Alam newspaper, Rabat, 1964-85, also bd. dirs. Mem. exec. com. Istiglal Party, 1978—; M.P. from Istiglal group, 1984-85. Ambassador of Kingdom of Morocco in Brazil, 1985—. Mem. Moroccan Writers Union (sec. gen. 1964, 69, 72), Fedn. Arab Journalists (vice sec.), Assn. for Spoken Spanish Journalists (pres. 1981), Moroccan Syndicate Journalists (1st vice sec. 1984).ts (1st vice sec. 1984). Office: Al-Alam Newspaper, 11 Ave Allah Ben Abdullah, Rabat Morocco

MESSER, ELI, airline executive; b. Ramat-Gan, Israel, Mar. 1, 1939; s. Walter and Regina (Schmuelewitz) M.; m. Ilana Goldenberg, Jan. 30, 1945; children: Odelia, Yael. Grad. high sch., Israel, 1957. Booking clk. Ganim Tours, Ramat-Gan, 1960-64; sales rep. Austrian Airlines, Tel Aviv, 1964-69, sales mgr., 1969-74, regional mgr., 1974—. Served to capt. Israel Def. Forces. Club: SKAL (Tel Aviv). Home: 1 Bassola, Tel Aviv Israel Office: Austrian Airlines, 17 Ben Yehuda St, Tel Aviv Israel

MESSER, THOMAS M., museum director; b. Bratislava, Czechoslovakia, Feb. 9, 1920; came to U.S., 1939, naturalized, 1944; s. Richard and Agatha (Albrecht) M.; m. Remedios García Villa, Jan. 10, 1948. Exchange student, Inst. Internat. Edn., 1939; student, Thiel Coll., Greenville, Pa., 1939-41; B.A., Boston U., 1942; degree, U. Sorbonne, Paris, 1947; M.A., Harvard U., 1951; D.F.A. honoris causa, U. Mass., 1962. Dir. Roswell (N.Mex.) Mus., 1949-52; asst. dir. Am. Fedn. Arts, N.Y.C., 1952-53; dir. exhbns. Am. Fedn. Arts, 1953-55, dir., 1955-56, trustee, 1972—; dir. Inst. Contemporary Art, Boston, 1957-61, Solomon R. Guggenheim Mus., N.Y.C., 1961—; adj. prof. Harvard U., 1960, Barnard Coll., 1966, 71; mem. exec. com. Am. Arts Alliance, Washington; pres. The MacDowell Colony Inc., 1977-78. Author: Edvard Munch, 1973; Contbr. to mus. catalogues, art jours. Trustee Wooster Sch. Spl. fellow for study in Brussels Belgian-Am. Ednl. Found., 1953; sr. fellow Center Advanced Studies, Wesleyan U., 1966; decorated knight Royal Order St. Olav. Mem. Assn. Art Mus. Dirs. (pres. 1974-75). Clubs: Met. Opera (N.Y.C.), Century Assn. (N.Y.C.) (admissions com. 1973-76). Office: Solomon R Guggenheim Mus 1071 Fifth Ave New York NY 10128 *

MESSERVY, SIR (RONEY) GODFREY (COLLUMBELL), business executive; b. Nov. 17, 1924; s. Roney Forshaw Messervy and Bertha (Collumbell) Crosby; m. Susan Particia Gertrude Nunn, 1952; 3 children. Student, U. Cambridge, Eng.; DSc (hon.), U. Aston, Birmingham, Eng., 1982, City U., 1986. Trainee CAV, mem. Lucas Group, 1949, dir. equipment sales, 1963, dir., gen. mgr., also dir. various Lucas subs.), 1966, mng. dir., 1974, dep. chmn., 1979, chmn., chief exec., 1980-87; chmn. Costain Group plc, 1987—; bd. dirs. Joseph Lucas Ltd., Joseph Lucas (Industries) Ltd. Mem. council Birmingham C. of Industry and C., 1979—, v.p., 1980-82, pres., 1982-83; mem. council SMMT, 1980—, mem. exec. com., v.p., 1984, pres., 1987-88; mem. council CBI, 1982—, BOTB, 1984—; mem. Engring. Industries Council, 1980—, Nat. Def. Industries Council, 1980-87. Served with Brit. mil., 1943-47. Decorated Knight, 1986. Mem. Worshipful Co. of Ironmongers (freeman 1977, liveryman 1979). Office: Costain Group plc, 111 Westminster Bridge Rd, London SE1 7EU, England *

MESSIAEN, OLIVIER, composer, educator; b. Avignon, France, Dec. 10, 1908; s. Pierre and Cecile (Sauvage) M.; student Etudes classiques au Conservatoire de Paris, 1919, Etudes de la rhythmique hindoue, 1935, Etudes d'ornithologie, 1943; Dr.h.c., Cath. U. Am., 1972; m. 2d, Yvonne Loriod, July 1, 1961; 1 son by previous marriage, Pascal. Prof. harmony Conservatory Paris, 1942—, prof. rhythmic and analysis, 1947—, prof. of composition, 1966—; organist Trinité, Paris, 1931—; concert tours throughout Europe, S.Am., Japan, U.S.; cours de compositions, Budapest, Darmstadt, Buenos Aires, Tanglewood, Mass. Decorated grand cross Legion d'Honneur; grand cross Order of Merit; comdr. Arts and Letters of France; comdr. Mérite fédéral Allemagne; recipient Erasme prize, 1971. Sibelius prize, 1971; Von Siemens prize, 1975; Leonie Sonning prize, 1977; Liebermann prize, 1983; Wolf Found. prize, 1983; grandprize Académie Berlin, 1984; Prix Inamori de Kyoto, 1985; grand prize Ville de Paris, 1985. Mem. acads. Baviere, Berlin, Rome, Hamburg, London, Stockholm, Madrid, Nat. Acad. Arts and Letters. Composer: L'Asension (orch.), 1933; Nativité du Seigneur (organ), 1935; Poèmes pour mi, 1936; Quatuor pour la fin du Temps, 1941; Visions de l'Amen (2 pianos), 1943; Vingt Regards (piano), 1944; Trois petites Liturgies, 1943; Turangalîla-Symphonie, 1948; Livre d'Orgue, 1952; Catalogue d'Oiseaux, for piano, 1958; Chronochromie for orch., 1960; Sept Haï-Kaï for piano and small orch., 1963; Et exspecto resurrectionem mortuorum, pour cuivres, bois, percussions métalliques, 1964; Meditations sur le Mystère de la Sainte Trinité, pour orgue, 1969; Transfiguration de N.S. Jesus Christ (choir, 7 solos and grand orch.), 1969; La Fauvette des jardins, for piano, 1970; Des Canyons aux Étoiles, piano and orch., 1970-74; Saint François d'Assise (opera), 1975-83, (pour orgue) Livre du Saint Sacrement, 1985, (piano) Petites Esquisses D'Oiseaux, 1986.

MESSNER, KATHRYN HERTZOG, civic worker; b. Glendale, Calif., May 27, 1915; d. Walter Sylvester and Sadie (Dinger) Hertzog; B.A., UCLA, 1936, M.A., 1951; m. Ernest Lincoln, Jan. 1, 1942; children—Ernest Lincoln, Martha Allison Messner Cloran. Tchr. social studies Los Angeles schs., 1937-46; mem. Los Angeles County Grand Jury, 1961. Mem. exec. bd. Los Angeles Family Service, 1959-62; dist. atty.'s adv. com., 1965-71, dist. atty.'s adv. council, 1971-82; mem. San Marino Community Council; chmn. San Marino chpt. Am. Cancer Soc.; bd. dirs. Pasadena Rep. Women's Club, 1960-62, San Marino dist. council Girl Scouts U.S.A., 1959-68, Am. Field Service, San Marino, 1983—; pres. San Marino High Sch. PTA, 1964-65; bd. mem. Pasadena Vol. Placement Bur., 1962-68; mem. adv. bd. Univ. YWCA, 1956—; co-chmn. Dist. Atty.'s Adv. Bd. Young Citizens Council, 1968-72; mem. San Marino Red Cross Council, 1966—, chmn., 1969-71, vice chmn., 1971-74; mem. San Marino bd. Am. Field Service; mem. atty. gen.'s vol. adv. com., 1971-80; bd. dirs. Los Angeles Women's Philharm. Com., 1974—, Beverly Hills-West Los Angeles YWCA, 1974-85, Los Angeles YWCA, 1975-84, Los Angeles Lawyers Wives Club, 1974—, Pacificulture Art Mus., 1976-80, Reachout Com., Music Center, Vol. Action Center, West Los Angeles, Calif., 1980-85, Stevens House, 1980—, Pasadena Philharm. Com., 1980-85, Friends Outside, 1983—, Internat. Christian Scholarship Found., 1984—; hon. bd. dirs. Pasadena chpt. ARC, 1978-82. Recipient spl. commendation Am. Cancer Soc., 1961; Community Service award UCLA, 1981. Mem. Pasadena Philharmonic, Las Floristas, Huntington Meml. Clinic Aux., Nat. Charity League, Pasadena Dispensary Aux., Gold Shield (co-founder), Pi Lambda Theta (sec. 1983—), Pi Gamma Mu, Mortar Bd., Prytanean Soc. Home: 1786 Kelton Ave Los Angeles CA 90024

MESSNER, ZBIGNIEW, prime minister of Poland, economist, politician; b. Stryj, Poland, Mar. 13, 1929; married; 2 children. Grad. Higher Sch. of Econs., Katowice, 1951, M. Econs., Higher Sch. Econs., Cracow, 1952, Dr. Econs., 1961, Dr. Habilitatis, 1969. Extraordinary prof. of econs., 1972, Ordinary prof. econs, 1977. Tchr., Higher Sch. of Econs. (now Acad. Econs.), Katowice, asst., 1950-54, lectr., 1954-68, pro-rector, 1968-75, rector, 1975-81; dir. Inst. Data Processing Orgns., 1972-77; chmn. Voivodship People's Council, Katowice, 1980-83; mem. Polish United Workers' Party, 1953—, mem. Cen. Com. and Polit. Bur., 1981—, mem. Cen. Com. Commn. for Investigation into Social Conflicts in the History of Polish People's Republic, 1981-84, first sec. Voivodship PUWP com., 1982-83, vice-chmn. Council of Ministers, 1983-85, chmn., (prime minister), 1985-88; dep. chmn. Commn. for Econ. Reform, 1984-86, chmn., from 1986. Author numerous publs. in field. Decorated Comdrs. Cross of Polonia Restituta, 1973, First Class Banner of Labour, 1984; recipient Prizes of Ministry of Sci., Higher Edn. and Tech., Nat. Edn. Commn. medal, 1973, award Meritorious Tchr. of People's Poland, 1974; named Hon. Miner of Polish People's Republic, 1983. Mem. Polish Econ. Soc. (v.p. main bd. 1971-81). Address: Urzad Rady Ministrow, Al Ujazdowskie 1/3, 00-583 Warsaw Poland

MESTAN, ANTONIN, language educator; b. Prague, Czechoslovakia, Aug. 29, 1930; s. Frantisek and Magda (Sarboch) M.; m. Vera Horalek. PhD, Charles U., Prague, 1953. Sci. worker Acad. Scis., Prague, 1954-66; langs. instr. U. Freiburg, Fed. Republic of Germany, 1966-69, lectr. Slavics, 1966-74; prof. State U., Amherst, Mass., 1974; prof. U. Freiburg, Fed. Republic of Germany, 1974-81, prof. Slavics, 1981—. Author: History of Czech Literature, 1984, Czech Literature 1785-1985, 1987; editor: Lodereckers Vocabulary, 1984, Czech-Polish Relations, 1986, Czech-German Vocabulary so K.H. Macha May, 1988. Roman Catholic. Home: Kapplerstr 49, 7800 Freiburg Federal Republic of Germany Office: Univ Freiburg, 7800 Freiburg Federal Republic of Germany

MESTIRI, MAHMOUD, minister of foreign affairs, Tunisia; b. Tunis, Tunisia, Dec. 25, 1929; s. Mohamed and Sohra Lasram M.; divorced; one s. Student, Inst. dÉtudes Politiques, France, Univ. de Lyons, France. Tunisian del. UN, N.Y.C., alt. del., 1958-59; head of Tunisian Spl. Diplomatic Mission to Congo Leopoldville, 1960; asst. to personal Rep. of UN Sec.-Gen. Belgium, 1961; dep. permanent rep. of Tunisia UN, N.Y.C., 1962-65; sec.-gen. for fgn affairs Tunis, 1965-67; permanent rep. UN, Tunisia, 1967-69; chmn. spl. com. on granting of independence to colonial countries and peoples UN, 1968-69; Tunisian ambassador Federal Republic of Germany, 1971-73, USSR and Poland, 1973-76; Tunisian permanent rep. UN, N.Y.C., 1976-80; minister of fgn. affairs Tunis, Tunisia, 1987—. Office: Office of Minister of Fgn Affairs, Tunis Tunisia *

MESTMÄCKER, ERNST-JOACHIM, lawyer, educator, academic administrator; b. Hameln, Fed. Republic of Germany, Sept. 25, 1926; m. Theresia Poll; children: Iris, Margaret. D of Law, Frankfurt (Fed. Republic Germany) U., 1953; cert. in habilitation, Frankfurt (Fed. Republic Germany), 1958; D of Econs. (hon.), U. Cologne, Fed. Republic Germany, 1980. Asst. Frankfurt (Fed. Republic Germany) U., 1954-58; prof. law Saarbrücken (Fed. Republic Germany) U., 1959-63, Münster (Fed. Republic Germany) U., 1963-69; prof. law Bielefeld (Fed. Republic Germany) U., 1969-78, rector, 1968-71; dir. Max Planck Inst. for Fgn. and Internat. Pvt. Law, Hamburg, Fed. Republic Germany, 1979—; spl. advisor Commn. European Communities, Brussels, 1963-72; vis. prof. Law Sch. U. Mich., Ann Arbor, 1965, 67, 75; chmn. German Monopolies Commn., Cologne, 1973-78. Editor jours., monograph series, symposia, various publs.; contbr. articles to scholarly jours. Mem. Council Econ. Advisors to German Ministry Econs., Bonn, Fed. Republic Germany, 1962—; bd. dirs. Deutscher Juristentag e.V., Bonn, 1983—. Recipient Wirtschaftspublizistik award Ludwig-Erhard-Stiftung, 1980, Cross of Merit Fed. Republic Germany, 1981; named hon. senator Bielefeld U., 1984. Mem. Gesellschaft Für Wirtschafts- und Sozialwissenschaften, Gesellschaft Für Rechtsvergleichtung, Max Planck Soc. Advancement Sci. (v.p. 1984). Club: übersee. Lodge: Rotary (Hamburg). Office: Max Planck Inst, Mittelweg 187, D-2000 Hamburg Federal Republic of Germany

MESTRE, JORGE, government analyst; b. Havana, Cuba, June 19, 1942; came to U.S., 1960, naturalized, 1969; s. Jose F. and Maria Cecilia (Folchs) M.; m. Matilde P. Valines, May 19, 1968; 1 son, Jorge H. B.A., Columbus Coll., Havana, 1960; M. Bus. and Pub. Adminstrn., Southwestern U., 1982, Ph.D. in Mgmt., 1983. Social scientist, Social Security Adminstrn., Alexandria, Va., 1966-72; program mgr. U.S. Customs Service, Washington, 1972-77, Drug Enforcement Adminstrn., Washington, 1977-80; sr. analyst U.S. Nuclear Regulatory Commn., Washington, 1980—. Commr. Human Rights Commn., Fairfax County, Va., 1977-85. Served with U.S. Army, 1964-66. Mem. Am. Soc. Personnel Adminstrn., Acad. Polit. Sci., Am. Judicature Soc., Nat. Assn. Fed. Investigators, Mensa. Roman Catholic. Home: 4344 Ashford Ln Fairfax VA 22032 Office: US Nuclear Regulatory Commn MNBB-7217 Washington DC 20555

MESTRE, MANUEL, architect; b. Mexico City, July 18, 1955; s. Manuel Mestre and Dolores (Noriega) De Mestre. B, Inst. Cumbres, Mexico City, 1979; grad. architect, U. Anahuac, Mexico City, 1982; cert. old bldgs. restorer, Colegio de Arquitectos, Mexico City. Cert. hotel planner Instituto Superior de Arquitectura Mexico City, 1988. Dir. design Constructora Monarca, Mexico City, 1978-79; pres. Manuel Mestre Arquitectos, Mexico City, 1979—; project mgr. Bosques de Reforma, Mexico City, 1981-82. Clubs: Sta. Maria (Valle de B.); Raqueta (Mexico City). Home and Office: Reforma 2009, 11000 Mexico City Mexico

MÉSZÁROS, ERNŐ, meteorologist, researcher; b. Budapest, Hungary, Apr. 12, 1935; s. Lajos and Julianna (Gréci) M.; m. Ágnes Nagy, Aug. 5, 1957 (dec. June 1986); 1 child, Lörinc. Degree in meteorology, L. Eötvös U., Budapest, 1957, Dr. rer. nat., 1961; D Earth Scis., Acad. Scis., Budapest, 1970; D H.C., U. Bretagne Occidente, Brest, France, 1983. Research scientist Aerol. Observatory of Nat. Meteorol. Service, Budapest, 1957-64, head div., 1964-71; dep. dir. Inst. Atmospheric Physics Nat. Meteorol. Service, Budapest, 1971-76, dir. Inst. Atmospheric Physics, 1976—; prin. Tng. Ctr. World Meteorol. Orgn. on Air Pollution Monitoring, Budapest, 1976. Author: Atmospheric Chemistry, 1981, (manual) Air Pollution Monitoring, 1985; author, editor: Physical Meteorology, 1982; contbr. chpt. to Environmental Warfare, 1984. Recipient Silver medal Order of Labor Presdl. Council of Hungary, 1976, Gold medal Order of Labor, 1982, ProNatura award nat. Environ. Agy., 1987. Mem. Hungarian Acad. Scis. (chmn. meteorol. com. 1978—, v.p. dept. earth scis. 1985—, Acad. prize 1979), Meteorol. Soc. Hungary (sci. bd. 1980—, medallion 1975), European Assn. for Sci. of Air Pollution (v.p. 1985). Home: 3 Peterhalmi, 1181 Budapest Hungary Office: Inst for Atmospheric Physics, 1 Peterhalmi, PO Box 36, H-1675 Budapest Hungary

METCALF, LYNNETTE CAROL, naval officer, journalist, educator; b. Van Nuys, Calif., June 22, 1955; d. William Edward and Carol Annette (Keith) M.; m. Scott Edward Hruska, May 16, 1987. BA in Communications and Media, Our Lady of Lake, 1978; MA in Human Relations, U. Okla., 1980; MA in Mktg. Webster U., 1986. Enlisted U.S. Air Force, 1973, advanced through grades to sgt., 1975; intelligence analyst, Taiwan, Italy and Tex., 1973-76; historian, journalist, San Antonio, 1976-78; commd. officer U.S. Navy, 1978, advanced through ranks to lt. comdr., 1988; pub. relations officer, Rep. of Panama, 1979-81; mgr. system program, London, 1981-82; ops. plans/tng., McMurdo Sta., Antarctica, 1982-84; exec. officer transient personnel unit Naval Tng. Ctr., Great Lakes, Ill., 1984-86, comdg. officer transient personnel unit, 1986-87; asst. prof. naval sci. U. Notre Dame NROTC, 1987—; nat. coordinator Seapower/Maritime Affairs curriculum, 1987—; anchorwoman USN-TV CONTACT, 1986-87. Contbr. articles to profl. jours.; editor Naval Station Anchorline, 1979-81, WOPN Caryatides, 1985-86; author: Winter's Summer, 1983. Sec. San Vito Dei Normanni theatre group, Italy, 1975-76; coordinator Magic Box Theater, Zion, Ill., 1984-86; dir. "Too Bashful for Broadway" variety show, Naval Tng. Ctr., 1986-87. Decorated Antarctic Service medal, 1983, Sec. Navy Letter of Commendation, 1984, Navy Commendation, 1987, Expert Marksman medal, 1985, Antarctic Service medal, 1983, Navy Commendation medal, 1987. Mem. Nat. Assn. Female Execs., Women Officers' Prof. Network. (communications chair 1985-86, programs chair 1986-87), Patron Michiana Arts & Scis. Council, Ladies of Notre Dame. Clubs: McMurdo; Soc. of South Pole. Avocations: golf, scuba diving, travel, reading, writing, performing. Office: Notre Dame U Dept Naval Sci South Bend IN 46556

METCALFE, ROBERT DAVIS, III, lawyer; b. Bridgeport, Conn., July 2, 1956; s. Robert Davis Jr. and Barbara Ann (Peaslee) M. BA summa cum laude, U. Conn., 1978, JD, 1981; MA, Trinity Coll., 1982. Bar: Conn. 1981, U.S. Supreme Ct. 1986. Judge adv. USN, Norfolk, Va., 1982-85; spl. asst. U.S. atty. U.S. Dept. Justice, Norfolk, 1985; trial atty. U.S. Dept. Justice, Washington, 1985—. Instr. ARC, Hartford, Conn., 1976-80; legis. asst. Conn. Gen. Assembly, Hartford, 1977. Served to lt. USN, 1982-85. Mem. Fed. Bar Assn., Conn. Bar Assn., Judge Adv. Assn., Mensa, Phi Beta Kappa. Republican. Episcopalian.

METEVELIS, PETER JOEL, humanities educator; b. Tacoma, Nov. 5, 1943; arrived in Japan, 1980; s. Themistocles and Dorothy (Dalrymple) M. BA, UCLA, 1973, MA, 1980; MA, Ind. U., 1980. Test mechanic rocket engine engring. Rocketdyne div. N.Am. Aviation, Los Angeles, 1964-68; part-time tchr., textbook writer Inst. Intercultural Studies, Los Angeles, 1979-80; tchr. Niikawa High Sch., Uozu City, Toyama, Japan, 1980-81; lectr. Wayo Women's Coll., Ichikawa, Chiba, Japan, 1981-84; prof. Tokoha Gakuen U., Shizuoka, Japan, 1984—; part-time lectr. Meijigakuin U., Tokyo, 1982-87; speaker 30th Internat. Conf. Orientalists in Japan, Tokyo, 1985, 31st Internat. Congress Human Scis. in Asia and North Africa, Kyoto, 1983; discussant 14th ann. conf. Prof.s' World Peach Acad., Baguio, Philippines, 1985. Author: (books) How to Write an English Essay, 1982, MS-DOS Fairu Seirigaku, 1986, MS-DOS Batchi Puroguramu Shu, 1987; editor: The Academician, Tokyo, 1984-85; columnist The Basic, Tokyo, 1987—; contbr. articles to profl. jours. Research fellow Kyoto (Japan) U., 1974-75; research scholar Japanese Ministry Edn., 1974. Mem. Assn. Asian Studies, Folklore Soc. Japan, Japan Found., Asiatic Soc. Japan, Toho Gakkai. Greek Orthodox. Home: 4-17-1 Toshinden, Shizuoka 421-01, Japan

METRA, MARCO, physician; b. Parma, Italy, Sept. 13, 1957; s. Ettore and Giovanna (Brighenti) M.; m. Paola Radaelli, June 27, 1987. MD, U. Parma, Italy, 1981. Vis. researcher clin. pharmacology U. Chgo., 1985; cardiology researcher U. Brescia, Italy, 1986—. Contbr. articles to profl. jours. Italian Ministry Edn. grantee Univ. Chgo., 1985. Home: Via Garzetta 17, 25100 Brescia Italy Office: Spedali Civili, Piazza Spedali Civili, 25060 Brescia Italy

METTLER, RUBEN FREDERICK, electronics and engineering company executive; b. Shafter, Calif., Feb. 23, 1924; s. Henry Frederick and Lydia M.; m. Donna Jean Smith, May 1, 1955; children: Matthew Frederick, Daniel Frederick. Student, Stanford, 1941-43; BSEE, Calif. Inst. Tech., 1944, MS, 1947, PhD in Elec. and Aero. Engring, 1949. Registered profl. engr., Calif. Assoc. div. dir. systems research and devel. Hughes Aircraft Co., 1949-54; spl. cons. to asst. sec. def. U.S. Dept. Def., 1954-55; asst. gen. mgr. guided missile research div. Ramo-Wooldridge Corp., 1955-58; pres. Space Tech. Labs., Inc., Los Angeles, 1962-65, TRW Systems Group, 1965-68; exec. v.p. TRW Inc. (formerly Thompson Ramo Wooldridge, Inc.), 1965, asst. pres., 1968-69, pres., chief operating officer, 1969-77, chmn. bd., chief exec. officer, 1977—, also bd. dirs.; bd. dirs. Bank Am. Corp., Merck & Co.; past vice-chmn. ind. adv. council Dept. Def.; chmn. Pres.'s Sci. Policy Task Force, 1969; mem. Pres.'s Blue Ribbon Def. Panel, 1969-70, Emergency Com. for Am. Trade. Author reports on airborne electronic systems; patentee interceptor fire control systems. Nat. campaign chmn. United Negro Coll. Fund, 1980-81; chmn. Nat. Alliance Bus., 1978-79; chmn. bd. trustees Calif. Inst. Tech.; trustee Com. Econ. Devel., Cleve. Clinic Found.; bd. dirs. Nat.

Action Council for Minorities in Engring. Served with USNR, 1942-46. Named one of Outstanding Young Men of Am., U.S. Jr. C. of C., 1955, So. Calif.'s Engr. of Year, 1964; recipient Meritorious Civilian Service award Dept. Def., 1969, Nat. Human Relations award NCCJ, 1979, Excellence in Mgmt. award Industry Week Mag., 1979. Fellow IEEE, AIAA; mem. Sci. Research Soc. Am., Bus. Roundtable (chmn. 1982-84), Conf. Bd. (trustee 1982—), Bus. Council (vice chmn. 1981-82, chmn. 1986-87), Nat. Acad. Engring., The Japan Soc. (bd. dirs.), Sigma Xi, Eta Kappa Nu (Nation's Outstanding Young Elec. Engr. 1954), Tau Beta Pi, Theta Xi. Clubs: Cosmos (Washington); Union, 50 (Cleve.). Home and Office: TRW Inc 1900 Richmond Rd Cleveland OH 44124 also: TRW Space & Def Sector 1 Space Park Redondo Beach CA 90278 *

METZ, WOLFGANG, historian, educator; b. Hildesheim, Fed. Republic Germany, Apr. 12, 1919; s. Ernst Christoph and Erika (Bornemann) M.; m. Lieselotte Welt. PhD, U. Göttingen, Fed. Republic Germany, 1947. Librarian State Library, Kassel, Fed. Republic Germany, 1947-51, U. Münster, 1952-53, State Library, Hannover, Fed. Republic Germany, 1954-64; chief librarian State Library, Speyer, Fed. Republic Germany, 1964-82; lectr. U. Göttingen, 1960-64; lectr. U. Mainz, Fed. Republic Germany, 1968-83, prof., 1971—. Author: Das Karolingische Reichsgut, 1960, Staufische Güterverzeichnisse, 1964, Erforschung des Karolingischen Reichsguts, 1971, Das Servitium Regis, 1978. Home: Albert Schweitzerstrasse 14, D 6720 Speyer Federal Republic of Germany

METZENBAUM, HOWARD MORTON, U.S. senator; b. Cleve., June 4, 1917; s. Charles I. and Anna (Klafter) M.; m. Shirley Turoff, Aug. 8, 1946; children: Barbara Jo, Susan Lynn, Shelley Hope, Amy Beth. B.A., Ohio State U., 1939, LL.D., 1941. Chmn. bd. Airport Parking Co. Am., 1958-66, ITT Consumer Services Corp., 1966-68; chmn. bd. ComCorp, 1969-74, after 1975; U.S. senator from Ohio 1974, 77—; Mem. War Labor Bd., 1942-45, Ohio Bur. Code Rev., 1949-50, Cleve. Met. Housing Authority, 1968-70, Lake Erie Regional Transit Authority, 1972-73, Ohio Ho. of Reps., 1943-46, Ohio Senate, 1947-50; mem. Ohio Democratic Exec. Com., from 1966, Ohio Dem. Finance Com., from 1969. Trustee Mt. Sinai Hosp., Cleve., 1961-73, treas., 1966-73; bd. dirs. Council Human Relations, United Cerebral Palsy Assn., Nat. Council Hunger and Malnutrition, Karamu House, St. Vincent Charity Hosp., Cleve., St. Jude Research Hosp., Memphis; nat. co-chmn. Nat. Citizens' Com. Conquest Cancer; vice-chmn. fellows Brandeis U. Mem. Am., Ohio, Cuyahoga, Cleve. bar assns., Am. Assn. Trial Lawyers, Order of Coif, Phi Eta Sigma, Tau Epsilon Rho. Office: US Senate 140 Russell Senate Bldg Washington DC 20510 *

METZGER, DARRYL EUGENE, mechanical and aerospace engineering educator; b. Salinas, Calif., July 11, 1937; s. August and Ruth H. (Anderson) M.; m. Dorothy Marie Castro, Dec. 16, 1956; children: Catherine Ann, Kim Marie, Lauri Marie, John David. BS in Mech. Engring., Stanford U., 1959, MS, 1960, PhD, 1963. Registered profl. engr., Ariz. Asst. prof. mech. engring Ariz. State U., Tempe, 1963-67, assoc. prof., 1967-70, prof., 1970—, prof., chmn. dept., 1974—, dir. thermosci. research, 1980—; cons. Pratt & Whitney Aircraft, East Hartford, Conn., 1977—, Pratt & Whitney Aircraft Can., 1979—, Garrett Turbine Engine Corp., Phoenix, 1966-77, NASA Lewis Research Ctr., NASA Office of Aeronautics and Space Tech., USAF Aeropropulsion Lab., Worthington Turbine Internat., Solar Turbine Internat., Allied Chem. Corp., Office of Naval Research, Sundstrand Aviation, AT&T, Bell Labs., Calspan Advanced Tech. Ctr., Rocketdyne div. Rockwell Internat., Ishikawajima-Harima Heavy Industries Co., Ltd., Tokyo; keynote address NATO Adv. Group for Aerospace Research and Develop., Norway, 1985; U.S. del. U.S./China Binat. Workshop on Heat Transfer, Beijing, Xian, Shanghai, 1983, NSF U.S./China Program Dev. Meeting, Hawaii, 1983, NSF/Consiglio Nazionale delle Ricerche Italy Joint Workshop on Heat Transfer and Combustion, Pisa, Italy, 1982; mem. U.S. sci. com. Internat. Heat Transfer Conf., 1986; mem. NASA Space Shuttle Main Engine Rev. Team, 1986-87, NASA Space Engring. Program Externat. Task Team, 1987. Contbr. articles to profl. jours.; editor: Regenerative and Recuperative Heat Exchangers, 1981, Fundamental Heat Transfer Research, 1980, Heat and Mass Transfer in Rotating Machinery, 1983, Heat Transfer in Gas Turbine Engines, 1987; mem. editorial bd. Internat. Jour. Exptl. Heat Transfer, 1987—. Ford Found. fellow, 1960; NSF fellow, 1961, ASEE/NASA fellow, 1964-65; recipient Alexander von Humboldt sr. research scientist award Fed. Republic Germany, 1985, 86, 87, achievement award for research in rotating machinery Am. Soc. Mech. Engrs., Japan Soc. Mech. Engrs., 1985, Faculty Achievement award Ariz. State U. Alumni Assn., 1987; Sonderforschungsbereich grantee, 1988—. Fellow ASME (mem. gas turbine com., chmn. heat transfer div. 1982-84, mem. com. on faculty quality 1986), Ariz. State U. Alumni Assn.; mem. AIAA, Soaring Soc. Am., Fed. Aero. Inst. (Internat. Diamond award), Phi Beta Kappa, Sigma Xi, Tau Beta Pi, Pi Tau Sigma, Phi Kappa Phi. Home: 8601 N 49th St Paradise Valley AZ 85253 Office: Ariz State U Mech and Aerospace Engring Dept Tempe AZ 85287

METZGER, H(OWELL) PETER, publicist, essayist; b. N.Y.C., Feb. 22, 1931; s. Julius Radley and Gertrude (Fuller) M.; m. Frances Windham, June 30, 1956 (div. July 1987); children: John, James, Lisa, Suzanne. B.A., Brandeis U., 1953; Ph.D., Columbia U., 1965. Mgr. advanced programs Ball Bros. Research Corp., Boulder, 1968-70; research assoc. Dept. Chemistry, U. Colo., Boulder, 1966-68; sr. research scientist N.Y. State Psychiat. Inst., N.Y.C., 1965-66; syndicated columnist N.Y. Times Syndicate, 1972-74, Science Critic, Newspaper Enterprise Assn., 1974-76; sci. editor Rocky Mt. News, Denver, 1973-77; mgr. public affairs planning Public Service Co. Colo., Denver, 1977—; cons. Environ. Instrumentation, 1970-72; dir. Colspan Environ. Systems, Inc., Boulder, Colo., 1969-72. Author: The Atomic Establishment, 1972; Contbr. articles in field to profl. jours., nat. mags. Pres. Colo. Com. for Environ. Info., Boulder, 1968-72; mem. Colo. Gov.'s State Health Planning Council, 1969-72, Colo. Gov.'s Adv. Com. Underground Nuclear Explosions, 1971-74; mem. spl. project on energy policy mgmt. Heritage Found., 1980; mem. 1981 Presdl. Rank Rev. Bd. U.S. Office Personnel Mgmt., 1981; Bd. dirs. Wildlife-2000, 1970-72, Colo. Def. Council, 1972—. USPHS fellow, 1959-65; prin. investigator, 1968; archivee Hoover Instn. Stanford U., 1982. Mem. ACLU (state bd. 1968-71), Sigma Xi, Phi Lambda Upsilon. Clubs: Denver Athletic, Denver Press; Am. Alpine (N.Y.C.). Address: 2595 Stanford Ave Boulder CO 80303

METZGER, JEAN MARC, rheumatologist; b. Strasbourg, France, Mar. 27, 1948; s. Pierre Henri and Odette Germaine (Weill) M. Diploma in Aeronautics, Med. U., Nancy, 1975; Diploma of Sport Medicine, Sch. Med. U., Besancon, 1977; Diploma Climatology and Hydrology, Sch. Med. U. Nancy, France, 1976, diploma in Rheumatology, 1978; MD, Med. U. Strasbourg, France, 1978. Resident U. Hosp. of Besancon, 1973-78; cons. Service of Rheumatology CHU Hautepierre, Strasbourg, 1978-88. Author: Acunpuctur and Tobacco, 1977, Cervical Lesions in Rheumatoid Arthritis Study of 100 Cases, 1978, Relations Between Biological Rythms and Chinese Med., 1976. Gen. sec. France-Israel Friendship, 1979—, Europe-Israel Parlementary Assn., 1982. Mem. French Organ. Against Rheumatism, Rheumatology Soc. of NE France, French Soc. Ozonotherapy, Ozonstudies and Med. Research Assn. Jewish. Lodge: B'nai Brith. Office: Cabinet de rheumatology, 28 Ave des Vosges, 67000 Strasbourg France

METZGER, VERNON ARTHUR, educator; b. Baldwin Park, Calif., Aug 13, 1918; s. Vernon and Nellie C. (Ross) M.; B.S., U. Calif., Berkeley, 1947, M.B.A., 1948; m. Beth Arlene Metzger, Feb. 19, 1955; children—Susan, Linda, 1 step-son, David. Estimating engr. C. F. Braun & Co., 1949; prof. mgmt. Calif. State U. at Long Beach, 1949—, founder Sch. Bus.; mgmt. cons., 1949—. Mem. Fire Commn. Fountain Valley, Calif., 1959-60; pres. Orange County Democratic League, 1967-68; mem. State Dept. mgmt. task force to promote modern mgmt. in Yugoslavia, 1977; mem. State of Calif. Fair Polit. Practices Commn., Orange County Transit Com. Served with USNR, 1942-45. Recipient Outstanding Citizens award Orange County (Calif.) Bd. Suprs. Fellow Soc. for Advancement of Mgmt. (life; dir.); mem. Acad. Mgmt., Orange County Indsl. Relations Research Assn. (v.p.), Beta Gamma Sigma, Alpha Kappa Psi, Tau Kappa Upsilon. Home: 1938 Balearic Dr Costa Mesa CA 92626 Office: 1250 Bellflower Blvd Long Beach CA 90804

METZGER-CAMPBELL, LINDA ARLENE, educator; b. Orange, Calif., Nov. 15, 1957; d. Vernon Arthur and Beth Arlene (Wilson) Metzger; m. James Lee Campbell, Nov. 26, 1983. A.A., Orange Coast Community Coll., 1976; B.A., Long Beach State U., 1978; M.A., Azusa Pacific U., 1985. Tchr., Santa Ana Unified Schs. (Calif.), 1979—, tchr. 1st grade health curriculum, 1983, trainer gifted and talented individuals, 1985-86, master tchr., 1987—. Mem. Kappa Delta Pi (social v.p. 1979).

METZLER, DIETER ERNST LOUIS, ancient history educator; b. Muenster, Germany, May 18, 1939; s. Ernst and Mathilde (Meyer) M.; 1 dau., Irina. Dr.Phil., U. Muenster, 1966. Researcher, Mus. Karlsruhe (W.Ger.), 1967; asst. U. Cologne (W.Ger.), 1968, U. Muenster (W.Ger.), 1970-77; fellow Darwin Coll., Cambridge, Eng., 1977; prof. ordinarius U. Muenster (W.Ger.), 1977—. Author: Portraet und Gesellschaft, 1971; Ancient Iran, 1977; contbr. articles on ancient history and classical archaeology to profl. jours. Home: Kellermannstr 3, 4400 Muenster Federal Republic of Germany Office: U Muenster Fliednerstr 21, 4400 Muenster Federal Republic of Germany

METZLER, YVONNE LEETE, travel agt.; b. Bishop, Calif., Jan. 25, 1930; d. Ben Ford and Gladys Edna (Johnson) Leete; student U. Calif., Berkeley, 1949; m. Richard Harvey Metzler, June 2, 1950; children: David Grant, Regan M., Erin E. Student Empire Coll., 1988—. Vocat. instr. Ukiah (Calif.) Jr. Acad., 1962-63; bookkeeper Sid Beamer Volkswagen, Ukiah, 1963-64; acct. Ukiah Convalescent Hosp., 1964, Walter Woodard P.A., Ukiah, 1964-66; asso. dir. Fashion Two Twenty, Ukiah, 1966-67, dir., Santa Rosa, Calif., 1967-71; acct. P.K. Marsh, M.D., Ukiah, 1971-72, Walter Woodard P.A. and Clarence White C.P.A., Ukiah, 1972-74; partner, travel agt. Redwood Travel Agy., Ukiah, 1973-76; owner, mgr. A-1 Travel Planners, Ukiah, 1976—; owner A-1 Travel Planners of Willits, Calif., 1979-88. Commr., Ukiah City Planning Commn., 1979-84 , chmn., 1981-83; rep. Mendocino County Visitors and Conv. Bur., 1988—, Pvt. Industry Council, 1988—; mem. Republican County Central Com., 1978-80. Mem. Ukiah C. of C. (1st v.p. 1980, pres. 1981-82), Mendocino County C. of C. (dir. 1981). Clubs: Soroptimist (pres. 1977-78), Bus. and Profl. Women (treas. 1977-78, named Woman of the 80's). Office: 505 E Perkins St Ukiah CA 95482

MEYBERG, JOERG-DIETRICH JOHANNES, psychologist, psychotherapist, researcher; b. Hemeringen, Niedersachsen, Fed. Republic Germany, June 24, 1951; s. Werner-Friedrich and Adelheid Louise (Grzegorzewski) M. Degree in Teaching, Pedagogic U., Aachen, Fed. Republic Germany, 1977, Pedagogic U., Borken, Fed. Republic Germany, 1978; M in Psychol. Scis., U. Muenster, Fed. Republic Germany, 1984. Cert. psychologist. Tchr. Primary Sch., Borken, 1977-78; pvt. practice psychology Muenster, 1984—; researcher U. Muenster, 1984—. Served with German Air Force, 1972-73. Evangelical. Home: Steinfurterstrasse 14-16, PO Box 5503, 4400 Muenster Federal Republic of Germany

MEYER, ARMIN HENRY, retired diplomat, author, educator; b. Ft. Wayne, Ind., Jan. 19, 1914; s. Armin Paul and Leona (Buss) M.; m. Alice James, Apr. 23, 1949; 1 dau., Kathleen Alice. Student, Lincoln (Ill.) Coll., 1931-33; A.B., Capital U., 1935, LL.D., 1957; M.A., Ohio State U., 1941, LL.D., 1972; LL.D., Wartburg Coll., S.D. Sch. Mines and Tech., 1972. Faculty Capital U., Columbus, Ohio, 1935-41; staff OWI, Egypt, Iraq, 1942-46; U.S. pub. affairs officer Baghdad, Iraq, 1946-48; pub. affairs adviser U.S. Dept. State, 1948-52; sec. Am. embassy, Beirut, Lebanon, 1952-55; dep. chief mission Kabul, Afghanistan, 1955-57; dep. dir. Office South Asian Affairs Dept. State, 1957-58, dep. dir. Office Near Eastern Affairs, 1958-59, dir. Office New Eastern Affairs, 1959-61, dep. asst. sec. of state for Nr. Eastern and South Asian Affairs, 1961; U.S. ambassador to Lebanon, 1961-65, Iran, 1965-69, Japan, 1969-72; spl. asst. to sec. state, chmn. Cabinet Com. to Combat Terrorism 1972-73; vis. prof. Am. U., 1974-75; dir. Ferdowsi project Georgetown U., 1975-79, adj. prof. diplomacy, 1975-86; Woodrow Wilson vis. fellow, 1974—, cons., Middle East, 1975—. Author: Assignment Tokyo: An Ambassador's Journal, 1974; co-author: Education in Diplomacy, 1987. Hon. mem. Lincoln Sesquicentennial Commn., 1959; bd. dirs. Washington Inst. Fgn. Affairs, 1979—, pres., 1988—. Recipient Meritorious service award Dept. State, 1958, Superior Honor award, 1973; decorated Order of Rising Sun, 1st class (Japan), 1982. Mem. Sigma Psi. Lutheran. Home: 4610 Reno Rd NW Washington DC 20008

MEYER, BETTE EUNICE, historian, museologist, preservationist; b. Chgo., Apr. 18, 1930; d. Henry Hahneman and Pearl Eunice (Kane) Wagner; m. Robert Edward Meyer, Feb. 3, 1951; children—Robert Daniel, Kathleen Lynn, Susan Joan. B.A., De Paul U., Chgo., 1956; M.Ed., Eastern Wash. U., Cheney, 1967, B.A. magna cum laude, 1971; postgrad. Wash. State U., 1981—. Curator history and edn. Eastern Wash. State Hist. Soc., Spokane, 1967-71; chief Office of Archeology and Historic Preservation, Wash. State Parks, Olympia, 1971-73; exec. dir. Congress of Valley Agys., Livermore, Calif., 1975-77; historic preservation planner Benton-Franklin Govtl. Conf., Richland, Wash., 1978-79; researcher Wash. State U. Found., Pullman, 1981-84; devel. and mktg. coordinator Holy Names Ctr. at Ft. George Wright Historic Dist., Spokane, 1984-87; exec. com. Wash. State Geog. Names Bd., Olympia, 1971-73. Author: Ainsworth: A Railroad Town, 1983; also articles. Chmn. Pullman Civic Arts Commn., 1981-82; mem. Wash. Land Use Plan Commn., Olympia, 1971-72, adv. com. Wash. State U. Mus., 1981-84; active local philanthropic orgns. NEH fellow. Mem. Am. Assn. Mus., Am. Assn. State, Local History (grantee, bd. dirs.), Can. Mus. Assn., Nat. Trust Historic Preservation, Whitman County Hist. Soc. (bd. dirs. 1981-83). Mont. Hist. Soc., AAUW (pub. info. chmn. Wash. div. 1972), Washington Trust for Historic Preservation, Council Am.'s Mil. Past, Victorian Soc. Am. Home: W 903 Westover Rd Spokane WA 99218

MEYER, CHARLES HOWARD, lawyer; b. St. Paul, Aug. 1, 1952; s. Howard Joseph and Helen Evangeline (Ericson) M.; m. Patti Jo Graf, Sept. 11, 1981; 1 child, Joseph Charles. BS in Bus. with high distinction, U. Minn., 1974; JD magna cum laude, Harvard U., 1977. Bar: Minn. 1977, U.S. Dist. Ct. Minn. 1977, U.S. Ct. Appeals (8th cir.) 1981, U.S. Claims Ct. 1987; CPA, Minn. Staff acct. Deloitte Haskins & Sells, Mpls., 1974, 75; ptnr. Oppenheimer Law Firm, St. Paul/Mpls., 1976, 77-85, 1988—; sr. tax atty. Cargill, Inc., Mpls., 1985-88; lectr. continuing legal edn. seminars. Mem. ABA, Minn. State Bar Assn., Hennepin County Bar Assn., Harvard Law Sch. Assn., Am. Inst. CPA's (Elijah Watt Sells gold medal), Nat. Accts. Assn., Am. Accts. Assn., Minn. Soc. CPA's (Harold C. Utley award 1974). Lutheran. Clubs: Harvard, North Oaks Golf (Minn.). Home: 5879 Royal Oaks Dr Shoreview MN 55126 Office: Oppenheimer Law Firm 3400 Plaza VII 45 South 7th St Minneapolis MN 55402

MEYER, FRED WILLIAM, JR., memorial parks exec.; b. Fair Haven, Mich., Jan. 7, 1924; s. Fred W. and Gladys (Marshall) M.; m. Jean Hope, Aug. 5, 1946; children—Frederick, Thomas, James, Nancy. AB, Mich. State Coll., 1946. Salesman Chapel Hill Meml. Gardens, Lansing, Mich., 1946-47; mgr. Roselawn Meml. Gardens, Saginaw, Mich., 1947-49; dist. mgr. Sunset Meml. Gardens, Evansville, Ind., 1949-53; pres., dir. Memory Gardens Mgmt. Corp., Indpls., Hamilton Meml. Gardens, Chattanooga, Covington Meml. Gardens, Ft. Wayne, Ind., Chapel Hill Meml. Gardens, Grand Rapids, Mich., Forest Lawn Memory Gardens, Indpls., Lincoln Memory Gardens, Indpls., Sherwood Meml. Gardens, Knoxville, Tenn., Chapel Hill Meml. Gardens, South Bend, Ind., White Chapel Meml. Gardens, Springfield, Mo., Nebo Meml. Park, Martinsville, Ind., Mercury Devel. Corp., Indpls., Quality Marble Imports, Indpls., Quality Printers, Indpls., Am. Bronze Craft, Inc., Judsonia, Ark. Mem. C. of C., A.I.M., Nat. Sales Execs., Am. Cemetery Assn., Sigma Chi, Phi Kappa Delta. Clubs: Athenaem Turners, Columbia, Meridian Hills Country, Woodland Country. Lodge: Elks. Home: 110 E 111th St Indianapolis IN 46280 Office: 3733 N Meridian St Indianapolis IN 46208

MEYER, GARY MILTON, artist; b. Boonville, Mo., May 13, 1934; s. Milton Simon and Anna Margaret (Davis) Meyer; m. Hiroko Julie Ii, Feb. 26, 1960; 1 son, Allan Gary Yoshio. B.P.A. with honors, Art Ctr. Coll. Design, Pasadena, Calif., 1959; postgrad. Chouinard Art Inst., 1962. Prodn. illustrator Universal Studios, Universal City, Calif., 1966-68; illus. Macco, Newport Beach, Calif., 1968-69; v.p. Recretects, Costa Mesa, Calif., 1970-71; illus., prin. Gary Meyer Illustration, Santa Monica and Burbank, Calif., 1972-78; pres. Gary Meyer Inc., Santa Monica, 1978—; documentary artist U.S. Air Force, 1967—. One man shows: Burbank Bd. Edn., 1952, J. Walter Thompson, Chgo., 1984; numerous group shows, including N.Am. Sculpture Exhbn., Golden, Colo., 1981, 83, Illus. West, Los Angeles County Mus. Sci. and Industry, 1983, Ill. West, 1984, Keys Art Exhbn., 1984; represented in permanent collections Smithsonian Air and Space Mus., USAF, Washington; prin. works include Roaring Head bronze sculpture (N.Am. Sculpture exhbn. Art Castings of Colo. award 1981), Fathead bronze sculpture (N.Am. Sculpture exhbn. Beyond Bronze award 1983). Served to sgt. USMC, 1952-55; Korea. Recipient 1st and 3d Pl. awards Tech. Illustration Mgmt. Assn., 1962, 1st Pl. award Tech. Illustration Mgmt. Assn., 1963, award of excellence CA-80, Communication Arts Mag., 1980, 1st prize European category Hollywood Reporter Mag. Key Arts Awards, 1983, Silver medal Illustration West 24 mag., 1985, Founders award Am. Soc. Aviation Artists, 1987, also numerous award certs. Mem. Soc. Illustrators, Soc. Illustrators Los Angeles (v.p., 2 Spl. Judges awards 1982, Best of Show award 1983, Best of Category award 1983, Spl. Judges award 1983, Best of Category award), Soc. Art Ctr. Alumni (sec. 1974-75). Democrat. Mem. Unity Ch. Home and Studio: 227 W Channel Rd Santa Monica CA 90402

MEYER, HAROLD LOUIS, mechanical engineer; b. Chgo., June 25, 1916; s. Norman Robert and Martha (Stoewsand) M.; m. Charlotte Alene Tilberg, June 21, 1941 (dec. 1951); 1 child, John C. Nelson. Student, Armour Inst. Tech., Chgo., 1934-42, U. Akron, 1942-44; BA in Natural Sci., Southwestern Coll., Winfield, Kans., 1951; student, Ill. Inst. Tech., 1955-73. Sales engr. Olsen & Tilgner, Chgo., 1938-39; project engr. Gen. Electric X-Ray, 1939-42, field engr., 1944-46; project engr. Goodyear Aircraft, 1942-44; chief x-ray technologist and therapist William Neton Meml. Hosp., Winfield, 1946-51; sr. design cons. Pollak and Skan, Chgo., 1952-58, cons. design specialist, 1963-68; project engr. Gaertner Scientific Co., Chgo., 1958-63; sr. design specialist Am. Steel Foundries, Chgo., 1969-74; cons. Morgen Design, Milw., 1974-76; proprietor Meyersen Engring., Addison, Ill., 1981—, also bd. dirs.; cons. dir. Miller Paint Equipment, Addison, 1976-87; design cons. R.R. Donnelley, Kraft Foods. Inventor: box sealing sta., 1939, chest X-ray equipment, 1942, G-2 airship, 1944, space program periscope, 1962, reactor test sta. periscope, 1962, beer can filling machine, 1963, atomic waste handling vehicle, 1965, ry. freight car trucks, 1974, hwy. trailer 5th wheels, 1974, motorized precision paint colorant dispensing machines, 1986. Sponsered a family of Cambodian Chinese refugees; mem. Norwood Park (Ill.) Norwegian Old Peoples Home; mem. Family Shelter Service, Glen Ellyn, Ill. Served with USNR, 1949-52. Recipient Appreciation award Lioness Club, Glendale Heights, 1985. Mem. AAAS, Chem. Engring. Product Research Panel, Ill. Inst. Tech. Alumni Assn. (new student recruiter 1985-87, Recognition award 1986, 87), Am. Registry of X-Ray Techs., Phi Kappa Sigma. Republican. Presbyterian. Lodges: Masons, Lions (dir. 1985-86). Office: Meyerson Enging PO Box 248 Addison IL 60101

MEYER, IRWIN STEPHAN, lawyer, accountant; b. Monticello, N.Y., Nov. 14, 1941; s. Ralph and Janice (Cohen) M.; m. Leslie J. Mazor, July 10, 1977; children—Kimberly B., Joshua A. B.S., Rider Coll., 1963; J.D., Cornell U., 1966. Bar: N.Y. 1966. Tax mgr. Lybrand Ross Bros. & Montgomery, N.Y.C., 1966-71; mem. firm Ehrenkranz, Ehrenkranz & Schultz, N.Y.C., 1971-74; prin. Irwin S. Meyer, 1974-77, 82—; mem. firm Levine, Honig, Eisenberg & Meyer, 1977-78, Eisenberg, Honig & Meyer, 1978-81, Eisenberg, Honig, Meyer & Fogler, 1981-82. Served with U.S. Army, 1966-71. C.P.A., N.J. Mem. ABA, N.Y. Bar Assn., Am. Assn. Atty.-C.P.A.s, N.Y. Assn. Atty.-C.P.A.s, Am. Inst. C.P.A.s, N.J. Soc. C.P.A.s. Home: 19 Woodhaven Dr New City NY 10956 Office: One Blue Hill Plaza Pearl River NY 10956

MEYER, JEAN-CLAUDE, psychoanalyst, psychotherapist; b. Thann, France, May 10, 1937; 2 children. Degree in psychiatrie, Strasbourg U., 1968; degree in psychoanalysis and haptotherapie, Internat. Soc. Research Devel. Haptonomy, OMS, France, 1987. Pvt. practice psychoanalysis Mulhouse, France. Home: 45 Rue Wanne, 68100 Mulhouse France Office: 10 Rue de Ferrette, 68100 Mulhouse France

MEYER, JEAN-PIERRE, psychiatrist; b. Paris, Apr. 3, 1949; s. Henry Jules and Jacqueline Suzanne (Roux).; m. Marie Elisabeth Buisan, June 25, 1977; children: Arnaud Jean, Gauthier Henri. MD, Broussais U., Paris, 1975; Cert. of Maritime Medicine, 1976; Cert. of Med. Expertise, Cochin U., Paris, 1978; specialist in psychiatry, Necker U., Paris, 1978. Intern Fontainebleau (France) Hosp., 1974, Enfants Malades Hosp., 1975, Melun (France) Hosp., 1976, Mohamed V Hosp., Rabat, Morocco, 1976, Lagny (France) Hosp., 1977; intern psychiatrist infirmary of police Paris, 1977, sole practice medicine, specializing in psychiatry, 1979—; cons. Paris Hosp., 1986—, expert cons. Securite Sociale, Paris and Civil, 1984 expert cons. Ct. of Appeals, Paris, 1988; archbishopric, Paris, 1979—. Author: Relaxation Therapeutique, 1986; co-author: Le Projet en Psychotherapie, 1983, Abrege de Neuro-Psychiatrie. Contbr. articles to profl. jours. V.p. Mutual Ins.'s, Paris, 1972—. Mem. Intergroupe de Formation en Relaxation, Med. Assn. Paris. Roman Catholic. Office: 16 Rue des Sablons, 75116 Paris France

MEYER, JOHN CHRISTEN EDVARD, diplomat; b. Hesselager, Denmark, Oct. 21, 1923; s. Edvard and Augusta (Rasmussen) M.; m. Birthe Nielsen, June 21, 1952; children—Jens, Birgitte, Henrik. Propr., Meyco Emballage A/S, Denmark, 1941—, Tubenfabrik Burg-AG, W.Ger., 1941—; pres. bd. dirs. com. Glud & Marstrands Fabriker A/S, A/S Ernst Voss Fabrik, De danske Bomuldsspinderier A/S, A/S Grenaa Dampvaeveri, Denmark, 1968-78; bd. dir. Codan and Codan Liv ins. cos., 1973-82; Danish consul gen. in Monaco, 1966—. Bd. dirs. I.C. Hempel Found., Denmark, 1973-86. Decorated Order of Dannebrog, Knight's Cross 1st class (Denmark). Address: 11 Blvd. Albert Monaco

MEYER, LAWRENCE GEORGE, lawyer; b. East Grand Rapids, Mich., Oct. 2, 1940; s. George and Evangeline (Boerma) M.; children from previous marriage: David Lawrence, Jenifer Lynne; m. 2d. Linda Elizabeth Buck, May 31, 1980; children: Elizabeth Tilden, Travis Henley. BA with honors, Mich. State U., 1961; JD with distinction, U. Mich., 1964. Bar: Wis., Ill. 1965, U.S. Supreme Ct. 1968, D.C. 1972. Assoc., Whyte, Hirschboeck, Minahan, Hardin & Harland, Milw., 1964-66; atty. antitrust div. U.S. Dept. Justice, 1966-68; legal counsel U.S. Senator Robert P. Griffin from Mich., 1968-70; dir. policy planning FTC, 1970-72; ptnr. Patton, Boggs & Blow, Washington, 1972-85, Arent, Fox, Kintner, Plotkin & Kahn, Washington, 1985—. Recipient Disting. Service Award, FTC, 1972. Mem. ABA, D.C. Bar Assn. Clubs: U.S. Senate Ex S.O.B.'s City Tavern, Congl. Country, Pisces (Washington); The Bayhill (Orlando). Contbr. articles on antitrust and trial practice to law jours.; asst. editor. U. Mich. Law Rev., 1960-61. Home: 8801 Belmart Rd Potomac MD 20854 Office: 1050 Connecticut Ave Washington DC 20036

MEYER, LEE GORDON, attorney, fuel company executive; b. Washington, Oct. 22, 1943; s. Edmond Gerald and Betty (Knobloch) M.; m. Lynn Nix, Mar. 14, 1980; children—Veronica, Victoria, David. B.S. in Chemistry, U. Wyo., 1966, M.B.A., 1969, J.D. (hon.), 1973. Bar: Wyo. 1973, Tex. 1973, Ohio 1981, Ky. 1982, Colo. 1985, U.S. Patent Office, U.S. Supreme Ct. Patent atty. Texaco Corp., Austin, Tex., 1974-77; chief patent and trademark counsel Alcan Aluminum Co., Cleve., 1977-79; gen. counsel Donn, Inc., Cleve., 1979-81; asst. gen. counsel Diamond Shamrock Co., Lexington, Ky., 1981-83; v.p. fin. and adminstrn. Fort Union Coal Co., Denver, 1983-84; pres., chief exec. officer Carbon Fuels Corp., Denver, 1984—. Patentee in field. Mem. ABA, Am. Mgmt. Assn., Am. Chem. Soc., Licensing Exec. Soc., Ops. Research Soc., Denver C. of C. Republican. Home: 10487 E Ida Ave Englewood CO 80111 Office: Carbon Fuels Corp 5105 DTC Pkwy #317 Englewood CO 80111

MEYER, LORENZO FRANCISCO, university dean; b. Mexico City, Feb. 24, 1942; s. Lorenzo Raymundo and Rosa Maria (Cossio) M.; m. Argentina Terán, Aug. 10, 1971 (div.); m. Romana Gloria Falcón, Mar. 18, 1976; children: Lorenzo, Román. BA, El Colegio de Mexico, 1963, PhD, 1967; MA, U. Chgo., 1970. Prof. Ctr. for Internat. Studies at El Colegio de Mexico, Mexico City, 1970—, dir., 1977-81; acad. dean El Colegio de Mexico, Mexico City, 1985—; vis. fellow Oxford U., 1980; vis. prof. U. Tex., Austin, 1972-73, Colo. Coll., Colorado Springs, 1975-76, U. Chgo., 1981-82. Author: Mexico and the U.S. in the Oil Controversy, 1977, (with others) The United States and Mexico, 1985; editorial collaborator Excélsior newspaper, Mexico City, 1981—. Recipient Social Scis. award Mexican Acad. Sci. Research, 1974. Mem. Latin Am. Studies Assn. (exec. com. 1986—). Office: El Colegio de Mexico, Camino al Ajusco 20, Mexico City Mexico

MEYER, MARION M., editor; b. Sheboygan, Wis., July 14, 1923; d. Herman O. and Viola A. (Hoch) M.; B.A., Lakeland Coll., 1950; M.A., N.Y.U., 1957. Payroll clk. Am. Chair Co., Sheboygan, 1941-46; tchr. English and religion, dir. athletics Am. Sch. for Girls, Baghdad, Iraq, 1950-56; mem. edn./publ. staff United Ch. Bd. for Homeland Ministries, United Ch. Press/Pilgrim Press, 1958-64, sr. editor, 1965—; cons. to religious orgns. on editorial matters, copyrights, hymnals. Incorporating mem. Contact Phila., Inc., 1972, bd. dirs., 1972-75, v.p., chmn. com. to organize community adv. bd., chmn. auditing com., editor newsletter, 1972-74, pres., 1974-75, assoc. mem., 1977—. Mem. ofcl. bd. Old First Reformed Ch., Phila., 1984—; deacon United Ch. Christ, 1984—, mem. Mid.-East Com. of Pa. SE Conf. United Ch. Christ, 1986—. Honored as role model United Ch. of Christ, 1982, 85. Mem. AAUW. Contbr. articles to various publs. Home: 1900 J F Kennedy Blvd Philadelphia PA 19103 Office: 132 W 31st St New York NY 10001

MEYER, PHILIP GILBERT, lawyer; b. Louisville, June 26, 1945; s. Henry Gilbert and Adele (Gutermuth) M.; m. Jackie Darlene Watson, Jan. 30, 1971 (div. Apr. 1976); m. Sylvia Saunders, Oct. 9, 1976. B.B.A., U. Mich., 1967; J.D., U. Tex. 1970. Bar: Tex. 1970, Mich. 1971, U.S. Tax Ct. 1972, U.S. Dist. Ct. (ea. dist.) Mich. 1971, U.S. Ct. Appeals (6th cir.) 1972, U.S. Dist. Ct. (no. dist.) Ohio 1976. Clk., Wayne County Cir. Ct., Detroit, 1970-72; atty. Leonard C. Jaques, Detroit, 1972; assoc. Christy & Robbins, Dearborn, Mich., 1972-73; ptnr. Foster, Meadows & Ballard, Detroit, 1973-79; of counsel Christy, Rogers & Gantz, Dearborn, 1979-81, Rogers & Gantz, Dearborn, 1981-86, prin. Philip G. Meyer and Assocs., 1986—; adj. prof. U. Detroit Sch. Law, 1979. Mem. ABA (com. vice chmn. rules and procedure 1982—), Maritime Law Assn. U.S., Mich. Bar Assn. (vice chmn. admiralty sect. 1978), Tex. Bar Assn., Detroit Bar Assn. Republican. Club: Propeller-Port of Detroit (pres. 1984-85).). Home: 5905 Independence Ln West Bloomfield MI 48322 Office: 5767 W Maple Rd Suite 100 West Bloomfield MI 48322

MEYER, RICHARD E(DWARD), music, film and video producer/executive, former advertising and cosmetics executive; b. Cin., May 8, 1939; s. Joseph H. and Dolores C. (Daley) M.; m. Julia I. Kallish; children: Donna, Valerie. AB in Journalism, Advt. and Mktg with hons., U. Mich., 1961. Mgr. auto staff advt. dept. Chgo. Tribune, 1961-63; account supr., v.p. London & Assos., Chgo., 1963-64; founder, pres., chmn. bd. Meyer & Rosenthal, Inc. (formerly Richard E. Meyer, Inc.), Chgo., 1965-74; exec. v.p., gen. mgr. Jovan Inc., Chgo., 1974-75; pres., chief operating officer Jovan Inc., 1975-79, pres., chief exec. officer, 1980-85; pres., chief exec. officer Yardley of London, Lancaster, 1980-85, Beecham Cosmetics, 1980-85, Omni Cosmetics, 1980-85, Parfums Hermes U.S.A., 1980-85; pres., chmn. bd. Red Entertainment Inc., Chgo., 1983-86, Red Label Records Inc., Chgo., 1983-86; past pres. Fragrance Found., 1985. Writer, producer various feature videos/films including Super Bowl Shuffle (RIAA Gold and Platinum awards 1986, Grammy nominee 1986,87), Mike Ditka's Grabowski Shuffle (RIAA Gold and Platinum video awards, 1987); patentee various product designs. Recipient numerous awards N.Y. Advt. Club, Chgo. Advt. Club, Designers and Art Dirs., TV commls., Print Casebook, First Advt. Agy. Network; recipient Communication Arts awards Printing Industry Am. Mem. Nat. Acad. Recording Arts and Scis., Am. Film Inst., Acad. Motion Picture Arts and Scis., Delta Upsilon (trustee 1961—). Clubs: U. Mich. of Chgo.

MEYER, ROSALIND STERLING, educational advisor; b. Melbourne, Victoria, Australia, Mar. 4, 1930; d. Douglas Gordon and Margaret Burns (Sterling) Bain; m. John William Gibson Meyer, Oct. 7, 1955 (div. Nov. 1975); children—Elizabeth Gay, William Duncan. B.A. with honors, U. Melbourne, 1951; M.A., U. Oxford, 1954. Head, English studies Marydale Convent, Hampshire, Eng., 1964-69; tutor dept. English Monash U., Melbourne, 1975-78; advisor lang. and learning strategies Deakin U., Geelong, Australia, 1979—. Author: Where Might Is Write, 1980; (with P.A. Caldwell) Sentence Performance, 1982. Contbr. articles and papers to profl. jours. Mem. com. World Wild Life, Winchester, Eng., 1971-73; hot-line helper Samaritans, Southampton, Eng., 1971-73. Mem. Lady Margaret Hall, Oxford (sr.), U. Melbourne Alumni Assn., Higher Edn. Research and Devel. Soc. of Australasia, Kipling Soc. (v.p. Melbourne). Mem. Uniting Ch. Australia. Avocations: theatre, amateur acting, body-surfing, driving elderly Alfa-Romeos. Office: Deakin U, 3217 Victoria Australia

MEYER, THOMAS ROBERT, TV product executive; b. Buffalo, Apr. 20, 1936; s. Amel Robert and Mildred Lucille M.; m. Dawn E. Shaffer, 1985. Student Purdue U., 1953-55, Alexander Hamilton Inst. Bus., 1960-62, West Coast U., 1969-72; B in Math., Thomas Edison State Coll., 1988; children—Helen, Robyn, Sharon, Robert. Sect. chief wideband systems engring. Ground Elec. Engring. and Installation Agy., Dept. Air Force, 1960-66; product mgr., systems engr. RCA Corp., Burbank, Calif., 1966-71; systems cons. Hubert Wilke, Inc., Los Angeles, 1971-72; product mgr. Telemation, Inc., Salt Lake City, 1972-77; v.p. engring. Dynair Electronics, San Diego, 1977—. Served with USAF, 1955-59. Decorated Legion of Merit; recipient Bronze Zero Defects award Dept. Air Force, 1966. Fellow Soc. Motion Picture and TV Engrs. (chmn. subcom. digital control, co-chmn. SMPTE/European Broadcast Union task force for remote control); sr. mem. Soc. Broadcast Engrs., Soc. St. Paul; mem. Computer Soc. of IEEE, Am. Electronics Assn., Tau Beta Pi. Republican. Episcopalian. Research and publs. on color TV tech. and optics, TV equipment and systems, application of computer to TV systems. Office: Dynair Electronics PO Box 84378 San Diego CA 92138

MEYER MALDONADO, EDUARDO ARTURO, physician, surgeon, education administrator; b. Guatemala City, Guatemala, Dec. 31, 1936; s. Pedro Meyer and Berta Maldonado; m. Ilda Meyer De Sosa; children—Rosana, Eduardo, Monica Meyer. B.S., Colegio de Infantes, 1955; M.Orthopedics, Georgetown U., 1974; D.Sc., Taiwan Nat. U., 1983. Mem. faculty Med. Sch., U. San Carlos, Guatemala City, from 1968, rector univ., from 1982, gen. sec. med. sch., 1974-78; chief dept. orthopedics San Juan de Dios Hosp., Guatemala City, from 1970; chmn. Ministry of Edn., Guatemala. Contbr. articles to profl. jours. Vice-pres., State Council, 1979, advisor, 1979. Mem. Guatemala Med. Fedn., Guatemala Orthopedia Nat. Assn., Hand Surgery Assn., Med., Physics and Natural Scis. Acad. Guatemala. Roman Catholic. Clubs: American, Dante Allighieri (Guatemala City). Avocations: reading; film. Home: 20 Avenida A 12-87, Guatemala 11 Guatemala Office: Ministry of Edn, Palacio Nacional, Guatemala City Guatemala *

MEYERS, ANTHONY JAMES, lawyer, legal educator; b. Seattle, July 7, 1950; s. Henry Joseph and Catherine Luella (McGeough) M. B.A. in Philosophy and Polit. Sci. magna cum laude, Seattle U., 1972; M.A. in Polit. Sci., Boston Coll., 1973; J.D., U. Wash., 1976. Bar: Wash. 1977, U.S. Dist. Ct. Wash. 1977, U.S. Ct. Appeals (9th cir.) 1979, U.S. Supreme Ct. 1981. Grad. research asst. Boston Coll.; law clk. presiding justice Superior Ct., King County, Seattle, 1978; assoc. Joseph S. Kane, Seattle, 1977-78; ptnr. Kane & Meyers, Seattle, 1978-81, pres. Kane & Meyers, Inc., P.S., Seattle, 1981—; legal instr. City U. of Seattle; judge pro tem King County Superior Ct., Seattle; judge pro tem Seattle Mcpl. Ct. Mem. ABA, Seattle-King County Bar Assn., Wash. State Trial Lawyers Assn., Am. Trial Lawyers Assn., Nat. Assn. Criminal Def. Attys., Am. Soc. Internat. Law, Nat. Assn. Criminal Def. Lawyers, Phi Alpha Delta, Alpha Sigma Nu. Roman Catholic. Office: Kane & Meyers Inc PS 607 3d Ave 306 Lyon Bldg Seattle WA 98104

MEYERS, CHRISTINE LAINE, publishing and media executive, consultant; b. Detroit, Mar. 7, 1949; d. Ernest Robert and Eva Elizabeth (Laine) M.; 1 child, Kathryn Laine. BA, U. Mich., 1968. Editor, indsl. relations Diesel div. Gen. Motors Corp., Detroit, 1968; nat. advt. mgr. J.L. Hudson Co., Detroit, 1969-76, mgr. internal sales promotion, 1972-73, dir. pub., 1973-76; nat. advt. mgr. Pontiac Motor div., Mich., 1976-78; pres., owner Laine Meyers Assocs., Troy, Mich., 1978—; dir. Internat. Inst. Met. Detroit, Inc. Contbr. articles to profl. publs. Mem. bus. adv. council Cen. Mich. U., 1977—. Named Mich. Ad Woman of Yr., 1976, One of Top 10 Working Women, Glamour mag., 1978, One of 100 Best and Brightest, Advt. Age, 1987. Mem. Women in Communications (Vanguard award 1986), Internat. Assn. Bus. Communicators, Adcraft Club, Women's Advt. Club (1st v.p. 1975), Women's Econ. Club (pres. 1976-77), Internat. Women's Forum Mich. (pres. 1986—), Internat. Inst. of Detroit (bd. dirs. 1986—), Detroit C. of C., Mortar Board, Quill and Scroll, Pub. Relations Com. Women for United Found., Founders Soc. Detroit Inst. Arts, Fashion Group, Pub. Relations Soc. Am., First Soc. Detroit (exec. com. 1970-71), Kappa Tau Alpha. Home: 1780 Kensington Bloomfield Hills MI 48013 Office: Laine Meyers Inc 3645 Crooks Rd Troy MI 48084

MEYERS, GEORGE EDWARD, plastics company executive; b. N.Y.C., June 26, 1928; s. Sol and Ethel (Treppel) M.; student Sampson Coll., 1948-49, Columbia, 1949-50; m. Marianna Jacobson, Dec. 8, 1955; children—Deborah Lynn, Joanne Alyssa. Technician Manhattan Project, 1944; tech. rep. Mearl Corp., 1952-56; student Sampson Coll., Geneva, N.Y., 1948-50, Columbia U., N.Y.C., 1949-50. tech. rep. Mearl Corp., N.Y.C., 1952-56; sales mgr. Rona Labs., Bayonne, N.J.1956-59; v.p. Dimensional Pigments Corp., Bayonne, 1959-60; pres. Plastic Cons. Internat., Inc., Dix Hills, N.Y., 1959—, Tech. Machinery Corp., Plainview, N.Y., 1963-69; pres. Extrudyne, Inc., Amityville, N.Y., 1970-77, also dir.; dir. research and devel. Homeland Industries, Bohemia, N.Y., 1977-80; dir. ops. Aqua-Sol, Inc., Deer Park, N.Y., 1980-85; tchr., staff cons. N.Y.C. Bd. Higher Edn., Bronx Community Coll., 1966-70; lectr. N.Y.U., Technion, Haifa, Israel. Served with CIC, AUS, 1946-48. Mem. Soc. Plastics Engrs. (sr. mem., v.p. N.Y. sect. 1967-68), Soc. Plastics Industry (profl. mem.), Am. Ordnance Assn., Aircraft Owners and Pilots Assn, Nat. Rifle Assn. (life mem.), Am. Chem. Soc., Internat. Assn. Housing Sci. (charter mem.), Internat. Assn. Soilless Culture. Contbr. articles to profl. jours. Patentee in field; lectr.; seminar conductor in plastics and hydroponics and seminar leader Modern Plastics Mag. courses. Avocations: flying, numismatics, pistol shooting, antique collector. Home and Office: 25 Penn Dr Dix Hills NY 11746

MEYERS, JAMES FRANK, electronics engineer; b. Binghamton, N.Y., Sept. 9, 1946; s. Edwin Fox and Louise (Okrepkie) M.; B.E.E., U. Louisville, 1969, M.E., 1972; postgrad. George Washington U. Instr. elec. engring lab. U. Louisville, 1968-69; engring coop. technician Langley Research Center, NASA, Hampton, Va., 1966-69, aerospace technologist, 1969—. Mem. IEEE (sect. chmn. 1975), Turnberry Two Owners Assn. (pres., dir. 1979-82), Sports Car Club Am. (div. rallye exec. 1982-86), Eta Kappa Nu, Tau Beta Pi, Sigma Tau. Contbr. articles to profl. jours.; patentee in field. Office: NASA Langley Research Ctr M/S 235A Hampton VA 23665

MEYERS, LYNN BETTY, architect; b. Chgo., Dec. 2, 1952; d. William J. and Dorothy (King) M.; m. Dana Terp, May 17, 1975; children: Sophia, Rachel. Student, Royal Acad. Architecture, Copenhagen, Denmark, 1971; BArch, Washington U., St. Louis, 1974, MArch, 1977. Registered architect, Ill. Architect Holabird & Root Architects, Chgo., 1973, 76, Hist. Pullman Found., Chgo., 1975, Jay Alpert Architects, Woodbridge, Conn., 1976, City of Chgo. Bur. Architects, 1978-80; sole practice architecture Chgo., 1980-82; prin., architect Terp Meyers Architects, Chgo., 1982—. Exhbns. include: Centre George Pompidou, Paris, 1978, Fifth Internat. Congress Union Internat. Des Femmes Architects, Seattle, 1979, Frumkin Struve Gallery, Chgo., 1981, Art. Inst. Chgo., 1983, Inst. Francais d'Architecture, Paris, 1983, Mus. Sci. and Industry, Chgo., 1985; pub. in profl. jours. including Progressive Architecture, Modo Design, Los Angeles Architect; work featured in various archtl. books; exhibited 150 Yrs. of Chgo. Architecture, Mus. Sci. and Industry, Chgo., 1985. Recipient Progressive Architecture mag. award, 1980; First Place Los Angeles AIA Real Problems Competition, 1986. Mem. AIA (task force com. for 1992 World's Fair), Union Internat. Des Femmes Architects, Chgo. Women in Architecture (v.p. 1980-81, Allied Arts award 1974), Young Chgo. Architects. Office: Terp Meyers Architects 919 N Michigan Ave Chicago IL 60611

MEYERS, MORTON ALLEN, physician, educator; b. Troy, N.Y., Oct. 1, 1933; s. David and Jeanne Sarah (Dunn) M.; m. Beatrice Applebaum, June 1, 1963; children—Richard, Amy. M.D., SUNY, Upstate Med. Coll., 1959. Diplomate: Am. Bd. Radiology. Intern Bellevue Hosp., N.Y.C., 1959-60; resident in radiology Columbia-Presbyn. Med. Center, N.Y.C., 1960-63; fellow Am. Cancer Soc., 1961-63; prof. dept. radiology Cornell U. Med. Center, N.Y.C., 1973-78; prof., chmn. dept. radiology SUNY Sch. Medicine, Stony Brook, 1978—; vis. investigator St. Mark's Hosp., London, 1976; speaker Radiol. Soc. N.Am., 1986. Author: Diseases of the Adrenal Glands: Radiologic Diagnosis, 1963, Dynamic Radiology of the Abdomen: Normal and Pathologic Anatomy, 1976, 2d edit., 1982, 3d edit., 1988, Iatrogenic Gastrointestinal Complications, 1981; series editor: Radiology of Iatrogenic Disorders, 1981—; editor: Computed Tomography of the Gastrointestinal Tract: Including the Peritoneal Cavity and Mesentery, 1986; founding editor-in-chief: Gastrointestinal Radiology, 1976—; contbr. chpts. to med. textbooks, articles to med. jours.; speaker in field. Served to capt. M.C. U.S. Army, 1963-65. Fellow Am. Coll. Radiology; mem. Radiol. Soc. N. Am., Am. Roentgen Ray Soc., Assn. Univ. Radiologists, N.Y. Roentgen Ray Soc., Am. Gastroenterol. Assn., Soc. Gastrointestinal Radiologists, AAAS, Soc. Uroradiology, N.Y. Acad. Gastroenterology, Phila. Roentgen Soc., Harvey Soc., N.Y. Acad. Scis., Soc. Chmn. Acad. Radiology Depts., L.I. Radiologic Soc., Alpha Omega Alpha. Home: 14 Wainscott Ln East Setauket NY 11733 Office: SUNY Health Scis Ctr Sch Medicine Dept Radiology Stony Brook NY 11794

MEYERSON, STANLEY PHILLIP, lawyer; b. Spartanburg, S.C., Apr. 13, 1916; s. Louis A. and Ella Meyerson; m. Marion Legg, Feb. 6, 1941; children—Marianne Martin, Camilla Jurskis, Margot Ellis, Stanley P. A.B., Duke U., 1937, J.D., 1939. Bar: S.C. 1939, N.Y. 1940, Ga. 1945. Ptnr. Johnson Hatcher & Meyerson, Atlanta, 1945-55, Hatcher, Meyerson, Oxford & Irvin, Atlanta, 1955-78, Westmoreland, Hall, McGee, Oxford & Meyerson, Atlanta, 1978—; former adj. prof. Ga. STate U.; dir., officer various corps. Mem. Am. Coll. Mortgage Attys., Atlanta Estate Planning Council. Contbr. legal jours. Served to lt. cmdr. USNR, 1941-45. Mem. Duke Alumni Assn. (former pres. Atlanta chpt.).

MEYERSTEIN, DAN, chemistry educator, library administrator; b. Jerusalem, Oct. 7, 1938; s. Rolf and Hermine (Fried) M.; m. Naomi Rishpon, June 24, 1962; children: Michal, Ronit, Ruth, Gil. MS, Hebrew U., 1961, PhD, 1965. Researcher Soreq Nuclear Research Ctr., Rehovoth, Israel, 1961-65; postdoctoral fellow Argonne (Ill.) Nat. Lab., 1965-67; mem. faculty Ben Gurion U. Negev, Ben Sheva, Israel, 1968—, prof. chemistry, dir. library, 1979—, dir. Coal Research Ctr., 1986—. Mem. editorial bd. Israel Jour. Chemistry, 1982—. Fellow Royal Soc. Chemistry (assoc.); mem. Israel Chem. Soc. (pres. 1988—), Am. Chem. Soc. Home: 12 Arava St, Omer Israel Office: Ben Gurion U Chemistry Dept, Beer Sheva Israel

MEYLER, WILLIAM ANTHONY, financial executive; b. Newark, Oct. 29, 1944; s. Raymond Francis and Margaret (Loveless) M.; B.S., St. Joseph's Coll., 1966; M.B.A., Fairleigh Dickinson U., 1974; m. Dana Irene Brennan, May 3, 1975. Sr. acct. Ernst & Whinney, Trenton, N.J., 1970; dir. acctg. Baker Industries, Inc., Parsippany, N.J., 1971-72; mgr. corp. acctg. Witco Chem. Corp., N.Y.C., 1973-75, asst. to controller, 1976-79, asst. controller world-wide ops., 1977-82, asst. controller mgmt. info. systems, 1982-84; ptnr. Letters, Meyler & Co., C.P.A.s, 1984—; sr. v.p. Investment Technologies, Inc.; adj. prof. Monmouth Coll., 1983—; bd. dirs. Investment Techs. C.P.A., N.J. Fellow N.J. Soc. C.P.A.s; mem. Am. Inst. C.P.A.s, Am. Acctg. Assn., Middletown C. of C. Lodge: Rotary. Home: 30 Southview Terr S Middletown NJ 07748 Office: 277 Park Ave New York NY 10017

MEYLOR, COLLEEN BETH, product specialist, educator; b. Milw., Nov. 29, 1957; d. Michael Bernard and Karole Joan (Kabbeck) M. BSCE, U. Wis., Madison, 1979; MBA, Baldwin Wallace Coll., 1987. Devel. engr. Foseco, Inc., Cleve., 1980-82, foundry product specialist, 1982-85, sr. product devel. specialist, 1985-86, steelmill product specialist, 1986-88, product mgr. evaporative casting products, 1988—; instr. Cast Metals Inst., Am. Foundry Soc., Chgo., 1984—; bd. dirs. Foseco Employees Fed. Credit Union, 1983—, treas. 1986. Mem. Profl. Engring. Soc., Am. Foundryman's Soc., Am. Women in Metal Industries, Nat. Assn. Female Execs., Iron & Steel Soc., U. Wis. Alumni Assn. Avocations: piano, sports. Home: 32747 Willowbrook Ln North Ridgeville OH 44039 Office: Foseco Inc 20200 Sheldon Rd Cleveland OH 44142

MEYNARD, JEAN-YVES, research administrator; b. Tunis, Tunisia, Apr. 22, 1944; s. Claude and Carmen (Fontaine) M.; m. Marie N. Dutriez, Dec. 19, 1969; children—Olivier, Aude. Engr., Ecole de Chimie, Besancon, France, 1967, B.S., Faculte de Chimie, Besancon, France, 1966, Sc.D., 1971. Engr., Siplast, Chartres, France, 1971-72, chief labs., Mondoubleau, 1972-77, dir. research, 1977-84; dir. for Europe, SIPSY, Avrille, France, 1984—. Patentee waterproofing materials, bituminous-polymer blends. Mem. Chambre Syndicale de l'etanchéité, Joint Com. CIB-RILEM, NRCA, NBS. Office: SIPSY, 49240 Avrille France

MEYNINGER, RITA, civil engineer; b. 1935 Newark; B.S. in Civil Engring., Newark Coll. Engring., 1958; MS in Civil Engring., NYU, 1973; candidate DEng, N.J. Inst. Tech. With Clinton Bogert & Assos., Ft. Lee, N.J., 1970-74; v.p., gen. mgr. Resource Planning div. Hydrosci., Inc., Emerson, N.J., 1974-78; regional dir., region II, Fed. Emergency Mgmt. Agy., N.Y.C., 1979-81; fed. coordinating officer in emergency declaration at Love Canal, N.Y. State, 1980; fed. coordinating officer in drought emergency declaration in N.J., 1980; sr. v.p. Envirespone, Inc., subs. Foster Wheeler Corp., Livingston, N.J., 1980-88; pres. pres. Environ. Systems Mgmt. and Design, Fort Lee, N.J., 1988—. Recipient Alumni Honor Roll award N.J. Inst. Tech., 1980; named Eminent Engr. Mem., Tau Beta Pi, 1986. Mem. ASCE, Am. Water Works Assn., Water Pollution Control Fedn. Home: 300 Winston Dr Cliffside Park NJ 07010

MEYROWITZ, ALVIN A(BRAHAM), retired mgmt. exec.; b. N.Y.C., Dec. 16, 1917; s. Jacob Norman and Anne (Bader) M.; A.B., Cornell U., 1938; M.B.A., N.Y.U., 1941; law sch. George Washington U., 1948-50; m. Ruth Liberman, Feb. 1, 1942; children—Linda Jean, Jack Norman. Asso. bus. research dept. U. Newark, 1937-38; market analyst Miller Franklin Co., 1938-41; chief copper br. Office Civilian Supply W.P.B., 1941-46; dir. basic materials NHA, 1946-49; asst. dir. copper div. NPA, 1949-51; v.p. H. Kramer & Co., gen. mgr. Calif. div., El Segundo, Calif., 1951-62, v.p. H. Kramer & Co., El Segundo, 1964-82, cons., 1982-85; pres. Metals Refining Co., Inc., Los Angeles, 1962-64; dir. Mchts. Petroleum Co. Cons. Copper Policy, Wash., 1951-61; bd. dirs. Calif. Tech. Systems, Inc., Glendale; bd. advisers Mfrs. Bank, Los Angeles. Exec. reservist Bus. and Def. Services Adminstrn., Dept. Commerce, 1956—; vice chmn. So. Calif. Nat. Def. Exec. Res. Trustee City of Hope, Duarte, Calif. Rotarian. Mem. Am. Marketing Assn., Am. Statis. Assn. Am. Econ. Assn., Am. Ordnance Assn., A.I.M., Air Pollution Control Assn., Los Angeles, El Segundo chambers commerce, Sigma Alpha Mu. Clubs: Canyon country (Palm Springs, Calif.). Home: 10450 Wilshire Blvd Los Angeles CA 90024 also: 2470 Playa Circle Palm Springs CA 92264

MEYSTEL, ALEXANDER MICHAEL, electrical engineering educator; b. Leningrad, USSR, Feb. 25, 1935; came to U.S., 1978, naturalized, 1984; s. M.L. and C.S. (Cotliar) M.; m. Marina Selitsky, Feb. 26, 1971; 1 child, Misha. MSEE, Poly. Inst., Odessa, USSR, 1957; PhD, ENIMS, Moscow, 1965. Project leader Design Office Machines, Odessa, USSR, 1957-63; sr. researcher Exptl. Sci. Research Inst. Metalcutting Machines, Moscow, 1963-65, head lab., Erevan, 1965-69, sr. scientist, Moscow, 1969-73; head dept. Informelecto, 1973-77; sr. staff scientist Gould, Inc., Chgo., 1978-79; research/devel. dir. Hyperloop, Inc., Chgo., 1980-81; assoc. prof. elec. engring. U. Fla., Gainesville, 1980-84; prof. elec. engring. and computer engring. Drexel U., Phila., 1984—; cons. in field. Contbr. articles to profl. jours.; author: Automated Positioning Controls, 1970, Engineering Computations and Design of Automated Machines, 1976, Computer Aided Decision Making, 1976; me. editorial bd. Jour. Robotics and Adaptive Control. Developed and demonstrated mobile autonomous system; patentee in field. Recipient medals for engring. innovations All-Union Exhbn. of Indsl. Achievements, Moscow, 1962-70. Mem. IEEE (sr., chmn. internat. symposium intelligent control), N.Y. Acad. Sci., Soc. Indsl. and Applied Math., Am. Assn. Artificial Intelligence, Sigma Xi. Jewish. Office: Drexel U Dept Elec Engring Philadelphia PA 19104

MEZA, ROBERTO, ambassador; b. Santa Ana, El Salvador, Nov. 25, 1937; s. Jose and Blance (Delgado) M.; m. Maruca Perez; children: Maria Beatriz, Roberto, Luis, Juan Pablo, Maria Luisa, Claudia. MS in Civil Engring., U. El Salvador. Interim mayor of San Salvador 1969; v.p. Cen. Elections Council, El Salvador, 1982-83; minister Ministry Pub. Works, 1984-85; ambassador UN, N.Y.C., 1986—. Pres. Christian Family Movement, San Salvador; bd. dirs. Christian Dem. Party, San Salvador, info. Constrn. Chamber, 1970. Mem. Asociacion Salvadoreña de Engenieros (v.p. 1970). Roman Catholic. Club: Club Deportivo Intermat. (San Salvador). Office: Permanent Mission of El Salvador to the UN 46 Park Ave New York NY 10016

MEZIE-OKOYE, JOHN-JOE ODILI, mechanical engineer; b. Oraukwu, Anambra State, Nigeria, June 11, 1946; s. Hyacinth Ekemezie and Juliana Nwakaife Okoye-Ogbachalu; m. Margaret-Mary Ifeoma Ogujawa, Aug. 5, 1978; children: Dumebi, Uche, Somto, Chibuzor. BSME with honors, U. Nigeria, 1974; M Engring. in power plants, U. Liverpool, Eng., 1976. Contract engr. Drake and Skull Ltd., Lagos, Nigeria, 1976-79; prin. engr. U. Port Harcourt, Nigeria, 1979-83, chief engr., 1983—; engring. cons. Cath. Inst. West Africa, Port Harcourt, 1982—; chmn. bd. dirs. Bonitas Investments Ltd., Port Harcourt, 1985—. Mem. Instn. Mech. Engrs., Chartered Instn. Bldg. Services Engrs., Am. Soc. Heating, Refrigerating and Air Conditioning Engrs. Lodges: Rotary, Knights St. John (1st v.p Port Harcourt Commandery 1987—). Office: U Port Harcourt, Port Harcourt Nigeria

MIALL, DAVID STEPHEN, English educator; b. Brighton, Eng., Jan. 11, 1947; s. Stuart and Margaret (Peyton) M.; m. Valerie Kennedy, Aug. 8, 1967 (div. Jan. 1981); 1 child, Laurence; m. Sylvia Christine Chard, Dec. 30, 1982. Associate, Guildhall Sch. Music, London, 1967; BA with honors, Stirling U., Scotland, 1976; PhD, Univ. Coll., U. Wales, Cardiff, 1980. Tutorial fellow Univ. Coll., Cardiff, 1976-79; lectr. in English Coll. St. Paul and St. Mary, Cheltenham, Eng., 1979-81, sr. lectr., 1981-86, prin. lectr., 1986—, research dir. arts, 1985—; mem. English bd. Council for Nat. Acad. Awards, London, 1983—, specialist advisor on computing and humanities, 1987—. Editor: Metaphor: Problems and Perspectives, 1982; contbr. articles to profl. jours. Postdoctoral fellow Ctr. for Study Reading U. Ill., Urbana-Champaign, 1982-83. Mem. Nat. Council Tchrs. English, Brit. Soc. Aesthetics, Assn. Literary and Linguistic Computing, Friends Coleridge in Somerset (founder, chmn. 1987—). Office: Coll St Paul and St Mary, The Park, Cheltenham, Gloucestershire GL50 2RH, England

MIAN, MUHAMMAD ARIF, civil engineer; b. Sialkot, Pakistan, May 1, 1950; s. Muhammad Sadiq and Iqbal Begum M.; m. Nargis Bano, June 14, 1982; 1 child, Alim Arif. BS in Civil Engring., West Pakistan U. Engring. and Tech., 1972; postgrad., Alexander Hamilton Inst., N.Y.C., 1981, Mgmt. Games Inst., Larchmont, N.Y., 1980. Registered profl. engr. Pakistan, cons. engr. specialist hwys. and bridges, Pakistan. Apprentice engr. The Architects Bur., Pakistan, 1972-73, cons. engr., 1973-75; jr. engr. Nat. Constrn. Ltd., Pakistan, 1973; structural engr. Nat. Engring. Services, Pakistan, 1973-75; area mgr. M?S Interconsult, Riyadh, Saudi Arabia, 1973-80; project mgr. Bin Jarallah Establishment, Khamis Mushayt, Saudi Arabia, 1980-81, tech. dir., 1981—; tech. advisor So. Region Rd Dept. Ministry of Communicatons, Saudi Arabia, 1977—. Contbr. articles in field to profl. jours. Joint sec. Adara Khidmat Khalak, Lahore, Pakistan, 1970-72; chmn. Silkot Engring. Welfare Soc., 1973-75. Saigol Found. Scholar, 1968. Mem. ASCE (recipient medal 1980), Soc. Am. Mil. Engrs., Am. Concrete Inst., Internat. Soc. Soil Mechanics, Inst. Engrs. Pakistan (recipient medal 1975). Muslim. Clubs: Jamkhana, Officers (Lahore). Home: Muhammad Pura, Sialkot Pakistan Office: Bin Jarallah Establishment, PO Box 72, Khamis Mushayt Saudi Arabia

MICALE, FRANK JUDE, lawyer; b. Pitts., Jan. 10, 1949; s. Frank Jacob and Catherine Anna (Wagner) M. B.A., Duquesne U., 1971, J.D., 1977. Bar: Pa. 1977, U.S. Dist. Ct. (we. dist.) Pa. 1977, U.S. Ct. Appeals (3d cir.) 1978; U.S. Supreme Ct., 1986. Law clk. judge U.S. Ct. Appeals (3d cir.), 1977-78; law clk. to judge U.S. Dist. Ct. (we. dist. Pa.), 1978-79; assoc. Egler & Reinstadtler, Pitts., 1979-80; dep. atty. gen., sr. dep. atty. gen. in charge torts litigation sect. western region Office of Atty. Gen., Commonwealth of Pa., 1980—; Mem. ABA, Pa. Bar Assn., Allegheny County Bar Assn. Home: 555 S Negley Ave No 9 Pittsburgh PA 15232 Office: 400 Manor Bldg Pittsburgh PA 15219

MICALLEF, GODWIN CHARLES, tobacco company executive; b. Floriana, Malta, May 29, 1938; s. Anthony and Adelina (Marmara) M.; m. Beatrice Roseanne Pullicino, Apr. 28, 1963; 1 son, Kenneth. Bus. Studies cert., Coll. of Arts, Sci. and Tech., Valletta, Malta, 1967. Various positions accounts dept. BP Malta Ltd., Valletta, 1956-66, mktg. asst., 1967-68, sect. head accounts, 1969-73; acct. Agio Tobacco Co. Ltd., Zejtun, Malta, 1973-77, controller fin. and adminstrn., 1978—; dir. Mercury Publicity Services Ltd., Valletta, 1967—; cons. to various firms, Malta, 1974—, also Cana Movement, Floriana, 1970—. Fellow Inst. Prodn. Control U.K.; mem. Tobacco Industry Council-Malta, Malta C. of C., Fedn. Industries-Malta (sr. v.p. 1988). Office: Agio Tobacco Co Ltd, B9 Bulebel Industrial Estate, Zejtun Malta

MICCOLI, PAOLO ANTONIO, surgeon; b. Livorno, Toscana, Italy, June 7, 1947; s. Francesco and Liliana (Montano) M.; m. Gabriella Puntoni, Dec. 22, 1973; children: Francesco, Mario. MD, Scuola Normale Univ. Pisa, Italy, 1972. Resident in gen. surgery U. Pisa, 1973-78, asst. prof., 1974-83, assoc. prof., 1983-86, prof. surgery, 1986—. Editor: (jour.) Sports and Medicine. Mem. Internat. Assn. Endocrine Surgeons, Assn. Italiana Chirurgia Endocrina, Assn. Italiana Richerche Chirurgia, Soc. Internat. de Chirurgie. Liberal. Roman Catholic. Office: U Pisa Clinica Chirurgica, Via Roma 57, 56100 Pisa Italy

MICHAEL, CAROL LYNN, computer executive; b. Chgo., Feb. 2, 1953; d. Jay Holden Simpson and Mabel (Blevins) French; m. Gregory Clark Michael, Jan. 1, 1984; children: Jillian Nicole, Lowell Evan. AS in Computer Sci., Pikes Peak Community Coll., 1978; cert. profl. mgmt. Mountain States Employer Council, 1982; BS in Tech. Mgmt., Regis Coll., 1986. Programmer City of Colorado Springs, 1978-79; programmer, analyst Colo. Dept. of Correction, Colorado Springs, 1979-80 software specialist Digital, Colordo Springs, 1980-81, sr. systems analyst, 1981-82, project mgr., 1983, staff mgr., 1983, mgr. of info. systems, 1983-87, engring mgr. Sun Microsystem, 1987—; speaker Colo. State Bd. Edn., Colorado Springs, 1983, Colo. State Edn. Adv. Council, Colorado Springs, 1982; condr. bus. seminar for profl. sales people, Colorado Springs, 1978. Host SAT-UP Breakfast Local Bus. Community, Colorado Springs, 1978. Recipient Outstanding Achievement in Data Processing award Pikes Peak Community Coll., 1977-78, Exemplary Student award, 1978, Outstanding Bus. Student award, Wall Street Jour., 1978, Software Services Excellence award Digital, 1981, Achievement award Digital Info. Systems, 1984, 85; named Outstanding Young Woman of Am., 1984. Mem. Assn. Computing Machinery, Data Processng Mgmt. Assn. (bd. dirs.), Nat. Assn. Female Execs., Salesman with a Purpose, Phi Theta Kappa. Home: 935 Moreno Ave Palo Alto CA 94303

MICHAEL, DOROTHY ANN, nurse, naval officer; b. Lancaster, Pa., Sept. 20, 1950; d. Richard Linus and Mary Ruth (Hahn) Michael. Diploma, R.N., Montgomery Hosp. Sch. Nursing, Norristown, Pa., 1971; BS Nursing, George Mason U., 1980; MS in Nursing U. Tex. Health Sci. Ctr., 1985. Commd. ensign U.S. Navy, 1970, selected to rank of comdr. Nurse Corps, 1988; staff nurse Nat. Naval Med. Ctr., Bethesda, Md., 1971-73; charge nurse Naval Hosp., Guantanamo Bay, Cuba, 1973-74, Naval Regional Med. Ctr., Phila., 1974-76, Naval Hosp., Keflavik, Iceland, 1977, Naval Hosp., Bethesda, 1980-84, sr. nurse, asst. officer-in-charge Br. Med. Clinic, Naval Weapons Ctr., China Lake, Calif., 1986—; splty. advisor to dir. Navy Nurse Corp., Navy Med. Command, Washington, 1983-84. V.p. Deepwood Homeowners Assn., Reston, Va., 1978-82; advisor, com. mem. Reston Found., 1979. Mem. Calif. Soc. for Nursing Service Adminstrs., Am. Public Health Assn., Vietnam Vets Am., Nat. Assn. Female Execs., Nat. Assn. Quality Assurance Profls., Am. Nurses Assn. (cert. nursing adminstrn.), Sigma Theta Tau. Roman Catholic. Home: 136 N Gwen Dr Ridgecrest CA 93555

MICHAELI, DAN MOSHE, internist, medical center director; b. Jerusalem, June 10, 1933; s. Abraham Sholom and Bilha (Kosovsky) M.; m. Miriam Montag, Mar. 31, 1963; children: Adi, Meirav. B in Medicine, U. Geneva, Switzerland, 1953; MD, Hebrew U., Jerusalem, 1958. Cert. internal medicine, health care mgmt. Resident in internal medicine Tel Hashomer Hosp., Ramat Gan, Israel, 1960-66, dir. dept. medicine and infectious diseases, 1970-73; research fellow infectious diseases N.Eng. Med. Ctr. Hosp. Tufts U., Boston, 1968-70; med. comdr. Israel Def. Forces, 1966-68, dep. surgeon gen., 1974-75, brig. gen., surgeon gen., 1975-79; dir. Tel Aviv (Israel) Sourasky Med. Ctr., 1980-84, dir. gen., 1986—; dir. gen. Israel Ministry of Health, 1984-86; assoc. prof. internal medicine Sackler Faculty of Medicine, Tel Aviv U., 1980. Contbr. numerous articles to profl. jours. Fellow Infectious Disease Soc. Am. (affiliate); mem. Israel Soc. Internal Medicine, Internat. Soc. Internal Medicine. Israel Med. Assn. Home: 13 Herzog St, Givatayim 53600, Israel Office: Ichilov Hosp Tel Aviv Med Ctr, 6 Weizman St, Tel Aviv 64239, Israel

MICHAELI, HANS WILHELM, patent lawyer; b. Berlin, Germany, Feb. 24, 1921; s. Wilhelm and Sophie (Goldstein) M.; m. Tove T. Michaeli Kviat, Sept. 27, 1955; children: Eva, Ruth, Dan. MS in Econs., Stockholm Sch. Bus. Adminstrn., Sweden, 1954. Patent lawyer Dr. Ludwig Brann Patentbyra AB, Stockholm, 1957—. Mem. Assn. Swedish Patent Attys. (pres. 1986-88). Office: Dr Ludwig Brann Patentbyra AB, Kungsgatan 3, S-103 92 Stockholm Sweden

MICHAELIDES, DOROS NIKITA, internist; b. Nicosia, Cyprus, Jan. 7, 1936; came to U.S., 1969; s. Nikita P. and Elpinike (Taliadorou) M.; m. Eutychia J. Loizides, Feb. 27, 1965; children: Nike-Elsie, Joanna-Doris. M.D. cum laude (Royal Greek Govt. scholar), U. Athens, 1962; D.T.M. and H. (Greek State Scholarship Found. scholar), U. Liverpool (Eng.), 1967; M.Sc. in Clin. Biochemistry and Endocrinology (Greek State Scholarship Found. scholar), U. Newcastle-upon-Tyne (Eng.), 1969. Clk., intern U. Uppsala (Sweden), 1962; resident Nicosia Gen. Hosp., 1963-66; fellow U. Liverpool Hosps., 1967; fellow internal and clin. medicine Royal Infirmary, U. Edinburgh, 1967-68; research fellow Royal Victoria Infirmary, U. Newcastle-upon-Tyne, 1968-69; resident internal medicine Bapt. Meml. Hosp., Memphis, 1969-72; fellow in chest diseases Western Okla. Chest Disease Hosp., 1970-71; chief clin. immunology and respiratory care center, Erie, Pa.; chief respiratory care center VA Med. Center, Erie, 1972-84, acting chief dept. medicine, 1980-81; asst. clin. prof. medicine Hahnemann Med. Coll. Phila., 1977—; asst. clin. prof. medicine Gannon U., Erie, 1977—; mem. staff internal medicine Hamot Med. Center, immunology & chest diseases Metro Health Ctr., Erie; preceptor medicine St. Vincent's Health Center. Recipient citation for outstanding services to vets. DAV, 1975, citation Adminstr. U.S. Vets. Affairs, 1978. Diplomate Am. Bd. Family Practice, Am. Bd. Allergy and Immunology; cert. in infectious diseases and immunochemistry, Eng. Fellow ACP (life), Am. Assn. Cert. Allergists, Am. Coll. Allergists (com. autoimmune diseases), Am. Assn. Clin. Immunology and Allergy (pulmonary com.). Am. Coll. Chest Physicians (life; critical care com.), Royal Soc. Medicine, Am. Coll. Angiology, N.Y. Acad. Scis., Am. Coll. Clin. Pharmacology, Am. Assn. Cert. Allergists. Democrat. Greek Orthodox. Author: The Occurrence of Proteolytic Inhibitors in Heart and Skeletal Muscle, 1969; Blood Gases, Acid-Base and Electrolytes Disturbances, 1980; Immediate Hypersensitivity: The Immunochemistry and Therapeutics of Reversible Airway Obstruction, 1980; The Equivalent Potency of Corticosteroid Preparations used in Reversible Airway Obstruction, 1981; contbr. articles to med. jours. Home: 4107 State St Erie PA 16508 Office: Metro Health Ctr Allergy Immunology & Chest Diseases 1611 Peach St Suite 220 Erie PA 16501

MICHAELS, GORDON JOSEPH, copper company executive; b. Williamsport, Pa., May 9, 1930; s. Scott Joseph and Gloria Jean M.; m. Cleo Arlene Lela Tietbohl, June 12, 1954; children: Cathryn, Cheryl, Carole. BSEE, Bucknell U., 1959. Tool engr. Ternstedt div. Gen. Motors, Warren, Mich., 1950-59, sr. facilities engr., 1959-65; div. mgr. rectifiers M & T Chem. div. Am. Can Co., Rahway, N.J., 1965-71; v.p. mfg. and engring. Ullrich Copper Co., Kenilworth, N.J., 1971—; pres. Golld Truck Inc., Dorgo Products Inc. Bd. dirs. Tech. Machinery Inst., Union, N.J.; active Jr. Achievement, Elizabeth, N.J.; mem. Nat. Trust Hist. Preservation. Served with AUS, 1954-56. Mem. IEEE, Soc. Mining Engrs., Am. Electroplaters Soc., Soc. Mfg. Engrs., AAAS, Nat. Rifle Assn., Cryogenic Soc. Am., Internat. Platform Assn., Am. Legion, Smithsonian Assn. (assoc.), Nat. Trust for Historic Preservation, Nat. Wildlife Fedn. Republican. Lutheran. Home: Star Route Trout Run PA 17771 Office: HC64 PO Box 318 Trout Run PA 17771

MICHAELS, HOWARD BRIAN, medical physicist, educator, hospital administrator; b. Toronto, Ont., Can., May 29, 1949; s. Isaiah and Rosalind (Rosenberg) M.; m. Lois S. Kwitman, Mar. 15, 1980; 1 child, Elie David (dec.). B.A.Sc., U. Toronto, 1971, M.Sc., 1973, Ph.D. in Med. Biophysics, 1976. Registered profl. engr., Ont. Postdoctoral fellow Ont. Cancer Inst., Toronto, 1976; research fellow in radiation medicine Mass. Gen. Hosp., 1976-78; research fellow in radiation therapy Harvard Med. Sch., Boston, 1976-78; asst. radiation biophysicist and asst. prof. radiation therapy, 1978-81; chief physicist, dir. med. physics Ont. Cancer Found., Toronto-Bayview Regional Cancer Ctr., 1981—; asst. prof. depts. med. biophysics and radiology, U. Toronto, 1981—; depts. oncology and radiology (Sunnybrook Med. Centre), 1981—. Contbr. articles to profl. jours. Nat. Cancer Inst. Can. K.M. Hunter fellow, 1975-76; Radiation Research Soc. awardee, 1974, 76, 78, 79, 83, 87. Mem. Am. Assn. Physicists in Medicine, Can. Assn. Physicists, Radiation Research Soc., Assn. Profl. Engrs. Ont. Office: Ont Cancer Found, 2075 Bayview Ave, Toronto, ON Canada M4N 3M5

MICHAELS, JOHN PATRICK, JR., investment banker, media broker; b. Orlando, Fla., May 28, 1944; s. John Patrick and Mary Elizabeth (Slemons) M.; grad. Jamaica Coll., Kingston, 1961; B.A. magna cum laude, Tulane U., 1966; M.A. in Communications (ABC fellow), U. Pa., 1968; student London Sch. Econs., U. London, 1964; m. Ingeborg D. Theimer, May 2, 1970; 1 dau., Kimberly Lynn. With Times Mirror Co., 1968-72, v.p. mktg. and devel. TM Communications Co., 1968-72; v.p. Cable Funding, N.Y.C., 1973; founder, chmn. Communications Equity Assos., cable TV investment bankers, 1973—; Atlantic Am. Holdings, Tampa, Fla. Tulane scholar, 1962-66; Tulane fellow, 1963-66. Fellow Inst. Dirs. (London); mem. Nat. Cable TV Assn., Community Antenna TV Assn., Am. Mktg. Assn., Royal TV Soc., Phi Beta Kappa, Phi Eta Sigma. Clubs: Univ.; Two Rivers Hounds. Home: 3024 Villa Rosa Park Tampa FL 33611 Office: 851 Lincoln Ctr 5401 W Kennedy Blvd Tampa FL 33609

MICHAELS, PATRICK FRANCIS, broadcasting company executive; b. Superior, Wis., Nov. 5, 1925; s. Julian and Kathryn Elizabeth (Keating) M.; A.A., U. Melbourne, 1943; B.A., Golden State U., 1954; Ph.D., London U., 1964; m. Paula Naomi Bowen, May 1, 1960; children—Stephanie Michelle, Patricia Erin. War corr. CBS; news editor King Broadcasting, 1945-50; war corr. Mid-East Internat. News Service, 1947-49; war corr. MBS, Korea, 1950-53; news dir. Sta. WDSU-AM-FM-TV, 1953-54; fgn. corr. NBC, S. Am., 1954-56; news dir. Sta. KWIZ, 1956-59; commentator ABC, Los Angeles, 1959-62; fgn. corr. Am. News Services, London, 1962-64; news commentator McFadden Bartell Sta. KCBQ, 1964-68; news commentator ABC, San Francisco, 1968-70; news dir. Sta. KWIZ, Santa Ana, Calif., 1970-74, station mgr., 1974-81; pres. Sta. KWRM, Corona, Calif., KQLH, San Bernardino, Calif., 1981—. Bd. dirs. Econ. Devel. Corp. Mem. Calif. Broadcasters Assn. (bd. dirs.), Nat. Assn. Radio Broadcasters (legis. liaison com.), Am. Fedn. TV and Radio Artists, Orange County Broadcasters Assn. (pres.), Sigma Delta Chi (ethics com.). Republican. Clubs: Rotary, Balboa Bay (bd. govs.), South Shore Yacht, Internat. Yachting Fellowship of Rotarians (staff commodore). Home: 4521 Cortland Dr Corona del Mar CA 92625 Office: Sta KQLH FM Box 100 Corona CA 91718

MICHAELS, RICHARD EDWARD, lawyer; b. Chgo., June 10, 1952; s. Benjamin and Lillian (Borawski) Mikolajczewski; m. Karen Lynn Belau Michaels, May 17, 1980; children: Jonathan R., Timothy R. BS in Commerce summa cum laude, DePaul U., 1973; JD, Northwestern U., 1977. Bar: Ill. 1977, U.S. Dist. Ct. (no. dist.) Ill. 1977, U.S. Ct. Appeals (7th cir.) 1977; CPA, Ill. Acct. Touche Ross & Co., Chgo., 1973-74; assoc. Schuyler, Roche & Zwirner and predecessor firm Hubachek & Kelly Ltd., Chgo., 1977-83; ptnr. Schuyler, Roche & Zwirner, Chgo., 1983—. Mem. Northwestern U. Law Rev., 1976-77. Mem. mission bd. St. Andrews Luth. Ch., Park Ridge, Ill., 1983—. Mem. ABA, Internat. Bar Assn., Ill. Bar Assn., Chgo. Bar Assn., Beta Gamma Sigma, Pi Gamma Mu, Beta Alpha Psi, Phi Eta Sigma, Delta Epsilon Sigma, DePaul U. Alumni Assn., DePaul U. Boosters, Chgo. Athletic Assn. Lutheran. Clubs: Plaza, Northwestern U. (Chgo.). Home: 832 Wilkinson Pkwy Park Ridge IL 60068 Office: Schuyler Roche & Zwirner 3800 Prudential Plaza Chicago IL 60601

MICHALSKY, WALTER, educator; b. Siret, Romania, Jan. 19, 1947; s. Ioan and Miroslava (Maikovski) M.; m. Anna Irene Dyba, July 24, 1971; children—Alyssa Katrina, Alena Kristina (dec.). B.A., McMaster U., Hamilton, Ont., Can., 1970; M.A., U. Western Ont., London, Ont., Can., 1971; M.Ed., U. Toronto, Ont., Can., 1974. Teaching asst. U. Western Ont., 1971-72; tchr. Hamilton Bd. Edn., Ont., 1973—, chmn. profl. devel., 1979-80, adv. Students' Council, 1984-86; writer Remedial Studies Project, 1974-75. Contbr. articles to profl. jours., mags., newspapers. Advisor, Ukranian Parents Com., Hamilton, 1984-85. Mem. Am. Humanist Assn., Can. Humanist Assn., Ont. Secondary Schs. Tchrs. Fedn. Clubs: Chess, Tennis. Avocations: photography; table-tennis; book collecting. Office: Hill Park Secondary Sch, 465 E 16th St, Hamilton, ON Canada L9A 4K6

MICHAM, NANCY SUE, information systems executive; b. Toledo, May 15, 1956; d. Charles Edward and Dorothy Ruth (Bittner) Linker; m. Donald Thomas Kerner, June 20, 1975 (div. June 1980); m. Ray David Micham, III, May 19, 1984; 1 child, Brittni Mae. AS with high honors, U. Toledo, 1980; BSM cum laude, Pepperdine U., 1983. Cert. systems profl. Programmer, Owens-Ill., Toledo, 1973-80; programmer analyst Smith Tool Co., Irvine, Calif., 1980-82; systems analyst Denny's, Inc., La Mirada, Calif., 1982-83; sr. corp. systems analyst, mgr. corp. systems group Libbey-Owens-Ford Co., Toledo, 1983-86, pres. Seagate Systems Cons., 1986—. Participant ToledoScape. Mem. Nat. Mgmt. Assn., Assn. Systems Mgmt., Inst. for Cert. of Systems Profls., Nat. Assn. Female Execs. Republican. Roman Catholic. Avocations: travel, backpacking, bicycling, aerobics teaching.

MICHANEK, ERNST NATANAEL, ambassador; b. Stockholm, Sept. 27, 1919; s. Gustav V. and Selma A. (Andersson) M.; m. Annika E. Hedlund, June 24, 1943; children—Elisabeth Kristina, Katarina, Gunnar. B.A., U. Uppsala, 1944, Ph.D. (hon.), 1972. Journalist, Sweden, 1944-47; advisor welfare policies Ministry Social Welfare and Labor, Stockholm, 1948-56, under-sec. state, 1956-64; dir.-gen. Swedish Internat. Devel. Authority, Stockholm, 1964-79; ambassador Fgn. Ministry, Stockholm, 1979-87; del. or ind. advisor UN System, 1951—. Chmn., Dag Hammarskjold Found., 1965—, Swedish Commn. Internat. Econ. Tech. Coop., 1979—, Stockholm Internat. Peace Research Inst., 1986-87; vice chmn. Internat. Def. and Aid Fund for So. Africa, London, 1982—. Mem. Royal Swedish Acad. Scis. Lutheran. Club: Royal Commonwealth Soc. Home: Petersbergs W 76, S-12657 Stockholm Sweden

MICHAU, JEAN-LOUIS, management consultant; b. Paris, May 29, 1951; s. Christian and Nicole (Bedel) Michau-Dumesnil; m. Patricia De Nicolay, Dec. 20, 1980; children: Jean-Baptiste, Axel. M in Sociology, U. Paris I, 1973; PhD in Econs., U. Chgo., 1979. Chmn. Labs. Osiris, Paris, 1980—; sr. cons. Bossard Cons., Paris, 1981—. Author: Horaire Modulaire, 1981 (Prix Harvard Expansion Best Mgmt. Book of Yr. 1982), Strategie Du Temps Remunere, 1983, Entree Dans La Vie Active, 1984, Sortir De La Vie, 1985, Liberer Le Temps, 1987. Mem. Inst. de L'Entreprise (pres. commn. 1982—). Roman Catholic. Clubs: Automobile (Paris), Racing. Home: 53 Ave Kleber, 75116 Paris France Office: Lab Osiris, 4 Rue des Bourdonnais, 75001 Paris France

MICHEL, FRANCOIS CLAUDE, French ambassador; b. Saint Denis, France, July 30, 1928; s. Claude and Marie Emilie (Cabane de Laprade) M.; m. Jeanine Maurice, June 1, 1953; children—Xavier, Arnaud, Pascale, Jerome. Licence en Droit, U. Paris, 1958; Brevet, Ecole Nat. de la France d'Outre-Mer, 1959. Civil service officer Colonial Ministry, Cameroon, 1951-58; asst. minister of fgn. affairs, Paris, 1959-60; sec., counselor French embassy, Cameroon, Turkey, Ethiopia, Malagasy, and Ireland, 1960-75; dir. cultural affairs Ministry Fgn. Affairs, Paris, 1976-83; ambassador French embassy, Port-au-Prince, Haiti, 1983-86; dir. staff, Fgn. Sec. State's Dept., Paris, 1986-87; ambassador Frnch Embassy, Addis-Ababa, Ethiopia. Decorated Mérite Camerounais (Cameroon); Mérite Francais Legion d'Honneur (France). Roman Catholic. Avocation: swimming. Home: 57 rue du Docteur Blanche, Paris 75016 France Office: Embassy of France, PO Box 1464, Addis-Ababa Ethiopia

MICHEL, HENRY LUDWIG, civil engineer; b. Frankfurt, Fed. Republic of Germany, June 18, 1924; s. Maximilian Frederick and Loschka (Hepner) M.; m. Mary Elizabeth Strolis, June 5, 1954; children—Eve Musette, Ann Elizabeth. B.S.C.E., Columbia U., 1949. Registered profl. engr., Colo., N.Y., Ohio, Pa., Va., Mass., Conn., N.J., Mont. Chief engr. and gen. mgr. Panero-Weidlinger-Salvadori (cons. engrs.), Rome, 1960-62; pres., chief engr. Engring. Cons., Internat., Rome, 1962-65; partner Parsons Brinckerhoff Quade & Douglas, N.Y.C., 1965—; sr. v.p. Parsons Brinckerhoff Quade & Douglas, 1965-75, pres., 1975—, chief exec. officer, 1975—, dir., 1969—; dir. Parsons Brinckerhoff, Inc.; chmn. Parsons Brinckerhoff Internat. ; guest lectr. Grad. Sch. Mgmt., Colo. State U., 1975-76; advisor Office Tech. Assessment, The White House; chmn. Design Profl. Coalition. Contbr. numerous articles on mgmt. and transp. engring. to engring. jours. Fellow ASCE, Soc. Am. Mil. Engrs.; mem. Am. Cons. Engrs. Council , Internat. Road Fedn. (vice chmn., dir. 1977—), Nat. Assn. Corp. Dirs., N.Y. Soc. Profl. Engrs., Columbia U. Engring. Sch. Alumni Assn. (Egleston medal 1982, pres. 1986—), Am. Inst. Mgmt. (pres.'s council 1976), Am. European Community Assn. (dir. 1983—), Newcomen Soc. N.Am. Club: University. Home: 35 Sutton Pl New York NY 10022 Office: Parsons Brinckerhoff Inc 250 W 34th St New York NY 10119

MICHEL, JAMES, government official of Seychelles; b. Seychelles, Aug. 16, 1944. Ed. secondary sch., Victoria, Seychelles, 1959. Tchr. primary and secondary schs., Anse Boileau, 1960-61; with Cable & Wireless Ltd., 1961-71, Hotel des Seychelles, 1971-74; mem. exec. com. Seychelles People's United Party, 1974, editor ofcl. partt newspaper The People, 1974—; now chief of staff Seychelles People's Liberation Army and minister of edn. and info.; dep. sec. gen. Seychelles People's Progressive Front, 1984—. Office: Ministry Edn Info and Youth, Victoria Seychelles

MICHEL, JAMES H., government official, lawyer; b. St. Louis, Aug. 25, 1939; s. Paul J. and Margaret K. (Scheitlin) M.; m. Conception L. Trejo, Sept. 10, 1960; children—Mark, Kurt, Linda, Paul. J.D., St. Louis U., 1965. Bar: D.C., Mo. Atty. Dept. State, Washington, 1965-74, asst. to legal adviser, 1974-78, dep. legal adviser, 1978-83, dep. asst. sec. for Inter-Am. affairs, 1983-87; ambassador to Guatemala, 1987—. Pres. St. Thomas More Fed. Credit Union, Arlington, Va., 1970—. Recipient Meritorious Exec. award Pres. Carter, 1980, Disting. Exec. award Pres. Reagan, 1982, Superior award Dept. State, 1983. Mem. Fed. Bar Assn. (Tom C. Clark award 1982), D.C. Bar Assn., Mo. Bar Assn., Am. Soc. Internat. Law, Inter-Am. Bar Assn. Roman Catholic. Office: US Ambassador to Guatemala care Dept State Washington DC 20520 *

MICHEL, LUC YVES, chemical company executive; b. Strasbourg, Alsace, France, Apr. 22, 1937; s. Marcel François and Emilie (Singer) M.; m. Doris Marlyse Knobloch, July 6, 1967; children—Véronique-Chantal, Stéphanie-Valérie. Degree in Pharmacy, Univ., Strasbourg, 1960, degree in Biochemistry, 1964, degree in Scis., 1964. Microbiologist Pharm. U., Strasbourg, France, 1960-64, 66-68; mgr. quantitative analysis Eli Lilly Co., Strasbourg, 1968-70, dir. gen. pharmacist in charge, 1970-74; with Allcaps, Waiblingen, W. Ger., 1974-76; dep. dir. gen. Capsugel, Colmar, France, 1976-79, dir. gen., 1979—, pres. directeur général, dir. research-devel. and applied technologies, 1986—. Vice pres. Union Stes Art Dramatique de l'Est, Nancy, 1985—; pres. Comediens du Rhin, Strasbourg, 1970—.Served with French Army Res., 1964-66. Mem. Chambre Syndicale Chimie (adminstr. 1979—), Colmar C. of C. and Industry (del.). Roman Catholic. Home: 15 Rue de l'Ill, 67640 Fegersheim France

MICHEL, RICHARD CHRIS, economist; b. Rochester, N.Y., Dec. 25, 1945; s. James Peter and Dina (Noun) M.; A.B., Syracuse (N.Y.) U., 1967; M.P.A., Wharton Sch., U. Pa., 1975. Assoc. analyst Congressional Budget Office, Washington, 1975-76; sr. research assoc. Urban Inst., Washington, 1976-77, 79—, dir. Income Security and Pension Policy Ctr., 1983—; sr. economist Office Sec. HEW, 1977-79. Mem. Am. Econ. Assn., Western Econ. Assn., So. Econ. Assn., Assn. Pub. Policy and Mgmt. Democrat. Mem. Greek Orthodox Ch. Clubs: Wharton Alumni, Syracuse Alumni (Washington). Contbr. articles to profl. publs. Home: 7512 Rambling Ridge Dr Fairfax Station VA 22039

MICHEL, ROBERT EMORY, wholesale company executive; b. Balt., Dec. 19, 1911; s. Ambrose Emory and Mary Elizabeth (Wood) M.; LL.D., U. Balt., 1935; m. Mary Ellen Michel, Dec. 29, 1934 (dec. 1975); children—Suzanne Michel Twells, Robert E., Greer Michel Haines, John W. H.; m. 2d, Cecile H. Meers, July 10, 1981. Bar: Md. 1936. Pres. R.E. Michel Co., Inc., Balt., 1950—, now chmn. bd., also dir. Bd. govs. Balt. Symphony Orch.; bd. dirs., pres. Star Spangled Banner Flag House Assn.; bd. dirs. U.S. Frigate Constellation Found.; mem. maritime com. Md. Hist. Soc., Balt. Mem. Balt. C. of C. Republican. Episcopalian. Clubs: Balt. Country, Md., Gibson Island. Home: 217 Paddington Rd Baltimore MD 21212 Office: 2801 W Patapsco Ave Baltimore MD 21230

MICHEL, THOMAS FRANCIS, religion educator; b. St. Louis, Feb. 5, 1941; s. Victor James and Bernadette Bridget (Fox) M. BA, Cardinal Glennon Coll., 1963; M Religious Edn., Kenrick Sem., 1967; PhD, U. Chgo., 1978. Mem. Soc. of Jesus (Jesuits). Lectr. Northwestern U., Evanston, Ill., 1974-75; asst. prof. Columbia U., N.Y.C., 1977-78; prof. Inst. Filsafat Teologi, Yogyakarta, Indonesia, 1978-85, Gregorian U., Rome, 1986-88; official Vatican Secretariat for Non-Christians, Vatican City, 1981-87; vis. prof. St. Paul Sem., Davao, The Philippines, 1982-83, Dansalan Coll., Marawi City, The Philippines, 1983; counsellor for Islamic affairs, Soc. Jesus, Rome, 1984-88. Author: A Muslim Theologian's Response to Christianity, 1985, Analytical Index of Bulletin, 1987; editor: Islam: Continuity and Change, 1987; author 65 articles in field. Fulbright Hays research/Am. Research Ctr. grantee, Egypt, 1976; Fulbright teaching fellow Ankara U. and Dokuz Eylul U., Turkey, 1986-88. Democrat. Roman Catholic. Home: Borgo S Spirito 5, 00193 Rome Italy Office: Pontifical Council, Interreligious Dialogue, 00120 The Vatican Vatican City

MICHEL BARBOSA, LUIS FERNANDO, architect, educator; b. Irapuato, Guanajuato, Mex., Nov. 13, 1951; s. Fernando Michel Alvarez and Emma Barbosa Ochoa de Michel; m. Ingrid Niehus, Jan. 17, 1976; children—Ingrid, Luisa Womti, Luis Fernando, Claire. Lic. Architecture U. Guanajuato, 1970, M.S., 1975, M.S. in Monuments Restoration, 1979. Constrn. resident Expo Fresas, Irapuato, 1975-77; projects, constrn. coordinator Flooding Emergency Plan, Irapuato, 1973-74; resident, appraiser City Remodling Plan, Irapuato, 1975-76; assoc. prof. U. Guanajuato Sch. Architecture, 1977—; exec. dir. Michel & Assocs., Irapuato, 1978—; lic. real estate appraiser Somex and Comermex Bank S.N.C., Irapuato, 1984—, mem. cons. council Comermex Bank S.N.C., 1984—; cons. Irapuato Constrn. Regulation City Plan, 1983—. Archtl. designer Mérida City pub. fountain, 1972, Hidalgo recreational park, Irapuato, 1975; designer constrn. Pepsi Cola factory, Irapuato, 1976; designer constrn. Cerveceria Modelo warehouses and offices, 1982-86. Com. mem. Expo Fresa Fair, 1975-77; tech. cons. city Orphanat, 1975-77. Fellow Irapuato Architects Collegiate; mem. Assn. Architects (treas. 1975-77, 81-84), Ateneo de Artes, Letras, Ciencia y Tecnologia, Nat. Banking System Commn. Roman Catholic. Club: Irapuato Golf, Santa Margarita Golf. Lodge: Rotary. Avocations: photography; tennis; swimming; travel. Home: Volcan N 180, Irapuato, 36660 Guanajuato Mexico Office: Volcan N 178, Irapuato, 36660 Guanajuato Mexico

MICHELIS, MICHAEL FRANK, physician; b. Bklyn., Dec. 11, 1938; s. Michael and Gisella (Gammer) M.; B.A., Columbia U., 1959; M.D., George Washington U., 1963; m. Mary Ann Wolak, July 28, 1973; children—Elizabeth Ann, Katherine Clare. Intern, Resident Lenox Hill Hosp., N.Y.C., 1963-65; resident Hosp. Med. Coll. Pa., Phila., 1965-67; fellow in renal disease dept. medicine U. Pitts. Sch. Medicine, 1969-70, asst. prof. medicine, 1971-75; chief renal diagnostic unit VA Hosp., Pitts., 1971-75; asst. prof. clin. medicine N.Y.U. Med. Sch., 1975—; asso. prof. clin. medicine N.Y. Med. Coll., 1980-87, prof., 1987—; chief nephrology sect. Lenox Hill Hosp., N.Y.C., 1975—; spl. lectr. Georgetown U. Med. Sch., 1973—; lectr. Western Pa. Continuing Edn. for Physicians, 1972-75, vis. prof., 1976; mem. merit rev. bd. VA, 1973-76; cons. clin. fellowship rev. com. NIH, 1981—; mem. exec. com. End Stage Renal Disease Network, N.Y.C., 1981-85; mem. med. adv. bd. Nat. Kidney Found. of N.Y./N.J., 1987—. Served to maj. M.C., AUS, 1967-69. Decorated Army Commendation medal, 1969; grantee Health, Research and Services Found., 1970, 72. 74. Mem. AMA (invited lectr. 1973-75). ACP, Am. Fedn. Clin. Research, Am. Soc. Nephrology, Internat. Soc. Nephrology, Central Soc. Clin. Research. Greek Orthodox. Contbr. articles to profl. jours. and textbooks. Asst. editor Clin. Nephrology, 1979—; assoc. editor Geriatric Nephrology, 1986. Home: 16 Woodland Park Dr Tenafly NJ 07670 Office: Lenox Hill Hosp 100 E 77th St New York NY 10021

MICHELLE, SIMONE, dance educator; b. Paris, May 10, 1917; arrived in Eng., 1945; d. Marcel Herman and Marguerite (Wagen) Moser; m. Soukop Willi, Jan. 5, 1907; children: M. Soukop, Anita Cox. Diploma, Jooss-Leeder Sch. Dance, 1940. Profl. dancer U.S., France, Switzerland; tchr. Sigurd Leeder Sch. Dance, 1948-61, co-dir., 1961-68; tchr. opera sch., Eng., 1958-69, acting sch., 1958-69; sr. lecgr. Laban Ctr. Movment and Dance, London, 1965—; dance theater coordinator, 1983—. Home: 26 Greville Rd, London NW6 5JA, England Office: Laban Ctr Movement and Dance, Laurie Grove, London SE14, England

MICHELS, DAVID BARRY, physiologist, engineer; b. Chgo., Feb. 21, 1942; s. Charles Bernard and Ethelyn (Leven) M.; m. Lynnell Roberta Spitza, June 21, 1964; children—Melinda Relayne, Tamara Joy. BS, UCLA, 1964, MS, 1967, PhD, 1975. Engr. Bendix, North Hollywood, Calif., 1964-65; engr. Hughes Aircraft, Culver City, Calif., 1965-69, sr. staff mem., Canoga Park, Calif., 1980—; research scientist Tech. Service Corp., Santa Monica, Calif., 1969-72; researcher UCLA, 1972-75; faculty researcher U. Calif.-San Diego, 1975-80; cons., 1980—. Contbr. articles to profl. jours. Chmn. Nobel Jr. High Adv. Council, Northridge, Calif., 1983-87; pres. Parents Heart Assn., Los Angeles, 1985-87. Mem. Am. Physiol. Soc., IEEE. Republican. Jewish. Current work: Effects of weightlessness and gravity on the lung, first chest x-rays and measurements of gas and blood distributions during weightlessness, designed analyser to test astronauts' lungs aboard space shuttle, designed radar angle processor for Strategic Defense Initiative Delta 180 intercept. Subspecialties: Pulmonary medicine, Systems engineering. Home: 10828 Amigo Ave Northridge CA 91326

MICHIE, DONALD, research scientist; b. Rangoon, Burma, Nov. 11, 1923; s. James Kilgour and Marjorie Crain (Pfeiffer) M.; M.A., Oxford U., 1949, D.Phil., 1953, D.Sc., 1971; m. Zena Marguerite Davis; 1 son, Christopher; m. Anne McLaren; children—Susan, Jonathan, Caroline; m. Jean Elizabeth Hayes, Mar. 1, 1971. Research asso. U. London, 1952-58; sr. lectr., reader dept. surg. sci. U. Edinburgh, Scotland, 1958-64, dir. exptl. programming unit, 1965, chmn. dept. machine intelligence and perception, 1967, dir. machine intelligence research unit, 1974-84, prof. machine intelligence, 1967-84, prof. emeritus, 1985—; prof. computer sci. U. Strathclyde, Eng., 1985—; exec. dir. Turing Inst., 1983-84, chief scientist, 1985—; tech. dir. Intelligent Terminals Ltd., 1984—. Fellow Zool. Soc., Royal Soc. Edinburgh, Brit. Computer Soc.; mem. London Math. Soc., Brit. Soc. Artificial Intelligence and Simulation of Behavior, Royal Instn. Club: Atheneum, New (Edinburgh). Author: Computing Science in 1964; A Pilot Study of the State of University-based Research in UK, 1965; On Machine Intelligence, 1974, 2d edit., 1986; Machine Intelligence and Related Topics, 1982; co-author: The Creative Computer, 1984. Office: The Turing Inst, Glasgow G1 2AD, Scotland UK

MICHLER, MARKWART WALDEMAR, orthopedist, historian of medicine, surgeon; b. Breslau, Silesia, German Dem. Republic, Apr. 30, 1923; s. Waldemar Karl-Arthur and Leonie Frieda (Olleck) M.; student U. Breslau, 1942-44, U. Berlin, 1946-49; Dipl. in surgery, 1957, Dipl. in orthopaedics, 1958, M.D., 1958; m. Inge Stemmler, Dec. 20, 1957; children: Waldemar, Karl-Friedrich; Intern, Städt. Krankenhaus Berlin Neukölln, 1950-51; resident Städt. Auguste-Viktoria-Krankenhaus Berlin-Schöneberg, 1951-56; orthopedic clinician Evangelisches Waldkrankenhaus, Berlin-Spandau, 1956-61, chief physiotherapy Orthopedic Clinic, 1958-61; sci. asst., lectr. med. history Inst. Friedrich Wilhelms U. Bonn, Fed. Republic Germany, 1961-64; lectr. Med. History Inst., U. Hamburg, Fed. Republic Germany, 1964-65, habilitation history medicine, 1965; prof. history of medicine Justus Liebig U., Giessen, Fed. Republic Germany, 1965-73, ret., 1973; pvt. practice as orthopedist and spa physician, Bad Brückenau, Fed. Republic Germany, 1974—; dir. Inst. History of Medicine Justus Liebig U. Giessen and leader Ludwig Schunk Meml. Library, 1965-73. Served with Tank Corps, German Army, World War II. Mem. Deutsche Gesellschaft für Geschichte d Medizin d Naturwissenschaften und der Technik; Gesellschaft f Wissenschaftsgeschichte, Schweizerische Ges Geschichte d Med und d Naturwissenschaften, History of Sci. Soc., AAAS, Société Internat. d'Histoire de la Médecine, N.Y. Acad. Scis., Internat. Acad. History Medicine, Deutsche Gesellschaft für Orthopädie und Traumatologie, Société Internat. de Chirurgie Orthopédique et de Traumatologie. Author: numerous books; contbr. articles to profl. jours. Home: 36 Ernst Putz Str, D-8788 Bad Brückenau Federal Republic of Germany Office: Elisabethenhof Bad, D-8788 Brückenau D-8788 Federal Republic of Germany

MICHON, JOHN ALBERTUS, psychology educator; b. Utrecht, The Netherlands, Oct. 29, 1935; s. Jaap J. and Sophia Ch. A. (De Ruyter) M.; m. Hetty Sommer, July 5, 1960; children: Job, Annet. MA, U. Utrecht, 1960; PhD, U. Leyden, The Netherlands, 1967. Research scientist Inst. Perception TNO, Soesterberg, The Netherlands, 1960-69, sr. scientist, 1969-73; prof. exptl. psychology and traffic U. Groningen, Haren, The Netherlands, 1971—, head dept. psychologyy, 1983-86; chmn., dir. Traffic Research Ctr. U. Groningen, 1977—; vis. prof. Carnegie-Mellon U., Pitts., 1986-87; cons. Ministry Transport, Edn., Dept. Transport, Gt. Britain. Author: Timing in Temporal Tracking, 1967, Beinvloeding van Mobiliteit, 1980; editor: Handbook of Psychonomics, 1976, 79, Time, Mind and Behavior, 1985, Guyau and the Idea of Time, 1988. Pres. Netherlands Psychomomics Found., 1975-80; vice-chmn. Nat. Road Safety Council, The Hague, Netherlands, 1977-86; chmn. adv. com. on Info. Mgmt., The Hague, 1982-84; bd. dirs. Royal Netherlands Touring Club ANWB, The Hague, 1981—. Served to 1st lt. Dutch army, 1962-63. Sci. fellow NATO, 1965-66, fellow Netherlands Inst. for Advanced Studies, 1975-76. Mem. Royal Netherlands Acad. Arts and Scis., Netherlands Inst. Psychologists, Am. Psychol. Assn. (affiliate), European Soc. for Cognitive Psychology (sec. 1985—). Lodge: Rotary. (pres. local club 1979-80). Office: U Groningen, Kerklaan 30, 9751 NN Haren The Netherlands

MICKEL, HUBERT SHELDON, neurologist; b. Bridgeton, N.J., Aug. 27, 1937; s. Ralph Andrew and Lillian Almeda (Burkett) M.; B.S. summa cum laude, Eastern Nazarene Coll., 1958; M.D., Harvard U., 1962; m. Betty Jane Harris, Oct. 2, 1961 (div. Dec. 1971); children—Paul David, Deborah Elizabeth, Pamela Marie; m. Julie L. Moll, June 4, 1979; children: John Christopher Frederick, Joseph Erich Alexander. Intern, Mary Fletcher Hosp., Burlington, Vt., 1962-63; resident internal medicine Royal Victoria Hosp., Montreal, Que., Can., 1963-64; resident neurology, neurol. unit Boston City Hosp., 1964-67; NIH spl. fellow in chemistry Harvard U., 1967-68; practice medicine specializing emergency medicine and neurology, Boston, 1970-83, Concord, Mass., 1971-73, New Bedford, Mass., 1975-79, Fairfax, Va., 1979-81, Boston, 1981-83, Bethesda, Md., 1983—; NIH spl. expert lab. of experimental neuropathology, Nat. Inst. Neurol. Communicative Disorders, and Stroke, 1987—; vis. scientist Dept. Neuropathology Armed Forces Inst. Pathology, 1987-88; instr. neurology Harvard Med. Sch., Boston, 1970-71, asst. prof. neurology, 1971-77, asst. clin. prof. neurology, 1977-83; instr. neurology Boston U. Sch. Medicine, 1970-79; clin. asst. prof. neurology Georgetown U., 1981—; clin. assoc. prof. neurology, Uniformed Services U. of Health Scis., Bethesda, 1985—, reappointed, 1987-88, 88-89; instr. advanced trauma life support, 1981—, advanced cardiac life support, 1983; research assoc. neurosurgery Children's Hosp. Med. Center, Boston, 1970-71, asst. neurology, 1970-77, asso. in neurology, 1977-83; dir. Wrentham State Sch. div., dept. neurology Children's Hosp. Med. Center, Boston, 1973-76; asst. neurology Beth Israel Hosp., Boston, 1971-76; sr. resident pre-med. adviser Leverett House, Harvard U., Cambridge, Mass., 1971-79, hon. research asso., dept. chemistry, 1977-79; chief physician, dir. med. research Wrentham (Mass.) State Sch., 1973-76; emergency med. physician Fairfax Hosp., Falls Church, Va., 1979, Commonwealth Hosp., Fairfax, 1979-80, Greater S.E. Community Hosp., Washington, 1980; fellow in shock-trauma Washington Hosp. Center, 1981; dir. emergency dept. Carney Hosp., Boston, 1981-82. Served to maj. M.C., USAF, 1968-70; to lt. col. USAR, 1982-87. Diplomate Am. Bd. Psychiatry and Neurology, Am. Bd. Emergency Medicine (examiner). Fellow Internat. Biog. Assn., Am. Coll. Emergency Physicians; mem. AMA, Am. Acad. Neurology, N.Y. Acad. Sci., AAAS, Assn. Research in Nervous and Mental Diseases, Assn. Harvard Chemists, Mass. Med. Soc., Am. Chem. Soc., Am. Oil Chemists Soc., Internat. Soc. Fat Research, Undersea Med. Soc., Pan Am. Med. Soc. (N.Am. v.p. sect. neurology), Am. Coll. Emergency Physicians, Soc. Tchrs. of Emergency Medicine, Univ. Assn. Emergency Medicine, Am. Heart Assn. (Stroke Council), Internat. Platform Assn., Robert Schumann Gesellschaft, Brahms Gesellschaft. Office: PO Box 41046 Bethesda MD 20814

MICKELSON, GEORGE S., governor of South Dakota; b. Mobridge, S.D., Jan. 31, 1941; s. George T. and Madge Mickelson; m. Linda McCahren; children: Mark, Amy, David. BS, U. S.D., 1963, JD, 1965. Ptnr. McCann, Martin and Mickelson, Brookings, S.D., 1968-83, Mickelson, Erickson and Helsper, Brookings, 1983-86; state's atty. Brookings County, 1970-74; mem. S.D. Ho. of Reps., Pierre, 1975-80, speaker pro tempore, 1977-78, speaker, 1979-80; gov. State of S.D., 1986—; chmn. S.D. Bd. Charities and Corrections, 1980-84. Served to capt. U.S. Army, 1963-67, Vietnam. Mem. ABA, S.D. Bar Assn., Assn. Trial Lawyers Am., S.D. Trial Lawyers Assn., Am. Judicature Soc., VFW, Am. Legion. Republican. Methodist. Office: Office of the Gov 500 E Capitol Pierre SD 57501

MICKSCH, (ROLF) JURGEN, educational administrator; b. Breslau, Fed. Republic Germany, Jan. 20, 1941; s. Rudolf and Ursula (Muller) M. Theologian, U. Berlin, 1965; PhD, U. Erlangen/Munster, Fed. Republic Germany, 1971. Reverend Protestant Ch., Regensburg, Fed. Republic Germany, 1965; study inspector Theol. Student House, Erlangen, Fed. Republic Germany, 1965-66; sci. asst. Fgn. Office Protestant Chs. Germany, Frankfurt, Fed. Republic Germany, 1971-73, dir. immigrants, 1974-84; study dir. Evangelische Akademie Tutzing, Fed. Republic Germany, 1984—; chmn. ecumenical commn. for support orthodox priests Instn. Pub. Law in Fed. Republic Germany, Munich, 1980—; moderator working group on racism Chs. Com. on Migrant Workers in Europe, Brussels, Belgium, 1982—; chmn. immigrant working group Dirs. Protestant Acads. in Fed. Republic Germany, Frankfurt, 1984—. Author: Youth and Leisure in the German Dem. Republic, 1972, Christians and Muslims in Dialogue, 1982, The Life with Immigrants, 1984; editor: Living with Muslims, 1980, AIDS-Fate and Chance, 1988, others; contbr. articles to profl. jours. Chmn. Ecumenical Com. for Week of Immigrants in Fed. Republic Germany, Frankfurt, 1974—; chmn. Pro Asyl Orgn. for Refugees in Fed. Republic of Germany, Frankfurt, 1986—. Mem. Ecumenical Assn. of Acads. and Laity Ctrs. in Europe (mem. exec. com. 1984—). Lutheran. Office: Evangelische Akademie Tutzing, SchloBstr 2 and 4, 8132 Tutzing Federal Republic of Germany

MIDDLEBROOKS, EDDIE JOE, environmental engineer; b. Crawford County, Ga., Oct. 16, 1932; s. Robert Harold and Jewel LaVerne (Dixon) M.; m. Charlotte Linda Hardy, Dec. 6, 1958; 1 child, Linda Tracey. B.C.E., U. Fla., 1956, M.S., 1960; Ph.D., Miss. State U., 1966. Diplomate: Am. Acad. Environmental Engrs.; Registered profl. engr., Ariz., Miss., Utah registered land surveyor, Fla. Asst. san. engr. USPHS, Cin., 1956-58; field engr. T.T. Jones Constrn. Co., Atlanta, 1958-59; grad. teaching asst. U. Fla., 1959-60; research asst. U. Ariz., 1960-61; asst. prof., asso. prof. Miss. State U., 1962-67; research engr., asst. dir. San. Engrng. Research Lab., U. Calif.-Berkeley, 1968-70; prof. Utah State U., Logan, 1970-82; dean Utah State U. (Coll. Engring.), 1974-82; Newman chair natural resources engring. Clemson U., 1982-83; provost, v.p. acad. affairs Tenn. Tech. U., 1983-88; provost, v.p. acad. affairs, prof. chem. engring. U. Tulsa, 1988—; mem. nat. drinking water adv. council EPA, 1981-83; cons. EPA, UN Indsl. Devel. Orgn., Calif. Water Resources Control Bd., also numerous indsl. and engring. firms. Author: Modeling the Eutrophication Process, 1974, Statistical Calculations-How To Solve Statistical Problems, 1976, Biostimulation and Nutrient Assessment, 1976, Water Supply Engineering Design, 1977, Lagoon Information Source Book, 1978, Industrial Pollution Control, Vol. 1: Agro-Industries, 1979, Wastewater Collection and Treatment: Principles and Practices, 1979, Water Reuse, 1982, Wastewater Stabilization Lagoon Design, Performance and Upgrading, 1982, Reverse Osmosis Treatment of Drinking Water, 1986, Pollution Control in the Petrochemicals Industry, 1987, Natural Systems for Waste Management and Treatment, 1988; mem. editorial adv. bd. Lewis Pubs. Inc., Envionment Internat.; contbr. tech. articles to profl. jours. Fellow ASCE; mem. AAAS, Water Pollution Control Fedn. (Eddy medal 1969, dir. 1979-81), Assn. Environ. Engrng. Profs. (pres. 1974), Utah Water Pollution Control Assn. (pres. 1976), Internat. Assn. on Water Pollution Research, Am. Soc. Engring. Edn., Am. Soc. Limnology and Oceanography, Sigma Xi, Omicron Delta Kappa, Phi Kappa Phi, Tau Beta Pi, Sigma Tau. Home: 1115 E 20th St Tulsa OK 74120 Office: U Tulsa Office of Provost 600 S College Ave Tulsa OK 74104

MIDDLEDITCH, BRIAN STANLEY, biochemistry educator; b. Bury St. Edmunds, Suffolk, Eng., July 15, 1945; came to U.S., 1971; s. Stanley Stafford and Dorothy (Harker) M.; m. Patricia Rosalind Nair, July 18, 1970; 1 dau., Courtney Lauren. B.Sc., U. London, 1966; M.Sc., U. Essex, 1967; Ph.D., U. Glasgow, 1971. Research asst. U. Glasgow, Scotland, 1967-71; vis. asst. prof. Baylor Coll. Medicine, Houston, 1971-75; asst. prof. U. Houston, 1975-80, assoc. prof., 1980—. Author: Mass Spectrometry of Priority Pollutants, 1981; editor: Practical Mass Spectrometry, 1979, Environmental Effects of Offshore Oil Production, 1981, Analytical Artifacts, 1986. Grantee Nat. Marine Fisheries Service 1976-80, Sea Grant Program, 1977-81, NASA, 1980—, IBM, 1985—, NIH, 1988—, Tex. Advanced Research Program, 1988—. Mem. Am. Chem. Soc., Am. Soc. Mass Spectrometry, World Mariculture Soc. Home: 4101 Emory Ave Houston TX 77005 Office: U Houston Dept Biochemistry Houston TX 77204

MIDDLEKAUFF, ROGER DAVID, lawyer; b. Cleve., May 6, 1935; s. Roger David and Ella Marie (Holan) M.; m. Gail Palmer, Apr. 19, 1963; children: Roger David, Arthur Henry. BChemE, Cornell U., 1958; JD cum laude, Northwestern U., 1964. Bar: Ohio 1964, D.C. 1966, U.S. Supreme Ct. 1974. Assoc., Roetzel & Andress, Akron, Ohio, 1964-66, Kirkland, Ellis & Rowe, Washington, 1966-69; assoc. Thompson, and Middlekauff and predecessor firms, Washington, 1969-72, ptnr., 1973-83; ptnr. McKenna, Conner & Cuneo, 1983—; mem. adv. com. extension service project Dept. Agr., 1976; mem. adv. com. solar energy project ERDA, 1975; indsl. observer Codex Alimentarius Commn., FAO/WHO and com. meetings; project rev. group control tech. assessment of fermentation processes, Nat. Inst. Occupational Safety and Health. Contbr. articles to legal jours.; editor handbooks, Practising Law Inst.; mem. editorial bd. Jour. Regulatory Pharmacology and Toxicology; co-editor: The Impact of Chemistry on Biotechnology, 1988. Vice chmn. bur. Greater Washington Bd. Trade; trustee Internat. Life Scis. Inst., Nutrition Found., Inc.; chmn. Arthur S. Flemming Awards Commn., 1969-70; vol. gen. counsel Episcopal Found. for Drama, 1976-77, Scotland Community Devel. Assn., 1971-73, Congregations United for Shelter, 1971-73, Iona House, 1974-77; sr. warden St. Columbia's Episc. Ch., Washington, 1975-77; sec., bd. dirs. Episc. Ch. Homes, Washington; mem. lawyers' panel Pres. Ford's Com., 1976; chmn. pres.'s chpt. Nat. Capital Area council Nat. Eagle Scout Assn. Served with USN, 1958-61. Recipient Silver Wreath award local chpt. Boy Scouts Am. Mem. ABA (chmn. subcom. on food and color additives and pesticide residues, food, drug and cosmetic com. 1977-82), Bar Assn. D.C. (chmn. corp. and bus. law com. 1977-82), Am. Chem. Soc. (sec., treas. biotech. secretariat, 1986—), Inst. Food Technologists (exec. com. div. toxicology and safety evaluation, 1987—), Order of Coif. Episcopalian. Clubs: Metropolitan, Rotary. Office: McKenna Conner & Cuneo 1575 Eye St NW Washington DC 20005

MIDDLETON, ANTHONY WAYNE, JR., urologist, educator; b. Salt Lake City, May 6, 1939; s. Anthony Wayne and Dolores Caravena (Lowry) M.; BS, U. Utah, 1963; MD, Cornell U., 1966; m. Carol Samuelson, Oct. 23, 1970; children: Anthony Wayne, Suzanne, Kathryn, Jane, Michelle. Intern, U. Utah Hosps., Salt Lake City, 1966-67; resident in urology Mass. Gen. Hosp., Boston, 1970-74; practice urology Middleton Urol. Assos., Salt Lake City, 1974—; mem. staff Primary Children's Hosp., staff pres., 1981-82; mem. staff Latter-Day Saints Hosp., Holy Cross Hosp.; asst. clin. prof. surgery U. Utah Med. Coll., 1977—; vice chmn. bd. govs. Utah Med. Self-Ins. Assn., 1980-81, chmn. 1985-87. Bd. dirs. Utah chpt. Am. Cancer Soc., 1978-86; bishop Ch. Jesus Christ Latter-day Saints; vice chmn. Utah Med. Polit. Action Com., 1978-81, chmn., 1981-83; chmn. Utah Physicians for Reagan, 1983-84; mem. U. Utah Coll. Medicine Dean's Search Com., 1983-84; bd. dirs. Utah Symphony, 1985—. Served as capt. USAF, 1968-70. Mem. ACS, Utah State Med. Assn. (pres. 87—), Am. Urologic Assn., AMA (socioecons. com. 1987—), AMA, Salt Lake County Med. Assn. (sec. 1965-67, pres. liaison com. 1980-81, pres.-elect 1981-83, pres. 1984), Utah Urol. Assn. (pres. 1976-77), Salt Lake Surg. Soc. (treas. 1977-78), Phi Beta Kappa, Alpha Omega Alpha, Beta Theta Pi. Republican. Contbr. articles to profl. jours. Home: 2798 Chancellor Pl Salt Lake City UT 84108 Office: 1060 E 1st S Salt Lake City UT 84102

MIDDLETON, CAROLE FOSTER, insurance broker, consultant; b. Weymouth, Mass., Dec. 24, 1946; d. David Warren and Hazel Margaret (McRae) Foster; B.A., Coll. St. Catherine, 1968; B.S., Rutgers U., 1974; MA, Webster U., 1987; m. Finley N. Middleton, II, Mar. 23, 1974. Claims supr. Allstate Ins. Co., 1969-74; asst. account exec. Johnson & Higgins, Brazil, 1974-76; new bus. prodn. mgr. Edward Lumley & Sons, South Africa, 1976-77; asst. v.p. Johnson & Higgins, N.Y.C., 1977-81; asst. v.p. Alexander & Alexander, N.Y.C., 1981-83; pres. Lynmar Internat., Yonkers, N.Y., 1983—, Foxberry Press, Gourmet Internat., Shopping & Mailing Internat. (all subs.); adj. faculty mem. Webster U., Leiden campus; speaker on sales techniques, internat. ins., fgn. investment in the U.S., women in ins., women's networking, multinat. corps. Bd. dirs. Bklyn. YWCA, 1980-83, chmn. fin. com., treas., 1982; chair Republicans Abroad-Netherlands, 1987-88. Mem. Nat. Assn. Ins. Women, Am. Mgmt. Assn., Nat. Fedn. Bus. and Profl. Women, Assn. Profl. Ins. Women (adv. bd. 1982-83), Women's Econ. Round Table, Am. Women's Club Denmark (pres. 1986-87). Presbyterian. Clubs: Wall St. Bus. and Profl. Women's (past pres.); Women's Nat. Rep. Columnist Wall St. Woman, 1979-80; editor Chronicle mag., 1984-86; author: Managing Foreign Risks, 1988.

MIDDLETON, DAVID, physicist, applied mathematician, educator; b. N.Y.C., Apr. 19, 1920; s. Charles Davies Scudder and Lucile (Davidson) M.; m. Nadea Butler, May 26, 1945 (div. 1971); children: Susan Terry, Leslie Butler, David Scudder Blakeslee, George Davidson Powell; m. Joan Bartlett Reed, 1971; children: Christopher Hope, Andrew Bartlett, Henry H. Reed. Grad., Deerfield Acad., 1938; AB summa cum laude, Harvard U., 1942, AM, 1945, PhD in Physics, 1947. Teaching fellow electronics Harvard U., Cambridge, Mass., 1942, spl. research assoc., radio research lab., 1942-45, NSF predoctoral fellow physics, 1945-47, research fellow electronics, 1947-49, asst. prof. applied physics, 1949-54; cons. physicist Cambridge, 1954—, Concord, Mass., 1957-71, N.Y.C., 1971—; adj. prof. elec. engring. Columbia U., 1960-61; adj. prof. applied physics and communication theory Rensselaer Poly. Inst., Hartford Grad. Ctr., 1961-70; adj. prof. communication theory U. R.I., 1966—; adj. prof. math. scis. Rice U., 1979—; U.S. del. internat. conf. Internat. Radio Union, Lima, Peru, 1975; lectr. NATO Advanced Study Inst., Grenoble, France, 1964, Copenhagen, 1980, Luneburg, W. Ger., 1984; Naval Research Adv. Com., 1970-77; Supercomputer Research Ctr. Sci. Adv. Bd.; cons. physicist numerous cos., instns. and research ctrs. Author: Introduction to Statistical Communication Theory, 1960; Russian edit. Soviet Radio Moscow 2 vols., 1961, 62, Topics in Communication Theory, 1965 (Russian edit. 1966); sci. editor: English edit. Statistical Methods in Sonar (by V.V. Ol'shevskii), 1978; mem. editorial bd.: Info. and Control, Advanced Serials in Electronics and Cybernetics, 1971-82; contbr. articles to tech. jours. Recipient award (with W.H. Huggins) Nat. Electronics Conf., 1956; Wisdom award of honor, 1970; First prize 3d Internat. Symposium on Electromagnetic Compatibility Rotterdam, Holland, 1979; awards U.S. Dept. Commerce, 1978. Fellow Am. Phys. Soc., IEEE (life; several prize paper awards 1977, 79), AAAS, Explorers Club, Acoustical Soc. Am.; mem. Optical Soc. Am., Am. Math. Soc., Soc. Indsl. and Applied Math., AAUP, N.Y. Acad. Sci., Authors Guild Am., U.S. Naval Inst., Inst. Math. Stats., Phi Beta Kappa, Sigma Xi. Clubs: Harwich Port Tennis Assn.; Harvard (N.Y.C.); Cosmos (Washington). Home and Office: 127 E 91st St New York NY 10128 also: 35 Concord Ave Cambridge MA 02138 also: 13 Harbor Rd Harwich Port MA 02646

MIDDLETON, DEREK THOMAS, immunologist; b. Belfast, No. Ireland, Sept. 30, 1946; s. Thomas and Ena (Watson) M.; m. Verna Lyttle; children: Richard, Christopher. BSc in Microbiology, Queen's U., Belfast, 1968, PhD, 1981. Research officer dept. microbiology Queen's U., 1968-71; scientist No. Ireland Tissue Typing Lab., City Hosp., Belfast, 1971-73, sr. scientist, 1973-77, prin. scientist, 1977-83, cons. scientist, 1983—. Author numerous papers on tissue-typing. Organizer British Bone Marrow Donor Appeal, No. Ireland. Mem. British Transplantation Soc. (treas.), No. Ireland Alliance Party. Mem. Alliance Party. Office: City Hosp, No Ireland Tissue Typing Service, Belfast BT9 7AD, Northern Ireland

MIDDLETON, HERMAN DAVID, SR., theater educator; b. Sanford, Fla., Mar. 24, 1925; s. Arthur Herman and Ruby Elmerry (Hart) M.; m. Amelia Mary Eggart, Dec. 1, 1945; children—Herman David, Kathleen Hart. B.S., Columbia U., 1948, M.A., 1949; Ph.D., U. Fla., 1964; postgrad., N.Y. U., 1950, Northwestern U., 1951. Instr., dir. drama and speech Maryville (Tenn.) Coll., 1949-50; instr., designer, tech. dir. theatre U. Del., 1951-55; asst. prof., head dept. drama U. N.C., Greensboro, 1956-59; asso. prof., head dept. drama and speech U. N.C., 1959-65, prof., head dept., 1965-74, prof., 1974-79, Excellence Fund prof. dept. communication and theatre, 1979—; designer Chucky Jack, Great Smokey Mountains Hist. Soc., Gatlinburg, Tenn., 1956, designer, dir., 1957; communications cons. N.C. Nat. Bank, 1968, Jefferson Standard Life Ins. Co., Greensboro, N.C., 1969, Gilbarco, Inc., Greensboro, 1969-70, 73. Drama critic, columnist: Sunday Star, Wilmington, Del., 1952; theatre editor: Players Mag, 1959-61; theatre columnist: Sunday editions Greensboro Daily News, 1959-62; contbr. articles to profl. jours. Mem. N.C. Arts Council Commn., 1964-66, Guilford County Bi-Centennial Celebration Commn., 1969-70; pres. Shanks Village Players, Orangeburg, N.Y., 1947-48, Univ. Drama Group, Newark, Del., 1954-55; bd. dirs. Broadway Theatre League Greensboro, 1958-60, Greensboro Community Arts Council, 1964-67, 69-72, Greensboro Community Theatre, 1983-86; organizer-cons. The Market Players, West Market St. United Meth. Ch., 1979-82. Served with USN, 1943-46. Recipient O. Henry award Greensboro C. of C., 1966; Gold medallion Amoco Oil Co., 1973; Suzanne M. Davis award Southeastern Theatre Conf., 1975. Mem. Am. Nat. Theatre and Acad. (organizer, exec. v.p. Piedmont chpt. 1957-60), Am. Theatre Assn. (chmn. bd. nominations 1971-72), Am. Coll. Theatre Festival (regional festival dir. 1973, 80, regional dir., mem. nat. com. 1978-80), Assn. for Theatre in Higher Edn. (founding mem. 1986-87), Speech Communication Assn. Am., Nat. Collegiate Players, Southeastern Theatre Conf. (bd. dirs. 1963-68, 87—, pres. 1965, pres. pro-tem 1966), Carolina Dramatic Assn. (bd. dirs. 1958-59), N.C. Drama and Speech Assn. (pres. 1966-67), N.C. Theatre Conf. (co-organizer 1971, bd. dirs. 1984—, pres. 1987-88), Assn. for Theater in Higher Edn., Phi Delta Kappa, Phi Kappa Phi, Theta Alpha Phi, Alpha Psi Omega. Democrat. Methodist. Home: 203A Village Ln Greensboro NC 27409 Office: U NC Dept Communication and Theatre Greensboro NC 27412

MIDDLETON, NORMAN GRAHAM, social worker, psychotherapist; b. Jacksonville, Fla., Jan. 21, 1935; s. Norman Graham and Betty (Quina) M.; m. Judy Stephens, Aug. 1, 1968; stepchildren—Monty Stokes, Toni Stokes. B.A., U. Miami (Fla.), 1960; M.S.W., Fla. State U., 1962. Casework counselor Family Service, Miami, 1962-64; psychiat. social worker assoc. firm Drs. Watson, Steele, Wiener, Sarasota, Fla., 1964-66; marriage, family counselor, Sarasota, 1966—. Instr. Manatee Jr. Coll., Bradenton, Fla., 1973-76. Author: The Caverns of My Mind, 1985. Pres. Council on Epilepsy, Sarasota, 1969-70. Served with USAF, 1954-58. Fellow Fla. Soc. Clin. Social Work (pres. 1978-80); mem. Nat. Assn. Social Workers, Am. Assn. Marriage and Family Therapists, Am. Group Psychotherapy Assn., Am. Assn. Sex Educators and Counselors (cert. sex educator), Acad. Cert. Social Workers. Democrat. Episcopalian. Home: 16626 Winburn Dr Sarasota FL 34240 Office: 1857 Floyd St Sarasota FL 34239

MIEGE, JEAN CHARLES, perfume company executive; b. Lille, France, Sept. 22, 1952; s. Jean and Jeannine (Cellot) M.; m. Frederique Haie, July 7, 1973; children—Anthony, Laureline. Baccalaureat Mathematique, Lille, 1970; grad. Ecole des Cadres, Paris, 1976. Export mgr. Schiaparelli, Paris, 1976-78; comml. mgr. Leonard, Paris, 1978-79; pres. JCM Parfums, Paris, 1979—, BULGARI Parfum, 1984—; comml. art dir. Al Hadi Ltd., London, 1982-86; v.p. OR MEC S.A., Lille, 1977-86. Editor movie and book: The Pilgrimmage to Mecca, 1983, The Holy Cities, 1983. Recipient award Fragrance Found., 1982; named Couseiller du Commerce Exterieur de la France, 1987. Address: Bd Kellermann 102, 75013 Paris France

MIELE, JOEL ARTHUR, SR., civil engineer; b. Jersey City, May 28, 1934; s. Jene Gerald Sr., and Eleanor Natale (Bergida) M.; m. Faith Roseann Trombetta, July 21, 1952 (div. 1954); m. 2d Josephine Ann Cottone, Feb. 14, 1959; children—Joel Arthur, Jr., Vita Marie, Janet Ann. B.C.E., Poly. Inst. Bklyn., 1955. Registered profl. engr., N.Y., N.J.; profl. planner, N.J. Civil engr. Yudell & Miele, Queens, N.Y., 1955-57; chief engr. Jene G. Miele Assocs., Queens, 1960-68; prin., chief exec. officer Miele Assocs., Queens, 1968—. Patentee masonry wall constrn. Pres. bd. visitors Creedmoor State Hosp., 1979—; v.p., bd. dirs. Peninsula Hosp. Ctr.; v.p., dir. Peninsula Nursing Home; chmn. Community Bd. 10, Queens, 1978—; trustee, treas. Queens Pub. Communications Corp., 1983—; trustee Queens Borough Pub. Library, 1979—. Served to Lt. (j.g.), USN, 1957-60; served to capt. USNR, 1960—. Named Italian-Am. of Yr., Ferrini Welfare League, Queens, 1980; Outstanding Community Leader award Boy Scouts Am., 1987. Fellow ASCE; mem. ASTM, Nat. Soc. Profl. Engrs., N.Y. State Soc. Profl. Engrs. (v.p. 1984-86, pres. 1988, nat. dir. 1987—, Engr. of Yr. 1983, pres. Queens chpt. 1980-82), Soc. Am. Mil. Engrs., N.Y. State Assn. of Professions (founding), Ozone Howard C. of C. (pres. 1980-84, 86—), Am. Parkinson Disease Assn. (dir. 1985—, exec. com. 1987—). Democrat. Congregationalist. Office: Miele Assocs 81-01 Furmanville Ave Middle Village NY 11379

MIELKE, CLARENCE HAROLD, JR., hematologist; b. Spokane, Wash., June 18, 1936; s. Clarence Harold and Marie Katherine (Gillespie) M.; B.S., Wash. State U., 1959; M.D., U. Louisville, 1963; m. Marcia Rae, July 5, 1964; children—Elisa, John, Tina. Intern, San Francisco Gen. Hosp., 1963-64; resident in medicine Portland VA Hosp., 1964-65, San Francisco Gen. Hosp., 1965-67; fellow in hematology U. So. Calif., 1967-68; teaching fellow, asst. physician, instr. Tufts-New Eng. Med. Center Hosps., Boston, 1968-71; sr. scientist, dir. hematology Inst. Med. Scis., San Francisco, 1971—; chief hematology Presbyn. Hosp., San Francisco, 1971—; asst. clin. prof. medicine U. Calif. Sch. Medicine, San Francisco, 1971-80, assoc. clin. prof., 1979—, dir. Inst. Cancer Research; trustee, bd. dirs. Med. Research Inst. San Francisco. NIH grantee, 1973—. Fellow ACP, Internat. Soc. Hematology, Am. Coll. Angiology; mem. Am. Soc. Internal Medicine, Internat. Soc. Thrombosis and Hemostasis, Am. Heart Assn., N.Y. Acad. Scis., AMA, San Francisco Med. Soc., Am. Thoracic Soc., AAAS, Internat. Soc. Angiology. Editor emeritus, Jour. Clin. Apheresis, 1981; contbr. chpts. to books, articles to med. jours. Office: Inst of Cancer Research 2200 Webster St San Francisco CA 94115

MIESSE, MARY ELIZABETH (BETH), educator; b. Amarillo, Tex.; M.Ed. in Guidance and Counseling, M.A., W. Tex. State U., Canyon, 1952, M.B.A., 1960; M.Personnel Service, U. Colo., Boulder, 1954. With various bus. firms and radio stas., 1940-47; prof. Amarillo (Tex.) Coll., 1947-63; tchr. pvt. and pub. schs., also TV work, 1963-78; spl. edn. cons., writer, 1978—. Mem. NEA, Nat Fed. State Poetry Socs., Poetry Soc. Tex., Tex. State Tchrs. Assn., Bus. Profl. Womens Assn., Toastmistress Internat., Am. Psychol. Assn., North Plains Assn. for Children with Learning Disabilities, AAUP, AAUW. Pioneered in ednl. TV in West Tex.; recipient awards in typewriting and ednl. TV; elected to Top Ten Women of Yr., Am. Bus. Women's Assn. Certified in spl. edn. supr., spl. edn. counselor, ednl. diagnostician, spl. edn. (lang. and/or learning disabled, mentally retarded) tchr., profl. counselor, profl. tchr., supt., prin., Tex. Editor, Tex. Jr. Coll. Tchrs. Assn. publ., 7 yrs. Producer radio poetry show. Home and Office: PO Box 3133 Valle de Oro TX 79010

MIFUNE, TOSHIRO, actor, film producer; b. Chintago, Japan, Apr. 1, 1920; s. Tokuzo and Sen M.; children—Shiro, Takeshi. Film actor, 1947—; films include These Foolish Times, 1947, Drunken Angel, 1948, The Seven Samurai, Rashamon, 1950, The Legend of Musashi, 1954, The Rickshawman, 1958, The Hidden Fortress, 1958, The Three Treasures, 1959, Yojimbo, 1961, The Storm of the Pacific, Grand Prix, Rebellion, 1965, Admiral Yamamoto, 1968, Hell In The Pacific, 1968, Furinkazan, 1969, Red Sun, 1971, Paper Tiger, 1974, The Battle of Midway, 1975, Shogun, 1981, The Equals, 1981, Inchon, 1982, The Challenge, 1982, others; pres. Mifune Prodns. Co. Ltd. Clubs: Hunting, Yacht, Flying. Office: Mifune Prodns Co Ltd, 9-30-7 Seijyo Setagaya-ku, Tokyo Japan *

MIGLIETTI, MARIO, psychoanalyst, publisher; b. Torino, Piemonte, Italy, Mar. 18, 1946; s. Luigi and Angela (Pavesi) M.; m. Silvia Camodeca; children: Elisa, Cecilia. D in Architecture, U. Torino, 1974; D in Psychology, U. Padua (Italy), 1985. Registered architect, Italy. Vice-chmn. Synectic Cons., Lagos, Nigeria, 1976-81; expert Italian Ministry Fgn. Affairs, Rome, 1981; cons. Lega Coop., Torino, 1981-84; chmn. Castalia, Torino, 1984—; Cons. Archtl. and Engring. State Cons., Accra, Ghana, 1977-81, Biennale Di Venezia, Italy, 1981-82; psychoanalyst Studio Medico, Torino, 1985—. Author: Esperienze di Progettazione, 1981, Repertorio Delle Tipologie Residenziali, 1983, NTR, 1983; editor: (book) Il Flauto Magico, 1985. Fellow Italian Soc. Psychology; mem. Italian Inst. Architects. Roman Catholic. Home: Via Principi d' Acaja 20, I-10138 Torino Italy Office: Studio Medico, Corso Peschiera 327, I-10141 Torino Italy

MIGNANI, ROBERTO, physics educator and researcher; b. Messina, Italy, Jan. 28, 1946; s. Pietro and Maria Antonietta (Parise) M.; m. Rosa Amato, June 17, 1976; children: Ruggero, Diana. PhD in Physics, U. Palermo (Italy), 1970. Fellow, Inst. for Theoretical Physics, Catania U. (Italy), 1971-73, dept. physics, Università" La Sapienza", Rome, 1974, assoc. prof. physics, 1977-80, prof. electrodynamics, 1981—; assoc. prof. dept. physics L'Aquila U. (Italy), 1975-76; prof. theoretical physics Inst. for Basic Research, Cambridge, Mass., 1981—; research assoc. Sicilian Ctr. for Nuclear Physics and Structure of Matter, Catania, 1971-74, Italian Nat. Inst. for Nuclear Physics (INFN), Rome, 1971—, Italian Nat. Orgn. for Nuclear Energy (ENEA), Rome, 1984. Contbr. articles on physics to profl. jours.; editor Hadronic Jour.; (book) Selected Papers of Italian Physicists: Piero Caldirola vols. I-IV, 1986. Fellow Italian Phys. Soc. Office: I Universita di Roma, LaSapienza P le A Moro 2, 00185 Rome Italy

MIGNAULT, JEAN, finance company executive; b. Montreal, Quebec, Can., Nov. 3, 1950; s. Jack and Giselle (Miron) M.; m. Diane Filiatrault; children: Marc, Andre, Philippe. B in Civil Law, McGill U., Montreal, 1972; MBA, Western Ont. U., London, Ont., 1976. Dir. personnel, indsl. relations Ciment nd. Inc., Montreal, 1976-79; pres. Miron Group Inc., Laval, Que., 1979—. Mem. Can. Bar Assn., Que. Bar Assn., Laval C. of C. (v.p. 1986—). Club: St. Denis. Home: 61 Les Chenes, Laval, PQ Canada Office: Miron Group Inc, 1755 Cunard, Laval, PQ Canada H75 2B4

MIHAILOVIC, MIHAILO, chemist, educator; b. Belgrade, Yugoslavia, Jan. 22, 1924; s. Ljubomir and Bozana (Bartos) M.; B.Sc., U. Belgrade, 1950; D.Sc., Serbian Acad. Sci. and Arts, 1953; m. Miroslava Cvetincanin, May 9, 1948; children—Ljubomir, Milan. Asst., Serbian Acad. Sci. and Arts, Belgrade, 1950-54; asst. prof. dept. chemistry Faculty of Sci., U. Belgrade, 1955-61, asso. prof., 1961-68, prof., 1968—; vis. prof. U. Wis., Cornell U., 1967; sci. cons.; pres., mem. exec. council Inst. Chemistry, Tech. and Metallurgy, Belgrade, 1967-71. Recipient Dec. prize Serbian Govt., 1957; Oct. prize City of Belgrade, 1969; 7th July prize Serbian Republic, 1978; AVNOJ prize Yugoslavia, 1983; prize d'Aumale, French Acad. Scis., 1985. Mem. Serbian Chem. Soc. (hon.; exec. council 1961—, v.p. 1962-65, pres. 1978—), Serbian Acad. Sci. and Arts, Yugoslav Acad. Sci. and Arts, Slovenian Acad. Sci. and Arts, Croatian Chem. Soc., N.Y. Acad. Sci. Am. Chem. Soc., Swiss Chem. Soc., Royal Soc. Chemistry (London), French Chem. Soc., German Chem. Soc., Royal Netherlands Chem. Soc., Internat. Soc. Heterocyclic Chemistry, European Photochemistry Assn. Assn. Swiss Chemists; cons. editor Tetrahedron, Tetrahedron Letters, 1986—, contbr. articles to profl. jours; author: (with V.M. Micovic) Lithium Aluminum Hydride in Organic Chemistry, 1955; (with Z. Cekovic) Intramolecular Oxidative Cyclization of Alcohols with Lead Tetraacetate, 1970; (with Z. Cekovic) Oxidation and Reduction of Phenols, 1971; (with R.E. Partch) Alcohol Oxidation by Lead Tetraacetate, 1972; cons. editor Tetrahedron, 1986—, Tetrahedron Letters, 1986—; discoverer functionalization of remote nonactivated carbon atoms by the lead tetraacetate reaction, 1959, 5L10-secosteroids, 1964, vitamin D3 derivatives, 1977, aromatization of steroids and equilenin-type compounds, 1977-82, cyclization of alcohols, 1978—; diseco-steroids (containing 14- and 15-membered rings), 1985—, others. Home: 6 Marsala Tita, 11000 Belgrade Yugoslavia Office: Dept Chemistry Faculty Sci, 16 Studentski trg, 11001 Belgrade Yugoslavia

MIHAJLOV, MIHAJLO N., educator, human rights activist, writer; b. Pancevo, Serbia, Yugoslavia, Sept. 24, 1934; came to U.S., 1978; s. Nicholai F. and Vera A. (Danilov) M. BA, U. Zagreb, Yugoslavia, 1959, MA, 1961. Asst. prof. U. Zagreb, 1963-66; freelance writer western press 1965-66, 70-74, imprisoned, 1966-70, 70-74, lectr. U.S.A., Europe and Asia, 1978-79; fellow Nat. Humanities Ctr., N.C., 1980-81; vis. lectr. Yale U., 1981; vis. prof. Russian lit. and philosophy U. Va., Charlottesville, 1982-83; prof. Middlebury (Vt.) Summer Russian Sch., 1983; vis. prof. Ohio State U., Columbus, 1983—. Author: Moscow Summer, 1965, Russian Themes, 1968, Underground Notes, 1976, 82, Unscientific Thoughts, 1979; mem. editorial bd. Kontinent, 1975—, Forum, 1982—, Tribuna, 1983—. Co-chmn. TDI Com. to Aid Yugoslav Dem. Dissidents, N.Y.C., 1973—; chmn. bd. Democracy Internat., Washington, 1980—. Served with Yugoslavia Army, 1961-62. Recipient ann. award Council Against Communist Aggression, 1975, 78, Internat. League for Human Rights, 1978, Humanistic Perspective in Contemporary Soc. award Ford Found., 1980. Mem. Am. Assn. for Advancement of Slavic Studies, Am. Polit. Sci. Assn., Am. Assn. Tchrs. Slavic Lang. and Lit., Helsinki Assn. (dir. 1980—). Russian Orthodox. Office: Ohio State U Slavic Dept Columbus OH 43210

MIHALY, ANDRAS, composer, educator; b. Budapest, Nov. 6, 1917; s. Dezsö Mauthner and Erzsebet (Grosz) M.; student Berzsenyu Gymnasium and F. Liszt Conservatoire of Music, Budapest; student cello with Adolf Schiffer; student chamber music with Leo Weiner and Imre Waldbauer; m. 2d Klara Pfeifer, 1951, m. 3d, Csilla Varga; 3 sons. Violoncello solo in orch. Budapest Opera House, 1946-47; gen. sec. Budapest Opera, 1948-49; prof. chamber music F. Liszt Conservatorie, Budapest, 1950—; reader contemporary music dept. musical Hungarian Broadcasting Corp., 1959—; leader New Hungarian Chamber Ensemble; dir. Hungarian State Opera, from 1978; composer: Concerto for Violoncello and Orch., 1953, Concerto for Pianoforte and Orch., 1954, Fantasy for Wind Quintet and String Orch., 1955, Songs on the Poems of James Joyce, 1958, Concerto for Violin and Orch., 1959, String Quartet, 1960, Symphony, 1962, Together and Alone, 1965, Musica per 15, 1974, String Quartet # 3, 1975, Musica per Viola, 1975. Recipient Kossuth prize, 1955, Erkel prize 1950, 65, Liszt prize, 1972, Labour order Merit Golden Degree, 1970, Eminent Artist of Hungary, For Socialist Hungary Order Merit, 1977. Address: Vérhalom tér 9b, 1025 Budapest II Hungary other: Budapest Chamber Ensemble, vi Nepkoztarsasagu u 22, 1025 Budapest II Hungary *

MIJAJLOVIC, ZARKO DUSAN, mathematics educator, logician; b. Prokuplje, Serbia, Yugoslavia, July 1, 1948; s. Dusan Sretko and Ljiljana Petar (Pavicevic) M.; m. Svetlana Milorad Pavlovic, Nov. 28, 1971; children—Aleksandar, Ivana. Grad. U. Belgrade, Yugoslavia, 1971, M.S., 1973, Ph.D., 1977; postgrad. U. Wis.-Madison, 1973-74. Asst. U. Belgrade, 1971-78, docent in math., 1979-86 , head logic seminar Math. Inst., 1977—, assoc. prof. math., 1986—. Co-author: Group Theory, 1983; Hilbert's Problems and Logic, 1985; author An Introduction to Model Theory, 1987; also articles. Recipient 1st prize for paper Balkan's Union Math., 1977; Fulbright scholar U. Wis.-Madison, 1973-74; hon. fellow U. Wis.-Madison, 1978. Mem. Assn. Symbolic Logic, Am. Math. Soc. Avocation: astronomy. Home: Tomasa Jeza 6, 11000 Belgrade Yugoslavia Office: U Belgrade Faculty Sci, Inst Math Studentski trg 16, 11000 Belgrade Yugoslavia

MIKALOW, ALFRED ALEXANDER, II, deep sea diver, marine surveyor; b. N.Y.C., Jan. 19, 1921; student Rutgers U., 1940; M.S., U. Calif.-Berkeley, 1948; M.A., Rochdale U. (Can.), 1950; m. Janice Brenner, Aug. 1, 1960; children—Alfred Alexander, Jon Alfred. Owner, Coastal Diving Co., Oakland, Calif., 1950—, Divers Supply, Oakland, 1952—; dir. Coastal Sch. Deep Sea Diving, Oakland, 1950—; capt. and master research vessel Coastal Researcher I; mem. Marine Inspection Bur., Oakland. marine diving contractor, cons. Mem. adv. bd. Medic Alert Found., Turlock, Calif., 1960—. Served to lt. comdr. USN, 1941-47, 49-50. Decorated Purple Heart, Silver Star. Mem. Divers Assn. Am. (pres. 1970-74), Treasury Recovery, Inc. (pres. 1972-75), Internat. Assn. Profl. Divers, Assn. Diving Contractors, Calif. Assn. Pvt. Edn. (no. v.p. 1971-72), Authors Guild, Internat. Game Fish Assn., U.S. Navy League, U.S. Res. Officers Assn., Tailhook Assn., Explorer Club (San Francisco), Calif. Assn. Marine Surveyors (pres. 1988—). Clubs: Masons, Lions. Author: Fell's Guide to Sunken Treasure Ships of the World, 1972; (with H. Rieseberg) The Knight from Maine, 1974. Office: 320 29th Ave Oakland CA 94601

MIKELL, VERNON TERRY, marketing manager; b. Ithaca, N.Y., Sept. 21, 1937; s. Pearce and Marie (Boone) M.; B.A., Pace U., 1970; M.S., L.I. U., 1972; Ph.D., Fordham U., 1981; m. Barbara Dalton, Mar. 26, 1974; children—Toli Pierce, Star Marie. With Am. Tel. & Tel. Co., Morristown, N.J., 1964—, now staff mgr. mktg. Served with USN, 1955-59. Mem. N.Y. Acad. Sci., Am. Personnel and Guidance Assn., Telephone Pioneers, AAAS, Nat. Soc. for Performance and Instruction. Author: Black-White Differences in Manifest Needs and Satisfactions in an Affirmative Action Environment, 1981. Home: 9 Center Ln Succasunna NJ 07876 Office: Bedminster NJ 07921

MIKES, ANDRIJA, physician, educator; b. Garesnica, Yugoslavia, Feb. 12, 1918; s. Aladar and Irma (Kastl) M.; m. Vera Barta, 1942 (div.); children—Djordje, Miroslav; m. 2d Vera Bratic, Jan. 1956; 1 son, Dragan. M.D., Med. Faculty of Belgrade, 1946, Specialist in Internal Medicine, 1952, D. Med. Sci., Sarajevo (Yugoslavia), 1969. Asst., Med. Faculty of Sarajevo, 1951-54; head dept. internal medicine Banjaluka U., 1954-69, 79-83, prof. internal medicine, 1979—; dir. Gen. Hosp., Banjaluka, 1965-66; head dept. Inst. for Chest Diseases, Sremska Kamenica, Novi Sad, 1969-76, asst. prof., 1976-78, head Inst. of Oncology, 1976-79. Mem. Yugoslav Assn. Hematology, Internat. Soc. Hematology, Assn. d'Europe d'Medicine Interne d'Ensamble. Contbr. numerous articles to profl. jours.; contbr. chpt. on hematology to Internal Medicine. Home: Zije Dizdarevica 5, 78000 Banjaluka Yugoslavia

MIKES, MELANIE, language educator, researcher; b. Novi Sad, Yugoslavia, July 31, 1924; d. Oskar and Giselle (Quittner) Spreitzer; children: Bence, Ester, Etel. BA, Faculty Philosophy, Zagreb, Yugoslavia, 1951; D Linguistics, Faculty Philosophy, Novi Sad, 1965. Tchr. secondary schs. Yugoslavia, 1952-68; researcher Inst. Hungarian Studies U. Novi Sad, 1969—, dir. project on child linguistics, 1970-76, project on multilingualism, 1974-83. Author books on lang. acquisition, contrastive linguistics; contbr. numerous articles to profl. jours. Mem. Internat. Assn. Applied Linguistics (pres. Yugoslav affiliation 1973-76), Internat. Soc. Applied Psycholinguistics, Internat. Assn. Study of Child Lang. Home: Boška Buhelo B, Novi Sad Vojvodina Yugoslavia Office: Filosofski Fakultet, Stevana Musića bb, Novi Sad Vojvodina Yugoslavia

MIKESELL, MARY (JANE), therapist; b. Rockledge, Fla., Oct. 29, 1943; d. John and Mary C. (Leighty) Wagner. B.A., Calif. State U.-Northridge, 1967; M.A., Pacific Oaks Coll., 1980; postgrad. Calif. Grad. Inst. Psychology, 1984—, Tchr., Los Angeles pub. schs., 1966-69; photog. lab. dir. Oceanograficos de Honduras, Roatan, 1969-70; supr. Los Angeles Life Ins. Co., 1970-72; customer service rep. Beverly Hills Fed. Savs. & Loans, Calif., 1972-73; mem. staff counseling ctr. Calif. State U.-Northridge, 1974-78; head office services Pacific Oaks Coll., Pasadena, Calif., 1978-79; prodn. supr. Frito-Lay, Inc., Los Angeles, 1979-81; circulation supr. Daily News, Van Nuys, Calif., 1981-82; ednl. therapist/MFCC intern Barr Counseling Ctr., 1982-86 and Victory-Tampa Psychol. Ctr. (now Reseda Psychol. Ctr.), San Fernando Valley, Calif., 1982—; project coordinator Carlson Rockey & Assocs., Brentwood, Calif., 1983-84; staff mem Southland Olympic News Bur., Sub-Ctr. Steward, Press Ops., Olympic Water Polo Venue, LAOOC, 1983-84; project coordinator/communications and systems specialist Student Ins. div. William F. Hooper, Inc., Brentwood, 1985-87; cons. Designer Collection by Pingy, 1985, others. Photographer. Mem. Nat. Assn. Female Execs., Planetary Soc., Calif. Scholarship Fedn., Calif. Inst. Psychology Grad. Student Assn. (v.p. 1985-88). Democrat. Club: CSUN Anthropology. Avocations: photography; writing; laser research; astronomy; sports. Office: CGI Counseling Ctr 1100 Glendon Ave 11th Floor Los Angeles CA 90049

MIKHAEL, YAHYA SAAD, cardiologist, educator; b. Mansura, Dakahlia, Egypt, Feb. 18, 1932; s. Hanna Saad and Matilda Nasr(Mankabady) M.; m. Nadia Fahmy Messeiha, Jan. 28, 1965; children: Hala Y.S., Hadia Y.S. MB, BCh, Kasr el Eini, 1953; diploma medicine, Cairo U., 1956, diploma cardiology, 1959, MD, 1961. Intern Cairo U. Hosps., 1954-55, resident in medicine, 1955-57; clin. demonstrator Faculty of Medicine Cairo U., 1958-63, lectr. in medicine, 1963-70, assoc. prof. cardiology, 1970-75, prof., 1975-85, head dept. cardiology faculty medicine; cons., chief Al-Salam Hosp., Cairo, 1980—. Asst. editor Jour. Egyptian Med. Assn., 1963, Bull. Egyptian Soc. Cardiology, 1960. CIS grantee, Paris, 1969, Internat. Soc. Cardiology fellow, Orsay, France, 1973. Fellow Am. Coll. Cardiology. Mem. Nat. Party. Mem. Christian Coptic Orthodox Ch. Club: Gezira Sporting (Cairo). Home: 4 Dr Handoussa St, Garden City, Cairo Egypt

MIKHAIL, WILLIAM MESIHA, economist, educator; b. Fayoum, Egypt, May 31, 1935; s. Mesiha M. and Foutnah Mikhail; m. Nariman Marei, Dec. 23, 1983; 1 son, Fadi. Ph.D. in Stats., London Sch. Econs., 1969. Assoc. prof. Cairo U., 1970-76; prof. econometrics Am. U., Cairo, 1976—; cons. in field. Mem. Econometric Soc., Am. Statis. Assn., Egyptian Statis. Assn. Author articles in field. Home: PO Box 623, Cairo Egypt Office: 113 Kasr El-Aini St, Cairo Egypt

MIKHALKOV, SERGEY VLADIMIROVICH, poet, playwright; b. Moscow, Mar. 12, 1913; Author: (with El-Registan) Soviet Anthem, 1943; publs. include: Dyadya Styopa, 1936, Collected Works (poems, stories, plays), From Carriage to Space Ship, 1975, Jolly Hares, 1969; film script: Frontline Friends, 1941; plays: Tom Kenti, 1938, Red Neckerchief, 1947, Ilya Golovin, Y khochu domoi, 1949, Lobsters, 1952, Zaika-Zaznaika, 1955, Basni Mikhalkova, 1957, Sombrero, 1958, A Monument to Oneself, 1958, Dikari, 1959, Green Grasshopper, 1964, In the Museum of Lenin, 1968, Fables, 1970, Disobedience Day, 1971. Mem. Communist Party, 1950—; Com. Youth Affairs, Soviet Nationalities. Recipient 3 Orders of Lenin, Hero Socialist Labour, 1973, Red Banner, Red Banner of Labour, Red Star, Lenin prize, 1970. Mem. Union Writers (1st sec. Moscow br., 1965-70, chmn. union, 1970—). Address: USSR Union Writers, ul Vorovskogo 52, Moscow USSR

MIKKELSEN, RICHARD, central banker; b. Copenhagen, Apr. 27, 1920; s. Martin and Julie (Schultz) M.; m. Ester Overgaard, Feb. 27, 1944. M in Econs. Banker Slagelse og Omegn, 1937-45; asst. Danmarks Nat. Bank, 1945-54, asst. head div., 1954-61; attaché Danish OEEC-Delegation, Paris, 1955-57; asst. head dept. Danmarks Nat. Bank, 1961, head dept., 1961, dir., 1966, dep. gov., 1971, gov., 1982—; bd. dirs. European Monetary Agreement, 1970-72, Indsl. Mortgage Fund, 1971-81, Export Fin. Corp., 1975—, Employees Capital Pension Fund, steering com. 1980—, Indust. Mortgage Credit Fund, 1981—, Monetary Com. EEC, 1982—, Nordic Com. Fin. Matters, 1982—; supr. Mortgage Credit Council, 1972-81. Office: Danmarks Nationalbank, Havnegade 5, 1093 Copenhagen Denmark

MIKO, ANDRAS, opera producer, educator; b. Budapest, Hungary, June 30, 1922; s. Strelinger Karoly and Maria (Kriser) M.; m. Eva Rehak. Producer State Opera, Budapest, 1946—; prof. Acad. Music, Budapest, 1950—. Producer of operas at Covent Garden, London, Teato Colon, Buenos Aires, Copenhage, Helsinki, Savonlinna, Finland, Moscow, East Berlin, Teatro Regio, Torino, Genva, Cologne, Warsaw, others. Home: 1 Uri utca 44/46, 1014 Budapest Hungary Address: Hungarian State Opera, Nepkoztarsasag utja 22, Budapest VI, Hungary

MIKOLAIZYK, DEBORAH FRANSISCO, pharmacist; b. Detroit, Mar. 15, 1956; d. Theodore Joseph and Phyllis Irene (VanZant) F.; m. Gerald John Norris, Aug. 21, 1976 (div. May 1981); m. Michael Gene Mikolaizyk, Feb. 11, 1987. BS in Pharmacy, Ferris State Coll., 1978. Pharmacist, asst. mgr. Cunningham Drug Stores, 6 stores in met. Detroit area, 1978-81; cons. Specialized Pharmacy Services, Livonia, Mich., 1981-83; ptnr. Village Pharmacies, Harrison and Beaverton, Mich., 1983—. Mem. Cen. Mich. Pharmacists Assn. (sec. 1983-85), Nat. Assn. Retail Druggists. Republican. Avocations: cross country skiing, sailing. Home: 192 Hillcrest Harrison MI 48625 Office: Village Pharmacy 158 N 1st St Harrison MI 48625

MIKOLAYCAK, CHARLES, illustrator; b. Scranton, Pa., Jan. 26, 1937; s. John and Helen (Gruscelak) M.; m. Carole Kismaric, Oct. 1, 1970. BFA, Pratt Inst., 1958. Illustrator Atelier Du Crot, Hamburg, Fed. Republic Germany, 1959; picture editor Time/Life Books, N.Y.C., 1963-76; guest instr. book illustration Syracuse (N.Y.) U., 1976—. Author, illustrator: The Boy Who Tried To Cheat Death, 1970, Babushka, 1984 (N.Y. Times Best Illustrated Book award 1984); illustrator: The Great Wolf and The Good Woodsman, 1967, In The Morning of Time, 1970, The Tall Man From Boston, 1975, Tam Lin, 1990, I Am Joseph, 1980, Peter and the Wolf, 1982, The Highwayman, 1983, A Child is Born, 1983, The Man Who Could Call Down Owls, 1984, He Is Risen, The Changing Maze, 1985, The Lullaby Songbook, 1986, Exodus, 1988 (Nat. Jewish Book award 1988), The Rumor of Pavel and Paali, 1988, A Gift From St. Nicholas, 1988, Voyages: Selected Poems by Walt Whitman; designer: Prelude To War, 1976, Cats of Africa, 1968. Served with U.S. Army, 1960-62. Recipient Soc. Illustrators Gold medal, 1971, Promotion and Graphics Design award, 1980, Golden Kite Honor Book award for illustrations Soc. Children's Book Writers, 1986, Kerlan award U. Minn., 1987. Home and Office: 64 E 91st St New York NY 10128

MIKULIC, BRANKO, Yugoslavian government official; b. Gornji Vakuf, Bosnia and Herzegovina, Yugoslavia, 1928. Grad. Sch. of Bus. Active Nat. Liberation Struggle, from 1943; mem. League of Communists of Yugoslavia, 1945—, mem. Presidency, 1969-78, elected mem. presidency of central com. at XI Congress, later apptd. pres. central com.; now prime ministerformerly sec. Communist Assembly coms. in various dists. and pres. Dist. Sarajevo; elected sec. central com. League of Communists of Bosnia and Herzegovina, 1964, later elected sec. of exec. com. of central com., pres. central com., 1969-78; elected pres. exec. council Assembly of Bosnia and Herzegovina, 1967; also mem. Yugoslavian Presidency from Bosnia and Herzegovina; pres. fed. exec. council, 1986—. Recipient various Yugoslavian and fgn. decorations. Office: Savez Komunista Jogoslavije, Bul Lenina 6, Novi Beograd Yugoslavia *

MIKULSKI, BARBARA ANN, senator; b. Balt., July 20, 1936; d. William and Christina Eleanor (Kutz) M. B.A., Mt. St. Agnes Coll., 1958; M.S.W., U. Md., 1965; LL.D. (hon.), Goucher Coll., 1973, Hood Coll., 1978. Tchr. Mt. St. Agnes Coll., 1969; tchr. Community Coll. Balt., 1970-71, VISTA Tng. Ctr., 1965-70; with Balt. Dept. Social Services, 1961-63, 66-70, York Family Agy., 1964, Assoc. Catholic Charities, 1958-61; former mem. Balt. City Council; mem. 96th-99th congresses from 3d Md. Dist., 1979-87, mem. interstate and fgn. commerce com., mcht. marine com.; mem. U.S. Senate appropriations environment and pub. works, labor and human relations, small bus. coms. 100th Congress, 1987—; mem. Congl. Steel Caucus, Congresswomen's Caucus, Democratic Study Group, Environ. Study Conf., Mems. Congress for Peace Through Law; cons. Nat. Ctr. Urban Ethnic Affairs, others. Contbr. articles to mags. and newspapers. Bd. dirs. Valley House; nat. bd. dirs. Urban Coalition; mem. Polish Women's Alliance, Polish Am. Congress, Citizens Planning and Housing Assn., S.E. Community Orgn.; chmn. com. community devel. Archdiocesan Urban Commn.; mem. nat. com. Muskie for Pres., 1971-72; chmn. com. del. selection and party structure Dem. Nat. Com.; Dem. nominee U.S. Senate, 1974, Ho. of Reps., 1976; mem. Dem. Nat. Strategy Council. Named Woman of Yr. MS. mag., 1987. Mem. Nat. Women's Polit. Caucus, Nat. Bus. and Profl. Women's Assn., Am. Fedn. Tchrs., Nat. Assn. Social Workers, LWV. Office: US Senate 320 Hart Office Bldg Washington DC 20510-2003

MIKUZ, JURE, art gallery director; b. Ljubljana, Slovenia, Yugoslavia, Apr. 23, 1949; s. Metod and Zlata (Vidmar) M. BFA, U. Ljubljana, 1972, MFA, 1975, PhD, 1983. Curator Nat. Mus. Revolution, Ljubljana, 1972-74; curator, researcher Nat. Gallery Modern Art, Ljubljana, 1975-86, dir., 1986—; adj. prof. U. Ljubljana, 1985—. Author: The Image of the Hand, 1983, Fritz Lang, 1985. Office: Moderna Galerija, Tomsiceva 14, 61000 Ljubljana Yugoslavia

MILACK, GARY PAUL, podiatric physician and surgeon; b. Floral Park, N.Y., May 7, 1949; s. Paul Philip and Ruth (Fogelson) M.; B.S., Coll. Emporia, 1971; D.P.M., Ohio Coll. Podiatric Medicine, 1975; m. Deborah A. Stitz, May 25, 1980; children: Justin Paul, Tiffany Joy, Bradley Ray. Diplomate Am. Inst. Foot Medicine. Resident Md. Podiatry Residency Program,

Balt., 1975-76; pvt. practice podiatric medicine, Shoreham, N.Y., 1978—; staff Kings Park Psychiat. Hosp. Center, 1978—, Central Suffolk Hosp., Riverhead, N.Y., 1982; founder, exec. dir. Nat. Soc. Conscious Sedation in Podiatric Medicine; instr. conscious sedation techniques. Recipient Salvation Army Outstanding Service in Clinic award, 1975; March of Dimes award for service, 1979; Presdl. award for fitness walking, 1977. Fellow Suffolk Acad. Medicine, Am. Soc. Podiatric Dermatology, Acad. Ambulatory Foot Surgeons, Nat. Soc. Conscious Sedation in Pediatric Med. (founder, exec. dir.), Am. Soc. Podiatric Medicine, Am. Assn. Hosp. Podiatrists; mem. Am. Podiatric Med. Writers Assn. (trustee), Am. Med. Writers Assn., Am. Acad. Administrn., Soc. Dental Anesthesiology (affiliate), Rocky Point C. of C. Contbg. editor Current Podiatry Dermatology Sect; editor-in-chief Jour. Current Podiatric Medicine, Derma-Prints newsletter; contbg. editor Podiatry Products Report. Contbr. articles to profl. jours. Office: 45 Route 25A Suite D-1 Shoreham NY 11786

MILANESI, MAURIZIO, accounting company executive; b. Milan, Apr. 25, 1938; s. Giulio and Marina (Del Conte) M.; m. Sigrid Schworer, May 4, 1963; children: Roberta, Federica. Grad., U. Milan, 1956. Acct. Arthur Andersen Co., Milan, 1960-65, audit mgr., 1965-70, ptnr., 1970-80; mng. ptnr. Milan office Arthur Andersen Co., 1980-83; mng. ptnr. for Italy Arthur Andersen Co., Milan, 1983—. Contbr. articles to various newspapers. Mem. Assn. Nat. Direttori Amministrativi Fimamziari (pres. bd. auditors 1970). Roman Catholic. Home: Via Biondi 1, 20154 Milan Italy Office: Arthur Andersen & Co, Via della Moscova 3, 20121 Milan Italy

MILES, (ARNOLD) ASHLEY, physician, microbiologist; b. Mar. 20, 1904; S. Harry Miles; M.A., M.D., Cambridge (Eng.) U. and St. Bartholomews Hosp., London, m. Ellen Margerite Dahl. Demonstrator in bacteriology London Sch. Hygiene, 1929; demonstrator in pathology U. Cambridge, 1931; reader in bacteriology Brit. Postgrad. Med. Sch., London, 1935; prof. bacteriology U. London, 1937-45, prof. exptl. pathology, 1952-71, now prof. emeritus; acting dir. Graham Med. Research Labs., Univ. Coll. Hosp. Med. Sch., 1943-45; dir. Med. Research Council wound infection unit Nat. Inst. Med. Research, 1942-46; dep. dir., 1947-52, dir. dept. biol. standards, 1946-52; dir. Lister Inst. Preventive Medicine, 1952-71; dep. dir. dept. med. microbiology London Hosp. Med. Coll., 1976—; cons. in field. Created knight, 1966. Fellow Royal Soc., Royal Coll. Physicians, Royal Coll. Pathologists, Soc. Gen. Microbiology (hon.) mem. Acad. de Medicine de Belgique (fgn. corr.), Am. Soc. Microbiology, Am. Assn. Pathologists, Deutsche Gesellschaft für Hygiene und Mikrobiologie, others. Author: (with Wilson) Topley and Wilson's Principles of Bacteriology and Immunity, 1945, 55, 64, 75, 84; contbr. articles to profl. jours. Address: Dept Med Microbiology, London Hosp Med Coll, Turner St, London E1 2AD England Other: care Royal Soc, 6 Carlton House Terrace, London SW1Y 5AG England *

MILES, CHARLES JOHN, business consultant; b. Cape Town, Republic of South Africa, Mar. 10, 1931; s. William Albert and Dora (Oneil) M.; m. Yvonne Joan Miles, Dec. 22, 1951; children: Margaret, Michael, Rosemary, Charles, Barbara, Shelagh, Lorraine. Grad. in Acctg., U. Johannesburg, Republic of South Africa. Mng. dir. Pegasus Cons., Ltd., Johannesburg, 1969—. Contbr. articles to profl. jours. Sir William Thorne scholar Cape Tech. Coll., 1962. Fellow Faculty Corp. Secs.; mem. Inst. Dirs., Inst. Mgmt., Inst. Internal Auditors. Roman Catholic. Club: Johannesburg. Home: 24 Tony St, Edenvale Transvaal 1610, Republic of South Africa Office: Pegasus Cons Ltd, PO Box 854, Edenvale Transvaal 1610, Republic of South Africa

MILES, GEORGE THOMAS, aerospace engineer, educator; b. Gillingham, Kent, Eng., Mar. 29, 1925; came to U.S., 1953; s. George J. and Rosina M. (Roper) M.; divorced; children: Glenn Tracey, Kathryn Yvonne, Ronald George. BS, U. London, 1947; AA, Mt. San Antonio Coll., 1965. Cert. community coll. tchr., Calif. Design analyst Jet Propulsion Lab., Pasadena, Calif., 1960-62; chief standards engr. Aerojet-Gen., Azusa, Calif., 1963-68; sr. engr. Westinghouse, Sunnyvale, Calif., 1969-72; configuration mgr. TRW, Hawthorne, Calif., 1973-79; mgr. engring. services BASF, Fountain Valley, Calif., 1980-83; tchr. CEDU Sch., Running Springs, Calif., 1984; tchr. El Camino Coll., Torrance, Calif., 1975—, Cerritos (Calif.) Coll., 1980-83; counselor/tchr. Coop. Career Edn., Torrance, 1982; rep. Nat. Aerospace Standards Com. and E20 Com. Soc. Automotive Engrs., 1963, 68. Editor LASER, 1964. Bd. dirs. Hawthorne C. of C., 1978; mem. Coll. Adv. Coms., Torrance, 1982—. Served with ednl. corps English Army, 1947-49. Recipient Founding Mem. award Vocat. Indsl. Clubs Am., 1975, Cert. Appreciation, Calif. Indsl. Edn. Assn., 1978. Mem. Standards Engrs. Soc. (publicity chmn. 1964), U.S. Metric Assn. (Cert. Appreciation, 1964). Republican. Episcopalian. Home: 1349 W 135th St #12 Gardena CA 90247 Office: El Camino Coll 16007 Crenshaw Blvd Torrance CA 90506

MILES, JEREMY JOHN, corporate executive; b. London, Jan. 1, 1933; s. Frederick George and Maxine Frances Mary (Blossom) Forbes-Robertson M.; m. Susan Miles; 1 child, Jonathon Gaston. Student, Harrow Sch. Comml. dir. Link-Miles, Ltd., Eng., 1965-70, Miles Hivolt, Ltd., Eng., 1970-75; chmn. Vanderhoff Internat., Ltd., Eng., 1976-85; dir. Vanderhoff pLc, Eng., 1985—; bd. dirs. Hunting Hivolt Ltd.; chmn. Persona pLc, 1986—. Served to sub-lt. Royal Naval Res., 1951-53.

MILES, MICHAEL ARNOLD, food company executive; b. Chgo., June 22, 1939; s. Arnold and Alice (Morrissey) M.; m. Pamela L. Miles; children: Michael Arnold Jr., Christopher. B.S., Northwestern U., 1961. Various mgmt. positions to v.p., account supr. Leo Burnett Co., Inc., 1961-71; with Heublein, Inc., 1971-82, sr. v.p. mktg. Ky. Fried Chicken, 1971-72, v.p. gen. mgr. grocery products, 1972-75, internat., 1975-77, v.p. group exec. Internat. group, chmn. foodservice and franchise group Ky. Fried Chicken, 1977-81, sr. v.p. foods, Louisville, 1981-82; pres., chief operating officer Kraft, Inc., Glenview, Ill., 1982—; dir. Capital Holding Corp., Citizens Fidelity Corp., Dart & Kraft, Inc. Bd. dirs. Lyric Opera Chgo.; mem. adv. council J.L. Kellogg Grad. Sch. Mgmt. Northwestern U., Evanston, Ill. Office: Kraft Inc Kraft Ct Glenview IL 60025 *

MILES, PATRICK AUSTIN, marketing and career development consultant; b. Croxley, Herts., Eng., Sept. 5, 1928; s. Thomas Frank and Elsie Sarah (New) M.; m. Catherine Rosemary, Sept. 5, 1967. B.A., Trinity Coll., Dublin U., 1953, M.A., 1960. Shipping mgr. P & O Group U.K., Arabian Gulf, 1956-65; export mgr. Seagrams U.S.A., Africa and Middle East, 1965-71; nat. accts. mgr. Scottish and Newcastle Breweries, Edinburgh, U.K., 1971-77; cons. Middle East Consultants, London, 1978-82; mktg. mgr. Cosmoplast Ind. Co., Sharjah, United Arab Emirates, 1982-87; mktg. cons., 1987—. Author: (poetry) Tomorrows Poets, 1970, Wisdom Smiling, 1988. Served to lt. Brit. Army, 1946-49. Fellow Royal Soc. Arts. Mem. Conservative Party. Anglican. Clubs: Royal Overseas League (London), Moor Park Golf. Lodges: Rosicrucian Order Amorc (San Jose). Home: BM Lattice, London WC1 England

MILES, PETER RICHARD, English literature educator; b. Heathfield, Sussex, England, July 15, 1949; s. George Bertram and Winifred Olive (Eade) M.; m. Kathleen Jane Tierney, Sept. 11, 1976. BA in English, U. Birmingham, 1970, MA in English, 1972. English lectr. Saint David's U. Coll., Lampeter, Dyfed, Eng., 1973—; editorial advisor Trivium, Lampeter, 1976—; external examiner W. Midlands Coll., Walsall, 1983-86. Author: (with others) Cinema, Literature and Society, 1987; co-editor: The Woman in White, 1982, Framley Parsonage, 1984; reviews editor jour. The Powys Rev., 1980—; contbr. articles to profl. jours. Charles Grant Robertson scholar U. Birmingham, 1970. Mem. Bibliog. Soc., Powys Soc., Assn. Univ. Tchrs. Office: St Davids U Coll, Dept English Lit, Lampeter Dyfed SA48 7ED, Wales

MILES, ROGER EDMUND, research statistician; b. Chipping Norton, Oxfordshire, English, Apr. 27, 1935; arrived in Australia, 1967; s. Leonard and Winifred (Hackett) M. BA, Cambridge U., Eng., 1958, MA, 1963, PhD, 1964. Instr. dept. math. Princeton (N.J.) U., 1961-62; instr. dept. stats. U. Calif., Berkeley, 1962-63; fellow Emmanuel Coll., Cambridge, 1963-64; lectr. dept. stats. U. Coll. Wales, Aberystwyth, 1964-66; sr. research fellow dept. stats. Inst. Advanced Studies Australian Nat. U., Canberra, 1967-71; fellow Australian Nat. U., 1971-72, sr. fellow, 1972—. Contbr. numerous articles on geometrical probability, stereology and scoring systems to profl. jours. Fellow Royal Statis. Soc., Internat. Soc. Stereology (pres. 1984-87); mem. Australian Conservation Found. (life). Home: RMB 345, 2620 Queanbeyan, New South Wales Australia

MILES, THOMAS RICHARD, psychologist, educator; b. Sheffield, Yorkshire, Eng., Mar. 11, 1923; s. Richard and Alice (Miller) M.; m. Elaine Armstrong, Aug. 23, 1951; 1 child, Patrick. MA, Oxford (Eng.) U., 1949; PhD, U. Wales, 1963. Lectr. psychology U. Coll. North Wales, Bangor, Gwynedd, 1949-63, prof., 1963-87. Author: Religion and the Scientific Outlook, 1959, Eliminating the Unconscious, 1966, Dyslexia, The Pattern of Difficulties, 1983, Understanding Dyslexia, 1987; (with others) Conceptual Issues in Operant Psychology, 1978, Dyslexia at College, 1986. Mem. Working Party Needs of Dyslexic Adult, 1973-77, Working Party Dyslexia, Dept. Edn. Sci., 1980-86. Served to lt. Royal Arty., 1942-45. Fellow Brit. Psychol. Soc. (life); mem. Brit. Dyslexia Assn. (life, v.p.), Exptl. Psychology Soc. (life). Mem. Soc. Friends. Club: Penn (London). Home: Llys-y-Gwynt, Llandegfan Menai Bridge, Gwynedd LL59 5YD, Wales Office: U Coll North Wales, Bangor Gwynedd LL57 2DT, Wales

MILGRIM, FRANKLIN MARSHALL, merchant; b. N.Y.C., Aug. 24, 1925; s. Charles and Sally (Knobel) M.; m. Carol E. Kleinman, Sept. 2, 1945; children: Nancy Ellen, Catherine. Grad. with honors, Woodmere (N.Y.) Acad., 1943; B.S. in Econs. with honors, Wharton Sch. U. Pa., 1949. Asst. mgr. Milgrim, Cleve., 1949-50; merchandiser, buyer H. Milgrim Bros., Inc., N.Y.C., 1950-52; v.p., dir., gen. merchandiser H. Milgrim Bros., Inc., 1952-57; pres., dir. Milgrim, Inc., Cleve. and Columbus, Ohio, 1957—; v.p., dir. Milgrim, Inc. (Mich.), Detroit, 1962-66, The 9-18 Corp., Cleve., 1969—; pres., treas., dir. Milgrim Suburban, Inc., 1963—, Milo, Inc., Columbus, 1966—, The Milgrim Co., Cleve., 1966—; pres., dir. Frankly Paul Bailey Inc., Cleve., 1965—; Dir., v.p. M and M Receivers Assn., Cleve., 1959-68. Pres. Severance Center Mchts. Assn., Cleveland Heights, 1963-66; Pres., bd. dirs. Greater Cleve. Area chpt. Nat. Council on Alcoholism, 1973—; chmn. bd. Alcoholism Services of Cleve., 1977—; fin. chmn. adv. council Salvation Army Harbor Light Complex, 1976—, chmn. bd. adv. council, 1981—; mem. Greater Cleve. adv. bd. Salvation Army, 1981—; founding bd. dirs. Sister Mary Ignatia Gavin Found.; foreman Cuyahoga County Grand Jury, 1986. Served with USNR, 1943-46. Clubs: Oakwood Country (Cleve.), Cleveland Mid-Day (Cleve.), City (Cleve.); Cleveland Playhouse; Turnberry (North Miami Beach, Fla.). Home: 1 Bratenahl Pl Bratenahl OH 44108 also: 4000 Towerside Terrace #1908 Miami FL 33138 Office: 1310 Huron Rd Cleveland OH 44115

MILHORAT, THOMAS HERRICK, neurosurgeon; b. N.Y.C., Apr. 5, 1936; s. Ade Thomas and Edith Caulkins (Herrick) M.; children: John Thomas, Robert Herrick. BS, Cornell U., 1957, MD, 1961. Intern, asst. resident in gen. surgery N.Y. Hosp.-Cornell Med. Ctr., 1961-63; clin. assoc., dept. surg. neurology Nat. Inst. Neurol. Diseases and Blindness, Bethesda, 1963-65; asst. resident, chief resident in neurosurgery N.Y. Hosp.-Cornell Med. Ctr., 1965-68, asst. neurosurgeon NIH, 1968-71; assoc. prof. neurol. surgery, assoc. prof. child health and devel. George Washington U. Sch. Medicine, Washington, 1971-74; prof. child health and devel. George Washington U., Washington, 1974-81, prof. neurol. surgery, 1974-81; chmn. dept. neurosurgery Children's Hosp. Nat. Med. Ctr., Washington, 1971-81; prof. neurol. surgery, dept. chmn. SUNY Health Sci. Ctr. at Bklyn., 1982—; neurosurgeon-in-chief Kings County Hosp., Univ. Hosp., L.I. Coll. Hosp., 1982—. Author: Hydrocephalus and Cerebrospinal Fluid, 1972, Pediatric Neurosurgery, 1978, Cerebrospinal Fluid and the Brain Edemas, 1987, (with M.K. Hammock) Cranial Computed Tomography in Infancy and Childhood, 1981; contbr. 150 articles to sci. publs. and chpts. to books. Chmn. bd. Internat. Neurosci. Found. Served to lt. comdr. USPHS, 1963-65. Awarded 1st prize in Pathology, Cornell U. Med. Sch. Dept. Ob-Gyn, 1960, Charles L. Horn prize Cornell Med. Sch., 1961, Best Paper award ann. combined meeting N.Y. Acad. Medicine/N.Y. Neurosurg. Soc./N.Y. Soc. Neurosurgery. Mem. Nat. Council Scientists NIH, AAAS, Internat. Soc. Pediatric Neurosurgery, Am. Assn. Neurol. Surgery, Am. Assn. Neurol. Surgery, Am. Acad. Pediatrics (surg. sect.), Soc. Pediatric Research, N.Y. Soc. Neurosurgery, Soc. Neurosci., Internat. Soc. Neurosci., Med. Club. Bklyn. Office: SUNY Health Sci Ctr at Bklyn 450 Clarkson Ave PO Box 1189 Brooklyn NY 11203

MILINOVICH, THOMAS GEORGE, accountant, managing tax director; b. Pitts., Mar. 23, 1948; s. Michael Andrew and Anne Marie (Koss) M., m. Debra Mae Burnett, May 18, 1974; children: Karen Marie, Timothy Michael. BS, Duquesne U., 1970. CPA, Pa. Staff acct. Arthur Anderson & Co., Pitts., 1970-71, Milinovich & Co., Waynesburg, Pa., 1971-74; tax sr. Milinovich & Co., Waynesburg, 1974-78, mng. tax dir., 1978—, pres., 1981—; dir., sec. W.F. Baird, M.D., Assocs., Waynesburg, 1972-84. Chmn. adv. com. Green County Area Vocat.-Tech. Sch., Waynesburg, 1980-84. Mem. Pa. Inst. CPA's (chmn. mems. services and benefits com. 1983-86), Estate Planning Council Southeastern Pa. (treas. 1981-83). Democrat. Roman Catholic. Lodges: Elks, Rotary (pres. Waynesburg 1975-76, dist. gov. 1983-84). Home: 1575 6th St Waynesburg PA 15370

MILITELLO, SAMUEL PHILIP, lawyer; b. Buffalo, Dec. 16, 1947; s. Samuel Anthony and Katherine (Pesono) M.; m. Anne Little, May 27, 1972; children: Matthew Samuel, Rebecca Anne, Caitlin Frances. BA, Canisius Coll., 1969; JD, SUNY-Buffalo, 1972. Bar: N.Y. 1972, U.S. Ct. Mil. Appeals 1973, U.S. Ct. Claims 1977, U.S. Supreme Ct. 1977, U.S. Dist. Ct. (we. dist.) N.Y. 1986. Assoc., Williams & Katzman, Watertown, N.Y., 1978-79; legal counsel Parsons Corp., Pasadena, Calif., 1979-84, mgr. litigation, 1981-84; gen. counsel, sec. Envirogas, Inc., Hamburg, N.Y., 1984-86 ; sole practice, Watertown, 1986-87; assoc. Bond, Schoeneck & King, Watertown, 1987—; counsel Parsons Gilbane, New Orleans, 1979-81; gen. counsel Graham Constrn. & Maintenance Corp., Watertown, 1979—, Law Bros. Contracting Corp., 1986—, C&C Infared, 1986—. Served to capt. JAGC, U.S. Army, 1973-78. Decorated Army Commendation medal with one oak leaf cluster, Meritorious Service medal. Mem. ABA (pub. contracts sect. oil and gas), Fed. Bar Assn., N.Y. State Bar Assn., Am. Judicature Soc., No. N.Y. Builders Exchange, Assoc. Gen. Contractors Am., Associated Bldg. Contractors, Am. Legion. Republican. Roman Catholic. Lodge: KC (advocate 1978-79). Office: 215 Washington St PO Box 6158 Watertown NY 13601

MILLÁN-FUERTES, JOSÉ ANTONIO, Spanish language educator; b. Valencia, Spain, Dec. 5, 1936; s. Antonio and Joaquina (Fuertes) Millan; m. Zoila Gómez, Dec. 27, 1967; children—Yumi, Pilar Isabel. B. Sci. and Lit., Nat. High Sch. Inst., 1953; Mercantile Expert, Nat. Commerce Profl. Zaragoza, Spain, 1956; Mercantile prof. Nat. Commerce Profl. Zaragoza, 1960. Lectr., Takushoku U., Tokyo, 1963-65, Fgn. Lang. U., Tokyo, 1966-67, Kanagawa U., Yokohama, Japan, 1964-67, tchr., 1967-74, asst. prof., 1974-83, prof. Spanish lang., 1983—; Spanish lang. cons., translator Toyota Motor Corp., 1964—. Author: Journalistic News in Spanish, vol. 1, 1976, vol. 2, 1983; contbr. articles to profl. jours. Mem. Japan Hispanic Assn., Japan Hispanist Inst., Kanagawa U. Humanities Inst., Kanagawa U. Ctr. for Lang. Studies. Office: Kanagawa U Rokkaku-bashi 3-27, Yokohama, Kanagawa-Ken Kanagawa-ken 221, Japan

MILLAR, ALAN, educator; b. Edinburgh, Scotland, Dec. 14, 1947; s. John and Pearl (McMurtrie) M.; m. Rose-Mary Millar, July 7, 1972; 1 child, Stephane David. MA in Mental Philosophy with honours, U. Edinburgh, Scotland, 1969; PhD, U. Cambridge, Eng., 1974. Lectr. in philosophy and religious studies U. Stirling, Scotland, 1971—. Joint editor; Scots Philos. Monograph Series, 1984-86, Macmillan Studies in Contemporary Philosophy, 1987—; contbr. articles to profl. jours. Office: U Stirling, Stirling FK9 4LA, Scotland

MILLAR, CESAR ABADILLA, surgeon; b. Lucena, Quezon, Philippines, Oct. 5, 1925; s. Fabian Rabe and Angela (Abadilla) M.; m. Josefina Coscolluela, Dec. 19, 1959; children: Gisela, Gabriel, Cesar, Angela, Jose Fabian. AA, U. Philippines, Manila, 1944, MD, 1949. Diplomate Philippine Bd. Surgery, Philippine Bd. Thoracic and Cardiovascular Surgery, Philippine Coll. Chest Physicians. Med. officer schistosomiasis research Dept. Health, Manila, 1949-51; resident in gen. surgery Hosp. St. Raphael, New Haven, Conn., 1951-55; resident in thoracic surgery Kings County Hosp., SUNY, Bklyn., 1955-57; instr. surgery Ramon Magsaysay Meml. Med. Ctr., U. The East, Quezon City, Philippines, 1957-72, prof., 1972—, chmn. dept. surgery, 1982-86; chmn. dept. surgery Med. City Gen. Hosp., Greenhills, Philippines, 1969—, Lung Ctr. Philippines, Quezon City, 1986—; cons. in thoracic surgery Our Lady of Lourdes Hosp., Manila, 1957—; clin. prof. surgery U. Philippines, Manila, 1982—. Contbr. articles to profl. jours. Fellow Am. Coll. Surgeons, Philippine Coll. Surgeons (regent 1980-82); mem. Philippine Assn. Thoracic and Cardiovascular Surgeons (charter mem., pres. 1966-67, 85-86, chmn. 1987—). Roman Catholic. Home: 9 Celedonio Salvador St, Quezon City Philippines Office: Med City Gen Hosp, Greenhills, Mandluyong, Metro Manila Philippines

MILLARD, JAMES KEMPER, marketing and advertising executive, consultant; b. Lexington, Ky., Oct. 28, 1948; s. Lyman Clifford and Cora Spence (Carrick) M., Jr.; m. Linda Madelyn Hooper, Nov. 26, 1983; children: Lyman Clifford III, Sean Duffy, James Kemper Jr., Caroline Carrick. B.A. in Polit. Sci., Transylvania U., 1971. Corr. AP, 1970-71; prodn. asst. Sta. WLEX-TV, Lexington, Ky., 1970; floor dir., asst. news dir., 1971-73, producer, reporter, 1974-76; producer, dir. Ky. Dept. Pub. Info., Lexington, 1973; successively admissions counselor, dir. promotional services, dir. univ. relations, assoc. dir. devel. Transylvania U., Lexington, 1973-79; field mktg. mgr. Abbott Advt. Agy., Inc., Lexington, 1979-80, account exec., 1980-81, account supr., 1981-85; dir. mktg. Steak 'n Shake, Inc., Indpls., 1985; dir. field mktg. Nutri/System, Inc., Phila., 1985-88, v.p. communications, 1988—; bd. dirs., mem. advt. com., chmn. Bluegrass chpt. Ky. Restaurant Assn.; mem. acad. adv. com. mass communications Eastern Ky. U., also guest lectr. Sec., treas. Bluegrass Integrated Pest Mgmt. Coop.; deacon Cen. Christian Ch., Lexington. Recipient Addy (Bronze) award Lexington Advt. Club, 1976, Addy (Best of Show, Gold, Silver, Bronze, Merit) award, 1982; Addy (Silver, Bronze, Merit) award Am. Advt. Fedn., 1981, 83; Gt. Menu. Gold award Nat. Restaurant Assn., 1982; Louie (Merit) award Louisville Advt. Club, 1976; named Key Man of 1981, Jerrico, Inc.; Best Children's Menu, Fla. Restaurant Assn., 1982; Hon. Order Ky. Cols. Mem. Delta Sigma Phi. Democrat. Mem. Disciples of Christ. Club: Columbia (Indpls.). Home: 21 Wetherburn Dr Downingtown PA 19335-3346 Office: Nutri System Inc 3901 Commerce Ave Willow Grove PA 19090

MILLARD, LAVERGNE HARRIET, free-lance artist; b. Chgo., July 8, 1925; d. Lewis and Julia (Smolk) Bassmire; student Chgo. Art Inst., 1937-39; m. Samuel Costales, 1943 (div. 1957); m. Bailey Millard, Mar. 9, 1958 (div.); children—Bryan Lewis Costales, Julianne, Juanita Crump, Candace Lynn Millard. Cocktail waitress Verdis, Grant Street, Concord, Calif., 1955-61; mgr. used book shop Joyce Book Shop, Concord, 1964-79, seller art works, own prints; freelance artist, 1979—. Recipient ribbons local fairs, art shows. Republican. Copyright holder for pastel art work. Home and Office: 1890 Farm Bureau Rd Apt 11 Concord CA 94519

MILLARD, NEAL STEVEN, lawyer; b. Dallas, June 6, 1947; s. Bernard and Adele (Marks) M.; m. Holly Ann Hinman, Dec. 30, 1970. BA cum laude, UCLA, 1969; JD, U. Chgo., 1972. Bar: Calif. 1972, U.S. Dist. Ct. (cen. dist.) Calif. 1973, U.S. Tax Ct. 1973, U.S. Ct. Appeals (9th cir.) 1987. Assoc. Willis, Butler & Schiefly, Los Angeles, 1972-75; ptnr. Morrison & Foerster, Los Angeles, 1975-84, Jones, Day, Reavis & Pogue, Los Angeles, 1984—; instr. Calif. State Coll., San Bernardino, 1975-76; lectr. Practising Law Inst., N.Y.C., 1983—, Calif. Edn. of Bar, 1987—. Mem. citizens adv. com. Los Angeles Olympics, 1982-84; trustee Altadena (Calif.) Library Dist., 1985-86; bd. dirs. Woodcraft Rangers, Los Angeles, 1982—, pres., 1986-88. Served to capt. U.S. Army, 1970-72. Mem. ABA, Calif. Bar Assn., Los Angeles County Bar Assn. (trustee 1985-87), Pub. Counsel (bd. dirs. 1984-87), U. Chgo. Law Alumni Assn. (So. Calif. chpt. bd. dirs. 1981—), Phi Beta Kappa, Pi Gamma Mu, Phi Delta Phi. Club: Altadena Town and County. Office: Jones Day Reavis & Pogue 355 S Grand Ave Suite 3000 Los Angeles CA 90071

MILLARD, PETER HENRY, geriatric medicine educator; b. Arundel, Sussex, Eng., July 18, 1937; s. Edward Joseph and Thelma Fanny (Burrows) M.; m. Alys Gillian Thomas, Jan. 27, 1962; children: Paul William, Stephen Edward, David Christopher. MBBS with honors, Univ. Coll. Hosp., London, 1960; MRCP, Royal Coll. Physicians, 1966. Med. officer Cameroon Devel. Corp., West Cameroon, 1962-63; med. registrar Nat. Temperance Hosp., London, 1964-66; sr. registrar Univ. Coll. Hosp., London, 1966-68; cons. physician St. George's Hosp., London, 1968-75, sr. lectr. St. George's Hosp. Med. Sch., London, 1975-78, Eleanor Peel prof. geriatric medicine, 1978—, also U. London, 1978—; hon. med. adviser Assn. Carers, 1982-87, Counsel and Care for the Elderly, 1979-87; gov. Age Concern Eng., 1983, Ctr. Policy on Aging, 1986. Contbr. articles to profl. jours.; author: The Dwarfs and Their King, 1950. Gov., Linacre Ctr., London, 1981-86. Fellow Royal Coll. Physicians, British Assn. Service to Elderly (pres. 1983—), British Geriatrics Soc. (past sec., mem. council), British Soc. Research on Aging (exec. 1979-83), Royal Inst. Pub. Health and Hygiene (chmn. edn. com. 1983—). Roman Catholic. Home: 12 Cornwall Rd, Cheam, Surrey SM2 6DR, England Office: St George's Hosp Med Sch, Geriatric Teaching and, Research Unit, London England

MILLER, ALWIN VERMAR, educational advisor, consultant; b. Dardanelle, Ark., Oct. 12, 1922; s. William Marshall and Ollie Vernice (Green) M.; m. Patricia Jane Knox, Dec. 31, 1945; children—Carol, Alwin, William, Patricia, Thomas. A.A., Ark. Poly. Inst., 1939; B.S., B.A. with honors, UCLA, 1947, M.Ed., 1948, Ed.D., 1956; cert. Internat. Inst. Ednl. Planning (UNESCO), 1967-68. Instr. Chico State Coll., Calif., 1948-49; assoc. prof. So. Oreg. Coll., Ashland, 1949-57; edn. advisor AID, Washington, 1957-75; cons. on internat. devel., Upper Marlboro, Md., 1975—. Served to lt. col. USAF, 1942-46. Mem. Soc. Internat. Devel., Am. Soc. for Tng. and Devel., Internat. Soc. Ednl. Planning, Reserve Officers Assn. (v.p. D.C. dept. 1986-87), Res. Officers Assn. (v.p. D.C. dept. 1986-87), Phi Delta Kappa. Democrat. Mem. Ch. of Christ. Lodge: Lions, Masons, Shriners, K.T. Office: PO Box 4066 Upper Marlboro MD 20775

MILLER, ARTHUR, playwright, author; b. N.Y.C., Oct. 17, 1915; s. Isadore and Augusta (Barnett) M.; m. Mary Grace Slattery, Aug. 5, 1940 (div.); children: Jane Ellen, Robert; m. Marilyn Monroe, June 1956 (div.); m. Ingeborg Morath, Feb. 1962; 1 dau. AB, U. Mich., 1938, LHD, 1956. assoc. prof. drama U. Mich., 1973-74. Playwright: Man Who Had All the Luck, 1944, Situation Normal, 1944, All My Sons, 1948 (N.Y. Drama Critics award); motion picture Death of a Salesman (N.Y. Drama Critics Circle award, Pulitzer prize 1949); The Crucible, 1953 (Tony award); motion picture View from the Bridge, 1955; Collected Plays, 1958, After the Fall, 1963, Incident at Vichy, 1964, A Memory of Two Mondays, 1955, The Price, 1956, Up From Paradise, The Archbishop's Ceiling, The American Clock, 1981; screenplay Playing For Time, 1981, stage version, 1985; one-act plays: Clara, 1985, I Can't Remember Anything, 1985; author: novel Focus, 1945; novel (later screenplay) The Misfits, 1960; The Price, 1968, The Creation of the World and Other Businesses, 1972, In Russia, 1969; also story collection I Don't Need You Anymore, 1967; (with Inge Morath) Chinese Encounters, 1979, (memoir) Salesman in Beijing, 1984, (autobiography) Time-Bends, 1987. Recipient Hopwood award for Playwriting U. Mich., 1936, 37; Theatre Guild Nat. Award, 1938; Antoinette Perry Award, 1953; Gold Medal for drama Nat. Inst. Arts and Letters, 1959; Creative Arts award Brandeis U., 1970; Anglo-Am. award, 1966. Office: care ICM 40 W 57th St New York NY 10019

MILLER, ARTHUR HAROLD, lawyer; b. Plainfield, N.J., Sept. 21, 1935; s. Leon Daniel and Bertha Zelda (Madoff) M.; m. Lynn Fieldman, Aug. 24, 1958; children—Jennifer, Jonathan. B.A., Princeton U., 1957; J.D., Columbia U., 1960. Bar: N.Y. 1961, U.S. Supreme Ct. 1965, N.J. 1969. Assoc. Wachtel & Michaelson, N.Y.C., 1961-65, Netter, Lewy, Dowd, N.Y.C., 1965-67, Dannenberg Hazen & Lake, N.Y.C., 1967-69; ptnr. Clarick, Clarick & Miller, New Brunswick, N.J., 1971-78, Miller & Littman, New Brunswick, 1979—; chmn. Middlesex County Legal Services Corp., New Brunswick, 1975-83. Mem. Sch. Bd. Highland Park, N.J., 1981-84. Democrat. Jewish. Mem. N.J. Bar Assn. (chmn. availibility legal services com. 1983-85, lawyer referral com. 1986-88), N.Y. State Bar Assn., Middlesex County Bar Assn. (trustee 1987—). Home: 145 N 9th Ave Highland Park NJ 08904 Office: Miller & Littman 96 Paterson St New Brunswick NJ 08901

MILLER, BILL, management and marketing consultant; b. Jersey City, Mar. 6, 1933; Children: Valerie, Lynn, Lori, Michael, Billy Joe. MBA, La Jolla U., 1980. Cert. (life) coll. level tchr. psychology, bus. mgmt. and mktg., mgmt. orgn. and human relations, Calif. Enlisted USMC, 1948, ret., 1967; instr. karate, judo and mob control N.J. and Calif. Police Depts.; dist.

sales mgr. Syntex Labs., Palo Alto, Calif., 1968-75; owner, pres. Bill Miller and Assocs., Inc., 1976—, Mgmt. Dynamics; cons. to mgmt. in healthcare, exec. search; presenter mgmt. seminars; instr. psychology, bus. mgmt. and mktg., mgmt. orgn. and human relations U. Calif.-La Jolla and Nat. U., San Diego. Sponsor, founder Ann. Rancho Bernardo (Calif.) Half Marathon. Home: 12696 Pacato Circle N Rancho Bernardo CA 92128

MILLER, BRIAN PETER, sports psychologist; b. London, Oct. 29, 1957; s. Horace David and Jean (Kirk) M.; m. Rachel Mary Ormerod, July 12, 1980. BEd with honors, U. Wales, Cardiff, 1980; MA, U. Birmingham, Eng., 1981. Lectr. sports psychology Bed. Coll. Higher Edn., Bedfordshire, Eng., 1981-84; sports psychologist Australian Inst. Sport, Canberra, Australia, 1984—; Australian team psychologist Commonwealth Games, Edinburgh, 1986, World Univ. Games, Zagreb, 1987, Olympic Games, Seoul, 1988. Author: Sport Psychology and Running, 1987; contbr. articles to profl. jours. Mem. Internat. Soc. Sport Psychology, Australian Psychol. Soc., Australian Sports Medicine Fedn., Brit. Assn. Sports Scis. Office: Australian Inst Sport, PO Box 176, Belconnen 2616, Australia

MILLER, BRUCE RICHARD, employee benefits executive; b. Hazleton, Pa., Mar. 16, 1944; s. Robert Joseph and Marguerite Marie (Fritz) M.; B.A. in Polit. Sci., Pa. State U., 1971. Supr. salary adminstrn. Govt. Employees Ins. Co., Chevy Chase, Md., 1971-73; asst. to personnel dir. MCI Telecommunications, Inc., Washington, 1973-74; wage and salary adminstr. Kay Jewelers, Inc., Alexandria, Va., 1974, dir. personnel, 1974-84, div. v.p. personnel, 1981-85; founder, pres., chief exec. officer Employee Benefits Corp. Am., Fairfax, 1984—. Pa. State U. Presdl. assoc.; contbr. articles to profl. jours. Mem. Alexandria Human Rights Commn., 1982-85, Active Back the Lions Club. Served with U.S. Army, 1966-70. Mem. Am. Soc. Personnel Adminstrn., Fairfax County C. of C., Cen. Fairfax C. of C., Arlington C. of C., Met. Washington Bd. Trade, Alexandria C. of C., George Mason U. Patriots Club, Pa. State U. Alumni Assn., Pa. State U. Nittany Lion Club (bd. dirs., mem. adv. council), Pa. State U. Club of Greater Washington, Nat. Capital Area Nittany Lion (bd. dirs.), Nat. Assn. Life Underwriters. Home: 5402 Ives Pl Springfield VA 22151 Office: 3607 Chain Bridge Rd Suite A Fairfax VA 22030

MILLER, CAREY BRENT, oil company executive, geologist; b. Chickasha, Okla., Aug. 23, 1949; s. Roy Lee and Wilma LaVelle (Smith) M.; m. Margie Jean Broaddus, June 7, 1969; 1 child, Derrik Brent. BS in Geology, U. Okla., 1978; BS in Math., Okla. Coll. Liberal Arts, 1970. dist. sales rep. United Foam Corp., Shawnee, Okla., 1975-76; researcher Environ. Res. Devel. Assn., U. Okla., Norman, 1976-77; dist. geologist Grace Petroleum Corp., Oklahoma City, 1977-80, Western Pacific Petroleum, Oklahoma City, 1980-82; pres. Hold Exploration Co., Oklahoma City, 1982-85, BriCar Resources, Inc., Oklahoma City, 1982—, also bd. dirs.; bd. dirs. Blue Pine Pottery Corp., Oklahoma City, Park Loan Co., Inc., v.p. 1987—; bd. dirs. Roy-Al Corp., Oklahoma City. Served to 1st lt. U.S. Army, 1971-74. Mem. Am. Assn. Petroleum Geologists, Soc. Exploration Geophysicists, Oklahoma City Geol. Soc., Geophys. Soc. Oklahoma City, Oklahoma City C. of C., Phi Gamma Lambda (pres. 1969-70), Sigma Gamma Epsilon. Republican. Baptist. Home: 2910 Meadow Ave Norman OK 73072 Office: BriCar Inc 1207 Sovereign Row Oklahoma City OK 73108

MILLER, CAROLYN M. FORIS, histotechnologist; b. N.Y.C., Mar. 13, 1937; d. John Stephen and Caroline Bernice (Banoff) Foris; m. Herbert J. Miller. A.A., Thomas A. Edison Coll., 1979. Technician dept. Hosps. of City of NY., 1959-68; instr. histology Allen Sch. for Med. Tech.; supr. histology Wycoff Heights Hosp., 1968-70; mgr. tissue pathology lab. Metpath, Inc., Teterboro N.J., 1970-84; staff analyst Wood Hull Med. and Mental Health Ctr., Bklyn. Coordinator legis. adv. bd. dirs. for chmn. health for N.Y. State, 1974-75; moderator of community discussion sessions on drug abuse, 1973; bd. govs. Mid Queens Regular Democratic Orgn., 1965-75, sec., v.p., also campaign coordinator for candidates of this orgn., editor newsletter; coordinator Anatomical Pathology services, Woodhill Med. and Mental Health Ctr., Bklyn., 1985-86. Recipient certs. Merit and Appreciation, N.Y. State Assemblymen. Mem. Nat. Soc. for Histotech. (charter mem. pub. relations com.), N.Y. Soc. for Histotech. (charter mem., co-editor newsletter 1975-76), N.J. Soc. for Histotech. (charter mem.), Am. Soc. Clin. Pathology (assoc. and affiliate member). Roman Catholic.

MILLER, CHARLES LESLIE, chemical engineer, planner, consultant; b. Tampa, Fla., June 5, 1929; s. Charles H. and Myrle Iona (Walstrom) M.; m. Roberta Jean Pye, Sept. 9, 1949; children—Charles Henry, Stephen, Jonathan, Matthew. BCE, MIT, 1951, MCE, 1958. Registered profl. engr., Mass., Fla., Tenn., N.H., R.I., P.R. Successively field engr., project engr., exec. engr. Michael Baker, Jr., Inc. (cons. engrs.), Rochester, Pa., 1951-55; asst. prof. surveying, dir. photogrammetry lab. Mass. Inst. Tech., 1955-59, asso. prof. civil engring., head data engring. div., 1959-61, prof. civil engring., 1961-77, head dept., 1961-70, dir. urban systems lab., 1968-75, dir. civil engring. systems lab., 1961-65, dir. inter-Am. program civil engring., 1961-65, asso. dean engring., 1970-71; cons. engr. 1955—; chmn. bd., sr. cons., pres. CLM Systems, Inc., C.L. Miller Co., Inc.; adviser Commonwealth of P.R; dir. Geo-Transport Found.; Chmn. Pres.-elect's Task Force on Transp., 1968-69. Author tech. papers. Recipient Outstanding Young Man of Greater Boston award. Fellow Am. Acad. Arts and Scis.; mem. ASCE, N.Y. Acad. Scis., Am. Inst. Cons. Engrs., Am. Soc. Engring. Edn. (George Westinghouse award), Am. Soc. Photogrammetry, Am. Congress Surveying and Mapping, Am. Rd. Builders Assn., Transp. Research Bd., Assn. Computing Machinery, Sigma Xi, Chi Epsilon, Tau Beta Pi. Office: CL Miller Company 4023 S Dale Mabry Tampa FL 33611

MILLER, DAVID EDMOND, physician; b. Biscoe, N.C., June 6, 1930; s. James Herbert and Elsie Dale (McGlaughon) M.; m. Marjorie Willard Penton, June 4, 1960; children: Marjorie Dale, David Edmond. AB, Duke U., 1952, MD, 1956. Diplomate Am. Bd. Internal Medicine (subspecialty bd. cardiovasular disease). Internmed. ctr. Duke U., Durham, N.C., 1956-57, resident in internal medicine, 1957-58, 59, 60, research fellow cardiovascular disease, 1958-59, 61, assoc. internal medicine and cardiology, 1963-79, clin. asst., prof. medicine cardiology, 1979—; practice medicine specialising in internal medicine Durham, 1964—; attending physician internal medicine div. cardiology Watts Hosp., Durham, 1964-76, chief medicine, 1975-76; attending physician cardiology div. internal medicine Durham County Gen. Hosp., 1976—, chmn. dept. internal medicine, 1976-82, pres. med. staff, 1980-81; adv. com. Duke Med. Ctr. Contbr. articles to profl. jours. Council clin. cardiology N.C. chpt. Am. Heart Assn., 1963—. Served to lt. comdr. USNR, 1961-63. Fellow ACP, Am. Coll. Cardiology; mem. AMA, So. Med. Assn., N.C. Med. Soc. (del. ho. of dels. 1981, 82, 83), N.C. Durham-Orange County Med. Soc., Am. Soc. Internal Medicine, N.C. Soc. Internal Medicine (exec. council), Am. Fedn. Clin. Research. Methodist. Clubs: Capitol City, Hope Valley Country. Home: 1544 Hermitage Ct Durham NC 27707 Office: 2609 N Duke St Suite 403 Durham NC 27704

MILLER, DAVID FRANCIS, retail executive; b. Jacksonville, Fla., June 1, 1929; s. Frank Holten and Verna (Sharp) M.; m. Gloria Parks, June 13, 1952; children—David F., Clara, Elizabeth, Jane. B.S.B.A., U. Fla., 1951. With J.C. Penney Co., Inc., 1953—, mdse. mgr. Dallas regional office, 1964-66, mktg. mgr. women's fashions, 1966-69, dist. mgr., Atlanta, 1969-70, asst. to dir. regional ops., N.Y.C., 1970-72, dir. regional coordination, 1972-74, v.p., 1974-76, regional v.p. Eastern region, 1976-79, sr. v.p., dir., 1980-83; pres. J.C. Penney Stores and Catalog, 1983—, vice chmn., chief operating officer, 1988—. Mem. adv. com. Women's Prison Assn., 1974-76; mem. adv. council Coll. Bus. Adminstrn., U. Fla.; mem. ofcl. bd. United Meth. Ch., Huntington, N.Y., 1976; chmn. comml. div. United Way, N.Y.C., 1982. Served with USAF, 1951-53. Republican. Club: Huntington Country. Office: JC Penney Co Inc PO Box 659000 Dallas TX 75265 *

MILLER, DEANE GUYNES, styling salon exec.; b. El Paso, Tex., Jan. 12, 1927; d. James Tillman and Margaret (Brady) Guynes; degree in bus. adminstrn. U. Tex., El Paso, 1947; m. Richard George Miller, Apr. 12, 1947; children—J. Michael, Marcia Deane. Owner four Merle Norman Cosmetic Studios, El Paso, 1967—; pres. The Velvet Door, Inc., El Paso, 1967—; dir. Mountain Bell Telephone Co. Pres. bd. dirs. YWCA, 1967; v.p. Sun Bowl Assn., 1970; bd. dirs. El Paso Symphony Assn.; bd. dirs., treas. El Paso Mus. Art; chmn. bd. El Paso Internat. Airport; bd. dirs., sec. Armed Services YMCA, 1987. Named Outstanding Woman field of civic endeavor, El Paso Herald Post. Mem. Women's C. of C. (pres. 1969, now dir.), Pan Am. Round Table (dir., pres. 1987). Home: 1 Silent Crest St El Paso TX 79902 Office: 122 Thunderbird St El Paso TX 79912

MILLER, DONALD LANE, publishing executive; b. Pitts., May 14, 1918; s. Donald Edwin and Arvilla (Lane) M.; A.B., Kenyon Coll., 1940; Russian interpreter cert. U. Colo., 1946; postgrad. U. Pitts., 1947-48; m. Norma Reno, Feb. 2, 1951. Reporter, Pitts. Sun-Telegraph, 1940-42, Washington Post, 1946; with pub. relations dept. Westinghouse Electric Corp., Pitts., 1947-51; reporter Billboard and Tide, 1953; pub. relations dir. Nat. Agrl. Chem. Assn., Washington, 1954-58; sec. Donald Larch & Co., Washington, 1958-61; pres. Asso. Pub. Relations Counselors, Washington, 1961-77; chmn. bd. Braddock Communications, Inc., Washington, TMS Imports, Irvington, Va. and and N.Y.C.; chmn. bd. Children's Aid Internat.; exec. dir. All Am. Conf., Washington, 1962-75. Editor, GOP Nationalities News, Rep. Nat. Com., 1960; pub. relations nationalities div. Rep. Nat. Com., 1964; coordinator life underwriters sect. Citizens for Nixon-Agnew, 1968. Served from ensign to lt., USNR, 1942-46; from lt. to lt. comdr., 1951-53. Decorated Knight of Europe. Mem. English Speaking Union, SAR, Phi Beta Kappa, Delta Tau Delta. Clubs: Nat. Press, Army & Navy; Indian Creek Yacht and Country. Author: Strategy for Conquest, 1966 Braddock's Presidential Quotations; Braddock's Quotations on Peace and Conflict. Home: 429 Irvington Rd Box 1978 Kilmarnock VA 22482 Office: 1001 Connecticut Ave NW Washington DC 20036

MILLER, DUANE KING, health and beauty care company executive; b. N.Y.C., Mar. 1, 1931; s. Henry Charles and Helen Marion (King) M.; A.B. in Econs. and Fin., NYU, 1951; m. Nancy L. Longley, June 6, 1954; children—Cheryl L., Duane L. Vice pres. mktg. Warner-Chilcott div. Warner Lambert Co., Morris Plains, N.J., 1970-72, pres. div., 1973-77, exec. v.p. Am. Optical div. and pres. Am. Optical Internat. div., Southbridge, Mass., 1978; pres. biol. and proprietary products divs., v.p. Revlon Health Care Group, Revlon Corp., Tuckahoe, N.Y., 1978-80, pres. ethical, proprietary and vision care divs., 1981—, corp. v.p. parent co., 1982, pres. Revlon Health Care Group, 1983—, corp. exec. v.p. parent co., 1984—, pres. Revlon Health Beauty Care and Internat. Group, 1988—; cons. in field. Mem. Republican Nat. Com. Mem. Pharm Mfrs. Assn. (bd. dirs.), Nat. Pharm. Council, Am. Mgmt. Assn., Am. Mktg. Assn. (pres. N.J. chpt. 1967-68), Sales Exec. Club N.Y. Clubs: Princeton N.Y.; Roxiticus (N.J.) Golf; Clubs of Ocean Pines (Md.); Masons, Shriners. Author: (with others) Marketing Planning for Chief Executives and Planners, 1966. Home: PO Box 63 Brookside NJ 07926 Office: Revlon Inc 767 Fifth Ave New York NY 10022

MILLER, E. WILLARD, geographer; b. Turkey City, Pa., May 17, 1915; s. Archie Howard and Tessie Bernella (Master) M.; m. Ruby Skinner, June 27, 1941. M.A., U. Nebr., 1939; Ph.D., Ohio State U., 1942. Instr. Ohio State U., 1941-43; asst. prof. geography and geology Western Res. U., 1943-44; asso. prof. geography Pa. State U., University Park, 1945-49; prof. Pa. State U., 1949—, chief div. geography, 1945-53, head dept. geography, 1954-63; asst. dean for resident instrn. Coll. Earth and Mineral Scis., 1964-72, asso. dean, 1972-80, asst. dean for resident instrn. and continuing edn., 1967-69; dir. Acad. Year Inst., Earth Scis., NSF, 1967-71; geographer OSS, Washington, 1944-45; spl. research on Arctic environ. problems for Q.M. Gen., U.S. Army, 1947-50; geographic adviser Thomas Y. Crowell Co. Author: Careers in Geography, 1948 (rev. 1955), (with others) The World's Nations: An Economic and Regional Geography, 1958, A Geography of Manufacturing, 1962, An Economic Atlas of Pennsylvania, 1964, (with G. Langdon) Exploring Earth Environments: A World Geography, 1964, Energy Resources of the United States, 1968, Mineral Resources of the United States, 1968, A Geography of Industrial Location, 1970, A Socio-Economic Atlas of Pennsylvania, 1974, Manufacturing: A Study of Industrial Location, 1977, Industrial Location: A Bibliography, 1978, Physical Geography: Earth Systems and Human Interactions, 1985, Pennsylvania: A Keystone to Progress, 1986, (with Ruby M. Miller) During Business In and With Latin America, 1987, (with Ruby M. Miller) Economic, Political and Regional Aspects of the World's Energy Problems, 1979, The Third World: Natural Resources, Economics, Politics and Social Conditions, 1981, Africa: A Bibliography on the Third World, 1981, Northern and Western Africa: A Bibliography on the Third World, 1981, Tropical Eastern and Southern Africa: A Bibliography on the Third World, 1981, The American Coal Industry: Economic, Political and Environmental Aspects, 1980, Manufacturing in Nonmetropolitan Pennsylvania, 1980; (with Ruby M. Miller) Latin America: A Bibliography on the Third World, 1982, South America: A Bibliography in the Third World, 1982, Middle America: A Bibliography on the Third World, 1982, Industrial Location and Planning: Theory, Models and Factors of Localization: A Bibliography, 1984, Industrial Location and Planning: Localization, Growth and Organization: A Bibliography, 1984, Industrial Location and Planning: Regions and Countries: A Bibliography, 1984; Pennsylvania: Architecture and Culture: A Bibliography, 1985, United States' Foreign Relation: Western Europe, 1987, United States' Foreign Relations: Soviet Union and Eastern Europe, 1987, United States' Foreign Relations: Middle East, 1987, United States' Foreign Relations: Africa, 1987, United States Foreign Relations: East Asia, South Asia and Oceania, 1987, United States' Foreign Relations: Latin America, 1987, United States' Foreign Relations: United States and Canada, 1987, Industrial Parks, Export Processing Zones, and Enterprise Zones: A Bibliography, 1987, The 1976 Presidential Elections: A Bibliography, 1987, The 1980 Presidential Election: A Bibliography, 1987, The 1984 Presidential Election: A Bibliography, 1987, The Third World: Economic Development, 1988, The Third World: Government and Political Relations, Social Conditions, Population, Urbanization, Education, and Communications, 1988, The Third World: Economic Activities, 1988, Natural Resources and Commerical Policy, 1988, others; editorial dir.: Earth and Mineral Scis. Bull, 1967-69; editor: (with S. K. Majumdar) Pennsylvania Coal: Resources, Technology and Utilization, 1983, Hazardous and Toxic Wastes: Management and Health Effects, 1984, Solid and Liquid Wastes: Managment Methods and Socioeconomic Considerations, 1984, Management of Radioactive Materials and Wastes: Issues and Progress, 1985, Environmental Consequences of Energy Production, 1987, Ecology and Restoration of the Delaware River Basin, 1988; assoc. editor: The Pennsylvania Geographer; media materials editor: Jour. Geography, 1981-84; contbg. editor: Producers Monthly Mag; contbr. articles to sci. jours. Recipient certificate of merit from OSS; Whitback award Nat. Council Geog. Edn., 1950; Pa. Gov.'s citation for contbn. to Commonwealth, 1975; Pa. Dept. Commerce Sec.'s Meritorious Services award, 1975. Fellow Explorers Club, Am. Geog Soc., AAAS, Nat. Council Geog. Edn.; mem. Am. Inst. Mining, Metall. and Petroleum Engrs., Am. Soc. Profl. Geographers (pres. 1948), Assn. Am. Geographers, Pa. Geog. Soc. (pres. 1962-63, dir. 1965—, Meritorious Service award 1974, 84), Pa. Acad. Sci. (pres. 1966-68, editorial bd. Procs. 1985—, Spl. Services award 1976, 87), Sigma Xi, Pi Gamma Mu, Beta Gamma Sigma. Home: 845 Outer Dr State College PA 16801

MILLER, EDGAR, psychologist; b. Manchester, Eng., Jan. 13, 1939; s. Lawrence Kennedy and Olive Mary (Robson) M.; married; children: Andrew, Johanna, James. BS, Hull U., Eng., 1964; M in Philosophy, London U., 1966; PhD, Hull U., Eng., 1972. Lectr. U. Hull, Eng., 1967-71; sr. lectr. U. Southampton, Eng., 1971-77; vis. prof. Queen's U., Kingston, Ont., 1975-76; chief psychologist Cambridge (Eng.) Health Authority, 1977—; assoc. lectr. U. Cambridge, Eng., 1980—. Author: Abnormal Aging, 1977, Recovery and Management of Neuropsychological Impairments, 1985; author: (with S.T. Morley) Investigating Abnormal Behavior, 1986. Machin Meml. lectr. U. Hull, Eng., 1987—. Fellow Brit. Psychol. Soc.; mem. Exptl. Psychology Soc. Home: 54 West Dr, Caldecote, Cambridge CB3 7NY, England Office: Addenbrooke's Hosp, Dept Clin Psychology, Cambridge CB2 2QY, England

MILLER, ELVA RUBY CONNES (MRS. JOHN R. MILLER), civic worker; b. Joplin, Mo.; d. Edward and Ada (Martin) Connes; student Pomona Coll., part-time, 1936-56; m. John R. Miller, Jan. 17, 1934 (dec. Nov. 1968). Entertainer various night clubs, supper clubs, also Hollywood Bowl, 1967; TV appearances; rec. artist Capitol Records, 1966—, Amaret Records, 1969—; appeared in motion pictures. Active Girl Scouts U.S.A., 1933-58; hon. mem. Mayor's Com. for Sr. Citizens, Los Angeles, 1966; mem. Disabled Am. Vets., Comdrs. Club, Music Ctr. Los Angeles County. Recipient awards including Thanks badge Girl Scouts U.S.A., 1956, Key to City, Mayor San Diego, 1967, plaque Dept. of Def. for trip to Vietnam, 1967. Mem. Gen. Alumni Assn. U. So. Calif. (life). Republican. Presbyterian. Home: 9585 Reseda Blvd Northridge CA 91324

MILLER, EMERSON WALDO, accountant, tax, financial, business and management consultant; b. Green Island, Jamaica, W.I., Jan. 27, 1920; s. Adolphus Eustace and Catherine Sarah (Dixon) M.; m. Olive Claire Ford, Apr. 10, 1945; children—Cheryll, Hellena, Emerson, Oliver, Donald, Selwyn. Student U. Toronto, (Ont., Can.), 1938-41, U. Calif.-Berkeley, 1950-61. Came to U.S., 1950, naturalized, 1957. Cost accountant Poierier & McLane Corp., N.Y.C., 1941-42; prin. Emerson Miller & Co., Kingston, Jamaica, 1942-49; lectr. accounting and bus. law Jamaica Sch. Commerce, Kingston, 1945-48; tax examiner, conferee Internat. Revenue Service, San Francisco, 1963-64; chief financial and accounting aspects transp. and communications services programs Gen. Services Adminstrn., San Francisco, 1965-70, chief maj. segment financial mgmt. activities, 1970-84; prin. Emerson W. Miller Tax, Fin., Bus. and Mgmt. Services, 1984—; instr. govt. accounting, 1966-69. Fed. Govt. Accountants Assn. rep. mgmt. improvement com. Fed. Exec. Bd., San Francisco, 1973-74. Chmn. credit com. VARO Fed. Credit Union, San Francisco, 1969-81, treas., dir., 1981—. Recipient Disting. Service award Toastmasters Internat., 1968, Commendable Service award Gen. Services Adminstrn., 1968, Spl. Achievement award, 1969; Faithful Service award VARO-SF Fed. Credit Union, 1974. Mem. Am. Accounting Assn., Nat. Assn. Accountants, Fed. Govt. Accountants Assn. (chpt. pres.), Am. Mgmt. Assn., Financial Mgmt. Assn., Brit. Inst. Mgmt., Am. Judicature Soc., Royal Econ. Soc. (Cambridge), U. Calif. Alumni Assn., Internat. Platform Assn., Acad. Polit. and Social Sci., AAAS, N.Y. Acad. Scis. Clubs: Toastmasters Internat. (ednl. v.p.), (San Francisco), No. Calif. Cricket (San Anselmo); Brit. Social and Athletic (Los Angeles). Home: 505 Coventry Rd Kensington CA 94707 Office: PO Box 471 Berkeley CA 94701

MILLER, GENEVIEVE, medical historian; b. Butler, Pa., Oct. 15, 1914; d. Charles Russell and Genevieve (Wolford) M. A.B., Goucher Coll., 1935; M.A., Johns Hopkins U., 1939; Ph.D., Cornell U., 1955. Asst. in history of medicine Johns Hopkins Inst. of History of Medicine, Balt., 1943-44, instr., 1945-48, research assoc., 1979—; asst. prof. history of medicine Sch. Medicine, Case Western Res. U., Cleve., 1953-67, assoc. prof., 1967-79, assoc. prof. emeritus, 1979—; research assoc. in med. history Cleve. Med. Library Assn., 1953-62, curator Howard Dittrick Mus. of Hist. Medicine, 1962-67, dir. Howard Dittrick Mus. Hist. Medicine, 1967-79. Author: William Beaumont's Formative Years: Two Early Notebooks 1811-1821, 1946; The Adoption of Inoculation for Smallpox in England and France (William H. Welch medal Am. Assn. for History of Medicine 1962), 1957; Bibliography of the History of Medicine of the U.S. and Canada, 1939-1960, 1964; Bibliography of the Writings of Henry E. Sigerist, 1966; Letters of Edward Jenner and Other Documents Concerning the Early History of Vaccination, 1983; assoc. editor Bull. of History of Medicine, 1944-48, acting editor, 1948, mem. adv. editorial bd. 1960—; mem. bd. editors Jour. of History of Medicine and Allied Scis., 1948-65; editor Bull. of Cleve. Med. Library, 1954-72; editor newsletter Am. Assn. for History of Medicine, 1986—; contbr. articles in field to profl. jours. Am. Council Learned Socs. fellow, 1948-50; Dean Van Meter fellow, 1953-54. Alumna trustee Goucher Coll., Balt., 1966-69. Hon. fellow Cleve. Med. Library Assn.; mem. Am. Assn. for History of Medicine (pres. 1978-80, mem. council 1960-63), Am. Hist. Assn., Internat. Soc. for History of Medicine, Soc. Archtl. Historians, Phi Beta Kappa; corr. mem. fgn. socs. for history of medicine. Democrat. Home and Office: Judson Manor 1890 E 107 St Apt 816 Cleveland OH 44106

MILLER, GLORIA M., management consultant; b. Mercer County, Pa., Oct. 24, 1940; d. Cecil F. and Edith H. (Bittler) Gill; divorced; 1 son, Mark William. B.S. in Bus. Adminstrn., Youngstown (Ohio) State U., 1966. Sr. acct. Mort-Bohn Assos., C.P.A.s, Sharon, Pa., 1963-67; asst. controller Hynes Steel Products Co., Youngstown, 1967-70; exec. dir. Crawford County Community Action Agy., Meadville, Pa., 1970-73; planning and devel. dir. Multi-County Human Resources Corp., Meadville, 1973-76; adminstr., chief exec. officer Mercer County Consortium Services, Inc., Clark, Pa., 1976-83, NW Pa. Tng. Ptnrship. Consortium, Inc., 1983-85; owner, chief exec. officer G. M. Miller Assocs., 1985—, Mgmt. Devel. Ctr.; bd. dirs., regional rep. Nat. Assn. County Employment and Tng. Adminstrn., 1978-81; bd. dirs., sec. Mercer County Area Agy. Aging, 1976-82; v.p. Mid-Atlantic Manpower Profl. Assn., 1979-80; gen. adv. com. Mercer County Area Vocat. Tech. Sch., Mercer, 1979-85, Venango County Area Vocat. Tech. Sch., Oil City, Pa., 1981-85; bd. dirs. Greenville Area Econ. Devel. Corp., 1984—; mem. Greenville Bus. Incubator Oversight and Adv. Com., 1985—; treas., bd. dirs. Pa. Incubator Network Assn., 1985—. Recipient various certs. appreciation. Mem. Am. Mgmt. Assn., Am. Soc. Tng. and Devel., Pa. Assn. Service Delivery Area Adminstrs. (chmn. 1982-84). Presbyterian. Home: PO Box 171 12 N Main St Greenville PA 16125 Office: PO Box 171 12 N Diamond St Greenville PA 16125 also: 201 Power St New Castle PA 16102

MILLER, HARVEY ALFRED, educator; b. Sturgis, Mich., Oct. 19, 1928; s. Harry Clifton and Carmen (Sager) M.; m. Robin Bovard Huck, Jan. 25, 1980; children: Valerie Yvonne, Harry Alfred, Emily Luce Huck. B.S., U. Mich., 1950; M.S., U. Hawaii, 1952; Ph.D., Stanford U., 1957. Instr. botany U. Mass., 1955-56; instr. botany Miami U., 1956-57, asst. prof., 1957-61, assoc. prof., curator herbarium, 1961-67; prof., chmn. program in biology Wash. State U., 1967-69; vis. prof. botany U. Ill., 1969-70; prof., chmn. dept. biol. scis. Fla. Tech. U., 1970-75, prof., 1975—; v.p. Marine Research Assocs. Ltd., Nassau, 1962-65; assoc. Lotspeich & Assocs., natural systems analysts, Winter Park, Fla., 1979—; botanist U. Mich. Expdn. to Aleutian Islands, 1949-50; prin. investigator Systematic and Phytogeol. Studies Bryophytes of Pacific Islands, NSF, 1959, Miami U. Expdn. to Micronesia, 1960; dir. NSF-Miami U. Expdn. to Micronesia and Philippines, 1965; prin. investigator NSF bryophytes of So. Melanesia, 1983-86; research assoc. Orlando Sci. Ctr., Orlando; vis. prof. U. Guam, 1965; cons. tropical botany, foliage plant patents, also designs for sci. bldgs.; adj. prof. botany Miami U., 1985—. Author: (with H.O. Whittier and B.A. Whittier) Prodromus Florae Muscorum Polynesiae, 1978, Prodromus Florae Hepaticarum Polynesiae, 1983; editor: Florida Scientist, 1973-78; contbr. articles to sci. jours. Mem. exec. bd. and chmn. scholarship and grant selection com. Mercury Seven Found., 1985—. Recipient Acacia Order of Pythagoras; recipient Acacia Nat. award of Merit; Guggenheim fellow, 1958. Fellow AAAS, Linnean Soc. London; mem. Pacific Sci. Assn. (chmn. sci. com. for botany 1975-83), Assn. Tropical Biology, Council Biology Editors, Am. Inst. Biol. Scis., Am. Bryol. Soc. (v.p. 1962-63, pres. 1964-65), Brit. Bryol. Soc., Bot. Soc. Am., Electron. Microscopy Soc. Am., Internat. Assn. Plant Taxonomists, Internat. Assn. Bryologists, Mich. Acad. Sci. Arts and Letters, Hawaiian Acad. Sci., Am. Soc. Plant Taxonomists, Fla. Acad. Sci. (exec. sec. 1976-83, pres. 1980), Nordic Bryol. Soc., Acacia, Explorers Club, Sigma Xi, Phi Sigma, Beta Beta Beta. Home: Box 4413 Winter Park FL 32793 Office: U Central Fla Orlando FL 32816

MILLER, H(ARVEY) CRANE, lawyer; b. Manchester, Conn., May 21, 1935; s. Jacob F. and Mary Jane (Crane) M.; m. Jane Lincoln, June 15, 1957; children—Seth, Alden, Christopher, Caleb, Deborah. A.B., Williams Coll., 1957; LL.B., U. Va., 1960. Bar: Va. 1960, D.C. 1965. Atty. Dept. of Navy, Washington, 1960-65; asst. gen. counsel Smithsonian Instn., Washington, 1965-70; counsel com. on commerce U.S. Senate, Washington, 1970-72; sole practice, Washington, 1972-78, 82—; gen. counsel Sheaffer & Roland, Inc., Chgo., 1978-82; legal advisor Presdl. Commn. Marine Sci., Engring and Resources, 1968-70. Contbr. articles to profl. jours. Mem. Commn. on Ministry, Episc. Diocese of Washington, 1984—, chmn., 1986—; bd. dirs. several not-for-profit charitable and ednl. orgns. Mem. D.C. Bar Assn., Va. Bar Assn., Earthquake Engring. Research Inst., Nat. Acad. Scis. (mem. several panels and coms.). Democrat.

MILLER, HARVEY STOKES SHIPLEY, medical company executive; b. Phila., Sept. 28, 1948; s. Frank Leroy and Betty Charlotte (Elfont) M. B.A., Swarthmore Coll., 1970; J.D., Harvard U., 1973. Bar: N.Y. 1973. Assoc., Debevoise & Plimpton, N.Y.C., 1973-75; curator and dir. dept. collections and spl. exhbns. Franklin Inst., Phila., 1975-81; v.p. Energy Solutions, Inc., N.Y.C., 1982-84; pres., chief exec. officer, dir. Daltex Med. Scis., Inc., N.Y.C., 1983-86; chief operating officer, vice chmn., 1986—. Author: Milton Avery: Drawings and Paintings, 1976; It's About Time, 1979; author, editor New Spaces: Exploring the Aesthetic Dimensions of Holography, 1979. Mem. vis. com. on photography George Eastman House, Rochester,

N.Y., 1976-78; v.p. Milton and Sally Avery Arts Found., N.Y.C., 1983—; assoc. trustee U. Pa., 1981—; trustee Phila. Mus. Art, 1985—; bd. govs. Print Club, Phila., 1976-87; bd. overseers U. Pa. Sch. Nursing, 1981—, Edith C. Blum Art Inst. Bard Coll., 1984-87; bd. dirs., mem. corp. MacDowell Colony, N.Y.C., 1982-85; exec. bd. dirs. Fabric Workshop, Phila., 1976-86; mem. prints and drawings and photographs trustees adv. com. Phila. Mus. Art, 1974—, trustee, 1985—; bd. assocs. Swarthmore Coll. Libraries, Phila., 1978-86; treas. Arcadia Found., Norristown, Pa., 1981—; chmn. adv. bd. Inst. Contemporary Art U. Pa., 1982-84; trustee Phila. Coll. Art, 1978-86, Pa. Acad. Fine Arts, 1982—; trustee, vice chmn. Coms. on Instrn.; trustee N.Y. Studio Sch., 1974-80; mem. exec. bd. Citizens for Arts in Pa., 1980, Friends of Moore Coll., 1981-83; bd. dirs. Once Gallery, Inc., 1974-75; chmn. collections and exhibitions commn. Pa. Acad. Fine Arts, 1985-87; mem. Mayor's Cultural Adv. Council, Phila., 1987—. Recipient Noble award Swarthmore Coll., 1968. Mem. ABA, N.Y.C. Bar assn., Athenaeum, Library Co. Phila., Am. Philos. Soc., Hist. Soc. Pa., Phi Sigma Kappa. Republican. Clubs: Harvard, Union League, Rittenhouse (assoc.), Peale. Home: Moorhope Mathers Ln Fort Washington PA 19034 Office: Daltex Medi-Scis Inc 414 Eagle Rock Ave West Orange NJ 07052

MILLER, HERBERT DELL, petroleum engineer; b. Oklahoma City, Sept. 29, 1919; s. Merrill Dell and Susan (Green) M.; B.S. in Petroleum Engring., Okla. U., 1941; m. Rosalind Rebecca Moore, Nov. 23, 1947; children—Rebecca Miller Friedman, Robert Rexford. Field engr. Amerada Petroleum Corp., Houston, 1948-49, Hobbs, N.Mex., 1947-48, dist. engr., Longview, Tex., 1949-57, sr. engr., Tulsa, 1957-62; petroleum engr. Moore & Miller Oil Co., Oklahoma City, 1962-78; owner Herbert D. Miller Co., Oklahoma City, 1978—. Served to maj., F.A., AUS, 1941-47; ETO. Decorated Bronze Star with oak leaf cluster, Purple Heart (U.S.); Croix de Guerre (France). Registered profl. engr., Okla., Tex. Mem. AIME, Petroleum Club. Republican. Episcopalian (pres. Men's Club 1973). Clubs: Oklahoma City Golf, Country. Home: 6708 NW Grand Blvd Oklahoma City OK 73116 Office: 1236 First National Ctr W 120 N Robinson Oklahoma City OK 73102

MILLER, HOWARD, architect; b. Ft. Wayne, Ind., Mar. 18, 1944; s. Marcus and Ida (Henry) M.; m. Margot Hare, Nov. 25, 1977; 1 dau., Jessica. B.Arch., Miami U., Oxford, Ohio, 1968; M.S., Heriott-Watt U., Scotland, 1974. Registered architect. Estimator, William Duprey & Son, North Conway, N.H., 1977-78; project mgr. P. Mirski Architect, Laconia, N.H., 1978-79; designer W M Design Group, Center Harbor, N.H., 1979; assoc. S. Stokes Architect, Laconia, 1980-83; prin. Architects Plus, Ossipee, N.H., 1983, also treas. Mem. Zoning Bd., Laconia, 1981-83; Planning Bd., Conway, 1984—. Served to lt. USN, 1969-73. Recipient Henry Adams award, Miami U., 1968, cert. for Pub. Works Engring., USN, 1970. Mem. AIA. Democrat. Unitarian. Home: Winding Ln South Conway NH 03813 Office: Red Barn Complex Rt 16 Box 3182 North Conway NH 03860

MILLER, JACK EVERETT, lawyer; b. Monroe, La., Dec. 10, 1921; s. Herman M. and Sybil (Harrison) M.; m. Vivian G., May 13, 1945; m. 2d, Kathryn G., Dec. 23, 1970; children—Jack Everett, John A. Attended Ga. Inst. Tech., Gilbert Johnson Law Sch. Bar: U.S. Ct. Claims, U.S. Tax Ct., U.S. Ct. Mil. Appeals, U.S. Supreme Ct. Assoc. Lewis & Sullivan, Savannah, Ga., 1948-52; ptnr. Glass & Miller, Savannah, 1954-57; ptnr. Duffy, Miller & Duffy, Savannah, 1957-69; sole practice, Savannah, 1969—. Served with JAGC, USAF, 1952-54. Decorated Meritorious Service medal. Mem. Ga. Bar Assn., Am. Bus. Clubs (pres. 1959, dist. gov. 1964), Nat. Bus. Clubs. Home: 2 Stillwood Ct Savannah GA 31406 Office: 122 E Oglethorpe Ave Savannah GA 31401

MILLER, JAMES EDWARD, computer scientist, educator; b. Lafayette, La., Mar. 21, 1940; s. Edward Gustave and Orpha Marie (DeVilbis) M.; m. Diane Moon, June 6, 1964; children—Deborah Elaine, Michael Edward. B.S., U. La.-Lafayette, 1961, Ph.D., 1972; M.S., Auburn U., 1964. Systems engr. IBM, Birmingham, Ala., 1965-68; asst. prof. U. West Fla., Pensacola, 1968-70, chmn. systems sci., 1972-86; grad. researcher U. La.-Lafayette, 1970-72; computer systems analyst EPA, Washington, 1979; prof., chmn. computer sci. and stats. U. So. Miss., Hattiesburg, 1986—; program evaluator Computer Sci. Accreditation Commn., 1986—, cons., lectr. in field. Author numerous articles for tech. publs. Mem. Assn. Computing Machinery (editor Computer Sci. Edn. spl. interest group bull. 1982—), Data Processing Mgmt. Assn. (dir. edn. spl. interest group 1985-86). Democrat. Methodist. Lodge: Rotary. Avocations: Research on computer crime, computer sci. edn. Office: Univ of So Miss So Sta PO Box 5106 Hattiesburg MS 39406

MILLER, JEANNE-MARIE ANDERSON (MRS. NATHAN J.), educator, administrator; b. Washington, Feb. 18, 1937; d. William and Agnes Catherine (Johns) Anderson; B.A., Howard U., 1959, M.A., 1963, Ph.D., 1976; m. Nathan John Miller, Oct. 2, 1960. Instr. dept. English Howard U., Washington, 1963-76, asst. prof., 1976-79, assoc. prof., 1979—, also asst. dir. Inst. Arts and Humanities, 1973-75, asst. acad. planning office v.p. for Acad. Affairs, 1976—; cons. Am. Studies Assn., 1972-75, Silver Burdett Pub. Co., Nat. Endowment for Humanities, 1978—; adv. bd. D.C. Library for Arts, 1973—, John Oliver Killens Writers Guild, 1975—, Afro-Am. Theatre, Balt., 1975—. Mem. Washington Performing Arts Soc., 1971—, Friends of Sta. WETA-TV, 1971—, Mus. African Art, 1971—, Arena Stage Assos., 1972—, Washington Opera Guild, 1982—, Wolf Trap Assocs., 1982—, Ford Found. fellow, 1970-72; So. Fellowships Fund fellow, 1972-74; Howard U. research grantee, 1975-76; Am. Council Learned Socs. grantee, 1978-79; Nat. Endowment Humanities grantee, 1981-84. Mem. Nat. Council Tchrs. of English, Coll. English Assn., Am. Studies Assn., Am. Theatre Assn., AAUP, AAUW, D.C. LWV, Common Cause, ACLU, Am. Acad. Polit. and Social Sci., Coll. Lang. Assn., MLA, Am. Assn. Higher Edn., Nat. Assn. Women Deans, Adminstrs. and Counselors, Friends Kennedy Center for Performing Arts, Pi Lambda Theta. Democrat. Episcopalian. Editor, Black Theatre Bull., 1977—; Realism to Ritual: Form and Style in Black Theatre, 1983; asso. editor Theatre Jour., 1980-81; contbr. articles to profl. jours. Home: 1100 6th St SW Washington DC 20024

MILLER, JEFFREY HAROLD, designer; b. Wilkes-Barre, Pa., Aug. 27, 1942; s. Milton and Irma (Ganz) M.; children: Jacob Milton, Erin Fitzpatrick, Benjamin David Ganz, Jonathan Peter Desmond. BA, Pa. State U., 1964, postgrad., 1964-65, postgrad., Harvard U., 1965. Pres., Jeff Miller Assos., New Rochelle, N.Y., 1964-65, MG Assocs., Alexandria, Va., 1969-71, Hunter/Miller & Assocs., Design Cons., Alexandria, 1971—; mem. fed. portfolio rev. panel U.S. CSC; cons. Nat. Endowment for Arts; mem. Fed. Hwy. Adminstrn. Task Force on Transp. Graphics and Communications; mem. adv. panel Interior Design Mag. Mem. adv. bd. Va. Water Resources Research Ctr., Richmond, 1987. Served to lt. USN, 1965-69. Decorated Navy Achievement medal; recipient Design Rev. award Indsl. Design Mag., 1970, Achievement award Va. Travel Council, 1973. Mem. Fed. Design Council, Constrn. Specifications Inst., Washington Bd. Trade, Am. Craftsmen's Council, Design Giants Adv. Bd. Club: Belle Haven Country (Alexandria). Home: 410 Prince St Alexandria VA 22314 Office: Hunter/Miller and Assocs 225 N Fairfax St Alexandria VA 22314

MILLER, JOE LEON, manufacturing company executive; b. Lyons, Kans., May 23, 1931; s. William Alexander and Jenny Marie (Chapin) M.; m. Katheryn Patricia Brent, Nov. 16, 1966; children: Sean Peter, Timothy Alexander. B.A. in Econs. with honors, San Jose (Calif.) State U., 1958; M.B.A., U. Hartford, 1973. Dir. mgmt. info. systems Kaman Aerospace Corp., Bloomfield, Conn., 1967-74; with Aeronca, Inc., Charlotte, N.C., 1974—. Chmn. Aeronca Found. Served with USAF, 1951-54. Mem. Nat. Assn. Accts., Fin. Execs. Inst., Aerospace Industries Assn. Republican. Clubs: Union League (N.Y.C.); Carmel Country (Charlotte); Quail Hollow Country, Charlotte Tower. Home: 4413 St Ives Pl Charlotte NC 28211

MILLER, JOHN ANTON, financial and managment consultant; b. Monrovia, Calif., May 18, 1948; s. Anton George and Wilda Joyce (Reed) M.; m. Kathy Little, Dec. 23, 1973; children: Lisa, Michael. BA in Acctg., San Diego State U., 1970. CPA Calif., Tex. Audit mgr. Arthur Andersen & Co., San Diego, 1970-77; chief fin. officer Servco div. Smith Internat., Inc., Gardena, Calif., 1977-79; dir. fin. and ops. planning corp. hdqrs. Smith Internat., Inc., Newport Beach, Calif., 1979-85; v.p. bus. devel. Smith Drilling Systems div. Smith Internat., Houston, 1985—; prin. Miller-Newlin & Co. Bus. Cons., Houston, 1986—. Author mgmt. review and petroleum mgmt. mags. Chmn. accts. sect. United Way, 1976. Mem. Am. Inst. CPA's, Tex. Soc. CPA's, Soc. Petroleum Engrs., Am. Mgmt. Assn., Houston Bankruptcy Forum. Republican. Home: 67 Night Song Ct The Woodlands TX 77381 Office: 12941 I-45 North Suite 606 Houston TX 77060

MILLER, JOHN LEED, lawyer; b. Geneva, Ill., May 7, 1949; s. John Axel and Martha Mary (Masilunis) M. B.A., Northwestern U., 1971; J.D., U. Chgo., 1975. Bar: Ill. 1975. Assoc. counsel Profl. Ind. Mass-Mktg. Adminstrs., Chgo., 1975-76; legis. counsel to minority leader Ill. Ho. of Reps., Chgo. and Springfield (Ill.), 1977-80; chief legal counsel, 1980, chief counsel to speaker of Ho. of Reps., 1981-83; ptnr. Shaw and Miller, P.C., Chgo., 1981-84, Theodore A. Woerthwein, P.C., 1984-85, Woerthwein & Miller P.C., 1985—. Statewide chmn. Ill. Young Voters for the Pres., 1972; dir. Ill. Ho. Republican campaign com., 1976, 78, cons., 1982. Served with USNG, 1969-75. James scholar, 1970. Mem. ABA, Inter-Am. Bar Assn., Lawyers for the Creative Arts, Primitive Art Soc. Chgo. (treas. 1984-86, v.p. 1987—, pres. 1988—), Phi Eta Sigma, Phi Beta Kappa. Lutheran. Clubs: S.Am. Explorers (Lima, Peru), Elks (DeKalb, Ill.). Home: 1030 N State Apt 9D Chicago IL 60610 Office: Woerthwein & Miller 401 S LaSalle St Suite 1200 Chicago IL 60605

MILLER, JOHN T., JR., lawyer, educator; b. Waterbury, Conn., Aug. 10, 1922; s. John T. and Anna (Purdy) M.; m. Dorothy Shaen Dawe; children: Kent, Lauren, Clare, Miriam, Michael, Sheila, Lisa, Colin, Margaret. A.B. with high honors, Clark U., 1944; J.D., Georgetown U., 1948; Docteur en Droit, U. Geneva (Switzerland), 1951; postgrad. U. Paris, 1951. Bar: Conn. 1949, D.C. 1950, U.S. Ct. Appeals (3d cir.) 1958, U.S. Ct. Appeals (D.C. cir.) 1952, U.S. Ct. Appeals (5th cir.) 1957, U.S. Supreme Ct. 1952. With Econ. Cooperation Adminstrn., Am. embassy, London, 1950-51; assoc. Covington & Burling, 1952-53; Gallagher, Connor & Boland, 1953-62; sole practice, Washington, 1962—; adj. prof. law Georgetown U. Law Center, Washington, 1959—; mem. Panel on Future of Internat. Ct. Justice. Trustee Clark U., 1970-76; bd. advs. Georgetown Visitation Prep. Sch., 1972—; former fin. chmn. troop 46 Nat. Capital Area council Boy Scouts Am. Served with U.S. Army, 1943-46, to 1st lt. C.E., 1948-49. Recipient 10 yr. teaching award Nat. Jud. Coll., 1983. Mem. ABA (council mem., chmn. adminstrv. law sect.), D.C. Bar Assn., Fed. Energy Bar Assn. (v.p. 1988—), Internat. Bar Assn., Internat. Law Assn., AAUP. Republican. Roman Catholic. Clubs: International (Washington), Congressional Country (Bethesda, Md.). Co-author: Regulation of Trade, 1953, Modern American Antitrust Law, 1948, Major American Antitrust Laws, 1965; author: Foreign Trade in Gas and Electricity in North America: A Legal and Historical Study, 1970, Energy Problems and the Federal Government: Cases and Material, 1979, 2d edit. 1981; contbr. articles, book revs. to legal publs. Home: 4721 Rodman St NW Washington DC 20016 Office: 1001 Connecticut Ave NW Washington DC 20036

MILLER, JONATHAN WOLFE, theater and film director, physician; b. London, July 21, 1934; m. Helen Rachel Collet, 1956; 3 children. Ed. St. John's Coll., Cambridge U.; M.B., B.Ch., Univ. Coll. Hosp. Med. Sch., London; D.Litt. (hon.), U. Leicester, 1981; Dr. (hon.), Open U., 1983. Dir. Nottingham Playhouse, 1963-69; assoc. dir. Nat. Theatre, 1973-75; mem. Arts Council, 1975-76; vis. prof. drama Westfield Coll., U. London, 1977-78. Co-author, actor in Beyond the Fringe, 1961-64; dir. Under Plain Cover, Royal Ct. Theatre, 1962, The Old Glory, N.Y.C., 1964, Prometheus Bound, Yale Drama Sch., 1967, Oxford and Cambridge Shakespeare Co. prodn. of Twelfth Night, on tour in U.S., 1969; dir. for Nat. Tehatre, London: The Merchant of Venice, 1970, Danton's Death, 1971, The School for Scandal, 1972, The Marriage of Figaro, 1974; other prodns. include: The Tempest, London, 1970, Prometheus Bound, London, 1971, The Taming of the Shrew, Chichester, Eng., 1972, The Seagull, Chichester, 1973, The Malcontent, Nottingham, Eng., 1973, The Family in Love, Greenwich Season, 1974, (opera) Arden Must Die, 1974, The Importance of Being Earnest, 1975, The Cunning Little Vixen, 1975, All's Well That Ends Well, Measure For Measure, Greenwich Season, 1975, Three Sisters, 1977, The Marriage of Figaro at English Nat. Opera, 1978, (opera) Arabella, 1980, (opera) Falstaff, 1980, 81, (opera) Othello, 1982, (opera) Rigoletto, 1982, 84, (opera) Fidelio, 1982, 83; (Broadway play) Long Day's Journey into Night, 1986; films: Take a Girl Like You, 1969; TV films include: Whistle and I'll Come to You, 1967, Alice in Wonderland, 1967, The Body in Question series, 1978, Henry the Sixth, part one, 1983, States of Mind series, 1983; exec. producer Shakespeare TV series, 1979-81; author: The Body in Question, 1978. Decorated Order Brit. Empire; named dir. of Yr., Soc. West End Theatre Awards, 1976; recipient Silver medal Royal TV Soc., 1981; fellow Univ. Coll. London; hon. fellow St. John's Coll., Cambridge U.; research fellow in history of medicine Univ. Coll., London U., 1970-73. Address: 63 Gloucester Crescent, London NW1 England *

MILLER, JOSEPH IRWIN, automotive manufacturing company executive; b. Columbus, Ind., May 26, 1909; s. Hugh Thomas and Nettie Irwin (Sweeney) M.; m. Xenia Ruth Simons, Feb. 5, 1943; children: Margaret Irwin, Catherine Gibbs, Elizabeth Ann Garr, Hugh Thomas, II, William Irwin. Grad., Taft Sch., 1927; A.B., Yale U., 1931, M.A. (hon.), 1959, L.H.D. (hon.), 1979; M.A., Oxford (Eng.) U., 1933; LL.D., Bethany Coll., 1956, Tex. Christian U., Ind. U., 1958, Oberlin Coll., Princeton, 1962, Hamilton Coll., 1964, Columbia, 1968, Mich. State U., 1968, Dartmouth, 1971, U. Notre Dame, 1972, Ball State U., 1972, Lynchburg Coll., 1985; L.H.D. (hon.), Case Inst. Tech., 1966, U. Dubuque, 1977; Hum.D., Manchester U., 1973, Moravian Coll., 1976. Asso. Cummins Engine Co., Inc., Columbus, Ind., 1934—; v.p., gen. mgr. Cummins Engine Co., Inc., 1934-42, exec. v.p., 1944-47, pres., 1947-51, chmn. bd., 1951-77, chmn. exec. and fin. com., 1977—; pres. Irwin-Union Bank & Trust Co., 1947-54, dir., 1937—, chmn., 1954-75; chmn. exec. com. Irwin Union Corp., 1976—; mem. Commn. Money and Credit, 1958-61, Pres.'s Com. Postal Reorgn., 1968, Pres.'s Com. Urban Housing, 1968; chmn. Pres.'s Com. on Trade Relations with Soviet Union and Eastern European Nations, 1965, Nat. Adv. Commn. on Health Manpower, 1966; vice chmn. UN Commn. on Multinat. Corps., 1974; adv. council U.S. Dept. Commerce, 1976; mem. Study Commn. on U.S. Policy Toward So. Africa, 1979-81. Pres. Nat. Council Chs. of Christ in U.S.A., 1960-63; trustee Nat. Humanities Ctr.; mem. central and exec. coms. World Council Chs., 1961-68; trustee Ford Found., 1961-79, Yale Corp., 1959-77, Urban Inst., 1966-76, Mayo Found., 1977-82; fellow Branford Coll. Served to lt. USNR, 1942-44. Recipient Rosenberger award U. Chgo., 1977, 1st MacDowell Colony award, 1981; hon. fellow Balliol Coll., Oxford (Eng.) U.; Benjamin Franklin fellow Royal Soc. Arts. Fellow Am. Acad. Arts and Scis.; mem. Am. Philos. Soc., AIA (hon.), Ind. Acad., Bus. Council, Conf. Bd. (sr.), Phi Beta Kappa, Beta Gamma Sigma. Mem. Christian Ch. (Disciples of Christ) (elder). Clubs: Yale, Century, Links (N.Y.C.); Chicago; Indpls. Athletic, Columbia (Indpls.). Office: Cummins Engine Co Inc 500 Jackson St Box 3005 Columbus IN 47202

MILLER, KARL A, management counselor; b. Reading, Pa., Feb. 27, 1931; s. Harvey and Kathleen Schwartz (Bechtel) M.; B.S. Indsl. Engring, Pa. State U., 1953; M.S. Indsl. Mgmt., M.I.T., 1963; m. Carol Joann Mickle, July 28, 1956; children—Dawn Alison, Kevin Bryan. Bus. mgr. Gen. Electric Co., Evendale, Ohio, 1953-55, Lynn, Mass., 1956-63; asst. to pres. Burn & Roe, N.Y.C., 1964-65; cons. George Armstrong Co., N.Y.C., 1966-68; sr. cons. H.B. Maynard Co., N.Y.C., 1968-70; mng. partner Kamid Assocs., mgmt. cons. to newspapers, electronic media, agribus., govt., architects, engrs., constrn., mfg. and health care delivery firms, Yonkers, N.Y., 1971—; owner David Goliath Ltd.; arbitrator Better Bus. Bur. of N.Y.C., 1982-84; lectr. fin. profitability and mktg. Bucknell U., Pa., Mercy Coll., N.Y., Dominican Coll., Blauvelt, N.Y., 1981-82; speaker in field. Pres. men's brotherhood Collegiate Ch. of N.Y.C., 1970-72; pres. Westchestertowne Houses Condominium, Yonkers, 1971-76, Council of Condominiums of N.Y. State, 1972-76; commr. of deeds City of Yonkers, 1976, chmn. citizens' budget adv. com., 1975-76. Recipient Speak Up award Peabody (Mass.) Jr. C. of C., 1960, Minuteman citation, 1960. Mem. Yonkers C. of C. (pres.'s. club 1975-78), M.I.T. Alumni Center N.Y.C. (gov. 1970-81), Air Force Assn., U.S. Naval Inst., Friends of Hist. Hudson Valley, Triangle Frat., Sigma Tau. Republican. Mem. Protestant Dutch Reformed Ch. Author: The Farm Machinery Market, 1973; also articles. Editor: Jet Engine Newsletter, 1955-56. Home: 412-21 N Broadway Yonkers NY 10701 Home: 546 S Richard St Bedford PA 15522 Office: PO Box 63 Yonkers NY 10703

MILLER, KENNETH EDWARD, mechanical engineer, consultant; b. Weymouth, Mass., Dec. 24, 1951; s. Edward Francis and Lena Joan (Trotta) M.; m. Florence Gay Wilson, Sept. 18, 1976; children: Nicole Elizabeth, Brent Edward. BSME, Northeastern U., 1974; MS in Systems Mgmt., U. So. Calif., 1982. Registered profl. engr., N.Y., N.H., Ariz., Nev.; registered land surveyor, Ariz. Test engr. Stone & Webster Engring., Boston, 1974-76; plant engr. N.Y. State Power Authority, Buchanan, 1976-80; maintenance engr. Pub. Service Co. of N.H., Seabrook, 1980-82; cons. engr. Helios Engring. Inc., Litchfield Park, Ariz., 1982-87; sr. supervisory service engr. Quadrex Corp., Coraopolis, Penn., 1987—. Republican. Roman Catholic. Home and Office: 131 W Elm St Pembroke MA 02359

MILLER, L. MARTIN, accountant, financial planning specialist; b. N.Y.C., Sept. 17, 1939; s. Harvey and Julia (Lewis) M.; m. Judith Sklar, Jan. 21, 1962; children—Philip, Marjorie. B.S., Wharton Sch., U. Pa., 1960. C.P.A.; accredited fin. planning specialist. Jr. acct. Deloitte, Haskins & Sells, N.Y.C., 1960-62, sr. acct., Phila., 1962-64; mng. partner Cogen, Sklar, Levick & Co., Phila., 1964—; treas. Coronet Container Co., Inc., Phila., Val Mar Realty Corp., N.Y.C.; dir. Penn Internat. Trading Co., Phila., 1964—; mng. dir. C.P.A. Tax Forum, 1966-69; underwriting mem. Lloyds of London, 1978—; lectr., discussion leader on fin. and taxation; columnist Montgomery and Bucks County Dental News. Mem. Phila. Rep. com., 1963-67; chmn. Lower Merion Twp. scholarship fund, 1975-78; bd. dirs. Penn Valley Civic Assn., 1973-79; mem. Lower Merion Planning Commn., 1978-82; mem. Gov.'s Tax Study Commn.; pres. Mensa Edn. and Research Found., 1984-86 ; mem. SEC Forum on Small Bus. Capital Formation, 1983; apptd. to Pa. State Bd. Accountancy, 1985-89. Served with U.S. Army, 1961-62. Recipient Outstanding Achievement award Germantown Civic Assn., 1965. Mem. Pa. Inst. C.P.A.s (edn. com. 1975-78, bd. dirs. 1979-81, by-laws chmn. 1980-83), Nat. Assn. State Bds. Accountancy (edn. com. 1987—), Am. Inst. C.P.A.s (nat. tax commn. 1979-82, exec. com. self regulation div. for C.P.A. firms, acctg. and rev. services com. 1985—), Little 10 Acctg. Assn. (edn. chmn. 1980-84), Mensa (internat. fin. officer 1970-74), Beta Alpha Psi. Clubs: Masons (past master) Plays and Players (treas. 1978-79). Author: Accountants Guide to S.E.C. Filings, 1968; contbr. articles to profl. jours. Home: 204 Dove Ln Haverford PA 19041 Office: Cogen Sklar & Levick 225 City Line Ave Philadelphia PA 19004

MILLER, LARRY THOMAS, accountant; b. Omaha, Oct. 24, 1940; s. Elmer Thomas and Lucile Valentine (Hammon) M. Student U. Omaha, 1958-63. With accounting dept. Union Pacific R.R. Co., Omaha, 1959—, tax acct., 1969—. Mem. nat. adv. bd. Am. Security Council. Served with U.S. Army, M.P., 1965-67. Mem. Am. Acctg. Assn. Republican. Office: Union Pacific RR 1416 Dodge Omaha NE 68179

MILLER, MARY JEANNETTE, office management specialist; b. Washington, Sept. 24, 1912; d. John William and David Evengeline (Hill) Sims; m. Cecil Miller, June 17, 1934 (dec.); children—Sylvenia Delores Doby, Ferdi A., Cecil Jr. Student Howard U., 1929-30, U. Ill., 1940-42, Dept. Agr. Grad. Sch., 1957-59, U. Md., 1975; cert. in Vocat. Photography, Prince George's Community Coll., 1986. Chief mail processing unit Bur. Reclamation, Washington, 1940-57; records supr. AID, Manila, Korea, Mali, Guyana, Dominican Republic, Indonesia, Laos, 1957-71; office engr. Bechtel Assos., Washington, 1976-79; real estate asso; tchr. English as 2d lang. Ministry of Edn., Seoul, Korea, 1960-61, Ministry of Fin., Laos, 1968-70; cons. to Ministry of Fin. Royal Lao Govt., 1971-74; cons. AID missions to Yemen, Sudan, Somalia, 1982; records mgmt. cons. AID, Monrovia, Liberia, 1980-81, Sri Lanka, 1984; docent Mus. African Art Smithsonian Inst., Washington, 1986—. Author handbooks on office mgmt. Mem. Mayor's Internat. Adv. Council. Mem. Soc. Am. Archivists, Am. Mgmt. Assn., Montgomery County Bd. Realtors, Am. Fgn. Service Assn., Nat. Trust Hist. Preservation, Zeta Phi Beta. Roman Catholic. Home and Office: 1008 Avery Pl Largo MD 20772

MILLER, MILTON ALLEN, lawyer; b. Los Angeles, Jan. 15, 1954; s. Samuel C. and Sylvia Mary Jane (Silver) M. AB with distinction and honors in Econs., Stanford U., 1976; JD with honors, Harvard U., 1979. Bar: Calif. 1979, U.S. Ct. Appeals (9th cir.) 1979, U.S. Dist. Ct. (cen., no. and so. dists.) Calif. Law clk. U.S. Ct. Appeals (9th cir.), Sacramento, 1979-80; assoc. firm Latham & Watkins, Los Angeles, 1979-86, ptnr., 1986—. Articles editor Harvard Law Rev., 1978-79. Mem. Am. Cancer Soc., Los Angeles. Mem. ABA, Calif. State Bar Assn. (com. on profl. responsibility), Los Angeles County Bar Assn. (profl. responsibility and ethics com.), Assn. Trial Lawyers Am., Phi Beta Kappa. Home: 1674 Clear View Dr Beverly Hills CA 90210 Office: Latham & Watkins 555 S Flower St Los Angeles CA 90071

MILLER, NANCY ELLEN, health care administrator; b. Long Beach, N.Y., Aug. 20, 1947; d. Jerome H. and Kathy P. M. BA, NYU, 1969; MA, Harvard U., 1970; PhD, U. Chgo., 1978; cert. Washington Sch. Psychiatry, 1981; postgrad. Washington Psychoanalytic Inst., 1981—. Clin. psychologist City of Chgo. Dept. Mental Health, 1971-77; research asst. dept. psychiatry U. Chgo., 1972-75, research asso., 1975-77; exec. sec. Sci. Rev. Group NIMH, 1977-79, chief clin. research program Center for Studies of Mental Health Aging, 1977-86, chief clin. research program Mental Disorders Aging Research Br., 1986—; instr. clin. geriatric psychiatry Georgetown U. Sch. Medicine; clin. faculty psychiatry dept., Navy Med. Command, Nat. Capital Region; adj. assoc. prof. dept. psychiatry Uniformed Services U. Health Scis.; del. White House Conf. on Aging, 1981. Author: (with Gene Cohen) Clinical Aspects of Alzheimer's Disease and Senile Dementia, 1981, Schizophrenia and Aging: Schizophrenia, Paranoia and Schizophreniform Disorders in Late Life, 1987, (with E. Erlenmeyer-Kimling) Life-Span Research on the Prediction of Psychopathology, 1986; mem. editorial bd. Jour. Ednl. Gerontology, 1976-80, Neurobiology of Aging, 1980-86, Profl. Psychology, 1980—, Psychoanalytic Psychology, 1983-88, Clin. Gerontologist, 1983—, Am. Jour. Orthopsychiatry, 1985—; contbr. numerous articles in field. USPHS fellow, 1972-76; HEW fellow, 1975-77; recipient Alcohol, Drug Abuse and Mental Health Adminstrn. Honor award, U.S. Pub. Health Service Spl. Recognition award. Mem. AAAS, Am. Orthopsychiat. Assn., Am. Psychoanalytic Assn., Am. Psychol. Assn., Boston Soc. Gerontologic Psychiatry, D.C. Psychol. Assn., Washington Psychoanalytic Soc., Gerontol. Soc. Am., Internat. Assn. Gerontology, Internat. Brain Research Orgn., Internat. Neuropsychol. Soc., Internat. Psychogeriatric Assn., Soc. Neurosci., Soc. Psychotherapy Research, Phi Delta Kappa, Pi Lambda Theta. Home: 9 Logan Circle NW Washington DC 20005 Office: NIMH Mental Disorders Aging Research Branch Rm #11-C-03 Rockville MD 20857

MILLER, PATRICK MICHAEL, research and development company executive; b. Maple City, Mich., June 2, 1936; s. William Aloysius and Evelyn Nesbit (Svoboda) M.; B.S., Mich. State U., 1957; M.S., 1960, Ph.D., 1966; m. Dolores Anne Osterman, Dec. 28, 1957; children—Mary, Brenda, Suzanne, P. Michael. Tchr. math. high sch., East Lansing, Mich., 1957-60; research engr. Ford Motor Co., Dearborn, Mich., 1960-62; asst. dir. edn. Soc. Mfg. Engrs., Dearborn, Mich., 1962-63; instr. engring. mechanics Mich. State U., East Lansing, 1963-66; asst. head dept. Calspan Corp. (formerly Cornell Aero. Lab.), Buffalo, 1966-77; pres. MGA Research Corp., 1977—; lectr., cons. in field; witness before congl. coms., govt. task forces on automotive transp.; former mem. transp. adv. com. Fed. Energy Adminstrn. Mem. ASME, Soc. Automotive Engrs., Phi Kappa Phi, Sigma Xi. Roman Catholic. Home: 910 Virginia Dr Alden NY 14004 Office: 12790 Main Rd PO Box 71 Akron NY 14001

MILLER, PAUL ALBERT, diversified holding company executive; b. San Francisco, Oct. 30, 1924; s. Robert W. and Elizabeth (Folger) M.; children: Robert L., Charles B., Christian F., Gordon E., Alejandro C., Juan J. BA, Harvard U., 1946. Staff aide So. Calif. Gas Co., Los Angeles, 1948-52; treas., dir. Pacific Enterprises, San Francisco, 1952-58; v.p., treas. Pacific Lighting Corp., San Francisco, 1958-66, exec. v.p., 1966-68, pres., chief exec. officer, 1968-72, chmn. bd., chief exec. officer, 1972—; bd. dirs. Wells Fargo & Co., Wells Fargo Bank, Newhall Mgmt. Corp.; trustee Mut. Life Ins. Co. N.Y. Bd. dirs. Civic Light Opera Assn., Los Angeles World Affairs Council, United Way, Los Angeles, Calif. Bus. Roundtable ; trustee Am. Enterprise Inst., Washington, U. So. Calif.; dir. John Douglas French Found. for Alzheimer's Disease. Served with U.S. Army, 1943-46. Mem. Calif. C. of C. (bd. dirs.). Clubs: Pacific Union, Bohemian (San Francisco); Brook, Racquet and Tennis (N.Y.C.); The Regency; Regency Whist. London, Portland; White's. Office: Pacific Enterprises 801 S Grand St Los Angeles CA 90017

MILLER, PETER PUTNAM, lawyer; b. N.Y.C., May 11, 1938; s. Robert Floyd and Dolores Madeleine (Putnam) M.; m. Gloria Jean Everson, July 26, 1968; children: Jonathan Putnam, Kristen Iversen. BA, Yale U., 1960; JD, Stanford U., 1968. Bar: N.Y. 1969. Assoc. Sullivan & Cromwell, N.Y.C., 1968-74; counsel Mobil Oil Corp., N.Y.C., 1974; counsel Mobil Producing NW Europe div. Mobil Oil Corp., London, 1974-76; gen. counsel Exploration Norway div. Mobil Oil Corp., Stavanger, 1976-79; gen. counsel Mobil Oil Indonesia div. Mobil Oil Corp., Jakarta, 1979-83; asst. gen. counsel E & D div. Mobil Oil Corp., N.Y.C., 1983-87; sr. counsel Mktg. and Refining div. Mobil Oil Corp., N.Y.C., 1987—; lectr. numerous internat. bar assn. seminars; co-founder Indonesian Assn. Petroleum Lawyers, 1982-83. Cubmaster Cub Scouts Am., Jakarta, 1980-83, Darien, Conn., 1984-86, Weston, Conn., 1986—. Served to capt. U.S. Army, 1962-67, Vietnam. Recipient Dist. Award of Merit, Boy Scouts Am., Jakarta, 1983. Mem. ABA, Internat. Bar Assn. (officer oil and gas com. energy law sect. 1986—). Episcopalian. Home: 10 Cedar Ln Weston CT 06883 Office: Mobil Oil Corp 150 E 42d St New York NY 10017

MILLER, RICHARD JEROME, banker; b. Erie, Pa., May 8, 1939; s. Richard A. and Irene (Strahl) M.; children by previous marriage—E. Scott, Lisa Ann, Sondra Lynn; m. Suzanne Marie Johnson, Oct. 22, 1983. B.S., Lehigh U., 1961; M.A., New Sch. N.Y.C., 1964; postgrad. NYU, 1964-68. With Chase Manhattan Bank, N.Y.C., 1961-82, v.p., 1974-82; v.p. E.F. Hutton Credit Corp./Chrysler Capital Corp., Greenwich, Conn., 1982-88, Mfrs. Hanover Trust Co., N.Y.C., 1988—. Mem. Waldwick Bd. Edn., N.J., 1968-72, v.p., 1971-72. Mem. Am. Econ. Assn., Western Fin. Assn. Democrat. Roman Catholic. Club: NYU (N.Y.C.). Home: The Columbia 2E 275 W 96th St New York NY 10025 Office: Mfrs Hanover Trust Co 270 Park Ave New York NY 10017

MILLER, RICHARDS THORN, naval architect, engineer; b. Jenkintown, Pa., Jan. 31, 1918; s. Herman Geistweit and Helen Buckman (Thorn) M.; B.S. in Naval Architecture and Marine Engring., Webb Inst. Naval Architecture, 1940; Naval Engr., MIT, 1951; m. Jean Corbat Spear, Sept. 13, 1941; (dec.); children—Patricia (Mrs. Charles G. Fishburn), Linda (Mrs. John X. Carrier); m. 2d, Alice Johnson Houghton, May 19, 1984. Commd. ensign U.S. Navy, 1940, advanced through grades to capt., 1960; specialized work design oceanographic research ships, mine sweepers, torpedo boats, destroyers; ret., 1968; mgr. ocean engring. Oceanic div. Westinghouse Electric Corp., 1969-75, adv. engr., 1975-79; cons. naval architect and engr., 1968—; mem. com. naval architecture Am. Bur. Shipping, 1960-63, mem. tech. com., 1978—, mem. ship structure com., 1966-68. Decorated Navy Legion of Merit; recipient William Selkirk Owen award, 1983. Fellow Soc. Naval Architects and Marine Engrs. (chmn. S.E. sect. 1965-66, chmn. marine systems com. 1970-77, chmn. tech. and research steering com. 1977-78, chmn. small craft com. 1983-87, v.p. tech. and research 1979-81, hon. v.p. (life), 1981—, mem. council 1976—, mem. exec. com. 1977-81; Capt. Joseph H. Linnard prize 1964); mem. Am. Soc. Naval Engrs. (mem. council 1976-78), U.S. Naval Inst., Sigma Xi. Clubs: N.Y. Yacht (N.Y.C.), Annapolis Yacht, Sailing of the Chesapeake. Author: (with R.G. Henry) Sailing Yacht Design, 1963; also sects. in books, articles. Home and Office: 957 Melvin Rd Annapolis MD 21403

MILLER, ROBERT ERIC, construction executive; b. Jacksonville, Fla., May 4, 1919; s. Robert E. and Uldene (Sheppard) M.; m. Katharine Connell, Nov. 6, 1971 (dec. 1977); children—Marsha Helen, Robert Eric, Deborah Paull, Andrew Hines; m. Lilyan James Privott, Jan. 29, 1978. Student U. Ga., 1936-39. Mgr. personnel and labor relations H.K. Ferguson Co., Cleve., 1941-56; v.p. Bechtel Corp., San Francisco, 1956-80; pres., dir. Pacific Internat. Computing Corp., 1973-75, pres., dir. Fluor Constructors Inc., 1980-85; chmn., chief exec. officer, dir. Miller-Kerr Inc., Houston, 1985—, Orfatex, Inc.; bd. dirs. ORFA Corp. of Am.; mem. services adv. com. to U.S. trade rep., 1980—. Contbr. articles to profl. jours. Bd. dirs. Industry dn. Council Calif., 1974-75; trustee Golden Gate U. San Francisco, 1974-75, San Francisco Met. YMCA, 1969-71, Am. Sch. in London, 1965-67. Mem. Assoc. Gen. Contractors Am. (past v.p. Cleve.), Nat. Constructors Assn. (pres. Washington 1972). Episcopalian. Clubs: Meadow (Fairfax, Calif.); Olympic (San Francisco); Brae-Burn Country (Houston); 1925 F St., Univ., George Town (Washington) Columbia Country (Chevy Chase, Md.); Saint Simons Island (Ga.). Home: 3 Riverway Suite 900 Houston TX 77056 Office: 3 Riverway Suite 1570 Houston TX 77056

MILLER, ROBERT FARNHAM, political scientist; b. Boston, Dec. 10, 1932; arrived in Australia, 1973; s. Harry Leonard and Lilyon (Waratt) M.; m. Mary Ellen Driggers, July 25, 1958; children: Juliet Olivia, Katherine Elizabeth. AB, U. Mich., 1957; AM, Harvard U., 1959, PhD, 1965. Asst. prof. Washington U., St. Louis, 1964-67, SUNY, Stony Brook, 1967-69; assoc. prof. U. Ill., Urbana, 1969-73; fellow in polit. sci. Australian Nat. U., Canberra, 1973-75, sr. fellow in polit. sci., 1975—. Author: 100,000 Tractors, 1970; co-editor Khrushchev and the Communist World, 1984, Gorbachev at the Helm, 1987; contbr. articles to profl. jours. Woodrow Wilson Found. fellow, 1957. Mem. Am. Assn. for Advancement of Slavic Studies, Australasian Assn. for Study of Socialist Countries (pres. 1985-88), Australasian Polit. Studies Assn. Jewish. Lodge: B'nai B'rith. Home: 10 Miller St, 2601 O'Connor Australia

MILLER, ROBERT HYLAND, optical physicist; b. Balt.; s. Theodore Hyland and Emma Louise (Kahmer) M.; B.A. in Physics, Johns Hopkins U., 1962; M.S., Stevens Inst. Tech., N.J., 1968. Supr. lab. Keuffel & Esser Co., Morristown, N.J., 1962-72; tech. dir. Valtec Corp., Holliston, Mass., 1972-77; sr. research scientist Optical Coating Lab., Inc., 1977-80; sr. optical physicist Nanometrics, Sunnyvale, Calif., 1980-81; pres. Stanford Tech. Assoc., Santa Rosa, Calif., 1981-84; process devel. physicist 3M Co. (optical recording), Mountain View, Calif., 1984—; cons. to cos. including LTV Corp., Allied Corp., Teledyne, and Siemens. Recipient Hon. Sci. award Bausch & Lomb, 1956. Mem. Optical Soc. Am., Am. Vacuum Soc., Materials Research Soc., Soc. Photo-Optical Instrumentation Engrs., IEEE, Mus. Soc. San Francisco. Home: 1816 Arroyo Sierra Ct Santa Rosa CA 95405 Office: 420 Bernardo Ave Mountain View CA 94043

MILLER, ROBERT SCOTT, not-for-profit organization administrator, social worker; b. Seattle, Dec. 12, 1947; s. Bert Lester and Carol Theresa (Gustafson) M.; m. Karen Ann Staake, Nov. 12, 1977; children: Sarah, Megan, Emily. BA in Sociology, Seattle Pacific U., 1970; AM in Social Work, U. Chgo., 1972; MA in Human Resources Mgmt., Pepperdine U., 1977. Registered counselor, Wash. Br. supr. Wash. State Dept. Social and Health Services, Oak Harbor and Anacortes, 1975-78; supr. casework Everett, 1973-75; lectr., coordinator rural community mental health project U. Wash., Seattle, 1978-83; exec. dir. Armed Services YMCA, Oak Harbor, 1984-86; area dir. United Way of Island County, Oak Harbor, 1986-88, exec. dir., 1988—; part-time instr. Chapman Coll., Orange, Calif., 1988—. Contbr. articles to profl. jours. Recipient outstanding service award Armed Services YMCA of U.S., Dallas, 1985, two program merit awards McDonald's Corp., Oak Harbor, 1986. Mem. Nat. Assn. Social Workers (cert., bd. dirs. Wash. chpt. 1982-85), Wash. Assn. Social Welfare (pres. 1975-76), Bus. and Profl. Women (v.p. Oak Harbor chpt. 1985-86, pres. 1986-87), Internat. Platform Assn., Navy League. Lutheran. Lodge: Lions (sec. North Whidbey chpt. 1987-88, v.p. 1988—). Home: 2450 S Rocky Way Coupeville WA 98239 Office: United Way of Island County Navy Family Service Ctr Seaplane Base Bldg 20 PO Box 798 Oak Harbor WA 98277

MILLER, ROBERT STEVENS, JR., automobile manufacturing company executive; b. Portland, Oreg., Nov. 4, 1941; s. Robert Stevens and Barbara (Weston) M.; m. Margaret Rose Kyger, Nov. 9, 1966; children—Christopher John, Robert Stevens, Alexander Lamont. A.B. with distinction, Stanford U., 1963; LL.B., Harvard U., 1966; M.B.A., Stanford U., 1968. Bar: Calif. bar 1966. Fin. analyst Ford Motor Co., Dearborn, Mich., 1968-71; spl. studies mgr. Ford Motor Co., Mexico City, 1971-73; dir. fin. Ford Asia-Pacific, Inc., Melbourne, Australia, 1974-77, Ford Motor Co., Caracas, Venezuela, 1977-79; v.p., treas. Chrysler Corp., Detroit, 1980-81, exec. v.p. fin., 1981-85, vice chmn. bd., 1985—; dir. Moore-Oregon Lumber Co., Coos Bay, Oreg. Bd. dirs. United Found., Detroit. Mem. Calif. Bar Assn.

MILLER, ROBERT WARBURTON, psychologist, consultant; b. Bellefonte, Pa., Nov. 23, 1921; s. Joseph Frederick and Mary (Warburton) M.; A.B., Pa. State U., 1942; M.A., Redlands U., 1951; Ph.D., U. So. Calif., 1957; J.D., Loma Linda Coll. Law, 1983; m. Joyce Larayne Maxey, Mar. 24, 1946; children—Pamela Joyce Larayne, Robert Brent Warburton, Page Layne Warburton. Grad. mgr. Asso. Student Body, San Bernardino Valley Coll., 1946-51; lectr. U. So. Calif., Los Angeles, 1956-57; pvt. practice psychology and speech pathology, San Bernardino, Calif., 1954—; staff clin. psychologist San Bernardino County Gen. Hosp., 1968-75; dir. Mojave Valley Mental Health Services, 1970-72; cons. Grand Terrace Convalescent Hosp., 1965—, Citrus Care Convalescent Hosp., 1968—; lectr., U. Redlands, 1958-59, Loma Linda U., 1963; adj. prof. Eastern Wash. State U., 1974—; instr. U. So. Calif. Inst. Safety and Systems Mgmt., 1984; adj. prof. Chapman Coll., 1986; mem. Calif. Licensing Com. for Speech Pathologists, 1959-61; mem. psychol. exam. com. Calif. Bd. Med. Examiners, 1970-74, chmn. subcom. legislation, 1971-73, chmn. subcom. statistics and evaluations, 1972-74; owner, supr. Tao-Teh-King Farms, 1953—; owner, adminstr. Warburton Profl. Office Bldgs., 1959-71; chmn. bd. dirs. San Bernardino and Riverside Counties Investment Corp., 1958-70; pres., dir. Colton Profl. Bldg., Inc.; pres. Avora Corp., 1973—; dir. E. Pioneer Water Co., 1972—, v.p., 1974-80, pres., 1980—; adj. prof. communications and applied psychology U. So. Calif., Eastern Wash. U. Dep. sheriff San Bernardino County, 1961-68; troop com. chmn. San Bernardino Boy Scouts Am., 1964-65; mem. fruit rack com. Nat. Orange Show, 1957-64; adv. bd. San Bernardino Area Mental Health Assn., 1965, chmn. speakers bur., 1964-66; bd. dirs. San Bernardino Goodwill Industries, 1963—, exec. com. Inland Counties, 1965-71, pres., 1968-70, hon. mem. bd., 1972; v.p., then pres. bd. dirs., trustee San Bernardino chpt. City of Hope Hosp.; mem. community redevel. citizens adv. com., 2d ward rep., 1978-84; bd. dirs. metro bd. YMCA, 1986—. Served to lt. USNR, 1942-46, to lt. comdr., 1951-53; capt. Res. Recipient George Washington medal Freedoms Found. at Valley Forge, 1970, 72, 73; Disting. Pub. Service award Inlands So. Calif. Psychol. Assn., 1976. Fellow Am. Assn. Marriage Counselors; mem. Calif., Inland (pres. 1973-74) psychol. assns., U. Redlands Fellows, Soc. Am. Mil. Engrs., San Bernardino Civic Light Opera Assn., S.A.R. (chpt. v.p. 1965-66, state pres. 1967-69, nat. trustee 1970-71, v.p. gen. 1971-73, nat. exec. com. 1972-76, nat. sec. gen. 1974-76, chmn. nat. soc. 1976-77), Nat. Congress Parents and Tchrs., Naval Res. Officers Assn. (pres. Arrowhead chpt. 1973-74), San Bernardino C. of C. (dir. 1975—), Navy League of the U.S. (pres. San Bernardino council 1980-87), Pi Lambda Sigma, Kappa Sigma, Tau Kappa Alpha. Methodist. Clubs: Carriage (pres. 1965-67, dir.), Wilsonian (San Bernardino), Masons. Author: (with Joyce L. Miller) Dealing With The Behavioral Problems In The Elementary School, 1968, A Therapy Guide For The Families of Adult Aphasics, 1972. Contbr. articles to profl. jours. Office: Warburton House 6836 Palm Ave Highland CA 92346

MILLER, RUSSELL TUTTLE, realtor; b. Spokane, Dec. 10, 1922; s. Russell Tuttle and Claudia (Lewis) M.; B.S., Mass. Inst. Tech., 1948; postgrad. Colo. Sch. Mines, 1950; m. Georgette Thioliere, Apr. 17, 1948. Pres., Golden West Enterprises, Cambridge, Mass., 1939-48;pres., New World Exploration Corp., Los Angeles, 1948-56; cons. mineral engring., Los Angeles, 1956-58; pres. Tech. Mktg. Assos., Los Angeles, 1959-73; pres. Titan Realty Corp., Los Angeles, 1959—, Worldwide Properties, Ltd., Newport Beach, Calif., 1976—, Sepol, Ltd., Irvine, Calif., 1976—, Internat. Fin. Cons., Newport Beach, Calif., 1972—. Served in U.S. Army, 1942-45. Decorated Purple Heart. Mem. Am. Inst. Mining and Metall. Engrs., Am. Inst. Mining Engrs., Am. Inst. Chem. Engrs., Soc. Exploration Geophysicists. Episcopalian. Clubs: Calif. Yacht, Riviera Country, Marina City, Balboa Bay. Home and Office: 5 Tanglewood Irvine CA 92714

MILLER, SHELBY ALEXANDER, chemical engineer, educator; b. Louisville, July 9, 1914; s. George Walter and Stella Katherine (Cralle) M.; m. Jean Adele Danielson, Dec. 26, 1939 (div. May 1948); 1 son, Shelby Carlton; m. Doreen Adare Kennedy, May 29, 1952 (dec. Feb. 1971). B.S., U. Louisville, 1935; Ph.D., U. Minn., 1944. Registered profl. engr., Del., Kans., N.Y. Asst. chemist Corhart Refractories Co., Louisville, 1935-36; teaching, research asst. chem. engring. U. Minn., Mpls., 1935-39; devel. engr., research chem. engr. E.I. duPont de Nemours & Co., Inc., Wilmington, Del., 1940-46; assoc. prof. chem. engring. U. Kan., Lawrence, 1946-50; prof. U. Kan., 1950-55; Fulbright prof. chem. engring. King's Coll. Durham U., Newcastle-upon-Tyne, Eng., 1952-53; prof., chem. engring. U. Rochester, 1955-69, chmn., 1955-68; asso. lab. dir. Argonne (Ill.) Nat. Lab., 1969-74; dir. Center Ednl. Affairs, 1969-79, sr. chem. engr., 1979-84; ret. sr. chem. engr., cons. 1984—; vis. prof. chem. engring. U. Calif., Berkeley, 1967-68; vis. prof. U. of Philippines, Quezon City, 1986. Editor: Chem. Engring. Edn. Quar, 1965-67; sect. editor: Perry's Chem. Engring. Handbook, 5th edit., 1973, 6th edit., 1984; contbr. articles to tech., profl. jours. Sec. Kans. Bd. Engring. Examiners, 1954-55; mem. adv. com. on tng. Internat. Atomic Energy Commn., 1975-79; Treas. Lawrence (Kans.) League for Practice Democracy, 1950-52. Fellow AAAS, Am. Inst. Chemists, Am. Inst. Chem. Engrs. (past chmn. Kansas City sect.); mem. Am. Chem. Soc. (past chmn. Rochester sect.), Soc. Chem. Industry, Am. Soc. Engring. Edn. (past chmn. grad. studies div.), Am. Nuclear Soc., Filtration Soc., Triangle, Sigma Xi, Sigma Tau, Phi Lambda Upsilon, Tau Beta Pi, Alpha Chi Sigma. Presbyn. Home: 825 63d St Downers Grove IL 60516 Office: Chem Technology Div Argonne Nat Lab Argonne IL 60439

MILLER, STEPHEN HERSCHEL, surgery educator; b. N.Y.C., Jan. 12, 1941; s. Morris Louis and Mildred Lily (Beller) M.; m. Carol Susan Shapiro, Dec. 18, 1965; children: Mark, David. BS, UCLA, 1960, MD, 1964. Diplomate Am. Bd. Surgery, Am. Bd. Plastic Surgery (mem. exec. com. 1985—, chmn. written examination sect. 1985—, bd. dirs. 1984—). Asst. prof. surgery U. Calif., San Francisco, 1973-74; from asst. prof. to prof. surgery Milton S. Hershey Med. Ctr., Hershey, Pa., 1974-78; chief div. plastic surgery Oreg. Health Scis. U., Portland, 1979—. Physician advisor Boy Scouts Am., dist. chmn. scoutmaster exec. council, 1983-84; bd. dirs. Temple Beth Israel, Portland, 1984-86. Recipient Physician Recognition award, 1976; grantee Med. Research Found. of Oreg., 1980, Oreg. Health Scis. U., 1980. Mem. ACS (chmn. program com. 1983—), Am. Soc. Plastic and Reconstructive Surgery (bd. dirs. 1980—, v.p. 1985-86, pres.-elect 1986-87, pres. 1987-88, grantee 1976), Am. Assn. Plastic Surgeons (chmn. research com. 1983-84), Assn. Acad. Chmn. Plastic Surgery (sec./treas. 1985—). Home: 3 Dover Way Lake Oswego OR 97034 Office: Oreg Health Scis U 3181 SW Sam Jackson Park Rd Portland OR 97206

MILLER, STEVEN JEFFREY, lawyer; b. Chgo., Feb. 13, 1954; s. Hadley A. and Carol J. (Prince) M.; m. Mona Deutsch, Aug. 21, 1977. BA magna cum laude, U. Pa., 1974; JD, Stanford U., 1977. Bar: Calif. 1977, U.S. Supreme Ct. 1982, U.S. Ct. Appeals (9th cir.) 1979, U.S. Ct. Appeals (10th cir.) 1981, U.S. Dist. Ct. (cent. dist.) Calif. 1978, U.S. Dist. Ct. (so. dist.) Calif. 1982, U.S. Dist. Ct. (no. and ea. dists.) Calif., 1987. Assoc. Lawler, Felix & Hall, Los Angeles, 1977-84, Wyman, Bautzer, Christensen, Kuchel & Silbert, Los Angeles, 1984-86; of counsel Law Offices of Peter J. McNulty, Bel Air, Calif., 1986—. Mem. ABA, State Bar of Calif., Los Angeles County Bar Assn., Am. Judicature Soc., Internat. Assn. Jewish Lawyers and Jurists, Assn. Bus. Trial Lawyers, Assn. Trial Lawyers Am., Calif. Trial Lawyers Assn., Phi Beta Kappa. Office: Law Offices of Peter J McNulty 827 Moraga Dr Bel Air CA 90049

MILLER, STEWART RANSOM, lawyer; b. Dallas, June 11, 1945; s. Giles Edwin and Betty Jane (Stewart) M.; m. Ann Wilson Pugh, Dec. 7, 1963; children—Rhett, Ross, Christi. B.B.A., Austin Coll., 1968; J.D., U. Tex., 1970. Bar: Tex. 1970, U.S. Dist. Ct. (ea. dist.) Tex. 1971, U.S. Dist. Ct. (no. dist.) Tex. 1972, U.S. Dist. Ct. (so. dist.) Tex. 1980, U.S. Tax Ct. 1977, U.S. Ct. Appeals (5th cir.) 1977, U.S. Ct. Appeals (11th cir.) 1981, U.S. Supreme Ct. 1977, U.S. Dist. Ct. (no. dist.) Okla. 1987. Assoc., Wade & Thomas, Dallas, 1970, 71, Sammons Enterprises, Inc., Dallas, 1971-78; ptnr. Smith, Miller & Carlton, Dallas, 1978—; dir. Legal Security Life Ins. Co., Dallas, 1971-78. Mem. Charter Commn., Town of Highland Park; bd. dirs., sec. Aberrant Behavior Ctr., Inc., Dallas, 1978—, Behavioral Research Ctr., Inc., Dallas, 1980—. Named Outstanding Student Delta Theta Phi, 1970; cert. comml. real estate law specialist Tex. Bd. Legal Specialization. Mem. State Bar Tex., Dallas Bar Assn., Dallas Bus. Assn. (past pres.). Episcopalian. Home: 3219 Mockingbird Dallas TX 75205 Office: Miller & Miller 5080 Spectrum Dr LB 103 Dallas TX 75248

MILLER, SUSAN CHRISTINE, marketing manager, educator; b. Canton, S.D., Mar. 5, 1955; d. Roger Donald and Nordis Kathryn (Hansen) Mortensbak; m. Mike E. Miller, Jan. 7, 1972 (div. 1977); children: Mandy Shane, Christine Kathryn. BS in Bus. and Mktg., Nat. Coll., Rapid City, S.D., 1981; MBA, U. S.D., 1985; MPA, U. Okla., 1987. Tourism asst. Rapid City C. of C., 1978-79; copywriter Rapid City Jour., 1979-81; account exec. The Guide Newspaper, Rapid City, 1981-82, Okla. County Newspaper Group, Midwest City, 1982-83, Daily Oklahoman & Times, Oklahoma City, 1983-84; mktg. dir. Crossroads Mall, Oklahoma City, 1984-87; mktg. mgr. Homart Devel., Chesapeake, Va., 1987—; instr. Tidewater Community Coll., 1987—, Chesapeake. Contbr. articles to profl. jours. Div. leader YMCA Fundraiser, 1987, pres., founder Okla. Mall Mktg. Assn., 1986. Bus. Profl. Women acad. scholar, 1979; named Outstanding Civilian Supporter 3d Combat Com. Group, 1986, one of Outstanding Young Women Am. Outstanding Young Ams., 1986. Mem. Internat. Council Shopping Ctrs. (state chmn. Kids Identification Sign-up, Okla., 1986, pub. service program Kids Say Know to Drugs 1987), Nat. Assn. Female Execs., A.F. Assn. (asst. v.p. membership), Okla. City C. of C. (co-chmn. mil. affairs, 1985-87, speaker 1986-87, conv. tourism bur. 1986-87), Hampton Roads Co. of C. (media chmn. Chesapeake Jubilee 1988). Republican. Mennonite. Club: Toastmasters. Home: 1249 A Ivystone Way Chesapeake VA 23320 Office: Homart Devel 1401 Greenbrier Pkwy Chesapeake VA 23320

MILLER, SUSAN HEILMANN, newspaper publishing executive; b. Yuba City, Calif., Jan. 13, 1945; d. Paul Clay and Helen Christine (Sterud) Heilmann; m. Allen Clinton Miller III, June 24, 1967. BA, Stanford U., 1966; MS, Columbia U., 1969; PhD, Stanford U., 1976. Info. officer Montgomery County Schs., Rockville, Md., 1970-71, Palo Alto Schs., Calif., 1969-70, 71-73; news-features editor Bremerton Sun, Wash., 1976-80; night city editor Peninsula Times Tribune, Palo Alto, 1980-81; exec. editor News-Gazette, Champaign, Ill., 1981-85; dir. editorial devel. Scripps Howard Newspapers, Cin., 1985—. Contbr. articles to profl. jours. Bd. dirs. Vol. Illini Projects, U. Ill., 1983-85, Washington Journalism Ctr., 1985—, New Directions for News, 1988—; mem. Pulitzer Prize Nominating Jury, 1986-87, accrediting com. Accrediting Council on Journalism and Mass Communication. Mem. Am. Soc. Newspaper Editors (bd. dirs. 1985—), Assoc. Press Mng. Editors (bd. dirs.1984—), Ill. AP Mng. Editors (bd. dirs. 1984-85). Clubs: Executive (Champaign, Ill.) (bd.dirs. 1984-85); Bankers (Cin.). Office: Scripps Howard Newspapers 1100 Central Trust Tower Cincinnati OH 45202

MILLER, SYDELL LOIS, cosmetics executive, marketing professional; b. Cleve., Aug. 10, 1937; d. Jack Harvey Lubin and Evelyne (Saltzman) Brower; m. Arnold Max Miller, Oct. 19, 1958; children: Lauren Beth, Stacie Lynn. Student, U. Miami, 1955-56. Mgr. Hair Salon, Cleve., 1958-60; pres., owner Women's Retail Store, Cleve., 1960-72; exec. v.p. Ardell, Inc., Solon, Ohio, 1972-84; exec. v.p. and owner Matrix Essentials, Inc., Solon, 1980—; pres. Lauren Stacy Mktg., Inc., Solon, 1972—. Editor ednl. books and newsletter, Salons, 1981—. Mem. Mt. Sinai Hosp. Aux., Cleve., 1972—, Beachwood (Ohio) Mus., 1981—, Cleve. Fashion Group. Mem. Am. Beauty Assns. (bd. dirs. 1988—, named Woman of Yr. 1985), Beauty and Barber Supply Inst., Inc., Cosmetic, Toiletry and Fragrance Assn., Inc. Office: Matrix Essentials Inc 30601 Carter St Solon OH 44139

MILLER, TED ROBERT, management consultant; b. Perth Amboy, N.J., Sept. 17, 1947; s. Marvin Lester and Carolyn Ruth (Guttman) M.; BS in Engring., Case Western Res. U., 1968; MS in Operations Research, M in City Planning, U. Pa., 1970, PhD in Regional Sci., 1975. Ops. research analyst U.S. Dept. Commerce, Nat. Bur. Standards and HEW, Washington, 1971-75; staff dir. task force on Nat. Blood Data Center and com. for commonality in blood banking automation Am. Blood Commn., Rosslyn, Va., 1975-77; asst. dir. urban and econ. devel. Nat. Inst. Advanced Studies, Washington, 1977-78; v.p. Granville Corp., Washington, 1978-84; sr. research assoc. Urban Inst., Washington, 1984—. Mem. Bd. Proprs. Eastern N.J., 1974—; pres. Adelphi Ter. Condominium Assn., 1979-81. Mem. Am. Inst. Cert. Planners, Nat. Assn. Housing and Redevel. Ofcls., Am. Public Health Assn., Ops. Research Soc. Am., Regional Sci. Assn., AAAS, Am. Econ. Assn., World Future Soc., Pi Delta Epsilon. Democrat. Contbr. articles to profl. jours. Office: 2100 M St NW Washington DC 20037

MILLER, THOMAS ALLEN, surgery educator; b. Harrisburg, Pa., July 7, 1944; s. Joseph E. and Marion R. (Corpman) M.; m. Janet Ruth Walters, Dec. 28, 1968; children: David Allen, William James, Laurie Ann. B.S. cum laude, Wheaton (Ill.) Coll., 1966; M.D., Temple U., 1970. Instr. dept. biology Wheaton(Ill.) Coll., 1966; intern in surgery U. Chgo. Hosps., 1970-71; resident in Surgery U. Mich. Hosps., 1971-75; instr. dept. surgery, postdoctoral research fellow in gastrointestinal hormone physiology U. Tex. Med. Branch, Galveston, 1975-76; instr. dept. surgery & physiology, postdoctoral research fellow in gastrointestinal physiology U. Tex. Med. Sch., Houston, 1976-77, asst. prof. surgery, 1977-79, assoc. prof., 1979-84, prof., 1984—, dir. acad. affairs, resident tng., 1981-82, dir. grad. surg. edn., 1982—, assoc. chmn. dept. surgery, 1985—; cons. on gastrointestinal research Procter and Gamble & Co., Cin., 1985—, Upjohn Co., Kalamazoo, Mich., 1986—; grant reviewer VA Merit Rev. Bd., Washington, 1984—; mem. steering com. NIH Concensus Panel on Gastric Injury and Protection, 1986-87; mem. surgery and bioengineering study sect. Nat. Inst. of Health, 1987— . Editor: The Physiologic Basis of Modern Surgical Care, 1988; co-editor: (with S.J. Dudrick) The Management of Difficult Surgical Problems, 1981; contbr. articles to profl. jours. Upjohn Co. grantee, 1977-78; Distilled Spirits Council grantee, 1977-78; U. Tex. grantee, 1978-79; NIH grantee, 1979—. Fellow ACS (com. on surg. edn. 1985—); mem. AAAS, Am. Digestive Disease Soc., Am. Fedn. Clin. Research, Am. Gastroent. Assn., AMA, Am. Physiol. Soc., Am. Soc. Parenteral and Enteral Nutrition, Assn. Acad. Surgery (chmn. com on legis. issues 1978-79, com. on issues 1979-81, nominating com. 1983-84), Coll. Internat. Chirugiae Digestivae, Harris County Med. Soc. (cancer com. 1980—), Houston Gastroent. Assn., Houston Surg. Soc., N.Y. Acad. Scis., Pancreatic Club Inc., Soc. Internat. de Chirurgie, Soc. Exptl. Biology and Medicine, Soc. Surgery of Alimentary Tract (nominating com. 1982, auditing com. 1983), Soc. Univ. Surgeons (councilman-at-large 1983-86), Splanchnic Circulation Group, Tex. Med. Assn., Surgery Biology Club III, Tex. Surg. Soc. Republican. Presbyterian. Home: 10618 Shady River Houston TX 77042 Office: U Tex Med Sch Dept Surgery 6431 Fannin Room 4266 Houston TX 77030

MILLER, THOMAS EUGENE, legal editor, writer; b. Bryan, Tex., Jan. 4, 1929; s. Eugene Adam and Ella Lucille (Schroeder) M. B.A., Tex. A&M U., 1950; M.A., U. Tex., 1956, J.D., 1966; postgrad. U. Houston, 1957-58, U Calif.-Berkeley, 1983. Bar: Tex. 1966. Research technician M.D. Anderson Hosp., Houston, 1956-58; claims examiner trainee Soc. Security Adminstrn., New Orleans, 1964; trademark examiner trainee Dept. Commerce, Washington, 1966; editor Bancroft-Whitney Co., San Francisco, 1966—. Author book under pseudonym. Contbg. mem. Democratic Nat. Com., 1981-88. Fellow Internat. Biog. Assn. (life, dep. dir. gen.), Am. Biog. Inst. (life, Grand Ambassador of Achievement award); mem. ABA, Internat. Platform Assn., Phi Kappa Phi, Psi Chi, Phi Eta Sigma. Methodist. Clubs: Nat. Writers, Press, Commonwealth. Home: 2293 Turk Blvd Apt 5 San Francisco CA 94118 Office: Bancroft-Whitney Co 3205 Van Ness Ave San Francisco CA 94109

MILLER, THOMAS W. C., human resources consultant; b. Phila., May 28, 1938; s. Thomas and Almira Wilson (Gregory) M.; m. Marjorie Lane Billings, Oct. 2, 1965 (div. 1973); children—Thomas Wilson Caulkins, Jason Evans Billings; m. Loraine Laughlin MacDougall, July 22, 1977; children—Elizabeth Gregory Miller, Katherine Allen Miller. Student Haverford Coll., Columbia U. Mgmt. trainee Md. Casualty Ins. Co., Balt., 1961-63; pres. Capital Analysis, Morristown, N.J., 1963-69; v.p., div. mgr. Amax Fin. Services, Pitts., 1969-77; v.p. Profl. Career Counselors, N.Y.C., 1977-83; v.p. Goodrich & Sherwood, N.Y.C., 1983—. Served with USAR, 1959-65. Mem. Am. Soc. Personnel Adminstrs., Inst. for Application of Psychol. Types, Am. Mgmt. Assn., N.Y. Personnal Mgmt. Assn., Pa. Horse Breeders Assn. Clubs: Union of N.Y.; The Duquesne (Pitts.); Rolling Rock (Ligonier, Pa.); Misquamicut (Watch Hill, R.I.); Church of N.Y., Adirondack Mountain, Nat. Steeplechase and Hunt Assn., Am. Driving Soc., Brit. Driving Soc. Club: Watch Hill Yacht. Lodge: Military Order of Loyal Legion. Avocations: sports; folk art; antique collecting. Home: 161 E 90 St New York NY 10128 Office: The Goodrich and Sherwood Co 521 Fifth Ave New York NY 10017

MILLER, THOMAS WAINWRIGHT, JR., consulting engineer, state official; b. Clearwater, Fla., Nov. 28, 1927; s. Thomas Wainwright and Grace Ellen (Gilbert) M.; B.C.E., Ga. Inst. Tech., 1952, D in Bus. Adminstrn., Carson-Newman Coll., 1988; m. Mavis Stinson, Dec. 25, 1952; 1 son, Thomas Wainwright III. Regional engr. Fla. State Bd. Health, 1952-56; dir. Lee County Mosquito Control Dist., Ft. Myers, Fla., 1956—; engr.-in-charge Lee County Hyacinth Control Dist., 1961—; pres. T.W. Miller & Assos., Inc., 1962—; dir. First Fed. Savs. & Loan Assn. Ft. Myers. Trustee, pres., chief exec. officer Price Found.; trustee Bapt. Found., Palm Beach Atlantic Coll., Edison Community Coll. Endowment Corp.; bd. dirs. Lee Meml. Hosp.; Served with AUS, 1946-47. Registered profl. engr., Fla., La., Mass. Fellow Fla. Engring. Soc., Met. Ft. Myers C. of C. (pres. 1983, dir.); mem. Bus. Devel. Corp. Southwest Fla., Council on Founds. Clubs: Fort Myers Rod and Gun (pres. 1969, now dir.); Royal Palm Yacht. Lodges: Masons, Shriners, Rotary (pres. 1975). Contbr. articles to profl. jours. Office: Lee County Mosquito Control Dist PO Box 06005 Fort Myers FL 33906

MILLER, W(ALTER) GORDON, water conditioning company executive; b. Havre, Mont., July 6, 1932; s. Walter Wesley and Vivian (Vagg) M.; m. Gayle Highberg, Dec. 29, 1954; children—Peggy, Debby, David. B.A. in Psychology, Carleton Coll., 1954; M.S. in TV, Syracuse U., 1955. Pres., Cleanwater Corp. Mich., Marlette, 1958—, Culligan Water Conditioning Co., Marlette, 1958—, LaCrosse, Wis., 1974—; v.p. dir. U.S. Water Co., Mpls., 1978—; dir. NBD Sandusky Bank, Mich.; pres. WQA Employee's Benefit Corp., Lisle, Ill. Chmn., Sanilac County (Mich.) Mental Health Bd., 1971—; chmn. bd. Marlette Community Hosp., 1971—; sec. Sanilac County Bldg. Authority, 1972—. Recipient Key award Water Quality Assn., 1977, award of merit, 1987. Mem. Mich. Water Conditioning Assn. (founder, pres.), Internat. Water Conditioning Assn. (pres.). Republican. Presbyterian. Office: 3099 Main St Marlette MI 48453

MILLER, WALTER RICHARD, JR., banker; b. N.Y.C., Nov. 20, 1934; s. Walter Richard and Ann M. (Phelan) M.; m. Joan M. Groark; children: Kathryn A., Margaret E., Jennifer M., Walter Richard III. AB, Dartmouth Coll., 1955; MBA, Columbia U., 1957; PhD, NYU, 1965. Dir. mktg., v.p. Mellon Nat. Corp., Pitts., 1965-78; sr. v.p. First Atlanta Corp., 1979-81; exec. v.p. Norwest Corp., Mpls., 1981-86; pres., chief exec. officer First Constn. Fin. Corp., New Haven, 1986—, also bd. dirs.; pres., chief exec. officer First Constn. Bank, also bd. dirs.; vice chmn. CIRRUS System Inc. Contbr. articles, chpts. to profl. pubs. Bd. dirs. St. Paul Chamber Orch., Minn. Pub. Radio, Sci. Mus. Minn., Quinnipiac (Conn.) Coll., The Mus. of Am. Theatre, Orchestra New England. Served with USAF, 1958. Teaching fellow NYU, N.Y.C., 1960; Ford Found. fellow NYU, 1962. Mem. Interbank Card Assn. (internat. chmn.), Am. Mktg. Assn. (contbg. editor), Bank Mktg. Assn. (bd. dirs., chmn. mktg. planning council, chmn. mktg. mgmt. council). Clubs: Minneapolis; Somerset (St. Paul); New Haven Country, Quinipiac (New Haven). Home: 2 Marshall Rd Hamden CT 06517 Office: First Constn Fin Corp 80 Elm St New Haven CT 06510

MILLER, WAYNE DUNBAR, speech pathologist, audiologist; b. Brockton, Mass., Dec. 26, 1934; s. Wilford Eugene and Doris Mae (Dunbar) Miller; ; m. Helen Louise Grant; children: Valerie-Gail, Wilford Gordon. BA in Speech Pathology, Staley Coll., Brookline, Mass., 1958; ME in Counseling, Psychotherapy, Suffolk U., 1971. Certs. in clin. competence speech pathology, lang. pathology and audiology; lic. speech pathologist, audiologist; Mass. Tchr. English, Mendon (Mass.) High Sch., 1958-59; acad. clin. practicum in aphasiology Holy Ghost Hosp., Cambridge, Mass., 1959-61; pvt. practice speech pathology, 1961—; supr. speech therapy and hearing Paul A. Dever State Sch., Taunton, Mass., 1961-70; practice neuro-communi-pathology (aphasiology) Goddard Meml. Hosp., Stoughton, Mass., 1966—, Sturdy Meml. Hosp., Attleboro, Mass., 1970—; speech pathologist Attleboro public schs., 1970—; founder Speech, Lang. and Hearing Clinic Morton Hosp., 1968. Deacon, Covenant Congl. Ch., North Easton, Mass., 1979-81, 87; mem. profl. adv. bd. and utilization rev. com. Stoughton Pub. Health Com., 1980—; sustaining mem. Rep. Nat. Com., 1981—. Served with Army N.G., 1953-61. Clin. fellow Parson (Kans.) State Hosp., 1964. Mem. Am. Speech and Hearing Assn., Am. Audiology Soc., Mass. Speech and Hearing Assn., NEA, Mass. Edn. Assn., Attleboro Edn. Assn., U.S. Naval Inst., Am. Legion . Lodges: Masons, Shriners, DeMolay (chpt. adv. council 1980—, rainbow adv. bd. 1987—). Home and Office: 76 Short St South Easton MA 02375 also: Goddard Meml Hosp 909 Sumner St Stoughton MA 02072

MILLER, WENDELL SMITH, chemist, consultant; b. Columbus, Ohio, Sept. 26, 1925; s. Wendell Pierce and Emma Josephine (Smith) M.; B.A., Pomona Coll., 1944; M.S., U. Calif. at Los Angeles, 1952; m. Dorothy Marie Pagen, Aug. 18, 1949; children—William Ross, Wendell Roger. Chemist U.S. Rubber Co., Torrance, Calif., 1944; sr. chemist Carbide & Carbon Chemicals Corp., Oak Ridge, 1944-48; partner Kellogg & Miller, Los Angeles, 1949-56; patent coordinator Electro Optical Systems, Inc., Pasadena, Calif., 1956-59; v.p. Intertech. Corp. optical and optoelectronic system devel., North Hollywood, Calif., 1960-66, dir., 1966— ; assoc. Ctr. for Study of Evolution and Origin of Life, UCLA. Commr., Great Western Council Boy Scouts Am., 1960-65. Served with AUS, 1944-46. Decorated Army Commendation medal. Mem. Los Angeles Patent Law Assn., IEEE, AAAS, 20th Century Round Table, Sigma Xi, Phi Beta Kappa, Pi Mu Epsilon. Numerous patents in field. Home: 1341 Comstock Ave Los Angeles CA 90024

MILLER, WILBUR CASTEEL, former university president; b. Des Moines, Aug. 26, 1923; s. Cecil S. and Laura M. (Kesterson) M.; m. Viretta A. Shaw, Mar. 30, 1946; children—W. Kent, Jill M. Student, Drake U., 1941-43, St. Louis U., 1943-44; BS in Bus. Adminstrn, U. Denver, 1948, MA, 1949, PhD, 1953, LLD, 1972. Faculty dept. psychology U. Denver, 1949-72, prof., 1963-72, dean grad sch., 1964-65, vice chancellor acad. affairs, dean faculty, 1965-72, acting chancellor, 1966-67; pres. Drake U., Des Moines, from 1972, pres. emeritus, 1985—; Chester M. Alter endowed prof. and chair in adminstrn. Loretto Heights Coll., Denver, 1986—; cons. USAF Acad., 1957; co-dir. research project in maladaptive behavior U. Colo. Med. Sch., 1960-72; Ford Found. cons. to Venezuela, 1968-69. Author: Personality Social Class and Delinquency, 1966; contbg. author: New Viewpoints in the Social Sciences, 1958, Readings in Child Development and Personality, 1970. Served with AUS, 1943-46. U. Mich. postdoctoral fellow, 1963-64. Fellow Am. Psychol. Assn.; mem. Colo. Psychol. Assn. (past pres.), Rocky Mountain Psychol. Assn. (past pres.), Phi Beta Kappa, Sigma Xi. Office: Loretto Heights Coll 3001 S Federal Blvd Denver CO 80236

MILLER, WILBUR HOBART, business diversification consultant; b. Boston, Feb. 15, 1915; s. Silas Reuben and Muriel Mae (Greene) M.; B.S., U. N.H., 1936, M.S., 1938; Ph.D. (univ. fellow, 1940-41), Columbia U., 1941; m. Harriett I. Harmon, June 20, 1941; children: Nancy Iber Miller Harray, Warren Harmon, Donna Sewall Miller Davidge. Research chemist Am. Cyanamid Co., Stamford, Conn., 1941-49, Washington tech. rep., 1949-53, dir. food industry devel., 1953-57, tech. dir. products for agr. Cyanamid Internat., N.Y.C., 1957-60; sr. scientist Dunlap & Assos., Darien, Conn., 1960-63, sr. asso., 1963-66; coordinator new product devel. Celanese Corp., N.Y.C., 1966-67, mgr. comml. research, 1967-68, dir. corp. devel., 1969-84; bus. diversification cons., 1984—; lectr. on bus. and soc. Western Conn. State Coll., 1977-79. Chmn. Stamford Forum for World Affairs, 1954-87, hon. chmn. 1987—; mem. adv. bd. Center for the Study of the Presidency, 1980—; bd. Stamford Symphony, 1974-80, v.p., 1978-80; pres. Council for Continuing Edn., Stamford, 1962, bd., 1960-70; elder United Presbyn. Ch., nominating com., 1960-63; pres. Interfaith Council of Stamford, 1973; internat. fellow U. Bridgeport, 1985—; mem. pres.'s council U. N.H., 1982—. Recipient outstanding achievement award Coll. Tech., U. N.H., 1971, Am. Design award, 1948, Golden Rule Award J.C. Penney & Co., 1986. Fellow AAAS, Am. Inst. Chemists (councillor N.Y. chpt. 1984-85); mem. Am. Chem. Soc. (news service adv. bd., 1948-53), N.Y. Acad. Scis., Societé de Chimie Industrielle (v.p. fin. Am. sect. 1980-84, dir. 1984—), Inst. Food Tech., Soc. for Internat. Devel., Am. Acad. Polit. and Social Scis., Sigma Xi. Club: Chemists (treas. 1982-84) (N.Y.C.). Contbr. sci. papers to profl. jours.; patentee in field. Home: 19 Crestview Ave Stamford CT 06907

MILLER, WILLIAM CHARLES, lawyer; b. Jacksonville, Fla., Aug. 6, 1937; s. Charles and Mary Elizabeth (Kiger) M.; m. Hadmut Gisela Larsen, June 10, 1961; children: Monica Lee, Charles Andreas. B.A., Washington and Lee U., 1958, LL.B., 1961; LL.M., N.Y. U., 1963; postgrad., Harvard Bus. Sch., 1978. Bar: Fla. 1961, Calif. 1984, U.S. Supreme Ct. 1968, Ind. 1987. Counsel to electrochem., elastomers and internat. depts. E.I. duPont de Nemours & Co., Wilmington, Del., 1963-66; counsel S. Am. ops. Bristol-Myers Co., N.Y.C., 1967-69; internat. counsel Xerox Corp., Stamford, Conn., 1969-79; assoc. gen. counsel Xerox Corp., 1979-80; v.p., gen. counsel, sec. Max Factor & Co., Hollywood, Calif., 1981-85, Boehringer Mannheim Corp., Indpls., 1985—. Bd. dirs. Southwestern Legal Found., 1975-85. Fulbright scholar, 1959-60; Ford Found. fellow, 1961-62; Hague Acad. fellow, 1963; German Govt. grantee, 1962-63; Kappa Sigma scholar, 1959. Mem. Internat. Bar Assn., ABA, Calif. Bar Assn., Fla. Bar Assn., Ind. Bar Assn., Phi Beta Kappa, Phi Eta Sigma, Delta Theta Phi. Republican. Mem. Christian Ch. (Disciples of Christ). Lodges: Masons, Elks. Home: 32 Cool Creek Ct Carmel IN 46032 Office: Boehringer Mannheim Corp 9115 Hague Rd Indianapolis IN 46250

MILLER, WILLIAM DAWES, metals and energy company executive; b. Buffalo, Feb. 14, 1919; s. William S. and Hazel (Sands) M.; m. Celeste M. Fain, Nov. 20, 1943 (dec. 1970); 1 child, Elizabeth F.; m. Anne J. Johnson, Dec. 20, 1972. BS in Mech. Engring., Carnegie Inst. Tech., 1942. Prodn. engr. Wright Aero. Corp., Cin., 1942-44; with AEC, 1944-53, dep. chief Oak Ridge Prodn. div., 1944-49, chief ops. div. Paducah Area, 1949-51, dep. mgr. Paducah Area, 1951-53; v.p., chief engr. Continental Copper & Steel Industries, Inc., N.Y.C., 1953-60; v.p. Consol. Aluminum Corp., Jackson, Tenn., 1960, exec. v.p., 1960-61, pres., chief exec. officer, 1961-69; chmn. bd. AIAG Metals, Inc., Jackson, 1961-69; pres., chief exec. officer Gulf Coast Aluminum Corp., 1967-69, Independence Energy Co., Inc., 1979—, Metvest Inc., 1988—; dir. mfg. planning and devel. Anaconda Co., N.Y.C., 1969-71, v.p., 1971-79; pres. Anaconda Jamaica, 1971-73; v.p. Anaconda Aluminum Co., 1969-73; v.p. Mitsui-Anaconda Corp., 1973-78; bd. dirs. Habanero Corp., Pioneer Fund; mem. adv. bd. Alexander Proudfoot Co., 1985-88. Clubs: Met. (gov., pres., chief exec. officer 1985—), Doubles, Shinnecock Hills Golf, Meadow Tennis, Southampton (Southampton); Beach, Mayacoo Golf, Old Guard Soc. (Palm Beach, Fla.). Home and Office: 35 E 75th St New York NY 10021

MILLER, WILLIAM ELWOOD, mining co. exec.; b. Bend, Oreg., May 9, 1919; s. Harry Adelbert and Sarah (Heyburn) M.; B.A., Stanford, 1941, M.B.A., 1947; m. Constance Alban Crosby, July 2, 1955; children—William, Constance, Harold, Mary, Sarah Crosby, Charles Crosby, Helen, Harry. Owner and operator Central Oregon Pumice Co., Bend, 1948—; pres. The Miller Lumber Co., Bend, The Miller Ranch Co., Bend. Commr., City of Bend, 1959-62, mayor, 1960. Bd. dirs. Central Oreg. Coll.; pres. Central Oreg. Coll. Found., 1956-57; dir. Central Oregon Coll. Area Ednl. Dist., 1961-65, chmn., 1964-65; bd. govs. Ore. Dept. Geology and Mineral Industries, 1971-75. Served with A.C., USNR, 1942-45. Decorated D.F.C., Air medal. Mem. Central Oreg. (v.p. 1954), Bend (pres. 1954) chambers commerce, Kappa Sigma. Republican. Episcopalian. Rotarian (dir. Bend 1955-56). Club: Bend Golf. Home: 527 NW Congress St Bend OR 97701 Office: 5 NW Greenwood Ave Bend OR 97701

MILLER, ZOYA DICKINS, civic worker; b. Washington, July 15, 1923; d. Randolph and Zoya Pavlovna (Klementinovska) Dickins; grad. Stuart Sch. Costume Design, Washington, 1942; student Sophie Newcomb Coll., 1944, New Eng. Conservatory Music, 1946; grad. Internat. Sch. Reading, 1969; m. Hilliard Eve Miller, Jr., Dec. 6, 1943; children: Jeffrey Arnot, Hilliard Eve III. Fashion coordinator, cons. Mademoiselle mag., 1942-44; instr. Stuart Summer Sch. Costume Design, Washington, 1942; fashion coordinator Julius Garfinckel, Washington, 1942-43; star TV show Cowbelle Kitchen, 1957-58, Flair for Living, 1958-59; model mags. and comml. films, also nat. comml. recs., 1956—; dir. program devel. Webb-Waring Lung Inst., Denver, 1973—. Mem. exec. com., bd. dirs. El Paso County chpt. Am. Lung Assn., 1954-63; mem. exec. com. Am. Lung Assn. Colo., 1965-84, bd. dris. 1965-87, chmn. radio and TV council, 1963-70, mem. med. affairs com., 1965-70, pres., 1961-68, procurer found. funds, 1965-70; developer nat. radio ednl. prodns. for internat. use Nat. Tb and Respiratory Disease Assn., Am. Lung Assn., 1963-70, coordinator statewide screening programs Colo., other states, 1965-72; chmn. benefit fund raising El Paso County Cancer Soc., 1963; founder, coordinator Colorado Springs Debutante Ball, 1967—; coordinator Nat. Gov.'s Conf. Ball, 1969; mem. exec. com. Colo. Gov.'s Comprehensive Health Planning Council, 1967-74, chmn., 1972-73; chmn. Colo. Chronic Care Com., 1969-73, chmn. fund raising, 1970-72, chmn. spl. com. congressional studies on nat. health bills, 1971-73; mem. Colo.-Wyo. Regional Med. Program Adv. Council, 1969-73; mem. Colo. Med. Found. Consumers Adv. Council, 1972-78; mem. decorative arts com. Colorado Springs Fine Arts Ctr., 1972-75; founder, state coordinator Nov. Noel Pediatrics Benefit Am. Lung Assn., 1973-87; founder, state pres. Newborn Hope, 1987. Recipient James J. Waring award Colo. Conf. on Respiratory Disease Workers, 1963; Zoya Dickins Miller Vol. of Yr. award established Am. Lung Assn. of Colo., 1979; Nat. Pub. Relations award Am. Lung Assn., 1979, Gold Double Bar Cross award, 1980, 83; named Humanitarian of Yr., Am. Lung Assn. of Colo., 1987. Lic. pvt. pilot. Mem. Nat. (chmn. nat. father of year contest 1956-57), Colo., El Paso County (pres. 1954, TV chmn. 1954-59) cowbelle assns., Colo. Assn. Fund Raisers. Club: Broadmoor Garden (ways and means chmn. 1967-69, civic chmn. 1970-71, publicity chmn. 1972) (Colorado Springs, Colo.). Contbr. articles, lectures on health care systems and fund raising. Home: 74 W Cheyenne Mountain Blvd Colorado Springs CO 80906

MILLERD, PATRICK RIVERSDALE, financial director; b. Johannesburg, Transvaal, Republic of South Africa, May 28, 1948; s. Michael Riversdale and Margaret Ella (Hughes) M.; m. Mary Theresa Pretorius, 1974; children: Andrew, David, Mark. BS in Econs., Natal U., 1970; BSc with honors, U.N.I. S. Africa, 1981. Cost acct. Feltex, Ltd., Durban, Republic of South Africa, 1970-74; fin. dir. David Whitehead and Sons Ltd., Tongaat, 1974—. Contbr. several articles to profl. jours. Councillor, Borough of Ballito, Republic of South Africa, 1986-88. Mem. South African Prodn. and Inventory Control Soc. Mem. Progressive Fed. Party. Club: Maidstone Country. Home: 2 Alde Crescent Westbrook, Tongaat Natal, Republic of South Africa Office: David Whitehead and Sons Ltd, P Bag 14, Tongaat Natal 4400, Republic of South Africa

MILLIE, HAROLD RAYMOND, editor; b. Mpls., July 19, 1930; s. Odin Larsen and Aagot (Skaftun) M.; B.A., Claremont Men's Coll., 1955, M.A., 1960; m. Elena Gonozalez, Aug. 8, 1969. Resident teaching fellow Brown U., Providence, 1961-63; research asso. Nat. Planning Assn., Washington, 1964-65; ops. research analyst Nat. Bur. Standards, Washington, 1965-70, GSA, Washington, 1971-73; editor Bur. Mines, Dept. Interior, Washington, 1974-79; internat. petroleum trade specialist U.S. Dept. Energy, 1979—. Served with U.S. Army, 1949-50. Mem. AIME. Episcopalian. Editor: Minerals and Materials/A Monthly Survey, 1976-79. Home: 5152 Manning Pl NW Washington DC 20016 Office: 1000 Independence Ave SW Washington DC 20585

MILLIGAN, MICHAEL LEE, dentist; b. Kenton, Ohio, Sept. 5, 1952; s. Robert L. and Lena R. (Chiesa) M.; m. Karen S. Nice, Sept. 20, 1975; children: Kristen, Patrick, Lyndsey, Marisa. BS, U. Houston, 1975; DMD, So. Ill. U., 1978. Gen. practice dentistry Bloomington, Ill., 1978—; co-developer Eastland Profl. Bldg., Bloomington, 1987-88. Mem. ADA, Ill. Dental Soc., McLean County Dental Soc. (pres. 1987—). Lodges: KC. Home: 208 Grandview Dr Normal IL 61761 Office: 1404 Eastland Dr Suite 101 Bloomington IL 61701

MILLIGAN, ROBERT LEE, JR., computer company executive; b. Evanston, Ill., Apr. 4, 1934; s. Robert L. and Alice (Connell) M.; B.S., Northwestern U., 1958; m. Susan A. Woodrow, Mar. 23, 1957; children—William, Bonnie, Thomas, Robert III. Account rep. IBM, Chgo., 1957-66; sr. cons. L.B. Knight & Assocs., Chgo., 1966-68; v.p. mktg. Trans Union Systems Corp., Chgo., 1968-73; sr. v.p. sales mktg., sec. Systems Mgmt. Inc., Rosemont, Ill., 1973-87, dir., 1980-87; pres., chief exec. officer, owner Target Data, Inc., Northbrook, Ill., 1987—; treas. Systems Mgmt. Inc. Service Corp.; dir. Nanofast, Inc., Chgo., 1982-84. Div. mgr. N. Suburban YMCA Bldg., 1967; area chmn. Northfield Twp. Republican Party, 1965-71. Bd. dirs. United Fund, Glenview, Ill., 1967-69, Robert R. McCormick Chgo. Boys Club, 1974—; pres. bd. mgrs. Glenview Amateur Hockey Assn., 1974-79, gen. mgr. Glenbrook South High Sch. Hockey Club, 1973-78. Served with AUS, 1953-55. Mem. Data Processing Mgmt. Assn., Consumer Credit Assn. (dir., sec. 1969-70), Phi Kappa Psi. Presbyterian. Clubs: Northwestern (dir. 1973-75) (Chgo.); Glen View (Ill.). Home: 1450 Lawrence Ln Northbrook IL 60062 Office: Target Data Inc 630 Dundee Rd Suite 125 Northbrook IL 60062

MILLIKAN, LARRY EDWARD, dermatologist; b. Sterling, Ill., May 12, 1936; s. Daniel Franklin and Harriet Adeline (Parmenter) M.; m. Jeanine Dorothy Johnson, Aug. 27, 1960; children: Marshall, Rebecca. B.A., Monmouth Coll., 1958; M.D., U. Mo., 1962. Intern Great Lakes Naval Hosp., Ill., 1962-63; housestaff in tng. U. Mich., Ann Arbor, 1967-69, chief resident, 1969-70; asst. prof. dermatology U. Mo., Columbia, 1970-74, assoc. prof., 1974-81; chmn. dept. dermatology Tulane U., New Orleans, 1981—; cons. physician Charity Hosp., New Orleans, Lallie Kemp Charity Hosp., Tulane U. Hosp., New Orleans, VA Hosp., Biloxi, Miss., Huey P. Long Hosp., Pineville, St. Tammany Parish Hosp., Covington, La., Alexandria VA Hosp., La., New Orleans VA Hosp., Student Health Service, Gunn Clinic. Assoc. editor Internat. Jour. Dermatology, 1980—; mem. editorial bd. Current Concepts in Skin Disorders, Am. Jour. Med. Scis., Jour. Am. Acad. Dermatology, Postgraduate Medicine; contbr. articles to med jours. Served with USN, 1960-67. Nat. Cancer Inst. grantee, 1976—. Fellow ACP; mem. Am. Acad. Dermatology (bd. dirs. 1986-90), Am. Dermatol. Assn., Am. Dermatol. Soc. for Allergy and Immunology (pres., bd. dirs.), Soc. for Investigative Dermatology (past pres. South Sect.), So. Med. Assn. (vice chmn. dermatology sect. 1984), Coll. Physicians Phila., Assn. Profs. Dermatology (bd. dirs. 1984-86), AMA, Orleans Parish Med. Soc., La. State Med. Soc., AAAS, Pan Am. Med. Assn. (council), Am. Soc. Dermatol. Surgery, Internat. Soc. for Tropical Dermatology, South Central Dermatologic Congress (sec. gen. 1982-86, pres. 1986-90), Nat. Bd. Med. Examiners, Mo. Allergy Assn. (past pres.), Mo. Dermatol. Assn. (past pres.), Sigma Xi, Alpha Omega Alpha, Alpha Tau Omega. Home: Lacombe LA 70445 Office: Tulane Univ Sch Medicine Dept of Dermatology Suite 355Y New Orleans LA 70112

MILLIKEN, JOHN GORDON, research economist; b. Denver, May 12, 1927; s. William Boyd and Margaret Irene (Marsh) M.; m. Marie Violet Machell, June 13, 1953; children: Karen Marie, Douglas Gordon, David Tait, Anne Alain. B.S., Yale U., 1949, B.Eng., 1950; M.S., U. Colo., 1966, D.B.A., 1969. Registered profl. engr., Colo. Engr. U.S. Bur. Reclamation, Denver, 1950-55; asst. to plant mgr. Stanley Aviation Corp., Denver, 1955-56; prin. mgmt. engr., dept. mgr. Martin-Marietta Aerospace Div., Denver, 1956-64; mgmt. engr. Safeway Stores, Inc., Denver, 1964-66; sr. research economist, prof., assoc. div. head U. Denver Research Inst., 1966-86; pres. Univ. Senate, 1980-81; prin. Milliken Chapman Research Group, Inc., Littleton, Colo., 1986-88, Milliken Research Group, Inc., Littleton, 1988—; vis. fellow sci. policy research unit U. Sussex, Eng., 1975-76; dir. Sci. Mgmt. Corp., Cogenco Internat., Inc., LIK Securities, Inc.; cons. mgmt. engr. Author: Aerospace Management Techniques, 1971, Federal Incentives for Innovation, 1974, Recycling Municipal Wastewater, 1977, Water and Energy in Colorado's Future, 1981, Technological Innovation and Economic Vitality, 1983, Metropolitan Water Management, 1981; others; contbr. articles to profl. jours. Bd. dirs. Southeast Englewood Water Dist., 1962—, South Englewood San. Dist., 1965—, South Suburban Met. Recreation and Park Dist., 1971—; chmn. Democratic Com. of Arapahoe County, 1969-71, 5th Congl. Dist. Colo., 1972-73, 74-75; mem. exec. com. Colo. Faculty Adv. Council, 1981-85; mem. Garrison Diversion Unit Commn., 1984; trustee Colo. Local Govt. Liquid Asset Trust, 1986—. Served with M.C. AUS, 1945-46. Recipient Adlai E. Stevenson Meml. award, 1981. Mem. Acad. Mgmt., Nat. Assn. Bus. Economists, Yale Sci. and Engring. Assn., Am. Water Works Assn., Sigma Xi, Tau Beta Pi, Beta Gamma Sigma, Sigma Iota Epsilon. Congregationalist. Home: 6502 S Ogden St Littleton CO 80121 Office: Milliken Research Group Inc 6631 S University Blvd Littleton CO 80121

MILLMAN, SANDY KEITH, public relations consultant; b. Poughkeepsie, N.Y., Mar. 23, 1930; s. Morris and Rosalie (Josephson) M.; AB in Publicity, U. Miami, 1952; postgrad. SUNY, New Paltz, 1953, New Sch. Social Research, 1963, MA, NYU Grad. Sch. Journalism, 1985; m. Ellin S. Bainder, Aug. 30, 1953; children: Jode Susan, Stuart Lawrence. With public relations Pan Am. World Airways, 1952; pub. relations cons. to Govt. Japan, 1958-70; pres. Nat. Athletic Products, N.Y.C., 1962—, Tempo Golf & Tennis, Inc., 1976—; v.p. Weimann Internat, Inc., N.Y.C., 1963—; mktg. cons. to commr. trade Honduras UN Trade Commn., 1966—. Intelligence team U.S. State Dept., 1947. Mem. U.S. Power Squadron, Aircraft Owners and Pilots Assn., Mid-Hudson Power Squadron, U.S. Trotting Assn., N.Y. State Sheriff's Assn., Public Relations Soc. Am., Radio and TV News Dirs. Assn., Golf Writers Assn. Am., Profl. Journalism Soc., Alpha Delta Sigma. Clubs: Atrium, Publicity (N.Y.C.). Home: 7 Adriance Ave Poughkeepsie NY 12602 Office: 201 E 28th St New York NY 10010

MILLOY, FRANK JOSEPH, JR., physician; b. Phoenix, June 26, 1924; s. Frank Joseph and Ola (McCabe) M.; student Notre Dame U., 1942-43; M.S., Northwestern U., 1949, M.D., 1947. Intern, Cook County Hosp., Chgo., 1947-49, resident, 1953-57; practice medicine, specializing in surgery, Lake Forest, Ill., 1958—; asso. attending staff Presbyn.—St. Lukes Hosp.; attending staff Cook County Hosp.; mem. staff U. Ill. Research Hosp.; clin. asso. prof. surgery, U. Ill. Med. Sch.; asso. prof. surgery Rush Med. Sch. Cons. West Side Vet. Hosp. Served as apprentice seaman USNR, 1943-45; lt. M.C., USNR, 1950-52; PTO. Diplomate Am. Bd. Surgery and Thoracic Surgery. Mem. A.C.S., Chgo. Surg. Soc., Internat. Soc. Surgery, Am. Coll. Chest Physicians, Soc. Thoracic Surgeons, Phi Beta Pi. Clubs: Metropolitan, University (Chgo.). Home: 574 Jackson Ave Glencoe IL 60022 Office: 800 Westmoreland Dr Lake Forest IL 60045

MILLS, BRIAN WILLIAM, technology finance consultant; b. Reigate, Surrey, Eng., Apr. 30, 1933; s. William John and Elsie Ella (Spencer) M.; m. Bronwen Mary Newton, Nov. 19, 1960; children—Deryn Mary, Alison Myfanwy. B.A., U. Bristol, 1956. Systems mgr. Leo Computers Ltd., London, 1957-60, sales mgr., Johannesburg, S.Africa, 1960-63; cons. mgr. Coopers & Lybrand, London, 1964-67; mng. services dir. P&O Group, London, 1967-70; chief exec. mgmt. services BOC Internat., London, 1970-75; chmn. Datasolve Ltd., London, 1975-80, Datastream Internat., London, 1977-80, Abtex Systems Ltd., Aberdeen, 1984—; dir. Advanced System Architectures (Holdings) Ltd., London. Gov., Royal Marsden Hosp., London, 1980—; chmn. Thames Cancer Registry, London, 1981—; mem. MidSurrey Community Health Council, 1974-80. Served to lt. Brit. Army, 1951-53. Fellow Chartered Assn. Cert. Accts., Brit. Computer Soc.; vice-chmn. Patients Assn. London, 1988—; mem. Bond and Share Soc. (treas. 1978—). Avocations: scripophily; industrial history. Home and Office: PO Box 9, Tadworth Surrey KT20 7JU, England

MILLS, CARROLL BING, physicist, consultant; b. Huntington, W.Va., Aug. 8, 1916; s. Otto Herbert and Edith Marie (Bing) M.; m. Anita Margery Hodgson, Feb. 17, 1944; children—Kenneth, Elissa, Ivy, Valerie. AB, Marshall U., 1938; MS, U. Hawaii, 1941. Physicist U.S. Engring. Dept., Honolulu, 1941-43, U. Calif.-Berkeley, 1943-47, Oak Ridge Nat. Lab., 1947-54, Curtiss Wright Corp., Woodridge, N.J., 1954-56, Los Alamos Nat. Lab., 1956-74, cons., Santa Fe, 1974—; cons. Energy Conversion Systems, Ottawa, Ont., Can., 1974—. Contbr. articles to profl. pubs. Patentee in field. Mem. Am. Phys. Soc., Am. Nuclear Soc. (chmn. Trinity sect. 1966), AAAS (hon.). Republican. Mem. Ch. of Jesus Christ of Latter-day Saints. Club: Toastmasters dist. gov. 1966). Home and Office: PO Box 802 155 Greene St Kenwood CA 95452

MILLS, FREDERICK VANFLEET, art educator, watercolorist; b. Bremen, Ohio, June 5, 1925; s. Frederick William and Juanita Ellen (VanFleet) M.; m. Lois Jean Rademacher; children: Mark Steven (dec.), Michael Sherwood, Mollie Sue, Merre Shannon, Randal Dean, Susan Lynn, Todd Patrick, Shondra Marie. B.S., Ohio State U., 1949; M.S., Ind. U., 1951, Ed.D., 1956; postgrad., U.S. Army Staff and Command Coll., 1973-76. Tchr. art, supr. Celina (Ohio) Public Schs., 1949-51; instr. univ. high sch. Ind. U., 1951-55, from asst. prof. art to prof., 1955-65; vis. prof. U. Tex.-Austin, 1965; chmn. design dept. U. Tenn., 1966-68; chmn. dept. art Ill. State U., 1968-85; pres. Western Arts Assn., 1964-66; research reader Humanities br. HEW, 1968-69; cons., resource person Rockefeller Panel, 1977; cons. Latin Am. Scholarship Program (Brazil) Harvard U., 1981-82; mem. com. Ill. Fine Arts Rev. for Capital Devel. Bd., 1987—, planning com. Nat. Inst. Advanced Studies in Art and Design and Archives of Am. Art Sch., 1988—; trustee Ill. Summer Sch. for the Arts, 1988—. Author, editor: The Status of the Visual Arts in

Higher Education, 1976, New Perspectives in Visual Arts Administration, 1977, Issues in the Administration of Visual Arts, 1978, Politics and the Visual Arts, 1979, The Visual Arts in the Ninth Decade, 1980; contbr. to profl. jours.; watercolors exhibited, Suzette Schochet Gallery, Newport, R.I. Pres. Ill. Alliance Art Edn., 1975-77; mem. Tenn. Arts Commn., 1967-68. Served to maj. USAR; Col. Ill. Militia. Recipient Recognition award Alliance for Arts Edn., 1984. Mem. Nat. Council Art Adminstrs. (dir. 1973-79, sr. research editor 1979-81), Nat. Assn. Schs. Art (nat. com. 1979-81), Coll. Art Assn., Nat. Art Edn. Assn. (dir. 1964-66), Scabbard and Blade, Phi Delta Kappa, Delta Tau Delta, Delta Phi Delta. Club: Rotary Internat. Office: Ctr for Visual Arts 119 Normal IL 61761

MILLS, GEORGE MARSHALL, state official, insurance executive; b. Newton, N.J., May 20, 1923; s. J. Marshall and Emma (Scott) M.; m. Dorothy Lovilla Allen, Apr. 21, 1945; children: Dianne (Mrs. Thomas McKay III), Dorothy L.A. (Mrs. Edward Sphatt). BA, Rutgers U., 1943; MA, Columbia U., 1951, profl. cert., 1952. CLU; CPCU; chartered fin. cons. Pres. George M. Mills Inc., North Brunswick, N.J., 1946-75; pres. CORECO, Inc., Newark, 1960-78; risk mgr. N.J. Hwy. Authority, Woodbridge, 1978—; cons. Govs.'s Com. on Bus. Efficiency in Pub. Schs., 1979-80. Bd. dirs. Alpha Chi Rho Ednl. Found.; dir. workshop Easter Seal Soc.; mem. Gov.'s Task Force on Sound Mcpl. Govt., 1981-82; pres. Nat. Interfrat. Conf., 1979-80. Served with USNR, 1943-46. Mem. Am. Coll. Life Underwriters, Am. Coll. Property Liability Underwriters, Internat. Bridge Tunnel and Turnpike Assn. (chmn. risk mgmt. com., mem. bus. ins. risk mgmt. bd. 1988—), New Brunswick Hist. Soc., English Speaking Union, Alpha Chi Rho (nat. councillor 1964-70, nat. pres. 1970-73, nat. treas. 1975-87), Kappa Kappa Psi, Tau Kappa Alpha, Phi Delta Phi. Mem. Reformed Ch. Am. Club: Rutgers U. Alumni-Faculty (New Brunswick, N.J.). Home: 1054 Hoover Dr North Brunswick NJ 08902 Office: US Route 9 Woodbridge NJ 07095

MILLS, OTTO HARRY, JR., pharmacologist, researcher; b. Phila., July 1, 1941; s. Otto H. and Mary A. Mills; m. Carol Smith, Aug. 7, 1968; 1 child, Jeffrey K. B.A., Central High Sch., 1959; B.S., Kutztown U., 1963; M.S., Calif. Coast U., 1976, Ph.D., 1976. Research asst. U. Pa. Grad. Group, Phila., 1965-66, U. Pa. Vet. Sch., 1966-67; research assoc. U. Pa. Sch. Medicine, Phila., 1967-84; dir. dermatology research div. U. Medicine and Dentistry of N.J.-Robert Wood Johnson Med. Sch., New Brunswick, N.J., 1984—; dir. div. dermal research Hill Top Research, Inc., East Brunswick, N.J., 1984—. Contbr. chpts. to books and articles to profl. jours. Served with USAFR, 1966-72. Recipient Stelwagon prize Coll. Physicians Phila., 1971, Merit cert. Med. Soc. N.J., 1975. Fellow Royal Soc. Medicine, Am. Coll. Clin. Pharmacologists; mem. Am. Acad. Dermatology (faculty ann. meetings 1976—, Silver award 1970, 85, Bronze award 1981), Am. Fedn. for Clin. Research, Soc. for Exptl. Biology and Medicine, Soc. for Investigative Dermatology, Am. Soc. for Clin. Pharmacology and Therapeutics, AAAS, N.Y. Acad. Sci., Princeton U. Chapel Fellowship, Bucks County Hist. Soc., Phila. Master Track Assn., Am. Dermatol. Health Assn. Republican. Avocations: tennis; running. Office: UMDNJ-Robert Wood Johnson Med Sch Div Dermatology 1 Penn Plaza New Brunswick NJ 08901

MILLS, ROBERT A., lawyer; b. Kansas City, Mo., Jan. 14, 1934; s. William N. and Mary Aileene (Arnold) M.; m. Jan. 14, 1956 (div. Apr. 1978); children—Thomas B., James A., John M.; m. Anita Hickey, Feb. 12, 1983; 1 child, Christopher Robert. B.S., U. Mo., 1955; J.D., Washington U., St. Louis, 1960. Bar: Calif. Trial atty. U.S. Dept. Justice, Washington, 1960-62; assoc. Lewis & Roca, Phoenix, 1962-65, McCutchen Doyle Brown & Enersen, San Francisco, 1965-70; ptnr. McCutchen Doyle Brown & Enersen, 1970—. Editorial cons. Calif. Legal Systems, Wills & Trusts, 1983. Served to 1st lt. U.S. Army, 1955-57. Fellow Am. Coll. Probate Counsel; mem. State Bar Calif. (chmn. probate and trust law com. 1975-76), ABA, Fed. Bar Assn. (chpt. pres. 1964), Internat. Acad. Estate and Trust Law (pres. 1988-89). Clubs: Bankers, Olympic (San Francisco). Home: 15 Rancheria Rd Kentfield CA 94904 Office: McCutchen Doyle et al Three Embarcadero Center San Francisco CA 94111

MILLSAPS, FRED RAY, investor; b. Blue Ridge, Ga., Apr. 30, 1929; s. Samuel Hunter and Ora Lee (Bradshaw) M.; m. Audrey Margaret Hopkins, June 22, 1957; children: Judith Gail, Stephen Hunter, Walter Scott. A.B., Emory U., 1951; postgrad., U. Wis. Sch. Banking, 1955-57, Harvard Bus. Sch., 1962. Auditor Fed. Res. Bank, Atlanta, 1953-58, asst. v.p., 1958-62, v.p., 1962-64; fin. v.p. Fla. Power & Light Co., 1965-69; pres., dir. First Nat. Bank of Ft. Lauderdale, Fla., 1969-73; chmn., pres. Landmark Banking Corp. of Fla., Ft. Lauderdale, 1971-78; chmn. Landmark Union Trust Bank of St. Petersburg, Fla., 1976-78, Compupix Tech., Inc.; Dir. Fla. Nat. Bank, Shipp Corp., Toronto, Ont. Chmn. com. of 100 Broward County (Fla.) Indsl. Devel. Bd., 1972-77; chmn. South Fla. Coordinating Council, 1976-78, WPBT Community TV Found. of South Fla., 1973-75, Fla. So. Coll., Lakeland, Honda Classic, Holy Cross Found.; mem. Fla. Council of 100. Methodist. Clubs: Tower, Eagle Trace Country, Inverrary (Fort Lauderdale).

MILLSAPS, KNOX, aerospace engineer, educator; b. Birmingham, Ala., Sept. 10, 1921; s. Knox Taylor and Millie Mae (Joyce) M.; m. Lorraine Marie Hartle, June 12, 1956 (div. Nov. 1980); children—Melinda Marie, Mary Charmaine, Catherine Marie, Knox Taylor. B.A., Auburn U., 1940; Ph.D., Calif. Inst. Tech., 1943. Asso. prof. aero. engring. Ohio State U., Columbus, 1946-48; mathematician Office Air Research, 1948-49; prof. physics Auburn (Ala.) U., 1949-50, 51-52; research physicist Flight Research Lab., Wright Air Development Center, 1950-51; chief mathematician Aero. Research Lab., 1952-55; prof. mech. engring. Mass. Inst. Tech., Cambridge, 1955-56; chief sci. Air Force Missile Devel. Center, 1955-60; exec. dir. Air Force Office Sci. Research, 1960-63; research prof. aerospace engring. U. Fla., Gainesville, 1963-68, chmn. dept. engring. sci., 1973-86, prof. engring. sci., 1986—; head prof. mech. engring. Colo. State U., Fort Collins, 1968-73. Mem. Am. Phys. Soc., Am. Math. Soc., Math. Assn. Am., Soc. Indsl. and Applied Math., Soc. Engring. Sci., Am. Inst. Aeros. and Astronautics, Sigma Xi. Clubs: Cosmos, Gainesville Golf and Country. Home: PO Box 13857 Gainesville FL 32604 Office: U Fla Dept Engring Sci Gainesville FL 32611

MILLY, RAYMOND ANTHONY, lawyer; b. Pitts., Aug. 29, 1930; s. Paul Peter and Juliana (Yavorsky) M. B.A., Duquesne U., 1956; J.D., Loyola U., New Orleans, 1974. Bar: La. 1975, U.S. Dist. Ct. (ea. dist.) La. 1975, U.S. Supreme Ct. 1978, U.S. Ct. Appeals (5th cir.) 1982. Sole practice, Metairie, La., 1985—. Served with USMC, 1948-52. Democrat. Roman Catholic. Office: 117 Focis St Suite 202 Metairie LA 70005

MILNE, GEORGE RICHARD ALOYSIOUS, manufacturing company official; b. Cin., Jan. 10, 1936; s. James A. and Elizabeth (Padur) M.; m. Lorraine V. Kraus, Sept. 21, 1963 (div.); children—James R., John E.; m. Mary Ruth Jenkins, Mar. 20, 1982. Student in commerce U. Cin., 1959-62, NOMA grad. fellow cert. in mgmt. adminstrv. services; B.S. in Bus. and Commerce, U. Louisville, 1963. Supr. engring. services and records Am. Radiator and Standard San. Corp., Cin., 1958-60, product liaison engr., 1960-61, ops. supr., 1961-62, buyer, Louisville, 1962-64, supr. purchases and services, 1964, purchasing agt., 1965; purchasing agt. Mascon Toy Co. div. Masco Corp., Lorain, Ohio, 1966-69, mgr. purchasing youth and recreational products div. Leisure Group, Inc. (formerly Masco Corp.), 1969-70; purchasing agt. plumbing products div. Delta Faucet Co., Taylor, Mich. and Greensburg, Ind., 1970-75, divisional purchasing agt., 1975-76, divisional purchasing mgr., Indpls., 1976-78, divisional mgr. purchasing internat., 1978-88, v.p. purchasing, 1988—. Lectr. purchasing and economy. Bd. dirs. YMCA; active Nat. Alliance Businessmen. Served with USAF, 1955-58. Mem. Nat. Assn. Purchasing Mgmt. (Devel. Man of Yr. 1974-75, pres. 1982-83), Purchasing Mgmt. Assn. Indpls., Am. Copper Council (bd. dirs.), Copper Club. Republican. Roman Catholic. Lodge: Fraternal Order of Foresters. Contbr. articles to profl. jours. Home: 9635 Greentree Dr Carmel IN 46032 Office: 55 E 111th St Indianapolis IN 46280

MILNE, SIR JOHN (DRUMMOND), business executive; b. Aug. 13, 1924; s. Frederick John and Minnie Elizabeth Milne; m. Joan Akroyd, 1948; 4 children. Student, U. Cambridge, Eng. Mgmt. trainee APCM (now Blue Circle Industries), 1948, dir., 1964, mng. dir., chief exec., 1975; chmn. Blue Circle Industries plc, 1983—; asst. to dir. Overseas Investments, 1953; pres. Ocean Cement, Vancouver, Can., 1957; chmn., mng. dir. BCI, 1983; non-exec. chmn. DRG (formerly The Dickinson Robinson Group) plc, 1987—; bd. dirs. Royal Ins. plc. Served Brit. mil., 1943-47. Decorated Knight, 1986. Clubs: Boodle's, MCC, Berkshire Golf. Office: Chilton House, Chilton Candover, Hants England *

MILNE, JOHN STEWART, physician; b. Port Stanley, Falkland Islands, July 18, 1921; s. John and Isabella (Atkins) M.; m. Elizabeth Irons, Jan. 27, 1944; children—Jennifer, Roy, John, Veronica (dec. 1987). MB, ChB, U. Edinburgh, 1944, BSc, 1952, MD, 1973, DSc, 1982. Gen. practice medicine, Ormiston, East Lothian, Scotland, 1946-66; research fellow Scottish Home and Health Dept., Edinburgh, 1967-74, assoc. specialist in psychiatry Royal Victoria Hosp., Edinburgh, Scotland, 1973-75, cons. physician in geriatrics East Fortune Hosp., North Berwick, East Lothian, 1976-82; sr. research fellow Edinburgh U., 1982-85; ret., 1985; mem. sci. staff Med. Research Council, Edinburgh, 1971-73; cons. physician geriatric unit Royal Victoria Hosp., Edinburgh. Author: Clinical Effects of Aging; A Longitudinal Study, 1985. Contbr. articles to profl. jours. Fellow Soc. Antiquaries (Scotland), Royal Coll. Physicians (Edinburgh); mem. Brit. Med. Assn. Presbyterian. Avocations: English literature, archaeology. Home: 8 Macnair Ave, North Berwick, Lothian EH39 4QY, Scotland Office: Royal Victorian Hosp, Edinburgh Scotland

MILNER, ANTHONY CROTHERS, historian, educator; b. Melbourne, Victoria, Australia, Dec. 10, 1945; s. Norman and Audrey Ellen (Crothers) M.; m. Claire Shirley Dexter. BA, Monash U., Melbourne, 1967; MA, Cornell U., 1971, PhD, 1977. Lectr. Cornell U., Ithaca, N.Y., 1974-75; lectr. U. Kent, Canterbury, Eng., 1975-79, head dept. SE Asian studies, 1979-81; lectr. Australian Nat. U., Canberra, 1981-84, sr. lectr., 1985—; pres. Canberra br. Australian Inst. Internat. Affairs, 1986—. Author: Kerajaan: Malay Political Culture, 1982; co-author: Perceptions Of The Haj, 1984; editor: Southeast Asia From 9th to 14th Centuries, 1986. Fellow Royal Asiatic Soc.; mem. Assn. Asian Studies (editor Asian Studies Review 1985—). Club: Commonwealth (Canberra). Home: Maybrook, 2622 Braidwood Australia Office: Australian Nat U, 2000 Canberra Australia

MILO, FRANK ANTHONY, manufacturing executive; b. Bristol, Conn., Aug. 19, 1946; s. Frank Raymond and Helen Ellen Milo; BS in Indsl. Engring., Gen. Motors Inst., 1970. Abrasives supr. New Departure-Hyatt Bearings div. Gen. Motors Corp., Bristol, 1964-72; sales engr. air tools Ingersoll Rand Co., Liberty Corners, N.J., 1972-74; process engr. Electric Boat div. Gen. Dynamics, Groton, Conn., 1974-75; regional sales mgr. Unbrako Chem. Products div. SPS Tech., 1975-78; nat. sales mgr. Permabond Internat., Englewood, N.J., 1978-80; v.p. sales and mktg. world-wide Pacer Tech. & Resources, Campbell, Calif., 1980-84; pres., founder Firecat Tech., Mountain View, Calif., 1984—; bus. devel. mgr. Alembic Chems. U.S.A., Mountain View, 1986—; mktg. mgr. Penn Internat. Chem., Mountain View, 1986—. Mem. Sigma Nu. Democrat. Roman Catholic. Office: Penn Internat Chems 943 Stierlin Rd Mountain View CA 94043 also: Firecat Tech 928 Wright Ave Unit 902 Mountain View CA 94043

MILO, PATRICIA MARIE, advertising executive; b. Chgo., June 8, 1951; d. William James and Mary Lou (Terrill) Mainzer; m. Francis James Casey, May 28, 1977 (div. Jan. 1985); m. Timothy Steven Milo, March 21, 1987. BA, So. Ill. U., 1973; postgrad., Lake Forest Coll., 1987—. Graphic artist Lawson Products, Des Plaines, Ill., 1975-78; advt. coordinator Diversey Chem. Co., Des Plaines, 1978-79; advt. mgr. ACCO Internat., Inc. USA, Wheeling, Ill., 1979-81; pres., owner Prism Communications, Inc., Des Plaines, 1982—; account exec. Images Photography, Des Plaines, 1982—. Designer/editor monthly bull. Norwood Gospel Chapel. Tchr. Sunday sch., Norwood Gospel Chapel, Chgo., 1977-80; active Evang. Free Ch. of Des Plaines. Mem. Greater O'Hare Assn., Bus./Profl. Advt. Assoc. Avocations: aerobics, running, body building, reading, ballroom dancing. Office: Prism Communications Inc 4370 N Stoneharbor Dr Suite 100 Hoffman Estates IL 60195

MILOSZ, CZESLAW, poet, author, educator; b. Lithuania, June 30, 1911; came to U.S., 1960, naturalized, 1970; s. Aleksander and Weronika (Kunat) M. M.Juris, U. Wilno, Lithuania, 1934; Litt.D. (hon.), U. Mich., 1977. Programmer Polish Nat. Radio, 1935-39; diplomatic service Polish Fgn. Affairs Ministry, Warsaw, 1945-50; vis. lectr. U. Calif., Berkeley, 1960-61; prof. Slavic langs. and lits. U. Calif., 1961-78, prof. emeritus, 1978—. Author: The Captive Mind, 1953, Native Realm, 1968, Post-War Polish Poetry, 1965, The History of Polish Literature, 1969, Selected Poems, 1972, Bells in Winter, 1978, The Issa Valley, 1981, Separate Notebooks, 1984, The Land of Ulro, 1984, The Unattainable Earth, 1985. Recipient Prix Littéraire Européen Les Guildes du Livre, Geneva, 1953, Neustadt Internat. prize for lit. U. Okla., 1978, citation U. Calif., Berkeley, 1978, Nobel prize for lit., 1980; Nat. Culture Fund fellow, 1934-35; Guggenheim fellow, 1976. Mem. Am. Inst. Arts and Scis., Polish Inst. Letters and Scis. in Am., PEN Club in Exile. Office: U Calif Dept Slavic Langs and Lits Berkeley CA 94720 *

MILOV, LEONID VASILJEVICH, historian, educator; b. Moscow, July 28, 1929; s. Vasilij Vasiljevich and Olimpiada Nicolaevna (Parfentjeva) M.; m. Irina Vladimirovna Gravve, May 28, 1953; 1 child, Olga Leonidovna. Student, Lomonosov State U., Moscow, 1953, grad. in history, 1958; Dr. in History, Inst. of History Acad. Scis., Moscow, 1974. Sci. employee Inst. Slavistic Acad. Scis. USSR, Moscow, 1956-60; asst., docent Lomonosov State U., 1960-66, docent, 1976-77, prof., mem. sci. council hist. faculty, 1977—; chief lab. quantitative methods Inst. History Acad. Scis. USSR, Moscow, 1971-76. Author: Study of Economic Note General Survey, 1965; co-author: All-Russian Agrarian Market XYIII-beg. XX, 1974, Tendency of Agrarian Development in Russian State I Half XYII, 1986; asst. editor in chief Jour. History USSR, 1966-71, mem. editorial staff, 1966-75. Communist. Office: Hist Faculty Lomonosov State U, Leninskie gory, 117234 Moscow USSR

MILOVANOVIC, GRADIMIR V., mathematics educator, consultant; b. Zorunovac, Yugoslavia, Jan. 2, 1948; s. Vukasin and Vukadinka (Savic) M.; m. Dobrila Lazic, Sept. 8, 1967; 1 child, Irena. BS in Computer Sci., U. Nis, 1971, MS in Math., 1974, PhD in Math., 1976. Asst. dept. math. faculty electronic engring. U. Nis, Yugoslavia, 1971-76, asst. prof., 1976-81, assoc. prof., 1982-85, prof., 1986—, head dept. math., 1983—, chmn. bd. grad. studies 1982-87; vis. prof. S. Markovic U., Kragujevac, Yugoslavia, 1981-84; head researcher project Regional Assoc. Sci., Nis, 1982—;chmn. organizing com. Conf. Numerical Methods and Approximation Theory, 1984, 87. Author 6 books and textbooks, 70 papers on numerical analysis, 1979—; editor: Numerical Methods and Approximation Theory, 1984, 88; editor-in chief Facta Universitatis-Ser. Mathematics and Informatics univ. jour.; mem. editorial bd. Jour. Univ. Beograd. Publ. Elektrotehn Fak. Ser. Mat. Fiz; reviewer math. reviews. Grantee Rep. Sci. Found, Belgrade, 1986—. Mem. Societe Mathematique de France, Am. Math. Soc., GAMM, University Tchrs. Recipient Anniversary award Faculty Electronic Engring., 1981. Home: B Adzije 26/10, 18000 Nis Yugoslavia Office: Faculty Electronic Engring, Beogradska 14, PO Box 73, 18000 Nis Yugoslavia

MILSTEIN, CÉSAR, molecular biologist; b. Oct. 8, 1927; s. Lázaro and Máxima Milstein; m. Celia Prilleltensky, 1953. Ed. Colegio Nacional De Bahia Blanca, U. Nacional de Buenos Aires, Fitzwilliam Coll., Cambridge. Brit. Council fellow, 1958-60; staff Instituto Nacional de Microbiologia, Buenos Aires, 1957-63, head Div. de Biologia Molecular, 1961-63; mem. staff M.R.C. Lab. of Molecular Biology, 1963—, mem. gov. bd., 1975-79. Recipient Royal medal Royal Soc., 1982, Nobel prize for medicine, 1984; Rozenberg prize, 1979, Mattia award, 1979, Gross Howit prize, 1980, Koch prize, 1980, Wolf prize in medicine, 1980, Wellcome Found. medal, 1980, Gimene Dia medal, 1981, Sloan prize Gen. Motors Cancer Research Found., 1981, Gardner award Gardner Found., 1981. Contbr. articles to profl. jours. Fellow Royal Coll. Physicians (hon.); mem. Nat. Acad. Scis. (fgn. assoc.). Avocation: cooking. Office: Med Research Council Centre, Hills Rd, Cambridge England *

MILSTEIN, FREDERICK, mechanical engineer, materials scientist, educator; b. N.Y.C., May 14, 1939; s. Herman and Fay (Schatz) M.; B.S., UCLA, 1962; M.S. (Ford Found. fellow), 1963, Ph.D. (NASA predoctoral traineeship), 1966; m. Ester Aida Gleizer, Aug. 28, 1960; children—Michael David, Deborah Sue, Lawrence Joshua. Scientist, Centre National de la Recherche Scientifique, Grenoble, France, 1966-67; research scientist RAND Corp., Santa Monica, Calif., 1967-69; acting asst. prof. UCLA, 1969-70; asst. prof. U. Calif., Santa Barbara, 1970-73, asso. prof., 1973-78, prof., 1978—, asso. dean Coll. Engring., 1973-75; chmn. dept. mech. and environ. engring., 1981-82; lectr. and guest lectr. UCLA, 1968-69; resident cons. RAND Corp., 1969-71, Mission Research Corp., 1985-87. Sr. fellow Weizmann Inst. Sci., Rehovot, Israel, 1975-76; Guggenheim fellow dept. applied math. and theoretical physics U. Cambridge, Eng., summer 1975, 76, also vis. fellow Clare Hall, Cambridge; Guggenheim Meml. fellow, 1975-76; NATO sr. fellow, 1976-77; sr. disting. fellow Am. Soc. Engring. Edn., 1988. Mem. Am. Phys. Soc., ASME, Am. Soc. for Metals, Am. Soc. Engring. Edn., AAUP, N.Y. Acad. Sci., Sigma Xi. Contbr. articles profl. jours. Home: 456 Braemar Ranch Ln Santa Barbara CA 93109 Office: U Calif Mechanical Engring Dept Santa Barbara CA 93106

MILSTEIN, NATHAN, concert violinist; b. Odessa, Russia, Dec. 31, 1904; came to U.S.,, naturalized, 1942; s. Miron and Maria (Bluestein) M.; m. Therese Weldon, 1945; 1 dau., Maria Bernadette. Student, of P. Stoliarsky, Odessa, of Leopold Auer at Conservatory Music St. Petersburg, of Eugene Ysaye at Brussels. Extensive tours of native country, 1920-26; ann. tours all European countries, U.S. and Can. since 1929, interrupted by World War.; several tours, S.Am., Cuba, Mex., North Africa. Recipient Grammy award for classical-instrumental soloist, 1975, Kennedy Ctr. award for Lifetime Achievement, 1987; decorated comdr. Legion of Honor (France); Cross of Honor (Austria). Mem. Acad. St. Cecilia (Italy). Address: care Shaw Concerts Inc 1995 Broadway New York NY 10023 *

MILTON, ARTHUR GREGORY, newspaper executive; b. Bklyn., Jan. 24, 1911; s. Joseph and Elsie (Broedel) M.; m. Marie F. Landis, Apr. 5, 1942; children—Donald Landis, Patricia Ann. With N.Y. World, 1930-31; exec. N.Y. Mirror, 1931-34, 40-63, N.Y. Am., 1934-37; exec. N.Y. Jour. Am., 1963-66, World Jour. Tribune, N.Y.C., 1966-67; asso. pub., v.p. El Tiempo, 1967-68; pres., pub. Levittown (N.Y.) Tribune, 1968-72; exec. L.I. Press, 1972-77, The Trib, 1977-78; pub. Dateline mag., 1959-79; exec. v.p. Mid Island Tribune Co., Inc., 1968-81. Mem. N.Y. State Fair Trial-Free Press Conf., 1968-79. Trustee Overseas Press Club Edward R. Murrow Found., 1963-68, 72-79, treas., 1972-75; trustee Bob Considine Scholarship Fund. Served as capt. AUS, World War II; ETO. Mem. Overseas Press Club (sec. 1965-66, gov. 1973-74, 77-79, v.p. 1974-76, award for meritorious service 1959-61, 76), Soc. Silurians, Banshees, 4th Inf. Div. Assn., N.Y. Press Assn., Phoenix Press Club, Sigma Delta Chi, Deadline Club (exec. council 1968-78, treas. 1975-79). Club: L.I. Athletic. Home: 18823 129th Ave Sun City West AZ 85375

MILTON, JAMES, public relations executive; b. Dublin, Ireland, Sept. 21, 1945; s. Thomas James and Phillomena Mary (O'Neill) M.; m. Carmel Barron, July 13, 1947; children: Donal Aoife,Tara Ciaran. Post master's gen. cert., Kevin State Vocat. Coll., 1963. Trainee journalist Bus. and Fin. Mag., Dublin, 1964-65, journalist, 1966-68, dep. editor, 1968-69, editor, 1970-73; dir. Murray Cons., Dublin, 1974—; non-exec. dir. Belenos Publs., Dublin, 1975-84; dir. Fourel Investments, Dublin. Bd. dirs. Friends St. Luke's Hosp., Dublin, 1982—; mem. Appeal's Com. of Hospice for Dying-Harold's Cross, 1987. Mem. Mktg. Inst. Ireland, Pub. Relations Inst. Ireland. Roman Catholic. Home: 79 Terenure Rd W, Dublin 6 Ireland Office: Murray Cons, 35 Upper Mount St, Dublin 2 Ireland

MILTON, ROBERT MITCHELL, chemical company executive; b. St. Joseph, Mich., Nov. 29, 1920; s. Clare Leon and Frances Thornton (Mitchell) M.; m. Mary Wills Bridges, June 22, 1946; children—Mrs. M. Gillian Sanders, Mrs. Suzanne M. Padilla, David Wills. B.A., Oberlin Coll., 1941; M.A., Johns Hopkins U., 1943, Ph.D., 1944. C.Y. War Project Johns Hopkins U., Balt., 1943-45, research assoc., 1945-46; with Union Carbide Corp., 1946-85, research chemist, 1946-51, research supr., 1951-54, mgr. devel. lab., 1954-58, asst. mgr. new products, 1958-59, asst. dir., then dir. research Linde div., 1959-73, exec. v.p. Showa UNOX, Showa Union Gosei div., 1973-77, dir. agrl. bus. devel., v.p. Keystone Seed Co. div., 1977-79; assoc. corp. dir. product safety and liability Union Carbide Corp., Danbury, Conn., 1980-85; pres. R. Milton Assocs., Inc., 1986—; cons. U.S. Naval Tech. Mission to Europe, 1945; mem. adv. bd. hyperbaric medicine SUNY, 1966-73; mem. nat. research council panel on environ. protection, safety and hazardous materials of Com. on Chem. Engring. Frontiers, 1985-87. Inventor Linde molecular sieve adsorbents and catalysts, hi-flux tubing; patentee in field. Mem. AAAS, Am. Chem. Soc. (Jackob F. Schoelkopf medal 1963), Am. Inst. Chem. Engrs., Am. Inst. Chemists (Chem. Pioneer award 1980, dir. at large 1982-87, pres.-elect 1988—), Phi Beta Kappa, Sigma Xi. Clubs: Wawashkamo Golf (pres.); Mackinac Island (Mich.) Yacht; Johns Hopkins. Home and Office: 5991 Set-N-Sun Pl Jupiter FL 33458 also: PO Box 326 Mackinac Island MI 49757

MILUTINOVIČ, VELJKO M., computer science educator; b. Belgrade, Yugoslavia, May 4, 1951; came to U.S., 1982; s. Milan M. and Simonda D. (Dodič) M.; m. Dragana Panajotovič; children: Dusan, Milan, Goran. BS in Elect. Engring., U. Belgrade, 1975, MS in Engring, 1978, PhD, 1982. Teaching/research asst. U. Belgrade, 1975-76; proj. leader Michael Pupin Inst., Belgrade, 1967-82; asst. prof. Fla. Internat. U., Miami, 1982-83, Purdue U., West Lafayette, Ind., 1983—; cons. RCA, Moorestown, N.J., 1984—, NCR, Dayton, Ohio, 1987—. Contbr. articles to profl. jours.; papers in field. Mem. IEEE, European Assn. for Microprocessing of Microprogramming (bd. dirs 1977—), Yugoslav. Assn. for Elect. Engring., Internat Soc. Mini and Micro Computer Systems. Home: 725 Northridge Dr West Lafayette IN 47906 Office: Purdue U Sch Elect Engring West Lafayette IN 47907

MILWARD, ALAN STEELE, economic history educator, consultant; b. Stoke-on-Trent, Eng., Jan. 19, 1935; s. Joseph Thomas and Dorothy (Steele) M.; m. Claudine Jeanne Lemaitre, Nov. 25, 1963; children: Colette, Victoire, Zoe. BA, U. Coll., London, 1956; PhD, London Sch. Econs., 1960; MA, U. Manchester, 1976. Lectr. econ. history U. Edinburgh, Scotland, 1960-65; sr. lectr. social studies U. East Anglia, Norwich, Eng., 1965-68; vis. prof. econs. Stanford U., 1966-67, assoc. prof., 1969-71; vis. prof. econs. U. Ill., Urbana, 1978-79; guest prof. Inst. Sozialwissenschaften U. Siegen, Fed. Republic Germany, 1980; prof. European studies U. Manchester, Eng., 1971-83; prof. contemporary history European U. Inst., Florence, Italy, 1983-86; prof. econ. history London Sch. Econs., 1986—; external prof. European U. Inst., Florence, 1986—; dir. d'etudes Ecole de Hautes Etudes en Sci. Sociales. Author: The German Economy at War, 1965, The New Order and the French Economy, 1970, War Economy and Society, 1977, The Reconstruction of Western Europe, 1986; contbr. articles to profl. jours. Mem. Archives Adv. Com. European Community. Brit. Acad. fellow 1987. Mem. Univ. Assn. Contemporary European Studies (pres. 1980-83), Econ. History Assn., German History Soc., Assn. Profs. History contemporary aspiér Communanté Européene. Office: London Sch Econs, Houghton St, London WC2, England

MIMAROGLU, SAIT KEMAL, management executive; b. Siirt, Turkey, Aug. 24, 1929; s. Abdullah and Feride Mimaroglu; m. Esma Bilge Calguner, July 8, 1972; children—Feride Idil, Emre Kemal, Cem Kemal. B.S., Faculty Polit. Scis. and Law (Turkey), 1952; LL.D., Faculty of Law (Turkey), 1956. Asst. prof. Faculty Polit. Scis., Ankara, Turkey, 1956-60, assoc. prof., 1960-67, prof., 1967—; chmn., chief exec. officer Tobank, Ankara, 1963-87 ; bd. dirs. Aymar, Istanbul, Turkey, 1978—, Ardem, Istanbul, 1978-87 , Sark, Istanbul, 1978-87; chmn. chief exec. office Mekas, Ankara, 1987—. bd. dirs. Güris, Ankara. Author: Foreigner's Real Estate Ownership in Turkey, 1956; Collective Bargaining in Turkish Law, 1964, Treaty of Business Law, 1967. Active Inst. Internat. de Droit d'Expression Francaise, Paris, R.B.A., Global Econ. Action Inst., N.Y.C. Served to lt. Turkish Army, 1954-56. Mem. Internat. Bankers Assn. (v.p. 1974-76, exec. com. 1976-78), Tüsiad (Turkish Industrialists and Businessmen's Assn.) Home: Saf Saf Sokak #24 Emirgan, Istanbul Turkey

MIMS, THOMAS JEROME, insurance executive; b. Sumter County, S.C., Dec. 12, 1899; m. Valma Gillespie, 1926; children: Thomas Jerome, G. Frank. B.A., Furman U., 1921. With Rec. and Statis. Corp. N.Y., 1921-29; asst. mgr. Rec. and Statis. Corp. N.Y., Phila., 1922-25; mgr. Rec. and Statis. Corp. N.Y., Indpls., 1925-27, Boston, 1927-29; ins. spl. agt. State of N.J., 1931-32; mgr. Wm. R. Timmons Agy., Greenville, S.C., 1933—; v.p., sec. Canal Ins. Co., Greenville, 1942-48; pres., dir. Canal Ins. Co., 1948—, Canal Indemnity Co., Greenville; partner Valetep, Greenville, 1975—; mem. Legis.

Com. To Study Automobile Liability Ins., 1969-70. Emeritus mem. adv. council Furman U., from 1974; mem. adv. bd. S.C. Safety Council, 1969-84, pres., 1970-75, 81-84; bd. dirs. United Way of Greenville, 1970-88, campaign vice chmn., 1975, chmn., 1976, v.p., 1977, pres., 1978, chmn. bd., 1979, hon. bd. dirs., 1981; bd. dirs. S.C. United Way, 1981-84; mem. fin. com. 1st Bapt. Ch., Greenville, 1971—, past pres. men's Bible class; pres. Rotary Charities, Inc., 1964-65; past mem. bd. dirs. Met. Arts Council; mem. Greenville Little Theatre Council, 1951-85, bus. mgr., 1951-53, 64-66, v.p., 1956-57, 72-73, pres., 1957-58, 73-75; bd. dirs. Greenville Area Mental Health Ctr. Named Boss of Yr., Greenville Jaycees, 1964, Boss of Yr., Greenville Assn. Ins. Women, 1977; S.C. Vol. of Yr., United Way, 1979; Ins. Co. Man of Yr., Ind. Ins. Agts. S.C., 1980; recipient Service award Internat. Ins. Soc., Paris, 1098. Fellow Pres.'s Council AIM; mem. Greenville C. of C. (chmn. community relations com. 1964-69, dir. 1969-74, pres. 1973, pres. Found. 1973), S.C. C. of C., U.S. C. of C. (ins. com. 1959-61, 64-68), Internat. Ins. Soc. (chmn. bd. dirs. 1983-84, bd. electors, registrar 1984-85, past other coms., named to Hall of Fame, Service award 1980), Nat. Assn. Ins. Agts., S.C. Assn. Ins. Agts., Greenville Assn. Ins. Agts. (v.p. 1950-51, pres. 1951-52, chmn. exec. com. 1952-53), Am. Mgmt. Assn., President's Assn., Motor Transp. Assn. (dir. 1973-75, chmn. ins. com. 1951-63), Assn. S.C. Property and Casualty Ins. Cos. (1st v.p. 1961-62, 71-72, pres. 1962-63, 72-73, exec. com. 1961-74), Truck and Heavy Equipment Claims Council (charter mem., chmn. membership com.), Internat. Platform Assn., Newcomen Soc., Conf. Bd. Clubs: World Trade (Atlanta); Poinsett (emeritus), Commerce, Greenville Touchdown, (charter, pres. 1963-64), Clemson IPTAY, City, Furman Paladins (Greenville); Palmetto, Summit (Columbia, S.C.); Short Snout. Lodge: Rotary (pres. Greenville 1963-64, v.p. 1964-65). Office: Canal Ins Co PO Box 7 Greenville SC 29602

MINAC, VLADIMIR, writer, screenwriter, linguist, literary critic; b. Klenovec, Czechoslovakia, Aug. 10, 1922; s. Jan and Zuzana (Karkuš) M.; m. Méria Denesova, Nov. 14, 1949; children: Vladimír, Galina, Verona. B of Philosophy, Comenius U., Bratislava, Czechoslovakia, 1944. Editor Obrana Tudu, Bratislava, 1946-49; chief editor Kultúrny Život, Bratislava, 1951-55, Slovenské Pohlady, Bratislava, 1955-56; profl. writer Bratislava, 1957—; chmn. Matica Slovenské, Bratislava, 1974—. Author: (compiled essays) Time and Books, 1962, Paradoxes, 1966, Blowing in the Embers, 1970, On Literature, 1972, Selected Disputes of J.M. Hurban, 1974, Texts and Contexts, 1982, Coherences, 1986; (general non-fiction) Death Strikes in the Mountains, 1948, Yesterday and Tomorrow, 1949, Breakthrough, 1950, At the Turn, 1954, (trilogy) The Long Time of Waiting, 1958, Living and the Dead, 1959, The Bells Ring For a Day, 1961, (general non-fiction) You Are Never Alone, 1962, Records, 1964, Who Marches Along the Road, 1966, The Happiness-Maker, 1966, Portraits, 1986; screenwriter Czech films The Fight Will End Tomorrow, 1951, Méria Justinové, 1951, Untilled Fields, 1954, Captain Dabač, 1959. Mem. cen. com. Communist Party of Slovakia, 1971—; dep. Slovak Nat. Council, 1971—. Recipient numerous national and international awards and honours. Mem. Czechoslovak Fgn. Inst. (chmn. 1982—), Union Slovak Writers, Union Czechoslovak Writers. Home: Vazovova 17, 81107 Bratislava Czechoslovakia Office: Matica Slovenska, Pugacevova 2, 812 51 Bratislava Czechoslovakia

MINAH, FRANCIS MISHECK, politician for the Republic of Sierra Leone; b. Pujehum, Sierra Leone, Aug. 19, 1929; m. Gladys Emuchay; 6 children. Grad. Methodist Boys Sch., 1948; LLB with honors Kings Coll., U. London, 1963, LLM S. OAS., 1965. Civil service clk., Sierra Leone, 1949-55, asst. social devel. officer, 1955-59, pres. Student's Union of Great Britain and Ireland, 1960-62, mem. Ho. of Reps., Sierra Leone, from 1967-87 , minister of Trade and Industry, 1973-75, minister of Fgn. Affairs, 1975-77, atty. gen. and minister of Justice, 1977-79, 82-84, minister of Finance, 1979-82, 1st v.p., 1984-87. Decorated Order of the Republic, Sierra Leone, 1977, Comdr, of Rep., Sierra Leone 1986; UNESCO fellow to study community devel. in India and Liberia. Address: Office of the, 1st Vice President, Freetown Sierra Leone *

MINAHAN, DANIEL FRANCIS, manufacturing company executive; b. Orange, N.J., Dec. 3, 1929; s. Alfred A. and Katherine (Kelly) M.; m. Mary Jean Gaffney, May 2, 1953; children: Daniel Francis, John Alfred. AB magna cum laude, U. Notre Dame, 1951; JD magna cum laude, U. Conn., 1964; grad., Advanced Mgmt. Program, Harvard, 1975. Bar: Conn. 1964, U.S. Supreme Ct 1964, U.S. Ct. of Appeals, U.S. Dist. Ct. Conn. 1967. Mgr. indsl. engring. Uniroyal, Inc., Naugatuck, Conn., 1952-59, mgr. indsl. relations, 1959-64; dir. labor relations Uniroyal, Inc., N.Y.C., 1964-66; v.p. indsl. relations and labor counsel Phillips Van Heusen Corp., N.Y.C., 1966-69; v.p. personnel-adminstrn. Broadway-Hale Stores, Inc., Los Angeles, 1969-70; v.p. employee relations, sec. Magnavox-N.Am., Philips Corp., 1970-73, v.p. ops., group exec., 1973-83, sr. v.p. adminstrn., 1984—. Co-author: The Developing Labor Law, 1971. Pres. Magnavox Found.; chmn. bd. Internat. Fedn. Keystone Youth Orgns., London and Chgo.; trustee U. Conn. Law Sch. Served with USMCR. Mem. ABA, Conn. Bar Assn., Assn. Bar City N.Y., NAM, Research Inst. Am., Harvard Advanced Mgmt. Assn., Japan Soc., Bur. Nat. Affairs, Internat. Platform Assn., Electronic Inst. Am. Clubs: Harvard, Bd. Room (N.Y.C.); Club Internat. (Chgo.); Belfrey (London); Landmark. Office: N Am Philips Corp 100 E 42d St New York NY 10017

MINAMI, NAOYUKI, architect; b. Tokyo, Oct. 22, 1953; s. Naoji and Kiiko Minami. BArch, Tokyo Met. U., 1977, MArch, 1979. Registered architect, Tokyo. Archtl. engr. Yachiyo Engring. Co., Ltd., Tokyo, 1979—. Home: 1-8-5 Azabu-juban Minato-ku, Tokyo 106, Japan Office: Yachiyo Engring Co Ltd, 1-10-21 Nakameguro Megurolen, Tokyo 153, Japan

MINCH, VIRGIL ADELBERT, civil and sanitary engineer; b. Cleve., Dec. 24, 1924; s. Henry Joseph and Mary (Terlaak) M.; BS, N.D. State U., 1946; SM in San. Engring., Mass. Inst. Tech., 1948; m. Elma Queen, Jan. 6, 1947; children—David, Philip. Research asso. Mass. Inst. Tech., 1948-49; sr. san. engr. USPHS, Cin., 1949-53; staff engr. Mead Corp., Chillicothe, Ohio, 1953-55, group leader, 1956-59, mgr. pollution control activities, 1960-65, asso. dir. tech. services, 1966-68, coordinator environmental resources, 1969-73; v.p., dir. Asso. Water and Air Resources Engrs., Nashville, 1972-74; project mgr. Stanley Cons., Muscatine, Iowa, 1974, v.p., 1974-77; v.p. John J. Harte Assocs., Inc., Atlanta, 1977-78; SE regional mktg. mgr. Environ. Research and Tech., Atlanta, 1978-80; engr., design mgr. Fluor Daniel, Inc., Greenville, S.C., 1980-83, project mgr., 1983-86; pres. VAMCO Engring. Exec. Search Group, 1986—; engr. dir. USPHS Res., 1980—. Recipient Indsl. liaison service award Ohio River Valley Water Sanitation Commn., 1959. Registered profl. engr. Ga., N.J. Mem. Scioto Conservancy dist. (v.p., dir. 1959—), Am. Meteorol. Soc., Am. Water Works Assn., Water Pollution Control Fedn., Air Pollution Control Assn., TAPPI, Ga. Pulp and Paper Assn. (sec. 1955-65), Nat. Council Air and Stream Improvement (chmn. S. Central region 1963-69), Nat. Rivers and Harbors Congress (chmn. S.E. Ohio sect. 1968-72), Sigma Xi, Tau Beta Pi, Sigma Phi Delta. Contbr. articles profl. jours. Patentee plastic film trickling filter. Home: 3146 Smokecreek Ct Atlanta GA 30345 Office: 3000 Langford Rd Suite 700 Norcross GA 30071

MINDEL, LAURENCE BRISKER, restaurateur; b. Toledo, Oct. 27, 1937; s. Seymour Stewart and Eleanor (Brisker) M.; B.A., U. Mich., 1959; m. Deborah Dudley, Oct. 20, 1978; children: Katherine Dudley, Nicolas Laurence; children by previous marriage—Michael Laurence, Laura Beth, Anthony Jay. Gen. mgr. Western Coffee Instants, Inc. Burlingame, Cal., 1962-64, dir., partner, 1964, chmn., chief exec. officer Caswell Coffee Co., San Francisco, 1964-70; v.p., dir. Coffee Instants, Inc., Long Island City, N.Y., 1966-70; v.p. Superior Tea and Coffee Co., 1968-70; chmn., chief exec. officer Spectrum Foods, Inc., 1970-85; pres. Restaurant Group Saga Corp., Menlo Park, Calif., 1985-86; chmn., chief exec. officer Il Fornaio (Am.) Corp., 1987—. Trustee The Branson Sch. Mem. San Francisco Mus. Art, Young Pres. Orgn. Internat. Club: The Concordia-Argonaut (San Francisco). Home: 86 San Carlos Ave Sausalito CA 94965 Office: Il Fornaio Am Corp 725 Greenwich St San Francisco CA 94133

MINDELL, EARL LAWRENCE, nutritionist, pharmacist, author; b. St. Boniface, Man., Can., Jan. 20, 1940; s. William and Minerva Sybil (Galsky) M.; came to U.S., 1965, naturalized, 1972; BS in Pharmacy, N.D. State U., 1963; PhD in Nutrition, Pacific We. U., 1985; m. Gail Andrea Jaffe, May 16, 1971; children: Evan Louis-Ashley, Alanna Dayan. Pres. Adanac Mgmt. Inc., 1979—, Compact Disc-Count, Inc.; instr. Dale Carnegie course; lectr. on nutrition, radio and TV. Mem. Beverly Hills, Rancho Park, Western Los Angeles (dir.) regional chambers commerce, Calif., Am. pharm. assns., Am. Acad. Gen. Pharm. Practice, Am. Inst. for History of Pharmacy, Am. Nutrition Soc., Internat. Coll. Applied Nutrition, Nutrition Found., Nat. Health Fedn., Am. Dieticians Assn., Orthomolecular Med. Assn., Internat. Acad. Preventive Medicine. Clubs: City of Hope, Masons, Shriners. Author: Earl Mindell's Vitamin Bible, Earl Mindell's Vitamin Bible for your Kid, Earl Mindell's Quick and Easy Guide to Better Health, Earl Mindell's Pill Bible, Earl Mindell's Shaping Up with Vitamins, Earl Mindell's Unsafe At Any Meal; columnist Let's Live mag., The Vitamin Supplement (Can.), The Vitamin Connection (U.K.), Better Health and Living mag.; contbr. articles on nutrition to profl. jours. Home: 709 N Hillcrest Rd Beverly Hills CA 90210 Office: 10739 W Pico Blvd West Los Angeles CA 90064

MINDER, GABRIEL GEORGE, management consultant; b. Budapest, Hungary, Aug. 4, 1936; arrived in Switzerland, 1943; m. Wanda S. Magaloff, Sept. 23, 1967; children: Raphael, Xenia. MS, ETH, Zurich, Switzerland, 1959, PhD, 1969. Registered indsl. engr., Switzerland. Planning engr. Schmidheiny & Co., Zurich, 1960-62; sr. adminstrn. officer CERN, Geneva, 1963-72; v.p. Schindler, Lucerne, Switzerland, 1972-75; cons. mgmt. Geneva, 1976—; bd. dirs. The Intelligent Office Co., London. Author: (with others) Ratios for EDP, 1977. Served to capt. Swiss Arty. Res. Mem. Schweizer Verein Datenverarb (founding mem.), Brit. Computer Soc. (affiliate mem.), Swiss Computer Cons. Assn. (bd. dirs. 1986—).

MINDES, GAYLE DEAN, educator; b. Kansas City, Mo., Feb. 11, 1942; d. Elton Burnett and Juanita Maxine (Mangold) Taylor; BS, U. Kans., 1964; MS, U. Wis., 1965; EdD, Loyola U., Chgo., 1979; m. Marvin William Mindes, June 20, 1969 (dec.); 1 son, Jonathan Seth. Tchr. public schs., Newburgh, N.Y., 1965-67; spl. educator Ill. Dept. Mental Health, Chgo., 1967-69; spl. edn. supr. Evanston (Ill.) Dist. 65 Schs., 1969-74; lectr. Northeastern Ill. U., Chgo., 1974, Loyola U., Chgo., 1974-76, Coll. St. Francis, Joliet, Ill., 1976-79, North Park Coll., Chgo., 1978; cons. Chgo. Head Start, 1978-79; asst. prof. edn. Oklahoma City U., 1979-80; vis. asst. prof., research assoc. Roosevelt U. Coll. Edn., Chgo., after 1983; dir. research and devel., dir. tchr. edn., asst. prof.; cons. Arts Council Oklahoma City, Okla. Indian Affairs Commn., 1979-80, Lincolnwood (Ill.) Pub. Schs., Chgo. Pub. Schs., Atwood Sch. Dist, Chgo. Assn. Reatrded Citizens, Nat. Assn. Tech. Tng. Schs., Ill. State Bd. Edn., Itasca Pub. Schs., Decatur Pub. Schs., edn. orgns. Assoc. editor Ill. Sch. Research and Devel.; editor Ill. Div. Early Childhood Edn. Adv. Com. to Ill. Bd. Edn.; contbr. articles to profl. jours. Bd. dirs. North Side Family Day Care, 1981; mem. edn. adv. com. Okla. Dept. Edn., 1979-80; mem. planning com. Lake View Citizens Council Day Care Center, 1978-79, Lake View Mental Health Adv. Bd., 1986-88, local planning council Ill. Dept. Child and Family Services, Florence G. Heller JCC membership com., Harold Washington Coll. Child Devel. Adv. Bd., Cerebral Palsy Assn. scholar, 1965; U. Wis. fellow in mental retardation, 1964-65; U. Kans. scholar, 1960. Fellow Am. Orthopsychiat. Assn.; mem. Assn. Supervision and Curriculum Devel., Assn. Children with Learning Disabilities, Nat. Assn. Edn. Young Children, Am. Ednl. Research Assn., Council for Exceptional Children, Ill. Council for Exceptional Children, Council for Adminstrs. Spl. Edn., Council on Children with Behavioral Disorders, AAUP, Soc. for Research in Child Devel., Alpha Sigma Nu, Phi Delta Kappa, Pi Lambda Theta. Office: Roosevelt U Coll Edn Chicago IL 60605

MINEMURA, KATSUHIRO, mathematics educator; b. Takada, Niigata, Japan, June 2, 1945; s. Katsuya and Aiko Minemura; m. Yuriko Yamazaki; children: Tomohiro, Satoko. Bachelor's degree, U. Tokyo, 1968, Master's degree, 1970, DSc, 1974. Research asst. Hiroshima (Japan) U., 1971-74; lectr. Japan Women's U., Tokyo, 1974-75, assoc. prof., 1975—; research asst. The Inst. for Advanced Study, Princeton, N.J., 1977-78. Contbr. articles to profl. jours. Office: Japan Women's U, 2-8-1 Mejirodai Bunkyo-ku, Tokyo 112, Japan

MINER, JOHN BURNHAM, industrial relations educator, writer; b. N.Y.C., July 20, 1926; s. John Lynn and Bess (Burnham) M.; children by previous marriage: Barbara, John, Cynthia, Frances; m. Barbara Allen Williams, June 1, 1979; children: Jennifer, Heather. AB, Princeton U., 1950, PhD, 1955; MA, Clark U., 1952. Lic. psychologist, Ga., N.Y. Research Assoc. Columbia U., 1956-57; mgr. psychol. services Atlantic Refining Co., Phila., 1957-60; faculty mem. U. Oreg., Eugene, 1960-68; prof., chmn. dept. organizational sci. U. Md., College Park, 1968-73; research prof. Ga. State U., Atlanta, 1973-87; pres. Organizational Measurement Systems Press, Buffalo, 1976—; prof. Human Resources SUNY, Buffalo, 1987—; cons. McKinsey & Co., N.Y.C., 1966-69; vis. lectr. U. Pa., Phila, 1959-60; vis. prof. U. Calif., Berkeley, 1966-67, U. South Fla., Tampa, 1972. Author many books and monographs including Personnel Psychology, 1969; Personnel and Industrial Relations, 1969, 73, 77, 85; The Challenge of Managing, 1975; (with Mary Green Miner) Policy Issues in Personnel and Industrial Relations, 1977; (with George A. Steiner) Management Policy and Strategy, 1977 (James A. Hamilton-Hosp. Adminstrs. Book award) 1982, 86; (with M.G. Miner) Employee Selection Within the Law, 1978; Theories of Organizational Behavior, 1980; Theories of Organizational Structure and Process, 1982; People Problems: The Executive Answer Book, 1985; The Practice of Management, 1985; Organizational Behavior: Performance and Productivity, 1988; contbr. numerous articles, papers to profl. jours. Served with AUS, 1944-46, ETO. Decorated Bronze Star, Combat Infantryman's Badge; named Disting. Prof. Ga. State U., 1974. Fellow Acad. Mgmt. (editor Jour. 1973-75, pres. 1977-78), Am. Psychol. Assn., Soc. for Personality Assessment; mem. Indsl. Relations Research Assn. Republican. Club: Princeton (N.Y.C.). Home: 11054 Howe Rd Akron NY 14001 Office: SUNY Dept Orgn & Human Resources Jacobs Mgmt Ctr Buffalo NY 14260

MINER, THOMAS HAWLEY, international consultant; b. Shelbyville, Ill., June 19, 1927; s. Lester Ward and Thirza (Hawley) M.; m. Lucyna T. Minciel, July 22, 1983; children: Robert Thomas, William John. Student, U.S. Mil. Acad., 1946-47; BA, Knox Coll., 1950; JD, U. Ill., 1953. Bar: Ill. 1954. Atty. Continental Ill. Nat. Bank & Trust Co., Chgo., 1953-55; pres. Harper-Wyman Internat. (S.A.), Venezuela and Mex., 1955-58, Hudson Internat. (S.A.), Can. and Switzerland, 1958-60, Thomas H. Miner & Assoc., Inc., Chgo., 1960—; chmn. Miner, Fraser & Gabriel Pub. Affairs, Inc., Washington, 1982-88, Miner Systems, Inc., 1981—; bd. dirs. Lakeside Bank; vice-chmn. Ill. dist. export council U.S. Dept. Commerce, 1971-76; sec. Consular Corps Chgo., 1986-88. Bd. dirs. Sch. of Art Inst. Chgo., 1977-81; bd. govs., life mem., sustaining fellow Art Inst. Chgo.; former chmn. UN Assn. Chgo.; pres., founder Mid-Am. Com., 1968—; former bd. dirs. UNICEF; trustee 4th Presbyterian Ch., Chgo.; bd. advisors Mercy Hosp. Served in USNR, 1945-46; to capt. U.S. Army, 1946-47. Decorated commendatore Ordine al Merito della Repubblica Italiana; named One of Chgo.'s 10 Outstanding Young Men, 1962, Chicagoan of Year Chgo. Assn. Commerce and Industry, 1968; hon. consul Republic of Senegal, 1970-88. Mem. Am. Mgmt. Assn., Chgo. Assn. Commerce and Industry, Mid-Am.-Arab C. of C. (past dir.), Chgo. Bar Assn., Chgo. Com., Chgo. Concil Fgn. Relations (past dir.), Council of Ams., Internat. Bus. Council (past dir., past pres.), Japan-Am. Soc., Nat. Council U.S.-China Trade, English Speaking Union (dir., past chmn.), U.S.-USSR Trade and Econ. Council, Mus. Contemporary Art, Newcomen Soc. N.Am., Thomas Minor Soc., Phi Delta Phi, Phi Gamma Delta. Clubs: Chicago, Economic, Mid-Am (Chgo.); International, Desireé (Washington); University (Milw.); Tryall Golf and Beach (Jamaica). Lodge: Rotary. Office: 150 N Michigan Ave Chicago IL 60601 other: Miner Fraser & Gabriel Pub Affairs Inc 1025 Connecticut Ave NW #700 Washington DC 20036

MINETTE, DENNIS JEROME, fin. computing cons.; b. Columbus, Nebr., May 18, 1937; s. Lawrence Edward and Angela Ellen (Kelley) M.; B.S.E.E., U. Nebr., 1970; M.B.A., Babson Coll., 1978; m. Virginia Rae Jordan, Oct. 27, 1961; children—Jordan Edward, Lawrence Edward II. Brokerage systems designer Honeywell Info. Systems, Mpls. and Wellesly, Mass., 1970-75; devel. mgr. Investment Info., Inc., Cambridge, Mass., 1975-77; product support mgr. Small Bus. Systems div. Data Gen. Corp., Westboro, Mass., 1977-81; pres. Minette Data Systems, Inc., Sarasota, Fla., 1981—. Capital improvement programs committeeman Town of Medway (Mass.), 1978-79, mem. town fin. com., 1979-80. Served with USN, 1956-60, 61-67, served to lt. commdr. res., 1967-87. Mem. IEEE, IEEE Computer Soc., Data Processing Mgmt. Assn. (cert.), Naval Res. Assn. (life), Res. Officers Assn., Am. Legion, U. Nebr. Alumni Assn. (life), Eta Kappa Nu, Sigma Tau. Republican. Roman Catholic. Office: Minette Data Systems Inc PO Drawer 15435 Sarasota FL 34277

MINGAY, GORDON RDMUND, agrarian history educator; b. Long Eaton, Derbyshire, Eng., June 20, 1923; s. William Edmund and Florence Mabel (Tuckwood) M.; m. Mavis Tippen, May 1, 1948. BA with 1st class honors, U. Nottingham, Eng., 1952, PhD, 1958. Lectr. London Sch. Econs., 1957-65; reader U. Kent, Canterbury, 1965-68, prof. agrarian history, 1968-86, emeritus prof. agrarian history, 1987—. Author: (monograph) English Landed Society in 18th Century, 1963; (text) (with J.D. Chambers) The Agricultural Revolution 1750-1880, 1966; editor Agrl. History Rev., 1973-83. Served to lt. comdr. Royal Navy, 1942-47. Mem. Brit. Agrl. History Soc. (pres. 1986—). Office: Univ Kent, Canterbury Kent England

MINGERS, ANNEMARIE GERTRUD, pediatrician, educator; b. Duelmen, Germany, Aug. 18, 1930; d. Adolf Josef and Gertrud Franziska (Roessing) M. Student Med. U. Cologne, Düsseldorf, 1957-62; M.D., U. Duesseldorf, 1962; habilitation, U. Wuerzburg, 1975, prof., 1980. Intern, resident Univ. Pediatric Clinic, Wuerzburg, asst. physician, 1966-75, sr. asst., 1975-78, sr. physician, 1978—, prof., 1980—; physician various hosps., Ratingen, Datteln, Recklinghausen, 1962-66; pediatric cons. to legal authorities, Würzburg, 1970—. Mem. editorial bd. Jour. Social Pediatrics, 1979-85, Child Abuse and Neglect, the Internat. Jour., 1983-86. Contbr. articles to profl. jours. Mem. German Pediatric Soc., German Soc. Social Pediatrics, Internat. Soc. Prevention of Child Abuse and Neglect. Roman Catholic. Office: U Kinderklinik, Josef-Schneider-Strasse 2, D-8700 Wuerzburg Federal Republic of Germany

MINKEL, HERBERT PHILIP, JR., lawyer; b. Boston, Feb. 11, 1947; s. Herbert Philip and Helen (Sullivan) M. A.B., Holy Cross Coll., 1969; J.D., NYU, 1972. Bar: Mass. 1973, N.Y. 1976, U.S. Dist. Ct. Mass. 1973, U.S. Dist. Ct. (so. dist.) N.Y. 1976. Law clk. U.S. Dist. Ct. Mass., Boston, 1972-73; assoc. Milbank, Tweed, Hadley & McCloy, N.Y.C., 1973-79; ptnr. Fried, Frank, Harris, Shriver & Jacobson, N.Y.C., 1979—; adj. prof. NYU Law Sch., 1987-88; mem. adv. com. on bankruptcy rules Judicial Conf. U.S. Contbg. editor 5 Collier on Bankruptcy, 15th edit. 1979-88; contbr. articles to profl. jours.; author American Bankers Association Bankruptcy Manual, 1979. Root-Tilden scholar, NYU, 1969-72. Mem. Nat. Bankruptcy Conf., ABA, N.Y. Bar Assn., Assn. of Bar of City of N.Y. Home: 330 E 46th St New York NY 10017 Office: Fried Frank Harris Shriver & Jacobson 1 New York Plaza New York NY 10004

MINKLEY, SUZANNE SAWYER, educator; b. Middletown, Ohio, May 15, 1915; d. Clifford Louis and Harriett May (Logan) Sawyer; A.B., John B. Stetson U., 1937, M.A., 1942; B.L.S., George Peabody Coll. of Vanderbilt U., 1940; postgrad. Manatee Jr. Coll., 1960, Fla. So. Coll., 1966, U. South Fla., 1966-67; m. Carl Henry Minkley, Apr. 3, 1943; children—Elizabeth Suzanne Jarrard, Philip Carl. Tchr., librarian Mt. Dora High Sch., 1937-41, Leesburg High Sch., 1941-43, Delray Beach High Sch., 1943-45, Samsula Elem. Sch., 1955-56, Sarasota High Sch., 1956-57; reading specialist Bayshore Jr. High Sch., 1963-74, chmn. lang. arts dept. Bayshore Middle Sch., 1967-74; tchr. social studies Bradenton Middle Sch., 1974-84; cons. tchr. tng. program Edn. Professions Devel. Act of U.S. Dept. Edn., 1970-71; parliamentarian Manatee County Edn. Assn., 1968-72; mem. Volusia County Continuing Council on Edn., 1954-56; parliamentarian Bradenton Middle Sch. PTA, 1976-78. Chmn. bd. Deland (Fla.) Children's Mus., 1954-56; state bd. dirs. Am. Cancer Soc., 1954-61. Recipient citation Am. Cancer Soc., 1952-55; cert. of profl. acceptance NEA, 1966-67. Mem. Volusia County Fedn. Women's Clubs (legis. chmn. 1952-54), Fla. Fedn. Women's Clubs (chmn. radio and TV 1962-66), DAR, NEA, Fla. Edn. Assn., AAUW (chmn. edn. com. Deland br. 1943-45, Sarasota br. 1960-62), Am. Inst. Parliamentarians (cert. mem. Gulfcoast chpt., pres. 1984-85), Nat. Assn. Parliamentarians (pres. Sarasota unit 1973-77, 79-82, membership chmn. Sarasota unit 1982-84, parliamentarian Bradenton unit 1982-84, edn. chmn. Bradenton unit 1980-82), Fla. Assn. Parliamentarians, Gen. Fedn. Women's Clubs, Leonardy Gaveliers (pres. 1972-73), Mu Omega Xi, Sigma Kappa. Democrat. So. Baptist. Clubs: Primrose Garden (pres., founder 1953-55), Orange Blossom Garden (pres. 1962-63), DeLand Women's (pres. 1951-53), Woman's of Sarasota (pres. 1960-61), Fla. Fedn. Women's Clubs (dist. dir. 1960-63, parliamentarian dist. 1963-65). Coordinator Have Gavel, Will Travel panels for civic and social orgns., 1959-65. Home: 2540 Hibiscus St Sarasota FL 33579

MINKOFF, HARRY, product sampling company executive; b. Bklyn., Mar. 28, 1918; s. Louis and Lena (Zausner) M.; B.B.A., CCNY, 1940; m. Ruth Blumenfeld, Nov. 9, 1940; children—George Robert, Lawrence Alan, Jane Barbara Minkoff Hodes. Founder, pres. Gift-Pax, West Hempstead, N.Y., 1948—; mem. advt., mktg. faculty CCNY, 1945-49. Vice pres., bd. govs., chmn. membership com. Fedn. Jewish Philanthropies Commn. on Synagogue Relations, N.Y.C.; trustee Harvard U. Center Jewish Studies and Hebrew Library; chmn. bd. trustees L.I. Ednl. TV Council, Inc.; past v.p. L.I. Anti-Defamation League, 1975-80, mem. nat. planning com., 1980—; past v.p. L.I. Am. Jewish Com., mem. nat. inter-religious com., 1980—; bd. dirs. Hewbrew Acad. Nassau County (N.Y.), Hope for Youth, Westbury, N.Y.; bd. dirs., 1978—, past chmn. bd. Eglevsky Ballet Co., New Hyde Park, N.Y.; pres. Gt. Neck (N.Y.) Orch. Soc., 1975-80, life mem. bd. dirs., 1980—; adv. council Hofstra U., 1970—, past v.p.; hon. mem. bd. dirs. Centra Nassau YM and YWHA, Franklin Square, N.Y.; asso. mem. bd. dirs. Temple Beth-El, Gt. Neck; N.Am. exec. com. mem. World Union for Progressive Judaism; chmn. bd. Friends of the Arts, 1985, now pres. Served with U.S. Army, 1941-44. Recipient Alumni Achievement award CCNY, 1965; Outstanding Leadership award Gt. Neck Symphony Soc., 1977. Mem. CCNY Sch. Bus. Alumni Assn. (pres. 1963-65, life mem. bd. dirs. 1966—), Baruch Coll. Alumni Assn. (dir.). Club: Hofstra U. (dir.). Home: 28 Wildwood Dr Great Neck NY 11024 Office: 25 Hempstead Gardens Dr West Hempstead NY 11552

MINNE, JEAN-FRANCOIS, business executive; b. Paris, Jan. 29, 1944; s. Henri Georges and Marguerite (Saule) M.; m. Dumont de Chassart, July 10, 1971 (div. Apr. 1977); m. Termingnon Catherine, Dec. 31, 1981. Lic., Institut Droit des Affaires, Paris, 1967; grad., Institut d'Administration des Entreprises, Paris, 1968, Institut Hautes Etudes Publicitaires, Paris, 1967. Account exec. Oscar PUblicité, Paris, 1970-72; account dir. D'Arcy MacManus & Masius, Paris, 1972-75, gen. mgr., 1976-80, chmn., 1980-84; chmn. TBWA France, Paris, 1984—; internat. bd. dirs. TWBA Group, Paris, 1984—. Mem. CNPF, Paris, 1987, Espace Liberal, Paris, 1987. Home: 63 rue Jacques Dulud, 92000 Neuilly France Office: TWBA, 25 rue de Pont-Neuf, 75001 Paris France

MINNELLA, CORRADO, publishing company executive; b. Rome, Nov. 27, 1943; s. Renato and Hilda Minnella; m. Roberta Ponzi, July, 1976; children: Federica, Gianluca. Degree in Physics, Milan U., 1967; postgrad., Harvard U., 1985. Dep. gen. mgr. Helene Curtis Co., Milan, 1971-80; exec. dir., v.p. S. Paolo-Publiepi, Milan, 1981—. Served to lt. Italian Navy, 1962-66. Home: Via Albani 5, 20149 Milan Italy Office: S Paolo-Publiepi, Via Grotto 36, 2014 Milan Italy

MINNEMANN, HELMUTH MARQUES, government official; b. Porto, Portugal, Nov. 29, 1924; s. Johannes Christian and Adelia (Marques) M.; B.S., U. Porto, 1943-47; degree in physics and chemistry U. Coimbra, 1948; m. Anna Lucia Kraft, July 31, 1955; children—Manuel, Reiner, Elisabeth. Lectr., Portuguese lang., U. Hamburg (W. Ger.), 1951; mem., chancellor Portugese Legation, Bonn, W. Ger., 1951-55; chemist Badische Anilin und Soda-Fabrik, Ludwigshafen, W. Ger., 1956-58; with Portuguese Govt. Trade Office in Germany, Bonn, Hamburg, Munich, 1958—, dir., 1958—; comml. counselor Portuguese Embassy, Bonn, 1961—. Decorated comdr. Order of Henry the Navigator (Portugal), 1978; Cross of Merit 1st class (W.Ger.). Mem. Circulo Eca de Queiroz, Lit. Assn. Lisbon. Roman Catholic. Club: Am. Embassy (Bonn). Contbr. articles to profl. jours. Home: 7 Rhenusallee, 5300 Bonn 3 Federal Republic of Germany Office: 78 Ubierstrasse, 5300 Bonn 2 Federal Republic of Germany

MINNIE, MARY VIRGINIA, social worker, educator; b. Eau Claire, Wis., Feb. 16, 1922; d. Herman Joseph and Virginia Martha (Strong) M. BA, U.

Wis., 1944; MA, U. Chgo., 1949, Case Western Reserve U., 1956. Lic. clin. social worker, Calif. Supr. day care Wis. Children Youth, Madison, 1949-57; coordinator child study project Child Guidance Clinic, Grand Rapids, Mich., 1957-60; faculty, community services Pacific Oaks Coll., Pasadena, Calif., 1960-70; pvt. practice specializing in social work various cities, Calif., 1970-78; cons., educator So. Calif. Health Care, North Hollywood, Calif., 1978—; med. social worker Kaiser Permanente Home Health, Downey, Calif., 1985-87; assoc. Baby Sitters Guild, Inc., 1987—; cons. Home Health, 1987—; pres. Midwest Assn. Nursery Edn., Grand Rapids, 1958-60; bd. dirs., sec. So. Calif. Health Care, North Hollywood; bd. dirs., v.p. Baby Sitters Guild Inc., South Pasadena; cons. project Head Start Office Econ. Opportunity, Washington, 1965-70. Mem. Soc. Clin. Social Workers, Nat. Assn. Social Workers, Nat. Assn. Edn. Young Children (1960-62). Democrat. Club: Altrusa (Laguna Beach, Calif.) (pres. 1984-87). Home and Office: 1622 Bank St S Pasadena CA 91030

MINO, SHIGEKAZA, business executive; b. Oct. 12, 1923. Grad., Kobe Keigai U., 1948. With Kubota Ltd., Osaka, Japan, 1948—, mng. dir., 1975, now pres. Home: 1-10 Kitsuyama-cho, Nishinomiya, Hyogo 662 Japan Office: Kubota Ltd, 2-47 Shikit Suhigashi 1-chome, Namiwa-ku Japan *

MINOGUE, VALERIE PEARSON, French literature educator; b. Llanelli, Dyfed, Wales, Apr. 26, 1931; d. Frederick George and Martha (Pearson) Hallett; m. Kenneth Robert Minogue, June 16, 1954; children: Nicholas, Eunice. BA with honors, Cambridge U., 1952, MLitt, 1956. Asst. lectr. French and Italian U. Coll., Cardiff, Wales, 1952-53; part-time lectr. London U., 1958-61, asst. lectr., 1962-64, lectr., 1964-75, sr. lectr., 1975-81; prof. French, Head Dept. Romance Studies U. Coll. Swansea, Wales, 1981-88, research prof., 1988—; contbr. Cambridge Italian Dictionary, 1956-61; vis. fellow Australian Nat. U., Canberra, 1976; vis. lectr. various univs. in Eng., Australia, New Zealand, /France, and Italy. Author: Proust: Du Côté de Chez Swann, 1973, Nathalie Sarraute: The War of the Words, 1981; editor Romance Studies jour., 1982—; contbr. articles to profl. jours. Mem. Assn. Univ. Tchrs., Assn. Univ. Profs. French. Anglican. Home: 92 Eaton Crescent, Swansea West Glamorgan SA1 4QP, Wales Office: Univ Coll Swansea, Singleton Park, Swansea West Glamorgan SA2 8PP, Wales

MINOR, DAVID MICHAEL, lawyer; b. Bowie, Tex., Apr. 21, 1946; s. David Ritchie and Lillian (Ervin) M. B.A., Tex. Christian U., 1969; J.D., South Tex. Coll. Law, 1976. Bar: Tex., U.S. Tax Ct. Asst. county atty. Hale County (Tex.), 1978-79; asst. criminal dist. atty. Kaufman County (Tex.), 1979-81; ptnr. Chitty, Minor & Archer, Terrell, Tex., 1982—. rep. client, gen. counsel Shroud of Turin Research Project Inc. Mem. ABA, State Bar Tex., Tex. County and Dist. Attys. Assn. Democrat. Roman Catholic. Home: PO Drawer 610 Terrell TX 75160 Office: Brin Opera House Bldg 3d Floor 102 E Moore Terrell TX 75160

MINOR, PHILIP CURTIS, electronics engineer; b. Ada, Okla., Aug. 24, 1947; s. Elmo Carlton and Zella Mae (Pennington) M.; student E. Central State U., 1965-68; B.S. cum laude with honors in Physics, U. Ark., 1970; M.S., U. Utah, 1972; postgrad. U. No. Colo., 1977, George Washington U., 1979, Cornell U., 1984; m. Mary Ellen Bounds, Nov. 27, 1968; 1 dau., Rose Mary. Electronic engr. U.S. Army Communications Electronics Engring. Installation Agy., Ft. Huachuca, Ariz., 1973-78; program mgr. Systems Devel. div., SRI Internat., Arlington, Va., 1978—. Served with U.S. Army, 1972-74. Decorated Army Commendation medal; recipient Civil Service Outstanding Performance award, 1976; Armed Forces Communications Electronics Assn. Disting. Service citation, 1975; Teaching Assts. Evaluation Com. award, U. Utah, 1972. Mem. Armed Forces Communications Electronics Assn., Planetary Soc., Assn. Old Crows, Okla. State Soc., Thomas Minor Soc. Contbr. articles to profl. jours. Home: 7807 Wendy Ridge Ln Annandale VA 22003 Office: 1611 N Kent St Arlington VA 22209

MINSKER, ROBERT STANLEY, consultant, former personnel executive; b. Pitts. Jan. 1, 1911; s. Theodore Kuhne and Isabella Lavinia (Trumbor) M.; B.S., U. Ill., 1934; postgrad. Pa. State U., 1938-39; m. Marion Elizabeth Warner, May 29, 1937; children: Norma (Mrs. Leo Jerome Brown II), Robert S., James. D. With Owens-Ill., Inc., Toledo, Ohio, 1934-76, personnel dir. Clarion (Pa.) plant, 1936-40, personnel dir. Columbus (Ohio) plant, 1940-44, mgr. indsl. relations Alton, 1945-72, adminstr. workmen's compensation, safety and health Ill. and pub. affairs Ill. Plants, 1972-76; dir. Germania Fin. Corp., 1963-82, Germania Bank 1953-82, hon. dir., 1982—; assoc. faculty So. Ill. U., 1959-64. Lectr., cons. Chmn. Madison County Savs. Bond Campaign, 1959-61; active Boy Scouts Am.; pres. Piasa Bird Council, 1949-51, mem. exec. bd., 1945—; mem. grievance com. panel State of Ill. Dept. Personnel, 1967-80; vice chmn. Higher Edn. Coordinating Council Met. St. Louis, 1966-70; founder Board Pride, Inc., 1966—. Mem. Bd. Edn., 1957-70, pres. 1961-70. Bd. dirs., treas., sec., exec. com. Alton Meml. Hosp., 1969-88, dir. emeritus 1988—, bd. dirs. Alton Meml. Hosp. Found., 1986——; Jr. Achievement, United Fund.; bd. dirs. Community Chest, v.p., 1949-54, 61-66, gen. chmn., 1949-50; adminstr. Alton Found., sec., 1955—; trustee Lewis and Clark Community Coll., sec. bd., 1970-77; bd. dirs. McKendree Coll., 1981—; mem. pres. council U. Ill. Found. Recipient Silver Beaver award Boy Scouts of Am., 1951; Achievement award U.S. Treasury Dept., 1951; Hall of Fame award Piasa Bird Council, 1969, Alton Citizens' award, 1988; named to Lewis and Clark Hall of Fame, 1977. Mem. Alton C. of C. (chmn. pub. relations 1951-54), U. Ill. Varsity "I" Assn., U. Ill. Alumni Assn., Nature Conservation Assn. (a founder), Acacia, Alpha Phi Omega. Methodist. Clubs: Masons, (32 deg.), K.T., Shriners. Home: 2018 Chapin Pl Alton IL 62002

MINTOFF, DOMINIC, architect, former prime minister of Malta; b. Cospicua, Aug. 6, 1916; s. Lawrence and Concetta (Farrugia) M.; B.Sc., U. Malta, 1937, B.E.&A., A.&C.E., 1939; M.A. in Engring. Sci. (Govt. Travelling scholar, Rhodes scholar), Oxford U.; m. Moyra de Vere Bentick, Nov. 22, 1947; children—Ann, Joan. Gen. sec. Malta Labour Party, 1936-37, leader, 1949—; civil engr., U.K., 1941-43; practice of architecture, Malta, 1943—; elected to council of govt. and exec. council, 1945, mem. Legis. Assembly, 1947—; dep. leader Labour Party, also dep. prime minister and minister of works and reconstrn., 1947-49; prime minister and minister of fin. 1955-58, resigned to lead Maltese Liberation Movement, 1958; opposition leader, 1962-71; prime minister, 1971-84, minister commonwealth and fgn. affairs, 1971-76; minister fgn. affairs, minister of interior, 1976-81; mem. Labour dels. to U.K., 1945, 47, 48, 49. Contbr. articles to sci., lit. and artistic publs. Home: The Olives, Tarxien Malta

MINTURN, WILLIAM OLIVER, physician, surgeon; b. Chgo., June 16, 1926; s. Benjamin Earl and Jeannette (Tate) M.; student Wichita State U., 1942-43, St. Mary's Coll., Minn., 1943-44, Friends U., 1948, B.S., Trinity Coll., Conn., 1948; M.D., Yale U., 1952; m. Shirley Alice Moseley, June 15, 1952; children—Sarah Louise, David Bruce, Laura Ann. Diplomate Nat. Bd. Med. Examiners. Intern, Cook County Hosp., Chgo., 1952-53; instr. surgery Wayne U., Detroit, 1953-57; resident in gen. surgery Detroit Receiving Hosp., 1953-57; resident in chest surgery Ingham Chest Hosp., Lansing, Mich., 1957-58, Roswell Park Cancer Inst. and Buffalo Children's Hosp., 1958-59; chief thoracic surgery VA Hosp., Phoenix, 1959-60; chief surgery Glendale (Ariz.) Samaritan Hosp., 1961-70; pvt. practice medicine, specializing in gen. and chest surgery, Sun City, Ariz., 1961—; founder, pres. Sun City Med. Clinic, 1961—; mem. staffs Boswell Meml., Glendale Samaritan, Maryvale Samaritan, Phoenix Bapt., John C. Lincoln Hosps. Bd. dirs. Sun City chpt. Am. Cancer Soc. Served with USNR, 1943-45. Recipient merit award as founding mem. Boswell Hosp., Sun City, 1976; Faces in Crowd award Sports Illustrated mag., 1981. Diplomate Am. Bd. Surgery. Fellow Am. Coll. Chest Physicians; mem. AMA (named to Over-50 Sports Hall of Fame, 1984), Phoenix, Ariz. surg. assns., Pan Am. Med. Assn., SAR, Ariz. Marathon Soc., Delta Phi, Alpha Kappa Kappa. Republican. Episcopalian. Clubs: Rotary; Medics, Match Point Tennis (Phoenix); Prescott Country. Contbr. articles to Road Racers Am., Yale Medicine. Home: 6034 N 38th Pl Paradise Valley AZ 85253 Office: 10222 Coggins Dr Sun City AZ 85351

MINTZ, M. J., lawyer; b. Phila., Oct. 29, 1940; s. Arthur and Lillian (Altenberg) M.; divorced; children—Robert A., Christine L.; m. Judith E. Held. B.S., Temple U., 1961, J.D., 1968. Bar: D.C.; C.P.A., Pa., D.C. Proprietor, operator M.J. Mintz & Co., CPA, Phila., 1964-68, atty. adv. to judge U.S. Tax Ct., Washington, 1968-70; asst. gen. counsel Cost of Living Council, Washington, 1971-73; ptnr. Dickstein, Shapiro & Morin, Washington, 1973—; adj. prof. George Mason U. Law Sch., Va., 1974-78; adv. Employee Retirement Income Security Act of 1974, Adv. Council, Washington, 1982-85. Contbr. articles to profl. jours. Apptd. by Pres. Reagan to advisory com. Pension Benifit Guaranty Corp., 1987; rep. candidate Fairfax County Bd. of Suprs., 1971. Fellow Nat. Assn. Watch & Clock Collectors; mem. ABA, Am. Inst. C.P.A.s, Antuquarian Horological Soc. (London). Clubs: Cosmos, Belle Haven Country, Chappaquiddick Beach, Capitol Hill. Avocations: antiquarian horologist.

MINTZ, STEPHEN ALLAN, financial services company executive, lawyer; b. N.Y.C., May 21, 1943; s. Irving and Anne (Medwick) M.; m. Dale Leibson, June 19, 1966; children: Eric Michael, Jaclyn Leibson. AB, Cornell U., 1965; JD cum laude, Harvard U., 1968. Bar: N.Y. 1969. Assoc. Proskauer, Rose, Goetz & Mendelsohn, N.Y.C., 1968-76, ptnr., 1976-80; v.p. Integrated Resources, Inc., N.Y.C., 1980-84, 1st. v.p., 1984-86, sr. v.p., chmn. Resources Hotel Mgmt. Services Div., 1986—. Mem. ABA, N.Y. State Bar Assn., Assn. Bar City N.Y. Democrat. Jewish. Avocation: amateur radio operator. Home: 11 Eve Ln Rye NY 10580 Office: Integrated Resources Inc 666 3d Ave New York NY 10017

MINTZER, EDWARD CARL, JR., lawyer; b. Phila., Sept. 17, 1949; s. Edward Carl and Jean Marie (McGinnis) M.; m. Colleen Anne Marie Hanratty, June 6, 1975; children: Catherine Marie, Elizabeth Seton, Edward Carl III, Conor Andrew. BA, St. Charles Coll., 1971; MA, Villanova U., 1974; JD, Temple U., 1979. Bar: Pa. 1979, U.S. Dist. Ct. (ea. dist.) Pa. 1979, U.S. Ct. Appeals (3rd cir.) 1980, U.S. Supreme Ct. 1982. Exec. dir., program dir. Programs for Exceptional People, Inc., Phila., 1973-78; assoc. McWilliams and Sweeney, Phila., 1979-82; ptnr. McWilliams and Mintzer, Phila., 1982—. chmn. bd. CATCH, Inc., Phila., 1981—, C.M.S., Inc., 1715 Properties, Inc. Mem. Pa. Bar Assn., Phila. Bar Assn. (med. and legal subcom.), Pa. Trial Lawyers Assn., Phila. Trial Lawyers Assn. Democrat. Roman Catholic. Office: McWilliams & Mintzer PC 260 S Broad St Atlantic Bldg Suite 610 Philadelphia PA 19102

MIR, M(OHAMMAD) AFZAL, physician, educator; b. Trehgam, Kashmir, May 6, 1936; came to U.K., 1964, naturalized, 1972; s. M. Abdullah and Taja (Bhutt) M.; m. Zarifa War, Jan. 8, 1962 (div. 1970); 1 child, Farooq; m. Lynda Green, Mar. 7, 1977; children—Deborah Tabassum, Joanne Taj. M.B.B.S., U. Ujjain, India, 1962; D.C.H., U. London, 1965; F.Sc. (hon.), Sri Pratap Coll., 1956. Med. officer Agy. Hosp. Gilgit, Kashmir, 1962-64; sr. house officer Alder Hey Children's Hosp., Liverpool, Eng., 1964-65; med. registrar Withington Hosp., Manchester, Eng., North Ormsby Hosp., Midlesbrough, Eng., Queen Mary's Hosp., Sidcup, Eng., 1965-72; med. registrar Manchester Royal Infirmary, 1972-74, sr. med. registrar, 1974-77; sr. lectr., cons. physician Coll. Medicine, U. Wales, Cardiff, 1978—, video educator, 1980—, chmn. editorial bd. video edn. in postgrad. medicine, 1985—. Author: An Aid to Membership of Royal Coll of Physicians Short Cases, 1986; also articles on metabolic disorders in acute leukemia, sodium transport in red blood cells, obesity, respiratory diseases, and med. edn. to profl. publs. Brit. Heart Found. European traveling fellow, London, 1977. Fellow Royal Coll. Physicians; mem. Med. Research Soc., Brit. Diabetic Assn., Brit. Cardiac Soc. (Young Investigators award 1976), Brit. Soc. Cardiovascular Research, Brit. Hypertension Soc., Am. Soc. Hypertension, N.Y. Acad. Scis., Assn. Physicians in Wales, Welsh Diabetic Group, Cardiff Med. Soc., Cardiff Lung Fedn. Avocations: music; literature; hiking; writing; bridge. Home: Iscoed, Old Mill Rd, Lisvane, Cardiff CF4 5XP, Wales Office: U Wales Coll Medicine, Heath Park, Cardiff CF4 4XN, Wales

MIR, MOHD AKRAM, physician; b. Dadyal, Pakistan, Nov. 5, 1948; s. Mohd Sharif and Safoora Begum M.; m. Hafeeza Mir, Oct. 25, 1975; five children. M Medicine and Sci., Nishtar Med. Coll., Multan, Pakistan, 1972; diploma in acupunture, Beijing, China, 1983. Practice medicine, med. dir. Sharif Clinic, Dadyal, 1973—. Mem. Pakistan Med. and Dental Council. Muslim. Home: House #302 Sector 3, Dadyal District, Mirpne AK Pakistan Office: Sharif Clinic, Dadyal Pakistan

MIRA, JOHN FRANCIS, psychiatrist, educator; b. Emporium, Pa., June 19, 1945; s. Dominic Earnest and Josephine Leona M.; married. M.D., Creighton U., 1970. Diplomate Am. Bd. Psychiatry and Neurology. Intern, St. Paul and Parkland hosps., Dallas, 1970-71; resident Strong Meml. Hosp., Rochester, N.Y., 1971-74; staff psychiatrist Naval Regional Med. Center, Phila., 1974-76; chief inpatient staff psychiatrist Albert Einstein Med. Center, No. div., Phila., 1976-79, acting chmn. adult psychiatry, 1978-79; dir. inpatient psychiatry Carlisle (Pa.) Hosp., 1979-82; acting med. dir. Helen Stevens Community Mental Health Center, Carlisle, 1979-80; pvt. practice psychiatry, Carlisle, 1979-83, Camp Hill (Pa.), 1983—; chmn. psychiatry Harrisburg (Pa.) Hosp., 1983-86; asst. prof. psychiatry Hershey Med. Ctr., Pa. State U., 1983—; med. dir. Harrisburg Inst. Psychiatry, 1983-86. Served with USN, 1974-76. Mem. Am. Psychiat. Assn., Nat. Assn. Residents and Interns. Office: 890 Poplar Church Rd #204 Camp Hill PA 17011

MIRACLE, GORDON ELDON, educator; b. Olympia, Wash., May 28, 1930; s. Gordon Tipler and Corine Adriana (Orlebeke) M.; m. Christa Stoeter, June 29, 1957; children—Gary, Gregory, Glenn. B.B.A., U. Wis., 1952, M.B.A., 1958, Ph.D., 1962. Case officer, civilian intelligence analyst U.S. Army, W. Ger., 1955-57; instr. commerce Grad. Sch. Bus., U. Wis., Madison, 1958-60; instr., then asst. prof. mktg. U. Mich., Ann Arbor, 1960-66; assoc. prof. advt. Mich. State U., East Lansing, 1966-70; prof. advt. Mich. State U., 1970—, chmn. dept., 1974-80; vis. prof. mktg. mgmt. N. European Mgmt. Inst., Oslo, 1972-73; cons., lectr. in field. Author: Management of International Advertising, 1966; co-author: International Marketing Management, 1970, Advertising and Government Regulation, 1979, Instructor's Manual for International Marketing Management, 1971, European Reguation of Advertising: Supranational Regulation of Advertising in the European Economic Community, 1986, Voluntary Regulation of Advertising: A Comparative Analysis of the United Kingdom and the United States, 1987; contbr. articles to scholarly and profl. jours.; editor: Marketing Decision Making: Strategy and Payoff, 1965, Sharing for Understanding, Proc. Ann. Conf. Am. Acad. Advt., 1977. Served with AUS, 1952-55. Ford Found. fellow, 1961-62, 64; Am. Assn. Advt. Agys. fellow Marsteller, Inc., 1967; Advt. Ednl. Found. fellow McCann-Erikson Hakuhodo, 1985; Fulbright research fellow Waseda U., Tokyo, 1985. Mem. Am. Acad. Advt. (treas., exec. com. 1978-79), Acad. Internat. Bus. (sec., exec. com. 1973-75), Am. Mktg. Assn., Internat. Advt. Assn., Adcraft Club Detroit. Home: 1461 Cheboygan Rd Okemos MI 48864 Office: Mich State U Dept Advt East Lansing MI 48824

MIRANDA, CARLOS SA, food products company executive; b. Fall River, Mass., Nov. 16, 1929; s. Carlos Sa and Annette (Pratt) M.; m. Natalie Cardoso, Jan. 5, 1949; children—Carla, Lucy, John. B.S. in Mech. Engring., Marquette U., 1956. With internat. div. Kellogg Co., Battle Creek, Mich., 1964-65, gen. mgr., Brazil, 1965-80, gen. mgr. Kellogg's Spain, 1983-84, v.p. Kellogg Internat., Battle Creek, 1980—. Recipient Pero Vaz Caminha award, Brazil, 1976; conferred title Comdr. of Legion of Honor of Marshal Rondon, Brazil, 1971. Mem. ASME. Republican. Roman Catholic. Office: Kellogg Co One Kellogg Square PO Box 3599 Battle Creek MI 49016

MIRANDA, FRANK JOSEPH, dentist, educator; b. Erie, Pa., June 30, 1946; s. Joseph Francis and Vivian Mary (Lewis) M.; m. Joan Ethel Antes, Oct. 7, 1976; children—Cory Michael, Erin Christine. Student, UCLA, 1964-67, DDS, 1971; MEd summa cum laude, Central State U., Edmond, Okla., 1976, MBA summa cum laude, 1979. Assoc. dentist UCLA Sch. Dentistry, 1971-74; pvt. practice dentistry Lynwood (Calif.) Children's Found., 1971-72; asst. prof. operative dentistry Okla. U. Coll. Dentistry, 1974-80, assoc. prof., 1980-87, prof., 1987—, dir. continuing edn., 1986-88; mem. adj. faculty Oscar Rose Jr. Coll., 1980—; cons. odontologist Okla. Chief Med. Examiner, 1975-80 ; pvt. practice dentistry, 1974—; chmn. operative subcom. Central Regional Dental Testing Service, 1982-84. Contbr. articles to profl. jours.; author teaching syllabi, 1980; editorial adviser Dental Student Jour., 1983, Dentist mag. Mem. Okla. Hispanic Assn. for Higher Edn., Oklahoma City, 1981; panelist Sta.-KTVY Unity Program, Oklahoma City, 1981; bd. dirs. Okla. U. Health Sci. Center Fed. Credit Union, 1982, treas., 1983-84, sec., 1984-87; trustee Okla. Dental Found., 1985—; mem. vol. faculty Free Dental Clinic, Good Shepherd Ministries, 1st Baptist Ch., 1982—; vice chmn. Affirmative Action Council, Oklahoma City, 1982. Named Outstanding Tchr. Okla. U. Coll. Dentistry graduating srs., 1978, 80, 81, Best Clin. Instr., 1983, 85, 87, others; Regents scholar UCLA, 1964-67; Acad. Gen. Dentistry fellow, 1980; Acad. Dentistry Internat. fellow, 1981; Acad. Internat. Dental Studies fellow, 1982; Am. Coll. Dentists fellow, 1983. Mem. Internat. Assn. Dental Research (mem. dental materials group 1982-86), Am. Assn. Dental Research (pres. chpt. 1980-82, sec.-treas. 1985-86), Acad. Operative Dentistry, ADA, Okla. Dental Assn. (assoc. editor jour. 1983), Oklahoma County Dental Soc. (bd. dirs. and ho. of dels. 1984—, v.p. 1987-88), Am. Assn. Dental Schs. (chmn. exec. com. 1982-83), Conf. Operative Dentistry Educators (nat. sec. 1974-79, nat. coordinator 1986—), Apollonians, Omicron Kappa Upsilon, Kappa Delta Pi. Home: 6645 Whitehall Dr Oklahoma City OK 73123 Office: U Okla Coll Dentistry 1001 Stanton L Young Blvd Oklahoma City OK 73190

MIRANDA PAZ, LETICIA ELENA, decorating company executive, consultant; b. El Paso, Tex., Aug. 19, 1937; came to Mex., 1939; d. Fausto R. Miranda and Conchita (Paz Cordero) M.; m. Jorge de la Macorra, Apr. 16, 1958 (div. 1980); children—Jorge Enrique, Leticia, Laura, Gerardo, Rodrigo, Jeronimo, Ximena. Degree in Humanities, Colegio Regina (Mex.), 1956. Tchr. Colegio Regina, 1956-58; tchr. Colegio Vista Hermosa, Mex., 1971-74, English dept. prin., 1974-81; cons. Children's Press, Mex., 1980-85; landscaper, decorator Funtanet Enterprise, 1972-82, Simon Enterprise, 1980—; gen. mgr. Decoraciones y Jardines, Lemi, Mex., 1980—; cons. Club de Golf, Santa Fe, 1985. Author: Vista Hermosa's Grammar Book, 1976-77; also articles, play. Treas. Jr. League Mex., Mexico City, 1970; active Am. Sch. PTA Art Fair, Mexico City, 1983, 85. Roman Catholic. Avocations: reading; jogging; squash; music; art exhibitions; travel. Home: Reforma 3009, 05000 Mexico City Mexico Office: Decoraciones y Jardines Lemi, 05000 Mexico City Mexico

MIRAZIZ, JOHN LEON, architect; b. Palestine, Dec. 5, 1940; s. Leon Gabriel and Farha Salim (Abu Amsha) M.; m. Laila Elias Marzouka, Aug. 23, 1981; children: Lina Ann, Charles Paul, Elizabeth John. BSc in Architecture, Baghdad U., Iraq, 1965; MArch in Urban Design, Rice U., 1975. Design architect Kuwait Engrs. Office, 1966-70, sr. design architect, 1970-75, sr. assoc., 1975-80; gen. mgr., sr. architect Kuwati Archtl Cons., Kuwait, 1980—. Prin. works include Dasman Complex, Kuwait, 1976, Kuwait Embassy, Jordan, 1978, Al-Wataniya, Kuwait, 1979, Palm Horticulture Ctr., Kuwait, 1986, Kuwait Embassy, North Yemen, 1988. Mem. Union Iraqi Engrs., Kuwait Soc. Engrs. Home: Maydan Hawalli, Hmoud Al Naser St, Tukhaim Bldg Apt #1, 13041 Kuwait Kuwait Office: Kuwaiti Archtl Cons, PO 4002 Safat, 13041 Kuwait Kuwait

MIRCEA, MALITA, mathematics educator; b. Oradea, Romania, Feb. 20, 1927; s. Pavel and Veturia Mircea; married; 3 children. Diploma in Math., U. Bucharest, Romania, 1949, PhD. Dir. library Romanian Acad., 1950-56; dep. minister fgn. affairs 1962-70, minister edn., 1970-72; adviser to Pres. Romania, 1972-77; ambassador to Switzerland, 1980-82, U.S.A., 1982-85; prof. math. U. Bucharest, 1985—. Author: Chronicle of the Year 2000, Diplomacy: Schools and Institutions, Romanian Diplomacy: A Historical Outlook, Grey Gold, 3 Vols., Theory and Practice of Negotiations, Ideas in March, The Wall and the Ivy, Mathematical Approaches to International Relations, 3 Vols., Mathematics of Organization, Coalition and Connections in Games. Mem. Romanian Writers' Union, Romanian Acad. Social and Polit. Studies, Romanian Acad. (corr., chmn. com. future studies), World Acad. Art and Sci., World Future Studies Fedn., European Ctr. Research and Documentation in Social Scis., Internat. Found. Devel. Studies, Internat. Council Sci. Policy Studies, N.Y. Acad. Scis. Club: Rome. Address: 24 Kiseleff, Bucharest Romania

MIRGHANI, AHMAD ALI AL-, Sudanese government official. Mem. Dem. Unionist Party; pres. Sudan Governing Council, Khartoum, 1986—; chmn. State Council, Khartoum, 1987—. Address: Democratic Unionist Party, Khartoum Sudan *

MIRKIN, GEORGE, petroleum geologist; b. Leningrad, USSR, Mar. 21, 1936; came to U.S., 1978, naturalized, 1985; s. Rakhmuel and Goda (Kunin) M.; m. Inessa Berlin, Mar. 14, 1958; children: Marina, Daniel. MS, Mining Inst., Leningrad, 1959; PhD, Nat. Exploration Petroleum Research Inst., Leningrad, 1967; cert. Nat. Inst. Patent Law, Leningrad, 1977. Cert. petroleum geologist. Geologist Nat. Exploration Petroleum Research Inst., 1959-67, research assoc., 1967-70, research adv., 1970-78; research specilist Exxon Prodn. Research Co., Houston, 1979-86; cons. geologist, Houston, 1986 ; pres. Quanto Internat. Co. Ltd. 1987—; cons. U. Moscow, 1976-78, Northwest Regional Dept. Mingeo, USSR, Leningrad, 1976-78, Sci. Dept. Mingeo USSR, Moscow, 1973. Author: Morphostructural Methods of Studying Oil-Bearing Regions, 1968; Instruction of Optical Processing of Geological Data, 1977. Contbr. articles to profl. jours. Patentee in field. Pres.'s Assn. Immigrants from USSR, Houston, 1979-80. Recipient honor rank Inventor of USSR, State Com. Inventions and Discovering USSR, 1975; honor diploma All Union Exhbn. Achievements in Sci. and Tehcnique, 1974. Mem. Am. Assn. Petroleum Geologists (adv. bd., treatise of petrol. geology 1987—, mem. geosat com. 1986—). Avocations: painting; sports. Home: 5514 Yarwell Houston TX 77096 Office: Quanto Internat Co Ltd 5514 Yarwell Houston TX 77096

MIRSKY, ELLIS RICHARD, lawyer; b. San Diego, Nov. 22, 1947; s. Jacob Joseph and Lucille (Albert) M.; m. Renee Grundstein, Apr. 18, 1970; children—Jason, Lauren. B.Engring., CCNY, 1969, M.Eng., 1971; J.D., Fordham U., 1976. Bar: N.Y. 1977, U.S. Dist. Ct. (so. and ea. dists.) N.Y. 1978, U.S. Supreme Ct. 1986. Engr., Curtiss-Wright Corp., Woodridge, N.J., 1969-73, Ebasco Services, Inc., N.Y.C., 1973-75; assoc. Rosenman Colin Freund Lewis & Cohen, N.Y.C., 1975-83; asst. gen. counsel Combustion Engring., Inc., Stamford, Conn., 1983-87, head litigation dept., 1985-87, v.p. chief litigation dept., 1987—. NSF grantee, 1968. Mem. Assn. Bar City of N.Y., ASME (assoc.), Engrs. Club (trustee 1976), Fedn. Ins. and Corp. Counsel. Home: 10 Cupsaw Ct Nanuet NY 10954 Office: Combustion Engring Inc 900 Long Ridge Rd Stamford CT 06902

MIRZA, FIDA ALI, mercantile and marine financial executive; b. Srinagar, India, Feb. 14, 1949; came to Pakistan, 1951; s. Mirza Mohammad Husain and Hajra (Mirza) Mirza; m. Zeenat Mirmohammadi, Aug. 6, 1976; 1 child, Nida. B.S., D.J. Govt. Sci. Coll., 1969; B.B.A. with honors, Inst. Bus. Adminstrn., U. Karachi, 1972, M.B.A., 1974. Dept. mgr. mgmt. info. systems Fed. Light Engring. Corp. Ltd., Karachi, Pakistan, 1975-79, State Engring. Corp. Ltd., Karachi, 1979-80; mgr. fin. Gulfeast Ship Mgmt. Ltd., Hong Kong, 1980-82; mgr. fin. and adminstrn. Merc. and Marine (Middle East) ltd., Sharjah, United Arab Emirates, 1982—. Islam. Avocations: reading; magazines. Home: 108-J Block II PECHS, Karachi, Sind Pakistan Office: Mercantile and Marine, (Mid East) Ltd, PO Box 2066, Sharjah United Arab Emirates

MIRZA, MUHAMMAD AYUB, pediatrician; b. Mirpur, Kashmir, Pakistan, May 21, 1929; s. Fazal Ilahi and Begum (Fatima) M.; m. Shirin Gul, Sept. 3, 1957; children: Amjad Ayub, Alina Ayub, Sarmad Ayub. FSc, D.A.V. Coll., Jullundur, Pakistan, 1948; BS, Gordon Coll., Rawalpindi, Pakistan, 1949; MBBS, Dow Med. Coll., Karachi, Pakistan, 1956; diploma in child health, Royal Faculty Physicians and Surgeons, 1962. Various positions Nat. Health Service Hosps., Eng., 1957-63; sr. house surgeon Children's Hosp., Nottingham, Eng., 1963; practice medicine specializing in pediatrics Rawalpindi, Pakistan, 1964—; lectr. in field. Author: We, The Strangers, 1977, Rainvow in Blood, 1982, Net of a Wave, 1986; translator: Mei Hai Eminesco's Poems, 1981. Sec. gen. All Pakistan World Youth Festival Com., Karachi, 1953-54; founder, sec. gen. Pakistan-China Friendship Soc., Rawalpindi and Islamabad, Pakistan, 1966-68, pres., 1968-78. Mem. Pakistan Med. Assn. (sec. gen. 1964-65, v.p. 1973-75, cen. councillor 1968-76), Brit. Med. Assn., All Pakistan-China Friendship Assn. (v.p. 1984-87, sr. v.p. 1987—). Muslim. Club: Islamabad. Home: 15-8 Harley St, Rawalpindi, Punjab Pakistan Office: P-212 Jami Masjid Rd, Rawalpindi, Punjab Pakistan

MIRZOYAN, EDVARD MIKHAILOVICH, music educator, composer; b. Gory, Georgia, U.S.S.R., May 12, 1921; s. Mikhail Ivanovich and Lucy Bogdanovna (Pershangy) M.; m. Elena Mamikonovna Stepanyan, Apr. 20, 1927; children: Zara, Arshac. Diploma, State Conservatory, Yerevan, U.S.S.R., 1941, Mus. Studio, Moscow, 1948. Instr. State Conservatory, Yerevan, 1948-57, asst. prof., 1957-65, prof., 1965—, head dept. music, 1975-

87. Composer String Quartet, 1947, Symphony, 1961, Cello Sonate, 1967; author (poetry) Epitaph, 1988. Dep. Town Soviet, Yerevan, 1950-55, Supreme Soviet of Armenian Soviet Socialist Republic, Yerevan, 1959—. Named to Order Badge of Honour, Supreme Soviet of Moscow, 1956, Honoured Art Worker, Yerevan, 1958, People's Artist, Yerevan, 1963, Order of Lenin, 1971, People's Artist, U.S.S.R., 1981, Order of Kirill and Mefody, Bulgaria, 1981. Home: Demirchyan Str 25 Apt 9, 375000, Yerevan Armenia SSR USSR Office: Composers Union, Demirchyan Str 25, 375000, Yerevan Armenian SSR USSR

MISHIMA, YOSHITSUGU, nuclear metallurgist, emeritus educator; b. Tokyo, Aug. 5, 1921; s. Tokushichi Kijyu and Fumiko M.; B.Engring., U. Tokyo, 1944, Dr. Engring., 1956; m. Tsuneko Momoshima, Jan. 21, 1945; children—Yoshikazu, Yoshinao. Assoc. prof., U. Tokyo, Hongo Tokyo, Japan, 1949-63, prof. nuclear metallurgy, 1963-82, prof. emeritus, 1982—; tech. advisor Japan Atomic Energy Research Inst.; councillor PNC (Power Reactor and Nuclear Fuel Devel. Corp.), 1983—, Atomic Energy Commn., Japan; mem. reactor safety adv. com. Nuclear Regulatory Commn. Japan, 1959—, vice chmn., 1968-79, chmn., 1979—, chmn. fuel safety research planning com., 1960; dir. Nuclear Power Engring. Test Ctr., 1977—; top adv., gen. mgr. Nuclear Power Gen. Safety Ctr. Chmn. higher duty fuel devel. com. Ministry of Internat. Trade and Industry, 1967—, chmn. fuel cycle specialist com., 1968—; mem adv. com. postal services Ministry of Postal Services. Recipient Nuclear Safety award Nuclear Regulatory Commn. Japan, 1982; Maejima award for postal services Ministry Postal Services, 1984; W.J. Kroll Internat. award, 1986; Murakami award, 1986. Mem. Japan Inst. Metals (dir., award 1964), Nuclear Safety Research Assn. (v.p. 1979—), Japan Atomic Indsl. Forum (dir.), Sci. Council Japan, Atomic Energy Soc. JApan (v.p. 1986, 87, pres. 1988), All Japan Coll. Baseball Fedn. (exec. dir. 1982—), Internat. Soc. Japanese Philately (dir. 1952—), AIME, Am. Philatelic Soc., ASTM (Russ Ogden award 1986), Japan Nuclear Soc. (award 1971, v.p. 1986-87), Iron and Steel Inst. Buddhist. Author: Postage Stamp Production, 1943; Engrineering Metals, 1958; Less-common Metals, 1961; Science in Philately, 1965; Nuclear Fuels, 1971; Baseball for the Ten Million, 1977; Nuclear Energy Through Postage Stamps, 1983; editor Modern Philately, 1975—. Home: 3-30-11 Matsunoki Suginami-ku, Tokyo 116, Japan

MISHRA, BRAJESH CHANDRA, diplomat; b. Sept. 29, 1928. With Indian Fgn. Service, 1951—; 3d sec. Karachi, Pakistan; 2d sec. Rangoon, Burma; 1st sec. Brussels; under-sec. Ministry of Fgn. Affairs Govt. of India, 1956-57, dep. sec., 1957-60; first sec., then counsellor Permanent Mission to UN, N.Y.C., 1964-69; minister and chardé d'affaires Indian Embassy, Peking, People's Republic China, 1969-73; ambassador and permanent rep. to UN Geneva, 1973-77; ambassador to Indonesia 1977-79, permanent rep. to UN, 1979-81, cons. to UN from Govt. of India, 1981—, UN commr. for Namibia and asst. sec.-gen., 1982—. Office: Permanent Mission of India to the UN 750 Third Ave 21st Floor New York NY 10017 *

MISITI, AURELIO, engineering educator; b. Melicucco, Italy, Jan. 3, 1935; s. Nicodemo and Pasqualina M.; m. Marta La Porta, Feb. 2, 1962; children: Marina, Nicola. Laurea in Engring., U. Rome, 1961. Prof. hydraulic engring. U. Rome, 1975-81, prof. sanitary engring., 1981—; chmn. Azienda Comunale Energia e Ambiente, Rome, 1983-87, C.G.I.L., Lazio, Rome, 1975-81; dir. Dept. Hydraulics, Transp. S. and Roads U. Rome, 1987—. Author: Idraulica, 1976; editor Ingegneria Sanitaria, 1982—. Mem. Associazione Naz. Ingegneria Sanitaria, Associazione Idrotecnica Italiana. Mem. P.C.I. Pol. Party. Home: Via Licia 19, 00183 Rome Italy Office: U Rome Dept Hydraulics, Transp S & Roads, Via Eudossiana 18, 00184 Rome Italy

MISKOVSKY, GEORGE, SR., lawyer; b. Oklahoma City, Feb. 13, 1910; s. Frank and Mary (Bourek) M.; m. Nelly Oleta Donahue, Dec. 30, 1932; children: George, Gary, Grover, Gail Marie. LL.B., U. Okla., 1936. Bar: Okla. 1936. Sr. partner firm Miskovsky, Sullivan, Taylor & Manchester, Oklahoma City, 1936—; pub. defender Oklahoma City, 1936; county atty. Oklahoma County, 1943-44; of counsel Col. John Embry. Mem. Okla. Ho. of Reps., 1939-42; mem. Okla. Senate, 1950-60; pres., dir. Economy Square Inc. Mem. Am., Okla., Oklahoma County bar assns., Am. Judicature Soc., Am. Trial Lawyers Assn., Nat. Assn. Criminal Def. Lawyers, Am. Acad. Matrimonial Lawyers, U. Okla. Law Assn., Oklahoma City C. of C., Order of Coif, Pi Kappa Alpha, Phi Alpha Delta. Democrat. Episcopalian. Clubs: Lions, Oklahoma City Golf and Country, Sooner Dinner, Masons, Shriners, Pair de la Chaine, Bailli Honoraire d'Okla, Confrerie de la Chaine des Rotisseurs. Home: 1511 Drury Ln Oklahoma City OK 73116 Office: Miskovsky Sullivan Taylor & Manchester 302 Hightower Bldg Oklahoma City OK 73102

MISKUS, MICHAEL ANTHONY, electrical engineer, consultant; b. East Chicago, Ind., Dec. 10, 1950; s. Paul and Josephine Miskus; BS, Purdue U., 1972; AAS in Elec. Engring. Tech., Purdue U., Indpls., 1972; cert. mgmt. Ind. U., 1972, Ind. Central Coll., 1974; m. Jeannie Ellen Dolmanni, Nov. 4, 1972. Service engr. Reliance Electric & Engring. Co., Hammond, Ind., 1972-73; maintenance supr., maintenance mgr. Diamond Chain Co./AMSTED Industries, Indpls., 1973-76; primary and facilities elec. engr. Johnson & Johnson Baby Products Co., Park Forest South, Ill., 1976-81; prin. Miskus Cons., indsl./comml. elec. cons., 1979—; plant and facilities engring. mgr. Sherwin Williams Co., Chgo. Emulsion Plant, Chgo., 1981-85; with Miscon Assocs., Riverside, Calif., 1985—; acting dir. plant and facilities engring. Bourns Inc., 1982—; instr., lectr. EET program Moraine Valley Community Coll., Palos Hills, Ill., 1979; lectr. energy engring., bldg. automation systems Prairie State Coll., Chicago Heights, Ill., 1980—; mem. adj. faculty, faculty adv. bd. Orange Coast Coll., Costa Mesa, Calif.; mem. Elec. Industry Evaluation Panel. Mem. faculty adv. bd. Moraine Valley Community Coll., 1980—. Mem. IEEE, Assn. Energy Engrs., Assn. Energy Engrs. (sr., So. Calif. chpt.), Illuminating Engring. Soc. N.Am., Internat. Platform Assn., Riverside C. of C. Club: Purdue of Los Angeles. Office: Miscon Assocs PO Box 55353 Riverside CA 92517

MISLEJ, JORGE L., construction company executive; b. Santiago, Chile, Aug. 9, 1949; s. Jorge A. Mislej and Yolanda C. Musalem; m. Maria A. Anania, July 25, 1956; children: Jorge, José Antonio, M. Antonieta, Luis Alberto. MBA, Cath. U. of Santiago, 1972. Asst. to minister Ministry of Econs., Santiago, 1974-77; vice chmn. Lan Chile Airlines, Santiago, 1977-81; dir. Banco Osorno, Santiago, 1981-83, Procesac S.A., Santiago, 1981-84, Banco Concepcion, Santiago, 1983-85; pres. PHS Chile Ltd., Santiago, 1982-86; chmn. Zumasa S.A., Santiago, 1986—; chmn. bd. PHS Internat. Corp., Santiago, 1981—; prof. Cath. U., Santiago, 1972-85, Mil. High Sch., 1976-87; cons. Mislej and Co., Santiago, 1973-87. Bd. dirs. Ski Patrol, Chile, 1969-87, Santiago-Club Aereo, 1986-87, Radio Ham Club Santiago, 1985-87. Mem. Engrs. Assn. Chile. Roman Catholic. Office: Zumasa SA, Vicuña Mackenna 1865, Santiago Chile

MISNER, ROBERT DAVID, electronic engineer; b. Waynesville, Ill., May 1, 1920; s. Oscar and Elizabeth (Nyren) M.; student Ill. Wesleyan U., 1939-42; B.S. in Physics, George Washington U., 1946; postgr. U. Md., 1948; m. Virginia Fuehrer, June 4, 1949; children—Robin Beth, Christie Marie. Mem. staff U.S. Naval Research Lab., Washington, 1942-44, 46—, br. head signal exploitation br., 1965—; cons. Served in USNR, 1944-46. Recipient Disting. Civilian Service award USN, 1970; others. Mem. IEEE (sr.), Assn. Old Crows, Sigma Xi. Contbr. articles to profl. jours. Home: 7107 Sussex Pl Alexandria VA 22307 Office: 4555 Overlook Ave Washington DC 20375

MISRACH, RICHARD LAURENCE, photographer; b. Los Angeles, July 11, 1949; s. Robert Laskin and Lucille (Gardner) M.; m. Debra Bloomfield, Jan. 18, 1981 (div. 1987); 1 son, Jacob Luke. A.B. in Psychology, U. Calif., Berkeley, 1971. Instr. Assoc. Students Studio, U. Calif., Berkeley, 1971-77; vis. lectr. U. Calif.-Berkeley, 1982; lectr. U. Calif.-Santa Barbara, 1984; juror Nat. Endowment Arts, 1986. Exhbns. include Musée Art Moderne, Paris, 1979, Mus. Modern Art, N.Y.C., 1978, Whitney Mus. Am. Art, N.Y.C., 1981, Grapestake Gallery, San Francisco, 1979, 81, Young-Hoffman Gallery, Chgo., 1980, Centre Georges Pompidou, Paris, 1983, Oakland Mus., 1982, San Francisco Mus. Modern Art, 1983, Centre Georges Pompidou, Paris, 1983, Los Angeles County Mus. Art, 1984, Fraenkel Gallery, San Francisco, 1985, Oakland Mus., 1987, Min Gallery, Tokyo, 1975-87, numerous others; books include: Telegraph 3 A.M, 1974, Grapestake Gallery, 1979, (A Photographic Book), 1979, Hawaii portfolio, 1980, Graecism dye-transfer portfolio, 1982, Desert Cantos, 1987, (Internat. Ctr. of Photography award, 1988), Houston Ctr. for Photography, 1985, Light Gallery, N.Y.C., 1985, Martin Gallery, Washington, 1985, Richard Misrach, 1988. Guggenheim fellow, 1978; Ferguson grantee, 1976; Nat. Endowment for Arts grantee, 1973, 77, 84; AT&T commn., 1979.

MISSAN, RICHARD SHERMAN, transportation executive, lawyer; b. New Haven, Oct. 5, 1933; s. Albert and Hannah (Hochberg) M.; m. Aileen Louise; children—Hilary, Andrew, Wendy. B.A., Yale U., 1955, J.D., 1958. Bar: N.Y. 1959, U.S. Dist. Ct. (so. and ea. dists.) N.Y. 1979. Assoc. Kaye, Scholer, Fierman, Hays & Handler, N.Y.C., 1962-67; ptnr. Schoenfeld & Jacobs, N.Y.C., 1968-78, Walsh & Frisch, N.Y.C., 1979-80, Gersten, Savage & Kaplowitz, N.Y.C., 1980-87, v.p., gen. counsel, Avis, Inc., 1987—. Mem. ABA, N.Y. State Bar Assn., Fed. Bar Council, Assn. Bar City N.Y. (com. on corrections, chmn. subcom. on legis., com. on juvenile justice, chmn. subcom. on juvenile facilities, past com. corrections, com. on atomic energy, mem. com. on mcpl. affairs, com. on housing and urban devel.). Club: Yale (N.Y.C.). Office: Avis Inc 900 Old Country Rd Garden City NY 11530

MISSONG, ALFRED, ambassador; b. Vienna, Austria, 1934; s. Alfred and Juliana (Riepl) M.; m. Roswitha Kuehnert; children: Lucas, Alexandra, Thomas. D of Law, U. Vienna, 1959. Free-lance journalist Vienna, 1953-58; officer civil service Austrian Fgn. Office, Vienna, 1958-60, chief press dept., 1974-77; attachè Austrian embassy, Belgrade, 1960-63, Vienna, 1963-65; press attachè Moscow, 1965-68; counsellor London, 1968-72; Austrian ambassador to Mex., 1977-82, Caracas, Venezuela, 1982-86; dir. Diplomatic Acad., Vienna, 1986—. Roman Catholic. Office: Diplomatic Acad, Favoritenstrasse 15, 1090 Vienna Austria

MISTRY, NASSIRUDHIN HASSANALY, management executive; b. Bombay, India, Sept. 21, 1944; arrived in Pakistan, 1950; s. Hassanaly Abdullah and Shereen (Hassanaly) M.; m. Nasim N. Mistry, Feb. 20, 1971; children: Nadya N., Shamshuddin N. BS in Engring., Karachi (Pakistan) U., 1968. Trainee Karachi Gas Co. Ltd., 1969; engr. Noor Silk Mills, Karachi, 1969-70, J & P Coats Ltd., Karachi, 1970-76; successively instrument engr., project engr. then mgr. power and instrumentation Javedan Cement Ltd., Karachi, 1976-81; from elec. engr. to chief engr. Pakland Cement Ltd., Karachi, 1981-82, gen. mgr. factory, 1982-85, gen. mgr. coordination, 1985—; founder, then pres. Aga Khan Nazimabad Shoes and Pani Co., Karachi; lectr. in field. Tchr. religion H.R.H. The Aga Khan Nazimabad Religious Night Sch., Karachi, 1961-63; enumerator, dir. Nazimabad and Sultanabad areas edn. study team H.R.H. The Aga Khan Ismailia Edn. Bd., Karachi, 1971-72; mem. H.R.H. The Aga Khan Garden Ismailia Local Council, Karachi, 1972-76, mem. jud. and instn. coms., 1973, mem., then co-convenor propaganda and publicity com., also convenor instn. com., 1973-76; convenor stalls sub-com., mem. policy and main com. H.S.H. Prince Ali S. Khan Garden Rovers Crew Idd-ul-Fitr Athletic Meet and Fete, Karachi, 1974; mem. planning com. H.R.H. The Aga Khan Econ. Planning and Grants Council for Ismailis, Karachi, 1975-76; mem. burial bus. donation com. H.R.H. The Aga Khan Garden Local Council, Karachi, 1975-76; enumerator socio-welfare need study com., mem. garden local study com. H.R.H. The Aga Khan Ismailia Fed. Council, Karachi, 1976-77, in-charge garden local scrutiny com., 1977; chmn. H.R.H. The Aga Khan Nazimabad Edn. Promotion Com., 1977-80; chmn., group scout master H.S.H. Prince Ali S. Khan Nazimabad Coordinating Council for Scouts, Guides and Orch., Karachi, 1977-78; mem. constrn. com. H.R.H. The Aga Khan Nazimabad Jamat Khana, 1978-80; hon. worker The Aga Khan Maternity Home, 1980-81; mem. H.H. Prince Aga Khan Shia Imami Regional Council, Karachi and Baluchistan, India, 1984-87, mem. jud. com., 1984-85; convenor socio-econ. upliftment com. H.H. Prince Aga Khan Shia Imami Ismailia Regional Council, Karachi and Baluchistan, 1985-87, convenor graveyard com., 1986-87; mem. resources mobilization contact com., mem. core com. on manpower issue H.H. Prince Afa Khan Shia Imami Ismailia Fed. Council, Pakistan, 1986—; mem. Shia Imami Ismailia Tariqah and Religious Edn. Bd., Pakistan, 1987—. Fellow Inst. Elec. Engrs. Pakistan; mem. Ismaili Engrs. and Architects Assn. (founder, mem. mng. com.), Pakistan Inst. Engrs., Pakistan Engring. Council, IEEE, Instrument Soc. Am., Tech. Assn. Pulp and Paper Industry. Clubs: Karchi Golf, Karachi. Home: B 196 Block C, North Nazimabad, Karachi, Sind Pakistan Office: Pakland Cement Ltd, A-14 Trade Ctr Shahrea Faisai, Karachi, Sind Pakistan

MITA, KATSUSHIGE, electronic and electrical equipment company executive; b. Tokyo, Apr. 6, 1924; s. Yoshitaro and Fuji M.; B.E., U. Tokyo, 1949; m. Toriko Miyata, May 27, 1957; children—Yoko, Makiko. With Hitachi, Ltd., Tokyo, 1949—, gen. mgr. Kanagawa works, 1971-76, group exec. computer group, 1976-77, exec. mng. dir., 1977-79, sr. exec. mng. dir., 1979-80, exec. v.p., 1980-81, pres., 1981—, also dir. Mem. Communication Industries Assn. Japan, Electronic Industries Assn. Japan. Buddhism. Office: 4-6 Kanda-Surugadai, Chiyoda-ku, Tokyo 101, Japan

MITCHAM, BOB ANDERSON, lawyer; b. Atlanta, July 16, 1933; s. George Anderson and Pearl (Bing) M.; m. Lupe M. Vazquez, Dec. 6, 1969; children—Robert Anderson, Tamara Lynn, Matthew Vazquez. B.S., Fla. So. Coll., Lakeland, 1959; J.D., Stetson U., 1962. Bar: Fla. 1963, U.S. Dist. Ct. (mid. dist.) Fla. 1963, U.S. Ct. Apls. (5th cir.) 1965, U.S. Ct. Apls. (11th cir.) 1983. Ptnr., Mitcham & Honig, Tampa, Fla., 1963-66, Mitcham, Leon & Guito, Tampa, 1966-68; sole practice, Tampa, 1968-82; ptnr. Mitcham, Weed & Barbas, Tampa, 1982—; lectr. Oxford U., Eng., 1981, U. London, 1987. Contbr. articles to profl. jours. Pres. Young Democrats of Fla., Tampa, 1968. Served with USAF, 1952-59. Perry Nicholas Trial scholar, 1961. Mem. Criminal Def. Lawyers of Hillsborough County (pres. 1981-82), Hillsborough County Bar Assn. (dir. 1981-85), Ybor City C. of C. (dir. 1981-82, chmn. Super Bowl XVIII). Democrat. Mem. Ch. of God. Office: Mitcham Weed Barbas et al 1509 E 8th Ave Tampa FL 33605

MITCHELL, ANN MARGARET, historian, records manager, archivist; b. Melbourne, Victoria, Australia, Apr. 15, 1938; d. Albert Percy and Dorothy Elaine (Exelby) M. BA, U. Melbourne, 1964, MA, 1967, PhD, 1973. Asst., Gaston Renard Antiquarian Bookseller, Melbourne, 1960-63; resident tutor Univ. Women's Coll., Melbourne, 1964-67; historian Alfred Hosp., Melbourne, 1967-71; adminstrv. asst. U. Leeds (Eng.), 1973-76; historian Sydney Hosp. (Australia), 1976-86; officer-in-charge records adminstrn. Monash U., Melbouirne, 1988—. Author: The Hospital South of the Yarra, 1977; contbr. articles to various publs., including Australian Dictionary of Biography. Recipient Dennis Wettenhall Postgrad. prize in History, U. Melbourne, 1967. Mem. Australian Hist. Assn., Australian Fedn. Univ. Women, Australian Soc. Authors, Med. History Soc., Profl. Historians Assn. NSW, Royal Australian Hist. Soc., Australian Soc. Archivists (assoc.). Address: GPO Box 1784, 2001 Sydney New South Wales 2001, Australia Office: Sydney Hosp, Macquarie St, Sydney 2000, Australia

MITCHELL, AUSTIN VERNON, member of parliament; b. Sept. 19, 1934. BA, Manchester U., 1956; MA, Nuffield Coll., Oxford, 1957. Lectr. history Otago U., Dunedin, New Zealand, 1959-63; sr. lectr. politics U. Canterbury, Christchurch, New Zealand, 1963-67; fellow Nuffield Coll., Oxford, 1967-69; journalist Yorkshire TV Leeds, 1969-71, Sta. BBC TV, 1972; presenter Yorkshire TV, 1973; mem. of parliament Great Grimsby, 1977—. Author: Whigs in Opposition 1815-30, People and Politics in New Zealand, Westminster Man, The Case for Labour. Opposition spokesman for Trade and Industry, 1987—. Mem. Labour Party. Mem. Ch. of Eng. Home: 15 New Cartergate Rd, Grimsby England Office: House of Commons, Westminster England

MITCHELL, DONALD WAYNE, management consultant, investment manager, lawyer, cattle breeder; b. San Bernardino, Calif., Nov. 1, 1946; s. Donald Wardell and Edith Felice (Wood) M.; m. Carol Bruckner, Nov. 11, 1984; children: Donald Weyland, Mark De Saussure, Mandy Sara, Janis Felicia. AB magna cum laude, Harvard U., 1968, J.D., 1971. Bar: Mass. 1971. Project mgr. Boston Cons. Group, 1971-74; dir. strategic planning, Heublein, Inc., Farmington, Conn., 1974-77; mng. dir. Mitchell and Co., Weston, Mass., 1977—; pres. Mitchell Investment Mgmt. Co., Inc., Weston, 1981—, DMMJ Cattle Breeding Corp., 1986—, DMMJ Cattle Feeding Corp., 1986—; bd. dirs. Money Tree Prodns. Inc. Vice chmn. law sch. fund, Harvard U., Cambridge, 1981-82, chmn. law sch. fund 10th ann. gift campaign, 1980-81, chmn. law sch. class of 1971 15th reunion, 1985-86, cochmn. class of 1968 20th reunion Harvard U., 1986-88; cons. Greater Hartford Arts Council, 1975-77; bd. dirs. Newton Soccer Assn., 1985—. Mem. Harvard Alumni Assn. (bd. dirs. 1986-88), Harvard Law Sch. Assn. (mem. centennial com. 1984-86, treas. 1987—). Clubs: Brae Burn Country (West Newton, Mass.). Office: Mitchell and Co 9 Riverside Rd Weston MA 02193

MITCHELL, GEORGE JOHN, lawyer, senator; b. Waterville, Maine, Aug. 20, 1933; s. George J. and Mary (Saad) M. B.A., Bowdoin Coll., 1954; LL.B., Georgetown U., 1960. Bar: Maine bar 1960, D.C. bar 1960. Trial atty. U.S. Dept. Justice, Washington, 1960-62; exec. asst. Senator Muskie, 1962-65; partner firm Jensen & Baird, Portland, Maine, 1965-77; U.S. atty. Maine, 1977-79; U.S. dist. judge 1979-80; U.S. Senator from Maine, 1980—; Chmn. Maine Democratic Com., 1966-68; nat. committeeman, Maine, 1968-77. Served with U.S. Army, 1954-56. Office: 176 Russell Senate Bldg Washington DC 20510

MITCHELL, GEORGE TRICE, physician; b. Marshall, Ill., Jan. 20, 1914; s. Roscoe Addison and Alma (Trice) M.; m. Mildred Aletha Miller, June 21, 1941; children: Linda Sue, Mary Kathryn. BS, Purdue U., 1935; MD, George Washington U., 1940. Intern Meth. Hosp., Indpls., 1940-41; gen. practice medicine Marshall, 1946—; mem. courtesy staff Union and Regional Hosps., Terre Haute, Ind.; clin. assoc. Sch. Basic Medicine U. Ill.; chmn. bd. dirs. First Nat. Bank, Marshall. Mem. adv. council premedicine Eastern Ill. U., 1965-69; alt. del. Rep. Conv., 1968, del., 1972; trustee Lakeland Jr. Coll. Served from 1st lt. to lt. col. USAAF, 1941-45. Fellow Am. Acad. Family Physicians; mem. AMA, Ill. Med. Soc. (2d v.p. 1980-81), Clark County Med. Soc. (pres.), Aesculapian Soc. of Wabash Valley (pres. 1965), Clark County Hist. Soc. (pres. 1968-70). Methodist. Lodges: Masons (32 degree), Shriners. Home: RFD 2 Marshall IL 62441 Office: 410 N 2d St Marshall IL 62441

MITCHELL, GLENN WHITTAKER, physician, army officer; b. New Haven, Feb. 23, 1946; s. Roy Glenn and Bernice Wakelee (Jacobs) M.; Sc.B. in Physics, Brown U., 1967, Sc.M. in Elec. Engring. (NDEA fellow), 1969, M.D. (Univ. fellow), 1975; m. Jane Ann Hathaway; children—Bradford Roy, Brewster Scot. 1 dau. by previous marriage, Heather Flynn. Diplomate Am. Bd. Emergency Medicine. Instr. elec. engring. U. Bridgeport (Conn.), 1968-69; dir. test facility Technik, Inc., N.Y.C., 1969-71; intern R.I. Hosp., Providence, 1975-76; resident Butler Hosp., Providence, 1976-77; emergency physician Warwick and North Providence (R.I.) hosps., 1977-78; mem. staff gen. medicine and emergency medicine Venice (Fla.) Hosp., 1978-80; emergency physician R.I. Hosp., 1981-82; dir. emergency dept. Meml. Hosp., Pawtucket, R.I., 1983-84; researcher U.S. Army Aeromed. Research Lab., Ft. Rucker, Ala., 1984—; pres. Microcomputer Engring. Inc., Venice, 1979-82; pres. The Computer Prescription, Inc., 1983-84; med. dir. emergency services Sarasota County (Fla.) 1979-80; med. dir., dir. emergency services R.I. Dept. Health, 1981-84; chmn. coordinating bd. R.I. Ambulance Service, 1981-84. Fellow Am. Coll. Emergency Physicians (chmn. nat. com. on disaster medicine 1983-85, pres. Govt. Services chpt. 1985-86), Aerospace Med. Assn. (assoc.); mem. Assn. Mil. Surgeons U.S., Soc. U.S. Army Flight Surgeons (life), Sigma Xi, Zeta Psi (elder). Home: 12 Faith Ln Fort Rucker AL 36362 Office: US Army Aeromed Research Lab Box 577 Fort Rucker AL 36362

MITCHELL, JAMES FITZALLEN, prime minister of St. Vincent and the Grenadines, agronomist, hotelier; b. Bequia, Grenadines, 1931; s. Reginald Fitzgerald and Lois M. Grad. Imperial Coll. of Tropical Agr., Trinidad, 1954; student U. B.C., 1954-56. Chief research officer, St. Vincent, 1958-60; editor pest control articles and news summaries Ministry of Overseas Devel., London, 1965-66; M.P. for the Grenadines, 1966—; Minister of Trade, Agr., Labour and Tourism, 1967-72; premier of St. Vincent, 1972-74; prime minister of St. Vincent and the Grenadines, 1984—, now also minister of fgn. affairs . Pres., founder New Democratic Party. Address: Prime Minister's Office, Kingstown Saint Vincent *

MITCHELL, JERE HOLLOWAY, researcher, physiologist, medical educator; b. Longview, Tex., Oct. 17, 1928; s. William Holloway and Dorothea (Turner) M.; m. Pamela Battey, Oct. 1, 1960; children: Wendy O'Sullivan, Laurie Clemens M., Amy Dewing M. BS with honors, Va. Mil. Inst., 1950; MD, Southwestern Med. Sch., 1954. Intern Parkland Meml. Hosp., Dallas, 1954-55, resident in internal medicine, 1955-56; asst. prof. medicine and physiology U. Tex. Southwestern Med. Ctr., Dallas, 1962-66, dir. Weinberger Lab. for Cardiopulmonary Research, 1966—, assoc. prof., 1966-69, prof., 1969—, dir. Harry S. Moss Heart Ctr., 1976—, holder Frank M. Ryburn Jr. chair in heart research, 1982—. Established Investigator, Am. Heart Assn., 1962-67. Recipient Career Devel. award USPHS, 1968-73; Donald W. Seldin Research award U. Tex. Southwestern, 1978. Attending physician Parkland Meml. Hosp., 1963—, St. Paul Med. Ctr., 1966—, VA Med. Ctr. Dallas, 1969—. Mem. Internat. Union Physiol. Soc. (commn. on cardiovascular physiology 1977—), Applied Physiol. Orthopedics Study Sect., NIH, 1979-81; Respirat. Appl. Physiol. Study Sect., NIH, 1981-82; Council of Caridac Rehab. of Internat. Soc. & Fed. Cardiol., 1981—; Sci. Adv. Bd., USAF, 1986—; Med. Sci. Com. AAAS, 1988—. Mem. editorial bd. Am. Jour. Physiology, 1972-76, Circulation, 1978-81, Am. Jour. Cardiology, 1965-74, 82-84, Cardiovascular Research, 1979-87, Jour. Cardiopulmonary Rehab., 1981—, Clin. Physiology, 1981—, Jour. Applied Physiology, 1978-82, 84—. Fellow Am. Coll. Cardiology (Young Investigator award 1961), Am. Coll. Sports Medicine (Citation award 1983, Honor award 1988); mem. Am. Heart Assn. (Award of Merit 1984, pres. Dallas div. 1977-78, pres. Tex. affiliate 1983-84), Am. Fedn. Clin. Research (emeritus), Am. Soc. Clin. Investigation (emeritus), Assn. Am. Physicians, Am. Physiol. Soc. (cardiovascular sect.), Assn. Univ. Cardiologists, Alpha Omega Alpha. Office: U Tex Southwestern Med Ctr Harry S Moss Heart Ctr 5323 Harry Hines Blvd Dallas TX 75235-9034

MITCHELL, JOHN FRANCIS, electronics company executive; b. Chgo., Jan. 1, 1928; s. William and Bridie (Keane) M.; B.S. in Elec. Engring., Ill. Inst. Tech., 1950; m. Margaret J. Gillis, Aug. 26, 1950; children—Catherine (Mrs. Edward Welsh III), John, Kevin. Exec. v.p., asst. chief operating officer Motorola Inc., Schaumburg, Ill., 1953-80, pres., 1980—, chief operating officer, 1986-87, vice chmn., 1987—, also bd. dirs. Served to lt. (j.g.) USNR, 1950-53. Mem. IEEE (sr.). Club: Inverness (Ill.) Country. Patentee in field. Office: Motorola Inc 1303 E Algonquin Rd Schaumburg IL 60196 *

MITCHELL, JOSEPH BRADY, mil. historian, author; b. Ft. Leavenworth, Kans., Sept. 25, 1915; s. William A. and Margery (Brady) M.; B.S., U.S. Mil. Acad., 1937; m. Vivienne French Brown, Aug. 20, 1938; children—Sherwood N., J. Bradford. Mem. ops. div. War Dept. Gen. Staff, 1945-49; chief historian Am. Battle Monuments Commn., 1950-61, hist. cons., 1969—; curator Ft. Ward Mus. and Park, Alexandria, Va., 1964-77. Served from 2d lt. to lt. col., 5th inf. div., AUS, 1937-45; ETO. Decorated Bronze Star; recipient Am. Revolutionary Round Table prize for best book in field, 1962. Mem. Alexandria Hist. Soc. (pres. 1981-83), Soc. of Cin., Civil War Round Table Alexandria (past pres., Joseph B. Mitchell award named in honor of birographee), Civil War Round Table D.C. (past pres., Bruce Catton award), Am. Revolution Round Table D.C. (past pres.), SCV (comdr.-in-chief 1980-82, chmn. nat. affairs com. 1982—). Episcopalian. Author: Decisive Battles of the Civil War, 1955; Decisive Battles of the American Revolution, 1962; Twenty Decisive Battles of the World, 1964; Discipline and Bayonets, 1967; The Badge of Gallantry, 1968; Military Leaders in the Civil War, 1972; contbr. articles to encys. and mags. Home: 601 Wilkes St Apt 102 Alexandria VA 22314

MITCHELL, JOSEPH PATRICK, architect; b. Bellingham, Wash., Sept. 29, 1939; s. Joseph Henry and Jessie Delila (Smith) M.; student Western Wash. State Coll., 1957-59; B.A., U. Wash., 1963, B.Arch., 1965; m. Marilyn Ruth Jorgenson, June 23, 1962; children—Amy Evangeline, Kirk Patrick, Scott Henry. Asso. designer, draftsman, project architect Beckwith Spangler Davis, Bellevue, Wash., 1965-70; prin. J. Patrick Mitchell, AIA & Assoc./Architects/Planners/Cons., Kirkland, Wash., 1970—. Chmn. long range planning com. Lake Retreat Camp, 1965—; bldg. chmn. Northshore Baptist Ch., 1980—, elder, 1984—; mem. bd. extension and central com. Columbia Baptist Conf., 1977-83. Cert. Nat. Council Archtl. Registration Bds. Mem. AIA, Constrn. Specification Inst., Interfaith Forum Religion, Art, and Architecture, Nat. Fedn. Ind. Bus., Unltd. Hydroplane Hall of Fame Mus.

Christian Camping Internat., Woodinville C. of C. Republican. Office: 12620 120th Ave NE Suite 208 Kirkland WA 98033

MITCHELL, JOSEPH (QUINCY), journalist, writer; b. Fairmont, N.C., July 27, 1908; s. Averette Nance and Elizabeth Amanda (Parker) M.; m. Therese Dagny Engelsted Jacobsen, Feb. 27, 1931; children: Nora (Mrs. John L.R. Sanborn), Elizabeth (Mrs. Henry Curtis). Student, U. N.C., 1925-29. Reporter N.Y. World, N.Y.C., 1929-30, N.Y. Herald Tribune, 1930-31, N.Y. World Telegram, 1931-38; writer New Yorker mag., N.Y.C., 1938—. Author: My Ears Are Bent, 1938, McSorley's Wonderful Saloon, 1943, Old Mr. Flood, 1948, The Bottom of the Harbor, 1960, Joe Gould's Secret, 1965, (with Edmund Wilson) Apologies to the Iroquois, With a Study of the Mohawks in High Steel, 1960. Vestryman Grace Ch., N.Y.C., 1978-84; mem. N.Y.C. Landmarks Preservation Commn., 1982-87; mem. restoration com. South Street Seaport Mus., 1972-80. Recipient Gold medal for lit. State N.C., 1984. Mem. Am. Acad. and Inst. Arts. and Letters (sec. 1972-74), Soc. Archtl. Historians, Soc. Indsl. Archeology, Friends of Cast-Iron Architecture, James Joyce Soc., Gypsy Lore Soc. (Eng.). Club: Century Assn. (N.Y.C.). Home: 44 W 10th St New York NY 10011 Office: The New Yorker 25 W 43d St New York NY 10036

MITCHELL, MAURICE B., publishing executive; b. N.Y.C., Feb. 9, 1915; s. Jacob and Beatrice (Weinstein) M.; m. Mildred Roth, Mar. 1937; 1 child, Lee Mark; m. Mary V. Rowles, Nov. 1951; children: Keith Edward, Deborah Irene. Student, NYU, 1932-35; LL.D. (hon.), U. Denver, 1958, W.Va. Wesleyan U., 1978; L.H.D. (hon.), Nat. Coll. Edn., 1969; Litt.D. (hon.), Colo. State U., 1971. With N.Y. Times, 1935-36; editor Gouverneur (N.Y.) Press, 1936-37; asst. pub. Ogdensburg (N.Y.) Jour., 1938-39, Rochester (N.Y.) Times-Union, 1940; nat. advt. mgr. Albany (N.Y.) Knickerbocker-News, 1941-43; with CBS, Washington, also N.Y.C., 1945-48, Nat. Assn. Broadcasters, Washington, 1948-49; mng. dir. Broadcast Advt. Bur./TVB, N.Y.C., 1949-50; with NBC, 1953; v.p., assoc. program service div. Muzak Corp., N.Y.C., 1950-53; dir. Muzak Corp., 1953-58; pres., dir. Ency. Brit. Films, Inc., 1953-62; pres. Ency. Brit., Inc (Chgo. and all subs.), 1962-67; dir. Ency. Brit. Ednl. Corp., 1977—; chancellor U. Denver, 1967-77; pres. Center for Study Democratic Instns./Fund for the Republic, 1977-78; chmn. Pacific Basin Inst., Santa Barbara, Calif., 1978—; dir. Washington program communication policy studies Annenberg Schs. Communication, 1983-85, cons., 1986—; chmn. Internat. Acad., Santa Barbara, Calif., 1988—; co-founder, chmn. Westview Press, Boulder, Colo., 1975-83; owner, pub. Rocky Mountain Herald, 1975-78; chmn. Denver br. Fed. Res. Bank, 1971-76, dir. Kansas City br., 1976-77. Contbr. articles on edn. and communications to profl. jours. Mem. U.S. Commn. on Civil Rights, 1968-74; chmn. Calif. Ednl. Tech. adv. com., 1981-83, Denver Community Edn. Council on Integration Pub. Schs., 1974-76; trustee Freedoms Found.; chmn. Colo. com. Rhodes Scholarship Trust, 1974-77, Calif. Commn., 1978-80; citizens bd. U. Chgo.; mem. adv. com. U.S. Army Command and Gen. Staff Coll., Dept. Army, 1975-78; chmn. Western Regional Judges Truman Scholarships, 1976-82; dir. Nat. Public Radio, 1977-82, chmn., 1979-82; bd. assos. Nat. Coll. Edn.; trustee Com. Econ. Devel., 1957-62; bd. dirs. Fgn. Policy Assn., World Affairs Center and Nat. Citizens on Internat. Coop., 1966-71, chmn., 1980; bd. dirs., Inst. Internat. Edn., 1978-85, African Student Aid Fund; trustee Nat. U., San Diego. Recipient George Washington medal Freedoms Found., 1969; VFW medal of Merit, 1970; Cert. of Recognition for disting. service to edn. Phi Delta Kappa, 1971; Golden Plate award Am. Acad. Achievement, 1972; Civis Princeps award Regis Coll., Denver, 1973; Meritorious award Denver Met. NAACP, 1973; Malcolm Glenn Wyer award Adult Edn. Council Met. Denver, 1975; B'nai B'rith award, 1976; Human Relations award Beth Joseph Synagogue, Denver, 1976; award NCCJ, 1974. Mem. Colo. State Hist. Soc. (dir.), Phi Beta Kappa, Beta Alpha Psi, Omicron Delta Kappa, Beta Gamma Sigma, Alpha Kappa Psi. Clubs: Cosmos (Washington), Univ. (Denver), Chgo., Mid-Am. (Chgo.), Santa Barbara (Calif.). Lodge: Masons. Home: 1455 E Mountain Dr Montecito CA 93108

MITCHELL, MICHAEL DENNIS HENRY, aerospace marketing consultant; b. Brussels, May 3, 1950; s. Sir Dennis and Mireille (Countess Cornet de Ways Ruart) M.; m. Countess Diane D'Avernas, Sept. 1, 1978; children: Hugh, Caroline, Dennis. MA, Dublin U., 1972. Exec. James F. Fox Inc., N.Y.C., 1972-73; dir. Aero Systems, OHain, Belgium, 1975—; cons. Lockheed Corp., Calif., 1980—, British Aerospace, U.K., 1976—, Westland Helicopters, U.K., 1976—, Marconi Def. Systems, U.K., 1987—. Contbr. articles to James Def. Weekly, 1986. Served as 2d lt. Belgian Grenadier Guards, 1974-75. Roman Catholic. Club: Royal Golf de Belgique, Cercle Gaulois (Brussels). Office: Aero Systems, Chemin des Chasseurs, 1328 Ohain Belgium

MITCHELL, MICHAEL EUGENE, electronics engineer, business executive; b. Kalamazoo, June 29, 1930; s. Otto Eugene and Helen Elaine (Mullins) M.; student Western Mich. U., 1948-51; B.S. in E.E., U. Mich., 1953, B.S. in Engring. Math., 1953; m. Joan Hortense Beard, Sept. 13, 1953; children—Michael T., Donald G., Nicole M. Mem. tech. staff Bell Telephone Labs., Whippany, N.J., 1953-57; communications systems engr., cons. engr. Gen. Electric Co., Ithaca, N.Y., Okalahoma City and Syracuse, N.Y., 1957-75; sr. staff engr. communications systems div. Hughes Aircraft Co., Fullerton, Calif., 1975—; pres. Opportunityland Inc., Fullerton, 1981—. Kalamazoo Citizens grantee 1949; Jaycees scholar, 1948; Joseph Boyer scholar, 1952; recipient AIEE-IRE award U. Mich., 1953. Mem. IEEE (past treas., chmn. chpt.), Sigma Xi, Eta Kappa Nu, Tau Beta Pi, Phi Kappa Phi, Kappa Rho Sigma, Kappa Alpha Psi. Author govt. reports and articles in profl. jours.; patentee in field. Office: 1861 N Euclid Suite 180 Fullerton CA 92635

MITCHELL, MICHAEL JAMES, data processing executive; b. Phila., June 21, 1945; s. Walter J. and Ruth (Hutchins) M. B.S., Nebr. Wesleyan, 1968; cert. in systems analysis design with distinction U. Minn., 1975. Cert. systems profl., cert. data processer. Systems analyst FBI, Washington, 1969-71, Norwest Computer Services, Mpls., 1971-75, Daytons, Mpls., 1975-78, Nat. Car Rental, Mpls., 1978-79; cons. Technalysis, Mpls., 1979-86; chief exec. officer Michael J. Mitchell Inc., 1986— . Served to E-5 USN, 1968-69. Mem. Assn. Systems Mgmt. Republican. Club: Lemans. Lodge: Masons. Avocations: skiing; sailing. Home and Office: 5628 Logan Ave S Minneapolis MN 55419

MITCHELL, PAUL BLACKBURN, JR., carpet manufacturing executive; b. Bryson City, N.C., Apr. 6, 1940; s. Paul Blackburn and Mary Frances (Sawyer) M.; m. Geraldine Loretta Lombardi, May 11, 1974; children: Paul B. III, Mary Catherine, John Thomas, Julie Ann. BS in Textile Engring., N.C. State U., 1966. Devel. mgr. Rohm & Haas, Phila., 1966-70; internat. prodn. mgr. Rohm & Haas, Miami, 1970-79; asst. to pres. Schlegel, Rochester, N.Y., 1979-80; mktg. mgr. Ralston Purina, St. Louis, 1980-85; owner Carpeting Concepts, Mascoutah, Ill., 1985—; cons. PM Tex, Collinsville, Ill., 1975—. Author: Flocking, 1973, Coatings, 1974, Chemical Formulas, 1975; patentee textiles and carpets. Coordinator, Ill. Cub Scout chmn. Boy Scouts Am., 1981-86. Mem. Am. Assn. Textile Chemists and Colorists, Tech. Assn. of Pulp and Paper Industry, Theta Chi. Republican. Baptist. Home: 2003 Ravenwood Dr Collinsville IL 62234 Office: Carpeting Concepts 1410 Eisenhower St Mascoutah IL 62258

MITCHELL, PAULA RAE, nursing educator; b. Independence, Mo., Jan. 10, 1951; d. Millard Henry and E. Lorene (Denton) Gates; m. Ralph William Mitchell, May 24, 1975. BS in Nursing, Graceland Coll., 1973; MS in Nursing, U. Tex., 1976; postgrad. N.Mex. State U. RN, Tex., Mo.; cert. childbirth educator. Commd. capt. U.S. Army, 1972; ob-gyn nurse practitioner U.S. Army, Seoul, Korea, 1977-78; resigned, 1978; instr. nursing El Paso Community Coll. (Tex.), 1979-85, dir. nursing, 1985—, acting div. chmn. health occupations, 1985-86, div. chmn., 1986—, curriculum facilitator, 1984-86; ob-gyn nurse practitioner Planned Parenthood, El Paso, 1981-86, mem. med. com., 1986-87. Founder, bd. dirs. Health-C.R.E.S.T., El Paso, 1981-85; mem. pub. edn. com. Am. Cancer Soc., El Paso, 1983-84. Decorated Army Commendation medal, Meritorious Service medal. Contbr. articles to profl. jours. Mem. Nat. League for Nursing (mem. resolutions com. Assocs. Degree council, 1987—), Am. Soc. for Psychoprophylaxis in Obstetrics, Nurses Assn. of Am. Coll. Obstetricians and Gynecologists (cert. in ambulatory women's health care; chpt. coordinator 1979-83, nat. program rev. com. 1984-86, correspondent 1987-88), Advanced Nurse Practitioner Group El Paso (coordinator 1980-83 legislative committee 1984), Orgn. for Advancement of Assoc. Degree in Nursing (Tex. membership chmn. 1985—), Am. Vocat. Assn., Am. Assn. Women in Community and Jr. Colls., Nat. Council Occupational Edn. (mem. articulation task force), Nat. Council of Instructional Adminstrs. Sigma Theta Tau. Mem. Christian Ch. (Disciples of Christ). Home: 4616 Cupid Dr El Paso TX 79924 Office: El Paso Community College PO Box 20500 El Paso TX 79998

MITCHELL, PETER DENNIS, biochemist; b. Mitcham, Surrey, Eng., Sept. 29, 1920; s. Christopher Gibbs and Kate Beatrice Dorothy (Taplin) M.; B.A., Jesus Coll., Cambridge U., 1943, Ph.D., 1950, Sc.D. (hon.), 1985; Dr.rer.nat. (hon.), Tech. U. Berlin, 1976; D.Sc. (hon.), Exeter U., 1977, U. Chgo., 1978, U. Liverpool, 1979, U. Bristol, 1980, U. Edinburgh, 1980, U. Hull, 1980, U. East Anglia, 1981, U. York, 1982; m. Patricia Helen Mary ffrench, Nov. 1, 1958; children—Julia, Jeremy, Vanessa, Daniel, Jason, Gideon. With dept. biochemistry Cambridge U., 1943-55, demonstrator, 1950-55; dir. chem. biology unit, dept. zoology U. Edinburgh (Scotland), 1955-63, sr. lectr., then reader, 1961-63, James Rennie Bequest lectr., 1980; dir. research Glynn Research Inst., Bodmin, Cornwall, 1964-87; chmn. hon. dir. Glynn Research Found., 1987—; Sir Hans Krebs lectr. Fedn. European Biochem. Socs., 1978; Fritz Lipmann lectr. German Soc. Biol. Chemistry, 1978; Humphry Davy meml. lectr. Royal Inst. Chemistry and The Chilterns and Middlesex sect. of Chem. Soc., 1980; Croonian lectr. The Royal Soc., 1987. Recipient Louis and Bert Freedman Found. award N.Y. Acad. Scis., 1974; Wilhelm Feldberg prize Feldberg Found. Anglo/German Sci. Exchange, 1976; Lewis S. Rosenstiel award Brandeis U., 1977; Nobel Prize in chemistry, 1978; Medal of Honor, Athens (Greece) Mcpl. Council; co-recipient Warren Triennial prize Mass. Gen. Hosp., Boston, 1974; fellow Jesus Coll., Cambridge. Fellow Royal Soc. (Copley medal 1981); hon. fellow Royal Soc. Edinburgh; mem. Biochem. Soc. (CIBA medal 1973), Econ. Research Council, European Molecular Biology Orgn.; fgn. assoc. U.S. Nat. Acad. Scis.; hon. mem. Soc. Gen. Microbiology, Am. Soc. Biol. Chemists, Am. Acad. Arts and Scis., Japanese Biochem. Soc. Author: Chemiosmotic Coupling in Oxidative and Photosynthetic Phosphorylation, 1966, Chemiosmotic Coupling and Energy Transduction, 1968; also papers. Hon. adv. editor Biosci. Reports. Office: The Glynn Research Found Ltd, Glynn House, Bodmin Cornwall PL30 4AU, England

MITCHELL, ROBERT JAMES, petroleum co. exec.; b. Montour Falls, N.Y., Mar. 16, 1925; s. Robert Bowlby and Helen (Bates) M.; student Ga. Inst. Tech., 1944, U. Richmond, 1945, Sampson Coll., 1947-48; student Valparaiso U., 1948, J.D., 1953; m. Pearl Kohnken, Aug. 30, 1947; children—Susan E., LuAnne, Robert James II. Adjuster, State Farm Mut. Auto Ins., Valparaiso, 1953-54; dist. rep. life ins. Aid Assn. for Lutherans, Hoffman, Ill., 1954-57; with dept. of devel. Valparaiso (Ind.) U., 1957-58; oil producer, Hoffman, 1958-64; founder Ego Oil Co., Inc., 1964, pres., 1964—, also dir. Bd. dirs. Law Sch. Alumni Bd., 1970-73. Served with USNR, 1941-46, 50-52. Mem. Ind. Petroleum Assn. Am. (dir. 1976—), Delta Theta Phi. Rotarian. Home: PO Box 87 Hoffman IL 62250 Office: 123 S Locust St PO Box 787 Centralia IL 62801

MITCHELL, ROY DEVOY, industrial engineer; b. Hot Springs, Ark., Sept. 11, 1922; s. Watson W. and Marie (Stewart) M.; m. Jane Caroline Gibson, Feb. 14, 1958; children: Michael, Marilyn, Martha, Stewart, Nancy. BS, Okla. State U., 1948, MS, 1950; B of Indsl. Mgmt., Auburn U., 1960. Registered profl. engr., Ala., Miss. Instr. Odessa (Tex.) Coll., 1953-56; prof. engring. graphics Auburn (Ala.) U., 1956-63; field engr. HHFA, Community Facilities Adminstrn., Atlanta and Jackson, Miss., 1963-71; area engr. Met. Devel. Office, HUD, 1971-72, chief architecture and engring., 1972-75, chief program planning and support br., 1975, dir. archtl. br., Jackson, 1975-77, chief archtl. br. and engring. br., 1977-84, community planning and devel. rep., 1984-88; prin. Mitchell Mgmt. and Engring., 1988—; cons. Army Ballistic Missile Agy., Huntsville, Ala., 1957-58, Auburn Research Found., NASA, 1963; mem. state tech. action panel Coop. Area Manpower Planning System. Mem. Cen. Miss. Fed. Personnel Adv. Council; mem. House and Home mag. adv. panel, 1977; trustee, bd. dirs. Meth. Ch., 1959-60. Served with USNR, 1943-46. Recipient Outstanding Achievement award HUD, Commendation by Sec. HUD. Mem. NSPE, Am. Soc. for Engring. Edn., Miss. Soc. Profl. Engrs., Nat. Assn. Govt. Engrs. (charter mem.), Jackson Fed. Execs. Assn., Cen. Miss. Safety Council, Am. Water Works Assn., Iota Lambda Sigma. Club: River Hills (Jackson). Home and Office: HUD 706 Forest Point Dr Brandon MS 39042

MITCHELL, RUSSELL HARRY, dermatologist; b. Erie, N.D., Oct. 19, 1925; s. William John and Anna Lillian (Sögge) M.; B.S., B.A., U. Minn., Mpls., 1947, B.M., M.D., 1951; postgrad. U. Pa. Med. Sch., 1968-69; m. Judith Lawes Douvarjo, May 24, 1968; children: Kathy Ellen, Gregory Alan, Jill Elaine, Crystal Anne. Intern, Gorgas Hosp., C.Z., 1951-52; resident in dermatology U.S. Naval Hosp., Phila., 1967-70; asst. chief out-patient dept. Gorgas Hosp., 1955-64; chief med. and surg. wards Ariz. State Hosp., Phoenix, 1965; commd. lt. (j.g.) M.C., U.S. Navy, 1953, advanced through grades to capt., 1968; service in Vietnam; ret., 1981; practice medicine specializing in dermatology, Leesburg, Va., 1978—; cons. dermatologist Prince William Hosp., 1974-85; mem. staff Loudoun Meml. Hosp., 1975—; dermatologist Nat. Naval Med. Center, Bethesda, Md., 1973-81; asst. prof. Georgetown U. Med. Sch., 1975-85. Pres. Archaeol. Soc. Panama, 1962-64. Decorated Bronze Star with combat V; Vietnam Gallantry Cross with palm and clasp; Caballero Orden de Vasco Nuñez de Balboa (Panama); diplomate Am. Bd. Dermatology. Fellow Am. Acad. Dermatology, Am. Acad. Physicians, Explorers Club; mem. AMA, Assn. Mil. Surgeons, Assn. Mil. Dermatologists (life), Soc. Am. Archaeology, Royal Soc. Medicine, Pan Am. Med. Assn., Loudoun County Med. Soc., Dermatology Found., Marine's Meml. Club (assoc.), Internat. Platform Soc., Phi Chi. Contbr. articles to med. and archaeol. publs. Home: Rural Rt 2 Box 99 Leesburg VA 22075 Office: 821-D S King St Leesburg VA 22075

MITCHELL, VERNICE VIRGINIA, nurse, poet, author; b. Scott, Miss., Mar. 11, 1921; d. Isaiah and Martha Magdalene (Edwards) Smith; m. Willis Mitchell, Aug. 17, 1940; children: Elaine, Kenneth, Liethia, John, Ransom, Paul. Diploma, Princeton Continuation Coll., 1955. Lic. practical nurse Cook County Sch. Nursing, Chgo., 1951-59, U. Ill. Hosp., Chgo., 1959-67, Grant Hosp., Chgo., 1967-78, Northwestern Meml. Hosp., Chgo., 1979-84; Aetna Nurse's Registry U. Ill. Hosp., Chgo., 1984—. Author: The Book Success Through Spiritual Truths, 1987, (poems) A Women, Chicago, The 12 Months; also numerous poetry and musical lyrics; guest poet on Dial-A-Poem, Chgo., 1988-89. Recipient merit cert. Am. Poetry Assn., 1982, World of Poetry, 1983, 85; Golden Poet award World of Poetry, 1985. Club: 6700 Emerald Ave. Block (pres. 1971—).

MITCHELL, WAYNE LEE, educator, social worker; b. Rapid City, S.D., Mar. 25, 1937; s. Albert C. and Elizabeth Isabelle (Nagel) M.; B.A., U. Redlands (Calif.), 1959; M.S.W., Ariz. State U., 1970, Ed.D., 1979. Profl. social worker various county, state, and fed. agencies, 1962-70, Bur. Indian Affairs, Phoenix, 1970-77, USPHS, 1977-79; asst. prof. Ariz. State U., 1979-84; with USPHS, Phoenix, 1984—. Bd. dirs. Phoenix Indian Community Sch., 1973-75; bd. dirs. Phoenix Indian Center, 1974-79, Community Service award, 1977; mem. Phoenix Area Health Adv. Bd., 1975; mem. Community Behavioral Mental Health Bd., 1976-80; lectr. in field. Bd. dirs. Central Ariz. Health Systems Agy.; mem. Fgn. Relations Com. Phoenix. Served with USCG, 1960-62. Recipient Community Service award Ariz. Temple of Islam, 1980. Mem. UN Assn., Nat. Assn. Social Workers, Am. Orthopsychiat. Assn., NAACP, Internat. Platform Assn., Asia Soc., U.S.-China Assn., Kappa Delta Pi, Phi Delta Kappa, Chi Sigma Chi. Congregationalist. Democrat. Contbr. articles to publs. Home: PO Box 61 Phoenix AZ 85001 Office: 4212 N 16th St Phoenix AZ 85016

MITCHELL, WILLIAM STANLEY, personnel director; b. New Haven, June 15, 1930; s. William S. and Anna A. (Neit) M.; m. Barbara Jane Johnson, Aug. 16, 1958; children—Christopher, Kathryn. B.A., Conn. Wesleyan U., 1951; grad. U.S. Army Command and Gen. Staff Coll., 1978. Fellow Life Mgmt. Inst.; cert. adminstrv. mgr. Analyst, Met. Life Ins. Co., N.Y.C., 1958-64, cons., 1965-69, mgr., 1970-73, div. mgr., 1974-80, dir. personnel, 1981-85; corp. personnel dir. Formosa Plastics Corp., Florham Park N.J., 1986—; cons. N.Y.C. Econ. Devel. Council, 1976; conf. speaker. Author articles in field. Membership chmn. Manalapan Twp. (N.J.) Citizens Com., 1964-66. Served to lt. col. USAR, 1958-78. Recipient profl. awards. Mem. Life Office Mgmt. Assn. (com. chmn. 1979-81, council 1980-81), Acad. Cert. Adminstrv. Mgrs., Am. Soc. Tng. and Devel., Phi Sigma Kappa. Methodist. Home: 7 Juniper Ave Englishtown NJ 07726 Office: 66 Hanover Dr Florham Park NJ

MITHAL, MANISH BHOODHAR, corporate executive; b. Bulawayo, Zimbabwe, Sept. 9, 1961; s. Bhoodhar and Rasvanti (Parmar) M. B in Engring., Sardar Patel U., Gujarat, India, 183. Dir. Kara Sons, Zimbabwe, 1983-85, mng. dir., 1985—; bd. dirs. Kara Sons Properties. Club: Leo. Home: 60 Leander Ave Hillside, Bulawayo Zimbabwe Office: Kara Sons, 135 Jameson St, Bulawayo Zimbabwe

MITIN, MARK BORISOVICH, philosopher; b. Zhitomir, Ukraine, July 5, 1901. Ed. Inst. Red Profs., Moscow. In party work, 1929-36; sci. worker Inst. Philosophy, 1936-44; lectr. Higher Party Sch., 1945-50; chief editor For a Lasting Peace, For a People's Democracy, Bucharest, Romania, 1950-56, Question of Philosophy, 1960-67; dep. to USSR Supreme Soviet, 1952-58; mem. staff All-Union Soc. Znania (Knowledge), 1956-60; chmn. sci. council on problems of fgn. ideological movements Acad. Scis. USSR, 1967-87. Author: Hegel and the Theory of Dialectical Materialism, 1932; For Materialist Biological Sciences, 1949; Philosophy of the Contemporary World, 1960; V.I. Lenin and the Pressing Problems of Philosophy, 1971; Philosophy Today, 1975; Problems of Ideological Combat Today, 1976; Philosophy and Progress, 1979. Mem. central com. Communist Party Soviet Union, 1939-61. Decorated Order of Lenin (three times), Order of Red Banner of Labor (three times), Order of Oct. Revolution, Order of Friendship of Peoples; recipient State prize, 1943. Mem. Acad. Scis. USSR. Address: 14 Ul Volkhonka, Moscow USSR

MITLEHNER, WOLFGANG, internist; b. Berlin, Sept. 16, 1948; s. Kurt and Irmgard (Trugasel) M.; m. Martina Mentzendorff, Aug. 2, 1980; children: Till, Hans Casper. Student, Canisius Coll., Berlin, 1968, Free U., Berlin, 1972; MD, Free U., Berlin, 1976. Intern, resident Krankenhaus Urban, Berlin, 1977-83, asst. med. dir., 1984—. Office: Kraukenhaus Urban, Dieffenbachst 61, Berlin Federal Republic of Germany

MITRA, ASOKE NATH, physicist, educator; b. Rajshahi, India, Apr. 15, 1929; s. Jatindra Nath and Rama Rani (Bose) M.; m. Anjali Ghosh, Nov. 27, 1956; children—Bani, Gargi. B.A. with honors in Math., Ramjas Coll., Delhi, 1947, M.A. in Math., 1949; Ph.D. in Physics, Delhi U., 1952, Cornell U., 1955. Lectr. physics U. Delhi, 1949-52; central state scholar Govt. India, Cornell U., Ithaca, N.Y., 1952-55; reader in physics Aligarh Muslim U., India, 1955-60, Delhi U., 1960-62; vis. prof. physics Ind. U., Bloomington, 1962-63; prof. physics Delhi U., 1963-69, sr. prof., 1969—; profl. cons. Rutherford Lab., 1968; vis. scientist UCLA, 1967, CERN, 1968, 83, 85, U. Tex.-Austin, 1971, Bonn, 1974, U. Paris, 1977, Deutsche Elektronen Synchrotron, 1979, Internat. Ctr. for Theoretical Physics, Trieste, 1962, 65, 67, 68, 69, 70, 71, 74, 77, 83, Tubingen, 1985, Ind. U., Bloomington, 1986; nat. lectr. Univ. Grants Commn., India, 1973; vis. prof. U. Ill., Chgo., 1986-87; vis. lectr. Nuffield Found., Australia, 1973; mem. internat. adv. coms. for successive internat. conf. series on few body problems in nuclear and particle physics and other internat. confs.; convenor, organizer 7th Internat. Conf. on Few Body Problems, Delhi U., 1975-76; sr. exchange visitor U.S. univs., Indo-U.S. Joint Program, 1976; sr. exchange visitor Brit. univs., Indian Nat. Sci. Acad. Royal Soc. Exchange Programme, 1979. Editor: Few Body Dynamics, 1976; Niels Bohr-A Profile, 1985. Bd. editors: Few Body Systems, 1985. Contbr. articles and revs. to profl. jours. Mem. physics panel Univ. Grants Commn., India, New Delhi, 1974-76, 80-82; mem. council Raman Research Inst., Bangalore, India, 1978—; mem. Nat. Bd. for Higher Maths., Bombay, 1982—; mem. phys. adv. com. dept. sci. and tech. Govt. India, 1982—; mem. physics coms. Council for Sci. and Indsl. Research, New Delhi, 1974-78, 81—; mem. nat. accelerator com. Dept. Atomic Energy, India, 1979-83. Recipient S. S. Bhatnagar award Council for Sci. and Indsl. Research India, New Delhi, 1969, Meth Nad Saha award Univ. Grants Commn., New Delhi, 1975; nat. fellow Univ. Grants Commn., 1975-78; assoc. Internat. Ctr. for Theoretical Physics, Trieste, 1967-70, sr. assoc., 1972-77, hon. assoc., 1978-83. Fellow Indian Nat. Sci. Acad. (sec. 1975-79, editor publ. 1983—, S.N. Bose medal 1986), Indian Acad. Sci. (council 1975-78), Am. Phys. Soc. Avocations: stamp and coin collecting; philosophy of science. Home: 244 Tagore Park, Delhi 110009 India Office: U Delhi, Dept Physics, Delhi 110007 India

MITRA, SANTOSH, oncologist; b. Calcutta, West Bengal, India, Dec. 5, 1922; s. Ramaprased and Sarajubala M.; m. Manjari Ghosh, Apr. 20, 1951; 1 child, Sunirmal. MB, Calcutta U., 1947; D in Clin. Pathology, Faculty STM, Calcutta, 1957; PhD in Cancerology, Calcutta U., 1965. Resident R.G. Kar Med. Coll. Hosp., Calcutta, 1947-48, Remount Rd. Hosp., Calcutta, 1949-50; pathologist and blood bank officer Chittaranjan Cancer Hosp., Calcutta, 1951-56, cons. chemotherapist, 1970—; head dept. exptl. leukemia Chittaranjan Nat. Cancer Research Ctr., Calcutta, 1957-82, dir., 1968-72. Assoc. editor Indian Jour. Cancer Chemotherapy, 1979—, Indian Jour. Cytology, 1984—; contbr. over 60 papers in field. Fulbright scholar USEFI, 1960; postdoctoral fellow Leukemic Soc. Inc., N.Y.C., 1960. Mem. Indian Assn. Cancer Chemotherapists (founder, sec. 1976—), Indian Soc. Oncology, Indian Cancer Soc., Indian Med. Assn., Indian Acad. Cytology. Club: Calcutta. Lodge: Rotary (past pres. South Calcutta chpt.). Home: 26/I Garishat Rd, Calcutta West Bengal 700 029, India Office: Eveland Nursing Home, 6 Southern Ave, Calcutta West Bengal 700 026, India

MITRA, SUBRATA KUMAR, political science educator; b. Gunupur, Orissa, India, June 16, 1949; arrived in Eng., 1985; s. Haripada and Kalyani (Mitra) M.; m. Marie-Paule Mitra, June 26, 1976; 1 child, Emilie-Kalyani. MA in Polit. Sci., Delhi U., 1971; MPhil., Jawaharlal Nehru U., 1972; PhD in Polit. Sci., U. Rochester, 1976. Lectr. polit. sci. Delhi U., India, 1971-72; teaching fellow U. Rochester, N.Y., 1972-76; research assoc. Ctr. for Study Developing Socs., Delhi, 1976-79, Institut Francais d'Opinion-Pubiques, Paris, 1982-85; research fellow Maison des Sciences de l'Hommes, Paris, 1979-80; postdoctoral fellow Alexander von Humboldt-Stiftung, Bonn, 1980-82; lectr. Indian politics U. Hull, Eng., 1985—; cons. UNESCO, Paris, 1984-85, East Yorkshire Health Authority, 1985-86. Author: Governmental Instability in Indian States, 1979, Participation in Development, 1982, The State in India; contbr. articles to profl. jours. Nat. scholar Govt. of India, 1965-71, Fulbright scholar, 1972 Indo-French exchange scholar, 1979-80. Mem. Brit. Assn. South Asian Studies (nat. exec. com.), Polit. Studies Assn., Assn. Francaise Sciences Politiques, Indian Polit. Sci. Assn. (life). Home: 76 Victoria Ave, Hull HU5 3DS, England Office: U Hull Dept Politics, Cottingham Rd, Hull HU6 7RX, England

MITSIS, FOTIS JOHN, dentist, educator; b. Phiniki, Filiaton, Greece, Sept. 1, 1926; s. John Gregory and Efterpi (Lagou) M.; D.D.S., U. Athens, 1951, M.D., 1964; Sc.D. in Dentistry, U. Pa., 1962, cert. in endodontics and periodontics, 1965; 1 child, Evi. Asst. dept. dental pathology and therapeutics Dental Sch., U. Athens (Greece), 1956-62, assoc., 1962-66, assoc. prof., 1966-69, prof., 1969—, dean Dental Sch., 1975-77, 83-88, pres. Gen. Hosp. Evangelismos, 1987— , rector U. Athens, 1978-81; vis. prof. Tufts U., 1977-78; mem. Nat. Council Health; mem. Adv. Com. on Dental Tng. in EEC. Served with Greek Army, 1952-55. NIH fellow USPHS, 1965. Mem. Am. Acad. Periodontology, Am. Assn. Endodontists, Fedn. Dentaire Internat., Internat. Assn. Dental Research, AAAS, Greek Assn. Odontostomatol. Research (pres. 1970-72). Author: Atlas of Dental Histology, 1963; Dental Pathology and Therapeutics, 1971; Oral Embryology and Histology, 1974; Introduction in Dentistry and History of Dentistry, 1975; Periodontology, 1979; Endodontics, 1981; contbr. sci. papers to profl. confs. and internat. and Greek jours.; research in field. Office: Athinisin Ethnikon, Kai Kapodistriakon, Panepistimion O dos, Panepistimiou 30, 143 Athens Greece

MITSOTAKIS, CONSTANTIN, government official of Greece, lawyer; b. Chania, Greece, Oct. 18, 1918; s. Kyriakos and Stavroula (Ploumidakis) M.; m. Marika Giannoykoy, June 6, 1953; children—Dora, Alexandra, Catherine, Kyriakos. Degree in Law and Econs., Athens U., 1943. Cert. lawyer. M.P., Liberal Party, Chania, Greece, 1941-61, Center Union, 1961-67; under the Colonel's Junta was arrested, released and escaped Greece, 1967-74; pres., M.P., Neoliberal Party, Greece, 1977; M.P., NEA Democratia Party, Greece, 1981-84, pres., opposition leader, 1984—, sec. of state for fin. Greece, 1951; acting minister for communication and public works, minister of fin., 1963-64, minister of coordination, 1965, 78-80, minister of fgn. affairs, 1980-81. Office: Nea Demokratia, Odos Rigillis 18, 106 74 Athens Greece

MITSUI, YOSHIYUKI, architectural educator; b. Tokuyama, Yamaguchi, Japan, Aug. 6, 1940; s. Toshiharu and Masu (Hayashi) M.; m. Ryoko Kobayashi, Dec. 27, 1970; children: Daisuke, Motoko, Mitsui. B in Engring., Osaka U., 1964, M in Engring., 1966, DEngr, 1974. Registered architect, Japan. Research assoc. Osaka U., Japan, 1968-72; lectr. Kumamoto U., Japan, 1972-74, assoc. prof., 1974-83, prof., 1983—; Commr. Japan Steel-Rib Fabricators Assn., 1984—; legal advisor Kumamoto Dist. Ct., 1981—. Author: Design Recommendations for Tubular Structures, 1980. Mem. Archtl. Inst. Japan (commr. 1967—), Soc. Naval Architects of Japan, Japan Welding Soc. Home: Musashigaoka 1-224, 862 Kumamoto Japan Office: Kumamoto U, Kurokami 2-39-1, 860 Kumamoto Japan

MITSUO, MITSUISHI, trading company executive; b. Nishinomiya, Hyogo, Japan, Mar. 29, 1937; s. Unosuke and Haru Mitsuishi; m. Kayoko Mitsuishi; 1 child, Masako. Grad. English sch., Palmore Inst., Kobe, Japan, 1959. With Kawasaki Heavy Industries Co., Inc., Kobe, Japan, 1951-58, Tomei Co. Ltd., Osaka, Japan, 1958-70, Mitsuishi Shoji Co., Ikoma, Nara, Japan, 1971—. Home: 19-14 Kitashin-machi, 630-02 Ikoma Japan Office: Mitsuishi Shoji Co, 1955 Tanida-cho, 630-02 Ikoma Japan

MITTEL, JOHN J., economist, corporate executive, consultant; b. L.I., N.Y.; s. John and Mary (Leidolf) M.; 1 child, James C.; B.B.A., CUNY. Researcher econs. dept. McGraw Hill & Co., N.Y.C.; mgr., asst. to pres. Indsl. Commodity Corp., J. Carvel Lange Inc. and J. Carvel Lange Internat., Inc., 1956-64, corp. sec., 1958—, v.p., 1964-80, exec. v.p., 1980—; pres. I.C. Investors Corp., 1972—, I.C. Pension Adv., Inc., 1977—; dir. several corps.; plan adminstr., trustee Combined Indsl. Commodity Corp. and J. Carvel Lange Inc. Pension Plan, 1962—, J. Carvel Lange Internat. Inc. Profit Sharing Trust, 1969—, Combined Indsl. Commodity Corp. and J. Carvel Lange Inc. Employees Profit Sharing Plan, 1977—. Mem. grad. adv. bd. Bernard M. Baruch Coll., City U. N.Y., 1971-72. Mem. Conf. Bd., Am. Statis. Assn., Newcomen Soc. N.Am. Club: Union League (N.Y.C.). Co-author: How Good A Sales Profit Are You, 1961; The Role of the Economic Consulting Firm; also numerous market surveys.

MITTELSTADT, CHARLES ANTHONY, advertising executive; b. Eau Claire, Wis., Mar. 19, 1918; s. Frederick William and Pearl (White) M.; m. Angelica Farber, Feb. 20, 1957; children—Nancy Lee, Charles Anthony II, Monica, Simone. B.S., U. Wis., 1942, postgrad., 1945-47; grad., Advanced Mgmt. Program, Harvard, 1960. Radio announcer sta. WIBA, Madison, Wis., 1945-47; account exec. Foote, Cone & Belding, Chgo., 1948-52, Campbell-Mithun, Chgo., 1953-54; mktg. dir. Tatham-Laird, Chgo., 1955-56; exec. v.p. McCann-Marschalk, N.Y.C., 1957-64, also bd. dirs.; chmn. plans bd., mgr. Interpub. Group Cos., Inc., Frankfurt, Germany, 1964-66; pres., chief operating officer Erwin Wasey, Inc., Los Angeles, 1967-69; sr. v.p., mgr. Ctr. for Advt. Services Interpub. Group of Cos., Inc., 1969—. Trustee N.Y. Foundling Hosp., 1979—. Clubs: Wisconsin Alumni, Harvard Alumni, N.Y. Athletic (N.Y.C.); Westchester Country (bd. govs. 1988—, Rye); Am. Yacht. Home: Griswold Rd Rye NY 10580 Office: Interpublic Group of Cos Inc 1271 Ave of the Americas New York NY 10020

MITTELSTADT, RUSSELL JAMES, lawyer; b. Eau Claire, Wis., Jan. 12, 1931; s. Frederick William and Pearl Hazel (White) M.; m. Marlys Rudd, June 28, 1953; children—Mary K., Marcus J., Miles S. B.S., U. Wis., 1952, J.D., 1960; grad. U.S. Army Command and Gen. Staff Coll., U.S. Army War Coll., U.S. Indsl. Coll. Bar: Wis. 1960, U.S. Supreme Ct. 1966, U.S. Dist. Ct. (we. dist.) Wis. 1960, U.S. Ct Appeals (7th cir.) 1962. Assoc. Spohn, Ross, Stevens & Pick, Madison, Wis., 1960-62; judge Dane County (Wis.), 1966-72; sole practice, Madison, 1962-66, 72-76; pres. Russell J. Mittelstadt Law Offices, S.C., Madison, 1976—. Treas., 2d Dist. Republican Com., 1981-83, chmn., 1983-85; del. Rep. Nat. Conv.; bd. dirs. Rep. Com. Dane County, 1981-82, treas., 1965-66, bd. dirs., 1962-66; founder Vols. in Probation in Dane County, 1970. Served with U.S. Army, 1952-57; to col. Res. Decorated Meritorious Service medal; named Disting. Mil. Grad., U. Wis., 1952; recipient Service awards Am. Legion, 40 and 8, CD, others; Rennebohm scholar, 1952; Wis. Law Alumnae scholar, 1959. Mem. State Bar Wis., Res. Officers Assn. (jr. v.p. 1966, nat. v.p. 1970, nat. Army com. 1967-69), Mil. Order World Wars (comdr. Madison chpt. 1973-84), VFW, Am. Legion. Wis. nat. councilman 1980-85, Wis. pres. 1965). Lutheran. Clubs: Exchange (past pres.), Madison.

MITTENDORF, THEODOR HENRY, paper mfg. cons.; b. Clay Center, Kans., Jan. 14, 1895; s. Theodor Henry and Antonie (Carls) M.; B.S., Okla. State University, 1917; m. Dorothy E. Solger, May 18, 1919 (dec. Mar. 29, 1979); 1 dau., Laone M. (Mrs. D. R. Hoerl); m. 2d, Marguerite E. McLean, Oct. 3, 1980 Lectr. extension div. Okla. State U., 1917; lectr., free lance writer, 1919-20; dept. supt. Armour & Co., Chgo., 1920-22; sec., dir. sales and advt. Mid-States Gummed Paper Co., Chgo., 1922-38; v.p. charge sales Industrial Training Inst., 1938-39, v.p., gen. mgr. The Gummed Products Co., Troy, Ohio, 1940-48; v.p. charge sales Hudson Pulp and Paper Corp., N.Y.C., 1948-56, exec. v.p., 1956-58, cons., 1958—; pres. Mitt Industries, Inc., Mount Dora, Fla., 1972—; dir. 5 East 71st St. Corp. Dir. Muscular Dystrophy Assn. Served from 2d lt. F.A. to 1st lt. AS, U.S. Army, World War I, AEF. Named to Okla. State U. Alumni Hall of Fame, 1961. Mem. Kraft Paper Assn. (dir., mem. exec. com. 1951-58), Gummed Industries Assn. (pres. 1955-56), Paper Bag Inst. (pres. 1955-56), Paper Club N.Y., Am. Legion, Symposiarchs, Kappa Sigma, Alpha Zeta, Pi Kappa Delta. Republican. Methodist. Clubs: Masons, Order Eastern Star. Mount Dora (Fla.) Golf, Mount Dora Yacht; Ponte Vedra (Fla.); African Safari of Fla., Okla. State U. President's (life), Okla. State U. Henry G. Bennett Soc. (life), Okla. State U. Alumni Assn. (life). Avocation: big game hunting. Home: Box 1138 Mount Dora FL 32757 Office: PO Box 1138 Mount Dora FL 32757

MITTER, PARTHA, educator; b. Calcutta, West Bengal, India, 1938; arrived in Eng., 1962; s. Rabindra Nath and Pushpa Lata (Dé) M.; m. Swasti Sanyal, Aug. 7, 1960; children: Rana Shantashil Rajyeswar, Pamina Radha. BA with honors, Presidency Coll., Calcutta, 1954-58, London U., 1962-65; PhD, London U., 1965-70; MA, Cambridge U., Eng., 1968. Jr. research fellow Churchill Coll. Cambridge U., 1968-69, research fellow Clare Hall, 1970-74; lectr. in history Sussex U., Brighton, Eng., 1974—. Author: Much Maligned Monsters, 1977; compiler and author exhbn. History of Indian Photography, London, 1982; contbr. articles to profl. jours. Reader of the Brit. Acad., 1985-87; Mellon fellow Inst. for Advanced Study, Princeton, 1981-82. Fellow Royal Soc. of Arts. Mem. Labour Party. Home: 25 Norfolk Rd, Brighton Sussex BN1 3AA, England

MITTERMAYER, HELMUT WOLFGANG, physician, clinical microbiologist; b. Linz, Austria, July 13, 1947; s. Helmut O.W. and Marianne Mittermayer; MD, U. Vienna (Austria), 1972; m. Liselotte Ambos, July 13, 1972; children: Ursula, Fritz, Werner. Tng. in microbiology and hygiene Hygiene Inst., U. Vienna, 1972-75; splty. tng. in lab. medicine Elisabethinen Hosp., Linz, 1976-80, hosp. hygienist, chmn. infection control com., 1976—, in charge clin. microbiology, 1977—, cons. for chemotherapy 1977—, head dept. med. microbiology and hygiene, 1984—; asst. prof. hygiene, microbiology and preventive medicine U. Vienna, 1987—; lectr. in postgrad. med. edn.; presenter papers to sci. meetings. Mem. Austrian Soc. Hygiene, Microbiology and Preventive Medicine (chmn. working group for clin. microbiology), Am. Soc. for Microbiology, Austrian Soc. Clin. Chemistry, Assn. Italian Clin. Microbiologists, Hosp. Infection Soc. (London), Paul Ehrlich Soc. Chemotherapy, German Soc. for Hygiene and Microbiology, European Soc. for Clin. Microbiology, European Study Group on Antibiotic Resistance (com. mem.). Contbr. articles on infection control, clin. microbiology, anaerobic bacteria to med. jours. Office: Elisabethinen Hosp, 1 Fadingerstrasse, A-0410 Linz Austria

MITTERRAND, FRANÇOIS MAURICE MARIE, president of France; b. Oct. 26, 1916; s. Joseph and Yvonne Lorain; ed. U. Paris; m. Danielle Gouze, Oct. 28, 1944; children: Jean-Christophe, Gilbert. Dep. to French Parliament, 1946-58, 62—; minister for ex-service men, 1947-48; sec. state for info., 1948-49; minister for overseas ters., 1950-51; chmn. Union Démocratique et Socialiste de la Résistance, 1951-52; del. Council of Europe, 1953; minister of interior, 1954-55; minister state for justice, 1956-57; senator, 1969-62; pres. Fedn. Democratic and Socialist Left, 1965-68; 1st sec. Socialist Party, 1971-81; vice chmn. Socialist Internat., after 1972; pres. France, 1981—; polit. dir. Le Courier de la Nièvre. Served with French Forces, 1939-40; prisoner of war, escaped, later active French Resistance; sec.-gen. Orgn. for Prisoners of War, War Victims and Refugees, 1944-46. Decorated Great Cross Légion d'Honneur, Croix de Guerre, Rosette de la Résistance. Author: Le coup d'état permanent, 1964; Ma part de vérité, 1969; Un socialisme du possible, 1970; L rose au poing, 1973; L paille et le grain, 1975; Politique I (in 3 parts), 1977; L'abeille et l'architecte, 1978; Ici et Maintenant, 1980, Politique II, 1981. Office: Palais del L'Elysee, 75008 Paris France

MITTON, JOHN ROGER, computer science educator; b. Lancaster, Eng., Nov. 11, 1946; s. Alfred and Lily (Clarke) M.; m. Roslyn Anne Hastings, Sept. 28, 1947; children: Rayhana, George, Edward. BA in Psychology and Philosophy, Oxford (Eng.) U., 1968, diploma in computer sci., 1982. Researcher, author N. Kensington Family Study, London, 1969-71; dep. dir. Lesotho Distance Teaching Ctr., Maseru, 1974-77; sr. research officer Inst. Community Studies, London, 1978-81; researcher Birkbeck Coll., London, 1984-86, lectr., 1986—. Author: Practical Research in Distance Teaching, 1982; co-author: A Community Project in Notting Dale, 1972, Unemployment, Poverty and Social Policy in Europe, 1983; contbr. articles to profl. jours. Address: Birkbeck Coll, Dept Computer Sci, Malet St, London WC1E 7HX, England

MITZ, VLADIMIR, plastic surgeon; b. Vielikoie Selo, USSR, Mar. 3, 1943; came to France, 1949, naturalized, 1957; s. Hersz Jumen and Maria (Mincberg) M.; 1 child, Illitch. M.D., 1973. Intern, Lariboisiere Hosp., Paris, 1967; resident Jackson Meml. Hosp., Miami, Fla., 1975; chief clinic Assistance Publique, Paris, 1973-78, mem. staff, 1980—; prof. anatomy Faculty Medicine, Paris, 1970-74; dir. micro vascular lab. Bovcicaut Hosp., Paris, 1980—. Author: Operation Beaute, 1984; Lambeaux Musculo Cutanes, 1984. Producer movie Operation Verite, 1982. Pres. Mouvement de Recherche en Plastique Humaine, Paris, 1972. Mem. Brazilian Soc. Plastic Surgery (assoc.), French Soc. Plastic Reconstructive Aesthetic Surgery. Avocation: painting. Home: 12 Rue du Renard, 75004 Paris France Office: 176 Blvd St Germain, 75006 Paris France

MIURA, TOKUHIRO, educator; b. Sukumo, Japan, May 30, 1928; s. Harukichi and Sueno (Enoki) M.; student Kochi (Japan) Tchrs. Coll., 1945-48, Waseda U., Tokyo, 1949-51, 52-53; BA, U. Calif., Berkeley, 1956; MA, NE Mo. State U., 1959; m. Masako Matsumoto, Nov. 5, 1959; children: Tokutaka, Yuri. Reporter and mem. editorial staff Japan Times, Tokyo, 1960-63; instr. English, Hosei U., Tokyo, 1961-65, prof. English and Am. lit., 1965—, chmn. dept. English, 1981-85. Mem. MLA, English Lit. Soc. Japan, Am. Lit. Soc. Japan. Buddhist. Author: Robinson Jeffers' Quest in The Double Axe, 1967; Poetics of Robinson Jeffers, 1977; Literary Phenomena: A Conceptual Framework of Literature, 1979; Selected Poems of Robinson Jeffers (in Japanese translation), 1986. Home: 23-28 4-chome, Naruse-dai, Machida-shi, Tokyo 194, Japan Office: 17-1 2-chome Fujimi-cho, Chiyoda-ku, Tokyo 102, Japan

MIWA, MAKIKO, service company executive, lecturer; b. Tokyo, Jan. 18, 1951; d. Masahiro and Nobue (Ichimura) M.; m. Ichinowatari Katsuhiko, Oct. 21, 1983. B.A., Japan Women's U., Tokyo, 1973; M.L.S., U. Pitts., 1978; Ph.D., Keio U., Tokyo, 1983. Asst. researcher Social Sci. Info. Utilization Lab., Pitts., 1978; lectr. Sch. Library and Info. Sci., Keio U., Tokyo, 1980—; info. specialist U. Tsukuba Sci. Info. Processing Ctr., Ibaraki, Japan, 1981-83; info. cons. Epoch Research Co., Tokyo, 1983—; mem. Com. Establishment of Info. Ctr., Nat. Olympic Youth Ctr., Tokyo, 1982-83, Info. Research Com. Human Devel. Ctr., Tokyo, 1982—. Author: Introduction to Library and Information Science, 1983; Introduction to Eric Database, 1983. Mem. editorial bd. Informediary. Mem. Mita Soc. Library and Info. Sci., Japan Documentation Soc., Japan Soc. Library Sci., Am. Soc. Info. Sci. Home: 7-12 Nakano 2 chome Apt 106, Nakano-Ku, Tokyo 164, Japan Office: Keio U Sch Library and Info Sci, 15-14 Mita 2 chome Minato-Ku, Tokyo 108, Japan

MIXON, ROSALIE WARD, social work consultant; b. Maysville, Mo., Feb. 17, 1908; d. Luther Thomas and Mary (Bray) Ward; A.B., Park Coll., 1929; postgrad. (Univ. scholar 1929-30, 32-35), U. Chgo., 1929-34; M.S.W., U. So. Calif., 1944; postgrad. UCLA, 1965, Riverside, 1970, San Diego, 1975-76; m. John Lewis Mixon, Dec. 20, 1929; children—Rosemary Mixon Snow, John Lindley, David Lewis, Robert Nelson. Dir. med. social service Children's Meml. Hosp., Chgo., 1951-52; researcher in religious demography, 1952-58; instr. social work La Verne Coll. (Calif.), 1958-59; with Calif. Dept. Mental Hygiene, San Bernardino and Pomona, 1959-66, 69-74; Fulbright lectr., cons. psychiat. and med. social work Med. Sch., Pahlavi U., Shiraz, Iran, 1966-67; lectr. Sch. Social Work, Teheran, Iran, 1966-67; social researcher Meth. Bd. World Missions, Lima, Peru, 1968-69; pvt. practice psychiat. social work cons., Redlands, Calif., 1974—; vis. prof. Alaska Pacific U., Anchorage, 1978-79. Active Chgo. Community Fund Adv. Com., 1951, Claremont Community Services Com., 1960-75, Redlands A.B.L.E. Com., 1975—. Lic. clin. social worker, Calif. Mem. Nat. Assn. Social Workers, Nat. Acad. Cert. Social Workers, Register Clin. Social Workers, Soc. Internat. Devel. Club: Browser's Book. Author: The Methodist Churches of Arizona, 1966; The Barriadas of Lima, Peru, 1969; contbr. chpt. to Choice and Change, 1966. Address: 716 Plymouth Rd Claremont CA 91711

MIYAGAWA, ICHIRO, physicist; b. Hiratsuka, Kanagawa, Japan, Mar. 5, 1922; s. Shigejiro and Tsuma (Itoh) M.; m. Mitsuko Yamada, Feb. 10, 1950; children: Shigeru, Haruyo, Mari. BS, Nagoya (Japan) U., 1945; DSc, U. Tokyo, 1954. Asst. prof. U. Tokyo, 1959-62; vis. asst. prof. Duke U., Durham, N.C., 1963-65; asst. prof. physics U. Ala., Tuscaloosa, 1965-66, assoc. prof., 1966-70; prof. U. Ala., 1970-80, Univ. Research prof. physics, 1980—; cons. Redstone Arsenal, 1966-72. Contbr. articles to profl. jours. USPHS grantee; EPA grantee; NIH grantee. Fellow Am. Phys. Soc.; mem., AAAS, Sigma Xi. Home: 4905 10th Ct E Tuscaloosa AL 35405 Office: U Ala PO Box 1921 Tuscaloosa AL 35487

MIYAGAWA, TAKAO, life produce company executive; b. Suzaka City, Japan, Apr. 17, 1955; s. Shozo and Kazuko M. B Econs., Hosei U., Tokyo, 1979. Bus. editor KCC Inc., Nagano City, Japan, 1979-84; with Sakurai Kanseido Inc., Obuse Cho, Japan, 1984-87; mgmt. cons., ins. agt. Suzaka City, 1987—; councillor Self-Image Devel. Lab., Yamatokoriyama, 1977—; br. chief Touring Club Japan, Tokyo, 1987—, Hunger Project, 1988—. Home and Office: 1176 Takahashi Cho, Suzaka City Nagano Pref, Japan

MIYAKE, SHIGEMITSU, banker; b. Osaka, Feb. 27, 1911; s. Shigetaka and Fumi (Ito) M.; m. Hina Inoue, 1935; 3 children. Ed. Tokyo Imperial U. With Bank of Japan, 1933-67, dir., 1962-67, advisor, 1974-82; dep. pres. Tokai Bank Ltd., 1967-68, pres., 1968-69, chmn. and pres., 1969-75; chmn., 1975-86, chmn. bd., 1986-88, chmn. emeritus, 1988—; chmn. Cen. Japan Railway Co., Ltd., 1987—. Decorated Order of the Sacred Treasure, 1st class, 1982, Blue Ribbon medal, 1974. Mem. Japan Mgr. Orgn. (exec. dir. 1970—), Fedn. Japan Econ. Orgns. (exec. dir. 1971-87), Nagoya C. of C. and Industry (pres. 1974-81, advisor 1981—), Japan C. of C. and Industry (v.p. 1974-81). Address: Tokai Bank Ltd, 3-21-24 Nishiki 3-chome, Naka-ku, Nagoya 460, Japan

MIYAKODA, TOORU, landscape architect; b. Seoul, Republic of Korea, Aug. 3, 1941; s. Tatsuaburo and Fukue Miyakoda; m. Yoshiko Yamanaka, Aug. 1, 1975; children: Kinoto, Aya. MS, U. Osaka Prefecture, Sakai, Japan, 1967; BS, U. Berkeley, 1971; degree in design, Harvard U., 1972. Lic. cons. engr. Landscape architect Zion & Breen Assocs., Inc., N.J., 1973; sr. landscape architect Kajima Corp., Tokyo, 1974-85; prin. Keikan Sekkei Co., Ltd., Tokyo, 1986—. Author: Total Landscape Elements, 1988; contbr. articles to profl. jours. Fellow Soc. Japanese Landscape Architecture (Design award 1984), Soc. Japanese Architecture (mem. design award com. 1985); mem. Japan Cons. Engr. Assn. Lodge: Kiyosato no Mori. Home: 5-8-15 Kitashinagawa #314, Shinagawa-ku, Tokyo 141, Japan Office: Keikan Sekkei Co Ltd, 3-18-3 Higashigotanda, Shinagawa-ku, Tokyo 141, Japan

MIYAMOTO, RICHARD TAKASHI, otolaryngologist; b. Zeeland, Mich., Feb. 2, 1944; s. Dave Norio and Haruko (Okano) M.; m. Cynthia VanderBurgh, June 17, 1967; children—Richard Christopher, Geoffrey Takashi. B.S. cum laude, Wheaton Coll., 1966; M.D., U. Mich., 1970; M.S. in Otology, U.So. Calif., 1978. Diplomate Am. Bd. Otolaryngology. Intern Butterworth Hosp., Grand Rapids, Mich., 1970-71, resident in surgery, 1971-72; resident in otolaryngology Ind. U. Sch. Medicine, 1972-75; fellow in otology and neurotology St. Vincent Hosp. and Otologic Med. Group, Los Angeles, 1977-78; asst. prof. Ind. U. Sch. Medicine, Indpls., 1978-83, assoc. prof., 1983-88; prof. 1988—;chmn. 1987, chief Otology and Neurotology dept. Otolaryngology, Head and Neck Surgery, Ind. U., 1982—; chmn. dept. Otolaryngology, 1987—; chief Otolaryngology, Head and Neck Surgery Wishard Meml. Hosp., 1979—. Contbr. articles to profl. jours. Served to maj. USAF, 1975-77. Named Arilla DeVault Disting. investigator Ind. U., 1983. Fellow Am. Acad. Otolaryngology (gov. 1982—), ACS, Am. Otological, Rhinological, and Laryngological Soc. (Thesis Disting. for Excellence award), Am. Neurotology Soc. Am. Auditory Soc. (mem. exec. com. 1985—); Am. Otol. Soc. Republican. Presbyterian. Avocation: tennis. Office: Riley Hosp 702 Barnhill Dr Suite A-56 Indianapolis IN 46223

MIYASAKI, SHUICHI, lawyer; b. Paauilo, Hawaii, Aug. 6, 1928; s. Torakichi and Teyo (Kimura) M.; m. Pearl Takeko Saiki, Sept. 11, 1954; children—Joy Michiko, Miles Tadashi, Jan Keiko, Ann Yoshie. B.S.C.E., U. Hawaii-Honolulu, 1951; J.D., U. Minn., 1957; LL.M. in Taxation, Georgetown U., 1959; grad. Army War Coll., 1973. Bar: Minn. 1957, Hawaii 1959, U.S. Supreme Ct. 1980. Examiner, U.S. Patent Office, 1957-59; dep. atty. gen. State of Hawaii, 1960-61; mem., dir., treas. Okumura Takushi Funaki & Wee, Honolulu, 1961—; atty. Hawaii Senate, 1961, chief counsel ways and means com., 1962, chief counsel judiciary com., 1967-70; civil engr. Japan Constrn. Agy., Tokyo, 1953-54; staff judge adv., col. USAR, Ft. DeRussy, Hawaii, 1968-79; local legal counsel Jaycees, 1962. Legis. chmn. armed services com. C. of C. of Hawaii, 1973; intl. rep. Aloha council Boy Scouts Am., 1963-78; exec. com., sec., dir. Legal Aid Soc. Hawaii, 1970-72; state v.p. Hawaii Jaycees, 1964-65; dir., legal counsel St. Louis Heights Community Assn., 1963, 65, 73; dir., legal counsel Citizens Study Club for Naturalization of Citizens, 1963-68; life mem. Res. Officers Assn. U.S. Served to 1st lt., AUS, 1951-54. Decorated Meritorious Service medal with oak leaf cluster. Mem. ABA, Hawaii Bar Assn., U.S. Patent Office Soc., Hawaii Estate Planning Council, Phi Delta Phi. Clubs: Central YMCA, Waikiki Athletic, Army Golf Assn. Lodges: Elks, Rotary. Address: 1552 Bertram St Honolulu HI 96816

MIYASHIRO, YOSHINOBU, newspaper publishing executive; b. Tokyo, Mar. 19, 1944; s. Minekazu and Hana M.; m. Noriko Aoyama, Nov. 3, 1972; children: Kenichi, Yasuko, Masako, Junko. Grad., Chuo U., Tokyo, 1967. Mem. staff textile div. Nissho Corp., Tokyo, 1967-69; media rep. de Grassi and Assocs., Tokyo, 1969-74, v.p., 1974-77; mgr. Japan div. Fin. Times Newspaper, Tokyo, 1977—; mem. Makuhari Met. Devel. Com., 1986-87. Mem. Liberal Democratic Party. Buddhist. Club: Foreign Correspondent (Tokyo). Home: 3-5-2 Nakakasai Edogawa Ku, Tokyo 134, Japan Office: The Fin Times Kasahara Bldg, 1-6-10 Uchikanda Chiyoda ku, Tokyo 101, Japan

MIYATA, TERUO, chemist; b. Kawasaki, July 17, 1931; s. Katsuzo and Masu M.; m. Chizuko Takada, Mar. 23, 1958; children—Masumi, Takeshi. B.S., Tohoku U., 1954; Ph.D., Tokyo U., 1970. Research assoc. Research Lab. Nippi, Tokyo, 1954-77; sr. research assoc. Cornell Med. Coll., N.Y.C., 1973-77; sr. mng. dir. Koken Co., Tokyo, 1977—, dir. Koken Bioschi. Inst., 1977—, Tokyo. Lectr., Tokyo Med. Dental Coll., Tokyo, 1972-73, Kyoto U., 1978—, Kitasato U., Tokyo, 1981—, Tokyo U. Agr. and Tech., 1983—. Co-author: Collagen, 1973; Biomaterials, 1982. Patentee collagen application. Mem. Japanese Polymer Sci. Assn., Japanese Artifical Organs Assn., Japanese Biomaterials, Am. Chem. Soc., Am. Artificial Internal Organs. Avocations: golf; skiing; sports. Office: Koken Bioscience Inst, 2 11 21 Nakane Meguro Ku, Tokyo 152, Japan

MIYAUCHI, YOSHIHIKO, leasing company executive; b. Hyugo Prefecture, Japan, 1935. BA in Commerce, Kansei Gakuin U., Japan, 1958; MBA, U. Wash., 1960. With Nichimen and Co. Ltd., 1960-64; charter mem. Orient Leasing Co., 1964, bd. dirs., 1970—, mng. dir., 1973, sr. mng. dir., 1976, exec. v.p., 1979, pres., 1980—; pres. Family Consumer Credit Co., Ltd., Budget Rent a Car Co., Ltd.; bd. dirs. U.S. Leasing Internat. Inc., Rubloff Inc.; vice-chmn. Japan Leasing Assn. Author: An Introduction to Leasing, 1970. Office: Orient Leasing Co Ltd, 4-1 Hamamatsucho 2-chome, Minato-ku, Tokyo 105 Japan *

MIYAZAKI, KEN-ICHI, mathematics educator; b. Hiroshima, Japan, Apr. 29, 1930; s. Shunji and Masako (Inada) M.; m. Hideko Yoshimura, Dec. 18, 1960; children: Takehiko, Kazuhiko. MS, Hiroshima U., 1955, DSC, 1974. Asst. Hiroshima U., 1961-62; lectr. Kagoshima (Japan) U., 1962-65; asst. prof. Kyushu Inst. Tech., Kitakyushu, Japan, 1965-74, prof. math., 1974, head evening session, 1987—. Mem. Math. Soc. Japan (councillor 1974-75, 87—), Am. Math. Soc. Home: 3-27-302 Sensui-cho, Kitakyushu, Fukuoka 804, Japan Office: Kyushu Inst Tech, 1-1 Sensui-cho, Kitakyushu 804, Japan

MIYAZAKI, NAGAO, electronics company executive; b. Kobe City, Japan, Jan. 15, 1931; s. Chuichi and Tomoko Miyazaki; m. Hisako Miyazaki, Mar. 15, 1956; children: Yoshiko, Yuko, Junko. B of Engring., Osaka City (Japan) U., 1954. With Fujitec Ltd., Osaka, Japan, 1954-58; with Amano Miyasaki & Co. Ltd., Osaka, 1958-72, pres., 1972—; pres. Japan Electronics Industry Ltd., Osaka, 1962—. Mem. Osaka C. of C. and Industry, Osaka Indsl. Assn., Japan System House Assn., Kansai Employers Assn. Lodge: Rotary. Home: 2-16-10 Nishiyama-Dai, Osakasayama, Osaka 589, Japan Office: Japan Electronics Industry Ltd, 3-13-25 Katuyamakita Ikunoku, Osaka 544, Japan

MIYAZAWA, KIICHI, Japanese politician; b. Tokyo, Oct. 8, 1919; married; 2 children. Grad., Tokyo Imperial U., 1941. With Japanese Fin. Ministry, 1942-52, govt. rep. to San Francisco Peace Conf., 1951, mem. House of Councillors, 1953-65, parliamentary vice-minister of edn., 1959-60, minister of state, dir.-gen. Econ. Planning Agy., 1962-64, 66-68, 77-78, mem. Ho. of Reps., 1967—, minister internat. trade and industry, 1970-71, minister of fgn. affairs, 1974-76, minister of state, chief cabinet sec., 1980-82, minister of fin. 1986—, dep. prime minister, 1987—; chmn. exec. council Liberal Dem. Party, 1984—. Author: Tokyo-Washington Secret Talk, 1956; Challenge for Beautiful Japan, 1984. Address: Ministry of Fin, Tokyo Japan

MIYOKAWA, TSUNEJI, ceramics company executive, auditor; b. Tokyo, May 8, 1924; s. Kunijiro and Kuniko Miyokawa; m. Tsuneko Miyokawa, Jan. 6, 1953; children: Haruo, Akio. B in Econs., Keio U., 1946. Gen. mgr. strategic planning, Toshiba Ceramics Co., Ltd., Tokyo, 1981-83; statutory auditor Toshiba Monofrax Co., Ltd., Tokyo, 1983-85, Toshiba Ceramics Co., Ltd., Tokyo, 1985—. Home: 23-7 Egota 1-chome, Nakano-ku, 165 Tokyo Japan

MIYOSHI, KIYOSHI (KAWAKAMI), designer, television art director; b. Tokyo, Dec. 15, 1929; s. Tamaziro and Kayo (Kawakami) M.; m. Aoi Miyoshi, May 3, 1968. B in Engring. and Architecture, Waseda U., Tokyo, 1951; student, Theatrical Arts Coll., Tokyo, 1954. Designer NHK Japan Broadcasting Co., Tokyo, 1956-71, sr. art dir. stage and design div., 1971-82; chief art dir. Osaka regional Headquarters 1982—; lectr. Osaka U. of Arts, 1982—; bd. dirs. Korean Munha Broadcasting Co., Seoul, 1969-79. Author: A Scope of Image Art, 1987. Fellow Japan Soc. Image Arts and Scis.; mem. Tomon Architects Assn., Japan Stage and TV Designers Assn. (standing dir. 1970-74, bd. dirs. Osaka br., 1982—). Office: Nat Bunraku Theater Stage, Sect 1-12-10 Nipponbashi, Minami-Ku, 542 Osaka Japan

MIYOSHI, TAKEO, mathematician, educator; b. Matsuyama, Ehime, Japan, May 8, 1936; s. Nobukazu and Shima (Yamauchi) M.; m. Michiko Sato, Dec. 16, 1967; children—Tatsuhiko, Maiko. B.S., Sci. U. Tokyo, 1962, M.S., 1964. Assoc. prof. math. Nihon Inst. Tech., Saitama, Japan, 1967-69, Ehime U., Matsuyama, 1969—. Mem. Math. Soc. Japan, Deutsche Mathematiker Vereinigung, Math. Assn. Am. Buddhist. Avocation: systems analysis. Home: 1-23 Kuwabara, 1-chome, Matsuyama, Ehime 790, Japan Office: Ehime U, Dept Math, Bunkyo-cho 3, Matsuyama, Ehime 790 Japan

MIZON, GRAYHAM ERNEST, econometrics educator; b. Rochdale, Lancashire, Eng., Nov. 29, 1942; s. Ernest and Emily Sykes (Smith) M.; m.

Elizabeth Rigg, July 29, 1972; children: Guy Andrew, Helen Rachel. BS, London Sch. Econs., 1965, MS, 1966, PhD, 1972; MA, Oxford U., 1971. Mgr. Unilever Ltd., London, 1968-70; sr. cons. Commodities Research Unit, London, 1970-71; research fellow St. Catherine's Coll., Oxford, Eng., 1971-74; lectr. in stats. London Sch. Econs., 1974-77; Leverhulme prof. econometrics Southampton (Eng.) U., 1977—, chmn. dept., 1980-82; vis. fellow dept. stats. Australian Nat. U., Canberra, 1977, 82; vis. prof. U. Calif., San Diego, 1977, 86-87; mem. econs. com. Social Sci. Research Council, London, 1979-83;. Asst. editor Rev. Econ. Studies, 1980-82, mng. editor, 1982-86; contbr. articles to profl. jours. Research grantee Social Sci. Research Council, 1976-79, Advanced Studies Com., Southampton, 1979-80, Econ. and Social Research Council, 1983-86; research fellow Ctr. Econ. Policy Research, London, 1983—. Home: 18 Greenbank Crescent, Bassett Southampton SO1 7FQ, England Office: Southampton U, Dept Econs, Southampton SO9 5NH, England

MIZRAHI, ABRAHAM MORDECHAY, physician, cosmetics and health care company executive; b. Jerusalem, Israel, Apr. 16, 1929; came to U.S., 1952, naturalized, 1960; s. Solomon R. and Rachel (Haliwa) M.; m. Suzanne Eve Glasser, Mar. 15, 1956; children: Debra, Judith, Karen. B.S., Manchester Coll., 1955; M.D., Albert Einstein Coll. Medicine, 1960. Diplomate: Am. Bd. Pediatrics, Nat. Bd. Med. Examiners. Intern U. N.C., 1960-61; pediatric resident Columbia-Presbyn. Med. Center, N.Y.C., 1961-63; NIH fellow in neonatology Columbia-Presbyn. Med. Center, 1963-65; assoc. dir. Newborn Service Mt. Sinai Hosp., N.Y.C.; also dir. Newborn Service Elmhurst Med. Center, 1965-67; staff physician Geigy Pharm. Corp., N.Y.C., 1967-69; head cardio-pulmonary sect. Geigy Pharm. Corp., 1969-71; sr. v.p. corp. med. affairs USV Pharm. Corp., Tuckahoe, N.Y., 1971-76; v.p. health and safety Revlon, Inc., N.Y.C., 1976—; assoc. in pediatrics Columbia U., 1963-67; cons. neonatology Misericordia-Fordham Med. Center, 1967—; clin. affiliate N.Y. Hosp.; clin. asst. prof. Cornell U. Med. Coll., 1982—. Contbr. articles to profl. jours. Trustee Westchester (N.Y.) Jewish Center. Mem. AMA, N.Y. State and County Med. Soc., Am., N.Y. acads. medicine, Am. Soc. Clin. Pharmacology and Therapeutics, Am. Pub. Health Assn., Am. Occupational Med. Assn. Home: 7 Jason Ln Mamaroneck NY 10543 Office: 767 Fifth Ave New York NY 10022

MIZROCH, JOHN F., lawyer; b. Norfolk, Va., Sept. 28, 1948; s. Solomon B. and Muriel G. Mizroch; m. Martha Melissa Bankston; children: Zachary, Elliott, Brandon. BA, U. Va., 1970, MA, 1972; JD, Coll. of William and Mary, 1975. Bar: Va. 1975, D.C. 1977, Colo. 1980, Tex. 1985. Asst. commonwealth atty. Commonwealth Atty. Office, Arlington, Va., 1975-76; fgn. service officer USIA, Washington, 1976-79; pvt. practice real estate devel., Winter Park, Colo., 1980-84; v.p., counsel VCMI, Dallas, 1984-86; gen. counsel W.O. Bankston, Enterprise, Dallas, 1986-87; dep. asst. sec. commerce Office of Trade Adjustment Assistance, Dept. Commerce, Washington, 1987—. Town councilman Winter Park Town Council, 1982-84. Mem. ABA. Home: 4825 V St NW Washington DC 20007 Office: Commerce Dept 14th St NW Washington DC 20230

MIZUNO, RYUCHI JEROME, management information system consultant; b. Nyuzen, Japan, Oct. 17, 1962; s. Ryosuke and Michiko M. LLB, Sophia U., Tokyo, 1985. Head dealing dept. Mikei Real Estate Agy., Tokyo, 1983-85; cons. Arthur Andersen and Co., Tokyo, 1985—. Chief conductor Tokyo Youth Orch., 1979—. Anglican. Home: Mokko-House, 3-3-11-201 Arai, Ichikawa, Chiba 272-01, Japan Office: Arthur Andersen and Co, Nissei Akasaka Bldg 8-1-19, Akasaka, Minato Tokyo Japan

MIZUTANI, MASAKI, marketing executive; b. Tsurumi, Kanagawa, Japan, July 16, 1948; s. Kazutoshi and Yoshiko (Kitazawa) M.; m. Fiona Margaret Fitzpatrick, May 15, 1976; children: Thomas Joseph, James Gerald, John Robert. BSEE, Tokyo Inst. Tech., 1971; postgrad., Tokyo U. Agr. and Tech., 1972-73. Engr. sales dept. Toyo Corp., Tokyo, 1971-72; design engr. NEC Sanei Instruments Ltd., Tokyo, 1975-78; mgr. European liaison office Starnberg, Fed. Republic of Germany, 1979-86; dep. mgr., exec. mktg. gen. merchandise dept. Mitsui & Co., London, 1986—. Office: Mitsui & Co, Temple Ct, 11 Queen Victoria St, London EC4N 4JB, England

MKAPA, BENJAMIN WILLIAM, Tanzanian Minister for foreign affairs; b. Ndanda, Nov. 12, 1938; s. William Matwani and Stephania Nambanga; m. Anna Joseph Maro, 1966; 2 children. Ed., Makerere U. Coll. Adminstrv. officer, 1962, fgn. service Officer, 1963; mng. editor Tanzania Nationalist and Uhuru, 1966, The Daily News and Sun News, 1972; press sec. to pres., 1974; founding dir. Tanzania News Agy., 1976; Minister fgn. affairs, Tanzania, 1977-80, 84—, minister info. and culture, 1980-82, high commr. to Canada, ambassador to U.S., 1982-84, mem. Parliament, 1985—; mem. nat. exec. com. Chama Cha Mapinduzi, 1987—. Address: Ministry Fgn Affairs, Dar Es Salaam Tanzania

MLADENOV, PETER TOSHEV, Bulgarian minister foreign affairs; b. Toshevtsi, Vidin, Bulgaria, Aug. 22, 1936; grad. Suvorov Cadet Coll., 1954; postgrad. Sofia U., Inst. of Internat. Relations, Moscow 1957-63. Diplomate internat. relations. Sec., Vidin dist. com. League of Young Communists, 1963, 1st sec., 1964, head internat. relations dept. cen. com., 1966, sec. cen. com., 1966-69; 1st sec. Vidin dist. com. Bulgarian Communist Party, 1969-71, mem. politboro Cen. Com., 1971—, alt. mem., 1974, dep. to nat. assembly, minister fgn. affairs, 1971—. Address: Ministry of Fgn Affairs, 2 Alexander Zhendov St, Sofia Bulgaria *

MLELE, THOMAS JOHNSON JOSEPH, psychiatrist, consultant; b. Iringa, Tanzania, July 25, 1948; s. Joseph William and Tulikala (Mungongo) M.; m. Catherine Rodden Ngota; m. Jan. 8, 1983; children: Jema Claire, Brian Williard. MD, U. Dar Es Salaam, Tanzania, 1974; DPM, Inst. Psychiatry, London, 1979. Medical officer Mirembe Mental Hosp., Dodoma, Tanzania, 1975-77; clin. asst. Inst. Psychiatry, London, 1978-79; registrar Maudsley Hosp., Bethlehem Royal Hosp., London, 1979-81; sr. registrar Stoke Park Group Hosps., Bristol, Eng., 1981-85; cons. psychiatrist West Midlands Regional Health Authority, Birmingham, Eng., 1985—; clin. tutor mental health U. Bristol, 1985. Contbr. articles to profl. jours. Mem. Royal Coll. Psychiatrists. Anglican. Home: 13 Dale Close, Great Barr, Birmingham B43 6A8, England Office: St Margarets Hosp, Great Barr Park, Birmingham B43 7EZ, England

MMAHAT, ARLENE CECILE, steel company executive, civic activist; b. New Orleans, Oct. 5, 1943; d. John Alden and Margaret Therese (Nuccio) Montgomery; m. John Anthony Mmahat, Aug. 12, 1967; children—Arlene, Amy, John Anthony, Jr. B.A., La. State U., 1965. Clk., Shell Oil Co., New Orleans, 1965; claims rep. Social Security, New Orleans, 1966-67; chmn. bd. New Era Tubulars, New Orleans, 1979-84; chief exec. officer Olympia Tubular Corp., New Orleans, 1984—. Bd. dirs. New Orleans Symphony, 1983-86 , chmn. musicians adv. com., 1984, 85, membership chmn., 1985, oil and gas chmn. devel. com., 1983, devel. chmn. pub. sector, 1984; mem. Houston Bus. Council, 1980—, Dallas Regional Bus. Council, 1987—, New Orleans Mus. Art Odyssey, 1987; Ind. Women's Orgn., 1968—steering com. Internat. Gastroenteroly Research Fellowship Fund, Tulane U. Med. Ctr.; mem. adv. bd. Kennedy Ctr. for Performing Arts, 1980, Loyola U. Sch. Music, 1982—, New Orleans Mus. Art, 1986— ; fin. advisor New Orleans Symphony Soc. Jr. Com., 1977-79, fin. chmn., 1976; bd. dirs. Young Audiences, Inc., 1985—; mem. nat. adv. bd. on tech. and the disabled U.S. Dept. HHS; bd. dirs. Leukemia Soc. Am., Inc., 1978, corp. del., 1979; founder Ladies Leukemia League, Nat. Assn. Women Bus. Owners chpt. 1980; Odyssey Weekend chmn. New Orleans Mus. Art, 1985, fellows, 1983; mem. adv. com. St. Michael's Sch. for Spl. Students, 1978—, fin. chmn., 1977, mem. fin. com., 1973-76; fin. chmn. La. Landmarks Soc., 1973-75; bd. dirs. Preservation Resource Ctr., 1980, ways and means com., 1979, Christmas Benefit advisor, 1975, 76, mem. Women in Bus./ Women in Politics, Acad. Sacred Heart Adv. Study Com. Assoc. producer Film Am., Inc. Gottschalk, A Musical Portrait, 1986. Named One of 10 Outstanding Persons, New Orleans Inst. Human Understanding, 1977; One of 83 People to Watch in 1983, New Orleans Mag.; recipient Vol. Activist award Germain Monteil and D.H. Holmes Co., Ltd., 1977. Democrat. Roman Catholic. Home: 1239 1st St New Orleans LA 70130 Office: Olympia Tubular Corp 348 Baronne St Suite 602 New Orleans LA 70112

MMUSI, PETER, government official. V.p. and minister of fin. and planning Botswana. Office: Office of Vice Pres, Gaborone Botswana *

MO, XIAO HUI, trading company executive; b. Malaysia, Sept. 13, 1942; arrived in Singapore, 1945; Founder, dir. Mdse. Trading Pvt. Ltd, Singapore, 1983—. Office: Mdse Trading Pvt Ltd, 08-11/12 Asia Ins Bldg, 2 Finlayson Green, Singapore 0104, Singapore

MOATS, MICHAEL EMBRY, dentist; b. Akron, Ohio, Sept. 22, 1947; s. O. Embry and Helen Louise (Whitelaw) M.; m. Gloria Jean Vanderborg, Nov. 24, 1984; 1 child, Colin Robert Moats. BS, Davidson Coll., 1969; DDS, Loyola U., 1977. Lic. dentist, Ill. Sci. tchr. New Trier West High Sch., Northfield, Ill., 1969-73; asst. clin. prof. Loyola U. Sch. Dentist, Maywood, Ill., 1977-78; gen. practice dentistry, Buffalo Grove, Ill., 1977—. Chmn., bd. dirs. Midwest Epilepsy Ctr., Lombard, Ill., 1983—; consecrated lay minister Long Grove (Ill.) Community Ch., 1981, deacon, 1983-87; treas. Christ Ch. of Long Grove, 1988—; pres. bd. dirs. Prairie Christian Sch., 1988—; bd. dirs. Am. Cancer Soc., Buffalo Grove, 1983-84; bd. dirs. Wheeling/Buffalo Grove (Ill.) United Way, 1986, OMNI Youth Services, 1986—; chmn. Family Life Conf. I and II Chgo., 1986-88. Recipient Acad. Gen. Dentistry award, 1977. Paul Harris fellow, 1986; recipient Presdl. citation Rotary Internat., 1985. Mem. ADA, Ill. State Dental Soc., Chgo. Dental Soc. (mem. NW suburban br. peer review com., 1988—), Soc. Occlusal Studies, Arlington Dental Study Club, Sigma Chi. Republican. Mem. Christian Ch. Lodge: Rotary (local pres. 1984-85, 1988-89, bd. dirs. 1985-87). Avocations: jogging, scuba diving, photography. Office: 1401 W Dundee Rd Suite 212 Buffalo Grove IL 60089

MOATTI, CLAUDE-ROSE, history educator; b. Miliana, Algeria, Feb. 19, 1954; arrived in France, 1962.; d. Jean Moatti and Denise Bitoun Stephan; 1 child, Thomas. Licence lettres, U. Paris IC, 1974, Maitrise, 1976; postgrad., Ecole Normale Superieure, Paris, 1974-79; Dr Histoire, U. Paris I, 1987. Asst. U. Le Mans (France), 1981-84, U. Caen (France), 1985-86; prof. history Ecole Française de Rome, 1986—; editor Books-Garnier, Paris, 1979-81, Gallimard, Paris, 1980-84. Author: Comment Vivaient les Romains, 1986; contbr. articles to profl. publs.; co-producer Virgile, 1985-86. Jewish. Home: Via Sforza Pallavivini 11, 00193 Rome Italy Office: Ecole Francaise de Rome, Piazza Farnese 67, 00186 Rome Italy

MOBBS, KENNETH WILLIAMS, musician; b. Higham Ferrers, Northants, Eng., Aug. 4, 1925; s. George William and Grace Elsie (Pack) M.; m. Barbara Joyce McNeill, Sept. 2, 1950 (div. Apr. 1979); children: Sheelagh, Barbara, Patricia; m. Mary Jeanette Randall, May 18, 1979. MusB, Cambridge U., 1949, MA in Natural Scis. and Music, 1950; Licentiate in Pianoforte, Royal Acad. Music, Eng., 1941. Asst. lectr. music U. Bristol, Eng., 1950-53, lectr., 1953-64, sr. lectr., 1964-83; mus. dir. Bristol Opera Sch., 1954-64, Bristol Intimate Opera, 1981-84; freelance performer, lectr., 1983—; dir. Mobbs Keyboard Collection and Keyboard Photog. Archive, Bristol, 1976—. Contbr. articles on keyboard instruments to profl. publs.; composer, arranger Engaged!, 1963. Organ scholar Clare Coll., Cambridge, 1943, hon. scholar, 1948; fellow Royal Coll. Organists, 1949. Mem. Galpin Soc. for Study Mus. Instruments (mem. com. 1986—), Inc. Soc. Musicians, Assn. Univ. Tchrs., Musicians Union, Fellowship Makers and Restorers Hist. Mus. Instruments. Home: 16 All Saints Rd, Bristol BS8 2JJ, England

MOBERLY, LINDEN EMERY, educational administrator; b. Laramie, Wyo., Jan. 4, 1923; s. Linden E. and Ruth (Gathercole) M.; B.S., Coll. Emporia, 1952; M.S., Kans. State Tchrs. Coll., 1954; m. Viola F. Mosher, Apr. 29, 1949. Tchr. sci., Florence, Kans., 1952-54, Concordia, Kans., 1954-56, Grand Junction, Colo., 1957-60; asst. prin. Orchard Mesa Jr. High Sch., Grand Junction, 1960-66, prin., 1967-84; field cons. Nat. Assn. Secondary Sch. Prins., 1985—. Served to sgt. USMC, 1941-46. Recipient Outstanding Secondary Prin. award Colo. Assn. Sch. Execs., 1978. Mem. NEA, Nat. Assn. Secondary Prins. (dir. 1979-83), Colo. Edn. Assn. (dir. 1968-71), Colo. North Central Assn. Colls. and Secondary Schs., Colo. Assn. Secondary Sch. Prins. (dir. 1974-77). Club: Lions. Home: 2256 Kingston Rd Grand Junction CO 81503

MOBILLE, GEORGE THOMAS, lawyer; b. South Bend, Ind., July 27, 1925; s. Thomas George and Anne N. (Psillas) M.; m. Diana Mezines; children—Jane, Barbara, Thomas, John. B.S. in Chem. Engring., U. Notre Dame, 1948; LL.B., Cornell U., 1951. Bar: N.Y. 1951, D.C. 1952. Assoc. Cushman, Darby & Cushman, Washington, 1951-55, ptnr., 1955—, sr. ptnr., 1965—; vis. lectr. patent and antitrust law Cath. U. Am. Law Sch., 1953-56. Served with USNR, 1943-45. Republican. Greek Orthodox. Clubs: Capitol Hill, Metropolitan. Contbr. articles to profl. jours. Home: 5210 Portsmouth Rd Bethesda MD 20816 Office: Cushman Darby & Cushman 1615 L St NW Washington DC 20036

MOBLEY, JOHN HOMER, II, lawyer; b. Shreveport, La., Apr. 21, 1930; s. John Hinson and Beulah (Wilson) M.; m. Sue Lawton, Aug. 9, 1958; children—John Lawton, Anne Davant. A.B., U. Ga., 1951, J.D., 1953. Bar: Ga. 1952, U.S. Dist. Ct., D.C. Mem. firm Kelley & Mobley, Atlanta, 1956-63, Gambrell & Mobley, 1963-83; sr. ptnr., Sutherland, Asbill & Brennan, 1983—. Served to capt. JAGC, USAF, 1953-55. Mem. State Bar Ga., ABA, Atlanta Bar Assn., Am. Judicature Soc., Atlanta Lawyers Club, Phi Delta Phi. Clubs: Atlanta Athletic, Atlanta Country, Commerce, Piedmont Driving, Georgian. (Atlanta); N.Y. Athletic, World Trade (N.Y.C.); Metropolitan (Washington). Home: 4348 Sentinel Post Rd Atlanta GA 30327 Office: Sutherland Asbill & Brennan 3100 First Atlanta Tower Atlanta GA 30383

MOBUTU SESE SEKO, president of Zaire; b. Oct. 14, 1930; ed. Mbandaka and Kinshasa. Sgt.-maj. accountancy dept. Force Publique, Belgian Congo, 1949-56; journalist in Kinshasa; course Inst. Social Studies, Brussels, Belgian, then journalist in Leopoldville; mem. Mouvement Nat. Congolaise; del. Brussels Round Table Conf. on Congo Independence, 1959-60; sec. state for nat. def. Lumunba cabinet, 1960; chief staff Congo Army, 1960; took over supreme power in name of army, suspended all polit. activity for 3 months, 1960; apptd. coll. high commnrs. to take over govt.; maj. gen., comdr.-in-chief Congolese forces, 1961-65; lt.-gen., pres. of Zaire, 1965—; now also state commr. for fgn. affairs and internat. cooperation. Founder nat. party Mouvement Populaire de la Revolution, 1967; restored name of Zaire to the country. Address: Office of the Pres, Kinshasa Zaire *

MOCAK, VALER, architect; b. Michalovce, Czechoslovakia, July 2, 1932; came to U.S., 1969; s. Ladislav and Zlatica (Ferkova) M.; m. Juliana Tomasova, Dec. 29, 1956; children—Ladislav, Jana, George. M.Arch., Technol. Univ., Bratislava, Czechoslovakia, 1955, postgrad., Brno, 1963-64. Registered architect, N.Y., N.J. Chief architect, ptnr. Stavoprojekt, Presov, Czechoslovakia, 1953-69; staff architect I.M. Pei & Ptnrs., N.Y.C., 1969-70, Fleagle & Kaeyer, Yonkers, N.Y., 1973-75; asst. project mgr. Ferrenz & Taylor, N.Y.C., 1976-80; project architect Haines Lundberg Waehler, N.Y.C., 1980-83; cons. Skidmore Owings Merrill, N.Y.C., 1985—; pres. Internat. Consulting and Design Ctr., Yonkers, 1970—; instr. architecture, urban design, U. Presov. Prin. projects include Concentrated Housing Devel. in Michalovce, Bardejov, Humenne, Presov, Czechoslavakia; designer skylobbies, structures in future skyscrapers interconnected by bridge-like malls; author The Prognosis of the Development of Some Regions of Eastern Slovakia Up to the Year 2000, Skylobbies as Interconnecting Links Amid the Cluster of Skyscrapers. Mem. regional adv. bds. on urban design and planning, Czechoslovakia, 1955-69. Mem. AIA, N.Y. State Assn. Architects, Inst. Urban Design. Home: 187 Grassy Sprain Rd Yonkers NY 10710

MOCHARLA, RAMAN, research microbiologist and molecular biologist, educator; b. Mattigiri, Karnataka, India, Sept. 19, 1953; came to U.S. 1981; s. V. Krishnarao and Savithramma Mocharla; m. Hanna Tialowska, Jan. 15, 1983; 1 child, Robert Michael. BS in Biology, U. Agra, 1972; MS in Microbiology, GBP U., India, 1976; PhD in Microbiology, U. Kurukshetra, India, 1980; cert. in microbiology UNESCO/WHO and Czechoslavak Acad. Sci., Prague, 1981. Research asst. G.B.P. U., 1972-74; Scientist S-1 Indian Council Agr. Research, New Delhi, 1977-80; UNESCO/WHO fellow Czechoslovak Acad. Sci., Prague, 1980-81; postdoctoral fellow U. Okla., Norman, 1981-83; assoc. research scientist Okla. Med. Research Found., Oklahoma City, 1983-84, S.R. Noble Found., Ardmore, Okla., 1984-86; research assoc. Ind. U. Sch. Medicine, Indpls. Contbr. articles to profl. jours. Fellow Dayalbagh U., 1970-72, Council Sci. and Indsl. Research New Delhi, 1974-77, Nat. Inst. Gen. Med. Sci., 1981-83, Nat. Dental Research Inst., 1986—. Mem. AAAS, Am. Soc. Biol. Chemists, Nat. Geographic Soc., Am. Soc. Indusl. Microbiology, Ind. Acad. Sci., Australian Soc. Microbiology, Am. Soc. Microbiology, Am. Assn. Immunologists, Inst. Biology London, N.Y. Acad. Scis. (life), Sigma Xi (life), Phi Lambda Upsilon (life). Avocations: music; travel; cooking; outdoor games. Home: 3138 Shadow Brook Dr Indianapolis IN 46214 Office: Ind U Sch Medicine Dept Med Genetics 702 Barnhill Dr Indianapolis IN 46223

MOCK, ALOIS, government official; b. Euratsfeld, Austria, June 10, 1934; m. Edith Partik, 1963. LLD, U. Vienna, 1957; postgrad., U. Bologna, Italy, 1957-58, U. Brussels, 1960-61. Mem. Ministry of Edn., Austria, 1958, Fed. Chancellery, Austria, 1961; mem. Austrian del. Orgn. Econ., Coop. and Devel., Paris, 1962-66; sec. to Fed. Chancellor, Austria, 1966; minister of edn. Austria, 1969-70; mem. Nationalrat, Austria, 1970—; exec. chmn. Asterreichische Volkspartei, Austria, 1978; fed. chmn. Asterreichische Volkspartei, 1979; vice chancellor, minister fgn. affairs 1987—. Mem. Austrian Fedn. Workers and Employees (chmn. 1971—), European Dem. Union (pres. 1979—), Internat. Dem. Union (pres. 1983—). Office: Office of Vice Chancellor, Vienna Austria *

MOCK, DAVID CLINTON, JR., internist; b. Redlands, Calif., May 6, 1922; s. David Clinton and Eithel (Benson) M.; m. Marcella Enriqueta Fellin, Nov. 13, 1952. A.B., U. So. Calif., 1944; M.D., M.H.D., Hahnemann Med. Coll., 1948. Intern Hahnemann Hosp., Phila., 1948-49; resident San Mateo (Calif.) County Hosp., 1949-51, 54, VA Hosp., Oklahoma City, 1954-55; research fellow in exptl. therapeutics U. Okla., Oklahoma City, 1956-57, L.N. Upjohn fellow, 1958, dir. exptl. therapeutics unit, 1959-62, assoc. prof. medicine, 1963-72, prof., 1972-84, emeritus prof. medicine, 1984—, assoc. dean med. student affairs, 1970-76, assoc. dean postdoctoral edn., 1976-82, dir. continuing med. edn., 1980-83, dir. Transitional Yr. program, 1976-84, dir. History of Medicine program, 1982-84; assoc. mem. Faculty of Homeopathy Royal London Homeopathic Hosp., Eng.; pres. Coachella Valley Fruit Co., Inc., Indio, Calif. Surgeon USPHS, 1951-53; now med. dir. Res. Fellow ACP; mem. Am. Fedn. Clin. Research, N.Y. Acad. Scis., Am. Theatre Organ Soc. Home: 570 Alameda Blvd Coronado CA 92118

MOCK, MELINDA SMITH, nurse, medical consultant; b. Austell, Ga., Nov. 15, 1947; d. Robert Jehu and Emily Dorris (Smith) Smith; m. David Thomas Mock, Oct. 20, 1969. A.S. in Nursing, DeKalb Coll., 1972. R.N., Ga.; cert. orthopedic nurse specialist. Nursing technician Ga. Baptist Hosp., Atlanta, 1967, staff nurse, 1979; asst. corr. Harcourt, Brace & World Pub. Co., Atlanta, 1968-69; receptionist-sec. Goodbody & Co., Atlanta, 1969-70; nursing asst. DeKalb Gen. Hosp., Decatur, Ga., 1970-71; staff nurse Doctor's Meml. Hosp., Atlanta, 1972-73; staff nurse Shallowford Community Hosp., Atlanta, 1973, relief charge nurse, 1973, charge nurse, 1973-76, head nurse, 1976-79, orthopedic specialist emergency room, 1979; rehab. specialist Internat. Rehab. Assocs., Inc., Norcross, Ga., 1981, sr. rehab. specialist, 1981, rehab. supr., 1981-82; cons., founder, propr. Healthcare Cost Cons., Alpharetta, Ga., 1982-83; cons., founder, pres. Healthcare Cost Cons., Inc., Alpharetta, 1983—; mem. legis. com. of adv. council Ga. Bd. Nursing, Atlanta, 1984-85; mem. adv. council Milton High Sch. Coop. Bus. Edn., 1986—; active Congressman Patrick Swindall's Sr. Citizen Adv. Council, Nat. Fedn. Specialty Nursing Orgns. Task Force on Profl. Liability Ins., 1987—, Dep. voter registrar Fulton County Voter Registration Dept., Atlanta, 1983-87. Recipient Nat. Disting. Service Registry award, 1987; Named one of Outstanding Young Women Am., 1984. Mem. Nat. Assn. Orthopedic Nurses (nat. policies com. 1981-82, chmn. govt. relations com. 1987—, Washington intern 1987, legislative contbr. editor NAON NEWS), Orthopedic Nurses Assn. (nat. bd. dirs. 1977-79, nat. treas. 1979-81, Council Splty. Nursing Orgns. Ga. (nominating com. 1976-77), Assn. Rehab. Nurses (bd. dirs. Ga. chpt. 1980-81, del. people-to-people program to People's Republic China 1981), Nat. Fed. Independent Businesses, Nat. Assn. Female Execs., Ga. Jaycees (dist. 4C rep. Ga. Jaycee Legis. 1984, 85, adminstrv. asst. 1985), North Fulton C. of C. (vice chmn. health service effectiveness alliance 1984-85, chmn. 1985-86, co-chmn./editor periodical 1985), Alpharetta Jaycees (adminstrv. v.p. 1984-85), internal v.p. 1985-86), Alpharetta Jaycee Women (bd. dirs. 1983). Baptist. Avocations: reading, boating, community service activities. Home: 424 Michael Dr Alpharetta GA 30201 Office: HealthCare Cost Cons Inc 26 Milton Ave Suite W-4 Alpharetta GA 30201

MOCK, ROBERT CLAUDE, architect; b. Baden, Fed. Republic of Germany, May 3, 1928; came to U.S., 1938, naturalized, 1943; s. Ernest and Charlotte (Geismar) M.; m. Belle Carol Bach, Dec. 23, 1952 (div.); children: John Bach, Nicole Louise; m. Marjorie Reubenfeld, Dec. 20, 1964. B.Arch., Pratt Inst., 1950; M. Arch., Harvard U., 1953. Registered architect, N.Y., Conn., N.J., Nat. Council Archtl. Registration Bds. Architect George C. Marshall Space Center, Huntsville, Ala., 1950-51; archtl. critic Columbia Sch. Architecture, N.Y.C., 1953-54; dir. facility design Am. Airlines, N.Y.C., 1955-60; founder Robert C. Mock & Assocs. (architects and engrs.), N.Y.C., 1960—; Mem. Mayor's Panel of Architects, N.Y.C. Prin. works include: Shine Motor Inn, Queens, N.Y., 1961 (recipient 1st prize motel category Queens C. of C. 1961), temporary terminal bldg. Eastern Air Lines , La Guardia Airport, N.Y.C., 1961, cargo bldgs United Airlines and Trans World Airlines, Kennedy Airport, N.Y.C., Bridgeport (Conn.) Airport, 1961, Eastern Air Lines Med. Ctr., Kennedy Airport, 1962, ticket office Trans World Airlines Fifth Ave., N.Y.C., 1962, terminal bldgs. Eastern Air Lines and Trans World Airlines , La Guardia Airport, N.Y.C., 1963, 7 bldgs. Mfrs. Hanover Trust Co. , 1964-66, kitchen and commissary bldg. Lufthansa German Airlines, 1964, Ambassador Club, La Guardia Airport, 1964, Happyland Sch., N.Y.C., 1965, cargo bldgs. Alitalia and Lufthansa German Airlines, Kennedy Airport, 1965, FAA-Nat. Prototype Air Traffic Control Tower, 1966; Lufthansa German Airlines; Irish Internat. Airlines, El Al Israel Airlines, Varig Brazilian Airlines; passenger terminals Kennedy Airport, 1970; Swiss Air Cargo Terminal, Lufthansa German Airlines, cargo terminals El Al Israel airline cargo terminal, Kennedy Airport, 1972, passenger terminal Aerolineas Argentina, 1974, N.Am. hdqrs. Aerolineas Argentinas, N.Y.C., 1974, corp. hdqrs. Am. Airlines, 1977, N.Am. hdqrs. Varig Brazilian Airlines, N.Y.C., 1977, Norel-Ronel Indsl. Pk., Hollywood, Fla., 1979, N.Am. hdqrs. Irish Internat. Airlines , N.Y.C., 1979, corp. hdqrs. Bankers Trust Co., N.Y.C., 1980, cargo terminal Air India, cargo terminal Flying Tiger, Kennedy Airport, 1982, 2 flight kitchen bldgs. Ogden Food Corp., Kennedy Airport, 1984, 88 and LaGuardia Airport, 1987, Greenwich Assn. Retarded Citizens Sch., 1983, passenger terminal extension Varig Brazilian Airlines , 1985, 3 restaurants La Guardia Airport, 1987. Recipient United Way Vol. of Yr. award, 1984. Mem. Am. Arbitration Assn. Clubs: City, Harvard. Office: 185 Byram Shore Rd Greenwich CT 06830

MOCKRIDGE, NORTON, writer, editor; b. N.Y.C., Sept. 29, 1915; s. Frank Walter and Fredricka (Apfel) M.; m. Margaret Gleason, 1946 (div. 1961); m. Valborg Palmer, 1963; children—Phillip, Nancy Mockridge Miner. John. Student, pub. schs., Mt. Kisco, N.Y. Journalist Mt. Kisco Recorder, N.Y., 1933-36; journalist White Plains Daily Reporter, N.Y., 1936-40; with World-Telegram & Sun, N.Y.C., 1940-66, city editor, 1956-63, humor columnist, 1963-66; with World Jour. Tribune, 1967; syndicated humor columnist Scripps-Howard newspapers and United Feature Syndicate, 1963-80; editor Customized Communications div. Med. Econs. Co., Litton Publs., Oradell, N.J., 1971-81; fgn. corr. Ind. News Alliance div. United Feature Syndicate, 1980—; pres. Valnor Prodns., Inc., 1981—. Author: 17 books including This is Costello, 1951, The Big Fix, 1954, Costello on the Spot, 1957, Fractured English, 1965, A Funny Thing Happened, 1966, Mockridge, You're Slipping, 1967, The Scrawl of the Wild, 1968, Eye on the Odds, 1976, Types of Medical Practice: Making Your Choice, 1982; contbr. articles to mags.; author numerous film story outlines; tech. adviser film Teacher's Pet, 1957; lectr. Keedick Lecture Bur.; host daily radio show Sta.-WCBS, 1963-64, CBS radio network, 1964-70. Served to 1st lt. AUS, 1942-45. Recipient Christopher award the Christophers, 1949; Pulitzer prize (with World-Telegram city news staff), 1963; Jesse H. Neal award, 1974. Mem. 7th Regt. Vets. Assn. (life), Silurian Soc., N.Y. Vet. Police Assn., Sigma Delta Chi. Episcopalian. Clubs: Players, Dutch Treat, River, Coffee House, Regency, Casino (Chgo.); Cuernavaca Croquet (Mex.), Balboa Beach. Office: Valnor Prodns Inc 2509 N Campbell Ave Tucson AZ 85719

MODAK, TRIDIB KUMAR, engineering company executive, researcher; b. Calcutta, W. Bengal, India, Feb. 2, 1948; s. Jiban Chandra and Sneha Lata Modak; married Aug. 13, 1975. BEE, Jadavpur U., Calcutta, 1972; RHP diploma, 1984. Elec. engr. C.P.W.D., Durgapur, 1973-76, Jorhat, 1976-78; service engr. JYOTI Ltd., Gauhati, 1978-81; officer in charge JYOTI Ltd., 1981-83, branch mgr., 1983-87; branch mgr. JYOTI Ltd., Bangalore, 1987—; hydel cons. Electricity Bds., N.E. States, 1978-87. Mem. Inst. Engrs. Office: Jyotti Limited, 132 RV Rd VV Puram, Bangalore, Karnataka 560004, India

MODARRESS SADEGHI, JAAFAR, writer; b. Isfahan, Iran, May 19, 1954. Author: Children Are Not Playing, 1977, A Play, 1980, Gáv-khooni, 1984, The Other Ones' Spare and Other Stories, 1986. Home and Office: 1-8 Farihan Bldg, Behshahr St S Kheradmand St, Tehran 15849, Iran

MODERO, ANTONIO, diversified mining and investment company executive; b. Mexico City, June 4, 1937; s. Enrique and Beatriz (Bracho) M.; m. Teresa Pinson, Mar. 3, 1962; children: Antonioo, Eugenio, Marisa. Degree in mining engring., U. Mex., 1959; MBA, Harvard U., 1961. Exec. DuPont, Mexico City, 1961-68; pres. Industrias Penoles, Mexico City, 1968-78; chmn. IEM, Mexico City, 1979—, Woolworth Mex., Mexico City, 1981—; chmn., chief exec. officer Industrias Luisman S.A., Mexico City, 1979—; bd. dirs. Mexico Fund Inc., N.Y.C. Named Businessman of Yr., Executivos de Ventas y Mercadotecnia A.C., 1983. Mem. Mexican Mining Industry Assn. (chmn.), Mexican Bus. Council (Bd. dirs.). Roman Catholic. Clubs: University, Bankers (Mexico City). Office: Campos Eliseos #400, Lomas de Chapultepec, 11000 Mexico City Mexico

MODERY, RICHARD GILLMAN, marketing and sales executive; b. Chgo., Sept. 20, 1941; s. Richard Gustave Modery and Betty Jane (Gillman) Perok; m. Kay Francis Whitby, July 31, 1966 (div. July 1977); children: Stacey Lynn, Marci Kay; m. Anne-Marie Lucette Arsenault, Feb. 27, 1979. Student, Joliet (Ill.) Jr. Coll., 1959-61, Aurora (Ill.) Coll., 1963-65, Davenport Bus. Coll., Grand Rapids, Mich., 1969-71, Northwestern U., Evanston, Ill., 1987. Mktg. products mgr. Rapistan, Inc., Grand Rapids, 1964-75; mgr. estimating, project mgmt., customer service E.W. Buschman Co., Cin., 1975-78; exec. v.p. Metzgar Conveyor Co., Grand Rapids, 1979-84; mng. dir. Metzco Internat (cen. and S.Am.), Granp Rapids, Mich., 1981-84, Transfer Technologies, Inc., Grand Rapids, 1984-87; gen. ptnr., pres., chief exec. officer Nat. Monument Co., Grand Rapids, 1986—; v.p. Translogic Corp., Denver, 1987—; cons. in field. Patentee in field. Commr. City of East Grand Rapids, Mich. Traffic Commn., 1983-86. Served with USNG, 1963-69. Mem. Internat. Material Mgmt. Soc., Am. Mgmt. Assn., Material Handling Inst. (speaker nat. confs.). Lodge: Masons (32 degree).

MODESITT, FRITZY DAL, lawyer; b. Brazil, Ind., Nov. 11, 1942; s. Chester D. Modesitt and Josephine (Haviland) Harrison; m. Mary Kathryn Sapp, June 12, 1965; children—Chad, Leslie. B.A. in Bus. Mgmt., Ind. State U., 1972; J.D., Ind. U., 1976. Bar: Ind., U.S. Dist. Ct. (so. dist.) Ind., U.S. Claims Ct., U.S. Tax Ct., U.S. Ct. Internat. Trade, U.S. Ct. Appeals (fed. and 7th cirs.), U.S. Mil. Ct. Appeals, U.S. Supreme Ct., U.S. Ct. Internat. Trade, U.S. Tax Ct. Microwave technologist AT&T Corp., Inpls., 1966-76; pros. atty. 13th Judicial Cir., Brazil, Ind., 1979—; sole practice, Brazil, 1976—. Mem. ABA, Nat. Dist. Attys. Assn., Ind. Trial Lawyers Assn., Assn. Trial Lawyers Am., Ind. Bar Assn., Clay County Bar Assn., Exchange (Brazil). Lodge: Masons. Democrat. Home: Rural Rt 14 Brazil IN 47834

MODI, JAGDISH JAMNADAS, computer company executive; b. Kakamega, Kenya, Nov. 10, 1956; arrived in Eng., 1968; s. Jamnadas Gordhandas and Champaben (Khimji) M. BSc with honors, Aston U., Birmingham, Eng., 1978; postgrad. diploma, Cambridge (Eng.) U., 1979; PhD, London U., 1982. Research asst. Oxford (Eng.) U., 1983-84; research assoc. Cambridge U., 1984—; mng. dir. Parallel Computing Corp., London and Cambridge, 1986—. Author: Parallel Algorithms and Matrix Computation, 1988; contbr. articles to profl. jours. Fellow Inst. Math. and Applications, Cambridge Philos. Soc. Home: 7 Rushy Close, Leicester LE4 7PT, England Office: Cambridge U Dept Engring, Trumpington St, Cambridge CB2 1PZ, England

MODIANO, PATRICK JEAN, author; b. Boulogne-Billancourt, July 30, 1945; s. Albert and Luisa (Colpyn) M.; m. Dominique Zehrfuss, 1970; 2 children. Ed. coll. in Paris. Author: La place de l'etoile, 1968; La ronde de nuit, 1969; Les boulevards de ceinture, 1972; (screenplay) Lacombe Lucien, 1973; (novel) Villa triste, 1975; (novel) Livret de famille, 1977; Rue des boutiques obscures, 1978; Une Jeunesse, 1981; Memory Lane, 1981; Poupée Blonde, 1983; (novel) De si Braves Garcons, 1982, Quartier Perdu, 1985, Dimanches d'Aout, 1986. Recipient prix Roger Nimier, 1968, prix Felix Feneon, 1969, Grand prix d l'Academie Francaise, 1972, prix goncourt, 1978. Office: care Editions Gallimard, 5 rue Sebastien Bottin, 75007 Paris France

MODICA, ALFRED JOSEPH, marketing communications management company executive; b. Riverdale, N.Y., Jan. 22, 1925; s. Vincent J. and Agatha S. (Nicosia) M.; certificate Morton Schs. Real Estate, N.Y.C., 1963; cert. Henry George Sch. Social Sci., N.Y.C., 1966; LL.B., Blackstone Sch. Law, Chgo., 1965, J.D., 1968; B.S. in Bus. Adminstrn., Empire State Coll. State U. N.Y., 1976; M.B.A. with distinction, L.I. U., 1979; m. Teresa D. O'Donnell, Sept. 7, 1947; children—Christopher, Stephen, Eugene. Sales mgr. Electrolux Corp., N.Y.C., 1946-49; free-lance mktg. dir., 1949-54; pres., dir. Meadowstone, Inc., N.Y.C., 1954-62; mktg. communications cons. on franchise programming, 1962-66; exec. v.p. Seltz Franchising Devel., Inc., N.Y.C., 1967-69; pres., dir. OFI Corp., Maspeth, N.Y., 1969—, Lee Myles Assos. Corp., Maspeth, 1970—; exec. v.p., dir. Lee Myles Corp., Maspeth, 1970—, Alfred J. Modica Assos., 1974—; prof., area dir. mgmt. Mercy Coll., 1974—, also ednl. workshop sessions for minority groups, workshop sessions and seminars for fed. and state govts., bus., 1970—; mem. faculty, seminar leader mgmt., div. bus. and mgmt. N.Y. U. Sch. Continuing Edn. Served with USMCR, 1943-46. Mem. Inst. for Applied Communications (dir.), Am. Acad. Cons., Am. Soc. Personnel Adminstrs., Mid-Hudson Inst., Nat. Small Bus. Assn., C. of C. U.S., Internat. Platform Assn., Alpha Psi Omega, Kappa Delta Pi. Asso. editor Franchising Around the World mag., 1970—. Contbr. articles to profl. publs. Office: 36 Sandrock Ave Dobbs Ferry NY 10522

MODIGLIANI, FRANCO, economics and finance educator; b. Rome, June 18, 1918; came to U.S., 1939, naturalized, 1946; s. Enrico and Olga (Flaschel) M.; m. Serena Calabi, May 22, 1939; children: Andrea, Sergio. D.Jurisprudence, U. Rome, 1939; D.Social Sci., New Sch. Social Research, N.Y.C., 1944; LL.D. ad honorem, U. Chgo., 1967; D. honoris causa, U. Louvain, Belgium, 1974, Istituto Universitario di Bergamo, 1979; L.H.D., Bard Coll., 1985, Brandeis U., 1986; DCS, U. Hartford, 1988. Instr. econs. and statistics N.J. Coll. Women, New Brunswick, 1942; instr., then asso. econs. and statistics Bard Coll., Columbia, 1942-44; lectr., asst. prof. math. econs. and econometrics New Sch. Social Research, 1943-44, 46-48; research asso., chief statistician Inst. World Affairs, N.Y.C., 1945-48; research cons. Cowles Commn. Research in Econs., U. Chgo., 1949-54; asso. prof., then prof. econs. U. Ill., 1949-52; prof. econs. and indsl. adminstrn. Carnegie Inst. Tech., 1952-60; vis. prof. econs. Harvard U., 1957-58; prof. econs. Northwestern U., 1960-62; vis. prof. econs. MIT, 1960-61, prof. econs. and finance, 1962—, Inst. prof., 1970—; Fellow polit. economy U. Chgo., 1948; Fulbright lectr. U. Rome, also, Palermo, Italy, 1955. Author: The Collected Papers of Franco Modigliani, 3 vols, 1980; co-author: National Incomes and International Trade, 1953, Planning Production, Inventories and Work Forces, 1960, The Role of Anticipations and Plans in Economic Behavior and Their Use in Economic Analysis and Forecasting, 1961, New Mortgage Designs for Stable Housing in an Inflationary Environment, 1975, Mercato del Lavoro, Distribuzione del Reddito e Consumi Privati, 1975, The Debate Over Stabilization Policy, 1986, Il Caso Italia, 1986. Mem. macro econs. policy group Ctr. for European Policy Studies, 1985—. Recipient Nobel prize in econ. sci., 1985, Graham and Dodd award, 1975, 80, James R. Killian Jr. Faculty Achievement award, 1985. Fellow Econometric Soc. (council 1960, v.p. 1961, pres. 1962), Am. Econ. Assn. (v.p. 1975, pres. 1976), Internat. Econ. Assn. (v.p. 1977-83, hon. pres. 1983—), Am. Acad. Arts and Scis.; mem. Nat. Acad. Scis., Am. Fin. Assn. (pres. 1981). Home: 25 Clark St Belmont MA 02178 Office: MIT Sloan Sch of Mgmt Cambridge MA 02139

MÖDINGER, WERNER, university director; b. Waiblingen, Germany, Feb. 15, 1940; arrived in Republic South Africa, 1964; s. Willy Friedrich and Emma Klara (Frank) M.; m. Joan Magda Clark, Dec. 15, 1970; children: Heinrich, Thomas George. MSc. in Math., U. Stellenbosch, S. Africa, 1965; D. in Math., U. Stuttgart, Federal Republic of Germany, 1977. Tchr. Stuttgart High Schs., Fed. Republic Germany, 1968-69; lectr. U. Stellenbosch, 1969-75; sr. lectr. U. Transkei, Republic South Africa, 1976-77, math. prof., Dean of Sci., 1978-81; dir. U. Qwaqwa, Republic South Africa, 1982—; research scientist Council for Sci. and Industrial Research, Pretoria, Republic South Africa, 1979; exchange scientist Deutsche Forschungsgemeinschaft, Moscow, USSR, 1966; ednl. cons various private and govt. orgns., 1978—. contbr. numerous articles to various profl. jours. Mem. Math. Assn. Am., S. African Math. Soc. Office: U Qwaqwa, Prvt Bag X13, 9866 Phuthaditjhaba Republic of South Africa

MODLIN, HOWARD S., lawyer; b. N.Y.C., Apr. 10, 1931; s. Martin and Rose Modlin; m. Margot S., Oct. 18, 1956; children—James, Laura, Peter. A.B., Union Coll., Schenectady, 1952; J.D., Columbia U., 1955. Bar: N.Y. 1956, D.C. 1973. Assoc., Weisman, Celler, Spett & Modlin, N.Y.C., 1956-61, ptnr., 1961-76, mng. ptnr., 1976—; sec., dir. Fedders Corp., Peapack, N.J., Gen. DataComm Industries, Inc., Middlebury, Conn.; dir. Trans-Lux Corp., Norwalk, Conn., Fischbach Corp., N.Y.C., Am.-Book-Stratford Press, Inc., Jersey City, N.J. Chmn. bd. dirs. Daus. of Jacob Geriatric Ctr., Bronx, N.Y. Mem. ABA, Assn. Bar City N.Y., D.C. Bar Assn. Office: Weisman Celler Spett & Modlin 320 Park Ave New York NY 10022

MOE, MAGNE RAGNAR, pharmacist; b. Ørsta, Norway, Jan. 1, 1913; s. Olav and Marna (Kjeldseth) M.; m. Ingrid F. Grønneberg; children: Kari Winther, Marna, Anne Elisabeth Lofterød. Degree in pharmacy, U. Oslo, 1936. Provisor Mjøndalen (Norway) Apotek, 1937-47; sales mgr. Tollef Bredal A/S, Oslo, 1947-54; mng. dir. Norsk Medisinaldepot, Oslo, Bergen, Trondheim, Harstad, Norway, 1954-83, cons., 1983—. Chmn. bd. Pharm. Hist. Mus., Oslo, 1984—, Univ. for Pensjonists, Asker, Norway, 1985—. Recipient honors King of Norway, 1982. Mem. Norges Apotekerforening (hon.). Home: Askerjordet 50, 1370 Asker Norway

MOELLER, BEVERLEY BOWEN, agribusiness executive; b. Long Beach, Calif., Oct. 12, 1925; d. George Walter and Agnes Ruth (Coffey) Bowen; B.A., Whittier Coll., 1956; M.A., UCLA, 1965, Ph.D., 1968; m. Roger David Moeller, Dec. 11, 1955; children: Roger Bowen Shelton, Wendell Shelton, Claire Agnes, Barbara Bowen, Thomas David. Writer, Valley News and Green Sheet, Van Nuys, Calif., 1961-64; scholar-tchr. Valley Coll., Los Angeles, 1968-69, UCLA, 1970; instr. Petróleos Brasileiros, Salvador, Bahia, Brazil, 1972-73; pres. Nova Pioneira Agroindustrial Ltda., Belém Pará, Brazil, 1982—; dir. Associacão Cultural Brasil-Estados Unidos, 1972-73. Mem. Calif. Regional Water Quality Control Commn., 1970-71; bd. dirs. Dallas Council World Affairs, 1988—. Mem. Dallas Arboretum and Bot. Soc., Dallas Zool. Soc., Internat. Soc. Tropical Foresters, Forest History Soc., Kappa Kappa Gamma. Republican. Author: Phil Swing and Boulder Dam, 1971. Home: 7802 Glenn Eagle Dallas TX 75248

MOELLER, HORST, historian; b. Breslau, Germany, Jan. 12, 1943; s. Theodor and Elisabeth (Neuwirth) M.; m. Hildegard von der Bank; 2 children. Staatsexamen, Free U., Berlin, 1969, Ph.D., 1972, habilitation, 1978. Lectr. Free U., Berlin, 1969-77, Bundespraesidialamt, Bonn, Fed. Republic Germany, 1978; dep. dir. Inst. fuer Zeitgeschichte, Munich, Fed. Republic Germany, 1979-82; prof. history U. Erlangen-Nuernberg, Fed. Republic Germany, 1982—; vis. fellow St. Antony's Coll., Oxford, Eng., 1986; vis. prof. Sorbonne, Paris, 1988. Author: Aufklaerung in Preussen, 1974; Exodus der Kultur, 1984; Weimar. Die unvollendete Demokratie, 1985; Parlamentarismus in Preussen, 1919-1932, 1985, Vernunft und Kritik. Deutsche Aufklaerung im 17. und 18. Jahrhundert, 1986; also articles. Mem. Historische Kommission zu Berlin, Kommission fuer Geschichte des Parlamentarismus und der Politischen Parteien, Bonn. Roman Catholic. Office: Univ Erlangen-Nuernberg, Kochstrasse 4, 852 Erlangen Federal Republic of Germany

MOELLER, ROBERT CHARLES (BUD), management consultant; b. Washington, Sept. 5, 1954; s. Charles Edward and Ann Joan (Federico) M.; m. Carol Elizabeth Buchanan, June 19, 1976; children: Melaine Elizabeth, Robert Kehne. BChemE, Ga. Inst. Tech., 1976; MBA, Harvard U., 1978. Cons. ERT, Concord, Mass., 1977-78; assoc. Booz, Allen & Hamilton, Bethesda, Md., 1978-81, sr. assoc., 1981-83; prin. Booz, Allen & Hamilton, San Francisco, 1983—; chmn. bd. dirs. Nat. Capital YFC, Olney, Md., 1981-83. Contbr. articles to energy pubs. Chmn. bd. dirs. East Bay Youth for Christ, Concord, Calif., 1983—; mem. Rep. Presdl. Task Force, Washington, 1984-86; adv. Montgomery County (Md.) Health Dept., 1981. Mem. Am. Inst. Chem. Engrs., Ferrari Owners Club, Mensa. Republican. Mem. Evangelical Free Ch. Club: HBS (San Francisco). Home: 225 Clyde Dr Walnut Creek CA 94598 Office: Booz Allen & Hamilton 555 Montgomery St San Francisco CA 94111

MOELLERING, ROBERT CHARLES, JR., internist, educator; b. Lafayette, Ind., June 9, 1936; s. Robert Charles and Irene Pauline (Nolde) M.; m. Mary Tigg Johnston, June 14, 1964 (div. 1987); children: Anne Elizabeth, Robert Charles, Catherine Irene; m. Mary Jane Ferraro, July 11, 1987. B.A., Valparaiso U., 1958, D.Sc., 1980; M.D. cum laude, Harvard U., 1962. Diplomate: Am. Bd. Internal Medicine. Intern Mass. Gen. Hosp., Boston, 1962-63, resident, 1963-64, postdoctoral fellow in infectious diseases, 1967-70, resident, 1966-67, mem. infectious disease unit and asst. physician, 1970-76, assoc. physician, 1976-83, hon. physician, 1983—, cons. bacteriology, 1972—; instr. medicine Harvard U. Med. Sch., Boston, 1970-72, asst. prof., 1972-76, assoc. prof., 1976-80, prof., 1980—; chmn. dept. medicine, physician-in-chief New Eng. Deaconess Hosp., 1981—; Shields Warren-Mallinckrodt prof. clin. research Harvard U. Med. Sch., Boston, 1981—; mem. subcom. on susceptibility testing Nat. Com. for Clin. Lab. Standards, 1976—; mem. subcom. on antimicrobial agts. and chemotheraph, 1978—, subcom. on antimicrobiol disc. diffusion suceptibility testing, 1980—. Mem. editorial bd. New Eng. Jour. Medicine, 1977-81, Antimicrobial Agts. and Chem. Therapy, 1977-81, European Jour. Clin. Microbiology, 1981—, Jour. Infectious Deseases, 1981-85, Infectious Disease Alert, 1981—, Pharmacotherapy, 1982—, Antimicrobial Agts. Annual, 1984—, Zentralblatt Fur Bacteriologie, Microbiologie und Hygiene, 1984—, Jour. of Infection, 1986—, Innovations, 1986—, Residents Forum in Internal Medicine, 1988—; editor Antimicrobial Agts. and Chemotherapy, 1982-85, Les Infections, 1983; editor-in-chief Amtimicrobial Agts. and Chem. Therapy, 1985—, editor; Antimicrobial Agents Ann., 1984—; cons. editor: Infectious Disease Clinics N.Am., 1986—; contbr. articles to profl. jours. Served with USPHS, 1964-66. Grantee USPHS. Fellow ACP, Infectious Diseases Soc. Am.; mem. Am. Soc. Microbiology, Am. Clin. and Climatol. Assn., Internat. Soc. Chemotherapy, Am. Soc. Clin. Investigation, European Soc. Clin. Microbiology, Am. Fedn. Clin. Research, Roxbury Clin. Records Club, Mass. Med. Soc., Alpha Omega Alpha, Phi Kappa Psi. Home: 16 Breakwater Dr Chesla MA 02150 Office: New Eng Deaconess Hosp Dept Medicine 110 Francis St Boston MA 02215

MOEMEKA, ANDREW AZUKAEGO, communications educator, development communication specialist; b. Aniocha, Bendel, Benin, Nigeria, Nov. 30, 1940; came to U.S. 1983; s. Moemeka Oti and Margaret (Jideonwo) M.; m. Helen Obiageli Onwudili, June 18, 1963; children—Nwachukwu, Chukwugoziem, Chinye, Ekene, Okechukwu, Nnebuchi. B.A. with honors, Lagos U., 1972; M.Sc., Edinburgh U., Scotland, 1976. Programme producer broadcasting, Lagos, Nigeria, 1966-72; lectr. Ahmadu Bello Varsity, Zaria, 1973-79; lectr. SUNY-Albany, 1985—; sr. lectr. Lagos U., 1979—, assoc. prof., 1986—; cons. in field; mem. UNESCO Right to Communicate, Paris, 1978—. Author: Reporter's Handbook, 1980, Local Radio/Education, 1981. Contbr. articles to profl. jours. Named Outstanding Tchr., SUNY-Albany, 1984, Internat. Communication Assn., 1985; African Literacy Soc. grantee, 1980, SUNY Albany grantee, 1985; recipient Disting. Doctoral Dissertation Presdl. award SUNY, 1988. Mem. Internat. Communications Assn., Internat. Inst. Communications, African Council on Communications Edn. (trustee), East-West Communication Inst. (profl. assoc.). Nigerian Mass Communication Assn. Mem. Christian Ch. Home: U Lagos, 8 Bayajjida Close, Akoka-Yaba, Lagos Nigeria Office: U Lagos, Dept Communications, Akoka-Yaba, Lagos Nigeria

MOERDIJK, ALPHONSUS MARIA FRANCISCUS JOSEPHUS, lexicographer; b. Roosendaal, The Netherlands, Dec. 12, 1944; s. Alphonse Marie Clement and Dymphna Maria (Lyppens) M.; m. Yvonne Wilhelmina Arons, July 2, 1969; children: Martijn, Aukje, Michiel. DLitt, Cath. U., Nijmegen, The Netherlands, 1979. Tchr. Carolus Borromeus Coll., Helmond, The Netherlands, 1969-75, Nutsacademie, Rotterdam, 1976-84; prin. sci. officer Inst. for Dutch Lexicogaphy, Leiden, 1975—. Author: Continentaalwestgermaanse en Central Romaanse Heteroniemen voor Hec Begrippencomplex Rok-Onderrok-Jurk, 1979; editor Woordenboek der Nederlandsche Taal; contbr. articles on lexicography, lexicology, etymology, dialectology, morphology and semantics to profl. jours. Mem. Maatschappij Nederlandse Letterkunde. Home: Akkerhoornbloem 45, 2317 KS Leiden The Netherlands Office: Inst for Dutch, Lexicography, Postbus 9515, 2300 RA Leiden The Netherlands

MOERDLER, CHARLES GERARD, lawyer; b. Paris, Nov. 15, 1934; came to U.S., 1946, naturalized, 1951; s. Herman and Erna Anna (Brandwein) M.; m. Pearl G. Hecht, Dec. 26, 1955; children: Jeffrey Alan, Mark Laurence, Sharon Michele. B.A., L.I.U., 1953; LL.B., J.D., Fordham U., 1956. Bar: N.Y. 1956. Asso. firm Cravath, Swaine & Moore, N.Y.C., 1956-65; spl. counsel coms. City of N.Y. and judiciary N.Y. State Assembly, 1960-61; commr. bldgs. City of N.Y., 1966-67; sr. partner Stroock & Stroock & Lavan, N.Y.C., 1967—; bd. dirs. N.Y. Post Co. Inc.; cons. housing, urban devel. and real estate to mayor City N.Y., 1967-73; commr. N.Y. State Ins. Fund, 1978—, vice chmn., 1986—. Mem. editorial bd. N.Y. Law Jour., 1985—; assoc. editor Fordham Law Rev., 1956. Pres. N.Y. Young Republican Club, 1965; asst. dir. Rockefeller nat. presdl. campaign com., 1964; adv. bd. Sch. Internat. Affairs, Columbia U., 1977-80; bd. govs. L.I. U., 1966, trustee, 1985—; chmn. Community Planning Bds. 8 and 14, Bronx County, 1977-78; nat. bd. govs. Am. Jewish Congress, 1966; bd. overseers Jewish Theol. Sem. Am., 1983—; trustee St. Barnabas Hosp., Bronx, N.Y., 1985—. Recipient Tristam Walker Metcalf award L.I.U., 1966, cert. N.Y.C. Planning Commn., 1979; named Riverdale (N.Y.) Man of Year Riverdale Community Council, 1980. Mem. Am. Bar Assn., N.Y. State Bar Assn., N.Y. County Lawyers Assn., Bar Assn. City N.Y., Free Sons of Israel. Club: World Trade Center (N.Y.C.). Home: 7 Rivercrest Rd Riverdale NY 10471 Office: Stroock & Stroock & Lavan 7 Hanover Sq New York NY 10004

MOERINGS, BERT JOSEPH, stockbroker; b. Lobith, Holland, Oct. 11, 1946; came to U.S., 1950; s. Nicolaas A. and Betty J. M.; m. Marsha Rinker, Mar. 15, 1980; children: Nicholas, Lauren. BS in Econs., Spring Hill Coll., 1980. Stockbroker E.F. Hutton, Vero Beach, Fla., 1972-73, Merrill Lynch, Palm Beach, Fla., 1973-79, Alan Bush Brokerage Co., Palm Beach, 1979-86; pres., chief exec. officer CMC Services, Inc., Palm Beach, 1986—; bd. dirs. Money Concepts, Dominick Mgmt. Corp.; so. regional v.p. Dominick and Dominick, Inc. Served to capt. U.S. Army, 1968-71. Decorated Bronze Star. Mem. Palm Beach County Amatuer Golf Assn. (bd. dirs., vice-chmn.). Republican. Home: 2329 Prosperity Bay Ct Palm Beach Gardens FL 33410

MOESHART, HERMAN JAN, curator; b. nr. Amstel, The Netherlands, Aug. 24, 1937; s. Hermanus Ebertus and Dymphna Johanna (Smeltzer) M.; m. Miyako Yamada, Nov. 19, 1971; children: Herman Yoshinobu, Kumi Joanne. Student, U. Leiden, The Netherlands, 1959—. Asst. curator photography collection U. Leiden, 1974—; researcher 19th century Japanese history; pres. Mus. Coop., Leiden, 1982-88. Author: Diary of a Dutch Consul in Japan (1957-69), 1987; co-author: Yomigaeru Bakumatsu, 1986 (Internat. prize Photographic Soc. Japan 1987); contbr. articles to profl. jours. Served to cpl. Civilian Pub. Service, 1957-59. Mem. European Assn. Japanese Studies, Dutch Assn. Japanese Studies, Dutch-Japanese Soc., Von Siebold Research Soc. Japan, Asiatic Soc. Japan, Assn. Studies of the Early State, Deutsche Gesellschaft für Photographie (corr.). Mem. French Reformed Ch. Home: Zwenkgras 16, 2318 TH Leiden The Netherlands Office: Printroom U Leiden, Rapenburg 65, 2311 GJ Leiden The Netherlands

MOFFETT, FRANK CARDWELL, architect; b. Houston, Dec. 9, 1931; s. Ferrell Orlando and Jewell Bernice (Williams) M.; B.Arch., U. Tex., 1958; m. Annie Doris Thorn, Aug. 1, 1952 (div.); children: David Cardwell (dec.), Douglas Howard; m. Darlene Adele Alm Sayan, June 7, 1985. Architect with archtl. firms, Seattle, Harmon, Pray & Detrich, Arnold G. Gangnes, Ralf E. Decker, Roland Terry & Assos., 1958-64; partner Heideman & Moffett, AIA, Seattle, 1964-71; chief architect Wash. State Dept. Hwys., Olympia, 1971-77, Wash. State Dept. Transp., 1977-87; owner The Moffett Co., Olympia, 1974—; founder, treas. The Architects' Alliance Inc., Olympia, 1987—; advisor Wash. State Bldg. Code Adv. Council, 1975—; instr. civil engring. tech. Olympia Tech. Community Coll., 1975-77; adv. mem. archtl. barriers subcom. Internat. Conf. Building Ofcls.; archtl. works include hdqrs. Gen. Telephone Directory Co., Everett, Wash., 1964; Edmonds Unitarian Ch., 1966; tenant devel. Seattle Hdqrs. Office, Seattle-First Nat. Bank, 1968-70; Wash. State Dept. Transp. Area Hdqrs. Offices, Mt. Vernon, Selah, Raymond, Colfax and Port Orchard 1973-87, Materials Lab., Spokane, Wash., 1974, Olympic Meml. Gardens, Turnwater, Wash., 1988; archtl. barriers cons. State of Alaska, 1978. Chmn. Planning Commn. of Mountlake Terr., Wash., 1963, 64, mem., 1961-67; mem. State of Wash. Gov.'s Task Force on Wilderness, 1972-75, Heritage Park Task Force, Olympia, Wash., 1986—; trustee Cascade Symphony Orch., 1971; incorporating pres. United Singles, Olympia, 1978-79. Served with USN, 1951-54. Registered architect, Alaska, Calif., Wash., profl. engr., Wash.; cert. Nat. Council Archtl. Registration Bds., U.S. Dept. Def., Fallout Shelter Analysis, environ. engring. Mem. AIA (dir. S.W. Wash. chpt. 1980-82, pres.-elect 1985, pres. 1986, dir. Wash. council 1986, architects in govt. nat. com. 1978-87), Am. Public Works Assn., Inst. Bldgs. and Grounds, ASCE, Constrn. Specifications Inst., Am. Arbitration Assn. (invited panelist), Gen. Soc. Mayflower Descs. (gov. Wash. Soc. 1982-83), Nat. Huguenot Soc. (pres. Wash. Soc. 1981-83, 85-87), Olympia Geneal. Soc. (pres. 1978-80), SAR (state treas. 1984-85), SCV, Sons and Daus. of Pilgrims, (gov. Wash. Soc. 1984), Order of Magna Charta. Republican. Unitarian. Clubs: Rotary Internat. (pres. Edmonds, 1969-70), Coll. of Seattle, Olympia Yacht, Olympia Country and Golf. Co-author: An Illustrated Handbook for Barrier-Free Design, 2d edit., 1984, 3d edit., 1987. Home: PO Box 2422 Olympia WA 98507 Office: PO Box 2422 Olympia WA 98507

MOFTAH, MOUNIR, mechanical design engineer; b. Cairo, Egypt, Nov. 22, 1922; s. Amin and Rose (Seweha) M.; m. Marcelle Alfonse Elmahmoudy, Aug. 6, 1950; children—Magued, Maha, Medhat, Monica. B.M.E., Cairo U., 1948; chartered engr., Instn. Mech. Engrs. (London), 1970. Engr. Ministry Mcpl. and Rural Affairs, Egypt, 1949-56; dir. works Ministry Housing and Utilities, Egypt, 1955-66; mgr. transport and workshops United Distbn. Co., Egypt, 1966-67; dir. mech. fleet sector Ministry Housing and Utilities, Egypt, 1967-68; design engr. Water Authority of W. Australia, Perth, 1969—; cons. Upper Egypt Gen. Contraction Co., Cairo, 1964-68; lectr. Tng. Centre Ministry Housing and Utilities, Egypt, 1965-68. Author: Factors Governing Yield of Wells in Egypt, 1956; Gas Turbine Performance Under Varying Ambient Temperature, 1971. Mem. Civil Service Assn., ASME, Instn. Mech. Engrs., Instn. Engrs. Australia. Club: Met. Water Authority Social. Avocations: chess; tennis; walking; reading. Office: Water Authority of West Australia, Newcastle St, Leede, rville 6007, Australia

MOGAS, GUILHERME YSENBOUT, telecommunications executive; b. Luanda, Angola, June 10, 1951; s. Armando Ferreira and Willemina (Ysenbout) M.; m. Filomena Godinho Monteiro, Dec. 23, 1986. Student, U. Angola, 1975. Sound operator Emissora Oficial Angola, Luanda, 1969-74; emisson supr. Radio Nacional Angola, Luanda, 1974-77, chief dept., 1977-83, dir.-gen., 1983—. Inventor Image Transducer for Blind People, 1977, Safety Light Switch, 1979, Vehicle Wight Meter, 1980. Home: Largo de Cambambe 14, Luanda Angola Office: Rádio Nacional de Angola, Rua Comandante Jika, Luanda 1329, Angola

MOGENSEN, GUNNAR VIBY, social science educator; b. Braedstrup, Denmark, Sept. 22, 1934; s. Antonius and Kathrine (Petersen) M.; m. Paula Maria Laforce (div. 1970); children: Klaus Viby, Stine Viby; m. Karin Annette Fogtmann, May 29, 1971; children: Niels Viby, Rasmus Viby. MA in Econs., U. Copenhagen, 1963. Researcher Danish Nat. Inst. Social Research, Copenhagen, 1963-69, program dir., 1976—; asst. prof. econs. U. Copenhagen, 1969-76. Author: Social Change in Rural Areas, 1970, The Underground Economy, 1985, The Methodology of Economic History, 1987, 8 other books; contbr. numerous articles to profl. publs. Mem. Nat. Research Bd. Social Scis. Office: Danish Nat Inst Social Research, 28 Borgergade, 1300 Copenhagen Denmark

MOGRIDGE, MARTIN JOHN HENRY, transportation researcher, consultant; b. Welwyn, Eng., Dec. 2, 1940; s. Henry George and Maisie (Elliott) M.; m. Jacqueline Wesley, July 25, 1981. BSc, Univ Coll., London, 1962, PhD, 1966. Profl. officer Greater London Council, 1966-68, prin. planner, 1973-78; PSO Ctr. Environ. Studies, London, 1968-73; assoc. sr. research fellow Univ. Coll., London, 1978—; propr. Martin Mogridge Assocs., 1978—; co-chmn. 5th Internat. Conf. Travel Behavior, La Baume-Lès-Aix, France, 1987. Author: The Car Market, 1983; patentee in field; contbr. articles to profl. jours. Fellow Brit. Interplanetary Soc.; mem. Inst. Patentees and Inventors, World Univ. Home: 75 Camberley House, Redhill St, London NW1 4AX, England Office: Univ Coll London, Gower St, London WC1E 6BT, England

MOHAMED, ASHIK ALTAF, Guyanese diplomat; b. De Kinderen, Guyana, Mar. 3, 1933; s. Yakub and Zaitun (Badal) M.; m. Bibi Farida Ali, Aug. 10, 1958; children—Reza, Ferial, Arshad. Student in econs. U. London, 1959-61; Diploma in Pub. Adminstrn., U. P.R., 1962. Adminstrv. cadet Govt. Guyana, Georgetown, 1959-61, adminstrv. asst., 1961-64, asst. permanent sec., 1964-66; 2d sec. Guyana High Commn., London, 1966-69, 1st sec., 1969-72; dir. econ. dept. Ministry of Fgn. Affairs, Georgetown, 1972-74, dir., gen. Dept. for Asia, Africa, Middle-East and Internat. Orgns., 1980-81; permanent sec. Ministry of Info. and Culture, Georgetown, 1974-76; minister-counsellor Embassy of Guyana, Beijing, 1976-80; ambassador of Guyana to People's Republic of China, Japan, Pakistan and Democratic People's Republic of Korea, 1981—. Chmn. Nat. Trust, Georgetown, 1974-76, Bd. Film Censors, 1974-76; sec.-Gen. Muslim League of Guyana, Georgetown, 1953-66, Muslim Youth Orgn., 1958-66; chmn. edn. bd. United Sad'r Islamic Anjuman, Georgetown, 1972-76.

MOHAMED, ASHMEER, confectionary company executive; b. Couva, Trinidad, July 6, 1956; s. Sheriff and Ashroon (Khan) M.; m. Albeadea Hamid; children: Rubeena, Ateesha. Diploma, Omardeen's Sch. Acctg., San Fernando, Trinidad, 1977. Accounts clk. K.C. Confectinary Ltd., Couva, 1973-76, sec. bd. dirs., 1976-80, bd. dirs. Mem. Customs Brokers and Customs Clks. Assn., Nat. Geographic Soc. Club: Couva Sports (v.p. 1987—). Office: KC Confectinary Ltd, Southern Main Rd, Couva Trinidad

MOHAMED ARIFF, ABDUL WAHAB BIN, pediatrician; b. Penang Island, Malaysia, Dec. 24, 1919; s. Mohamed Ariff Ghouse Meah and Sharifah Aminah binti Syed Mohamed; married twice; children: Ahmad Fathil, Rohani, Nazli, Mohzani. LMS, U. Malaya and Coll. Medicine, Singapore, 1949; DCH, DPH; LM, 1959; student Mahidol U., Bangkok, Thailand, 1976; DS (hon.), 1985. Fed. dir. Health Services Malaysia, 1970-71; fed. dir. planning and devel. Ministry Health Malaysia, 1971-74; dean medicine, prof., head dept. social and preventive medicine Nat. U. Malaysia, 1975-78; practice medicine specializing in pediatrics, Penang Island, 1981—. Author: Medical Students During the Jpanese Invasion of Singapore 1941-42, 1987. Nat. chmn. Mayasian Com. for Man and the Biosphere Programme, 1971-74. Recipient awards King of Malaysia, Sultan Brunei, Kelantan, 1964, 72, Gov. Penang State, Malaysia, 1977; Malayan Govt. Queen's fellow, 1955, WHO fellow, 1967. Fellow Royal Inst. Pub. Health and Hygiene (life), Royal Soc. Health London; mem. Malaysian Med. Assn. (life), Nat. Heart Assn. Malaysia, Med. Practitioners Soc., Penang Malay Assn. (life). Home and Office: 543-B Jalan Tanjong Bunga, 11200 Penang Malaysia

MOHAMMAD, BAWANI, physician; b. Junagadh, India, Jan. 4, 1938; arrived in Pakistan, 1948; s. Ismail Mohammad and Aisha Bawani; m. Roshan Ara, Sept. 11, 1958; children: Nargis, Mahfooza, Naseem, Waseem, Aseem. MBBS, Liaquat Med. Coll., Pakistan, 1963. Intern Liaquat Med. Coll. Hosp., Pakistan, 1963-64; gen. practice medicine Tando-Adam, Pakistan, 1965—. Pakistan Ministry of Edn. scholar, 1956-63. Mem. Pakistan Med. Assn. (sec.-treas.); exec. mem. Memon Jamat (Tando-Adam). Lodge: Rotary. Home: Asendas Para, Tanao-adam, Sanghar Pakistan Office: Liaquat Bazar, Tando Adam, Sanghar Pakistan

MOHAMMAD, KAZI WALI, physician; b. Kharpur, Sind, Pakistan, Apr. 4, 1946; s. Mr. and Mrs. Kazi Peer Mohammad; m. Waseem Wali Kazi, May 3, 1975. MB, BS, Liaquat Med. Coll., Hyderabad, Pakistan, 1971. Staff surgeon Combined Military Hosp., Hyderbad, Sind, Pakistan, 1973-74; staff surgeon, gen. med. duty officer Combined Military Hosp., Bannu, Pakistan, 1975 76; resident med. officer Wapda Hosp., Guddu, Sind, Pakistan, 1976-83; med. supr. Wapda Hosp., Quetta, Baluchistan, Pakistan, 1983-84; sr. med. officer Area Electricity Bd., Hyderabad, 1984-86; resident med. officer Wapda Hosp., Guddu, 1986—. Served to capt. Med. Service Corp., 1975-76. Mem. Pakistan Med. and Dental Assn. Islamabad, Pakistan Med. Assn. Guddu (v.p. 1986-87). Clubs: Gymkhana (Hyderabad), Officers (Guddu)(sports sec. 1987). Home: Kazi Mohalla, Gambat, Khairpur Sind, Pakistan Office: Wapda Hosp, Officers Colony, Guddu Sind, Pakistan

MOHAMMAD DOKHT MARAGHEH, RAHIM, economist; b. Maragheh, Azarbaijan, Iran, Aug. 10, 1950; came to Holland in 1985.; s. Seifali and Malahat (Azarbarzin) M.; m. Charlotte Elaine Andrews, Apr. 21, 1980; children: Ammar, Tarlan, Ayeh. BA, Nat. U., Tehran, Iran, 1974; Grad. studies, U. Tex., Dallas, 1979. Adminstr. Jorjani Hosp., Tehran, Iran, 1970-75; fin. adminstr. consul Red Crescent, Tehran, 1979-80; librarian U. Tex., Dallas, 1975-79; instr. U. Tehran, 1985-86; fin. analyst NIIO, Tehran, 1981-85; investment cons. IPDIC, Tehran, 1983-86; mgr. Osva Alhavi, Tehran, 1980-86, LAL Enterprise, The Hague, Holland, 1986—; cons. D.P., Tehran, 1987—. Contbr. articles to profl.jours.; editor profl. jours. Islamic.

MOHLER, TERENCE JOHN, psychologist; b. Toledo, July 8, 1929; s. Edward F. and Gertrude A. (Aylward) M.; m. Carol B. Kulczak, Oct. 1, 1955; children—Renee, John, Timothy. B.E., Toledo U., 1955, M.E., 1966, Ed.S. in Psychology and Counseling, 1975, postgrad., 1981-82; Ph.D., Walden U., 1979; PhD, Union Grad. Sch., 1987. Psychologist, Toledo Bd. Edn., 1969—; sr. partner Psychol. Assocs., Maumee, Ohio, 1970—; assoc. fellow Inst. for Advanced Study in Rational Psychotherapy, N.Y.C. Served with AUS, 1951-53; Korea. Lic. psychologist, Ohio. Mem. Am., Ohio, Northwestern Ohio, Maumee Valley psychol. assns., Soc. Behaviorists, Toledo Acad. Profl. Psychology, Nat. Registry Mental Health Providers, Am. Personnel and Guidance Assn., Ohio Personnel and Guidance Assn., Council for Exceptional Children, Kappa Delta Phi. Lodge: Rotary. Home: 1113 Winghaven Rd Maumee OH 43537 Office: 5757 Monclova Rd Maumee OH 43537

MOHOLY, NOEL FRANCIS, clergyman; b. San Francisco, May 26, 1916; s. John Joseph and Eva Gertrude (Cippa) M.; grad. St. Anthony's Sem., Santa Barbara; S.T.D., Faculte de Theologie, Universite Laval, Quebec, Que., Can., 1948. Joined Franciscan Friars, 1935; ordained priest Roman Catholic Ch., 1941; tchr. fundamental theology Old Mission Santa Barbara, 1942-43, sacred theology, 1947-58; tchr. langs. St. Anthony's Sem., 1943-44; Am. adminstr. (handling affairs of the cause in U.S.) Cause of Padre Junipero Serra, 1950-55, vice postulator, 1958—; retreat master San Damiano Retreat, Danville, Calif., 1964-67. Mem. Assay Commn. U.S. Mint, 1964. Occupied numerous pulpits, assisted in several Franciscan Retreat Houses; condr. series illustrated lectrs. on cause of canonization of Padre Junipero Serra to students of all Franciscan study houses in U.S., summer 1952, also speaker in field at various clubs of Serra Internat. in U.S., Europe and Far East, on NBC, CBS, ABC broadcasts and conducted own local TV series. Exec. dir., treas. Old Mission Restoration Project, 1954-58; mem. Calif. Hist. Landmarks Adv. Com., 1962-71, Calif. Hist. Resources Commn., 1971-76, Calif. Bicentennial Celebration Commn., 1967-70; pres. Serra Bicentennial commn., 1983-86. Nat. and internat. authority on mariology, Calif. history (particularly history of Father Serra). Decorated Knight comdr. Order of Isabella the Catholic. Pres. Father Junipero Serra 250th Anniversary Assn., Inc., 1964—. Named hon. citizen Petra de Mallora, 1969, Palma de Mallorca, 1976. Mem. Mariol. Soc. Am., Native Sons Golden West, Associacion de los Amigos de Padre Serra, K.C., Calif. Missions Study Assn. Author: Our Last Chance, 1931; Saint Irenaeus; the Father of Mariology, 1952; The California Mission Story, 1975; The First Californian, 1976; co-author (with Don DeNevi) Junipero Serra, 1985; producer phonograph records Songs of the California Missions, 1951, Christmas at Mission Santa Barbara, 1953, St. Francis Peace Record, 1957; producer The Founding Father of the West, 1976. Home: St Boniface Friary 133 Golden Gate Ave San Francisco CA 94102 Office: Serra Cause Old Mission Santa Barbara CA 93105-3697

MOHR, HANS ULRICH, English and American literature educator; b. Mulhouse, Alsace, Sept. 15, 1943; s. Alfred Eduard and Johanna Christiana (Hoyer) M.; m. Christine Rosemarie Steiner, June 27, 1970; 1 child, Guido Thomas. MA, Free U. Berlin, 1969. Lectr. U. Konstanz, Fed. Republic Germany, 1970-75; co-editor, sci. advisor Open U. U. Tübingen, Fed. Republic Germany, 1976-78; asst. prof. U. Bielefeld, Fed. Republic Germany, 1978-86; prof. English and Am. Lit. U. Bielefeld, 1986—. Author: Afro-American Texts and Social Processes, Social History of Gothic Fiction; contbr. articles on social history of lit. to learned publs. Mem. MLA, Anglistentag, Shakespeare Soc. Fed. Republic Germany, German Assn. Am. Studies. Lutheran. Home: 90 Spandauer Allee, D-4800 Bielefeld 1 Federal Republic of Gemany Office: U Bielefeld, Fac f Ling & Lit, Universitätsstrasse, D-4800 Bielefeld 1, Federal Republic of Germany

MOHR, JAY PRESTON, neurologist; b. Mar. 5, 1937; s. John G. and Marguerite F. Mohr; A.B., Haverford Coll., 1958; M.S., U. Va., 1963, M.D., 1963; m. Joan L. Seal, Mar. 10, 1962; children—Thea, Gregory. Intern, then asst. resident in medicine Mary Imogene Bassett Hosp., Cooperstown, N.Y., 1963-65; asst. resident in neurology N.Y. Neurol. Inst., Columbia-Presbyn. Med. Ctr., N.Y.C., 1965-66; fellow in neurology Mass. Gen. Hosp., Boston, 1966-69; instr. neurology Johns Hopkins U. Med. Sch., also U. Md. Med. Sch., 1969-71; assoc. neurologist Mass. Gen. Hosp., also asst. prof. Harvard U. Med. Sch., 1972-78; prof. neurology, chmn. dept. U. South Ala. Med. Sch., Mobile, 1978-83; Sciarra prof. clin. neurology Columbia U. Coll. Physicians and Surgeons, N.Y.C., 1983—; dir. cerebrovascular research N.Y. Neurol. Inst., N.Y.C., 1983—. Served as maj. M.C., U.S. Army, 1969-72. Diplomate Am. Bd. Neurology and Psychiatry. Fellow Am. Acad. Neurology; mem. Am. Neurol. Assn., Am. Heart Assn. (stroke council), Sigma Xi. Democrat. Quaker. Contbr. articles to med. jours. Home: PO Box 1014 Shelter Island Heights NY 11965 Office: NY Neurol Inst 710 W 168th St New York NY 10032

MOHR, JOHN LUTHER, biologist, environmental consultant; b. Reading, Pa., Dec. 1, 1911; s. Luther Seth and Anna Elizabeth (Davis) M.; m. Frances Edith Christensen, Nov. 23, 1939; children: Jeremy John, Christopher Charles. A.B. in Biology, Bucknell U., 1933; student, Oberlin Coll., 1933-34; Ph.D. in Zoology, U. Calif. at Berkeley, 1939. Research asso. Pacific Islands Research, Stanford, 1942-44; research asso. Allan Hancock Found., U. So. Calif., 1944-46, asst. prof., 1946-47, asst. prof. dept. biology, 1947-54, asso. prof., 1954-57, prof., 1957-77, prof. emeritus, 1977—, chmn. dept., 1960-62; marine borer and pollution surveys harbors So. Calif., 1948-51, arctic marine biol. research, 1952-71; chief marine zool. group U.S. Antarctic research ship Eltanin in Drake Passage, 1962, in South Pacific sector, 1965; research asso. malacology Los Angeles County Mus. of Natural History deontology in sci. and academia, problems with offshore drilling discharges and oil spill dispersants, 1978—. Mem. Biol. Stain Commn., 1948—, trustee, 1971-81, emeritus trustee, 1981—, v.p., 1976-80; bd. dirs. Calif. Natural Areas Coordinating Council. Recipient Guggenheim fellowship, 1957-58. Fellow AAAS (council 1964-73), So. Calif. Acad. Sci., Sigma Xi (exec. com. 1964-67, 68, 69, chpt.-at-large bd. 1968-69); mem. Marine Biol. Assn. U.K. (life), Am. Soc. Parasitologists, Am. Micros. Soc., Western Soc. Naturalists (pres. 1960-61), Soc. Protozoologists, Am. Soc. Tropical Medicine and Hygiene, Am. Soc. Zoologists, Ecol. Soc. Am., Planning and Conservation League, Calif. Native Plants Soc., Am. Inst. Biol. Scis., San Francisco Bay Assn., Common Cause, Huxleyan, Phi Sigma, Theta Upsilon Omega. Home: 3819 Chanson Dr Los Angeles CA 90043

MOHR, ROBERT JAMES, aeronautics company executive; b. Tiffin, Ohio, May 1, 1932; s. Glenn Orland and Catherine Francis (Crist) M.; m. Roberta Joyce Tank, May 1, 1955; children—Scott Aaron, Todd Darren, Lynne Annette. B.S. in Aero. Engring., Calif. Poly. State U., 1959; cert. bus. UCLA, 1972. Project engr. McDonnell Douglas Astronautics Co., Sacramento, Calif. and Huntington Beach, Calif., 1959-70, configuration mgr., Huntington Beach, 1970-72, program integration mgr., 1972-83, test mgr., Alexandria, Va., 1983-85, program mgr., 1985, CBS TV network Apollo 11 MDAC rep., Los Angeles, 1969, tech. team dir., Huntsville, Ala., 1969, 70. Vice chmn., then chmn. Inst. Aero. Scis., San Luis Obispo, Calif., 1957-59; coordinator, coach Youth Basketball League, Mission Viejo, Calif., 1970-76; pres., v.p. Little League Baseball, Mission Viejo, 1970-71; elder local Presbyn. Ch., dir. Homeowners Assn., Springfield, Va.; mem. mil. assistance advisor team Salamanca, Spain, 1954. Served with USAF, 1951-55. Mem. Naval Inst. Republican. Avocations: golf; tennis; jogging; civil war literature; aircraft. Home: 8703 Sheridan Farms Ct Springfield VA 22152 Office: McDonnell Douglas Astronautics PO Box 19109 Alexandria VA 22320

MOHRI, HITOSHI, surgeon, educator; b. Taihoku City, Japan, July 28, 1930; s. Tetsuo and Sonoko (Oda) M.; M.D., Tohoku U., 1955, Ph.D., 1962; m. Yoko Murayama, Mar. 28, 1963; children: Alidé, Chihiro, Alvin Chikafusa, Melissa June. Asst., dept. surgery Tohoku U., Sendai, Japan, 1959-63; chief cardiothoracic surgery Katta Gen. Hosp., Shiroishi, Japan, 1963-64; vis. scientist dept. surgery U. Wash., Seattle, 1964-68, asst. prof., 1968-71, asso. prof., 1971-76; asso. prof. cardiothoracic surgery Tohoku U., Sendai, Japan, 1976-79, prof., chmn. cardiothorac surg. dept., 1987—; prof., chmn. 1st dept. surgery Yamaguchi U., Ube, Japan, 1979-87; established investigator Am. Heart Assn., 1970-75. Wash. Heart Assn. fellow, 1967-70; grantee NIH, 1968-75, Japanese Dept. Edn., 1962, 77-79, 81. Mem. Am. Assn. Thoracic Surgery, Internat. Cardiovascular Soc., Société Internationale de Chirurgie, N.Y. Acad. Sci., Japanese Soc. Pediatric Surgery, Japanese Soc. Artificial Organs, Japan Surg. Soc., Japanese Assn. Thoracic Surgery, Sigma Xi. Author: Hypothermia for Cardiovascular Surgery, 1981; adv. editorial bd. Jour. Cardiovascular Surgery, 1983—; contbr. articles to profl. jours. Home: 20-3 Moniwadai, 5-chome, Sendai 982-02, Japan Office: 1-1 Seiryomachi, Sendai 980, Japan

MOHYDIN, MOHAMMED ABU ZAFAR, physician, government official; b. Kasur, Pakistan, Sept. 1, 1928; s. Ghulam and Sardar (Begum) M.; m. Gulshan Ara Begum; children: Asim, Aliya, Bilal Shaikhu. MBBS, K.E. Med. Coll., Lahore, Pakistan, 1951; MRCP, Royal Coll. Physicians, London, 1959; FRCP, Royal Coll. Physicians, Edinburgh, Scotland, 1966; FCPS, Coll. Physicians and Surgeons, Pakistan, 1973. Med. specialist Combined Mil. Hosps., Lahore, 1961-63; personal physician to the Pres. and Prime Minister Pakistan, 1963-75; sr. instr. medicine Armed Forces Med. Coll., Pakistan, 1964-75; dir., prof. Postgrad. Med. Inst., Lahore, 1975-79; chmn., dean, prof. and head div. medicine, cons. physician Armed Forces Pakistan, Rawalpindi, 1979-84; head div. Armed Forces Med. Coll., Rawalpindi, 1979-84; dean, head dept. medicine Postgrad. Med. Inst., Lahore, 1984-86, Shaikh Zayed Postgrad. Med. Inst., Lahore, 1986—; chmn. Pakistan Med. Research Council, Lahore, 1976—; mem. adv. com. on biomed. research WHO and European Med. Research Orgn., 1984—. Editorial bd. Medicines Internat. Oxford, Islamic World Med. Jour. Served as lt. gen. Pakistan Armed Forces, 1984—. Recipient French Order of Merit, 1965. Mem. Pakistan Acad. Scis., Pakistan Cardiac Soc. Home: 16 Jail Rd, OPP-APWA College, Shadman, Lahore Pakistan Office: Shaikh Zayed Med Inst, Lahore Pakistan

MOI, DANIEL ARAP, president of Kenya; b. Sacho, Baringo Dist., Kenya, 1924; ed. African Mission Sch., A.I.M. Sch., Govt. African Sch. Tchr., 1945-57; head tchr. Govt. African Sch., Kabarnet, Kenya, 1946-48; 55-57; tchr. Tambach Tchr. Tng. Sch., Kabarnet, 1948-54; African rep. mem. Legis. Council, 1957-63; chmn. Kenya African Dem. Union, 1960-61; mem. Ho. of Reps., 1961—; Parliamentary sec. Ministry of Edn., 1961; minister of edn., 1961-62, minister of local govt., 1962-64, minister of home affairs, 1964-67; pres. Kenya African Nat. Union for Rift Valley Province, 1966-67, 82—; v.p. of Kenya, 1967-78, former minister of home affairs; pres. of Kenya, comdr.-in-chief of Armed Forces, 1978—. Mem. Rift Valley Edn. Bd., Kalenjin Lang. Com.; chmn. Rift Valley Provincial Ct. Address: Office of the Pres, PO Box 30510, Nairobi Kenya *

MOILANEN, THOMAS ALFRED, construction equipment distributor, funeral director; b. Hancock, Mich., Sept. 3, 1944; s. A. Edward and Elsie E. (Karkanen) M.; m. Kathleen Ann Maibach, Sept. 18, 1965; children: Todd Alan, Karl Edward. Cert., Wayne State U., 1967. Licensed funeral dir., Mich. Funeral dir. Ross B. Northrop & Son, Inc., Redford, Mich., 1967-68; sales mgr. Cloverdale Equipment Co., Oak Park, Mich., 1971; v.p., gen. mgr. Cloverdale Equipment Co., Oak Park, 1972-78, pres., chief exec. officer, bd. dirs., 1978—; pres., chief exec. officer, bd. dirs. Hasper Equipment Co., Muskegon, Mich., 1980—, SunBelt Crane & Equipment, Sarasota, Fla., 1982—, Armstrong/Cloverdale Equipment Co., Columbia, S.C., 1987—. Treas., bd. dirs. Livonia Hockey Assn., 1981-82. Mem. Associated Equipment Dealers Am. (equipment distbn. com. 1984), Mich. Constrn. Equipment Dealers Assn. (pres. 1983, 88), Concrete Improvement Bd. (bd. dirs. 1978-79). Republican. Lodge: Kiwanis (bd. dirs. Redford 1967-69, pres. 1969-70). Home: 18332 Laraugh Northville MI 48167 Office: Cloverdale Equipment Co 13133 Cloverdale Oak Park MI 48237

MOINET, ERIC EMIL, tax specialist; b. Paris, Mar. 17, 1952; s. Emil and Marguerite (Baccon) M.; m. Glynis Carol Moinet, May 6, 1980; children: Danielle Louise, Nicolette Anne. Assoc. in Applied Sci., Queensborough Community Coll., 1982; BBA, Baruch Coll., 1988. Jr. acct. Jason & Berman, CPA's, N.Y.C., 1982-84; sr. asst. internat. tax specialist KPMG, Peat, Marwick, Main & Co., CPAs, N.Y.C., 1984-88, Raleigh, N.C., 1988—. Mem. Nat. Assn. Accts., N.Y. State Assn. CPA Candidates, Inc. (chmn. pub. relations, recruiting, and career coms. 1985-87, bd. dirs. 1985-87, v.p. 1986-87), Fin. and Econs. Soc. (rec. sec.), Club for Accts. Seeking Heights (pres., advisor, founding mem.), Queensborough Community Coll. Alumni Assn., Baruch Coll. Acctg. Soc., Alpha Beta Gamma. Republican. Roman Catholic.

MOISE, STEVEN KAHN, lawyer; b. Lubbock, Tex., July 28, 1944; s. Joseph J. and Marguerite K. Moise; B.A., U. Colo., Boulder, 1966, J.D., 1969; m. Beth Maxwell, June 2, 1968; children—Adam M., Grant S. Admitted to Colo. bar, 1969, N.Mex. bar, 1971; atty. firm Rothgerber, Appel & Powers, Denver, 1969-71; atty. firm Sutin, Thayer & Browne, P.C., Albuquerque, 1971—, pres., chief exec. officer 1984—, also bd. dirs.; bd. dirs. Southwest Nat. Bank, Albuqerque, 1974-85; N.Mex. Symphony Orch., 1973-78, pres., 1977-78; trustee Presbyn. Health Care Found., Albuquerque, 1980-87, U. Colo. Found., 1969-79, 87—, United Way, 1979-84, Congregation Albert, Albuquerque, 1977-85, v.p., 1979-80, pres., 1981-82; trustee Manzano Day Sch., Albuquerque, 1979-86, U. N.Mex. Robert O. Anderson Sch. Mgmt. Found., 1979-85, Albuquerque Econ. Devel., 1982—, sec., 1984-86, v.p. 1986-88, pres., 1988—; trustee, v.p. Albuquerque Community Found., 1982-84, pres., 1984—; sec. Albuquerque All Seasons Corp., 1986—; N.Mex. Amigos, 1986—. Mem. ABA, N.Mex. Bar Assn., Colo. Bar Assn., Albuquerque Bar Assn., Denver Bar Assn. Democrat. Home: 6611 Guadalupe Trail NW Albuquerque NM 87107 Office: PO Box 1945 Albuquerque NM 87103

MOISEYEV, IGOR ALEKSANDROVICH, choreographer; b. Kiev, Russia, Jan. 21, 1906; s. Alersandr Michajlovich and Anna Aleksandrovna (Gren) M.; m. Tamara Akekseevna Seifort, July 8, 1918; 1 child, Olga Igorevna; m. Irina Alekseevna Chagadaeva. Student, Bolshoi Theater Ballet Sch., Moscow, Univ. of Art, Moscow. Soloist Bolshoi Theater, Moscow, 1924-37; artistic dir. State Acad. Ensemble of Folk Dance, Moscow, 1937—. Recipient Lenin prize, 1967, State prize 1942, 47, 52, 81; named Honored Artist of USSR, 1953, Hero of the Socialist Labour, 1976. Home: Sersphimovicha 2 flat 382, Moscow USSR Office: Moiseyev Dance Co, 20 Ploshchad Mayakovskogo, Moscow USSR

MOJSOV, LAZAR, Yugoslavian government official, journalist, diplomat; b. Negotino, Macedonia, Dec. 19, 1920; s. Dono and Efka Mojsov; grad. Belgrade U. Law Sch.; m. Liljiana Jankov, 1945; 2 children. Mem. Yugoslav Communist Party, 1940—; joined Nat. Liberation struggle 1941—; govt. ofcl. Republic of Macedonia after World War II; pub. prosecutor, minister of justice, 1953-58; pres. Supreme Ct., 1953; dir. Inst. for Study of Horlier's Movement, 1961-62, "Nova Makedonija" pub. house, 1953-58; dir., chief edn. BORBA, 1962-64; pres. Internat. Com. of Fed. Conf. Socialist Alliance of Working People of Yogoslavia, from 1965; ambassador to USSR and Mongolia, 1958-61; ambassador to Austria, 1967-69; rep. Internat. Atomic Energy Agy., 1967-69; permanent Yugoslav rep. to UN, 1969-74; ambassador to Guyana and Jamaica, 1969-74; pres. UN Gen. Assembly, 1977-78, and spl. session of Gen. Assembly on Disarmament, 1978; dep. fed. sec. for Fgn. Affairs, 1974-78, fed. sec. for Fgn. Affairs, 1982-84; mem. Presidency, 1984—; mem. central com. League of Communists of Yugoslavia, 1979—, pres. of the Presidency central com., 1980-81; pres. of the Presidency of the Socialist Fed. Republic of Yugoslavia (SFRY), 1987-88; mem. of Presidency of the SFRY, 1988—. Decorated Partisan Commemoration medal, numerous others. Author: The Bulgarian Working Party (Communist) and the Macedonian National Question, 1948; Vasil Glarrinov, First Propagator of Socialism in Macedonia, 1949; Concerning the Question of the Macedonian National Minority in Greece, 1954. Office: Office of the Member of the Presidency, of the SFR of Yugoslavia, Federation Palace, New Belgrade Yugoslavia

MOJZER, MIKLOS, gallery curator; b. Budapest, Hungary, Nov. 7, 1931; s. Antal and Lucia (Regenhart) M.; m. Eva Kovacs, Sept. 20, 1958; 1 child, Anna. Degree, Lorand Eotvos U., Budapest, 1955. Keeper, Christian Mus., Esztergom, Hungary, 1955-57, Mus. of Fine Arts, Budapest, 1957-74; keeper Hungarian Nat. Gallery, Budapest, 1974—, curator, 1977—. Contbr. articles to profl. jours. Recipient Ferenc Mora prize Hungarian Ministry of Culture, 1983. Mem. Regeszeti es Muveszettorteneti Tarsulat (mem. com.). Roman Catholic. Avocation: interior decorating. Home: Eotvos Lorand u 10 III 14, H-1053 Budapest Hungary Office: Hungarian Nat Gallery, Budavari Palota, H-1250 Pf31 Budapest Hungary

MOK, CARSON KWOK-CHI, structural engineer; b. Canton, China, Jan. 17, 1932; came to U.S., 1956, naturalized, 1962; s. King and Chi-Big (Lum) M.; B.S. in Civil Engring., Chu Hai U., Hong Kong, 1953; M.C.E., Cath. U. Am., 1968; m. Virginia Wai-Ching Cheng, Sept. 19, 1959. Structural designer Wong Cho Tong, Hong Kong, 1954-56; bridge designer Michael Baker Jr., Inc., College Park, Md., 1957-60; structural engr., chief design engr., asso. Milton A. Gurewitz Assos., Washington, 1961-65; partner Wright & Mok, Silver Spring, Md., 1966-75; owner Carson K.C. Mok, Cons. Engr., Silver Spring, 1976-81, pres., 1982—; facility engring. cons. Washington Met. Area Transit Authority, 1985-86; pres. Transp. Engring. and Mgmt. Assocs., P.C., Washington, 1986—; adj. asst. prof. Howard U., Washington, 1976-79, adj. assoc. prof., 1980-81. Sec., N.Am. bd. trustees, China Grad. Sch. Theology, Wayne, Pa., 1972-74, pres., 1975-83, v.p., 1984—; elder Chinese Bible Ch. Md., Rockville, 1978-80; chmn. Chinese Christian Ch. Greater Washington, 1958-61, 71, elder, 1972-76. Recipient Outstanding Standard of Teaching award Howard U., 1980; registered profl. engr., Md., D.C. Mem. ASCE, ASTM, Constrn. Specification Inst., Nat. Assn. Corrosion Engrs., Concrete Reinforcing Steel Inst., Am. Concrete Inst., Am. Welding Soc., Prestressed Concrete Inst., Post-Tensioning Inst., Soc. Exptl. Mechanics., Internat. Assn. Bridge and Structural Engring. Contbr. articles to profl. jours. Home: 4405 Bestor Dr Rockville MD 20853 Office: 9001 Ottawa Pl Silver Spring MD 20910

MOKLER, PAUL HELMUT, physicist, educator; b. Aalen, Germany, May 3, 1941; m. Hannelore Klein, 1968; children: Annette V., Florian T. Degree, U. Heidelberg, Fed. Republic Germany, 1968; PhD in Physics, U. Heidelberg, Fed. Republic Germany, 1969; Venia Legendi, U. Köln, Fed. Republic Germany, 1973. Sci. asst. Max-Planck-Inst. für Kernphysik, Heidelberg, 1968-69; scientist Kernforschungsanlage, Jülich, Germany, 1969-73; staff scientist Gessellschaft für Schwerionenforschung, Darmstadt, Germany, 1973—; honorary prof., U. Giessen, 1984—; privat dozent, U. Cololgne, 1973-80, Tech U. Darmstadt, 1980-84. co-editor: jour. on physics (Z. Physics D). Mem. German Phys. Soc., Internat. Conf. on Physics of Electronic and Atomic Collisions (gen. com. 1974-81). Office: GSI, Planck Str 1, 6100 Darmstadt Federal Republic of Germany

MOKRZYNSKI, JERZY BOGUSKAW, architect; b. Rzeszów, Poland, Sept. 22, 1909; s. Joseph and Helen (Tabaczkowska) M.; m. Mary Potczynska-Armötowicz, Apr. 6, 1945; 1 child, Teres. Degree in (architecture), Polytechnic Sch., Warsaw, 1935. Diplomate in architecture. Pvt. practice architecture 1936-39; with Architectonic State Office, 1945-80, Marszalkowska. Author: Tourist Facilities, 1962, 72, Vacation Houses, 1977, Architecture of the Leisure Time, 1988; prin. works include Free U., Lódz, Poland, Bank of Investment, Poznan, Poland, Recreation Center, Romanowo, Poland, Philharmonic Hall and Music Sch., Rzeszów, Poland, Labour Party Bldg., Warsaw, Hotel and Mus. Biatowieza, Poland, Railway Stn., Katowice, Poland, Puppet Theatre, Bialystok, Mus. Contemporary Art, Skopje, Yugoslavia, Polish Pavillions, New Delhi and Thesaloniki, Greece. Recipient Golden Badge Rebuilding Warsaw award, 1957, Officer's Cross of

Polonia Restituta, 1957, Order Banner of Labour, 1969, Golden Medal Ministry of Bldg., 1975, State Art awards grade III, 1951, grade II, 1955, grade I, 1974, Hon. Badge Activist of Culture, 1978. Mem. Polish Assn. Architects (v.p. 1952-56), Assn. Authors. Roman Catholic. Home: ul Marszalkowska 140 m 18, 00 061 Warsaw Poland

MOLANDER, SOLE HANNA KAISA, economist; b. Helsinki, Finland, Jan. 15, 1945; d. Eero and Kaisa I. (Pelkonen) Mustakallio; m. Ahti I. Molander, 1977 (div. 1983); children: Riku P., Kati M. MA, Turku U., Finland, 1968, Harvard U., 1971; Licentiate, Helsinki U., 1977. Instr. U. Hawaii, Honolulu, 1967-68; asst. Harvard U., Cambridge, Mass., 1970-72; officer 1st Nat. Bank of Boston, London, 1972-75; researcher Nat. Bd. Trade and Consumer, Helsinki, 1976-77; economist Okobank, Helsinki, 1977—. Contbr. articles to newspapers. Chmn. Helsinki Women Ceter Party, 1986—; mem. Parliamentary Equal Rights Com., 1987—; mem. Ministry of Environment Housing Com., 1987—; mem. Helsinki Bd. of Taxation, 1980—. Yrso Jahnsson Found. grantee, 1987. Mem. Finish Econ. Assn., Finnish Soc. Econ. Research. Home: Paasitie 15, SF-00830 Helsinki Finland

MOLEDO, LEONARDO, journalist, researcher, novelist; b. Buenos Aires, Argentina, Feb. 20, 1947; s. Santiago Moledo and Ida Zelicovich; married, 1972; children: Fernando, Lucia. Licenciado in Math., U. Buenos Aires, 1967. Researcher Conicet, Argentina. Author: La Mala Guita, 1976, Verídico Informe, 1985; contbr. articles on math. and lit. to profl. jours. Home: Francisco A Figueroa 719, 1180 Buenos Aires Argentina

MOLIN, KARL ERIK LENNART, educator; b. Stockholm, Dec. 5, 1944; s. Lennart and Ann-Mari (Nyqvist) M.; m. Berit Rönnstedt, June 16, 1973; children: Maria, Erika. MA, Stockholm U., 1964, PhD, 1974. Asst. prof. Stockholm U., 1974-80, Uppsala U., Sweden, 1980—; research dir. spl. project Uppsala U., 1980-86; organizer 1990 Alfred Nobel Symposion on 'Conceptions on Nat. History'. Author: Defense, Welfare and Democracy, 1974, The Domestic War, 1982; editor and contributor of several books on modern Swedish and Scandinavian polit. and social history; contbr. articles to profl. jours. Nat. sec. Internat. Commn. History Representative and Parliamentary Instns., 1974-86. Home: Brantinsgatan 56, S-11535 Stockholm Sweden Office: Uppsala U, S t Larsgatar 2, S-75220 Uppsala Sweden

MOLINARI, JOSEPH FRANCIS, optometrist; b. Worcester, Mass.; s. Wallace F. and Antoinette M. (Tortora) M. AA, Cen. New Eng. Coll., 1972; BS, New Eng. Coll., 1973, OD, 1974; MEd, Mercer U., 1979. Staff optometrist Lahey Clin. Med. Ctr., 1977-79; asst. prof. U. Ala., 1979-82; gen. practice optometry, Panama City Beach, Fla., 1982—; cons. USAF, Tyndall AFB, 1980—. Contbr. articles to profl. jours.; item writer Nat. Bd. Optometry, Washington, 1980-83. Pres. Harbour Villas Assn., Inc., 1985-86, Gulf of Mex. Optics Inc., Panama City Beach, 1984-88; chmn. Bay Point Anterior Segment Symposium Inc., 1984-88. Served to maj. USAFR, 1974—. Recipient Spurgeon Eure award Am. Optometric Found., 1978, 81-82, Dallos Contact Lens Research award Brit. Contact Lens Assn., 1984. Fellow Am. Acad. Optometry, Am. Coll. Optometric Physicians (diplomate); mem. Fla. Optometric Assn. (del. 1984-85), Neuro-optometry Soc. (chmn. 1985-88), Am. Coll. Optometry Physicians. Lodges: Lions, Sons of Italy. Office: 10010 Middle Beach Rd Panama City Beach FL 32407

MOLL, CLARENCE RUSSEL, university chancellor; b. Chalfont, Pa., Oct. 31, 1913; s. George A. and Anna A. (Schmidt) M.; m. Ruth E. Henderson, Nov. 19, 1941; children: Robert Henderson, Jonathan George. BS, Temple U., 1934, EdM, 1937; LHD, Pa. Mil. Coll., 1949; PhD, NYU, 1955; LLD, Temple U., 1963; ScD, Chungang U., Seoul, Korea, 1969; LLD, Swarthmore Coll., 1970, Gannon U., 1981; LittD, Delaware Valley Coll., 1976; PedD, Widener U., 1981. Instr. physics and chemistry Conshohocken (Pa.) High Sch., 1935-37; instr. sci. Freehold (N.J.) High Sch., 1937-38; instr. physics, chemistry Memorial High Sch., Haddonfield, N.J., 1938-42; instr. electronics and radar U.S. Navy, Phila., 1942-43; asso. prof. physics Pa. Mil. Coll., Chester, Pa., 1943-45; registrar, coordinator engring. program Pa. Mil. Coll., 1945-47, dean admissions, student personnel, prof. edn., 1947-56, v.p., dean personnel services, 1956-59, pres. coll., 1959-72; pres. Widener U. (formerly PMC Colls.), 1972-81, chancellor, 1981—; instr. electronics Temple U., 1944-46; headmaster Pa. Mil. Prep. Sch., 1945-47; bd. dirs. Fedders Corp., Ironworkers Savs. Bank, RDC, Inc. Author: numerous mag. articles. History of Pennsylvania Military College. Chmn. Pa. Commn. Ind. Colls., 1969, Found. For Ind. Colls. Pa., 1970; chmn. Com. for Financing Higher Edn. in Pa., 1975; bd. dirs. Tirlawyn, Tyler Arboretum, Crozer Chester Med. Ctr.; trustee Pa. Inst. Tech., 1982—; mem. Am. Assn. Homes for Aging, Continuing Care Accrediting Commn. Recipient Horatio Alger award, 1962, Disting. Alumnus award Temple U., 1964, B'nai B'rith Citizen Service award, 1966, Distinguished Citizen award, 1971, Themis award Del. County Bar, 1976, Good Citizenship award Phila. Bar, 1976, Exec. of Yr. award Soc. Advancement Mgmt., 1978. Mem. Assn. Mil. Colls. and Schs. (pres. 1969), Pa. Assn. Colls. and Univs. (pres. 1970), Am. Soc. Engring. Edn., Tau Beta Pi, Phi Delta Kappa, Alpha Sigma Lambda, Phi Kappa Phi. Lutheran. Clubs: Masons; Springhaven (Wallingford, Pa.); University (N.Y.C.); Racquet, Sunday Breakfast (Phila.); University (Wilmington, Del.). Home: 1960 Dog Kennel Rd Media PA 19063 Office: Widener U Chester PA 19013

MOLL, DON L., ecologist, educator, researcher; b. Peoria, Ill., Oct. 3, 1949; s. Edward and Bessie I. (Kennedy) M.; m. Barbara Kay Rogers, Mar. 17, 1972; children—Jane Elisabeth, Bryan Christopher. B.S., Ill. State U., 1971; M.S., Western Ill. U., 1973; Ph.D., Ill. State U., 1977. Asst. prof. biology S.W. Mo. State U., Springfield, 1977-82, assoc. prof., 1982-88, prof., 1988—; cons. Mo. Dept. Conservation, Jefferson City, 1980—, U.S. Fish and Wildlife Service, Washington, 1980, World Wildlife Fund, 1983, Internat. Union Conservation Nature and Natural Reources, Gland, Switzerland, 1981—; cons. on endangered species Ill. Dept. Transp., 1985-88. Contbr. numerous articles to profl. jours., books. S.W. Mo. State U. grantee, 1982, 83, 85; World Wildlife Fund grantee, 1984; Fauna and Flora Preservation Soc. grantee, 1984. Mem. Am. Soc. Icthyologists and Herpetologists, Herpetologists League, Soc. Study Amphibians and Reptiles, Mo. Acad. Sci., Nat. Audubon Soc., Bobby Witcher Soc., Alligator-Snapper Soc., Sigma Xi (assoc.). Research on paleoecology, ecology, and conservation of reptiles and amphibians, principally freshwater and marine turtles; foraging ecology and interactions in aquatic vertebrate communities. Home: 2455 S Aspen Springfield MO 65807 Office: Southwest Mo State U Dept Biology 901 S National Springfield MO 65804

MOLLEL, PAUL LUCAS, construction company executive; b. Arusha, Tanzania, Nov. 5, 1947; s. Lucas and Ruth Mollel; diploma in architecture 1967; Internat. Corr. Schs. Diploma, Inst. Brit. Engrs., 1973. Registered tech. engr., Eng. Archtl. asst. French & Hastings, Brit. Architects, Dar es Salaam, 1968-69; regional archtl. asst. East African Posts and Telegraph Corp., Dar es Salaam, 1970-74; bldg. supt. Williamson Diamond Mine, Mwadui, 1975-77; bldgs. estates mgr. Inst. Devel. Mgmt., Morogoro, 1977-79; sr. project engr. Equator Constrn. Co., Arusha, Tanzania, 1980-84; sr. asst. engr. Wade Adams British Contractors, 1984—. Mem. Tanzania Inst. Engrs., Archtl. Assn. Tanzania, Inst. Bldgs. Lutheran. Club: Badminton. Office: Box 982, Arusha Tanzania

MOLLENHOFF, CLARK RAYMOND, journalist, educator, writer; b. Burnside, Iowa, Apr. 16, 1921; s. Raymond Eldon and Margaret Pearl (Clark) M.; m. Georgia Giles Osmundson, Oct. 13, 1939 (div. Jan. 1978); children: Gjore Jean, Jacquelin Sue Mollenhoff Montgomery, Clark Raymond; m. Jane Cook Schurz, July 12, 1981. Student, Webster City Jr. Coll., 1938-41; LL.B., Drake U., 1944; Nieman fellow, Harvard U., 1949-50; LL.D., Colby Coll., 1959; L.H.D., Cornell Coll., 1960; Litt.D., Drake U., 1961, Iowa Wesleyan Coll., 1966, Simpson Coll., 1974. Bar: Iowa 1944, D.C. 1970, U.S. Supreme Ct. 1970, Fed. Ct. 1944. Reporter, Des Moines Register and Tribune, 1941-50; with Washington bur. Cowles Publs., 1950-69; spl. counsel to Pres. U.S., 1969-70; bur. chief Des Moines Register, Washington, 1970-77; prof. journalism and law Washington and Lee U., Lexington, Va., 1976—; Oxford exchange fellow Univ. Coll., 1980, 85; dir. Inst. on Polit. Journalism, Georgetown U., 1988—. Author: Washington Cover-Up, 1962, Tentacles of Power, 1965, Despoilers of Democracy, 1965, The Pentagon, 1967, George Romney Mormon in Politics, 1968, Strike Force, 1972, Game Plan for Disaster, 1976, The Man Who Pardoned Nixon, 1976, The President Who Failed, 1980, Investigative Reporting: From Courthouse to White House, 1981, Atanasoff: Forgotten Father of the Computer, 1988. Served to lt. (j.g.) USNR, 1944-46. Recipient nat. SDX award, Washington corr., 1953, 55, pub. service award, 1958; Raymond Clapper award, 1956; Heywood Broun award, 1956; Pulitzer prize for nat. reporting, 1958; Eisenhower exchange fellowship for study Africa, Middle East and Europe, 1960; Elijah Parish Lovejoy fellow, 1959; Nat. Headliner Award (mag. writing), 1960; John Peter Zenger award U. Ariz., 1962; William Allen White Meml. award U. Kansas, 1964, Alumnus of Yr. award Drake U., 1986; Nat. Am. Legion Fourth Estate award, 1965, George Mason/Virginia SPJ-SDX award, 1987; Soc. Profl. Journalists-Sigma Delta Chi fellow, 1980. Mem. ABA, Iowa Bar Assn., Investigative Reporters and Editors, Inc. (bd. dirs. 1979-84), Omicron Delta Kappa, Sigma Delta Chi. Roman Catholic. Clubs: Nat. Press (Washington) (bd. govs. 1956-64); Gridiron. Office: Washington and Lee Univ 207 Reid Hall Lexington VA 24450

MOLLER, AAGE RICHARD MOLLER, physiologist; b. Finderup, Denmark, Apr. 16, 1932; s. Jens and Kristine Marie (Pedersen) M.; m. Margareta Bjuro, July 26, 1977; children: Peter, Jan. Cand. med., Karolinska Inst., Stockholm, 1975, PhD, 1965. Research assoc., asst. prof., research fellow Swedish Med. Research Council, Karolinska Inst., 1966-77; assoc. prof. otolaryngology U. Gothenburg, Sweden, 1977-78; research prof. otolaryngology and physiology U. Pitts. Sch. Medicine, 1978-83, research prof. neurol. surgery, 1983-88, prof., 1988—; sr. lectr. Carnegie Mellon U., Pitts., 1980—; dir. research Internat. Ctr. Insect Physiology and Ecology, Nairobi, Kenya, 1970-76. Author of profl. books; contbr. articles to profl. jours.; editor-in-chief Hearing Research, Elsevier, Holland, 1977—. Served as cpl. Danish Army, 1951-53. Fellow Acoustical Soc. Am.; mem. Swedish Physiol. Assn., Swedish Acoustical Soc., Soc. Occupational and Environ. Health, Soc. Neurosci., N.Y. Acad. Sci., Assn. Research in Otolaryngology, AAAS, Am. Physiol. Soc., Am. Acad. of Clin. Neuro-Physiology. Home: 5427 Northumberland St Pittsburgh PA 15217 Office: 9402 Presbyterian U Hosp 230 Lothrop St Pittsburgh PA 15213

MØLLER, HENRIK, acoustic engineering educator; b. Aarhus, Denmark, Feb. 26, 1951; s. Holger and Ruth Binderup (Christiansen) M.; m. Grethe Lyndgaard Andersen, Sept. 25, 1976 (div. 1984). BEE, Danish Engring. Acad., Aalborg, Denmark, 1974; PhD in Acoustics, Aalborg U., 1984. Devel. engr. Bruel & Kjaer, Naerum, Denmark, 1974-76; research engr., project leader Aalborg U., 1976-79, asst. prof. acoustics, 1979-80, assoc. prof., 1980-82, 84—, sr. research engr., 1982-84; organizer Conf. on Low Frequency Noise and Hearing, Aalborg, 1980, Nordic Acoustical Meeting, Aalborg, 1986. Author: Effects of Infrasound on Man, 1984; contbr. articles to profl. jours.; mem. editorial bd. Jour. Low Frequency Noise and Vibration, London, 1982—. Recipient Rockwool Sound prize Rockwool Internat. A/S, Copenhagen, 1979; A. R. Angelos grantee, Copenhagen, 1986. Mem. Danish Engring. Soc., Danish Acoustical Soc., Audio Engring. Soc., IEEE, Danish Biomed. Soc., Danish Standards Orgn./Acoustics, Internat. Standardization Orgn./Frequency Weighing. Home: Vejgaard Bymidte 83, DK-9000 Aalborg Denmark Office: Aalborg U Inst Electronic Systems, Fredrik Bajers Vej 7, DK-9220 Aalborg Denmark

MOLLER, MAERSK MCKINNEY, shipowner; b. Copenhagen, July 13, 1913; s. Arnold Peter and Chastine Estelle (Mc-Kinney) M.; m. Emma Marie Neergaard Rasmussen; children: Leise, Kirsten, Ane. Ptnr. A.P. Møller, 1940-65, sr. ptrn. 1965—; chmn. Steamship Co. 1912 Ltd., Steamship Co. Svendborg Ltd., Steamship Co. 1960 Ltd., Odense Steel Shipyard Ltd., Maersk Olie og Gas A/S. Dansk Industri Syndikat A/S. Address: 50 Esplanaden, DK-1098 Copenhagen K Denmark

MOLLIN, RICHARD ANTHONY, mathematics educator, photographer; b. Kingston, Ont., Can., Dec. 12, 1947; s. Anthony Mollin and Bertha Olivine (LaLonde) Wilson; m. Kristen Elizabeth Kallstrom, Dec. 31, 1980. B.A., U. Western Ont., 1971, M.A., 1972; Ph.D., Queen's U., 1975. Postdoctoral fellow Concordia U., Montreal, Que., Can., 1975-76; sessional lectr. U. Victoria, B.C., Can., 1976-77; research assoc. U. Toronto, Ont., Can., 1977-78; asst. prof. McMaster U., Hamilton, Ont., 1978-79, U. Lethbridge, Alta., Can., 1979-81; asst. prof., research fellow Queen's U., Kingston, Ont., 1981-82; asst. prof. math. U. Calgary, Alta., 1982-83, assoc. prof., 1983—. Contbr. articles to profl. jours. Photographer, interviewer of actors. Reviewer Zentralblatt fur Math., Fed. Republic Germany, 1977—, Am. Math. Soc., 1985—. Can. Council fellow, 1974-75; Natural Scis. and Engring. Research Council of Can. grantee, 1978-82, fellow, 1981-82. Mem. Can. Math. Soc., Am. Math. Soc. Clubs: Riverside (Calgary), Faculty U. (Calgary). Avocations: squash; bicycling; hiking, chess. Office: U Calgary Dept Math, 2500 University Dr NW, Calgary, AB Canada T2N 1N4

MOLONY, MICHAEL JANSSENS, JR., lawyer; b. New Orleans, Sept. 2, 1922; s. Michael Janssens and Marie (Perret) M.; m. Jane Leslie Waguespack, Oct. 21, 1951; children—Michael Janssens III, Leslie, Megan, Kevin, Sara, Brian, Ian, Duncan. J.D., Tulane U., 1950. Bar: La. 1950, D.C. 1979. Practice law New Orleans. Ptnr., Molony & Baldwin, 1950; assoc. ptnr. Jones, Flanders, Waechter & Walker, 1951-56; ptnr. Jones, Walker, Waechter, Poitevent, Carrere & Denegre, 1956-75, Milling, Benson, Woodward, Hillyer, Pierson & Miller, 1975—; instr., lectr. Med. Sch. and Univ. Coll., Tulane U., 1953-59; mem. Eisenhower Legal Com., 1952. Bd. commrs. Port of New Orleans, 1976-81, pres., 1978, vice-chmn. past pres.' council, 1985—; bd. dirs. La. World Expn. Inc., 1974-84; bd. dirs., exec. com. New Orleans Tourist and Conv. Commn., 1971-74, 78, chmn. family attractions com. 1973-75; chmn. La. Gov.'s Task Force on Space Industry, 1971-73; chmn. Gov.'s Citizens' Adv. Com. Met. New Orleans Transp. and Planning Program, 1971-77; mem. La. Gov.'s Task Force Natural Gas Requirements, 1971-72; mem. Goals Found. Council and ex-officio mem. Goals Found., Met. New Orleans Goals Program, 1969-72, vice chmn. ad hoc planning com. Goals Met. New Orleans, 1969-73; vice chmn. Port of New Orleans Operation Impact, 1969-70; mem. Met. Area Com., New Orleans, 1970-84; trustee Pub. Affairs Research Council La., 1970-73; bd. dirs., mem. exec. com. Met. Council Continuing Higher Edn., U. New Orleans, 1980—; Mayor's Council on Internat. Trade and Econ. Devel., 1978; trustee Gulf South Research Inst., 1980—; trustee Loyola U., New Orleans, 1985—; bd. visitors Loyola U. Sch. Bus. Adminstrn., 1981—; bd. dirs., mem. exec. com. Internat. Trade Mart, chmn. internat. bus. com., 1983-85; chmn. Task Force on Internat. Banking, 1982; Acad. Sacred Heart, 1975-77, Internat. House, 1985—, Times-Picayune Loving Cup for civic contbrs., 1986. Served with AUS, USAAF, 1942-46, PTO. Mem. Fed. Bar Assn., ABA (mgmt. co-chmn. com. devel. law union adminstrn. and procedures 1969), La. Bar Assn. (past sec.-treas., gov. 1959-60, editor jour. 1957-59, sec. spl. supreme ct. com. on drafting code jud. ethics), New Orleans Bar Assn. (dir. legal aid bur. 1954, vice chmn. standing com. pub. relations 1970-71), Am. Judicature Soc., La. Law Inst. (asst. sec.-treas. 1958-79), Am. Arbitration Assn. (bd. dirs., chmn. La. adv. council), So. Inst. Mgmt. (founder), World Trade Ctr.-New Orleans (bd. dirs. 1978—), AIM, U.S. C. of C. (urban and regional affairs com. 1970-72), La. C. of C. (bd. dirs. 1963-66), New Orleans Area C. of C. (v.p. met. devel. and urban affairs 1969, past chmn. council, bd. dirs. 1970-78, pres.-elect 1970, pres. 1971, exec. com. 1972), Sigma Chi (pres. alumni chpt. 1956). Roman Catholic. Clubs: Internat. House, Plimsoll, So. Yacht Serra, Lakewood Country, Pickwick, Bienville, City (New Orleans). Home: 3039 Hudson Pl New Orleans LA 70131 Office: 909 Poydras St Suite 2300 New Orleans LA 70112-1017

MOLSKI, BOGUSLAW ANDRZEJ, botanist; b. Kosow Lacki, Poland, Jan. 5, 1932; s. Mieczyslaw and Elenora M.; B.Forestry, Agrl. U. Waszawa, 1955, M.Forestry, 1957, Dr.Sc., 1964; m. Irena Pogorzelska, Mar. 30, 1968; children—Leszek, Kasia, Asia. Asst. lectr. in botany Agrl. U. Waszawa, 1955-60, lectr., 1960-64; lectr. U. Nigeria, Naukka, 1964-66; sr. lectr. in botany, 1966-67; head Dept. Tropical Forestry, Krakow, Poland, 1968-70; organizer, 1st dir. Bot. Garden of Polish Acad. Scis., Warsaw, 1970—, prof. botany, 1980—; organizer World Rye Gene Bank, Warsaw; mem. 3d Polish Antarctic Expdn., 1978-79; high level expert UNEP for environ. problems of wars, Geneva, 1983; sci. writer for newspaper Trybuna Ludu, Warsaw, 1963-85. Decorated Polonia Restituta Cross. Grantee, U. Helsinki, 1959, Mich. State U., 1965, Polish Acad. Scis., 1968-70, FAO, 1983. Mem. Internat. Assn. Bot. Gardens, Internat. Assn. Plant Taxonomy, Polish Bot. Soc., Internat. Soc. Hort. Sci., Fedn. European Soc. Plant Physiology, Polish Forestry Soc. Contbr. articles in field to profl. jours.; editor Dendrology Jour., 1978—, Botanic Gardens Jour., 1979—; builder 1st greenhouse in Antarctica, 1978. Home: 11a Orezna, 02-938 Warszawa Poland Office: Prawdziwka 2, 00 979 Warszawa Poland

MOLSTAD, RUNAR, engineer; b. Oslo, Jan. 11, 1964; s. Egil and Berit Wendela (Kleven) M. Freelance technician Oslo, 1982-84; customer engr. NCR Norge AS, Oslo, 1984-85, sr. rework engr., 1985-86, sr. engr., 1986—. Served with Norwegian cav., 1983-84. Fellow Human-Etisk Forbund; mem. Internat. Airline Passenger Assn., Internat. Humanist and Ethical Union. Democrat. Home: Bjerregaards Gate 22, N-0172 Oslo Norway Office: NCR Norge AS, Waldemar Thraner Gate 98, N-0131 Oslo Norway

MOLYNEAUX, JAMES HENRY, politician; b. Aug. 27, 1920; s. William Molyneaux. Grad., Aldergrove Sch. Vice-chmn. mng. com. Eastern Spl. Care Hosp., Ireland, 1966-73; hon. sec. S. Antrim Unionist Assn., Ireland, 1964-70; v.p. Ulster Unionist Council, 1974; mem. No. Ireland Assembly, 1982-86; leader Ulster Unionist Party House of Commons, 1974—; M.P. from Antrim South 1970-83, M.P. from Lagan Valley, 1983—. Served with Royal Air Force, 1941-46. Decorated Grand Master of Orange Order, Hon. PGM of Can., Sovereign Grand Master. Office: Aldergrove, Crumlin Co, Antrim Northern Ireland *

MOMIROVICČ, KONSTANTIN, statistics and computer science professor; b. Tetovo, Yugoslavia, Jan. 13, 1932; s. Nikola and Aleksandra (Galič) M.; m. Neda Ostoič, Feb. 1956 (div, 1970); 1 child, Aleksandar; m. Ankica Hosek, Oct. 4, 1975. BS in Psychology, U. Zagreb, Yugoslavia, 1955, PhD, 1964. Lab. chief Zagreb Mil. Hosp., 1955-59, Inst. for Genetic Psychology, Zagreb, 1960-65; asst. U. Zagreb, Yugoslavia, 1960-63, asst. prof., 1963-66, assoc. prof., 1966-71, prof., 1971—; gen. dir. U. Computing Ctr., 1979-83, sci. cons., 1971-79, 1983—. Author: Analysis of Change, 1987, Quantitative Methods, 1984, Statistical Systems, 1983, Multivariate Data Analysis, 1978. Pres. State Council for Informatics, 1973-78. Recipient genetic research award Soviet Assoc. for Genetics, 1986, Ramiro Bujas Croatian Psychol. Assn., 1985. Mem. Internat. Assn. for Computational Statistics, Psychometric Soc., Internat. Assn. for Applied Phychology, European Anthro. Assn., Internat. Assn. for Genetics and Somatol (v.p. 1982—). Home: Brace Domany 4, 41000 Zagreb Yugoslavia Office: Faculty of Physical Culture, Horvačćanski Zavoj 15, 41000 Zagreb Yugoslavia

MOMMSEN, HANS, historian; b. Marburg, Hessen, Fed. Republic of Germany, Nov. 5, 1930; s. Wilhelm and Marie-Therese (Iken) M.; m. Margaretha Reindl, 1966. PhD, U. Tübingen, Fed. Republic Germany, 1958-60. Asst. at hist. seminar U. Tübingen, 1958-60; mem. Inst. for Zeitgeschichte, Munich, 1960-61; asst. at hist. seminar U. Heidelberg, Fed. Republic of Germany, 1962-67; prof. Modern European history Ruhr U. Bochum, Fed. Republic of Germany, 1968—, dir. Inst. for History of Labour Movement, 1977-83; vis. prof. Harvard U., Cambridge, Mass., 1974, U. Calif., Berkeley, 1978, Hebrew U. of Jerusalem, 1980, Georgetown U., Washington, 1982; vis. mem. Inst. for Advanced Study, Princeton, N.J., 1974. Contbr. articles to profl. jours. and chpts. to books. Fellow Inst. for Advanced Study, Berlin, 1983-84. Home: Askulapweg 16, 4630 Bochum 1 Federal Republic of Germany Office: Ruhr U Bochum, Universitatstrasse 150, 4630 Bochum Federal Republic of Germany

MOMMSEN, WOLFGANG JUSTIN, historian; b. Marburg, Fed. Republic of Germany, Nov. 5, 1930; s. Wilhelm and Marie Therese (Iken) M.; m. Sabine von Schalburg; children: Hans, Kai, Kerstin, Johanne. Student, Marburg U., 1951-52; PhD, Cologne U., 1958; postgrad., Leeds (Eng.) U.; DLitt (hon.), U. East Anglia, Norwich, Eng. Vis. prof. Tech. U., Karlsruhe, Fed. Republic of Germany, 1967; prof. U. Düsseldorf, Fed. Republic of Germany, 1968—; dir. German Hist. Inst., London, 1977-85. Author: Das Zeitalter des Imperialismus, 1961, Theories on Imperialism, 1979, Max Weber and German Politics, 1986 (UP award 1986), The Political and Social Theory of Max Weber—Collected Essdays, 1989. Mem. Verband der Historiker Deutschlands (treas. 1986—), Internat. Commn. History of Historiography (sec.-gen.), Historical Assn. (hon. mem.), German History Soc. Lodge: Rotary. Home: Leuchtenberger Kirchweg 43, 4000 Dusseldorf 31 Federal Republic of Germany Office: Univ Dusseldorf, Universitatsstrasse 1, 4000 Dusseldorf Federal Republic of Germany

MOMOH, JOSEPH SAIDU, president of the Republic of Sierra Leone, army officer; b. Binkolo, Sierra Leone, Jan. 26, 1937; m. Hannah Victoria Wilson; 2 children. Cambridge Sch. Cert., West African Methodist Collegiate Sch., Freetown, 1955; LL.D. (hon.), U. Sierra Leone, 1985. Mem. Sierra Leone Civil Service until 1958; mil. tng., Ghana, 1962-63, Mons Officers Cadet Sch., Aldershot, U.K., 1963, mil. tng. dept., Zaria, Nigeria, 1963, commd. 2d lt. Royal Sierra Leone Mil. Forces, 1963, advanced through grades to brigadier and force comdr. Republic of Sierra Leone Mil. Forces, 1973, now major gen.; mem. Parliament, Sierra Leone, 1973-85, minister of State, 1973-85, pres. Republic of Sierra Leone, 1985—, now also minister def. Patron, Bus. House Football League; mem. Sierra Leone Overseas and Olympic Games Com.; patron Sierra Leone/Liberian Friendship Soc., Sierra Leone Boy Scouts Assn. Decorated Order Brit. Empire, 1970; Nat. Order of the Rokel, 1981; Order of the Nat. Security Merit, Govt. of the Republic of Korea, 1984. Address: Office of the Pres, Freetown Sierra Leone *

MON, LOURDES GAGUI, school principal; b. Bangar, Philippines, Mar. 6, 1944; came to U.S., 1967; d. Crispin Yabut and Josefa Vergara (Agas) Gagui; m. Francis Lopez Mon, July 17, 1968; children: Catherine, Joey. BS in Elem. Edn., U. of East, Manila, 1963; MEd, Loyola U., Chgo., 1976. Tchr. San Sebastian Coll., 1963-64, St. Joseph's Coll., Philippines, 1964-67, Beloit (Wis.) Pub. Schs., 1967-69, Immaculate Conception Sch., Chgo., 1969-83; prin. St. Josaphat Sch., Chgo., 1983—; ex-officio mem. St. Josaphat Sch. Bd., 1983—; coordinator U.S. State Dept. Confs. for Minorities and Women. Contbg. editor: Maynila mag., 1983-85; contbg. writer: T M Herald, 1983-85; assoc. editor: VIA Times mag., 1984-86, columnist, 1984—, sr. editor, 1986—. Pres. Asian Human Services, Chgo., 1986-88; active Am. Profls. Civic Alliance; vol. Immigration and Naturalization Program, 1985—; exec. dir. immigration program Am. Filipino Profls. Civic Alliance; mem. Filipino Am. Council Bd., 1983-85; co-founder, bd. dirs. Sining Kayumanggi Theatre Group. Named Outstanding Asian of Yr., Asian Am. Coalition Chgo., 1986. Mem. Assn. for Supervision and Curriculum Devel., Archdiocesan Prins. Assn., Nat. Cath. Edn. Assn., Filipino Am. Women's Network (chmn. Ill. chpt. 1987—). Republican. Roman Catholic. Lodge: Lions (v.p. Chgo. chpt. 1984—). Office: St Josaphat Sch 2245 N Southport Ave Chicago IL 60614

MONACO, DANIEL JOSEPH, lawyer; b. Easton, Pa., May 12, 1922; s. Federico and Maria (Romano) M.; m. Marian P. Monaco, June 25, 1953 (div.); children—Denise E., Mimi D. A.B., Lafayette Coll., 1943; M.A., U. Chgo., 1946; J.D., Stanford U., 1951; postgrad., U. Mich., 1944-45. Bar: Calif. 1951, U.S. Dist. Ct. (no. dist.) Calif. 1951, U.S. Sup. Ct. 1961. Faculty U. Miami, Fla., 1946-47; founder, sr. ptnr. Monaco, Anderlini & Finkelstein, San Mateo, 1953—; inheritance tax appraiser State of Calif., 1963-67. Chmn. San Mateo County Democratic Central Com., 1960-61, mem. Calif. State Exec. Bd.; founder, pres. Circlon Internat., 1980-81; chmn. World Peace Through Law Conf. com. to establish a Citizens World Ct. Served with M.I. U.S. Army, 1943-46; served to lt. USAR, 1946-50. Mem. Calif. State Bar Assn., San Mateo County Bar Assn., Assn. Trial Lawyers Am., Calif. Trial Lawyers Assn., (bd. govs.), San Mateo County Trial Lawyers Assn. (pres.), Am. Bd. Trial Advocates, Am. Soc. Internat. Law, World Peace through Law. Club: Peninsula Golf and Country (San Mateo). Home: 295 Darrell Rd Hillsborough CA 94010 Office: 400 S El Camino Real #700 San Mateo CA 94402

MONAGHAN, PETER WILLIAM, retail company director; b. Edinburgh, Scotland, Aug. 25, 1947; s. James and Elizabeth (Dick) M.; m. Ann Stewart, July 18, 1970; children: James, Adam, Rachel. BA in Commerce, Heriot-Watt U., Edinburgh, 1970; grad. Program for Mgmt. Devel., Harvard U., 1985. Mdse. mgr. Marks and Spencer, London, 1970-76; devel. mgr. John Menzies, Edinburgh, 1976-81; area mgr. J. Sainsbury, London, 1981-83; dir. Coopers & Lybrand, London, 1983-86, Citibank, London, 1986-87; group mktg. dir. Dollond & Aitchison, Yardley, Eng., 1987—. Office: Dollond & Aitchison Group, 1323 Coventry Rd, Yardley Birmingham B25 8LP, England

MONAHAN, LEONARD FRANCIS, musician, singer, composer, publisher; b. Toledo, Aug. 19, 1948; s. Leonard Francis and Theresa Margaret (Geraldo) M.; m. Elaine Ann Welling, Oct. 14, 1978. B.S. in Psychology and Philosophy, U. Toledo, 1980. Musician, writer Len Monahan Prodns., Toledo, 1971-75; musician, composer, publisher World Airwave Music, Toledo, 1975—; founder Red Dog Records Label. Recipient Internat. Recognition of Christmas Music. Mem. Broadcast Music Inc., Internat. Platform Assn., Nat. Assn. Independent Recording Distbrs. Author: If You Were Big and I Were Small, 1971, The Land of Echoing Fountains, 1972, Sending You My Thoughts, 1987, Another Road, 1987, Tapping at Your Window, 1988; composer numerous songs. Office: 9967-US-A20 Delta OH 43515

MONARCHI, DAVID EDWARD, management scientist, information scientist, educator; b. Miami Beach, Fla., July 31, 1944; s. Joseph Louis and Elizabeth Rose (Muller) M.; B.S. in Engring. Physics, Colo. Sch. of Mines, 1966; Ph.D. (NDEA fellow), U. Ariz., 1972; 1 son by previous marriage, David Edward. Asst. dir. of Bus. Research Div., U. Colo., Boulder, 1972-75, asst. prof. mgmt. sci./info. systems, 1972-75, assoc. prof. mgmt. sci. and info. systems, 1975-84; assoc. dir. Bus. Research Div., 1975-80, dir. Div. Info. Sci. Research, 1982-84; prin. investigator of socio-econ. environ. systems for govtl. agys., and local govt. orgns., State of Colo., also info. systems for pvt. firms, 1972-77. Mem. Gov.'s Energy Task Force Com., 1974. Mem. IEEE, Inst. for Mgmt. Sci., Assn. Computing Machinery, Am. Assn. Artificial Intelligence. Contbr. numerous articles on socio-econ. modeling to profl. jours. Avocations: modeling, artificial intelligence. Home: 32 Benthaven Place Boulder CO 80303 Office: U Colorado Grad Sch Business Boulder CO 80309

MONBIOT, RAYMOND GEOFFREY, soup company executive; b. Garlinge, Kent, Eng., Sept. 1, 1937; s. Maurice Ferdinand and Ruth (Salmon) M.; m. Rosalie Vivien Gresham Cooke, Dec. 8, 1961; children—George, Katherine, Eleanor. Student London Bus. Sch., 1970. Jr. mgmt. trainee J. Lyons & Co., Ltd., London, 1956-62; nat. sales and dist. mgr. Lyons Bakery Ltd., London, 1962-69; mng. dir. SFK Ltd., J. Lyons & Co., London, 1969-73, Lyons Catering Supplies, London, 1973-75, H. Telfer Ltd., J. Lyons & Co., London, 1975-78; mng. dir. Assoc. Biscuits Ltd., Huntley & Palmer Foods, Reading, Berkshire, Eng., 1978-82; chmn. Campbell's U.K. Ltd., Campbell Soup Co., Reading, 1982—. Author: How to Manage Your Boss, 1980; regular contbr. articles to trade jours. Chmn., pres. Henley Conservative Assn. (Oxfordshire, Eng.), 1975—; chmn. Upper Thames Euro Constituency, Reading, Berkshire, 1982-84, Ox & Bucks Euro Constituency, 1984—, Duke of Edinburgh Award Indsl. Council, 1976-86. Mem. Conservative Party Nat. Exec., 1987—; chmn. Conservative Party Nat.Trade and Industry Forum, London Bus. Sch. Liaison Com., 1984-88; past pres. Reading Regatta. Decorated Order of Brit. Empire. Fellow Mktg. Soc., Inst. Meat; mem. Inst. Dirs. Conservative. Mem. Ch. of Eng. Club: Leander (Henley). Home: Peppard House, Peppard Common, Henley on Thames, Oxfordshire RG9 5JE, England Office: Campbell's UK Ltd, Kennet House 80 King's Rd, Reading, Berkshire England

MOND, BERTRAM, mathematician, educator; b. N.Y.C., Aug. 24, 1931; arrived in Australia, 1969; s. Isaac and Mollie (Turk) M.; m. Judy Edna Porush, July 1957 (dec. Oct. 1969); children: Daniel, Michelle; m. Chaya Lorberbaum, Sept. 23, 1970; 1 child, Michael. BA, Yeshiva U., N.Y.C., 1951; MA, Bucknell U., 1959; PhD, U. Cin., 1963. Prof. math. LaTrobe U., Bundoora, Australia, 1969—, dean sch. phys. scis., 1976-78, chmn. math. dept., 1970-82, dep. chair acad. bd., 1987. Presenter, contbr. over 100 papers to sci. jours.; editor Australian Jour. Math., 1969-74; assoc. editor Jour. Info. and Optimization Scis., Indian Jour. Mgmt. Systems. Pres. Hillel Found. Victoria, Melbourne, 1980-81. Served to 1st lt. USAF, 1956-57. Mem. Am. Math. Soc., Australian Math. Soc. (editor jour.), Math. Programming Soc. Office: Latrobe U Dept Math, Bundoora 3083, Australia

MONDALE, WALTER FREDERICK, lawyer, former vice president U.S.; b. Ceylon, Minn., Jan. 5, 1928; s. Theodore Sigvaard and Claribel Hope (Cowan) M.; m. Joan Adams, Dec. 27, 1955; children: Theodore, Eleanor, William. B.A. cum laude, U. Minn., 1951, LL.B., 1956. Bar: Minn. 1956. Pvt. practice law 1956-60; atty. gen. State of Minn., 1960-64; U.S. senator from Minn. 1964-77; v.p. U.S., 1977-80; mem. Nat. Security Council, 1977-81; mem. firm Winston & Strawn, 1977—; Democratic nominee for pres. U.S., 1984. Author: The Accountability of Power-Toward a Responsible Presidency, 1976. Mem. Democratic Farm Labor Party.; Democratic Candidate for Pres. U.S., 1984; regent Smithsonian Instn. Served with AUS, 1951-53. Presbyterian. Office: Dorsey & Whitney 2200 First Bank Pl E Minneapolis MN 55402 *

MONDOLFO, PAOLO, management consultant; b. Alexandria, Egypt, Aug. 12, 1943; arrived in Italy, 1960; s. Gastone Ubaldo and Elda (Forte) M.; m. Ada Grillo, Apr. 4, 1970; children: Silvia, Sergio. BSEE, Poly. Milan, 1970. Material mgr. GTE Telecomunicazioni, Milan, 1970-74; sr. cons., mgr. Authur Andersen and Co., Milan, 1974-81; pvt. practice mgmt. cons. Milan, 1981—; dir. Coopers and Lybrand Assocs. Europe, London, 1984—; prin. Booz-Allen & Hamilton, Milan, 1987—; speaker in field, 1982—. Author, editor Logistica D'Impresa mag., 1981—. Served to lt. Italian air force, 1969-70. Mem. Am. Prodn. and Inventory Control Soc., Assn. Italiana per la Gestione Industriale (founder, pres. 1981—), World Congress for Prodn. and Inventory Control (bd. dirs. 1985—). Home: via LB Alberti 8, 20149 Milan Italy

MONDRAGON, ALFONSO BALLESTEROS, physicist, educator; b. Toluca, Mexico, Mar. 14, 1932; s. Joaquin Mondragon-Forgues and Rebeca Ballesteros-Garibay; m. Myriam Garcia Ceballos, Dec. 16, 1955; children—Ricardo, Alfonso, Raul Javier, Myriam. M.S. in Physics, U. Nacional Autonoma, Mexico City, 1955; Ph.D. in Math. Physics, U. Birmingham, Eng., 1960. Cert. physicist, Mexico. Asst. prof. physics U. Nacional Autonoma, 1953-56, asst. researcher, 1954-56, prof., 1961—, head dept. theoretical physics, 1986— ; cons. Inst. Nuclear Research, Mexico City, 1961—; research fellow Internat. Centre for Theoretical Physics, Trieste, Italy, 1969-70. Author: La Unidad de la Naturaleza en el Pensamiento de Einstein, 1981; La Fisica Nuclear, 1983; editor: La obra Cientifica de M.S. Vallarta, 1979, Semblanza de Manuel Sandoval Vallarta, 1988; contbr. articles to profl. jours. Recipient Ignacio Manuel Altamirano Prize, Mexico, 1957; Disting. Service medal U. Nacional Autonoma, 1979; Jose Antonio Alzate prize, Mexico, 1984. Fellow Academia de la Investigacion Cientifica Mexico, Sistema Nacional de Investigadores; mem. Sociedad Mexicana de Fisica, Am. Phys. Soc., AAAS, N.Y. Acad. Scis. Roman Catholic. Home: Retorno de Correggio 8, Mixcoac, 03730 Mexico City Mexico Office: Instituto de Fisica, U Nacional Autonoma, Apdo Postal 20-364, 01000 Mexico City Mexico

MONEGHAN, JOHN EDWARD, aerospace engineer; b. Fremont, Ohio, Oct. 13, 1950; s. Edward Eugene and Mary Ann (Meyers) M.; m. Christine Dawn Moneghan, Feb. 14, 1987; 1 child, Kathleen Dawn. B.S. in Geology, U. Notre Dame, 1972, B.S. in Engring., 1973; M.B.A., Nat. U., 1977. sr. engr. Pacer Systems, Fort Washington, Pa., 1980-83; space systems engr. Gen. Electric Co., Valley Forge, Pa., 1983—. Instr. ARC, Notre Dame, Ind., 1970-73, Fremont, 1968-73. Served to lt. comdr. USN, 1973-79, comdr. USNR, 1979—. Recipient N.Am. Rockwell Aviation award, Naval Air Tng. Command USN, 1973 and various military decorations; Sikorsky Winged S award. Mem. AIAA, ASCE, Nat. Helicopter Assn., Naval Res. Assn. Home: 1955 Rangerbrook Circle Warrington PA 18976

MONEY, ALEXANDER, airline company executive; b. Manchester, Eng., Mar. 26, 1958; s. Alexander and Joan (Mayoh) M. Student pub. schs., Manchester. With cargo reservations dept. SAS Scandinavian Airlines, Manchester, 1977-78, with cargo ops. dept., 1978-79, supr. cargo ops., 1979-82; cargo sales rep. SAS Scandinavian Airlines, Birmingham, Eng., 1982-83; cargo sales mgr. SAS Scandinavian Airlines, Midlands, Eng., 1983-84; passenger sales mgr. SAS Scandinavian Airlines, East Midlands, Eng., 1984-85; mgr. passenger and cargo dist. sales, SAS Scandinavian Airlines, East Midlands and East Anglia, Eng., 1985—; cons. investigator Internat. Air Transport Assn., Midlands, 1984—. Wrestling coach YMCA, Manchester, 1974-87. Mem. Leicester C. of C. and Industry. Mem. Ch. of England. Clubs: Midlands Interline, Skal of Nottingham. Home: 17 Pares Way, Ockbrook Derby DE7 3TJ, England Office: Scandinavian Airlines System, 52-3 Conduit St, London W1R 0AY, England

MONFORT, ELIAS RIGGS, III, management consultant; b. Chgo., Sept. 6, 1929; s. Elias Riggs and Elizabeth (Sebald) M.; B.S., Purdue U., 1952; m. Hathalie Jean Ward, June 8, 1957; children—Stephen, Scott, Jonathan, Christoper. Liaison engr. Douglas Aircraft Co., Santa Monica, Calif., 1952; internat. regional mgr. Cessna Aircraft Co., Wichita, Kans., 1958-64; long-range planning service Stanford Research Inst., Sunnyvale, Calif., 1964-77, strategic mgmt., 1978-87; mng. prin. Monfort Mgmt., 1988—. Bd. regents Cogswell Engring. Coll. Served to capt. USAF, 1952-57; Korea. Mem. Soc. Automotive Engrs., Exptl. Aircraft Assn., Internat. Aerobatic Club, Corp. Planners Assn. (founding), Planning Forum (contbg. editor). Republican. Episcopalian. Clubs: Sequoia Woods Golf and Country. Home: 1609 Honfleur Dr Sunnyvale CA 94087

MONGEON, MARCEL DYDZAK, real estate developer; b. Hamilton, Ont., Can., Dec. 28, 1956; s. Marcel Louis and Joyce (Dydzak) M.; m. Patricia Louise Dodge, July 13, 1984. B of Commerce, McGill U., Montreal, Can., 1978, LLB, BCL, 1982. Lawyer Heenan Blaikie, Montreal, 1984-86; chief operating officer Joymarmon Group, Inc., Hamilton, 1986—. Bd. mem. Hamilton Apt. Assn., 1986—. Mem. Law Soc. Upper Can., Barreau Que., Hamilton Lawyers Assn., Inst. Cert. Computer Profls., Hamilton Dist C. of C. Roman Catholic. Club: University (Montreal). Office: 400 E 42d St, Suite 108, Hamilton, ON Canada L8T 3B1

MONIBA, HARRY FUMBA, vice president of Liberia; b. Ngihema, Kolahun Dist., Lofa County, Liberia, Oct. 22, 1937; came to England, 1981; s. Janga (Sando) M.; m. Minita Kollie, Feb. 28, 1969; children: Harry, Paul Lynn, Alicia Bendu, Gladys Koisay, Clarence Kpehe. B.Sc.Ed. cum laude, Cuttington U. Coll., Suacoco, Liberia, 1964; M.Sc.Ed., SUNY-New Paltz, 1967; Ph.D., Mich. State U., 1975. Tchr. jr. and sr. high schs. Holy Cross Mission, Bolahun, 1965, tchr., registrar, vice prin., 1968-70; research and teaching asst. Mich. State U., East Lansing, research asst., 1972, grad. teaching asst. African Studies Ctr., 1973, research asst., 1973; spl. asst., coordinator for curriculum and research Ministry of Edn., Monrovia, Liberia, 1975-76, dir. research, 1976, sr. dir. internat. corps. Ministry Fgn. Affairs, 1976; first sec., consul Embassy of the Republic of Liberia, Ottawa, Can., 1977-80, Washington, 1976-80; asst. minister European affairs Ministry Fgn. Affairs, Monrovia, Liberia, 1980-81; Liberian ambassador to Gt. Brit. and No. Ireland, Liberian ambassador to Holy See, Rome, 1981-86; v.p. Second Republic of Liberia, 1986—. Recipient All-round Student award Cuttington U. Coll., 1962, Alumni Cert. of award, 1982. Assoc. mem. Liberian Studies Assn., African Studies Assn., Lofa County Tchrs. Assn., Tau Sigma. Episcopalian. Home: Coombe Hill House 176, Coombe Ln W, Kingston-upon-Thames, Surrey KT2 7DE, England Office: Office Vice Pres, Monrovia Liberia *

MONIER, JEAN-MARIE SÉBASTIEN, mathematics educator; b. Marseilles, France, Apr. 19, 1952; s. François Pierre and Marie-Thérèse Monier; m. Pascale Marie Vannet, July 16, 1981; children: Sophie, Hélène. Prof. math. Lycee la Martiniere, Lyon, France, 1978—; cons. Ecole Superieure de Commerce de Lyon, France, 1984-87; prof. Inst. de Chimie et Physique Indsl., Lyon, 1985-87. Author: Les Cahiers De Prepa, 1984, 87. Mem. Math. Assn. Am., Union des Profs. de Speciales. Home: 7 Rue Pascal, 69003 Lyon France Office: Lycee la Martiniere, 41 Rue Antoine Lumiere, 69008 Lyon France

MONJO, JOHN CAMERON, foreign service officer; b. Stamford, Conn., July 17, 1931; s. Ferdinand Nicolas, Jr. and Mayme (Holden Bahin) M.; m. Sirkka Orvokki Kortelainen, Feb. 28, 1964; children: Christina Cameron, Rolf Kortelainen. B.S., U. Pa., 1953. Joined Fgn. Service, Dept. State, 1957; fgn. service officer Phnom Penh, Cambodia, 1958-61; with econ.-comml. sect. Dept. State, Tokyo, 1961-64; with econ.-comml. sect. Dept. State, Washington, 1967-71, country dir. Philippines, 1978-79, dep. asst. sec., 1983-87; detail to U.S. Army, Naha, Okinawa, Japan, 1963-67; polit. officer U.S. embassy, Jakarta, Indonesia, 1971-76, dep. chief of mission, 1982-83; prin. officer U.S. Consulate Gen., Casablanca, Morocco, 1976-78; dep. chief of mission U.S. embassy, Seoul, South Korea, 1979-82; prin. dep. asst. sec. East Asia Bur. Dept. State, 1983-87; U. S. ambassador to Malaysia, Washington, DC, 1987— . Served to lt. USN, 1953-56. Office: Dept of State Kuala Lumpur Washington DC 20520

MONK, SAMUEL HOLT, II, judge; b. Anniston, Ala., July 14, 1946; s. Richard Hunley and Marjorie Louise (Schneider) M.; m. Mary Lou Gibbins, June 11, 1971; children—Carolyn Elizabeth, William Gibbins. B.A., Jacksonville State U., 1969; J.D., U. Ala., 1975. Bar: Ala. 1975, U.S. Dist. Ct. (no. dist.) Ala. 1976, U.S. Supreme Ct., U.S. Tax Ct. 1978, U.S. Supreme Ct. Sole practice, Anniston, 1975-78; asst. dist. atty. 7th Jud. Cir., Anniston, 1977-78, judge, 1979—; dist. judge Calhoun-Cleburne Counties, Anniston, Ala., 1978-79. Bd. dirs. YMCA, Anniston, 1979-86, Choccolocco council Boy Scouts Am., 1980—, Voluntary Action Agy., Anniston, 1981-87; pres. Am. Cancer Soc., Calhoun County, 1984-86, bd. dirs., 1984—; pres, Vol. and Info. Ctr., Calhoun County, 1986. Served to capt. USAR, 1969-72, Vietnam. Mem. ABA, Ala. State Bar Assn., Calhoun County Bar Assn., Ala. Cir. Judges Assn., Ala. Jud. Coll. Faculty Assn., Order of Coif. Democrat. Episcopalian. Clubs: Rotary. Lodges: Masons. Home: 614 Ayers Dr Anniston AL 36201 Office: Cir Ct 7th Cir Ala PO Box 636 Anniston AL 36202

MONNINGER, ROBERT HAROLD GEORGE, ophthalmologist, educator; b. Chgo., Nov. 5, 1918; s. Louis Robert and Katherine (Lechner) M.; m. Anna Evelyn Turnen, Sept. 1, 1944; children—Carl John William, Peter Louis Philip. A.A., North Park Coll., 1939; B.S., Northwestern U., 1941, M.A., 1945; M.D., Loyola U., Chgo., 1953, Sc.D. (hon.), 1968. Diplomate Am. Bd. Cosmetic Plastic Surgery. Intern St. Francis Hosp., Evanston, Ill., 1953-54; resident Presbyterian-St. Luke's, U. Ill. Research and Eye, Va. hosps., 1954-57; mem. leadership council Ravenswood Hosp. Med. Ctr.; instr. chemistry Lake Forest Coll., Ill., 1946-47; instr. biochemistry, physiology Loyola U. Dental Sch., 1948-49; clin. assoc. prof. ophthalmology Stritch Sch. Medicine, Loyola U., Maywood, Ill., 1957-72; practice medicine specializing in ophthalmology Lake Forest, 1957—; prof. dept. surgery Univ. Health Scis. Univ. Health Scis. Chgo. Med. Sch., chmn. dept. Ophthalmology; guest lectr. numerous univs. med. ctrs. U.S., Can., Europe, Central and S.Am., Orient; resident lectr. Klinikum der Goethe-Universitat, Fed. Republic Germany, 1981; mem. panel Nat. Disease and Therapeutic Index; cons. Draize eve toxicity test revision HEW, cons. research pharm. cos. Nat. Assoc. Smithsonian Instn.; bd. dirs. Eye Rehab. and Research Found.; postgrad. faculty Internat. Glaucoma Congress; lectr. Hopital Dieu, Paris; lectr. postgrad. courses for developing nations physicians WHO; life mem. Postgrad. Sch. Medicine U. Vienna; cons. Nat. Acad. Sci.; adv. bd. Madera Del Rio Found. Cons. author Textbook of Endocrinology. Editorial bd. Clin. Medicine, 1958—, EENT Digest, 1958—, Internat. Surgery, 1972—, profl. jours. Served with USMCR, 1941-44. Recipient citation Gov. Bahamas, 1960, Ophthalmic Found. award, 1963, Sci. Exhibit award Ill. State Med. Soc., 1966, Franco-Am. Meritorious citation, 1967, Paris Port No. 1 Am. Legion award, 1967, citation Pres. Mexico, 1968, Sightsaving award Bausch & Lomb, 1968, exhibit award Western Hemisphere Congress Internat. Surgeons, 1968, Research citation Japanese Soc. Ophthalmology, 1969; Barraquer Gold Medallion; Physician's Recognition award AMA, Bicentennial citation Library of Congress Registration Book; meritorious citation Gov. Ill., citation and medal Lord Mayor of Rome, also Pres. of Italy, 1981, Civic Ctr. of Evanston, Ill., 1981, commendation and citation Ill. Gen. Assembly, 1982, cert. of accomplishment Loyola U. Alumni Assn., Chgo., 1983; Catherine White Scholarship fellow, 1945-46. Fellow Internat. Coll. Surgeons (postgrad. faculty continuing edn.), Am. Coll. Angiology, Oxford Ophthal. Congress and Soc. (lectr. 1960-61), Royal Soc. Health, Internat. Acad. Cosmetic Surgery (editorial bd.), Sociedad Mexicana Ortopedia (hon.), C. Puestow Surg. Soc.; mem. AAAs, Internat. Soc. Geog. Ophthalmology (program course coordinator, lectr. ocular electrophysiology VI Internat. Congress, Rio de Janiero), Pan Am. Assn. Ophthalmology, Assn. for Research Ophthalmology, Am. Assn. Ophthalmology, Am. Soc. Contemporary Ophthalmology, Internat. Glaucoma Soc., Ill. Soc. for Med. Research, Ill. Assn. Ophthalmology, Internat. Soc. clin. electrophysiology of Vision (hon., lectr. 1978), Brazilian Soc. Ophthalmology (hon. corr.), German Ophthal. Soc., Internat. Fedn. Clin. Chemists (lectr.), Primum Froum Ophthalmologicum (lectr.), European Ophthal. Soc. (lectr.), Internat. Congress Anatomists (lectr.), Assn. des Diabetologues Francise (lectr.), German Soc. for Internal Medicine (lectr.), Met. Opera Guild, Fedn. Am. Scientists, N.Y. Acad. Scis., Ill. Acad. Scis., AAUP, Nat. Soc. Lit. and Arts, Nat. Hist. Soc., Rush Med. Sch.-Presbyn. St. Luke's Alumni Assn., Sociedad Poblana Oftalmologia (hon, silver placue, commemorative prestige lectr. 1982) (Mex.), Internat. Platform Assn., Cousteau Soc., Sigma Xi, Sigma Alpha Epsilon, Phi Beta Pi, Theta Kappa Psi. Office: 320 E Vine St Lake Forest IL 60045 also: 734 S Oak Knoll Dr Lake Forest IL 60045

MONROCHE, ANDRÉ VICTOR JACQUES, physician; b. Saumur, France, May 31, 1941; s. Maurice and Thérèse (Chevreau) M.; m. Bodet-Pasquier, July 8, 1966; children: Benoît, Sabine, Hélène, Matthieu. MD, Faculté de Médecine, Angers, France, 1970; Degree in Rheumatology, Faculté de Médecine, Paris, 1972. Gen practice spa medicine Villa Forestier, Aix-les-Bains, France, 1970-72; gen. practice rheumatology and sports medicine Cabinet Med., Angers, 1973—. Author: Eléments de Rhumatologie, 1975, Eau et Sport pour votre Santé, 1988; editor-in-chief review Cinésiologie 1980. Club: Panathlon Internat. (Paris) (v.p. 1986, 88). Office: Cabinet Medical, 1 rue d'Alsace, 49100 Angers France

MONROE, BROOKS, investment banker; b. Greenville, S.C., July 24, 1925; s. Clarence Jennings and Edith (Johnson) M.; m. Hilda Marie Meredith, June 30, 1956. B.S. in Commerce, U. Va., 1948, J.D., 1951; grad., Inst. Investment Banking, U. Pa., 1959. Dir. pub. relations Scott, Horner & Co., Lynchburg, Va., 1951-53; sales mgr. Scott, Horner & Co., Richmond, Va., 1953-56; v.p., gen. sales mgr. Scott, Horner & Co., Lynchburg, 1956-59; sales mgr. nat. and underwriting Francis I. duPont & Co., N.Y.C., 1959-61; gen. partner Francis I. duPont & Co., 1961-66, Paine, Webber, Jackson & Curtis, N.Y.C., 1966-69; pres., chief exec. officer Brooks Monroe & Co., Inc., N.Y.C., 1969—; chmn. HHM Corp., Wilmington and Beverly Hills, Calif., 1969—, Bargeland Corp., Phila., 1970—, IGAS Corp., Pitts., 1975—; chmn. PPM Internat., Inc., Spartanburg; S.C.founder, chmn. Execs. Guardian Co., N.Y.C., 1971—; Tchr. U. Va., 1949-51; asso. mem. Am., N.Y. stock exchanges, 1961-72; mem. Pacific Stock Exchange, 1962-66, Chgo. Bd. Trade, 1962-66. Bd. dirs. McIntire Sch. Commerce U. Va. Served with USAAF, 1943-46, PTO. Mem. U. Va. Alumni Assn. (N.Y. pres. 1978-81), Sigma Chi, Delta Sigma Rho, Pi Delta Epsilon, Omicron Delta Kappa, Delta Theta Pi. Republican. Presbyterian. (trustee). Clubs: Boar's Head Sport, (Charlottesville, Va.), Farmington Country (Charlottesville); Bond, City Midday, Union League (N.Y.C.); Quogue (N.Y.) Field, Quogue Beach; Clan Munro (Scotland and U.S.). Home: Ednam Forest Charlottesville VA 22901 Office: #2 Boar's Head Place Charlottesville VA 22901

MONROE, EDWIN WALL, physician, university dean; b. Laurinburg, N.C., Mar. 10, 1927; s. Robert Andrew and Berrie (Bryant) M.; m. Nancy Laura Gaquerel, Mar. 14, 1953; 1 dau., Martha Lynn. Student, U. Louisville, 1945-46; B.S., Davidson Coll., 1947; post grad., U. N.C. Sch. Medicine, 1947-49; M.D., U. Pa., 1951. Intern Med. Coll. Va. Hosp., Richmond, 1951-52; resident internal medicine N.C. Meml. Hosp., U. N.C., 1952-56, chief resident, asst. in medicine, 1955-56, instr. medicine, 1956-57; practice medicine specializing in internal medicine Greenville, N.C., 1956-68; dean Sch. Allied Health and Social Professions, 1968-71; dir. health affairs East Carolina U., 1968-71, vice-chancellor health affairs, 1971-79; asso. dean East Carolina U. (Sch. Medicine), 1979-86; mem. staff Pitt County Meml. Hosp.; exec. dean East Carolina U. Sch. of Medicine, 1986—; mem. regional adv. group N.C. Regional Med. Program, 1970-76; mem. facilities adv. com. N.C. Div. Vocat. Rehab., 1969-74; mem. Gov.'s Adv. Council Comprehensive Health Planning, 1974, Coastal Plains Mental Health Authority, 1969-74; pres. Eastern Area Health Edn. Center, 1974-82, exec. dir., 1982—; mem. N.C. Health Coordinating Council, 1977-85. Del. White House Conf. on Aging, 1981; mem. N.C. Commn. Jobs and Econ. Growth, 1986—, State Health Coordinating Council, Raleigh, 1977-86; Nat. Adv. Environ. Health Scis. Council, Washington, 1980-84. Served with USNR, 1945-46. Recipient Priestly prize U. Pa. Sch. Medicine, 1951. Mem. Pitt County (pres. 1968), N.C. med. soc. (2d v.p. 1986-87), AMA, Assn. Am. Med. Colls., Am. Coll. Physicians (fellow), Sigma Xi. Democrat. Protestant. Club: Greenville (N.C.) Country. Home: 104 W Longmeadow Rd Greenville NC 27858 Office: East Carolina U Sch Medicine Greenville NC 27858

MONROE, GEORGE EASOM, consultation executive; b. Stafford, Va., Aug. 10, 1925; s. George Easom and Elizabeth (Harding) M.; B.S., U. Va., 1954; m. Nancy Lynn Delima, Nov. 20, 1969. Head, calibrations sect. Naval Weapons Lab., Dahlgren, Va., 1947-52; mem. Office of Ordnance Research, Durham, N.C., 1952-53; dep. dir. Electro-Mechanical Labs, White Sands Missile Range, N.Mex., 1953-58; with Planning Research Corp., McLean, Va., 1958-87 , v.p., 1978-87; pres. Gemsys Corp., Melbourne Beach, Fla., 1987—; bd. dirs. Systems Tech. Assocs., Envisions Corp. Served with USN, 1942-46. Mem. Nat. Council Profl. Service Firms (past pres.), Nat. Council Tech. Services Industries. Club: Capitol Hill. Office: 208 E Eau Gallie Blvd Suite 13 Indian Harbour Beach FL 32937

MONROE, HASKELL M., JR., university chancellor; b. Dallas, Mar. 18, 1931; s. Haskell M. and Myrtle Marie (Jackson) M.; m. Margaret Joan Phillips, June 15, 1957; children: Stephen, Melanie, Mark, John. B.A., Austin (Tex.) Coll., 1952, M.A., 1954; Ph.D., Rice U., Houston, 1961. From instr. to prof. Tex. A&M U., 1959-80; asst. dean Tex. A&M U. (Grad. Sch.), 1965-68, asst. v.p. acad. affairs, 1972-74, dean faculties, 1974-80, assoc. v.p. acad. affairs, 1977-80; pres. U. Tex., El Paso, 1980-87; chancellor U. Mo., Columbia, 1987—; instr. Schreiner Inst., Kerrville, Tex., summer 1959; vis. lectr. Emory U., summers 1967, 72; faculty lectr. Tex. A&M U., 1972; alumni lectr. Austin Coll., 1980; dir. Southwestern Bell Telephone Co. Contbr. articles, revs.; editor: Papers of Jefferson Davis, 1964-69; adv. editor: Texana, 1964—; bd. editorial advisers: Booker T. Washington Papers, 1965-85 . Bd. dirs. Brazos Valley Rehab. Center, 1975-77, Salvation Army, El Paso, 1984-87,m Columbia, 1988—, Crime Stoppers of El Paso; trustee Bryan Hosp., 1976-79, chmn., 1979; bd. ch. visitors Austin Coll., 1977-78; deacon First Presbyn. Ch., Bryan, 1961-63, elder, 1965-67, 69-71, 73-74, clk. of session, 1973-74, chmn. pulpit nominating com., 1971-72; mem. presbytery's council Presbytery of Brazos, 1969-71, mem. resources for the 80s steering com., 1978-80. Served with USNR, 1954-56. Recipient Disting. Alumnus award Austin Coll., 1978; also numerous teaching and achievement awards; grantee Social Sci. Research Council; grantee Tex. A&M U.; grantee Huntington Library. Mem. Am. Hist. Assn., Orgn. Am. Historians, So. Hist. Assn., Hist. Found. Presbyn. and Reformed Chs. (pres. 1970-72), So. Conf. Deans Faculties and Acad. Vice Presidents (pres. 1978). Clubs: Country of Mo., Rotary of El Paso (hon.). Home: 3200 Westcreek Circle Columbia MO 65205 Office: U Mo Office of the Chancellor Columbia MO 65211

MONSON, CAROL LYNN, osteopathic physician, psychotherapist; b. Blue Island, Ill., Nov. 3, 1946; d. Marcus Edward and Margaret Bertha (Andres) M.; m. Frank E. Warden, Feb. 28, 1981. B.S., No. Ill. U., 1968, M.S., 1969; D.O., Mich State Coll. Osteo. Medicine, 1979. Lic. physician, Mich., diplomate Am. Bd. Osteo. Gen. Practitioners, Am. Bd. Osteo. Gen. Practice. Expeditor-psychotherapist H. Douglas Singer Zone Ctr., Rockford, Ill., 1969-71; psychotherapist Tri-County Mental Health, St. Johns, Mich., 1971-76; pvt. practice psychotherapy, East Lansing, Mich., 1976-80; intern Lansing Gen. Hosp., Mich., 1979-80; pvt. practice osteo. medicine, Lansing, 1980—; mem. staff Ingham Med. Hosp., Lansing Gen. Hosp., chmn. gen practice, 1987—; field instr. Sch. Social Work, U. Mich., 1973-76; clin. instr. Central Mich. Dept. Psychology, 1974-75; clin. prof. Mich. State U., 1980—; mem. adv. bd. Substance Abuse Clearinghouse, Lansing, 1983-85, Kelly Health Care, Lansing, 1983-85, Americor Health Services, Lansing, 1984—; chairperson dept. gen. practice Lansing Gen. Hosp. Mem. Am. Osteo Assn., Internat. Transactional Analysis Assn., Mich. Assn. Physicians and Surgeons, Ingham County Osteo. Assn., Nat. Assn. Career Women (conv. com. 1984—), Lansing Assn. Career Women. Lodge: Zonta (chmn. service com. Mid Mich. Capital Area chpt.). Avocations: gardening; orchid growing; antique collecting. Office: 3320 W Saginaw St Lansing MI 48917

MONTAG, DAVID MOSES, computer company executive; b. Los Angeles, Apr. 30, 1939; s. Gustave and Esther (Kessler) M.; student UCLA, 1957-61; m. Beverly Edythe Bowden, Sept. 24, 1967; children: Daniel Gershon, Esther Yael, Michael Menachem. Tech. writer L.H. Butcher Co., Los Angeles, 1961; phys. sci. lab. technician East Los Angeles Coll., Monterey Park, 1961—, planetarium lectr., 1963—; owner EDUCOMP, Monterey Park, Calif.,

1980—; mktg. cons. Aquinas Computer Corp.; ednl. cons. for computer-assisted instrn. Bd. dirs. Or Chadash, Inc., Monterey Park, 1968—; v.p., bd. dirs. Coll. Religious Conf., 1968—. Mem. Assn. of Orthodox Jewish Scientists, Laser Inst. Am., AIAA. Home: 729 N Spaulding Ave Los Angeles CA 90046 Office: Box 384 Monterey Park CA 91754

MONTAG, RUDOLF CURT, translator, consultant; b. Mt. Vernon, N.Y., June 6, 1942; s. Rudolf and Margaret Marion (Noll) M.; A.B., Columbia U., 1964; m. Beatrice Liliane Daverio, June 8, 1968; children: Valerie Helen, Carine Beatrice, Paul Rudolf. Documentation cons. missile div. Aerospatiale, Les Mureaux, Paris, 1971-73; translator, cons. mil., space and aeros. div. Compagnie Internat. pour l'Informatique, Vélizy, Paris, 1972—, CII-Honeywell Bull, Paris, 1976—, Compagnie Française des Petroles, 1977—, IBM France/World, 1977—, Siemens France, 1978—, Thomson-CSF T-VT div., 1978—, Electronique Marcel Dassault, 1978-83, Electronique Serge Dassault, 1983—, Honeywell S.A., 1979—, Société d'Etudes des Systèmes d'Automation, 1979—, Société Européenne de Mini-Informatique et de Systèmes, 1979—, Internat. Computers Ltd., 1979-81, La Radiotechnique-Compelec, 1980—, Thomson-CSF-Informatique, 1980—, Sligos, 1982—. Served with AUS, 1965-67. Mem. Assn. Computing Machinery, IEEE, Brit. Computer Soc. (assoc.). Home: Chateau de Brecy, 18220 Les Aix d'Angillon France Office: 22 Ave Mozart, 75016 Paris France

MONTAGNIER, LUC ANTOINE, oncologist; b. Chabris, Indre, France, Aug. 18, 1932; 3 children. Cert. of Studies on Natural Scis., U. Poitiers, France, 1953, BS, 1955; MD, U. Paris, 1960. Asst. Faculté des Scis, Paris, 1955-60; attaché de recherche CNRS, Paris, 1960-63, chargé de recherche, 1963-67, maitre de recherche, 1967-72, dir. research, 1974—; head lab. Institut du Radium, Orsay, France, 1965-72; head viral oncology unit Institut Pasteur, Paris, 1972—, head virology dept., 1982-85, prof., 1974—; dir. virology course Institut Pasteur, 1980-85; mem. responsible research team CNRS; discovered HIV-1 virus, 1983 and HIV-2 virus, 1985. Author: Vaincre le Sida, 1987. Named Chevalier de la Légion d'Honneur, 1984, Commandeur de l'Ordre Nat. du Mérite, 1986. Office: Institut Pasteur, 25 rue du Dr Roux, 75015 Paris France

MONTALENTI, GIUSEPPE, geneticist, former educator; b. Asti, Italy, Dec. 13, 1904; s. Paolo and Bertola Ida M.; m. Luciana Fratini, Mar. 19, 1964 (dec. Oct. 1980). D. Natural Scis., U. Rome, 1926. Asst. prof. zoology U. Rome, 1926-37, U. Bologna, 1937-39; chief dept. zoology Zool. Sta., Aquarium of Naples, 1939-44; prof. genetics U. Naples, 1940-60; prof. genetics U. Rome, 1960-75, prof. emeritus, 1975—; pres. Accademia Nazionale dei Lincei, Rome, 1981-85. Author books including: Storia della biologia e della Medicina, 1962; Introduzione alla Genetica, 1972; L'Evoluzione, 1982. Contbr. articles to profl. jours. Mem. Internat. Union Biol. Scis. (pres. 1958-61). Office: Accademia Nazionale dei Lincei, via della Lungara 10, 00165 Rome Italy

MONTAÑA, JORDI, marketing educator; b. Barcelona, Spain, June 20, 1949; s. Francesc and Carmen (Matosas) M.; 1 child, Roger. Grad., E.T.S.I.I.B., Barcelona, 1971; MBA, Escuela Superior Adminstracion y Direc. Empresas, Barcelona, 1976. V.p. CIT Ballve, Textiles, Barcelona, 1971-75; ptnr. Holdstaff, Cons., Barcelona, 1975-78; prof. mktg. Escuela Superior Administracion y Direc. Empresas, 1976—, assoc. dean, 1982-86, chmn. mktg. dept., 1985—; head. tech. dept. B.C.D. Design Ctr., Barcelona, 1978-80; pres. QUOD, Barcelona, 1983—; vis. prof. Ecole Haute Etudes Commerciales, Paris, 1986—, U. Centro Americana, Managua, Nicaragua, 1986—, San Salvador, El Salvador, 1987—; bd. dirs. CODEH, Barcelona, 1985—; expert UN Indsl. Devel. Orgn., Vienna, 1987—; journalist Diari de Barcelona, 1987. Author: Marketing Policy, 1983, The White Book on Design, 1984, Design Policy and Competitive Advantages, 1986, How to Design a Product, 1988. Active Red Cross Orgn., 1982—. Miro Found. fellow, Barcelona, 1980—. Mem. Colegio Ingenieros Industriales, Am. Mktg. Assn., Acad. Mktg. Sci. (chmn. III world congress 1986), Foment Decorative Arts. Clubs: Centre Excursion, Real Tennis (Barcelona). Office: ESADE, Avenida Pedralbes 60-62, 08034 Barcelona Spain

MONTAND, YVES (YVES LIVI), actor, singer; b. Oct. 13, 1921; m. Simone Signoret, 1951 (dec. 1985). Ed. primary sch., Marseilles, France. Interpreter of numerous famous songs; stage performances in straight plays and variety; films include: Les portes de la nuit, 1946; Marguerite de la nuit, 1955; Aimex-vous Brahms, 1961, My Geisha, 1962, Is Paris Burning, 1966, Grand Prix, 1967, Wages of Fear, 1956, Let's Make Love, 1960, Where the Hot Wind Blows, 1960, Z, 1969, On a Clear Day You Can See Forever, 1970, Tout va bien, 1972, Cesar et Rosalie, 1972, Etat de Siège, Le fils, 1973, Le hasard et la violence; Vincent, François, Paul et les autres, 1974, Le grand escogriffe, 1976, I comme Icare, 1979, Clair de femme, 1979, Le choix des armes, 1981, Tout feu tout flamme, 1981, Garçon, 1983, Jean De Florette, 1986, Manon Des Sources, 1986; author memoirs: Du soleil plein la tete, 1955. Office: 15 place Dauphine, 75001 Paris France *

MONTAUT, ANNIE, linguist, educator; b. Clermont, France, Mar. 7, 1951; d. Montaut Jacques and Hélène (Bourgeade) M.; 1 child, Aurore. BA, MA, U. Paris Sorbonne, 1973; Agregation Lettres, Ecole Normale Superieure Lettres, Tunis, 1974; PhD, Queen's U., 1981. Asst. prof. linguistics Ecole Normale Superieure Lettres, Tunis, 1974-76; tchr. secondary sch. France, 1976-77; asst. prof. lingusitics, lit. theory Jawaharlal Nehru U., New Dehli, India, 1981-87; cons. Ministry of Edn., New Dehli, 1983-85; translator Indian Council Cultural Relations, New Dehli, 1983-87. Co-author: Les Litteratures de L'Inde, 1987; contbr. articles to profl. jours. Gen. sec. Intersyndical Assn., New Dehli, 1983-86; active Groupe de Recherche Relations Actancielles Linguistique, Ctr. de Recherche et d'Etude sur le sous Continent Indien. Mem. Assn. Profs. FrançaisU. Can., Assn. Semiotic Studies, Assn. Les Amis de Cerisy, Assn. Etude Celiniennes, Soc. de Linguistique de Paris, Dhrupad Soc. Office: Inalco, Pl Mal Delattre de Tassigny, 75016 Paris France

MONTE, SALVATORE JOSEPH, polymer chemicals manufacturing company executive; b. Bklyn., Sept. 18, 1939; s. Michael Salvatore and Antoinette A. (Gentile) M.; B.C.E., Manhattan Coll., 1961; M.S. in Polymeric Materials, Poly. Inst. N.Y., 1969; m. Erika Gertraud Spiegelhalder, Oct. 14, 1961; children—Michelle Marie, Deborah Frances, Denise Christine, Eric Michael. Asst. supt. Turner Constrn. Co., N.Y.C., Phila., 1961-64; project mgr. Blaize Constrn. Co., Eastchester, N.Y., 1964-66; v.p. Kenrich Petrochems., Inc., Bayonne, N.J., 1966-69, exec. v.p., 1969-79, pres., 1980—, trustee pension fund, 1976—; mgmt. trustee Oil, Chem. and Atomic Workers Local 8-406 Welfare Fund. Bd. dirs. United Fund, 1970, Jobs of Bayonne, 1980; v.p., sec. South Ganon-Forest Hills Home-owners Assn., 1971-74. Registered profl. engr., N.Y. State, N.J. Mem. Soc. Plastics Engrs. (div. dir. 1980), Soc. Plastics Industries, Am. Chem. Soc. (rubber div.), N.Y. Federated Soc. Coatings Tech., N.Y. (chmn. bd. 1976), Phila., Boston, Blue Ridge, S.E. Ohio rubber groups, Soc. Rheology, Am. Def. Preparedness Assn., AAAS, Bayonne C. of C., Phi Kappa Theta, Chi Epsilon. Republican. Roman Catholic. Clubs: Richmond County Country; Bayonne Rotary (dir. 1974-77, pres. 1981). Contbr. numerous articles to profl. publs. and mags., chpts. to books on interfacial tech. Patentee in U.S. and 22 fgn. countries on monoalkoxy, chelated, coordinated and neoalkoxy titanate and zirconate coupling agts., cumyl phenol derivatives.

MONTERO, DARREL MARTIN, sociologist, social worker; b. Sacramento, Mar. 4, 1946; s. Tony and Evelyn (Hash) M.; m. Tara Kathleen McLaughlin, July 6, 1975; children: David Paul, Lynn Elizabeth, Laura Ann. AB, Calif. State U., 1970; MA, UCLA, 1972, PhD, 1974. Postgrad. researcher Japanese-Am. Research Project UCLA, 1971-73, dir. research, 1973-75; assoc. head Program on Comparative Ethnic Studies, Survey Research Ctr. UCLA, 1973-75; asst. prof. sociology Case Western Res. U., Cleve., 1975-76; asst. prof. urban studies, research sociologist Pub. Opinion Survey, dir. urban ethnic research program U. Md., College Park, 1976-79; assoc. prof., dir. urban ethnic research program Ariz. State U., Tempe, 1979—; cons. research sect. Viewer Sponsored TV Found., Los Angeles, Berrien E. Moore Law Office, Inc., Gardena, Calif., 1973, Bur. for Social Sci. Research, Inc., Washington. Author: Japanese Americans: Changing Patterns of Ethnic Affiliation Over Three Generations, 1980, Urban Studies, 1978, Vietnamese Americans: Patterns of Resettlement and Socioeconomic Adaptation in the United States, 1979, Social Problems; mem. editorial bd. Humanity and Society, 1978—; contbr. articles to profl. jours. Served with U.S. Army, 1966-72. Mem. Am. Sociol. Assn., Am. Assn. Pub. Opinion Research (exec. council, standards com.), Am. Ednl. Research Assn., Council of Social Work Edn., Soc. Study of Social Problems, D.C. Sociol. Soc., Am. Soc. Pub. Adminstrn., Nat. Assn. Social Workers, Pacific Sociol. Assn. Home: 1444 W Kiva Ave Mesa AZ 85202 Office: Ariz State U Sch Social Work Tempe AZ 85281

MONTGOMERY, G. CRANWELL, U.S. ambassador to Oman; b. Chattanooga, Aug. 24, 1944; s. George Donaldson and Mary Elizabeth (Cranwell) M.; divorced; 1 child, Erynn Elizabeth. B.A., U. Va., 1966; J.D., Vanderbilt U., 1975. Bar: U.S. Ct. Appeals (D.C. cir.). Legis. staff Senator Howard Baker, 1975-80; spl. counsel Senate Majority Leader, 1980-85; U.S. ambassador to Oman 1985—. Served with USN, 1966-72; capt. Res. Mem. ABA, D.C. Bar Assn., Sigma Chi. Office: US Ambassador to Oman care US State Dept Washington DC 20520

MONTGOMERY, HENRY IRVING, financial planner; b. Decorah, Iowa, Dec. 18, 1924; s. Harry Biggs and Martha Grace (Wilkinson) M.; m. Barbara Louise Hook, Aug. 14, 1948; children—Barbara Ruth, Michael Henry, Kelly Ann, Andrew Stuart. Student U. Iowa, 1942-43, 47-48; B.B.A., Tulane U., 1952, postgrad., 1952; postgrad. U. Minn., 1976. Cert. fin. planner, Colo. Field agt. OSS, SSU, CIG, CIA, Central Europe, 1945-47; pres. Nehi Bottling Co., Decorah, Iowa, 1952-64; prin. Montgomery Assocs., Mktg. Cons., Trieste, Italy and Iowa, 1965-72; pres. Planners Fin. Services, Inc., Mpls., 1972—. Author: Race Toward Berlin, 1945. Served with U.S. Army, 1943-46; ETO. Mem. Inst. Cert. Fin. Planners (bd. dirs. 1977-82, pres. 1980-81, chmn. 1981-82, Cert. Fin. Planner of Yr. 1984, chmn. Nat. Products Standards Bd. 1984-88), Nat. Assn. Securities Dealers Dist. Coms., Internat. Assn. Fin. Planning (internat. dir. 1976-81), Mpls. Estate Planning Council, Met. Tax Planning Group (pres. 1984-87), Twin City Fin. Planners (pres. 1976-78), Twin Cities Soc. of Inst. Cert. Fin. Planners, Am. Legion, Beta Gamma Sigma. Lodge: Elks (Decorah). Italian and German langs. Office: Planners Fin Services Inc 3500 W 80th St 670 Minneapolis MN 55431

MONTGOMERY, JOHN WARWICK, legal educator, theologian; b. Warsaw, N.Y., Oct. 18, 1931; s. Maurice Warwick and Harriet (Smith) M.; m. Joyce Ann Bailer, Aug. 14, 1954; children—Elizabeth Ann, David Warwick, Catherine Ann. A.B. with distinction in philosophy, Cornell U., 1952; B.L.S., U. Calif., Berkeley, 1954, M.A., 1958; B.D., Wittenberg U., 1958, M.S.T., 1960; Ph.D., U. Chgo., 1962; Docteur de l'Université, mention Théologie Protestante, U. Strasbourg, France, 1964; LLB, LaSalle Extension U., 1977; diplôme cum laude, Internat. Inst. Human Rights, Strasbourg, 1978; M. Phil. in Law, U. Essex, Eng., 1983. Bar: Va. 1978, Calif. 1979, D.C. 1985, U.S. Supreme Ct. 1981, Eng. 1984; cert. law librarian; diplomate Med. Library Assn.; ordained to Ministry Lutheran Ch., 1958. Librarian, gen. reference service U. Calif. Library, Berkeley, 1954-55; instr. Bibl. Hebrew, Hellenistic Greek, Medieval Latin Wittenberg U., Springfield, Ohio, 1956-59; head librarian, mem. federated theol. faculty Swift Library Div. and Philosophy, U. Chgo., 1959-60; assoc. prof., chmn. dept. history Wilfred Laurier U. (formerly Waterloo Luth. U.), Ont., Can., 1960-64; prof., chmn. div. ch. history, history of Christian thought, dir. European Seminar program Trinity Evang. Div. Sch., Deerfield, Ill., 1964-74; prof. law and theology George Mason U. Sch. Law (formerly Internat. Sch. of Law), Arlington, Va., 1974-75; theol. cons. Christian Legal Soc., 1975-76; dir. studies Internat. Inst. Human Rights, Strasbourg, France, 1979-81; dean, prof. jurisprudence, dir. European program Simon Greenleaf Sch. Law, Anaheim, Calif., 1980—; vis. prof. Concordia Theol. Sem., Springfield, Ill., 1964-67, DePaul U., Chgo., 1967-70; hon. fellow Revelle Coll., U. Calif., San Diego, 1970; rector Freie Fakultaten Hamburg, Federal Republic Germany, 1981-82; lectr. Research Scientists Christian Fellowship Conf. St. Catherines Coll., Oxford U., 1985; Pascal lectr. on Christianity and the Univ., U. Waterloo, Ont., Can., 1987; numerous other invitational functions. Author: The Writing of Research Papers in Theology, 1959; A Union List of Serial Publications in Chicago Area Protestant Theological Libraries, 1960; A Seventeenth-Century View of European Libraries, 1962; Chytraeus on Sacrifice: A Reformation Treatise in Biblical Theology, 1962; The Shape of the Past: An Introduction to Philosophical Historiography, 1962, rev. edition, 1975; The Is God Dead Controversy, 1966; (with Thomas J.J. Altizer) The Altizer-Montgomery Dialogue, 1967: Crisis in Lutheran Theology, 2 vols., 1967, rev. edit., 1973; Es confiable el Christianismo?, 1968; Ecumenicity, Evangelicals, and Rome, 1969; Where is History Going?, 1969; History & Christianity, 1970; Damned Through the Church, 1970; The Suicide of Christian Theology, 1970; Computers, Cultural Change and the Christ, 1970; In Defense of Martin Luther, 1970; La Mort de Dieu, 1971; (with Joseph Fletcher) Situation Ethics: True or False?, 1972; The Quest for Noah's Ark, 1972, rev. edit., 1974; Verdammt durch die Kirche, 1973; Christianity for the Toughminded, 1973; Cross and Crucible, 2 vols., 1973; Principalities and Powers: The World of the Occult, 1973, rev. edit., 1975; How Do We Know There is a God?, 1973; Myth, Allegory and Gospel, 1974; The Inerrant Word of God, 1974; Jurisprudence: A Book of Readings, 1974, 2d edit., 1980; The Law Above the Law, 1975; Cómo Sabemos Que Hay un Dios?; 1975; Demon Possession, 1975; The Shaping of America,11976; Faith Founded on Fact, 1978; Law and Gospel: A Study for Integrating Faith and Practice, 1978, rev. edit., 1986; Slaughter of the Innocents, 1981; the Marxist Approach to Human Rights: Analysis & Critique, 1984; Human Rights and Human Dignity, 1986. Editor: Lippincott's Evangelical Perspectives, 7 vols., 1970-72; International Scholars Directory, 1973; contbg. editor: Christianity Today, 1965-84; Films: Is Christianity Credible?, 1968; In Search of Noah's Ark, 1977; Defending the Biblical Gospel, 1985 (11 videocassette series) Contbr. articles to acad., theol., legal encys. and jours., chpts. to books. Nat. Luth. Ednl. Conf. fellow, 1959-60; Can. Council postdoctoral sr. research fellow, 1963-64; Am. Assn. Theol. Schs. faculty fellow, 1967-68. Fellow Académie de Gastronomie Brillat-Savarin (Paris); Victoria Inst. (London), Am. Sci. Affiliation (nat. philosophy sci. and history sci. commn. 1966-70); mem. World Assn. Law Profs., Am. Soc. Internat. Law, ABA, Internat. Bar Assn., Calif. Bar Assn. (human rights commn. 1980-83), Union Internat. des Avocats, Nat. Assn. Realtors, Tolkien Soc. Am., N.Y. C.S. Lewis Soc., Am. Hist. Assn., Soc. Reformation Research, Creation Research Soc., Luth. Acad. for Scholarship, Tyndale Fellowship (Eng.), Am. Theol. Library Assn., Bibliog. Soc. U. Va., Evang. Theol. Soc., Middle Temple and Lincoln's Inn (barrister mem.), Internat. Wine and Food Soc., Société des Amis des Arts (Strasbourg), Chaîne des Rôtisseurs (chevalier), Wig & Pen (London), Club des Casseroles Lasserre, Ordre des Chevaliers du Saint-Sepulcre Byzantin (commandeur), Phi Beta Kappa, Phi Kappa Phi, Beta Phi Mu. Address: 1 rue de Palerme, 67000 Strasbourg France also: 3855 E LaPalma Ave Anaheim CA 92807 also: Flat 9, 4 Crane Ct, Fleet St, London EC4, England

MONTGOMERY, LARRY DALE, biologist; b. Longview, Wash., Feb. 24, 1950; s. Edward Dale and Wanda Lea (Collins) M.; m. Linda Fay Hensley, Nov. 17, 1978 (div. Dec. 1980). BA in Biol. Scis., Cen. Wash. State Coll., 1973. Lic. fissionable material handler; cert. pool/spa operator. Radiochemistry technician Westingtonhouse Hanford, Richland, Wash., 1974-76; research asst. Pacific Northwest Labs., Richland, 1976-81; prin. code enforcement officer Municipality of Anchorage, 1982-83, environ. sanitarian, 1985-86; engring. tech. Alaska Environ. Control Services, Anchorage, 1983, dir. environ. service, 1984-85; sanitarian dist. Municipality of Anchorage, 1986-87; with dept. Health Services Environ. Health Services, Albany, Ore., 1988—. Contbr. articles to profl. jours. Mem. Internat. Assn. Milk, Food, and Environ. Sanitarians, AAAS, Am. Pub. Health Assn., Nat. Environ. Health Assn. (registered sanitarian), Nat. Geog. Soc., N.Y. Acad. Scis., Conf. for Food Protection. Democrat. Baptist. Home: 4987 Powers Ave NW Albany OR 97321

MONTGOMERY, ROBERT LEW, psychology educator; b. Grayson, Ky., July 2, 1941; s. Everett DeForest and Ruth Agnes (Glass) M.; m. Sallie Stewart Meier, Sept. 6, 1966 (dec. Feb. 1978); m. Frances Marie Haemmerlie, June 16, 1979; children—Melissa, John. B.A., Bethany (W.Va.) Coll., 1964; M.S., Okla. State U., 1967, Ph.D., 1968. Research asst. Okla. State U., 1964-68; asst. prof. psychology U. Mo.-Rolla, 1968-73, assoc. prof., 1973-78, prof., 1978—, head dept. psychology, 1975-81; vis. prof. U. Fla., 1974-75. Contbr. articles to profl. jours. Recipient Phi Kappa Phi Disting. Service award U. Mo.-Rolla, 1975; Nat. Cambell fellow, 1963-64; NDEA fellow, 1967-68; U. Mo.-Rolla Asst. Prof. grantee, 1969, 71. Mem. Am. Psychol. Assn., Psychonomic Soc., Midwestern Psychol. Assn. (local rep. 1981—), Southwestern Psychol. Assn. (council 1984), Mo. Psychol. Assn. Episcopalian. Club: Oak Meadows (Rolla). Home: Route 4 Box 322 Rolla MO 65401 Office: U Mo Dept Psychology Rolla MO 65401

MONTGOMERY, ROBERT LOUIS, systems engineer, physical chemist; b. San Francisco, Nov. 20, 1935; s. Louis Clyde and Fay Elythe (Myers) M.; m. Patricia Helen Cook, Mar. 17, 1962; children: Cynthia Elaine, Jeanette Louise, Cecelia Irene, Howard Edwin. BS in Chemistry, U. Calif., Berkeley, 1956; PhD in Phys. Chemistry, Okla. State U., 1975. Registered profl. engr., Kans., Tex., Colo. Phys. chemist U.S. Bur. Mines, Reno, 1956-62; NSF predoctoral fellow Okla. State U., Stillwater, 1963-66; sr. engr. Boeing Co., Wichita, Kans., 1966-75; postdoctoral fellow Rice U., Houston, 1975-77, sr. research assoc., 1982-84; tech. data engr. M.W. Kellogg Co., Houston, 1977-82; staff engr. Martin Marietta, Denver, 1984—. Contbr. articles to profl. jours. Mem. Am. Chem. Soc., Profl. Engrs. Colo., Am. Soc. for Metals, AIAA, Sigma Xi. Lodge: Moose. Home: 9933 Fairwood St Littleton CO 80125 Office: Martin Marietta Astronautics Group PO Box 179 Denver CO 80201

MONTIAGUE, CIRIACO MONSALE, surgeon; b. Miagao, Iloilo, Philippines, June 18, 1924; parents: Gerardo Jalandoni Montiague and Nicolasa Monsale; m. Fe Rodrigues Montiague, June 25, 1964; children: Maria Lynda, Reynaldo, Lowella, Raul. MD, U. St. Tomas, Manila, Philippines, 1953. Resident gen. practice MacNeal Meml. Hosp., Berwyn, Ill., 1956; resident, surgery St. Joseph Hosp., Lexington, Ky., 1960; med. dir. Adecor Emergency Hosp., Maco, Davao, Philippines, 1961-78; dir. med. services U. Mindanao, Davao City, Philippines, 1978—; instr. legal medicine and med. jurisprudence U. Mindanao, Coll. Law, Davao City, 1986—; bd. dirs. Rural Bank of Mabini, Maco, Davao, 1976—. Recipient Philippine Govt. and Vet. Legion award, 1967, Merit award U. St. Tomas Alumni Assn., 1978, Testimonial of Service award Davao Med. Soc., 1985. Mem. Philippine Med. Assn. (Plaque of Merit award for Outstanding Physician Davao del Norte, 1973), Philippine Occupational and Indsl. Med. Assn. (pres. Davao chpt. 1986-88; Presdl. award, 1981), Acad. Family Physicians of Philippines (Family Physician of the Yr. award, 1987), Davao del Norte Med. Soc. (pres. 1971-73). Roman Catholic. Lodge: Rotary (pres. Central Davao club, 1987-88; Rotarian of the Yr. award, 1985). Home: 1 Ruby St, Marfori Subdiv, Davao City Philippines Office: UM Multitest & Med Ctr, P Reyes St, Davao City Philippines

MONTY, IB, museum director; b. Frederiksberg, Denmark, Dec. 10, 1930; s. Erik and Anne (Michelsen) M.; m. Lise Mørck, Nov. 26, 1955; children: Kristine, Kasper. MA, U. Copenhagen, 1956. Asst. curator Danish Film Mus., Copenhagen, 1957-60, dir., 1960—; critic (newspaper) yllands-Posten, Arhus, Denmark, 1958—; asst. tchr. U. Copenhagen, 1963-66; mem. The Film Bd., Copenhagen, 1965-69. Editor-in-chief Kosmorama, 1960-67; editor, translator: Leonardo da Vinci: Notes, 1953; editor (3 vol. anthology) Se-det er film I-III, 1964-66; contbr. articles to profl. jours. Home: Vesterbrogade 15A, DK-1620 Copenhagen V Denmark Office: Det Danske Filmmuseum, Store Søndervoldstrede, DK-1419 Copenhagen K Denmark

MONYAK, WENDELL PETER, pharmacist; b. Chgo., Sept. 14, 1931; s. Wendell and Mary Elizabeth M.; m. Lorraine Mostek, Aug. 29, 1964. BS in Chemistry, Roosevelt U., 1957; BS in Pharmacy, St. Louis Coll. Pharmacy, 1961. Asst. chief pharmacist Little Co. of Mary Hosp., Chgo., 1961-66; chief pharmacist MacNeal Meml. Hosp., Berwyn, Ill., 1966-72; dir. pharmacy Ill. Masonic Med. Ctr., Chgo., 1972, dir. pharm. services, 1972-87; dir. pharmacy services St. Anne's Hosp., Chgo., 1987—; teaching assoc. U. Ill., 1972-87. Author: Hospital Formulary and Therapeutic Guide for Residents and Interns, 1974, 3d edit. 1986. Pres., chmn. bd. dirs. Bohemian Home for Aged, 1986. Served with M.C., AUS, 1955-57. Mem. Am. Pharm. Assn., Am. Soc. Hosp. Pharmacists, Ill. Pharm. Assn. (Spl. Recignition award), No. Ill. Soc. Hosp. Pharmacists, Chgo. Hosp. Council. Club: Oakbrook Executive. Home: 19 W 059 Chateau N Oak Brook IL 60521 Office: 4950 W Thomas Chicago IL 60651

MONYAKE, LENGOLO BURENG, minister of works Lesotho; b. Thabana Morena, Lesotho, Apr. 1, 1930; s. Bureng Lengolo and Leomile (Kuali) M.; m. Molulela Mapetla, July 13, 1957; children: Bonang, Mophato, Bureng Thabo. B.Sc., Fort Hare, 1950; postgrad. U. Toronto, Can., 1963-64, Carleton U., Can., 1964-65; M.Sc., London Sch. Econs., 1967. Tchr. Transvaal Edn. Dept., Evaton, 1952-61; dir. stats. Lesotho Govt., Maseru, 1969-74, permanent sec., 1974-76, dep. sr. permanent sec., 1976-78, ambassador of Lesotho to Belgium, Brussels, 1979-83, also non-residential ambassador to Luxembourg and the Netherlands; mng. dir. Lesotho Nat. Devel. Corp., Maseru, 1984-87; minister of fgn. affairs, Maseru, 1987-88, minister of works, 1988—; cons. Econ. Commn. for Africa, 1976, UNFPA, N.Y., 1978; dir. Lesotho Bank, Maseru, 1975-78, Lesotho Airways, Maseru, 1976-78. Avocations: tennis; photography; music. Home: PO Box 526, Maseru 100 Lesotho Office: Ministry of Fgn Affairs, Maseru Lesotho

MONZON, CARLOS MANUEL, physician; b. Guatemala, C.A., Dec. 16, 1949; came to U.S., 1977; s. Carlos Manuel and Amparo (Letona) M.; m. Evelyn David, Sept. 26, 1975; children—Carlos Rodolfo, Juan Pablo. M.D., U. San Carlos, Guatemala, 1976. Diplomate Am. Bd. Pediatrics, Am. Bd. Pediatric Hematology and Oncology. Resident in pediatrics U. San Carlos, Guatemala, 1976-77, U. Mo.-Columbia, 1977-80; fellow in pediatric hematology and oncology Mayo Grad. Sch. Medicine, Rochester, Minn., 1980-82; instr. pediatrics U. Mo.-Columbia, 1982-83, asst. prof. child health, 1983—. Contbr. articles to med. jours. Recipient Fritz Kenny Meml. award in pediatric research, Midwest Soc. Pediatric Research, 1981. Fellow Am. Acad. Pediatrics. Home: 4038 Sonora Ct Columbia MO 65201 Office: U Mo Health Scis Ctr Dept Child Health 1 Hospital Dr Columbia MO 65201

MOODY, ANTHONY DAVID, literature educator; b. Shannon, Manawatu, N.Z., Jan. 21, 1932; s. Edward Tabrum and Nora (Gordon) M. BA, U. N.Z., 1951, MA with 1st honors, 1952; BA with 1st class honors, Oxford U., 1955, MA, 1962. Lectr. in English Melbourne U., Australia, 1958-63, sr. lectr. in English, 1964-65; lectr. in English U. York, Eng., 1966-72, sr. lectr. in English, 1972-80, reader in English, 1980-84, prof. lit., 1984—. Author: Virginia Woolf, 1963, The Merchant of Venice, 1964, T.S. Eliot: Poet, 1979, At the Antipodes, 1982, The El Salvador Sequence, 1984. U. N.Z. Shirtcliffe fellow, 1953-55, Nuffield Found. travelling fellow, 1965. Mem. Assn. U. Tchrs., Nat. Poetry Found. Office: U York Dept English, Heslington, York YO1 5DD, England

MOODY, DAVID THOMAS, petroleum company executive; b. Nashville, Jan. 19, 1941; s. David Woodward and Mary Rebecca (Nicks) M.; m. Julia Marcy Mason, Oct. 17, 1981; 1 child, Marcy Nicks. BA, Vanderbilt U., 1963, JD, 1966. Bar: Tenn. 1966, Tex. 1969. Assoc. Baker & Botts, Houston, 1968-76, ptnr., 1977-82; sr. v.p. The Charter Co., Jacksonville, Fla., 1983-84, exec. v.p., 1984-85, pres., chief exec. officer, 1986—, also bd. dirs.; bd. dirs. Am. Banks of Fla. Inc., Jacksonville. Mem. ABA, State Bar Tex., Sigma Chi, Phi Delta Phi. Presbyterian. Clubs: The River, Fla. Yacht (Jacksonville).

MOODY, ELIZABETH ANNE, physicist; b. Portland, Me., Oct. 29, 1948; d. Earl Louis and Margaret Mary (Downing) M. A.B., Simmons Coll., 1971; postgrad., Harvard U., 1973. Data analyst Smithsonian Astrophys. Obs., Cambridge, Mass., 1969; research cons. M.I.T. Instrumentation Lab., Cambridge, 1973-74, Ind. Cons., Boston, 1975-76; research scientist Aerodyne Research, Burlington, Mass., 1977-78, Sci. Applications, Bedford, Mass., 1979-80, U.S. Air Force Geophysics Lab., Bedford, 1981; design/devel. engr. Raytheon Co., Bedford, 1982—; cons. Contbr. articles to profl. jours. Recipient Woman of Future citation Mass. Dept. Edn., 1965; award for courage, honor, leadership Am. Legion, 1966; Community Service commendation United Community Services Mass., 1965; Scholastic Achievement award Mass. Dept. Edn., 1970. Mem. Am. Astron. Soc., Am. Phys. Soc., Astron. Soc. Pacific, Assn. Women in Sci., ACLU, NAACP, NOW, People for Am. Way, Anti-Defamation League, Meml. Soc. N. Eng., Harvard Alumni Kirkland Cosmology (liaison officer). Mem. Ch. of Larger Fellowship, Unitarian Universalist. Home: PO Box 5546 Beverly Farms MA 01915 Office: MSD MS M27-3 Hartwell Rd Bedford MA 01730

MOODY, EVELYN WILIE, consulting geologist; b. Waco, Tex.; d. William Braden and Enid Eva (Holt) Wilie; student Baylor U., 1934-35; B.A. with honors in geology and edn. U. Tex., 1938, M.A. with honors in geology, 1940; children—John D., Melissa L., Jennifer A. Geologist, Ark. Fuel Oil Co., Shreveport, La., New Orleans and Houston, 1942-45; teaching asst. Colo. Sch. Mines, Golden, 1946-47; exploration cons. geologist Gen. Crude

Oil Co., Houston, 1975-77; ind. cons. geologist, Houston, 1977—; exploration cons. geologist Shell Oil Co., Houston, 1979-81; faculty dept. continuing edn. Rice U., Houston, 1978. Cert. profl. geologist. Treas., Sipes Found., 1984, pres., 1985, treas., 1984, editor Sipes Bulletin, 1983-1985 . Recipient Sipes Found. Nat. award for Outstanding Service, 1988, Sipes Houston Chpt. Chmn. award for Outstanding Service to Sipes, 1986. Mem. Am. Assn. Petroleum Geologists, Soc. Ind. Profl. Earth Scientists (sec. 1978-79, vice chmn. 1979-80, chpt. chmn. 1980-81, nat. dir. 1982-85), Geol. Soc. Am., Watercolor Soc. Houston, Art Students League N.Y.C., Art Assn., Am. Inst. Profl. Geologists, Houston Geol. Soc., Pi Beta Phi (nat. officer 1958-60, 66-68), Pi Lambda Theta. Republican. Presbyterian. Contbr. articles to profl. jours.; editor: The Manual for Independence, 1983, The Business of Being a Petroleum Independent (A Road Map for the Self Employed), 1987. author: How (To Try) To Find An Oil Field, 1981. Office: 956 The Main Bldg 1212 Main St Houston TX 77002

MOODY, FLORENCE ELIZABETH, education educator, college dean; b. Penn Yan, N.Y., Sept. 29, 1932; d. James William Southby and Rebecca (Worrall) M.; B.S., SUNY, Geneseo, 1954; M.S., Syracuse (N.Y.) U., 1961; Ed.D. (NDEA fellow), U. Rochester (N.Y.)., 1969. Elem. sch. tchr., N.Y. State, 1954-64, 66-68; coordinator profl. devel. Eastern Regional Inst. Edn., Syracuse, 1969-71; mem. faculty SUNY, Oswego, 1971—, prof. elem. edn., 1978—, asso. dean profl. studies State U. Coll. at Oswego, 1981-86, dean profl. studies, 1986—; mem. N.Y. State Tchr. Edn. Cert. and Practice Bd., 1983—; mem. Tchr. Edn. Conf. Bd., 1982-84. Nat. sec. Nat. Women's Party, 1974-76; bd. dirs. Oswego County Extension Service, 1974-76. Danforth asso., 1978—. Mem. Am. Assn. Colls. Tchr. Edn. (pres. N.Y. State chpt. 1983-84), Assn. Tchr. Educators, Assn. Supervision and Curriculum Devel., Am. Ednl. Research Assn., N.Y. State Assn. Tchr. Educators (sec., exec. bd. 1976-78), Kappa Delta Pi, Pi Lambda Theta, Phi Delta Kappa, Delta Kappa Gamma. Presbyterian. Club: Order Eastern Star. Author reports, curriculum materials in field. Home: 5143 Franklin Ave Oswego NY 13126 Office: SUNY Div Profl Studies Oswego NY 13126

MOODY, GEORGE FRANKLIN, banker; b. Riverside, Calif., July 28, 1930; s. William Clifford and Mildred R. (Scott) M.; m. Mary Jane Plank, Jan. 19, 1950; children: Jeffrey George, Jane Ellen Moody Fowler, John Franklin, Joseph William. Student, Riverside City Coll., 1948-50; grad. with honors, Pacific Coast Banking Sch., 1963. Bus. officer U. Calif., Riverside, 1950-52; with Security Pacific Nat. Bank, Los Angeles, 1953—, dir. personnel, v.p., 1970-71, sr. v.p. inland div. adminstrn., 1971-73, exec. v.p., 1973-78, vice chmn., 1978-80, pres., chief exec. officer, 1985; pres., chief operating officer Security Pacific Corp., Los Angeles, 1985—, also bd. dirs. Chief prin. officer, mem. nat. bd. govs., ARC, chmn. exec. com. 1979-80; bd. dirs. Found., U.S. Olympic Com., chmn. Western region, 1981-84; trustee Calif. Neighborhood Housing Service Found., Jr. Achievement So. Calif.; trustee, mem. exec. com. Pomona Coll.; pres. Los Angeles area council Boy Scouts Am., 1980—; past bd. dirs. Los Angeles Music Ctr. Operating Co., Los Angeles United Way, Calif. Econ. Devel. Corp.; past. bd. dirs., past v.p. Hollywood Presbyn. Med. Ctr., Calif. Econ. Devel. Corp.; past chmn. Music Ctr. Unified Fund, Invest-In-Am.; past trustee Calif. Mus. Found., Com. for Econ. Devel., Washington; past. mem. bd. govs. Calif. Community Found. Mem. Los Angeles C. of C. (past pres.), U.S. C. of C. (bd. dirs.), Colorado River Assn. (pres.), Am. Bankers Assn. (bd. dirs.), Calif. Bankers Assn., Assn. Res. City Bankers, Merchants and Mfrs. Assn. (past chmn.), Performing Arts Council (former gov.). Republican. Clubs: California, Los Angeles Country, Hacienda Country. Office: Security Pacific Corp 333 S Hope St Los Angeles CA 90071 *

MOODY, LAMON LAMAR, JR., civil engineer; b. Bogalusa, La., Nov. 8, 1924; s. Lamar Lamon and Vida (Seal) M.; B.S. in Civil Engring., U. Southwestern La., 1951; m. Eve Thibodeaux, Sept. 22, 1954; children—Lamon Lamar III, Jennifer Eve, Jeffrey Matthew. Engr., Tex. Co., N.Y.C., 1951-52; project engr. African Petroleum Terminals, West Africa, 1952-56; chief engr. Kaiser Aluminum & Chem. Corp., Baton Rouge, 1956-63; pres., owner Dyer & Moody, Inc., Cons. Engrs., Baker, La., 1963—, also chmn. bd., dir. Chmn., Baker Planning Commn., 1961-63. Trustee La. Council on Econ. Edn., 1987-88. Served with USMCR, 1943-46. Decorated Purple Heart; registered profl. engr., La., Ark., Miss., Tex. Fellow ASCE, Am. Congress Surveying and Mapping (award for excellency 1972); mem. La. Engring. Soc. (dir., v.p. 1980-81, pres. 1982-83, Charles M. Kerr award for public relations 1971, A.B. Patterson medal 1981, Odom award for distinguished service to engring. profession, 1986), Profl. Engrs. in Pvt. Practice (state chmn. 1969-70), La. Land Surveyors Assn. (pres. 1968-69, Land Surveyor of Yr. award 1975), Cons. Engrs. Council, Engrs. Joint Council, Research Council of La. (exec. com., trustee public affairs), Baker C. of C. (pres. 1977, Bus. Leader of Yr. award 1975), NSPE (nat. dir. 1982-83), Blue Key. Democrat. Baptist. Clubs: Masons (32 deg., K.C.C.H. 1986), Kiwanis (dir. 1964-65). Home: 3811 Charry Dr Baker LA 70714 Office: 2845 Ray Weiland Dr Baker LA 70714

MOODY, RON, actor, writer; b. London, Jan. 8, 1924; s. Bernard and Kate (Ogus) Moodnick; B.Sc. in Econs., U. London, 1953. Appeared in plays: 6 Years Revue, 1959, Candide, 1960, Oliver, as Shylock in Merchant of Venice, 1967, as Polonius in Hamlet, 1972, as Richard in Richard III, 1978, Iago in Othello, 1981, as Harpagan in Moliere's The Miser; (films) Oliver, 1967, Twelve Chairs, 1970, Dogpound Shuffle, 1973, Wrong is Right, 1981, Where is Parsifal?, 1983; on TV as Inspector Hart in Nobody's Perfect, ABC-TV, 1980, Dial M for Murder, 1981. Served with RAF, 1943-48. Recipient Golden Globe award, 1968; Moscow Golden Bear award as best actor, 1970. Mem. Am. Acad. Motion Picture Arts and Scis., Variety Club of Great Brit., Actors Equity, Screen Actors Guild, Clowns Internat. (pres. 1984), Performing Rights Soc. Author musical comedies: Joey, 1966; Saturnalia, 1970; Move Along Sideways, 1971; The Showman, 1976. Author: The Devil You Don't, 1980; Very Very Slightly Imperfect. Home: Ingleside 41, The Green, London N14, England Office: Eric Glass Ltd, 28 Berkeley Sq, London W1, England *

MOODY, WILLIS ELVIS, JR., ceramic engineer; b. Raleigh, N.C., Mar. 30, 1924; s. Willis Elvis and Inez Marie (McDade) M.; m. Mary Susan McAfee, Mar. 22, 1947 (div. June 1967); children: Susan E., Michael T., Peggy A., Willis Elvis, III, William S.; m. Mildred Elizabeth Smith, Apr. 11, 1987. B.S. in Ceramic Engring, N.C. State U., Raleigh, 1948, M.S., 1949, Ph.D., 1956; postgrad. in Nuclear Metallurgy, Iowa State U., 1957; J.D., Woodrow Wilson Coll. Law, 1979. Bar: Ga. bar; registered profl. engr., Ga. Ceramic engr. Spark Plug div. Electric Auto Lite Co., Fostoria, Ohio, 1949-50; ceramic engr. Lab. Equipment Corp., St. Joseph, Mich., 1950-51; instr. ceramic engring. and metallurgy N.C. State U., Raleigh, 1951-56; faculty Ga. Inst. Tech., Atlanta, 1956-85; prof. ceramic engring. Ga. Inst. Tech., 1960-85; retired 1985; research participant Oak Ridge Nat. Lab., summers 1954-55; cons. to clay and ceramic industries, 1951—. Contbr. articles to tech. jours. Served with AAC, 1943-46, ETO. Decorated Air medal with 2 oak leaf clusters. Fellow Orton Ceramic Found., Am. Ceramic Soc. (trustee 1965-68, dir. Southeastern sect. 1962); mem. Ceramic Ednl. Council (pres. 1963), Am. Soc. Engring. Edn. (chmn. materials div. 1971), Am. Phys. Soc., AAAS, Assn. Applied Solar Energy, Nat. Inst. Ceramic Engrs. (pres. 1980), Am. Assn. Engring. Socs. (gov. 1979-81), Clay Minerals Soc. (councillor 1969-71), Keramos, Sigma Xi, Sigma Pi Sigma, Tau Beta Pi. Home: 1062 N Driud Hills Cir Decatur GA 30033

MOOERS, CHRISTOPHER NORTHRUP KENNARD, physical oceanographer, educator; b. Hagerstown, Md., Nov. 11, 1935; s. Frank Burt and Helen (Miner) M.; m. Elizabeth Eva Fauntleroy, June 11, 1960; children: Blaine Hansen MacFee, Randall Walden Lincoln. BS, U.S. Naval Acad., 1957; MS, U. Conn., 1964; PhD, Oreg. State U., 1969. Postdoctoral fellow U. Liverpool (Eng.), 1969-70; asst. prof. U. Miami (Fla.), 1970-72, assoc. prof., 1972-76; assoc. prof. U. Del., Newark, 1976-78, prof., 1978-79; prof., chmn. dept. oceanography Naval Postgrad. Sch., Monterey, Calif., 1979-86; dir. Stemmis Space Ctr. Inst. for Naval Oceanography, 1986—. Contbr. articles to profl. jours. Served with USN, 1957-64. NSF fellow, 1964-67; NATO fellow, 1969-70; Sr. Queen Elizabeth fellow, 1980. Mem. Am. Geophys. Union (former pres. ocean sci. sect.), Eastern Pacific Oceanic Conf. (chmn. 1979-86), Am. Meterol. Soc., Acoustical Soc. Am., Challenger Soc., Marine Tech. Soc., AAAS, Sigma Xi. Home: 5353 Camp St New Orleans LA 70115 Office: Inst for Naval Oceanography SSC Station MS 39529

MOOLLAN, CASSAM ISMAEL, chief justice of Mauritius; b. Port Louis, Mauritius, Feb. 26, 1927; s. Moollan Ismael Mohamed Moollan and Fatima Nazroo; m. Rassoulbibie Adam, Nov. 12, 1954; children—Oomar, Aisha, Naseem. LL.B., U. London, 1950. Admitted to bar Lincoln's Inn, 1951; created Queen's Counsel, 1969. Dist. magistrate, Mauritius, 1955-58, crown counsel, 1958-64, sr. crown counsel, 1964-66, solicitor gen., 1966-70, judge supreme ct., 1970-78, sr. judge supreme ct., 1978-82, chief justice, 1982—. Collaborating editor Law Reports of Mauritius, 1981—. Acting gov. gen. of Mauritius, 1984, 85, 85-86. Named knight bachelor (U.K.). Club: Port Louis Gymkhana (pres. 1970-75). Avocations: biographies; Indian music; tennis; bridge. Office: Supreme Court, Jules Koenig St, Port Louis Mauritius *

MOON, GORDON AMES, II, former magazine editor; b. Jesup, Ga., Oct. 13, 1915; s. Robert Percy and Clara Barbara (Bowman) M.; B.S. in Chem. Engring., Auburn U., 1938; M.S. in Journalism, U. Wis., 1962; student Coll. of William and Mary, 1959-60, U. Md., 1958-59, U. Ky., 1938, U. Colo., 1962-63; grad. U.S. Army Command and Gen. Staff Coll., 1948; m. Ruby Aileen Thigpen, 1937 (div. Apr. 1953); children: Mrs. Edmund D. Dixon, Mrs. Wilbur H. Hinton; m. Chantal Henriette Mathieu, July 22, 1953; children: Gilberte Moon Suehiro, Nellie Moon Dytrych, Helene Moon Moy, Robert, Nicole Moon. Mem. staff dept. metallurgy U.S. Steel Corp., Ensley, Ala., 1938-40; active duty commn. 2d lt. U.S. Army, 1940, advanced through grades to col., 1954; comdr. 4th F.A. Bn., South Pacific, 1943-45; gen. staff Hdqrs. Army Ground Forces, 1945-47; faculty USAF Command and Staff Sch., 1948-50; gen. staff Allied Forces Central Europe, NATO, 1951-55; faculty U.S. Army Command and Gen. Staff Coll., 1955-58; exec. officer 7th Div. Arty., Korea, 1958-59; press officer Hdqrs. Allied Forces Central Europe-NATO, 1964-67, Hdqrs. Fifth Army, 1967-68; retired, 1968; dir. pub. relations Chgo. Heart Assn., 1969-70; asso. editor Commerce Mag., Chgo., 1971, editor, 1972-82; ret., 1982; tchr. English as second lang. Ill. Sch. Dist. 113 and Arroyave Acad. Decorated Legion of Merit, Bronze Star. Mem. Ret. Officers Assn., Am. Philatelic Soc. Contbr. articles in mil., bus. field to periodicals. Home: 1163 Ridgewood Dr Highland Park IL 60035

MOON, LYNNE HARA, personnel and training executive; b. Honolulu, Dec. 3, 1950; d. James and Gladys (Nakama) Hara. B.A. in Communications and Sociology magna cum laude, U. Wash., 1972; M.A., U. Hawaii, 1979. Research assoc. Hawaii Employers Council, Honolulu, 1976-77; personnel/tng. mgr. Liberty House, Honolulu, 1979-80, employee relations mgr., 1980-81; employee relations and mgmt. devel. mgr. Duty Free Shoppers, Honolulu, 1981-82, corp. dir. tng. and devel., 1982—. Bd. dirs. Jr. Achievement, Honolulu, 1982-84, advisor, 1976; coach J. Roger Basketball League, Honolulu, 1973. Wash. Advt. Scholar, 1972; East-West Ctr. degree scholar, 1972-74. Mem. Women in Communications, Am. Soc. Personnel Adminstrs., Am. Soc. Tng. and Devel., Internat. Platform Assn., Phi Beta Kappa, Alpha Kappa Delta, Alpha Lambda Delta. Democrat. Address: 5340 Liwai St Honolulu HI 96821 Office: Duty Free Shoppers 655 Montgomery 18th Floor San Francisco CA 94111 Office: 655 Montgomery St 18th Floor San Francisco CA 94111

MOON, WILLIAM BYRD, clinical psychologist; b. Athens, Ga., July 7, 1943; s. Paul Sanders and Betty (Winn) M.; children from previous marriage: M. Michelle, William M.; m. Frances Lynn Richards, Nov. 19, 1983; children: Whitney Anne, Paul Eugene. AB, Armstrong State Coll., Savannah, Ga., 1970; MSW, U. Ga., 1972; PhD, Fla. Inst. Tech., 1984. Asst. dir. Chatham County Day Ctr., Savannah, 1972-73; dir. social services Anneewakee Hosp., Douglasville, Ga., 1973-75; dir. child and adolescent service Pineland MH/MR Programs, Statesboro, Ga., 1975-78, dir. M.H. services, 1978-81; exec. dir. Youth Estate, Inc., Brunswick, Ga., 1981-84; staff psychologist Anneewakee Hosp., Douglasville, Ga., 1984-86; pvt. practice Smyrna and Dallas, Ga., 1986—; cons. Bulloch Meml. Hosp., Statesboro, 1977-79; instr. St. Leo Coll., Hinesville, Ga., 1979, Ga. So. Coll., Statesboro, 1980, Armstrong State Coll., Savannah, Ga., 1972-73, Tift Coll., Annewakee Ctr., Douglasville, 1984—. Served to E-5 U.S. Army, Vietnam. Mem. Am. Psychol. Assn., Ga. Psychol. Assn., Soc. Personality Assessment. Episcopalian. Lodge: Optimist. Home: 3394 Spinnaker way Acworth GA 30101 Office: 4015 S Cobb Dr Suite 140 Smyrna GA 30080

MOONEY, LORI, county official; b. Atlantic City, Aug. 22, 1929; d. Joseph Aloysius and Alice Marie Inemer; m. Charles H. Calvi (div.); children: Joseph P., Stephen C., Christina L.; m. Thomas Christopher Mooney; children: Thomas C., Timothy C. Service rep. Bell Telephone Co., Atlantic City, 1950-58; sr. evaluator U.S. Census Bur., N.J., 1960-63; coordinator Nat. Small Bus. Com. for Johnson and Humphrey, Washington, 1964; owner, mgr. Lori Mooney & Co., Realtors, Atlantic County, N.J., 1965-77; commr. Atlantic County Bd. Elections, from 1970, also chmn. 5 yrs.; county clk. County of Atlantic, Mays Landing, 1978—; mem. Active Corps Execs., Nat. SBA; chmn. county clk. liaison com. N.J. Supreme Ct., 1984-86. Del. Democratic Nat. Conv., 1972, 76, 84, 88; mem. study team N.J. Div. Youth and Family Services, 1982; mem. U.S. Senator Bill Bradley's Citizen Adv. Com. Recipient Woman of Achievement award N.J. Fedn. Bus. and Profl. Women, 1985. Mem. Internat. Platform Assn., Internat. Assn. Clks., Recorders, Election Ofcls. and Treas. (N.J. dir. 1988—), Atlantic County Realtors Assn., Bus. and Profl. Women Atlantic County (scholarship chmn. 1982-85), County Officers Assn. N.J. (bd. dirs. 1978—), N.J. Assn. County Clks. (chmn. 1984-86), N.J. Assn. Realtors, Nat. Assn. Realtors, N.J. League Municipalities, Assn. Records Mgrs. and Administrs., Atlantic City Women's C. of C., Nat. Assn. Female Execs. Home: 62 E Wright St Pleasantville NJ 08232 Office: Atlantic County Clks Office Main St Mays Landing NJ 08330

MOONEY, PATRICK JOSEPH, research gerontologist, biochemist; b. Chgo., July 21, 1930; s. Hugh Nicholas and Dorothy (Montgomery) M.; B.Sc., Roosevelt U., Chgo., 1965; children—Mary Kimera, Michael Kevin, Mary Kathleen. Constrn. and devel. engr., Chgo., 1950-64; archtl. supt. U. Ill., Chgo., 1964-67; bus. mgmt. systems cons., Chgo. and San Diego, Calif., 1969-76; co-founder, pres. Supernutrition Life-Extension Research, Inc., San Francisco, 1976—, Forever Young, San Francisco, 1977—; research and teaching assoc. Am. Inst. Biosocial Research, Tacoma, 1979—; founder, dir. Inst. Human Ecology, San Francisco, 1980-81; cons. balancing body chemistry for life-extension. Recipient award for outstanding contbns. to field of nutrition, Internat. Coll. Applied Nutrition, 1980, Manilla Med. Soc., 1984. Author: Supernutrition, the Answer to Aging, Wrinkles and the Degenerative Diseases, 1978; (with Hans J. Kugler) A Computerized Diet Analysis and Health Risk Evaluation, 1979.

MOOR, JOAN THORNTON ROTHWELL (MRS. EDGAR JACQUES MOOR), biochemist; b. Lynn, Mass., Feb. 19, 1921; d. Paul Taylor and Adeline (Magrane) Rothwell; A.B., Vassar Coll., 1942; S.M., Mass. Inst. Tech., 1945; m. Edgar Jacques Moor, Aug. 5, 1950. Instr., Vassar Coll., Poughkeepsie, N.Y., 1946; research asst. Children's Hosp., Boston, 1947-48; research asst. New Eng. Deaconess Hosp., Boston, 1949-51; staff div. sponsored research M.I.T., Cambridge, 1952-77; cons., author, 1977—; treas., dir. Multinational Bus. Assos., Inc., Cambridge, 1967-80. Fellow Internat. Acad. Law and Sci.; mem. Am. Chem. Soc., AAAS, Boston Council Fgn. Relations, Inc. New Eng. Council Latin Am. Studies (hon.), Sigma Xi. Republican. Roman Catholic. Contbr. articles to profl. jours. Home: Box 655 Lincoln MA 01773

MOORCOCK, MICHAEL JOHN, author; b. Mitcham, Surrey, Eng., Dec. 18, 1939; s. Arthur and June (Taylor) M.; m. Hilary Bailey, 1962; children—Sophia, Katherine, Max. Editor, Tarzan Adventures juvenile mag., 1965-68; editor, writer Sexton Blake Library, 1959-61; editor, phamphleteer Liberal Party Eng., 1962-63; editor, pub. New Worlds, 1969-74; author many sci. fiction books and edited collections, also short stories; recent novels: Byzantium Endures, 1981, The Entropy Tango, 1981, The Warhouse and the World's Pain, 1981, The Brothel in Rosenstrasse, 1982, The Bane of the Black Sword, 1984, The Silver Warriors, 1985, The Dragon in the Sword, The End of All Swords, The Ice Schooner, The Sword of the Dawn, The Vanishing Tower, Stormbringer, others; series include the Dancers at the End of Time group, The History of Runestaff. Recipient Nebula award for Behold the Man, 1967; Brit. Fantasy Soc. award, Arts Council Great Britain award for New Worlds, 1967; Derleth award for Knight of Swords, 1974, for The King of the Swords, 1973, Jade Man's Eyes, 1974, Sword and the Stallion, 1975, The Hollow Lands, 1976; numerous other awards for excellence in writing. *

MOORE, ALMA C., publishing executive; b. Cin.; d. Henry Paul and Helena Anne (Link) Clausing; m. Roy Moore, Jan. 14, 1961. Student, Stephens Coll., Parsons Sch. Design, New Sch. Social Research, N.Y.C. Women's editor TV Guide mag., N.Y.C., 1962-70; dir. advt., promotion and pub. relations Yves Saint Laurent Parfums, 1971-72; v.p., promotion and editorial dir. Viva/Omni mags., 1974-80; dir. mktg. communication Redbook mag., 1980-83; editor, pub. Woman Entrepreneur mag., 1983-85; pres. Alma C. Moore, Mag. Cons., N.Y.C., 1983—. Mem. ind. jud. screening panel N.Y.C. Civil Ct. Judges Democratic Com., 1985. Mem. Nat. Trust Hist. Preservation, Advt. Women N.Y., Women in Communications (N.Y. chpt.), NOW, Nat. Women's Polit. Caucus, League of Women Voters, Civil Liberties Union. Democrat. Club: Women's City of N.Y. (bd. dirs.). Home and Office: 319 E 53rd St New York NY 10022

MOORE, A(LVIN) C(RAWFORD), JR., investment analyst; b. Sylva, N.C., Sept. 14, 1943; s. Alvin Crawford and Breyl (Hooper) M.; m. Susan Bryson, Aug. 12, 1966 (div. 1970); m. Joan Lorberbaum, Dec. 29, 1971; 1 child, Brett Crawford. B.B.A., Wake Forest U., 1964; J.D., U. N.C., 1967. Bar: N.C. 1967. Dir. instl. research Reynolds Securities, Inc., N.Y.C., 1968-75; pres. Dunvegan Assocs., Inc., N.Y.C., 1975-85; sr. v.p., dir. research Argus Research Corp., N.Y.C., 1985—; dir. Dunvegan Assocs.; gen. ptnr. Sylva Ptnrs., 1979—; bd. dirs. Biltmore Capital Corp. Served with USAF, 1966-70. Mem. ABA, N.Y. Soc. Security Analysts, Nat. Assn. Security Dealers, Oil Analyst Group of N.Y., U.S. Tae Kwon Do Assn. Republican. Lutheran. Clubs: Union League, Metropolitan, N.Y. Stock Exchange Luncheon. Avocations: fitness, music, automobiles. Home: Box 318 Rt 1 Sherman CT 06784 Office: Argus Research Corp 17 Battery Pl New York NY 10004

MOORE, ARCH A., JR., governor of West Virginia; b. Moundsville, W.Va., Apr. 16, 1923; s. Arch A. and Genevieve (Jones) M.; m. Shelley S. Riley, 1949; children—Arch A. III, Shelley Wellons Moore Capito, Lucy St. Clair Moore Durbin. Student, Lafayette Coll., 1943; A.B., W.Va. U., 1948, LL.B., 1951. Bar: W.Va. Practice law W.Va., 1951—; mem. W.Va. Ho. of Dels., 1952, 85th-90th Congresses W.Va., 1957-69; gov. State of W.Va., 1969-77, 85—. Republican party candidate for U.S. Senate, 1978, for gov. of W.Va., 1980. Mem. ABA, W.Va. Bar Assn. Office: Office of Gov State Capitol Charleston WV 25305

MOORE, BILLIE LEE, transportation executive; b. Denison, Tex., Sept. 15, 1931; s. Emery Wood and Bethel (Jackson) M.; m. Doris Stringer, Nov. 4, 1951; children: Sondra Clare, James Curtis. BBA with honors, U. North Tex. (name formerly North Tex. State U)., 1957, MBA, 1971. Supply officer GSA, Ft. Worth, 1958-62, inventory mgr., 1963-68, mgmt. analyst, 1969-79; traffic mgr. GSA, 1980-84, zone mgr., 1984—; instr. bus. Tarrant County Jr. Coll., Ft. Worth, 1972—; Execs. on Campus speaker North Tex. State U., 1988. Mem. Friends of Weatherford Pub. Library, 1986, Nature Conservancy, Austin, Tex., 1986. Recipient Community Service award United Fund. Mem. Fed. Bus. Assn. (chmn. pub. affairs 1964, chmn. pub. relations com. 1965, cert. of Achievement, 1964), Fine Arts Assn., Sierra Club, Nat. Wildlife Fedn. Lutheran. Clubs: Whirl-A-Ways (Weatherford) (pres. 1979-80), Toastmasters (Ft. Worth) (v.p. 1974-75).

MOORE, BOB STAHLY, communications executive; b. Pasadena, Calif., July 3, 1936; s. Norman Hastings and Mary Augusta (Stahly) M. Student, U. Mo., 1954-58, MIT, 1958-62. News dir. WPEO, Peoria, Ill., 1958-60, KSST, Davenport, Iowa, 1960-62, WIRE, Indpls., 1962-64, WCFL, Chgo., 1964-67; White House corr. Metromedia, Inc., Washington, 1967-71; news dir. Gateway Communications, Altoona, Pa., 1972-74; Washington Bur. chief MBS, 1974-76; v.p. news MBS, Arlington, Va., 1976-78; White House corr. MBS, 1978-81; dir. communications Fed. Home Loan Bank Bd., Washington, 1981-85; spl. asst. to bd. govs. Fed. Res. System, Washington, 1985—. Active ARC. Served with USAF, 1961-63. Recipient profl. awards Ind. News Broadcasters, 1963, Ill. News Broadcasters, 1965, UPI, 1960, 63, 65, AP, 1956, 58, 61, 65, 67, Mo. News Broadcasters, 1956, 61. Mem. Radio and Television News Dirs. Assn. (Profl. award), White House Corrs. Assn., State Dept. Corrs. Assn., Radio-Television Corrs. Gallery (U.S. Capitol), Chgo. Council on Fgn. Relations, Pub. Relations Soc. Am., Nat., Washington, Chgo. press clubs, U.S. Jr., Mo., Ill. chambers commerce, Sigma Delta Chi. Presbyterian. Home: 817 Crescent Dr Alexandria VA 22302 Office: 20th and Constitution NW Washington DC 20551

MOORE, BRIAN, writer; b. Belfast, No. Ireland, Aug. 25, 1921; came to U.S., 1960; s. James Bernard and Eileen (McFadden) M.; m. Jean Denney, Oct. 1967; 1 son, Michael. Grad., St. Malachy's Coll., 1939. Author: The Lonely Passion of Judith Hearne, 1955, The Feast of Lupercal, 1957, The Luck of Ginger Coffey, 1960, An Answer From Limbo, 1962, The Emperor of Ice-Cream, 1965, I Am Mary Dunne, 1968, Fergus, 1970, The Revolution Script, 1971, Catholics, 1972, The Great Victorian Collection, 1975, The Doctor's Wife, 1976, The Mangan Inheritance, 1979, The Temptation of Eileen Hughes, 1981, Cold Heaven,1983, Black Robe, 1985, The Color of Blood, 1987. Recipient Que. Lit. prize, 1958, U.S. Nat. Arts and Letters award, 1961, Fiction award Gov.-Gen. Can., 1961, 75, W.H. Smith award, 1973, James Tait Black Meml. award, 1975, Heinemann award Royal Soc. Lit., 1986; Sunday Express Book of Yr. award, 1987; Guggenheim fellow, 1959; Can. Council sr. fellow, 1962, 76; Scottish Arts Council Internat. fellow, 1983. Office: care Curtis Brown 10 Astor Pl New York NY 10003

MOORE, DANIEL EDMUND, educational administrator; b. Pitts., Dec. 31, 1926; s. John Daniel and Alma Helen (Goehring) M.; B.S.Ed., Duquesne U., 1949, M.Ed., 1952; postgrad. California (Pa.) State Coll., 1954-56, U. Pitts., 1958-59, Mt. Mercy Coll., 1959-60, Cath. U. Am., 1966, W.Va. U., 1970-72; m. Rose Marie Blunkosky, Nov. 11, 1949; children—Catherine, Claire Marie Moore Caveney, Mary Moore Brilmyer, Suzanne Moore Gray, Elizabeth Moore Sullivan. Tchr. math. Cecil Twp. Sch. Dist., McDonald, Pa., 1949-52, Pitts. Public Schs., 1952-53; with Mt. Lebanon Twp. (Pa.) Sch. Dist., 1953—, psychologist, 1954-71, dir. pupil personnel services, 1971—; lectr. ednl. psychology Grad. Sch. Edn. Duquesne U., 1957—; ednl. cons. St. Francis Schs. Nursing, New Castle and Pitts., 1959—; psychol. cons. Peters Twp. Sch. Dist., McMurray, Pa., 1961—; mem. test adv. bd. Ednl. Records Bur., 1976—; hearing officer Right to Edn. Office, Dept. Edn., Harrisburg, Pa., 1975—; inservice adv. bd. Pa. Dept. Edn. Hearing Officers. Mem. Chartiers Valley Sch. Dist. Bd., 1963-86, pres., 1971; mem. Pkwy. West Tech. Sch. Bd., 1965-67; bd. dirs. secondary sch. research program Ednl. Testing Service, Princeton, 1971—; bd. dirs. Robert E. Ward Home for Children, 1975—. Served with USNR, 1945-48. Henry C. Frick grantee, 1970, 73; named Jaycee Educator of Yr. for South Hills Area, Ward Home Outstanding Community Leader, 1984. Mem. Am., Pa. psychol. assns., Council Exceptional Children (pres. 1957), Phi Delta Kappa (pres. chpt. 1974-75, Service Key award 1985). Roman Catholic. Home: 213 Station St Bridgeville PA 15017 Office: Mt Lebanon Sch Dist 7 Horseman Dr Pittsburgh PA 15228

MOORE, DAVID MORESBY, botanist, educator; b. Barnard Castle, Durham, Eng., July 26, 1933; s. Moresby George and Elizabeth (Grange) M.; m. Ida Elizabeth Shaw, July 26, 1957; children: Wayne Peter, Lloyd Randal. B.Sc., Univ. Coll., U. Durham, 1954, Ph.D., 1957, D.Sc., 1984. Research officer div. plant industry Commonwealth Sci. and Indsl. Research Orgn., Canberra, Australia, 1957-59; research botanist UCLA, 1959-61; lectr. dept. botany U. Leicester (Eng.), 1961-68; reader in plant taxonomy U. Reading (Eng.), 1968-76, prof., 1976—. Royal Soc. London grantee, 1963, 68, 71, 75; Nat. Environ. Research Council grantee, 1970, 75, 78, 86. Mem. Soc. Study Evolution, Brit. Ecol. Soc., Bot. Soc. British Isles, Sociedad Botánica de Argentina, Linnean Soc. London. Author: Vascular Flora of Falkland Islands, 1968; Plant Cytogenetics, 1977; Flora of Tierra del Fuego, 1982; (with A.R. Clapham and T.G. Turin) Flora of the British Isles, edit. 3, 1987. Editor: (with others) Flora Europaea, Vols. 1-5, 1963-80; Green Planet, 1982; (with V.H. Heywood) Current Concepts in Plant Taxonomy, 1984; (with O. Boelcke and F.A. Roig) Transecta Botánica de la Patagonia Austral, 1985. Office: Botany Dept, U Reading Whiteknights, Reading RG6 2AS England

MOORE, DONALD WILLIAM, engineer, consultant; b. Rochester, Victoria, Australia, Oct. 22, 1941; s. Reginald Eric and Alys Mary (Donaldson) M.; m. Dawn Aileen Hicks, Apr.14, 1969; children: Anne Louise, Ian Bruce. A in Civil Engring., Royal Melbourne Inst., Victoria, Australia,

1961. Engr. Clive Steel Assocs., Melbourne, 1961-65, sr. engr., 1965-69; dir. Charlett and Moore Pty. Ltd., Melbourne, 1969-80; mng. dir. Don Moore and Assocs. Pty. Ltd., Melbourne, 1980—, also bd. dirs.; bd. dirs. Scheme Australia Proprietory Ltd., Melbourne, Insulboard Ltd., Melbourne, Bardon Corp. Proprietory Ltd., Grangecorp Proprietory Ltd., Northstar Proprietory Ltd., Moores Proprietory Ltd., Charlett & Moore Proprietory Ltd., Armanebe Proprietory Ltd. Fellow Instn. Engrs. Australia, Instn. Structural Engrs. London. Home: 16 Westminster Ave, Bulleen 3105 Victoria Australia Office: Don Moore and Assocs Pty Ltd, 11/663 Victoria St, Abbotsford 3067 Victoria Australia

MOORE, FAY LINDA, computer programmer; b. Houston, Apr. 7, 1942; d. Charlie Louis and Esther Mable (Banks) Moore; m. Noel Patrick Walker, Jan. 5, 1963 (div. 1967); 1 child, Trina Nicole Moore. Student, Prairie View Agrl. and Mech. Coll., 1960-61, Tex. So. U., 1961. Instr. Internat. Bus. Coll., Houston, 1965; keypunch operator IBM Corp., Houston, 1965-67, sr. keypunch operator, 1967-70, programmer technician, 1970-72, asst. programmer, 1972-73, assoc. programmer, 1973-84; sr. assoc. programmer, 1984-87, staff programmer, 1987—. Mem. Internat. Platform Assn., Booker T. Washington Alumni Assn., Ms. Found. for Women, Inc., Data Processing Mgmt. Assn., Nat. Assn. Female Execs. Inc. Democrat. Roman Catholic. Club: First Osborne Group. Avocations: personal computing, board games. Office: IBM Corp 3700 Bay Area Blvd MC 6402A Houston TX 77058-1199

MOORE, G(EORGE) PAUL, speech pathologist, educator; b. Everson, W. Va., Nov. 2, 1907; s. George B. and Emma (Ayers) M.; m. Gertrude H. Conley, June 10, 1929 (dec.); children—Anne Gertrude Moore Dooley, Paul David; m. 2d, Grace MacLellan Murphey, Mar. 1, 1981. A.B., W. Va. U., 1929, D.Sc. (hon.), 1974; M.A., Northwestern U., 1930, Ph.D., 1936. Faculty dept. communicative disorders, Sch. Speech, Northwestern U., 1930-62, dir. voice research lab., 1940-62, dir. voice clinic, 1950-62; lectr. in otolaryngology Northwestern Med. Sch., 1953-62, dir. research lab. Inst. Laryngology and Voice Disorders, Chgo., 1957-62; prof. speech U. Fla., Gainesville, 1962-77, chmn. dept. speech, 1962-73, dir. communicative scis. lab., 1962-68, disting. service prof., 1977, acting chmn. dept. speech, 1977-78, disting. service prof. emeritus, 1980, adj. prof. elec. engring., 1981—; vis. faculty U. Colo., summer 1948, 51, 67, U. Minn., 1963, U. Witwatersrand, Johannesburg, S.Africa, summer 1971; co-chmn. Internat. Voice Conf., 1957; mem. communicative scis. study sect. NIH, 1959-63; mem. speech pathology and audiology adv. panel, Vocat. Rehab. Adminstrn., HEW, 1962, 64; mem. rev. panel speech and hearing, Neurol. and Sensory Disease Service Program, Bur. State Services, HEW, 1963-66, adv. com., 1964-67; mem. communicative disorders research tng. com. Nat. Inst. Neurol. Diseases and Blindness, NIH, 1964-68; mem. communicative disorders program project rev. com. Nat. Inst. Neurol. diseases and Stroke, 1969-73, chmn. 1971-72, mem. nat. adv. neurol. and communicative disorders and stroke council, 1973-77; mem. Am. Bd. Examiners in Speech Pathology and Audiology, 1965-67. Recipient merit award Am. Acad. Ophthalmology and Otolaryngology, 1962; Gould award William and Harriet Gould Found., 1962; Barraquer Meml. award Smith, Miller and Patch, 1969; Disting. Faculty award Fla. Blue Key, 1975; Tchr. Scholar award U. Fla., 1976; honors Ill. Speech, Lang. and Hearing Assn., 1979; Fellow Am. Speech-Lang.-Hearing Assn. (pres. 1961; Honors of Assn. award 1966); mem. Fla. Speech and Hearing Assn. (honor award 1977), So. Speech Assn., Speech Communication Assn. (Golden Anniversary award for scholarship 1969), Internat. Coll. Exptl. Phonology, Internat. Assn. Logopedics and Phoniatrics, Am. Assn. Phonetic Scis., AMA (spl. affiliate), Sigma Xi. Republican. Presbyterian. Club: Kiwanis. Author: Organic Voice Disorders, 1971; patentee laryngoscope, 1975; contbr. chpts. to books, articles to profl. jours. Home: 2234 NW 6th Pl Gainesville FL 32603 Office: U Fla 63 Dauer Hall Gainesville FL 32611

MOORE, HELEN ELIZABETH, freelance reporter; b. Rush County, Ind., Dec. 19, 1920; d. John Brackenridge and Mary Amelia (Custer) Johnson; m. John William Sheridan, July 6, 1942 (dec. Jan. 1944); m. Harry Evan Moore, May 15, 1954; 1 child, William Randolph. BS, Ind. U., 1972, MS, 1973. Ofcl. ct. reporter 37th Jud. Cir., Brookville, Ind., 1950-60; freelance reporter Rushvile, Ind., 1960—; conv. reporter various assns. Served with USMC, 1943. Recipient Sagamore of the Wabash award Gov. Ind., 1984. Mem. Women Marines Assn. (charter, nat. pres. 1966-68), Am. Legion Aux. (various offices 1950—, pres. Ind. dept. 1966-67, conv. reporter), Bus. and Profl. Women (dist. dir., various offices 1967—), Nat. Shorthand Reporters Assn., (registered profl. reporter), Ind. Shorthand Reporters Assn. (state treas., edit. Hoosier Reporter, chmn. Legal directory), Ind. German Heritage Soc. (state bd. dirs. 1984-86, recording sec.). Democrat. Methodist. Home and Office: PO Box 206 Rushville IN 46173

MOORE, JACQUELYN CORNELIA, labor union ofcl., editor; b. Balt., Dec. 25, 1929; d. James C. and Harriette I. (Conaway) Thomas; m. Clarence Carbin Moore, Jan. 19, 1947 (dec. Feb. 1970); children—Clarence Joseph, Janet Elizabeth Moore Oliver. Mail clk. U.S. P.O., Phila., 1966—; editor Local 509 Newsletter, Nat. Alliance of Postal and Fed. Employees, Washington, 1969-74, editorial newsletter chmn., 1969-74, sec. Dist. 5, 1972-74, nat. editor Nat. Alliance, 1974—, mem. exec. bd., 1974—, union photographer, 1974—, dir. 202 Housing for Elderly Corp. bds., Chattanooga, New Orleans, 1981—, Atlanta, 1988—, sec. supervisory com. Nat. Fed. Credit Union, 1977-82, 84—. Vol. D.C. Voting Rights Corp., Washington, 1979—; sustaining mem. Dem. Nat. Com., 1977—. Mem. Coalition of Labor Union Women. Roman Catholic. Clubs: Capitol Press, Nat. Bus. and Profl. Women's, Nat. Press. Home: 1102 R St NW Washington DC 20009 Office: 1628 11th St NW Washington DC 20001

MOORE, JAMES EVERETT, JR., lawyer; b. Georgetown, Del., July 23, 1950; s. James Everett Sr. and Dorothy (Wilson) M.; m. Deborah Chafin, June 9, 1973; children: Jennifer, Lara, Jaime, J. Everett III (Trey). AA, U. Del., Georgetown, 1970; BA, U. Del., Newark, 1972; JD, Marshall-Wythe Sch. Law, 1975. Bar: D.C. 1976, Del. 1976, U.S. Dist. Ct. Del. 1977. Assoc. Robert C. Wolhar, Jr., Georgetown, 1976; ptnr. Wolhar & Moore, Georgetown, 1976-84; dir. J. Everett Moore, Jr., P.A., Georgetown, 1984-86; ptnr. Moore & Hitchens, P.A., Georgetown, 1986—; issuing agt. Ticor Title, 1st Am. Title, Meridian Title. Pres. Active Young Reps., Sussex County, Del., 1976; chmn. Sussex County Rep. Exec. Com., 1985—; del. State Rep. Conv., 1976, 86—. Named one of Outstanding Young Men Am., 1979. Mem. Sussex County Bar Assn., Del. Bar Assn., ABA. Methodist. Lodges: Masons, Elks. Home: RFD 5 Box 22 Georgetown DE 19947 Office: 108 N Bedford St Georgetown DE 19947

MOORE, JAMES YOUNG, retail executive; b. Florence, Ala., Jan. 24, 1913; s. Charles Wallace and Ada Jane (Young) M.; student U. Tenn., N.Y.U.; m. Elizabeth Lumpkin, Jan. 8, 1938 (dec. 1985); children—James Young, Mary Jane (Mrs. Timothy J. Cambias), Elizabeth Diane (Mrs. James D. Cone), Susan Wallace (Mrs. Kenneth Daniel Wilson), Molly Ann; m. Olive Lusty, June 3, 1987. Systems adminstr. Bell S. Services; chmn. bd. Jim Moore Co., Lawrenceburg, Tenn., 1939—; owner Double M Ranch, 1972—. Participant 1st Nat. Conf. Jud. Selection and Tenure, 1974. Past internat. dir. Boy Scouts Am.; past dir. Am. Cancer Soc.; exec. com. Citizens for Ct. Modernization. Presdl. elector at large for Tenn., 1936; nat. committeeman Young Republican Fedn., 1939-48; del. Rep. Nat. Conv., 1940, bd. dirs. Rep. Nat. Com. Charter mem. Fellows Menninger Found., Rep. Senatorial Inner Circle, Rep. Presdl. Task Force mem. nat. advisory council Am. Security Council; sponsor Young Ams. for Freedom, Nat. League POW-MIA Families; mem. nat. steering com. Korean War Mem. Named Hon. Citizen Boy's Town, Nebr. Mem. C. of C. (past nat. counselor, past dir.), Internat. Platform Assn., Farm Bur., Am. Judicature Soc., Menswear Retailers Am., Hospitalized Vets. Delta Tau Delta (life). Republican. Mem. Ch. of Christ. Clubs: Tennessee Wally Byam Caravan, U.S. Senatorial (founding mem.), Heritage Found. Pres. Home: 1301 S Locust Ave Lawrenceburg TN 38464 Winter Address: PO Box 5469 Saddle Bag Lake Resort Lake Wales FL 33853 Office: 39 NW Public Square Lawrenceburg TN 38464

MOORE, JEAN OLIVER, lawyer; b. Wichita, Kans., July 25, 1925; s. Jesse Lee and Olive F. (Bryant) M.; m. Arline Louise Watkins, June 9, 1947 (div.); children—Susan Moore Jackson, Rossanne Moore Thomson, Colin B.; m. 2d, Helen Leoti Fritz, Aug. 21, 1979. B.A., U. Kans., 1957, LL.B., 1949, J.D., 1968. Bar: Kans. 1949, U.S. Ct. Appeals (10th cir.) 1954, U.S. Supreme Ct. 1972. Practice in Wichita, 1949—; sr. mem. Jean Oliver Moore, Wichita, 1961—; lectr. Wichita State U., 1951-71; instr. U. Kans. Extension Div., 1951-52, Am. Inst. Banking, 1954—; pres. Great Western Trading Corp., Wichita, 1972—; dir. Karefree Nursing Centers, Inc., numerous other corps. Sub-local chmn. March of Dimes, 1967, 69. Mem. Assn. Trial Lawyers Am., Fed. Bar Assn., Kans. Bar Assn., Wichita Bar Assn. (chmn. criminal law com. 1982-85), Nat. Assn. Criminal Def. Lawyers (Kans. chmn. 1977-78, pres.; Pres.'s award 1977), Wis. Criminal Defense Lawyers Assn. (life), Am. Judicature Soc., Okla. Criminal Def. Lawyers Assn. Recipient Wisdom award of Honor Wisdom Soc., 1971. Republican. Club: Masons. Author: The Ancient Law, 1954; contbr. articles to legal jours. Office: 1044 N Waco St Wichita KS 67203 Office: 1311 North Terr Wichita KS 67208

MOORE, JOANNE, postal superintendent; b. Newport News, Va., Nov. 1, 1943; d. Joseph and Mable (Williams) Jackson; m. Calvin Louis Moore, June 28, 1969; children: Nikisha Terri, Calvin Louis. BA, U. Md.-Balt., 1982. Mgr., U.S. Postal Service, Balt., 1978-84, quality control specialist, 1984-88, detailed tour superintendant, Wilmington, Del., 1988—. Active local Apostolic ch.; pres. youth dept. United House of Prayer for All People, Balt., 1971-81; bd. dirs. McCollough Day Care Ctr., 1983-86; finalist Mrs. America Pageant, Balt., 1983; chairperson Md. State Mistress Ceremony, 1979-88. Mem. Network, Nat. Assn. Female Execs., Am. Bus. Women's Assn., Nat. Assn. Postal Suprs. (newsletter editor 1983-84, area v.p. 1985-86), U. Md. Alumni Assn. Democrat. Avocations: writing, bowling, singing, fishing. Home: 7100 Hull Ct Baltimore MD 21207 Office: US Postal Service 147 Quigley Blvd Wilmington DE 19850-9997

MOORE, JOE FARNHAM, management consultant; b. Duncan, Okla., Dec. 11, 1929; s. Joe David and Lauraleen (Farnham) M.; m. Glenna Sue Killian, Dec. 31, 1949; children: Ellen Patrice Miller Moore, Joe Farnham, Randall Burris, Michael Lewis, Jane Elizabeth Kampschmidt Moore. S.B. in Chem. Engring, MIT, 1952. Diplomate: Registered profl. engr., Tex. Chem. engr. Humble Oil Refining Co., Baytown, Tex., 1952-56; founder 1957; since chief exec. officer, dir. Bonner & Moore Assos. BMAG- Wiesbaden F..R.W.G., Houston; pres., dir. WinPro Co.; mem. corp. MIT, energy lab. adv. bd.; cons. indsl. engring. dept. U. Houston. Author articles computer tech., world energy econs., mgmt. Trustee endowment fund Houston, dir. Sch. for Deaf Children; bd. dirs. Houston Symphony Orchestra. Recipient Presdl. citation MIT, 1975, Bronze Beaver award, 1976. Mem. Am. Inst. Chem. Engrs., Nat., Tex. socs. profl. engrs., MIT Alumni Assn. (pres. 1978-79, chmn. nat. selection com.). Clubs: River Oaks Breakfast Assn, Lakeside Country, Heritage; Blue Lake Golf, Horseshoe Bay Country (Marble Falls, Tex.); Captains (London).

MOORE, JOHN CORDELL, lawyer; b. Winchester, Ill., July 20, 1912; s. John Clayton and Winifred (Peak) M.; m. Pauline Ruyle, July 29, 1939 (dec. 1979); m. Wilma K. Smith Jackson, Aug. 1981. A.B., Ill. Coll., 1936, LL.D., 1967; LL.B., Georgetown U., 1949, J.D., 1967; postgrad., Am. U., 1955-57. Bar: Tenn., U.S. Supreme Ct. Rep. Universal Credit Co., St. Louis, 1937-39; tchr. Capitol Page Sch.; also clk. to mem. Ho. of Reps., 1939-41; examiner Metals Res. Co., 1941-42; exec. dir. Fgn. Liquidation Commn. for S. and C. Am., Balboa, C.Z., 1946-47; with Office Alien Property, Dept. Justice, 1947-50; asst. dir. property mgmt. Interior Dept., 1950-52, dir. security for dept., 1952-61; adminstr. Oil Import Adminstrn., 1961-65, asst. sec. for mineral resources, 1965-69; now lawyer, also internat. energy cons.; U.S. rep. oil and energy com. OECD, Paris, 1965-69; former dir. Clark Oil, Milw. Served to comdr. USNR, 1942-46; capt. Res. Mem. Fed. Bar Assn., Tenn. Bar Assn., Nat. Rifle Assn. (life); mem. Am. Legion, VFW, Delta Theta Phi. Democrat. Methodist. Clubs: Illini Country (Springfield, Ill.); Army-Navy; Nat. Lawyers (Washington); Jacksonville Country (Ill.). Home: 15 Inverness Dr Springfield IL 62704

MOORE, JOSEPH, retired lawyer, foundation executive; b. Bluefield, W.Va., May 18, 1920; s. Hugh Paul and Mary Elizabeth (Simpson) M.; m. Barbara Tracy Finkelstein, June 15, 1942; children: Steven, Sandra. JD, Columbia U., 1958, U. Ariz., 1970. Enlisted USN, 1942, advanced through grades to 1st lt., resigned, 1955; assoc. Linscott, Sloan, N.Y.C., 1959-66; sole practice N.Y.C., 1966-77; ptnr. Moore-Henry, Washington, 1977-81; researcher, placement officer Creative Mgmt., Washington, 1981-83; chmn. bd. J&D Meml. Found. Inc., Spencer, W.Va., 1983—; pres., chief exec. officer Creative Prodns. Author: No Time for Tears, 1968, For Fear We Shall Perish, Hold Back the Night, Battered Children; producer Christian films. Mem. White House Conf. on Children. Republican. Jewish. Home: Ashley Manor Box 150 Spencer WV 25276 Office: J & D Meml Found Inc PO Box 357 Spencer WV 25276

MOORE, KURT RICHARD, anthropologist, art historian; b. Scott AFB, Ill., Oct. 9, 1955; s. Richard Vernal and Irmgard Ludwiga (Bennewitz) M. AB, U. Ill., 1976, BFA, 1976; MA, So. Ill. U., 1981, postgrad., 1984-85. Grad. teaching asst. So. Ill. U. Field Sch. Archaeology, Carbondale, 1977, Center Continuing Edn., 1978, archaeol. field/lab. asst. Center Archaeol. Investigations, 1978-79, grad. research asst., 1979-80; archaeologist Ill. State Mus. Soc., Springfield, Ill., 1980-82; research archaeologist Am. Resources Group, Ltd., Carbondale, Ill., 1982-85; mgr. tech. support TSG, Inc., Carbondale, 1985-86; dir. corp. and found. relations, Le Moyne Coll., Syracuse, N.Y., 1986-87; asst. dir. corp. devel. Cornell U., Ithaca, 1987—. Contbr. articles to profl. jours; author monographs. Edmund J. James scholar U. Ill., Urbana, 1972-73, John T. Rusher Meml. scholar, 1975-76; So. Ill. U. scholar, 1981-87. Mem. Mo. Archeol. Soc., Nat. Assn. Practice of Anthropology (charter), Am. Anthrop. Assn., Artist Blacksmith Assn. N. Am., Current Anthropology (assoc.), Soc. Am. Archaeology, Vols. in Tech. Assistance, Cen. States Anthrop. Soc., Phi Kappa Phi, Am. Amateur Racquetball Assn., N.Y. State Racquetball Assn. Republican. Roman Catholic. Avocations: racquetball, art. Home: 8 E Main St Cortland NY 13045 Office: Cornell U Office Corp Devel 726 University Ave Ithaca NY 14853

MOORE, LAURENCE JOHN, business educator; b. Greeley, Colo., May 7, 1938; s. John Herold and Ruth Anderson M.; m. Nancy Kay Hibbert, Aug. 31, 1963; children: Rebecca Ann, John Andrew, Stefani Ruth. B.A. in Econs, Monmouth Coll., Ill., 1962; M.S. in Econs, Ariz. State U., 1965, D.B.A. in Mgmt. Sci, 1970. Dist. mktg. rep. Standard Oil Co. (Ind.), Chgo., 1962-63; sr. analyst long range and capital planning 1964-66; head quantitative studies Continental Ill. Bank, Chgo., 1966-67; mem. faculty dept. mgmt. sci. Coll. Bus. Va. Poly. Inst. and State U., Blacksburg, 1970—; prof. Coll. Bus. Va. Poly. Inst. and State U., 1977-85, C&P Disting. prof. bus., 1985—, head dept. Coll. Bus., 1976-83, dir. univ. fin. planning and analysis, 1983-84; cons. in field. Author: (with S.M. Lee, B.W. Taylor) Management Science, 1981, (with S.M. Lee) Introduction to Decision Sciences, 1975, (with E.R. Clayton) GERT Modeling and Simulation: Fundamentals and Applications, 1976. Served with U.S. Army, 1957-59. Recipient Disting. Service award SE region Am. Inst. Decision Scis., 1977. Fellow Am. Inst. Decision Scis. (pres. 1983-84, Disting. Service award 1986); mem. Inst. Mgmt. Sci. (Disting. Service award SE region), Ops. Research Soc. Am., Inst. Indsl. Engrs., Alpha Iota Delta, Beta Gamma Sigma, Omicron Delta Epsilon, Sigma Iota Epsilon. Presbyterian. Home: 6109 Tall Oaks Dr Blacksburg VA 24060 Office: Va Poly Inst and State U Dept Mgmt Sci 107 Pamplin Hall Blacksburg VA 24061

MOORE, LAWRENCE JACK, oil company executive, lawyer; b. Brownwood, Tex., Jan. 24, 1926; s. Lawrence Houston and Lena Emily (Grantham) M.; m. Eloise Camille Dickinson, May 24, 1947; children: John L., James D., Jane E. Moore Horner. Student Howard Payne U., 1946-47, Tarleton State U., 1942-43; LLB, U. Tex., 1949. Bar: Tex. 1949, N.Y. 1980. Sole practice, 1949-57; city atty., Ballinger, Tex., 1950, 55-57; county atty. Runnels County, Tex., 1951-54; atty. Texaco Inc., 1957-70, assoc. gen. counsel, 1970-79; v.p., gen. counsel Caltex Petroleum Corp., Dallas, 1979—; adv. bd. Internat. and Comparative Law Ctr., Internat. Oil and Gas Ctr. of Southwestern Legal Found.; devel. bd., U. Tex., Dallas. Served to cpl. AUS, 1944-46. Mem. ABA, Am. Soc. Internat. Law, Internat. Bar Assn., Internat. Law Assn., State Bar Tex., Dallas Bar Assn., Assn. Bar City N.Y. Republican. Methodist. Clubs: University (N.Y.C.); Country of Darien (Conn.); Northwood, Dallas Petroleum, University (Dallas). Lodge: Masons. Office: Caltex Petroleum Corp PO Box 619500 Dallas TX 75261-9500

MOORE, MARY FRENCH (MUFFY), potter, community activist; b. N.Y.C., Feb. 25, 1938; d. John and Rhoda (Teagle) Walker French; B.A. cum laude, Colo. U., 1964; m. Alan Baird Minier, Oct. 9, 1982; children—Jonathan Corbet, Jennifer Corbet, Michael Corbet. Ceramics mfr., Wilson, Wyo., 1969-82, Cheyenne, Wyo., 1982—; commr. County of Teton (Wyo.), 1976-83, chmn. bd. commrs., 1981, 83, mem. dept. public assistance and social service, 1976-82, mem. recreation bd., 1978-81, water quality adv. bd., 1976-82. Bd. dirs. Teton Sci. Sch., 1968-83, vice chmn., 1979-81, chmn., 1982; bd. dirs. Teton Energy Council, 1978-83; mem. water quality adv. bd. Wyo. Dept. Environ. Quality, 1979-83; Democratic precinct committeewoman, 1978-81; mem. Wyo. Dem. Central Com., 1981-83; vice chmn. Laramie County Dem. Central Com., 1983-84, Wyo. Dem. nat. committewoman, 1984-87; chmn. Wyo. Dem. Party, 1987—; del. Dem. Nat. Conv., 1984, 88, mem. fairness commn. Dem. Nat. Com., 1985, vice-chairwoman western caucus, 1986—; chmn. platform com. Wyo. Dem. Conv., 1982; mem. Wyo. Dept. Environ. Quality Land Quality Adv. Bd., 1983-86; mem. Gov.'s Steering Com. on Troubled Youth, 1982, dem. nat. com. Compliance Assistance Commn., 1986-87; legis. aide for Gov. Wyo., 1985, 86; project coordinator Gov.'s Com. on Childrens' Services, 1985-86; bd. dirs. Wyo. Outdoor Council, 1984-85. Recipient Woman of Yr. award Jackson Hole Bus. and Profl. Women, 1981. Mem. Jackson Hole Art Assn. (bd. dirs., vice chmn. 1981, chmn. 1982), Pi Sigma Alpha. Home: 8907 Cowpoke Rd Cheyenne WY 82009

MOORE, MAURICE MALCOLM, investment advisor; b. Mpls., Oct. 16, 1920; s. Maurice Malcolm and Olive (Brown) M.; m. Marian Adelaide Zierold, Aug. 15, 1953; children: Malcolm M., Mary Melissa, Marian Elizabeth Lindblad. BA, Williams Coll., 1942; MBA, Harvard U., 1946. Dir. Flint Aero. Corp., Detroit, 1952-54; sales mgr. Lithium Corp. Am., Chgo., 1959-65; sr. account exec. Glore Forgan Corp., Chgo., 1965-70; officer A.G. Becker & Co., Chgo., 1970-80; stock broker, v.p. Vincent, Chesley & Co., Chgo., 1980-84, Prescott, Ball and Turben, Chgo., 1984—. Served to lt. USNR, 1943-46, 51-52, PTO. Republican. Clubs: Indian Hill (Winnetka, Ill.); Metropolitan (Chgo.). Office: Prescott Ball & Turben 230 W Monroe Chicago IL 60606

MOORE, MCPHERSON DORSETT, lawyer; b. Pine Bluff, Ark., Mar. 1, 1947; s. Arl Van and Jesse (Dorsett) M. BS, U. Miss., 1970; JD, U. Ark., 1974. Bar: Ark. 1974, Mo. 1975, U.S. Patent and Trademark Office 1977, U.S. Dist. Ct. (ea. dist.) Mo. 1977, U.S. Ct. Appeals (8th, 10th and Fed. cirs.). Design engr. Tenneco, Newport News, Va., 1970-71; assoc. Rogers, Eilers & Howell, St. Louis, 1974-80; ptnr. Rogers, Howell, Moore & Haferkamp, St. Louis, 1981—. Bd. dirs. Legal Services of Eastern Mo., 1984—. Served with USAR, 1970-76. Mem. ABA, Bar Assn. Met. St. Louis (chmn. young lawyers sect. 1981-82, sec. 1984-85, v.p. 1985-86, chmn. trial sect. 1986-87, pres. 1988—), Ark. Bar Assn., St. Louis County Bar Assn., Am. Intellectual Property Law Assn., Phi Delta Theta Alumni (treas. St. Louis chpt. 1987-88, sec. 1988—). Episcopalian. Club: University (St. Louis). Home: 49 Godwin Ln Saint Louis MO 63124 Office: Rogers Howell Moore & Haferkamp 7777 Bonhomme Ave Suite 1700 Saint Louis MO 63105

MOORE, MICHAEL, psychologist; b. Budapest, Hungary, Sept. 19, 1942; s. Jeno and Anna (Foldes) Mohos; m. Jolanta Henner, Sept. 4, 1963; children—Karen, Raphael. B.A., Hebrew U., 1965; M.A., Wayne State U., 1970, Ph.D., 1971. Asst. prof. U. Calif., Davis, 1971-73, vis. prof., 1988—; sr. lectr. Technion, Haifa, Israel, 1975, asso. prof. psychology, 1983—, head dept. gen. studies, 1986-88; cons. Council on Criminal Justice, Sacramento, 1971-73, Acad. for Hebrew Lang., Jerusalem, 1974-80, Center for Ednl. Adminstrn., Haifa, 1975-80, Dept. Edn., Sacramento, 1981. Contbr. articles to profl. jours. Served to 2d lt. Israel Def. Force, 1965-67. Wayne State U. grad. fellow, 1969-70; U. Calif. faculty grantee, 1972-73; Technion Faculty grantee, 1973—. Mem. Am. Psychol. Assn., Israeli Psychol. Assn., Israeli Ednl. Research Assn. (vice chmn. 1979-80). Office: Technion, Haifa 32000, Israel

MOORE, PEGGY SUE, corporation financial executive; b. Wichita, Kans., June 16, 1942; d. George Alvin and Marie Aileene (Hoskinson) M. Student, Wichita State U., 1961-63, Wichita Bus. Coll., 1963-64. Controller Mears Electric Co., Wichita, 1965-69; exec. v.p., sec., treas., chief fin. officer CPI Corp., Wichita, 1969—, also bd. dirs.; Trustee Fringe Benefits Co., Kansas City, Mo., 1984-85. Mem. Rep. Nat. Com., Washington, 1985-86, task force 1986—; bd. dirs. Good Shepherd Luth. Ch., Wichita, 1980-85. Mem. Nat. Assn. Female Execs. Inc, Wichita C. of C., Women's Nat. Bowling Assn. (bd. dirs., pub. com. 1969-76), Internat. Platform Assn., DAR. Office: CPI Corp 816 E Funston Wichita KS 67211

MOORE, PHYLLIS CLARK, library consultant; b. Binghamton, N.Y., Jan. 31, 1927; d. John Oscar and Gladys Jeanette (Tilbury) Clark; BA, Hartwick Coll., 1949; MLS, Syracuse U., 1954 ; PhD, U. Wis., 1971; LittD, Colo. State U., 1973; DLS (hon.) Marquis Giuseppe Scicluna Internat. U., Malta, 1987; m. R(oberts) Scott Wellington Moore, Sept. 14, 1954 (dec. 1979); m. Donald S. Wolfe, Feb. 16, 1980. Librarian Free Library Phila., 1954-57; Librarian-adminstr. GS-9 main reference/Interloan Center, dir. 22 spl. services libraries met. Stuttgart, Fed. Republic Germany, U.S. Govt. Spl. Services Europe, 1957-62; dept. Head young adult, fine arts, audiovisual, reference Yonkers (N.Y.) Pub. Library, 1962-67; dir. Hastings-on-Hudson (N.Y.) Pub. Library, 1967-68; cons. audio-visual services Westchester County (N.Y.) Library System, 1968-72; dir. Falls Church (Va.) Pub. Library, 1972-77; city librarian Alameda Free Library; dir. Alameda (Calif.) Free Library, 1978-84; library supr. Ojai (Calif.) Unified Sch. Dist., 1984-87; cons. library, 1987—; research dir. Underwater Sealabs, Bremerhaven, W. Ger., 1960-61; tech. advisor Community Action Program Yonkers, N.Y., 1965-68. Chancel choir Ojai Presbyn. Ch. Active Nat. Humane Soc., Recording Service for Visually Handicapped. Mem. ALA (exec. council 1975-79), Internat. Oceanographic Found., Nat. Assn. Sch. and Media Librarians, Mask and Lute (pres. 1974), Nat. Health and Welfare Assn. (exec. bd.), Defenders of Wildlife (adv. council), Greenpeace, U.S.A., Bay Area Library and Info. System (chairperson 1978-79), Audio Philharmonic Soc. (pres. 1983-84), Ojai Valley Hist. Mus. Author: Beneath the Sea, 1974; Command Performance, 1975; Blues in the Bibliotheque, 1979; A Catchy Title, 1980; Beyond the Blues, 1981; Girls of Yesteryear, 1983-84 (nat. TV prodn. award). Contbr. articles to profl. publs. Home: 25 Juniper Ln Ojai CA 93023 Office: 1975 Maricopa Hwy Ojai CA 93023

MOORE, RAYBURN SABATZKY, educator; b. Helena, Ark., May 26, 1920; s. Max Sabatzky and Sammie Lou (Rayburn) M.; m. Margaret Elizabeth Bear, Aug. 30, 1947; children: Margaret Elizabeth, Robert Rayburn. A.B., Vanderbilt U., 1942, M.A., 1947; Ph.D., Duke U., 1956. Vice pres. Interstate Grocer Co., Helena, 1947-50; research and grad. asst. Duke U., 1952-54; asst. prof. English, Hendrix Coll., Conway, Ark., 1954-55; asso. prof. Hendrix Coll., 1955-58, prof., 1958-59; asso. prof. U. Ga., Athens, 1959-65; prof. U. Ga., 1965—, dir. grad. studies in English, 1964-69, chmn. Am. studies program, 1968—, chmn. div. lang and lit., 1975—; vis. scholar Duke U., 1958, 64. Author: Constance Fenimore Woolson, 1963, For the Major and Selected Short Stories of Constance Fenimore Woolson, 1967, Paul Hamilton Hayne, 1972, A Man of Letters in the Nineteenth-Century South: Selected Letters of Paul Hamilton Hayne, 1982; sr. editor: History of Southern Literature, 1985, Selected Letters of Henry James to Edmund Gosse (1882-1915): A Literary Friendship, 1988; mem. editorial bd. U. Ga. Press, 1972-74, Ga. Rev., 1974-82, chmn., 1980-82; contbr. articles to profl. jours. Mem. troop com. Boy Scouts Am., Athens, 1973-75; deacon, elder Presbyterian Ch., 1962—. Served to capt. U.S. Army, 1942-46, PTO. Mem. Soc. Study So. Lit. (exec. com. 1968, 74-79, 85—, v.p. 1981-82, pres. 1983-84), MLA (exec. com. Gen. Topics VI 1972-75), South Atlantic Grad. English Coop. Group (exec. com. 1969-79, chmn. 1971-72), South Atlantic Modern Lang. Assn. (exec. com. 1975-77, nominating com. 1985-87), Blue Key, Phi Beta Kappa, Sigma Chi. Office: U Ga 130 Park Hall Athens GA 30602

MOORE, ROBERT IAN, historian, educator; b. Enniskillen, Northern Ireland, May 8, 1941; s. Thomas and Elsie (Ellis) M.; m. Wendy Elizabeth Jenrick, Aug. 10, 1968; children: Olivia C., Richard T., Gerald P. BA, U. Oxford, Eng., 1962, MA, 1966. Lectr. U. Sheffield, Eng., 1964-78, sr. lectr., 1978—. Author: The Birth of Popular Heresy, 1975, The Origins of European Dissent, 1977, The Formation of a Persecuting Society, 1987; editor: Hamlyn Historical Atlas, 1981, (monograph series) New Perspectives on the Past, 1983—. Fellow Royal Hist. Soc.; mem. Ecclesiastical Hist. Soc. (mem. com. 1977-80). Mem. Liberal Party.

MOORE, ROBIN JAMES, historian educator; b. Melbourne, Victoria, Australia, Apr. 29, 1934; s. Frederick Ernest and Alma Winifred (Hicks) Moore; m. Rosemary Hope Sweetapple, 1976. BA with honors, U. Melbourne, 1954, MA, 1958; PhD, U. London, 1964, D. of Literature, 1980. Exec. Containers Ltd., Melbourne, 1955-60; cons. Arthur Andersen, Melbourne, 1960; exec. Western Mining Corp., Melbourne, 1960-62; lectr. Sch. Oriental and African Studies, London, 1964-71; prof. Flinders U., Adelaide, South Australia, 1971—, dean Sch. Social Scis., 1988—. Author, editor and contbr. articles on History of British India. Gov. Adelaide Festival of Arts, Inc., 1980—. Recipient Fulbright Sr. award, Tulsa, 1987. Fellow Australian Acad. of Humanities (council mem. 1986-88); mem. Australian Hist. Assn. (pres. 1983-84). Club: Adelaide. Home: Palm St, 5081 Medindie Australia Office: Flinders U, 5042 Bedford Park Australia

MOORE, ROGER ALLAN, lawyer; b. Framingham, Mass., Aug. 8, 1931; s. Ralph Chester and Mabelle (Taft) M.; AB cum laude, Harvard U., 1953, JD, 1956; m. Barbara Lee Wildman, July 4, 1955; children—Marshall Christian, Elizabeth Lee, Taft Hayden Davis, Allan Baron. Admitted to Mass. bar, 1956, since practiced in Boston; assoc. Ropes & Gray, 1956-66, ptnr., 1967—. Chmn. bd. Nat. Rev., Inc.; gen. counsel Republican Nat. Com., 1981—; gen. counsel del. Rep. Nat. Conv., 1988; gen. counsel, del. Rep. Nat. Commendation, 1988; mem. Electoral Coll., 1984; spl. parliamentarian Adminstrv. Conf. of U.S., 1981—; gen. counsel Pres.'s Reelection Com., 1984; chmn. U.S. presdl. delegation to Haiti's 1987 elections; sec. Harvard Med. Ctr.; sec. Harvard Med. Ctr.; clk. L.S. Starrett Co., Wrentham Steel Products Co. Pres. Harvard Young Rep. Club, 1953-54; former chmn. bd. dirs. Beacon Hill Civic Assn.; former mem. Bd. Fgn. Scholarships, Dept. State; bd. dirs. Historic Boston, Salzburg Sem. in Am. Studies, Austria, 1954-66; bd. dirs., clk. Corp. Maintaining Editorial Diversity in Am.; bd. dirs., clk. Bostonian Soc. Recipient Endicott Peabody Saltonstall prize Harvard U., 1953, Boylston prize, 1952. Mem. ABA (adv. commn. standing com. on law and the electoral process), Mass. Bar Assn., Boston Bar Assn., Old South Assn. (past pres.), Mass. Hist. Soc., Commanderie de Bordeaux. Episcopalian (sr. warden). Clubs: Somerset, Harvard (Boston and N.Y.C.); Country (Brookline, Mass.); Metropolitan (Washington); Harvard Faculty. Home: 26 W Cedar St Boston MA 02108 Office: Ropes & Gray 225 Franklin St Boston MA 02110

MOORE, SHIRLEY THROCKMORTON (MRS. ELMER LEE MOORE), accountant; b. Des Moines, July 4, 1918; d. John Carder and Jessie (Wright) Throckmorton; student Iowa State Tchrs. Coll., summers 1937-38, Madison Coll., 1939-41; M.C.S., Benjamin Franklin U., 1944; m. Elmer Lee Moore, Dec. 19, 1946; children—Fay, Lynn Dallas. Asst. bookkeeper Sibley Hosp., Washington, 1941-42, Alvord & Alvord, 1942-46, bookkeeper, 1946-49, chief accountant, 1950-64, fin. adviser to sr. partner, 1957-64; dir. Allen Oil Co., 1958-74; pvt. practice acctg., 1964—. Mem. sch. bd. Takoma Acad., Takoma Park, Md., 1970—. Recipient Disting. Grad. award Benjamin Franklin U., 1961. C.P.A., Md. Mem. Am., D.C. (pub. relations com. 1976—) insts. C.P.A.s, Am. Women's Soc. C.P.A.s, Am. Soc. Women Accts. (legislation chmn. 1960-62, nat. dir. 1952-53, nat. treas. 1953-54), Bus. and Profl. Women's Club (treas. D.C. 1967-68), Benjamin Franklin U. Alumni Assn. (Disting. Alumni award 1964, charter, past dir.), D.A.R., Md. Assn. C.P.A.s (charter chmn. membership com. Montgomery Prince George County 1963-64, chmn. student relations com. 1964-67, pres. 1968-69, mem. fed. tax com. 1971-73). Mem. Seventh Day Adventist Ch. Contbr. articles to profl. jours. Home and Office: 1007 Elm Ave Takoma Park MD 20912

MOORE, SIMON JAMES, marine zoologist; b. Pembury, Kent, Eng., Mar. 18, 1948; s. Geoffrey Edward Henry and Jean Elizabeth (Darton) M.; m. Jennifer Audrey Monk, May 22, 1948. Ed., Paddington Tech. Coll., London, 1971-72. Asst. sci. officer Brit. Mus. Natural History, London, 1968-74, sci. officer, 1974-81, higher sci. officer, 1981—; contbg. editor Nat. Knife Collecting Assn., Chattanooga, 1983—. Author: English Spoons 1650-1930, 1987, Penknives and Other Folding Knives, 1988; contbr. articles to profl. jours. Mem. Brit. Arachnological Assn., Inst. Sci. Tech. (cert.), Biol. Curator's Group, Museums Assn., London Fedn. Museums and Art Galleries. Anglican. Clubs: Silver Study Group (North London); Player Piano Group (Middlesex). Office: British Museum Natural History, Cromwell Rd, London SW7 5BD, England

MOORE, TERRIS, educator; b. Haddonfield, N.J., Apr. 11, 1908; s. Robert Thomas and Selma Helena (Muller) M.; m. Katrina Eaton Hincks, June 17, 1933; children—Katrina, Henry Winslow (dec.). Grad., Storm King Sch., Cornwall, N.Y.; B.A., Williams Coll., 1929, LL.D. (hon.), 1979; M.B.A., Harvard Grad. Sch. Bus. Adminstrn., 1933, Doctor Comml. Sci., 1937; LL.D., U. Alaska, 1967. Treas. and dir. William R. McAdams, Inc., Boston, 1940-49; with Patterson, Teale and Dennis (accountants), Boston, 1945; instr. finance U. Calif. at Los Angeles, 1937-39; pres. Boston Mus. of Sci., 1945-48, life trustee, 1972—; pres. U. Alaska, 1949-53, hon. prof. of univ., 1954-72, prof., pres. emeritus, 1973—; dir. indsl. cooperation U. Maine, 1954-55; vis. prof. bus. adminstrn. Colby Coll., Waterville, Maine, 1955-57; cons. Quartermaster Research & Engring. Center, Natick, Mass., 1957-69, Army Sci. Adv. Panel, 1959-69, (U.S. Army Test and Evaluation Command), 1963-69. Author: chpt. in Modern Airmanship, 1957, Mt. McKinley, the Pioneer Climbs, 1967; Co-author: chpt. in Men Against the Clouds, 1934; Contbr. articles to various mags. and jours. Sec., research coodinator of Maine Coll.-Community Research Program, 1954-57; mem. overseers vis. com. in biology Harvard U., 1946-49; Mem N.E. Govs.' Com. Pub. Transp., 1954-57. Served as expert cons. to quartermaster gen. 1942-44; cons. Aero. Research Found., 1956. Recipient certificate of appreciation for outstanding contbn. war effort Q.M. Gen., 1944, Distinguished Service award USAF for; C.A.P. Fellow Royal Geog. Soc., Am. Geog. Soc. (councillor 1967-88); mem. N.Y. Acad. Scis. (life), Am. Geophys. Union, AAAS, Alpha Kappa Psi, Delta Phi. Clubs: Explorers (N.Y.); St. Botolph (Boston); The Alpine (London); American Alpine (hon.), Harvard Travellers (hon.), Appalachian Mountain (hon.), Pioneers of Alaska (hon.), Mountaineers of Seattle (hon.). Home: Borestone Mountain Monson ME 04464 Office: 123 Brattle St Cambridge MA 02138

MOORE, THOMAS JUSTIN, JR., former utility company executive, lawyer; b. Richmond, Va., Apr. 15, 1925; s. Thomas Justin and Carrie (Willingham) M.; m. Mary Elizabeth Pearson, Oct. 22, 1954 (dec. Mar. 1983); children: Mary Elizabeth, Thomas Justin III; m. Jeanette S. Bray, Sept. 29, 1984. AB, Princeton U., 1947; LLB, U. Va., 1950. Bar: Va. 1949. Assoc. Hunton, Williams, Gay, Gibson & Powell, Richmond, 1950-54; mem. firm Hunton, Williams, Gay, Gibson & Powell, 1955-67; with Va. Electric & Power Co., 1967-85, pres., 1970-78, vice chmn., 1978, chmn. bd., chief exec. officer, 1978-85, also dir.; counsel Hunton and Williams, Richmond; dir. Central Fidelity Bank, GTE Corp., Philip Morris Inc. Campaign chmn. Richmond United Givers Fund, 1962, chmn. bd. trustees, 1973; bd. assocs. U. Richmond; trustee Colonial Williamsburg Found.; bd. dirs. Atomic Indsl. Forum, 1975-77, Southeastern Elec. Exchange, 1979-84, Edison Electric Inst., 1979-84; mem. Va. Found. Ind. Colls., chmn., 1973-75; chmn. Va. Coll. Bldg. Authority, 1973-75, Richmond Renaissance, 1982—. Served to lt. (j.g.) USNR, 1943-46, PTO. Mem. ABA, Va. Bar Assn. (chmn. exec. com. 1967), Richmond Bar Assn. (pres. 1966), Bar Assn. City N.Y., Conf. Bd., Met. Richmond C. of C. (dir.), Phi Alpha Delta, Omicron Delta Kappa. Episcopalian. Clubs: Princeton, Brook (N.Y.C.); Metropolitan (Washington); Country of Virginia, Commonwealth, Downtown (Richmond). Home: 214 S Wilton Rd Richmond VA 23226 Office: PO Box 1535 Richmond VA 23219

MOORE, VIRGINIA BRADLEY, librarian, educator; b. Laurens, S.C., May 13, 1932; d. Robert Otis Brown and Queen Esther (Smith) Bradley; m. David Lee Moore, Dec. 27, 1957 (div. 1973). B.S., Winston-Salem State U., 1954; M.L.S., U. Md., 1970. Cert. in library sci. edn. Tchr., John R. Hawkins High Sch., Warrenton, N.C., 1954-55, Happy Plains High Sch., Taylorsville, N.C., 1955-58, Young and Carver elem. schs., Washington, 1958-65; librarian Davis and Minor elem. schs., Washington, 1965-72, Ballou Sr. High Sch., Kramer Jr. High Sch., Washington, 1972-75, 78-80, Anacostia Sr. High Sch., Washington, 1975-77, 80—; class, club sponsor, 1975—; chmn. competency-based curriculum D.C. Pub. Schs., 1978—; speaker, presenter Ch. and Synagogue Library Assn., 1975, 80, 83; dir. ch. library workshops Asbury United Methodist Ch., Washington, 1972-74, 76; mem. 1st library and info. sci. del. to People's Republic China, 1985. Author: (bibliography) The Negro in American History, 1619-1968, 1968; TV script for vacation reading program, 1971, sound/slide presentation D.C. Church Libraries' Bicentennial Celebration, 1976; video script and tchr.'s guide for Nat. Library Week Balloon Launch Day, 1983; bibliography Black Literature/Materials, 1987. Rec. sec. Washington Pan-Hellenic Council, 1975; librarian Mt. Carmel Baptist Ch., Washington, 1984. Recipient certs. of award D.C. Pub. Library, 1980, D.C. Pub. Schs., 1983; NDEA scholar Central State Coll., Edmond, Okla., 1969, U. Ky., 1969; scholar Ball State U., 1969; grad. fellow U. Md., 1969. Mem. NEA (life), LWV, Internat. Assn. Sch. Librarians, Am. Assn. Sch. Librarians (coms. 1973-83), D.C. Assn. Sch. Librarians (pres. 1971-73, citation 1973, newsletter editor 1971-75, 83, Soc. Sch. Librarians, Freedom to Read Found., ALA (councilor-at-large 1983-91), D.C. Library Assn., Md. Ednl. Media Orgn., Internat. Platform Assn., Prince Georges County LWV, Zeta Phi Beta (v.p. chpt. 1972-74), Delta Kappa Gamma. Democrat. Club: S.E. Neighbors. Home: 2100 Brooks Dr Apt 721 Forestville MD 20747 Office: Anacostia Sr High Sch 16th and R Sts SE Washington DC 20020

MOORE, WILLIAM BLACK, JR., retired aluminum company executive; b. Jackson, Miss., Sept. 18, 1924; s. William Black and May Isom (Whitten) M.; m. Lillian Wells, Sept. 14, 1946; children—Kathryn Ramsey Moore Dannels, William Black III, Bethany Moore Richmond. B.S. in Chem. Engring., U. Louisville, 1945, M.S. in Chem. Engring., 1947. Registered profl. engr., Ky. Chem. engr. U. Louisville Research Inst., 1947-49; mktg. mgr. Reynolds Metals, Louisville, 1949-58, dir. mktg., Richmond, Va., 1958-61, regional gen. mgr., St. Louis, 1961-69, v.p., Richmond, 1969-80, ret. Contbr. articles to profl. jours. V.p. bd. dirs. Rappahannock Found. Served to lt. USNR, 1943-47. Mem. Ky. Soc. Profl. Engrs., AIA (hon.). Baptist. Clubs: Indian Creek (Kilmarnock, Va.); Country of Va. (Richmond). Avocations: fishing; farming. Home: PO Box 1300 Kilmarnock VA 22482

MOORE, WILLIAM ESTILL, JR., land management and financial executive; b. Bowling Green, Ky., Dec. 19, 1920; s. William E. and Carolyn (Elkin) M.; m. Margaret Jackson Shanks, Mar. 12, 1952; children: Carrol Meteer, William Estill III, Marilyn Taylor, Thomas Edwin III, James Rogers. B.A., Stanford, 1947. Asst. to pres. Tejon Ranch Co., Bakersfield, Calif., 1947-48, v.p., 1948-58, exec. v.p., 1958-60, pres., 1960-70, chmn. exec. com., 1963-70, exec. cons., 1970—; v.p. Chandler-Sherman Corp., 1949-56, pres., bd. dirs., 1956-70; pres., bd. dirs. Rowland Land Co., 1955-70; chmn. bd. dirs. Heritage Investment Corp., 1973—; bd. dirs., mem. exec. com., mem. investment com. T.I. Corp. and Title Ins. & Trust Co., 1956-84; founding dir. Heritage Savs. & Loan Assn., chmn. bd., 1973-79; bd. dirs. San Joaquin Valley Oil Producers, Pacific Western Industries Inc. Bd. dirs. Tejon-Castac Water Dist., 1961-70; sec. Calif. Water Resources Assn., 1960-74, pres., 1974-78, chmn. bd., 1978-87, also bd. dirs. and mem. exec. com.; sec. Wheeler Ridge-Maricopa Water Dist., Kern County, Arvin-Edison Water Dist., 1952-72, Kern County, Calif. Irrigation Dist. Assn., Feather River Project Assn., 1955-66; bd. dirs. Kern County Water Commn., 1956—, pres., 1966-76; bd. dirs., exec. cons. Kings County Devel. Corp.; bd. dirs. No. Kern Water Dist., 1972—, sec., 1977—. Served to lt. col. USMCR, 1940-46. Decorated Navy Cross, Silver Star medal, Purple Heart. Mem. Philharmonic Assn. Los Angeles, Kern County Water Assn. (pres. 1970-73, dir. 1955—), Calif. Farm Bur., Calif. Cattlemen's Assn., Calif. C. of C., Bakersfield C. of C., Los Angeles C. of C., Navy League (v.p., dir. Bakersfield). Republican. Presbyn. Clubs: Commonwealth (San Francisco); Annandale (Pasadena, Calif.); Food and Wine Soc. (London, Eng.). Address: 2930 22d St Bakersfield CA 93301

MOORE, WOODVALL RAY, librarian; b. Flatwoods, Ky., May 19, 1942; s. Clyde Raymond and Erma (Gallion) M.; A.A., So. Bible Coll., Houston, 1963, B.S., 1965; M.S. in L.S., U. Ky., 1972; m. Sarah Ellen Markham, Dec. 14, 1963; children—Tamra Sheri, Woodvall Allen. Dir. library So. Bible Coll., 1968-76; dir. library services Evangel Coll., Springfield, Mo., 1976—; bd. dirs. Mo. Library Network Corp.; past pres. adv. council Southwestern Mo. Library Network; chaplain Greene County Sheriff Dept.; presenter Assemblies of God Marriage Encounter Inc.; ordained Assemblies of God Ch., 1969. Precint chmn. Republican Party, Houston, 1972-76. Mem. ALA, Mo. Library Assn. (computer and info. tech. com.), Assn. Christian Librarians (dir. 1979—, pres. 1983-84, dir. pub. relations 1988—), Springfield Librarians Assn. Republican. Office: 1111 N Glenstone St Springfield MO 65802

MOORER, DOUGLASS CHARLES, educator; b. Birmingham, Ala., May 5, 1951; s. Charles and Lou Ethel (Thornton) M.; BS, Ala. State U., 1975; MS U.S. Sports Acad., 1987. Instr., Lawson State Community Coll., Ala., 1974-76; Tchr. Corps Project community coordinator Miles Coll., Fairfield, Ala., 1976-77; elem. sch. tchr. Birmingham Bd. Edn., 1977—; athletic trainer Summer Youth Sports program, Miles Coll., 1977-82, G.W. Carver High Sch., 1978—. Vol. water safety instr. ARC, 1969-82; Boys' Club worker, 1969-73, 78-81. Recipient Vol. Service award ARC, 1980, 81, 85, 86, Service award Upward Bound Program, 1979. Mem. Assn. for Secondary Curriculum Devel., Nat. Assn. Sports Ofcls., Nat. Fedn. Interscholastic Ofcls. Assn., Nat. Athletic Trainers Assn. (assoc.), AAHPERD. Democrat. Roman Catholic. Lodge: Foresters, Knights of St. Peter Claver. Home: 3140 Spaulding St SW Birmingham AL 35221 Office: Birmingham Bd Edn 4311 Court J Birmingham AL 35208

MOORHEAD, THOMAS EDWARD, lawyer; b. Owosso, Mich., Aug. 27, 1946; s. Kenneth Edward and Lillian Jane (Becker) M.; B.A. in Communication Arts, Mich. State U., 1970; J.D., Detroit Coll. Law, 1973; m. Marjorie E. Semans, Sept. 9, 1967; children—Robert Scott, Kristine Elizabeth. Admitted to Mich. bar, 1973; legal counsel Legis. Service Bur., State of Mich., Lansing, 1973-74; ptnr. firm Des Jardins & Moorhead, P.C., Owosso, 1974-85; sole practice, Owosso, 1985—. Pres., Bentley Sch. PTO, Owosso; mem. adminstrv. bd. 1st United Meth. Ch., Owosso; bd. dirs. Shiawassee Arts Council; treas. Cub Scout Pack 67 Boy Scouts Am.; mem. Community Prayer Breakfast Com.; mem. Shiawassee County Republican Exec. Com. Mem. Am. Bar Assn., Assn. Trial Lawyers Am., Shiawassee County Bar Assn. (past pres.), State Bar of Mich., Mich. State U. Alumni Assn., Owosso Jaycees (pres.; named Outstanding Local Pres. by state assn. 1977). Republican. Home: 1265 Ada St Owosso MI 48867 Office: 217 N Washington St Suites 105-107 Owosso MI 48867

MOORHEAD, WILLIAM DAVID, III, lawyer; b. Knoxville, Tenn., Aug. 13, 1952; s. William David and Virginia (Wood) M.; m. Thelma Rogena Murray, Sept. 4, 1976; children—John Murray, Virginia Salima. B.B.A., U. Ga., 1973, J.D., 1976. Bar: Tenn. 1976, U.S. Dist. Ct. (ea. dist.) Tenn. 1976, Ga. 1977, U.S. Tax Ct. 1977, U.S. Ct. Claims, 1985, U.S. Supreme Ct. 1985. Assoc. Stophel, Caldwell & Heggie, Chattanooga, 1976-77; ptnr. Murray & Moorhead, Americus, Ga., 1977-80, Vansant, Corriere & Moorhead, P.C., Albany, Ga., 1981-85, Hall & Moorhead, P.C., Albany, 1985—; pres. Continental Consol. Corp., Albany, 1983—, W.D. Moorhead & Co., Albany, 1984—; Del. Ga. Dem. Com., 1978. Vassar Wooley scholar, 1973-76. Mem. ABA, Tenn. Bar Assn., Ga. Bar Assn., Dougherty County Bar Assn., Albany Estate Planning Council (v.p. 1982-83). Baptist. Home: 3509 Old Dawson Rd Albany GA 31707 Office: Hall & Moorhead PC 314 Residence Ave Albany GA 31701

MOORTY, S. S., English language educator; b. Madanapalle, India; came to U.S., 1970, naturalized, 1984; s. Lakshmi N. and Annapoorna (Ayyagari) Sikha; m. Vijayalakshmi Viswanatha, May 16, 1968; children—Naresh, Neela. B. Commerce, Osmania U., 1956; M.A., Delhi U., India, 1966; Ph.D. in English, U. Utah, 1976. Adminstrv. asst. Council of Sci. and Indsl. Research, New Delhi, India, 1957-67; lectr. English, Shri Ram Coll. Commerce, Delhi U., 1967-70; teaching asst. dept. English, U. Utah, Salt Lake City, 1970-74; instr. English, Westminster Coll., Salt Lake City, 1970-71; asst. prof. English, So. Utah State Coll., Cedar City, 1975-80, assoc. prof., 1980-88, prof., 1988—, dir. composition, 1982-85, 87-88, chmn. English dept., 1985-87; faculty adviser lit. mag., 1977-82; lectr. Shakespeare high schs., community groups, Elder Hostel mems., faculty groups; panelist on new approaches tp Shakespearean comedy World Shakespeare Congress, West Berlin, Germany, 1986. Author poems in anthology; contbr. articles, book revs. to profl. jours.; contbr. poetry to jours. Assoc. mem. South Asian Area Ctr., U. Wis. Recipient numerous awards for debating, writing, poetry, and acad. excellence; Am. Studies Research Ctr. grantee, 1970; postdoctorate summer fellow NEH, Cornell U., 1984; recipient Disting. Faculty Honor Lecture award So. Utah State Coll., 1984. Mem. MLA (dir. Asian Langs. and Lit. sect), Rocky Mountain MLA (dir. Asian Langs. and Lit. sect.), Utah Acad. Scis., Arts and Letters (sect. leader gen. lit. 1977, 80, 85, 88, Disting. Coll. Teaching award 1986), Western Lit. Assn., Western Social Sci. Assn., European Assn. Commonwealth Lang. and Lit., Internat. Shakespeare Assn. (Stratford-upon-Avon), Shakespeare Assn. Am., Frank Norris Soc., Soc. Narrative Lit., Assn. Mormon Letters, Phi Delta Kappa (pres. So. Utah chpt. 1984-85, newsletter editor). Hindu. Home: 1178 Mountain View Dr Cedar City UT 84720 Office: So Utah State Coll Dept English Lang and Lit Cedar City UT 84720

MOOS, EDWARD A., securities executive; b. N.Y.C., July 17, 1937; s. Henry H. and Dorothy E. (Warren) M.; B.A. in History, Houghton Coll., 1959; postgrad. Sch. Fgn. Affairs, George Washington U., 1959-60, Grad. Sch. Bus., NYU, 1961-63; m. Louise E. Wheadon, Dec. 26, 1964; children—Philip, Antonia. With Smith Barney, N.Y.C. 1961-63; exec. v.p. Weeden Co., N.Y.C. 1963-77, mem. exec. com. 1975-77, mgr. mcpl. bond dept., U.S. govt. bond dept. and internat. bond dept., 1977-78; chmn. bd., chief exec. officer E.A. Moos & Co. Inc., Summit, N.J., 1978—. Bd. dirs. Cheshire Home, A. Gary Shilling and Co. Served with U.S. Army, 1960-61. Mem. Pub. Securities Assn., Mcpl. Bond Club N.Y. (gov.). Republican. Clubs: Short Hills, Racquet of Short Hills. Home: 19 Moraine Pl Short Hills NJ 07078 Office: 350 Springfield Ave Summit NJ 07901

MOOS, GILBERT ELLSWORTH, chemistry educator; consultant; b. Hasbrouck Heights, N.J., May 1, 1915; s. Bernard and Florence Margaret (Dalrymple) M.; m. Ruth Carolyn Feinthel, June 17, 1944 (dec. 1983); children—Carolyn Ruth, Walter Hamilton. B.S. with honors St. Lawrence U., 1936; M.S., M.I.T., 1937, Ph.D., 1939. Instr. chemistry Rollins Coll., 1939-40; research assoc. M.I.T., 1940; research chemist, group leader Am. Oak Leather Co., 1941-42; research chemist, group leader, sect. head Celanese Corp. Am., 1942-52; asst. prof., assoc. prof. chemistry St. Lawrence U., Canton, N.Y., 1952-63; chmn. dept. chemistry State Univ. Coll., Fredonia, N.Y., 1963-68, prof. chemistry, 1963-83, prof. emeritus, 1983—; cons. Howard Smith Paper Mills, Ltd., Cornwall, Ont., Can., 1955-61, Chemstrand Corp., Decatur, Ala., 1958, Seton Leather Co., Newark, N.J., 1958, McGraw-Hill Book Co., Inc., N.Y.C., 1961-62, D. Van Nostrand Co., Inc., Princeton, N.J., 1960-66. Author: Natural and Synthetic Fibers, 1980; Chemistry of Cancer, 1982; Essays on Biochemistry (7 vols.), 1969-75. Editor The Test Tube newsletter, 1953; mem. editorial bd. The Chemist, 1986—. Patentee in field. Contbr. articles to profl. jours. Dir. Allegheny Mountain Sci. Fair, N.Y., Pa., 1975-77, bd. dirs. 1966-83; chmn. Lake Shore Area Am. Cancer Soc., Chautauqua County, N.Y., 1969; pub. lectr. various clubs, schs., socs., etc., N.Y., N.J., Pa., Md., 1969—. Recipient Dale Carnegie award, 1951. Recipient numerous research grants, 1954-80. Fellow AAAS, Am. Inst. Chemists (cert.); mem. Am. Chem. Soc. (sec., chmn. local sect. 1952-68, 50 yrs.), AAUP (St. Lawrence U. chpt. v.p., pres.), N.Y. Acad. Scis., United Univ. Professions. Republican. Episcopalian. Avocations: stamp collecting, coin collecting, walking. Home: 34 Middlesex Rd Fredonia NY 14063 Office: SUNY Dept Chemistry Fredonia NY 14063

MOOSA, IBRAHIM RASHEED, educational administrator; b. Maldive Islands, Mar. 18, 1951; s. Moosa Hassan and Hussain Hajar Moosa; m. Shamiya Latheef Rasheed, Feb. 12, 1976; children: Razeen, Razna, Razan, Risal. BS in Math. with honors, Azhar U., Cairo, Arab Republic Egypt, 1975. Math. tchr. Majeediya Sch., Male, Rep. Maldives, 1975-78, Sci. Edn. Ctr., Male, Rep. Maldives, 1978-80; asst. dir. Inst. Islamic Studies, Male, Rep. Maldives, 1980-83, dir., 1983—; cons. Republic Maldives Ministry of Edn., 1982—; translator Nat. Council for Linguistic and Hist. Research, 1986-87. Radio commentator Voice of Maldives, 1986—; ednl. scriptwriter for Maldives radio and TV programs, 1985—; editor and columnist religious and current affairs; author various ednl. texts. Mem. Nat. Council for Mosques (sec.-gen. 1986—). Islamic. Home: H Meerubahuruge-Aage, Male 2005, Republic of Maldives Office: Inst of Islamic Studies, Sosun Magu, Male 2006, Republic of Maldives

MOOSE, BRIAN DAVID, artist, art director; b. San Mateo, Calif., July 30, 1958; s. Irvin Russel and Gene (Thompson) M. AA in Comml. Art, Coll. of San Mateo, 1981; BFA in Illustration, Calif. State U., Long Beach, 1984. Pvt. practice illustrator San Mateo, 1977-81, Long Beach, 1981—; creative cons. Walt Disney Prodns., Anaheim, Calif., 1981-84; sr. model builder Walt Disney Co., Washington, 1984—; art dir. Am. Space Meml. Found. Inc., Washington, 1986—; cons., designer Toyota, 1986—, Design Sci. Internat., Los Angeles, 1986—, Quadrant Group Inc., Los Angeles, 1986—, Cook Design, Silicon Valley, Calif., 1988—. Represented in permanent collection Smithsonian Inst., 1984; exhibited in shows of N.Y. Soc. Illustrators, N.Y.C., 1985, The Soc. of Illustrators (Illustrators 27), Genre Art Pubs. Ltd., Burbank, Calif. Mem. Graphic Artist Guild, Western Art Dirs. Club, OASIS L5 Soc., Montage Arts Group. Republican. Home: 134 McLellan Ave San Mateo CA 94403 Office: Walt Disney Co 1313 Harbor Blvd Anaheim CA 92803

MOOSE, GEORGE E., government official; b. N.Y.C., June 23, 1944; s. Robert and Ellen Amanda Lane (Jones) M.; m. Judith Roberta Kaufmann, Jan. 3, 1981. BA, Grinnell Coll., 1966; postgrad., Syracuse U., 1967. Spl. asst. to under sec. for polit. affairs Dept. of State, Washington, 1977-78, dep. dir. for South Africa, 1978-79, U.S. ambassador to Benin, from 1983, U.S. ambassador to Senegal, 1988—, now with mgmt. ops.; dep. polit. counselor U.S. Mission to UN, Washington, 1980-83. Recipient Superior Honor award Dept. of State, Grenada, 1974, 79, Meritorious Honor award, Washington, 1975; fgn. affairs fellow Council on Fgn. Relations, N.Y.C., 1979-80. Mem. Am. Fgn. Service Assn. Home and Office: Dept of State 2201 C St NW Washington DC 20520 *

MOOTS, KENNETH LEE, agricultural company executive; b. Ness City, Kans., Dec. 12, 1929; s. Alvie Ray and Ethel (Patterson) M.; m. Bernice Fackler, June 20, 1955 (div. 1979); children: Gloria, Jaque, James, Heather; m. Ann Windsor, Apr. 2, 1980. BS, Colo. A&M U., 1952; MA, Kans. State U., 1955. Co-owner, pres. Sunnyside Inc., Cottage Grove, Oreg., 1955-60; nat. mgr. mktg. devel., also other dist.-level positions Chevron Chem. Co., San Francisco, 1960-73; project mgr. Checci Co., Kabul, Afghanistan, 1973-75, Jordan Valley Authority, Amman, 1979-80, Harrod (Saudi Arabia) Agr. Project, 1980; v.p., gen. mgr. Western Farm Service, San Francisco, 1975-79; chief party Internat. Fertilizer Devel. Ctr., Dacca, Bangladesh, 1981—; bd. dirs. Western AG, Fresno, Calif., Creative Engring., Phoenix, Polo Verde Inc.; advisor Nat. Agrl. Council, Kabul, 1973; cons. Bangladesh Fertilizer Policy Rev., 1981—. Contbr. articles to profl. jours. Named 1st citizen Burlington (Wash.) City Council, 1964; recipient agrl. gold award of yr. Afghanistan Nat. Council, 1973. Mem. Am. Mgmt. Assn., Agr. Devel. Council (bd. dirs.), Internat. Tng. Inst. (bd. dirs.), Western Agr. Chem. Assn. (bd. dirs. 1975). Republican. Clubs: Dhaka, Bengal (Calcutta, India). Home: GPO Box 3044, Dhaka Bangladesh Office: Internat Fertilizer Devel, GPO Box 3044, Dhaka Bangladesh

MORADEYO, ISRAEL OLUFEMI, company executive; b. Abeokuta, Nigeria, Mar. 11, 1941; s. John Ogunsina and Emily (Osalola) M.; m. Margaret Mopelola Ogundipe, July 28, 1968; children: Kolawole, Femi, Tope. Student, African Ch. Gramma Sch., Abeokuta, 1956-60; diploma in nursing, Long Grove Hosp., Epsom-Surrey, Eng., 1967; diploma in mktg., S.W. London Coll., 1969. Registered mental nurse, London. Staff nurse Long Grove Hosp., Epsom-Surrey, Eng., 1967-68; dep. charge nurse St. John's Hosp., London, 1968-70; med. sales mgr. Nimesco Nigeria Ltd., Lagos, 1970-71, Sonnar Nigeria Ltd., Lagos, 1972-74; owner Femope Mktg. Co., Lagos, 1975-85; chief exec. Femope Ltd., Lagos, 1985—; coordinator distbn. USAID Donated Family Planning Projects Commodities in Nigeria, U.S., 1981—; project dir. Jhpiego Equipment Maintenance Ctr. in Nigeria, Balt., U.S.A., 1981—; Nigerian fin. agt. for Internat. Project Assistance Services, N.C., U.S.A., 1987—, Population Crisis Com., N.Y., U.S.A., 1987—; coordinator Kuje Awuwo Community Devel. Council, Lagos, 1979—. African Anglican. Clubs: 57/62 (treas. 1985—). Office: Femope Ltd, 83 Palm Ave, PO Box 1543, Mushin, Lagos Nigeria

MORADI-ARAGHI, AHMAD, research chemist; b. Tehran, Iran, Mar. 23, 1943; came to U.S., 1968, naturalized, 1985; s. Rajabali and Kobra (Bakhtiari) M.; m. Anita Mendoza, Feb. 2, 1974; children: Kevin, David, Michael. BS, U. Tehran, 1965; MS, Tenn. Tech. U., 1971; PhD, North Tex. State U., 1976. Postdoctoral fellow N. Tex. State U., Denton, 1976-77; asst. prof. Jundi Shapur U., Ahwaz, Iran, 1977-78; postdoctoral fellow Tex. Christian

U., Ft. Worth, 1978-80; research chemist Phillips Petroleum Co., Bartlesville, Okla., 1980-86, sr. research chemist, 1986-; sr. chemist Nat. Inst. Petroleum and Energy Research, Bartlesville, 1988—. Contbr. articles to profl. jours. Patentee in field. Served to 2d lt. Iranian Army, 1965-67. Robert A. Welch Found. fellow, 1973-76, 76-77, 78-80. Mem. Am. Chem. Soc. (polymeric materials sci. and engring. div.), Soc. Petroleum Engrs., Alpha Xi Sigma. Democrat. Islam. Club: Tulsa Zoo Friends. Avocations: photography, gardening, woodworking. Home: 1931 Windstone Dr Bartlesville OK 74006 Office: Phillips Petroleum Co 229 GB PRC8 Bartlesville OK 74004

MORAGODA, A. M., holding company executive. Mng. dir. Mercantile Credit Group, Colombo, Sri Lanka. Office: Mercantile Credit Group, Mercantile House 55, Jandhipathi Mawatha, Colombo 1 Sri Lanka

MORAIN, MARY STONE DEWING, assn. exec.; b. Boston, Mar. 18, 1911; d. Arthur S. and Frances (Hall Rousmaniere) Dewing; student Radcliffe Coll., 1930-33; BS, Simmons Sch. Social Work, 1934; MA, U. Chgo., 1937; cert. social work U. So. Calif., 1941; m. Lloyd L. Morain, July 6, 1946. Social worker, Calif., N.Y.C., 1941-45; tchr. social scis. Keuka Coll., N.Y., 1945-46; v.p. LWV, Boston, 1946-53; bd. dirs., v.p. Planned Parenthood League Mass., 1948-52; bd. dirs., pres. Planned Parenthood Assn. San Francisco, 1953-60; bd. dirs. Internat. Humanist and Ethical Union, 1953-65; bd. dirs., v.p. Assn. Vol. Sterilization, 1963-77, 79—, UNESCO Assn. U.S.A., 1977—, Monterey YWCA, 1975-80, UN Assn. San Francisco, 1961-69; pres. Internat. Soc. Gen. Semantics, 1976—; bd. dir. Tor House Found., 1984—, Hidden Valley Inst. of the Arts, 1983—. Fellow World Acad. Art and Sci.; mem. Am. Assn. Social Workers. Club: Altrusa. Author: (with Lloyd Morain) Humanism as the Next Step, 1954; contbr. articles to profl. jours. Editor: Teaching General Semantics, 1969; Classroom Exercises in General Semantics, 1980; Bridging Worlds through General Semantics, 1984; Enriching Professional Skills Through General Semantics, 1986. Home: PO Box 7190 Carmel CA 93921 Office: PO Box 2469 San Francisco CA 94126

MORAIS, AULO PRADO, auditor; b. Paraguaçu, Brazil, Nov. 6, 1940; s. José Armando and Heloisa Prado Morais; m. Marcia Almeida Morais, June 26, 1965; children: Aulo Márcio, Mariluse, Marcelo, Mariane, Cristiane. B in Acctg., Cath. U., Belo Horizonte, Brazil, 1967, BBA, 1968; grad. in Auditing, Fed. U., Belo Horizonte, 1973, NYU, 1975. Acct. Banco Mercantil de Minas Gerais, Belo Horizonte, 1961-68, Planotec, Belo Horizonte, 1968-70; fin. mgr. Hidrominas, Belo Horizonte, 1970-73; auditor Orplan-Ind. Auditors, Belo Horizonte, 1973-74; auditor/mgr. Construtora Mendes Jr., S.A., Belo Horizonte, 1975—. Mem. Inst. Internal Auditors, Inst. de Auditors Internal Brazil. Home: Rua Inspetor Nilo Seabra 85, 31 170 Cidade Nova, Belo Horizonte Brazil Office: Construtora Mendes Jr SA, Av Prof Mario Werneck 1685, 30 430 Belo Horizonte Brazil

MORALES, ARMANDO, psychotherapist, mental health educator; b. Los Angeles, Sept. 18, 1932; s. Roberto Torres and Lupe (Acevedo) M.; m. Rebecca Gonzales, Aug. 27, 1955 (div. Apr. 1980); children: Roland Victor, Gary Vincent. AA, East Los Angeles Jr. Coll., 1955; BA, Los Angeles State Coll., 1957; MSW, U. So. Calif. Sch. Social Work, 1963, DSW, 1971. Gang group worker Los Angeles Times Boys Club, 1954-57; sr. dep. probation officer Los Angeles County Probation Dept., 1957-63, Las Palmas Sch. for Girls, Los Angeles County Probation Dept., 1963-66; supervising psychiat. social worker, mental health cons. Los Angeles County Dept. Mental Health, 1966-71; prof., chief clin. social work dept., dir. Spanish speaking psychosocial clinic, dir. intern tng. program Neuropsychiat. Inst. UCLA Sch. Medicine, 1971—; cons. Calif. Youth Authority, East Los Angeles, 1977—; speaker in field. Author: Ando Sangrando: A Study of Mexican American-Police Conflict, 1972, Social Work: A Profession of Many Faces, 1977, 80, 83, 86, 88; co-editor The Psychosocial Development of Minority Group Children, 1983; composer ethnic songs. pres. Western Ctr. on Law and Poverty, Inc., Los Angeles, 1975-77, bd. dirs., 1968-78; vice chmn. Citizens Adv. Council, Calif. Dept. Mental Health, 1977-82. Served as sgt. USAF, 1951-54. Appointed to Pres.' Commn. on Mental Health Task Panel on Legal and Ethical Issues, 1977-78; fellow NIMH, 1962, 69, 77; named Far East Air Force Bantamweight Champion, 1952, 53. Mem. Nat. Assn. Social Workers (cert.), Trabajadores de La Raza, Council on Mental Health Western Interstate Commn. for Higher Edn., 1976-78 (chmn.), Commn. Human Relations (commr., v.p. 1975-78). Democrat. Roman Catholic. Office: UCLA Sch Medicine Neuropsychiatric Inst 760 Westwood Plaza Los Angeles CA 90024

MORALES, ENRIQUE C. MIGUEL, engineer, teacher; b. Alcazar de S. Juan, Ciudad Real, Spain, Nov. 11, 1949; s. Licinio and Antonia (Campo) M.; m. Debra Collins, Nov. 26, 1972 (div. 1981); 1 dau., Coral Sue. B.S. in Petroleum Engring. with honors, U. Tulsa, 1972; M.S. in Petroleum Engring., Stanford U., 1975, M.S. in Ops. Research, 1976; Petroleum Engr. (reval.), Central U. Venezuela, 1979. Well site engr. Shell Venezuela, Lagunillas, 1972-73, heavy oil reservoir engr., 1973-74; research engr. Chevron, La Habra, Calif., 1976-77; sr. reservoir engr. Shell Internat./Maraven, Caracas, Venezuela, The Hague, Holland, 1977-81, head of short term planning, Caracas, 1982-83, project leader, The Hague, 1983-86; head onshore oil reservoir engring., NAM, Holland, 1986—; asst. prof. Calif. State U.-Fullerton, 1976-77, Cen. Univ. Grad. Div., Caracas, 1978-80. Shell Oil Co. scholar, 1968-72, 74-76. Mem. Soc. Petroleum Engrs. Roman Catholic. Avocations: sailing, tennis, stamp collecting, horseback riding. Home: de Vallei 86, 9405 KL Assen Holland Office: Nederlandse Aardolie, Maatschappij, PO Box 28, Assen Holland

MORALES-GALARRETA, JULIO, child psychoanalyst, psychiatrist, child psychiatrist; b. Trujillo, Peru, Dec. 1, 1936; came to U.S., 1973; s. Julio Morales-Fernandez and Lidia (Galarreta) Morales; m. Lourdes Tincopa, Dec. 3, 1966; children: Lourdes Lydia, Julio Fernando. MD, U. Trujillo, 1966; grad., St. Louis Psychoanalytic Inst., 1984, grad. in child psychoanalysis, 1985. Diplomate Am. Bd. Psychiatry and Neurology; cert. psychoanalyst.; cert. child psychoanalyst. Resident in psychiatry Ministry of Pub. Health, Peru, 1965-68; supr. psychiat. tng. program Ministry Pub. Health, Peru, 1970-72; physician and surgeon U. Trujillo, 1966; instr. psychaitry St. Marcos U., Peru, 1968-72; resident in psychiatry Fairfield Hills Hosp., Newtown, Conn., 1972-74; fellow in child psychiatry Washington U., St. Louis, 1974-76, instr. child psychiatry, 1976-82; dir. child devel. project St. Louis Psychonalytic Inst., 1982—; asst. clin. prof. psychiatry and pediatrics St. Louis U., 1983—; faculty psychoanalysis and child analysis St. Louis Psychoanalytic Inst., 1984—. Fellow Peruvian Psychiat. Assn.; mem. St. Louis Met. Med. Soc., Am. Psychiat. Assn., Am. Acad. Child Psychiatry, Am. Psychoanalytic Assn., Am. Soc. Adolescent Psychiatry, Assn. Child Psychoanalysis. Home: 7415 Byron Pl Saint Louis MO 63105 Office: 141 N Meramec Ave Saint Louis MO 63105

MORALES-LEZCANO, VICTOR M., historian, educator; b. Las Palmas, Spain, Jan. 30, 1939; s. Morales Miranda and Lezcano Garcia. MA in History, U. Madrid, 1961, PhD in History, 1965. Asst. U. Madrid, 1963-64, U. La Laguna, Canary Islands, Spain, 1964-65; vis. lectr. Wilmington (Ohio) Coll., 1966-67; researcher U. Paris, 1968-70; lectr. U. Madrid, 1972-82; prof. history Spanish Open U., Madrid, 1982—; lectr. Diplomatic Sch., Madrid, 1981—. Author: Spain in the War Years (1939-45), 1980, Relations Between Spain and North of Africa, 2d edit., 1986; contbr. articles to profl. jours. Salzburg (Austria) Seminar fellow, 1972; grantee Brit. Council. Mem. Assn. Española of Africanistas (v.p. 1982—), Reunion Bienal España-Africa En Las Palmas (bd. dirs. 1984—). Home: Dracena 27 1B, 28016 Madrid Spain

MORAN, DERMOT BRENDAN, philosopher, educator, broadcaster; b. Dublin, Ireland, June 21, 1953; s. Patrick and Nora (O'Sullivan) M. BA, U. Coll., Dublin, 1973; MA, Yale U., 1974, M.Phil., 1976, PhD, 1986. Teaching asst. Yale U., New Haven, Conn., 1974-78, prof. philosophy, 1986—; lectr. Queen's U., Belfast, Northern Ireland, 1979-82, Maynooth Coll., County Kildare, Ireland, 1982—; vis. prof. Yale U., 1986-87. Author: The Philosophy of John Scottus Eriugena, 1988; editor Irish Writers Coop., 1977-79, Crane Bag Jour., 1977-86; contbr. articles to profl. jours.; broadcaster Radio Telefis Eireann, Dublin, 1984—. Recipient New Irish Writing award Hennessy/Irish Press, 1970; Yale U. fellow, 1973. Mem. Irish Philos. Soc. (sec. 1985-87), Irish Fedn. Univ. Tchrs., Irish Aikido Fedn. Office: Maynooth Coll, Dept Philosophy, Kildare Ireland

MORAN, HAROLD JOSEPH, retired lawyer; b. N.Y.C., Feb. 21, 1907; s. Thomas J. and Leonore M.F. (Geoghegan) M.; A.B. cum laude, Holy Cross Coll., 1928; LL.B., Fordham U., 1932; J.D., 1968; m. Geraldine D. Starkey, July 12, 1956. Admitted to N.Y. bar, 1934; practiced in N.Y.C., 1934-42, Bklyn., 1949-57, Malverne, N.Y., 1977—; law dept. Title Guarantee & Trust Co., Bklyn., 1945-48; sr. atty. real property bur. N.Y. State Law Dept., Albany, 1957-63, N.Y.C., 1963-77, ret., 1977; spl. dep. atty. gen. election frauds, 1973. Title closer City Title Co., Bklyn., 1949-52; U.S., P.R. mortgage loan examiner Cadwalader, Wickersham & Taft, N.Y.C., 1952-56, 63—, 9th Fed. Savs. & Loan Assn., N.Y.C., 1971—; instr. law St. John's U. Sch. Commerce, Jamaica, N.Y., 1956-57. Served with AUS, 1942-45. Knight Holy Sepulchre. Mem. Am. Bar Assn., Bar Assn. Nassau County, Am. Judicature Soc., N.Y. County Lawyers Assn., Catholic Lawyers Guild. Democrat. Roman Catholic. Club: Southward Ho Country. Home: 407 Hamlet Ave Carolina Beach NC 28428

MORAN, JAMES B., ambassador; b. Port Angeles, Wash., Apr. 30, 1924; s. Edward George and Johanna (Linehan) M.; m. Jean Elton, Apr. 14, 1953; children: Johanna Jean, Thomas Elton, Robert James, John Frederic. BA, U. Wash., 1950; student, Indsl. Coll. of Armed Forces, 1969-70. Exec. trainee Union Oil of Calif., 1949-50; purser Puget Sound Nav. Co., 1950-52; various positions U.S. Fgn. Service, Tehran, Rangoon, Moscow, Saigon, Beijing, Washington, 1952-57; U.S. ambassador to Seychelles U.S. Fgn. Service, Victoria, 1987—. Served to 1st lt. USAF, Pacific. Recipient Meritorious & Superior Honor awards Dept. of State, 1964, 80, 83, Performance Pay award Sr. Fgn. Service, 1982, 84, Presdl. Pay award, Sr. Fgn. Service, 1986.. Mem. Am. Fgn. Service Assn., U. Wash. Alumni Assn., Alpha Tau Omega Alumni Assn. Home: 6001 Thomas Dr Springfield VA 22150 Office: Am Embassy Victoria Box 148APO New York NY 09030

MORAN, JOHN GERARD, physician; b. Dublin, Ireland, June 9, 1926; arrived in Brunei, 1962; s. Lawrence Moran and Susan McCormack. D.P.H. with high honors, Nat. U. Ireland, 1951; Diploma in Tropical Medicine, U. London, 1959. House surgeon Ashford Hosp., Kent, Eng., 1949-50; intern Syracuse (N.Y.) Gen. Hosp., 1950-51; resident surgeon East Orange (N.J.) Gen. Hosp., 1951-52; asst. health officer Town of Bristol, Eng., 1957-59; full-time Royal Army service doctor 1959-83; med. officer Royal Brunei Malay Regiment, 1964—. Author: Juvenile Delinquency, 1959. Served with Royal Brit. Army, 1955-57. Decorated Officer Order Brit. Empire, Officer 1st Class Most Honorable Order Crown of Brunei; accorded equivalent title of Lord by the Sultan of Brunei; recipient Sultan's Personal Medal. Fellow Royal Coll. Physicians Ireland, Royal Coll. Surgeons Ireland; mem. Brit. Med. Assn. Roman Catholic. Clubs: Wig and Pen (London); Royal Brunei Yacht, Royal Brunei Polo. Home and Office: Bandar Seri Begawan Brunei

MORAN, MARTIN JOSEPH, fund raising company executive; b. Bklyn., Nov. 3, 1930; s. Dominick and Mary (Lydon) M.; m. Mary Therese Schofield, June 5, 1954; children: Martin Joseph, John P., Maureen M., Thomas S., Robert P., William M., Maria M. BA, St. John's U., 1952. Profl. fund raising cons., 1956—; founder Martin J. Moran Co., Inc., N.Y.C., 1964, pres., 1964-74, chmn. bd., 1974—. Mem. Cardinal's Com. for Edn., N.Y.C., 1970-79, Cardinal's Com. for Laity Archdiocese N.Y., 1979—, Am. Revolution Bicentennial Commn., Oyster Bay, N.Y.; mem. Massapequa Park (N.Y.) Bd. Zoning Appeals, 1972-84, chmn., 1978-84; mem. Massapequa Park Ethics Commn., 1969-72; trustee Notre Dame Coll., S.I., 1969-72, La Salle Acad., N.Y.C., 1971-87; mem. pres.'s council Cath. U.P.R., Ponce, 1966-71. Served as aviator USNR, 1952-56. Decorated knight Order Holy Sepulchre, Pope Paul VI, 1968, Knight of Malta, Pope Paul VI, 1973; recipient Pietas medal St. John's U., N.Y., 1988. Mem. Navy League, Navy Hist. Assn., Am. Assn. Fund Raising Counsel (bd. dirs. 1970—), Friendly Sons of St. Patrick. Roman Catholic. Club: Madison Square Garden (N.Y.C.); Lost Tree Village Golf (North Palm Beach, Fla.). Lodge: KC. Home: 1300 Lake Shore Dr Massapequa Park NY 11762 Office: One Penn Plaza New York NY 10119

MORAN, PHILIP DAVID, lawyer; b. Lynn, Mass., June 3, 1937; s. J. Francis and Margaret M. (Shanahan) M.; m. Carole A. Regan, May 12, 1962; children—Maura F., Philip David. A.B., Holy Cross Coll., 1958; Ed.M., Salem State Coll., 1961; J.D., Suffolk U., 1968. Bar: Mass. 1968, U.S. Dist. Ct. Mass., 1972, U.S. Supreme Ct., 1988. House counsel Viatron Computer Systems Corp., Burlington, Mass., 1968-71; ptnr. Kane & Moran, Lynn, Mass., 1972-78; sole practice Salem, Mass., 1978—; asst. dist. atty. Essex County (Mass.), 1974-78. Bd. dirs. Nat. Right to Life Inc., 1977-83, 87—, treas., 1981-83; mem. Salem Conservation Commn., 1980—, chmn., 1982—; mem. pres.'s council Holy Cross Coll., 1985—; mem. Nat. Inst. Trial Advocacy U. Colo., 1973. Served with U.S. Army, 1960-66. Mem. Mass. Bar Assn., Salem Bar Assn., Lynn Bar Assn., Am. Trial Lawyers Assn. Home: 415 Lafayette St Salem MA 01970 Office: 32 Lynde St Salem MA 01970

MORAN, THOMAS HARRY, university administrator; b. Milw., Oct. 21, 1937; s. Harry Edward and Edna Agnes Moran; B.S., U. Wis., 1964, M.A., 1972, Ph.D., 1974; m. Barbara Ellen Saklad, June 10, 1969; children—David Thomas, Karen Ellen. Dir. capital budgeting Wis. Dept. Adminstrn., 1962-64; exec. dir. Wis. Higher Ednl. Aids Bd., 1964-69; spl. cons. tax policy Wis. Dept. Revenue, 1973-74; dep. dir. Wis. Manpower Council, Office of Gov., 1974-76; v.p. bus. and fin., treas. U. Detroit, 1976-78; exec. assoc. v.p. health affairs U. So. Calif., Los Angeles, 1979-87; v.p. bus. affairs, 1988—. USN fellow, 1957-59; U.S. Office Edn. research fellow, 1973. Mem. Am. Assn. Higher Edn., Phi Kappa Phi. Office: U So Calif 349 Adminstrn Bldg University Park Los Angeles CA 90007

MORANDO, JEANNE BUTLER, savings and loan association executive; b. Crystal River, Fla., Feb. 17, 1928; d. James Taylor and Lucile (Sparkman) Butler; student St. Helen's Hall Jr. Coll., 1945, U. Oreg. Extension Center, Portland, 1949-51, San Joaquin Delta Coll., 1963-65; m. Herbert O. Hope, June 12, 1951 (dec. 1958); m. 2d, Sil S. Morando, Jan. 13, 1961; children—Marta Lucile Hope Morando, James William Hope Morando. Asst. buyer Olds & Kings Western Dept. Stores, Inc., Portland, 1948-51; gen. mgr. Hadley's Inc., Stockton, Calif., 1958-61; with World Savs. and Loan Assn., 1972-77, regional mgr., Oakland and Stockton, Calif., 1974-76, mktg. coordinator, Oakland, 1977; v.p., savs. adminstr., mktg. dir. Stockton Savs. & Loan Assn., 1977—; pres. 1987, Stockton Advt., Mktg. Media Club, Inc., Bd. govs. Stockton Civic Theatre, 1967-69, chmn. public relations and publicity, mem. steering com., 1967-69, 71-72, trustee, 1982-86; mem. adv. bd. U. Coll. of U. Pacific; bd. dirs. San Joaquin County (Calif.) United Way, 1979—, v.p., 1981-85, pres. and 1st v.p., 1985-86, pres., 1986-87, chmn. bd. trustees, 1987—; bd. dirs., v.p. Friends of Chamber Music, sec. Jr. Achievement San Joaquin County, 1984—; mem. San Joaquin County Crime Awareness and Prevention Com., 1980; trustee Friends of Chamber Music, 1983—, bd. dirs., chmn. Artist Selection com. and booking. Lic. real estate broker, Calif. Mem. Savs. Instn. Mktg. Soc. Am. (basic mktg. sch. cert.), Stockton Opera Guild, Stockton Symphony League, San Joaquin County Zool. Soc. (life). Republican. Lutheran. Club: Exec. Women (Stockton). Home: 1202 McClellan Way Stockton CA 95207 Office: 131 N San Joaquin St Stockton CA 95201

MORAVIA, ALBERTO (ALBERTO PINCHERLE MORAVIA), author; b. Rome, Nov. 28, 1907; s. Carlo and Teresa de (Marsanich) M.; m. Elsa Morante, Apr. 21, 1941 (dec. 1985); m. Carmen Lelera, 1986. Author: (novels) Gli indifferenti (The Indifferent Ones), 1929, Le Ambizioni Sbagliate (Mistaken Ambitions), 1935, La Mascherara (The Fancy Dress Party), 1941, Agostino (Corriere Lombardo prize 1945), 1944, La Romana (The Woman of Rome), 1947, La Disubbidienza, 1948, L'Amore Coniugale (Conjugal Love), 1949, Il Conformista (The Conformist), 1951, Il disprezzo (A Ghost at Noon), 1954, La Ciociara (Two Women), 1957, La noia (The Empty Canvas) Viareggio prize 1961), 1961 L'Attenzione (The Lie), 1965, Io e Lui (Two: The Phallis Novel), 1970, La Vita Interiore, 1978; (plays) Teatro, 1958, Beatrice Cenci, 1965, Il mondo e quello che e (The World As It Is), 1966, Il dio Kurt, 1967, La Vita e Gioco, 1970; (short stories) La bella vita, 1935, L'Imbroglio, 1937, I Sogni del Pigro, 1940, L'Amante infelice, 1943, L'Epidemia, 1945, Due Cortigiane, 1945, Racconti Romani (Roman Tales), 1945, I Racconti, 1954, Nuovi Racconti Romani (More Roman Tales), 1959, L'Automa (The Fetish), 1963, L'Uomo come fine, e altri saggi (Man as an End: A Defense of Humanism), 1965, Una cos e una cosa, 1966, Il Paradiso (Paradise and Other Stories), 1970, Un' altra Vita, 1973, A quale tribu appartieni, 1974, Boh, 1975, Impegno Controvoglia, 1980; (travel) La revoluzione culturale in Cina, 1967, The Voyeur, 1987; film critic L'Espresso, 1965—; editor for publishing house; guest Dept. State, U.S., 1955; lectr. Queens Coll., City U. N.Y. and other schs., 1964, 68; visited China, 1967. Decorated chevalier Legion d'Honneur (France); recipient Strega Lit. prize, 1952, Marzotto award for fiction, 1954. Mem. PEN, Am. Acad. Arts and Letters (hon.), Nat. Inst. Arts and Letters (hon.). *

MORAWSKI, MICHAK, transportation executive; b. Warsaw, Poland, Nov. 16, 1945; s. Edward Osóbka and Wiska (Pankiewicz) M.; m. Maria Quoos. M of Law, Warsaw U., 1968; cert. Legal Counsel, Regional Ct. Warsaw, 1972. IATA officer Lot Polish Airlines, Warsaw, 1968-73; mgr. Denmark Lot Polish Airlines, Copenhagen, 1973-77; IATA and tariffs mgr. Lot Polish Airlines, Warsaw, 1977-86, 87—; mgr. Norway Lot Polish Airlines, Oslo, 1986-87. Contbr. articles on civil aviation to Polityka mag. Recipient Medal of Merit Warsaw State Council, 1979. Mem. Country Music Assn. (v.p. 1980-85). Club: Skål (Copenhagen and Oslo). Home: Lowicka 51/56, Warsaw Poland Office: Lot Polish Airlines, 17 Stycznia 39, Warsaw Poland

MORE, PHILIP JEROME, archeologist, art and antiquities company executive; b. Chgo., Dec. 11, 1911; s. Louis Eli and Anna Leah (Kahn) M.; m. Sylvia Sally Bernstein, Oct. 16, 1937 (div. 1977); children: Andrea More Williams, Michael E., William M. B.S., Heidelberg (Germany) U., 1933; postgrad., Ill. Inst. Tech., 1936; LL.D. (hon.), Roosevelt U., 1967; M.B.A., Columbia Pacific U., 1980, Ph.D. in Archeology, 1981. Owner, pres. Feris Flying Service, Chgo., 1936-38; metallurgist Standard Dental Labs., Chgo., 1938-39; project design engr. Birtman Electric Co., Chgo., 1939-50; sr. design engr. Hotpoint div. Gen. Electric Co., Cicero, Ill., 1950-68; dir. purchasing Modern Maid, McGraw Edison, Chattanooga, 1968-76; pres. Choo-Choo Indsls., 1977-79, Things of Beauty, 1979—; cons. on primitive monies to museums and univs.; sponsor numis. studies Roosevelt U., 1966-67; chmn. Roosevelt U. Numis. Library Project. Author: The Lure of Primitive Money, 1960, Odd and Curious Monies of the World, 1963, Primitive Money of the World, Fact and Fantasy, 1981; editorial adv. bd.: Appliance Mag.; contbr. articles on monies and engring. design to profl. jours. Presdl. appointee Assay Commn., 1965; chmn. Engrs. for Senator Baker, 1972—; Chmn. Engrs. for Pres. Carter, 1976; patron Ednl. Libraries to Exodus Trust, San Francisco, Columbia Pacific U., Petaluma, Calif., Hunter Mus. of Art, Mitzpah Congregation, Chattanooga (Ten.) Afro-Am. Mus. Served to comdr. USNR, 1950-58. Decorated Navy Cross; recipient citation for cost saving Gen. Electric Co., 1966. Mem. Gas Appliance Engring. Soc. (pres. 1970-71), Am. Soc. Gas Engrs. (nat. pres. 1975), Indsl. and Sci. Conf. (adv. council appliance design and mfg.), North Shore Coin Club (founder, pres. 1950-58), Chgo. Coin Club (pres. 1964-65), Central States Numis. Soc. (pres. 1965-66), Am. Assn. Ret. Persons (pres. regional br. 1986.). Address: PO Box 4864 Chattanooga TN 37405

MORE, SYVER WAKEMAN, geologist; b. Washington, Jan. 27, 1950; s. John William and Virginia (Wakeman) M.; m. Judith Ann Bessler, May 25, 1974; children—Kristin Elisabeth, Andrew Alan. B.S. in Geoscis., U. Ariz., 1972, M.S. in Geoscis., 1980. Registered geologist, Ariz. Asst. exploration geologist Continental Oil Co., Tucson, 1972-73; mine devel. geologist Conoco Minerals, Florence, Ariz., 1973-75; exploration geologist Exxon Co. U.S.A., 1976; exploration geologist Amax Exploration Inc., Tucson, 1979, Billiton Exploration U.S.A., Tucson, 1980-86; sr. minerals geologist Billiton Minerals USA Inc., Lancaster, Calif., 1986-88; sr. geologist Atlas Precious Metals, Las Vegas, 1988—. DuVal Corp. fellow, 1977. Mem. Geol. Soc. Am., Soc. Mining Engrs. of AIME, Soc. Econ. Geologists, Am. Inst. Profl. Geologists, Nat. Rifle Assn. (life). Republican. Club: Tucson Rod and Gun. Research or work interests: Exploration and development of base-and precious-metal deposits; exploration program design and management. Subspecialties: Geology; Mineral exploration and development. Office: Atlas Minerals 743 Horizon Ct #202 Grand Junction CO 81506

MOREAU, HUGUES ANDRE, physician; b. Limoges, France, July 17, 1948; s. Jacques and Colette (Hugues) M.; m. Martine Houles, Sept. 15, 1972 (div. 1980); children: Gilles, Eva; m. Josette Denise Roy, Sept. 24, 1984; 1 child, Martial. Grad., Lycee Gay Lussac, 1966, postgrad. in math., 1967; MD, U. Limoges, 1975. Intern Centre Hosp. Regional, Gueret, France, 1974; gen. practice medicine Limoges, 1975—. Served as chief med. officer French Air Force, 1974-75. Mem. Confedn. Syndicates Med. Francais (pres. dept. 1985), Assn. Conferal Formation Medicine (regional counsel 1984), Syndicat Autonome de Haute Vienne (pres. 1985—). Roman Catholic. Home: 197 Ave du General Leclerc, 87100 Limoges France Office: Cabinet Med La Bastide 2, 14 Allee Seurat, 87100 Seurat France

MOREAU, JEANNE, actress; b. Jan. 23, 1928; ed. College Edgar-Quinet, Conservatoire national d'art dramatique; d. Anatole Desire and Kathleen (Buckley) M.; m. Jean-Louis Richard, 1949; 1 son, Jerome; m. 2d, William Friedkin, 1977 (div.). Stage actress Comedie Francaise, 1948-52, Theatre National Populaire, 1953; other stage appearances include: L'heure eblouissante, La machine infernale, Pygmalion, La chatte sur un toit brulant, La bonne soupe, La chevauchee sur le lac de Constance, films include: Touchez pas au grisbi, Le salaire du peche, Ascensuer pour l'echafaud, Les amants, Moderato Cantabile, Les liaison dangereuses, Dialogue des Carmelites, Jules et Jim, Eve, The Victors, La baie des anges, Peau de banane, Le train, Le journal d'une femme de chamber, Mata Hari—H21, The Yellow Rolls-Royce, Viva Maria, 1965, Mademoiselle, 1965, Chimes at Midnight, 1966, The Sailor from Gibraltar, 1967, The Bride Wore Black, 1967, The Great Catherine, 1968, Le corps de Diane, 1970, Une histoire immortelle Monte Walsh, L'humeur vagabonde, Comptes rebours, 1971, Chere Louise, 1972, Jeanne, la Francaise, 1972, Nathalie Granger, 1972, Je t'aime, 1973, Les valseuses, 1973, La race des seigneurs, 1973, Pleurs, 1974, Le jardin qui bascule, 1974, Souvenirs d'en France, 1974, Lumiere (also dir.), 1976, The Last Tycoon, 1976, Mr. Klein, 1976, Le Petit Theatre de Jean Renoir, 1976, L'adolescente, 1978, Plein Sud, 1981, Mille Milliards de Dollars, 1982, La Truite, 1982, Querelle, 1983, Lillian Gish, 1984, Le Recit de la servante Zerline, 1987 (Best Actress award Moliere French theatre, 1988); pres. Cannes Film Festival, 1975, Paris Internat. Film Festival, 1975. Decorated chevalier Legion d'honneur, commandeur and National du Merite chevalier des Arts et Lettres. Editor-in-chief In mag., 1971-72. Address: care Bur Georges Beaume, 3 quai Malaquais, 75006 Paris France Other: care Artmedia, 10 Ave George V, 75008 Paris France *

MOREAU, MARC JEAN, research director; b. Nantes, Loire Atlantique, France, Aug. 3, 1948; s. Paul and Jeanine (Leclerc) M.; m. Baudouin Francoise, July 22, 1972; children: Remi, Bruno. B, Lycies Victor Hugo, Nantes, 1967; Theisis of Doctrat, U. Paris, France, 1981. With Nat. Ctr. Scientific Research, Roscoff, France, 1975—; dir. research Nat. Ctr. Scientific Research, Roscoff, 1987—. Home: 3 Rue Des Corsaires, 29211 Roscoff France Office: Cen Nat Recher Scientifique, Biol Station, 29211 Roscoff France

MOREIRA, FAUSTO ROGERIO GIRIO, pharmaceutical publishing executive; b. Lisbon, Portugal, Apr. 17, 1936; s. Joaquim Pacheco and Maria Helena (Gírio) M.; m. Albina Rosa, Aug. 4, 1957; children: Paulo Manuel, Pedro Lúcio. Degree in Pharm. Doctoring, Pharmacy Faculty, Oporto, Portugal, 1967. Diplomate in Pharmacy. Indsl. researcher Lab. Normal (Ciba-Geigy), Lisbon, 1957-60; market research Lab. Normal (Ciba-Geigy), Oporto, 1960-67, promotion mgr., 1967-74, mktg. dir., 1974-78; chmn. Giefarma, Ltd., Oporto, 1978—, periodicals dir., 1978—; mktg. cons. E. Merck, Lisbon, 1960-67, Citécnica Editors, Lisbon, 1975-78. Author: (periodical) Noticias Terapeuticas; editor (periodical) Interfarma; contbr. articles to profl. jours. Mem. Portuguese Soc. Mktg., Industry Coll. Pharm. Soc. Presbyterian. Office: Giefarma Ltd, R Constituicao 814-4S25, P-4200 Oporto Portugal

MOREIRA RATO, DIOGO CORREIA, product specialist; b. Lisbon, Portugal, Oct. 23, 1960; s. Pedro Joaquim da Costa Moreira Rato and Maria Victoria Deslandes Correia. BSBA cum laude, Boston U., 1982. Asst. product mgr. Johnson & Johnson Profl. Div., Lisbon, 1982-83, jr. product mgr., 1983-84, full product mgr., 1984-86, sr. product mgr., 1986-87, sr. product specialist, 1987-88, group product mgr. surgical div., 1988—. Recipient Valuable Contribution to Microsurg. Learning award, Phila., 1987. Roman Catholic. Home: Rua do Alcaide, 9, 2750 Cascais Portugal Office: Johnson & Johnson Profl Div, Apt 17, 2746 Queluz Codex Portugal

MORELAND, WILLIAM JOHN, real estate broker; b. Chgo., Feb. 21, 1916; s. James C. and Izora M. (McCabe) M.; A.B., U. Ill., 1938; student Northwestern U., 1937. With James C. Moreland & Son, Inc., real estate and home building, Chgo., 1938—, pres., 1952—; pres. Moreland Realty, Inc., Chgo., 1952-72. Builder, operator Howard Johnson Motor Lodge, Chgo., 1960-72. Helped develop model housing community, El Salvador, Central Am., 1960's. Presidential appointment to commerce com. for Alliance for Progress, 1962-64. Served to lt. USNR, 1941-46. Mem. Home Bldrs. Assn. Chicagoland (pres. 1961-62), Chgo. Assn. Commerce and Industry, Chgo., N.W. Real Estate Bds., N.W. Bldrs. Assn., Nat. Assn. Home Bldrs. (hon. life dir. 1972—), Chi Psi. Republican. Roman Catholic. Office: 5717 Milwaukee Ave Chicago IL 60646

MORELL, WILLIAM NELSON, JR., foreign trade association executive; b. Takoma Park, Md., July 13, 1920; s. William N. and Louise (Cox) M.; student Coll. William and Mary, 1938-40; A.B., George Washington U., 1942; M.A., U. Pa., 1948; student Am. U., 1950-51; grad. Nat. War Coll., 1956; m. Patricia Leonhard, Apr. 3, 1943; 1 dau., Lynn. Jr. economist Bur. Labor Stats., 1941; asst. prof. fin. George Washington U., 1941; mem. U.S. mil. mission to Moscow, 1944-46; asst. prof. Drexel Inst. Tech., 1946-48; instr. U. Pa., 1947-48; with CIA, 1949-68; chmn. spl. study group NSC Planning Bd., 1960; econ. counselor Am. embassy, Moscow, 1960-61; dep. asst. dir. office research and reports CIA, 1962-66, dir. Office Econ. Research, 1966-67, mem. U.S. econ. def. adv. com., adv. com. export policy, 1966-67; lectr. on Communist econs., 1960-68; faculty Nat. War Coll., 1968; econ. counselor Am. embassy, Taipei, Taiwan, 1968-73; spl. asst. to sec. treasury 1973-77; treasury mem. U.S. Intelligence Bd., 1973-77; mng. dir. USA-ROC Econ. Council, Crystal Lake, Ill., 1977-78, pres., 1979—; cons. pvt. firms, 1979—; author, lectr. on Taiwan economy. Served to lt. (s.g.) USNR, 1942-46. Decorated Order Brilliant Star (Republic China), 1973, Order Brilliant Star with Violet Grand Cordon, 1986; recipient Superior Achievement award, medal of merit CIA, Exceptional Service medal Treasury Dept., Nat. Intelligence Disting. Service award. Mem. Artus. Episcopalian (lay reader). Clubs: Congressional Country (Potomac, Md.); Ocean Reef (Key Largo, Fla.). Home: 1530 W Old Mill Rd Lake Forest IL 60045 Office: 200 Main St Crystal Lake IL 60014

MORELLI, BRUNO M., diamond mining executive; b. Lazzaro Di Savena, Bologna, Italy; s. Cesare and Baratta Angela M.; children: Marco, Claudia, Cesar, Giulia, Lucio. Dr. of Geol. Scis., U. Bologna, 1956. Chef de mission adjoint Soc. Miniere Du Beceka, Zaire, 1956-60; head mines, exploration dept. Soc. Miniere De Bakwanga, Zaire, 1960-65, mgr., mng. dir., chmn., 1965-73, délégué général adjoint, 1973-75, mng. dir., 1978-86, v.p., 1987—; pres. Sibradiam, Brésil, 1978—, Remica, 1986—; mgr. dept. mines Sibeka, Belgium, 1975-86, mng. dir., 1986—; bd. dirs. Sibinter, Luxembourg, 1978—, Sogeti, Belgium, 1983—, Exmin, U.S., 1986—, Diamant Boart, Belgium, 1987—. Collaborator Le diamant-Flammarion, 1979. Office: Sibeka, Rue Royale 52, 1000 Brussels Belgium

MORELLI, CARMEN, lawyer; b. Hartford, Conn., Oct. 30, 1922; s. Joseph and Helen (Carani) M.; m. Irene Edna Montminy, June 26, 1943; children: Richard A., Mark D., Carl J. BSBA, Boston U., 1949, JD, 1952. Bar: Conn. 1955, U.S. Dist. Ct. Conn. 1958. Sr. ptnr. Morelli & Morelli, Windsor, Conn.; mem. Conn. Ho. of Reps., 1959-61; rep. Capitol Regional Planning Agy., 1965-72; atty. Town of Windsor, 1961; asst. prosecutor Town of Windsor, 1957-58. Mem. Windsor Town Com., 1957-82, chmn. 1964-65, treas., 1960-64, mem. planning and zoning commn., 1965-74, mem. charter revision com., 1963-64, Rep. Presdl. Task Force. Served with USN, 1943-45. Mem. ABA, Conn. Bar Assn., Hartford Bar Assn., Windsor Bar Assn. (pres. 1979), Windsor C. of C. (v.p. 1978), Am. Arbitration Assn. Roman Catholic. Club: Elks, Rotary. Home: 41 Farmstead Ln Windsor CT 06095 Office: 66 Maple Ave Windsor CT 06095

MORELOCK, JAMES CRUTCHFIELD, mathematician; b. Martin, Tenn., Feb. 7, 1920; s. Joseph Fletcher and Lura Martha (Crutchfield) M.; student Bethel Coll., McKenzie, Tenn., 1937-39; B.S., Memphis State Coll., 1941; M.A., U. Mo., 1948; Ph.D. (fellow), U. Fla., 1952; m. Eugenia Scott Browne, Apr. 29, 1945 (dec.); children—Elinor Morelock Smith, Constance Morelock Grear (dec.), Diana Morelock Brown. Instr. astronomy and math. U. Fla., Gainesville, 1949-52; asst. prof. math. Auburn (Ala.) U., 1952-56; head math. dept. King Coll., Bristol, Tenn., 1956-60; mathematician U.S. Naval Computation Lab., Dahlgren, Va., 1960-61; mem. staff Computation Center Gen. Electric, Huntsville, Ala., 1961-63; mathematician computation lab. Marshall Space Flight Center, Huntsville, Ala., 1963-78, ret., 1978. Instl. rep. to Boy Scouts, Civitan Club, Auburn, 1952-56; v.p. Huntsville Concert Band, 1963—. Served with USAAF, 1941-45; PTO. Manning scholar, 1940-41; recipient U.S. Treasury award, 1968, NASA 10 year Achievement award, 1969, NASA Apollo Achievement award, 1969. Mem. Am. Math. Soc., Math. Assn. Am., Assn. Computing Machinery, Bristol Astronomy Soc. (pres. 1956-60). Methodist. Club: Pistol. Home: 2917 Garth Rd SE Huntsville AL 35801

MOREN, CHARLES VERNER, lawyer, judge; b. Webster, Wis., Jan. 29, 1920; s. John Arthur and Jennie Marie (Anderson) M.; m. Sylvia Jene Smith, Mar. 15, 1946 (div.); m. Donna Rae McFarland, Sept. 22, 1982; children—Marie, Leslie, Stephen, James, John, Daniel. B.A., U. Minn., 1942, LL.B., 1948. Bar: Minn. 1948, Wash. 1954, U.S. Dist. Ct. (we. dist.) Wash. 1956. Trial atty. Mpls. St. Ry. Co., 1948-50; sole practice, Anoka, Minn., 1951-52; assoc. Bundlie, Kelley, Finley & Maun, St. Paul, 1952-53; asst. city atty. City of Seattle, 1954-55; atty. Gen. Ins. Co., Seattle, 1955-56; ptnr. Keller, Rohrback, Waldo, Moren & Hiscock, Seattle, 1957-75, Moren Lageschulte & Cornell, Seattle, 1975-88, Moren Cornell & Hansen, 1988—; city atty. City of Lake Forest Park, Wash., 1963-65, judge mcpl. ct., 1970—. Co-founder City of Lake Forest Park, Seattle, 1963. Served to lt. USN, 1942-46, PTO. Mem. ABA, Minn. Bar Assn., Wash. State Bar Assn., Am. Arbitration Assn., Assn. Trial Lawyers Am., Full Gospel Businessmens Fellowship (bd. dirs. Seattle chpt. 1975-78). Republican. Home: 1213 SW 174th St Seattle WA 98166 Office: Moren Cornell & Hansen 11320 Roosevelt Way NE Seattle WA 98125

MORENO BARBERA, FERNANDO, architect; consultant; b. Ceuta, Spain, June 22, 1913; s. Fernando and Francisca (Barbera Ferrer) Moreno Calderon; m. Margarita von Hartenstein, Feb. 16, 1946 (div.); 1 son, Fernando; m. Carmen Cavengt. Diploma in Architecture, Escuela Superior de Arquitectos, Madrid, 1940; postgrad. Tech. Hochschule, Berlin, 1941, Tech. Hochschule, Stuttgart, 1942; Dr. Architect, Escuela Superior de Arquitectos, Madrid, 1966. Architect Prof. Paul Bonatz, Berlin/Stuttgart, Germany, 1941-43, Ministerio de Educacion, Madrid, 1940-75; exec. pres. M.B. Consultants, Madrid, 1944—; attache Spanish Embassy, Berlin, 1941-43; prof. scenography Escuela Ofcl. de Cinematograffa, Madrid, 1947-49; exec. dir. Empresa Nacional de Turismo, Madrid, 1954-65; prof. Escuela Superior de Arquitectos, Madrid, 1971-72. Restorer and rehabilitator: Hostal Reyes Catolicos, Santiago de Compostela, Spain, 1964, Hostal San Marcos, Leon, Spain, 1956, Palacio Villahermosa, Madrid (Juan de Villanueva award 1979), 1976, Casa del Cordon Burgos (Cert. Engring. Ops. Exec. award 1987); supr. Univ. Laboral de Cheste, Valencia, Spain, 1969, P.P.O. Bldg, Madrid, 1973, Premio Colegio de Arquitectos, 1974, Univ. Campus, Kuwait, 1978. Humbolt Stieftung grantee, 1940; Internat. Coop. Adminstrn. grantee, 1959; recipient Silver Hexagon award Habitation Space Internat., 1979. Fellow Colegio Ofcl. Arquitectos de Madrid, Hermandad de Arquitectos. Roman Catholic. Clubs: Real Puerta de Hierro, de Campo, Real Automovil. Home: El Espinarejo, Manzanares el Real, Madrid Spain Office: M B Cons, Paseo de la Habana 15, 28036 Madrid Spain

MOREY, LARRY WAYNE, nuclear training facility administrator; b. Cedar Rapids, Iowa, Apr. 22, 1949; s. Eugene Austin and LaVonne Elsie (Fritz) M.; m. Rosellen Louise Murley, Jan. 3, 1976 (div. Apr. 1980); m. Ann Marie Johnson, Oct. 16, 1982; 1 child, Sean Michael. PhD in Human Resources Devel., Pacific Western U., 1986. Nationally cert. fire service instr. Prodn. scheduler Square D Mfg. Co., Cedar Rapids, Iowa, 1967-72; security cons. Vets. Pub. Safety, Cedar Rapids, 1972-77; nuclear security cons. Iowa Electric Light and Power Co., Cedar Rapids, 1977-78, security tng. instr., 1978-80, facility adminstr., 1980—; mem. Industry Edn. Council, Cedar Rapids, 1986—. Author: (book) Fire Brigade Training for DAEC, 1983, DAEC Fire Plan, 1984, ARC Disaster Plan, 1984. Chmn. first aid ARC, Cedar Rapids, 1982, chmn. disaster, vol. cons. 1984. Served to sgt. USAF, 1969-72. Mem. Disabled Am. Vets., Internat. Soc. Fire Service Instrs., Iowa Soc. Fire Service Instrs., Iowa Firemans Assn. Democrat. Methodist. Lodges: Masons, Order of Eastern Star, Shriners. Home: 3808 Blue Mound Dr NE Cedar Rapids IA 52402 Office: Iowa Electric Light & Power Co IE Tower Cedar Rapids IA 52401

MORGAN, AUDREY, architect; b. Neenah, Wis., Oct. 19, 1931; d. Andrew John Charles Hopfensperger and Melda Lily (Radtke) Anderson; m. Earl Adrian Morgan (div.); children: Michael A., Susan Lynn Heiner, Nancy Lee, Diana Morgan Lucio. B.A., U. Wash., 1955. Registered architect, Wash.; cert. NCARB. Project mgr. The Austin Co., Renton, Wash., 1972-75; med. facilities architect The NBBJ Group, Seattle, 1975-79; architect constrn. rev. unit Wash. State Dept. Social and Health Services, Olympia, 1979-81; project dir., med. planner John Graham & Co., Seattle, 1981-83; pvt. practice architecture, Seattle, 1983—, also health care facility cons., code analyst. Contbr. articles to profl. jours. and govt. papers; prin. works include quality assurance coordinator for design phase Madigan Army Med. Ctr., Ft. Lewis, Wash.; med. planner and code analyst Rockwood Clinic, Spokane, Wash.; med. planner facilities for child, adult, juvenile and forensic psychiatric patients., States of Wash. and Oreg. Cons. on property mgmt. Totem council Girl Scouts U.S.A., Seattle, 1969-84, troop leader, cons., trainer, 1961-74. Mem. AIA (subcoms. codes and standards, health planning and mental health of nat. com. on architecture for health 1980—, and numerous other coms., founding mem. Wash. council AIA architecture for health panel 1981—,recorder 1981-84, vice chmn., 1987, chmn. 1988, bd. dirs. S.W. Wash. chpt. 1983-84), Nat. Fire Protection Assn., Soc. Am. Value Engrs., Am. Hosp. Assn., Assn. Western Hosps., Wash. State Hosp. Assn., Seattle Womens Sailing Assn., Audubon Soc., Alpha Omicron Pi. Lutheran. Clubs: Coronado 25 Fleet 13 (Seattle) (past sec., bull. editor); GSA 25 Plus. Home and Office: 4216 Greenwood Ave N Seattle WA 98103

MORGAN, BARRIE SCOTT, geography educator; b. Cardiff, Wales, Aug. 5, 1943; s. Thomas John and Hilda Lilian (Merry) M.; m. Christine Maralyn Woolley, Sept. 26, 1970 (div. 1978); m. Jean Sarah De'Ath, Sept. 3, 1982; children—Thomas Rhys, Tegwen Clare. B.Sc., Exeter U., Eng., 1964, Ph.D., 1970. Asst. lectr. U. Leeds, Eng., 1966-67; lectr. King's Coll. London, 1967-86; dir. N.Am. Programmes King's Coll., London, 1986—. Contbr. articles to profl. jours. Recipient research award Brit. Acad., 1983. Mem. Inst. Brit. Geographers, Geog. Assn. Avocations: opera; sports. Home: 28 Burnt Ash Ln, Bromley, Kent BR1 4DH, England Office: King's Coll London, Strand, London WC2R 2LS, England

MORGAN, BRIAN LESLIE G., educator, author; b. Gillingham, Eng., Jan. 6, 1947; came to U.S., 1975; s. Sydney W.G. and Grace H. (Milner) M.; m. Roberta Eddye Goldin, Apr. 8, 1973. B.Sc., London U., 1972, M.Sc., 1973, Ph.D., 1975. Postdoctoral fellow Columbia U., N.Y.C., 1975-78, staff assoc., 1978-79, asst. prof., 1979—; cons. Self mag., N.Y.C., 1983—. Author: The Lifelong Nutrition Guide, 1983; The Carbohydrate Miracle Diet Book, 1983; Drug-Nutrient Interaction Guide, 1986; Brain Food, 1986; Nutrition Prescription, 1987; contbr. articles to profl. jours. Mem. Am. Inst. Nutrition, Brit. Nutrition Soc., N.Y. Acad. Scis. (animal com. 1981—, conf. com. 1984—); Harvey Soc., N.Am. Assn. for Study of Obesity. Episcopalian.

MORGAN, BRUCE RAY, international consultant; b. Los Angeles, Oct. 28, 1932; s. Francis Raymond and Rose Hall (Black) M.; m. Bette Jeanne Moore, Oct. 7, 1957; children: Michael John, Brian Leo, Jeanne Ann. A.A., Sacramento Jr. Coll., 1952; B.S., U. Calif.-Berkeley, 1954, LL.B., 1957. Bar: Calif. 1957. Judge adv. USAF, Saudi Arabia and Morocco, 1958-61; atty. firm Thelen, Marrin, Johnson & Bridges, San Francisco, 1961-67; dep. dir. Peace Corps, Nepal, 1967-68; dir. Peace Corps, 1968-70; exec. dir. Center Research and Edn., Denver, 1971-75; dir. U.S. representation to Saudi Arabia-U.S. Joint Commn. on Econ. Coop., Riyadh, 1975-76; pres. Morgan-Newman Assocs., Inc., Washington, 1976—. Editor: Calif. State Bar Jour. Legis. Rev, 1957. Served with USAF, 1958-61. Mem. U.S., Calif. bars. Office: Morgan-Newman Assocs 1010 N Glebe Rd Suite 500 Arlington VA 22201 also: 3 Paddington St, London W1N 3LA, England

MORGAN, CHARLES RUSSELL, lawyer; b. New Orleans, Oct. 15, 1946; s. Charles and Marian E. (Wetzel) M.; 1 child, Charles Bradford. BA, U. N.C., 1968; JD, Columbia U., 1971. Bar: N.Y. 1973, Ill. 1981. Law clk. to presiding judge U.S. Ct. Appeals (D.C. cir.), Washington, 1971-72; atty. Davis, Polk & Wardwell, N.Y.C., 1972-80; sr. staff counsel Household International, Inc., Prospect Heights, Ill., 1980-83; v.p., asst. gen. counsel Kraft, Inc., Glenview, Ill., 1983-85; v.p., sr. corp. counsel Kraft, Inc., Glenview, 1985-88; v.p., gen. counsel Chiquita Brands, Inc., Cin., 1988—; Bd. advisors Law Dept. Mgmt., Bus. Laws, Inc. Contbg. editor The Corp. Counselor, 1986—. Mem. ABA (chmn. corp. counsel com. 1983-86, chmn. communications com. 1986—), Legal Club Chgo. Presbyterian. Club: Army-Navy. Office: Chiquita Brands Inc 250 E 5th St Cincinnati OH 45202

MORGAN, DENNIS RICHARD, lawyer; b. Lexington, Va., Jan. 3, 1942; s. Benjamin Richard and Gladys Belle (Brown) M. B.A., Washington and Lee U., 1964; J.D., U. Va., 1967; LL.M. in Labor Law, NYU, 1971. Bar: Ohio 1967, Va. 1967, U.S. Ct. Appeals (4th cir.) 1968, U.S. Ct. Appeals (6th cir.) 1971, U.S. Supreme Ct. 1972. Law clk. to chief judge U.S. Dist. Ct. Ea. Dist. Va., 1967-68; mem. Marshman, Snyder & Seeley (now Marshman, Snyder & Corrigan), Cleve., 1971-72; dir. labor relations Ohio Dept. Adminstrv. Services, 1972-75; asst. city atty. Columbus, Ohio, 1975-77; dir. Ohio Legis. Reference Bur., 1979-81; assoc. Clemans, Nelson & Assocs., Columbus, 1981; sole practice, Columbus, 1978—; lectr. in field; guest lectr. Central Mich. U., 1975; judge moot ct. Ohio State U. Sch. Law, 1981, 83, grad. div., 1973, 74, 76, Baldwin-Wallace Coll., 1973; legal counsel Dist. IV Communications Workers Am. Vice chmn. Franklin County Democratic Party, 1976-82, dem. com. person Ward 58, Columbus, 1973—; chmn. rules com. Ohio State Dem. Conv., 1974; co-founder, trustee Greater West Side Dem. Club; negotiator Franklin County United Way, 1977-81; regional chmn. ann. alumni fund-raising program U. Va. Sch. Law; mem. Friends of the Library, Franklin County, 1976—. Robert E. Lee Research scholar, summer, 1965; recipient Am. Jurisprudence award, 1967. Served to capt. U.S. Army, 1968-70. Mem. Indsl. Relations Research Assn., ABA, Fed. Bar Assn., Am. Judicature Soc., Pi Sigma Alpha. Roman Catholic. Clubs: Shamrock, Columbus Metroplitan (charter). Home: 1261 Woodbrook Ln #G Columbus OH 43223

MORGAN, ERIC LEE, aquatic ecologist; b. Hickory, N.C., Feb. 17, 1940; s. Karl Ziegler and Helen Lee (McCoy) M.; married July 13, 1965 (div. 1975); children: Sean K., Eric L. Jr. (dec. 1971). B.S., Middle Tenn. State U., 1964, M.S., 1969; Ph.D., Va. Polytech. Inst. & State U., 1973. Research asst. U. Ga. Savannah River Ecol. Lab., 1965-67; research assoc. Dept. Energy Comparative Animal Physiology Lab., 1967-68; asst. prof. U. Tenn., Chattanooga, 1969-70; asst. prof., dir. environ. biology research program Tenn. Tech. U., Cookeville, 1972-79; assoc. prof., dir. environ. biol. research program, 1979—, dir. upper Cumberland Biol. Sta., 1981-83; assoc. AWARE, Inc., Nashville, 1973—, ERM-Southeast, Inc., Brentwood, Tenn., 1980—, Advent Group, Inc., Brentwood, Tenn., 1985—; ptnr. Young-Morgan & Assocs. Inc. Environ. Cons., 1987—; mem. peer rev. panel for Environ. Biology EPA, 1985—. Contbr. numerous articles to sci. jours., chpts. to books. Tenn. Acad. Sci. fellow; served as prin. investigator in charge of numerous research grants and contracts for indsl. and govtl. sources. Mem. Cave Research Found., AAAS, Ecol. Soc. Am., Internat. Assn. Water Pollution Research, Soc. Internat. Limnologiae, Internat. Water Resources Assn., Soc. Environ. Toxicology and Chemistry, ASTM, Am. Soc. Limmology and Oceanography, Beta Beta Beta, Phi Sigma Xi. Democrat. Lutheran. Home: 1570 Forrest Rd Cookeville TN 38501

MORGAN, ETHEL B., accountant; b. N.Y.C., Jan. 16, 1914; d. Morris and Dina Branman; B.S., U. Ala., 1964; m. Donald Arol Morgan, Mar. 14, 1936; children—Margaret Voelkel, Barbara Weeks, John T., Janet Katich, Ethel Lynn. Mathematician, Army Missile Command, Redstone Arsenal, Ala., 1964-67, computer specialist, 1967-71, lead engr. air def. system command control software, 1971-73; pvt. practice acctg., fin. cons., Huntsville, Ala., 1974—. Pres., Huntsville-Madison County Council on Aging, 1980-82; vice chmn. Citizens Adv. Com. to Small Claims Ct., 1980-83; bd. dirs. Madison County Sr. Center, 1979-83; bd. dirs. Madison County Council on Aging, 1978-82. Mem. Nat. Soc. Pub. Accts., Nat. Assn. Enrolled Agts. Ala. Soc. Public Accts., Ala. Soc. Enrolled Agts. (treas. 1983—), AAUW, Phi Beta Kappa. Office: PO Box 4312 Huntsville AL 35815

MORGAN, EVELYN BUCK, nursing educator; b. Phila., Nov. 3, 1931; d. Kenneth Edward and Evelyn Louise (Rhineberg) Buck; m. John Allen McGeary, Aug. 15, 1958 (div. 1964); children—John Andrew, Jacquelyn Ann McGeary Keplinger; m. Kenneth Dean Morgan, June 26, 1965 (dec. 1975). R.N., Muhlenberg Hosp. Sch. Nursing, 1955; B.S. in Nursing summa cum laude, Ohio State U., 1972, M.S., 1973; Ed.D., Nova. U., 1978. R.N., N.J., Ohio, Fla., Calif.; cert. specialist Am. Nurses Assn. Psychiat.-Mental Health Clin. Specialists; advanced R.N. practitioner Fla. Bd. Nursing. Staff nurse Muhlenburg Hosp., Plainfield, N.J., 1955-57; indsl. nurse Western Electric Co., Columbus, Ohio, 1957-59; supr. Mt. Carmel Hosp., Columbus, 1960-65; instr. Grant Hosp. Sch. Nursing, 1965-72; cons. Ohio Dept. Health, 1972-74; prof. nursing Miami (Fla.)-Dade Community Coll., 1974—; family therapist Hollywood Pavilion Hosp., 1977-82; pvt. practice family therapy, Ft. Lauderdale, Fla., 1982—. Sustaining mem. Democratic Nat. Com., 1975—. Mem. Am. Nurses Assn., Fla. Council Psychiat.-Mental Health Clin. Specialists, Am. Nurses Found., Am. Holistic Nurses Assn., Sigma Theta Tau. Democrat. Roman Catholic.

MORGAN, JO VALENTINE, JR., lawyer; b. Washington, June 26, 1920; s. Jo. V. and Elizabeth Parker (Crenshaw) M.; A.B. magna cum laude, Princeton U., 1942; LL.B., Yale U., 1947; m. Norma Jean Lawrence, May 22, 1943; children—Carol Jo, Jo Lawrence, Susan Leigh. Admitted to D.C. bar, 1948, Md. bar, 1948; mem. firm Whiteford, Hart, Carmody & Wilson, Washington, 1948-85, partner, 1953-76, sr. partner, 1976-85; mem., dir. Jackson & Campbell, P.C., 1985—; dir. Dist. Realty Title Ins. Corp. Chmn. Bethesda USO, 1949-52; pres. Summer Citizens Assn., 1958-61; pres. Westmoreland Citizens Assn., 1956-57. Bd. dirs., gen. counsel Internat. Soc. Protection Animals; pres., bd. dirs. Montgomery County Humane Soc. Served from 2d lt. to capt., AUS, 1942-45, ETO. Decorated D.F.C., Purple Heart, Air medals (AAC). Fellow Am. Coll. Trial Lawyers; mem. Am. Bar Assn., Bar Assn. D.C. (bd. dirs. 1958-60, 73-75), D.C. Lawyers Club, Order of Coif, Phi Beta Kappa. Democrat. Episcopalian. Clubs: Chevy Chase, Metropolitan, Princeton, The Barristers; Wesley Heights Community (pres. 1964-67). Home: 5120 Westpath Way Bethesda MD 20816 Office: 1120 20th St NW Washington DC 20036 also: 200 A Monroe St Rockville MD 20850

MORGAN, JOHN AUGUSTINE, university executive, consultant; b. Medford, Mass., Feb. 4, 1936; s. John Augustine and Mary Frances (Maley) M.; m. Jean Marie Doyle, Jan. 8, 1959 (div. 1980); 1 child, John Patrick. B.S., Boston U., 1956; M.S., U. Colo., 1963; diploma War Coll., 1967; Ed.D., Nova U., 1980. Commd. 2d lt. U.S. Air Force, 1956, advanced through grades to col., 1978; served various Air Force ops., combat, Viet Nam and world-wide, 1954-72; dir. planning Def. Indsl. Ctr., Phila., 1970-73, dir. ops., 1973-74; dir. weapon system U.S. Air Force, Belleville, Ill., 1974-76; v.p. Piedmont Tech. Coll., Greenwood, S.C., 1978-84, exec. v.p., 1984—; pvt. practice as cons., Greenwood, 1978—; doctoral adv. Nova U., Ft. Lauderdale, Fla., 1983—. Author: Retrenchment in the 80s, 1981 (Nat. Practicum of Yr. award 1981). Contbr. articles to profl. jours. Chmn. Piedmont Found. Fund Dr., Greenwood, 1985. Decorated Purple Heart, Legion of Merit, Silver Star, Bronze Star, Republic Viet Nam Gallantry Cross; named Educator of Yr. S.C. Tech. Assn., 1981, 1986, 1987, Leadership S.C., 1988. Mem. Am. Assn. Community Jr. Colls., S.C. Assn. Govt. Purchasing Ofcls., S.C. Assn. State Planning Ofcls., C. of C., Greenwood Running Club, Greenwood Riding Hunt Club, Am. Legion. Lodges: Kiwanis, Elks. Home: Gatewood 101 Hawthorne Ct Greenwood SC 29646 Office: Piedmont Tech Coll Box 1467 Greenwood SC 29648

MORGAN, LEONARD EUGENE, medical and commercial illustrator; b. Princeton, Ind., Dec. 12, 1948; s. Billy Gene and Ester June (Wright) M.; m. Frances Elizabeth Airdo, Jan. 31, 1970; children—Natalie Jean, Lindsay Ann. B.S. in Med. Art, U. Ill. Med. Ctr., 1974. Free-lance illustrator Bolingbrook, Ill., 1976—; guest speaker U. Ill. Med. Ctr. Chgo., 1980—. Speaker Assn. Med. Illustrators Annual Meeting, Norfolk, Va., 1986. Contbr. articles to profl. jours. Work appeared in Illustrators 27 Annual, 1985, Am. Illustration III Annual, 1985, 1985 Print's Regional Design Annual, 1985, Studio Mag's The Creative Decade, 1976-86, Communication Arts Ann., 1987, The One Show, 1987, The Rx Club Show, NYC, 1987. Recipient DESI award, 1985, Prints Regional Design Annual award, 1987. Mem. Assn. Med. Illustrators (1st and 2d place awards in advt. 1985), Midwest Med. Illustrators Assn. (speaker regional meeting), Artists Guild Chgo. (silver medal 1984), Graphic Artists Guild N.Y. Avocations: Fishing, travel, family activities, air brush design innovations. Home: 730 Victoria Ct Bolingbrook IL 60439

MORGAN, M. JANE, computer systems consultant; b. Washington, July 21, 1945; d. Edmond John and Roberta (Livingstone) Dolphin; 1 child, Sheena Anne. Student U. Md., 1963-66, Montgomery Coll., 1966-70; BA in Applied Behavioral Sci. with honors, Nat. Coll. Edn., 1987. With HUD, Washington, 1965-84, computer specialist, 1978-84; pres., chief exec. officer Systems and Mgmt. Assocs., 1983-87; dir. systems engring. Advanced Technology Systems, Inc., Vienna, Va., 1984-86; chief tech. staff Tech. and Mgmt. Services, Inc., 1986—. Mem. Am. Mgmt. Assns. Episcopalian. Club: Order Eastern Star. Office: Care Systems and Mgmt Assocs 10252 Cherry Walk Ct Oakton VA 22124

MORGAN, MAGNUS NILS IVAR, executive search company executive; b. Nyköping, Sweden, Feb. 3, 1940; s. Bertil and Anna Britta (Björklund) Löfström; M.B.A. with honors, Boston U., 1976; m. Anne Morgan, Dec. 23, 1977. Public relations dir. ITT Norden AB, Standard Radio & Telefon AB, Sweden, 1965-70; bus. planning mgr. ITT Europe Inc., Belgium, 1970-78; asst. dir. Thyssen Bornemisza S.A.M., Monaco, 1978-80; sr. partner Houdiniere & Morgan Internat., Paris, 1980-83, Morgan & Ptnrs. Exec. Search, Monaco, 1983—. Mem. Am. C. of C. Clubs: Monte Carlo (Monaco). Toastmasters (Brussels). Home: Trocadero, 43 Ave de Grande Bretagne, Monte Carlo 98000, Monaco Office: 22 Ave de la Costa, MC 98000 Monaco

MORGAN, MARK BRYAN, evangelist, business and communications translator; b. Sinton, Tex., June 8, 1957; came to Chile, 1977; s. Phillip Roy and Betty Jean (Barnes) M.; m. Ximena del Carmen Fernandez, Dec. 27, 1980; children: Lindsay Star, Kristopher Mark, Kaylee Rianne, Ana Paulina (foster dau.). Student, Fla. Coll., 1975-76, Centro Estudios y Servicios Internat., 1979, Ariz. Inst. Banking, 1982, Phoenix Coll., 1982, Baxter Inst., 1985, U. Austral, 1986, U. Catolica de Santiago, 1988. Evangelist Ch. of Christ, Phoenix, 1975-76, Chile and Argentina, 1977-78, Chile and Colombia, Valparaiso-Quillota, Chile, 1979-80, Valdivia, Chile, 1983—; translator TV sta., Cath. U., Valparaiso, 1980; translator legal dept. Cemento Melon/Blue Circle Corp., La Calera, Chile, 1981; with pub. relations dept., TV commentator Municipality of Vina del Mar, Chile, 1981; researcher Valley Nat. Bank, Phoenix, 1982; pres. Morgan Enterprises, 1983—. Translator, editor: Fellowship, To Teach a Teacher, Training for Service, Bible Authority, The Finger of God, Basic Principles of Christ I and II, Hebrews, 1988, Now That I'm a Christian, 1987. Democrat. Home: Geromino Urmeneta, 202 Valdivia Chile Office: Church of Christ, Casilla 37, 202 Geronimo Urmeneta Chile

MORGAN, RALPH, business executive; b. Elkhart, Ind., Feb. 23, 1924; s. Ralph Samuel and Jeanette Rae (Randall) M.; m. Doris Kathleen (Hayward), Sept. 2, 1945 (div. Jan. 1974); children: Christopher Alan, Carol Jane; m. Georgia Lou Teach, Feb. 9, 1975. Student, Wayne State U., 1942-43, 46-47. Apprentice mouthpiece maker J.J. Babbitt Co., Elkhart, 1935-36; profl. woodwind musician various dance bands, Ind., Mich., 1936-52; owner, dir. band Music by Morgan, Detroit, 1943; woodwind technician The Linton Band Instrument Co., Elkhart, 1948-50; woodwind technician The Selmer Co., Elkhart, 1950-52, mgr. SE dist. sales, 1952-68, mgr. nat. band instrument, 1970-74, chief woodwind designer, 1974-80; owner, operator Morgan Music Co., Tampa, 1968-70; prin. Morgan Enterprises, Springfield, Ohio, 1980—; lectr., clinician U. Ky. Music Sch., Louisville, 1986, 87, Clarfest '85 Duquesne U., Pitts., 1985, U. Pitts. Music Dept., 1985, Ind. State U., Terre Haute, 1983. Author, editor Colonial Currency, 1976; patentee in field. Bd. dirs. COMACS, Inc., Champaign, Ill., 1988—. Served to T/sgt. USAF, 1943-45, 45 combat missions. Republican. Lodge: Optimist (v.p. Springfield club 1982-83, pres. 1983-84). Home and Office: 490 Forest Dr Springfield OH 45505

MORGAN, RAY ELLINGWOOD, JR., journalist; b. Topeka, June 11, 1922; s. Ray Ellingwood and Vala Marie (McClenny) M.; m. Mary Grace Burkhardt, July 21, 1946; children: Stephen Ray, Mary Susan, Sally Ann, Cynthia Louise, Scott Ellingwood. B.A., Washburn U., 1946; postgrad., U. Kans., 1946. Reporter Topeka Daily Capital, 1946-51; reporter Kansas City (Mo.) Star, 1951-64, Kans. editor, 1964-77, spl. projects dir., 1977-78, columnist, 1978-85; columnist Squire Publs., Inc., Shawnee Mission, Kans., 1986—; polit. commentator Sta. KCTV, 1986—; staff Center for Sci. and Internat. Affairs, Harvard U., 1982-83; mem. Kans. Lottery Commn., 1987—;. Contbr. articles to newspapers and mags. Del. White House Conf. on Natural Beauty, 1964; mem. Shawnee (Kans.) Sch. Bd., 1964-67; active Friends of Art, William Rockhill Nelson Gallery of Art, Friends of Johnson County Library; trustee William Allen White Found., Washburn U.; mem. adv. bd. Eagleton Inst. Politics, Rutgers U., 1966-76; adv. com. Center for Study of Presidency; mem. adv. com. Harry S. Truman Good Neighbor Award Found.; mem. Johnson County Commn. on Aging, 1987—; bd. dirs. Johnson County Mental Health Assn. Served with AUS, 1942-43. Named Communicator of Year Women in Communications, Inc., 1978, Man of Year DAR, 1972, Man of Year DAV, 1982; recipient Press award Fleet Res. Assn., 1982; Disting. Service award DAV, 1985, Fed. Exec. Council Greater Kansas City, 1985; hon. fellow Harry S. Truman Inst. Fellow Smithsonian Instn.; mem. Am. Adventurers Assn., Kans. Hist. Soc. (life), Shawnee Mission Indian Hist. Soc., Am. Mus. Natural History (assoc.), U.S. Capitol Hist. Soc., Circus Fans Am. Assn., Nat. Intelligence Study Ctr., Assn. of Former Intelligence Officers, Am. Security Council (adv. bd.), Earthwatch, Sigma Delta Chi, Phi Delta Theta. Republican. Congregationalist. Clubs: Kansas City Press (bd. dirs.); Overland Park Swim. Lodge: Masons (32 deg.). Home and Office: 6815 Flint St Shawnee Mission KS 66203

MORGAN, ROBERT GEORGE, accounting educator, researcher; b. Sanford, Maine, Feb. 20, 1941; s. George Andrew and Katherine (Gray) M.; m. Jacqueline Buhl, Jan. 2, 1965; children—Robert George, Katherine Neva. B.A., Piedmont Coll., Demorest, Ga., 1969; M.Acctg., U. Ga., 1971, Ph.D., 1974. C.P.A., N.C., Tenn. Asst. prof. acctg. U. Wyo., Laramie, 1974-76, Drexel U., Phila., 1976-80; assoc. prof. acctg. U. N.C.-Greensboro, 1980-83; prof. acctg. Loyola Coll., Balt., 1983-85; chmn. dept. acctg. East Tenn. State U., Johnson City, 1985—. Editor Jour. The Mgmt. Rev., 1983-85. Contbr. articles to profl. jours. Treas., Running Brook PTA, Columbia, Md., 1984-85. Mem. Am. Inst. C.P.A.s, Nat. Assn. Accts., Am. Acctg. Assn., Acad. Acctg. Historians, Beta Gamma Sigma, Beta Alpha Psi. Methodist. Avocation: golf. Home: 1 Townview Dr Johnson City TN 37604 Office: E Tenn State U Dept Acctg PO Box 23800-A Johnson City TN 37614-0002

MORGAN, WILLIAM JAMES, psychologist; b. Rochester, N.Y., Apr. 30, 1910; A.B., U. Rochester, 1933; Ph.D., Yale, 1937; m. Antonia Mary Farquharson Bell, Nov. 2, 1944; children—William James, Jean Elizabeth, Robert Macnair. Chief clinician Vineland (N.J.) Tng. Sch., 1936-38; psychologist Bd. Edn. Rochester, 1939-41; dir. Psychol. Test Bur., Rochester, 1941-42; dep. chief tng., chief psychol. assessment CIA, 1947-52; mem. Psychol. Strategy Bd., White House, 1952-53; pres. Aptitude Assocs., Merrifield, Va., 1953—; dir. Strategic Power Analysis Corp.; mem. Army Research Com.; cons. Dept. Justice, Dept. Def., other agys. Mem. Va. Bd. Certification Clin. Psychologists. Trustee Va. Psychol. Found. Served from pvt. to maj. AUS, 1942-47; OSS, ETO. Diplomate in clin. psychology Am. Bd. Examiners Profl. Psychology. Mem. Va. Psychol. Assn. (pres. 1957-58), Sigma Xi. Author: Spies and Saboteurs (Gollancs-London), 1955; The O.S.S. and I, 1957; numerous articles and tests. Home: 2816 Gallows Rd Vienna VA 22180

MORGAN, WILLIAM JOHN HENRY, newspaper executive; b. Schoetmar, Fed. Republic Germany, July 24, 1954; s. William Clifford Morgan and Rosemary Georgina (Rogers) Beckett; m. Susan Anne Tierney. BA in German with honors, U. Reading, Eng., 1976. Media exec. Ted Bates, London, 1976-80; media mgr. BBDO, London, 1980-81; advt. mgr. The Economist, London, 1981-85, Frankfurt, Fed. Republic Germany, 1981—. Mem. Internat. Advt. Assn. Office: Economist Newspaper Ltd, Friedrichstrasse 34, 6000 Frankfurt Federal Republic of Germany

MORGAN, WILLIAM WILSON, astronomer, educator; b. Bethesda, Tenn., Jan. 3, 1906; s. William Thomas and Mary McCorkle (Wilson) M.; m. Helen Montgomery Barrett, June 2, 1928 (dec. 1963); children: Emily Wilson, William Barrett; m. Jean Doyle Eliot, 1966. Student, Washington and Lee U., 1923-26; B.S., U. Chgo., 1927, Ph.D., 1931; D.Honoris Causa, U. Cordoba, Argentina, 1971; D.Sc. (hon.), Yale U., 1978. Instr. Yerkes Obs., U. Chgo., Williams Bay, Wis., 1932-36; asst. prof. Yerkes Obs., U. Chgo., 1936-43, asso. prof., 1943-47, prof., 1947-66, Bernard E. and Ellen C. Sunny Distinguished prof. astronomy, 1966-74, prof. emeritus, 1974—, chmn. dept. astronomy, 1960-66; dir. Yerkes and McDonald Observatories, 1960-63; mng. editor Astrophys. Jour., 1947-52; Henry Norris Russell lectr. Am. Astron. Soc., 1961. Author: (with P.C. Keenan, Edith Kellman) An Atlas of Stellar Spectra, 1943, (with H.A. Abt and J.W. Tapscott) Revised MK Spectral Atlas for Stars Earlier than the Sun, 1978; contbr. research articles to profl. publs. Recipient Bruce gold medal Astron. Soc. Pacific, 1958, Henry Draper medal Nat. Acad. Scis., 1980. Mem. Am. Acad. Arts and Scis., Nat. Acad. Scis.; mem. Pontifical Acads. Scis.; Mem. Royal Danish Acad. Scis. and Letters, Royal Astron. Soc. (assoc. Herschel medal), Nat. Acad. Scis. Argentina, Soc. Royale des Sciences de Liege. Congregationalist. Office: Yerkes Observatory Box 258 Williams Bay WI 53191

MORGANOFF, ABRAHAM DAVID, neurologist; b. N.Y.C., June 28, 1949; s. Harry and Gloria M.; m. Fern Roth, May 6, 1978; children—Gregory Neil, Jessica Hope, Michelle Melanie. B.S., CCNY, 1971; M.D., Autonoma Med. Sch. Guadalajara (Mex.), 1975. Intern in medicine N.Y. Med. Coll.-Misericordia Hosp., 1975-76; resident in medicine N.J. Coll. Medicine, 1976-77; resident in neurology N.Y. Med. Coll.-Met. Hosp., 1977-80, chief resident neurology, 1979-80; practice medicine specializing in neurology, Plainfield, Union and Somerset, N.J., 1980—; mem. staff Muhlenberg, Somerset, Meml. Gen. hosps.; cons. Carrier Clinic, Runnells Hosp.; clin. instr. neurology Rutgers U. Med. Sch. Treas., bd. dirs. Mountain Jewish Community Center, 1981—. Recipient Physicians Recognition award AMA, 1976—. Mem. Internat. Acad. Sci., Am. Acad. Neurology, AMA, Am. EEG Soc., Am. Heart Assn., Am. Psychosomatic Assn., Acad. Medicine N.J., Neurol. Assn. N.J. (chmn. ethics com., rec. sec., treas.), Union Somerset County Med. Soc., Plainfield Assn. Physicians (pres.), N.J. Multisplty. Soc. Office: 5 Mountain Blvd Warren NJ 07060 also: 441 Chestnut St Union NJ

MORGANROTH, MAYER, lawyer; b. Detroit, Mar. 20, 1931; s. Maurice Jack Morganroth and Sophie (Reisman) Blum; m. Sheila Rubinstein, Aug. 16, 1958; children: Lauri, Jeffrey, Cherie. JD, Detroit Coll. Law, 1954. Bar: Mich. 1955, Ohio 1958, U.S. Ct. Appeals (6th cir.) 1968, U.S. Supreme Ct. 1971, N.Y. 1985, U.S. Tax Ct. 1985, U.S. Ct. Appeals (4th cir.) 1985, U.S. Ct. Claims 1986, U.S. Ct. Appeals (2d cir.) 1986. Sole practice Detroit, 1955—, N.Y.C., 1983—; cons. to lending instns.; lectr. on real estate NYU, 1980—, bus. entities and structures Wayne State U., 1981—. Served with USN, 1948-50. Mem. ABA, N.Y. State Bar Assn., Southfield Bar Assn., Assn. Trial Lawyers Am., Am. Judicature Soc., Nat. Criminal Def. Assn. Republican. Jewish. Clubs: West Bloomfield (Mich.) Country; Fairlane (Dearborn, Mich.); Knollwood, Sky High Health (Boston); Edgewood Athletic (pres. 1963-65). Office: 28588 Northwestern #444 Southfield MI 48034 also: 99 Park Ave New York NY 10016

MORGENSTERN, MATTHEW, computer scientist; b. N.Y.C.. BSEE, Columbia U., 1968, MSEE and Computer Sci., 1970; MS in Computer Sci. and Mgmt., MIT, 1975, PhD in Computer Sci., 1976. Asst. prof. computer sci. Rutgers U., New Brunswick, N.J., 1976-82; research computer scientist Info. Scis. Inst., U. So. Calif., Los Angeles, 1982-84; sr. computer scientist SRI Internat., Menlo Park, Calif., 1984—. Contbr. articles to profl. jours. Mem. IEEE, Am. Assn. Artificial Intelligence, Assn. Computing Machinery, Sigma Xi, Tau Beta Pi, Eta Kappa Nu. Office: SRI Internat 333 Ravenswood Ave Menlo Park CA 94025

MORGENSTERN, SUSIE HOCH, university educator, writer; b. Newark, Mar. 18, 1945; arrived in France, 1967; d. Meyer and Sylvia (Needelman) Hoch; married; children: Aliyah, Mayah. BA, Rutgers U., 1967; MA, U. Nice, France, 1969, PhD, 1972. Instr. U. Nice, 1972—; literary critic numerous mags. and newspapers; writer Ecole des Loisirs, Gallimard, Paris. 1979—. Editor: It's Not Fair, 1982, Terminale Tout le Monde Descend, 1985, Premier Amour, Dernier Amour, 1987; (picture book) La Grosse Patate, 1986. Recipient Grand Prix, Ministry Youth, 1981, Prix Loisirs Jeunes, 1983, Prix Mille Jeunes Lecteurs, Bibliotheque pour tous, 1985, Prix Alice, Ministry Women's Rights, 1986. Jewish. Office: Faculte des Sci, Nice France

MORGISON, F. EDWARD, investment broker; b. Clay Center, Kans., Oct. 4, 1940; s. Fred and Lena Edna (Chaput) M.; B.A. in Math., Emporia State U., 1963; M.S. in Bus. Adminstrn., U. Mo., Columbia, 1964; M.S. in Acctg. candidate U. Mo., Kansas City, 1981—; m. Karen Lorene Herdman, Nov. 21, 1964; 1 dau., Diana Michelle. Computer programmer U. Mo. Med. Center, Columbia, 1964-65; adminstrv. and budget analyst Urban Renewal Project, Independence, Mo., 1965-66; account exec., bank broker Stifel Nicolaus & Co., Kansas City, Mo., 1966-73; pres., chief exec. officer Will-Mor Investment Systems, Kansas City, Mo., 1973-75; br. mgr. Edward Jones & Co., 1975; editorial and exec. asst. to Morgan Maxfield, candidate for U.S. Congress, Kansas City, 1976; sr. account exec., merger and acquisitions specialist R. Rowland & Co., Kansas City, Mo., 1976-77; chmn. bd., pres., chief exec. officer Mo. Securities Inc., Kansas City, 1977-78; v.p., regional mgr. Charles Schwab & Co., Kansas City, 1978-79; v.p. Profl. Assistance, 1979-81; registered agt. Offerman & Co., Kansas City, 1979-81; chief exec. officer Morgison & Assos., Kansas City, 1979-81; fiscal dir. Housing Authority of Kansas City, 1981; exec. v.p. J. Penner & Assocs., 1981-82; pres. J. Penner & Co., 1982-83; account exec., registered broker Lowell H. Listrom & Co., 1981-84; pres., chief exec. officer First Allen Securitis Inc., 1983—; dir., sec. Hubach Group Inc., 1987—; bd. dirs., treas. Skytrader Corp., 1986—, Emergency Systems Services, 1986—; bd. dirs. Internat. Tex. Industries, Inc., San Antonio; chmn. bd., treas. Masters' Mark, Inc., 1986—. Recipient Bausch and Lomb Sci. award, 1959; Sci. award Lambda Delta Lambda, 1962; registered account exec. N.Y. Stock Exchange, Am. Exchange, registered securities agt., Mo., Kans., Ill., gen. securities prin., fin. and ops. prin., mcpl. securities prin. Mem. U. Mo. (life), Emporia State U. (life) alumni assns., Nat. Rifle Assn. (life), U.S. Chess Fedn. (life), Mensa (life). Home: 1000 NE 96th Terr Kansas City MO 64155 Office: 6505 N Prospect St Suite 101 Gladstone MO 64119

MORGNER, AURELIUS, economist, educator; b. N.Y.C., May 23, 1917; s. Oscar A. and Anna G. (Hoffmeister) M. B.S. in Bus. Adminstrn., U. Mo., 1938, M.A. in Econs., 1940; Ph.D., U. Minn., 1955. Investigator Dept. Labor, 1941; project dir. Employment Stblzn. Research Inst., 1941-42; instr. bus. adminstrn. U. Minn., 1942-46; lectr. Northwestern U., 1946-47; assoc. prof. Tex. A&M U., 1947-56, prof., 1956-58; vis. prof. U. São Paulo, Brazil, 1958-60; dir. grad. studies U. São Paulo, 1959-60; prof. econs. U. So. Calif., Los Angeles, 1960—; chmn. dept. U. So. Calif., 1962-69; prof. internat. econs. Sch. Internat. Relations, 1960—; Pub. panel mem. Chgo. Regional War Labor Bd., 1943-45; pub. rep. minimum wage com. Dept. Labor, 1942, 43; cons. Govt. Eucador, 1965-68, Govt. Guyana, 1968, state Nev., 1970, Philippines, 1971-72, Yemen Arab Republic, 1974-75; U.S. State Dept. vis. lectr., Brazil, summer 1966. Co-author: Local Labor Markets, 1948, Problems in Economic Analysis, 1948, Problems in the Theory of Price, 1954 (trans. Spanish 1965, Portuguese 1967). Ford faculty fellow Columbia U., 1954-55. Mem. So. Calif. Econ. Assn. (pres. 1965-66), Am. Econs. Assn., Western Econ. Assn., Am. Arbitration Assn., Internat. Studies Assn. Office: U of So Calif Economics Dept Los Angeles CA 90089-0035

MORI, HIDEO, chemical company executive; b. Osaka, Japan, Apr. 1, 1925; s. Shigekazu and Ikue M.; m. Masako Mori Okano; children: Hideto, Yujiro. LLB, Kyoto Imperial U., 1947. Dir. Sumitomo Chem. Co. Ltd., Oasaka, 1977-80, mng. dir., 1980-82, sr. mng. dir., 1982-85, pres., 1985—; bd. dirs. Nihon Oxirane Co. Ltd., Tokyo, Nihon Singapore Polyolefin Co. Ltd., Tokyo; bd. dirs. Japan Aldehyde Co. Ltd., Osaka, Chiba Chlorine & Alkali Co. Ltd., Osaka, vice chmn. Petrochemical Corp. of Singapore Ltd. Mem. Japan Fedn. Employers' Assn. (standing dir.), Kansai Econ. Fedn. (standing dir.), Kansai Com. for Econ. Devel. (bd. dirs.), Japan Chem. Industry Assn. (v.p.), Osaka Indsl. Assn. (bd. dirs.), Japan Petrochemical Industry Assn. (chmn.), Kansai Chem. Industry Assn. (pres.), Japan Tariff Assn. Office: Sumitomo Chem Co Ltd, 7-9 Nihonbashi 2-chome, Chuo-ku, Tokyo 103, Japan

MORI, KEI, economist, system engineer; b. Kyoto, Japan, Nov. 20, 1932; s. Taikichiro and Hanako (Idogawa) M.; m. Yoko Arisawa, Apr. 2, 1963; children—Mariko, Asuka. B.A., Keio U., Tokyo, 1955, M.A., 1958, Ph.D., 1968. Asst. prof. dept. adminstrn. engring., faculty engring. Keio U., Tokyo, 1958-64, asst. prof., 1964-68, assoc. prof., 1968-73, prof. dept. adminstrn. engring., faculty sci. and tech., Yokohama, 1973—; research assoc. Wharton Sch., U. Pa., 1968-70; inventor, dir. inst. LaForet Engring., Tokyo, 1978—, chmn. bd., 1985—; cons. IBM Japan, Tokyo, 1960-73; organizing engr. life maintenance module of Space Sta., NASA, Tokyo, 1982—; com. chmn. light energy transmission Opto Electronic Industry Devel. Assn., Tokyo, 1982, com. chmn. local area optical network, 1983; counselor Database Promotion Ctr., Japan, 1985—; chmn. bd. dirs. Office Research on Bldgs. & Info. Tech., 1987—; com. mem. The Japan Legal Info. Ctr., Inc., 1987—; mem. exec. com. Marine Biotech. Inventor solar ray collector and transmission system, 1980, spectrum selection and light emission for biol. applications, 1981; exec. editor Jour. Info. Processing Japan, 1960-67, 73-75. Exec. dir. Assn. Computer Edn. for Pvt. Univs., Tokyo, 1977—; project leader Redevel. Project of ARK Hills in Center City of Tokyo, 1982—. Mem. Econs. and Econometric Soc. Japan, Info. Processing Soc. Japan, Japan Soc. Aero. and Space Scis., Illuminating Engring. Inst. Japan, Japan Rheumatism Assn., Japan Inst. for Macro-Engring. Club: Blue Red and Blue (Tokyo). Buddhist. Home: 3-16-3-501 Kaminoge Setagaya-ku, Tokyo Japan Office: La Foret Engring, 2-7-8 Toranomon Minato-ku, Tokyo Japan

MORIMOTO, CARL NOBORU, computer system engineer; b. Hiroshima, Japan, Mar. 31, 1942; came to U.S., 1957, naturalized, 1965; s. Toshiyuki and Teruko (Hirano) M.; m. Helen Kiyomi Yoshizaki, June 28, 1969; children: Matthew Ken, Justin Ray. B.A., U. Hawaii, 1965; Ph.D., U. Wash., 1970. Research assoc. dept. chemistry Mich. State U., East lansing, 1970-72; postdoctoral fellow dept. biochemistry and biophysics Tex. A&M U., College Station, 1972-75; sr. sci. programmer Syntex Analytical Instruments Inc., Cupertino, Calif., 1975-78; prin. programmer analyst, software engring. mgr. Control Data Corp., Sunnyvale, Calif., 1978-83; mem. profl. staff Space System div. Gen. Electric Co., San Jose, Calif., 1983—. Mem. Am. Crystallographic Assn., Assn. Computing Machinery, Am. Chem. Soc., Sigma Xi. Am. Baptist. Home: 4003 Hamilton Park Dr San Jose CA 95130

MORIMOTO, SHINPEI, endocrinologist; b. Kamioka, Gifu Prefecture, Japan, July 23, 1930; s. Kikunosuke and Miyo Morimoto; M.D., Kanazawa U., 1956, D.M.Sci., 1961; m. Reiko Kaino, Oct. 6, 1962; children—Shinji, Mutsumi, Takashi. From asst. to lectr. 2d dept. internal medicine Kanazawa U. Hosp., 1961-73; assoc. prof. medicine Kanazawa Med. U., 1973-81, prof. medicine, 1981—. Grantee Japanese Sci. Research Fund, 1973—, Japanese Ministry Health and Welfare, 1981—. Mem. Japanese Endocrine Soc. (councilor 1969—), Japanese Soc. Hypertension (councilor 1978—), Japanese Soc. Internal Medicine, Japanese Diabetic Soc. (councilor 1969—), N.Y. Acad. Scis. Contbr. articles to med. jours. Home: 8-59 Kasamai-1-Chome, Kanazawa 920, Japan Office: Kanazawa Med U Div Encocrinology, Dept Internal Medicine, 1-1 Daigaku Uchinada, Ishikawa 920-02, Japan

MORIN, BERNARD PAUL, computer company executive; b. Avionon, France, Dec. 25, 1943; s. Louis and Juliette (Marin) M.; m. Nicole Hurabielle-Pere, Dec. 28, 1964; children—Laurence, Thierry. Engr., Ecole Poly., Paris, 1964. Research engr. French AEC, Cadarache, France, 1965-69; sales rep. IBM France, Paris, 1970-73; sales mgr. Control Data France, Paris, 1973-85; sales mgr. Info. Internat., Runois, France, 1986—; mktg. cons., Marne Vallee, France, 1980-86; sales mgr. Informatique Internationale, Rkungis, France, 1986-87; sales rep. Network System, Nevilly, France, 1987—. Office: Network Systems France, 185 AV Gen de Gaulle, 92000 Neuilly France

MORIN, JEAN-PIERRE, roofing company executive; b. Neuilly, France, Aug. 27, 1948; s. Pierre Andre and Marie Louise (Langlois) M.; m. Danièle Pion Goureau; children: Alexandra, Pierre Antoine, Juliette. B, LTE Jules-Ferry, Versailles, France, 1966; ingenieur, Ensam, Paris, 1971; M in Constrn., Stanford U., 1973. Comml. engr. Bouygues SA, Clamart, France, 1973-75; dir. agy. Spapa SA, Vitry, France, 1976-78; bd. dirs. IE Holding SA, Calais, ISO Entreprises SA, Ballainvillers, France, Nord Asphalte, Gondecourt, France, IE Cobanor, St. Amand Les Eaux, France, SAITRE, Abidjan, Ivory Coast. Served to lt. French Air Force, 1971-72. Roman Catholic. Office: IE Holding, 1 Rue Des Salines, F-62100 Calais France

MORIN, SYLVIA CRANE, neuro-psychiatrist, electro-encephalographer; b. Los Angeles, Oct. 24, 1922; arrived in France, 1948; d. Samuel and Ruth Jean (Zarenda) Smith; m. Georges Laurent Morin, Mar. 30, 1948; children—Christiane Andree, Andre Samuel, Thierry Georges. B.A., U. So. Calif., 1944; M.D., Bordeaux Med. Faculty, France, 1961; diploma neuropsychiatry, EEG, Paris Med. Faculty, 1969. Neuro psychiatrist, St. Brieuc, France, 1962—; co-owner pvt. Psychiat. Hosp., Yffiniac, France, 1965—; electroencephalographer Salpetriere Hosp., Paris, 1974-76; bd. dirs. Franco-Am. Inst., Rennes, France, 1967—, sec., 1985. Contbr. numerous articles on epilepsy to profl. jours. Mem. French Speaking EEG Soc. and Clin. Neuro-Physiology (titular), French and Internat. Leagues Against Epilepsy. Roman Catholic. Avocations: sailing, archery, swimming. Home and Office: Clinique du Val Josselin, 22120 Yffiniac Cotes-Du-Nord France

MORIO, MICHIO, anesthesiology educator; b. Onomichi, Hiroshima, Japan, Apr. 19, 1931; s. Ryoichi and Yasuko (Sakihara) M.; m. Akiko Nakatani, Oct. 21, 1957; 1 dau., Tomoko. M.D., Hiroshima U., 1956; Ph.D., Kyoto U., 1961. Diplomate Japanese Bd. Anesthesiology. Instr., Kyoto U. Hosp., 1961-62; asst. prof. anesthesiology Hiroshima U. Hosp., 1962-65, assoc. prof., 1965-66, prof., chmn. dept. anesthesiology, 1967—, councilor, 1979-84, 88—, dir. Univ. Hosp., 1980-84; dean Sch. Med. Hiroshima U., 1988—; vis. prof. anesthesiology Albert Einstein Coll. Medicine, 1971-72. Editor-in-chief Hiroshima Jour. Anesthesia, 1965—; Jour. Hiroshima Med. Assn., 1982—. Examinar, Japanese Ministry of Health and Welfare, 1979-81; head bd. Japanese Ministry of Prefectural Govt., 1979-82; councilor Radiation Effect Found., Hiroshima; 1980-83. Japanese Ministry of Edn. grantee, 1974-76, 77-78, 78-80, 79-83, 84-86, 87—. Fellow Japan Soc. Promotion of Sci. (vis. grantee 1981), Japanese Ministry of Edn., Sci. and Culture (vis. grantee 1971-72); mem. Am. Soc. Cardiovascular Anesthesia, Japanese Soc. Anesthesiology, Japanese Assn. Acute Medicine, Japanese Med. Assn.; hon. mem. Yugoslavian Soc. Anesthetists, Bulgarian Soc. Anesthesiology Resuscitation (hon.). Clubs: Numata Tennis, Diners, Prince. Home: Midori 2-27-34, Minami-ku, Hiroshima 734, Japan Office: Hiroshima U Sch Med, Dept Anesthesiology, Kasumi 1-2-3, Minami-ku, Hiroshima 734, Japan

MORISHIMA, TOZO, manufacturing executive; b. Jan. 8, 1920; m. Tomiko Morishima. Grad., Tokyo U., 1941. With Japan Indsl. Bank, from 1942, v.p., from 1975; currently pres. Toyo Soda Kogyo, Tokyo; bd. dirs. Shin Osaka Kyowa Sekiyu Kagaku. Home: 15-10-1005 Yoyogi, 5-chome Shibuya-ku, Tokyo 151, Japan Office: Toyo Soda Kogyo, Toso Bldg 1-7-7 Aksaka, Minato-ku, Tokyo 107, Japan *

MORITA, AKIO, electronics company executive; b. Nagoya, Japan, Jan. 26, 1921; s. Kyuzaemon and Shuko (Toda) M.; m. Yoshiko Kamei, May 13, 1950; children: Hideo, Masao, Naoko. Grad. in physics, Osaka Imperial U., 1944. Co-founder Tokyo Telecommunications Engring. Corp. (now Sony Corp.), Tokyo, 1946, exec. v.p., 1959-71, pres., 1971-76, chmn., chief exec. officer, 1976—; pres. Sony Corp. Am., 1960-66, chmn. bd., 1966-72, chmn. fin. com., 1972-74, 77-81, chmn. exec. com., 1974-77, 81—; mem. internat. council Morgan Guaranty Trust Co.; vice chmn. Keidanren, chmn. Com. on Internat. Indsl. Coop. Recipient Medal of Honor with Blue Ribbon, Royal Soc. Arts Albert medal. Home: 5-6 Aobadai 2-chome Meguroku, Tokyo 153 Japan Office: Sony Corp, Tokyo Int Box 5100, Tokyo Japan 100-31 also: Sony Corp of America 9 W 57th St New York NY 10019 *

MORITA, JAMES MASAMI, banker, lawyer; b. Kealakekua, South Kona, Hawaii, July 18, 1913; s. Ushima and Kichi (Yamamoto) M.; m. Aiko Nagakura, Jan. 12, 1957; children: Caryn Sami, Marie Michiko. B.A., U. Hawaii, 1936; LL.B., Georgetown U., 1940; grad., Stonier Grad. Sch. Banking, 1970. Bar: Hawaii, D.C. 1940, U.S. Supreme Ct. 1949. Partner firm Fukushima & Morita, Honolulu, 1941-50; 1st asst. pub. prosecutor Honolulu, 1951-52; atty. City-County Honolulu, 1953-55, spl. counsel, 1956-57; atty. Morita, Kamo & Sakai, Honolulu, 1960-70; chmn. bd., chief exec. officer City Bank; Chmn. bd., pres. CB Bancshares, Inc.; bd. dirs. Citibank Properties, All Hawaii Investment Corp., New Otani Kaimana Beach Hotel, Tony Hawaii Corp, Pacific Olds GMC, Kanebo Cosmetics Hawaii, Inc., Huntington Beach Imports, Tony Calif., Ltd. Nat. trustee Nat. Jewish Hosp. and Research Ctr., 1977, Hawaii Loa Coll., 1980; active Boy Scouts Am.; mem. campaign exec. com. Japanese Cultural Ctr. Hawaii. Decorated Order of Rising Sun 3d class (Japan); recipient Outstanding award Nat. Jewish Hosp., 1976; recipient 75th Anniversary Rainbow award to disting alumni U. Hawaii, 1982, Freedom Symbol award Sertoma Club, 1983. Mem. Bar Assn. Hawaii, Am. Bankers Assn. (Stonier adv. bd.), Hawaii Bankers Assn., Mid-Pacific Alumni Assn., Georgetown U. Alumni Assn., Japan-Hawaii Econ. Council, Japan-Am. Soc. Honolulu., Hawaii Soc. Corp. Planners, Hawaii C. of C. (bd. dirs), U. Hawaii Alumni Assn. Democrat. Clubs: Waialae Country, 200, Honolulu Country, U. Hawaii Pres.'s, Plaza, Mid-Pacific, All Winners, Mynah. Office: 810 Richards St City Bank Box 3709 Honolulu HI 96811

MORITA, KATSURA, chemist; b. Osaka-fu, Japan, May 6, 1925; s. Keijiro and Sueno M.; m. Mitome Morita; children: Atsuko Matsumura, Hiroshi. BS, Kyoto U., Japan, 1948; PhD, Kyoto U., 1960. Mgr. new product planning and devel. div. Takeda Chem. Industries, Ltd., Japan, 1974-75; gen. mgr. cen. research div. Takeda Chem. Industries, Ltd., 1982-85, also bd. dirs., mng. dir., 1985-86, sr. mng. dir., 1986—; dir. cen. research div. Medicinal Research Labs., Takeda, 1975-81; bd. dirs. Protein Engring. Research Inst., Tokyo. Author: Discovery of Lenthionine, Tetrahedron Letters, 1966; Editor: Dictionary of Organic Compounds, The Soc. Synthetic Organic Chemistry, Japan, 1985. Chmn. com. for dev. of tech. The Kansai Keizai Doyukai, 1987—. Recipient Yakuji-koro-sho, Osaka-fu, 1986. Fellow Bioindustry Devel. Ctr.; mem. Chem. Soc. Japan, Pharm. Soc. Japan. Home: 2-11-18 Toyoshima-kita, IKeda-shi, Osaka-fu 563, Japan Office: Takeda Chem Industries Ltd, 2-27 Doshomachi, Osaka-shi 541, Japan

MORITA, MASAMI, literature educator; b. Nagasaki, Japan, Dec. 1, 1927; s. Hikoichi and Sumi M.; m. Masue Okuhara, Nov. 17, 1963; children—Yuichiro, Fumie, Tomoe. B.A., Waseda U., Tokyo, 1951, M.A., 1961. Lectr., Takasaki City Coll. Econs., Gunma, Japan, 1967-68, assoc. prof., 1968-74, prof., 1974-87, prof. Kanda U. of Internal. Studies, Chiba, Japan, 1987—; part-time lectr. Waseda U., 1978—; vis. scholar U. Cambridge, Eng., 1973-74; vis. fellow Yale U., New Haven, 1983-84. Contbr. articles to learned jours. Grantee for study and research abroad Japanese Ministry Edn., 1973-74; Fulbright fellow Japan-U.S. Ednl. Commn., 1983-84. Mem. MLA, English Literary Soc. Japan, Am. Lit. Soc. Japan, Comparative Lit. Soc. Japan. Club: Cambridge Soc. (Eng.). Avocations: music, travel. Home: 662-3 Shokanji, Takasaki 370, Gunma Japan Office: Kanda U of Internat Studies, 1-4-1 Wakaba, Chiba 260, Japan

MORITZ, MILTON EDWARD, telephone company executive; b. Reading, Pa., Sept. 5, 1931; s. Edward Raymond and Anna May M.; student U. Md., 1950-51, Fla. State U., 1959-60; m. Elizabeth Ann Walls, June 6, 1952; children: Betsy Ann Moritz Koppenhaver, Stephen Edward, Sandra E. Enlisted in U.S. Army, 1963, served as spl. agt. M.I.; ret., 1970; safety and security dir. Harrisburg (Pa.) Hosp., 1970-72; security mgr. United Telephone Systems, Carlisle, Pa., 1972—; lectr., instr. Harrisburg Area Community Coll. Pres., Greater Harrisburg Crime Clinic, 1974. Decorated Bronze Star with oak leaf cluster. Mem. Am. Soc. Indsl. Security (past pres., chmn. bd. dirs.), Assn. Former Intelligence Officers, Internat. Narcotic Enforcement Officers Assn., Pa. Crime Prevention Assn. (bd. dirs.). Republican. Lutheran. Home: 7723 Avondale Terr Harrisburg PA 17112 Office: 1170 Harrisburg Pike Carlisle PA 17013

MORK, GORDON ROBERT, historian, educator; b. St. Cloud, Minn., May 6, 1938; s. Gordon Matthew and Agnes (Gibb) M.; m. Dianne Jeannette Muetzel, Aug. 11, 1963; children: Robert, Kristiana, Elizabeth. Instr. history U. Minn., Mpls., 1966; lectr., asst. prof. U. Calif., Davis, 1966-70; mem. faculty Purdue U., West Lafayette, Ind., 1970—; assoc. prof. Purdue

U., West Lafayette, 1973—, dir. honors program in the humanities, 1985-87, dir grad. studies in history, Am. studies, 1987—; resident dir. Purdue U.-Ind. U. Program, Hamburg, Fed. Republic Germany, 1975-76; research fellow in humanities U. Wis., Madison, 1969-70. Author: Modern Western Civilization: A Concise History, 2d edit., 1981, Instructor's Manual: A History of Civilization, 1988; mem. adv. bd. Teaching History, 1983—, History Teacher, 1986—. Mem. citizens task force Lafayette Sch. Corp., 1978-79; bd. dirs. Ind. Humanities Council, 1986—; bd. dirs., sec. Murdock-Sunnyside Bldg. Corp., 1980—. Mem. Am. Hist. Assn., Conf. Group on Cen. European History, Soc. History Edn., Leo Baeck Inst., Conf. Group on German Politics, Internat. Soc. for History Didactics, Phi Beta Kappa. Home: 1521 Cason St Lafayette IN 47904 Office: Purdue U Dept History West Lafayette IN 47907

MORK, LAURA LUNDE, refrigeration executive; b. Seattle, Dec. 5, 1956; d. Marvin Conrad and Mary Anna (Bowman) Lunde; m. Loren Leslie Mork, Dec. 23, 1980. BS in Chem. Engring., U. Wash., 1980. Engring. intern EPA, Seattle, 1977-78; fuel engr. Bethlehem Steel Corp., Seattle, 1980-85; control engr. Seattle Steel Corp., 1985; utility engr. Lederle Labs., Pearl River, N.Y., 1985-87; head refrigeration dept., 1987—. Rep. precinct committeeman, Seattle, 1980; mem. com. Assn. of Wash. Bus., Olympia, 1983-85. Mem. Assn. Energy Engrs., ASHRAE, Am. Inst. Chem. Engrs., Soc. Women Engrs., Instrument Soc. Am., Nat. Assn. Female Execs.

MØRLAND, BERIT SOFIE, medical research council executive, researcher; b. Trondheim, Norway, Mar. 7, 1942; d. Ottar and Elsa Ytrehus; m. Jørg Morland, Dec. 28, 1962; children: Henning, Jon, Anders, Hans Jørgen. Degree in dentistry, U. Oslo, 1964; PhD, U. Tromsø, 1980. Gen. practice dentistry Oslo, 1964-74; research fellow U. Tromsø, Norway, 1974-77, asst. prof. morphology, 1977-80; asst. prof. immunology U. Oslo, 1980-86; product mgr. Apotheernes Lab., Oslo, 1986-87; deputy dir. Med. Research Council, Oslo, 1987—. Contbr. 50-60 articles on immunology cell biology to profl. jours. Home: Grimelundshaugen 12 D, 0374 Oslo 3 Norway Office: Med Research Council NAVF, Sandakerveien 99, 0483 Oslo 4 Norway

MORLEY, HARRY THOMAS, JR., real estate executive; b. St. Louis, Aug. 13, 1930; s. Harry Thomas and Celeste Elizabeth (Davies) M.; m. Nelda Lee Mulholland, Sept. 3, 1960; children: Lisa, Mark, Marci. BA, U. Mo., 1955; MA, U. Denver, 1959. Dir. men's student activities Iowa State Tchrs. Coll., 1955-57; dir. student housing U. Denver, 1957-60; pvt. practice psychol. consulting St. Louis, 1960-63; dir. adminstrn. County of St. Louis, Mo., 1963-70; regional dir. HUD, Kansas City, Mo., 1970-71; asst. sec. adminstrn. HUD, 1971-73; pres. St. Louis Regional Commerce and Growth Assn., 1973-78; partner Taylor, Morley, Simon, Inc., St. Louis, 1978—; teaching cons.-lectr. Washington U., St. Louis, 1962-70. Bd. dirs., mem. exec. com. St. Louis Coll. Pharmacy; mem. exec. com. Better Bus. Bur.; chmn. Mo. Indsl. Devel. Bd., Mo. State Hwy. Commn.; bd. dirs. St. Luke's Hosps., Downtown St. Louis, Inc., Laclede's Landing Redevel. Corp. Served with USN, 1951-53. Mem. Am. C. of C. Execs., Nat. Assn. Homebuilders, St. Louis Homebuildres Assn. (exec. com.), St. Louis Advt. Club. Republican. Methodist. Clubs: Mo. Athletic, St. Louis, Noonday, Castle Oak Country, Round Table. Home: 14238 Forest Crest Dr Chesterfield MO 63017 Office: 1227 Fern Ridge Pkwy Saint Louis MO 63141-4451

MORLEY, MICHAEL WILLIAM, drama educator, researcher, reviewer; b. Christchurch, Canterbury, N.Z., June 4, 1943; s. Roy William and Iris Joan (Brosnahan) M.; m. Pamela Louise Falkiner, Sept. 3, 1965 (div. 1980); children—Stephanie Joanne, Nicola Louise, Vanessa Jane; m. Caroline Ann Rich, May 17, 1986; 1 child, Jessica Frances. B.A., Auckland U., 1962, M.A. with 1st class honors, 1963; B.Litt., Christ Church, Oxford, 1968. Lectr. German, Auckland U., N.Z., 1968, sr. lectr., 1970-75; sr. lectr. drama Flinders U., Adelaide, South Australia, Australia, 1975-81, reader, 1982-84, prof., 1984—; theatre critic The Advertiser, Adelaide, 1976, Theatre Australia, Sydney, New South Wales, 1977-82, The Nat. Times, Sydney, 1983-86, The Australian Fin. Review, 1986—; mem. playreading panel State Theatre Co., Adelaide, 1979—, Nat. Playwright's Conf., Canberra, Australian Capital Territory, 1985. Author: Brecht: A Study, 1977. Contbr. articles on Brecht's poetry and theatre to profl. jours. Mus. dir., pianist theatre prodns. Never the Twain, 1977, Threepenny Opera, 1981. Mem. Internat. Brecht Soc., Australasian Drama Studies Assn. (com. 1982—). Avocations: cricket; rugby; tennis; classical music; cinema. Home: 8 Alma Rd, Fullarton, 3073 Adelaide, South Australia Australia Office: Flinders U, Drama Discipline, Bedford Park, Adelaide, South Australia Australia

MORLEY, NICHOLAS H., real estate and development executive; b. Sofia, Bulgaria, July 11, 1929; came to U.S., 1956, naturalized, 1961; s. Joseph and Regina M. (Levy) M.; m. Adelaida Padron; children—Melvin Y., Manuel F., Ady Mary, Odette M., Judith M. Dir. internat. div. Gen. Devel. Corp., Miami, Fla., 1960-63; chmn. bd., chief exec. officer Interterra, Inc., 1970—, Interterra Developers, Ltd., 1963—, Morley Realty Corp., 1963—, Gen. Real Estate, Ltd., 1963—, Grand Bahama Mortgage Corp., 1963—, U.S. Devel. Corp., Alaska, 1966—, Geneva Investment, Ltd., 1967—, U.S. Devel. Corp. Hawaii, 1968—, Regina Interiors, Inc., 1969—, Vanguard Investment, Ltd., 1970—, Corp. Econ. Devel., 1970—, U.S. Devel. Corp. Del., 1971—, N.H. Morley & Co., 1973—, Interterra Funding Corp., 1974—, U.S. Investment Services, Inc., 1974—, Interterra Realty Corp., 1975—, Interterra (N.A.), 1975—, Interterra Panama (S.A.), 1976—, Brickmore Inc., 1977—. Chmn. fin. com. Fla. Republican Party, 1977—; mem. at large SBA Nat. Adv. Council, spl. U.S. ambassador to, Venezuela and Brazil, 1974, hon. vice consul of, Panama; founder, trustee Mt. Sinai Hosp., Miami; bd. dirs. Mt. Sinai Med. Center Found., Martin Tech. Inst., Statue of Liberty, Ellis Island Centennial Commn.; trustee Fla. Internat. U. Found., St. Thomas U. founder Fla. Internat. U., Miami Jewish Home and Hosp. for the Aged; exec. bd. South Fla. council Boy Scouts Am.; former bd. dirs. U.S. Com. for Refugees; former mem. Fla. Council of 100; mem. U. Miami Soc. of Founders, NCCJ, Fla. Commn. on Ethics, 1978; del. Rep. Nat. Conv., 1976, 84. Decorated Chevalier of Order of St. Alexander, Order of Francisco Miranda, Order of St. John of Jerusalem, Knights of Malta; hon. mayor City of Port Charlotte (Fla.); Nicholas H. Morley Loyalty Park Port, St. Lucie (Fla.), and Ambassador Nicholas H. Morley Law Ctr. at St. Thomas U. named in his honor. Mem. The Vizcayans (life), Soc. Protection of Ancient Bldgs. (Eng.), NCCJ. Clubs: 200 (Miami); The Italians. Home: 1581 Brickell Ave Villa Regina Miami FL 33131 Office: Interterra Realty Co 1200 Brickell Ave Interterra Bldg 20th Floor Miami FL 33131

MORLEY, PATRICIA ANN, English and Canadian studies educator, writer; b. Toronto, Can., May 25, 1929; d. Frederick Charles and Mabel Olive (Winsland) Marlow; divorced; children: Lawrence, Patricia, Christopher, David. BA with honors, U. Toronto, 1951; MA, Carleton U., 1967; PhD, U. Ottawa, 1970. Lectr. U. Ottawa, 1971-72; asst. prof. Sir George Williams U., Montreal, 1972-75; assoc. prof. English and Can. studies Concordia U., Montreal, 1975-80, prof., 1980—; fellow Lonergan Coll., 1979-84, Simone de Beauvoir Inst., 1979-87; Shastri lectr. Shastri Indo-Can. Inst, India, 1983. Author: The Mystery of Unity: Theme and Technique in the Novels of Patrick White, 1972, The Immoral Moralists: Hugh MacLennan and Leonard Cohen, 1972, Robertson Davies, 1976, The Comedians: Hugh Hood and Rudy Wiebe, 1977; editor: Ernest Thompson Seton, 1977, Morley Callaghan, 1978, Margaret Laurence, 1981, Kurelek: A Biography, 1986; contbr. numerous articles to lang. and lit. jours; book reviewer Ottawa Jour., 1971-80, Ottawa Citizen, 1981—, Birmingham News, 1982-87. Can. Council fellow, 1969-70, Humanities Research Council Can. grantee, 1971, Social Sci. Research Council Can. grantee, 1972, Ottawa Carleton Literary award, 1986-87. Mem. Internat. Fedn. Modern Lang. and Lit. Home: Box 137, Manotick, ON Canada KOA 2NO

MORLEY, WILLIAM JOHN, finance executive; b. Itarsi, India, Oct. 28, 1911; s. Gilbert Anthony and Winifred Florence (Purvis) M.; m. Bernadette Mary Nolan, Sept. 16, 1961; children: Patrick Thomas, Robert Frederick. Owner, mgr., cons. fin. and indsl. W.J. Morley Fin. Consultancy, London. Mem. Conservative Party. Roman Catholic. Clubs: Royal Naval (London); Western Turf (Scotland). Home: 106 Village Rd, Enfield EN1 2EX, England Office: 46/47 Pall Mall, London SW1Y 5JG, England

MORNER, NILS-AXEL, geologist, educator; b. Stockholm, Mar. 17, 1938; s. Stellan and Moussia M.; m. Ulla Wilander, July 6, 1961; children—Jonas, Ninna, Philip. B.Sci., Stockholm U., 1962, Fil. lic., 1965, Ph.D., 1969. With Swedish Nat. Research Council, U. Stockholm, 1970—, research scientist geology, 1969—; guest prof., Brazil, 1979; vis. scientist, France, 1980-81. Editor: Earth Pheology, Isostasy and Eustasy, 1980; Climatic Changes on a Yearly to Millennial Basis, 1984. Contbr. over 280 articles to sci. jours. Patronus Skytheanum Found., Uppsala, Sweden; chmn. Esplunda Found., Örebro, Sweden. Postdoctoral fellow, Can., 1969-70. Fellow Geol. Soc. Am.; mem. Internat. Union Quaternary Research (pres. Neotectonics com.). Office: Geol Inst, S-10691 Stockholm Sweden

MORONEY, ROBERT EMMET, retired stock and bond broker-dealer, investment banker, appraiser of non-marketable securities; b. Dallas, Feb. 15, 1903; s. William Joseph and Lelia (Rodgers) M.; m. Jessie Dew Robinson Coolidge, 1940; children: Linda (Muffie), June. Student, U. Dallas, 1920, Georgetown U., 1921; AB, U. Wis., 1923. With Texpolite Bldg. & Loan Assn., Dallas, 1924, Anchor Savings Bldg. & Loan Assn., Madison, Wis., 1924, Guaranty Co. of N.Y., N.Y.C. and Chgo., 1925-26, Dunn & Carr and successors Carr, Moroney & Co., Moroney & Co., Moroney, Beissner & Co., Inc., Houston, 1927-62; bus. mgr. St. John The Divine Episcopal Ch., Houston, 1963-64; v.p. investments Capital Nat. Bank, Houston, 1965-67; ind. fin. cons. Houston, 1966-68; salesman Moroney, Beissner & Co., Inc., Houston, 1968-74; v.p. valuation Rotan Mosle Inc., Houston, 1974-82, retired, 1982; Co-founder, past nat. committeeman Nat. Security Traders Assn.; co-founder, past gov. Investment Bankers Assn. of Tex.; past chmn., past gov. Tex. group Investment Bankers Assn. of Am. Past bd. dirs. Houston Found. for Ballet, Houston Grand Opera Assn., Soc. for Performing Arts, Diocesan Devel. Bd., Church Found. at Rice U., Sheltering Arms, Intercontinental Airport Inter-faith Chapel, Assn. for Community TV, Retina Research Found.; former vol. driver ARC, Christian Community Service Ctr., Houston Met. Ministries' Meals-on-Wheels. Served with USNR, 1943-45. Recipient Driver #1 award Houston Met. Ministries' Meals-on-Wheels, 1984, Sr. award Houston Met. Ministries' Meals-on-Wheels, 1985. Mem. Houston Soc. Fin. Analysts, Fin. Analysts Fedn., Phi Delta Theta. Episcopalian. Clubs: Houston Stock and Bond (hon. mem. #1), Houston, River Oaks Country. Home: The Hallmark 4718 Hallmark Ln Apt 201 Houston TX 77056

MORONEY, STEVEN PETER, marketing professional; b. Halifax, Yorkshire, Eng., Mar. 15, 1955; s. Bernard and May (Stork) M.; m. Pamela Waldron, Dec. 3, 1977; children: Kerry Joanne, Christopher James. Compositor Halifax Evening Courier, Yorkshire, Eng.; rep. sales Hardy Printers, Castleford, Yorkshire, Eng.; mgr. sales Spectrum Computer Supplies, Bradford, Yorkshire, Eng., 1981-83; mgr. div. Spectrum Computer Supplies, Bradford, 1983-84, dir. div., 1984-85, dir. sales and mktg., main bd. dirs., 1985—, mng. dir., 1988—. Methodist. Home: 1 Heathfield Pl, Skircoat-green Rd, Halifax HX3 0BX, England Office: Spectrum Computer Supplies, 27 E Parade, Bradford BD1 5RJ, England

MOROSANI, GEORGE WARRINGTON, real estate developer, realtor; b. Cin., July 20, 1941; s. Remy Edmond and Virginia Caroline (Warrington) M.; B.A., Rollins Coll., 1964, M.B.A., 1965; m. Judith Clontz, July 3, 1980; children by previous marriage—Katherine Carmichael, Elizabeth Warrington. Fin. mgr. Lunar Orbitor and Minuteman Programs, Boeing Co., Cape Canaveral, Fla., 1965-68; controller Equitable Leasing Co., Asheville, N.C., 1968— ; founder, pres., treas. Western Carolina Warehousing Co., Asheville, 1969-86; co-founder, pres. Asheville Jaycee Housing, Inc., 1971-77; founder, pres., treas. A Mini Storage Co., Fletcher, N.C., 1976—; co-founder, treas. Accent on Living Co., Asheville, 1978-81; founder, pres., treas. G.M. Leasing, Asheville, N.C. 1986—, The Kingswood Co., Fletcher, N.C., 1986—; gen. partner Pine Needle Apts., Arden, N.C., 1978—, Pine Ridge Apts., Skyland, N.C., 1980—, Morganton Heights Apts., Morganton, N.C., 1981—, Maiden (N.C.) Apts., 1981—, Valley View Shopping Ctr., Candler, N.C., 1982-86, Meadow Garden Apts., Hendersonville, N.C., 1983—, Drexel Apts., N.C., 1983—, Heritage Hill Apts., Marion, N.C., 1983—, Cavalier Arms Apts., Waynesville, N.C., 1986—, Gwenmont Arms Apts., Murphy, N.C., 1986—, Nicol Arms Apts., Sylva, N.C., 1986—, Meadowwood Arms Apts., Gray, Tenn., 1986—, 4 Seasons Apts., Erwin, Tenn., 1986—, M. Realty, Asheville, 1986—, Woods Edge Apts., North Wilksboro, N.C., 1987—, Deer Park Apts., Cleve., N.C., 1987—; ptnr. Laurel Ridge Realty, Litchfield, Conn., 1973—, Laurel Properties, Rochester, Vt., 1978—, Ashland Assocs., Asheville, N.C., 1985—, Airport Assocs., Asheville, 1986-87; owner George W. Morosani Indsl. Realtor, Fletcher, 1981—. Bd. dirs. Jr. Achievement Greater Asheville Area, 1977—; mem. Regional Housing Adv. Com., Land-of-Sky Regional Council, 1981-86; mem. Council Rural Housing and Devel., 1982—; co-founder, treas. N.C. Council Rural Rental Housing, 1985—, sec., 1986—. Named Man of Yr., Asheville Jaycees, 1976. Mem. Sales and Mktg. Execs. Asheville (dir. 1974-76, 1982-84, chmn. membership com. 1976-77), Western N.C. Traffic Club (dir. 1973-74, sec.-treas. 1974-76, pres. 1976-77, dir. 1977-79), Asheville Bd. Realtors, Hendersonville Bd. Realtors, Real Estate Securities and Syndication Inst., Nat. Assn. Realtors, N.C. Assn. Realtors (property mgmt. div.). Mem. Asheville Comml. and Investment Realty Assn. (v.p. programs 1986-88, sec.-treas. 1988—), Nat. Mini-Storage Inst., W.N.C. Exchangers, Am. Rental Assn., Greater Asheville Apt. Assn., Council Ind. Bus. Owners, Better Bus. Bur. Asheville/Western N.C. (dir. 1988—), Self-Service Storage Assn., Asheville Area C. of C. (chmn. indsl. relations 1978-79). Episcopalian. Clubs: Biltmore Forest Country, Asheville Downtown City. Lodge: Civitan (dir. 1975-77). Home: 260 Cane Creek Rd Fletcher NC 28732 Office: Forest Ctr Suite 201 932 Hendersonville Rd Asheville NC 28803

MOROSCO, B. ANTHONY, lawyer; b. Yonkers, N.Y., Nov. 29, 1936; s. Ben and Rita (Farrelly) M. m. Laurie Lee Scott, Nov. 12, 1983; children—Marina, Edith, Anthony, Benson, Lenore. A.B., Fordham U., 1958; LL.B., Columbia U., 1961. Bar: N.Y. 1962, Va. 1963, U.S. Ct. Mil. Appeals 1963, U.S. Dist. Ct. (so. dist.) N.Y. 1971, U.S. Ct. Appeals (2d cir.) N.Y. 1973, U.S. Supreme Ct. 1975. Asst. dist. atty., Westchester County, N.Y., 1965-78, chief of appeals, 1971-78; ptnr. Aurnou, Rubenstein, Morosco & Kelligrew, White Plains, N.Y., 1978-80; ptnr. Morosco & Cunard, White Plains, 1980—; counsel to spl. dist. atty. Dutchess County (N.Y.), 1981—; adj. assoc. prof. law Pace U., Pleasantville, N.Y. Editor Columbia Law Rev. Served to capt. JAGC, U.S. Army, 1962-65. Mem. N.Y. State Bar Assn., Westchester County Bar Assn. (bd. dirs. 1975-77), Yorktown Bar Assn. (pres. 1977-78), N.Y. State Dist. Attys. Assn. (legis. sec. 1969-78). Republican. Roman Catholic. Club: K.C. Author: Prosecution and Defense of Sex Crimes, 1976; chpts. in books. Office: 99 Court St White Plains NY 10601

MORPURGO, ATTILIO RUDOLPH (ANDY), economics development consultant; b. Trieste, Italy, Feb. 22, 1920; s. Ignatius and Olga (Schaur) M., m. Maria Antoinette Bignolini, Dec. 31, 1942; children—Ondina Christine, Lucina Olga. Engineer, Tech. State Inst., Trieste, 1939. Civil engr. railways, Perth, W. Australia, 1950-54; engr. roads and bridges, Port Moresby, New Guinea, 1954-56, MMM Cons., Toronto, Ont., Can., 1957-58; sr. regional planner Govt. of Ont., Thunder Bay, 1959-72; ministry of Treasury div. No. Econ. Devel., Ontario, 1972-77; dir. fin. Ministry of Northern Affairs, Toronto, 1977-81, dir. strategic planning, 1981-84; now cons. Contbr. articles to profl. jours. Mem. Can. Inst. Planners, Am. Planning Assn., Can. Mining Inst., Inst. Pub. Adminstrn., Ontario Land Economists (pres. 1981-82). Lodge: Rotary. Home: 8 Windy Golfway, Don Mills, ON Canada M3C 3A7

MORREL, WILLIAM GRIFFIN, JR., banker; b. Lynchburg, Va., Aug 25, 1933; s. William Griffin and Virginia Louise (Baldwin) M.; m. Sandra Virginia Coats, Jan. 31, 1959; children: William Griffin, John Coats, Elisabeth White, Jere Coleman. BS, Yale U., 1955; postgrad. Rutgers U., 1965-67. With Md. Nat. Bank, Balt., 1955-84, asst. v.p., 1959, v.p., 1964, sr. v.p., 1975-84, chmn. internat. loan com., others; pres., bd. dirs. Md. Nat. Overseas Investment Corp.; chmn. bd. London Interstate Bank Ltd.; chmn. bd. dirs. Md. Internat. Bank; sr. v.p., chief operating officer Abu Dhabi Internat. Bank, Inc., 1984-86, pres., chief exec. officer, Heritage Internat. Bank, 1986—; consul of the Netherlands at Balt., 1978—. Mem. Balt. Consular Corps, 1978—; chmn. Md. World Trade Efforts Commn., 1983-85; mem. Md. Trade Policy Council, 1985—; vice chmn. Dist. Export Council, 1983—. Contbr. articles to profl. jours. Sr. fellow Ctr. for Internat. Banking Studies, Darden Grad. Bus. Sch. U. Va., 1978—. Served with U.S. Army, 1956-58. Mem. Bankers Assn. for Fgn. Trade (bd. dirs. 1975-78), Robert Morris Assocs. (nat. bd. dirs. 1984—), Internat. Lending Council (bd. dirs., chmn., 1978-80), Md. Hist. Soc. (trustee), Balt. Council Fgn. Relations (trustee), Econ. Devel. Council. Republican. Presbyterian. Clubs: Yale, Farmington Country, Elkridge, Merchants, Ctr. Home: 6 Beechdale Rd Baltimore MD 21210 Office: Heritage Internat Bank 7126 Wisconsin Ave Bethesda MD 20814

MORRELL, JAMES BOWES, science history educator; b. Bradford, Eng., Nov. 24, 1933; s. Lewis and Caroline Annie (Bowes) M.; m. Janet Yorke, Dec. 29, 1962; children: Elizabeth, Margaret Jane. BSc, U. Birmingham, 1954; MA, Oxford U., 1957; Cert. Edn., U. Bristol, 1958. Schoolmaster Haberdashers Aske's Sch., London, 1958-59, Queen Elizabeth Grammar Sch., Wakfield, Eng., 1959-63; lectr. history of sci. U. Bradford, Yorkshire, Eng., 1964-83; reader U. Bradford, Yorkshire, 1983—; vis. prof. U. Pa., 1970. Author: (with A.W. Thackray) Gentlemen of Science, 1981, (with I. Inkster) Metropolis and Province, 1983; contbr. articles to profl. jours. Fellow Royal Hist. Soc.; mem. Brit. Soc. History of Sci. (pres. 1982-84). Office: U Bradford, Sch European Studies, Bradford, Yorkshire BD7 1DP, England

MORRELL, JAMES FRANCIS, management consultant; b. Niagara Falls, N.Y., July 9, 1931; s. James H. and Frances Catherine (Downey) M.; B.B.A., LeMoyne Coll., 1952; m. Mary Anne Boessneck, Apr. 18, 1959; children—James C., Lisa A., Diane M. With Price Waterhouse & Co., N.Y.C., 1954-62; methods analyst Niagara Mohawk Power Corp., Syracuse, 1962-63, supr. research and stats., 1963-64, staff asst., 1964-65, adminstrv. asst., 1965-67, asst. controller, 1967-71, controller, 1971-73, v.p. corp. planning, 1973-87; cons. Power Mgmt. Assocs., Columbia, Md., 1987—, cons. Burns and Roe Co., Dradell, N.J., 1988—; lectr. Syracuse U., Rensselaer Poly. Inst., SUNY. Served with USAF, 1952-54. C.P.A., N.Y. Mem. Am. Cons. League, Nat. Assn. Bus. Economists, N.Y. Assn. Bus. Economists, Soc. for Strategic and Long Range Planning, Planning Forum, Bus. Week Corp. Planning 100, Am. Inst. C.P.A.s, Edison Electric Inst. (chmn. strategic planning com., exec. adv. com.), Am. Gas Assn. (strategic planning com.), N.Y. State Soc. C.P.A.s. Republican. Roman Catholic. Home: 213 Thornton Circle S Camillus NY 13031

MORRELL, WAYNE BEAM, JR., artist; b. Clementon, N.J., Dec. 24, 1923; s. Wayne Beam and Martha L. (Plack) M.; student Drexel Inst., Phila. Sch. Indsl. Art.; grad. Famous Artist Sch., Westport, Conn.; m. Lillian Eunice Major, July 14, 1952; children—David Wayne (dec.), Lisa Anne. Exhibited one-man show Washington County Art Mus., Hagerstown, Md., 1973; exhibited nat. group shows including NAD, Conn. Acad. Fine Arts, Wadsworth Atheneum, Addison Gallery Am. Art, Mus. Fine Arts, Columbus, Ga., New Britain Mus., Smithsonian Inst., Expn. Intercontinental, Monaco, France, Gateway Art Gallery, Palm Beach, Fla., Bleich Galleries, Carmel, Calif., Mus., Bombay, India, 1967, City Hall, Hong Kong, 1975-76; indsl. exhibitor, designer John Oldham Studios, 1955-58, art dir., 1958-61; designer Paris and Brussells Worlds Fairs, other maj. exhibits; designer cover Reader's Digest, 1967, Yankee mag., 1980. Served with AUS, 1949-52. Recipient Louis Seley purchase award; Gold medal Rockport Art Assn., 1969; Gold medal Jordan Marsh, Boston; award Council Am. Art Socs., 1971; Canelli Gold Medal award Academic Artists Assn., 1974; others. Mem. Allied Artists Am. (Jane Peterson award 1969, 74), Am. Artists Profl. League, Am. Vet. Soc. Artists, Springfield Acad. Artists (past council), Rockport Art Assn. (William Mariboe award, Harriet Mattson award, award for Winter Marshes 1980), North Shore Art Assn., Americana Gallery, Golden Web, Santa Fe, Merrill Gallery, Taos, O'Brien's Emporium, Scottsdale, Ariz., Montcrest Gallery, Chattanooga, Grand Central Art Galleries, Newman Galleries Phila. and Bryn Mawr, Pa., Dassin Gallery, Los Angeles, Salmagundi Club (Gwynne Lennon prize 1971, Phillip J. Ross award 1971, 1st hon. mention 1971). Home: 1 Squam Hollow Rockport MA 01966 Office: 25 Main St Rockport MA 01966

MORRICE, NORMAN ALEXANDER, ballet company director; b. Agua Dulce, Mexico, Sept. 10, 1931; s. Norman and Helen (Vickers) M.; attended Rambert Sch. Ballet. Joined Ballet Rambert as dancer, 1952, became prin. dancer, 1958, asst. dir., 1966-70, dir., 1970-74, also choreographer ballets; free-lance choreographer, 1974-77; dir. Royal Ballet Co., London, 1977-86 ; first success as choreographer with Two Brothers, 1958; second ballet Hazana (premiere, Sadler's Wells Theatre, London), 1958; ballet Hazard, Bath (Eng.) Festival, 1967; ballets choreographed include: 1-2-3, Them and Us, Pastorale Variee, Ladies, Ladies, Spindrift, numerous others. Recipient Elizabeth II Coronation award. Office: Royal Ballet, Royal Opera House, Covent Garden, London WC2E 7QA, England *

MORRICE, RUTH FILL, educator, writer, consultant; b. Tonawanda, N.Y., Feb. 15, 1914; d. William Louis Allen and Grace Lillian Maude (Bates) Fill; m. Charles Elmer Conklin, Dec. 8, 1930; 1 dau., Mary Ruth Fill Conklin Mailey; m. John Buchan Morrice, Oct. 19, 1946; children: John Fill Morrice, Christina Forbes Morrice Reynolds, Eleanor Wylde Morrice, George Niven Morrice. BA, Boston U., 1942, MA, 1943, postgrad., 1945-47; postgrad., Monterey Coll., San Jose State U., U. Calif.-Santa Cruz, U. Calif.-Berkeley. Asst. to English dept. Boston U., 1942-47; tchr. Hinsdale (Ill.) High Sch., 1943-45, head dept. English; instr. English Coll. William and Mary, Williamsburg, Va., 1947; instr. English and creative writing Culver Stockton Coll., Canton, Mo., 1948-49; faculty English and social studies Hartnell Coll., Salinas, Calif., 1967; teaching prin., counselor Olympia Sch., San Benito County, Calif., 1969-70; spl. tchr. Pacific Grove (Calif.) Unified Sch. Dist., 1964-76; ednl. cons., counselor, Carmel, Calif.; free lance writer, artist; sec. to Edward Rowe Snow, 1946, 47. Author: The Poetry of George Santayana, 1943, A Definition of the Novel 1920 to present, 1981, A Study of Santayana and Ruskin, 1981, ...Personal Biography, 1981; editor: A Pilgrim Returns to Cape Cod (Edward Rowe Snow), 1946-47, Photographs and Thoughts from My Journeying in the Orient, 1979. Bd. dirs., supt. Bible Sch., Tustin (Calif.) Congl. Ch., 1964; den mother, pack and dist. leader San Fernando Valley council Boy Scouts Am.; mem. sch. bd. Montague Sch., Los Angeles; active parent groups, Heart Fund, ch. and other choirs. Mem. AAUP, Coll. English Assn. (sec. to treas. 1947-48), Nat. Tchrs. Assn., Calif. Tchrs. Assn., Alpha Phi. Republican. Congregationalist. Home and Office: 3508 Trevis Way Carmel CA 93923

MORRIN, THOMAS HARVEY, engineering research company executive; b. Woodland, Calif., Nov. 24, 1914; s. Thomas E. and Florence J. (Hill) M.; m. Frances M. Von Ahn, Feb. 1, 1941; children: Thomas H., Diane, Linda, Denise. B.S., U. Calif., 1937; grad., U.S. Navy Grad. Sch., Annapolis, Md., 1941. Student engr. Westinghouse Electric Mfg. Co., Emeryville, Calif., 1937; elec. engr. Pacific Gas & Electric Co., 1938-41; head microwave engring. div. Raytheon Mfg. Co., Waltham, Mass., 1947-48; chmn. elec. engring. dept. Stanford Research Inst., 1948-52, dir. engring., research, 1952-60, gen. mgr. engring., 1960-64, vice pres. engring., sci., 1964-68; pres. University City Sci. Inst., Phila., 1968-69, Morrin Assos., Inc., Wenatchee, Wash., 1968-72. Trustee Am. Acad. Transp. Served as officer USNR, 1938-58, comdr. USN, 1945-48. Decorated Bronze Star. Fellow IEEE, AAAS; mem. Sci. Research Soc. Am. Club: Marine Meml. (San Francisco). Address: 654 23d Ave San Francisco CA 94121

MORRIS, ALPHA LOCKHART, sociology educator, researcher; b. Taylor, Miss., Mar. 17, 1932; d. Odeal William and Ruby (Smith) Lockhart; m. Jesse Anderson Morris Sr., Dec. 25, 1952 (dec. 1980); children—Jesse Anderson Jr., Patricia Alpha. B.S., Alcorn State U., 1952; M.A., Mich. State U., 1955; Ph.D., Miss. State U., 1978. Cert. secondary tchr., Miss. Tchr. home econs. Union County Schs., New Albany, Miss., 1952-53, Clairborne County, Port Gibson, Miss., 1964-70; instr. social sci. Alcorn State U., Lorman, Miss., 1970-78, asst. prof. sociology, 1978—; dir. Lilly Endowment Project, Lorman, 1984—; cons. Miss. Council on Aging, McComb, 1984—; guest speaker Claiborne County Schs., Port Gibson, 1981—. Contbr. articles to profl. jours. Mem. exec. com. Miss. Cultural Crossroads, Port Gibson, 1980—, Clairborne County Democratic Party, Port Gibson, 1984—; participant nat. study of black family Nat. Assn. Equal Opportunity Minorities Higher Edn. Recipient People to People Internat. award U. Neb., 1982; Fulbright-Hays scholar, 1984. Mem. Am. Sociol. Assn., Mid-South Sociol. Assn. (nominations com. 1984), Claiborne County Ushers Assn.; Sociologists for Women in Soc. (area reporter 1981), So. Sociol. Soc. (minorities com. 1983—), Alcorn Nat. Alumni Assn. (Alumnus of Yr. 1987), Phi Delta Kappa, Delta Sigma Theta (pres. 1981—), Alpha Kappa Delta. Baptist. Home: Route 2 Box 30 Lorman MS 39096

MORRIS, BENJAMIN HUME, lawyer; b. Louisville, Sept. 25, 1917; s. Benjamin Franklin and Mary (Hume) M.; m. Lacy Hibbs Abell, July 7, 1942; children—Benjamin Hume, Lacy Wayne; m. 2d, Mary Frances Fowler Gatlin, Nov. 9, 1968. J.D., U. Louisville, 1941. Bars: Ky. 1940, U.S. Supreme Ct. 1966. Assoc., Doolan, Helm, Stites & Wood, Louisville, 1941-50; atty. Brown-Forman Distillers Corp., Louisville, 1950-56; resident counsel, 1956-64, v.p., resident counsel, 1964-73, v.p., gen. counsel 1973-81, corp. sec. 1981; pres., dir. Canadian Mist Distillers, Ltd., Collingwood, Ont., Can., 1971-81; of counsel Morris, Nicolas, Welsh & Vandeventer, Louisville, 1982-86, Ray & Morris, 1986—. Trustee, sec. W. L. Lyons Brown Found., 1964—; trustee City of Riverwood, Ky., 1977-81; chmn. Jefferson County Social Service Adv. Com., 1959-62; bd. govs. Jefferson Alcohol and Drug Abuse Ctr., 1983—; past. bd. dirs. Ky. C. of C., Better Bus. Bur. Louisville. Served to capt. USAF, 1941-45; col. Res. ret. Decorated Air medal with oak leaf cluster; recipient Disting. Alumni award, U. Louisville, 1981. Mem. Ky. Bar Assn., Ky. Soc. S.A.R. (pres., 1978), Nat. Soc. S.A.R. (v.p. 1980, chancellor gen. 1982-83, sec. gen. 1984, pres. gen. 1985, Minuteman award 1984, Gold Good Citizenship medal 1986), Ky. Distillers Assn. (chmn. 1969), Distilled Spirits Council U.S. (pres. 1973, chmn. 1973-74, chmn. emeritus 1982—), Assn. Canadian Distillers (bd. dirs. 1971-81), Soc. Colonial Wars, Soc. of the War of 1812, Soc. Sons and Daus. of the Pilgrims, Mil. Order of World Wars. Republican. Presbyterian. Clubs: Louisville Boat, Filson, Army and Navy. Reviser, Corp. sect. Banks-Baldwin's Ky. Legal Forms Book, 1982. Address: 2005 High Ridge Rd Louisville KY 40207

MORRIS, CLIVE SYDNEY, patent lawyer; b. Leeds, Eng., Dec. 24, 1943; arrived in Switzerland, 1968; s. Sydney and Dorothy Mary (Daniels) M.; m. Bronwyn Mary Harrington, June 8, 1973; children: Jonathan, Colette, Laura. BSc, U. Nottingham, Eng., 1965; Grad., Chartered Inst. Patent Agts., 1973. Patent examiner Patent Office, London, 1965-68; patent agt., head pharm. patents div. Sandoz AG, Basle, Switzerland, 1968—; also dep. dir. Sandoz AG, Basle. Home: Steingrubenweq 162, 4125 Riehen Switzerland

MORRIS, EARLE ELIAS, JR., state official, business executive; b. Greenville, S.C., July 14, 1928; s. Earle Elias and Bernice (Carey) M.; m. Jane L. Boroughs, Apr. 12, 1958; children: Lynda Lewis, Carey Mauldin, Elizabeth McDaniel, Earle Elias III; m. Carol Telford, Oct. 4, 1972; 1 son, David Earle. B.S., Clemson Coll., 1949, LL.D.; D.Public Service, U. S.C., 1980, Dr. Med. Sci.; LL.D., The Citadel; H.H.D., Lander Coll., Francis Marion Coll., 1984. Pres., chmn. bd. Morris & Co., Inc. (wholesale grocers), Pickens, S.C.; v.p., dir. Pickens Bank, 1956-69, Bankers Trust S.C., Pickens, 1968-75; pres. Gen. Ins. Agy., Pickens, 1970—; sec. Carolina Investors, Inc.; ptnr. Morris Realty Co., Pickens; mem. S.C. Ho. of Reps., 1950-54, S.C. Senate, 1954-70; lt. gov. State of S.C., 1971-75, comptroller gen., 1976—; chmn. bd. Santee Cooper Fisheries (Far East) Ltd., Hong Kong, Tai Pan Technologies, Ltd., Hong Kong; dir. Brunswick Worsted Mills, S.C. Devel. Corp., Pickens Savs. & Loan Assn. S.C. rep. and chmn. So. Regional Commn. Mental Health; mem. Crippled Children's Soc. S.C., Gov. S.C. Adv. Group Mental Health Planning, Nat. Adv. Mental Health Council, 1965-69, S.C. Interagy. Council Mental Retardation, S.C. Mental Health Commn., 1975-76; bd. dirs. Clemson U. Found., pres., 1984-85; del. S.C. Democratic Conv., 1950-84, Nat. Dem. Com., 1952, 56, 68, 72; chmn. S.C. Dem. Com., 1966-68; trustee Fin. Acctg. Found.; state dir. Selective Service System. Served to col. S.C. N.G. Named Disting. Alumnus Clemson Coll.; recipient Algernon Sydney Sullivan award, 1980, Donald L. Scantlebury award, 1985. Mem. Nat. Assn. State Comptrollers (pres. 1982), Nat. Assn. State Auditors, Comptrollers and Treasurers (v.p. 1988), S.C. Nat. Guard Assn. (pres. 1980-81), S.C. Jr. C. of C., S.C. Rehab. Assn. (v.p.), Blue Key, Sigma Alpha Epsilon, Phi Kappa Phi. Presbyterian (elder, former deacon, synod trustee). Clubs: Palmetto, Faculty (Columbia); Poinsett (Greenville). Lodges: Masons, Shriners, Lions. Home: 159 Lake Murray Terr Lexington SC 29072

MORRIS, ELIZABETH TREAT, physical therapist; b. Hartford, Conn., Feb. 20, 1936; d. Charles Wells and Marion Louise (Case) Treat; B.S. in Phys. Therapy, U. Conn., 1960; m. David Breck Morris, July 10, 1961; children—Russell Charles, Jeffrey David. Phys. therapist Crippled Children's Clinic No. Va., Arlington, 1960-62, Shriners Hosp. Crippled Children, Salt Lake City, 1967-69, Holy Cross Hosp., Salt Lake City, 1970-74; pvt. practice phys. therapy, Salt Lake City, 1975—. Mem. Am. Phys. Therapy Assn., Am. Congress Rehab. Medicine, Salt Lake Area C. of C., Friendship Force Utah, U.S. Figure Skating Assn. Home: 4177 Mathews Way Salt Lake City UT 84124 Office: 2178 So 900 East Suite 3 Salt Lake City UT 84106

MORRIS, HENRY MADISON, JR., educator, college president; b. Dallas, Oct. 6, 1918; s. Henry Madison and Ida (Hunter) M.; m. Mary Louise Beach, Jan. 24, 1940; children: Henry Madison III, Kathleen Louise, John David, Andrew Hunter, Mary Ruth, Rebecca Jean. B.S. with distinction, Rice Inst., 1939; M.S., U. Minn., 1948, Ph.D., 1950; LL.D., Bob Jones U., 1966. Registered engr., Tex. Jr. engr. Tex. Hwy. Dept., 1938-39; from jr. engr. to asst. engr. Internat. Boundary Commn., El Paso, 1939-42; instr. civil engring. Rice Inst., 1942-46; from instr. to asst. prof. U. Minn., Mpls., also research project leader St. Anthony Falls Hydraulics Lab., 1946-51; prof., head dept. civil engring. Southwestern La. Inst., Lafayette, 1951-57, Va. Poly. Inst., Blacksburg, 1957-70; v.p. acad. affairs Christian Heritage Coll., San Diego, 1970-78, pres., 1978-80; dir. Inst. for Creation Research, 1970-80, pres., 1980—. Author: (with Richard Stephens) Report on Rio Grande Water Conservation Investigation, 1942, That You Might Believe, 1946, 2d edit., 1978, (with Curtis Larson) Hydraulics of Flow in Culverts, 1948, The Bible and Modern Science, 1951, rev. edit., 1968, (with John C. Whitcomb) The Genesis Flood, 1961, Applied Hydraulics in Engineering, 1963, The Twilight of Evolution, 1964, Science, Scripture and Salvation, 1965, 2d edit., 1971, Studies in the Bible and Science, 1966, Evolution and the Modern Christian, 1967, Biblical Cosmology and Modern Science, 1970, The Bible has the Answer, 1971, Science and Creation: A Handbook for Teachers, 1971, (with J.M. Wiggert) Applied Hydraulics, 1972, A Biblical Manual on Science and Creation, 1972, The Remarkable Birth of Planet Earth, 1973, Many Infallible Proofs, 1974, Scientific Creationism, 1974, 2d edit., 1985, Troubled Waters of Evolution, 1975, The Genesis Record, 1976, Education for the Real World, 1977, 2d edit., 1983, The Scientific Case for Creation, 1977, The Beginning of the World, 1977, Sampling the Psalms, 1978, King of Creation, 1980, Men of Science, Men of God, 1982, Evolution in Turmoil, 1982, The Revelation Record, 1983, History of Modern Creationism, 1984, The Biblical Basis for Modern Science, 1984, Creation and the Modern Christian, 1985, Science and The Bible, 1986, Days of Praise, 1986, The God Who is Real, 1988, The Remarkable Record of Job, 1988; (with Martin Clark) The Bible Has The Answer, 1987, 2d edit., 1987; (with Gary E. Parker) What is Creation Science, 1982, 2d edit., 1987; research bulls., tech. articles, reports and booklets. Fellow AAAS, ASCE, Am. Sci. Affiliation; mem. Am. Soc. Engring. Edn. (sec.-editor civil engring. div. 1967-70), Trans-Nat. Assn. Christian Schs. (pres. 1983—), Creation Research Soc. (pres. 1967-73), Am. Geophys. Union, Geol. Soc. Am., Am. Assn. Petroleum Geologists, Geochem. Soc., Gideons (pres. La. 1954-56), Phi Beta Kappa, Sigma Xi, Chi Epsilon, Tau Beta Pi. Baptist. Home: 6733 El Banquero San Diego CA 92116

MORRIS, HENRY MADISON, III, religious organization administrator; b. El Paso, Tex., May 15, 1942; s. Henry Madison and Mary Louise (Beach) M.; B.A. summa cum laude, Christian Heritage Coll., 1976; M.Div., Luther Rice Sem., 1977, D.Min., 1978; postgrad., Pepperdine U., 1988—; m. Janet Deckman, July 25, 1964; children: Henry M., Scotta Marie. Regional mgr. Integon Ins. Co., Greenville, S.C., 1969-75; ordained to ministry Bapt. Ch., 1968; pastor Hallmark Bapt. Ch., Greenville, 1969-75; assoc. prof. Bible, Christian Heritage Coll., El Cajon, Calif., 1977-78, adminstrv. v.p., 1978-80; pastor First Bapt. Ch., Canoga Park, Calif., 1980-86; chief adminstrv. officer Wismer Assocs., Inc., Canoga Park, 1986—; lectr. in field. Served with U.S. Army, 1959-66. Republican. Author: Baptism: What is It?, 1977; Explore the Word, 1978; Churches: History and Doctrine, 1980. Office: 22134 Sherman Way Canoga Park CA 91306

MORRIS, JAMES ALOYSIUS, economist, educator; b. Lawrence, Mass., May 25, 1918; s. George Thomas and Elizabeth (Reardon) M.; m. Marjorie Leila Frampton, May 30, 1942; children: Stephen Frampton, Elizabeth Harvey. B.A. with high honors, Northeastern U., 1942, LL.D., 1968; A.M., Harvard U., 1947, Ph.D., 1951; Litt.D., Coll. Charleston, 1970; L.H.D., Lander Coll., 1971, Francis Marion Coll., 1982. Adj. prof. U. S.C., Columbia, 1947-51; assoc. prof. U. S.C., 1951-56, prof. econs., dir. grad. studies Sch. Bus. Adminstrn., 1956-61, dean Sch. Bus. Adminstrn., 1961-66, v.p. advanced studies and research, dean Grad. Sch., 1966-68, chmn. faculty com. on admissions and athletics, Disting. prof., 1972-77; econ. cons. 1977—; commr. S.C. Commn. on Higher Edn., 1968-72; chmn. bd. dirs., exec. com. S.C. Blue Cross-Blue Shield; former vice chmn. Gov.'s Productivity Council; former chmn. Charlotte br. Fed. Res. Bank., Republic Nat. Bank; labor arbitrator Fed. Mediation Service, Am. Arbitration Assn., 1948—; vis. research prof. Nuffield Coll., Oxford U., 1953-54; cons. to dir. ICA, 1955; spl. econ. adviser to dir. USOM, Turkey, 1956-57; past chmn. S.C. Regional Export Expansion Council; mem. Gov.'s Task Force on the Economy, Gov.'s Adv. Group on Health Planning; past chmn. Gov.'s Adv. Group on Mental Health Planning; chmn. bd. S.C. Econ. Advisers Council, S.C. Law Inst. Author: Woolen and Worsted Manufacturing in the Southern Piedmont, 1952; contbr. articles and revs. to profl. jours. Bd. dirs. United Community Services; pres. U. S.C. Ednl. Found.; past chmn. bd. Nat. Lab. For Higher Edn.; mem. corp. Northeastern U.; mem. Nat. Alumni Council Northeastern U.; trustee Episc. Div. of Upper S.C., 1988—. Served to lt. col. U.S. Army, 1940-41, 42-46. Mem. Am., So. econ. assns., Nat. Assn. Bus. Economists, Am. Arbitration Assn., Nat. Acad. Arbitrators. Episcopalian (sr. warden, lay reader). Clubs: Forum, Forest Lake Country, Palmetto, Summit. Lodge: Rotary. Home: 1718 Madison Rd Apt 403 Columbia SC 29204 Office: U SC Columbia SC 29208

MORRIS, JAMES MALACHY, lawyer; b. Champaign, Ill., June 5, 1952; s. Walter Michael and Ellen Frances (Solon) M.; m. Mary Delilah Baker, Oct. 17, 1987. Student Oxford U. (Eng.), 1972; B.A., Brown U., 1974; J.D., U. Pa.-Phila., 1977. Bar: N.Y. 1978, U.S. Dist. Ct. (so. and ea. dists.) N.Y. 1978, Ill. 1980, U.S. Tax Ct. 1982, U.S. Sup. Ct. 1983; admitted to Barristers Chambers, Manchester, Eng., 1987. Assoc., Reid & Priest, N.Y.C., 1977-80; sr. law clk. Sup. Ct. Ill., Springfield, 1980-81; assoc. Carter, Ledyard & Milburn, N.Y.C., 1981-83; sole practice, N.Y.C., 1983-87 counsel FCA, Washington, 1987—; cons. Internat. Awards Found., Zurich, 1981—, Pritzker Architecture Prize Found., N.Y.C., 1981—, Herbert Oppenheimer, Nathan & VanDyck, London, 1985—. Contbr. articles to profl. jours. Mem. ABA, Ill. Bar Assn., N.Y. State Bar Assn., N.Y. County Lawyers Assn., Assn. Bar City N.Y., Brit. Inst. Internat. and Comparative Law. Office: Georgetown Station Box 25723 Washington DC 20007

MORRIS, JAN, writer; b. Oct. 2, 1926. Mem. editorial staff The Times, 1951-56, The Guardian, 1957-62. Fellow Royal Soc. Literature; mem. Acad. Gymreig. Author: (as James Morris) Coast to Coast, 1956; Sultan in Oman, 1957; The Market of Seleukia, 1957; Coronation Everest, 1958; South African Winter, 1958; The Hashemite Kings, 1959; Venice, 1960; The Upstairs Donkey (for children), 1962; The Road to Huddersfield, 1963; Cities, 1963; The Presence of Spain, 1964; Oxford, 1965; Pax Britannica, 1968; The Great Port, 1970; Places, 1972; Heaven's Command, 1973; Farewell the Trumpets, 1978; (as Jan Morris) Conundrum, 1974; Travels, 1976; The Oxford Book of Oxford, 1978; Spain, 1979; Destinations, 1980; The Venetian Empire, 1980; My Favourite Stories of Wales, 1980; The Small Oxford Book of Wales, 1982; The Spectacle of Empire, 1982, Stones of Empire, 1983, Journeys, 1984, The Matter of Wales, 1984, Among the Cities, 1985, Last Letters from Hav, 1985, Manhattan '45, 1987, Hong Kong, 1988.

MORRIS, JANE ELIZABETH, home economics educator; b. Marietta, Ohio, Nov. 28, 1940; d. Harold Watson and LaRue (Graham) M. Student, U. Ky., 1960; BS, Marietta Coll., 1962, postgrad., 1963; MA, Kent State U., 1970, postgrad., 1985-87; postgrad., Coll. Mt. St. Joseph, 1984-86, John Carroll U., 1986, Ashland Coll., 1987. Cert. high sch. tchr., Ohio. Tchr. home econs. Chagrin Falls (Ohio) Mid. and High Sch., 1962—; head cheerleading advisor, Chagrin Falls High Sch., 1970-80, freshman class advisor, 1981-82, head Fine and Practical Arts Dept., 1982-84, sophomore class advisor, 1982-85, 87-88, prin.'s cabinet, 1987-88. Vice chmn. The Elec. Women's Round Table, Inc., Cleve., 1968, chmn. 1969-70; treas. Trees Condominum Assn., 1981-83; active Chagrin Falls chpt. Am. Heart Assn., Am. Cancer Soc. Mem. NEA, Career Edn. Assn., Ohio Edn. Assn., Northeast Ohio Edn. Assn., Chagrin Falls Tchrs. Assn. (bldg. rep. 1986, 87, 88), Alpha Xi Delta. Methodist. Office: Chagrin Falls Schs 77 E Washington St Chagrin Falls OH 44022

MORRIS, JOHN E., lawyer; b. N.Y.C., Sept. 30, 1916; s. John and Honora C. (Long) M.; m. Patricia E. Grojean. A.B., CCNY; A.M., Columbia U.; J.D., Harvard U. Bar: N.Y. 1942, U.S. Dist. Ct. (so. and ea. dists.) N.Y. Trial lawyer Clarke & Reilly, 1946-50; ptnr. Morris & Duffy, N.Y.C., 1950—. Served to lt. USCG, 1942-46; ETO. Mem. ABA, N.Y. State Bar Assn., Airplane Owners & Pilots Assn., N.Y. County Lawyers Assn., Internat. Assn. Ins. Counsel. Roman Catholic. Clubs: Harvard, N.Y. Athletic (N.Y.C.), Great Dane Club Am. (bd. dirs.). Office: 233 Broadway 18th Floor New York NY 10279

MORRIS, JOHN THEODORE, planning official; b. Denver, Jan. 18, 1929; s. Theodore Ora and Daisy Allison (McDonald) M.; B.F.A., Denver U., 1955; m. Dolores Irene Seaman, June 21, 1951; children—Holly Lee, Heather Ann, Heidi Jo, Douglas Fraser. Apprentice landscape architect S.R. DeBoer & Co., Denver, summer 1949, planning technician (part-time), 1954-55; sr. planner and assoc. Trafton Bean & Assocs., Boulder, Colo., 1955-62; prin. Land Planning Assocs., planning cons., Boulder, 1962-65; planning dir. and park coordinator Boulder County, 1965-67; sch. planner Boulder Valley Sch. Dist., 1967-84, also dir. planning and engring., 1967-84, supr. facility improvement program, 1969-84; pvt. sch. planning cons., 1984—; cons. U. Colo. Bur. Ednl. Field Services, 1974. Bd. dirs. Historic Boulder, 1974-76; mem. parks and recreation adv. com. Denver Regional Council Govts., 1975-84. Served with USCG, 1950-53. Mem. Am. Inst. Cert. Planners, Am. Planning Assn., Council of Ednl. Facility Planners Internat. Home and Office: Jamestown Star Rt 7647 N 32d St Boulder CO 80302

MORRIS, J(OSEPH) ANTHONY, public interest organization official; b. nr. Marboro, Md., Sept. 6, 1918; s. Charles Lafayette and Essie (Stokes) M.; B.S., Cath. U. Am., 1940, M.S., 1942, Ph.D., 1947; m. Ruth Savoy, Nov. 1, 1942; children—Carol Ann, Marilyn T., Joseph A., Larry A. Asst. scientist Josiah Macy, Jr. Found., N.Y.C., 1943-44; virologist, Depts. Agr., Interior, Laurel, Md., 1944-47; virologist, chief hepatitis virus research Walter Reed Army Inst. Research, Washington, 1947-56; virologist, asst. chief, dept. virus and rickettsial diseases U.S. Army Med. Command, Japan, 1956-59; virologist chief sect. respiratory viruses, div. biologics standards NIH, Bethesda, Md., 1959—, dir. slow, latent and temperate virus br. FDA, Bethesda, 1972-76; lectr. dept. microbiology U. Md., College Park, 1977-79; vice-chmn. Bell of Atri, Inc., College Park, 1979-82, chmn., 1983; cons. Commn. on Influenza, Armed Forces Epidemiologic Bd., 1960—, Nat. Inst. Neurol. Diseases and Blindness, 1962—. Mem. Soc. Tropical Medicine and Hygiene, Soc. Am. Microbiologists, Soc. Exptl. Biology and Medicine, Am. Assn. Immunologists, N.Y. Acad. Sci. Discoverer of respiratory sycytial virus; research on infectious hepatitis, respiratory diseases of virus etiology and zoonosis. Home: 23-E Ridge Rd Greenbelt MD 20770

MORRIS, JOSEPH GETEHMNAH, university administrator; b. Kpoomkpala, Bong County, Liberia, Nov. 11, 1929; s. Keamu and Neagar (Gonlellel) Gayne; m. Cecelia Adelaide Morris, Apr. 11, 1959; children: Joseph Jr., Clement, Charlene, Rachel, Genelaide, Barbara, Cecelia. BA, U. Liberia, 1954; MS in Edn., U. Wis., 1958; postgrad., Pa. State U., 1959; PhD, Cornell U., 1968. Edn. aide in-service tchr. tng. AID, Monrovia, Liberia, 1955-57; dir. tchr. edn. Ministry of Edn., Monrovia, 1959-64, exec. sec. for UNESCO, 1969-70, asst. minister, 1972-75, dep. minister, 1976-77; Liberian ambassador to Sierra Leone, 1978-84; pres. U. Liberia, 1985-87; del. UNESCO Conf. on Ednl. Needs of Africa, Addis Ababa, Ethiopia, 1961, 16th Session of Gen. Conf. UNESCO, Paris, 1970, Conf. of Chief Tech. Advisors, UNESCO, Paris, 1975, 4th Ordinary Session of Ministerial Council of Mano River Union, Freetown, Sierra Leone, 1977, Am. Assn. State Colls. and Univs. Conf., Washington, 1985; participant Internat. Dialogue in Africa, Buoake, Ivory Coast, 1969, Khumasi, Ghana, 1975. Mem. Liberian Nat. Population Commn., 1986—, Pres. Tolbert's Party on a State visit to Uganda, 1976; chmn. Liberian Nat. Commn. for Internat. Yr. of Peace, 1986, A.M.E.Ch. Recipient Ofcl. UN Commemorative medal, 1986, various nat. edn. awards. Mem. Assn. African Univs., Internat. Assn. Univ. Presidents (head High Commn. for Peace 1985), West African Examinations Council, Liberian Research Assn., Nat. Tchrs. Assn. Liberia, Am. Assn. Sch. Adminstrs., Phi Delta Kappa. Office: Ministry of Edn, World Bank Project, Implementation Unit, PO Box 9012, Monrovia Liberia

MORRIS, KENNETH PAUL, advertising executive; b. Chgo., Mar. 12, 1948; s. Melville and Bette Lou (Levy) M. BA, U. Louisville, 1970. Account exec. Al Paul Lefton Co., N.Y.C., 1970-77; Metromail Corp., N.Y.C., 1977-80; dir. direct mktg. Gen. Electric Credit Corp., Stamford, Conn., 1980-82; v.p. mktg. Yourdon, Inc., N.Y.C., 1982-84; pres. Morris Direct Mktg., Inc., Tuckahoe, N.Y., 1984—; cons. Am. Mgmt. Assn., 1984—, other direct mktg. orgns. Mem. Direct Mktg. Assn. Avocations: tennis, golf, Metropolitan Opera Guild. Office: Morris Direct Mktg Inc 14 Westview Ave Tuckahoe NY 10707

MORRIS, LOIS LAWSON, educator; b. Antoine, Ark., Nov. 27, 1914; d. Oscar Moran and Dona Alice (Ward) Lawson; m. William D. Morris, July 2, 1932 (dec.); 1 child, Lavonne Morris Howell. B.A., Henderson U., 1948; M.S., U. Ark., 1951, M.A., 1966; postgrad. U. Colo., 1954, Am. U., 1958, U. N.C., 1968. History tchr. Delight High Sch., Ark., 1942-47; counselor Huntsville Vocat. Sch., 1947-48; guidance dir. Russellville Pub. Sch. System, Ark., 1948-55; asst. prof. edn. U. Ark., Fayetteville, 1955-82, prof. emeritus, 1982—; ednl. cons. Ark. Pub. Schs., 1965-78. Mem. Commn. on Needs for Women, 1976-78; pres. Washington County Hist. Soc., 1983-84. Named Ark. Coll. Tchr. of Year, 1972; recipient Plaque for outstanding services to Washington County Hist. Soc., 1984. Mem. Ark. Council Social Studies (sec.-treas.), Washington County Hist. Soc. (exec. bd. 1977-80), NEA, Nat. Council Social Studies, Ark. Edn. Assn., Ark. Hist. Assn., AAUW, U. Ark. Alumni Assn., LWV, Phi Delta Kappa, Kappa Delta Pi, Phi Alpha Theta. Democrat. Episcopalian. Address: 1601 W 3d St Russellville AR 72801

MORRIS, MAX KING, foundation executive, former naval officer; b. Springfield, Mo., Oct. 23, 1924; s. Lee Howard and Aldyth (King) M.; m. Mary Jane Bull, June 19, 1952; children: Jane, William, Mary. B.S., U.S. Naval Acad., 1947; M.A. in Internat. Law, Tufts U., 1960, M.A. in Internat. Econs., 1961, Ph.D., 1967. Commd. ensign U.S. Navy, 1947, advanced through grades to rear adm., 1972; carrier pilot with combat duty in Korea and Vietnam 1947-71, comdr. jet squadron U.S.S. America, 1965-67, maj. command at sea, 1969-70, comdt. U.S. Naval Acad., 1971-73, Joint Chiefs of Staff rep. UN Law of Sea Conf., 1973-77, ret., 1977; pres. Thalassa Research Co., Jacksonville, Fla., 1977—; exec. dir. Arthur Vining Davis Founds., Fla., 1979—. Author: Politico-Military Coordination in the Armed Forces, 1968; Contbr. numerous articles to naval and legal jours. Served with arty. U.S. Army, 1942-44. Decorated D.S.M., Legion of Merit (2), Air medal (5). Mem. Internat. Inst. Strategic Studies (London), Council on Fgn. Relations, Middle East Inst., U.S. Naval Inst. Clubs: N.Y. Yacht, Fla. Yacht; Belfry (London); Ponte Vedra (Fla.). Home: 4123 Duval Dr Ponte Vedra Beach FL 32250

MORRIS, PETER WILLIAM GRINDAL, educator; b. Southport, Lancashire, Eng., June 2, 1947; s. Edmund Grindal and Edith Betty (Gelder) M.; m. Carolyn Elizabeth McLellan, Apr. 19, 1975; children: Simon A G, David E T, Charlotte E. BS, U. Manchester, Eng., 1968, MS, 1970, PhD, 1972. Engr. Sir Robert MacAlpine & Sons Ltd., London, 1968-69, 72-75; cons. Booz Allen & Hamilton, Paris, 1975-79; sr. cons. Arthur D. Little, Cambridge, Mass., 1979-84; mem. faculty U. Oxford, Eng., 1985—; exec. dir. major projects assn. Templeton Coll., Oxford, 1986—; bd. advisors Project Mgmt. Program Carolina U., 1985—. Author: The Anatomy of Major Projects, 1987; contbr. articles to profl. jours. Research Fellow Templeton Coll., Oxford, 1984-86. Mem. Chartered Inst. Bldg. (cert.), Royal Inst. Tech. (vis. fellow, Stockholm 1987—), Arthur D. Little Mgmt. Edn. Inst. (faculty 1979—). Clubs: United Oxford and Cambridge. Office: Major Projects Assn, Templeton Coll, Kennington OX1 5NY, England

MORRIS, ROBERT JOHN, insurance company executive; b. London, Jan. 22, 1934; arrived in Philippines, 1965; s. E. Hugh F. and Muriel Pamela (Cashmore) M.; divorced; children: Maria Pamela, William Henry A.T.; m. Helen Lim; children: Alexandria, Anna, Hugh Robert. Salesman Mfrs. Life Ins. Co., Malaya, 1957-59, dist. mgr., 1959-62; life underwriter Mfrs. Life Ins. Co., London, 1962-65; mgr. for the Philippines Mfrs. Life Ins. Co., Manila, 1965-83; exec. v.p. Pioneer Life Assurance Corp., Manila, 1983—; bd. dirs. Papa Securities Corp. Clubs: Manila Polo, Casino Español. Office: Pioneer Life Assurance Corp, 108 Paseo de Roxas, Makati, Metro-Manila The Philippines

MORRIS, SIDNEY ALLEN, mathematician, educator, researcher; b. Brisbane, Queensland, Australia, Nov. 24, 1947; s. Victor Joseph M.; m. Elizabeth Morris, Dec. 10, 1973. B.Sc. with honors, U. Queensland, Brisbane, 1969; Ph.D., Flinders U., Adelaide, South Australia, Australia, 1970. Lectr. U. Adelaide, 1970; postdoctoral fellow U. Fla., Gainesville, 1970-71; from lectr. to sr. lectr. U. New South Wales, Sydney, Australia, 1971-75; reader in math. LaTrobe U., Melbourne, Victoria, Australia, 1976-88; prof., dept. head math., stats., computing sci., U. New England, 1988—; higher sch. cert. examiner Victorian Inst. Secondary Edn., Melbourne, 1983-85; U.K. Sci. Research Council sr. vis. fellow, Bangor, Wales, 1974. Author: Pontryagin Duality, 1977; also numerous research papers on topological groups. Pres. B'nai B'rith Hillel Found. Victoria, Melbourne, 1983-84. Recipient Lester R. Ford award Math. Assn. Am. Mem. Australian Math. Soc. (council 1975-88, editor bull. 1979-84, editor-in-chief lecture series 1983—). Avocations: television; squash; swimming. Office: Univ New England, Dept Math Statistics, and Computer Sci, Armidale NSW 2351, Australia

MORRISH, JOHN HERBERT, coal mining company executive; b. Cherrywood, Ont., Aug. 6, 1930; s. A. Roy and M. Ella (Milroy) M.; m. Elizabeth Anne Lunn; children: Catherine, David. BS in Applied Sci., U. Toronto, 1952. Registered profl. engr., Ont. With various engring. positions CP Rail, Toronto, Montreal, Schreiber, Moose Jaw, Winnipeg, Can., 1952-66; mgr. mktg., sales CP Rail, Vancouver, B.C., 1966-69; system mgr. mktg. CP Rail, Montreal, Que., 1969-71, gen. mgr. market devel., 1971-74, v.p. mktg., sales, 1974-77; pres., chief exec. officer Fording Coal, Ltd., Calgary, Alta., 1977—, also bd. dirs.; bd. dirs. Great West Steel Industries, Coal Assn. Can. (chmn.). Appointed by Govt. of Can. Coal Industry Adv. Bd. Internat. Energy Agy., 1979—. Mem. Coal Assn. Can. (bd. dirs., exec. com., past chmn.), Internat. Coal Devel. Inst. (bd. dirs. 1985—), Can. Taiwan Bus. Assn. (chmn. 1986—), Can. Japan Businessmen's Coop. Com. (bd. dirs. 1985—). Office: Fording Coal Ltd, #200 9th Ave SE, Calgary, AB Canada

MORRISON, GLEN WARREN, accountant; b. Montgomery, Ala., Sept. 20, 1934; s. Marcus and Gladys (Deavers) M.; m. Joyce Lannom, July 12, 1958; 1 son, Gregg. B.S., U. Ala., 1961; J.D., Jones Law Sch., 1972. C.P.A., Ala., Ga., Miss., Mo. Staff acct. J. Bradley Haynes & Co., Rome, Ga., 1961-64; sr. acct. Dudley, Hopton-Jones, Sims & Freeman, Birmingham, Ala., 1964-68, ptnr., 1968—, mem. exec. com., 1982—. Mem. Am. Inst. C.P.A.s, Ala. Soc. C.P.A.s (audit com. 1975—), Assoc. Acctg. Firms Internat. (audit com. 1973—), Commerce Exec. Soc., Inst.Cert. Fin. Planners, Internat. Assn. Fin. Planners, Commerce Exec. Soc. Club: Tip-Off (Birmingham, Ala.). Lodges: Masons, Vestavia Hills Lions (past pres.). Home: 1804 Laurel Rd Birmingham AL 35216 Office: Dudley Hopton-Jones et al 3d Floor 2101 Magnolia Ave S Birmingham AL 35205

MORRISON, IAN ALASTAIR, human services executive b. Glasgow, Scotland, Apr. 22, 1924; came to U.S., 1932, naturalized, 1937; s. William John and Alexandrina (Smith) M.; B.A. (Grad. fellow 1948), Wagner Coll., S.I., N.Y., 1948, L.H.D., 1968; M.A., Columbia U., 1950, M.S., 1958, Ed.D., 1961; L.H.D., Bard Coll., 1968; m. Naida Brown, Apr. 19, 1946; children—Craig William, Sheila Elise. Assoc. prof. history, dean students Wagner Coll., 1949-56; exec. Inter Royal Corp., N.Y.C., 1956-57; exec. sec. Greer Sch., Millbrook, N.Y., 1958-61, exec. dir., 1961-72; pres. Greer-Woodycrest Children's Service, N.Y.C., 1972—, Greer Crest retirement community, 1984—; dir. Greer Inst.; dir. Bank of Millbrook. Pres. Eastchester (N.Y.) Bd. Edn., 1962-66, Unionvale (N.Y.) Bd. Edn., 1969-87; mem. adv. council Dutchess County Coll.; mem. long-range com. Columbia U. Div. Geriatrics and Gerontology; vice chmn., bd. dirs. St. Francis Hosp., Poughkeepsie, N.Y., 1981—, vice chmn., 1987—; bd. dirs. Conservation and Human Resources, Millbrook, 1980-85. Served with AUS, World War II; ETO. Decorated Purple Heart (2). Mem. N.Y. State Assn. Child Care

Agencies (pres. 1969), N.Y. State Assn. Children's Inst. (chmn. edn. com. 1961-68, pres. 1968), Nat. Assn. Homes for Children (dir. 1975—, pres. 1977-79, chmn. pub. affairs com. 1975-87, dir. 1975-84, author code of ethics), Nat. Assn. Sr. Living Industry (founding mem.), Child Welfare League Am., Fgn. Policy Assn., St. Andrews Soc., Nat. Assn. Homes for Children, Am. Assn. Homes for Aged, Nat. Assn. Fundraisers, English Speaking Union, St. Andrews Soc. N.Y. Democrat. Clubs: Union League (N.Y.C.); Millbrook Golf and Tennis; Bradenton (Fla.) Yacht. Author: Higher Education in World War II, 1950; American Political Parties: Political Science Handbook, 1953; Foster Care in the United States, 1975; editor MAHC Pub. Affairs Bull., 1975-87; editor, Continuing Care Retirement Communities: Social, Political and Financial Issues; pub. Residential Group Care quar.; also articles and pub. affairs newsletter. Address: Box 2000 Millbrook NY 12545 also: 723 Hillcrest Dr Bradenton FL 33505

MORRISON, PAUL LESLIE, corporate director, retired educator; b. Hartsville, Ind., Nov. 25, 1899; s. James H. and Effie (Mahaffey) M.; B.A., Depauw U., 1921, LL.D., 1949; Ph.D., Northwestern U., 1927, M.B.A., 1922; C.P.A., Ill., 1923; m. Carolyn L. Rosemeier, Dec. 31, 1924; children—Paul Leslie, James Frederick. Partner, Kohler, Pettengill & Co., accountants, Chgo., 1925-27; partner Sheridan, Farwell & Morrison, Inc., investment counsellors, Chgo., 1933-40; mgr. investment dept., bus. office Northwestern U., 1941-42; mem. faculty Northwestern U., 1923-58, prof. finance, chmn. finance dept., dir. grad. div. Sch. Commerce, adminstrv. officer; dir., past chmn. exec. com. Calif. Cold Storage & Distbg. Co.; ret. dir. Harris Trust & Savs. Bank, Chgs.; former mem. Am. adv. bd. (dir., exec. com. Am. subsidiaries) Zurich Ins. Co. (Switzerland). Mem. diplomatic missions on German and Japanese peace treaties, 1951-52; spl. asst. to Pres. U.S., also mem. planning bd. Nat. Security Council, 1953-54; asst. dir. Bur. Budget, 1953-54. Life trustee DePauw U.; past pres., dir. Owen L. Conn Found. Served as pvt., inf., U.S. Army, 1918; commd. capt., finance dept., 1942, disch. lt. col., 1946; chief central fiscal office China Theater, 1944-45; recalled to active duty, 1950 as col., gen. staff, serving as asst. comptroller army internat. affairs, 1950-52. Decorated Legion of Merit; recipient commendation sec. army. Mem. Am. Econ. Assn., Phi Beta Kappa, Alpha Tau Omega, Beta Gamma Sigma. Methodist. Clubs: University, Investment Analysts (past pres.) (Chgo.); Lauderdale Yacht, Tower (Ft. Lauderdale, Fla.); Westmoreland Country (Wilmette). Author: (with E.L. Kohler) Principles of Accounting, 2d edit., 1931. Author profl. articles. Address: One Arbor Ln Apt #404 Evanston IL 60201

MORRISON, ROBERT H., writer, publisher; b. San Bernardino, Calif., Jan. 28, 1938; s. Charles Hugh and Sarah Inez (Morrison-Rutledge) M.; m. Patricia L. Seefried, Apr. 12, 1980; children: Robert Hugh, Jeri L., Donna D., Debra M., James C., Shawn C., Jordan C. AA, Pasadena City Coll., 1958. Various engring. and acctg. positions 1957-61; pres. Fin. Mgmt. Assocs., Inc., Phoenix, 1961-78, Outward Bound, Ltd., Phoenix, 1978—. Author: My Hobby As a Business, 1973, The Fraud Report, 1975, Why S.O.B.'s Succeed and Nice Guys Fail in Small Business, 1976, Contracting Out, The Pawns, The Moneylenders, The Rulemakers, Stalemate, How to Steal a Job, 1977-78, How to Survive and Prosper in the Next American Depression, War or Revolution, 1979, Promoter's Gold, 1979, Divorce Dirty Tricks, 1979, The Greedy Bastard's Business Manual, 1981, Gambler's Gold, 1982, The New Venture Planner, 1982, Tax Navigation, 1983, How to Win, Delay, Reduce or Eliminate Lawsuits for Money Without a Lawyer, 1983, How to Steal a Business, 1983, Getting Money For Your Business, 1983, How to Make Yourself, Your Product, or Your Company Famous, 1983, How to Sell Every Word You Write, 1983, How to Get Blood From a Turnip, 1983, Computer Entrepreneur, 1985, Automatic Income Making System (13 vols.), 1987. Mem. Nat. Assn. Accredited Tax Accts., Honolulu Exec. Assn. Republican. Club: Elks. Office: Morrison Peterson Pub Inc PO Box 25130 Honolulu HI 96734

MORRISON, ROBERT STIER, medical administrator, nephrologist; b. Kansas City, Mo., Aug. 3, 1922; s. Guy Thornton and Florida Elizabeth (Stier) M.; m. Marie Day Townsend, May 12, 1951; children—Robert T., Diane D., Nancy E., Ann R., Scott C. A.B., U. Mo., 1946; M.D., Harvard Med. Sch., 1950. Diplomate Am. Bd. Internal Medicine. Fellow in nephrology Peter Bent Brigham Hosp., Boston, 1953-55; chief nephrology Lemuel Shattuck Hosp., Boston, 1955-77, chief profl. services, 1972-77; chief medicine Kaiser Hosp., Honolulu, 1978-81; chief nephrology St. Louis U. Hosp., 1981-84; chief medicine VA Med. Ctr., Leavenworth, Kans., 1984-87; assoc. prof. medicine Tufts Med. Sch., Boston, 1955-77; prof. medicine U. Hawaii, Honolulu, 1978-81; St. Louis Sch. Medicine, 1981-84. Contbr. chpts. to books, articles to profl. jours. Chmn. sci. adv. com. Mass. Kidney Found., 1974; sec. med. adv. com. Nat. Kidney Found., Boston, 1975; chmn. Bd. Health, Hingham, Mass., 1976; sci. adv. com. St. Louis Kidney Found., 1984. Recipient Teaching 25 Yrs. award Harvard U., 1977; Service to Commonwealth award Mass. Dept. Health, 1977; Dialysis Unit named in honor at Lemuel Shattuck Hosp., 1977; 11 Yrs. of Service award Hingham Bd. Health, 1977. Mem. Am. Soc. Nephrology, Am. Soc. Artificial Internal Organs, AMA, Mass. Med. Soc., Kansas City Geriatrics Soc. Democrat. Avocations: photography; camping; swimming. Home: 469 n u Rd Apt 1104 Honolulu HI 96815

MORRISON, ROGER BARRON, geologist; b. Madison, Wis., Mar. 26, 1914; s. Frank Barron and Elsie Rhea (Bullard) M.; B.A., Cornell U., 1933, M.S., 1934; postgrad. U. Calif.-Berkeley, 1934-35, Stanford U., 1935-38; Ph.D., U. Nev., 1964; m. Harriet Louise Williams, Apr. 7, 1941; children—John Christopher, Peter Hallock and Craig Brewster (twins). Geologist U.S. Geol. Survey, 1939-76; vis. adj. prof. dept. geoscis. U. Ariz., 1976-81, Mackay Sch. Mines, U. Nev., Reno, 1984—; cons. geologist Morrison and Assocs., 1978—; prin. investigator 2 Landsat-1 and 2 Skylab earth resources investigation projects NASA, 1972-75. Fellow Geol. Soc. Am.; mem. AAAS, Internat. Assn. Quaternary Research (past mem. Holocene and pedology commns.), Am. Soc. Photogrammetry, Am. Soc. Agronomy, Soil Sci. Soc. Am., Internat. Soil Sci. Soc., Am. Quaternary Assn., Sigma Xi. Club: Colorado Mountain. Author 2 books, co-author one book; editor 1 book; co-editor 2 books; also co-editor Catena, 1973—; contbr. more than 100 articles to profl. jours. Home and Office: 13150 W 9th Ave Golden CO 80401

MORRISON, SCOTT DAVID, telecommunications engineer; b. Duluth, Minn., May 8, 1952; s. Robert Henry and Shirley Elaine (Tester) M.; m. Jana Louise Bergeron, May 29, 1976; children—Robert Scott, Matthew John. Cert. in welding, Duluth Area Inst. Tech., 1971; student U. Wis.-Superior, 1976-77, BA Concordia Coll., 1988. Cert. in quality tech., Am. Soc. Quality Control and St. Paul Tech. Vocat. Inst., 1985; lic. vocat. instr., Minn., 1984. Assoc. in Mfg. Mgmt., North Hennepin Community Coll., 1985; cert. welder Litton Ship Systems, Pascagoula, Miss., 1971-72, Barko Hydraulics, Superior, Wis., 1972-76; welder and cert. level II non-destructive examination inspector Am. Hoist and Derrick Co., Mpls., 1978-80; quality supr. Colight Inc., Mpls., 1980, Tol-O-Matic, Inc., Mpls., 1980-82; quality assurance engr. ADC Telecommunications, Mpls., 1982-84, design assurance engr., 1985-86, product assurance engr., 1986-1987, sr. product assurance engr., quality improvement facilitator, 1987—; engr. in devel. test procedures for telecommunications equipment Brit. Telcom Test Labs., Ipswich, West Midlands, Eng., 1986, sr. product assurance engr., 1987—. Judge, U.S. Amateur Boxing Fedn., Mpls., 1978—. Mem. Am. Soc. Quality Control (cert. quality engr., chmn. host and attendance subcom. 1986-87), Am. Welding Soc., Soc. Mfg. Engrs., Internat. Platform Assn. Roman Catholic. Home: 4034 Regent Ave N Minneapolis MN 55422 Office: ADC Telecommunications 4900 W 78th St Minneapolis MN 55435

MORRISON, WALTON STEPHEN, lawyer; b. Big Spring, Tex., June 16, 1907; s. Matthew Harmon and Ethel (Jackson) M.; m. Mary Lyon Bell, Dec. 19, 1932. Student Tex. A&M U., 1926-28; J.D., U. Tex., 1932. Bar: Tex. 1932. Asso., Morrison & Morrison, Big Spring, 1932-36, ptnr., 1939, 46; atty. County of Howard, 1937-39, judge, 1941-42, 47-48; atty. City of Big Spring, 1949-58; sole practice, Big Spring, 1953—; lectr. Am. Inst. Banking. Served with USAF, 1942-46. Fellow Tex. Bar Found., Am. Coll. Probate Counsel; mem. Tex. City Attys. Assn. (pres. 1955-56), Am. Judicature Soc., Tex. Bar Assn., ABA. Baptist. Clubs: Rotary (pres. 1949), Masons, Shriner. Home: 1501 E 11th Pl Big Spring TX 79720 Office: 113 E 2d St PO Box 792 Big Spring TX 79720

MORRISS, PETER RICHARD, educator; b. Woking, Surrey, July 11, 1947; s. William Henry and Eva Ilona (Magyar) M. BA in Politics, Essex U., 1971; PhD, Manchester U., 1979. Temporary lectr. Manchester U., Eng., 1977-78, Essex U., Colchester, Eng., 1979-80; lectr. politics Liverpool (Eng.) U., 1980—. Author: Power: A Philosophical Analysis, 1987; contbr. articles to profl. jours. Mem. Polit. Studies Assn., Soc. for Applied Philosophy, Hastings Ctr. (N.Y.). Office: U Liverpool, Liverpool L69 3BX, England

MORRISSEY, MICHAEL JAMES TERENCE, writer; b. Auckland, New Zealand, Mar. 22, 1942; s. Michael Joseph and Evelyn May (King) M.; m. Dorothy Payne, 1967 (div. 1975); childrn: Duretta Ann, Hayley. Student (hon. fellow in writing), U. Iowa, 1985. Feature writer New Zealand Herald, Auckland, 1987; organizer Waiheke Summer Writing Sch., Auckland, 1983—. Author: Make Love in all the Rooms, 1978, Closer to the Bone, 1981, The Fat Lady and teh Astronomer, 1981, She's Not the Child of Sylvia Plath, 1981, Dreams, 1981, Taking in the View, 1986, Silver Brains, 1987, You Were Always Going To Be There, 1988; editor: The Globe Tapes, 1985, The New Fiction, 1985. Recipient Writer's Bursary, New Zealand Lit. Fund, 1977, Tom Gallon Trust award, 1979, Te Awamutu Festival Arts Poetry Competition award, 1979, Auckland Speech Tchrs. Assn. Short Story Competition award, 1980, Fulbright Cultural Travel award, 1981, Best First Book of Prose award, 1982, Auckland Star Short Story Competion award, 1985, Lilian Ida Smith poetry award, 1986, Te Awamutu Short Story Competition award, 1986. Mem. PEN Internat., Writers Guild, Journalists Union. Home: Box 39-288, Auckland West, Auckland New Zealand

MORROW, TIMOTHY T(ITUS), importer-retailer; b. Chgo., July 4, 1911; s. Albert and Donna Carnilia (Domaini) Gazzeri (changed name from Titus T. Gazzeri to Timothy T. Morrow, May 4, 1942); privately educated; 1 dau., Collette Gail (Mrs. William Van Dree). Prodn. mgr. Critchfield & Co., Chgo., 1925-29, Buchen Co., 1929-31; art dir. Rosenow Co., 1931-36; advt. and sales promotion mgr. Transparent Package Co., 1936-40; pres. Pioneer Mfg. Co., 1940-42; account exec. Bozell & Jacobs, Inc., 1942-46; v.p. and account exec. W. W. Garrison & Co., 1946-48; established Tim Morrow Advt., 1948, pres., 1948-56, merger 1956; v.p. Henri, Hurst & McDonald, 1956-58; v.p. MacFarland Aveyard & Co., 1958-60; v.p., supervising dir., mem. bd. The Biddle Co., 1960-63; owner La Casa Rosa restaurant and mail order bus., San Juan Bautista, Calif., 1963-64; owner The Gallery Ltd., Lahaina, Maui, Hawaii. Chmn. Lahaina Improvement Com.; mem. nat. host com. Western region Exhbn. of People's Republic of China, 1980. Mem. Maui C. of C. (dir.), West Maui Businessmen's Assn., Lahaina Art Soc. (co-founder, 1st pres.), Am. Soc. Appraisors (sr. mem.). Clubs: Lahaina Yacht, Lahaina Canoe (charter). Producer: Tin Pan Alley of the Air (won Am. Fed. Advt. award as best musical of 1945), 1945-46; Of Men in Music, 1947; television: Of Men and Music, 1949; Shirley and Bedelia, Stories in the Sand, Bible Stories, Sit or Miss, 1950-51. Home: PO Box 7 Lahaina HI 96761 Office: The Gallery Ltd Front St Lahaina HI 96761

MORROW, WINSTON VAUGHAN, lawyer, business executive; b. Grand Rapids, Mich., Mar. 22, 1924; s. Winston V. and Selma (von Egloffstein) M.; m. Margaret Ellen Staples, June 25, 1948; children: Thomas Christopher, Mark Staples. AB cum laude, Williams Coll., 1947; JD, Harvard U., 1950. Bar: R.I. 1950. Assoc. atty. Edwards & Angell, Providence, 1950-57; exec. v.p., asst. treas., gen. counsel, bd. dirs. Avis, Inc. and subs., 1957-61; v.p., gen. mgr. Rent A Car div. Avis, Inc., 1962-64, pres., bd. dirs., 1964-75; chmn., chief exec. officer, bd. dirs. Avis, Inc. and Avis Rent A Car System, Inc., 1965-77; chmn., pres., bd. dirs. Teleflorists Inc. and subs., 1978-80; pres. Ticor, Los Angeles, 1981—, chief exec. officer, 1984—, also bd. dirs.; pres., chief exec. officer New TC Holding Corp., 1983—, also bd. dirs.; chmn., chief exec. officer Ticor Title Ins. Co., 1982—, also bd. dirs.; chmn. Ticor Realty Tax Services, also bd. dirs.; bd. dirs. S&L Holdings, Inc., MPB Corp.; cons. Flowtrans Internat., 1977; mem. Pres.'s Industry and Govt. Spl. Travel Task Force, 1968, travel adv. bd. U.S. Travel Service, 1968-76, Los Angeles City-wide Airport Adv. Com., 1983-85; co-chmn. Los Angeles Transp. Coalition. Mem. juvenile task force Nat. Council Crime and Delinquency, 1985-86, Los Angeles Mayor's Bus. Council, 1983-86, Housing Roundtable, Washington, 1983-85; bd. dirs. Police Found., Washington, 1983—; trustee Com. for Econ. Devel., Washington, 1987—. Served as technician, M.C. AUS, 1943-46. Decorated Stella Della Solidarieta Italy, Gold Tourism medal Austria). Mem. Fed. Bar Assn., R.I. Bar Assn., Car and Truck Rental and Leasing Assn. (nat. pres. 1961-63), Los Angeles Area C. of C. (bd. dirs. 1983—), Calif. Bus. Roundtable, Phi Beta Kappa, Kappa Alpha. Clubs: Pacific Union (San Francisco), Bald Peak Colony (N.H.), Racquet and Tennis, Williams (N.Y.C.), Internat. (Washington); Calif., Los Angeles Tennis, Lincoln Los Angeles, Centre Santa Ana. Home: 2315 Bronson Hill Dr Los Angeles CA 90068 also: Cushing Corners Rd Freedom NH 03836 Office: 6300 Wilshire Blvd Suite 2100 Los Angeles CA 90048

MORSE, SIR CHRISTOPHER JEREMY, bank executive; b. Dec. 10, 1928; s. Francis John and Kinbarra (Armfield-Marrow) M.; m. Belinda Marianne Mills, 1955; 5 children. Grad., U. Oxford, Eng., 1953. Trainee Glyn, Mills and Co.; exec. dir. Bank of Eng., 1965-72; dep. chmn. Lloyds Bank Internat., 1975-77, chmn., 1977—; chmn. Lloyds Merchant Bank Holdings, 1985—; chmn. Deputies of Com. of Twenty, IMF, 1972-74, Com. of London Clearing Bankers, 1980-82; mem. Council of Lloyd's, 1987—; pres. Institut Internat. d'Etudes Bancaires, 1982-83, Internat. Monetary Conf., 1985-86; mem. NEDC, 1977-81; bd. dirs. Alexanders Discount Co. Ltd., 1975-84; gov. Henley Mgmt. Coll., 1966-85; alt. gov. for U.K. of IMF, 1966-72. Chmn. trustees Beit Meml. Fellowhips for Med. Research, 1976—; chmn. City Arts Trust, 1976-79; FIDE Internat. Judge for chess compositions, 1975—; dep. chmn. Bus. in the Community. Served with Brit. mil., 1948-49. Decorated KCMG, 1975; named Freeman, City of London, 1978. Mem. Brit. Overseas Bankers' Club (pres. 1983-84), London Forex Assn. (pres. 1978—), Brit. Chess Problem So. (pres. 1977-79). Club: Athenaeum. Office: Drayton Gardens, London SW10, England *

MORSE, F. D., JR., dentist; b. Glen Lyn, Va., Apr. 5, 1928; s. Frank D. and Ida Estell (Davis) M.; B.S., Concord Coll., 1951; D.D.S., Med. Coll. Va., 1955; m. Patsy Lee Apple, Feb. 4, 1967; children—Fortis Davis, Pamela Marie. Free lance photographer, 1950-56; practice dentistry, Pearisburg, Va., 1958—; mem. staff Giles Hosp., Pearisburg, 1958-86. Served from asst. dental surgeon to sr. asst. dental surgeon USPHS, 1955-57; assigned to USCG, 1957-58. Mem. Am., S.W. Va. dental assns., Assn. Mil. Surgeons, AAAS Nat. Assn. Advancement Sci., Fedn. Dentaire Internat., Internat. Platform Assn., W.Va. Collegiate Acad. Sci., Beta Phi. Kiwanian. Home: Bicuspid Acres Pearisburg VA 24134 Office: Giles Profl Bldg Pearisburg VA 24134

MORSE, JOHN JOSEPH, educator; b. Framingham, Mass., Sept. 30, 1938; s. John Thomas and Elizabeth Marie (Pakus) M.; BA magna cum laude, Coll. Holy Cross, 1960; MBA with distinction, Harvard U., 1966, D in Bus. Adminstrn., 1969. Mem. faculty Grad. Sch. Mgmt., UCLA, 1969-80, prof. orgnl. behavior and psychology, 1969-80, vice chmn., 1975-77; prof. mgmt. and orgnl. behavior Fla. Internat. U., Miami, 1984—, assoc. dean continuing exec. edn., 1986—; cons. Xerox Corp., U.S. Postal Service, Blue Cross-Blue Shield, So. Calif. Edison, U.S. Navy, U.S. Airfoce Lockheed Aircraft, Boston Cons. Group, Raytheon Co., Coulter Electronics, Cordis Corp., numerous hosps. and public health care orgns.; tchr. Instituto de Administracion Cientifica de las Empresas, Mexico City; researcher, adviser Los Angeles County Govt. Served with USN, 1960-64. Recipient Distinguished Tchr. award U. Calif. at Los Angeles, 1972, Ryder System prof., 1987; NDEA fellow, 1966-69. Mem. Am. Sociol. Assn., Assn. Humanistic Psychology, Acad. Mgmt., Decision Scis. Inst., Harvard Bus. Sch. Assn. Author: Organizations and Their Members, 1974; also numerous articles; reviewer and referee for numerous scholarly jours. and publs. Office: Fla Internat U Coll Bus Adminstrn Univ Park Campus Miami FL 33199

MORSE, LEON WILLIAM, distribution management executive; b. N.Y.C., Nov. 13, 1912; s. Benjamin and Leah (Shapiro) M.; m. Goldie Kohn, Mar. 30, 1941; children: Jeffrey W., Saul J. BS, NYU, 1935; grad. Acad. Advanced Traffic, 1937, 1954; DBA, Columbia Pacific U., 1979. Registered practitioner ICC, Fed. Maritime Commn. Individual bus., traffic mgmt. cons., Phila., 1950-58; gen. traffic mgr. W.H. Rorer, Inc., Ft. Washington, Pa., 1958-77; adj. prof. econs. of transp., logistics Pa. State U., Ogontz campus, 1960-83; owner Morse Assocs.; course leader seminars in traffic mgmt., phys. distbn. mgmt. and transp. contract negotiations, Am. Mgmt. Assn., others. Author: Practical Handbook of Industrial Traffic Management, 1980, 87, (manuals) Job of the Traffic Manager, Effective Traffic Management, Fundamentals of Traffic Management, Transportaion Contract Negotiations. Served to capt. Transp. Corps, AUS, World War II. Recipient Del. Valley Traffic Mgr. of Yr. award, 1963. Mem. Traffic and Transp. Club of Phila., Traffic Club of Phila., Traffic Club of Norristown, Am. Soc. Internat. Execs. (past pres., bd. dirs., sec., cert.), Assn. Transp. Practitioners, Am. Soc. Transp. and Logistics (emeritus), Council Logistics Mgmt., Transp. Research Forum, Drug and Toilet Preparations Traffic Conf. (pres. 1973-75, chmn. bd. 1975-77), Roosevelt Sr. Security Assn. (bd. dirs.). Lodge: Mason (Shriner).

MORSE, LOWELL WESLEY, banking executive; b. West Palm Beach, Fla., May 1, 1937; s. Alton and Blanche (Yelverton) M.; B.S., U. Santa Clara, 1968; grad. Def. Lang. Inst., Monterey, Calif., 1959; m. Vera Giacalone, June 22, 1958; children—Lowell Wesley, Stephen D., Michael S. Russian linguist U.S. Army Security Agy., 1957-60; asst. city mgr. City of Pacific Grove (Calif.), 1961-66; city mgr. Town of Los Altos Hills (Calif.), 1967-69; chmn. Morse & Assos., Inc., Carmel, Calif., 1972—; founder, dir. Plaza Bank of Commerce, San Jose, 1979—. Served with U.S. Army, 1957-60. Home: PO Box 222980 Carmel CA 93922 Office: 26619 Carmel Center Place Suite 201 Carmel CA 93923

MORSE, WILLIAM FRANCIS, clergyman; b. Western Springs, Ill., Aug. 25, 1899; s. Francis William and Phoebe A. (Kelsey) M.; student Eugene Bible U., 1920-23; Lingield Coll., 1940-41; m. Mary Quintila Shirley, Feb. 22, 1929; children—William George, Patricia Anne. Farmer Harrisburg, Oreg., 1923-26; retail salesman Chase Gardens, Eugene, 1927; mgr. Sunnyside Greenhouses, Portland, Oreg., 1928; owner, operator florist bus. Newberg, Oreg., 1928-40; mgr. relief work east end Yamhill County, Newberg, 1932-33; opened ch. Mt. Top, Newberg, 1932-40; ordained to ministry Christian Ch., 1935; pastor Ch. of Christ, Amity, Oreg., 1940-44, 48-50, Seaside (Oreg.) Christian Ch., 1944-48; organizer Wi-Ne-Ma Christian Camp, Inc., Cloverdale, Oreg., 1944, pres., 1944-69, gen. mgr., 1950-67, trustee, 1944-70; pastor Wi-Ne-Ma Christian Ch., 1951-70; research and geneal. work, 1970—; pres. Morse Soc., 1973—. Trustee Turner Meml. Home, 1946-80, trustee emeritus, 1980—; chmn. bd. trustees Oretown Cemetery Assn., 1970-78, trustee, 1979—. Mem. Newberg Park Commn., 1933-40, Sch. Bd., 1936-40; chmn. Area Agy. on Aging, Dist. 1, Tillamook-Clatsop County, Oreg., 1976-79, mem. exec. bd., 1976-82; bd. dirs. Am. Indian Evangelism Assn., 1977-86 . Served with U.S. Army, World War I. Mem. Nesctucca Ministers Fellowship (pres. 1966-67), Oretown Grange, Vets. World War I. Home and Office: 42880 Ocean View Dr Cloverdale OR 97112

MORTENSEN, ARVID LEGRANDE, insurance company executive, lawyer; b. Bremerton, Wash., July 11, 1941; s. George Andrew and Mary Louise (Myers) M.; m. Elaine Marie Mains, Aug. 2, 1968; children: Marie Louise, Anne Catherine, Joseph Duncan. BS in English and Psychology, Brigham Young U., 1965, MBA in Mktg. and Fin., 1967; JD cum laude, Ind. U., 1980. Bar: Ind. 1980, U.S. Supreme Ct. 1983, Mo. 1985, D.C. 1985; CLU. Agt. Conn. Mut. Life Ins. Co., Salt Lake City, 1967-68, agt. and br. mgr., Idaho Falls, Idaho, 1968-74; with Research and Rev. Service Am., Inc./Newkirk Assos., Inc., Indpls., 1974-83, sr. editor, 1975-79, mgr. advanced products and seminars, 1979-80, sr. mktg. exec., 1980-83; tax and fin. planner, Indpls., 1980-85, St. Louis and Chesterfield, Mo., 1985—. mem. sr. mgmt. com., v.p. Allied Fidelity Corp., 1983-85, Allied Fidelity Ins. Co., 1983-85, Tex. Fire and Casualty Ins. Co., 1983-85; v.p., bd. dirs. Gen. Am. Ins. Co., St. Louis, 1985-86; v.p. Gen. Am. Life Ins. Co., St. Louis, 1985—; sole practice, Indpls., 1980-85, St. Louis and Chesterfield, Mo., 1985—; active with Ch. Jesus Christ of Latter-day Saints, Idaho Falls, Idaho, Indpls., St. Louis, 1949—. Mem. Assn. Advanced Life Underwriting, ABA, Mo. Bar Assn., Bar Assn. Met. St. Louis, D.C. Bar Assn., Am. Soc. CLU's, Nat. Assn. Life Underwriters, Mo. Assn. Life Underwriters, St. Louis Assn. Life Underwriters, Internat. Assn. Fin. Planners. Author: Employee Stock Ownership Plans, 1975, Fundamentals of Corporate Qualified Retirement Plans, 1975, 78, 80; Buy-See Agreements, 1988; (with Norman H. Tarver) The IRA Manual, 1975-87 edits.; (with Norman H. Tarver) The Keogh Manual, 1975, 77, 78, 80 edits.; (with Norman H. Tarver) The Section 403 (b) Manual, 1975, 77, 78, 80, 84, 85, 87 edits.; (with Leo C. Hodges) The Life Insurance Trust Handbook, 1980; contbr. articles to profl. jours.; editor-in-chief various tax and fin. planning courses; bd. editors Ind. Law Rev., 1977-78. Home: 480 Hunters Hill Dr Chesterfield MO 63017 Office: 700 Market St PO Box 396 Saint Louis Mo 63166

MORTIER, GERARD, opera director; b. Ghent, Belgium, Nov. 25, 1943. Student law U. Ghent, 1961-66, journalism and communications, 1966-67. Adminstrv. asst. Flanders Festival, 1968-72; artistic planner Deutsche Oper am Rhein, Düsseldorf, 1972-73; asst. adminstr. Oper der Stadt Frankfurt am Main, 1973-77; dir. artistic prodn. Hamburg Staatsoper, 1977-79; tech. program cons. Théâtre National de l'Opéra de Paris, 1979-81; dir. gen. Opéra National, Brussels, 1981—. Office: Opéra National, Leopold 4, 1000 Brussels Belgium

MORTIER, JEAN PIERRE, orthopedic surgeon; b. Paris, May 28, 1936; s. Armand and Odette Mortier; m. Marie-Aline Siestronck, Sept. 9, 1967; children: Aurelie, Olivia, Jeremy. MD, U. Paris, 1960. With Externe Hopitaux Paris, 1960-65, intern, 1965-70; asst. chief and clinician, cons. Hopital Rothschild, Paris, 1970-74; surgeon Clinique Mont-Louis, Paris, 1974—. Contbr. articles to med. jours. Mem. Societe Francaise Chiurgie Orthopedique, Group Etude Main. Home: 71 Rue Claude Bernard, 75007 Paris France Office: Clinique Mont-Louis, 8 Rue de la Folie Regnault, 75011 Paris France

MORTON, CHARLES BRINKLEY, bishop, former state legislator; b. Meridian, Miss., Jan. 6, 1926; s. Albert Cole and Jean (Brinkley) M.; m. Virginia Roseborough, Aug. 26, 1948; children—Charles Brinkley, Mary Virginia. JD with distinction, U. Miss., 1949; MDiv optime merens, U. South, 1959, DD, 1982. Bar: Miss. 1949, Tenn.; ordained to ministry Protestant Episcopal Ch. as deacon and priest, 1959. Sole practice Senatobia, Miss., 1949-56; mem. Thomas & Morton, Senatobia, Miss., 1952-56, Miss. Ho. of Reps., 1948-52, Miss. Senate, 1952-56; priest-in-charge Ch. of Incarnation, West Point, Miss., 1959-62; rector Grace-St. Luke's Ch., Memphis, 1962-74; dean Cathedral of Advent, Birmingham, Ala., 1974-82; bishop Episcopal Diocese of San Diego, 1982—. Contbr. articles to law and hist. jours. Mem. Miss. Commn. Interstate Coop., 1952-56, Miss. State Hist. Commn., 1952-56; chmn. bd. Bishop's Sch., La Jolla, Calif., Episcopal Community Services, San Diego; trustee Berkeley Div. Sch., Yale U.; active numerous civic and cultural groups. Served with AUS, World War II, Korea; col., chaplain Res. ret. Decorated Silver Star, Bronze Star medal with cluster, Purple Heart, Combat Inf. Badge; recipient Freedoms Found. Honor medal, 1967, 68, 72. Mem. Mil. Order World Wars, Am. Legion (past post comdr.), Phi Delta Phi, Tau Kappa Alpha, Omicron Delta Kappa, Phi Delta Theta. Lodge: Rotary. Office: Episcopal Diocese of San Diego 2728 Sixth Ave San Diego CA 92103

MORTON, DONALD LEE, surgery educator; b. Richwood, W.Va., Sept. 12, 1934; s. Howard Jennings and Mary Gertrude (Boggs) M.; m. Wilma Miley (dec. Aug. 1982); children: Diana Lynn, Laura Ann, Donald Jr., Christen Helene. BA, U. Calif., Berkeley, 1955; MD, U. Calif., San Francisco, 1958. Diplomate Am. Bd. Surgery, Am. Bd. Thoracic Surgery; lic. surgeon Calif. State Bd. Med. Examiners. Intern U. Calif. Med. Ctr., San Francisco, 1958-59, resident in surgery, 1959-60, surg. fellow, 1962-66; clin. assoc. surgeon Nat. Cancer Inst., NIH, Bethesda, Md., 1960-62; sr. investigator Nat. Cancer Inst., NIH, Bethesda, 1966-69, sr. surgeon, head tumor immunology sect., 1969-71; chief surgery VA Hosp., Sepulveda, Calif., 1971-74, chief oncology sect., surg. services, 1974-81; prof. surgery, chief surg. oncology div. UCLA, 1971—, chief gen. surgery div., 1977-82; hon. med. staff surgery Cedars-Sinai Med. Ctr., Los Angeles, 1981—; mem. immunology adv. segment Nat. Cancer Inst., 1969-71, search com., 1974, bd. sci. counselors, 1974-78, surg. oncology research devel. subcom. 1979-84; mem. com. for objective 6 Nat. Cancer Plan, 1971, chmn. surg. onconolgy research program planning, 1974; sci. adv. council Cancer Research Inst. 1974, bd. sci. advisors, 1974-80; sci. adv. bd. Wash. U., St. Louis, 1974-80; exec. policy com. Jonsson Comprehensive Cancer Ctr., UCLA, 1981—, ad hoc peer rev. com. 1984—. Mem. editorial bd. Jour. Nat. Cancer Inst., Jour. Surg.

Oncology, Seminars in Oncology, Jour. Surg. Research, Surgery, Cancer Immunology and Immunotherapy; editorial adv. bd. Cancer Research, Clin. Orthopaedics Related Research. Served with USPHS, 1960-69. Recipient Superior Service award HEW, 1970, Esther Langer award U. Chgo., 1978, Golden Scalpel Teaching Excellence award, 1983-84, Cancer Immunology award Cancer Research Inst. Mem. AAAS, ACS, AMA, Am. Assn. Cancer Edn., Am. Assn. Cancer Research, Am. Assn. Thoracic Surgery, Am. Assn. Immunologists, Am. Radium Soc., Am. Soc. Exptl. Pathology, Am. Soc. Clin. Oncology (chmn. nominating com. 1976-77), Am. Soc. Microbiology, Am. Surg. Assn., Assn. Acad. Surgery, Bay Surg. Soc., Los Angeles County Med. Assn., Los Angeles Surg. Soc., Naffziger Surg. Soc., Pacific Coast Surg. Assn., Pan-Pacific Surg. Assn., Physician's Aid Assn., Reticuloendothelial Soc., Societe Internationale de Chirurgie, Soc. Head and Neck Surgeons, Soc. Surg. Oncology (ad hoc com. clin. research 1976-81, chmn. govt. relations com. 1978-81, long range planning com. 1981-84, exec. com. 1981-82, clin. research and govt. relations com. 1984-85), Soc. Univ. Surgeons, Transplantation Soc., Western Med. Research Assn., Western Thoracic Surg. Soc., Am. Coll. Chest Physicians. Office: UCLA Sch Medicine Div Surg Oncology Louis Factor Bldg Los Angeles CA 90024

MORTON, EDWARD JAMES, insurance company executive; b. Ft. Wayne, Ind., Nov. 8, 1926; s. Clifford Leroy and Clara Marie (Merklein) M.; m. Jean Ann McClernon, Apr. 30, 1949; children: Marcia Lynn, Anne; m. Matthild Schneider, Sept. 19, 1986; 1 child, Katharine. B.A., Yale U., 1949. With John Hancock Mut. Life Ins. Co., Boston, 1949—, v.p., then sr. v.p., 1967-74, exec. v.p., 1974-82, pres., chief operating officer, 1982-86, chmn., chief exec. officer, 1987—. Trustee Boston Plan for Excellence in the Pub. Schs., Mus. Fine Arts; bd. overseers Boston Symphony Orch., Children's Hosp., Mem. Corp., Ctr. for Blood Research, Northeastern U.; active Bd. Jobs for Mass.; dir. New Eng. Council. Served with USAAF, 1945. Fellow Soc. Actuaries; mem. Nat. Assn. Security Dealers (prin.), Actuaries Club Boston, Phi Beta Kappa. Clubs: Comml. (Boston), Algonquin (Boston). Office: John Hancock Mut Life Ins Co PO Box 111 Boston MA 02117

MORTON, JEROME HOLDREN, school psychologist; b. Duluth, Minn., July 30, 1942; s. Jerome Raefield and Svea (Holdren) M.; m. Anna Mary Moore, June 9, 1964; children: Scot, Jeanette. BA, Centre Coll., 1964; MS, Miami U., Oxford, Ohio, 1966; PhD, U. Tenn., 1973. Psychologist Pinellas County Sch. System, Clearwater, Fla., 1969-71; dir. psychol. and spl. edn. services Little Tenn. Valley Ednl. Coop., Lenoir City, Tenn., 1973-76, exec. dir., 1977—; ptnr., Psychol. and Ednl. Cons., Knoxville, Tenn., 1985—; due process hearing officer State Tenn. Dept. Edn., Nashville, 1974-86; hon. asst. prof. psychology dept. U. Tenn., Knoxville, 1978—; cons. S.W. Va. Consortium for a Coop. Services Orgn., Big Stone Gap, 1983-86. Co-chmn. East Tenn. Coalition for Children, 1983-84, chmn., 1984-85; dir. Alternative Ctr. for Learning, Knoxville, 1985—. Served with U.S. Army, 1966-69. Mem. Tenn. Assn. Psychology in Schs. (pres. 1976-77), Tenn. Psychol. Assn. (v.p. 1976-77), Nat. Assn. Sch. Psychology, Am. Psychol. Assn. Home: 7309 Bonny Kate Dr Knoxville TN 37920 Office: Rt 9 Box 316 Lenoir City TN 37771

MORTON, RANDALL EUGENE, nuclear engineer, aerospace products company executive, consultant; b. Portland, Oreg., May 4, 1950; s. Eugene Randall and Kathryn Hazel (Myers) M.; m. Lori Kay Turner, Mar. 23, 1979; children: Nicole Ashley, Colin Tyler. BS in Elec. Engring., U. Wash., Seattle, 1972; MS in Nuclear Engring., 1974; PhD, 1979. Registered nuclear engr., Wash. Exec. cons. Holloran & Assocs., Bellevue, Wash., 1977-81; corp. cons. AGA Cons., Bellevue, 1981-82; sr. mfg. systems analyst Eldec Corp., Lynnwood, Wash., 1982-83, sr. engr. research and devel. staff, 1983-85, engring. mgr. advanced product devel., 1985—; owner Innovative Concepts, Redmond, Wash., 1984—. Contbr. articles to profl. jours.; inventor. Mem. Soc. Automotive Engrs. (mem. aerospace avionics and integration standards com.), Soc. Photo-Optical Instrumentation Engrs., Am. Nuclear Soc. (vice. chmn. Puget Sound chpt. 1981-82, chmn. 1982-84), IEEE, Optical Soc. Am., Wash. State Soccer League (Over-30 All-Star Club). Home: 10320 181st St NE Redmond WA 98052 Office: Eldec Corp 1522-217th Pl SE Bothell WA 98041-3006

MOSBACHER, EMIL, JR., real estate investor, independent oil and gas producer; b. White Plains, N.Y., Apr. 1, 1922; s. Emil and Gertrude (Schwartz) M.; m. Patricia Ryan, Nov. 24, 1950; children: Emil III, Richard Bruce, John David. Grad. cum laude, Choate Sch., 1939; B.A., Dartmouth Coll., 1943, M.A. (hon.), 1963; LL.D. (hon.), L.I. U., 1969. dir. Chubb Corp., Fed. Ins. Co., Vigilant Ins. Co., Chem. Bank and Chem. N.Y. Corp., Putnam Trust Co., Greenwich, Conn., Avon Products Inc., Amax Gold Inc.; chief protocol Dept. of State, Washington, 1969-72; chmn. N.Y. State Racing and Wagering Bd., 1973-74. Co.-chmn. ARC, N.Y.C., 1962-63, bd. dirs., 1977-79; hon. trustee Lenox Hill Hosp.; hon. trustee Choate Sch., Wallingford, Conn., 1968-75, former chmn. Choate Fathers Assn.; former pres. Fathers Assn. Rye Country Day Sch.; past trustee Mystic Seaport; bd. dirs. Hoover Instn. War, Revolution and Peace, chmn., 1979, 82-85; mem. N.Y. Med. Coll. adv. council; mem. adv. bd. Dartmouth Inst.; mem. adv. bd. Dartmouth Inst., 1975-81, former mem. adv. bd. Dartmouth Alumni Council, chmn. Dartmouth Third Century Dr.; gen. chmn. United Hosp. Fund of N.Y., 1977, 78; chmn. Operation Sail, 1964, 76, 86; bd. govs. Ronald Reagan Presdl. Found.; elected bd. adv. Naval War Coll., 1987. Served to lt. USNR, 1942-45. Mem. Ind. Petroleum Assn. Am., Yacht Racing Assn. L.I. Sound, U.S. Yacht Racing Union, U.S. Internat. Sailing Assn., N.Am. Yacht Racing Union, Choate Assos., Pilgrims of U.S., U.S. Srs. Golf Assn., Gamma Delta Chi. Republican. Clubs: Blindbrook (Rye Brook, N.Y.); The Brook (N.Y.C.);Mashomack Fish and Game Preserve; Round Hill, Indian Harbor Yacht (Greenwich, Conn.); Bohemian (San Francisco); Indian Creek Country (Miami, Fla.); Chevy Chase, Metropolitan (Washington), Royal Corinthian (Cowes, Eng.), N.Y. Yacht (past commodore, trustee); Bal Harbour Yacht (Fla.); Storm Trysail. Home: Greenwich CT 08630 Office: Meridian Bldg 170 Mason St Greenwich CT 06830

MOSBAKK, KURT MALVIN, government official; b. Orkland, Norway, Nov. 21, 1934; s. Henrik and Jenny (Traasdahl) M.; m. Else Kulsrud (div. 1971); children: Ketil, Eirik, Kjersti; m. Grete Mosbakk. Degree in econs. and bus. adminstrn., Norway U., Bergen, 1958. Jr. exec. officer Accts.' Dept., NSB, Oslo, Norway, 1959-60; exec. officer Municipality of Oslo, 1960-61, Telecommunication Adminstrn., Oslo, 1961-68; personal asst. to minister of def. Office Ministry of Def., Oslo, 1964-65; head div. Norwegian Fedn. Trade Unions, 1969-74; dep. gov. Finnmark County, Vadsoe, Norway, 1974-75, exec., 1976-86; minister trade and shipping Govt. of Norway, Oslo, 1986-88. Mem. cen. com. Norwegian Labour Party, Oslo, 1969-73; vice mayor Loerensuog (Norway) Community, 1981-75; dep. mem. Norwegian Parliament, Oslo, 1983-77. UNESCO scholar, 1961, Norwegian Council of Disarmament scholar, 1965-66.

MOSCA, PIERRE ROGER, physician, angiologist; b. Metz, Moselle, France, Jan. 17, 1926; s. Charles Felix and Madeline (Dangreau) M.; married July 19, 1962 (div. 1981); 1 child; m. Anne Jullien, Aug. 27, 1983. MD, U. Lille, 1954; cert. vascular pathology, U. Paris, 1970. Cert. tchr. of vascular diseases. Externe Hosp. St. Sauveur, Lille, 1948-50, Hosp. Charité, Lille, 1950-53; intern Lens Hosp., France, 1953-54; gen. practice medicine Lille, 1954-70, practice medicine specializing in vascular diseases, 1970—; hospitable vacation Cité Hosp., Lille, 1971—, Hosp. Victor Provo, Roubaix, France, 1972—. Author: Lympphatic Microcirculation, 1970, 2d edit. 1972, Syndrome of Lash's Stroke, 1975, Arteries as Pearls's Necklace, 1976, Doppler and Veinous Thrombosis, 1979, Recidivans Varix and Doppler, 1982. Sporting diploma Acad. Lille, 1943-44. Mem. Assn. des Angiologues du Nord de la France (pres.), Soc. Française de Phlébologie, Coll. Français de Pathologie Vasculaire, Soc. Française d'Angéilogie. Roman Catholic. Office: Blvd Carnot 51, 59800 Lille France

MOSCHOS, DEMITRIOS MINA, lawyer; b. Worcester, Mass., Jan. 8, 1941; s. Constantine Mina and Vasiliky (Strates) M.; m. Celeste Thomaris, Sept. 28, 1975; children—Kristin M., Thomas W. B.A. magna cum laude, U. Mass., 1962; J.D. magna cum laude, Boston U., 1965; grad. basic course U.S. Army JAG Sch., Charlottesville, Va., 1966. Bar: Mass., 1965, U.S. dist. ct. Mass. 1975, U.S. Ct. Mil. Apls. 1966. Exec. asst. to city mgr., also spl. legal csl. City of Worcester (Mass.), 1968-75, asst. city mgr. and spl. legal csl., 1975-80; assoc. Mirick, O'Connell, DeMallie & Lougee, Worcester, 1980-81, ptnr., 1982—; lectr. labor relations Worcester State Coll., 1975—; lectr. labor relations Clark U., 1978—; bd. dirs. Consumers Savs. Bank, Bank of New Eng., Worcester. Chmn. Worcester Housing Com., 1968-78, Worcester Energy Com., 1978-80; mem. Mass. Joint Labor Mgmt. Com., 1978-80; trustee United Way Hellenic Coll. and Mechanics Hall, Worcester, bd. dirs. Cath. Charities of Worcester. Served to capt. JAGC, U.S. Army, 1966-68. Decorated Army Commendation medal; recipient Alumni Acad. Achievement award Boston U. Law Sch., 1965; named Outstanding Young Man of Worcester County, Worcester County Jaycees, 1969; named in resolution of commendation Worcester City Council, 1980. Mem. ABA, Mass. Bar Assn. (Community Service award 1987), Worcester Bar Assn., Nat. Sch. Bds. Assn. Council Sch. Attys. Greek Orthodox. Club: Tatnuck Country. Drafter adminstrv. codes; contbr. articles to profl. jours. Office: 1700 Mechanics Bank Tower Worcester MA 01608

MOSELEY, JAMES FRANCIS, lawyer; b. Charleston, S.C., Dec. 6, 1936; s. John Olin and Kathryn (Moran) M.; m. Anne McGehee, June 10, 1961; children: James Francis Jr., John McGehee. A.B., The Citadel, 1958; J.D., U. Fla., 1961. Bar: Fla. 1961, U.S. Supreme Ct. 1970. Pres. Taylor, Moseley & Joyner, Jacksonville, Fla., 1963—; chmn. jud. nominating com. 4th Jud. Cir., 1978-80. Contbr. articles on admiralty, transp. and ins. law to legal jours. Pres. Civic Round Table, Jacksonville, 1974, United Way, 1979, Greater Jacksonville Community Found.; chmn. bd. trustees Jacksonville Pub. Library;bd. trustees Library Found., sec., 1987—; chmn. Southeastern Admiralty Law Inst., 1980; dir. Nat. Young Life Found., 1987—. Fellow Am. Coll. Trial Lawyers, Am. Bar Found.; mem. Jacksonville Bar Assn. (pres. 1975), Fla. Council Bar Pres. (chmn. 1979), Maritime Law Assn. (exec. com. 1978-81, chmn. navigation com. 1981-88del. Comite Maritime Internat. on Collision 1984—), Fed. Ins. Corp. Counsel (chmn. maritime law sect.), Internat. Assn. Def. Counsel. Clubs: Deerwood, River, Downtown Athletic (N.Y.C.), India House (N.Y.C.), St. John's Diner (pres.). Home: 7780 Hollyridge Rd Jacksonville FL 32217 Office: Taylor Moseley & Joyner 1887 Bldg 501 W Bay St Jacksonville FL 32202

MOSER, DEAN JOSEPH, accountant; b. San Francisco, Apr. 5, 1942; s. Joseph Edward and Velma Ida (Cruz) M.; B.S., U. San Francisco, 1964, postgrad. Law Sch., 1964-66; MA in taxation, Golden Gate U., 1988; m. Michele Patrice Cicerone, June 16, 1963; children—Jay, Lynele, Todd. CPA, Calif.; cert. fin. planner; lic. real estate broker, Calif. Owner, acct. DJM Bookkeeping Service, 1962-65; asst. controller Dymo Industries, Internat., Berkeley, Calif., 1965-67; mgr. taxes Arthur Andersen & Co., San Francisco, 1967-76; owner, mgr. Contadora Ltd., Novato, Calif., 1981—, Esprit Realty Co., Novato, 1981—; Dean J. Moser Accountancy Corp., Novato, 1981—, Stellar Properties; gen. ptnr. Galli Sq.; founding dir., treas., chief fin. officer Novato Nat. Bank, NorthBay Bancorp. Asst. scout master Boy Scouts Am.; past bd. dirs. Novato Human Needs Center. C.P.A., Calif. Mem. Calif. Soc. CPA's. Republican. Roman Catholic. Club: Rotary (Paul Harris fellow, pres. Ignacio and pres. Marin pres.'s council). Office: 94 Galli Dr Novato CA 94949

MOSER, LEO JOHN, foreign service officer; b. Los Angeles, Jan. 19, 1929; s. Carl and Rosa Elizabeth (Wininger) M.; m. Helen Ann Kropff, Aug. 17, 1952; children: Mark William, Ann Elizabeth, Carol Marie, Robert Dodd. A.B., U. So. Calif., 1951, M.A., 1952, Ph.D., 1957; M. in Pub. Adminstrn., Harvard U., 1960; diploma in Russian lang. and area specialization, Fgn. Service Inst., 1958-60, diploma in Chinese lang. and area specialization, 1965-67; student, Nat. Def. Coll. Can., 1970-71. With Air Express Internat., Los Angeles, 1949-50; instr. Los Angeles City Sch. System, 1952-53; instr. polit. sci. Compton Coll., 1953-54; joined U.S. Fgn. Service, 1954; vice consul Hong Kong, 1954-56; mgmt. analyst Dept. State, 1956-58; 2d sec. cultural affairs sect. Am. embassy, Moscow, USSR, 1960-62; consul Frankfurt-am-Main, Fed. Republic Germany, 1962-63; dep. chief polit. sec. Caracas, Venezuela, 1963-65; 1st sec. Am. embassy, Taipei, China, 1967-69; counselor polit. affairs Am. embassy, 1969-70; Am. embassy, Ottawa, Can.; detailed Nat. Def. Coll., Kingston, Ont., Can., 1970-71; country dir. for Republic of China Dept. State, Washington, 1971-73; dir. for Australia, New Zealand and Pacific Island affairs Dept. State, 1973-74, dir. Australia, New Zealand, Papua New Guinea and Pacific affairs, 1974-75; diplomat-in-residence, also vis. prof. Calif. State U. at Sacramento, 1975-76; polit. adviser Pacific Command Bur. Polit. Mil. Affairs, Dept. State, Honolulu, 1976-79; chargé d'affairs, chief of mission U.S. Embassy, Vientiane, Laos, 1979-81; minister-counselor 1981—; dir. Ctr. for Study of Fgn. Affairs Dept. State, 1982-85, acting asst. sec. state, sr. dep. asst. sec. Bur. Human Rights and Humanitarian Affairs, 1985-86; diplomat in residence Mansfield Ctr., 1986—; Mansfield prof. modern Asian affairs U. Mont., 1987—; mem. U.S. del. to ANZUS Counsel, Wellington, N.Z., 1974, 77, Washington, 1975, 78, Canberra, 1976, 79, Inauguration of 2d Republic, Monrovia, Liberia, 1986; mem. U.S. presdl. del. to independence of Tuvalu with rank spl. ambassador, 1978, mem. U.S. del. to Budapest Cultural Forum, 1985. Author: The Technology Trap: Survival in a Man-made Environment, 1979, The Chinese Mosaic: The People and the Provinces of China, 1983, Toward a Better Understanding: U.S.-Japan Relations, 1986. Bd. dirs. Taipei Am. Sch., 1969-70; sec. Harvard Club China, 1969-70; Teaching fellow polit. sci. U. So. Calif., 1951-54. Recipient Meritorious Service award Dept. State, 1977, Open Forum award Sec. State, 1985. Mem. Am. Fgn. Service Assn., Internat. Inst. for Strategic Studies, World Future Soc., Am. Assn. for Artificial Intelligence, Assn. for Asian Studies, Am. Wildlife Fedn. Unitarian. Office: Dept of State Washington DC 20520 also: U Mont Mansfield Ctr Missoula MT 59812

MOSER, MICHAEL JOSEPH, lawyer; b. N.Y.C., Aug. 31, 1950; s. Joseph Georg and Patricia Ann (Robertson) M.; m. Yvonne Yi-Feng Wei, Aug. 17, 1978; children: Yeone, Anna Sieglinde, Christa. BS, Georgetown U., 1972; MA, Columbia U., 1974, Phd, 1981; JD, Harvard U., 1980. Bar N.Y., 1981. Vis. scholar Academia Sinica, Taiwan, Republic of China, 1974-76; research assoc. Kyoto comperative law ctr. Doshing U., Japan, 1978-79; assoc. Coudert Bros., Hong Kong, 1980-82, Peking, People's Republic of China, 1982-83; assoc. Baker and MacKenzie, 1983-87; ptnr. Baker and MacKenzie, Hong Kong, 1987—. Author: Law and Social Change in a Chinese Community, 1982, Business Strategies for the People's Republic of China, 1986, (with others) China Tax Guide, 1987; editor: (book) Foreign Trade Investment and the Law in the People's Republic of China, 1983. V.p. Am. C. fo C., Peking, 1983. Mem. ABA, N.Y. State Bar Assn. Roman Catholic. Office: Baker and MacKenzie, 14/F Hutchison House, Harcourt Rd, Hong Kong Hong Kong

MOSER, ROBERT HARLAN, physician, educator; b. Trenton, N.J., June 16, 1923; s. Simon and Helena (Silvers) M.; m. Stella Margot Neeson, June 17, 1948; children: Steven Michael, Jonathan Evan. BS, Loyola U., Balt., 1944; MD, Georgetown U., 1948. Diplomate Am. Bd. Internal Medicine. Commd. 1st lt. U.S. Army, 1948, advanced through grades to col., 1966, intern D.C. Gen. Hosp., 1948-49, fellow pulmonary disease D.C. Gen. Hosp., 1949-50; bn. surgeon U.S. Army, Korea, 1950-51; asst. resident Georgetown U. Hosp. U.S. Army, 1951-52, chief resident Georgetown U. Hosp., 1952-53; chief med. service U.S. Army Hosp. U.S. Army, Salzburg, Austria, 1953-55, Wurzburg, Fed. Republic Germany, 1955-56; resident in cardiology Brooke Gen. Hosp. U.S. Army, 1956-57, asst. chief dept. medicine Brooke Gen. Hosp., 1957-59, chief Brooke Gen. Hosp., 1967-68, fellow hematology U. Utah Coll. Medicine, 1959-60, asst. chief U.S. Army Tripler Gen. Hosp., 1960-64, chief William Beaumont Gen. Hosp., 1965-67, chief Walter Reed Gen. Hosp., 1968-69, ret., 1969; chief of staff Maui (Hawaii) Meml. Hosp., 1969-73, chief dept. medicine, 1975-77; exec. v.p. Am. Coll. Physicians, Phila., 1977-86; v.p. med. affairs The NutraSweet Co., Deerfield, Ill., 1986—; assoc. prof. medicine Baylor U., 1958-59; clin. prof. medicine Hawaii U., 1969-77, Washington U., 1970-77, Abraham Lincoln Sch. Medicine, 1974-75; adj. prof. medicine U. Pa., 1977-86, Northwestern U., 1987—; adj. prof. Uniformed Services U. Health Scis., 1979—; flight controller Project Mercury, 1959-62; cons. mem. med. evaluation team Project Gemini, 1962-66; cons. Project Apollo, 1967-73, Tripler Gen. Hosp., 1970-77, Walter Reed Army Med. Ctr., 1974-86; mem. cardiovascular and renal adv. com. FDA, 1978-82; bd. dirs. Pub. Service Satellite Commn., 1980-86; chmn. life scis. adv. com. NASA, 1984-87, mem. adv. council, 1983-88, chmn. gen. med. panel Hosp. Satellite Network, 1984-86; mem. adv. com. Space Sta., 1988—; mem. Dept. Def. Com. on Grad. Med. Edn., 1986-87, mem. Life Scis. Strategic Planning Study Group, 1986-88. Author: Diseases of Medical Progress, 1955, rev. edit., 1969, House Officer Training, 1970; co-author: Adventures in Medical Writing, 1970; editor, chief div. sci. publs. Jour. AMA, Chgo., 1973-75; contbg. editor Med. Opinion and Rev., 1966-75; chmn. editorial bd. Diagnosis mag., 1986—; mem. editorial bd. Hawaii Med. Jour., Family Physicians, Archives of Internal Medicine, 1967-73, Western Jour. Medicine, 1975-87, Chest, 1975-80, Med. Times, 1977-84, Quality Rev Bull., 1979—; contbr. over 150 articles to med. sci. jours and med. books. Master Am. Coll. Physicians (exec. v.p. 1977-86). Fellow Am. Coll. Cardiology, Royal Coll. Physicians and Surgeons Can. (hon.), Am. Clin. and Climatol. Assn.; mem. Am. Med. Writers Assn., Am. Therapeutic Soc., Am. Osler Soc., Inst. Med., AMA (adv. panel registry of adverse drug reactions 1960-67, council on drugs 1967-73), Coll. Physicians Phila., Soc. Med. Cons. to Armed Forces, Alpha Sigma Nu, Alpha Omega Alpha. Democrat. Jewish. Home: 24605 Kelsey Rd Barrington IL 60010 Office: 1751 Lake Cook Rd Deerfield IL 60015

MOSES, NANCY LEE HEISE, dance educator; b. Burlington, Iowa, July 5, 1947; d. Harris Rolyn and Margaret Eileen (Mitchell) H.; m. Bradley Lynn Moses, Dec. 21, 1969; 1 child, Scott Frederick. B.S., Iowa State U., 1969, M.S., 1972; Ed.D., Boston U., 1980. Dance educator Ames Soc. for Arts, Iowa, 1969-73, Iowa State U., Ames, 1970-73, dir., performer, choreographer Iowa Dance Ensemble, performer Iowa State Dance Co.; movement specialist Scituate Montessori, Mass., 1981-82; dance educator Boston State Coll., 1973-82, dir. Boston State Coll. Dance Co., Boston U., 1979-84; dance educator, asst. prof. Depts. Speech Communication, Theatre Arts and Communication Disorders and Health, Physical Edn. and Recreation, Bridgewater State Coll., Mass., 1984—; dir., adv. Bridgewater Dance Club, 1985; cons. Ctr. for Health & Healing, Norwell, Mass., 1979—; dance specialist, performer of Sacred Dance United Ch. Christ, Norwell, 1973-85. Contbr. articles to profl. jours. Choreographer Cough Concerto, 1972, We Tendu Anything, 1976, Pulling, 1986, Theme & Variations, 1987, Backstage, 1988, A Time for Every Purpose, 1988. Mem. ch. com. Amnesty Internat., Norwell, 1980; mem. Bd. Christian Edn., Norwell, 1979-84; bd. dirs. Ctr. Health & Healing, Norwell, 1976-85, Iowa Arts Council; advisor Explorer Scouts Am., Norwell, 1979. Iowa Arts Council grantee, 1970. Mem. Dance and Child Internat. (treas. U.S. 1982-85), Mass. Assn. Health, Phys. Edn., Recreation and Dance (v.p. dance 1981-84), Ea. Dist. Assn., v.p., 1988, Nat. Dance Assn., New Eng. Theatre Conf., Internat. Dance Exercise Assn. (gold cert.), Eastern Dist. Assn. (v.p. dance 1988-89; council for conventions 1987-88), Am. Alliance Health, Phys. Edn., Recreation and Dance, Sigma Alpha Iota, Phi Kappa Phi, Sigma Kappa, Delta Kappa Gamma, Pi Lambda Theta. Club: P.E.O. (treas. 1983-85). Avocations: singing; leader prayer support group; needlework. Home: 32 Hawthorne Rd Hanover MA 02339 Office: Bridgewater State Coll Bridgewater MA 02324

MOSHER, SALLY EKENBERG, lawyer; b. N.Y.C., July 26, 1934; d. Leslie Joseph and Frances Josephine (McArdle) Ekenberg; m. James Kimberly Mosher, Aug. 13, 1960 (dec. Aug. 1982). MusB, Manhattanville Coll., 1956; postgrad., Hofstra U., 1958-60, U. So. Calif., 1971-73; JD, U. So. Calif., 1981. Bar: Calif., 1982. Musician, pianist, tchr. 1957-74; music critic Pasadena Star-News, 1967-72; mgr. Contrasts Concerts, Pasadena Art Mus., N.Y., Los Angeles, 1971-72; rep. Occidental Life Ins. Co., Pasadena, 1975-78; v.p. James K. Mosher Co., Pasadena, 1961-82, pres., 1982—; pres. Oakhill Enterprises, Pasadena, 1984—; assoc. White-Howell, Inc., Pasadena, 1984—. Contbr. articles to various publs. Bd. dirs. Jr. League Pasadena, 1966-67, Encounters Concerts, Pasadena, 1966-72, U. So. Calif. Friends of Music, Los Angeles, 1973-76, Pasadena Arts Council, 1986—, I Cantori, 1988—; bd. dirs., treas. Armory Ctr. for the Arts, Rep. Assocs.; mem. Citizen's Com. on Pub. Fin., Pasadena, 1985—, v.p. Pasadena Chamber Orchestra, 1986—; v.p., bd. dirs. Pasadena Chamber Orch., 1986—, pres., 1987-88; mem. Calif. 200 Council for Bicentennial of U.S. Constn., 1987—. Manhattanville Coll. hon. scholar, 1952-56. Fellow Fellows of Contemporary Art (Los Angeles); mem. ABA, Calif. Bar Assn., Los Angeles Bar Assn., Pasadena Bar Assn., Nat. Assn. Realtors, Am. Assn. Realtors, Calif. Assn. Realtors, Pasadena Bd. Realtors, Assocs. of Calif. Inst. Tech., Kappa Gamma Pi, Mu Phi Epsilon, Phi Alpha Delta. Republican. Club: Athenaeum. Home: 1260 Rancheros Rd Pasadena CA 91103 Office: 711 E Walnut St Suite 407 Pasadena CA 91101

MOSHOESHOE, HIS MAJESTY II (CONSTANTINE BERENG SEEISO), King of Lesotho (Basutoland); b. Mokhotlong, Lesotho, May 2, 1938; s. Seeiso Griffith and Mofumahali MaBereng; ed. Roma Coll., Oxford (Eng.) U., 1948-54, Benedictine Coll., Yorkshire, Eng., 1954-57, Corpus Christi Coll., 1957; m. Tabitha Constance Christina Masentle, 1962; children: Letsie David, Seeiso Semeone, Sebueng. Paramount chief of Basutoland, 1960-66; king upon restoration of Lesotho's independence, 1966—; exiled from Lesotho, Apr. 1970, returned from exile as head of state, Dec. 1970; chancellor Nat. U. Lesotho, 1971. Address: Royal Palace, PO Box 524, Maseru Lesotho *

MOSIER, FRANK EUGENE, oil company executive; b. Kersey, Pa., July 15, 1930; s. Clarence R. and Helen I. Mosier; m. Julia M. Fife, Sept. 2, 1961; children: Terry F., Patrick E., Kathleen R. BSCE, U. Pitts., 1953. With Standard Oil Co., Cleve., 1953—, mgr. planning and devel. mktg. and refining dept., 1968-71, v.p. supply and distbn., 1972-76, v.p. supply and transp., 1976-77, sr. v.p. mktg. and refining, 1977-78, sr. v.p. supply and transp., 1978-82, sr. v.p. downstream petroleum dept., 1982-85, exec. v.p., 1985-86, pres., chief. operating officer, 1986-88, vice-chmn., 1988—, also bd. dirs.; sr. v.p. Downstream Petroleum, 1982-84, exec. v.p., 1985-86, also bd. dirs.; bd. dirs. Society Corp., Cleve., Centerior Energy Corp., Cleve., BP Am., Inc., pres., 1987—;. Trustee U. Pitts., John Carroll U., Cleve., Fairview Gen. Hosp., Cleve. Served with U.S. Army, 1953-55. Mem. Am. Inst. Chem. Engrs., Am. Petroleum Inst., Nat. Petroleum Refiners Assn. Roman Catholic. Clubs: Cleve. Yachting, Mid-Day, Pepper Pike Country, Union, Westwood Country. Office: Standard Oil Co 200 Public Sq Cleveland OH 44114

MOSIER, OLIVE, arts administrator; b. Elizabeth, N.J., Mar. 24, 1952; d. Robert Joseph and Mary Malson (Rice) M. B.F.A., Howard U., 1974; M.A., Am. U., 1984. Sr. fin. editor Arthur Andersen & Co., Chgo., 1975-82; publs. assoc. Cultural Alliance, Washington, 1983-84; exec. dir. Nat. Artists Equity Assn., Washington, 1984—; exec. dir. U.S. Com. Internat. Assn. Art, Washington, 1984—; dir. Dance Constrn. Co., Washington, 1985. Contbr. articles to profl. jours. Charlotte W. Newcombe Found. grantee, 1983. Office: Nat Artists Equity Assn 1116 F St NW Suite 401 Washington DC 20004

MOSK, STANLEY, state justice; b. San Antonio, Sept. 4, 1912; s. Paul and Minna (Perl) M.; m. Edna Mitchell, Sept. 27, 1937 (dec.); 1 child, Richard Mitchell.; m. Susan Hines, Aug. 27, 1982. Student, U. Tex., 1931; Ph.B., U. Chgo., 1933; postgrad., U. Chgo. Law Sch., 1935, Hague Acad. Internat. Law, 1970; LL.D., U. Pacific, 1970, U. San Diego, 1971, U. Santa Clara, 1976, Calif. Western U., 1984, Southwestern U., 1987. Bar: Calif. 1935, U.S. Supreme Ct. 1956. Practiced in Los Angeles until 1939; exec. sec. to gov. Calif., 1939-42; judge Superior Ct. Los Angeles County, 1943-58; pro tem justice Dist. Ct. Appeal, Calif., 1954; atty. gen. Calif, also head state dept. justice, 1959-64; justice Supreme Ct. Calif., 1964—; mem. Jud. Council Calif., 1973-75, Internat. Commn. Jurists. Chmn. San Francisco Internat. Film Festival, 1967; mem. Dem. Nat. Com., Calif., 1960-64; bd. regents U. Calif., 1940; pres. Vista Del Mar Child Care Service, 1954-58; bd. dirs. San Francisco Law Sch., 1971-73, San Francisco Regional Cancer Found., 1980-83. Served with AUS, World War II. Recipient Disting. Alumnus award U. Chgo., 1958. Mem. Nat. Assn. Attys. Gen. (exec. bd. 1964), Western Assn. Attys. Gen. (pres. 1963), ABA, Calif., Los Angeles, Santa Monica, San Francisco bar assns., Am. Legion, Manuscript Soc., Calif. Hist. Soc., Am. Judicature Soc., Inst. Jud. Adminstrn., U. Chgo. Alumni Assn. No. Calif. (pres. 1957-58, 67), Order of Coif, Phi Alpha Delta. Mem. B'nai B'rith. Clubs: Hillcrest Country (Los Angeles); Commonwealth, Golden Gateway Tennis (San Francisco); Beverly Hills Tennis. Office: Calif Supreme Ct 455 Golden Gate Ave #4250 San Francisco CA 94102 also: Calif Supreme Ct Sacramento CA 95814

MOSKIN, JOHN ROBERT, editor, writer; b. N.Y.C., May 9, 1923; s. Morris and Irma (Rosenfeld) M.; m. Doris Marianne Bloch, Oct. 7, 1948 (div. 1978); children: Mark Douglas, David Scott, Nancy Irma; m. Lynn Carole Goldberg, Apr. 10, 1986. Grad., Horace Mann Sch., 1940; B.S., Harvard U., 1944; M.A., Columbia U., 1947. Reporter Boston Post, 1941-42, Newark News, 1947-48; asst. to gen. mgr. N.Y. Star, 1948-49; editor Westport (Conn.) Town Crier, 1949; med. editor Look mag., N.Y.C., 1950-

51; articles editor Look mag., 1951-53, sr. editor, 1956-66, fgn. editor, 1966-71; mng. editor Woman's Home Companion, 1953-56; sr. editor Collier's, 1956; editor at large Saturday Rev., 1972-75; sr. editor World Press Rev., 1976-87, contbg. editor, 1987—; editorial dir. Aspen Inst. Humanistic Studies, 1977-83; lectr. at numerous universities, 1951—; communications advisor Commonwealth Fund, 1983, editorial dir., 1984-87, sr. editorial advisor, 1987—. Author: (with others) The Decline of the American Male, 1958, Morality in America, 1966, Turncoat, 1968, The U.S. Marine Corps Story, 1977, 82, 87, Among Lions, 1982; Contbr. numerous articles to mags.; Editorial adv. com.: Dimensions mag, 1970-71, Present Tense, 1973—. Trustee Scarsdale Adult Sch., 1965-72, chmn., 1969-70; mem. Dana Reed Prize com. Harvard, 1947—; mem. com. Class of 1944, 1943—; mem. communications screening com. Council Internat. Exchange of Scholars, 1974-77; bd. dirs. SIECUS, 1972-80, Jerusalem Found., 1977—, Marine Corps Hist. Found., 1979-82, Faculty for Continuing Med. Edn., 1983-86. Served with AUS, 1943-46. Recipient Benjamin Franklin gold medal for pub. service Woman's Home Companion, 1955, Page One award Newspaper Guild N.Y., 1965, Sidney Hillman Found. award, 1965; National Headliners award, 1967; Overseas Press Club award, 1969; citation for excellence, 1971; Disting. Service award Marine Corps Combat Corrs. Assn., 1978; Nat. Jewish Book award, 1983. Mem. Am. Hist. Assn., Authors Guild, Fgn. Editors Group (chmn. 1970-71), Sigma Delta Chi (mem. nat. freedom of info. com. 1964, 71). Clubs: Nat. Press (Washington); Overseas Press (N.Y.C.) (gov. 1975-79), Century (N.Y.C.), Harvard (N.Y.C.), Lotos (N.Y.C.) (bd. dirs. 1988—), University (N.Y.C.). Home: 945 Fifth Ave New York NY 10021 also: Jerusalem Rd Tyringham MA 01264

MOSLER, HERMANN, law educator, former judge International Court of Justice; b. Hennef, Germany, Dec. 26, 1912; LL.D., Bonn U., 1937; Dr. Iur. h.c., U. Brussels, 1969, U. Saarbrucken, 1982; m. Anne Pipberger, Dec. 23, 1939; 5 children. Research fellow Kaiser Wilhelm Inst. for Fgn. Pub. Law and Pub. Internat. Law, 1937; barrister-at-law, Bonn, 1946; privat docent pub. internat. law, constl. law and adminstrv. law U. Bonn, 1946; prof. pub. law U. Frankfurt, 1949; vis. prof. internat. law Georgetown U., 1950; head legal dept. Fed. Ministry Fgn. Affairs, 1951-53; prof. U. Heidelberg, 1954; dir. Max Planck Inst. for Fgn. Pub. Law and Pub. Internat. Law, 1954-76; mem. Permanent Ct. of Arbitration, 1954-86; judge European Ct. Human Rights, Strassburg, 1959-81, v.p., 1974-77; ad hoc judge Internat. Ct. Justice, The Hague, 1968-69, judge, 1976-85. Mem. Heidelberg Acad. Scis. (pres. 1982-86), Austrian Acad. Scis. (corr.), Inst. Internat. Law, Curatorium of Hague Acad. Internat. Law, German Soc. Internat. Law (hon. pres. 1985). Office: Berlinerstr 48, 6900 Heidelberg 1 Federal Republic of Germany

MOSLER, KARL CLEMENS, statistics and economics educator; b. Bonn, Fed. Republic Germany, July 10, 1947; s. Hermann and Anne (Pipberger) M.; m. Susanne Duden, July 31, 1971; children: Katharina, Gioia. Diploma in math., U. Munich, 1972, PhD in Math., 1975. Habilitation U. Bundeswehr, 1981. Asst. U. Bundeswehr, Hamburg, Fed. Republic Germany, 1975-85, prof. statistics and quantitative econs., 1985—. Author: Optimum Transportation Networks, 1976, Decision Criteria Under Risk, 1982, Continuous Location of Transportation Networks, 1987; co-editor: Operations Research and Economic Theory, 1984. Recipient August Lösch Regional Sci. award Heidenheim/Brenz, 1976. Office: U Bundeswehr, Holstenhofweg 85, D-2000 Hamburg 70 Federal Republic of Germany

MOSLEY, SIMON JAMES, lawyer; b. London, Apr. 8, 1927; s. John Arthur and Caroline Edith Sutton (Timmis) Mosley/Dugdale; m. Maria Zeris, Dec. 17, 1957; children—George C., Claire A. B.A., Oxford U., 1951, M.A., 1952. Solicitor, 1957. Articles clk. Frere Cholmeley, London, 1953-57, ptnr., 1957-87, cons. 1987—; dept. chmn. Octavian Group Ltd., 1984—; chmn. Trinity Internat. Holdings PLC, 1985—; vice chmn. Inc. Council Law Reporting in England and Wales, 1979-84. Mem. U.K. Govt. Joint Select Com. for Improvement of Legislation in Eng. and Wales, 1973-75. Served to lt. Coldstream Guards, 1945-48. Bd. govs. Coll. Law, 1974—. Mem. Holborn Law Soc. (pres. 1969-70), Law Soc. (council 1970-81), Kensington and Chelsea Jr. C. of C. (pres. 1958). Club: Guards and Cavalry. Mem. Ch. of Eng.

MOSLEY, WILLIAM FIELDING, III, accountant; b. Munich, Mar. 2, 1948; came to U.S., 1950; s. William Fielding Jr. and Martha Frank (Bufkin) M.; m. Pamela Jane Fox, Aug. 1, 1970 (div. Nov. 1982); children: Ryan Scott, Todd William. BBA, North Tex. State U., 1970. CPA, Tex. Acct. Coopers & Lybrand, Dallas, 1970-73, A.H. Gardes & Co., Houston, 1973-76; v.p. Leavitt, Mosley & Co., Houston, 1976-79; pres. Mosley & Co., Houston, 1980—; instr. North Texas State U., Denton, 1971; bd. dirs. Inter-Continental Cons., Inc., Houston, SW Commerce, Inc., Houston, Scottson, Inc., Houston; dir. Fellowship Christian Fin. Advisors of Houston. Publicity chmn. Greater Houston Mayor's Prayer Breakfast, 1987, 88. Served with USAFR, 1967-73. Mem. Am. Inst. CPA's, Tex. Soc. CPA's, Houston Soc. CPA's, Christian Bus. Men's Com., Pi Kappa Phi. Baptist. Home: 394 Wilcrest Dr Houston TX 77042 Office: Mosley & Co Inc 3847 San Felipe Suite 4355 Houston TX 77057

MOSS, AMBLER HOLMES, JR., university dean, lawyer, former ambassador; b. Balt., Sept. 1, 1937; s. Ambler Holmes and Dorothea Dandridge (Williams) M.; m. Serena Welles, May 6, 1972; children: Ambler H., Benjamin Sumner, Serena Montserrat, Nicholas George Oliver. B.A., Yale U., 1960; J.D., George Washington U., 1970. Bar: D.C., Fla. Joined Fgn. Service Dept. State, 1964; vice consul Barcelona, 1964-66; adviser U.S. del. to OAS, 1966-69; Spanish desk officer 1968-70; assoc. firm Coudert Bros., Washington, 1971-73; resident atty. Coudert Bros., Brussels, Belgium, 1973-76; mem. U.S. Negotiating Team for Panama Canal treaties, 1977; dep. asst. Sec. of State, Washington, 1977-78; ambassador to Panama, 1978-82; of counsel Greenberg, Traurig, Askew, Hoffman, Lipoff, Quentel, Wolff P.A.; dean Grad. Sch. Internat. Studies, prof. U. Miami, Fla. Served with USN, 1960-64. Mem. ABA, Bar Assn. D.C., Am. Soc. Internat. Law, Am. Fgn. Service Assn., Council Fgn. Relations; mem. Greater Miami C. of C. (gov. 1983-86); Mem. Am. Legion. Clubs: Army and Navy, Navy League. Address: 5711 San Vicente St Coral Gables FL 33146

MOSS, CHARLES NORMAN, physician; b. Los Angeles, June 13, 1914; s. Charles Francis and Lena (Rye) M.; A.B., Stanford U., 1940; M.D., Harvard U., 1944; cert. U. Vienna, 1947; M.P.H., U. Calif.-Berkeley, 1955; Dr.P.H., UCLA, 1970; m. Margaret Louise Stakias; children—Charles Eric, Gail Linda, and Lori Anne. Surg. intern Peter Bent Brigham Hosp., Boston, 1944-45, asst. in surgery, 1947; commd. 1st lt. USAF, M.C., USAAF, 1945, advanced through grades to lt. col., USAF, 1956; Long course for flight surgeon USAF Sch. Aviation Medicine, Randolph AFB, Tex., 1948-49, preventive medicine div. Office USAF Surgeon Gen., Washington, 1955-59; air observer, med., 1954, became sr. flight surgeon 1956; later med. dir., Los Angeles div. North Am. Rockwell Corp., Los Angeles; chief med. adv. unit Los Angeles County, now ret. Decorated Army Commendation medal (U.S.); Chinese Breast Order of Yun Hui. Recipient Physicians Recognition award AMA, 1969, 72, 76, 79, 82. Diplomate in aerospace medicine and occupational medicine Am. Bd. Preventive Medicine. Fellow Am. Pub. Health Assn., AAAS, Am. Coll. Preventive Medicine, Royal Soc. Health, Am. Acad. Occupational Medicine, Western Occupational Med. Assn., Am. Assn. Occupational Medicine; mem. AMA, Mil. Surgeons U.S., Soc. Air Force Flight Surgeons, Am. Conf. Govt. Hygienests, Calif. Acad. Preventive Medicine, (dir.), Aerospace Med. Assn., Calif., Los Angeles County med. assns., Assn. Oldetime Barbell and Strongmen. Research and publs. in field. Home: 7714 Cowan Ave Los Angeles CA 90045

MOSS, MORTON HERBERT (MOSS HERBERT), newspaper columnist, editor, poet; b. N.Y.C., Mar. 21, 1914; s. Carl and Rose (Schnur) M.; student Columbia U., 1930-32; m. Ruth Miller, Feb. 19, 1939; 1 son, Eric. Sports writer N.Y. Post, N.Y.C., 1932-37, Internat. News Service, N.Y.C., 1937-40; sports editor, columnist Los Angeles Examiner (now Herald Examiner), 1941-61, asst. sports editor, columnist, 1962-68, TV editor, columnist, 1969-77, news wire editor, 1978-79. Mem. Nat. Acad. TV Arts and Scis., Los Angeles World Affairs Council, Greater Los Angeles Press Club, Poetry Soc. Am., Acad. of Am. Poets. Represented in Best Sports Stories, E.P. Dutton & Co., Inc., 1952, 1960, 61, 62, 64, 65, 66, 67. Author: In Sight of the Invisible, 1987; contbr. articles to various mags.; contbr. poetry to mags. Lyric, Ariz. Quar., Coastlines, Am. Poet, Global Architecture, also anthologies The Golden Year, 1960, The Various Light, 1964, Ipso Facto, 1975. Creator Simplified Five, the boxing scoring system adopted by Calif. State Athletic Commn., 1960-70. Home: 1909 N Normandie Ave Los Angeles CA 90027

MOSS, RICHARD, business machines distributor; b. Tokyo, Sept. 9, 1922; s. Robert Faulkner and Sybil Williams (Howard) M.; m. Maria Stella Ferreira, Apr. 15, 1950; children: Robert Faulkner III, William Chandler, Richard Howard. BA, Amherst Coll., 1943; grad. Advanced Mgmt. Program, Harvard Bus. Sch., 1967. Salesman then exec. asst. NCR Corp., N.Y.C. and Dayton, Ohio, 1946-53; dir. fin. S. A. Comercial Manuel Ferreira, Asunción, Paraguay, 1953-56; pres., chief exec. officer Máquinas de Comercio S.A., Quito, Ecuador, 1956—; dir. Labs. L.I.F.E., 1965—, Centros Comerciales del Ecuador S.A., 1970-76, 81-86, Hosp. Metropolitano, Quito, 1986—, Fundación Metrofraternidad, Quito, 1986—; cons. in field; participant U.S. Dept. Def. Joint Civilian Orientation Conf., 1966; hon. consul Japan in Guayaquil, Ecuador, 1958-65, hon. consul gen., 65-86. Chancelor, treas. Episcopal Ch. Ecuador. Served as officer USMCR, 1942-46. Decorated Order Sacred Treasure 3d class, Japan, 1969. Mem. Quito C. of C. (dir. 1970-72, 75-77, 81-83), Ecuadorian-Am. C. of C. (founder 1974, v.p. 1975-77). Clubs: Quito Tennis and Golf, Quito Executive; Guayaquil Country. Lodge: Rotary. Home: 2038 Ave 12 de Octubre, Quito Ecuador Office: 957 Versalles, PO Box 165-A, Quito Ecuador

MOSS, SANDRA HUGHES, law firm administrator; b. Atlanta, Dec. 24, 1945; d. Harold Melvin and Velma Aileen (Norton) H.; m. Marshall L. Moss, May 1, 1965; children—Tara Celise, Justin Hughes. Student W. Ga. Coll., 1964-65. Legal sec. Smith, Cohen, Ringel, Kohler & Martin, Atlanta, 1965-78; real estate salesman Century 21-Phoenix, College Park, Ga., 1978-80; office mgr./personnel dir. Smith, Cohen, Ringel, Kohler & Martin, Atlanta, 1980-85; dir. adminstrn. Smith, Gambrell & Russell, Atlanta, 1985—. Bd. dirs., sec. North Clayton Athletic Assn., Riverdale, Ga., 1981-83; sec. E.W. Oliver PTA, Riverdale, 1981; exec. com. E.W. Oliver and N. Clayton Jr. PTA, Riverdale, 1980, 81, 82; den leader Cub Scouts, Pack 959, Riverdale, 1984. Mem. Am. Soc. Personnel Adminstrs, Assn. Legal Adminstrs. (sec. Atlanta chpt. 1988). Home: 200 Deer Forest Trail Fayetteville GA 30214 Office: Smith Gambrell & Russell 2400 First Atlanta Tower 2 Peachtree St Atlanta GA 30383

MOSSAKOWSKI, STANISLAW-MARIA-ZYGMUNT, art historian; b. Sambor, Poland, Aug. 26, 1937; s. Stanislaw-Radoslaw and Maria-Urszula (Sroczynski) M.; MA, Jagiellonian U., Cracow, Poland, 1958, PhD, 1964; m. Wanda Zabietto, Aug. 4, 1962. Asst., Jagiellonian U. Library, 1958-67; asst. Inst. Art History, Polish Acad., Warsaw, 1967-71, asst. prof. art history, 1971-79, prof., 1979—, dep. dir. inst., 1973-78, dir. inst., 1978—. Decorated Golden Cross of Merits Poland, Knight Order Polonia Restituta; Bologna (Italy) U. grantee, 1965-66. Mem. Com. Internat. d'Histoire de l'Art, Polish Nat. Com., Soc. Scientiarum Varsaviensis, Socio Straniero di Ateneo Veneto at Venice. Roman Catholic. Author: (in Polish) Tilman van Gameren/The Architect of Polish Baroque, 1973; Sztuka jako swiadectwo czasu, 1981; chief editor Polish Art Studies, 1979-82, Biuletyn Historii Sztuki, 1981-1987. Office: Dtuga 28, 00-950 Warsaw Poland

MÖSSBAUER, RUDOLF L., physicist, educator; b. Munich, Germany, Jan. 31, 1929; s. Ludwig and Erna M.; ed. Technische Hochschule, Munich; D.Sc. (hon.), Oxford U., 1973, U. Leicester (Eng.), 1975; Dr. h.c., U. Grenoble (France), 1974; 3 children. Research asst. Max-Planck Inst., Heidelberg (W. Ger.), 1955-57; research fellow Technische Hochschule, Munich, 1958-60; research fellow Calif. Inst. Tech., 1960, sr. research fellow, 1961, prof. physics, 1961; prof. exptl. physics Tech. U. Munich, 1964-72, 77—; dir. Inst. Max von Laue, Grenoble, France and German-French-Brit. High Flux Reactor, 1972-77. Recipient Research Corp. award, 1960; Röntgen prize U. Giessen, 1961; Elliott Cresson medal Franklin Inst., Phila., 1961; Nobel prize for physics, 1961; Guthrie medal Inst. Physics (London), 1974; Lomonossovmedal Acad. Sci. USSR, 1984; Einstein medal Albert Einstein Soc., Bern, 1986. Mem. Deutsche Physikalische Gesellschaft, Deutsche Gesellschaft der Naturforscher, Leopoldina, Am. Phys. Soc., European Phys. Soc., Indian Acad. Scis., Am. Acad. Sci. (fgn.), Am. Acad. Arts Scis. (fgn), Nat. Acad. Scis. (fgn. assoc.), Bavarian Acad. Scis., Academia Nazionale dei XL Roma, Pontifical Acad. Scis., Acad. Sci. USSR (fgn.). Author publs. on recoilless nuclear resonance absorption and neutrino physics. Office: Tech U Munich, Dept Physics, 8046 Garching Federal Republic of Germany

MOSSE, PETER JOHN CHARLES, precious metals company executive; b. Mtarfa, Malta, Sept. 8, 1947; came to U.S., 1977; s. John Herbert Charles and Barbara Haworth (Holden) M. BA, Oxford U., 1969; MBA, U. Pa., 1971, postgrad., 1977—. Bank officer N.M. Rothschild & Sons Lt., London, 1971-76; spl. projects officer banking Bumiputra Mcht. Bankers Berhad, Kuala Lumpur, Malaysia, 1976-77; v.p., treas., sec. NMR Metals Incorp., N.Y.C., 1977-79, exec. v.p., 1979-83; sr. v.p. Rothschild Inc., N.Y.C., 1983—. Mem. The Gold Inst. (co. rep., bd. dirs. 1985—), The Silver Inst. (co. rep.), The Newcomen Soc. U.S., The Copper Club, Soc. Mining Engrs., Can. Inst. Mining and Metallurgy, Prospectors and Developers Assn. Can., Internat. Platform Assn., Commodity Exchange, Inc. Episcopalian. Home: 353 E 72d St 33D New York NY 10021 Office: Rothschild Inc 1 Rockefeller Plaza New York NY 10020

MOSSER, MARLA BIANCO, management consultant; b. Easton, Pa., July 20, 1953; d. Thomas S. and Alvera (Tomaino) Bianco; m. Bart H. Mosser, Feb. 23, 1979. BS in Edn. cum laude, West Chester U., 1975, MA in Psychology, 1977; M in Mgmt., Northwestern U., 1986. Teaching asst. psychology dept. West Chester (Pa.) U., 1975-76, psychology intern Counseling Ctr., 1976-77; counselor-therapist Devereux Found., Exton, Pa., 1976-77, psychotherapist, 1977-78; cons. Crawford Rehab. Services, Phila., 1978-79, Boston, 1979-80; v.p. J.M. Boros and Assoc., Ltd., Chgo., 1980-86; cons. Marla B. Mosser Assocs., 1987—; lectr. in field. Bd. dirs. Ctr. for Grieving Children, 1988—; mem. planning com. Maine State Council for Vols., 1988; active steering com.State Conf. in Volumteerism; bd. mem. Ctr. for Grieving Children. Mem. Women in Mgmt. (career devel. com. Chgo. chpt. 1983-84), Am. Soc. Personnel Adminstrs., Northwestern U. Profl. Women's Assn., Kappa Delta Pi, Psi Chi.

MOSTAFA, HASSAN MAHMOUD, otolaryngologist; b. Benisuif, Egypt, Feb. 10, 1930; s. Mahmoud Mostafa and Tafeda Mohamed Aly; married; children: Sherin, Mona, Dina. MB, BCH in Medicine, Cairo F. Medicine, 1952, diploma in ear, nose and throat, 1955, diploma in gen. surgery, 1956, MD in Ear, Nose and Throat, 1958. Practice medicine specializing in ear, nose and throat Kuwait, 1956-57, Misr Spinning & Weaving Co., Mahalla Kubra, Egypt, 1957-67; asst. prof. otolaryngology Tanta F. Medicine, Egypt, 1967-72, chmn. prof. otolaryngology, 1972—, dean, 1974-81; v.p. Tanta U., Egypt, 1981-85. Clubs: Gezira Sporting, Tawfikia Tennis, Shooting (Cairo). Home: PO Box 181 Orman, Cairo Egypt Office: 26 July St No 26-12, Cairo Egypt

MOTAMEDI, AHMAD, lawyer; b. Esfahan, Iran, Feb. 6, 1943; s. Mohammad Hassan and Batool (Mazoochian) M.; divorced; 1 child, Setareh. BA in Law and Criminology, Tehran (Iran) U., 1967, MA in Law, 1969. Sole practice law Tehran, 1967—; cons. various firms and govt. instns., 1972—; legal commentator Radio Tehran until 1979. Contbr. articles to newspapers, profl. jours. Mem. Internat. Lawyers Union, Internat. Lawyers Congress, Iranian Bar Assn. Moslem. Home: 10 Tir St, Mahmoodieh Ave Shemiran, Tehran Iran Office: 2/4 Pirooz, Bldg #270, Mohtasham St and Arv Ave, Tehran Iran

MOTHERSHEAD, ALICE BONZI (MRS. MORRIS WARNER MOTHERSHEAD), retired college administrator, civic worker; b. Milan, Italy, Dec. 25, 1914; came to U.S. 1920, naturalized 1925; d. Ercole and Alice (Spalding) Bonzi; pvt. pupil music and art; student Pasadena City Coll., 1958-60; m. Morris Warner Mothershead, Sept. 15, 1935; children: Warner Bonzi, Maria (Mrs. Andrei Rogers). Partner Floal Toy Co., Pasadena, Calif., 1942-44; community adv. Fgn. Student Program, Pasadena City Coll., from 1952, past dir. Community Liaison Center. Chmn., Am. Field Service Internat. Scholarships, Pasadena, 1953-55; mem. West Coast adv. com. Inst. Internat. Edn., San Francisco, 1957-70. Vice pres. San Rafael Sch. PTA, Pasadena, 1945-46; active Community Chest, ARC, Pasadena; chmn. Greater Los Angeles Com. Internat. Student and Visitor Services, 1962; mem. Woman's Civic League Pasadena, chmn. city affairs com., 1985, pres., 1986-87; bd. dirs. Fine Arts Club of Pasadena, 1983-85, Friends of Caltech Y, 1984—, Pasadena City Coll. Found., 1983-85; commr. City of Pasadena Cultural Heritage Commn., 1984—. Decorated knight Govt. of Italy, 1975. Mem. Nat. Assn. Fgn. Student Affairs (life, chmn. community sect. and v.p. 1964-65, chmn. U.S. study abroad com. 1969-70), Am. Assn. UN (chpt. 2d v.p. 1964), Soc. Women Geographers, Am. Friends Middle East, Zonta Internat., Omicron Mu Delta. Club: International (Pasadena). Author: Social Customs and Manners in the United States, 1957; Dining Customs Around the World, 1982; co-author: 15 Years of the Foreign Student Program at Pasadena City College, 1965. Editor: Students to People to Future, 1971. Lodge: Lions. Home: 675 Burleigh Dr Pasadena CA 91105

MOTIWALLA, DADI NOSHIR, advertising photographer, computer graphics producer, consultant; b. Bombay, Maharashtra, India, Nov. 26, 1954; s. Noshir Dadabhoy and Pilloo Minocher (Kutar) M.; m. Nurelle Subjally, July 17, 1985. Student Sydenham Coll. Commerce and Econs., Bombay, 1972-75; B.A., Brooks Inst. Photog. Art and Sci., 1981. Owner, mgr. Motiwalla Photo/Graphics, Dubai, United Arab Emirates, 1981—; participant seminar Rochester Inst. Tech., N.Y., 1981; lectr. Art Soc. Dubai, 1984; cons. in field. Brooks Inst. scholar, 1981. Mem. Internat. Advt. Assn., Apple Computer Club. Zoroastrian. Club: Chaine des Rotisseurs (chevalier 1984—); Zoroastrian. Avocations: computer graphics; music; travel; painting. Home: Intercontinental Plaza Apt 7F, Dubai Al-Maktoum St, Dubai United Arab Emirates Office: Motiwalla PhotoGraphics, Al-Maktoum St PO Box 1579, Dubai United Arab Emirates

MOTONO, HIDEO, banker; b. Ashiya, Hyogo, Japan, July 9, 1926; s. Keiji and Fumi Motono; m. Fumiko Motono, Oct. 2, 1954; children: Eiichi, Keiko Sasaki. LLB, Tokyo U., 1953. Mgr. lending dept. Mitsubishi Trust and Banking Corp., Tokyo, 1968-70, dep. gen. mgr. fgn. div., 1970-72, sr. dep. gen. mgr., 1972-76, gen. mgr., 1976-78, gen. mgr. internat. div., 1980-81; mng. dir. Australia-Japan Internat. Fin., Ltd., Hong Kong, 1978-80; sr. mng. dir. Dainichi Invest Co., Ltd., Kobe, Japan, 1981-85; spl. advisor Union Bank of Switzerland, Tokyo, 1985-86; sr. mng. dir. Union Bank of Switzerland (Trust and Banking) Ltd., Tokyo, 1986—. Home: 7-14 Sakurajosui 3-chome, Setagaya-ku, Tokyo 156, Japan Office: Union Bank of Switzerland Ltd, Hibiya Kokusai Bldg, 2-3 Uchisaiwaicho 2-chome, Chiyoda-ku, Tokyo 100, Japan

MOTOZUNA, KAZUMICHI, shipbuilding company executive, naval architect; b. Tokyo, Mar. 6, 1932; s. Kazuroku and Osana M.; m. Saeko Motozuna, Jan. 25, 1960; 1 child, Masamichi. Degree in Engring., Tokyo U., 1954. Gen. mgr. Ishikawajima-Harima Heavy Industries Co., Ltd., Tokyo, 1980-85, assoc. dir., 1985—; lectr. Tokyo U., 1983-87. Co-author various symposiums. Mem. Soc. Naval Architects Japan (dir.), The Marine Engring. Soc. Japan. Home: 3-15-9 Maruyamadai Konanku, Yokohama 233, Japan Office: Ishikawajima-Harima Heavy Industries Co Ltd, 1-6-2 Marunouchi Chiyodaku, Tokyo 100, Japan

MOTRO, MICHEL JOSEPH, publishing company executive; b. Toulouse, France, Aug. 30, 1943; s. Henri and Lucienne (Mordoh) M.; m. Marie France Crosnier, Dec. 28, 1968; children: Denis, Bernard. M.S., INSA, Lyon, 1965; M.B.A., I.A.E., U. Dauphine, Paris, 1971. Design engr. Thomson-CSF, Paris, 1967-69; br. mgr. Tex. Instruments France, Nice, 1969-75; mktg. dir. Europe, Tex. Instruments Consumer Group, Nice, 1975-82; chmn. Vifi Internat., Paris, 1983-86; sr. v.p. C.E.P., Paris, 1983-86, Internat. Thomson Components; pres., chief exec. officer IDC France, Paris; v.p. semicondrs. activities IDC Corp., Paris; chmn. TC DIS Thomson Components Ltd. U.K., Thomson Kom. Sweden; bd. dirs. INSEC Japan, THOMINTEX France Thomson Far East Ltd . Decorated chevalier des Arts et Lettres, 1986. Author movie: Les Bakotas, 1966; Centre Culturel Français du Gabon, 1966. Pres. European Sci. Film Festival, Lyon, 1964, 65. Office: IDC France, 12 Avenue Georges 5, 75008 Paris France

MOTSCH, WOLFGANG, linguist; b. Berlin, Apr. 11, 1934; married; 2 children. Diploma in German Lang. and Lit., Humboldt U., 1956. Sci. cooperator Acad. Scis. Germin Democratic Republic, Berlin, 1956-62; dept. head Cen. Inst. Linguistics, Berlin, 1963—. Author: Structuralistic Linguistics, 1974; co-author: German Grammar, 1981; contbr. articles to profl. jours. Mem. Internat. Pragmatics Assn. (adv. bd. 1987—). Office: Acd Scis, German Democratic Republic, Prenzlauer Promenade 149/151, 1100 Berlin German Democratic Republic

MOTT, SIR NEVILL (FRANCIS), physicist, educator, author; b. Leeds, Eng., Sept. 30, 1905; s. C.F. and Lilian Mary (Reynolds) M.; M.A., St. John's Coll., Cambridge, Eng., 1929; hon. degrees: D.Sc., U. Sheffield, London, Louvain, Grenoble, Paris, Poitiers, Bristol, Ottawa, Liverpool, Reading, Warwick, Lancaster, Heriot Watt, Bordeaux, St. Andrews, Essex, Stuttgart, Sussex, William and Mary, Marburg, Bar Ilan, Lille, Rome, Lisbon; D.Tech., Linkoping; m. Ruth Horder, Mar. 21, 1930; children: Elizabeth, Alice. Lectr. math. Cambridge U., 1930-33, Cavendish prof. exptl. physics, 1954-71, master Gonville and Caius Coll., 1959-66; prof. physics U. Bristol, 1933-54, also dir. H.H. Wills Phys. Lab., 1948-54; Page-Barbour lectr. U. Va., 1956. Mem. central adv. council Ministry of Edn., 1956-59; chmn. com. physics edn. Nuffield Found., 1965-75. Sci. adviser to Anti Aircraft Command, also supt. theoretical research in armaments Armament Research Dept., World War II. Decorated knight bachelor; recipient Nobel prize for physics, 1977. Fellow Royal Soc. (Hughes medalist 1941, Royal medal 1953, Copley medal 1972), Phys. Soc. of Great Britain (pres. 1956-58); mem. Nat. Acad. Scis., Am. Acad. Arts and Scis. (corr.), Inst. Physics (hon. fellow), Internat. Union Pure and Applied Physics (pres. 1951-57), Modern Langs. Assn. (pres. 1955), Société Française de Physique (hon.). Author: An Outline of Wave Mechanics, 1930; (with H.S.W. Massey) The Theory of Atomic Collisions, 1933; (with H. Jones) The Theory of the Properties of Metals and Alloys, 1936; (with R. W. Gurney) Electronic Processes in Ionic Crystals, 1940; Wave (with I. N. Snedden) Wave Mechanics and Its Applications, 1948; Elements of Wave Mechanics, 1952; Atomic Structure and the Strength of Metals, 1956; (with E. A. Davis) Electronic Processes in Non-crystalline 1971, 2d edit, 1979; Elements of Quantum Mechanics, 1972; Metal-Insulator Transitions, 1974; (autobiography) A Life in Science, 1986.

MOTTELSON, BEN R., physicist; b. Chgo., July 9, 1926; naturalized Danish citizen, 1971; s. Goodman and Georgia (Blum) M.; B.Sc., Purdue U., 1947; Ph.D., Harvard U., 1950; hon. degrees Purdue U., U. Heidelberg (Germany); m. Nancy Jane Reno, 1948 (dec. 1975); 3 children. Fellow, Inst. Theoretical Physics, Copenhagen, 1950-51; U.S. AEC fellow, Copenhagen, 1951-53; with theoretical study group European Orgn. for Nuclear Research, Copenhagen; prof. Nordic Inst. for Theoretical Atomic Physics, Copenhagen, from 1957; physicist Bohr Inst.; dir. Nordita, 1980—; vis. prof. U. Calif., Berkeley, 1959. Recipient Nobel prize for physics, 1975. Author: Nuclear Structure, vol 1, 1969, vol. 2 (with A. Bohr), 1975; numerous other publs. in field. Mem. Nat. Acad. Scis. (fgn. assoc.). Address: Nordita, Blegdamsvej 17, DK-2100 Copenhagen Denmark *

MOTTOLA, KARI MATIAS, political scientist; b. Kokkola, Finland, Aug. 24, 1945; s. Tatu Matias and Greta Linnea Margareta (Rusten) M.; m. Liisa Marjatta b. Ruutu, June 13, 1970; children: Matias, Hanno, Anna. MA Polit. Sci., U. Helsinki, 1969. Mem. fgn. news staff Helsingin Sanomat, 1965-72; info. sec. Finnish Inst. Internat. Affairs, 1972-73, dir., 1973—. Editor-in-chief Ulkopolitiikka, Yearbook of Finnish Fgn. Policy. Editor, co-author books. Contbr. articles to profl. jours. Sec., Paasikivi Soc., Helsinki, 1973-84. Served to lt. Finnish Army, 1964-65. Lutheran. Office: Finnish Inst Internat Affairs, Pursimiehenkatu, 00150 Helsinki Finland

MOTYKA, OLGA OSTROWSKYJ, physician; b. Adelaide, Australia, Oct. 18, 1952; d. Michael and Dunia (Kyrylenko) Ostrowskyj; m. Wolodymyr Motyka, Jan. 28, 1979; children—Olena, Danylo and Oleksander (twins). B. Medicine, U. Adelaide, 1975, B. Surgery, 1975. Intern Canberra Hosp., Australia, 1976-77; resident med. officer St. George Hosp., Sydney, Australia, 1977-78, Adelaide Children's Hosp., 1978-79; sch. med. officer Health Commn. of N.S.W., Newcastle, Australia, 1979-84; gen. practice medicine, Newcastle, 1984—; physician Family Planning Assn., Newcastle, 1979—; med. editor Ukrainian Radio Program, Sta. 2NUR-FM, Newcastle, 1982-84. Mem. Med. Women's Soc. N.S.W., (pres. Newcastle br. 1984-85), Ukrainian Med. Assn. Australia. Mem. Ukrainian Orthodox Ch. Avocations: gourmet cooking; embroidery; Pysanky writing; Ukrainian language. Office: 52 Ridley St, Charlestown 2290, Australia

MOTZFELDT, JONATHAN, prime minister of Greenland; b. Qagssimiut, Julianehaab, Greenland, Sept. 25, 1938; s. Søren M.; m. Margit Motzfeldt, Dec. 18, 1965. Vicar Sydprøven, Greenland, 1966-69, Jullianehaab, 1969-79; mem. Provincial Council Greenland, 1971-79; chmn. Landsting, 1979—, Landsstyre, 1979—, Siumut Party, 1977—; now prime minister, sec. adminstrn. Greenland. Named Knight of the Order of the Dannebrog. Address: Office Prime Minister, Nuuk Greenland *

MOUJAES, RABIH EMILE, financial analyst; b. Beirut, Mar. 7, 1954; s. Emile Philippe and Fulvia (Dallal) M. Diplome d'expert comptable, Inst. Comml. Scis., La Salle, Beirut, 1976; MBA, Boston U., 1983. Chief acct. Unifert Hellas, Piraeus, Greece, 1976-77; acctg. mgr. O.T.R.A.C.O., Piraeus, 1977-78; fin. exec. United Chems. NV, Brussels, 1978-79; sr. analyst Unifert Internat. SA, Brussels, 1980-86; fin. exec. Fertimar SA, Brussels, 1984—; fin. cons. TJA and Assocs., Middle East, 1983. Designed software for computer applications in shipping, 1987 (lic. agreement to market, 1988); contbr. articles to profl. jours. Fellow Inst. Chartered Accts.; mem. Cercle des Experts Comptables et Reviseurs de Comptes (pres., founder 1976-77), Boston U. Alumni Assn. (v.p. 1983-87). Home: 70000 Meerlaan, 1900 Overijse Belgium Office: Fertimar SA, 44 Ave des Arts, 1040 Brussels Belgium

MOULAERT, FRANK ADELINUS, economics educator; b. Brugge, Belgium, Apr. 5, 1951. B in Applied Econs., U. Faculteiten Sint-Ignatius te Antwerpen, 1972; MA in Econs., Katholieke Univ. Leuven, 1974, D in Econs., 1983; MA in Regional Sci., U. Pa., 1977, PhD in Regional Sci., 1979. Assoc. prof. Nat. Sch. Architecture and Town Planning, Antwerp, 1982—, Limburg Bus. Sch., Hasselt, Belgium, 1983-87; assoc. dir. Centre Europeen Johns Hopkins, France, 1984-86; assoc. prof., dir. cerie U. Lille I, France, 1986—. Author: (with R. Bollen) Racists are Wrong, 1984; (with F. Vandenbroucke) Making the Economic Crisis Worse, 1982; editor: (with P. Wilson) Regional Analysis and the New International Division of Labor, 1982, The Role of the State in Regional Industrial Development, 1988; (with A. Martens) Buitenlandse Minderheden in Naanderen-België, 1985; contbr. numerous articles and papers to profl. jours. and confs. Recipient several research grants. Mem. Regional Sci. Assn., European Econ. Assn., World Univ. Arts and Scis., Union for Radical Polit. Economy, Studiekring Post-Keynesiaanse Economie (past councillor). Office: U Lille I, Ufr Des Sciences Econ, Batiment C6, Villenueve d'Ascq, 59650 Lille France

MOULAISON, ROBERT LARRY, electronics engineer; b. Clearwater, Fla., Dec. 16, 1944; s. John Raymond and Victoria Beatrice (Curry) M.; m. Nancy Rosalie Knoten, Sept. 26, 1970 (div.); 1 dau., Heather Lea; m. Judith Ann Cutler, Sept. 4, 1983; stepsons, Michael H. Koren, Jeffrey P. Koren. B.S.E.E., U. Me., 1967. Assoc. field engr. to sr. field engr. Westinghouse Elec. Corp., Balt., 1967-81, sr. engr., 1982—; elec. engr. U.S. Naval Oceanographic Office, Bay St. Louis, Miss., 1981-82. Mem. IEEE, Armed Forces Communications and Electronics Assn., Assn. Old Crows, Tau Alpha Pi. Republican. Home: 9209 Allenswood Rd Randallstown MD 21133 Office: Westinghouse Electric Corp PO Box 1693 MS 4260 Baltimore MD 21203

MOULAY HASSAN BIN EL MEHDI, PRINCE, Moroccan diplomat; b. Aug. 14, 1912; s. Moulay El Mehdi Alaoui and Khnata Bent Mohamed Soussi. Caliph No. Zone of Morocco, 1925; ambassador to U.K. 1957-64, ambassador to Italy, 1964-67; gov. Banque du Maroc, 1969-84. Decorations include Ouissam Alaoui, Charles I Medal, Great Mil. Ouissam, Great Medal of Portugal, Great Dominican Medal, Great Naval Medal, Great Mahdaoui Medal, Great Houssni Medal. Address: care Banque du Maroc, PO Box 445, 277 ave Mohammed V, Rabat Morocco *

MOULDEN, BERNARD PAUL, university reader; b. Bristol, Eng., Jan. 15, 1945; s. Richard George Thomas and Joyce Rita (Webb) M.; m. Hilary Jayne Marks; children from previous marriage: Fiona Clare, Mark Richard. BA, U. Durham, Eng., 1966; PhD, U. Reading, Eng., 1974. Demonstrator U. Bristol, Eng., 1968-69; lectr. U. Reading, 1969-87, reader, 1987—. Office: U Reading, Psychology Dept, Earley Gate Whiteknights, RG6 2AL Reading England

MOULIN, ANNE MARIE, biology researcher; b. Clermont, Puy de Dome, France, Nov. 28, 1944; d. Charles H. and Yvette A. (Aurisse) M.; 1 child, Remy J. Bouallegue. MA in Philosophy, U. Paris, 1967; Cert. in Parasitology, Paris, 1975; MD, Paris U., 1979, MS in Human Biology, 1982; PhD in Philosophy, Lyon, France, 1986. Teaching asst. U. Clermont, Ferrand, France, 1970-78; researcher Nat. Ctr. Sci. Research, Paris, 1979—, research coordinator, 1982-84; fellow Wissenschafts Coll., Berlin, 1983-84; vis. scholar Harvard U., MIT, Boston U., Boston, 1984-87; assoc. researcher John's Hopkins U., 1987-88; cons. U. Hosp., Paris, 1979-83; fgn. office expert, Taiz, N. Yemen, 1982; mem. Nat. Ctr. Sci. Research, Paris. Co-author (with Pierre Chuvin): L'Islam au Peril des Femmes, 1982; contbr. articles to various profl. jours. Mem. Commn. for Life Scis. and Soc. Scis.

MOULTON, EDWARD QUENTIN, educator; b. Kalamazoo, Nov. 16, 1926; s. Burt Frederick and Esther (Fairchild) M.; m. Joy Wade, Jan. 2, 1954; children: Jennifer Fairchild, Charles Wade, David Frederick II, Alison Joy. B.S., Mich. State U., 1947; M.S., La. State U., 1948; Ph.D., U. Calif.-Berkeley, 1956; D.Sc. (hon.), Wittenberg U., 1980; LL.D. (hon.), Xavier U., 1983, Wilmington Coll., 1983. Registered profl. engr., Ohio. Instr. civil engring Mich. State U., 1947; hydraulic engring. fellow La. State U., 1947-48; engr. U.S. Waterways Expt. Sta., C.E., Vicksburg, Miss., 1948; research fellow U. Wis., 1948-49; asst. prof. civil engring. Auburn U., 1949-50; lectr. civil engring. U. Calif.-Berkeley, 1950-54; asst. prof. civil engring. Ohio State U., 1954-58, assoc. prof., 1958-64; asst. dean Ohio State U. (Grad. Sch.), 1958-62, assoc. dean Grad. Sch., Coll. Arts and Scis., chmn. geodetic sci., 1962-64, dean off-campus edn., asso. dean faculties for personnel budget, prof. engring. mechanics, 1964-66; dir. Coll. Sci. and Engring. Dayton campus Miami U.-Ohio State U., 1963-66; pres. U. S.D., 1966-68; exec. asst. to pres. Ohio State U., 1968-69, sec. trustees, 1968-79, prof. civil engring., 1968-79, v.p. adminstrv. ops., 1969-70, exec. v.p. adminstrv. ops., 1970-71, exec. v.p., 1971-73, v.p. bus. and adminstrn., 1973-79, v.p., sec. emeritus, 1984—; chancellor Ohio Bd. Regents, 1979-83, chancellor emeritus, 1984—; exec. v.p. Cranston Securities Co., 1983-84; pres. Lake Erie Coll., 1985-86; pres., gen. mgr. Columbus Symphony Orchestra, 1986-88; cons. Author articles, reports, bulls. on environ. engring. Trustee Blue Cross Central Ohio, 1971-77, 80-82; mem. nat. adv. council for small bus. to U.S. Sec. Treasury, 1975-76; mem. steering com. Devel. Com. Greater Columbus, 1970-80, chmn., 1978-79; mem. nat. adv. council SBA, 1973-76; bd. dirs. Columbus Safety Council, 1970-79, Greater Columbus Arts Council, 1970-78, Mid-Ohio Health Planning Commn., 1973-74, Am. Univs. for Research in Astronomy, 1972-79, Ohio Transp. Research Center, 1979-83; trustee Columbus Symphony Orch., 1980-85; trustee Riverside Meth. Hosp., 1979—, chmn. fin. and assets com., 1983—, treas. 1988—; vice chmn. Ohio Higher Edn. Facilities Commn., 1979-83; mem. Ohio Sch. and Coll. Bd. Registration, 1979-83, Ohio Ednl. TV Commn., 1979-83; chmn. Columbus Symphony Grand Ball, 1983; chmn. judging Internat. Sci. and Engring. Fair, 1984; mem. Midwest Edn. Bd., 1979-85. Served with USNR, 1945-46. Fellow ASCE; mem. Ohio Hist. Soc. (bd. dirs.), State Higher Edn. Exec. Officers (exec. com. 1981-83), Ohio Commodore, Sigma Xi, Tau Beta Pi, Pi Mu Epsilon, Chi Epsilon, Delta Omega, Romophos, Sigma Alpha Epsilon. Congregationalist. Clubs: Scioto Country, Capital, Faculty (Columbus), Athletic. Home: 1303 London Dr Columbus OH 43221

MOULTON, PAUL DOUGLAS (PETE), infosystems engineering consultant; b. Binghamton, N.Y., Sept. 1, 1944; s. Fredrick Douglas and Helene Marjorie (Cole) M.; B.S. in Math., Clarkson Coll. Tech., 1966, M.S. in Indsl. Mgmt., 1968; (N.Y. Regent scholar); children—Susan Jenifer, Jeremy Matthew. Instr. indsl. mgmt. Clarkson Coll. Potsdam, N.Y., 1967-68; tech. staff Sanders Data Systems, Inc., Nashua, N.H., 1968-71; grad. asst. Pa. State U., University Park, 1971-72; computer specialist Nat. Weather Service, Silver Spring, Md., 1972; mgr. Info. and Communication Applications, Inc., Rockville, Md., 1972-75; mgr. Rehab. Group, Inc., Arlington, Va., 1975-77; supr. spl. projects U.S. Senate, Washington, 1977-80; sr. cons. specialist telecommunications policies and programs Gen. Electric Info. Services Co., Rockville, Md., 1980; dir. Moulton, Minasi and Co., 1981—; internat. lectr., cons. in microcomputers and telecommunications. Mem. Assn. Computing Machinery, IEEE, Am. Inst. Indsl. Engrs. (sr.). Contbr. chpts. to books, articles to profl. jours. Home and Office: 7146 Rivers Edge Rd Columbia MD 21044

MOULTRIE, JOHN WESLEY, JR., state official; b. Marion, S.C., May 23, 1904; s. John Wesley and Missouri (Crockett) M.; A.B., Allegheny Coll., Meadville, Pa., 1927; postgrad. Harvard Law Sch., 1927-28, U. Mich. Law Sch., 1929-30, U. Minn., 1935-36, 38-39; M.A., Roosevelt U., 1967; m. Alice Gibson, Oct. 1, 1939 (dec. Nov. 1962); children—John Wesley III, Stanton Randolph. Prin. rural sch., Jacksonville, Fla., 1932-33; editor-in-chief The Spotlight, Chgo., 1934-35; dir. Consumer Center, Phyllis Wheatley House, Mpls., 1941-42; interviewer, unit supr. Minn. State Employment Service, Mpls., 1942-54; interviewer, counselor Gen. Indsl. Office, Ill. State Employment Service, Chgo., 1959-65, counseling supr., 1965-69, program coordinator, 1969-81, asst. mgr. local office, 1981-85 ; real estate broker, Chgo., 1955-88, ins. broker, Chgo., 1956-88. Mem. Internat. Assn. Personnel in Employment Security. Methodist (pres. ch. credit union). Home: 4330 S Martin Luther King Dr Chicago IL 60653

MOUMIN, AMINI ALI, ambassador; b. Mustamudu, Anjouan, Comoros, Aug. 30, 1944; arrived in Can., 1986; s. Ali Moumin Al Ahmed and Maridhia (Ali) Mzuri; m. Sarah Aboubacar, Sept. 9, 1974; children: Naissun, Shamsa, Mohamed-Lamin, Arafat. BA, Kuwait U., 1973; degree in diplomacy, Cambridge (Eng.) U., 1974; MA in Internat. Relations, Ileri U., Paris, 1976. Advisor to pres. Comoros, 1978-79; dir. for Africa Ministry Fgn. Affairs, Comoros, 1979-82, dir. gen. polit., 1982-86; ambassador to U.S. and Can. N.Y.C., 1986—. Named Officer, Star of Comoros. Home: 401 E 34th St S16K New York NY 10016 Office: Permanent Mission of Comoros 336 E 45th St New York NY 10017

MOUNDS, LEONA MAE REED, educator; b. Crosby, Tex., Sept. 9, 1945; d. Elton Phillip and Ora Lee (Jones) Reed; m. Aaron B. Mounds Jr., Aug. 21, 1965 (div.); 1 dau., Lisa Nichelle. B.S. in Elem. Edn., Bridgewater State Coll., 1973; M.A. in Mental Retardation, U. Alaska, 1980. Cert. tchr. Alaska, Colo., Tex., Mass., cert. adminstrv. prin. 1985. Tchr., Sch. Dist. 11, Colorado Springs, Colo., 1973-75; tchr. Anchorage Sch. Dist., 1976-78, 80—, mem. math. curriculum com., reading contact tchr., mem. talent bank. Tchr. Del Valle (Tex.) Sch. Dist., 1979-80. Bd. dirs. Urban League, 1974; 1st v.p. PTA, Crosby, Tex.; del. Tex. Democratic Conv., 1980, dist. 13 chair Dem. party, Anchorage; bd. dirs. C.R.I.S.I.S. Inc.; tchr. religious edn., lay Eucharist minister St. Martin De Pores Roman Cath. Ch., St. Patrick's Ch. Served with USAF, 1964-66. Alaska State Tchr. Incentive grantee, 1981; Ivy Lutz scholar, 1972. Mem. NEA (human relations coordinator Alaska chpt., region 6 bd. dirs., Alaska chpt. bd. dirs., vice chmn. women's caucus), Anchorage Edn. Assn. (minority chmn. 1982—, mem. Black Caucus polit. action com., v.p. programs 1986-88), Black Educators of Pikes Peak Region (pres. 1974), Anchorage Edn. Assn. (v.p. programs com. 1986-87, women's caucus), Assn. Supervision and Curriculum Devel., Alaska Women in Adminstrn., Council for Exception Children, NAACP.

MOUNOUD, PIERRE, child psychologist, researcher; b. Le Locle, Switzerland, Nov. 28, 1940; s. Jean-Claude and Ida (Varidel) M. Lic. in Psychology, U. Geneva (Switzerland), 1963, diplome in psychology, 1964, Ph.D. in Psychology, 1968; cert. in neurophysiology, U. Marseille, France, 1969. Assoc. prof. psychology U. Lausanne (Switzerland), 1973-76; extraordinary prof. U. Geneva, 1975-81, ordinary prof., 1981—; invited prof. U. Bruxelles (Belgium), 1978-79; research fellow CNRS, Marseille, France, 1968-70; vis. lectr. U. Varsovie, Pologne, 1981; invited fellow Brit. Psychol. Soc., 1983; vis. lectr. U. Minn., Mpls., 1984. Author: Structuration de l'Instrument, 1970; editor: Reconnaissance de son image, 1981; La Psychologie (Encyclopédie de la Pléiade, Gallimard), 1986; editor Cahiers de Psychologie Cognitive, 1980-87. Active Swiss Nat. Fund, Berne, 1972—. Mem. Swiss Psychol. Soc., Assn. de Psychologie Scientifique de Langue Francaise, Internat. Soc. Study of Behavioral Devel., Soc. for Research in Child Devel. Office: U of Geneva, Gen Dufour 24, 1211 Geneva 4 Switzerland

MOUNT, WARD (PAULINE WARD), painter, sculptor; b. Batavia, N.Y., Jan. 8, 1898; d. Fred Kendall and Nellie L. (Dowsey) Ward; m. Elmer M. Mount, M.D.; 1 son, Marshall. Grad., Flushing High Sch.; student, New York Univ., Art Students League; pupil of, Gertrude Gardner, Kenneth Hayes Miller, Albert P. Lucas, Joseph P. Pollia. Former head of dept., oil painting and sculpture N.J. State Tchrs. Coll.; founder, former dir. of art classes at the Jersey City Med. Center, N.J.; dir., instr. Ward Mount Art Classes. Represented by paintings and sculptures in permanent collections pvt. colls., art museums, U.S. and fgn., including, N.A.D., Library of Congress, Nat. Sculpture Soc., Archtl. League N.Y., Allied Artists Am., Allied Arts Mus., N.Y.C., Acad. Allied Arts, N.Y.C., Am. Brit. Art Center, Kearny Mus., Mont Clair Art Mus., Audubon Artists, Pa. Acad., Westchester Art Assn., Mus. Modern Art, N.Y.C., Macy Galleries, Smithsonian Inst., The Carlebach Galleries, N.Y.C., Worlds Fair N.Y., Meddallic Art, Lever House, N.Y. Hist. Soc., Columbia U. Library, Marquis Biog. Library, Chgo., Riverside Mus., Nat. Arts Club, Am. Heart Assn., Trenton State Mus., Audubon Artists, Hudson River Mus., Delgado Mus., Jersey City Mus., Provincetown Art Gallery, Bergen County (N.J.) Mus.; Designed: bronze Medal of Honor for, Painters and Sculptors Soc. N.J., 1947; Christmas card for, Am. Heart Assn., 1971. Hon. fellow J.F. Kennedy Found. Recipient numerous awards and prizes for sculpture and painting, including Gold medal Woman of Achievement, Jersey Jour., 1971; Plaque of Honor, Jersey City Mus., 1980, citation Jersey City Hist. Assn., 1987; named Artist of Yr., Hudson Artists, 1984; honoree at Statue of Liberty Gala, 1986. Fellow Royal Soc. of Arts (Eng.), Internat. Inst. Arts and Letters; mem. Painters and Sculptors Soc. N.J., Inc (founder, hon. pres.), Artists Equity, Internat. Platform Assn., DAR, Women of the Arts Mus. (charter), Acad. of Italy (gold medal mem.), several other artists and sculptors assns.

MOUNTCASTLE, KENNETH FRANKLIN, JR., stockbroker; b. Winston-Salem, N.C., Oct. 8, 1928; s. Kenneth Franklin and May M.; B.S. in Commerce, U. N.C., Chapel Hill, 1950; m. Mary Katharine Babcock, Sept. 1, 1951; children—Mary Babcock, Laura Lewis, Kenneth Franklin, Katharine Reynolds. With Mountcastle Knitting Co., Lexington, N.C., 1952-55, Reynolds & Co., N.Y.C., 1955-71; with Reynolds Securities Inc. (co. name changed to Dean Witter Reynolds 1978), N.Y.C., 1971—, sr. v.p., 1974—. Trustee, New Canaan (Conn.) Country Sch., 1962-68, Ethel Walker Sch., Simsbury, Conn., 1973-74; trustee Coro Found., 1980—, nat. chmn., 1986—; bd. dirs., past pres. Mary Reynolds Babcock Found., Winston-Salem, N.C.; bd. visitors U. N.C., Chapel Hill; bd. dirs. Inform, N.Y.C., Fresh Air Fund, N.Y.C., Sears-Roebuck Found. Served with U.S. Army, 1950-52. Republican. Presbyterian. Clubs: Country of New Canaan; Wee Burn Country (Darien, Conn.); Old Town (Winston-Salem, N.C.); Racquet and Tennis, City Midday, Bond, Stock Exchange Luncheon, Madison Sq. Garden (N.Y.C.). Home: 37 Oenoke Ln New Canaan CT 06840 Office: Dean Witter Reynolds 5 World Trade Ctr New York NY 10048

MOURAD, ATEF M., contracting company executive; b. Anout, Lebanon, Apr. 2, 1944; s. Mohammed Ali and Farida (Saad) M.; m. Maha Elhajt; children: Tania, Olfa, Yara, Rabia. BArch., U. Montreal, Que., Can., 1972, MA, 1977. Architect Montreal, 1972-80; tech. dir. Fast Contracting Co., Jeddah, Saudi Arabia, 1980-86; dir. tech. dept. Saudi Co. for Recreation Ctrs., Jeddah, 1986—. Devel. touristic cities and amusement parks. Mem. Ordre des Architects du Que., Assn. des Ingenieur du Liban. Address: Saudi Co for Recreation Ctrs, PO Box 9632, Jeddah Saudi Arabia

MOURAVIEFF-APOSTOL, ANDREW, association executive; b. Cannes, France, Feb. 7, 1913; s. Wladimir and Nadine (Tereschenko) M.; m. Ellen Marion Rothschild, Nov. 12, 1956; children: Michael, Nicholas, Christopher A. Student, Cambridge U., 1930-32; BS, Geneva (Switzerland) U., 1935. Paris and Berlin corr. London Daily Telegraph, 1936-40; columnist Evening Standard, London, 1940-48; refugee resettlement officer UN World Council, Geneva, 1949-67; sec.-gen. Internat. Fedn. Social Workers, Geneva, 1975—; appeals dir. Her Majesty's Fund for Air Raid Victims, 1941; corr. U.S. Office War Info., N.Y.C., 1941-42; liaison officer French. Mil. Mission, Washington, 1942; dir. info. P.C./UNESCO, London, 1946-48; UN manpower advisor to Govt. Peru, 1951-52. Decorated Bailiff Grand Cross Order of St. John of Jerusalem; Grand Cross Order of St. Saba; Order Homayun (Iran); Order of Merit (Chile), 1959. Mem. Internat. Assn. Conf. Translators. Mem. Anglican Church. Club: Naval (London). Lodge: Royal Soc. St. George (life gov.). Home: 31 Rue de l'Athenee, 1206 Geneva Switzerland

MOUSA, MOUSTAFA WAFEY, business executive; b. Alexandria, Egypt, Feb. 27, 1947; s. Wafey Abdelrahman Mousa and Souad Awad Gamda. LL.B., Faculty of Law. Personel officer Egypt Transport, Alexandria, 1968-73; sole practice, Alexandria, 1974-77; legal counsel Arab Comml. C., Doha-Qatar, 1977-80; dir. personel Hamad Hosp., Doha-Qatar, 1980-82; human resources mgr. Dar Al Maal Al Islami, Geneva, 1982-84; v.p. Kamel Corp., Geneva, 1984—; bd. dirs. Arab Fin. Group, Panama, 1983—; mgmt. cons. Performance Mgmt., Geneva, 1982—. Mem. Egyptian Bar Assn., Mediterranean Congress Young Lawyers, Internat. Commn. Jurists (assoc., sponsor). Home: 10 ch de la Tourelle, 1209 Geneva CH Switzerland Office: Kamel Corp SA, PO Box 839, 1200 Geneva Switzerland

MOUSHOUTAS, CONSTANTINE MICHAEL, diplomat; b. Nicosia, Cyprus; s. Michael and Elpiniki M.; B.A., Bklyn. Coll., 1957; LL.B., Bklyn. Law Sch., 1960, J.D., 1964; m. Christina, July 30, 1961; children—Michael, Joy. Consul gen. of Permanent Mission of Cyprus to UN, 1960-75; minister fgn. affairs Cyprus, Nicosia, 1976; high commr. Canberra, 1976-82; permanent rep. of Cyprus to UN, N.Y.C., 1982—. Office: Perm Mission of Cyprus to UN 13 East 40th St New York NY 11016

MOUSSAVI, HUSSEIN (MIR HOSEIN MUSAVI-KHAMENEI), prime minister of Iran; b. Iran, 1942. Ed., Nat. U., Teheran, Iran. Joined Islamic Soc. at Nat. U., since active in Islamic Socs.; imprisoned for opposition to Shah of Iran, 1973; founder, mem. Islamic Republican Party, 1979; chief editor newspaper Islamic Rep. Party, 1979; fgn. minister, Iran, 1981, prime minister, 1981—. Address: Office of the Prime Minister, Teheran Iran *

MOUSSEAU, DORIS NAOMI BARTON, elementary school principal; b. Alpena, Mich., May 6, 1934; d. Merritt Benjamin and Naomi Dora Josephine (Pieper) Barton; m. Bernard Joseph Mousseau, July 31, 1954. AA, Alpena Community Coll., 1954; BS, Wayne State U., 1959; MA, U. Mich., 1961, postgrad., 1972-75. Profl. cert. ednl. adminstr., tchr. Elem. tchr. Clarkston (Mich.) Community Schs., 1954-66; elem. sch. prin. Andersonville Sch., Clarkston, 1966—, Bailey Lake Sch., Clarkston, 1979—. Cons., research com. Youth Assistance Oakland County Ct. Services, 1968—; leader Clarkston PTA, 1967—; chairperson Clarkston Sch. Dist. United Way Campaign, 1985, 86; mem. allocation com. Oakland County United Way, 1987-88. Recipient Outstanding Service award Davisburg Jaycees, Springfield Twp., 1977, Vol. Recognition award Oakland County (Mich.) Cts., 1984. Fellow Assn. Supervision and Curriculum Devel., MACUL (State Assn. Ednl. Computer Users); mem. NEA (del. 1964), Mich. Assn. Elem. and Middle Sch. Prins. (treas., regional del. 1982—, pres.-elect region 7 1988, pres. 1988—), Mich. Edn. Assn. (pres. 1960-66, del. 1966), Clarkston Edn. Assn. (author, editor 1st directory 1963), Women's Bowling Assn., Phi Delta Kappa, Delta Kappa Gamma (pres. 1972-74, past state and nat. chmn., Woman of Distinction 1982). Republican. Club: Spring Meadows Golf. Lodge: Elks. Home: 6825 Rattalee Lake Rd Clarkston MI 48016 Office: Clarkston Community Schs Bailey Lake Sch 8051 Pine Knob Rd Clarkston MI 48016

MOUTON, JOHN OLIVIER, physicist, geophysics and computer design company executive; b. Lafayette, La., Aug. 9, 1944; s. Ralph Canedo and Amy (Roche) M.; B.A. in Math. and Physics with highest honors, UCLA, 1966, M.S. in Physics, 1967, Ph.D. in Math. Physics (NSF trainee), 1972; m. Carole Jean Davis, Mar. 29, 1974; children—Jeremy Alistair, Ian Alexandre, Andre Ryan. Sect. head Missile Systems div. Hughes Aircraft Co., Canoga Park, Calif., 1970-79; asst. research geophysicist Inst. Geophysics and Planetary Physics, UCLA, 1972-75; research specialist Exxon Prodn. Research Co., Houston, 1979-80; exec. v.p. Cyberan Corp., Houston, 1980-82; sr. v.p. Landmark Graphics Corp. Recipient Norman W. Akins award UCLA, 1967. Mem. Soc. Exploration Geophysicists, Phi Beta Kappa, Sigma Pi Sigma, Pi Mu Epsilon. Republican. Contbr. articles on physics and geophysics to profl. jours. Home: 802 Piedmont Dr Sugar Land TX 77478 Office: 333 Cypress Run Suite 100 Houston TX 77094

MOUTSOPOULOS, EVANGHELOS ANASTASIOS, philosopher, educator; b. Athens, Greece, Jan. 25, 1930; s. Anastasios C. and Victoria (Spinoula) M. BA, U. Athens, Greece, 1954; PhD, U. Paris, France, 1958. Assoc. prof. U. Aix-Marseilles, France, 1958-65; prof. U. Thessaloniki, Greece, 1965-69; prof. U. Athens, Greece, 1969—, pres., rector, 1977—. Author 36 vols. on philosophy. Chevalier De La Légion D' Honneur, 1980. Mem. Athens Acad. Scis., Acad. des Sci. Morales et Politiques, Inst. de France, Internat. Inst. de Philosophie, Fedn. Internat. des Soc. de Philosophie, Pres.'s Found. Research and Editions of Neohellenic Philosophy, Internat. Ctr. Platonic Aristotelian Studies, Mediterranean Soc. Philosophy. Greek Orthodox. Home: 40 Hypsilantou St, 11521 Athens Greece

MOWAT, FARLEY MCGILL, writer; b. Belleville, Ont., Can., May 12, 1921; s. Angus McGill and Helen (Thomson) M.; m. Frances Elizabeth Thornhill, Dec. 21, 1947; children: Robert Alexander, David Peter; m. Claire Angel Wheeler, 1965. B.A., U. Toronto, 1949, LL.D., 1973; D.Litt. (hon.), Laurentian U., 1970; LL.D., U. Lethbridge, Alta., 1973, U. P.E.I., 1979; D.Litt., U. Victoria, B.C., 1982, Lakehead U., Thunder Bay, Ont., 1986. Arctic exploration, sci. work 1947-48, writer, 1950—. Author: People of the Deer, 1952, The Regiment, 1955, Lost in the Barrens, 1956, The Dog Who Wouldn't Be, 1957, Coppermine Journey, 1958, The Grey Seas Under, 1958, The Desperate People, 1959, Ordeal By Ice, 1960, Owls in the Family, 1961, The Serpents Coil, 1961, The Black Joke, 1962, Never Cry Wolf, 1963, Westviking, 1965, The Curse of the Viking Grave, 1966, Canada North, 1967, The Polar Passion, 1967, (with John deVisser) This Rock Within the Sea, 1968, The Boat Who Wouldn't Float, 1969, The Siberians, 1971, A Whale for the Killing, 1972, Tundra, 1973, (with David Blackwood) Wake of the Great Sealers, 1973, The Snow Walker, 1975, Canada North Now, 1976, And No Birds Sang, 1979, The World of Farley Mowat, 1980, Sea of Slaughter, 1984, My Discovery of America, 1985, Woman in the Mist, 1987. Served to capt. inf. Canadian Army, 1939-45. Recipient Pres. Medal Univ. Western Ont., 1952, Anisfield Wolfe award, 1954, Gov. Gen.'s medal, 1957, Book of Yr. Medal Can. Library Assn., 1958, Hans Christian Anderson Internat. award, 1958, 65, Can. Women's Clubs award, 1958, Boys Clubs Am. award, 1962, Nat. Assn. Ind. Schs. award, 1963, Can. Centennial medal, 1967, Stephen Leacock medal for humor, 1970, Leacock Medal for Humour, 1970, Vicky Metcalf award, 1970, Mark Twain award, 1971, Book of Yr. award, 1976, Curran award, 1977, Queen Elizabeth II Jubilee medal, 1978, Knight of Mark Twain, 1980, Can. Author's award, 1981, 85; decorated officer Order of Can., 1981; L'Etoile de la Mer (France). Office: care Writers Union of Can, 24 Ryerson Ave, Toronto, ON Canada M4T 2P3

MOWERY, BOB LEE, librarian; b. Charlotte, N.C., June 22, 1920; s. Kerr Lee and Ella (Holman) M.; B.A., Catawba Coll., 1941; B.S. in L.S., U. Chgo., 1947, M.A., 1951; m. Peggy Setzer, Sept. 9, 1945; children—Margaret Mowery Paul, Mary Mowery Stephens, Robert, John. Catalogue librarian Dickinson Coll., 1947-50; librarian, head dept. library sci. Murray State Coll., 1951-53; librarian McNeese State Coll., 1953-58, Stetson U., 1958-64; dir. libraries Wittenberg U., 1964-83, prof., dir. libraries emeritus, 1983—; cons., acting dir. library Davis & Elkins Coll., 1986-87; founder, pres. Thoms Lit. Press. Chmn. com. parish edn. Fla. synod Lutheran Ch. Am., 1962-64, chmn. com. local arrangements constituting conv., 1962; mem. hist. work com. N.C. Synod., Luth. Ch. Am., 1983-87; chmn. com. library resources Regional Council Internat. Edn.; del. Seminar Current Trends Edn., Yugoslavia, Aug. 1966. Trustee DeLand (Fla.) Pub. Library, Newberry Coll., 1962-64, Springfield Art Center, 1976-81; bd. dirs., treas. Ohio Coll. Library Ctr., 1969-74; trustee Ohionet, 1978-83, trustee Friends of the Henderson County Pub. Library, pres., 1984-86; bd. dirs. Friends of N.C. Pub. Libraries, 1987—, v.p., pres. elect 1988-89. Served with AUS, 1942-46; maj., ret. Nat. Def. Fgn. Lang. fellow, 1967. Fellow Am. Council Learned Socs.; mem. Am., N.C. Library Assn., Bibliog. Soc., Bibliog. Soc. Am., Arthur Machen Soc. (Eng.) (life mem., pres. 1965-83), Assn. Coll. and Research Libraries (pres. Tri-state chpt. 1974-75), Acad. Library Assn. Ohio (pres. 1975-76). Democrat. Lutheran. Club: Univ. (Springfield). Lodge: Rotary (bd. dirs. Deland club 1961-63). Contbr. to profl. jours., encys.; editor La. Library Bull., 1955-58. Address: Box 218 Saluda NC 28773

MOWERY, JOHN HENRY, retired psychologist; b. Cin., Jan. 22, 1920; s. John Henry and Minna Henrietta (Hageman) M.; BA, Bowling Green State U., 1950; MA, Kent State U., 1951; m. Carolyn Rubel, June 4, 1960. Clin. psychologist Ind. Mental Health Div., Indpls., 1952; personnel psychologist Aero Mayflower Transit Co., Indpls., 1952-55; personnel adminstr. Am. Legion Nat. Hdqrs., Indpls., 1955-56; psychologist Am. Legion State Hdqrs., Indpls., 1956; asst. personnel dir. Hook Drugs Inc., Indpls., 1956-60; staff psychologist Psychol. Service Center, Toronto, Ont., Can., 1960-62; pvt. practice clin. psychologist, Mpls., 1963-87 ; cons. psychologist Lutheran Social Service Minn., 1970-85 . Served with USAAF, 1942-46. Mem. Am. Psychol. Assn. (life), Minn. Psychol. Assn (life), Psi Chi, Theta Chi. Methodist. Clubs: Mason, Statesman's, Regency. Home: 3101 E Calhoun Pkwy Minneapolis MN 55408

MOWINCKEL, JOHN WALLENDAHL, retired foreign service officer, public relations consultant; b. Genoa, Italy, July 7, 1920 (parents U.S. citizens); s. John A. and Cathe (Wallendahl) M.; B.A., Princeton U., 1943; m. Letizia Crostarosa, Oct. 18, 1947; 1 son, John C. Regional corr. U.S. News and World Report mag., Rome, 1946-48, Paris, 1948-49; editorial specialist ECA, Rome, 1950-53; info. officer USIA, Rome, 1953, program officer European area, Washington, 1954-57, dep. public affairs officer, Paris, 1957-61, public affairs officer, 1961-64; public affairs officer, Kinshasa, Zaire, 1964-67; minister-counselor public affairs, Rio de Janeiro, 1967-71; minister, dep. chief mission Am. embassy, Vienna, Austria, 1971-75; cons. public relations, Paris, 1975-83; dir. Ingram Internat., Monaco, 1983—. Served from 2d lt. to 1st lt., USMCR, 1943-46; OSS, Europe. Decorated Silver Star, Bronze Star; Croix de Guerre. Clubs: Racquet and Tennis (N.Y.C.), Travellers (Paris), Yacht (Monte Carlo). Address: 11 Ave Princesse Grace, MC98000 Monte Carlo Monaco

MOXHAM, PETER DERRICK, marketing executive; b. Chingford, Essex, Eng., Oct. 29, 1936; s. Arthur Edward and Lillian (Jones) M.; m. Pamela Olive Coulter, Feb. 14, 1959; children: Kim, Alan, Roger. Student pub. schs. Ops. dir. Thurston Aviation Ltd., Stansted, Eng., 1969-77; mktg. exec. CSE Aviation Ltd., Oxford, Eng., 1978—; chief exec. Air Taxi Ops. Assn., London, 1973-78, vice chmn., 1979—; mem. Brit. Civil Aviation Standing Conf., 1978—. Home: 9 Phillips Rd, Broadway, Worcestershire WR12 7EY, England Office: CSE Aviation Ltd, Oxford Airport, Kidlington, Oxford OX5 1RA, England

MOYA, (JOHN) HIDALGO, architect; b. Los Gatos, Calif., May 5, 1920; s. Hidalgo and Lilian (Chattaway) Moya; m. Jeniffer Innes Mary Hall, 1947; one son, two daus. Student, Royal W. of Eng. Coll. Art and Archtl. Assn. Sch. Architecture. Pvt. practice architect, 1946-76; ptnr. firm Powell, Moya and Ptnrs., London, 1976—. Major works include: Churchill Gardens flats, Westminster, 1948-62; Skylor, Festival of Britain, 1951; 1951; Mayfield Sch. Putney, 1955; Brasenose Coll. and Corpus Christi Coll., Oxford extensions, 1961; Chichester Festival Theatre, 1962; Plumstead Manor Sch., Woolwich, 1970; Brit. Pavilion Expo 70, Osaka, Japan, Mus. of London, 1977. Decorated comdr. Order Brit. Empire. Fellow Royal Inst. Brit. Architects (Winning Design award 1946, 1950, Bronze medal 1950, 58, 61, Festival of Britain award 1951, Mohlg Good Design in Housing award 1953, 54, Civic Trust awards 1961, Archtl. Design Project award 1965, Archtl. award 1967, Royal Gold medal 1974. *

MOYA VALGAÑON, JOSÉ GABRIEL, museum curator; b. Sajazarra, Spain, Nov. 3, 1939; s. Augusto Moya de Mena and Maria Luisa Valgañon Martinez de Salinas ; m. Maréa Concepción Yanguela; children: Angel, José Gabriel, Elena. Licenciado, U. Zaragoza, Spain, 1963, MD, 1978. Prof. art history U. Zaragoza, 1963-69; curator Mus. of Logroño, Spain, 1969-71, Sevilla (Spain) Mus. Fine Arts, 1971-73, Sorolla Mus., Madrid, 1973-74, Prado Mus., Madrid, 1974-81, Ministerio Cultura, Madrid, 1981-83; curator Mus. Applied Arts, Madrid, 1983—, also bd. dirs.; dir. artistic info. Direccion General de Bellas Artes, Madrid, 1973-79. Author: Inventario Artístico, 3 vols., 1976, Arquitectura del Siglo 17, 2 vols., 1981, Documentos Santo Dominico, 1986; contbr. articles to profl. jours. Roman Catholic. Office: Museo Nat de Artes Decorativas, Calle Montalban 12, 28014 Madrid Spain

MOYES, THERESA, clinical psychologist; b. Birkenhead, Merseyside, Eng., May 13, 1958; d. Gilbert and Eileen Lucy (Williams) M. BA with honors, U. Keele, Eng., 1981, postgrad. cert. in edn., 1982; M in Clin. Psychology, Liverpool (Eng.) U., 1986. Research psychologist St. Andrews Hosp., Northampton, Eng., 1982-83, probationer clin. psychologist, 1983-84; probationer clin. psychologist Merseyside Regional Health Authority, 1984-86; clin. psychologist community, child and adolescent services Nat. Health Service, Northumberland, Eng., 1986-87; sr. clin. psychologist community mental health team Nat. Health Service, Southport and Formby, Eng., 1987—. Mem. Brit. Psychol. Soc., Brit. Assn. Behavioral Psychotherapy, Psychology and Psychotherapy Assn., Assn. Child Psychologists and Psychiatrists. Office: Hesketh Park Hosp, Dept Clin Psychology, 51-51 Albert Rd, Southport, Merseyside PR9 0LT, England

MOYLAN, JAMES JOSEPH, lawyer; b. Forest Hills, N.Y., Feb. 3, 1948; s. James Gerard and Jessie Cora (Geary) M.; m. Barbara Chesrow, Aug. 29, 1970; children—James C., Joseph O., Alicia G. B.S.B.A., U. Denver, 1969, J.D., 1971. Bar: Colo. 1972, D.C. 1972, Ill. 1975, U.S. Dist. Ct. Colo. 1972, U.S. Supreme Ct. 1975. Trial atty. SEC, Washington, 1972-75; assoc. gen. counsel Chgo. Bd. Options Exchange, Ill., 1975-77; assoc. Abramson & Fox, Chgo., 1977-80; ptnr. Bowen, Knepper & Moylan Ltd., Chgo., 1980-82; ptnr. Moylan & Early, Ltd., Chgo., 1983-84; prin. James J. Moylan and Assocs., Ltd., Chgo., 1984—; adj. prof. law IIT Chgo. Kent Coll. Law, 1976—; former pub. dir. MidAm. Commodity Exchange div. Chgo. Bd. Trade, Chgo. Contbr. articles to profl. jours. Precinct capt. Ann M. Stepan Campaign, Chgo., 1983. Mem. Ill. State Bar Assn. (sect. council mem.), Chgo. Bar Assn., D.C. Bar Assn., ABA (sect. corp., banking and bus. law, sect. litigation). Republican. Roman Catholic. Club: Chgo. Athletic Assn.

MOYNIHAN, DANIEL PATRICK, U.S. senator, educator; b. Tulsa, Mar. 16, 1927; s. John Henry and Margaret Ann (Phipps) M.; m. Elizabeth Therese Brennan, May 29, 1955; children: Timothy Patrick, Maura Russell, John McCloskey. Student, CCNY, 1943; B.A. cum laude, Tufts U., 1948; M.A., Fletcher Sch. Law and Diplomacy, 1949, Ph.D., 1961, LL.D. (hon.), 1968; Fulbright fellow, London (Eng.) Sch. Econs. and Polit. Sci., 1950-51; A.M. (hon.), Harvard U., 1966; LL.D. (hon.), La Salle Coll., 1966, Seton Hall Coll., 1966, Catholic U. Am., 1968, Ill. Inst. Tech., 1968, New Sch. Social Research, 1968, Duquesne U., 1968, St. Louis U., 1968, U. Calif., 1969, U. Notre Dame, 1969, Fordham U., 1970, St. Bonaventure U., 1972, U. Ind., 1975, St. Anselm's Coll., 1976, Boston Coll., 1976, Ohio State U., 1976, Adelphi U., 1976, Hebrew U., 1976; D.Pub. Adminstrn. (hon.), Providence Coll., 1967; L.H.D. (hon.), U. Akron, 1967, Hamilton Coll., 1968; D.S.Sc. (hon.), Villanova U., 1968; D.H. (hon.), Bridgewater State Coll., 1972; D.Sc. (hon.), Mich. Tech. U., 1972; D.Sc. (hon.) numerous others. With Internat. Rescue Com., 1954; successively asst. to sec., asst. sec., acting sec. to gov. State of N.Y., 1955-58; mem. N.Y. State Tenure Commn., 1959-60; dir. N.Y. State Govt. Research Project, Syracuse U., 1959-61; spl. asst. to sec. labor 1961-62, exec. asst. to sec., 1962-63, asst. sec. labor, 1963-65; dir. Joint Center for Urban Studies, Mass. Inst. Tech. and Harvard, 1966-69; prof. edn. and urban politics Kennedy Sch. Govt., Harvard, 1966-73, sr. mem., 1966—, prof. govt., 1973—; asst. for urban affairs to Pres. U.S. 1969-70; counsellor to Pres. U.S., mem. Cabinet, 1969-70, cons. to Pres. U.S., 1971-73; mem. U.S. del. 26th Gen. Assembly, UN, 1971, Pres.'s Sci. Adv. Com., 1971-73; ambassador to India New Delhi, 1973-75; U.S. permanent rep. to UN, N.Y.C., 1975-76; U.S. senator from N.Y. 1977—; Vice chmn. Pres.'s Temp. Commn. on Pennsylvania Avenue, 1964-73; chmn. adv. com. traffic safety dept. HEW; fellow Center Advanced Studies, Wesleyan U., 1965-66; hon. fellow London Sch. Econs. and Polit. Sci., 1970—; Sec. pub. affairs com. N.Y. State Democratic Com., 1958-60; del. Dem. Nat. Conv., 1960, 76. Author: Maximum Feasible Misunderstanding, 1969, The Politics of a Guaranteed Income, 1973, Coping: On the Practice of Government, 1974, A Dangerous Place, 1978, Counting Our Blessings, 1980, Loyalties, 1984, Family and Nation, 1986; co-author: Beyond the Melting Pot, 1963 (Anisfield award 1963); Editor: The Defenses of Freedom, 1966, On Understanding Poverty, 1969, Toward a National Urban Policy, 1970; co-editor: On Equality of Educational Opportunity, 1972, Ethnicity: Theory and Experience, 1975; Editorial bd.: Pub. Interest; Contbr. articles to profl. publs. Vice chmn. Woodrow Wilson Internat. Center for Scholars, 1971—; chmn. bd. trustees Joseph H. Hirshhorn Mus. and Sculpture Garden, 1971-85. Served with USN, 1944-47. Recipient Centennial medal Syracuse U., 1969. Mem. Am. Philos. Soc., Nat. Acad. Pub. Adminstrn., AAAS (vice chmn. 1971, dir. 1972-73), Am. Acad. Arts and Scis. (chmn. seminar on poverty). Clubs: Century, Harvard (N.Y.C.). Address: 464 Russell Senate Bldg Washington DC 20510 *

MOZER, DORIS ANN, writer; b. July 10, 1929; d. Charles Ross and Mary Margaret (Redmiles) Werner; B.A., N.Mex. State U., 1963, M.A. in English, 1970; postgrad. in English, U. Md., 1982; div.; children—Stephen, Judith, Mary Catherine, Laura, John. Grad. asst. N.Mex. State U., 1963-65, instr., 1969-75; free-lance editor, 1969—; editor Sibyl-Child, women's arts and cultural jour., 1976—; grad. asst. U. Md., College Park, 1976-78, dir. Writing Center, 1978-80, acad. adviser, internship coordinator, 1980-82; tech. writer Environ. Satellite Data, Inc., Suitland, Md., 1982-84, RCA, Moorestown, N.J., 1984—. Vice pres., publicity chmn. Las Cruces (N.Mex.) Children's Theatre, 1968; pres., publicity chmn. Las Cruces Theater Guild, 1969. Folger Shakespearean Inst. fellow, 1979. Mem. Phi Kappa Phi. Democrat. Unitarian. Author: (poetry) The Quickest Promise Home. Home: 102 Fourth Ave 2R Mount Ephraim NJ 08059 Office: RCA Advanced Tech Labs Moorestown NJ 08057

MOZO, WILLIAM BRANTLY, JR., dentist; b. Cheyenne, Wyo., Jan. 9, 1950; s. William Brantly and Naomi Ruth (Berry) M.; D.D.S., U. Mo., 1975; m. Elizabeth Faria, June 27, 1976; children—Adam, Jason, Rebecca. Resident, Englewood (N.J.) Hosp., 1975-76; pvt. practice dentistry, South Plainfield, N.J., 1976—; mem. staff Muhlenberg Hosp., Rahway Hosp.; pres. Mozo Enterprises; instr. oral pathology Middlesex County Coll., 1978. Chmn. dental div. United Way, 1977-81. Mem. Am., N.J., Central dental socs., Acad. Gen. Dentistry, Warren Jaycees. Methodist. Club: South Plainfield Rotary. Home: 9 Claire Dr Warren NJ 07060 Office: 1550 Park Ave S Plainfield NJ 07080

MPELKAS, CHRISTOS CHARLES, plant physiologist; b. Lynn, Mass., Apr. 16, 1920; s. Charles and Katherine (Thomas) M.; m. Angela Vlahakis, June 8, 1947; children—Charles, John, William, Katherine. A.S., Essex A. and T. Inst., Mass., 1942; B.S., U. Mass., 1949; M.S., U. Conn., 1950. Research produce mgr. Star Supermarkets, Newtonville, Mass., 1950-52; research technician Mass. Agrl. Expt. Sta., Waltham, 1952-53; head vegetable crops dept. Essex A. and T. Inst., Hathorne, Mass., 1953-61; with Sylvania Lighting Products, Danvers, Mass., 1961-71, sr. applications engr., 1971-77; resource devel. specialist U. Mass., Amherst, 1971-77; plant physiologist, mgr. Hort. Lighting Tech. div. GTE Sylvania, 1977—; with Lynn Conservations Service, 1974—. Served with USAF, 1943-46. Mem. AAAS (biol. scis. sect.), Am. Soc. Agrl. Engrs., Am. Inst. Biol. Scis., Am. Soc. Plant Physiologists, Am. Soc. Photobiologists, Am. Soc. Hort. Sci., Bot. Soc. Am., Illuminating Engring. Soc. Nat. Elec. Mfrs. Assn. (photobiology com.), Assn. U.S. Army. Greek Orthodox. Clubs: Nahant Lions; Amity Masons (Danvers, Mass.); Aleppo Shriner. Home: 12 Mansfield St Lynn MA 01904 Office: 100 Endicott St Danvers MA 01923

MROCZEK, WILLIAM JOSEPH, research physician; b. N.Y.C., Aug. 9, 1940; s. William and Helena (Federowicz) M.; B.A., Seton Hall U., 1962; M.D., N.J. Coll. Medicine, 1966; m. Christine Landegger, Apr. 7, 1979; children: Ashley Elizabeth, Natasha Elena, Phoebe Victoria, Matthew Alexander; children by previous marriage—Michelle Anne, Melissa Lynn. Intern, St. Michael Hosp., Newark, 1966-67; resident Georgetown U. med. div. D.C. Gen. Hosp., 1967-69; fellow in cardiovascular disease Georgetown U. Sch. Medicine, 1969-70, asst. prof. medicine, 1972-77; chief dept. hosp. clinics Ft. Campbell, Ky., 1970-72; assoc. prof. medicine Howard U., Washington, 1977-82; dir. hypertension and hemodynamics lab. D.C. Gen. Hosp., 1972-82. Pres. No. Va. chpt. Am. Heart Assn., 1983-84; dir. Cardiovascular Ctr. No. Va., 1983—; mem. exec. com. Jefferson Hosp., Alexandria, Va. Served to maj. U.S. Army, 1970-72. Diplomate Am. Bd. Internal Medicine. Fellow Am. Coll. Cardiology, Am. Coll. Clin. Pharmacology, Am. Coll. Angiology, Am. Coll. Geriatrics, Am. Coll. Clin. Pharmacology (bd. regents); mem. Internat. Soc. Hypertension, Am. Soc. Hypertension, Am. Fedn. Clin. Research, Am. Soc. Nephrology, Am. Soc. Clin. Pharmacology and Therapeutics, Nat. Kidney Found., N.Y. Acad. Scis., AMA. Contbr. numerous articles to med. jours. Office: 6043-6045 Arlington Blvd Falls Church VA 22044

MSOSA, ANDERSON JOSUFAT, accountant; b. Malawi, Oct. 31, 1950; s. Josufat David and Falesi (Chilembwe) M.; m. Anastasia Maliwichi, Oct. 25, 1975; children: Angela, Alan, Yamiko, Trinitas, Lewis, Vanessa. BS, Chancellor Coll., Zomba, Malawi, 1975; diploma in acctg., Southampton (Eng.) Coll. Tech., 1978, Slough Coll., Buckinghamshire, Eng., 1980. Trainee acctg. Portland Cement Co., Blantyre, Malawi, 1975-77; systems acct. Air Malawi Ltd., Blantyre, 1977-79, expenditure acct., 1979-84; dep. group acct. Mandala Ltd. div. African Lakes Corp., Blantyre, 1984—. Mem. Ch. of Cen. Africa. Office: Mandala Ltd, PO Box 49, Blantyre Malawi

MSWATI, HIS MAJESTY III, King of Swaziland; (born Makhoseitive); b. 1968; s. King Sobhuza II and Ntombi. Educated in Eng. King of Swaziland, 1986—. Office: Ngwenyama/Lozi-Thentiezl, Mbabane Swaziland other: Univ of Swaziland, Private Bag 4, Kwaluseni Swaziland *

MTEWA, MEKKI, foundation adminstrator; b. Sungo, Mangochi, Malawi, Apr. 13, 1946. BA, Chapman Coll., 1974; MA in Polit. Sci., Calif. State U., Fullerton, 1975; postgrad., Miami U., Oxford, Ohio, 1975-76; diploma in exec. law and leadership studies, LaSalle Extension U., Chgo., 1977; PhD in Pub. Adminstrn. and Pub. Policy, Claremont Grad. Sch., 1979; postdoctoral in legal studies, Vrije U., Brussels, 1985-86. Regional adminstrv. sec. Agrl. Devel. and Mktg. Corp., Limbe, Malawi, 1964-66; adminstrv. sec. United Transport (Malawi) Ltd., Blantyre, 1966-67; legal asst. Lilley, Wills & Co., Limbe, 1968-70; exec. dir., founder Assn. for Advancement Policy, Research and Devel. in the Third World, 1981—; exec. v.p., dep. dir. POS Inst., Washington, 1982—; chmn., chief exec. officer Internat. Devel. Found. Inc., 1984—; chmn. Malawi Inst. Internat. Affairs, 1987—; research asst. Calif. State U., Fullerton, 1974-75, adj. prof., spring 1978-79; research asst. Polit. Sci. Dept. Miami U., Oxford, Ohio, 1975-76; adj. asst. prof. polit. sci. and mgmt. U. D.C., 1982-85; asst. prof. polit. sci. Howard U., Washington, 1979-85; cons. in field; lectr. in field. Author: Public Policy and Development Politics: The Politics of Technical Expertise in Africa, 1980, The Consultant Connexion: Evaluation of the Federal Consulting Service, 1981, Malawi Democratic Theory and Public Policy: A Preface, 1986; editor: Science Technology and Development: Options and Policies, 1982, Perspectives in International Development, 1986, Contemporary Issues in African Adminstration and Development Politics, 1987, International Development and Alternative Futures: The Coming Challenges, 1988; contbr. articles to profl. jours., chpts. to books; mem. adv. bd. CHANGE: The Internat. Tech. newspaper; guest editor Jour. Ea. African Research and Devel.; various TV and radio appearances; subject of articles. Dep. br. sec. Malawi Congress party, 1965-66; com. chair S.W. Scholarship Fund, S.S. Neighborhood Assembly, Washington; chair election com. Rosemary Coop. Housing project. Grantee Sci. and Tech. in So. Africa Devel. Coordination Conf., 1982, Peace Corps Coll. project, 1982; fellow Midwestern U. Consortium, Miami U., Alpha Assn. Phi Beta Kappa Alumni in So. Calif.; recipient Seminar award Fgn. Student Council. Mem. Internat. Services Assn. (bd. dirs.), Sci. Soc. Chile (bd. dirs.), Phi Sigma Alpha. Office: Internat Devel Found PO Box 70257 Washington DC 20024-1534

MUBARAK, MUHAMMAD HOSNI, president of Egypt; b. Karf al-Musailha, Minufiya, Egypt, May 4, 1928; grad. Mil. Acad. Egypt, 1949, Air Acad. Egypt, 1950; m. Susan Sabet; 2 sons. Head mil. del. to USSR, 1964-65; sta. comdr. Egyptian Air Force, Cairo West Airfield, 1966, chief staff, 1969-72, air vice marshal, 1969-74, air marshal, from 1974, commdr., 1972-75; appointed dep. minister war Govt. of Egypt, 1972, maj. gen., 1973-75, v.p., 1975-81, pres., 1981—, dir. gen. Egyptian Arms Procurement Agy., 1975—. Vice chmn. Nat. Democratic Party, from 1980, sec. gen., 1980-82, chmn., 1982—. Mem. Higher Council Nuclear Energy. Office: Office of Pres, Cairo Arab Republic of Egypt *

MUBBASHAR, MALIK HUSSAIN, psychiatrist, educator; b. Lahore, Punjab, Pakistan, Aug. 1, 1945; s. Miraj-ud-din and Shahzadi (Anwar) Malik; m. Yasmin Ihsan Mubbashar, Dec. 30, 1973; children: Sabooh, Aamna, Zainab, Saima, Fatima, Maryam, Imtiaz. MBBS, King Edward Med. Coll., Lahore, 1968; D of Psychiat. Medicine, Guy's Hosp. Med. Sch., London, 1971. Resident surgeon Malik Jalal Ud Din WAQF Hosp., Lahore, 1968, Mayo Hosp., Lahore, 1968-69; sr. house officer, registrar Kingston Gen. Hosp., London, 1969-70; Brit. council fellow Royal Postgrad. Med. Sch., London, 1970; registrar psychiatry Guy's Hosp. Med. Sch., 1971-72; Smith and Nephew fellow Inst. Neurology, London, 1973; cons. psychiatrist Gen. Govt. Hosp., Rawalpindi, Pakistan, 1974-77; assoc. prof. psychiatry Rawalpindi Med. Coll., 1977-82, prof., 1982—; head dept. psychol. medicine Rawalpindi Gen. Hosp., 1982—; vis. prof. St. John's U., Nfld., Can., 1973, Saskatoon U., Can., 1973; hon. prof. psychiatry and nervous system Armed Forces Med. Coll., Rawalpindi, 1974—; nat. coordinator program for mental health WHO, Pakistan, 1977—, fed. coordinator program for drug abuse control, 1975-80, mem. WHO adv. panel on mental health, dir. Collaborating Ctr. for Mental Health Research and Tng., 1987—, WHO Collaborating Ctr.; chmn. sci. session Pan-Pacific Conf. on Alcohol and Drug Abuse, Canberra, Australia, 1980; sec. com. on mental health and legislation Govt. of Pakistan. Author: NAFSIATI-WA-ZEHNI IMRAZ, 1981, A Text Book of Psychiatry, 1982, Liaison Psychiatry, 1983, Drug Dependence, 1984, Diagnosis and Therapy in Psychogeriatrics, 1985, A Case for the Mentally Ill, 1985, Community Mental Health, 1986; also articles; editor: Rawal Med. Jour., Rawalpindi. Founder Patern Soc. for Rehab. Mentally Ill, Rawalpindi, 1975—; mem. gen. body Chambelli Inst. for Mentally Retarded, Rawalpindi, 1976—; advisor Forces Career Inst., Rawalpindi, 1977—; innovator community mental health programs. Serving as hon. lt. col. Pakistan Med. Service, 1986—. Recipient Civil award of Pakistan, 1986. Fellow Royal Soc. Medicine (hon.), Am. Psychiat. Assn. (corr.), RCP, Royal Coll. Psychiatrists; mem. Internat. Brain Research Orgn., Internat. Council for Alcohol and Addictions, N.Y. Acad. Scis., Internat. Assn. Traffic Medicine, Brit. Assn. Psycho-Pharmacology. Muslim. Club: Islamabad (Pakistan). Home: H #11 St #2, F 8/3 Islamabad Pakistan Office: Rawalpindi Gen Hosp, WHO Collaborating Ctr, Dept Psychiatry, Rawalpindi Pakistan

MUCHNICK, RICHARD STUART, ophthalmologist; b. Bklyn., June 21, 1942; s. Max and Rae (Kozinsky) M.; BA with honors, Cornell U., 1963, MD, 1967; m. Felice Dee Greenberg, Oct. 29, 1978; 1 child, Amanda Michelle. Intern in medicine N.Y. Hosp., N.Y.C., 1967-68, now assoc. attending ophthalmologist, chief Pediatric Ophthalmology Clinic; resident in ophthalmology, 1970-73; practice medicine, specializing in ophthalmology, notably strabismus and ophthalmic plastic surgery N.Y.C., 1974—; attending surgeon, chief Ocular Motility Clinic, Manhattan Eye, Ear and Throat Hosp., N.Y.C.; clin. assoc. prof. ophthalmology Cornell U., N.Y.C., 1984—. Served with USPHS, 1968-70. Recipient Coryell Prize Surgery Cornell U. Med. Coll., 1967. Diplomate Am. Bd. Ophthalmology, Nat. Bd. Med. Examiners. Fellow A.C.S., Am. Acad. Ophthalmology; mem. Am. Soc. Ophthalmic Plastic and Reconstructive Surgery, Am. Assn. Pediatric Ophthalmology and Strabismus, Internat. Strabismological Assn., N.Y. Soc. Clin. Ophthalmology, AMA, N.Y. Acad. Medicine, Manhattan Ophthal. Soc., N.Y. Soc. Pediatric Ophthalmology and Strabismus, Alpha Omega Alpha, Alpha Epsilon Delta. Clubs: Lotos, 7th Regt. Tennis. Clin. researcher strabismus, ophthalmic plastic surgery, 1973—. Office: 69 E 71st St New York NY 10021

MUCKLE, DAVID SUTHERLAND, surgeon, educator; b. Weardale, Durham, Eng., Aug. 30, 1939; s. John L. and Ruth J. (Sutherland) M.; m. Christine Haymonds; children: Carolyn Jane, Deborah Christine. B.Med., U. Durham, 1963, B.Surgery, 1963, M.D., 1981, M.Surgery, 1971. Surgeon, Oxford, 1970-77, Middlesbrough Gen. Hosp., Cleveland, 1977—; cons. orthopedic surgeon, 1977—; med. advisor Fédération Internationale de Football Assn., Switzerland, 1977—; surgeon, mem. med. com. Football Assn., 1983—; surgeon Nuffield Hsp., Cleveland, 1981—. Author: Femoral Neck Fracture, 1977; Injuries in Sport, 1982; An Outline of Fractures, 1985; An Outline of Orthopaedic Practice, 1986. Fellow Brit. Orthopedic Assn., Brit. Orthopedic Research Soc. (com. mem. 1979), Royal Coll. Surgeons. Avocations: writing, natural history, poetry, all sports. Home: Redcroft 72 The Grove, Marton Middlesbrough TS7 8AJ, England Office: Middlesbrough Gen Hosp, Ward 14, Middlesbrough TS5 5AZ, England

MUDD, JOHN PHILIP, lawyer, real estate executive; b. Washington, Aug. 22, 1932; s. Thomas Paul and Frances Mary (Finotti) M.; m. Barbara Eve Sweeney, Aug. 10, 1957; children: Laura, Ellen, Philip, Clare, David. B.S.S., Georgetown U., 1954; J.D., Georgetown Law Center, 1956. Bar: Md. bar 1956, D.C. bar 1963, Fla. bar 1964, Calif. bar 1973. Individual practice law Upper Marlboro, Md., 1956-66; v.p., sec., corporate atty. Deltona Corp., Miami, Fla., 1966-72; sec. Nat. Community Builders, San Diego, 1972-73; gen. counsel Continental Advisers (adviser to Continental Mortgage Investors), 1973-75, sr. v.p., gen. counsel, 1975-80; sr. v.p., corp. atty. Am. Hosp. Mgmt. Corp., Miami, 1980—; pres. Tropic Devel. Corp., 1979—. Former mem. Land Devel. Adv. Com. N.Y. State; chmn student interview com. Georgetown U.; bd. dirs. Lasalle High Sch., Miami; bd. dirs., corporate counsel Com. of Dade County, Fla. Mem. ABA, Fla. Bar Assn., Calif. Bar Assn., Md. Bar Assn, D.C. Bar Assn., Fla. State Bar (exec. com. of corp. counsel com. 1978—). Democrat. Roman Catholic. Home: 1211 Hardee Rd Coral Gables FL 33146 Office: 9405 NW 41st St Miami FL 33178

MUDHOLKAR, GOVIND SHRIKRISHNA, statistician, educator; b. Aurangabad, India, Jan. 5, 1934; s. Shrikrishna Shrinivas and Saraswati (Panse) M.; m. Charlotte Anne Poythress, Dec. 28, 1968; children: Ashok G., Anil G. B.Sc. with honors, U. Poona, India, 1956, M.Sc., 1957; Ph.D., U. N.C., 1963. Prof. U. Poona, 1957-60; mem. faculty dept. stats. and biostats. U. Rochester, N.Y., 1963—; prof. U. Rochester, 1972—; vis. prof. Stanford U., Cath. U. Louvain (Belgium). Contbr. articles to profl. jours. Recipient numerous grants NSF, numerous grants NIH. Fellow Inst. Math. Stats.; mem. Am. Statis. Assn., Biometric Soc. Hindu. Home: 97 Woodland Rd Pittsford NY 14534 Office: U Rochester Dept Statistics Rochester NY 14627

MUDOOLA, DAN MUGUWA, political scientist, researcher; b. Iganga, Uganda, May 12, 1942; s. Yowasi Muguwa and Evereni (Bakyekoose) M.; m. Irene Nabuguzi, Sept. 9, 1977; children: Daniel Gumula, Susan Wandawa, Yowasi Muguwa, Eric Mutaisa. BA, U. East Africa, Uganda, 1967; MA in Econs., U. Manchester, Eng., 1968; PhD, Makerere U., Uganda, 1974. Lectr. in Polit. Sci. Makerere U., Kampala, Uganda, 1969-77, assoc. prof., 1984—; assoc. prof. Dar-es-Salaam U., Tanzania, 1977-83; exec. dir. Makerere Inst. Social Research, Kampala, 1984—; cons. World Bank, 1984-86. Editor Mawazo Jour., 1985; contbr. chpts. to several books. Fulbright scholar UCLA African Studies Center, 1983-84; Commonwealth traveling fellow, 1986. Mem. African Acad. Scis., Orgn. for Social Scis. Research in Eastern Africa. Home and Office: PO Box 16022, Kampala Uganda

MUECKE, WALTER GERHARD, marketing professional; b. Hofheim, Bavaria, Fed. Republic of Germany, May 24, 1946; s. Erwin Ernst and Edith (Adler) M.; m. AnneMarie Weinberg, Nov. 22, 1968; children: Thomas, Ruediger, Claudia. MS, U. Furtwangen (Fed. Republic Germany), 1976; BA, U. Konstanz (Fed. Republic Germany), 1977. System analyst Dept. Research and Tech., Stuttgart, Fed. Republic Germany, 1974-76; lectr. ELEKLUFT/AEG, Bonn, Fed. Republic Germany, 1977-78; project mgr. EDP NCR Corp., Augsburg, Fed. Republic Germany, 1978-80, software cons., 1980-82, gen. retail system mgr., 1982-83, product mktg. mgr., 1984—; system-service mgr. Kleindienst, Augsburg, Fed. Republic Germany, 1983-84. Contbr. articles to profl. jours. Parent rep. high sch., Mering, Fed. Rep. Germany, 1983. Served with Fed. Republic Germany Air Force, 1966-73. Mem. Augsburg C. of C. (lectr. 1987—). Clubs: Capital (Hamburg), Mktg. (Augsburg). Home: Garmischer Allee 38, D 8901 Kissing Federal Republic of Germany Office: NCR Gmbh, Ulmer Strasse 160, D8900 Augsburg Federal Republic of Germany

MUEHLBERG, NANCY RUTH, psychologist; b. Flint, Mich., Sept. 30, 1943; d. John Robert and Harriet Winifred (Quick) Muehlberg; B.A., State U. N.Y. at Buffalo, 1967, M.A., 1969, Ph.D., 1971; m. Edmund J. Sullivan, 1975. Psychologist child devel. program Children's Hosp., Buffalo, 1968-73, psychologist Speech and and Hearing Clinic, 1972—, psychologist Child Psychiatry Clinic, 1973—; psychologist Buffalo Hearing and Speech Center,

1972-73, cons., 1973—. Mem. Am. Psychol. Assn. Home: 32 Grant Rd Buffalo NY 14226 Office: 32 Grant Rd Snyder NY 14226

MUEHLENTHAL, CLARICE KELMAN, travel consultant; b. Cleve., Nov. 16, 1924; d. William and Ann (Teitel) Kelman; m. Arnold G. Muehlenthal, Dec. 17, 1950 (dec. Sept. 1980); children—Shelley Muehlenthal Mitchell, David M. Cert., Draughons Bus. Coll., 1945; cert. travel counselor, Inst. Cert. Travel Agts., 1980. Owner, Cee-Jay Bus. Service, Riverhead, N.Y., 1952-55; travel cons. Journey House Travel, Dallas, 1967-73; ptnr. Alpha Travel, Dallas, 1973-76; owner World Wide Travel Service, Dallas, 1976—. Round Table chmn. Dallas North dist. Boy Scouts Am., 1971-73; charter mem. Tex. Cultural Alliance, 1975—; courier Hands Around the World, Tex., 1975—. Recipient Dist. Award of Merit, Boy Scouts Am., Circle Ten, Dallas, 1973; Internat. Fellowship, Tex. Cultural Alliance, Dallas, 1982; named Ambassador of Goodwill, State Tex., 1975. Mem. Am. Soc. Travel Agts., The 3020 Soc. (sec.-treas. 1982—), Inst. Cert. Travel Agts. (study group leader 1983, life 1982), Assn. Retail Travel Agts., Travel Agy. Council N. Tex. (sec. 1981-83), Phi Sigma Alpha. Address: PO Box 59327 Dallas TX 75229 Office: World Wide Travel Service 2860 Walnut Hill Ln Suite 106 PO Box 52327 Dallas TX 75229

MUELLER, CHARLES BARBER, surgeon, educator; b. Carlinville, Ill., Jan. 22, 1917; s. Gustav Henry and Myrtle May (Barber) M.; m. Jean Mahaffey, Sept. 7, 1940; children: Frances Ann, John Barber, Richard Carl, William Gustav. A.B., U. Ill., 1938; M.D., Washington U., St. Louis, 1942; LHD (honoris causa), Blackburn Coll., 1987. Intern, then resident in surgery Barnes Hosp., St. Louis, 1942-43, 46-51; asst. prof. Washington U. Med. Sch., 1951-56; prof. surgery, chmn. dept. State U. N.Y. Med. Sch., Syracuse, 1956-67; prof. surgery McMaster U. Med. Sch., Hamilton, Ont., Can., 1967—; chmn. dept. McMaster U. Med. Sch., 1967-72. Contbr. articles to med. jours. Served with USNR, 1943-46. Decorated Purple Heart with 2 oak leaf clusters, Bronze Star; Jackson Johnson fellow, 1938-42; Rockefeller postwar asst., 1946-49; Markle scholar, 1949-54; recipient Alumni Achievement award Washington U., 1987. Mem. Am. Surg. Assn., Central Surg. Assn., Soc. Univ. Surgeons, Assn. Acad. Surgery, A.C.S. (v.p. 1987-88, Disting. Service award 1984), Royal Coll. Physicians and Surgeons, Phi Beta Kappa, Sigma Xi, Alpha Omega Alpha, Phi Kappa Phi. Home: 139 Dalewood Crescent, Hamilton, ON Canada L8S 4B8 Office: 1200 Main St W, McMaster U, Hamilton, ON Canada L8S 4J9

MUELLER, HERBERT JOSEPH, dental research associate, consultant; b. Milw., Feb. 17, 1941; s. Herbert L. and Ann S. (Gmeiner) M. BME, Marquette U., 1964; MS, Northwestern U., 1966, PhD, 1969. Research fellow Northwestern U., 1964-69, postdoctoral fellow, 1977-80; asst. prof., chmn. dept. Loyola U., 1968-71; research assoc. ADA, Chgo., 1980—. Contbr. articles to profl. jours., chpts. in book. Nat. Inst. Dental Research grantee. Mem. Am. Soc. Metals, Internat. Assn. Dental Research, Soc. Biomaterials, Acad. Dental Materials, Electrochem. Soc., Materials Research Soc., N.Y. Acad. Scis., Sigma Xi, Pi Tau Sigma, Tau Beta Pi. Research on interactions between biomaterials and saliva in terms of tarnish, corrosion, and electrochemical reactions of alloys; binding of ions to protein and absorption of protein to materials; development of improved dental amalgams and casting investments; fracture toughness and differential scanning calorimetry evaluations of dental materials. Home: 3533 W Lakefield Dr Milwaukee WI 53215 Office: Am Dental Assn 211 E Chicago Ave Chicago IL 60611

MUELLER, JAMES STEPHEN, project engineer; b. Chgo., Sept. 9, 1951; s. Frank Joseph and Lorraine Eileen (Anderson) M.; m. Virginia Hodges Rumely, Nov. 22, 1986; children: Jennifer and Scott (twins). BS in Engring., U. Ill.-Chgo., 1973. Acct. Bell & Howell, Chgo., 1969-79; sr. project engr. Dynascan, Chgo., 1979-87, Maxtec Internat. Corp., Chgo., 1987—. cons. Dynaphonics, Northbrook, Ill., 1982—. Mem. Planetary Soc., U. Ill. Alumni Assn., Internat. Platform Assn., Am. Biog. Inst. (research bd. advs.). Avocations: personal computing, tennis, golf, canoeing. Home: 9350 Hamilton Ct Dr Des Plaines IL 60016 Office: Maxtec Internat Corp 6470 W Cortland St Chicago IL 60635

MUELLER, KLAUS WOLFGANG, educator; b. Mannheim, Germany, June 6, 1933; s. Reinhold and Sophie (Eichenberg) M. Dr. Laws, U. Heidelberg, 1959, Dr. habilitation, 1964; prof. honoris causa, U. Stuttgart, 1967. Referendar, State of Germany, 1955-59, assessor, 1959-64; privat dozent U. Heidelberg, 1964-66; ordinary prof. U. Mainz, 1966—; justice Supreme Dist. Ct. Zweibrüchen, 1967—. Author: Der Sachveerstaendige, 1978, Genossenschaftsreicht, 3 vols., 1980, Sachenrecht, 1988, Rürgerliches Gesetzbuch, 2. Auflage, 1988;. Mem. Zivilrechtlehrer-Vereinigung, 1966—. Home: 10 Collinistrasse, 6800 Mannheim Federal Republic of Germany Office: Univ Mainz, 21 Saaratrasse, 6500 Mainz Federal Republic of Germany

MUELLER, LOIS M., psychologist; b. Milw., Nov. 30, 1943; d. Herman Gregor and Ora Emma (Dettmann) M.; B.S., U. Wis.-Milw., 1965; M.A., U. Tex., 1966, Ph.D., 1969. Postdoctoral intern VA Hosp., Wood, Wis., 1969-71; counselor, asst. prof. So. Ill. U. Counseling Center and dept. psychology, Carbondale, 1971-72, coordinator personal counseling, asst. prof., 1972-74, counselor, asst. prof., 1974-76; individual practice clin. psychology, Carbondale, 1972-76, Clearwater, Fla., 1977—; owner, dir. Adult and Child Psychology Clinic, Clearwater, 1978—; staff mem. Med. Center Hosp., Largo, Fla., 1979—; mem. profl. adv. com. Mental Health Assn. Pinellas County, 1978, Alt. Human Services, 1979-80; cons. Face Learning Center, Hotline Crisis Phone Service, 1977—; advice columnist Clearwater Sun newspaper, 1983—; pub. speaker local TV and radio stas., 1978, 79; talk show host WPLP Radio Sta., Clearwater, 1980-83, WTKN Radio Sta., Tampa Bay, 1988—. Campaign worker for Sen. George McGovern presdl. race, 1972. Lic. psychologist, Ill., Fla. Mem. Am., Fla., Ill., Pinellas (founder, pres. 1978) psychol. assns., Assn. Advancement Psychology, Am. Soc. Clin. Hypnosis, Fla. Soc. Clin. Hypnosis, Acad. Family Psychology, Bus. and Profl. Women of Clearwater, Assn. Women in Psychology. Contbr. articles to profl. jours. Office: 2901 US 19 N Suite 202 Clearwater FL 34621

MUELLER, MARK CHRISTOPHER, lawyer, accountant; b. Dallas, June 19, 1945; s. Herman August and Hazel Deane (Hatzenbuehler) M.; m. Linda Jane Reed. BA in Econs., So. Meth. U., 1967, MBA in Acctg., 1969, JD, 1971. Bar: Tex. 1971, U.S. Dist. Ct. (no. dist.) Tex. 1974, U.S. Tax Ct. 1974; CPA, Tex. Acct. Arthur Young & Co., Dallas, 1967-68, A.E. Krutilek, Dallas, 1968-71; sole practice law, Dallas, 1971—; assoc. L. Vance Stanton, Dallas, 1971-72; instr. legal writing and research So. Meth. U., Dallas, 1970-71, instr. legal acctg., 1975. Leading articles editor Southwestern Law Jour., 1970-71. Mem. ABA, Tex. Bar Assn., Tex. Soc. CPA's, Sons Republic Tex., Nat. Rifle Assn., Order of Coif, Sons Rep. Tex., Beta Alpha Psi, Phi Delta Phi, Sigma Chi. Club: Rock Creek Barbeque. Lodges: Masons, Shriners, Grotto. Home: 7310 Brennans St Dallas TX 75214 Office: 9854 Plano Rd Suite 100 Dallas TX 75238

MUELLER, MRS. G. O. W. See ADLER, FREDA SCHAFFER

MUELLER, PAUL HENRY, corporate director, bank executive; b. N.Y.C., June 24, 1917; s. Paul Herbert and Helen (Cantwell) M.; m. Jean Bonnel Vreeland, Sept. 10, 1949; 1 child, Donald Vreeland. B.S., NYU, 1940; A.B., Princeton U., 1941; Litt.D. (hon.), Heriot-Watt U., Edinburgh, Scotland. Page Citibank (N.A.), 1934; on leave 1939-46, asst. cashier, 1947-52, asst. v.p., 1952-58, v.p., 1958-65, sr. v.p., 1965-74, chmn. credit policy com., 1974-82; chmn. bd. Saab-Scania Am. Inc., 1982—; dir. Atlas Copco AB, Stockholm, 1982—; Skandinaviska Enskilda Banken, N.Y.C., 1983—; entered U.S. Fgn. Service, served in Panama, Cairo, Washington, 1941-43; asst. adminstrv. sec. UN Monetary and Fin. Conf., Bretton Woods, N.H., 1944; divisional asst. Dept. State, 1946; sec. West Indian Conf., 2d session, St. Thomas, V.I., 1946; vis. lectr. U. Va., 1980—; founding chmn., sr. fellow Center Internat. Banking Studies. Contbg. author: Offshore Lending by U.S. Commercial Banks, 1975, Bank Credit, 1981, Classics in Commercial Bank Lending, 1981, Vol. II, 1985; author: (with Leif H. Olsen) Credit and the Business Cycle, 1978, Learning from Lending, 1979, Credit Doctrine for Lending Officers, 1976, 81, Credit Endpapers, 1982, Perspective on Credit Risk, 1988; editorial rev. bd. Encyclopedia of Banking and Finance, 9th edit. Trustee Bloomfield Coll., N.J., 1983—, vice chmn., 1987-88, chmn. 1988—; treas. Marcus Wallenberg Found., 1984—. Served from 2d lt. to capt. USMCR, 1944-45. Recipient Alumni award Grad. Sch. Credit and Fin. Mgmt., Dartmouth Coll., Disting. Service award Robert Morris Assocs.; decorated Royal Order Polar Star (Sweden). Mem. Bankers Assn. Fgn. Trade (hon., v.p. 1976), Pilgrims, SAR, Beta Gamma Sigma. Republican. Presbyterian. Club: University (N.Y.C.). Home: 75 Rotary Dr Summit NJ 07901 Office: SAAB-Scania of Am Inc SAAB Drive Orange CT 06477

MUELLER, PETER STERLING, psychiatrist, educator; b. N.Y.C., Dec. 28, 1930; s. Reginald Sterling and Edith Louise (Welleck) M.; m. Ruth Antonia Shipman, Aug. 9, 1958; children: Anne Louise, Peter Sterling, Paul Shipman, Elizabeth Ruth. A.B., Princeton U., 1952; M.D., U. Rochester, 1956. Am. Cancer Soc. student fellow Francis Delafield Hosp., N.Y.C., summer 1955; intern Bellevue Hosp., Columbia U., N.Y.C., 1956-57; asst. resident in psychiatry Henry Phipps Psychiat. Clinic, Johns Hopkins Hosp., Balt., 1963-66; asst. prof. psychiatry Sch. Medicine, Yale U., New Haven, 1966-72; asso. prof. psychiatry Coll. Medicine and Dentistry of N.J., Rutgers Med. Sch., Piscataway, 1972-76; clin. prof. psychiatry Coll. Medicine and Dentistry of N.J., Rutgers Med. Sch., 1976-82; cons. for Rehab. Unit and Center for Indsl. Human Resources, Community Mental Health Center, 1973—; mem. courtesy staff dept. psychiatry Princeton Med. Center, 1976—; cons. in psychotherapy Conn. Valley Hosp., Middletown, 1966-72; cons. in psychiatry Carrier Clinic, Belle Mead, N.J., 1973—, VA Hosp., Lyons, N.J., 1975-78. Contbr. writings in field to profl. publs., U.S., Brit., papers to profl. confs. Served with USPHS, 1957-63. Mem. Am. Psychosomatic Soc., Am. Psychiat. Assn., AAAS, Amyotrophic Lateral Sclerosis Found. (adv. bd.), Sigma Xi. Episcopalian. Home: 182 Snowden Ln Princeton NJ 08540 Office: 601 Ewing St Princeton NJ 08540

MUELLER, ROBERT CLARE, lawyer; b. Sioux City, Iowa, May 17, 1946; s. Clare Robert and Betty Louise (Abker) M.; m. C. Brenda Rowland, Jan. 21, 1977; children—Martin, Clinton, Mitchell. A.B., U. S.D., 1968; J.D., Duke U., 1971; LL.M., George Washington U., 1974. Bar: Iowa 1971. Counsel to judge U.S. Ct. Mil. Appeals, Washington, 1975-80, counsel to chief judge, 1980—; mem. Joint-Service Com. Mil. Justice, Washington, 1977—, Working Group to Mil. Justice Act of 1983 Adv. Commn., Washington, 1984-85; judge Cath. U. Law Sch. Moot Ct. Competition, Washington, 1985-87. Co-author: Manual for Courts-Martial, U.S., 1984; Military Rules of Evidence; contbg. author World Book Encyclopedia, 1988; contbr. articles to profl. publs. Editor Fed. Bar News & Jour., 1984, 86 (Disting. Service award 1984, 86). Sec. Mil. Law Inst., 1986—; mem. County Supr.'s Zoning Rev. com., Fairfax County, Va., 1982. Served to capt. U.S. Army, 1971-75. Decorated Meritorious Service medal; recipient Outstanding Achievement award Sec. Def., 1976—. Mem. Fed. Bar Assn. (cir. v.p. 1983-85, nat. membership chmn. 1985-87, dep. chmn. judiciary sect. 1985-86, chmn. mil. law com. 1985-86; chmn. career service sect., 1986—; Disting. Service award 1985, nat. council mem. 1983—). Clubs: Nat. Lawyers, Washington Duke Law (bd. dirs. 1984—). Home: 5446 Midship Ct Burke VA 22015 Office: US Ct Mil Appeals 450 E St NW Washington DC 20442

MUELLER, ROY CLEMENT, graphic arts company and direct mail executive; b. Weehawken, N.J., Aug. 15, 1930; s. Adam and Bertha M.; student Rochester Inst. Tech., 1976; m. Patricia Robinson, Sept. 3, 1970; children—Eric, Janet, Debra, Gregory. Mgr. estimating/billing dept., Editors Press, Hyattsville, Md., 1962-66; v.p., gen. mgr. Peninsula Press div. A.S. Abell Corp., Salisbury, Md., 1968-70; owner, mgr. Crown Decal & Display, Co., Bristol, Tenn., 1972—; pres. Bristol Screen, Inc. (Va.), 1977—, Southmark div., 1985—; v.p., gen. mgr. Venture One, Bristol, 1988—. Recipient Ad award Tri City Advt. Fedn., 1975, internat. exhbn. award Screen Printing Assn., 1977. Mem. Screen Printing Assn., Mail Advt. Service Assn., Internat., Am. Philatelic Soc. Lodge: Rotary Internat. Republican. Lutheran. Home: 202 Forest Dr Bristol TN 37620 Office: 200 Delaware Ave Bristol TN 37620

MUELLER, RUDOLF WENDELIN, electronics company executive; b. Wuerzburg, Germany, Sept. 14, 1935; m. Hannelore Mueller, June 23, 1965; children: Christine, Bernhard. Degree math., physics, U. Wurzburg, Fed. Republic Germany, 1962. Devel. engr. UHER-Tape Recorders, Munich, 1963-65, dep. research mgr., 1965-72, head patent office, 1972-80; mgr. measuring tech. Agfa Gevaert AG, Munich, 1980-86, mgr. tech. service, 1987—. Mem. German Standards Commn., Inst. Electrotechnical Commn., Audio Engring. Soc. Home: Jm Ried 13, D8132 Traubing, Bavaria Federal Republic of Germany

MUELLER, STEPHAN, geophysicist, educator; b. Marktredwitz, Ger., July 30, 1930; s. Hermann Friedrich and Johanna Antonie Fanny (Leuze) M.; Dipl.-Phys., Inst. Tech. Stuttgart, 1957; M.Sc. in Elec. Engring., Columbia U., 1959; Dr.rer.nat., U. Stuttgart, 1962; m. Doris Luise Pfleiderer, July 31, 1959; children—Johannes Christoph, Tobias Ulrich. Lectr. geophysics U. Stuttgart, 1962-64; vis. prof. S.W. Center Advanced Studies, Richardson, Tex., 1964-65; prof. geophysics U. Karlsruhe, 1964-71, dean Faculty Natural Scis., 1968-69; vis. prof. U. Tex., Dallas, 1969-70; prof. Swiss Fed. Inst. Tech., 1971—, U. Zurich, 1977—; dean Sch. Natural Scis., Swiss Fed. Inst. Tech., 1978-80; dir. Swiss Earthquake Service, 1971—; pres. Swiss Geophys. Commn., 1972—, European Seismol. Commn., 1972-76, Internat. Commn. Controlled Source Seismology, 1975-83; chmn. governing council Internat. Seismol. Centre, 1975-85; chmn. European-Mediterranean Seismol. Centre, 1976-82. German Acad. Interchange scholar, 1954-55. Fellow Royal Astron. Soc., Am. Geophys. Union; mem. Internat. Assn. Seismology and Physics of Earth's Interior (pres. 1987—), European Geophys. Soc. (pres. 1978-80, hon. mem. 1984—), European Union Geoscis., German Geophys. Soc., Soc. Exploration Geophysicists, European Assn. Exploration Geophysicists, Seismol. Soc. Am., Seismol. Soc. Japan, Acoustical Soc. Am., Swiss Geophys. Soc. (pres. 1977-80), Swiss Soc. Natural Sci., Sigma Xi. Co-editor Pure and Applied Geophysics, 1974-83; editor-in-chief Annales Geophysicae, 1982-87; editorial bd. Jour. Geophysics, 1969-87, Tectonophysics, 1971-77, 84—, Bolletino di Geofisica Teorica ed Applicata, 1978—, Jour. Geodynamics, 1983—. Office: ETH-Geophysics, CH-8093 Zurich Switzerland

MUELLER-HEUBACH, EBERHARD AUGUST, medical educator, obstetrician-gynecologist; b. Berlin, Feb. 24, 1942; U.S., 1968; s. Heinrich G. and Elisabeth (Heubach) Mueller; m. Cornelia R. Uffmann, Feb. 6, 1968; 1 son, Oliver Maximilian. Abitur, Lichtenbergschule, Darmstadt, W.Ger., 1961; M.D., U. Cologne (W.Ger.), 1966. Diplomate: Am. Bd. Ob-Gyn (maternal-fetal medicine). Intern U. Cologne, 1967-68; intern Middlesex Gen. Hosp., New Brunswick, N.J., 1968-69; research fellow Columbia U., N.Y.C., 1969-71; resident and chief resident Sloane Hosp. for Women, N.Y.C., 1971-75; asst. prof. U. Pitts. Sch. Medicine/Magee-Women's Hosp., 1975-81, assoc. prof., 1981—. Reviewer: Am. Jour. Ob-Gyn, 1978—, Obstetrics and Gynecology, 1979—; contbr. chpts. to books, articles to profl. jours. Fellow Am. Coll. Obstetricians and Gynecologists (Hoechst award 1972); mem. Tri-State Perinatal Orgn. (v.p. 1981), Pa. Perinatal Assn. (pres.-elect 1982-84, pres. 1984-86), Soc. Gynecologic Investigation, Soc. Perinatal Obstetricians, Am. Fedn. Clin. Research, Pitts. Ob-Gyn Soc. (v.p. 1985-86, pres. 1986-87). Research on animal studies in fetal and maternal physiology; diabetes mellitus in pregnancy, high risk obstetrics. Office: U Pitts Sch Medicine Magee-Womens Hosp Pittsburgh PA 15213

MUGABE, ROBERT GABRIEL, president of Zimbabwe; b. Kutama, Feb. 21, 1924; B.A., Ft. Hare U., (S. Africa), 1951; B.Ed.; B.Sc. (Econ.), U. London, B.Admin., LL.B., LL.M.; hon. Dr., Ahmadu Bello U.; m. Sarah Hayfron; 1 son (dec.). Tchr., Driefontein Roman Cath. Sch., Umvuma, 1952, Salisbury S. Primary Sch., 1953, Gwelo, 1954, Chalimbana Tchr. Tng. Coll., Zambia, 1955-58, St. Mary's Tchr. Tng. Coll., Takoradi, Ghana, 1958-60; publicity sec. Nat. Democratic Party, 1960-61; publicity sec. Zimbabwe African People's Union, 1961-62; detained, 1962, 63, escaped to Tanzania, 1963; co-founder Zimbabwe African Nat. Union, 1963, sec.-gen., 1963, pres., 1977—; detained in Rhodesia, 1964-74; joint leader Patriotic Front (with Joshua Nkomo), 1976-80; leader Zimbabwe African Nat. Union del. Geneva Constl. Conf. on Rhodesia, 1976, Malta Conf., 1978, Lancaster House Conf., 1979-80; prime minister Zimbabwe, 1980-87, minister of def., 1980-87, exec. pres., 1988—. Recipient Newsmaker of Yr. award S. African Soc. Journalism, Internat. Human Rights award Howard U., Africa Prize, 1988. Address: Office of Pres, Harare Zimbabwe *

MUGEMANA, JEAN MARIE VIANNEY, minister of justice of Rwanda; b. Gitanwa, Rwanda, Oct. 10, 1951; s. Léonidas Munyarukato and Bélina Nyirakoma; m. Xavérina Niwemutoni; 2 sons. Diplome de candidat en droit, Universite Catholoque de Louvain, Belgium, 1973, Diplome de licence en Droit, 1976; cert. law Institut International des Droits de l'Homme, Strasbourg, France, 1979. Sec. of adminstrn. Ministry of Civil Service and Employment, Republic of Rwanda, 1976-79, dir. gen. pub. adminstrn., 1979-81, sec. gen. Ministry Youth and Sports, 1981-82; atty. gen. Rwanda Ct. of Appeal, 1982-84; minister of justice Republic of Rwanda, Kigali, 1984—. Office: Ministry of Justice, Box 160, Kigali Rwanda *

MUGFORD, ALFRED GEORGE, machine company executive; b. Everett, Mass., Sept. 7, 1928; s. James and Emmie (Boone) M.; m. Martha Black, Nov. 25, 1983; children—Holly Anne Montgomery Nye, Edward du Mee Montgomery, III; children by previous marriage—Janet Anne Sprague, Nancy Anne, George Edward. B.S., Bentley Coll., 1950. With Jerguson Gage & Valve Co., Burlington, Mass., 1947-64; controller Jerguson Gage & Valve Co., 1963-64; treas., controller Sarco Co., Inc., Allentown, Pa., 1964-66; v.p. finance Whitin Machine Works, Whitinsville, Mass., 1966-68; v.p., gen. mgr. Whitin Machine Works, 1967-68, corp. staff, 1968; with White Consol. Industries, Cleve., 1963-87; v.p., corp. staff, group v.p. White Consol. Industries, 1969-76, exec. v.p., 1976-84, sr. exec. v.p., 1984-87; cons. to mfg. industry Bay Village, Ohio, 1987—; v.p., bd. dirs. Alpha Assocs., Inc., Mpls. Chmn. Burlington Finance Bd., 1958-62, New Bldg. and Capital Fund Raising Com., 1960-63. Mem. Burlington Jr. C. of C. (charter mem., v.p. 1956-58), MAPI. Presbyterian (chmn. bd. trustees 1961-63). Clubs: Avon Oaks Country (fin. com. 1974-75, trustee, pres. 1977-78, bd. dirs. 1986—), Duquesne, Lions. Home and Office: 30529 Ednil Dr Bay Village OH 44140

MUGGERIDGE, MALCOLM, editor, writer; b. Sanderstead, Surrey, Eng., Mar. 24, 1903; s. Henry Thomas and Annie (Booler) M.; m. Katherine Dobbs, Sept. 1927; 4 children. Student, Selwyn Coll., Cambridge. Lectr. Egyptian U., Cairo, 1927-30; editorial staff Manchester Guardian, 1930-32, Moscow corr., 1932-33; asst. editor Calcutta Statesman, 1934-35; editorial staff Evening Standard, 1935-36; Washington corr. Daily Telegraph, 1946-47, dep. editor, 1950-52; editor Punch, 1953-57; rector Edinburgh U., 1967-68. Author: Three Flats (production Stage Soc.), 1931, Autumnal Face, 1931, Winter in Moscow, 1933, The Earnest Atheist, a Life of Samuel Butler, 1936, In a Valley of this Restless Mind, 1938, The Thirties, 1940, Ciano's Papers, 1948, Affairs of the Heart, 1949, (with Paul Hogarth) London à la Mode, 1966, Tread Softly for You Tread on my Jokes, 1966, Jesus Rediscovered, 1969, Something Beautiful for God, 1971, (with Alec Vidler) Paul-Envoy Extraordinary, 1972, Chronicles of Wasted Time, Vol. I-The Green Stick, 1972, Vol. II-The Infernal Grove, 1973, Jesus-The Man Who Lives, 1975, The Third Testament, 1976, Christ and the Media, 1977, The End of Christendom, 1980, My Life in Pictures, 1987, (essays) Conversion: A Spiritual Journey, 1988; editor: (with Alec Vidler) English edit. Ciano's Diary, 1947. Served as maj. intelligence corps. Brit. Army, 1939-45. Decorated Legion of Honor, Croix de Guerre with Palm, Medaille de la Reconnaissance France). Address: Park Cottage, East Sussex, Robertsbridge England also: 10 Bouverie St, London EC4, England *

MÜHLANGER, ERICH, ski company executive; b. Liezen, Austria, Aug. 26, 1941; came to U.S., 1971, naturalized, 1975; s. Alois and Maria (Stückelschweiger) M.; m. Gilda V. Oliver, July 13, 1973; 1 child, Erich. Assoc. Engring., Murau Berufsschule Spl. Trade, Austria, 1959; student Inst. Tech. and Engring., Weiler Im Allgau, Germany, 1963-65. Salesman, Olin Ski Co. (Olin-Authier), Switzerland, 1965-67, mem. mktg. dept., 1967-69, service and mfg., 1969-71, quality control insp., Middletown, Conn., 1971-77, supr., 1977-78, gen. foreman, 1978-83, process control mgr., 1983-88; dir. mfg. Entech Corp., 1988—. Charter mem. Presdl. Task Force, trustee; preferred mem. of U.S. Senatorial Club. Served to cpl. Austrian Air Force, 1959-60. Mem. Screenprinting Assn. Am., Am. Mgmt. Assn. Roman Catholic. Club: Mgmt. Home: 13 Clemens Ct Rocky Hill CT 06067 Office: 475 Smith St Middletown CT 06457

MUHLENBRUCH, CARL W., civil engineer; b. Decatur, Ill., Nov. 21, 1915; s. Carl William and Clara (Theobald) M.; m. Agnes M. Kringel, Nov. 22, 1939; children: Phyllis Elaine (Mrs. Richard B. Wallace), Joan Carol (Mrs. Frederick B. Wenk). BCE, U. Ill., 1937, CE, 1945; MCE, Carnegie Inst. Tech., 1943. Research engineer Aluminum Research Labs., Pitts., 1937-39; cons. engring. 1939-50; mem. faculty Carnegie Inst. Tech., 1939-48; assoc. prof. civil engring. Northwestern U., 1948-54; pres. TEC-SEARCH, Inc. (formerly Ednl. and Tech. Consultants Inc.), 1954-67, chmn. bd., 1967—; Pres. Profl. Centers Bldg. Corp., 1961-77. Author: Experimental Mechanics and Properties of Materials; Contbr. articles engring. publs. Treas., bd. dirs. Concordia Coll. Found. Recipient Stanford E. Thompson award, 1945. Mem. Am. Econ. Devel. Council (certified indsl. developer), Am. Soc. Engring. Edn. (editor Educational Aids in Engring.), Nat. Soc. Profl. Engrs., ASCE, Sigma Xi, Tau Beta Phi, Omicron Delta Kappa. Lutheran. Club: University (Evanston). Lodge: Rotary (dist. gov. 1980-81). Office: Tec-Search 1000 Skokie Blvd Wilmette IL 60091

MUHLNICKEL, ISABELLE, mental health counselor; b. Strong, Colo., May 11, 1931; d. Albert and Frances (Martinez) Quintana; m. Ludwig Albert Muhlnickel, Jan. 13, 1952; children: Ludwig Albert, Elizabeth, Mary Karolyn. BA in Sociology, Met. State Coll.-Denver, 1980. Lic. psychiat. technician, Colo. Ednl. loan officer Lowry Fed. Credit Union, Denver, 1972-76; mgr., dir. Teamsters Credit Union, Denver, 1980-81; psychiat. technician State of Colo., Wheatridge, 1981—; del. to China Research Soc. Modernization of Mgmt., The China Assn. Sci. and Tech., People to People Internat., People's Republic China, 1988.; founder, exec. dir. Fathers Crisis Center, Denver, 1984—. Met. State Coll. Colo. Scholars award, 1977, 78, 79. Mem. Nat. Assn. Female Execs., Inst. Internat. Edn. Democrat. Roman Catholic. Avocations: travel, photography, skiing, hiking, painting.

MUJAGIC, CHRISTOPHE ALEXANDRE, business executive; b. Doboj, Bosnia, Yugoslavia, June 27, 1940; s. Avdo M. and Asima (Hazic) M.; m. Colette Michele Feste, Nov. 6, 1965. MBA, U. Zagreb, 1963, U. Aix en Provence, 1968; cert. sr. execs. MIT, 1982. Mktg. devel. mgr. Corning Glass Works (N.Y.), 1977-79; gen. mgr. consumer products South Europe, Corning France, Neuilly, 1979-81; v.p., gen. mgr. consumer products Corning Europe, Neuilly, 1981-86; bd. dirs. Corning France, Corning Ltd., Sunderland, Eng.; chmn. Corning Benelux, Brussels, Corning SPA, Milan, Corning Iberica, Madrid, 1986; gen. mgr. Boussac St. Freres S.A. Served to lt. Yugoslavian Army, 1963-64. Mem. MIT Club Paris, Am. Mktg. Assn. Home: 55 Rue des Galons, 92190 Meudon France Office: Boussac Saint Freres, 11 Rue François ler, 75008 Paris France

MUJICA, BARBARA LOUISE, foreign language educator, author; b. Altoona, Pa., Dec. 25, 1943; d. Louis and Carol Freida (Kline) Kaminar; A.B., UCLA, 1964; M.A., Middlebury Coll., 1965; Ph.D., N.Y. U., 1974; m. Mauro E. Mujica, Dec. 26, 1966; children: Lillian Louise, Mariana Ximena, Mauro Eduardo Ignacio. Tchr. French, UCLA, 1963-64; assoc. editor modern langs. Harcourt Brace Jovanovich, N.Y.C., 1966-73; instr., asst. prof. Romance langs. CUNY, 1973-74; assoc. prof. Spanish, Georgetown U., Washington, 1974—. Penfield fellow, 1971; NEH summer Inst. faculty, 1980, Spanish Govt. grantee, 1987. Dir. El Retablo, Spanish lang. theater. Mem. Writers Center, Brazilian Am. Cultural Inst., Am. Assn. Tchrs. Spanish and Portuguese, MLA, Women's Caucus MLA, South Atlantic MLA, N.E. MLA, AAUP, Annual Symposium on Spanish Golden Age Drama (editor Proceedings, 1987, 88), Philological Assn. Pacific Coast, Assn. Tchrs. Spanish Classical Drama. Author: A-LM Spanish, Levels I-IV, 1969-74; Readings in Spanish Literature, 1975; Calderon's Characters: An Existential Point of View, 1980; Pasaporte, 1980, rev. edit., 1984; Aquí y ahora, 1979; Entrevista, 1982; Iberian Pastoral Characters, 1986; editor, pub. Verbena: Bilingual Rev. of the Arts, 1979-85; sr. assoc. editor, bd. dirs. Washington Rev.; contbr. articles to profl. jours., newspapers, lit. mags. Home: 8807 Fox Hills Trail Potomac MD 20854 Office: Georgetown U Dept Spanish Washington DC 20057

MUJICA, MAURO E., architect; b. Antofagasta, Chile, Apr. 20, 1941; came to U.S., 1965, naturalized, 1970; s. Mauro Raul and Graciela (Parodi-Blayfus) M.; m. Barbara Louise Kaminar, Dec. 26, 1966; children: Lillian Louise, Mariana Ximena, Mauro Eduardo Ignacio III. MArch, Columbia U., 1971. Head designer Columbia U. Office Archtl. Planning, N.Y.C., 1966-71; project mgr. Walker, Sander, Ford & Kerr, Architects, Princeton, N.J., 1971-72; prin. Mauro E. Mujica, Architect, N.Y.C., 1972-74; dir. internat. div. Greenhorne & O'Mara, Inc., Riverdale, Md., 1974-78; partner Mujica & Reddy Architects, Washington, 1978-80; prin. Mauro E. Mujica, Architect, Washington, 1980-81; partner Mujica & Berlin Investment Bankers, Washington, 1982-85, Mujica Keppie Henderson Internat., Washington and Glasgow, Scotland, 1981-83, Mujica-Seifert Architects, Washington and London, 1983-87; pres., chief exec. officer The Pace Group, Washington, 1987—. Prin. works include: Tennis Clubhouse, Columbia U., Nat. Hosp., Puerto Barrios, Guatemala, Plaza Hotel interiors, La Paz, Bolivia. Fellow Inst. Dirs. (London); mem. AIA, Columbia U. Archtl. Alumni Assn. Republican. Home: 8807 Fox Hills Tr Potomac MD 20854 Office: 1300 New York Ave NW Washington DC 20005

MUJTABA, SAYEEDA KHATOON, surgeon; b. Samber, India, June 1, 1938; d. Syed Imdad and Zakiri (Khatoon) Hussain; m. Shah Syed Mujtaba, Mar. 22, 1964; children: Syed Mubtagha Shah, Syed Muntiq Shah. Faculty of Sci., U. Chitagong, Dacca, Bangladesh, 1965; B in Med. and Surgery, Fatima Jinnah Med. Coll., Lahore, Pakistan, 1962. House job in surgery Services Hosp. Lahore, 1962-64; mng. dir. Mansab Clinic, Lahore, 1964—. Mem. Pakistan Med. Assn. Islam. Office: Mansab Clinic, 3 Fane Rd, Lahore Pakistan

MUJTABA, SHAH SYED, anesthesiologist; b. Rohtak, Punjab, India, Dec. 30, 1935; s. Shah Mahmood and Hameeda (Begum) Syed; m. Sayeeda Khatoon, Mar. 22, 1964; children: Mahnaz Shah, Syed Mubtagha Shah, Syed Muntiq Shah. Faculty of Sci., U. Punjab, Pakistan, 1954; B. in Medicine and Surgery, King Edward Med. Coll., Lahore, Pakistan, 1960. Intern Mayo Hosp., Lahore, 1961, registrar anasthesiologist, 1962-67; anasthesiologist Lady Walington Hosp., Lahore, 1967-68; dir. Mansab Clinic, Lahore, 1968—. Mem. Coll. Physicians and Surgeons, Pakistan Med. Assn. Islam. Club: Lahore Gymkhana. Office: Mansab Clinic, 3 Fane Rd, Lahore Pakistan

MUKA, BETTY LORAINE OAKES, lawyer; b. McAlester, Okla., Jan. 30, 1929; d. Herbert La Fern and Loraine Lillian (Coppedge) Oakes; m. Arthur Allen Muka, Sept. 6, 1952; children: Diane Loraine, Stephen Arthur, Christopher Herbert, Martha Ann, Deborah Susan. Student Monticello Coll., 1946-47; BS, Okla. U., 1950; MS, Cornell U., 1953, MBA, 1970; JD, Syracuse U. 1980. Bar: R.I. 1983, U.S. Dist. Ct. R.I. 1984. Mgr. dining room Anna Maude's Cafeteria, Oklahoma City, 1950-51; faculty dining room mgr. V.P.I., Blacksburg, Va., 1955-56; owner, mgr. The Cottage Restaurant, 1959-60; lectr., lab. instr. foods and organic chemistry Cornell U., 1961; owner, mgr. student housing, 1965-68; jr. acct. Maxfield, Randolph & Carpenter, CPA's, Ithaca, N.Y., 1970-71; income tax cons. H & R Block, Ithaca, 1971-73; atty. pro se, 1972—; hostess-bookkeeper Holiday Inn, Ithaca, 1972-73; salesperson Investors Diversified Services, Ithaca, 1972-73, NASD, 1973; agt. Inventory Control Co., 1975-78; law clk. 1978-79; sole practice, Providence, 1983-85; lectr. in fin. Tompkins Cortland Community Coll. Leader various youth groups, Ithaca, 1964-71. Mem. ABA, N.Y. State Bar Assn., R.I. Bar Assn., R.I. Trial Lawyer's Assn., Assn. Trial Lawyers Am., Mortar Bd., Delta Delta Delta Alumnae (pres. 1974), Phi Delta Phi (bd. dirs. 1980, J. Mark McCarthy award 1980), Sigma Delta Epsilon. Club: Toastmasters. Home and Office: 113 Kay St Ithaca NY 14850

MUKETE, NFON VICTOR E., traditional ruler and statesman; b. Kumba, Cameroon, Nov. 15, 1918; s. Abel Mukete and Maria DiGo; m. Hannah Ntoh Makia, Apr. 19, 1947; children: Michael, Abel, Godfrey, Diko, Ebarko, Ekale, Akpo, Ekoko. Diploma in Agrl., Higher Coll. Yaba, Lagos, 1943; BS with honors, Manchester U., Eng., 1951; postgrad., Christ Coll. Cambridge U., 1951-52. Chmn., mng. dir. Mukete Plantations, Ltd., Cameroon, 1968—; fed. minister of research and info. Fed. Govt. Nigeria, 1958-59, fed. minister without portfolio, 1955-57; chmn. Cameroon Devel. Corp., 1960-82; Paramount chief Kumba, Cameroon, 1968—; chmn. Mukete Estates, Ltd., Cameroon, 1987—; mem. econ. and social council Cameroon, 1975—; judge Ct. of Impeachment, Cameroon, 1975—. 1st v.p. C. of C. Industry and Mines, Cameroon, 1963-82; mem. Nat. Council of Credit, 1963-73; mem. West Cameroon Police Service Commn., 1964-66; co-founder The Cameroon Times, 1960—. Decorated knight ofcl. Humane Order of African Redemption (Liberia); officer Cross Order of Merit (Fed. Republic of Germany); knight and officer Order of Agrl. Merit, Order of Valour. Mem. Cameroon People's Dem. Movement (cen. com. 1985—), Cameroon Nat. Union Party (cen. com. 1983-85), Kamerun United Nat. Congress (gen. sec. 1953-54), Greater Kumba Planning Authority, Nigerian Fed. Ho. of Reps. Home: Nfon's Palace, Kumba Cameroon Office: Office of the Nfon and, Kumba Traditional Council, PO Box 1, Kumba Cameroon

MUKHTAR, ABDUL MUHYI, mechanical engineer; b. Azare, Bauchi, Nigeria, May 30, 1944; s. Mukhtar Abdallah and Hajia (Asama'u) M.; married, Sept. 1976; children: Nuraddeen, Naguib, Mufawud, Zayyan. Nat. diplomas in Mech./Elec. Engring., Kaduna Poly., Nigeria, 1968, 70. Adminstrv. mgr. Mansa Constrn. Co. Ltd., Kano, Nigeria, 1970-75; mng. dir. SAA Group Cos., Kano, Bauchi, 1975—; chmn. Cailytimes Group Cos., 1984-85; bd. dirs. B.S.U.U., 1986—; chmn. Daily Times Group of Cos., 1985-86. Mem. Nigerian Constrn. Reviewing Com., 1987-88; councillor Shira Local Govt. Bauchi State, 1979-82. Moslem. Home and Office: #19 Kano Rd, PO Box 84, Azare Bauchi Nigeria

MUKOYAMA, JAMES HIDEFUMI, JR., securities executive; b. Chgo., Aug. 3, 1944; s. Hidefumi James and Miye (Maruyama) M.; m. Kyung Ja Woo, June 20, 1971; children: Sumi Martha, Jae Thomas. BA in English, U. Ill., 1965, MA in Social Studies, 1966; honor grad. U.S. Army Inf. Sch., 1966; grad. U.S. Army Command and Gen. Staff Coll., 1979, U.S. Army War Coll., 1984. Registered prin., sr. registered options prin. Nat. Assn. Securities Dealers. Asst. dept. mgr. Mitsui & Co. (USA), Inc., Chgo., 1971-74; mem. Chgo. Bd. Options Exchange, 1974-75; v.p. 1st Omaha Securities, Chgo., 1975-76, Heartland Securities, Chgo., 1976—; allied mem. N.Y. Stock Exchange; v.p. Lefta Advt., Chgo., 1976—. Mem. exec. bd. Hillside Free Meth. h., Evanston, Ill., 1982—. Served with U.S. Army, 1965-70; brigadier gen. Res., 1971—. Decorated Silver Star, Purple Heart, 3 Bronze Stars; Vietnamese Army Cross of Gallantry; Japanese Army Parachutist badge; recipient cert. of merit Korean Army, others. Mem. U. Ill. Alumni Assn. (life), Assn. U.S. Army, Mil. Order Purple Heart, Am. Legion, Res. Officers Assn., Sr. Army Res. Commdrs. Assn. Home: 4009 Tracey Ct Glenview IL 60025 Office: Heartland Securities Inc 208 S LaSalle St Chicago IL 60604

MUKRAM SHEIKH, MUHAMMED MUBASHIR, government official, marketing executive; b. Kasur, Pakistan, Feb. 22, 1950; arrived in Botswana, 1980; s. Muhammed Rafiq Akram and Amatush Shakoor (Akram) S.; m. Musarrat Mukram, Sept. 24, 1972 (dec. 1975); m. Zainib Mukram, June 6, 1976; children: Tahira Uzma, Saad Mubashir, Shahid Mubashir, Sajid Mubashir, Abid Mubashir. BA in Econs. and Stat., Govt. Coll., 1969; MA in History, Punjab (Pakistan) U., 1972, MA in Polit. Sci., 1973, PhD in Econs. and Mktg. (hon.), 1984, PhD in Bus. Adminstrn., 1986. Exec. editor Weekly Islami, Jamhooria, Pakistan, 1972-74; mng. proprietor Naeem Printing Agy., Lahore, Pakistan, 1974-76; mgr. mktg. and sales Roti Corp. Pakistan, Lahore, 1976-80; UNV on fgn. trade UNCTAD; assigned to Ministry of Commerce and Industry, Gaborone, Botswana, 1980-82, chief trade officer, 1982—, chief publs., publicity, trade and investment info. services, and pub. relations Trade and Investment Promotion Dept., 1984—. Mng. editor Botswana Bus. News, 1982—; contbr. articles to profl. jours. Sec. Bazm-E-Abad-O-Amal, Lahore, 1970-72; pres. Anjman Farogh-e-Quaran, Lahore, 1974-75; registrar Pak Pioneers Boy Scouts troop, Lahore, 1974-75; chmn. Pak Pioneer Youth League, Lahore, 1976-80; vol. U.N. Conf. on Trade and Devel. Recipient St. John's Ambulance Assn. medal, 1969, Roll of Honor award Govt. Coll. Lahore, 1969, Ambulance Civil Def. award, 1969, Badges of Merit award. Fellow Inst. Commerce London, Brit. Soc. Commerce, Inst. Sales and Mktg. Mgmt., Brit. Inst. Mgmt., Internat. Inst. Social Econs.; mem. Inst. Mktg. Eng., Assn. MBA Execs. Home: Sham Kot Nau dist, Kasur Pakistan Office: Ministry of Commerce and Industry, PO Box 1974, Gaborone Botswana

MULCAHY, GEOFFREY JOHN, holding company executive; b. Sunderland, Eng., Feb. 7, 1942; s. Maurice F. and Kathleen (Blankinsop) M.; m. Valerie Elizabeth Mulcahy, Apr. 17, 1965; children—Robert J., Sarah E. B.Sc., U. Manchester, 1963; M.B.A., Harvard U., 1969. Fin. dir. Brit. Sugar Co., London, 1977-82; fin. dir. Woolworth Holdings, London, 1982-84, group mng. dir., 1984-86, chief exec., 1986—. Fellow Brit. Inst. Mgmt. Office: Woolworth Holdings, NW House, 119 Marylebone Rd, London NW1 5PX England

MULCAHY, RISTEARD, cardiologist; b. Dublin, Ireland, July 13, 1922; s. Richard and Mary Josephine (Ryan) M.; m. Aileen Hanton; children: Richard, David, Hugh, Tina, Barbara, Lisa. MB, BCh, U. Coll., Dublin, 1945, MD, 1948. Registrar St. John and St. Elizabeth Hosps., London, 1946-48; postgrad. Nat. Heart Hosp., London, 1948-50; cardiologist St. Vincent's Hosp., Dublin, 1950—, Coombe Lying-in Hosp., Dublin, 1950—; prof. preventive cardiology dept. U. Coll., Dublin, 1979—. Author: Heart Attack and Lifestyle, 1974, Beat Heart Disease, 1979; contbr. numerous articles on sci., revs. and editorials. Research grantee Brit. and Irish Heart Founds.; research grantee Med. Research Council of Ireland; grantee Unilver Trust. Fellow Royal Coll. Physicians (London and Ireland chpt.), Royal Soc. Medicine, Brit. Cardiac Soc., Royal Acad. Medicine Ireland; mem. Irish Cardiac Soc. Roman Catholic. Clubs: Corrigan; Fitzwilliam Lawn Tennis; Milltown Golf (capt. 1954-55) (Dublin). Office: St Vincents Hosp, Dublin 4, Ireland

MULDER, CHRISTIAAN, weed physiologist; b. Roodepoort, S. Africa, Apr. 27, 1941; s. Frederik Jacobus Mulder and Maria (Jordaan) Peach; m. Elizabeth Madelief Van Der Spuy, Oct. 2, 1965; children—Lizel, Christiaan, Pieter-Melt. B.Sc. in Agr., U. Pretoria, 1962, M.Sc. in Agrl., 1969; Ph.D., N.D. State U., 1977. Asst. profl. officer Dept. Agr., Barberton, S. Africa, 1962-63; officer in charge Cotton Research Sta., Barberton, 1963-65; agrl. researcher Bayer Co., Johannesburg, S. Africa, 1965-74; grad. research asst. N.D. State U., Fargo, 1974-76, research asst., 1976-77, research assoc., 1977-78; head research sta. BASF Nelspruit, S. Africa, 1978—. Contbr. articles to profl. jours. Chmn. divisional council Nat. Party, Edenvale, S.Africa, 1973; mem. sch. bd. City of Edenvale, 1973. Mem. S.African Soc. Crop Prodn., Weed Sci. Soc. Am., S.African Weed Sci. Soc. (pres.), S.African Council for Natural Scientists, Sigma Xi. Conservative. Mem. Dutch Ref. Ch. Lodge: Rapportryers. Home: 7 Kort St, Nelspruit, Travsvaal 1200, Republic of South Africa Office: BASF South Africa Ltd, PO Box 239, Nelspruit, Transvaal 1200, Republic of South Africa

MULDER, HENDRIK, IV, health services company executive; b. Kampen, The Netherlands, Oct. 23, 1934; s. Hendrik III and Annie (Leyssenaar) M.; m. Jantie Tiemens, Apr. 27, 1964; children: Ernst H., Marten G., Gert D. BEE, Tech. Coll., Haarlem, The Netherlands, 1956; MEE, Tech. Univ., Delft, The Netherlands, 1963. Design and devel. mgr. Philips Data-Systems, Apeldoorn, The Netherlands, 1963-71; info. systems mgr. Philips Corp. EDP, Eindhoven, The Netherlands, 1971-75; cen. planning mgr. Philips Med. Systems, Best, The Netherlands, 1975-79, mgr. integral logistics, 1979—, dir., chief logistics officer, 1983—. Chmn. Cen. Membership Registration, Delft, 1967—; chmn., supervisory bd. Dutch Reformed Ch., 1973-79. Served to 1st lt. Dutch Army S.C., 1956-58; maj. civil def., 1971. Fellow Am. Prodn. and Inventory Control Soc., Royal Inst. Engrs., Orde van Organisatie Adviseurs, Nederlandse Vereniging voor Logistiek Mgmt. Home: Europalaan 12, Son en Breugel 5691 EN, The Netherlands

MULDER, HERMAN, banker; b. The Hague, Netherlands, June 7, 1946; s. Herman and Wilma (Prijs) M.; m. Hillegien Fenna Horring, May 15, 1970; children—Alexander, Jan-Maarten, Michiel, Olivier. Master at Law, Leiden U., 1969; Bachelor Bus. Econs., Rotterdam U., 1972. Asst. treas. Pakhoed/Paktank, Rotterdam, 1972-74, project mgr. M8A, 1975-76; mgr. new bus. devel. Pakhood USA, Blue Bell, 1977-79; mgr. energy relationship AmRo Bank, Amsterdam, 1980-81, head of project finance, 1982, head of project fin./export fin., 1983-86; with mgmt. team corp. banking div., 1983—, head credit workout/restructuring dept., 1987—, sr. v.p., 1985—; guest lectr. Internat. Petroleum Econs. Seminaf/IMI, Geneva, 1983—. Contbr. articles to profl. jours. Mem. Assn. Fin.-Econ. Mgmt. Liberal. Avocations: tennis, hockey, skiing. Home: 42 Koningslaan, 1406 KH Bussum The Netherlands

MÜLDER, JURGEN BERNHARD, executive search firm executive, executive search consultant; b. Celle, Germany, Sept. 14, 1937; m. Annekatrin Merks; children—Philip, Annabel, Jochen. M.S. in Mining Engring., Techn. Hochschule Clausthal-Zellerfeld, 1964, Ph.D. in Comparative Law, 1968; M.B.A., European Inst. Bus. Adminstrn., Fontainebleau, France, 1968. Mgr., prin. Spencer Stuart & Assocs., Mgmt. Cons., 1968-77; mng. ptnr. Mulder & Ptnr. Unternehmensberatung GmbH, Frankfurt/Main, W.Ger., 1978—; bd. dirs. AMROP Internat. Office: Mülder & Ptnr Unternehmensberatung, GmbH Frankfurt Airport Ctr, 6000 Frankfurt/Main 75 Federal Republic of Germany

MULET, JEAN-PIERRE, physician; b. La Ciotat, Provence, France, Aug. 22, 1946; s. François and Paule (Sarrouh) M.; m. Catherine Morand, Sept. 17, 1970; children: Florence, Sophie, Jean-Phillipe, Marie. C.P.E.M., U. Lyon, France, 1966, C.E.S. in Médecine Aéronautique, 1977; MD, U. Lyon, Lyon, France, 1972. Diplomate Aeronautic and Spatial Med. Gen. practice medicine Francheville, France, 1975—. Served as cooperant in the French Mil. Service, 1973-75. Mem. Rassemblement pour la République party. Roman Catholic. Home: Allee Florian 5, 69160 Tassin France Office: 29 Ave du Chater, 69340 Francheville France

MULFORD, DONALD LEWIS, publisher; b. Montclair, N.J., Apr. 22, 1918; s. Vincent S. and Madeleine (Day) M.; A.B., Princeton, 1940; m. Frances Root, Aug. 9, 1940 (div. Apr. 1954); children—Marcia M., Sally E., Sandra D. (dec.); m. 2d, Josephine M. Abbott Davisson, Apr. 23, 1954 (dec. Mar. 1956); stepchildren—Lee, Joanne, Sue; m. 3d, Emily L. Enbysk, Dec. 29, 1958. With Montclair Times Co., 1940—, exec. v.p., 1950—, asso. pub., 1956-71, pres., co-pub., 1971-79, pres., pub., 1979—; pres., pub. Verona-Cedar Grove Times, 1979—. Mem. N.J. Press Assn. (pres. 1980-81, chmn. bd. 1981-82), Phi Beta Kappa. Rotarian. Clubs: Princeton, Montclair Golf; Nat. Press (Washington); Nassau (Princeton, N.J.). Home: 260 Highland Ave Upper Montclair NJ 07043 Office: 114 Valley Rd Montclair NJ 07042

MULFORD, ROBERT IRWIN, management consultant; b. Taft, Calif., Oct. 17, 1935; s. Donald Milton Mulford and Jean (Stevens) Mulford Albrecht; m. Nancy Colleen Spencer, Mar. 4, 1960 (div. 1979); m. Martha June Whiteley, Apr. 21, 1979; children: Jennifer Lynn, Stephanie Ann. BBA, Woodbury U., 1960; cert. indsl. relations UCLA, 1965. Dir. personnel Computer Sci. Corp., Washington, 1969-72; v.p. personnel and adminstrn. Unionamerica, Inc., Los Angeles, 1972-76; mgmt. cons. in pvt. practice, San Francisco, 1977-78; mgr. employment Intel Corp., Santa Clara, Calif., 1978-80; corp. mgr. employment and tng. Signetics Corp., Sunnyvale, Calif., 1980-83; exec. v.p. Robert S. Blake Assocs., Cupertino, Calif., 1983-84, pres., 1985-86. Pub. safety commr., Saratoga, Calif., 1984—; pres. Mulford Moreland Assocs., Inc., San Jose, Calif., 1986—; bd. dirs. United Cerebral Palsy, Los Angeles, 1975-76; bd. dirs., v.p. Exceptional Children's Found., Los Angeles, 1974-76. Served with U.S. Army, 1955-58, Europe. Mem. Am. Soc. Personnel Adminstrn., Outplacement Internat. Employment Mgmt. Assn., Assn. Outplacement Cons. Firms. Republican. Office: Mulford Moreland & Assocs Inc 101 Metro Dr San Jose CA 95110-1314

MULIANTO, HAJI SINDHU, cigarette company executive; b. Salatiga, Indonesia, Sept. 6, 1940; s. Mohadi Karsodikromo and Sutijah Sukemi; m. Titiek Qodariah; children: E. Palupi R., D.I. Handayani, N. Prabawani, M.B. Ikhsani, Diana I., Arum Aqlima. Student, Acad. of Leather Tech., Yogyakarta, Indonesia, 1964; BS, Cordwainers Tech. Coll., London, 1969; MS, State Inst. of Industrial Mgmt., Jakarta, Indonesia, 1980. Technician P.T. Setia Ciliwung, Jakarta, 1964-65; group foreman P.T. Sepatu Bata, Jakarta, 1966-70, buyer, 1970-72; floor mgr. P.T. Sepatu Bata, 1973-75, mgmt. devel. mgr., 1975-77, factory mgr., 1977-80; tech. advisor Bata Shoe Co., Dacca, Bangladesh, 1972-73; tng. mgr. P.T. BAT, Jakarta, 1981-87; human resources devel. mgr. PT. BAT, 1987-88; prodn. and tech. dir. PT. Ruri Safira, 1988—; lectr., prof. Inst. Industrial Mgmt., 1985—; dir., cons. Bina Manajemen Trg. Inst., Jakarta, 1987—; chmn. Yayasan Bina Insustria Indonesia, 1986—. Author: Manager as a Leader, 1985, 2nd. ed. 1987, Manager as an Interviewer, 1985. Chmn. Muhammadiyah dist. br., Jakarta, 1985—. Mem. Indonesian Assn. for Tng. and Devel., London Inst. Tng. and Devel., Indonesian Personnel Mgmt. Assn., Indonesian Quality Mgmt. Assn., Industrial Soc. (London). Islam. Home: Kp Melayu Kecil I, Gg XII/29, 12840 Jakarta Indonesia Office: PT Ruri Safira, Jl Senopati 114 Keb. Baru, 11410 Jakarta Indonesia

MULJONO, WINAR HARTONO, pharmaceutical company executive; b. Malang, East Java, Indonesia, Nov. 5, 1943; s. Janto and Sarna (Lies) M.; m. Adriana Wirianata, July 15, 1972; children: Lukas, Mark. BA, U. Trisakti, 1969; MM, Grad. Sch. Mgmt., Jakarta, 1971; MBA, Inst. for Mgmt. Edn. and Devel., Jakarta, 1985. Supr. CV Beringin, Jakarta, 1967-69; chief comml. dept. PT Bayer Farma Indonesia, Jakarta, 1971-74; purchasing exec. PT B.A.T., Jakarta, 1974; materials control mgr. PT Warner Lambert Indonesia, Jakarta, 1975—, S.E.A. purchasing coordinator, 1980—; mgmt. cons., Jakarta, 1980—. Mem. Himpunan Mktg. Execs. Indonesia, Masyara kat Alumni Pendidikan Manajemen Terpadu LPPM (treas. 1983), Keluarga Alumni MBA-IPPM. Home: Jalan Cideng Barat 50, Jakarta 10150, Indonesia

MULLAN, IDA VIRGINIA, accountant; b. South Tunnell, Tenn., Feb. 5, 1926; d. Huldy and Virginia (Parker) Johnston; student Purdue U. Extension, 1944-45, U. Calif. Extension, San Francisco, 1946, Mary Hardin-Baylor Coll., 1960, Lamar State Coll. Tech., 1961-62, Ind. U. Extension, 1964; m. William Harvey Mullan, Oct. 2, 1943 (div. 1972); 1 dau., Carmen Maria. Mgr., sec.-treas. Belco Industries, Inc., St. Louis, 1949-59; acct. with J. Marvin Campbell, C.P.A., Port Arthur, Tex., 1961-62; dist. mgr. Nat. Acceptance Co. Am., Atlanta, 1962; public acct., Port Arthur, 1962-63; acct. Spann & Rassmann, Inc., Indpls., 1963-64; sr. acct., auditor Elmer Fox & Co., C.P.A., 1965-67; asst. controller Univ. Computing Co., Dallas, 1967-70; sr. v.p. fin. and adminstrn. Bell Equipment Corp., N.Y.C., 1970, Los Angeles, 1971-73; v.p. fin. Scope Industries, Los Angeles, 1973-87; organizer, dir. First Women's Bank Calif., Los Angeles. C.P.A., Tex., Ind. Mem. Am. Inst. C.P.A.s, Tex., Ind., Am. Woman's socs. C.P.A.s, Am. Soc. Women Accts. Roman Catholic. Club: Toastmistress. Home: 2505 McCoy Rd Carrollton TX 75006

MULLANI, NIZAR ABDUL, medical educator researcher; b. Daressalaam, Tanzania, Oct. 22, 1942; s. Abdulshamsh Husein and Noorbanu Jiwan-Hirjee M.; m. Linda Kay, June 21, 1975; 1 son, Ethan. B.S., Washington U., St. Louis, 1967. Research asst. biomed computer lab. Washington U., 1970-80, research assoc. div. radiation scis. Mallinckrodt Inst. Radiology, Sch. Medicine, 1976-80; asst. prof. medicine, tech. dir. positron diagnostic and research ctr. U. Tex. Health Sci. Ctr., Houston, 1980-85, assoc. prof. medicine, 1985—, tech. dir. ctr. cardiovascular and imaging research 1985—. Mem. site visit rev. com. NIH and Dept. Energy; reviewer Jour. Nuclear Medicine, IEEE Transactions on Nuclear Sci., Jour. Computer Assisted Tomography. Contbr. articles to profl. jours. Grantee Am. Heart Assn. Mem. IEEE Nuclear Sci. Soc. (sr.), Soc. Nuclear Medicine, AAAS. Moslem. Office: 6431 Fannin Houston TX 77025

MULLEN, THOMAS EDGAR, real estate consultant; b. Hackensack, N.J., Feb. 10, 1936; s. Luke B. and Jean (Edgar) M.; m. Sarah Lee Huff, Aug. 17, 1984. BS in Engring., Va. Poly. Tech., 1954; grad mgmt. program, Harvard U., 1964. Cons. in field. Mgr. mktg. Eastern Airlines, N.Y.C., 1954-69; pres. Profl. Sprits Mktg., N.Y.C., 1969-72, Shelter Devel. Corp. Am., N.Y.C., 1972-79; supr. ops. Gen. Mills, Orlando, Fla., 1980-86; cons., exec., realtor A.H.M. Graves Co. Inc., Indpls., 1986—. Inventor TV Guider Holder, patent, 1971. Fund raiser Am. Cancer Soc., Miami, 1967-70, Weschester Hosp., N.Y.C., 1967-70. Mem. Met. Bd. Realtors, Nat. Assn. Realtors. Republican. Roman Catholic. Home: 6251 Behner Way Indianapolis IN 46250 Office: AHM Graves Co Inc Carmel IN 46032

MÜLLER, ANSELM WINFRIED, philosopher, educator; b. Berlin, Federal Republic of Germany, Apr. 27, 1942; s. Josef and Maria (Röper) M. PhD, U. Fribourg, Switzerland, 1966; Habilitation, U. Trier, 1978. Lectr. philosophy Balliol Coll., Oxford, Eng., 1967-69; fellow Australian Nat. U., Canberra, 1970; lectr. U. Trier and Braunschweig, Fed. Republic Germany, 1972-74; asst. prof. U. Trier, 1974-79, prof., 1979—; Mem. Wissenschaftl. Beirat Möhler-Inst. für Ökumenik, Paderborn, 1979—. Author: Ontologie in Wittgensteins Tractatus, 1967, Praktisches Folgern, 1982; contbr. articles to profl. jours. Monk of the Benedictine Abbey of St. Matthias, Trier, 1961—. Home: Matthiasstr 85, D5500 Trier Federal Republic of Germany Office: Trier U, D5500 Trier Federal Republic of Germany

MULLER, CHARLES, diplomat; b. Zurich, Switzerland, July 4, 1922; s. Hans Martin and Clara (Meyer) M.; m. Marlise Brugger, July 25, 1950. Lic. ès sci. polit. internat. U. Geneva, 1946. With Swiss Ministry Fgn. Affairs, 1946—, ambassador to Indonesia and Vietnam, 1970-73, head Europe-N.Am. div., 1973-75, sec.-gen. European Free Trade Assn., Geneva, 1976-81, ambassador to Fed. Republic Ger., Bonn, 1981-87.

MULLER, CHARLES ALISTER, insurance company executive; b. Frome, Eng., May 16, 1925; s. Charles James and Enid Daphne (Swinscow) M.; student Brit. schs.; m. Mary Nelson Exton, Aug. 25, 1950; 4 children. Engaged in ins. broking, London, 1942—; del. Internat. Commn. Large Dams. Mem. council Royal Borough of Kensington and Chelsea, London, 1949-78, mayor, 1968-69, alderman, 1969-78; chmn. S. Kensington Young Conservative Assn., 1948-49; Fellow Royal Geog. Soc., trustee ERAS Found. Asso. Corp. Ins. Brokers; mem. Am. Underground Space Assn. Club: City Univ. (London). Author articles in field. Home: Flat 3, 12 Abercorn Pl, London NW8, England Office: Andrew Weir Ins Brokers Ltd, 17A-18 Bevis Marks, London EC3A 7BB, England

MULLER, SIR CLAUS DELOSEY (LORD GARRYHILL), security consulting company executive; b. Portrush, No. Ireland, Aug. 28, 1941; arrived in Fed. Republic Germany, 1955; s. Carl Michael and Lady Caroline (DeLosey) M.; m. Evelyn Buchwald, Nov. 13, 1968 (div. 1977); 1 child, Jens. Student pub. schs., No. Ireland, Germany, Switzerland. with quality control com. IHK Bonn 1976; translator-interpretor IHK Dortmund, 1986; lectr. photography, arts, 1987—. Journalist Westdeutsches Tageblatt, Dortmund, Fed. Republic Germany, 1959-63; freelance journalist, photographer Austria, Luxembourg, Switzerland, Fed. Republic Germany, 1966-70; mgmt. trainee Tyne Canoes Ltd., Twickenham, Eng., 1971-72; export mgr. Coleraine (No. Ireland) Canoe Ctr., 1972-73, mng. dir., 1973-74; mng. dir. Project Mgmt., Portrush, 1974-75, Cedem Internat., Ballynakill, Garryhill, Ireland, 1975—; gen. mgr. SecurConsult, Dortmund, 1978—. Patentee integral kayak rudder device. Recipient gold, silver, bronze medals Brit., Irish, Swedish, Danish, German canoe unions, 1970—, hon. Silver medal German Canoe Union, 1975; touring Bronze medal Internat. Canoe Fedn., 1975, touring Silver medal, 1978. Fellow Inst. Sales and Mktg. Mgmt.; mem. Am. Mgmt. Assns. Internat., Liberals Internat., Irish/German Circle (sec. gen. 1980—). Club: Liberal (London). Home: The Lodge, Ballynakill/Garryhill Ireland Office: SecurConsult, Rheinlanddamm 3, D-4600 Dortmund Federal Republic of Germany

MULLER, DOROTHEA ROSALIE, retired educator; b. Bklyn., Oct. 29, 1924; d. William Thomas and Anna (Zataracz) Muller; B.A. cum laude, Hunter Coll., 1946; M.A. (scholar 1946-47), U. Wis., 1948; Ph.D. (fellow 1951-53), NYU, 1956. Temporary tutor Hunter Coll., N.Y.C., 1948-50, 56; tchr. N.Y.C. Public Schs., 1950-53, White Plains (N.Y.) High Sch., 1953-54; mem. faculty C. W. Post Coll. of L.I. U., Greenvale, N.Y., 1957-82, asst. prof., 1957-62, assoc. prof., 1962-71, prof. history, 1971-82. Recipient Founders Day award NYU, 1956; AAUW fellow, 1964-65. Mem., Am. Hist. Assn., Orgn. Am. Historians, Western History Assn., Am. Soc. Church History, Wyo. State Hist. Soc. Contbr. articles to profl. jours.

MULLER, FRANK B., advertising executive; b. Copenhagen, Denmark, Nov. 25, 1926; s. Herman B. and Johanne M. (Ammentorp) M.; m. Judith Hunter, Apr. 14, 1956; children—Mark W., Hunter J., Frank B. Student, Harvard U., 1944; B.N.S. in Naval Sci., Tufts Coll., 1946; B.S. in Mech. Engring., Tufts U., 1948. Account supr. advt. dept. Gen. Electric Co., 1948-55; exec. v.p. Muller Jordan Weiss Inc., N.Y.C., 1955—. Served to lt. (j.g.) USNR, 1944-47. Mem. ASME. Republican. Congregationalist. Clubs: N.Y. Yacht (N.Y.C.); Saugatuck Harbor Yacht (Westport, Conn.) (bd. govs. 1965-75, 79-80, commodore 1970-71). Home: 46 Marion Rd Westport CT 06880 Office: Muller Jordan Weiss 666 Fifth Ave New York NY 10103

MULLER, JEROME KENNETH, art dealer, editor, psychologist; b. Amityville, N.Y., July 18, 1934; s. Alphons and Helen (Haberl) m.; m. Nora Marie Nestor, Dec. 21, 1974. BS, Marquette U., 1961; postgrad., Calif.

State U., Fullerton, 1985-86; MA, Nat. U., San Diego, 1988; postgrad., Newport Ctr. for Psychoanalytic Studies, 1988—. Comml. and editorial photographer N.Y.C., 1952-55; mng. editor Country Beautiful mag., Milw., 1961-62, Reprodns. Rev. mag., N.Y.C., 1967-68; editor, art dir. Orange County (Calif.) Illustrated, Newport Beach, 1962-67, art editor, 1970-79, exec. editor, art dir., 1968-69; owner, chief exec. officer Creative Services Advt. Agy., Newport Beach, 1969-79; founder, chief exec. officer Mus. Graphics, Costa Mesa, Calif., 1978—; tchr. photography Lindenhurst (N.Y.) High Sch., 1952-54; tchr. comic art U. Calif., Irvine, 1979; guest curator 50th Anniversary Exhbn. Mickey Mouse, 1928-78, The Bowers Mus., Santa Ana, Calif., 1978; organized Moving Image Exhbn. Mus. Sci. and Industry, Chgo., Cooper-Hewitt Mus., N.Y.C., William Rockhill Nelson Gallery, Kansas City, 1981; collector original works of outstanding Am. cartoonists which are exhibited at major mus. One-man shows include Souk Gallery, Newport Beach, 1970; Author: Rex Brandt, 1972; contbr. photographs and articles to mags. Served with USAF, 1956-57. Recipient two silver medals 20th Ann. Exhbn. Advt. and Editorial Art in West, 1965. Mem. Profl. Photographers West, Newport Harbor Art Mus., Mus. Modern Art (N.Y.C.), Met. Mus. Art, Art Mus. Assn. Am., Laguna Beach Mus. Art, Newport Harbor C. of C., Alpha Sigma Nu. Clubs: Los Angeles Press, Orange County Press. Home: 2438 Bowdoin Pl Costa Mesa CA 92626 Office: PO Box 10743 Costa Mesa CA 92627

MÜLLER, JORGE ERNESTO, physicist, researcher; b. Buenos Aires, Mar. 3, 1943; arrived in Fed. Republic Germany, 1980; s. Emil and Fryda (Bilgrei) M.; m. Christine Kunigunda Wehr, Apr. 28, 1983; 1 child, Hanna Naemi. MS in Engring., U. Buenos Aires, 1968; MS in Physics, U. Chile, Santiago, 1973; PhD in Physics, Cornell U., 1979. Lectr. U. Chile, 1970-73; teaching and research asst. Cornell U., Ithaca, 1974-79; researcher in theoretical physics Kernforschungsanlage Jülich, Fed. Republic Germany, 1980—. Contbr. articles to profl. jours. Office: Kernforschungsanlage Jülich, Postfach 1913, D-5170 Jülich Federal Republic of Germany

MÜLLER, K. ALEX, physicist, researcher; b. Apr. 20, 1927. PhD in Physics, Swiss Fed. Inst. Tech., 1958; DSc (hon.), U. Geneva, 1987, Tech. U. Munich, 1987, U. Studi di Pavia, Italy, 1987. Project mgr. Battelle Inst., Geneva, 1958-63; lectr. U. Zurich, Switzerland, 1962—, titular prof. physics, 1970—; researcher solid-state physics IBM Zurich Research Lab., Rüschlikon, Switzerland, 1963-73, mgr. dept. physics, 1973-82, fellow, 1982-85; researcher Switzerland, 1985—. Contbr. over 200 articles to tech. publs. Recipient Marcel-Benoist Found. prize, 1986, Nobel prize in physics, 1987, (with J. Georg Bednorz) Fritz London Meml. award, 1987, Dannie Heineman prize Acad. Scis. Göttingen, Fed. Republic of Germany, 1987, Robert Wichard Pohl prize German Phys. Soc., 1987, Europhysics prize Hewlett-Packard Co., 1988. Fellow Am. Phys. Soc. (Internat. prize for new materials research 1988); mem. European Phys. Soc. (mem. ferroelectricity group), Swiss Phys. Soc., Zurich Phys. Soc. (pres. 1968-69), Groupement Ampère. Office: IBM Zurich Research Lab, Saumerstrasse 4, CH-8803 Ruschlikon Switzerland *

MÜLLER, KLAUS RICHARD, scientist; b. Greiz, Thüringen, Germany, Jan. 29, 1932; divorced; 1 child. PhD, Humboldt U., Berlin, 1962; PhD, Habilitation, Humboldt U., 1970. Asst. Humboldt U., Berlin, 1954-59; sci. collaborator Akademie Wissenschaften DDR, Berlin, 1959—; tchr. Humboldt U., Berlin, 1953-72, Pädagogische Hochschule Karl Liebknecht, Potsdam, 1957-75. Author: Die Beseeltheit in der Grammatik der russischen Sprache der Gegenwart und ihre historische Entwicklung, 1965; co-editor: O Bojan, du Nachtigall der alten Zeit, 1965, 67, 75, 82; editor, co-author: Zur Ausbildung der Norm der deutschen Literatursprache auf der lexikalischen Ebene (1470-1730), 1976, 89; editor Fjodor Tjutschew, 1988; author: (with others) Deutsch-Russisches Wörterbuch, 1983, Etymologisches Wörterbuch des Deutschen, 1988; editor: Albrecht von Eyb, Ehebüchlein, 1986, Itineraria rossica, 1986, Altrussisches Hausbuch Domostroi, 1987, Fjodor Tjutschew, 1988; contbr. articles to profl. jours. Mem. Kommission für Lexikologie und Lexikographie beim Internat. Slawistenkomitee. Home: AchtermannstraBe 51, 1100 Berlin German Democratic Republic

MULLER, ROLF HUGO, chemist; b. Aarau, Switzerland, Aug. 6, 1929; came to U.S., 1957, naturalized, 1967; s. Wilhelm and Alice Louise (Schmid) M.; m. Dorothy Leah Donaldson, July 18, 1962; children: Wilhelm Karl, Alice Barbara. MS in Natural Sci., Fed. Inst. Tech., Zurich, Switzerland, 1953, teaching cert., 1955, PhD in Natural Sci., 1957; postgrad., U. Calif., Berkeley, 1960-61. Asst. in phys. chemistry Fed. Inst. Tech., 1955-56; research and devel. chemist E.I. DuPont de Nemours, Parkersburg, W.Va., 1957-60; research assoc. dept. chem. engring. U. Calif., Berkeley, 1961-62; staff scientist Lawrence Berkeley Lab., 1962-66, prin. investigator, 1966—, asst. div. head., 1970-86, assoc. div. head, 1987—, staff sr. scientist, 1978—; lectr. univ. dept. chem. engring., 1966—; sec. Nat. Battery Adv. Com. to Dept. Energy adhoc, Planning Subcom. 1977-85. Editor several books; contbr. articles to profl. jours. Mem. AAAS, Electrochem. Soc. (sect. chmn. 1971, councilor 1976, sec., treas. phys. electrochemistry div. 1985-86), Internat. Soc. Electrochemistry (div. co-chmn. 1973-77, plenary lectr. Zurich 1976, chmn. tech. program 1984), Swiss Chem. Soc., Optical Soc. Am., U. Calif. at Berkeley Faculty. Home: 36 Highgate Rd Berkeley CA 94707 Office: U Calif Lawrence Berkeley Lab Materials and Chem Scis div 62-203 Berkeley CA 94720

MULLER, SIEGFRIED WOLFGANG, export executive; b. Essen, Germany, May 9, 1942; came to France, 1968; s. Eduard and Juliane (Grahli) M.; m. Maria Ines Munoz Gomez, Dec. 14, 1979; children: Juliana, Klaus. BS, Calif. Coast U., 1985. Programmer, Eurocomp, Minden, Fed. Republic Germany, 1963-65; sales engr. CAE, Frankfurt, Fed. Republic Germany, 1965-68; area mgr. export Telemecanique, Rueil, France, 1968-76; area mgr. export SEMS, Louveciennes, France, 1976-81; export mgr. Orega, Auxonne, France, 1981-87, Videocolor, Paris, 1987. Home: 2 Rue des Pepinieres, 92330 Sceaux France Office: Videocolor, 7 Bd Romain Rolland, 92128 Montrouge France

MULLER, STEVEN, university president; b. Hamburg, Germany, Nov. 22, 1927; came to U.S., 1940, naturalized, 1949; s. Werner Adolph and Marianne (Hartstein) M.; m. Margie Hellman, June 19, 1951; children: Julie, Elizabeth. B.A., UCLA, 1948; B.Litt. (Rhodes scholar), Oxford (Eng.) U., 1951; Ph.D., Cornell U., 1958. Asst. prof. Haverford (Pa.) Coll., 1956-58; mem. faculty and adminstrn. Cornell U., 1958-71; dir. Cornell U. (Center Internat. Studies), 1961-66, v.p. pub. affairs, 1966-71; provost Johns Hopkins U., 1971-72, pres., 1972—; also trustee Johns Hopkins U. and Hosp.; pres. Johns Hopkins Hosp., 1972-83; cons. Dept. Def., 1962-67, ACDA, 1962-67; bd. dirs. CSX Corp., Orgn. Resources Counselors Inc., Millipore Corp., Beneficial Corp., Alex. Brown, Inc. Author: Documents on European Government, 1963, also articles.; bd. editors: Daedalus. Bd. dirs. German Marshall Fund of U.S., Consortium for Advancement Higher Edn., Balt. Mus. Art., Md. Acad. Scis. Served with U.S. Army, 1954-55. Decorated comdr. Order of Merit Fed. Republic of Germany). Mem. Am. Acad. Arts and Scis., Com. for Econ. Devel., Council Fgn. Relations, Am. Polit. Sci. Assn., Internat. Inst. Strategic Studies, Am. Assn. Rhodes Scholars, Phi Beta Kappa. Clubs: Cosmos (Washington); Center (Balt.). Office: Johns Hopkins Univ Charles & 34th Sts Baltimore MD 21218

MÜLLER, WERNER E.G., biochemist; b. Sprendlingen, Germany, Aug. 19, 1942; s. Jakob A. and Marie (Bopp) M.; m. Isabel Zahn, Dec. 28, 1971; 1 child, Claudia. Ph.D., U. Mainz, 1967. Med. Faculty U. Mainz, Fed. Republic Germany, 1971—, prof. biochemistry, 1972—, head dept. Angewandte Molekularbiologie, 1977—. Author: Chemotherapie von Tumoren, 1975; The Antibiotic Bleomycin, 1977. Editor: Biochemical and Morphological Aspects of Aging, 1981, Progress in Molecular and Subcellular Biology, 1983. Contbr. articles to profl. jours. Recipient Boehringer Ingelheim prize, 1972, Johann Georg Zimmermann prize, 1977, Bürger prize, 1980. Fellow N.Y. Acad. Scis.; mem. Deutsche Gesellschaft für Biologische Chemie, Deutsche Krebsgesellschaft, Gesellschaft für Naturforscher und Ärzte, European Assn. Cancer Research. Home: Semmelweisstrasse 12, 6200 Wiesbaden Federal Republic of Germany Office: U Mainz, Inst für Physiologische Chemie, Duesbergweg, 6500 Mainz Federal Republic of Germany

MÜLLER-KARPE, MICHAEL, archaeologist, researcher; b. Munich, Feb. 4, 1955; s. Hermann and Renate (Ausfeld) M.-K.; m. Sárika Petrás, Dec. 17, 1985; children: Monika, Zoltán. D. in Philosophy, U. Heidelberg, Fed. Republic Germany, 1987. Curator Vortaunus Mus., Oberursel, Fed. Republic Germany, 1973-74; mem. Uruk-Warka expedition German Inst. Archaeology, Baghdad, Iraq, 1974-75; mem. Merimde expedition German Inst. Archaeology, Cairo, 1977; head Tell Uqair expedition U. Heidelberg and State Orgn. Antiquities, Iraq, 1978; head exhibition Uruk-Warka Collection, Heidelberg, Fed. Republic Germany, 1985—. Author: Metal Vessels in Iraq, 1987. Recipient scholarship for Iraq DAAD, 1979. Mem. Hist. Soc. Oberursel (bd. dirs. 1973-74), Am. Inst. for Yemeni Studies. Office: Inst für Ur-und Frühgeschichte, Marstallhof 4, D-6900 Heidelberg Federal Republic of Germany

MÜLLER-MERBACH, HEINER ERICH, educator; b. Hamburg, Fed. Republic of Germany, June 28, 1936; s. Erich Müller and Gertrud Müller-Merbach; m. Uta Schade, May 16, 1969; children: Jens, Mareile. Diploma Wirtschaftsingenieur, Technische Hochschule, 1960, PhD, 1962. Prof. U. Mainz, Fed. Republic of Germany, 1967-71, Technische Hochschule, Darmstadt, Fed. Republic of Germany, 1971-83, U. Kaiserslautern, Fed. Republic of Germany, 1983—; hon. prof. Tongji U., Shanghai, Peoples Republic of China, 1986. Author: Operations Research, 1969; editor-in-chief (jour.): Technologie & Management. Mem. Internat. Fedn. Operational Research Socs. (pres. 1983-85, past pres. 1986-88), Inst. Mgmt. Scis. (council mem. 1986-88), Verband Deutscher Wirtschaftsingenieure (pres. 1985-87). Home: Am Löwentor 11, D-6100 Darmstadt Federal Republic of Germany Office: U Kaiserslautern, PO Box 3049, D-6750 Kaiserslautern Federal Republic of Germany

MULLER-VAN SANTEN, JULIA JOHANNA GERTRUD, English educator; b. The Hague, The Netherlands, Oct. 18, 1937; d. Fred and Bettie C.S. (Richter) Van Santen; m. Frans Muller, May 24,1932; children: Martin J., Felix, Emmy H. 2d teaching degree, Nutsseminarium U., Amsterdam, The Netherlands, 1972; 1st teaching degree, Vrije Leergangen, Amsterdam, 1976—, Drs. cum laude, 1978. Tchr. English Montessori Lyceum, Amsterdam, 1972-74, Barlaeus Gymnasium, Amsterdam, 1974-76; lectr. Vrije U., Amsterdam, 1985—, Hogeschool Holland, Diemen, The Netherlands, 1986—; mem. legal dept. Tchrs. Union Higher Edn., The Hague, 1975—, bd. dirs., sec., 1976—; pres. emancipation com.Higher Edn. Council, The Netherlands, 1982-84; mem. legal dept. Union Higher Civil Servants, The Hague, 1982—. Author: Max van Egmond, Setting the Tone, 1984; translator: Sexual Behavior, 1965, Encyclopedia of the Classical World, 1965, Games People Play, 1967. Active Govt. Equal Rights Com., The Netherlands, 1984—; pres. Tchr. and Student Council Vrije Leergangen, Amsterdam/Diemen, 1984-87; organizer, Aemstelrande Concerts, Amsterdam. Home: Amsteldijk 89, 1074 JB Amsterdam The Netherlands Office: The Hogeschool Holland, Dept English, Wildenborch 6, 1112 XB Diemen The Netherlands

MULLETTE, JULIENNE PATRICIA, research astrologer, author, lecturer, television personality and producer, editor, holistic health center administrator; b. Sydney, Australia, Nov. 19, 1940; came to U.S., 1953; d. Ronald Stanley Lewis and Sheila Rosalind Blunden (Phillips) M.; m. Fred Gillette Sturm, Nov. 24, 1964 (div. Dec. 1969); m. Kenneth Walter Gillman, Dec. 27, 1971 (div. Dec. 1978); children—Noah Khristoff Mullette-Gillman, O'Dhaniel Alexander Mullette-Gillman. B.A., Western Coll. for Women, Oxford, Ohio, 1961; postgrad. Harvard U., 1964, U. Sao Paulo, Brazil, 1965, Inst. do Filosofia, Sao Paulo, 1965, Miami U., Oxford, 1967-69. Tchr. English, High Mowing Sch., Wilton, N.H., 1962-64, Stoneleigh-Prospect Hill Sch., Greenfield, Mass., 1964; seminar dir. Western Coll., Oxford, Ohio, 1967-69; pres. Family Tree, The Home Univ., Montclair, N.J., 1978-80; dir. Pleroma Holistic Health Ctr., Montclair, 1980—; dir. Astrological Research Ctr., Sydney, Australia, 1983; hostess You and the Cosmos talk show WFMU, East Orange, N.J., 1985, The Juliette Mullette Show, Connections TV, Newark, 1985—, The Juliette Mullette Show WFDU-FM, Fairleigh Dickinson U., N.J., 1986—; founder Spiritual Devel. Research Group 1986—, Spvt. astrology counselor, 1962—; lectr., speaker worldwide, 1968—; guest on radio and TV shows, U.S. and Can., 1962—; host syndicated radio talk show The Juliette Mullette Show, N.Y., N.J., 1987—; owner, pres. Moonlight Pond, Woodbourne, N.Y., 1988—; founder The Spiritual Devel. Ctr., 1986—. Author: The Moon— Understanding the Subconscious, 1973; also articles, 1968—. Founding editor KÓSMOS mag., 1968-78, The Jour. of Astrological Studies, 1970. Founder local chpt. La Leche League, Montclair, 1974. Mem. AAUW (chair cultural affairs Montclair chpt.), Spiritual Devel. Group (founder 1987), Internat. Soc. Astrological Research (founding pres. 1968-78), Am. Fedn. Astrologers (cert.), Societé Belge d'Astrologie, Am. Assn. Humanistic Psychology, AAUW (dir. cultural affairs 1987—), Nat. Assn. Female Execs., Internat. Llamas Assn. Avocations: competitive tennis, local theatre, singing, breeding and training of llamas, alpacas and other exotic animals. Home: 89 A Star Rt Woodbourne NY 12788

MULLIGAN, JOHN THOMAS, lawyer; b. Phila., Dec. 28, 1934; s. Martin A. and Mary Katherine (Glennon) M.; m. Marie A. Pinter, Aug. 22, 1959; children—Mary T., Lisa M. B.S. in Polit. Sci., St. Joseph's U., 1956; J.D. cum laude, U. Pa., 1959. Bar: N.Y. 1960, Pa. 1963, U.S. Dist. Ct. (so. and ea. dists.) N.Y. 1962, U.S. Dist. Ct. (ea. dist.) Pa. 1964, U.S. Tax Ct. 1962, U.S. Ct. Appeals (3d cir. 1965), U.S. Supreme Ct. 1965. Assoc. Dewey, Ballantine, Bushby, Palmer & Wood, N.Y.C., 1959-62; sr. atty. Western Electric Co., N.Y.C., 1962-63; ptnr. Lord & Mulligan, Media, Pa., 1963—; solicitor Marple Twp., Broomall, Pa., 1970-71, Haverford Twp., Havertown, Pa., 1972-73, Radnor-Haverford-Marple Sewer Authority, Wayne, Pa., 1974-83; panel mem. Fed. Ct. Arbitration, Phila., 1977—. Mem. Haverford Twp. Adult Sch., Haverford, Pa., 1965-66; fin. chmn. Haverford Twp. Democratic Com., Havertown, 1965-70. Recipient Commendation U.S. Dist Ct. (ea. dist.) Pa. 1983. Mem. Assn. Trial Lawyers Am., ABA, Pa. Trial Lawyers Assn., Pa. Bar Assn., N.Y. State Bar Assn., Delaware County Bar Assn., Assn. Bar City of N.Y. Democrat. Roman Catholic. Clubs: Llanerch Country (Havertown, Pa.) (sec. 1977-81); Atlantic City Country (Northfield, N.J.); Overbrook Country (Bryn Mawr, Pa.). Home: 2728 N Kent Rd Broomall PA 19008 Office: Lord and Mulligan 15 W Front St Media PA 19063

MULLIGAN, WILLIAM G(EORGE), lawyer; b. N.Y.C., July 16, 1906; s. William George and Agnes (Murphy) M.; m. Dorothy K. Zimmer, Jan. 27, 1928 (dec.); 1 dau., Maura Elaine; m. Mary Luciel McGookey, Sept. 6, 1942; children—Don John (dec.), Luciel Laurene; m. Elinor Patterson O'Connor, Dec. 6, 1975. A.B., Hamilton Coll., 1927; LL.B., Harvard U., 1930. Bar: N.Y. 1931, N.J. 1976. Asst. Wickersham Crime Commn., 1929-30; asst. to Hon. Hiram C. Todd, spl. dep. N.Y. atty. gen. pros. jud. frauds, 1930-31; asst. Hon. Samuel Seabury in proceedings before N.Y. State Gov. Franklin D. Roosevelt to remove James J. Walker as mayor of N.Y. City, 1931-32; assoc. White & Case, 1932-34; asst. corp. counsel City N.Y., 1934-38; chief div. transit 1936, chief div. franchises, 1938; asso. counsel Bd. Transportation, 1939-40; sr. ptnr. various law firms since 1940; now Hall, McNicol, Hamilton & Clark; defended N.Y. Curb Exchange in all litigations brought against it, 1943-50; gen. counsel War Materials, Inc. (fed. material procurement agy.), Pitts., 1942-43. Author: Expert Witnesses: Direct and Cross-examinations, 1987; lectr. on legal topics. Mem. Assn. Bar City N.Y., Am. Coll. Trial Lawyers, N.Y. County Lawyers Assn., Am., N.Y. State, N.J. bar assns., S.A.R. (chancellor N.Y. chpt.), Theta Delta Chi (grad. treas. grand lodge 1964-66). Roman Catholic. Clubs: Union League (N.Y.C.), Harvard (N.Y.C.); Panther Valley Golf and Country (Allamuchy, N.J.); Baltusrol Golf (Springfield, N.J.). Office: Hall McNicol Hamilton & Clark News Bldg 220 E 42d St New York NY 10017 Also: Mulligan Mulligan & Gavin 480 Hwy 517 Hackettstown NJ 07840

MULLIN, RONALD CLEVELAND, mathematics educator; b. Guelph, Ont., Can., Aug. 15, 1936; s. William C. and Edna Mae (Rachar) M.; m. Janet Elizabeth Simpson, Aug. 12, 1971; children—Kimberley, Jaime-Anne. B.A., U. Western Ont., London, 1959; M.A., U. Waterloo, Ont., 1960, Ph.D., 1964. Prof. math. U. Waterloo, 1969—; pres. Cryptech Inc., Waterloo, 1985—; cons. Communications Research Centre, Ottawa, Ont., 1982—. Co-author: Mathematical Theory of Coding, 1975. Patentee in field. Grantee Nat. Sci. and Engring. Research Council, 1965—. Fellow Inst. Math. and its Applications. Home: 533 Twin Oaks Crescent, Waterloo, ON Canada N2L 3G1 Office: U Waterloo, Waterloo, ON Canada N2L 3G1

MULLINS, RICHARD AUSTIN, chemical engineer; b. Seelyville, Ind., Apr. 22, 1918; s. Fred A. and Ethel (Zenor) M.; B.S. in Chem. Engring., Rose Poly. Inst., 1940; postgrad. Yale, 1942-43; m. Margaret Ann Dellacca, Nov. 27, 1946 (dec. Nov. 1982); children—Scott Alan, Mark Earl. Chemist, Ayrshire Collieries Corp., Brazil, Ind., 1940-49; chief chemist Fairview Collieries Corp., Danville, Ill., 1949-54; preparations mgr. Enos Coal Mining Co., Oakland City, Ind., 1954-72, Enoco Collieries, Inc., Bruceville, Ind., 1954-62; mining engr. Kings Station Coal Corp.; mgr. analytical procedures Old Ben Coal Corp., 1973-84; ret., 1984. Am. Mining Congress cons. to Am. Standards Assn. and Internat. Orgn. for Standards, 1960-74; mem. indsl. cons. com. Ind. Geol. Survey, 1958-72; mem. organizing com. 5th Internat. Coal Preparation Congress, Pittsburgh, 1966. Mem. exec. bd. Buffalo Trace council Boy Scouts Am., also mem. speakers bur. Bd. dirs. Princeton Boys Club. Served with AUS, 1942-46; ETO. Decorated Medaille de la France Liberee (France); recipient Eagle Scout award, Boy Scouts Am., 1935, Silver Beaver award, 1962, Wood Badge Beads award, 1960; Outstanding Community Service award Princeton Civitan Club, 1964; Engr. of Year award S.W. chpt. Ind. Soc. Profl. Engrs., 1965; Prince of Princeton award Princeton C. of C., 1981. Registered profl. engr., Ind., Ill. Mem. AIME (life mem.), ASTM (sr. mem., R.D. Glenn award 1985), Am. Chem. Soc., Nat. Soc. Profl. Engrs. (life mem.), Ind., Ill. mining insts., Ind. Coal Soc. (pres. 1958-59), Am. Mining Congress (chmn. com. coal preparation 1964-68), Am. Legion (past commn. chmn.), VFW (past co. comdr., 40 & 8 VFW), Ind. Soc. Profl. Land Surveyors, Rose Tech. Alumni Assn. (pres. 1976-77, Honor Alumnus 1980), Order of Ring, Sigma Nu. Methodist (lay speaker). Mason, Elk. Contbr. articles to profl. jours. Home: Rural Route 4 Box 159 Princeton IN 47670

MULRONEY, (MARTIN) BRIAN, prime minister Canada; b. Mar. 20, 1939; s. Benedict and Irene (O'Shea) M.; m. Mila Pivnicki, 1973; 4 children. B.A., St. Francis Xavier U., LL.D. (hon.), 1979; LL.L., U. Laval, Que.; LL.D. (hon.), Meml. U., 1980. Ptnr. Ogilvy, Renault, Montreal, Que., 1965-76; pres. Iron Ore Co. of Can., 1976-83; mem. Parliament Can. from Central Nova Scotia, Ottawa, Ont., 1983-84; mem. Parliament Can. from Manicouagan 1984—, leader of Her Majesty's Loyal Opposition, 1983-84, prime minister Can., 1984—; royal commr. Cliche Commn. investigating violence in Que. constrn. industry, 1974. Author: Where I Stand, 1983. Clubs: Mt. Royal (Montreal); Albany (Toronto); Garrison (Quebec). Office: House of Commons, Office of Prime Minister, Ottawa, ON Canada K1A 0A2 *

MULRYAN, HENRY TRIST, mineral company executive; b. Palo Alto, Calif., Jan. 6, 1927; s. Henry and Marian Abigail (Trist) M.; m. Lenore Hoag, Aug. 25, 1948; children: Patricia T., James W., Carol. Student, Yale U., 1945-46; AB in Econs., Stanford U., 1948; postgrad., Am. Grad. Sch. Internat. Bus., 1949, Columbia U., 1983. V.p. mktg. Sierra Talc Co., South Pasadena, Calif., 1955-65; v.p. mktg. United Sierra, Trenton, N.J., 1965-67, v.p., gen. mgr., 1967-70, pres., 1970-77; v.p. Cyprus Mines Corp., Los Angeles, 1978-80; sr. v.p. ops. Cyprus indsl. minerals div. Amoco Minerals Co., Englewood, Colo., 1980-85; pres. Cyprus Indls. Minerals Co., Englewood, 1985-87; v.p. Cyprus Minerals Co., Englewood, 1985-87, sr. v.p. mktg., corp. adminstr., 1987—; chmn. Nihon Mistron Co., Tokyo. Served with U.S. Army, 1944-46. Clubs: Jonathan (Los Angeles); Met. (Englewood, Colo.). Lodge: Rotary (pres. South Pasadena club 1964-65) (bd. dirs. Princeton, N.J. club 1969-75). Office: Cyprus Minerals Co 9100 E Mineral Circle Englewood CO 80112

MULUKA, EVANS ADAM PESSA, psychiatry educator; b. Kakamega, Kenya, July 4, 1945; s. Samuel and Rosah (Waka) M.; m. Nellie Anzazi Mwendar, Dec. 30, 1972; children: Eric, Alan, Samuel. MB, ChB, U. Nairobi, 1974. Med. officer Ministry of Health, Mombasa, Kenya, 1974-75; tutorial fellow U. Nairobi, 1976-79, lectr. in psychiatry, 1983—; resident in psychiatry Maudsley Hosp., London, 1980-82; cons. Kenyatta Nat. Hosp., 1983—, Mathari Mental Hosp., Nairobi, 1983—, Aga Khan Hosp., Nairobi, 1984—. Editor: East Africa Med. Jour., 1985—; contbr. articles to profl. jours. Mem. Royal Coll. Psychiatrists, Kenya Med. Assn. Mem. Kenya African Nat. Union Party. Office: U Nairobi Kenyatta Nat Hosp, Nairobi Kenya

MUMMA, ALBERT G., retired naval officer, manufacturing company executive, management consultant; b. Findlay, Ohio, June 2, 1906; grad. U.S. Naval Acad., 1926; D.Eng., Newark Coll. Engring., 1970; m. Carmen Braley, 1927; children—Albert G., John S., David B. Commd. ensign USN, 1926, advanced through grades to rear adm.; head tech. intelligence div. Naval Forces Europe, World War II; comdr. David Taylor Model Basin, Mare Island Naval Shipyard, also chief Bur. Ships, U.S. Navy, 1955-59; builder nuclear high speed submarines, U.S.S. Enterprise, Long Beach, Bainbridge and Polaris submarines, 1957; ret., 1959; v.p., group exec. Worthington Corp., 1964, exec. v.p., dir. in charge all domestic ops., 1967, pres., chief operating officer, 1967, chmn. bd., 1967-71; chmn. Am. Shipbldg. Commn., 1971-73. Trustee emeritus Drew U., Madison, N.J. Recipient Adm. Jerry Land Gold medal; awarded Knight Grand Officer of Orange Nassau by the Queen of the Netherlands. Fellow Soc. Naval Architects and Marine Engrs. (hon.; past pres.); mem. Am. Soc. Naval Engrs. (hon.; past pres.), Nat. Acad. Scis. (past mem. research council; past chmn. numerous coms.), Nat. Acad. Engring. (life). Clubs: Army and Navy, Army and Navy Country (Washington); N.Y. Yacht (N.Y.C.); Baltusrol Golf (Springfield, N.J.); Mountain Lake (Lake Wales, Fla.). Home: Bald Peak Colony Club Box 405 Melvin Village NH 03850

MUMMA, ALBERT GIRARD, JR., architect; b. Long Beach, Calif., July 2, 1928; s. Albert Girard and Carmen (Braley) M.; m. Janeal Thomas Woolf, Dec. 24, 1973; children by previous marriage—Eugenia M. Villagra, Albert Girard III, Peter Brenaman. B.Arch., U. Va., 1951. Designer McLeod & Ferrara, Architects, Washington, 1951-56; assoc. Deigert & Yerkes, Architects, 1956-62; prin. Mumma & Assocs., Washington, 1962—; archtl. designer hotel div. Marriott Corp., 1980-82. Prin. archtl. works include: Nat. Arboretum Hdqrs. Bldg, 1961, Finnmark Sq., Silver Spring, Md., 1964, Inverness townhouses, Potomac, Md., 1971, Post Office and Fed. Bldg., Elkins, W.Va., 1971, U.S. Trade Fairs in Spain, Finland, Japan, El Salvador, Poland 1963-72, Fallswood housing project, Falls Church, Va., 1972, Bristow Village townhouses, Annandale, Va., 1972-73, Marriott Hotel, Dayton, Ohio, 1982, Plaza Venetia, Biscayne Bay, Miami, Fla., 1983, Houston Med. Ctr. Hotel, Newark Airport Hotel, 1984, pvt. residences, subdivision and townhouse projects, Washington, Md., Va., Pa., 1962—. Served with USMCR, 1945-47. Recipient Design award Washington Bd. Trade, 1964; winner Newark Airport Hotel Competition, 1981. Mem. AIA (medal 1951). Presbyterian. Club: Rappahannock River Yacht (Irvington, Va.). also: P O Box 205 Merry Point VA 22513

MUMMERY, PETER, publishing company executive; b. London, Oct. 10, 1930; s. William Lance and Dawn (Liddell) M.; m. Sandra Bingley, June 8, 1963; children: Steven, Piers, Nicola. MB, Cambridge (Eng.) U., 1944-49. Advt. mgr. Rootes, London, 1955-59, Rootes Motors, N.Y.C., 1959-63, Time, London, 1963-68, 73-77, Johannesburg, South Africa, 1968-73; pub. dir. Far East Trade Press, Hong Kong, 1977-79; dist. mgr. Businessweek, London, 1979—. Served to lt. Brit. Army, 1949-51. Mem. Ch. of Eng. Clubs: Marylebone Cricket, Royal Automobile (London). Office: Businessweek, 34 Dover St, London W1X 4BR, England

MUNAR, MICHELE, physician; b. Dijon, Côte D'Or, France, Apr. 27, 1949; d. Antoine-Philippe and Madeleine (Decrette) M.; m. Patrick Lecour, June 20, 1984; 1 child, Anne-Gaelle. Doctorate, Medicine Faculty Internat. Med., Dijon, 1976; diploma, Acupunture and Stimulo-Therapy Soc., Paris, 1983. Labour dr. Unic-Fiat, Fourchambault, Nievre, France, 1976; physician, acupunctor Chateauroux, Indre, 1977—; part-time chief dr. Cure Home Gireugne, Saint-Maur, Indre, 1978-79; maternal and infantile protection dir. Direction Dept. Affaires Sanitaires et Sociales, Chateauroux, 1977-79. Office: 16 rue Eugene Delacroix, 36000 Chateauroux, Indre France

MUNDENDE, DARLINGTON CHONGO, geography educator; b. Mporokoso, Zambia, July 24, 1954; s. Jackson Mwenya Mundende Chifuta and Monica Lombe (Mangu) Mwenya; m. Grace Bertha Chikaka, May 6, 1979; children: Chongo, Mulenga Chonya, Mwenya Chifuta. BA, U. Zambia, 1978; MA, U. Alta., Can., 1981; postgrad., Mich. State U., 1984—. Tutor, demonstrator U. Zambia, Lusaka, 1978-79, staff devel. fellow, 1979-81, lectr., 1982—, sr. research fellow, 1984-88; cons. Cen. Statis. Office, Lusaka, 1982-83. Contbr. articles to profl. jours. Grad. fellow The Population Council, N.Y.C., 1987-88. Mem. Internat. Union for the Sci. Study of Population, Assn. Am. Geographers, Zambia Geog. Assn. (asst. editor 1983-84), Population Reference Bur. Seventh-Day Adventist. Office: U Zambia Dept Geography, Box 32379, Lusaka Zambia

MUNDIA, NALUMINO, diplomat, former prime minister of Zambia; b. Namanda Village, Kalabo Dist., Zambia, Nov. 21, 1927; m. Cecilia Sithole, 1964; 6 children. Ed. Shri Ram Coll. Commerce, U. Delhi (India), Atlanta U. Tchr. in Zimbabwe and Namibia; founding mem., dep. nat. treas., dir. elections United Nat. Ind. Party, 1961-65; minister of local govt., commerce, industry and tourism, labour and social devel. Zambia, 1964-66; M.P. from Kabwe, Zambia, 1967; M.P., dep. pres. Parliament, African Nat. Congress, 1969; M.P., 1981—, minister of fin., 1983-84; mem. central com. United Nat. Ind. Party, 1978—, chair subcom. youth and sports, 1979-81, vice chair Nat. Commn. for Devel. Planning; prime minister of Zambia, 1984-86; ambassador to U.S., Washington, 1986—, Brazil, Peru and Venezuela. Author: Grim Peep into the North.Avocations: gardening, swimming. Office: Embassy Republic Zambia 2419 Mass Ave NW Washington DC 20008

MUNGER, ELMER LEWIS, civil engineer, educator; b. Manhattan, Kans., Jan. 4, 1915; s. Harold Hawley and Jane (Green) M.; m. Vivian Marie Bloomfield, Dec. 28, 1939; children: John Thomas, Harold Hawley II, Jane Marie. B.S., Kans. State U., 1936, M.S., 1938; Ph.D., Iowa State U., 1957. Registered profl. engr., Nebr., Kans., Iowa, Vt. Rodman St. Louis-Southwestern Ry., Ark., Mo., 1937-38; engr. U.S. Engr. Dept., Ohio, Nebr., 1938-46; missionary engr. Philippine Episcopal Ch., 1946-48; engr. Wilson & Co., Salina, Kans., 1948; tchr. Iowa State U., 1948-51, 54-58; engr. C.E., U.S. Army, Alaska, 1951-54; from tchr. to dean Norwich U., Northfield, Vt., 1958-69; prof. gen. engring. U. P.R., Mayagüez, 1969-75; prof. civil engring. Mich. Tech. U., 1975-80; cons. engr. 1980—; Mem. spl. com. on engring. Inter-Am. Devel. Bank, U. W.I., 1971. Author: (with Clarence J. Douglas) Construction Management, 1970. Fellow ASCE, Soc. Am. Mil. Engrs.; mem. Nat., Vt. socs. profl. engrs., Am. Soc. Engring. Edn., Phi Kappa Phi, Sigma Tau, Tau Beta Pi, Chi Epsilon. Episcopalian. Clubs: Masons, Shriners. Home: 21028 Tucker Ave Port Charlotte FL 33954

MUNIER, JACQUES JEAN GILBERT, electronics executive; b. Casablanca, Morocco, July 25, 1928; s. Henri Constant and Noelle Marie (Gerardin) M.; m. Gisèle Marie Prieur, Mar. 20, 1952; children: Jacques-Henri, Hubert, Jean-Marc, Catherine. Diploma, Ecole Superieure d'Electricite, Paris, 1948. Electronic engr. tech. Atelier Indsl. de L'Air, Casablanca, 1948-57, Canadair, Montreal, Que., Can., 1957-64; sales engr. Aerel, Paris, 1964-68; dir. tech. Seuri, Paris, 1968—. Home: 10 ter, Chemin du Parc, 95220 Herblay France Office: Seuri, 36 Ave Hoche, 75008 Paris France

MUNIM, FAZLE KADERI MUHAMMAD ABDUL, chief justice of Bangladesh; b. Dhaka, Bangladesh, Dec. 1, 1924; s. Muhammad Abdul Khaliq Munim and Shayesta Khatun; m. Syeda Nurun Nahar, Nov. 9, 1953; children: Ahsan Mahbub, Hussain Mahmud, Junaid, Zubayr, Saad. BA with honors, U. Calcutta, 1945; MA, U. Dhaka, 1947, LLB, 1949; LLM, U. London, 1958, PhD in Constl. Law, 1960. Barrister of the Lincoln's Inn. Advocate High Ct. of Dhaka, 1951-64; sr. judge advocate Supreme Ct. of Pakistan, 1964-69; legal advisor Indsl. Devel. Bank Pakistan, 1969-70; advocate-gen. of East Pakistan 1970-72; judge High Ct. Dhaka, 1970—; chief justice Bangladesh 1982—; dep. sec. Ministry of Law and Parliamentary Affairs Govt. Bangladesh, 1972-73; judge High Ct. Bangladesh, 1972-76; judge appellate div. Supreme Ct. Bangladesh 1976-82; mem. Internat. Law Commn. UN, 1976-77; chmn. Judicial Tng. Mgmt. Bd., 1985—, Bangladesh Jail Reforms Commn., 1979-81; mem. Expert Com. for Drafting Statute for Internat. Islamic Ct. Justice-Orgn. Islamic Conf., 1981. Author: Rights of the Citizen under the Constitution and Law, 1975, Legal Aspects of Martial Law, 1988. Mem. Syndicate of the U. Dhaka, 1972-75, Syndicate of the U. Jahangirnagar, Bangladesh, 1972-78. Mem. Bangladesh Inst. Law and Internat. Affairs (founder, pres., chmn.), East Pakistan Bar Council, Pakistan Bar Council. Home: 19 Hare Rd, Dhaka Bangladesh Office: Supreme Ct, Dhaka Bangladesh

MUNOZ, MARIO ALEJANDRO, civil engineer; b. Havana, Cuba, Feb. 27, 1928; s. Ramón and Concepción (Bermudo) M.; came to U.S., 1961, naturalized, 1968; M.Arch., U. Havana, 1954; postgrad. City Colls. Chgo., 1974; m. Julia Josephine Garrofe, Jan. 17, 1970. Owner, Muñoz Bermudo-Construcciones, Havana, 1954-61; designer various cos., Chgo., 1961-65; designer Chgo. Transit Authority, Mdse. Mart, Chgo., 1965-69; civil engr. Dept. Water and Sewers, City of Chgo., 1969-79, supervising engr. Dept. of Sewers, 1979-85, coordinating engr., 1985-88, asst. chief engr., 1988—; mem. central area subway system utilities com. City of Chgo., 1974—, mem. computer graphics com., 1977-78. Mem. Am. Pub. Works Assn., Western Soc. Engrs., Chgo. Architecture Found., Chgo. Council Fgn. Relations. Roman Catholic. Clubs: Ground Hog, Execs. (speaker's table com.) (Chgo.); Oak Brook Polo. Home: 5455 N Sheridan Rd Apt 1912 Chicago IL 60640 Office: 121 N LaSalle St Chicago IL 60602

MUÑOZ RUIZ, EMILIO, biochemist, researcher; b. Valencia, Spain, Jan. 13, 1937; s. Emilio and Ana (Ruiz Montalt) Muñoz Orts; m. Angeles Van Den Eynde, Dec. 28, 1964; children: Victor, Ana. MS in Pharmacy, U. Madrid, 1960, PhD in Microbial Biochemistry, 1964. Fellow Consejo Superior Sci. Investigations, Madrid, 1960-66, research asst., 1966-67, sr. researcher, 1971-84, prof. research, 1984—; research asst. Liege (Belgium) U., 1964-67, vis. lectr., 1969; research assoc. NYU, N.Y.C., 1967-68; vis. prof. Los Andes U., Merida, Venezuela, 1972, 75; gen. dir. sci. policy unit, Madrid, 1982-86, gen. dir. sci. and tech. research, 1986-87; exec. Gen. Secret Interministerial Com. Sci. and Tech., Madrid, 1987—. Co-editor: Mechanisms of Protein, 1972; co-author: Apuntes para Una, 1982, Science and Technology, 1986; contbr. articles to profl. jours. Named Premio Periodismo Cientifico, Sci. and Cultural Found., 1982; Juan March Found. fellow, 1963. Mem. Spanish Microbiology Soc., Spanish Biochemistry Soc., Spanish Soc. Terapeutical Chemistry, European Molecular Biochemistry Orgn., Found. Valenciana Estudios Avanzados (corr.), Real Acad. Pharmacy (corr.). Mem. Socialist Party. Roman Catholic. Office: CSIC R&D Nat Plan Sect, Rosario Pino 14-16, 28020 Madrid Spain

MUÑOZ VEGA, PABLO CARDINAL, archbishop; b. Mira, del Carchi, Ecuador, May 23, 1903; s. Antonio Muñoz and Josefa Vega; B.Humanities and Classics, Colegio Loyola, Quito, 1922; Filosofía y Ciencias, Colegio Máximo de San Ignacio, Quito, 1927; D.Filosofía, Facultad de Teologia en Oña, Spain, 1931; Licencia y Grado Doctoral de Magister Aggregatus, Gregoriana U., Rome, 1938. Ordained priest Roman Catholic Ch., 1933; prof. philosophy Gregoriana U., 1938-45, prof. theology, 1945-50; rector Pontificio Colegio Pio-Latino-Americano, 1955-57; rector Pontifical Gregorian U., Rome, 1957-64; titular bishop of Ceramo, 1964-67; archbishop of Quito, from 1967, now archbishop emeritus; elevated to Sacred Coll. of Cardinals, 1969; mem. Sacred Congregation Cath. Edn., Sacred Congregation Religious Life. Author: Introducción a la síntesis de San Agustin, 1945; Causalidad filosófica y determinismo científico, 1946; El estudio del hombre como introducción al problema de o sobrenatural, 1948; Los Problemas de la experiencia mística a la luz del pensamiento agustiniano en Augustinus Magister, 1954; Fe e inteligencia en los orígenes de la ciencia moderna, 1965; Fe y Politica, 1986 Address: Casilla 16-0234 CEQ, Apartado 106, Quito Ecuador

MUNRO, IAN HYSLOP, physicist; b. Manchester, Eng., May 25, 1937; s. Robert and Christina White (Hunter) M.; m. Joan Elizabeth Speight, Oct. 15, 1960; children: Robert Speight, Elizabeth Hunter, Neil Harland, Janet Crawford. BS in Physics with honors, U. Manchester, 1958, PhD in Physics, 1962. Lectr. in physics Manchester U., 1964-75; vis. scientist NRC Ottawa, Can., 1967-69; sr. vis. scientist Stanford (Calif.) Med. Ctr., 1977-79; sr. prin. sci. officer Daresbury Lab., Warrington, Eng., 1980—; hon. prof. physics Aberdeen U., 1985—. Contbr. articles to profl. publs. Mem. council Manchester Literary and Philos. Soc. Fellow Inst. Physics, Royal Micros. Soc.; mem. Am. Phys. Soc., Assn. Radiation Research, European Photochemistry Assn. Presbyterian. Home: 12 Kingston Rd, Didsbury, Manchester M20 8RZ, England Office: Daresbury Lab, Warrington WA4 4AD, England

MUNRO, J. RICHARD, publishing company executive; b. 1931; (married). B.A., Colgate U., 1957; postgrad., Columbia U., NYU; Litt. D. (hon.), Richmond U., 1983. With Time, Inc., 1957—; pres. Pioneer Press, Inc., subs. Time, 1969; pub. Sports Illus., 1969-71; v.p. Time Inc., 1971-75, group v.p. for video, 1975-79, exec. v.p., 1979-80, pres., 1980-86, chief exec. officer, 1980—, chmn., 1986—, also dir.; dir. IBM Corp. Mem. Pres.' Council on Phys. Fitness and Sport; trustee Experiment in Internat. Living, Brattleboro, Vt., Northfield Mount Hermon Sch., Colgate U.; bd. dirs. Urban League of Southwestern Fairfield County (Conn.), Jr. Achievement, United Negro Coll. Fund; bd. dirs., chmn. edn. com. N.Y.C. Partnership. Served with USMCR., Korea. Decorated Purple Heart with 2 clusters. Clubs: Country of New Canaan (Conn.), River, Winter of New Canaan. Office: Time Inc Time & Life Bldg New York NY 10020 *

MUNRO, SANFORD STERLING, JR., investment banking company executive; b. Madison, Wis., Mar. 2, 1932; s. Sanford Sterling and Dorothea Irene (Spears) M.; m. Valerie Gene Halbert, Apr. 4, 1956; children—Sanford Sterling, Margaret, Mary, Elizabeth, Peter, Matthew, Andrew. B.A., George Washington U., 1957. Mem. profl. staff U.S. Senate, Washington, 1953-61; adminstrv. asst. U.S. Senator Henry M. Jackson, 1961-75; chief of staff Jackson for Pres. Com., 1975-76; govtl. affairs cons. Wenatchee, Wash., 1977; adminstr. Bonneville Power Adminstrn., U.S. Dept. Energy, Portland, Oreg., 1978-81; v.p., nat. dir. pub. power John Nuveen & Co., Inc., Seattle and Chgo., 1981—; bd. dirs. Cen. Wash. Bank, Wenatchee. Bd. dirs. U.S. nat. com. World Energy Conf.; chmn. U.S. Entity for Columbia River Treaty; mem. Pacific N.W. River Basins Commn., 1978-81; trustee Cen. Wash. U., 1977-83, 85—; v.p. Henry M. Jackson Found. Served with U.S. Army, 1952-53. Mem. Electric Power Research Inst. (vice chmn. bd. 1978-81), Electric Club Oreg. Democrat. Episcopalian. Clubs: Portland City, Wash. Athletic, Wenatchee Swim and Tennis. Home: 1202 South Hills Dr Wenatchee WA 98801

MUNROE, GEORGE BARBER, business executive; b. Joliet, Ill., Jan. 5, 1922; s. George Muller and Ruth (Barber) M.; m. Elinor Bunin, May 30, 1968; children by previous marriage: George Taylor, Ralph W. Taylor. AB, Dartmouth Coll., 1943; LLB, Harvard U., 1949; BA (Rhodes scholar), Christ Church, Oxford (Eng.) U., 1951, MA, 1956; DHL (hon.), No. Ariz. U., 1981. Bar: N.Y. 1949. Assoc. firm Cravath, Swaine & Moore, N.Y.C., 1949; atty. Office Gen. Counsel, U.S. High Commn. Germany, Frankfurt and Bonn, 1951-53; justice U.S. Ct. Restitution Appeals, Allied High Commn. Germany, Nuremberg, 1953-54; assoc. firm Debevoise, Plimpton & McLean, N.Y.C., 1954-58; with Phelps Dodge Corp., 1958—, v.p., 1962-66, pres., 1966-75, 80-82, chief exec. officer, 1969-87, chmn. bd., 1975-87, chmn. fin. com., cons., 1987—, also dir.; dir. AMAX, Inc., Mfrs. Hanover Corp., N.Y. Life Ins. Co., N.Y. Times Co., Manville Corp., Santa Fe So. Pacific Corp. Trustee, chmn. Dartmouth Coll., Met. Mus. Art; pres., dir. N.Y. Internat. Festival of Arts. Served to lt. (j.g.) USNR, 1943-46. Mem. Council on Fgn. Relations, Am. Inst. Mining, Metall. and Petroleum Engrs. (assoc.), Acad. Polit. Sci. (dir.), Mining and Metall. Soc. Am. Clubs: River, Sky, University (N.Y.C.). Office: Phelps Dodge Corp 300 Park Ave New York NY 10022

MUNSON, NANCY KAY, lawyer; b. Huntington, N.Y., June 22, 1936; d. Howard H. and Edna M. (Keenan) Munson. Student, Hofstra U., 1959-62; JD, Bklyn. Law Sch., 1965. Bar: N.Y. 1966, U.S. Supreme Ct. 1970, U.S. Ct. Appeals (2d cir.) 1971, U.S. Dist. Ct. (ea. and so. dists.) N.Y. 1968. Law clk. to E. Merritt Weidner Huntington, 1959-66, sole practice, 1966—; mem. legal adv. bd. Chgo. Title Ins. Co., Riverhead, N.Y., 1981—. Trustee Huntington Fire Dept. Death Benefit Fund; pres., trustee, chmn. bd. Bklyn. Home for Aged Men Found. Mem. ABA, Suffolk County Bar Assn., Bklyn. Bar Assn., N.Y. State Bar Assn., Nat. Rifle Assn. Republican. Christian Scientist. Club: Soroptimist (past pres.). Office: 197 New York Ave Huntington NY 11743

MUNSTER, ANDREW MICHAEL, medical educator, surgeon; b. Budapest, Hungary, Dec. 10, 1935; came to U.S., 1965; s. Leopold S. and Marianne (Barcza) M.; m. Joy O'Sullivan, Dec. 7, 1963; children—Andrea, Tara, Alexandra. M.D., U. Sydney (Australia), 1959. Diplomate Am. Bd. Surgery. Research fellow Harvard U. Med. Sch., Boston, 1966-67; asst. prof. surgery U. Tex.-San Antonio, 1968-71, assoc. prof. surgery Med. U. S.C., Charleston, 1971-76; assoc. prof. Johns Hopkins U., Balt., 1976-85, prof. surgery, 1985—; dir. burn ctr. Balt. City Hosp., 1976—; v.p. Chesapeake Physicians, Balt., 1978-84. Author: Surgical Anatomy, 1971; Surgical Immunology, 1976; Burn Care for House Officers, 1980; contbr. numerous articles to med. jours. Pres., Chesapeake Ednl. Research Trust, Balt., 1980-84, Charleston Symphony, 1974-75, Charleston TriCounty Arts Council, 1975-76. Served to lt. col. U.S. Army, 1968-71. Recipient John Hunter prize U. Sydney, 1959; named Hunterian prof. Royal Coll. Surgeons, 1974. Fellow Royal Coll. Surgeons of Eng., Royal Coll. Surgeons of Edinburgh (Scotland), Am. Assn. Surgeons of Trauma, Colombian Coll. Surgeons (hon.); mem. Soc. Surg. Assn., Soc. Univ. Surgeons, Am. Surg. Assn. Office: Balt City Hosps 4940 Eastern Ave Baltimore MD 21224

MUNTANER-I-PASCUAL, JOSEP M., banker, economist, journalist; b. Barcelona, Spain, Apr. 27, 1939; s. Joaquim and Carme (Pascual) Muntaner; m. Núria Aramon-i-Stein, Dec. 11, 1970. M in Econ. Scis., U. Barcelona, 1961; B in Info. Scis., Autonomous U. Barcelona, 1983. Econ. advisor Harris & Bosch Aymerich, Madrid, 1962-63; researcher econs. Assn. Investigación Empresas Confeccionistas, Barcelona, 1963-64; gen. mgr. Cedec S.L., Barcelona, 1964-73; mng. dir. Europa de Inversiones and Europa Inversiones y Leasing, Barcelona, 1973-83; econ. research mgr. Banco de Europa, Barcelona, 1973-83; first gen. mgr. Inst. Català del Crèdit Agrari, Spain, 1984-85; first chmn. and gen. mgr. Inst. Català de Fins., 1985—; asst. prof. U. Barcelona, 1961-66, Autonomous U. Barcelona, 1971-73; prof. Escola Superior Adminstrn. Direcció Empreses and Inst. Catòlic Estudis Socials, 1966-69, U. Perpignan, France, 1983—; lectr. Mem. Report of Spanish Regional Devel., 1972-75, Commn. Spanish Urban Structures, 1972-75; mng. dir. Cercle Agermanament Occitano-Català, 1978—, Omnium Cultural, 1980—. Author: Cap una Economia dels Països Catalans, 1979, also 6 others; (with others) Essay-Band Katalonien, 1983, also 8 others; editor Desenvolupament de Girona, 1973, also 16 others; mng. dir. Avui newspaper, Barcelona, 1983-88; program dir. TV Española, Barcelona, 1982-83; contbr. articles on econs. to periodicals. Social Council fellow Poly. U. Catalonia, 1985—, Council TV de Catalunya, 1985—. Fellow Inst. d'Estudis Catalans of Union Acad. Internat.; mem. Soc. Catalana d'Economia (chmn. 1977-85), Collegi d'Economistes de Catalunya. Office: Inst Català de Fins, Carrer de Pau Claris 138, 2n, E-08009 Barcelona Catalonia, Spain

MUNTEAN, GEORGE, historian, literary critic, researcher, folklorist; b. Bilca, Romania, Nov. 17, 1932; s. Atanasie and Varvara (Tărîtă) M.; m. Adela Popescu, Mar. 8, 1956. BA in Philology and Lit., U. Bucharest, 1959. Journalist, editor Contemporanul Bucharest, Romania, 1959-68; researcher G. Călinescu Inst. Lit. History and Theory, Bucharest, Romania, 1960, prin. researcher, 1969; prin. researcher, editor-in-chief Rev. Lit. History and Theory, Bucharest, Romania, 1973-78. Author, editor collections of folklore, essays, articles, dialectology, chronicles, book revs. and anthologies. Recipient prize Romanian Acad., 1977. Fellow Romanian Writers Union. Home: Sos Mihai Bravu 98-106, Apt 142, 73266 Bucharest Romania Office: C Calinescu Inst Lit History and Theory, Ba Schitu Magureanu 1, 70626 Bucharest Romania

MUNTZING, JONAS, pharmaceutical company executive, physiology educator; b. Lund, Sweden, May 9, 1940; s. Arne and Gudrun (Lewis Johsson) M.; m. Gunilla Ann-Mari Akesson, Jan. 2, 1965; children: Martina, Kristina. PhD, U. Lund, 1971. Instr. U. Lund, 1964-67, asst. prof. physiology, 1977—; with AB Leo, Helsingborg, Sweden, 1972—, dir. cancer chemotherepeutics, 1987—; com. sec. Cen. U. Bur., Stockholm, 1966-67. Mem. editorial bd. Jour. The Prostate, N.Y.C., 1979—; contbr. articles to profl. jours. and books. Roswell Park Meml. Inst. research assoc., 1972-73, 75-76. Mem. Soc. Experimental Biology and Medicine, Endocrine Soc., Am. Assn. Cancer Research, European Assn. Cancer Research, Swedish Oncology Soc. Office: Pharmacia Leo AB, PO Box 941, S-251 08 Helsingborg Sweden

MUNYON, WILLIAM HARRY, JR., architect; b. Panama City, Panama, Feb. 20, 1945 (parents Am. citizens); s. William Harry and Ruth (Hyde) M.; m. Cheryl Lynn Guess, Dec. 31, 1987; B.A., Tulane U., 1967; postgrad. U. Hawaii, 1972-73; B.Arch. with high distinction, U. Ariz., 1978; postgrad. U.S. Naval War Coll., 1984, Armed Forces Staff Coll., 1985. Elec. designer Ohlsen-Mitchell, Inc., New Orleans, 1966-67; research cons. hist. preservation U. Ariz., Tucson, 1974-75; cons. hist. preservation State of Ariz., Phoenix, 1974-75; mktg. dir., programmer, designer Architecture One, Ltd., Tucson, 1975-78; mng. prin. Artistic License II, graphics and design, 1975-86, Aardvark Graphics, 1986—; dir. mktg. Hansen Lind Meyer, P.C., Iowa City and Chgo., 1978-79; v.p. John F. Steffen Assos., Inc., subs. Turner Constrn., St. Louis, 1979-80; sr. asso., dir. corp. devel. Rees Assos., Inc., Oklahoma City, 1980-82; mktg. dir., asst. to pres., dir. planning, dir. interior architecture SHWC, Inc., Dallas, 1982-84; dir. justice facilities program Henningson, Durham & Richardson Inc., Dallas, 1984-87; dir. justice and security facilities Kaplan/McLaughlin/Diaz Architects, San Francisco, 1987—; mktg. cons., 1979—; vice chmn., chief exec. officer Program Mgmt. Assocs., 1987—; mem. adv. bd. Interior Design mag., 1978-79; mem. Bldg. Energy Performance Standards Adv. Panel, 1979-81. Active U. Ariz. Fund for Athletic Devel., 1977—; sponsor Dallas 500; mem. Naval War Coll. Found. Served with USN, 1967-73; capt. Res. Recipient Producer's Council prize for design excellence, 1977. Mem. AIA (architecture for justice com. 1978—, Henry Adams award 1978, regional design awards), Nat. Trust Hist. Preservation, Naval Res. Officers Assn., Soc. Archtl. Historians, Am. Planning Assn., Am. Correctional Assn., Am. Jail Assn., Naval Inst., Soc. Mktg. Profl. Services, Res. Officers Assn. U.S., Mensa, Lionel Collectors Club Am., Brit. Model Soldier Soc., Nat. Rifle Assn., Profl. Services Mgmt. Assn., Dallas Mus. Art, Assn. Former Intelligence Officers, Navy League, Tulane U. Alumni Assn., Blue Key, Scabbard and Blade, Phi Kappa Phi (life), Sigma Chi (life). Roman Catholic. Clubs: La Cima, 65 Roses Sports. Founder ann. archtl. history prize U. Ariz., 1979—, ann. mil. leadership award Tulane U., 1985—. Home: 9 Mara Vista Ct Tiburon CA 94920

MUNZ, PETER, history educator; b. Chemnitz, Germany, May 12, 1921; came to N.Z. 1940; s. Leo and Agnes Carlotta (Lichtenstein) M.; m. Keelah Anne Vickerman, Sept. 19, 1950; 1 child, Jacob. M.A., Canterbury U.-N.Z., 1943; Ph.D., Cambridge U.-Eng., 1948. Prof. history Victoria U., Wellington, N.Z., 1966—. Author: The Place of Hooker in the History of Thought, 1952, Problems of Religious Knowledge, 1959, The Origin of the Carolingian Empire, 1960, Relationship and Solitude, 1964, Frederick Barbarossa, 1969, Life in the Age of Charlemagne, 1969, When the Golden Bough Breaks, 1973, The Shapes of Time, 1977, Our Knowledge of the Growth of Knowledge, 1985, (with G. Ellis) Boso's Life of Pope Alexander III, 1973. Translator books. Contbr. articles to profl. jours. Avocations: tennis; skiing. Home: 128 Ohiro Rd, Wellington New Zealand Office: Victoria U, Private Bag, Wellington New Zealand

MUNZER, STEPHEN IRA, lawyer, real estate syndicator; b. N.Y.C., Mar. 15, 1939; s. Harry and Edith (Isacowitz) M.; m. Patricia Eve Munzer, Aug. 11, 1965; children—John, Margaret. A.B., Brown U., 1960; J.D., Cornell U., 1963. Bar: N.Y. 1964, U.S. Supreme Ct. 1974, U.S. Dist. Ct. (so. dist.) N.Y. Formerly assoc. Finley, Kimble & Underburg; formerly ptnr. Pincus Munzer Bizar & D'Alessandro; real estate investor; pres. Simcor Mgmt. Corp., N.Y.C. Served to lt., USNR, 1965-75. Mem. Assn. Bar City N.Y., N.Y. State Bar Assn. Jewish. Club: City Athletic (N.Y.C.). Home: 850 Park Ave New York NY 10021 Office: One Citicorp Ctr New York NY 10022

MURAD, JOSÉ ELIAS, pharmacologist, university administrator; b. Lavras, Brazil, Oct. 31, 1924; s. Elias and Labibe Murad; m. Therezinha Myrtes Costa, July 10, 1954; 1 son, Mario Stefano Costa (dec.). Degree in Pharmacy, Sch. of Pharmacy, Belo Horizonte, Brazil, 1948; degree in Chemistry, Philosophy Sch., Belo Horizonte, 1950; degree in medicine, Sch. of Medicine, Belo Horizonte, 1955; hon. degree in Pharmacology U. Paris Med. Sch., 1960; hon. degree in brain biochemistry U. Tex.-Dallas, 1965. Chmn. pharmacology Med. Scis. Sch., Belo Horizonte, 1963—, dean med. sch., 1973-87; chmn. pharmacy Pharmacy Sch., Belo Horizonte, 1968-83, dean pharmacy sch., 1975-78; dir. Drug Orientation Ctr., Belo Horizonte, 1980-87; pres. Fuliban-Lebanese Found. MG State, Belo Horizonte, 1980-83. Author: What You Must Know about Psychotropics/The One-Way Trip, (1st prize 1972), 1972, How to Fight The Drug Abuse, 1985, The Therapeutical Jungle in Brazil, 1986; contbr. articles to profl. jours. Pres. S. Bento's Neighborhood Assn., 1976, Fuliban-Lebanese Found., 1980-83, Tchr's. Assn. MG State, 1963, 65; honor citizen Mcpl. Chamber of Belo Horizonte, 1983. U. Paris grantee, 1959-60; U. Tex. Med. Sch. grantee, 1964-65, Am. Coll. Physicians Drug Abuse Treatment Ctrs. grantee, 1982; recipient Big Medal of Inconfidencia Minas Gerais Govt. State, 1983; elected congressman (fed. dep.) Brazilian Constn., 1987—. Mem. Brazilian Federal Council on Narcotics, AAAS, Soc. Franç aise Therapeutique and Pharmacod, Brazilian Assn. Advancement Scis., Assn. Lebanese Cultural Mundial (Khalil Gibran medal). Roman Catholic. Clubs: Rotary, Pic. Home: Av Consul Antonio Cadar, 327 Belo Horizonte, 30000 Minas Gerais Brazil Office: Sch Med Scis, Al Ezequiel Dias 275, Belo Horizonte, 30000 Minas Gerais Brazil

MURADIAN, VAZGEN, composer, viola d'amore player; b. Ashtarak, Armenia, Oct. 17, 1921; came to U.S., 1950, naturalized, 1956; s. Grigor and Arusiak (Vardanian) M.; m. Arpi Kirkyasharian, Aug. 29, 1964; children: Vardges, Armen. Grad., Benedetto Marcello State Conservatory Music, Venice, 1948; student composition, Gabriele Bianchi; student composition violin, Luigi Ferro. Tchr. violin, solfeggio and theory of music Collegio Armeno, Venice, Italy, 1945-50; pvt. tchr. viola d'amore. Composer numerous works including 6 symphonies, 55 concertos for all classical instruments and many concertos for rare instruments, 4 moto perpetuos for violin and orch., 7 sonatas for solo violin, 6 sonatas for violin and piano, 2 sonatas for piano, sonata for viola d'amore, 2 quartets, 2 trios for violin, violoncello and piano, 56 songs with orch. and 8 songs for chorus and orch. on works of Shakespeare, Goethe, Dante, Hugo, others; author articles in field; debut, N.Y. Lincoln Center, 1972; violist with various U.S. orchs. including New Orleans Philharmonic, Wagner Opera Co.; appeared as viola d'amore soloist, U.S. and abroad, compositions performed throughout Europe and Am. Recipient Tekeyan prize, 1962. Mem. ASCAP, Viola D'amore Soc. Home: 269 W 72d St New York NY 10023

MURAKAMI, HARUO, physician; b. Sapporo, Japan, June 16, 1930; s. Teikichi and Shizue Kuranami; m. Hiroko Murakami, May 27, 1959; children—Keiko, Tomoko, Chiharu. M.D., Tokyo Med. and Dental U., 1957. Fellow 1st Clinic of Internal Medicine, Tokyo Med. and Dental U., 1957-67; chief Ichikawa Daiichi Hosp., Tokyo, 1967-77; dir. Murakami Clinic, Tokyo, 1977—. Contbr. articles to med. jours. Mem. Japanese Soc. Internal Medicine, Japan Med. Assn., Chofu Med. Assn. (dir. 1980—). Liberal Democrat. Bhuddist. Home: 5-11-7 Minami-Yukigaya, Ohta-ku, Tokyo 145, Japan Office: Murakami Clinic, 5-11-7 Minami-Yukigaya, Ohta ku, Tokyo 145, Japan

MURAKAWA, HIRONORI, trading company executive; b. Takamatsu, Japan, Feb. 14, 1938; s. Masaichi and Sumi Murakawa; m. Takako Murakawa, Oct. 8, 1966. BA, U. Kagawa, 1962. Sect. chief Kanematsu-Gosho Ltd., Osaka, Japan, 1962-77; div. mgr. Descente Ltd., Osaka, 1978-87; mng. dir. Mation Ltd., Osaka, 1987—. Buddhist. Home: 10-205 No 1, Shinkanaoka-3 cho, Sakai, Osaka 591, Japan Office: Mation Ltd, 54 Higashi Shimizu-machi, Minami-ku, Osaka 542, Japan

MURAKHOVSKIY, VSEVOLOD SERAFIMOVICH, Soviet government official; b. Ukraine, USSR, Oct. 20, 1926. Grad., Stavropol Pedagogical Inst., 1954. Dep. to Council of the Union, USSR Supreme Soviet, 1979—; mem. Cen. Com. Communist Party Soviet Union, 1981—; dep. chair Mandate Commn., 1984-85; now 1st dep. chair USSR Council Ministers, Moscow; chair USSR State Agro-Indsl. Com. Served with Soviet Army, 1944-50. Decorated Order of October Revolution, Order of Lenin, Hero Socialist Labour. Address: Council Ministers, Office 1st Dep Chmn, Moscow USSR *

MURASHKO, GALINA PAVLOVNA, historian educator; b. Tejkovo, Ivanovskaja, USSR, Jan. 3, 1932; d. Rezonov Pavel Ivanovich and Kosareva Ecaterina Nikolajevna; m. Alfred Murashko, Apr. 3, 1956; m. Florja Boris Nikolajevich, Mar. 13, 1976. Postgrad., Inst. Slavon Balkan, Moscow, 1954-59, D in Sci., 1980. Scientist Inst. Slavon Balkan, 1959—. Author: six books including Put Chehoslovatskogo Krestjanstva, 1972, Velikij Oktjabr i Revolucii 40 Godov, 1977, Politicheskaja Borba, 1986; contbr. articles in field. Communist. Office: Inst Slavon Balkan, Leningradskij prosp 7, Moscow USSR

MURASKI, ANTHONY AUGUSTUS, lawyer; b. Cohoes, N.Y., July 28, 1946; s. Adam Joseph and Angeline Mary (Vozzy) M.; m. Janice Kay Selberg, Nov. 25, 1978; children: Adam Peter, Emily Jo. BA, MA in Speech/Hearing, Sacramento State Coll., 1970; PhD in Audiology/ Hearing Sci., U. Mich., 1977; JD, Detroit Coll. Law, 1979. Bar: Mich. 1980, U.S. Dist. Ct. (ea. dist.) Mich. 1981, U.S. Ct. Appeals (6th cir.) 1982. Asst. Kresge Hearing Research Inst. U. Mich., Ann Arbor, 1971-77; asst. prof. Wayne State U. Med. Sch., Detroit, 1979-82; assoc. Kitch, Suhrheinrich, Saurbier & Drutchas, Detroit, 1982-83; assoc. prof. Detroit Coll. Law, 1983-85; mng. ptnr. Muraski & Sikorski, Ann Arbor, 1985—; cons. audiology Ministry of Environment, Ont., Can., 1980-81; trustee Deaf, Speech and Hearing Ctr., Detroit, 1981—; legal adv. on air WWJ Radio, Detroit, 1984—; mem. mental health adv. bd. on deafness Dept. Mental Health, 1984, vis. com. U. Mich. Sch. Edn., 1986—. Author: Legal Aspects of Audiological Practice, 1982, Hearing Conservation in Industry: Licensure, Liability and Forensics, 1985. Mem. ABA, Mich. Bar Assn., Washtenaw County Bar Assn., Am. Speech-Lang.-Hearing Assn. (sci. merit award, 1981), Ann Arbor C. of C. Home: 1603 Westminster Pl Ann Arbor MI 48104 Office: Muraski & Sikorski 300 N Fifth Ave Suite 240 Ann Arbor MI 48104

MURATA, AKIRA, manufacturing executive; b. Mar. 25, 1921; m. Shizue Murata. Ed. pub. schs., Kyoto, Japan. Founder Murata Mfg. Co., Ltd., 1944; pres. Fukui Murata Mfg Co. Ltd., 1950-55; pres. Murata Mfg. Co., Ltd., from 1955, now chmn.; chmn. Murata Erie NA div. Murata Mfg. Co., Ltd., Smyrna, Ga. Decorated Medal of Honor with Blue Ribbon, 1980. Home: 15 Maruyama, Kamiueno-cho, Muko, Kyoto Japan Office: Murata Erie NA Inc 2200 Lake Park Dr Smyrna GA 30080-7604 also: Murata Mfg Co Ltd, 266-10 Tenjin, 2-chome Nagaokakyoshi, Kyoto Japan *

MURATA, YASUO, economics educator; b. Osaka, Japan, Jan. 26, 1931; s. Masao and Sadae (Morii) M.; m. Hiroko Sakurai, Feb. 7, 1960; 1 dau., Akiko. B.A., Kobe U. (Japan), 1953, M.A., 1955, D. Econs., 1958; Ph.D., Stanford U., 1965. Lectr., Kobe U. Commerce, 1958-60, assoc. prof., 1960-68, prof., 1968-71; prof. Dalhousie U., Halifax, N.S., Can., 1971-74; prof. econs. Nagoya City U. (Japan) 1974-86. Author: (with Michio Morishima) Working of Econometric Model, 1972; Mathematics for Stability and Optimization of Economic Systems, 1977; Optimal Control Methods for Discrete-Time Economic System, 1982; Modern Macroeconomics (in Japanese), 1984; editorial bd. Optimal Control Applications and Methods, 1984-88. Grantee Fulbright Commn., 1962, Japan Econ. Research Found., 1979, Mishima Meml. Found., 1982. Mem. Am. Econ. Assn., Econometric Soc., Japan Assn. Econs. and Econometrics (trustee 1980-86), Japan Assn. Automatic Control. Home: 1-16-17 Karatodai Kitaku, Kobe 651-13, Japan Office: Kansai U, Dept Econs, Suita, Osaka Prefecture 564, Japan

MURATA, YOSHIO, architectural engineer; b. Tokyo, June 25, 1933; s. Eiichiro and Takako (Yamada) M.; m. Hiroko Ohshima, May 30, 1961. BS in Structural Engring., U. Tokyo, 1956, MS in Structural Engring., 1958, PhD in Structural Engring., 1961. With Yamashita Architects and Engrs., Inc., Tokyo, 1961-67; with Nihon Architects, Engrs. and Cons., Inc., Tokyo, 1967—, mgr. structural engring. div., 1974-76, dir., 1976-83, mng. dir., exec. sec., 1983—; pres. Nihon Engring. System, Inc., Tokyo, 1984—. Co-author: Design of Concrete Structures, 1983, Seismic Design of Steel Structures, 1984. Mem. Archtl. Inst. Japan, Japan Architects Assn., Japan Structural Cons. Assn. (bd. dirs. 1985—). Buddhist. Home: 6-16-10-505 Shimouma, Setagaya-ku, Tokyo 154, Japan Office: Nihon Architects Engrs & Cons, Shinjuku Mitsui Bldg 2-1-1, Nishi-Shinjuku, Tokyo 163, Japan

MURAY, ALFONSO, architect; b. Orizaba, Veracruz, Mex., Nov. 3, 1939; s. Kenichi and Shige (Kobory) M.; m. Graciela Abe, Oct. 8, 1966; children: Alfonso, Eduardo, Mauricio. B.Arch., U. Mex., 1963. Mgr. gardening dept. Flores y Regalos Matsumoto, Mexico City, 1965-73; gen. mgr. Jardineria Matsumoto, S.A., Mexico City, 1973-75; pres., gen. dir. Muray Arquitectos, S.A., Mexico City, 1975—; pres. Muray, Villegas, Arquitectos, S.C., Mexico City, 1987—; past pres. Inst. Cultural Mexicano Japonés, A.C., Mexico City, 1985—, fellow, 1987—. Fellow Assn. Nisei de Mex., A.C., Mexico City, 1975—. Mem. Interior Plantscape Assn. (merit award 1979, honor award 1980 (2), highest honor award 1983, 84, merit award 1985), Associated Landscape Contractors Am. (merit award 1981, grand award 1983, merit award 1986), Sociedad de Arquitectos Paisajistas de Mex. (pres. 1987—), Colegio de Arquitectos de Mex., Internat. Fedn. Landscape Architects. Roman Catholic. Avocations: lecturing, photography, reading, travel. Home: Prol Rio San Angel 382, DF 01760 Mexico City Mexico Office: Muray Arquitectos SA, 16 de Septiembre #21, DF 04260 Mexico City Mexico

MURAYAMA, HIROMI, architect; b. Sept. 8, 1941; s. Katsumi and Chizuko (Kameda) M.; m. Kiyoko Matsuzaki, Apr. 8, 1970; 1 child, Rei. BArch, Waseda U., 1966; MArch, Tokyo U. Arts, 1968. Registered 1st class architect. Sr. architect Nikken Sekkei, Tokyo, 1968—. Author: The Shinjuku Green Tower Building: An Example of Urban Redevelopment, 1987, (with others) Planning and Detailing of Intelligent Buildings, 1987. Recipient award for Pola Cosmetics Co. Archtl. Inst. Japan, 1972, award for Shinjuku Green Tower Bldg. Japan Sign Design Assn., 1986, award for Shinjuku Green Tower Bldg. Japan Color Research Inst., 1988. Mem. Archtl. Inst. Japan. Buddhist. Home: 2-27-7 Nishi Rokugo, Ota-ku, Tokyo 144, Japan Office: Nikken Sekkei, 1-4-27 Koraku, Bunkyo-ku, Tokyo 112, Japan

MURAYAMA, MAKIO, biochemist; b. San Francisco, Aug. 10, 1912; s. Hakuyo and Namiye (Miyasaka) M.; children: Gibbs Soga, Alice Myra. B.A., U. Calif., Berkeley, 1938, M.A., 1940; Ph.D. (NIH fellow), U. Mich., 1953. Research biochemist Children's Hosp. of Mich., Detroit, 1943-48, Harper Hosp., Detroit, 1950-54; research fellow in chemistry Calif. Inst. Tech., Pasadena, 1954-56; research asso. in biochemistry Grad. Sch. Medicine, U. Pa., Phila., 1956-58; spl. research fellow Nat. Cancer Inst. at Cavendish Lab., Cambridge, Eng., 1958; research biochemist NIH, Bethesda, Md., 1958—. Author: (with Robert M. Nalbandian) Sickle Cell Hemoglobin, 1973. Fellow Am. Inst. Chemists; mem. Am. Chem. Soc., Am. Soc. Biol. Chemists, AAAS, Assn. Clin. Scientists, Internat. Platform Assn., W.African Soc. Pharmacology (hon.), Sigma Xi. Home: 5010 Benton Ave Bethesda MD 20814 Office: NIH Bldg 6 Room 129 Bethesda MD 20892

MURAYAMA, TOSHIO, engineering company executive; b. Sept. 23, 1920. Grad. high sch., Nagasaki, Japan. V.p. Hitachi Shipbuilding and Engring. Co., Ltd., Osaka, Japan, also bd. dirs.; pres. Hitachi Zosen Corp., Osaka; bd. dirs. Onami Unyo Soko. Home: 5-10 Fujishirodai, 2-chome Suita, Osaka 565, Japan Office: Hitachi Zosen Corp, 6-14 Edobori, 1-chome Nishi-ku, Osaka 550, Japan *

MURCHISON, DAVID CLAUDIUS, lawyer; b. N.Y.C., Aug. 19, 1923; s. Claudius Temple and Constance (Waterman) M.; m. June Margaret Guilfoyle, Dec. 19, 1946; children—David Roderick, Brian, Courtney, Bradley, Stacy. Student, U. N.C., 1942-43; A.A., George Washington U., 1947, J.D. with honors, 1949. Bar: D.C. 1949, Supreme Ct. 1955. Asso. Dorr, Hand & Dawson, N.Y.C., 1949-50; partner Howrey, Simon, Baker & Murchison, Washington, 1956—; legal asst. under sec. army, 1949-51; counsel motor vehicle, textile, aircraft, ordnance and shipbldg. divs. Nat. Prodn. Authority, 1951-52; asso. gen. counsel Small Def. Plants Adminstrn., 1952-53; legal adv. and asst. to chmn. FTC, 1953-55. Served with AUS, 1943-45. Mem. ABA (chmn. com. internat. restrictive bus. practices, sect. antitrust law 1954-55, sect. adminstrv. law, sect. litigation), Fed., D.C., N.Y. bar assns., Order of Coif, Phi Delta Phi. Republican. Clubs: Metropolitan, Chevy Chase. Home: 5409 Spangler Ave Bethesda MD 20816 Office: 1730 Pennsylvania Ave NW Washington DC 20006

MURDHANI, (LEONARDUS) BENNY, Indonesian government official. Head intelligence Ministry Def., 1976—; dep. chief. Bakin, 1976—; head Nat. Strategic Intelligence Ctr., 1979—; comdr. Indonesian Armed Forces, 1983—; head Konkamtib, 1983—; minister def. and security Indonesia, Jakarta, 1988—. Address: Ministry Def and Security, Jalan Merdeka, Barat 13 Jakarta Pesat, Indonesia *

MURDOCH, (KEITH) RUPERT, publisher; b. Melbourne, Australia, Mar. 11, 1931; came to U.S., 1974, naturalized, 1985; s. Keith and Elisabeth Joy (Greene) M.; m. Anna Maria Torv, Apr. 28, 1967; children: Prudence, Elisabeth, Lachlan, James. M.A., Worcester Coll., Oxford, Eng., 1953. Chmn. News Am. Pub. Inc. (pubs. New York Post, New York mag. and Village Voice), 1977—, 1974—; Chmn. News Am. Pub. Inc. (pubs. Boston Herald, N.Y. Post, London Times), News Am. Pub. Inc. (pubs. Chgo. Sun-Times), 1983-86; chmn. News Internat., Ltd. Group, London; chief exec., mng. dir. News, Ltd. Group & Asso. Cos., Australia.; chmn. 20th Century Fox Prodns., 1985—; owner, pub. numerous newspapers, mags. and TV stas. in Australia and U.K. 1983—. Home: 1 Virginia St, London E1 9XN, England Office: care News Corp Ltd 210 South St New York NY 10002 *

MURDOCK, ALVIN EDWIN, counselor; b. Sand Springs, Tex., Jan. 3, 1918; married, 5 children. M.S. in Agr., Sam Houston State U., Huntsville, Tex., 1947, M.A. in Agr., 1949. Counselor, Victoria (Tex.) Ind. Sch. Dist., 1960-61, Tyler (Tex.) Ind. Sch. Dist., 1961-64, Llano (Tex.) Ind. Sch. Dist., 1964-66, Anderson County Coop., Palestine, Tex., 1966-86; ret., 1986; supr-counselor Night Adult Basic Edn., 1974-76. Scout master Boy Scouts Am., 1953-55; sustaining mem. Republican Nat. Com., 1980-81. Served with USMC, 1943-45. Mem. Tex. Small Schs. Assn., Tex. Personnel and Guidance Assn., Am. Security Council (adv. bd. 1980-81). Baptist. Club: U.S. Senatorial. Test cons. for Tex. Edn. Agy.; coop. coordinator for crime prevention and drug edn. Tex. Edn. Assn.

MURDOCK, PHELPS DUBOIS, JR., marketing and advertising agency executive; b. Kansas City, Mo., May 5, 1944; s. Phelps Dubois and Betty Jane Murdock; student U. Mo., Kansas City, 1962-66; m. Nancy Jane Winfrey, June 7, 1977; children—Susan, Kathleen, Mark, Brooks, Phelps DuBois III, Molly. Sales service mgr. Sta.-KCMO-TV, Kansas City, Mo., 1965-66; account exec. Fremerman-Papin Advt., Kansas City, Mo., 1966-71, TV prodn. mgr., 1966-70, v.p., 1970-71; mng. ptnr. New Slant Prodns., Kansas City, Mo., 1971-73; v.p., creative dir. Travis-Walz-Lane Advt., Kansas City, Mo. and Mission, Kans., 1973-76; pres., chief exec. officer Phelps Murdock Mktg. and Advt., Inc., Kansas City, Mo., 1977—; guest lectr. colls., univs. Active Heart of Am. United Way, 1966-80, mem. exec. bd., 1976, bd. dirs., 1976-80; active Help Educate Emotionally Disturbed, Inc., Kansas City, Mo., 1968-80, pres. bd. dirs. HEED Found., 1979-80; active Heart of Am. council Boy Scouts Am., 1975-85, bd. govs. Bacchus Ednl. and Cultural Found., Kansas City, Mo., 1973-76, found. chmn., 1975; mem. Kansas City Bicentennial Commn., 1975-76, Union Sta. Commn., 1987—, Com. for Union Sta., 1987—, v.p., 1988—, and many others; Internat. Platform Assn., 1987—; vol. coach, local youth leagues, 1975-83; cons. Com. for County Progress Campaigns, Charter Campaign, Jackson County, Mo., 1970; Kansas City Magnet Schs., 1986-88. Recipient various awards including United Way Nat. Communications award, 1975; Effie citation N.Y. Mktg. Assn., 1975; 1st Place Print Ad award and 1st Place Poster award 9th Dist. Addy Awards, 1975, 1st Place Regional-Nat. TV Campaign award, 1976; Omni award, 1980-82, 86, 87; Silver award KCAD, 1981; 1st Place TV Campaign award KCAF Big One Show, 1976; Best-of-Show and Gold medal award Dallas Soc. Visual Communications, 1976; Gold medal Kansas City Litho Craftmen, 1988; named Mic-O-Say hon. warrior, 1978. Mem. Advt. and Sales Execs. Found., Am. Advt. Fed. Democrat. Author numerous TV, radio commls., film, TV and radio musical compositions; film and television direction; creator "Modulatin' With McCall" NBC, 1976-77; film with Walter Cronkite, Union Station is US., 1988. Home: #1 Chartwell Kansas City MO 64114 Office: 21 E 29th St Kansas City MO 64108

MURDOCK, WILBERT QUINC, biomedical engineer; b. N.Y.C., July 3, 1958; s. William Quinc and Rosa (Washington) M. B.S.E.E., Poly. Inst. of N.Y., 1980, M.S. in Bioengring., 1983. Research fellow Poly. Inst. of N.Y., N.Y.C., 1980-82; adj. prof. elec. engring. N.Y.C. Tech. Coll., 1981-82; adj. prof. computer sci. Baruch Coll., N.Y.C., 1982-83; pres. Computers for Sports, Inc. (now Motiontronics for Sci. Inc.), N.Y.C., 1983—. Author: Voice Recognition System for Handicapped, 1983. Inventor knee alignment monitoring device, real-time motion analysis system, biofeedback device to keep drivers awake, computer-driven laser system for dentistry, biofeedback device for hearing loss prevention, others. Mem. IEEE. Subspecialties: Biomedical engineering; Real-time video motion analysis. Home: 1118 E 215th St Bronx NY 10469

MURER, MICHAEL ANTON, lawyer, consultant; b. Joliet, Ill., Sept. 3, 1944; s. Sergio Arthur and Helen Ilene (Bolos) M.; m. Cherilyn G. DiSpirito, Nov. 19, 1966; children: Jeffrey, Sasha. BA, Purdue U., 1965; JD, Georgetown U., 1968. Bar: Ill. 1968. Ptnr. Vinson, Singer & Murer, Joliet, 1969-74, Murer, Bolden, Koslowski & Polito, Joliet, 1975-80; sole practice Joliet, 1980—; 1st asst. pub. defender Will County, 1970-78; adj. faculty Lewis U., Lockport, Ill., 1975-79; cons. Murer Cons., Joliet, 1980—; spl. asst. atty. gen. Ill., 1984; adj. faculty St. Francis Coll., 1985. Mem. founding com. Lewis U. Sch. Law, Glen Ellyn, Ill., 1976-78; nominee 4th congl. dist. Ill. U.S. Congress, 1980-82; bd. dirs. Spanish Ctr., Joliet. Mem. ABA, Ill. Bar Assn., Will County Bar Assn., Ill. Trial Lawyers Assn. Democrat. Roman Catholic. Home: 62 W Washington St Joliet IL 60432 Office: 81 N Chicago St Joliet IL 60431

MURERWA, HERBERT, diplomat of Zimbabwe; b. Harare, Zimbabwe, May 31, 1941; 5 children. BA, George Williams Coll., 1972; MEd, Harvard U., 1973, EdD, 1978. Econ. affairs officer UN, Addis Ababa, Ethiopia, 1978-80; permanent sec. Zimbabwe Govt., 1980-84; high commr. for Zimbabwe to U.K., London, 1984—; mem. governing bd. ILO, Geneva, 1982-84. Mem. council U. Zimbabwe, 1981-83. Home: 321 Ard-na-lea Close, Glen Lorne, Harare Zimbabwe Office: Zimbabwe House, 429 Strand, London WC 2, England

MURKOWSKI, FRANK HUGHES, senator; b. Seattle, Mar. 28, 1933; s. Frank Michael and Helen (Hughes) M.; m. Nancy R. Gore, Aug. 28, 1954; children—Carol Victoria Murkowski Sturgulewski, Lisa Ann Murkowski Martell, Frank Michael, Eileen Marie Murkowski Van Wyke, Mary Catherine, Brian Patrick. Student, Santa Clara U., 1952-53; BA in Econs, Seattle U., 1955. With Pacific Nat. Bank of, Seattle, 1957-58; with Nat. Bank of Alaska, Anchorage, 1959-67; asst. v.p., mgr. Nat. Bank of Alaska (Wrangell br.), 1963-66; v.p. charge bus. devel. Nat. Bank of Alaska (Wrangell br.), Anchorage, 1966-67; commr. dept. econ. devel. State of Alaska, Juneau, 1967-70; pres. Alaska Nat. Bank of the North, Fairbanks, 1971-80; U.S. Senator from Alaska, 1981—; mem. Energy and Natural Resources Com.; ranking mem. Vets. Affairs Com.; mem. Fgn. Relations Com., Indian Affairs Com. former vice pres. B.C. and Alaska Bd. Trade; Rep. nominee for U.S. Congress from Alaska, 1970. Served with USCGR, 1955-57. Mem. Am. Bankers Assn, Alaska Bankers Assn. (pres. 1973), Young Pres.'s Orgn., Alaska C of C (pres. 1977), Anchorage C of C (dir. 1966), B.C. C of C, Fairbanks C of C (dir. 1973-78). Clubs: Elks, Lions, Washington Athletic. Office: 709 Hart Senate Bldg Washington DC 20510

MUROBUSE, FUMIRO, publishing company executive; b. Kawasaki, Kanagawa, Japan, Apr. 1, 1925; s. Hidehira and Miki (Yajima) M.; m. Fuyumi Nakazato, Nov. 8, 1960. M in Econs., Tokyo U., 1949. Editor Nihon Keizai Shimbun, Inc., Tokyo, 1949-57; corr. N.Y.C., 1957-60; chief editor econ. dept. Osaka, Japan, 1960-63; gen. sec. Japan Econ. Research Ctr., Tokyo, 1964-68; dir. Nikkei Bus. Publs. Inc., Tokyo, 1969—; pres. 5, Tokyo, 1980—; mgmt. advisor Nihon Keizai Shimbun, Tokyo, 1985—. Co-author: Japan's Economy in 1985, 1964; translator: New Business Journalism, 1981. Grantee Ford Found., N.Y.C., 1968. Mem. Japan Futurology Assn. Buddhist. Clubs: New Otani Spa (Tokyo); Kawagoe (Saitama). Home: Apt 1303, 2-3-1 Ohtsuka, Bunkyo-ku, Tokyo 112, Japan Office: Nikkei Bus Publs Inc, 1-1 Kanda Ogawamachi, Tokyo 101, Japan

MUROFF, LAWRENCE ROSS, physician; b. Phila., Dec. 26, 1942; s. John M. and Carolyn (Kramer) M.; m. Carol R. Savoy, July 12, 1969; children: Michael Bruce, Julie Anne. A.B. cum laude, Dartmouth Coll., 1964, B.M.S., 1965; M.D. cum laude, Harvard U., 1967. Diplomate Am. Bd. Radiology, Am. Bd. Nuclear Medicine. Intern Boston City Hosp., Harvard, 1968; resident in radiology Columbia Presbyn. Med. Center, N.Y.C., 1970-73, chief resident, 1973; instr., asst. radiologist 1973-74; dir. dept. nuclear medicine, computed tomography and magnetic resonance imaging Univ. Community Hosp., Tampa, Fla., 1974—; clin. asst. prof. radiology U. South Fla., 1974-78, clin. assoc. prof., 1978-82, clin. prof., 1988—. Contbr. articles to profl. jours. Served to lt. comdr. USPHS, 1968-70. Fellow Am. Coll. Nuclear Medicine (disting. fellow, Fla. del.), Am. Coll. Nuclear Physicians (regents 1976-78, pres.-elect 1978, pres. 1979, fellow 1980), Am. Coll. Radiology (councilor 1979-80, chancellor 1981-87, chmn. commn. on nuclear medicine 1981-87, fellow 1981); mem. Am. Assn. Acad. Chief Residents Radiology (chmn. 1973), AMA, Boylston Soc., Fla. Assn. Nuclear Physicians (pres. 1976), Fla. Med. Assn., Hillsborough County Med. Assn., Radiol. Soc. N.Am., Soc. Nuclear Medicine (council 1975—, trustee 1980-84, 86—, pres. Southeastern chpt. 1983, vice chmn. correlative imaging council 1983), Fla. Radiol. Soc. (exec. com. 1976—, treas. 1984, sec. 1985, v.p. 1986, pres. elect 1987, pres. 1988—), West Coast Radiol. Soc., Soc. Mag. Resonance Imaging (bd. dirs. 1988—, chmn. ednl. program 1988), Phi Beta Kappa, Alpha Omega Alpha. Office: 13550 N 31st St Tampa FL 33612

MUROTA, TAKESHI, professor of economics; b. Takasaki, Gumma, Japan, Oct. 8, 1943; s. Toyoji and Yoshiko (Yoshizawa) M.; m. Kiyoko Tachibana; 2 children. BS in Physics, Kyoto (Japan) U., 1967; MA in Econs., Osaka (Japan) U., 1969; PhD in Econs., U. Minn., 1976. Lectr. econs. U. Ill., Urbana, 1973-74, Kokugakuin U., Tokyo, 1975-78; assoc. prof. Hitotsubashi U., Tokyo, 1978-87, prof. econs., 1987—; cons. Japan Assn. Wood Carbonization, Tokyo, 1985—; exhibition dir. INAX Galleries, Tokyo and Osaka, 1986. Author: Economics of Energy and Entropy, 1979, Economics of Water-Soil Matrix, 1982, Four Seasons of Waterwheels, 1983, Economics of Coppice, 1985; co-editor: Entropy, 1985, The New Economics of Nuclear Power, 1986, Environmental Economics, 1987, The Ptolemaic Econoics, 1988. Rep. Watermill Hamlet Assn., Fujieda, Shizuoka, 1981—. Grantee European Coordination Ctr. Research and Documentation in Social Scis., Vienna, 1987. Mem. Japan Assn. Econs. and Econometrics, Japan Assn. Indsl. Archeology, Soc. for Studies on Entropy. Office: Hitotsubashi U, Dept Econs, Naka 2-1, Kunitachi, Tokyo 186, Japan

MURPHY, BEN CARROLL, engineering company executive; b. Rome, Miss., Aug. 21, 1931; s. Benjamin Franklin and Effie (Lett) M.; B.S., Delta State U., 1969, M.B.A., 1974; grad. United Electronic Inst., 1972; m. Vivian Inez Hancock, Mar. 3, 1950; children—Lanny Carroll, Debra Kay Murphy Snead, Kathy M. Murphy David, Gregory Lynn, Jon Patrick. With U.S. Gypsum Co., Greenville, Miss., 1951-54, 55-56, Atlantic & Pacific Tea Co., Greenville, 1954-55; cost acct. Baxter Labs., Cleveland, Miss., 1966-69; project engr. mfg. U.S. Gypsum Co., Danville, Va., 1969-72; plant personnel and safety mgr. Cook Industries, Inc., Memphis, 1972-73, div. safety dir., plant personnel mgr., 1973-75, corp. compensation sr. analyst, 1976, div. indsl. relations and personnel mgr., 1975-76, corp. compensation mgr., 1976-79; div. asst. personnel mgr. Mitchell Engring. Co., Columbus, Miss., 1979-80, structural supt., 1980-82, mgr. prodn. control systems, 1982—. night instr. bus. and econs. N.W. Jr. Coll., Southaven, Miss., 1975-79, Golden Tri-Angle Vo-Tec, 1980—; cons. in compensation S.E. Memphis Mental Health Center, 1978-82. Mem. Mid-South Compensation and Benefits Assn. (dir. 1977-80, mem. organizing team 1976), Univ. for Women (adv. com. for extended studies of Miss. U.), Am. Compensation Soc., Soc. Mfg. Engrs. (sr., 3d v.p. chpt.), Miss. Mfg. Assn., Am. Mgmt. Compensation Soc. Baptist. Lodge: Masons (32 degree). Home: PO Box 1103 Batesville MS 38606 Office: PO Drawer 911 Columbus MS 39701

MURPHY, DENNIS PATRICK, hotel executive; b. Buffalo, N.Y., Jan. 12, 1958; s. Dennis Charles and Dorothy E. Murphy. B in Hospitality Mgmt., Fla. Internat. U., 1980. Mgr. hotel ops. Marriott Corp., Washington, 1979-80; dir. food and beverage Mariner Corp., Houston, 1980-83; corp. dir. Innco Hospitality, Wichita, Kans., 1984-86; ops. exec. Clubhouse Inns of Am., 1986-88; pres. JLH Lodge Corp., Amherst, N.Y., 1988—, bd. dirs.; bd. dirs. Humanitech Inc., N.Y., 1983—; nominated Esquire mag. register, 1985; mem. rev. com. Ednl. Inst. Am. Hotel Assn., 1988—. Chmn. Gov.'s Youth Traffic Safety Com., N.Y., 1977-79; mem. Nat. Youth Safety Council, Washington, 1978. recipient Elsworth Statler award The Statler Found., 1978-79, Eugene Fitzsimmons award Internat. Assn. Hospitality Accts., 1980. Mem. Nat. Restaurant Assn., Soc. Wine Educators (pubs. com. 1977-79), Am. Hotel Motel Assn. (mem. publ. com. ednl. inst.). Home: 505 N Rock Rd #1304 Wichita KS 67206 Office: 3380 Sheridan Dr Suite 390 Amherst NY 14226

MURPHY, EUGENE FRANCIS, consultant, retired government official; b. Syracuse, N.Y., May 31, 1913; s. Eugene Francis and Mary Grace (Thompson) M.; m. Helene M. Murphy, Dec. 31, 1955; children: Anne F., Thomas E. M.E., Cornell U., 1935; M.M.E., Syracuse U., 1937; Ph.D., Ill. Inst. Tech., 1948. Teaching asst. Syracuse U., 1935-36; engr. Ingersoll-Rand Co., Painted Post, N.Y., 1936-39; instr. Ill. Inst. Tech., 1939-41; from instr. to asst. prof. U. Calif., Berkeley, 1941-48; staff engr. Nat. Acad. Scis., Washington, 1945-48; adv. fellow Mellon Inst., Pitts., 1947-48; with VA, N.Y.C., 1948-83; chief research and devel. div. Prosthetic and Sensory Aids Service, 1948-73; dir. Research Center for Prosthetics, 1973-78; dir. Office of Tech. Transfer, 1978-83, sci. advisor, 1983-85; Mem. council Alliance for Engring. in Medicine and Biology, 1969—; mem. adv. com. U. Wis., 1978-82, Case Western Res. U., 1981, Am. Found. for Blind, 1981-83; cons. disability and rehab. research, 1987. Contbg. author: Human Limbs and their Substitutes, 1954, Orthopaedic Appliances Atlas, vol. 1, 2, Human Factors in Technology, 1963, Biomedical Engineering Systems, 1970, Critical Revs. in Bioengring, 1971, CRC Handbook of Materials, Vol. III, 1975, Atlas of Orthotics, 1976, 2d edit., 1985, Therapeutic Medical Devices: Application and Design, 1982, McGraw-Hill Ency. Sci. and Tech. Yearbook, 1985; contbr. to Wiley Encyclopedia of Medical Devices and Instrumentation, 1988; editor: Bull. Prosthetics Research, 1978-82; contbr. articles profl. jours. Recipient Silver medal Paris, France, 1961; Meritorious Service award VA, 1971; Disting. Career award VA, 1983; Biomedical Engring. Leadership award Alliance for Engring. in Medicine and Biology, 1983; citation Outstanding Handicapped Fed. Employee, 1971; Profl. Achievement award Ill. Inst. Technology, 1983; Fulbright lectr. Soc. and Home for Cripples, Denmark, 1957-58. Fellow AAAS, ASME, Internat. Soc. for Prosthetics and Orthotics, Assn. for Advancement of Rehab. Tech.; assoc. fellow N.Y. Acad. Medicine; mem. Nat. Acad. Engring., N.Y. Acad. Sci., Acoustical Soc. Am., Optical Soc. Am., Sigma Xi, Tau Beta Pi, Phi Kappa Phi. Home: 511 E 20th St New York NY 10010

MURPHY, FRANCIS SEWARD, journalist; b. Portland, Oreg., Sept. 9, 1914; s. Francis H. and Blanche (Livesay) M.; B.A., Reed Coll., 1936; m. Clare Eastham Cooke, Sept. 20, 1974. With The Oregonian, Portland, 1936-79, TV editor, Behind the Mike columnist, 1952-79. Archeol. explorer Mayan ruins, Yucatan, Mex., 1950—, mem. Am. Quintana Roo Expdn., 1965, 66, 68. Served with AUS, 1942-46. Mem. Royal Asiatic Soc., Royal Hong Kong Jockey Club. Democrat. Congregationalist. Clubs: City (bd. govs. 1950, 64-66); Explorers, Am. Club of Hong Kong. Home: 4213 NE 32d Ave Portland OR 97211 Home: 1102 Tavistock,, 10 Tregunter Path,, Hong Kong Hong Kong

MURPHY, FRANKLIN DAVID, physician, educator, publisher; b. Kansas City, Mo., Jan. 29, 1916; s. Franklin E. and Cordelia (Brown) M.; m. Judith Joyce Harris, Dec. 28, 1940; children: Judith (Mrs. Walter Dickey), Martha (Mrs. Craig Crockwell), Carolyn Murphy Milner, Franklin. A.B., U. Kans., 1936; M.D., U. Pa., 1941. Diplomate: Am. Bd. Internal Medicine. Intern Hosp. U. Pa., 1941-42, instr., 1942-44; instr. medicine U. Kans., 1946-48, dean Sch. Medicine, assoc. prof. medicine, 1948-51, chancellor, 1951-60; chancellor UCLA, 1960-68; chmn. bd., chief exec. officer Times Mirror Co., 1968-81, chmn. exec. com., 1981-86; trustee J. Paul Getty Trust; dir. emeritus Times-Mirror Co. Chmn. Kress Found., Nat. Gallery of Art.; trustee Los Angeles County Mus. Art. Served to capt. AUS, 1944-46. Named One of Ten Outstanding Young Men U.S. Jr. C. of C., 1949; recipient Outstanding Civilian Service award U.S. Army, 1967. Fellow A.C.P.; mem. Phi Beta Kappa, Sigma Xi, Alpha Omega Alpha, Beta Theta Pi, Nu Sigma Nu. Episcopalian. Home: 419 Robert Ln Beverly Hills CA 90210 Office: Times Mirror Co Times Mirror Sq Los Angeles CA 90053

MURPHY, GRETA WERWATH, retired college official; b. Milw., Aug. 24, 1910; d. Oscar and Johanna (Seelhorst) Werwath; m. John Heery Murphy, Sept. 18, 1941. Ed. Ohio State U., 1943-45. With Milw. Sch. Engring., 1928—, head admissions dept., 1931-42, dir. pub. relations, 1945-66, v.p. pub. relations and devel., 1966-77, v.p., cons., 1978—, regent emeritus, 1985—. Mem. Milw. County Planning Commn., 1966—, vice chmn., 1974-75, chmn., 1976-77. Mem. Pub. Relations Soc. Am. (founder, past pres. Wis.

chpt.), Am. Coll. Pub. Relations Assn. (past dir., sec., trustee), Women's Advt. Club (pres.). Club: Womans of Wis. Home: 1032 Malaga Ave Coral Gables FL 33134 Other: 5556 S Cedar Beach Belgium WI 53004

MURPHY, JAMES HENRY, priest, educator; b. Dublin, Ireland, May 15, 1959; s. Philip Patrick and Barbara Mary (O'Hare) M. BA, Nat. U. Ireland, 1980; BDiv, U. London, 1983; diploma in Pastoral Studies, All Hallows Coll., Dublin, 1984; higher diploma in Edn., Dublin U., 1987. Joined Congregation of Mission, 1976, ordained priest Roman Catholic Ch., 1985. Dir. adult edn., mem. retreat team All Hallows Coll., 1984-85; tchr. English and Religious Studies, dir. liturgy Castleknock Coll., Dublin, 1985—. Home and Office: Castleknock Coll, Dublin 15, Ireland

MURPHY, JAMES JOSEPH, organization development consultant, speaker; b. Bridgeport, Conn., Dec. 29, 1944; s. William Oliver and Martha Frances (Bukovick) M.; m. Ellen Joann Duane, Jan. 22, 1977; children—Kavan Duane, James Michael. B.S. in Bus. Adminstrn. King's Coll., Wilkes-Barre, Pa., 1966. Personnel mdse. mgr. Montgomery Ward & Co., Chgo., 1966-74; regional personnel mgr. Caldor Inc., Norwalk, Conn., 1974-77; tng., devel. dir. Morse Shoe Inc., Canton, Mass., 1977-85; pres. The Listening Ctr., Buzzards Bay, Mass., 1985—; chmn. Bourne-Sandwich Small Bus. Cons. Group, N.E. Pa. Bus. Machine Computer Show, Wilkes-Barre, Pa., 1966; lectr. in field. Bd. dirs. Bourne-Sandwich C. of C. Served with USN, 1967-69. Recipient Outstanding Citizenship award United Fund, Albany, N.Y., 1970, U.S. Savs. Bond Program award U.S. Sec. Treasury, 1971. Mem. Am. Soc. Tng. and Devel. Roman Catholic. Home: 4 Vicki Circle Bourne MA 02532 Office: PO Box 561 Buzzards Bay MA 02532

MURPHY, JOHN ARTHUR, tobacco and brewing company executive; b. N.Y.C., Dec. 15, 1929; s. John A. and Mary J. (Touhey) M.; m. Carole Ann Paul, June 28, 1952; children: John A., Kevin P., Timothy M., Kellyann, Robert B., Kathleen. B.S., Villanova U., 1951; J.D., Columbia U., 1954. Bar: N.Y. 1954. Since practiced in N.Y.C.; ptnr. firm Conboy, Hewitt O'Brien & Boardman, 1954-62; asst. gen. counsel Philip Morris, Inc., N.Y.C., 1962-66, v.p., 1967-76, exec. v.p., 1976-78, group exec. v.p., 1978-84, pres., 1984—, also bd. dirs.; asst. to pres. Philip Morris Internat., 1966-67, exec. v.p., 1967-71; pres., chief exec. officer Miller Brewing Co., Milw., 1971-78, chmn. bd., chief exec. officer, 1978-84; dir. Nat. Westminster Bank USA. Trustee North Shore Univ. Hosp., Marquette U., Alverno Coll.; dir., mem. exec. com. Keep Am. Beautiful Inc. Decorated Knight of Malta. Mem. ABA, N.Y. State Bar Assn. Office: Philip Morris Cos Inc 120 Park Ave New York NY 10017

MURPHY, JOHN JOSEPH, manufacturing company executive; b. Olean, N.Y., Nov. 24, 1931; s. John Joseph and Mary M.; m. Louise John; children: Kathleen A. Murphy Bell, Karen L. Murphy Rochelli, Patricia L. Murphy Smith, Michael J. AAS in Mech. Engring., Rochester Inst. Tech., 1952; MBA, So. Meth. U. Engr. Clark div. Dresser Industries, Olean, 1952-67; gen. mgr. roots blower div. Clark div. Connersville, Ind., 1967-69; pres. crane, hoist and tower div. Muskegon, Mich., 1969-70; pres. machinery group Houston, 1970-75; sr. v.p. ops. Dallas, 1980, exec. v.p., 1982, pres., 1982—, chmn. bd., chief exec. officer, 1983—; bd. dirs. PepsiCo, Inc.; mem. Pres.'s Export Council. Chmn. bd. trustees St. Bonaventure (N.Y.) U.; bd. dirs. Tex. Research League. Bus. Served with U.S. Army, 1954-56. Mem. Am. Council for Capital Formation (bd. dirs.), U.S. C. of C. (bd. dirs.), Machinery and Allied Products Inst. (exec. com.). Office: Dresser Industries Inc 1600 Pacific Bldg PO Box 718 Dallas TX 75221

MURPHY, JOSEPH JAMES, II, utilities executive; b. N.Y.C., Jan. 14, 1939; s. Joseph James and Margaret Mary (Russell) M.; m. Grace Patricia Kiernan, June 8, 1963; children—Joseph, Daniel, Craig. B.B.A., Iona Coll., 1961, M.B.A., 1976. Sr. acct. Price Waterhouse , N.Y.C., 1964-67; sr. fin. analyst Atlantic Richfield Corp., N.Y.C., 1967-69; controller, chief fin. officer Cavitron Corp., N.Y.C., 1969-71; v.p. fin., chief fin. officer Conn. Energy Corp., Bridgeport, 1971-79; exec. v.p., chief fin. officer The Hydraulic Co., Bridgeport, 1979—, dir., 1981-83; ptnr. High St. Assocs., 1986—; dir. Stamford Water Co. (Conn.), Timco, Inc., Pittsfield, N.H., Main St. South Corp., Bridgeport; mem. adv. counsel Fairfield U., 1980-82. Contbr. articles to profl. jours. Bd. dirs. Boys'/Girls' Club, Bridgeport, 1980-82; treas. Pop Warner Football, Fairfield, Conn., 1978-83. Served to 1st lt. USMC, 1961-64; Caribbean. Mem. Am. Water Works Assn., Nat. Assn. Water Cos. (vice chmn. fin. com.). Roman Catholic. Club: Patterson (Fairfield). Office: Hydraulic Co 835 Main St Bridgeport CT 06601

MURPHY, JOSEPH S., university chancellor, educator; b. Newark, Nov. 15, 1933; m. Susan Crile, 1984; children by previous marriage—Lisa, Susanne, Peter. Student, U. Colo., 1951-53; A.B., Olivet Coll., Mich., 1955; Graham Kenan fellow, Woodrow Wilson fellow, U. N.C. at Chapel Hill, 1955-56; M.A., Brandeis U., 1959, Ph.D., 1961. Teaching fellow, instr., asst. prof. Brandeis U., 1957-65; dir. V.I. Peace Corps Tng. Center, St. Croix, 1965-66; asst. Office Sec. HEW, Washington, 1966-67; assoc. dir. Job Corps, OEO, Washington, 1967-68; dir. U.S. Peace Corps, Ethiopia, 1968-70; vice chancellor for higher edn. State of N.J., 1970-71; pres. Queens Coll., prof. polit. sci. Grad. Faculty, CUNY, 1971-77, chancellor, 1982—; pres. Bennington (Vt.) Coll., 1977-82; cons. V.I. Econ. Opportunity Program, 1965-66; mem. N.Y. State Martin Luther King Commn., 1985—, Gov's. Task Force on Higher Edn., 1975-76; chmn., bd. dirs. research found. CUNY, 1984—; chmn. Nat. Coalition for Aid to Part-Time Students, 1983—, Nat. Pell Grant Coalition, 1982—, City Council Pres. Commn. on Adult Edn., 1974-76; chmn. governance and coordination com. N.Y. State, 1975-76; chmn. adv. bd. Chem. Bank, N.Y., 1974-76; mem. AFL-CIO Higher Edn. Council, 1983—; pres. Coll. Pub. Agy. Council, N.Y.C., 1973-74. Author: The Theory of Universals in Eighteenth Century British Empiricism, 1961, Political Theory: A Conceptual Analysis, 1968; contbr. articles to profl. jours. Bd. dirs. Phelps Stokes Fund, 1986—, N.Y. Urban League, N.Y.C., 1984—, AM. Red Cross, N.Y.C., 1972-76, Ralph Bunche Inst. on UN, 1974, Operation Sail Bicentennial Celebration, N.Y.C., 1975-76; bd. advisors Sta. WNET-TV, N.Y.C., 1984; trustee Queens County Art and Cultural Ctr., 1972-76, Mt. Sinai Med. Ctr.; vice chmn. Regents Regional Coordinating Council for Postsecondary Edn. in N.Y.C., 1973-75. Recipient Merit award U.S. Fgn. Service, 1965. Mem. Am. Assn. Higher Edn., Am. Philos. Assn., Am. Polit. Sci. Assn., Am. Orthopsychiatric Assn., AAAS, AAUP. Office: CUNY Office of the Chancellor 535 E 80th St New York NY 10021

MURPHY, MARGARETTE CELESTINE EVANS, educator, writer; b. Chgo., June 25, 1926; d. Crawford and Ethel Hazel (Cartman) Evans; Ph.B., U. Chgo., 1945, M.A., 1949, postgrad., 1950-79, Ph.D., Colo. Christian Coll., 1972; m. Robert H. Murphy, Sept. 25, 1949; children: Linda, Michelle. Tchr., English, Spanish and French, Willard Elem. Sch., 1950-52, McKinley High Sch., 1952-60, chmn. fgn. langs. dept. Crane High Sch., 1960-64, Harlan High Sch., Chgo., 1967—; tchr. TESL, Chgo. City Jr. Colls., 1976—. Mem. Women's Share in Pub. Service, Brazilian Soc. Chgo., Am. Security Council (nat. adv. bd.), U. Chgo. Alumni Assn., AAUW, Esperanto Soc. Chgo., Alpha Kappa Alpha. Republican. Roman Catholic. Club: 1200 of Chgo. Author: Note on Martinez Zuviria, Argentinian Novelist, 1949. Home: 8214 S Evans Ave Chicago IL 60619 Office: care Mrs Eva C Martin and Linda M Murphy 907 Polk Ave Memphis TN 38104

MURPHY, MARY KATHLEEN CONNORS, college administrator, writer; b. Pueblo, Colo.; d. Joseph Charles and Eileen E. (McDermott) Connors; m. Michael C. Murphy, June 6, 1959; children—Holly Ann, Emily Louise, Patricia Marie. AB, Loretto Heights Coll., 1960; MEd, Emory U., 1968; PhD, Ga. State U., 1980. Tchr. English pub. schs., Moultrie, Ga., 1959, Sacramento, 1960, Marietta, Ga., 1960-65, DeKalb County, Ga., 1966; tech. writer Ga. Dept. Edn., 1966-69; editorial asst. So. Regional Edn. Bd., Atlanta, 1969-71; dir. alumni affairs The Lovett Sch., Atlanta, 1972-75, dir. publs. and info. services, 1975-77; coordinator summer series in aging Ga. State U., 1979; dir. devel. found. relations Ga. Inst. Tech., 1980-87; dir. devel., 1987—; state coordinator for Ga., Am. Council on Edn. nat. identification program for women in higher edn. adminstrn., 1983-85; presenter profl. confs.; freelance edn. writer, 1968—; contbr. and contbg. editor numerous articles on teaching, secondary edn., higher edn., and fund raising to profl. publs.; columnist Daily Jour., Marietta, 1963-67, The Atlanta Constn., 1963-68. Bd. advisors Bridge Family Counseling Center, 1981-86, Northside Sch. Arts, 1981-83; bd. dirs. Atlanta Women's Network, 1982-84, v.p., 1983-84; bd. dirs. Sch. Religion, Cathedral of Christ the King, 1979-84; publicity chmn. Phoenix Soc. Atlanta, 1981—, adv. com., 1988—; mem. allocations com., exec. com. United Way Met. Atlanta, 1983; bd. counseling Fulton Service Ctr., Met. Atlanta chpt. ARC, 1982-83; mem. Leadership Atlanta, class of 1983-84; group facilitator, 1984-85, co-chmn. edn. program, 1987. NDEA fellow, 1965-66; Adminstrn. of Aging fellow, 1977-79; recipient Image Maker award Atlanta Profl. Women's Directory, Inc. 1984. Mem. Council for Advancement and Support of Edn. (publs. com., alumni adv. com., dist. III bd. 1981—, chmn. corp. and found. support conf., N.Y.C., 1985, maj. donor research conf. N.Y.C. 1985, dist. III conf. chmn. 1986) Nat. Assn. Ind. Schs. (publs. com.), Edn. Writers Assn., Am. Vocat. Assn., Nat. Soc. Fund Raising Execs. (v.p. chpt. 1985, pres. 1986-87, mem.-at-large nat. bd. 1985—, chmn. pub. relations com. 1985-87, asst. treas., mem. exec. com. 1988—), Phi Delta Kappa, Kappa Delta Pi (pres. 1980-81). Co-author: Fitting in as a New Service Wife, 1966; editor handbook on found. fund raising, 1988. Home: 2903 Rivermeade Dr NW Atlanta GA 30327

MURPHY, PAUL KERNS, advertising executive; b. Phila., Feb. 7, 1938; s. John Joseph and Anna (Reigart) M.; A.B., Harvard U., 1960; m. Patricia Ann Petrus, Jan. 22, 1966; children—Scott Kerns, Brooke Calder. Account exec. Gallup & Robinson, Inc., Princeton, N.J., 1963-66; research account supr. Compton Advt., Inc., N.Y.C., 1966-69; v.p., research dir. TV Testing Co., N.Y.C., 1969-71, pres., 1971-76; asso. research dir. Young & Rubicam, Inc., N.Y.C., 1976-79, v.p., research dir., Chgo., 1979-82, sr. v.p., research dir. Splty. Group of Cos., N.Y.C., 1982-83; sr. v.p., dir. mktg. services Dentsu Young & Rubicam, N.Y.C., 1984-86; exec. v.p. dir., prin. Airport Interviewing & Research, Inc., Hartsdale, N.Y., 1986-88, sr. v.p., gen. mgr. N.Y. Office of The Wirthlin Group, N.Y.C., 1988—. Served with USMC, 1960. Columbia U. research grantee, 1962-63. Mem. Am. Mktg. Assn., SAR. Republican. Club: Harvard (N.Y.C.). Home: 15 Lorrie Ln Lawrenceville NJ 08648 Office: 420 Lexington Ave New York NY 10017

MURPHY, PRESTON VINCENT, electronics company executive; b. East Chicago, Ind., Mar. 3, 1930; s. Lester and Angelique (Molloy) M.; m. Vaucel Marie-Claire; children: Patrick, Lorraine, Valérie, Melanie. B.S. in Chemistry, U. Notre Dame, 1951; A.M. in Radio Chemistry, Washington U., St. Louis, 1954, Ph.D. in Radio Chemistry, 1956. Pres., Panoramic Research Inc., Palo Alto, Calif., 1962-65; mgr. Thermo Electron Corp., Waltham, Mass., 1965-73, gen. mgr., Barcelona, Spain, 1973-76; pres., Lectret S.A., Geneva, 1976—. Contbr. tech. articles to profl. publs. Patentee in field. Mem. Brit. Phys. Soc., Internat. Soc. Hybred Microelectronics, Am. Phys. Soc., Audio Engring. Soc. Office: Lectret, 25 Champs Frechets, Meyrin, 1217 Geneva Switzerland

MURPHY, RALPH EDGAR, financial consultant, former business executive; b. Manchester, N.H., Aug. 14, 1931; s. Charles Joseph and Dorothy May (Leslie) M.; B.S. in Edn., Plymouth State Coll. (U. N.H.), 1956; m. Marjorie Anne Miller, July 4, 1964 (div. Nov. 1977); 1 child, Margaret Leslie. Bus. instr. Anne Arundel County, Md., 1956-58; traffic specialist Chemstrand Corp., N.Y.C., 1958-60, Greenville, S.C., 1960-61, transp. mgr., N.Y.C., 1961-64; audit supr. Monsanto Co., St. Louis, 1964-70; audit supr. Microdot Inc., Greenwich, Conn., 1970-74, asst. to v.p. operational analysis, 1974-75; dir. fin. Malco, a Microdot Co., Montgomeryville, 1975-77; controller, asst. sec. Malco Mfg. Can. Ltd., acting controller Microdot Ltd., Tokyo; controller Microdot connector group, Montgomeryville, Pa., 1977-79; asst. controller Ingredient Tech. Corp., N.Y.C. and Darien, Conn., 1979-82, corp. sec., Pelham Manor, N.Y., 1982-85; fin. cons., 1985—. Cert. internal auditor, Conn., Pa. Mem. Inst. Internal Auditors Am. Soc. Corp. Secs. Home: PO Box 10779 Stamford CT 06904-1779

MURPHY, RANDALL KENT, consultant; b. Laramie, Wyo., Nov. 8, 1943; s. Robert Joseph and Sally (McConnell) M.; student U. Wyo., 1961-65; M.B.A., So. Meth. U., 1983; m. Cynthia Laura Hillhouse, Dec. 29, 1978; children—Caroline, Scott, Emily. Dir. mktg. Wycoa, Inc., Denver, 1967-70; dir. Communications Resource Inst., Dallas, 1971-72; account exec. Xerox Learning Systems, Dallas, 1973-74; regional mgr. Systema Corp., Dallas, 1975; pres. Performance Assocs.; pres., dir. Acclivus Corp., Dallas, 1976—; founder, chmn. Acclivus Inst., 1982—. Active, Dallas Mus. Fine Arts, Dallas Hist. Soc., Dallas Symphony Assn. Served with AUS, 1966. Mem. Am. Soc. Tng. and Devel., Sales and Mktg. Execs. Internat., Inst. Mgmt. Scis., Soc. Applied Learning Tech., Nat. Soc. Performance and Instrn., Assn. M.B.A. Execs., Internat. Platform Assn., Assn. Mgmt. Cons., World Futre Soc., Am. Assn. Higher Edn., World Future Soc., Soc. for Intercultural Edn., Tng. and Research, Internat. Fedn. Tng. and Devel. Orgns., So. Meth. U. Alumni Assn. U. Wyo. Alumni Assn. Roman Catholic. Club: University. Author: Performance Management of the Selling Process, 1979; Coaching and Counseling for Performance, 1980; Managing Development and Performance, 1982; Acclivus Performance Planning System, 1983; (with others) BASE for Sales Performance, 1983; Acclivus Coaching, 1984; Acclivus Sales Negotiation, 1985; BASE for Effective Presentations, 1987; co-inventor The Randy-Band, multi-purpose apparel accessory, 1968. Home: 6540 Crestpoint Dr Dallas TX 75240

MURPHY, ROBERT BLAIR, management consulting company executive; b. Phila., Jan. 19, 1931; s. William Beverly and Helen Marie (Brennan) M.; B.S., Yale, 1953; m. Elise McBryde, July 10, 1981; children by previous marriage—Stephen, Emily, Julia, David, Catherine. Indsl. engr. Dupont Corp., Aiken, S.C., 1953-55; mgr. sales can div. Reynolds Metals Co., Richmond, Va., 1955-69; gen. mgr. corrugated div. Continental Can Co., N.Y.C., 1969-73; v.p. and gen. mgr. beverage div. Am. Can Co., Greenwich, Conn., 1973-75; asso. Heidrick & Struggles, Inc., N.Y.C., 1976-78, v.p., 1978; v.p., mng. dir. Stamford office Spencer Stuart & Assocs., 1978-84, ptnr., 1982-84; co-founder Sullivan-Murphy Assocs., 1984—. Clubs: Round Hill, Riverside Yacht (Greenwich); Yale (N.Y.C.); Merion Cricket (Haverford, Pa.). Home: 11 Indian Mill Rd Cos Cob CT 06807 Office: 6 Landmark Sq Stamford CT 06901

MURPHY, THOMAS FRANCIS (TODD), wholesale distribution company executive; b. Burlington, Vt., Sept. 11, 1942; s. Edmund Joseph and Rosella (Juve) M.; A.B.A., Champlain Coll., 1964; OPM, Harvard Bus. Sch., 1983; m. Jane Christie, Apr. 30, 1966; children—Kara, Glenn. Brian. Pres., Burlington News Agy., Inc., Burlington, 1964—, Lake Champlain Yacht Sales, Inc., Burlington, 1971-76, European Auto, Inc., 1972-74, owner Bookglenn, 1968-72; pres. Daytona News, Inc., Daytona Beach, Fla., 1976—, Plattsburgh News Co., 1982—; dir. Mchts. Nat. Bank. Chmn. Burlington St. Commn., 1972-75; chmn. Burlington Water Pollution Control Bd., 1972-75; trustee emeritus Champlain Coll.; mem. Bank of Vermont Council, 1974—. Mem. Atlantic Coast Ind. Distbrs. Assn. (dir. 1966-85). Roman Catholic. Clubs: Ethan Allen, Mallets Bay Boat. Home: 5 Driftwood Ln Burlington VT 05401 Office: Hercules Dr Colchester VT 05446

MURPHY, WILLIAM BEVERLY, business executive; b. Appleton, Wis., June 17, 1907; s. S.W. and Hilma (Anderson) M.; m. Helen Brennan, May 28, 1930; children: Robert Blair, Ann Pollock, John Huston, Eric Stevens. B.S. in Chem. Engring., U. Wis., 1928; L.H.D., Pa. Mil. Coll., 1960; LL.D., Lawrence U., 1954, U. Wis., 1963, St. Joseph's Coll., 1965, Rutgers U., 1973; Sc.D., Ursinus Coll., 1970; Engring.D., Drexel U., 1970. Exec. v.p. A.C. Nielsen Co., Chgo., 1928-38; with Campbell Soup Co., 1938-72, exec. v.p., 1949, dir., 1950-80, pres., chief exec. officer, 1953-72; dir. Merck & Co., Inc., 1959-80, AT&T, 1961-78, Internat. Paper Co., 1969-80. Author: Fifty Active Years (Gantt medal 1979). Chmn. Radio Free Europe Fund, 1960-61, Nutrition Found., 1964-65, Bus. Council, 1965-66, Bus. Roundtable, 1972-73; mem. Pub. Adv. Com. on U.S. Trade Policy, Pres.'s Adv. Com. on Labor-Mgmt. Policy, 1964-68, Commn. on Food and Fiber, 1966-67, Commn. on Postal Orgn., 1967-68; mem. hazard adv. com. EPA, 1971-72; hon. trustee Phila. Mus. Art, chmn. capital devel. campaign, 1971-74; chmn. pub. edn. com. Greater Phila. Movement, 1973-74; hon. trustee Acad. Natural Scis. of Phila.; life mem. exec. com. MIT, 1966-72, 76-82, co-chmn. steering com. leadership campaign, 1976-80; life mem. Wis. Alumni Research Found., pres., 1982-86; bd. dirs. Phila. Soc. Promoting Agr., 1981—, pres., 1985-86. Served WPB, 1942-45. Decorated Presdl. medal for Merit, 1946. Mem. Delta Upsilon, Tau Beta Pi. Republican. Presbyterian. Clubs: Merion Cricket, Philadelphia, Buck Harbor Yacht. Home: 110 Maplehill Rd Gladwyne PA 19035 Office: PO Box 40 Haverford PA 19041

MURRAY, ALAN, engineering manager; b. Newcastle upon Tyne, Eng., Aug. 21, 1949; s. Gavin Murray and Hilda Brook; m. Marie Jane Walker, Mar. 8, 1973; children: Lloyd Kennedy, Aidan Taylor. Higher Nat. Cert. Mech., Newcastle Poly., Newcastle upon Tyne, 1970; Nat. Cert. Bus. Studies, Coll. Art and Tech., Newcastle upon Tyne, 1985. Draughtsman design Sir Howard Grubb Parsons & Co. Ltd., Newcastle upon Tyne, 1966-75, C.A. Parsons & Co. Ltd., Newcastle upon Tyne, 1975-77, Grubb Parsons & Co. Ltd., Newcastle upon Tyne, 1977-78, Am. Air Filters, Cramlington, Eng., 1978, Winthrop Labs. Ltd., Newcastle upon Tyne, 1978; mfg. liaison engr. on line inspection Brit. Gas Corp., Cramlington, 1978-80; engr. product design and devel. Elmwood Sensors Ltd., Tyne, Eng., 1980-85, mgr. product engring., 1985—. Patentee in field. Fellow Inst. Bus. and Tech. Mgmt.; mem. Brit. Inst. Mgmt. (assoc.). Home: 23 Yarmouth Dr, Northumberland NE23 9TS, England Office: Elmwood Sensors Ltd, Elm Rd, North Shields, Tyne NE29 8SA, England

MURRAY, ALLEN EDWARD, oil company executive; b. N.Y.C., Mar. 5, 1929; s. Allen and Carla (Jones) M.; m. Patricia Ryan, July 28, 1951; children: Allen, Marilyn, Ellen, Eileen, Allison. B.S. in Bus. Adminstrn, NYU, 1956. Trainee Pub. Nat. Bank & Trust Co., N.Y.C., 1948-49; acct. Gulf Oil Corp., 1949-52; various fin. positions Socony-Vacuum Overseas Supply Co. (Mobil), 1952-56; with Mobil Oil Corp. subs. Mobil Corp., 1956—, v.p. planning N.Am. div., 1968-69, v.p. planning, supply and transp. N.Am. div., 1969-74, exec. v.p. N.Am. div., 1974, pres. U.S. mktg. and refining div., exec. v.p., 1975-82, pres. worldwide mktg. and refining, 1979-82, corp. pres., 1983-84, chief operating officer, 1984-86, chief exec. officer, chief operating officer, chmn. exec. com., 1986—, chmn. bd., 1986—, also dir., 1976—; pres., chief operating officer Mobil Corp., N.Y.C., 1984-86, chmn., chief exec. officer, 1986—, dir., 1977—; dir. Met. Life Ins. Co. Mem. adv. council Columbia U. Grad. Sch. Bus.; trustee Presbyn. Hosp., N.Y.C. Served with USNR, 1946-48. Mem. Nat. Fgn. Trade Council (dir.), Am. Petroleum Inst. (dir.), Council on Fgn. Relations. Club: Huntington Country. Office: Mobil Corp 150 E 42d St New York NY 10017 *

MURRAY, ANGIE ANNA ALICE, government official; b. Thibodaux, La., July 6, 1949; d. Edward Justin Paul and Anna Angelina (Himmler) Hebert; m. Walter Thomas Murray, Mar. 21, 1970; children: Thomas Joseph, Anthony Michael. Speedwriting Cert., Sawyer Secretarial Sch., 1974. Mem. customer service staff European Exchange System, Ramstein, Ger., 1967-68; buyer, expeditor Thurow Electronics, Tampa, Fla., 1968-70; quotation clk. Thomas & Betts Co., Elizabeth, N.J., 1970-75; cost acct., girl Friday, Fulton Shirt Co., Elizabeth, 1975-76; office sec. Rapides Parish Police Jury, Alexandria, La., 1977-81, parish sec., 1981—; sec. Rapides Parish Stormwater Mgmt. and Drainage Dist., 1983—. Recipient Journalism award Noncommd. Officers Wives Club, 1967. Mem. Am. Soc. Notaries, Sec.-Treas. Orgn. of La. (region 8 exec. bd.), VFW Aux. Democrat. Roman Catholic. Avocations: reading; handicrafts. Home: PO Box 187 Elmer LA 71424 Office: Rapides Parish Police Jury PO Box 1150 Alexandria LA 71309

MURRAY, ANITA JEAN, data processing executive, consultant; b. Pitts., May 22, 1943; d. Julius and Nancy (Betza) Czujko; m. Christopher H. Murray, Apr. 6, 1968 (div. 1976). BS in Psychology, U. Pitts., 1964; MS in Stats., Stanford U., 1967. Cert. data processor. Systems analyst Pan Am. World Airways, N.Y.C., 1967-69; asst. controller Bunge Corp., N.Y.C., 1969-79; prin. nat. office Arthur Young & Co., N.Y.C., 1979-82; v.p. mgmt. info. systems Murjani Internat. Ltd., Saddle Brook, N.J., 1982-85; pres. Amston Mgmt., Inc., N.Y.C., 1985—; seminar leader Am. Mgmt. Assn., N.Y.C., 1979-82. Author: Minicomputer Bus. Solutions, 1981. Pres. Married Ams. for Tax Equality, N.Y.C., 1973-76; chmn. office mgmt. com. Community Bd. 1, N.Y.C., 1983. Mem. Data Processing Mgmt. Assn. (speaker 1981-82), Internat. Platform Assn., Am. Women Entrepreneurs. Club: Skating of N.Y. Avocations: photography, design. Office: Amston Mgmt Inc 52 Laight St New York NY 10013

MURRAY, CHARLES ANDREW, chemical company executive; b. Franklin County, Ind., Oct. 9, 1911; s. Archibald K. and Maude M. (Stafford) M.; m. Marguerite Jensen (dec.), Sept. 3, 1938; children—Bonnie Christine, Lance Kerr, Robin Elo, Jamie Andrew; m. 2d, Eleanor Chapman Laughridge, June 10, 1979; 1 stepdau., Linda. B.S. in Chem. Engring, Purdue U., 1934; M.S., U. Mich., 1936, Ph.D., 1940. Chemist E.I. du Pont de Nemours & Co., Deepwater, N.J., 1934-35, Central Soya Co., Decatur, Ind., 1940-42; pilot plant supr. Reichold Chems. Co., Inc., Ferndale, Mich., 1942-46, plant mgr., Tuscaloosa, Ala., 1946-48, dist. sales mgr., New Orleans, 1948-55; mgr. paint and varnish dept. Crosby Forest Products Co., Picayune, Miss., 1955-60; dir. research Cordo Chem. Corp., Mobile, Ala., 1960-63; pres. M&W Enterprises, Inc., Savannah, Ga., 1963-67; product devel. mgr. Cordo div. Ferro Corp., Mobile, 1967; tech. dir. Mobile Rosin Oil Co., Mobile, 1968—, dir., v.p., 1968—; del. conf. on coatings Argentina Bur. Standards, 1959. Active CAP, Boy Scouts Am. Mem. Am. Chem. Soc., Fedn. Soc. Coatings Tech. (gulf coast sect.), Aircraft Owners and Pilots Assn., Sigma Xi, Phi Lambda Upsilon, Alpha Chi Sigma. Presbyterian. Club: Lake Forest Yacht and Country (Daphne, Ala.). Contbr. numerous articles to profl. jours. Home: PO Box 635 Spanish Fort AL 36527 Office: Mobile Rosin Oil Co PO Drawer 70107 Mobile AL 36607

MURRAY, CHRISTOPHER CHARLES, III, architect; b. Bklyn., July 6, 1950; s. Christopher Charles and Gertrude Rose (Marr) M.; m. Ann Herring, Nov. 16, 1974. BArch, U. Notre Dame, 1973. Registered architect, N.Y., Md., D.C., Va. Project architect Hibner Architects, Garden City, N.Y., 1973-76; project mgr. BBM Architects, N.Y.C., 1976-79; project dir. Gensler & Assocs., N.Y.C., 1979-84, office dir., v.p., mem. nat. mgmt. com., 1984—. Prin. works include interior design Covington & Burling bldg., 1983, First Am. Bancshares, 1985. Mem. Greater Washington Bd. Trade, 1986. Mem. AIA, N.Y. Soc. Architects, Md. Soc. Architects, N.Y. Bldg. Congress. Roman Catholic. Club: Notre Dame (Washington). Home: 12517 Knightsbridge Ct Potomac MD 20850 Office: Gensler & Assocs 1101 17th St NW Washington DC 20036

MURRAY, FREDERICK FRANKLIN, lawyer; b. Corpus Christi, Tex., Aug. 1, 1950; s. Marvin Frank and Suzanne Louise Murray; m. Susan McKeen. BA, Rice U., 1972; JD, U. Tex., 1974. Bar: Tex. 1975, N.Y. 1987, D.C. 1987, U.S. Dist. Ct. (so. dist.) Tex. 1976, U.S. Dist. Ct. (no. and we. dists.) Tex. 1986, U.S. Ct. Claims 1976, U.S. Tax Ct. 1976, U.S. Ct. Appeals (5th and D.C. cirs.) 1976, U.S. Supreme Ct. 1978, U.S. Ct. Internat. Trade 1985, U.S. Dist. Ct. (ea. dist.) Tex. 1987; CPA, Tex. Ptnr. Chamberlain, Hrdlicka, White, Johnson & Williams, Houston, 1985—; mem. Tax Law Adv. Commn. Tex. Bd. Legal Specialization, 1984—, vice chmn., 1987—; mem. Commn. of Tax Law Examiners, 1984—; adj. prof. U. Houston Law Ctr., 1984—, U. Tex. Sch. Law, 1987—; faculty lectr. Rice U. Jones Grad. Sch. Adminstrn., 1987—; speaker various assns. and univs. Author various publs.; mem. bd. advisers Houston Jour. Internat. Law, 1986—, chmn., 1987—. Del. Bishop's Diocesan Pastoral Council, 1979-80; chmn. parish council Sacred Heart Cathedral, Cath. Diocese Galveston-Houston, 1979-81, mem. Red Mass Steering Com., 1986—; mem. exec. com., bd. dirs., 1987—, chmn. deferred giving com. Houston Symphony Soc., 1984-88, chmn. pub. affairs com., 1988—; co-trustee Houston Symphony Soc. Endowment Fund, 1987—; mem. fund council Rice U., 1987—, exec. com. 1988—, chmn. Major Gifts Com., 1988—.Mem. Am. Arbitration Assn. (panels comml. and internat. arbitrators 1980—), ABA (officer various coms.), Internat. Bar Assn., Houston Bar Assn., State Bar of Tex. (various coms.), N.Y. State Bar Assn., D.C. Bar Assn., Am. Inst. CPA's, Tex. Soc. CPA's, Internat. Tax Forum of Houston (sec. 1981-84, pres. 1984—), Internat. Fiscal Assn., Am. Soc. Internat. Law., Am. Fgn. Law Assn., Union Internationale Des Avocats. Office: Citicorp Ctr 1200 Smith St Suite 1400 Houston TX 77002

MURRAY, GILMAN YOST, engring.-constrn. co. exec.; b. Springfield, Mass., Dec. 26, 1923; s. Arthur F. and Barbara (Gilman) M.; student Lehigh U., 1941-43; B.S. in Chem. Engring., Mass. Inst. Tech., 1944, M.S. in Metallury, 1948; postgrad. Cornell U., Ithaca, N.Y., 1945, N.C. State Coll., 1945; m. Winifred Jean Tipping, June 15, 1947; children—Scott Tipping, Craig Arthur, Victoria Anne. Research engr. Allis-Chalmers Co., Milw., 1948-50, Los Angeles, 1950-52, San Francisco, 1952-54; mgr. bus. devel. Western-Knapp Engring. Co., San Francisco, 1954-61; v.p. Bradberry Assos., 1961-67, merged with Bendix Corp., 1967, v.p., 1967-68; v.p. Hallanger & Assos. subs. Zapata Orgn., San Francisco, 1968-71; v.p., gen. mgr. Fluor Utah, Inc., San Mateo, 1971-74, sr. v.p., 1974-78; sr. v.p., div. mgr., dir. Ralph M. Parsons Co., Pasadena, Calif., 1978-79; pres., dir. Lurgi Corp., Belmont, Calif., 1979-85, pres., dir., chief exec. officer, Unipon Group, Inc., Mountain

View, Calif., 1985—. Served to lt. (j.g.), USNR, 1943-46. Recipient award merit Colo. Mining Assn., 1959. Registered profl. engr., Calif. Mem. Am. Inst. Mining Engrs., Am. Mining Congress, Mining and Metall. Soc. Am., MIT Club No. Calif., Sigma Xi, Alpha Chi Sigma, Delta Sigma Phi. Elk. Clubs: Monterey Peninsula Country Club (Pebble Beach, Calif.); Bankers, Engrs., Commonwealth of San Francisco, Univ. (Pasadena). Home: 12355 Stonebrook St Los Altos Hills CA 94022 Office: 1134 W El Camino Real Mountain View CA 94040

MURRAY, GRAHAM CHRISTOPHER, computer company executive; b. Ladysmith, South Africa, July 26, 1948; came to Australia, 1970; s. Hugh Molyneux and Dagmar Oxley (Oxland) M.; m. Rebecca Emily Gauci, Feb. 11, 1983; children: David Hugh, Stuart Alexander. BSc, U. Auckland, New Zealand, 1968, MSc with honors, 1969. Cons. W.D. Scott & Co., Sydney, Australia, 1970-71; lectr. N.S.W. Inst. Tech., Sydney, 1972; mng. dir. Chris Murray & Assocs. Pty. Ltd., Sydney, 1973-78, Quickplan Inc. Pty. Ltd., Sydney, 1979-81; pres. Qicplan Support, San Francisco, 1980—; mng. dir. Qicplan Australia Pty. Ltd, Sydney, 1981-86, Streamline Systems Pty. Ltd., Sydney, 1986—; cons. various companies in Australia, New Zealand, U.S., Can., U.K., 1973-87. Inventor software, 1974-87. Mem. Ch. of Eng. Home: 13 Plunkett Rd, Balmoral Beach 2088, Australia Office: Streamline Systems Pty Ltd, 600 Military Rd, Mosman 2088, Australia

MURRAY, JAMES ALAN, municipal official, financial executive; b. Evansville, Ind., Oct. 2, 1942; s. William Dewey and Dorothy Marie (Gleason) M.; B.S., U. N.Mex., 1964; M.B.A., Harvard U., 1969; M.A. (NDEA fellow), U. Oreg., 1971, Ph.D., 1972; m. Amber Lee Tootle; children—Heidi Lynn, Paul Alan, Kendra Leigh. Dir. fin. City of Boulder (Colo.), 1972-73, dir. adminstrv. services, 1973-74; v.p. Briscoe, Maphis, Murray & Lamont, Inc., Boulder, 1974-78, pres., 1978-84, also dir.; dir. fin. City and County of Denver, 1984-86, chief exec. officer, 1986-87, asst. to mayor, 1987—; adj. assoc. prof. Grad. Sch. Public Affairs, U. Colo., Boulder, 1972-80, Denver, 1985—. Mem. open space adv. com. City of Boulder, 1972-74; bd. dirs. Met. Denver Sewage Authority, 1984-85. Mem. Am. Econ. Assn., Western Econ. Assn., Am. Soc. Pub. Adminstrn., Water Pollution Control Fedn., Kappa Mu Epsilon, Pi Alpha Alpha. Home: 99 S Downing #602 Denver CO 80209 Office: 350 City and County Bldg Denver CO 80202

MURRAY, JAMES DICKSON, mathematical biology educator; b. Moffat, Scotland, Jan. 2, 1931; s. Peter and Sarah Jane (Black) M.; m. Sheila Todd Campbell, Oct. 1959; children: Mark Woodeaton, Sarah Corrine. BSc in Math. with 1st class honors, U. St. Andrews, Scotland, 1953, PhD in Applied Math., 1956; MA, U. Oxford, Eng., 1961, DSc in Math., 1968. Lectr. applied math. King's Coll. Durham U., Newcastle, Eng., 1955-56; Gordon McKay lectr. and research fellow Harvard U., Cambridge, Mass., 1956-59, research assoc. engring., applied physics, 1963-64; lectr. Univ. Coll., London, 1959-61; fellow in math. Hartford Coll. U. Oxford, 1961-63, reader, 1972-86, prof. math. biology, 1986—; prof. engring. mechanics U. Mich., Ann Arbor, 1965-67; prof. math. NYU, N.Y.C., 1967-70; Dir. Ctr. for Math. Biology U. Oxford, 1983—; vis. prof. applied math. MIT, 1979, U. Utah, Salt Lake City, 1979, 85, Cal. Tech. U., 1983; vis. research prof. Nat. Tsing Hua U., Republic of China, 1975, U. Florence, Italy, 1976, Winegard Guelph U., 1980; guest lectr. U. B.C., Vancouver, 1979,; guest prof. U. Heidelberg, Fed. Republic Germany, 1980; disting. vis. prof., Scott Hawkins lectr. So. Meth. U., Dallas, 1984; vis. scholar ULAM Los Alamos Nat. Lab., 1985. Author: Asymptotic Analysis, 1974, Russian translation, 1987-88, Nonlinear Differential Equation Models in Biology, 1977, Russian translation, 1983, Theories of Biological Pattern Formation, 1981, Modelling Patterns in Space and Time, 1983, Mathematical Biology, 1988; contbr. numerous articles to learned jours. Recipient Heineman Stiftung award NATO, 1980; vis. fellow St. Catherine's Coll. U. Oxfors, 1967, Guggenheim fellow, 1967-68; Stanislaw Vis. scholar U. Calif., 1985. Fellow Royal Soc., Royal Soc. Edinburgh. Office: U Oxford, Math Inst, 24-29 St Giles, Oxford OX1 3LB, England

MURRAY, JAMES DOYLE, accountant; b. Rochester, N.Y., July 24, 1938; s. William Herbert and Mildred Frances (Becker) M.; m. Mary Louise Goodyear, June 22, 1962; children—William, Robert. B.S., U. Rochester, 1961. C.P.A., N.Y. With Ernst & Whinney, Rochester, N.Y., 1963—, ptnr., 1977-86; ptnr. Siebert, Dunay & Murray, CPA's, Rochester, 1986—; mem. faculty Found. for Acctg. Edn., N.Y.C., 1979—. Contbr. articles to profl. jours. Treas. William Warfield Scholarship Fund, 1987—; active fund raising Boy Scouts Am., Rochester Philharm., Rochester Mus. and Sci. Ctr.; bd. dirs., treas. Downstairs Cabaret, 1985; mem. Eagle bd. of rev. Boy Scouts Am.; deacon Presbyn Ch., 1987—. Served to lt. USN, 1961-63. Mem. Am. Inst. C.P.A.s, N.Y. State Soc. C.P.A.s (pres. Rochester chpt. 1982-83), Nat. Assn. Accts. (bd. dirs. 1978-80), Mcpl. Fin. Officers Assn. (assoc.), Health Care Fin. Mgmt. Assn. (assoc.). Republican. Presbyterian. Clubs: Genesee Valley, University (Rochester). Home: 42 Black Watch Trail Fairport NY 14450 Office: Siebert Dunay & Murray 26 Broadway Rochester NY 14607

MURRAY, JAMES MICHAEL, law librarian, legal educator, lawyer; b. Seattle, Nov. 8, 1944; s. Clarence Nicholas and Della May (Snyder) M.; m. Linda Monthy Murray; M.Law Librarianship, U. Wash., 1978; J.D., Gonzaga U., 1971. Bar: Wash., 1974. Reference/reserve librarian U. Texas Law Library, Austin, 1978-81; assoc. law librarian Washington U. Law Library, St. Louis, 1981-84; law librarian, asst. prof. Gonzaga U. Sch. Law, Spokane, 1984—; cons. in field. Bd. dirs. ACLU, Spokane chpt., 1987—; Wash. Vol. Lawyers for the Arts, 1976-78. Mem. Am. Assn. Law Libraries, Western Pacific Assn. Law Libraries, ABA, Wash. State Bar Assn (law sch. liaison com., 1986—). Mem. state adv. bd. National Reporter on Legal Ethics and Professional Responsibility, 1982—; author: (with Reams and McDermott) American Legal Literature: Bibliography of Selected Legal Resources, 1985; editor Texas Bar Jour. (Books Appraisals Column), 1979-82; author revs., acknowledgements and bibliographies in field. Home: W 921 29th Spokane WA 99203 Office: Gonzaga U Sch Law Library E 600 Sharp Ave Spokane WA 99202

MURRAY, JAMES WILLIAM, retired clothing manufacturing executive; b. Hawick, Scotland, Apr. 3, 1917; s. William Allan Murray and Helen Beattie. Cert. knitwear tech., Henderson Tech. Coll., Hawick, 1937. In knitwear trade Hawick, 1932-39; prin. J.W. Murray & Ptnrs., Hawick, 1946-80. Dist. councillor Roxburgh, Scotland, 1977-88. Served with Royal Arty., 1940-45. Mem. Inst. Pub. Relations.

MURRAY, JOHN JOSEPH, historian, educator; b. Bath, Maine, July 2, 1915; s. John Joseph and Ida (King) M.; m. Helen Elizabeth Tomson, Jan. 30, 1942; children: John Joseph III, Michael Tomson. A.B., U. Maine, 1937; M.A., Ind. U., 1938; Ph.D., UCLA, 1942. Editor Douglas Aircraft, 1938-45; instr. history Ohio State U., 1945; instr. Northwestern U., 1945-46; asst. prof. Ind. U., 1946-49, assoc. prof., 1949-54; prof. Coe Coll., 1954—, chmn. history dept., 1955—, Henrietta Arnold prof., 1977-80, Arnold prof. emeritus, 1980—; vis. assoc. prof. UCLA, summer 1949; vis. prof. U. B.C., summer 1956; historian Iowa Light and Power Co., 1980—. Author: A Student Guidebook to English History, 1947, An Honest Diplomat at the Hague, 1956, Amsterdam in the Age of Rembrandt, 1967, George I, the Baltic and the Whig Split, 1969, Antwerp in the Age of Plantin and Breughel, 1970, It Took All of Us, 1982, Flanders and England: The Influence of the Low Countries on Tudor-Stuart England, 1984; editor: Essays in Modern European History, 1952, The Heritage of the Middle West, 1958; contbr. articles, book revs. to Am., fgn. hist. jours.; author, narrator TV scripts for comml. TV. Fulbright research scholar U. Leiden, Netherlands, 1951-52; fellow Folger Shakespeare Library, Washington, 1954, summer 1959, sr. research fellow, 1973-74; Social Science fellow to Eng., 1960-61; fellow Newberry Library, summer 1963; faculty fellow Assoc. Colls. of Midwest-Newberry Library Seminar in Humanities, 1965-66; John Simon Guggenheim fellow, 1968-69; Mercator Fonds fellow Belgium, summer 1973; decorated knight Order of Belgian Crown, 1981; recipient Most Outstanding Career prize 50th reunion U. Maine Class of 1937, 1987. Fellow Royal Hist. Soc. (Eng.), Historisch Genootschop (Netherlands), Karolinska Förbundet (Sweden); mem. Cedar Rapids Art Assn., Am. Hist. Assn., Kappa Sigma, Blue Key, Sr. Skull, Phi Kappa Phi. Congregationalist. Clubs: Cedar Rapids Country, Cosmos. Home: 1508 Circa Del Lago B-211 Lake San Marcos CA 92069

MURRAY, LAWRENCE, management consultant; b. N.Y.C., May 10, 1939; s. Gilbert and Edna (Blatt) M.; B.A., Cornell U., 1961; M.B.A., U. Okla., 1966; children—Robert, David, Daniel. Account exec. Merrill Lynch, Paramus, N.J., 1965-69; chmn., pres. Murray, Lind & Co., Inc., Jersey City, 1969-72; dir. investor relations IU Internat. Corp., Phila., 1972-73, dir. spl. projects, 1974-75; dir. fin. communications ARA Services, Inc., Phila., 1975-78; chmn., chief exec. officer Century Mgmt. and affiliated cos., West Chester, Pa., 1976-82; chmn., chief exec. officer Creative Mgmt. Corp., Bala Cynwyd and West Chester, Pa., 1982-87; underwriter Jefferson Standard Life Ins. Co., Greensboro, N.C., 1982-83; chmn., chief exec. officer Fin. Mgmt. Profl. Corp., West Chester, 1983—; v.p. Venture Frontiers Co., Denver, 1984—; bd. dirs. Exelaris Corp.; lectr. bus. orgn. and mgmt. Bergen Community Coll., 1971-72. Pres., Congregation Beth Israel, Media, Pa., 1977-78, Parents Without Partners, Valley Forge, Pa., 1982-83; v.p. Cornell U. Class of 1961, 1981-86. Served to 1st lt. arty., U.S. Army, 1963-64. Mem. Nat. Investor Relations Inst. (pres. Phila. chpt. 1976-78), Internat. Council Shopping Centers. Author: The Organized Stockbroker, 1970; A New Era in Mergers and Acquisitions, 1974; Communications: Management's Newest Marketing Skill, 1976; contbr. articles to profl. jours. Home: 924 Hollyview Ln West Chester PA 19380 Office: 402 Barker Circle Suite 5 West Chester PA 19380

MURRAY, MICHAEL EDMUND, economist; b. Auckland, New Zealand, Mar. 6, 1945; s. John McGregor and Norma Beryl (Spearman) M.; m. Jillian Munro, Feb 1968; children: Conrad, Charlotte, Emma, Edward. BS in Econs. and Computer Sci., U. Canterbury, 1974. Commd. Royal New Zealand Air Force, 1963, navigator, 1964, ret., 1974; ops. research analyst New Zealand Nat. Airways Corp., 1975-76; corp. exec. Shell Group of Cos., New Zealand, 1976-80; comml. exec. Bay of Plenty Harbour Bd., New Zealand, 1980-82; founder, owner, cons. McGregor & Co., Tauranga, New Zealand, 1982—. Contbr. articles to profl. jours. Bd. govs. Tauranga Boys Coll., New Zealand, 1983-88. Mem. Royal Aero. Soc., Royal Inst. Navigation, Chartered Inst. Transport. Lodge: Rotary (Tauranga). Office: McGregor & Co, 12th Ave & Christopher St, PO Box 2288, Tauranga New Zealand

MURRAY, NANCY SIEGEL, marketing executive; b. Chelsea, Mass., Nov. 20, 1947; d. Edward Isaac and Bertha (Greenberg) Siegel; m. Ronald Francis Murray, Aug. 8, 1976. B.A., Vassar Coll., 1970; M.Ed., Columbia U., 1975; M.B.A., So. Meth. U., 1980; cert. in COBOL programming, Columbia U., 1983. Cert. rehab. counselor, N.Y. Counseling intern Neurol. Inst., N.Y.C., 1974; supr. counseling Hosp. for Joint Diseases, N.Y.C., 1975-78; market research analyst Acclivus Corp., Dallas, 1980, Suburban Assocs., Ridgewood, N.J., 1981; sr. market research analyst/internat. mktg. Mfrs. Hanover Trust Co., N.Y.C., 1982-84; mktg. officer Marine Midland Bank, N.Y.C., 1984-86, asst. v.p. and market research dir., 1987—. Mem. Am. Mktg. Assn., Bank Mktg. Assn., Am. Soc. Tng. and Devel., Nat. Rehab. Assn. Democrat. Club: Vassar. Home: 183 Lake Rd Morristown NJ 07960

MURRAY, PETER, metallurgist, manufacturing company executive; b. Rotherham, Yorks, Eng., Mar. 13, 1920; came to U.S., 1967, naturalized, 1974; s. Michael and Ann (Hamstead) M.; m. Frances Josephine Glaisher, Sept. 8, 1947; children: Jane, Paul, Alexander. B.Sc. in Chemistry with honors, Sheffield (Eng.) U., 1941, postgrad., 1946-49; Ph.D. in Metallurgy, Brit. Iron and Steel Research Bursar, Sheffield, 1948. Research chemist Steetley Co., Ltd., Worksop, Notts, Eng., 1941-45; with Atomic Energy Research Establishment, Harwell, Eng., 1949-67; head div. metallurgy Atomic Energy Research Establishment, 1960-64, asst. dir., 1964-67; tech. dir., mgr. fuels and materials, advanced reactors div. Westinghouse Electric Corp., Madison, Pa., 1967-74; dir. research Westinghouse Electric Europe (S.A.), Brussels, 1974-75; chief scientist advanced power systems divs. Westinghouse Electric Corp., Madison, Pa., 1975-81; dir. nuclear programs Westinghouse Electric Corp., Washington, 1981—; mem. divisional rev. coms. Argonne Nat. Lab., 1968-73; Mellor Meml. lectr. Inst. Ceramics, 1963. Contbr. numerous articles to profl. jours.; editorial adv. bd.: Jour. Less Common Metals, 1968—. Recipient Holland Meml. Research prize Sheffield U., 1949. Fellow Royal Inst. Chemistry (Newton Chambers Research prize 1954), Inst. Ceramics; mem. Brit. Ceramics Soc. (pres. 1965), Am. Ceramic Soc., Am. Nuclear Soc., Nat. Acad. Engring. Roman Catholic. Home: 20308 Canby Ct Gaithersburg MD 20879 Office: Westinghouse Electric Corp 1801 K St NW Washington DC 20006

MURRAY, RICHARD DEIBEL, physician; b. Youngstown, Ohio, Dec. 25, 1921; s. Thomas Henry and Olive (Deibel) M. BS, U. Notre Dame, 1942; MD, Georgetown U., 1946; MS, U. Pa., 1953. Intern Youngstown Hosp. Assn., 1946-47; mem. attending staff, chief plastic surgery service, resident plastic surgery Kings County Hosp., Bklyn., 1952-54; practice medicine specializing in plastic surgery Youngstown, 1955—; mem. courtesy staff St. Elizabeth hosp., cons. staff. Salem City Hosp.; cons. plastic surgery Hosp. of Our Lady of Maryknoll, Kowloon, Hong Kong; Louis Guerrera Meml. lectr. Santo Tomas U., Manila, 1964; clin. asst. prof. plastic surgery Northeastern Ohio U. Author: The Rise and Fall of the State, 1967, The Key to Nostradamus, 1975, Signs and Wonders, 1979; contbr. articles to profl. jours.; sculptor marble Orpheus fountain, Youngstown; other sculptures exhibited group shows Am. Physicians Art Assn., Butler Art Inst., Am. Soc. Cleft Palate Rehab. Served to lt. (j.g.) USMC, 1947-49, USNR. Decorated Order St. John of Jerusalem; recipient Frank Purnell award City of Youngstown, Physician of Yr. award City of Youngstown, 1979. Mem. Am. Soc. Plastic and Reconstructive Surgery, Robert Ivy Soc. Phila., Ohio Valley Plastic Soc., Kings County Soc., AMA, Mahoning County Med. Soc. Clubs: Youngstown Country; N.Y. Athletic. Lodges: Rotary, Elks. Home and Office: 2125 Glenwood Ave Youngstown OH 44511

MURRAY, RICHARD MAXIMILIAN, insurance executive; b. Vienna, Austria, Nov. 21, 1922; came to U.S., 1955, naturalized, 1961; s. and Elizabeth Helen Peiker. Grad. in world commerce studies, U. Vienna; postgrad., Columbia U. Asst. sec. Sterling Offices Ltd. (reins. intermediaries), London, Toronto, N.Y.C., 1951-59; v.p. Guy Carpenter, Inc. (reins. intermediaries), N.Y.C., 1959-68; v.p. Travelers Ins. Cos., 1968-87, ret., 1987; mng. dir. La Metropole Ins. Co., Brussels; bd. electors Ins. Hall of Fame, dir. Unity Fire & Fen. Ins. Co., N.Y.C., Gen. Security Ins. Corp. N.Y., Urbaine Life Reins. Co., N.Y.C., Rockleigh Mgmt. Corp., N.Y.C. Contbr. articles to profl. publs. Decorated for promotion of pvt. ins. (Peru); Knight Order of St. John, Knights of Malta (ambassador at large). Mem. Internat. Ins. Adv. Council. Clubs: Hartford Golf, 20th Century. Home: 30 Woodland St Hartford CT 06105 Office: 80 John St New York NY 10038

MURRAY, ROBERT FOX, lawyer; b. Burlington, Vt., Feb. 28, 1952; s. Robert and Mary (Fox) M. BA, Colgate U., 1974; JD, Boston U., 1978. Bar: Mass. 1978, U.S. Dist. Ct. Mass. 1979. Assoc. Law Offices of George Howard, Dedham, Mass., 1978-80, from assoc. to ptnr. Fairbanks & Silvia Koczera, Fountain, Murray, New Bedford, Mass., 1980-84; sole practice, New Bedford, 1984—. Bd. dirs., clk. New Bedford Downtown Bus. Assn., Inc. Mem. New Bedford C. of C., Waterfront Hist. Area League, Assn. Trial Lawyers Am., Mass. Acad. Trial Attys., Mass. Bar Assn., New Bedford Bar Assn., Bristol County Bar Assn., Bristol County Bar Advs. Democrat. Office: 22 Centre St New Bedford MA 02740

MURRAY, WILLIAM BARLOW, meat processing company executive; b. Ripon, Wis., Mar. 11, 1941; came to Colombia, 1965; s. John Barlow and Nellie (Weiss) M.; m. Lois Thompson, Aug. 29, 1964; children—Margaret Courtney, Grant Thompson. B.A., Swarthmore Coll., 1963; M.B.A., Harvard U., 1965. Fellow, MIT, Cambridge, 1965-68; pres. Rica Rondo, S.A., Cali, Colombia, 1968—. Bd. dirs. Colombian Inst. Mgmt. Edn., Cali, 1979—, Colegio Bolivar, Cali, 1979-80, Centro Colombo Americano, Cali, 1975-78. Recipient Indsl. Merit medal Colombian Presidency Recongnition, 1988. Mem. Am. Soc. (pres. 1970-72), Nat. Industrialists Assn. (v.p. 1979—). Clubs: Colombia, Campestre. Home: Avenida La Maria #33 Pance, Aptdo Aereo 4842, Cali Valle Colombia Office: Rica Rondo SA, Aptdo Aereo, 4842 Cali Valle Colombia

MURRAY, WILLIAM MICHAEL (MIKE), lawyer; b. Ottumwa, Iowa, Dec. 28, 1947; s. William Bernard and Thelma Jean (Hart) M.; m. Ann Elizabeth Wawzonek, Oct. 11, 1973; children—Kathleen Elizabeth, Daniel Webster. BA, U. Iowa, 1970, JD, 1973. Bar: Iowa 1973, U.S. Dist. Ct. (so. dist.) Iowa 1976, U.S. Dist. Ct. (no. dist.) Iowa 1978, U.S. Ct. Appeals (8th cir.) 1978. Staff counsel Iowa Civil Rights Commn., Des Moines, 1973-76; assoc. Bertroche & Hagen, Des Moines, 1976-78; ptnr. Murray, Davoren & Jankins, Des Moines, 1978—. Bd. dirs. Iowa Civil Liberties Union, Des Moines, 1978-83, pres., 1982-83; bd. dirs. Polk County Legal Aid Soc., Des Moines, 1984—. Mem. Assn. Trial Lawyers Am., Assn. Trial Lawyers Iowa, ABA, Iowa State Bar Assn., Polk County Bar Assn. Democrat. Club: Des Moines Jaycees (bd. dirs. legal counsel 1980-81). Home: 600 SW 42d St Des Moines IA 50312 Office: Murray Davoren & Jankins 5601 Hickman Rd Suites 3 & 4 Des Moines IA 50310

MURRAY, WILLIAM PETER, lawyer; b. Albany, N.Y., June 29, 1924; s. James Ryan and Hazel Mary (Kilroy) M. B.A., Siena Coll., 1948; J.D., Cath. U., 1951. Bar: D.C. 1951, U.S. Ct. Appeals D.C. 1951, N.Y. 1952, U.S. Dist. Ct. (so. dist.) N.Y. 1953, U.S. Ct. Appeals (2d cir.) 1973, U.S. Ct. Mil. Appeals 1956, U.S. Supreme Ct. 1980. Sole practice, N.Y.C. and Washington, 1951-69; assoc. McNally O'Brien & K, N.Y.C., 1951-56, Robert G. Burkhardt, Esq., N.Y.C., 1962-63, Donald F. Mooney, Esq., N.Y.C., 1967-68; counsel in charge and acting corp. counsel Water Supply Unit, N.Y.C. Law Dept., Kingston, 1969-79; sole practice, Kingston, 1979—. Casenote editor Cath. U. Am. Law Rev., 1950-51; contbr. articles to profl. jours. Spl. dep. atty. gen. Dept. Law, State of N.Y., 1952-57. Founding mem., law sch. rep. Cath U. Am. Grad. Student Council, 1951. Served with U.S. Army, 1943-45. Decorated Combat Infantryman's badge, Bronze Star, European-African-Mid. Eastern campaign medal with Bronze Arrowhead and 5 Battle Stars. Mem. D.C. Bar Assn. Roman Catholic. Club: Century.

MURRELL, TURNER MEADOWS, finance and insurance company executive, lawyer; b. Greensboro, N.C., Feb. 5, 1923; s. James Robert and Sallie Frances (Page) M.; B.A., Washburn U., 1948, J.D., 1949; m. Patricia L. Shortall, Dec. 4, 1975; children—Gregory S., Leslie Ann, Todd G.; stepchildren—John J., Janis Lynn, Kathleen A., Lisa M. Shortall. Admitted to Kans. bar, 1949, U.S. Supreme Ct. bar, 1950; individual practice law, Topeka, 1949—; ptnr. Baker, Doherty & Murrell, Topeka, 1952-53; judge City of Topeka, 1953-56; ptnr. Meyer, Gault, Marshall, Hawks & Murrell, 1954-61, Murrell, Scott & Quinlan, 1961-69; pres., chmn. Am. Investors Life Ins. Co., Inc., Topeka, 1965—; chmn. Nat. Investment Corp., Inc., 1968—, Internat. Investors Life Ins. Co., Ic., 1969-77; pres. Am. Option and Equity Fund, Inc., 1968-78; dir. Commerce Bank and Trust, Topeka, 1978—; chmn., chief exec. officer Am. Vestors Fin. Corp., 1986—; lectr. Tulane U., New Orleans, 1951-52. Mem. Kans. Ho. of Reps., 1957-61, majority floor leader, 1959-61; trustee Washburn U., 1978—. Served with USN, 1943-46. Recipient Young Man of Yr. award U.S. C. of C., 1957; Disting. Service award City of Topeka, 1957. Mem. ABA, Kans. Bar Assn., Topeka Bar Assn., Delta Theta Phi. Clubs: Topeka Country, Masons, Shriners. Home: 421 Danbury Ln Topeka KS 66606 Office: 415 SW 8th St Topeka KS 66601

MURRY, RICHARD PORTER, retired judge, lawyer; b. Clayton, N. Mex., July 19, 1912; s. Hub and Merle (Davis) M.; children—Terri, Lilla, Portia. Student, Mo. Sch. of Mines, 1931-34; J.D., U. Ariz., 1940. Bar Ariz. 1940. Sole practice, Clifton, Ariz., 1940-43; atty., Greenlee County (Ariz.), 1943-50; atty., Towns of Clifton and Duncan (Ariz.), 1944-50; judge Superior Ct. Greenlee County, 1951-71; judge Maricopa, Yavapai, Pima, Gila, Mohave Counties (Ariz.), 1971-77; spl. master U.S. Dist. Ct., Phoenix, 1977—. Vice chmn. Ariz. Young Democrats, 1949-50; v.p. central com. Ariz. Dem. 1949-50; v.p. Three-G council Boy Scouts Am.; bd. dirs. Ariz. Acad. Mem. ABA, Ariz. Bar Assn., Ariz. State Judges' Assn., (past pres.), Presbyterian. Clubs: Clifton Rotary (pres.), Clifton Elks (exalted ruler 1946-47). Home: 4615 E Orange Dr Phoenix AZ 85018

MURSTEN, HARRY, construction company executive; b. Buffalo, Nov. 11, 1930; s. Sidney and Ruth (Lunenfeld) M.; m. Linda Fenton (div.); children—David, Pamela, Amy, Michael; m. 2d, Margaret Brown Feldman, Sept. 24, 1967; children—Jacqueline, Scott. B.S. in Bus. Adminstrn., U. Buffalo, 1953. Cert. gen. contractor, Fla. Chief exec. officer Retail Store, Buffalo, 1953-59; pres. Barlin Constrn. Co., Miami, Fla., 1960-70; pres., chief exec. officer Mursten Constrn., Miami, 1971—; faculty mem. Nova U., Ft. Lauderdale, Fla., 1984-87; tech. presenter People's Republic China, 1982. Chmn. Com. 100, Hialeah, Fla., 1983-84; pres. Northwest Dade Regional YMCA, Miami, 1983-84, Metro YMCA, 1985; pres. Learning Disabilities Found., Miami, 1978-79; v.p. Profit, Inc., 1986-87, pres. 1987. Recipient Community Service award Dade County Pub. Schs., 1977. Mem. Am. Inst. Constructors, Constrn. Specifications Inst., Associated Builders & Contractors (nat. asst. sec. 1984, pres. Fla. chpt. 1982-83, Member of Year award Washington, 1982, Member of Year award Boca Raton, 1982, 79, nat 3d v.p. 1985, nat. 2d v.p., 1986), Northwest Dade C. of C. (dir. 1982-86, sec. 1986-87, treas. 1987-88), Ctr. for Curative Research (dir. 1987). Lodge: United Craft.

MURTAUGH, GORDON MATTHEW, consultant; b. N.Y.C., Mar. 20, 1924; s. George Edward and Rose Mary (Meeske) M.; m. Lois Betty Koch, Sept. 6, 1952; children: Gordon, Joan Murtaugh Borstell, Kathryn Murtaugh Ross, Thomas, Patricia. ME, Stevens Inst. Tech., 1945; MBA, NYU, 1954. Process engr. M. W. Kellogg, Jersey City, 1946-51; prodn. supt., plant controller AMF, Long Island, N.Y., 1951-66; corp. staff mem. ITT, N.Y.C., 1966-69, asst. to exec. v.p., 1969-71; product line mgr. Levitt & Sons, Long Island, 1971-73, sr. v.p., 1973-75; pres. Palm Cable, Palm Coast, Fla., 1975-84; pres. Palm Coast Utility, 1975-84; v.p. Admiral Corp., Palm Coast, 1975-84. Mem. sch. system adv. bd. Flagler County Sch. Curriculum Com., Fla., 1979-81. Served with USAAF, 1945-46. Republican. Home and Office: 102 Windlake Ct Niceville FL 32578

MURTHA, FRANCIS BRIAN, photographer, minister; b. Bklyn., Mar. 23, 1915; s. Francis Pierre and Hazel Beatrice (Greenvault) M.; grad. high sch.; m. Helen L. Braner, July 31, 1968; children—Patricia L. (Mrs. Gary Shepard), Terry, Kevin, Jack. With North Plainfield (N.J.) Police Dept., 1936-52; chief detective bur., 1941-52; with Harolds Club, Reno, 1952-72, chief of photography, 1960-72; photographer, photo lab. technician U. Nev., Reno, from 1973, ret.; ordained minister Candlelight Gospel Mission, Reno. Pres. local 85, North Plainfield (N.J.) Patrolmen's Benevolent Assn., 1937-39, del. to N.J. Legislature, 1939-42; with Nev. wing CAP, 1953-69, dep. wingcomdr., 1964-69, Distinguished award, 1965. Served with USAF, 1942-45. Mem. Profl. Photographer of Am. (mem. nat. council 1972-76). Lion. Home: 949 Del Mar Way Reno NV 89502 Office: 655 N Virginia St Reno NV 89501

MURTHY, C. K. N., TV consultant; b. Bangalore, Karnata, India, Dec. 20, 1927; parents V. Krishna Murthy and Savithriamma; married, Apr. 26, 1951; children: C.N.S. Murthy, C.N. Sashi Murthy, C.N. Giridhar Murthy. B in Electrical Engr., U. Coll. Engring. Bangalore, India, 1949. Asst. engr. All India Radio Govt. India, 1949-81, sta. engr., 1981-85; supr. engr. Door Darshan TV, Bangalore, India, 1985-86; cons. Freelance, Bangalore, 1986—. Fellow Inst. Electronics and Telecommunication Engrs. Hindu. Office: 585 Block II (110 II Main), Rajajinagar Bangalore, Karnatako 560010, India also: 9520 Hinton Dr Santee CA 92071

MURTON, PETER MURRAY, computer executive; b. Swan Hill, Victoria, Australia, May 21, 1929; m. Valmai Phillips, Mar. 6, 1954; children: David, Sandra. BEE, Melbourne U., Australia, 1951. Engr. Telcom Australia, Melbourne, 1952-54; planning mgr. Colonial Mut. Life Ins. Co., Melbourne, 1954-63, data processing mgr., 1963-72, mgr. adminstrn., 1972-83, computer, communication mgr., 1983-86, cons. mgr., 1986—. Fellow Australian Computer Soc. (hon. life, sec. 1972—, gov. internal affairs 1984—, v.p. 1988—); mem. Instn. Engrs., Standards Assn. Com. on Info. Systems (chmn. 1970—). Home: 110 Powlett st, 3002 East Melbourne Australia Office: Colonial Mut Life Ins Co, 330 Collins St, 3000 Melbourne Australia

MURZEWSKI, JANUSZ WLADYSLAW, civil engineer, educator; b. Tarnopol, Poland, May 17, 1928; s. Wladyslaw and Janina (Pelczarska) M.; m. Barbara Krawczykowska, May 7, 1955; children: Wladyslaw, Bozena. M of Engring., Mining and Metall. Acad., Krakow, Poland, 1951; DSc, Krakow Politechnika, 1956; postgrad., Brown U., 1959-60. Teaching asst. Krakow Politechnika, 1950-55, asst. prof., 1960-67, prof. civil engring., 1967—, vice dean civil engring., 1962-74, chmn. dept. math., 1964-70, head metal structures, 1970—; research assoc. Polish Acad. Scis., Warsaw, 1955-59; internat. expert UN Indsl. Devel. Orgn., Rio de Janeiro, Brazil, 1977-78; cons. Mine Constrn. Devel. Ctr., Myslowice, Poland, 1973-77. Author: Safety of Building Structures, Polish edit., 1970, German edit., 1974; editor: 4

vols. of proceedings for Structural Reliability Conf., 1972, 77, 82, 87; mem. editorial bd. Internat. Jour. Structural Safety; contbr. over 200 papers and 400 revs. to profl. jours. Recipient Sci. award Minister of Sci. and Higher Edn., 1970, 72, 80, 83, Knight's cross Council of State, 1972, Golden medal for bldg. Minister of Bldg., 1981, medal of nat. edn. Minister of Edn., 1984. Fellow Internat. Sci. Orgn. (mem. adv. com.); mem. Polish Acad. Scis. (sect. v.p. 1978, mem. civil engring. com.), Polish Soc. Theoretical and Applied Mechanics (founder, v.p. 1972-76), Am. Math. Soc., Internat. Assn. for Structural Safety and Reliability, Polish Math. Soc. Home: ul Zaleskiego 44/6, 31-525 Crakow Poland Office: Crakow Politechnika, ul Warsawska 24, 31-155 Crakow Poland

MUSACCHIO, KIRK ANTHONY, lawyer, financial and real estate consultant; b. Fresno, Calif., Nov. 11, 1955; s. Theodore Alphonsus and Darlene June (Mirigian) M.; m. Stephane-Leigh Haines, Sept. 22, 1984. BA cum laude, U. San Francisco, 1977; JD, U. Santa Clara, 1980. Bar: Calif. 1982, U.S. Dist. Ct. (no. dist.) Calif. 1982. Legal writer Matthew Bender & Co., San Francisco, 1981-82; sr. v.p., legal counsel Centennial Savs. and Loan, Santa Rosa, Calif., 1983-84, exec. v.p., gen. counsel, asst. sec., 1984, exec. v.p. and gen. counsel/adminstrn., 1984-85; pres. KTM Corp., San Francisco, 1986—. Comments editor and mem. law rev. bd., U. Santa Clara, 1980. Assoc. com. mem. Boys' Town of Italy, San Francisco, 1986. Mem. ABA, Commonwealth Club Calif., Triple X fraternity. Republican. Roman Catholic. Lodge: Masons. Home: 1475 Balhan Dr 108 Concord CA 94521 Office: KTM Corp 130 El Dorado Ct San Francisco CA 94066

MUSACCHIO, THEODORE ALPHONSUS, international business consultant; b. Fresno, Calif., Aug. 11, 1934; s. Anthony and Constance (Ambrogio) M.; B.A., Fresno State Coll., 1956; postgrad. U. Calif. Sch. Law-San Francisco, 1959-61; m. Darlene June Mirigian, Mar. 20, 1955; 1 child, Kirk Anthony. Exec. trainee Bank of Am., NT & SA, Fresno, 1956-59; exec. Wells Fargo Bank, San Francisco, 1961-64; adminstrv. v.p. Columbus Savs. & Loan Assn., San Francisco, 1964-72; sr. v.p. Imperial Savs. and Loan Assn., San Francisco, 1972-76; dir., pres., chief exec. officer Columbus-Marin Savs. and Loan Assn., TAM Fin. Corp., Marcent Fin. Corp. and Columbus Fin. Corp., 1976-85; chmn. bd. and chief exec. officer KTM Corp., 1986—. Mem. exec. com. Boys' Towns of Italy, 1965—; pres. San Francisco Columbus Day Celebration, 1968. Mem. Fin. Instns. Mktg. Assn. (charter), Musicians' Union, Internat. Assn. Machinists, Am. Savs. and Loan Inst. (past pres. San Francisco chpt.), Il Cenacolo, Order Sons of Italy in Am., Italian Fedn. Calif. (past bd. dirs.), Sigma Pi. Clubs: Commonwealth of Calif., Family, Villa Taverna (San Francisco). Lodges: Masons (32 deg.), Shriners. Home and Office: 130 El Dorado Ct San Bruno CA 94066

MUSAMBACINE, BWALYA, United Nations official; b. Chikubi's Village, Luapula, Zambia, Feb. 17, 1936; s. Noah Bwalya and Serah (Kundapupe) M.; m. Jennifer Mulenga; children: Kasalwe, Bwalya, Chomba, Chabala, Bupe, Kunda, Bwalya, Mambwe, Mwansa, Mwelwa. BA, U. Zambia, 1969; MA, U. Manchester, 1975; diploma in project mgmt., pub. adminstrn., higher tchr.'s tng., Cafrad U., Nairobi. Tchr. Zambia Ministry Edn., Chingola, 1955-66; mgr. Indeco Steelbldg. Zambia Clay Ltd., Kitwe, 1969-73; lectr. Nat. Inst. Pub. Adminstrn., Lusaka, Zambia, 1973-75, sr. lectr., 1975-78; adminstrv. officer Staff Tng. Ctr. UN Econ. Commn. for Africa, Addis Ababa, Ethiopia, 1978—. Author: Training for Results, 1978, Management Made Simple, 1982. Mem. Brit. Inst. Mgmt., European Inst. for Trans-Nat. Studies in Group and Organizational Devel., Alexander Hamilton Inst. Exec. Devel. Mgmt. Office: UNECA Staff Tng Ctr, PO Box 60090, Addis Ababa Ethiopia

MUSAVI-KHAMENEI, MIR HOSEIN See MOUSSAVI, HUSSEIN

MUSCARELLA, GIUSEPPE, oil and gas exploration company executive; b. Palermo, Italy, Oct. 6, 1928; s. Alessandro and Concetta (Furetta) M.; m. Aurora Faso, Nov. 22, 1948; children—Concetta, Assia, Alessandro, Giorgio, Roy M.Mech. Engring., U. Palermo, 1951. Shop mgr. Ansaldo S.p.A., Genoa, Italy, 1952-58; project mgr. AGIP S.p.A., Milan, Italy, 1958-61; comml. mgr. AGIP U.S.A., Inc., N.Y.C., 1962-66; v.p. AGIP Petroleum Co., Inc., Houston, 1967-68; engring. mgr. AGIP SpA, Milan, Italy, 1969-70, exec. v.p., dir., 1981-84, chmn. bd., chief exec. officer, 1984—; mng. dir. Tecnomare, Venice, Italy, 1971-80. Office: AGIP SpA, 1-20097 San Donato Milanese Italy Other: care EJ Malonis AGIP US Rep 666 5th Ave New York NY 10103

MUSCH, ELIZABETH, advertising executive; b. Utrecht, The Netherlands, Aug. 25, 1952; came to U.S., naturalized, 1965, arrived in France, 1979; d. Otto Eduard and Pauline (Lefeber) M. BA in Internat. Affairs, U. So. Calif., 1973; MA in Internat. Politics, Tufts U., 1974. Mktg. specialist Netherlands C. of C., Los Angeles, 1974-75; account exec. Benton and Bowles, N.Y.C., 1976-79; account supr., account dir. Paris, 1979-83, dir. client services, 1983-85; dep. mng. dir. D'Arcy, Masius, Benton and Bowles, Paris, 1985-87, mng. dir., 1987—. Mktg. advisor Care, Paris, 1987-88. Democrat. Roman Catholic. Home: 10 quai Henri IV, 75004 Paris France Office: D'Arcy Masius Benton & Bowles, 10 Blvd du Parc, 92521 Neuilly France

MUSE, MARK DANA, psychologist; b. Pasadena, Calif., Mar. 1, 1952; s. Harry Lee and Nelda Hayward (Evans) M.; m. Michele Standish, Sept. 10, 1970 (div. 1975); 1 child, Dana Michele; m. Gloria Frigola, Aug. 15, 1978. BS, No. Ariz. U., 1973, MA, 1978, EdD, 1980; Ldo., U. Barcelona, Spain, 1984. Lic. psychologist, Md., also Spain. Dir. Pain Clinic, Sacred Heart Hosp., Cumberland, Md., 1982-87, Wellness Counseling, Cumberland, 1986-87; dir. Centre Mensana, Girona, Spain, 1987—. Author: Stress y Relax, 1983; Exercise for the Chronic Pain Patient, 1984. Contbr. numerous articles to profl. jours. Mem. Am. Psychol. Assn., World Fedn. Mental Health, Sociedad Interamericana de Psicologia, Collegi Oficial de Psicologs de Catalunya. Research on post traumatic stress disorder in chronic pain syndromes. Home: Migdia 16, 21502 Girona Spain Office: Centre Mensana, Apartat de Correus 437, 17002 Girona Spain

MUSE, STEPHEN H., lawyer, retirement community developer; b. Mesa, Ariz., Nov. 20, 1947; s. H.H. Muse and Moneta (Leavitt) Hill; m. Colleen Lloyd, Jan. 26, 1973; children—Melissa, Jessica, Sara. B.S., U.S. Mil. Acad., 1970; M.B.A., U. Hawaii, 1974; J.D., Brigham Young U., 1977. Bar: Utah 1977, Okla. 1979, U.S. Ct. Mil. Appeals 1978, U.S. Ct. Appeals (D.C. cir.), U.S. Ct. Claims 1980, U.S. Supreme Ct. 1980, U.S. Tax Ct. 1980, Tex. 1984. Commd. 2d lt. U.S. Army, 1970, advanced through grades to maj. U.S. Army Res., 1983; asst. staff judge advocate U.S. Army, Ft. Sam Houston, Tex., 1977-83; ptnr. Duterroil, Muse & Shackelford, San Antonio, Tex., 1983-85; vice-chmn. Towers at Ft. Sam Houston, San Antonio, 1982-85; pres., chmn. Advanced Living Techs., Inc., San Antonio, 1987—. Recipient Lamp award ABA, 1984. Mem. Am. Inst. C.P.A.s, Am. Bar Assn., Am. Assn. Realtors (broker mem.). Democrat. Mormon. Home: 5919 Winding Ridge Dr San Antonio TX 78239-2136 Office: Advance Living Techs Inc 1100 NE Loop 410 Suite 900 San Antonio TX 78209

MUSEVENI, YOWERI KAGUTA, president of Uganda, b. 1944; married; 4 children. Grad., Econs. and Polit. Sci., U. Coll. Dar es Salaam, Tanzania, 1970. Formerly tchr. Tech. Coll., then research officer of intelligence unit; in polit. exile, Tanzania, 1971-79, creator, head guerilla force, Front for Nat. Salvation; minister defense, Uganda, 1979-80, 86—, guerilla leader, 1981-86, pres., Uganda, 1986—. Office: Office of the Pres, Kampala Uganda *

MUSHEN, ROBERT LINTON, ophthalmologist; b. Klamath Falls, Oreg., Mar. 4, 1943; s. Samuel Albert and Beulah (Gore) M.; B.S. in Chemistry (Nat. Merit scholar), Stanford U., 1964; M.D., U. Oreg., 1968; m. Deborah Campbell, July 5, 1969; children—Melanie, Gregory, Timothy. Intern, Santa Clara Valley Med. Center, San Jose, Calif., 1968-69; resident in ophthalmology Brooke Army Med. Center, San Antonio, 1972-75; chief service Kerrville (Tex.) VA Hosp., 1975-76; mem. staff Madigan Army Med. Center, Tacoma, 1976-77; chief of staff and eye service Kadlec Hosp., Richland, Wash., 1977—; pres. Richland Eye Clinic, 1977—; cons. in field. Served with M.C., U.S. Army Res., 1969-75. Recipient award Oreg. Mus. Sci. and Industry, 1960; Nat. Eye Found. fellow, 1974-75. Mem. A.C.S., Am. Acad. Ophthalmology, Am. Intraocular Implant Soc., Soc. Eye Surgeons, AMA, Wash. Med. Assn., Wash. Acad. Ophthalmology, Benton-Franklin County Med. Soc., Alpha Omega Alpha. Republican. Co-author: Neuroanatomy Guide, 1967; contbr. articles to med. jours. Inventor bifocal trial lens. Home: 1302 Brentwood Richland WA 99352-9699 Office: Kadlec Hosp 948 Stevens Dr Richland WA 99352

MUSHTAQ, QAISER, mathematics educator; b. Punjab, Pakistan, Feb. 28, 1954; s. Mushtaq Ali and Saghira Akhter; m. Aileen Tan, Jan. 10, 1985. B.Sc., Gordon Coll., Rawalpindi, 1972; M.Sc., Islamabad U., 1976; M.Phil., Quaid-I-Azam U., Islamabad, 1978; D.Phil., Oxford U., 1983. Lectr., Multan U., Pakistan, 1978-79; lectr. Quaid-I-Azam U., Islamabad, 1979-80, asst. prof. math., 1983—; Royal scholar Oxford U., 1980-83. Contbr. articles to sci. jours. Pres., Oxford Union Islamic Soc., 1983. Recipient Chowla medal Kans. State U./Govt. Coll., Lahore, 1977; Royal Commn. Exhbn. of 1851 scholar, 1980. Mem. Pakistan Math. Soc., Oxford Soc., London Math. Soc., Am. Math. Soc., Math. Soc. Punjab, SE Asian Math. Soc., Pakistan Stat. Soc. Office: Quiad-I-Azam U, Dept Math, Islamabad Pakistan

MUSICUS, MILTON, management consultant; b. Russia, Feb. 23, 1913; s. Boris and Sofia (Dorfman) M.; B.S., CCNY, 1933; M.A., Columbia U., 1934; M.P.A., N.Y. U., 1941; m. Marjorie E. Fine, July 5, 1940; children—Josephine N., Barbara J. Exam. asst. N.Y.C. CSC, 1937-42; asst. dir. salary standardization N.Y. State CSC, Albany, 1942-49; asst. commr. adminstrn. N.Y. State Dept. Edn., 1949-59, 61-63; asst. sec. to gov. for adminstrn., Albany, 1959-61; exec. dir. N.Y. State Health Facilities Corp., Albany, 1964-70; adminstr. mcpl. services N.Y.C., 1970-74, dir. city constrn., 1970-74; pres. Milton Musicus, Ltd., 1979—; vis. prof. SUNY, Albany, 1974-80, St. Rose Coll., 1980-81; cons. adminstrn. Dominican Govt., Ecuador, Honduras, P.R., Turkey, N.Y. State Charter Revision Commn.; cons. on energy N.Y. Senate Finance Minority Com., N.Y. State Emergency Fuel Office, 1974; asso. Inst. Public Adminstrn., N.Y.C., 1974; asso. Clapp and Mayne, Inc., P.R., 1974-86; cons. UN, 1978. First v.p. Council Community Services, Albany, 1968-69; mem. Gov.'s Constrn. Adv. Com., Interdepartmental Com. on Mgmt. Improvement, State Adv. Purchasing Council, N.Y. State Salary Standardization Bd.; chmn. N.Y.C. Mayor's Interdeptl. Com. Public Utilities, 1970-74; chmn. Mayor's Flatbush Task Force, 1970-74; mem. City Univ. Constrn. Fund, 1970-72. Bd. govs. Bldg. Congress, 1970-74. Recipient A.E. Smith award outstanding public adminstrn., 1959; award for outstanding contbr. to profl. service in N.Y. State, Rockefeller Coll. Pub. Affairs, 1985. Mem. Am. Soc. Public Adminstrn. (dist. pres. 1956, dir. nat. council 1957), Phi Delta Kappa, Phi Beta Kappa. Home: 4 Harvard Ave Albany NY 12208

MUSIHIN, KONSTANTIN K., electrical engineer; b. Harbin, China, June 17, 1927; s. Konstantin N. and Alexandra A. (Lapitsky) M.; came to U.S., 1967, naturalized, 1973; ed. YMCA Inst., 1942, North Manchurian U., 1945, Harbin Poly. Inst., 1948; m. Natalia Krilova, Oct. 18, 1964; 1 son, Nicholas. Asst. prof. Harbin Poly. Inst., 1950-53; elec. engr. Moinho Santista, Sao Paulo, Brazil, 1955-60; constrn. project mgr. Caterpillar-Brazil, Santo Amaro, 1960-61; mech. engr. Matarazzo Industries, Sao Paulo, 1961-62; chief of works Vidrobras, St. Gobain, Brazil, 1962-64; project engr. Brown Boveri, Sao Paulo, 1965-67; sr. engr. Kaiser Engrs., Oakland, Calif., 1967-73; sr. engr. Bechtel Power Corp., San Francisco, 1973-75; supr. power and control San Francisco Bay Area Rapid Transit, Oakland, 1976-78; chief elec. engr. L.K. Comstock Engring. Co., San Francisco, 1978-79; prin. engr. Morrison Knudsen Co., San Francisco, 1979-84; prin. engr. Brown and Caldwell, Cons. Engrs., Pleasant Hill, Calif., 1984-85; cons. engr. Pacific Gas and Electric Co., San Francisco, 1986—. Registered profl. engr., Calif., Colo., N.Y., N.J., Pa., Ill., Wash. Mem. IEEE (sr.), Instrument Soc. Am. (sr.), Am. Mgmt. Assn., Nat., Calif. socs. profl. engrs., Nat. Assn. Corrosion Engrs., Instituto de Engenharia de Sao Paulo. Mem. Christian Orthodox Ch. Clubs: Am.-Brazilian, Brit.-Am. Home: 320 Park View Terr Unit 207 Oakland CA 94610

MUSOKOTWANE, KEBBY SILILO KAMBULU, prime minister of Zambia; b. Musokotwane, Zambia, May 5, 1946; m. Muzya Regina Bulowa, Dec. 18, 1967; 5 children. Student David Livingstone Teachers Training Coll., 1963-64, U. Zambia, 1971. Primary sch. tchr., 1965, demonstration tchr., 1965-71, dep. headteacher, 1968-69, headteacher, 1970; lectr., 1972-73; elected mem. Parliament, 1973; minister of water and natural resources, 1977-78, minister of youth and sport, 1979; apptd. minister of fin. and tech. cooperation, 1983; apptd. minister of gen. edn. and culture, 1983-85; prime minister Republic of Zambia, 1985—. Office: Office of the Prime Minister, Lusaka Zambia *

MUSSCHOOT, ANNE MARIE, language educator; b. Gent, Belgium, July 16, 1944. PhD, State Univ. of Gent, Belgium, 1971. Prof. Dutch lit. State Univ. of Gent, 1983—; vis. prof. Univ. Pa., Phila., 1986. Author books on modern Dutch lit. and theory of lit.; contbr. articles to profl. jours. Recipient lit. criticism awards. Mem. Internat. Vereinigung Für Germanistik. Office: Rijksuniversiteit, Blandynberg 2, 9000 Gent Belgium

MUSSELMAN, LARRY L., chemical engineer; b. Erie, Pa., Aug. 16, 1947; s. Lloyd H. and Lyda M.; student (Scholar) Malone Coll., 1966-67; B.S. in Chem. Engring. magna cum laude (scholar), Akron U., 1971, M.S. in Engring., 1972; m. Susan E., Nov. 25, 1966; children—Cheri A., Jason L., Lucy A., Gavin A., Lauren A. Research engr. Timken Co., 1971-77; sr. research engr. Alcoa Co., Alcoa Center, Pa., 1977-79, sr. scientist, 1979-81, staff engr., 1981-83, tech. service mgr., 1983-86, tech. mgr., 1986— ; mem. tech. adv. com. Ohio Legislature. Mem. ASME (sect. dir.), Am. Soc. Lubrication Engrs., Soc. Plastics Engrs., Am. Soc. for Testing and Materials (fire testing coms.), Fire Retardant Chems. Assn., Soc. Plastics Industry Coms., Sigma Xi, Sigma Tau, Alpha Chi Sigma. Contbr. articles on polymers and fire retardants to profl. jours.; patentee in field. Office: Alcoa Tech Ctr Alcoa Center PA 15069

MUSSER, C. WALTON, physical scientist, consultant; b. Mt. Joy, Pa., Apr. 5, 1909; s. Ezra Nissley and Cora Grace (Weidman) M.; m. Edna Mae Hoak, June 23, 1937; children—Lila Darle (Mrs. Richard Hackman), Yvonne Duane (Mrs. Harold Graham), Stanley Walton. Student, Chgo. Tech. Coll., 1926-28, Leavitt Sch. Psychology, 1928-29, Wharton Sch. Finance and Commerce, 1929-30, U. Pa., 1930-32, Mass. Inst. Tech., 1957. Chief engr. product devel. Indsl. Improvement Corp., Phila., 1936-41; research adviser Dept. Def., 1941-56; pres., dir. research Sci. Research, Inc., Glenside, Pa., 1945-52; pvt. practice cons., adviser in research and devel. 1936—. Holder of over 162 U.S. Patents in 32 different classes and more than 60 patents in over 28 countries. Recipient Exceptional Civilian Service award for First Working Recoilless Weapon, Sec. of War, 1945; John C. Jones medal for Disting. Service, Am. Ordnance Assn., 1951; Machine Design award ASME, 1968; named to Ordnance Hall of Fame. Mem. Acad. Applied Scis., Am. Def. Preparedness Assn. (hon. life), Nat. Soc. Profl. Engrs., Sigma Xi. Address: 1206 Lela Ln Santa Maria CA 93454

MUSSER, ROBERT DANIEL, JR., resort hotel operator; b. Circleville, Ohio, Apr. 29, 1932; s. Robert Daniel and Elizabeth (Woodfill) M.; B.A., Dartmouth Coll., 1955; m. Amelia Maverick Epler, Nov. 30, 1957; children—Robin Epler, Margaret Stewart, Robert Daniel. With Grand Hotel Co. subs. Musser-Mackinac Holding Co., Inc., Mackinac Island, Mich., 1957—, pres., chief exec. officer, gen. mgr., 1962—, pres., owner holding co., 1979—, pres. Grand Hotel Mgmt. Services, Inc., chief exec. officer, chmn. bd. dirs. Grand Hotel Co.; dir. D & N Savs. Bank. Served with AUS, 1955-57. Mem. Mich., Am. hotel and motel assns., Hotel Sales Mgmt. Assn., Mackinac Island C. of C. Episcopalian. Clubs: Mackinac Island Yacht, Country of Lansing, Automobile (Lansing). Home: 13855 Peacock Rd Laingsburg MI 48848 Office: Grand Hotel Mackinac Island MI 49757 also: Grand Hotel Co 116 W Ottowa Lansing MI 48933

MUSSHOFF, KARL ALBERT, radiation oncologist; b. Wuppertal, Germany, June 11, 1910; s. Gustav and Amalie Kauls M.; M.D., U. Munich (Germany), 1935; m. Margarethe Herbst, Aug. 25, 1951; children—Stephan, Renate. Univ. lectr. medicine and radiology U. Freiburg (W. Ger.), 1960; prof., 1966—, emeritus dir. sect. radiotherapy Radiol. Centre Albert Ludwigs U., Freiburg, 1977—. Recipient W.C. Röntgen Plakette of Remscheid-Lennen, Girth-town of Röntgen, 1983; Leopold Freund Medaille of Österreichische gesellschaft für Radionologie, Radiobiologie, Medizinishe Radiophysik, 1985. Mem. Group European Radiotherapists (hon., pres. 1973), European Soc. Therapeutic Radiology and Oncology, German Cancer Soc. (hon.), German Radiation Soc., S.W. German Radiation Soc. (pres. 1972), German Soc. Internal Medicine, German Soc. Hematology and Oncology, Soc. German Physicists and Doctors, Am. Coll. Radiology (hon. fellow), Beirat der Deutschen Krebshilte (adv.). Co-editor Jour. Cancer Research Clin. Oncology, Strahlentherapie, Jour. Radiation Oncology Biol. Physics, Pneumonologie-Pneumonology. Home: 33 Eichenweg, 7573 Sinzheim-Vormberg, Baden Federal Republic of Germany Office: Medizinische Fakultät, Albert-Ludwigs-U, 7800 Freiburg Federal Republic of Germany

MUSSIL, STEPHAN ARTHUR, cinematographer; b. Vienna, Austria, July 16, 1952; s. Herbert Waldemar and Hertha Maria (Vukovits) M.; m. Bigi Egger, May 12, 1979; children: Joseph Mathias, Jakob Michael. Producer ORF, Vienna, 1974-80; operator EAV, Vienna, 1980-85; mgr. prodn. Mussil Films, Vienna, 1985—. Mem. Austrian Assn. Cinematographers. Home: Schalkgasse 5, Vienna Austria Office: Herbeckstr 47, Vienna Austria

MUSSMAN, WILLIAM EDWARD, lawyer, oil company executive; b. Mpls., Feb. 10, 1919; s. William Edward and Vera Marie (Chamberlain) M.; m. Janet Jonn Skittone, Dec. 19, 1948; children: William Edward III, Ann C. B.S. in Law, U. Minn., 1941, J.D., 1946. Bar: Minn. 1946, Calif. 1950, U.S. Supreme Ct. 1960. Asst. prof. law U. Minn., 1946-49; vis. prof. U. Calif., Berkeley, 1949; assoc. firm Pillsbury, Madison & Sutro, San Francisco, 1949-56; partner Pillsbury, Madison & Sutro, 1956-74; v.p., legal, dir. Standard Oil Co. of Calif., San Francisco, 1974-84. Served with USMCR, 1942-45. Decorated D.F.C. Fellow Southwestern Legal Found.; mem. ABA, Am. Arbitration Assn. Office: Three Embarcadero Ctr Suite 1060 San Francisco CA 94111

MUSSMAN, WILLIAM EDWARD, III, lawyer; b. San Francisco, Jan. 31, 1951; s. William Edward and Janet Jonn (Skittone) M.; m. Carol Lynne Johnson, Jan. 9, 1988; B.S., Stanford U., 1973; J.D., U. Calif.-San Francisco, 1976. Bar: Calif. 1976, U.S. Dist. Ct. (no. dist.) Calif. 1976,, U.S. Dist. Ct. (cen. dist.) Calif. 1982, U.S. Ct. Appeals (9th cir.) 1987, U.S. Supreme Ct., 1986. Assoc. Lasky, Haas, Cohler & Munter, San Francisco, 1980-82, Pillsbury, Madison & Sutro, San Francisco, 1982-84; assoc. Carr & Mussman, San Francisco, 1984—. Sustaining mem. Yosemite Area council Boy Scouts Am., 1981—; missionary Ch. Jesus Christ Latter Day Sts., Tokyo, 1977-78. Mem. ABA, San Francisco Bar Assn., Latter Day Saints Bus. Club (pres. 1982-84), Brigham Young U. Mgmt. Soc. (bd. dirs., 1984-88, v.p. 1984-86, pres. 1986-87), Stanford Alumni Assn. (life), Tau Beta Pi. Office: Carr & Mussman 3 Embarcadero Ctr Suite 1060 San Francisco CA 94111

MUSSO, GIANNI LUCA, metal processing executive; b. Turin, Piedmont, Italy, Nov. 9, 1958; s. Giovanni Antonio and Piera Maria (Perinetto) M. Cert. in edn., Royal Charles-Albert Coll., Moncalieri, Italy, 1976; cert. in proficiency and alliance, Lemania Coll., Lausanne, Switzerland, 1978, diploma in commerce, 1980; hautes etudes commerciales, U. of Lausanne, 1982. Sales mgr. Musso srl, Turin, 1982-83; lab and research mgr. Avita spa, San Gillio T., Italy, 1983-84; admnistrn. gen. mgr. Fondac spa, San Gillio T., 1984-87; research and new tech. mgr. Iramtec srl, San Gillio T., 1985-87; gen. mgr. Musso Holding, Turin, 1987. Author: The Thermoshock Process, 1988. Mem. ASSOFOND, Indsl. Union of Turin, Italian Assn. Metallurgy, Assn. Technique de Fonderie, Am. Foundrymen Assn. Lodge: Rotaract. Clubs: Garlenda Golf (Italian Riviera), Golf Crans (Switzerland), Yacht (Alassio). Office: Musso Holding, 47 Via Valdellatorre, 10040 San Gillio T Italy

MUSTACCHI, PIERO, physician, educator; b. Cairo, Egypt, May 29, 1920; came to U.S., 1947; naturalized, 1952; s. Gino and Gilda (Rieti) M.; m. Dora Lisa Ancona, Sept. 26, 1948; children—Roberto, Michael. B.S. in Humanities, U. Florence, Italy, 1938; postgrad. in anatomy, Eleve Interne, U. Lausanne, Switzerland, 1938-39; M.B., Ch.B., Fouad I U., Cairo, Egypt, 1944, grad. in Arabic lang. and lit., 1946; D Medicine and Surgery, U. Pisa, 1986. Lic. physician Egypt, 1946. Diplomate, Am. Bd. Internal Medicine. House officer English Hosp., Ch. Missionary Soc., Cairo, Egypt, 1945-47; clin. affiliate U. Calif., San Francisco, 1947-48; intern Franklin Hosp., San Francisco, 1948-49; resident in pathology U. Calif., San Francisco, 1949-51; resident in medicine Meml. Ctr. Cancer and Allied Diseases, N.Y.C., 1951-53; research epidemiologist Dept. HEW, Nat. Cancer Inst., Bethesda, Md., 1955-57; cons. allergy clinic U. Calif., San Francisco, 1957-70, clin. prof. medicine and preventive medicine, 1970—, head occupational epidemiology, 1975—, head div. internat. health edn. dept. epidemiology and internat. health, 1985—; med. cons., vis. prof. numerous ednl. and profl. instns. including U. Calif.-San Francisco, U. Marseille, 1981, 82, U. Pisa, Italy, 1983, U. Gabon, 1984, U. Siena, Italy, 1985, U. Calif.-San Francisco Ctr. for Rehab. and Occupational Health, 1984—, Work Clinic, 1975—; cons. numerous govtl. agys. throughout the world. Contbr. chpts. to books, articles to profl. jours. Editorial bd. Medecine d'Afrique Noire, Ospedali d'Italia. Served with USN, USPHS, 1953-55. Decorated Order of Merit (Italy), Ordre de la Legion d'Honneur (France), Medal of St. John of Jerusalem, Sovereign Order of Malta, Order of the Republic (Egypt); Scroll, Leonard da Vinci Soc., San Francisco, 1965; award Internat. Inst. Oakland, 1964; Hon. Vice Consul. Italy, 1971—. Fellow Am. Soc. Occupational Medicine, ACP; mem. AAAS, Am. Soc. Environ. and Occupational Health, Am. Assn. Cancer Research, Calif. Soc. Allergy and Immunology, Calif. Med. Assn., San Francisco Med. Soc., West Coast Allergy Soc. (founding mem.), Mexican Congress on Hypertension (corr.), Assn. Internationale pour la Recherche Medicale et l'Edn. Continue (U.S. rep.). Democrat. Clubs: Villa Taverna (San Francisco), Accademia Italiana della Cucina. Home: 3344 Laguna St San Francisco CA 94123 Office: U Calif Parnassus Ave San Francisco CA 94143

MUSTAFA, SHAMS, chemist, consultant; b. Karachi, Pakistan, Oct. 8, 1952; came to U.S., 1977, naturalized, 1984; s. Mustafa Hasan Zuberi and Shaista Shakri Mustafa; m. Naheed Shams Mustafa, Apr. 23, 1982; children: Adeel, Shariq. B.S., Punjab U., Lahore, Pakistan, 1969, honors, 1970, M.S. in Inorganic and Analytical Chemistry, 1972. Sr. chemist Ace Labs., Karachi, 1972-77, cons., 1972-77; chemist Am. Standards Testing Bur., N.Y.C., 1977-79; scientist in charge grain and vegetable oil lab. Caleb Brett (USA), New Orleans, 1979-88, chief chemist agrl. lab. Caleb Brett (USA). Author: Carbohydrate Chemistry; translator scientific texts from English to Urdu. Fellow Am. Inst. Chemists; mem. Am. Oil Chemists Soc. (cert., referee, Smalley award 1986-87), Am. Inst. Chem. Engrs., Am. Chem. Soc., Internat. Union Pure and Applied Chemistry, Union Concerned Scientists, Assn. Ofcl. Analytical Chemists, ASTM, AAAS, N.Y. Acad. Scis., Nat. Soybean Processors Assn. (ofcl. chemist), Nat. Cottonseed Products Assn. Republican. Islam. Avocations: reading, travel, physical fitness, home improvement. Home: 1417 Meeker Loop Laplace LA 70068 Office: Caleb Brett (USA) Inc 4927 Jefferson Hwy Jefferson LA 70121

MUSTAIN, DOUGLAS DEE, lawyer; b. Shreveport, La., Nov. 2, 1945; s. Reginald K. and Dorothy J. (Green) M.; m. Sharon L. Tegarden, Aug. 19, 1967; children—Kristi Kaye, Kari Dee, Kenton Douglas, Kyle Robert, Kirk Stephen, Kali Elizabeth. Student Knox Coll., 1963-64, Murray State U., 1964-66; B.S., U. Ill., 1971; J.D., U. Iowa, 1974. Bar: Iowa 1974, Ill. 1974; U.S. Dist. Ct. (cen. dist.) Ill. 1974, U.S. Ct. Appeals (7th cir.) 1980, U.S. Supreme Ct. 1986. Law clk. Shulman, Phelan, Tucker, Boyle & Mullin, Iowa City, 1972-74; assoc. Stuart, Neagle & West, Galesburg, Ill., 1974-76; ptnr. West, Neagle & Williamson, Galesburg, 1977—; instr. real estate law Carl Sandburg Coll., Galesburg, 1977-81. Chmn. Citizens Referendum Com., Galesburg, 1983, 1987-88; bd. dirs. YMCA, Galesburg, 1983—, Cottage Hosp. Care Corp., Galesburg, 1984—; trustee 1st Presbyn. Ch., Galesburg, 1984; commr. Galesburg Pub. Transp. Commn., 1985—; pres., founder Galesburg Pub. Sch. Found., 1987—. Served to SP5 U.S. Army, 1966-69, Vietnam. Decorated Army Commendation with oak leaf cluster. Mem. Knox County Bar Assn. (pres. 1980-82), ABA (comml. litigation com. 1981—), Assn. Trial Lawyers Am., Ill. Trial Lawyers Assn. Republican. Home: 1234 N Prairie St Galesburg IL 61401 Office: West Neagle & Williamson 58 S Cherry St Galesburg IL 61401

MUSTAPHA, ALHAJI MOHAMED SANUSI, transportation executive; b. Freetown, Sierra Leone, June 1, 1903. Grad., Prince of Wales Sch., Freetown, 1925. With Sierra Leone Civil Service, 1926; joint sec. Foulah Town Mosque Com., 1933; founder Mustapha Bros., 1946; reader law Lincoln's Inn, London, 1947-50; minister Ministry of Works and Transport, 1953, Ministry of Natural Resources, 1957, Ministry of Fin., 1958-59; dep. prime minister Republic of Sierra Leone, 1959, mem. governing council, cen.

com., 1978; minister Ministry of Trade and Industry, 1962, Ministry of Social Welfare, 1963-64; mem. Sierra Leone Parliament, 1969; acting 2d v.p. Sierra Leone Airlines, Freetown, 1979-80, chmn., 1982—; apptd. lic. buying agt. Sierra Leone Produce Mktg. Bd., 1950, pres. assn. lic. buying agts., 1967; del., advisor to Sierra Leone Constl. Conf., London, 1960. Asst. sec. Sierra Leone Muslim Congress, 1932, chmn. bd. govs. Secondary Sch., 1965-69, pres., 1974; hon. sec. East Ward Rate Payers Assn., 1935; nat. treas. sierra Leone Peoples' Party, mem. exec. com., 1950; mem. legis. council, exec. council Freetown East Electoral Dist., 1951; bd. govs. Ahmadiyya Secondary Sch., 1965-70; chmn. bd. govs. Prince of Wales Sch., 1967-70. Served as cpl. Sierra Leone Defence Corps, 1939-45. Decorated comdr. Brit. Empire, comdr. Order of Rokel; recipient Sierra Leone Independence medal, 1961. Mem. Old Prince Waleans Assn., Royal Commonwealth Soc. Office: Sierra Leone Airlines, 21/23 Siaka Stevvens St, Freetown Sierra Leone also: PO Box 285, Freetown Sierra Leone

MUSTAPHA, TAMTON, gastroenterologist; b. Calicut, Kerala, India, Oct. 17, 1941; s. Mahamood and Asmabi (Tamton) Thoosikannan; student Malabar Christian Coll., India, 1958; M.D., Calicut Med. Coll., 1963; m. Rahma Marikar, June 15, 1969; children—Monisha, Mumtaz. Resident in internal medicine VA Hosp., Bklyn., 1967-68, Grasslands Hosp., Valhalla, N.Y., 1968-70; resident in gastroenterology Montefiore Hosp., Bronx, 1970-72; practice medicine, specializing in gastroenterology, Hudson, N.Y., 1972—; attending physician Columbia Meml. Hosp., Hudson, 1972—Greene County Hosp.; instr. medicine Albany Med. Center, 1972—; bd. dirs., chmn. auditing assurance Hudson Valley PSRO; bd. dirs. regional heart assn. Paul Harris fellow, Rotary Internat., 1979—; mem. town planning bd. Kudehok, 1987—; diplomate Am. Bd. Internal Medicine, Am. Bd. Gastroenterology. Fellow Am. Coll. Gastroenterologists; mem. Columbia County Med. Soc., N.Y. State Med. Soc., AMA, Am. Gastroent. Assn., ACP, Am. Soc. Internal Medicine, Acad. Scis., Am. Heart Assn. (bd. dirs.), Columbia and Dutches Lung Assn., Assn. for Mentally Retarded, Am. Assn. Physicians and Dentists of India (pres. Capital dist. 1986). Republican. Lodge: Rotary (dir. 1976-78, pres.-elect 1986-87, pres. 1987—), Mason (master). Home: Brindhaven RD 1 Valatie NY 12184 Office: 848 Columbia St Hudson NY 12534

MUSTION, ALAN LEE, pharmacist; b. Oklahoma City, Feb. 6, 1947; s. Granville E. and Iris E. (Graham) M.; children: Jeffrey Alan, Jennifer Chere; m. Mary Jane Bozek, Dec. 4, 1982. BS in Pharmacy, Southwestern Okla. State U., 1970. Staff pharmacist VA Med. Ctr., Oklahoma City, 1970-74, dir. pharmacy, Saginaw, Mich., 1974-76, asst. dir. pharmacy, Richmond, Va., 1976-77, dir. pharmacy, Iowa City, Iowa, 1977—; clin. instr. clin./hosp. div. U. Iowa, 1977—. Contbr. articles to profl. jours. Served to maj. USAR. Recipient VA Spl. Achievement awards, 1973, 77, 86, 87, VA Suggestion awards, 1979, 81, 83, VA Cost Reduction award, 1983, VA Contbr. award, 1987; research grantee Travenol Labs., 1980-87, VA HSR&D grantee, 1984, 88. Mem. Am. Soc. Hosp. Pharmacists, Iowa Soc. Hosp. Pharmacists, Assn. Mil. Surgeons of U.S., Am. Assn. Colls. Pharmacy, Res. Officers Assn., Kappa Psi. Methodist. Home: 821 Spencer Dr Iowa City IA 52240 Office: VA Med Center Hwy 6 West Iowa City IA 52240

MUSTO, DAVID FRANKLIN, physician, historian, consultant; b. Tacoma, Wash., Jan. 8, 1936; s. Charles Hiram and Hilda Marie (Hanson) Mustoe; m. Emma Jean Baudendistel, June 2, 1961; children: Jeanne Marie, David Kyle, John Baird, Christopher Edward. B.A., U. Wash., 1956, M.D., 1963; M.A., Yale U., 1961. Lic. physician, Conn., Pa. Intern. Pa. Hosp., Phila., 1963-64; resident Yale Med. Ctr., New Haven, 1964-67; spl. asst. to dir. NIMH, Bethesda, Md., 1967-69; vis. asst. prof. Johns Hopkins U., 1968-69; asst. prof. Yale U., 1969-73, assoc. prof., 1973-78, sr. research scientist, 1978-81, prof., 1981—, Exec. fellow Davenport Coll., 1983—; mem. adv. editorial com. Yale Edits. Private Papers James Boswell, 1975—; cons. Exec. Office of Pres., 1973-75; mem. White House Strategy Council, 1978-81; mem. panel on alcohol policy Nat. Acad. Scis., Washington, 1978-82; cons. White House Conf. on Families, 1979-80. Historian Pres.'s Commn. on Mental Health, 1977-78; adv. U.S. Del. to UN Commn. Narcotic Drugs, Geneva, 1978-79; mem. nat. council Smithsonian Instn., Washington, 1981—; hist. cons. Presdl. Commn. Human Immuno-deficiency Virus Epidemic, 1988. Served with USPHS, 1967-69. mem. New Haven County Med. Assn. (chmn. bicentennial com. 1983), Am. Inst. History of Pharmacy (chmn. Urdang Medal com. 1978, Kremers award), Am. Hist. Assn., Am. Assn. History of Medicine (chmn. edn. com. 1985-86, William Osler medal), Soc. of the Cincinnati in the State of Conn. Clubs: Cosmos (Washington); Yale (N.Y.C.); Athenaeum (London); Beaumont Med. (pres. 1985-87). Office: Yale U 333 Cedar St New Haven CT 06510

MUSYANI, MARCEL RANWELL, railways executive; b. Isoka, Zambia, Aug. 19, 1938; s. Sabangwa Whitemore and Musyani and Elizabeth Enala Nantambo; m. Ernestina Namufungwe, Nov. 13, 1959; children: Agatha, Clement, Martha Bernard, Dennis, Justin, Gertrude, Catherine. Diploma in Accountantcy, Evelyn Hone Coll., Lusaka, Zambia, 1978; cert. in transport mgmt., Brit. Transport Staff Coll., London, 1982. Comml. clk. Zambia Rys., 1964-67, sta. master, 1967-69, sub. acct., 1969-75; asst. acct. Zambia Rys., Kabwe, 1975-78, sr. internal auditor, 1980—. Sect. sec. United Independence Party, Moto-Moto br., Kabwe, 1979; chmn. PTA, St. Paul Secondary Sch., Kabwe, 1981-84; treas. Sacrad Heart Parish Council, Kabwe, 1982-84. Mem. Inst. Internal Auditors. Roman Catholic. Home: 6 Limulunga Pl, Kabwe Zambia 81633 Office: Zambia Rys, Kabwe Zambia 80935

MUTA, HIROMITSU, economist, educator; b. Amagi, Fukuoka, Japan, Dec. 20, 1946; s. Hideo and Michiko (Hirai) M.; m. Emiko Iwata, Dec. 7, 1975; children: Yukako, Hirokazu, Risako. BA, U. Tokyo, 1971, MA, 1973. Sr. researcher Nat. Inst. Ednl. Research, Tokyo, 1974-85; assoc. prof. Tokyo Inst. Tech., 1985—. Author: Contemporary School Systems, 1976, Theory and Research of Audiovisual Education, 1979. Nitobe fellow Internat. House Japan, 1980-82. Mem. Japan Soc. Sociology of Edn. (assoc. editor 1984—), Japan Soc. Ednl. Adminstrn. (assoc. editor 1986—), Japan Soc. Sci. Edn. (research com. 1986—). Home: 3-24-10 Denenchofu, Otaku 145, Japan Office: Tokyo Inst Tech, 2-12-1 Ohokayama Meguroku, Tokyo 152, Japan

MUTHAYYA, BOPPANDA CUTTAYYA, psychologist, institute administrator, researcher; b. Virajpet, Karnataka Coorg. Dist., India, Sept. 11, 1934; s. Cuttayya and Neelamma Cuttayya; m. Rani Muthayya, May 19, 1963; children: Praveen, Nayan. BA in Psychology with honors, U. Mysore, 1955, MA in Psychology, 1956; PhD in Psychology, U. Madras, 1961. Lectr. in psychology Sri Venkateswara U., Tirupati, Andhra Pradesh, India, 1960-61; reader in psychology Sri Venkateswara U., Tirupati, 1968; dir. psychology Nat. Inst. Rural Devel., Hyderabad, Andhra Pradesh, 1968—, dean-in-charge, 1977-78, dir.-gen.-in-charge, 1982; vis. lectr. in psychology Indian Inst. Tech., Madras, 1963; hon. chief testing officer Juvenile Guidance Bur., Madras, 1962-65, hon. dir., 1965-68; mem. adminstrv. personnel selection com. Govt. Andhra Pradesh, Hyderbad, 1974-75; coordinator course in rural devel. Cen. U. Hyderbad, 1978-80; dir. course on research methodology for women Asian and Pacific Ctr. for Women's Devel., Bangkok, 1980; coordinator FAO regional council on improving nutrition of rural poor, 1982; huest lectr. various tng. instns. in adminstrn., rural devel.; participant profl. confs. Author numerous research reports; contbr. numerous articles to profl. jours.; mem. editorial bd. Jour. Psychol. Research, Indian Jour. Applied Psychology. Fellow UN Asian and Pacific Devel. Inst., 1978. Mem. Indian Sci. Congress Assn., Indian Psychol. Assn., Indian Acad. Applied Psychology (exec. council 1968-72, regional pres. 1977), Indian Soc. Criminology (exec. council 1971, 72, 75), Madras Psychology Soc., Indian Soc. Tng. and Devel. Office: Nat Inst Rural Devel, Hyderbad, Andhra Pradesh 500 030, India

MUTHIG, KLAUS PETER, psychology educator; b. Krefeld, Fed. Republic Germany, Apr. 12, 1949; s. Gerhard and Katharina (Ferdinand) M. BS in Psychology, U. Bonn, 1972, MS in Psychology, 1974, PhD in Psychology, 1978. Research asst. dept. psychology U. Bonn, Fed. Republic Germany, 1975-77; asst. prof. dept. psychology Free U. Berlin, Fed. Republic Germany, 1977-81, U. Tübingen, Fed. Republic Germany, 1981—; guest scientist IBM Sci. Ctr., Heidelberg, Fed. Republic Germany, 1984-86. Author: Constructional Experimental Design, 1979, Theory, Experiment and Experimental Design, 1981; contbr. articles to sci. jours. Mem. Deutsche Gesellschaft fIr Psychologie, Am. Psychol. Assn. (fgn. affiliate), Gesellschaft für Informatik. Office: Univ Tübingen Dept Psychology, Friedrichstrasse 29, 7400 Tübingen Federal Republic of Germany

MUTHU, FRANCIS SAVARI, county agency administrator; b. Tamil Nadu, India, June 3, 1934; came to U.S., 1969; s. C. Savarimuthu and Nayagammal; m. Regina Roseline Gabriel, May 3, 1967; children: Anna, Sharon. Vidvan, Madras U., India, 1957; B of Oriental Learning, Annamalai U., India, 1962, BEd, 1964; MA, Loyola U., Chgo., 1972, PhD, 1978. Tchr., head Tamil language dept. St. Anns High Sch., Tamil Nadu, 1957-60, St. Bede's High Sch., Tamil Nadu, 1964-69; lectr. Tamil language and literatures Loyola Coll, Madras, India, 1957-59; correctional counselor Cook County Jail, Chgo., 1969-73; counselor, supr. Manpower Cook County office Employment Tng., Chgo., 1973-76, planner Manpower, 1976-80; regional mgr. Cook County office Employment Tng., Maywood, Ill., 1980—; prof. Loyola U., Chgo., 1980-85, adj. prof. of Sociology, Triton Coll., 1987—. Editor: Thozhan, 1958-60; sub-editor Poochendu, 1960-64; editorial bd. Thondan, 1964-69; translator Biblical Commn. of Tamil Nadu, 1964-68. Mem. humanities adv. com. Triton Coll. Arthur J. Schmitt Found. doctoral fellow, Chgo., 1974-75; named Outstanding New Citizen, Citizenship Council Met. Chgo., 1983; recipient Outstanding Citizenship and Americanism award Kiwanis Internat. and The Des Plaines Times, 1984. Mem. Ill. Employment and Tng. Assn. (editorial bd.). Roman Catholic (parish leadership). Club: Chgo. Tamil Sangam (pres. 1983-84). Home: 920 Leahy Circle E Des Plaines IL 60016 Office: Cook County Office Employment Tng 1311 Maybrook Dr Rm 205 Maywood IL 60153

MUTI, RICCARDO, orchestra conductor; b. Naples, Italy, July 28, 1941. Ed., Milan Conservatory; MusD (hon.), U. Pa., Mt. Holyoke Coll.; LLD (hon.), Warwick U., Eng.; Doctor Honoris Causa, Princeton U. Prin. condr. Orch. Maggio Musicale Florentino, Florence, Italy, 1969-80; guest condr. numerous orchs., Europe and U.S.; music dir. Philharmonia Orch., London, 1973-82, prin. guest condr. Phila. Orch., 1977-78, music dir., 1980—; music dir., La Scala, 1986—, prin. condr., 1973-82; concerts at Salzburg, Edinburgh, Lucerne, Flanders, Vienna and Berlin Festivals; condr. operas at Vienna, La Scala, Milan, Munich. (Recipient numerous internat. prizes for recordings). Decorated officer of merit Republica Tedesca, Commendatore and Grand Ufficiale Della Republica Italiana; winner Guido Cantelli prize, 1967; recipient Verdienst Kreuz, Fed. Republic of Germany. Hon. mem. Royal Acad. Music, Acad. Santa Cecilia, Acad. Luigi Cherubini. Office: care Phila Orch 1420 Locust St Philadelphia PA 19102 *

MUTO, KIYOSHI, structural company executive; b. Ibaraki, Japan, Jan. 29, 1903; m. Yoshi Sano, Feb. 23, 1929. D of Engring., Tokyo U., 1929. Prof. Tokyo U., 1935-63, prof. emeritus, 1963—; exec. v.p. Kajima Corp., Tokyo, 1963-77, hon. adv., 1977—; pres. Muto Inst. Structural Mechanics, Inc., Tokyo, 1965-86; chmn. Muto & Assocs. Ltd., Tokyo, 1986—. Author: The Aseismic Design of Structures (6 vols.), 1963-77; prin. works include bldg. 1st highrise in Japan, Kasumigaseki Bldg. Recipient Person of Cultural Merit award Minister of Edn., Japan, 1979. Mem. Internat. Assn. Earthquake Engring. (orgainizer 1963), Japan Acad. (Emperor's prize 1964), Am. Concrete Inst. Japan (hon. mem.), Nat. Acad. Engring. (fgn. assoc.), Order of Culture. Home: 3 13 10 Nishiochiai, Shinjuku-ku, Tokyo 161, Japan Office: Muto & Assocs, Shinjuku Mitsui Bldg 2 1 1, Nishishinjuku Shinjuku-ku, Tokyo 163, Japan

MUTTALIB, KALAM, lawyer; b. Cleve., Apr. 21, 1943; s. Roy and Ruby (Pitts) Mathis; m. Bashirah, Dec. 12, 1970 (div. Jan. 1977); children—Khabir, Rasool; m. Kimetta Ann Davis, Sept. 12, 1980; children: Kalam, Aliyah, Meira, Ahmed Selim. BA, Cleve. State U., 1971; JD, Case Western Res. U., 1974. Bar: Ohio 1974, U.S. Dist. Ct. (no. dist.) Ohio 1975, U.S. Ct. Appeals (6th cir.) 1980, U.S. Supreme Ct. 1980. Research technician Glidden Durkee div. of SCM Cleve., 1966-75; assoc. Carl J. Character Co. L.P.A., Cleve., 1975-78; sole practice, 1978-80, 84—; housing ct. referee Cleve. Municipal Ct., 1980-84. Editor, compiler: Cleveland Municipal Housing Court Rules, 1983; editor Vindicator, 1970; founding editor Kuwais, 1971. Mem. Big Bros. Greater Cleve., 1975, United Negro Coll. Fund, Cleve., 1983. Recipient Martin Luther King award Friends of East Side News, Cleve., 1982. Mem. NAACP, Norman S. Minor Bar Assn. (pres. 1981-82), Friends of Karamu, John Harlan Law Club (2d v.p. 1977-78), Young Lawyers Council, Cleve. Bar Assn. (bd. mem. 1976-79). Democrat. Muslim. Home: 3693 Berkeley Cleveland Heights OH 44118 Office: 3500 Terminal Tower Cleveland OH 44113

MUTZIGER-BECK, JUDY LYNN, advertising executive; b. Mitchell, S.D., Oct. 7, 1947; d. Leslie Daniel and Rita Rose (Weber) M.; m. Serge Beck, June 4, 1983. Grad. high sch., Etha, S.D.; cert. exec. sec., Nat. Coll. Bus., Rapid City, S.D., 1966. Sec. GTI Corp. Scientific Software, Denver, 1966-68; waitress, ski-bum Red Lion Inn, Vail, Colo., 1968-70, Kulm Hotel, St. Moritz, Switzerland, 1971-73; real estate agt. Paris Placement, France, 1973-75; data bank cons. World Econ. Forum, Geneva, Switzerland, 1976-82; advt. exec. Vert Pomme, Montricher, Switzerland, 1982—.

MUZENDA, SIMON VENGAI, vice president Republic of Zimbabwe; b. Gutu, Masvingo Province, Zimbabwe, Oct. 28, 1922; diploma in carpentry Marianhill Coll., South Africa, 1948; m. Maude Muzenda; 8 children. Instr., Mazenod Sch., Mayville, South Africa, 1948-50; carpenter, Bulawayo twp. of Barbourfields, from 1953, also Umvuma; co-founder Barbourfields Tenants Assn.; co-founder Nat. Democratic Party; chmn. Umvuma br., organizing sec. for Masvinso province, 1960-61, party banned, 1962; adminstrv. sec. Masvingo, Zimbabwe African People's Union, 1962, dep. organizing sec. 1st Congress Zimbabwe African Nat. Union; dep. adminstrv. sec. Zambia, 1975-76, minister fgn. affairs, 1980-81; with Zimbabwe African Nat. Liberation Army, 1977-80; minister energy and water resources Republic of Zimbabwe, from 1984, dep. prime minister, 1980-88, v.p., 1988—. Office: Office of Dep Prime Minister, Pvt Bag 7700, Harare Zimbabwe

MUZOREWA, ABEL TENDEKAYI, Zimbabwean ecclesiastic and politician; b. Old Umtali, Zimbabwe, Apr. 14, 1925; m. Margaret Muzorewa. Student Old Umtali Secondary Sch., Nyadiri United Meth. Mission, Central Meth. Coll., Fayette, Mo., Scarritt Coll., Nashville, Tenn. Pastor, Chiduku N. Circuit, 1955-57, Old Umtali Mission, 1963; dir. youth work Rhodesia Ann. Conf., 1965; joint dir. of youth work Rhodesia Christian Council, 1965; travelling sec. Student Christian Movt, 1965; resident bishop United Meth. Ch., Rhodesia, 1968—; pres. African Nat. Council, 1971-85, rep. Geneva Conf. on Rhodesia, 1976, contested Mar. 1980 election as leader of African Nat. Council; mem. Transitional Exec. Council to prepare transfer to majority rule in Rhodesia, 1978-79; prime minister of Zimbabwe Rhodesia, minister of def. and combined ops., 1979. Author: Manifesto for African National Council, 1972; Rise Up and Walk (autobiography) 1978. Recipient UN prize for outstanding achievement in human rights, 1973. Office: United Meth Ch, PO Box 8293, Causeway, Harare Zimbabwe *

MWAI, GEORGE KANGONGA, manufacturing executive; b. Central Kenya, Dec. 22, 1934; s. Richard and Zipora (Mwai) Munge; m. Annah Ngima Wanjihia Mwai, Sept. 20, 1958; children—Sam Mwai, Margaret V. Wairimu, Ivy Marjorie Nyawira, Kimutia Wanjihia, Jaine Waruguru. Student pub. schs., Kenya. Officer, Ministry of Social Services and Community Devel. and Rehab., Kenya, 1955-57; African affairs officer Aberdare County Council, Kenya, 1957-60; exec. trainee to mng. dir. Unga Ltd., Kenya, 1960-80; group mng. dir. Mercat Ltd., Nairobi, Kenya, 1980—. Mem. Kenya African Nat. Union, 1976. Fellow Brit. Inst. Mgmt., Inst. Dirs.; mem. Kenya Inst. Mgmt., Am. Mgmt. Assn., Inst. Profl Mgrs. Clubs: Muthaiga Country, Mt. Kenya Safari, Karen Country, Muthaiga Golf, Rift Valley Sports, Nyen Golf. Avocations: golf; jogging; farming. Home: Box 46964, Nairobi Kenya Office: PO Box 30096, Nairobi Kenya

MWAIKAMBO, GIBBONS, insurance company executive; b. Tukuyu, Mbeya, Tanzania, Oct. 14, 1938; s. James Elli Paddy and Agnes (Mbete) M.; m. Esther Mariki, Aug. 1967; children: James, Gwamaka, Mkundwe. MS in Econs., Friendship U., Moscow, 1967; cert. ins., Coll. of Ins., N.Y.C., 1970. With Nat. Ins. Corp., Dar-es-Salaam, Tanzania, 1970—; Chmn., dir. Tanzania Investment Bank, Dar-es-Salaam, 1970-85. Elected mem. Tanzania Parliament, Dar-es-Salaam, 1980-85. Fellow Inst. Dirs. United Kingdom. Office: National Insurance Corp, PO Box 9264 DSM, Dar es Salaam Tanzania

MWAMWENDA, TUNTUFYE SELEMANI, psychology educator; b. Mbeya, Tanzania, Apr. 14, 1945; s. Selemani Mwamwenda and Rahabu Songwe; m. Bernadette Bazarirwaki, Apr. 14, 1972; children: Escort, Anthony, Asiimwe, Eddie. BA, Spicer Coll., Poona, India, 1971; MS, SUNY, Plattsburg, 1976; MA, U. Ottawa, Can., 1978; PhD, U. Alta., Edmonton, Can., 1981. Tchr. Simbi Primary Sch., Kendu Bay, Kenya, 1967, Gendia Secondary Sch., Kendu Bay, 1967, Bugema Adventist Coll., Kampala, Uganda, 1971; Tchr. Kitante Hill Secondary Sch., Kampala, 1972-74; research asst. U. Alta., 1978-81, visiting prof., 1986—; lectr. U. Botswana, Gaborone, 1981-83; assoc. prof. U. Transkei, Umtata, 1984-86. Author: (with others) Educational Psychology from an African Perspective: An Educational Psychology for African Schools, 1986; contbr. articles to profl. jours. Mem. Brit. Psychol. Soc., Am. Psychol. Assn., Internat. Cross Cultural Psychology Assn. Adventist. Office: U Transkei, PB X1 Unitra, Umtata, Transkei Republic of South Africa

MWINYI, ALI HASSAN, president United Republic of Tanzania; b. Dar es Salaam, Tanzania, May 8, 1925; s. Hassan and Asha Sheikh M.; m. Mtumwa Yusuf, Mar. 14, 1947 (div. Aug. 1958); 1 child, Asha; m. Siti Abdala, Sept. 29, 1960; 1 child, Fatma. Ed. Tchrs.' Coll., Dole, Zanzibar, 1943-44. Prin. Perm. Sec. Edn., Zanzibar, 1963-64; asst. gen. mgr. Zanzibar State Trading Corp., 1964; minister of state, United Republic of Tanzania, 1970, minister of health, 1972, minister home affairs; former Tanzanian ambassador to Egypt; minister natural resources and tourism United Republic of Zanzibar, 1982-83, minister of state attached to v.p. office for union affairs, 1983-84; v.p. United Republic of Tanzania, 1984-85, pres., 1985—, also chmn. Revolutionary Council Zanzibar, from 1984, pres. Zanzibar, 1984-85. Muslim. Office: Office of the Pres, Dar es Salaam Tanzania *

MYAMBO, KATHLEEN ANN, psychologist, educator; b. Pitts., May 6, 1943; d. Guido and Dorothy Marie (Picelli) Meneghini; m. Simon Myambo, Aug. 1, 1968; children—Melissa Tandiwe, Temai Tongai. B.A. cum laude, Pa. State U., 1964, M.S., 1965; Ph.D., Syracuse U., 1978. Asst. prof. psychology U. Malawi, Blantyre, 1968-72; psychologist Rome Devel. Ctr., N.Y., 1974-77, Syracuse Devel. Ctr., N.Y., 1977-78; unit chief Skills for Living Program Hutchings Psychiat. Ctr., Syracuse, 1978-80; sr. lectr. psychology U. Zambia, Lusaka, 1980-82; assoc. prof. psychology U. Zimbabwe, 1982—; mem. faculty Onondaga Community Coll., 1973-74. Contbr. articles to profl. jours. Mem. Am. Psychol. Assn., Phi Beta Kappa, Phi Kappa Phi, Pi Gamma Mu, Alpha Lambda Delta. Office: U Zimbabwe, Dept Psychology, PO Box MP 167, Harare Zimbabwe

MYEROWITZ, P. DAVID, cardiac surgeon; b. Balt., Jan. 18, 1947; s. Joseph Robert and Merry (Brown) M.; B.S., U. Md., 1966, M.D., 1970; M.S., U. Minn., 1977; m. Susan Karen Macks, June 18, 1967 (div.); children—Morris Brown, Elissa Suzanne, Ian Matthew. Intern in surgery U. Minn., Mpls., 1970-71, resident in surgery, 1971-72, 74-77; resident in cardiothoracic surgery U. Chgo., 1977-79; practice medicine, specializing in cardiovascular surgery, Madison, Wis., 1979—; asst. prof. thoracic and cardiovascular surgery U. Wis., Madison, 1979-85, assoc. prof., 1985, chief sect. cardiac transplantation, 1984-85, Karl P. Klassen prof., chief thoracic and cardiovascular surgeon Ohio State Univ. and Hosps., Columbus, 1985—. Served with USPHS, 1972-74. Mem. ACS, Am. Coll. Cardiology, Assn. for Acad. Surgery, Soc. Univ. Surgeons, Soc. Thoracic Surgeons, ASAIO, Am. Coll. Chest Physicians, Am. Heart Assn., Internat. Soc. Heart Transplantation, Internat. Soc. Cardiovascular Surgery, Am. Assn. Thoracic Surgeons. Jewish. Contbr. articles to profl. jours. Office: Ohio State Univ Hosps Doan N-825 Columbus OH 43210

MYERS, ALFRED FRANTZ, state education official; b. Crooked Creek State Park, Pa., Feb. 19, 1936; s. Jacob Alfred Jr. and Ida Gertrude (Schaeffer) M.; BA, Lehigh U., 1958, MA, 1966; postgrad. George Peabody Coll., 1971-72. Instr., Grand River Acad., Austinburg, Ohio, 1966, Culver Mil. Acad. (Ind.), 1966-68, Kiskiminetas Springs Sch., Saltsburg, Pa., 1968-71; asst. prof. social studies Ind. State U., Terre Haute, 1972-73; div. trainer Ency. Britannica, Rochester, N.Y., 1973-75; mgr. Rupp's, Kittanning, Pa., 1976-77; criminal justice system planner Pa. Commn. on Crime and Delinquency, Harrisburg, 1977-80; research assoc. Pa. Dept. Edn., Harrisburg, Pa., 1980—. Social work Dominican Rep., 1958. Served to 1st lt. with USAF, 1958-63. Mem. AAUP, Nat. Council Social Studies, Am. Acad. Polit. and Social Sci., Am. Evaluation Assn., Am. Sociol. Assn., Assn. for Supervision and Curriculum Devel., Am. Ednl. Research Assn., Am. Hist. Assn., Caribbean Studies Assn., Assn. Am. Geographers, Am. Assn. for Adult and Continuing Edn., Am. Polit. Sci. Assn., Am. Statis. Assn., Acad. Polit. Sci., Council Basic Edn., Nat. Council Geog. Edn., Mid. States Council for Social Studies (pres. 1987-88), Nat. Braille Assn., ACLU, People for Am. Way., Am. Legion, Orgn. Am. Historians, Am. Geog. Soc., Phi Beta Kappa, Phi Delta Kappa. Home: PO Box 11604 Harrisburg PA 17108-1604

MYERS, CAROLE ANN, health transportation service executive; b. Henderson, Ky., June 14, 1938; d. James Newton and Rosalene Alberta (Eakins) Wade; m. Lawrence William Myers, Dec. 28, 1957 (dec. Feb. 1980); children: Patti Myers Crisler, Nancy Myers Allen, Sandra Myers Kowalski, Mark William. Cert., St. Francis Hosp., 1971; student, Butler U., 1979. Cert. emergency med. tech., paramedic. Pres., chief exec. officer Myers Ambulance Service, Greenwood, Ind., 1966—. Bd. dirs. Greenwood Sr. Citizens Ctr.; mem. Rep. Sen. Inner Circle, Washington, 1984. Named Disting. Hoosier by Gov. of Ind., 1984. Mem. Ind. Ambulance Assn. (pres. 1983-85, treas. 1986—), Ind. Emergency Med. Services Commn., Am. Ambulance Assn. (sec. 1983-84, treas. 1985-86, v.p. 1987—, pres.-elect, woman of yr. 1983), Greater Greenwood C. of C. (bd. dirs., sec. 1988).. Home: 150 N Madison Ave Greenwood IN 46142 Office: Myers Ambulance Service Inc 325 W Wiley St Greenwood IN 46142

MYERS, EUGENE EKANDER, art consultant; b. Grand Forks, N.D., May 5, 1914; s. John Q. and Hattye Jane (Ekander) M.; m. Florence Hutchinson Ritchie, Sept. 9, 1974. BS in Edn., U. N.D., 1936, MS in Edn., 1938; postgrad., U. Oreg., 1937; MA, Northwestern U., 1940, Columbia U., 1947; grad., Advanced Mgmt. Program, Harvard U., 1953; cert., Cambridge (Eng.) U., 1958; postgrad., U. Md., 1958-61, Oxford (Eng.) U., 1964; diploma, various mil. schs. Student asst. U. N.D., 1935-36, instr. summer sessions, 1936, 37, asst., 1936-37; prof., head dept. N.D. Tchrs. Coll., 1938-40; instr. Columbia U. Tchrs. Coll., 1940-41; vis. prof. U. Vt., summers, 1941, 42; commd. 1st lt. USAAF, 1942, advanced through grades to col., 1951; dir. personnel plans and tng. Hdqrs. Air Force Systems Command Washington, 1959-60; dir. personnel research and long-range plans Hdqrs. Air Force Systems Command 1960-62; head dept. internat. relations Air War Coll., Air U. Maxwell AFB, Ala., 1962-63; dir. curriculum, dean (Air War Coll., Air U.) 1963-65; dir. res. affairs Hdqrs. Air Res. Personnel Center Denver, 1965-66; ret. 1966; dean Corcoran Sch. Art, Washington, 1966-70; founder Corcoran Sch. Art Abroad, Leeds, Eng., 1967; v.p. mgmt. Corcoran Gallery Art, Washington, 1970-72; vis. art dir. Washington, also Palm Beach, Fla.; art cons. 1972—; adv. Washington chpt. Nat. Soc. Arts and Letters.; bd. assos. Artists Equity. Author: (with Paul E. Barr) Creative Lettering, 1938, (with others) The Subject Fields in General Education, 1939, Applied Psychology, 1940; contbr. articles, reports to mags. and profl. pubs. Bd. dirs. Columbia (Md.) Inst. Art; bd. dirs. World Arts Found., N.Y., Court Art Center, Montgomery, Ala. and Palm Beach, Fla., Order of Lafayette, Boston, English-Speaking Union, Palm Beach, mem. Hamilton St. Vol. Fire Dept. and Lit. Soc., Balt., Pundits, Palm Beach. Recipient Sioux award U. N.D., 1978. Mem. Internat. Communication Assn. (hon.), U. N.D. Alumni Assn. (pres. Washington chpt. 1959), Mil. Classics Soc., Titanic Soc., Mil. Order Carabao, Order of St. John of Jerusalem, Knightly Assn. St. George the Martyr, Co. Mil. Historians, Mil. Order World Wars, Ancient Order United Workmen, Saint Andrews Soc., Clan Donnachaidh (Perthshire, Scotland), Soc. Friends St. Andrews (Scotland) U., Delta Omicron Epsilon, Lambda Chi Alpha, Delta Phi Delta, Phi Delta Kappa, Phi Alpha Theta. Republican. Presbyterian. Clubs: Union (Manchester, Eng.) (hon.); Royal Scottish Automobile (Glasgow, Scotland); Royal Overseas (London); New (Edinburgh, Scotland) (assoc.); Army and Navy (Washington), Nat. Aviation (Washington), City Tavern (Washington), Harvard Business School (Washington); Army and Navy Country (Arlington, Va.); Metropolitan (N.Y.C.), Wings (N.Y.C.), Explorers (N.Y.C.) (fellow), Harvard (N.Y.C.); Minneapolis; Everglades (Palm Beach, Fla.), Beach (Palm Beach, Fla.), Sailfish of Fla. (Palm Beach, Fla.); Fairmont (W.Va.) Field Country, Lions; Little (Gulf

Stream, Fla.). Home: 1 Royal Palm Way Palm Beach FL 33480 also: 3320 Volta Pl NW Washington DC 20007

MYERS, JAMES OLEON, banker, insurance and leasing company executive; b. Emporia, Kans., Aug. 25, 1945; s. John Edgar and Mildred Fontaine (Perkins) M.; m. Carolyn Rae Colaw, Sept. 17, 1965 (div. 1966); m. Carole Ann Perkins, Nov. 9, 1974; 1 stepchild, Kelli Renea Sandburg; 1 adopted child, Christine Lynn Myers. Student gen. bus. Emporia State U., 1965; grad. with honors Alexander Hamilton Inst., Tulsa, 1970; diploma Sch. Ins., U. Kans., 1977; diploma comml. lending U. Okla., 1982. Cert. consumer credit exec. Br. mgr. Pacific fin. loans div. Transam. Corp., Los Angeles, 1965-72; gen. sales mgr. Emporia Volkswagen, Inc., 1973-75; resident v.p. Kans., Ins. Enterprises, Inc., St. Louis, 1975-77; asst. v.p. Admire Bank and Trust, Emporia, 1977-79, v.p., 1979-81, pres., chief exec. officer, trust officer, 1981—, dir., 1981—; pres., chief exec. officer, Admire BancShares Inc., 1987; dir. Kans. Devel. Credit Corp., Topeka, Am. Fin. Services, Inc., Emporia. Adminstrv. bd., 1st United Methodist Ch., Emporia, 1983—, trustee, 1987—; adminstr. corp. relations United Way of Emporia, 1979—; bd. dirs. Lyon County chpt. Am. Cancer Soc.; state dir. Kans. Small Bus. Devel. Network, 1985. Commd. adm. Navy of state of Nebr. Col. Kans. Calvary. Mem. Kans. Bankers Assn., Kans. Consumer Credit Assn. (dir. 1983—), Internat. Consumer Credit Assn. (exec. mem.), Kans. C. of C. and Industry (econ. devel. council 1984—), Emporia C. of C. (ambassador 1983—, vice chmn. Chmn.'s Club 1984, bd. dirs. 1984—). Republican. Lodges: Lions (dir. Emporia 1973-75), Rotary, Elks (treas. 1967), Eagles. Home: PO Box 19 Emporia KS 66801-0019 Office: Admire Bank and Trust PO Box 1047 Emporia KS 66801-1047

MYERS, NORMAN, environmental and development consulting company executive, economist, ecologist, educator; b. Whitewell, Eng., Aug. 24, 1934; s. John and Gladys (Haworth) M.; m. Dorothy M. Halliman, Dec. 11, 1965; children: Malindi Elizabeth, Mara Rosalind. BA, Oxford U., Eng., 1957, MA, 1959; PhD, U. Calif., Berkeley, 1973. Dist. officer Kenya Adminstrn., 1958-61; tchr. high sch. Nairobi, Kenya, 1961-66; freelance writer, photographer, lectr., broadcaster on conservation African Wetlands 1966-69; surveyor of leopard and cheetah Internat. Union Conservation Nature and Natural Resources/World Wildlife Fund, 1972-73; sr. assoc. Gland, Switzerland, 1986—; wildlife and parks officer for Africa FAO, 1974-75; mem. project on threatened species and genetic resources Rockefeller Bros. Fund, 1976-78; surveyor on conversion rates in tropical moist forests U.S. Nat. Acad. Scis., 1978-79; policy synthesizer World Bank, Kenya, 1979; project on priority-ranking strategy for threatened species World Wildlife Fund, 1980-81; prin. Norman Myers Consultancy Ltd., Oxford, Eng., 1981—; cons., lectr., adj. prof. various univs.; sr. adviser World Commn. Environ. and Devel., Geneva, 1985-87; vis. fellow World Resources Inst., Washington, 1986—. Author: The Long African Day, 1972, The Sinking Ark, 1979, A Wealth of Wild Species, 1983, numerous others; contbg. author, editor numerous profl. jours, also newspapers and mags., including Internat. Wildlife, Jour. Forest Ecology and Mgmt. Mem. council African Wildlife Found., Soc. Conservation Biology; bd. dirs. Ctr. Conservation Biology. Recipient Gold medal World Wildlife Fund Internat., 1983, N.Y. Zool. Soc., 1986, Spl. Achievement award Sierra Club, 1987, Disting. Achievement award Soc. Conservation Biology, 1987. Mem. Internat. Assn. Ecology, Internat. Soc. Tropical Ecology, Internat. Soc. Tropical Foresters, Internat. Soc. Social Econs., Am. Assn. Environ. and Resource Economists, Internat. Assn. Agrl. Economists, Internat. Council Environ. Law, Nat. Assn. Sci. Writers U.S., Assn. Brit. Sci. Writers, Internat. Platform Assn. Address: Upper Meadow Old Rd, Headington Oxford OX3 8SZ, England

MYERS, PHILLIP FENTON, business executive; b. Cleve., June 24, 1935; s. Max I. and Rebecca (Rosenbloom) M.; m. Hope Gail Strum, Aug. 13, 1961. B.I.E., Ohio State U., 1958, M.B.A., 1960; D.B.A., Harvard U., 1966. Staff indsl. engr. Procter & Gamble Co., Cin., 1958; sr. cons. Cresap, McCormack & Paget, N.Y.C., 1960-61; staff assoc. Mitre Corp., Bedford, Mass., 1961; cons. Systems Devel. Corp., Santa Monica, Calif., 1963-64; corp. asst. long range planning Electronic Specialty Co., Los Angeles, 1966-68; chmn. Atek Industries, 1968-72; pres. Myers Fin. Corp., 1973—, Steel Fuels Corp., 1976-77; chmn. Amvid Communication Services, Inc., 1975-79, Gen. Hydrogen Corp. Am., 1976-79, Omni Resources Devel. Corp., 1979-83; chmn., pres. Am. Internat. Mining Co., Inc., 1979-83; pres. Whitehall Internat. Mgmt. Co., Inc., 1982 , Global Bond Mktg Services, Inc., 1987—; gen. ptnr. Pacific Internat. Devel. Co., 1985—; pres. Global Bond Mktg. Services, Ltd., 1987—; founding dir. Warner Ctr. Bank, 1980-83; lectr. bus. adminstrn. U. So. Calif., Los Angeles, 1967-74; prof. Pepperdine U. Grad. Sch. Bus. Adminstrn., 1974-81. Trustee, treas. Chamber Symphony Soc. Calif., 1971-78; pub. safety commr. City of Hidden Hills, Calif., 1977-83, chmn., 1982-83; co-chmn. budget adv. com. Las Virgenas Sch. Dist., 1983-86; mem. Mayor's Blue Ribbon Fin. Com., 1981-82; mem. dean's select adv. com. Coll. Engring., Ohio State U., 1984—. Served to capt. USAF, 1958-60. Ford Found. fellow, 1961-64. Mem. Harvard Bus. Sch. Assn., Ohio State Alumni Assn. Club: Harvard of So. Calif. (bd. dirs. 1970-74, treas. 1971-73). Home and Office: 5819 Fitzpatrick Rd Suite 1000 Calabasas CA 91302

MYERS, ROBERT EUGENE, educator, writer; b. Los Angeles, Jan. 15, 1924; s. Harold Eugene and Margaret (Anawalt) M.; A.B., U. Calif., Berkeley, 1955; M.A. (Crown-Zellerbach fellow), Reed Coll., 1960; Ed.D., U. Ga., 1968; m. Patricia A. Tazer, Aug. 17, 1956; children—Edward E., Margaret A., Hal R., Karen I. Employed in phonograph record business, 1946-54; tchr. elem. sch., Calif., Oreg., Minn., 1954-61; research asst. U. Minn., 1961-62; asst. prof. Augsburg Coll., 1962-63, U. Oreg., 1963-66; elem. tchr., Eugene, Oreg., 1966-67; asso. prof. U. Victoria, 1968-70; asso. research prof. Oreg. System of Higher Edn., 1970-73; film maker, producer ednl. filmstrips, books and recs., 1973-77; with Oreg. Dept. Edn., Salem, 1977-81, learning resources specialist, 1977-81, with Linn-Benton Edn. Service Dist., Albany, Oreg., 1982—. Mem. exec. bd. Nat. Assn. for Gifted Children, 1974-77. Served with U.S. Mcht. Marine, 1944-45. Recipient CINE Golden Eagle award Council Internat. Non-theatrical Events, 1973. Mem. Internat. Reading Assn. Democrat. Author: (with E. Paul Torrance) Creative Learning and Teaching (Pi Lambda Theta award 1971), 1970, Can You Imagine?, 1965, Invitations to Thinking and Doing, 1964, Invitations to Speaking and Writing Creatively, 1965, Plots, Puzzles, and Ploys, 1966, For Those Who Wonder, 1966; Timberwood Tales, Vol. II, 1977; Wondering, 1984, Imagining, 1985. Home: 440 NW Elks Dr Corvallis OR 97330 Office: 905 4th Ave Albany OR 97321

MYERS, RODMAN NATHANIEL, lawyer; b. Detroit, Oct. 27, 1920; s. Isaac Rodman and Fredericka (Hirschman) M.; m. Jeanette Polisei, Mar. 19, 1957; children: Jennifer Sue, Rodman Jay. BA, Wayne State U., 1941; LLB, U. Mich., 1943. Bar: Mich. 1943, U.S. Supreme Ct. 1962. Agt. IRS, Detroit, 1943; ptnr. Butzel, Keidan, Simon, Myers & Graham, Detroit, 1943—; bd. dirs. Mich. Nat. Bank North-Metro. Bd. dirs. United Community Services of Met. Detroit, 1978—, v.p., 1981—, chmn. social services div., 1982—; bd. dirs. Children's Ctr. of Wayne County (Mich.), 1963—, pres., 1969-72; founding mem., trustee Detroit Sci. Ctr.; pres., trustee Mich. chpt. Leukemia Soc. Am., nat. trustee; commr. Detroit Mcpl. Parking Authority, 1963-71; former trustee Temple Beth El, Birmingham; former trustee Jewish Vocat. Service and Community Workshop. Mem. ABA, State Bar Mich. (chmn. atty. discipline panel, past vice chmn. unauthorized practice of law com., past mem. character and fitness com.), Detroit Bar Assn. Clubs: Renaissance, Fairlane. Home: 3833 Lakeland Ln Bloomfield Hills MI 48013 Office: 2490 1st Nat Bldg Detroit MI 48226

MYERS, SAMUEL, lawyer; b. Phila., Oct. 1, 1934; s. Saul and Mollie (Levin) M.; m. Myrna Reva Norwitz, Mar. 11, 1962; children: Caren Margo, Claudia Emmanuelle. BS in Econs., U. Pa., 1956; JD, Yale U., 1960. Bar: N.Y. 1961; conseil juridique, France 1966. Assoc. Kaye, Scholer, Fierman, Hays & Handler, N.Y.C., 1961-70; head Paris office Kaye, Scholer, Fierman, Hays & Handler, 1966-69; European counsel, v.p. legal affairs Gulf & Western Inc., Rome and Paris, 1971-84; European counsel Paul, Weiss, Rifkind, Wharton & Garrison, Paris, 1985-88; sole practice Paris, 1988—; bd. dirs. Lupac S.A., Brussels. Author various handbooks; editor Yale Law Rev., 1958-60. Chmn. Am. sect. Lycee Internat., St. Germain en Laye, France, 1982-84; bd. dirs. Union Liberale Israelite de France, Paris, 1981-85. Mem. N.Y.C. Bar Assn., N.Y. County Bar Assn., N.Y. State Bar Assn., ABA, Internat. Bar Assn., Assn. Conseils Juridiques. Democrat. Jewish. Clubs: American, Yale, Wharton (Paris). Lodge: Masons. Home: 18 Ave de Louveciennes, 78170 La Celle Saint Cloud France Office: 25 Quai Voltaire, 75007 Paris France

MYERS, WILLIAM OSGOOD, thoracic and cardiovascular surgeon; b. Hastings, Nebr., Aug. 19, 1929; s. Joy Uberto and Lena C. (Osgood) M.; B.A., Hastings Coll., 1951; M.D., Northwestern U., 1955; m. Lois Mae Payne, Dec. 26, 1952; children—Jessica, Wendell, Inez, John, Michael. Intern, City Detroit Receiving Hosp., 1955-56, resident in anesthesiology, 1956-57; gen. practice medicine, Blue Hill, Nebr., 1959-62; cons. in anesthesia, anesthesiologist, Mary Lanning Meml. Hosp., Hastings, Nebr., Webster County Hosp., Red Cloud, Nebr., and Smith County Hosp., Smith Center, Kans., 1959-62; surg. resident Sacred Heart Hosp., Yankton, S.D., 1962-65; instr. anatomy U. S.D. Med. Sch., Vermillion, S.D., 1963-65; resident in gen. surgery U. Kans. Med. Center, Kans. City, 1965-66; fellow thoracic and cardiovascular surgery U. Kans. Med. Center, 1966-68; cardiovascular surgeon Marshfield Clinic, Marshfield, Wis. and St. Joseph's Hosp., Marshfield, 1968—, chmn. sect. thoracic and cardiovascular surgery, 1972-76, chmn. dept surgery, 1974-79, asst. chmn. surg. services, 1981-85; clin. assoc. prof. surgery U. Wis., 1981—; prin. investigator Coronary Artery Surgery Study, Nat. Heart, Lung and Blood Inst., 1973—; bd. dirs. Marshfield Med. Found., 1978-84 . Active Boy Scouts Am.; mem. respiratory therapy adv. com. Midstate Tech. Inst., Marshfield, 1975—; elder 1st Presbyn. Ch., Marshfield, 1974—; chmn. research com. Marshfield Med. Found., 1985—; mem. council Wis. Surgical Assn. Council Wis. Chpt. ACS, 1987—; council on Cardiovascular Surgery AHA . Served with USAF, 1957-59. Diplomate Am. Bd. Surgery, Am. Bd. Thoracic Surgery. Mem. Wis., Wood County med. socs, AMA, Wis. Surg. Soc., A.C.S., Am. Coll. Cardiology, Am. Thoracic Soc., Am. Assn. Thoracic Surgery, Frederick A. Coller Surg. Soc., Central Surg. Assn., Western Surg. Assn. Contbr. articles to profl. jours. Home: 1110 Balsam Ave Marshfield WI 54449 Office: 1000 N Oak Ave Marshfield WI 54449

MYERSON, GERALD, mathematician; b. N.Y.C., July 10, 1951; arrived in Australia, 1987; s. Louis and Betty (Wolf) M.; m. Teresa Petrzelka, June 23, 1985; 1 child, Sarah. AB, Harvard U., 1972; MS, Stanford U, 1975; PhD, U. Mich., 1977. Asst. prof. SUNY, Buffalo, 1977-85, S.W. Tex. State U., 1986; lectr. Macquarie U., North Ryde, Australia, 1987—; vis. asst. prof. U. B.C., Vancouver, 1982-83, U. Tex., 1985-86. Contbr. articles to prof. jours. Faculty research fellow State SUNY, 1978, 82. Mem. Am. Mathematical Soc., Mathmatical Assn. Am., Australian Mathematical Soc. Democrat. Judaism. Office: Macquarie U, Sch Math, North Ryde 2109, Australia

MYHRMAN, BO OLOF WALTER, banker; b. Gothenburg, Sweden, July 16, 1936; s. Walter and Nada (Holmquist) M.; m. Gunnel Elisabeth Nyman, Sept. 11, 1960; children—Elisabeth, Olof. Dist. atty. degree, U. Stockholm, 1959; police commr. degree, Nat. Swedish Police Coll., 1960; B.Law Degree, U. Stockholm, 1961. Asst. dist. atty. Office of Pub. Prosecutor, County of Malmohus, Sweden, 1960-62; asst. judge Dist. Ct., Helsingborg, Sweden, 1962-64; bank lawyer, sr. bank lawyer Skandinaviska Banken, Gothenburg, 1965-72; asst. v.p. and v.p. Skandinaviska Enskilda Banken, Gothenburg, 1973-76, gen. mgr., gen. counsel, 1977—, mem. mgmt. com., 1977—, sr. v.p., 1980—; dir. Tor Line AB, Gothenburg, 1983—, Dickson Constant Nordiska AB, Gothenburg, 1983—, Hefa AB, 1987—; dir., sec. Halmstad Group Found., Sweden, 1976—; mem. European adv. council Salzburg Seminar Am. Studies, 1976-81. Mem. Internat. Bar Assn., Internat. Fiscal Assn. Avocations: languages; history; genealogy; travel. Home: Husfrejagatan 3, S442 39 Kungalv Sweden Office: Skandinaviska Enskilda Banken, Ostra Hamngatan 24, S405 04 Gothenburg Sweden

MYKKELTVEIT, JOHANNES, mathematician, engineer; b. Evanger, Hordaland, Norway, Dec. 28, 1941; s. Jørgen and Anna (Norheim) Mykkeltveit. MS, U. Bergen, Norway, 1967, PhD, 1977. Sci. research asst. U. Bergen, 1968-71, 72-78; cons. Kommunedata Vestlandet, Bergen, 1978-81; research engr. Rogaland Research Inst., Stavanger, Norway, 1981—. Contbr. articles on computers and information to profl. jours. Research fellow Calif. Inst. Tech., Pasadena, 1971-72. Mem. Soc. Indsl. and Applied Math. Office: Rogaland Research Inst, Ullandhaug, N4004 Stavanger Norway

MYLONAKIS, STAMATIOS GREGORY, chemist; b. Athens, Greece, Aug. 18, 1937; came to U.S., 1963; s. Gregory and Vassiliki (Charalampopoulos) M.; m. Pamela H. Morton, May 15, 1965 (dec. Mar. 1978); 1 son, Gregory John. BS in Chemistry, U. Athens, 1961; MS in Phys. Organic Chemistry, Ill. Inst. Tech., 1964; PhD in Phys. Organic Chemistry, Mich. State U., 1971. Research scientist Brookhaven Nat. Lab., Upton, N.Y., 1965-68; instr. U. Calif., Berkeley, 1971-73; group leader Rohm and Haas Co., Springhouse, Pa., 1973-76; supr. DeSoto Inc., Des Plaines, Ill., 1976-79; staff scientist Borg-Warner Chems., Inc. Des Plaines, 1979-81, research and devel. mgr., 1981-87, dept. head EniChem Ams. Inc., Princeton, N.J., 1988— . Author numerous research papers; patentee in polymer synthesis and applications fields. Mem. tech. adv. bd. Case Western Res. U., PhD thesis adv. com. Lehigh U. Served as lt., Greek Army, 1961-63. Ill. Inst. Tech. fellow, 1963-64; Mich. State U. fellow, 1968-71. Mem. Am. Chem. Soc., Sigma Xi. Office: EniChem Ams Inc 2000 Princeton Pk Monmouth Junction NJ 08852

MYLONAS, THEODORE P., banker; b. Athens, Greece, Nov. 19, 1947; s. Pavlos and Helen (Antoniou) M.; m. Nikoletta Ioakim, June 23, 1982. BA in Polit. Sci., U. Athens, 1973, BA in Pub. Adminstrn., 1982. With P. Mylonas & Co., Athens, 1961-63; messenger Am. Express Bank, Athens, 1963-65, deposit clk., 1965-67, loan clk., 1969-70; asst. head deposits dept. Am. Express Bank, 1970-72, asst. head loans dept., 1972-74, head loans dept., 1974-78, asst. br. mgr., 1978-79, corp. account officer, 1979-81, br. mgr., sr. corp. account officer, 1981—. Served with Greek mil., 1967-69. Scholar State Found., 1972, Ministry of Labor, 1972. Club: Marine (Piraeus). Home: 8 Saki Karagiorga Str, Glyfada 16675, 153 41 Athens Greece Office: Am Express Bank Ltd, 13 Skouze St, 185-35 Piraeus Greece

MYLVAGANAM, KANAGA SABA PATHY, electrical engineering scientist; b. Jaffna, Sri Lanka, Aug. 31, 1951; arrived in Norway, 1983; s. Murugesu and Siva Anantha Nayagi (Thiru Gnana Sampanthar) M.; m. Haima Chellappah, Nov. 2, 1983; children: Janani, Thulasi. B.Sc. with honors in Engring., U. Sri Lanka, 1974; Diploma in Engring., Tech. U. Berlin, 1978, Doctorate in Engring., 1986. Chartered engr., chartered physicist. Asst. lectr. U. Sri Lanka, Moratuwa, Colombo, 1974-76; tutor Tech. U. Berlin, Fed. Republic Germany, 1977-78, sci. and research fellow, 1978-83; sr. scientist, project leader Christian Michelsen Inst., Bergen-Fantoft, Norway, 1983—; cons. to industry, oil firms. Contbr. articles to profl. jours. Friedrich Naumann Stiftung scholar Fed. Republic Germany, 1977-78; recipient travel scholarship to U.S., Norwegian Sci. Research Council, 1987. Mem. Instn. Elec. Engrs. London, IEEE (sr.), Internat. Soc. for Optical Engring., Inst. Physics (London), Am. Math. Soc., Soc. Indsl. and Applied Math., N.Y. Acad. Scis., Verein Deutscher Elektrotechniker, Deutsche Gesellschaft fuer Sonnenenergie., Norske Sivilingeniores Forening. Hindu. Avocations: photography; paintings; languages; archaeology. Home: Nordasvegen 183, N5041 Bergen-Nordas Norway Office: Christian Michelsen Inst, Dept Sci and Tech, Fantoftvegen 38, N-5036 Bergen-Fantoft Norway

MYRDAL, JAN, author; b. Stockholm, July 19, 1927; 2 children. D.Litt. (hon.), Upsala (N.J.) Coll., 1980. Columnist, Stockholms-Tidningen, 1963-66, Aftonbladet, 1966-72; chmn., pub. Folket i Bild/Kulturfront, 1971-72, columnist, 1972—. Author: Hemkomst, 1954; Jubelvar, 1955; Att bli och vara, 1956; Badrumskranen, 1957; Karriä r, 1975; playwright: Folkets Hus, 1953; Moraliteter, 1967; Garderingar, 1969; B. Olsen, 1972; (films) Myglaren, 1966; Hjalparen, 1968; Balzac or the triumphs of realism, 1975; (TV documentaries) Democratic Kampuchea, 1978-79; Guerilla Base Area of Democratic Kampuchea, 1979; China, 1979; 13 films on history of polit. caricature, 1982; (in English) Report from a Chinese Village, 1965; Chinese Journey, 1965; Confessions of a Disloyal European, 1968; Angkor: as essay on art and imperialism, 1970; China: the Revolution Continued, 1971; Gates to Asia, 1971; Albania Defiant, 1976; The Silk Road, 1979; China Notebook 1975-78, 1979; Return to a Chinese Village, 1984; India Waits, 1984. *

MYRÉN, PER-OLOF, infosystems specialist, director; b. Stockholm, May 21, 1952; s. Bengt Olof and Ingrid (Wikner) M.; m. Birgitta Korfitsen, June 27, 1980. BEE, Royal Inst. Tech., Stockholm, 1976; MBA, Stockholm U., 1977. Dir., owner Beslutsmodeller AB, Stockholm, 1977—; ptnr. Digitech Computersysteme GmBH, Vienna, Austria, 1987; com. mem. LKD Computer Supplier Orgn., 1984—. Served as sgt. Swedish Marine Corps, 1978. Office: Beslutsmodeller AB, PO Box 681, S-131 00 Nacka Sweden

MYSLOBODSKY, MICHAEL S., psychology, neurology educator; b. Vilna, Poland, Jan. 2, 1937; came to Israel, 1973; s. Simon and Paula (Glick) M.; m. Alexandra Parmet, Oct. 6, 1960. M.D. summa cum laude, Charkow Med. Sch., USSR, 1960; Ph.D. (C.Sci), Moscow Inst. of Higher Nervous Activity, 1965, D.Sc., 1971. Resident Neuropsychiatry Hosp. USSR, 1960-62; jr. research asst. to sr. researcher Inst. Higher Nervous Activity and Neurophysiology, Moscow, 1962-73; assoc. prof. dept. psychology Tel-Aviv U., Ramat Aviv, Israel, 1974-78, prof., dir. psychobiology research unit, 1978—; vis. scientist NIMH, Bethesda, Md., 1985-87. Editorial bd. Internat. Jour. Psychophysiology, 1983—. Co-author: Seizure Acitivity, 1970; author: Hypersynchronous Activity of the Brain, 1973; Petit Mal Epilepsy, 1976. Editor; Hemisyndromes, 1983.; editor: (with A. Mirsky) Elements of Petit Mal Epilepsy, 1988. Contbr. articles to profl. jours. Mem. Israel Med. Assn., Psychobiol. Soc. Israel, Soc. Neuroscis. U.S. (fgn.), Academia Rodinensis Pro Remediatione.

MYSYROWICZ, ANDRÉ, physicist; b. Luck, Poland, Feb. 17, 1939; came to Switzerlnd, 1940; s. Zbigniew and Laure (de Chelminska) M.; m. Clotilde Ferrand, June 24, 1972; children: Constance, Ladislas, Rose. Degree in physics Inst. Tech., Zurich, 1963; PhD, U. Strasbourg, France, 1968. Maître de recherches CNRS, Paris, 1972-84, dir. research, 1984—; vis. scientist U. Calif.-Berkeley, 1973-74, U. Ind., Bloomington, 1981-82; vis. prof. ISSP, Tokyo, 1980, 87, Brown U., 1986; adj. prof. Optical Scis. Ctr., Tucson. Contbr. numerous articles to sci. jours. Mem. Optical Soc. Am., Am. Phys. Soc., SFP. Roman Catholic. Avocations: skiing, tennis, music. Home: 15 rue Clement Marot, 75008 Paris France Office: GPS, Ecole Normale Supè, rieure 2 place Jussieu, 75005 Paris France also: ENSTA, Ecole Polytechnique, Palaiseau France

MYTTON, DAVID ROBERT, metallurgic engineer; b. Rickmansworth, Eng., Feb. 9, 1928; s. Reginald and Violet Marwood (Troughton) M.; m. Stephne Von Backström Bosman, Dec. 28, 1954; children: John, Richard, Caroline. Student, Camborne Sch. of Mines, Cornwall, Eng. Sr. v.p. LCMC Philippines, 1966-76; mng. dir. DM & Assocs., Philippines, 1976-77; cons. engr. RCM Lusaka Zambia, 1977-79, Philipp Bros. N.Y., N.Y.C., 1979-82, Philippine Govt., 1982-86; gen. mgr. Zambia Engring. Service Ltd. (now Techpro), Zambia, Eng., 1986-88; bd. dirs. Enterprise Ashford, Yts Kent, Itec Ashford, Cotechnik. Fellow Instn. of Mining and Metallurgy. Home: Quince Cottage, Bilsington Ashford Kent, England TN25 7J2 Office: Techpro, International House, Dover Place TN23 1EX, England

MZWINILA, MAURICE OARABILE, electrical engineer, computer engineer, consultant; b. Tonota, June 20, 1951; s. Daniel and Joyce (Monei) M.; m. Nosho Mirandah Mphoeng, Nov. 13, 1975; children: Chewingie Kefentse, Kebuileng Hayden, Kutlwano Maurice. Student Norwood Tech. Coll., London, 1969-70, Derby (Eng.) Dist. Coll. Art and Tech., 1970-73; B.S. in Elec. Engring. magna cum laude, N.C. A&T State U., Greensboro, N.C., 1983. Asst. mgr. Everglo Electric, Francistown, Botswana, 1973-74, maintenance electrician Water Utilities Corp., Shashe, Botswana, 1974-75, stores supr., buyer Botswana Power Corp., Gaborone, Botswana, 1975-79; parts mgr. Motor Distbrs., Gaborone, 1984-85; engr. Botswana Vaccine Inst., Gaborone, 1985-86, dep. chief engr., 1986-87, cons. engr. A.R. Edwards and Assocs., Gaborne, 1988— . Mem. IEEE, Eta Kappa Nu, Tau Alpha Tau, Phi Sigma Eta. Mormon. Avocations: computer programming; observation of our environment; reading.

NAADIMUTHU, GOVINDASAMI, industrial engineering educator; b. Sirkali, India, Aug. 9, 1947; s. Ganapathi Govindasami and Saraswathi Bala Mudaliar; m. Amirtha Doraiswamy Naadimuthu, Aug. 17, 1975; children—Revathi, Sathish. B.E., U. Madras (India), 1968; D.I.I.T., Indian Inst. Tech., Madras, 1969; M.S., Kans. State U., 1971, Ph.D., 1974. Grad. research asst. Kans. State U., Manhattan, 1969-73; asst. prof. Calif. Poly. State U., San Luis Obispo. 1973-74; asst. prof. indsl. engring. Fairleigh Dickinson U., Teaneck, N.J., 1974-78, assoc. prof., 1978-83, prof., 1983—, chmn. dept. indsl. engring., 1982—. Contbr. articles to profl. jours. Mem. Am. Inst. Indsl. Engrs. (sr.), AAUP, Sigma Xi, Tau Beta Pi, Alpha Pi Mu, Phi Kappa Phi. Hindu. Home: 631 Colonial Blvd Westwood NJ 07675 Office: Fairleigh Dickinson U 1000 River Rd Teaneck NJ 07666

NABHOLTZ, ANDRE, retired nuclear medicine physician; b. Brieulle, France, Sept. 8, 1924; s. Jules and Marid (de Land'huy) N.; m. Jacqueline Escriba, Apr. 27, 1954; children: Jean-Marc, Franz-Olivier. MD, Faculte Medicin Paris, 1950; Lic. et Sci., Faculte Sorbonne, Paris, 1964; diploma in nuclear physics, Faculte des Sci., Orsay, France, 1965. Doctor Overseas Service, Vietnam, 1951-53, Congo, Algeria, Madagascar, 1953-65; mgr.radiation protection service Atomic Energy Commn., Tahiti, 1965-68, Hydro-Quebec, Canada, 1968-73. Mem. Health Physics Soc. Home and Office: 28 Rue Hubert Languet, 21350 Vitteaux France

NABI, GHULAM, physician; b. Amratsar, India, Oct. 1, 1943; s. Ch.Lal Din and Doulat Bibi; children from previous marriage: Riffat Yasmeen, Nighat Yasmeen, Akhlaq Ahma, Rizwan Ahmad; m. Jamila Akhter, March 21, 1980. MBBS, Liaqat Med. Coll., Jamshoro, Pakistan, 1968. Practice med. Chiniot Sheikh Assn. Hosp., Faisalabad, Pakistan, 1969-72, Rehmania Clinic, Faisalabad, 1972—. Club: Chenab. Home: 174B Sadar Bazar, Faisalabad Punjab, Pakistan Office: 174B Sadar Bazar, Ghulam Muhammad Abad, Faisalabad Punjab, Pakistan

NABOKOV, DMITRI, operatic bass, translator; b. Berlin, May 10, 1934; came to U.S., 1940, naturalized 1945; s. Vladimir and Vera (Slonim) N. AB cum laude, Harvard U., 1955; student, Longy Sch. Music, 1955-57. Leading Bass roles, Teatro Liceo, Barcelona, Phila. Lyric, bologna Opera, Conn. Opera, N.J. Opera, Toledo Opera, Cin. Summer Opera, Portland Opera, New Orleans Opera, Lyon, Grenoble, Rouen, Geneva, French radio and TV, Israel State radio, and others, 1967—; translator numerous works of Vladimir Nabokov, 1957—, and others; contbr. articles and essays to various collections and periodicals; recs. classical and operatic music, 1963—; participant award winning recording Madrigals by Gesualdo, 1963. Served with AUS, 1957-59. Winner internat. opera contests Reggio Emilio, 1960, Parma, 1966. Mem. Offshore Powerboat Racing Assn. Clubs: Am. Alpine, Ferrari of Switzerland. Home: 12 Via Leopardi, 20052 Monza Italy also: Montreux-Palace Hotel, 1820 Montreux Switzerland

NACHMAN, NORMAN HARRY, lawyer; b. Chgo.; s. Harry and Mary (Leibowitz) N.; m. Anne Lev, June 19, 1932; children—Nancy Nachman Laskow, James Lev, Susan. Ph.B., U. Chgo., 1930, J.D., 1932. Bar: Ill. 1932, U.S. Dist. Ct. (no. dist.) Ill. 1932, U.S. Dist. Ct. (we. dist.) Tex. 1978, U.S. Ct. Apls. (5th cir.) 1978, U.S. Ct. Apls. (7th cir.) 1942, U.S. Sup. Ct. 1942. Assoc. Michael Gesas, Chgo., 1932-35; assoc. Schwartz & Cooper, Chgo., 1936-40, ptnr., 1940-46; sole practice, Chgo., 1947-67; founder, sr. ptnr. Nachman, Munitz & Sweig, Ltd., Chgo., 1967—; mem. adv. com. bankruptcy rules Jud. Conf. U.S., 1960-76, 78—; mem. Nat. Bankruptcy Conf., 1957—, chmn. com. bankruptcy reorganization plans and securities problems, 1977—; mem. faculty numerous bankruptcy seminars throughout U.S. Chmn. appeals bd. Chgo. Dept. Environ. Control, 1960—. Served to lt. USN, 1943-46. Mem. ABA (past chmn. comml. bankruptcy com.), Chgo. Bar Assn. (pres. 1963-64), Ill. Bar Assn. Clubs: Standard, Bryn Mawr Country, Law, Mid-Day (Chgo.). Jewish. Contbg. editor: Collier on Bankruptcy, 1981. Office: Winston & Strawn 1 First Nat Plaza Suite 5000 Chicago IL 60603

NACHMAN, RONALD JAMES, research chemist; b. Takoma Park, Md., Feb. 1, 1954; s. Joseph Frank and Rosemary (Anderson) N.; m. Lita Rose Wilson, Dec. 18, 1976 (div. 1987). BS in Chemistry, U. Calif., San Diego, 1976; PhD in Organic Chemistry, Stanford U., 1981. Research asst. Scripps Inst. Oceanography, La Jolla, Calif., 1974-76; chemist Western Regional Research Ctr., USDA, Berkeley, Calif., 1981—; vis. scientist The Salk Inst., La Jolla, 1985, Research Inst. Scripps Clinic, La Jolla, 1988. Contbr. sci. articles to profl. jours. Recipient USDA Cert. Merit, 1988. Fellow Sci. and Humanities Symposia; mem. AAAS, Am. Chem. Soc., N.Y. Acad. Scis.,

Sigma Xi. Home: 7 Peak Ct Hercules CA 94547 Office: USDA Western Regional Research Ctr 800 Buchanan St Berkeley CA 94710

NACHTRIEB, NORMAN HARRY, chemist, educator; b. Chgo., Mar. 4, 1916; s. Norman David and Minnie (Barnard) N.; m. Marcia Binford, Aug. 22, 1953; 1 dau., Marianna C. B.S., U. Chgo., 1936, Ph.D., 1941. Chemist Ill. Geol. Survey, Urbana, 1937-38, Pitts. Plate Glass Co., Barberton, Ohio, 1941-43; research chemist Manhattan dist. U.S. C.E., U. Chgo., 1943-44; alternate group leader Los Alamos Sci. Lab., 1944-46; asst. prof. chemistry U. Chgo., 1946-48, assoc. prof., 1948-53, prof., 1953-84, prof. emeritus, 1984—, chmn. dept., 1962-71, head phys sci. sect. coll., 1958-59, 60-62, assoc. dean phys. scis. div., 1973-76, master phys. scis. collegiate div., assoc. dean coll., 1973-76; vis. prof. chemistry U. Ill., Chgo., 1985—. Author: Principles and Practice of Spectrochemical Analysis, 1950, Principles of Modern Chemistry, 1986; adv. editor: Ency. Brit, 1955—; assoc. editor: Jour. Chem. Physics, 1956-58; mem. editorial adv. bd.: Analytical Chemistry, 1958-61. Mem. policy bd. SPE div. NSF, 1964-66; mem. adv. bd. edn. div. 1967-69, Consol. High Sch. Dist. 230 Bd. Edn. Recipient Quantrell award U. Chgo., 1962, 77; J.T. Baker fellow analytical chemistry, 1940-41; NSF sr. postdoctoral fellow, 1959-60. Fellow Am. Phys. Soc.; mem. Am. Chem. Soc. (adv. bd. petroleum research fund 1967-70). Office: 5735 Ellis Ave Chicago IL 60637

NACHWALTER, MICHAEL, lawyer; b. N.Y.C., Aug. 31, 1940; s. Samuel J. Nachwalter; m. Irene, Aug. 15, 1965; children—Helynn, Robert. B.S., Bucknell U., 1962; M.S., L.I. U., 1967; J.D. cum laude, U. Miami, 1967; LL.M., Yale U., 1968. Bar: Fla. 1967, D.C. 1979, U.S. Dist. Ct. (so., middle dists.) Fla., U.S. Ct. Appeals (5th and 11th cirs.), U.S. Supreme Ct. Law clk. U.S. Dist. Ct. (so. dist.) Fla.; ptnr. Kelly, Black, Black & Kenney; now ptnr. Kenny Nachwalter & Seymour, Miami; lectr. Law Sch. U. Miami. Mem. Fla. Bar Assn., ABA, Fed. Bar Assn., Dade County Bar Assn., Fla. Bar. (bd. govs.), Omicron Delta Kappa, Phi Kappa Phi, Phi Delta Phi, Iron Arrow, Soc. Wig and Robe. Democrat. Editor in chief U. Miami Law Rev., 1966-67. Office: 400 Edward Ball Bldg 100 Chopin Plaza Miami FL 33131

NACOL, MAE, lawyer; b. Port Arthur, Tex., June 15, 1944; d. William Samuel and Ethel (Bowman) N.; children—Shawn Alexander Nacol, Catherine Regina Nacol. B.S., Rice U., 1965; student, So. Tex. Coll. Law. Bar: Tex. 1969, U.S. Dist. Ct. (so. dist.) Tex. 1969. Diamond buyer/appraiser Nacol's Jewelry, Houston, 1961—; sole practice, Houston, 1969—. Chmn. bd., nat. dir. A.R.M.S. of Am. Ltd., Houston, 1984-85. Recipient Mayor's Recognition award City of Houston, 1972; Ford Found. fellow So. Tex. Coll. Law, Houston, 1965. Mem. Houston Bar Assn. (chmn. candidate com. 1970, chmn. membership com. 1971, chmn. lawyers referral com. 1972), Tex. Trial Lawyers Assn., Nat. Assn. Women Lawyers, Am. Judicature Soc. Presbyterian. Office: Nacol & Assoc 500 Jefferson #1915 Houston TX 77002-7334

NADELL, ANDREW THOMAS, psychiatrist; b. N.Y.C., Nov. 3, 1946; s. Samuel Tyler and Bertha Elaine (Trupine) N. MA, Columbia U., 1968; MSc, U. London, 1973; MD, Duke U., 1974. Diplomate Am. Bd. Psychiatry and Neurology. Resident in psychiatry U. Calif., Davis, 1974-77; clin. instr. psychiatry Stanford (Calif.) U. Sch. Medicine, 1979-84, clin. asst. prof. psychiatry, 1984—. Fellow Royal Soc. Medicine; mem. Am. Psychiat. Assn., Am. Assn. History of Medicine, Am. Osler Soc., Bay Area History Medicine Soc. (sec. 1984-88, v.p. 1988—), Soc. for Social History Medicine, Assn. Internat. de Bibliophilie, Soc. Internat. d'Histoire de la Médecine, Stanford U. Libraries Assocs. (adv. council 1988—). Clubs: Grolier (N.Y.C.); Roxburghe, Colophon, Commonwealth, Book of Calif. (San Francisco). Office: 1828 El Camino Real Burlingame CA 94010

NADITCH, RONALD MARVIN, lawyer; b. Balt., Oct. 3, 1937; s. Albert I. and Marion Naditch; m. Phyllis K. Naditch, Dec. 31, 1968; children—Robyn, Allison. B.A., Dickinson Coll., 1959; J.D. with honor, U. Md., 1962. Bar: Md. 1962. Law clk. to assoc. judge Md. Ct. Appeals, 1962-63; assoc. Goodman and Bloom, 1964-65; part-time asst. states atty. Anne Arundel County, Md., 1966—; atty. Anne Arundel County Dept. Social Services, 1979-85; sole practice, Annapolis, Md., 1964—; mem. grievance rev. bd. State of Md.; lectr. continuing legal edn. Served with USCG. Mem. ABA, Md. Bar Assn., Md. Trial Lawyers Assn., Am. Trial Lawyers Assn., Nat. Dist. Attys. Assn. (lectr.), Md. Dist. Attys. Assn. (lectr.). Assoc. editor Md. Law Rev. Home: 44 Southgate Ave Annapolis MD 21401 Office: 49 Cornhill St Annapolis MD 21401

NADZICK, JUDITH ANN, accountant; b. Paterson, N.J., Mar. 6, 1948; d. John and Ethel (McDonald) N.; B.B.A. in Acctg., U. Miami (Fla.), 1971. Staff accountant, mgr. Ernst & Whinney, C.P.A.s, N.Y.C., 1971-78; asst. treas. Gulf & Western Industries, Inc., N.Y.C., 1979-83, asst. v.p., 1980-82, v.p., 1982-83; v.p., corp. controller United Mchts. and Mfrs. Inc., N.Y.C., 1983-85, sr. v.p., 1985-86, exec. v.p., chief fin. officer, 1986—, also bd. dirs. 1987—. C.P.A., N.J. Mem. Am. Inst. C.P.A.s, Nat. Assn. Accts., N.Y. State Soc. C.P.A.s, U. Miami Alumni Assn., Delta Delta Delta. Roman Catholic. Home: 2 Lincoln Sq Apt 15G New York NY 10023

NAFTALIS, GARY PHILIP, lawyer; b. Newark, Nov. 23, 1941; s. Gilbert and Bertha Beatrice (Gruber) N.; m. Donna Arditi, June 30, 1974; children: Benjamin, Joshua, Daniel, Sarah. AB, Rutgers U., 1963; AM, Brown U., 1965; LLB, Columbia U., 1967. Bar: N.Y. 1967, U.S. Supreme Ct. 1974, U.S. Ct. Appeals (2d cir.) 1968, U.S. Ct. Appeals (3d cir.) 1973, U.S. Dist. Ct. (so. dist.) N.Y. 1969. Law clk. to judge U.S. Dist. Ct. So. Dist. N.Y., 1967-68; asst. U.S. atty. So. Dist. N.Y., 1968-74, asst. chief criminal div., 1972-74; spl. asst. U.S. atty. for V.I., 1972-73; spl. counsel U.S. Senate Subcom. on Long Term Care, 1975; spl. counsel N.Y. State Temp. Commn. on Living Costs and the Economy, 1975; ptnr. Orans, Elsen, Polstein & Naftalis, N.Y.C., 1974-81, Kramer, Levin, Nessen, Kamin & Frankel, N.Y.C., 1981—; lectr. in law Columbia U. Law Sch., 1976—; vis. lectr. Harvard U. Law Sch., 1979; mem. deptl. disciplinary com. Appellate div. 1st Dept., 1980-86. Author: (with Marvin E. Frankel) The Grand Jury: An Institution on Trial, 1977, Considerations in Representing Attorneys in Civil and Criminal Enforcement Proceedings, 1981, Sentencing: Helping Judges Do Their Jobs, 1986; editor: White Collar Crimes, 1980. Trustee, Boys Brotherhood Republic, 1978—, Blueberry Treatment Center, 1981—. Mem. ABA, N.Y. City Bar Assn. (com. criminal cts. 1980-83, com. judiciary 1984-87, com. on criminal law 1987—, council on criminal justice 1985—), Fed. Bar Council (com. cts. of 2d cir. 1974-77), N.Y. State Bar Assn. (com. state legis. 1974-76). Home: 336 West End Ave Apt 18-C New York NY 10023 Office: 919 3rd Ave New York NY 10022

NAFZIGER, JAMES ALBERT RICHMOND, lawyer, educator; b. Mpls., Sept. 24, 1940; s. Ralph Otto and Charlotte Monona (Hamilton) N.; B.A., U. Wis., 1962, M.A., 1969; J.D., Harvard U., 1967. Bar: Wis. 1967. Law clk. to chief judge U.S. Dist. Ct. (ea. dist.) Wis., 1967-69; fellow Am. Soc. Internat. Law, Washington, 1969-70, adminstrv. dir., 1970-74; exec. sec. Assn. Student Internat. Law Socs., 1969-70; lectr. Sch. Law, Cath. U. Am., Washington, 1970-74; vis. assoc. prof. Sch. Law, U. Oreg., 1974-77; vis. prof. Nat. Autonomous U. Mex., 1978; assoc. prof. law Coll. Law, Willamette U., Salem, Oreg., 1977-80, prof., 1980—, assoc. dean, 1985-86, dir. China program, 1984—; scholar-in-residence Rockeller Found. Ctr., Bellagio, Italy, 1985; lectr., tutor Inst. Pub. Internat. Law and Internat. Relations, Thessaloniki, Greece, 1982; mem. bd. advisors Harvard Internat. Law Jour., Denver Jour. Internat. Law and Policy, Am. Jour. Comparative Law (bd. dirs. 1985—). Served to 1st lt. U.S. Army, 1962-64. Mem. Am. Soc. Internat. Law (exec. council 1983-86, co-chmn. western region), Am. Assn. for Comparative Study of Law (bd. dirs.) Internat. Law Assn. (exec. com. 1986—, chmn. human rights com. Am. br. 1983—, UNA-USA pres. Oreg. Div. 1987—), Washington Fgn. Law Soc. (v.p. 1973-74), Internat. Studies Assn. (exec. bd. 1974-77, internat. law sect.), ACLU (pres. chpt. 1980-81, mem. state bd. 1982-88 , sec. 1983-87), Assn. Am. Law Schs. (chmn. law and arts sect. 1981-83, chmn. internat. law sect. 1984-85, bd. dirs. N.W. Regional China Council 1987—), Am. Law Inst., Oreg. Internat. Council (exec. com. 1985—, dir. 1982—), Phi Beta Kappa, Phi Kappa Phi. Editor Procs. of Am. Soc. Internat. Law, 1977; Am. author: Conflict of Laws: A Northwest Perspective, 1985, International Sports Law, 1988; contbr. articles to profl. jours. Home: 3775 Saxon Dr S Salem OR 97302 Office: Willamette U Coll Law Salem OR 97301

NAG, SUBIR K., radiation oncologist; b. Calcutta, India, Dec. 10, 1951; came to U.S., 1977; s. Sunil K. and Bela R. (Dawn) N.; m. Sima Dutta, Mar. 9, 1982; children—Sunita, Sumona. .M.B.B.S., All India Inst. Med. Sci., New Delhi, 1975. Diplomate Am. Bd. Radiology, Resident in radiotherapy Montefiore Hosp., Bronx, N.Y., 1977-79, chief resident, 1978-79; fellow in radiotherapy Meml. Sloan Kettering Cancer Ctr., N.Y.C., 1980, spl. brachytherapy fellow, 1980-81; asst. prof. radiation oncology U. Tenn. Hosp., Memphis, 1981-86, chief radiation oncology, 1983-86; staff radiation oncologist City of Memphis Hosp., 1981-86; cons. St. Judes Childrens Research Hosp., Memphis, 1982-86; clin. dir. radiation oncology Vanderbilt U., Nashville, 1986-87; clin. dir. Southeastern Cancer Inst., Chattanooga, 1987—. Contbr. articles to profl. jours. Mem. Am. Soc. Therapeutic Radiologists, Radiol. Soc. N.Am., AMA, Am. Coll. Radiology, Am. Soc. Clin. Oncologists, Radiation Research Soc., Am. Assn. Cancer Edn. Home: 1309 Darlene Circle Chattanooga TN 37412 Office: 2339 McCallie Ave Suite 411 Chattanooga TN 37404

NAGAI, KUNIO, food products executive; b. Tokyo, Mar. 25, 1915; s. Matsuzo and Sueko (Yanagiya) N.; m. Kuniko Mitani, May 5, 1946; children: Naoko Kazusa, Motoo. LLB, Tokyo Imperial U., 1940. From clk. to sect. chief Indsl. Bank of Japan, Tokyo, 1940-60, mgr., 1960-64, dir., 1964-67; mng. dir. Toyo Soda Mfg. Co. Ltd., Tokyo, 1967-69, sr. mng. dir., 1969-75, v.p., 1975-77; dir., pres. Japan Organo Co., Ltd., Tokyo, 1977-87, chmn., 1987—. Served to lt. comdr. Japanese Navy, 1940-45. Mem. Doyu Econ. Assn. (chmn. 1987). Club: Tokyo Kiwanis (pres. 1984). Home: 4 16 27 Seijo, Setagaua ku, Tokyo 157, Japan Office: Japan Organo Co Ltd, 28 23 Hongo 1 chome, Bunkyo ku, Tokyo 113, Japan

NAGAO, HIROSI, mathematician, educator; b. Kure, Hiroshima, Japan, Feb. 25, 1925; m. Takako Yamashita, Nov. 7, 1955; children: Ikuko Matsuyama, Jun Nagao. BS, Osaka U., Japan, 1946, PhD, 1955. Assoc. prof. math. Osaka City U., 1953-63, prof., 1963-68; prof. math. Osaka U., 1968-88, dean Faculty of Sci., 1985-88, prof. emeritus, 1988—; prof. Tezukayama U., 1988—. Author: Group Theory, 1965, Groups and Designs, 1974, Representations of Finite Groups, 1987. Mem. Math. Soc. Japan, Am. Math. Soc. Home: 1-7-5 Kunokidai, Tpdabayashi, Osaka 584, Japan Office: Tezukayama U, 7-1-1 Tezukayama, Nara 631, Japan

NAGDA, KANTI, community center executive; b. Changa, Saurastra, India, May 1, 1946; came to U.K., 1972; s. Vershi Bhoja and Zaviben N.; m. Bhagwati Desai, Nov. 9, 1972; children—Dipen, Rupen. Student Coll. Future Edn., Chipenham, U.K., 1967, East African U., Kampala, Uganda, 1969. Tchr., City High Sch., Kampala, 1969-72; acct. Hollander Hyams Ltd., London, 1972-82; mgr. Community Centre, Harrow, U.K., 1982—; dir. Anglo-Indian Circle, Harrow, 1974. Author: Muratiyo Ke Nokar, 1967; editor: Oshwal News, 1981; contbr. articles in field to profl. jours. and newspapers. Sec. gen. Confederation Indian Orgns. U.K., 1975; hon. editorial cons. Internat. Asian Guide and Who's Who, U.K., 1975; mem. Harrow Crime Prevention Panel, U.K., 1983. Club: Indian Nat. Lodge: Lions (Pres. Greenford Willow Tree chpt. 1988—). Home: 170 Tolcarne Dr, Pinner, Middlesex HA5 2DR, England Office: London Borough of Harrow, Station Rd, Harrow, Middlesex HA1 2UL, England

NAGEL, MARY JANE, home entertainment retail company executive; b. New Rochelle, N.Y., July 15, 1952; d. Lawrence William, Jr. and Frances Theresa (Meehan) N.; student public schs., New Rochelle. Mail order div. mgr. Citadel Record Club, Larchmont, N.Y., 1968-71; record store mgr. Longines Symphonette Stereo, Larchmont, 1971-74; divisional mgr. Sam Goody, Inc., Maspeth, N.Y., 1974-78, record/tape buyer, 1978-81, softgoods adminstrn. mgr., Edison, N.J., 1981-83, dir. field merchandising, 1984, field ops. mgr., 1985-86; regional dir. Musicland Group, Mpls., 1987—. Mem. Nat. Assn. Female Execs. Roman Catholic. Office: Musicland Group 7500 Excelsior Blvd Minneapolis MN 55426

NAGELGAST, ELSIE BLANCHE, museum curator; b. Cathcart, South Africa, June 10, 1931; d. Alexander Daniel Peter and Elsje Johanna (Beukes) Jubber; m. Laurence Bertie Hughes, Aug. 23, 1957 (div. Jan. 1968); m. 2d, Edward Johann Dirk, July 3, 1971. BA, Witwatersrand U., Johannesburg, S. Africa, 1949, diploma Librarianship, 1962; diploma teaching Coll. Edn., Johannesburg, 1950. Tchr., King Edward VII Preparatory, Johannesburg, 1951-55; tchr. schs., London, 1956-57; tchr. Indian Girls High Sch., Pietermaritzburg, 1958-59; tchr. schs., London, 1959-60; librarian Pub. Library, Johannesburg, 1963-76; asst. curator Africana Mus., Johannesburg, 1976-80, curator, 1980—; adv. mem. Nat. Adv. Com. for Museums, 1981-86. Author: Personal Reminiscences of Early Johannesburg, 1966; contbr. chpts. to books; editor: Africana Notes & News, 1980—. Anglican. Home: 1 Hamlin St, Johannesburg 2192, Republic of South Africa Office: Africana Mus, Pub Library Bldg, Market Sq, Johannesburg 2001, Republic of South Africa

NAGI, MOSTAFA HELMEY, social scientist, educator; b. Samalig, Egypt, June 15, 1934; came to U.S., 1964, naturalized, 1975; s. Faried and Hamida (Shenishen) N.; m. Wiam Youssif Abdualahad, Aug. 15, 1977; 1 child, Suhair. B.Sc., Cairo U., 1958; M.A., Bowling Green State U., 1967; Ph.D., U. Conn., 1970. Specialist, Council Pub. Services and Ministry of Agr., Egypt and Syria, 1958-64; asst. prof. sociology Bowling Green (Ohio) State U., 1969-71, assoc. prof., 1972-80, prof., 1980—, chair Dept. Sociology, Anthropology and Social Work, Kuwait U., 1985-87 ; sr. cons. Govt. of Iraq, Arab Project and Devel. Inst., Lebanon, 1974-75; cons. Kuwait Inst. Sci. Advancement, 1986-87, Amiri Diwan, Kuwait, 1984-85, Ministry of dn., Kuwait, 1986-87; vis. prof. Kuwait U., 1977-79, 84-86; referee NSF, profl. jours. and pub. cos. NSF grantee, 1979; NIH grantee, 1972. Mem. Am. Sociol. Assn., Population Assn. Am., N.Y. Acad. Sci., Am. Gerontol. Soc., AAAS, Ohio Acad. Sci., North Central Sociol. Assn., Soc. for Sci. Study Religion, Acad. Polit. Sci., Internat. Platform Assn. Contbr. articles to profl. jours. Home: 1127 Clark St Bowling Green OH 43402 Office: Dept Sociology Bowling Green State U Bowling Green OH 43403

NAGI, SAAD Z(AGHLOUL), sociologist, educator; b. Samalig, Menufia, Egypt, Apr. 30, 1925; came to U.S., 1953, naturalized, 1963; s. Faried and Hamida (Shineishin) N.; m. Kay Gonder, Sept. 15, 1957; children: Karima, Mazen, Omar. B.Sc., Cairo U., 1947; M.Sc., U. Mo., 1954; Ph.D., Ohio State U., 1958. Research specialist Egyptian Govt., Cairo, 1947-53; research asst. Ohio State U., Columbus, 1953-57, asst. prof., 1958-63, assoc. prof., 1963-64, prof. sociology, 1964—, prof. phys. medicine, 1969—, Mershon prof. sociology and pub. policy, 1971—, chmn. dept. sociology, 1982—; mem. peer rev. com. Social Security Adminstrn., Balt., 1963-66, Maternal and Child Health Services, Rockville, Md., 1967-72; chmn. peer rev. com. Vocat. Rehab. Adminstrn., Washington, 1965-68, Office Child Devel., Washington, 1971-75; cons. WHO, Geneva, 1972-75, GAO, Washington, 1984—. Author: Disabiltiy and Rehabilitaion, 1969, Child Maltreatment in the United States, 1977; co-author: Disablility: From Social Problem to Social Program, 1980; co-editor: The Social Context of Research, 1972. Recipient Outstanding Research Contbns. award Nat. Rehab. Assn., Washington, 1970; recipient Disting. Research award Ohio State U., 1982; Fulbright fellow, 1953-54. Mem. Am. Sociol. Assn., AAAS, Am. Pub. Health Assn. Office: Ohio State U 190 N Oval Mall Columbus OH 43210

NAGORSKI, ZYGMUNT, political scientist; b. Warsaw, Poland, Sept. 27, 1912; came to U.S., 1948, naturalized, 1953; s. Zygmunt Julian and Maria Nagorski; m. Marie Bogdaszewski, Nov. 22, 1938; children—Maria, Andrew, Teresa. M.A., U. Cracow (Poland), 1935; postgrad. U. Geneva, 1937-38, Internat. Inst. Trade and Patents, Berne, Switzerland, 1937-38, Reporter, Chattanooga Times, 1948; editor-in-chief Fgn. News Service, Inc., N.Y.C., 1949-56; chief Internat. Br. Office Research, USIA, Washington, 1956-59; fgn. service officer, Cairo, 1959-61, Seoul, 1961-64, Paris, 1964-66; spl. asst. to pres. Fgn. Policy Assn., Inc., N.Y.C., 1966-68; mem. profl. staff Hudson Inst., Inc., 1968-69; dir. Members Meetings Program, Council on Fgn. Relations, N.Y.C., 1969-78; v.p. Lehrman Inst., 1978-80; spl. adv. Aspen Inst.; adj. asst. prof. polit. sci. dept. Queens Coll., 1974-75; v.p. Human Resource Services, Inc., 1980-81; guest lectr. Wilton Park, Sussex, Eng., Fgn. Service Inst., Center for Study Human Values, Tanglewood, N.C., Experiment in Internat. Living (Vt.), also numerous univs.; v.p., dir. exec. seminars programs Aspen Inst. Humanistic Studies, 1981- 85; pres. Ctr. for Internat. Leadership, N.Y.C., 1986—. Pres., Am. Friends of Wilton Park, 1967-70, Mid-Atlantic Club of New York, 1972—; bd. dirs. Scarsdale Adult Sch., 1968-72, Internat. U. Found. Served with Polish Army, 1939-45 under French and British Command. Decorated Brit. War medal, officer's cross Order of Merit (W. Ger.); recipient Outstanding Fgn. Born Am. award Internat. Ctr. of N.Y., 1988; comdr. Order of Leopold II (Belgium); recipient Meritorious Service award USIA, 1965, Internat. Ctr. of N.Y. Ann. Fgn. Born Ams. award, 1988. Mem. Am. Acad. Polit. Sci., Council on Fgn. Relations, Am. Polit. Sci. Assn., Internat. Studies Assn., Polish Inst. Arts and Scis., Am. Fgn. Service Assn. Democrat. Roman Catholic. Club: University (N.Y.C.). Author: Armed Unemployment, 1945; The Psychology of East-West Trade, 1975. Contbr. articles to newspapers and mags. Home: 91 Central Park W New York NY 10023 Office: Ctr for Internat Leadership 333 W 86th St New York NY 10024

NAGSEVI, CHAROENCHAI, personnel and adminstration executive; b. Bangkok, Thailand, Oct. 14, 1931; s. Chai and Tham (Promprakai) N.; m. Boon ying Ratanawimol, May 8, 1958; children—Chaturonchai, Montip, Anavaj, Chaturachoke. Diploma in acctg. Thamasat U., Bangkok, 1954, B.Com., 1955; M.B.A., Inst. Adminstrn., Karachi, Pakistan, 1962. Commd. arty. officer Royal Thai Army, 1955, advanced through grades to capt., 1962; personnel and adminstrv. officer, Bangkok, 1962-66, ret., 1966; personnel adminstrn. mgr. Diethelm & Co., Ltd., Bangkok, 1967-78; indsl. relations div. mgr. Dole Thailand Ltd., Hua Hin, Thailand, 1978-81; sr. mgr. East Asiatic Co., Thailand, Bangkok, 1981-84; gen. affairs dir. Johnson & Johnson (Thailand) Ltd., Bangkok, 1984—. Editor Jour. Personnel Mgmt. Assn. of Thailand, 1970. Arbitrator Labour Dept., Thailand, 1981—; mem. com. Social Security Working Group, Pub. Welfare Dept., Thailand, 1977, Labour Law Revision Com., Labour Dept., Thailand, 1973. South East Asia Treaty Orgn. scholar, 1960-62. Mem. Thailand Mgmt. Assn. (life; sec. Personnel Mgmt. Group, 1970, chmn. 1973). Avocation: reading. Office: Johnson & Johnson (Thailand) Ltd, 106 Chalongkrung Lat Krabang, Bangkok 10520, Thailand

NAGUCKA, RUTA RAFAELA, linguist, educator, consultant; b. Zebrzydowice, Poland, Mar. 23, 1930; d. Adam and Emilia (Pustówka) Sikora; m. Anthony Nagucki, Apr. 2, 1966. MA, The Jagiellonian U., Kraków, Poland, 1952, PhD, 1963, Dr. habilitation, 1968. Asst. Jagiellonian U., 1955-57, sr. asst., 1957-63, adiunkt, 1963-68, docent, 1968-78, assoc. prof., 1978-84, prof., 1984—. Author: The Syntactic Component of Chaucer's Astrolabe, 1968 (minister higher edn. award, 1969), Negatively Phrased Utterances in English, 1978 (minister higher edn. award, 1979), An Integrated Analysis of Syntax and Semantics of Obsolete English Constructions, 1984 (minister higher edn. award, 1985); contbr. articles to profl. jours. Recipient Golden Cross Merit, Polish Govt. 1975, Cross Polonia Restituta, Polish Govt., 1978, Com. Nat. Edn. medal, Minister Higher Edn., 1983. Mem. Linguistic Soc. Am., Polish Linguistic Soc., Internat. Assn. Univ. Profs. English, Soc. Linguistica Europaea. Lutheran. Home: Dzierzynskiego 30 m5, 30-052 Krakõw Poland Office: The Jagiellonian U, Golebia 24, 31-007 Krakõw Poland

NAGUIB, MOHSEN SOBHY, psychiatrist; b Assuit, Egypt, May 22, 1949; came to U.K. 1978; s. Sobhy and Aida (Gergis) N.; m. Nayera Nicola, Aug. 22, 1983; children—Justine, Mina. M.B., Ch.B., Ain Shams U., Cairo, 1973; M.R.C. Psychiatry, London, 1981, D.P.M., 1981; postgrad. London U. Various posts in medicine and psychiatry, Cairo, 1974-78; registrar in psychiatry St. Bartholomew's Med. Sch., London, 1978-79, Maudsley Hosp., London, 1979-80, sr. registrar, 1983—; research worker Inst. of Psychiatry, London, 1980-83, lectr., 1983—; cons., sr. lectr. psychiatry of old age St. Mary's Med. Sch. and St. Charles Hosps., London, 1985—; hon. sr. lectr. psychiatry Royal Postgrad. Med. Sch. Hammersmith Hosp., London, 1986—; recognized tchr. psychiatry London U., 1987; clin. tutor psychiatry postgrad. trainees St. Mary's Hosp. Med. Sch., 1987—. Contbr. articles to profl. jours. Mem. Royal Coll. Psychiatrists, U.K., Alzehimer's Disease Soc. Coptic Orthodox Christian, Internat. Psychogeriatric Assn. Avocations: photography; music; playing the violin and lute. Home: 12 Mulgrave Rd, Ealing, London W5 1LE, England Office: St Charles' Hosp, Exmoor St, London W10, England

NAGURSKI, JAN STEPHEN, controller; b. Long Beach, Calif., Sept. 23, 1944; s. Stephen and Edna Mae (Hart) N.; m. Bernadette Esther Barrett, Apr. 23, 1976; children: Mark, Brian, Kevin. BA in English, Calif. State U., Long Beach, 1967; degree in civilian club mgmt. with honors, Air Force Inst. Tech., Wright-Patterson AFB, Ohio, 1971; MBA, Pepperdine U., 1983. Commd. 2d lt. USAF, 1967, advanced through grades to capt., 1970, resigned, 1975; acct. Sta. WBAP/KSCS, Ft. Worth, 1975-76; mgmt. acct. Adria Ltd., Strabane, Ireland, 1976-78; gen. mgr. Bundoran (Ireland) Holidays, 1978-81; corp. fin. planning mgr. Luxfer USA, Riverside, Calif., 1981-87; controller Superform USA, Inc., Riverside, 1987—; cons., controller Superform USA, Riverside, 1985—. Author, editor newsletter Smudgepot, 1984-86. Cubmaster Boy Scouts Am., Canyon Lake, Calif. Recipient Gold Medal Menu award Nat. Restaurant Assn., Ft. Worth, 1973. Mem. Nat. Assn. Accts. (pres. 1985-86), Data Processing Mgmt. Assn., Inst. Adminstrv. Acctg., U.K. Republican. Roman Catholic. Home: 30820 Emperor Dr Canyon Lake CA 92380 Office: Superform USA Inc 6825 Jurupa Ave PO Box 5375 Riverside CA 92517-5375

NAGY, STEVEN, biochemist; b. Fords, N.J., Apr. 7, 1936; s. Steven and Martha (Moberg) N.; m. Suzanne Nagy; children: Lacey, Nicolette, Steven. BS in Chemistry, La. State U., 1960; MS in Physiology and Biochemistry, Rutgers U., 1962, PhD in Biochemistry, 1965; MEngring. in Indsl. Engring., U. South Fla., 1977. Analytical chemist USPHS, Metuchen, N.J., 1962-65; research asso. Lever Bros., Edgewater, N.J., 1965-67; research chemist Dept. Agr., Winter Haven, Fla., 1968-79; processing research coordinator Fla. Dept. Citrus, Lake Alfred, 1979—; adj. prof. U. Fla., 1979—. Mem. Am. Chem. Soc. (chmn. div. agrl. and food chemistry), Phytochem. Soc. N. Am., Inst. Food Technologists, Am. Soc. for Hort. Sci., Internat. Soc. Citriculture, Fla. Hort. Soc., Sigma Xi. Republican. Author: Citrus Science and Technology, 2 vols., 1977; Tropical and Subtropical Fruits, 1980; Citrus Nutrition and Quality, 1980; Fresh Citrus Fruits, 1986, Adulteration of Fruit Juice Beverages, 1988; contbr. articles to profl. jours. Home: 103 Arietta Shores Dr Auburndale FL 33823 Office: 700 Experiment Sta Rd Lake Alfred FL 33850

NAHAS, GABRIEL GEORGES, pharmacologist, educator; b. Alexandria, Egypt, Mar. 4, 1920; came to U.S., 1947, naturalized, 1962; s. Bishara and Gabrielle (Wolff) N.; m. Marilyn Cashman, Feb. 13, 1954; children: Michele, Anthony, Christiane. BA, U. Toulouse, France, 1937, MD, 1944; MS, U. Rochester, 1949; PhD, U. Minn., 1953; D (hon.), U. Uppsala, 1988. Rockefeller Found. fellow U. Rochester, 1947-48; Mayo Found. fellow Mayo Clinic, 1949-50; research fellow U. Minn., 1950-53; staff Marie-Lannelongue Hosp., Paris, 1953-55; mem. faculty U. Minn., 1955-57; staff Walter Reed Army Inst. Research, 1957-59; faculty George Washington U. Med. Sch., 1957-59; faculty Columbia Coll. Physicians and Surgeons, 1959—, prof. anesthesiology, 1962—; Fulbright scholar, 1966; adj. prof. anesthesiology (research) U. Paris, 1968-71; Fellow Council Circulation and Basic Sci., Am. Heart Assn., 1961—; com. on trauma NRC, 1964-66; adv. bd. Cousteau Soc.; cons. U.N. Commn. on Narcotics; dir. research INSERM, Paris, 1972—. Author: Marihuana, Deceptive Weed, 1973, 2d edit., 1984 , Keep Off the Grass, 1976, 3d edit., 1985, The Cocaine Wars, 1987; editor: (with W.D.M. Paton) Marihuana: Biological Effects, 1979, (with H.C. Frick) Drug Abuse in the Modern World, 1981. Served as spl. agt. French Underground, 1941-44; as 1st lt. M.C., French Army, 1944-45. Decorated Presdl. Medal of Freedom with gold palm U.S.; comdr. Legion of Honor, Croix de Guerre with 3 palms (France), Order Brit. Empire, Order Orange Nassau Netherlands, Silver medal City of Paris; recipient Medal of Honor, Statue of Liberty Centennial, 1986. Fellow AAAS, N.Y. Acad. Sci.; mem. Am. Physiol. Soc., Harvey Soc., Am. Soc. Pharmacology and Exptl. Therapeutics, Am. Soc. Clin. Pharmacology, Soc. Physiol. Langue Française, French Acad. Medicine (laureate), Brit. Pharm. Soc., Sigma Xi. Home: 114 Chestnut St Englewood NJ 07631 also: 59 Rue de Babylone, Paris France Office: Columbia Coll Physicians & Surgeons 630 W 168th St New York NY 10032 also: INSERM, Inst Toxicologie, 200 Faubourg St Denis, Paris France

NAHMIAS, BERNARD ALFRED, stomatologist; b. Toulouse, France, Apr. 10, 1945; s. Elie and Henriette (Carrie) N. MD, U. Paris, 1974. Attache Pub. Assistance Dept., Paris, 1975-80, Hosp. Argenteuil, Paris, 1980-85; practice medicine specializing in stomatology Sannois, France, 1985—.

Served to maj. M.C. French Army, 1972-73. Home: 19 Blvd Gabriel Peri 10, 95110 Sannois France Office: 2 Promenade des 2 Puits, 95110 Sannois France

NAHON, GERARD, French historian, university professor; b. Paris, Jan. 19, 1931; s. Joseph Sauveur and Yvette (Kenoui) N.; m. Maryvonne Rouret, Dec. 23, 1954; children: Myriam, Jacques, Ariel, Elisabeth. BA in Philosophy, 1949; cert. in Hebrew, Inst. Nat. Langues et Civilisations Orientales, 1953. Researcher Ctr. Nat. la Recherche Sci., Paris, 1965-78; lectr. Inst. Nat. Langues et Civilisations Orientales, Paris, 1969-80; dir. of studies Ecole Pratique Hautes Etudes Sect. Scis. Religieuses, 1977—; dir. Rev. des Etudes Juives, Paris, 1965—; lectr. Séminaire Israélite de France, Paris, 1972—; dir. Equipe Recherche 208 Nouvelle Gallia Judaica; sec. Soc. Etudes Juives, 1965—. Author: Les Hebreux, 1963, Les Nations Juives Portugaises du Sud-Quest de la France 1684-1791, Documents, 1981, Inscriptions HébraÉques et Juives en France Médiévale, 1986. Decorated Medaille d'argent de l'Inst. de France, 1987. Home: 28 rue de la Chabourne, Le Mesnil Saint Denis, Yvelines France Office: EPHE Religieuses, Sorbonne 45, rue des Ecoles, 75005 Paris France

NAIF IBN ABDULAZIZ, PRINCE, Saudi Arabian minister of interior; b. Mecca, Saudi Arabia, 1933; s. King Abdul-Aziz. Former gov., Riyadh, Saudi Arabia, former gov. of Meddina; former acting minister of interior; state minister for interior affairs, until 1975; minister of interior, 1975—. Office: Ministry of Interior, Riyadh Saudi Arabia *

NAIK, RAMA NARAYAN, health care company executive; b. Kumta, Karnataka, India, July 13, 1929; s. Narayan and Honnamma N.; m. Malati Naik, Jan. 14, 1940; children: Rajesh, Namrata, Yogita. BS, Karnatak Coll., Dharwar, India, 1950, MS, 1953; LLB, R.L. Law Coll., Belgaum, India, 1952. Analytical chemist Parke Davis India, Bombay, 1954-56; sr. scientific asst. Atomic Engergy Establishment, Bombay, 1956-58; chief analyst, quality control mgr. Johnson and Johnson Ltd, Bombay, 1958-65; chief chemist, dep. works mgr. Richardson Hindustan Ltd., Bombay, 1965-75; mgr. gen. works Johnson and Johnson Ltd., Bombay, 1975—. Home: 10 Ahiya Apts 16th Rd, Santa Cruz W Bombay, Maharashtra 400054, India Office: Johnson and Johnson Ltd, 30 Forjett St Bombay, Maharashtra 400036, India

NAIL, ZELMA ELAINE FAIRBANKS, school counselor; b. San Angelo, Tex., Feb. 26, 1933; d. Clannie Albert and Eva Lena (Coulter) Fairbanks; m. James C. Nail, Aug. 25, 1957; children: Ronald James, Daniel Albert. BA, Trinity U., San Antonio, 1954, MEd, 1957. Cert. nat. counselor, cert. profl. educator; lic. profl. counselor, Tex. Secondary sch. tchr., San Antonio, 1954-57; sec. B'nai Brith Hillel Found., College Station, Tex., 1957-58; bookkeeper Terry Farm Supply Co., Brownfield, Tex., 1965-68; elem. sch. tchr., Brownfield, 1968-70; secondary sch. counselor Matthews Jr. High Sch., Lubbock, Tex., 1970—; sec./treas. Save-Alert Co. Pres. Friends of Library, Terry County, Tex., 1966-68, United Presbyn. Women's Orgn., Brownfield, 1967; mem. Tex. Fedn. of Women's Clubs, 1965-70, Lubbock County Emergency First Aid Team, 1974-76; mem., dist. coordinator Counselors Legis. Involvement Com. for Tex., 1985-87, recorder, 1986-87 . Life mem. NEA, Tex. State Tchrs. Assn., Tex. Classroom Tchrs. Assn.; mem. Am. Assn. Counseling and Devel., Tex. Assn. Counseling and Devel. (conv. coordinator 1979, pub. relations com. 1980-85, sec. 1988—, pub. relations com. 1980-85, 88, fin. com. 1988—, legis. com. 1987-88), West Tex. Assn. Counseling and Devel. (pres. 1978-80, sec./treas. 1976-78, Counselor of Yr. 1986), Am. Sch. Counselors Assn., Tex. Sch. Counselors Assn. (Rhosine Fleming Meml. outstanding counselor of Tex. award 1980, senator 1987-88), AAUW, Lubbock Classroom Tchrs. Assn., Lubbock Educators Assn., Tex. Career Guidance Assn., Nat. Congress Parents and Tchrs., Tex. Assn. for Multicultural Counseling and Devel., Lubbock Cotton Aux., Friends of Lubbock County Library, Alpha Omega Study Club, Brownfield, 1965-70. Presbyterian. Home: 5426 80th St Lubbock TX 79424 Office: 417 N Akron St Lubbock TX 79415

NAIMI, SHAPUR, cardiologist; b. Tehran, Iran, Mar. 28, 1928; s. Mohsen and Mahbuba (Naim) N.; came to U.S., 1959, naturalized, 1968; M.B., Ch.B., Birmingham (Eng.) U., 1953; m. Amy Cabot Simonds, May 11, 1963; children—Timothy Simonds, Susan Lyman, Cameron Lowell. House physician Royal Postgrad Med. Sch. London, 1955; sr. house officer Inst. Diseases of the Chest, London, 1956; fellow in grad. tng. New Eng. Med Center and Mass. Inst. Tech., 1961-64; cardiologist Tufts New Eng. Med. Center, Boston, 1966-—, dir. intensive cardiac care unit, 1973-—, asso. prof. Med. Sch., 1970-—. Recipient Distinguished Instr. award, 1972, Teaching citation, 1976, Excellence in Teaching award, 1982 (all Tufts Med. Sch.); diplomate Royal Coll. Physicians London, Royal Coll. Physicians Edinburgh, Am. Bd. Internal Medicine (subsplty. bd. cardiovascular disease). Fellow Royal Coll. Physicians (Edinburgh), A.C.P., Am. Coll. Cardiology; mem. Am. Soc. Exptl. Biology and Medicine, Am. Heart Assn., Mass. Med. Soc. Clubs: Country Brookline; Cohasset Yacht. Contbr. to profl. jours. Home: 265 Woodland Rd Chestnut Hill MA 02167 Office: 171 Harrison Ave Boston MA 02111

NAIPAUL, VIDIADHAR SURAJPRASAD, author; b. Trinidad, W.I., Aug. 17, 1932. Student, Queen's Royal Coll., Trinidad, 1943-48; B.A., University Coll., Oxford, Eng., 1954; D.Litt. (hon.), St. Andrews Coll., Scotland, 1979, Columbia U., 1981, Cambridge U., 1983. Author: Miguel Street, 1959, A House for Mr. Biswas, 1961, An Area of Darkness, 1964, In A Free State, 1971, Guerrillas, 1975, A Bend in the River, 1979, Among the Believers, 1981, The Enigma of Arrival, 1987. Office: Gillon Aitken Aitken & Stone Ltd, 29 Fernshaw Rd, London SW10 0TG, England also: care Andre Deutsch Ltd, 105 Grat Russell St, London WC1, England

NAIR, CHEMMAT SIVASANKARAN, pump company executive; b. Trichur, Painkulam, India, Sept. 21, 1951; s. Raghavan and Meenakshyamma Nair; m. Indira Kokoori, Nov. 13, 1974; 1 child, Jayashree Sivasankaran. Grad. high sch., Chelakara, India. Stenographer The Cen. Pulp Mills, Ltd., Fort Songad, India, 1968-72, Papco Mills, Ltd., Khopeli, India, 1972-73; imports officer KSB Pumps Ltd., Pune, India, 1973—. Home: Gawade Vasahath Ln, Chinchwadgaon, 411033 Pune India

NAIR, SIVAN CHANDRASEKHARAN, director of photography, producer, director; b. Harippad, India, May 15, 1932; s. Gopala Pillai and Bhavani Amma; m. B. Chandramoni Sivan, June 12, 1953; children: Sangeeth Sivan, Santosh Sivan, Sanjeev Sivan, Saritha Sivan. Proprietor Sivans Studio, Trivandrum, Kerala, India, 1959; pres. Sivan Studio Art Gallery, Trivandrum, 1962; dir. Sarith Films, Trivandrum, 1972; pres. Yuva Chaithanya, Harippad, Kerala, 1977, Nat. Ctr. for Visual Arts, Trivandrum; dir. Film Line Corp., Trivandrum, 1975—; jury mem. Kerala State Film Awards, Trivandrum, 1982, Nat. Film Festival, New Delhi, 1986. Producer: (feature film) Swapnam, 1972 (state nat. award 1972); producer, dir.: (documentary) Know Thyself, 1977 (internat. award 1977); producer, dir. photography: (feature) Yagam, 1981 (nat. and state awards 1982). Mem. Am. Film Inst. (nat.), South Indian Film C. of C., Cine Technicians Assn., Producers Guild Assn. Home: Sivans Bldgs, Trivandrum Kerala, India 695 011 Office: Film Line Corp, MG Rd, Trivandrum Kerala 695 001, India

NAIR, VELAYUDHAN, pharmacologist, medical educator; b. India, Dec. 29, 1928; came to U.S., 1956, naturalized, 1963; s. Parameswaran and Ammini N.; m. Jo Ann Burke, Nov. 30, 1957; children: David, Larry, Sharon. Ph.D. in Medicine, U. London, 1956, D.Sc., 1976. Research assoc. U. Ill. Coll. Medicine, 1956-58; asst. prof. U. Chgo. Sch. Medicine, 1958-63; dir. lab. neuropharmacology and biochemistry Michael Reese Hosp. and Med. Center, Chgo., 1963-68; dir. therapeutic research Michael Reese Hosp. and Med. Center, 1968-71; vis. asso. prof. pharmacology Chgo. Med. Sch., 1963-68, vis. prof., 1968-71, prof. pharmacology, 1971—, vice chmn. dept. pharmacology and therapeutics, 1971-76; dean Chgo. Med. Sch. (Sch. Grad. and Postdoctoral Studies), 1976—. Contbr. articles to profl. publs. Recipient Morris Parker award U. Health Scis./Chgo. Med. Sch., 1972. Fellow AAAS, N.Y. Acad. Scis.; mem. Internat. Brain Research Orgn., Internat. Soc. Biochem. Pharmacology, Am. Soc. Pharmacology and Exptl. Therapeutics, Am. Soc. Clin. Pharmacology and Therapeutics, Radiation Research Soc., Soc. Toxicology, Am. Chem. Soc., Brit. Chem. Soc., Royal Inst. Chemistry (London), Pan Am. Med. Assn. (council on toxicology), Soc. Exptl. Biology and Medicine, AAUP, Soc. Neurosci., Internat. Soc. Chronobiology, Am. Coll. Toxicology, Internat. Soc. Developmental Neurosci., Sigma Xi, Alpha Omega Alpha. Club: Cosmos (Washington). Office: 3333 Green Bay Rd North Chicago IL 60064

NAISH, PETER LAWRENCE NORMAN, psychologist, educator; b. London, Jan. 15, 1945; s. Norman Harry and Marjorie Florence (Thring) N.; m. Margarita Guzman-Juarez, Apr. 16, 1977; children: Ileana, Andrew. BS in Physics and Chemistry, U. London, 1966; BS in Pyschology, U. Reading, 1976; DPhil, Oxford U., Eng., 1981. Postdoctoral research fellow dept. exptl. psychology Oxford U., 1981-87; lectr. psychology Somerville Coll., 1985-87; tutor psychology, cons. Open U., Milton Keynes, Eng., 1985—; prin. psychologist Royal Aerospace Establishment, Farnborough, Eng., 1987—. Author: What Is Hypnosis, 1986; contbr. articles to profl. jours.; inventor electro-mech. shutter. Social Sci. Research Council research grantee, 1981, Home Office research grantee, 1984. Mem. Brit. Psychol. Soc. (assoc.), Exptl. Psychology Assn., Brit. Soc. Exptl. and Clin. Hypnosis (mem. council 1982—, asst. editor 1982—, librarian 1985—), Radio Soc. Gt. Britain, Oxford Bach Choir. Mem. Ch. Eng. Home: 29 Silverthorne Dr, Caversham Reading RG4 7NR, England Office: Royal Aerospace Establishment, F131 Bldg, Farnborough England

NAJERA, RAFAEL, virologist; b. Córdoba, Spain, Feb. 19, 1938; s. Luis and María (Morrondo) N.; M.B., Madrid U., 1962, M.D., 1967; M.Sci., Birmingham (Eng.) Med. Sch., 1967, postgrad., 1967-68; D.P.H., Sch. Public Health Madrid, 1965; m. Margarita Vázquez de Parga, July 1, 1965; children—Isabel, Gonzalo. Assoc. chief, service respiratory and exanthematic viruses Nat. Center for Virology, Majadahonda, Madrid, 1963-72, chief service, 1972-80; med. officer virus diseases unit WHO, Geneva, 1980-81; assoc. prof. virology Madrid Faculty Medicine, 1970-73; dir. Nat. Center Microbiology, 1982-86, Gen. Inst. Health "Carlos III", 1986—, WHO Collaborating Ctr. for AIDS. Decorated knight comdr. Civil Order Sanidad. Mem. Spanish Soc. Microbiology (sec., pres. virology group 1970—), Spanish Soc. Virology (pres. 1988—), Soc. Gen. Microbiology, Am. Soc. Microbiology, Internat. Assn. Biol. Standardization, European Teratology Soc., Internat. Epidemiol. Assn., Am. Public Health Assn., others. Contbr. articles in field to profl jours. Office: Instituto de Salud Carlos III, Majadahonda, 28220 Madrid Spain

NAJIBULLAH, S'AYID MOHAMMAD, head of state of Democratic Republic of Afghanistan, army officer and party official; b. Kabul, Afghanistan, 1947; married; 1 dau. Student Kabul U., 1964. Head of KHAD Secret Police, Afghanistan, 1980, head security forces and armed forces, 1985—; mem. People's Dem. Party, Afghanistan, 1965, mem. Cen. Com., 1977, gen. sec. 1986—; ambassador to Iran, 1979; pres. Revolutionary Council, 1987—; pres. Republic of Afghanistan, 1987—. Office: care Hdqs Central Com, People's Dem Party Afghanistan, Kabul Afghanistan *

NAKACHE, MARGARET ANN, artist; b. Hartford, Conn., Dec. 17, 1932; d. Joseph Charles and Alice Mable (Coyle) Lynch; B.F.A., R.I. Sch. Design, 1954; French cert. L'Ecole Nationale Superieure Des Beaux-Arts, Paris, 1954-56; m. Fernand Robert Nakache, Aug. 17, 1957; children—Catherine, Patricia. Artist, Universal Films, N.Y.C., 1956-57; designer Girl Scouts U.S.A., N.Y.C., 1959-62; one-woman shows: retrospective exhbn. Palos Verdes (Calif.) Gallery, 1971, La Gallerie du Meridien, Paris, 1975, 77, 79, Prince Royal Gallery, Alexandria, Va., 1978, Hunter House, Vienna, Va., 1982, retrospective exhbn. Georgetown U. Hosp., Washington, 1985, 87; group shows include: Art Barn, Washington, 1978, Cape Cod Art Assn., West Barnstable, Mass., 1979, 83, Colvin Mill Run, Va., 1980; represented in permanent collections: L'Ambassade du Liban, Paris, Prince Royal Gallery, Our Lady of Victory Ch., Centerville, Mass., Georgetown U. Hosp., Washington, Sandscape Gallery, Munson Meeting, Chatham, Mass. Mem. Vienna Arts Soc. Roman Catholic. Home: 1448 Woodacre McLean VA 22101

NAKAGAMI, HIDETOSHI, science administrator, research manager; b. Bizen, Okayama, Japan, Mar. 11, 1945; s. Hideo Nakagami and Seiko (Takamatsu) N.; m. Miyoko Hayakwa, Nov. 6, 1970; children: Wakana, Hidehiro. BA in Engring., Yokohama Nat. U., Japan, 1968, M in Engring., 1970; postgrad., U. Tokyo, 1970-73. Pres. Jyukankyo Research Inst., Tokyo, 1973—; mem. com. Sci. and Tech. Agy., Tokyo, 1976-84, Econ. Planning Agy., Tokyo, 1980-82, Ministry Internat. Trade and Industry, Tokyo, 1985-86. Co-author: (with others) Energy Analysis, 1980 (Energy Forum award 1980), Energy, 1984; contbr. articles to profl. jours. Mem. Japan Soc. Energy and Resources, Archtl. Inst. Japan. Buddhist. Home: 1-1-16 C308 Meguro, 153 Meguro-ku, Tokyo Japan Office: Jyukankyo Research Inst Inc, #2 Mitomo Blvd, 2-2-8 Ebisunishi, 150 Shibuyaku, Tokyo Japan

NAKAI, TAKASHI, agricultural engineer; b. Japan, May 3, 1941; s. Isojirou and Ayako (Kawada) N.; m. Kazue Komatsu, Feb. 10, 1969; children: Kei, Yasumi, Shin. B of Agr., Kyushu U., Fukuoka, Japan, 1964, D of Agr, 1982. Ind. researcher Gov. Forest Experiment Sta., Tokyo, 1964-72, 73-78; guest researcher Div. of Bldg. Research CSIRO, Melbourne, Australia, 1972-73; head of engring. properties of wood unit Forestry and Forest Products Research Inst., Tsukuba City, Japan, 1978—. Co-author: Wood Handbook, 1982, Timber Engineering Book, 1985; editor: Jour. Tropical Forestry, 1982—, (newsletter) Jour. JWRS. Mem. Archtl. Inst. of Japan, Japan Wood Research Soc. (editor newsletter 1981-85), Forest Products Research Soc., Timber Research and Devel. Assn., Am. Soc. for Testing and Materials D-7 on Wood. Home: 2 3 32 Umezone, 305 Tsukuba City Ibaraki, Japan Office: Forestry and Forest Products Research Inst, 1 Matsuno-sato, 305 Kukizaki Ibaraki, Japan

NAKAJIMA, HAJIMU, architectural educator; b. Mariyama, Shiga, Japan, Nov. 22, 1925; s. Masasaburo and Kinu (Hinoue) N.; m. Yuriko Nakajima, May 2, 1951. Student, Nagoya Inst. Tech., Japan, 1947. Architect Takenaka Komuten Co. Ltd., Nagoya, 1947-48, Dept. Architecture Shiga Prefecture, Otu, Japan, 1948-63; asst. prof. Nagoya Inst. Tech., 1963-67; prof. Aichi Inst. Tech., Toyota, 1967—; dir. Nakajima study Dept. Architecture Inst. Tech., Nagoya, Hikone, 1967—; chmn. Archtl. Judgement Com., Okazaki, Aichi, 1981—; vice chmn. Environment Council Com., Hikone, Shiga, 1985-86, Architect Judgement Com., Otu, Shiga, 1984—, City Planning Com., Seto, Aichi, 1983—. Author: Architectural Design, 1972, Building Consruction, 1972, Town Planning, 1974, General Remarks of Architecture, 1975. Mem. Archtl. Inst. Japan (councilor), Archtl. Assn. Japan (councilor), Japan Ergonomics Research Soc. (councilor). Club: Nagoya Meito R.C. Home: Matsubara-cho, 522 Hikone, Shiga Japan Office: Aichi Inst Tech, Yakusa-cho, 470-03 Toyota, Aichi Japan

NAKAJIMA, HIROSHI, educator; b. Hiroshima, Japan, June 12, 1923; s. Iwao and Tamae (Takenaka) N.; student Nishogakusha Coll., 1942-44; B.A., Waseda U., 1950, M.A., 1954; m. Sei Sakao, May 2, 1966; children: Akihiko, Takehiko. Asst. prof. Japan Women's Coll. Econs., 1954-59; lectr. Waseda U., 1954-63; vis. prof. U. Helsinki, 1962-63; asst. prof. Waseda U., Tokyo, 1963-68, prof. comparative and internat. edn., 1968—. Mng. dir. Japanese Inst. Social Studies on Sweden, 1978—; vice-chmn. youth com. Higashikurumeshi, 1978-83; councilor mem. bd. edn. Higashikurumeshi, 1983—. Served with Japanese Army, 1943-46. Recipient Acad. Hon. Medal, U. Helsinki, 1963. Mem. Japan Comparative Edn. Soc. (mng. dir. 1972—), Comparative and Internat. Edn. Soc., Finnish Soc. Study Edn., Finnish Acad. Sci. and Letters (fgn. mem.). Author: The Development of American Educational Thought, 1959; Education in the Welfare States, 1965; School Education in the World, 1981. Home: 1-4-37 Minamisawa, Higashikurumeshi, Tokyo 203, Japan Office: 1-24-1 Toyama, Shinjyuku-ku, Tokyo 162, Japan

NAKAKUKI, MASAFUMI, physician, psychiatry educator; b. Shimotsuma, Ibaragi, Japan, Mar. 1, 1930; came to U.S., 1969, naturalized 1975; s. Keisuke and Toi (Saito) N.; m. Ritsuko Oka, May 25, 1957; children: Mari, Emma. MS, U. Ibaragi, 1949; MD, U. Tokyo, 1953. Diplomate Am. Bd. Psychiatry and Neurology. Intern U. Tokyo Hosp., 1953-54, dir. psychiat. inpatient service, 1966-69; resident in psychiatry U. Tokyo, 1954-60, U. Colo.-Denver, 1962-66; asst. prof. psychiatry U. Colo. Med. Ctr., Denver, 1969-73; staff psychiatrist Ft. Logan Mental Health Ctr., Denver, 1973-74, Arapahoe Mental Health Ctr., Englewood, Colo., 1974-76; med. dir. Park East Mental Health Ctr. Denver, 1977-83; pres. Masafumi Nakakuki, M.D., P.C., Denver, 1977—; pres. med. staff Bethesda Hosp., Denver, 1982-83; psychiat. cons. Asian Pacific Devel. Ctr., Denver, 1983—. Author: Textbook of Psychiatry for the General Practitioner, 1968; New Parenting and Culture, 1982. Bd. dirs. Asian Human Service Assn., Denver, 1982. Fulbright scholar, 1961. Fellow Am. Psychiat. Assn.; mem. Colo. Med. Soc., AAAS, N.Y. Acad. Scis. Office: 4770 E Iliff Ave Denver CO 80222

NAKAMURA, HIROMICHI, architect, consultant; b. Tokyo, Apr. 24, 1942; s. Kohki and Hirono N.; m. Hiroko Ohmata, Sept. 12, 1971. Grad., Tokyo U., 1966. Asst. architect Takeo Sato & Assocs. Architects, Minato-Ku, Tokyo, 1966-68, Masato Ohtaka & Assocs. Architects, Shibuya-ku, Tokyo, 1968-71; mng. dir. Kenzo Tange & Urtec, Minato-Ku, Tokyo, 1971-87, Hiromichi Nakamura Architect and Assocs., Shibuya-ku, 1987—. Mem. Japan Inst. Architects (com. mem.), Architect Inst. Japan. Club: Seizyo Loan Tennis. Home: 2-28-15 Kamisoshgiaya, Setagaya-ku, 157 Tokyo Japan Office: Hiromichi Nakamura, 30-1 Kamiyama-cho, Sibuya-ku, 107 Tokyo Japan

NAKAMURA, HIROMU, psychologist; b. Los Angeles, Nov. 6, 1926; s. Genjiro and Misao (Kamura) N.; A.B., U. Redlands, 1948; M.A., UCLA, 1951; Ph.D., U. So. Calif., 1973; m. Tamaye Yumiba, Mar. 27, 1955; children—Glenn Vernon, Colleen Patricia. Clin. psychology intern Massillon (Ohio) State Hosp., 1951-52; clin. psychologist Patton (Calif.) State Hosp., 1952-58; clin. psychologist Lanterman State Hosp. and Developmental Center (formerly Pacific State Hosp.), Pomona, Calif., 1958-—, program dir., 1971-—. Mem. Am., Calif. psychol. assns., Am. Assn. Mental Deficiency, AAAS, Am. Pub. Health Assn., Nat. Geographic Soc., Town Hall Calif., Los Angeles World Affairs Council, World-wide Acad. Scholars, N.Y. Acad. Scis., Psi Chi. Presbyterian. Home: 3861 Shelter Grove Dr Claremont CA 91711 Office: PO Box 100 Pomona CA 91766

NAKAMURA, HISAO, corporate professional; b. Kyoto, Japan, Nov. 11, 1923; s. Kinjiro and Masao N.; m. Fusako Nagai, 1955; children: Takashi, Reiko. Degree in Econs., Kyoto U., 1948, postgrad. degree, 1950. With Kurray Co. Ltd., Osaka, Japan, 1950-72; dir. Kurray Co. Ltd., Osaka, 1972-76, mng. dir., 1976-81, exec. v.p., 1981-85, pres., 1985—; pres. Kyowa Gas Chem. Co. Ltd., Tokyo, 1985—; chmn. Kuraray Trading Co. Ltd., Osaka, 1984—. Chmn. Saijo (Japan) Cen. Hosp, 1986—; bd. dirs. Aizenen Hosp., Osaka, 1984—, Ohara Mus. Art, Kurashiki, Japan, 1985—. Mem. Japan Chem. Fibers Assn., Kansai Econ. Fedn. (bd. dirs. 1985—), Japan Fedn. Econ. Orgns. (bd. dirs. 1985—). Clubs: Okayama (Japan) Mitsu Country; Imabashi (Osaka). Home: 52 Nigawa-dai, Takarazuka Hyogo 665, Japan Office: Kuraray Co Ltd, 1-12-39 Umeda Kita Ku, Osaka 530, Japan

NAKAMURA, KAZUO, vacuum company executive; b. Chichibu, Japan, Sept. 27, 1919; s. Hisakichi and Yasu (Asami) N.; m. Masuko Ukita, May 4, 1946; children—Yutaka, Machiko Mise, Kumiko Usuda. B.S., Tokyo U., 1942. Researcher, Naval Engring. Research Inst., Tokyo, 1942-45; ednl. ofcl. dept. physics Tokyo U., 1946-49, 69; lectr., asst. prof. Toyo U., 1951-53; gen. engring. mgr. and dir. Tokuda Seisakusho Co., Tokyo, 1949-59; dir. Ulvac Corp., Chigasaki, Japan, 1959-79, auditor, 1983—; pres. Shinkuriko Co. subs. Ulvac, Yokohama, Japan, 1969-72; chmn. Ulvac Coating Corp. subs. Ulvac, Chichibu, Japan, 1979-83. Author: Vacuum Technology and Freeze Drying, 1954; An Introduction to Vacuum Industry, 1964; (with others) Ency. of Aeromech. Engring., 1955; patentee in field. Served to lt. Japanese Navy, 1942-45. Mem. Vacuum Soc. of Japan, Japan Solar Energy Soc., Am. Vacuum Soc., Japan Soc. Sci. Policy and Research Mgmt. Assn. Research Inst. Sci. and Tech. (dir.). Home: 2 33 6 Okusawa Setagaya-Ku, Tokyo 158, Japan Office: Ulvac Corp Kanagawa Prefecture, 2500 Hagizono, Chigasaki 253, Japan

NAKAMURA, KIKONOSHIN, patent documentalist; b. Tsuruoka, Yamagata, Japan, Oct. 24, 1933; s. Shichiro and Ei (Hiwatashi) N.; m. Kazuko Yamaguchi, Nov. 24, 1965; children: Aya, Maki. BS, Tohoku U., Sendai, Japan, 1957, MS, 1959, PhD, 1962. Researcher Cen. Research Labs., Ajinomoto Co., Kawasaki, Kanagawa, Japan, 1962-65, asst. mgr. patent dept., 1982—; patent documentalist Cen. Research Labs., Ajinomoto Co., Tokyo, Kyobashi, 1965-81; chief mem. patent info. com. Japan Patent Assn., Chiyoda, Tokyo, 1981-87. Author, editor: Search Report on Patent Documentation Activities in Europe and U.S.A., 1981. Office: Ajinomoto Co Inc, Patent Dept, Suzuki-Cho 1-1, Kawasaki, Kanagawa 240, Japan

NAKAMURA, MASAMI, physician; b. Yokohama, Japan, Nov. 18, 1934; s. Seiichi and Wasako N.; m. Yuriko Yamashita, Jan. 26, 1963; children—Mari, Hiromi. M.D., Tokyo U., 1959; D.Med. Scis., 1965. Mem. med. staff Tokyo U., 1965-66, 69-72; research fellow U. Minn., Austin, 1966-69; dir. Nakamura Clinic, Yokohama, 1972—; dir. The Kanagawa-ku Med. Assn., Yokohama, Japan, 1979—. Mem. Japanese Soc. Internal Medicine, Japanese Soc. Gastroenterology, Japanese Soc. Alcohol Studies, N.Y. Acad. Scis. Club: Kanagawa-East Rotary (Yokohama). Home: 59-8 Sawatari Kanagawa-Ku, Yokohama 221, Japan Office: Nakamura Clinic, 2-16 Kamitanmachi, Yokohama 221, Japan

NAKAMURA, YASUHIDE, marketing executive; b. Utsunomiya, Tochigi, Japan, Feb. 7, 1950; s. Yasuichi and Taeko Nakamura; m. Tokuko Nakamura, Oct. 8, 1972; children: Jun, Masaki. Degree in organic chem., Toyo U., Tokyo, 1972. Chemist Funakoshi Pham, Tokyo, 1972-74; with staff waters chromato div. Nihon Millipore Ltd., Tokyo, 1975-80, sales mgr., then dir., 1981-85; area mgr. br. sales waters chromato div. Nihon Millipore Ltd., Japan, 1986-87, dir. mktg., 1987—. Home: 1-21-21 Kamiimaizumi, 243-04 Ebina Kanagawa Japan Office: Nihon Millipore Ltd, Water Chromato Div, 1-3-12 Kitashinagawa, Shinagawa-ku Tokyo 140, Japan

NAKANISHI, KOJI, chemistry educator, research institute administrator; b. Hong Kong, May 11, 1925; came to U.S., 1969; s. Yuzo and Yoshiko (Sakata) N.; m. Yasuko Abe, Oct. 25, 1947; children: Keiko, Jun. B.Sc., Nagoya U., Japan, 1947; DSc (hon.), Williams Coll., 1987; Ph.D., Nagoya U., 1954; DSc (hon.), Williams Coll., 1987. Asst. prof. Nagoya U., 1955-58; prof. Tokyo Kyoiku U., 1958-63, Tohoku U., Sendai, Japan, 1963-69; prof. chemistry Columbia U., N.Y.C., 1969-80; centennial prof. chemistry Columbia U., 1980—; dir. research Internat. Ctr. Insect Physiology and Ecology, Nairobi, Kenya, 1969-77; dir. Suntory Inst. for Bioorganic Research, Osaka, Japan, 1979—. Author: Infrared Spectroscopy—Practical, 1962, rev. edit., 1977, Circular Dichroic Spectroscopy—Exciton Coupling in Organic Stereochemistry, 1983. Recipient Asahi Cultural award Asahi Press, Tokyo, 1968, E.E. Smissmann medal U. Kans., 1979, H.C. Urey award Phi Lambda Upsilon chpt. Columbia U., 1980, Alcon award in ophthalmology, 1986; Paul Karrer gold medal U. Zurich, 1986. Mem. Chem. Soc. Japan (soc. award 1954, 79), Am. Chem. Soc. (E. Guenther award 1978, Remsen award, Md. sect. 1981), Brit. Chem. Soc. (Centenary medal 1979), Am. Acad. Arts and Scis., Am. Soc. Pharmacognosy (research achievement award 1985). Home: 560 Riverside Dr New York NY 10027 Office: Dept Chemistry Columbia U 116th St Broadway New York NY 10027

NAKARAI, CHARLES FREDERICK TOYOZO, musicologist; b. Indpls., Apr. 25, 1936; s. Toyozo Wada and Frances Aileen N.; B.A. cum laude, Butler U., 1958, Mus.M., 1967; postgrad. U. N.C., 1967-70. Organist, dir. choirs Northwood Christian ch., Indpls., 1954-57; minister music Broad Ripple Christian Ch., Indpls., 1957-58; asst. prof. music Milligan Coll., Tenn., 1970-72; pvt. instrn. organ, piano, Durham, 1972—. Served with USAF, 1958-64. Mem. Am. Musicol. Soc., Coll. Music Soc., Am. Guild Organists, Music Tchrs. Nat. Assn., Music Library Assn., Durham Music Tchrs. Assn. Composer: Three Movements for Chorus, 1971, Bluesy, 1979. Address: 3520 Mayfair St Apt 205 Durham NC 27707

NAKASHIO, TATSUYA, land development auditor; b. Kure, Hiroshima, Japan, Jan. 1, 1921; s. Tsutaichi and Katsuno (Murao) N.; m. Hisako Koike, Feb. 28, 1945; children—Noburu, Kazumi. Student Tokyo U., 1942-44. With personnel div. Mitsui Mining Co., Tokyo, 1944-49; with planning sect. Econ. Investigation Agy., Tokyo, 1949-52; govt. orgn. officer Adminstrv. Mgmt. Agy., Tokyo, 1952-75; chief of regional office, auditor Land Devel. Pub. Corp., Tokyo, 1975-79, cons., 1979-81. Author: Modernization of Administrative Management, 1959; Government Management, 1970, 2d edit., 1980. UN fellow, 1956-57. Avocations: golf; dancing. Home: 30-13 Ikebukuro Naka-ku, Yokohama Kanagawa-ken 231, Japan

NAKASONE, YASUHIRO, former prime minister of Japan; b. Takasaki City, Gunma Prefecture, Japan, May 27, 1918; m. Tsukato Kobayashi, 1945;

children: Michiko, Mieko, Hirofumi. Grad., U. Tokyo, 1941. With Ministry of Home Affairs, Japan, 1941, 45-47; head Police Adminstrn. Dept. Kagawa Prefectural Govt.; insp. Tokyo Mt. Police Dept., to 1947; mem. Ho. of Reps. of Japan Tokyo, 1947—; minister of state, dir. gen. Sci. and Tech. Agy., 1959-60; minister of transport 1967-68; minister of state, dir. gen. Def. Agy., 1970-71; minister of internat. trade and industry 1972-74; minister of state, dir. gen. Adminstrn. Mgmt. Agy., 1980-82; prime minister 1982-87; exec. council Liberal Dem. Party of Japan, 1971-72, 77-78, sec. gen., 1974-76, pres., until 1987. Served to lt. comdr. Imperial Navy, 1941-45. Office: care Liberal Democratic Party, Tokyo Japan *

NAKATA, TERUKO, educator; b. Osaka City, Osaka, Japan, Feb. 20, 1935; d. Hajime and Asako Yuno; m. Minoru Nakata, Mar. 20, 1960; children: Kazuyo, Shoichi,Shinji. BSociology, Nanzan U., Japan, 1957. Lic. social studies tchr. Researcher human relationship gen. research group Med. Dept. Nagoya U., Nagoya City, Japan, 1957-59; asst. Aichiprefectural U., Nagoya City, 1959-81; asst. prof. social studies Nagoya City Women's Jr. Coll., 1981-88, prof., 1988—. Author: Women's Independence and Domestic Science, 1981, Modern Family and Raising Children, 1986, Working Women in Nagoya, 1987; author, editor: Women's Work and a Nursery School, 1987. Mem. Nagoya City Conf. Women's Problems, 1976-77; mem. ops. council Nagoya Women Workers' Ctr., 1980-81; pres. Nagoya City Pub. Nursery Sch. Parents Assn., 1945-49, Aichi Nurture Groups Liaison Conf., 1949-55. Mem. Japan Social Welfare Soc. (mem. editorial staff 1987), Aichi Women Research Workers' Assn. Home: 2-11-12 Shinnishi Chikusa-ku, Nagoya Aichi-ken 464, Japan

NAKATANI, SHIGEYUKI, hotel and restaurant executive; b. Kanazawa, Ishikawa, Japan, Nov. 16, 1947; s. Tokio and Teruko Nakatani; m. Yuko Nakatani; children: Gruen, Miyo. B of Polit. Sci., Waseda U., 1972; post-grad., Ariz. State U., 1976; M of Profl. Studies, Cornell U., 1981. Dir. personnel dept. Sanby Devel. Co., Tokyo, 1971-73; exec. dir. Habusui Hotel Co., Kanazawa, 1974-79; pres. Maisonde Rose Co., Kanazawa, 1982—; lectr. dept. English Kanazawa Women's Coll., 1985—. Author: Japanese Inns, 1981. Mem. Kanazawa Japanese Inns Assn. (bd. execs. 1987). Club: Saigawa Forum (Kanazawa). Lodge: Rotary (chmn. internat. friendship com. 1986).

NAKATSUJI, TERUYUKI, construction company executive; b. Sakai, Japan, Nov. 8, 1947; s. Yoshio and Yaeko (Shinkuma) N.; m. Kazuko Koide, Oct. 10, 1975; children: Shunichiro, Hirotaka, Yuki. BS, Osaka (Japan) U., 1971, MS, 1973, PhD, 1982. Researcher Shimizu Corp., Tokyo, 1973-85, sr. researcher, 1985-86, mgr. tech. div., 1986—; dir. Nefcom Corp., Tokyo, 1987—. Author: Welding Joints of Buildings, 1983, Structural Reliability, 1988, Welding Dynamics, 1988; patentee concrete reinforcement. Fellow Stud Welder Authorizing Com.; mem. Japan Inst. Welding, Archtl. Inst. Japan. Buddhist. Home: 12 15 Imagawa 1 Chome, Suginami ku, Tokyo 167, Japan Office: Shimizo Corp, 15 13 Shibaura 4 Chome, Minato ku, Tokyo 108, Japan

NAKAZAWA, OKUTO, architectural design company executive, architect; b. Itabashi-ku, Tokyo, Japan, Oct. 28, 1954; s. Toyoshi and Kii (Kumakura) N.; m. Ikuko Shimizu, Nov. 20, 1983. BArch, Sci. U. of Tokyo, 1980, MS in Engring., 1982. First class architect, Japan. Asst. instr. Sci. U. of Tokyo, 1982-87; pres. Space produce OCToi OCT, Tokyo, 1986—; architect Akira Yamashita & Assocs., Inc., Boston, 1987—; vis. researcher Japan System Devel. Found., Tokyo, 1984; vis. architect Takeo Sato & Assocs., Inc., Tokyo, 1985. Recipient award Meml. Library Sci. U. of Tokyo, 1981, SD Rev. 1984, 1984. Mem. Archtl. Inst. of Japan, Bldg. Climatology Subcom. of Kanto (physiol. and psychol. problems subcom. 1986—, area dist. research com. 1985-89). Home: NIC-heim 803 1-6-2, Azumabashi Sumida-ku, 130 Tokyo Japan Office: Space produce OCToi OCT, 301, 1-12-2 Hanakawado, Taito-ku, 111 Tokyo Japan

NAKHOSTEEN, JOHN ALEXANDER, pulmonary internist, educator; b. Isfahan, Iran, Mar. 3, 1937; s. Adle Benjamin and Margaret (Badal) N.; m. Gabriele Krebs, July 12, 1968; children: Benjamin, Sandra, Nicola. BA, Claremont (Calif.) Men's Coll., 1959; MD, U. Cologne, Fed. Republic Germany, 1970. Intern, resident Marienhosp., Kerpen, Fed. Republic Germany, 1970-72; resident in surgery Nikolaushops., Rheinberg, Fed. Republic Germany, 1972-73; resident in internal medicine Generalhosp., Krefeld, Fed. Republic Germany, 1973-77; resident in pulmonary medicine Ruhrlandklinik, Essen, Fed. Republic Germany, 1977-80, pulmonary cons., 1980-81; resident in allergy and immunology Inst. Immunology, Univ. Hosp., Essen, Fed. Republic Germany, 1981-83; chief pulmonary dept. Augusta Teaching Hosp., Bochum, Fed. Republic Germany, 1983—; assoc. prof. medicine Univ. Hosp., Essen, 1982—; vis. prof. pulmonary div. UCLA Health Ctr., 1984—; chmn. commn. Quality Control Bronchology, Bochum, 1985—. Author: Atlas-Manual Bronchoscopy, 1983; editor: Bronchology, 1981; mem. bd. editors Pneumologie Thieme, Stuttgart, Fed. Republic Germany, 1986—; contbr. numerous articles to sci. publs.; creator teaching models, bronchoscopy, heart-lung model. Grantee German Sci. Inst. Fellow Am. Coll. Chest Physicians, Am. Coll. Chest Physicians, German Cen. Com. Tuberculosis (bd. dirs. commn. of experts 1986—), Assn. Clin. Pulmonology (chmn. 1985—), German Pulmonary Assn.; mem. World Assn. Bronchology (bd. dirs. 1985—). Republican. Anglican. Office: Augusta Teaching Hosp, Pulmonary Dept, Bergstrasse 26, 4630 Bochum Federal Republic of Germany

NALCIOGLU, ORHAN, radiological science educator; b. Istanbul, Feb. 2, 1944; U.S., 1966, naturalized, 1974; s. Mustafa and Meliha N. B.S., Robert Coll., Istanbul, 1966; M.S., Case Western Res. U., 1968; Ph.D., U. Ore., 1970. Postdoctoral fellow dept. physics U. Calif.-Davis, 1970-71; Research assoc. dept. physics U. Rochester, N.Y., 1971-74; Research assocs. dept. physics U. Wis., Madison, 1974-76; sr. physicist EMI Med. Inc., Northbrook, Ill., 1976-77; prof. depts. radiol. scis., elec. engring. and medicine U. Calif.-Irvine, 1977—, head div. physics and engring., 1985—; cons. UN, 1980-81. Contbr. articles to profl. jours. Mobil scholar, 1961-66. Fellow IEEE; mem. Am. Phys. Soc., Am. Assn. Physicists in Medicine. Democrat. Subspecialty: Medical physics. Office: Dept Radiol Sci Univ Calif Irvine CA 92717

NALIMOV, VASILII VASILYEVICH, mathematician, educator, philosopher; b. Moscow, Nov. 4, 1910; s. Vasilii Petrovich and Nadezhda Ivanovna (Totubalina) N.; m. Irina Vladimirovna Usova (dec.); m. Jeanna Aleksandrovna Drogalina. Student in math., Moscow U., 1929-30; D of Engring. Scis. (hon.), Inst. Meterology, Leningrad, USSR, 1964. Researcher All-Union Inst. Electric Tech., Moscow, 1931-34, Inst. Instruments Constrn., Moscow, 1934-36; researcher metall. plant Kazakhstan, USSR, 1949-56; researcher Inst. Rare Metals, Moscow, 1959-65; prof., head lab. Moscow State U., 1965—. Author: The Application of Mathematical Statistics to Chemical Analysis, 1963, Statistical Methods for Design of Extremal Experiments, 1968, Measurement of Science. Study of the Development of Science as Information Process, 1971, In the Labyrinths of Language: A Mathematician's Journey, 1981, Faces of Science, 1981, Realms of the Unconscious: The Enchanted Frontier, 1982, Space, Time and Life. The Probabilistic Pathways of Evolution, 1985, others; editor: Viniti, USSR Acad. Scis., Moscow, 1956-59; mem. editorial bd.: Indsl. Lab. jour., Moscow, 1961—; cons. editor Scientometrics jour., Budapest, 1980—; contbr. numerous papers to sci. jours. Recipient Derek de Solla Price medal Internat. Jour. Scientometrics, 1987. Home: ul Udaltsova 4 kv 327, 117 415 Moscow USSR Office: Moscow State U, Lab Bldg A, 119 899 Moscow USSR

NAM, JUNG WAN, mathematics educator; b. Chinju, Korea, Apr. 21, 1927; s. Eok Man Nam and Uh Ik Choi; children: Sukyong, Likyong, Hyonchel, Mikyong. BS, Seoul Nat. U., 1956; MS, Kyungpook Nat. U., 1971; PhD, Pusan Nat. U., 1979. chief dept. math. Gyeongsang Nat. U., 1970-80, dean coll., 1980-84, dean grad. sch. edn., 1984-87; com. of edn. Gyeongnam Edn. Bd., Changwon, Korea, 1984—. Recipient Edn. Merit award Korean Edn. Fedl., 1983, Nation award Govt. of Korea, 1986. Home: 297-7 Sangdae-dong, 660-320 Chinju Republic of Korea Office: Gyeongsang Nat U, 900 Kazoa-dong, 660-701 Chinju Republic of Korea

NAM, SANG BOO, physicist; b. Kyung Nam, Korea, Jan. 30, 1936; came to U.S., 1959, naturalized, 1978; s. Sai Hi and Boon Hi (Kim) N.; m. Wonki Kim, June 1, 1969; children—Sae Woo, Jean Ok. B.S., Seoul Nat. U., Korea, 1958; M.S., U. Ill., 1961, Ph.D., 1966. Research assoc. U. Ill., Urbana, 1966; research fellow Rutgers U., New Brunswick, N.J., 1966-68; asst. prof. physics U. Va., Charlottesville, 1968-71; vis. prof. physics Seoul Nat. U., 1970, Belfer Grad. Sch., Yeshiva U., N.Y.C., 1971-74; sr. research fellow in physics Nat. Acad. Sci.-NRC, Washington, 1974-76; research prof. physics U. Dayton, Ohio, 1976-80; sr. research physicist Grad. Research Ctr., Wright State U., Dayton, 1980—. Served with Korean Army, 1958-59. U. Ill. fellow, 1961. Fellow Am. Phys. Soc., Korean Phys. Soc.; mem. AAAS, N.Y. Acad. Scis., Sigma Xi. Home: 7735 Peters Pike Dayton OH 45414

NAMALIU, RABBIE, Papua New Guinea government official. Prime minister Papua New Guinea, Port Moresby, 1988—. Address: Office of Prime Minister, Port Moresby Papua New Guinea *

NAMBA, TATSUJI, physician, researcher; b. Changchun, China, Jan. 29, 1927; came to U.S., 1959, naturalized, 1968; s. Yosuke and Michino (Hinata) N. M.D., Okayama U., Japan, 1950, Ph.D., 1955. Asst., lectr. medicine Okayama U. Med. Sch. and Hosp., 1955-62; research assoc. Maimonides Med. Ctr., Bklyn., 1959-66; dir. neuromuscular labs. Maimonides Med. Ctr., 1966-70, dir. neuromuscular disease div., head electromyography clinic, 1966—; instr., asst. prof., assoc. prof. medicine State U. N.Y., Bklyn., 1959-76; prof. State U. N.Y., 1976—; mem. med. adv. bd. Myasthenia Gravis Found., 1968—. Recipient commendation for research and clin. activities on insecticide poisoning Minister Health and Welfare, Japanese Govt., 1958. Fellow A.C.P.; mem. A.M.A., Am. Acad. Neurology, Am. Soc. Pharmacology and Exptl. Therapeutics, Am. Soc. Clin. Pharmacology and Therapeutics, Am. Assn. Electromyography. Office: 4802 10th Ave Brooklyn NY 11219

NAMDARI, BAHRAM, surgeon; b. Oct. 26, 1939; s. Rostam and Sarvar Namdari; M.D., 1966; m. Kathleen Diane Wilmore, Jan. 5, 1976; 3 children. Resident in gen. surgery St. John's Mercy Med. Ctr., St. Louis, 1969-73; fellow in cardiovascular surgery with Michael DeBakey, Baylor Coll. Medicine, Houston, 1974-75; practice medicine specializing in gen. and vascular surgery and surg. treatment of obesity, Milw., 1976—; mem. staff St. Mary's, St. Luke's, St. Michael, Good Samaritan, Trinity Meml., St. Anthony, Family, St. Francis hosps. (all Milw.); founder, pres. Famous Mealwaukee Foods Enterprises. Diplomate Am. Bd. Surgery. Fellow ACS, Internat. Coll. Surgeons; mem. Med. Soc. Milwaukee County, Milw. Acad. Surgery, Wis. Med. Soc., Wis. Surg. Soc., Royal Soc Medicine Eng. (affiliate), Am. Soc. for Bariatric Surgery, AMA, World Med. Assn., Internat. Acad. Bariatric Medicine (founding mem.), Michael DeBakey Internat. Cardiovascular Soc. Contbr. articles to med. jours.; patentee med. instruments and other devices. Office: Great Lakes Med and Surg Ctr 6000 S 27th St Milwaukee WI 53221

NAMIAS, ALEXIS, dermatologic surgeon, consultant; b. Paris, Mar. 25, 1952; s. Gustave and Rose (Gottheff) N.; m. Laura Barbero, July 15, 1977; children: Jonathan, Raphaël. MD, U. Paris VII, 1981. Cons. Hosp. St. Louis, Paris, 1982, Hosp. de Passy, Paris, 1982-85; practice medicine specializing in dermatologic surgery, Paris, 1985—; instr. U. Paris VII, 1985-86. Contbr. articles on surgery and dermatology to med. jours. Served to lt. French Navy, 1980. Mem. Soc. Française de Chirurgie Dermatologique, Soc. Française de Médecine Esthétique. Club: Forest Hills Tennis (Paris). Home: 75 Bis Ave de Wagram, 75017 Paris France Office: Cabinet de Chirurgie Dermatologique, 28 Place St Ferdinand, 75017 Paris France

NAMIKAWA, YASUO, architect; b. Kyoto, Japan, Feb. 1, 1919; s. Unosuke and Seki (Akasaki) N.; m. Toshiko Matsuo, Feb. 1, 1955; children: Chikage, Chiharu. Engring. cert., Japanese Imperial Navy, Yokosuka, 1942. Lic. architect and builder, Kyoto Prefecture, 1950. Apprentice builder Yamazaki Constrn. Co., Kyoto, 1931-40; master builder, owner Namikawa Constrn. Co., Kyoto, 1951—; guest lectr. Kyoto U., 1982—, Japan Architects' Assn., 1985, Seibu Developers Inc., 1985. Asst. editor, essayist Hiroba Archtl. Jour., 1955—; Contbr. essays to newspapers, 1977—. Asst. fireman Kyoto Fire Dept., 1938—; cons. Kyoto Prefecture Inst. for Promotion Traditional Bldg., 1982—. Served with the Japanese Navy, 1940-46. Recipient award for promotion traditional ceremonies Mayor of Kyoto, 1979, award for preservation traditional architecture Mayor of Kyoto, 1987. Mem. Japanese Architects' Found. (traditional craftsmen's award 1983), Japan Architects' Soc., Japan Archtl. Hist. Soc. Buddhist. Home and Office: Namikawa Constrn Co, 46 Anenishi, Sanjo-Omiya Nishi-Iru Agaru, Nakagyo-Ku, Kyoto 604, Japan

NAMKUNG, WON, plasma physicist; b. Mokpo, Korea, Oct. 13, 1943; came to U.S., 1971; s. Hyung and Namchul (Kim) N.; m. Cookie Whang, Dec. 27, 1969; children—Ju, Young-Nan. B.S. in Physics, Seoul Nat. U. (Korea), 1965; Ph.D. in Physics, U. Tenn., 1977. Research assoc. U. Tenn.-Knoxville, 1978, U. Md., College Park, 1978-80, asst. prof., 1980-84; research physicist Naval Surface Weapons Ctr., White Oak, Md., 1984—. Contbr. articles to profl. jours. Dept. Energy grantee, 1982-85; Air Force Office Sci. Research grantee, 1981-84; Strategic Def. Initiative Orgn. grantee, 1986—. Mem. Am. Phys. Soc., IEEE. Roman Catholic. Current work: Microwave generation, particle beam physics, RF plasma heating, pulsed power engineering, accelerator physics. Subspecialties: Plasma physics; Electrical engineering. Home: 8601 Briarwood Ct Laurel MD 20708

NAMPHY, HENRI, former head of state Republic of Haiti, army officer; b. Nov. 2, 1932; married; 2 children. Grad., Haitian Mil. Acad. Army officer, Haiti, 1954-88, brig. gen., 1981-84, lt. gen., from 1984, chief of staff of Armed Forces; mem. Mil. Junta and head of state, 1986-88, pres. Nat. Council of Govt., 1986-88. Address: Nat Council Govt, Office of President, Port-au-Prince Haiti *

NANCE, MARY JOE, educator; b. Carthage, Tex., Aug. 7, 1921; d. F. F. and Mary Elizabeth (Knight) Born; B.B.A., North Tex. State U., 1953; postgrad. Northwestern State U. La., 1974; M.E., Antioch U., 1978; m. Earl C. Nance, July 12, 1946; 1 child, David Earl. Tchr., Port Isabel (Tex.) Integrated Sch. Dist., to 1979; tchr. English, Splendora (Tex.) High Sch., 1979-80, McLeod, Tex., 1980-81, Bremond, Tex., 1981-84. Served with WAAC, 1942-43, WAC 1945. Recipient Image Maker award Carthage C. of C., 1984; cert. bus. educator. Mem. Nat. Bus. Edn. Assn., NEA, Tex. Tchrs. Assn., Tex. Bus. Tchrs. Assn. (cert. of appreciation 1978), Nat. Women's Army Corps Vets. Assn., Air Force Assn. (life), Assn. Supervision and Curriculum Devel., Council for Basic Edn., Nat. Hist. Soc., Tex. Council English Tchrs. Baptist.

NANDA, DAVE KUMAR, geneticist; b. Mandibahuddin, India, Mar. 15, 1938; s. Chaman Lal and Ganga Devi (Sehgal) N.; B.Sc., Delhi U., 1958; M.S., Indian Agrl. Research Inst., 1960; Ph.D. in Agronomy and Genetics, U. Wis., 1964; m. Connie Kalra, Sept. 17, 1966; children—Arvin Kumar, Paul Kalra. Internat. trainee DeKalb Ag Research (Ill.), 1964-65; dir. research Edward J. Funk & Sons, Inc., Kentland, Ind., 1965-68; Eastern area research dir. Pfizer Genetics, Inc., Windfall, Ind., 1968-80; dir. research O's Gold Seed Co., Parkersburg, Iowa, 1980-82, v.p. research, 1982-86; v.p. research Seed Tec Internat., Inc., pres. India Assn. Cedar Falls-Waterloo, 1983-84. Research asst. maize, millets collecting unit leader The Rockefeller Found.,1960-61. Mem. Am. Soc. Agronomy, Crop Sci. Soc. Am., Soil Sci. Soc. Am., Am. Seed Trade Assn., Ind. Seed Producers Assn. Ind. (past pres.), Sigma Xi. Contbr. articles to profl. jours. Home: 148 Rhinegarten Dr Florissant MO 63031 Office: Seed Tec Internat Inc Carrollton IL 62016

NANDADASA, PUWAKDANDAWE NARAYANA, manufacturing company executive; b. Matara, Sri Lanka, Dec. 6, 1944; s. Puwakdandawe Narayana and Athuraliya Welandagoda (Jemonona) Handy Silva; m. Devasurendra Mallika, Feb. 5, 1969; children: Roshini Indika, Nayomi Niroshi, Gothami Shironee, Dinu Deep. Student, Ceylon Tech. Coll., Sri Lanka, 1962-64, City and Guilds London Inst., 1967-70, Stanford U., 1985. Spl. apprentice engring. Colombo (Sri Lanka) Port Commn., 1964-67; progress asst. Ceylon Transport Bd., Colombo, 1967-69; mech. engr. State Timber Corp., Colombo, 1969-74, project engr., 1974-80; founding mem. Flexport Little Three Daughters, Colombo, 1980—; chmn., mng. dir. Flexport Ltd., Colombo and Nugegoda, 1980—; chmn. Flexport Group of Cos., Colombo, 1980—; design cons. Priministers Tower Hall Found., Sri Lanka, 1985-87, Arthur C. Clarke Ctr. Modern Tech., 1985-87, Jaycees, Sri Lanka, 1980-87, Lions, Sri Lanka, 1982-87. Designer and creator Dr. Arthur C. Clarke Trophy Satellite Communication, 1985; inventor stone carving by chems., 1985, alluminium printing, 1987. Recipient Ten Outstanding Persons award Jaycees, 1982; Export Devel. Bd. scholar, 1985. Mem. Photo Chem. Machining Inst., Am. Electroplater's & Surface Finishing Soc., Assn. Interior Designers. Buddhist. Home: 127 Jambugasmulla Mawatha, Nugegoda Sri Lanka Office: Flexport Little Three Daughters', 69 Old Kesbawa Rd, Rattanapitiya, Boralasgamuwa Sri Lanka

NANUT RIES, LUCIA NEDA, public relations executive; b. Banya Luka, Bosnia, Yugoslavia, Nov. 6, 1938; d. Carlo and Maria (Tyman) N.; m. Bernard Jean Ries, May 16, 1983. Degree in elec. engring., U. Elec. Engring., Zagreb, Yugoslavia, 1958; degree in Serbo Croate, U. Langs., Zagreb, 1958. Dir. Ries Engring. Share Co., Addis Abeba, Ethiopia, Nyala Motors Share Co., Addis Abeba, Paul Ries and Sons Ethiopia Ltd. Share Co., Addis Abeba, 1974-88. Club: Internat. Womens (Addis Abeba). Home: 19 Ave Santa Maria, 06590 Port La Galere, Theoule France

NANZ, CLAUS ERNEST, economist, management consultant; b. Stuttgart, June 14, 1934. B. Commerce (Dipl. rer. pol.) U. Frankfurt; Doctor's degree (Dr. rer. oec.), U. Mannheim. Gen. mgr., bd. dirs. various German holding cos.; pres., owner Eurofound Internat. Mgmt. Cons., 1976—. Author: Fluktuation: Das Problem und betriebliche Massnahmen seiner Minderung. Recipient Best Thesis award Univ. Mannheim and Rhein-Main C. of C. Avocations: climbing, skiing, scientific travelling, languages. Address: Mittelberg 244 D 8986, Federal Republic of Germany

NAOHIKO, OKUBO, member House of Representatives; b. Tokyo, Oct. 4, 1936. MA, Weseda U., Tokyo, 1959. With Eguchi Ins. Co., Tokyo, 1956-61, Seikyo Press, Tokyo, 1961-65; sec.-gen. Min-on, Tokyo, 1965-69; member House of Representatives, Tokyo, 1969—; sec.-gen. Komeito (Clean Government Party), Tokyo, 1986—. Dir. Standing Com. Foreign Affairs, 1970, Standing Com. Diet Policy, 1972, Youth Bur.; chmn. Diet Policy Com., 1977; mem. Standing Com. Budget. Office: Komeito, 17 Minamimoto-machi, Shinjuku-ku, Tokyo 160, Japan

NAPIER, BURTON GEORGE, bank executive; b. Toronto, Ont., Nov. 11, 1940; s. George Burton and Elizabeth Barr (Canning) N.; m. Gillian Janice Renton; children: Mark Paul, Tracy Joyce. Student, U. Toronto Conservatory Music, 1955; diploma in computer sci., Humber Coll., 1970; M in Program Mgmt., Harvard U., 1980. Mktg. mgr. Indsl. Acceptance Corp., Toronto, Ont., 1963-67; mgmt. cons. Sigma Mgmt. Ltd., Toronto, Ont., 1967-69; computer mgr. Can. Imperial Bank Commerce, Toronto, Ont., 1970-72; computer mgr. Toronto Dominion Bank, Toronto, Ont., 1972-79, dir. strategic planning, 1979-80, asst. gen. mgr. info. systems, 1980-83, v.p. info. systems, 1983-86, sr. v.p. info. systems, 1986—; lectr. IBM Can., Bell Can., Northern Telecom, UNISYS. Advisor Govt. of Can. Auditor Gen., Ottawa, 1987—; vice chmn. Humber Coll., Toronto, 1982—. Home: 30 Wellington St E, Suite 901, Toronto, ON Canada M5E 1S3

NAPIER, DOUGLAS WILLIAM, lawyer, county attorney; b. Alexandria, Va., Sept. 11, 1951; s. William Wilson and Leo Elizabeth (Moore) N.; m. Kathy Gwen Talbert, Aug. 24, 1974; children—Brian Douglas, Adam Scott, Brooke Elizabeth. B.S., Va. Poly. Inst. and State U., 1973; J.D., Wake Forest U., 1976. Bar: Va. 1976, U.S. Ct. (ea. and we. dist.) Va. 1978, U.S. Ct. Appeals (4th cir.) 1983. Assoc., Ambrogi, Mote & Ritter, Winchester, Va., 1976-77; ptnr. Napier & Napier, Front Royal, Va., 1977—; county atty. Warren County (Va.), 1978—; atty. Chem. Abuse Task Force, 1983—. Author: The Cross, 1982. Mem. staff, contbr. Wake Forest Law Rev., 1976. Bd. dirs. United Way, Front Royal, 1978; parliamentarian Warren County Republican Com., 1981; cons. Council Domestic Violence, 1984; del. People to People Citizen Ambassador Program's Legal Del. to China, 1987. Mem. Warren County Bar Assn. (v.p., pres.), Va. Bar Assn., Va. Trial Lawyers Assn., ABA, Front Royal C. of C. (bd. dirs., v.p. 1986-88, pres. 88—), Internat. Platform Assn. Baptist. Clubs: Optimist Internat. (sec. 1980-81, Achievement award 1980), Isaac Walton League. Home: 115 Accomac Rd Royal VA 22630 Office: Napier & Napier 10 Court House Sq Front Royal VA 22630

NAPIER, JOHN HAWKINS, III, historian; b. Berkeley, Calif., Feb. 6, 1925; s. John Hawkins and Lena Mae (Tate) N.; B.A., U. Miss., 1949; M.A., Auburn U., 1967; postgrad. Georgetown U., 1971; m. Harriet Elizabeth McGehee (dec.). m. Cameron Mayson Freeman, Sept. 11, 1964. Journalist, tchr. Picayune (Miss.) High Sch., 1946; commd. 2d lt. U.S. Air Force, 1949, advanced through grades to lt. col., 1966, ret., 1977; staff dir. Congressional Com. on S.E. Asia, 1970; faculty Air War Coll., 1971-74; Air U. Command historian, 1974-77; asst. to exec. dir. Ala. Commn. on Higher Edn., Montgomery, 1977-78; adj. history faculty Auburn U., Montgomery, 1980-85; columnist Montgomery Advertiser, 1980-87; lectr. in field. Pres., Montgomery Opera Guild, 1974-75, Montgomery Community Concert Assn., 1974-76, Old S. Hist. Soc., 1977-78. Served with USMC, 1943-46. Decorated Legion of Merit, also others; recipient award of Merit, Ala. Hist. Commn., 1976, Order of St. John of Jerusalem, Sovereign Mil. Order of Temple of Jerusalem; Merit award English-Speaking Union U.S., 1983; Taylor Medal and grad. fellow U. Miss., 1949; Storrs scholar Pomona Coll., 1942-43. Mem. English-Speaking Union (pres. 1978-87, nat. dir. 1980-86, 87—), Newcomen Soc., Ala. Hist. Assn. (pres. 1979-80), Soc. Pioneers Montgomery (pres. 1980-81), Soc. Colonial Wars, SCV (vice comdr. Ala. 1979-80), Soc. War of 1812 (pres. Ala. 1980-82), St. Andrews Soc., S.R., SAR (pres. 1974-75), Clan Napier in N.Am. (lt. to chief 1985—), Order 1st Families Va., Jamestowne Soc., Sigma Chi, Phi Kappa Phi, Omicron Delta Kappa, Phi Alpha Theta, Pi Sigma Alpha, Scabbard and Blade. Democrat. Episcopalian. Clubs: Montgomery Country, Capital City, Aztec 1847, Mil. Order Carabao; Victory Services (London). Author: Lower Pearl River's Piney Woods: Its Land and People, 1985; The Air Force Officers Guide, 27th edit., 1986. Contbr. articles to profl. jours. Home: Kilmahew Box 614 Rt 2 Ramer AL 36069-9231

NAPIER, ROBERT JON, architect; b. Bklyn., Dec. 2, 1934; s. John and Anna Constance (Turuta) N.; BArch, Pratt Inst., 1957, MArch, 1959; m. Fada S. Cumbridge, Jan. 29, 1981; children from previous marriage: Jason, Kristina Anne, Julia Anne. pvt. practice architecture, University Park, Pa., 1963-66; assoc. William N. Breger Assocs., architects, N.Y.C., 1966-69; prin. Unger/Napier Assocs., N.Y.C., 1970-73; v.p. project devel., chief architect Kraus Enterprises, Inc., N.Y.C., 1973-81; architect, real estate devel. cons., N.Y.C., 1981—; sr. assoc., cons. Wank Adams Slavin Assn. Architects, Planners, Engrs., 1986—; dir. devel., design and bldg. ops. Procida Constrn. Corp., Inc., 1982-84; univ. chief architect, archtl. unit mgr. office facilities Planning and Mgmt., CUNY, 1984-86; asst. prof. architecture Pa. State U., 1959-66, vis. lectr. dept. public info., 1960-65; vis. critic dept. architecture Pratt Inst., 1967-69; adj. asst. prof. CUNY, 1972-73; cons. several radio, TV stas. Mem. AIA, AAUP, N.Y. State Soc. Architects. Home: 250 Mercer St New York NY 10012 Office: 2 Astor Pl New York NY 10003

NAPOLITANO, MIGUEL JUAN CARLOS, pharmaceutical company executive; b. Buenos Aires, Jan. 25, 1947; s. Miguel Juan and Itala Ana (Chionetti) N.; m. Maria Matilde Di Salvo, 1975; children: Miguel Juan Carlos, Maria Eugenia. Diploma with high proficiency, Argentinian Assn. English Culture, Buenos Aires, 1960-66; MD, Buenos Aires U., 1972. Psychiatrist Hosp. C.G. Durand, Buenos Aires, 1972-78; sci. dir. Astra S.A.F.P. and Q., Buenos Aires, 1973-81; pharmacologist med. sch. U. Buenos Aires, 1975-78; scientific dir. Boehringer Argentina S.A., Buenos Aires, 1981—; adj. asst. prof. Psychiatry C.G. Durand Hosp., 1974-78. Guest lectr. Rotary Club, Buenos Aires, 1987. Recipient Golden Rat award Leprological Research Inst., Rosario, Argentina, 1985; Roemmers Found. grantee, Buenos Aires, 1986. Mem. Ctr. Studies for Pharm. Industry Devel. in Argentina, Pharm. Industry Physicians Assn. (bd. dirs. 1977-81), Argentine Med. Assn., Argentine Soc. Pharmacology and Therapy, Argentine Soc. Cardiology, Argentine Soc. Diabetes, Argentine Soc. Psychiatry. Club: Italiano (Buenos Aires). Home: Gorriti 4128, 1172 Buenos Aires Argentina Office: Boehringer Argentina SA, Viamonte 2213, 1056 Buenos Aires Argentina

NAQVI, IQBAL MEHDI, electrical engineering educator, consultant; b. New Delhi, India, Jan. 6, 1939; came to U.S., 1958; s. Mehdi Hasan and Nazar Amna (Zaidi) N.; m. Alice L. Smith, Dec. 19, 1964 (div. May 1975); children—Javed Iqbal, Jasmin Noor. B.S., U. Punjab, Pakistan, 1958; B.E., Youngstown U., 1960; M.S., U. Pa., 1961; Ph.D., Cornell U., 1970. Sr. prin. engr. Honeywell Inc., Waltham, Mass., 1961-66; asst. prof. U. Hawaii, Honolulu, 1970-73; mem. research staff Fairchild Semiconductor, Palo Alto, Calif., 1973-75; mem. sr. tech. staff Rockwell Internat., Anaheim, Calif., 1975-78; head device engring. Hughes Aircraft Co., Newport Beach, Calif., 1978-82; vis. lectr. Calif. State U.=Fullerton, 1977, Calif. State Poly. U., 1978, U. Calif.-Irvine, 1981—; sr. cons. engr., head VLSI devel. MAI Basic Four, Tustin, Calif., 1982-85; cons. Western Digital Corp., Irvine, 1985—; lectr. tech. presentation Device Research Conf., 1968, 70; moderator panel discussion Engring. Workstations, 1984, Silicon compilers, 1985. Contbr. articles to tech. jours. Research scholar U. Pa., 1961; research fellow Cornell U., 1966-69; research grantee U. Hawaii, 1971-73. Mem. IEEE (chmn. Orange County sect. 1988—, program chmn. Orange County 1984-85, edn. chmn. 1984-85, chmn. circuits and systems/electron devices chpt. 1985-86), Computer Soc., Circuits and Systems Soc., Electron Devices Soc. Clubs: Sierra (San Francisco). Current work: Directing microelectronic chip development activity for computer applications; responsible for computer-aided design; lecturer, organizer of profl. courses and workshops; device physics. Subspecialties: Electronics; Computer-aided design. Home: 14771 Doncaster Rd Irvine CA 92714

NARAYAN, RAJ, metallurgical engineer, educator; b. Muzaffar Nagar, India, Sept. 12, 1941; s. Ram and Prakash (Vati) N.; B.Sc., Agra (India) U., 1958; B.E.in Metall. Engring., Indian Inst. Sci., Bangalore, 1961; Ph.D. in Metall. Engring., U. Newcastle Upon Tyne (Eng.), 1970; m. Vibha, Jan. 19, 1964; children—Anshu, Amit. With Directorate of Industries, Kanpur, India, 1961-62; incharge marine corrosion research sta., Digha, India; scientist Nat. Metall. Lab., Jamshedpur, India, 1962-65; lectr. in metall. engring. U. Roorkee (India), 1965-66; research asso. U. Newcastle Upon Tyne, 1966-69; research fellow Univ. Coll., Swansea, Wales, 1970-71; sect. leader for metallurgy research and devel. C.A. Parsons & Co., Ltd., Newcastle Upon Tyne, 1971-74; asst. prof. metall. engring. Indian Inst. Tech., Kanpur, 1974-80, prof. metall. engring., 1980—; guest prof. metall. engring. Cath. U., Leuven, Belgium, 1984; cons. in field; mem. adv. com. as corrosion and coatings expert Builder's Friend. Recipient IAEC Golden Jubilee award for contbns. in field of corrosion, 1981. Fellow Soc. Advancement Electrochem. Sci. and Tech. Hindu. Author: An Introduction to Metallic Corrosion and Its Prevention, 1982; contbr. numerous articles to profl. jours. Home: 477 Indian Inst Tech Campus, Kanpur 208016, India Office: Indian Inst Tech, Dept Metallurgy, Kanpur 208016, India

NARINS, CHARLES SEYMOUR, lawyer, instrument co. exec., hosp. ofcl.; b. Bklyn., Mar. 12, 1909; s. Joshua and Sarah E. (Levy) N.; LL.B., Yale U., 1932; B.S., N.Y. U., 1929; m. Frances D. Kross; children—Lyn Ross, Joyce Hedda. Admitted to N.Y. bar, 1933, Mass. bar, 1955; atty. Curtin & Glynn, N.Y.C., 1932-34, Glynn, Smith & Narins, 1934-37, Probst & Probst, 1937-47; pres., dir., counsel C. L. Berger & Sons, Inc., 1947-68; div. chmn. Berger Instruments div. High Voltage Engring. Corp., Boston, 1968-74; dir., chmn. med. planning New Eng. Sinai Hosp., Stoughton, Mass., 1974—. Trustee Boston Ballet Co., Boston Opera; bd. dirs. Boston Civic Symphony, 1975-76; bd. dirs., 1st v.p. Greater Palm Beach Symphony; mem. corp. Norfolk House, Boston. Mem. Am., N.Y., Mass., Boston bar assns., Assn. Bar City N.Y., N.Y. County Lawyers Assn., Am. Congress Surveying and Mapping, Am. Judicature Soc., Boston C. of C., Assn. Yale Alumni (law sch. rep.), Internat. Cultural Soc., Pi Lambda Phi. Clubs: Univ., Yale (Boston); Boston Yacht (Marblehead, Mass.); Yale, Poinciana (Palm Beach); Yale, N.Y. U. (N.Y.C.); Kernwood Country (Salem, Mass.); Palm Beach (Fla.) Country (bd. govs., sec.). Home: 150 Bradley Pl Palm Beach FL 33480 Summer: 24 Skinners Path Marblehead MA 01945

NARJES, KARL-HEINZ, government official; b. Soltau, Fed. Republic of Germany, 1924. LLD, U. Hamburg, 1952. Joined German Fgn. Service, 1955, then counselor; dep. chef de cabinet of the pres. Commn. of the European Communities, 1958, chef de cabinet, 1963, dir. gen. press and info., 1968-69, v.p. indsl. affairs, info. tech., 1981, also v.p. research and sci., 1985—; minister for economy and transport German Fed. Parliament, Schleswig-Holstein, 1972-81; chmn. econ. affairs com. German Fed. Parliament, 1972-76. Served with German Armed Forces; prisoner of war in Can. and Eng. during World War II. Office: co Comm of European Communities, 200 rue de la Loi, 1049 Brussels Belgium *

NARLIKAR, JAYANT VISHNU, astrophysicist, educator; b. Kolhapur, India, July 19, 1938; s. Vishnu Vasudeo and Sumati Vishnu (Huzurbazar) N.; B.Sc., Banaras Hindu U., 1957; M.A., Cambridge (Eng.) U., 1964, Ph.D., 1963, Sc.D., 1976; m. Mangala Sadashiv Rajwade, June 21, 1966; children—Geeta, Girija, Leelavati. Berry Ramsey fellow, also sr. research fellow King's Coll., Cambridge, 1963-72, mem. staff Inst. Theoretical Astronomy, Cambridge U., 1967-72; prof. Tata Inst. Fundamental Research, Bombay, 1972—; mem. sci. adv. council to prime minister of India, 1986—. Jawaharlal Nehru fellow, 1973-75; recipient Smith prize Cambridge U., 1962, Adams prize, 1967; Padmabhushan award Govt. India, 1965; Bhatnagar award, 1978; Rashtrabhushan award, 1983; Rathindra award, 1985. Fellow Cambridge Philos. Soc., Indian Nat. Sci. Acad., Indian Acad. Scis.; mem. Royal Astron. Soc. (fgn. assoc.), Astron. Soc. India (pres. 1982-85), Indian Assn. Gen. Relativity and Gravitation (pres. 1982-84), Indian Physics Assn. Club: Cambridge Union. Author: The Structure of the Universe: General Relativity and Cosmology; Introduction to Cosmology; The Lighter Side of Gravity; Violent Phenomena in the Universe; From Black Clouds to Black Holes; co-author: Action at a Distance in Physics and Cosmology; The Physics-Astronomy Frontier; (with T. Padmanabhan) Gravity, Gauge Theories and Quantum Cosmology, 1986; contbr. articles to profl. jours. Office: Tata Inst Fundamental Research, Bombay 400 005 India

NAROD, ARNOLD S., financial planner; b. Phila., Dec. 11, 1946; s. Manuel and Betty Narod; B.A., Temple U., Phila., 1968; C.L.U., 1977; diploma Coll. Fin. Planning, 1977; m. Bonnie Orlove, June 30, 1968; children—Jennifer Rose, Scott Farrell. Social worker Crime Prevention Assn. Phila., 1968-72; ins. agt., King of Prussia, Pa., 1972—; pres. Pa. Pension Cons., Inc., King of Prussia, 1977—, South Jersey Pension Cons., Atlantic City, 1977—; founder, 1977, since fin. planner Investment Search, Inc.; founder, chief exec. officer Investment Search Internat.; founder Auto Lease, Ltd., 1987—. Mem. Am. Soc. C.L.U.s, Soc. Cert. Fin. Planners, Nat. Assn. Fin. Cons., Ind. Ins. Agts. Assn., Pa. Ins. Assn., Phila. Assn. Life Underwriters, Phila. Estate Planning Council, Montgomery County Estate Planning Council, Res. Officers Assn. U.S. Home: PO Box 471 King of Prussia PA 19406 Office: 1643 Atlantic Ave Atlantic City NJ 08401

NARROWE, MORTON HERMAN, rabbi; b. Phila., Mar. 15, 1932; arrived in Sweden, 1965; s. Morris and Sarah Ruth (Lisack) N.; m. Judith Luba Halpren, June 15, 1958; children: Joshua Avraham, Elizabeth Ann, David Isaac. BA, Yeshiva U., 1954; MA, Jewish Theol. Sem. Am., 1959, DD, 1984. Ordained rabbi, 1959. Rabbi Temple Beth Sholom, Satellite Beach, Fla., 1962-65; rabbi Jewish community Stockholm, 1965—; chief rabbi Jewish community 1975—; v.p. World Council Synagogues, 1975—. Contbr. articles to theol. publs. Mem. Nat. Bible Commn. Sweden (bd. dirs. 1976—), Internat. Council Christians and Jews (v.p. Swedish br. 1980—), Swedish Friends Red Star of David (pres. 1983-87), Zionist Fedn. Sweden, Jewish Community Ctr. Stockholm (bd. dirs.). Served to lt. USN, 1959-62. Lodge: B'nai Brith. Home: Torstenssonsgatan 4, S-11456 Stockholm Sweden Office: Judiska Forsamlingen Wahrendorffsgatan, 3 Box 7427, S-10391 Stockholm Sweden

NARUO, SHINJI, infosystems engineer; b. Kitakyushu, Fukuoka, Japan, Sept. 24, 1959; s. Kazutoshi and Setsuko Naruo. Degree in Law, Shimane U., Japan, 1982; M. of Econs., Okayama U., Japan, 1984. Circulating system engr. Nomura Computer System Co., Tokyo, 1984-86, with internat. securities, fin. system dept., 1986—; leader Data Base Security Com., Tokyo, 1987, Internat. Corp. Legal Problem Com., Tokyo, 1987. Mem. Living Circumstance Protection, Kitakyushu City, Japan, 1986. Mem. Japan Data Base Assn. Home: 28-20 Kakinokidai Midoriku, Yokohama Kanagaya 227, Japan Office: Nomura Research Inst, 4-29 Yotsuya Shinjuku, Tokyo 151, Japan

NARUSIS, REGINA GYTÉ FIRANT, lawyer; b. Kaunas, Lithuania, Oct. 12, 1936; came to U.S., 1949, naturalized, 1955; d. Victor and Eugenia S. (Cesnavicius) Firant; m. Bernard V. Narusis, June 19, 1959; children: Victor John, Ellen Marie, Susan Marie. BA, U. Ill., 1957, JD, 1959. Bar: Ill. 1960. Ptnr. Narusis & Narusis, Cary, Ill., 1961—; atty. City of McHenry (Ill.), 1973—; village atty. Fox River Grove, Ill., 1967-73; asst. state's atty., McHenry County, Ill., 1968-75, head juvenile div., 1968-75. Mem. McHenry County Bd. Health, Woodstock, Ill., 1964-75, McHenry County Welfare Services Com., 1968-75; mem., pres. Dist. 46 Sch. Bd., McHenry County, 1964-79; mem. adminstrv. council, mem. exec. bd. Marian Cen. Cath. High Sch., 1981—; bd. dirs. Cath. Found. for People of Diocese of Rockford, Ill., 1988—. Mem. Ill. Bar Assn., McHenry County Bar Assn., Women's Bar Assn., Am. Judicature Soc., Nat. Dist. Attys. Assn., Kappa Beta Pi. Address: 213 W Lake Shore Dr Cary IL 60013

NASALLI ROCCA DI CORNELIANO, MARIO CARDINAL, clergyman; b. Piacenza, Italy, Aug. 12, 1903. Ordained priest Roman Catholic Ch., 1927; titular archbishop of Anzio, 1969; elevated to Sacred Coll. of Cardinals, 1969; titular ch. St. John the Baptist; mem. Congregation of Sacraments and Divine Worship, Congregation Causes of Saints, Secretariat of Non-Believers. Office: Piazza della Vitta Leonina 9, 00193 Rome Italy *

NASH, CHARLES EDWARD, physics educator; b. London, Oct. 22, 1948; arrived in Ireland, 1955; s. John and Anne Cecilia (Osborn) N.; m. Edna Mary Gallagher, Feb. 23, 1974; children: Elise Anne, Oliver Charles, Mary Carmen, Nicholas Conal. BA in Theoretical Physics, Trinity Coll., Dublin, Ireland, 1970; PhD in Theoretical Physics, Christ's Coll., Cambridge, Eng., 1973. Research fellow Imperial Coll., London, 1973-75; research fellow, lectr. Trinity Coll., Dublin, 1975-79; lectr. St. Patrick's Coll., Maynooth, Ireland, 1979-84, sr. lectr., 1984—; external examiner Dept. Math., Trinity Coll., 1985—. Author: Relativistic Quantum Fields, 1978, Topology and Geometry for Physicists, 1983; referee Oxford U. Press, Academic Press, 1979—; referee various research jours., United Kingdom, U.S., 1972—; contbr. articles to profl. jours. Mem. Dublin Symphony Orch. Mem. Internat. Assn. Math. Physicists, Irish Math. Soc. Office: St Patrick's Coll, Dept Math and Physics, Maynooth Kildare Ireland

NASH, FREDERICK COPP, lawyer; b. Media, Pa., Mar. 19, 1908; s. Fred J. and Maebelle W. (Copp) N.; A.B., Yale U., 1930; LL.B., U. Mich., 1933; m. Carolyn Coffin, Sept. 23, 1933; children—Howard C. (dec.), Judith A., Cynthia J. Admitted to Mich. bar, 1933; asso. with Bodman Longley, Bogle, Middleton & Farley and successor firms, Detroit, 1933-41; partner firm Bodman, Longley, & Dahling, and predecessor firms, Detroit, 1941-56, 59—; gen. counsel Dept. Commerce, 1956-59. Treas., Mich.-Ohio Nav. Co., Detroit, 1954-56; sec., dir. Detroit Lions, Inc., 1964—; dir. Detroit, Toledo & Ironton R.R., 1971-80, Ann Arbor R.R., 1971-73. Mem. Rochester (Mich.) Village Council, 1953-55, Avon-Rochester Planning Commn., 1950-56; pres.-dir. Grand Lawn Cemetery, Detroit, 1954-56; bd. dirs. Oakland Citizens League, 1959-80; bd. govs. Cranbrook Schs. div. Cranbrook Ednl. Com., 1959-81, gov. emeritus, 1981—; trustee, Matilda R. Wilson Fund, pres., 1982—. Served to lt. USNR, World War II. Mem. Am. Bar Assn., Detroit Bar Assn., State Bar Mich., Greater Detroit Bd. Commerce, Phi Beta Kappa. Presbyterian (elder). Clubs: Detroit Athletic, Detroit, Renaissance, Yondotega. Address: 4760 E Michigan Ave Au Gres MI 48703

NASH, HENRY WARREN, marketing educator; b. Tampa, Fla., Sept. 19, 1927; s. Leslie Dikeman and Mildred (Johnson) N.; m. Frances Lora Venters, Aug. 20, 1950; children: Warren Leslie, Richard Dale. B.S. in Bus. Adminstrn. U. Fla., 1950, M.B.A., 1951; postgrad., Ind. U., 1951-53; Ph.D., U. Ala., 1965. Student asst. U. Fla., 1948-50, grad. asst., 1950-51; grad. asst. Ind. U., 1951-53; salesman Field Enterprises, Inc., Chgo., 1953; asso. prof. bus. and econs. Miss. Coll., 1953-57; asso. prof. marketing Miss. State U., 1957-66, prof., head dept., 1966—; partner Southland Cons. Assos., 1968—; bd. dirs. Govt. Employees Credit Union, 1969—, v.p., 1969-73, pres., 1973-78. Author: (with others) Principles of Marketing, 1961. Served with USNR, 1945-46. Loveman's Merchandising fellow U. Ala., 1961-62. Mem. Am. Marketing Assn., Am. Acad. Advt., Acad. Internat. Bus., So. Econ. Assn., So. Marketing Assn. (sec. 1974-75, pres. 1976-77), Sales and Marketing Execs. (internat. chmn. educators com. 1967-70), Miss. Retail Mchts. Assn. (bd. dirs.), Pi Sigma Epsilon (nat. educator v.p. 1967-69, nat. pres. 1967-71), Beta Gamma Sigma, Omicron Delta Kappa, Mu Kappa Tau (nat. v.p. 1977-79, 86-88, pres. 1979-81, 88—), Alpha Kappa Psi, Phi Kappa Phi, Blue Key. Baptist (tchr., deacon). Club: Kiwanian (Starkville) (treas. 1969-70, v.p. 1973-74, pres. 1974-75, lt. gov. 1977-78, gov. 1982-83). Home: 114 Forest Hill Dr Starkville MS 39759 Office: Miss State Univ Dept of Mktg Mississippi State MS 39762

NASH, JAY ROBERT, III, author, playwright, publisher; b. Indpls., Nov. 26, 1937; s. Jay Robert and Jerrie Lynne (Cosur) N.; m. Janice Patricia Schwartz, Sept. 15, 1962 (div.); children: Lee Travis, Andrea Lynne; m. Judith Anne Anetsberger, Sept. 10, 1983; 1 child, Jay Robert IV. B.A. in Lit. U. Paris, France, 1958. Editor Milw. Lit. Times, 1961; editor Antioch (Ill.) News, 1962; mng. editor Am. Trade Mags., Chgo., 1962-66; editorial dir. PRM Corp., Chgo., 1967; editor-in-chief Chgo. Land Mag., 1967-70; freelance writer Chgo., 1970—; editor-in-chief, pub. Cine Books, Inc., Chgo., 1984-86, Crime Books, Inc., Wilmette, Ill., 1987—; editor, pub. Lit. Times (jour. of fine arts), Chgo., 1961-70. Author: Lost Natives & Expatriates, 1965, Dillinger: Dead or Alive?, 1970, Citizen Hoover, 1972, Bloodletters and Badmen, A Narrative Encyclopedia of American Criminals from the Pilgrims to the Present, 1973, On All Fronts, 1974, Hustlers and Con Men, 1976, Darkest Hours, 1976, Among the Missing, 1978, Murder America, A Social History of Homicide in the United States from the Revolution to the Present, 1980, Almanac of World Crime, 1981, A Crime Story, 1981; play Last Rites for the Boys, 1979; Look for the Woman, A Narrative Encyclopedia of Female Criminals from Elizabethan Times to the Present, 1981, The Innovators, 1981, True Crime Quiz Book, 1981, People to See, A History of Chicago's Makers and Breakers, 1981, The Dark Fountain, 1982, Murder Among the Mighty, 1982, Zanies, A Narrative Encyclopedia of the World's Greatest Eccentrics, 1982, Crime Movie Quiz Book, 1983, The Dillinger Dossier, 1983, Open Files: A Narrative Encyclopedia of the World's Greatest Unsolved Crimes, 1983, The Toughest Movie Quiz Book Ever, 1983, Jay Robert Nash's Crime Chronology: A Worldwide Record, 1900-1983, 1983, The Mafia Diaries, 1984, Makers and Breakers of Chicago, 1985; author, editor, pub. The Motion Picture Guide (12 vol. film ency.), 1986, Crime Jour. Served with Intelligence Service AUS, 1956-58. Mem. Authors Guild Inc. Office: PO Box 512 Wilmette IL 60091-1630

NASH, JONATHON MICHAEL, mechanical engineer; b. Little Rock, Aug. 10, 1942; s. Bertram B. and Nora B. (Shed) N.; B.S.M.E., U. Miss., 1966, M.S. in Engring. Sci., 1970, Ph.D. in Engring. Sci., 1973; m. Meta W. Smith, Aug. 12, 1972; children—Lillian Kendrick, Caroline Michael. Jr. engr. IBM Fed. Systems div., Huntsville, Ala., 1967-68, sr. asso. engr., 1973-74, staff engr., 1975-77, project engr., 1977-78, devel. engr., Gaithersburg, Md., 1978-80, adv. engr., 1980-81, tech. planning mgr., 1981-83, sr. engr. FAA programs, Rockville, Md., 1983—; research assoc. U. Miss., 1970-72, adj. assoc. prof. mech. engring., 1983—; aerospace engr., sci. intern NASA Manned Space Craft Center, summers 1970, 71; instr. U. Ala., Huntsville, 1977-78. Bd. dirs. Arts Council of Frederick City and County, Md., 1981-84, v.p., 1982-83; mem. Lafayette County (Miss.) Republican Exec. Com., 1972-73. Served with C.E., U.S. Army, 1968-70, Vietnam; maj. USAR. Decorated Bronze Star. Recipient NASA New Tech. award, 1979; NASA Apollo Achievement award 1971; Ala. Young Engr. of Yr. award, Nat. Soc. Profl. Engrs., 1978; Tudor medal for engring. contbns. Soc. Am. Mil. Engrs., 1978; Engring. Achievement award, Huntsville chpt. Soc. Am. Mil. Engrs., 1977; Outstanding Young Engr. of Yr. award Huntsville chpt. Ala. Soc. Profl. Engrs., 1976, others; U. Miss. fellow, 1970-73; registered profl. engr., Ala., Miss., Md. Fellow ASME (exec. com. Solar Energy Div. 1981-86, sec./treas. 1982-83, vice chmn. 1983-84, chmn. 1984-85, mem. operating bd. Energy Resources Group 1984—, Cert. of Appreciation, Solar Engery div. 1982, 85, chptr. chmn., 1978, vice chmn. 1977-78, treas. 1976-77, mem. Nat. Bur. Standards Interaction Com.), Am. Inst. Chem. Engrs., ASHRAE (nat. tech. com. on solar energy utilization 1977-80), Soc. Am. Mil. Engrs. (chpt. pres. 1976-77, dir. 1977-78), Md. Engring. Soc., Nat. Soc. Profl. Engrs., Ala. Soc. Profl. Engrs. (chpt. dir. 1978), Internat. Solar Energy Soc., Ala. Solar Energy Assn. (chpt. dir. 1978), AIAA (assoc. fellow), Am. Def. Preparedness Assn., Sigma Xi (chpt. pres. 1977-78), Omicron Delta Kappa, Alpha Tau Omega (pres. Huntsville alumni 1976-77), VFW, Res. Officers Assn. Editor: (with Smok, Thomas and Jenkins) Modeling, Simulation, Testing and Measurements for Solar Energy Systems, 1978; assoc. editor: (jour.) Applied Mechanics Revs., 1985-87, Mfg. Rev., 1987—; contbr. articles to profl. jours.; inventor in field. Home: 300 Rockwell Terr Frederick MD 21701 Office: 9201 Corporate Blvd Rockville MD 20850

NASH, (CYRIL) KNOWLTON, journalist, broadcast executive; b. Toronto, Ont., Can., Nov. 18, 1927; s. Cyril Knowlton and Alys (Worsley) N.; m. Lorraine Thomson; 1 child, Anne. Sports writer Globe and Mail mag., Toronto, 1946; fiction mag. editor Toronto, 1946, editor weekly newspaper, 1947; bur. mgr. Brit. United Press, Halifax, N.S., Vancouver, B.C., Toronto, 1947-51; dir. info. Internat. Fedn. Agrl. Producers, Washington and Paris, 1951-58; Washington corr. CBC, Fin. Post, others, 1958-69; dir. TV Info. Programs CBC, 1969-76, dir. TV News and Current Affairs, 1976-78, chief corr., anchor, 1978—; rapporteur various UN coms., 1951-58. Author: History on the Run, Prime Time at Ten, others. Past chmn. Toronto bf. Can. Mental Health Assn. Mem. Can. Corrs. Assn. (former pres.), CBC Corrs. Assn. (former pres.), White Ho. Corrs. Assn., Overseas Writers Club. Clubs: Nat. Press. (Washington); Toronto Press. Home: 66 Collier St, Toronto, ON Canada M4W 1L9 Office: Box 500 Terminal A, Toronto, ON Canada E4

NASH, RICHARD MARK, minister; b. Detroit, May 1, 1958; s. Richard Taylor and Joyce Elaine (Jansen) N.; m. Elizabeth Keller, June 21, 1980. BA in History cum laude, Harvard U., 1980; ThM, Dallas Theol. Seminary, 1985. Ordained minister Free Will Bapt. Ch., 1985. Instr. in lay inst. Dallas Theol. Seminary, 1983; prof. Free Will Bapt. Bible Coll., 1985; minister of Christian edn. Cen. Free Will Bapt. Ch., Royal Oak, Mich., 1986-87; assoc. pastor for adult edn. Community Ch. of Greenwood, Ind., 1987—; curriculum writer Randall House, Nashville, 1985-86, cons., 1985. Contbr. articles to profl. jours. and the Open Bible. Named One of Outstanding Young Men of Am., 1979, 80. Mem. Fellowship Evangelical Community Chs. Home: 1199 Pilgrim Rd Greenwood IN 46142 Office: Community Ch of Greenwood 1477 W Main St Greenwood IN 46142

NASH, STEPHEN MICHAEL, chemist, hazardous materials compliance representative; b. Spencer, Ind., Jan. 24, 1947; s. William Christian Nash and Juanita (Brown) Foley; m. Deanna Faye Wood, Mar. 29, 1983; children: Christopher Jon and Brian Michael (twins). BS in Chemistry, Ind. U., 1969; MS in Chemistry, Purdue U., Indpls., 1972. Tech. assoc. Lilly Research Labs., Indpls., 1968-69, assoc. organic chemist, 1969-73, organic chemist, 1973-78, asst. sr. organic chemist, 1978-80; hazardous materials compliance rep. Eli Lilly & Co., Indpls., 1980—; advisor Chemtrec, Washington, 1985—; bd. dirs. Hazardous Materials Adv. Council, Washington, 1986—. Contbr. articles to profl. jours.; patentee in field. Mem. nat. adv. bd. Findlay Coll., 1988—. Fellow Am. Inst. Chemists; mem. AAAS, Am. Chem. Soc., Internat. Union Pure and Applied Chemistry (affiliate), Internat. Platform Assn., N.Y. Acad. Scis., Ind. U. Alumni Assn. Club: Royal Oak Country. Office: Eli Lilly and Co Lilly Corp Ctr Indianapolis IN 46285

NASON, DORIS ELNORA, emeritus educator; b. North Girard, Pa., Apr. 25, 1913; d. Roy B. and Emma (Dean) Nason; student Edinboro (Pa.) State Coll., 1930-32; B.S. in Edn., Boston U., 1947, M.Ed., 1948, Ed.D., 1951. Elementary tchr. Union Twp., Pa., 1932-35, Union City, Pa., 1935-42, Millcreek Twp., Pa., 1942-43, 45-47; Link Trainer instr. USN, Sanford, Fla., 1943-45; teaching fellow elementary edn. Boston U., 1948-50, lectr. edn., summers 1948-50; asst. prof. edn. U. Conn., 1950-61, asso. prof. edn., 1961-70, prof., 1970-75, acting dir. reading-study center, 1969-72, dir., 1972-75, dir. Reading Resources Network Center in Conn., 1970-75, prof. emeritus, 1975—; adj. prof. Stetson U., 1978—; cons., lectr. in reading field; cons. for reading diagnosis in-service audio cassette program Scholastic Mags., 1975. Mem. Conn. Assn. Reading Research, Nat. Conf. Research English, Internat., New Eng. (mem. exec. bd., 1964-68, pres. 1966-67, pres. Eastern Conn. council 1974-75) reading assns., Fla. State Reading Council (disabled reader group), AAUW (pres. Daytona Beach br. 1979-81), NOW, Internat. Platform Assn., Pi Lambda Theta (adviser Beta Sigma chpt., life mem., faculty sponsor), Phi Delta Kappa. Democrat. Mem. United Ch. of Christ. Author (with Robert Norris, Herbert Tag and Richard Neville) Foundations for Elementary School Teaching, 1963; contbg. author: Educational Innovation, 1975. Editor: Teacher Education Quar., 1957-58; mem. editorial bd. 1952-66. Contbr. articles to profl. jours. Home: 8 Hieleah Dr Apt 201 Holly Hill FL 32017

NASR, AMIN MARWAN, ophthalmologist; b. Beirut, Lebanon, Aug. 1, 1953; s. Marwan Michael and Badr (Nassar) N.; m. Rola Bahije Naamani; 1 child, Karim Amin. BS II in Math., Internat. Coll., Beirut, 1971; BS, Am. U., Beirut, 1974, MD, 1978; MD in Ophthalmic Surgeon, Am. U. Med. Ctr., Beirut, 1981; MD in Oculoplastic Surgeon, Harvard U. Med. Sch., 1982; diploma in ophthalmic ultrasound, U. Iowa, 1983. Clin. assoc. Dept. Ophthalmology U. Iowa, Iowa City, 1983; cons. surgeon King Khaled Eye Specialist Hosp., Riyadh, Saudi Arabia, 1984, chief oculoplastic surgery, 1984-85, dir. ultrasonography and anaplastology, 1985—, chmn. pharmacy and therapeutic, 1985-87. Editorial bd. Pakistan Jour. Ophthalmology, 1986—, Saudi Bull. Ophthalmology, RIyadh, 1987—, Modern Medicine, 1987—; contbr. articles to profl. jours. Chief sr. scouts Lebanese Scouts Assn., 1974-79; bd. dirs. Greek Orthodox Ch., Mt. Lebanon, 1982-83. Recipient Red Cross award Lebanese Red Cross Assn., 1972, Resident of Yr. award Ophthalmology Alumni Assn. Am. U., San Francisco, 1982. Fellow Internat. Coll. Surgeons, Internat. Contact Lens Soc.; mem. Internat. Soc. Orbital Disorders, Am. Acad. Ophthalmology, Internat. Soc. Ophthalmic Ultrasound, Am. Inst. Ultrasound in Medicine. Clubs: C.K. Beyer Study (Boston); Lumni Aub (Beirut). Office: King Khaled Eye Specialist Hosp, PO Box 7191, Riyadh 11462, Saudi Arabia

NASR, KHALIL ANIS, banker; b. Amman, Jordan, Aug. 16, 1953; s. Anis Khalil and Laila Ibrahim (Nazha) N.; m. Ghada S. Sahawneh, Jan. 19, 1986; 1 child, Anis. Student U. Jordan, 1972-76. Acct. Chase Manhattan Bank, Amman, 1976-77, credit analyst, 1978-79, asst. mgr., 1980-82, mgr. credit and mktg., 1982-84, 2d v.p., 1984-86; mgr. Bank of Jordan/Amman, 1986—. Greek Orthodox. Avocation: sports. Home: PO Box 9368, Jabal Al-Weibdeh, Amman Jordan Office: Bank of Jordan, First Circle - Jabal Amman, PO Box 20191, Amman Jordan

NASRU, OMAR, sales professional; b. Addis Ababa, Ethiopia, Aug. 8, 1945; Omar Suleiman and Khadija Saeed.; m. Ferida Abdullahi; children: Hayat, Wedad and Hanan (twins). Diploma in acctg., U. Addis Ababa, 1976. Reservation agt. Ethiopian Airlines, Addis Ababa, 1967-70, ticket agt., 1970-74, sales rep., 1974-84, supr. sales, 1984-86, sales mgr., 1986—. Lodges: Toasmasters (local sec. 1980-81), Lions (local officer 1986—). Home: PO Box 4539, Addis Ababa Ethiopia Office: PO Box 1755, Addis Ababa Ethiopia

NASSAU, MICHAEL JAY, lawyer; b. N.Y.C., June 3, 1935; s. Benjamin and Belle (Nassau) N.; m. Roberta Bluma Herzlich, June 26, 1971; children—Stephanie Ellen, William Michael. B.A. summa cum laude, Yale U., 1956, LL.B. cum laude, 1960. Bar: N.Y. 1960, U.S. Dist. Ct. (so. dist.) N.Y. 1978, U.S. Tax Ct. 1963, U.S. Ct. Appeals (2d cir.) 1963, U.S. Supreme Ct. 1965. Asst. instr. in constl. law Yale U., 1959-60; law clk. to judge U.S. Ct. Appeals 2d Cir., 1960-61; assoc. tax dept. Paul, Weiss, Rifkind, Wharton & Garrison, N.Y.C., 1961-73; ptnr. Kramer, Levin, Nessen, Kamin & Frankel, and predecessor, N.Y.C., 1974—; mem. adv. bd. Matthew Bender Fed. Pension Law Service, 1975-76; mem. adv. com. NYU Ann. Inst. Employee Plans and Exec. Compensation, 1976-79; mem. steering com. Am. Pension Conf., 1981-83; lectr. in field; panelist various seminars on employee benefits. Mem. N.Y. State Bar Assn. (co-chmn. employee benefits sect. taxation 1976-78, mem. exec. com. sect. taxation 1976-79), Assn. Bar City N.Y. (chmn. sub-com. pension legis. of com. taxation 1975-76), Phi Beta Kappa. Contbr. chpts., articles to law publs.; panelist Pension Video Seminar, 1983.

NASSBERG, RICHARD T., lawyer; b. N.Y.C., Mar. 30, 1942; s. Jules and Rhea (Steinglass) N.; m. Kathryn J. Schultz, May 2, 1981; children—Schuyler M. L., Kathryn Cupp. B.S. in Econs., Wharton Sch., U. Pa., 1963; J.D., U. Pa., 1968. Bar: N.Y. 1969, U.S. Ct. Appeals (2d cir.) 1970, Pa. 1972, Tex. 1983. Assoc. Milbank, Tweed, Hadley & McCloy, N.Y.C., 1968-70; assoc. Baer & McGoldrick, N.Y.C., 1970-71; assoc. Schnader, Harrison,

Segal & Lewis, Phila., 1971-78, ptnr., 1978-82; ptnr. Mayor, Day & Caldwell, Houston, 1982—; planning chmn. courses of study on banking and comml. lending law Am. Law Inst.-ABA, 1979—, mem. adv. com. to sub-com. on continuing legal edn., 1982—. Served with Army N.G., 1963-65, USAR, 1965-66, USAFR, 1966-69. Mem. Am. Law Inst., ABA (adv. group on comml. law 1985—), Tex. Bar Assn., Houston Bar Assn. Clubs: Racquet, Franklin Inn (Phila.); Houston (Houston). Author: The Lender's Handbook, 1986; editor resource books on banking law; contbr. articles on banking law to profl. publs.; editor U. Pa. Law Rev., 1967-68, assoc. editor, 1966-67. Office: Mayor Day & Caldwell 1900 Republic Bank Center Houston TX 77002

NASSER, ESSAM, electrial engineer, physicist; b. Cairo, Feb. 3, 1931; s. Abdelaziz Hassan and Aida (Darwish) N.; m. Fawkeya Shaker; children—Nadya, Mona. B.E.E., Cairo U., 1952; Dipl-Ing., Tech. U. West Berlin, 1955, Dr.-Ing., 1959. Research engr., group leader Siemens Co., Fed. Republic Germany, 1958-61, 62-63; asst. prof. physics U. Calif.-Berkeley, 1961-62; prof. elec. engring. Engring Research Inst., Iowa State U., Ames, 1963-71, 73-77; vis. prof. elec. engring. Am. U. Beirut, 1971-73; vis. prof. power engring. Tech. U. Denmark, Lyngby, 1972; vis. prof. physics Am. U., Cairo, 1974-76; head Dar Al-Handash Cons., Cairo, 1977-80; pres. Middle East Cons., Cairo, 1980—; cons. U.S. Dept. Interior, Washington, Ministry Electric Power, Cairo; nat. chmn. Working Group on Insulator Contamination, N.Y.C., 1967-74. Author: Fundamentals of Gaseous Ionization and Plasma Electronics, 1971; Transmission Line Corona Effects, 1972; The Structure of the electric Energy System, 1974. Contbr. articles to profl. jours. Patentee in field. Recipient award Senate of West Berlin, 1958; grantee Office Naval Research, Washington, 1961, NSF, Washington, 1968-70. Fellow IEEE, Power Engring. Soc.; mem. Am. Phys. Soc., Conf. on Large Electric Networks, Paris, AAUP, Sigma Xi. Lodge: Rotary. Home: 9 Giza St, Giza Arab Republic of Egypt Office: PO Box 181, Dokki Arab Republic of Egypt

NASSIF, THOMAS ANTHONY, ambassador; b. Cedar Rapids, Iowa, July 22, 1941; s. George Joseph and Clara Christine (Nofal) N.; m. Zinetta Marie Meherg, Sept. 14, 1968; children—Jaisa Diane, Matthew Christian. B.S., Calif. State U.-Los Angeles, 1965; J.D., Calif. Western Sch. Law, 1969. Assoc., then ptnr. Gray, Cary, Ames & Frye, El Centro, Calif., 1980-81; dep. and acting chief of protocol Dept. State, Washington, 1981-83; dep. asst. sec. Bur. Near Eastern and South Asian Affairs, Dept State, Washington, 1983-85; U.S. ambassador to Morocco, 1985—. Active campaign Reagan for Pres., 1980; mem. Calif. State Republican Central Com. Served with U.S. Army and U.S.N.G., 1960-67. Recipient Disting. Profl. Achievement award Attiyeh Benevolent Soc. Office: Dept of State US Ambassador to Morrocco Washington DC 20520 also: Am Embassy APO New York NY 09284-5000

NASSONOVA, VALENTINA A., rheumatologist; b. Dnepropetrovsk, Ukraine, USSR, July 6, 1923; d. Alexander Joseph Karnaushenko and Eugenia (Gavrilovna) Tkacheva; 1 child, Eugene Nassonov. Student, Russia Ministry of Health, Moscow, 1946. Clin. intern Russia Ministry of Health, 1946-51; asst. Moscow Med. Inst., 1951-58; sr. investigator Inst. of Rheumotology, Moscow, 1958-61, head clin. dept., 1961-70, dir., 1970—; cons. WHO, 1978-88; academician, sec. dept. clin. medicine USSR Acad. Med. Sci., 1985—. Author: Systemic Lupus Erythematosus, 1972, Pathogenetic Therapy of Rheumatic Disease, 1983, Systemic Allergic Vasculitis, 1980; editor: The Importance of Age and Sex in RD, 1985, Rheumatoid Arthritis, 1983. Pres. European League against Rheumatic Disease., 1979-81. Home: Begovaja Str 11-182, 125284 Moscow USSR Office: Inst Rheumatology, 115522 Kashirskoye shosse, 34-a Moscow USSR

NASU, TADAMI, paper company executive; b. Apr. 12, 1919; married. G-rad., Tokyo U., 1941. With Indsl. Bank of Japan, from 1942; previously mng. dir., now pres. Sanyo-Kokusaku Pulp Co. Ltd., Tokyo; auditor Chiyoda Shigyo Kabushiki Kaisha. Home: 8-5 Seijo, 5-chome Setagaya-ku, Tokyo 157, Japan Office: Sanyo-Kokusaku Pulp Co Ltd, 1-4-5 Marunauchi, Chiyoda-ku, Tokyo Japan *

NATALE, ANTHONY PAUL, government agency administrator; b. Trenton, N.J., June 17, 1925; s. Domenic Anthony and Maria Josephine (Porfirio) N.; B.S., Villanova U., 1973; M. in Adminstrn., Rider Coll., 1976; m. Frances Daloisio, July 1, 1951; children—Robert Alan, John Anthony. With U.S. Steel Corp., Trenton, N.J., asst. to works engr., appropriations engr., wire rope prodn. foreman, 1951-70; budget coordinator N.J. Dept. Transp., 1970; adminstrv. asst. bus. and fin. Trenton State Coll., 1971-74, purchasing officer, 1974-78, asst. dir. bus. services, 1978-81, coadj. faculty, 1977-82, adj. faculty Sch. Bus., 1982—, also mem. speakers bur., 1985-87; asst. dir Property and Facilities Mgmt., Gen. Services Administrn., facilities mgr. Justice complex Div. Purchasing and Property, Gen. Services Adminstrn., State of N.J., 1982-85, relocation coordinator engring., div. property and facilities mgmt.; student assessment evaluator, mem. program adv. com. Edison Coll., Trenton. Bd. dirs. Lower Bucks Regional Confraternity of Christian Doctrine Roman Cath. Ch., 1974-78, asst. prin. adminstrn., 1978-82; v.p. Mercer Musical Theatre, 1982-84. Served with AUS, 1943-46, 50-51, N.J. N.G., 1947-50. Decorated Combat Infantrymans Badge. Mem. DAV, Am. Def. Preparedness Assn., Internat. Personnel Mgmt. Assn., Am. Soc. Public Adminstrn., Acad. Polit. Sci., Purchasing Agts. Club Trenton, Villanova U., Rider Coll. alumni assns., Bldg. Owners and Mgrs. Assn. Internat., Smithsonian Assocs., Assn. Govt. Accts., Cousteau Soc. Club: KC. (3d deg.). Home: 653 Teich Dr Yardley PA 19067 Office: State Office Bldg Room 202 135 W Hanover St Trenton NJ 08625

NATALE, SAMUEL MICHAEL, educator, psychotherapist, clergyman; b. Phila., May 5, 1943; s. Samuel and Anne (Vanore) N. D.Phil., Oxford (Eng.) U., 1972. Ordained priest Roman Catholic Ch., 1979; lic. psychologist Md.; exec. dir. Archdiocesan Consultation Center, Washington, 1975-76; dir. tng. Nat. Found. for Ednl. Research, Eng., Wales, 1971-72; prof. psychology Grad. Sch. Religion, Fordham U., 1978; assoc. prof. mgmt. St. John's U., N.Y.C., 1978-81; asso. prof. mgmt. U. Bridgeport, Conn., 1981—, Iona Coll., N.Y., 1986—; pvt. practice psychotherapy and pastoral counseling 1978—; cons. Archdiocese of Balt., Newark and Phila., Allentown, Diocese of Richmond, Erie, Pa., 1973—; vis. scholar St. Edmund House, Cambridge U., 1985; research fellow Warborough Trust, Oxford, Eng. Author: An Experiment in Empathy, 1972, Pastoral Counselling, 1977, Motivation and Perception, 1983, Business Ethics and Morals, 1983, Loneliness and Religious Growth, 1986, Education in Religious Understanding, 1987, Psychology of Religion and Pastoral Care, 1987; editor: International Journal of Value-Based Management; contbr. numerous articles to profl. jours. Fellow Royal Soc. Arts; mem. Am. Psychol. Assn., Brit. Psychol. Soc., Internat. Council Psychologists, Acad. of Mgmt., Human Factors Soc., Am. Assn. Pastoral Counselors (cert. clin.), Am. Acad. Psychotherapists. Home: 549 Colonial Rd Franklin Lakes NJ 07417

NATELLO, GREGORY WILLIAM, physician; b. Phila., Mar. 30, 1954; s. Americo Vespucci and Catherine (Logan) N. AB in Biology, Gettysburg COll., 1976; DO, Phila. Coll. Osteo. Medicine, 1980. Diplomate Nat. Bd. Examiners Osteo. Physicians and Surgeons, Am. Bd. Internal Medicine. Intern Detroit Osteopathic Hosp., 1980-81; gen. practice medicine Pennsauken, N.J., 1981-82; resident in internal medicine Cleve. Clinic Found., 1982-85; fellow in geriatrics Case Western Res. U. Sch. Medicine, Cleve., 1985-86; assoc. in cardiovascular diseases U. Ala., Birmingham, 1986—; instr. physical diagnosis sch. medicine Case Western Res. U., 1984-85. Recipient award of Merit for Outstanding Achievement, Detroit Osteo. Hosp., 1981, Disting. Sr. Resident award Cleve. Clinic Found., 1985. Mem. AMA, Am. Coll. Physicians, Am. Coll. Chest Physicians, Phila. Coll. Osteopathic Medicine Alumni Assn. (life), Eisenhower Soc. Gettysburg, Am. Geriatric Soc., Phi Kappa Psi. Republican. Roman Catholic.

NATERSTAD, TORMOD, chemist; b. Seimsfoss, Kvinnherad, Norway, Nov. 9, 1942; s. Bjarne and Engelina (Dalland) N.; m. Brynhild Livik, July 13, 1969; children: Endre, Aslaug, Sigve, Tarje. MS, U. Trondheim, Norway, 1967, PhD, 1974. Research asst. U. Trondheim, 1969-70, fellow, 1970-72, acting asst. prof., 1972-73; postdoctoral fellow Iowa State U., Ames, 1974-75; project engr. Ardal OG Sunndal Verk AS, Ardalstangen, Norway, 1976-77, section research and devel. fellow, 1977-79, mgr. research and devel., 1979-86; mgr. tech. Hydro Aluminum AS, Oslo, Norway, 1987—. Co-author: Understanding of The Hall-Heroult Process, 1976; contbr. articles to profl. jours.; patentee in field. Mem. Metall. Soc. of AIME. Home: JR Wilhelmsens Vei 42, 1370 Asker Norway Office: Hydro Aluminum AS, Drammensveien 134, 03 Oslo Norway

NATH, SUNIL BARAN, planner, researcher, state agency administrator; b. Silchar, Assam, India, Mar. 31, 1937; s. Sarat Chandra and Sarada (Devi) N.; came to U.S., 1968, naturalized, 1977; B.A., Visva-Bharati Internat. U., Sriniketan, India, 1960; M.A. in Sociology, Agra (India) U., 1964, Ph.D. candidate in Sociology, 1967; M.A. candidate in Pub. Adminstrn., Fla. State U., 1978, Ph.D. candidate in Criminology, 1978—, student in Bus. Law, 1978—, grad. cert. in pub. adminstrn., 1978; M.B.A. and Ph.D. candidate Calif. Coast U., 1983—; m. Abha Rani Barua, Dec. 3, 1967; children—Subrata (Bobby), Sunita, Lipika. Asst. prof. sociology B.V. Rural Higher Inst., Agra, 1964-67; instr., field dir. Survey Data Center, Polit. Research Inst., Fla. State U., Tallahassee, 1969-70, research asso., field dir., 1970-71; statistician Fla. Parole and Probation Commn., Tallahassee, 1971, project dir. Fla. intensive probation and parole projects, 1971-73, dir. research planning and statistics, 1973-74, dir. planning and evaluation, 1974-76; planner, evaluator Dept. Offender Rehab., Tallahassee, 1976-79; civil rights adminstr. Fla. Dept. Transp., Tallahassee, 1978-81, supr. budget and planning, 1981-83, ops. and mgmt. cons. II, asst. bur. chief minority programs, 1983—; co-dir. Fla. Conf. on Evaluation Research; owner Nath Auto Super Mktg. Services, Tallahassee, 1977—; cons. Human Research & Devel. Services, Inc., Univ. Research Corp., Inc., Washington; a founding mem. Good Life Gen. Store, Tallahassee, 1979—; sub-agt. A Tour Travel Agy., Chgo. and Travel Connection, Inc., Miami, 1978—. Cubmaster Cub Scouts, 1979-80; active Boy Scouts Am., 1976—; mem. Gov.'s Adult Reform Plan, 1972-73; project dir. L.E.E.A. grant, 1972-74; 4-H Club community leader, 1979—. Mem. Am., Fla., So. States correctional assns., Am., So. sociol. assns., Am. Judicature Soc., Am. Acad. Polit. and Social Scis., Internat. Platform Assn., Nat., Fla. councils on crime and delinquency, Assn. for Correctional Research and Statistics, Internat. Howard League for Penal Reform (Eng.), Am. Soc. Pub. Adminstrn., Conf. Minority Pub. Adminstrs., Nat. Assn. Ams. of Asian Indian Descent (nat. exec. bd. 1980—), Am. Soc. Tng. and Devel. (treas. 1987—), India Assn. Tallahassee pres. 1983-84), Delta Tau Kappa, Alpha Kappa Delta. Democrat. Hindu. Club: Toastmasters (pres. 1979-80, gov. Suwannee div. 1985—) (Tallahassee). Lodge: Kiwanis. Contbr. articles to profl. jours. Home: 431 Victory Garden Dr Tallahassee FL 32301 Office: 605 Suwannee St Tallahassee FL 32301

NATH, VISHWA, publisher, editor; b. Lahore, India, Apr. 27, 1920; s. Raj Pal and Saraswati Devi Nath; m. Veena Malhotra; children: Sudhir, Kapil, Meera Johri. MA in Econs., Panjab (India) U., 1942. Mng. ptnr. Rajpal and Sons, Delhi, 1948—; chmn. Vision Books Pvt. Ltd., Delhi, 1974—. Editor: (jour.) Naya Sahitya, 1960. Mem. Fedn. Indian Pub. (pres. 1980-81), All India Hindi Pub. Assn. (pres.), D.A.V. Trust and Mng. Soc. (v.p.). Lodge: Rotary (pres., dist. sec.). Home: 5 Racquet Ct Rd, Delhi 110 054, India Office: Rajpal and Sons, Kashmere Gate, Delhi 110 006, India

NATHAN, OVE, physicist, university official; b. Copenhagen, Jan. 12, 1926; s. Frits and Amelie (Friedmann) N.; m. Marianne Wandall, Apr. 7, 1956; children: Marietta, Camilla; MSc Techn. U., Denmark, 1952, D.Ph. in Physics, U. Copenhagen, 1964. Prof. physics, U. Copenhagen, 1970—, rector magnificus, 1982—. chmn. bd. trustees Copenhagen Sci. Park, Denmark, 1986—; mem. Groupe de Bellerive, Royal Danish Acad. Scis. and Letters, Danish Acad. Tech. Scis., Commn. European Communities Com. for European Devel. Sci. and Tech., Brussels, 1987—. Contbr. articles to profl. jours. Author books on sci.-tech. relations, articles on nuclear physics. Recipient Gottlieb Ernst Clausen, Gads legat, 1969, Jens Rosenkjaer-prisen, 1974. Office: Kobenhavns Universitet, Copenhagen K, PO Box 2177 10 Noerregade, DK 1017 Copenhagen Denmark

NATHANS, DANIEL, biologist; b. Wilmington, Del., Oct. 30, 1928; s. Samuel and Sarah (Levitan) N.; m. Joanne E. Gomberg, Mar. 4, 1956; children: Eli, Jeremy, Benjamin. B.S., U. Del., 1950; M.D., Washington U., 1954. Intern Presbyn. Hosp., N.Y.C., 1954-55; resident in medicine Presbyn. Hosp., 1957-59; clin. assoc. Nat. Cancer Inst., 1955-57; guest investigator Rockefeller U., N.Y.C., 1959-62; prof. microbiology Sch. Medicine, Johns Hopkins, 1962-72, prof., dir. dept. microbiology, 1972-82, Univ. prof., 1982—; sr. investigator Howard Hughes Med. Inst., 1982—. Recipient Nobel prize in physiology or medicine, 1978. Fellow Am. Acad. Arts and Scis.; mem. Nat. Acad. Scis. Office: Johns Hopkins Univ Dept Molecular Biology & Genetics 725 N Wolfe St Baltimore MD 21205 *

NATHANSON, A. LYNN, broadcasting executive; b. Sydney, N.S., Can., Dec. 4, 1955; came to U.S., 1970, permanent resident, 1978; d. Norris Lionel and Reva (Brook) N.; m. Mark Joseph Pandiscio, Oct. 8, 1978; 1 child, Jennifer Cara. AB in Music and French, Brown U., 1977. Program mgr., announcer Sta. CJCB-FM, Sydney, 1978; floor dir., asst. dir. Sta. WJAR-TV, Providence, R.I., 1979-80; devel. officer Boston Biomed. Research Inst., 1980-81; concert mgr. Mus. Fine Arts, Boston, 1980-81, mgr. Remis Auditorium, 1981-82; sr. v.p. Sta. WCRB, Charles River Broadcasting, Waltham, Mass., 1982-87; sr. v.p., gen. mgr., 1987—; cons. Stas. CJCB-AM, CKPE-FM, Sydney. Chmn. Flights of Fancy Gala fundraiser Dana Farber Cancer Inst., Boston, 1986; bd. dirs. Friends of Dana Farber Cancer Inst., 1985—; mem. benefit com. Pro Arte Chamber Orch., 1986. Mem. Classic Music Broadcasters Assn., Concert Music Broadcasters Assn. (bd. dirs. 1987—, v.p. 1988—, v.p., bd. dirs. 1988—), Assn. for Classical Music, Advt. Club of Boston, Boston Symphony Assn. Vols. Jewish. Avocations: piano, singing, swimming, skiing. Home: 241 Perkins St J-202 Boston MA 02130 Office: Sta WCRB Charles River Broadcasting 750 South St Waltham MA 02254

NATHANSON, LINDA SUE, technical writer, software training specialist, systems analyst; b. Washington, Aug. 11, 1946; d. Nat and Edith (Weinstein) N.; m. James F. Barrett. BS, U. Md., 1969; MA, UCLA, 1970, PhD, 1975. Tng. dir. Rockland Research Inst., Orangeburg, N.Y., 1975-77; asst. prof. psychology SUNY, 1978-79; pres. Cabri Prodns., Inc., Ft. Lee, N.J., 1979-81; research supr. Darcy, McManus & Masius, St. Louis, 1981-83; mgr. software tng., documentation On-Line Software Internat., Ft. Lee, 1983-85; pvt. practice cons. Ft. Lee, 1985-87; founder, exec. dir. The Edin. Group, Inc., Gillette, N.J., 1987—. Author: (with others) Psychological Testing: An Introduction to Tests and Measurement, 1988; contbr. articles to mags. and profl. jours. Recipient Research Service award 1978; Albert Einstein Coll. Medicine Research fellow, 1978-79. Mem. Am. Psychol. Assn., Ind. Computing Cons.'s Assn. (editor Interface newsletter of N.Y./N.J. chpt.). Jewish. Home and Office: 102 Sunrise Dr Gillette NJ 07933

NATHANSON, MORTON, neurologist, educator; b. N.Y.C., May 31, 1918; s. Nathan and Celia N.; m. Margret Regina Maier, Dec. 16, 1948; children—David, Madlyn, Laura. AB, U. Mich., 1939; MD, La. State U., New Orleans, 1943. Diplomate Am. Bd. Neurology Resident neuropathology Columbia Coll. Physicians and Surgeons, 1967; resident N.Y.U. Bellevue, 1946-49 dir. Multiple Sclerosis research program, 1950-54, instr. neurology, 1950-54, asst. prof., 1954-60, assoc. prof., 1960-67; clin. prof. neurology Mt. Sinai Sch. Medicine, N.Y.C., 1967-72, profl. lectr., 1973—; prof. neurology Sch. Medicine SUNY-Stony Brook, 1972—; adj. prof. neuropsychology Queens Coll., City U. N.Y., 1978—; doctoral faculty City U. N.Y. Grad. Sch., 1979—; chief neurology Long Island Jewish Med. Center, New Hyde Park, N.Y., 1972—, chmn. emeritus, 1985—. Contbr. chpts. to books, numerous articles to profl. jours. Served with M.C. U.S. Army, 1944-46. Recipient NIH contract award, 1978—. Fellow Am. Acad. Neurology; mem. Am. Neurol. Assn., Assn., Univ. Profs. Neurology, Am. Fedn. Clin. Research, Am. Assn. History Medicine, Soc. Neuroscience N.Y. Acad. Sci., N.Y. Acad. Medicine, Brit. Brain Research Assn., European Brain and Behavior Soc., Internat. Soc. for History Medicine, Soc. Neurosci., Harvey Soc., Sigma Xi. Home: 1 Pebble Ln Roslyn Heights NY 11577 Office: L I Jewish Med Ctr Dept of Neurology New Hyde Park NY 11042

NATHANSON, SUSAN DEE DIAMOND, speech pathologist; b. N.Y.C., Mar. 4, 1942; d. Charles Herbert and Hana (Mackler) Diamond; BA, Adelphi U., 1963, postgrad., 1977; MA, Bklyn. Coll., 1966; postgrad. U. Ky., 1966-67, NYU, 1978, C.W. Post Coll., 1983; m. Barry Frank Nathanson, Aug. 21, 1966; children: Richard Andrew, Laurie Jill. Speech improvement tchr., N.Y.C. pub. schs., 1963-66; speech pathologist United Cerebral Palsy, Lexington, Ky., 1966-67; clin. supr. Speech Ctr., U. Ky., Lexington, 1966-67; speech pathologist Orthopedically Handicapped unit Bur. for Speech Improvement, N.Y.C. Bd. Edn., 1967-70; pvt. practice, N.Y.C., 1970-74; tchr. lang. arts orthopedic unit, N.Y.C., 1974-75; tchr. deaf, speech pathologist Herricks public schs., New Hyde Park, N.Y., 1975-84; speech pathologist Herrick Pub. Sch., 1984—; drama tchr. Denton Ave. Sch., 1985—; pvt. practice, 1980—; Recipient Jenkins Meml. award N.Y. State Congress of Parents and Teachers, 1988; mem. Herricks Arts Council, 1988—. Mem. Am. Speech and Hearing Assn., N.Y. State Speech Language and Hearing Assn., L.I. Speech, Hearing and Lang. Assn. Office: Herricks Pub Schs New Hyde Park NY 11040

NATION, HORACE HENDRIX, III, circuit court judge; b. Birmingham, Ala., Oct. 8, 1948; s. Horace Hendrix Nation Jr. and Lucy Faye (Diesker) Bearden; m. Jean Marie Lawley, Dec. 30, 1970; children—Horace Hendrix, IV, James Leighton. B.S., U. Ala., 1971; J.D., Cumberland Law Sch., 1974. Bar: Ala. 1974. Asst. dist. atty. Walker County, Jasper, Ala., 1975-77; judge dist. ct. State of Ala., Jasper, 1977-80, cir. ct., 1980—; instr. Walker Coll. Mem. ABA, Ala. State Bar Assn., Walker County Bar Assn., Law Enforcement Planning Agy. (adv. bd.), Ala. Assn. Cir. Judges, Phi Delta Phi. Democrat. Mem. Disciples of Christ Ch. Lodge: Rotary. Home: 2300 Acadian Pl Jasper AL 35501 Office: Presiding Cir Judge PO Box 1442 Jasper AL 35502

NATION, STEPHEN HINES, business executive; b. Basingstoke, Hampshire, Eng., Aug. 13, 1946; m. Susan Margaret Bagshaw, June 6, 1981; children: Kate Alice, Matthew Alan. Student, Watford (Eng.) Coll. Tech., 1967-70. Printing apprentice Nat. Children's Home, Harpenden, Eng., 1963-67; printing technologist Metal Box Co. Ltd., London, 1970-73; asst. printing mgr. Westminster Press, Watford, 1973-74, Kendall, Eng., 1974-76; mgr. tech. services Link Paper Ltd., London, 1977-81; mgr. tech. services Barnett's Ltd., London, 1981-87, mgr. tech. sales, 1987—. Editor Paper Choice, 1981—; contbr. articles to tech. publs. Mem. Inst. Printing, Brit. Inst. Mgmt. Mem. Ch. of England. Office: Barnett's Ltd, Britannia Rd, Waltham Cross, Herts EN8 7RQ, England

NATISS, GARY MITCHELL, lawyer; b. N.Y.C., Dec. 12, 1956; s. Marvin and Suzanne E. (Brodie) N.; m. Lisa Sue Maller, Sept. 6, 1981; 1 child, Lauren Beth. BS, Union Coll., Schnectady, N.Y., 1978; JD, N.Y. Law Sch., 1981. Bar: N.Y. 1982, Fla. 1982, U.S. Dist. Ct. (ea. and so. dists.) N.Y. 1982. Assoc. Natiss, Ferenzo & Barrocas P.C., Roslyn Heights, N.Y., 1981-83, Garbarini, Scher & DeCicco P.C., N.Y.C., 1983-87; of counsel Weinreb, Weinreb & Weinreb, West Babylon, N.Y., 1987—. Mem. ABA, Fla. Bar Assn., N.Y. State Bar Assn., Nassau County Bar Assn., Assn. Trial Lawyers Am., Suffolk County Bar Assn., N.Y. State Trial Lawyers Assn. Republican. Jewish. Office: Weinreb Weinreb & Weinreb 475 Sunrise Hwy PO Box 1579 West Babylon NY 11704

NATSIOS, NICHOLAS ANDREW, retired foreign service officer; b. Lowell, Mass., July 31, 1920; s. Andrew and Fanny (Papageorgiou) N.; m. Mitzi Peterson, Sept. 2, 1951; children: Christine Daphne, Deborah Diane, Valerie Sophia, Alexandra Roxanne. Student, Lowell Technol. Inst., 1939-40; B.A. cum laude, Ohio State U., 1948; M.A.L.D., Fletcher Sch. Law and Diplomacy, 1983. Civilian spl. adviser polit. problems U.S. Mil. Mission, Salonika, Greece, 1948-50; polit. adviser mil. secretariat U.S. Mil. Mission in, Athens, Greece, 1951-56; polit. officer, 1st sec. embassy, spl. asst. to ambassador Am. embassy, Saigon, Viet Nam, 1956-60; attache Am. embassy, Paris, 1960-62; spl. asst. to ambassador Am. embassy, Seoul, 1962-65; 1st sec. American embassy, Buenos Aires, Argentina, 1965-69; spl. asst. to ambassador Am. embassy, The Hague, The Netherlands, 1969-72; regional affairs officer. Am. embassy, Tehran, Iran, 1972-74; mgmt. cons. 1977—. Served to capt. AUS, 1942-47; comdg. officer Italian Frontier Control Detachment, U.S. Occupation Forces, 1945-47, Milan, Italy. Decorated medal of Merit; decorated Bronze Star U.S.; knight comdr. of Italy; Knight comdr. Order of St. George; medal of Mil. Valor Italy; D.S.C. 1st class Knights of Malta; Order of Eagle Yugoslavia; Distinguished Service medal Greece; Order of Service Merit Korea). Mem. Phi Beta Kappa, Phi Eta Sigma. Address: 77 Lincoln Pkwy Lowell MA 01851

NATSUME, WILLIAM SHIRO, self-improvement publications company executive; b. Shanghai, People's Republic of China, Feb. 2, 1928; s. Son-Min and Tsun-In (Sze) Hoa; m. Yu Chang, Feb. 2, 1945 (div. 1956); children: Peter, Paul; m. Aiko Takahashi, Feb. 2, 1969; 1 child, Margaret. V.p. Far Eastern Trading Co., Tokyo, 1952-56; pres. Orient Art Co., Tokyo, 1952-56, Maywu & Yang Co. of Japan, Tokyo, 1956-60; mng. dir. Kung's Shipping, Tokyo, 1960-62; sales mgr. Encyclopedia Brittanica, Inc., Japan, 1962-69; pres. Success Unltd., Japan, 1967-78, T.B.R., Inc., Tokyo, 1978—. Author 9 books and software programs on positive mental attitudes, 1977—; translator 6 books by Dr. Robert H. Schuller, 1983; editor: (with Dr. Robert H. Schuller) Possibility Thinking, Japanese version, 1983. Chmn. Possibility Thinkers Soc., Japan, 1981—. Mem. Full Gospel Businessmen's Fellowship Internat. (life). Club: Tokyo Am. Lodges: Lions. Office: TBR Inst Inc, 1-17-1 Kakinokizaka, Meguro-ku, 152 Tokyo Japan

NATTA, ALESSANDRO, politician, educator; b. Imperia, Italy, Jan. 7, 1918. Active mem. Communist Party of Italia, 1945—; mem. town council of Imperia, 1946-60; elected M.P., 1948; re-elected mem. nat. direction and pres. parliamentary group, 1953, 58, 63, 68; re-elected, 1972-76; re-elected mem. of Def. Com., 1979-83; mem. central com., secretariat and nat. direction of Communist Party of Italia, leader, gen. sec., 1984-88. Office: Partito Comunista Italiano, Via Delle, Botteghe Oscure 4, 00186 Rome Italy *

NAUERT, ROGER CHARLES, health care consultant; b. St. Louis, Jan. 6, 1943; s. Charles Henry and Vilma Amelia (Schneider) N.; B.S., Mich. State U., 1965; J.D., Northwestern U., 1969; M.B.A., U. Chgo., 1979; m. Elaine Louise Harrison, Feb. 18, 1967; children—Paul, Christina. Bar: Ill. 1969. Asst. atty. gen. State of Ill., 1969-71; chief counsel Ill. Legis. Investigating Commn., 1971-73; asst. state comptroller State of Ill., 1973-77; dir. adminstrn. and fin. Health and Hosps. Governing Commn. Cook County, Chgo., 1977-79; nat. dir. health care services Grant Thornton, Chgo., 1979—; vis. lectr. health adminstrn. Vanderbilt U.; vis. lectr. econs., fin. and health U. Chgo., 1978—; preceptor Wharton Sch., U. Pa., cons. health care mktg. Am. Mktg. Assn., 1977—. Fin. commr. Village of Bloomingdale (Ill.). Ford Found. grantee, 1968-69. Mem. Am. Hosp. Assn., Am. Public Health Assn., Am. Coll. Healthcare Execs., Am. Assn. Healthcare Cons., Nat. Health Lawyers Assn., State Bar Ill., Health Care Fin. Mgmt. Assn. (faculty mem.), Alpha Phi Sigma, Phi Delta Phi, Delta Upsilon. Clubs: Plaza, LaGrange Country. Author: The Comptroller—Illinois' Chief Fiscal Control Officer, 1976; A Sociology of Health, 1977; The Demography of Illness, 1978; Proposal for a National Health Policy, 1979; Health Care Feasibility Studies, 1980; Health Care Planning Guide, 1981; Health Care Strategic Planning, 1982; Overcoming the Obstacles to Planning, 1983; Principles of Hospital Cash Management, 1984; Healthcare Networking Arrangements, 1985; Strategic Planning for Physicians, 1986; HMO's: A Once and Future Strategy, 1987, Mergers, Acquisitions and Divestitures, 1988. Home: 6505 Cherokee Dr Indian Head Park IL 60525 Office: 6th Floor Prudential Plaza Chicago IL 60601

NAVA-CARILLO, GERMÁN, minister of foreign affairs; b. Maracaibo, Venezuela, Aug. 21, 1930; married; 2 children. Student, Universidad Central de Venezuela. Joined Ministry of Fgn. Affairs, Venezuela, 1955; Minister Plenipotentiary, Chargeé d'Affairs London, 1967; Asst. Dir.-Gen. Int. Politics and Chief Div. of Inter-Am. Affairs Ministry of Fgn. Affairs, 1967-69; Minister-Counsellor, Perm. Mission UN, 1967-69, Ambassador and Dep. Perm. Rep., 1969-70; Ambassador to Egypt, Ethiopia 1970-72; dir. protocol Ministry of Fgn. Affairs, 1972-74; Ambassador to Costa Rica 1974-75; dir. of internal politics Ministry of Fgn. Affairs, 1975-78; gen. dir. internal politics and vice-minister 1978-79; perm. rep. UN, 1979-81; vice-minister Ministry of Fgn. Affairs, 1984-88, minister, 1988—; rep. of Venezuela to several UN and other internat. confs. Office: care Ministerio de Relaciones, Exteriores, Casa Amarilla, Esq Principal, Caracas Venezuela *

NAVAJAS-MOGRO, HUGO, diplomat; b. Tarija, Bolivia, Aug. 1, 1923; s. Jorge and Emma (Mogro) Navajas; m. Dorothy Bennett, Aug. 1, 1949; children: Marcia N. Carlisle, Hugo W. Navajas. MA, NYU, 1958. Officer Bolivian Fgn. Office, 1943-46, dir. dept., 1950-51; 2d sec. Bolivian Embassy, Washington, 1946-49; 1st sec. Bolivian Mission to UN, N.Y.C., 1951-52; mem. staff UN, N.Y.C., 1952-53; dep. rep. Tech. Asst. Bd. UN, Argentina,

1963-66; sr. polit. advisor UN Sec. Gen. Mission, Dominican Rep., 1966; resident rep. UN Devel. Program, Dominican Rep., Uruguay, Argentina, 1966-80; dir. policy div. UN Devel. Program, N.Y.C., 1980-83, regional dir. for Latin Am. and Caribbean, 1983-87; ambassador Permanent Mission of Bolivia to UN, N.Y.C., 1988—. Club: Jockey (Buenos Aires). Home: 6 Salem Ln Port Washington NY 11050

NAVARRE, YVES HENRI MICHEL, author; b. Condom, France, Sept. 24, 1940; s. Rene and Adrienne (Bax) Navarre. Ed. Lycee Pasteur, Neuilly-sur-Seine, Ecole des Hautes Etudes Commerciales du Nord, U. of Lille. Publicity editor Havas Agy., 1965; creative editor Synergie, 1966-67; head of design Publicis, 1968-69; design dir. B.B.D.O., 1969-70. Author novels including Lady Black, 1971; Evolene, 1972; Les Loukoums, 1973; Le coeur qui cogne, 1974; Killer, 1975; Niagarak, 1976; Le petit galopin de nos corps, 1977; Kurvenal, 1977; Je vis où je m'attache, 1978; Portrait de Julien devant la fenetre, 1979; Le temps voulu, 1979; Le jardin d'acclimatation, 1980; Biographie, 1981; Romances sans paroles, 1982; Premiè res pages, 1983; L'Espé rance de beaux voyages, No. 1, 1984, No. 2, 1985; Louise, 1986; Une vie de chat, 1986; Fête Des Mêres, 1987: Romans Un Roman, 1988; playwright: Il pleut, si tuait papalmaman, 1974; Dialogue des sourdes, 1974; Freaks Society, 1974; Champagne, 1974; Les valises, 1974; Histoire d'amour, 1976; La guerre des piscines, 1976; Lucienne de Carpentras, 1976; Les dernieres clientes, 1976; Happy End, 1980; Villa des fleurs, 1986. Decorated chevalier de l'ordre des Arts et des Lettres, chevalier de l'ordre du Mé rite, chevalier de la Légion d"Honneur; recipient Prix Goncourt, 1980.

NAVARRETE, JORGE EDUARDO, ambassador; b. Mexico City, Apr. 29, 1940; s. Gabriel and Lucrecia (Lopez) N.; m. Marie Bolaños, 1965 (dec. Sept. 1985); 1 child, Federico Navarrete Linares; m. Angeles Salceda, July 31, 1986. BA in Econs., U. Mexico, 1970. Head econ. studies Nat. Fgn. Trade Bank, Mexico City, 1967-72; Mexican ambassador to Venezuela, 1972-75, Austria, 1976, Yugoslavia, 1977-78; Mexican ambassador to UN, 1979; undersec. econ. affairs Ministry Fgn. Affairs, Mexico City, 1979-85; ambassador to Eng. London, 1986—. Author: Latin American External Debt, 1987. Office: Embassy of Mexico, 8 Halkin St, London SW1X 7DW England

NAVARRO, ANDREW JESUS, educator; b. Havana, Cuba, Sept. 11, 1946; came to U.S. 1951, naturalized 1968; s. Andrew Jesus and Carmen Caridad (Torres) N.; m. Deborah Anne Goodman, Aug. 3, 1968 (div. July, 1985); children—Andrew Robert, Laurie Lee; m. Karyl K. Carlson, June 24, 1986. Student Fla. State U., 1964-67; B.Ed, U. Miami, 1968; M.Ed., Fla. Atlantic U., 1971, postgrad., 1972-78. Cert. tchr., Fla. Varsity debate coach Miami Norland High Sch., Fla., 1973-82, varsity tennis coach, 1976-83, asst. prin., 1978-79, dept. chmn., 1980—; coordinator exec. internship program, 1986—, ct. intern program, 1986—; asst. principal, No. Miami Beach (Fla.) Sr. High Sch., 1988—; instr. Miami-Dade Community Coll., 1984—; supervising tchr. Dade County Schs., Miami, 1982, 85-88, directing tchr., 1972-73, 76. Author: (jour.) Notes From the Lecturn, 1977. Editor jours. Perspectives, 1976, Reflections, 1977, Charles Merrill Pub.; The Human Experience, 1987. Co. Chmn. Dade County Instructional Materials Council, Miami, 1985—; mem. Dade County Exam. Rev. Panel, 1986; coordinator Close-Up Found., Washington, 1979, 82-83; mem. Young Americans for Freedom, Miami, 1965-66, Broward County Bi-Centennial Com., Fla., 1975-76. Recipient Outstanding Spokesman for Freedom award VFW, 1976, 79, 81, Diamond Key award Nat. Forensic League, 1977, Barkley Forum Membership award Emory U., 1976, Voice of Democracy award VFW, 1977. Mem. Nat. Council Social Studies, Nat. Forensic League, Sigma Phi Epsilon. Republican. Avocations: tennis; gardening; camping; various animal welfare orgns. Home: 1078 Laguna Springs Dr Fort Lauderdale FL 33326 Office: North Miami Beach Sr High Sch 1247 NE 167 St North Miami Beach FL 33162

NAVARRO, ARMANDO SALOVICZ, ballet director; b. Buenos Aires, Argentina, Apr. 24, 1930; immigrated to Netherlands, 1962, naturalized, 1978; s. Herman and Elvira (Navarro) Salovicz; diploma as dance prof., Conservatorio Nacional de Musica y Arte Escenico, 1946; m. Marianne Sarstadt, Feb. 7, 1961; 1 dau., Rachel. Dancer, Teatro Colon, Buenos Aires, 1947-49, 1953-55; dancer, then soloist Ballet Alicia Alonso, 1950-52, 1st character dancer, 1952; 1st dancer Ballet Vasili Lambrinos, Buenos Aires, 1956-62; dancer Ballet du Marquis de Cuevas, 1956-62, soloist, then 1st character dancer, 1958-62; ballet master Scapino Ballet, Amsterdam, Netherlands, 1962-64, asst. artistic dir., 1965-70, artistic dir., 1970—, choreographer: Ghost-Castle, 1968, Coppelia, 1971, Half Symphony, 1974, The Nutcracker, 1975, Cinderella, 1978, Duet, 1979, Clowns, 1980, Humoresque, 1981, Willem Van Oranje, the History of a Prince, 1984. Roman Catholic. Office: Scaplino Ballet, Luchtvaartstraat 2, 1059 Amsterdam CA The Netherlands

NAVID, DANIEL BAN, lawyer; b. Racine, Wis., Apr. 14, 1950; s. Barry B. and Helen (Ban) N.; m. Jacqueline Skozek, Apr. 26, 1975; children—Anna, Emily, Steven. B.A., U. Mich., 1971; J.D., Northwestern U., 1975. Bar: Ill. 1975. Asst. to dir. Ill. Dept. Conservation, Chgo., 1974-75; asst. legal officer IUCN Environ. Law Ctr., Bonn, Ger., 1975-78; exec. officer law Internat. Union Cons. Nature, Bonn, 1979-81, exec. officer environ. planning, Gland, Switzerland, 1981-83, exec. asst. to dir. gen., 1984-85, head internat. relations, 1985-87; sec.-gen. Internat. Wetland Conv., 1988—; environ. law cons. UNESCO, div. Ecol. Scis., Paris, 1982, 83. Editor: Multilateral Environ. Convs., 1976-81. Mem. State Ill. Endangered Species Protection Bd., 1974-76; mem., legal counsel Internat. Council Environ. Law, 1977—. Office: Sec Gen, Convention on Wetlands, on Internat Importance, Ave du Mont Blanc, 1196 Gland Switzerland

NAVON, YITZHAK, deputy prime minister, minister of education and culture, former president of Israel; b. Jerusalem, April 9, 1921; s. Yosef Navon and Miriam Ben-Atar; m. Ofira Reznikov-Erez; 2 children; student Hebrew U., Jerusalem; Formerly tchr. Jerusalem elem. and secondary schs.; dir. Arabic dept. Hagana, Jerusalem, 1946-49; 2d sec. Israeli embassy, Argentina and Uruguay, 1949-50; polit. sec. to fgn. minister Israel, 1951-52, head bur. to prime minister, 1952-63; dir. dept. of culture, ministry edn. and culture, 1963-65; mem. Knesset, 1965-78, former speaker and chmn. def. and fgn. affairs com.; pres. of Israel, 1978-83, now dep. prime minister, minister edn. and culture. Chmn. World Zionist Council, 1973-78, Wolf Found. Mem. Mapai Party, 1951-65, Rafi, 1965-68, Israel Labour Party, from 1968. Mem. Labour Party. Avocations: theatre, folklore and cantorial music. Office: Ministry Edn and Culture, Jerusalem Israel *

NAVRATILOVA, MARTINA, professional tennis player; b. Prague, Czechoslovakia, Oct. 18, 1956; came to U.S., 1975, naturalized, 1981; d. Miroslav Navratil and Jana Navratilova. Student, schs. in Czechoslovakia. Profl. tennis player 1975—. Author: (with George Vecsey) Martina, 1985. Winner Czechoslovak Nat. singles, 1972-74, U.S. Open singles, 1983, 84, 87 U.S. Open doubles, 1977, 78, 80, 83, 84, 87, U.S. Open mixed doubles, 1987, Va. Slims Tournament, 1978, 83, 84, 85, 86, Wimbledon singles, 1978, 79, 82, 83, 84, 85, 86, 87, Wimbledon women's doubles, 1976, 79, 81, 82, 83, 84, 86, Wimbledon mixed doubles, 1985, French Open singles, 1982, 84, Australian Open singles, 1981, 83, 85, Grand Slam of Women's Tennis, 1984; named Hon. Citizen of Dallas, AP Female Athlete of Yr., 1983. Mem. Women's Tennis Assn. (dir., exec. com.). Office: care Sargent Hill 525 Bailey Fort Worth TX 76107 *

NAYLOR, GEORGE LEROY, lawyer, railroad executive; b. Bountiful, Utah, May 11, 1915; s. Joseph Francis and Josephine Chase (Wood) N.; student U. Utah, 1934-36; student George Washington U., 1937; J.D. (Bancroft Whitney scholar), U. San Francisco, 1953; m. Maxine Elizabeth Lewis, Jan. 18, 1941; children—Georgia Naylor Price, RoseMaree Naylor Hammer, George LeRoy II. Admitted to Calif. bar, 1954, Ill. bar, 1968; v.p., sec., legis. rep. Internat. Union of Mine, Mill & Smelter Workers, CIO, Dist. Union 2, Utah-Nevada, 1942-44; examiner So. Pacific Co., San Francisco, 1949-54, chief examiner, 1955, asst. mgr., 1956-61; carrier mem. Nat. R.R. Adjustment Bd., Chgo., 1961-77, chmn., 1970-77; atty. Village of Fox River Valley Gardens, Ill., 1974-77; practice law, legal cons., Ill. and Calif., 1977—; gen. counsel for Can-Veyor, Inc., Mountain View, Calif., 1959-64; adj. instr. dept. mgmt. U. West Fla., 1981. Served with AUS, World War II. Mem. ABA, Ill. Bar Assn., Calif. Bar Assn., Chgo. Bar Assn., San Francisco Bar Assn. Mormon. Author: Defending Carriers Before the NRAB and Public Law Boards, 1969, Choice Morsels in Tax and Property Law, 1966, Underground at Bingham Canyon, 1944; National Railroad Adjustment Board Practice Manual, 1978. Office: Round Barn Station PO Box 6323 Champaign IL 61821-8323 also: 2976 Camargo Ct San Jose CA 95132

NAYLOR, JONATHAN MICHAEL, veterinary educator; b. York, Yorkshire, Eng., Apr. 5, 1951; s. John Edward and Joyce Parker (Watson) N.; m. Carolyn Ann Mathias; children: Matthew, Michael. BS, U. Bristol, Eng., 1972, B in Vet. Sci., 1975; PhD, U. Pa. Diplomate Am. Coll. Vet. Internal Medicine, Am. Coll. Vet. Nutrition. Intern, then resident U. Pa., Phila., 1975-76, Phila. Found. Scholar, 1978-81; assoc. prof. U. Sask., Saskatoon, Can., 1981-87, prof., 1987—; examiner Am. Coll. Vet. Medicine, 1983-86, 88—; reviewer Canadian J. Veterinary Research, 1986—. Mem. Royal Coll. Vet. Surgeons, Can. Vet. Med. Assn., Soc. Exptl. Biology and Medicine, Shock Soc. Office: U Sask, WCVM, Saskatoon, SK Canada S7J 3W2

NAYMIK, JAMES JOHN, process design engineer; b. Youngstown, Ohio, July 9, 1946; s. Joseph and Mary (Petrisin) N. B.S.M.T., Cleve. State U., 1974; M.B.A., Baldwin Wallace U., 1977. Project engr. Davy McKee Corp., Cleve., 1974-82; application engr. AGA Gas, Inc., Cleve., 1982-83; cons. traffic accident reconstrn., Cleve., 1983-84; sr. process design engr. Clevite Industries, Inc., 1984-87, J.P. Industries, Inc., 1987—. Served to cpl. USMC, 1968-70. Mem. ASME, Soc. Automotive Engrs. Eastern Orthodox. Home and Office: 6614 Crossview Rd Cleveland OH 44131

NAZARBAYEV, NURSULTAN ABISHEVICH, Soviet state official; b. Kazakhstan, 1940. Grad. Higher Tech. Ednl. Inst. of Karaganda Metall. Combine, 1967, Communist Party Soviet Union Central Com. Higher Party Corres. Sch., 1976. Worker Karaganda Metall. Plant, 1960-64, 65-69; 1st sec. of Temir-Tau City Com. Komsomol, 1969-71; 2d sec. of Temir-Tau City Com. Kazakh Communist Party, 1971-73; sec. of party com. of Karaganda Metall. Combine, 1973-77; sec. 2nd sec. of Karanganda Oblast Com. Kazakh Communist Party, 1977-79; sec. of Central Com. and mem. Bur. Central Com. Kazakh Communist Party, 1979— , chmn. Kazakh SSR Council of Ministers, 1984—; mem. Central Auditing Com. Communist Party Soviet Union, 1981—. Address: Kazakh SSR, Council of Ministers, Alnia-Ata, Kazakhstan USSR *

NAZE, ANDRE GERARD, business manager; b. Mechelen, Antwerp, Belgium, Dec. 21, 1950; s. Jean Jacques and Clara (Wille) N.; m. Josee Maria Rams, Aug. 8, 1975; children: Sophie, Veronique. Salesman Procter and Gamble, Belgium, 1974-76; from asst. sales mgr. to sales dir. Biscuits Delacre, Belgium, 1976-86; gen. mgr. C.V. Joyvalle, Grimbergen, Belgium, 1986—. Home: Marnxdrreef 4, B-2500 Lier Antwerp, Belgium Office: CV Joyvalle, S-Gravenmolenstraat 10, B-1850 Grimbergen Belgium

NAZER, ABDUL FATTAH MOHIDDIN, contracting company executive; b. Jeddah, Saudi Arabia, 1945; s. Mohiddin Mohammed Omar and Zakiyah Nazer; B.Sc. with honors in Chemistry, Riyadh U., 1965; Ph.D., U. Birmingham (Eng.), 1973; m. Iman A. Turki, 1974; children—Tai, Seba, Tamara, Mohiddin, Mohammad. Instr., then asst. prof. chemistry Faculty Sci., Riyadh U., 1965-77; comptroller gen. Dallah Avco Trans Arabia Co., Jeddah, 1977-78, dir. gen., 1978-84; dir. gen. Larsen & Nielsen Saudi Arabia, Jeddah, 1981-85, chmn. bd., 1981—; vice chmn. bd. Arabian Aircraft Services Co., 1981—; vice chmn. bd. Dowty-Arabasco, 1984—; v.p. for investment Dallah Group Co., 1984—; pres., chmn. bd. Al Ittihad Club, 1985-87, hon. mem., 1987—; dir. Saudi Pub. Transport Co., Tihama for Advt., Pub. Relations and Mktg., Nat. Operation Indsl. Services Co., Chmn. sports com. King Saud U., 1973-77. Mem. Saudi Arabian Football Fedn. Author articles in field. Address: Dallah Group Co, Box 430, Jeddah 21411 Saudi Arabia

NAZER, HISHAM M., Saudi Arabia government official; b. Jeddah, Saudi Arabia, Aug. 31, 1932; s. Mohiddin N.; m. Amira H. Badawi; children: Jawaher, Loay H., Tal, Fehr, Nud, Mudar. Grad., Victoria Coll., Alexandria, Egypt, 1953; BA in Internat. Relations with honors, U. Calif., 1957, MA in Polit. Sci., 1958. Advisor Directorate Gen. Oil and Mineral Affairs, Saudi Arabia, 1958-60; dir. gen. pub. affairs Ministry Petroleum and Mineral Resources, Saudi Arabia, 1960-62, dep. minister, 1962-86, acting minister, 1986, minister, 1986—; minister planning Saudi Arabia, 1986—, acting minister planning, 1986—; 1st gov. representing Saudi Arabia OPEC Bd. Govs., 1961; pres. Cen. Planning Orgn., Saudi Arabia, 1968; minister state, mem. Council Ministers, Saudi Arabia, 1971; vice chmn. Royal Commn. for Jubail and Yanbu, 1975—. Address: Ministry Petroleum and, Mineral Resources, PO Box 247, Riyadh 11191, Saudi Arabia *

NAZIR-AHMED, VELLORE SHERIF, librarian; b. Madras, India, Oct. 27, 1929; s. Mohammed Shariff and Rahimunisa Begum Vellore; m. Razia Nazir Mahbub Sultana; children: Amtul Rahim, Khalid Ahmed, Umai Habiba, Fathima Humera, Tanvir Fathima, Sheriff Ahmed. BA, Nizam Coll., Hyderabad, 1952, LLB, 1954; B in Library Sci., Delhi U., 1955. Librarian Rly. Test and Research Ctr., Lucknow, India, 1955-59, Heavy Electircals, Ltd., Bhopal, India, 1959-65, Indian Inst. Tech., Madras, 1965-75; UNESCO expert Nat. Document Ctr., Khartoum, Sudan, 1976-78; sr. librarian Indian Inst. Tech., Madras, 1978—; bd. studies dept. library sci. Calicut U., 1975-76, Madurai-Kamaraj U., 1979-81, Madras U., 1982-84. Author: Handbook of Library Administration, 2 Vols., 3d edit., 1986; editor Union Catalogue Periodicals and Serials, 1972, SDI and Library Info. Bulletin, 1972-76. Fellow Netherlands Govt., 1967, Deutscher Akademischer Austauschdienst, 1967, Internat. Assn. Tech. Univ. Libraries, 1973, UNESCO, 1975. Mem. Indian Nat. Sci. Documentation Ctr. (adv. council 1982-84), Indian Assn. Spl. Libraries and Info. Ctr. (exec. 1973-75). Home: B 3/2 Delhi Ave, IIT Campus, Madras 600 036, India Office: Indian Inst Tech, Madras 600 036, India

NAZLIS, DIMITRI GEORGE, aeronautical engineer; b. Athens, July 1, 1937; s. George Dimitros and Elisabeth (Sakizlis) N.; m. Maria Athan Rigopoulou, May 23, 1968 (div. 1983); children: George, Elizabeth; m. Yiota Emmanuel Prevelaki, Oct. 28, 1985. BSc Aero. Engring., Hellenic A.F. Acad., Athens, 1961; BA Econs., Athens U.; BBA, Deere-Pierce Coll., Athens; postgrad., Cranfield Inst. Tech., U.K. Maintenance officer various positions Hellenic A.F., 1961-75; quality assurance dep., Greek minister of def., war industries directorate, logistics dep. Hellenic A.F., Volos, 1982-83; operational analyst Hellenic Nat. Def. Gen. Staff, 1975-79; v.p. systems and mgmt. Bionica S.A., Athens, 1983-85; mng. dir. Mediterranean Engring. Co., Athens, 1986—; Author: Basic Principle of Management, 1977, 2d edit., 1978. Mem. Gen. Assembly Greek Boy Scouts, Athens, 1977-87. Decorated Golden Cross of the Phoenix Order, Medal of Military Merit. Mem. Royal Aero. Soc., Hellenic O.R. Soc., Hellenic Bus. Mgmt. Assn., Hellenic Aerospace Engrs. Soc. (pres. 1987—). Mem. New Democracy Party. Christian Orthodox. Home: Karvela 23 AG Parasuevi, 153 42 Athens Greece Office: Mediterranean Engring Co, Academias 61, 106 79 Athens Greece

NAZOS, DEMETRI ELEFTHERIOS, obstetrician, gynecologist; b. Mykonos, Greece, July 20, 1949; came to U.S., 1967, naturalized, 1983; s. Eleftherios D. and Anousso (Grypari) N.; m. Dorothea A. Lazarides, Dec. 3, 1977; children—Anna D., Elliot D. B.S., Loyola U., Chgo., 1971; M.D., U. Athens, 1976. Diplomate Am. Bd. Ob-Gyn. Intern U. Athens Hosps., 1975-76; resident Harper Grace Hosp., Wayne State U., Detroit, 1976-80; practice medicine specializing in ob-gyn., Livonia, Mich., 1980-81, Joliet, Ill., 1981—; mem. staff St. Joseph Med. Ctr., Silver Cross Hosp.; pres., chief exec. officer Amsurg Surg. Ctr. Sustaining mem. Rep. Nat. Com. Presdl. Task Force. Fellow Am. Coll. Ob-Gyn., Am. Fertility Soc.; mem. Royal Soc. Medicine-Eng., AMA, Greek Med. Assn., Am. Assn. Laparoscopists, Ill. Med. Assn., Southeastern Surg. Soc. Mich., Will-Grundy County Med. Soc., Am. Mgmt Inst., Nat. Rifle Assn., Ill. State Rifle Assn. Clubs: Senatorial; Joliet Country; Lincoln Skeet and Trap. Greek Orthodox. Lodge: Rotary. Avocations: photography; hunting; gun collecting. Home: 24436 Woodridge Way Rt 1 Joliet IL 60436 Office: 330 N Madison St Joliet IL 60435

NDAM, SHADRACK NJAH, United Nations official, adviser; b. Mundum I, Mezam, Cameroon, May 18, 1942; came to Austria, 1969; s. Marcus Tebo and Magdalena Ngum Ndam; m. Phebe Ngum; children—Marilyn Bih, Kingsley Nibahfor, Carlson Njih, Shirley Ngum. B.Sc. in Chem. Engring., U. R.I., 1968, M.Sc. in Chem. Engring., 1969. Registered profl. engr. Prodn. and process control officer Cameroon Devel. Corp., Bota/Tiko, 1969; indsl. devel. officer UN Industrial Devel. Orgn., Vienna, 1969-77, tech. asst. to dep. exec. dir., 1978-82, chief, coordination unit for Indsl. Devel. Decade for Africa, 1983—; UN Indsl. Devel. Orgn. adviser to Orgn. of African Unity, Addis Ababa, Ethiopia, 1980; adviser to African, Asian and Latin Am. govts. and orgns., 1971-83. Editor: Industrial Research Institutes: Organization for Effective Research, Technical and Commercial Services; Programme for the IDDA, 1982; Development of Industrial and Technological Manpower in Africa, 1984; cons. Lagos Plan of Action and Final Act of Lagos, 1980; editor reports on 3d world industrialization and Africa. Scout master World Scout Assn., Owerri, Nigeria, 1961-62. Mem. Tau Beta Pi, Am. Inst. Chem. Engring. (vice-chmn. chpt. 1968-69), Cameroon Nat. Union. Lodge: Lions. Home: Grossbauerstrasse 83, A-1210 Vienna Austria Office: UN Industrial Devel Orgn, Wagrammerstrasse 5, A-1220 Vienna Austria

NDETEI, DAVID MUSYIMI, psychiatrist, educator, consultant, researcher; b. Machakos, Kenya, Jan. 1, 1948; s. John and Esther (Kamba) N.; m. Rose Mbithe Mulwa; children: Mutindi, Nzuki, Wayua, Mulwa. MB, ChB, U. Nairobi, Kenya, 1974; MD, U. Nairobi, 1985; DPM, U. London, 1978. Cert. psychiatrist, family-marital-sex therapist. Intern Ministry of Health, Kenya, 1975-76, resident in psychiatry, 1976-77; registrar in psychiatry Inst. Psychiatry, London, 1977-81; lectr. psychiatry U. Nairobi, 1981-83, sr. lectr., 1983-88, prof., 1988—; cons. Kenyatta Nat. Hosp., Mathare Hosp., Nairobi Hosp., 1981—. Columnist weekly med. column Kenyan Daily Nation; contbr. articles to internat., profl. jours. Mem. Kenya Med. Assn. (dir. Voice of Kenya Health Program), Kenya Psychiat. Assn., African Psychiat. Assn., African Assn. Family and Sex Therapists, Royal Coll. Psychiatrists U.K. Office: U Nairobi Dept Psychiatry, PO Box 30588, Nairobi Kenya

NDIAYE, BABACAR, banker; b. Conakry, Guinea, Nov. 6, 1936; married; 7 children. BSBA, Toulouse (France) Ecole Supérieure de Commerce, 1961; grad. in banking devel., Ctr. Fin. and Banking, Paris, 1964; grad. in econ., Institut de Sciences Politiques, Paris, 1964; grad. acctg. with Diplome d'Etat d'Expertise Comptable, Paris, 1966. Fin. asst. African Devel. Bank, Paris, 1965-67, project fin. analyst, 1967-70, chief pub. utilities section, 1971-72, head internal auditing, 1973-74, asst. dir. fin. dept., 1974-75, dep. dir. fin. dept., 1976-78, dir. fin. dept., 1978-80, v.p., 1980-85, pres., 1985—. Active African Priority Program for Econ. Recovery. Named Banker of Yr. Internat. Fin. Review London, 1984. Mem. French Inst. Chartered Accts. Office: African Devel Bank, 01 BP 1387, Abidjan 01 Ivory Coast

NDINGA-OBA, ANTOINE, minister of foreign affairs and cooperation of The People's Republic of The Congo, educator; b. Owando, People's Republic of Congo, 1941; married; 6 children. C.E.E.G., 1965; Licence, 1965; Masters, 1969; Doctorate 3d cycle, 1972; Diploma of Pedagogic Adviser; Diploma for Instrn. Living Langs.; Cert. Intercultural Psychology; also educated in ednl. scis. UNESCO, Paris, Geneva, Brussels. Dir. Nat. Inst. Research and Pedagogic Activity, 1972-74, Superior Inst. Ednl. Scis., 1974-76; rector U. Brazzaville (now U. Marien Ngouabi), People's Republic of Congo, 1976-77, linguistic instr., from 1972, prof. 2d category, 4th echelon, and active mem. FETRASEIC, 1972—, asst. master linguistics, 6th echelon, 1978—, adj. prof. and master linguistic conf., 1981—; minister of nat. edn. People's Republic of Congo, Brazzaville, 1977-84, minister of fgn. affairs and cooperation, 1984—; sec.-gen. Conf. African Univ. Rectors, 1976-77; pres. exec. com. African Office Ednl. Scis., 1976-81. Mem. central com. Parti Congolais du Travail, 1979—, mem. polit. bur., 1984—. Office: Ministry of Fgn Affairs, and Cooperation, Brazzaville People's Republic of Congo *

N'DONG, LEON, diplomat; b. Libreville, Gabon, Feb. 15, 1935; s. Jean-Martin Bikegne and Marthe Kemaboune; m. Chantal Annette BeKale; children—Yannick, Loic, Tatiana, Thierry. Licencie in Law and Polit. Sci., Faculte de Droit de Rennes, France, 1967, Diploma in Modern Lit., 1964; Diploma, Inst. Universitaire de Hautes Etudes Internationales, Geneva, 1968, Diploma in Diplomatic Studies, 1968; LL.D. (hon.), South Eastern Theol. Sem., New Haven, 1983; docteur honoris causa Southeastern U., New Haven. Sec. gen. Ministry of Fgn. Affairs and Cooperation, Libreville, 1969-72; asst. Ecole Nat. d'Adminstrn., 1969-72; ambassador from Gabon to Central African Republic and Sudan, 1972-73; ambassador to Morocco, 1973-74; permanent rep., ambassador from Gabon to UN, Geneva, 1974-76, N.Y.C., 1976-80; permanent rep. from Gabon to UN Security Council, 1978-79, pres., 1978; ambassador to Great Britain, 1980-86, to Fed. Republic Germany, 1986—, to Sweden during 1987, to Norway and Denmark during 1988; rep. from Gabon to numerous internat. confs. Decorated comdr. de l'Etoile Equatoriale, comdr. de l'Ordre National du Merite (Gabon); comdr. de l'Ordre de la Pleiade (France); comdr. de l'Ordre du Nilen (Sudan); Grand Cordon de l'Etoile Brillante de Chine; comdr. de l'Ordre National du Dahomey; comdr. de l'Ordre de la Devotion; comdr. de l'Ordre Diplomatique de la Republique de Coree. Mem. Parti Democratique Gabonais. Roman Catholic.

NEAL, CONSTANCE ANN TRILLICH, lawyer, librarian, minister; b. Chgo., Apr. 16, 1949; d. Lee and Ruth (Goodhue) Trillich; m. Robert Dale Neal, Dec. 25, 1972 (div. 1988); 1 son, Adam Danforth. BA in French, U. Tenn., 1971, cert. Sorbonne, 1970; MLn, Emory U., 1979; JD, Mercer Law Sch., 1982. Bar: Ga. 1982; cert. Reiki therapist level II. Reservationist AAA, Tampa, Fla., 1971-72; library tech. asst. I, Mercer U., Macon, Ga., 1973-74, library tech. asst. II, 1974-78; teaching asst. Mercer Law Sch., Macon, 1981; asst. prof. Mercer Med. Sch., Macon, 1980-82; sole practice, Macon, 1982-86; minister Ch. Tzaddi, 1986—; minister Alliance of Divine Love, 1988—; research asst. Ctr. Constl. Studies, Macon, 1983; instr. bus. Wesleyan Coll., Macon, 1982. Bd. dirs. Unity Ch., Middle, Ga., 1987, Sec., 1987. Bd. dirs. Macon Council World Affairs, 1981-82; mem. Friends Emory Libraries, Atlanta, 1980—; mem. Friends Eckerd Coll. Library, St. Petersburg, Fla., 1980—. Mem. ABA, Am. Soc. Law and Medicine, Am. Judicature Soc., DAR (Kaskaskia chpt.), Mercer U. Women's Club (treas. 1974, pres. 1986, bd. dirs. 1987), Am. Assn. U. Women, Friends of the Library, Mid. Ga. Gem and Mineral Soc., Macon Mus. Arts and Scis., La Leche League (sec. 1985), Phi Alpha Delta. Republican.

NEAL, PATRICIA, actress; b. Packard, Ky., Jan. 20, 1926; d. William Burdette and Eura Mildred (Petrey) N.; m. Roald Dahl, July 2, 1953 (div.); children: Olivia Twenty (dec. 1962), Tessa Sophia, Theo Mathew Roald, Ophelia Magdalene, Lucy Neal. Student, Northwestern U., 1943-45. Appeared in Broadway prodns.: Another Part of the Forest, 1946 (N.Y. Critics, Antoinette Perry, other awards 1946), Children's Hour, 1952, Roomful of Roses, 1955, Suddenly Last Summer, 1958, The Miracle Worker, 1960; films include: The Fountainhead, 1948, The Hasty Heart, 1948, The Breaking Point, 1949, Three Secrets, 1949, Bright Leaf, 1950, Raton Pass, 1951, Operation Pacific, 1951, The Day the Earth Stood Still, 1951, Weekend with Father, 1951, Diplomatic Courier, 1952, Washington Story, 1952, Something for the Birds, 1952, Face in the Crowd, 1956, Hud, 1963 (N.Y. Film Critics award 1964, Acad. Motion Picture Arts and Scis. award 1964, Best Fgn. Actress award Brit. Acad. 1964), Psych 59, 1964, In Harm's Way, 1965, The Subject Was Roses, 1968, The Night Digger, 1970, Baxter, 1973, Happy Mother's Day, Love, George, 1973, Widows Nest, 1976, The Passage, 1978, Ghost Story, 1981; TV appearances, 1952—, including mini-series The Bastard, 1978, TV movie All Quiet on the Western Front, 1979, The Homecoming; also TV commls.; lectr.; author: (autobiography) As I Am, 1988. Com. mem. Internat. Help for Children, Eng.; hon. bd. dirs. Nat. Found. Encephalitis Research; mem. Washington Speakers Bur., 1978—. Named Most Outstanding Woman from Tenn. under 40, 1963; recipient Gold medal Nat. Inst. Social Scis., 1983; Patricia Neal Rehabilitation Hosp. named in her honor, Knoxville, Tenn. Mem. Actors Studio, Pi Beta Phi, Phi Beta. Mem. Ch. of England.

NEAL, WILLIAM DOUGLAS, data processing company executive; b. Frederick, Md., Feb. 16, 1943; s. Bascom Slemp and Thelma Irene (Crummitte) N.; B.S. in Commerce and Engring., Drexel U., 1966; M.S. in Indsl. Mgmt., Ga. Inst. Tech., 1973; m. Carolyn Routh Pollard, Apr. 4, 1982; children by previous marriage: W. Douglas, Elizabeth Anne, Georgia Irene. Dir., founder, prin. stockholder Sophisticated Data Research, Inc., Atlanta, 1973—; guest lectr. Emory U., 1978-86, Ga. State U., 1977—, Ga. Inst. Tech., 1985—. Served to maj. U.S. Army, 1966-77. Decorated Meritorious Service medal, Purple Heart (2), Bronze Star medal with V (5), Army Commendation medal (3), Air medal (6). Mem. Am. Mktg. Assn. (pres. Atlanta chpt. 1982-83, dir. 1980-81, mem. Speakers Bur; regional v.p. and bd. dirs.

1984-86, div. v.p. and bd. dirs. 1987—), Sigma Pi. Republican. Home: 1855 Moores Mill Rd Atlanta GA 30318 Office: 2251 Perimeter Park Dr Atlanta GA 30341

NEALE, F. BRENT, V, investment banker; b. N.Y.C., Aug. 28, 1919; s. G. Brent and Sophie Hill (Hamilton) N.; student N.Y. Inst. Fin., 1938-41, St. Peter's Coll., 1950, NYU Grad. Sch. Bus., 1954-58, Coll. Fin. Planning, 1978-80; m. Elizabeth M. Rowan, Apr. 25, 1953. Asst. syndicate mgr. Loeb Rhoades Co., N.Y.C., 1945-54; syndicate mgr. Parrish & Co., N.Y.C., 1954-58; salesman Lehman Bros., N.Y.C., 1958-62; sales mgr. and v.p. Blair Granbery Marache & Co., N.Y.C., 1962-64; assoc. mem. N.Y. Stock Exchange, 1962-64; asst. v.p. sales E.F. Hutton Co., N.Y.C., 1965-71; instl. salesman Riter Pyne Kendall & Hollister, Inc., N.Y.C., 1971-72; instl. sales Hayden Stone Co., N.Y.C., 1972-74; investment banking and instl. sales Hoppin Watson Inc., N.Y.C., 1974-76; salesman Smith Barney, Harris Upham & Co., Inc., Tinton Falls, N.J., 1976-79; investment adv., fin. planner, ins. agt.; mgr. Sands Point South Condominium, Monmouth Beach, N.J., 1980-81; dir. Pkwy. Plastics Co., Piscataway, N.J., 1960—, Neale Assocs., 1978—, AGCO Sales, Inc., Union City, N.J., 1984—; mgr. tobacco farm, 1945-54. Chmn. Monmouth (N.J.) Ocean Damage Control Bd., 1958-64; chmn. Central Rd.-Seaview Ave.-Monmouth Beach Project, 1975-81; mem. planning bd. Boro of Monmouth Beach, 1976-77, 78-81, commr. revenue and fin., 1977-78, mayor, 1978-81; campaign mgr. Monmouth County Republican primary candidates, 1958, 62; mem. Monmouth County Mayor's Beach Erosion Com., 1978-81, chmn., 1981; trustee Ch. of Precious Blood, Monmouth Beach; spl. Eucharist Minister Bishop Trenton. Served with AUS, 1941-45. Decorated Purple Heart, Bronze Star, Combat Infantryman's Badge with 7 battle stars; recipient citations Fairleigh Dickinson U., 1954, 56, Kiwanis Internat., 1950, Internat. Lions Clubs, 1951; Cath. Action medal, 1950. Registered investment adviser. Mem. Internat. Assn. Fin. Planning (treas., dir. Central N.J. chpt. 1982-84, Cert. of Appreciation 1984), Md. Soc., N.Y. Soc. (pres. 1951-54, 70-74, pres. emeritus 1983—), So. Soc. (trustee 1970-74), Wall Streeters (pres. 1958-76), SAR, Order Magna Charta (baron), Order Descs. Charlemagne, Sovereign Order Temple Jerusalem (Knight Immacula), Manor Lords Md., Channel Club, Money Marketeers, Soc. 1st Div., Cath. War Vets. (N.J. trustee 1948-50, comdr. Hudson County 1949-50), Monmouth Beach Bus. Men's Club. Clubs: K.C., Monmouth Beach Bath and Tennis (trustee 1972-75). Home: 94 Ocean Ave Monmouth Beach NJ 07750 Office: PO Box 215 Monmouth Beach NJ 07750-0215

NEALS, FELIX, lawyer, parapsychologist; b. Jacksonville, Fla.; children—Felix R., Felice, Julien. B.S., Idaho State U., 1955; J.D., Washburn U., 1958. Bar: Kans. 1958, N.Y. 1961. Atty., adminstr. ITT, N.Y.C., 1964-67; adminstr. RCA, N.Y.C., 1967-69; gen. counsel Lovable Co., N.Y.C., 1969-74; sole practice, N.Y.C., 1975-80; adminstrv. law judge N.Y. State Dept. of State, N.Y.C., 1980—; owner, founder Jazz Hall of Fame Club. Author: Psychosystematics—A Method of Mental Control, 1975. Chmn. housing com. N.J. Gov's. Bi-Partisan Com. Equal Opportunity, 1965; mem. U.S. Vice-Pres.'s Spl. Task Force Edn., and Employment, 1968; co-chmn. Mayor's Com. on Edn., East Orange, N.J., 1975; arbitrator Community Dispute Service, Am. Arbitration Assn., N.Y.C., 1983. Served with U.S. Army, 1946-49, PTO. Mem. Nat. Bar Assn., Assn. of N.Y. State Civil Service Attys. Office: NY State Dept of State 270 Broadway New York NY 10007 Office: 21 Hudson St New York NY 10013

NEAR, HENRY, university educator; b. London, May 23, 1929; arrived in Israel, 1955; s. Ezekiel and Leah (Segal) N.; m. Aliza Goldenberg, 1952; children: Yael, Shulamit, Eitan, Daniella. BA in Litterae Humaniores, Oxford U., Eng., 1953, MA, 1967; PhD in Polit. Sci., Hebrew U., Jerusalem, 1977. Agrl. worker Kibbutz Beit Ha'emek, Israel, 1955-59, 62-70, sec., 1959, 66-68; ednl. dir., emissary World Habonim, Israel and Eng., 1959-62; dir. youth dept. Ichud Hakvutzot Vehakibbutzim, Israel, 1971-73; lectr. dept. Jewish History Oranim U., Israel, 1974—; lectr. dept. land of Israel studies Haifa U., Israel, 1974—. Author: The Kibbutz and Society, 1974; editor: The Seventh Day, 1970; contbr. articles on history and philosophy of the kibbutz to jours. Home: Kibbutz Beit Ha'emek, Western Galilee 25 115, Israel Office: Univ Dept, Oranim, PO Tiv'on 36 910, Israel

NEAS, JOHN THEODORE, petroleum company executive; b. Tulsa, May 1, 1940; s. George and Lillian J. (Kasper) N.; BS, Okla. State U., 1967, MS, 1968; m. Sally Jane McPherson, June 10, 1966; children: Stephen, Gregory, Matthew. With acctg. dept. Rockwell Internat., 1965; with controller's dept. Amoco Prodn. Co., 1966-67; mem. audit and tax staff Deloitte, Haskins & Sells, 1968-75; pres. Nat. Petroleum Sales, Inc., Tulsa, 1975—, Port City Bulk Terminal, Inc., Tulsa, 1976—, McPherson Fuels & Asphalts, Inc., 1981—, John Neas Tank Lines, Inc., 1986—, BSC Tulsa, Inc., 1986—, Triple T Services, Inc., 1986—; asst. instr. U. Tulsa, 1974. CPA, Okla. Mem. Nat. Assn. Accts. (v.p. membership 1976-77), Am. Inst. CPA's, Okla. Soc. CPA's, Am. Petroleum Inst., McClellan-Kerr Arkansas River Navigation System Hist. Soc. Republican. Lutheran. Clubs: Petroleum, Oil Marketers, Transportation (Tulsa); Propeller, Oaks Country, Okla. State U. President's, Okla. State U. Bus. Adminstrn. Assocs., Golf (Okla.). Home: 2943 E 69th St Tulsa OK 74136 Office: 5401 S Harvard Suite 200 Tulsa OK 74135

NEASE, HOWARD C., marketing company executive; b. Kingman, Kans., Feb. 9, 1934; s. Francis H. and Lena B. N.; grad. Baker U., 1953; M.H.D., U. Metaphysics, Los Angeles, 1982; m. Johnie Lois Miller, Dec. 12, 1954; children—Ricky H., Randy F., Gregory L., Debra A., Jeffery T. Salesman, Mut. of Omaha, Kans., 1954-60, unit mgr., 1960-69, sales dir., 1967-69, agy. mgr. Toledo, 1969-74; founder, pres. Personal Dynamics, Inc., Toledo, 1974—, Product Devel. Inst., Inc., Toledo, 1976—, Neaco Mktg. Systems, Toledo, 1982—; pres. Briteway Products, Toledo, 1978—, Global Labs, Inc., Toledo, 1979—; founder, pres. Howard Nease & Assocs., 1976—; Mem. adv. com. for small bus. mgmt. program, Penta County Vocat. Sch., Perrysburg, Ohio, 1975; mem. state adv. com. for nurses tng. Owens Tech. Coll., Toledo. Mem. Am. Mgmt. Assn., Toledo Area Better Bus. Bur., Toledo Area C. of C. Republican. Researcher, author various indsl. tng. programs including Holiday Inn, Midwest Towel; inventor Wind Jennie. Home: 4551 Carskaddon Toledo OH 43615 Office: 5151 Monroe St Suite 240 Toledo OH 43623

NEAVE, HENRY ROBERT, mathematical statistics educator, researcher, consultant, writer; b. Norwich, Norfolk, Eng., July 14, 1942; s. George Robert and Hettie Rose (Woodhouse) N.; m. Bette Jane Cox, July 4, 1970 (div. Feb. 1976). B.Sc., U. Nottingham (Eng.), 1963, Ph.D., 1967. Tutorial asst. U. Nottingham, 1963-66, asst. lectr. math. statistics, 1966-67, lectr., 1968—; asst. prof. U. Wis., Madison, 1967-68; research fellow McGill U., Montreal, Que., Can., 1970; founder, dir. Research British Deming Assn., 1987; statis. quality cons. Nashua Corp., Bracknell, Berkshire, Eng., 1981-83, PPG Industries, France, 1984—. Author: (with E. Foxley) Programming in Algol 60, 1968; Statistics Tables, 1978; Elementary Statistics Tables, 1981, (with P.L.B. Worthington) Distribution-Free Tests, 1988, (with John S. Dowd) Simple Charting Methods for Quality Improvement, 1989; contbr. articles in field to profl. jours. Mus. dir. Beeston Operatic Soc., Nottingham, 1976-83, West Bridgford Operatic Soc., Nottingham, 1983—. Fellow Royal Statis. Soc. (sec. E. Midlands br. 1972-74, vice chmn. 1974—); mem. Inst. Math. Statistics, Am. Statis. Assn., Am. Soc. for Quality Control. Home: 168 Melton Rd, West Bridgford, Nottingham NG2 6FJ England

NEAVES, WILLIAM BARLOW, cell biologist, educator; b. Spur, Tex., Dec. 25, 1943; s. William Fred and Revvie Lee (Hefner) N.; m. Priscilla Wood, Jan. 28, 1965; children: William Barlow, Clarissa D'laine. A.B. magna cum laude, Harvard U., 1966; postgrad., Med. Sch., 1966-67, Ph.D., 1969. Lectr. vet. anatomy U. Nairobi, 1970-71, vis. prof., 1978; lectr. anatomy Harvard U., 1972; asst. prof. cell biology U. Tex. Health Sci. Center, Dallas, 1972-74; asso. prof. U. Tex. Health Sci. Center, 1974-77, prof., 1977—; dean U. Tex. Health Sci. Center (Grad. Sch. Biomed. Scis.), 1980-88; interim dean. U. Tex. Health Sci. Ctr. Southwestern Med. Sch., 1986-88; exec. v.p. U. Tex. Southwestern Med. Ctr., 1988—; research asso. herpetology Los Angeles County Mus., 1970-73; vis. lectr. U. Chgo., 1976-77. Asso. editor The Anatomical Record, 1975-87; mem. editorial bd. Biology of Reproduction, 1983-86, mem. editorial bd. Jour. of Andrology, 1987— ; contbr. chpts. to books, articles to profl. jours. Bd. dirs. Damon Runyan-Walter Winchell Cancer Fund, 1986—. Rockefeller Found. fellow, 1970-71; Milton Fund grantee, 1970-71; Population Council grantee, 1973-75; NIH grantee, 1973—; Ford. Found. grantee, 1976-78. Mem. AAAS, Am. Assn. Anatomists, Am. Soc. Andrology (Young Andrologist award 1983), N.Y. Acad. Sci., Soc. Study Reprodn., Sigma Xi. Methodist. Office: 5323 Harry Hines Blvd Dallas TX 75235

NEBENZAHL, ERNST ITZHAK, lawyer, public official; b. Frankfurt, Main, Germany, Oct. 24, 1907; arrived in Israel, 1933; s. Leopold and Betty (Hirsch) N.; m. Hildegard Hollander, Apr. 27, 1933; children: Avigdor, Plia, Isaiah, Shulamit. JD summa cum laude, Goethe U., 1929; PhD (hon.), Bar-Ilan U., Ramat Gan, Israel, 1982. Asst. law faculty Goethe U., Frankfurt, 1930-32; legal advisor pvt. bank Jerusalem, 1934-44; dir. dept. Jewish Agy., Jerusalem, 1949-51; chmn. adv. council and adv. bd. Bank Of Israel, 1954, mem., 1957; state comptroller State of Israel, 1961-81, commr. pub. complaints, 1971-81; mem. Commn. on Yom Kippur War 1973-75; pres. Jerusalem Coll. Tech., 1982-85, chancellor, 1985—; chmn. pub. com. for determining salary of Knesset mems., 1984-86; bd. dirs. Bar-Ilan U., Shaare Zedek Hosp., Jerusalem, 1982—; mem. governing bd. Internat. Orgn. Supreme Audit Instns., 1965-80, pres. 1965-68. Served as officer Israeli Def. Force, 1948-51. Decorated Royal Swedish Order of Wasa, 1st class; named Hon. Consul of Sweden, 1952, Consul Gen. of Sweden, 1954. Lodge: B'nai Brith (pres. 1951-53). Home: Batei Machse 9, Old City, Jerusalem 97500, Israel

NEBERGALL, DONALD CHARLES, investment executive; b. Davenport, Iowa, Aug. 12, 1928; s. Ellis W. and Hilda (Bruhn) N.; m. Shirley Elaine Williams, Apr. 12, 1952; children: Robert W., Nancy L. Nebergall Bosma. BS, Iowa State U., 1951. With Poweshiek County Nat. Bank, 1958-72, sr. v.p., to 1972; founding pres. Brenton Bank and Trust Co., Cedar Rapids, Iowa, 1972-82, chmn. bd., 1982-86; v.p. Chapman Co., 1986—; bd. dirs. Telephone & Data Systems, Inc., Iowa Automated Clearing House; vice-chmn. ITS, Inc. (both subs. Iowa Bankers Assn.). V.p., bd. dirs. Iowa 4-H Found., 1972-76; div. campaign chmn. United Way; bd. dirs. ARC, Boy Scouts Am.; bd. dirs., treas., past pres. Methwick Manor Retirement Home; founding trustee Cedar Rapids Community Sch. Dist. Found. Served with AUS, 1946-48. Recipient Ptnr. in 4-H award Iowa 4-H, 1983. Mem. Cedar Rapids Greater Downtown Assn. (pres., bd. dirs.), Alpha Zeta, Gamma Sigma Delta, Delta Upsilon. Republican. Methodist. Lodge: Rotary. Office: 2919 Applewood Place NE Cedar Rapids IA 52401

NEBIL, CORINNE ELIZABETH, artist; b. Varmland, Sweden, Apr. 30, 1918; came to U.S., 1920, naturalized, 1942; d. Eric and Elisabet (Tillstrom) Erickson; student NAD, 1954, Traphagen Sch. Fashion, 1955-56, Art Students League, N.Y.C., 1949-52, Whitney Sch. Art, 1948, U. Bridgeport, 1955; m. Roland Nebil; 1 dau., Ninette. Co-owner The Little Gallery, Bridgeport, Conn., 1954-60; art dir. Kid Stuff mag., 1964; free lance fashion illustrator, 1966-81; one-woman shows: Westport Country Playhouse, 1955, Chappalier Gallery, N.Y.C., 1958, Radio City Music Hall, N.Y.C., 1955, others; group shows: Art-U.S.A., Madison Sq. Garden, N.Y.C., 1948, Pastel Soc. Am., N.Y.C., 1982, Smithsonian Instn., Washington, 1965, Lincoln Ctr., Avery Fischer Hall, 1982, Swedish-Am. Artists travelling show, 1967, also others; represented in numerous pvt. collections; instr. art Famous Artists Schs. Internat., Westport, Conn., 1975-76, Central Fla. Jr. Coll., 1981—, Silvermine Sch. Art, Norwalk, Conn., 1980, Bridgeport Art League and Conn. Classic Arts Workshop, 1981-82. Recipient numerous awards, latest being best portrait award Conn. Show, 1982. Mem. Nat. League Am. Penwomen, Conn. Classic Arts, Pastel Soc. Am. Designer, painter ceiling mural St. Joseph's Ch., Bridgeport, Conn., 1958. Home: 853 NE 10th Ave Ocala FL 32670

NECESSARY, GWENDOLYN SMOOT, pharmacist; b. Man, W.Va., June 3, 1958; d. Ivory and Hazel M. (Gilliam) Smoot; m. Robert Clark Necessary, July 25, 1982; 1 child, Jillian Leigh. B.S., W.Va. U., 1980. Pharmacist, mgr. Rite Aid Pharmacy, Man, 1980-87, Adkins Pharmacy, Gilbert, W.Va., 1987—; relief pharmacist Adkins Pharmacy, Gilbert, W.Va., 1984—. Sec., v.p. Hemlock Hills Garden, Man, 1983—; historian Triadelphia Woman's Club, Man, 1983—, parliamentarian, 1986. Mem. W.Va. Pharmacists Assn., Am. Pharm. Assn., W.Va. U. Alumni Assn., W. Va., Nat. Assn. Parliamentarians, Lambda Kappa Sigma. Democrat. Methodist. Avocations: travel; cooking; playing piano; volunteer work. Home: PO Box 47 Lorado WV 25630 Office: Adkins Pharmacy Drawer H Gilbert WV 25621

NEDERLANDER, JAMES MORTON, theatre executive; b. Detroit, Mar. 31, 1922; s. David T. and Sarah L. (Applebaum) N.; m. Charlene Saunders, Feb. 12, 1969; children: James Laurence, Sharon, Kristina. Student, Detroit Inst. Tech. Chmn., former pres. Nederlander Orgn., Inc. (formerly Nederlander Producing Co. Am., Inc., N.Y.C. Owner numerous theatres including: Palace, Lunt-Fontanne Theatre, Nederlander Theatre, Brooks Atkinson Theatre, Gershivia Theatre, Neil Simon Theatre, Mark Hellinger Theatre, N.Y.C., Greek Theatre, Pantages Theatre, Wilshire Theatre, Pacific Amphitheatre, Los Angeles, Fox Theatre, San Diego, Curran Theatre, Golden Gate Theatre, Orpheum, San Francisco, Fisher Theatre, Pine Knob Mus. Theatre, Masonic Temple, Detroit, Arie Crown Theatre, Chgo., Poplar Creek, Hoffman Estates, Ill., Merriweather Post Pavilion, Columbia, Md., Concord Pavilion, Calif., Aldwych Theatre, London, Palace West Theatre, Phoenix; producer numerous shows for Broadway including Nicholas Nickleby, Little Johnny Jones, Annie, La Cage aux Folles, Nine, Applause, Hello Dolly, Not Now Darling, See Saw, Oliver, Abelard and Heloise, Sherlock Holmes, Treemonisha, Habeus Corpus, Otherwise Engaged, Whose Life is it Anyway?, Betrayal, Woman of the Year, Lena Horne: The Lady and Her Music, The Dresser, Noises Off, Merlin, Night and Day, My Fat Friend, Shirley MacLaine on Broadway, Sweet Charity Benefactors, 1985-86, Breaking The Code, 1986; numerous road show prodns.; touring revivals: Peter Pan, Hello Dolly Porgy and Bess, The Music Man, I Do! I Do!, Oklahoma, On a Clear Day You Can See Forever, Fiddler on the Roof. Office: 810 7th Ave 2d Floor New York NY 10019

NEDOM, H. ARTHUR, petroleum consultant; b. Lincoln, Nebr., Aug. 19, 1925; s. Henry Arthur and Pearle Bertrick (Swan) N.; m. Patricia Margaret Rankin, July 4, 1974; children: Richard A., Robert L., Nicole C. B.S., U. Tulsa, 1949, M.S., 1950; postgrad. in bus. adminstrn., Northwestern U., Evanston, Ill., 1968. Chief engr. Amerada Petroleum Corp., Tulsa, 1961-65; v.p. Amerada Petroleum Corp., 1965-70, Natomas Co., San Francisco, 1971-74; also dir.; pres. Norwegian Oil Co., Houston, 1974-75; pres., mng. dir. Weeks Petroleum Ltd., Westport, Conn., 1975-82; cons. 1982—; chmn. bd. arbitration Prudhoe Bay Unit 1983-84; chmn. Offshore Tech. Conf., 1971; bd. dirs. Engrs. Joint Council, 1978. Contbr. articles to profl. jours. Served with inf. U.S. Army, 1943-45, ETO. Decorated Bronze Star; named Disting. Alumnus U. Tulsa, 1972. Mem. Soc. Petroleum Engrs. (dir. 1965-68, pres. 1967, Disting. Lectr. 1973, Disting. Service award 1978, DeGolyer Disting. Service medal 1981 Disting. mem. 1983), AIME (dir. 1966-69, 76-79, pres. 1977, Hon. mem. 1982), Am. Assn. Engring. Socs. (dir. 1980-82, chmn. 1981, Spl. award 1979, Engring. Service award 1980), Am. Assn. Petroleum Geologists, Am. Petroleum Inst. (citation for service 1961). Episcopalian. Home: 21 Deerwood Ln Westport CT 06880

NEEDLES, BELVERD EARL, JR., accounting educator; b. Lubbock, Tex., Sept. 16, 1942; s. Belverd Earl and Billie (Anderson) N.; B.B.A., Tex. Tech U., 1964, M.B.A., 1965; Ph.D., U. Ill., 1969; m. Marian Powers, May 23, 1976; children—Jennifer Helen, Jeffrey Scott, Annabelle Marian. C.P.A., Ill.; cert. mgmt. acct. Asst. prof., assoc. prof. acctg. Tex. Tech U., Lubbock, 1968-72; dean Coll. Bus. and Adminstrn., Chgo. State U., 1972-76; prof. acctg. U. Ill., Urbana, 1976-78; dir. Sch. Accountancy, DePaul U., Chgo., 1978-86, prof. acctg., 1978—. Author: Accounting and Organizational Control, 1973, Modern Business, 2d edit., 1977, Principles of Accounting, 1980, 3d edit., 1987, Financial Accounting, 1982, 2d edit., 1986, The CPA Examination: A Complete Review, 7th edit., 1986, Comparative International Auditing Standards, 1985, Financial and Managerial Accounting, 1988; editor Accounting Instructor's Report, 1981—, The Accounting Profession and the Middle Market, 1986, Creating and Enhancing The Value of Post-Baccalareate Accounting Education, 1988. Treas., bd. dirs. C.P.A.s for Pub. Interest, 1978-86. Gen. Electric fellow, 1965-66; Deloitte Haskins and Sells fellow, 1966-68; named Disting. Alumnus Tex. Tech U., 1986; recipient Award of Merit DePaul U., 1986. Fellow Am. Acctg. Assn. (sec. internat. sect. 1984-86, vice chmn. 1986-87, chmn. 1987-88); mem. Fedn. Schs. Accountancy (dir. 1980-87, pres. 1986), Am. Inst. C.P.A.s, Acad. Internat. Bus., Ill. C.P.A. Soc., European Acctg. Assn. (exec. com. 1986—), Fin. Execs. Inst., Nat. Assn. Accts., Phi Delta Kappa, Phi Kappa Phi, Beta Alpha Psi, Beta Gamma Sigma. Club: Chgo. Athletic.

NEEL, LOUIS EUGENE FELIX, physicist; b. Lyons, France, Nov. 22, 1904; s. Louis Antoine and Marie Antoinette (Hartmayer) N.; Agrégé de l'Université, Ecole Normale Supé rieure, 1928; Docteur es-Sciences, Strasbourg, France, 1932; m. Hélène Hourticq, Sept. 14, 1931; children—Marie-Francoise, Marguerite Gué ly, Pierre. With Faculté des Sciences, Strasbourg, 1928-45, prof., 1937-45; prof. Faculté des Sciences Grenoble, France, 1945-76; dir. Lab. Electrostatics and Physics of Metal, 1940-71; pres. Institut Nat. Polytechnique, Grenoble, 1970-76; dir. Centre d'Etudes Nuclé aires, Grenoble, 1957-71; French rep. sci. council NATO, 1960-82; pres. Conseil Sup. Sûreté nucléaire, 1973-86. Decorated grand croix Legion of Honor, Gold medal Nat. Center Sci. Research; Nobel prize in physics, 1970. Mem. French Acad. Sci., acads. sci. Moscow, Halle, Royal Soc. London, Romanian Acad., Royal Netherlands Acad. Scis., Am. Acad. Arts and Scis., French Soc. Physics (hon. pres.), Internat. Union Pure and Applied Physics (hon. pres.). Research and numerous publs. on magnetic properties of solids; introduced sci. ideas of ferrimagnetism and antiferromagnetism; discoveries of certain magnetic properties of fine grains and crystals, directional order of magnetism, magnetic after effect. Home: 15 rue Marcel-Allégot, 92190 Meudon-Bellevue France

NEELY, HORACE HOLLIS, experimental physicist; b. Sabinal, Tex., Aug. 12, 1932; s. Hollis Hubert and Phylea Ann (Seabourn) N.; m. Norma Jean Warner, July 30, 1950; children—Karen Marie, Vic Allen, Rich Aaron. B.S., West Coast U., 1965. Mem. tech. staff Atomics Internat., Canoga Park, Calif., 1952-69; sr. cyclotron engr. UCLA, 1969-74; sr. staff engr. Rockwell Internat., Canoga Park, Calif., 1974—. Contbr. articles to profl. jours. Recipient ETEC Engr. of Yr. award, 1984. Mem. Am. Nuclear Soc., Am. Soc. for Nondestructive Testing, ASME, Am. Inst. Metall. Engrs., Sigma Xi. Club: Trail Dusters (Woodland Hills, Calif.) (pres. 1970-72). Current work: Study of LMFBR steam generator leak dynamics and inservice inspection; fusion reactor first wall liquid flow studies. Subspecialties: Nuclear fission; Heat transfer.

NEELY, ROBERT ALLEN, physician; b. Temple, Tex., Mar. 1, 1921; s. Jubal A. and Almeida (Fordtran) N.; B.A., U. Tex., 1942, M.D., 1944; postgrad. Washington U., 1951-52; m. Eleanor V. Stein, June 29, 1944; children—Byron D., Warren F. Intern, also resident Hermann Hosp., Houston, 1944-45, 55-57; gen. practice medicine, 1946-51, specializing in ophthalmology, Bellville, Tex., 1955—; trustee, staff mem. Bellville Hosp., Inc.; pres. Mid-Tex. Nursing Homes, Inc.; chmn. bd. dirs. 1st Nat. Bank of Bellville. Mem. Bellville Ind. Sch. Dist. Sch. Bd., 1948-53; past pres. Bellville Area United Fund; adv. bd. mem. Sam Houston Area council Boy Scouts Am., past mem. nat. council; mem. chancellor's council U. Tex. System. Served with USNR, 1943-46, 53-55. Recipient Silver Beaver award Boy Scouts Am. Fellow Am. Acad. Ophthalmology; mem. AMA, Austin-Grimes-Waller Counties (past pres.), Ninth Dist. (past pres.) med. soc., Tex. Med. Assn., Tex. Ophthal. Assn., Houston Ophthal. Soc., Tex. Soc. Opthalmology and Otolaryngology, Bellville C. of C., VFW (life). Republican. Lutheran. Clubs: Bellville Golf (past pres.), Doctors, Lions (past pres.). Home: 105 E Hacienda Ln Bellville TX 77418 Office: Bellville Clinic Bldg Bellville TX 77418

NEER, CHARLES SUMNER, II, orthopaedic surgeon, educator; b. Vinita, Okla., Nov. 10, 1917; s. Charles Sumner and Pearl Victoria (Brooke) N.; m. Patricia Stainton, Aug. 28, 1947; children: Charlotte Marguerite, Sydney Victoria. BA, Dartmouth Coll., 1939; MD, U. Pa., 1942. Intern U. Pa. Hosp., Phila., 1942-43; asso. in surgery N.Y. Orthopedic-Columbia-Presbyn. Med. Center, N.Y.C., 1943-44; instr. in surgery Coll. Physicians and Surgeons, Columbia U., N.Y.C., 1946-47; instr. orthopaedic surgery Coll. Physicians and Surgeons, Columbia U., 1947-57, asst. prof. clin. orthopaedic surgery, 1957-64, asso. prof., 1964-68, prof. clin. orthopaedic surgery, 1968—; attending orthopaedic surgeon Columbia-Presbyn. Med. Ctr., N.Y.C.; chief adult reconstructive service N.Y. Orthopaedic Hosp.; chief shoulder and elbow clinic Presbyn. Hosp.; chmn. 4th internat. Congress Shoulder Surgeons. Contbr. articles to books, tech. films, sound slides. Served with U.S. Army, 1944-46. Fellow ACS (sr. mem. nat. com. on trauma), Am. Acad. Orthopaedic Surgeons (com. on upper extremity, shoulder com.); mem. Am. Bd. Orthopaedic Surgeons (Disting. Service award 1975, bd. dirs. 1970-75), Am. Shoulder and Elbow Surgeons (inaugural pres.), Am. Assn. Surgery of Trauma, Am. Orthopaedic Assn., N.Y. Acad. Medicine, Allen O. Whipple Surg. Soc., AMA, N.Y. State Med. Soc., N.Y. County Med. Soc., Pan Am. Med. Assn., Am. Trauma Soc., Sociedad Latino Americana de Ortopedia y Traumatologia, Internat. Soc. Orthopaedic Surgery and Traumatology, Va. Orthopaedic Soc. (hon.), Carolina Orthopaedic Alumni Assn. (hon.), Conn. Orthopaedic Club (hon.), Internat. Congress Shoulder Surgeons, Société Francaise de Chirurgie Orthopdique et Traumatologique (hon.), Alpha Omega Alpha, Phi Chi. Home: 223 Glenwood Rd Englewood NJ 07631 Office: Columbia U Coll Physicians and Surgeons 161 Fort Washington Ave New York NY 10032

NEFF, FRED LEONARD, lawyer; b. St. Paul, Nov. 1, 1948; s. Elliott and Mollie (Poboisk) N. BS with high distinction, U. Minn., 1970; JD, William Mitchell Coll. Law, 1976. Bar: Minn. 1976, U.S. Dist. Ct. Minn. 1977, U.S. Ct. Appeals (8th cir.) 1985, U.S. Supreme Ct. 1985, Wis. Supreme Ct. 1986. Tchr. Hopkins (Minn.) Pub. Schs., 1970-72; instr. Inver Hills Community Coll., St. Paul, 1973-76, U. Minn., Mpls., 1974-76; sole practice, Mpls., 1976-79; asst. county atty. Sibley County, Gaylord, Minn., 1979-80; mng. atty. Hyatt Legal Services, St. Paul, 1981-83, regional ptnr., 1983-85, profl. devel. ptnr., 1985-86; owner, dir. Neff Law Firm, Edina, Mpls. and St. Paul, 1986—; counsel Am. Tool Supply Co., St. Paul, 1976-78; cons. Nat. Detective Agy., Inc., St. Paul, 1980-83; lectr., guest intr. U. Wis., 1976-77; spl instr. Hamline U., 1977; vis. lectr. Coll. Saint Scholastica, 1977; bd. dirs. Acceptance Ins. Holdings, Inc., 1987—. Author: Fred Neff's Self-Defense Library, 1976, Everybody's Self-Defense Book, 1978, Karate Is for Me, 1980, Running Is for Me, 1980, Lessons from the Samurai, 1986, Lessons from the Art of Kempo, 1986, Lessons from the Western Warriors, 1986. Adviser to bd. Sibley County Commrs., 1979-80; speaker before civic groups, 1976-82; mem. Hennepin County Juvenile Justice Panel, 1980-82, Hennepin County Pub. Def. Conflict Panel, 1980-82, 86—, Hennepin Bar Assn. Advice Panel Law Day, 1987, Panel Union Privilege Legal Services div. AFL-CIO, 1986—, Montgomery Wards Legal Services Panel, 1986—, Edina Hist. Soc.; charter mem. Commn. for the Battle of Normandy Mus.; founding sponsor Civil Justice Found., 1986—. Recipient St. Paul Citizen of Month award, Citizens Group, 1975, Student Appreciation U. Minn. award, 1978, Commendation award Sibley County Attys. Office, 1980, Leadership award Hyatt Legal Services, 1984, Mgn. Attys. Guidance award 1985, Justice award 1986, Creative Thinker award regional staff 1986, Good Neighbor award WCCO Radio, 1985, Lamp of Knowledge award Twin Cities Lawyers Guild, 1986, numerous other awards and honors. Fellow Roscoe Pound Found., Nat. Dist. Attys. Assn.; mem. ABA, Assn. Trial Lawyers Am., Minn. Bar Assn., Hennepin County Bar Assn., Wis. Bar. Assn., Ramsey County Bar Assn., Am. Judicature Soc., Minn. Martial Arts Assn. (pres. 1974-78 Outstanding Instr. award 1973), Nippon Kobudo Rengokai (dir. N.Central States 1972-76), Edina C. of C., Sigma Alpha Mu. Lodge: Masons, Kiwanis. Home: 7380 France Ave S Suite 100 Edina MN 55435 Office: 701 4th Ave S Suite 500 Minneapolis MN 55415 also: 345 St Peter St Suite 800 Saint Paul MN 55102 also: 5930 Brooklyn Blvd Suite 100 Brooklyn Center MN 55429

NEFF, ROBERT CLARK, lawyer; b. St. Marys, Ohio, Feb. 11, 1921; s. Homer Armstrong and Irene (McCulloch) N.; m. Betty Baker, July 3, 1954; children—Cynthia Lee Neff Schifer, Robert Clark, Abigail Lynn (dec.); m. 2d, Helen Picking, July 24, 1975. B.A., Coll. Wooster, 1943; postgrad. U. Mich., 1946-47; LL.B., Ohio No. U., 1950. Bar: Ohio 1950, U.S. Dist. Ct. (no. dist.) Ohio 1978. Sole practice, Bucyrus, Ohio, 1950—; law dir. City of Bucyrus, 1961—. Chmn. blood program Crawford County (Ohio) unit ARC, 1955—; mem. adv. bd. Salvation Army, 1962—; clk. of session 1st Presbyterian Ch., Bucyrus, 1958—. Served with USNR, World War II; comdr. Res. ret. Mem. Ohio Bar Assn., Crawford County Bar Assn., Naval Res. Assn., Ret. Officers Assn., Nat. Inst. Mcpl. Law Officers, Am. Legion, Bucyrus Area C. of C. (bd. dirs., recipient Outstanding Citizen award, 1973), Bucyrus Citizen of Yr., 1981. Republican. Clubs: Kiwanis (past pres.), Masons. Home: 1085 Mary Ann Ln Box 406 Bucyrus OH 44820 Office: 840 S Sandusky Ave Box 406 Bucyrus OH 44820

NEFF, THOMAS JOSEPH, executive search firm executive; b. Easton, Pa., Oct. 2, 1937; s. John Wallace and Elizabeth Ann (Dougherty) N.; m. Susan Culver Paull, Nov. 26, 1971 (dec.); children: David Andrew, Mark Gregory, Scott Dougherty. BS in Indsl. Engring., Lafayette Coll., 1959; MBA, Lehigh U., 1961. Assoc. McKinsey & Co., Inc., N.Y.C. and Australia, 1963-66; dir. mktg. planning Trans-World Airlines, N.Y.C., 1966-69; pres. Hosp. Data Scis., Inc., N.Y.C., 1969-74; prin. Booz, Allen & Hamilton, Inc., N.Y.C., 1974-76; regional ptnr. N.Am.; bd. dirs. Spencer Stuart & Assos., N.Y.C., 1976-79; pres., bd. dirs. Spencer Stuart & Assocs., N.Y.C., 1979—; bd. dirs. Macmillan, Inc., Lord Abbett & Co. Mut. Funds, Affiliated Fund. Served with U.S. Army, 1961-63. Republican. Roman Catholic. Clubs: Links, Yale, Sky, Racquet and Tennis; Blind Brook; Quogue (N.Y.) Beach, Quogue Field; Round Hill. Home: 96 Round Hill Rd Greenwich CT 06831 Office: Spencer Stuart and Assocs Park Ave Plaza 55 E 52d St New York NY 10055

NEGAHBAN, EZATOLLAH, archaeologist; b. Ahwaz, Iran, Mar. 1, 1926; s. Abdol Amir and Roghieh (Dideban) N.; m. Miriam Lois Miller, May 1955; children: Ali, Bahman, Mehrdad, Babak, Daryus. BA, U. Tehran, Iran, 1948; MA, U. Chgo. Oriental Inst., 1954; Doctorate, Council of Edn., Tehran, Iran, 1956. Assoc. prof. U. Tehran, 1956-62, prof., 1962-78, dir. Inst. Archaeology, 1957-78, head dept. archaeology, 1968-75, dean faculty of letters, 1975-78; tech. dir. Iranian Archaeol. Service, Tehran, 1960-65; tech. advisor to Ministry of Culture, Tehran, 1965-79; dir. Iran Bastan Mus. 19, Tehran, 1966-68; vis. curator, vis. prof. Univ. Mus., U. Pa., 1980—; sec. gen. Internat. Congress of Iranian Art and Archaeology and dir. 5th Congress, Tehran-Shiraz, 1968; dir. excavation of Mehranabad, 1961, Marlik, 1961-62, Haft Tepe, 1966-78, Qazin Plain Expdn. (Zaghe, Qabrestan, Sagzabad, 1970-78), Archaeol. Survey of N.E. Iran, 1965, Mazandaran highlands, 1975. Author: Buffware Sequence in Khuzistan, 1954, Preliminary Report on Marlik Excavation, 1964, Metal Vessels from Marlik, 1983, Excavation of Haft Tepe. Mem. Deutsches Archaeologische Inst., Internat. Congress of Pre and Protohistory. Moslem. Home: 5226 Rexford Rd Philadelphia PA 19131 Office: U Pa Dept Anthropology 325 Univ Museum Philadelphia PA 19104-6398

NEGI, SHARAD SINGH, author, administrator; b. Agra, India, Apr. 1, 1957; s. Bejai Singh and Shakuntala N.; m. Manju Thakur, Nov. 29, 1983. B.Sc., Garhwal U., India, 1976, M.Sc., 1978, Ph.D., 1981. Asst. conservator forests Himachal Pradesh Govt., Nurpur, India, 1982, Rajgarh, India, 1982-83; dep. conservator forests, Rajgarh, 1983-85; dep. conservator forests Nat. Forest Acad., Dehra Dun, 1985—. Author: Environmental Problems in the Himalaya, 1982, Geology for Foresters, 1982, Scientific Management of Forests, 1984, Silviculture of Indian Trees, 1985, Managing the Himalayan Environment, 1986, Operation Pushpak, 1986, Forest Working Plan, 1988; author other books on forestry, conservation and silviculture; editor Indian Jour. Forestry, 1985-86; contbr. numerous papers and articles to profl. jours. Council Sci. and Indsl. Research fellow, 1979. Recipient Nilgiri Wildlife award Indian Forest Coll., 1982, Indo-German Soc. Freiburg award, 1986. Mem. Indian Sci. Congress Assn., Indian Environ. Soc., Asian Environ Soc., Ctr. for Sci. and Environment. Hindu. Avocation: trekking. Home: 24-C Lytton Rd, Dehradun 248001 Uttar Pradesh India Office: Nat Forest Acad, New Forest, Dehradun 248006 Uttar Pradesh India

NEHAUL, PATRICK DAMON, construction company executive; b. Bridgetown, Barbados, West Indies, Feb. 17, 1954; s. George Bhagwandas and Gloria Patricia (Bullen) N.; m. Noor Rafza Rahaman, Jan. 3, 1981; children: Jihad-Raza, Nur Zakiya. B.Comm. with honors, U. Windsor, Ont., Can., 1977. Mng. dir. Nehaul Constrn. Co., Barbados, 1977—; dir. Hotel Investors, Barbados, Century 21 Ltd., Barbados. Lodge: Rotary (pres. local club 1983-84). Home: 6 Brighton Beach, Black Rock, Saint Michael Barbados Office: Nehaul Constrn Co Ltd, 4th Ave Rendezvous Gardens, Christ Church Barbados

NEHER, LESLIE IRWIN, engineer, former air force officer; b. Marion, Ind., Sept. 15, 1906; s. Irvin Warner and Lelia Myrtle (Irwin) N.; m. Lucy Marion Price; 1 son, David Price; m. Cecelia Marguerite Hayworth, June 14, 1956; B.S. in Elec. Engring., Purdue U., 1930. Registered profl. engr., Ind., N.Mex. Engr. high voltage research, 1930-32; engr. U.S. Army, Phila., 1933-37; heating engr. gas utility, 1937-40; commd. 2d lt. U.S. Army, 1929, advanced through grades to Col., 1947; dir. tng., Tng. Command, Heavy Bombardment, Amarillo AFB, Tex., 1942-44; dir. mgmt. tng., 15th AF, Colorado Springs, Colo., 1945-46; mgr. Korea Electric Power Co., Seoul, 1946-47, ret., 1960; engr. Neher Engring. Co., Gas City, Ind., 1960—. Chmn. Midwest Indsl. Gas Council, 1969; historian Grant County, Ind., 1985—. Named Outstanding Liaison Officer, Air Force Acad., 1959; Ambassador for Peace, Republic of Korea, 1977; recipient Republic of Korea Service medal, 1977. Mem. Ind. Soc. Profl. Engrs. (Outstanding Engr. 1982, Engr. of Yr. Ind. 1986), Nat. Soc. Profl. Engrs., Midwest Indsl. Gas Assn. (chmn. 1969), Am. Assn. of Reitred Persons (pres. Grant County chpt. 1986,87). Republican. Methodist. Lodge: Kiwanis (Disting. sect. 1979-85, lt. gov. 1964; Disting. Service award 1962).

NEHLIN, NILS GUSTAF OSSIAN, administrative director; b. Säffle, Värmland, Sweden, Aug. 11, 1923; s. Harald and Lilly (Andersson) N.; m. Britta Ahnquist, Apr. 4, 1954; children: Gunilla, Christina, Magnus. MS, Stockholm Sch. Econs., 1951. Auditor Price Waterhouse Co., Stockholm, 1952-57; chief acct. AB Nordiska MetallduksVäveriet, Uppsala, Sweden, 1957-65; fin. dir. AB Nordviror, Uppsala, 1965—. Served to capt. Swedish mil. Lodges: Lions (pres. 1972-73), Masons. Home: Norra Parkvägen 9, S-75245 Uppsala Sweden Office: PO Box 69, S-75103 Uppsala Sweden

NEIDLINGER, GUSTAV, baritone; b. Mar. 21, 1910; s. Gustav and Margarete (Wagner) N.; m. Elisabeth Hartmann, 1936; 2 children. Student, Humanistisches Gymnasium, Mainz, Opernschule, Frankfurt/Main. Performer Stadttheater, Mainz and Plauen, Fed. Republic Germany, Staatsoper, Hamburg and Stuttgart, Fed. Republic Germany, Bayreuth Festival, Fed. Republic Germany, Deutsche Oper, Berlin, Fed. Republic Germany, La Scala, Milan, Covent Garden, London, Grand Opera, Paris, Teatro La Fenice, Venice, Italy, Rome Opera, Staatsoper, Vienna, Austria, Met. Opera, N.Y.C., Lyric Opera, Chgo., Theatro Colon, Buenos Aires, Argentina, Opera San Carlo, Naples, Italy, Staatsoper, Stuttgart. Recipient Grosses Verdienstkreuz des Verdienstordens der Bundesrepublik Deutschland 1974, Ehrenmitglied der Staatsoper Stuttgart 1977; Gutenbergplakette der Stadt Mainz 1985. Address: 5427 Lahnstrasse 57, Bad Ems Federal Republic of Germany

NEIL, LAVERNE, textile design executive; b. Cherokee, Iowa; d. John R. and Anie (Brownlie) N. A.B., U. Colo., 1923; student Chgo. Acad. Fine Arts, 1925-26, N.Y. U., 1927-28. Decorator, Lord & Taylor, N.Y.C., 1928-30; adviser Hearns, 1930-32, Gimbel's, 1933-34; gen. mdse. coordinator Sloane Stores, 1934-53; style cons. S.M. Hexter Co., 1953-71; v.p., dir. styling and pub. relations F. Schumaker, 1971-83, dir. designing and producing printed textiles. Recipient honor award The Decorators Club, 1985. Mem. Fashion Group (v.p. 1950-52), Nat. Home Fashion League (v.p. 1948, pres. 1949, 50) (trail blazer award, 1985), Upholstery and Decorative Fabrics Assn. Am. (v.p. 1964-66). Club: Three Arts (pres. 1929-30) (N.Y.C.). Home: 2 W 67th St New York NY 10023 Office: F Schumacher & Co 919 3d Ave New York NY 10022

NEILD, ROBERT RALPH, economist, educator; b. Peterborough, U.K., Sept. 10, 1924; s. Ralph and Josephine Neild; m. Elizabeth W. Griffiths; 5 children. Ed. Charterhouse and Trinity Coll., Cambridge. Sec. UN Econ. Commn. for Europe, Geneva, 1947-51; mem. staff econ. sect. Cabinet Office (later Treasury), 1951-56; lectr. econs., fellow Trinity Coll., Cambridge U., 1956-58, prof. econs., 1971-84; mem. staff Nat. Inst. Econ. and Social Research, 1958-64; econ. adviser to Treasury, 1964-67; mem. Fulton Com. on Civil Service, 1966-68; dir. Stockholm Internat. Peace Research Inst., 1967-71, mem. governing bd., 1972—; lectr. in field. Author: Pricing and Employment in the Trade Cycle, 1964; The Measurement and Reform of Budgetary Policy (with T.S. Ward), 1978; How to make up your mind about the Bomb, 1981. Mem. governing body Queen Elizabeth Coll., Oxford, 1978—. Served with RAF, 1943-45. Office: 5 Cranmer Rd, Cambridge England *

NEILL, DENIS MICHAEL, government relations consulting company executive; b. Grand Rapids, Mich., Apr. 27, 1943; s. Thomas Patrick and Agnes Josephine (Weber) N.; m. Mary Kathleen Golden, June 11, 1966; children: Mark, Erin. AB cum laude, St. Louis U., 1964, JD cum laude, 1967. Bar: Mo. 1967, D.C. 1969. Gen. atty. Office of Asst. Regional Counsel IRS, Newark, 1967-68; assoc. Arent, Fox, Kintner, Plotkin & Kahn, Washington, 1969-71, Morgan, Lewis & Bockius, Washington, 1971-72; atty. advisor office gen. counsel AID, Washington, 1972-73, asst. gen. counsel legis. and policy coordination, 1973-75, asst. adminstr. legis. affairs, 1975-77; sr. v.p., gen. counsel Aeromaritime Internat. Corp., Washington, 1977-81; counsel Surrey & Morse, Washington, 1981-82; ptnr. Neill, Mullenholz & Shaw, Washington, 1982—; pres. Neill & Co. Inc., Washington, 1982—; bd. dirs. Fed. City Nat. Bank, Washington. Bd. dirs. Barker Found. Served to lt. USCG, 1968-71. Recipient Superior Unit Citation AID, 1976, Disting. Honor award, 1977. Mem. ABA, Fed. Bar Assn., D.C. Bar Assn., Mo. Bar Assn., Nat. Security Indsl. Assn. (bd. dirs. 1982—). Democrat. Roman Catholic. Clubs: Capitol Hill, Army and Navy, Internat. (Washington); Columbia Country (Chevy Chase, Md.). Home: 5945 Searl Terr Bethesda MD 20816 Office: Neill & Co 900 17th St NW Suite 400 Washington DC 20006

NEILL, LAQUITA JOYCE BELL, educator, home economist, librarian; b. Humphreys County, Miss., Aug. 10, 1930; d. Clarence Marvin and Dorothy (Parker) Bell; m. Robert Wood Neill, Apr. 29, 1956; 1 child, Robert Wood, Jr. BS in Home Econs., Delta State U., Cleve., 1952, MLS, 1977; grad. Miss. Ednl. Adminstrn. Leadership Inst. for Women U. So. Miss., 1987. Asst. home economist Panola County, Miss. Cooperative Extension Service, Batesville, 1952-54, home economist Carroll County, Carrollton, Miss., 1954-57; bookkeeper, teller Peoples Bank & Trust Co., North Carrollton, 1959-61; instr. home econs. Leflore County, Greenwood, Miss., 1961-62, Carroll County, Carrollton, 1962-77; media dir. Leflore County High Sch., Itta Bena, Miss., 1977-78, Winona Elem. Sch., Miss., 1978-79, J.Z. George Sch., North Carrollton, 1979—; ptnr. Bell Farms, Tchula and Belzoni, Miss.; dir. Neill Forest Products, Inc., Carrollton, Neill Realty, Inc., Carrollton. Trustee, mem. adminstrv. bd. Carrollton United Methodist Ch. Named Regional Star Tchr. Miss. Econ. Council, 1973. Mem. Miss. Library Assn., Miss. Assn. Media Educators, ALA, Miss. Archeol. Assn. (Cottanlandia chpt.), Miss. Assn. Educators, NEA, Delta State Univ. Alumni Assn., UDC (The H. D. Money chpt.), Carroll Soc. for Preservation of Antiquites, Internat. Bell Soc. (bd. govs.), Bell Family Assn. of U.S. (charter mem.), Clan Bell Descendants, Council of Scottish Clan Assns., Zeta State (Alpha Phi chpt.), Delta Kappa Gamma. Club: Cherokee Rose Garden. Home: 204 Washington St Carrollton MS 38917 Office: PO Box 264 Carrollton MS 38917

NEILL, (FRANCIS) PATRICK, lawyer, educator, college administrator; b. England, Aug. 8, 1926; s. Sir Thomas and Lady Annie Strachan (Bishop) N.; m. Lady Caroline Susan, 1954; children—Timothy, Robin, Jonathan, Harriett, Matthew, Emma. Ed. Highgate Sch., Magdalen Coll., Oxford U.; LL.D. (hon.), U. Hull; D.C.L. (hon.), Oxford U. Called to the Bar, Gray's Inn, 1951. Fellow All Souls Coll., Oxford U., 1950-77, sub-warden, 1972-74, warden, 1977—, univ. vice chancellor, 1983; recorder of Crown Ct., 1975-78; judge Ct. of Appeal of Jersey and Guernsey, 1977—; chmn. Justice All Souls Com. for Rev. Adminstrv. Law, 1978, Press Council, 1978—, Council for Securities Industry, 1978-85, Benchers Gray's Inn, 1971; mem. Bar Council, 1967-71, vice chmn., 1973-74, chmn., 1974-75; chmn. Senate of Inns of Ct. and the Bar, 1974-75. Served with Rifle Brigade, 1944-47, G.S.O., III (Tng.) Brit. Troops Egypt, 1947. Gibbs Law Scholar, 1949; Eldon Law Scholar, 1950. Clubs: Athenaeum, Garrick, Beefsteak. Office: All Souls Coll, High St, Oxford, Oxfordshire OX1 4AL, England

NEILSON, JAMES, journalist; b. West Ewell, Surrey, England, Nov. 2, 1940; s. James and Flora Stuart (MacQuarrie) N.; m. Julia Helena Caballero, Dec. 1, 1970; children: Gwendolen, Derek, Moira, Ingrid. Columnist leader writer Buenos Aires Herald, 1966-74, editor-in-chief, 1979-86; columnist leader writer The Province, Vancouver, British Columbia, Can., 1974-75, Rio Negro, Argentina, 1986-87; free-lance writer 1987—. Contbr. thousands of articles to worldwide publs. Home: Santiago De Compostela, 28035 Madrid Spain

NEILSON, JOHN WILBERT TENNANT, research company executive, consultant, educator; b. Oakland, Calif., May 9, 1944; s. Donald Wilbert Tennant and Mary Vera (Peart) N.; divorced; children—Sean Wilbert Tennant, Kimberly Mary. B.S. in Edn., So. Oreg. State Coll., 1969, M.S. in Gen. Studies, 1972. Registered sanitarian trainee Oreg. State Dept. Health, 1973. Dept. chmn. Days Creek (Oreg.) High Sch., 1969-70; chmn. biology dept. South Umpqua High Sch., Myrtle Creek, Oreg., 1970-75; microbiologist, chemist Umpqua Research Co., Myrtle Creek, Oreg., 1973-76, field rep., 1976-78; prof. sci. Lane Community Coll., Eugene, Oreg., 1976-78; salesman Jewett Office Supply, Medford, Oreg., 1978-80, Truscott Office Products, Medford, 1978-82, chief exec. officer pres. Neilson Research Medford, 1976—; lab. analyst, cons. drinking water; chief exec. officer, pres. Am. Lab. Network, Medford, 1986—; mktg. lab. services. Served with U.S. Army, 1962-65, USAR, 1976—. Mem. Am. Soc. Microbiology, Am. Water Works Assn., Assn. Ofcl. Analytical Chemists, Water Pollution Control Fedn. Republican. Episcopalian. Club: Rotary. Author: Northwestern CB Log Book, 1976.

NEIMAN, LEROY, artist; b. St. Paul, June 8, 1927; s. Charles and Lydia (Serline) Runquist; m. Janet Byrne, June 22, 1957. Student, Sch. Art Inst. Chgo., 1946-50, U. Ill., 1951, DePaul U., 1951; Litt.D., Franklin Pierce Coll., 1976; hon. Doctorate, St. John's U., 1980, Iona Coll., 1985. Instr. Sch. Art Inst. Chgo., 1950-60, Saugatuck (Mich.) Summer Sch. Painting, 1957-58, 63, Sch. Arts and Crafts, Winston-Salem, N.C., 1963; instr. painting Atlanta Youth Council, 1968-69; printmaker-graphics 1971—; ofcl. artist Olymics, ABC-TV, Munich, 1972, Montreal, 1976; ofcl. artist U.S. Olympics, 1980, 84, CNN-TV Goodwill Games, Moscow, 1986; computer artist CBS-TV (Superbowl), New Orleans, 1978. Exhibited one-man shows, Oehlshlaeger Gallery, Chgo., 1959, 61, O'Hana Gallery, London, Gallerie O. Bosc, Paris, 1962, Hammer Gallery, N.Y.C., 1963, 65, 67, 70, 72, 76, 78, 79, 81-83, 85-87, Huntington-Hartford Gallery Modern Art, N.Y.C., 1967, Heath Gallery, Atlanta, 1969, Abbey Theatre, Dublin, Ireland, 1970, Museo de Bellas Artes, Caracas, Indpls. Inst. Arts, 1972, Hermitage Mus., Leningrad, Tobu Gallery, Tokyo, 1974, Springfield (Mass.) Mus. Fine Arts, 1974, 84, Knoedler Gallery, London, 1976, Casa gratica, Helsinki, 1977, Renée Victor, Stockholm, 1977, Okla. Art Ctr., Oklahoma City, 1981, Harrod's, London, 1982, retrospective show, Minn. Mus. Art, St. Paul, 1975, Meredith Long Galleries, Houston, 1978, Hanae Mori Gallery, Tokyo, 1988, New State Tretyakov Mus., 1988, Santa Monica (Calif.) Heritage Mus., 1988; two-man show, Neiman-Warhol, Los Angeles Inst. Contemporary Art, 1981; exhibited in group shows, Art Inst. Chgo., 1954-60, Carnegie Internat., 1956, Corcoran Gallery Am., Washington, Walker Art Center, Mpls., 1957, Ringling Mus., Sarasota, Fla., 1959, Salon d'Art Mus., Paris, 1961, Nat. Gallery Portraiture, Smithsonian Instn., Washington, Minn. Mus. Art, 1969, Rotunda Della Basana, Milan, Italy, 1971, Royal Coll. Art, London, 1971, Minn. Mus. Art Nat. Tour, 1976-77, Whitney Mus., 1985 Master Prints of 19th and 20th Centuries, Hammer Galls., N.Y., 1987; represented in permanent collections, Mpls. Inst. Arts, Ill. State Mus., Springfield, Joslyn Mus., Omaha, Wodham Coll., Oxford, Eng., Nat. Art Mus. Sport, N.Y.C., Museo De Ballas Artes Caracas, Hermitage Mus., Indpls. Inst. Arts, U. Ill., Balt. Mus. Fine Art; executed murals at, Merc. Nat. Bank, Hammond, Ind., Continental Hotel, Chgo., Swedish Lloyd Ship S.S. Patricia, Stockholm, ceramic tile mural, Sportsmans Park, Chgo.; sculptor 3-piece horse racing motif, 1977; Harlequin, 1983; Defiant Stallone, 1987, Vigilant Panther, 1987; Author: LeRoy Neiman—Art and Life Style, 1974, Horses, 1979, LeRoy Neiman. Posters, 1980, LeRoy Neiman. Catalogue Raisonné, 1980, Carnaval, 1981, LeRoy Neiman: Winners, 1983, Japanese translation, 1985, Monte Carlo Chase, 1988; illustrator: 12 paintings deluxe edit. Moby Dick, 1975. Served with AUS, 1942-46. Recipient 1st prize Twin City Show, 1953, 2d prize Minn. State Show, 1954, Clark Meml. prize Chgo. Show, 1957, Hamilton-Graham prize Ball State Coll., 1958, Municipal prize Chgo. Show, 1958, Purchase prize Miss. Valley Show, 1959, Gold medal Salon d'Art Modern Paris, 1961; award of merit as nation's outstanding sports artist AAU, 1976; Olympic Artist of Century award, 1979, Gold Medal award St. John's U., 1985. Address: 1 W 67th St New York NY 10023

NEIMAN, ROBERT LEROY, management consultant; b. Chgo., Feb. 9, 1930; s. Maurice and Shirley (Albin) N.; B.S. in Communications with honors, U. Ill., 1951, M.A. in Social and Behavioral Scis., 1952; m. Marlene Kaufman (dec. Mar. 1972); m. Barbara Milkes (dec. Mar. 1983); 1 dau., Debra Bea. Asst. to pres. Utility Plastic Packaging Co., Chgo., 1953-54; from dept. mgr. to v.p. Castle and Assos., Chgo., 1954-73; v.p. Mendheim Co., Chgo., 1973-77, sr. v.p., 1977-86, pres. Neiman & Assocs, 1986— ; guest radio speaker on cancer research fund raising, 1984. Chmn. Marlene K. Neiman Meml. Found. of Am. Cancer Soc., 1972-75, chmn. Barbara J. Neiman Meml. Found. for Lung Cancer, 1983; bd. dirs. Morton Grove, Ill. unit Am. Cancer Soc. Served as 1st lt. USAF, 1951-53. Recipient Presdl. citation; Joggers award Lehmann Sports Club. Mem. Am. Personnel and Guidance Assn., Am. Inst. Indsl. Engrs., Soc. Mfg. Engrs., Am. Mgmt. Assn., Nat. Assn. Corp. and Profl. Recruiters, Air Force Assn., North Shore Assn. for Retarded, Sigma Delta Chi, Sigma Delta Pi. Club: Skokie Valley Kiwanis (program chmn.). Author articles in field. Home: 9401 Natchez Ave Morton Grove IL 60053 Office: 9401 N Natchez Morton Grove IL 60053

NEIMAN, TANYA MARIE, lawyer; b. Pitts., June 28, 1949; d. Max and Helen (Lamaga) N. AB, Mills Coll., 1970; JD, U. Calif.Hastings Coll. of Law, San Francisco, 1974. Bar: Calif. 1975. Law assoc. Boalt Hall U. Calif., Berkeley, 1974-76; pub. defender State of Calif., San Francisco, 1976-81; assoc. gen. counsel, dir. vol. legal services Bar Assn. San Francisco, 1982—. Mem. ABA (speaker 1985—, Harrison Tweed award 1985), Calif. Bar Assn. (exec. com. 1984—, legal services sect.), Golden Gate Bus. Assn. Found. (v.p. grant making 1985—), Nat. Conf. Women and Law (speaker 1975—)Nat. Lawyers Guild. Office: Bar Assn San Francisco 685 Market St San Francisco CA 94105

NEIMARK, PHILIP JOHN, financial consultant, editor; b. Chgo., Sept. 13, 1939; s. Mortimer William N. ; m. Vassa Lynn; children: Tanya Lee, Joshua Daniel. Student U. Chgo., 1956-58, Northwestern U., 1958-59; D in Bus. Mgmt. (hon.), Ricker Coll., Houlton, Maine, 1976. Mem. Chgo. Mercantile Exchange, 1968-74; owner Josephson Neimark Trading Co., Chgo., 1972-73; ptnr. Rosenthal & Co., Chgo., 1973-77; owner, prin. Philip J. Neimark Investments, Miami, Fla., 1977-79, Chgo., 1979—; pres. Neimark Fin. Pub. Co., 1985—; editor, pub. Philip J. Neimark Viewpoint, N.Y.C., 1976-85, editor Pro Trade, 1984—, Low Priced Stock Edit., 1984—; fin. editor Money Maker mag., 1979-85; mem. Internat. Monetary Market, 1971-74, N.Y. Mercantile Exchange, 1973-74, Chgo. Bd. of Options Exchange, 1973-75; editor, Low Priced Stock Edition, 1984—, Pro Trade, 1985—. Author: How to Be Lucky, 1975; contbg. editor Consumers Digest mag., 1977-85. Bd. dirs. Luth. Gen. Med. Found., Principal Vassa Internat. Mem. Fla. Exec. Planning Assn., South Fla. Fin. Planners Assn., Investment Co. Inst., Nat. Paso Fino Assn. (founder). Office: 224 E Ontario Chicago IL 60611

NEINER, ANDREW JOSEPH, financial planning executive; b. Ft. Scott, Kans., Feb. 15,1950; s. Andrew W. and Celeste H. (Beck) N.; m. Linda M. Koenig, Aug. 16, 1969; children: Carrie L., Christine M., Joseph M., Elizabeth A. BSBA, U. Mo., St. Louis, 1972; MBA, St. Louis U., 1976. Fin. analyst Chrysler Corp., St. Louis, 1972-75; fin. mgr. Gen. Cable Corp., St. Louis, 1975-79; controller Consol. Aluminum, St. Louis, 1979-80, group controller, 1980-83, ops. controller, 1983-85, corp. controller, 1985, dir. corp. planning, 1986, v.p. fin., 1986—; condr. fin. workshop Alusuisse Ltd., Zurich, Switzerland, 1985; instr. St. Louis Jr. Coll., 1978-80, U. Mo., St. Louis, 1978. Mem. Am. Mgmt. Assn., Fin. Exec. Inst., Electors Savs. Credit Union (bd. dirs. 1988). Roman Catholic. Home: 15104 Appalachian Trail Chesterfield MO 63017 Office: Consol Aluminum 11960 Westline Industrial Dr Saint Louis MO 63146

NEINFELDT, GERALD OTTO, educational administrator; b. Janesville, Wis., Dec. 1, 1937; s. Otto E. and Freda C. (Gackstaetter) N.; B.E., U. Wis., Whitewater, 1959; M.S. in Bus. Edn., U. Wis., Madison, 1967; m. Judith A. Kehl, Nov. 8, 1958; children—Laurie, Timothy, Jennifer. Instr. bus. edn. Pittsville (Wis.) Pub. Schs., 1959-60, Wisconsin Rapids (Wis.) Vocat. Sch., 1959-60; instr. bus. edn. Elkhorn (Wis.) Sch. Dist., 1960-67, bus. mgr., 1967—; adult evening supr. Gateway Tech. Inst., Elkhorn, Wis., 1979-81. Registered sch. bus. adminstr.; cert. tchr., sch. bus. ofcl., Wis. Mem. Am. Assn. Sch. Adminstrs., Assn. Sch. Bus. Ofcls., Am. Mgmt. Assn., Wis. Assn. Sch. Bus. Ofcls. (dir. 1983-85), Delta Kappa, Phi Pi Epsilon. Lutheran. Home: 519 N Edgewood Ave Elkhorn WI 53121 Office: Adminstrv Service Center 1887 Building Elkhorn WI 53121

NELIPOVICH, SANDRA GRASSI, artist; b. Oak Park, Ill., Nov. 22, 1939; d. Alessandro and Lena Mary (Ascareggi) Grassi; m. John Nelipovich Jr., Aug. 19, 1973. BFA in Art Edn., U. Ill., 1961; postgrad., Northwestern U., 1963, Gonzaga U., Florence, Italy, 1966, Art Inst. Chgo., 1968; diploma, Accademia Universale Alessandro Magno, Prato, Italy, 1983. Tchr. art Edgewood Jr. High Sch., Highland Park, Ill., 1961-62, Emerson Sch. Jr. High Sch., Oak Park, 1962-77; batik artist Calif., 1977—; illustrator Jolly Robin Publ. Co., 1988—; supr. student tchrs., Oak Park, 1970-75; adult edn. tchr. ESL, ceramics, Medinah, Ill., 1974; mem. curriculum action group on Human Dignity, EEO workshop demonstrator, Oak Park, 1975-76; guest lectr. Muckenthaler Ctr., Fullerton, Calif., 1980; fabric designer for fashion designer Barbara Jax, 1987. One-woman shows include Lawry's Calif. Ctr., Los Angeles, 1981-83, 1982, Whittier (Calif.) Mus., 1985-86, Anaheim (Calif.) Cultural Ctr., 1986-88, Ill. Inst. Tech., Chgo., 1988; also gallery exhibits in Oak Brook, Ill., 1982, La Habra, Calif., 1983; represented in permanent collections McDonald's Corp., Oak Brook, Ill., Glenkirk Sch., Deerfield, Ill., and in galleries in Laguna Beach, Calif., Maui, Hawaii; fashion designer for Barbara Jax, 1987; illustrator for Jolly Robin Pub. Co., Anaheim, 1988—. Recipient numerous awards, purchase prizes, 1979—. Mem. AAUW (hospitality chmn. 1984-85), Oak Park Art League, Orange Art Assn. (jury chairperson 1980), Anaheim Art Assn., Muckenthaler Ctr. Circle. Roman Catholic. Club: Anaheim Hills Women's. Home and Office: 5922 Calle Cedro Anaheim CA 92807

NELISCHER, MAURICE PAUL, landscape architecture educator; b. Edmonton, Alta, Can., Jan. 2, 1951; s. Joseph Edward and Irene (Burghart) N. B.Sc. with honors, Carleton U., 1975; M. Landscape Architecture, U. Guelph, 1978. Prof. landscape architecture U. Calgary, Alta., Can., 1978-79, U. Guelph, Ont., Can., 1979—; cons., designer, developer M.P. Nelischer & Assocs., Guelph and Toronto, 1978-85. Author: Treas, Shrubs & Groundcovers, 1980; Sir G. Jellicoe, 1983; Handbook of Landscape Architectural Construction, 1985. Vice pres.'s research fellow U. Guelph, 1983, Agrl. Can. research grantee, 1981-84. Mem. Council Educators in Landscape Architecutre (dir. 1983-85), Ont. Assn. Landscape Architects, Can. Assn. Landscape Architects, Am. Soc. Land Architects. Avocations: carpentry; skiing; windsurfing. Home: 75 Martin Ave, Guelph, ON Canada N1G 2A3 Office: U Guelph, Dept Landscape Architecture, Guelph, ON Canada N1G 2W1

NELLEMOSE, KNUD, sculptor; b. Copenhagen, Mar. 12, 1908; s. Aage and Anna Nellemose; m. Pia Bendix, 1950; 3 sons. Educated Royal Acad. Art, Copenhagen. First exhbn. of sculpture, 1931; represented at Venice Biennale, 1950, other internat. exhbns.; prin. works include: busts of Their Majesties King Frederik, Queen Ingrid and Queen Margrethe II of Denmark; statues of Soren Kierkegaard, King Frederick IX; represented in permanent collections State Gallery of Copenhagen, other Danish museums, Nat. Mus. Stockholm, Nat. Mus. Oslo, Nat. Mus. Auschwitz, Poland; sculptor marble bust of Hans Andersen for 150th anniversary celebrations. Mem. State Art Found., 1958-64. Decorated knight Order of Dannebrog; recipient Eckersberg medal, 1944; Kai Nielsen Bequest, 1947; Carlsberg Travelling scholar, 1947-48; Thorvaldson medal, 1968.

NELLES, MAURICE, mechanical engineer, author; b. Madison, S.D., Oct. 19, 1906; s. Hubert Tilman and Anne (Benson) N.; m. Cecelia Nelson, Aug. 28, 1929; 1 son, Maurice Tilman; foster daus., Sally Sue Hopkins, Merrill Sherwin. A.B., U. S.D., 1927, A.M., 1928; Ph.D., Harvard, 1932; D.Sc., U. S.D., 1955. Prof. physics Columbus Coll., 1928-29; instr. chemistry U. S.D., 1929-30; research chemist Nat. Aniline Chem. Co., 1932-34, Union Oil Co., 1934-36; camp dir. Civilian Conservation Corps, Ft. Lewis, 1936-37; research engr. Riverside Cement Co., 1937-39; engr. Permanente Corp., 1939-40; staff asst. Lockheed Aircraft, 1940-46; prof. aero. engring., mgr. Allan Hancock Found., U. So. Calif., 1947-50; prof. dir. engring. expt. sta. Pa. State U., 1950-51; dir. research Borg-Warner, also v.p. petro-mechanics div., 1951-54; dir. research and diversification, mgr. graphic arts div. Technicolor Corp.,

1954-57; v.p. engring. Crane Co., Chgo., 1957-59; v.p. Am. Electronics, Inc., 1959-62, Quail Products, Inc.; pres. Corwith Co. div. Crane Co., Locked-Lattice Steel Co.; dir. Merd Corp., Lamb-Weston, Inc., Scientia Corp., Hydro-Aire Co., Crane, Ltd., Can., Western Optics, Inc., Radix Corp.; Rust prof. bus. adminstrn. U. Va.; exec. dir. Tayloe Murphy Inst.; prof. Grad. Sch. Bus. Adminstrn., 1966-70, Christian Heritage Coll.; cons. Nat. Acad. Sci.; Dep. dir. WPB; mem. war metall. com. NACA; dir. Sch. Ministry World Evangelism, Inc., 1977-81; chief engr. Office Prodn. Research and Devel. Author: Satan's 20th Century Strategy, 1971, Precious Christian Thought Patterns, 1973, The Deal, 1976, also articles mgmt. research and engring., new research technique. Trustee Midwest Research Inst., Marine Studies Inst.; commr. to synod United Presbyn. Ch. Charles Coffin fellow; George H. Emerson scholar; Harvard U. fellow. Fellow Am. Inst. Chemists; mem. Am. Soc. M.E., Soc. Automotive Engrs., Inst. Aero. Scis., I.E.E.E., Am. Chem. Soc., Am. Soc. Naval Engrs., Am. Soc. Metals, AIAA, Am. Soc. Motion Picture and TV Engrs., Internat. Soc. Visual Literacy, Optical Soc. Am., Am. Mgmt. Assn., A.A.A.S., Sigma Xi, Tau Beta Pi, Alpha Tau Omega, Tau Kappa Alpha, Sigma Phi Delta, Gamma Alpha, Alpha Chi Sigma. Presbyn. (elder, mem. San Diego Presbytery). Clubs: Mason, Los Angeles Athletic; Montecito (Santa Barbara); Chemists (N.Y.C.); Farmington Country (Charlottesville, Va.). Home: 5522 Rutgers Rd La Jolla CA 92037

NELLI, DONALD JAMES, business school executive, accountant; b. Seneca Falls, N.Y., Feb. 19, 1917; s. Thomas and Vita N.; m. Victoria Margaret Serino, Aug. 31, 1941 (dec. May 1980); children: Thomas, Diane, Joseph, John; m. 2d, Carmel L. Dowd, Sept. 19, 1981; BS, Syracuse U., 1948. CPA, N.Y. Staff acct. Seidman & Seidman, N.Y.C., 1948-49, Stover, Butler & Murphy, Syracuse, N.Y., 1949-55; instr. Syracuse U., 1953; instr. acctg. Central City Bus. Inst., Syracuse, 1955-58, pres., 1958—, also pvt. practice acctg., Syracuse. Served with USNR, 1943-46. CPA, N.Y. Mem. Am. Inst. CPAs, N.Y. State Soc. CPAs, Am. Acctg. Assn., AAUP. Roman Catholic. Clubs: Lakeshore Yacht and Country (Clay, N.Y.), Italian Am. Athletic (Syracuse). Home: 7929 Boxford Rd Clay NY 13041 Office: 953 James St Syracuse NY 13203

NELLIGAN, KATE (PATRICIA COLLEEN NELLIGAN), actress; b. London, Ont., Can., Mar. 16, 1951; d. Patrick Joseph and Alice (Dier) N. Ed., York U., Toronto, Cen. Sch. Speech and Drama, London, Eng. Appeared in plays in Bristol, London, and New York: Barefoot in the Park, 1972, Misalliance, A Streetcar Named Desire, The Playboy of the Western World, London Assurance, Lulu, Private Lives, Knuckle, 1974, Heartbreak House, 1975, Plenty, 1975, As You Like It, A Moon for the Misbegotten, 1984, Virginia, 1985; films include: The Count of Monte Cristo, 1979, The Romantic Englishwoman, 1979, Dracula, 1979, Patman, 1980, Eye of the Needle, 1980, Agent, 1980, Without a Trace, 1983, Eleni, 1985; TV appearances include: The Onedin Line, The Lady of the Camellias, Licking Hitler, Measure for Measure, Therese Raquin, 1980, Forgive Our Foolish Ways, 1980. Recipient Best Actress award Evening Standard, 1978. Office: Larry Dalzell Assocs, 3 Goodwin's Ct, London WC2, England *

NELLIS, MURIEL GOLLON, author, literary agent; b. N.Y.C., Sept. 13, 1931; d. Abraham and Sara (Fried) Gollon; m. Joseph Leon Nellis, Dec. 12, 1964; children—Barbara, David M.; m. Howard S. Pressman, 1950 (div. 1962); children—Adam J., Amy E. Student New Sch. Social Research 1947, Hofstra U., 1948. Continuity dir. WLNA Radio, Peekskill, N.Y., 1949-50; traffic mgr. WGNR Radio, New Rochelle, N.Y., 1950; women's continuity dir. WIP Radio, Phila., 1955-56; traffic/sales dir. WDAS Radio, Phila., 1956-57; pres., pub. Murette/M&N Publishers, Chester, Pa. and N.Y.C., 1960-65; pub., creator Let's Color in (fgn.) Languages, 1960-64; on-air person Panorama, WTTG-TV, Washington, 1970; pres., chief exec. officer NRCA Inc., Washington, 1972—; prin. Lit./Creative Artist Agy., Washington, 1982—; author: The Female Fix, 1980; pub., mng. editor Lady's Circle mag., 1963-65; editor, writer Drug Abuse Education, 1972; contbr. articles various mags.; cons. NIMH, coms. on crime, health and human resources U.S. Ho. of Reps. Bd. dirs. LWV, Washington, 1967; mem. Task Force Drug Abuse in Schs., Washington, 1973; cons. Gov.'s Com. on Substance Abuse, Hawaii, 1977; nat. dir. Alliance Regional Coalitions, 1976-78; mem. panel Presdl. Commn. on Mental Health, 1978; designer, mgr. Internat. Conf. Drugs, Alcohol, Womens Health, Washington,/Fla., 1975; cons., editor NIMH, 1972; juror media awards Am. Psychol. Assn., 1981—. Named Hon. Citizen New Orleans, 1979. Mem. ABA (assoc.), Am. Booksellers Assn., Am. Pub. Health Assn. Club: Hadassah (life). Home: 3539 Albemarle St NW Washington DC 20008

NELSEN, DAVID HALL, aerospace company executive; b. Aurelia, Iowa, Sept. 1, 1942; s. Andrew Skosen and Marjorie May (Hall) N.; B.S., Morningside Coll., Sioux City, Iowa, 1965; m. Carol Deanne Johnson, Aug. 4, 1973; children—Wayne Thomas, Jodi Christine. Coop. advt. asst. Amana Refrigeration, Inc., Iowa, 1965-68; sr. cost acct. Owens Co., Iowa City, Iowa, 1968-71; advt. asst. Barber-Colman Co., Rockford, Ill., 1971-72; energy systems div. sr. contract and fin. budget adminstr. Sundstrand Corp., Rockford, 1972—. Advisor Sundstrand Jr. Achievement, 1972-75; active Rockford Horn Choir; vol. Contact Teleministries Rockford, 1972—, facilitator trainer, 1974; bd. dirs. P.A. Peterson Home, Rockford. Served with USAR, 1965-71. Mem. Am. Mgmt. Assn., Nat. Assn. Accts., Nat. Contract Mgmt. Assn., Sigma Tau Delta, Alpha Phi Gamma, Phi Beta Mu, Tau Kappa Epsilon. Republican. Lutheran. Lodge: Masons (32 degree). Home: 707 Parkside Dr Rockford IL 61108 Office: 4747 Harrison Ave Rockford IL 61101

NELSON, ALAN JAN, entertainment company executive; b. Los Angeles, Sept. 18, 1944; s. Arthur Leonard and Laura Nelson; A.A., Los Angeles Valley City Coll., 1965; B.S., San Franando Valley State Coll., 1967; M.S., Calif. State Coll., Los Angeles, 1969. Actor, 1962—, screen writer, 1978—, comic, 1965—, stuntman, 1975—, film producer, 1979—; asst. adminstr. Oak Hill Learning Services, Lakeview Terrace, Calif., 1970; dir. community services City of South El Monte (Calif.), 1971; v.p. Ev Gray Lighting Co., Van Nuys, Calif., 1972-75; hosp. adminstr. Los Angeles Met. Hosp., 1976; exec. dir. Search Consortium, West Los Angeles, 1977-79; pres. AGVA, N.Y.C., 1979-83; pres. L & N Prodns. Inc., Van Nuys, 1975—; pres. A.J.N. Hallelujah, Inc., 1981—; 4th v.p. Theatre Authority Inc., 1980-83; corp. cons. entertainment field, 1975-78; evangelist, 1975—. Vice pres. West Los Angeles Coordinating Council, 1977; mem. El Monte Coordinating Council, 1971. Recipient Mid-Wilshire Optimists Outstanding Service award, 1980, Outstanding Service plaque AGVA, 1981, citation for advancement of variety artist State of N.J., 1981, Golden Mask award Hollywood Appreciation Soc., 1982. Mem. Screen Actors Guild, Actors and Artists Am. Assoc. (5th v.p. 1980-83). Democrat. Club: Friars. Home: 6356 Ventura Canyon Van Nuys CA 91401

NELSON, ALBERT LOUIS, III, finance executive; b. St. Louis, Apr. 29, 1938; s. Albert Louis and Mildred Mary (Bischoff) N.; m. Pamela Eakins, Mar. 14, 1970; children: Holly Reid, Amy Bischoff. BS in Mech. Engring., Washington U., St. Louis, 1960, MBA, 1962; LLB, George Washington U., 1964. Exec. v.p. Equity Research Assocs., Inc., N.Y.C., 1967-69; pres. The Westwood Group, Inc., Los Angeles, 1969-73; dir. chem. plastics Gen. Tire & Rubber Co., Akron, Ohio, 1973-75; sr. v.p., dir. corp. service dept. Prescott, Ball & Turben, Cleve., 1975-86; pres. Albert Nelson Investment Co., Inc., Fairlawn, Ohio, 1986—. Served with U.S. Army, 1964-66. Clubs: N.Y. Stock Exchange Lunch; Portage Country.

NELSON, ARTHUR HUNT, corporate executive; b. Kansas City, Mo., May 21, 1923; s. Carl Ferdinand and Hearty (Brown) N.; A.B., U. Kans., 1943; J.D., Harvard, 1949; m. Eleanor Thomas, Dec. 27, 1954; children—Carl F., Frances, Pamela. Staff radiation lab. Mass. Inst. Tech., 1943-44; sr. engr., cons. Raytheon Mfg. Co., Boston, 1948-52; admitted to Mass. bar, 1949, practiced in Boston; v.p., treas., dir. Gen. Electronic Labs., Inc., Cambridge, Mass., 1951-64, chmn. bd., 1959-63; treas., dir. Sci. Electronics, Inc., Cambridge, 1955-64; treas., dir. Assos. for Internat. Research, Inc., 1954—, pres., 1968-—; treas., dir. Victor Realty Devel., Inc., 1959-76, pres., 1972-76, gen. ptnr., 1976—; gen. ptnr. Prospect Hill Exec. Office Park, 1977—; dir. Internat. Data Group, Inc. Pres., trustee Tech. Edn. Research Centers, Inc., 1965—; trustee Winsor Sch., Boston, 1978—, treas., 1978-82; bd. dirs. Charles River Mus. Industry, Boston, 1986—. Served from ensign to lt. (j.g.), USNR, 1944-46. Mem. Am., Mass., Boston bar assns., Boston Computer Soc. (bd. dirs. 1985—), Greater Boston C. of C., Phi Beta Kappa, Sigma Xi, Beta Theta Pi. Club: Harvard (Boston). Home: 75 Robin Rd Weston MA 02193 Office: 200 5th Ave Waltham MA 02154

NELSON, BRYAN EUGENE, lawyer; b. Salina, Kans., Sept. 21, 1946; s. Merle Theodore and Winona Jean (Parsons) N. Student Kans. State U., 1968-72; B.S. in Polit. Sci., U. Kans., 1973, J.D., 1976. Bar: Kans. 1976, U.S. Dist. Ct. Kans. 1976, U.S. Ct. Appeals (10th cir.) 1981, U.S. Supreme Ct. 1981. Cert. civil trial adv. Nat. Bd. Trial Advocacy. Assoc. Weeks, Thomas, Lysaught, Bingham & Mustain, Overland Park, Kans., 1976, Alder & Zemites, Overland Park, 1977; ptnr. Alder Nelson & McKenna, Overland Park, 1978—; lectr. seminars. Served with USAF, 1976-79. Mem. Def. Research Inst., ABA, Kans. Bar Assn., Wyandotte County Bar Assn., Johnson County Bar Assn., ACLU, Kans. Assn. Def. Counsel, Kansas City Claims Assn. Republican. Methodist. Office: 6900 College Blvd Suite 430 Overland Park KS 66210

NELSON, DAVID STUART, manufacturing company executive; b. Waltham, Mass., Oct. 8, 1946; s. Stanley Walter Fredrick and Grace Elizabeth (Stewart) N.; m. Mary Sharon Wells, Dec. 30, 1967; children: Michele Marie, Heather Christine. BS, Clarkson U., Potsdam, N.Y., 1969. Indsl. engr. Colgate-Palmolive Co. Inc., Jersey City, 1969-71, foreman, 1971, warehouse and shipping supr., 1971-75; mgr. purchasing, planning and distbn. Colgate-Palmolive Co. Inc., San Juan, P.R., 1975-82; plant dir. mfg. for Panama and Costa Rica Colgate-Palmolive Co. Inc., Panama City, 1982-85; plant mgr. Colgate-Palmolive Co. Inc., Boksburg, Republic South Africa, 1985—. Mem. Am. Soc. Johannesburg (pres. 1986-87), Delta Upsilon. Office: Colgate Palmolive Co, PO Box 213, 528 Commissioner St, Boksburg 1460, Republic of South Africa

NELSON, DONALD ALBERT, paper company executive; b. Murray, Nebr., Dec. 28, 1922; arrived in Venezuela, 1948; s. Bror Harry and Selma Louise (Johnson) N.; m. Maria Elena Lavie, Apr. 7, 1951; children: Maria Elena, Juan Alberto, Patricia Luisa, Donald Harry Bror. BSBA, U. Nebr., 1943. Export exec. Banton Corp., San Francisco and N.Y.C., 1946-48; head land and legal Tex. Petroleum Co., Venezuela, 1948-57; pres. Papeles Venezolanos, C.A., Venezuela, 1957—; pres. Papeles Nacionales Flamingo, Venezuela, 1979—, Prevalco, C.A., Venezuela, 1980—, Propaca, Venezuela, 1985—; bd. dirs. Naviera Lavinel, C.A. Served to 1st lt. inf. Venezuelan Army, 1943-46, CBI. Recipient Worker Merit award Venezuelan Govt., 1983, Francisco de Miranda award, 1986. Mem. Delta Sigma Pi. Roman Catholic. Clubs: Playa G. Yachting (bd. dirs. 1955-61), Lagunita Country (Venezuela). Home: #228 Calle Lindero, Urb Cerro Verde, 1061 Caracas Venezuela Office: Centro Gerencial Mohedano, Ave Mohedano, La Castellana, Caracas Venezuela

NELSON, EDWARD SHEFFIELD, lawyer, former utility company executive; b. Keevil, Ark., Feb. 23, 1941; s. Robert Ford and Thelma Jo (Mayberry) N.; m. Mary Lynn McCastlain, Oct. 12, 1962; children: Cynthia, Lynn (dec.), Laura. BS, U. Cen. Ark., 1963; LLB, Ark. Law Sch., 1968; JD, U. Ark., 1969. Mgmt. trainee Ark. La. Gas Co., Little Rock, 1963-64; sales engr. Ark. La. Gas Co., 1964-67, sales coordinator, 1967-69, gen. sales mgr., 1969-71, v.p., gen. sales mgr., 1971-73, pres., dir., 1973-79, pres., chmn., chief exec. officer, 1979-85; ptnr., chmn. bd., chief exec. officer House, Wallace, Nelson & Jewel, Little Rock, 1985-86; sole practice Sheffield Nelson P.A., Little Rock, 1986—; bd. dirs. Fed. Res. Mem. N.G., 1957-63; Bd. dirs. U. Ark., Little Rock, vice-chmn. bd. visitors, 1981; bd. dirs. Philander Smith Coll., 1981; chmn. Ark. Indsl. Devel. Commn., 1987; immediate past chmn. Little Rock br. Fed. Res. Bd. St. Louis; chmn. Econ. Expansion Study Commn., 1987—; bd. dirs. Ark. Ednl. TV Found., Ark. Game and Fish Commn. Found. Named Ark.'s Outstanding Young Man Ark. J. C. of C., 1973; One of Am.'s Ten Outstanding Young Men U.S. Jr. C. of C., 1974; Citizen of Yr. Ark. chpt. March of Dimes, 1983; Humanitarian of Yr. NCCJ, 1983; Best Chief Exec. Officer in Natural Gas Industry Wall Street Transcript, 1983. Mem. Am., Ark., Pulaski County bar assns., Ark. C. of C. (dir.), Little Rock C. of C. (dir., pres. 1981), Sales and Mktg. Execs. Assn. (pres. 1975, Top Mgmt. award 1977), U. Ark. Law Sch. Alumni Assn. (pres. 1980). Democrat. Methodist. Office: 1610 Tower Bldg Little Rock AR 72201

NELSON, GORDON LEIGH, chemist, educator; b. Palo Alto, Calif., May 27, 1943; s. Nels Folke and Alice Virginia (Fredrickson) N. BS in Chemistry, U. Nev., 1965; MS, Yale U., 1967, PhD, 1970. Staff research chemist corp. research and devel. Gen. Electric Co., Schenectady, N.Y., 1970-74; mgr. combustibility tech. plastics div. Gen. Electric Co., Pittsfield, Mass., 1974-79, mgr. environ. protection plastics div., 1979-82; v.p. materials sci. and tech. Springborn Labs. Inc., Enfield, Conn., 1982-83; prof., chmn. dept. polymer sci. U. So. Miss., Hattiesburg, 1983—; cons. in field. Author: Carbon-13 Nuclear Magnetic Resonance For Organic Chemists, 1972; editor books on coatings sci. tech.; contbr. articles to profl. jours. Mem. Am. Inst. of Chemists, Soc. Plastics Engrs., Am. Chem. Soc. (pres. 1988, bd. dirs. 1977-85, 87-89, Henry Hill award 1986), Computer and Bus. Equipment Mfrs. Assn. (chmn. Plastics Task Group), ASTM (E5 cert. of appreciation 1985), So. Soc. for Coatings Technology, Nat. Fire Protection Assn., IEC (U.S. tech. adv. group on info. processing equipment), Structural Plastics div. Soc. of the Plastics Industry (mem. exec. com., chmn. combustibility com., Man of Yr. 1979), Miss. Acad. Scis., Yale Chemists Assn. (pres. 1981—), Nev. Hist. Soc., Sigma Xi. Republican. Presbyterian. Office: U So Miss Dept Polymer Sci Southern Station Box 10063 Hattiesburg MS 39406-0063

NELSON, GRANT STEEL, lawyer, educator; b. Mitchell, S.D., Apr. 18, 1939; s. Howard Steel and Clara Marie (Winandy) N.; m. Judith Ann Haugen, Sept. 22, 1962; children: Mary Elizabeth, Rebekah Anne, John Adam. B.A. magna cum laude, U. Minn., 1960; J.D. cum laude, 1963. Bar: Minn. 1963, Mo. 1971. Assoc. firm Faegre & Benson, Mpls., 1963-67; mem. law faculty U. Mo., Columbia, 1967—; asso. prof. U. Mo., 1970-72, prof., 1972—, Enoch H. Crowder prof. law, 1974—; bd. legal advs. Great Plains Legal Found., 1978—; vis. asst. prof. law U. Mich., Ann Arbor, 1969-70, Brigham Young U., Salt Lake City, summer 1976; vis. prof. law U. Minn., Mpls., 1981-82; disting. vis. prof. Pepperdine (Calif.) U., 1987-88; commr. Nat. Conf. Commrs. Uniform State Laws. Author: (with Van Hecke and Leavell) Cases and Materials on Equitable Remedies and Restitution, 1973, (with Whitman) Cases and Materials on Real Estate Finance and Development, 1976, Cases and Materials on Real Estate Transfer, Finance and Development, 1981, (with Osborne and Whitman) Real Estate Finance Law, 1979, (with Leavell and Love) Cases and Materials on Equitable Remedies and Restitution, 1980, (with Whitman) Land Transactions and Finance, 1983; (with Whitman) Real Estate Finance Law, 1985, (with Leavell and Love) Cases and Materials on Equitable Remedies, Restitution and Damages, 1986, (with Whitman) Cases and Materials on Real Estate Transfer, Finance and Development, 1987, (with Whitman) Land Transactions and France, 1988; contbr. articles to profl. jours. Served to 1st lt. AUS, 1964-65. Recipient award for meritorious service and achievement U. Mo. Law Sch. Found., 1974; recipient Disting. Faculty Service award U. Mo.-Columbia Alumni Assn., 1978, Disting. Faculty award, 1986. Fellow Am. Bar Found.; mem. Am., Boone County bar assns., Mo. Bar (vice chmn. property law com. 1974-75, chmn. property law com. 1975-77), Assn. Am. Law Schs. (sect. chmn. 1976-77), Am. Law Inst., Order Coif, Phi Beta Kappa, Phi Delta Phi. Home: 1905 Woodhollow Dr Columbia MO 65203 Office: 234 Tate Hall U Mo Columbia MO 65211

NELSON, HARRY WILLIAM, author, poet, artist; b. N.Y.C., June 9, 1908; s. Nels William and Alma Constance (Svenson) N.; student Brown U., 1926-28; A.B. cum laude, Yale, 1933; postgrad. U. N.H., summer 1939, Lafayette U., summer 1951, U. Conn., 1950-51; studied under Harve Stein, 1949-59, Clarence Brodeur, 1963-70, Beatrice Cuming, 1964-67, Art Students League, Lyman Allyn Mus., 1948-70, Robert A. Cale, 1974, 77. Tchr. English, R.E. Fitch Sr. High Sch., Groton, Conn., 1934-64, dir. dramatics, 1942-52; innovator, nat. spokesman for dramatic choric odes. Founder, 1st pres. Indian and Colonial Research Center, Old Mystic, Conn., 1965-70, lectr. 20th ann. address, 1985. Recipient Leander Leitner award Am. Lit. Assn., 1940, Cora Smith Gould Meml. award, 1946; Monday prize Poetry Soc. Ga., 1969; Suffield (Conn.) Conf. Poetry award, 1971, 1st prize ann. contest Mass. State Poetry Soc., 1986; finalist Chase Going Woodhouse poetry competition Mohegan Coll., 1974; named Most Accomplished Poet, recipient Excellence of Performance award Greater Hartford Civic and Arts Festival Poetry Contest, 1976; hon. mention Carlisle (Pa.) Poets award, 1978; 1st award in poetry Conn. Writers Competition, Conn. Writers League, 1980, 1st prize Paul Mellon Arts Center, Wallingford, Conn. Spring Poetry Festival, 1981; 1st prize Mass. State Poetry Soc., 1986; State of Conn. Medal 350th Commemorative, 1985; elected to Educators' Hall of Fame, 1987. Mem. Living Heritage Guild Groton (pres. 1965-67), New London Art Students League (pres. 1965-68), Poetry Soc. Am. (nominee governing bd. preservation of soc. 1978, ind. 1980), Mystic Art Assn. (Wimpfheimer award 1979, Maxwelton award for aquamedia, 1981), Essex Art Assn. (bd. dirs. 1987, E. Gould Chalker award 1985), Conn. (publs. com. 1977 1st and 3d awards Ann. Yellow Pad Competition 1979, asso. editor Conn. River Rev. 1979-82), Pa. poetry socs., Shelley Soc. N.Y., Internat. Platform Assn., Gungywamp Soc., Chi Delta Theta. Author: Startled Flight (poems, included in spl. Am. lit. collection Beinecke Rare Book and Manuscript Library, Yale), 1930; Impelling Reminiscence (poems) (Leitner award), 1940; Ours is the Work (dramatic choric ode), 1942; The Years of the Whirlwind (poems, dramatic choric ode), 1943; The Moon is Near (also illustrator; narrative poem), 1944; Never to Forget This (dramatic choric ode), 1944; The Fever in the Drum (poems), 1945; From Moon-Filled Sky (songs), 1947; Look to the Horizon Within (dramatic choric ode), 1948; The Winter Tree (poems; 1971 Suffield Conf. Poetry award), 1972; Not of This Star Dust (poems), 1973; Blame the Skulk of Night, 1974; Wolf Stone, Wolf Stone (poems), 1976; Encounter at the Aquarium (poems), 1978; Command Performance (poems), 1980, A Catch of Creation, 1984; others; poems pub. in various lit. revs., also Hartford Courant, 1968-—; poetry readings schs., colls., various orgns.; guest poet Williams Sch., 1974, 75, 78, 79, 81, Housatonic Community Coll., Bridgeport, 1980, Stamford Radio WSTC, 1981, Groton Library, 1985, Celebration of Arts program U. Conn. and Groton Arts Com., 1986. Exhibited one-man show Lyman Allyn Mus., 1968, Groton Playhouse Gallery, 1956, Hartford Nat. Bank, 1964-68, Waterford Library, 1971, Woodworth Hall, Conn. Coll., 1972, retrospective Lawrence Meml. Hosp., New London, 1973, 80, 82, Groton Public Library, 1980, 87, Conn. Bank & Trust, 1983; group shows at Boston Mus. Fine Arts, Sterling Library Yale, Lyme Art Gallery, 1968-—, Mystic Art Gallery, 1950-—, Essex Art Gallery, 1964-—, Converse Gallery, Cummings Art Center, Conn. Coll., 1973; Bicentennial Commn., Mystic Art Assn., 1976, prints exhbn., 1979, others; one-man retrospective show Liberty Bank, Old Mystic, 1977, 50th Anniversary Exhbn. The Early Years: Mystic Art Assn., 1981, Eastern Conn. Symphony Orch. Old Lyme Exhibit, 1981, Invitational New Eng. Art Show, U.S. Coast Guard Acad., 1981, New Eng. South Shore Artists, Westerly Library, 1984; represented in permanent collections at Lyman Allyn Mus., Groton Library, pvt. collections. Recipient Silver trophy Am. Cancer Art Exhbn., Mitchell Coll., 1968, Spl. award for monotypes, 1970, Spl. prize design and graphics, 1971; 1st prize for tech. excellence U. Conn. Avery Point Art Exhbn., 1969, 1st prize unltd. media, 1971; awards East Haddam, 1969, 71, New London Mall, 1971, Southington, 1971, 1st in show, Montville, 1973, best in show, Colchester, 1974; others. Cons. art Groton Library, 1984-86; ind. film maker, showing and lecturing colls., schs., museums, orgns., 1958-—; Shakespeare Celebration lectr. Groton Arts Com., Groton Library, 1981, Michelangelo, 1983, Waterford Library, 1984; films include The Research Paper, The Tall Ships, Fleet and One Tuna, Our Walden, Puppet and Camera, The Edge of Winter, The Eternal Prelude, Vain Carrousel, This Autumn Day. Home: 213 Pleasant Valley Rd Groton CT 06340

NELSON, HARVEY FRANS, JR., foreign service officer; b. Long Beach, Calif., Jan. 26, 1924; s. Harvey Frans and Marian (Norris) N.; m. Celia Anne Kendrick, June 27, 1947 (dec. June 1985); children—Erik Frans, Kai David, Peter Norris, Annika Di Vittorio; m. Esta Harrie de Fossard, May 31, 1987. B.A., Occidental Coll., 1948; postgrad., Stockholm U., 1948-49; M.A., Fletcher Sch. Internat. Law and Diplomacy, Medford, Mass., 1950. Commd. fgn. service officer Dept. State, 1951; dep. chief of mission Am. embassy, Pretoria, Republic of South Africa, 1976-79; diplomat in residence Ariz. State U., Tempe, 1979-80; dep. commandant U.S. Army War Coll., Carlisle, Pa., 1980-84; ambassador Am. embassy, Mbabane, Swaziland, 1985—. Served to lt. (j.g.) USN, 1942-46. Home and Office: Dept of State US Ambassador to Swaziland Washington DC 20520

NELSON, JACK ODELL, JR., lawyer; b. Dallas, Oct. 8, 1947; s. Jack Odell and Rose Mary (Trepoy) N. B.B.A., Tex. Tech U., 1969; J.D., U. Tex., 1972. Bar: Tex. 1972, U.S. Dist. Ct. (no. dist.) Tex. 1973, U.S. Ct. Appeals (5th cir.) 1974, U.S. Supreme Ct. 1981. Assoc. firm Garner, Boulter, Jesko & Purdom and successor firms, Lubbock, Tex., 1972-76, 77-80, firm Gardere, Porter & DeHay, Dallas, 1976-77; ptnr. firm Nelson & Nelson, Lubbock, 1981—. Mem. Tex. Bar Assn. (dist. 16 grievance com.), Lubbock County Bar Assn., Tex. Assn. Def. Counsel, Internat. Assn. Def. Counsel, Sigma Chi, Phi Delta Phi. Mem. Disciples of Christ Ch. Club: Lubbock. Lodge: Rotary. Office: Nelson & Nelson 1220 1st Repub Bank Bldg 916 Main St Lubbock TX 79401

NELSON, JAY SCOTT, lawyer; b. Chgo., Sept. 5, 1941; s. J.O. and Genevieve (Monson) N.; m. Gertrude Sturhahn, Aug. 29, 1970; children: Erik, Thea. BA, Parsons Coll., 1964; MBA, U. Iowa, 1967; JD, John Marshall Law Sch., 1975. Bar: Ill. 1975, U.S. Dist. Ct. (no. dist.) Ill. 1975, U.S. Ct. Appeals (7th cir.) 1978, U.S. Dist. Ct. (no. dist. trial) Ill. 1985. Auditor E.I. duPont Co., Wilmington, Del., 1969-71; assoc. Schaffenegger, Watson & Peterson Ltd., Chgo., 1975-85, ptnr., 1985—. Served to sgt. U.S. Army, 1968-69. Mem. ABA, Ill. State Bar Assn., Chgo. Bar Assn., Trial Lawyers Club Chgo. Presbyterian.

NELSON, JOHN CARL, statistician, consultant; b. Sterling, Ill., Feb. 11, 1958; s. Carl Harold and Esther Mae (Stern) N. B.S. in Math., Kans State U., 1980, M.S. in Stats., 1981; M. Engring. Mgmt., Northwestern U., 1985. Statistician, Travenol Labs., Inc., Morton Grove, Ill., 1981-83; cons. ZS Assocs., Evanston, Ill., 1984-85; founder, prin. Applied Research Co., Chgo., 1985—. Co-editor: The Commodity Option Analyst, 1985. Mem. Am. Statis. Assn., Inst. Mgmt. Sci., Pi Mu Epsilon. Club: U.S. Tennis Assn. Office: Applied Research Co 53 W Jackson Suite 318 Chicago IL 60604

NELSON, LARRY DEAN, telecommunications and computer systems company executive, consultant; b. Newton, Kans., Aug. 5, 1937; s. Carl Aaron and Leta V. (Van Eaton) N.; m. Linda Hawkins, June 2, 1972. B.A., Phillips U., 1959; M.S., Kans. State U., 1962; Ph.D., Ohio State U., 1965. From research asst. to research assoc. Research Found., Ohio State U., Columbus, 1962-65; mathematician II, Batelle Meml. Inst., Columbus, 1962-65; from mem. tech. staff to supr. math. dept. and data systems devel. Bellcomm, Inc., Washington, 1965-72; supr. mgmt. info. systems dept. Bell Telephone Labs., Murray Hill, N.J., 1972-77; supr. rate and tariff planning div. AT&T, N.Y.C., 1977-79; dep. adminstr. research and spl. programs adminstrn. U.S. Dept. Transp., Washington, 1979-81; pres. MCS, Inc., Washington, 1981—; supr. govt. communications ctr. AT&T Bell Labs., 1985—; cons. Contel Info. Systems, Denver, 1982-85, Martin Marietta Corp., Denver, 1982-85. Contbr. articles to profl. jours. Organizer, sponsor Odd Jobs Club, Washington, 1967-72; pres. Mountain County Condominiums Assn., Dillon, Colo., 1975-83, 85—; treas. Chris' Landing Condominium Assn., 1986—; mem. Am. del. 5th Meeting of U.S.-USSR Joint Commn. on Cooperation in Field of Transp., Moscow, 1979; head Am. del. 5th Meeting of U.S.-USSR Working Group on Transport of Future, Moscow, 1979. Mem. IEEE (sec. D.C. sect. 1982, cert. appreciation 1968), Systems, Man and Cybernetics Soc. (sec. 1981, v.p. 1982-83), Math. Programming Soc., Am. Math. Soc., N.Y. Acad. Scis., Assn. Computing Machinery, Sigma Xi, Phi Kappa Phi, Pi Mu Epsilon. Democrat. Mem. Deciples of Christ. Current work: Analysis, design and development of computer and telecommunication secure information movement and management systems, networks and management networks, data base systems. Subspecialties: Distributed systems and networks; Systems engineering. Office: ATT-Bell Labs Holmdel NJ 07733

NELSON, LAWRENCE OLAF, educator; b. Hartford, Conn., Feb. 1, 1926; s. Lawrence Olaf and Gerda Amelia Elizabeth (Hanson) N.; m. Kathleen Alice Brito, Aug. 26, 1950; children: Scott Laurence, Adam Foster. B.S., Central Conn. State U., 1949; M.A., U. Conn., 1953; Ph.D., Mich. State U., 1960. Tchr. pub. schs. Stamford, Conn., 1949-52; asst. dir. U. Conn., 1952-55; asst. to pres. State Coll., Moorhead, Minn., 1956-57; dean of adminstrn. State Coll., 1957-58; cons. Office of Edn., HEW, Washington, 1960; mem. faculty Purdue U., Lafayette, Ind., 1960-74; adminstrv. dean Purdue U., 1967-74; dean Purdue U. (Ft. Wayne Campus), 1969-70, asst. to provost,

1974; prof. higher edn., dean continuing edn. U. Ariz., Tucson, 1974-81; prof. ednl. founds., adminstrn. and higher edn. U. Ariz., 1974—; cons. in field. Mem. planning com. Ind. Gov.'s Regional Correction Center, 1969-71; mem. adv. panel Ind. Higher Edn. Telecommunications System, 1971-74; adv. bd. Midwestern Center, Nat. Humanities Series, 1972-74; mem. Ind. Com. for Humanities, 1972-74, Tucson Com. on Fgn. Relations, 1975-85; bd. dirs. Continuing Edn. for Deaf, 1975-81, Ariz. Consortium for Edn. in Social Services, 1977-81. Author: Cooperative Projects Among Colleges and Universities, 1961. Mem. Am. Assn. Higher Edn., Assn. Continuing Higher Edn., Nat. Assn. Student Personnel Administrators, NEA, Nat. Univ. Continuing Edn. Assn., Nat. Univ. Extension Assn. (award 1971, dir. 1978-80), Phi Delta Kappa, Epsilon Pi Tau, Delta Chi. Clubs: Kiwanis of Greater Lafayette (pres. 1967), Kiwanis of Moorhead (dir. 1957-58), Rotary of Tucson (dir. 1979-80, pres. 1980-81). Home: 1330 Indian Wells Rd Tucson AZ 85718 Office: 629 Education Bldg U Ariz Tucson AZ 85721

NELSON, MICHAEL EDWARD, journalist; b. Bromley, Kent, Eng., Apr. 30, 1929; s. Thomas Alfred and Dorothy Pretoria (Bevan) N.; m. Helga Johanna Den Ouden, Mar. 26, 1960; children—Patrick, Paul, Shivaun. B.A. with honors in Modern History, Magdalen Coll., Oxford U., Eng., 1952. Journalist, Reuters Ltd., London and Far East, 1952-62, mgr. econ. services, 1962-76, gen. mgr., 1976, joint dep. mng. dir., gen. mgr., 1976-81, dep. mng. dir., gen. mgr., 1981—, dep. mng. dir., gen. mgr. Reuters Holdings Plc, London, 1984; chmn. Visnews Ltd., London. Club: Garrick (London). Office: Reuters Ltd, 85 Fleet St, London EC4P 4AJ, England

NELSON, NANCY ELEANOR, pediatrician, educator; b. El Paso, Apr. 4, 1933; d. Harry Hamilton and Helen Maude (Murphy) N. B.A. magna cum laude, U. Colo., 1955, M.D., 1959. Intern, Case Western Res. U. Hosp., 1959-60, resident, 1960-63; practice medicine specializing in pediatrics, Denver, 1963—; assoc. clin. prof. U. Colo. Sch. Medicine, Denver, 1977—, asst. dean Sch. Medicine, 1982—. Mem. Am. Acad. Pediatrics, AMA, Denver Med. Soc. (pres. 1983-84), Colo. Med. Soc. (bd. dirs. 1985—). Home: 1265 Elizabeth Denver CO 80206 Office: 4200 E 9th Ave Denver CO 80262

NELSON, NANCY MELIN, editor, consultant; b. Cleve., Feb. 15, 1941; d. Myron Alexander and Irma (Sell) M.; m. Milo Gabriel Nelson, Feb. 15, 1980. BA, Mt. Union Coll., Alliance, Ohio, 1962; MA, Wayne State U., 1972; MLS, Simmons Coll., 1972. Serials librarian U. Vt., Burlington, 1972-75, Central Mich. U., Mt. Pleasant, 1975-78; library systems analyst Research Library Group, Stanford, Calif., 1979, Online Computer Library Ctr., Columbus, Ohio, 1980; serials librarian CUNY Grad. Ctr., N.Y.C., 1981-82; editor-in-chief Library Hi Tech, 1982-83, Library Hi Tech News and Library Software Rev., 1982-88, Serials Rev., 1978-83, Ref. Services Rev., 1980-83, Small Computers in Libraries, 1984—, CD-Rom Librarian, 1987—, prin. Nelson Assocs., 1982—. Editor: Serials Collection, 1982; Serials Management in an Automated Age, 1982; International Subscription Agents, 1978; Serials and Microforms, 1983; Library Standards 1984; CD-Roms in Print, 1987; author: Essential Guide to the Library IBM PC, 1985, vols. 1, 8, 1987; contbr. articles to profl. jours. Mem. ALA. Democrat.

NELSON, PATRICIA SWEAZEY, international management consultant, executive coach, psychotherapist; b. Seattle, Mar. 5, 1927; d. Manley Earl and F. Pauline (Pickard) S.; m. Russell Paul Nelson; children—Cynthia, Andrea, Barry. BA magna cum laude, U. Wash., 1971; postgrad. Whitworth Coll., 1985. Interpreter Italian prisoners of war U.S. Army, Seattle, 1944-45; interpreter, adminstr. trouble-shooter Pomona Valley Community Hosp., 1951-53; lead tchr. of Kindergarten, program developer, co-dir. Alpental Kinderschule, Seattle Day Nursery, 1956-69; export/import mgr. Warn Internat., Seattle, 1971-72; trainer computer transition and corp. hdqrs. mgmt. devel. team Unigard Ins., Seattle, 1972-74; dir. Nelson Internat. Assocs., Seattle, 1974—; researcher/cons. Swissair Transport, 1982—, field counselor expatriate families abroad, 1980—. Author: Guide to Girl Scout Backpacking, 1965. Council cons. in Alpine travel Girl Scouts U.S.A., Seattle, 1960-67, also trainer, leader, explorer advisor; designer, dir. commissary program, bd. dirs. King County Search and Rescue Assn., 1967-74; dir. sites, program developer, Lichtenfeld Backpacking Encampment, 1964-67; adj. faculty City Univ. Seattle, 1975-79, Cen. Washington Univ., 1978—. Mem. Assn. for Tng. and Devel., Soc. for Internat. Edn., Tng. and Research.

NELSON, RICHARD MARTIN, medical association executive; b. Grand Rapids, Mich., Mar. 24, 1918; s. Martin and Bertha L. (Campbell) N.; student Grand Rapids Jr. Coll., Calvin Coll., 1938, U. Mich., 1939-40; m. Ruth Margaret Parsons, Oct. 16, 1948; children—Richard Martin, Robert Dwight. Mem. staff Mich. Farm Bur., 1947-49, Calif. Farm Bur. Fedn., 1949-53, Wash. State Farm Bur., 1953-55; dir. program devel. Am. Farm Bur. Fedn., 1955-58; field rep. AMA, 1959-67, dir. program devel., 1967-68; exec. dir. Philadelphia County Med. Soc., Phila., 1969-83. Mem. Pres.'s Commn. on Fitness Am. Youth, 1957, Gov.'s Council on Youth, 1956; mem. Phila. Adult and Aging Services, 1976-80; mem. council on services to the aging Delaware County, 1983-88, pres., 1985-87; active Boy Scouts Am. Recipient citations Med. Soc. State N.C., 1964, Med. Assn. Ga., 1965, P.R. Med. Assn., 1966, Strittmatter award, 1982. Mem. U.S.-Yugoslavian Med. Assn. (sec.-treas. 1972-73), Med. Club Phila. (exec. sec. 1973—). Home: 303 N Sproul Rd Broomall PA 19008-2028

NELSON, ROBERT JOHN, publisher; b. Cumberland, Wis., Apr. 5, 1926; s. Arthur N. and Alma O. (Johnson) N.; m. Constance Joan Wollan, Sept. 24, 1955 (div. 1970); children: Kevin, Pamela, Cynthia. BA cum laude, U. Minn., 1949. Section mgr. Powers Dept. Store, Mpls., 1950-51; agt. Res. Life Ins. Co., Mpls., 1951-52; rep., editor James C. Fifield Co., Mpls., 1952-67; founder, owner The Nelson Co., Hopkins, Minn., 1967—. Editor, publisher: Nelson's Law Office Directory, 1967—. Served with USAAF, 1944-45. Republican. Lutheran. Home: 5300 Vernon Ave Edina MN 55436 Office: The Nelson Co PO Box 309 Hopkins MN 55343

NELSON, RUSSELL MARION, surgeon, educator; b. Salt Lake City, Sept. 9, 1924; s. Marion C. and Edna (Anderson) N.; m. Dantzel White, Aug. 31, 1945; children: Marsha Nelson McKellar, Wendy Nelson Maxfield, Gloria Nelson Irion, Brenda Nelson Miles, Sylvia Nelson Webster, Emily Nelson Wittwer, Laurie Nelson Marsh, Rosalie Nelson Ringwood, Marjorie Nelson Helsten, Russell Marion, Jr. B.A., U. Utah, 1945, M.D., 1947; Ph.D. in Surgery, U. Minn., 1954; Sc.D. (hon.), Brigham Young U., 1970. Diplomate: Am. Bd. Surgery, Am. Bd. Thoracic Surgery (dir. 1972-78). Intern U. Minn. Hosps., Mpls., 1947; asst. resident surgery U. Minn. Hosps., 1948-51; first asst. resident surgery Mass. Gen. Hosp., Boston, 1953-54; sr. resident surgery U. Minn. Hosps., Mpls., 1954-55; practice medicine (specializing in cardiovascular and thoracic surgery), Salt Lake City, 1959-84; staff surgeon Latter-day Saints Hosp., Salt Lake City, 1959-84; dir. surg. research lab. Latter-day Saints Hosp., 1959-72, chief cardiovascular-thoracic surg. div., 1967-72, also bd. govs., 1970-84, vice chmn., 1979—; staff surgeon Primary Children's Hosp., Salt Lake City, 1960; attending in surgery VA Hosp., Salt Lake City, 1955-84, Univ. Hosp., Salt Lake City, 1955-84; asst. prof. surgery U. Utah Med. Sch., 1955-59, asst. clin. prof. surgery, 1959-66, asso. clin. prof. surgery, clin. prof., 1966-69, research prof. surgery, 1970—; staff services Utah Biomed. Test Lab., 1970-84; dir. tng. program cardiovascular and thoracic surgery at Univ. Utah affiliated hosps., 1967-84; mem. policyholders adv. com. New Eng. Mut. Life Ins. Co., Boston, 1976-80. Contbr. articles to profl. jours. Mem. White House Conf. on Youth and Children, 1960; Bd. dirs. Internat. Cardiology Found.; bd. govs. L.D.S. Hosp., 1970—, Deseret Gymnasium, 1971-75, Promised Valley Playhouse, 1970-79. Served from 1st lt. to capt. M.C. AUS, 1951-53. Markle scholar in med. scis., 1957-59; Fellowship of Medici Publici U. Utah Coll. Medicine, 1966; Distinguished Alumni award, 1967; Gold Medal of Merit, Argentina, 1974. Fellow A.C.S. (chmn. adv. council on thoracic surgery 1973-75), Am. Coll. Cardiology, Am. Coll. Chest Physicians; mem. Am. Assn. Thoracic Surgery, Am. Soc. Artificial Internal Organs, AMA, Dirs. Thoracic Residencies (pres. 1971-72), Utah Med. Assn. (pres. 1970-71), Salt Lake County Med. Soc., Am. Heart Assn. (exec. com. cardiovascular surgery 1972, dir. 1976-78, chmn. council cardiovascular surgery 1976-78), Utah Heart Assn. (pres. 1964-65), Soc. Thoracic Surgeons, Soc. Vascular Surgery (sec. 1968-72, pres. 1974), Utah Thoracic Soc., Salt Lake Surg. Soc., Samson Thoracic Surg. Soc., Western Soc. for Clin. Research, Soc. U. Surgeons, Am., Western, Pan-Pacific surg. assns., Inter. Am. Soc. Cardiology (bd. mgrs.), Phi Beta Kappa, Sigma Xi, Alpha Omega Alpha, Phi Kappa Phi, Sigma Chi. Mem. Ch. of Jesus Christ of Latter-day Saints (pres. Bonneville Stake 1964-71, gen. pres. Sunday sch. 1971-79, regional rep. 1979-84, Quorum of the Twelve Apostles 1984—). Home: 1347 Normandie Circle Salt Lake City UT 84105 Office: 47 E S Temple Salt Lake City UT 84150

NELSON, SARAH JANE, financial executive; b. Louisville, Sept. 14, 1927; d. Charles Lionel and Edith (Morgan) M.; m. Troy Lee Roman, Dec. 12, 1950; children: Ann, Paul, Cynthia. BS, Harvard U., 1948, MBA, 1949. Securities analyst Harris Trust & Savs. bank, Chgo., 1949-51; with B.F. Goddrich Co., 1951-68; controller Perkin Elmer Corp., 1961-62, marketing mgr., 1962-68; v.p. finance Interco Inc., 1968-78, exec. v.p., chief fin. officer, 1979—; dir. Cone Mills Corp., Holly Corp. Bd. visitors Washington U., St. Louis, 1981—; trustee St. Louis Art Mus.; bd. dirs. St. Louis Opera Theatre. Served with USNR, 1944-46. Mem. Financial Execs. Inst. Club: Cherry Valley Country (St. Louis). Home: Werik Towers 321 E Sunshine St Springfield MO 65807

NELSON, TED L(ONG), distributor; b. Independence, La., Jan. 22, 1927; s. Henry L. and Johnnie (Warren) N.; m. Lula Mae Robertson, Dec. 26, 1957 (div.); children: Cynthia Dianne, Pamela Sue, John Christian, Hyacinth Fern, Ted Barry. Student, Southeastern La. U., 1947-49. Factory rep. Mac's Super Gloss Co., Inc., 1954-56; owner, operator Nelson Distbg. Co., Bunkie, La., 1957—; vol. distbr. cucuzzi seeds. Mem. La. Ho. Reps., 1956-60. Served with USN, 1943-45. Democrat. Baptist. Lodges: Masons, Lions. Author legislation to regulate hydraulic brake fluid in La., later became fed. law. Office: Nelson Distbg Co 504 S Holly Bunkie LA 71322

NELSON, THOMAS ADAMS, electrical engineer, transportation consultant; b. Berkeley, Calif., Aug. 26, 1921; s. Thomas Fleming and Mabel Margaretta (Adams) N.; m. Mary Anne Mares, July 12, 1958. A.A., Los Angeles City Coll., 1942; B.S., U. So. Calif., 1949, M.S., 1953; cert. bus. mgmt. UCLA, 1970. Registered profl. engr., Calif. Design engr. Los Angeles Dept. Water and Power, 1950-53, quality assurance engr., U.S., Europe and Japan, 1953-65, asst. chief quality assurance engr., Los Angeles, 1965-68, chief quality assurance engr., 1968-72, mgr. communications, transmission lines, sta. maintenance and distbn. trouble, 1972-80; rail transp. cons., Ariz. and Nev., 1973-79, rep. to Calif. Power Pool, 1975-77; cons. engr., transp. cons., Los Angeles, 1980—; reviewer rail transit plans So. Calif. Rapid Transit Dist., Los Angeles County Transp. Commn., Orange County Transit Dist., Caltrans, San Diego Transp. Devel., 1978-87. Editor, major author Railroad Chronology Compendium, 1976, 50 Years of Railroading in Southern California, 1987; editor Jour. Pacific R.R. Soc., 1980-84, 87—. Contbr. articles to profl. jours. Mem. Citizens Adv. Commn. for Met. Rail, Hollywood, Calif., 1982-84, Met. Rail CORE Forum, 1987. Served to capt. USAAF, 1942-45, ETO. Mem. IEEE (sr.), Pacific R.R. Soc. (bd. dirs. 1977-80, 82-85, v.p. 1986, pres. 1987—), Eta Kappa Nu, Tau Beta Pi, Phi Kappa Phi.

NELSON, VITA JOY, editor, publisher; b. N.Y.C., Dec. 9, 1937; d. Leon Abraham and Bertha (Sher) Reiner; m. Lester Nelson, Aug. 27, 1961; children: Lee Reiner, Clifford Samuel, Cara Ritchie. BA, Boston U., 1959. Promotion copywriter Street & Smith, N.Y.C., 1958-59; asst. to mng. editor Mademoiselle Mag., N.Y.C., 1959-60; mcpl. bond trader Granger & Co., N.Y.C., 1960-63; founder, editor, publisher Westchester Mag., Mamaroneck, N.Y., 1968-80, L.I. Mag., 1973-78, Moneypaper, Larchmont, N.Y., 1981—. Bd. dirs. Westchester Tourism Council, Westchester County, N.Y., 1974-75, Sackerpath council Girl Scouts U.S.A., White Plains, N.Y., 1976-79; bd. govs. v.p. Am. Jewish Com., Westchester, N.Y., 1979—. Recipient citation Council Arts, 1972; Media award Pub. Relations Soc. Am., 1974. Mem. Women in Communications (Outstanding Communicator award 1983), Sigma Delta Chi. Democrat. Home: Pleasant Ridge Rd Harrison NY 10528 Office: Temper of the Times Communications 930 Mamaroneck Ave Mamaroneck NY 10543

NELSON-REES, WALTER ANTHONY, geneticist, educator, art dealer, writer; b. Havana, Cuba, Jan. 11, 1929; came to U.S., 1948; s. Julius Maria and Dora Belle (Nelson) R. BA, Emory U., 1951, MA, 1952; PhD, U. Calif., Berkeley, 1960. Fulbright research scholar Max Planck Inst. Marine Biology, Tübingen, Fed. Republic Germany, 1961-62; research assoc. genetics dept. U. Calif., Berkeley, 1960-61, asst. research geneticist Sch. Pub. Health, 1961-67, assoc. research geneticist Sch. Pub. Health, 1967-73, 1973-81; chmn. VI Conf. Mammalian Cytology and Somatic Cell Genetics, 1967; lectr. Sch. Pub. Health U. Calif., Berkeley, 1970-73; assoc. chief cell culture lab. U. Calif. Naval Bioscis. Lab., Oakland, Calif., 1969-77; chmn. cell culture dept., 1977-81; adj. faculty W.A. Jones Cell Sci. Ctr., Lake Placid, N.Y., 1977-78; cons. to Univ., Nat. and Internat. Insts. on Cell Culture and Cytogenetics; cons. Breast Tumor Task Force, Nat. Cancer Inst., NIH, 1975-77; lectr. in field. contbr. scientific articles to profl. jours; author of biographies on artists Lillie May Nicholson, 1981, John O'Shea (Silver medal Commonwealth Club of Calif. 1986), 1985 and Albert Thomas DeRome, 1988; prepared catalogues for exhbns. of works by numerous artists. Ptnr. WIM Fine Arts, Oakland; mem. hist. art com. Art Guild Oakland Mus., chmn. 1983-84, sec. 1984-85; co-dir. exhbns. Monterey Peninsula Mus. Art., 1981, 83; active mem. Bay Area Program for Smithsonian Instns. Bicentennial Inventory Am. Paintings Executed Prior to 1918. Served with Chem. Corps U.S. Army, 1953-56. Recipient NIH tng. grantee, 1960-61. Mem. Internat. Hospitality Ctr., San Francisco Bay Area, XIII Internat Congress Genetics (chmn. organizing com.), Genetic Soc. Am. XIV Internat. Congress Genetics (vice chmn. travel and lodging, fin. com. 1978). Reviewing editor In Vitro 1977-78. Tissue Culture Assn. (chmn. constn. and by laws com., chmn. organizing com. 1966, v.p. 1978-80), Oakland Mus. Assn. (bd. dirs. 1979-80). Home and Office: 6000 Contra Costa Rd Oakland CA 94618

NEMEC, JAROSLAV, industrial engineering educator; b. Horazdovice, Klatovy, Czechoslovakia, Mar. 15, 1927; s. Karel and Bohuslava (Kropsbauerova) N.; m. Zdenka Havlova, Aug. 19, 1921. Degree in Engring., Tech. U. Prague, Czechoslovakia, 1947; D of Scis., Tech. U. Prague, 1955. Design engr. CKD Praha Works, Prague, 1942-45; dir. dept. research CKD Praha Sokolovo, Prague, 1945-53; prof. Coll. of Transport, dean Tech. U. Prague, 1953-55, prof., vice rector, 1953-59, 1975-79; head dept. materials, prof. nuclear and physical engring. CVUT, Prague, 1969-86; dir. academics Inst. Theoretical and Applied Mechanics, Prague, 1979—. Author: Strength of Pressure Vessels Under Different Operational Conditions, Toughness and Strength of Steel Parts, (with Acad. Serensen) Failure of Strength of Plastics, (with Prof. Valenta) New Methods of Calculations of Rigidity and Strength of Machines, The Problem of Nuclear Equipment, Dynamics and Life-time of Locomotives, others; contbr. numerous articles to profl. jours; about 20 individual art expositions in Czechoslavakia and abroad. Recipient Kaplan medal, 1958, Klement Gottwald State prize, 1965, 74, Felber medal, 1971, Krizik medal, 1976, Order of Labour award, 1981, Nat. prize, 1985, Komensky medal, 1986. Fellow Internat. Conf. on Fracture (hon., v.p. 1984, treas. 1966, past bd. dirs.); mem. Internat. Assn. Shell and Spatial Structures, Welding Soc., Czech Acad. Scis. Home: Letohradska 60, 7 Prague 17000, Czechoslovakia Office: Acad Scis, Karlova 2, 1 Prague 11000, Czechoslovakia

NEMETH, KAROLY, president Hungarian People's Republic; b. Paka County Zala, Dec. 14, 1922. Student Party Acad., 1952-54. Meat industry worker, 1939-42, joined Communist Party, 1945, first sec. County Csongrad Party Com., 1954-60; head Dept. Agr., Cen. Com., 1960-62; first sec. Budapest Party Com., Hungarian Socialist Workers' Party, 1965-74, sec. cen. com., 1962-65, from 1974, dep. sec. gen., 1985-87, mem. polit. com., 1970—, head econ. bd. Cen. Com., 1975-78; mem. Pres. Council, 1967—, pres. 1987-88; M.P., 1958—. Author: Tettekkel-felelosseggel (Acts Responsibilities), 1974, A magasabb kovetelmenyek utjan (On the Road of Higher Requirements), 1979, Party, Society, Politics, 1986. Recipient Labour Order of Merit, 1955, 59; decorated Order Hungarian People's Republic. Address: Hungarian Socialist, Workers' Party, 1054 Budapest, Szechenyi rkp 19 Hungary *

NEMETZ, PETER NEWMAN, policy analysis educator, economics researcher; b. Vancouver, B.C., Can., Feb. 19, 1944; s. Nathan Theodore and Bel Nemetz. B.A. in Econs. and Polit. Sci., U. B.C., 1966; A.M. in Econs., Harvard U., 1969, Ph.D. in Econs., 1973. Teaching fellow, tutor Harvard U., Cambridge, Mass., 1971-73; lectr. Sch. Planning, U. B.C., Vancouver, 1973-75, asst. prof., assoc. prof. policy analysis, 1975—, chmn., 1984—; postdoctoral fellow Westwater Research Centre, Vancouver, 1973-75; vis. scientist, dept. med. stats. and epidemiol. Mayo Clinic, 1986-88, sr. visiting scientist Dept. of Health Scis. Research Mayo Clini, 1988-89; cons. consumer and corp. affairs, Can., 1977-80. Editor Jour. Bus. Adminstrn., 1978—. Contbr. articles to sci. jours. Grantee Natural Scis. and Engring. Research Council Can., 1976—, Consumer and Corp. Affairs Can., 1978-80, Econ. Council of Can., 1979-80, Max Bell Found., 1982-84. Mem. Am. Econ. Assn., AAAS, Assn. Environ. and Resource Economists, Internat. Epidemiol. Assn. Liberal. Jewish. Clubs: Harvard of B.C. (pres. 1986—), University (Vancouver). Avocations: swimming; photography. Office: Univ British Columbia, Faculty of Commerce, Vancouver, BC Canada V6T 1Y8

NEMIR, DONALD PHILIP, lawyer; b. Oakland, Calif., Oct. 31, 1931; s. Philip F. and Mary (Shavor) N.; A.B., U. Calif. at Berkeley, 1957, J.D., 1960. Admitted to Calif. bar, 1961; sole practice San Francisco, 1961—; pres. Law Offices Donald Nemir. Mem. ABA (litigation com.), Calif. State Bar Assn. (litigation com.). Phi Delta Phi. Club: Univ. (San Francisco). Office: 2 Embarcadero Ctr Suite 740 San Francisco CA 94111

NEMIRO, BEVERLY MIRIUM ANDERSON, writer, educator; b. St. Paul, May 29, 1925; d. Martin and Anna Mae (Oshanyk) Anderson; m. Jerome Morton Nemiro, Feb. 10, 1951 (div. May 1975); children: Guy Samuel, Lee Anna, Dee Martin. Student Reed Coll., 1943-44; B.A., U. Colo., 1947; postgrad., U. Denver. Tchr., Seattle Pub. Schs., 1945-46; fashion coordinator, dir. Denver Dry Goods Co., 1948-51; fashion model, Denver, 1951-58, 78—; fashion dir. Denver Market Week Assn., 1952-53; free-lance writer, Denver, 1958—; moderator TV program Your Preschool Child, Denver, 1955-56; instr. writing and communications U. Colo. Denver Ctr., 1970—, U. Calif., San Diego, 1976-78, Met. State Coll., 1985—; dir. pub. relations Fairmont Hotel, Denver, 1979-80; free lance fashion and TV model; author: The Complete Book of High Altitude Baking, 1961, Colorado a la Carte, 1963, Colorado a la Carte, Series II, 1966, (with Donna Hamilton) The High Altitude Cookbook, 1969, The Busy People's Cookbook, 1971 (Better Homes and Gardens Book Club selection 1971), Where to Eat in Colorado, 1967, Lunch Box Cookbook, 1965, Complete Book of High Altitude Baking, 1961, (under name Beverly Anderson) Single After 50, 1978, The New High Altitude Cookbook, 1980. Co-founder, pres. Jr. Symphony Guild, Denver, 1959-60; active Denver Art Mus., Denver Symphony Group. Recipient Achievement Rewards for Coll. Scientists, Sante Fe Opera, Denver Ear Inst., Top Hand award Colo. Authors' League, 1969, 72, 79-82, 100 Best Best Books of Yr. award N.Y. Times, 1969, 71; named one of Colo.'s Women of Yr., Denver Post, 1964. Mem. Pub. Relations Soc. Am., Am. Soc. Journalists and Authors, Nat. Writers Club, Colo. Authors League (dir. 1969—), Authors Guild, Authors League Am., Friends Denver Library, Sigma Delta Chi, Kappa Alpha Theta. Address: 420 S Marion Pkwy Apt 1003 Denver CO 80209

NENASHEV, MIKHAIL FEDOROVICH, Soviet government official; b. 1929. Grad., Magnitogorsk Pedagogical Inst., 1952, D Hist. Sci., 1979. Asst. prof. Magnitogorsk Pedagogical Inst., 1961; 2d sec. Magnitogorsk City Com., 1963-67; sec. Cheliabinsk Oblast Com., 1968-75; dep. chief propoganda dept. Cen. Com. Communist Party Soviet Union, Moscow, 1975-78; editor-in-chief Sovetskaia Rosiia, 1978—; mem. Cen. Com. Communist Party Soviet Union, 1981—, now chmn. state com. pub. houses. Office: State Com for Pub Houses, Office Chmn, Moscow USSR *

NENNO, SOJI, metallurgist, educator; b. Osaka, Japan, Dec. 9, 1924; s. Sokichi and Haru (Hayakawa) N.; B.S., Osaka U., 1947, D.Eng., 1961; Ph.D., Northwestern U., 1959; m. Hisako Harada, Jan. 6, 1952. Asst., Osaka U., 1952-62; assoc. prof. Marquette U., Milw., 1962-64; prof. dept. materials sci. and engring. Osaka U., 1964-88, prof. emeritus, 1988—. Recipient Service award Northwestern U. Alumni Assn., 1982. Mem. Japan Inst. Metals, Phys. Soc. Japan, Iron and Steel Inst. Japan, Am. Inst. Mining and Metall. Engrs. Contbr. articles to profl. jours. Patentee in field. Home: A27-102 3-Chome, Fujishirodai Suita, Osaka 565, Japan Office: Osaka Univ2-1, Yamadaoka Suita, Dept Materials Sci & Engring, Osaka 565, Japan

NENONEN, TARMO OLAVI, computer software company executive, horsebreeder; b. Helsinki, Finland, Oct. 3, 1946; s. Otto and Helga Tuulikki (Olkkonen) N.; m. Auli Marjatta Salovuori, May 5, 1971; children: Meri Tuulia, Tero Roope. Grad. economist, Sch. Econs., Helsinki, 1977; postgrad., Kallion Yhteiskoulu, Helsinki, 1968. Programmer analyst Finnish State Computer Ctr., Helsinki, 1968-70; systems analyst Tietotehdas Oy, Espoo, Finland, 1970-71; chief systems analyst Finnish Air Force, Helsinki, 1971-73; systems mgr. Oy Wilh. Schauman Air Base, Almay, Helsinki, 1973-82; mgr. dir. Myyr-Data & Co., Nurmijarvi, Finland, 1982—; v.p. Common Suomi for IBM/3X's. Helsinki, 1981-83; lectr. on Cobol-lang., Query-lang., 1973, 76, 77. Author booklet, Query-language, 1973. Served as lt. Finnish Air Force, 1966-67. Recipient Bronze plate Riding Assn. Finland, 1986. Mem. Finnish Computer Assn., Finnish Arab Horse Soc. (pres. 1986—), Finnish Ridinghorse Breeders (v.p. 1982—), Warmlood Ridinghorse Breeders (bd. dirs. 1987—). Clubs: S.H. Golf (Luukkaa, Finland); Finnish DX (Helsinki). Office: Myyr-Data & Co, Aspiniituntie, SF-01900 Nurmijarvi Finland

NEOH, CHOO KEONG, physician; b. Alor Star, Kedah, Malaysia, Jan. 16, 1941; s. Boo Liat and Lim Khin N.; m. Helen Loo Sak Ngor, Apr. 11, 1969; children: Eu Gene, Eu Rick, Eu Bryan, Eu Bjorn. B in Medicine and Surgery, U. Singapore, 1967. House officer Gen. Hosp., Penang, Malaysia, 1967-68; med. officer Dist. Hosp., Kedah, Malaysia, 1968-70; med. officer trainee Univ. Hosp., Kuala Lumpur, Malaysia, 1970-72; gen. practitioner Neoh Klinik (Neoh Clinic), Kedah, Malaysia, 1973—. Mem. Malaysian Med. Assn. Buddhist. Club: Royal Kedah (Alor Star). Office: Neoh Klinik G05 Kompleks MPKS, Jalan Kolam Air, 05000 Alor Star, Kedah Malaysia

NEPOMUCENO, LUIS, film producer; b. Manila, July 24, 1930; s. Jose and Isabel (Acuña) N.; m. Amparo Bomediano, June 12, 1954; children: Jose Luis, Miguel, Amparo, Joaquin, Jaime, Lucia, Jacobo. Diploma in photography, N.Y. Inst. Photography, N.Y.C., 1952. V.p. Nepomuceno Prodns., Inc., Manila, 1953-59, pres., 1960—; pres. L. Nepomuceno and Sons, Inc. and Fame, Inc., Manila, 1965—; bd. dirs. Malussa Internat. Ltd., Hong Kong. Producer/dir.: Because of a Flower, 1967 (Gran Prix award), The Beggar, 1969 (Gran Prix award); producer: Manila, Open City, 1968 (Gran Prix); producer/dir./writer: Igorota, 1969 (Best Film and Best Dir. awards); designer various product advt. promotions, Proctor and Gamble; producer and dir. over 1000 theatrical and TV films and commls.; film editor and screenplay writer for various feature films; editor: GLOW mag. Chmn. Inner Glow Mission, 1982-87; pres. Legion of Little Souls, 1984—; condr. Marian Year projects, Santuario de San Antonio, Makati; organizer Family Rosary Crusade, Santuario de San Antonio. Mem. Royal Photographic Soc. (assoc. 1965), MENSA Internat. Roman Catholic. Clubs: Manila Polo, Baguio Country. Home: 518 Buendia Ave, Forbes Park N, Makati 1200, Philippines Office: Nepomuceno Prodns Inc, ADC PO Box 7450, Manila Internat Airport 1300, Philippines

NEPOMUCENO, PETER GOMEZ, utility company executive; b. Angeles, Philippines, June 29, 1936; s. Juan D. and Teresa (Gomez) N.; m. Wilma Sandoval. BS in Lit., Ateneo de Manila, Quezon City, Philippines, 1956; BCE, Mapua Inst. Tech., Manila, 1959. Lic. civil engr. Pres., gen. mgr. Angeles Electric Corp., Metro Manila, 1958—, T. G. N. Realty Corp., Angeles City, Philippines, 1962—, Juan D. Nepomuceno Sons Inc., Angeles City, 1969—, AKAI Philippines Inc., Pasig, Metro Manila, 1981—, Teresa Waterworks Inc., Angeles City, 1985—; vice-chmn. Holy Angel U., Angeles City, Kressler Internat. Philippines Inc., Makati, Metro Manila. Chmn. ACCCI-Found. for Econ. Devel., Angeles City; mem. bd. advisors Kapampangan Devel. Found., Angeles City, mem. Kawayan Group, Angeles City. Served to lt. col. Philippine AFR. Mem. Angeles City C. of C. and Industry. Office: Angeles Electric Corp, 717 State Financing Ctr Bldg, Ortigas Ave, Mandaluyong Metro Manila Philippines

NERFIN, MARC, publisher; b. Geneva, Sept. 26, 1930; s. Marcel and Simone (Lacroix) N.; m. Francoise Lentillon, Sept. 5, 1953 (div. 1970); children: catherine Monod, Sophie; m. Catherine Svanberg, Jan. 13, 1973; children: Edouard Olof, Louise Ylva. Licence in History, U. Geneva, 1955. Journalist La Voix Ouvriere, Geneva, 1952-58; tchr. Ministry Edn., Tunisia, 1958-62; advisor UN Econ. Commn. for Africa, Addis Ababa, 1963-65, UN under-sec. gen. for econ. and social affairs, N.Y.C., 1966-68, UN commr. for study UN devel. system, Geneva, 1968-70; exec. asst. to sec. gen. UN Conf.

on Environment, Geneva, 1970-72; dir. Dag Hammerskjöld project on Devel. and Internat. Cooperation, Geneva, 1973-75; pres. Interant. Found. for Devel. Alternatives, Nyon, Switzerland, 1976—; mem. exec. com. Latin Am. Inst. for Transnat. Studies, Santiago, Mex. and Buenos Aires, Communications for Devel. Found., Malta; assoc. mem. Third World Forum, Cairo; sec.-treas. Christopher Eckenstein Found. for Study Relations with Third World, Geneva. Author: Entretiens avec Ahmed Ben Salah sur la Dynamique Socialiste dans la Tunisie des Anneës 60, 1974, German edit., 1976, Arabic edit., 1980; editor: Another Development: Approaches and Strategies, 1977, Mex. edit., 1978; editor periodical IFDA Dossier, 1978—; mem. editorial com. Devel. Dialogue, 1975—; contbr. articles to profl. jours. Mem. World Future Studies Fedn., World Social Prospects Assn. Office: IFDA, 4 Pl du Marche, 1260 Nyon Switzerland

NERLICH, GRAHAM CHARLES, philosophy educator; b. Adelaide, South Australia, Australia, Nov. 23, 1929; s. Alfred Hugo and Mona Pearl (Burdon) N.; m. Susan Kaye Vickerman, Jan. 24, 1966 (dec. June 1986); children: Andrew, David, Stephen. BA with honors, U. Adelaide, 1954, MA, 1955; B. Phil, Oxford U., Eng., 1958. Lectr. Leicester U., Eng., 1958-61; sr. lectr. U. Sydney, New South Wales, Australia, 1962-68, assoc. prof., 1968-72, prof., 1972-73; Hughes prof. philosophy U. Adelaide, South Australia, 1974—. Author: Shape of Space, 1976; contbr. articles to profl. jours. Fellow Australian Acad. Humanities, mem. Logic Methodology and Philosophy of Sci. (mem. council Internat. Union for History and Philosophy of Sci.). Home: 21 Hill St, North Adelaide 5006, Australia Office: U Adelaide Dept Philosophy, Box 498 GPO, Adelaide 5001, Australia

NERRIERE, JEAN-PAUL, data processing executive; b. Cherbourg, France, Mar. 18, 1940; s. Paul and Reneé N.; m. Michele Constantin, Aug. 31, 1963. Degree in Engring., Ecole Cen., Paris, 1963. Various mktg. positions IBM France, Paris, Lille, Grenoble, Marseille, 1965-77; adminstrv. asst. to chmn. IBM Corp. Hdqrs., Armonk, N.Y., 1977-79; dir. orgn. IBM Europe, Paris, 1979-80; div. dir. IBM France, Paris, 1980-83; dir. ops. in Eng. and Italy IBM Europe, Paris, 1983-86, asst. gen. mgr., 1984-85; asst. gen. mgr. mktg. and services IBM France, Paris, 1985-87; v.p. profl. services IBM Europe, Paris, 1988—. Served with French Navy, 1964-65. Named Knight in the Nat. Order of Merit Pres. of the Republic., 1986. Mem. Ecole Cen. Gen. Mgrs. Club. Office: IBM Europe Tour Pascal, La Defense, 92075 Paris France

NERSESSIAN, VREJ NERSES, curator, vicar; b. Teheran, Armenia, Dec. 15, 1948; arrived in London, 1968; s. David and Sandoukht Nersessian; m. Leyla Althounyan, Aug. 1, 1979; children: Tiran, Zhirayr. ThM, Theol. Sem., 1968; PhD and BD, U. London, 1975. Curator Christian Middle Eastdept. The Brit. Library, London, 1975—; ecumenical chaplin Cathedral St. Albans, Eng., 1984—; chief examiner for modern and classical Armenian, U. London, 1985—; mem. com. Anglican-Consultative Com., London, 1986—. Author: Theology and History, 1978, Bibliography, 1980, Biblical Exegesis, 1981, Art History & Theology, 1987. Mem. Soc. for Armenian Studies, Assn. Internat. des Etudes Armeniennes. Mem. Armenian Orthodox Ch. Home: 32 Beechwood Ave, South Harrow HA2 8BY, England Office: The Brit Library, 14 Store Street, London WC1E 7DG, England

NESBIT, DOUGLAS CHARLES, educator; b. London, Eng., Oct. 4, 1926; s. Charles Henry Fletcher and Constance Elspeth (Bruce) N.; B.A., U. Toronto, 1949, Ont. Coll. Edn., 1950; postgrad. U. Western Ont., 1962, 64, 67. Tchr., Bruce Mines (Ont., Can.) Continuation Sch., 1950-51; tchr., later head geography dept. Banting Meml. High Sch., Alliston, Ont., 1951-84; pres. bd. dirs. Brit. Israel World Fedn., 1984—. Pres., Alliston br. Canadian Bible Soc. Served with RCAF, 1943-44. Fellow Am. Geog. Soc., Nat. Council Geog. Edn.; mem. Ont. Assn. Geog. and Environmental Edn., Canadian Assn. Geographers, Assn. Am. Geographers, AAAS, Brit. Israel World Fedn. (pres.), Scottish Tartans Soc. (life), Royal Can. Legion, Royal Commonwealth Soc., Monarchist League Can., Can. Inst. Internat. Affairs. Club: Empire of Can. Home: Box 89, Alliston, ON Canada L0M 1A0

NESBIT, RICHARD ANDREW, public health advisor; b. Adelaide, Australia, Oct. 3, 1947; s. Francis Randolph and Winifred Jean (Young) N.; m. Kay Margaret Wilson, Apr. 10, 1974 (div. 1980). MB, BS, U. Adelaide, 1970; D.T.P.H., U. Sydney, 1982. Lectr. Royal Hosp. St, Bartholomew, London, 1976; sr. resident Cancer Control Agy. of B.C., Vancouver, Can., 1977-78; sr. registrar Ludwig Inst. for Cancer Research, Sydney, Australia, 1979; physician Tom Dooley Heritage, Thailand, 1980; med. coordinator Catholic Relief Services, Surin, Thailand, 1981; physician Internat. Com. Red Cross, Thailand, 1983; med. dir. Internat. Rescue Com., Peshawar, Pakistan, 1983-85; med. advisor U.N. High Commr. for refugees, Sudan, 1983-87; med. coordinator U.N. High Commr. for refugees, Islamabad, Pakistan, 1987—. Med. advisor Movie Prodn. The Killing Fields, Thailand, 1983. Fellow Royal Soc. Tropical Medicine & Hygiene, Royal Australian Coll. Physicians; mem. Am. Pub. Health Assn., Nat. Council Internat. Health, Royal Coll. Physicians. Office: UN High Commr Refugees, Case Postal 2500, CH 1211 Geneva Switzerland

NESBIT, ROBERT GROVER, consultant; b. Scranton, Pa., Feb. 8, 1932; s. George Archibald and Mildred Maude (Bohl) N.; m. Nancy Elizabeth Wilson, June 17, 1961; children: Robert, Jonathan. B.S., U. Scranton, 1957; M.S., NYU, 1958. Asst. to dean NYU, N.Y.C., 1960-64; mdse. mgr. Associated Merchandising Corp., N.Y.C., 1964-67; dir. corp. mktg. Genesco, Inc., Nashville, 1968-77; v.p., div. gen. mgr. Levi Straus & Co., San Francisco, 1977-79; sr. partner Korn/Ferry Internat., N.Y.C., 1979—; lectr. NYU, 1980. Served with U.S. Army, 1953-55. Mem. Nat. Retail Mchts. Assn., Am. Apparel Mfrs. Assn., Sigma Nu. Presbyterian. Club: N.Y. Athletic. Home: 239 Putnam Rd New Canaan CT 06840 Office: 237 Park Ave New York NY 10017

NESBITT, FRANK WILBUR, lawyer; b. Miami, Okla., Dec. 26, 1916; s. Frank Wilbur and Nelle M. (Grayson) N.; m. Delores M. Shaw, 1950 (div. 1978); children: Mary Nelle Pearson, Kathleen Marie Smith; m. Mary Louise Turner Gardner, Aug. 22, 1982. AB, Okla. U., 1937; JD, U. Tex., 1939. Bar: Tex. 1939, U.S. Dist. Ct. (so. dist.) Tex. 1939, U.S. Ct. Appeals (5th cir.). Sole practice, Corpus Christi, Tex., 1939-41; asst. city atty. Corpus Christi, 1941-42; ptnr. King & Nesbitt, Corpus Christi, 1946-54, Wood & Burney, Corpus Christi, 1954—. Served to capt. AUS, 1942-46. Mem. ABA, State Bar Tex., Nueces County Bar Assn., Am. Coll. Trial Lawyers, Tex. Bar Found. Democrat. Episcopalian. Office: Wood & Burney One Shoreline Plaza 300 N Tower Corpus Christi TX 78403

NESBITT, JOHN ARTHUR, educator; b. Detroit, Mar. 29, 1933; s. John Jackson and Anna Maye (Hartley) N.; m. Dolores Antonia Gutierrez, Apr. 8, 1961; children: John Arthur, Victoria Bowen. Student, Olivet Coll., 1952-53; B.A., Mich. State U., 1955; M.A., Tchrs. Coll., Columbia U., 1961, Ed.D., 1968. Registered hosp. recreation dir.; cert. therapeutic recreation specialist. Program dir. Jaycees Internat., Miami, Fla., 1957-60; recreation leader Inst. Rehab. Medicine, NYU-Bellevue Med. Center, 1960-61; dir. World Commn. on Vocat. Rehab., Internat. Soc. Rehab. of Disabled, N.Y.C., 1961-63; dep. dir. gen. Internat. Recreation Assn., N.Y.C., 1964-65; asst. sec. gen. Internat. Soc. for Rehab. of Disabled, N.Y.C., 1966-68; asst. prof., coordinator rehab. services San Jose State U., 1968-69; assoc. prof., dir. Inst. Interdisciplinary Studies, 1969-72; assoc. prof., chmn. dept. leisure studies U. Iowa, Iowa City, 1972-76; prof. recreation edn. program U. Iowa, 1976-85, prof., chmn. dept. leisure studies, 1986-87; pres. Spl. Recreation, Inc.; dir. com. for handicapped People to People Program, 1964—; chmn. com. recreation and leisure U.S. Pres.'s Com. on Employment of Handicapped, 1972-81. Author, editor books in field; editor: Alert Mag., 1956, Jaycees Internat. World, 1957-60, Internat. Rehab. Rev, 1965-68, Therapeutic Recreation Jour, 1968-70, Jour. Iowa Parks and Recreation, 1974-76, Play, Recreation and Leisure for People Who Are Disabled, 1977, Fed. Funding for Spl. Recreation, 1978, New Concepts and New Processes in Spl. Recreation, 1978, New Horizons in Profl. Tng. in Recreation Service for Handicapped Children and Youth, 1983, Nisbet/Nesbitt Soc. Newsletter, 1983-86, Special Recreation Digest, 1984—, Spl. Recreation Compendium, 1986; sr. editor Recreation and Leisure Service for Disadvantaged, 1979; editor, compiler Spl. Recreation Compendium of 1,000 Resources for Disabled People, 1986. Bd. dirs., treas. United Cerebral Palsy Assn., San Mateo and Santa Clara County, 1970-72; bd. dirs. Harold Russell Found., 1971-73, Goodwill Industries Santa Clara County, 1969-72, rehab. counselor, master therapeutic recreation specialist. Served with USAF, 1955-57; maj. Ret. Recipient numerous awards and citations for work with handicapped. Mem. Nat. Therapeutic Recreation Soc. (pres. 1970-71), Nat. Rehab. Assn., Am. Assn. Leisure and Recreation (dir.), Nat. Consortium on Phys. Edn. and Recreation for Handicapped (pres. 1976-77), Nat. Forum Comml. Recreation and Handicapped (chmn. 1979), AAHPER, Iowa Parks and Recreation Assn. (dir.), Nat. Rehab. Counseling Assn., Council Exceptional Children, Pi Sigma Epsilon. Presbyterian. Office: U Iowa Coll Liberal Arts Dept Leisure Studies FH 426 Iowa City IA 52242

NESBITT, LEROY EDWARD, inventor, design specialist; b. Phila., Sept. 14, 1925; s. Lonnie Reynolds and Josephine Elvira N.; student Temple U., 1965-69; m. Vivian Elizabeth Lee, June 27, 1952; 1 son, Warren Eric. Founder, pres. Incentives, Inc., Wilmington, Del., 1975—; design specialist Sperry Corp., Blue Bell, Pa. Served with U.S. Army, 1943-46. Decorated Bronze Star (4). Home and Office: 6213 Gardenia St Philadelphia PA 19144

NESS, ALBERT KENNETH, artist; b. St. Ignace, Mich., June 21, 1903; s. Albert Klingberg and Violet Matilda (Sutherland); m. Lenore Consuelo Chrisman, Aug. 4, 1926; children—Peter, James Kenneth, Jane Lenore. Student U. Detroit, 1923-24, Detroit Sch. of Applied Art, 1924-26, Wicker Sch. of Fine Art, 1926-28; Diploma, Sch. of Art Inst., 1932. Show-card writer, window display man S.S. Kresge Co., Detroit, 1923-24; artist poster and advt. Cunningham Drugs, Detroit, 1924-26; artist layout lettering and design W.L. Flemming Studios, Detroit, 1926-28, McAleer Displays, Chgo., 1929-32; artist, design asst. Layman-Whitney Assocs., 1933 World's Fair, Chgo.; layout artist, poster designer Elevated Advt. Co., Chgo., 1934-37; instr., art dir. Sch. of Applied Art, Chgo., 1938-40; Carnegie resident artist U. N.C., Chapel Hill, 1941-43, dir. War Art Ctr., 1942-43, resident artist, assoc. prof. art, 1943-49, acting head, dept. art, acting dir. Person Hall Art Gallery, 1944-45, resident artist, prof. art, 1949-73, acting head dept. of art, acting dir. Person Hall Art Gallery, 1955, 57-58, resident artist, prof. emeritus, 1973—. One man shows include: Chester Johnson Galleries, Chgo., 1932, Evanston Art Ctr., Ill., 1940, Person Hall Art Gallery, 1941, N.C. Art Soc. Gallery, Raleigh, 1942, Duke U. Art Gallery, Durham, N.C., 1955, Louisburg Coll. Gallery, N.C., 1964, Ackland Art Mus., U.N.C. Chapel Hill, 1973; Internat. Water Color Exhbn. Chgo. Art Inst., 1934-39; Golden Gate Internat. Exposition, San Francisco, 1939, exhibited in group shows: Whitney Mus., N.Y.C., 1933, U. Chattanooga, Tenn., 1946, Centennial Exhbn. U. Fla., Gainesville, 1953, Jacksonville Art Mus, Fla., 1960; exhibited nationally Am. Artists' Anns., Chgo. Art Inst., 1935-37, Butler Art Inst., Youngstown, Ohio, 1951, Pa. Acad. Am. Annuals, Phila., 1953-54, others; works in pub. collections include: N.C. Mus., Raleigh, Ackland Art Mus., Reynolds Found., Winston Salem, Duke U. Art Mus., Durham. Contbr. to local and state newspapers. Editor, designer, photographer: A brochure on art study, 1964. Recipient Jenkins Meml. prize 38th Ann. Chgo. Artists' Exhbn., 1934, Purchase award N.C. Artists' Ann., Raleigh, 1953; 2-Star award Movie Maker Competition, London, 1970, N.C. award in Fine Arts, 1973, Purchase award Reynolds Competition, Winston Salem, 1977.

NESSELRATH, HEINZ-GUENTHER, classicist, educator; b. Titz-Roedingen, Fed. Republic Germany, Nov. 9, 1957; s. Martin and Magdalene (Baerenz) N. PhD, U. Cologne, Fed. Republic Germany, 1981; degree, U. Cologne, 1983. Asst. researcher, Inst. for Studies in Classical Antiquity U. Cologne, 1981—. Author: Lukians Parasitendialog, 1985. Mem. Mommsen Gesellschaft, British Classical Assn. Roman Catholic. Office: U Koeln Inst Altertumskunde, Albertus Magnus Pl, 5000 Koeln 41 Federal Republic of Germany

NESSEN, WARD HENRY, typographer, lawyer; b. Empire, Mich., Nov. 29, 1909; s. Henry L. and Louise (Stecher) N.; m. Jane Randall, Apr. 4, 1959. AB, U. Mich., 1931; JD, John Marshall Law Sch., Chgo., 1937; course in acctg. Northwestern U. Grad. Sch., 1946. Bar: Ill. 1937. With trust dept. No. Trust Co., Chgo., 1934-41; sales planning Am. Home Products, 1946-51; sales exec. Permacel Tape Corp., 1951-55; pres. The Highton Co., Newark, 1955-75; sr. v.p. Arrow Typographers, Newark, 1975-84; chmn. Coll. Communications Seminar, 1973. Mem. Civic Clubs Council Greater Newark Area, 1957-59, Bd. Comml. Arbitration N.Y.C., 1982-86; chmn. selection com. Advt. Hall of Fame of N.J., 1983. Served from 2d lt. to lt. col. AUS, 1941-46, ETO, assigned SOS. Decorated Bronze Star with oak leaf cluster, Army Commendation medal; recipient Elmer G. Voigt award, 1975. Mem. Typographers Internat. Assn. (pres. 1970-71), N.J. Typographers Assn. (pres. 1957-59), Printing Industries N.J. (pres. 1967-69), Printing Industries N.Y. (bd. govs. 1967-69), Order of John Marshall, Sigma Phi. Republican. Episcopalian. Clubs: Type Dirs.; Advt. N.J. (bd. govs 1972-84). Home: 11 Euclid Ave Summit NJ 07901

NESTERENKO, YEVGENIY YEVGENIYEVICH, singer, vocal art educator; b. Moscow, Jan. 8, 1938; s. Yevgeniy Nikiforovich Nesterenko and Velta Voldemarovna Baumann; m. Yekaterina Dmitrievna Alexeyeva; 1 child, Maxim Yevgeniyevich. Diploma in engring., Engring and Bldg. Inst., Leningrad, USSR, 1961; grad., Rimsky-Korsakov Conservatoire, Leningrad, 1965. Engr. Lensovnarkhoz, Leningrad, 1961-62; soloist Maly Theatre Opera and Ballet, Leningrad, 1963-67, Kirov Theatre Opera and Ballet, Leningrad, 1967-71, Bolshoy Theatre, Moscow, 1971—; vocal tchr. Leningrad Conservatoire, 1967-72, Musical-Pedagogical Inst. Gnessin, Moscow, 1972-75; tchr., chmn. dept. Tchaikovsky Conservatoire, Moscow, 1975—, prof., 1981. Author: Thoughts on My Profession, 1985. Mem. presidium Soviet Cultural Found., Moscow, 1986—; pres. opera sect. Musical Soc. USSR, 1987—. Named People's Artist Govt. USSR, 1976, Hero of Labour Govt. USSR, 1988; recipient Grammy award Am. Acad. Recording Artists, 1979, Lenin prize, 1982, Giovanni Zenatello prize City of Verona, Italy, 1986, Viotti d'Oro prize City of Vercelli, Italy, 1981. Home: Frunzenskaya nab 24/1-178, 119146 Moscow USSR Office: Bolshoy Theatre, Marx Prospect 8/2, 103009 Moscow USSR

NETANYAHU, BENJAMIN, Israeli diplomat; b. Tel Aviv, Oct. 21, 1949; s. Benzion and Cela (Segal) N. B.Sc., MIT, 1974, M.Sc., 1976. Cons. Boston Cons. Group, 1976-78; dir. Jonathan Inst., Jerusalem, 1978-80; dir. mktg. Rim Industries, Jerusalem, 1980-82; minister Israeli embassy, Washington, 1982-84; ambassador Israeli Mission to UN, N.Y.C., 1984—. Editor: The Letters of Jonathan Netanyahu, 1979; International Terrorism: Challenge and Response, 1981, Terrorism: How the West Can Win, 1986. Contbr. articles to newspapers. Served to capt. Israel Def. Force, 1967-72. Jewish.

NETHERCOTE, JOHN RAYMOND, government official; b. Sydney, New South Wales, Australia, Mar. 1, 1948; s. Arthur William and Dorothy Isabel (Steward) N. BA, U. Sydney, 1969. Project officer Royal Commn. Australian Govt. Adminstrn., Canberra, 1974-76; sr. advisor policy Can. Pub. Service Commn., Ottawa, Ont., 1979; acting dir. research Pub. Service Bd., Canberra, 1980-81, project officer, 1982-84, dir. info., 1985-87; sec. Senate Standing Com. Fin. Pub. Adminstrn., Canberra, 1987—; cons. Dept. Fgn. Affairs, Canberra, 1981; research officer Def. Rev. Com., Sydney, 1981-82; sec. Nat. Inquiry Local Govt. Fin., 1984-85. Mng. editor Royal Australian Inst. Pub. Administrn., Australian Studies in Pub. Adminstrn., 1984—; editor Parliament and Bureaucracy, 1982; contbg. editor Australian commonwealth Adminstrn., 1984, 86. Mem. Royal Australian Inst. Pub. Adminstrn. (dep. pres. 1987—, div. councillor 1973-76, 80), Australian Inst. Internat. Affairs, Australian Inst. Polit. Sci., Australasian Polit. Studies Assn., Inst. Pub. Adminstrn. Can. Home: PO Box E113, Queen Victoria Terrace 2600, Australia Office: The Senate, Parliament House, Canberra 2600, Australia

NETHERCUT, WILLIAM ROBERT, classicist, educator, baritone; b. Rockford, Ill., Jan. 11, 1936; s. Robert C. and Constance E. (Stanley) N.; m. Jane Lillian Swann, July 27, 1977; children: William Andrew, Amanda Jane, Robert Christopher, Jason Scott. A.B. magna cum laude, Harvard U., 1958; student, New Eng. Conservatory of Music, 1959-60; M.A. (Henry Drisler fellow, Pres.'s fellow), Columbia U., 1961, Ph.D., 1963. Instr., Greek and Latin Columbia U., 1961-66, asst. prof., 1966-67, Lawrence H. Chamberlain fellow, 1967; assoc. prof. classics U. Ga., Athens, 1967-72; prof. U. Ga., 1972-75; prof. classics U. Tex., Austin, 1975—; undergrad. adv. U. Tex., 1977-82; vis. fellow classics U. New Eng., Armidale, Australia, 1985; vis. prof. Brigham Young U., 1986; NEH vis. lectr. Inst. on Vergil Miami U., 1986; announcer radio sta. WROK, Rockford, 1957-58; cons. on Greece and Rome Pathescope Ednl. Films, N.Y.C., 1965-66; appearance ednl. program TV sta. WGTV, Athens, 1970-72; lectr. 1st Internat. Conf. on Ovid, Constanta, Rumania, 1972, Internat. Soc. Homeric Studies, Athens, Greece, 1973, 74, 3d Internat. Congress S.E. European Studies, Bucharest, 1974, Conf. on Ancient Novel, Bangor, Wales, 1976. Soloist, New Eng. Opera Theatre, Boston, 1958-59; debut as Figaro in: Barber of Seville, 1958; soloist recital, Carnegie Hall, N.Y.C., 1966, Atlanta Opera Co., 1968, Austin Lyric Opera Theatre, 1987-88; translator: De Praestigiis Daemonum (Johan Weyer), 1964, Almanach Perpetuum Celestium Motuum (Rabbi Abraham Zacuto), 1973; editor: Tex. Classics in Action, 1976-82; asso. editor The World and Its Peoples, Italy, 1964, Latina et Graeca, 1974, Helios, Jour. Classical Assn. Southwestern U.S, 1977-81; author: A Course in the Derivation of English Words from Greek and Latin, 1981; contbr. articles on classical lit., antiquity to profl. jours. Coach community youth soccer and baseball, 1985—; chmn. com. for chaplaincy Breckenridge Hosp., Austin, Tex., 1985. Am. Council Learned Socs. grantee, 1972; recipient U. Tex. Alumni award for teaching excellence, 1982. Mem. Rocky Mountain Modern Lang. Assn. (sec. classics 1986, pres. classics 1987), Am. Philol. Assn. (campus adv. service 1975-78), Archaeol. Inst. Am. (pres. Athens chpt. 1972-74), Vergilian Soc. Am. (life mem., trustee 1974-79, 1st v.p. 1981-82, pres. 1983-84, dir. Egypt, Greece, Italy 1983), Classical Assn. Southwestern U.S., Classical Assn. Middle West and South (nat. com. for promotion of Latin 1978-81), Tex. Classical Assn. (pres. 1979-81, hon. life mem. 1983—), Am. Classical League. Clubs: Harvard, University, Explorers of N.Y.C. Lodges: Masons; KT. Home: 1003 High Rd Austin TX 78746

NETTELBECK, COLIN WILLIAM, language educator; b. Streaky Bay, Australia, Mar. 29, 1938; s. Harry William George Nettelbeck and Christina May (Montgomery-Ross) Mundy; m. Carol Emily Membrino; children: Alexander John, Jennifer Maria, Bridget Christina. BA with honors, Adelaide U., Australia, 1960; diploma phonetique, Inst. de Phonetique, Paris, 1962; D with honors, U. Paris, 1964. Asst. prof. U. Calif., Berkeley, 1963-70; sr. lectr. Monash U., Clayton, Victoria, Australia, 1971-86, assoc. prof., 1986—, head French dept., 1983-86. Author: Les Personnages De Bernanos, Romancier, 1970, Patrick Modiano, 1986, French and Second World War, 1987; editor: Cahiers Celine V, 1979; contbr. articles to profl. jours. Named Palmes Académiques officier French Govt., 1985; U. Adelaide scholar, 1960-63. Mem. Modern Lang. Assn., Australian Lang. and Lit. Assn., Soc. des. Etudes Celiniennes, Alliance Francaise (pres. 1980-85), Alliance Francaise Australian Fedn. (pres. 1985—). Roman Catholic. Home: 33 Dalgety Std Rd, 3182 Saint Kilda Australia Office: Monash U, 3168 Clayton Australia

NETTLES, JOHN BARNWELL, physician, educator; b. Dover, N.C., May 19, 1922; s. Stephen A. and Estelle (Hendrix) N.; m. Eunice Anita Saugstad, Apr. 28, 1956; children: Eric, Robert, John Barnwell. B.S., U. S.C., 1941; M.D., Med. Coll. S.C., 1944. Diplomate: Am. Bd. Obstetrics and Gynecology. Intern Garfield Meml. Hosp., Washington, 1944-45; research fellow in pathology Med. Coll. Ga., Augusta, 1946-47; resident in obstetrics and gynecology U. Ill. Research and Ednl. Hosps., Chgo., 1947-51; instr. to asst. prof. obstetrics and gynecology U. Ill. Coll. Medicine, Chgo., 1951-57; asst. prof., asso. prof., prof. obstetrics, gynecology U. Ark. Med. Center, Little Rock, 1957-69; dir. grad. edn. Hillcrest Med. Center, Tulsa, 1969-73; prof. ob-gyn Coll. Medicine, U. Okla., Oklahoma City, 1969—; chmn. dept. gynecology and obstetrics U. Okla.-Tulsa Med. Coll., 1975-80, prof., 1980—, mem. council on residency edn. in obstetrics, gynecology, 1974-79; dir. Tulsa Obstet. and Gynecol. Edn. Found., 1969-80; Coordinator med. edn. Nat. Def., Ark., 1961-69; mem. S.W. regional med. adv. com. Planned Parenthood Fedn. Am., 1974-78; mem. adv. com. Health Policy Agenda Am. People, 1982—, rev. com. Accrediation Council for Continuing Med. Edn., 1987—. Contbr. articles on uterine malignancy, kidney biopsy in pregnancy, perinatal morbidity and mortality, human sexuality sch. age pregnancy to profl. jours. Served as lt. (j.g.) M.C. USNR, 1945-46; as lt. 1953-54. Fellow Am. Coll. Obstetricians and Gynecologists (dist. sec.-treas. 1964-70, dist. chmn. exec. bd. 1970-73, v.p. 1977-78), A.C.S. (bd. govs. 1969-71, program com. 1970-71, Surg. forum 1977-84, adv. com. gyn/ob 1985—), Royal Soc. Health, Royal Soc. Medicine; mem. Ark. Obstet. and Gynecol. Soc. (exec. sec. 1959-69), Central Assn. Obstetrics and Gynecology (exec. com. 1966-69, pres. 1978-79), Internat. Soc. Advancement Humanistic Studies in Gynecology, Assn. Mil. Surgeons U.S., AMA (sect. council on obstetrics and gynecology 1975—, chmn. 1982—, del. from Am. Coll. Obstetricians and Gynecologists 1987—), Nurses Assn. Am. Coll. Obstetricians and Gynecologists (exec. bd. 1970-73, assoc. 1980—), So. Med. Assn. (chmn. obstetrics 1973-74), Okla. Med. Soc., Tulsa County Med. Soc., Chgo. Med. Soc., Am. Assn. for Maternal and Infant Health, Assn. Am. Med. Colls., Am. Public Health Assn., Am. Assn. Sex Edn. Counselors and Therapists (S.W. regional bd. 1976—), Soc. for Gynecol. Investigation, AAAS, Am. Soc. for Study Fertility and Sterility, Internat. Soc. Gen. Semantics, Aerospace Med. Assn., So. Gynecol. and Obstet. Soc. (pres. 1981-82), Am. Cancer Soc. (pres. Okla. div. 1979-83), Com. on In-Tng. Exam. in Obstetrics and Gynecology, Am. Coll. Nurse Midwives (governing bd. examiners 1979—), Sigma Xi, Phi Rho Sigma. Lutheran. Office: U Okla Tulsa Med Coll 2808 S Sheridan Rd Tulsa OK 74129

NEUBER, FRIEDEL, banker; b. Duisburg-Rheinhausen, Germany, July 10, 1935. Indsl. apprentice Fried. Krupp Huttenwerke A.G., Essen, W.Ger., 1953-61; chief exec. Bertha Hosp., Duisburg, 1961-69; pres. Rhineland Sparkassen and Giro Assn., Dusseldorf, 1969-81; chmn. mng. bd. Westdeutsche Landesbank, Dusseldorf, 1981—; dep. state parliament North Rhine-Westphalia, 1962-75. Office: Westdeutsche Landesbank, Girozentrale, Herzogstrasse 15, PF 1128 4000 Dusseldorf 1 Federal Republic of Germany

NEUENSCHWANDER, FREDERICK PHILLIP, management professional; b. Akron, Ohio, Mar. 19, 1924; s. Willis Lee and Esther (Mayer) N.; student Franklin and Marshall Coll., 1942-43, U. Akron, 1946-48; m. Mary Jane Porter, Mar. 19, 1948 (dec.); children—Carol, Frederick Philip, Lynn, Dean, Richard. Chief insp. Retail Credit Co., Akron, 1948-55; exec. v.p. Wadsworth (Ohio) C. of C., 1955-62, Wadsworth Devel. Corp., 1955-62, Wooster (Ohio) C. of C., 1962-63, Wooster Expansion, Inc., 1962-63; dir. devel. dept. State of Ohio, Columbus, 1963-71; exec. v.p. James A. Rhodes & Assos., Columbus, 1971-74; prin. F.P. Neuenschwander & Assos., Worthington, Ohio, 1975—. Mem. adv. council Small Bus. Adminstrn., Ohio Scenic Rivers Commn.; exec. dir. Wadsworth United Fund, Inc., 1956-62; pres. Templed Hills, Inc.; pres. Central Ohio exec. bd. Boy Scouts Am.; vice-chmn. Ohio Water Commn., Ohio Expns. Commn.; chmn. Ohio Water and Sewer Rotary Fund Commn.; mem., past chmn. Midwest Gov.'s Adv. Council; sec. Ohio Devel. Council, Ohio Devel. Finance Commn. Adv. council Rio Grande Coll.; 1st chmn. bd. trustees Ohio Transp. Research Center; trustee Eden Theological Seminary; bd. dirs. League Against Child Abuse, United Ch. Bd. for World Ministries. Served with AUS, 1943-46. Named Outstanding Young Man of Year, Wadsworth Jr. C. of C., 1958; recipient SIR award for directing outstanding state indsl. devel. program N. Am., 1966, 68, Ohio Gov.'s award 1967. Mem. Am., Gt. Lakes Indsl. Devel. Councils, C. of C. Execs. of Ohio, Huguenot Soc. Am., Am. Legion, Ohio Soc. N.Y. (res. v.p.). Mem. United Ch. of Christ (property mgmt. com. Ohio Conf.). Club: Worthington Hills Country. Home: 5614 Chapman Rd Delaware OH 43015-9203 Office: 7870 Olentangy River Rd Worthington OH 43235

NEUMANN, ALFRED, East German politician; b. Berlin, Dec. 15, 1909; emigrated to USSR, 1934, returned to Germany, 1941. Ed. elem. sch. Carpenter by trade; active mem. labor movement, 1928—; mem. Community Party (KPD), 1929; mem. Internat. Brig. in Spain, 1938-39; imprisoned in Germany, 1942-45; mem. KPD, 1945-46, Socialist Unity Party (SED), from 1946; first sec. Greater Berlin Dist. SED, 1953-57, mem. SED Central Com., 1954—, candidate mem. Politburo, 1954-58, mem., 1958—, sec. SED Central Com., 1957-61; pres. Econ. Council, 1961-65, minister of materials, 1965-68, first dep. chmn. Council of Ministers, 1968—; mem. Volkskammer (People's Chamber), 1954. Decorated Vaterlandischer Verdienstorden in gold (2), Karl-Marx-Orden (2) others. Office: Office of First Deputy Chairman, care Ministerrat, Berlin German Democratic Republic *

NEUMANN, BERNHARD HERMANN, mathematician; b. Berlin-Charlottenburg, Germany, Oct. 15, 1909; s. Richard and Else (Aronstein) N.; m. Hanna von Caemmerer, Dec. 22, 1938 (dec. Nov. 1971); children—Irene Brown, Peter, Barbara Cullingworth, Walter, Daniel; m. Dorothea Zeim, Dec. 24, 1973. Student U. Freiburg, Germany, 1928-29;

Dr.phil., U. Berlin, 1932; Ph.D., Cambridge U., Eng., 1935; D.Sc., U. Manchester, Eng., 1954; D.Sc. (hon.), U. Newcastle, Australia, 1974, Monash U., Australia, 1982; D. Math. (hon.), U. Waterloo, 1986. Lectr., Univ. Coll., Hull, Eng., 1946-48; faculty U. Manchester, Eng., 1948-61; prof., head dept. math. Inst. Advanced Studies, Australian Nat. U., Canberra, 1962-74, hon. univ. fellow, 1975—; hon. research fellow div. Math. and Stats. Commonwealth Sci. and Indsl. Research Orgn., Canberra, 1978—. Contbr. numerous articles to math. jours. Editor Houston Jour. Math., 1974—. Served with Brit. Armed Forces, 1940-45. Recipient prize Wiskundig Genootschap, Amsterdam, Netherlands, 1949; Adams prize U. Cambridge, 1952, 53. Fellow Royal Soc., Australian Acad. Sci. (v.p. 1969-71, Matthew Flinders lectr. 1984); mem. London Math. Soc. (v.p. 1959-61, editor proc. 1959-61), Australian Math. Soc. (v.p. several terms, pres. 1964-66, hon. mem. 1981—, editor bull. 1969-79, hon. editor 1979—), many other profl. orgns., also chess and musical clubs and socs. Avocations: classical music (cello), chess, cycling. Home: 20 Talbot St, Forrest ACT 2603, Australia Office: Australian Nat U, GPO Box 4, Canberra ACT 2601, Australia also: CSIRO-DMS, CPO Box 1965, Canberra ACT 2601, Australia

NEUMANN, GERWIN WILHELM WALTER, neurosurgeon; b. Riga, Latvia, Apr. 21, 1938; came to U.S., 1970; s. Kurt Wilhelm Ernst and Eugenie Elvira (Konow) N.; student German Inst., Osorno, Chile, 1949-56; M.D., U. Concepcion, Chile, 1962; m. Karin Rosemarie Kempe, Oct. 30, 1965; children—Antje Karin, Tamara Andrea, Renate Dagmar, Birgit Lorena. Intern, Clin. Regional Hosp., Concepcion, 1963; resident in neurosurgery Cath. U. Clin. Hosp., Santiago, Chile, 1964-68; fellow in neurosurgery Lahey Clinic, Boston, 1968-69; chief neurosurgery Regional Hosp. of Talca, Chile, 1969-71; prof. neurophysiology U. Chile, Talca, 1969-70, prof. neurology and neurosurgery, 1969-70; fellow New Eng. Bapt. Hosp., Boston, 1971, active staff, 1972—; practice medicine specializing in neurosurgery, Boston, 1972—. Elder, Lutheran Ch. of the Newtons, 1973, v.p., 1974, pres., 1975, 76, del. Eastern Synod, 1975, 76. Mem. Interam. Coll. Physicians and Surgeons, Am. Soc. Regional Anesthesia, Internat. Med. Services Boston (pres.), Chilean Med. Coll., Med. Soc. Ctr., AMA, Mass. Med. Soc., Norfolk Dist. Med. Soc., New Eng. Neurosurg. Soc., Latin Am. Med. Soc. (pres. 1976-77), Internat. Assn. Study of Pain (founding), Am. Pain Soc. (founding), Eastern Pain Soc. (founding), New Eng. Pain Assn. (founding), AMA Vienna, Internat. Fedn. Neurol. Surgery, Found. for International. Edn. in Neurol. Surgery, Am. Assn. Algology (founding), Mass. Neurosurg. Soc., World Med. Soc., AAAS, Schlaraffia Bostonia. Home: 37 Woodridge Rd Wayland MA 01778 Office: 125 Parker Hill Ave Boston MA 02120

NEUMANN, HANS-JOACHIM, chemist, educator; b. Forst, Prussia, Germany, Oct. 25, 1930; s. Max and Dora (Mueller) N.; m. Waldtraut Brandes; children: Klaus Dietrich, Ute Mund, Juergen, Eckhard, Silke. Diploma in Chemistry, Tech. U., Braunschweig, Federal Republic of Germany, 1956, Dr. rer. nat., 1959; Dr.habil., Tech. U. Clausthal, Republic of Germany, 1983. Sci. asst. Inst. Chem. Tech. Tech. U., Braunschweig, Republic of Germany, 1959-69; dep. dir. German Inst. Petroleum Research, Clausthal-Zellerfeld, Republic of Germany, 1969—; head inst. 1970-75; pvt. docent Tech. U., Braunschweig, 1969-76, prof., 1976-83; lectr. Tech. U., Clausthal, Republic of Germany, 1970-76, prof., 1976—. Author: Composition and Properties of Petroleum, 1981, Petroleum Refining, 1984; editor: Bitumen and seine Anwendung, 1981; contbr. articles to profl. jours. Warden Evang. Luth. Ch., Wolfenbuettel, Republic of Germany, 1963-72. Recipient first prize, Tech. U. Braunschweig, 1956, plaque, Tech. Metall. Faculty U., Belgrade, Yugoslavia, 1986. Mem. Soc. German Chemists, German Sci. Soc. Petroleum, Natural Gas and Coal (advisor 1970-76), Colloid Soc. Club: Lions (pres. 1987-88) (Oberharz, Republic of Germany). Home: Einersberger Blick 3, D3302 Clausthal-Zellerfeld Federal Republic of Germany Office: Inst Petroleum Research, Walther-Nernst Str 7, D3392 Clausthal-Zellerfeld Federal Republic of Germany

NEUMANN, VACLAV, symphony conductor; b. Prague, Sept. 29, 1920; ed. Prague Conservatoire. Former viola player Smetana Quartet; mem. Czech Philharm. Orch.; deputized for Rafael Kubelik, 1948; later conducted orchs. in Karlovy Vary and Brno; condr. Prague Symphony Orch., 1956-63, Czech Philharm., 1964-68; chief condr. Komische Oper, Berlin, 1957-60; conducted 1st performance of The Cunning Little Vixen (Janacek); condr. Leipzig Gewandhaus Orch., also gen. music dir. Leipzig Opera House, 1964-67; condr. Czech Philharm. Orch., 1967-68, chief condr., 1968 ; chief condr. Stuttgart Opera House, 1970-73; condr. 1987 Vienna Philharm.; regularly conducts Vienna Symphonic Orch.; condr. Munich Opera Ensemble, Sweden, 1960, 1970, 71, 72, 74, Romania, 1951, 71, 73, Fed. Republic of Germany, 1962, 65, 67, 71, 73, 74, 75, Yugoslavia, 1970, Bulgaria, 1975, Belgium, 1970, Switzerland, 1970, 75, Spain, 1975, Finland, 1975; conducted many European orchestras including Berlin Philharm., Orchestre National de France, Royal Philharm., Hamburg Philharm., Boston Symphony, N.Y. Philharm. Recipient Nat. prize German Democratic Republic, 1966, honored artist, 1967, nat. artist, 1971, Order of Labour, 1980. Mem. Mahler-Gesellschaft (hon.), Gesellschaft der Musikfreunde (hon.). Address: Czech Philharmonic Orch, Alsovo Nabrezi 12, 11001 Prague 1 Czechoslovakia

NEUMULLER, HEINZ, photographic company executive; b. Merseburg, W. Ger., May 1, 1920; s. Kurt and Friedel (Hö lken) N.; student Grunewald Gymnasium Berlin; m. Petra Funcke, Mar. 10, 1977; children—Christiane, Tim, Caroline, Alexander. Bus. mgr., ptnr. Carl Wöltje, Photo-Film-TV, Oldenburg, W. Ger., 1948—, Vereinigte Cewe-Color Betriebe, Oldenburg, Hamburg, Bremen, Lübeck, Nürnberg, Munich, Mönchengladbach, Paris and Freiburg, W. Ger. Served with German Submarine Corps, 1938-45. Decorated Iron Cross. Recipient Order of Merit, 1st class, Fed. Republic Germany. Chmn. Arbeitgeber-Verband Oldenburg e.v. Mem. Deutscher Photo-Kinohandler-Bund, Deutsche Gesellschaft for Photography e.v. (Cologne, W. Ger.), Chamber of Industry and Commerce (adv. bd. Oldenburg). Home: Vossbergweg 66B, 2904 Sandkrug Federal Republic of Germany Office: Meerweg 30-32, 2900 Oldenburg Federal Republic of Germany

NEUSCHEL, ROBERT PERCY, educator, former management consultant; b. Hamburg, N.Y., Mar. 13, 1919; s. Percy J. and Anna (Becker) N.; m. Dorothy Virginia Maxwell, Oct. 20, 1944; children—Kerr Anne Ziprick, Carla Becker Neuschel Wyckoff, Robert Friedrich. B.A., Denison U., 1941; M.B.A., Harvard U., 1947. Indsl. engr. Sylvania Elec. Products Co., Inc., 1947-49; with McKinsey & Co., Inc., 1950-79, sr. partner, dir., 1967-79; prof. corp. governance J. L. Kellogg Grad. Sch. Mgmt.; dir. Transp. Center, Northwestern U.; bd. dirs. Butler Mfg. Co., Combined Ins. Co. Am., Templeton, Kenly & Co.; lectr. in field; mem. McKinsey Found. Mgmt. Research, Inc.; transp. task force Reagan transition team. Contbr. to profl. jours. Pres. Bd. Edn., Lake Forest, Ill., 1965-70; rep. Nat. council Boy Scouts Am., 1970—, mem. N.E. exec. council, 1969—; chmn. bd. Lake Forest Symphony, 1973; bd. dirs. Loyola U., Chgo., Chgo. Boys' Club, Nat. Center Voluntary Action, Inst. Mgmt. Consultants; trustee N. Suburban Mass Transit, 1972-73, Loyola Med. Ctr.; mem. adv. council Grad. Sch. Mgmt., Northwestern U; White House conferee Drug Free Am.; mem. Nat. Pet. Council Trans. and Supply com. Served to capt. USAAF, World War II. Fellow Acad. Advancement Corp. Governance; mem. Transp. Assn. Am. Presbyterian (ruling elder). Clubs: Harvard Bus. Sch. (pres. 1964-65), Economic, Executive, Chicago, Mid America, Mid-Day (Chgo.); Onwentsia (Lake Forest). Home: 101 E Sunset Pl Lake Forest IL 60045 Office: 1936 Sheridan Rd Evanston IL 60201

NEVADOMSKY, JOSEPH JOHN, anthropology educator; b. Shenandoah, Pa., Oct. 24, 1942; s. Zigmund Stanley and Julia Olga (Vislosky) N.; m. Rebecca Nogieru Agheyisi, Mar. 31, 1973; 1 child, Jason. BA, U. San Diego, 1964; MA, U. Calif., Berkeley, 1968, U. Calif., Berkeley, 1973; PhD, U. Calif., Berkeley, 1977. With Provincial Tchr.'s Coll., Peace Corps, Abudu, Nigeria, 1964-66; lectr. U. Lagos, Nigeria, 1973-75; lectr. U. Benin, Benin City, Nigeria, 1975-80, research fellow, 1980-84, research assoc. prof., 1984-87, assoc. prof., 1987—; vis. scholar U. Kans., Lawrence, 1981; head cultural research Centre for Social, Cultural and Environ. Research, Benin City, 1980-87. Photographer photomural Nat. Mus. of African Arts Smithsonian Inst., 1987; contbr. articles to profl. jours. Fellow NIMH, 1970-74; Fulbright scholar U. Delhi, India, 1967-68. Fellow Royal Anthropol. Inst., Am. Anthropol. Assn.; mem. Inst. African Studies. Roman Catholic. Club: Benin (Benin City). Office: Univ Benin, Ugbowo Campus, Benin City Nigeria

NEVELOFF, JAY A., lawyer; b. Bklyn., Oct. 11, 1950; s. Cydelle (Weber) Elrich; m. Arlene Sillman, Aug. 26, 1972; children: David, Kevin. BA, Bklyn. Coll., 1971; JD, NYU, 1974. Bar: N.Y. 1975, U.S. Dist. Ct. (so. and ea. dists.) N.Y. 1975, U.S. Ct. Appeals (2d cir.) 1975, U.S. Supreme Ct. 1982. Assoc. Marshall, Bratter, Greene, Allison & Tucker, N.Y.C., 1974-82; assoc. Rosenman, Colin, Freund, Lewis & Cohen, N.Y.C., 1982-83, ptnr., 1983—. Editor N.Y. Real Property Service. Mem. Am. Law Inst., N.Y. State Bar Assn. (condominium and cooperative law com. 1983—), Assn. of Bar of City of N.Y. (real property law com. 1984—, chmn. subcom. to prepare condominium unit resale contract 1984—, lectr. 1988), Practising Law Inst. (lectr. 1985), N.Y. County Lawyers Assn. (lectr. 1984-88), Community Assns. Inst. (lectr. 1986). Home: 134 Alder Dr Briarcliff Manor NY 10510 Office: Rosenman & Colin 575 Madison Ave New York NY 10022

NEVES, GUILHERME PEREIRA DAS, historian, educator; b. Rio de Janeiro, Brazil, May 27, 1950; s. Paulo Pereira and Gilda Pereira (Castagnoli) N.; m. Lúcia Bastos. B in History, U. Fed. Rio de Janeiro, 1973, lic. in history, 1976; M in Brazilian Hist, U. Fed. Fluminense, Niterói, Brazil, 1984. Prof. U. Fed. Fluminense, Niterói, 1977—; coordinator undergrad. programs U. Fed. Fluminense, Rio de Janeiro, 1985-87. Contbr. articles about late XVIIIth century Brazilian history/theory and methodology of history to profl. jours. Mem. Soc. Brasileira Pesquisa Histórica. Office: U Fed Fluminense, Rua São Paulo, 30/320, 24210 Niterói Brazil

NEVILLE, JOHN, actor, director; b. London, May 2, 1925; s. Reginald and Mabel L. (Fry) Neville; m. Caroline Hooper, 1948; 6 children. Ed. Royal Acad. Dramatic Art; Dr. Dramatic Arts (hon.), Lethbridge U., Alta., Can., 1979; D.F.A. (hon.) N.S. Coll. Art and Design, 1981. With Bristol Old Vic Co., London, 1953, Chichester Theatre Co., 1962; dir. Nottingham Playhouse, 1963-68, Newcastle Playhouse, 1967; hon. prof. drama, Nottingham U., 1967—; drama adviser Howard and Wyndham, Ltd.; artistic dir. Citadel Theatre, Edmonton, Alta., Can., 1973-78, Neptune Theatre, Halifax, N.S., 1978-83; artistic dir., Stratford Shakespearean Festival, Stratford, Ont., Can., 1985—; actor films: Mr. Topaz, Oscar Wilde, Billy Budd, A Study in Terror, Adventures of Gerrard, lead role Adventures of Baron Munchausen, 1987. Decorated knight Order Brit. Empire.

NEVIN, JOHN JOSEPH, tire and rubber manufacturing executive; b. Jersey City, Feb. 13, 1927; s. Edward Vincent and Anna (Burns) N.; m. Anna Filice, June 16, 1951; children: Stanley James, John Joseph, Richard Charles, Paul Edward, Gerald Patrick, Mary Anne. B.S., U. Calif., 1950; M.B.A., Harvard U., 1952. Various positions fin., product planning and mktg. Ford Motor Co., Dearborn, Mich., 1954-71; v.p. mktg. Ford Motor Co., 1969-71; pres. Zenith Radio Corp., Chgo., 1971-76; chmn. Zenith Radio Corp., 1976-79; pres. Firestone Tire & Rubber Co., Akron, Ohio, 1979-82, chief exec. officer, 1980—, chmn., 1981—. Gen. chmn. Summit County United Way, 1983. Served with USNR, 1945-46. Office: Firestone Tire & Rubber Co 205 N Michigan Ave Suite 3800 Chicago IL 60601

NEVO, DAVID, education educator; b. Sokal, Poland, June 22, 1939; came to Israel, 1949, naturalized, 1949; s. Arie and Bela (Grosman) Schiffenbauer; children—Aviv, Ziv, Arbel. B.A., Hebrew U., Jerusalem, 1967; M.A., Tel Aviv U., 1972; Ph.D., Ohio State U., 1974. Assoc. prof. edn. Tel Aviv U., 1975—. Author: The Gifted Disadvantaged, 1979. Editor: Theory and Research in Educational Practice, 1977; Evaluation Roles in Education, 1981, Evaluation in Decision Making, 1988, Useful Evaluation, 1988; contbr. articles, research reports to profl. publs. Served to capt. Israeli Army, 1957-77. Mem. Internat. Assn. for Evaluation of Ednl. Achievement (mem. gen. assembly, rep. for Israel), Am. Edn. Research Assn., Am. Evaluation Assn. Jewish. Office: Tel Aviv U Sch Edn, Tel Aviv 69978 Israel

NEW, LAURENCE ANTHONY WALLIS, lieutenant governor, military officer; b. London, Feb. 15, 1932; s. Stanley William and Constance Mary (Marshal) N.; m. Anna Doreen Vérity, Aug. 11, 1956; children: Amanda, Richard, Deborah Ann, Richard. Student, Royal Mil. Acad., Sandhurst, Eng., 1952, Army Staff Coll., Camberley, Eng., 1963; attended, Joint Services Staff Coll., Latimer, Eng., 1968, Royal Coll. Defence Studies, London, 1980. Commd. 2d lt. Brit. Army, 1952, advanced through ranks to maj. gen., 1982; sec. def. policy staff Brit. Army, U.K., 1970-71, col. gen. staff, 1977-79; brigade maj. 20th Armoured Brigade, Fed. Republic Germany, 1968-69; comdg. officer 4th Royal Tank Regt., Fed. Republic Germany, U.K., 1971-73; defence, mil. attaché Brit. Embassy, Tel Aviv, 1976-77; col. gen. staff operational requirements Army Dept., U.K., 1977-79, brig. gen. staff, 1980-83, asst. chief staff operational requirements, 1983-84; asst. chief def. staff Ministry Def., London, 1984-85; lt. gov., pres. Tynwald Parliment, Isle of Man, U.K., 1985—; col. commandant Royal Tank Rgmt., 1985—. Decorated companion Order Bath, commander Brit. Empire, knight Order St. John. Mem. Brit. Inst. Mgmt. (companion). Club: Army and Navy (London). Address: Govt House, Tynwald Isle of Man

NEWBERG, HERBERT BARKAN, lawyer; b. Phila., July 18, 1937; s. Samuel A. and Lillian (Barkan) N.; m. Babette Josephs, Jan. 28, 1962; children: Lee Aaron, Elizabeth. B.S., U. Pa., 1958; J.D., Harvard U., 1961. Bar: Pa. 1962, U.S. Dist. Ct. (ea. dist.) Pa. 1962, U.S. Ct. Appeals (3d cir.) 1962, U.S. Supreme Ct. 1966, U.S. Ct. Appeals (2d, 5th, 6th, 10th, 11th, D.C. cirs.) 1981-85. Asst. city solicitor City of Phila., 1962-64; assoc., then ptnr. firm Cohen, Shapiro, Berger, Polisher & Cohen, Phila., 1964-70; ptnr. firm David Berger Profl. Assn., Phila., 1971-72, cons., 1972—; ptnr. Herbert B. Newberg Law Offices, Phila., 1975-78; counsel Barrack, Rodos & McMahon, 1978-81; pres. Herbert B. Newberg, Esq. P.C., Phila., 1982—; cons., expert in field; mem. faculty Temple U. Law Sch., 1975; mem. faculty Advanced Advocacy Coll., Assn. Am. Trial Lawyers, 1977; bd. dirs. Phila. Community Legal Services, 1976, 78, Pa. Law Coordination Ctr., 1981—. Author: Newberg on Class Actions, 8 vols., 1977, 2d edit., 5 vols., 1985, Attorney Fee Awards, 1986, Action Decisions Checklist, 1977; editor: Court Awarded Fees in Public Interest Litigation, 1978; others. Bd. dirs. Pa. ACLU, 1982-84; bd. dirs. Sr. Citizens Judicare Project, 1978-85, Am. Jewish Com., Phila., 1970-85, Jewish Community Relations Council, 1976-86; pres. Lawyers Alliance for Nuclear Arms Control, Phila., 1982—. Served with USAR, 1961-66. Beta Gamma Sigma scholar, 1958; Beta Alpha Psi scholar, 1958. Mem. ABA, Pa. Bar Assn., Phila. Bar Assn., Am. Law Inst., Fed. Bar Assn., Assn. Am. Trial Lawyers. Office: 227 S 6th St Suite 200 Philadelphia PA 19106

NEWBERRY, ELIZABETH CARTER, owner greenhouse and floral company; b. Blackwell, Tex., Nov. 25, 1921; m. Weldon Omar Newberry, Sept. 24, 1950 (dec. Nov. 1984); 1 child. Student Hardin Simmons U., 1938-39. Office mgr. F. W. Woolworth, Abilene, Tex., 1939-50; acct. Western Devel. & Investment Corp., Englewood, Colo., 1968-72; owner, operator Newberry Bros. Greenhouse and Florist, Denver, 1972—; bd. dirs. Western Devel. and Investment Corp. Englewood, Colo., 1979-87. Pres. Ellsworth Elem. Sch. PTA, Denver, 1961-62; v.p. Hill Jr. High Sch. PTA, Denver. Home: 201 Monroe Denver CO 80206 Office: Newberry Bros Greenhouse 201 Garfield Denver CO 80206

NEWBOLD, HERBERT LEON, JR., internist, writer; b. High Point, N.C., Nov. 3, 1921; s. Herbert Leon and Mary Temperance (Sherrod) N.; children: Lucile Newbold Corley, Susan. Student, U. Chgo., 1941, Coll. William and Mary, 1941; B.S., Duke U., 1945, M.D., 1945; postgrad., Northwestern U., 1951, New Sch. Social Research, 1960-61. Intern U. Chgo. Clinics, 1945-46, U. Minn., 1949-50; resident Woodlawn Hosp., Chgo., 1946; resident in internal medicine Vanderbilt U. and associated VA Hosp., Nashville, 1946-47; resident in psychiatry U. Ill. and associated VA Hosp., Hines, Ill., 1955-58; practice medicine specializing in internal medicine Newton, N.C., 1947-48; practice medicine specializing in psychiatry Chgo., 1950-55, 1958-60; Asheville, N.C., 1961-70; N.Y.C., 1970-76, pvt. practice specializing in med. nutrition, 1976—; instr. neurology and psychiatry Sch. Medicine, Northwestern U., Chgo., 1958-61. freelance writer, 1950—; novels include 1/3 of an Inch of French Bread, 1961, Long John, 1979, Dr. Cox's Couch, 1979; others under pseudonym, 1950-60; sci. books include text Psychiatric Programming of People, 1972, Mega-Nutrients for Your Nerves, 1975, Dr. Newbold's Revolutionary New Discoveries about Weight Loss,How to master the hidden allergies that make you fat, 1977, Physicians Handbook on Orthomolecular Medicine, 1977, Vitamin C Against Cancer, 1979, Meganutrients, 1987; numerous appearances radio and TV; contbr. articles to profl. jours. Served with U.S. Army, 1943-45, 46-47. Fellow Am. Acad. Environ. Medicine; mem. AMA. Address: 115 E 34th St New York NY 10016

NEWBORN, JUD, cultural anthropologist, writer; b. N.Y.C., Nov. 8, 1952; s. Solomon and Rita (Cohen) N. BA magna cum laude in Anthropology and English, NYU, 1974; postgrad., Clare Hall, Cambridge U., 1974-75; MA in Anthropology, U. Chgo., 1977, PhD in Anthropology, 1988. Freelance writer N.Y.C., Munich, Chgo., 1974—; publicist Oxford U. Press, N.Y.C., 1975-76; sr. researcher, scholar-in-residence Mus. Jewish Heritage (N.Y. Holocaust Meml. Commn.), N.Y.C., 1986—; cons. Sci. Inst. for Pub. Info., N.Y.C., 1987—; cons., speaker, lectr. in field. Author: Shattering the German Night the Story of the White Rose Anti-Nazi Resistance, 1986; German translator for numerous articles for profl. jours. Fulbright fellow, 1980-82; Newcombe fellow, 1984-85. Mem. Am. Anthrop. Assn., The Authors' Guild, Phi Beta Kappa. Office: c/o Elaine Markson Lit Agy 44 Greenwich Ave New York NY 10011

NEWBY, (PERCY) HOWARD, novelist; b. Crowborough, Eng., June 25, 1918; s. Percy and Isobel Clutsam (Bryant) N.; grad. St. Paul's Coll., Cheltenham, 1938; m. Joan Thompson, July 12, 1945; children—Sarah Jane Newby Schenk, Katharine Charlotte. Lectr., Cairo U., 1942-46; freelance writer, 1946-49; with BBC, 1949—, mng. dir. BBC Radio, 1976-78; chmn. English Stage Co., 1978-85; author numerous books, 1945—, including: A Journey to the Interior, 1945; The Picnic at Sakkara, 1955; The Barbary Light, 1962; Something to Answer For, 1968; A Lot to Ask, 1973; Kith, 1977; The Egypt Story, 1979; Warrior Pharaohs, 1980; Feelings Have Changed, 1981; Saladin in his Time, 1983; Leaning in the Wind, 1986. Served with Brit. Army, 1939-42. Decorated comdr. Order Brit. Empire; recipient Rockefeller-Atlantic award lit., 1946; Somerset Maugham prize, 1948; Yorkshire Post Fiction award, 1968; Booker prize, 1969. Mem. Soc. Authors. Home: Garsington House, Garsington, Oxford OX9 9AB England

NEWELL, GREGORY JOHN, ambassador; b. Geneseo, Ill., Aug. 30, 1949; s. Eugene Earl and Ima Delores (Stamper) N.; m. Candilyn Jones, Oct. 2, 1978; children: David, Kendall, Catherine, Michael, Mattson. Student, Brigham Young U., Laie, Hawaii, 1967-68, Brigham Young U., Provo, Utah, 1971-72, 73-74. Field dir. Com. to Re-elect the Pres., Washington and Detroit, 1972; planning analyst Alexander Hamilton Life Ins. Co., Farmington Hills, Mich., 1974-75; staff asst. to Pres. White House, Washington, 1975-77, spl. asst. to Pres., 1981-82; coordinator lang. evaluation Brigham Young U., Provo, Utah, 1977-78; dep. adminstrv. asst. Office of Gov., Harrisburg, Pa., 1979-81; asst. sec. of state Dept. State, Washington, 1982-85; U.S. ambassador to Sweden Dept. State, 1985—. Republican. Mormon. Home: Strandvagen 101, 115-27 Stockholm Sweden Office: Dept of State US Ambassador to Sweden Washington DC 20520-5750 *

NEWELL, LEONARD JACKSON, JR., university dean, educator; b. Dayton, Ohio, Oct. 11, 1938; s. Leonard J. and Henrietta (Wahlenmaier) N.; m. Linda King, June 15, 1963; children—Christine, Jennifer, Eric, Heather. Student Deep Springs Coll., Calif., 1956-59; B.A. in History, Ohio State U., 1961, Ph.D. in Higher Edn., 1972; M.A. in History, Duke U., 1964. Instr. history Deep Springs Coll., Calif., 1965-67, mem. bd. trustees, 1987—; asst. dean Coll. Liberal Arts, U. N.H., 1967-70; assoc. dir. Univ. Council for Ednl. Adminstrn., Columbus, Ohio, 1970-74; successively asst. prof., assoc. prof., prof. higher edn., U. Utah, Salt Lake City, 1974—, dean student affairs 1974-78, dean liberal edn., 1974—; vis. prof. Anglican Mgmt. Ctr., Danbury, Essex, Eng., 1978; prin. investigator curricular devel. fund for improvement of post-secondary Nat. Inst. Edn., 1981-83; Co-author: A Study of Professors of Education Administration, 1973, A History of Thought and Practice in Educational Administration, 1987, The Educational Administration Professionate, 1988; contbr. numerous articles to profl. jours.; editor Rev. of Higher Edn., 1986—; Thought, 1982-88 ; bd. editors Jour. Gen. Edn., 1983—. Bd. dirs. Utahns United Against Nuclear Arms Race, Salt Lake City, 1982—; voting dist. chmn. Democratic Orgn., Salt Lake City, 1975-77; scoutmaster Boy Scouts Am., Salt Lake City, 1984—. Thomas Holy fellow, Ohio State U., 1971. Mem. Assn. for Gen. and Liberal Studies (pres. 1988—), Am. Ednl. Research Assn. (assoc. program chmn. 1986—), Assn. for Study of Higher Edn., Assn. Am. Colls. (instl. rep. 1983—), Phi Beta Kappa, Phi Kappa Phi (chpt. pres. 1985), Phi Alpha Theta, Phi Delta Kappa. Home: 1218 Harvard Ave Salt Lake City UT 84105 Office: U Utah 40 Olpin Union Salt Lake City UT 84112

NEWMAN, ANITA NADINE, physician; b. Honolulu, June 13, 1949, d. William Reece Elton and Margie Ruth (Pollard) Newman; m. Frank Ellis Burkett, Dec. 30, 1978; children—Justin Ellis, Chelsea Newman, Andrew Frank. AB, Stanford U., 1971; MD, Dartmouth Coll., 1975. Diplomate Am. Bd. Otolaryngology. Intern, resident in gen. surgery Northwestern Meml. Hosp., Chgo., 1975-77, resident in otolaryngology, 1977-78; resident UCLA Hosp. and Clinics, 1979-82, asst. prof., 1982—; staff surgeon Wadsworth VA Hosp., Los Angeles, 1982-84; research fellow in neurotology UCLA, 1984—. Contbr. articles to med. jours. Mem. alumni admissions support com. Darmouth Med. Sch. Alumni Council, 1983—. Mem. Am. Acad. Otolaryngology, Am. Med. Women's Assn., Los Angeles County Med. Women's Assn., Assn. Research in Otolaryngology, Stanford Women's Honor Soc. Democrat. Office: UCLA Hosp and Clinics Div Head and Neck Surgery Westwood CA 90024

NEWMAN, BARRY I., banker; b. N.Y.C., Mar. 19, 1932; s. M.A. and T.C. (Weitman) N.; B.A., Alfred U., 1952; J.D., N.Y. U., 1955; m. Jean Short, Mar. 6, 1965; children: Suzanne, Cathy, David. Admitted to N.Y. State Bar, 1957, Ohio bar, 1957, U.S. Supreme Ct. bar, 1967; practiced in N.Y.C., 1957; partner firm Shapiro Persky Marken & Newman, Cleve., 1957-63; asst. v.p. Meinhard & Co. (now Meinhard Comml. Corp.), N.Y.C., 1963-65; v.p. Amsterdam Overseas Corp., N.Y.C., 1966-68; pres. No. Fin. Corp., Los Angeles, 1968-72; sr. v.p. Aetna Bus. Credit, Inc., Hartford, Conn., 1972-78; exec. v.p. Security Pacific Fin. Group, San Diego, 1978-81, chmn., pres., chief exec. officer, 1981-82; sr. exec. v.p. Gt. Am. First Savs. Bank, 1982—; chmn. bd. dirs. San Diego County Capital Asset Leasing Corp. Served with U.S. Army, 1955-57. Recipient Distinguished Service award Cleve. Jr. C. of C., 1961. Mem. ABA, N.Y. State Bar Assn., Ohio Bar Assn., San Diego Bar Assn., San Diego Taxpayers Assn. (bd. dirs.). Republican. Club: Fairbanks Ranch Country; Univ. Club of San Diego (pres.). Lodge: Masons. Home: 3308 Avenida Sierra Escondido CA 92025 Office: Gt Am 1st Savs Bank 600 B St San Diego Fed Bldg San Diego CA 92183

NEWMAN, CHARLES ANDREW, lawyer; b. Los Angeles, Mar. 18, 1949; s. Arthur and Gladys (Barnett) N.; m. Joan Kathleen Meskiel, Aug. 8, 1971; children: Anne R., Elyse S. BA magna cum laude, U. Calif., 1970; JD, Washington U., 1973. Bar: Mo. 1973, U.S. Dist. Ct. (ea. dist.) Mo. 1973, U.S. Ct. Appeals (8th cir.) 1973, U.S. Supreme Ct. 1976, D.C. 1981, U.S. Tax Ct. 1981, U.S. Claims Ct. 1981. From assoc. to ptnr. Thompson & Mitchell, St. Louis, 1973—; lectr. law Washington, U., St. Louis, 1976-78. Mem. United Jewish Appeal Young Leadership Cabinet, N.Y.C., 1985—; v.p. Repertory Theatre of St. Louis, 1986—; bd. dirs. Ctr. for Study of Dispute Resolution, 1985—, Legal Services Eastern Mo., 1985—, Planned Parenthood of St. Louis, 1986—, Jewish fedn. of St. Louis, 1986—. Recipient Lon O. Hocker Meml. Trial award Mo. Bar Found., 1984. Mem. ABA, Mo. Bar Assn., Bar Assn. Met. St. Louis (Merit award 1976). Democrat. Club: Mo. Athletic (St. Louis). Office: Thompson & Mitchell One Mercantile Ctr Saint Louis MO 63101

NEWMAN, DANIEL JOSEPH, political consultant, journalist; b. Cleve., Oct. 23, 1959; s. Arthur Jerome and Ruth (Davis) N.; m. Silvia Fabiani, May 31, 1986. BA, Swarthmore Coll., 1981. Asst. to dir. Trilateral Commn., N.Y.C., 1981-84; dir. fellowships/program ASPEN Inst., Washington, 1984-85, Aspen Italia, Rome, 1986; asst. to pres. Banca Nazionale dell'Agricoltura, Rome, 1985—; columnist Internat. Courier, Rome, 1985-86. Home: Via Labicana 80, 00184 Rome Italy

NEWMAN, DAVID WILLIAM, plant physiology and biochemistry educator; b. Pleasant Grove, Utah, Oct. 26, 1933; s. Frank Byrd and Edna (Holdaway) N.; m. JoAnne Marie Slighting, May 16, 1956; 1 child, Steven D. BS, U. Utah, 1955, MS, 1957, PhD, 1960; postgrad. Oak Ridge Inst. Nuclear Studies. Research fellow U. Utah, 1956-59; asst. prof. Miami U., Oxford, Ohio, 1960-66, assoc. prof., 1966-74, prof. dept. botany, 1974-87, prof. emeritus, 1987—. Co-author: Eco-physiology Plant Membrane

L.P.A.'s; editor: Instrumental Methods of Experimental Biology, 1964; co-editor: (3 vols.) Models in Plant Physiology and Biochemistry; contbr. articles and photographs to profl. jours., mags. and textbooks. Served with U.S. Army, 1957-62. NSF grantee, indsl. research grantee; finalist nat./internat. photog. contests. Fellow Ohio Acad. Scis.; mem. AAAS, Am. Chem. Soc., Am. Soc. Plant Physiologists, Am. Oil Chemists Soc., Société Francaise de Physiologie Vegetaie, Friends of Photography, Calumet Photog. Soc. (charter), Internat. Platform Assn., Sierra Club, Phi Beta Kappa, Sigma Xi, Phi Kappa Phi, Phi Sigma. Editor: Instrumental Methods of Experimental Biology, 1964; contbr. articles to profl. jours. Home: 4836 Butterfly Dr Prescott AZ 86301 Office: Botany Dept Miami U Oxford OH 45056

NEWMAN, ELLEN MAGNIN, consultant; b. San Francisco, Apr. 19, 1928; d. Cyril Isaac and Anna Smithline Magnin; student Stanford U., 1945-48; m. Walter Simon Newman, Sr., Oct. 15, 1950; children—Walter Simon, Robert Magnin (dec.), John Donald. With Joseph Magnin Co., San Francisco, 1948-69, women's apparel buyer, 1948-54, developer sales tng., 1954-60, dir. product devel., 1960-64, dir. new products and new brs., 1964-69; spl. asst. to pres. Joseph Magnin, San Francisco, 1969-72; in house cons. consumer affairs Amfac, Honolulu, 1972-74; pres. Ellen Newman Assos., San Francisco, 1974—; dir. Wells Fargo & Co., Wells Fargo Bank, San Francisco. Mem. Mayor's Fiscal Adv. Com. City San Francisco; v.p. bd. govs. San Francisco Symphony; council mem. SRI Internat.; mem. adv. council Grad. Sch. Bus., Stanford U.; chair U. Calif. San Francisco Found. Mem. Com. 200, Women's Forum West, San Francisco C. of C. (v.p., bd. dirs.). Clubs: Metropolitan, City (bd. govs.). Office: 323 Geary St Suite 507 San Francisco CA 94102

NEWMAN, HARRY RUDOLPH, educator, urologist; b. Russia, Sept. 10, 1909; naturalized, 1919, came to U.S., 1935, naturalized, 1944; s. Abraham and Mary (Rudolph) N.; m. Lillian Lear, Aug. 18, 1942; children: Nancy Ellen, Robert Lear, Suzanne Mary. M.D., U. Toronto, 1935; M.S., U. Pa., 1940. Diplomate: Am. Bd. Urology. Resident urology U. Minn. Hosps., 1936-37, All Saints Hosp., London, Eng., 1937-38; sr. resident urology N.Y. Postgrad. Med. Sch. and Hosp., 1939-40, Boston Long Island Hosp., 1941-42; resident surgery N.Y. Postgrad. Hosp., 1942; resident gen. surgery Prince of Wales Hosp., Plymouth, Eng.; attending urologist Yale New-Haven Hosp.; attending univ. service Yale U., asst. clin. prof. urology, 1949—; dir. urology Albert Einstein Coll. Medicine, also clin. prof. surgery, chief urology, 1957—, clin. prof. urology, 1957-62, prof. urology, 1963-65, 66-80, emeritus prof. urology, 1980—, chmn. dept., 1966-80; now prof. history; chief urology Bronx Mcpl. Hosp., 1966—; chief urology community div. Grace New Haven Hosp., 1965-66; cons. urologist Stamford (Conn.) Hosp., St. Joseph Hosp., Stamford, 1965—; former asst. clin. prof. urology NYU; dir. urology City N.Y. Bronx Mcpl. Med. Center, 1954-65; chief urology Regional Hosp., Hunter Field, Savannah, Ga. Served from capt. to maj. USAAF, 1942-46. Fellow ACS, N.Y. Acad. Medicine; mem. Soc. Univ. Urologists, Sigma Xi. Clubs: Masons (New Haven) (32 deg.), Shriners (New Haven), Yale (New Haven); Woodbridge (Conn.) Country. Home: 95 Broadfield Rd Hamden CT 06517 Office: 2 Church St S New Haven CT 06510

NEWMAN, JAMES MICHAEL, lawyer; b. Bklyn., Apr. 3, 1946; s. Sheldon and Ethel (Silverman) N.; m. Lee Galen; children—Danielle Cari, Matthew Evan, Merrie Lee, Cindy Joy, Bradley Curtis. B.A., Queens Coll., 1966; J.D., NYU, 1969, LL.M., 1975. Bar: N.Y. 1970, N.J. 1977. Assoc., Kramer, Marx, Greenlee & Backus, N.Y.C., 1970-73, Forsyth, Decker, Murray & Broderick, N.Y.C., 1973-74; ptnr. Goldzweig, Reilly, Grossman & Newman, Marlboro, N.J., 1978-79, Tommaney & Newman, N.Y.C., 1975-82, Canarick & Newman, Freehold, N.J., 1982-84; pub. defender Marlboro Twp. (N.J.), 1984-86. Dep. mayor Marlboro Twp., 1975-79, dir. econ. devel., 1975-79, dir. commuter affairs, 1974; interim commr. Western Monmouth Utilities Authority, 1977; 1975-79; pres. Marlboro Democratic Club, 1978, trustee, 1979-81; pres. Marlboro Dem. Orgn., 1982; mem. Central N.J. Transp. Bd., 1974-76; judge Marlboro Twp, 1986—. Mem. ABA, New York County Lawyers Assn., Monmouth County Bar Assn., N.J. Bar Assn. Jewish. Lodge: Masons. Office: 64 W Main St Freehold NJ 07728

NEWMAN, JAY, philosopher, philosophy educator; b. Bklyn., Feb., 28, 1948; s. Louis and Kate (Rothbaum) N. B.A., Bklyn. Coll., 1968; M.A., Brown U., 1969; Ph.D., York U., Toronto, 1971. From lectr. to assoc. prof. U. Guelph, Ont., Can., 1971-82, prof. philosophy, 1982—; hon. research fellow U. Birmingham, Eng., 1981, vis. research fellow Calgary Inst. for Humanities U. Calgary, 1988—. Author: Foundations of Religious Tolerance, 1982; The Mental Philosophy of John Henry Newman, 1986; Fanatics and Hypocrites, 1986, also articles. Mem. Can. Philos. Assn., Can. Theol. Soc., Am. Cath. Philos. Assn., Am. Acad. Religion, Phi Beta Kappa. Home: 524 Woolwich St, Guelph, ON Canada N1H 3X8 Office: Univ Guelph, Dept Philosophy, Guelph, ON Canada N1G 2W1

NEWMAN, JULIAN CLISSOLD, information technology educator; b. Edinburgh, Scotland, May 15, 1942; s. Sidney Thomas Mayow and Joy (Pickering) N.; m. Rhona Louisa McBride, Sept. 3, 1965; children: Simon Thomas McBride, Sigrid Julia. BA, Oxford U., Eng., 1963; BA with 1st class hons., London U., 1970. Tech. author Internat. Computers Ltd., London, 1967-72; research fellow Heriot-Watt U., Edinburgh, Scotland, 1972-73, 80-81; lectr. Glasgow Coll. Tech., Scotland, 1973-75; sr. lectr. Ulster Poly., Belfast, No. Ireland, 1975-80; prin. lectr. info. tech. City Poly., London, 1981—; panel mem. Computer Law and Security Report, 1986—. Contbr. articles to profl. jours. Mem. Brit. Computer Soc. (human computer interaction group), Assn. of Poly. Tchrs. (nat. council 1976-77). Office: City Poly Office, Tech Dept, London England

NEWMAN, LAWRENCE WALKER, lawyer; b. Boston, July 1, 1935; s. Leon Bettoney and Hazel W. (Walker) N.; m. Cecilia Isette Santos, Nov. 29, 1975; children: Reynaldo W., Timothy D., Virginia I.S., Isabel B., Thomas H. A.B., Harvard U., 1957, LL.B., 1960. Bar: D.C. 1961, N.Y. 1965. Atty. U.S. Dept. Justice, 1960-61, Spl. Study of Securities Markets and Office Spl. Counsel on Investment Co. Act Matters, U.S. SEC, 1961-64; asst. U.S. atty. So. Dist. N.Y., 1964-69; assoc. Baker & McKenzie, N.Y.C., 1969-71, ptnr., 1971—; mem. internat. adv. com. World Arbitration Inst., 1984-87, corp. counsel com. of Am. Arbitration Assn., 1987—, U.S. Council for Internat. Bus., 1987—; mem. adv. com. Asia Pacific Ctr. Resolution of Internat. Trade Disputes, Litigation, 1987—. Co-author: column N.Y. Law Jour., 1982—, U.S. Iranian Claimants Com. (chmn. 1982—). Mem. ABA (com. internat. litigation, com. internat. arbitration), Internat. Bar Assn. (com. dispute resolution, com. constrn. litigation), Inter-Am. Bar Assn., Fed. Bar Council, Am. Fgn. Law Assn., Maritime Law Assn. U.S., Assn. of Bar of City of N.Y. (mem. com. on arbitration 1977-79, mem. com. on fgn. and comparative law 1987—), Am. Arbitration Assn. (corp. counsel com. 1987—), U.S. Council Internat. Bus. Home: 1001 Park Ave New York NY 10028 Office: Baker & McKenzie 805 3d Ave New York NY 10022

NEWMAN, LEONARD JAY, retail jewel merchant, gemologist; b. Milw., Oct. 25, 1927; s. David and Pia Goldie (Smith) N.; m. Louise Shainberg, Jan. 14, 1951; children—Shelley, Marty, Alan, Heidi, Dee. B.S., Purdue U.; postgrad. Washington U., St. Louis. Owner, mgr. Newman's Diamond Ctr., Jasper, Ind., 1951—; tchr. The Jasper Ctr., Ind., 1970-80. Bd. dirs. VUJC Found., State Bd. Health Systems Agy., sub area Health Systems Agy.; 1st v.p. Vincennes Univ. Found.; past pres. Jasper Community Arts Commn.; pres. Friends of Arts; commnr. Boy Scouts Am.; mem. Dubois County Mental Health Assn., lay adv. bd. Convent Immaculate Conception Sisters of St. Benedict, Ferdinand, Ind., Jasper Hist. Soc., German Club, Young Abe Lincoln Soc.; bd. dirs. Dubois County Crippled Children's Soc., Bloomington (Ind.) Symphony; pres. Jasper Edn. Fund. Recipient Outstanding Citizenship award Purdue U. Alumni Assn., 1980. Mem. Nat. Assn. Jewelry Appraisers (sr.), Ind. Jewelers Orgn. Am., Retail Jewelers Am., Jasper C. of C., Jaycees (Rooster, past pres., past nat. bd. dirs., Disting. Service award 1957), Purdue Agrl. Alumni Assn. (hon.), Skull and Crescent (hon.), Hadassah, Sigma Alpha Mu, Alpha Phi Omega. Lodges: Lions, Masons, Shriners (past pres.), B'nai Brith. Home: 923 McArthur Jasper IN 47546 Office: Newman's Diamond Ctr 3D Plaza Jasper IN 47546

NEWMAN, LINNAEA ROSE, horticulturist; b. Milw., Sept. 23, 1953; d. Arthur Fred and Katherine Elnora (Cook) N. BS, U. Wis., 1977. Cert. interior horticulturist, cert. performax cons. Grower Shroeder's Flowerland, Green Bay, Wis., 1977-78; with installation Tropical Plant Rentals, Inc., Prarie View, Ill., 1978, with spl. service, 1978-84, mgr. edn. and research, 1984—; bd. govs. Nat. Council Interior Horticulture Cert., 1982-85, vice chmn., 1985-86, chmn., 1987—. Author: (with others) Retail Store Planning and Design Manual, 1986; contbr. articles to profl. jours. Named one of Outstanding Young Women Am., 1985. Mem. Entomol. Soc. Am., Internat. Soc. Arboriculture, Ohio Florists Assn. (mem. planning com. 1983—), Assoc. Landscape Contractors Am. (interior plantscape div. com., 1987—, edn. com. 1987—), Nat. Assn. Women in Horticulture (v.p. 1986-87). Home: 1051 Midlothian Rd Mundelein IL 60060 Office: Tropical Plant Rentals Inc 15671 Aptakisic Rd Prairie View IL 60069

NEWMAN, LOUIS BENJAMIN, educator, physician; b. N.Y.C.; s. Morris and Mollie (Banzuly) N.; m. Rose Manilow, Jan. 21, 1951. M.E., Ill. Inst. Tech., 1921; M.D., Rush Med. Coll., 1933. Diplomate Am. Bd. Phys. Med. and Rehab. Intern Cook County Hosp., Chgo., 1932-33; practice of medicine, specializing rehab. medicine Chgo., 1933—; prof. rehab. medicine Northwestern U. Sch. Medicine, 1946—; chief rehab. medicine VA Hosp., Hines, Ill., 1946-53, VA Research Hosp., Chgo., 1953-66; cons. rehab. medicine VA hosps. and several community hosps. Chgo., 1967—; professorial lectr. rehab. medicine Coll. Medicine, U. Ill., Loyola U. Stritch Med. Sch., U. Health Scis.-The Chgo. Med. Sch.; mem. drs. adv. com. Shaare Zedek Hosp. and Med. Center, Jerusalem, Israel; cons. Loyola U. Hosp.; Mem. med. adv. and cons. bd. Armour Research Fedn. of Ill. Inst. Tech. Contbr. articles to med. jours. Health div. com. on handicapped Welfare Council of Met. Chgo.; med. adv. bd. Research Project on Rehab. Met. Chgo., Vis. Nurse Assn., United Parkinson Found., Am. Rehab. Found., Nat. Found., Inc., Am. Assn. Rehab. Therapists, Assn. Phys. and Mental Rehab., Nat. Multiple Sclerosis Soc.; Founding mem. Hebrew U. Jerusalem, 1970—; founding mem. Magen David Adom-Israeli Red Cross, 1978—; mem. Chgo. com Weizmann Inst. Sci., Rehovot, Israel, 1970—; mem. com. Israel Inst. Tech., Technion City, 1970—; v.p. Am. Mus. Phys. Medicine and Rehab., Chgo., 1982—. Served as comdr. M.C. USNR, World War II; head dept. phys. medicine and rehab. Naval Hosps., Oakland, Calif.; head dept. phys. medicine and rehab. Naval Hosps., also Seattle. Recipient B'nai B'rith award in recognition services for rehab. hospitalized vets., 1952; commendation Pres.'s Com. on Employment of Physically Handicapped, 1956; John E. Davis award for outstanding service phys. medicine and rehab. Assn. Phys. and Mental Rehab., 1956; disting. service award Ill. Inst. Tech., 1957; named Civil Servant of Year Fed. Personnel Council Chgo., 1958; meritorious service award VA, 1958; Citation Pub. Service as Useful Citizen U. Chgo., 1959; commendation from adminstr. vets. affairs for success Crusade of Mercy Drive at VA Research Hospital Chgo., 1962; Disting. Service key Am. Congress of Rehab. Medicine, 1963; Nat. Rehab. Citation for outstanding services Am. Legion, 1967; Disting. Achievement award Assn. Med. Rehab. Dirs. and Coordinators, 1967; award for outstanding devotion and achievements in rehab. Ill. and Chgo. Socs. Phys. Medicine and Rehab., 1986; Louis B. Newman Disting. Service award established by Ill. Soc. Phys. Medicine and Rehab., 1980; represented in archives Armed Forces Med. Library, 1956, 80. Fellow Am. Geriatrics Soc.; mem. Am. Congress Rehab. Medicine (v.p.; chmn. midwestern sect. 1948-49), AMA (past chmn. sect. on phys. medicine), Ill. Soc. Phys. Medicine and Rehab. (founding mem., 1st pres., recognition award 1986), Inst. Medicine Chgo. (rehab. com.), Nat. Multiple Sclerosis Soc. (med. adv. bd.), Internat. Soc. Rehab. of Disabled, World Med. Assn., Ill., Chgo. med. socs., Am. Acad. Phys. Medicine and Rehab. (pres.), Chgo. Heart Assn. (rehab. com.), Ill. Assn. Professions (charter mem.), Vis. Nurse Assn. (mem. med. adv. com. 1967—), Am. Assn. Electromyography and Electrodiagnosis, Am. Inst. Ultrasonics in Medicine. Address: 400 E Randolph St - 3219 Chicago IL 60601

NEWMAN, MARC ALAN, electrical engineer; b. Jasper, Ind., Nov. 21, 1955; s.Leonard Jay and P. Louise (Shainberg) N.; m. Shelley Jane Martin, Aug. 13, 1977. BSEE, Purdue U., 1977, MSEE, 1979. Sr. elec. engr. Sperry Corp. Flight Systems, Phoenix, 1979-85; staff engr. Motorola Inc., Tempe, Ariz., 1985-88, Quincy St. Corp., Phoenix, 1988—; prolog expert Motorola Inc., Tempe, 1985—. Mem. IEEE, Am. Assn. Artificial Intelligence, Ariz. Artifical Intelligence Assn. (founder), Internat. Platform Assn., Phi Sigma Kappa, Eta Kappa Nu. Home: 18414 N 46th Dr Glendale AZ 85308 Office: Motorola Inc Govt Electronics Group 2100 E Elliot Rd Tempe AZ 85282

NEWMAN, MAURICE STANLEY, accountant, educator; b. Southchurch, Eng., July 12, 1917; came to U.S., 1931, naturalized, 1939; s. David S. and Mabel (Campbell-Everden) N.; B.B.A., CCNY, 1947; M.B.A., N.Y. U., 1966, Ph.D., 1972; m. Ann Marie Schwartz, July 22, 1943; children—James William, David Frederick, Nancy Louise Newman Limata, Susan Catherine Newman Schmierer, John Campbell, Sarah Jane Hughes. Asst. office mgr. Bank Manhattan Co., N.Y.C., 1936-43; chief acct. consumer fin. div. Irving Trust Co., N.Y.C., 1945-47; mgr. Arthur Andersen & Co., N.Y.C., 1947-51; mgmt. cons. Cresap, McCormick & Paget, N.Y.C., 1952-56; partner Deloitte Haskins & Sells, N.Y.C., 1956-77; bd. visitors research prof. Coll. Commerce and Bus. Adminstrn., U. Ala., University, 1976—. Served to lt. (j.g.) USN, 1943-46. C.P.A., N.Y., Calif., Ill., Wis., Iowa, La. Mem. Am. Inst. C.P.A.s, Ala. Soc. C.P.A.s, Calif. Soc. C.P.A.s, Nat. Assn. Accts., Am. Mgmt. Assn. Presbyterian. Clubs: Masons. Shriners; North River Yacht: Hot Springs (Va.) Golf and Tennis, Princeton. Home: 38 Ridgeland Tuscaloosa AL 35406 Office: PO Drawer AC University AL 35486

NEWMAN, MICHAEL RODNEY, lawyer; b. N.Y.C., Oct. 2, 1945; s. Morris and Helen Gloria (Hendler) N.; m. Cheryl Jeanne Anker, June 11, 1967; children—Hillary Abra, Nicole Brooke. B.A., U. Denver, 1967; J.D., John Marshall Law Sch., 1970. Bar: Calif. 1971, U.S. Dist. Ct. (cen. dist.) Calif. 1972, U.S. Dist. Ct. (no. dist.) Calif. 1975, U.S. Dist. Ct. (so. dist.) Calif. 1979, U.S. Dist. Ct. (ea. dist.) Calif. 1983, U.S. Ct. Appeals (9th cir.) 1974, U.S. Tax Ct. 1979, U.S. Supreme Ct. 1978. Assoc., David Daar, 1971-76; ptnr. Daar & Newman, 1976-78, Miller & Daar, 1978-88, Miller & Daar & Newman, 1988— ; judge pro tem Los Angeles Mcpl. Ct., 1982—. Lectr. Eastern Claims Conf., Eastern Life Claims Conf., Nat. Health Care Anti-Fraud Assn., AIA Conf. on Ins. Fraud; Mem. Los Angeles Citizens Organizing Com. for Olympic Summer Games, 1984, mem. govtl. liaison adv. commn. 1984; mem. So. Calif. Com. for Olympic Summer Games, 1984; cert. ofcl. Athletics Congress of U.S., bd. dirs. So. Pacific Assn. Recipient NYU Bronze medal in Physics, 1962; U.S. Navy Sci. award in Math., 1963. Mem. ABA (multi-dist. litigation subcom., com. on class actions), Los Angeles County Bar Assn., Conf. of Ins. Counsel. Office: 11500 W Olympic Blvd Suite 600 Los Angeles CA 90064

NEWMAN, MILTON, dentist, hypnotist; b. Bklyn., Dec. 29, 1930; s. Joe and Ruth (Yormark) N.; B.S., Purdue U., 1951; postgrad. N.Y.U., 1951-52; D.D.S., U. Pa., 1956; M.S., L.I. U., 1979; m. Phyllis Hershkowitz, Dec. 28, 1952; children—Renee Holly, Eileen Sharon, Jeffrey Mark. Pvt. practice dentistry, hypnosis, counseling, Peekskill, N.Y., 1958—; mem. gen. adv. bd. Bd. Coop. Ednl. Services, Yorktown, N.Y., 1978-85, chmn. dental adv. bd., 1966-85; sec. dental dept. Peekskill Community Hosp., 1962-79. Mem. parents exec. com. Purdue U., 1978-82, mem. pres.'s council, 1982—; pres. bd. dirs. Hand to Mouth Players, Garrison, N.Y., 1986-88; bd. dirs. Yorktown Players, 1988—. Served with USAF, 1956-58. Recipient merit cert. Bd. Coop. Ednl. Services, 1976; diplomate Am. Bd. Hypnosis in Dentistry, 1971. Mem. ADA, Am. Personnel and Guidance Assn., Am. Mental Health Counselors Assn., Am. Soc. Clin. Hypnosis, Soc. Clin. and Exptl. Hypnosis, N.Y. Soc. Clin. Hypnosis, Dental Soc. State N.Y., Ninth Dist. Dental Soc., Peekskill-Yorktown Dental Soc. (pres. 1964). Contbr. articles to profl. jours. Club. Deans. Home and Office: 2 Gallows Hill Rd RFD 2 Box 2 Peekskill NY 10566

NEWMAN, PETER JOHN, interior design company executive; b. Brisbane, Queensland, Australia, Feb. 23, 1944; s. Robert Willmot and Gladys Morgans N. Degree in arts, Queensland Tech. Inst., Brisbane, 1960-62. Artist Graphic Advt. Proprietary, Ltd., Brisbane, 1962-63; asst. art dir. T. Hilken Waite Proprietary, Ltd., Brisbane, 1963-65; art dir. McCann-Erickson Proprietary, Ltd., Sydney, Australia, 1965-66; art dir. Ling-McCann-Erickson, Ltd., Bangkok, 1966-68, Hong Kong, 1968-73; project dir. Avant Garde Designs, Ltd., Hong Kong, 1974-77; mng. dir. Design 2000 (Design World Ltd.), Hong Kong, 1977—; promotion sponsor Hong Kong for Cotton Council, Inc., Washington, 1984, 85. Author: (newspaper series) Dwelling on Design, 1979-80. Mem. Royal Soc. Prevention Cruelty to Animals, Alzheimers Disease and Disorders Assn. Recipient Best Poster Design Queensland Govt. State Library, 1961, Best Art Direction Art Dirs. Assn. Thailand, 1968. Mem. Am. Soc. Interior Designers. Mem. Liberal National Party. Clubs: American (Hong Kong), H.L.Y. Country (Hong Kong). Lodges: Roscicrucian, Knights Templars of Aquarius. Office: Design 2000 (Design World Ltd), 363-370 Ocean Ctr, Kowloon Hong Kong

NEWMAN, PHYLLIS, counselor, therapist, hypnotist; b. N.Y.C., Aug. 20, 1933; d. Max and Frieda Yetta (Pechter) Hershkowitz; B.S., Mercy Coll., 1977; M.S., L.I.U., 1979; m. Milton Newman, Dec. 28, 1952; children—Renee Holly, Eileen Sharon, Jeffrey Mark. Pvt. practice hypnosis and therapy, Peekskill, N.Y., 1977—; lectr. in field; lectr. Pepsico Fitness Ctr., Purchase, N.Y., 1984, Purdue U., 1986, 88, Girl Scouts' Council, local radio; dir. counseling Hypnosis Group, 1979—. Mem. parents exec. bd. Purdue U., 1978-83, mem. pres.' council, 1983—; mem. Hand to Mouth Players, Garrison, N.Y. Mem. Am. Assn. Counseling and Devel., Am. Mental Health Counselors Assn., N.Y. Soc. Ericksonian Hypnosis, Am. Assn. Profl. Hypnotherapists. Contbr. articles to profl. jours. Club. Deans. Address: 2 Gallows Hill Rd RFD Box 2 Peekskill NY 10566

NEWMAN, RALPH GEOFFREY, literary scholar historian; b. Chgo., Nov. 3, 1911; s. Henry and Dora (Glickman) N.; m. Estelle Hoffman, 1934 (div.); children: Maxine (Mrs. Richard G. Brandenburg), Carol (Mrs. Parry); m. Patricia Lyons Simon, 1972. Litt.D., James Milliken U. (Lincoln Coll.), 1950, Knox Coll., Rockford Coll.; LL.D., Iowa Wesleyan Coll.; Litt. D., Meisei U., Tokyo. Founder Abraham Lincoln Book Shop, Inc., Chgo., 1933-84; pres. Americana House, Inc., from 1959, Lincoln's New Salem Enterprises, Inc., from 1952, Ralph Geoffrey Newman, Inc., 1967—, Civil War Enterprises, Inc., 1985—. Author: (with Otto Eisenschiml) The American Iliad, 1947, Abraham Lincoln: An Autobiographical Narrative, 1970; Editor: The Diary of a Public Man, 1945, The Railsplitter, 1950, (with Otto Eisenschiml, E.B. Long) The Civil War, 1956; radio series The Abraham Lincoln Story, 1958-59; Lincoln for the Ages, 1960, (with Otto Eisenchiml) Evewitness, 1960, (with E.B. Long) The Civil War Digest, 1960, Pictorial Autobiography of Abraham Lincoln, 1962, Time-Table for the Lincoln Funeral, 1965, Abraham Lincoln: His Story in His Own Words, 1975, Abraham Lincoln's Last Full Measure of Devotion, 1981; mem. editorial bd.: Civil War History, 1955-70. Chmn. Ill. com. N.Y. World's Fair, 1963-65; chmn. Ill. Sesquicentennial Commn., 1965-69; mem. Ill. Spl. Events Commn., 1969-73; past pres. Adult Edn. Council Greater Chgo.; bd regents Lincoln Acad. Ill.; city archivist, City of Chgo., 1979-80; pres. bd. dirs. Chgo. Public Library, 1964-79; trustee Lincoln Coll.; past chmn. bd. dirs. Ford's Theatre Soc., Washington; pres. Urban Libraries Council, 1970-78. Served with USNR, 1944-45. Recipient diploma of honor Lincoln Meml. U., 1952; Am. of Year award Independence Hall Assn., 1958; Nevins-Freeman award, 1975; laureate Lincoln Acad. Ill., 1983, Barondess award Lincoln Group of N.Y., 1987. Mem. Civil War Round Table Chgo. (founder 1940, Harry S. Truman award Kansas City chpt. 1966), Royal Arts Soc. (London), Abraham Lincoln Assn. (dir.), Stephen A. Douglas Assn. (pres.), Ulysses S. Grant Assn. (pres.), Am., Ind., Ill., Iowa, Kans., Chgo. hist. socs., Am. Legion, ALA, Am. Booksellers Assn., Bibliog. Socs. Am., U.S. Info. Agy. (book and library com.), Soc. Am. Historians, Newberry Library Assocs. Chgo., Phi Alpha Theta. Clubs: Arts, Caxton, Barclay, Carleton, Internat. (Chgo.); Sangamo (Springfield, Ill.).

NEWMAN, SAMUEL, trust company executive; b. N.Y.C., Mar. 12, 1938; s. Aaron and Rachel (Hershkowitz) N.; m. Carolyn Gropper, Oct. 27, 1963; children—Marci Ann, Jodi Robin, Michael David. BBA, CUNY, 1971; grad. Advanced Mgmt. Program, Harvard U., 1982. Methods analyst Bankers Trust Co., N.Y.C., 1960-67; project leader Clark O'Neill SVC Corp., Fairview, N.J., 1967-68; sr. v.p. Irving Trust Co., N.Y.C., 1968-85, Mfrs. Hanover Trust, N.Y.C., 1985—; chmn. bd. dirs. S.W.I.F.T. Terminal Services; chmn. N.Y. Clearing House funds transfer com.; speaker industry confs. Contbr. articles to profl. jours. Served with U.S. Army, 1957-60. Mem. Soc. Worldwide Fin. Telecommunication (bd. dirs. 1978—). Office: Manufacturers Hanover Trust Co 4 New York Plaza 22nd Floor New York NY 10015

NEWMAN, SCOTT DAVID, lawyer; b. N.Y.C., Nov. 5, 1947; s. Edwin Stanley and Evaline Ada (Lipp) N.; m. Judy Lynn Monchik, June 24, 1972; 1 child, Eric. B.A. magna cum laude, Yale U., 1969; J.D., Harvard U., 1973, M.B.A., 1973; LL.M. in Taxation, NYU, 1977. Bar: N.Y. 1974, U.S. Dist. Ct. (so. and ea. dists.) N.Y. 1975, U.S. Ct. Appeals (2d cir.) 1975, U.S. Ct. Claims 1976, U.S. Tax Ct. 1979. Assoc. Dewey, Ballantine, Bushby, Palmer & Wood, N.Y.C., 1973-76, Stroock & Stroock & Lavan, N.Y.C., 1976-78; assoc., ptnr. Zimet, Haines, Moss & Friedman, N.Y.C., 1978-81; tax counsel Phibro-Salomon Inc., N.Y.C., 1981-84; ptnr. Baer, Marks & Upham, N.Y.C., 1984-87; ptnr. Wiener, Zuckerbrot, Weiss & Newman, N.Y.C., 1987—. Co-author tape cassettes: New Tax Reform Act of 1976, Tax Reform' '78, 1978. Tax Reform Act of 1984, 1986, Tax Reform Act of 1986, 1986; contbr. article to profl. jour. Mem. Phi Beta Kappa. Home: 21 Kipp St Chappaqua NY 10514 Office: Wiener Zuckerbrot Weiss & Newman 260 Madison Ave New York NY 10016

NEWMAN, SHELDON OSCAR, computer company executive; b. N.Y.C., June 25, 1923; s. Morris and Anna (Schlanger) N.; m. Miriam Jasphy, July 30, 1950; children—Barry Marc, Amy Stacy, Andrew Eric. B.S.E.E., CUNY, 1944. Project engr. NASA, Sunnyvale, Calif., 1946-47; gen. mgr. info. and communications div. Sperry Corp., Gt. Neck, N.Y., 1947-67; chmn. bd., chief exec. officer Algorex Corp., Syosset, N.Y., 1968—. Chmn. bd. trustees Orthopaedic Inst., Hosp. for Joint Diseases, N.Y.C.; bd. dirs. HJD Research and Devel. Found.; pres. Pine Lake Park Coop. Assn., Peekskill, N.Y. Patentee in field. Served to lt. (j.g.), USN, 1944-46. Mem. IEEE, Archaeol. Inst. Am. (pres.), North Shore Soc., Tau Beta Pi, Eta Kappa Nu. Lodge: Masons.

NEWMAN, STANLEY RAY, oil refining company executive; b. Milo, Idaho, Mar. 5, 1923; s. Franklin Hughes and Ethel Amelda (Crowley) N.; student Tex. A&M U, 1944-45; B.S., U. Utah, 1947, Ph.D., 1952. m. Rosa Klein, May 27, 1961; children—Trudy Lynn, Susan Louise, Karen Elizabeth, Paul Daniel, Phillip John. With Texaco Research Center, Beacon, N.Y., 1951-82, technologist, 1973-77, sr. technologist research mfg.-fuels, 1977-82, profl. cons. on fuels and chems., 1983—. Chmn., Planning Bd., Village of Fishkill, N.Y., 1973- 77; mem. Dutchess County Solid Waste Mgmt. Bd., 1974-76. Served with inf. U.S. Army, 1944, Signal Corps, 1944-46. Mem. N.Y. Acad. Sci., AAAS, Dutchess County Geneal. Soc. (pres. 1981-87, exec. v.p. 1987—), N.Y. Fruit Testing Assn., Sigma Xi (pres. Texaco Research Center br. 1980-81). Republican. Mormon. Patentee in field. Home: 24 Virginia Ave Fishkill NY 12524

NEWMAN, THOMAS DANIEL, clergyman, school administrator; b. London, Eng., May 12, 1922; s. Frederick and Margaret (O'Leary) N.; m. Louise Johannah Albertano, Apr. 1, 1963; 1 dau., Susan (Mrs. Alan J. Rennie). Student, Glasgow Sch. Accounting, 1946, Unity Sch. Christianity, 1962-66, Harvard Div. Sch., 1967—; DSc, Alma Coll., 1975. Mng. dir. Thomas Newman (Printers) Ltd., 1945-49; mng. dir. H. & M.J. Pubs. Ltd., 1947-49, Forget-Me-Not Greeting Cards Ltd., 1949-61, Diplomat Greetings Ltd., 1957-61, Nevill's Ltd., 1955-57; ordained to ministry Christ's Ch., 1966; pastor Christ's Ch., Springfield, Mo., 1966-67, Longwood, Brookline, Mass., 1967—; adminstrv. dir. Am. Schs. Oriental Research, 1968, treas., 1970—, trustee, 1972—; founder Carthage Research Inst., Khereddine, Tunisia, 1975, Cyprus Archaeol. Research Inst., Nicosia, 1977; cons. Joint Archeol. Expdns. to, Ai, 1969-73, to; Tell-El-Hesi, 1970-73, to, Idalion, 1970-73; mem. Joint Archeol. Expdn. to, Caesarea Maritima, 1971, to; Carthage, 1975; dir. Logistics Survey Qu'Rayyah, Saudi Arabia, 1973; pub. cons. (Dead Sea Scrolls Com.), 1968-73; Trustee Allbright Inst. Archeol. Research, Jerusalem.; Am. Center Oriental Research, Amman, Jordan. Served with RAF, 1940-45. Mem. Archeol. Inst. Am., Soc. Bibl. Lit., Soc. O.T. Studies. Clubs: Mason, Harvard Faculty; University (Boston) (Sarasota). Home: 8 Club Acre Ln Bedford NH 03102 Office: Colchester and Chapel Sts Brookline MA 02146

NEWMAN, TILLMAN EUGENE, JR., food company executive; b. Greenwood, Ark., Feb. 13, 1938; s. Tillman Eugene and Theresa Christine (Simmons) N.; m. Linda Gail Childers, Feb. 13, 1983; children—James Barton Langley, Robert, John, Michael, Kristen Newman. B.S. in Chem. Engring., U. Ark., 1963. Registered profl. engr., Ark., Iowa, Mo. Plant mgr.

Ralston Purina, St. Louis, 1963-67, project mgr., 1967-71; v.p. Huxtable-Hammond, Kansas City, Mo., 1971-79; dir. engring. Tyson Foods, Russellville, Ark., 1979—; bd. dirs. Mech. Controllers of Iowa, 1976-78; mem. Ark. Allied Industries, Little Rock, 1980—. Bd. dirs. Ark. Fedn. Water and Air, 1984—. Served to sgt. USNG, 1956-65. Mem. Nat. Soc. Profl. Engrs., Am. Inst. Chem. Engrs., Am. Soc. Mech. Engrs., Russellville C. of C. Baptist. Avocations: fishing; boating. Office: Tyson Foods PO Box 847 Russellville AR 72801

NEWMARK, MARILYN, sculptor; b. N.Y.C., July 20, 1928; d. Edward Ellis and Mabel (Davies) Newmark; student Adelphi Coll., 1945-47, Alfred U., 1949; m. Leonard J. Meiselman, Mar. 15, 1952. Sculptor, specializing in horses, equestrian figures, dogs in sporting scenes; exhibited in group shows: sculpture exhbn. Ky. Derby Mus., Calif. Acad. Sci., NAD, Nat. Arts Club, Nat. Art Mus. of Sport (all N.Y.C.), James Ford Bell Mus., Wis., Smithsonian Instn., Washington, Pa. Acad. Natural Scis., Calif. Acad. Scis., Port of History Mus., Pa.; represented in permanent collections Nat. Mus. Racing, Saratoga, N.Y., Internat. Mus. of Horse, Ky. Horse Park, Nat. Art Museum of Sport, also pvt. collections of Harvey Firestone, Whitney Stone, Ogden Phipps, A.B. Hancock Jr., Peggy Agustus, Morgan Firestone, A. Werk Cook. Recipient Anna Hyatt Huntington award, 1970, 71, 72, 75, 78, 80, 81, 82, 83, 86, gold medal, 1973; award Council Am. Artists Socs., 1972, 73, 79, 80; Hudson Valley John Newington award, 1973, 77, gold medal, 1979; NAD Ellin P. Speyer award, 1974, Artist Fund award, 1982. Fellow Nat. Sculpture Soc. (council 1973-75, rec. sec. 1976, sec. 1977-79, council 1981-83, Bronze medal 1986), Am. Artists Profl. League (Gold medal 1974, 77, Medal of Honor 1987); mem. Allied Artists Am. (Gold medal 1981), Pen and Brush Club (gold medal 1977, Solo award 1974, 78, 80), Soc. Animal Artists (jury of admissions 1972-75), Nat. Acad. Equine Artists (founding mem.), Nassau Suffolk Horsemans Assn. (dir., corr. sec.). Clubs: Catherine Lorillard Wolfe Art (jury of admissions N.Y.C. 1972-74); Smithtown Hunt, Nat. Steeplechase and Hunt Assn., Past Meadowbrook Hunt (L.I., N.Y.). Address: Woodhollow Rd East Hills NY 11577

NEWMARK, MILTON MAXWELL, lawyer; b. Oakland, Calif., Feb. 24, 1916; s. Milton and Mary (Maxwell) N.; m. Marion Irene Johnson, July 31, 1941; children—Mari Newmark Anderson, Lucy Newmark Sammons, Grace Newmark Lucini. A.B., U. Calif.-Berkeley, 1936, J.D., 1947. Bar: Calif. 1940, U.S. Supreme Ct. 1944. Ptnr. Milton Newmark, San Francisco, 1941-56; sole practice, 1956-62; sole practice, Lafayette, Calif., 1962-80, Walnut Creek, Calif., 1980—; lectr. bankruptcy State Bar of Calif. Continuing Edn. Program. Served with U.S. Army, 1942-46; to lt. col. USAR. Mem. Alameda County Rep. Cen. Com., 1940-41; pres. Alameda Rep. Assembly, 1950. Mem. Am. Legion, ABA, San Francisco Bar Assn., Contra Costa Bar Assn., Alameda County Bar Assn., Scabbard and Blade. Lodges: Masons, Shriners, Rotary. Home: 609 Terra California Dr No 6 Walnut Creek CA 94595 Office: 1900 Olympic Blvd Suite 103 Walnut Creek CA 94596

NEWPHER, JAMES ALFRED, JR., management consultant; b. New Brighton, Pa., Nov. 14, 1930; s. James Alfred and Olive Myrtle (Houlette) N.; B.S., U. Pa., 1952; M.B.A., Wharton Sch. U. Pa., 1957; m. Mildred Taylor, Aug. 23, 1953. Indsl. engr., Corning Glass Works (N.Y.), 1957-58, plant supr., 1958-60, prodn. supt., 1960-61, plant mgr., 1961-63, dept. mgr. advance products, 1963-64; asso. Booz, Allen & Hamilton, Inc., Chgo., 1964-69; v.p., mng. officer Lamalie Assos., Chgo., 1969-73; pres., chief exec. officer Newpher & Co., Inc., Chgo., 1973—; dir. Design Tech., Inc. Served with USN, 1951-56. Decorated Purple Heart. Mem. Naval Res. Assn., Inst. Mgmt. Cons., Res. Officers Assn. Presbyn. Club: Metropolitan Chgo. Home: 1655 We-Go Trail Deerfield IL 60015 Office: 2215 York Rd Suite 202 Oak Brook IL 60521

NEWPORT, WALTER AUGUSTUS, III, language educator; b. Hays, Kans., Dec. 18, 1945; came to Japan, 1983; s. Walter Augustus and Mildred L. (Albertson) N.; m. Sally Ann Flickinger, Aug. 29, 1969; children—Sarah Albertson, Nathaniel Todd. B.S., Iowa State U., 1969; B.A., U. Minn., 1976; M.A., Middlebury Coll., 1977; specialist credential U. Calif.-Irvine, 1979. Cert. tchr., Calif. Spanish instr. Cerritos Coll., Norwalk, Calif., 1978, Chapman Coll., Orange, Calif., 1979; ESL coordinator Dana Hills High Sch., Dana Point, Calif., 1979-83; Spanish instr. Saddleback Coll., Mission Viejo, Calif., 1977 83; lectr. English and Spanish, Toyama Coll. Fgn. Langs., Japan, 1984—; co-founder, cons. Toyama Internat. Ctr., 1984—. Chmn. welcome com. Christian Ch. (Disciples of Christ), Anaheim, Calif., 1982; organizing mem. Saddleback Christian Ch., Mission Viejo, 1982-83. Served to lt. comdr. USNR, 1969-79. Phi Kappa Phi scholar, 1976; Middlebury Coll. scholar, Madrid, 1976-77. Mem. MLA, Am. Ednl. Research Assn., Am. Tchrs. of Spanish and Portuguese. Avocations: sports; classical music. Home: 2-38 Fujinokidai, Toyama City 930 Japan

NEWSOM, CARROLL VINCENT, retired educator; b. Buckley, Ill., Feb. 23, 1904; s. Curtis Bishop and Mattie F. (Fisher) N.; A.B., Coll. Emporia, 1924, L.H.D., 1957; M.A., U. Mich., 1927, Ph.D., 1931, LL.D., 1974; recipient 25 hon. degrees; m. Frances J. Higley, Aug. 15, 1928; children—Jeanne Carolyn (Mrs. W.A. Challener, III), Walter Burton, Gerald Higley. Mem. faculties U. Mich., U. N.M., Oberlin Coll., 1944-48; asst. commr. for higher edn. State N.Y. 1948-50, asso. commr. for higher and profl. edn., 1950-55; exec. v.p. N.Y. U., 1955-56, pres., 1956-62; pres. Prentice-Hall, Inc., Englewood Cliffs, N.J., 1962-64, vice chmn. bd., 1962-65, pres., 1964-65; chmn. bd. Hawthorn Books, 1964-65; chmn. exec. com. Random House, Inc., 1967-70, dir., 1967-70; ednl. cons. RCA, 1965-66, v.p., 1966-69, dir., 1961-71; edn. cons. instns. in France, Turkey, India, Ethiopia. Mem. and former mem. bds. several orgns. in field of edn., math. and internat. affairs; bd. dirs. Nat. Assn. Ednl. Broadcasters; mem., dir. N.Y. World's Fair Corp., 1959-64; bd. dirs. Guggenheim Found., 1962-76, chmn., 1974-76; mem. several other coms. and bds. Decorated chevalier Legion of Honor (France); recipient Pasteur medal. Fellow AAAS (pres. S.W. div. 1940-41, nat. council 1945-46); Benjamin Franklin fellow Royal Soc. Arts (London); mem. and sometime officer several, nat. profl. assns. and orgns. including Phi Beta Kappa. Author or co-author several books in field math., gen. edn., latest being: (with Howard Eves) Foundations and Fundamental Concepts of Mathematics, 1958; Mathematical Discourses, 1964; The Roots of Christianity, 1979; Problems are for Solving, 1984; also articles profl. jours. Contbr. yearbook Nat. Soc. for Study of Edn., 1952. Editor: A Television Policy for Education, 1952, Am. Math. Monthly, 1947-51. Home: 6000 Riverside Dr Apt B-413 Dublin OH 43017

NEWSOM, DOUGLAS ANN JOHNSON, journalist, educator; b. Dallas, Jan. 16, 1934; d. J. Douglas and R. Grace (Dickson) Johnson; BJ cum laude, U. Tex., 1954, BFA summa cum laude, 1955, M in Journalism 1956, PhD, 1978; m. L. Mack Newsom, Jr., Oct. 27, 1956 (dec.); children: Michael Douglas, Kevin Jackson, Nancy Elizabeth, William Macklemore. Gen. publicity State Fair Tex., 1955; advt. and promotion Newsom's Women's Wear, 1956-57; publicity Auto Market Show, 1961; lab. instr. radio-tv news-writing course U. Tex., 1961-62; local publicist Tex. Boys Choir, 1964-69, nat. publicist, 1967-69; pub. relations dir. Gt. S.W. Boat Show Dallas, 1966-72, Family Fun Show, 1970-71, Horace Ainsworth Co., Dallas, 1966-76; pres. Profl. Devel. Cons.'s, Inc., non-profit seminar prodn.; faculty Tex. Christian U., Ft. Worth, 1969—, prof. dept. journalism, chmn. dept., 1979-86, adviser yearbook and mag., 1969-79; dir. ONEOK Inc., diversified energy co. Sec.-treas., Public Relations Found. Tex., 1979-80, also trustee; public relations chmn. local Am. Heart Assn., 1973-76, state public relations com. 1974-82, chmn., 1980-82; trustee Found. for Pub. Relations Research and Edn., 1985—; mem. Gas Research Adv. Council, 1981—. Mem. Assn. Edn. in Journalism (pres. public relations div. 1974-75, nat. pres. 1984-88), Women in Communications (nat. conv. treas. 1967, nat. public relations chmn. 1969-71), Public Relations Soc. Am. (nat. edn. com. 1975, chmn. 1978, nat. faculty adviser, chmn. edn. sect.), Tex. Public Relations Assn. (dir. 1976-84, v.p. 1980-82, pres. 1982-83), Am. Women in Radio and TV, Delta Delta Delta, Mortar Bd. Alumnae (adviser Tex. Christian U. 1974-75). Episcopalian. Author: (with Alan Scott) This is PR, 1976, 3d edit., 1984, (with Bob Carrell) Writing for Public Relations Practice, 1981, 2d edit., 1986, (with Jim Wollert) Media Writing, 1984, 2d edit., 1988; editorial bd. Public Relations Rev., 1978-82. Home: 4237 Shannon Dr Fort Worth TX 76116 Office: Tex Christian U Dept Journalism PO Box 32930 Fort Worth TX 76129

NEWSOM, MICKEY BRUNSON, management and political consultant; b. Columbia, Miss., July 26, 1941; s. James Hezzie and Opal Eugenia (Prescott) N.; A.A., Hartnell Coll., 1961; B.B.A., Golden Gate U., 1964, M.B.A., 1976; m. Rose Marie Christensen, May 25, 1963. Mgr., Roy's Restaurants, Salinas, Calif., 1964-67; prin. Humboldt County Schs., Redcrest, Calif., 1967-69; educator Bur. Indian Affairs, Wide Ruins, Ariz., 1969-71; owner Hardware Auto Store, Columbus, Miss., 1971-80, Newsom & Co., 1971—; cons. State of La., 1981—. Polit. cons. various state and nat. candidates; mem. Mcpl. Democratic Exec. Com., 1977-80; bd. dirs. County Assn. Retarded Citizens, 1979-80. Mem. East Miss. Council (dir. 1977-80), Forest Farmers Assn., Nat. Assn. Suggestion Systems. Democrat. Lutheran. Clubs: Columbus Civitan (pres. 1977-78, lt. gov. Miss. North dist. 1978-79); Commonwealth of Calif. Lodge: Kiwanis. Mailing Address: PO Box 2455 Chalmette LA 70044

NEWSON, LLOYD JAMES, choreographer; b. Albury, New South Wales, Mar. 2, 1957; s. Owen James and Gloria Marie (Faulkiner) N. Hon. Degree in Psychology/BSW, U. Melbourne, Victoria, Australia, 1979; student, London Sch. Contemporary Dance, 1980-81. Dancer, choreographer Modern Dance Ensemble, Victoria, 1976-77, Impulse Dance Theatre/ New Zealand Ballet Co., Wellington, 1979, Extemporary Dance Theatre, London, 1981-85; freelance dancer, choreographer Eng., 1985-86; artistic dir. D.V.8 Phys. Theatre, London, 1986—; choreographer dance creation; various commns. Arts Council Gt. Britain, 1986-87. Recipient Tng. award Arts Council Great Britain, 1984, Choreographic Bursary Greater London Arts, 1985, Dance award Manchester Evening News Theatre, 1987, Dance award Digital Equipment Co., 1986-88. Mem. Actors Equity Assn. (rep. 1982-85), Nat. Orgn. for Dance/Mime. Office: DV8 Physical Theatre, 17 Dukes Rd, London WC1, England

NEWSTEAD, ROBERT RICHARD, urologist; b. Detroit, Sept. 16, 1935; s. Oran Henry and Agnes Audery (Lewandowski) N.; m. Marie Carmela LiPuma, Aug. 5, 1961; children: Elizabeth Marie, Peter Joseph, Angela Agnes, Paul Michael. Student, Coll. Idaho, 1955-57, Quincy Coll., 1957-58; MD, Loyola U., Chgo., 1963. Intern Walter Reed Gen. Hosp., Washington, 1963-64; resident U. Iowa, Iowa City, 1967-71; urologist Urology Clinic Yakima, Wash., 1971-84, pres., 1984—; chief of surgery St. Elizabeth Med. Ctr., Yakima, 1980-81, Yakima Valley Hosp., 1978-79. Bd. dirs. St. Elizabeth Found., Yakima, 1983—, The Capital Theater, 1987—, Boy Scouts Am., Yakima, 1982-86. Served to capt. U.S. Army, 1962-67. Fellow Am. Cancer Soc., Iowa City, 1969-70, Am. Cancer Soc., 1961; named one of Outstanding Young Men Am., 1968. Fellow Am. Bd. Urology, ACS, Am. Urol. Assn., Wash. State Urol. Bd.; mem. AMA, Rubin Flocks Soc. (pres. 1985-86), Yakima Surgical Soc. (pres. 1982-83), Yakima County Med. Soc. (pres. elect 1988-89). Roman Catholic. Lodge: Rotary. Home: 814 Conestoga Blvd Yakima WA 98908 Office: Urology Clinic Yakima 206 S 11th Ave Yakima WA 98902

NEWTON, ALICE FAYE, health services company executive; b. Brownsville, Ind., Nov. 2, 1937; d. Richard Smith and Myrtle Mae (Hill) Adams; m. Edward Leo Newton, June 7, 1957; children: Kevin L., Teri Newton Whitehead, Christopher Edward. Grad. high sch., Broadhead, Ky., 1955. Sec. to pres. Humana Inc., Louisville, 1966-70, asst. corp. sec., 1970-80, corp. sec., 1980—. Mem. Am. Soc. Corp. Secs. Democrat. Baptist. Office: Humana Inc 500 W Main St Humana Bldg Louisville KY 40202

NEWTON, GEORGE ADDISON, investment banker, lawyer; b. Denver, Apr. 2, 1911; s. George Addison and Gertrude (Manderson) N.; m. Mary Virginia Powell, Sept. 18, 1937; children: George Addison IV, Nancy Ella, Virginia Powell. A.B., U. Colo., 1933; LL.B., Harvard U., 1936. Bar: Ill. 1937, Mo. 1946. Asso. firm Scott, MacLeish & Falk, Chgo., 1936-42; partner G.H. Walker & Co., St. Louis, 1946-62; mng. partner G.H. Walker & Co., 1962-72; chmn. bd. Stifel Nicolaus & Co., Inc., St. Louis, 1972-82, chmn. emeritus, 1982—; chief exec. officer Stifel Nicolaus & Co., Inc., 1974-78. Bd. govs. Greater St. Louis Community Chest; mem. Council on Civic Needs; bd. dirs. Episcopal Home for Children, St. Luke's Hosp.; bd. dirs. Goodwill Industries, 1963—, chmn. bd., 1980-82; bd. dirs. U. Colo. Improvement Corp., U. Colo. Found., St. Louis Conservatory Music; dir. devel. fund U. Colo., 1954-55, chmn., 1955; trustee Fontbonne Coll., 1972-80, chmn., 1974-77; trustee Govtl. Research Inst.; trustee, Whitfield Sch., 1978—, pres. 1986—. Served to maj. USAAF, 1942-45. Recipient C. Fobb award U. Colo., 1955, alumni recognition award, 1958; named to C Club Hall Fame, 1968; silver ann. All Am. award Sports Illustrated, 1957, Norlin award U. Colo., 1968; U. Colo. medal, 1984. Mem. Investment Bankers Assn. Am. (pres. 1961), Nat. Assn. Securities Dealers (gov. 1954-56, vice chmn. 1956), Assn. Stock Exchange Firms (gov. 1969-72), Sales Execs. Assn. (dir. 1955-60), U. Colo. Assn. Alumni (dir. 1965-67), Japan-Am. Soc. St. Louis (dir. 1980—, pres. 1982-85), Phi Beta Kappa, Phi Gamma Delta. Episcopalian (treas. diocese of Mo., 1958-69; sr. warden; trustee diocesan investment trust). Clubs: Racquet (St. Louis), Noonday (St. Louis), St. Louis (St. Louis), Bellerive Country (St. Louis); Denver Country; Legal (Chgo.); Boulder (Colo.) Country; Links (N.Y.C.). Home: 6428 Cecil Ave Saint Louis MO 63105 Office: 500 N Broadway Saint Louis MO 63102

NEWTON, RICHARD WARD, pediatric neurologist; b. Cleethorpes, Eng., Dec. 27, 1950; s. John Richard and Barbara Ward (Duckles) N.; m. Judith Alison Hyde, Oct. 4, 1980; children: Sarah Louise, Michael John. MB BS, Kings Coll. Hosp. Med. Sch., 1973. Cert. child and adolescent neurology. Physician King's Coll. Hosp., London, 1973-74; gen. practice trainee Humberside Vocat. Tng. Scheme, Hull on Humberside, Eng., 1974-77; registrar pediatrics Hull Royal Infirmary, 1977-78; tutor and registrar in child health U. Manchester (Eng.) St. Mary's Hosp., 1978-79; sr. registrar pediatric neurology Children's Hosp. Manchester, 1979-83; cons. in child and adolescent neurology Manchester Childrens Hosp., 1983—; cons. in child and adolescent neurology Booth Hall Children's Hosps., Manchester. Contbr. articles to profl. jours. Mem. Royal Coll. Physicians UK (standing com. 1979-84), Soc. Reproductive and Infant Psychology (chmn. 1986—), Manchester Pediatric Club, Manchester Med. Soc., British Pediatric Neurology Assn. Anglican. Office: Royal Manchester Childrens Hosp, Hosp Rd, Pendlebury M27 1HA, England

NEWTON-SMITH, WILLIAM HERBERT, philosopher; b. Orillia, Ont., Can., May 25, 1943; s. John William and Kathleen Elizabeth (Tinbombe) N.; m. Doris Heffron, June 29, 1968 (div. 1980); children: Apple Casey, Raine Kelly. BA, Queen's Coll., Ont., 1966; MA, Cornell U., N.Y., 1969; PhD, Oxford U., Eng., 1974. Sr. tutor Balliol Coll. Oxford U., 1978-81, sr. proctor, 1984-85; curator Bodleian Library, Oxford, 1985—; bd. dirs. Oxcom Ltd., Oxford; editor Routledge & Kegan Paul, London, 1982—. Author: The Structure of Time, 1980, The Rationality of Science, 1981, Logic, 1984. Trustee Jan Hus Ednl. Found., London, 1981—. Fairfax fellow Balliol Coll., Oxford, 1970—, Hon. fellow Champlain Coll., Ont., 1981, Hon. Prof. Keele U., Eng., 1986. Mem. Labour party. Home: 92 Lonsdale Rd, Oxford OX2 7ER, England Office: Balliol Coll, Broad St, Oxford OX1 3BJ, England

NEYER, JOSEPH, educator, writer, lecturer; b. New Rochelle, N.Y., Mar. 8, 1913; s. Louis and Tillie (Berzon) N.; m. Friderika Ginsberg, July 26, 1966. A.B. magna cum laude, Harvard U., 1934, A.M., 1935, Ph.D., 1942; student, U. Paris, 1936-37. Asst. philosophy Harvard U., 1937-38, 39-40; research asst. anthropology U. Chgo., 1938-39; instr. philosophy Vassar Coll., 1940-42; Rockefeller fellow 1946-47; mem. faculty Rutgers U., 1947—, prof. philosophy, 1963-75, prof. emeritus, 1975—, chmn. dept., 1953-65. Author articles in social and polit. philosophy, sociology, psychoanalysis, recent Middle East history.; mem. editorial bd.: Middle East Review; adv. bd.: Jerusalem Quar. Served with AUS, 1942-46. Mem. Am. Profs. for Peace in Middle East (mem. nat. steering com.), Am. Acad. Assn. Peace in Middle East (vice-chmn. bd. dirs.), Am. Sociol. Assn., Am. Philos. Soc., Phi Beta Kappa. Home: 55 W 11th St New York NY 10011 Office: Dept Philosophy Rutgers Univ New Brunswick NJ 08903

NEZONDET, PIERRE L., trading company executive; b. Paris, June 25, 1947; s. Raymond L. and Louise (Bergeron) N.; m. Marie-Jean Cusin; children: Carine V., Romain R. Grad. in Engring., Arts et Metiers, Paris, 1971; grad. in Mgmt., Cesa, Jouy en Josas, France, 1980. Sales area mgr. Ingersoll, Paris, 1973-76; product mgr. Hahn and Kolb, Paris, 1974-77, mng. dir. asst., 1977-81; mng. dir. Omnitechnique, Paris, 1981—, Hi-Tec, Paris, 1981—. Served with French mil., 1971-72. Home: 37 Parc D'Ardenay, 91120 Palaiseau France Office: Omnitechnique, 33 Rue Charles de Gaulle, 91400 Orsay France

NG, CHI-FAI RAYMOND, transportation company executive; b. Hong Kong, July 28, 1947; s. Yan Kee and Kit Young (Chan) N.; m. Po-Ping Tang; children: Salina, Betty, Michael. Student, Hong Kong Poly. Coll., 1967-69. Accts. and gen. mgr. Walter Isbrandtsen & Assocs., Hong Kong, 1970-73; dir. Gyro Shipping Ltd., Hong Kong, 1973—. Mem. com. Hong Kong Chinese Fine Arts Assn., 1986—. Mem. Brit. Inst. Mgmt. (chartered sec. and adminstr.), Assn. Internat. Accts. Club: Hilltop Country. Office: Kentex Container Services Co Ltd, Ste 403 The Centre Mark, 287-299 Queen's Rd, Central Hong Kong Hong Kong

NG, LAWRENCE MING-LOY, cardiologist; b. Hong Kong, Mar. 21, 1940; came to U.S., 1967, naturalized, 1977; s. John Iu-cheung and Mary Wing (Wong) N.; B.Med., U. Hong Kong, 1965, B.Surg., 1965; m. Bella May Ha Kan, June 25, 1971; children—Jennifer Wing-mui, Jessica Wing-yee. House physician Queen Elizabeth Hosp., Hong Kong, 1965-66, med. officer, 1966-67; resident physician Children's Hosp. of Los Angeles, 1967-68; resident physician Children's Hosp. Med. Center, Oakland, Calif., 1968-70, fellow in pediatric cardiology, 1970-72, now mem. teaching staff; practice medicine, specializing in pediatrics and pediatric cardiology, San Leandro, Calif., 1972—, Oakland, Calif., 1982—; chief of pediatrics Oakland Hosp., 1974-77; chief of pediatrics Vesper Meml. Hosp., 1977-79, sec. staff, 1984, v.p. staff, 1985; chief pediatrics Meml. Hosp., San Leandro, 1986-88. Active Republican Party. Diplomate Am. Bd. Pediatrics. Fellow Am. Acad. Pediatrics; mem. AMA, Calif. Med. Assn., Am. Heart Assn., Los Angeles Pediatric Soc., East Bay Pediatric Soc., Smithsonian Assos., Nat. Geog. Soc., Orgn. Chinese Ams. (chpt. pres. 1984), Chinese-Am. Physicians Soc. (co-founder, sec. 1980, pres. 1983), Oakland Mus. Assns., Oakland Chinatown C. of C. (bd. dirs. 1986—). Buddhist. Club: Bay-O-Vista. Office: 345 9th St Suite 204-205 Oakland CA 94607 Other: 1234 E 14th St Suite 401 San Leandro CA 94577

NG, RICHARD FOOK SANG, audio consultant; b. Singapore, Dec. 2, 1947; s. Chee Yan and Foong(Oh) Ng Shum. B.Sc., U. Singapore, 1971. Materials planner Texas Instruments Co., Singapore, 1971-75; audio visual mgr. Rank O'Connor's, Singapore, 1975-79; exec. dir. Audio Synergy Pte Ltd., Singapore, 1979-82, mng. dir., 1982—; freelance microcomputer and software cons., 1987—; physical fitness cons., 1987—. Contbr. articles to profl. jours. Mem. Audio Engring. Soc. N.Y., Acoustical Soc. Am. (assoc.). Lodge: Rosicrucians. Home and Office: 5 Lorong 33, Geylang, Singapore 1438 Singapore

NG, SIK-HUNG, psychology educator; b. Hong Kong, Nov. 17, 1946; came to N.Z., 1976; s. Chew and Sau Mui (Chan) Ng; m. Grace Fung-Mo Yan, July 8, 1972; 1 son, Hallmian Victor. B.Soc.Sc. with honors, U. Hong Kong, 1970, M.Soc.Sc., 1974; Ph.D., U. Bristol, 1978. Research asst. U. Hong Kong, 1970-72; tutor The Chinese U. Hong Kong, 1973; lectr. U. Otago, Dunedin, N.Z., 1976-83, sr. lectr. dept. psychology, 1983—; vis. lectr. The Chinese U., Hong Kong, 1982. Author: The Social Psychology of Power, 1980; contbr. articles in field to profl. jours. Interpretor, Dunedin Chinese Ch., 1979-. Recipient bursary Am. Women's Assn., Hong Kong, 1967-70, Hunter award, 1986; scholarship Brit. Council, Hong Kong, 1973-74; post-grad. scholarship U. Bristol, Eng., 1974-76; research grantee U. Otago Research Com., 1976—, Social Sci. Research Fund Com., 1983-87, C. C. Ding Research Fund, 1985, N.Z. Health Dept., 1987—. Mem. Internat. Assn. Cross-cultural Psychology, Internat. Assn. Applied Psychology, British Psychol. Soc., European Assn. Exptl. Social Psychology, Royal Soc. N.Z. Office: Psychology Dept, U Otago, PO Box 56, Dunedin New Zealand

NGAI, YIN LEUNG STEPHEN, dermatologist; b. Hong Kong, June 24, 1949; s. Lam Sai and Pui Lan (Cheung) N.; m. Hei Pun, Aug. 30, 1982; children: Yue Ching Eugene, Yue Yan Ian. MB, BS, U. Hong Kong, 1973; Diploma in Dermatology, U. London, 1979. Intern Queen Mary Hosp., Hong Kong, 1973-74; resident in gen. medicine and dermatology Auckland Hosp. Bd., New Zealand, 1974-78; practice medicine specializing in dermatology Hong Kong, 1979—; staff dermatologist St. Teresa's Hosp., Hong Kong, 1980—, Our Lady of Maryknoll Hosp., Hong Kong, 1982—; cons. dermatologist Fedn. Trade Unions, Hong Kong, 1984—, Hong Kong Stockbrokers Assn., 1982, Cathay Pacific Airways, 1980—. Contbr. articles to profl. jours. Fellow Hong Kong Coll. Physicians; mem. Royal Coll. Physicians (U.K.), Hong Kong Assn. Dermatology (hon. sec. 1985-87, vice chmn. 1987—), Asian Dermatol. Assn. Home: 8A 45 Conduit Rd, Hong Kong Hong Kong Office: Room 807 Hang Shing Bldg, 363 Nathan Rd, Kowloon Hong Kong

NGARUKIYINTWALI, FRANÇOIS, minister of foreign affairs and cooperation of Rwanda; b. Janje, Rwanda, Dec. 5, 1940; married; 5 children. Student Universite d'Etat de Liege, Belgium, 1962-64. First sec. Rwanda Embassy, Kinshasa, Zaire, 1964-66, charge d'affaires, 1966-68; dir. gen. external relations Ministry Fgn. Affairs and Cooperation Rwanda, Kigali, 1968-73, sec. gen., 1973-76, minister fgn. affairs and cooperation, 1979—; ambassador of Rwanda to Fed. Republic Germany, Switzerland and Austria, Bonn, Fed. Republic Germany, 1976-79; permanent rep. of Rwanda to UN, Geneva, 1976-79, to UN Orgn. for Indsl. Devel., 1976-79; mem. central com. Nat. Revolutionary Movement Rwanda, from 1980; mem. Prefectorial Council Rwanda, 1981—; dep. Nat. Council Devel. Rwanda, 1982—. Decorated comdr. Nat. Order of the Revolution; various fgn. hon. distinctions. Office: Ministry Fgn Affairs, Kigali Rwanda *

NGEI, PAUL, politician; b. Machakos, Kenya, 1923. BSc in Econs., Makerere Coll., Kampala, Uganda. Founder Wasya wa Mukamba newspaper and Uhuru wa Mwafrika, 1950; dep. gen. sec. Kenya African Union, 1951-52; pres. Kenya African Farmers' and Traders' Union, 1961; founder African People's Party, 1962; chair Maize Mktg. Bd., 1963-64; minister co-operatives and mktg. Kenya Govt., 1964-65, minister housing and social services, 1965-66, minister for housing, 1966-74, minister local govt., 1974-75, M.P. for Kagunda, 1976—, minister of co-operative devel., 1976-79, minister of works, 1979-82, minister of livestock devel., 1982-83, minister of lands and settlement, 1983-84, minister of environment and nat. resources, 1984-85, minister of water devel., from 1985, minister of culture and social services, 1988—; mng. dir. Akamba Carving and Indsl. Co. Office: Ministry of Culture and, Social Services, Nairobi Kenya *

NGOERAH, I GOESTI NGOERAH GDE, neurologist, educator; b. Denpasar, Bali, Indonesia, Mar. 31, 1923; s. I Gusti Made Oka.; m. I Gusti Ayu Oka Arwati, Mar. 18, 1953; 8 children. MD, U. Indonesia, 1948. Student asst. U. Indonesia, Jakarta, 1945-48, asst. neurologist, 1950-53; with Indonesian Red Cross, 1945-50; gen. practice medicine Bdung area, Indonesia, 1953-59; dir. Wangaya Hosp., 1959-65; dean faculty of medicine Udayana U., Denpasar, 1964-68, assoc. prof. neurology, 1965-68, prof., 1968—, head dept., 1964—, pres. of univ., 1968-77; vis. prof. various univs. India, U.K., Australia, 1970-77. Author: The Principles of Neurology, 1988; contbr. numerous articles to profl. jours. Mem. Provisional Peoples Consultative Assembly; chmn. Bali regional com. Provisional Peoples Assembly, 1968-72. Decorated Satya 2d class, Indonesia; recipient Alma Anugrah award for excellent service Udayana U., 1987. Mem. Indonesian Med. Assn., Indonesian Neurol. Assn., N.Y. Acad. Scis. Mem. Golongan Karya Party. Hoome: Jalan Jendral Sudirman 14, Denpasar, Bali 80113, Indonesia Office: Udayana U Dept Neurology, RSU Wangaya Jalan Kartini 109, Denpasar, Bali Indonesia

NGUGI, WA THIONG'O (JAMES), author; b. Limuru, Kenya, 1938. Educated Makerere Univ. Coll., Uganda and Leeds, U., Eng. Lectr. lit. U. Nairobi, 1967-69; fellow in creative writing Makerere U., 1969-70; vis. assoc. prof. Northwestern U., Evanston, Ill., 1970-71; former sr. lectr. and chmn. lit. dept. U. Nairobi. Books include: Weep Not Child, 1964; The River Between, 1965; A Grain of Wheat, 1967; Petals of Blood (novel), 1977; Devil on the Cross, 1978; (with Micere Mugo) The Trial of Dedan Kimati, 1977; Detained: A Writer's Prison Diary, 1981; Maitu Njugira, Devil on the Cross, 1982; Homecoming (essays), 1972; Secret Lives (short stories), 1973; plays include: The Black Hermit, 1962; (with others) I'll Marry When I Choose, 1981. *

NGUJO, GRACE TAGHOY, dentist, educator; b. Cebu City, Philippines, Apr. 20, 1960; d. Tiburcio B. and Carmen Sierras (Taghoy) N.; m. George Uy Chang, Sept. 18, 1983; 1 child, Geff Henderson. DDM, Southwestern U, 1983. Sales rep. Cebu Far Eastern Drug, Inc., Cebu City, Philippines, 1983—; instr., mem. profl. staff Cebu Doctors Coll. Dentistry, 1984—. Mem. Philippine Dental Assn., Cebu Dental Soc. Roman Catholic. Home: Bayanihan Village, Basak Pardo, Cebu City 6000, Philippines Office: Cebu Far Eastern Drug Inc, 99 101 Juan Luna St, Cebu City 6401, Philippines

NGUYEN, ANN CAC KHUE, pharmaceutical and bioorganic chemist; b. Sontay, Vietnam; came to U.S., 1975; naturalized citizen; d. Nguyen Van Soan and Luu Thi Hieu. BS, U. Saigon, 1973; MS, San Francisco State U., 1978; PhD, U. Calif., San Francisco, 1983. Teaching and research asst. U. Calif., San Francisco, 1978-83, postdoctoral fellow, 1983-86; research scientist U. Calif., 1987—. Contbr. articles to profl. jours. Recipient Nat. Research Service award, NIH, 1981-83; Regents fellow U. Calif., San Francisco, 1978-81. Mem. Am. Chem. Soc., AAAS, Bay Area Enzyme Mechanism Group, Nat. Coop. Drug Discovery Group. Roman Catholic. Home: 1488 Portola Dr San Francisco CA 94127 Office: U Calif Dept Pharmaceutical Chemistry San Francisco CA 94143

NGUYEN, CHARLES CUONG, engineering educator, researcher; b. Danang, Vietnam, Jan. 1, 1956; came to U.S., 1978, naturalized, 1984; s. Buoi and Tinh Thi Nguyen. Diplom Ing. Konstanz U., Fed. Republic Germany, 1978; M.S. with distinction, George Washington U., 1980, D.Sc. with superior performance, 1982. Engr. Siemens Corp., Erlangen, Fed. Republic Germany, 1977-78; lectr. George Washington U., Washington, 1978-82; asst. prof. engring. Cath. U. Am., Washington, 1982-87, assoc. prof. elec. engring., 1987—; dir. Ctr. for Artificial Intelligence and Robotics, 1985—. Contbr. numerous papers IEEE Transaction of Automatic Control, Internatl Jour of Control. NASA and Am. Soc. Elec. Engrs. fellowship, 1985, 86; recipient Research Initiation award Engring. Found., 1985. Mem. IEEE (v.p. Washington chpt.), Internat. Soc. Mini- and Microcomputers, Sigma Xi, Tau Beta Pi. Roman Catholic. Avocations: guitar, singing, tennis, skiing, ping pong.

NGUYEN, MICHAEL X.N., computer scientist; b. Saigon, Vietnam, July 23, 1959; arrived in Can., 1975; s. Van Trang and Thi Quy N. Diploma coll. studies, Dawson Coll., Montreal, 1979; BS, McGill U., Montreal, 1982. Programmer The Mercantile Bank Can., Montreal, 1981-83; programmer analyst Assumption Mut. Life, Moncton, Can., 1983-85, info. ctr. mgr., 1985-86; sr. cons. ScotiaTech, Bedford, Can., 1986—. Fellow Life Mgmt. Inst.; mem. Assn. Inst. Cert. Computer Profls. Office: ScotiaTech, 3 Bedford Hills Rd, Bedford, NS Canada B4A1J5

NGUYEN, PAUL DUNG QUOC, lawyer; b. Hung Yen, Vietnam, Feb. 2, 1943; came to U.S., 1975; s. Trac Trong and Do Thi (Vu) N.; m. Kim-Dung T. Dang, Dec. 26, 1967; children: Theresa Thu, Catherine Bao-Chau, Jonathan Hung. LLB, Hue Law Sch., Vietnam, 1965; MA in Pub. Policy Adminstrn., U. Wis., 1973. Bar: N.Y. 1979, U.S. Dist. Ct. (so. and ea. dists.) N.Y. 1979, U.S. Tax Ct. 1979. Prof. law Hue & Can Tho Law Schs., Vietnam, 1973-75; assoc. Proskauer, Rose, Getz & Mendelsohn, N.Y.C., 1979-80; sole practice N.Y.C., 1980-81; corp. law specialist City of New York, 1981—. Bd. dirs. N.Y.C. Indochinese Refugees, 1980—. Recipient Nat. Legion Honor award Office of Pres., Saigon, 1970. Mem. ABA, Assn. of Bar of City of N.Y. (Outstanding Performance prize com. on mcpl. affairs 1986). Office: NYC Law Dept Office Corp Counsel 100 Church St New York NY 10007

NGUYEN, PHAN TUAN, otolaryngologist; b. Hanoi, Vietnam, Nov. 21, 1936; arrived in France, 1953.; s. Hop Gian and Thi Dang (Phan) N.; m. Monique Ligot, Dec. 16, 1967; children: Stéphane, Philippe, Hervé. Degree in physics, chem., biology, Sci. U., Paris, 1955; MD, Faculté de Médécine, Paris, 1964. Intern Orleans' (France) Hosp., 1963-66; physician chief substitute Hosp. Chateaudun, France, 1964-65; physician Infant and Mother Protection, Orleans, 1966-67; practice specializing in oto rhino laryngology Orleans, 1967—; physician Surgery Clinic Jeanne d'Arc, Orleans, 1967—, also bd. dirs., 1983—; cons. dept. oto rhino laryngology Head and Neck Surgery Hosp., Orleans, 1983. Contbr. articles to profl. jours. Mem. USO, Orleans, 1973. Mem. Ctrs. Soc. Otolaryngology, Otorhinolaryngology Nat. French Syndicate. Home: 40 Rue Alsace Lorraine, 45000 Orleans France Office: 32 Blvd Marie Stuart, 45000 Orleans France

NGUYEN, SON VAN, research scientist, engineer; b. Ho Chi Minh City, Vietnam, Mar. 18, 1956; came to U.S., 1974; s. Khai Van and Hoa Thi (Bui) N. B.A., SUNY-Plattsburgh, 1978; Ph.D., Brown U., 1981; postgrad. U. Vt., 1983. Research chemist Exxon Research and Engring., Baytown, Tex., 1980; research scientist, engr. IBM Corp., Essex Junction, Vt., 1981—. Contbr. articles to profl. jours. Mem. N.Y. Acad Sci., Electrochem. Soc., Am. Chem. Soc., Sigma Xi. Home: PO Box 324 Essex Junction VT 05453

NGUYEN, VAN-HUAN PHILIPPE, physician; b. Hanoi, Republic of Vietnam, Nov. 7, 1923; s. Nguyen Van-Dang and Pham Thi-Ty N.; m. Maix Jacqueline, July 21, 1953; children: Pascale, Philippe, Bernard, Sylvie. MD, U. Hanoi, 1950; Laureate, Inst. Polit. Sci., Paris, 1954; MD, U. Tours, France, 1975. Violinist Conservatory of Music Orch., Paris, 1954-55; mem. staff Office of Pres. of South Vietnam, 1955-60; dir. info. Govt. of Saigon, Vietnam, 1960-64; guest prof. Stanford U. in France, Tours, 1964-66; journalist Nouvelle Republique, Tours, 1964-75; physician Ctr. L. Sevestre, Tours, 1975-77; practice medicine, Tours, 1977—. Club: Beauregard Tennis (Tours). Home: Cochard, Fondettes Luynes, 37230 Tours France Office: Cabinet Medical, De Grammont Ave, 37000 Tours France

NGUYEN, VIET TAN, aircraft maintenance company exeuctive; b. Kampot, Cambodia, June 18, 1928; came to U.S., 1975; s. Tan Van Nguyen and Men Thi Doan; m. Muoi Nguyen, Mar. 15, 1956; children: Tien, Thach, Tung, Vu, Yen, Oanh. BMath, U. Paris, 1951, MAero Engring., 1953. Dir. air transport Vietnam Directorate Civil Aviation, 1955-56; tech. dir. Air Vietnam, 1958-65, pres., 1965-69; advisor indsl. devel. Investment Bank for Devel., Vietnam, 1970-75; dir., prin. tech. PanAm Tap Air Zaire, 1976-77; gen. mgr. ops. and tech. Gulf Air, Bahrain, 1977-86, Gulf Aircraft Maintenance Co., Abu Dhabi, United Arab Emirates, 1986—. Club: Gamco Social (Abu Dhabi). Home: 5414 Southampton Dr Springfield VA 22151-1436

NGUYEN CO THACH, minister foreign affairs Socialist Republic Vietnam. Assigned Vietnamese embassy, India, 1956-60; participant Geneva Peace Talks, 1962; chmn. Com. to Investigate U.S. War Crimes, 1966; minister fgn. affairs Govt. Socialist Republic Vietnam, 1980—; alt. mem. Politburo, 1982—. Address: Ministry of Fgn Affairs, Hanoi Socialist Republic of Vietnam *

NGUYEN HUU THO, vice chairman State Council of Vietnam; b. Cholon, July 10, 1910. Chmn., Nat. Liberation Front Central Com., 1962—, Presidium of Central Com., 1964—; chmn. consultative council Provisional Revolutionary Govt. Republic of South Vietnam, 1969-76; v.p. Socialist Republic of Vietnam, 1976-80, acting pres.,1980-81, chmn. standing com. Nat. Assembly, 1981-87, vice chmn. State Council, 1981—; v.p. Council of State, 1981-84. Decorated Order of Friendship among Nations, Order of Friendship of the People (USSR). Address: care State Council, Hanoi Vietnam *

NGUYEN VAN LINH, government official; b. Hai Hung Province, Vietnam, July 1, 1915. Joined Indochinese Communist Party, 1936; mem. local party exec. com. Indochinese Communist Party, Saigon, 1939; sec. Saigon Party Com., 1945; mem. standing com. Regional Party Com., 1949; acting sec. Cen. Party Commn. for the South, 1957-60; mem. Party Cen. Com., 1960, then sec. and dep. sec.; sec. Ho Chi Minh City Party Com., 1976; head socialist transformation, head commn. for mass agitation Party Cen. Com., 1976; also mem. Polit. Bur. and Secretariat; also pres. Fedn. of Trade Union; mem. polit. bur. 1986; permanent mem. secretariat Party Cen. Com., 1986; gen. sec. cen. com. Communist Party of Vietnam, 1986. Office: Dang Cong San Viet-Nam, 1 Hoang Van Thu St, Hanoi Socialist Republic of Vietnam *

NGUZ A KARL-I-BOND, government official from Zaire; b. Musumba, 1938. Grad., U. Louvain, Belgium. Announcer Radio Lubumbashi, 1957-60, Radio Kinshasa, 1964; mem. Congolese Embassy, Brussels, 1964-66; govt. commr. Union Miniere, 1965-68; counsellor, Congolese del. to UN N.Y.C, 1966-68; minister, then ambassador and permanent rep. to UN Geneva, 1970-72; state commr. for Fgn. Affairs 1972-74, 76-77, 79-81; ambassador from Zaire Washington, 1986-88; state commr. for Fgn. Affairs and Internat. Cooperation Zaire, 1988—. Mem. Political Bur. of the Mouvement Populaire de la Revolution, 1972-77, 79-81, Nat. Security Council, 1979-81, bd. dirs. 1974-77; v.p. exec. council Polit., Econ. and Fin. Commn., 1977; arrested 1977; accused of treason and sentenced to death, sentence commuted to life imprisonment, Sept., 1977, reinstated, 1979; resigned posts while in Brussels, 1981; in exile, 1982; returned to Zaire, 1985. Office: Ministry of Fgn Affairs, BP 7100, Kinshasa-Gombe Zaire *

NIBBI, FILIPPO, writer; b. Cortona, Tuscany, Italy, Feb. 1, 1935; s. Italo and Giuseppina (Angori) N.; m. Paola Vaccari, Nov. 25, 1965; children: Pietro, Nicola. B in Math. and Physics, U. Degli Studi, Bologna, Italy, 1962. Author: Antifascisti ad Arezzo, 1974, Guida Storica di Arezzo, 1982; (poetry books) Parlando di mio Nonno Polifemo, 1973, O/lezzo di Poeta, 1983, Dopo la Polonia, 1985; co-author: Esercizi di Fantasia, 1981; editor: All'insegna dell'A-Ztèco; founder Titus Quaderni di Poesa, 1984. Mem. Nat. Sindicate Writers. Roman Catholic. Home: Via Guido Monaco 15, 52100 Arezzo Italy

NICANDROS, CONSTANTINE STAVROS, oil company executive; b. Port Said, Egypt, Aug. 2, 1933; came to U.S., 1955, naturalized, 1963; s. Stavros Constantine and Helen (Lianakis) N.; m. Tassie Boozalis, May 24, 1959; children: Steve Constantine, Vicky Ellen. Diplome, HEC Ecole des Hautes Etudes Commerciales, 1954; license en droit, Law Sch. U. Paris, 1954, doctorate in economic sci, 1955; M.B.A., Harvard U., 1957. With planning dept. Conoco Inc., Houston, 1957-61; With planning dept. Conoco Inc., N.Y.C., 1961-64, land acquisition internat. exploration-prodn. dept., 1964-65, mgr. planning eastern hemisphere, 1966-71, gen. mgr. supply and transp., eastern hemisphere, 1971-72, v.p. supply and transp. eastern hemisphere, 1972-74, exec. v.p. eastern hemisphere refining, mktg. and supply and transp., 1974-75; exec. v.p. worldwide supply and transp. Conoco Inc., Stamford, Conn., 1975-78; group exec. v.p. petroleum products Conoco Inc., Houston, 1978-83, pres. petroleum ops., 1983-87, pres., chief exec. officer, 1987—, also bd. dirs.; dir. and exec. v.p., mem. exec. com. E.I. duPont de Nemours & Co.; bd. dirs. Tex. Commerce Bancshares, Inc., Tex. Commerce Bank-Houston. Bd. dirs. Houston Symphony Soc., Am. Heart Assn.; mem. adv. com. Houston Ballet Found.; bd. trustees Houston Lyric Theater Found., United Way of the Tex. Gulf Coast (campaign chmn. Houston United Way campaign), Baylor Coll. Medicine; bd. trustees, mem. exec. com. Houston Grand Opera, Baylor Coll. Medicine. Mem. Am. Petroleum Inst. (dir.), Tex. Research League, Inst. Internat. Edn. (so. regional adv. bd.), Internat. Inst. Strategic Studies (adv. bd. ctr. strategic and internat. studies), The Forum Club (bd. govs., exec. com.). Greek Orthodox. Office: Conoco Inc PO Box 2197 Houston TX 77252

NICCOLINI, DIANORA, photographer; b. Florence, Italy, Oct. 3, 1936; d. George and Elaine (Augsbury) Niccolini; came to U.S., 1945, naturalized, 1960; student Hunter Coll., 1955-62, Art Students League, 1960, Germain Sch. Photography, 1962. Med. photographer Manhattan Eye, Ear and Throat Hosp., 1963-65; organizer med. photography dept., 1st chief med. photographer Lenox Hill Hosp., 1965-67; organizer, head dept. med. and audio visual edn. St. Clare's Hosp., N.Y.C., 1967-76; mem. Third Eye Gallery, N.Y.C., 1974-76; owner Dianora Niccolini Creations, 1976—; instr. photography Camera Club N.Y., 1978-79, Germaine Sch. Photography, 1978-79, N.Y. Inst. Photography, 1981-83; one woman shows 209 Photo Gallery, Top of the Stairs Gallery, Third Eye Gallery, 1974, 75, 77, West Broadway Gallery, N.Y.C., 1981, Camera Club N.Y., 1982, Photographics Unltd. Gallery, N.Y.C., 1981; project dir. Photography over 65, N.Y.C., 1978; pub. portfolios. Mem. Women Photographers N.Y. (founder 1974), Biol. Photog. Assn., Assn. Ind. Video and Filmmakers, Internat. Center Photography, Am. Soc. Mag. Photographers, Am. Soc. Picture Profls., Profl. Women Photographers (coordinator 1980-84), Unity Center Practical Christianity. Author: Women of Vision, 1982; Men in Focus, 1983; editor: P.W.P. Times, 1981-82; contbr. to photog. books, 1979, 80; contbg. editor Functional Photography, 1979-80, N.Y. Photo Dist. News, 1980. Home: 356 E 78th St New York NY 10021 Office: 2 W 32d St Suite 200 New York NY 10001

NICHELSON DEL CANTO, WINSTON VICTOR, pharmaceutical companies executive; b. Santiago, Chile, Aug. 3, 1943; s. Miguel Nichelson and Raquel Merrinia (del Canto) Cuitino; m. Sonia Aida Martinez, Mar. 17, 1967 (div. 1985); children: Victor Marcelo, Carolina Beatriz, Constanza Grazia, Miguel Alejandro; m. Maria Victoria Prado Scott, Sept. 17, 1985. BS, Grange Sch., Santiago, 1960; PhD in Chem., U. Chile, Santiago, 1965. Registered pharmaceutical chemist, Santiago. Pres. Soc. Inrobiliaria Sta., Santiago, 1983, Unversione y Rentas Sta. Carolina, Santiago, 1983; pharm. chemist Laboratorio Norpine, Santiago, 1967, dir. and exec. mgr., 1970-82, pres., 1982—; gen. mgr. Laboratorio Cosneqar, Santiago, 1973—; bd. dirs., cons. and legal rep. numerous holding companies. Contbr. articles to sci. jours., 1967, 68. Cons. to govt. agys., 1980. Recipient Internat. Am. Quality award Editoria Ofice, N.Y., Can., Rio de Janeiro, Lima, Peru, 1984-86. Fellow Pharm. Chem. Assn., Chem. Industry Soc., Chem. Cosmetic Soc., Santiago. Roman Catholic. Club: Dehesa Golf, Granadicha Country (Vina del Mar). Office: Laboratorio Norgine SA, Casilla 3457 Correo 1, Santiago 3457, Chile

NICHOLAS, H.G., historian; b. Treharris Glamorgan, Wales. MA, U. Oxford, 1938; DCL (hon.), U. Pitts., 1968. Fellow Exeter Coll., Oxford, Eng., 1946-51; fellow New Coll., Oxford, Eng., 1951-78, fellow emeritus, 1978—; faculty fellow Nuffield Coll., Oxford, 1948-57; prof. Am. history insts. Oxford U., 1969-78. Author: The American Union, 1948, The British General Election, 1950, 2d edit., 1951, The United Nations, 1959, 5th revised edit., 1975, The Nature of American Politics, 1980, 2d edit., 1986. Fellow British Acad. Club: Athenaeum (London). Home: New College, Oxford OX1 3BN, England

NICHOLAS, JAMES A., orthopedic surgeon, hospital official; b. Portsmouth, Va., Apr. 15, 1921; s. Harry and Julia N.; m. Kiki Chris, June 14, 1952; children—Philip Duncan, Stephen James, Nicole Hambro. B.A., NYU, 1942; M.D., Downstate Med. Ctr., 1945. Diplomate Am. Bd. Orthopedic Surgery. Resident, various hosps. especially Hosp. Spl. Surgery, N.Y.C., 1946-52, asst. dir. research, 1952-60; dir. dept. orthopedic surgery Lenox Hill Hosp., N.Y.C., 1970—, dir. Inst. Sports Medicine and Athletic Trauma, 1973—, founding dir. Nicholas Inst. Sports Medicine, 1973—; dir. Gulf & Western Corp., N.Y.C., 1983—; cons. U.S. Army Hosp., West Point, N.Y., 1960—, Bert Bell Retirement Plan, N.Y.C., 1984—; orthopedic cons. Nat. Football League, N.Y.C., 1968—; mem. Presdl. Council Phys. Fitness in Sports, Washington, 1979-82, cons., 1983—; prof. orthopedic surgery N.Y. Med. Coll., Valhalla, 1984—; assoc. prof. orthopedic surgery Cornell Med. Coll., N.Y.C., 1970—. Editor 15 books including: Injuries to the Spine and Lower Extremity in Sports Medicine, 1986; patentee manual muscle tester. Trustee ctr. council Cornell U. Med. Ctr. N.Y. Hosp., 1986—. Served to capt. M.C. U.S. Army, 1945-46, 50-51, Korea. Spingold Found. grantee in sports medicine, 1976—; recipient Frank Babbott Disting. Alumnus award, 1985, Royal Order of Phoenix, Greek Govt. Service, 1970; named Health Am. Fitness Leader, Jaycees, 1982. Fellow ACS, Am. Orthopedic Assn.; mem. Orthopedic Research Soc. (sec. treas. 1968-69), Am. Orthopedic Soc. for Sports (pres. 1980-81), N.Y. Acad. Medicine (pres. 1974). Greek Orthodox. Clubs: Mill Reef (Antigua, West Indies), Hellenic Univ., Westchester Country. Avocations: astronomy; golf; beach walking; finance study. Home: 22 Cayuga Rd Scarsdale NY 10583 Office: 130 E 77th St Lenox Hill Hosp New York NY 10021

NICHOLAS, LAWRENCE BRUCE, import company executive; b. Dallas, Nov. 9, 1945; s. J. W. and Helen Elouise (Whiteacre) N.; B.B.A., So. Meth. U., 1968; m. Virginia Pearl Farmer, Aug. 5, 1967; children—Helen Brooke, John Lawrence, Alexis Bradlee. Mem. sales staff Nicholas Machinery Co., Dallas, 1963-69; sales mgr. Indsl. and Comml. Research Corp., Dallas, 1969-74; v.p. Precision Concepts Corp., Dallas, 1974-76, gen. mgr., 1976-78, pres., Addison, Tex., 1978-86, dir., 1974-86 ; pres. INCOR Inc., Addison, 1974—, dir., 1972—; pres. INCOR Internat., Dallas, 1981—; pres., dir. Multiple Axis Machine Corp., 1986—. Served as officer Ordnance Corps, U.S. Army, 1968, N.G., 1968-74. Mem. Nat. Sporting Goods Assn., Nat. Assn. Diecutters and Diemakers, Nat. Rifle Assn., Nat. Shooting Sports Found., Safari Club Internat, Game Conservation Internat., Dallas Council on World Affairs (dir.), Internat. Trade Assn. of Dallas. Club: Bent Tree Country. Office: PO Box 918 Addison TX 75001

NICHOLAS, NICHOLAS JOHN, JR., communications company executive; b. Portsmouth, N.H., Sept. 3, 1939; s. Nicholas John N.; B.A. magna cum laude, Princeton U., 1962; M.B.A., Harvard U., 1964; m. Llewellyn Jones, May 27, 1972; children: Charlotte, John, Hilary, Alexander, Alexandra. Dir. fin. analysis Time Inc., N.Y.C., 1964-69, asst. to pres., 1970, asst. treas., 1971-73, v.p., from 1975, now pres., chief operating officer, dir. ; pres. Manhattan Cable TV, 1973-76; pres. Home Box Office, N.Y.C., 1976-80, chmn., 1979-81, chief fin. officer, 1982—. Office: Time Inc Time & Life Bldg Rockefeller Ctr New York NY 10020 *

NICHOLAS, ROBERT JON, agricultural company executive; b. Sonoma, Calif., June 19, 1942; s. George A. and Eleen M. (Johnson) N.; B.S. in Agrl. Econs., U. Calif., Davis, 1964; J.D., U. Calif., Berkeley, 1967; m. Janet H. Gross, May 4, 1969; children—Laura Christene, Kimberly Ann. With Nicholas Turkey Breeding Farms, Inc., Sonoma, 1969—, pres., 1974-82, chmn., 1982—; mem. Calif. Agrl. Export Adv. Commn., 1974-85, U.S. Dept. Agr. Poultry Health Com., 1975-80; 1st alt. Sec. of State Calif., 1981-83; dir. P. Leiner Nutritional Products, 1986—. Mem. Calif. Lt. Gov.'s Commn. on Agr., 1979-83; mem. policy adv. council Coll. Agr. and Environ. Sci., U. Calif., 1982—; mem. Sonoma County Republican Central Com., 1976-80, mem. Calif. Rep. State Central Com., 1977—; del. Rep. Nat. Conv., 1980-84; adv. council Nat. Conservative Polit. Action Com., 1980-83; co-founder Sebastiani Fair Reapportionment Plan, 1982-83; mem. devel. council Sonoma State U., 1980-84. Served with AUS, 1967-69. Mem. Poultry Breeders Am. (dir. 1971-84, 1st v.p. 1975-76, pres. 1976-77), Calif. Turkey Fedn. (dir. 1971—), Calif. Turkey Industry Bd. (chmn. 1976, 77, 85-86), Nat. Turkey Fedn. (dir. 1972—, mem. exec. com. 1980-83), Pacific Egg and Poultry Assn. (dir. 1974-76), World Turkey Fedn. (pres. 1978—). World Record holder flycasting, mountain whitefish Internat. Game Fish Assn. Clubs: Commonwealth, Capitol Hill. Home: 17500 Norrbom Rd Sonoma CA 95476 Office: PO Box Y Sonoma CA 95476

NICHOLLS, GRANT TELFER, financial planner; b. East Meadow, N.Y., Mar. 22, 1946; s. Russell E. and Marjorie G. N.; m. Linda Eicher, Sept. 23, 1967; children: Russell E., Debora J. BS in Edn., Lebanon Valley Coll., Annville, Pa., 1969. Agt., agy. tng. dir. Penn Mut. Life Ins. Co., Cherry Hill, N.J., 1970-72; gen. agt. Beneficial Standard Life Ins. Co., New Lisbon, N.J., 1972-74; adminstrv. asst., dir. sales Colonial Life Ins. Co. Am., East Orange, N.J., 1974-80; supt. agys. Bankers Security Life Ins. Soc., N.Y.C., 1980-83; pres. Personal Fin. Advisors, Hackettstown, N.J., 1983-88, Bus. Transfer Services, Inc., Hackettstown, 1987—. Exec. bd. N.J. First Aid Council, 1972-74, vice chmn. 22d Dist., 1973; mem. Burlington County Adv. Council Task Force on Emergency Med. Services, 1972-74; asst. chief Presdl. Lakes First Aid Squad, 1973; v.p. Brown Mills Emergency Squad, 1974; mem. Warren County adv. council Regional Health Planning Agy. of No. N.J., 1978-88; mem. Allamuchy Twp. Planning Bd., 1979-88, vice chmn., 1980-81, chmn., 1981-86, twp. councilman, 1986-87, coordinator emergency mgmt., 1986—; alumni ambassador Lebanon Valley Coll., 1977—, trustee, 1984—; mem. Annville Cleona Jaycees, 1967-69; mem. Comprehensive Health Planning Council South N.J.; mem. Warren County (N.J.) Solid Waste Adv. Council, 1980-83; mem. Rep. County Com., 1981-85; trustee Warren County Community Coll. Commn., 1982-86; chmn. bd. Dialysis Ctr. N.W. Jersey, 1982-86; trustee Warren County Pollution Control Fin. Authority, trustee, 1987—; mem. adminstrv. bd. Trinity United Meth. Ch., 1986—. Decorated Knight of Malta, Order St. John Jerusalem; named Man of Yr., Camden Gen. Agts. and Mgrs. Conf., 1972. Mem. Lebanon Valley Coll. Alumni Assn. Republican. Club: Fraternal Order Police (1st v.p. 1973-74). Lodge: Rotary (Hackettstown) (treas. 1984, v.p. 1986-87, pres. 1987-88). Home: Walnut Hill Farm PO Box 216 Allamuchy NJ 07820 Office: PO Box 550 128 Maple Ave Hackettstown NJ 07840

NICHOLLS, RICHARD AURELIUS, obstetrician, gynecologist; b. Norfolk, Va., Aug. 12, 1941; s. Richard Beddoe and Aurelia (Gill) N.; m. Geri Bowden, Feb. 24, 1986. B.S. in Biology, Stetson U., 1963; M.D., Med. Coll. Va., 1967. Diplomate Am. Bd. Ob-Gyn. Intern, Charity Hosp., Tulane div., New Orleans, 1967-68, resident in ob-gyn, 1968-71; asst. prof. ob-gyn Tulane Med. Sch., New Orleans, 1973-74, clin. asst. prof., 1974-83; practice medicine specializing in ob-gyn, Pascagoula, Miss., 1974—; mem. staff Singing River Hosp., chmn. surg. and ob-gyn depts., 1979-80. Bd. dirs. Miss. Racing Assn. Served to maj. US. Army, 1971-73. Fellow Am. Coll. Ob-Gyn, ACS; mem. Miss. State Med. Soc., Singing River Med. Soc., Am. Fertility Soc., Am. Assn. Gynecol. Laparoscopists, Am. Med. Soc., So. Med. Soc., New Orleans Grad. Med. Assembly, New Orleans Ob-Gyn Soc., Gulf Coast Ob-Gyn Soc., Conrad Collins Ob-Gyn Soc., Am. Venereal Disease Soc., Am. Cancer Soc. (bd. dirs Jackson County Br.). Contbr. articles to med. jours.

NICHOLS, ALAN HAMMOND, lawyer; b. Palo Alto, Calif., Feb. 14, 1940; s. John Ralph and Shirley Weston (Charles) N.; children—Alan Hammond, Sharon Elizabeth, Shan Darwin; m. Nancy A. Mattlingly, Mar. 28, 1988; stepchildren: Christopher, McCade. B.A., Stanford U., 1951, J.D., 1955; D.S. (hon.), Calif. Coll. Podiatric Medicine, 1980. Bar: Calif. 1955, U.S. Dist. Ct. (no. dist.) Calif. 1955, U.S. Dist. Ct. (cen. dist.) Calif. 1969, U.S. Dist. Ct. (ea. dist.) Calif. 1978, U.S. Dist. Ct. Ariz. 1978, U.S. Dist. Ct. Minn. 1979, U.S. Dist. Ct. (so. dist.) Calif. 1980, U.S. Tax Ct. 1981. Assoc. Lillick, Geary, Wheat, Adams & Charles, San Francisco, 1955-61; pres. Nichols & Rogers, San Francisco, 1961-74; pres. Nichols Law Corp., San Francisco, 1974-83, Nichols, Doi & Rapaport, San Francisco, 1983-87; Nichols, Doi, Papaport& Chan, San francisco, 1987—; prof. forensic medicine Calif. Coll. Podiatric Medicine, 1975-77. Mem. San Francisco Library Commn., 1962-65; v.p. San Francisco Council Chs., 1965-68; pres. sch. bd. San Francisco Unified Sch. Dist., 1967-71; exec. com. Council Great City Schs. of U.S.; del. Calif. Sch. Bd. Assn. Assembly; mem. Civil Grand Jury, San Francisco, 1975-76; pres. Young Republicans San Francisco, 1957, Calif.; 1959, mem. Rep. Central Com., San Francisco, 1961—, pres., 1976; trustee City Coll. San Francisco, 1966-71, pres. bd. trustees, 1970-71; trustee Calif. Coll. Podiatric Medicine, 1973-85, Cathedral Sch., 1973-74, vice-chmn., 1983—; past trustee Prescott Center Coll. Served to lt. AUS, 1951-54. Decorated Commendation medal with 4 clusters; named Young Man of Yr., San Francisco newspapers, 1961. Mem. ABA (local govt. sect., real property probate and trust law sect., urban, state and local govt. sect., corp., banking and bus. law sect., forum com. on health law), San Francisco Bar Assn., State Bar Assn. Calif. (estate planning, trust and probate law sect.), Am. Arbitration Assn. (arbitrator), Phi Beta Kappa, Phi Delta Phi, Sigma Nu. Club: Bohemian. Author: (with Harold E. Rogers, Jr.) Water for California, 2 vols., 1967; (poetry) To Climb a Sacred Mountain, 1979, San Francisco Commuter, 1970; (play) Siddartha, 1977; A Gift from the Master, 1978; contbr. articles to profl. jours. including Stanford Law Rev., UCLA Law Rev., Am. Bar Rev. Office: Nichols Doi Rapaport & Chan 1032 Broadway San Francisco CA 94133

NICHOLS, CALEB LEROY, lawyer, educator; b. Sedley, Va., Oct. 19, 1947; s. Alfred Manry and Sylvia Lee (Young) N.; B.A., Norfolk State U., 1970; J.D., U. Conn., West Hartford, 1973; LL.M., Georgetown U., 1977. Bar: Pa. 1974, U.S. Ct. Customs and Patent Appeals 1974, U.S. Ct. Mil. Appeals, 1974, U.S. Ct. Claims 1974, U.S. Customs Ct. 1974, U.S. Tax Ct. 1974, U.S. Supreme Ct., 1977, U.S. Dist. Ct. (ea. dist.) Pa. 1977, U.S. Ct. Appeals (9th cir.) 1977, U.S. Ct. Appeals (4th cir.), 1978, U.S. Ct. Internat. Trade 1981. Legal asst. First Nat. Bank, Portland, Oreg., 1977-78; securities examiner Corp. Commn., Salem, Oreg., 1978-79; examiner atty. Nat. Assn. Securities Dealers, Chgo., 1979-80; legal asst. Legal Service Corp. Iowa, Des Moines, 1980; asst. counsel Pa. Dept. Revenue, Harrisburg, 1981-83; dir. Conn. Dept. Banking, Hartford, 1983-87; prof. Western Conn. State Coll., Danbury, 1987—; assoc. prof. Ancell Sch. Bus. Western Conn. State U., 1987—; mem. task force Bd. Accountancy Conn. Sec. of State; mem. World Affairs Ctr., Hartford, 1987. Mem. bd. adv. inst. fin. planning Quinnipiac Coll., 1987. Served to lt. USCG, 1973-77. Mem. N.Am. Securities Adminstrs. Assn., (chmn. disclosure com. 1983-85), Nat. Assn. Securities Dealers, Inc. (arbitrator 1982—), Westchester-Fairfield Corp. Counsel Assn.,

Practising Law Inst., Inst. Fin. Planning (bd. advisers). Fed. Bar Assn. Democrat. Home: 67 Rowan St Apt 3 Danbury CT 06810

NICHOLS, CHARLES WALTER, III, banker; b. N.Y.C., Aug. 25, 1937; s. Charles Walter and Marjorie (Jones) N.; B.A., U. Va., 1959; m. Anne Sharp, Aug. 8, 1959; children—Blair, Sandra, Walter, Hope. Vice pres. Citibank, N.Y.C., 1962-78, Morgan Guaranty Trust Co. N.Y., N.Y.C., 1979—. Bd. dirs. Nichols Found., Inc., 1969—, pres. 1988—; Choate Rosemary Hall, 1972-77, 82—, Greenwich House, 1972—, pres., 1984—, Lower Hudson (N.Y.) chpt. Nature Conservancy, 1978-87, hon. trustee, 1988—, John Jay Homestead, 1980—, Nat. Audubon Soc., 1983-87, pres. council, 1988—; mem. adv. bd. N.Y. Zool. Soc. (Bronx Zoo), 1987—. Served to 1st lt. U.S. Army, 1960-62. Decorated Army Commendation medal. Mem. Am. Sunbathing Assn., Naturist Soc. Clubs: Bedford (N.Y.) Golf and Tennis, Pilgrims of U.S. Office: Morgan Guaranty Trust Co NY 9 W 57th St New York NY 10019

NICHOLS, DAVID ARTHUR, state justice; b. Lincolnville, Maine, Aug. 6, 1917; s. George E. and Flora E. (Pillsbury) N. A.B. magna cum laude, Bates Coll., 1942; J.D., U. Mich., 1949. Bar: Maine bar 1949, Mass. bar 1949, U.S. Supreme Ct 1954. Practice in Camden, Maine, 1949-75; justice Maine Superior Ct., 1975-77, Maine Supreme Jud. Ct., 1977—; Mem. Maine Exec. Council, 1955-57; moderator Lincolnville Town Meeting, 1950-74. Contbr. to legal and gen. publs. Chmn. Maine Republican Com., 1960-64; mem. Rep. Nat. Com., 1960-68; chmn. Maine council Young Reps., 1950-54; New Eng. council Young Reps., 1952-54; trustee, past pres. Penobscot Bay Med. Center. Served with USAAF, 1942-45. Fellow Am. Bar Found., Am. Coll. Trial Lawyers; mem. Camden-Rockport C. of C. (past pres.), Maine Hist. Soc., Camden Hist. Soc. (past pres.), Camden Bus. Men's Assn. (past pres.), ABA (bd. govs. 1960-63, ho. dels. 1957-78), Maine Bar Assn., Am. Judicature Soc. (dir. 1960-64), New Eng. Historic Geneal. Soc. (trustee), Bates Coll. Alumni Assn. (past pres.), Maine Trial Lawyers Assn. (past pres.), Phi Beta Kappa, Delta Sigma Rho. Clubs: Odd Fellow, Rotary (past pres.). Home: Box 76 Lincolnville ME 04849 Office: Knox County Courthouse PO Box 867 Rockland ME 04841-0867

NICHOLS, EUGENE DOUGLAS, mathematics educator; b. Rovno, Poland, Feb. 6, 1923; came to U.S., 1946, naturalized, 1951; s. Alex and Anna (Radchuk) Nichiporuk; m. Alice Bissell, Mar. 31, 1951. B.S., U. Chgo., 1949, postgrad., 1949-51; M.Ed., U. Ill., 1953, M.A., 1954, Ph.D., 1956. Instr. math. Roberts Wesleyan Coll., North Chili, N.Y., 1950-51, U. Ill., 1951-56; asso. prof. math. edn. Fla. State U., 1956-61, prof., head dept., 1961-73; dir. Project for Mathematical Devel. of Children, 1973-77; dir. math program NSF, summers 1958-61; dir. Math. Inst. Elem. Tchrs., 1961—; Chmn. U. Ill. Com. on Sch. Math., 1954-55; cons. editor math McGraw-Hill Book Co., summer 1956. Co-author: Modern Elementary Algebra, 1961, Introduction to Sets, 1962, Arithmetic of Directed Numbers, 1962, Introduction to Equations and Inequalities, 1963, Introduction to Coordinate Geometry, 1963, Introduction to Exponents, 1964, Understanding Arithmetic, 1965, Elementary Mathematics Patterns and Structure, 1966, Algebra, 1966, Modern Geometry, 1968, Modern Trigonometry, 1968, Modern Intermediate Algebra, 1969, Analytic Geometry, 1973, Holt Algebra 1, 1974, 78, 82, 86, Holt Algebra 2, 1974, 78, 82, 86, Holt Geometry, 1974, 78, 82, 86, Holt School Mathematics, 1974, 78, 81, Holt Mathematics, 1981, 85, Pre-Algebra Mathematics, 1980, 86, Elementary School Mathematics and How to Teach It, 1982; author: Pre-Algebra Mathematics, 1970, College Mathematics for General Education, rev. edit, 1975, Introductory Algebra for College Students, 1971, Mathematics for the Elementary School Teacher, 1971, College Mathematics, 1975. Named Fla. State U. Distinguished Prof., 1968-69; recipient Distinguished Alumni award U. Ill. Coll. Edn., 1970. Mem. Am. Math. Soc., Math. Assn. Am., Sch. Sci. and Math. Assn., Nat. Council Tchrs. Math., Council Basic Edn., Pi Mu Epsilon, Phi Delta Kappa. Home: 3386 W Lake Shore Dr Tallahassee FL 32312

NICHOLS, HENRY ELIOT, lawyer, savings and loan executive; b. N.Y.C., Jan. 3, 1924; s. William and Elizabeth (Lisse) N.; m. Frances Griffin Morrison, Aug. 12, 1950 (dec. July 1978); children: Clyde Whitney, Diane Spencer; m. Mary Ann Wall, May 31, 1987. B.A., Yale U., 1946; J.D., U. Va., 1948. Bar: D.C. 1950, U.S. Dist. Ct. 1950, U.S. Ct. Appeals 1952, U.S. Supreme Ct. 1969. Assoc. Frederick W. Berens, Washington, 1950-52; sole practice, Washington, 1952—; real estate columnist Washington Star, 1966-81; pres., gen. counsel Hamilton Fed. Savs. & Loan Assn., 1971-74; vice chmn. bd. Columbia 1st Fed. Savs. & Loan Assn., Washington, 1974—; pres. Century Fin. Corp., 1971—; regional v.p. Preview, Inc., 1972-78; dir., exec. com. Columbia Real Estate Title Ins. Co., Washington, 1968-78; dir. Greater Met. Bd. Trade, 1974-78, Dist. Realty Title Ins. Co., 1978-86. Nat. adv. bd. Harker Prep. Sch., 1975-80; exec. com. Father Walter E. Schmitz Meml. Fund, Cath. U., 1982=83; bd. dirs. Vincent T. Lombardi Cancer Research Ctr., 1979-84; del. Pres. Johnson's Conf. Law and Poverty, 1967; vice chmn. Mayor's Ad Hoc Com. Housing Code Problems, Washington, 1968-71; mem. Commn. Landlord-Tenant Affairs Washington City Council, 1970-71; vice chmn. Washington Area Realtors Council, 1970; exec. com., dir. Downtown Progress, 1970; bd. dirs. Washington Mental Health Assn., 1973, Washington Med Ctr., 1975. Served to capt. USAAF, 1942-46. Mem. Am. Land Devel. Assn., Nat. Assn. Realtors, Nat. Assn. Real Estate Editors, Washington Bd. Realtors (pres. 1970, Realtor of Yr. 1970, Martin Isen award 1981), Greater Met. Washington Bd. Trade (bd. dirs. 1974-80), U.S. League Savs. Assns. (attys. com. 1971—), Washington Savs. and Loan League, ABA, D.C. Bar Assn., Internat. Real Estate Fedn., Omega Tau Rho. Episcopalian. Clubs: Yale, Cosmos, Rolls Royce, Antique Auto, St. Elmo. Patentee med. inventions; contbr. articles profl. jours. Address: 1 Kittery Ct Bethesda MD 20817 Office: 1122 Connecticut Ave NW Washington DC 20036

NICHOLS, JAMES RICHARD, civil engineer, consultant; b. Amarillo, Tex., June 29, 1923; s. Marvin Curtis and Ethel (Nichols) N.; m. Billie Louise Smith, Dec. 24, 1944; children: Judith Ann, James Richard Jr., John M. B.S. in Civil Engring., Tex. A&M U., 1949, M.S. in Civil Engring., 1950. Registered profl. engr., Tex., Okla., N.Mex. Ptnr. Freese & Nichols, Inc., Cons. Engrs., Fort Worth, 1950-76; pres. Freese & Nichols, Inc., Cons. Engrs., 1977-88, chmn., 1988—; chmn. exec. com., bd. dirs. MBank Fort Worth. CHmn. Ft. Worth Conv. and Vis. Bur.; bd. dirs. United Way of Tarrant County, Pub. Communications Found. North Tex., North Tex. Commn.; trustee All Saints Episcopal Hosp., Fort Worth, Tex. A&M Research Found., Tex. Wesleyan Coll. Served with U.S. Army, 1943-46. Fellow Am. Cons. Engrs. Council; mem. Cons. Engrs. Council, ASCE, Nat. Soc. Profl. Engrs., Fort Worth C. of C. (bd. dirs., mem. adv. council), Newcomen Soc. Methodist. Clubs: Masons, Rotary, Fort Worth, Exchange. Home: 4821 Overton Woods Dr Fort Worth TX 76109 Office: Freese & Nichols Inc 811 Lamar St Fort Worth TX 76102

NICHOLS, ROBERT EDMUND, writer, editor, journalist; b. Daytona Beach, Fla., Feb. 14, 1925; s. Joe D. and Edna A. (Casper) N.; m. Diana R. Grosso; children by previous marriage: Craig S., Kim S., Robin K. Student, San Diego State Coll., 1942-43, St. John's Coll., 1944-45, George Washington U., 1948-49. Reporter San Diego Union, 1942-44; corr. Washington bur. N.Y. Herald Tribune, 1945-48, CBS, 1948-51, Time, Inc., 1951-61; contbg. editor, asst. edn. dir. Life mag., N.Y.C., 1951-52; corr. representing Time, Life, Fortune, Sports Illus. mags., San Diego area, 1952-61; Sunday editor San Diego Union, 1952-61; fin. editor Los Angeles Times, 1961-68, mem. editorial bd., 1965-68; spl. asst. to bd. govs. Fed. Res. System, 1968-70; v.p., dir. editorial services and pub. info. Bank of Am., 1970-73, v.p., dir. pub. relations, 1973-78, v.p., dir. policy and program devel., 1978-85; prin. Robert E. Nichols Communications, San Francisco, 1985—. Writer, dir. film and radio documentaries. Recipient Loeb Newspaper Spl. Achievement award, 1963, Loeb award disting. fin. reporting, 1964. Fellow Royal Geog. Soc., Explorers Club; mem. Calif. Scholarship Fedn. (hon. life), Soc. Am. Bus. Editors and Writers (pres. 1967-68), Soc. Profl. Journalists. Clubs: South Polar Press (Little Am. Antarctic); S.Am. Explorers (Lima). Home and Office: 38 Ord Ct San Francisco CA 94114

NICHOLS, RONALD LEE, surgeon, educator; b. Chgo., June 25, 1941; s. Peter Raymond and Jane Eleanor (Johnson) N.; m. Elsa Elaine Johnson, Dec. 4, 1964; children: Kimberly Jane, Matthew Bennett. M.D., U. Ill., 1966, M.S., 1970. Diplomate: Am. Bd. Surgery, Nat. Bd. Med. Examiners. Intern U. Ill. Hosp., Chgo., 1966-67, resident in surgery, 1967-72, instr. surgery, 1970-72, asst. prof. surgery, 1972-74; assoc. prof. surgery U. Health Scis. Chgo. Med. Sch., 1975-77, dir. surg. edn., 1975-77; Henderson prof. surgery Tulane U. Sch. Medicine, New Orleans, 1977—, prof. microbiology and immunology, 1979—, vice chmn. dept. surgery, 1982—; staff surgeon Tulane U. Med. Ctr. Hosp., New Orleans, Charity Hosp. La., New Orleans; cons. surgeon VA Hosp., Alexandria, La., 1978—, Huey P. Long Hosp., Pineville, La., Lallie Kemp Charity Hosp., Independence, La., Touro Infirmary, New Orleans, Monmouth Med. Ctr., Long Branch, N.J.; mem. VA Coop. Study Rev. Bd. 1978-81, VA Merit Rev. Bd. in Surgery, 1979-82. Author: (with Gorbach, Bartlett and Nichols) Manual of Surgical Infection, 1984; mem. editorial bd. Current Surgery, 1977—, Hosp. Physician, 1980—, Infection Control, 1980—, Guidelines to Antibiotic Therapy, 1976-81, Am. Jour. Infection Control, 1981—, Internat. Medicine, 1983—, Confronting Infection, 1983-86, Current Concepts in Clinical Surgery, 1984—, Fact Line, 1984—, Host/Pathogen News, 1984—, Advances in Therapy, 1984—, Task Force Antibiotic Management System, 1985; contbr. chpts. to books, articles to med. jours. Elected faculty sponser graduating class Tulane Med. Sch., 1979, 80, 83, 85, 87, 88. Served to major USAR, 1972-75. Recipient House Staff teaching award U. Ill. Coll. Medicine, 1973, Research award Bd. Trustees U. Health Scis.-Chgo. Med. Sch., 1977, Owl Club Teaching award, 1980, 81, 82, 83, 84, 85, 86; named Clin. Prof. of Yr. U. Health Scis. Chgo. Med. Sch., 1977, Clin. Prof. of Yr., Tulane U. Sch. Medicine, 1979; Douglas Stubbs Lectr. Surg. Sect. Nat. Med. Assn., 1987. Fellow Infectious Disease Soc. Am., Am. Acad. Microbiology, Internat. Soc. Univ. Colon and Rectal Surgeons, ACS (chmn. operating room environment com. 1981-83, sr. mem. 1984-87, internat. relations com. 1987—); mem. Nat. Found. for Infectious Diseases (bd. dirs. 1988—), Joint Commn. on Accreditation of Health Care Orgn. (JCAH) Infection Control adv. group, 1988—, AMA, So. Med. Assn. (vice chmn. sect. surgery 1980-81, chmn. 1982-83), Assn. Acad. Surgery, N.Y. Acad. Sci., Warren H. Cole Soc. (pres.-elect 1988), Assn. VA Surgeons, Soc. Surgery Alimentary Tract, Inst. Medicine Chgo., Midwest Surg. Assn., Cen. Surg. Assn., Ill. Surg. Soc., European Soc. Surg. Research, Collegium Internationale Chirugiae Digestivae, Chgo. Surg. Soc., New Orleans Surg. Soc., Soc. Univ. Surgeons, Surg. Soc. La., Southeastern Surg. Soc., Alton Ochsner Surg. Soc., Am. Soc. Microbiology, Soc. Internat. de Chirugie, Surg. Infection Soc. (sci. study com. 1982-83, fellowship com. 1985-87, ad hoc sci. liaison com., 1986—, program com., 1987—), Soc. for Intestinal Microbial Ecology & Disease, Soc. Critical Care Medicine, Am. Surg. Assn., Kansas City Surg. Soc., Surg. Infection Soc. (ad hoc sci. liaison com. 1986—, program com. 1987—), Bay Surg. Soc. (hon.), Cuban Surg. Soc. (hon.), Panhellenic Surg. Soc. (hon.), Sigma Xi., Alpha Omega Alpha. Episcopalian. Home: 1521 7th St New Orleans LA 70115 Office: 1430 Tulane Ave New Orleans LA 70112

NICHOLS, THEODORE GEORGE, engineer; b. Chgo., July 27, 1927; s. Michael Feodor and Sophia (Lewandowski) N.; Student Wright Jr. Coll., 1950-53, Ill. Inst. Tech., 1956-61: m. Barbara McKillip, Mar. 14, 1975; children by previous marriage—Michael J., Julie Ann, Theodore George. Supt., Paschen Contractors, Ill. and Ind., 1947-56; dir. phys. plant Ill. Inst. Tech. Research Inst., Chgo., 1956-69; dir. engring. Rush Presbyn. St. Luke's Med. Center, Chgo., 1969—. Deacon, sec. council St. Andrews Ch., 1966-68; com. chmn., instl. rep. Chgo. Area Council Boy Scouts Am., 1967-68. Mem. Am. Hosp. Assn., Inst. Plant Maintenance, Western Soc. Engrs., Chgo. Supts. Assn. Supervised constrn. 1st indsl. nuclear reactor, 1955. Home: 111 Fernwood Dr Glenview IL 60025 Office: 1753 W Congress Pkwy Chicago IL 60612

NICHOLSON, EDNA ELIZABETH, retired public health official; b. Redwood Falls, Minn., Dec. 23, 1907; d. Ernest Crawford and Alma (Bordeaux) N.; A.B., U. Mich., 1930, M.S. in Pub. Health, 1931, cert. social work, 1931. Nat. Tb Assn. fellow in social research, 1930-31; med. social work ARC, U.S. Naval Hosp., Great Lakes, Ill., 1931-33; asst. dir. med. relief service Cook County Bur. Public Welfare, Chgo., 1933-35; instr. social aspects of nursing Cook County Sch. Nursing and asst. dir. social service Cook County Hosp., Chgo., 1935-37; dir. med. relief service Chgo. Relief Adminstrn., 1938-42; vis. lectr. Sch. Hygiene and Pub. Health, U. Mich., 1939; cons. on med. assistance, bur. pub. assistance Fed. Security Agency, 1942-44; dir. Central Service for Chronically Ill, Inst. Medicine, Chgo., 1944-54; exec. dir. Inst. Medicine of Chgo., 1955-64; sr. specialist program ops. and standards Med. Services Adminstrn., HEW, 1964-71; spl. lectr. program in hosp. adminstrn. Northwestern U., 1945-60; tech. adviser Commn. on Chronic Illness, 1949-56. Recipient Cancer Care award Nat. Cancer Found., 1955. Mem. Am. Public Health Assn., Phi Beta Kappa, Delta Omega, Sigma Kappa. Author: Terminal Care for Cancer Patients, 1950; Surveying Community Needs and Resources for Care of the Chronically Ill, 1950; The Nurse and Chronic Illness: Planning New Institutional Facilities for Longterm Care, 1956; A Comprehensive Community Plan for Meeting the Problems of Chronic Illness, 1959. Contbr. to profl. jours. Home: 315 N LaGrange Rd LaGrange Park IL 60525

NICHOLSON, LUTHER BEAL, fin. cons.; b. Sulphur Springs, Tex., Dec. 15, 1921; s. Stephen Edward and Elma (McCracken) N.; B.B.A., So. Meth. U., 1942, postgrad., 1946-47, Tex. U., 1947-48; diploma Southwestern Grad. Sch. Banking, 1967; m. Ruth Wimbish, May 29, 1952; children—Penelope Elizabeth, Stephen David. Controller, Varo, Inc., Garland, Tex., 1946-55, dir., 1947-72, v.p. fin., 1955-66, sr. v.p., 1966-67, exec. v.p., 1967-70, pres., 1970-71, chmn. bd., 1971-72, cons. to bd. dirs., 1972-75; gen. mgr. Challenger Lock Co., Los Angeles, 1956-58; dir. Varo Inc. Electrokinetics div., Varo Optical, Inc., Biometrics Instrument Corp., Varo Atlas GmbH, Micropac Industries, Inc., Gt. No. Corp., Garland Bank & Trust Co. Bd. dirs., exec. v.p. Harriett Stanton-Edna Murray Found. Served with AUS, 1942-46. Mem. Fin. Execs. Inst. (past pres.), Am. Inst. C.P.A.'s, AIM, Am. Mgmt. Assn., NAM. Home: 1917 Melody Ln Garland TX 75042 Office: 610 Main Garland TX 75040

NICHOLSON, MARION CRAWFORD, mayor, manufacturers representative; b. College Park, Ga., Jan. 31, 1917; s. William Malcolm and Marion Melissa (Neely) N.; m. Catherine Vaughn Wise, Apr. 5, 1948; children: Catherine Marion, Barbara Ann. Cert. in aero. engring., Ga. Inst. Tech., 1940. With Atlanta Constn. Pub. Co., 1937-40; sta. mgr. Eastern Air Lines, Atlanta, St. Louis, Memphis and Lake Charles, La., 1940-53; owner, operator M.C. Nicholson & Assocs., mfrs. sales rep., St. John, Mo., 1953—, Aetna Metal Products Co., St. John, 1973-86 ; Councilman, St. John, 1974, mayor, 1974-77, 83—; pres. PTA council Normandy Sch. System, 1966-67; mem. St. Louis Bd. Elec. Trade. Mem. Mayors of Small Cities St. Louis County (pres.). Presbyterian. Address: 3901 Engler Ave Saint Louis MO 63114

NICHOLSON, MYREEN MOORE, researcher, artist; b. Norfolk, Va., June 2, 1940; d. William Chester and Illeen (Fox) Moore; m. Roland Quarles Nicholson, Jan. 9, 1964 (div. 1978); children: Andrea Joy, Ross; m. Harold Wellington McKinney II, Jan. 18, 1981; 1 child, Cara Isadora. BA, William and Mary Coll., 1962; MLS, U. N.C., 1971; postgrad. Old Dominion U. 1962-64, 75—, The Citadel, 1968-69, Hastie Sch. Art, 1968, Chrysler Mus. Art Sch., 1964. English tchr., Chesapeake, Va., 1962-63; dept. head, Portsmouth (Va.) Bus. Coll., 1963-64; tech. writer City Planning/Art Commn., Norfolk, 1964-65; art tchr. Norfolk pub. schs., 1965-67; prof. lit., art Palmer Jr. Coll., Charleston, S.C., 1968; librarian Charleston Schs., 1968-69; asst. to asst. dir. and dir. City Library Norfolk, 1970-72, art librarian, 1972-75, research librarian, 1975-83, asst. head fiction, 1983—; dir. W. Ghent Arts Alliance, Norfolk, 1978—. Poet-in-schs., Virginia Beach, Va., 1987. Book reviewer Art Book Revs., Library Jour., 1973-76; editor, illustrator Acquisitions Bibliographies, 1970—; contbr. art and poetry to various publs. Mem. Virginia Beach Arts Ctr., 1978—, Peninsula Art Ctr., 1983—; bd. dirs. W. Ghent Art/Lit. Festival, 1979. Recipient various art and poetry contests; Coll. William and Mary art scholar, 1958; Nat. Endowment Arts grantee, 1975. Mem. ALA (poster sessions rev. com. 1985-87, pub. relations judge, subcom. communications 1988-90), Pub. Library Assn. (com. bylaws and orgns 1988-90), Va. Library Assn. (pub. relations com. 1984-86, grievance and pay equity com. 1986-88, Logo award 1985), Southeastern Library Assn. (Rothrock award com. 1986-88), Poetry Soc. Va. (eastern pres. 1986—) Art Libraries Soc. N.Am., Tidewater Artists Assn., Southeastern Coll. Art Assn., Acad. Am. Poets, Internat. Platform Assn. (artists assn., selected judge speaking ladder 1987—), Old Dominion U. Alumni Assn. (artistic dir.), Southeastern Soc. Archtl. Historians, Ikara (pres. 1986—). Home: 1404 Gates Ave Norfolk VA 23507 Office: Norfolk Pub Library 301 E City Hall Ave Norfolk VA 23510

NICHOLSON, ROY STEPHEN, community college president; b. Radford, Va., Mar. 4, 1926; s. Roy S. and Ethel Dovie (Macy) N.; m. Carol Nicholson, 1987; 1 child, Suzanne Carpenter. A.B., Marion Coll., 1950; M.A., Syracuse U., 1956; Ph.D., Mich. State U., 1971. Acad. dean Lansing Community Coll., 1966-69; pres. Daley Coll., Chgo., 1969-71, Clark County Community Coll., 1971-76, Mt. Hood Community Coll. Dist., 1976-85; chancellor Oakland Community Coll., 1985—. Mem. Mayor's Manpower Adv. Council, 1972-76; bd. dirs. Portland (Oreg.) Involvement Corp., 1976-79, PIC Multnomah-Wash., Mercy Corps, 1985—; mem. exec. com. Explorer Olympic Program, 1979; chief investigator HEW small research project, 1970-71; chmn. bd. Project Global Village, Inc., 1982-85; bd. dirs. Pontiac Devel. Authority, 1988. Served with USN, 1943-46. Mem. Am. Assn. Community and Jr. Colls. (pres. Pres.'s Acad. 1982, bd. dirs. 1985-87), N.W. Assn. Community and Jr. Colls. (pres. 1976), Am. Sch. Adminstrs. Assn., Am. Sociology Assn., Am. Acad. Polit. and Social Scis., Gresham C. of C. (dir. 1977-79), Japan-Am. Soc., World Affairs Council, Am. Futurist Soc., Phi Delta Kappa. Club: Rotary (pres. 1983, Paul Harris fellow 1986). Home: 6805 Chimney Sweep Ct West Bloomfield MI 48322 Office: 2480 Opdyke Rd Bloomfield Hills MI 48013

NICHOLSON, STUART ADAMS, lawyer, ecologist and environmental scientist; b. Albany, N.Y., May 24, 1941; s. Kenneth Gerald and Gladyce (Wenz) N.; children: Laura Ellice, Paul Michael. BS in Biology, SUNY-Albany, 1964, MS in Biology, 1965; PhD in Botany, U. Ga., 1970; JD, U. N.D., 1983. Bar: N.D. 1983, Minn. 1984. Research assoc. atomospheric sci. SUNY-Albany, 1970-71; asst. prof. biology State U. Coll., Fredonia, N.Y., 1971-75; ecologist Environment Cons. Inc., Mayville, N.Y., 1975-76; lectr. biology U. So. Pacific, Suva, Fiji, 1976-78; sr. research analyst St. Lawrence-Eastern Ont. Commn., Watertown, N.Y., 1979-80; sr. research scientist U. N.D., Grand Forks, 1980-82, assoc. dir., 1982-83, program dir., 1983-84; atty. various law firms, Mpls., 1984—; cons. firms, corps., 1973-79; sr. practitioner Legal Aid Assn. N.D., Grand Forks, 1982-83; mem. Voluntary Income Tax Assistance, Grand Forks, 1981; tchr. U. Ga., State U. Coll., Fredonia, U. South Pacific, Empire State Coll., 1965-67, 71-79; advisor govtl. orgns., 1972-84; ecology resource advisor N.Y. State Dept. Environ. Conservation, Albany, 1973; bd. dirs. Chautauqua County Environ. Def. Council, Jamestown, 1973-75, Grand Forks Food Coop., 1984; organizer Chautauqua Lake Biology Symposium, 1974. Contbr. articles to profl. jours.; reviewer Bull. of Torrey Bot. Club, 1974, 83. Grantee U. South Pacific, 1976-78, NSF grantee, 1974; State U. Coll. fellow, 1972-75; N.D. Pub. Service Commn. research contract 1983, Office Surface Mining research contract, 1982. Mem. ABA, Minn. State Bar Assn., State Bar Assn. N.D., Ecol. Soc. Am., Brit. Ecol. Soc., Sigma Xi, Phi Sigma, Beta Beta Beta. Home: Box 201312 Bloomington MN 55420

NICKEL, ALBERT GEORGE, advertising agency executive; b. Pitts., July 12, 1943; s. Frank George and Dorothy (Wefling) N.; m. Margery Flanders, May 31, 1968; children: Melissa, Mark. AB, Washington and Jefferson Coll., 1965; MBA, Ind. U., 1967. Mktg. research analyst Pfizer, Inc., N.Y.C., 1967, profl. service rep., 1967-68, mktg. research mgr., 1968-69, product mgr., 1969-70; product mgr. USV Internat., Tuckahoe, N.Y., 1970-71; account exec. J. Walter Thompson (Deltakos), N.Y.C., 1971-72, account supr., 1972-73; account supr. Sudler & Hennessey, N.Y.C., 1973-77; sr. v.p. mgmt. group supr. Young and Rubicam, N.Y.C., 1977-79; exec. v.p./dir. ops. Dorritie & Lyons, Inc., N.Y.C., 1979—. Trustee Wilton YMCA; bd. dirs., exec. com. Wilton LaCrosse Assn., Wilton High Sch. Long Range Planning Team. Served to capt. USAF, 1969. Mem. Pharm. Advt. Council, Mkdwest Pharm. Adv. Council. Club: Wilton Riding (pres.), Shore and Country, Silver Spring Country. Home: 97 Keelers Ridge Rd Wilton CT 06897 Office: Dorritie & Lyons Inc 655 3d Ave New York NY 10017

NICKEL, HERMAN WILHELM, ambassador, journalist; b. Berlin, Oct. 23, 1928; emigrated to U.S., 1947; s. Walter and Wilhelmine (Freund) N.; m. Phyllis Fritchey, May 24, 1958; 1 son, Clayton A. Abitur, Arndt Gymnasium, Berlin, 1946; B.A., Union Coll., 1951; J.D., Syracuse U., 1956. Reporter Die Neue Zeitung, Berlin, 1946-47; polit. reporter U.S. High Commn., Berlin, 1951-53; corr. Time-Life News Service, Washington, London, Johannesburg, South Africa; bur. chief Time-Life News Service, Bonn, W.Ger., Tokyo, London, 1958-77; bd. editors Fortune mag., Washington, 1977-81; U.S. ambassador to South Africa Dept. State, Pretoria, 1982-86; diplomat-in-residence Johns Hopkins U. Fgn. Policy Inst., Washington, 1986—. Contbr.: articles to Time, Fortune, N.Y. Times mag., Fgn. Policy Quar., SAIS Review, Orbis. Union Coll. scholar, 1947-51; Syracuse U. Coll. Law scholar, 1953-56. Mem. NAACP (local bd. mem. 1949-51). Home: 4448 Hawthorne St NW Washington DC 20016 Office: Johns Hopkins Fgn Policy Inst 1619 Massachusets Ave NW Washington DC 20036

NICKERSON, JOHN MITCHELL, political science educator; b. Lewiston, Maine, July 1, 1937; s. Elmer Winfield and Marion Gertrude (Howard) N. B.A., U. Maine, 1959; M.A., Wash. State U., 1966; Ph.D., U. Idaho, 1971. Research assoc. Bur. Pub. Adminstrn. U. Maine, Orono, 1967-68, assoc. prof., polit. sci., 1970-81, prof., 1981—; prof. U. Maine, Augusta, 1981—, also mem. grad. faculty, developer Baccalaureate program in pub. adminstrn.; dir. New Eng. Govtl. Research Inst., Inc., Waterville, Maine, 1971—; lectr. Colby Coll., Waterville, Maine, 1979, Maine State Dedimus Justice; cons. in field. Author: The Control of Civil Disturbances, 1968, Municipal Police in Maine - A Study of Selected Personnel Practices with Emphasis on Recruit Selection and Training, 1969, (with others) A Study of Policy-Making: The Dynamics and Adaptability of the U.S. Federal System, 1971; editor, author foreward: Is the Municipality Liable for Insufficiently Trained Police? (James P. Murphy), 1968; contbr. articles to profl. jours. Mem. Maine State Police Planning Adv. Group, Maine State Bd. Assessment Rev., Maine Hwy. Safety Com.; vice chmn. adv. bd. Salvation Army, Augusta; trustee, treas. Lithgow Library. Dept. Justice grantee, 1967. Mem. AAUP, Am. Polit. Sci. Assn., New Eng. Polit. Sci. Assn., Northeastern Polit. Sci. Assn., Acad. Polit. Sci. (life), Am. Acad. Polit. and Social Sci. (life), Am. Soc. for Pub. Adminstrn., ACLU (life), Kennebec Hist. Soc. (life), Kennebec Valley Humane Soc. (life), Maine Civil Liberties Union (life, legis. com.), Pi Sigma Alpha, Pi Alpha Alpha. Lodge: Rotary. Home: 190 Capitol St Augusta ME 04330 Office: U Maine University Heights Augusta ME 04330

NICKLE, DENNIS EDWIN, electronics engineer; b. Sioux City, Iowa, Jan. 30, 1936; s. Harold Bateman and Helen Cecilia (Killackey) N.; B.S. in Math., Fla. State U., 1961. Reliability mathematician Pratt & Whitney Aircraft Co., W. Palm Beach, Fla., 1961-63; br. supr. Melpar Inc., Falls Church, Va., 1963-66; prin. mem. tech. staff Xerox Data Systems, Rockville, Md., 1966-70; sr. tech. officer WHO, Washington, 1970-76; software quality assurance mgr. Melpar div. E-Systems Corp., Falls Church, 1976—; ordained deacon Roman Catholic Ch., 1979. Chief judge for computers Fairfax County Regional Sci. Fair, 1964—; mem. Am. Security Council; scoutmaster, commr. Boy Scouts Am., 1957—; youth custodian Fairfax County Juvenile Ct., 1973-87; chaplain No. Va. Regional Juvenile Detention Home, 1978—; moderator Nocturnal Adoration Soc. Served with arty. U.S. Army, 1958-60. Recipient Eagle award, Silver award, Silver Beaver award, other awards Boy Scouts Am.; Ad Altare Dei, St. George Emblem, Diocese of Richmond. Mem. Assn. Computing Machinery, Old Crows Assn., Rolm Mil-Spec Computer Users Group (internat. pres.), Nat. Security Indsl. Assn. (convention com. 1985—, software quality assurance subcom., regional membership chmn. 1981—), IEEE (sr.)(mem. standards working group in computers 1983—), Computer Soc., Hewlett Packard Users Group, Smithsonian Assn., Internat. Platform Assn., Nat. Rifle Assn. (life), Alpha Phi Omega (life), Sigma Phi Epsilon. Club: KC (4 deg.). Co-author: Handbook for Handling Non-Productive Stress in Adolescence. Office: 7700 Arlington Blvd Falls Church VA 22046

NICKLES, DON, senator; b. Ponca City, Okla., Dec. 6, 1948; s. Robert C. and Coeweene (Bryan) N.; m. Linda L. Morrison, Sept. 5, 1968; children—Donald Lee II, Jennifer Lynn, Kim Elizabeth, Robyn Lee. B.A. in Bus. Adminstrn, Okla. State U., 1971. Owner, operator Don Nickles Profl. Cleaning Service, Stillwater, Okla., 1968-71; v.p., gen. mgr. Nickles Machine Corp., Ponca City, 1972-80; mem. Okla. Senate, 1979-80; mem. U.S. Senate from Okla., 1981—, mem. com. on energy and natural resources, com. on appropriations and budget; mem. U.S. Senate arms control observer group. Bd. dirs. Ponca City United Way; mem. Kay Council for Retarded Children, Ponca City, St. Mary's Roman Cath. Parish Council; mem. adv. bd. Salvation Army, Ponca City. Served with USNG, 1970-76. Named one of Outstanding Young Men of Am., U.S. Jaycees, 1983. Mem. Fellowship Christian Athletes, Ponca City C. of C. Republican. Club: Rotary. Office: Office of Senate 713 Hart Senate Bldg Washington DC 20510 *

NICOL, DAVIDSON SYLVESTER HECTOR WILLOUGHBY, Sierra Leonean diplomat, scientist, educator; b. Freetown, Sept. 14, 1924; 5 children. B.A. with 1st class honors, Christ's Coll., Cambridge, 1946; several hon. degrees. Sr. pathologist Sierra Leone Govt., 1958-60, hon. cons. pathologist, 1960—; guest lectr. numerous Am. univs.; prin. Fourah Bay Coll., Univ. Coll. Sierra Leone, Freetown, 1960-67; vice chancellor U. Sierra Leone, 1966-68; chmn. Conf. of Inter-Univ. Cooperation in West Africa, 1961, needs and priorities com., U. East Africa, 1963, Sierra Leone Nat. Library Bd.; pres. Sierra Leone Nat. Red. Cross Soc., 1963-65, W. African Sci. Assn., 1963-65; dir. Central Bank Sierra Leone, 1963-68; permanent rep. to UN, 1969-71, mem. econ. and social council, 1969-70, security council, 1970-71 (pres. 1970), chmn. spl. com. on decolonization, 1970-71; high commr. to U.K. and ambassador to Denmark, Sweden, Finland, Norway, 1971-72; under-sec. gen. UN and exec. dir. UNITAR, 1972-82, hon. sr. fellow, 1982—; pres. World Fedn. of UN Assns., 1983-87, hon. pres., 1987; Commonwealth lectr., Cambridge, 1975; chmn. UN Interagy. Humanitarian Mission to Angola, 1976, UN Human Rights Commn., Ethiopia, 1979, 80; dir. Cen. Bank of Sierra Leone, Consolidated African Selection Trust Ltd., London; fellow Christ's Coll. (hon.), Cambridge, Royal Coll. Pathologists, London, W. African Coll. Physicians, W. African Coll. Surgeons. Recipient Margaret Wrong prize for lit. in Africa, 1952; Independence medal, Sierra Leone; decorated grand comdr. Order of Rokel; grand comdr. Star of Africa (Liberia); companion Order St. Michael and St. George (U.K.). Author: The Structure of Human Insulin, 1960; Africa, A Subjective View, 1964; African Self-Govt. 1865, the Dawn of Nationalism, 1969; The Truly Married Woman and Other Stories, 1965; New and Modern Role for the Commonwealth, 1977; The United Nations and Decision Making: the role of Women, 1978; Nigeria and the Future of Africa (Ilorin Lectures), 1980; Regionalism and the New International Economic Order, 1981; The United Nations Security Council: Towards Greater Effectiveness, 1981; Creative Women, 1982. Address: Christ's College, Cambridge England

NICOL, KLAUS, biomechanics educator; b. Mindelheim, Germany, May 27, 1939; s. Ernst and Carola (Bannick) N.; m. Uth Waltraud, May 30, 1961; children—Natascha Birgit, Sven-Boris, Cornelia Martina Yvonne. Abitur, Liebig-Gymnasium, Frankfurt, W.Ger., 1959; diploma of physics, Goethe U., Frankfurt, 1967, Ph.D. in Physics, 1971. Wissenschaftlicher Mitarbeiter, Inst. for sport and sport scis. Goethe U., 1972-73, Akademischer Rat, 1973-79; prof. dept. sport scis. Wilhelms U., Munster, W.Ger., 1979—, mem. and chmn. 10 univ. commns., 1979—; dir. Inst. Phys. Edn., 1982, vice dean dept. sports scis., 1982-85, dean dept. sports sci., 1987—. Patentee in field of measuring techniques; contbr. articles to profl. jours. Mem. Internat. Soc. Biomechanics, Deutscher Verband fur Sportwissenschaft. Mem. Free Democratic Party. Lutheran. Club: Beruflich und Soziale Rehabilitation. Home: Adelheidstrasse 13, 6000 Frankfurt 50 Federal Republic of Germany Office: FB 20 der Universitat, Horstmarer Landweg 62 B, 4400 Munster Federal Republic of Germany

NICOL, MARJORIE CARMICHAEL, research psychologist; b. Orange, N.J., Jan. 6, 1926; d. Norman Carmichael and Ethel Sarah (Siviter) N.; BA, Upsala Coll., MS, 1978; MPh, PhD, CUNY, 1988. Art dir. Finneran Advt. Co., N.Y.C., 1944-47; mgr. advt. prodn. RCA, Harrison, N.J., 1948-58; advt. mgr., writer NPS Advt., East Orange, N.J., 1960-67; pres. measurement and eval., chief exec. officer, psychol. evaluator F.L. Merritt, Inc., Montclair, N.J., 1967—, chief exec. officer., dir. Rafiki, Essex County, N.J., 1965—; officer Montclair Rehab. Orgn., 1981-86; founder Met. Opera at Lincoln Center. Republican. Presbyterian. Author: Nicol Index. Home: 89 Linden St Millburn NJ 07041 Office: PO Box 111 Millburn NJ 07041

NICOLAISEN, BJORN, aquaculture company executive; b. Oslo, June 5, 1952; s. Harald and Betty Mary (Cohen) N.; m. Berit Weibust, Aug. 25, 1973; children: Thomas, Beate. Grad. Law Sch., U. Oslo, 1978. Bar: Norway. Cons. Ministry of Environment, Oslo, 1978-80; judge Dist. Ct., Eidsvoll, Norway, 1980-81; barrister Atty. Gen. for Civil Cases, Oslo, 1981-83; assoc. Wikborg Rein & Co., Oslo, 1983-86; v.p. legal dept. Noraqua A/S, Oslo, 1985—. Home: Allergodtvn 2A, Jessheim 2050, Norway Office: Noraqua A/S, Fridthjof Nansens vei 19, Oslo 3 0369, Norway

NICOLAS, JEAN-MARIE XAVIER, computer scientist; b. Mens, France, June 29, 1945; s. Auguste B. and Marcelle L. (Reymond) N.; m. Ginette Labatut, Feb. 14, 1970; children—Emmanuelle, Gaelle. M.A.Sc. in Computer Sci., U. Grenoble, 1969; D.Sc., U. Toulouse, 1973, Ph.D., 1979. Research asst. U. Toulouse, 1969-70, research engr., lectr. ENSAE-CERT, 1973-84; mem. faculty Ecole Nationale Superieure de Aeronautique de l' Esp ace, 1970-73; research group leader European Computer-Industry Research Ctr., Munich, 1984—; cons. and lectr. on computer sci. Mem. editorial bd. numerous profl. jours. Contbr. articles to profl. jours. Home: 43 Wesendonkstrasse, D8000 Munich Federal Republic of Germany Office: 17 Arabellastrasse, D8000 Munich Federal Republic of Germany

NICOLAU, JOSE MIGUEL QUINTAS, electrical engineer; b. Beira, Mozambique, June 15, 1956; s. Jose Nicolau and Maria Victoria de Carvalho Quintas; m. Carla Maria Cardoso Raposo Pereira, May 12, 1979; children: Patricia Raposo Pereira Nicolau, Joana Raposo Pereira Nicolau. Elec. Engr., U. Maputo, Mozambique, 1976. Instr. U. Maputo, 1976-77; planning dir. Electricity Commn., Maputo, 1977-80, project dir. Cabora Bassa HP, 1980—, personnel dir., 1983—; county rep. So. Africa Devel. Coordination Conf. Energy Sector, Maputo, 1982—; small hydro power promoter Electricity Commn., Maputo, 1981-87; mem. Permanent Joint Com. on Cahora Bassa hydroelectric power between govts. of Mozambique, South Africa, and Portugal, 1987. Office: Electricidade de Mocambique, Avenida 25 de Setembro 1218, Maputo Mozambique

NICOLESCU, BASARAB, physicist; b. Ploiesti, Prahova, Romania, Mar. 25, 1942; s. Anton and Anghelichi (Anastasiade) N.; m. Michelle Moreau, Dec. 27, 1975; children: Daria, Matthieu-Vlad. D. U. Paris, 1972. Research asst. Ctr. Nat. de la Recherche Sci., France, 1970-74, dir. research, 1974—; vis. scientist Lawrence Berkeley (Calif.) Lab., 1976-77, Sci. Research Council, 1979. Author: Ion Barbu-Cosmologia Jocului Secund, 1968, Nous, la Particule et le Monde, 1985 (Silver medal Acad. Française 1986), (with J. Tran Thahn Van) Elastic and Diffractive Scattering, 1986. Counselor Conf. on Sci. and Boundaries of Knowledge: The Prologue of Our Cultural Past, UNESCO, Venice, 1986. Am.-Romanian Acad. award Am.-Romanian Acad. Arts and Scis., U.S., 1987. Mem. Internat. Ctr. for Transdisciplinary Research (founding) (pres. 1987—). Office: Inst de Physique Nucleaire, B P 1, 91406 Orsay France

NICOLETTI, FRANCOIS-XAVIER, banker; b. San Giovanni in Fiore, Italy, Nov. 30, 1936; s. Giovanni and Angela (Mangone) X.; m. Annick Rouez, Sept. 22, 1962; 1 son, Laurent. B.A., Columbia Pacific U., 1981, M.B.A, 1982, Ph.D. in Internat. Bus. Adminstrn., 1984. Area acct. Borini Prono Nigeria Ltd., Lagos, 1960-64; asst. adminstrn. mgr. Sté . Francaise Dragages Travaux Publics (Paris), Beira, Mozambique, 1965-67, fin. acct., Kitwe, Zambia, 1967-68; acct. Finacor, Paris, France, 1968-69; adminstrn. mgr. Kefinco Ltd., Nairobi, Kenya, 1969-70; asst. mgr. fgn. exchange and internat. dept. Banque Europeenne de Financement, Paris, 1970-72; mgr. fonde de pouvoirs internat. dept. Banque Canadienne Nationale (Europe), Paris, 1972-73; with Am. Express Internat. Banking Corp., 1973-79, dir. gen. adjoint Paris br., 1977-79, dir. Amex Bank Ltd., London, 1977-78, v.p., N.Y.C., 1978-79; dir. internat. fin. dept. Midland Bank France S.A., Paris, 1979-81; adminstr.-dir. gen. Overland Trust Fin. S.A., Geneva, 1981-87; dir. internat. fin. ops. Finorsud S.A., Geneva, 1987—. Author: Professional Work: Financing Exports With Promissory Notes, 1977 Recipient Silver medal Arts, Sciences et Lettres, 1976. Mem. Am. Mgmt. Assn. Internat., Club des Directeurs de Banques (Paris), Maxim's Bus. (Paris), Cercle Interallié (Paris). Roman Catholic. Home: 52 Route de Florissant, 1206 Geneva Switzerland Office: Finorsud SA, 1 place du Port, 1204 Geneva Switzerland

NICOLIN, CURT RENÉ, Swedish heavy industry manufacturing company executive; b. Stockholm, Mar. 10, 1921; s. Felix and Anna-Lisa N.; m. Ulla Sanden, 1946; 5 children. Ed. Royal Inst. Tech., Stockholm; Dr. Tech. h.c., 1974. With STAL Finspong, 1945-59, v.p. and tech. dir., 1953-55, pres., 1955-59; pres. Turbin AB de Laval Ljunstrom, Finspong, 1959-61; interim pres. Scandinavian Airlines System (SAS), 1961-62, now Swedish chmn. SAS; pres. ASEA AB, Vasteras, 1961-76, chmn. bd., 1976—; chmn. Swedish Employers Fedn., 1976-83; chmn. Swedish Match Co., 1985—. Decorated comdr., Order of Vasa, 1st class, 1974. Author: Private Industry in a Public World, 1973. Address: ASEA, Box 7373, 10391 Stockholm Sweden also: Swedish Match AB, V Tradgardsgatan 15, Box 16100, S-10322 Stockholm Sweden *

NICOLIS, GREGOIRE, science educator; b. Athens, Greece, Sept. 11, 1939; s. Stamatios and Catherine (Siganou) N.; m. Catherine Rouvas, Aug. 21, 1966; children: Helen, Stamatios. BEE, Nat. Tech. U., Athens, 1962; PhD in Physics, U. Brussels, 1965. Research asst. U. Brussels, 1964-66, asst. prof., 1968-72, assoc. prof., 1973-86, prof., 1986—; postdoctoral fellow, research assoc. U. Chgo., 1966-67; vis. prof. U. Tex., Austin, 1972, U. Oreg., 1976, U. Paris, 1975-77, 86, U. Geneva, 1979. Author: Self-organization in Nonequilibrium Systems, 1977, Exploring Complexity, 1987; co-editor: Membranes, Dissipative Structures and Evolution, 1975, Order and Fluctuations in Equilibrium and Nonequilibrium Statistical Mechanics, 1981, Aspects of Chemical Evolution, 1984, Chemical Instabilities, 1984, Irreversible Phenomena and Dynamical Systems Analysis in Geosciences, 1987, From Chemical to Biological Organization, 1988; assoc. editor: Bull. Math. Biology, 1975, Biophys. Chemistry, 1975,Jour. Nonequilibrium Thermodynamics, 1978, Advances in Chem. Physics, 1978, Jour. Statis. Physics, 1982, Dynamics and Stability of Systems, 1986. Mem. N.Y. Acad. Sci., Am. Phys. Soc., European Phys. Soc., AAAS, Belgian Acad. Sci. (fgn. assoc.), European Acad. Sci. (corr.). Home: 26 ave de l'Uruguay, 1050 Brussels Belgium Office: ULB CP, 231 Blvd du Triomphe, 1050 Brussels Belgium

NICOLOPULOS, THANIA, writer; b. Pernambuco, Brazil, Jan. 12, 1924; arrived in Mexico, 1924; d. Elias Nicolopulos Pablopulos and Georgina (Joanides) Reissis; m. Ricardo Farias Rosas, Dec. 26, 1942; children: Ricardo Farias, Georgina Farias Nicolopulos de Arellano. Grad., La Prensa, Mexico, 1945. Founder, editor Centro Editorial Mexicano Osiris, Mexico, 1974; freelance writer Mexico City, 1960—. Author: Interpretacion de los Suenos, 1965, Antologia del Pensamiento, 1973, Tlaltelolco Presente, 1974, El Despertar de los Sentidos, 1975, Metaforas y Paradojas, 1975, Dream Interpretation, 1978, El Magico Lenguaje de los Suenos, 1967, Interpretacion de las Manos, 1980, Sebastiana la Medium, 1981, El Verano de la Vida, 1982, La Ofrenda, 1983, Reminicencias, 1983; contbr. numerous articles and poems on astrology internationally. Fellow Altrusas, Red Cross, Fedn. Internat. Vols.; mem. Assn. Escritores Poetas Mexicanos, Soc. Autores Compositories S. de A. de I.P., Anthropology Mus. Mexico, S.O.G.E.M. Home: Sierra Ventana 545, 11000 Mexico City Mexico

NICOPOULOS, GEORGE, account director; b. Athens, Greece, Aug. 14, 1960; s. Nicolaos and Constantina Nicopoulos. Grad., Athens Coll., 1979; BS in Advt. and Pub. Relations, Emerson Coll., Boston, 1986; MS in Advt. and Pub. Relations suma cum laude, Emerson Coll., 1987. With traffic dept. Producta SA, Athens, 1979-81, media buyer, 1981-82, jr. account, 1982-84; account exec. Producta/Univas SA, Athens, 1984-85; account exec. internship Arnold & Co., Boston, 1986-87; account dir. Producta SA Advt., Athens, 1987—; cons. Akademos Ltd. Advt., Athens, 1985—. Home: 1 Evias St, 113 62 Athens Greece Office: Producta SA, 224 Syngrou Ave, 176 72 Athens Greece

NIEDEREHE, HANS JOSEF, Romance linguistics educator; b. Cologne, Fed. Republic Germany, May 28, 1937; s. Adam and Caecilie (Breuer) N.; m. Silvia Hackmann, July 31, 1964; children: Georg, Matthias, Christiane. Staatsexamen, U. Cologne, 1964, PhD, 1966; habilitation, U. Hamburg, 1973. Research asst. Centre Recherche pour un Tresor de la Langue Francaise, Nancy, France, 1964; asst. prof. U. Hamburg, 1965-72; prof. U. Trier, Fed. Republic Germany, 1974—; bd. dirs. Que.-Archiv., 1978—. Author: Alfonso x el sabio y la Lingustica, 1987; editor Historiographia Linguistica, 1976—, Zeitschrift der Gesellschaft Kanada Studien, 1984—. Home: Hauptstr 135, D5501 Mertesdorf Federal Republic of Germany Office: FB II (Romanistik), Universitat, 5500 Trier Federal Republic of Germany

NIEDERHAUSER, WILHELM, electrical engineer; b. Wolfern, Austria, May 12, 1949; arrived in United Arab Emirates, 1980; s. Rudolf and Maria (Strasser) N.; m. Clarita B. Diaz, May 31, 1987; children: Dannabel, Christoph. Degree in elec. engring., Fed. Coll. Tech., Steyr, Austria, 1968. Designer Sprecher & Schuh, Linz, Austria, 1970; engr. Howe Richardson Scale, Johannesburg, Republic of South Africa, 1971; project engr. HMS Automation, Wolfern, 1971-75; sr. engr., cons. Dynamic Projects Ltd., Johannesburg, 1975-80; gen. mgr. Gulf Dynamic Switchgear, Sharjah, United Arab Emirates, 1980—. Served with Austrian Army, 1968-69. Mem. United Arab Emirates Engrs. Soc. Home: PO Box 6155, Sharjah United Arab Emirates Office: Gulf Dynamic Switchgear, PO Box 6155, Sharjah United Arab Emirates

NIEDERMAN, JAMES CORSON, physician; b. Hamilton, Ohio, Nov. 27, 1924; s. Clifford Frederick and Henrietta (Corson) N.; m. Miriam Camp, Dec. 12, 1951; children—Timothy Porter, Derrick Corson, Eliza Orton, Caroline Noble. Student, Kenyon Coll., 1942-45, D.Sc. (hon.), 1981; M.D., Johns Hopkins U., 1949. Intern Johns Hopkins Hosp., Balt., 1949-50; asst. resident in medicine Yale-New Haven Med. Center, 1950-51, assoc. resident, 1953-55; practice medicine specializing in internal medicine and clin. epidemiology New Haven, 1955—; instr. Yale U., 1955-58, asst. prof., 1958-66, assoc. prof., 1966-76, clin. prof. medicine and epidemiology, 1976—; mem. herpes adv. team Internat. Agy. for Research in Cancer, WHO; mem. Nat. Council for Johns Hopkins Medicine. Trustee Kenyon Coll.; bd. counselors Smith Coll., 1970-77. Served to 1st lt. M.C. U.S. Army, 1951-53. Fellow Silliman Coll., Yale U. Fellow Am. Coll. Epidemiology; mem. AMA, Am. Fedn. Clin. Research, Infectious Diseases Soc. Am., Am. Epidemiol. Soc., Johns Hopkins Med. and Surg. Assn., Sigma Xi. Democrat. Episcopalian. Clubs: Yale (N.Y.C.); New Haven Lawn. Home: 429 Sperry Rd Bethany CT 06525 Office: 333 Cedar St New Haven CT 06510

NIEDERREITER, HARALD GUENTHER, mathematician, researcher; b. Vienna, June 7, 1944; s. Simon and Erna (Emig) N.; m. Gerlinde Hollweger, Aug. 30, 1969. PhD, U. Vienna, 1969. Asst. prof. So. Ill. U., Carbondale, 1969-72, assoc. prof., 1972-73; mem. Inst. Advanced Study, Princeton, N.J., 1973-75; vis. prof. UCLA, 1975-76; prof. U. Ill., Urbana, 1976-78, U. W.I., Kingston, Jamaica, 1978-81; researcher Austrian Acad. Scis., Vienna, 1981—. Author: Uniform Distribution of Sequences, 1974, Finite Fields, 1983, Introduction to Finite Fields and Their Applications, 1986; contbr. over 100 research articles to math. jours.; assoc. editor Mathematics of Computation, 1988—. Named hon. prof. U. Vienna, 1986. Mem. Am. Math. Soc., Math. Assn. Am., Austrian Math. Soc., Internat. Assn. Cryptologic Research. Home: Sieveringer Str 41, A1190 Vienna Austria Office: Austrian Acad Scis, Dr Ignaz-Seipel-Platz 2, A1010 Vienna Austria

NIEDLING, HOPE HOTCHKISS, dietitian; b. Meriden, Ill.; d. Bert and Myrle Glenn (Vaughn) Hotchkiss; student North Central Coll., 1939-40; B.S., U. Ill., 1943; M.S. in Food Sci. and Nutrition, U. Wis. 1974; m. Ivan Martin Niedling, June 26, 1948. Teaching dietitian Univ. Hosp., Balt., 1944; dietitian public sch. cafeterias, Balt., 1944-48; dir. admisions Thomas Sch. Retailing, Phila., 1954-55; instr. foods U. Wis., Stevens Point, 1967-68; food service supr., instr. Mid-State, N.Central and Fox Valley Tech. Insts., Wis., 1973-75; cons. dietitian nursing homes in Wis., 1973—. Chmn. Village of Plover Cancer Fund Drive, 1977-78; bd. dirs. Stout Found., U. Wis., 1977-87; sec.-treas. Joint Com. Edn. State of Wis., 1978—. Recipient Loyalty award U. Ill., 1978, award of merit U. Ill. Home Econs. Assn., 1979. Mem. Am. Dietetic Assn. (ho. of dels. 1974-77), Wis. Dietetic Assn., No. Wis. Dietetic Assn. (pres. 1971-73), Soc. Nutrition Edn., Nutrition Today Soc., Nutritionists in Bus., Wis. Assn. Registered Parliamentarians (state corr. sec. 1978-80), Wis. Fedn. Women's Clubs (1st v.p. 1978-80), U. Ill. Home Econs. Alumni Assn. (bd. dirs. 1972-78), Daus. Am. Colonists, Nat. Assn. Registered Parliamentarians, Wis. Public Health Assn. (mem. aging com. 1974-78), Portage County Humane Soc. (sec. 1973-84), Wis. Fedn. Women's Clubs (pres. 1980-82), Gen. Fedn. Women's Clubs (sec.-treas. region 1982-84, chmn. internat. aid div. 1982-84, pres. Gt. Lakes region 1984-86, fundraiser chmn. Gt. Lakes Regional 1986-88), Colonial Dames XVII Century (chpt. 1st v.p. 1981-83, chpt. pres. 1983—), DAR (sec. 1977-80, 1st vice regent 1980-83, state regent 1983-86, chpt. regent 1972-77, chpt. registrar 1977—, pres. Wis. state officers club 1976-77, nat. bd. mgmt. 1983—, v.p. gen. 1987-90, pres. v.p. gens. club, 1988—, nat. chmn. lineage research com. 1986-89, nat. social mem. commn. 1986—), AAUW (pres. br. 1968-72, state corr. sec. 1970-72), U. Ill. Alumni Assn. (dir. 1973), NCCJ (disting. merit citation 1976; vice chmn. Wis. region 1975—; Portage County chmn. Nat. Brotherhood Week 1972—), Portage County Bicentennial of Const. of U.S., Wis. Soc. Children Am. Revolution (sr. state corr. sec. 1984-86, sr. state 1st v.p. 1986—), Wis. Soc. Am. Revolution (state organizing sec.), Children of the Am. Revolution, Nat. Soc. Women Descendants Ancient and Honorable Artillery Co., Nat. Soc. Daughters Founders and Patriots of Am., Soc. Descendants Washington's Army at Valley Forge, Hereditary Order of First Families of Mass., Wis. Fedn. Republican Women (dist. chmn. 1969-74), Gamma Sigma Delta, Epsilon Sigma Omicron. Methodist. Clubs: Stevens Point Area Woman's (pres. 1972-74, 76-78). Lodge: Order Eastern Star, Order of Amaranth, Order White Shrine of Jerusalem. Address: 1008 3rd St Stevens Point WI 54481

NIEDZIELSKI, JAMES PETER, engineer; b. Bay City, Mich., Jan. 19, 1939; s. Clement John and Eleanore (Craves) N.; m. Anne Wazbinski, Sept. 3, 1960; children: Nancy, Nickalee, Aaron. Grad., Devry Tech. Inst., Chgo., 1963. Engr. Laser Systems Corp., Ann Arbor, Mich., 1963-69; prodn. mgr. Photon Sources, Inc., Livonia, Mich., 1969-75; v.p. engring. Phoenix Laser, Livonia, 1975-79; sales mgr. Rob-Con Inc., Livonia, 1979-83; chief engr. Laser Techs., South Lyon, Mich., 1983—; cons., 1980—. Contbr. devel. 1st pulsed carbon dioxide laser, packing for 1st indsl. laser; designer 1st laser used for glaucomia surgery, 1st program-controlled robot, 1st double arm indl. robot. Mem. Soc. Mfg. Engrs. Club: Round Table (Plymouth, Mich.). Home: 8383 Rushton Rd South Lyon MI 48178 Office: Laser Techs 10131 Colonial Industry South Lyon MI 48178

NIEHOUSE, OLIVER LESLIE, management consultant; b. St. Louis, July 25, 1920; s. Oliver Lewis and Edythe Mae (Burch) N.; m. Ellen Verdell Sims, Apr. 1, 1945; 1 child, Daniel Lee (dec.). BS, Sir George Williams U., Montreal, 1957; MBA, U. Chgo., 1963; postgrad. NYU, 1968-78; MS, Calif. Am. U., 1979. With Olin Industries Inc., East Alton, Ill., 1941-51, research and devel. supr., 1947-51, mgr. tech. sales, N.Y.C., 1951-55; mgr. advt. and sales devel. TCF of Can., Ltd., Montreal, P.Q., 1955-58; dir. sales Yardley of London Ltd., Toronto, Ont., 1958-60; gen. mgr. Sunbeam Corp., Chgo., 1960-65; v.p., dir. Sunbeam A.G., Zug, Switzerland, 1965-67; mng. dir. Sunbeam Electric Ltd., East Kilbride, Scotland, and London, 1965-67; v.p., gen. mgr. Pantasote Co. of N.Y., N.Y.C., 1967-70; pres. subsidiaries, exec. v.p. Polypump Ltd., Toronto, Ont., 1970-71; asst. prof. Hofstra U., Hempstead, N.Y., 1971-78; pres. Niehouse & Assocs. Inc., Forest Hills, N.Y., 1971—; vis. assoc. prof. Mktg. NYU, 1988—; dir. ctr. for mgmt. devel., disting. lectr. in mgmt. Coll. of Bus., Rochester Inst. Tech., 1986-87. Patentee in field. Editorial bd. Management Solutions jour.; contbr. articles to profl. jours. Recipient Disting. Teaching award Hofstra U., 1975. Mem. Nat. Speakers Assn., Acad. of Mgmt., Am. Mktg. Assn., Am. Soc. for Tng. and Devel., Am. Chem. Soc. Home: 175 Kellogg Dr Wilton CT 06897 Office: Niehouse and Assocs Inc 109-23 71st Rd Forest Hills NY 11375

NIEHUSS, MERITH, historian, educator; b. Bielefeld, Fed. Republic of Germany, Feb. 13, 1954; s. Joachim and Annemarie (Tappert) N. MA, U. Munich, 1978, Diploma in Social Scis., 1980, PhD, 1982. Academic counselor Inst. New History, Munich, 1982—. Author: Arbeiter in Krieg und Inflation, 1983; co-author Wahlen im Kaiserreich, 1980, Wahlen in der Bundesrepublik, 1987. Mem. Verband der Historiker Deutschlands, 1982—. Office: U Inst New History, Trautenwolfstrasse 3, 8000 Munich 40, Federal Republic of Germany

NIEKAMP, ALBERT, publishing company auditing director; b. Brummen, Netherlands, Sept. 5, 1930; s. Egbertus and Hendrika Johanna (Harmsen) N.; m. Jacoba Bertha Verschleuss, Nov. 9, 1963; children—Egbert Gerrit, Gerard Esse. Registered acct. Netherland Inst. Registered Accts. Asst. auditor Moret & Starke, Rotterdam, 1952-54; asst. auditor KLM, Amsterdam, also N.Y.C., 1959-62; sr. auditor Arthur Andersen & Co., The Hague, 1962-67; internal auditor Holland-Amerika Line, Rotterdam, 1967-70, S.H.V., Utrecht, 1970-79; dir. auditing Elsevier nv, Amsterdam, 1979—; expert-examiner auditing Free U., Amsterdam, 1979—. Contbr. articles to profl. jours. Mem. editorial bd. Corp. Crime and Security Bull.-Oxford, 1980. Bd. dirs. Nat. Mus. Mus. Clocks and Street Organs, Utrecht, 1974. Served with Dutch Royal Air Force, 1950-52. Fellow Nat. Inst. Register accountants, Inst. Internal Auditors, Inst. EDP auditors, Nat. Assn. Accountants. Christian Democrat. Dutch Reformed. Club: Bunnik Lawn Tennis. Home: Camminghalaan 5, Bunnik, Utrecht 3981 GD The Netherlands Office: Elsevier, PO Box 470, 1000 AL, Amsterdam The Netherlands

NIELSEN, AAGE ROSENDAL, educational association administrator; b. Stagstrup, Thy, Denmark, June 30, 1921; s. Emanuel and Maren Svankjaer (Jensen) N.; m. Laurel Caldwel, July 24, 1949 (div. June 1960); children: Rasmus, Kim, Rosendal, Denny. Student, Sorø Acad., Denmark, 1941-44, Grandview Coll., Des Moines, Iowa, 1947-48, Hartford (Conn.) Sem., 1948-49. Tchr. various schs., Denmark, 1944-50; rector Nordenfiord World U., Thy, 1972—; pres. Assn. World Edn., Thy, 1978—; founder, bd. dirs. Scandinavian Seminar for Cultural Studies, Copenhagen; traveling salesman Lisle Fellowship, Mich., 1952-53; cons. Assn. World Edn. UN, N.Y., 1978—; organizer 2 Assn. World Edn. Congresses, India and Denmark, 1975-86. Author: Lust for Learning, 1970, World Education, 1971, United Nations University, 1975; contbr. 40 articles to profl. jours. Founder Coop. among Transnationals, 1986—; co-founder UN Univ. Ctr., Thy, 1974; chmn. UNúNGO com. UN Univ. for Peace, N.Y.C., 1980—; minister Universal Life ch., Inc., Calif., 1969—; bd. dirs. Globale Folkeligheds, 1986—. Named an Assn. World Edn. Peace Messenger, UN, 1987. Lodge: Masons. Home: Skyumvej 101, 7752 Snedsted Thy Denmark Office: Assn World Edn, Skyumvej 1010, 7752 Snedsted Thy Denmark

NIELSEN, DIANE TAPPEN, mathematician; b. N.Y.C., July 4, 1947; d. Aage William and Belinda Willmira (Tappen) Nielsen. Student Lasell Jr. Coll., 1965-66; B.A. in Sociology, Am. U., 1969; B.A. in Math., George Washington U., 1983. Computer specialist U.S. Geol. Survey, Reston, Va., 1972-79, mathematician U.S. Geol. Survey, 1979; asst. to natural resources advisor Inter-Am. Devel. Bank, Washington, 1979-85 ; mathematician U.S. Geol. Survey, Reston, 1985—; collaborator with Dr. B.F. Grossling, in petroleum resource assessments of developing countries, 1973—. Co-author: In Search of Oil, vols. 1 and 2, 1985. Mem. Soc. Indsl. and Applied Math., N.Y. Acad. Scis, Internat. Assn. Energy Econonmists, Nat. Computer Graphics Assn. Episcopalian. Office: US Geol Survey Nat Ctr 12201 Sunrise Valley Dr Reston VA 22092

NIELSEN, ERLAND KOLDING, library director; b. Frederiksberg, Denmark, Jan. 13, 1947; s. Olav and Anna (Kolding) N.; m. Anne Birthe van Holck, 1969 (div. 1981); children: Gudrun, Jens Christian; m. Inger SØrensen, 1982. MA in History, PhD, U. Copenhagen, 1973. Lectr. Royal Sch. Librarianship U. Copenhagen, 1971-80, asst. prof. Inst Contemporary History, 1973-83, head dept. humanities and social scis., 1980-86, head Edn. Research Librarians and Documentalists Royal Sch. Librarianship, 1984-86; dir. gen. Royal Library, Copenhagen, 1986—. Author 3 books in history and library sci.; contbr. articles to profl. jours. Mem. Research Librarian's Council (sec. 1975-79, chmn. 1979-82), Danish Research Libraries Assn. (bd. dirs. 1987—), Adv. Council Research Libraries (bd. dirs. 1987—), Library Sect. Nat. Union Academics (chmn. 1977-85), Conf. Dirs. Nat. Libraries, Danish Nat. Bd. Protection Cultural Values, Arnamagnean Commn. Home: Egholmsvej 1, DK-2830 Virum Denmark Office: Royal Library, Christians Brygge 8, DK-1302 Copenhagen Denmark

NIELSEN, HANS FREDE, historical linguist; b. Bramming, Denmark, May 20, 1943; s. Frede and Sonja (Schultz) N.; m. Helene Boile Kristjansen, Jan. 5, 1979. BA, Trinity Coll., Cambridge, Eng., 1968; Mag. Art., Copenhagen U., 1971; Dr. Phil., Odense (Denmark) U., 1982. Assoc. prof. hist. linguistics Dept. English Odense U., 1975—, chmn., 1984-86; vis. prof. Univ. Coll. London, 1984; guest lectr. various univs., Engl., U.S., the Netherlands, Denmark; external examiner in English Copenhagen Sch.

Econs., 1977—, U. Copenhagen, U. Aarhus, 1984—. Author: De germanske sprog, 1979, Old English and the Continental Germanic Languages, 1981; co-author: Irregularities in Modern English, 1986; editor NOWELE Jour., 1983—, PEO, 1983—; co-editor Friserstudier, 1980—; cons. editor Jour. English Linguistics, 1984—; contbr. articles to profl. jours. Mem. Conf. Editors of Learned Jours. Home: Esbern Snaresvej 1, DK-4180 Sorø Denmark Office: Odense U Dept English, Campusvej 55, DK-5230 Odense Denmark

NIELSEN, JOERGEN MOELLER, transportation company finance executive; b. Horsens, Denmark, Apr. 7, 1959; s. Boerge Moeller and Kamma Moeller (Stoevlback) N. BS in Econs., Handelshoejskolen U., Aarhus, Denmark, 1981, MS in Econs., 1983. Market researcher Dansk Supermarked A/S, Aarhus, 1982; mgmt. asst. Priess & Co. A/S, Glyngoere, Denmark, 1983-84; controller Danfoss A/S, Nordborg, Denmark, 1984-86; fin. dir. EHJ Transport & Spedition A/S, Padborg, Denmark, 1986—; bd. dirs. Transnordic Data A/C., Padborg. Mem. Foreningen af Danske Civilekonomer. Office: EHJ Transport & Spedition A/S, Industrive 13, 6330 Padborg Denmark

NIELSEN, KIRSTEN, theology educator; b. Svendborg, Fyn, Denmark, Oct. 12, 1943; d. Verner Gustav Thorvald and Else Marie (Foss) Schroll; m. Leif Nielsen, July 29, 1967. MA in Religious Studies, French, Aarhus U., Denmark, 1970, PhD in Theology, 1976, D in Theology, 1985. Asst. prof. Inst. Religionsstudier, U. Aarhus, 1971-76, assoc. prof., 1976—; dean of faculty U. Aarhus, 1984 ; mem. Com. for Translating the Old Testament into Modern Danish, 1976—. Mem. Danish Bible Soc. (bd. dirs.), Religionsvidenskabeligt Tidsskrift (bd. dirs.). Lutheran. Home: Vågøgade 5, 8200 Aarhus N, Jutland Denmark Office: Det Teologiske Fakultet, Nordre Ringgade, 8000 Aarhus C, Jutland Denmark

NIELSEN, NIELS-AAGE, banker; b. Copenhagen, Oct. 13, 1933; s. Hans Andersen Nielsen and Signe (Nielsen) Hoyer-Nielsen; m. Lucy Ann Dudman, Dec. 17, 1960; children—Vibeke, Pia, Erik. M.Econs., U. Aarhus (Denmark), 1959. Cons., Danish Savs. Banks Assn., 1961-63; mng. dir. Sav. Banks Data Ctrs., 1963-73; mng. dir. Nordic Sav. Data, 1969-73; dep. gen. mgr. Sparekassen SDS, Copenhagen, 1973-77, gen. mgr., 1977—; dir., vice chmn. Money Instns. Payment Ctr., Copenhagen, 1971-84; dir. Danish Export Credit Council, 1975-80; vice chmn. Eurocard-Denmark, 1977-83; vice chmn. Money Instns. Debit and Credit Card Co., Copenhagen, 1979-83; dir. London Interstate Bank, 1981. Rotary Internat. fellow, 1959-60. Mem. Danish Assn. Stockbroking Cos. (bd. dirs. 1987). Office: Sparekassen SDS, Kongens Nytorv 8, 1050 Copenhagen Denmark

NIELSEN, STEVEN JEROME, dentist; b. Amery, Wis., Apr. 21, 1947; s. Gordon P. and Betty Lu (Olson) N.; m. Joan E. Geiser, Jan. 30, 1971; children—Stephanie Rae, Lindsay Joan. Student Gustavus Adolphus Coll., 1965-67; B.S., D.D.S., U. Minn., 1971. Intern W.Va. U., 1971-72; practice dentistry, Golden Valley, Minn., 1972—; pres. Bassett Creek Dental, Golden Valley, 1980—; cons. nursing homes. Mem. ADA, Minn. Dental Assn., Mpls. Dist. Dental Soc., Am. Acad. Dental Group Practice, W.Va. Soc. Hosp. Dentists. Republican. Lutheran. Lodge: Lions (pres. 1980-81, 100% Pres.'s award 1981). Avocations: boating; sailboarding; skiing; racquetball. Home: 3300 Carman Rd Excelsior MN 55331 Office: 5851 Duluth St Golden Valley MN 55422

NIELSON, WILLIAM PAUL, insurance executive; b. Plandome, N.Y., Feb. 8, 1929; s. Paul A. and Marquerite (Morgenthaler) N. B.A., Randolph-Macon Coll., 1950; postgrad. U. Edinburg, 1951. Pres. Paul A. Nielson & Son, Inc., Manhasset, N.Y., 1952—. Treas. St. Mary's Hosp. for Children, Bayside, N.Y., 1985; v.p. Vis. Home Health Service of Nassau, Manhasset, 1982-85; trustee Vincent Smith Sch., Port Washington, 1975-80. Republican. Episcopalian. Clubs: Port Washington Yacht (commodore 1988), North Hempstead Country. Avocation: sailing. Office: Paul A Nielson & Son Inc 19 Park Ave Manhasset NY 11030

NIEMANN, RÜDIGER ERNST WALTER, lawyer; b. Kö ln, Germany, June 6, 1936; s. Walter Adolf Hermann and Ingeborg Dorothea (Mickel) N.; m. Marianne Weindorf, Dec. 30, 1964; children—Fabian, Saskia. LL.B., U. Kö ln. Barrister, Kö ln, 1966-68; legal adv. BDZV German Newspaper Assn., Bonn, 1968-72, dir., Bonn, 1972-85, chief mgr., 1986—; mng. dir. M. DuMont Schauberg pub. Decorated Cross Order of Merit (Fed. Republic Germany). Home: 12 Am Sonnenhang, Bonn Federal Republic of Germany Office: 70 Breite Strasse, Köln Federal Republic of Germany

NIEMCZYK, JULIAN MARTIN, U.S. ambassador to Czechoslovakia; b. Fort Sill, Okla., Aug. 26, 1920; married. B.A., U. Philippines, 1955. Enlisted U.S. Army, 1940, served as tech. sgt. to 1st lt., 1940-44, capt. Office Strategic Services, Burma and China, 1944-45, capt. Joint Operation Crossroads, atomic bomb test, 1946, capt. Combat Info. Ctr., Balt., 1947-49, maj. Office Spl. Investigations, Washington, 1949-50, maj. Far East Air Force, 1950-52, lt. col. Air Attache Office, U.S. Embassy, Manila, Philippines, 1952-56, lt. col. tng. for new assignment, 1956-57, lt. col., air attache U.S. Embassy, Warsaw, 1958-60, col. Nat. Security Agy., 1960-65, col. tng. for new assignment, 1965-67, col., def. and air attache, U.S. Embassy, Prague, Czechoslovakia, 1967-69, col. Internat. Security Affairs, Office Sec. Def., Washington, 1969-71, ret. as col., USAF, 1971; dir. heritage groups div. Republican Nat. Com., Washington, 1972-75, exec. dir. Heritage Groups Council, 1975-81; chief exec. officer People to People Internat., 1983-86; U.S. Ambassador to Czechoslovakia, 1986—. Office: Am Embassy, Trziste, 15-12548 Prague Czechoslovakia also: Dept of State US Ambassador to Czechoslavakia Washington DC 20520 *

NIEMEYER, OSCAR, architect; b. Rio de Janeiro, Dec. 15, 1907; s. Oscar Niemeyer Soares; m. Anita Niemeyer; 1 dau. Grad., Escola Nacional Belas Artes, Rio de Janeiro. With Office of Lúcio Costa, 1935. Prin. works include Ministry of Edn. and Health Bldg., Rio de Janeiro,1937-43, Brazilian Pavilion, N.Y. World Fair, 1939, Bienal Exhbn. Hall, São Paulo, French CP bldg., Paris, 1966, Palace of Arches, Brasília; with others UN Bldg., N.Y.C., 1947; dir. architecture for new capital of Brasília, 1957—. Recipient Lenin Peace prize, 1963, Prix Internat. de l'Architecture d'aujourd'hui, 1966; co-recipient Pritzker prize, 1988. Address: 3940 ave Atlântica, Rio de Janeiro RJ, Brazil *

NIEMI, (ERKKI) JUSSI, linguist, educator; b. Pori, Finland, Feb. 10, 1950; s. Kauko Jussi and Kyllikki Emilia (Varjomaa) N.; m. Eva Sinikka Buss, July 27, 1975; 1 child, John. MBA, Turku (Finland) U., 1976, licentiate of philosophy, 1978, PhD, 1984. Research asst. U. Turku, 1976-77; asst. U. Joensuu, Finland, 1977-79, sr. lectr., 1979—; assoc. prof. pro tem U. Jyväskylä, Finland, 1983-84; prin. investigator research project Neurolinguistic study of Finnish aphasics, Joensuu, 1982—. Contbr. numerous articles to profl. jours. Grantee Fulbright Found., 1977, Acad. Finland, 1983—. Mem. Linguistic Soc. Am., Internat. Soc. Applied Psycholinguistics, Nordic Assn Linguists, Assn. Computational Linguistics, Internat. Neuropsychol. Soc. Office: U Joensuu, PO Box 111, 80101 Joensuu Finland

NIEMI, TAPIO JUHANI, investment banker; b. Helsinki, Finland, June 18, 1949; s. Erkki Kalervo and Linda Borghild (Pelin) N.; m. Tuija Irene Koskinen, Mar. 14, 1975; children: Lassi Tapio Viljami, Jussi Antti Ilmari. BSc in Econs., Helsinki Sch. Econs. and Bus. Adminstrn., 1973. Security dealer stock exchange dept. Kansallis-Osake-Pankki, Helsinki, 1973-78, mgr. stock exchange dept., 1978-84, sr. mgr. securities dept., 1984-86, 1st v.p. investments and new issues div., 1986-87; 1st v.p. investment banking Sales, Trading and Investor Services, 1987—. Mem. Neles 30 Yr. Found. (bd. dirs. 1986—), Finnish Assn. for Allergic Diseases (fin. com. 1986—). Office: Kansallis-Osake-Pankki, Aleksanterinkatu 42, SF-00100 Helsinki Finland

NIEMOLLER, ARTHUR B., engineer; b. Wakefield, Kans., Oct. 4, 1912; s. Benjamin Henry and Minnie Christine (Carlson) N.; m. Ann Sochor, May 29, 1937 (dec. June 1982); children: Joanna Matteson, Arthur D. BSEE, Kans. State U., 1933. Registered profl. engr., N.Y., N.J., Pa., Ill., Ohio. Engr. Westinghouse, Newark, Hillside, N.J., 1937-59, Chgo., 1959-61, Pitts., 1961-65, Cin., 1965-77; pvt. practice engr. Montgomery, Ohio, 1977—. Patentee in field. Served with USN, 1933-37. Mem. IEEE, NSPE. Republican. Presbyterian. Home and Office: 7888 Mitchell Farm Ln Cincinnati OH 45242

NIERMAN, LEONARDO MENDELEJIS, artist; b. Mexico City, Nov. 1, 1932; s. Chanel and Clara (Mendelejis) N.; m. Esther Ptak, Feb. 16, 1957; children: Monica, Daniel, Claudia. BS in Physics and Math, U. Mexico; degree in bus. adminstrn., U. Mex., 1959, degree in music, hon. degree, 1960. One-man shows, Proteo Gallery, 1958, 60, C.D.I. Gallery, 1956, Misrachi Gallery, 1964, Galeria Merkup, 1969, Mus. Modern Art, 1972, all Mexico City, Galeria Sudamericana, N.Y.C., 1958, Hammer Galleries, N.Y.C., 1960, I.F.A. Galleries, Washington, 1952, 62, 65, 68, 71, Edgardo Acosta Gallery, Beverly Hills, Calif., 1961, Art Collectors Gallery, Beverly Hills, 1966, Main St. Gallery, Chgo., 1961, Doll & Richard Gallery, Boston, 1963, Pucker Safrai Gallery, Boston, 1969, El Paso (Tex.) Mus Art, 1964, 71, Wolfard's Gallery, Rochester, N.Y., 1964, Pub. Library Rockville Centre, N.Y., 1964, Little Gallery, Phila., 1964, Neusteters Gallery Fine Arts, Denver, 1965, Judah L. Magnes Meml. Mus., Berkeley, Calif., 1967, Galerie Katia Granoff, Paris, 1969, Little Gallery, Phila., 1970, Aalwin Gallery, London, 1970, Gallery Modern Art, Scottsdale, Ariz., 1971, Mus. Contemporary Arts, Bogota, Colombia, 1973, 74, Galerie Dresdnere, Ont., Can., Casa de la Cultura, Cucuta, Colombia, 1974, also mus., galleries, Haifa, Israel, Rome, Italy, Toronto, Ont., Can., Paris, France, 1962—; exhibited group shows mus., Caracas, Venezuela, 1958, Mexico City, 1958—, Havana, Cuba, 1959, Tokyo, Japan, 1963, Paris, France, 1961, Nagoya, Japan, 1963, Kyoto, Japan, 1963, Osaka, Japan, 1963, Bogota, 1963, Santiago, Chile, 1963, Buenos Aires, Argentina, 1963, Rio de Janeiro, Brazil, 1963, Costa Rica, 1963, Panama, 1963, Oslo, Norway, 1965, Warsaw, Poland, 1965, Madrid, Spain, 1965, Stockholm, Sweden, 1966, Brussels, Belgium, 1966; also exhibitions at the Mus. Contemporary Art, Bogota, Colombia (diploma d'honneur of fine arts in Monaco), 1976, B. Lewin Galleries, Los Angeles, 1977, I.F. A. Galleries, Washington, 1977, Merrill Chase Galleries, Chgo., 1977, Am. Mus., Hayden Planetarium, N.Y.C., 1978, Cumberland Mus. of Sci. Ctr., Nashville, 1978, Fernback Sci. Ctr., Atlanta, 1978, Nahan Galleries, New Orleans, 1980, Broward Galleries, Pompano Beach, Fla., 1980, Mus. Sci. and Industry, Chgo., 1980, Galeria de Arte Misrachi, Mexico City, 1982, Calif. Mus. Sci. and Industry, 1982, Museo de Arte e Historia, Ciudad Juarez, Mexico, 1984, Centro de Artes Visuales e Investigaciones Esteticas, Mexico, 1984, Barbara Gillman Gallery, Miami, 1984, MIT Mus., Boston, 1984; also exhibited Expo, 1958, also numerous mus., univs., Eastern and Western U.S., Can., 1958—; executed murals, Sch. Commerce University City, Mexico, 1956, Bank San Francisco, 1965, physics bldg., Princeton, 1969; also executed stained glass windows, Mexican synagogues, 1968-69; represented in permanent collections, Mus. Modern Art in Mexico, Atlanta Mus., Mus. Modern Art Haifa, Gallery Modern Art, N.Y.C., Phoenix Art Mus., Pan Am. Union, Washington, Detroit Inst. Arts, Bogota Mus. Contemporary Arts, Mus. Contemporary Arts, Madrid, Acad. Fine Arts, Honolulu, Tucson Art Center, Tel-Aviv Mus., Israel Mus., Jerusalem, Kennedy Art Center, Washington, Boston Mus. Fine Arts, U. Va., No. Ill. Univ., Chgo. Art Inst., other mus. and galleries. (Recipient 1st prize Mexican Contemporary Art, Art Inst. Mexico 1964, Palme d'or Beaux Arts, Monaco 1969, gold medal Tomasso Campanella Found. 1972). Recipient Gold medal Internat. Parliament for Safety and Peace-U.S.A.-Italy, 1983; named Accademico D'Europe, Centro Studi di Ricerchi L'Accademia D'Europa, Italy; European Banner of Arts Prize, Italy, 1984, Oscar D'Italia, 1984; winner of world-wide competition to do a sculpture for U. Cen. Fla., Orlando, 1986. Life fellow Royal Soc. Arts (London, Eng.). Office: Amsterdam 43 PH, Mexico City 11, Mexico also: Str Reforma 16 Bis, Mexico City 20, Mexico *

NIERSTE, JOSEPH PAUL, software engineer; b. Marion, Ind., Feb. 20, 1952; s. Louis Lemuel and Mary Catherine (Dragstrem) N.; m. Deborah Mae Goble, Sept. 20, 1986. BA Applied Piano, Bob Jones U., 1975; MM in Musical Performance, Ball State U., 1977, MS in Computer Sci., 1984. Instr. Marion Coll., 1983-84, Ball State U., Muncie, Ind., 1983-84; software engr. Tokheim Corp., Ft. Wayne, Ind., 1984, Delco Electronics, Kokomo, Ind., 1984—. Mem. Pi Kappa Lambda. Republican. Baptist. Home: 832 W Woodland Ave Kokomo IN 46902 Office: Delco Electronics Corp CT-40-D Kokomo IN 46902

NIES, FRIEDRICH HEINRICH, language educator; b. Ludwigshafen, Fed. Republic Germany, Feb. 13, 1934; s. Fritz and Lilli P. (Gutmann) N.; m. Hildegard A. Hansen, Dec. 29, 1959; children: Axel, Barbara A., Charlotte. Grad., U. Heidelberg, Fed. Republic Germany, 1959, PhD, 1961. Asst. d'allemand College Coubebevoie, France, 1957-58; lecteur d'allemand U. Rennes, France, 1959-61; lectr., Akademischer Rat U. Heidelberg, 1961-70; prof. U. Dusseldorf, Fed. Republic Germany, 1970—, dean faculty, 1977-78; vis. prof. U. Nanterre, France, 1981; pres. Fachausschuss D.F.G., 1980-84. Author: Poesie in prosaischer Welt, 1964, Gattungspoetik, 1972 (prix Strasbourg 1973), Genres Mineurs, 1978; editor: 28 books, 4 jours.; contbr. articles to profl. pubs. Named officer de Palmes Acad., 1985. Mem. Deutscher Romanistenverband (pres. 1984-87), Akademisches Auslandsamt Universitat (pres. 1974—), Societe des Etudes Romantiques. Home: Morikestrasse 28, 4044 Kaarst 1 Federal Republic of Germany Office: Univ Dusseldorf, Universitatsstrasse 1, 4000 Dusseldorf Federal Republic of Germany

NIETO, JUAN MANUEL, physician; b. Alpine, Tex., Sept. 24, 1949; s. Edmundo Miguel and Socorro (Herrera) N.; BS, U. Notre Dame, 1970; MD, U. Colo., 1974; children: Ana Raquel, Cristina Marie. Intern, Los Angeles County, U. So. Calif. Med. Ctr., 1974-75; physician Community Health Found., Los Angeles, 1975-77, Emergency Dept. Physicians Med. Group, Marina Del Ray, Calif., 1977-78; resident in emergency medicine Denver Gen.-St. Anthony Hosp. Systems, 1978-80; mem. staff North Colo. Med. Center, Greeley, Colo., 1980-83; emergency physician, med. dir. emergency dept. Brackenridge Hosp., Austin, Tex., 1984-85; practice medicine, Austin, 1983—; emergency physician Emergency Physicians Affiliates, 1986—; mem. planning com. Starflight Helicopter Air Transport, 1985; instr. advanced cardiac life support, 1977; bd. dirs. Nat. Chicano Health Orgn., 1971-74; adv. E. Los Angeles Hypertension Screening Program, 1978; med. adv. Weld County Ambulance Service, 1980-83; med. dir. Air Life, 1980-83. del. Colo. Med. Soc., 1983. Fellow Am. Coll. Emergency Physicians; mem. Am. Coll. Emergency Physicians, Am. Public Health Assn., Tex. Med. Assn., Travis County Med. Soc., Acad. Polit. Sci., Amnesty Internat. Lodge: Optimists.

NIETO-ROIG, JUAN JOSE, mathematician, educator; b. Madrid, Spain, Sept. 27, 1958; s. Ruperto and Maria (Concepción) N.; m. Angela Torres-Iglesias, July 13, 1985. M.Math., U. Santiago, Spain, 1980; D.Math., 1983. Teaching asst. U. Santiago, Spain, 1980, prof. math., 1983—; vis. prof. U. Tex.-Arlington, 1981-83. Contbr. articles to math. jours. Recipient Best Student award Matematicas Univ., Santiago, 1980. Research fellow U. Santiago, 1981-83. Mem. Am. Math. Soc., Soc. Indsl. and Applied Math., Assn. Computing Machinery. Office: Universidad De Santiago, Facultad Matematicas, Santiago, La Coruna Spain

NIEUWDORP, HENRICUS (HANS) MARIUS JOSEPH, museum curator; b. Rotterdam, Netherlands, June 19, 1944; came to Belgium, 1952; s. Adriaan M. J. and Elza (Spitzen) N.; m. Beatrijs X.A.G. Van Ongeval, Nov. 26, 1969; children—Eva, Nicolaas, Maarten. Licence in History of Art with high distinction Cath. U., Louvain, Belgium, 1968. Sci. asst. Hist. Mus., Antwerp, Belgium, 1968-69, Royal Mus. Fine Arts, Brussels, Belgium, 1969-76; asst. curator Mus. Mayer V.D. Bergh, Antwerp, Belgium, 1976-80; curator, dir. Art Mus., Antwerp, 1980—; sec. Belgian Nat. Com., Internat. Mus., 1977-80; bd. dirs. Mus. Assn., Belgium, 1974—; docent Inst. Art History, Antwerp, 1978-81. Author: Textiles/Museum Mayer V. D. Bergh, 1979; Museum Mayer V. D. Bergh, 1980; contbr. articles on sculpture to profl. jours. Mem. Nat. Mus. Council (pres. 1987—). Roman Catholic. Home: Lorkenlaan 7, B-2508 Nylen-Kessel Belgium Office: Mus Mayer van den Bergh, Lange Gasthuisstraat 19, B-2000 Antwerp Belgium

NIEVES-RODRIGUEZ, MIGUEL ANGEL, mercantile executive; b. Penuelas, P.R., May 8, 1913; s. Vicente Cosme Nieves and Gertrudis Rodriguez; m. Ana Maria Rodriguez, Dec. 10, 1934; children—Maria del Rosario, Miguel Angel, Ana Teresa, Carmen Luisa, Jose Randolph. Student U. P.R., 1967. Office mgr. Bosch Bros., Ponce, P.R., 1930; corr. El Imparcial newspaper, P.R., 1933; columnist various local newspapers, P.R., 1932-74; announcer, script writer Sta. WPRP, Ponce, 1934-47; founder Federacion Deportiva, Mercedita-Ponce, P.R., 1933-41; sales mgr. Colgate-Palmolive Co., San Juan, P.R., 1964; gen. mgr. and asst. v.p. Spanish Am. Trading, San Juan, 1966; exec. dir. Bd. Trade of P.R., San Juan, 1967—; 1st v.p. Inst. Psicopedagogico of P.R., 1957. P.R. del. Internat. Symposium on Mental Retardation, Bombay, India, 1979; apptd. personal escort to rep. of Pope Paul VI, Mariologic Congress, Santo Domingo, Dominican Republic, 1964, recieved Holy Communion from Pope John Paul II, 1984; bd. dirs. P.R. council Boy Scouts Am., 1963. Served with N.G., 1940. Recipient cross medal Pro Ecclesia et Pontifice, 1983, spl. diploma for Golden Wedding Anniversary, 1984, Merit award Bd. Trade of P.R., 1975, Merit award Broadcasters Associates of P.R., 1978, spl. award Camara Comerciantes Mayoristas P.R., 1986, other merit awards from K.C., Lions Club, Penuelas Mcpl. Govt., P.R. Ho. of Reps. Mem. Hist. Assn. P.R., Am. Assn. of Mental Deficiency. Roman Catholic. Clubs: Peñolano (past navigator), K.C. (hon. life, 4th degree, bd. dirs.).

NIGHTINGALE, EARL CLIFFORD, radio commentator, writer; b. Los Angeles, Mar. 12, 1921; s. Albert Victor and Gladys Fae (Hamer) N.; m. Mary Peterson, July 21, 1942 (div. 1960); children: David Alan, Pamela; m. Lenarda Certa, May 17, 1962 (div. 1976); 1 son, Earl Clifford.; m. Diana Lee Johnson, May 15, 1982. Writer, announcer Sta. KTAR, Phoenix, 1946-49, CBS, Chgo., 1949-50; formed own co. Earl Nightingale, Inc., Chgo., 1950; chmn. bd. Earl Nightingale, Inc., 1950-59; writer, producer own radio program WGN, Chgo., 1950-56; (merged with Lloyd Conant and Splty. Mail Services), Chgo., 1959; forming Nightingale-Conant Corp., Chgo., 1959; chmn. bd. Nightingale-Conant Corp., 1959-87, chmn. emeritus, 1987—. Writer, narrator daily radio program broadcast world-wide; author: This is Earl Nightingale, 1969, Earl Nightingale's Greatest Discovery: The Strangest Secret Revisited, 1987. Active various civic and cultural affairs; Hon. trustee Broward Community Coll., 1974-75. Served with USMC, 1938-46. Inducted into Radio Hall of Fame, 1986; recipient Gold medal Napoleon Hill Found., 1987. Home and Office: Fort Myers FL 33902 Mailing Address: 5446 E Desert Jewel Dr Paradise Valley AZ 85253

NIGHTINGALE, EDMUND JOSEPH, clinical psychologist; b. St. Paul, Jan. 10, 1941; s. Edmund Anthony and Lauretta Alexandria (Horejs) N.; student Nazareth Hall Prep. Sem., 1959-61; A.B., St. Paul Sem., 1963; A.B. magna cum laude, Catholic U. of Louvain (Belgium), 1965, M.A., 1967, S.T.B. cum laude, 1967; postgrad. U. Minn., 1971; M.A., Loyola U., Chgo., 1973, Ph.D. in Clin. Psychology, 1975; m. Marie Arcara, Apr. 9, 1978; 1 son, Edmund Bernard. With Cath. Archdiocese of St. Paul and Mpls., 1967-73; intern in clin. psychology Michael Reese Hosp. and Med. Center, Chgo., 1973-74, W. Side VA Hosp., Chgo., 1974-75; staff psychologist, student counseling center, Loyola U., Chgo., 1975; staff psychologist and clin. coordinator of inpatient unit, drug dependency treatment center Hines (Ill.) VA Hosp., 1975-79, acting chief drug dependency treatment center, 1979-80; chief psychology VA Med. Ctr., Danville, Ill., 1980-86; chief psychology VA Med. Ctr. Mpls., 1986—; mem. personnel bd. Archdiocese of St. Paul and Mpls., 1968-70; lectr. psychology, Loyola U., Chgo., 1975; asst. professorial lectr. psychology, St. Xavier Coll., Chgo., 1975-78; adj. asst. prof. psychology in psychiatry, Abraham Lincoln Sch. Medicine, Med. Center U. Ill., Chgo., 1977-82; adj. prof. psychology Purdue U., 1981-87; asst. prof. psychiatry Med. Sch., U. Minn., 1987—, clin. assoc. prof. psycholgy Coll. Liberal Arts, 1986—; clin. asst. prof. U. Ill. Sch. Medicine, Urbana/Champaign, 1982-87; mem. grad. faculty in counseling psychology Ind. State U., Terre Haute, 1983-86. Bd. dirs. Inst. Postgrad. Studies, Ill. Psychol. Assn., Registered psychologist, Ill.; lic. cons. psychologist, Minn.; certified Nat. Registry of Health Service Providers in Psychology. Mem. Am. Psychol. Assn. (clin. psychology, public service, and psychotherapy divs.), Ill. Psychol. Assn. (clin. psychology and acad. sects.; sec. 1982-83, pres.-elect 1983-84, pres. 1984-85), AAAS, Assn. for Advancement of Psychology, Am. Group Psychotherapy Assn., Am. Soc. Clin. Hypnosis, Minn. Psychol. Assn., Am. Evaluation Assn., Am. Assn. Univ. Profs., Assn. VA chief Psychologists (sec.-treas. 1987—). Founding editor: Louvain Studies, 1966; editor: VA Directory of Psychology Staffing and Services, 1982, 83, 84, 85, 87. Home: 2281 Ocala Ct Mendota Heights MN 55120 Office: VA Med Center Minneapolis MN 55417

NIGHTINGALE, GEOFFREY JOSEPH, communications company executive, consultant; b. New Haven, Conn., Sept. 5, 1938; s. Louis M. and Evelyn G. (Carr) N.; m. Gisela I. Staats, Apr. 7, 1961; children: Alyssa M., Christopher G. BA, CCNY, 1963. Editor Trench Pubs., N.Y.C., 1961-64; pub. relations AE W. Alec Jordan Assocs., N.Y.C., 1964-68; pub. relations AE Burson-Marsteller, N.Y.C., 1968-71, group mgr., v.p. pub. relations, 1971-73, creative dir. pub. relations, v.p., 1973-78, exec. v.p., worldwide creative dir., 1983—; mng. dir. Syner Genics div. Burson-Marsteller, N.Y.C., London, Frankfurt, The Hague (The Netherlands), Brussels, 1986—; creative cons. N.Y.C., 1978-83; cons. Port of Galveston, Tex., 1984-86. Contbr. articles to profl. jours. Cons. Conservative Party, 1977-78, USA for Africa, 1985-86. Served with U.S. Army, 1958-60. Mem. Internat. Assn. Bus. Communicators, Corp. Communication Cons., World Future Soc. Republican. Unitarian-Universalist. Office: Burson-Marsteller Syner Genics div 230 Park Ave S New York NY 10003

NIGHTINGALE, WILLIAM JOSLYN, management consulting company executive; b. Mpls., Sept. 16, 1929; s. William Issac and Gladys (Joslyn) N.; B.A., Bowdoin Coll., 1951; M.B.A., Harvard U., 1953; children—Paul, Sara, William Joslyn, Margaret. Mktg. mgr. Gen. Mills Inc., Mpls., 1957-66; sr. asso. Booz, Allen & Hamilton Inc., N.Y.C., 1966-68; v.p. fin. Hanes Corp., Winston-Salem, N.C., 1969; pres. Bali Co. Inc., N.Y.C., 1970-75; pres. Nightingale & Assocs. Inc., New Canaan, Conn., 1975—; dir. Ring's End Lumber Inc., Evans Asset Holdings; trustee Short Term Asset Res. Money Market Fund. Active numerous charitable orgns.; vestryman St. Luke's Episcopal Ch., 1975-78; mem. Darien Representative Town Meeting, 1971-74. Served to lt. (j.g.) USNR, 1953-57. Republican. Clubs: Wee Burn Country; Harvard (N.Y.C.); Coral Beach, Noroton (Conn.) Yacht. Home: Villager Pond 23 Norman Lane Darien CT 06820-1718 Office: 3 Forest St New Canaan CT 06840

NIGL, ALFRED JAMES, psychologist, cons., researcher, author; b. Oshkosh, Wis., July 30, 1949; s. Alfred Joseph and Marion Jane (Roberts) N.; m. Terri S. Abbott, Feb. 19, 1982; children: William Scott, Geoffrey Alan, Brandon Abbott. BA in Psychology, U. Wis., 1971; MA in Clin. Psychology, U. Cin., 1973, PhD in Clin. Psychology, 1975. Diplomate Am. Acad. Behavioral Medicine; cert. Biofeedback Certification Inst. Am. Lic. psychologist, Wis., Calif. Clin. intern or grad. trainee Cin. Gen. Hosp., 1971, Rollman Psychiat. Clinic, Cin., 1971, U. Cin. Univ. Counseling Ctr., 1971, 73, U. Cin. Med. Ctr. Cen. Psychiat. Clinic, 1972, Cin. Ctr. Developmental Disorders, 1973-75, U. Cin. Crises Intervention Clinic, 1973-75, U. Cin. mental health program, 1974-75; acting dir. tng. and research, mental health program U. Cin. Student Health Program, 1974-75; cons. staff psychologist Psychol. and Mgmt. Cons. Services, S.C., Milw., 1975-76; cons. First Western Med. Group, So. Calif., 1986—, Sci. Trading Gmbh, Frankfurt, Fed. Republic Germany, 1981—; pres. Milw. Devel. Ctr., 1975-78; chief psychologist Jackson Psychiat. Ctr., Milw., 1978-80; dir. child and adolescent services Oxnard (Calif.) Mental Health Ctr., 1980-81; cons., dir. biofeedback Kaiser-Permanente Healthwise, 1982-83; dir. rehab. psychology Grossmont Dist. Hosp., 1983-85; pvt. practice psychology, 1985—; cons. Calif. Regional Ctrs. for Developmentally Disabled; staff psychologist Luth. Hosp. Milw., 1978-70, dept. psychiatry Waukesha Meml. Hosp., 1978-80; dir. biofeedback, family practice residency program Waukesha Meml. Hosp. affiliated with Med. Coll. Wis., 1980; adj. clin. prof. Grad. Sch. Pub. Health, San Diego State U., 1983—; pres. Biofeedback Soc. Wis., 1979-80. Bd. dirs. Big Bros./Big Sisters, Ventura County, Calif., 1981-82, Ventura County Rape Crisis Ctr., 1982. U. Cin. Gradn. sch. Council research grantee, 1974; Am. Psychol. Assn. Overseas travel grantee, 1982. Mem. Am. Acad. Behavioral Medicine, AAAS, Am. Psychol. Assn., N.Y. Acad. Scis., Acad. Psychosomatic Medicine, Biofeedback Soc. Am. (rep. to Council State Biofeedback Socs. 1980), Internat. Assn. Study of Pain, Ventura County Psychol. Assn. (bd. dirs. 1982-83). Author: (with Fischer-Williams and Sovine) A Textbook of Biological Feedback, 1981, revised 1986, The Development of Children's Understanding of Spatial Relations, vol. 62 of European Univ. Studies-Psychology, 1981, Biofeedback and Behavioral Strategies in Pain Treatment, 1984; research, publs. in field. Office: 1662 E Main St Suite 216 El Cajon CA 92021

NIGRO, GIOVANNI, pediatric educator; b. Eboli, Italy, Mar. 10, 1945; s. Carmine Antonio and Adalgisa (Tedesco) N.; m. Gloria Taliani, July 5, 1953; 1 child, Veronica. MD, U. Rome, 1970, postgrad., 1972, 74, 77. Asst. prof. U. Rome, 1975-84, prof. pediatrics, 1984—; Italian del. European Soc. Against Virus Diseases. Contbr. articles to profl. jours. Mem. European Group for Rapid Virus Diagnosis, European Soc. for Pediatric Infectious Diseases, Italian Soc. of Pediatrics, Assn. Med. Researchers (del. 1987). Home: Via Parenzo 1, 00198 Rome Italy Office: Via Alessandria 91, 00198 Rome Italy

NIHILL, KAREN BAILEY, nursing home executive, nurse clinician; b. Erie, Pa., Mar. 15, 1947; d. William C. and Eleanor (Danielson) Bailey; R.N., Hamot Med. Center, Erie, 1968; postgrad. U. Pa., 1974—; 1 son, Liam H. Critical care nurse Hamot Med. Center, 1968-71, VA Hosp., Phila., 1974-77; dir. nursing Chapel Manor and Nursing Home, Phila., 1977—, also Phila. Protestant Home and Elmira Jeffries Nursing Home. Active Lutheran Ch. Women's Orgn. Served to lt. Nurse Corps, U.S. Navy, 1971-73. VA grantee, 1974. Mem. Am. Assn. Critical Care Nurses, Pa. Nurses Assn. Republican. Home: 10984 South Shore Ave Northeast PA 16428

NIHMURA, MASAZUMI, food company executive; b. Matsumoto, Nagano Prefecture, Japan, Mar. 12, 1939; s. Chihiro and Yae (Fukao) N.; m. Sumiko Matsuura, Oct. 26, 1969. B, Tokyo U., 1961, PhD in Agr., 1974. Researcher Ajinomoto Co., Inc., Kawasaki, Japan, 1961-73; mgr. lab. Ajinomoto Co., Inc., Tokyo and Yokohama, 1973-80; deputy mgr.cen. research labs. Ajinomoto Gen. Foods, Inc., Suzuka, Japan, 1980-83, mgr., 1983—; also bd. dirs. Ajinomoto Gen. Foods, Inc. Contbr. articles to profl. jours.; inventor in field.

NIHOUL, JACQUES CHARLES-JOSEPH, marine engineer, educator; b. Ans, Belgium, June 6, 1937; s. Victor Marcel and Louise (Ghenne) N.; Ingenieur Physicien, Liege U., 1960; M.S., M.I.T., 1961; Ph.D., Cambridge (Eng.) U., 1965; m. Anne Marie Respentino, May 13, 1966; children—Arnaud, Gaetane. Prof. fluid mechanics U. Louvain (Belgium), 1965—; prof., holder chair of mechs. U. Liege (Belgium), 1966—; Perrin Galpin vis. prof. U. Calif., 1970; Belgian vis. prof. U. London, 1981; sci. adv. Minister for the Walloon Region in water mgmt., 1978—. Served with Air Force Meteo, 1963-64. Ford Found. fellow, 1959; Belgium Am. Ednl. Found. fellow, 1960; NATO Sci. Com. fellow, 1961, 62; recipient Francqui Prize, 1978. Mem. Comite Natl. d'Oceanologie, Comite Nat. de Geodesie et Geophysique Academie, Am. Geophys. Union, Internat. Assn. Hydraulic Research, Internat. Assn. Phys. Scis. of the Ocean, Sci. Com. Oceanic Research, NATO Oceanography Com. Roman Catholic. Author: Modelling of Marine Systems, 1975; Bottom Turbulence, 1977; Hydrodynamics of Estuaries and Fjords, 1978; Marine Forecasting, 1979; Magnetohydrodynamique, 1980; Marine Turbulence, 1980; Ecohydrodynamics, 1981; Hydrodynamics of Semi-Enclosed Seas, 1982; Hydrodynamic Models of Shallow Continental Seas, 1982; Hydrodynamics of the Equatorial Ocean, 1983; Remote Sensing of Shelf Seas Hydrodynamics, 1984; Coupled Ocean-Atmosphere Models, 1985; Marine Interfaces Ecohydrodynamics, 1986, Three-Dimensiional Models of Marine and Estuarine Dynamics, 1987, Small-scale Turbulence and Mixing in the Ocean, 1988. Home: 18 Chemin du Moulin, B4157 Saint Severin Belgium Office: B6 Sart Tilman, B4000 Liege Belgium

NIITU, YASUTAKA, pediatrician, educator; b. Nagano Prefecture, Japan, Aug. 3, 1920; s. Shusuke and Tsuruji N.; m. Tokiko Komuro, Dec. 8, 1952; children—Hidetaka, Iwayasu, Munetaka. Igakushi, Tohoku Imperial U., 1943, M.D. (Igakuhakase), 1949. Research fellow Research Inst. for Tb and Leprosy, Tohoku U., Sendai, Japan, 1943-54, asst. prof. dept. pediatrics, 1954-63, Univ. prof. pediatrics Research Inst. for TB and Cancer, 1964-84, prof. emeritus, 1984—; dr. Miyagi br. Japan Anti TB Assn., 1984-86; pres. Sendai Kosei Hosp., 1986—; adviser Japan Sarcoidosis com. Served to capt. M.C., Japanese Army, 1943-45. Mem. Japan Soc. Pediatric Pneumology (pres. 1980—), Internat. Orgn. Mycoplasmology, Japan Soc. Chest Diseases, Soc. Japanese Virologists, Soc. Paediatrica Japonica, Japanese Soc. Tb, Japan Soc. Pediatric. Co-author books in Japanese, including: Virus and Diseases, 1969; Routine Pediatric Diagnosis and Treatment, 1971; New Virology, 1972; Pediatric X-Ray Diagnosis, 1972; Handbook of Clinical Pneumology, 1977; Present Pediatrics, 1978; Clinical Virology, 1978; Sarcoidosis, 1979; Practice of Pediatric Infections, 1980; Mycoplasma, 1981; Illustrations of Mycoplasma, 1981; Illustrations of Pediatric Diagnosis and Treatment, 1981; Illustrated Pediatric Chart 1982; Topics of Infections, 1983. Mem. editorial bd. Pediatric Pneumonology. Contbr. 300 articles to profl. jours. Home: Higashikatsuyama 1-5-6, 981 Sendai Japan Office: Sendai Kosei Hosp, Hirosemachi 4-12, 980 Sendai Japan

NIKAS, ARISTIDES JAMES, III, geologist; b. San Francisco, Dec. 10, 1956; s. A. James and Theresa Dorothy (Steilberg) N. B.A., San Francisco State U., 1979; postgrad. Golden Gate U., 1982—. Instr. Calif. Acad. Scis., San Francisco, 1972-73; lab. technician Brit. Petroleum, San Francisco, 1974-80; geologist Standard Oil of Ohio, San Francisco, 1980-84; dir., pres. New World Expressions, San Rafael, Calif., 1983—, Video Properties King County, Inc., Bellevue, Wash., 1984-85; pres. GeoMarketing, San Francisco, 1984—; venture analyst Internat. Tech. Consortium Corp., San Jose, Calif.; fin. cons., San Francisco. Mem. Am. Assn. Petroleum Geologists, Soc. Econ. Paleontologists and Mineralogists, Coast Geol. Soc., No. Calif. Geol. Soc. Republican. Greek Orthodox.

NIKLES, DAVID EUGENE, chemist; b. Akron, Ohio, July 3, 1954; s. Edward Eugene and Anna Lucile (Willis) N.; m. Jacqueline A. Werstler, June 16, 1979. B.S., U. Akron, 1977; Ph.D., Case Western Res. U., 1982. Lab. technician Firestone Synthetic Rubber and Latex Co., Akron, 1972-77; sr. research chemist Hoechst Celanese Advanced Tech. Group, Summit, N.J., 1982—. Contbr. articles to profl. jours. Mem. Am. Chem. Soc., Materials Research Soc., Electrochem. Soc., Soc. Photo-Optical Instrumentation Engrs., Optical Soc. Am. Current work: Materials science; polymeric materials for use in optical storage of information; optical characterization of materials. Subspecialties: Inorganic chemistry; Laser data storage and reproduction.

NIKODEM, KAZIMIERZ, mathematician; b. Bedzin, Poland, Feb. 3, 1953; s. Tadeusz and Teresa (Trefon) N.; m. Jadwiga Martyniak; children: Joanna, Mateusz. MS, Silesian U., Katowice, Poland, 1977, PhD, 1981. Asst. Silesian U., 1977-79, asst. lectr., 1979-81, tutor, 1981-84; tutor Tech. U. Looz', Bielsko-Biala, Poland, 1984—. Reviewer Math. Revs., Ann Arbor, Mich., 1984—, Zentralblatt für Mathematik, Karlsrue, 1986—; contbr. articles to profl. jours. Mem. Polskie Towarzystwo Matematyczne, Am. Mathematical Soc. Roman Catholic. Home: Skosna 9/22, 43-300 Bielsko-Biala Poland Office: Tech U Dept Math, Findera 32, 43-300 Bielsko-Biala Poland

NIKOLIC, GEORGE, cardiologist, consultant; b. Belgrade, Yugoslavia, Feb. 7, 1945; came to Australia, 1964; s. Ilija and Sofija (Rajic) N.; m. Annette Courtney Smith, Feb. 7, 1978; children: Alexandra Courtney, John George. MB, BS with honors, Sydney U., 1971. Diplomate Am. Bd. Internal Medicine, Am. Bd. Cardiology Med. resident St. Vincent's Hosp., Sydney, Australia, 1971-72, med. registrar, 1973-74, cardiology registrar, 1975; med. and cardiology registrar Woden Valley, Canberra, Australia, 1976-77, dir. intensive care, 1978, 1982—; cardiology fellow St. Vincent Hosps., S.I., Worcester, 1979-82; asst. prof. medicine U. Mass., Worcester, 1981-82, instr. phys. diagnosis, 1980—. Contbr. articles in field to med. jours. Fellow Royal Australasian Coll. Physicians (sec. Australian capital Territory br., Canberra 1983), Am. Coll. Cardiology, Am. Coll. Chest Physicians; mem. Australia-N.Z. Intensive Care Soc., Critical Care Soc., Cardiac Soc. Australia and New Zealand. Office: Woden Valley Hosp, PO Box 11, Woden ACT, Australia 2605

NIKONOV, VIKTOR PETROVICH, Soviet government official; b. 1929. Grad., Azovo-Chernomorsky Agrl. Inst., 1950. Mem. Communist Party Soviet Union, 1954—; dep. dir., then dir. of a machine and tractor sta. 1950-58; head agrl. dept. Krasnoyarsk regional com. Communist Party Soviet Union, 1958-61, 2d sec. Tartar Autonomous Soviet Socialist Republic dist. com., 1961-67, 1st sec. Mari Autonomous Soviet Socialist Republic dist. com., 1967-79; dep. to USSR Supreme Soviet, Moscow, 1962—; candidate mem. Cen. Com. Communist Party Soviet Union, 1971-76, mem., 1976—, mem. sec., 1985—; dep. minister agr. USSR, 1979—; mem. Politburo 1987—. Decorated Order of Oct. Revolution. Office: Communist Party Soviet Union, Politburo, Moscow USSR *

NIL, GÜVEN, finance company executive, banking advisor; b. Istanbul, May 20, 1944; s. Mehmet and Hayriye (Colakoğlu) N.; m. Vicdan Alaybek, Sept. 19, 1970; children: Eren, Emil. BSc, Robert Coll., Istanbul, 1967; MBA, Robert Coll., 1969. Gen. mgr. Vigi AS, Istanbul, 1973-79; pres. Erem Ltd., Istanbul, 1980—; rep. Petrabank, Jordan, 1984—. Mem. Istanbul C. of C. Home: Kisikli CAD 118, Camlica, Istanbul Turkey Office: Erem Ltd, Ortaklar CAD 2/16 Mecidiyekoy, 80290 Istanbul Turkey

NILAND, MERVYN EUGENE ARTHUR, chemical company executive; b. Benoni, Transvaal, South Africa, Nov. 3, 1936; s. Norman Wayne and Sally (White) N.; m. Beryl Jean McLaren, Nov. 29, 1958; children—Tracey, Donovan, Katy-Lee, Sally-Anne. B.Sc., Wits U., Johannesburg, South Africa, 1955-57. Instr., Dale Carnegie Tng. Sch., Johannesburg, 1979—; founder, dir. Advanced Leadership Workshop, Johannesburg, 1981—; founder, mng. dir. Harvard Chem. Industries, Benoni, 1959—; dir. Success Inst., Benoni, 1983—, Parent Effectiveness Tng., Benoni, 1983—. Author scriptures translations Swinging Scriptures, 1978. Patentee hand cleaner. Marathon capt. Benoni Harriers, 1978-80; mem. Am. Entrepreneur, Los Angeles, 1979; bd. dirs. Christian Fellowship and Service. Recipient Bronze Comrades Medals Comrades Marathon Assn., 1979-85, Washie 100 miler trophy, Buffalo Club, 1985. Methodist. Clubs: Benoni Northerns Athletic (founder, pres. 1981—), Benoni Country. Avocations: marathon running, photography, motor racing, squash, canoeing cycling. Home: 67 Miles Sharp St, Benoni, Transvaal 1500, Republic of South Africa Office: PO Box 445, Luton Rd, Indsl Sites, Benoni, Transvaal 1500, Republic of South Africa

NILES, THOMAS MICHAEL TOLLIVER, U.S. ambassador to Canada; b. Lexington, Ky., Sept. 22, 1939; s. John Jacob and Rena (Lipetz) N.; m. Carroll C. Ehringhaus, July 22, 1967; children: John Thomas, Mary Chapman. BA, Harvard U., 1960; MA, U. Ky., 1962. Commd. fgn. service officer Dept. State, Washington, 1962; U.S. ambassador to Can. Dept. State. Recipient Superior Honor award Dept. State, 1982, 85. Mem. Phi Beta Kappa. Office: US Embassy, 100 Wellington St, Ottawa, ON Canada K1P 5T1 Office: Dept of State US Ambassador to Canada Washington DC 20520 *

NILL, CARL JONATHAN, publishing executive; b. Dayton, Ohio, Sept. 7, 1938; s. Carl M. and Winifred N.; student Wheaton Coll., 1957-58; grad. Am. Inst. Banking, Chgo., 1964; D.D. (hon.), N. Fla. Bapt. Theol. Sem., 1986; m. Suzanne Jacobsen, July 1, 1960; 1 son, Kevin Jonathan. Asst. cashier Bank of Naperville (Ill.), 1960-64; asst. v.p. Am. Nat. Bank Jacksonville, 1964-68; v.p. State Bank Jacksonville, 1968-71; chmn., pres. Fla. Equity and Mortgage Investors, Jacksonville, 1972-73; pvt. investments, Jacksonville, 1973-74; co-owner Home & Land Publ. Corp., Tallahassee, Fla., 1974—, Ea. regional sales dir., owner Harmony House Pub., Jacksonville, 1980—. Bd. dirs. Campus Crusade for Christ, Jim Ponder Ministries, Christian Light Found., Luther Rice Sem. Republican. Baptist. Clubs: Deerwood, University, Bent Tree, Marsh Landing-Sawgrass, Tournament Players. Tenor, vocal rec. artist also TV and radio appearances. Home: 8006 Green Glade Rd Jacksonville FL 32256 Office: 8421 Baymeadows Way Suite 1 Jacksonville FL 32256

NILSEN, HELGE NORMANN, language educator; b. Bergen, Norway, July 29, 1937; s. Alf Normann Nilsen and Bergljot (Skjellanger) Fischer; m. Berit Knutsen, 1962 (div. 1967); m. Kirsten Sirene Flatøy, 1969; children: Alf Normann, Tarjei. PhD, U Bergen, 1969. Research asst. U. Bergen, 1967-70; prof. Am. lit. U. Trondheim, Norway, 1970—. Author: Hart Crane's Divided Vision: An Analysis of The Bridge, 1980. Home: Ole Nordgatds Vei 47, 7049 Trondheim Norway Office: U Trondheim, Dragvoll, 7055 Trondheim Norway

NILSON, STEN SPARRE, retired political scientist, educator; b. Oslo, Norway, Feb. 3, 1915; s. Robert and Ebba (Sparre) N.; m. Bodil Hals Bakke, July 22, 1945; children—Ellen, Ebba, Haaken. M.A. in Econs., U. Oslo, 1940, Dr. Philosophy, 1975. With Norwegian Pub. Service, 1940-45, 1950-65; research assoc. Michelsen Inst., Bergen, Norway, 1947-50; mem. faculty Inst. Polit. Sci., U. Oslo, 1966-86, prof., 1978-86; vis. prof. La. State U., Baton Rouge, 1964, U. Md., College Park, 1976, McGill U., Montreal, 1985; research assoc. Ctr. Internat. Studies, Princeton U., 1966-67. Mem. Norwegian Polit. Sci. Assn., Norwegian Economists Assn. Author: Histoire et sciences politiques, 1950; Knut Hamsun und die Politik, 1964. Lutheran. Home: Dalsvei 45A, Oslo 3 Norway

NILSSEN, PER ARNLJOT, airline executive; b. Hisoey, Arendal, Norway, Mar. 7, 1936; s. Arnljot and Helene (Thygesen) N.; m. Turid Riska, Feb. 5, 1966; children: Siv Helen, Sten Idar. Student, Horten Tech. U., 1960; PhD, Ness Tech. Acad., 1962. Project engr. Borregaard Paper Mill, Sarpsborg, Norway, 1960-63; devel. engr. Braathens Safe, Stavanger, Sweden, 1963-71; supt. airframe and systems engring. Braathens Safe, Stavanger, Norway, 1971-78, mgr. staff engring., 1978-85, sta. mgr., 1985—. Served with Norwegian Royal A.F., 1958-60. Mem. Norwegian Assn. Profl. Engrs., Norwegian Assn. Engrs. (bd. dirs.). Lodge: Rotary (Hafrsfjord, Stavanger). Club: Skål (Stavanger). Home: Erik Werenskjoldsvei 4, 4023 Stavanger Norway Office: Braathens Safe Stavanger, Airport, 4055 Sola Norway

NILSSON, BIRGIT, soprano; b. Karup, Sweden, May 17, 1918; d. Nils P. and Justina (Paulsson) Svensson; m. Bertil Niklasson, Sept. 10, 1948. Student, Royal Musical Acad., Stockholm; Mus.D. (hon.), Amherst U., Mass., Andover U., Manhattan Sch. Music, 1982, Mich. State U., 1982. Appeared opera and concert houses in, Europe, N.Am., S.Am., Japan and Australia; most famous roles include: Isolde, Brünnhilde, Turandot, Elektra. Decorated 1st comdr. Order of Vasa Sweden; Austrian and Bavarian Kammersaengerin; named Swedish Royal Court Singer. Hon. mem. Royal Acad. Music London, Royal Acad. Music Stockholm, Vienna State Opera. Office: care Eric Semon Assocs Inc 111 W 57th St New York NY 10019 also: PO Box 527, Stockholm C Sweden *

NILSSON, HANS WOLMAR, financial executive; b. Stockholm, Sweden, Aug. 29, 1941; s. Erik Wolmar and Anna Birgit (Gustafsson) N.; m. Ingrid Kristina (Karlsson), Feb. 29, 1944; children: Mats, Christian, Ann-Sofie, Catharina. MBA, U. Stockholm, 1966. Dep. group controller Ericsson, 1966-79; v.p. Pripp's Breweries, Stockholm, Sweden, 1979-83; exec. v.p. SIAB AB, Stockholm, 1983—. Office: SIAB AB, Tegeluddsvagen 21, S115 Stockholm 86, Sweden

NILSSON, NIC, union executive; b. Lund, Sweden, Nov. 1, 1933; s. Jons Olof and Hanna Linnea (Nilsdotter) N.; m. Aina Ingrid Andersson, June 10, 1955 (div. 1972); 1 child, Sven Niclas; m. Ulla Ingegerd Carlson, Mar. 27, 1976. Student, Scandinavian Sch., Geneva, 1967, Brit.-Nordic Sch., Manchester, Eng., 1971. Policeman Molndals, Sweden, 1955-60; ombudsman Stockholm SSU Dist., 1960-63, Swedish Tenants Union, Stockholm, 1963—; gen. sec. Internat. Tenants Union, Stockholm, 1985—. Author: Space for Play, 1969, Play for All, 1975, Together in the Block, 1978, Play Everywhere, 1987; contbr. articles to various publs. Mem. Stockholm Leisure Bd., 1967—, Swedish Play Council, 1971—; pres. Internat. Falcon Movement, socialist edn., Brussels, 1979—. Served with Swedish Army, 1950-55. Authors Soc. grantee, 1981. Mem. Internat. Assn. for Child's Right to Play (pres. 1981—), European Leisure and Recreation Assn. (council 1972—), Internat. Fedn. Park and Recreation Assn. (bd. dirs. 1985—). Home: Norrtullsgatan 12B X, S-11327 Stockholm Sweden Office: Internat Union Tenants, PO Box 7514, S-10392 Stockholm Sweden

NILSSON, STEFAN K., automotive company executive, researcher; b. Kungälv, Sweden, Jan. 23, 1954; s. Lennart Nils Enar and Solveig (Bengtsson) N. MS in Engring., Chalmers U. Tech, Goteborg, Sweden, 1978. Mgr. design office Nordverk, Uddevalla, Sweden, 1978-79; biomechanics specialist Volvo Car Corp., Goteborg, 1979-83, mgr. tech. devel., 1983—. Contbr. articles to profl. jours. Mem. Soc. Automotive Engrs., Am. Assn. Automotive Medicine. Mem. Liberal Party. Club: Marstrand Yacht (Sweden). Home: Foreningsgatau 1B, S41127 Goteborg Sweden Office: Volvo Car Corp, Dept 93550 PV22, S40508 Goteborg Sweden

NIMPOENO, HARJO, international trade center administrator; b. Amsterdam, The Netherlands, Feb. 10, 1927; s. Raden Mas Soedono and Johanna Maria (Lensink) N.; m. Tilly Deinges-Bruyninga, 1946 (div. 1953); children: Roswita, Ardjono; m. Gerda Julia Awuy; children: Irani, Indra. Student, Vrye U., Amsterdam, 1948-49. Mgr. pub. relations, internal services Garuda Indonesian Airways/KLM, Jakarta, Indonesia, 1949-54; night editor Aneta News Agy., Jakarta, 1954-55; pvt. practice ins. agt. Jakmed, Indonesia, 1955-59; mng. dir. PT Deli Travel Service, Medan, Jakarta, 1959-64; regional mgr. Investors Overseas Services, Geneva, Indonesia, 1964-71; pvt. practice fin. and ins. cons. Jakarta, 1971-83; pres., dir. PT Asuransi Gadjah Mada, Jakarta, 1983-85; exec. dir. World Trade Ctr. Jakarta, 1985—; cons. Balfour, Williamson (London Bank) Jakarta, 1975-80, Arbuthnot, Latham (London Bank), Jakarta, 1980-82. Served to sgt. Netherlands Marine Corps, 1945-48. Recipient Ereteken Voor Orde en Vrede, Netherlands Govt., 1947, Oranje Nassau medal with swords, Netherlands Govt., 1947. Lodge: Rotary (Kuningan, Jakarta club pres. 1988—). Office: World Trade Ctr Jakarta, JL Sudirman Kav 31, 12920 Jakarta Indonesia

NIMS, CHARLES FRANCIS, minister, Egyptologist; b. Norwalk, Ohio, Oct. 19, 1906; s. Joel Benjamin and Grace (Wildman) N.; student U. Toledo, 1924-25; A.B., Alma Coll., 1928; B.D., McCormick Theol. Sem., 1931; Ph.D., U. Chgo., 1937; m. Myrtle Eileen Keillor, Apr. 18, 1931. Ordained to ministry Presbyn. Ch., 1931; pastor, First Ch., Eldorado, Ill., 1940-43; research asst. Oriental Inst., 1934-40; staff Sakkarah Expdn., Egypt, 1934-36; staff Epigraphic Survey, 1937-39; Egyptologist Epigraphic Survey, 1946-63, field dir., 1964-72; research asso. dept. Oriental lang. U. Chgo., 1948-67, faculty mem., 1960-61, assoc. prof., 1967-70, prof., 1970-72, emeritus, 1972—; staff mem. Chgo. Archeol. Expdn., Tolmeita, Libya, 1954, 56, 57, 58; lectr. adult edn. Field Mus. Natural History, 1976. Mem. Soc. Bibl. Lit., Am. Photog. Soc., Mil. Chaplains Assn. U.S., AAUP, L'Association Internationale pour l'Étude du Droit Pharaonique (hon. pres.); ordinary mem. Deutsches Archaologisches Instut; assoc. mem. L'Institut d' Egypte; mem. Phi Beta Kappa. Served as chaplain (capt.) U.S. Army, 1943-46. Author: (with H.H. Nelson et al) Medinet Habu IV, 1940; (with Prentice Duell) Mastaba of Mereruka, 1938; (with G.R. Hughes) Reliefs and Inscriptions in Karnak, III, 1954; Medinet Habu V-VIII (with G.R. Hughes), 1957-70; Thebes of the Pharoahs, 1965; (with E.F. Wente) The Tomb of Kheruef, 1980, The Temple of Khonsu, I, 1979; (with William Murnane) The Temple of Khonsu, II, 1981. Contbr. articles to profl. jours. Home: 5540 Blackstone Ave Chicago IL 60637 Office: Oriental Inst U Chgo Chicago IL 60637

NINEHAM, DENNIS ERIC, retired theology educator; b. Southampton, Eng., Sept. 27, 1921; s. Stanley Martin and Bessie Edith (Gain) N.; m. Ruth Corfield Miller, Aug. 13, 1946; children: Elizabeth, Clare, Hugh, Christopher. BA, Oxford U., 1943, MA, 1947; BD, Cambridge U., 1964; DD (hon.), Yale U., 1965, BDS, 1965; DD (hon.), U. Birmingham, Eng., 1972; DD, Oxford U., 1978. Fellow, chaplain Queen's Coll., Oxford, Eng., 1946-54; prof. London U., 1954-64; regius prof. Cambridge U., 1964-69; fellow Emmanuel Coll., Cambridge, 1964-69; warden Keble Coll., Oxford, 1969-79; prof. Bristol U., Eng., 1980-86. Author: The Gospel of St. Mark, 1963, The Use and Abuse of the Bible, 1976, Explorations in Theology, 1977; editor: Studies in the Gospels, 1955, 2d. edit. 1957, The Church's Use of the Bible, 1963. Proctor Ch. of Eng. Assembly, 1955-70, Ch. of Eng. Gen. Synod, 1970-76. Fellow King's Coll. U. London, 1961, hon. fellow Keble Coll. Oxford U., 1980, fellow King Edward VI Sch. Southampton U., 1986. Home: 4 Wootten Dr, Iffley Turn, Oxford OX4 4DS, England

NINOMIYA, KEIKO, pediatric cardiologist; b. Kikuna, Yokohama, Japan, Jan. 2, 1955; d. Kazuya and Yoko (Koyama) Hirano; m. Junichi Ninomiya, May 26, 1979; 1 child, Kazuhiro. MD, Nippon Med. Sch., Tokyo, 1979, DMed Sci., 1983. Research fellow Nippon Med. Sch. Hosp., 1979, research fellow, 1981-83, fellow, 1983-84; resident in pediatric cardiology 1984, 1984—; observer Hosp. for Sick Children, Toronto, 1980-81, Tokyo Women's Coll. Hosp., 1984. Author: Pediatric Cardiology, 1986; contbr. articles to med. jours. Mem. Japan Pediatric Soc., Japan Circulation Soc., Societus Caldiologica Paediatrica, Japan Soc. Ultrasonics in Medicine, Japan Applied Physiol. Soc. Home: 1-19-12 Yutenji Meguro-ku, 153 Tokyo Japan Office: Nippon Med Sch Hosp, 3-5-5 Iidabashi Chiyoda-ku, 102 Tokyo Japan

NIPITELLA, ALFIO MARQUIS OF CASTIGLIONE, artist; b. Lentini, Sycile, June 22, 1913; s. Filadelfo and Salvatrice (Marchioness of Castiglione Di Pietro) Marquis of Castiglione; student Acad. Fine Arts, Rome, 1937; m. Maria Minnucci, Oct, 23, 1946; children—Gabriella, Rosalba, Giovanna Isabelle. Tchr. design and history art Italian State High Schs., 1938; one-man shows: Mus. Modern Art, N.Y.C., 1975, Waldorf Astoria, N.Y.C., 1975, Tate Gallery, London, 1975; group shows include: Galerie des 20Jahunderts, Berlin, 1976, Tokio Kukuritsu Kindaj Bijutsukan, 1976, Nat. Gallery Victoria, 1976, Nat. Gallery Can., Ottawa, Ont., 1976; represented in permanent collections: Adler Fielding Galleries, Johannesburg, Musé e d'Art Moderne, Paris, Nat. Mus. Stockholm, Gallery of Art Estense of Ferrare, Gallery of Art La zattera, Viareggio. Served with mil., 1934-36, 40-44. Recipient Gold and Silver medal awards art shows. Mem. Acad. Tiberina, Rome, Acad. of the 500, Acad. Artis Templum Internat. Acad. (regional del.), Acad. of Atrs and Scis. of N.Y., Acad. Scis. Letters, and Arts, The Marzocco Florence Internat. Acad. (regional del.), Free World Internat. Acad., European Community Artists, Club Artists Foggia, Homo Electus Ducati Extensis Ferrara, Gallery of Artists Siracuse, The Pipire. Roman Catholic. Club: KC. Lodge: Chavalier de la Legion d'Honour. Home: 55 Via Regina, Elena, 65122 Pescara Italy

NIPKOW, KARL-ERNST HEINRICH, theologian; b. Bielefeld, Fed. Republic Germany, Dec. 19, 1928; s. Ernst and Margarete (Spiekerkötter) N.; m. Rosemarie Ingrid Kowalzyk, June 4, 1954; children: Renate Dorothea, Markus Friedemann. PhD, U. Marburg, Fed. Republic Germany, 1959. Cert. tchr. Tchr., secondary, grammar schs. Bielefeld, 1955-61; lectr. U. Marburg, 1961-65; prof. Tchr. Tng. Coll., Hannover, Fed. Republic Germany, 1965-68, U. Tuebingen, Fed. Republic Germany, 1968—; commr. World Council Chs., Geneva, 1968-83; chmn. Comenius Inst., Muenster, Fed. Republic Germany, 1969—; commr. edn. Evang. Ch. Germany, Hannover, 1969—. Author: Schule und Religionsunterricht im Wandel, 1971, Grundfragen der Religionspaedagogik, 3 vols., 1975-82; contbr. articles to profl. jours. Mem. Deutsche Gesellschaft fuer Erziehungswissenschaft, Gesellschaft fuer Wissenschaftliche Theologie, The Religious Edn. Assn. Lutheran. Home: 49 Weiherstrasse, 7400 Tuebingen 9 Federal Republic of Germany Office: Evangelical Theol Faculty, Hoelderlinstrasse 16, 7400 Tuebingen Federal Republic of Germany

NIRENBERG, MARSHALL WARREN, biochemist; b. N.Y.C., Apr. 10, 1927; s. Harry Edward and Minerva (Bykowsky) N.; m. Perola Zaltzman, July 14, 1961. B.S. in Zoology, U. Fla., 1948, M.S., 1952; Ph.D. in Biochemistry, U. Mich., 1957. Postdoctoral fellow Am. Cancer Soc. at NIH, 1957-59; postdoctoral fellow USPHS at NIH, 1959-60; mem. staff NIH, 1960—; research biochemist, chief lab. biochem. genetics Nat. Heart, Lung and Blood Inst., 1962—. Recipient Molecular Biology award Nat. Acad. Scis., 1962, award in biol. scis. Washington Acad. Scis., 1962, medal HEW, 1964, Modern Medicine award, 1963, Harrison Howe award Am. Chem. Soc., 1964, Nat. Medal Sci. Pres. Johnson, 1965, Hildebrand award Am. Chem. Soc., 1966, Research Corp. award, 1966, A.C.P. award, 1967, Gairdner Found. award merit Can., 1967, Prix Charles Leopold Meyer French Acad. Scis., 1967, Franklin medal Franklin Inst., 1968, Albert Lasker Med. Research award, 1968, Priestly award, 1968; co-recipient Louisa Gross Horowitz prize Columbia, 1968, Nobel prize in medicine and physiology, 1968. Fellow AAAS, N.Y. Acad. Scis.; mem. Am. Soc. Biol. Chemists, Am. Chem. Soc. (Paul Lewis award enzyme chemistry 1964), Am. Acad. Arts and Scis., Biophys. Soc., Nat. Acad. Scis., Washington Acad. Scis., Soc. for Study Devel. and Growth, Harvey Soc. (hon.), Leopoldina Deutsche Akademie der Naturforscher, Pontificial Acad. Scis. Office: Lab Biochem Genetics NIH 9000 Rockville Pike Bethesda MD 20892 *

NIRULA, DEEPAK, foodservice executive; b. New Delhi, India, Apr. 3, 1952; s. Madan and Satya (Mehta) N.; m. Ramni Bhalla, Dec. 20, 1985; 1 child, Tara. BS in Hotel Mgmt., Cornell U., 1974. Banquet mgr. Thunderbird Inn at the Quay, Vancouver, Wash., 1974, mgr. rooms, 1975; gen. mgr. Thunderbird Gov. House, Olympia, Wash., 1975-77; tech. advisor

Nirulas Corner House Pvt. Ltd., New Delhi, 1977-79, dir., 1979-81, mgr. dir., 1981—; bd. dirs. Hotel and Foodservice Cons. Ltd., New Delhi. Mem. Nat. Restaurant Assn. India (sec. gen. 1982-86, trustee 1987—, treas. 1987—). Home: A/14 Anand Niketan, New Delhi India Office: Nirulas Corner House Pvt Ltd, 1 Block Connaught Circus, New Delhi 110 001, India

NISHIDA, KOHZO, business administration educator; b. Nagoya, Japan, Nov. 1, 1938; s. Norihiro and Toki (Utani) N.; m. Junko Murase, Nov. 3, 1968; children: Kazuhiko, Kimito. PhD in Bus. Adminstrn., Kobe U., Japan, 1971. With Matsushita Electric Indsl. Co., Ltd., Osaka, Japan, 1961-63; asst. prof. Aichi U., Toyohashi, Japan, 1968-71; prof. Nagoya City U., Japan, 1971—; vis. prof. Internat. Inst. for Studies and Tng., Fuzinomiya, Japan, 1971-82. Author 14 books; editor 2 books; contbr. articles to profl. jours. Home: 3-2 Nekogohora-dori, 464 Nagoya Japan Office: Nagoya City U Faculty Econs, 1 Yamanohata Mizuho-cho, 467 Nagoya Japan

NISHIGUCHI, HIROSHI, manufacturing executive; b. Amagsaki, Hyogo, Japan, Oct. 7, 1939; s. Eiji and Hideko (Onobori) N.; m. Katsu Kusama, Dec. 14, 1963; children: Kaori, Noriko, Tetsu. B, Nagoya Inst. Tech., Japan, 1962. With mktg. dept. Mitsui & Co., Ltd., Osaka, Japan, 1962-67; with exporting dept. J/V project in Taipei Mitsui & Co., Ltd., Osaka, 1967-74; with mktg. dept. plants and machinery Mitsui & Co., Ltd., Taipei, Seoul, 1974-79; with med. system, sect. gen. mgr. Mitsui & Co., Ltd., Osaka, 1980-86; with satelite telecommunication dept. dep. gen. mgr. Mitsui & Co., Ltd., Tokyo, 1982—; mem. cooperation com. Japan-Korea Machinery Industries, Tokyo, Seoul, 1980-86; lectr., mem. Project 21st Century, Osaka, 1981-86. Mem. editorial staff Aggressologic Systems Council for Metabolic Info. & Control System., 1985-87. Mem. coaching staff soccer Nishinomiya City, 1984-86. Home: 1-47-24 Kita-Karasuyama, 157 Setagaya-ku, Tokyo Japan Office: Mitsui & Co Ltd, 1-2-1 Ohtemachi, 100-91 Chiyoda-ku, Tokyo Japan

NISHIMURA, MASARU, manufacturing company executive; b. Tokyo, Japan, Mar. 4, 1922; s. Ben and Kiyoko (Yamaguchi) N.; m. Kazuko Shindo, Nov. 11, 1951; children: Misako, Mineko. B of Law, Keio U., 1945. Mem. staff M. Nagano Law Office, 1946-47; gen. mgr. chem. plants sales and devel. Kawasaki Heavy Industries, Tokyo, 1967-77, exec. gen. mgr., Iran Office, 1977-79; gen. mgr. machinery and ships div. Kawasho Corp., Tokyo, 1979-83; v.p. Calista Internat. Corp. (U.S.A.), resident rep. Tokyo Office, 1983-85; sr. ptnr. Rim Pac Assocs., 1985—. Served as lt. Japanese Air Forces, 1943-45. Mem. Japan Petroleum Inst., Am. Water Works Assn., Fuel Soc. Japan, Japan Tunneling Assn. Clubs: Tokyo American, Clipper, Ambassador, Top Flight, Nikko Country. Home: 3 8 38 309 Minami Aoyama, Minato-ku, 107 Tokyo Japan Office: 3-8-38-309 Minami Aoyama, Minato-ku, 107 Tokyo Japan

NISHINO, TSUTOMU, electrical engineering educator; b. Taiwan, Jan. 1, 1930; arrived in Japan, 1946; s. Takanori and Oyoshi (Hongo) T.; m. Toshiko Sanbe, Oct. 18, 1959; children: Toru, Kanae Amano. BS, U. Osaka, Japan, 1954, D, 1974. Researcher Matsushita Research Inst., Tokyo and Kawasaki, 1961-83; prof. elec. engring. Takamatsu Nat. Coll. Tech., Japan, 1983—. Mem. Inst. Electronics Info. and Communication Engrs. Japan, Inst. Elec. Engrs. Japan, Inst. TV Engrs. Japan. Club: Yashima Tennis (Takamatsu). Home: Yashima Nisui Machi, 2445-12-B102 Takamatsu 761-01, Japan Office: Takamatsu Nat Coll Tech, 355 Chokushicho, 761 Takamatsu Japan also: Minami Kibogaoka, 97 Asahi-ku, 241 Yokohama Japan

NISHIYAMA, CHIAKI, economist, educator; b. Fukuoka-ken, Japan, Aug. 9, 1924; s. Michiki and Teruko (Tsuji) N.; m. Shigeko Okabe, June 9, 1957; children—Keita, Mikiko. B.A. in Econs., Rikkyo U., Tokyo, 1950; M.A. in Polit. Sci., U. Chgo., 1952, Ph.D. in Social Thought, 1960, postgrad. in econs., 1959-60. Lectr. U.Chgo., 1957-61; assoc. prof. Rikkyo U., 1962-64, prof. econs., 1964—; sr. research fellow Hoover Instn., Stanford U., 1978—; lectr. Tng. Inst., Ministry Trade and Industry, Japanese Govt., 1964-66, Gakushuin U., 1970-71, Waseda U., 1972-74; exec. dir. Assembly on U.S.-Japan Econ. Policy, 1972-76; prime minister's spl. envoy to U.S., 1971, 75; specialist counselor Japan Employers' Assn., 1975-85; del. European Assembly, Strasbourg, France, 1982; world travel for Japanese Ministry Fgn. Affairs, Japan External Trade Orgn., 1968-82; lectr. various univs., U.S. and Europe, 1976-83. Author numerous books, including: Lecture on Modern Economics, 1964; Free Economy, Its Policies and Principles, 1974; The Price for Prosperity, 1974; A Monetary History and Analysis of the Japanese Economy, 1868-1970, 1974; Reflection on Japanese Economy, 1976; Monetarism, 1976; The Last Chance for Creativity, Liberty and Prosperity, 1981; Human Capitalims, 1982; The Fourth Philosophy, Vol. I, 1982, Vol. II, 1983; No Limits to Growth, 1984; The Essence of Hayek, 1984, The Japanese Economy, 1987, Panadigm Shift, 1987, Japanese Economy and Life Tomorrow, 1988; editorial bd. Jour. Internat. Money and Fin., 1981—. Bd. dirs. Inst. Econ. Affairs, London, 1976—; adv. bd Econ. Inst. Paris, 1984—. Recipient Japan Econ. Lit. award Japan Econ. Jour., 1974; Earhart fellow, 1957-61; E. C. Nef fellow, 1958-59; fellow Woodrow Wilson Internat. Ctr. for Scholars, 1976-77; grantee Relm, 1964-67, Ford, 1965-66, Lilly, 1966-67, Bank of Japan, Bankers Assn. Japan, other fin. orgns., 1978-83. Mem. Am. Enterprise Inst. (adj. scholar), Am. Econ. Assn., Theoretical Econs. Assn., Internat. Econ. Assn., Statis. Soc., Mont Pelerin Soc. (pres. 1980-82, sr. v.p. 1982-85, hon. v.p. 1986—. Episcopalian. Home: 5-15-18 Kamiuma, Setagaya-ku, 154 Tokyo Japan Office: Nishiyama-Kenkyushitsu, 5-15-18 Kamiuma, Setagaya-ku, 154 Tokyo Japan

NISHIYAMA, KEN'ICHI, computer economist, educator. B.S., Kyoto U., 1966, M.S., 1968, Sc.D., 1972. Research assoc. Kyushu U., Fukuoka, Japan, 1971-77; research assoc. U. Tokyo, 1977-80, assoc. prof., 1980-81; prof. computer econs. Teikyo U., Tokyo, 1981—; group leader Research Devel. Corp. Japan, Tokyo, 1984—. Home: 8-308 Tate 2-1, 353 Shiki, Saitama Japan

NISHIYAMA, TOSHI YUKI, physics educator; b. Osaka, Japan, Jan. 31, 1922; s. Ushinosuke and Ko-o (Yamanaka) N.; m. Sawako Handa, Mar. 15, 1953; 2 daus., Ayami Nishiyama Kobayashi, Yuri Nishiyama Kamino-o. B.Sc., Osaka U., 1945, D. Sc., 1954. Research assoc Osaka U., 1945-55, assoc. prof., 1955-58, prof., 1958-85, prof. emeritus, 1985—; prof. Osaka Inst. Tech., 1985—; asst. prof. U. Md., College Park, 1961-62; prof. faculty sci. Osaka U., 1959-61, Inst. Plasma Physics Nagoya U., Japan, 1963. Contbr. articles to profl. jours. Yukawa Meml. fellow Osaka U., 1951; Weizmann Meml. fellow Weizmann Inst., Israel, 1960. Mem. Phys. Soc. Japan (dir. Osaka br. 1977-78), Am. Phys. Soc., N.Y. Acad. Scis., Sigma Xi. Lodge: Rotary Internat. (Toyonaka). Home: 2-14-55 Minami, Okamachi, Toyonaka, 560 Osaka Japan Office: Osaka Inst Tech. 5-16-1 O-omiya, Asahiku, 535 Osaka Japan

NISKANEN, PAUL MCCORD, travel company executive; b. Bend, Oreg., July 6, 1943; s. William Arthur and Nina Elizabeth (McCord) N.; m. Christine Campbell; 1 son, Tapio. Student U. Freiburg, W. Ger., 1963-64; B.A., Stanford U., 1965; M.B.A., U. Chgo., 1966. Fin. analyst Kimberly-Clark Corp., Neenah, Wis., 1966-68; bus. mgr. Avent Inc. subs. Kimberly-Clark Corp., Tucson, 1968-70; v.p., gen. mgr. Pacific Trailways Bus. Line, Portland, Oreg., 1970-81; chmn. bd., owner Niskanen & Jones, Inc., Moab, Utah, 1982—, Perspectives, Inc., Portland. Appointed counsel for Finland, 1980—; Mem. Gov.'s Travel Adv. Com., Salem, Oreg., 1976-81; 1st pres. Oreg. Hospitality and Visitors Assn., Portland, 1977-78; bd. dirs. Suomi Coll., Hancock, Mich., 1981—; nat. co-chmn. Dole for Pres. Com., 1987. Mem. Travel Industry Assn. Am., Am. Assn. Travel Agts., Pacific Northwest Travel Assn. (chmn. 1978-79), Scandinavian Heritage Found. (bd. dirs. 1984). Republican. Home: 4366 SW Hewett Blvd Portland OR 97221 Office: Niskanen & Jones Inc 452 N Main St Moab UT 84532

NISS, MOGENS ALLAN, mathematician, educator; b. Frederiksberg, Denmark, Nov. 1, 1944; s. Darling and Asta Johanne (Sørensen) N.; m. Kirsten Hunosøe, July 28, 1966; children: Henning, Martin. PhD, U. Copenhagen, Denmark, 1968. Scholar, math. dept. U. Copenhagen, 1968-71; asst. prof. Danish Acad. Engring., 1971-72; assoc. prof. Roskilde U. Ctr., Denmark, 1972—, dean faculty of sci., 1976-78, mem. senate, 1976-78, 84—; com. chmn. Ministry of Edn., Denmark, 1973-74, com. mem., 1975. Author: Matematisk Analyse, 1972, Beskaftigelsesmodellen i SMEC III, 1982, Talsystemets Opbygning, 1985; editor: Mathematics and the Real World, 1979. Mem. Albertslund (Denmark) Mcpl. Sch. Bd., 1978—. Mem. Internat. Commn. on Math. Instrn. (exec. com. 1987—). Home: Galgebakken Over 6-1B, 2620 Albertslund Denmark Office: Roskilde U Ctr, PO Box 260, 4000 Roskilde Denmark

NISSAN, SORIN JAACOB, metallurgical engineer; b. Bucharest, Romania, June 4, 1948; arrived in Can., 1970; s. Jaacob and Julia (Glükmann) Schwartz-Neagu; m. Victoria Lucia Kaplan, Dec. 1, 1972; children: Oded, Erik. Degree in Mech. Engring., Inst. Tech., Bucharest, Romania, 1970; MSc in Materials Engring., Inst. Tech., Technion, Haifa, Israel, 1974. Registered profl. engr., Ont., Can. Project engr. Israel Aircraft Industries, Tel Aviv, 1977-78; metallurgical engr. Hydro-Research Div., Toronto, Ont., 1978-80; sr. materials engr. aircraft div. Canadair Ltd., Montreal, Que., Can., 1980-82; materials cons. Bristol Aerospace Ltd., Winnipeg, Man., 1983—. Contbr. articles to profl. jours. Served to 1st lt. Israel Def. Forces, 1974-77. Mem. Soc. Advancement Materials and Processes, Ont. Assn. Profl. Engrs., Soc. Plastic Engrs., Am. Inst. Aero. Astronautics. Home: 11-524 Kenaston Blvd, Winnipeg, MB Canada R3N 1Z1 Office: Bristol Aerospace Ltd, 660 Berry St, PO Box 874, Winnipeg, MB Canada R3C 2S4

NISSIM, MOSHE, Israeli government official; b. Jerusalem, 1935; m. Ruth Korn, 1966; 4 daughters, 1 son. Law student, Hebrew U., Jerusalem, 1953-57. Bar: Israel 1964. Mem. Knesset, Jerusalem, 1959—; minister without portfolio Israel, Jerusalem, 1978-80, minister justice, 1980-86, minister fin., 1986—. Contbr. articles to profl. jours. Mem. Israel Bar Assn. Address: Ministry Finance, Jerusalem Israel *

NISTICÒ, GIUSEPPE, pharmacology educator; b. Cardinale, Calabria, Italy, Mar. 16, 1941; m. Maria Louise Hipwood; children: Steven, Robert. MD, Univ. Degli Studi, Naples, Italy, 1965. Asst. prof. Univ. Degli Studi, Naples, 1966-72; specialist in neurology and psychiatry Univ. Degli Studi, Modena, Italy, 1968; assoc. prof. Univ. Degli Studi, Messina, Italy, 1973-75, dir. Inst. Pharmacology, 1976-82, prof., 1980; dir. Inst. Pharmacology Univ. Degli Studi, Catanzaro, Italy, 1983. Author: Neurotransmitters and Anterior Pituitary Function, 1978, Farmacologia Comunicazione Sinaptica, 1986, Brain Messengers and the Pituitary Gland, 1988; co-editor: Progr. in Nonmammalian Brain Research, 1983, Neurotransmitters, Seizures and Epilepsy III, 1986, VII International Conference Tetanus, 1985; contbr. articles to profl. jours. Christian Democrat. Roman Catholic. Office: Inst Pharmacology, Via T Campanella, 88100 Cantanzaro CZ, Italy

NITSCHE, ERIK FREDI, graphic designer; b. Lausanne, Switzerland, July 7, 1908; came to U.S., 1934; naturalized, 1942.; s. George Franz and Else Ida (Schueren) N.; m. Margaret Homberger, July 7, 1932 (div. 1974); children—Marc Eric, John Paul; m. Renate Elisabeth Wulff, Nov. 19, 1976. Student, Switzerland, Munich, Germany, Paris. Designer 1929—. Works include designs for RCA, Ohrbach's, Dorland Internat., Decca Records, 20th Century Fox, Mus. Modern Art, Container Corp. Am., Rexall, Revlon, Hurd's, Harveys', Heublein, Bloomingdale's, Beck, Universal Pictures, Gen. Dynamics, Stern Mag., Paris Match, Hachette; most recent work designing postage stamps, Bonn, Fed. Republic Germany, 1984-1987; Unicover Corp., designing Philatelic First Day Covers, Cheyenne, Wyo., 1985; numerous exhibits, most recent being Stadt Museum, Munich, Fed. Republic Germany, 1983, Nat. Museum Modern Art, Kyoto, Japan, 1983, Centre Pompidou, Paris, 1988; designer numerous books; subject numerous books, book series and articles in profl. jours.; designed Dynamic Am., General Dynamics Corporate History, 20 Vol. History of Music, Épopée Mondiale d'un Siécle, 5 Vol. History of the Last Century; pub. 12 vol. history of sci. and tech. Recipient Direct Mail Merit award, 1948; gold medal award Art Dirs. Club, 1949, awards of distinctive merit, 1957-61. Fellow Internat. Inst. Arts and Letters; mem. Art Dirs. Club. Am. Inst. Graphic Arts. Alliance Graphique Internationale (Paris).

NITSCHE, JOHANNES CARL CHRISTIAN, mathematics educator; b. Olbernhau, Germany, Jan. 22, 1925; came to U.S., 1956; s. Ludwig Johannes and Irma (Raecke) N.; m. Carmen Dolores Mercado Delgado, July 1, 1959; children: Carmen Irma, Johannes Marcos and Ludwig Carlos (twins). Diplom für Mathematik, U. Göttingen, 1950; Ph.D., U. Leipzig, 1951; Privatdozent, Tech. U. Berlin, 1955. Asst. U. Göttingen, 1948-50; research mathematician Max Planck Institut für Strömungsforschung Göttingen, 1950-52; asst. Privatdozent Tech. U., Berlin, 1952-56; vis. asso. prof. U. Cin., 1956-57; asso. prof. U. Minn., Mpls., 1957-60; prof. math. U. Minn., 1960—; head Sch. Math., 1971-78; vis. prof. U. P.R., 1960-61, U. Hamburg, 1965, Tech. Hochschule Vienna, 1968, U. Bonn, 1971, 73, 77, 80, 81, U. Heidelberg, 1979, 82, 83, U. Munich, 1983, U. Florence, 1983. Author: Vorlesungen über Minimalflächen, 1975, Lectures on Minimal Surfaces, 1988; mem. editorial bd.: Archive of Rational Mechanics and Analysis, 1967—; editor: Analysis, 1980—; assoc. editor: Contemporary Math, 1980—; Contbr. articles to profl. jours. Mem. Am. del. joint Soviet-Am. Symposium on Partial Differential Equations, Novosibirsk, 1963, U.S.-Japan Seminar on Differential Geometry, Tokyo, 1977; speaker 750th Berlin Anniversary Colloquium, Free U. Berlin, 1987. Recipient Lester R. Ford award for outstanding expository writing, 1975; George Taylor Disting. Service award U. Minn. Found., 1980; Humboldt prize for sr. U.S. scientists Alexander von Humboldt Found., 1981; Fulbright research fellow Stanford, 1955-56; Keynote speaker Festive Colloquium, U. Ulm, June, 1986. Mem. AAAS, Am. Math. Soc., Circolo Matematico di Palermo, Deutsche Mathematiker-Vereinigung, Edinburgh Math. Soc., Gesellschaft für Angewandte Mathematik und Mechanik, Math. Assn. Am., N.Y. Acad. Scis., Österreichische Mathematische Gesellschaft, Soc. Natural Philosophy. Home: 2765 Dean Pkwy Minneapolis MN 55416

NITZE, PAUL HENRY, policy advisor; b. Amherst, Mass., Jan. 16, 1907; s. William A. and Anina (Hilken) N.; m. Phyllis Pratt, Dec. 2, 1932 (dec.); children—Heidi, Peter, William II, Phyllis. A.B. cum laude, Harvard U., 1928; LL.D., New Sch. Social Research, Pratt Inst., Johns Hopkins, Howard U. With Dillon, Read & Co. (investment bankers), N.Y.C., 1929-37; v.p. Dillon, Read & Co. (investment bankers), 1939-41; pres. P.H. Nitze & Co., Inc., 1938-39; U.S. govt. fin. dir. Coordinator Inter-Am. Affairs; chief metals and minerals br. Bd. Econ. Warfare; dir. fgn. procurement and devel. br. Fgn. Econ. Adminstrn; dir., then vice chmn. U.S. Strategic Bombing Survey, 1944-46; dep. dir. Office Internat. Trade Policy, Dept. State, 1946; dep. to asst. sec. state for econ. affairs 1948-49; dir. policy planning staff Dept. State, 1950-53; pres. Fgn. Service Ednl. Found., Washington, 1953-61; asst. sec. def. for Internat. Security Affairs, 1961-63; sec. of Navy 1963-67, dep. sec. of def., 1967-69; mem. U.S. del. Strategic Arms Limitation Talks, 1969-74; head U.S. negotiating team Arms Control Talks, Geneva, 1981-84; spl. advisor to pres. and sec. state on arms control matters 1984—. Author: U.S. Foreign Policy, 1945-1955. Recipient Medal for Merit, Medal of Freedom, George C. Marshall, Knight Comdrs. Cross (badge and star) Order of Merit of Fed. Republic of Germany. Home: 3120 Woodley Rd NW Washington DC 20008 Office: US Dept State 2201 C St NW Washington DC 20520

NIXON, EDWARD CALVERT, trade executive, consultant; b. Whittier, Calif., May 3, 1930; s. Francis Anthony and Hannah (Milhous) N.; m. Gay Lynne Woods, June 1, 1957; children—Amelie, Elizabeth. BS, Duke U., 1952; MS, N.C. State U., 1954. Lic. real estate broker, Wash. With comml. dept. Pacific N.W. Bell, Seattle, 1962-63, 67-68; tech. personnel supr. Bellcomm, Inc., Washington, 1964-67; cons., trustee Richard Nixon Found., Los Angeles, 1969-74; assoc. broker Harmon & Assocs., Seattle, 1975-77; exec. v.p. DNA Corp., Newport Beach, Calif., and Cairo, 1977-79; pres. Nixon World Enterprises, Inc., Lynnwood, Wash., 1980—; chmn. Great Circle Resources, Inc., 1986—. Mem. Wash. Republican Central Com., Olympia, 1968; co-chmn. Com. for Reelection of Pres., Washington, 1972; mem. sea grant adv. panel U. So. Calif., 1971. Served to capt. USNR, 1955-62. Mem. Am. Wind Energy Assn., Nat. Assn. Realtors, Am. Soc. Oceanography (bd. dirs. 1969-71), AIME. Mem. Soc. Friends. Clubs: Rainier, Wash. Athletic (Seattle); Pisces (Washington). Home: 1609 175th St SW Lynnwood WA 98037 Office: Great Circle Resources Inc One Union Sq Seattle WA 98104

NIXON, JOHN EDWIN, orthopedic surgeon, consultant; b. Hyde, Eng., Dec. 5, 1948; s. Edwin and Dorothy (Hall) N.; m. Bridget Anne Coulson; children: David John, Susannah Jane, Natasha Elizabeth. MD, Edinburgh (Scotland) Med. Sch., 1972; BChir, London, 1979; MA, Oxford (Eng.) U., 1983; M in Surgery, U. Edinburgh, 1987. Field coordinator in famine relief VSO Ethiopia, 1973-74; registrar integral surgery St. Bartholomew's Hosp., London, 1975-77; orthopaedic trainee Royal Postgrad. Med. Sch., London, 1978-80; lectr. orthopaedics Oxford U., 1980-83, clin. reader orthopaedic surgery, 1983-87; cons. orthopaedic surgery Kings Coll. Hosp. and Med. Sch., London, 1987—. Contbr. articles to profl. jours. Fellow Royal Soc. Medicine, Royal Coll. Surgeons, Girdlestone Orthopaedic Soc.; mem. British Med. Assn. Office: Kings Coll Hosp, Denmark Hill, London SE5 9RS, England

NIXON, RICHARD MILHOUS, former President of U.S.; b. Yorba Linda, Calif., Jan. 9, 1913; s. Francis A. and Hannah (Milhous) N.; m. Thelma Catherine Patricia Ryan, June 21, 1940; children: Patricia (Mrs. Edward Finch Cox), Julie (Mrs. Dwight David Eisenhower II). A.B., Whittier Coll., 1934; LL.B. with honors, Duke U., 1937. Bar: Calif. 1937, U.S. Supreme Ct. 1947, N.Y. State 1963-69. Practiced in Whittier, Calif., 1937-42; atty. Office Price Adminstrn., Washington, Jan.-Aug. 1942; mem. 80th-81st Congresses from 12th Calif. Dist.; U.S. senator from Calif. 1950-53, v.p. of U.S., 1953-61, Republican candidate for Pres. of U.S., 1960, Republican nominee for gov. Calif., 1962; counsel firm Adams, Duque & Hazeltine, Los Angeles, 1961-63; mem. firm Mudge, Stern, Baldwin & Todd, N.Y.C., 1963-64; ptnr. firm Nixon, Mudge, Rose, Guthrie & Alexander, N.Y.C., 1964-67, Nixon, Mudge, Rose, Guthrie, Alexander & Mitchell, N.Y.C., 1967-68; elected 37th Pres. of U.S. 1968, 72, inaugurated, 1969, 73, resigned, 1974. Author: Six Crises, 1962, RN, 1978, The Real War, 1980, Leaders, 1982, Real Peace, 1984, No More Vietnams, 1985, 1999: Victory Without War, 1988. Hon. chmn. Boy Clubs Am.; trustee Whittier Coll., 1939-68. Served to lt. comdr. USNR, 1942-46, PTO. Mem. Order of Coif. Mem. Soc. of Friends. Address: 142 E 65th St New York NY 10021 *

NIXON, ROBERT PLEASANTS, amateur tree gardener, former electric motor manufacturing company executive; b. Rome, Ga., Dec. 5, 1913; s. George Felton and Eunice (Adamson) N.; m. Helen May Hill, June 4, 1942; children: Robert H., Edward H., James R. Grad. summa cum laude, Darlington Sch., 1931; A.B. with honors in econs, Duke U., 1935. CPA. Treas. Bus. News Pub. Co., Detroit, 1935-48; asst. to v.p. Wachovia Bank & Trust Co., Winston-Salem, N.C., 1941; auditor Jacuzzi Bros., Inc., Richmond, Calif., 1948-52; v.p., 1st controller then sec.-treas. Franklin Electric Co., Inc., Bluffton, Ind., 1952-83; also dir. Franklin Electric and subs. in Can., Europe, S. Africa; sec. Oil Dynamics, Inc., Tulsa, 1967-83; dir. Quincy Post & Lumber Co. Bd. dirs. Caylor-Nickel Hosp., Bluffton, 1974-83; bd. dirs., exec. com. Allen-Wells Red Cross, 1980-82; pres. Wells County Found., 1972; mem. bd. vis. Ball State U., 1968-72. Served with USNR, 1941-45; lt. comdr. Res. 1951. Mem. NAM (environ. quality com.), Phi Beta Kappa, Omicron Delta Kappa, Alpha Kappa Psi, Phi Eta Sigma, Sigma Nu. Republican. Presbyterian (elder). Club: Parlor City Country (Bluffton). Home: 630 Elm Dr Bluffton IN 46714

NIZAMI, TAUFIQ AHMAD, political science educator; b. Meerut, U.P., India, Nov. 21, 1944; s. Aziz Ahmad and Syeda (Khatoon) N.; B.A., Muslim U., 1963, M.A., 1965; Ph.D., 1970; m. Naheed Mohsin, Oct. 23, 1974; 1 child, Ayaz A. Lectr. polit. sci. Muslim U., Aligarh, India, 1966; lectr. Coll. Gen. Studies, U.S.C., Columbia, 1971-73, also postdoctoral fellow; sr. lectr. polit. sci. U. Dar es Salaam, Tanzania, 1977-83; reader dept. polit. sci. Muslim U., Aligarh, India, 1983—. Merit scholar, 1961-65. Mem. Internat. Studies Assn., All India Polit. Sci. Assn., African Council Social Scis. Club: Internat. (U.S.). Author: Political Thought and Activity in India, 1969; The Communist Party and India's Foreign Policy, 1971; The Divided Left, 1972; editor: Asia in Perspective, 1974; Tanzania and the World, 1984; mem. editorial bd. Indian Jour. Politics. Home: Japan House, Marris Rd, Aligarh India Office: Dept Political Science, Muslim Univ, Aligarh UP, India

NIZAMUDDIN, GHULAM NIZAMUDDIN, oil company executive; b. Ghazipar, India, July 27, 1940; s. Malik Mohammad and Husan (Bano) Yusuf; m. Farzana Perveen, Sept. 30, 1966; children: Farah Nizam, Tariq Nizam Malik. BS, D.J. Sind Govt. Sci. Coll., Karachi, Pakistan, 1959; LLB, S.M. Law Coll., Karachi, 1962. Lectr. S.M. Govt. Sci. Coll., Karachi, 1959-65; adminstr. Haroon Oils Ltd., Karachi, 1965—, co. sec., 1980—; mem. editorial adv. bd. Custom and Excise Review, Karachi, 1980—. Author: Filing Requirements under the Companies Ordinance, 1984, Offenses, Offenders and Penalties under the Companies Ordinance, 1984. Fellow Inst. Chartered Secs. Adminstrs. (council mem., hon. sec. 1985—), Inst. Profl. Mgrs. and Adminstrs.; mem. British Inst. Mgmt., Corp. and Taxation Law Soc. (council mem. 1987—). Home: B-65 Block N North Nazimabad, Karachi, Sind Pakistan Office: Haroon Oils Ltd, 11 Dockyard Rd W Wharf, 4992 Karachi, Sind Pakistan

NIŽETIC, BRANKO Z., eye surgeon, research consultant; b. Belgrade, Yugoslavia, Mar. 1, 1925; s. Zdravko and Jelisaveta (Radojlovic) N.; m. Louise Masson, Feb. 27, 1963; children: Philip, Alexander. MD, U. Pavia, Italy, 1948. Resident in ophtalmology U. Geneva and U. Parma (Italy), 1951; dep. chmn. eye dept. U. Split Med. Sch., Yugoslavia, 1954-60; program mgr. communicable eye diseases and prevention of blindness WHO, Morocco, 1960-70; regional officer pub. health ophthalmology WHO, Denmark, 1970-76, regional officer coop. programs devel., 1976-78, regional officer research promotion and devel., 1978-81, chief research promotion and devel., 1981-85; prof. pub. health ophthalmology Free U., Brussels, 1985—; mem. Internat. Study Com. Teaching and Continuing Postgrad. Edn. in Ophthalmology, 1974, chmn. Internat. Symposium, Kyoto, Japan, 1978—, Com. on Info. Internat. Council Ophthalmology, Commn. Sci. Ctr. Preventitive Medicine, Nancy-les-Vandoeuvres, France; alt. mem. exec. bd. Internat. Agy. Prevention of Blindness, 1982-86; advisor ophthalmology Danish Internat. Devel. Agy., 1977, 79; sec. European adv. com. med. research WHO, 1978—; adj. prof. ophthalmology Cath. U., Rome, 1985—. Mem. editorial bd. Internat. Rev. Trachoma, Paris, 1976, Vision, Singapore, 1980—. Recipient Trachoma Golden medal Internat. Orgn. Against Trachoma and Ligue Contre le Trachome, 1977. Mem. Internat. Assn. Cataract Related Researches (v.p. 1984—), Internat. Soc. Geograph. Ophthalmology (hon. life), Asia-Pacific Acad. Ophthalmology (hon. advisor 1976—, Disting. Service award 1981). Mem. Christian Orthodox Ch. Office: Free U Sch Pub Health, 808 Route de Lennik, 1070 Brussels Belgium

NKALA, ENOS MZOMBI, government official; b. Filabusi, Zimbabwe, Aug. 23, 1932; Widowed; 3 children. Student, Eden Sch., Mzinyati, Zimbabwe; degree in law and commerce, dip. in accountancy, bus. mgmt. and pub. adminstrn. With Bantu Missor, Salisbury, Zimbabwe, 1952-55; in ins. 1956; active Youth League; caretaker sec.-gen. Nat. Dem. Party, Zimbabwe, then dep. sec.-gen., 1960; founding mem. Zimbabwe African Nat. Union, 1963; treas.-gen. Zimbabwe African Nat. Union, Gwelo, 1964; then minister home affairs Govt. of Zimbabwe, now minister of def. Office: Ministry of Def, Harare Zimbabwe *

NKOMO, JOSHUA, Zimbabwe politician; b. 1917; ed. Adam's Coll., Natal, U. South Africa, Johannesburg. Welfare officer Rhodesia Rys., Bulawayo, then organizing sec. Rhodesian African Ry. Workers Union, 1945-50; pres. African Congress; engaged in ins. and real estate bus.; pres.-gen. African Nat. Congress, 1957; pres. Nat. Democratic Party, 1960; pres. Zimbabwe African People's Union, 1961; pres. African Nat. Council, 1964-76, mem. exec., 1974-76, leader del. Geneva Conf. on Rhodesia, leader council, 1976—; leader Patriotic Front, 1976—; minister for home affairs Zimbabwe, 1980-82, sr. minister local govt., rural and urban devel. of pres.' office, 1988—, interim v.p., 1988; banished and imprisoned, 1964-74. Office: Patriotic Front, 48 Kenneth Kaunda Ave, Vanguard House, Harare Zimbabwe *

NKYA, SAID HASSAN, textile corporation executive; b. Moshi, Tanzania, Nov. 15, 1946; s. Hassan Mohamed and Aziza Hassan Nkya; m. Linael Lema, Oct. 18, 1975; children: Hassan, Yasmin, Fadhyl. BA in Stats./ Econs., U. Dar, Tanzania, 1971; MS in Mgmt., ADL Mgmt. Inst., 1974. Ops. officer Nat. Devel. Corp., Dar-es-Salaam, 1972-72; dep. dir. ops. Nat. Textile Corp., Dar-es-Salaam, 1975-76, dir. ops., 1977-78, mng. dir., chief exec. officer, 1978—; mem. Econ. Planning and Consultative Council, 1984—; chmn. bd. Kilimanjaro Textile Corp., Ltd., Tanganyika Dyeing and Weaving Mills, Ltd., Dar-es-Salaam, 1978, Polytex, Morogoro, 1981, Tanzania Sewing Thread Mfrs. Ltd., 1986—, Tanzanian Carpet Co. Ltd.; bd. dirs. The State Ins. Brokers Ltd., The Tanzania Indsl. Studies and Cons. Orgns., Bd. Internal Trade. Contbr. articles to profl. jours. Fellow Textile Inst., Inst. of Dirs., British Inst. Mgmt., Textile Inst. Manchester, U.K. (v.p. 1985—). Muslim. Clubs: Gymkhana, Moshi. Home: PO Box 21693, Dar-es-

Salaam Tanzania Office: Nat Textile Corp, Pamba Rd, PO Box 9531, Dar-es-Salaam Tanzania

NOBBS, KENNETH JOHN, camera company executive; b. Norfolk Island, Australia, Apr. 10, 1938; s. Charles Hebblethwaite Hasty and Sylvia Esther (Robinson) N.; m. Pamela Vicary, Oct. 15, 1960; children: Debbie Norma, Roy Anthony. Diploma in accountancy, Longburn Coll., New Zealand, 1955. Clk. Alex Harvey & Sons Pty. Ltd., Auckland, New Zealand, 1956-58; postmaster Posts and Telegraphs, Madang and Mt. Hagen, Papua New Guinea, 1958-64; salesman K.A. Prentice & Co., Norfolk Island, 1965-67; propr. Cameralines Ltd., Norfolk Island, 1967-70, mng. dir., 1970—; exec. dir. South Pacific Shipping Co. (N.I.) Ltd. Mem. Soc. Descendants Pitcairn Settlers. Lodge: Rotary (pres. 1980-81). Home: Peters Hwy, Norfolk Island Australia Office: Cameralines Ltd, PO Box 29 Burnt Pine, Norfolk Island Australia

NOBEL, PETER, lawyer, researcher; b. Stockholm, Dec. 8, 1931; s. Leif Jurij Nobel and Anna Elisabeth (Mellen) Molander; m. Agnes Waldenstrom. Oct. 7, 1961; children—Leif Jakob, Andreas, Jonas. Juris Kandidat, U. Uppsala, Sweden, 1963, J.D. (hon.), 1985. Bar: Sweden 1986. Assoc., Advokatfirman, Chrysander, Uppsala, 1963-68, ptnr., 1968-86; assigned expert Swedish Govt. Com. for Reform of Law on Arrest and Custody in Criminal Proceedings, 1974-80, 83-85, on Law of Asylum, 1985; lectr. Law Sch., Uppsala, 1964-69; apptd. ombudsman against ethnic discrimination Govt. of Sweden, 1986; cons. in field. Author: (with G. Melander), Invandrarrätt, 1984; Refugee Law in the Sudan, 1982; editor: Refugees and Development in Africa, 1987; (with G. Melander) African Refugees and the Law, 1971, International Legal Instruments of Refugees in Africa, 1979; editor: Advokaten, Tidskrift for Sveriges Advokatsamfund, 1973-86. Mem. Social Welfare Com., 1970-76; bd. dirs. Uppsala-Gavle Mcpl. Theatre, 1976-80; hon. treas., trustee European Human Rights Found., Amsterdam/London, 1981—. Mem. Swedish Bar Assn. (dep. bd. dirs. 1970-78), Internat. Inst. Humanitarian Law (San Remo). Home: Döbelnsgatan 28 B, S-752 37 Uppsala Sweden Office: S-10333 Stockholm Sweden

NOBLE, FRANCES ELIZABETH, educator, author; b. Chgo., Sept. 3, 1903; d. George William and Clara Louise (Lane) N. B.A. cum laude, Northwestern U., 1924, M.A., 1926, Ph.D., 1945. Mem. faculty Western Mich. U., Kalamazoo, 1931—, prof. French, head dept., 1955-73, prof. emerita, 1973—; French tchr. Fort Lauderdale (Fla.) Public Library, 1978—. Pres., Crippled Children's Guild of Broward County. Decorated palmes academiques, 1945. Author: (novel) Destiny's Daughter, 1980; The Political Ideas of Alfred de Musset, 1945; also articles. Mem. Alliance Française (past pres.), Am. Assn. Tchrs. of French, Phi Beta Kappa. Republican. Home: 2915 NE Center Ave Fort Lauderdale FL 33308

NOBLE, GEORGE COCHRAN, accountant, international corporate consultant; b. Douglas, Isle of Man, Dec. 19, 1944; s. Francis Alexander and Betty (White) N.; m. Elizabeth Jane Burnett, Dec. 20, 1976. Student, King Williams Coll., Castletown, Isle of Man, 1954-63. Chartered acct., Can. Articled pupil acctg. B. Sugden & Co., Douglas, 1963-69; internal auditor Coca Cola Export Corp., N.Y.C., 1969-71; asst. treas. Princess Properties Internat., Hamilton, Bermuda, 1972-73; insolvency specialist Coopers & Lybrand, Nassau, The Bahamas, 1973-76; prin. Noble & Co., Douglas, 1977—; chmn. Island Bus. Brokers, Douglas, 1978—, Abacus Advisers Ltd., Douglas, 1986—; official trustee in bankruptcy Isle of Man High Ct., Douglas, 1985—; chmn. Office Adminstrn. & Services Ltd., Douglas, 1980—; bd. dirs. Asset Global Funds Ltd., Douglas, Stronghold Internat. Mgmt. Ltd., Douglas; hon. consul Republic of Liberia, Isle of Man, 1987. Fellow Inst. Chartered Accts. in Eng. and Wales (chmn. Isle of Man 1985-86); mem. Can. Inst. Chartered Accts. (Bermuda Provincial Inst.). Mem. Ch. of Eng. Club: Ellan Vannin (Douglas) (treas. 1981-83). Lodge: Past Rotarians ((pres. Isle of Man 1987-88). Office: Noble & Co, Abacus House Mona St, Douglas Isle of Man

NOBLE, JAMES KENDRICK, JR., investment firm executive; b. N.Y.C., Oct. 6, 1928; s. James Kendrick and Orrel Tennant (Baldwin) N.; m. Norma Jean Rowell, June 16, 1951; children: Anne Rowell, James Kendrick III. Student, Princeton U., 1945-46; B.S., U.S. Naval Acad., 1950; M.B.A., NYU, 1961; postgrad., Sch. Edn., 1962-68. Commd. ensign USN, 1950; transferred to USNR 1957; advanced through grades to capt. USNR, 1973; asst. gunnery officer in U.S.S. Thomas E. Fraser 1950-51; student naval aviator USNR, 1951-52, pilot asst. ops. officer, 1952-55; student USN Gen. Line Sch., 1955-56; instr. U.S. Naval Acad., 1956-57, Officer Candidate Sch., Newport, R.I., 1958; asst. to pres. Noble & Noble, Pub., Inc., N.Y.C., 1957-60; dir. spl. projects Noble & Noble, Pub., Inc., 1960-62, v.p., 1962-65, exec. v.p., 1965-66, dir., 1957-65; dir., v.p. Translation Pub. Co., N.Y.C., 1958-65; cons. Translation Pub. Co., 1965-66; v.p., dir. Elbon Realty Corp., Bronxville, N.Y., 1960-65; cons. Elbon Realty Corp., 1965-66; comdg. officer NAIRU R2, 1968-70; staff NARS W2, 1970-71, NRID 3-1, 1971-74; comdg. officer NRCSG 302, 1974-76; sr. analyst F. Eberstadt & Co., 1966-69; sr. analyst Auerbach, Pollak & Richardson, 1969-75, v.p., 1972-75, mgr. spl. research projects, 1973-75, dir., 1975; v.p. research Paine, Webber, Jackson & Curtis, Inc., 1975-77, assoc. dir. research, 1976-77; v.p. Paine Webber, N.Y.C., 1977-79; 1st v.p. Paine Webber, 1979—; dir. Curriculum Info. Center, Inc., Denver, 1972-78; instl. investor All Am. Research Team, 1972—. Author: Ploob, 1949, rev., 1956; editor pub.: The Years Between, 1966; also articles in various kinds publs. Vice pres. Bolton Gardens Assn., 1959-61; mem. Bronxville Bd. Edn., 1968-74, pres., 1970-72; Republican co-leader 21st Dist., Eastchester, N.Y., 1961-65; Dir. Merit; cons., dir. Space and Sci. Train, 1962-63; trustee St. John's Hosp., Yonkers, N.Y., 1972—, com. chmn., 1980—. Fellow AAAS; mem. Info. Industry Assn. (disting. profl. mem.), Nat. Inst. Social Scis., N.Y. Soc. Security Analysts (mem. com. 1971—, dir. 1975-84, v.p. 1977-81, exec. v.p. 1981-82, pres. 1982-83), Am. Textbook Pub. Inst. (com. chmn. 1964-66), AIAA (mem. com. 1957-61), Printing and Pub. Industry Analysts Assn. (pres. 1969-71), Fin. Analysts Fedn. (dir. 1984-87), Chartered Fin. Analyst, Naval Res. Assn. (v.p. N.Y. Navy chpt. 1968-76), others. Mem. Reformed Ch. Clubs: Wings (N.Y.C.); Siwanoy Country (Bronxville, N.Y.). Home: 45 Edgewood Ln Bronxville NY 10708 Office: Paine Webber Inc 1285 Ave of the Americas New York NY 10019

NOBLE, RICHARD LLOYD, lawyer; b. Oklahoma City, Oct. 11, 1939; s. Samuel Lloyd and Eloise Joyce (Millard) N. AB with distinction, Stanford, 1961, LLB, 1964. Bar: Calif. 1964. Assoc. firm Cooper, White & Cooper, San Francisco, 1965-67; assoc., ptnr. firm Voegelin, Barton, Harris & Callister, Los Angeles, 1967-70; ptnr. Noble & Campbell, Los Angeles, San Francisco, 1970—; dir. Langdale Corp., Los Angeles, Gt. Pacific Fin. Co., Sacramento; lectr. Tax Inst. U. So. Calif., 1970; Treas. Young Republicans Calif., 1960-62; Bd. govs. St. Thomas Aquinas Coll.; mem. Colo. River Bd. of Calif. Contbr. articles to legal jours. Recipient Hilmer Oehlman Jr. award Stanford Law Sch., 1962; Benjamin Harrison Fellow Stanford U., 1964. Mem. Am., Los Angeles, San Francisco bar assns., State Bar Calif., Pi Sigma Alpha, Delta Sigma Rho. Republican. Clubs: Commercial (San Francisco), Commonwealth (San Francisco); Stock Exchange (Los Angeles), Petroleum (Los Angeles); Beach Tennis (Pebble Beach, Calif.); Capitol Hill (Washington). Home: 2222 Ave of Stars Los Angeles CA 90067 Office: Noble & Campbell Uhler 888 W 6th St Los Angeles CA 90017

NOBLE, STUART HARRIS, newspaper executive; b. Vancouver, B.C., Can., Jan. 11, 1941; s. Stewart Ian and Mina Rebecca (Harris) N.; m. Ann Rosalind Thorne, June 20, 1964 (dec. Dec. 1983); children: Kirsten Ann, Kenneth Stuart, William Frank, Catherine Marquerite; m. Susan Carmen Melnechuk, May 12, 1984; 1 child, Justin Arthur. BS in Forestry, U. B.C., Vancouver. From trainee to mgr. employee relations MacMillan Bloedel Ltd., Vancouver, 1965-77; dir. human resources Fording Coal Ltd., Calgary, Alta., Can., 1977-85; v.p. human resources Pacific Pres Ltd., Vancouver, 1985, v.p. human resources and ops., 1988—. Recipient Outstanding Service award Big Bros. of B.C., 1973. Mem. Indsl. Relations Mgmt. Assn., Can. and Am. Newspaper Assns., Vancouver Bd. Trade. Lodge: Rotary (sec., treas. local chpt. 1974-76). Home: 6700 Whiteoak Dr, Richmond, BC Canada V7E 4Z9 Office: Pacific Press Ltd, 2250 Granville St, Vancouver, BC Canada V6H 3G2

NOCENT, PIERRE-HENRY, endocrinologist; b. Dax, France, Nov. 15, 1943; m. Marie-Paule Bodart, Dec. 26, 1968; children: Bénédicte, Mathieu, Guillaume. MD, U. Paris, 1974. Pvt. practice medicine specializing in endocrinology Poitiers, France, 1975—; cons. Jean Bernard Hosp., Poitiers, 1975. Lodge: Lions. Home and Office: 54 Ave De La Liberation, 86000 Poitiers France

NOCTON, FRANÇOIS GERARD, pediatrician; b. Survilliers, Val D'Oise, France, Oct. 12, 1934; s. Jean and Marie-Louise (Feuilliatre) N.; m. Nicole Chevillard, Apr. 28, 1960; children: Bénédicte, Laurent, Veronique, Vincent. Docteur en Médecine, Faculté de Médecine, Paris, 1965, CES Pediatrie, 1966. Externe Hopitaux de Paris, 1956-59, intern, 1961-65; clinic chief Faculté de Médecine, Paris, 1965-67; chief of service Pediatrie-Hopital, Senlis, France, 1966-78, Pediatrie Centre Hospitalier Genèral, Creil, France, 1978—; pres. Ordre des Médecins Departemental, Oise, France, 1981—. Contbr. articles to profl. jours. Served to lt. Med. Corps French Army, 1959-61. Mem. Soc. Française Pediatrie. Roman Catholic. Home: 12 Rue Saint-Pierre, 60300 Senlis France Office: Centre Hospitalier Genèral, Boulevard Laënnec, 60100 Creil France

NOE, SALLY (SARA) WOODWORTH, educator, local history researcher; b. Kansas City, Mo., Mar. 18, 1926; d. Hugh Johnson and Katharine (McAntire) Woodworth; m. Robert Clark Noe, Aug. 14, 1945; children: Katharine Merry, Thomas Clark, William Dean. BA, U. N.Mex., 1969, MA, 1984. Cert. tchr., N.Mex. Elem. tchr. Morenci Pub. Schs., Ariz., 1946-47; elem. tchr. Gallup-McKinley County Sch. Dist., N.Mex., 1955-56, tchr. Office Navajo Edn. Opportunity, Concentrated Employment Practice, 1968-69, tchr. secondary social studies, 1969-87, chmn. dept. social studies, 1977-87; social studies evaluator, N.Mex. schs., 1975—; instr. N.Mex. history U. N.Mex., Gallup, 1986—; cons. Harcourt, Brace, Jovanovich, 1985-86. Author N.Mex. Council for Social Studies and State N.Mex. Dept. Edn. unit for Native Am. history, 1979; author Gallup centennial calendar, 1981. Head rug clk. InterTribal Indian Ceremonial, Gallup, 1976—; bd. dirs. N.Mex. Law Related Edn.; regional dir. N.Mex. History Day; mem. com. Ft. Wingate Preservation Task Force, 1984, Com. on Status of History in N.Mex. Pub. Schs., 1984; participant Navajo Nation History and Govt. Inst., 1987; bd. dirs. Inter-Tribal Indian Ceremonial Assn., 1987—; presenter Colloquium for Research on Women C.R.O.W. U. N.Mex., 1988; mem. U. N.Mex. Centennial Com., 1988. Recipient 3d Place award High Sch. div. econs. Kazanjian Found., 1970, Tchr.'s medal Freedom Found. at Valley Forge, 1973, Inst. for Am. Indian History award Newberry Library, 1978, Dorothy Woodward award for Edn. Hist. Soc. N.Mex., 1987; Ethnic Am. Coe fellow Stanford U., Calif., 1979; S.W. Inst. Research on Women fellow U. Ariz., 1983; Spl. Programs in Citizenship Edn. fellow Wake Forest U. Sch. Law, 1985. Mem. AAUW, N.Mex. Council for Social Studies (pres. 1980-81), N.Mex. Hist. Soc. (presenter), Nat. Council Social Studies, N.Mex. Archeol. Soc. (cert. crew mem., presenter state meeting 1986), N.Mex. Soc. for Preservation History, Gallup Hist. Soc., Delta Kappa Gamma (pres. Gallup chpt. 1979-80), Alpha Delta Pi. Democrat. Episcopalian. Lodges: Order Eastern Star, PEO. Home: PO Box 502 1911 Mark St Gallup NM 87301 Office: Gallup High Sch PO Box 39 Gallup NM 87301

NOECKER, CARL BLUE, lawyer; b. Lancaster, Ohio, Apr. 17, 1912; s. G.O. and Maude (Hedges) N.; J.D., Ohio State U., 1936; m. Ada Margaret Coon, Nov. 30, 1934 (dec. June 1962); children—Nadine, Daniel B.; Stepchildren: Karen, Scott; m. 2d, Virginia O. Simpson, Oct. 26, 1962 (dec. Mar. 1973); m. 3d, Eleanor M. Benson, Jan. 5, 1974. Admitted to Ohio bar, 1936, Calif. bar, 1949; practiced law, Columbus, Ohio, 1936-43, Walnut Creek, Calif., 1950—; real estate rep. Texaco, Inc., San Francisco, 1947-50. Mem. Calif. City, County, State People to People Delegation to Eng., Germany, Russia, Poland, Hungary, France, 1967. City atty., Walnut Creek, 1959-65. Bd. govs. Shriners Hosps. for Crippled Children, San Francisco. Served to lt. comdr. USNR, 1943-47. Mem. State Bar Calif., Am., Ohio, Contra Costa, Central Contra Costa (past pres.) bar assns., Walnut Creek Area C. of C. (past pres., dir.), Am. Arbitration Assn., Royal Order Jesters. Mason (Shriner). Clubs: Elks (Walnut Creek); Commonwealth of Calif. (San Francisco). Home: 3915 S Pearldale Dr Lafayette CA 94549 Office: 2363 Blvd Circle Highland Bldg Suite #3 Walnut Creek CA 94595

NOEHREN, ROBERT, organist, organ builder; b. Buffalo, Dec. 16, 1910; s. Alfred H. and Juliet (Egelhoff) N.; student Inst. Mus. Art, N.Y.C., 1929-30, Curtis Inst. Music, Phila., 1930-31; B.Mus., U. Mich., 1948; D. Mus. (hon.), Davidson Coll., 1957; m. Eloise Southern, Aug. 27, 1938; children—Judith, Arthur. Instr., Davidson Coll., 1946-49; prof., univ. organist U. Mich., 1949-77, prof. emeritus, 1977—; vis. prof. U. Kans., 1975; organ builder; important instruments include organ in St. John's Roman Cath. Cathedral, Milw., 1st Unitarian Ch., San Francisco, 1st Presbyn. Ch., Buffalo, St. Andrew's Episc. Ch., Newport News, Va., Calvary Episc. Ch., Rochester, Minn.; designer, cons., 1954—; concert tours of Europe, 1948—; soloist Phila. Orch., Philharmonia Hungarica, New Sinfonia; rec. artist Lyrichord, Urania, Orion, Delos records; spl. research old organs Europe, 17th and 18th century organs in France. Recipient Grande Prix du Disque. Contbr. articles profl. jours. Composer pieces for organ, piano, voice, chorus. Patentee combination action for organs. Home: 17605 Drayton Hall Way San Diego CA 92128

NOEL, PATRICK PAUL, glass company executive; b. Rousies, France, Jan. 28, 1946; s. Jean Leon and Elise (Munier) N.; m. Yvonne Marcelle Drancourt, May 24, 1969; children: Luc, Elise. Dip. in Engring., Ctr. d'Etudes Supérieures des Tech. Industrielles, Paris, 1969; MBA, Inst. Supérieures des Affairs, Jouy-en-Josas, 1971. Registered profl. engr. Project mgr. Richier-Ford, Paris, 1972-79, Rank-Xerox, Paris, 1979-81; mfg. mgr. OTP-Xerox, Gonesse, France, 1981-85; info. services mgr. Corning France, Avon, 1985—. Roman Catholic. Home: 14 Villa D'este, F-75648 Paris France Office: Corning France, 44 Ave De Valvins, F-77210 Avon France

NOELLE, HORST CARL, physician, medical educator; b. Wilhelmshaven, Germany, Feb. 2, 1924; s. Heinrich Wilhelm and Anna Maria (Neubert) N.; student U. Berlin, 1942-43, U. Wü rzburg, 1943-44; M.D., U. Hamburg, 1949. Intern, Town-Hosp., Bremerhaven, 1949-50, resident, 1950-52; resident Med. U. Clinic, Hamburg, 1953-54, Town-Hosp., Emden, 1954-55, Med. U.-Clinic, Kiel, 1955-60; resident Med. U.-Clinic Giessen, 1960-64, head dept. neurology, 1964-68; mem. Inst. Nutrition & Research, 1968; head State Dietitians Coll. at U. Kiel and Giessen, 1955-68; asst. prof. Justus Liebig U., Giessen, 1966-68, research prof., 1968-75, hon. prof., 1975—; now med. supt. Med. Clinic, Central Hosp. Reinkenheide, Bremerhaven; pres. adv. council for Nutritional Sci. to German fishing industry. Served to capt. German Air Force, 1941-46. Lutheran. Contbr. articles to med. jours. Home: 24 von Glahn Str, 2850 Bremerhaven Federal Republic of Germany Office: Central Hospital, Reinkenheide, 2850 Bremerhaven Federal Republic of Germany

NOER, HAROLD ROLF, surgeon; b. Madison, Wis., Apr. 3, 1927; s. Harold R. and Blanche K. (Field) N.; m. Betty Schlegelmilch, Sept. 16, 1950; children—Harold Rolf III, Karen Marie, Carol Ann. B.A., U. Wis., 1946, M.D., 1948. Diplomate Am. Bd. Orthopaedic Surgery. Intern, Augustana Hosp., Chgo., 1948-49; fellow in anatomy Wayne U. Med. Coll., Detroit, 1949-50; fellow in surgery Detroit Receiving Hosp., 1949-50; resident Grace Hosp., Detroit, 1953-55; practice medicine specializing in orthopedic surgery Alexandria and Arlington, Va.; commd. lt. (j.g.) M.C., U.S. Navy, 1950, advanced through grades to comdr., 1961; flight surgeon USMC Air Sta., Cherry Point, N.C., 1952-53; resident orthopedic surgeon U.S. Naval Hosp., Oakland, Calif., 1955-57; asst. then acting chief orthopedics U.S. Naval Hosp., Camp Lejeune, N.C., 1958-61, U.S. Naval Hosp., St. Albans, N.Y., 1961-63; chief neurosurgery U.S. Naval Hosp., Camp Lejeune, 1958-61; sr. med. officer U.S. 6th fleet Mediterranean, 1962-65; orthopedic basic sci. dir. U.S. Armed Forces Inst. Pathology, Washington, 1965-67; resigned, 1967; cons. orthopedics U.S. Naval Hosp. Bethesda, Md., 1965-68, U.S. Dept. Transp., 1969—; former attending surgeon Crippled Children's Program, Arlington, Va., 1967-83; mem. staff Nat. Orthopedic and Rehab. Hosp., Arlington, 1967—, Alexandria (Va.) Hosp., 1967—, also Northern Va. Drs. Hosp., Alexandria Hosp. Decorated Purple Heart. Fellow ACS, Internat. Coll. Surgeons, Am. Acad. Orthopedic Surgery; mem. Alexandria Med. Soc., Soc. Mil. Orthopedic Surgeons, Washington Orthopedic Soc. (past pres.), Va. Orthopedic Soc. Club: West River Sailing. Episcopalian. Author: Navigator's Pocket Calculator Handbook, 1983; contbr. articles to profl. jours. Office: 5203 Leesburg Pike Suite 1601 Falls Church VA 22041

NOESJIRWAN, JENNIFER ANNE, social communication educator; b. Wellington, New Zealand, May 15, 1941; arrived in Australia, 1964; d. Lionel Paul and Onyx (Brenkley) Latham; m. Wan Noesjirwan, Mar. 19, 1963; children: Daman, Juston, Kynan. BA, Victoria U., 1963, MA, 1966; PhD, Macquarie U., 1978. Cons. Indonesia Dept. Edn., Jakarta, 1970-71; edn. research officer New South Wales Inst. Tech., Sydney, Australia, 1972; sr. tutor Macquarie U., Sydney, 1973-77; lectr. Kuring-Gai Coll. Advanced Edn., Sydney, 1978-81, coordinator community orgns. programs, 1985-88, cons., evaluator Dept. Environ. Planning, Sydney, 1982; lectr. Hawkesbury Agrl. Coll., 1984—; cons., author Local Govt. and Shires Assn., Sydney, 1983; research assoc. Am. Field Service, N.Y.C. Contbr. articles to profl. jours.; co-author: Simulation Game, 1980. Address: 27 Rothwell Rd, 2074 Turramurra, New South Wales Australia

NOETH, CAROLYN FRANCES, speech and language pathologist; b. Cleve., July 21, 1924; d. Sam Falco and Barbara Serafina (Loparo) Armaro; m. Lawrence Andrew Noeth Sr., June 29, 1946; children: Lawrence Andrew Jr. (dec.), Barbara Marie Heaney. AB magna cum laude, Case Western Res. U., 1963; MEd, U. Ill., 1972; postgrad., Nat. Coll. Edn., 1975—. Speech therapist Chgo. Pub. Schs., 1965; speech, lang. and hearing clinician J. Sterling Morton High Schs., Cicero and Berwyn, Ill., 1965-82, tchr. learning disabilities/behavior disorders, 1982, dist. ednl. diagnostician, 1982-84; Title I Project tchr., summers 1966-67, lang. disabilities cons., summers 1968-69, in-service tng. cons., summer 1970, dir. Title I Project, summers 1973-74, learning disabilities tchr. W. Campus of Morton, 1971-75, chmn. Educable-Mentally Handicapped-Opportunities Tchrs. Com., 1967-68, spl. edn. area and in-sch. tchrs. workshops, 1967—. Precinct elections judge, 1953-55; block capt. Mothers March of Dimes and Heart Fund, 1949-60; St. Agatha's rep. Nat. Catholic Women's League, 1952-53; collector for charities, 1967; mem. exec. bd. Morton Scholarship League, 1981-84, corr. sec., 1981-83; vol. Am. Cancer Soc., 1985—; vol. judge Ill. Acad. Decathlon, 1988—. First recipient Virda L. Stewart award for Speech, Western Res. U., 1963, recipient Outstanding Sr. award, 1963. Mem. Am. (certified), Ill. speech and hearing assns., Council Exceptional Children (div. for learning disabilities, chpt. spl. projects chmn., exec. bd. 1976-81, chpt. pres. 1979-80), Assn. Children with Learning Disabilities, Council for Learning Disabilities, Profls. in Learning Disabilities, Internat. Platform Assn., Kappa Delta Pi, Delta Kappa Gamma (chmn., co-chmn. chpt. music com. 1979—, mem. state program com. 1981-83, chpt. music rep. to state 1982—). Roman Catholic. Clubs: St. Norbert's Women's (Northbrook, Ill.), Case-Western Res. U., U. Ill. Alumni Assns., Lions (vol. Northbrook, 1966—). Chmn. in compiling and publishing Student Handbook, Cleve. Coll., 1962; contbr. lyric parodies and musical programs J. Sterling Morton High Sch. West Retirement Teas, 1972-83. Home and Office: 1849 Walnut Circle Northbrook IL 60062

NOGGLE, LAWRENCE WESLEY, mechanical engineer; b. Dayton, Ohio, Oct. 9, 1935; s. William Henry and Lula Evelyn (O'Dell) N.; B.M.E., Gen. Motors Inst., 1959; B.A., Simpson Coll., 1965; M.Sc., Ohio State U., 1972, Ph.D., 1973; postgrad. Indsl. Coll. of Armed Forces, 1980-81; postgrad. Fed. Exec. Inst., 1988; m. Alwilda June Yount, Nov. 20, 1952; children—Lawrence Wesley, Yvonne, Grant, Matthew, Dorinda. Coop. student, jr. project engr. Gen. Motors Corp., Indpls. and Oak Ridge, 1954-61; aerospace engr. USAF, Wright-Patterson AFB, Ohio, 1961-62; computer room supr. Wells Fargo Bank, San Franciso, 1962-65; research engr. Boeing Co., Seattle, 1965-66; aerospace engr., sr. aerospace engr., study mgr. aero. systems div. Wright Patterson AFB, 1966-86, program mgr., mission area planner, 1976-80, chief tactical devel. planning, 1981-83, dep. dir. joint tactical interopeability system program office, 1983-86, spl. asst., dep. for tactical warfare systems, spl. asst., dep. asst. sec. air force (acquisition), 1986—; tchr. Simpson Coll., 1962-63. Gen. Motors Corp. fellow, 1954-58, USAF fellow, 1970-71, ASD fellow, 1986-87; recipient Outstanding Performance award USAF, 1968, 69, 73, 74, 80-84, 85-87. Mem. AIAA (tech. com. air transp. systems 1978-81), Air Force Assn., Ohio State U. Alumni Assn., Gen. Motors Inst. Alumni Assn., ICAF Alumni Assn., Fed. Exec. Inst. Alumni Assn., Sigma Xi, Tau Beta Pi, Chi Alpha Omega. Mem. Christian and Missionary Alliance Ch. Contbr. articles to profl. jours. Home: 7009 Needwood Rd Rockville MD 20855 Office: Sec Air Force/AQ The Pentagon Rm 4D961 Washington DC 20330

NOGI, TIAKI, textile designer; b. Kyoto, Japan, Dec. 17, 1937; s. Shogo and Namie (Kumon) N.; m. Yoshie Seto, May 10, 1964; children—Yuko, Akiko. BA, Kansai U. (Japan), 1961. Studio mgr. Shogo Nogi Studio, Kyoto, 1969-75; owner, dir. Nogi Tiaki Designs, London and Kyoto, 1975—; designer wallcoverings, upholsteries, bedlinen. Roman Catholic. Avocations: coin collecting, Sunday carpentry, operas, classical music. Home: 23 Okamachi Misasagi, Yamasina, 607 Kyoto Japan Office: Nogi Tiaki Designs, 23 Okamachi Misasagi, 607 Kyoto Japan

NOGUCHI, HIDEO, insurance agency executive; b. Kyoto, Japan, Jan. 17, 1945; s. Tasao and Ishiko (Tsujii) N.; m. Eleanor Kazuko Horii, May 7, 1970; children—Mark H.Y., Mitchell H.Y. B.B.A., U. Hawaii, 1969. Buyer RCA Purchasing Co., Tokyo, 1969-73; ins. specialist Continental Ins. Agy., Honolulu, 1973-82; pres. Noguchi & Assocs., Inc., Honolulu, 1983—; cons. Recipient Nat. New Agt. Leadership award CNA Corp., 1974, Agt. of Yr. award Continental Ins. Agy., annually 1973-81, Key Club award CNA Co., 1975, 79-81. Mem. Nat. Assn. Life Underwriters, Honolulu Assn. Life Underwriters, Million Dollar Round Table. Lodge: Rotary (dir. Ala Moana, Honolulu club). Home: 3678 Woodlawn Terrace Pl Honolulu HI 96822 Office: 1314 S King St Suite 560 Honolulu HI 96814

NOGUCHI, HIROSHI, engineering educator; b. Tokyo, Japan, Aug. 9, 1946; s. Kou and Kimie (Ohtake) N.; m. Yoriko Ito, Jan. 8, 1982; children: Mariko, Eriko. B in Engring., U. Tokyo, 1970, M in Engring., 1972, D in Engring., 1976. Registered architect 1st class. Research architect U. Tokyo, 1976-77; asst. prof. Chiba (Japan) U., 1977-79, assoc. prof., 1979—; vis. researcher U. Toronto, 1984-85. Co-author: Shear Analysis of Reinforced Concrete Structures, 1983, Finite Element Analysis of Reinforced Concrete Structures, 1986. Mem. ASCE, Archtl. Inst. Japan, Japan Concrete Inst. (Meritorious Paper award, 1985), Tokyo Soc. Architects, Am. Concrete Inst., Internat. Assn. Bridges and Structural Engring. Home: 3-26-1-102 Yatsu, Narashino-shi, Chiba 275, Japan Office: Chiba U Dept Archtl Engring, 1-33 Yayoi-cho, Chiba 260, Japan

NOGUCHI, TERUO, oil company executive; b. Tokyo, Nov. 5, 1917; s. Eizaburo and Yae (Minakami) N.; m. Michiko Kohama, Oct. 20, 1948; children—Hideo, Yasuo. B.S., Osaka U., 1941, D.Sc., 1958. With Koa Oil Co., Ltd., Tokyo, 1944—, dir., 1961-64, mng. dir., 1964-67, chief mng. dir., 1967-73, pres., 1973—; chmn. Research Assn. Residual Oil Processing, 1979—; chmn. Research Assn. Petroleum Devel. Alternatives, 1980—, pres. 1980—, Japan Cooperation Ctr. Petroleum Industry Deve., 1981—; chmn. Research Assn. Utilization Light Oil, 1983— ; dir. Mitsui Petrochem. Industries, Tokyo Tanker Co., Ltd., Nippon Oil Staging Terminal Co. Ltd. Decorated Order of Blue Ribbon (Japan), Order of Rising Sun, Gold Rays with Neck Ribbon. Mem. Keidanren, Japan Petroleum Inst. (hon.). Lodge: Rotary. Home: 30 Minami-cho, Shinjuku-ku, 162 Tokyo Japan Office: Koa Oil Co Ltd, 2-6-2 Ohtemachi, Chiyoda-ku, 100 Tokyo Japan

NOGUCHI, YASUHIRO, photographic chemist; b. Kyoto, Japan, Dec. 30, 1941; s. Etsuo and Emi (Shimada) N.; m. Asako Ikeda, Mar. 29, 1970; children—Keiko, Yuhko. B.S., Kyoto U., 1965, M.S., 1967, Ph.D., 1985; postgrad. Mich. State U., 1974-75. Research chemist Fuji Photo Film Co., Asaka, Saitama, Japan, 1967-74, sr. researcher, Minamiashigara, Kanagawa, Japan, 1976-83, mem. sr. patent staff, 1983—; vis. scholar Columbia U., N.Y.C., 1975-76. Fuji Photo Film Co. Ltd. overseas study grantee Mich. State U., East Lansing, 1974-75, Columbia U., 1975-76. Mem. Am. Chem. Soc., Chem. Soc. Japan, Polymer chemistry Soc. Japan, Soc. Photog. Sci. and Engring., Gakushikai. Club: Ibaraki Country (Osaka, Japan). Home: 190-6 Kuno, Kanagawa 250 Odawara Japan Office: Fuji Photo Film Co Ltd, 210 Nakanuma, Minamiashigara, 250-01 Kanagawa Japan

NOGUERES, HENRI, lawyer, journalist, historian, author; b. Bages, France, Nov. 13, 1916; s. Louis and Madeleine Nogueres; m. Jacqueline Profichet, Nov. 4, 1939; 1 child, Dominique. Degree in Law, Univ. of Paris. Journalist Le Populaire, Paris, 1936-38; atty. Cts. of Paris, 1942-46; editor-in-chief Le Populaire, Paris, 1946-49; dir., editor-in-chief Central Press Agy., Paris, 1949-59; writer, dir., producer TV programs, series, French TV,

1960—; adminstrv. dir., dir. hist. collections Edits. Robert Laffont, Paris, 1962-66; co-dir. revue Janus, 1964-66, sec.-gen. Edits. Flammarion, 1966-76; advocate Ct. of Paris, 1976—. Author: Histoire de la Resistance en France, 5 vols.; La Vie quotidienne en France au temps du Front Populaire; La vie quotidienne des resistents. Pres. Ligue des Droits de l'Homme, 1975-84, hon. pres., 1984—. Served to lt. col. French Army, 1938-45. Decorated comdr. Legion d'honneur; Medaille Mil.; comdr., Ordre Nat. du Merite; Medaille de la Resistance; Croix de Guerre, 1939-45. Mem. Soutien Confraternel des journalistes (pres. 1960-74, hon. pres., 1974—). Address: Cabinet d'Avocats Associes, 70 Ave Marceau, 75008 Paris France

NOIR, ANDRE EMILE, shipping and telecommunications executive; b. Montrouge, France, July 3, 1929; s. Antoine Rene and Marcelle (Guenot) N.; m. Paulette David, Aug. 1, 1953; children—Francois, Philippe, Beatrice, Fabienne, Matthieu, Bertrand. B.S., Lycee Buffon, Paris, 1949; M.B.A., Sherbrooke U., Que., Can., 1971. Inspecteur, prin. adj. Ministere des Postes et Telecommunications, Paris, 1957-63; charge de mission Ministere Economie et Finances, Paris, 1963-65; inspecteur principal Ministere Postes et Telecommunications, Paris, 1966-70, Direction des Telecommunications du Reseau National, Paris, 1971-73; inspecteur principal, then dir. adjoint Dion Generale des Telecommunications, Paris, 1973-80; directeur adjoint Direction du Materiel de Transport, Paris, 1980—. Adminstr. Union Departementale des Associations Familiales des Haut De Seine, 1975; mem. Comite Technique des Transports, Paris, 1977; Comite Regional de Distribution du Gaz, Paris, 1982. Home: 22 Ave Emile Boutroux, Montrouge 92120, France Office: Direction du Materiel de Transport, 26 rue du Commandant, Rene Mouchotte, 75675 Paris France

NOJA, GIAN PAOLO, defense industry executive; b. Pavia, Italy, July 24, 1944; s. Giovanni and Maria (Vidali) N.; m. Lorraine Rowland, July 8, 1967; children: Gian Marcello, Gian Luca. Degree Physics, U. Genoa, 1966, Polit. Scis., 1969; Degree in Bus. Adminstrn., Inst. Superior Formation, 1971. Mng. dir. Gajon Inst. Tech., Genoa, 1971-74, chmn., 1974—; vice chmn. Italtraining Corp., Genoa, 1973-80; chmn. I.S.L. Corp., Genoa, 1980—, Cesedat Corp., 1982—, I.T.F. Corp., Genoa, 1982—, Assn. Industrialists-Electromechanics Industry, Genoa, 1981-83. Author: Horizontal and Vertical Administration, 1975, New Frontiers for Computer Aided Instruction, 1985, Eliminating the Gap Between Training and Maintenance, 1986; researcher, inventor def. computerized tng. and maintenance systems. Club: Internat. Yacht (Rapallo, Italy) (dir. 1978—). Office: Gajon Inst Tech, Via Piaggio 9, 16136 Genoa Italy

NOJGAARD, MORTEN, philologist, educator; b. Holback, Denmark, July 28, 1934; s. Niels and Annie (Bay) N.; m. Stina Lund, Sept. 13, 1962; children: Elisabeth, Andreas, Rasmus, Caroline. MA, U. Copenhagen, 1959, PhD, 1964. Prof. Rodovre Coll., Copenhagen, 1960-63; research fellow U. Copenhagen, 1963-66; prof. Romance philology U. Odense, Denmark, 1966—. Author: La Fable Antique I-II, 1964-67, Elévation et Expansion, les Deux Dimensions de Baudelaire, 1973, An Introduction to Literary Analysis, 1975; chief editor Orbis Litterarum, 1968—; contbr. articles to profl. jours. Judge City Ct., Odense, 1982—. Decorated Ordre du Merite, 1980. Mem. Danish Royal Acad. Scis., Lund Soc. Letters, Alliance Francaise (pres. Odense 1970—). Home: Alokken, DK-5250 Odense Denmark Office: U Odense, Campusvej 55, DK-5250 Odense Denmark

NOLAN, DAVID BRIAN, lawyer; b. Washington, Jan. 1, 1951; s. John Joseph and Mary Jane N.; m. Cheryl Ann Cottle, June 30, 1979; children: John Joseph II, David Brian II. BA, Duke U., 1973; MPA, Am. U., 1975; JD, U. San Fernando Valley, 1978; postgrad., Georgetown U., 1981—. Bar: Calif. 1978, U.S. Dist. Ct. (cen. dist.) Calif. 1979, U.S. Ct. Claims 1981, U.S. Tax Ct. 1981, U.S. Ct. Appeals (D.C. cir.) 1984. Asst. dir. research Younger-Curb Campaign, Los Angeles, 1978; assoc. L. Rob Werner Law Offices, Encino, Calif., 1979-80; atty. conflicts Office of Pres. Elect, Washington, 1980-81; staff atty. Office of counsel to the Pres. White House, Washington, 1981; staff asst. office of sec. U.S. Dept. Treasury, Washington, 1981-85; spl. asst. office gen. counsel U.D. Dept. Energy, Washington, 1985—. Assoc. editor New Guard Mag., 1983-85. Steering com. Los Angeles Reps., 1979-80, Reagan for Pres., Los Angeles, 1980; chmn. 39th assembly, Rep. Cen. Com., 1979-80; alt. del. 1972 Rep. Nat. Conv.; pres. N.C. Coll. Rep. Com. 1972-73; nat. treas., bd. dirs. Young Americans for Freedom, Sterling, Va., 1983-85; corp. dir., sec. Am. Sovereignty Task Force, Vienna, Va., 1984—, State Dept. Watch. Ltd., Vienna, 1984 . Charles Edison Youth Found. scholar, 1971; Named one of Outstanding Young Men Am., Jaycees, 1976-86. Mem. ABA, Fed. Bar Assn., D.C. Bar Assn. (chmn. ethics com. young lawyers div. 1985-87), Federalist Soc., U.S. Justice Found. (of counsel, co-founder 1979—), Nat. Lawyers Club. Club: Conservative (Washington). Home: 1805 Ingemar Ct Alexandria VA 22308 Office: US Dept Energy 1000 Independence Ave SW Washington DC 20585

NOLAN, FRANCIS PERRY, diplomat; b. Adelaide, Australia, Jan. 6, 1945; s. Francis Perry and Alice Adelaide (Wilson) N. B Laws, U. Adelaide, 1967. Barrister, solicitor South Australia and Australian Capital Ter. Third sec. Australian High Commn., Lagos, Nigeria, 1969-70; counsellor Australian High Commn., London, 1988—; asst. dir. legal div. Australian Dept. Fgn. Affairs, Canberra, 1971-72, dir. Mid. East sect., 1985—; 1st sec. Australian Embassy, Vienna, Austria, 1972-75; 1st sec. mission to UN Australian Embassy, N.Y.C., 1979-82; charge d'affairs Australian Embassy, Beirut, 1982-84; high commr. Australian Embassy, Mauritius, 1984; bd. dirs. Internat. Tech. Australia (ITOA) Ltd., Sydney. Decorated Order of Australia. Clubs: Royal Canberra Golf, Adelaide U. Boat. Home: 342 Moore Park Rd, 2021 Paddington New South Wales, Australia Office: Dept Fgn Affairs, Parkes, Canberra 2064, Australia

NOLAN, LOUISE MARY, school system administrator, author; b. Boston, Sept. 28, 1947; d. John Joseph and Helen (Spiers) Nolan; B.A., Regis Coll., 1969; M.Ed., Boston U., 1971 postgrad., 1981-82; postgrad Fitchburg State Coll., 1972-74, Salem State Coll., 1977-79; Ph.D., Boston Coll., 1986. Counselor, Camp Thoreau, Inc., Concord, Mass., 1964-68; tchr., chmn. sci. dept. John F. Kennedy Meml. Jr. High Sch., Woburn, Mass., 1969-86; asst. supt. schs. for curriculum and instrn. Woburn Pub. Schs., 1986—; co-owner Ruth and Louise Silkscreening, Lexington, Mass., Fancypants, Carlisle, Mass.; dir. ecology program Curry Coll., Milton, Mass., summer 1977. Active New Eng. League Mid. Schs., Nat. League Mid. Schs. Vice chmn. Mass. Sci. Fair Com. NSF grantee, 1972-73, 77-79, 81-82; chemistry fellow Boston U., 1983-84; For a Cleaner Environment grantee, 1984-86. Mem. Mass. Tchrs. Assn., NEA, AAAS, Nat. Assn. Sci. Tchrs., Mass. Assn. Sci. Tchrs., Nat. Assn. Biology Tchrs., Nat. Assn. Research in Sci. Teaching, Middlesex County Tchrs. Assn., Biology Roundtable, Woburn Tchrs. Assn., Mass. Supts. Assn., Beta Beta Beta, Pi Lambda Theta. Democrat. Roman Catholic. Clubs: Museum Fine Arts, Lit. Guild, Concord Art Assn., Mus. of Sci., Theatre Guild. Author: Y.E.S.-A Comprehensive Guide to Students Educating Youth in Environmental Sciences; Bioluminescence—An Experimental Guide; Marine Plankton; Heath Physical Science, 1983, 87; also papers. Home: 9 Stevens Rd Lexington MA 02173 Office: Joyce Jr High Sch Adminstrn Offices Locust St Woburn MA 01801

NOLAN, RICHARD THOMAS, educator, clergyman; b. Waltham, Mass., May 30, 1937; s. Thomas Michael and Elizabeth Louise (Leishman) N.; B.A., Trinity Coll., 1960; M.Div. Hartford Sem. Found., 1963; M.A. in Religion, Yale U., 1967; Ph.D., N.Y.U., 1973. Ordained deacon Episcopal Ch., 1963, priest, 1965; basic cert., Clin. Pastoral Edn., Conn. Valley Hosp., 1962. Instr. Hartford (Conn.) Sem. Found., 1967-68, asst. acad. dean, lectr. philosophy and edn., 1968-70; instr. Mattatuck Community Coll., Waterbury, Conn., 1969-70, asst. prof. philosophy and history, 1970-74, assoc. prof., 1974-78, prof. philosophy and social sci., 1978—; research fellow in med. ethics Yale U., 1978; vicar St. Paul's Parish, Bantam, Conn., 1974-88, Pastor Emeritus, 1988—; pres. Litchfield Inst. (Conn. and Fla.), 1984—; mem. Ethics Com. Waterbury Hosp. Health Ctr., 1984-88; research fellow in profl. and bus. ethics Yale U., 1987; adj. dir. exec. programs and prof. philosophy of religion and Christian ethics Fairfax U.; vis. prof. philosophy, theology and religious studies various colls. and univs. N.Y., Conn. and Fla., 1964—; adj. assoc. in continuing edn. Berkeley Div. Sch. Yale U., 1987—; Rabbi Harry Haplern Meml. lect., Southbury, Conn., 1987; guest preacher various chs., 1973—, including Cathedral of St. John the Divine, N.Y.C., Trinity Cathedral, Miami; assoc. for edn. Christ Ch. Cathedral, Hartford, Conn., 1988—; host: (audio-taped interviews with Yale Faculty and others) Converstaions With . ., 1987—; guest speaker for colleges, schools, various profl. and community orgns., 1973—. Mem. Am. Acad. Religion, Am. Philos. Assn., Author's Guild, Inst. Society, Ethics and Life Scis. Author: (with H. Titus, M. Smith) Living Issues in Philosophy, 7th edit., 1979, 8th edit., 1986; (with F. Kirkpatrick) Living Issues in Ethics, 1982; editor, contbr. Diaconate Now, 1968. Address: PO Box 483 Bristol CT 06010 also: 781 W Oakland Park Blvd Fort Lauderdale FL 33311-1797

NOLAND, PATRICIA HAMPTON, editor, writer, poet; b. New Orleans, Dec. 24, 1924; d. Leon Maxwell and Clara Hampton (Whittle) Noland. BA, U. Houston, 1981; Dr. Leadership in Poetry (hon.), Internat. Acad. Leadership, Philippines, 1969; DLH (hon.) Free U. Asia, 1973; diploma of merit in lit., U. Arts, Salsomaggiore Terme, Italy, 1982; postgrad., Rice U., 1987. Vol. Mental Health Ctr., St. Joseph's Hosp., Houston, 1970-71; founder, pres., editor monthly newsletter Internat. Poetry Inst., Houston, 1969—. Author: Poems, 1960; editor: Whoever Heard a Birdie Cry?, 1970. Chmn. music com. 1st Ch. of Christian Scientist, Houston. Named Hon. Internat. Poet Laureate, United Poets Laureate Internat., Manila, 1969. Mem. Am. Hort. Soc., Mus. Fin Arts Houston, Met. Opera Guild, Smithsonian Instn., Colonial Williamsburg Found., Nat. Trust Hist. Preservation, Cousteau Soc., Met. Mus. Art, Boston Mus. Fine Arts, Isabella Stewart Gardner Mus., Norton Gallery and Sch. Art, New Orleans Mus. Art, Mus. for Women in Art, Internat. Platform Assn., English-Speaking Union, Mus. of Art of Am. West, Chgo. Art Inst., L'Alliance Française. Democrat. Club: Jr. League Luncheon. Home: 2400 Westheimer Rd Apt 215W Houston TX 77098 Office: PO Box 53087 Houston TX 77052

NOLAND, WAYNE BARNETT, manufacturing executive; b. Spirit Lake, Iowa, Nov. 13, 1918; s. Fred Alvard and Nora Lucinda (Cook) N.; student pub. schs., Earlham, Iowa; m. Ruth Ellen Smith, June 2, 1941; children—Barbara Jo, Alice Marie, Gary Chester, Larry Fred. Engr., mgr. mfg. Woodford Mfg. Co., Des Moines, 1943-70; pres. Noland Mfg. Co., Inc., Carlisle, Iowa, 1970—. Mem. Soc. of Friends. Patentee in field. Home: 340 Crescent Dr Carlisle IA 50047 Office: 100 E School St Carlisle IA 50047

NOLEN, LYNN DEAN, lawyer; b. Wetumka, Okla., Sept. 16, 1940; s. James Everett and Ora Florence (Pierce) N.; m. Cynthia Kay Heath, May 7, 1971; children—Angela Kay, Jennifer Lynn. B.A., East Central State Coll., Ada, Okla., 1961; LL.B., U. Okla., 1964. Bar: Okla. Sole practice, 1964-69, 72—; asst. dist. atty. Muskogee County, Okla., 1971-72. Served to capt. JAGC, U.S. Army, 1968-72. Mem. Okla. Bar Assn. Democrat. Baptist. Clubs: Masons, Shriners, Odd Fellows. Address: 501 W Okmulgee Ave Muskogee OK 74401

NOLTE, GEORGE WASHINGTON, former investment company executive; b. nr. Woodbury, N.J., Apr. 2, 1904; s. Harry Kircher and Anna (Porch) N. BS, U. Pa., 1924. CPA, Pa. Acct. Lybrand, Ross Bros. & Montgomery, Phila., 1924-32; comptroller Atwater Kent Mfg. Co., Phila., Wilmington, Del., 1932-49, v.p., 1949-67, pres., 1972-81; v.p. Kent Co., Wilmington, 1972-81; treas. Kent Elec. Mfg. Corp., 1949-71; bd. dirs. Atwater Kent Mfg. Co. Cons. parks, recreation com. Bd. Chosen Freeholders, Gloucester County, N.J., 1965-66; pres., trustee Gloucester County Conservancy, Etlon Found. Served to comdr. USNR, 1942-46. Recipient Disting. Service award for outstanding community service Woodbury Jr. C. of C., 1965. Mem. Am. Inst. CPA's. Home: 801 Lake Shore Dr Lake Park FL 33403 Office: 3411 Silverside Rd Wilmington DE 19810

NOLTE, TIMOTHY JAMES, marketing professional; b. Waseca, Minn., Mar. 17, 1954; s. Donald S. and Marceline M. (Fairchild) N. Student, U.S. Air Force Acad., 1972-73; BEE, U. Minn., 1980. Engr. mktg. Hewlett Packard, Colorado Springs, Colo., 1980-83; engr. product mktg. Hewlett Packard, Colorado Springs, 1983-85; European product mgr. HP64000 Systems European Mktg. Ctr. Hewlett-Packard, Böeblingen, Federal Republic of Germany, 1985—. Contbr. articles to profl. jours. Office: Hewlett-Packard TSS-EMC, Herrenberger Str 130, 7030 Böeblingen Federal Republic of Germany

NOLTINGK, BERNARD EDWARD, physicist, consultant; b. Torquay, Eng., Mar. 4, 1918; s. Ludwig Bernhard and May Emma Kate (Dick) N.; m. Daphne Gwladys Williams, Oct. 19, 1940; children: Janet Daphne, Christopher Timothy, Ann Bridget. BSc, U. London, 1937, PhD, 1940. Head electronics Motor Industry Research Assn., London, 1941-47; head ultrasonics Mullard Research Labs., Surrey, Eng., 1947-52; head strata control Mining Research Estab., Middlesex, Eng., 1952-55; head electronics Tube Investments Research Lab., Cambridge, Eng., 1955-60; head instrumentation Ctl. Electricity Research Lab., Surrey, 1960-81; sole cons. Dorking, Eng., 1981—. Author: The Human Element in Research Management, 1959, The Art of Research, 1965, (with others) Ultrasonic Cavitation, 1950; editor: Instrument Technology, 1985—, Instrumentation Reference Book, 1988, contbr. numerous articles to profl. jours. Elder, United Reformed Ch. Fellow Inst. Physics, IEEE, Royal Soc. Arts. Mem. Social and Liberal Democrats. Home and Office: Windwhistle Nutcombe Ln, Dorking, Surrey RH4 3DZ, England

NOMURA, MIDORI, engineering educator; b. Saga, Japan, May 4, 1951; s. Shigekazu and Nobuko (Fukuda) N.; m. Kazuhiko Nishide, May 3, 1986. BE, Tokyo Met. U., 1974, D in Engring., 1987. Architect Research Inst. Sch. Bldgs., Tokyo, 1976-80; post doctoral fellowship Japan Soc. Promotion Sci., Tokyo, 1984-85; asst. Tokyo Met. U., 1985-86; lectr. Tokyo Met. Coll. Allied Med. Scis., 1986—. Research grantee The Toyota Found., 1986, Ministry of Edn., Sci. and Culture grantee, 1987. Mem. Archtl. Inst. Japan (mem. com. handicapped 1978—, mgr. com. sch. bldgs. 1984—), The Japanese Assn. Spl. Edn., Nippon Assn. Edn. 2002, The Japan Inst. Hosp. Architecture, Japan Ergonomics Research Soc. Home: 1-19-1-403 Kitaotsuka, Toshima-ku, 170 Tokyo Japan Office: Tokyo Met Coll Allied Med Scis, 7-2-10 Higashi-Ogu, Arakawa-ku, 116 Tokyo Japan

NONAKA, IKUJIRO, business educator; b. Tokyo, May 10, 1935; s. Asajiro and Iku N.; m. Sachiko Yokota, Apr. 29, 1960; children: Miho, Yukiho. BS, Waseda U., Tokyo, 1958; MBA, U. Calif., Berkeley, 1968, PhD in Bus. Adminstrn., 1972. Mem. corp. staff Fuji Electric Co., Tokyo, 1958-67; research asst. U. Calif., Berkeley, 1967-72; prof. Nanzan U., Nagoya, Aichi, Japan, 1977-79, Nat. Def. Acad., Yokosuke, Kanagawa, Japan, 1979-82, Hitotsubashi U., Kunitachi, Tokyo, Japan, 1982—. Author Organization and Market, 1974 (Nikkei prize, 1974), An Evolutionary Theory of the Firm, 1985; co-author Strategic vs. Evolutionary Management: A U.S.-Japan Comparison, 1983 (Acad. Assn. Orgnl. Sci. prize 1984), Essence of Failure, 1984. Mem. Acad. Assn. Orgnl. Sci. Home: 1-57-4 Kinugaoka, Hachioji 192 Tokyo Japan Office: Hitotsubashi U Inst Bus Research, 2-1 Naka, Kunitachi 186 Tokyo Japan

NONOYAMA, MEIHAN, biomedical research institute executive; b. Tokyo, Feb. 25, 1938; came to U.S., 1966; s. Hayakichi and Kie (Kasagi) N.; m. Keiko Sakaguchi, Jan. 19, 1969; 1 son, Akihisa. B.S., U. Tokyo, 1961, M.S., 1963, Ph.D., 1966. Research assoc. U. Ill.-Urbana, 1966-68; vis. scientist Wistar Inst., Phila., 1968-70; asst. prof. U. N.C.-Chapel Hill, 1970-73; assoc. prof. Rush Presbyn. St. Luke's Hosp. and U. Ill.-Chgo., 1973-76; dir. molecular virology Life Scis., Inc., St. Petersburg, Fla., 1976-81; pres. Showa U. Research Inst. for Biomedicine, 1981—; prof. U. South Fla. and Showa U., 1981—. Fulbright fellow, 1966; NIH grantee, 1973—; Am. Cancer Soc. grantee, 1975, 85; Leukemia Found. grantee, 1976. Mem. Am. Soc. Microbiology, Am. Soc. Virology, Am. Assn. Cancer Research, Soc. Exptl. Biology, Japanese Soc. Cancer. Contbr. articles to profl. jours. Office: 10900 Roosevelt Blvd N Saint Petersburg FL 33702

NOONAN, MICHAEL J., defense minister Ireland; b. Bruff, County Limerick, Ireland, Sept. 4, 1935; s. John and Hannah (Slattery) N.; m. Helen Sheehan, Nov. 28, 1961; children: Marie Noonan Madden, Ann, John, Cahterine, Carmel, Patrick. Student, Salesian Coll., Pallaskenry, County Limerick. Elected T.D. Dail Eireann, Dublin, Ireland, 1969—; opposition spokesman on agr. Fianna Fail Party, Dublin, 1983-87; minister for def. Ireland, Dublin, 1987—. Roman Catholic. Home: Crean Bruff, Kilmallock Couty Limerick, Ireland Office: Dept of Def, Parkgate, Dublin 8 Ireland

NOONAN, PATRICK FRANCIS, business executive, conservationist; b. St. Petersburg, Fla., Dec. 2, 1942; s. Francis Patrick and Henrietta (Donovan) N.; m. Nancy Elizabeth Peck, Aug. 15, 1964; children: Karen Elizabeth, Dawn Wiley. A.B., Gettysburg Coll., 1961-65; M.City and Regional Planning, Catholic U. Am., 1967; M.B.A., Am. U., 1971. Planner Md. Nat. Capitol Park and Planning Com., Silver Spring, 1965-68; investment counseler, real estate broker, appraiser Washington, 1967-69; dir. ops. The Nature Conservancy, Arlington, Va., 1969-73; pres. The Nature Conservancy, 1973-80; chmn. Conservation Resources Group, 1981—; pres. The Conservation Fund, 1985—; Exec. com. Natural Resources Council Am., 1973-75; mem. Appalachian Nat. Scenic Trail Adv. Council, 1974—. Trustee Cath. Youth Orgn. of Washington, 1975—, Gettysburg Coll., 1978—, Duke U. Sch. Forestry and Environ. Studies, 1979—, Ind. Sector, 1984—; chmn. Am. Farmland Trust, 1987—; mem. Pres.'s Comm. on Am. Outdoors, 1985-87. Recipient Conservation award Am. Motors Corp., 1974; Horace Marden Albright Scenic Preservation medal, 1974; Conservation award U.S. Dept. Interior, 1980; Disting. Conservationist award Natural Resources Council Am., 1983; Cynthia Pratt Lauglin conservation medal Garden Clubs Am., 1984; MacArthur Found. fellow, 1985-90. Mem. Am. Soc. Appraisers (sr.), Am. Inst. Cert. Planners, Am. Conservation Assn. (trustee 1986—, chmn.), Sigma Alpha Epsilon. Club: Congressional (Washington). Home: 11901 Glen Mill Rd Potomac MD 20854

NOOR, ISMAIL, management consultant; b. Muar, Johor, Malaysia, June 14, 1942; s. Haji Mohamed Noor and Ramlah (Abdul) Rahman; m. Marina Abdullah, Feb. 23, 1977; 1 child, Elina. BA, U. Malaya, Malaysia, 1967; M of Mgmt., Kensington (Calif.) U., 1979, PhD, 1983; grad. mgmt. program, U. Hawaii, 1985. Civil service officer Adminstrn. and Fgn. Service, Malaysia, 1967-74; gen. mgr. State Econ. Devel. Corp., 1970-74; dir. Korn/Ferry-PBC, Kuala Lumpur, Malaysia, 1976-80; exec. chmn. Norconsult K.L. SDN. BHD., Kuala Lumpur, 1976—; cons. Pacific Asian Mgmt. Inst., Hawaii, 1984-85, Penang Port Commn., Kuala Lumpur, 1983, Malaysian Airline System, Kuala Lumpur, 1983-85, Boustead, Kuala Lumpur, 1987. Contbr. articles to profl. jours. Fellow Inst. Mgmt. Cons.; mem. Malaysian Inst. Dirs. (councilor Kuala Lumpur chpt. 1984—), Malaysian Ins. Mgmt. (councilor Kuala Lumpur chpt. 1987), Singapore Inst. Mgmt., British Inst. Mgmt. Club: Toastmasters (adviser Kuala Lumpur club 1987, Internat. Taped Speech Contest Winner 1980). Home and Office: #28 Jalan 2/1 Tman Tar, 68000 Ampang Jaya Selangor, Malaysia

NOOR, MUHAMMED ASLAM, mathematics educator, researcher; b. Faisalabad, Pakistan, Mar. 20, 1945; s. Sher Muhammad and Rahmat (Bibi) Choudry; m. Khalida Inayat Noor, Dec. 13, 1970; children—Nauman, Sasan, Mona, Farhan. B.A., Punjab U., Lahore, Pakistan, 1965, M.A., 1967; M.Sc., Queen's U., Kingston, Can., 1971; Ph.D., Brunel U., London, 1975. Research fellow Islamabad U., Pakistan, 1967-68; sr. research fellow Italian Govt., Italy, 1968-69; asst. prof. Jundi Shapur U., Ahwaz, Iran, 1975-78; assoc. prof. Kerman U., Iran, 1978-80, Islamia U., Bahawalpur, Pakistan, 1980-81, King Saud U., Riyadh, Saudi Arabia, 1981-85, prof., 1985—; chmn. bd. grad. studies Islamia U., Pakistan, 1980-81, chmn. math. dept., 1980-81; staff reviewer Springer-Verlag, Berlin, 1976—; convener numerical analysis group math. dept. King Saud U., Riyadh, 1982—; reviewer for many math. jours. in fields of numerical analysis and related topics. Contbr. articles to profl. jours. Fellow Islamabad U., 1967, Italian Govt., 1968, Pakistan Govt., 1961-65. Fellow Institut of Math. and Its Applications (assoc); mem. Punjab Math. Soc., Soc. for Indsl. and Applied Math., Iranian Math. Soc., N.Y. Acad. Scis. Home: 70-P Gulberg, 2 Lahore Pakistan Office: King Saud Univ Coll Sci, PO Box 2455, Riyadh 11451 Saudi Arabia

NOPAR, ALAN SCOTT, lawyer; b. Chgo., Nov. 14, 1951; s. Myron E. and Evelyn R. (Millman) N. BS, U. Ill., 1976; JD, Stanford U., 1979. Bar: Ariz. 1979, U.S. Dist. Ct. Ariz. 1980, U.S. Ct. Appeals (9th cir.) 1980, U.S. Supreme Ct. 1982; CPA, Ill. Assoc. O'Connor, Cavanagh, Anderson, Westover, Killingsworth & Beshears P.A., Phoenix, 1979-85, ptnr., 1985-87; of counsel Tower, Byrne & Beaugureau, Phoenix, 1987—. Mem. Ariz. Rep. Caucus, Phoenix, 1984—. Mem. ABA (corp. banking and bus. law sect.), Ariz. Bar Assn. (corp. banking and bus. law sect.), Maricopa County Bar Assn. (corp. banking and bus. law sect.), Am. Inst. CPA's. Office: Tower Byrne & Beaugureau PC 2111 E Highland Ave Suite 255 Phoenix AZ 85016

NORA, JAMES JACKSON, physician, author; b. Chgo., June 26, 1928; s. Joseph James and May Henrietta (Jackson) N.; m. Barbara June Fluhrer, Sept. 7, 1949 (div. 1963); children: Wendy Alison, Penelope Welbon, Marianne Leslie; m. Audrey Faye Hart, Apr. 9, 1966; children: James Jackson Jr., Elizabeth Hart Nora. AB, Harvard U., 1950; MD, Yale U., 1954; MPH, U. Calif., Berkeley, 1978. Assoc. prof. pediatrics Baylor Coll. Medicine, Houston, 1965-71; prof. genetics, preventive medicine and pediatrics U. Colo. Sch. Medicine, Denver, 1971—; dir. preventive cariology U. Colo. Sch. Medicine, 1978—; dir. genetics rose Med. Ctr., Denver, 1980—; dir. pediatric cardiology and cardiovascular tng. U. Colo. Sch. Medicine, 1971-78; mem. task force Nat. Heart and Lung Program, Bethesda, Md., 1973; cons. WHO, Geneva, 1983—; mem. U.S.-U.S.S.R. Exchange Program on Heart Disease, Moscow and Leningrad, 1975. Author: The Whole Heart Book, 1980; (with F.C. Fraser) Medical Genetics, 1981, Genetics of Man, 1986. Com. mem. March of Dimes, Am. Heart Assn., Boy Scouts Am. Served to lt. USAAC, 1945-47. Grantee Nat. Heart, Lung and Blood Inst., Nat. Inst. Child Health and Human Devel., Am. Heart Assn., NIH; recipient Virginia Apgar Meml. award. Fellow Am. Coll. Cardiology, Am. Acad. Pediatrics; mem. Am. Pediatric Soc., Soc. Pediatric Research, Am. Heart Assn., Teratology Soc., Transplantation Soc., Am. Soc. Human Genetics, Authors Guild, Authors League, Acad. Am. Poets. Democrat. Presbyterian. Club: Rocky Mountain Harvard (Denver). Home: 6135 E 6th Ave Denver CO 80220 Office: U Colo Sch Medicine A-007 4200 E 9th Ave Denver CO 80262

NORBACK, JUDITH CAROL SHAUL, industrial psychologist, computer specialist, author; b. Rochester, N.Y., July 5, 1953; d. John Daley and Barbara (Bark) Shaul; BA magna cum laude (fellow), Cornell U., 1975; MA, Princeton U., 1977, PhD, 1979; m. Craig T. Norback, Oct. 12, 1976. Instr. psychology Cornell U., 1973-75, Princeton U., 1976-79, Rutgers U., 1981, spring 86, Fairleigh Dickenson U., summer 1986, 87; systems programmer McGraw-Hill Co., 1981-83, Princeton U. Computer Ctr., 1983-86, research assoc. Ednl. Testing Service, 1987—. Author: The Alcohol and Drug Abuse Yearbook/Directory, 1979; The Mental Health Yearbook/Directory, 1979; The Sourcebook of Aid for the Mentally and Physically Handicapped, 1983; The Sourcebook of Family Planning and Family Counseling, 1983; The Complete Guide to Computer Careers, 1987, Hazardous Chemicals on File, 1988. Mem. Am. Psychol. Assn., Mensa. Assn. Princeton Grad. Alumni; contbr. articles to profl. jours.

NORBOM, JON OLA, Norwegian government official; b. Baerum, Norway, Dec. 15, 1923; s. Harold and Ragna (Hauger) N.; m. Ellen Hook, Sept. 11, 1954; children—Ingrid, Susan. Cand. Econ., U. Oslo, 1949. Economist, Ministry of Industry Govt. Norway, 1950-54; economist Nat. Bur. Econ. Research, N.Y.C., 1954-55; statistician UN, N.Y.C., 1955-59; research economist, expert on Comml. Policy, Gatt, Geneva, 1959-67, 69-71; under-sec. state Fin. Ministry, Norway, 1967-69; dir. Internat. Trade Centre, Geneva, 1971-72, 73-83; minister of Fin., Norway, 1972-73; permanent sec. Ministry of Social Affairs, Norway, 1984—; chmn. Spl. Commn. on Financing Social Security and Health Care, Oslo, 1983-84; mem. UN Commn. on Social Policy, 1982-87. Home: Holgerlystvn 23C, 2 Oslo Norway

NORCLIFFE, JAMES SAMUEL, educator, writer; b. Greymouth, New Zealand, Mar. 3, 1946; s. Billy and Agnes (Smith) N.; m. Joan Melvyn King, Sept. 6, 1949; children: Thomas James, Elizabeth Jane, Zoë Claire (dec.). BA, Canterbury U., New Zealand, 1968; MA, Canterbury U., 1969. Tchr. Shirley Boys High Sch., Christchurch, New Zealand, 1969-78; head sr. English Mairehau High Sch., Christchurch, 1978-86; lectr. Nankai U., Tianjin, China, 1986—. Contbr. ency. New Zealand Heritage, 1972, New Zealand Nat. Heritage, 1975; contbr. articles to profl. jours.; author short stories, poetry. Mem. Canterbury English Tchrs. Assn. (chmn. 1985-86), Poets, Playwrights, Essayists, Novelists. Mem. New Zealand Labour Party. Club: Canterbury Film Soc. Home: 67 Albert Terrace, Christchurch 2, New Zealand Office: Mairehau High Sch, Christchurch New Zealand

NORCROSS, LAWRENCE JOHN, educational administrator; b. Peterborough, Northants, Great Britain, Apr. 14, 1927; s. Frederick Marshall and Florence Kate (Hedges) N.; m. Janet Margaret Wallace, Aug. 17, 1958; children—Matthew, Alastair, Joanna, Daniel. B.A. with honours, U. Leeds, 1957. Asst. tchr. Singlegate Sch., Surrey, Eng., 1957-61, Abbey Wood Sch., London, 1961-63; housemaster Battersea County Sch., London, 1963-74; dep. headmaster Highbury Grove Sch., London, 1974-75, headmaster, 1975-87; mem. Univ. Entrance and Schs. Exam. Council, London U., 1979-84; mem. adv. council Edn. Unit IEA. Author: The Ilea: A Case For Reform, 1983; contbr. articles to profl. jours.; broadcaster radio and TV. Trustee, mem. exec. com. Nat. Council for Ednl. Standards, London, 1975—, trustee Grant Maintained Schs. Trust, 1988— ; mem. ednl. study group Centre for Policy Studies, London, 1980—; trustee Ednl. Research Trust, 1985—. Served as leading signalman Royal Navy, 1942-49; East Indies. Decorated Order Brit. Empire Mem. Secondary Heads' Assn., HMC, Nat. Assn. Schoolmasters/Union of Women Tchrs. (exec. com. London chpt. 1975—, mem. headmasters' conf. 1985-87). Conservative. Mem. Ch. of Eng. Clubs: Surrey County, Cricket (London). Home: 3 St Nicholas Mansions, Trinity Cresent, London SW17 7AF, England Other: Crockwell Cottage, Crockwell St, Shipston-on-Stour, Warwickshire England

NORDAHL-HANSEN, ROLV, shipping company executive; b. Kristiansand, Vestagder, Norway, Jan. 19, 1923; s. Jacob and Margit N.H.; m. Aud Wilhelmine; children: Unni Grethe, Jacob. Diploma, Shipping Sch., London. Mgr. shipping dept. Eiving Kile A.S., Kristiansand, 1941-45; mgr. shipbroker dept. Savabini Shipping A.S., Oslo, Norway, 1952-70, pres., 1970-75; shipbroker ShipOwnerStorm, Copenhagen, Norway, 1975-76; mng. dir. Sea Service A.S., Oslo, 1976-84, A.S. Sibaco, Ltd., Oslo, 1975—. Home: Jonas Reinsgate, 0360 Oslo 3, Norway Office: AS Sibaco Ltd, PO Box 5372 MJ St, 0304 Oslo 3, Norway

NORDAL, JOHANNES, banker; b. Reykjavik, Iceland, May 11, 1924; s. Sigurour and Olof (Jonsdottir) N.; m. Dora Guojonsdottir, Dec. 19, 1953; children—Bera, Sigurour, Guorun, Salvor, Olof, Marta. B.Sc. in Econs., London Sch. Econs., 1950; Ph.D., U. London, 1953. Econ. adviser Nat. Bank of Iceland, Reykjavik, 1954-59, gen. mgr., 1959-61; gov. Central Bank of Iceland, Reykjavik, 1961—; gov. for Iceland Internat. Monetary Fund, Washington, 1965—; chmn. Nat. Power Co., 1965—. Editor jours.: Fjarmalatioindi fin., 1954—, Helgafell literary, 1955-59. Fellow Icelandic Sci. Soc.; mem. Sci. Fund Iceland (chmn. humanities div. 1965—). Home: Laugarasvegur 11, 104 Reykjavik Iceland Office: Central Bank of Iceland, Kalkofnsvegur 1, 150 Reykjavik Iceland

NORDBY, EUGENE JORGEN, orthopedic surgeon; b. Abbotsford, Wis., Apr. 30, 1918; s. Herman Preus and Lucille Violet (Korsrud) N.; m. Olive Marie Jensen, June 21, 1941; 1 child, Jon Jorgen. B.A., Luther Coll., Decorah, Iowa, 1939; M.D., U. Wis., 1943. Intern Madison Gen. Hosp., Wis., 1943-44, asst. in orthopedic surgery, 1944-48; practice medicine specializing in orthopedic surgery Madison, Wis., 1948—; pres. Bone and Joint Surgery Assocs., S.C., 1969—; chief staff Madison Gen. Hosp., 1957-63, bd. dirs., 1957-76; assoc. clin. prof. U. Wis. Med. Sch., 1961—; chmn. Wis. Physicians Service, 1979—; dir. Wis. Regional Med. Program; bd. govs. Wis. Health Care Liability Ins. Plan.; dir. Chgo. Madison and No. RR; chmn. trustees S.M.S. Realty Corp. Assoc. editor Clin. Orthopaedics and Related Research, 1964—. Pres. Norwegian Am. Mus., Decorah, Iowa, 1968—. Served to capt. M.C., AUS, 1944-46. Recipient Disting. Service award Luther Coll., 1964, Sr. Service award Internat. Rotary, 1987. Decorated knight 1st class Royal Norwegian Order St. Olav. Mem. Am. Acad. Orthopaedic Surgeons (dir. 1972-73), Clin. Orthopaedic Soc., Assn. Bone and Joint Surgeons (pres. 1973), Internat. Soc. Study Lumbar Spine, State Med. Soc. Wis. (chmn. 1968-76, treas. 1976—; Council award 1976), N.Am. Spine Soc., Internat. Intradiscal Therapy Soc. (sec. 1987—), Wis. Orthopaedic Soc., Dane County Med. Soc. (pres. 1957), Phi Chi. Lutheran. Club: Nat. Exchange. Home: 6234 Highlands Madison WI 53705 Office: 2704 Marshall Ct Madison WI 53705

NORDBY, REIDAR FRODE, food manaufacturing executive; b. Hamar, Norway, Apr. 5, 1948; s. Reidar Fritjof Norby and Ebba (Neuman) Melkild; m. Anne Marit Lehne, Aug. 5, 1972; children: Margrethe, Magnus. BS in Mech. Engring., Heriot-Watt U., 1975. Prodn. planner Sarpsborg Paa A.S., Norway, 1975-76; tech. dir. Ideal A/S, Hamar, 1976-81, v.p., 1981-86, pres., 1986-87; pres. Norsk Tipping A/S, Hamar, 1988—; bd. dirs. Den Norske Creditbank, Hamar; chmn. bd. dirs. Ideal Eiendom A/S, Hamar, 1987—, ATEK A/S, Hamar; vice chmn., mem. adv. bd. C. Tybring Gjedde, Oslo, 1987—. Chmn. econ. bd. Conservative Party, Hamar, 1986—; del. Conservative Party Conf., Tromso, Norway, 1987; mem. Hoyres Innlandsutvalg, 1987. Mem. Conf. Norwegian Industry (bd. dirs. 1985—), County Conf. Industry (chmn. 1985—), Roundtable. Lodge: Masons, Rotary. Home: Kvartsveien 2, 2322 Ridabu Norway Office: Norsk Tipping A/S, Jönsrudveien 21, 2300 Hamar Norway

NORDDAHL, BIRGIR VALSON, physicist, researcher; b. Reykjavik, Iceland, Feb. 11, 1947; s. Valur Gudmundsson and Karin Marie (Jensen) N.; m. Helle Bodil Damslund; children: Mette Maj, Jon Asger, Martin Halldor. BSc in Chemistry, U. Aathus, Denmark, 1971, MSc in Physics, 1974. Research fellow CERN, Geneva, 1972-74, Niels Bohr Inst., Copenhagen, 1974; faculty Midtfyn Mcpl. Coll., Ringe, Denmark, 1974-83, Svendborg (Denmark) Nursing Coll., 1975-77; researcher in chemistry and physics Roulunds Fabriker, Odense, Denmark, 1983-84, mgr. power transmission research and devel., testing and documentation, 1985-88; mgr. Dansk Miljo Tecnic Ltd., 1988—; project engr. Samfundsteknik, Odense, 1984; dir. Rudme Coop. Bank. Contbr. articles to profl. jours. Mem. Danish Physics Tchrs. Assn. (chmn. 1980-82), Danish Assn. Rubber Tech., Am. Assn. Physics Tchrs., Danish Assn. Academics. Home: Rudmevej 38, 5750 Ringe Denmark Office: Danish Bioprotein/Miljoteknik, Stenhuggervej 7-9, Odense Denmark

NORDEN, K. ELIS, management consultant; b. Stockholm, Feb. 27, 1921; s. Daniel Henrik and Ella Amanda (Larsson) N.; m. Astrid Margaretha Lethin, June 24, 1946; children: Jan-Hendrik, Gunilla, Carl-Magnus. BEE, Royal Inst. Tech., Stockholm, 1954. Devel. engr. Swedish Radio AB, 1940-44; chief radar devel dept. Royal Swedish Air Bd., 1944-54; founder, pres. Elenik Automation AB, Stockholm, 1955-64, Norden Automation Systems AG, Zurich, Switzerland, 1964-79, NAS Austria, Vienna, 1966-79, NAS Holland, Woudenberg, 1968-79; mgmt. cons. to airlines, iron, steel and chem. industry, specialist in motion wieghing, computer controlled material handling; course dir. modern electronic weighing Ctr. Profl. Advancement, East Brunswick, N.J.; tchr. Royal Swedish Air Force High Sch., 1955-64. Author: The Inventors Book, 1963, Pulp and Paper, 1968, Aufbereitungstechn, 1972, Electronic Weighing in Industrial Processes, 1984; patentee in field. Mem. Swedish Inst. Tech., Swedish Assn. Elec. Engrs., Assn. Instrument Tech., Verein Deutscher Eisen. Club: Sallskaper (Sweden); Nueva Andalucia Golf and Country (v.p.) (Spain). Home: Spitzackerstrasse 2, 7310 Bad Ragaz Switzerland also: P34 Calle 11D, Brisas del Golf Nueva, Andalucia, Marbella Spain Office: Alpenstrasse 2, PO Box 4535, CH-6304 Zug Switzerland

NORDENSTAM, RUNE BERTIL, botanist; b. Nykoping, Sweden, Feb. 20, 1936; s. Bengt Torgny and Greta Hulda Sofia (Lundh) N.; m. Gunilla Madeleine Lindberg, Apr. 5, 1966; 1 dau., Felicia. PhD candidate, U. Lund, 1958, Fil. Mag., 1958, Fil. Lic., 1966, PhD, 1968, Docent, 1969. Asst., U. Lund, Sweden, 1956-58, 61, 67, lectr., 1964-66, research asst., 1968-69; curator Swedish Mus. Natural History, Stockholm, 1969-74, 1st curator, 1974-80, prof., 1980—, dir. research div., 1982-84. Editor: Botaniska Notiser, 1965-66, sci. serial Opera Botanica, 1965-66. Contbr. articles to bot. jours. Bd. dirs. Swedish Natural Sci. Research Council, 1983-86, dir. biology com., 1980-86; mem. Univ. Library Bd., Stockholm 1981-87; mem. bd. Hedin Found., Stockholm, Swedish Linn Soc. Recipient Linnaeus prize in Botany, Royal Physiographic Soc., 1980; Smuts Meml. fellow Nat. Botanic Gardens, Kirstenbosch, South Africa, 1962-63. Mem. SW African Sci. Soc. (corr.), Bayerische Botanische Gesellschaft (corr.), World Wildlife Fund (v.p. Swedish chpt.), Royal Swedish Acad. Scis. (council), Swedish Nat. Com. Biology, Abisko Sci. Sta. (mem. bd.). Clubs: Travellers (vice chmn.), Idun Soc. Home: Krutvagen 4 Sollentuna, S-19155 Stockholm Sweden Office: Swedish Mus Natural History, Section of Botany PO Box 50007, S-10405 Stockholm Sweden

NORDHAGEN, HALLIE HUERTH, nursing home administrator; b. Sarona, Wis., Apr. 2, 1914; d. Mathias James and Ethel Elizabeth (Fann) Huerth; B.Ed., U. Wis., Superior, 1938, M.A., 1949; m. Carl E. Nordhagen, May 24, 1947; children—Bruce Carl, Brian Keith. Prin., tchr. Wis. Public Schs., 1932-46; supervising tchr. Wis. Community Coll., 1946-48; psychiat. adminstr. Trempealeau County Health Care Center, psychiat. nursing home, Whitehall, Wis., 1959—; mem. Wis. Nursing Home Adminstrs. Examining Bd.; fellow Menninger Clinic, Topeka, 1979-81. Recipient Disting. Service award in edn. and hosp. adminstrn., London, 1967, award for services to human services programs Wis. Assn. Human Services, 1972, award for outstanding services to exceptional children Assn. Retarded Children, 1978, award for accomplishments in human resources Trempealeau County Conservation Service, 1981; Wis. State Senate citation, 1983; citatioin Wis. Gov., 1984. Mem. Wis. Assn. County Homes, Wis. Edn. Assn., Wis. Assn. Human Services Programs, Internat. Platform Assn., Am. Lutheran Ch. Women. Clubs: Whitehall Country, Women's. Author: Wisconsin Indians, 1966. Home: 2220 Claire St Whitehall WI 54773

NORDLING, BERNARD ERICK, lawyer; b. Nekoma, Kans., June 14, 1921; A.B., McPherson Coll., 1947; student George Washington U., 1941-43; LL.B., J.D., Kans. U., 1949; m. Barbara Ann Burkholder, Mar. 26, 1949 . Clerical employee FBI, 1941-44; admitted to Kans. bar, 1949, U.S. Dist. Ct. Kans. 1949, U.S. Ct. Appeals (10th cir.) 1970; practiced in Hugoton, Kans., 1949—; mem. firms Kramer & Nordling, 1950-65, Kramer, Nordling, Nordling & Tate, 1966—; city atty., Hugoton, 1951-87; county atty. Stevens County (Kans.), 1957-63. exec. sec. S.W. Kans. Royalty Owners Assn., 1968-; Kans. mem. legal com. Interstate Oil Compact Commn., 1969—, mem. supply tech. adv. com. Nat. Gas Survey, FPC, 1975-77; mem. Kans. Energy Adv. Council, 1975-78, exec. com., 1976-78. Editor U. Kans. Law Rev. of Kans. Bar Jour., 1949. Mem. Hugoton Sch. Bds., 1954-68, pres. grade sch. bd., 1961-66; pres. Stevens County Library Bd., 1957-63. Trustee McPherson Coll., 1971-81, mem. exec. com., 1975-81; bd. govs. Kans. U. Law Soc., 1984-87. Served with AUS, 1944-46. Mem. ABA, Kans. Bar Assn., SW Kans. Bar Assn., Am. Judicature Soc., City Attys. Assn. of Kans. (exec. com. 1975-83, pres. 1982-83), Nat. Honor Soc., Nat. Assn. Royalty Owners (bd. govs. 1980—), Order of Coif, Phi Alpha Delta. Home: 218 N Jackson St Hugoton KS 67951 Office: 209 E 6th St Hugoton KS 67951

NORDLINGER, GERSON, JR., investor; b. Washington, Feb. 2, 1916; s. Gerson and Camille (Bensinger) N.; B.A., George Washington U., 1935; B.C.S., Benjamin Franklin U., 1939. Head, Navy Dept. Bur. Aeros. Budget, 1946-50; treas. Nordlinger Investment Corp., Washington, 1955—; dir. Washington Real Estate Investment Trust, 1961—. Chmn., D.C. Arts Commn., 1965-67; v.p. Nat. Symphony Orch. Assn., 1953-59, Nat. Ballet, 1966-70; pres. Prevention of Blindness Soc., 1960-67; treas. Friendship House, 1951-69; vice chmn. D.C. Recreation Bd., 1960-67; trustee Washington Performing Arts Soc., Mt. Vernon Coll., Washington Opera, Bacon House, Phillips Collection. Mem. state com. Republican party, 1952-64. Served to lt. comdr. Supply Corps., USNR, 1941-46; PTO. C.P.A., D.C. Mem. D.C. Inst. C.P.A.s. Clubs: Cosmos, Arts, Met., 1925 F St. Home: 3115 Cleveland Ave NW Washington DC 20008

NORDQUIST, STEPHEN GLOS, lawyer; b. Mpls., May 13, 1936; s. Oscar Alvin Nordquist and Georgiana (Glos) Ruplin; m. Cynthia Alexandra Turner, Aug. 16, 1958 (div. Aug. 1967); children: Darcy Alden, Timothy Turner; m. Regina Frances Stanton, Nov. 1, 1969; 1 child, Nicholas Alden. BA cum laude, U. Minn., 1958, LL.B cum laude, 1961. Bar: Minn. 1961, N.Y. 1962. Assoc. Dewey, Ballantine, Bushby, Palmer & Wood, N.Y.C., 1961-69, ptnr., 1969-85; sr. v.p. W.P. Carey & Co., Inc., N.Y.C., 1985-86, exec v.p., sec., 1986-87; jr. ptnr. Cole & Deitz, N.Y.C., 1988—; pres., bd. dirs. Carey Corp. Property, Inc., Carey-Longmont Inc., Carey-Longmont Real Property, Inc., N.Y.C., 1985-87, 520 East 86th Street, Inc. 1st v.p., dir. Seaview Assn. Fire Island (N.Y.), Inc. Republican. Congregationalist. Clubs: Knickerbocker (house com.), Club at World Trade Ctr. Home: 520 E 86th St Apt 3B New York NY 10028 Office: Cole & Deitz 175 Water St New York NY 10038-4981

NOREIKO, STEPHEN FRANCIS, language educator; b. London, Dec. 30, 1943; s. Joseph Francis and Muriel Edna (Dines) N.; m. Carole Rasch, July 11, 1973; 1 child, Joachim. BA, U. Southampton, Eng., 1965, M in Philosophy, 1977. Tchr. Ecole St.-Yves, Quimper, France, 1967-68; lectr. U. Rouen, France, 1968-69, U. Ulster, Derry, Coleraine, Ireland, 1969-74, U. Hull, Eng., 1974—. Author: À la Tienne, 1985, Making Sense of the French Language, 1988; mem. editorial com. Etudes sur le français contemporain, London, 1986—; contbr. articles to profl. jours.; author numerous computer programs. Coordinator Friends of Earth, Hull, 1978-81; corr. Cyclists' Rights Network, Hull, 1985—. Hull U. grantee, 1986. Mem. Assn. French Lang. Studies, Assn. Internat. d'Etudes Occitanes, Soc. for French Studies, Soc. pour l'Info. Grammaticale, Soc. de Linguistique Romane. Office: The University, Cottingham Rd, Hull HU6 7RX, England

NOREN, CARL ERIK, electronics company executive; b. Stockholm, Sweden, Nov. 7, 1957; s. Karl Erik and Maj Elisabeth (Henningsson) N.; m. Kari Fröseth, Apr. 8, 1981; children: Tom, Carl Wilhelm, Petra. Bus. Adminstrn., U. Stockholm, 1985. Exec. mem. Nortroll Svenska A.B., Nykoping, Sweden, 1985—; mng. dir. AB Noren & Co., Nykoping, Sweden, 1986—; bd. dirs. Nortroll A.S., Norway. Served as sgt. Swedish Army, 1978-79. Office: Nortroll Sv AB, PO Box 283, 61126 Nykoping Sweden

NORGREN, CHRISTIAN, banker; b. Stockholm, Jan. 26, 1941; arrived in Liechtenstein, 1981; s. Stig Oskar Christian and Elsa (Bergh) N.; m. Marie Bertheau, Apr. 17, 1965; children: Carl Christian, Marie Charlotte. BA, U. Stockholm, 1962; MBA, U. Lund, Sweden, 1964; diploma, IMEDE, Lausanne, Switzerland, 1969; diploma in mgmt., Stanford U., 1978. Treasury asst. L.M. Ericsson, Stockholm, 1964-65; asst. v.p. Skandinaviska Enskilda Banken, Stockholm, 1965-68, v.p., 1968-70, mng. dir., 1970-71; regional mgr. Scandinavian Bank Ltd., London, 1971-74; mgr. SE-Banken Rep. Office, Frankfurt, Fed. Republic Germany, 1974-76; mng. dir. Deutsch-Skandinavische Bank, Frankfurt, 1976-81; pres., chief exec. officer Prince of Liechtenstein Found., Vaduz, 1981—; chmn. Bank Liechtenstein AG, Vaduz, 1981—; bd. dirs. ASEA Brown Boveri, Crossair AG, Zurich, Switzerland, AB Export-Invest, Stockholm, Anglo-Elementar Ins., Vienna, Prospect Group Inc., N.Y.C., Voest-Alpine AG, Linz, Austria. Co-author: Swedish Industry-Structure and Change, 1970, Eurodollars-Eurobonds, 1972, Foreign Financing, 1974. Bd. dirs. World Scout Found., Geneva, 1986—, IMEDE, 1988—. Recipient Liechtenstein Service Cross and Star, Prince of Liechtenstein, 1985. Office: Prince Liechtenstein Found, PO Box 366, FL-9490 Vaduz Liechtenstein

NORGREN, JAN HELGE, advertising agency executive; b. Landskrona, Scania, Sweden, Jan. 25, 1935; s. Till Denna Fåfängans ; m. Marknad Soker; children: Bara, Inte, En, Asna, Utan, Hal, Flock. Sales promotion mgr. Philips Radio TV, Stockholm, 1956-59; product mgr. Husqvarna Ab, Huskvarna, Sweden, 1959-63; account exec. Gumaelius Advt. Agy., Jönköping, Sweden, 1963-67, Malmö, Sweden, 1967-78; mng. dir. Norgren Advt. Agy., Malmö, Sweden, 1978—. Office: Norgren Reklambyrå, Box 4132, S-203 12 Malmö Sweden

NORIEGA MORENO, MANUEL ANTONIO, military commander; b. Panama City, Republic of Panama, Feb. 11, 1940; s. Ricaurter Tomas Noriega and Maria Feliz Moreno; m. Felicidad Sieiro; children: Lorena, Sandra, Thays. Cert. lab. technician, Hosp. Nacional, Republic of Panama; cert. honoris causa, Escuela Militar de Chorrillos, Republic of Panama, 1984. Cert. mil. engr., Republic of Panama. Cartographer engr. Internat. Geodesic Service, Panama City, 1961-63; sub.-lt. Guardia Nacional, Panama City, 1963-69, chief combat units, 1969-70; chief mil. zone Guardia Nacional, Chiriqui, Republic of Panama, 1970; mem. joint chiefs of staff Guardia Nacional, Panama City, 1970-81, chief joint chiefs of staff, 1982-83; chief commander, gen. Panamanian Armed Forces, Panama City, 1983—; pres. Interpol Internat. Conf., 1974. Author: Inmortal Ayacucho, 1952. Planner Civic Action, Panama City, 1983; active League of Red Cross and Red Crescent Soc., Panama City, 1986, Folkloric Ensemble, Panama City, 1987. Decorated Shining Flag (Republic of China); Great Cross-José María Córdoba (Colombia); Gold medal (El Salvador); Great Cross, Peruvian Cross, Great Cross-Francisco Bolognesi (Peru); Great Cross-Mil. Merit (Argentina); Armed Forces Cross (Honduras); Legion of Honor knight comdr. (France); Victorious October (Nicaragua); Eagle Order (Republic of Panama); recipient honor placque DEA, 1979, honor medal Amateur Judo Fedn., 1982, distinction Govt. of Israel, 1982, cert.-honoris causa Peru Civil Guard, 1983, merit degree Argentinian Navy, 1983, honor guest degree, Guatemaia City, 1985, merit degree Govt. of Guatemala, 1985, Ton El medal Republic of Korea, 1985; 1st Class medal Govt. of Mex., 1987, honor degree Peruvian Polic Acad., 1987; named an honor ambassador Sports and Sea Scis. Acad.-Govt. of Italy, 1987. Mem. Mil. Engr. Soc. (hon. degree 1980), Peruvian Mil. Engr. Found., Bolivarian Soc., Judo Soc. Panama, Am. Moo Duk Kwan Tang Soo Do Assn. (1st dan). Roman Catholic. Office: Panamanian Armed Forces, Avenida B, Panama 3434 Zona 1, Republic of Panama

NORKIN, CYNTHIA CLAIR, physical therapist; b. Boston, May 6, 1932; d. Miles Nelson and Carolyn (Green) Clair; BS in Edn., Tufts U., 1954; cert. phys. therapy Bouve Boston Coll., 1954; MS, Boston U., 1973, EdD, 1984; m. Stanislav A. Norkin, Feb. 19, 1955 (dec. 1970); 1 child, Alexandra. Instr., Bouve-Boston Coll., 1954-55; staff phys. therapist New Eng. Med. Center, Boston, 1954-55; staff phys. therapist Abington Meml. Hosp., Abington, Pa., 1965-70, Eastern Montgomery County Vis. Nurse Assn., 1970-72; asst. prof. phys. therapy Sargent Coll., Boston U., 1973-84; assoc. prof. phys. therapy, dir. Sch. Phys. Therapy, Ohio U., Athens, 1984—; cons. Boston Center Ind. Living, Cambridge Vis. Nurse Assn., Mass. Medicaid Cost Effectiveness Project, 1978; sec. Health Planning Council Greater Boston, 1976-78. Trustee Brimmer and May Sch., 1980. Mem. Am. Phys. Therapy Assn., Mass. Phys. Therapy Assn. (chmn. Mass. quality assurance com. 1980-85), Am. Public Health Assn., AAAS, Mass. Assn. Mental Health, Athens County Vi. Nurse Assn. (sec. adv. council 1984—). Episcopalian. Author: (with others) Joint Structure and Function: A Comprehensive Analysis, 1983; (with D.J. White) Joint Measurement: A Guide to Goniometry, 1985.

NORLAND, ANDREAS, editor, author; b. Baerum, Norway, May 9, 1935; s. Realph Immanuel Ottesen and Aasta Sigrun (Saether) N.; m. Sonja Hammer, Sept. 10, 1959; children—Cecilie, Fredrik, Henrik, Thomas. Grad., Acad. Journalism, Oslo. Journalist, Toensbergs Blad, Toensberg, Norway, 1958-63, Aftenposten, Oslo, 1963-73; editor Verdens Gang, Oslo, 1973-74, editor-in-chief, 1977-87, Osloavisen A/S, 1987—, Adresseavisen, Trondheim, Norway, 1974-77; dir. Schibsted Pub. Group, Oslo, 1977—; chmn. bd. Schibsted Book Pub. Co., Oslo, 1982—. Author: Haarde Tider, 1973; Mord i Stortinget, 1981; Finansministeren er Myrdet, 1982. Bd. dirs. Norsk Journalistlag, Oslo, 1968-72, Adresseavisen, Trondheim, 1974-77; vice-chmn. Pressens Faglige Utvalg, Oslo, 1970-74, Norsk Redaktorforening, Oslo, 1980-82. Home: Pilestredet 99, Oslo 3 Norway Office: Osloavisen A/S, Grensen 18, 0159 Oslo 1 Norway

NORMAN, ALBERT GEORGE, JR., lawyer; b. Birmingham, Ala., May 29, 1929; s. Albert G. and Ila Mae (Carroll) N.; m. Catherine Marshall DeShazo, Sept. 3, 1955; children: Catherine Marshall, Albert George III. B.A., Auburn U., 1953; LL.B., Emory U., 1958; M.A., U. N.C., 1960. Bar: Ga. 1957. Assoc. firm Moise, Post & Gardner, Atlanta, 1958-60; partner Moise, Post & Gardner, 1960-62; ptnr. firm Hansell & Post, Atlanta, 1962-86, Long, Aldridge & Norman, Atlanta, 1986—; dir. Atlanta Gas Light Co. Served with USAF, 1946-49. Mem. Am., Ga., Atlanta bar assns., Lawyers Club Atlanta (pres. 1973-74), Am. Law Inst., Am. Judicature Soc. (dir. 1975-78). Club: Cherokee Town and Country. Home: 3381 Valley Circle NW Atlanta GA 30305 Office: Rhodes-Haverty Bldg Atlanta GA 30043-1863

NORMAN, HERBERT JOHN LA FRENCH, marketing executive; b. London, Jan. 15, 1932; s. Herbert La French and Hilda Caroline (West) N.; m. Jill Frances Sharp, Aug. 11, 1956; children: Elizabeth Mary, Sarah Jane, Bernard John. BS, London U., 1953; A, Royal Coll. of Sci., London, 1953. Organ builder Wm. Hill & Son and Norman & Beard Ltd., London, 1953-70, mng. dir., 1970-74; computer mktg. exec. IBM, UK, Ltd., London, 1974—; organ cons. Lancing Coll., Sussex, Eng., 1983-87, Mill Hill Sch., London, 1984-87, Sherborne Abbey, Dorset, Eng., 1984-88, English & Am. Ch., The Hague, Holland, 1985-88, Pershore Abbey, Worcestershire, Eng., 1988—; mem. organ adv. com. Council for the Care of Chs. Author: The Organ Today, 1966, The Organs of Britain, 1984; editor: Jour. The Organbuilder, 1983—, Musical Instrument Technology, 1965—; contbr. articles to profl. jour. Organist's Review, 1980—. Mem. St. Albans Diocesan Synod, 1980-86; ch. warden Holy Trinity Ch., Lyonsdown, New Barnet, 1986-87. Fellow Inst. Musical Instrument Tech., Inc. Soc. Organ Builders. Mem. Church of England. Club: 41 (Hornsey). Home: 15 Baxendale, London N20 OEG, England

NORMAN, JESSYE, soprano; b. Augusta, Ga., Sept. 15, 1945; d. Silas Sr. and Janie (King) N. B.M. cum laude, Howard U., 1967; postgrad., Peabody Conservatory, 1967; M.Mus., U. Mich., 1968; MusD (hon.), U. South, 1984, Boston Conservatory, 1984, U. Mich., 1987. Debut, Deutsche Oper, Berlin, 1969, Italy, 1970; appeared: in operas Die Walküre, Idomeneo, L'Africaine, Marriage of Figaro, Aida, Don Giovanni, Tannhauser, Gotterdammerung, Ariadne auf Naxos, Les Troyens, Dido and Aeneas, Oedipus Rex, Hérodiade, Les Contes d'Hoffmann; debut in operas, La Scala, Milan, Italy, 1972, Salzburg Festival, 1977, U.S. debut, Hollywood Bowl, 1972, appeared with, Tanglewood Festival, Mass., also Edinburgh (Scotland) Festival, debut, Covent Garden, 1972; appeared in 1st Great Performers recital, Lincoln Center, N.Y.C., 1973—; other guest performances include, Los Angeles Philharm. Orch., Boston Symphony Orch., Am. Symphony Orch., Chgo. Symphony Orch., San Francisco Symphony Orch., Cleve. Orch., Detroit Symphony, N.Y. Philharm. Orch., London Symphony Orch., London Philharm. Orch., BBC Orch., Israel Philharm. Orch., Orchestre de Paris, Nat. Symphony Orch., English Chamber Orch., Royal Philharm., London Phila. Orch., Milw. Symphony Orch., Stockholm Philharm. Orch., Vienna Philharm. Orch., Berlin Philharm. Orch.; tours, Europe, S. Am., Australia, numerous recs., Columbia, EMI, Philips Records. Recipient 1st prize Bavarian Radio Corp. Internat. Music Competition, 1968, Grand Prix du Disque Deutsche Schallplatten, Preis, Alumni award U. Mich., 1982, Outstanding Musician of Yr. award Musical Am., 1982, Grand Prix du Disque Academie Charles Cros, 1983, Commandeur de l'Ordre des Arts et des Lettres, France, 1984, Grammy awards, 1980, 82, 85, numerous other awards; named hon. life mem. Girl Scouts U.S., 1987. Mem. Royal Acad. Music (hon.), Alpha Kappa Alpha, Gamma Sigma Sigma, Sigma Alpha Iota, Pi Kappa Lambda. Club: Friday Morning Music (Washington). Office: care Shaw Concerts Inc 1900 Broadway New York NY 10023

NORMAN, JOHN EDWARD, independent petroleum landman; b. Denver, May 22, 1922; s. John Edward and Ella (Warren) N.; m. Hope Sabin, Sept. 5, 1946; children—J. Thomas, Gerould W., Nancy E., Susan G., Douglas E. BSBA, U. Denver, 1949, MBA, 1972. Clk., bookkeeper Capitol Life Ins. Co., Denver, 1945-46; salesman Security Life and Accident Co., Denver, 1947; bookkeeper Central Bank and Trust Co., Denver, 1947-50; automobile salesman H.A. Hennies, Denver, 1950; petroleum landman Continental Oil Co. (name changed to Conoco Inc. 1979), Denver, 1950-85; ind. petroleum landman, 1985—. Lectr. pub. lands Colo. Sch. Mines, 1968-85; lectr. mineral titles and landmen's role in oil industry Casper Coll., 1969-71. Mem. Casper Mcpl. Band Commn., 1965-71, mem. band, 1961-71, mgr., 1968-71; former musician, bd. dirs. Casper Civic Symphony; former bd. dirs. Jefferson Symphony, performing mem., 1972-75. Served with AUS, World War II. Mem. Am. Assn. Petroleum Landmen (dir. at large, chmn. publs. for regional dir.), Wyo. Assn. Petroleum Landmen (pres.), Denver Assn. Petroleum Landmen, Rocky Mountain Oil and Gas Assn. (pub. lands com. 1981—), Rocky Mountain Petroleum Pioneers. Episcopalian (mem. choir, vestryman, past dir. acolytes). Club: Elks. Home and Office: 2710 S Jay St Denver CO 80227

NORMAN, JOHN WILLIAM, oil co. exec.; b. Harrisburg, Ill., Sept. 4, 1910; s. Walter Jacob and Clarissa May (Bush) N.; student pub. schs., Saline County, Ill.; m. Marcella Mary Souheaver, July 2, 1937. Dist. mgr. Martin Oil Co., 1936-54; with Am-Bulk Oil Co. (name changed to Norman Oil Co., 1960), Lisle, Ill., 1949—, pres., 1960—. Served with USNR, 1943-44. Mem. VFW, Am. Legion. Home: 5 S 511 Columbian St Naperville IL 60540 Office: 1018 Ogden Ave Lisle IL 60532

NORMAN, RALPH LOUIS, physicist; b. Kingston, Tenn., Mar. 25, 1933; s. Walter Hugh and Helen Irene (Smith) N.; m. Agnes Irene Pickel, Sept. 5,

1964; children: Mark Alan, Max Alvin. B.S., U. Tenn., 1959; LL.B., Blackstone Sch. Law, 1967, J.D., 1971; certificate, Indsl. Coll. Armed Forces, 1969; M.A. in Pub. Adminstrn, U. Okla., 1971; D.Sci. (hon.), Apollo Research Inst., 1976. Engr. Chrysler Corp. Missile Div., Huntsville, Ala., 1959-60; physicist Army Rocket & Guided Missile Agy., Redstone Arsenal, Ala., 1960-61; asst. project mgr. Army Missile Command, Redstone Arsenal, 1961-62; project mgr. Army Missile Command, 1962—; faculty Athens (Ala.) Coll., 1970-71, Calhoun Jr. Coll., Decatur, Ala., 1971-74, 85—, U. Montevallo, Ala., 1973-74, U. Ala. at Huntsville, 1976-77, Columbia (Mo.) Coll., 1977-79; cons. firm Bishop and Sexton, 1973—, Athens (Ala.) State Coll.; reviewer NSF, 1974-76; FAA examiner. Contbr. articles profl. jours. Served with USN, 1951-55. Recipient Dept. Def. commendations, 1961, 65, Dept. Army commendation, 1972. Mem. N.Y. Acad. Scis., Assn. U.S. Army. Home: Route 1 Box 726 Harvest AL 35749 Office: Hdqrs US Army Missile Command Redstone Arsenal AL 35809

NORMAN, TRUDY, data processing executive; b. Carlinville, Ill., Mar. 12, 1936; d. Ralph Earl and Gladys Mae (Shade) Challans; student James Millikin U., 1968-70; children—Carol Lischalk, James Norman, Cheryl Spencer. Mgr. client services Central Computing Corp., Decatur, Ill., 1968-71; sr. systems analyst STAT:TAB Corp., Chgo., 1971-74; project mgr. Chgo. Bd. Edn., 1974-78; mgr. data services Central Telephone, Chgo., 1978-80; dir. system services, Advanced System Allications, Inc., 1978-80, dir. system services, dir. human resources, Bloomingdale, Ill., 1980—; cons. and speaker in field. Active Lakeview Citizens Council, 1979—, Riverview Neighbors, 1981—, Addams Center, 1975-82; mem. Met. Chgo. Air Force Community Council, Coll. Placement Council. Mem. Am. Mgmt. Assn., Data Processing Mgmt. Assn., Am. Soc. for Personnel Adminstrn., Am. Soc. for Tng. and Devel., Midwest Coll. Placement Assn., Met. Chgo. Community Council for Civic Leaders, BMW Owners Assn. Am. Club: Executives (Chgo.). Contbr. articles to profl. jours. Home: 3320 N Hamilton Ave Chicago IL 60618

NORMAN, WILLIAM GENE, food processing company executive; b. Fallbrook, Calif., Sept. 22, 1932; s. Hassel Sylvester Norman and Maude (Reed) Gilchrist; m. Nancy Claire Norman, Sept. 1, 1956 (div. Nov. 1980); children: Christoher Heald, Catherine Jean; m. Flavia del Favero, Apr. 14, 1981. BS, San Diego State U., 1956; MS, Am. Grad. Sch. Internat. Mgmt., 1957. Meat buyer, mgr. ops. I.B.E.C. Supermarkets, Caracas, Venezuela, 1957-63; sales mgr., v.p. mktg. W.M. Underwood Co., Caracas, 1964-67, pres., gen. mgr., 1968-72, 79-80; dir. Latin Am. div. W.M. Underwood Co., Westwood, Mass., 1981-86; prin. Good Guys Home Ctr., Fallbrook, 1973-76; pres. subs. Dr. Scholl, Mexico City, 1977-78; pres., gen. mgr., exec. v.p. Latin Am. subs. Pet Inc., Caracas, 1982—; bd. dirs. Aguarrem, Caracas, Diablitos Venezolanos C.A., Caracas. Served as sgt. U.S.M.C., 1950-52. Paul Harris fellow Fallbrook Rotary, 1975. Mem. Cafidea, VenAmCham, Aicar. Republican. Clubs: Valle Arriba, Caracas Raquet. Lodges: Masons, Shriners. Address: Jet Cargo Internat M-367 PO Box 020010 Miami FL 33102-0010 Office: Diablitos Venezolanos CA, Ed Onivas Piso 3/Ave Abraham Lincoln, Caracas Venezuela

NORMAND, JACQUES MARIE, neurologist; b. Vesoul, Haute-Saone, France, Jan. 22, 1936; s. Jacques and Jeanne (Weinmann) N.; m. Sylvie Lenfant, Dec. 11, 1982. MD, Faculte Medecine, Paris, 1962, grad. in phys. medecine, 1965. Diplomate French Bd. Medicine. Resident Hopitaux Civils, Paris, 1957-63; chief rehab. service Etablissements Helio-Marins, Berck-sur-Mer, France, 1963-72, chief dept. clin. neurophysiology, 1972—. Author: Paraplegia, 1980, Diaphragmatic Electromyography, 1987. Dep. mayor Town of Berck-sur-Mer, 1977—. Mem. Internat. Soc. Paraplegia. Home: Ave du Chat Noir 54, 62780 Cucq Pas de Calais France Office: Etablissements Helio-Marins, rue Calot 52, 62600 Berck-sur-Mer Pas de Calais France

NORODOM SIHANOUK, HIS ROYAL HIGHNESS PRINCE See **SIHANOUK, PRINCE NORODOM**

NORONHA, EDWARD FRANCIS, physician; b. Gaya, India, Mar. 10, 1937; s. Ernest Frank and Gertrude Francis (Paul) N.; m. Hooi Hoon Tan. M Medicine and Sci., Nat. Med. Coll., Calcutta, India, 1968. Resident Gen. Hosp., Kuala Lumpur, Malaysia, 1968-69; gen. practitioner Far Eastern Dispensary, Kuala Lumpur, 1969-70, 72-73; med. officer Assunta Hosp., Petaling Jaya, Malaysia, 1973—. Served to capt. Malaysian Army, 1970-72. Mem. Malaysian Indian Congress. Roman Catholic. Club: Royal Selangor. Home: 37 Jalan, 18114, 46000 Petaling Jaya Malaysia Office: Assunta Hospital, Jalan Templer, 46990 Petaling Jaya Malaysia

NORRBACK, JOHAN OLE, Finland government official; b. Övermark, Finland, Mar. 18, 1941; m. Vivi-Ann Lindquist, 1959. Tchr. 1966-67; dist. sec. Swedish People's Party, Ostrobothnia, Finland, 1967-71; exec. mgr. Provincial Union Swedish Ostrobothnia, 1971—; chmn. parliamentary group Swedish People's Party, 1983-87; polit. sec. to minister communications Finland, Helsinki, 1976-77, M.P., 1979—, minister def., 1987—. Mem. Vaasa City Council, Finland, 1981—. Address: Ministry Def, Et Makasiinikatu 8A, 00130 Helsinki Finland *

NORRBY, S. RAGNAR, medical educator; b. Gothenburg, Sweden, Mar. 29, 1943; s. K. Sven T. and Ina (Odin) N.; m. E. Ann-Sofie Bengston, May 28, 1966; children: A. Katarina , Anna U. PhD, U. Gothenburg, 1970, MD, 1971. Resident, fellow in clin. virology Gothenburg, 1964-70; resident in internal medicine and surgery and psychiatry Kristinehamn Hosp., Sweden, 1971; resident, fellow, assoc. prof. in infectious diseases East Hosp., Gothenburg, 1972-77, 79-80; sr. med. dir. Merck, Sharp & Dohme Research Labs., Rahway, N.J, 1977-79; prof., chmn. dept. infectious diseases Umeå (Sweden) U. Hosp., 1980-87, Lund (Sweden) U. Hosp., 1988—. Contbr. articles to profl. jours. Mem. Internat. Soc. for Chemotherapy (exec. com. 1987—), Infectious Diseases Soc. Am.., Scandinavian Soc. for Antimicrobial Chemotherapy (pres. 1984—). Office: U Lund, Dept Infectious Diseases, Lasarettet, S22185 Lund Sweden

NORREGAARD, ARNOLD, advertising executive; b. Mesinge, Funen, Denmark, Aug. 21, 1925; s. Carl H. and Thyra C. (Friis) N.; Ingrid Larsen, Aug. 3, 1952; children: Nils, Susanne. Sectional mgr. Gutenberghus Advt. Film, Copenhagen, 1954-63, chief acct., 1964-68, bus. mgr., 1968-75, mng. dir., 1975-84; pres. Bellevue Studio, Copenhagen, 1984—, also bd. dirs.; mem. Royal Danish Commn. Mass Media, Copenhagen, 1981-84; bd. dirs. Stofa, Horsens, Denmark. Served with Danish Army, 1947-48. Mem. Soc. Motion Picture and Tech. Engring., Internat. Tape/Disc Assn. (v.p., bd. dirs. 1980). Lodge: Rotary (pres. Taarnby chpt. 1975-76, chmn. Denmark Youth Program 1984—). Home: 2 C Finnedalsvej, DK-2770 Kastrup Denmark Office: Bellevue Studio AS, 71 Dortheavej, DK-2400 Copenhagen NV Denmark

NORRIS, BARBARA THERESA, financial manager, stockbroker, insurance broker; b. Bklyn., Nov. 20, 1948; d. William Valentine and Stella (Laskowski) N.; diploma, L.I. Coll. Hosp. Sch. Nursing, 1968; B.S. magna cum laude, City U. N.Y., 1982. Charge nurse medicine/surgery L.I. Coll. Hosp., Bklyn., 1968-69, asst. head nurse labor/delivery unit, 1969-72, asst. dir. nursing, 1972-74, staff devel. instr., 1974-79, staff cons. materials mgmt. and nursing recruitment, 1979-80, staff cons. materials mgmt., 1980-83; mktg. cons., 1982-83; pres. Barbara Norris, Inc. Recipient N.Y. State Regents Incentive award, 1966; Nursing Sch. scholar Women's Floral Assn., 1968; lic. nurse, N.Y. Mem. L.I. Coll. Hosp. Sch. Nursing Alumnae Assn., Am. Assn. Critical Care Nurses, N.Y. Heart Assn., Smithsonian Assocs., Nat. Mus. Women in the Arts (charter), Arline Shahmanesh Hodgkins Research Orgn. Editor Nursing Communications, 1976-79. Contbr. poetry to anthologies. Home: 51-A Douglass St Brooklyn NY 11231 Office: Allied Capital Group Inc 11 Broadway New York NY 10004

NORRIS, CHARLES HEAD, JR., lawyer, financial executive; b. Boston, Sept. 14, 1940; s. Charles Head and Martha Marie N.; B.A., U. Pa., 1963, J.D., 1968; M.A., U. Wash., 1965; m. Diana D. Strawbridge, July 27, 1974; 1 dau., Margaret Dorrance. Admitted to Pa. bar, 1968; mem. firm Morgan, Lewis & Bockius, Phila., 1968-77; pres., chief exec. Artemis Corp., 1978-79; chmn. bd., chief exec., 1979—; chmn. exec. com., vice chmn. bd. Remington Rand Corp., 1979-81; partner Artemis Energy Co., 1980—; bd. dirs. Del. Trust Co., Meridian Bancorp, Inc., Asprey & Co. Ltd., Artemis Corp., Sarasin Asset Mgmt., Inc., Artemis Holdings Ltd.; trustee maj. stockholders' voting trust group Campbell Soup Co. Bd. dirs. Margaret Dorrance Strawbridge Found. Pa. II, Elesabeth Ingalls Gillet Found., Soc. Four Arts; mem. Pa. Commn. Crime and Delinquency, 1980-84; mem. Thouron Award Selection Com., 1985—; mem. Pa. Electoral Coll., 1980; mem. West Pikeland Twp. Suprs., 1969-72; mem. bd. visitors Carnegie Mellon U. Sch. Urban and Pub. Affairs. Served with USAF, 1959. Mem. ABA, Pa. Bar Assn., Am. Econ. Assn. Clubs: Phila., Seminole Golf, Knickerbocker, Bath and Tennis (bd. dirs., officer), Union League, Vicmead Hunt, Everglades (bd. dirs.), Wilmington Country; Sunningdale Golf (Eng.); The Country (Brookline). Office: 125 Strafford Ave Wayne PA 19087

NORRIS, JOHN ANTHONY, commissioner, lawyer, businessman, manager, editor, spokesman; b. Buffalo, Dec. 27, 1946; s. Joseph D. and Maria L. (Suite) N.; m. Kathleen M. Mullen, July 13, 1969; children: Patricia Marie, John Anthony II, Joseph Mullen, Mary Kathleen, Elizabeth Mary. BA, U. Rochester, 1968; JD, MBA with honors, Cornell U., 1973; cert., Harvard U. Sch. Govt., 1986. Bar: Mass. 1973. Assoc. Peabody, Brown, Boston, 1973-75; assoc. Powers Hall, Boston, 1975-76, ptnr., mem. exec. com., 1976-80, v.p., dir., 1979-80, chmn. adminstrv. com., 1976-79, chmn. hiring com., 1979-80; chmn. bd., pres., chief exec. officer, founder Norris & Norris, Boston, 1980-85; dep. commr. and chief operating officer FDA, Washington, 1985-88, chmn. action planning and cap coms., 1985-88, chmn. reye syndrome com, 1985-87, chmn. trade legis. com., 1987-88; corporate exec. v.p. Hill and Knowlton, Inc., N.Y.C., 1988—; worldwide dir. Health Scis. Consulting Group Hill and Knowlton, Inc., Boston, 1988—; mem. faculty Tufts Dental Sch., 1974-79, Boston Coll. Law Sch., 1976-80, Boston U. Law Sch., 1979-83, Harvard U. Public Health Sch., 1988—; mem. bd. editors FDA Drug Bulletin and FDA Consumer Report, 1985-88. Founder, faculty editor-in-chief Am. Jour. Law and Medicine, 1973-81, emeritus 1981—; editor-in-chief Cornell Internat. Law Jour., 1971-73; reviewer New Eng. Jour. Medicine Law-Medicine Notes, 1980-81; assoc. editor Medicolegal News, 1973-75. Mem. U.S. Del. to Japan (chmn.), Austria, Saudi Arabia, 1987, mem., chmn. Finland, Denmark, Italy, 1986; chmn. Mass. Statuatory Adv. Com. on Regulation of Clin. Labs., 1977-83; chmn. Boston Alumni and Scholarship Com., U. Rochester, 1979-85; mem. trustees council U. Rochester, 1979-85; mem. exec. com. Cornell Law Sch. Assn., 1982-85; mem. Mass. Gov.'s Blue Ribbon Task Force on DON, 1979-80, bd. trustees Jordan Hosp., 1978-80, mem. exec. com., 1979-80, chmn., chief exec. officer search com., 1980; chmn. Joseph D. Norris Health, Law and Pub. Policy Fund, 1979—; chmn. bd. Boston Holiday Project, 1981-83; mem. Pres. Chernobyl Task Force, 1986, co-chmn. health affects sub-com.; mem. Intra-Govtl. AIDS Task Force, 1987; mem. IOM Drug Devel. Forum, 1986—, co-chmn. end points sub-com., 1987—, Fed. Pain Commn., 1984-85. Served with U.S. Army, 1972-73, with res. Fed. Comprehensive Health Planning fellow, 1970-73; recipient Kansas City Hon. Key award, 1988, Nat. Health Fraud Conf. award, 1988, TOYL award, 1982, FDA Award of Merit, 1987, 88. Mem. ABA (vice chmn. medicine and law com. 1977-80), Mass. Bar Assn., Am. Soc. Hosp. Attys., Nat. Health Lawyers, Am. Soc. Law and Medicine (1st v.p. 1975-80, chmn. bd. 1981-84, mem. award 1981), Soc. Computer Applications to Med. Care (mem. bd. 1984-85), Phi Kappa Phi. Home: 531 W Washington St Hanson MA 02341 Office: Hill & Knowlton Inc Health Scis Cons Group 30 Rowes Wharf Boston MA 02110

NORRIS, JOHN STEVEN, construction company executive; b. Chgo., Apr. 25, 1943; s. Norris Dale and Olive (Grissinger) N.; B.A., U. Ariz., 1967; B.F.T., Am. Grad. Sch. Internat. Mgmt., 1968; m. Susan Jean Armstrong, May 3, 1975; children—Lindsey Jean, Whitney Ann, John Scott. Inspection officer Citicorp, Brazil, Colombia, Mexico, 1968-72, asst. cashier, N.Y.C., 1972-74; pres., gen. mgr. Phoenix Athletic Club, 1974-76; bus. mgr. Phoenix Pub. Inc., 1976-77; project mgr. Environ. Constrn. Co., Phoenix, 1977-79; pres. AGN Devel. Corp., Phoenix, 1979—, Valley View Realty, Inc., 1981-87; exec. v.p., sec., pres. RGW Construction Co., Inc.; pres. Norris/Roberts Group, Inc., Phoenix, 1987—. Bd. dirs. Christian Care Inc. Mem. Phi Delta Theta. Republican. Mem. Christian Ch. (deacon). Home: 14643 N 15th Ave Phoenix AZ 85023 Office: Norris/Roberts Group 2929 E Camelback Suite 250 Phoenix AZ 85106

NORRIS, ROBERT ERNEST, insurance executive; b. Great Bend, Kans., Apr. 25, 1947; s. Clyde Duncan and Elizabeth Marjorie (Penner) N.; m. Constance Jeanette Steffen, July 15, 1967; children: Robert Dee, Christopher Dalton, Stephen Tanner. BBA, Wichita State U. Assoc. in claims, Ins. Inst. Am. Asst. br. mgr. Crawford & Co., Kansas City, Mo., 1970—; br. mgr. Crawford & Co., Lincoln, Nebr., 1988—. Mem dist. and council coms. Heart of Am. council Boy Scouts Am., 1981—. Mem. Lincoln Claims Assn., Exptl. Aircraft Assn., Aircraft Owners and Pilots Assn., Amateur Radio Relay League. Republican. Lodge: Masons, Shriners. Office: Crawford and Co 145 N 46th St Suite 1 Lincoln NE 68505

NORRISH, KENNETH VICTOR, architect; b. Hounslow, Eng., Feb. 24, 1923; s. Richard John and Harriet Madge (Crook) N.; m. Joyce Hilda Bowers, Sept. 28, 1946 (div.); children—Antonia, Sheila, Jacqueline, Brenda, John; m. 2d, Georgette Gloria Safadi, Aug. 11, 1967; stepchildren—Peter, Christine, Amanda Heney. Assoc. Royal Inst. Brit. Architects, Birmingham Sch. Architecture, 1949. Asst. architect Cherrington & Stainton, Birmingham, Eng., 1946-49, ptnr., 1950-56; ptnr. Norrish & Stainton, Birmingham, 1956-70; dep. city architect Dept. Architecture, Portsmouth, Eng., 1970-78, city architect, 1978-88. Served to capt. Brit. Army, 1942-46. Fellow Royal Inst. Brit. Architects (chmn. so. region 1982-84, council 1986), Royal Soc. Arts. Home: 1 Grand Parade, Old Portsmouth PO1 2NF England Office: 1 Grand Parade, Old Portsmouth England

NORSWORTHY, JOHN RANDOLPH, economist; b. Norfolk, Va., Aug. 26, 1939; s. John Tignor and Annie Vivian (Smith) N.; m. Elizabeth Krassovsky, June 24, 1961 (div. 1962); 1 child, Leonid. Alexander; m. Susan Foster, Aug. 15, 1964 (div. 1971); 1 child, Ann Randolph. BA with distinction, U. Va., 1961; PhD in econs., U. Va., 1966. NDEA fellow, U. Va., 1961-65; postdoctoral fellow econs. U. Chgo., 1965-66; asst. prof. econs. U. Ill.-Chgo., 1966-68; asst., then assoc. prof. Temple U., Phila., 1968-71; chief applied econs. div. Office of Emergency Preparedness, Exec. Office Pres., Washington, 1971-73; chief productivity research div. Bur. Labor Stats., Washington, 1973-82; chief ctr. for econ. studies Bur. Census, U.S. Dept. Commerce, Washington, 1982-85; cons. economist, 1985-86; prof. econ. and mgmt. Rensselaer Poly. Inst., 1986—; mem. Brookings Panel on Econ. Activity, 1979. Contbr. articles to profl. jours. Recipient Disting. Achievement Award for Research, U.S. Dept. Labor, 1980, Lawrence R. Gordon award for Grad. Teaching and Research in Econs. Rensselaer Poly. Inst., 1988. Mem. Econometric Soc., Am. Econ. Assn., Am. Statis. Assn., Conf. on Research in Income and Wealth (exec. com. 1981-85), Phi Beta Kappa, Phi Eta Sigma, Tau Kappa Epsilon.

NORTH, HENRY RINGLING, oil company and entertainment executive; b. Chgo., Nov. 12, 1909; arrived in Switzerland, 1976; s. Henry Whitestone and Ida Loraina Wilhelmina (Ringling) N.; m. Ada Mae Thornburg, 1936 (div. 1945); 1 child, John Ringling II; m. Gloria de la Feld, Dec. 14, 1959. AB, Yale U., 1933. V.p., dir. Rockland Oil Co., Ardmore, Okla., 1937—, Sarasota Oil Co., Ardmore, Okla., 1937—; v.p. Ringling Bros.-Barnum & Bailey Circus Inc., Sarasota, Fla., 1937-42, 48-68. Author (with Alden Hatch) The Circus Kings, 1960. Served to comdr. USNR, 1942. Decorated Silver Star. Republican. Mem. Church of Ireland. Clubs: Yale (N.Y.C.), Racquet and Tennis (N.Y.C.); Kildare Street (Dublin, Ireland), Stephens Green (Dublin), Players (N.Y.C.).

NORTH, KENNETH E(ARL), lawyer; b. Chgo., Nov. 18, 1945; s. Earl and Marion (Temple) N.; m. Susan C. Gutzmer, June 6, 1970; children: Krista, Kari. AA with high honors, Coll. of DuPage, Glen Ellyn, Ill., 1970; BA with high honors, No. Ill. U., 1971; JD, Duke U., 1974. Bar: Ill. 1974, U.S. Dist. Ct. (no. dist.) Ill. 1974, Guam 1978, U.S. Tax Ct., 1975, U.S. Ct. Appeals (7th cir.), 1978, U.S. Supreme Ct., 1978, U.S. Ct. Internat. Trade 1978, U.S. Ct. Appeals (9th cir.) Calif. 1979. Div. chief DuPage County State's Attys. Office, Wheaton, 1976-78; spl. asst. U.S. atty. Terr. of Guam, Agana, 1978-79, atty. gen., 1979-80; prin. Law Offices Kenneth E. North & Assocs.; pres., editor North Pub. Co.; adj. prof. law John Marshall Law Sch., Chgo., 1985—, Keller Grad. Sch. Mgmt. Northwestern U.; instr. Northwestern U. Traffic Inst., 1985—; cons. Terr. of Guam, 1980-81; lectr., cons. regarding computer-aided litigation support, 1985—; counsel to various fin. instns. and domestic corps. Co-author: Criminal and Civil Tax Fraud, 1986; bd. editors Attorneys' Computer Report, 1986—; contbr. articles to legal pubis. Trustee, mem. adv. bd. Ams. for Effective Law Enforcement, 1986—; v.p. Glen Ellyn Manor Civic Assn., 1981-84, pres., 1984—; police commr. Village of Glen Ellyn, 1982—. Mem. Assn. Trial Lawyers Am. (sec. criminal sect. 1986-87, 2d vice chair 1987—), ABA, Ill. Bar Assn., World Bar Assn., Chgo. Bar Assn., Chgo. Duke Bar Assn. (pres. 1986-87), Chgo. Council Fgn. Relations, Internat. Platform Assn., Mensa. Republican. Pioneer use of computer in ct. Office: 2311 W 22d St Suite 217 Oak Brook IL 60521

NORTH, MAXINE WOODFIELD, holding company executive; b. Salem, Oreg.; arrived in Thailand, 1950; d. Victor Edward and MaBelle Eileen (Norwood) W.; m. Robert Guilford North (dec. Dec. 1954). Grad., bus. coll., Salem, 1938; student in lang., George Washington U., Washington, 1943; student, Mahidol U., Bangkok, 1979—. Adminstrv. asst. to chief postal censor Office of Censorship, Washington, 1941-44; exec. sec. legal dept. Columbia Pictures Corp., Hollywood, Calif., 1946-50; mng. dir. Pure Gas Co., Ltd., Bangkok, 1953-60, North Star Co., Ltd., Bangkok, 1956-86; chmn. bd. Thai Celadon Co., Ltd., Bangkok, 1960—; mng. dir. Starwagon Holdings, Ltd., Bangkok, 1986—; bd. dirs. Aloe Vera, Ltd., Bangkok. Mem. Am. C. of C. in Thailand (founder 1956). Republican. Roman Catholic. Clubs: Royal Bkk Sports, Foreign Corrs. (recording sec. 1983, 87). Home: The Emerald, 99 Wireless Rd, 10500 Bangkok Thailand Office: Starwagon Holdings Ltd, Charn Issara Tower 22d Floor, 942/164 Rama IV Rd, Bangkok 10500, Thailand

NORTH, PHIL RECORD, business executive; b. Fort Worth, July 6, 1918; s. James M. and Lottie R. N.; m. Janis Harris, July 28, 1944; children: Phillip Kevin, Kerry Lawrence, Mairin Kathleen, Deirdre Aine. A.B., U. Notre Dame, 1939. With Fort Worth Star Telegram, 1937-62, exec. editor, 1956-62, asst. gen. mgr., 1959-62; v.p. Carter Publs., Inc., 1949-62; with Tandy Corp., Fort Worth, 1966-82; chief exec. officer Tandy Corp., 1978-81, pres., 1978-81, chmn. bd., 1978-82; chmn. bd. 1st City Nat. Bank, Ft. Worth, 1982-86; chmn. bd. dirs. Western Ins. Cos., Ft. Worth; bd. dirs. Del Norte Tech., Euless, Tex. Served to maj. AUS, 1940-46. Decorated Bronze Star. Roman Catholic. Clubs: Fort Worth, River Crest, Shady Oaks, San Antonio Country, Rockport Country, Rockport Yacht, Corpus Christi Yacht.

NORTHCUTT, CLARENCE DEWEY, lawyer; b. Guin, Ala., July 7, 1916; s. Walter G. and Nancy E. (Homer) N.; m. Ruth Eleanor Storms, May 25, 1941; children: Gayle Marie (Mrs. John J. Young), John E. A.B., U. Okla., 1939, LL.B., 1938. Bar: Okla. 1938. Practiced in Ponca City, 1938—; former gen. counsel Frontier Fed. Savs. and Loan Assn.; Mem. bd. visitors U. Okla. Served with AUS, 1941-46. Decorated Bronze Star, Air medal with oak leaf cluster., Order St. John of Jerusalem; named Outstanding Citizen of Ponca City, 1982. Fellow Am. Coll. Trial Lawyers, Am. Coll. Probate Counsel, Am. Bar Found.; mem. Acad. Univ. Fellows, Internat. Soc. Barristers, Am. Bd. Advocacy, Internat. Acad. Trial Lawyers, Okla. Bar Assn. (pres. 1975, bd. govs.), Ponca City C. of C. (past pres.). Democrat. Baptist. Clubs: Mason, Kiwanian. Home: 132 Whitworth St Ponca City OK 74601 Office: PO Box 1669 Ponca City OK 74601

NORTHCUTT, HELENE LOUISE BERKING (MRS. CHARLES PHILLIP NORTHCUTT), artist, educator; b. Hannibal, Mo., July 6, 1916; d. Robert Stanley and Alice Lee (Adkisson) Berking; student Christian Coll., Columbia, Mo., 1932-33; B.S., U. Mo., 1939, A.M., 1940, Ed.D., 1959; m. Charles Phillip Northcutt, June 4, 1938 (dec.); children—John Berking, Francois Lee Northcutt Hedeen. Art tchr., supr. Oakwood High Sch. and Elem. Sch., 1937-39; tchr. jr. high sch. U. Mo. Lab. Sch., 1939-40; tchr. elem. art, Memphis, Mo., 1941; county-fine arts supr., Ralls County, Mo., 1941-42; tchr. art high sch., Columbia, 1943-44; tchr. art jr. high sch., Hannibal, Mo., 1951-54; supr. art Ralls County Reorganized Sch. Dist. VI, New London, 1954-56; vis prof. U. Upper Iowa, 1956; instr. U. Mo., 1956-57; prof. art Eastern Mont. Coll. unit U. Mont., Billings, from 1957, now prof. emeritus, mem. grad. faculty; vis. prof. art U. B.C., Vancouver, 1965; cons. in curriculum in art edn.; cons. environ. edn., cons. on Indian edn., early childhood; exhibits fibers and paintings; state dir. Am. Art Week, Am. Artists Profl. League, 1963-65; exhibit chmn. E.M.C. Gallery Fine Arts; program chmn. Becky Thatcher council Girl Scouts U.S.A., 1946-48; bd. dirs., treas. United Christian Campus Ministry; bd. dirs. Growth Through Art. Recipient scholarship Delta Kappa Gamma, 1956-57; Nat. Press award Gen. Fedn. Women's Clubs, 1951; named Outstanding Honor Grad. U. Mo., 1968; citations for distinctive service Eastern Mont. Coll., Helene B. Northcutt Gallery named in her honor. Mem. Nat. Soc. Coll. Profs., AAUP, Mont. Edn. Assn. (past pres. Eastern Faculty unit; v.p. dept. higher edn. 1966-68, dept. pres. 1968-70) Nat., Mont. (sec. 1967-69) art edn. assns., AAUW (past chpt. pres.), Mont. Early Childhood Edn. Assn., Gen. Fedn. Women's Clubs (local past pres.), Delta Kappa Gamma (past chpt. pres., chmn. com., chmn. state world fellowship), Delta Phi Delta, Kappa Delta Epsilon. Methodist (mem. commn. higher edn. ministries, trustee Yellowstone Conf.). Club: Eastern Montana College Faculty (Billings, Mont.). Author: Creative Expression, 1964; Competency base Module-Methods and Materials, 1974; contbr. to publs. in field; reviewer, editor manuscripts on art and art edn. Home: M-3 Timbers Townhomes 3224 Granger Ave E Billings MT 59102

NORTHEN, REBECCA TYSON, orchid specialist, author; b. Detroit, Aug. 24, 1910; d. William Elisha and Elizabeth (Weems) Tyson; student Radcliffe Coll., 1930-33; B.A., Wayne State U., 1935; M.A., Mt. Holyoke Coll., 1937; m. Henry Theodore Northen, Aug. 9, 1937; children—Elizabeth Northen Lyons, Philip Tyson, Thomas Henry. Lectr. in field. Mem. Am. Orchid Soc. (gold medal 1979), Orchid Digest Corp., Sigma Xi. Author: Home Orchid Growing, 1950, 3d edit., 1970; Orchids as House Plants, 1955, 2d edit., 1976; Miniature Orchids, 1980; (with Henry Theodore Northen) Secret of the Green Thumb, 1954; Greenhouse Gardening, 1956, 2d edit., 1973; Ingenious Kingdom, 1970. Address: 1215 Drake Circle San Luis Obispo CA 93401

NORTHROP, STUART JOHNSTON, manufacturing company executive; b. New Haven, Oct. 22, 1925; s. Filmer Stuart Cuckow and Christine (Johnston) N.; m. Cynthia Stafford Daniell, Feb. 23, 1946; children: Christine Daniell, Richard Rockwell Stafford. B.A. in Physics, Yale U., 1948. Indsl. engr. U.S. Rubber Co., Naugatuck, Conn., 1948-51; head indsl. engring. dept. Am. Cyanamid Co., Wallingford, Conn., 1951-54; mfg. mgr. Linear, Inc., Phila., 1954-57; mgr. quality control and mfg. Westinghouse Electric Co., Pitts., 1957-58; mfg. supt. SKF Industries, Phila., 1958-61; v.p. mfg. Am. Meter Co., Phila., 1961-69; founder, v.p., gen. mgr. water resources div. Singer Co., Phila.; pres., dir. Buffalo Meter Co., Four Layne Cos.; dir. Gen. Filter Co., 1969-72; chmn., chief exec. officer Huffy Corp., Dayton, Ohio, 1972-85, chmn. exec. com., 1985—; bd. dirs. Lukens, Inc., Coatesville, Pa., Fischer & Porter, Phila., Union Corp., N.Y.C.; former dir. DPL (formerly Dayton Power & Light Co.), Duriron, Bank One Dayton, Danis Constrn., Carlisle Retailers. County fin. chmn. George Bush Presdl. campaign, 1980; presdl. appointee Pres.'s Commn. on Ams. Outdoors, 1985-86; chmn. nat. hwy. safety adv. com. Dept. Transp., 1986—. Served with USAAF, 1944-45. Named Chief Exec. Officer of Yr. for leisure industry Wall Street Transcript, 1980. Mem. Del. Valley Investors (past pres.), Interlocutors, Elihu, Am. Bus. Conf. (founding), Fin. Commn. of Fund Ams. Future, Delta Kappa Epsilon, KOA Soc. Club: Merion Cricket (Haverford, Pa.). Home: 226 Cheswold Ln Haverford PA 19041 Office: Huffy Corp 7701 Byers Rd Miamisburg OH 45342

NORTON, GEOFFREY ANDREW, resource economist, educator; b. Cardiff, Wales, Nov. 9, 1942; s. Hubert Arthur and Katherine Ivy (Curthoys) N.; m. Diane Pimblett, Sept. 21, 1968; children: Ceri, Sarah. BSc, U. Coll., North Wales, 1965; MSc in Econs., U. Coll., 1966, PhD in Econs., 1968; DSc, U. London, 1988. Postdoctoral fellow U. Man., Winnipeg, Can., 1968-70; lectr., sr. lectr. Imperial Coll., London, 1970—; dir. Silwood Ctr. Pest Mgmt., 1985—. Author: Resource Economics, 1984. Mem. Consortium Overseas Pest Experts (sec. 1985—). Office: Imperial Coll, Silwood Park, Ascot SL5 7PY, England

NORTON, H. GAITHER, food company executive; b. Bklyn., Aug. 16, 1918; s. Dwight Fanning and Jessie (Gaither) N.; m. Ann Lou Allen, Mar.

23, 1941; children: Priscilla Ann, Lou Elaine; m. 2d., Laura Louise Smith, July 26, 1950; children: Craig Gaither, Laura Marjorie, Scott Clark, Ellen Louise. Student Middlebury Coll., 1936-37, NYU, 1939-40, Lafayette Coll., 1938-39, Stevens Inst. Tech., 1941; AB in Econs. with honors, UCLA, 1952. With Continental Can Co., 1937-41, sales trainee, 1939-41; employment interviewer, Grumman Aircraft Corp., 1941-43; USMC personnel classification and rehab. interviewer, counsellor, 1943-46; F.W. Boltz Corp., Los Angeles, 1947-48, nat. sales mgr., 1948-50; asst. div. mgr. Northeast div. Welch's Grape Juice Co., N.Y.C., 1952-54; pres. H.G. Norton Co., Inc., New Milford, Conn., 1954—. Bd. dirs. Weantinoge Heritage Land Trust, Inc., New Milford, 1965-76, hon. bd. dirs., 1976-82, 1st v.p., 1966-76, 82-88; mem. zoning bd. appeals, New Milford, 1970, planning commn. to set up Commn. on Aging, New Milford, 1972, panel to examine town police needs, 1980; sec., bd. dirs. Sunny Valley Found., 1978-79; mem. New Milford Conservation Commn., 1981—, Rep. Town Com., New Milford, 1982-86, Econ. Devel. Commn., 1984—. Served with USMC, 1943-46. Mem. Nat. Assn. Specialty Food Trade (pres., 1962-63), Nat. Assn. Splty. Food and Confection Brokers (pres. 1972-74, chmn. Internat. Fancy Food and Confection Show 1969), Nat. Food Distbrs. Assn. (dir. mfrs. council 1974-75, 88—), Phi Beta Kappa, Pi Gamma Mu. Home: PO Drawer 269 New Milford CT 06776 Office: PO Drawer 269 New Milford CT 06776

NORTON, ROBERT LEO, SR., mechanical engineering educator, researcher; b. Boston, May 5, 1939; s. Harry Joseph and Kathryn (Warren) N.; m. Nancy Auclair, Feb. 27, 1960; children: Robert L., Jr., MaryKay, Thomas J. BS, Northeastern U., 1967; MS, Tufts U., 1970. Registered profl. engr., Mass, R.I., N.H. Engr. Polaroid Corp., Cambridge, Mass., 1959-67; project engr. Jet Spray Cooler, Inc., Waltham, Mass, 1967-69; research assoc. N.E. Med. Ctr., Boston, 1969-74; prof. Tufts U., Medford, Mass., 1974-79; sr. engr. Polaroid Corp., Waltham, 1979-81; prof. mech. engring., Worcester Poly., Mass., 1981—; pres. Norton Assocs., Norfolk, Worcester, 1970—. Patentee (13) in field; contbr. articles to profl. jours. Mem. ASME, Am. Soc. Engring. Edn. (J.F. Curtis award 1984), Inst. Elec. Engrs., Pi Tau Sigma, Sigma Xi. Democrat. Avocations: sailing, computers. Office: WPI 100 Institute Rd Worcester MA 01609

NOTE, PAUL DRUON MICHAEL, management consultant; b. Algiers, Algeria, Jan. 13, 1956; came to Switzerland, 1961; s. Aime Pierre and Micheline Paule (Jahier) N. Degree in Econs., U. Grenoble (France), 1978; degree Institut d'Etudes Politiques, Grenoble, 1978; Hautes Etudes Commerciales, Jouy en Josas, France, 1981. Controller Europe Sandoz Ltd. (Wander group), Berne, Switzerland, 1982-83; corp. controller Produtos Sandoz Lda., Lisbon, Portugal, 1983-85; mgmt. cons. Hayek Engring. A.G., Zurich, 1986—. Served to lt. French Cavalry, 1979-80. Roman Catholic. Avocations: sailing; windsurfing; skiing; golf; tennis; hunting. Home: Chemin des Rojalets, 1296 Coppet Vaud Switzerland

NOTHDURFT, HANS JAKOB, pharmaceutical company executive; b. Bruchsal, Ger., May 30, 1911; s. Jakob Georg and Susanna Elisabeth (Birkenmeier) N.; Dr. med. U. Heidelberg, 1937, Dr. med. habil., 1939, Prof., 1945; m. Aenn Mühe, July 21, 1978; children—Jutta Breuker, Hans-Dieter. Univ. lectr. U. Heidelberg, 1940-49; practicing physician, 1949-59; pharm. co. exec. Boehringer-Mannheim, 1959-76; v.p. cons. co., 1976—; cons. fed. agys. and sci. socs.; ofcl. cons. German Orthopedic Soc. Served with German mil. forces, 1939-44. Decorated Gold medal for submarine service. Mem. nat. and internat. sci. socs. Club: Lions of Viernheim (pres. 1978-79). Research, publs. in field; introduced concept fgn. body sarcoma, now called Nothdurft effect. Home: 63/65 VIII Rathausstrasse, D-6806 Viernheim Federal Republic of Germany Office: 6 Am Aufstieg, D-6242 Kronberg Federal Republic of Germany

NOTHMANN, RUDOLF S., legal researcher; b. Hamburg, W.Ger., Feb. 4, 1907; came to U.S., 1941, naturalized, 1943; s. Nathan and Henrietta G. (Heymann) N. Referendar, U. Hamburg, 1929, Ph.D. in Law, 1932; postgrad. U. Liverpool Law Sch. (Eng.), 1931-32. Law clk. Hamburg Cts., 1929-33; export, legal adviser, adviser ocean marine ins. various firms, Ger., Eng., Sweden, Calif., 1933-43, 46-47; instr. fgn. exchange, fgn. trade Extension div. UCLA, 1947-48, vis. assoc. prof. UCLA, 1951; asst. prof. econs. Whittier Coll., 1948-50, assoc. prof., 1950-51; contract work U.S. Air Force, U.S. Navy, 1953-59; contract negotiator space projects, space and missile systems orgn. U.S. Air Force, Los Angeles, 1959-77; pvt. researcher in internat. comml. law, Pacific Palisades, Calif., 1977—. Served with U.S. Army, 1943-45; ETO. Recipient Gold Tape award Air Force Systems Command, 1970. Mem. Internat. Bar Assn. (vice chmn. internat. sales and related comml. trans. com. 1977-82), Am. Econ. Assn., Calif. Bar Assn. (internat. law sect.), Am. Soc. Internat. Law. Author: The Insurance Certificate in International Ocean Marine Insurance and Foreign Trade, 1932; The Oldest Corporation in the World: Six Hundred Years of Economic Evolution, 1949. Club: Uebersee (Hamburg). Home: PO Box 32 Pacific Palisades CA 90272

NOTOWIDIGDO, MUSINGGIH HARTOKO, information systems executive; b. Indonesia, Dec. 9, 1938; s. Moekarto and Martaniah (Brodjonegoro) N.; m. Sihar P. Tambunan, Oct. 1, 1966 (dec. Nov. 1976); m. Joanne S. Gutter, June 3, 1979; children: Matthew Joseph, Jonathan Paul. BME, George Washington U., 1961; MS, NYU, 1966, postgrad., 1970. Cons. Dollar Blitz & Assocs., Washington, 1962-64; ops. research analyst Am. Can Co., N.Y.C., 1966-69; prin. analyst Borden Inc., Columbus, Ohio, 1969-70, mgr. ops. research, 1970-71, mgr. ops. analysis and research, 1972-74, asst. gen. controller, officer, 1974-77, corp. dir. info. systems/econ. analysis, officer, 1977-83; v.p. info. systems Wendy's Internat., 1983—; adj. lectr. Grad. Sch. Adminstrn. Capital U. Contbr. articles to profl. jours. Mem. Fin Execs. Inst. (chmn. MIS com.), Ops. Research Soc., Inst. Mgmt. Sci., Am. Mgmt. Assn., Nat. Assn. Bus. Economists, Long Range Planning Soc., Am. Statis. Assn., AAAS, World Future Soc., Data Processing Mgmt. Assn., Soc. Info. Mgmt., N.Y. Acad. Scis. Republican. Clubs: Capital, Racquet. Home: 1965 Brandywine Dr Upper Arlington OH 43220 Office: 4288 W Dublin-Granville Rd Dublin OH 43017

NOTOWIDJOJO, SUHENDRO EKOPUTRO, manufacturing and trading company chief executive; b. Semarang, Central Java, Indonesia, Apr. 11, 1931; m. Adisari Matohay, Aug. 15, 1956; children—Rianti, Farida, Lindarsih, Budidharma. B.B.A., Grad. Sch. Bus. Adminstrn., Jakarta, 1954; M.B.A., U. So. Calif., 1976; Ph.D., Century U. (Calif.), 1982. Pres., NV Sumera Trading Co., Jakarta, 1958—; mng. dir. PT Damatex Inds., Jakarta, 1964—; pres. PT Fumira Steel Sheet Inds., Semarang, 1969—; pres. PT Budidharma Steel Inds., Jakarta, 1974—; pres. PT Candrasari Chem. Inds., Jakarta, 1974—; pres. PT Sumber Sejahtera Distbrs., Jakarta, 1974—; chmn., PT Tosan Prima Steel Inds., Jakarta, 1981—; dir. PT Dharma Manunggal Textiles, Tangerang, 1976—. Author: Indonesia-Japan Economic Cooperation in the Private Sector, 1981. Mem. Indonesian Galvanized Sheet Mfrs. Assn. (chmn. 1974—), Indonesian Steel Bars Mfrs. Assn. (chmn. 1985—), Indonesian Billet Mfrs. Assn. (chmn. 1976—), Indonesian Reinforced Steel Bar Mfrs. Assn. (chmn. 1985—), C. of C. (chmn. basic industries com. 1983), Asean Iron and Steel Fedn. (v.p., 1983), South East Asia Iron and Steel Inst. (mng. dir. 1984). Buddhist. Lodge: Rotary (Menteng-Jakarta). Office: PT Budidharma Steel Mfg, Wisma Argo Manunggal 9th Floor, Jl Jen Gatot Sebroto Kav 22, Jakarta 12930, Indonesia

NOTTAY, BALDEV KAUR, microbiologist; b. Nairobi, Kenya, East Africa, Jan. 15, 1936; d. Santa Singh and Swaran (Kaur) N. B.S. with honors, U. Bombay, 1960; M.Sc., U. Bombay, 1964. Research student Polio Research Unit, Haffkine Inst., Bombay, India, 1962-63; assoc. head poliovirus research Virology Dept., Med. Research Lab., Nairobi, 1964-71; vis. assoc. viral reagents CDC Ctrs. Disease Control, Atlanta, 1972-74, vis. assoc. enteric virology br., 1974-78, research microbiologist molecular biology unit, respiratory and enterovirus br., div. viral diseases, 1978—. Contbr. articles to profl. jours. Home: 5574 Wylstream St Norcross GA 30093 Office: 1600 Clifton Rd Atlanta GA 30333

NOTTINGHAM, EDGAR JAMESON, IV, clin. psychologist; b. Richmond, Va., Nov. 11, 1951; s. Edgar Jameson, III and Anna Sue (Springfield) N.; B.A., Randolph-Macon Coll., 1974; M.S. in Clin. Psychology, Va. Poly. Inst. and State U., 1976, Ph.D., 1979. Approved supr. rational-emotive therapy. Staff psychologist, coordinator treatment, acting dir. forensic unit Southwestern State Hosp., Marion, Va., 1977-78; intern clin. psychology U. Tenn. Center Health Scis., Memphjs, 1978-79; clin. psychologist, dir. and coordinator tng. in psychology Memphis Mental Health Inst., 1979-81; cons. psychologist Lakeside Hosp., 1981-86; partner East Memphis Psychol. Assocs., 1979—, Germantown Psychol. Assocs., 1984—; clin. exec. dir. Germantown Pshychol. Assocs., 1986—, dir. psychol. services Parkwood Hosp., 1987—; clin. asst. prof. U. Tenn. Ctr. Health Scis., 1981—; mem. adj. faculty Memphis State U., 1980—. Mem. Am. Psychol. Assn., Inst. Advanced Study in Rational Psychotherapy, Southeastern Psychol. Assn., Tenn. Psychol. Assn., Memphis Area Psychol. Assn., Am. Assn. Marriage and Family Therapy (clin. mem.), Sigma Xi, Phi Kappa Phi, Psi Chi, Omicron Delta Kappa, Pi Gamma Mu, Sigma Phi Epsilon. Coauthor manual. Contbr. articles profl. jours. Office: 7516 Enterprise Ave Suite 1 Germantown TN 38138

NOTTKE, WILLIAM HARRY, packaging company executive; b. Kankakee, Ill., Aug. 27, 1951; s. William Harry and Adeline Mae (Brinkman) N.; m. Lora Leigh Kronsbein, Apr. 3, 1980; children—Crystal, Ashley. Student Kankakee Community Coll., 1970-72, Western Ill U., 1969-70. Customer service supr. Baker & Taylor Co., Momence, Ill., 1971-73; sales/service corr. Kankakee Container Corp. (Ill.), 1973-76; sales/service mgr. Keystone Container Corp., St. Louis, 1976-79; owner, pres. Riverdale Packaging Corp., St. Louis, 1979—, also chmn. bd. Mem. Assn. Ind. Corrugated Converters (pres. St. Louis chpt.). Methodist. Office: Riverdale Packaging Corp 11490 Warnen Rd Maryland Heights MO 63043

NOURI, ABDUL MOTEY MOHAMMED, government communications official; b. Makkah, Saudi Arabia, Jan. 27, 1941; s. Mohammed Soliman and Fatma Hashim (Mojahid) N.; m. Aishah Hussain, Feb. 10, 1963; children: Ahmad, Lubna, Hatim, Mohammed. BS, U. Cairo Engring. Faculty, 1968; PhD in Engring., Kennedy-Western U., 1985. Elec. engr. Saudi Arabian Ministry Post Telegraph & Telephone, 1969-74, chief network dept., 1974-78; dir. gen. Saudi Arabian Ministry Post Telegraph & Telephone, Riyadh, 1978—; vice chmn. study group 15 cons. com. ITU, Geneva, 1980-85, chmn., 1985—. Mem. IEEE (sr.), Optical Soc. Am. Home: PO Box 1423, Riyadh Saudi Arabia Office: Ministry Post Telegraph & Telephone, Maazar Rd, Riyadh Saudi Arabia

NOUVELLET, JEAN-PIERRE, sales executive; b. Pacaudiere, France, Feb. 17, 1947; s. Joseph Eugene and Huguette (Chamussy) N.; m. Odile Casati, Aug. 4, 1971; children: Axelle, Maïeule, Joseph, Vianney. Grad., U. Lyon, France, 1971. Prodn. asst. Recticel-France, Paris, 1971-74; sr. field salesman Dow Chem.-France, Lyon and Strasbourg, 1974-84; sales mgr. Marbo-France, Lyon, 1985—. Roman Catholic. Home: Bosvert, 42620 Saint Martin D'Estreaux France Office: Marbo France, 155 Rue Pierre Corneille, 69003 Lyon France

NOUWEN, JAN JOHANNES, publishing executive; b. Hillegersberg, Netherlands, June 11, 1932; m. Hanna Kolthoff, Apr. 1, 1960; children—Rutger Jan, Martine. Law degree, Leiden U., 1955. Sec. gen. Nederlandse Dagblad Pers, Amsterdam, 1959-68; mng. dir. Sijthoff Pers, Rijswijk, 1968—; pres. bd. dirs. Provinciale Zeeuwse Courant, Middelburg, 1981—. Bd. dirs. Stichting Liberaal Reveil, Hague, 1975—, Nederlandse Radar Proefstation, Noordwijk, 1985—; gen. bd. dirs. VNO, 1980-86. Decorated officer Royal Order of Oranje-Nassau (Netherlands); officer Order Finnish Lion. Mem. Internat. Fedn. Newspaper Pubs. (v.p. 1984-88, gen. sec. 1988—), Press Inst. (chmn. 1975—), Mediacouncil, Dutch Found. Communication Devel. Cooperation (pres. bd.). Office: Sijthoff Pers BV, PO Box 16050, 2500 AA The Hague The Netherlands

NOVACK, SHELDON, educator; b. Phila., Apr. 11, 1938; s. Ike and Jeannette (Garber) N.; B.S., Temple U., 1959, M.B.A., 1966; Ph.D., N.Y. U., 1973; m. Goldie Stein, Dec. 17, 1960; children—Seth, Lauren Anne; m. 2d, Barbara Gross, 1982. Vice pres. Communications Fin. Corp., Phila., 1966-71; prof. Coll. of Ins., N.Y.C., 1971-72; asso. prof., chmn. dept. fin., public policy and bus. econs. L.I. U., Bklyn., 1973-76; faculty Seton Hall U., South Orange, N.J., 1976-79, Widener U., 1979, St. Joseph U., 1982; cons. in field; mng. ptnr. Matrix Leasing, Jenkintown, Pa., 1987; dir. Congl. Life Ins. Co., Zim Computer Corp. Bd. dirs. Am. Jewish Cultural Found. Served with AUS, 1960-62. Marcus Nadler fellow, 1966-68. Mem. Am., Eastern fin. assns., Am., Eastern econ. assns., The Money Marketeers, Econ., Pa. hist. assns., Western Econs. and Fin. Assn., Omicron Delta Epsilon, Beta Gamma Sigma. Asso. editor The American Economist Jour., 1976—. Home: 1523 Woodland Rd Rydal PA 19046

NOVAK, ALBERT JOHN WITTMAYER, electronic systems and parts manufacturing company executive; b. Grand Rapids, Mich., Mar. 30, 1921; s. Albert Joseph and B. Joan (Wittmayer) N.; A.B. magna cum laude in Physics, Harvard U., 1941; postgrad. M.I.T., 1944, Case Inst. Tech., 1946-48; m. Patricia M. Henline, Mar. 25, 1950 (div. Oct. 22, 1980); children—Patricia Joan, Albert John Wittmayer, David Bruce, Loren Lee; m. Suzanne Stover Basye, Apr. 30, 1984. Indsl. engr. RCA, Camden, N.J., 1941-42; sales mgr. Brush Instruments div. Clevite Corp., Cleve., 1946-53, gen. mgr. Tex. div., Houston, 1955-57; mgr. sales and engring. Ansonia Wire & Cable Co., Ashton, R.I., 1957-59; gen. mgr. Electronics div. Hoover Co., Balt. and Pompano Beach, Fla., 1959-65; founder, pres., chmn. bd. Novatronics Group, Inc., Novatronics, Inc., Pompano Beach, 1965-85, Novatronics of Can., Ltd., Stratford, Ont., Novatronics South, Inc., Delray Beach, Fla.; cons., bd. dirs. Nedax Inc., 1985—; adv. bd. Barnett Banks. Chmn., Broward Indsl. Bd., 1967, 75, Broward County Community Relations Commn., 1974, South Fla. Dist. Adv. Council, SBA, 1978; pres. Ft. Lauderdale Symphony Assn., 1970-72; v.p. Opera Guild, 1985-86; bd. dirs. South Fla. Edn. Center, 1963-—, pres., 1970—; bd. dirs. United Way Broward County, 1975—, v.p., 1977—; mem. Gov.'s Mgmt. Adv. Council for Health and Rehab. Services, 1977—, chmn. Dist. X Health and Rehab. Services Adv. Council, 1977; trustee Mus. of Art; bd. dirs. Center for Pastoral Counseling and Human Devel., 1973—, pres., 1977-79. Served to lt. comdr. USNR, 1942-46. Named Industrialist of Yr., Pompano Beach, 1966-67, 75-76; recipient Outstanding Service award Nat. Elec. Mfrs. Assn., 1967. Mem. Broward Mfrs. Assn. (pres. 1966-67), Am. Electronics Assn. (bd. dirs.), Greater Ft. Lauderdale C. of C. (dir. 1973-74), Phi Beta Kappa. Club: Harvard (pres. 1976-78) (Broward County). Home and Office: PO Box 1980 Melbourne FL 32902-1980

NOVAK, MICHAEL (JOHN), JR., religion educator, author, editor; b. Johnstown, Pa., Sept. 9, 1933; s. Michael John and Irene (Sakmar) N.; m. Karen Ruth Laub, June 29, 1963; children: Richard, Tanya, Jana. A.B. summa cum laude, Stonehill Coll., North Easton, Mass., 1956; B.T. cum laude, Gregorian U., Rome, 1958; M.A., Harvard U., 1966; LL.D., Keuka (N.Y.) Coll., 1970, Stonehill Coll., Mass., 1977; L.H.D., Davis and Elkins (W.Va.) Coll., 1971, LeMoyne (N.Y.) Coll., 1976, Sacred Heart U., 1977, Muhlenberg Coll., 1979, D'Youville Coll., 1981, Boston U., 1981, New Eng. Coll., 1983, Rivier Coll., 1984, Marquette U., 1987. Teaching fellow Harvard U., 1961-63; asst. prof. Stanford U., 1965-68; assoc. prof. philosophy and religious studies State U. N.Y., Old Westbury, 1968-71; assoc. dir. humanities Rockefeller Found., N.Y.C., 1973-75; provost Disciplines Coll., SUNY, Old Westbury, 1969-71; vis. prof. Jan. session Carleton Coll., Northfield, Minn., 1970, Immaculate Heart Coll., Hollywood, Calif., 1971; vis. prof. U. Calif., Santa Barbara, 1972, Riverside, 1975; Ledden-Watson disting. prof. religion Syracuse U., 1977-79; vis. W. Harold and Martha Welch Prof. Am. Studies U. Notre Dame, 1987-88; journalist nat. elections Newsday, 1972; writer in residence The Washington Star, 1976, syndicated columnist, 1976-80, 84—; resident scholar in religion and public policy Am. Enterprise Inst., Washington, 1978—, George Frederick Jewett chair pub. policy research, 1983—; dir. social and polit. studies U. Notre Dame, Ind., 1987—, chmn. working seminar on family and Am. welfare policy, 1986-87; assoc. editor Commonweal mag., 1966-69; contbg. editor Christian Century, 1967-80, Christianity and Crisis, 1968-76, Jour. Ecumenical Studies, 1967—, This World, 1982—, Catholicism in Crisis, 1982—; religion editor Nat. Rev., 1979-86 ; judge Nat. Book awards, 1971, DuPont Broadcast Journalism awards, 1971-80; speechwriter nat. polit. campaigns, 1970, 72; mem. Bd. Internat. Broadcasting, 1983—; mem. Presdl. Task Force Project Econ. Justice, 1985-87, Council Scholars Library of Congress, 1986—; mem. monitoring panel UNESCO, 1984; vice chmn. Lay Commn. Cath. Social Teaching and U.S. Economy, 1984-86; U.S. Ambassador to Experts Meeting on Human Contacts of the Conf. On Security and Cooperation in Europe, Bern, Switzerland, 1986. Author: novel The Tiber was Silver, 1961, A New Generation, 1964, The Experience of Marriage, 1964, The Open Church, 1964, Belief and Unbelief, 1965, A Time to Build, 1967, A Theology for Radical Politics, 1969, American Philosophy and the Future, 1968, Story in Politics, 1970, (with Brown and Herschel) Vietnam: Crisis of Conscience, 1967; Politics: Realism & Imagination, 1971, Ascent of the Mountain, Flight of the Dove, 1971, A Book of Elements, 1972, All the Catholic People, 1971, Naked I Leave, 1970, The Experience of Nothingness, 1970, The Rise of the Unmeltable Ethnics, 1972, Choosing Our King, 1974, The Joy of Sports, 1976, The Guns of Lattimer, 1978, The American Vision, 1978, Rethinking Human Rights I and II, 1981, 82, The Spirit of Democratic Capitalism, 1982, Confession of a Catholic, 1983, Moral Clarity in the Nuclear Age, 1983, Freedom with Justice, 1984, Human Rights and the New Realism, 1986, Will It Liberate? Questions About Liberation Theology, 1986, Character and Crime, 1986, The New Consensus on Family and Welfare, 1987, Taking Glasnost Seriously: Toward an Open Soviet Union, 1988; numerous others articles and books transl. into all maj. langs. Kent fellow, 1961—; fellow Hastings Inst., 1970-76; named Most Influential Prof. Sr. Class Stanford U., 1967, 68; Man of Yr. Johnstown, Pa., 1978; recipient Faith and Freedom award Religious Heritage Am., 1978, Medal of Freedom, 1981; named Friend of Freedom, 1981; Newman Alumni award CCNY, 1984; George Washington Honor medal, 1984; award of Excellence, Religion in Media, 8th annual Angel Awards, 1985, Ellis Island Medal Honor, 1986, diploma as vis. prof. U. Francisco Marroquin, 1985; named acad. corr. mem. from U.S., Argentina Nat. Acad. Scis., Morals & Politics, 1985, K.M.G., Sovereign Mil. Order of Malta, 1987, others. Mem. Soc. Religion in Higher Edn. (central com. 1970-73), Am. Acad. Religion (program dir. 1968-72), Council Fgn. Relations, Council Religion and Internat. Affairs., Soc. Christian Ethics, Inst. Religion and Democracy (dir. 1981—), Nat. Ctr. Urban and Ethnic Affairs (dir. 1982—). Office: Am Enterprise Inst 1150 17th St Washington DC 20036

NOVAK, STEVEN PAUL, business director; b. Warwick, Eng., Aug. 19, 1957; s. Anthony Stanislav and Sandra Euphemia (Edwards) N.; m. Marion McCaffrey, Aug. 18, 1979 (separated); children: Iain Stanislav, Alan Steven. Cert. in Computer Studies, Mid-Kent U., 1982. Sr. tech. rep. Survey & Gen. Instrument Co., Kent, Eng., 1982-85; sales mgr. Integrated Vision Systems, Peterborough, Eng., 1985-87; dir. Bus. Devel., Peterborough, Eng., 1987—. Served as surveyor Royal Engrs., 1975-82. Mem. Mensa. Conservative. Mem. Anglican. Ch. Office: Bus Devel, PO Box 92, Peterborough PE4 5DZ, England

NOVÁK, VILÉM, mathematician; b. Bruntál, Czechoslovakia, June 21, 1951; s. Vilém and Nina (Krasilová) N.; m. Eliška Dokonalová, June 21, 1975 (div. 1987); children: David, Martin. MSc, Mining U., Ostrava, Czechoslovakia, 1975, Charles U., Prague, Czechoslovakia, 1982; PhD, Charles U., Prague, Czechoslovakia, 1988. Advance designer Automation of Mgmt., Ostrava, 1975-84; researcher Mining Inst., Czechoslovakia Acad. Scis., Ostrava, 1984—; educator Mining U., 1978-80. Author: Fuzzy Sets and Their Applications, 1986, rev. edit., 1988 (Czechslovakian Literal Fund award 1987); contbr. 40 articles to profl. articles. Mem. Soc. Czechoslovak Mathematicians and Physicists. Office: Czech Acad Scis Mining Inst, Studentska 1768, 70800 Ostrava 4 Czechoslovakia

NOVÁK, VLADIMÍR JAN AMOS, biologist, health science facility administrator; b. Praha, Bohemia, Czechoslovakia, Apr. 22, 1919; s. Vladimír Jan Novák and Olga (Eisenkholová) Nováková; m. Miloslava Dvořáková, Apr. 9, 1945; children: Ivan, Vladimír. Doctor rerum naturalium, Charles U., Prague, 1946; PhD, Czechoslovak Acad. Sci., Prague, 1956; DSc, Czechoslovakia Acad. Sci., Prague, 1968. Asst. prof. sci. faculty Charles U., 1946-53, prof. philosophy, 1970—; researcher Inst. Biology Czechoslovak Acad. Sci., 1953-60, researcher Inst. Entomology, 1961-75, corr. mem., 1972—, researcher Inst. Microbiology, 1975-84; dir. Labor Evolution Biology, Prague, 1985—; prof. sci. faculty U. J.E. Purkyne, Brno, Czechoslovakia, 1970—; lectr., mem. cen. com. Czechoslovak Socialist Acad., Prague, 1973—. Author: Principle of Sociogenesis, 1982, Insect Hormones, 1975, Principle of Reflection, 1985; editor proceedings Symposia Evolutionary Biology, 8 vols., 1975—. Recipient Czechoslovak Govt. prize, 1968. Mem. Internat. Soc. for Study Origin of Life, Internat. Congresses for Systematic and Evolutionary Biology, Internat. Endocrinology Soc., Czechoslovak Biol. Soc., Czechoslovak Zool. Soc., Czechoslovak Entomol. Soc., Czechoslovak Med. Soc., Czechoslovak Philos. Soc. Home: Rejskova 2, 120 00 Prague 2, Bohemia Czechoslovakia

NOVAKOVIČ, BILJANA, physician, researcher; b. Banoviči, Yugoslavia, Jan. 13, 1961; parents Mirko and Nadežda (Koncul) N. MD, U. Med. Sch., Zagreb, Yugoslavia, 1983, MS, 1986. Pediatric resident Case Western U., 1986—. Contbr. articles to med. jours. Research fellow Sch. Pub. Health, A. Stamapr Med. Sch., Zagreb, 1984-85, Inst. for Mother and Child Health Care, 1986—. Office: Inst for Mother and Child Health, Klaiceva 16, Zagreb 41000, Yugoslavia

NOVER, NAOMI (GOLL NOVER), journalist, editor, author; b. Buffalo; d. B.B. and Rebecca (Shane) Goll; m. Barnet Nover. Student, U. Buffalo; BS, N.Y. State Tchrs. Coll.; MA, George Washington U., 1951. News, features, editorial asst. Buffalo Times; tchr. pub., pvt. schs. Buffalo Park Sch. (demonstration sch. of U. Buffalo), Snyder, N.Y.; music critic Denver Post at Goethe Music Festival, Aspen, Colo.; news corr., columnist Washington Bur. Denver Post; editor, bur. chief Nover News Bur., Washington, 1972—; Corr. on mission to Europe Portland Oregonian, Italian Peace Treaty Conf., Luxembourg; attended various econ. summits; White House corr. Pres. Ford European tour, 1975, Pres. Ford trip to China and trips to South Korea, Indonesia, Japan, Philippines, Hawaii, 1978, Pres. Carter trip to India, Saudi Arabia, Israel, Egypt, S.Am., Africa, Eng., Europe, Japan, etc., 1978, Pres. Reagan trips to Peoples Republic of China, Europe, Cen. Am., Caribbean, Iceland, Bali, Indonesia, Finland, Iceland, London, 1988. Writer, dir. plays produced in, Buffalo; participated radio and television plays; producer: nationally syndicated radio program Views and Interviews; author: nationally syndicated feature stories and column Washington Dateline, 1952—; Contbr. articles to mags. Formerly active ARC, U.S Treasury War Bonds; chmn. Kalorama area Community Chest, 1947-49; originator embassy participation groups, jr. hostess, chmn., originator embassy tour Goodwill Industries; past chmn., producer program with 1,000 Girl Scouts at Pan Am. Union; past mem. council Girl Scouts U.S.A.; chmn. program com. Columbian Women of George Washington U., 1953-56; nat. chmn. War Nurses Meml.; mem. women's bd. George Washington U. Hosp. Recipient award pin U.S. Treasury Dept.; Silver Eagle award Girl Scouts U.S.A.; chosen to christen ship SS Syosset for vol. and charity activities. Mem. White House Corrs. Assn., State Dept. Corrs. Assn., Congl. Press Galleries Corrs. Assn. U.S. Capitol, AAUW, U.S. Capitol Hist. Soc., U.S. Supreme Ct. Hist. Soc., Nat. League Am. Pen Women, Smithsonian Assocs., U.S. Archives, Phi Beta Kappa Assocs., Women in Arts Mus., Am. Hist. Assn., Sigma Delta Chi, Welcome to Washington, Ikebana, Pi Lambda Theta (past corr. ofcl. publ., nat. scholastic honors). Clubs: National Press (Washington), Washington Press (Washington), Am. News. Women's (Washington), Overseas Writers (Washington); Wychmere Harbor (Chatham, Mass.). Office: Nat Press Bldg Washington DC 20045

NOVER, NAOMI (GOLL), journalist, editor, author; b. Buffalo; d. B. B. and Rebecca (Shane) Goll; student U. Buffalo; B.S., N.Y. State Tchrs. Coll.; M.A., George Washington U., 1951; m. Barnet Nover. News, features, editorial asst. Buffalo Times; tchr. public, pvt. schs. Buffalo Park Sch. of U. Buffalo, Snyder, N.Y.; music critic Denver Post at Goethe Music Festival, Aspen, Colo., 1949; news corr., columnist Washington bur. Denver Post, 1952-72; editor, bur. chief Nover News Bur., Washington, 1972—; corr. on mission to Europe, Conf. at Luxembourg Palace, Paris, Portland Oregonian; White House corr. Pres. Ford European tour and Helsinki Summit Conf., 1975, Pres. Ford China and trip to Indonesia, Japan, Philippines, Hawaii, 1975, Pres. Carter and Reagan tours to Europe, Middle East, India, Japan, Korea, Alaska, Africa, S. Am., numerous others, also summit confs.; writer, dir. plays produced in Buffalo; participated radio and TV plays; producer nationally syndicated radio program Views and Interviews; author nationally syndicated illustrated feature stories and column Washington Dateline, 1952—. Formerly active ARC, U.S. Treasury War Bonds; past chmn. Kalorama area Community Chest, originator embassy participation groups, jr. hostess, chmn., originator embassy tour Goodwill Industries; past chmn., producer program with 1,000 Girl Scouts at Pan Am. Union; past mem. council Girl Scouts U.S.A.; chmn. program com. Columbian Women for scholarship awards of George Washington U., 1953-56; nat. chmn. War Nurses Meml. Com. Mem. women's bd. George Washington U. Hosp. Recipient award pin U.S. Treasury Dept.; Silver Eagle award Girl Scouts U.S.A. Mem. White House Corrs. Assn., State Dept. Corrs. Assn., Congl. Press Galleries Corrs. Assn., U.S. Supreme Ct. Hist. Soc., U.S. Capitol Hist. Soc., U.S. Archives, Smithsonian Assos., Colo. State Soc., Mass. State Soc., AAUW, Nat. League Am. Pen Women, Phi Beta Kappa (asso.), Sigma Delta Chi, Welcome to Washington, Ikebana, Pi Lambda Theta (past corr. ofcl. publ.). Clubs: Nat. Press, Washington Press, Am. News Women's, Overseas Writers, Am. Fgn. Service (Washington); Wychmere Harbor (Chatham, Mass.). Past asso. editor, contbr. Tchrs. Mag.; contbr. articles to mags. Office: Nat Press Bldg Washington DC 20045

NOVEY, HAROLD SIDNEY, physician, educator; b. Balt., Sept. 20, 1926; s. Allen and Ree (Snyder) N.; m. Lindsay Mercedes Chance, A.B., Johns Hopkins U., 1946; M.D., U. So. Calif., 1951. Diplomate Am. Bd. Internal Medicine, Am. Bd. Allergy and Immunology. Resident, U.S. VA Hosp., Long Beach, Calif., 1951-52, acting chief allergy, 1957-58; resident U.S. VA Hosp., Los Angeles, 1952-53; fellow Mass. Gen. Hosp., Boston, 1955-56; clin. instr. UCLA, 1958-65, asst. clin. prof., 1965-71; chief allergy U. Calif.-Irvine, 1971-82, assoc. clin. prof., 1972-80, prof. medicine, 1980—. Contbr. articles to med. jours. Served as 1st lt. M.C., USAF, 1953-55. Fellow ACP, Am. Acad. Allergy; mem. Western Soc. Allergy-Immunology (bd. dirs. 1983—), Calif. Soc. Allergy (pres. 1972), Los Angeles Soc. Allergy (pres. 1967), Orange County Allergy Immunology (pres. 1980), We. Soc. Allergy-Immunology (pres. 1988—). Office: Dept of Medicine U Calif-Irvine 101 City Dr S Orange CA 92668

NOVICK, SHELDON M., author, lawyer; b. N.Y.C., June 19, 1941; s. Irving and Ruth (Rosenblatt) N.; m. Carolyn M. Clinton; children: Melia Bensussen, Michael Clinton. B.A., Antioch Coll., 1963; J.D., Washington U. Sch. Law, 1977. Adminstr. Center for Biology of Natural Systems, Washington U., St. Louis, 1966-69; assoc. editor Environment mag., St. Louis, 1964-69; editor Environment mag., 1969-77, pub., 1972-74; assoc. firm Milgrim Thomajan Jacobs & Lee, N.Y.C., 1977-78; regional counsel U.S. EPA, Phila., 1978-86; scholar in residence Vt. Law Sch., 1987—; dir. RMB, Inc. Author: The Careless Atom, 1969, The Electric War, 1976, Law of Environ. Protection, 1987; editor: (with Dorothy Cottrell) Our World in Peril, 1971. Home: South Strafford VT 05070

NOVINS, ALAN SLATER, lawyer; b. Rochester, N.H., Oct. 23, 1937; s. Murray H. and Celia D. (Raphael) N. A.B., Harvard U., 1961; J.D., Columbia U., 1964. Bar: N.H. 1964, D.C. 1970. Legis. counsel to U.S. Senator Thomas J. McIntyre, 1964-70; asst. counsel U.S. Senate Com. on Banking, Housing and Urban Affairs, Washington, 1971; ptnr. Lobel, Novins, Lamont & Flug, (formerly Lobel, Novins & Lamont) Washington, 1972—. Chmn. hearing com. 6 D.C. Bd. on Profl. Responsibility, 1982-88 . Mem. ABA, Fed. Bar Assn., N.H. Bar Assn., D.C. Bar Assn., D.C. Bar (chmn. com. on specialization 1975-76). Office: 1275 K St NW Suite 770 Washington DC 20005

NOVINSKY, ANITA WAINGORT, college educator; b. Stachov, Poland, Nov. 22, 1932; d. Samuel and Gitla (Buchwald) Waingort; m. Mauricio Novinsky, Oct. 12, 1952; children: Sonia, Ilana. BA, U. Saõ Paulo, 1956, PhD, 1970. Prof. U. Saõ Paulo, Brazil, 1977—; bd. dirs. Ctr. for Jewish Studies U. Saõ Paulo. Author: Cristaõs Novos Na Bahia, 1970, A Inquisicão, 1985, Inventarios de Bens Confiscados a Cristãos Novos no. Brasil, 1978. Named One of ten Women of Yr. Conselho Nacional das Mulherer do Brasil, 1970; research fellow John Carter Brown U. Library, R.I., 1987-88. Mem. Inst. Hist. e Geog. de Saõ Paulo. Jewish. Home: Rua Esco'cia 217, 01450 Sao Paulo Brazil Office: Univ Sao Paulo, Caixa Postal 8105, 05508 Sao Paulo Brazil

NOVITZ, CHARLOTTE, artist; b. Chgo., Feb. 13, 1938; d. Meyer and Dinah Yvonne (Weisman) N. Student, Sch. Art Inst. of Chgo., 1957-58, Ind. U., 1955-56, U. Ill., 1956-57, Bklyn. Mus. Sch., 1959. One-man shows include Bodley Gallery, N.Y.C., 1978, Librarie de Seine, Paris, 1981, Anziche, Florence, Italy, 1984, Marymount Manhattan Coll., N.Y.C., 1986, Syndicat d'Initiatives, Carces, France, 1988; exhibited in group shows at Davis Galleries, N.Y.C., 1963-65, Graham Gallery, N.Y.C., 1977, Galerie Horizon, Paris, 1979-80, Galerie Breheret, Paris, 1982-86; two-man show Centre d'Acceuil Socioculterel, Montfort sur Argens, France, 1986; author: Circle, 1972, A History of Dragons, 1973. Named Finalist Prix de Rome, 1965; recipient Second prize Oskar Kokoschka, 1959, First prize Oskar Kokoschka City of Salzburg, 1961. Home: Maurrefrey, 83570 Montfort-sur-Argens France

NOVOGROD, NANCY ELLEN, editor; b. N.Y.C., Jan. 30, 1949; d. Max and Hilda (Kirschbaum) Gerstein; m. John Campner Novogrod, Nov. 7, 1976; children—James Campner, Caroline Anne. A.B., Mt. Holyoke Coll., 1971. Reader The New Yorker, N.Y.C., 1973-76, sec. fiction dept., 1971-73; asst. editor Clarkson N. Potter, Inc., N.Y.C., 1977-78, assoc. editor, 1978-80, editor, 1980-83, sr. editor, 1984-86; exec. editor, 1987, editor House and Garden, N.Y.C., 1987-88, editor-and-chief, 1988—. Office: House and Garden 350 Madison Ave New York NY 10017

NOWACK, PETER PAUL GEORG, data communications/information systems company executive, consultant; b. Bautzen, Germany, Apr. 30, 1939; s. Alfred and Liesbeth (Fuegmann) N.; m. Helga Wagner, May 23, 1967; children—Stephan, Vanessa. B.S.E.E., Tech. Coll., Munich, 1960; postgrad. U. Minn., 1961-62. Systems analyst, cons. Control Data Europe, Frankfurt, West Germany, The Hague, Netherlands, Geneva, 1962-67; cons. Diebold Europe S.A., Frankfurt, 1967; mktg. mgr. Intercontinental Systems, Inc., Wiesbaden, W. Ger., 1967-69; mktg. and ops. mgr. Control Data GmbH, Frankfurt, 1969-80; mng. dir. O. D. Infosys GmbH, Wiesbaden, 1980-82; gen. mgr. Info. Systems Group Motorola GmbH, Darmstadt, W. Germany, GmbH., 1982-86, Dynatech GmbH, Friedrichsdorf, W.Ger., 1986—. Mem. Deutsche Telecom e.V. Office: Dynatech GmbH, 22 Max-Planck-Strasse, D-6382 Friedrichsdorf Federal Republic of Germany

NOWAK, EWA MARIA, biochemist, educator; b. Warsaw, Poland, May 6, 1941; d. Josef and Stefania (Jozwiak) N.; m. Mariusz Jerzy Olszewski, July 24, 1965. MS, U. Warsaw, 1964; PhD, Polish Acad. Scis., 1973. Jr. sci. worker Nencki Inst. Exptl. Biology, Warsaw, 1964-67, sr. sci. worker, 1967-73, asst. prof. biochemistry, 1973—; postdoctoral fellow Max Planck Inst. for Med. Research, Heidelberg, Fed. Republic of Germany, 1974-76, fellow, 1979, 81, 84-86; fellow Inst. Biophysics, Pushchino, USSR, 1972, 74; sec. Cen. Research Program on Biology, Warsaw, 1986—. Recipient awards Polish Acad. Scis., 1970, 74, 77, 83; grantee A.V. Humboldt Found., 1974, Max Planck Soc., 1979. Mem. Polish Soc. Biochemistry. Roman Catholic. Office: Nencki Inst Exptl Biology, 3 Pasteur St, 02 093 Warsaw Poland

NOWAK-KIELBIKOWA, MARIA JANINA, historian educator; b. Katowice, Silesia, Poland, Dec. 25, 1930; d. Wojciech Adalbert and Sabina (Stepniewska) Nowak; m. Aleksander Waclaw Kielbik, Oct. 18, 1958. M in History, U. Warsaw, Poland, 1955, D in History, 1968; D habilit. in History, U. Warsaw, 1987. Asst. U. Warsaw, 1953-64; tchr. Econ. Sch. for Adults, Warsaw, 1964-70; researcher Polish Acad. Scis., Warsaw, 1970—. Author: Poland-Great Britain from 1918-1923, 1975, (with others) Rebirth of Polish Second Republic, Selected Documents, 1981, 1984. Mem. Polish Hist. Soc. Roman Catholic. Home: Leszczynska 10 flat 32, 00-339 Warsaw Mazovia Poland Office: Polish Acad Scis, Rynek Starego Miasta 29/31, 00-272 Warsaw Poland

NOWORYTA, EUGENIUSZ, Polish diplomat; b. Krakow, Poland, Dec. 25, 1935; s. Marian Jozef and Anna (Korzeniak) N.; m. Alicja Zalewska, Dec. 21, 1957; 1 child, Agnieszka. M.A., Central Sch. Fgn. Service, Warsaw, Poland, 1958; M.A. in Law, U. Warsaw, 1961; Ph.D. in Polit. Sci., 1976. With Ministry of Fgn. Affairs, Warsaw, from 1958; including head dept. policy planning, 1973-77, Western Europe, 1981-85. ambassador, permanent rep. to UN, N.Y.C., 1985—; ambassador to Chile, 1971-73; ambassador to Spain, 1977-81. Author: The Chilean Experiences, 1977. Contbr. articles to profl. jours. Mem. Polish United Workers' Party, Warsaw, 1961—; organizer Polish Socialist Youth's Union, Warsaw, 1956-57. Decorated Cross of Merit. Avocations: skiing; reading. Office: Perm Mission of Poland to UN 9 East 66th St New York NY 10021

NOXON, MARGARET WALTERS, community volunteer; b. Detroit, Dec. 16, 1903; d. George Alexander and Ethelwyn (Taylor) Walters; grad., Liggett Sch. for Girls, Det., 1922; life teaching certificate Wayne State U., 1925; student Columbia Tchrs. Coll., 1939-40; m. Herbert Richards Noxon, July 15, 1926 (dec. Aug. 4, 1971). Bd. dirs. Coll. Club, Detroit, 1925-30; mem. Salvation Army Aux., Detroit, 1926—; mem. Coll. Club, Summit N.J., 1941—; historian D.A.R., N.Y.C., 1943-46, vice regent, 1946-49; dir. New Eng., Women, 1961-64; dir. Woodycrest-Five Points Child Care, 1961-77; bd. dirs. ARC, Summit, N.J., service com. chmn. uniforms and insignias, 1943-45; v.p. N.Y. Infirmary Aux., N.Y.C., 1948-58, bd. dirs., 1959-80. Recipient award for meritorious personal service ARC, 1945. Mem. Nat. Inst. Social Scis., Grand Jury Assn. N.Y. County, D.A.R. (dir. 1950-70), St. David's Soc. State N.Y., English-Speaking Union, Daus. Am. Colonists, AAUW, Southampton Colonial Soc., Nat. Woman's Farm and Garden Assn. (dir. met. br. 1975—, dir. N.Y. State div. 1978-80, mem. nat. council 1978-80), Ch. Women's League for Patriotic Service, Women's Bible Soc. N.Y., Alpha Sigma Tau. Republican. Presbyterian. Clubs: Southampton (N.Y.) Bath and Tennis, City Gardens (dir. 1963-68, mem. adv. com. 1968-74, dir. 1974-80, adv. bd. 1980-83), York (bd. govs. 1965-66, 73-77), Barnard (trustee 1979-81), Sorosis (v.p. 1979-81), Regency (N.Y.C.). Home: 1100 Madison Ave Apt 10C Box 86 New York NY 10028

NOYES, RICHARD FRANCIS, optometrist; b. Des Moines, May 8, 1952; s. Robert F. and Mary C. N.; children—Jennifer, Bethany. BS in Gen. Sci., U. Iowa, 1975; BS in Visual Sci., Ill. Coll. Optometry, 1976, O.D., 1978. Practice optometry specializing in Ocular Disease Diagnosis and Mgmt., Marion, Iowa, 1978—; lectr. in ocular disease, advanced diagnostic and treatment techniques and practice mgmt. Named one of Outstanding Young Men in Am., 1984, Outstanding Young Optometrist State Iowa, 1985. Dir. Haiti Med. Mission, 1978—. Fellow Am. Coll. Optometric Physicians; mem. Iowa Optometric Assn. (legis. com. 1984, bd. dirs. 1985—, sec.-treas. 1987-88, v.p. 1988—), Am. Optometric Assn., Jaycees, Beta Sigma Kappa. Republican. Lutheran. Lodge: Lions (bd. dirs. 1979—, Disting. Service award 1983, A. Melvin Jones fellow 1988), Sertoma (Outstanding Service to Mankind award 1987). Home: 1640 25th Ave Marion IA 52302 Office: 1065 East Post Rd Marion IA 52302

NOYES, ROBERT EDWIN, publisher, writer; b. N.Y.C., June 22, 1925; s. Clarence A. and Edith (LaDomus) N.; m. Janet Brown, Mar. 24, 1952 (div. June 1963); children—Keith, Steven, Mark, Geoffrey; m. Mariel Jones, July 24, 1964; children—Rebecca, Robert. B.S. in Chem. Engring, Northwestern U., 1945. Chem. engr. Am. Cyanamid Co., Pearl River, N.Y., 1947; sales exec. Titanium Pigment Corp., N.Y.C., 1948-55; market research mgr. U.S. Indsl. Chem. Co., N.Y.C., 1956-58; sales mgr. atomic energy Curtiss Wright Export, N.Y.C., 1958-60; founder, pres., chmn. bd. Noyes Data Corp., Park Ridge, N.J., 1960—; pub. Noyes Press, Noyes Publs., Park Ridge, 1961—. Author numerous books in fields of internat. fin., devel., tech. Served to lt. (j.g.) USNR, 1945-47. Mem. Am. Chem. Soc., Am. Inst. Chem. Engrs., Archaeol. Inst. Am. Episcopalian. Clubs: N.Y. Yacht, Chemists (N.Y.); Chatham Yacht (Mass.). Home: 224 W Saddle River Rd Saddle River NJ 07458 Office: Noyes Bldg Park Ridge NJ 07656

NOZAKI, MASAHIKO, thoracic surgeon; b. London, Aug. 19, 1927; s. Masami and Kimi (Hamada) N.; m. Kayoko Watanabe, Mar. 21, 1959; children—Kiyoko, Haruyuki, Toyoko. M.D., Keio U., 1952, Ph.D., 1960; postdoctorate UCLA Med. Ctr., 1964. Mem. staff Nat. Sanatorim Muramatsu-Seiranso, 1953-67, 69-72; advanced research fellow Los Angeles County Heart Assn., 1967-69; head dept. pulmonary and thoracic surgery Hoshigaoka Kosei-Nenkin Hosp., Osaka, 1973-85; vice med. dir. Johoku Hosp., 1986—; vis. prof. Kobe U. Med. Sch., 1974-78. Fellow Am. Coll. Cardiology, Am. Coll. Chest Physicians; mem. Japanese Assn. Thoracic Surgery (council), Japanese Med. Soc. Biol. Interface (trustee). Home: 2872-35 Senbacho, Mito Ibaraki 310, Japan Office: 1395 Ishizuka, Johoku Ibaraki 311-43, Japan

NOZAKI, MASAKO, pharmacologist; b. Eniwa, Hokkaido, Japan, Mar. 24, 1941; came to U.S., 1974; s. Kennosuke and Sumi Nozaki; Ph.D., Hirosaki U. Med. Coll., 1976. Vis. asso. Nat. Inst. on Drug Abuse Addiction Research Center, Lexington, Ky., 1974-77; research asso. dept. pharmacology Cornell U. Med. Coll., N.Y.C., 1977-78; vis. asst. prof. dept. pharmacology U. Ky. Coll. Medicine, Lexington, 1978-79, med. research scientist, 1979-80; asst. prof. dept. pharmacology Sch. Dentistry, Hokkaido U., Sapporo, Japan, 1980—. Mem. AAAS, Internat. Platform Assn., Sigma Xi. Contbr. articles to profl. publs. Home: 4-1-17 Kitanosawa, Sapporo Minami-ku, Japan Office: Hokkaido U Sch Dentistry, Dept Pharmacology, Sapporo Japan

NSEKELA, RODGERS MONDAY, insurance executive; b. Tukuyu, Mbeya, Tanzania, Sept. 27, 1948; s. Ngonile Reuben Nsekela and Syabumi Mugogo; m. Fiddie Mwamwaya, Aug. 2, 1981; children: Lusekelo Reuben, Bumi. BA in econs. with honors, U. Dar-es-Salaam, Tanzania, 1979, diploma of edn., 1981; cert., Nat. Inst. Productivity, Dar-es-Salaam, May, 1981 and Aug., 1982, East African Mgmt. Inst., Arusha, Tanzania, Aug.-Sept., 1982 and Aug., 1986, Swiss Ins. Tng. Ctr., Switzerland, 1986. High sch. tchr. Ministry of Edn., Tanzania, 1971, 72; mgmt. trainee Nat. Ins. Corp., Dar-es-Salaam, 1972-76, research mgr., 1979-85; regional mgr. Nat. Ins. Corp., Iringa, Tanzania, 1985—; vice chmn. econs. U. Dar-es-Salaam, 1976-77. Home and Office: Nat Ins Corp, PO Box 666, Iringa Tanzania

NSUBUGA, EMMANUEL CARDINAL, archbishop of Kampala; b. Kisule, Uganda, Nov. 5, 1914. Ordained priest Roman Catholic Ch., 1946; consecrated bishop of Kampala, 1966; now archbishop of Kampala; elevated to Sacred Coll. of Cardinals, 1976; titular ch. St. Maria Nuova; mem. Congregation of Evangelization of Peoples. Address: PO Box 14125, Mengo, Kampala Uganda *

NUCCITELLI, SAUL ARNOLD, civil engineer, consultant; b. Yonkers, N.Y., Apr. 25, 1928; s. Agostino and Antoinette (D'Amicis) N.; m. Concetta Orlandi, Dec. 23, 1969; 1 child, Saul A. BS, NYU, 1949, MCE, 1954; DCE, MIT, 1960. Registered profl. engr., N.Y., Mo., Colo., Conn., Mass.; lic. land surveyor, Mo., Colo., Conn., Mass. Asst. civil engr. Westchester County Engrs., N.Y.C., 1949-51, 53-54; project engr. H.B. Bolas Enterprises, Denver, 1954-55; asst. prof., research engr., U. Denver, 1955-58; mem. staff MIT, 1958-60; asst. prof. engring. Cooper Union Coll., N.Y.C., 1960-62; pvt. practice cons. engring., Springfield, Mo., 1962—; organizer Met. Nat. Bank, Springfield; adviser, dir. Farm & Home Savs. and Loan Assn. Contbr. articles to profl. jours. Chmn. Adv. Council on Mo. Pub. Drinking Water; bd. dirs. Community Found. Greene County, Mus. of Ozarks; past chmn. Bd. City Utilities, Springfield; past pres. Downtown Springfield Assn. Served with U.S. Army, 1951-53. Recipient Cert. of Appreciation, Mo. Mcpl. League, 1981; named Mo. Cons. Engr. of Yr., 1973. Fellow ASCE; mem. Nat. Soc. Profl. Engrs., Mo. Soc. Profl. Engrs. (past pres. Ozark chpt.), Boston Soc. Civil Engrs., Am. Concrete Inst., Am. Inst. Steel Constrn., Am. Welding Soc., ASTM, Am. Soc. Mil. Engrs., Springfield C. of C. (past v.p.). Home: 2919 Brentmoor Ave Springfield MO 65804 Office: 122 Park Central Sq Springfield MO 65806

NUJOMA, SAM DANIEL, executive political party; b. Ongandjera, Namibian, May 12, 1929; s. Utoni Daniel and Mpingana (Kondomboro) N. married; 11 children. LLD, Ahmadu Bello U., Zaria, Nigeria, 1982, Roma U., Maseru, Lesotho, 1983. Pres. SWAPO of Namibia, Windhoek, 1960—. Recipient Ho Chi Minh award World Peace Council, 1986, Master Degree Order of Brasilia Fed. Dist. Gov. Brasilia, 1987; named citizen of Silvester mayor, Calif.,1965. Office: SWAPO Hdqrs, PO Box 2603, Dar es Salam Tanzania

NULL, DOUGLAS PETER, lawyer; b. N.Y.C., Nov. 11, 1926; s. William H. and Florence (Ostrow) N.; m. Marcia Tabor, Jan. 27, 1985; children: Lisa A. Holdeman, William S., Michael C. BS, Harvard U., 1945; JD, NYU, 1949, LLM, 1954. Bar: N.Y. 1950, U.S. Supreme Ct. 1963. Assoc. Poletti, Diamond, Roosevelt, Freidin & McKay, N.Y.C., 1949-50; asst. dist. atty. N.Y. County, N.Y., 1950-54; ptnr. Levy, Gutman, Goldberg & Null, N.Y.C., 1956-61; assoc. counsel CIT Fin. Corp., N.Y.C., 1954-56; sr. dep. county atty. Nassau County, N.Y., 1961-62; sr. ptnr. Null & Null, Garden City, N.Y., 1962-82; v.p. adminstrn., gen. counsel, bd. dirs. Kleartone, Inc., Westbury, N.Y., 1982—. Chmn. Great Neck Zone Dem. Party, 1960-67; bd. dirs. United Jewish Y's of L.I., 1983—; chmn. cultural Arts Com., 1983-86, v.p., 1986—. Served to lt. USNR, 1944-46. Mem. ABA, N.Y. State Bar Assn., Nassau Bar Assn., N.Y. State Trial Lawyers Assn., N.Y. Dist. Attys. Assn. Club: NYU (N.Y.C.). Office: 695 Summa Ave Westbury NY 11590

NUMAN, YASIN SAID, chairman council of ministers, People's Democratic Republic of Yemen; b. 1948. Minister of Fish Resources, 1982-86, dep. prime minister, 1985-86, prime minister People's Democratic Republic of Yemen, 1986—. Address: Office of Chmn, Council of Ministers, Aden People's Democratic Republic of Yemen *

NUMMELA, ERIC CARL, mathematics educator; b. Bemidji, Minn., July 30, 1941; arrived in Eng., 1984; s. Eric Urho and Borghild Olga (Opsahl) N.; m. Pamela Matilda Tatnall, Oct. 9, 1976; children: Jeremiah Arvid, Elizabeth Anne, Samuel Uno. BA in Math., U. Nev., 1964, MS in Math., 1966; PhD in Math., Tulane U., 1970. Postdoctoral fellow U. Fla., 1970-71, asst. prof., 1971-77; asst. prof. St. Cloud (Minn.) State U., 1977-79; from assoc. prof. to prof. math. New Eng. Coll., Henniker, N.H., 1979-88; vis. prof. math. and stats. St. Cloud (Minn.) State U., 1988—; bd. dirs. Brit. Campus Near Eng. Coll., Arundel, 1984-88. Author: (with Hofmann and Mostert) Cohomology Theories for Compact Abelian Groups; contbr. articles to profl. jours. Mem. Am. Math Soc., Math. Assn. Am. (chmn. northeastern sect. 1983-84), Soc. Indsl. and Applied Math., London Mat. Soc. Liberal. Lutheran. Office: New Eng Coll, British Campus, Arundel, West Sussex BN18 0DA, England

NUNES, MANUEL JACINTO, economics educator; b. Lisbon, Portugal, Jan. 27, 1926; s. Jose and Lourenca (Conceicao) N.; m. Lutgarda S.R. Rodrigues, Jan. 14, 1950; 1 child, Maria Manuela R. B.A., U. Lisbon, 1948, M.A., 1950, Ph.D., 1957. Sec. of treasure Govt. of Portugal, Lisbon, 1955-59; dep. gov. Bank of Portugal, 1960-75, gov., 1980-85; assoc. prof. econs. U. Lisbon, 1961-63, prof., 1963—; chmn. Nat. Saving Bank, 1976-80, minister of fin., dep. prime minister, 1978-79, econ. adviser, 1985—. Author: Structure of Portuguese Economy, 1954; National Income and the Balance Budget, 1963; Development and Planning, 1970. Mem. Forum of Mgr., Portuguese Assn. Economists. Roman Catholic. Avocation: swimming. Home: S Francisco De Sales, 17-A-10 Esq, 1200 Lisbon Portugal Office: Caixa Geral De Depositos, R St Catarina 1, 1200 Lisbon Portugal also: Acad Das Ciencias De Lisboa, 1000 Lisbon Portugal

NUÑEZ, ESTUARDO, literature educator; b. Lima, Peru, Sept. 5, 1908; Widowed, 1980; children: Osvaldo, Javier, Rosario; m. Carlota Carvallo. Student, Colegio Aleman de Lima; D in Lit., U. San Marcos, Lima, 1931. Prof. U. San Marcos, prof. emeritus, 1980—; vis. prof. SUNY, Buffalo, 1968; dir. Nat. Biblioteca Peru, 1969-73; dir. Acad Peruana de la Lengua. Author 50 books on Peruvian and S.Am. Lit. Home: Las Mimosas 155 Barranco, Lima 4 Peru

NUNEZ-PORTUONDO, RICARDO, investment company executive; b. N.Y.C., June 9, 1933; s. Emilio and Maria (Garcia) N-P.; m. Dolores Maldonado, Sept. 7, 1963; children—Ricardo Jose, Emilio Manuel, Eduardo Javier. LL.D., U. Havana, Cuba; postdoctoral in law, U. Fla., 1975. Bar: Cuba, Fla. Editor Latin Am. div. USIA, Miami, Fla., 1961-71; editor Latin Am. div. USIA, Washington, 1961-71; nat. dir. Cuban Refugee Program, Washington, 1975-77; pres. Internat. Mktg. Realty, Miami, 1977—, Central Investment Trust, Coral Gables, Fla., 1977—; chmn. bd. Interstate Bank of Commerce, Miami, 1986—. Author: The Other Image of Cuba, 1965; A Critique on the Linowitz Report, 1975. dir. Nat. Hispanic Scholarship Fund, San Francisco, 1978—; dir. COSSMHO, Washington, 1980—; trustee emeritus Fla. Internat. U., 1984—; pres. Mercy Hosp. Found., Miami, 1985—; bd. dirs. ARC, Greater Miami. Recipient numerous awards for civic contbns. including day named in honor Ricardo Nunez Day, Miami, 1975. Mem. Cuban Lawyers Assn., Cuban Acad. History. Republican. Roman Catholic. Clubs: Metropolitan (N.Y.C.); Lyford Cay (Nassau); Ocean Reef (Key Largo); Key Biscayne Yacht, Big Five, 200 (Miami). Home: 675 Solano Prado Coral Gables FL 33156 Office: PO Box 520-954 Miami FL 33152

NUNN, LESLIE EDGAR, lawyer; b. Evansville, Ind., Oct. 10, 1941. BA, U. Evansville, 1964; JD, U. Denver, 1967. Bar: Colo. 1967, N.Mex. 1977. Lawyer, adminstr. Navajo Tribe of Indians, 1973-76; sole practice, Silverton and Cortez, Colo., 1977-78; ptnr. Nunn & Dunlap, Farmington, N.Mex., 1978-84; sole practice, Denver, 1984-87, Burlington, Colo., 1987—. Served with JAGC, USAF, 1967-73. Mem. ABA, Colo., N.Mex., S.W. Colo., San Juan County, Navajo Nation bar assns., World Peace Through Law Assn., World Assn. Lawyers (world chmn. law and agr. com.). Decorated Bronze Star. Contbr. articles to legal jours. Home: 5807 County Rd 47 Burlington CO 80807 Office: 415 14th St Burlington CO 80807

NUNN, SAM, U.S. senator; b. Perry, Ga., Sept. 8, 1938; s. Samuel Augustus and Elizabeth (Cannon) N.; m. Colleen O'Brien, Sept. 25, 1965; children: Michelle, Brian. Student, Ga. Tech. Coll., 1956-59; A.B., LL.B., Emory U., 1962. Bar: Ga. 1962. Legal counsel armed services com. U.S. Ho. Reps., 1963; mem. firm Nunn, Geiger & Rampey, Perry, Ga., 1964-73; mem. Ga. Ho. Reps., 1968-72; U.S. senator from Ga. 1973—; chmn. Armed Services Com.; mem. Govtl. Affairs Com., Small Bus. Com., Intelligence Com.; farmer Perry, from 1964. Named One of Five Outstanding Young Men in Ga., Ga. Jaycees, 1971; recipient Most Effective Legislator award Dist. Attys. Assn., 1972. Mem. Perry C. of C. (pres. 1964), Ga. Planning Assn. (dir. 1966, pres. 1971). Office: Office of the Senate Care of Postmaster Washington DC 20510

NUNN, THOMAS CALVIN, military officer; b. Stillwater, Okla., May 19, 1951; s. Thomas Calvin and Agnes Ruth (Zaletel) N.; m. Christine Marie DeMagistris, June 9, 1973; children: Thomas Calvin III, Mary Theresa, Emily Elizabeth. BS, U.S. Mil. Acad., 1973; MS in Engring., Rensselaer Poly. Inst., 1981. Commd. 2d. lt. U.S. Army, 1973, advanced through grades to maj.; co. commdr U.S. Army, Schofield Barracks, Hawaii, 1978-79; dep. chief propulsion system div. U.S. Army, Warren, Mich., 1981-82, aide-de-camp to commanding gen., 1982-83, weapon system mgr., 1983-84, dep. chief combat systems div., 1984-85; exec. officer CEBNW U.S. Army, Coevorden, The Netherlands, 1986—; adj. prof. Fla. Inst. Tech., Melbourne, Fla.; adj. lectr. U. Md.-U. Coll., Heidelberg, Fed. Republic Germany, 1986—. Mem. Soc. Automotive Engrs. Republican. Roman Catholic. Home: Roosje Vosstraat 2, 7749 RD Coevorden The Netherlands Office: HHD CEBNW APO New York NY 09292

NUNN, TREVOR ROBERT, director; b. Ipswich, Eng., Jan. 14, 1940; s. Robert Alexander and Dorothy May (Piper) N.; student Ipswich Coll., Downing Coll., Cambridge, Eng.; LLD, U. Warwick, 1982; MA (hon.), U. Newcastle-upon-Tyne, 1982. m. Janet Suzman, 1969 (div. 1985); 1 son; m. Sharon Lee Hill, 1986; 1 dau. Trainee dir. Belgrade Theatre, Coventry; asso. dir. Royal Shakespeare Co., Warwickshire, Eng., 1964-68, artistic dir., 1968—, joint artistic dir., 1978-86, also chief exec.; dir. plays including Tango, 1965, The Revenger's Tragedy, 1965, 69, The Taming of the Shrew, The Relapse, The Winter's Tale, 1969, Hamlet, 1970, Henry VIII, 1970, Roman Season: Antony and Cleopatra, Coriolanus, Julius Caesar, Titus Andronicus, 1970, Macbeth, 1974, 76, Hedda Gabler (own version) 1975, Romeo and Juliet, 1976, Comedy of Errors, 1976, The Alchemist, 1977, As You Like It, 1977, Every Good Boy Deserves Favour, 1977, Three Sisters, 1978, The Merry Wives of Windsor, 1979, Once in a Lifetime, 1979 (Evening Standard award best dir.), Juno and the Paycock, 1980, The Life and Adventures of Nicholas Nickleby, 1980 (Tony award 1981 for best dir., Evening Standard award best dir.), touring revival, 1985, Cats, 1981 (Tony award for best dir. 1982), All's Well That Ends Well, 1981, Henry IV (parts I and II), 1981, 82, Starlight Express, 1984, Les Miserables, 1985 (Tony award for best dir. 1987), Chess, 1986; (opera) Idomeneo, 1982, Porgy and Bess, The Fair Maid of the West; TV shows Include: Anthony and Cleopatra, 1975, Comedy of Errors, 1976, Every Good Boy Deserves Favour, 1978, Macbeth, 1978; writer, dir. Shakespeare Workshops Word of Mouth, 1979, The Three Sisters, 1982, Peter Pan (with John Caird), 1982; film: Hedda, Great Hamlets, 1983, Lady Jane, 1985. Recipient London Theatre Critics Best Dir. award, 1969; Soc. Film and TV Arts award, 1975, Ivor Novello award for best Brit. Musical, 1976; numerous others. Office: Homevale Ltd, 28/29 Southampton St, London WC2E 7JA, England

NUNO, JUAN ANTONIO, educator, writer; b. Madrid, Mar. 27, 1927; s. Guillermo and Julia (Montes) N.; m. Alicia Lopez, Dec. 22, 1953; children: Alicia, Ana. MA, Univ. Cen., Caracas, Venezuela, 1951, PhD, 1962. Prof. philosophy Univ. Cen., Caracas, Venezuela, 1960—, head dept., 1970-80. Author: La Dialectica Platonica, 1962, Logica Formal, 1975, Los MItos Filosoficos, 1985, La Filosofia de Borges, 1987. Mem. Inst. Internat. de Pholisophie. Home: PO Box 51-773, 1050A Caracas Venezuela

NUNOI, KEIJIRO, management consultant; b. Nagasaki, Japan, Mar. 21, 1930; s. Yasujiro and Raku Nunoi; divorced; children: Haruto, Keiko, Fred, Masako, Sumiko. Student, Fgn. Services Inst., 1959. Shipping clk. Jardine, Matheson and Co. Ltd., Kobe, Japan, 1954-58; consuler staff Am. Embassy, Tokyo, 1958-63; pres. Overseas Research Inst., Inc., Tokyo, 1964-77; owner Nunoi Adminstrv. Scrivners Office, Tokyo, 1977-83; pres. Nunoi Internat. Bus. Cons. Group, Inc., Tokyo, 1983—; cons. Small Bus. Corp., Japanese Govt., Tokyo, 1986—. Author: U.S. Immigration and Nationality Act, 1958. Chmn. bd. dirs. Nunoi Found., 1987—; regular mem. Am. C. of C. in Japan, 1988—. Recipient Dark Blue Ribbon medal Japanese Emperor, 1986. Mem. Am. Japan Soc., Internat. House of Japan, Tokyo Adminstrv. Scrivners Assn. (bd. dirs. 1978-80). Club: Izu Nirayama Country (Japan). Home: Keijiro Nunoi, Hyness Azabu Toriizaka 301, 5-11-38 Roppongi Minato-ku, Tokyo Japan Office: Nunoi Internat Office, Chiyoda Bldg, 2-9-4 Aakasaka Minato-ku, Tokyo Japan

NUREYEV, RUDOLF HAMETOVICH, ballet dancer, ballet company executive; b. USSR, 1938; defected 1961; Student ballet, Lenigrad (USSR) Ballet Sch.; hon. doctorate, Phila. Coll. Performing Arts., 1980. Dancer Kirov Ballet, Leningrad, 1955-61, soloist, 1958-61; dancer Ballet of Marquis de Cuevas, 1961; with Ruth Page and Chgo. Opera Ballet, 1962; artistic dir. Paris Opera Ballet, 1983—. London debut (with Margot Fonteyn and Royal Ballet) Giselle, 1962; Am. debut (with Maria Tallchief) on Bell Telephone Hour; has appeared as guest artist with 25 companies including Am. Ballet Theatre, Australian Ballet, Colón Theatre Ballet, Deutsche Opera Ballet, Berlin, Dutch Nat. Ballet, Nat. Ballet Can., Paris Opera Ballet, Royal Danish Ballet, others; choreographer: (ballets) Romeo and Juliet, La Bayadere, Raymonda, Swan Lake, Tancredi, Sleeping Beauty, Nutcracker, Don Quixote, Don Juan, Giselle, Manfred, The Tempest, (films) including Evening With Royal Ballet, 1963, Romeo and Juliet, 1966, I Am A Dancer, 1972, Don Quixote, 1972, Valentino, 1977, Exposed, 1983, Washington Square, Cinderella, 1986. Recipient Capezio Dance award, 1987. Address: Paris Opera Ballet, 8 Rue Scribe, 75009 Paris France also: care Gorlinsky Ltd, 35 Dover St, London W1 England *

NUTTALL, JACQUES JEAN, telecommunications engineer; b. Dinan, Britanny, France, Mar. 25, 1936; s. Henri Paul and Henriette (Mace) N.; m. Janet Anne Clarke, Dec. 14, 1974; children: Christophe Franççis Xavier, Benjamin. BEE, Ecole Superieure d'Electricité, Paris, 1959. Engr. Telecom Nat. Research Ctr., Paris, 1961-66; engr. Nuclear Research Ctr., Geneva, 1966-73; chief engr. Alcatel Cit, Lannion, Paris, 1973—. Contbr. several articles to profl. jours.; inventor telephone exchange tester and signaler. Served with French Mil., 1959-61. Roman Catholic. Office: Alcatel, Route de Perros, 22304 Lannion France

NUTZHORN, CARL ROBBINS, lawyer; b. Rockville Centre, N.Y., Sept. 13, 1927; s. Carl William and Lorena Waite (Robbins) N.; m. Marta RoseMarie Larsson, Feb. 1965 (div. 1966). BA cum laude, Princeton U., 1951; JD, Columbia U., 1955. Bar: N.Y. 1957, U.S. Dist. Ct. (so. and ea. dist.) N.Y. 1957, U.S. Supreme Ct. 1961, U.S. Ct. Appeals (2d cir.) 1962, U.S. Dist. Ct. (we. dist.) Okla. 1968, U.S. Dist. Ct. Colo. 1970, U.S. Ct. Appeals (10th cir.) 1971. Assoc. Carter, Ledyard & Milburn, N.Y.C., 1955-57; assoc. atty. to gen. counsel Am. Fore Loyalty Ins. Group, N.Y.C., 1959-60; assoc. Smith & Auslander, N.Y.C., 1960-61, Smith, Steibel & Alexander, N.Y.C., 1962-63; sole practice, Aspen, Colo., 1972-81; semi-retired, Ft. Lauderdale, Fla., 1983—; mem. U.S. Tenth Cir. Jud. Conf., 1973-81. Author: Wage-Price Spiral and the Presidential Tariff Power, 1958, Hydrogen-Oxygen Energy Systems, 1964, Constitutional Problems of Pardon for Presidential Crime, 1985. Mem. Pitikin County Bd. Adjustment, Aspen, 1972-80; auditor Summer Arms Control Workshops of Aspen Inst., 1976-82. Served with USMCR, 1945-46. Mem. Colo. Bar Assn., Am. Arbitration Assn. (panel of arbitrators), Phi Delta Phi. Democrat. Lutheran. Home: 1900 S Ocean Dr N #1101 Fort Lauderdale FL 33316

NWAKO, M. P. KWAKO, Botswana government official; b. Ngwata Dist., Botswana, 1923; student Tiger Kloof Secondary Sch. Treas., Bakwena and Bamangwato Tribal Administrn.; sec., treas. Moeng Coll., 1954-64; mem. African Adv. Council; dep. chmn. Wages Bd. of the BP Abbatoirs; mem. legislative assembly Govt. of Botswana, 1965, minister of agr., 1965-66, minister state, 1966-69, minister health, labour and home affairs, 1969-77, minister commerce and industry, 1977—. Office: Ministry Commerce and Industry, Gaborone Botswana *

NWAUKWA, KEN DOUGLAS CHINAZOM, journalist; b. Mbieri, Imostate, Nigeria, Nov. 19, 1946; s. Charles Awazieama and Janet (Ihugba) N.; m. Chinwendu Elizabeth, May 24, 1974; children: Ken Douglas Jr., Charles, Elizabeth. BS in Journalism, Loyola U., Paris, 1974, PhD in mass communications, 1976; DD, Sch. Ministry, Miami, Flda., 1982; Degreee in (Journalism), Reading Sch. Journalism, Eng. Cert. journalist Nigeria, Czechoslovakia. Reporter Daily Express, Lagos, Nigeria, 1970-73; correspondent AP, N.Y.C., 1974-76; freelance reporter various newspapers, 1976—; pres. Lillyshall Publicity, Mbieri, Imo State, Nigera; paster Ch. of Gospel Ministry. Author: Selected Reports of Ken Douglas; Editor: Dialing the Crime World, 1972, This Ministry I Want to Serve. Sec. gen. Internat. Helpless Children Soc., Lagos, Nigeria; registrar African Inst. Edn., Lagos; Publicity Sec.Amankuta-Mbieri Progressive Union, Nigeria. Recipient Sci. Journalism award, Verband du Journalism, 1973, Internat. Journalism award, Internat. Orgn. Journalists, 1983. Fellow Inst. Profl. Mgrs., Inst. Chartered Sales Mgmt. and Mktg.; mem. Nigerian Union Journalists, Nigeria Inst. Pub. Relations, Internat. Orgn. JOurnalists. Club: Ken Douglas Sports (Mbieri). Home: Umuamon Amankuta, Mbieri PO Box 75, Imo State Nigeria Office: Imo Community Concord Newspaper, 132 Wetheral Rd Owerri, Imo State Nigeria

NYABOYA, ISIDORE, civil engineer; b. Ntwaro, Burundi, Feb. 18, 1946; s. Damien Kayengeyenge and Cecile Baranzize; m. Julie Mukangara, Sept. 11, 1976; children: Nina, Donnel, Marcel, Vanessa. BCE, NYU, 1970, MS in Indsl. Engring., 1972. Various positions including mem. editorial bd. Natural Resources Forum publ. UN, N.Y.C., 1972-76; minister of public works, energy and mines Govt. of Burundi, Bujumbura, 1976—, M.P., 1982—. Mem. Uprona Party. Office: BP 745, Bujumbura Burundi

NYAGUMBO, MAURICE, government official; b. Rusape, Zimbabwe, Dec. 12, 1924; married; 5 children. Student, St. Faith's Mission, Zimbabwe, St. Augustine's, Penhalonga, Zimbabwe. Founder, sec. Cen. African Social Club, 1953; founder Youth League in Zimbabwe; sec. Rusape br. African Nat. Congress, 1957; organising sec. Zimbabwe African Nat. Union, 1962; then minister of mines, coop devel. Govt. of Zimbabwe, now sr. minister polit. affairs. Office: Office of the Pres, Ministry of Polit Affairs, Harare Zimbabwe *

NYALALI, FRANCIS LUCAS, jurist; b. Mwanza, Tanzania, Feb. 3, 1935; s. Lucas Makali and Salome (Sato) Madiya; m. Loyce Phares, Dec. 28, 1968; children—Emmanueli, Karoli, Victor, Lulu. B.A. with honors (London), Univ. Coll. of East Africa, Makerere, 1961. Mem. Lincoln's Inn, London, 1965. Bar: Tanzania. Resident magistrate Judiciary Dept., Tanzania, 1966-71, judge High Ct., 1974-77, chief justice, 1977—; chmn. labor tribunal, Labor Dept., Tanzania, 1971-74. Author: Aspect of Industrial Conflicts in Tanzania, 1978. Decorated Order of United Republic (Tanzania). Patron Tanzania Judges and Magistrates Assn. Avocations: reading; nature watching. Office: Tanzania Ct Appeal, PO Box 9004, Dar es Salaam Tanzania

NYBERG, OISTEIN, oil company executive, consultant; b. Stavanger, Norway, Nov. 26, 1942; s. Ingolf Kristian and Anna (Hviding) N.; m. Patricia Louise Palczewski, Jan. 25, 1969; children—Mikael Oistein, Tania Marie, Mark Erik. Stavanger Tech., Stavanger Tech. Sch., 1963; B.S.C.E., Sch. Mines and Tech., 1967. Land surveyor, Fredrikstad County, Fredrikstad, Norway, 1964-65; structural engr. The Boeing Co., Seattle, 1967-69; field engr. Schlumberger, Europe, Middle East, 1969-73, base mgr., Shiraz, Iran, 1973-74; petrophys. engr. Statoil, Stavanger, Norway, 1974-76, sect. mgr., petroleum engr., 1976-78, ops. mgr., 1978-79, corp. prodn. mgr., 1981-84; mng. dir. Smedvig IPR, Norway, 1984—; chmn. Smedcomals, 1985-87; chmn. LaSalle-IPR, 1988; supt. prodn., planning mgr. Superior Oil, Lafayette, La., 1979-81; bd. dirs. LaSalle PDS, Gasmet. Rover leader Norges Speiderforbund, Sola, Norway, 1981-83. Served to cpl. Signal Corps, Norwegian Army, 1963-64. Mem. Soc. Petrophys. Well Log Analysts, Soc. Petroleum Engrs. (dir. 1978). Lutheran. Club: Jarl (sec. 1963-65) (Stavanger). Home: Nedre Varden 14, 4050 Sola Norway Office: Smedvig IPR, Løkkeveien 103, 4001 Stavanger Norway

NYBERG, WILLIAM ARTHUR, lawyer; b. Chgo., Aug. 27, 1947; s. E. Arthur and Lyna Marie (Palmer) N.; m. Margery Ann Lissner, Mar. 11, 1984. A.B., U. Ill., 1969, J.D., 1975; M.B.A., Columbia U., 1976. Bar: Ill. 1975, U.S. Dist. Ct. (so. and no. dists.) Ill. 1975, U.S. Ct. Appeals (7th cir.) 1975, U.S. Supreme Ct. 1981. Assoc. Winston & Strawn, Chgo., 1976-77; atty. AMSTED Industries, Inc., Chgo., 1977-81, The Richardson Co., Des Plaines, Ill., 1981-82; sr. atty. John Morrell & Co., Northfield, Ill., 1982-84; v.p., gen. counsel United States Can Co., Oak Brook, Ill., 1984-86; assoc.Laser, Schostok, Kolman and Frank, Chgo., 1986—. Served with U.S. Army, 1969-72; Vietnam. Decorated Bronze Star, Joint Service Commendation Medal. Mem. ABA, Ill. State Bar Assn., Chgo. Bar Assn. Methodist. Home: 533 County Line Rd Highland Park IL 60035 Office: 30 N LaSalle St Suite 2500 Chicago IL 60602

NYCE, JOHN DANIEL, lawyer; b. York, Pa., Sept. 7, 1947; s. Harry Lincoln and Dorothy (Wagner) N.; m. Karen Martzolf, Dec. 28, 1974; children—Joshua David, Laura Kimberly. B.A., SUNY-Buffalo, 1970; J.D., U. Miami, 1973. Bar: Fla. 1973, U.S. Dist. Ct. (so. dist.) Fla. 1973, U.S. Dist. Ct. (middle dist.) Fla. 1973, U.S. Ct. Appeals (5th and 11th cirs.) 1986, U.S. Supreme Ct. 1984. Assoc. Ralph P. Douglas, Pompano Beach, Fla., 1974, Coleman, Leonard & Morrison, Ft. Lauderdale, Fla., 1975-78; ptnr. Nyce and Smith, Ft. Lauderdale, 1979; sole practice, Ft. Lauderdale, 1980—. co-founder, dir. Rutherford Inst.; Bd. dirs. Alliance for Responsible Growth, Inc., Habitat for Humanity of Broward County, Inc.; bd. dirs., co-founder Fla. Family Adoption, Inc.; mem. Social Register Ft. Lauderdale; mem. Broward County Right to Life; mem. exec. com. Broward County Republican Party; bd. dirs. Shepherd Care Ministries, Inc., co-founder Christian Adoption Services of Shepherd Care Ministries, Inc.; cert. trainer Evangelism Explosion III Internat., Inc. Mem. Christian Lawyer's Assn. (founder, past pres., bd. dirs.), Atty's. Title Ins. Fund, Christian Legal Soc., Conservative Caucus of Broward County, Fla. Tennis Assn., The Gideons. Republican. Presbyterian. Home: 5910 NE 21st Ln Fort Lauderdale FL 33308 Office: 4367 N Federal Hwy Fort Lauderdale FL 33308

NYDICK, DAVID, foundation executive, columnist; b. N.Y.C., Feb. 10, 1929; s. Irving and Minnie (Bilibom) N.; m. Gilda Pivnick, June 14, 1953; children—Leslie Ruth, Jay Scott. B.A., NYU, 1950, M.A., 1952, profl. Diploma, 1960, postgrad., 1960—. Tchr. pub. schs., Great Neck, N.Y., 1954-60; prin. asst. supt. Princeton Pub. Schs., N.J., 1961-65; asst. supt. Jericho Pub. Schs., N.Y., 1965-68, supt., 1968-84; exec. dir. Guide Dog Found., Smithtown, N.Y., 1984—; assoc. prof. L.I. U., 1975—, Hofstra U., 1976—, Pace U., 1978—; asst. prof. Bklyn. Coll., 1979—; syndicated columnist UPI, Copley News, DANY News, 1962—. Pres., East Plains Mental Health Ctr., 1964—. Served with U.S. Army, 1952-54. Recipient Edn. Achievement award NCCJ, 1975. Mem. N.Y.U. Alumni Assn. (pres. 1971-72), Am. Assn. Sch. Adminstrs., Ednl. Writers Assn. Club: Overseas Press. Lodge: Masons. Home: 22 Lesley Dr Syosset NY 11791 Office: Guide Dog Found 371 E Jericho Turnpike Smithtown NY 11787

NYE, JOHN ROBERT, furniture company executive, transportation consultant; b. Phila., Apr. 18, 1947; s. William E. and Mary B. (Brick) N.; m. Judy Burris, May 31, 1969 (div. Dec. 1977); children—Keith, Lanny, John; m. 2d, Grace M. Adams, Feb. 28, 1981; children—Annette, Mark. BA, N.C. State U.-Raleigh, 1969. Prodn. mgr. Highland House, Hickory, N.C., 1969-79; distbn. mgr. Hickory Chair Co., 1979—. Mem. Catawba Valley Traffic Club; vice-chmn. Catawba County Mayors Com. for Handicapped, 1987—. Mem. Met. Planning Assn. Republican. Lutheran. Home: PO Box 3136 Hickory NC 28603 Office: Hickory Chair Co 37 9th St Pl SE Hickory NC 28601

NYEGAARD, STIG ELLIOT, communications company executive; b. Copenhagen, Apr. 25, 1935; s. Axel Elliot and Anne Lise (Bartels) N.; m. Thomsen Kirsten, Sept. 24, 1967 (dec. Aug. 1973); 1 child, Lars; m. Agnette Wahl, June 17, 1978; 1 child, Laura. Student, NYU. Advt. mgr. 3M Co., Copenhagen, 1962-63; advt. cons. various agys. Copenhagen, 1963-65; mng. dir. Recla Internat., Copenhagen, 1965-72; communications cons. Hillerod, Frederiksburg County, Denmark, 1972-84; owner, founder Elliot CBO, Vedbaek, Denmark, 1984—. Author: To Sell Society to Oneself, 1973, Handbook in Public Communication, 1974, Society Communication in 25 Minutes, 1975, Pressure on the Press, 1975, When You Cannot Close Your Mouth, 1976, Practical Ideas in Public Communication, 1977, On Election, That's How You Will be Heard, 1978, Regional Planning, 1979, The Planning of Community Communication, 1980; editor: Directions for Danish Laws, 1981-82, Directions for Medical Information, 1982; co-editor: System Export, 1983, Cross Pressure and Interaction, 1988. Mem. Den Danske Publicistklub. Liberal. Lutheran. Home: Fagerdalen 16, DK2950 Vedbaek Denmark Office: Elliot CBO, Gongehusvej 234, 2950 Vedbaek Denmark

NYFLÖT, IVAR, publishing company executive; b. Oslo, June 30, 1948; m. Grethe Bliks öen, Mar 8, 1975. B, Copenhagen Sch. Econs. and Bus. Adminstrn., 1972, MBA, 1974. Product mgr. Case/David Brown Ltd., Roskilde, Denmark, 1974-78; export mgr. Norema Ltd., Oslo, 1978-79, mktg. mgr., 1979-80; mng. dir. Norema Denmark Ltd., Copenhagen, 1980-82; v.p. Pran & Torgersen Ltd., Oslo, 1982-87, Kunnskapsforlaget, Oslo, 1987—. Mem. Exomar, Kreativ Forum. Home: Maltrostvn 10C, 0390 Oslo 3 Norway Office: Kunnskapsforlaget, Sehesteds Gate 4, 0130, Oslo Norway

NYGREN, KARL FRANCIS, lawyer; b. Wilkes-Barre, Pa., Mar. 9, 1927; s. Elmer F. N. and Stella P. (Rozmarek) Gernand; m. Elizabeth J. Parsons, Dec. 26, 1949; children: Phillip K., James F., Anne E. Student, DePaul U., 1946-48; J.D., U. Chgo., 1951. Bar: Ill. 1950, U.S. Dist. Ct. (no. dist.) Ill. 1951, U.S. Supreme Ct. 1972, U.S. Appeals (7th cir.) 1980, Calif. 1985. Assoc. Kirkland & Ellis, Chgo., 1951-58, ptnr., 1959-86, of counsel, 1987—; adj. prof. Santa Clara U. Law Sch., 1987-88; cons. prof. Stanford U. Law Sch., 1988—. Bd. dirs. Chgo. Lung Assn., 1971-88, exec. com., 1979-87, pres., 1986-87; exec. com. Lawyers Com. for Civil Rights Under Law, 1964-76, co-chmn., 1972-74; mem. vis. com. Law Sch., U. Chgo., 1974-77; governing mem. Art Inst. Chgo., 1981-82, Chgo. Symphony, 1981-86; adv. bd. Chgo. Cath. Charities; trustee DePaul U., 1985—. Served with F.A. AUS, 1944-46. Mem. ABA, Ill. Bar Assn. (chmn. com. on fed. legis. 1965-66, vice chmn. antitrust sect. 1964-65), Chgo. Bar Assn., State Bar Calif., Am. Judicature Soc. (exec. com., chmn. 1987-88), U. Chgo. Law Sch. Alumni Assn. Republican. Roman Catholic. Clubs: Law (Chgo.), Mid-Am. (Chgo.), Commercial (Chgo.). Home: 360 Encinal Ave Menlo Park CA 94025 Office: Kirkland & Ellis Suite 5600 200 E Randolph Dr Chicago IL 60601

NYHOLM, KURT RAINER, German language educator; b. Munsala, Finland, June 17, 1932; s. Birger and Elin (Fogel) N.; m. Gretel Maria Backman, Dec. 28, 1958; children: Gerd Anna-Lisa, Anders Johan. Fil. mag., Åbo (Finland) Acad., 1957, fil. lic., 1957, fil. dr., 1965. Lectr. in German Åbo Acad., 1956-67, prof., 1967—, dean Faculty of Arts, 1972-74, rector, 1975-78. Author: A.v. Scharfenbergs Merlin, 1967, Studien zum sog gleblümten Stil, 1972; author, editor: Albrechts Jüngerer Titurel, 1968, 1985, Gralepen in U. Füetrers Bearbeitung, 1964. Decorated comdr. White Rose of Finland; recipient Alexander von Humboldt silver medal, 1975, Grimm prize Ministry of German Dem. Republic, 1985. Mem. Arthurian Soc., Inst. für Deutsche Sprache, Finnish Soc. Scis. Letters. Lutheran. Home: Osterlanggatan 37 A 3, SF-20700 Abo Finland Office: Tyska Inst Abo Acad, Fanriksgatan 3, SF-20500 Abo Finland

NYKOWSKI, IRENEUSZ JAN, mathematician; b. Vilno, Poland, June 28, 1930; s. Zygmunt Franciszek and Weronika (Musialik) N.; m. Maria Gerarda Olejasz, Jan. 3, 1956; children: Wojciech, Katarzyna. BS in Math., U. Warsaw, Poland, 1952, MS in Math., 1954; PhD in Econs., Cen. Sch. Planning and Stats., Warsaw, 1962, DSc in Econs., 1968. Sr. asst. Cen. Sch. Planning and Stats., 1954-63, asst. prof. math., 1963-68, assoc. prof., 1968-74, prof., 1974—, head dept. ops. research Inst. Econometrics, 1965-72, 80—, vice dean faculty fin. and stats., 1972-74, vice dir. Inst. Developing Economy, 1975-77, dir. Inst. Cybernetics and Mgmt., 1977-80, dir. Inst. Econometrics, 1982-84. Author: An Application of Linear Programming in Construction, 1964 (award 1965), (with others) Transportation Problem in Linear Programming, 1972, 2d. edit., 1974 (award 1975), Linear Programming, 1981, 2d. edit., 1984 (award 1981), (with others) Multiobjective Programming, 1987, also 3 others; contbr. articles to profl. pubs. Recipient Oskar Lange's award Polish Econ. Soc., 1970, 2d Deg. prize Minister Sci., 1973, 82; Council for Internat. Exchange Scholars Fulbright-Hays grantee, 1974-75. Mem. Stats. and Econometrics Polish Acad. Sci. (sr. council systems research, assoc. editor Stats. Rev. Quar. 1974-82, vice editor 1982—). Home: Kinowa 25 m 220, 04 030 Warsaw Poland Office: Cen Sch Planning & Stats, Al Niepodlegtosci 162, 02 554 Warsaw Poland

NYLÉN, BERTIL FREDRIK, management consultant; b. Härnösand, Sweden, Apr. 20, 1944; parents John A.S. and Anna-Lisa (Johansson) N. Degree, U. Stockholm, 1969; degree in Civ. Econs., Stockholm Sch. of Econs., 1973. Asst. mgr. Ostgotabanken, Stockholm, 1974-79; chief exec. officer Bertil Nylén Cons., Stockholm, 1979—; bd. dirs. to 14 cos., 1979—. Author: Kreditgivning Till Företag, 1987. Served with the Swedish army, 1965-66. Office: Hamnagatan 11, S-11147 Stockholm Sweden

NYLÉN, KJELL ANDERS, advertising consultant, journalist; b. Lidköping, Sweden, Sept. 22, 1932; s. Gunner and Lena (Berggren) N.; m. Gunnel (Åhman); children: Barbro Anna, Anders Nils. Degree in Econs., Bar-Lock Inst., Stockholm, 1955. Project mgr. with various agys., Gothenburg, Sweden, 1956-65; advt. producer Scania Vabis, Södertalje, Sweden, 1965-67; copy writer Norman, Craig & Kummel, Malmö, 1967-72; chief editor Maskinkonakt, Lidköping, 1972-85; owner, mktg. and advt. cons. INNOVEX, Lidköping, 1986—. Patentee anti-theft pick pocket device, 1985. Served with the Swedish Air Force, 1955-56. Club: Utveckling Framtagning Markandsfoering Inventor's. Home: Gardesvagen 5, 53157 Lidkoping Sweden Office: INNOVEX, PO Box 617, S 53116 Lidkoping Sweden

OAKIE, ALFRED UMBERTO, automobile association administrator; b. Collingwood, Ont., Can., July 22, 1920; s. Costantino and Chiara (Donatelli) O.; m. Laura Oakie (dec.); children: Janet, Donald, Robert, Denise, Geoffrey. Asst. to mgr.-sec. Rubber Assn. of Can., Toronto, Ont., 1945-54; asst. to exec. dir. Soc. Indsl. Accts. (now named Soc. Mgmt. Accts. of Can.), Hamilton, Ont., 1954-56; pres. Hamilton Automobile Club, 1956—. Columnist Hamilton Automobile Club newsletter. Pres. Hamilton Safety Council, 1959, Hamilton Visitors and Conv. Bur., 1959; founding pres. St. Joseph's Hosp. Found., 1968-78; provincial govt. advisor Spl. Trucking Commn. on Road Safety, 1982-83; provincial govt. Police Pursuit Com., 1984-85; chmn. bus. adv. council McMaster U., 1981-84; mem. steering com. McMaster U. Bldg. Fund, 1987; chmn. St. Joseph's Hosp. Bd. Trustees, 1978-80, Hamilton Social Planning Council, Loretto Acad. Adv. Bd., 1966; active St. Joseph's Villa Fund Drive, Nat. Bd. Big Bros. Assn., Hamilton-Wentworth Regional Tourism Study Com.; vice-chmn. bd. dirs. Hamilton Gallery of Distinction Com.; founding mem. Civic Pedestrian Safety Com.; chmn. pub. service div. Hamilton & Dist. United Appeal Campaign, Can. Co-ordination Sch. Patrols; initiator, chmn. Can. Sch. Patrol Jamboree and Can. Sch. Patrol Tng. Camps.; treas. Can. Football Hall of Fame Bldg. Com. Named Transp. Person of the Yr., Ontario, 1988. Fellow Soc. Mgmt. Accts. of Can.; mem. Inst. Assn. Execs., Am. Automobile Assn. (pub. and govt. policy adv. com., com. club ofcls., advisor to nat. bd. dirs., ins. and fin. services com.), Found. Traffic Safety (research and devel. com., chmn. and Ont. spokesman on govt. an pub. affairs). Home: 105 Wilson St W, Unit 9, Ancaster, ON Canada L9G 1N4 Office: Hamilton Automobile Club, 393 Main St E, Hamilton, ON Canada L8N 3T7

OAKLEY, CLARON LOUIS, editor, publisher; b. Provo, Utah, Oct. 1, 1924; s. Louis Terry and Inez (McDonald) O.; student Brigham Young U., 1943, 46-47; B.S.J., Northwestern U., 1950, M.S.J., 1951; m. Julia Hansen, June 19, 1950 (dec.); children—Ellen Elizabeth, Bradford James, Sara Julia. Co-founder, v.p., sr. v.p., editor Audio-Digest Found., 1953—; sci. info. officer Pan-Pacific Surg. Assn. Mobile, 1963-66, A.C.S. mobile S.Am. sessions, 1969—; dir. Pacific Magnetic Tape Equipment Co. Active Boy Scouts Am.; trustee Audio-Digest Found.; Served to sgt.-maj. AUS, 1945-46; ETO. Recipient disting. layman citation AMA, 1982. Mem. Am. Film Inst., Nat. Acad. Rec. Arts and Scis., Am. Med. Writers Assn., Blue Key, Sigma Delta Chi. Mem. Ch. Jesus Christ of Latter-day Saints (former bishop, incumbent counselor stake presidency). Rotarian. Contbr. articles to profl. jours. Home: 2150 Kinneloa Canyon Rd Pasadena CA 91107 Office: 1577 E Chevy Chase Dr Glendale CA 91206

OAKLEY, DAVID ARTHUR, psychology educator; b. Newcastle Under Lyme, Staffordshire, Eng., July 15, 1942; s. Arthur and Daisy Thorpe O.; m. Christine Mary Pitt, Aug. 21, 1965; children: Samuel David, Benjamin James, Daniel Henry. BSc in Psychology with honors, U. Coll. London, 1965, PhD, 1976. Researcher MRC Unit on Neural Mechanisms Behavior, London, 1968-76; lectr. in psychology The City U., London, 1976-78; lectr. in psychology U. Coll. London, 1978-87, admissions tutor in psychology, 1983-86, asst. tutor to sci. faculty, 1986—, sr. lectr., 1987—; mem. exec. com. acad. bd. Univ. Coll., 1988—; treas. Brit. Soc. for Exptl. and Clin. Hypnosis, 1981—. Author, editor: Brain and Mind, 1985; editor Brain, Behavior and Evolution, 1979; contbr. numerous articles to profl. jours. Fellow Brit. Psychol. Soc., Am. Psychol. Assn.; mem. Am. Psychol. Soc., Exptl. Psychol. Soc., European Brain and Behavior Soc. (com. 1978-80), Brain Research Assn. Office: U Coll London, Dept Psychology, Gower St, London WCIE 6BT, England

OBADIA, ANDRE ISAAC, surgeon; b. Oran, Algeria, Mar. 21, 1927; s. Sam and Marthe Marie (Bouchara) O.; m. Annie Judith Ziza, June 5, 1961; children—Dominique, Laurence, Olivia. S.P.C.N., Faculty of Scis., Algiers, 1945; B. Ethnology, Faculty of Scis., Paris, 1959, B. Anthropology, 1960; med. qualification Ednl. Council Fgn. Med. Grads., Evanston, Ill., 1961. Externe des hopitaux Assistance Publique, Paris, 1949-54, intern des hopitaux, 1957-61; attaché CNRS, Hopital Broussais, Paris, 1964; chef de clinique Faculty of Med., Paris, 1962-66; surgeon Clinique Sully, Maisons-Laffitte, 1964—, Poissy Hosp., France, 1965—; cons. Centre Hospitalier des Courses, 1978—; med. expert Cour d'Appel, Versailles, 1984—; prof. Nurses Tng. Sch., 1969—. Contbr. articles to profl. pubs. Donateur, Appel Unifie Juif de France, Paris; hon. mem. Orphelinat Mutualiste de la Police Nationale Pris. Served to lt. French Armed Forces, 1955-57. Ministere des Affaires Etrangeres grantee, 1958; Fulbright fellow, 1962. Mem. Assn. Francaise de Chirurgie, Coll. de Pathologie Vasculaire, Compagnie des Experts de Versailles, Union Nationale des Medecins de Reserve, Coll. Nat. des Chirurgiens Francais, Assn. des Membres de l'Ordre Nat. du Merite. Jewish. Avocations: ethnology, minerology, chess. Home: 20 rue Euler, 75008 Paris France Office: Clinique Sully, 2 Place Sully, 78600 Maison-Lafitte France

OBANDO BRAVO, MIGUEL CARDINAL, archbishop of Managua; b. La Libertad, Nicaragua, Feb. 2, 1926. Ordained priest Roman Catholic Ch., 1958. Titular bishop of Puzia di Bizavena and aux. bishop of Matagalpa, 1968—, archbishop of Managua, 1970—, elevated to Sacred Coll. of Cardinals, 1985. Address: Arzobispado, Apto 3058, Managua Nicaragua *

OBER, RUSSELL JOHN, JR., lawyer; b. Pitts., June 26, 1948; s. Russell J. and Marion C. (Hampson) O.; m. Kathleen A. Stein, Apr. 8, 1972; children—Lauren Elizabeth, Russell John III. B.A., U. Pitts., 1970, J.D., 1973. Bar: Pa. 1973, U.S. Dist. Ct. (we. dist.) Pa. 1973, U.S. Ct. Appeals (4th cir.) 1976, U.S. Supreme Ct. 1976, U.S. Dist. Ct. (ea. dist.) Pa. 1978, U.S. Ct. Appeals (3d cir.) 1979, U.S. Tax Ct. 1982, U.S. Ct. Appeals (D.C. cir.) 1985. Asst. dist. atty. Allegheny County, Pitts., 1973-75; ptnr. Wallace Chapas & Ober, Pitts., 1975-80, Rose, Schmidt, Hasley & DiSalle, Pitts., 1980—. Bd. dirs. Parent and Child Guidance Ctr., Pitts., 1983-88, treas., 1985-86, pres. 1986-88; mem. Mt. Lebanon Traffic Commn., 1976-81. Mem. ABA (discovery com. litigation sect. 1982-88, ho. of dels. young lawyers div. 1982-83), Nat. Bd. Trial Advocacy (diplomate), Pa. Bar Assn. (ho. of dels. 1983—), Acad. Trial Lawyers Allegheny County (fellow 1983—, bd. govs. 1988—), Allegheny County Bar Assn. (chmn. young lawyers sect. 1983, bd. govs. 1984, fin. com. 1984—), U. Pitts. Law Alumni Assn. (bd. govs. 1984—, v.p. 1985-86, pres.- elect 1986-87, pres. 1987-88). Clubs: Pitts. Athletic, Rivers, Chartiers Country. Home: 393 Parker Dr Pittsburgh PA 15216 Office: Rose Schmidt Hasley & DiSalle 900 Oliver Bldg Pittsburgh PA 15222

OBERHAUSEN, JOYCE ANN, aircraft company executive, artist; b. Plain Dealing, La., Nov. 12, 1941; d. George Dewey and Jettie Cleo (Farrington) Wynn; m. James J. Oberhausen, Oct. 15, 1966; 1 dau., Georgann; m. Dale Estein, Sept. 15, 1958 (div. 1960); children—Darla Renee Estein Oberhausen Minor, Dale Henry Estein Oberhausen. Student Ayers Bus. Sch., Shreveport, 1962-63, U. Ala., 1964-65. Stenographer, sec. Lincoln Nat. Life Co., Shreveport, 1965-66; sec. Baifield Industries, Shreveport, 1975-86; internat. art tchr., Huntsville, Ala., 1974—; v.p. Precision Splty. Co., Huntsville, 1966—, Mil. Aircraft, Huntsville, 1979—; pres. Wynnson Enterprises, Huntsville, 1983—; owner Wynnson Galleries Pvt. Collections, Florist, Meridianville, 1987. Mgr. basketball team Meridianville, 1985-86; founder Nat. Mus. Women in Arts. Mem. Internat. Porcelain Guild, Nat. Assn. Female Execs., People to People, porcelain Portrait Soc., United Artists Assn., Am. Soc. of Profl. and Executive Women Hist. Soc. Avocations: oil painting, antiques, handcrafts, gourmet cooking, horseback riding. Home: 156 Spencer Dr Meridianville AL 35759 Office: Precision Splty Corp 150 Wells Rd Meridianville AL 35759

OBERHAUSER, ALOIS, professor; b. St. Ingbert, Fed. Republic of Germany, Jan. 20, 1930; s. Karl and Cecilie (Wagner) O.; m. Christel Klosterkamp, May 29, 1958. Degree, U. Münster, 1955, U. Munich, 1962. Prof. Albert Ludwigs Univ., Freiburg, Fed. Republic of Germany, 1963—; mem. research adv. bd. Ministry of Fin. Author: Finanzpolitik und private Vermögensbildung, 1963, (with others) Eigentumsbildung in Wohnungsbau, 1982. Roman Catholic. Office: Inst für Finanzwissenschaft, Albert Ludwigs Univ, Europaplatz 1, D-7800 Freiburg Federal Republic of Germany

OBERHUBER, KONRAD JOHANNES, art museum curator, educator; b. Linz/Donau, Austria, Mar. 31, 1935; m. Marianne Liebknecht, 1964; children: Lukas, Nikolaus, Wanako, Mariella. Ph.D., U. Vienna, Austria, 1959, Dozent, 1971. Asst. U. Vienna; delegated as research fellow to Austrian Inst. in Rome, 1959-61; asst., then curator Albertina, Vienna, 1961-71; research curator Nat. Gallery Art, Washington, 1971-74; guest lectr. Fogg Art Mus., Harvard U., Cambridge, Mass., spring 1974; curator of drawings, prof. fine arts Fogg Art Mus., Harvard U., 1974-85, Ian Woodner curator of drawings, prof. fine arts, 1985-87; dir. Graphische Sammlung Albertina, Vienna, 1987—; Italian Ministry of Culture scholar, Rome, winter 1958; asst. prof. Smith Coll., 1964-65; Kress fellow Harvard Center for Renaissance Studies, Florence, Italy, 1965-66; guest prof. Cambridge (Eng.) U., 1968. Author: Raphael, Die Zechnungen, 1983; contbr. articles to profl. jours. fellow Inst. Advanced Study Princeton, N.J., 1974-75; Nat. Endowment Humanities grantee, 1979-80; Gerda Henkel Stiftung grantee, 1983-84. Mem. Print Council Am. Office: Graphische Sammlung Albertina, Augustinerstrasse 1, A-1010 Vienna Austria *

OBERMANN, C. ESCO, psychologist, rehabilitation consultant; b. Yarmouth, Iowa, July 31, 1904; s. Albert B. and Evalyne (Calloway) O.; m. Avalon F. Law, June 3, 1929. A.B., U. Iowa, 1926, M.A., 1931, Ph.D., 1938. Diplomate Am. Bd. Profl. Psychologists. Chief vocational edn. Rochester (Minn.) Schs., 1928-36; research fellow U. Iowa, Iowa City, 1938-40; asso. prof. psychology U. Iowa, 1966-70, U. Tex., Austin, 1946; dir. vocational rehab. VA, 1946-60; dir. St. Paul Rehab. Center, 1960-63; research fellow Vocational Rehab. Adminstrn., 1963-65; asso. prof. psychology Iowa Wesleyan Coll., Mt. Pleasant, 1965-66; rehab. cons. Hudson, Wis., 1970—; adj. prof. Mankato (Minn.) State U., 1977—; mem. adv. com. Univ. House, U. Iowa, 1979—; mem. com. handicapped People-to-People Program. Author: A History of Vocational Rehabilitation in America, 1965, Coordination of Services for Handicapped Children and Youth, 1963, (with others) Continuing Education for Rehabilitation Counselors, 1969; Editor: (with others) Basic Issues In Rehabilitation, 1972. Served to col. USAAF, 1940-46. Recipient Disting. Alumnus award U. Iowa, 1986. Fellow Am. Psychol. Assn., AAAS; mem. Nat. Rehab. Counseling Assn., Nat. Rehab. Assn. (pres. 1961-62), Minn. Rehab. Assn. (pres. 1954), Iowa Rehab. Assn. (pres. 1967), Am. Personnel and Guidance Assn., Am. Speech and Hearing Assn., Assn. Advancement of Psychology, Minn. Family Farm Inst. (bd. dirs.), Sigma Xi, Delta Upsilon. Episcopalian. Club: Mason. Home: Afton MN 55001 Office: Box 241 Hudson WI 54016

OBERMAYER, HERMAN JOSEPH, newspaper publisher; b. Phila., Sept. 19, 1924; s. Leon J. and Julia (Sinsheimer) O.; student U. Geneva (Switzerland), 1946; A.B. cum laude, Dartmouth, 1948; m. Betty Nan Levy, June 28, 1955; children—Helen Julia, Veronica O. Atnipp, Adele Beatrice, Elizabeth Rose. Reporter, L.I. Daily Press, Jamaica, N.Y., 1950-53; classified advt. mgr. New Orleans Item, 1953-55; asst. to publisher Standard-Times, New Bedford, Mass., 1955-57; editor, pub. Long Branch (N.J.) Daily Record, 1957-71, No. Va. Sun, Arlington, 1963-; dir. Moleculon Research Corp., Cambridge, Mass.; Pulitzer Prize juror, 1983, 84. Bd. dirs. Monmouth Med. Center, 1958-71; mem. exec. council Monmouth Boy Scouts Am., 1958-71, mem. exec. com. Nat. Capital council, 1971-79, v.p., 1974-77; mem. Va. Legis. Alcohol Beverage Control Study Commn., 1972-74; bd. dirs. Monmouth Mus., 1968-71, No. Va. Jr. League, 1981-86; trustee Arlington (Va.) Bicentennial Commn., Am. Jewish Com., 1984—, v.p. Washington chpt. (Community Service Award 1986). Served with AUS, 1943-46; ETO. Recipient Rhineland campaign star, Friends of Scouting Award, 1966, Silver Beaver, 1977. Mem. Am. Soc. Newspaper Editors, Am. Newspaper Pubs. Assn., So. Newspapers Pubs. Assn. (dir. 1981-84), White House Corrs. Assn., Soc. Profl. Journalists, Sigma Chi. Jewish. Rotarian. Clubs: Nat. Press (Washington); Washington Golf and Country (Arlington, Va.); Dartmouth (N.Y.C.). Contbr. column Editor's Viewpoint to No. Va. Sun; articles to Sat. Eve. Post, This Week, Japan Economic Jour., Pageant, Travel, Ebony, Mag. Digest, Everybody's Digest, others. Home: 4114 N Ridgview Rd Arlington VA 22207 Office: 1227 N Ivy St Arlington VA 22201

OBERREIT, WALTER WILLIAM, lawyer; b. Paterson, N.J., Oct. 7, 1928; s. William and Gertrud (Limpert) O.; m. Anne-Marie Gohier, July 6, 1955; children: Stephan, Alexis, Jerome. BA, U. Mich., 1951; diploma, U. Paris Inst. Polit. Studies, 1955; JD, Yale U., 1958. Bar: N.Y. Assoc. Cleary, Gottlieb, Steen & Hamilton, N.Y.C., 1958-62, Paris, 1962-66; assoc. Cleary, Gottlieb, Steen & Hamilton, Brussels, 1966-67, ptnr., 1967—. Contbr. articles to profl. jours., chpts. to books. Served to lt. (j.g.) USN, 1953-55. Mem. ABA, Assn. of Bar of City of N.Y. (co-chmn. com. on relations with European Bars 1981—), Am. Arbitration Assn., Internat. Fiscal Assn., Ctr. European Policy Studies, Inst. Royal Relations Internat., Am. Soc. Internat. Law, Union Internat. Des Avocats. Clubs: Cercle Royal Gaulois, Cercle Nations, Am. Common Market (Brussels). Home: Ave Geo Bernier 7, 1050 Brussels Belgium Office: Cleary Gottlieb Steen Hamilton, rue de la Loi 23, 1040 Brussels Belgium

OBERST, PAUL, law educator emeritus; b. Owensboro, Ky., Apr. 22, 1914; m. Elizabeth Durfee; children—Paul, James, George, Mary, John. A.B., U. Evansville, 1936; J.D., U. Ky., 1939; LL.M., U. Mich., 1941. Bar: Ky. 1938, Mo. 1942. Assoc. firm Ryland, Stinson, Mag & Thomson, Kansas City, Mo., 1941-42; asst. prof. law Coll. of Law, U. Ky., Lexington, 1946-47; prof. Coll. of Law, U. Ky., 1947-82, emeritus prof., 1982—; vis. prof. U. Chgo., 1954-55, Duke U., 1980; prof., dir. civil liberties program N.Y. U., 1959-61; mem. Nat. Commn. on Acad. Tenure, 1971-73. Contbr. articles to legal jours. Mem. Ky. Commn. on Corrections, 1961-65; mem. Ky. Commn. on Human Rights, 1962-66, 80—, chmn., 1966-70, 73-76; trustee U. Ky., Lexington, 1963-69, 72-75; mem. Ky. state adv. com. U.S. Civil Rights Commn., 1979—, chmn., 1982-86. Served to lt. USNR, 1942-46. Mem. Assn. Am. Law Schs. (exec. com. 1970-72), Am., Ky. bar assns., Am. Law Inst., Order of Coif, Phi Delta Phi. Home: 829 Sherwood Dr Lexington KY 40502 Office: U Ky Coll of Law Lexington KY 40506

OBERT, EDWARD FREDRIC, mechanical engineering educator; b. Detroit, Jan. 18, 1910; s. Edward and Jessie (Funderburg) O.; m. Helen Hadley Whitman, Jan. 2, 1982. B.S., Northwestern U., 1933, M.E., 1934; M.S., U. Mich., 1940. Engr. mfg. Western Electric Co., Chgo., 1929-30; staff Office Naval Inspection, Chgo., 1934-37; prof. mech. engring. Northwestern U., 1937-58; prof. mech. engring. U. Wis., 1958—, chmn. dept., 1963-67; propr. Profl. Engring. Cons.; cons. Nat. Acad. Scis., USAF Acad., Denver, Aeromed. Lab. Alaska.; Committeeman NRC-Nat. Acad. Scis. Author: Thermodynamics, 1948, rev. edit., 1963, Elements of Thermodynamics and Heat Transfer, 1949, rev. edit., 1962, 80, Internal Combustion Engines, 1950, rev. edit., 1968, 73, Concepts of Thermodynamics, 1960; cons. editor: mech. engr. series of Internat. Textbook Co; contbr. articles tech. jours. Recipient George Westinghouse award Am. Soc. Engring. Edn., 1953, G. Edwin Burks award, 1971; U.S. Army cert. of appreciation for patriotic civilian service, 1970; Benjamin Smith Reynolds award U. Wis., 1973. Fellow ASME; mem. Soc. Automotive Engrs., Internat. Mark Twain Soc. (hon.), Sigma Xi, Pi Tau Sigma, Tau Beta Pi, Triangle Frat. Home: 7843 Ox Trail Verona WI 53593 Office: Mech Engring Dept U Wis Madison WI 53706

OBIANG NGUEMA MBASOGO, TEODORO, president of Equatorial Guinea; b. June 5, 1942; ed. in Spain. Army officer; formerly minister of def.; overthrew former pres. in coup, pres., 1979—; head Supreme Mil. Council, 1979—. Office: Oficina del Presidente, Malabo Equatorial Guinea *

OBIORAH, GEOFFREY OKECHUKWU, marketing executive; b. Awka, Anambra State, Nigeria, Dec. 6, 1954; s. Chief Ozo Odili and Ojiefi Gold Agbonma (Anaekwe) O.; m. Christiana Ogoma Molokwu; children: Obiageli, Chukwugozie, Ugochukwu. DipM in Mktg., Inst. Mktg., London, 1980; HND in Mktg., Kaduna (Nigeria) Poly., 1981; finalist, Inst. Purchasing and Supply, London, 1984. Acct. Distran (Nigeria) Ltd., Kano, 1977, sales mgr., 1979-80; field sales mgr. Johnson Wax Nigeria Ltd., Kaduna, 1980-82; elec. engr. power div. ITT, Kaduna, 1982-83; mktg. and comml. mgr. Deepclean Products (Nigeria) Ltd., Kaduna, 1983—, also bd. dirs. Served to capt. Biafran Army, 1967-70. Mem. Brit. Inst. Mgmt., Nigerian Inst. Mgmt. (assoc.), Inst. Mktg., Internat. Inst. Bookkeepers (assoc.), Inst. Adminstrv. Accts. (assoc.). Club: Awka Social of Nigeria. Home: Plot TK 43A, Badiko North Layout, Box 4527, Kaduna Nigeria Office: Deepclean Products, (Nigeria) Ltd, Box 4527, Kaduna Nigeria

O'BLOCK, ROBERT PAUL, management consultant; b. Pitts., Mar. 9, 1943; s. Paul Joseph and Mary Elizabeth (Galicic) O'B.; m. Megan Marie. B.S.M.E., Purdue U., 1965; M.B.A. (Research fellow), Harvard U., 1967. Research and teaching fellow in fin., econs. and urban mgmt., Harvard U., 1967-70; assoc. in real estate mgmt. and fin. McKinsey & Co., Inc., N.Y.C., 1969-78, prin., 1979-84, dir., 1984— ; gen. and mng. partner Freeport Center, Clearfield, Utah, 1971—; vis. lectr. urban econs. Yale Law Sch., Princeton U.; cons. Mass., N.J. housing fin. agys., Rockefeller Assos., HUD, 1968-76; chmn. mgmt. com. Snowbird Lodge (Utah), 1974-86. Mem. nat. adv. bd. Snowbird Arts Inst., 1977-83; mem. budget com. N.Y. Public Library, 1977-79; mem. adv. bd. Internat. Tennis Hall of Fame, 1986—. Roman Catholic. Clubs: River (N.Y.C.); Devon Yacht, Maidstone (East Hampton, N.Y.); Nat. Golf Links Am. (Southampton, N.Y.); Alta (Salt Lake City); Algonquin, Badmitton and Tennis (Boston); Ogden (Utah) Golf; The Country (Brookline, Mass.). Contbr. articles to profl. jours. Office: 277 Dartmouth St Boston MA 02116

OBODOWSKI, JANUSZ, diplomat; b. Siedlce, Poland, Jan. 2, 1930; s. Antoni and Stanislawa (Bakinowska) O.; m. Grazyna Prawdzic-Rudzka, Feb. 20, 1954; 1 child, Ewa. M of Demography, Main Sch. Planning and Stats., Warsaw, Poland, 1954, M of Econs., 1964; D of Econ. Sci., Warsaw Tech. U., 1973. Sect. head State Com. Econ. Planning, Warsaw, 1954-57; dep. dept. dir. Ministry Labour and Social Welfare, Warsaw, 1957-60; dep. dir., then dir. Labour and Wages Com., Warsaw, 1960-68; team dir. Planning Com. Council of Ministers, Warsaw, 1968-72; under-sec. state Ministry Labour, Wages and Social Affairs, Warsaw, 1972-80; dep. chmn. Govt. Demographic Com., Warsaw, 1974-83; minister Ministry Labour, Wages and Social Affairs, Warsaw, 1980-81, dep. prime minister, 1981-85; Polish ambassador to German Dem. Republic Berlin, 1986—; chmn. econ. com. Council of Ministers, Warsaw, 1981-82, planning com., 1982-83; chmn. exec. com. Council for Mut. Econ. Assistance, Moscow, 1984-85. Author: Problems of Employment, 1959, Policy of Employment and Wages, 1964, (essays) Walk on Earth, 1987; contbr. over 150 articles to profl. jours. Dep. chair Youth Orgn. of Workers Univ. Soc. of the Polish Socialist Party, 1947. Decorated Order Polonia Restituta Council of State, Officer 1974, Commdr. 1979, recipient Star of Friendship of Nations, 1985. Mem. Polish Econ. Soc., Inst. Labor and Social Affairs, Ctr. Devel. Mgrs., Polish Acad. Scis. (mem. labor and social policy com. 1975-80), Sci. Orgn. and Mgmt. Soc. Office: Embassy Polish People's Republic, Unter den Linden 72-74, 1080 Berlin German Democratic Republic

OBOLENSKY, DIMITRI, historian; b. Petrograd, USSR, Apr. 1, 1918; arrived in Eng., 1937; s. Prince Dimitri and Mary (Shuvaloc) O. BA, U. Cambridge, Eng., 1940, PhD, 1943, MA, 1944; LittD, Oxford U.; D (hon.), U. Paris, Sorbonne, 1980, U. Birmingham. Lectr. U. Cambridge, 1946-49; reader U. Oxford, 1949-61, prof., 1961-85, emeritus prof., 1985—. Author: The Bogomils, 1948, The Byzantine Commonwealth, 1961, Byzantium and the Slavs, 1961, The Byzantine Inhabitance of Eastern Europe, 1982, Six Byzantine Portraits, 1988. Decorated knight, Queen Elizabeth, 1984. Fellow British Acad., Soc. Antiquarians, Royal Hist. Soc.; mem. Acad. Athens (corr.). Club: Athenaeum (London). Home: 29 Belsyre Ct Woodstock Rd, Oxford OX2 6HV, England Office: British Acad, 20-21 Cornwall Terrace, London NW1 4QP, England

OBOLENSKY, IVAN, investment banker, foundations consultant, writer, publisher; b. London, May 15, 1925; s. Serge and Alice (Astor) O. (parents Am. citizens); m. Claire McGinnis, 1949 (div. 1956); children—Marina Ava, Ivan Serge, David; m. Mary Elizabeth Morris, 1959; 1 child, Serge. A.B., Yale U., 1947. Dir., chmn., pres. Ivan Obolensky Inc., pubs., 1956-65; dir. Silver Bear Inc., Atlanta; ptnr. A.T. Brod & Co., investment bankers, Dominick & Dominick Inc., investment bankers, 1965-70, Middendorf Colgate, investment bankers, 1970-73; v.p. C.B. Richard, Ellis/Moseley Hallgarten, investment bankers, 1974-81, Sterling Grace & Co., investment bankers, N.Y.C., 1982-87; sr. v.p. Josephthal & Co., investment bankers, N.Y.C., 1987—; gen. ptnr. Astor Capital Mgmt. Assocs., 1980—; v.p. Protocol Services Ltd.; v.p., treas. Serge Obolensky Assocs.; cons. and lectr. in field; pres. Hotel Investments Inc., N.Y.C., 1950-58. Author: Rogues' March, 1956, numerous others; contbr. to Nikon Krizoi Shimbun, Tokyo, on precious metals, 1985—, program com. N.Y. Soc. of Security Analysts for publishing, oil and gas; contbr. articles to profl. jours. Bd. dirs. Children's Blood Found., N.Y. Hosp., 1952—, pres., 1981—; pres. Josephine Lawrence Hopkins Found., 1971—, Whitemarsh Found., 1980—, Soldier's, Sailor's and Airmen's Club, 1982—; bd. dirs. Police Athletic League, N.Y.C., 1975—, Musicians Emergency Fund, 1981—, pres. 1987—, U.S.O., 1987—. Served as lt. (jg) air corps USNR, 1943-45, ret., 1980. Mem. Am. Legion, Mil. Order Loyal Legion U.S. (sr. vice comdr. 1966, comdr. 1967-70), St. Elmo Soc., Met. Mus. Art (life mem.). Clubs: Knickerbocker, N.Y. Yacht, Union (N.Y.C.). Lodge: Masons (Holland #8 master, 1981, 1st Manhattan Dist. Dep. Grandmaster, 1983-84). Address: 425 E 79th St New York NY 10021

OBRAZTOVA, ELENA, mezzo-soprano; b. Leningrad, USSR, July 7, 1937; grad. Leningrad. Conservatory, 1964. Debut as Marina in Boris Godunov, Bolshoi Opera, 1965; prin. roles in Russian opera reportoery, also as Carmen and Azunena; Am. debut as Marina, also appearances as Amneris in Aida, Delilalah in Samson et Delilah; recitalist, tchr. voice, coach repertory. Recipient numerous awards including Lenin prize, 1976. Office: care ICM Artists 40 W 57th St New York NY 10019 also: Bolshaya Dorogo, Milovskaya 21, Moscow USSR *

OBREGON, ALEJANDRO, painter; b. Colombia, June 4, 1920; s. Pedro and Carmen Obregon; 4 children. Educated Stonyhurst Coll., Eng., Middlesex Sch., Concord, Mass., Mus. Sch. Fine Arts, Boston. Dir., Sch. Fine Arts, Bogota, Colombia, 1949-51, Barranquilla, Colombia, 1956-57; one-man shows: Bogota, Barranquilla, Cali, Paris, Milan, Washington, New York, Lima, Madrid, Barcelona, Munich, Sao Paulo, Rio de Janeiro; represented in permanent collections: Mus. Modern Art, N.Y.C., Guggenheim Mus., N.Y.C., Phillips Gallery, Washington, Museo Nacional, Bogata, Inst. de Arte Contemporaneo, Lima, Museo de Arte Moderno, Bogota, Museo Nacional, La Paz, Galerie Creuze, Paris, Galerie Buchholz, Munich, Vatican Mus., Rome, Galeria Profili, Milan, Inst. Cultura Hispanica, Madrid. Recipient 1st nat. prize Guggenheim Inst., 1959; Prize, Sao Paulo Biennial, 1967; numerous other awards. *

O'BRIEN, BRIAN BOLTON, scientist, engineer, lawyer; b. New Berlin, N.Y., Mar. 15, 1941; s. Austin A. and Adeleine E. (Bolton) O'B. BS, U. Rochester, 1967; JD, New Eng. Sch. Law, 1975. Registered profl. engr., Mass.; bar: Mass. 1976, Dist. Ct. Mass. 1976, U.S. Supreme Ct. 1979. Chief electronics engr. Willsea Works, Rochester, N.Y., 1967-68; staff engr. Analog Devices, Inc., Norwood, Mass., 1968-69; sr. staff engr. Philbrick-Nexus Research Co., Dedham, Mass., 1969; chief engr. Computer Devices, Inc., Burlington, Mass., 1969-70; project engr. Di-An Controls Inc., Dorchester, Mass., 1970-72; chief engr., dir. Syner-Data Inc., Andover, Mass., 1972-74; tech. adviser Centronics Data Computer, Hudson, N.H., 1974-75; sole practice law, Weston, Mass., 1976—; pvt. practice as inventor, designer, and developer of high tech. systems, products, instruments, and mechanisms, including X-ray and laser image scanning systems, computer instrumentation, Weston, Mass., 1975—. Contbr. articles on laser image scanning to various publs. Mem. AAAS, Optical Soc. Am., IEEE, Mass. Bar Assn., Boston Computer Soc., Aircraft Owners and Pilots Assn., Mensa. Office: PO Box 651 Weston MA 02193

O'BRIEN, CAROL JEAN, park district superintendent; b. Chgo., June 18, 1939; d. Charles August and Frances Carolyn (Reese) Boeck; m. Thomas Joseph McEvoy, Oct. 18, 1958 (div. Mar. 1982); 1 child, Corrine Marie McEvoy; John Patrick O'Brien, July 18, 1985. Grad. high sch., Maywood, Ill., 1957. Mfrs. rep. Midwest Cen., Chgo., 1969-71; supt. recreation Wood Dale (Ill.) Park Dist., 1977-87, bus. mgr., 1988—. Mem. Nat. Parks and Recreation Assn., Suburban Parks and Recreation Assn. (chairperson 1983-85, sec. 1985-86, spl. projects com. 1986—), Ill. Parks and Recreation Assn. Lutheran. Home: Rt 1 PO Box 244 Boarbonnais IL 60914 Office: Wood Dale Park Dist 533 N Wood Dale Rd Wood Dale IL 60191

O'BRIEN, CONOR CRUISE, writer, diplomat; b. Dublin, Nov. 3, 1917; s. Francis Cruise and Katherine (Shechy) O'B.; ed. Trinity Coll., Dublin; Litt.D., Bradford U., 1971, U. Ghana, 1974, U. Edinburgh, 1976, U. Nice, 1978, Coleraine U., 1981, U. Liverpool, 1987; m. Christine H. Foster, 1939 (div. 1962); 3 children; m. 2d Marie MacEntee, 1962; 2 adopted children. Entered Dept. External Affairs Govt. of Ireland, 1944, counselor, Paris, 1955-56, head UN sect. and mem. Irish Del. to UN, 1956-60, asst. sec. gen. dept. 1960; rep. Sec. Gen. of UN, Katanga, Congo (Now Shaba, Zaire), 1961; vice chancellor U. Ghana, 1962-65; Regents prof., holder Albert Schweitzer chair in humanities N.Y. U., 1965-69; mem. Dail Eireann, Dublin, 1969-77; minister of Posts and Telegraphs, 1973-77; senator Dublin U., 1977-79; editor in chief The Observer, London, 1978-81, cons. edn., 1981—; pro-chancellor U. Dublin, 1973—; author: Maria Cross, 1952, Parnell and his Party, 1957, To Katanga and Back, 1962, Conflicting Concepts of the United Nations, 1964, Writers and Politics, 1965, The United Nations: Sacred Drama, 1967, Concor Cruise O'Brien Introduces Ireland, 1969, Camus, 1969; (with Maire Cruise O'Brien) A Concise History of Ireland, 1972, The Suspecting Glance, 1972, States of Ireland, 1972, Herod's Reflections on Political Violence, 1978; editor: The Shaping of Modern Ireland, 1959, Power and Consciousness, 1969, Edmund Burke's Reflections on the Revolution in France, 1969; Play: Murderous Angeles, 1968. Recipient Valiant for Truth Media award, 1979; fellow St. Catherine's Coll., Oxford, 1978-81. Mem. Royal Irish Acad. Office: Whitewater, The Summit, Howth, Dublin Ireland *

O'BRIEN, EDNA, author; b. County Clare, Ireland, Dec. 15, 1930; d. Michael and Lena (Cleary) O'B.; divorced, 1964; children. Ed. Pharm. Coll. Ireland. Prin. works include: The Country Girls, 1960, The Lonely Girl, 1962, Girls in Their Married Bliss, 1963, August is a Wicked Month, 1964, Casualties of Peace, 1966, The Love Object, 1968, Night, 1972, Mother Ireland, 1976, Johnny I Hardly Knew You (novel), 1977, Arabian Days, 1977, Mrs. Reinhardt and other stories, 1978, The Dazzle (children's book), Returning: A Collection of New Tales, 1982; (short stories) A Scandalous Woman, 1974; Stories of Joan of Arc, 1984; plays include: A Pagan Place, 1971, Virginia, 1979, Home Sweet Home, 1984; screenplay The Wicked Lady, 1979; TV play The Hard Way, 1980, Flesh and Blood, 1987. Recipient Yorkshire Post Novel award, 1971; Kingsley Amis award. Office: care Fraser & Dunlop Scripts Ltd, 91 Regent St, London W1, England *

O'BRIEN, GEORGE DENNIS, university president; b. Chgo., Feb. 21, 1931; s. George Francis and Helen (Fehlandt) O'B.; m. Judith Alyce Johnson, June 21, 1958; children: Elizabeth Belle, Juliana Helen, Victoria Alyce. A.B. in English, Yale, 1952; Carnegie research fellow, U. Chgo., 1956-57, Ph.D. in Philosophy, 1961. Tchr. humanities U. Chgo., 1956-57; successively instr., asst. prof., asst. dean coll. Princeton, 1958-65; on leave in Athens, Greece 1963-64; spl. honors seminars LaSalle Coll., spring 1963, fall 1964, spring 1965; assoc. prof. philosophy Middlebury Coll., 1965-71, prof., 1971-76, dean of men, 1965-67, dean of coll., 1967-74, dean faculty, 1975-76; pres. Bucknell U., 1976-84, U. Rochester, 1984—; Fellow Am. Council Learned Socs., London, Eng., 1971-72. Author: Hegel on Reason in History, 1975, God and the New Haven Railway, 1986; Contbr. articles to profl. jours. Trustee LaSalle Coll., Phila., 1965—; bd. dirs. Union Theol. Sem., 1985—. Mem. Am. Philos. Assn., Phi Beta Kappa. Home: 630 Mt Hope Ave Rochester NY 14620 Office: U Rochester Office of Pres Rochester NY 14627

O'BRIEN, GRACE WILHELMINA EHLIG, psychologist, retired educational administrator, writer, lectr.; b. Los Angeles, Aug. 27, 1922; d. Max Carl and Janette (Rentchler) Ehlig; A.A., Pasadena City Coll., 1942; A.B., UCLA, 1944, postgrad., 1944-46; postgrad. Riverside City Coll., 1946; postgrad. Calif. State Coll. at Los Angeles, 1954-66, 68-78, M.A. in Guidance, 1964; m. Louis J. O'Brien, Nov. 8, 1947; children—Carol Jean, Lawrence John, Perry Lewis. Tchr., Perris (Calif.) Union High Sch., 1945-46; tchr., counselor, psychometrist Los Angeles City Schs., 1946-66, cons. counselor, sch. psychologist Elem. Secondary Edn. Act, Edn. and Guidance program, 1966-68; head counselor, asst. prin. Garden Gate Opportunity Sch., 1968-73; vice prin. Markham Jr. High Sch., 1973, Belvedere Jr. High Sch., 1974; asst. prin. Garfield High Sch., 1974-75, Mt. Vernon Jr. High Sch., Los Angeles, 1975-76; prin. Garden Gate High Sch., 1977-80, Johnson High Sch., 1980-84. Den mother chmn. Cub Scouts, 1964-66. Recipient spl. service award Boy Scouts, 1964. Mem. UCLA Alumni Assn., Sr. High Prins. Assn., Los Angeles Assn. Sch. Adminstrs., Calif. Assn. Sch. Adminstrs., DAR, Phi Delta Kappa, Pi Lambda Theta, Chi Delta Phi. Presbyterian (supt. Sunday sch. 1953-54). Home: 3880 Shadow Grove Rd Pasadena CA 91107 Office: 900 E 42d St Los Angeles CA 90011

O'BRIEN, JOHN WILLIAM, JR., investment management company executive; b. Bronx, N.Y., Jan. 1, 1937; s. John William and Ruth Catherine (Timon) O'B.; B.S., MIT, 1958; M.S., UCLA, 1964; m. Jane Bower Nippert, Feb. 2, 1963; children—Christine, Andrea, Michael, John William III, Kevin Robert. Sr. asso. Planning Research Corp., Los Angeles, 1962-67; dir. fin. systems group Synergetic Scis., Inc., Tarzana, Calif., 1967-70; dir. analytical services div. James H. Oliphant & Co., Los Angeles, 1970-72; chmn. bd., chief exec. officer, pres. O'Brien Assos., Inc., Santa Monica, Calif., 1972-77; v.p. A.G. Becker Inc., 1977-81; chmn., chief exec. officer Leland O'Brien Rubinstein Assos., 1981—. Served to 1st lt. USAF, 1958-62. Recipient Graham and Dodd award Fin. Analysts Fedn., 1970. Mem. Delta Upsilon. Home: Box 3159 Blue Jay CA 92317 Office: 523 W 6th St Suite 220 Los Angeles CA 90014

O'BRIEN, JOSEPH EDWARD, JR., lawyer; b. Keokuk, Iowa, July 27, 1933; s. Joseph Edward and Dorothy Maude (Dickinson) O'B.; m. Jeralyn Alice Nibler, Jan. 28, 1966; children—Joseph Edward III, Leslie Ann. B.S. cum laude, Georgetown U., 1955, J.D., 1963; M.B.A., Am. U., 1956. Bar: Md. 1964, D.C. 1964, U.S. Ct. Appeals (D.C. cir.) 1964, U.S. Tax Ct. 1973, U.S. Ct. Appeals (4th cir.) 1977. Law clk. Circuit Ct. Montgomery County, Md., 1963-64; assoc. Brodsky & Cuddy, Kensington, Md., 1964-66; sole practice Rockville, Md., 1966-79, Bethesda, Md., 1979—; judge Appeal Tax Ct. Montgomery County, 1967-69, chief judge, 1968-69; mem. Montgomery County Bd. Appeals 1969-87, chmn. 1969-71, 81-83, vice chmn., 1972-80, 84-87. Served to comdr. USN. Mem. Montgomery County Bar Assn., ABA, Am. Arbitration Assn., Soc. Mayflower Descendants, Phi Delta Phi, Phi Alpha Theta. Republican. Roman Catholic. Clubs: Congressional Country.

(chmn. legal com. 1977, chmn. legal com. Kemper Open Golf Tournament, 1981, 83-86). Address: 6105 Madawaska Rd Bethesda MD 20816

O'BRIEN, KEVIN BENJAMIN, business consultant; b. Wellington, N.Z., Oct. 19, 1925; s. Benjamin and Lucy Veronica (Conaghan) O'B.; m. Audrey Berenice Cook, May 7, 1955 (dec. 1981); children—Christine, Mark, Janet, Josephine, Anne, Clare, Meredith. B. Commerce, Victoria U., Wellington, 1947, M. Commerce, 1948, B.A., 1953, LL.D. (hon.), 1984. Asst. produce mgr. Burch & Co. Ltd., Wellington, 1946-49; purchasing officer J.J. McCaskey & Son Ltd., Wellington, 1949-53; gen. mgr. N.Z. Players Theatre, Wellington, 1954—; pvt. practice as bus. cons., Wellington, 1960—; chmn. Tiki Tape N.Z. Ltd., Wellington, 1975—, Newport Distbg. Co., Wellington, 1963-86; dir. Richmond Mall Ltd., 1987—. Mem. tariff and devel. bd. Wellington, 1962-75, chmn., 1972-75; chmn. Commerce Commn., Wellington, 1977-84; chancellor Victoria U., Wellington, 1975-84. Recipient Queens Silver Jubilee medal, 1977; Decorated companion Order of St. Michael and St. George. Mem. N.Z. Assn. Economists, Wellington C. of C. (pres. 1958-59), N.Z. Univ. Students Assn. (pres. 1951, life mem.), Ret. Execs. Assn. (chmn. 1985—), Mfrs. Assn. (mem. council 1985—). Roman Catholic. Home: 25 Medway St, Wellington New Zealand

O'BRIEN, LIBBY ATKINS, public relations exec.; b. N.Y.C., Mar. 17, 1913; d. Richard Travis and Alice Gordon (Quigley) Atkins; grad. Kendall Hall, 1931; m. Richard Thomas O'Brien, June 25, 1935 (dec.); children—Francis DeSales, Sarah Jane O'Brien Prezalor. Car rep. Brady Stannard Motors, Brewster, N.Y., Blanchard Motors, Greenwich, Conn., and Tolm Motors, Darren, Conn., 1940-46; producer TV show Libby O'Brien's Table Toppers, 1946-48; commentator, dir. women's programs WLAD, Danbury, Conn., 1948-51, WSTC, Stamford, Conn., 1951-53; asst. dir. public relations Save the Children Fedn., 1954-55; advt. mgr. Roux Distbg. Corp., 1956-57; public relations mgr. Lily Tulip Cup Corp., 1957-64; owner, mgr. Libby O'Brien Enterprises, Inc., 1964-69; owner, breeder, exporter O'Brien Donkey Farm, promoter of tourism in Kenmare, Ireland, 1969-76; sales person, Chatham, Mass., 1976—; book collaborator; active Utilizing Sr. Energy, Know Your Body-Am. Health Orgn.; publicity chmn. Greenwich Meals on Wheels. Collector, seller old N.Y.C. st. signs; exhibited yarn art in singles shows on the Cape and in Newport, R.I. Mem. Am. Women in Radio and TV, Public Relations Assn., Public Relations Inst. U.K. Republican. Home: Moorland Farm Pheasant House #3 Hammersmith Rd Newport RI 02840

O'BRIEN, MARK STEPHEN, pediatric neurosurgeon; b. West New York, N.J., Jan. 2, 1933; s. Mark Peter and Hannah (Dempsey) O'B.; m. Mary Morris Johnson, June 3, 1961 (div.); children: David, Marcia, Derek; m. Karen Marie Sampson, June 1, 1984; children: Blythe, Blake. A.B. cum laude, Seton Hall U., 1955; M.D., St. Louis U., 1959. Intern St. John's Hosp., St. Louis, 1959-60; resident in surgery St. John's Hosp., 1960; resident in neurology Charity Hosp., New Orleans, 1962-63; resident in neurosurgery St. Vincent's Hosp., N.Y.C., 1963-64; resident in surgery St. Vincent's Hosp., 1965; sr. resident, chief resident Cin. Children's Hosp., U. Cin., 1965-68, research fellow in neurosurgery, 1966-67, 67-68; NIH spl. fellow in neuroradiology Albert Einstein Coll. Medicine, N.Y.C., 1968-69; mem. faculty dept. surgery Emory U. Sch. Medicine, Atlanta, 1969—; prof. surgery, assoc. prof. pediatrics Emory U. Sch. Medicine, 1979—; chief neurosurgery Henrietta Egleston Hosp. for Children, Atlanta, 1971—, Scottish Rite Hosp. for Crippled Children, Atlanta, 1975—; trustee Elaine Clark Center for Exceptional Children; mem. med. adv. bd. Nat. Found., March of Dimes; trustee Henrietta Egleston Hosp. for Children; mem. profl. adv. panel Spina Bifida Assn. Am. Contbr. chpts. to books, articles to med. jours. Served with USNR, 1960-62. Mem. Am. Assn. Neurol. Surgeons, Soc. Neurol. Surgeons, Congress Neurol. Surgeons, Internat. Soc. Pediatric Neurosurgery, Greater Atlanta Pediatric Soc., Med. Soc. Atlanta, AMA, A.C.S., Ga. Neurosurg. Soc., Am. Acad. Pediatrics, Am. Soc. Pediatric Neurosurgery, Pediatric Oncology Group. Home: 49 Camden Rd NE Atlanta GA 30309 Office: 1365 Clifton Rd NE Atlanta GA 30322

O'BRIEN, MARY DEVON, communications company executive, strategic planning-consultant; b. Buenos Aires, Argentina, Feb. 13, 1944; came to U.S., 1949, naturalized, 1962; d. George Earle and Margaret Frances (Richards) Owen; m. Gordon Covert O'Brien, Feb. 16, 1962 (div. Aug. 1982); children—Christopher Covert, Devon Elizabeth; m. Christopher Gerard Smith, May 28, 1983. BS, Rutgers U., 1975, MBA, 1976. Controller manpower Def. Communications div. ITT, Nutley, N.J., 1977-80, adminstr. program, 1977-78, mgr. cost, schedule control, 1978-79, voice processing project, 1979-80; mgr. project Avionics div. ITT, Nutley, 1980-81, sr. mgr. projects, 1981—; cons. strategic planning, N.J., 1983—; lectr. in field, 1977—. Author: Pace: System Manual, 1979, Voices, 1982. Chmn. Citizens Budget Adv. Com., Maplewood, N.J., 1984-87, chmn. recreation, library, pub. services, 1982-83, chmn. pub. safety, emergency services, 1983-84, chmn. schs. and edn., 1984-85; bd. dirs., officer Civic Assn., Maplewood, 1984—; first v.p. MCA, 1987—; chmn. Maple Leaf Service award Com., 1987—, United Way of Essex and West Hudson Community Edn. Program, Community Service Council of Oranges and Maplewood Homelessness, Affordable Housing, Shelter Com., United Way Community Services Council bd. trustees, 1988—; nat. chmn. Project Mgmt. Jour. Survey; mem. Maplewood Zoning Bd., 1983—; officer, mem. exec. bd. N.J. Project Mgmt. Inst., 1985—, pres., 1987—, v.p., 1986; chmn. bd. dirs. Performance Mgmt. Assn. Charter Com.; chmn. Internat. Project Mgmt. Inst. Jour. and Membership survey, 1986-87, mktg. com., 1986-, long range planning and steering com., 1987—; adv. bd. Project Mgmt. Jour., 1987—, N.J. PMI Ednl., 1987—; mem. MCA/N.J.Blood Bank Drive. Recipient Anti-Shoplifting Program award Distributive Edn. Club Am., 1981, N.J. Fedn. of Women's Clubs, 1981, 82, Retail Mchts. Assn., 1981, 82; Commendation and Merit awards Air Force Inst. Tech., 1981; Pres.'s Safety award ITT, 1983; State award N.J. Fedn. of Women's Clubs Garden Show, 1982; Cert. Spl. Merit award N.J. Fedn. of Women's Clubs, 1982. Mem. Internat. Platform Speakers Assn., Grand Jury Assn., Telecommunications Group and Aerospace Industries Assn., Women's Career Network Assn., Nat. Security Indsl. Assn., Assn. for Info. and Image Mgmt., ITT Mgmt. Assn., LWV. Club: Maplewood Women's EMD (pres. 1980-82). Home: 594 Valley St Maplewood NJ 07040 Office: ITT Avionics 417 River Rd Nutley NJ 07110

O'BRIEN, ROBERT BROWNELL, JR., banker, savings and loan executive; b. N.Y.C., Sept. 6, 1934; s. Robert Brownell and Eloise (Boles) O'B.; m. Sarah Lager, Nov. 28, 1958; children: Robert Brownell, III, William Stuart, Jennifer. B.A., Lehigh U., 1957; postgrad., N.Y. U. Grad. Sch. Bus. Adminstrn., Am. Inst. Banking. Asst. treas., credit officer, br. locations officer Bankers Trust Co., N.Y.C., 1957-63; with George A. Murray Co., gen. contractors, N.Y.C., 1964; also v.p. Bowery Savs. Bank, 1964-69; dir., chief exec. officer Fed. Savs. & Loan Ins. Corp., Washington, 1969-71; chmn. exec. com. Fed. Home Loan Bank Bd., 1969-71; v.p. Bowery Savs. Bank, N.Y.C., 1972; exec. v.p. First Fed. Savs. & Loan Assn., N.Y.C., 1973-75; chmn., pres., chief exec. officer Carteret Savs. Bank, Newark, from 1975, also bd. dirs.; bd. dirs. Home Group Centenial Industries, Essex Life Co., Home Group, Inc. Contbr. articles to trade mags. Bd. govs. N.J. State Opera; bd. dirs. United Way, Neighborhood Housing Services Am.; trustee Trinity Pawling Sch.; trustee, past chmn. Community Found. of N.J., 1987—; mem. Nat. Commn. on Neighborhoods. Mem. Nat. Council Savs. Instns. (past chmn.), Essex County Savs. and Loan League (past chmn.), N.J. Savs. League (chmn.), N.J. Hist. Soc. (chmn.), Greater Newark C. of C. (dir.). Republican. Episcopalian. Clubs: Union League; Delray Beach Yacht; Ocean Reef; New York Yacht; Bay Head Yacht; Morris County Golf. Home: 2423 N Ocean Blvd Gulf Stream FL 33483 Office: Carteret Savs Bank FA 200 South St Morristown NJ 07960

O'BRIEN, ROBERT S., state official; b. Seattle, Sept. 14, 1918; s. Edward R. and Maude (Ransom) O'B.; m. Kathryn E. Arvan, Oct. 18, 1941 (dec. June 1984). Student public schs. With Kaiser Co., 1938-46; restaurant owner 1946-50; treas. Grant County, Wash., 1950-65, State of Wash., 1965—; chmn. Wash. Fin. Com., 1965—, Wash. Public Deposit Protection Commn., 1969—, Wash. Public Employees Retirement Bd., 1969-77, Law Enforcement Officers and Firefighters Retirement System, 1971-77, Wash. State Investment Bd., 1981—; mem. Wash. Data Processing Adv. Bd., 1967-73, Gov.'s Exec. Mgmt. and Fiscal Affairs Com., 1978-80, Gov.'s Cabinet Com. on Tax Alternatives, 1978-80; trustee Wash. Tchr.'s Retirement System, 1965—. Recipient Leadership award Joint Council County and City Employees-Fedn. State Employees, 1970, Eagles Leadership award, 1967. Mem. Nat. Assn. State Auditors, Comptrollers and Treasurers (pres. 1977), Nat. Assn. Mcpl. Fin. Officers, Nat. Assn. State Treasurers, Western State Treasurers Assn. (pres. 1970), Wash. County Treas. Assn. (pres. 1955-56), Wash. Assn. Elected County Ofcls. (pres. 1955-58), Olympia Area C. of C., Soap Lake C. of C. (pres. 1948). Democrat. Clubs: Elks (hon. life); Moose, Eagles, Lions, Olympia Yacht, Olympia Country and Golf; Empire (Spokane); Wash. Athletic (Seattle). Office: State Treas Legislative Bldg AS-23 Olympia WA 98504

O'BRIEN, ROBERT THOMAS, portfolio manager, investment analyst; b. Phila., Oct. 7, 1941; s. James Francis Sr. and Mildred Anita (Gomez); m. Aurora Carol Forsthoffer, Nov. 7, 1964; 1 child, Michael Joseph. Cert., N.Y. Inst. Fin., 1963; BS, St. Joseph's U., 1971. Securities trader Brown Bros. Harriman, Phila., 1964-69, portfolio mgr., 1969-77, investment officer, 1977-80, asst. mgr., investment adv., 1980-83; v.p. Newbold's Asset Mgmt., Phila., 1983-85, sr. v.p., 1985-87, mng. dir., 1987—. Served with USAF and Pa. Air N.G., 1960-67, Vietnam. Mem. Phila. Securities Assn. Republican. Roman Catholic. Clubs: Racquet (house com.), Sailing Assn. (commodore 1980-82); Lewes Yacht, Aronimink Golf, Idle Hour Tennis. Home: 665 Dodds Ln Gladwyne PA 19035 Office: W H Newbolds Son & Co Inc 1500 Walnut St Philadelphia PA 19102

O'BRIEN, WALTER JOSEPH, II, lawyer; b. Chgo., Apr. 22, 1939; s. Walter Joseph O'Brien and Lorayne (Stouffer) Steele; children: Kelly A., Patrick W., Kathleen; m. Sharon Ann Curling, July 8, 1978; 1 child, John Joseph. BBA, U. Notre Dame, 1961; JD, Northwestern U.-Chgo., 1964. Bar: Ill. 1965, U.S. Dist. Ct. (no. dist.) Ill. 1965, U.S. Supreme Ct. 1973. Assoc. Nicholson, Nisen, Elliott & Meier, Chgo., 1966-70; pres., Capstan Co., Chgo., 1970-73, Walter J. O'Brien II, Ltd., Oak Brook, Ill., 1973-78, O'Brien & Assocs., P.C., Oakbrook Terrace, Ill., 1978—; dir. Atty. Title Guaranty Fund, Inc., Champaign, Ill., 1979—. Contbr. articles to legal jours. Commr., Oak Brook Plan Commn., 1980-85 ; mem. Oak Brook Zoning Bd. Appeals, 1985-87; v.p. Oak Brook Civic Assn., 1972; trustee St. Isaac Jogues Ch., Hinsdale, Ill., 1975-76. Served as capt. Q.M.C., U.S. Army, 1964-66. Fellow Ill. Bar Found.; mem. Ill. State Bar Assn. (mem. assembly), ABA, DuPage Bar Assn. (bd. dirs. 1987-88). Roman Catholic. Club: Butterfield Country (bd. dirs. 1982—) (Oak Brook). Office: O'Brien & Assocs PC 17W200 22d St Oakbrook Terrace IL 60181

O'BROLCHAIN, MÁIRE ÚNA, social demographer; b. Dublin, Dec. 29, 1948; d. Ruairi Gabriel and Catherine Angela (Geary) O'Brolchain; m. Antoni Leszek Chawluk, Aug. 16, 1973 (div. 1980). BA in Psychology with honors, U. Coll. Dublin, 1970; MSc in Stats and Ops. Research, Trinity Coll. Dublin, 1971. Research officer Bedford Coll., London, 1971-73; research fellow London Sch. Hygiene and Tropical Medicine, 1978-86; prin. research officer London Research Ctr., 1987—. Editorial adviser European Sociol. Rev., 1985—; contbr. sci. articles to numerous publs. Fellow Royal Statis. Soc.; mem. Internat. Union Sci. Study Population, Brit. Soc. Population Studies. Roman Catholic. Office: London Research Ctr, County Hall, London SE1 7PB, England

O'BYRNE, NATALIE KWASNESKI, psychiatrist; b. Bklyn., Nov. 29, 1933; d. Julian Leon and Jeannette Pauline (Kowalski) Kwasneski; BS in Chemistry cum laude, St. John's U., 1955; MD, State U. N.Y., Bklyn., 1959; m. William O'Byrne, June 13, 1959; children: Cecily, Matthew, Stephanie, Gabrielle, Luke. Intern, Kings County Hosp., N.Y.C., 1960-61; resident in pediatrics Children's Hosp., San Francisco, 1962-63, adolescent medicine fellow, 1963-64; resident in adult psychiatry St. Mary's Hosp., San Francisco, 1964-66, in child psychiatry, 1966-68; practice medicine specializing in adult, child and adolescent psychiatry, Corte Madera, Calif., 1968—; assoc. clin. prof. U. Calif. (San Francisco); sr. supervising psychiatrist Langley-Porter Children's Service; bd. dirs. Threshold, Inc. Diplomate Am. Bd. Psychiatry and Neurology, Am. Bd. Adult and Child Psychiatry. Fellow Am. Psychiat. Assn., Am. Acad. Child Psychiatry; mem. AMA, Calif. Med. Assn., Marin, San Francisco med. socs., No. Calif. Psychiat. Assn., Regional Orgn. Child-Adolescent Psychiatry. Roman Catholic. Home: 715 Butterfield Rd San Anselmo CA 94960 Office: 1556 Redwood Hwy Corte Madera CA 94925

OBZINA, JAROMÍR, Czechoslovak government official, educator; b. Brodek, May 28, 1929; s. Frantisek and Zofie (Obzinova) O.; ed. Prerov Secondary Sch., Ph.D., Central Com. of CPSU Higher Edn. Coll., Moscow; m. Své tla Obzinová ; 2 children. Sec., Chrudim Dist. Com., CP of Czechoslovakia; 1st. sec. Policka and Pardubice Dist. Com.; instr. Pardubice regional com.; held positions Main Polit. Bd. Czechoslvok People's Army, 1953-56; comdr. Antonin Zapotocky Mil. Acad. Polit. dept., 1956-64; head div. sci. CP Central Com. Dept. Edn. and Sci., 1965-68; dep. comdr. Czechoslovak People's Army Inst. Sci. Affairs, 1968-69; head div. sci., dept. head Dept. Edn. Sci. and Sci., 1969-73; minister interior, 1973-83; mem. House of the People of Fed. Nat. Assembly, 1973—, also mem. CP Central com., 1973—; dep. prime minister, 1983—; chmn. State Commn. for Sci., Tech., and Investments, 1983—. Address: State Commn for Sci, Tech and Investments, Slezska 9, 12029 Prague 2 Czechoslovakia

OCCHETTO, ACHILLE, Italian government official; b. Turin, Italy, Mar. 3, 1936. M.P. Italy, Rome, 1976—, mem. fgn. affairs com., 1976, mem. edn. and fine arts com., 1979, mem. cen. com. and nat. directorate; vice sec. Italian Communist Party, until 1988, gen. sec., 1988—. Address: Italian Communist Party, Via delle Botteghe Oscure 4, 00186 Rome Italy *

OCHOA, LUIS ADRIAN, manufacturing company executive, consultant; b. Guadalajara, Mexico, Feb. 9, 1955; s. Luis and Gloria (Fregoso) O.; m. Estela Molina, Apr. 2, 1977; children—Luis, Diego, Marcos, Diana, Carlos. Civil Engr., U. Autonoma de Guadalajara, 1976; M. en C., U. Nacional Autonoma de Mexico, 1977. Chief of project FOA, S.C., Mexico City, 1977-78; founder, pres. Articulos De Aluminio, Guadalajara, Mexico, 1979-84; pres. Tauber de Mexico, S.A., Guadalajara, 1984—; dir. Union De Credito Indsl., Guadalajara, Metaco Mexico S.A., Guadalajara; cons. Administracion e Informatica S.A., Guadalajara. Patentee water filter, 1978, bonding machine. Club: Playas Del Chante (pres. 1984-85). Avocation: camping. Office: Tauber De Mexico SA de CV, Tlahuac 77, 45050 Guadalajara Mexico

OCHOA, SEVERO, biochemist; b. Luarca, Spain, Sept. 24, 1905; came to U.S., 1940, naturalized, 1956; s. Severo and Carmen (Albornoz) O.; m. Carmen G. Cobian, July 8, 1931. A.B., Malaga (Spain) Coll., 1921; M.D., U. Madrid, Spain, 1929; D.Sc., Washington U., U. Brazil, 1957, U. Guadalajara, Mexico, 1959, Wesleyan U., U. Oxford, Eng., U. Salamanca, Spain, 1961, Gustavus Adolphus Coll., 1963, U. Pa., 1964, Brandeis U., 1965, U. Granada, Spain, U. Oviedo, Spain, 1967, U. Perugia, Italy, 1968, U. Mich., Weizman Inst., Israel, 1982; Dr. Med. Sci. (hon.), U. Santo Tomas, Manila, Philippines, 1963, U. Buenos Aires, 1968, U. Tucuman, Argentina, 1968; L.H.D., Yeshiva Univ., 1966; LL.D., U. Glasgow, Scotland, 1959. Lectr. physiology U. Madrid Med. Sch., 1931-35; head physiol. div. Inst. for Med. Research, 1935-36; guest research asst. in physiology Kaiser-Wilhelm Inst. for Med. Research, Heidelberg, Germany, 1936-37; Ray Lankester investigator Marine Biol. Lab., Plymouth, Eng., 1937; demonstrator Nuffield research asst. biochemistry Oxford (Eng.) U. Med. Sch., 1938-41; instr., research asso. pharmacology Washington U. Sch. of Medicine, St. Louis, 1941-42; research asso. medicine N.Y. U. Sch. Medicine, 1942-45, asst. prof. biochemistry, 1945-46, prof. pharmacology, chmn. dept., 1946-54, prof., chmn. dept. biochemistry, 1954-76, prof., 1976—; distinguished mem. Roche Inst. Molecular Biology. Author publs. on biochem. of muscles, glycolysis in heart and brain, transphosphorylations in yeast fermentation, pyruvic acid oxidation in brain and role of vitamin B1; RNA and Protein biosynthesis; genetic code. Decorated Order Rising Sun Japan; recipient (with Arthur Kornberg) 1959 Nobel prize in medicine, Albert Gallatin medal N.Y. U., 1970, Nat. Medal of Sci., 1980. Fellow N.Y. Acad. Scis., N.Y. Acad. Medicine, Am. Acad. of Arts and Sci., A.A.A.S.; mem. Nat. Acad. Sci., Am. Philos. Soc., Soc. for Exptl. Biology and Medicine, Soc. of Biol. Chemists (pres. 1958, editor jour. 1950-60), Internat. Union Biochemistry (pres. 1961-67), Biochem. Soc. (Eng.), Harvey Soc. (pres. 1953-54), Alpha Omega Alpha (hon.); fgn. mem. German Acad. Nat. Scis., Royal Spanish, USSR, Polish, Pullian, Italian, Argentinian, Barcelona (Spain), Brazilian acads. sci., Royal Soc. (Eng.), Pontifical Acad. Sci., G.D.R. Acad. Scis., Argentinian Nat. Acad. Medicine. Office: Roche Inst Molecular Biol Nutley NJ 07110

OCHOA MEJIA, JOSE, banker; b. Cali, Colombia, Dec. 24, 1940; s. Jose and Victoria (Mejia) O.; B.Mech. Engr. (Dean's scholar), Cornell U., 1965; M.B.A., 1967; m. Jennifer C. Lowe, Aug. 4, 1973; children—Alexis David, Lucas Sebastian. Fin. analyst Celanese Corp., N.Y.C., 1967-69; project mgr. Internat. Life Ins. Co. Ltd., London, 1969-73; mgr. Rothschild Intercontinental Bank Ltd., London, 1973-77; sr. mgr. Libra Bank Ltd., London, 1977; asst. gen. mng. Scandinavian Bank, London, 1978-80, sr. v.p., rep., N.Y.C., 1980-83, gen. mgr., London, 84; mng. dir. Corporacion Privada de Inversiones de Centroamerica S.A., San Jose, Costa Rica, 1985; v.p. Citibank N.A., London, 1986—. Mem. Cornell U. Council. Clubs: Bentley Drivers. Home: Rectory Cottage, Woodmancote, Henfield BN5 9SR, England Office: Citibank NA, 41 Berkeley Sq, London WIX 6NA, England

OCHSNER, OTHON HENRY, II, importer, restaurant critic; b. Chgo., May 19, 1934; s. Othon Henry and Louise Catherine (Schlichenmaier) O. A.A., Chgo. City Coll., 1961. Pub. relations staff Walgreen Co., Chgo., 1961-65; sales mgr. Porsche Car Imports, Northbrook, Ill., 1966-67; nat. sales mgr. Pirelli Tire Corp., N.Y.C., 1968-73; pres., chief exec. officer Ochsner Internat., Chgo., 1974—; also bd. dirs.; pres. Swiss-U.S.A. Racing Team, Chgo., 1976—. Author: Ochsner Pocket Guide to the Finest Restaurants in the World, 5th edit., 1987, Ochsner Restaurant Newsletter, 1986—. Mem. Mus. Sci. and Industry Bus. Alliance, Chgo., 1984. Served with U.S. Army, 1957-59. Mem. Am. -Swiss C. of C., French-Am. C. of C., German-Am. C. of C., Chef of Cuisine Assn. Chgo., The Art Inst. Chgo., Swiss Gourmet Soc. (pres. U.S. chpt.). Republican. Baptist. Avocation: visiting and reviewing world class French and Swiss restaurants worldwide. Home: 5885 N Forest Glen Ave Chicago IL 60646 Office: The Ochsner Bldg 4341 W Peterson Chicago IL 60646

O'CONNELL, DANIEL WALTER, investment company executive; b. Chgo., July 31, 1946; s. David Walter and Gertrude Ann (Schmidt) O'C.; m. Paula Marie Williams, Sept. 26, 1981. BS in Chemistry with high honors, U. Ill., 1968; MBA, Harvard U., 1974; MSA with distinction, DePaul U., Chgo., 1983. Research chemist U.S. Gypsum, Des Plaines, Ill., 1968-69; fin. analyst 1st Chgo. Corp., 1974-75, ltd. market advisor, trust officer, asst. v.p., 1975-79, v.p., mgr. instl. venture capital fund, 1979-84; mng. ptnr. Alpha Capital Venture Ptnrs., Chgo., 1984—; advisor R.W. Allsop & Assocs., Cedar Rapids, 1981—; bd. dirs. Channel One Communications, Clayton, Mo., CarCare Enterprises, Chgo. Served as lt. (j.g.) USN, 1969-72. Mem. Nat. Assn. Small Bus. Investment Cos., Chgo. High Tech. Assn. Club: Harvard U. Bus. Sch. Chgo. (v.p. 1979-83). Office: 3 First Nat Plaza Suite 1400 Chicago IL 60670

O'CONNELL, FRANCIS JOSEPH, lawyer; b. Ft. Edward, N.Y., Mar. 19, 1913; s. Daniel P. and Mary (Bowe) O'C.; m. Adelaide M. Nagro, Sept. 27, 1937; children—Chris, Mary Gaynour Lavonas. A.B., Columbia U., 1934; J.D., Fordham U., 1938; S.J.D. summa cum laude, Bklyn. Law Sch., 1945. Bar: N.Y. 1938, U.S. Tax Ct. 1941, U.S. Dist. Ct. (so. dist.) N.Y. 1942. Counsel and asst. to chmn. exec. com. for labor law and litigation Allied Chem. Corp., N.Y.C., 1942-70; ptnr. Bill & O'Connell and predecessor, N.Y.C., 1970-76; sole practice, Garden City, N.Y. and Cutchogue, N.Y., 1976—; arbitrator, fact-finder, mediator Fed. Mediation and Conciliation Service, N.Y. State Mediation Bd., Am. Arbitration Assn., also N.Y. State, Nassau and Suffolk County public employment relations bds., 1970—; adminstrv. law judge N.Y. State Dept. Health, 1979—; instr. labor law and labor relations Cornell U. U.S. del. ILO, Geneva, 1948, 59, 69, 72; trustee Village of Garden City, 1948-50; mem. bd. edn. Diocese of Rockville Centre (N.Y.), 1972-80; pres. various civic orgns., 1942—. Mem. ABA (labor and internat. law sects.), N.Y. State Bar Assn. (labor com.), Bar Assn. Nassau County (labor and arbitration coms., former chmn. arbitration and labor law coms.), Mfg. Chemists Assn. (chmn. indsl. relations com.), U.S. C. of C. (indsl. relations com.). Republican. Roman Catholic. Author: Labor Law and the First Line Supervisor, 1945; Restrictive Work Practices, 1967; National Emergency Strikes, 1968.

O'CONNELL, FRANCIS V(INCENT), mfr.; b. Norwich, Conn., July 8, 1903; s. Thomas Francis and Isabelle (Gelino) O.'C.; LL.B., Blackstone Coll. Law, 1932, J.D., 1940, LL.M., 1942; m. Marie Louise Lemoine, Nov. 7, 1940. Textile screen printer U.S. Finishing Co. Norwich, 1921-30; foreman Ahern Textile Print Co., Norwich, 1930-36; pres., owner Hand Craft Textile Print Co., Plainfield, Conn., 1936—. Roman Catholic. Home: 25 14th St Norwich CT 06360 Office: Bishop's Crossing Plainfield CT 06374

O'CONNELL, HENRY FRANCIS, lawyer; b. Winthrop, Mass., Jan. 4, 1922; s. Henry F. and Anna (Cunning) O'C. B.A., Boston Coll., 1943, J.D., 1948. Bar: Mass. 1948, U.S. Supreme Ct. 1956. House counsel electronics div. Am. Machine & Foundry Co., Boston, 1951-54; sole practice, Boston, 1954-60; assoc. Glynn & Dempsey, Boston, 1960-70, Avery, Dooley, Post & Avery, 1970-88; asst. atty. gen. mcpls. affairs State of Mass., 1969-88. Mem. Winthrop Bd. Selectmen, 1958-64, 68-72, chmn. 1960-61, 68-69, 71-72. Served to lt. USCGR, World War II. Mem. Mass. Bar Assn., Nat. Boating Fedn. (past pres.), Mass. Selectmen's Assn., Mass. Bay Yachts Clubs Assn. (past commodore). Home: 20 Belcher St Winthrop MA 02152

O'CONNELL, PHILIP RAYMOND, paper company executive, lawyer; b. N.Y.C., June 2, 1928; s. Michael Joseph and Ann (Blaney) O'C.; m. Joyce McCabe, July 6, 1957; children: Michael, Kathleen, Jennifer, David. A.B., Manhattan Coll., 1949; LL.B., Columbia U., 1956; grad., Advanced Mgmt. Program, Harvard U., 1967. Bar: N.Y. State 1956, U.S. Supreme Ct. 1961, Conn. 1988. Assoc. Dewey, Ballantine, Bushby, Palmer & Wood, N.Y.C., 1956-61, 62-64; gen. counsel, sec. Laurentide Finance Corp., San Francisco, 1961-62; gen. counsel Wallace-Murray Corp., 1964-66, div. mgr., 1966-70; pres., chief exec. officer, dir. Universal Papertech Corp., Hatfield, Pa., 1970-71; sec. Champion Internat. Corp., Stamford, Conn., 1972—, v.p., 1979-81, sr. v.p., 1981—; mem. legal adv. com. N.Y. Stock Exchange, 1985—; chmn. lawyers steering com. corp. responsibility task force The Bus. Roundtable, 1981-87. Trustee Champion Internat. Found., 1979—; bd. visitors Fairfield U. Sch. Bus., 1981—, chmn., 1983—; bd. dirs. Kearney-Nat. Corp., 1975-78. Served with USNR, 1951-54. Mem. Am. Law Inst., ABA, Am. Soc. Corp. Secs. (chmn. 1988—). Office: Champion Internat Corp 1 Champion Plaza Stamford CT 06921

O'CONNELL, RICHARD (JAMES), poet, educator; b. N.Y.C., Oct. 25, 1928; s. Richard James and Mary Ellen (Fallon) O'C.; B.S., Temple U., 1956; M.A., Johns Hopkins, 1957; m. Beryl Evelyn Reeves, Nov. 14, 1978. Instr. English Temple U., Phila., 1957-61, asst. prof., 1961-69, asso. prof., 1969-86; sr. assoc. prof., 1986—; guest lectr. poetry dept. writing seminars Johns Hopkins U., 1961-74; participant Poetry in Schs. Program, Pa. Council Arts, 1971-73; Fulbright lectr. Am. lit. U. Brazil, Rio de Janeiro, 1960, U. Navarre, Pamplona, Spain, 1962-63. Served with USN, 1948-52. Recipient prize Contemporary Poetry Press, 1972. Mem. PEN, MLA, Asso. Writing Programs, Walt Whitman Poetry Center (dir. 1975-84), Lit. Fellowship Phila. Author: From an Interior Silence, 1961; Cries of Flesh and Stone, 1962; New Poems and Translations, 1963; Brazilian Happenings, 1966; Terrane, 1967; Thirty Epigrams, 1971; Irish Monastic Poems (transl.), 1975; The Word in Time (selected transl. of Antonio Machado), 1975; Sappho (selected transl.), 1975; Lorca (selected transl.), 1976; Middle English Poems (transl.), 1976; More Irish Poems (transl.), 1976; Epigrams from Martial (transl.), 1976; One Hundred Epigrams from the Greek Anthology (trans.), 1977; Hudson's Fourth Voyage, 1978; The Epigrams of Luxorius (transl.), 1984; Temple Poems, 1985; Hanging Tough, 1986; Battle Poems, 1987. Editor: Apollo's Day, 17th Century Songs, 1969; Atlantis Edits., 1962—, Poetry Newsletter, 1971—. Home: 1147 Hillsboro Mile #504S Hillsboro Beach FL 33062

O'CONNELL, WILLIAM PARNELL, JR., investor; b. San Antonio, July 8, 1939; s. William Parnell and Clarine (Browning) O'C.; m. Susanne Krause, Apr. 4, 1964; children—William Parnell III, Byron Trent, Jonathan Troy. B.S., Tex. A&I U., 1964; M.B.A., Pepperdine U., 1977. Sales rep. Sweeco, Inc., Corpus Christi, Tex., 1962-66, v.p., gen. mgr., 1966-72; v.p., gen. mgr. Vallen Corp., Houston, 1972-75, exec. v.p., chief operating officer, 1975-78, pres., chief exec. officer, 1978-84; pres. Wm. P. O'Connell Interests, Houston, 1984—. Served with USCGR, 1958-59. Teaching fellow Tex. A&I U., 1965-

66. Mem. Safety Equipment Distbrs. Assn. (pres. 1978-79), Houston Indsl. Dist. Assn. (pres. 1979-80), Young Pres. Assn. (sec. Houston chpt., 1984-85), Vets. of Safety, Assn. Corporate Growth (pres. Houston chpt. 1985-86), Assn. Chem. Industry of Tex. (dir. 1986-87). Republican. Roman Catholic. Clubs: Champions Golf; Lochinvar Golf (pres. 1985—); Coronado. Office: 3720 San Jacinto St PO Box 3347 Houston TX 77004

O'CONNOR, DORIS JULIA, oil company foundation executive; b. N.Y.C. Apr. 30, 1930; d. Joseph D. and Mary (Longinotti) Bisagni; m. Gerard T. O'Connor, Oct. 8, 1950 (div. Dec. 1972); 1 dau., Kim C. B.A. cum laude in Econs., U. Houston, 1975. Adminstrv. asst. Shell Cos. Found., Inc., N.Y.C., 1966-71, asst. sec., Houston, 1971-73, sec., 1973-76, sr. v.p., dir., mem. exec. com., 1976—. Corp. assoc. United Way of Am., Washington, 1976—; corp. advisor Bus. Com. of Arts, N.Y.C., 1976—; del. Bus. Com. of Arts, Houston, 1982-87; dir. Ind. Sector, Washington, 1981—, vice chmn., 1983-87; mem. contbns. council Conf. Bd., N.Y.C., 1976—; advisor Council of Better Bus. Burs., Washington, 1975—, 1983-87. Mem. Omicron Delta Epsilon. Club: Plaza (bd. govs. 1987—).

O'CONNOR, JAMES JOHN, utility company executive; b. Chgo., Mar. 15, 1937; s. Fred James and Helen Elizabeth (Reilly) O'C.; m. Ellen Louise Lawlor, Nov. 24, 1960; children: Fred, John (dec.), James, Helen Elizabeth. BS, Holy Cross Coll., 1958; MBA, Harvard U., 1960; JD, Georgetown U., 1963. Bar: Ill. 1963. With Commonwealth Edison Co., Chgo., 1963—, asst. to chmn. exec. com., 1964-65, comml. mgr., 1966, asst. v.p., 1967-70, v.p., 1970-73, exec. v.p., 1973-77, pres., 1977-87, chmn., 1980—, chief exec. officer, also bd. dirs.; bd. dirs. Corning Glass Works, Midwest Stock Exchange, Tribune Co., First Chgo. Corp., First Nat. Bank of Chgo., United Air Lines. Mem. Ill. com. United Negro Coll. Fund, Statue of Liberty-Ellis Island Centennial Commn., Christopher Columbus Quincentenary Jubilee Commn.; bd. dirs. Assocs. Harvard U. Grad. Sch. Bus. Adminstrn., Leadership Council for Met. Open Communities, Lyric Opera, Mus. Sci. and Industry, St. Xavier Coll., Reading Is Fundamental, Helen Brach Found., Leadership Greater Chgo.; chmn., dir. United Way Crusade Mercy, Chgo.; chmn. Citizenship Council of Met. Chgo., 1976—, Cath. Charities Chgo., 1986—, Chgo. Met. Area Savs. Bond Campaign; past chmn. Inst. Nuclear Power Ops.; trustee Adler Planetarium, Michael Reese Med. Ctr., Northwestern U., Coll. Holy Cross; bd. dirs., past chmn. Chgo. Urban League; bd. advisors Mercy Hosp. and Med. Ctr.; past chmn. bd. trustees Field Mus. Natural History; mem. exec. bd. Chgo. Area Council Boy Scouts Am.; exec. v.p. The Hundred Club Cook County; mem. citizens bd. U. Chgo. Served with USAF, 1960-63; civilian aide to Sec. Army 1978-80. Mem. Am., Ill., Chgo. bar assns., Chgo. Assn. Commerce and Industry (dir.). Roman Catholic. Clubs: Comml., Econ., Chgo., Chgo. Commonwealth, Met. (Chgo.). Home: 9549 Monticello Ave Evanston IL 60203 Office: Commonwealth Edison Co PO Box 767 1 First National Plaza Chicago IL 60690

O'CONNOR, JOHN CARDINAL, archbishop, former naval officer; b. Phila., Jan. 15, 1920; s. Thomas Joseph and Dorothy Magdalene (Gomple) O'C. M.A., St. Charles Coll., 1949, Catholic U. Am., 1954; Ph.D., Georgetown U., 1970; D.R.E., Villanova (Pa.) U., 1976. Ordained priest Roman Catholic Ch., 1945, elevated to monsignor, 1966, consecrated bishop, 1979, created cardinal, 1985; served in Chaplain Corps U.S. Navy, 1952, advanced through grades to rear adm.; assigned to Atlantic and Pacific fleets U.S. Navy, Okinawa and Vietnam; sr. chaplain U.S. Naval Acad.; chief chaplains U.S. Navy, Washington; aux. bishop, vicar gen. Mil. Vicariate, 1979-83; apptd. bishop of Scranton Pa., 1983-84; archbishop Archdiocese of New York, New York, NY, 1984—; Exec. bd. Nat. USO, Georgetown Center Strategic and Internat. Studies, Marine Corps Found. Author: Principles and Problems of Naval Leadership, 1958, A Chaplain Looks at Vietnam, 1969, In Defense of Life, 1981. Decorated DMS, Legion of Merit (3), Meritorious Service medal. Mem. Am. Polit. Sci. Assn. Office: Archdiocese of New York 1011 1st Ave New York NY 10022 *

O'CONNOR, JOHN JOSEPH, surgeon, clinic administrator; b. Gowanda, N.Y., June 19, 1941; s. William Robert and Ernestine Louise O'C.; B.A., U. Buffalo, 1962; M.D., SUNY, Buffalo, 1966; Ph.D. in Psychology, Century U. Calif., 1984; m. Patricia Ann, June 12, 1965; 1 dau., Erin Eileen. Asst. resident in surgery Millard Fillmore Hosp., Buffalo, 1966-69, chief resident in surgery, 1969-70, preceptor colon surgery, 1970-72, asso. intestinal and rectal surgery, treas., dir., 1972—; instr. surgery Georgetown U., Washington, 1972—; asst. prof. surgery George Washington U., Washington, 1977—; dir. proctology clinic Columbia Hosp. for Women, Washington, 1977—, fellow in laser surgery, 1986; guest instr. surgery Uniformed Services U. Health Scis., 1979; med. advisor Soc. Gastrointestinal Assts.; instr. dept. nursing Suburban Hosp., Bethesda, Md. Mem. Am. Soc. Colon Rectal Surgeons (Hermance award 1971, 72), ACS, Am. Coll. Colon Rectal Surgeons, Greater Met. Washington Colonoscopy Soc. (pres.), Gynecologic Laser Soc., Royal Soc. Medicine (London). Contbr. articles on proctology to med. jours. Office: 4801 Massachusetts Ave NW Suite 205 Washington DC 20016

O'CONNOR, NEIL, psychologist; b. Geraldton, Western Australia, Australia, Mar. 23, 1917; s. Herbert and Pansy Muriel (Langoulant) O'C; m. Margaret Edge, July 29, 1949; children: Gillian, Peter. BA, U. West Australia, 1937; MA, Oxford (Eng.) U., 1947; PhD, London, 1951. Research psychologist Med. Research Council Developmental Psychology Unit, London, 1947, 82—, dir., 1967-82. Author: contbr. numerous articles to profl. jours. Served to capt. Brit. Army, 1942-46. Fellow Brit. Psychol. Soc.; mem. Exptl. Psychology Soc. (past pres., Kennedy award). Office: 10E/Med Research Council, 18 Woburn Sq, London WC1H ONS, England

O'CONNOR, SANDRA DAY, justice U.S. Supreme Court; b. El Paso, Tex., Mar. 26, 1930; d. Harry A. and Ada Mae (Wilkey) Day; m. John Jay O'Connor, III, Dec. 1952; children: Scott, Brian, Jay. AB in Econs. with great distinction, Stanford U., 1950, LLB, 1952. Bar: Calif. Dep. county atty. San Mateo, Calif., 1952-53; civil atty. Q.M. Market Ctr., Frankfurt and Main, Fed. Republic of Germany, 1954-57; sole practice Phoenix, 1959-65; asst. atty. gen. State of Ariz., 1965-69; Ariz. state senator 1969-75, chmn. com. on state, county and mcpl. affairs, 1972-73, majority leader, 1973-74; judge Maricopa County Superior Ct., 1975-79, Ariz. Ct. Appeals, 1979-81; assoc. justice Supreme Ct. U.S., 1981—; referee juvenile ct., 1962-64; chmn. vis. bd. Maricopa County Juvenile Detention Home, 1963-64; mem. Maricopa County Bd. Adjustments and Appeals, 1963-64, Anglo-Am. Legal Exchange, 1980, Maricopa County Superior Ct. Judges Tng. and Edn. Com., Maricopa Ct. Study Com.; chmn. com. to reorganize lower cts. Ariz. Supreme Ct., 1974-75; faculty Robert A. Taft Inst. Govt.; vice chmn. Select Law Enforcement Rev. Commn., 1979-80. Mem. bd. editors Stanford (Calif.) U. Law Rev. Mem. Ariz. Personnel Commn., 1968-69, Nat. Def. Adv. Com. on Women in Services, 1974-76; trustee Heard Mus., Phoenix, 1968-74, 76-81, pres., 1980-81; mem. adv. bd. Phoenix Salvation Army, 1975-81; trustee Stanford U., 1976-80, Phoenix County Day Sch.; mem. citizens adv. bd. Blood Services, 1975-77; nat. bd. dirs. Smithsonian Assocs., 1981—; past Rep. dist. chmn.; bd. dirs. Phoenix Community Council, Ariz. Acad., 1970-75, Jr. Achievement Ariz., 1975-79, Blue Cross/Blue Shield Ariz., 1975-79, Channel 8, 1975-79, Phoenix Hist. Soc., 1974-77, Maricopa County YMCA, 1978-81, Golden Gate Settlement. Recipient Ann. award NCCJ, 1975, Disting. Achievement award Ariz. State U., 1980; named Woman of Yr., Phoenix Advt. Club, 1972. Lodge: Soroptimists. Address: Supreme Ct of the US 1 First St NE Washington DC 20543 *

O'CONNOR, WILLIAM JAMES, philanthropic investment executive, publisher; b. Hornell, N.Y., Nov. 25, 1921; s. Edward George and Grace Louise (Mosher) O'C.; C.D.E., Johns Hopkins U., 1941; B.A., Alfred (N.Y.) U., 1949, M.Ed., 1951; Ed.D., U. Buffalo, 1961; postdoctoral research Oxford (Eng.) U., 1971; m. Phyllis Elizabeth Ranger, June 12, 1943; children—Linda Louise O'Connor Borkowski, Bonnie Jeanne O'Connor McCluskey. Dir. admissions Alfred U., 1949-53, asst. to pres., 1958-63, vis. lectr., 1963; supr. employee services Westinghouse Electric Co., Elmira, N.Y., 1953-55; dir. residence services U. Buffalo, 1955-58, vis. lectr., 1967-68; exec. dir. U. Buffalo Found., 1963-68; cons. exec. br. U.S. govt., 1967-68; chmn. Fla. Consortium Colls. and Univs., also v.p. Lake City (Fla.) Community Coll., 1968-75; pres. Cecil Community Coll., North East, Md., 1975-78; chmn. bd., pub. Creativity Center-1, Inc., Hornell, N.Y., 1971—, chmn. bd., chief exec. officer, 1978—, dir., 1949—; sr. v.p. Brakeley, J.P.J., Inc., Stamford, Conn., 1978—; dir. Research Services, Inc., 1967-71; vis. lectr. U. Fla., U. S.Fla., 1972-74. Trustee, Village of Horseheads (N.Y.), 1954-55; Vestryman Christ Episcopal Ch., Hornell, 1959-63, St. James Episcopal Ch., Lake City, 1970-73; bd. advs. Villa Maria Coll., Buffalo, 1967-68; bd. govs. Inst. Religous Leadership, 1986—. Served with USAAF, 1941-45. Am. Council Edn. fellow, 1976. Fellow Creative Edn. Found.; life mem. Am. Def. Preparedness Assn. Democrat. Club: Hornell Rotary (past dir.). Editor President's Ideajour., 1967-70, pub., 1971—. Office: Brakeley JPJ Inc 1600 Summer St Stamford CT 06905

O'CONNOR, WILLIAM MATTHEW, lawyer; b. Pensacola, Fla., Apr. 5, 1955; s. William Francis and Rosalind (Shea) O'C.; m. Mary Patricia Keepnews, Oct. 13, 1984; children: William Lawrence, Thomas Patrick. B.S. in Psychology, Fordham Coll., 1977, J.D., 1980. Bar: N.Y. 1981, N.J. 1987, U.S. Dist. Ct. N.J. 1987, U.S. Dist. Conn. 1988, U.S. Dist. Ct. (so., ea., no. and we. dists.) N.Y., 1981, U.S. Ct. Appeals (2nd cir.) 1983. Intern, N.Y. Atty. Gen., N.Y.C., 1978-79; legis. intern Am. Lung Assn., N.Y.C., 1979; assoc. Keane & Butler, N.Y.C., 1979-81, Keane & Beane, White Plains, N.Y., 1981-83, Cooperman, Levitt & Winikoff, P.C., N.Y.C., 1983-86, sr. assoc. Sullivan, Donovan, Hanrahan & Silliere, N.Y.C., 1986-87; ptnr. Foyen & Peri, N.Y.C., 1987—. Author: Lobbying Guidebook Am. Lung Assn., 1979. Named to Jessup Moot Ct. team Fordham Law Sch., 1980. Contbr. articles to profl. jours. Mem. legis. com. pub. schs., White Plains, 1981-82; Democratic committeeman Village of Pelham Manor, N.Y., 1985—. Mem. Assn. Trial Lawyers Am., Fed. Bar Council, N.Y. State Bar Assn., Westchester Bar Assn. (editor in chief Jour. 1983, mem. labor law com. 1981—). Fordham ILJ Alumni Assn. (dir. 1984—, ethics com. 1987—), New Rochelle Bar Assn. Democrat. Roman Catholic. Club: N.Y. Roadrunners. Home: 933 Washington Ave Pelham Manor NY 10803 Office: Foyen & Peri 250 Park Ave New York NY 10177

ODA, SHIGERU, international justice; b. Japan, Oct. 22, 1924; s. Toshio and Mioko (Horiuchi) O.; LL.B., Imperial U., Tokyo, 1947; LL.M., Yale U., 1952, J.S.D., 1953; LL.D., Tohoku U., 1962; LL.D. (hon.), Bopal (India) U., 1980, N.Y. Law Sch., 1981; m. Noriko Sugimura, Mar. 3, 1950; children—Hiroshi, Yasuko. Assoc. prof. law Tohoku U., Sendai, Japan, 1953-59, prof., 1959-76, prof. emeritus, 1985—; spl. asst. to minister for fgn. affairs, 1973-76; judge Internat. Ct. Justice, The Hague, 1976—. Mem. Am. Assn. Internat. Law (hon.), Inst. de Droit Internat. (titulaire), Internat. Law Assn., Japanese Soc. Internat. Law. Clubs: Tokyo, Yale, Society, Haagsche Country. Author books, articles internat. law, law of sea. Office: care Internat Ct of Justice, Peace Palace, 2517KJ The Hague The Netherlands

ODA, TAKUZO, biochemist, educator; b. Shinichicho, Japan, Oct. 20, 1923; s. Ryoichi and Misu Oda; M.D., Okayama U., 1947, Ph.D., 1953; m. Kazue Matsui, Dec. 8, 1946; children—Mariko, Yumiko. Intern, Okayama U. Hosp., 1947-48, mem. faculty, 1949—, prof. biochemistry, 1965—, dir. Cancer Inst., from 1969; dean Okayama U. Med. Sch., 1985-87 ; postdoctoral trainee Inst. Enzyme Research, U. Wis., Madison, 1960-62. Fellow Rockefeller Found., 1959-60, grantee, 1964; USPHS grantee, 1963-68. Mem. Japanese Soc. Electron Microscopy (Seto prize 1966), Japanese Soc. Biochemistry, Am. Soc. Cell Biology, Japanese Soc. Cancer, Japanese Soc. Cell Biology, Japanese Soc. Histochemistry, Japanese Soc. Virology. Author: Biochemistry of Biological Membranes, 1969, Mitochondria, Handbook of Cytology; editor, writer: Cell Biology series, 1979—; chief editor Acta Medica Okayama, 1975-85 . Home: 216-38 Maruyama, 703 Okayama Japan Office: 2-5-1 Shikatacho, Dept Biochemistry Cancer, Cancer Inst Okayama U Med Sch, 700 Okayama Japan

ODA, TEIICHI (AUGUSTINUS), pediatrician, educator; b. Seoul, Korea, Sept. 22, 1928; s. Matazoh and Michiko (Ogino) O.; m. Scahiko Kano, May 5, 1954; children—Kazuo, Naoko, Yuko. M.D., Kyushu U. (Fukuoka, Japan), 1953, D.Msc., 1958. Mem. pediatric staff Kyushu Welfare Pension Hosp., Kitakyushu, Japan, 1956-63; research fellow Cardiovascular Inst. U. Calif.-San Francisco, 1965-66; lectr. Kyushu U., Fukuoka, Japan, 1963-73; assoc. prof., 1973-75; prof. Fukuoka U., 1975—, chmn. pediatrics, 1977—, dean Sch. Nursing, 1981-85. Author: Rheumatic Fever, 1969; Pediatric Cardiology, 1973; Pediatric Pulmonary Function, 1977. Fellow Am. Coll. Chest Physicians. Roman Catholic. Home: 2-9-24 Heiwa, Minami-ku, 815 Fukuoka Japan Office: Fukuoka U Sch Medicine, 7-45-1 Nanakuma, Johnan-ku, 814-01 Fukuoka Japan

ODA, TOSHITSUGU, hepatologist; b. Kanazawa, Japan, Mar. 16, 1922; s. June and Ko (Umeda) O.; m. Toyoko Matsumoto, May 20, 1955; children: Toshihiko, Toshiyuki. MD, U. Tokyo, 1944, DMS, 1957. Assoc. prof. faculty medicine U. Tokyo, 1962-74, prof., 1974-82, dean, 1979-81, prof. emeritus, 1982—; dir. U. Tokyo Hosp., 1975-77, Nat. Med. Ctr., Japan, Tokyo, 1982—; mem. U.S.-Japan Coop. Med. Com., 1988—. Editor: (books) Hepatitis Viruses, 1978, Therapeutic Plasmapheresis, 1981. Mem. Japan Soc. Hepatology (chmn. bd. 1980—), Japan Soc. Gastroenterology (bd. dirs. 1980—). Buddhist. Home: 6-9-14 Honcho, Koganei, 184 Tokyo Japan Office: Nat Med Ctr Japan, 1-21-1 Toyama Shinjuku-ku, 162 Tokyo Japan

ODAMTTEN, HELEN MARY, English language educator; b. Accra, Ghana; d. Solomon Edmund and Marion Adeline (Dove) O.; B.A. in History and English, U. Southampton, Eng., 1959; postgrad. U. London, 1959-60; M.A. in Applied Linguistics, U. Essex, Colchester, Eng., 1971; cert. in English phonetics Univ. Coll., London, 1981. Tchr. English and history, asst. housemistress Achimota Secondary Sch., 1960-62; producer, programme organizer in schs. broadcasting Ghana Broadcasting Co., 1963-66, head programme tng. sch., 1967-74; research fellow Lang. Centre, U. Ghana, Legon, 1974-84, sr. research fellow, 1984—. Life mem. Ghana Soc. for Blind. Mem. Internat. Phonetic Assn. (cert. in English phonetics), Linguistic Circle Accra, West African Linguistic Soc., Hist. Assn. Ghana, Ghana U. Tchrs. Assn., Legon Women's Soc., Internat. Assn. Women in Radio and TV. Research on TESL particularly in Ghana and other African nations. Home: D375 3 Cromer Rd, PO Box 438, Accra Ghana Office: Language Centre U Ghana, PO Box 119, Legon Ghana

ODAWARA, KEN'ICHI, economist, educator; b. Tokyo, Mar. 8, 1933; s. Tsuneo and Kimie (Nagazumi) O.; m. Tsuneko Kurosawa, Sept. 25, 1965; children—Junichi, Nobuo. B.A., Jochi (Sophia) U., 1955, M.A., 1957; M.A., Boston Coll., 1958; postgrad. Columbia U., 1957-58. Research asst. Jochi U., Tokyo, 1956-59, instr., 1959-65, asso. prof., 1965-70, prof. econs., 1970—; lectr. U. Tokyo, Komaba campus, 1973-84, Waseda U., Tokyo, 1988—; cons. UN. Bankok, Thailand, 1965-68, 69-70, 74; vis. prof. U. Pitts., 1977, U. Hawaii, 1978; vis. scholar Yale U., 1972, MIT, 1975, Hitotsubashi U., Tokyo, 1985-86. Author: The Great American Disease, 1980, The Economic Friction between the U.S., Europe and Japan, 1981; author/co-editor: The Textbook of World Economy, 1981, International Political Economy, 1988; author/editor: Report of Symposium on U.S.-Japan Telecommunications Trade, 1986; contbr. articles to profl. jours. Chief instr. Inst. Money & Banking for Indonesian Govt. Trainees, Japan Internat. Coop. Agy., 1961-62; expert advisor Sci. Council, Ministry Edn., Tokyo, 1980-82; interviewer Econs. com. Fulbright Program, 1985; mem. internat. econs. research coordinator com. Sci. Council Japan, 1985—; chmn. Islamic Econ. Research Council, Japan Indsl. Policy Research Inst., Ministry of Internat. Trade & Industry, 1979-81. Japan Found. grantee, 1978; Union Nat. Econ. Assns. Japan grantee, 1983. Mem. Japan Soc. Internat. Econs. (councillor 1972-78, editor proceedings 1974-76. dir., 1978-85, exec. dir. 1985—, sec.-treas. 1980—), Am. Econ. Assn. Roman Catholic. Home: 1-3-4 Fujigaya, Kugenuma, Fujisawa-shi, 251 Kanagawa-ken Japan Office: Jochi (Sophia) U, 7-1 Kioi-Cho, Chiyoda-ku, 102 Tokyo Japan

ODDI, SILVIO CARDINAL, Cardinal; b. Morfasso, Piacenza, Italy, Nov. 14, 1910; s. Agostino and Esther (Oddi) O.; Doctorate in Canon Law, Rome, 1936; Dr. honoris causa, U. Buenos Aires, 1944, St. John's U., N.Y.C., 1981, St. Charles Sem., Phila. Ordained priest Roman Catholic Ch., 1933; named archbishop titular of Mesembria, 1953, cardinal, 1969. Mem. Vatican Diplomatic Service, Iran, Lebanon, Syria, Palestine, Egypt, France, Yugoslavia, Belgium and Luxembourg, 1936-69; spl. missions to Central Africa, Latin Am., Philippines, Cuba and Dominican Rep., 1961-74; cardinal; mem. Congregations for Causes of Saints, Bishops, Oriental Chs. of Pub. Affairs of the Ch., Supreme Tribunal of Apostolic Segnatura, Amministrazionedel Patrimonio della Sede Apostolica, Congregation per l'Evangelizzazione dei Popoli, Sanctuaries of Loreto and Pompei; pontifical legate to Basilica and Convent of St. Francis (Assisi). Home: 21 Via Pompeo Magno, 00192 Rome Italy

ODEGAARD, BJORN SKAR, clinical psychotherapist, marketing consultant; b. Oslo, July 22, 1946; s. Haakon and Borghild (Skar) O.; m. Kari Lorentzen Styr; children: MArius, Anders, Henrik. PhD in Psychology, U. Oslo, 1973. Counselor, therapist County Med. Hosp., Kristiansand, Norway, 1975-78, State Ctr. for Children and Youth, Kristiansand, 1978-81; ind. counselor, therapist, presenter indsl. seminars Oslo, 1981-84; personal counselor, therapisto Mental Exec. Health, Oslo, 1984—. contbr. chpts. to books. Bd. dirs. Oslo Pub. Housing project, 1982, Union Colostomi Operated, 1981. Served with Norwegian Army, 1974-75. Mem. Norwegian Psychol. Assn. (sec. Oslo chpt. 1985—, bd. dirs. pvt. practice group 1984—), Norwegian Inst. Vegetotherapy (bd. dirs. 1987), Classic and Vet. Car Club Oslo (bd. dirs. 1983—). Social Democrat. Home and Office: Solveien 123B, 1170 Oslo 11 Norway

ODELL, HERBERT, lawyer; b. Phila., Oct. 20, 1937; s. Samuel and Selma (Kramer) O.; m. Valerie Odell; children: Wesley, Jonathan, James, Sarah. BS in Econs., U. Pa., 1959; LLB magna cum laude, U. Miami, 1962; LLM, Harvard U., 1963. Bar: Fla. 1963, Pa. 1968. Trial atty. tax div. U.S. Dept. Justice, Washington, 1963-65; assoc. Walton, Lantaff, Schroeder, Carson & Wahl, Miami, Fla., 1965-67; from assoc. to ptnr. Morgan, Lewis & Bockius, Phila., 1967—; adj. prof. U. Miami, Villanova U.; lectr. various tax insts. Contbr. articles to profl. jours. Ford fellow, 1962-63. Mem. ABA, Fla. Bar Assn., Pa. Bar Assn., Phila. Bar Assn., Pa. Economy League (bd. dirs. 1983-85), Phi Kappa Phi, Omicron Delta Kappa, Beta Alpha Psi. Club: Harvard. Office: Morgan Lewis & Bockius 2000 One Logan Sq Philadelphia PA 19103

O'DELL, JOAN ELIZABETH, business executive, lawyer; b. East Dubuque, Ill., May 3, 1932; d. Peter Emerson and Olive (Bonnet) O'dell; children: Dominique R., Nicole L. BA cum laude, U. Miami, 1956, JD, 1958. Bar: Fla. 1958, D.C. 1974, Ill. 1978, Va. 1987; lic. real estate broker. Trial atty. U.S. SEC, Washington, 1959-60; asst. state atty. Office State Atty., Miami, Fla., 1960-64; asst. county atty. Dade County Atty.'s Office, Miami, 1964-70; county atty. Palm Beach County Atty.'s Office, West Palm Beach, Fla., 1970-71; regional gen. counsel. U.S. EPA, Region IV, Atlanta, 1971-73, assoc. gen. counsel, Washington, 1973-77; sr. counsel Nalco Chem. Co., Oakbrook, Ill., 1977-78; v.p. Angel Mining, Tenn., 1979—; pres. South West Land Investments, Miami, Fla., 1979—. Bd. dirs. Tucson Women's Found., 1982-84, U. Ariz. Bus. and Profl. Women's Club, Tucson, 1981-85; bd. dirs. LWV Tucson, 1981-85, pres., 1984-86; bd. dirs. LWV Ariz., 1985-86, chmn. nat. security study; mem. AAUW; mem. Exec. Women's Council, Tucson, 1982-85. Mem. ABA, Fed. Bar Assn., Fla. Bar Assn., D.C. Bar Assn., Va. State Bar Assn. Home: 703 S Lake Dr Lantana FL 33462

ODENT, MICHEL-ROBERT, obstetrician; b. Bresles, Oise, France, July 7, 1930; s. Paul and Madeleine H. (Carpentier) O.; m. Nicole Toulat, Apr. 24, 1957; children—Sylvie, Christophe. M.D., Faculté de Paris, 1961. Obstetrician, chief of service Centre Hospitalier, Pithiviers, France, 1962—. Author: Bien Naitre 1976; Genese de l'Homme Ecologique, 1979; Birth Reborn, 1984; Primal Health, 1986. Contbr. articles to profl. jours. Served to lt. French Army, 1957-59. Fellow Internat. Coll. Surgeons; mem. Association Française de Chirurgie. Roman Catholic. Home: 47 Avenue de la Republique, 45300 Pithiviers France Office: Centre Hospitalier, 45300 Pithiviers France

ODESCALCHI, EDMOND PÉRY, financial and management executive, consultant; b. Budapest, Hungary, Oct. 11, 1928; came to U.S., 1950; s. Prince Béla and Princess Charlotte (De Bay) O.; m. Esther De Kando, Sept. 30, 1961; children: Daniel, Dominic. Student, Cornell U., 1951, U. Pa., 1956-57; MS in Econs., St. Andrews U., Scotland, 1959. Adminstrv. asst. French Govt., Baden, Fed. Republic Germany, 1948-50; world trade specialist IBM Corp., Poughkeepsie, N.Y., 1952-60, project mgr., 1960-74; devel. mgr. IBM Corp., East Fishkill, N.Y., 1974; pres. Global Tech., Inc., N.Y.C., 1975—; Internat. fin. cons. Author: The Global Arena, 1973, Faces of Reality, 1975; contbr. articles to profl. jours. Mem. Rep. Nat. Com., 1984—. Mem. Bus. Cons. Assn., Am. Mus. Natural History (assoc.), Internat. Platform Assn. Home: 6 Freedom Rd Pleasant Valley NY 12569 Office: Global Tech Inc 5 31 50th Ave Long Island City NY 11101

ODHIAMBO, THOMAS R., entomologist, educator. Chmn., prof. Kenya Nat. Acad. Scis., Nairobi; founder, dir. Internat. Ctr. of Insect Physiology and Ecology, Kenya. Co-recipient Africa Prize for Leadership, 1987. Office: Kenya Nat Acad of Scis, PO Box 47288, Nairobi Kenya *

ODIJK, THEO, physical chemist, educator; b. Rotterdam, The Netherlands, Sept. 30, 1952; s. Cornelus Theodorus Odijk and Johanna Maria Christina Kloos. Masters, State U. at Leiden, The Netherlands, 1978, Doctorate, 1983. Sci. asst. U. Leiden, 1978-82, postdoctoral grad., 1983-84, lectr., 1985-87; prof. Tech. U., Delft, The Netherlands, 1987—. Contbr. articles to profl. jours. Recipient Gold medal Royal Dutch Soc. Chemistry, 1986. Office: Tech U Faculteit der Scheikundige Tech, Postbus 5045, Julianalaan 136, 2600 GA Delft The Netherlands

O'DILLON, RICHARD HILL, physician; b. Watkinsville, Ga., Dec. 11, 1934; s. Herman Thomas and Elizabeth (Hill) O'D.; B.S., U. Ga., 1956; M.D., Med. Coll. Ga., 1960. Intern, Athens (Ga.) Gen. Hosp., 1960-61; resident Grady Meml. Hosp., Atlanta, 1963; practice medicine, specializing in clin. investigation, Rochester, N.Y., 1964—; asst. med. dir. Strasenburgh Labs., 1964-65, asso. med. dir., 1966; group dir. product devel., clin. research Merrell-Nat. Labs., Cin., 1966-75, group dir. gastrointestinal clin. research, 1975-78; dir. clin. research Duphar Labs., Inc., 1979-87. Served as capt. USAF, 1961-62. Mem. AMA, So. Med. Assn., N.Y. Acad. Scis., Am. Acad. Dermatology, Ohio Med. Assn., Acad. Medicine Columbus and Franklin County, Am. Geriatrics Assn., AAAS, Gamma Sigma Epsilon, Phi Eta Sigma, Alpha Epsilon Delta, Delta Phi Alpha. Home: 728 Bluffview Dr Worthington OH 43235

ODNOPOSOFF, RICARDO, violinist, educator; b. Buenos Aires, Feb. 24, 1914; s. Mauricio and Juana Tauba (Wainstein) O.; naturalized U.S. citizen, 1953; m. Irmtraut Baum, Mar. 20, 1965; 1 child by previous marriage, Henriette Helene. M.Mus., High Sch. Music, Berlin, 1932. Violinist, playing in concerts throughout the world, 1932—; tchr. U. Caracas, Venezuela, 1943-47; taught summer courses Mozarteum, Salzburg, 1956-60, Internat. Summer Acad., Nice, France, 1959-73; prof. High Sch. for Music, Vienna, 1956—, prof. emeritus, 1975—; tchr. High Sch. for Music, Stuttgart, Germany, 1964—, Music High Sch., Zurich, 1975-84. Decorated chevalier des Arts et Lettres, France, chevalier de l'Ordre Rose Blanche, Finland, comdr. Order of Leopold II, Belgium, Grosses Verdienstkreuz des Verdienstordens, Federal Republic of Germany, Mun Hwa Po Chang, Republic of South Korea, medal for Merit, Argentina, medal of Honor in Silver, City of Vienna, 1979, Ehrenkreuz fü r Wissenschaft und Kunst I. Klasse, Austria, Medal of Merit in gold Govt. Baden-Wü rttemberg, W.Ger., others. Lodge: Masons. Home: 27 Singerstrasse, 1010 Vienna Austria

ODONI, ROBERT WINSTON KEITH, professor of number theory; b. London, July 14, 1947; s. Walter Anthony and Lois Marie (Conner) O.; m. Josephine Ann Ding, 1972; children: Theresa, Martin, Russell. BSc with honors, U. Exeter, Eng., 1968; PhD in Math., U. Cambridge, 1972. Temp. lectr. U. Liverpool, Eng., 1971-72; research fellow U. Glasgow, Scotland, 1972-73; lectr. U. Exeter, 1973-79, reader in number theory, 1979-85, personal chair number theory, 1985—. Contbr. research articles in number theory and analysis to profl. jours. Fellow Cambridge Philos. Soc.; mem. London Math. Soc. (editorial adviser 1987), Am. Math. Soc., Soc. Mathématique de France. Home: 35 Prospect Park, Exeter, Devonshire EX4 6NA, England Office: U Exeter, Dept Math, North Park Rd, Exeter EX4 4QE, England

O'DONNELL, DAVID DANIEL, educational services company executive; b. Washington, Aug. 31, 1941; s. Ferd D. and Angelina O'Donnell; m. Carol Knackstead, June 14, 1965 (div. 1969); 1 son, David Sean; m. Kay Boughner, Oct. 27, 1970; children: Daniel Joseph, Richard Robert. Student East Carolina U., 1964, Am. U., 1965-66; BA, Colo. Tech. Coll., 1988. Ops.

mgr. Record Sales, Washington, 1956-61; v.p. sales Capitol Sewing Machine Co., Washington, 1967-70; cons. Macro Systems, Silver Spring, Md., 1970-71; sales mgr. Control Data Corp., Miami, 1971-73; key accounts mgr. Sealy, Miami, 1973-75; dir. mktg. ITT-ITT Ednl. Services, Inc., Indpls., 1975—; gen. mgr., v.p. ITT Employment and Tng. Systems, Inc., Indpls., 1985-86; pres., chmn. bd. Colo. Tech. Coll., 1986—; guest speaker, lectr., cons. Served with USMCR, 1961-65. Republican. Home: 13920 Wyandott Dr Colorado Springs CO 80908 Office: Colo Tech Coll 4435 N Chestnut St Colorado Springs CO 80907

O'DONNELL, JOHN BOWMAN, foreign service officer; b. Waialua, Hawaii, Oct. 15, 1935; s. Raymond John and Maile (Bowman) O'D.; m. Sharon Starrett, Sept. 30, 1972; children—Erin, Meghan; m. Karol Elterich (div. June 1971); children—Allison, Shauna, Ramsey. B.A., Stanford U., 1956; postgrad U. Hawaii, 1959-60, Cornell U., 1973-74. Asst. dir. indsl. relations Waialua Sugar Co., Hawaii, 1960-62; with AID, various locations, 1962—, dep. dir. Office Rural Devel., Guatemala, 1974-77, dir. Office Agr. and Rural Devel., Lima, Peru, 1977-82, dep. dir. Office Rural Devel., Washington, 1982-85, dir. Office Agr. and Rural Devel., Quito, Ecuador, 1985-87, dep. agy. dir. Human Resources, Washington, 1988—. Served with AUS, 1957-59. Decorated U.S. Army Commendation medal; Order of Merit (Vietnam), Order Agrl. Merit (Peru); recipient Meritorious Honor award AID, 1977, Superior Honor award, 1984. Republican. Roman Catholic. Avocations: tennis; travel. Home: 1402 Mayflower Dr McLean VA 22101 Office: S&T/HR Room 611 SA-18 AID Washington DC 20523

O'DONNELL, JOHN LOGAN, lawyer; b. Chgo., Mar. 6, 1914; s. William Joseph and Elizabeth (McLogan) O'D.; m. Mary Ellen Sipe, Sept. 2, 1939 (dec. Dec. 29, 1979); 1 son, John Logan; m. Michele G. Fischer, May 9, 1981. B.A., Williams Coll., 1934; J.D., Northwestern U., 1937. Bar: Ill. bar 1937, N.Y. bar 1943, D.C. bar 1977. Asso. firm Defrees, Buckingham, Jones and Hoffman, Chgo., 1937-38; staff atty. Office Gen. Counsel, SEC, 1938-41; instr. Cath. U. Law Sch., 1938-41; asso. firm Cravath, Swaine & Moore, N.Y.C., 1941-52; partner firm Olwine, Connelly, Chase, O'Donnell & Weyher, N.Y.C., 1952—. Bd. dirs. Near East Found., 1968-84. Fellow Am. Coll. Trial Lawyers; mem. Assn. Bar City N.Y., Am., Fed., N.Y. State, N.Y. County bar assns., Beta Theta Pi, Phi Delta Phi. Roman Catholic. Clubs: Union, Univ., Williams, Sky (N.Y.C.). Home: 181 E 73d St New York NY 10021 Office: 299 Park Ave New York NY 10171

O'DONNELL, MARK JOSEPH, accountant; b. St. Louis, Mar. 28, 1954; s. William E. and Jeanne M. (Collins) O'D.; m. Jane E. Wismann, Sept. 29, 1973; children: Sean, Mark Jr., Kyle. BSBA magna cum laude, U. Mo., 1977. CPA, Mo. Cost acct. Hunter Engring., St. Louis, 1973-76; acct. Gen. Dynamics, St. Louis, 1976-77; acct. Lester Witte & Co., St. Louis, 1977-80, mgr., 1980-82; ptnr. Bounds, Poger & O'Donnell, St. Louis, 1982-86, mng. ptnr., 1986—. Named one of Outstanding Young Men Am., U.S. Jaycees, 1978. Mem. Am. Inst. CPA's, Mo. Soc. CPA's. Roman Catholic. Office: Bounds Poger & O'Donnell 120 S Central Ave Suite 400 Saint Louis MO 63105

O'DONNELL, MICHAEL LAWRENCE, international business executive, consultant; b. San Diego, Oct. 27, 1949; s. Michael Daniel and Cherry Joy (Pratt) O'D.; m. Jan Lesna Ansel, Oct. 3, 1970; children—Arish, Tennyson, Katie, Michael, Mandy, Jeremy. A.A., Cypress Coll., 1969; B.A., Calif. Western U., 1982, M.B.A., 1984. Cert. purchasing mgr.; lic. pvt. pilot. Gen. mgr. Utah Parks Co., Cedar City, 1969-71; mgr. K.S.I., Inc., Cedar City, 1971-74; purchasing mgr. Brigham Young U. and Polynesian Cultural Ctr., Honolulu, 1974-77; purchasing mgr. Latter Day Saints Ch., Honolulu, 1977-80, materials mgmt. mgr., 1980-83, regional mgr., APIA, Western Samoa, 1983-86; dir. procurement Sheraton Corp., of Hawaii-Japan, Honolulu, 1986-88, also bd. dirs.; mgr. GTE Sylvania Hawaii, 1988—, also bd. dirs.; trustee Enterprise Trust Co., Independence, Mo., 1981—; bd. dirs. Watanabe Floral, Inc., Honolulu; chmn. bd. Bus. Specialists Internat. Inc., Honolulu, 1981—, Internat. Mgmt. Specialists Inc., Honolulu, 1976—. Author articles in field. Dist. commr. Aloha Council Boy Scouts Am., Honolulu, 1977-83; chmn. Deseret Mut. Benefit, Western Samoa, 1983-85. Recipient King Kamehameha award, Polynesian Cultural Ctr., Honolulu, 1977, David O. McKay award, Brigham Young U., Laie, Hawaii, 1979, R. Billings award, Billings Energy Corp. (Mo.), 1982. Mem. Nat. Assn. Ednl. Buyers, Nat. Assn. Purchasing Mgmt. (v.p. 1980-81, dir. 1981-83, award 1983). Purchasing Mgmt. Assn. Hawaii (pres. 1978-79, Cliff C. Dalen award 1980). Internat. Fedn. Purchasing and Material Mgmt. (rep. 1976-83). C. of C. APIA Western Samoa. Mormon. Home: 91-951 Kalapu St Ewa Beach HI 96706 Office: BSI Inc PO Box 2501 Ewa Beach HI 96706

O'DONNELL, ROBERT JOHN, lawyer, mediator, educator; b. Worcester, Mass., Aug. 3, 1943; s. Joseph C. and Nellie (Balrukaitis) O'D.; m. Joyce I. Thomas, June 30, 1969 (div. Feb. 1984); children: Gary T., Shaun K. BS in Bus. Adminstrn., U. Calif., Berkeley, 1965; JD, Boston Coll. Law, 1969; cert., Coro Found., San Francisco, 1969. Bar: Vt. 1970, U.S. Dist. Ct. Vt. 1970. Sole practice Woodstock, Vt., 1970—; adj. faculty Coll. Edn. and Social Services U. Vt.-Burlington, 1986—, Woodbury Coll., Montpelier, Vt., 1986—. Intern San Francisco Neighborhood Legal Assistance Found., 1967; assoc. Harvard Legal Aid bur., 1967-68; founding dir., pres. Boston Coll. Legal Assistance Bur., 1968-69; justice peace Windsor County, 1979; mem. planning commn. Town of Pomfret, Vt., 1980—, grand juror, 1985—; mem. council Episcopal Diocese of Vt., 1982-86; sch. dir. Woodstock Union High Sch., 1983—; bd. dirs. ARC Cen. Vt. chpt., 1983—; lay reader, vestryman St. James Episc. Ch., Woodstock, 1985—; sr. assoc. Nat. Ctr. Assocs., Inc., 1984—. Mem. Vt. Bar Assn. (fee arbitration com. 1974-80, alternative dispute resolution com. 1987—), Windsor County Bar Assn. (pres. 1971-72), Vt. Mediators Assn. (steering com. 1986-87, pres. 1987—), N.H. Mediators Assn., Soc. for Profl. in Dispute Resolution, Acad. Family Mediators, Assn. of Family and Conciliation Cts. Republican. Home: Donegal On the Stage Rd South Pomfret VT 05067 Office: 5 the Green Woodstock VT 05091

O'DONNELL, WALTER GREGORY, management educator; b. Cleve., Feb. 3, 1903; s. Walter Thomas and Margaret (McGee) O'D.; m. Angelina M. Oriti, June 10, 1940; children: Charles, Kathleen, Roger, Arleen. LL.B., John Marshall Law Sch., Cleve., 1932; B.A., Western Res. U., 1932, M.A., 1944; Ph.D., Columbia U., 1959. Bar: Fla. 1925, U.S. Supreme Ct. 1928. Practiced in Pinellas County, 1925-30, Tallahassee, 1947-48; tchr. Cleve. Pub. High Schs., 1930-35; assoc. prof. Notre Dame Coll., 1935-37; assoc. prof. econs. and polit. sci. John Carroll U., 1937-43; instr. econs. Ohio State U., 1943-47; assoc. prof. econs. Fla. State U., 1947-48; instr. econs. Columbia U., 1948-51; assoc. prof. indsl. relations U. Pitts., 1951-52; inst. leader NAM, 1950-51; dir. tng. and exec. devel. Nat. Foremans Inst., 1952-53; mgmt. cons., tng. specialist T.W.I. Found., 1953-54; staff specialist indsl. relations Lockheed Aircraft, Inc., 1954-56; prof. mgmt. U. Mass., 1956-73, prof. emeritus, 1973—; disting. vis. prof. Mgmt. Bowling Green State U., 1974-76, 78-81; prof. bus. adminstrn. in residence U. Conn., Storrs, 1976-78; vis. lectr. Ohio Wesleyan U., summer 1946; vis. assoc. prof. mgmt. Rutgers U., 1954-56; vis. prof., ednl. cons. U. P.R., summer 1961; vis. prof. U. Madrid, 1963; vis. prof. mgmt. U. N.Mex., 1967-68; vis. prof. Bklyn. Poly. Inst., 1968-70; disting. vis. prof. mgmt. Loyola Coll., Balt., 1973, Georgetown U., 1973-74; vis. prof. mgmt. Sch. Adminstrv. Sci., U. Ala.-Huntsville, 1982-86. Author monographs; contbr. articles in field of mgmt. sci. to profl. jours. Mem. Cuyahoga County Charter Commn., 1932, Ohio Post War Planning Commn., 1945-46. Fulbright grantee U. Madrid, 1963. Mem. AAAS, Am. Acad. Mgmt., Inst. Mgmt. Scis. (founder, chmn., exec. sec. Coll. Mgmt. Philosophy 1960-73, reorganizer Coll. Mgmt. Philosophy with series of mongraphs 1978-80). Democrat. Roman Catholic. Office: U Mass Dept Mgmt Sch Bus Adminstrn Amherst MA 01002

O'DONNELL, WILLIAM DAVID, construction firm executive; b. Brockton, Mass., Aug. 21, 1926; s. John Frank and Agnes Teresa (Flanagan) O'D.; m. Dixie Lou Anderson, Jan. 31, 1951; children—Craig Patrick, Ginger Lynn. BS, U. N.Mex., 1953. Registered profl. engr., Ill., 1958. Engr., State of Ill., 1953-59; with Gregory-Anderson Co., Rockford, Ill., 1959—, gen. mgr., 1960-61, sec., 1961-81, pres., 1981—; dir. 1st Nat. Bank & Trust Co. of Rockford, 1st Community Bancorp, Inc., Growth Enterprise, Starvision, Inc. Dir. St. Anthony Med. Ctr., Starvision, Inc.; bd. dirs. Rockford YMCA, pres., 1984. Served with USN, 1943-47. Recipient Friend of the Boy award Optimist Club, 1966, Excalibur award for community service Rockford Register Star, 1971; named Titan of Yr., Boylan High Sch., 1974. Fellow ASCE, Nat. Soc. Profl. Engrs.; mem. No. Ill. Bldg. Contractors, Aircraft Owners and Pilots Assn., Balloon Fedn. Am., Sigma Tau, Chi Epsilon, Tau Beta Pi. Clubs: Forest Hills Country (Rockford); Adventurers (Chgo.). Lodges: Elks, Rotary (Service Above Self award 1972; v.p. Rockford chpt. 1983, pres. 1984). Home: 2004 Bradley Rd Rockford IL 61107 Office: 2525 Huffman Blvd Rockford IL 61103

O'DONNELL, WILLIAM THOMAS, radar systems mktg. exec.; b. Latrobe, Pa., Feb. 22, 1939; s. William Regis and Kathryn Ann (Coneff) O'D.; student Eastern N.Mex. U., 1958-61; student in mktg. John Carroll U., 1961-65, Ill. Inst. Tech., 1965-66; B.S.B.A., U. Phoenix, 1982, M.B.A. with distinction, 1984; m. Judith Koetke, Oct. 1, 1965; children—William Thomas and William Patrick (twins), Allison Rose, Kevin Raymond. Various sales positions Hickok Elec. Instrument Co., Cleve., 1961-65, Fairchild Semicondr., Mpls., 1965-67; Transitron Semicondr., Mpls., 1967-69; Burroughs Corp., Plainfield, N.J., 1967-71; mktg. mgr. Owens-Ill. Co., 1972-73, v.p. mktg. Pantek Co., subs. Owens-Ill. Co., Lewistown, Pa., 1973-75, v.p. mktg., nat. sales mgr., Toledo, 1975-76; mktg. mgr., nat. sales mgr. Govt. Electronics div. group Motorola Co., Scottsdale, Ariz., 1976-80, U.S. mktg. mgr. radar positioning systems Motorola Govt. Electronics Group, 1981—; gen. mgr. J. K. Internat., Scottsdale, 1980-81; mgmt. cons.; adj. prof. Union Grad. Sch.; guest lectr. U. Mich. Grad. Sch. Bus. Adminstrn.; instr. U. Phoenix, Scottsdale Community Coll.; area chair-gen. mgmt. Union grad. sch. Maricopa Community Coll. Chmn., Rep. Precinct, Burnsville, Minn., 1968-70; city fin. chmn., Burnsville; dir. community devel. U.S. Jaycees, Mpls., 1968-69; mem. Scottsdale 2000 Com. Served with USAF, 1957-61. Recipient Outstanding Achievement award Govt. Electronics div. Motorola Co., 1976, also Mktg. Mgmt. award Motorola Co., 1983, Marketing Orgn. award Motorola Co., 1985, Citation for Faciliation Ability U. Phoenix, 1986, Excellence in Orgn. award Motorola, 1986; named to Million Dollar Club, Burroughs Co., 1969-71; hon. citizen, Donaldsville, La., 1978; others. Mem. Phoenix Execs. Club, Am. Mktg. Assn., U. Phoenix Faculty Club (officer). Roman Catholic. Clubs: North Cape Yacht, Scottsdale Racquet, Toftnees Country. Home: 8432 E Belgian Trail Scottsdale AZ 85258

O'DONOVAN, FRED-MICHAEL, producer, director, business executive; b. Dublin, Ireland, May 27, 1927; s. John and Kathleen (Connolly) O'D.; m. Sally Tennant; children—Fiona, Sally Ann, Freddie. Artistic dir. prodn. co., after 1956, then mng. dir., group mng. dir., to 1980; artistic dir. Gaiety Theatre Dublin; chmn. Nat. Concert Hall (An Ceolarus Naisunta), 1981; chmn. Radio Telefis Eireann the Nat. Broadcasting Orgn. of Ireland, Dublin, 1981—; dir. Murphy's Brewery (Ireland) Ltd.; chmn. Westsat Ireland Ltd., 1984—; organizer Internat. Festival of Poetry; lectr. on lit. figures and their association with Irish theatre to U.S. univ. students. Producer numerous radio shows; author, producer radio program on child refugees for UNICEF; producer rec.: Complete Works of Shakespeare; producer plays: Gaels of Laughter, Juno and the Paycock, Man and Superman, Alfie, Relatively Speaking, Who's Afraid of Virginia Woolf'9 , Prisoner of Second Avenue, Sunshine Boys, The Golden Years, The Sound of Music, The Caretaker, Annie; creater, author TV shows and films: At Home with O'Hagan, The Ed Sullivan Show, Ireland, The Bing Crosby Show, Ireland, Meet the Quare Fella, The Man Who Invented St. Patrick, Crystal Clear (Cannes Festival award), creater, producer Jury's Irish Cabaret, 1963-70; producer many internat. shows, including: Ireland On Parade Co-Founder Irish Cancer Soc.; gov. Nat. Children's Hosp. Recipient Lord Mountbattan award, 1987. Club: Internat. Variety (hon. life mem.). Office: Radio Telefis Eireann, Dublin Ireland

ODUNEWU, ISIAKA ALANI, transportation company executive; b. Abeokuta, Nigeria, Apr. 1, 1947; s. Yinusa Akanbi and Amudalatu (Taiwo) O.; m. Fausat Abeni, Aug. 22, 1977; children: Mafutau Olakunle, Ibrahim Olaleken. Diploma, Nigeria Sch. Freight Forwarding, 1973. Clearing mgr. Ben Agy. Services (Nigeria) Ltd., Lagos, 1973-74; clearing mgr. Oceanair Services (Nigeria) Ltd., Lagos, 1975-77, asst. gen. mgr., 1977-78, mng. dir., 1978—. Founder Shomolu Com. of Understanding. Mem. Inst. Freight Forwarders (assoc.), Inst. Traffic Adminstrn. (assoc.), Nigerian Clearing and Forwarding Assn., Lagos C. of C., Lagos Mfg. Assn. Muslim. Club: Egba Social. Home: 1 Durojaiye St, off Apata St, Shomolu, Lagos Nigeria Office: 13 Olorunsogo St, Palmgrove Shomolu, PO Box 1043 Mushin, Lagos Nigeria

ODUNMBAKU, ABIODUN OLATUNJI, architect; b. Agege, Nigeria, Dec. 26, 1952; s. Adesegun Oladosu and Elizabeth Ayodele (Coker) O.; m. Mercy Obamogie, June 25, 1980; children: Abisola, Adenike. Diploma civil engring., Polytechnic U., Nigeria, 1977; B.Arch., Howard U., 1981; M.Arch., Cath. U. Am., 1982; Ph.D., U. Pa., 1988. Asst. civil engr. Ove Arup & Ptnrs., Ibadan, Nigeria, 1974-75; quantity surveyor Julius Berger Ltd., Lagos, 1975; civil engr. Etteh Aro & Ptnrs., Enugu, 1977-78; architect Leroy Brown & Assocs., Washington, 1981; dir. Omdaf Nigeria Ltd., Lagos, 1982—; ptnr. Mittel-Bau Constrn. Ltd., Lagos, 1982—; pres. The ABOD Assocs., Md., 1986—; cons. Marriott Corp., Bethesda, Md., 1987-88; architect, Phila. Architect's Workshop, 1986. Pres., Poly. Students Union, Ibadan, 1975-76. Mem. AIA (assoc.), Am. Planning Assn., Inst. Tranp. Engrs., Transp. Research Bd., Tau Sigma Delta.

ODUYOYE, MERCY AMBA, religious educator; b. Asamankese, Ghana, Oct. 21, 1934; d. Charles Kwaw and Mercy Dakwaa (Turkson) Yamoah; m. Adedoyin Modupe Oduyoye, Dec. 9, 1968. BA in Religionwith honors, U. Ghana, Legon-Accra, 1963; BA in Theology with honors, Cambridge (Eng.) U., 1965, MA in Theology with honors, 1969. Cert. tchr. Tchr. Ministry Edn., Ghana, 1955-59; youth edn. sec. World Council Chs., Geneva, 1967-70; youth sec. All Africa Council of Chs., Ibadan, Nigeria, 1970-73; tchr. States Schs. Bd., Ibadan/Oyo State, 1973-74; lectr. U. Ibadan, Ibadan/Oyo State, 1974-80, sr. lectr., 1980-86; Ford scholar Women's Studies in Religion Harvard Divinity Sch., Cambridge, Mass., 1985-86; vis. prof. Union Theol. Sem., N.Y.C., 1986-87; vis. lectr. Harvard U., 1985-86; commr. Faith and Order Commns., World Council Chs., Geneva, 1976-87, dep. gen. sec., 1987—. Author: Youth Without Jobs, 1972, Flight From the Farms, 1973, Church Youth Work in Africa, 1973, Christian Youth Work, 1979, And Women, Where Do They Come In:, 1980, Hearing and Knowing: A Theological Reflection on Christianity in Africa; editor: The State of Christian Theology in Nigeria. Mem. Nigerian Assn. for the Study of Religions, West Africa Assn. Theol. Insts., Ecumenical Assn. African Theologians (former v.p.), Ecumenical Assn. Third World Theologians, Oxford Inst. Meth. Theol. Studies (mem. steering com.), Internat. Assn. Mission Studies. Home: 2 Alayande St Bodija Estate, Ibadan 0Y0 State Nigeria Office: care World Council of Churches, 150 route de Ferney POB 66, 1211 Geneva 20 Switzerland

ODZA, RANDALL M., lawyer; b. Schnectady, May 6, 1942; s. Mitchell and Grace (Mannes) O.; m. Rita Ginness, June 19, 1966; children—Kenneth, Keith. B.S. in Indsl. and Labor Relations, Cornell U., 1964, LL.B., 1967. Bar: N.Y. 1967, U.S. Ct. Appeals (2d cir.) 1970, U.S. Dist. Ct. (so. and ea. dists.) N.Y. 1969, U.S. Dist. Ct. (we. dist.) N.Y. 1970. Assoc. Proskauer, Rose, Goetz & Mendelsohn, N.Y.C., 1967-69; assoc. Jaeckle, Fleischmann & Mugel, Buffalo, 1969-72, ptnr., 1972—. Trustee, legal counsel, treas. Temple Beth Am. Recipient Honor award Western N.Y. Retail Mchts. Assn., 1980. Mem. Indsl. Relations Research Assn. Western N.Y., ABA, Erie County Bar Assn., N.Y. State Bar Assn. Office: Jaeckle Fleischmann & Mugel Norstar Bldg 12 Fountain Plaza Buffalo NY 14202

OEH, GEORGE RICHARD, electrical engineer; b. Tacoma, Aug. 29, 1936; s. George Kenneth and Elsie Linnea (Ness) O.; BEE, U. Wash., 1958, MS (teaching fellow 1960), 1962; m. Diane Manley, Aug. 18, 1962; children: Karen Michelle, Jason Robert. Instr., U. Wash., 1961-62; advanced devel. engr., Philco-Ford Co., 1963-64; mgr. electromagnetics dept. GTE-Sylvania Co., 1964-72; mgr. sales Watkins Johnson Co., Palo Alto, Calif., 1972-82; v.p. Dalmo Victor Singer, Belmont, Calif., 1982—. Mem. Sunnyvale Park and Recreation Bd., 1968-69; bd. dirs. Sunnyvale Little League, 1977-78. Served with USAF, 1958-60. Mem. IEEE (chmn. San Francisco chpt. 1970-71), Armed Forces Communications Electronics Assn., Assn. Old Crows (past officer and dir.), Assn. Former Intelligence Officers, Res. Officers Assn. Democrat. Clubs: Western World Trade, Elks. Author papers in field. Home: 1056 Firth Ct Sunnyvale CA 94087 Office: 1515 Industrial Way Belmont CA 94002

OEI, HONG DJIEN, tobacco company executive, physician; b. Magelang, Indonesia, Apr. 5, 1939; s. Kok Hie and Marie Giam Nio (Tjan) O.; M.D., U. Indonesia, 1964; m. Wilowati Soerjanto, July 22, 1977; children—Ignatius Igor Rahmanadi, Augustinus Omar Rahmanadi. Vol. Roman Catholic mission physician, Temanggung, Indonesia, 1964-66; resident in pathol. anatomy Pathol. Inst., Nymegen, Netherlands, 1966-68; owner, dir. Oei Kok Hie Trading Co., Magelang, 1968—. Mem. Indonesian Med. Assn. Office: Jl Jenggolo 10, Magelang Indonesia

OEI, TAT HWAY, lawyer; b. Madiun, Indonesia, Apr. 12, 1923; s. T.H. Oei and T.N. Tan; ed. U. Leiden (Netherlands) 1950; m. Liem Kiet Nio, June 28, 1948; children—Eileen, George, Juswo, Hendrik. Practice law firm Oei Tat Hway Patent and Trade Mark Attys., Djakarta, Indonesia, 1951—. Mem. bd. All Indonesia Swimming Assn. Mem. Assn. Internationale pour la Protection de la Propriété Industrielle. Home: 17 Djl Tanah Abang II, Djakarta Indonesia Office: 5 Djl Kali Besar, Barat/PO Box 2102, Jakarta DKT Indonesia

OELLERS, PETER NORBERT, educator; b. Ratingen, Germany, Oct. 8, 1936; s. Werner and Susanne (Beck) G.; m. Maria Elisabeth Rengier, July 29, 1964; children: Christoph, Michael. Student, Universities, Cologne, Munich, Bonn, 1956-65; PhD, U. Bonn, Fed. Republic of Germany, 1965, cert. in edn., 1973. Prof. German lit. U. Bonn, 1975—; pres. Deutscher Germanistenverband, Bonn, 1984-87. Editor: Schiller-Nationalausgabe, 1978—; contbr. articles to profl. jours. and authored books about German lit. Mem. Social Dem. Party of Germany. Roman Catholic. Home: Ruedigerstr 14, D-5300 Bonn 2 Federal Republic of Germany Office: U Bonn, Am Hof 1d, D-5300 Bonn Federal Republic of Germany

OELOFSE, JAN HARM, game rancher, wildlife management consultant; b. Burgersdorp, Cape Province, South Africa, July 12, 1934; s. Andries and Johanna (Vorster) O.; m. Birte Sorensen, Mar. 17, 1962. Diploma in agriculture, Agrl. Coll., Cradock Cape, South Africa, 1952. Animal and trapping staff Tanganykia Game Ltd., Arusha Tanganykia, 1954-63; sr. game warden game translocation Natal Praks Bd., Hlahluwe Gamereserve, Natal, South Africa, 1964-72; game rancher Farm Okonjati, Kalkfeld, South West Africa, Namibia, South Africa, 1974—; mem. Wilderness Leadership Sch., Durban, Natal, 1967—; mem. tourist bd. South West African Adminstrn., Windhoeck, South West Africa, 1984—. Discoverer technique to capture wild animals with plastic material; patentee in field. Named Most Outstanding Hunter of Yr., 1982. Mem. Safari Club Internat., Internat. Profl. Hunters Assn. Lodge: Etosha Otjiwarongo. Avocations: sculpture; wildlife photography. Home: Mount Etjo Safari Lodge, PO Box 81, Kalkfeld 9000, Namibia Office: Mount Etijo Safari Lodge, Box 81, Kalkfeld 9000, Namibia

OERTER, GEORG WILHELM, manufacturing company executive; b. Petricken, Germany (now USSR), Feb. 2, 1927; married; 3 children. Grad., U. Cologne, 1954. Mgr. cost acctg. dept. Siemens Glas AG, Nordrhein-Westfallen, Fed. Republic Germany, 1954-55; asst. to pres. Cyklop Internat. AG, Cologne, Fed. Republic Germany, 1956-65, mng. dir., 1966—, mng. bd.; gen. mgr. Cyklop Internat. Agy.; bd. dirs. OY Cyklop AB, Finland, Strapesa SA, Barcelona, Spain, Cyklop SA, Madrid, Burseryds Bruk AB, Sweden, Cyklop Emballering SA, Denmark, Cyklop do Brasil, Sao Paulo, Brazil, Cyklop Strapping Corp, Downingtown, Pa., Cyklop-Serpac, Brussels, Cyklop Transportverpakkingen B.V., Cyklop S.P.A., Milan. Office: Cyklop Internat AG, Emil-Hofmann Strasse 1, 5000 Koln 50 Federal Republic of Germany

OERTLI-CAJACOB, PETER JOHN, management consultant; b. Höri, Zürich, Switzerland, May 29, 1941; s. Fritz Maximilian and Liselotte (Haedenkamp) O.; m. Cilla Maria Cajacob, Sept. 2, 1972; children: Thomas M., Adrian P., Matthias M. MSc, Swiss Fed. Inst. Tech., Zürich, 1968, DSc, 1975. Control engr. Brown Boveri & Cie AG, Baden, Switzerland, 1968-70; sci. asst. Inst. Mgmt. Sci. Swiss Fed. Inst. Tech., Zurich, 1970-72; mgmt. systems mgr. Hilti AG Fastening Systems, Schaan, Principality of Liechtenstein, 1972-75; tech. dir. Hilti Equipment Ltd., Manchester, Eng., 1976; v.p. mktg. Maag Gear Wheel Co., Zürich, 1977-82; group mgmt. cons. Knight Wendling AG, Zürich, 1983-87; ptnr. St. Gall Cons. Group, Zürich, 1988—; pres. bd. Eltrans AG, Zürich, 1986—. Author: Cybernetics of Economic Systems, 1977, translation in Russian, 1983; contbr. articles in econs., cybernetics, mgmt., mktg., and logistics to profl. jour. Bd. dirs. Tech. Soc., Zürich, 1987—. Mem. Swiss Soc. Mgmt., Swiss Group Artificial Intelligence and Cognitive Sci., Swiss Soc. Engrs. and Architects, Swiss Soc. Info. Tech. Free Democrats. Club: Efficiency (Zürich). Office: SCG St Gall Cons Group, Zürich AG, Airport Bus Ctr, Schaffhauserstr 134 Postfach, CH-8152 Zürich Glattbrugg Switzerland

OESTHOL, ERIK, construction company executive; b. Rattvik, Sweden, Apr. 5, 1916; s. Anders and Anna O.; m. Dency Gullberg, Feb. 2, 1941; children—Gunilla, Eva. Degree in civil engring. Tech. High Sch., Stockholm, 1941. Constrn. engr. Vatven Byggnads-Byran VBB, Stockholm, 1940-41, Byggnadsstyrelsen, 1941-44; chmn. Anders Dios AB, Uppsala, Sweden, 1944—. Home: Villa Japan Haga, Solna Sweden

OETKEN, DIETER, sales professional; b. Bremen, Fed. Republic Germany, July 15, 1938; s. Heinz and Getrud (Brünjes) O.; m. Heidrun Hoppe; children: Alexander, Annika. Grad. high sch., Bremen. Asst. mgr. Kuhlenkamo Renken, Bremen, 1958-60; dep. mgr. Internat. Tobacco Ltd, Vaduz, Lichtenstein, 1860-61; exec. mgr. Experta SA, Asuncion, Paraguay, 1961-63; gen. mgr., mng. ptnr. Importex GmbH, Bremen, 1964—; exec. mgr. (hon.) Zapag AG-Oetwil, Switzerland. Evangelical. Office: Importex GmbH, PO Box 104529, Bremen Federal Republic of Germany

O'FAOLAIN, SEAN, author; b. Ireland, 1900; s. Denis Whelan; m. Eileen Gould, 1928; 2 children. Ed. Nat. U. Ireland, Harvard U. Prin. works include: There's a Birdie in the Cage, 1935; A Born Genius, 1936; Bird Alone, 1936; The Autobiography of Wolfe Tone, 1937; A Purse of Coppers, 1937; An Irish Journey, 1939; Come Back to Erin, 1940; Story of Ireland, 1943; Teresa, 1947; The Irish, 1948; The Short Story, 1948; Summer in Italy, 1949; South to Sicily, 1953; The Vanishing Hero, 1956; I Remember, I Remember, 1962; Vive Moi, 1965; The Talking Trees, 1970; And Again, (1979; biographies include: Constance Markievicz: a Biography, 1934; King of the Beggars, 1938; The Great O'Neill, 1942; Newman's Way, 1952; collected short stories include: The Stories of Sean O'Faolain, 1958; The Heat of the Sun, 1966; Foreign Affairs, 1975; Selected Stories of Sean O'Faolain, 1978; Collected Stories, 1980, 83; play: She Had to Do Something, 1938; lectr. in English, Boston Coll., 1929, St. Mary's Coll., Strawberry Hill, 1929-33. Bd. dirs. Arts Council of Ireland, 1957-59. Commonwealth fellow, 1926-28; John Harvard fellow, 1928-29. *

O'FARRILL, ROMULO, JR., television executive, newspaper publisher; b. Puebla Pue, Mex., Dec. 15, 1917; s. Romulo and Dolores (Naude) O'F.; m. Hilda Avila Camacho, May 9, 1942; children: Victor Hugo, Hilda Gloria, Jose Antonio, Roberto. Student, Modern Comml. Sch., Puebla, 1931-32, St. Anselm's Coll., Manchester, N.H., 1933-34, Bus. Inst., Detroit, 1934-36. Pres., editor-in-chief Novedades Editores, S.A., pubs. of Novedades, The News and other newspapers; chmn. bd. Televisa, S.A., operating 124 TV stas.; chmn. bd. Sistema de TV Mexicana, S.A., operating 42 TV stas.; retired bd. mem. Goodyear Tire & Rubber Co., P.I.P.S.A., Avon Products, Inc., Indsl. Minera, Eastern Air Lines de Mex., DESC Sociedad de Fomento Indsl.; chmn. bd. T.S.M., I.E.M.S.A. Hon. Consul of Ireland in Mex., 1966; pres. bd. Hosp. Infantil de Méx., Federico Gomez, Oct. 87, Univ. bd. mem. U. de las Ams. Puebla, 1988; pres. Touring and Automobile Club of Mex., 1960-64, exec. v.p. Pan Am. Road Race, 1950-53, exec. com., 1954; pres. organizing com. Grand Prix of Mex. Races, 1962; bd. dirs. Mex. Red Cross, 1960-64, v.p. 1965-67, 77. Decorated officer Legion d'Honneur (France); Great Merit Cross (Fed. Republic Germany); grand cross Isabel la Catolica (Spain); Grade of Chivalry, Mex. Red Cross. Mem. Inter Am. Press Assn. (life mem. adv. bd., past pres.), Mex. Assn. Sovereign, Mil. Order Malta, Mil. and Hospitaller Order St. Lazarus of Jerusalem, Chevaliers du Tastevin, Champanion De Burdeos, Brit. C. of C. Clubs: Marco Polo, Met. (N.Y.C.); Rolling Rock, Losange D'Or Yacht, Internat. des Anciennes Pilotes de Grand Prix Formula 1; Campestre Mexico, Campestre Puebla Club de Golf Mexico, Golf La Hacienda, Golf ChapultepecUniversity, Am. Mexico City, Yates de Acapulco, Leones de la Ciudad de Mexico. Home: Ave Contreras 229, Contreras Mexico Office: Televisa SA, Chapultepec 18 Mexico

OFFIT, SIDNEY, writer, educator; b. Balt., Oct. 13, 1928; s. Barney and Lillian (Cohen) O.; m. Avodah Crindell Komito, Aug. 8, 1952; children: Kenneth, Michael Robert. B.A., Johns Hopkins U., 1950. Editorial staff Mercury Publs., N.Y.C., 1952-53, Macfadden Publs., N.Y.C., 1953-54; contbg. editor Baseball mag., Washington, 1955-58; mem. faculty N.Y. U., 1964—, adj. prof. creative writing, 1977—; asso. editor Intellectual Digest, 1970-72, sr. editor, 1972-74; lectr. creative writing New Sch. Social Research, 1965—; curator George Polk Awards for Journalism, 1977—; mem. nat. bd. Nat. Book Com., 1973-75; commentator Channel 5 TV, N.Y.C., 1975-85. Author: He Had it Made, 1959, The Other Side of the Street, 1962, Soupbone, 1963, Topsy Turvey, 1965, The Adventure of Homer Fink, 1966, The Boy Who Made a Million, 1968; short stories Not All the Girls Have Million Dollar Smiles, 1971; Only a Girl Like You, 1972, What Kind of Guy Do You Think I Am?, 1977; series sports books for boys, 1961-65, also essays, revs., short stories; book editor: Politics Today, 1978-80. Mem. selection com. Dist. Sch. Bd., N.Y.C., 1968; Mem. exec. bd. Lexington Democratic Club, 1957-60, N.Y. Dem. County Com., 1966—; chmn. 19th Precinct Community Council of N.Y.C., 1964-80. Recipient Disting. Alumni award Valley Forge Mil. Acad., 1961, Otty Community Service award, 1975; Teaching Excellence award NYU, 1981; Commendation for achievement as teacher, scholar, communicator N.Y. State Legislature, 1983; Proclamation for contbns. to City N.Y.C. Council, 1983. Mem. Tudor and Stuart Club, Authors Guild (council 1970-77, 79—), Authors League (nat. council 1976-79), Am. Center of P.E.N. (exec. com. 1969-88, v.p. 1970-74, internat. del. 1971, 72, 74). Clubs: Century Assn. (N.Y.C.), Coffee House (N.Y.C.). Home: 23 E 69th St New York NY 10021

OFFORD, DEREK CLIVE, Russian studies educator; b. Sutton, Eng., June 13, 1946; s. Stanley and Dorothy Clare (Danger) O.; m. Dorinda Ann O'Reilly, Apr. 27, 1974. BA in Modern Langs., Cambridge (Eng.) U., 1968; PhD, U. London, 1974. Lectr. Russian U. Wales, Aberstwyth, 1974-75; lectr. Russian U. Bristol, Eng., 1975-86, sr. lectr., 1986-88, reader, 1988—; Mem. Russian Lang. Undergrad. Study Com., 1981-85, chmn. 1986—. Author: Portraits of Early Russian Liberals, 1985, The Russian Revolutionary Movement in the 1880's, 1986; co-author: A Documentary History of Russian Thought, 1987; contbr. articles to profl. jours. British Council scholar Moscow State U., 1972-73. Mem. British Univ.'s Assn. Slavists (past com. mem.), Assn. Tchrs. Russian. Office: U Bristol Russian Dept, 17 Woodland Rd, Bristol BS8 1TE, England

O'FIAICH, TOMAS CARDINAL, archbishop of Armagh; b. County Armagh, Ireland, Nov. 3, 1923; s. Patrick and Annie (Caraher) Fee; B.A., St. Patrick's Coll., Maynooth, 1943; M.A., Univ. Coll., Dublin, 1950; Lic. Hist. Sc., Catholic U. Louvain (Belgium), 1952. Ordained priest Roman Catholic Ch., 1948; mem. faculty St. Patrick's Coll., Maynooth, 1953-77, prof. modern history, 1959-74, pres., 1974-77; consecrated Archbishop of Armagh and primate of All Ireland, 1977; created cardinal, 1979; chmn. Irish Episcopal Conf., 1977—; archbishop of Armagh; pres. Irish Speaking Priests, 1955-67. Author: Gaelscrinte i gCein, 1960; Irish Cultural Influence in Europe, 1966; Imeacht na nIarlai, 1972; Ma Nuad, 1972; Art McCooey and His Times, 1973; Art MacCumhaidh: Dánta, 1973; Columbanus in His Own Words, 1974; Oliver Plunkett-Ireland's New Saint, 1975; Oilibhear Pluinceid, 1976; Art MacBionaid: Dánta, 1979; Gaelscrinte San Eoraip, 1986; editor: Seanchas Ardmhacha, 1953-77; also articles. Address: Ara Coeli, Armagh BT61 7QY, Northern Ireland

O'FLARITY, JAMES P., lawyer; b. Yazoo City, Miss., Oct. 15, 1923. B.S., Millsaps Coll., 1950; postgrad., Jackson Sch. Law, 1948, 53-54; J.D., U. Fla., 1965. Bar: Miss. 1954, U.S. Dist. Ct. (so. dist.) Miss. 1954, U.S. Supreme Ct. 1957, U.S. Ct. Mil. Appeals 1957, U.S. Ct. Appeals (5th Cir.) 1957, Fla. 1966, U.S. Dist. Ct. (so. and mid. dists.) Fla. 1966, U.S. Dist. Ct. (no. dist.) Fla. 1967, U.S. Ct. Appeals (11th cir.) 1981. Assoc. law firm Cone, Owen, Wagner, Nugent & Johnson, West Palm Beach, Fla., 1966-69; sole practice law Palm Beach, Fla., 1969—; mem. nat. panel arbitrators Am. Arbitration Assn., 1967—; mem. Supreme Ct. Matrimonial Law Commn. Fla., 1982—, procedure B com., 1982—; lectr. on marital and family la; observer family ct. proc. Nat. Jud. Coll., 1983; mem. U. Fla. Law Ctr. Council, 1972, mem. legal edn. com., 1973, chmn. membership and fin. com., 1977-78, mem. emeritus, 1978—; leader del. for legal exchange on family law to Ministry of Justice, Peoples Republic of China, 1984. Contbr. articles to profl. publs. Mem. U. Fla. Pres.'s Council; mem. Fla. Family Support Council Adv. Bd., 1976; mem. chmn.'s com. U.S. Senatorial Bus. Adv. Bd., 1980—; col. La. Gov.'s Staff, 1982—. Fellow Am. Bar Found. (life), Roscoe Pound-Am. Trial Lawyers Found. (life), Am. Acad. Matrimonial Lawyers (nat. pres. 1985-86, nat. bd. of govs. 1977-88, founding pres. Fla. chpt. 1976-80, bd. mgrs. Fla chpt. 1976—, hon. permanent pres. emeritus 1982—), Internat. Acad. Matrimonial Lawyers Convenor and Founder Trusler Soc.; mem. Internat. Soc. Family Law, Internat. Bar Assn. (assoc.), Inter-Am. Bar Assn., Am. Law Inst., ABA (chmn. coms. 1973-75, 78-81, 82-83, editor Family Law Newsletter 1975-77, mem. council family law sect. 1976-85, vice-chmn. sect. 1981-82, chmn. sect. 1983-84, mem. conf. sect. chairmen 1982-85, mem. adv. bd. jour. 1978-80), Assn. Trial Lawyers Am. (Fla. State committeeman 1973-75, 1st chmn. family law sect. 1971-72, 72-73), Am. Judicature Soc., Am. Soc. Legal History, Supreme Ct. Hist Soc., Fla. Council Bar Assn. Presidents (life mem.), Fla. Bar Found. (life, exec. dir. screening com. 1976, chmn. projects com. 1976-77, asst. sect. 1973-79, dir. 1977-81), U. Fla. Law Ctr. Assn. (life), Acad Fla. Trial Lawyers (dir. 1974-77, coll. diplomates 1977), Fla. Bar Assn. (exec. council 1973-84, sec.-treas. family law sect. 1973-74, chmn. family law sect. 1974-75, 75-76, guest editor spl. issue jour. 1978, chmn. jour. and news editorial bd. 1978-79, mem. bd. cert., designation and edn. 1982—), Palm Beach County Bar Assn. (circuit ct. civil adv. com. 1981, mem. circuit ct. juvenile domestic relations adv. com. 1971-80, 81-83, adv. com. chmn. 1974-78), Solicitor's Family Law Assn. (Eng.), Phi Alpha Delta (life), Sigma Delta Kappa. Club: Gov.'s Palm Beach (founder, life mem., gov.'s council). Home: 908 Country Club Dr North Palm Beach FL 33408 Office: 215 5th St Suite 108 West Palm Beach FL 33401

O'FLYNN, FRANCIS DUNCAN, government official of New Zealand; b. Greymouth, New Zealand, 1918; s. Francis E. O'Flynn; m. Sylvia Elizabeth Hefford, 1942; 4 children. B.A., LL.M., Victoria U. Bar: N.Z.; Queen's counsel. Sole practice law, N.Z., 1954—; mem. Otaki Borough Council, 1968-71, chmn. State Service Tribunals, 1970-72; M.P. for Viapiti, 1972-75, Island Bay, 1978-87; mem. Wellington (N.Z.) City Council, 1977-83; minister of def. N.Z., 1984-87, former minister of state, of rehab., also in charge of war pensions; past mem. opposition on Justice, past assoc. fgn. affairs; mem. Statutes Revision Com., Fgn. Affairs Select Com. Editor: New Zealand Law Reports, 1977-78. Chmn. bd. trustees Norman Kirk Meml. Trust Fund. Served to Lt. Royal N.Z. Air Force, 1942-46 Mem. St. Thomas More Soc. (past pres.). Office: 105 Grant Rd, Thorndon New Zealand *

OFNER, WILLIAM BERNARD, lawyer; b. Los Angeles, Aug. 24, 1929; s. Harry D. and Gertrude (Skoss) Offner; m. Florence Ila Maxwell, Apr. 13, 1953 (div. 1956). A.A., Los Angeles City Coll., 1949; B.A., Calif. State U., Los Angeles, 1953; LL.B., Loyola U., Los Angeles, 1965; postgrad. Sorbonne, 1951, certificate de Langue Francaise, 1987, U. So. Calif., 1966. Bar: Calif. 1966, U.S. Dist. Ct. Calif. 1966, U.S. Supreme Ct. 1972. Assoc., Thomas Moore and Assocs., Los Angeles, 1967-69; sole practice, Los Angeles, 1969-70, 74—; assoc. Peter Lam, Los Angeles, 1981-87; assoc. C.M. Coronel, 1986-87, Jack D. Janofsky, 1987—; pres. DT Mktg. Inc.; lectr. Van Norman U., 1975. Served with USNR, 1947-54. Mem. Inst. Gen. Semantics, Inst. for Antiquity and Christianity, Soc. Judgement, Shakespeare Soc. (bd. dirs. 1987). Democrat. Jewish. Clubs: Los Angeles Athletic, Soc. of Judgement, Toastmasters. Avocations: water color painting, photography, linguistics. Office: 1102 Brand N Blvd #24 Glendale CA 91202

OFSTAD, JARLE, internist, educator; b. Alesund, Norway, Apr. 1, 1927; s. Nils and Johanna (Selbekk) O.; m. Aslaug Overaas; children: Ingrid, Randi, Jon Erik. Degree in Medicine, Med. Facijlty, Oslo, 1957. Lic. D Medicinae, specialist in Internal Medicine. Assoc. prof. Med. Facijlty, Bergen, Norway, 1965-73, prof., 1973—, chief nephrologist med. dept., 1965—, chief of staff, 1977—. Author: Renal Oxygen Extraction, Photometry in Blood, 1965; contbr. numerous articles to profl. jours. Chmn. Med. Research Council, Norway, 1976-81, Commn. Med. Ethics, 1978—, Michelsens Inst., 1986—; bd. dirs. Norwegian Underwater Tech. Inst., 1980-85. Named Knight of St. Olav, Oslo, 1987. Mem. Royal Acad. Sci., Bergen Research Soc. (chmn. 1986—). Home: V Bjerknes Vei 87, Landaas, 5030 Bergen Norway Office: Univ Hosp, Bergen Norway

OFTEDAL, TORFINN, former Norwegian diplomat; b. Sandnes, Norway, Apr. 7, 1909; s. Olav Magnus and Charlotte Sofie (Refvem) O.; B.S., U. Trondheim, 1936; m. Gloria Grosvenor, June 1, 1942 (dec. 1972); children—Elsie Mabel Oftedal Doersam, Olav T. Joined Norwegian Fgn. Service, 1938; assigned embassy, Washington, 1938-46, 51-60, Ministry Fgn. Affairs, 1946-49; Norwegian del. OEEC, 1949-51; ambassador to Austria, minister to Czechoslavkia and Hungary, 1960-65; spl. counsellor Ministry Fgn. Affairs, 1965-66; ambassador to Can., 1966-72; ambassador to Czechoslovakia and Rumania, 1973-75, ret., 1975. Participant numerous Norwegian delegations to internat. meetings and orgns.; alternate exec. dir. for Scandinavian countries World Bank, 1956-57. Decorated comdr. Order St. Olav; Grand Cross Austrian Order Merit. Clubs: Norske Selskab (Oslo); Chevy Chase (Washington). Home: 3900 Cathedral Ave NW Washington DC 20016

ÖFVERHOLM, STEFAN, electrical engineer; b. Ludvika, Sweden, Nov. 21, 1936; s. Håkan and Ragnhild Gudrun (Andersson) O.; m. Eva Guy Tiselius, Sept. 9, 1966 (div. 1971); m. Ulrika Mathilda Marie Skaar, Oct. 10, 1975; children: Harald, Ingegerd. MSEE, Chalmers U. Tech., Gothenburg, Sweden, 1963. Engr. microwave systems devel. Ericsson AB, Mölndal, Sweden, 1963-66; mgr. microwave lab. Trelleborgplast AB, Ljungby, Sweden, 1966-67; mgr. process and prodn. control projects Ericsson AB, Stockholm, Sweden, 1967-71; head computer devel. dept. Ericsson AB, Mölndal, Sweden, 1974-77; head testing methods and tech. Ericsson AB, Stockholm, Sweden, 1977-81; mgr. design and devel. Asea Lme Automation AB, Västerås, Sweden, 1971-74; v.p., gen. mgr. hybrid div. Rifa AB, Stockholm, Sweden, 1981-85; gen. mgr. controls div. Tour & Andersson AB, Västerhaninge, Sweden, 1985—. Home: Erik Dahlbergsallen 11, S-11524 Stockholm Sweden Office: Tour and Andersson AB, Fabriksvagen 1, S-13737 Vasterhaninge Sweden

OGATA, KATSUHIKO, engineering educator; b. Tokyo, Jan. 6, 1925; came to U.S., 1952; s. Fukuhei and Teruko (Yasaki) O.; m. Asako Nakamura, Sept. 6, 1961; 1 son, Takahiko. B.S., U. Tokyo, 1947; M.S., U. Ill., 1953; Ph.D., U. Calif., Berkeley, 1956. Research asst. Sci. Research Inst., Tokyo, 1948-51; fuel engr. Nippon Steel Tube Co., Tokyo, 1951-52; mem. faculty U. Minn., 1956—, prof. mech. engring., 1961—; prof. elec. engring. Yokohama Nat. U., 1960-61, 64-65, 68-69. Author: State Space Analysis of Control Systems, 1967, Modern Control Engineering, 1970, Dynamic Programming, 1973, Ingenieria de Control Moderna, 1974, Metody Przestrzeni Stanow w Teorii Sterowania, 1974, System Dynamics, 1978, Engenharia de Controle Moderno, 1982, Teknik Kontrol Automatik, 1985, Discrete-time Control Systems, 1986, Gendai Seigyo Riron, 1986, Dinamica de Sistemas, 1987. Recipient Outstanding Adv. award Inst. of Tech., U. Minn., 1981. Mem. ASME, Sigma Xi, Pi Tau Sigma. Office: Dept Mech Engring U Minn Minneapolis MN 55455

OGAWA, KONOSUKE, architect; b. Tokyo, Dec. 2, 1939; s. Tatsuyuki and Shizu (Matsumoto) O.; m. Kazumi Imamura, Dec. 2, 1962; children—Shinosuke, Minori. Design degree, Nippon Design Sch., 1964. Pres. Alen, Inc., Tokyo, 1962—; cons. Matsushita Electronics Co., 1983—, Toyota, Tokyo, 1983—, Tobu Dept. Store, Tokyo, 1981—, Govt. Japan, 1974—. Author numerous design presentations. Prin. works include shopping ctr. Itoyokado (award 1979), Daiei, Osaka (award 1979), dept. store ToTobu (award 1984). Mem. Tokyo Chamber Commerce and Industry. Democrat. Buddhist.

OGAWA, MASSARU, journalist; b. Los Angeles, 1915; s. Kenji Ogawa and Mine Fuijioka; m. Ayame Fukuhara, 1942; 3 children. Ed. UCLA, Tokyo Imperial Coll., Columbia U.; D.Litt. (hon.), Lewis and Clark Coll., Portland, Oreg., 1979. With Domei News Agy., 1941-46, Kyodo News Service 1946-48, The Japan Times, 1948—, Chief polit. sect., 1949, asst. mng. editor, 1950, chief editor, 1952, mng. editor, 1958-64, dir., 1959—, exec. editor, 1964-68, sr. editor, 1968-71, chief editorial writer, 1969-71, editor, 1971-77, advisor, 1977—; chmn. bd. Asia-Pacific Mag., Manila, 1981-85; lectr. Tokyo U., 1954-58; mem. Yoshida Internat. Edn. Found., 1968—, exec. dir., 1972—; mem. Japan Broadcasting Co. overseas program consultative council, 1974-84; dir. Internat. Motion Picture Co., 1970, Am. Studies Found., 1980—, Yoshida Shigeru Meml. Found., 1980—; pres. Pacific News Agy., 1973—. Editorial bd. Media Mag., Hong Kong, 1974. Recipient Vaughn-Ueda prize, 1987. Mem. Japan Editors and Pubs. Assn., Internat. Press Inst., Am.-Japan Soc. (exec. dir. 1980—), Phi Beta Kappa. Avocations: reading; sport. Home: 2 14 banchi 5-chome, Mejiro Toshima-Ku, Tokyo Japan

OGAWA, OSAMU, manufacturing executive; b. Kanda, Miyako, Fukuoka, Japan, Apr. 5, 1945; s. Hisamitu and Tamayo Ogawa; m. Eiko Inomoto, May 18, 1972. B, Kyusyu Inst. Tech., Kitakyusyu, Japan, 1968. Registered profl. engr., architect, Tokyo. Researcher Tokyo Rope Mfg. Co., Ltd., Tokyo, 1968-84, mgr., cons., 1984—. Inventor in field. Mem. Japan Soc. Civil Engrs., Soc. Naval Architects Japan. Home: Miyawada 531-2-712, 300-15 Fujishiro-Machi Kitasouma Ibaragi, Japan Office: Tokyo Rope Mfg Co Ltd, Chuouku Nihonbashi 2-5-11, 103 Tokyo Japan

OGDEN, MYRON WALDO, retired educational administrator; b. Cambridge, Mass., July 8, 1917; s. Waldo M. and Florence (Newton) O.; B.S. in Edn., Boston U., 1949; M.S. in Spl. Edn., U. Wash., Seattle, 1966; children—David M., Darren R. Instr. history Peninsula Coll., Port Angeles, Wash., 1967-70; dir. adult edn. Neah Bay (Wash.) Schs., 1969-70, dir. spl. edn., 1973-76, ret., 1976. Rep. Sch. Community Council, 1970-76. Mem. NEA, Wash., Clallam County (past pres.) edn. assns., Pi Gamma Mu, Phi Delta Kappa. Home: Belvedere 702 35th Ave Seattle WA 98122

OGDEN, SYLVESTER O., coal company executive; b. Paris, Mo., Oct. 29, 1935; s. Lester and Anastasia Ogden; m. Martha Jane Peterman, Feb. 15, 1964; children: Stasia, John. AA, Hannibal (Mo.) LaGrange Coll., 1957; BSChemE, U. Mo., 1961; MSChemE, U. Mo., Rolla, 1964; MBA, Cen. Mich. U., 1971. Various positions Dow Chem., Midland, Mich., 1964-71; v.p. planning and devel. Youghiogheny & Ohio, Cleve., 1971-75; pres., chief exec. officer Colorado Westermoreland; v.p. Westmoreland Coal, Colorado Springs, Colo., 1975-78, Panhandle Eastern Corp., 1978-81; pres., chief exec. officer Sunedco Co., Denver, 1981-84; v.p. Occidental Petrol, Lexington, Ky., 1984—; also chmn. bd., chief exec. officer Island Creek Coal Corp.; dir. Nat. Coal Council, Washington, Island Creek of China Coal, Ltd.; mem. joint cen. com. An Tai Bao Surface Mine, People's Republic China, 1986—. Founding chmn., dir. Alliance Clean Energy, Washington, 1983—. Mem. Nat. Coal Assn. (dir. 1978—), Ohio Mining and Reclamation Assn. (dir. 1978-81), Ky. Coal Assn. (dir. 1984—).

OGG, ROBERT DANFORTH, corporate executive; b. Gardiner, Maine, June 10, 1918; s. James and Eleanor B. (Danforth) O.; m. Nancy Foote, Oct. 21, 1978; children by previous marriage—Richard Aasgaard, Robert Danforth, James Erling. Student U. Calif.-Berkeley, Stanford U. Utilities engr. State of Calif., 1946-48; gen. mgr. Danforth Anchors, Berkeley, 1948-51, pres., chief exec. officer, 1951-59; mng. dir. Danforth div. The Eastern Co., 1959-79, dir., 1972-80; dir. Hodgdon Bros., East Boothbay, Maine, 1961-65; pres. Brewers Boatyard, West Southport, Maine, 1963-65; v.p. Henry R. Hinckley Co., Manset, Maine, 1974-79; pres. Ogg Oceans Systems, 1980—; chmn. Alpha Ocean Systems, 1983—. Author: Anchors & Anchorin (8 editions). Contbr. chpts. to books, articles to profl. jours. Patentee: Danforth anchors; compasses, depth sounders; auto pilots; gas detectors; numerous others. Mem. adv. com. U. Calif. Research Expeditions Program, 1979, co-chmn., 1983—; trustee U. Calif.-Berkeley Found., 1981, exec. com., 1983—, chmn. audit com., 1984—; advisor Lawrence Hall Sci.; founder, sr. warden St. Ann's Episcopal Ch., Windham, Maine, 1976-79; contbr. to ABC and BBB documentaries on Pearl Harbor. Served with USN Intelligence, 1941-46. Fellow Explorers Club, Calif. Acad. Scis. (life); mem. Navy League (founder Marin council), Soc. Naval Architects & Marine Engrs., Am. Soc. Naval Engrs., Am. Boat & Yacht Council, Boating Writers Internat., Am. Geophys. Union, IEEE, U.S. Naval Inst., R.G. Sproul Assocs., Woodshole Assocs., Sierra Club, U. Calif.-Berkeley Alumni Assn., Engring. Alumni Assn. Clubs: N.Y. Yacht; Pacific Union; Elks; Bear Backers; Chancellor's Circle. Address: 11490 Franz Valley Rd Calistoga CA 94515

OGG, WILSON REID, poet, curator, publisher, lawyer, educator; b. Alhambra, Calif., Feb. 26, 1928; s. James Brooks and Mary (Wilson) O. Student Pasadena Jr. Coll., 1946; A.B., U. Calif. at Berkeley, 1949, J.D., 1952; Cultural D in Philosophy of Law, World Univ. Roundtable, 1983. Assoc. trust Dept. Wells Fargo Bank, San Francisco, 1954-55; admitted to Calif. bar; pvt. practice law, Berkeley, 1955-78; real estate broker, cons., 1974-78; curator-in-residence Pinebrook, 1964—; owner Pinebrook Press, Berkeley, Calif., 1988—; research atty., legal editor dept. of continuing edn. of bar U. Calif. Extension, 1958-63; psychology instr. 25th Sta. Hosp., Taegu, Korea, 1954; English instr. Taegu English Lang. Inst., Taegu, 1954. Trustee World U., 1976-80; dir. admissions Internat. Soc. for Phil. Enquiry, 1981-84; dep. dir. gen. Internat. Biographical Centre, Eng., 1986—; dep. gov. Am. Biographical Inst. Research Assn., 1986—. Served with AUS, 1952-54. Cert. community coll. instr. Recipient 5th Prize for poem "My Cat and I" Am. Poetry Assn., 1987. Fellow Internat. Acad. Law and Sci.; mem. ABA, State Bar Calif., San Francisco Bar Assn., Am. Arbitration Assn. (nat. panel arbitrators), World Univ. Round Table (cult. D. in Philosophy of Law 1983), World Future Soc. (profl. mem.), AAAS, Am. Assn. Fin. Profls., Am. Soc. Psychical Research, Calif. Soc. Psychical Study (pres., chmn. bd. 1963-65), Soc. for Phys. Research (London), Parapsychol. Assn. (asso.), 999 Soc., Internat. Soc. Unified Sci., Worldwide Acad. Scholars, Am. Acad. Polit. and Social Sci., World Acad. Arts and Culture, Inc., Artists Embassy Internat., Internat. Platform Assn., Intertel, Ina Coolbrith Circle, Am. Legion, VFW, Am. Mensa, Lawyers in Mensa, Psychic Sci. Spl. Interest Group, Am. Legion, VFW. Unitarian. Mason, Elk. Clubs: Faculty (U. Calif.), City Commons (Berkeley); Press (San Francisco); Commonwealth of Calif.; Town Hall Calif. Author: My Escaping Self, 1988, Sons Without End, 1988, Love's Cradle, 1988, We Hatch Our Embryo, 1988; editor: Legal Aspects of Doing Business under Government Contracts and Subcontracts, 1958, Basic California Practice Handbook, 1959; contbr. numerous articles profl. jours; contbr. poetry to various mags. including American Poetry Anthology Vol. VI Number 5, Hearts on Fire: A Treasury of Poems on Love, Vol. IV, 1987, New Voices in American Poetry, 1987, The Poetry of Life A Treasury of Moments An. Poetry Anthology, Vol. VII, 1988. Home: 1104 Keith Ave Berkeley CA 94708-1607 Office: Eight Bret Harte Way Berkeley CA 94708-1611

OGILVIE, LLOYD JOHN, clergyman; b. Kenosha, Wis., Sept. 2, 1930; s. Vard Spencer and Katherine (Jacobson) O.; m. Mary Jane Jenkins, Mar. 25, 1951. B.A., Lake Forest Coll., 1952, Garrett Theol. Sem., 1956; postgrad., New Coll., U. Edinburgh, Scotland, 1955-56; D.D., Whitworth Coll., 1973; L.H.D., U. Redlands, 1974; D.Humanities, Moravian Coll., 1975. Ordained to ministry Presbyn. Ch., 1956; student pastor Gurnee, Ill., 1952-56; first pastor Winnetka (Ill.) Presbyn. Ch., 1956-62; pastor 1st; Presbyn. Ch., Bethlehem, Pa., 1962-72, 1st Presbyn. Ch., Hollywood, Calif., 1972—; preacher Chgo. Sunday Evening Club, 1962—, also frequent radio and TV personality weekly syndicated TV program Let God Love You. Author: A Life Full of Surprises, 1969, Let God Love You, 1974, If I Should Wake Before I Die, 1973, Lord of the Ups and Downs, 1974, You've Got Charisma, 1975, Cup of Wonder, 1976, Life Without Limits, 1976, Drumbeat of Love, 1977, When God First Thought of You, 1978, The Autobiography of God, 1979, The Bush Is Still Burning, 1980, The Radiance of the Inner Splendor, 1980, Congratulations, God Believes in You, 1981, Life as it Was Meant to Be, 1981, The Beauty of Love, The Beauty of Friendship, 1981, The Beauty of Caring, The Beauty of Sharing, 1981, God's Best for My Life, 1981, God's Will in Your Life, 1982, Ask Him Anything, 1982, Commentary on Book of Acts, 1983, Praying with Power, 1983, Falling into Greatness, 1983, Freedom in the Spirit, 1984, Making Stress Work For You, 1984, The Lord of the Impossible, 1984, Why Not Accept Christ's Healing and Wholeness, 1984, If God Cares, Why Do I Still Have Problems?, 1985, The Other Jesus, 1986, 12 Steps to Living Without Fear, 1987; gen. editor: Communicator's Commentary of the Bible, 1982; host: (TV and radio program) Let God Love You. Bd. dirs. Hollywood Presbyn. Hosp. Office: 1760 N Gower St Hollywood CA 90028

OGILVIE THOMPSON, JULIAN, mining company executive; b. Cape Town, Republic of South Africa, Jan. 27, 1934; s. Newton and Eve (Wiener) O. T.; m. Tessa Mary Brand, July 24, 1956; children: Christopher William, Rachel Amanda, Anthony Thomas, Leila Katherine. Student, U. Cape Town, 1953; MA, Oxford (Eng.) U., 1956; LLD (hon.), Rhodes U., 1988. With Anglo Am. Corp. South Africa, Ltd., Johannesburg, 1957—, personal asst., 1957-61, mgr., 1965-70, dir., 1970-71, exec. dir., 1971-83, dep. chmn., 1983—, also bd. dirs.; dir. DeBeers Consol. Mines Ltd., Kimberley, Republic of South Africa, 1966-82, dep. chmn., 1982-85, chmn., 1985—; vice chmn. First Nat. Bank; chmn. Minerals and Resources Corp., 1982—. Bd. dirs. Urban Found., Johannesburg. Rhodes scholar, 1953. Clubs: Brook (N.Y.C.); Kimberley; White's (London); Rand (Johannesburg). Home: Froome St Athol Ext 3, 2196 Sandton, Transvaal Republic of South Africa Office: Anglo Am Corp South Africa Ltd, 44 Main St, 2001 Johannesburg Transvaal, Republic of South Africa

OGLEY, DAVID JEFFREY, finance executive; b. Lancashire, Eng., May 5, 1955; came to Australia, 1961; s. Geoffrey Frank and Prudence Lilly (Sherman) O.; m. Susan Marilyn Rosaman, Jan. 26, 1979. B of Bus. in Acctg., Western Australia Inst. Tech., 1980, B of Bus. in Secretarial, 1983. With Commonwealth Banking Corp., Perth, Australia, 1973-77, Lynas Motors Pty. Ltd., Perth, 1977-78, Macrobertson Miller Airline Services, Perth, 1978-80; acctg. assoc. Indsl. Sales Holdings Ltd., Perth, 1980; acct., office mgr. various holding cos., Perth, 1980-81; acct., office mgr. Whittakers Ltd., Welshpool, Australia, 1981-85, co. sec., fin. controller, 1985—. Fellow Inst. Chartered Secs. and Adminstrs.; mem. Australian Soc. Accts. (assoc., cert.), Australian Inst. Credit Mgmt. (assoc.). Anglican. Home: 13 Bullcreek Dr, Bullcreek Australia 6155 Office: Whitakers Ltd, 271 Treasure Rd, Welshpool Australia 6107

OGOUMA, SIMON IFEDE, statistician, diplomat; b. Cotonou, Benin, Dassa-Tanghe, Beninese, Nov. 21, 1935; m. Marie Ogouma; 5 children. Student U. Dakar, 1956-59, Nat. Inst. Stats. and Econ. Studies, Paris, 1959-62; Diplome, French Nat. Sch. Stats. and Econ. Adminstrn. Dir., Office Stats., 1963-67; dir. studies High Commn. for Planning, 1967-68; dir. Nat. Inst. Stats. and Econ. Analysis, 1968-74; prefect Benin's Province de l'Atlantique, 1974-80; people's commr. Nat. Revolutionary Assembly, 1979-84; Benin Minister for Fgn. Affairs and Cooperation, 1980-82; permanent rep. of Benin to UN, 1982-87; pres. com. external relations of Cen. Com. Party Popular Revolution of Benin, 1987—; mem. Central Com., Party of Popular Rebolution of Benin; participated in various fgn. missions. Office: Mission of the Peoples Rep of Benin to UN 4 East 73d St New York NY 10021

O'GRADY, JAMES FRANCIS, agricultural researcher; b. Tipperary, Ireland, Aug. 17, 1935; s. Michael and Kathleen (McKenna) O'G.; m. Mary Hanly, June 12, 1961; children: Deirdre, Clodagh, Michael, Brian, Catriona, Aoife. B in Agrl. Sci., Univ. Coll., Dublin, 1958; MSc, Univ. Coll., Cork, 1961, PhD, 1967. Research officer Agrl. Inst. Ireland, Fermoy, 1959-73, head dept., 1973-83, asst. dir., 1983-88, dep. dir., 1988—; dir. Grange Research Ctr., Dunsany, Ireland, 1983—; vis. fellow U. Alta., Can., 1970-71; pres. pig commn. European Assn. for Animal Prodn., Rome, 1984—; animal husbandry researcher EEC, Brussels, 1984—. Contbr. research papers to internat. profl. jours. Vis. fellow Royal Irish Acad., U.S. and France, 1967, 81. Mem. Brit. Soc. Animal Prodn. (v.p. 1988—), Nutrition Soc., Soc. Feed Technologists, Irish Grassland Assn. (pres. 1977-78), Royal Dublin Soc. (com. mem. 1987). Roman Catholic. Clubs: Royal Tara Golf, Fermoy Golf, Old Collegians Rowing, Fermoy Rowing. Home: 159 Georgian Village, Dublin 15, Ireland Office: Agrl Inst, Grange Research Ctr, Dunsany Meath Ireland

O'GREEN, FREDERICK WILBERT, multi-industry company executive; b. Mason City, Iowa, Mar. 25, 1921; s. Oscar A. and Anna (Heikkinen) O'G.; m. Mildred G. Ludlow, Mar. 21, 1943; children: Susan Renee, Jane Lynn O'Green Koenig, John Frederick, Eric Stephen. Student, Mason City Jr. Coll., 1939-40; B.S. in Elec. Engring, Iowa State U., 1943; M.S. in Elec. Engring, U. Md., 1949; LL.D. (hon.), Pepperdine U., 1977. Project engr. Naval Ordnance Lab., White Oak, Md., 1943-55; dir. Agena D project Lockheed Aircraft Co., Sunnyvale, Calif., 1955-62; v.p. Litton Industries, Inc., Beverly Hills, Calif., 1962-66, sr. v.p., 1966-67, exec. v.p., 1967-72, pres., 1972-81, chmn., 1981-88, chief exec. officer, 1981-87, also dir. Served with USNR, 1945. Recipient Meritorious Civilian Service award U.S. Navy, 1954; Outstanding Achievement award Air Force Systems Command, 1964; Disting. Achievement citation Iowa State U., 1973; Energy Exec. of Yr. award Third World Energy Engring. Congress, 1980. Mem. AIM, AIAA, U.S. C. of C., Assn. U.S. Army, Phi Kappa Psi, Phi Mu Alpha. Republican. Lutheran. Office: Litton Industries Inc 360 N Crescent Dr Beverly Hills CA 90210 *

OGUCHI, TOMOHIRO, electrical engineer; b. Tokyo, Japan, Jan. 2, 1932; s. Kanji and Masae (Hama) O.; BS, Keio U., 1956, PhD, 1965; m. Reiko Uchino, June 19, 1977; 1 dau., Natsuko. Research asst. Radio Research Labs., Ministry of Posts and Telecommunications, Tokyo, Japan, 1956-65, research officer, 1965-68; vis. research assoc. Ohio State U., Columbus, 1968-69; chief research officer Communications Research Lab., Ministry of Posts and Telecommunications, Tokyo, Japan, 1968-82, dir. Office Radio Physics, 1982—; vis. prof. space physics Wuhan U., Wuchang, Hubei, People's Republic of China, 1983—. Mem. Internat. Union Radio Sci. (mem. com. 1988—), IEEE, Am. Geophys. Union, Sigma Xi. Club: Isuzu Sports Car. Contbr. articles to tech. jours. Home: 3-57-8 Chuō, Musashi-Murayama, Tokyo 190-12, Japan Office: 4-2-1 Nukui-Kita Koganei, Tokyo 184, Japan

OGUIBENINE, BORIS LEONIDOVIČ, Sanskrit educator, reader in Vedic religion; b. Novosibirsk, USSR, Nov. 6, 1940; arrived in Austria, 1974, France, 1975; s. Leonid and Olga (Guinzbourg) O.; m. Catherine Marie-Christine Bloc-Duraffour, May 19, 1978; children: Elisabeth, Hélène, Agnès. Diploma, Moscow U., 1962; postgrad., USSR Acad. Scis., Moscow, 1966; LittD, France, 1985. Research scholar Inst. Oriental Studies, Moscow, 1961-74; reader in Indian and Baltic linguistics U. Vienna, Austria, 1974-75; reader in Indian religions École Pratique des Hautes Études, Paris, 1975—; research scholar Ctr. Nat. de la Recherche Scientifique, Paris, 1977-88. Author: Structure d'un Mythe, 1973, Ernst Neizvestny, 1975, Essais sur la Culture Védique et Indo-Européenne, 1985, La déesse Usas, 1988. Research scholar U. Cambridge, 1975, 77; Ind. U., 1976, Leiden U., 1984-86. Mem. Centre d'études de l'Inde et l'Asie du Sud. Home: 22 rue de Passy, 75016 Paris France Office: Inst d'Etudes Sud-asiatiques, U Scis Humaines de Strasbourg, 67084 Strasbourg Cedex France

OGURA, YOSHIAKI, architect; b. Tokyo, Dec. 23, 1937; parents Haruji Ohmori and Fukiko Ogura; m. Yoshiko Honjo, Mar. 18, 1975 (dec. Jan 1981); children: Aya, Chika. Bachelor's, U. Tokyo, 1962; Master's, Harvard U., 1968. Registered architect, Japan, Singapore. Project architect Nikken Seddei Ltd, Tokyo, 1962-82, mgr. design div., 1982-85, dep. office rep., 1985-87, prin., 1987—. Mem. Japan Inst. of Architecture, Archtl. Inst. of Japan (award 1982). Home: 4 8 11 702 Takanawa, 108 Minato-Ku Tokyo Japan Office: Nikken Sekkei Ltd, 1 4 27 KorakuBunkyo-Ku, 112 Tokyo Japan

OH, HARRY HAK-KEUN, consulting electrical engineer; b. Seoul, Korea, Oct. 3, 1935; s. Soo Young and Kyung Ja (Park) Oh; came to U.S., 1953, naturalized, 1963; B.S., U. Pa., 1958; M.E.E., George Washington U., 1961; m. Soon Jean Ahn; children by previous marriage—Richard C., Philip S.; Project engr. Kluckhuhn & McDavid Co., 1958-63; chief elec. engr. Thomas B. Bourne & Assos., 1963-65; v.p. Mech. Constrn. Mfg. Co., Rockville, Md., 1977—; pres. Hary K. Oh & Assos., Kensington, Md., 1965-79, Oh & Chen Assocs., Rockville, Md., 1979—, chmn., 1985—. Cons., Nat. Minority Research Center, Washington, 1977—; pres. Md. Korean Am. Citizens' Fedn., 1981—; chmn. Nat. Korean Am. Citizens' Fedn., 1981—, Korean Am. Baseball Assn., 1984—; co-chmn. Korean-Am. Republican Nat. Fedn., 1960—. Decorated Nat. medal (Korea). Registered profl. engr., Md. Mem. Nat. Soc. Profl. Engrs., Md. Soc. Profl. Engrs. Methodist. Office: 11900 Parklawn Dr Rockville MD 20852

OH, JA BOK, government official; b. Kaesong, Republic of Korea, June 16, 1930; m. Jung Ja Ahn, Dec. 27, 1958; children: Bo Hwan, Hyae Young. Grad., Myongji U., Seoul, Republic of Korea, 1969; MA in Pub. Adminstrn., Seoul Nat. U., 1982. Commd. 2d lt. Republic of Korea Army, 1951, advanced through grades to gen., 1979, various staff positions, 1951-71; commanding officer 39th Regiment 15th Div., 1971-73; commanding gen. 6th Div., 1979-80; dir. Def. Security Agy. Ministry of Nat. Def., 1980-82; commanding gen. V Corps 1982-83; Vice Chief of Staff Republic of Korea Army, 1983-84, commanding gen. 2d Army, 1984-86, chmn. Joint Chiefs of Staff, 1986-87; Minister of Nat. Def. Republic of Korea, 1988—. Decorated Chung-mu Mil. Merit Medal, 1966, Presdl. Individual Citation, 1980, Tong-il Merit Medal, 1985, Legion of Merit. Office: Ministry of Nat Def, 1 3-Ka Yongsan-dong, Yongsan-ku, Seoul 140023, Republic of Korea

OH, MATTHEW INSOO, lawyer; b. Seoul, Republic of Korea, Aug. 5, 1938; s. Young Whan and Jeom-soon (Kim) Oh; m. Young Ok, May 24, 1973; children: John Z., Amy J. LLB, Seoul Nat. U., 1963, LLM, 1968; LLM, Columbia U., 1972; JD, William Mitchell Coll. Law, St. Paul, 1982. Bar: Minn. 1982. Sr. planning researcher Ministry of Constrn., Seoul, 1968-71; planner Altamaha, Ga. Regional Planning Commn., 1972-74; sole practice St. Paul, Minn., 1982—. Legal advisor Korean Elderly Soc., St. Paul, 1984—; mem. North Korea Human Rights Project, Mpls., 1985—; chmn. State of Minn. Council on Asian-Pacific Relations, St. Paul, 1985-86; v.p. Minn. Asian Advocacy Coalition, St. Paul, 1983-85; bd. dirs. Urban Concern Workshop, Inc., St. Paul, 1985-86. Fulbright fellow Fulbright Commn., Seoul, 1971. Mem. ABA, Fed. Bar Assn., Minn. Bar Assn. (immigration law sect. 1987-88), Ramsey County Bar Assn. (Yogi Berra award), Am. Immigration Lawyers Assn. Presbyterian. Home: 720 Mercury Dr Shoreview MN 55126 Office: 1430 Meritor Tower 444 Cedar St Saint Paul MN 55101

OH, MAY BUONG YU LAU, lawyer; b. Singapore, May 20, 1940; d. Pai Hu Liu Lau and Uk Cung Liu Hu; m. Siew Leong Oh, May 22, 1965; children—Su Lin, Siang Peng. Student Anglo Chinese Jr. Coll., Singapore, 1958-59; Barrister-at-Law, Lincoln's Inn (London), 1964. Called to bar of Eng., 1965; called to bar of Singapore, 1967; Adv., solicitor Supreme Ct. Singapore, 1967. Cert. Am. and internat. bus. law and transactions, acctg., taxation. Legal asst. firm Lee & Lee, Singapore, 1966-67; legal officer Housing and Devel. Bd., 1967; mgmt. asst. Mobil Oil Malaysia Sdn. Bhd., 1967, apptd. co. sec., 1968; legal counsel Mobil East, N.Y.C., 1970, Mobil Europe, London, 1970; apptd. gen. counsel Mobil Oil Singapore Pte Ltd., 1970, apptd. exec. dir. bd. dirs., 1971 (first Asian appointee), assigned primary responsibilities for govt. affairs, Singapore, 1973, dir. legal/govt. affairs Mobil Oil Singapore Pte Ltd. with regional responsibilities for Singapore, Malaysia and Thailand, 1973-84; dir. Mobil Asia Pte Ltd., 1974-84; ptnr. May Oh & Co., 1984—; sr. ptnr. May Oh & Wee Advocates & Solicitors, 1985—; mem. adv. bd. Internat. Comparative Law Ctr., Dallas; participant, speaker profl. internat. confs., Singapore, U.S., Europe. Contbr. articles to pubis. Chmn. organizing com. Pvt. Investment in Asia and the Pacific, 1973; bd. govs. Methodist Girls' Sch., 1978—; pres. Meth. Girls' Sch. Alumnae Assn., 1981—. chmn. Internat. Energy Conf., Singapore and Jakarta, 1984, 85. Conf. fellow Acad. Am. and Internat. Lat, 1970. Mem. Am. Inst. Mgmt. (council fellow 1981—), Singapore Law Soc., Singapore Econ. Soc., Internat. and Comparative Law Center (U.S.), Singapore Am. Bus. Council, Internat. Bar Assn. (conf. host planning com. 1982), Law Assn. for Asia and Western Pacific (chmn. energy sect.). Methodist. Clubs: Singapore Island Country, Jurong Country, Tarylon. Home: 27 Ewart Park, Singapore 1027, Singapore Office: May Oh & Wee, 21 Collyer Quay #14-02, Hong Kong Bank Bldg, Singapore 0104, Singapore

OH, SUK-WHAN, neuropsychiatry educator; b. Seoul, Republic of Korea, Oct. 20, 1926; s. Dae-Kun and Hyun-Sook (Kim) O.; m. Jung-Sook Lee, Sept. 6, 1961; children: Sea-Joong, Whasun. MD in neuropsychiatry, Seoul U., 1951; PhD, Pusan (Republic of Korea) U., 1964. Prof., chmn. Pusan U. Med. Sch., 1962-78, dean, 1974-76; prof., chmn. Inje U. Med. Sch., Seoul, 1978—. Co-author 7 books; contbr. articles to profl. jours. Co-fellow Am. Psychiat. Assn.; mem. Korean Neuropsychiat. Assn. (pres. 1975, chmn. 1976), Korean Soc. Biol. Psychiatry (pres. 1987). Home: Banpo Apt 54-501, Banpo Kangnam, Seoul 135 Republic of Korea Office: Paik Hosp, 85 2-Ka Jurdong, Chung-Ku, Seoul 100 Republic of Korea

OH, TAI KEUN, business educator; b. Seoul, Korea, Mar. 25, 1934; s. Chin Young and Eui Kyung (Yun) O.; came to U.S., 1958, naturalized, 1969; B.A., Seijo U., 1957; M.A., No. Ill. U., 1961; M.L.S., U. Wis., 1965, Ph.D., 1970; m. Gretchen Brenneke, Dec. 26, 1964; children—Erica, Elizabeth, Emily. Asst. prof. mgmt. Roosevelt U., Chgo., 1969-73; assoc. prof. Calif. State U., Fullerton, 1973-76, prof. mgmt., 1976—; vis. prof. U. Hawaii, 1983-84, 86; advisor Pacific Asian Mgmt. Inst., U. Hawaii; cons. Calty Design Research, Inc. subs. Toyota Motor Corp. Merchants and Mfrs. Assn.; seminar leader and speaker. Named Outstanding Prof., Sch. Bus. Adminstrn. and Econs., Calif. State U., Fullerton, 1976, 78. NSF grantee, 1968-69, recipient Exceptional Merit Service award Calif. State U., 1984, Meritorious Performance and Profl. Promise award Calif. State U., 1987. Mem. Acad. Mgmt., Indsl. Relations Research Assn., Acad. Internat. Bus. Editorial bd. Acad. Mgmt. Rev., 1978-81; contbg. author: Ency. Profl. Mgmt., 1978, Handbook of Management 1985; contbr. articles to profl. jours. Home: 2044 E Eucalyptus Ln Brea CA 92621 Office: Calif State U Fullerton CA 92634

O'HANLON, REDMOND DOUGLAS, writer; b. Langton Matravers, Dorset, Eng., June 5, 1947. BA, Merton Coll., Oxford, Eng., 1969, MPh with distinction, 1971; MA, St. Anthony's Coll., Oxford, Eng., 1974, PhD, 1977. Sr. scholar St. Antony's Coll., 1971-74; research fellow St. Anthony's Coll., 1974; asst. editor lit. supplement Times Newspaper Ltd., London, 1981—; mem. literary panel The Arts Council of Great Britain, London, 1971-74; sr. visitor St. Antony's Coll., 1985—. Author: Joseph Conrad and Charles Darwin, 1984, Into the Heart of Borneo, 1984, In Trouble Again, A Journey Between the Orinoco and the Amazon, 1988; contbr. to profl. jours. Fellow Royal Geog. Soc.; mem. Soc. for History of Natural History, British Trust for Ornithology. Home: Pelican House, Ch Hanborough, Oxford OX7 2AE, England Office: The Times Lit Supplement, Priory House, St John's Ln, London EL1M 4BX, England

O'HARA, DAVID MICHAEL, lawyer, real estate broker; b. Springfield, Ill., Mar. 31, 1940; s. James Dennis and Angela Maud (Becker) O'H.; B.S. in Civil Engring., Bradley U., 1962; J.D., U. Calif., 1969; m. Sharon F. LePage, Feb. 19, 1977. Admitted to Calif. bar, 1970; asst. legal counsel Castle & Cooke, Inc., San Francisco, 1968-69; with firm Danaher, Fletcher & Gunn, Palo Alto, Calif., 1969-70, Quaresma, Benya, Hall, Connich, Ellis & O'Hara, 1970—; tchr. real estate law Ohlone Coll., Fremont, Calif., 1972-82; legal counsel Calif. Jaycees, 1973-74. Bd. dirs. Operation Amigo, Riverside, Calif., 1973-74, Calif. Jaycee Found., 1973-74, Community Drug Council, Fremont, 1971-87; chmn. bd. dirs. Community Counseling and Edn. Center, 1975-87; mem. Block Grant Commn., City of Fremont, 1981-85. Served to lt. comdr. USNR, 1962-66. Recipient Nat. Am. Legion Citizenship award, 1958; Outstanding Young Men of Am. award 1972-74; Jaycee of Yr. award, 1974. Mem. Calif., Alameda County, San Francisco bar assns., Washington Twp. Bar Assn (pres. 1987), Internat. Platform Assn., Mensa. Clubs: Barristers, Commonwealth, Lawyers (San Francisco); Berkeley Yacht; Mission San Jose Rotary (pres. 1987—); Washington Twp. Men's. Author: Nuclear Biological and Chemical Warfare-Offense, 1966; Nuclear Biological and Chemical Warfare-Defense, 1967; The Incarceration and Persecution of the Atom, 1969; syndicated newspaper columnist Very Common Law, 1973-75. Contbr. articles to law jours. Home: 43792 Excelso Dr Fremont CA 94539 Office: Quaresma Benya Hall Connich Ellis & O'Hara 37323 Fremont Blvd Fremont CA 94536

OHE, TAKERU, management consultant; b. Tokyo, Sept. 28, 1940; s. Seizo and Sumie (Ichikawa) O. BS, Nihon U., Tokyo, 1964; postgrad., Princeton U., 1968; PhD, U. Md., 1972; MBA, Columbia U., 1981. Dir. new bus. Dymo Industry, Tokyo, 1973-74; gen. mgr. Dymo Japan, Tokyo, 1974-75; pres. T. Ohe & Assocs., Tokyo, 1975—; cons. Technoventure K.K., Tokyo, 1981—; bd. dirs. LSI Logic K.K., Nihon Semiconductor K.K. Author: Scientific Revolution, 1982, Entrepreneurialship, 1987. Mem. Japan Elec. Engr. Assn., Fgn. Correspondent Club. Office: T Ohe & Assocs Inc, Akiya 4893-1, Yokosuka 240-01, Japan

OHGA, NORIO, electronics executive; b. Numazu, Japan, Jan. 29, 1930; m. Midori Ohga. Grad., Tokyo Nat. U. Fine Arts and Music, 1953, Kunst U., Berlin, 1957. Cons., advisor Tokyo Tsushin Kogyo (later Sony Corp.), 1953-59; gen. mgr. tape recorder div., product planning div., indsl. design div. Sony Corp., Tokyo, 1959, bd. dirs., 1964-72, mng. dir., 1972-74, sr. mng. dir., 1974-76, dep. pres., 1976-82, pres., chief operating officer, 1982—; rep. dir., chmn. bd. CBS/Sony Inc. Mem. Electric Home Appliance Fair Trade Assn. (pres.), Assn. Devel. Broadcasting Tech. (pres.), Assn. Electric Home Applicances (pres.). Office: Sony Corp, 6-7-35 Kita-Shinagawa, Shinagawa-Ku, Tokyo Japan 141

O'HIGGINS, NIALL JOHN, surgeon, educator; b. Dublin, Ireland, Jan. 28, 1942; s. Niall Bartholomew and Johanna (O'Shea) O'H.; m. Rosaleen Elizabeth Healy, Dec. 4, 1979; children—Amy Claire, Eoin Francis, Lisa Ann, Conor Niall. M.B., B.Ch., B.A.O. with honors, Nat. Univ. Ireland, 1965, B.Sc. in Anatomy with honors, 1967, M.Ch., 1974. Sr. registrar and tutor in surgery Royal Postgrad. Med. Sch., London, 1970-74; sr. lectr. surgery Univ. Coll., London, 1976-78; prof., chmn. surgery Univ. Coll. and St. Vincent's Hosp., Dublin, 1978—. Co-editor: Surgical Management, 1984; contbr. articles to profl. jours. Recipient James IV Traveller award James IV Assn. Surgeons Inc., 1982. Fellow Royal Coll. Surgeons Eng., Royal Coll. Surgeons Edinburgh, Royal Coll. Surgeons Ireland; mem. James IV Assn. Surgeons, Council Royal Coll. Surgeons Ireland, Assn. Surgeons Gt. Britain and Ireland, Internat. Surg. Soc., Surg. Research Soc., Internat. Surg. Group, Internat. Assn. Endocrine Surgeons. Club: Fitzwilliam Lawn Tennis (Dublin). Avocations: reading; cycling. Home: 7 Burleigh Mews, Burlington Rd, Dublin 4 Ireland Office: St Vincent's Hosp, Elm Park, Dublin 4 Ireland

OHKUBO, SATOSHI, automotive executive. Chmn., dir. Honda Motor Co., Ltd., Tokyo. Office: Honda Motor Co Ltd, 27-8 6 chome, Jingumae, Shibuya-ku, Tokyo Japan *

OHLMAN, DOUGLAS RONALD, lawyer, investment consultant; b. Rockville Centre, N.Y., Mar. 25, 1949; s. Maxwell and Miriam (Frucht) O.; m. Elat Menashe, Dec. 4, 1983. B.A., Columbia Coll., 1971; J.D., Hofstra U., 1974. Bar: N.Y. 1975, U.S. Dist. Ct. (so., ea., no. and we. dists.) N.Y. 1976, U.S. Tax Ct. 1978, U.S. Supreme Ct. 1978, U.S. Ct. Claims 1978, U.S. Customs Ct. 1978. Vice pres. Info. & Research Services, Inc., Roslyn, N.Y., 1975-81; assoc. Baer & Marks, N.Y.C., 1974-75, Rains, Pogrebin & Scher, Mineola, N.Y., 1975-76, Weisman, Celler, Spett, Modlin & Wertheimer, N.Y.C., 1976-79, Hoffberg, Gordon, Rabin & Engler, N.Y.C., 1979-80, Bergner & Bergner, Blum & Ruditz, N.Y.C., 1980-81; gen. counsel Greenfield Ptnrs., N.Y.C., 1981-86, gen. ptnr., 1982-86, dep. mng. ptnr., 1984-86, chief operating officer, sr. v.p., sec., dir. V.W. Investors, Inc., J.L. Investors, Inc., N.Y.C., 1985-88, dir. Track Data Corp., N.Y.C., 1983-87; allied mem. N.Y. Stock Exchange, Inc., 1982-88. Mem. radio news team WKCR-FM, N.Y.C. (Writers Guild award, Peabody nomination 1968); contbng. editor Hofstra Law Rev., 1973-74. Communications dir., dep. radiol. officer Nassau County Civil Def., Town of Roslyn, N.Y., 1964-74; mem. com. Nassau County Liberal Party, 1982. Mem. ABA, N.Y. State Bar Assn., N.Y. County Lawyers Assn., Assn. Bar City N.Y. Home: 7 E 14th St Apt 602 New York NY 10003

OHLSON, BJÖRN AXEL OLOF, marketing professional; b. Karlskrona, Sweden, Mar. 25, 1955; Bertil and Karin (Ljunge) O.; m. Kristina Norström, June 28, 1986. Ensign, Royal Naval Acad., Stockholm, 1975; AS, Augusta Coll., 1979; B in Bus., U. Stockholm, 1981. Ins. sales rep. Trygg-Hansa, Stockholm, 1982-83; mktg. analyst Curtis Industries, Eastlake, Ohio, 1983-84; mktg. mgr. Electrolux Internat. Sales, Stockholm, 1984—. Served to lt., Swedish Navy, 1974-75, now Res. Rotary scholar, 1977-78. Clubs: Gälö Boat, Friskis and Svettis. Home: Björkbacksvägen 49, S-161 30 Bromma Sweden Office: Electrolux Internat, Luxbacken 1, S-10545 Stockholm Sweden

OHNISHI, KYOJI, trading firm planner; b. Kobe Hyogo, Japan, Feb. 10, 1948; s. Kihachiro and Miyako (Kadowaki) O.; m. Emiko Kikuchi; children: Fumi, Heihachiro, Eisuke. B in Engring., Keio U., Tokyo, 1970, M in Engring., 1973. Cert. info. processing engr. System engr. C. Itoh & Co., Ltd., Tokyo, 1973-84, strategy planner, 1985—. Bd. dirs. Setagaya Football Assn., Tokyo, 1979—. Home: Tamaku Minami-Ikuta, 3 8 2 Kawasaki, 214 Kanagawa Japan Office: C Itoh & Co Ltd, Kita Aoyama, 2 5 1 Minatoku, 107 Tokyo Japan

OHNISHI, MINORU, film company executive; b. Mihara-cho, Japan, Oct. 28, 1925; s. Sokichi and Mitsu Ohnishi; m. Yaeko Yur, Nov. 13, 1951; children: Mitsuru, Masahiko. BS in Econs., Tokyo U., 1948. With sales dept. Fuju Photo Film Co., Ltd., Tokyo, 1948-68, mgr. export sales, 1968-72, dir., 1972-76, mng. dir., 1976-79, sr. mng. dir., 1979-80, pres., 1980—. Decorated comdr. Order of Orange-Nassau, The Netherlands, 1986. Mem. Photo-sensitized Materials Mfrs.' Assn. Japan (pres. Tokyo chpt. 1980—). Office: Fuji Photo Film Co Ltd, 26-30 Nishiazabu 2-chome, 106 Minato-ku, Tokyo Japan

OHNO, SUSUMU, research scientist; b. Seoul, Korea, Feb. 1, 1928; came to U.S., 1953; s. Kenichi and Toshiko (Saito) O.; m. Midori Aoyama, Jan. 7, 1951; children—Azusa, Yukali Takeshi. D.V.M., Tokyo U. Agr. and Tech., 1949; Ph.D., Hokkaido U., 1956, D.Sc., 1961; D. Humanity (hon.), Kwansei Gakuin U., 1983; Sc.D. (hon.), U. Pa., 1984. Research staff pathology Tokyo U., 1950-53; research assoc. City of Hope, Duarte, Calif., 1953-66, chmn. biology, 1966-81, disting. scientist, 1981—; vis. prof. Albert Einstein Med. Sch., Bronx, N.Y., 1969, Basel Inst. for Immunology, Switzerland, 1976. Author monographs. Recipient Kihara prize Genetic Soc. Japan, Tokyo, 1983. Fellow AAAS, Am. Acad. Arts and Scis. (Amory prize 1981); mem. Nat. Acad. Scis. Office: Beckman Research Inst City of Hope 1450 E Duarte Rd Duarte CA 91010

OHSATO, MASAMI, communications professional; b. Tokyo, Sept. 29, 1948; s. Katsuma and Eiko O.; m. Haruko Okada, Feb. 27, 1982; B.Econs., Keio U., Tokyo, 1972. Pub. relations officer NHK (Japan Broadcasting Corp.), Osaka, Japan, 1972-76, mgmt. planning officer, Tokyo, 1977-81, news dept. research and devel. group, 1981-83, mgmt. info. div., 1983-87; overseas broadcasting dept., 1987—; vis. researcher Cambridge U. (U.K.), 1977, Leicester Centre for Mass Communication Research (UK), 1976. Author, editor: Elebra, 1971; editor: Jour. Network Kinki, 1975, Radio Japan News, 1987; contbr. profl. reports. Recipient Broadcasting Gov. award NHK, 1983. Mem. Behaviormetric Soc. Japan. Club: Keio Computer Soc. (Tokyo). Office: NHK, 2-2-1 Jinnan Shibuyaku, Tokyo Japan

OHTA, MICHITAKA, oil company executive; b. Tokyo, Aug. 12, 1954; arrived in United Arab Emirates, 1984; s. Hiroaki and Yoshiko (Inoue) O.; m. Etsuko Ohta, June 22, 1980; 1 child, Takahide. BS in Econs., Keio U., Japan, 1977. From engr. planning to planning officer Japan Oil Devel. Co., Ltd., Tokyo, 1977-82; mgr. acctg. Abu Dhabi Marine Areas Ltd., London, 1982-84; chief acct. Umm Al-Dalkh Devel. Co., Abu Dhabi, United Arab Emirates, 1984-88; treas. Zakum Devel. Co., Abu Dhabi, 1988—. Mem. Soc. Petroleum Engrs. Office: Zakum Devel Co, PO Box 6808, Abu Dhabi United Arab Emirates

OHTA, MINORU, architectural educator; b. Fukuoka, Japan, Jan. 5, 1923; s. Ryoichi and Etsu Ohta; m. Yurie Mizoguchi, Nov. 4, 1958; children: Mitsuru, Miho. B in Engring., U. Tokyo, 1944, DEng, 1962. Registered architect. Assoc. prof. engring., architecture Hokkaido U., Sapporo, Japan, 1948-63, prof. architecture, faculty of engring., 1963-86, dean Grad. Sch. Environ. Sci., 1982-86, prof. emeritus, 1986—; prof., chmn. Hokkaido Inst. Tech., Sapporo, 1986—. Prin. works include Hokkaido Mus. Modern Art, Tomakomai Mus., Sapporo Olympic Village. Chmn. City Planning Conf. Hokkaido Prefecture, 1971—, Archtl. Conf. Tomakomai City, 1968—; sub-chmn. City Planning Conf. Sapporo City, 1971—. Recipient Sci. and Tech. award Hokkaido Prefecture, 1964, The Hokkaido Kenchiku Sho Archtl. award, 1979. Mem. Japan Inst. Architects, City Planning Inst. Japan (councilor). Club: Sapporo Korakuen Golf. Lodge: Rotary. Home: 1-1 Kashiwagaoka Makomanai, Minami-Ku, Sapporo 005, Japan Office: Hokkaido Inst Tech, 419-2 Teine Maeda, Teine-Ku, Sapporo 006, Japan

OHTAGAKI, TAKAMI, transportation executive; b. Akashi, Hyogo, Japan, Jan. 19, 1923; s. Shiro and Fuku Ohtagaki; m. Junko Ojtagaki; children: Atsuko, Hideshi. EE, Waseda U., Tokyo, 1946. Dir. Kita-Osaka-Kyuko Ry. Co., Ltd., Toyonaka, Osaka, Japan, 1974, pres., 1980—. Buddhist. Home: 2-11-1 Uenohigashi, 560 Toyonaka, Osaka Japan Office: Kita-Osaka-Kyuko Ry Co Ltd, 2-4-1 Terauchi, 560 Toyonaka, Osaka Japan

OINAS, FELIX JOHANNES, foreign language educator; b. Tartu, Estonia, Mar. 6, 1911; came to U.S., 1949, naturalized, 1955; s. Ernst and Marie (Saarik) O.; m. Lisbet Kove, July 10, 1935; children: Helina Oinas Piano, Valdar. MA, Tartu U., Estonia, 1937; postgrad., Budapest U., 1935-36, Heidelberg U., 1946-48; PhD, Ind. U., 1952. Lectr. Budapest U., 1938-40; vis. lectr. Estonian Baltic U., Hamburg, 1946-49; lectr. Slavic langs. Ind. U., 1952-53, instr., 1953-55, asst. prof., 1955-61, assoc. prof., 1961-65, prof. Slavic langs. and Uralic and Altaic studies, 1965-81, prof. emeritus, 1981—; fellow Folklore Inst., 1965—. Author, editor 21 books in field.; Contbr. articles to profl. jours. Guggenheim fellow, 1961, 66; Fulbright grantee, 1961; Fulbright-Hays grantee, 1964; Nat. Endowment for Humanities grantee, 1974; recipient Cultural award Found. Estonian Arts and Letters; 1st prize Dr. Arthur Puksow Found. Fellow Am. Folklore Soc., Finnish Literary Soc., Finno-Ugric Soc., Finnish Folklore Soc., Baltisches Forschungsinstitut (Bonn), Inst. Estonian Lang. and Lit. (Stockholm); mem. Estonian Learned Soc. Am. (hon.), Finnish Acad. Scis., Estonian Sci. Inst. in Sweden (hon.). Lutheran. Home: 2513 E 8th St Bloomington IN 47401 Office: Slavic Dept Indiana Univ Bloomington IN 47405

OISO, TOSHIO, medical nutritionist; b. Tokyo, Apr. 2, 1908; s. Yasoji and Fusako (Ishiyama) O.; Ph.D., Med. Faculty Kyoto Imperial U., 1935, M.D., 1942; m. Miyako Moribe, Apr. 20, 1940; children—Katsuyoshi, Masayoshi, Hisayoshi. Research mem. Inst. Nutrition, Tokyo, 1935-38; adminstrv. ofcl. Ministry Health and Welfare Japan, Tokyo, 1938-50, chief sect. nutrition, 1953-63, chief sect. health, safety, personnel authority, Tokyo, 1950-53; councillor sci. and tech. Minister's Secretariat, 1963-65; dir. gen. Nat. Inst. Nutrition, Tokyo, 1965-74; exec. dir. Internat. Med. Found. Japan, Tokyo, 1974-85, dir. gen., 1985—; mem. various profl. councils; lectr. U. Kyoto, 1962-74, U. Tokyo, 1968, also others; panelist U.S. Japan Corp. Med. Sci. Program, 1966-74; mem. adv. panel nutrition WHO, 1955—. Decorated 2d order Sacred Treasure; named Hon. Citizen, City of New Orleans, 1957; recipient Minister's award, 1953, 69, 76. Mem. Japanese Soc. Food and Nutrition, Japanese Soc. Public Health, Japanese Soc. Vitaminology, Japanese Soc. Pediatrics, Food and Nutrition Research Assn. (pres. 1976—), Internat. Union Nutrition Scis. (council 1978-81), Am. Inst. Nutrition (hon.), Fedn. Asian Nutrition Socs. (council 1980-83). Buddhist. Author books in field; research, publs. in field.

OJA, ERKKI, mathematician, computer scientist; b. Helsinki, Finland, Mar. 22, 1948; s. Aulis and Anna Eleonora (Halonen) O.; m. Marja Inkeri Ruohomäki, Oct. 4, 1975; children—Merja Anneli, Riitta Liisa. Diploma Engr., Helsinki U. Tech., 1972, D.Tech., 1977. Research assoc. Brown U., Providence, 1977-78; sr. research fellow Finnish Acad., Helsinki, 1979-81; assoc. prof. dept. computer sci. Kuopio U., Finland, 1981-87; prof., dept. info. tech. Lappeenranta U. Tech., Finland, 1987—; vis. research scholar Tokyo Inst. Tech., 1983-84. Author: Subspace Methods of Pattern Recognition, 1983. Contbr. articles to profl. jours. Matsumae Internat. Found. fellow, Tokyo, 1983. Mem. IEEE, Am. Math. Soc., Pattern Recognition Soc. Finland. Office: Lappeenranta U Tech, 53851 Lappeenranta Finland

OJECHEMA, ATTAH DIKKO, airline executive; b. Otukpa, Nigeria, May 11, 1949; s. Apeh and Ajari (Ocheje) O.; m. Elezabeth, Dec. 5, 1974; children: Egbi, Ajuma, Onyo-Owoicho, Oche, Ena, Ajari. BSc with honors, Ahmadu Bello U., Zaria, Nigeria, 1973; postgrad., U. London, 1987—. H.S.C. tutor Govt. Tchrs. Coll., Keffi, Nigeria, 1969-70; dep. editor Midwest Bull., Benin City, Nigeria, 1973-74; adminstrv. officer, asst. registrar Ahmadu Bello U., Zaria, Nigeria, 1974-75; dist. officer K/Ala Dekina L. Govt., Benue State, Nigeria, 1978-79; sec. Otukpo Local Govt., Benue State, Nigeria, 1977-78; prin. pvt. sec. to Mil. Gov.'s Office, Benue State, Nigeria, 1978-79; dep. co. sec. Nigeria Airways Ltd., Lagos, 1979-86, co. sec., 1986—. Mem. Benue Devel. Fund, Makurdi, 1984—, chmn. Otukpa Youth Orgn., Lagos, 1986. Recipient NYSC award Fed. Govt. Nigeria, 1974. Fellow Nat. Inst. Adminstrs. Club: Ugbicho (Lagos). Lodge: Rotary. Home: 14 Adeyemo Alakija St, Gra Ikeja, Lagos Nigeria Office: Nigeria Airways Ltd, Airways House Ikeja, Lagos Nigeria

OJEDA PAULLADA, PEDRO, Mexican government official, politician, lawyer; b. Mexico City, Jan. 19, 1934; s. Manuel Ojeda Lacroix and Adela Paullada de Ojeda; m. Olga Cárdenas, 1959; five children. Ed. Universidad Nacional Autonóma de México. Head of personnel, lawyer Técnica y

Fundación, S.A. de C.V., 1955, Sub-mgr., 1955-57; gen. mgr. Industria Química de Plásticos S.A., 1957-58; dep. dir.-gen. Juntas Federales de Mejoras Materiales, 1959-65; dir.-gen. legal affairs SCT, 1966-70; sec.-gen. Presdl. Sec., 1970-71; atty. gen., 1971-76; sec. Dept. Labour and Social Welfare, 1976-81; pres. Nat. Exec. Com. Instl. Revolutionary Party, 1981—; minister of fisheries, 1982—. Gen. coordinator Mexican Programme for Internat. Women's Yr., 1975; chmn. world conf., 1975; chmn. 64th Internat. Conf. ILO, 1978. Decorated Order of Merit, Italy, Gran Cruz al Merito, Italy, Order Isabel la Católica, Spain. Address: Dept of Fisheries, Mexico City DF, Mexico *

OJEDA-PEÑA, EDUARDO MANUEL, mathematics educator; b. Guadalajara, Mex., Sept. 12, 1942; s. Luis Ojeda Mendoza and Maria de los Angeles (Peña) Ojeda; m. Amparo Cortes; children: Amparo, Eduardo Manuel, Maria de los Angeles, Maria Eugenia, Ana Rosa, Maria Guadalupe, Monica Gabriela. Degree in engring., U. Autonoma Guadalajara, 1964; MA in Math., U. Ariz., 1968. Inst. math. Prep. Sch. (Autonoma), Guadalajara, 1960-66; mech. designer Nibco de Mex., Guadalajara, 1962-66; lectr. math. U. Autonoma Guadalajara, 1968-71, prof. math., 1971—, dir. sch. math., 1975—. Translator: Calculus with Analytical Geometry (Zill) 1987, Abstract Algebra (Herstein) 1987. Named Hon. Citizen City of Tucson, 1967. Mem. Math. Assn. Am., Soc. Math. Mexicana. Home: Clemente Orozco #362, 44660 Guadalajara, Jalisco Mexico Office: U Autonoma Guadalajara, Ave Patria #1201, 44100 Guadalajara, Jalisco Mexico

OJIKA, TAKEO, mathematics educator; b. Nagoya, Aichi, Japan, Jan. 7, 1939; s. Tsuyoshi and Ai Ojika; m. Junko Ito, May 11, 1969. B in Engring., Waseda U., Tokyo, 1962; M in Engring., Kyoto U., Japan, 1969, PhD, 1975, DSc, 1982. Engr. Mitsubishi Heavy Indsl. Co., Nagoya, Japan, 1962-67; lectr. Osaka Kyoiku U., Japan, 1967-75, assoc. prof., 1975-88; prof. Gifu U., 1988—; vis. researcher U. So. Calif., Los Angeles, 1978-79. Contbr. articles to profl. jours. The Ministry of Edn. grantee, 1978-81, 87—. Mem. N.Y. Acad. Scis., Pa. Soc. Indsl. & Applied Math., The Math. Soc. Japan, Info. Processing Soc. Japan. Club: Shorinji Kempo (Kyoto) (officer Kagawa 1986—). Home: Estate Taga #301, 244-1 Kurono, 501-11 Gifu Japan Office: Gifu U, Dept Electronics and Computer, 1-1 Yanagido, 501-11 Gifu Japan

OJUTKANGAS, REIJO ANTERO, physician, administrator; b. Kannus, Finland, June 27, 1934; s. Sulo Antero and Taimi Elina (Koskinen) O.; m. Terttu Anneli Koivisto, July 25, 1953 (div.); children: Erkki J.A., Pertti V.I., Leena M.A., Mika R.P. D in Pharmacy, U. Helsinki, 1957, Candidate of Natural Scis., 1962; MD, U. Hamburg, 1969. Lic. pharmacist, physician, Finland. Alcohologist, physician Helsinki Dist. Treatment Program, 1976-77; physician Onandjokwe Mission Hosp., SW Africa, 1977-78; alcohologist, physician Nordhem Clinic, Gothenburg, Sweden, 1978-79; indsl. physician Medicar Found., Gothenburg, 1980-81; med. dir. Kalliola Clinic, Helsinki, 1981-82; exec. dir. Ethanol-Media Ltd., Helsinki, 1982—; mission physician Red Cross, Salisbury, Rhodesia, 1979, Cambodia, Thailand, 1980. Contbr. articles to profl. jours. Served to lt. col. UN Emergency Force, 1975-76, Mid. East. Lutheran. Club: Rotary. Home: Taivaanvuohentie 5 B 20, 00200 Helsinki Finland Office: Ethanol-Media Ltd, Nahkahousuntie 6A 17, SF-00210 Helsinki Finland

OKA, HIDETAKA, architect; b. Tokyo, Dec. 24, 1937; s. Ryuichi and Kimi Oka; m. Sachie Takemoto, Nov. 16, 1963; children: Mayuko, Tessyu. B of Engring., Tokyo U., 1961, M of Engring., 1963, D of Engring., 1968. Architect 1st class, Japan. V.p. Oka Sekkei Architects and Engrs., Inc., Tokyo, 1965—. Author: Theory of Architectural Design, 1977, The Organization of the City, 1986. Recipient Cert. of Praise Bldg. Contractors Soc., Tokyo, 1987. Mem. Japan Inst. Architects, Archtl. Inst. Japan. Office: Oka Sekkei Inc, #11 1 5-chome Sendagaya, Shibuya-ku, Tokyo Japan

OKABAYASHI, TOYOKI, educator, former securities company executive; b. Wassamu, Kamikawa, Hokkaido, Japan, Apr. 16, 1925; s. Kameju and Suzumi Okabayashi; m. Fukuko Okamoto, Mar. 19, 1963; children: Hideki, Hiroki, Hatsue. BA, Otaru Commerce Coll., 1947; M in Econs. Tohoku U., Sendai, Japan, 1950; PhD in Econs., U. Oreg., 1960. Researcher Bank of Toyko, N.Y.C., 1960; sub-mgr. fgn. research dept. Nomura Securities Co., Tokyo, 1961-63, sub-mgr. underwriting dept., 1964-69, sub-mgr. instnl. dept., 1969-73, mgr. pub. corp. dept., 1973-78, mgr. instl. dept., Osaka, 1978-83, mgr. bond. dept., Tokyo, 1983—; prof. U. Kanto Gakuen, 1985—; head U.S. Fin. Mission, 1984, Europe and U.S. Fin. Mgmt. Studies Mission, 1985-86, Europe Fin. Mgmt. Studies Mission, Hong Kong Securities Mkt. Studies Mission, 1987; chmn. fin. mgmt. com. Japan Fin. Corp. for Mcpl. Fin. Enterprises, 1985-87; pres. Heights Forest Co. Ltd., 1986; com. mem. for Fin. Mgmt. Meetings of Pension Fund for Local Govt Employees in Japan, 1988—; lectr. Otaru U. Commerce, 1963, Osaka Municipal U., 1983, Am. Family Life Assurance Co., 1986. Vice chmn. PTA, Kogakuin U., Tokyo, 1987. Mem. Japan Edn. Mgmt. Assn., Japan Mgmt. Analysis Assn., Japan Mgmt. Philosophy Assn. Lodge: Rotary. Home: 2-38-10 Nishimachi, Kokubunji City, Tokyo 185, Japan Office: U Kanto Gakuen, 200 Fijia-ku, Ohta-shi Gunma ken 370-04, Japan

OKABE, JOHN HITOSHI, computer company executive; b. Miyagi, Japan, May 11, 1945; s. Saburo and Hana (Tomimori) O.; m. Milliam Mie Sato, Dec. 15, 1979. BA in Engring., Osaka (Japan) U., 1968. Registered profl. engr., Japan. Programmer Toray Industries, Inc., Tokyo, 1968-71; systems engr. Toray Engring. Co., Ltd., Osaka, 1971-83; dir. System Corp., Osaka, 1983—; trustee St. Paul's Coll., Osaka. Fellow Info. Processing Soc. Japan; mem. Nat. Computer Graphics Assn., U.S. Mem. Anglican-Episcopal Ch. Home: 6-35-13 OKA, Matsubara Osaka 580, Japan Office: 1-1-17 Asahi-machi, Abeno-Ku, Osaka-City 545, Japan

OKADA, FUMIHIKO, psychiatrist; b. Obihiro, Hokkaido, Japan, Nov. 6, 1940; s. Michimaro and Chieko (Saida) O.; m. Junko Takeda, Apr. 28, 1978; children: Takabumi, Mona. MD, Hokkaido U., Sapporo, 1964, postgrad., 1965-73. Intern Hokkaido U. Hosp., 1964-65, asst. prof. Health Adminstrn. Ctr., 1976-81, assoc. prof. Health Adminstrn. Ctr., 1981—. Contbr. articles to profl. jours. Research fellow Vanderbilt U., 1981-82. Fellow Japanese Assn. Autonomic Nerve; mem. Japanese Assn. Psychiat. Neurology, N.Y. Acad. Scis. Home: Chuo-ku S 10 W 18 1-3-304, 064 Sapporo, Hokkaido Japan Office: Hokkaido U Health Adminstrn Ctr, North 8 West 5, 060 Sapporo, Hokkaido Japan

OKADA, RYOZO, professor of medicine, researcher; b. Kiryu, Gummaken, Japan, July 20, 1931; s. Kenji and Sachi (Ishihara) O.; m. Shigeko Shindo, May 25, 1958; children: Kyoko, Taro. MD, Tokyo U., 1956, D of Med. Sci, 1961. Intern then residen; asst. Sch. Med. Tokyo Med., 1962-63; research fellow Hektoen Inst. Cook County Hosp., Chgo., 1963-66; attending physician Yoikuin Hosp., Tokyo, 1966-68; assoc. prof. Sch. Med. Juntendo U., Tokyo, 1968-83, prof., 1983—, dir. cardiovascular lab., 1985—; cons. Migita Hosp., Tokyo, 1968—, Cardiovascular Inst. Roppongi, Tokyo, 1976—. Contbr. articles to med. jours. Active group study specific intractable diseases Met. Office of Tokyo, 1972—, cardiomyopathies Ministry of Health and Welfare, Japan, 1974; bd. dirs. Shirane Kaizen Sch., Gumma, Japan. Fellow Am. Geriatrics Soc., Council Prevention of Heart Disease; mem. Japanese Circulation Soc. (councilor), Japanese Angiology Soc. (councilor), Japanese Geriatrics Soc. (councilor). Home: 53 Asahigoaka, Kanagawaku, 221 Yokohama Japan Office: Juntendo U Sch Medicine, 2-1-1 Hongo, Bunkyoku, 113 Tokyo Japan

OKAMOTO, SIGERU, mathematics educator; b. Noda, Chiba, Japan, Feb. 4, 1930; s. Masaichiro and Taka (Kawajiri) O.; m. Fusae Konuma, Jan. 5, 1961; 1 child, Hiroshi. BS, Tokyo U. Edn., 1955, MS, 1957; PhD, Osaka (Japan) City U., 1964. Asst. prof. math. Mie (Japan) U., 1960-64; asst. prof. Yamaguchi (Japan) U., 1964-70; prof. Ibaraki (Japan) U., 1970—. Inventor in field. Mem. Math. Soc. Japan, Am. Math. Soc., Info. Processing Soc. Japan. Home: 3-3-41 Higashihara, 310 Mito, Ibaraki Japan Office: Ibaraki U, 2-1-1 Bunkyo, 310 Mito, Ibaraki Japan

OKAMOTO, SUSUMU, business executive; b. Feb. 17, 1927. Grad., Keio (Japan) U., 1951. With Kanebo Ltd., Osaka, Japan, 1951—, pres., chief operating officer. Home: 13-48 Minoo 8-chome, Minoo, Osaka Japan Office: Kanebo Ltd, 5-90 Tomobuchi-cho, miyakojima-ku, Osaka Japan *

OKAMOTO, YOSHIRO, hotel company executive; b. Tokyo, May 3, 1928; s. Kumao and Yoshiko (Nemoto) O.; m. Yasu Yukawa, Nov. 20, 1950 (dec. Sept. 1984); children: Keiko, Takao. Front office mgr. Sanno Hotel, Tokyo, 1951-62; mgr. Hilton Reservation Service, Far East, 1962-64; asst. dir. sales Japan office Hilton Internat. and Hilton Hotels Corp., Tokyo, 1964-68; dir. sales Japan office Hilton Hotels Corp., Tokyo, 1968-74, asst. v.p., dir. sales Far East div., 1974—. Recipient Pres.'s E Cert. of Service for outstanding contbn. to export expansion program Sec. Commerce; recognition awards for air transp. devel. Delta Air Lines, Hughes Air West, Pan Am. Airways, Japan Creative Tours. Mem. Am. Soc. Travel Agts., Japan Assn. Travel Agts., Hotel Sales Mgmt. Assn., U.S. Travel Service (steering com.), Japan Rifle Assn. Home: Bunkyo 204, 1-3-1 Mukogaoka, Bunkyo-ku, Tokyo 113, Japan Office: Hilton Hotels Corp, Suite 315, Hibya Park Bldg, 1-8-1 Yurakucho, Chiyoda-ku Tokyo 100, Japan

O'KANE, HUGH OLIVER, cardiac surgeon; b. Belfast, No. Ireland, Nov. 21, 1935; s. Felix Thomas and Margaret Mary (McKeever) Kane; married; children: Aisling, Hugh, Garrett, Anna. BSc in Physiology with honors, Queens U., Belfast, 1957, MB, B of Surgery, BAO, 1960, M of Surgery, 1969. House officer Mater Hosp., Belfast, 1960-61; physiology demonstrator Queens U., 1961-62; sr. house officer City Hosp., Belfast, 1962-64; surg. registrar Hosps. Authority, No. Ireland, 1964-65, sr. surg. registrar, 1965-67; surg. research fellow Mayo Clinic, Rochester, Minn., 1967-69, resident in cardiothoracic surgery, 1969-71; asst. prof. surgery, mem. staff Washington U./Jewish Hosp., St. Louis, 1971-73; cons. cardiac surgeon Royal Victoria Hosp., Belfast, 1973—. Contbr. numerous articles to profl. jours. Mem. British Cardiac Soc., Irish Cardiac Soc., Soc. Cardiothoracic Surgeons of Gt. Britain and Ireland, European Assn. Cardiothoracic Surgeons, Mayo Clinic Alumni Assn. Roman Catholic. Office: Royal Victoria Hosp, Grosvenor Rd, Belfast Ireland

OKASHA, ELISABETH, English educator; b. Romiley, Eng., Jan. 13, 1942; d. James Webster and Elisabeth Beryl (Roebuck) Barty; m. Ahmed Yousri Kamel Okasha, 1967; children: Leila, Samir, Mona, Rami. MA with honors, U. St. Andrews, Eng., 1963; PhD, U. Cambridge, 1967. Asst. lectr. U. Aberdeen, Scotland, 1966-69; lectr. U. East Anglia, Norwich, Eng., 1969-72, U. Assiut, Egypt, 1973, Nat. U. Ireland, Cork, 1976—; tutor U. Dundee, Scotland, 1975-77, Open U., U.K., 1964-66, 1975-77. Author: Hand-List of Anglo-Saxon Non-runic Inscriptions, 1971; contbr. articles to lit. jours. Mem. Internat. Soc. Anglo-Saxonists, Soc. Medieval Archaeology. Office: Univ Coll, Dept of English, Cork Ireland

OKAWARA, YOSHIO, Japanese ambassador to U.S.; b. Gunma Prefecture, Japan, Feb. 5, 1919; LL.B., Tokyo (Japan) U., 1942; m. Mitsuko Terajima, Apr. 13, 1948; children: Akio, Nobuo, Tamio. 2d and 1st sec. Japanese embassy, London, 1954-56; 1st sec., Manila, 1956-58; fellow Center for Internat. Affairs, Harvard U., 1962; 1st sec. Japanese embassy, Washington, 1962-63, counsellor, 1963-65; dir. personnel div. Ministry Fgn. Affairs, Tokyo, 1965-67, dep. dir. gen. Am. affairs bur., 1967-71, dir. gen., 1972-74, dep. vice minister for adminstrn., 1974-76; envoy extraordinary and minister plenipotentiary Japanese embassy, Washington, 1971-72; ambassador extraordinary and plenipotentiary of Japan to Australia, 1976-80; ambassador of Japan to Fiji and Republic of Nauru, 1976-80; ambassador to U.S., 1980—; exec. advisor Ministry Fgn. Affairs, Japan Fedn. Econ. Orgn., Kobe Steel Co. Ltd. Clubs: Royal Canberra Golf, Commonwealth (Canberra, Australia); Melbourne (Australia); Met. (Washington). Office: Kobe Steel Ltd, 3-18 Wakihama Cho, 1 chome Chuo-ku, Kobe 651, Hyogo Japan *

OKEBUGWU, ANDREW NKASIOBI, industrial management executive, educator; b. Avor, Nigeria, Dec. 25, 1937; s. James Okebugwu Adiele and Agnes (Uriaruh) Okebugwu; m. Martina Adanma, Sept. 22, 1962; children—Chinonyerem T., Ugochi I., Chinaemenma B., Odochi C., Onyinyechi F., Andrew N. Jr., Chimazie Martin. Diploma Nat. Sch. Salesmanship, Eng., 1971. Head tchr. Cath. Sch., Nbawsi, Parish, Nigeria, 1955-64; conf. coordinator Continuing Edn. Centre, U. Nigeria, 1965-72; pvt. mgmt. cons., Nigeria, 1973-80; chief exec. officer, mng. dir. OAO Nigeria, Avor Imo State, 1979—; dir. Andy Comml. Coll., Avor Imo State, 1979—; cons. Edn. Dept. Adult Edn., 1982-84; mgmt. cons. Jah Bilmar, Eziama, 1984—. Sec. Coll. Bldg. Com., Ntigha, 1979-81, Keep Imo Clean Com., 1984—; nat. sec. Ntigha Progressive Union, 1979—; chmn. Idi N'otu Cultural Assn., 1980—; sec. Eze Gwungwuga Ntigha Cabinet, 1985—; sec. Ebiri Osoagu Umuerim; fin. controller Amato Ntigha Farmers Multi Purpose Co-op. Ltd. Recipient Philanthropic honor award Destitute Orphan Welfare, 1983. Mem. Am. Mgmt. Assn., Nigerian Inst. Mgmt. Roman Catholic. Lodge: Socrates (debating com. 1983). Avocations: gardening, lawn tennis. Home: Umuerim Avor Ntigha, PO Box 134, Nbawsi Nigeria Office: OAO Nigeria Enterprises, Avor Ntigha, PO Box 134, Nbawsi Nigeria

OKEBUKOLA, PETER AKINSOLA, biology educator; b. Ilesa, Nigeria, Feb. 17, 1948; s. Daniel Akinlade and Lydia Anike (Ajala) O.; m. Frances Foluso Fajemilehin, July 22, 1978; children: Peter Oluwaseyi, Lydia Olubusola, Marian Doyinsola. BEd, U. Ibadan, 1973, PhD, 1984. Account supr. Nigerian Explosives and Plastics Co., Lagos, 1969-70; tchr. sci. Holy Saviour's Coll., Mushin, Nigeria, 1970; head dept. sci. Ososo (Nigeria) Grammar Sch., 1973-74, C.A.C. Tchr.'s Coll., Efon-Alaye, Nigeria, 1974-78; sr. lectr. Oyo State Coll. Edn., Ilesa, Nigeria, 1978-84; dir. dept. sci. Lagos State U., 1984—. Author: Primary Science and Methods, 1981; contbr. articles to profl. jours. Mem. Governing council Lagos STate Poly., 1985-87. Mem. Sci. Tchrs. Assn. Nigeria (sec. gen. 1985—), Inst. Biology London, Nat. Assn. Research in Sci. Teaching U.S., Integrated Sci. Panel Stan. Home: 18 Oshidehin St, Ogba Lagos Agege, Lagos Nigeria Office: Faculty Edn Lagos State U, 1087 Apapa, Lagos Nigeria

O'KEEFE, KEVIN MICHAEL, lawyer; b. Vincennes, Ind., Sept. 24, 1946; s. Roy Daniel and Mildred (Pawlak) O'K.; m. Margaret Yvonne Green, Sept. 25, 1971; children—Kathleen, Kelly. B.S. in Communications, U. Ill., 1969; J.D., Ill. Inst. Tech., 1973. Bar: Ill. 1973, Fla. 1974. Assoc. O'Keefe, Ashenden, Lyons & Ward, Chgo., 1973-76; ptnr., 1976—; bd. dirs. Healthcorp Affiliates, Naperville, Ill. Bd. dirs. Central DuPage Hosp., Winfield, Ill., 1981—, B.R. Ryall YMCA, Glen Ellyn, Ill., 1979-81. Mem. Inst. Property Taxation, Internat. Assn. Assessing Officers. Democrat. Roman Catholic. Home: 389 Robinwood Ln Wheaton IL 60187 Office: O'Keefe Ashenden Lyons & Ward 1 1st National Plaza Suite 5100 Chicago IL 60603

OKELL, JOBYNA LOUISE, public health administrator, accountant; b. Miami, Fla., Nov. 21, 1937; d. George Shaffer and Evelyn Maude (Pottmyer) O. B.B.A., U. Miami-Fla., 1961; postgrad. U. Miami, 1962, Nova U., 1976—. Acct. Crippled Children's Soc., Miami, Fla., 1964-65, Am. Coll. Found., Miami, 1965-66; owner Jobyna's Miniatures, Coral Gables, Fla., 1978—; exec. dir./adminstr., corp. dir. Fla. Health Profl. Services, Inc., Coral Gables, 1967—. Dist. chmn. Young Democrats Dade County and Fla., 1956-68; vice regent DAR, Coral Gables chpt., 1968-87, active Irish Georgian Soc., English Speaking Union; treas., dir. Merrick Manor Found., 1974-75; active Friends of Library, U. Miami, 1974-87; adv. bd. channeling project Miami Jewish Home and Hosp. for Aged, 1982-87. Recipient Outstanding County Young Democrat award Young Dems. Fla., 1964; Truman award Outstanding Young Dem. Young Dems. Dade County, 1965; Outstanding Jr. DAR, 1972. Mem. Am. Pub. Health Assn., Nat. League Nursing, Am. Soc. Pub. Adminstrn., Dade/Monroe Assn. Home Health Agys. (pres./dir. 1974-76), Health Planning Council South Fla., Health Systems Agy. South Fla., Fla. Assn. Home Health Agys., South Fla. In-Home Services (pres. 1985-88), Red-Sunset Merchants Assn., Nat. Assn. Miniature Enthusiasts, Internat. Guild Miniature Artisans, Ocean Waves Guild, Am. Philatelic Soc., Hawaiian Philatelic Soc., Nat. Quilting Assn., Am. Quilter's Soc., Geneal. Soc. Greater Miami (treas. 1987-88), Gamma Alpha Chi, Alpha Delta Pi. Republican. Episcopalian. Home: 715 Palermo Ave Coral Gables FL 33134 Office: Fla Health Profl Services Inc 1510 Venera Ave Coral Gables FL 33146

OKER-BLOM, NILS CHRISTIAN EDGAR, academic administrator, virologist; b. Helsinki, Finland, Aug. 5, 1919; s. Edgar Alexander and Zea Margit (Bergroth) O.-B.; m. Constance Victorine Nordenswan; children: Teodora Marianne, Maximilian Bjarne Christian, Ernst Gustaf Christian. MB, U. Helsinki, 1941, MD, 1947, D in Medicine, 1948; D honoris causa, U. Uppsala, Sweden, 1967. Head Helsinki Mcpl. Bacteria Lab. U. Helsinki, 1951-57, prof. virology, head dept. virology, 1957-83, dean med. faculty, 1968-69, asst. rector, 1974-78, rector magnificus, 1978-83, chancellor, 1983-88; chmn. joint com. Nordic Med. Research Councils/Nordic Publ. Com. for Medicine, 1977-80. Editor immunology sect. Intervirology, 1972—; contbr. numerous articles to profl. jours. Mem. expert adv. panel on virus diseases WHO, 1964—; chmn. Finnish nominating com. NaT. Inst. Health, 1980—; mem. adv. com. European Centre of Higher Edn. UNESCO, 1982—. Served with Finnish mil., 1939-40, 41-44. Recipient Standertskiold award Finnish Med. Soc., 1960, J.W. Runeberg medal, 1981. Mem. N.Y. Acad. Scis., Royal Soc. Medicine, Soc. Gen. Microbiology, Assn. des Epidemiologistes de langue francaise, Finnish Assn. Physicians, Finnish Pathology Assn., Internat. Union Biol. Scis. (v.p. 1973-75, pres. 1976-79, past pres. 1979-82, com. for biol. edn. 1982-86), Com. for Arctic Arboviruses, Standing Conf. Rectors, Pres. and Vice-Chancellors of European Univs. (ad personam mem. permanent com. 1978-85). Home: Katajaharjuntie 22 H, 00200 Helsinki Finland Office: U Helsinki, Offices of the Chancellor, Hallituskatu 6, 00170 Helsinki Finland

OKHAI, KASSAM ABOO, electronics and hardware executive; b. Zomba, Malawi, Apr. 9, 1948; s. Aboo Sulemanaand Marium (Mussa) O.; grad. high sch.; m. Kulsum Kali, Aug. 18, 1968; children—Faizal, Zeenat, Shezad. Founder, chief exec. Okhai Electronics Ltd., 1966—, Electra Sales Ltd., 1978—; chief exec. Comet Hardware, 1979—; chmn. bd., dir. Aboo S. Okhai Ltd., Okhai Electronics Ltd., Electra Sales Ltd., Radio & Elec. Services Ltd.; dir. Superfreeze Ltd., Sunder Furniture Ltd., Technorand Industries, Energy & Minerals Devel. Co., Agro Chem. Co. Chmn. fin. com. C. of C., 1973-75, chmn. comml. com., 1987; chmn. Limbe Muslim Community, 1975—; mem. Young Muslim Brotherhood, 1972—. Clubs: Rotary of Blantyre (chmn. community service com. 1979-80); Limbe Country. Home: 3 Tsirinana Rd, Box 5317, Limbe Malawi Office: 1 Kamuzu Hwy, PO Box 51146, Limbe Malawi

OKISHIO, SOICHIRO, university professor, architect; b. Tokyo, Sept. 2, 1928; s. Masao and Aki (Hata) O.; m. Katsuko Hirano, 1959; 1 child, Masami. B of Engring., U. Tokyo, 1952. Registered profl. architect. Chief architect Kuwait Cons. Office Nippon Telegraph & Telephone Pub. Corp., 1965-69; sr. staff architect Architects and Engrs. Bur. Nippon Telegraph & Telephone Pub. Corp., Tokyo, 1969-71, chief design sect., 1971-75, sr. staff architect Maj. Projects Dept., 1975-77, dir., chief architect, 1977-80; prof. Sch. Architecture Sci. U. Tokyo, 1980—; mem. bldg. council Ministry of Constrn. Japan, Tokyo, 1985—; vice chmn. intelligent bldg. com. Bldg. Ctr. Japan, Tokyo, 1986-88; researcher Firesci. and Tech. Lab. Fire Sci. and Tech. lab., Sci. U. Tokyo, 1986—. Author: Design of Electronic Office, 1986; supr. book translation Design of Automated Office, 1985. Expert opinion on hotel New Japan fire Met. Police Dept., Tokyo, 1982, Zao hotel fire Yamagata Prefecture Police Dept., 1983; leader intelligent bldg. research mission to USA Ministry Constrn. Japan, 1987; chmn. office environment symposium Japan Mgmt. Assn., Tokyo, 1984-88. Recipient Aluminum Architecture Prize award Light Metal Assn. of Japan, 1973. Mem. Archtl. Inst. of Japan, Acoustical Soc. of Japan, Illuminating Engring. Inst. of Japan, Japan Facility Mgmt. Assn. (founder). Club: Internat. House of Japan (Tokyo). Home: 3-22-14 Nakaochiai, Shinjukuku, 161 Tokyo Japan Office: Sci U Tokyo, 1-3 Kagurazaka, Shinjukuku, 162 Tokyo Japan

OKITA, SABURO, academic administrator; b. Dalien, Japan, Nov. 3, 1914; s. Shuji and Hana (Kojima) O.; m. Hisako Kajii; children: Yoichi, Yuji, Ryozo, Haruko. B of Engring., Tokyo Imperial U., 1937; PhD in Econs., Nagoya (Japan) U., 1962; hon. degree, U. Mich., 1977, Australian Nat. U., 1982, U. B.C., Can., 1984, Princeton U., 1985. Dir. gen. planning bur. Econ. Planning Agy., Japan, 1957-62, dir. gen. developing bur., 1962-63; pres., chmn. Japan Econ. Research Ctr., 1964—; pres. Overseas Econ. Cooperation Fund, Japan, 1973-77; minister fgn. affairs Ministry of State, 1979-80, govt. rep. external econ. relations, 1980-81; chmn. Inst. for Domestic and Internat. Policy Studies, Tokyo, 1981—; pres. Internat. U. Japan, Tokyo, 1982-87, chancellor, 1987—; mem. UN Com. for Devel. Planning, 1965-80, World Bank's Commn. on Internat. Devel., 1968-69. Author several books. Chmn. World Wildlife Fund Japan, 1984—, UNICEF Japan, 1987—. Recipient Ramon Magsaysa award for internat. understanding, 1971, Britannica award, 1987. Mem. Am. Econ. Assn., Am. Acad. Arts and Scis., Japan Assn. for Planning Adminstrn. (pres.). Home: 13-12 Koishikawa 5-chome, 112 Bunkyo-ku, Tokyo Japan Office: Inst Domestic/Internat Policy Studies, Fukokuseimei Bldg 2-2, Uchisaiwaicho 2-chome, 100 Chiyoda-ku, Tokyo Japan

OKONG'O, OWINO, physiologist, educator; b. Akoko, Nyanza, Kenya, Jan. 15, 1937; s. Luka and Nora Omolo (Akuom) O.; m. Miriam Auma Bwana, July 25, 1970; children: Nora Anyango, Othieno, Ochieng', Okoth, Omondi. BA with honors, Brandeis U., 1964; MA in Edn., Putney-Antioc Coll., 1964; MA in Med. Sci., Boston U., 1966; PhD in Physiology, Biophysics, U. Vt., 1969. Instr. physiology U. Vt., Burlington, 1969; lectr. U. Nairobi, Kenya, 1969-73; sr. lectr. U. Zambia, Lusaka, 1973-78; assoc. prof. Addis Ababa U., Ethiopia, 1978—; med. officer, scientist WHO, Addis Ababa, 1978—; occassional WHO rep. to UN Econ. Commn., Orgn. for African Unity, Govt. of Ethiopia, 1980—; sec. core group pub. health tng. program Ethiopian Ministry Health, 1985—. Contbr. articles to profl. jours. Bd. govs. Sandford English Community Sch., Addis Ababa, 1979-83, chmn., 1980-82. Fellow USPHS Boston U. and U. Vt., 1965-69; Wien Internat. scholar Brandeis U., 1961-64. Mem. Nat. Goeg. Soc., Inst. Biology. Mem. Kenya African Union Party. Anglican. Club: United Kenya (Nairobi). Home: PO Box 14796, Nairobi Kenya Office: WHO, PO Box 3069, Addis Ababa Kenya

OKORO, EUGENE ODINDU, insurance company executive; b. Owerri, Nigeria, Nov. 25, 1938; s. Joseph Ugochukwu and Bernice Nwaobiara (Anyanwu-Dede) O.; m. Patience Onyemaechi Njoku, Apr. 20, 1968; children: Osondu, Chinyere, Chinedu, Chiaka, Chikodi, Kelechi. BSc in Bus. Adminstrn. with honours, U. Lagos, Nigeria, 1985. Clerical officer Assoc. Industries Ltd., Royal Exchange Assurance Ltd., Aba, Nigeria, 1958-64; mgmt. trainee Royal Exchange Assurance, London, 1964-65; exec. officer Aba, 1965-67; resident rep. Onitsha, Nigeria, 1967-71; motor supt. Lagos, 1971-72; asst. to accident mgr. Royal Exchange Assurance, Lagos, 1972-73; br. mgr. Apapa, Nigeria, 1973-76; mgr. orgn. and methods Lagos, 1976-78; asst. gen. mgr. orgn. and methods 1978—. Chmn. G. Close Residents Assn., 1986—; mem. ceremonial and protocol subcom. Nat. Polio Plus Campaign Fund, Lagos, 1987—. Mem. Nigerian Inst. Mgmt., Brit. Inst. Mgmt., Am. Inst. Mgmt. (exec. counsellor 1981), Inst. Dirs. (London), Nigerian Inst. Internat. Affairs. Roman Catholic. Clubs: Owerri Umunna (Lagos) (gen. sec. 1984—), Rotary of Isolo (Lagos) (pres. 1987—). Office: Royal Exchange Assurance, 31 Marina, PO Box 112, Lagos Nigeria

OKSENDAL, BERNT KARSTEN, mathematics educator; b. Fredrikstad, Norway, Apr. 10, 1945; s. Andreas Sandvand and Anthonie (Amundsen) O.; m. Eva Aursland; children: Elise, Anders, Karina. Cand. real., U. Oslo, 1970; PhD, UCLA, 1971. Forste amanuensis Agder Coll., Kristiansand, Norway, 1972-83, U. Oslo, 1983—; research fellow British Sci. Research Council, Edinburgh, Scotland, 1982; vis. assoc. prof. Calif. Inst. Tech., Pasadena, 1984, UCLA, 1985. Author: (with K. Sydsæter) Linear Algebra, 1977; Stochastic Differential Equations, 1985.; contbr. articles to profl. jours. Mem. Bd. Higher Edn., Agder Counties, 1976-77. Research fellow The Royal Soc., 1971. Mem. Norwegian Math. Soc. (pres. 1987—). Office: U Oslo Dept Math, Box 1053 Blindern, N-0316 Oslo Norway

OKUBO, TOSHITERU, health science facility administrator educator; b. Tokyo, Japan, June 6, 1939; s. Michitada and Sumiko (Yamaguchi) O.; m. Tomoko (Ogura) Okubo, Feb. 15,1967; children: Junko, Toshitada. MB, Keio U., Tokyo, 1966, MD, 1978. Instr. sch. medicine Keio U., 1962-77; assoc. prof. Jichi Med. Sch., Minamikawachi, Tochigi, Japan, 1977-83; vis. prof. sch. pub. health UCLA, Los Angeles, 1981; prof. U. Occupational Environ. Health, Kitakyushu, 1983—; cons. Sony Corp., Tokyo, 1971-87, Ministry of Labor, Tokyo, 1984—. Author: Introduction to Epidemiology, 1976. Fellow Japan Indsl. Health Assn., Japanese Hygiene Assn; mem. Internat. Commn. Occupational Health, Internat. Epidemiol. Assn., Biometric Soc. Home: 5-2-27 Takasuminami Wakamatsu, 808-01 Kitakyushu Fukuoka Japan Office: U Occupational Environ Health, 1-1 Iseigaoka Yahatanishi, 807 Kitakyushu Fukuoka Japan

OKUDA, KUNIO, emeritus medical educator; b. Tokyo, May 21, 1921; s. Kinmatsu and Hatsue (Hashida) O.; m. Hinae Katsumata, May 24, 1947; children: Hiroaki, Keiko. MD, Manchuria Med. Coll., 1944; DSc, Chiba Med. Coll., Japan, 1951; PhD, Fukuoka U., 1983. With med. staff Chiba (Japan) Nat. Hosp., 1945-51; asst. prof. Yamaguchi Med. Coll., Ube, Japan, 1951-53, assoc. prof., 1953-63; asst. prof. Johns Hopkins Sch. Medicine, Balt., 1958-60; prof. medicine Kurume U. Sch. Medicine, Japan, 1963-71; prof. medicine Chiba U. Sch. Medicine, 1971-87, emeritus prof., 1987—; past pres. Japanese Soc. Hepatology, Tokyo, 1977-78; v.p. Orgn. de Gastro-Enterologie, 1982-86, hon. pres., 1986—. Contbr. articles to profl. jours. Recipient Spl. award Japanese Med. Assn., 1967, Abbott award Japanese Nuclear Medicine Soc., Publ. and Translation Cultural award Japanese Publ. Soc., 1977. Mem. Japan Vitamin Soc. (pres. 1987—, Spl. award 1963), Orgn. Mondiale de Gastro-Enterologie (hon. pres. 1986—), Internat. Assn. Study of Liver (past pres. 1978-80), Asian Pacific Assn. Study of Liver (past pres. 1980-82), Am. Gastroenterological Assn. Lodge: Rotary.

OKUDAIRA, KOZO, architect, educator; b. Kure, Japan, Aug. 5, 1929; s. Minoru and Toshiko (Ohnogi) O.; m. Reiko Yamada, Nov. 8, 1959; children: Takahiro, Mayumi. M in Tech., Tokyo U., 1954, D in Tech., 1987. Registered architect. Mem. staff Kunio Maekawa, Architect, Tokyo, 1954-70; prin. Kozo Okudaira, Architect, Tokyo, 1970—; prof. Tokyo Inst. Polys., Atsugi, Japan, 1979—. Author: Design of Museums (Anthropology of Architecture series no. 30), 1983; tranlator: The Master Builders, 1963. Mem. Archtl. Inst. Japan, Japan Inst. Architechts. Home: Higashi 2-17-4, Kunitachi, 186 Tokyo Japan Office: Tokyo Inst Polys, 1583 Iiyama, 243-02 Atsugi Kanagawa Japan

OKUMA, MASATAKA, automotive company executive; b. Nov. 1, 1914; m. Yoko Okuma. Grad., Tokyo U., 1938. With Indsl. Bank Japan Ltd., 1938, Fuji Heavy Industries Ltd., Japan, 1955; exec. dir. Nissan Motor Co. Ltd., Japan, 1966; now advisor Nissan Motor Co. Ltd. Mem. Japan Automobile Mfrs. Assn. (trustee). Home: 19-10 Akazutsumi 1-chome, Setagoya-ku, Tokyo 156 Japan *

OKUMURA, ARIYOSHI, banker; b. Kobe, Japan, Feb. 15, 1931; s. Yoshiyasu and Hisako O.; m. Sachiko Watanabe, Dec. 14, 1959; children: Yatuka, Shigeru, Hiroshi. BA, Tokyo U., 1953, MA in Econs., 1955; postgrad., Columbia U., 1957-58, Harvard U., 1984. Gen. mgr., dir. indsl. reseach dept., treasury dept., engring. cons. dept., internat. fin. research dept.; bd. dirs., mng. dir.; mem. Trilateral Commn., Indsl. Structure Council. Fulbright scholar. Office: Indsl Bank Japan, Marunouchi 1-3-3, Tokyo 100, Japan

OKUMURA, TOSHIKATSU, engineer; b. Kobe, Hyogo, Japan, Aug. 16, 1938; s. Gihei and Fusae (Okumura) O.; m. Haruko Tateishi, Jan. 9, 1965; children: Katsuichiro, Masako. B, Himeji Tech. Coll., Hyogo, 1963. Staff engr. Sanyo Electric Co., Ltd., Moriguchi, Osaka, Japan, 1963-67; mgr. dept. Sanyo Electric Co., Ltd., Oizumi, Gunma, Japan, 1986—; staff engr. Tokyo Sanyo Electric Co., Ltd., Oizumi, 1968-71, sr. staff engr., 1971-78, mgr. section, 1978-85. Home: 1084-43 Iizuka Cho, Ohta Gunma 373, Japan Office: Sanyo Electric Co Ltd, 180 Sakata, Oizumi Machi Gunma 370-05, Japan

OKUNO, YOSHIO, business executive; b. Tokyo, June 19, 1921; d. Kei and Nobuko (Nagasawa) O.; m. Nami Kurihara, June 1, 1959; B.A. in Econs., Tokyo U., Hongo, Tokyo, 1945; M.B.A. in Internat. Fin., NYU, 1952. Br. mgr. Mitsubishi Bank Ltd., Tokyo, 1964-73; pres. Chase Manhattan Corp., Tokyo, 1973-78; fgn. mgr. Japan Diamond Corp., Ueno, Tokyo, 1978-82; internat. trade mgr. Microboards, Inc., Funabashi, Japan, 1983-87; counselor, agt., Meiji Life Ins. Co, Tokyo, 1984-87, Drexel, Burnham, Lambert (Asis) Ltd., Tokyo, 1987—; currencies forward trader Forex Club. Served to 1st lt. Japanese Naval Air Force, 1943-45. Fulbright scholar, 1974. Liberal Democrat. Buddhist. Lodges: Kuju Kuri-Chiba Lions (Wheelchair Camp award 1974). Avocations: sports. Home: 2709-2 Kamihongo, Matsudo City, Chiba 271 2709-02, Japan Office: Drexel Burnham Shoken, Imperial Tower, 1-1-1 Uchisaiwaicho Chiyodaku, Tokyo 100 273, Japan

ÖKÜTÇÜ, DAVUT, textile company executive; b. Diyarbakir, Turkey, May 15, 1946; s. Mehmet Salih and Serife (Değirmenci) Ö.; m. Zehra Nurhan Uçak, July 21, 1973. BSChemE, Robert Coll., Istanbul, Turkey, 1969; MS in Indsl. Engring., Syracuse U., 1971. Research engr. Agway Corp., Syracuse, N.Y., 1971; indsl. engr. Koç Holding, Istanbul, 1971-72; planning mgr. Bozkurt Textiles, Istanbul, 1974-76, indsl. engring. mgr., 1976-78, plant mgr., 1978-80, asst. gen. mgr. tech., 1980—. Mem. adv. bd. Türkish Ednl. Found., Istanbul, 1987. Served to lt. Turkish Navy, 1972-74. Fellow Am. Inst. Indsl. Engrs.; mem. Robert Coll. Alumnae Assn., Darüssafaka Alumnae Assn., Chamber of Chem. Engrs., Textile Inst. Club: Bizim Tepe (Istanbul). Lodge: Rotary (com. chmn. Suadiye 1987). Office: Bozkurt Mensucat Sanayii AS, Kosuyolu-Zeytinburnu, 34770 Istanbul Turkey

OKUYAMA, SHINICHI, physician; b. Yamagata, Japan, Dec. 4, 1935; s. Kinzo Okuyama and Asayo Hasegawa; m. Masako Fujii, Dec. 4, 1966 (dec.); children: Yuriko, Izumi, Takashi, Jun; m. Junko Hsun Chen, Mar. 21, 1983; children: Midori, Shaw. MD, Tohoku (Japan) U., 1961, PhD, 1966. Intern Saiseikan Hosp., Yamagata, 1961-62; resident in radiology Tohoku U. Research Inst., Sendai, Japan, 1962-66; research assoc. Tohoku U. Inst. Tb, Leprosy and Cancer, 1966-73, assoc. prof. radiology, 1974-80; dir. radiology Tohoku Rosai Hosp., Sendai, 1980—. Author: Diagnostic Bone Scintigraphy, 1974, Compton Radiography, 1979, Induction of Cancer Rediffer-entiation, 1983, Evolutionary Concepts of Cancer, 1988. Recipient Compton Tomography-Radiotherapy Planning award Japanese Ministry of Edn., 1980. Mem. Japanese Soc. Radiology, Japanese Soc. Nuclear Medicine, Japanese Soc. Reticuloendothelial Systems, N.Y. Acad. Scis. Home: Nakayama 3-15-38, Sendai 981, Japan Office: Tohoku Rosai Hosp, Dainohara 4-3-21, Sendai 980, Japan

OLAH, JUDITH AGNES, chemist; b. Budapest, Jan. 21, 1929; came to U.S., 1964, naturalized, 1969; d. Janos and Magaret (Kraus) Lengyel; M.S. in Chemistry, Tech. U. Budapest, 1955; m. George A. Olah, July 9, 1949; children—George John, Ronald Peter. Research chemist Central Research Inst., Hungarian Acad. Scis., 1955-56; research asso. Case Western Res. U., Cleve., 1966-77; adj. asst. prof. chemistry U. So. Calif., 1977-79, adj. asso. prof., 1979—. Mem. Iota Sigma Pi. Contbr. articles on organic chemistry to profl. jours., chpts. in books. Home: 2252 Gloaming Way Beverly Hills CA 90210 Office: U Southern Calif Dept Chemistry University Park Los Angeles CA 90007

OLANDER, DONALD EDGAR, chemist, engineering executive; b. Chgo., Aug. 12, 1929; s. Albert Edgar and Abbie (Snyder) O.; m. Dayle Neva Roberts, June 22, 1950 (div. Jan. 1973); children: Mark, Eric, Lauren, Paul, Lisa; m. Geraldine June Frere, Feb. 25, 1975; children: Russell, Basilio, Kimberly, Bebe. BS in Chemistry, Northwestern U., 1951; MS in Chemistry, St. Louis U., 1955; PhD in Engring., Calif. Coast U., 1980. Chemist Mallinckrodt Co., St. Louis, 1951-53; project engr. Universal Match Corp., Ferguson, Mo., 1959-67; engr., quality control mgr. Aerojet-Gen. Co., Nimbus, Calif., 1959-67; staff scientist Explosive Tech., Fairfield, Calif., 1967-69; v.p. Networks Electronic Corp., Chatsworth, Calif., 1969-72; staff scientist Hi-Shear Tech. Corp., Torrance, Calif., 1979-87; chief scientist, tech. dir. Hi-Shear Propulsion div. Hi-Shear Tech. Corp., Sparks, Nev., 1987—. Patentee in field; contbr. articles to profl. jours. Asst. scoutmaster Boy Scouts Am., Fair Oaks, Calif., 1959-65; active Fair Oaks Presbyn. Ch., 1959-71. Mem. ASTM, Am. Chem. Soc., Am. Def. Preparedness Assn. Home: 2490 W Moana Ln Reno NV 89509 Office: Hi-Shear Tech Corp 6000 Slattery Rd Sparks NV 89431

OLANDER, RAY GUNNAR, lawyer; b. Buhl, Minn., May 15, 1926; s. Olof Gunnar and Margaret Esther (Meisner) O.; m. Audrey Joan Greenlaw, Aug. 1, 1959; children—Paul Robert, Mary Beth. B.E.E. with distinction, U. Minn., 1949, B.B.A. with distinction, 1949; J.D. cum laude, Harvard U., 1959. Bar: Minn. 1959, Wis. 1962, U.S. Patent Office 1968. Elec. engr. M. A. Hanna Co., Hibbing, Minn., 1950-56; assoc. Leonard, Street & Deinard, Mpls., 1959-61; comml. atty. Becor Western Inc. (formerly Bucyrus-Erie Co.), South Milwaukee, Wis., 1961-70, dir. contracts, 1970-76, v.p. comml., 1976—, gen. atty., 1978-80, corp. sec., 1978—, gen. counsel, 1980—; vice chmn. Becor Western Inc. (formerly Bucyrus-Erie Co.), South Milwaukee, 1988—; bd. dirs. Bucyrus-Erie Co., B-E Holdings Inc., Bucyrus Internat., Inc., Bucyrus (Africa) (Proprietary) Ltd., Bucyrus (Australia) Proprietary, Ltd., Wis. Holdings Party Ltd., Equipment Assurance Ltd., Minserco Inc., Western Gear machinery Co. Bd. dirs. Ballet Found. Milw., Inc., 1978—, Pub. Expenditure Research Found., Inc., Madison, Wis., 1978—, Pub. Expenditure Survey Wis., Madison, 1978-82. Served with USN, 1944-46. Mem. ABA, Wis. Bar Assn., Wis. Intellectual Property Law Assn., Am. Soc. Corp. Secs., Inc., Am. Corp. Counsel Assn., VFW, Eta Kappa Nu, Tau Beta Pi, Beta Gamma Sigma. Republican. Roman Catholic. Clubs: Harvard (N.Y.C.), Harvard of Wis., University (Milw.), Tuckaway Country (Franklin, Wis.). Lodges: Masons, Shriners. Home: 5881 Fleming Ct Greendale WI 53129 Office: Bucyrus-Erie Co 1100 Milwaukee Ave South Milwaukee WI 53172

OLAUSSON, INGRID, editor; b. Stockholm, Sweden, Dec. 9, 1934; d. Nils Harald Nielsen and Marta Lovisa (Jansson) Brelen; m. Rune Olausson; children: Lena, Karin. Student, Göteborgs Högre Samskola, Sweden, 1953; Degree in (interior architecture), Konst Industriella Skolan, Sweden, 1958. Cert. interior architect. Interior architect various firms, Gothenburg, Sweden, 1958-66; Mgr. Swedish Design Ctr., Stockholm, 1967-70; editor Alltihemmet Ahlén Rakerlund, Stockholm, 1970-77, Svenska Dagbladet, Stockholm, 1977—; pub. Hagaberg AB, Stockholm, 1983—. Author: numerous books. Bd. mem. The Newthinkers, Stockholm, 1982—, mgr dir. Hagaberg. Mem. Swedish Pub. Assn.

OLAV V, HIS MAJESTY THE KING OF NORWAY, b. Appleton House, Eng., July 2, 1903; s. King Haakon VII and Queen Maud (d. King Edward VII of Eng.); m. Princess Märtha of Sweden, Mar. 21,1929 (dec. 1954); children: Crown Prince Harald, Princess Ragnhild (wife of Erling Lorentzen), Princess Astrid (wife of Johan Martin Ferner). Ed. Norwegian Mil. Acad., Balliol Coll., Oxford U. Cmdr.-in-chief Norwegian Forces, World War II; following death of father, succeeded to throne, Sept. 21, 1957. Address: HM the King of Norway, Royal Palace, N-0010 Oslo Norway

OLAYAN, HAMAD B., chemist; b. Rawadat Sidair, Saudi Arabia, 1957. BS, King Saud U., Riyadh, 1980; MA, Imam Mohammed U., Riyadh, 1985. Tech. planning evaluator Saudi Basic Industries Corp., Riyadh, 1980-81, product devel. mgr., 1982-85, tech. planning and evaluation mgr., 1986—, research dir., 1987—; bd. dirs. SABIC Mktg.Co., Ltd. Pub. 3 books; contbr. articles to Al-Riyadh newspaper. Mem. Am. Chem. Soc., The Plastics and Rubber Inst. London. Home: PO Box 15391, Riyadh 11444, Saudi Arabia Office: Saudi Basic Industries Corp, PO Box 15391, Riyadh 11444, Saudi Arabia

OLAYAN, SULIMAN SALEH, corporate executive; b. Onaiza, Saudi Arabia, Nov. 5, 1918; s. Saleh and Heya (Al Ghanem) O.; student public schs., Bahrain Islands; m. Mary Perdikis, Feb. 22, 1974; children—Khaled, Hayat, Hutham, Lubna. Research specialist Arabian Am. Oil Co., 1937-47; founder and chmn. Olayan Group, Saudi Arabia, 1947—, which includes Olayan Investments Co. Establishment, Olayan Saudi Holding Co. and Subs., Olayan Financing Co. and Affiliates, Arab Comml. Enterprises and Subs.; chmn. bd. The Saudi Brit. Bank, Riyadh, Saudi Arabia, 1977—; mem. adv. bd. Energy Internat.; adv. bd. Am. Internat. Group; mem. internat. council Morgan Guaranty Trust Co. N.Y.Appointed Knight Comdr. of Brit. Empire, 1987; recipient Great Cross of the Order of Merit, Spain, 1985, Medal of Honor, Madrid C. of C., 1985. Mem. internat. adv. council SRI Internat., San Francisco; alumnus mem. The Rockefeller U. Council, N.Y.C., 1978—; trustee Am. U. of Beirut, 1979-84; trustee Freedoms Found. of Valley Forge; co-chmn. U.S.-Saudi Arabian Businessmen's Dialogue under the U.S.-Saudi Arabian Joint Commn. on Econ. Cooperation; internat. councillor, mem. adv. bd. Georgetown U. Ctr. for Strategic and Internat. Studies. Mem. U.S.-Arab C. of C. (bd. dirs. Washington), Saudi C. of C. and Industry (vice chmn. council), Riyadh C. of C. and Industry (chmn. council), The Conf. Bd. of N.Y. (sr. mem., internat. counselor), Royal Inst. Internat. Affairs, London, Riyadh Handicapped Children Assn. (chmn.). Islam. Clubs: Knickerbocker, N.Y. Athletic (N.Y.C.); Pacific-Union (San Francisco); Royal Automobile (London). Office: Olayan Group of Companies, PO Box 8772, Riyadh Saudi Arabia

OLBRECHTS, GUY ROBERT, electrical engineer, consultant; b. Mechelen, Belgium, May 22, 1935; came to U.S., 1967, naturalized, 1978; s. Alphonse and Blanche (Van Coolput) O.; m. Andree Julia Van Nes, Oct. 19, 1961; children: Philippe, Ingrid, Dominique. Ingenieur civil electricien Catholic U. Leuven, Belgium, 1960; M.B.A., Seattle U., 1976. Lead engr. Ctr. D'Etudes Nucleaires, Mol, Belgium, 1962-65; quality control mgr., chief engr. for magnetics Sprague Electromag., Ronse, Belgium, 1965-67; sr. engr. Boeing Co., Seattle, 1967-79; sect. mgr. data systems engring. and product support Sundstrand Data Control Corp., Redmond, Wash., 1979-87; project engr. memory sytems Sundstrand Data Control; propr., cons., designer Gentronics, Bellevue, Wash., 1970—. Patentee gyro wheel speed modulator, 1981, integrated strapdown/airdata sensor system, 1981, slow-acting phase-locked loop, 1983. Served as cpl. Belgian Army, 1961-62. Recipient inventor award Boeing Co., 1978. Republican. Roman Catholic. Home: 4809 116th Ave SE Bellevue WA 98006 Office: Sundstrand Data Control Corp Overlake Indsl Park Redmond WA 98052

OLBY, ROBERT, philosopher, educator; b. Beckenham, Kent, Eng., Oct. 4, 1933; s. Cecil A. and Nesta M. (Paul) O.; m. E. Judith S. Potter, Sept. 1, 1962; children: Alastair, Louise, Natasha, Fleur, Peter. BS, Imperial Coll., London, 1955; PhD, Oxford U., 1962. Tchr. Magdalen Coll. Sch., Oxford, Eng., 1956-59; postgrad. tchr. Magdalen Coll. Sch., Oxford, 1960-62; librarian Botany Sch. Oxford U., 1962-69; lectr. philosophy dept. Leeds (Eng.) U., 1969-75, reader, 1975—. Author: Origins of Mendelism, 1966, 2d edit., 1985 (Choice award 1967), The Path to the Double Helix, 1974. Mem. Brit. Soc. History Sci. (council 1986—, edn. sect. chmn.), History of Sci. Soc. Home: Beaconstones Langbar, Ilkley LS29 OES, England Office: Leeds U, Leeds LS2 9JT, England

OLD, BRUCE SCOTT, chemical and metallurgical engineer; b. Norfolk, Va., Oct. 21, 1913; s. Edward H.H. and Eugenia (Smith) O.; m. Katharine G. Day, Oct. 7, 1939; children: Edward H., Randolph B., Lansing G., Ashlee Virginia, Barbara Stuart. B.S., U. N.C., 1935; Sc.D., M.I.T., 1938. Research engr. devel. and research dept. Bethlehem Steel Corp., 1938-41; with Arthur D. Little, Inc., Cambridge, Mass., 1946-78; v.p. Arthur D. Little, Inc., 1950-60, sr. v.p., 1960-78; pres. Bruce S. Old Assos., Inc., 1979—; pres., chmn. Cambridge Corp., 1952-53; pres. Nuclear Metals, Inc., 1954-57; dir. Mass. Investors Trust and 13 other mut. funds in MFS group, 1973-85; chief metallurgy and materials br., div. research AEC, 1947-49; mem. Sci. Adv. Com. to Pres., 1952-56. Co-author: The Game of Singles in Tennis, 1962, Stroke Production in the Game of Tennis, 1971, The Game of Doubles in Tennis, 1956, Tennis Tactics, 1983; Contbr. articles to profl. publs. Corporator Wentworth Inst., Deaconess Hosp., Boston, Emerson Hosp., Concord, Mass. Served to comdr. USNR, 1941-46. Fellow Am. Soc. Metals, Am. Inst. Chemists, AAAS; mem. N.Y. Acad. Scis., Nat. Acad. Engring., Sigma Xi, Tau Beta Pi. Clubs: Concord Country, Wianno (Mass.). Address: PO Box 706 Concord MA 01742

OLD, HAROLD EVANS, JR., state official; b. Mansfield, Ohio, Sept. 11, 1939; s. Harold Evans and Pearl Edna (Beaschler) O.; m. Georgia A. Bernath, June 9, 1962 (div. July 1982); children—Eric K., Philip E. B.S., Marquette U., 1961; M.A., Western Mich. U., 1970; Ph.D., Mich. State U., 1973; postgrad. Naval War Coll., 1982-83. Grad. asst. Western Mich. U., Kalamazoo, also Mich. State U., East Lansing, 1967-72; instr. U. Conn., Storrs, 1972-73; exec. mgr. Ponderosa Systems, Lansing, Mich., 1973-74; adminstr. Mich. Dept. Pub. Health, Lansing, 1974-79, Mich. Dept. Labor, Lansing, 1979—; pres. Cedar Wood Homes, Inc., Schaumburg, Ill., 1983—. Served to lt. USN, 1961-67; capt. Res. NROTC scholar, 1957. Mem. Am. Polit. Sci. Assn., Res. Officers Assn., Naval Inst., Am. Soc. Pub. Adminstrn. (pres. Lansing 1982-83), Naval Res. Assn. (pres. Lansing 1970-73, 75—), Navy League, Am. Def. Preparedness Assn., Blue Jackets Assn. Club: Mich. Comdrs.

OLDENBURG, CLAES THURE, artist; b. Stockholm, Sweden, Jan. 28, 1929; s. Gosta and Sigrid Elisabeth (Lindforss) O.; m. Patricia Joan Muschinski, Apr. 13, 1960 (div. Apr. 1970); m. Coosje van Bruggen, July 22, 1977. B.A., Yale, 1951; student, Art Inst., Chgo., 1952-54. One-man shows include Reuben Gallery, N.Y.C., 1960, Green Gallery, N.Y.C., 1962, Sidney Janis Gallery, N.Y.C., 1964-70, Galerie Ileana Sonnabend, Paris, 1964, Robert Fraser Gallery, London, 1966, Moderna Museet, Stockholm, 1966, 77, Mus. Contemporary Art, Chgo., 1967, 77, Irving Blum Gallery, Los Angeles, 1968, Mus. Modern Art, N.Y.C., 1969, U. Calif. at Los Angeles Art Gallery, 1970, Stedelijk Mus., Amsterdam, 1970, 77, Tate Gallery, London, 1970, Nelson-Atkins Mus., Kansas City, 1972, Art Inst. Chgo., 1973, Leo Castelli Gallery, N.Y.C., 1974, 76, 80, Kunstmus., Basel, 1975, Margo Leavin Gallery, Los Angeles, 1975, 76, 78, 83, Art Gallery of Toronto, Ont., 1976, Centre Georges Pompidou Musée National d'Art Moderne, Paris, 1977, Kröller-Muller Mus., 1979, Mus. Ludwig, Cologne, 1979, David Adamson Gallery, Washington, 1982, Wave Hill, Bronx, N.Y., 1984, numerous others, exhibited in group shows at, Martha Jackson Gallery, N.Y.C., 1960, 61, Dallas Mus. Contemporary Art, 1961, 62, Sidney Janis Gallery, 1962, 64, Inst. Contemporary Arts, London, 1963, Art Inst. Chgo., 1962, 63, Allen Art Mus. Oberlin (Ohio) Coll., 1963, Mus. Modern Art, N.Y.C., 1963, Washington Gallery Modern Art, 1963, Am. Pavilion, Venice, 1964, Moderna Museet, Stockholm, 1964, Gulbenkian Found. Tate Gallery, London, 1964, Rochester (N.Y.) Meml. Mus., 1964-65, Worcester (Mass.) Mus., 1965, Met. Mus. Art, N.Y.C., 1969, Walker Art Center, 1975, others, numerous commd. works, rep. permanent collections at, Mus. Modern Art, Albright-Knox Art Gallery, Buffalo, Centre Georges Pompidou, Stedelijk Mus., Tate Gallery, Mus. Ludwig, Moderna Museet, Rose Art Mus. Brandeis U., Waltham, Mass., Oberlin Coll., Nat. Gallery Art, Canberra, Art Gallery Ont., Toronto, Art Inst. Chgo., Hirshorn Gallery and Sculpture Gorden, Whitney Mus. Modern Art, N.Y.C., numerous others. (Recipient Creative Arts citation Brandeis U. 1971, Sculpture award Am. Ann., Chgo. Art Inst. 1976, medal AIA 1977, Wilhelm Lehmbruck Sculpture award 1981); Author: Store Days, 1967, Proposals for Monuments and Buildings, 1969, Notes in Hand, 1971, Raw Notes, 1973. Office: care Sidney Janis Gallery 15 E 57th St New York NY 10022 *

OLDENBURG, RICHARD ERIK, museum executive; b. Stockholm, Sweden, Sept. 21, 1933; came to U.S., 1936, naturalized, 1959; s. Gösta and Sigrid Elisabeth (Lindforss) O.; m. Harriet Lisa Turnure, Dec. 17, 1960. A.B., Harvard U., 1954. Mgr. design dept. Doubleday & Co., Inc., N.Y.C., 1958-61; mng. editor trade div. Macmillan Co., Inc., N.Y.C., 1961-69; dir. publs. Museum Modern Art, N.Y.C., 1969-72; dir. mus. Museum Modern Art, 1972—. Served with AUS, 1956-58. Mem. Assn. Art Mus. Dirs. Home: 447 E 57th St New York NY 10022 Office: Mus of Modern Art 11 W 53d St New York NY 10019

OLDERMAN, GERALD MYRON, medical device company executive; b. N.Y.C., July 16, 1933; s. Cass and Hilda (Klein) O.; m. Myrna Ruth Schwartz, Aug. 3, 1958; children: Sharon, Neil, Lisa. BS in Chemistry, Rensselaer Poly Inst., 1958; MS Phys. Chemistry, Seton Hall U., 1971, PhD, 1972. Research chemist Nat. Cash Register, Dayton, Ohio, 1958-61; tech. mgmt. positions Johnson & Johnson, New Brunswick, N.J., 1961-75, v.p. research and devel. Surgikos div., 1975-78; v.p. research and devel. Am. Convertors div. Am. Hosp. Supply Corp., Evanston, Ill., 1978-85, Am. Pharmaseal div. Am. Hosp. Supply Corp., Valencia, Calif., 1985—; bd. dirs. Am. Convertors. Served with USMC, 1954-56. Recipient Robert Wood Johnson medal, Johnson & Johnson, 1969. Fellow Am. Chem. Soc.; mem. Assn. Advancement Med. Instrumentation, Assn. Nonwovens Industry (bd. dirs., corp. rep. 1986, 87), Nat. Fire Protection Assn. (industry rep.), Am. Soc. Artificial Internal Organs. Home: 17300 Citronia St Northridge CA 91325 Office: Am Pharmaseal 27200 N Tourney Rd Valencia CA 91355

OLDFORD, RICHMOND WAYNE, statistics educator; b. Toronto, Ont., Can., May 4, 1954; s. Willis Clifford and Emma Louisa (Fillier) O.; m. Nancy Dawn Gapp, Aug. 7, 1976. B in Math., U. Waterloo, Ont., 1977; MSc, U. Toronto, 1979, PhD, 1983. Survey methodologist Statistics Can., Ottawa, Ont., 1977-78; research assoc. MIT, Cambridge, Mass., 1983-85, lectr., 1984-86, prin. research assoc., 1985-86; asst. prof. U. Waterloo, 1986—. Contbr. articles to profl. jours. Mem. Statis. Soc. Can., Am. Statis. Assn., Royal Statis. Soc., Assn. Computing Machinery, Inst. Math. Statistics. Office: U Waterloo, 200 University Ave W, Waterloo, ON Canada N2L 3G1

OLDHAM, ELAINE DOROTHEA, educator; b. Coalinga, Calif., June 29, 1931; d. Claude Smith Oldham and Dorothy Elaine (Hill) Wilkins. AB in History, U. Calif., Berkeley, 1953; MS in Sch. Adminstrn., Calif. State U., Hayward, 1976; postgrad. U. Calif., Berkeley, Harvard U., Mills Coll. Tchr. Piedmont Unified Sch. Dist., Calif., 1956—. Pres., bd. dirs. Camron-Stanford House Preservation Assn., 1979-86, adminstrv. v.p., bd. dirs., 1976-79; mem. various civic and community support groups; bd. dirs. Anne Martin Children's Ctr. Mem. Am. Assn. Museums, Am. Assn. Mus. Trustees, Internat. Council Museums, Inst. Internat. Edn., Am. Assn. State and Local History, Oakland Mus. Assn., DAR (Outstanding Tchr. Am. History award), Colonial Dames Am., Magna Charta Dames, Daus. of Confederacy, Hugeunot Soc., Plantagenent Soc., Order of Washington, Order St. George and Descs. of Knights of Garter, U. Calif. Alumni Assn. (co-chmn. and chmn. of 10th and 25th yr. class reunions), Prytanean Alumnae Assn. (bd. dirs.), Phi Delta Kappa, Delta Kappa Gamma. Republican. Episcopalian. Club: Harvard (San Francisco); Women's Athletic of Alameda County. Office: 780 Magnolia Ave Piedmont CA 94611

OLDHAM, MAXINE JERNIGAN, real estate broker; b. Whittier, Calif., Oct. 13, 1923; d. John K. and Lela Hessie (Mears) Jernigan; m. Laurance Montgomery Oldham, Oct. 28, 1941; 1 child, John Laurence. AA, San Diego City Coll., 1973; student Western State U. Law, San Diego, 1976-77, LaSalle U., 1977-78; grad. Realtors Inst., Sacramento, 1978. Mgr. Edin Harig Realty, LaMesa, Calif., 1966-70; tchr. Bd. Edn., San Diego, 1959-66; mgr. Julia Cave Real Estate, San Diego, 1970-73; salesman Computer Realty, San Diego, 1973-74; owner Shelter Island Realty, San Diego, 1974—. Author: Jernigan History, 1982, Mears Geneology, 1985. Mem. Civil Service Commn., San Diego, 1957-58. Mem. Nat. Assn. Realtors, Calif. Assn. Realtors, San Diego Bd. Realtors, San Diego Apt. Assn., Internationale des Professions Immobilieres (internat. platform speaker), DAR, Colonial Dames 17th Century, Internat. Fedn. Univ. Women. Republican. Roman Catholic. Avocations: music, theater, painting, geneology, continuing edn. Home: 3348 Lowell St San Diego CA 92106 Office: Shelter Island Realty 2810 Lytton St San Diego CA 92110

OLDSHUE, JAMES Y., manufacturing company executive; b. Chgo., Apr. 18, 1925; s. James and Louise (Young) O.; m. Betty Ann Wiersema, June 14, 1947; children: Paul, Richard, Robert. B.S. in Chem. Engring., Ill. Inst. Tech., 1947, M.S., 1949, Ph.D. in Chem. Engring., 1951. Registered engr., N.Y. With Mixing Equipment Co., Rochester, N.Y., 1950—; dir. research Mixing Equipment Co., 1960-63, tech. dir., 1963-70, v.p. mixing tech., 1970—. Author: Fluid Mixing Technology, 1983; contbr. chpts. and articles to books and jours. Chmn. budget com. Internat. div. YMCA; bd. dirs. Rochester YMCA. Served with AUS, 1945-47. Recipient 1st Disting. Service award NE YMCA Internat. Com., 1979; Victor Marquez award Interam. Confedn. Chem. Engrs., 1983; named Rochester Engr. of Yr., 1980. Fellow Am. Inst. Chem. Engrs. (pres. 1979, treas. 1983-87, Eminent Chem. Engr., 1983, Founders award 1981); mem. Am. Assn. Engring. Socs. (chmn. 1985, K.A. Roe award 1987), Am. Chem. Soc., Internat. Platform Assn., Nat. Acad. Engring. (adv. com. internat. activities), World Congress Chem. Engrs. (v.p. 1986), Sigma Xi. Mem. Reformed Ch. in Am. (gen. program council). Club: Travelers Century. Lodge: Rotary. Home: 141 Tyringham Rd Rochester NY 14617 Office: 135 Mt Read Blvd Rochester NY 14611

OLDSHUE, PAUL FREDERICK, banker; b. Chgo., Nov. 4, 1949; s. James Young and Betty Ann (Wiersema) O.; m. Mary Elizabeth Holl, July 12, 1975; children: Emily Jane, Andrew Armstrong, Abigail Anne. BA, Williams Coll., Williamstown, Mass., 1971; MBA, NYU, 1978. With Chem. Bank, N.Y.C., 1973-78, asst. sec., 1976-78; with Orbanco Fin. Services Corp., 1978-84, v.p., treas., 1980-83; exec. v.p. Oreg. Bank, Portland, 1984-88; v.p. syndications & participations PacifiCorp Credit Inc., 1988—. Mem. Fin. Execs. Inst., Robert Morris Assocs. Republican. Club: Univ. (Portland).

OLEARCHYK, ANDREW S., cardiothoracic surgeon, educator; b. Przemysl, Poland, Dec. 3, 1935; s. Simon and Anna (Kravéts) O.; m. Renata

M. Sharan, June 26, 1971; children: Christina N., Roman A., Adrian S. Grad., Med. Acad., Warsaw, Poland, 1961. Diplomate Am. Bd. Surgery, Am. Bd. Thoracic Surgery. Chief div. anesthesiology, asst. dept. surgery Provincial Hosp., Kielce, Poland, 1963-66; resident in gen. surgery Geisinger Med. Ctr., Danville, Pa., 1968-73; resident in thoracic, cardiac surgery Allegheny Gen. Hosp., Pitts., 1980-82; practice medicine specializing in cardiac, thoracic and vascular surgery Phila. and Cherry Hill, N.J.; assoc. div. cardiothoracic surgery Episcopal Hosp., Phila., 1984—, Grad. Hosp., Phila., 1987—; clin. asst. prof. dept. surgery (thoracic) R.W. Johnson Med. Sch., Univ. Med. and Dentistry N.J., 1984—. Contbr. articles to med. jours., also 4 monographs. Fellow ACS; mem. Soc. Thoracic Surgeons, Ukrainian Med. Assn. N. Am. Home: 129 Walt Whitman Blvd Cherry Hill NJ 08003

O'LEARY, PAUL ALISTAIR, civil engineer; b. Chester, Eng., Dec. 5, 1942; s. Daniel and Gwendoline (Dickie) O'L.; m. Vivien Emery, Sept. 19, 1968; children—Mark, Robert. B.A., Cambridge U., Eng., 1964, M.A., 1968; Sc.M., Brown U., 1966. Registered profl. engr., Singapore; chartered engr., Gt. Britain. Asst. engr. Kirk & Kirk, Ltd., London, Eng., 1965-69; engr. Harris & Sutherland, London, 1969-72, sr. engr., 1972-75, assoc. ptnr., 1975-80; mng. dir. Harris & Sutherland Pte., Ltd., 1980—, Harriland Perunding Teknologi Pembinaan Sdn. Bhd., 1987—; dir. Computer Consortium, Ltd., London, 1976-80, Charles Haswell Cons. Pte., Ltd., Singapore, 1986—. Vice chmn. Round Table Great Britain, Epping, Eng., 1979-80. Univ. scholar Inst. Civil Engrs., Cambridge/Brown Univs., 1961-65; fellow Brown U., Rhode Island, 1964-65. Mem. Inst. Civil Engrs., Singapore Concrete Inst. (bd. dirs. 1983-86), Inst. Hwys. and Transp., Inst. Engrs. Singapore, Assn. Cons. Engrs. Singapore (council 1983—). Clubs: Tanglin; British (Singapore). Advocations: Tennis; badminton; swimming. Home: 4 Oriole Crescent, Raffles Park Singapore 1128 Office: Harris and Sutherland Pte Ltd, 10 Anson Rd #22-07, Internat Plaza, Singapore 0207, Singapore

OLEBY, CHRISTER, international marketing executive; b. Stockholm, Jan. 30, 1942; came to Spain, 1968; s. Goesta and Inez (Karlson) O.; m. Isabel Garcia Delgado, Mar. 24, 1975; 1 dau., Cristina. M.B.A., U. Lund, 1968. Mng. dir. G.I.C.C.S.A., Madrid, 1969-72; pres. Telispan, S.A., Madrid, 1972-74; pres. Gullring Iberica, S.A., Madrid, 1974-77, bd. dirs. Gullring Iberica S.A., Daroca, Spain, 1974—; mktg. dir. Indsl. Barranquesa, S.A., Pamplona, Spain, 1977-85; pres. I.B. Flanges Internat., Gulfport, Miss., 1982-85; dir. Soc. for Devel. of Navarra, S.A., Pamplona, 1985—. Recipient Internat. trophy for tech., Frankfurt, Germany, 1981. Mem. Trade Leaders Club. Club Mktg. Home: Pio XII, 1, 1-5A, E-31002 Pamplona Spain Office: SODENA, Arrieta 8-7, E-31002 Pamplona Spain

OLEJAR, PAUL DUNCAN, former information science administrator; b. Hazelton, Pa., Sept. 13, 1906; s. George and Anna (Danco) O.; m. Ann Ruth Dillard, Jan. 6, 1933 (dec. Oct. 1978); 1 child, Peter; m. Martha S. Ross, Sept. 8, 1979. AB, Dickinson Coll., 1928. Dir. edn. W.Va. Conservation Commn., 1936-41; coordinator U.S. Fish and Wildlife Service, 1941-42; chief press and radio Bur. Reclamation, Dept. Interior, 1946-47; editor Plant Industry Sta. AGRI, 1948-51; chmn. spl. reports Agrl. Research Adminstrn., 1951-56; dir. tech. info. Edgewood Arsenal, Md., 1956-63; chief, tech. info. plans and programs Army Research Office, Washington, 1963-64; chmn. chem. info. unit NSF, Washington, 1965-70; dir. drug info. program Sch. Pharmacy, U. N.C., Chapel Hill, 1970-73, ret., 1973. Author: A Taste of Red Onion, 1981; newspaper columnist, editor AP, Pa. and W.Va.; editor Hanover Record-Herald, Pa. Served with AUS, 1942-46. Decorated Army Commendation medal. Mem. Ravens Claw, Theta Chi, Omicron Delta Kappa. Methodist. Home: 724 Port Malabar Blvd NE Palm Bay FL 32905

OLENA, ARNOLD THEODORE, lawyer; b. N.Y.C., Feb. 19, 1919; s. Alfred Douglas and Mildred McDonald (Armour) O.; m. Nathalie Hawthorne French, May 5, 1951; children—Laura O. Mixter, Douglas French, Kenneth Arnold, Stephen Randle, Marion Hawthorne. A.B., Amherst Coll., 1940; LL.B., Yale U., 1947. Bar: N.Y. 1948. Assoc., Hodgson, Russ, Andrews, Woods & Goodyear, Buffalo, 1947-51, ptnr., 1951—; tchr. Am. Inst. Banking, 1949-54; mem. adv. bd. N.Y. state Am. Arbitration Assn., 1982—. Active Cerebral Palsy Assn. Western N.Y., Children's Found. Erie County. Mem. ABA (past co-chmn. labor arbitration com.), N.Y. State Bar Assn., Erie County Bar Assn., Indsl. Relations Research Assn. (Man of Yr. award, 1987), Greater Buffalo C. of C. Democrat. Unitarian-Universalist. Club: Thursday (Buffalo). Home: 276 Maple Rd East Aurora NY 14052 Office: 1 M & T Plaza Suite 1800 Buffalo NY 14203

OLER, WESLEY MARION, III, physician, educator; b. N.Y.C., Mar. 8, 1918; s. Wesley Marion and Imogene (Rubel) O.; m. Virginia Carolyn Craemer, Dec. 8, 1951; children: Helen Louise (dec.), Wesley Marion IV, Stephen Scott. Grad., Phillips Andover Acad., 1936; A.B., Yale U., 1940; M.D., Columbia U., 1943. Intern Bellevue Hosp., N.Y.C., 1944; resident Bellevue Hosp., 1948-50; fellow Hosp. U. Pa., 1951; practice medicine specializing in internal medicine Washington, 1952—; sr. adv. staff vice chmn. dept. medicine Washington Hosp. Center, 1962-64, v.p. med. bd., 1971-72, trustee, 1973-81; clin. prof. medicine Med. Sch., Georgetown U. Contbr. articles on old musical instruments to jours. Founder, past pres. Washington Recorder Soc.; bd. dirs. Am. Recorder Soc. Served to maj. M.C. U.S. Army (paratroops), 1944-47. Fellow A.C.P. (gov. 1980-84); mem. Mensa, Osler Soc. Washington (past pres.). Republican. Episcopalian. Clubs: Met, Cosmos, Chevy Chase. Home: 4800 Van Ness St NW Washington DC 20016 Office: 3301 New Mexico Ave NW Washington DC 20016

OLER, WESLEY MARION, IV, investment advisor; b. Washington, Apr. 13, 1955; arrived in Switzerland, 1982; s. Wesley Marion and Virginia Carolyn (Craemer) O. BA cum laude, Yale U., 1978; postgrad., George Washington U., 1978, NYU, 1979-81, Boston U., 1986-87. Chartered fin. analyst. Investment officer Brown Bros. Harriman & Co., N.Y.C., 1978-82; dep. mgr. Brown Bros. & Harriman Services, Zurich, Switzerland, 1982—. Mem. Swiss Assn. Fin. Analysts, Am. Club Zurich (v.p. 1985-86, pres. 1988, mem. exec. com.), Chaîne des Rôtisseurs, Swiss-Am. C. of C. (fin. and investments chpt.). Republican. Episcopalian. Clubs: Golf and Country (Zurich), Yale (Switzerland) (pres. 1984—, chmn. alumni schs. com. 1985—), Chevy Chase (Md.). Office: Brown Bros Harriman Services, Stockerstrasse 38, 8002 Zurich Switzerland

OLESEN, DORTE MARIANNE, mathematician, educator; b. Hillerød, Denmark, Jan. 8, 1948; d. Knud Henning and Irene Mariane (Pedersen) O.; m. Gert K. Pedersen, Feb. 26, 1971; children: Just, Oluf, Marianne. MS, U. Copenhagen, 1973; PhD, U. Odense, Denmark, 1975; DSc, U. Copenhagen, 1981. Research assoc. U. Odense (Denmark), 1973-74; acad. sec. Ministry of Edn., Copenhagen, 1974-76; postdoctoral fellow U. Copenhagen, 1976-79, lectr., 1980-88; prof. U. Roskilde, Denmark, 1988—; with Math. Scis. Research Inst., Berkeley, Calif., 1984-85; dean Faculty of Natural Scis., Copenhagen, 1986-88. Contbr. articles to profl. jours. Mem. Danish Council for Research Policy and Planning, 1987—. Recipient Gold medal U. Copenhagen, 1973; travel grantee Tagea Brandt Com., 1987. Mem. Danish Math. Soc., Am. Math. Soc. Office: U Roskilde IMFUFA, PO Box 260, 4000 Roskilde Denmark

OLESEN, MOGENS NORGAARD, mathematics educator; b. Frederiksvaerk, Denmark, May 10, 1948; s. Niels Norgaard and Katrine (Rasmussen) O.; m. Lilly Groen Pedersen, July 14, 1974; children—Thomas Norgaard, Eva Groen, Morten Norgaard. Candidate Sci., U. Copenhagen, Denmark, 1976. Vis. researcher U. Calif., San Diego, 1977-78; assoc. prof. math. Coll. of Elsinore, Denmark, 1978—, Sch. Forests, Fredensborg, Denmark, 1979—, U. Copenhagen, 1982—. Author: The Exponential Functions and their Applications, 1982; Mathematical Problems and Their Solutions, 1983; The Great Belt Crossing During 100 Years, 1983; Our Solar System, 1984; Planar Curves, 1984; Practical Mathematics, 1985; Applied Mathematics, 1985; Halley's Comet and the History of Cosmology, 1985; The Ferries on the Kattegat, 1986; Danish Railway Steam Ferries, 1987; The History of the Rodby-Puttgarden Crossing, 1988. Copenhagen travelling grantee for mathematicians, 1976. Mem. Danish Math. Soc., Am. Math. Soc., World Ship Soc. Lutheran. Avocations: history of mathematics, science, ships and railways, classical music. Home: H P Christensensvej 18, DK-3300 Frederiksvaerk Denmark Office: U Copenhagen, Studiestraede 6, DK-1455 Copenhagen Denmark

OLGAARD, ANDERS, economics educator; b. Aabenraa, Denmark, Sept. 5, 1926; s. Axel O. and Anna Lebeck; m. Alice Christiansen, 1951; three children. Dr. Polit., Univ. Copenhagen, 1966. Civil servant Econ. Sec., 1953-60; prof. econs., Univ. Copenhagen, 1962—; adviser in Malaysia, Harvard U. Devel. Adv. Service, 1968-69; mem. Econ. Council, 1966-68, chmn., 1970-76. Author: Growth, Productivity and Relative Prices, 1966; The Danish Economy, EEC Economic and Financial Series, 1980. Mem. Danish Econ. Assn. (pres. 1983—). Home: 12 Lerbaekvej, 2830 Virum Denmark Office: U Copenhagen Inst of Econs, 6 Studiestraede, 1455 Copenhagen Denmark

OLHAGER, JAN ERIK, industrial management educator, consultant; b. Solna, Sweden, Sept. 3, 1955; s. Albert Erik Henry and Britta Maria (Ekelund) O. M of Engring., U. Calif., 1981; MS in Indsl. Mgmt., Linköping (Sweden) Inst. Tech., 1980; PhD in Prodn. Econs., Linköping (Sweden) Inst. Tech., 1986. Lectr. Dept. Prodn. Econs. Linköping Inst. Tech., 1982-86, asst. prof., 1986—; cons. Promana, Linköping, 1982—. Author: Efficient Manufacturing Planning and Control (in Swedish), 1985; contbr. articles to profl. jours. Pres. Prodn.-Econ. Research in Linköping Found., 1982—. Scholar Södertälje Soc. Tech., 1978, D Engring. Erik Johnson Found., 1980, 81, Fulbright Commn., 1980-81. Mem. Swedish Inst. Indsl. Engrs. (v.p. 1983, pres. 1984-86), Swedish Prodn. and Inventory Control Soc., Internat. Soc. Inventory Research, The Internat. Cim Soc. Office: Linköping Inst Tech, Dept Prodn Econ, S-58183 Linköping Sweden

OLIENSIS, SHELDON, lawyer; b. Phila., Mar. 19, 1922. A.B. with honors, U. Pa., 1943; LL.B. magna cum laude, Harvard U., 1948. Bar: N.Y. State bar 1949. Partner Kaye Scholer Fierman Hays & Handler, N.Y.C., 1960—. Pres.: Harvard Law Rev., 1948. Trustee Harvard Law Sch. Assn., 1973-77, 1st v.p., 1980-82, pres., 1982-84; trustee Harvard Law Sch. Assn. N.Y.C., 1962-65, v.p., 1972-73, pres., 1978-79; nat. chmn. Harvard Law Sch. Fund, 1973-75; mem. Harvard overseers com. to visit law sch., 1981-87; spl. master appellate div. 1st dept. N.Y. State Supreme Ct., 1983—; bd. dirs. Legal Aid Soc., 1969—, pres., 1973-75; vice-chmn. N.Y.C. Cultural Council, 1968-75; bd. dirs. Cultural Council Found., 1968-88, pres., 1968-72, v.p., 1972-82; bd. dirs. Park Assn. N.Y.C., Inc., 1963-73, exec. com., 1967-73, pres., 1965-67; bd. dirs. Gateway Sch., N.Y.C., 1968-83, chmn. bd. trustees, 1968-70; dir., officer Wiltwyck Sch. for Boys, Inc., 1951-71; bd. dirs. East Harlem Tutorial Program, 1972-80, Fund for Modern Cts., 1979—, N.Y. Laywers for Pub. Interest, 1980-85; bd. dirs. Vols. of Legal Service Inc., 1984—, pres., 1984-87. Fellow Am. Coll. Trial Lawyers, Am. Bar Found.; mem. Lawyers' Com. Civil Rights Under Law, ABA, N.Y. State Bar Assn., N.Y. County Lawyers Assn., Assn. of Bar of City of N.Y. (exec. com. 1961-65, v.p. 1974-75, 86-87, chmn. com. state legis. 1959-61, pres. 1988—, com. revision of constn. and by-laws 1965-66, com. electric power and environ. 1971-74, com. on grievances 1975-78, com. on access to legal services 1982-87 , com. on fee disputes and conciliation, 1987—, mem. com. on grievances 1966-69, com. judiciary 1969-71, environ. report 1972, ad hoc com. lawyer advt. 1977-78). Office: Kaye Scholer Fierman Hays & Handler 425 Park Ave New York NY 10022

OLIPHANT, CHARLES ROMIG, physician; b. Waukegan, Ill., Sept. 10, 1917; s. Charles L. and Mary (Goss) R.; student St. Louis U., 1936-40; M.D., 1943; postgrad. Naval Med. Sch., 1946; m. Claire E. Canavan, Nov. 7, 1942; children: James R., Cathy Rose, Mary G., William D. Intern, Nat. Naval Med. Ctr., Bethesda, Md., 1943; pvt. practice medicine and surgery, San Diego, 1947—; pres., chief exec. officer Midway Med. Enterprises; former chief staff Balboa Hosp., Doctors Hosp., Cabrillo Med. Ctr.; chief staff emeritus Sharp Cabrillo Hosp.; mem. staff Mercy Hosp., Children's Hosp., Paradise Valley Hosp., Sharp Meml. Hosp.; sec. Sharp Sr. Health Care, S.D.; mem. exec. bd., past. comdr. San Diego Power Squadron. Charter mem. Am. Bd. Family Practice. Served with M.C., USN, 1943-47. Fellow Am. Geriatrics Soc., Am. Acad. Family Practice, Am. Assn. Abdominal Surgeons; mem. AMA, Calif. Med. Assn., Am. Acad. Family Physicians (past pres. San Diego chpt., del. Calif. chpt.), San Diego Med. Soc., Public Health League, Navy League, San Diego Power Squadron (past comdr.), SAR. Clubs: San Diego Yacht, Cameron Highlanders. Home: 4310 Trias San Diego CA 92103

OLIPHANT, ERNIE L., safety educator, public relations executive, consultant; b. Richmond, Ind., Oct. 25, 1934; d. Ernest E. and Beulah A. (Jones) Reid; m. George B. Oliphant, Sept. 25, 1955; children—David, Wendell, Rebecca. Student, Earlham Coll., 1953-55, Ariz. State U., 1974, Phoenix Coll., 1974-78. Planner, organizer, moderator confs., programs for various women's clubs, safety assns., 1971-86; nat. field coordinator Operation Lifesaver, Inc., 1986—; assoc. dir. Operation Lifesaver Nat. Safety Council, Phoenix, 1978-86; cons. Fed. R.R. Adminstrn.; lectr. in field.; adviser Am. Ry. Engring. Assn., Calif. Assn. Women Hwy. Safety Leaders, numerous others. Mem. R.R./Hwy. grade crossing com. Ariz. Corp. Commn.; mem. transp. and system com. Ariz. Gov.'s Commn. on Environment; mem. Ariz. Gov.'s Council Women for Hwy. Safety; mem. motor vehicle traffic safety at hwy.-r.r. grade crossings com., roadway environment com., women's div. com. Nat. Safety Council; mem. Phoenix Traffic Accident Reduction Program; task force mem. U.S. Dept. Transp. on Grade Crossing Safety. Recipient Safety award SW Safety Congress, 1973; citation of Merit Adv. Commn. on Ariz. Environment, 1974; Gov.'s award for hwy. safety, 1978; Gov.'s Merit of Recognition Outstanding Service in Hwy. Safety, 1980. Mem. Assn. R.R. Editors, Nat. Assn. Female Execs., Inc., Pub. Relations Soc. Am., R.R. Pub. Relations Assn., committees Nat. Acad. Scis. (dir. transp. research, planning, adminstrn. of transp. safety com., r.r.-hwy. grade crossing safety com.), Women's Transp. Seminar, Ariz. Fedn. Women's Clubs (named pres. of yr. 1968), Ariz. Safety Assn. (safety recognition award 1975), Gen. Fedn. Women's Clubs (internat. bd. dirs.), Nat. Assn. Women Hwy. Safety Leaders, Phi Theta Kappa. Republican. Quaker. Author of tech. publs.

OLIVEIRA, HELENA SILVA DE, language educator; b. Rio de Janeiro, July 7, 1915; d. Alfredo Egydio and Carolina (Silva) O. B.A. in Elem. Teaching, Escola de Prof., Rio de Janeiro, 1936; Lic., U. Brazil, 1940; M.A., Vanderbilt U., 1947. Coordinator, County Sch., Rio de Janeiro, 1942-45; head English Lang. dept. Instituto Educacao, Rio de Janeiro, 1948-64; head dept. English Coll. FEUDUC, Caxias, Rio de Janeiro, 1971-74; chmn. scholarship dept. IBEU, Rio de Janeiro, 1971-74; head, chmn. dept. language Uni-Granrio, Caxias, Rio de Janeiro, 1974-86. Mem. MLA, Tchrs. English as Second Lang., Internat. Assn. Tchrs. English as Second Lang., Internat. Assn. Tchrs. English as Fgn. Lang., Assn. Brazil Edn., Assn. Brazil Profs. U. English, Soc. Brazil Cultural English. Office: AFE-Faculdades Uni-Granrio, R Marques Herval 1160 Duque, 1160 Duque De Caxias, Rio de Janeiro Brazil

OLIVEIRA-LIMA, TOMAS DE AQUINO, educational administrator; b. Santo Tirso, Portugal, Mar. 28, 1925; s. Tomas and Ana Andre (Sousa) O.; m. Maria Lisette Belchior, Jan. 28, 1978. Theology M., San Anselmo U., Rome, 1953; Philosophy M., Faculty of Letters, Oporto, Portugal, 1973, Pedagogy Bach., 1969. Tchr. philosophy Benedictine Sem., Singeverga, Santo Tirso, 1953-59; dir. Colé gio de Lamego, 1959-65; faculty philosophy Superior Inst. Human Sci., Oporto, 1966-72, Engring. Inst., Oporto, 1973-75; tutor Pires Lima Sch., Oporto, 1974, Leonardo Coimbra Sch., Oporto, 1975, Bartolomeu Sch., Viana do Castelo, 1976; pedagogic mgr. Escola Preparatoria, Senhora da Hora, Portugal, 1982—. Roman Catholic. Home: Rua S Joao de Brito 38-2d, 4100 Oporto Portugal

OLIVER, BONNIE BONDURANT, educational telecommunications company executive, consultant; b. St. Louis, Jan. 25, 1933; d. Benjamin Burns and Florence Mary (Spencer) Bondurant; m. Donald Edgar Wiese, June 19, 1954 (div. 1972); children: Kurt Rowland, Martha Jill Wiese Reid; m. Raymond Elliott Oliver, Dec. 8, 1972. BA, Monmouth Coll., Ill., 1954; MA, U. Mo., 1957; postgrad. U. Calif., Irvine, 1963-65. Lic. tchr., Calif.; lic. in ednl. adminstrn. Sci. TV tchr. Santa Ana Schs., Calif., 1966-70; dir. dist. media Santa Ana Unified Schs., 1970-72; adminstr. Regional Ednl. TV, Downey, Calif., 1973-78; mgr. edn. tech. unit Calif. Dept. Edn., Sacramento, 1978-81; dep. dir. Calif. Pub. Broadcasting Commn., Sacramento, 1981-83; pres. Oliver and Co., Los Angeles, 1983—; project dir. Sta. KCET-TV, Los Angeles; dir. Pub. Service Satellite Consort, Washington; cons. Calif. Dept. Edn., Sacramento, Ky. Ednl. TV, Lexington; mem. Los Angeles County, Los Angeles Pub. Library Adult Reading Project Coucnil. Recipient Achievement Commendation City of Los Angeles, 1987. Contbr. articles to popular mags. Mem. friends com. Orange Commn. on Status of Women, Santa Ana, 1976, Los Angeles Southwest Coll. Literacy Council, Friends com. Coro Found.; chmn. adv. com. Internat. Childrens TV, Washington, 1979; trustee Stanford Home for Children, Sacramento, 1980-84. C-Span Cable Network fellow, Washington, 1980; recipient Susan B. Anthony Communications award Hollywood chpt. Bus. and Profl. Women, 1987. Mem. Acad. TV Arts and Sci., Calif. Media Library Edn. Assn., Am. Mgmt. Assn., Kappa Kappa Gamma Alunae Assn. Republican. Avocation: running. Home: 1005 Dodson Ave San Pedro CA 90732 Office: KCET 4401 Sunset Blvd Los Angeles CA 90027

OLIVER, CLIFTON, JR., management educator; b. Amarillo, Tex., Dec. 3, 1915; s. Clifton and Laura Pearl (Hudson) O.; B.A., Tex. Tech U., 1935, M.A., 1936; postgrad. La. State U., 1937-38, U. Wis., 1938-39. Prof. mgmt. Tex. Christian U., Ft. Worth, 1939-43; prof. U. Fla., Gainesville, 1946-85, dir. Mgmt. Center, 1959-71; cons. in field. Served to lt., AUS, 1943-46. Recipient service award U. Fla. Athletic Assn., 1977, CADE award for service to track; elected to Fla. Track and Field Hall of Fame, 1979; track and field ofcl. 1984 Olympic Games; named hon. life mem. Fla. Sheriffs Boys Ranch and Assn. Mem. Acad. Mgmt., Am. Personnel Assn., Am. Soc. Tng. Dirs., Nat. Panel Am. Arbitration Assn., Mgmt. Assn. Gainesville (pres. 1969-86), Nat. Police Assn., Fla. Purchasing Assn. (life), Fla. Blue Key, Alpha Kappa Psi (Service award 1968), Alpha Tau Omega (trustee, Service award 1971), Alpha Chi, Pi Sigma Alpha, Pi Gamma Mu. Lodges: Elks, Kiwanis. Home: 1144 Northwood Lake Northport AL 35476

OLIVER, DALE HUGH, lawyer; b. Lansing, Mich., June 26, 1947; s. Alvin Earl and Jean Elizabeth (Stanton) O.; m. Mylbra Ann Chorney, Aug. 16, 1969; children—Nathan Corey, John Franklin. B.A., Mich. State U., 1969; J.D. cum laude, Harvard U., 1972. Bar: D.C. 1973, U.S. Dist. Ct. (D.C. dist.) 1973, U.S. Ct. Claims 1983, U.S. Ct. Appeals (D.C. cir.) 1976, U.S. Ct. Appeals (fed. cir.) 1983, U.S. Supreme Ct. 1980. Assoc., ptnr. Jones, Day, Reavis & Pogue, Washington, 1975-79; ptnr. Crowell & Moring, Washington, 1979-84; ptnr. Gibson, Dunn & Crutcher, Washington, 1984-87; ptnr. Jones, Day, Reavis & Pogue, Washington, 1987—. Contbr. articles to profl. jours. Editor jour. Pub. Contracts Law, 1980—. Spl. counsel 1980 Presdl. Inaugeral Com., Washington, 1980. Served to capt. USAF, 1973-75. Mem. ABA (com. chmn. pub. contract section 1979—), Nat. Contract Mgmt. Assn., Nat. Security Indsl. Assn., Harvard Law Sch. Assn. Club: Mich. State U. Alumni of Washington (pres., dir. 1984—). Home: 8403 Honeywood Ct McLean VA 22102 Office: Jones Day Reavis & Pogue 1450 G St NW Suite 600 Washington DC 20005

OLIVER, HAROLD HUNTER, theologian, educator; b. Mobile, Ala., Oct. 9, 1930; s. Alonzo E. and Amelee (Dunaway) O.; A.B., Samford U., 1951; B.D., So. Bapt. Theol. Sem., 1954; Th.M. Princeton Theol. Sem., 1955; Ph.D., Emory U., 1961; m. Martha Ann Maddox, Aug. 12, 1951, 1 dau., Daphne Ann. Instr., Southeastern Bapt. Theol. Sem., Wake Forest, N.C., 1957-61, asst. prof., 1961-62, asso. prof., 1962-65; assoc. prof. Boston U., 1965-70, prof. of philos. theology, 1970—, acting assoc. dean, 1984, dir. advanced professional studies, 1985—; vis. fellow Inst. Theoretical Astronomy, Cambridge U., 1971-72; Chavanne vis. prof. religious studies Rice U., Houston, 1980-81. Nat. panelist Nat. Endowment for Humanities. A.T.S. faculty fellow, 1963-64; Danforth postdoctoral fellow, 1971-72. Fellow Royal Astron. Soc. (London); mem. Am. Acad. Religion, Am. Theol. Soc., Am. Philos. Assn., Metaphys. Soc. Am., Internat. Soc. Metaphysics Soc. Values in Higher Edn. Author: A Relational Metaphysic, 1981; Relatedness: Essays in Metaphysics and Theology, 1984; mem. editorial adv. bd. ZYGON: Jour. of Religion and Sci.; bd. editorial cons. The Personalist Forum; contbr. articles to profl. jours. Home: 7 Marshall Rd Winchester MA 01890 Office: Boston U 745 Commonwealth Ave Boston MA 02215

OLIVER, JOYCE ANNE, journalist, editorial consultant; b. Coral Gables, Fla., Sept. 19, 1958; d. John Joseph and Rosalie Cecile (Mack) O. BA in Communications, Calif. State U., Fullerton, 1980, postgrad. sch. mgmt., 1988. Corp. editor Norris Industries Inc., Huntington Beach, Calif., 1979-82; pres. J.A. Oliver Assocs., La Habra Heights, Calif., 1982—; corp. editorial cons. ALS Corp., Anaheim, Calif., 1985, Gen. Power Systems, Anaheim, 1985, MacroMarketing, Costa Mesa, Calif., 1985-86, PM Software, Huntington Beach, Calif., 1985-86, CompuQuote, Canoga Park, Calif., 1985-86, Nat. Semicondr. Can. Ltd., Mississauga, Ont., Can., 1986, Frame Inc., Fullerton, Calif., 1987-88, The Johnson-Layton Co., Los Angeles, 1988, Corp. Research Inc., Chgo., 1988; mem. Research Council of Scripps Clinic and Research Found., 1987-88. Contbr. to Cleve. Inst. Electronics publ. The Electron, 1986-88; contbg. editor Computer Dealer mag., 1987-88; also contbr. to Can. Electronics Engring. Mag., PC Week, The NOMDA Spokesman, Electronic Servicing, Adminstrv. Mgmt., High-Tech Selling, Video Systems, Tech. Photography, Computing Canada, Stores. Mem. Internat. Platform Assn., IEEE, Soc. Photo-Optical Instrumentation Engrs., Inst. Mgmt. Scis., Nat. Writers Club (profl.), Sigma Delta Chi/Soc. Profl. Journalists. Republican. Roman Catholic. Office: 2045 Fullerton Rd La Habra Heights CA 90631

OLIVER, ROLAND ANTHONY, educator; b. Srinagar, Kashmir, Mar. 30, 1923; s. D.G. and Lorimer Janet (Donaldson) O.; m. Caroline Florence, 1947 (dec. 1983); 1 dau. Student, King's Coll., Cambridge U. Attached to Fgn. Office, 1942-45; R.J. Smith research studentship King's Coll., Cambridge, 1946-48; lectr. Sch. Oriental and African Studies, 1948-58; reader in African history U. London, 1958-63, prof., 1963-86; Franqui prof. U. Brussels, 1961; vis. prof. Northwestern U., 1962, Harvard U., 1967; organizer internat. confs. African history and archaeology, 1953-61. Author: The Missionary Factor in East Africa, 1952; Sir Harry Johnston and the Scramble for Africa, 1957; editor: The Dawn of African History, 1961; A Short History of Africa (with D. Fage), 1962; A History of East Africa (with Gervase Mathew), 1963; Africa since 1800 (with A.E. Atmore) The Jour. African History, 1960-73; (with B.M. Fagan) Africa in the Iron Age, 1975; (with A.E. Atmore) The African Middle Ages, 1981; gen. editor (with J.D. Fage) Cambridge History of Africa, 8 vols., 1975-86. Recipient Haile Sellassie prize trust award, 1966. Mem. African Studies Assn. (pres. 1967-68), Brit. Inst. Eastern Africa, Royal African Soc. (council mem.), Academie Royale des Sciences d'Outreme. Address: care Friesham Woodhouse, Newbury, Berkshire RG16 9XB, England *

OLIVER, STEVEN WILES, banker; b. Los Angeles, May 27, 1947; s. Frank Wiles and Hazel Gloria (Patton) O.; m. Susan Elizabeth Peace, Nov. 27, 1971; children: Andrew Wells, Elizabeth Patton, Laura Rice. AB cum laude, Claremont Men's Coll., 1969; JD, Vanderbilt U., 1972. From asst. mgr. to v.p. Citibank, N.A., s.e. Asia, 1972-80; mng. dir. Lazard Asia Ltd., Hong Kong, 1980-88; also bd. dirs. Lazard Asia Asset Mgmt. Ltd., Hong Kong; mng. dir. Lazard Freres & Co. Ltd., London, 1988—; ptnr. Lazard Frères & Co., N.Y.C., 1988—. Mem. Community Chest Employee Contbn., Hong Kong, 1986-87, Community Chest Corp. Contbn., Hong Kong, 1987—. Presbyterian. Clubs: Hong Kong Country; Penang (Malaysia); Leland Country (Mich.). Office: Lazard Frères & Co Ltd, 21 Moorfields, Conpon EC2P 2HT, England

OLIVER, TIMOTHY LOUIS HENRY, civil engineer; b. Dartford, Eng., Jan. 27, 1955; arrived in Malaysia, 1987; s. Harry L. and Eileen Marie (Le Gras) O.; m. Julie Ormerod, Jan. 22, 1977; children: James John, Thomas Henry, Stephen Andrew. BS (hon.), U. Leeds, Eng., 1976. Chartered civil engr. Design engr. Sir Alexander Gibb and Ptnrs., Reading, Eng., 1976-79, Nairobi, Kenya, 1979-80; dep. resident engr. Nairobi, 1980-82; area civil engr. Netlon Ltd, Worcestershire, Eng., 1982-84; pavement applications mgr. Netlon Ltd, Eng., 1984-87; area mgr. Kuala Lumpur, Malaysia, 1987—. Mem. Inst. Civil Engrs., Inst. Highways and Transp. Office: Netlon Ltd, 6th Floor Block G, Pusat Bandar Damansara, Jalan Damansara, 50490 Kuala Lumpur Malaysia

OLIVER LEAHY TINEN KAEHLER, JEANNETTE See LEAHY, JEANNETTE

OLIVER, JEAN CLAUDE (HENRI GERARD), physician; b. Marseille, Bouches du Rhône, France, Jan. 15, 1936; s. Louis Jean Gérard and Louise Micheline (Borgna) O.; m. Micheline Mauricette Michaud, June 25, 1964; children: Agnès, Philippe. MD, U. Marseille, 1962. Pvt. practice medicine Marseille, 1962—; ear, nose, and throat specialist functional testing inotology and otoneurology 1968—; cons. various hosps. Marseille, 1965; chargé de cours U. Marseille, 1980. Author: Mesures d'impédance en Audiometrie, 1971, 2d rev. edit. 1978; co-author: La prothèse auditive Encyclopéie d'Orl, 1983, Manuel de Diagnostic Neurotologique Coll. Fran230ais; contbr. articles tp profl. jours. Mem. Soc. Française d'Orl, Coll. Française d'Orl, Soc. Belge d'Orl, Internat. Soc. Audiology. Roman Catholic. Office: Med Office, 438 rue Paradis, 13008 Marseille, Bouches du Rhone France

OLIVIER, SIR LAURENCE KERR, actor, director; b. Dorking, Surrey, Eng., May 22, 1907; s. Gerard Kerr and Agnes Louise (Crookenden) O.; m. Jill Esmond, 1930 (div. 1940); 1 son, Simon Tarquin; m. Vivien Leigh, Aug. 30, 1940 (div. 1960); m. Joan Plowright, Mar. 17, 1960; children: Richard Kerr, Tamsin Agnes Margaret, Julie Kate. Student, St. Edward's Sch., Oxford, Eng.; MA (hon.), Tufts Coll., 1946; DLitt (hon.), Oxford U., U. Manchester, 1968, U. London, 1968, U. Sussex, 1978; LLD (hon.), Edinburgh U. Actor Birmingham Repertory Co., 1925-28, Old Vic Theatre Co., 1937-38, 44-46, 49; founder New Vic Theatre Co., 1944; toured Australia and N. Z., 1948; mgr., actor St. James' Theatre, 1950-51; producer, actor Festival of Britain, 1951-54; actor Shakespeare Meml. Theatre, 1955; 1st dir. Chichester Festival Theatre, Nat. Theatre Gt. Brit., 1963-73. Stage appearances include: Murder on the Second Floor; dir., actor King Lear, 1946; dir. Skin of Our Teeth, 1946; producer and dir. Born Yesterday, 1946; motion picture debut, 1930; films include: Murder for Sale, 1930, The Yellow Ticket, 1931, Friends and Lovers, 1931, Westward Passage, 1932, Perfect Understanding, 1933, No Funny Business, 1934, I Stand Condemned, 1936, As You Like It, Fire Over England, 1937, Divorce of Lady X, 1938, Wuthering Heights, Clouds Over Europe, 1939, Rebecca, 21 Days Together, Pride and Prejudice, 1940, That Hamilton Woman, 1941, Demi-Paradise, 49th Parallel, The Invaders, 1942, Adventure for Two, Henry V, 1945, Carrie, The Magic Box, 1952, Beggar's Opera, Devil's Disciple, 1959, Spartacus, 1960, The Entertainer, 1960, Term of Trail, 1963, Bunny Lake is Missing, 1965, Othello, 1965, Khartoum, 1966, Shoes of the Fisherman, 1968, Oh, What a Lovely War, 1969, Dance of Death, David Copperfield, 1970, Three Sisters, 1970, Nicholas and Alexandria, 1971, Sleuth, 1972, Lady Caroline Lamb, 1972, Marathon Man, 1975, The Seven Percent Solution, 1976, A Bridge Too Far, 1977, The Betsy, 1978, The Boys from Brazil, 1978, A Little Romance, 1978, Dracula, 1978, Clash of the Titans, 1979, Inchon, 1979, The Jazz Singer, 1980, Wagner, 1982, The Bounty, 1984, Wild Geese II, 1984; dir., producer and actor Hamlet, 1947, Venus Observed, 1950; dir., actor: Richard III, 1954, The Prince and the Showgirl, 1956, John Gabriel Berkman, 1958; TV appearances include: The Power and the Glory, John Gabriel Borkman, 1959, The Moon and Sixpence, Long Day's Journey Into Night, 1972, The Merchant of Venice, 1973, Love Among the Ruins, 1974, Jesus of Nazareth, Cat on a Hot Tin Roof, Hindle Wakes, The Collection (Emmy award), 1976, Come Back Little Sheba, Daphne Laureola, Saturday Sunday Monday, 1977, Brideshead Revisited, Granada TV, 1979, A Voyage Around My Father, 1982, King Lear, 1983, The Ebony Tower, 1984, The Last Days of Pompeii, miniseries Peter the Great, 1986; appearances with Nat. Theatre include: Uncle Vanya, The Recruiting Officer, 1963, The Master Builder, 1964, Love for Love, 1966, Dance of Death, 1966, Othello, 1963, 66, Flea in Her Ear, 1967, Home and Beauty, 1969, Merchant of Venice, 1969, John Gabriel Borkman, The Power and the Glory, World at War, 1973, Love Among the Ruins, A Voyage Round My Father, 1982, King Lear, 1982. Author: (autobiography) Confessions of an Actor, 1983, On Acting, 1986. Served with Brit. Fleet Air Army, 1940-43. Created knight by King George VI, lord by Queen Elizabeth; decorated comdr. Order Dannebrog, Denmark, officer Legion of Honour, grand officer Ordine al Merito della Repubblica, Italy, Order of Yugoslav Flag with Gold Wreath, 1971, Order of Merit, 1981; recipient Oscar award for best actor, Motion Picture Acad., 1948; award for directing, producing and acting in Hamlet, Brit. Film Industry; Emmy award for the Moon and Sixpence, 1960, For Long Day's Journey Into Night, 1973; Danish Sonning prize, 1966; Gold medallion Swedish Acad. Lit.; hon. Oscar for lifelong contbn. to art of film, 1979. Clubs: Garrick; Green Room, Marylebone Cricket. Office: care LOP Ltd, 33-34 Chancery Ln, London WC2A 1EW, England *

OLIVIERI, JEAN MARIE, physician; b. Chgontier, France, Feb. 21, 1925; s. Docteur and Madeleine Sauvage (Desplanques) O.; m. Michelle Breuil Jarrige, July 2, 1950 (div. 1979); 1 child, Patricia; m. Elyett du Reau de la Gaignonnière, Jan. 20, 1979; children: Laetitia, Marie-Colomba. MD, Medicine Sch., Paris, 1952. Gen. practice medicine St. Martin du Bois, France, 1953—. Ao-author L'europe et le Solialisme, 1967. Assn. Des Tennis Express (Angers). Home: Les Laricios, Sainte Martin du Bois 49500 Segre, France

OLLEY, JOHN WILLIAM, clergyman, educator; b. Sydney, Australia, July 26, 1938; s. John Jeffrey George and Dorothy Elizabeth Ellen (Allison) O.; m. Elaine Waugh, Jan. 20, 1962; children: David John, Linda Christine, Catherine Louise. BSc with honors, U. Sydney, 1959; BD with honors, Bapt. Theol. Coll., Eastwood, Australia, 1965; M in Theology, Melbourne (Australia) Coll. Div., 1975. Ordained to ministry Bapt. Ch. Pastor Bapt. Chs., New South Wales, Australia, 1963-68; missionary Am. Bapt. Chs., Hong Kong, 1968-78; head O.T. Dept. Bapt. Theol. Coll. Western Australia, Bentley, 1978—, vice prin., 1984—; lectr. Chinese U. Hong Kong, 1968-78, chmn. dept. religion, 1974-77; mem. council Evangelical Alliance Western Australia, Perth, 1979—; lectr. Curtin U., Bentley, part-time, 1981—; pres. Bapt. Chs. Western Australia, 1982-83; alt. mem. Lausanne Com. for World Evangelization, Singapore, 1983. Author: Righteousness in Isaiah LXX, 1979, What on Earth?, 1982; contbr. articles to profl. jours. Mem. Soc. Bibl. Lit., Australia and New Zealand Soc. for Theol. studies (com. mem. Western Australia chpt. 1981—), Am. Schs. Oriental Research (profl.), Internat. Assn. Mission Studies. Office: Bapt Theol Coll Western Australia, Hayman Rd, 6102 Bentley Australia

OLLEY, ROBERT EDWARD, economist, educator; b. Vendun, Que., Can., Apr. 16, 1933; s. Edwin Henry and Elizabeth (Reed) O.; m. Shirley Ann Dahl, Jan. 19, 1957; children—Elizabeth Anne, George Steven, Susan Catherine, Maureen Carolyn. B.A., Carleton U., Can., 1960; M.A., Queen's U., Can., 1961, Ph.D. in Econs., 1969. Vis. asst. prof. Queen's U., Kingston, Ont., Can., 1967-68; asst. prof. econs. U. Sask., Saskatoon, Can., 1963-67, 68-69, assoc. prof., 1969-71, 73-75, prof., 1975—; econ. adviser Bell Can., Montreal, Que., 1971-73, 78-79, Can. Telecommunications Carriers Assn., 1978-85, Sask. Power Corp., 1980-83; econ. adviser AT&T, 1980—; dir. research Royal Commn. on Consumer Problems and Inflation, 1967-68. Author, editor: Consumer Product Testing, 1979; Consumer Product Testing II, 1981; Consumer Credit in Canada, 1966; Economics of the Public Firm: Regulation, Rates, Costs, Productivity Analysis, 1983, Total Factor Productivity of Canadian Telecommunications, 1984. Bd. dirs. Can. Found. for Econ. Edn., 1974-82, Can. Gen. Standards Bd., 1977-81. Recipient Silver Jubilee medal, 1977. Mem. Royal Econ. History Soc., Royal Econs. Assn., Econ. History Assn., Am. Econ. Assn., Can. Econ. Assn., Consumers Assn. Can. (v.p. 1967-76), Can. Standards Assn. (dir., mem. exec. com. 1971—, vice chmn. 1985-87, chmn. 1987—). Home: 824 Saskatchewan Crescent E, Saskatoon, SK Canada S7N 0L3

OLLOR, WALTER GBUTE, economist; b. Eleme, Rivers, Nigeria, Dec. 20, 1950; s. Jonah Ollor and Cecilia Lale (Ngesia) Ollornta; m. Helen Yorowa Osarollor, Jan. 3, 1978; children: Nyimeawia, Ntefomi, Nkaatoaan. BSc, U. Ife, 1975; PhD, Iowa State U., 1980. Research asst. Iowa State U., Ames, 1977-80; lectr. U. Port Harcurt, Nigeria, 1980-85, sr. lectr., 1985—; cons. Econometric and Acctg. Assocs., Port Harcourt, 1980—; chmn. bd. dirs. Internat. Mcht. Bank, Lagos, Nigeria. Sec. Acad. Staff Union of Univs., U. Port Harcourt, 1983-84; chmn. Eleme Devel. Union, 1986—. Mem. Am. Econ. Assn., Econometric Soc., Nigerian Econ. Soc. Clubs: Eleme Social (pres. 1984-85); The Rivers Soc. (Port Harcourt) (sec. gen. 1984-86). Office: Internat Merchant Bank, 1 Akin Adesola St, Victoria Island, Lagos Nigeria

OLMSTEAD, FRANCIS HENRY, JR., electronics industry executive; b. Corning, N.Y., June 21, 1938; s. Francis Henry and Josephine (Andolino) O.; B.S., Detroit U., 1960; M.S., Purdue U., 1962; postgrad. program for mgmt. devel. Harvard, 1976; m. Mary Helen Nelson, Sept. 2, 1961; children—Kathleen, Ann, John. Foreman, Corning Glass Works, 1962, sect. foreman, 1963-64, dept. foreman, 1965-66, prodn. supt., 1967-69, plant mgr., 1970-71, mgr. mktg., 1972-73, gen. sales and mktg. mgr., 1973-75, bus. mgr. lighting products, 1976-79, bus. mgr. TV products, 1979-80, v.p., gen. mgr. TV products, 1981—, gen. mgr. elec. products div., 1982-83 ; exec. v.p. N.Am. Philips Lighting Corp., Bloomfield, N.J., 1984-86; exec. v.p., gen. mgr., Somerset, N.J., 1986—; instr. bus. adminstrn. Elmira Coll., 1972-73; vis. lectr. Purdue U., 1973. Mem. exec. bd. Steuben area council Boy Scouts Am., 1975—, v.p. fin., 1977-79, pres. Steuben Area council, 1979-84, bd. dirs. N.E. region, 1984—, pres. N.J. Area, 1985—. Served to capt. U.S. Army, 1961-62. Recipient Silver Beaver award Boy Scouts Am., Disting. Alumni award Purdue U. Mem. ASME, Illuminating Engring. Soc., Nat. Assn. Elect. Distbrs., Corning C. of C., Krannert Sch. Alumni Assn. Purdue U. (pres.), Tau Beta Pi, Pi Tau Sigma. Republican. Roman Catholic. Club: Corning Country. Home: 23 Lockhaven Ln Bedminster NJ 07921 Office: N Am Philips Lighting Corp Phillips Sq Somerset NJ 08873-6800

OLNEY, PETER JAMES STEVEN, zoologist; b. Bournemouth, Eng., Feb. 7, 1931; s. James and Margaret (Stephen) O. BSc, U. Durham, 1958, diploma in Edn., 1959. Research biologist Wildfowl Trust, 1959-64; head of research Royal Soc. Protection of Birds, 1964-69; curator of birds Zool. Soc. London, 1969—, curator of birds & reptiles, 1982—; mem. Survival Service Commn., Glans, Switzerland, 1974—. Editor: International Zoo Yearbook, 1976—; author/editor: Birds of the Western Palearctic, 1977, 80, 83, 85; author: Paintings of Henry James, 1987, children's books; contbr. Encylopedia Britannica, 1980—. Mem. Adv. Com. on Birds, London, 1985—. Fellow Inst. Biology, London, Linnean Soc.; mem. Internat. Council Bird Preservation (chmn. 1982), Brit. Ornithologist's Union (v.p. 1985). Social Democrat. Home: 3 Dukes Ave, London N3 2DE, England Office: Zool Soc London, Regent's Park, London NW1 4RY, England

OLSCHKI, ALESSANDRO, publisher; b. Florence, Italy, Feb. 12, 1925; s. Aldo Manuzio and Rita (Roster) O.; m. Gigliola Serroni, Mar. 26, 1949 (dec. 1985); children—Daniele, Costanza; m. Lydia Boretti, Nov. 20, 1985. Student, Coll. Alla Querce, Florence. Asst. head Leo S. Olschki Publs., Florence, 1944-63, head, 1963—. Author: Underwater Spearfishing, 1962, 65. Italian underwater spearfishing champion, 1956, World Champion, 1957, 60; hom. mem. several underwater Italian groups. Mem. Acad. Underwater Scis., Underwater Tech. and Sci. Research Group (pres. 1986—). Avocations: underwater scientific research. Home: Via di S Piero in Palco n3, 501216 Florence Italy Office: Casa Editrice Leo S Olschki,, Viuzzo del Pozzetto,, 50126 Florence Italy

OLSDER, GEERT JAN, mathematics educator; b. Muntendam, Groningen, The Netherlands, Jan. 1, 1944; s. Foppo Jan and Christina Jantina (Meijering) O.; m. Elke Henderiëtta Toxopeus, June 21, 1969; children: Rena, Theda, Christina. BSc, U. Groningen, 1964, MSc cum laude, 1968, PhD cum laude, 1971. Researcher, educator U. Groningen, 1967-71, Twente U. Tech., Enschede, The Netherlands, 1971-81; postdoctoral fellow Stanford (Calif.) U., 1972-73; research assoc. Harvard U., Cambridge, 1979-80; mathematician Hollandse Signaalapparaten, Hengelo, The Netherlands, 1981-83; prof. math. Delft (The Netherlands) U. Tech., 1983—; cons. Nat. Aerospace Lab., Amsterdam, 1984—; vis. prof. U. So. Calif., Los Angeles, 1984, Northeast U. Tech., Shenyang, People's Republic of China, 1986. Coauthor: Dynamic Noncooperative Game Theory, 1982; contbr. 70 articles to profl. jours. Bd. dirs. Tubantia, Hengelo, 1980-83. Grantee ZWO, The Hague, The Netherlands, 1972, USAF, 1984, Ministry Edn. and Sci., The Hague, 1986. Mem. IEEE, Royal Dutch Inst. Engrs., Dutch Soc. Mathematicians, Internat. Fedn. Automatic Control (vice chmn. 1978-87). Office: Delft U Tech, PO Box 356, Delft 2600 AJ, The Netherlands

OLSEN, ALFRED JON, lawyer; b. Phoenix, Oct. 5, 1940; s. William Hans and Vera (Bearden) O.; m. Susan K. Smith, Apr. 15, 1979. B.A. in History, U. Ariz., 1962; M.S. in Acctg, Ariz. State U., 1964; J.D., Northwestern U., 1966. Bar: Ariz. 1966, Ill. 1966; C.P.A., Ariz., Ill. cert. tax specialist. Acct. Arthur Young & Co., C.P.A.s, Chgo., 1966-68; dir. firm Ehmann, Olsen & Lane (P.C.), Phoenix, 1969-76; dir. Streich, Lang, Weeks & Cardon (P.C.), Phoenix, 1977-78; v.p. Olsen-Smith, Ltd., Phoenix, 1978—. Bd. editors: Jour. Agrl. Law and Taxation, 1978—, Practical Real Estate Lawyer, 1983—. Mem. Phoenix adv. bd. Salvation Army., 1973-81. Fellow Am. Coll. Probate Counsel, Am. Coll. Tax Counsel; Mem. Central Ariz. Estate Planning Council (pres. 1972-73), State Bar Ariz. (chmn. tax sect. 1977-78), ABA (chmn. com. on agr., sect. taxation 1976-78, chmn. CLE com. sect. taxation 1982-84), Am. Law Inst. (chmn. tax planning for agr. 1973—), Nat. Cattlemen's Assn. (tax com. 1979-88), Internat. Acad. Estate and Trust Law (academician), Sigma Nu Internat. (pres. 1986-88). Office: 3300 Liberty Bank Plaza 301 E Virginia Ave Phoenix AZ 85004

OLSEN, ARTHUR ROBERT, economist, educator, author; b. Bklyn., Dec. 1, 1910; s. Martin and Clara Anita (Hansen) O.; m. Helen Marie Fehleisen, June 25, 1938; 1 dau., Karen Marie Steadman. B.S., NYU, 1939, A.M., 1940, Ed D., 1942. Prin. Elwood Sch., L.I., N.Y., 1935-37; asst. prin., instr. No. Merrick Sch., L.I., 1937-43; instr. Pratt Inst., N.Y.C., 1943-44; statistician Rayonier Inc., N.Y.C., 1944-47; prof. Western Ill. U., 1947-70, now emeritus; disting. adj. prof. econs. Ariz. State U., 1981-82; economist, author Southwestern Publ. Co., Cin., 1957—; del. U.S. Nat. Commn. UNESCO, economist S.W. Mo. Council on Econ. Edn.; bd. dirs. Ill. Council Econ. Edn.; bd. dirs. Community Edn. project, Macomb, Ill., 1957-59; past dir. and moderator WKAI Round Table of the Air. Mem. Rep. Presdl. Task Force, 1982; v.p. Sun City Agrl. Club, 1982. Served with USNG, 1930-33. Recipient Alumnus of Yr. award SUNY, 1978; Vesterheim fellow Norwegian Am. Mus., 1987, Joint Council Econ. Edn. fellow, 1960. Mem. NEA (life), Am. Econ. Assn. (life), Ill. Council Social Studies (past pres.), Smithsonian Assocs., Nat. Geog. Soc., Phi Delta Kappa, Kappa Delta Pi, Omicron Delta Epsilon. Republican. Protestant. Clubs: N.Y.U., Sun City Country. Lodge: Masons (33d degree). Author: (with T.J. Hailstones), Economics, 10th edit., 1985; Economic Institutions, 1958; Readings on Marriage and Family Relations, 1953; Economics Transparancies, 1973; Beat the Market, 1973; contbr. articles to profl. jours. Home and Office: 9232 107th Ave Sun City AZ 85351

OLSEN, DONALD EMMANUEL, architect, educator; b. Mpls., July 23, 1919; s. Clarence Edward and Thea (Scharnell) O.; m. Helen Karen Ohlson, Apr. 2, 1944; 1 child, Alan Edward. B.Arch., U. Minn., 1942; M. Arch., Harvard U., 1946; postgrad. in civic design, U. Liverpool, Eng., 1953; postgrad. in philosophy of sci., London Sch. Econs., 1962-63, 68. Registered architect, Calif. Archtl. designer Saarinen, Swanson & Saarinen, Bloomfield Hills, Mich., 1946; project mgr. Skidmore, Owings & Merrill, San Francisco, 1948; designer, draughtsman Wurster, Bernardi & Emmons, San Francisco, 1949-51; pvt. practice architecture Berkeley, Calif., 1954—; prof. architecture U. Calif.-Berkeley, 1954—; guest prof. various univs., lectr. in field, U.S., Eng., Germany; nominator Carnegie Grant Personality Assessment and Research Creativity Study Architects, 1959; profl. adviser City of San Francisco, 1961-62; juror, critic, evaluator, various programs, projects. Contbr. articles, chpts. to profl. publs.; subject of numerous profl. publs. Numerous exhibits throughout U.S., Europe; prin. works include numerous design commns. Recipient awards, including nat. awards of Excellence Archtl. Record, Houses of 1966; scholar Harvard U., Cambridge, Mass., 1945-46; A. W. Wheelwright fellow Harvard U., 1953. Fellow AIA (2 nat. honor awards 1970, 7 various regional, local Honor, Excellence and Merit awards 1967-79); mem. Brit. Soc. for Philosophy of Sci., Soc. for Philosophy and Tech., Open Soc. and Its Friends. Home: 771 San Diego Rd Berkeley CA 94707 Office: Donald E Olsen & Assocs Architects 1349 Powell St Emeryville CA 94608

OLSEN, HENNING ARGYL, business economist, accountant; b. Copenhagen, Dec. 31, 1917; s. Christian A. and Anna (Clausen) O.; m. Apr. 2, 1942; children—Annette, Lise Lotte. Comml. Sci., Sch. Econs. and Bus. Adminstrn., Copenhagen, 1940. Registered acct. Bank clk. Koebmands Bank, Copenhagen, 1934-37; acct. Chartered Accts. O.K. Petersen-H.C. Clemmensen, Copenhagen, 1937-42; exec. com. mem. Lolland-Falster Revisionsselskab, Nykoebing F, 1942-46; supr. Zonen Ambulance and Fly Service, Copenhagen, 1946-48; owner H. Argyl Olsen, Nykoebing F, Denmark, 1947—; tchr. Tech. Sch., Nykoebing, 1948-73; dist. pres. Europe Movement in Denmark, Storstroms. Mem. Forening Af Registrerede Revisorer (dist. pres. 1970-81), Ler. Counsel of Liberal Profession (exec. com. 1975-81), Confederation Fiscale Europeenne (exec. com. Bonn, Fed. Republic Germany 1975-81), Danish Tax Advisors (exec. com. 1979), Dansk Skattevidenskabelig Forening, Danish Br. Internat. Fiscal Assn., Assn. Civilokonomer, Assn. Businessmen. Conservative. Club: Royal Yacht. Lodge: Danish Mason. Office: H A Olsen Cons, Kongensgade 6, DK-4800 Nykoebing F Denmark

OLSEN, JACK, writer; b. Indpls., June 7, 1925; s. Rudolph O. and Florence (Drecksage) O.; m. Su Peterson, 1966; children: John Robert, Susan Joyce, Jonathan Rhoades, Julia Crispin, Evan Pierce, Barrie Elizabeth, Emily Sara Peterson, Harper Alexander Peterson. Student, U. Pa., 1946-47. Newspaper reporter San Diego Union Tribune, 1947-48, San Diego Jour., 1949-50, Washington Daily News, 1950- 51; TV news editor and broadcaster sta. WMAL-TV, Washington, 1950-51; newspaper reporter New Orleans Item, 1952-53, Chgo. Sun-Times, 1954-55; corr. Time mag., 1956-58, Midwest chief, 1959-59; sr. editor Sports Illus. mag., 1960-70. Author: The Mad World of Bridge, 1960, (pseudonym Jonathan Rhoades) Over the Fence is Out, 1961, The Climb up to Hell, 1962, (with Charles Goren) Bridge Is My Game, 1965, Black is Best: The Riddle of Cassius Clay, 1967, The Black Athlete: A Shameful Story, 1968, Silence on Monte Sole, 1968, Night of the Grizzlies, 1969, The Bridge at Chappaquiddick, 1970, Aphrodite: Desperate Mission, 1970, Slaughter the Animals, Poison the Earth, 1971, The Girls in the Office, 1971, The Girls on the Campus, 1972, Sweet Street, 1973, The Man with the Candy, 1974, Alphabet Jackson, 1974, Massy's Game, 1976, The Secret of Fire Five, 1977, Night Watch, 1979, Missing Persons, 1981, Have You Seen My Son?, 1982, " Son" : A Psychopath and His Victims, 1983, Give a Boy a Gun, 1985, Cold Kill, 1987; work included in numerous anthologies. Served with OSS AUS, 1943-44. Recipient Page One award Chgo. Newspaper Guild; Nat. Headliners award; Wash. Gov.'s award; citations U. Ind., Columbia U.

OLSEN, JØRN, epidemiology educator; b. Odense, Denmark, May 20, 1946; s. Svend Aage and Irma (Lund) O.; m. Ulla Sig; children: Janne, Uffe, Ole. MD, U. Aarhus, Denmark, 1979, PhD, 1982. Prof. epidemiology U. Aarhus; mem. med. research council, Denmark, 1985, comac-Epid EEC, Belgium, 1986—, working party WHO/EEC, Belgium, 1988—. Editor Scand Social Medicine, 1984—; author books and numerous articles. Mem. IEA. Home: Kragelunds Alle 14, 8270 Hojbjerg Denmark Office: Inst Social Medicine, Hoegh-Guldbergsgade 8, 8000 Aarhus Denmark

OLSEN, KENNETH HARRY, manufacturing company executive; b. Bridgeport, Conn., Feb. 20, 1926; s. Oswald and Svea (Nordling) O.; m. Eeva-Liisa Aulikki Valve, Dec. 12, 1950. B.S. in Elec. Engring, MIT, 1950, M.S., 1952. Elec. engr. Lincoln Lab., MIT, 1950-57; founder Digital Equipment Corp., Maynard, Mass., 1957, now pres., dir.; dir. Polaroid Corp., Shawnut Corp., Ford Motor Co. Mem. Pres.'s Sci. Adv. Com., 1971-73; trustee, v.p. Joslin Diabetes Found.; mem. corp. Wentworth Inst., Boston, MIT, Cambridge; trustee Gordon Coll., Wenham, Mass. Served with USNR, 1944-46. Named Young Elec. Engr. of Year Eta Kappa Nu, 1960. Mem. Nat. Acad. Engring. Home: Weston Rd Lincoln MA 01773 Office: Digital Equipment Corp 111 Powdermill Rd Maynard MA 01754 *

OLSEN, NIELS-ERIK, accountant; b. Copenhagen, Dec. 15, 1948; s. Børge Thomas and Else Johanne (Andersen) O.; m. Debra Lynn Wagstaff, Dec. 23, 1983; 1 child, Anne Leigh. BS in Econs., Copenhagen Sch. Econ. and Bus. Adminstrn., 1972, MS in Econs., 1974. CPA, Calif.; authorized pub. acct., Denmark. Audit mgr. Coopers and Lybrand, CPA's, Copenhagen, 1974-80; audit supr. Coopers and Lybrand, CPA's, Los Angeles, 1980-83; asst. controller Ashton Tate, Inc., Los Angeles, 1983-84; ptnr. Real Estate Ptnrship, Copenhagen, 1984-85; corp. controller The East Asiatic Co., Ltd. A/S, Copenhagen, 1985—. Served to pvt. Danish Army, 1968-69. Mem. Danish Inst. State Authorized Pub. Accts. Office: The East Asiatic Co Ltd A/S, Holbersgade 2, DK-1099 Copenhagen Denmark

OLSEN, OLAF, archaeologist, museum director; b. Copenhagen, June 7, 1928; s. Albert and Agnete (Bing) O.; m. Jean Catherine Dennistoun Sword; 1 child, Morten; m. Rikke Agnete Clausen, May 21, 1971. Cand. mag., Copenhagen U., 1953, Dr. Phil., 1966. Asst. Nat. Mus. Copenhagen, 1950, asst. keeper, 1958-61, dir. mus., keeper nat. antiquities, 1981—; prof. medieval archaeology Aarhus U., Denmark, 1971-81; dir. Hielmsteirne-Rosencrone Found., 1980—; v.p. Det Kongelige Nordiske Oldskriftselskab, 1981—. Author: Horgr, hof and church, 1966; Five Viking Ships, 1969; Fyrkat, 1977. Contbr. articles to profl. jours. Recipient awards various Danish Founds. Fellow Soc. Antiquaries London (hon.); mem. Royal Danish Acad. Sci. and Letters (v.p.), Vetenskapssoc. i Lund (Sweden), Deutsche Archaeologische Institut. Office: Nat Mus, Prinsens Palae, Frederiksholms Kanal 12, DK1220 Copenhagen Denmark

OLSEN, ROBERT JOHN, savings and loan association executive; b. N.Y.C., July 8, 1928; s. Christian Marinius and Agnes Geraldine (Jensen) O.; B.S., Strayer Coll., Washington, 1956; m. Eleanor Marion Peters, June 19, 1981; 1 child, Philip John. Supervisory agt. Fed. Home Loan Bank Bd., N.Y.C., 1956-65; pres., dir. Keystone Savs. & Loan Assn., Asbury Park, N.J., 1965-82; chmn. bd., pres. Rapid Money Services, Inc., Deal, N.J., 1977-82; chmn. bd., pres. Elmora Savs. and Loan Assn., Elizabeth, N.J., 1982-88; pres. Ramsey (N.J.) Savs. and Loan Assn., 1988—, also bd. dirs.; pres. 2d Century Corp., Asbury Park, 1980-82; dir. Central Corp. of Savs. & Loans, Newark, 1976-82, Fed. Home Loan Bank N.Y., 1974-77. Councilman, Borough of Oceanport, N.J., 1971-73, 77-80, council pres., 1979; police commr. Oceanport, N.J., 1972-80; v.p. Econ. Devel. Corp., Asbury Park, N.J., 1972-81, Oceanport, N.J., 1974-77; mem. Zoning Bd. of Adjustment, Oceanport, 1969-70; mem. Citizens Adv. Council, Oceanport, 1975-76; dir. Monmouth and Ocean Devel. Council, Eatontown, N.J., 1974-82; trustee Savs. and Loan Found. of Washington, 1978-82; chmn. N.J. Electronic Funds Transfer Com., 1971-82; mem. Monmouth County Fair Housing Task Force, 1980-82, Monmouth County Vocat. Sch. Bd., 1981-83; pres. Paulinskill Lake Assn., 1987—. Served with USMC, 1946-48, 1950-56. Mem. N.J. Savs. League (pres. chpt. 1966-67), U.S. Savs. League (vice chmn. com. on internal ops., chmn. remote service unit com.), Nat. Assn. Review Appraisers and Mortgage Undewriters, Fin. Mgrs. Soc. (adv. council), Nat. Assn. Savs. and Loan Suprs., Nat. Soc. Fin. Examiners, Monmouth County, Eastern Union County Realtors Assn., Sussex County Realtors Assn., Internat. Union Bldg. Socs. and Savs. Assns., Navy League, Assn. U.S. Army. Clubs: World Trade (N.Y.C.); Channel (Monmouth Beach, N.J.); Provost Marshals Guild (Ft. Monmouth, N.J.); Wheelman's (Asbury Park, N.J.). Home: RD 6 Box 508 Newton NJ 07860 Office: 121 Broad St Elizabeth NJ 07201

OLSEN, SAMUEL RICHARD, JR., printing company executive; b. Hamilton, Ohio, May 1, 1938; s. Samuel Richard and Hazel Mildred (Berg) O.; Assoc. Applied Sci., Rochester Inst. Tech., 1961; children—Kristin, Erika, Samuel Richard III; m. Roberta Apa, June 1, 1974; children—Lonnie, Erik. Vice-pres. mfg. Datagraphic N.Y., Inc., Rochester, N.Y., 1965-68; pres., chief exec. officer Form Service, Inc., Schiller Park, Ill., 1968—; pres., chief exec. officer Dealers Press, Inc., Rosemont, Ill., 1973—, also dir; v.p., dir. Form Service West, Inc., Camarillo, Calif.; founder, chief exec. officer Bus. Form Service East, Inc., Balt., 1980, Omega Mgmt. Ltd., 1983—, Computer Preferred, Inc., 1984—, CFS, Inc., Balt., 1987—. Served with USMC, 1960-63. Recipient Voight award Graphic Arts Tech. Found., 1981; named Forms Profl. Yr. N.Am. Pub., 1986. Mem. Nat. Bus. Forms Assn. (officer, dir.), Forms Mfg. Credit Interchange (chmn. 1973-74), Printing Industries Am., Internat. Bus. Forms Industries, Nat. Assn. Printers and Lithographers. Home: 772 Halbert Ln Barrington IL 60010 Office: 9500 Ainslie St Schiller Park !L 60176

OLSEN, STEVEN KENT, dentist; b. Spanish Fork, Utah, Nov. 20, 1944; s. Earl Clarence and Adela (Faux) O.; m. Karin Hurst, Oct. 5, 1984. BS, Brigham Young U., 1969; DDS, U. Pacific, 1974. Ptnr., practice dentistry specializing in surg. and endodontic procedures Brooks & Olsen, Salt Lake City, 1974—; gen. practice dentistry Steven K. Olsen, D.D.S., San Francisco, 1974-75; pres. S.K. Olsen, P.C., San Francisco, 1975—; ptnr. Olsen, H. & P., San Francisco, 1977-83; instr. U. Pacific, San Francisco, 1978—; dir. Calif. Inst. for Continuing Edn., San Francisco, 1981—; chmn. bd. Am. Dentists Ins. Corp., Grand Cayman, W.I., 1978-81; instr. Stanford (Calif.) Inst., 1979-82; med. staff Latter-day Saints Hosp.; cons. Calif. Inst., San Francisco, 1981—; ptnr. John Berghoff Devel. Co.; ptnr. Russell Harris Restorations, Dale Westington Mgmt. Co., Dave Olsen & Co.; bd. dirs. Wilks & Topper, Inc., San Francisco. Author: Accolade, 1963, (play) Lancer Ballade, 1963, (acad. course) World Religions, 1979; editor corr. course Calif. Inst., 1981. Recipient Good Citizenship medal SAR, 1963. Mem. Assn. Coll. of Physicians and Surgeons, ADA, Calif. Dental Assn., Utah Dental Assn., Alpha Epsilon Delta. Club: Physicians and Surgeons (San Francisco). Home: 385 Old La Honda Rd Woodside CA 94062 Office: 1 Embarcadero Ctr 2205 San Francisco CA 94111

OL'SHANSKIY, NIKOLAY MIKHAYLOVICH, government official; b. USSR, 1939. Student, L'vov Poly. Inst., Cen. Com.'s Acad. for Social Scis. Dir. regenerator factory Ministry Chem. Rebuilding, Sumy, Ukraine, USSR; minister Ministry Mineral Fertilizer Industry, Moscow, 1986—. Office: Ministry Mineral Fertilizer, Industry, Moscow USSR *

OLSNES, ARILD, oil company executive; b. Dalewam, Norway, May 17, 1945; s. Helga (Jacobsen) O.; m. Signe Raundal, Sept. 27, 1969; children: Hanne, Kariann, Ole Jacob. MBA, Norwegian Sch. Econs. and Bus. Adminstrn., Bergen, 1970. Product sec. Bergensmeieriet, Bergen, 1971, export sec., 1972, export mgr., 1973-75, mktg. mgr., 1975-77; bus. mgr. Ghana Cement Works, Accra, Ghana, 1977-79; mng. dir. Ghana Cement Works, Accra, 1979-82; v.p. Norcem Anchor, Stavanger, Norway, 1982-84, pres., 1984—; bd. dirs. Anchor Drilling Fluids, Aberdeen, Scotland, Esbjerg, Denmark. Mem. Sola Sportsclub (chmn. 1987—). Office: AVER Drilling Fluids A/S, Plattformv 2-4, 4056 Tananger Norway

OLSON, BONNIE BRETERNITZ-WAGGONER (MRS. O. DONALD OLSON), civic worker; b. North Platte, Nebr., May 30, 1916; d. Floyd Emil and Edith (Waggoner) Breternitz; A.B., U. Chgo., 1947; m. O. Donald Olson, May 17, 1944; children—Pamela Lynne, Douglas Donald. Dep. clk. Dist. Ct., Lincoln County, Nebr., 1940-42; advt. researcher Burke & Assos., Chgo., 1942; contbg. newspaper columnist Chgo. Herald-Am., 1943; social worker A.R.C., Chgo., 1942-44, Sacramento, Calif., 1944, Amarillo, Tex., 1945; exec. sec. Econometrica, Cowles Commn. for Research in Econs., Chgo., 1945-47; interior designer, antique dealer. Col.; participant Chgo. Maternity Ctr. Fund Drive, 1953, Chgo. Council on Fgn. Relations, 1948-54; mem. Colo. Springs Community Council, 1956-58, chmn. children's div., 1956-58, mem. exec. bd., 1956-58, mem. budget com., 1957-58; mem. Colorado Springs Charter Assn., 1956-60, mem. exec. bd., 1957-59, sec., 1958; chmn. El Paso County PTA, Protective Services for Children, 1959-61; chmn. women's div. fund drive ARC, 1961; mem. League Women Voters, 1957—, mem. state children's law com., 1961-63; chmn. ad hoc com. El Paso County Citizens' Com. for Nat. Probation and Parole Survey, Juvenile Ct. Procedures and Detention, 1957-61; mem. children's adv. com. Colo. Child Welfare Dept., 1959-63, chmn., 1961; del. White House Conf. on Children and Youth, 1960, 70; sec. Citizens Ad Hoc Com. for Comprehensive Mental Health Clinic for Pikes Peak Region, 1966—; mem. Colorado Springs Human Relations Commn., 1968-71; sustaining mem. Symphony Guild, 1970-72, Fine Arts Ctr., 1957—; mem. Pikes Peak Mental Health Ctr., 1964-67 (bd. dirs.); Colo. observer White House Conf. on Aging, Colo. Gov.'s Conf. on Aging, 1981, Dist. Atty.'s Child Abuse Task Force, 1986. Recipient Lane Bryant Ann. Nat. Awards citation, 1971; alumni citation for pub. service U. Chgo., 1961. Mem. Am. Acad. Polit. and Social Sci., Nat. Trust Historic Preservation, Women's Ednl. Soc. Colo. Coll. (life), Council on Religion and Internat. Affairs. Episcopalian. Clubs: Quadranglar, University (Chgo.); Broadmoor Golf, Garden of the Gods (Colorado Springs). Home: 2110 Hercules Dr Colorado Springs CO 80906

OLSON, CARL ERIC, lawyer; b. Center Moriches, N.Y., May 19, 1914; s. August William and Sophie (Maiwald) O.; m. Ila Dudley Yeatts, May 31, 1945; children—Carl Eric, William Yeatts, Nancy Dudley. A.B., Union Coll., 1936; J.D., Yale, 1940. Bar: Conn. 1941, N.Y. 1947. Assoc. Clark, Hall & Peck, New Haven, 1940-41; assoc. Reid & Priest, N.Y.C., 1946-56, ptnr. 1956-80; sole practice, Palm Beach Gardens, Fla., 1981—. Served to maj. U.S. Army, 1941-45. Mem. ABA, N.Y. State Bar Assn., Assn. Bar City of N.Y., Inter-Am. Bar Assn., Internat. Bar Assn. Republican. Congregationalist. Clubs: Yale (N.Y.C.). Home and Office: 6 Surrey Rd Palm Beach Gardens FL 33418

OLSON, DENNIS OLIVER, lawyer; b. Seminole, Tex., Oct. 19, 1947; s. Edwin and Beulah Matilda (Strang) O.; m. Leonee Lynn Claud, Jan. 30, 1971; children—James Edwin, Stacy Rae. B.A. in English, U. Tex., 1969; J.D., Tex. Tech U., 1974. Bar: Tex. 1974, U.S. Ct. Mil. Appeals 1974, U.S. Dist. Ct. (no. dist.) Tex. 1978, U.S. Dist. Ct. (we. dist.) Tex. 1978, U.S. Ct. Appeals (5th cir.) 1984, U.S. Supreme Ct. 1985. Commd. U.S. Marine Corps, 1969, advanced through grades to capt., 1973; infantry officer various locations including Vietnam, 1969-74, judge advocate, various locations, 1974-78; resigned, 1978; assoc. Carr, Evans, Fouts & Hunt, and predecessor, Lubbock, Tex., 1978-81; ptnr., 1981-85; sole practice, Dallas, 1985—. Bd. dirs. Presbyterian. Ctr. Dr's Clinic, Lubbock, 1983-85, United Campus Ministry, Tex. Tech U., Lubbock, 1984-85; elder Churchill Way Presbyn. Ch., Dallas; treas. bd. dirs. Lubbock chpt. ARC, 1981-82, v.p., bd. dirs. Quantico (Va.) chpt. ARC, 1975-77; vol. Lubbock United Way, 1978-80. Decorated Bronze Star; named Outstanding Young Man of Am., 1983. Mem. Lubbock County Bar Assn. (bd. dirs. 1983-85), Tex. Young Lawyers Assn. (bd. dirs. 1981-83), Judge Advocates Assn. (bd. dirs. 1976-78), Tex. Assn. of Defense Counsel, ABA, Lubbock C. of C. (grad. Leadership Lubbock program 1981), Phi Delta Phi. Home: 407 Fall Creek Dr Richardson TX 75080

OLSON, DONALD GEORGE, computer services administrator; b. Minot, N.D., May 16, 1941; s. George James and Ellen (Ranta) O.; BME, U. N.D., 1963; MME, N.D. State U., 1968; 1 son, Todd B. Analyst, programmer Bur. Reclamation, Denver, 1963-66; asst. dir. computer center N.D. State U., Fargo, 1966-69; data processing mgr. U. Calif. Sci. Lab., Los Alamos, 1969-74; dir. data processing nat. assessment ednl. progress Edn. Commn. States, Denver, 1974-77; staff mgr. Mountain Bell, Denver, 1977-80; dir. computer services Mankato (Minn.) State U., 1980-86, assoc. v.p. computer services, 1986—; cons. in field. Mem. Mankato Area Execs. Assn. Registered profl. engr., certified data processor. Mem. AAAS, Assn. Computing Machinery, YMCA, Phi Delta Theta. Republican. Presbyterian. Club: Kiwanis. Home: 144 River Hills Park Mankato MN 56001 Office: Mankato State U Computer Services Box 45 Mankato MN 56001

OLSON, HAROLD ROY, manufacturing company executive; b. Escanaba, Mich., Apr. 8, 1928; s. Roy A. and Sara Calla Margarita (Carlson) O.; B.A. in Journalism and Advt., Mich. State U., 1950; m. Angela Davis Hennessy, Sept. 26, 1959. Mail clk. McCann Erickson Co., N.Y.C., 1950, 52-53; book promotion specialist, mgr. mag. promotion McGraw-Hill, N.Y.C., 1953-56; mgr. mag. promotion Reinhold Publishing Co., N.Y.C., 1956-58; space salesman McCall Corp., N.Y.C., 1959-60; pres. Visual Identity, Inc., N.Y.C., 1960-68; mktg. rep. Honeywell Info. Systems, Inc., N.Y.C., 1969-86; pres. Hal Olson's EDGE-BUY Express, Inc., 1986—. Served with U.S. Army, 1950-52. Republican. Episcopalian. Home: 12 Stony Point Rd Westport CT 06880 Office: 575 Broad St Bridgeport CT 06604

OLSON, JACK B., former ambassador, consultant; b. Kilbourn, Wis., Aug. 29, 1920; s. Grover and Jane (Zimmerman) O.; m. Eleanor Lang; children—Jill (Mrs. William Gaffney), Sally (Mrs. Alexander Brackett). Student, U. Wis., 1938-39; B.S., Western Mich. U., Kalamazoo, 1942. Pres. Olson Boat Co., Wisconsin Dells; dir. Bank Wisconsin Dells, Bur. Bus. Research, U. Hawaii, 1961; mem. Pres.'s Air Quality Control Adv. Bd., 1970—; U.S. ambassador to Bahamas, 1976-77; Pres. Wis. Vacationland Council, 1952-57; dir. Wis. Trade Mission Europe, 1964, ofcl. rep., 1965; exec. chmn. Wis. World's Fair Participation Corp., 1964-65; pres. No. Gt. Lakes Area Council, 1958, Greater Wis. Found., 1969; mem. Pres.'s Citizens Adv. Com. on Environ. Quality. Chmn. Wis. March of Dimes, 1965-66, Wis. Vols. for Nixon, 1963-64, lt. gov., Wis., 1963-64, 67-70, candidate for gov., 1970; bd. dirs. Wis. Good Roads Assn. Served to lt. (j.g.) USNR, 1942-46, ETO. Recipient Disting. Alumnus award Western Mich. U., 1964; Sports Illus. Silver Anniversary All Am. Football award, 1966. Mem. Am. Legion, VFW, Wisconsin Dells C. of C. (dir.), Western Mich. U. Alumni Assn. (dir.). Presbyn. Lodge: Rotary. Address: FC 23B Ocean Reef Club Key Largo FL 33037

OLSON, JAMES ROBERT, infosystems engineer; b. Columbus, Nebr., Nov. 23, 1940; s. Robert August and Jean Elizabeth Olson; 1 child, Eric Robert. Student, U.S. Naval Acad., 1962; BA, U. Nebr., 1965; MA, Cen. Mich. U.; diploma Nat. Def. U., 1981. Commd. ensign U.S. Navy, 1965, advanced through grades to comdr., 1980; service in Southwest Pacific, Philippines and Vietnam; designated Space Systems Ops. Subspecialist, 1982; ret., 1983; sr. systems engr. Gen. Electric Space Systems Div., Valley Forge, Pa., 1983—; mem. faculty Def. Intelligence Sch., 1970-71; mem. Naval Insp. Gen. Staff, 1982. Mem. Ry. and Locomotive Hist. Soc. (life), Am. Assn. Pvt. R.R. Car Owners (dir. S.E. region 1983-84), Colo. R.R. Hist. Found. (life), Gulf, Mobile and Ohio Hist. Soc., Am. Swedish Hist. Found., VASA Order of Am. Decorated Bronze Star with combat V, Air medal (5), Vietnam Service medal, Republic of Vietnam Cross of Gallantry, Def. Meritorious Service medal, numerous others. Mem. Naval Intelligence Profls., Nat. Rifle Assn. (life), Armed Forces Communications Electronics Assn., ASHRAE, Phi Alpha Theta. Methodist. Club: Army-Navy Country (Washington). Home: 1356 Nathan Hale Dr Phoenixville PA 19460 Office: GE Space Systems Div Valley Forge Space Ctr PO Box 8555 Philadelphia PA 19101

OLSON, JOHN FREDERICK, lawyer; b. Santa Monica, Calif., Dec. 24, 1939; s. Paul Frederick and Helen Elizabeth (Evans) O.; m. Elizabeth H. Callard, Feb. 22, 1966; children: Timothy Cooley, Peter Jacobus, Matthew Evans, Emily Merrell, Nicholas Porter. AB, U. Calif., Berkeley, 1961; LLB, Harvard U., 1964. Bar: Calif. 1965, U.S. Dist. Ct. (cen. dist.) Calif. 1965, D.C. 1977, U.S. Dist. Ct. (D.C.) 1977. Assoc. Gibson, Dunn & Crutcher, Los Angeles, 1964-71, ptnr., 1971—. Contbr. articles to profl. jours. Vestryman S. John's Ch., Lafayette Sq., Washington, 1981-86, chmn. Triennial Fund Drive, 1984; v.p. Combined Health Appeal Nat. Capital Area, Washington, 1985—; chmn. Lawyers Com. for Performing Arts, 1986—; mem. adv. com. to Senate Banking Com. on Insider Trading Legis., 1987—. Mem. ABA (chmn. task force regulation of insider trading 1983-87, chmn. subcom. civil liabilities and litigation 1985-87, com. on fgn. claims 1982-86, vice chmn. com. on fed. regulation securities 1987—), Fed. Bar Assn. (exec. council securities com. 1985—), D.C. Bar Assn. (gen. counsel 1983-85), Am. Coll. Investment Counsel (founding trustee 1981-85). Democrat. Episcopalian. Clubs: University, Fed. City (Washington). Home: 3719 Bradley Ln Chevy Chase MD 20815 Office: Gibson Dunn & Crutcher 1050 Connecticut Ave NW Suite 900 Washington DC 20036

OLSON, JOHN LEE, bottling company executive; b. Havre, Mont., Aug. 5, 1939; s. Everett William and Dorothy (Edwards) O.; m. Marilyn Louise Johnson, Apr. 17, 1966; children: Karen, J. Randall. BA, U. Mont., 1962. Tchr., coach Hysham (Mont.) Pub. Schs., 1962-64; sales rep. PepsiCo Inc., Purchase, N.Y., 1964-65; pres., owner Blue Rock Beverage Co., Sidney, Mont., 1978—, Blue Rock Products Co., Sidney, Mont., 1966—; chmn., bd. dirs. Admiral Beverage Corp., Worland, Wyo., 1970—; bd. dirs. MDU Resources Group, Inc., Bismarck, N.D., First United Bank, Sidney, Devel. Corp. Mont., Helena. Served to cpl. USMCR, 1957. Named one of Outstanding Young Men of Am. U.S. Jaycees, 1970. Mem. Pepsi-Cola Bottlers Assn. (pres. 1978-79), Sidney C. of C. (pres. 1971). Republican. Lutheran. Lodges: Elks, Moose, Kiwanis. Home: 530 5th St SE Sidney MT 59270 Office: Blue Rock Products Co PO Box 1708 Sidney MT 59270

OLSON, KENNETH BARRIE, physician, educator; b. Seattle, Jan. 21, 1908; s. Donald Barrie and Hattie (Palmer) O.; m. Emma Naomi Tallman, Apr. 3, 1937 (dec. Mar. 1986); children—Karen Barrie Mason, Kenneth Barrie Jr. B.S., U. Wash., 1929; M.D., Harvard U., 1933. Resident in pathology Boston City Hosp., 1933-34; intern in surgery Presbyn. Hosp., N.Y.C., 1934-36, asst. resident and resident surgery, 1936-39; clin. asst. in surgery Columbia U. Sch. Medicine, N.Y., 1939-40, Trudeau Sanatorium, N.Y., 1941; asst. physician, acting pathologist Olive View Sanatorium, Calif., 1941-43; dir. Tb Control and dir. Firland Sanatorium, Seattle, 1943-45; asst. physician Glenridge Sanatorium, Schenectady, 1947-50; from instr. to assoc. prof. Albany Med. Coll., Union U., N.Y., from 1950, prof. medicine and head div. oncology, until 1972, prof. emeritus, 1973—; chief diagnosis br. div. cancer biology and diagnosis Nat. Cancer Inst.; cons. Nat. Cancer Inst., Bethesda, Md., 1973-74, Fla. Cancer Council, Tampa, 1974-88, Halifax Hosp. Med. Ctr., Daytona Beach, Fla., 1974—; Contbr. articles to profl. jours., chpt. to book. Bd. dirs. Am. Cancer Soc., Daytona Beach, 1974-83. Recipient Faculty Research award Albany Med. Sch., 1967, Golden Apple award for teaching, 1958, 66; Kenneth B. Olson Cancer Teaching Day at Albany Med. Coll. named in his honor, 1986. Fellow ACP; mem. Am. Soc. Clin. Oncology (pres. 1971-72), Am. Assn. Cancer Edn. (chmn. 1958, Margaret Hay Edwards award 1987), Am. Assn. Cancer Research, Alpha Omega Alpha. Club: Smyrna Yacht. Current work: Chemotherapy of cancer; tumor markers. Subspecialties: Internal medicine, Chemotherapy, Blood Clotting.

OLSON, LAURA MAXINE, information scientist; b. Baker, Oreg., June 16, 1927; d. Arthur Vard and Retta Belle (Mercer) Olson; B.S., U. Oreg., 1949. Line-up editor True Detective mag., N.Y.C., 1949-50; promotion writer N.Y. Herald Tribune Snydicate, writer N.Y. Herald Tribune News service, 1950-52; counsellor for women U Oreg., 1952-53; news editor Cottage Grove (Oreg.) Sentinel, 1953-54; reporter, polit. writer Roseburg (Oreg.) News-Rev., 1954-56; research asst. to U.S. rep., 1957-60; press asst. to U.S. senator, 1961-62; asst. legis. asst. to U.S. senator, 1962-65, legis. asst., 1966-68; spl. cons. population problems U.S. Senate Govt. Ops. Subcom. on Fgn. Aid Expenditures, 1965-68; head info. office Nat. Endowment for Humanities, 1968-70; chief clearing house and info. sect., population div. UN Econ. and Social Commn. for Asia and Pacific, 1970-82, chmn. staff assn., 1971-73, co-editor staff bull., 1973-74, co-chmn. staff assn. welfare com., chmn. staff council souvenir com. 1977-79, advisor, 1980-81; mem. staff U.S. Congressman Jim Weaver, dist. office, Eugene, Oreg., 1983-86 . trustee Nat. Population Reference Bur., 1983—. Mem. Oreg. Democratic Central Com., chair state budget; bd. dirs. Wayne Morse Hist. Park Corp.; mem. steering com. Fgn. Student Friendship Found., U. Oreg. 1982-88; founding mem., sponsor, dir. Willamette World Affairs Council; mem. Vida-McKenzie Neighborhood Watch; mem. Oreg. Citizens Utility Bd., chair 1988; mem. Lane County Library Adv. Com., Lane County Rds. Adv. Com. Recipient plaque UN Econ. and Social Commn. for Asia and Pacific, 1982. Mem. Women in Communications, Fgn. Corrs. of Thailand, Satri Sakone, Women in Internat. Orgns. (founding), Common Cause, Walterville Grange, McKenzie River C. of C. (dir. 1986—, named woman yr. 1987), Delta Delta Delta. Democrat. Episcopalian. Clubs: Royal Bangkok Sports. Home: 45014 McKenzie Hwy Leaburg OR 97489

OLSON, MARIAN KATHERINE, federal agency administrator, publisher, information broker; b. Tulsa, Oct. 15, 1933; d. Sherwood Joseph and Katherine M. (Miller) Lahman; BA in Polit. Sci., U. Colo., 1954, MA in Elem. Edn., 1962; EdD in Ednl. Adminstrn., U. Tulsa, 1969; m. Ronald Keith Olson, Oct. 27, 1956. Tchr. public schs., Wyo., Colo., Mont., 1958-67; teaching fellow, adj. instr. edn. U. Tulsa, 1968-69; asst. prof. edn. Eastern Mont. State Coll., 1970; program assoc. research adminstrn. Mont. State U., 1970-75; on leave with Energy Policy Office of White House, then with Fed. Energy Adminstrn., 1973-74; with Dept. Energy, and predecessor, 1975—, program analyst, 1975-79, chief planning and environ. compliance br., 1979-83; regional dir. Region VIII Fed. Emergency Mgmt. Agy., 1987—; pres. Solar Sense of Colo., Bannack Pub. Co. Contbr. articles in field. Grantee Okla. Consortium Higher Edn., 1969, NIMH, 1974. Mem. Am. Soc. for Info. Sci., Am. Assn. Budget and Program Analysis, Women in Energy, Internat. Assn. Ind. Pubs., Kappa Delta Pi, Phi Alpha Theta, Kappa Alpha Theta. Republican. Home: 707 Poppy Dr Brighton CO 80601 Office: FEMA Denver Fed Ctr Bldg 710 PO Box 25267 Denver CO 80225-0267

OLSON, RICHARD DEAN, pharmacology educator; b. Rupert, Idaho, June 22, 1949; s. Emerson J. and Thelma Maxine (Short) O.; m. Carol Ann Dyba, Jan. 5, 1974; children: Stephan Jay, David Richard, Jonathan Philip. BS, Coll. Idaho, 1971; postgrad., Idaho State U., 1972-74; PhD, Vanderbilt U., 1978. Instr. Vanderbilt U., Nashville, 1980-81, asst. prof., 1982, head pediatric clin. pharmacology unit, 1982; asst. prof. U. S. Ala., Mobile, 1982-83; acting asst. prof. U. Wash., Seattle, 1984-85, research assoc. prof., 1985—; v.p. Olson, Wong and Walsh Labs., Inc., Lindenhurst, Ill., 1987—; chief cardiovascular pharmacology research VA Med. Ctr., Boise, Idaho, 1984—; hon. dir. cardiovascular research lab. Capital Inst. Medicine, Beijing, Peoples Republic of China, 1986; investigator Am. Heart Assn., Nashville, 1981, NIH, Mobile, 1982; bd. dirs. Idaho affiliate Am. Heart Assn. Contbr. articles to profl. jours. Pres. Fellowship Crusade for Christ, Inc., Nampa, Idaho, 1986. Grantee Am. Heart Assn., 1981, 83, 84, 86, 88, Am. Fedn. Aging Research, Inc., Boise, 1985; VA Merit Review grantee, 1985, 88; NIH trainee, 1975-78; NIH New Investigator 1982; fellow, Am. Fedn. Aging Research, Inc. 1985—, NIH U. Colo., Denver, 1978-80. Mem. AAAS, N.Y. Acad. Scis., Am. Soc. Pharmacology and Exptl. Therapeutics, Am. Heart Assn., Am. Fedn. for Clin. Research, Sigma Xi. Home: 425 N Benewah Nampa ID 83651 Office: VA Med Ctr #151 500 W Fort St Boise ID 83702

OLSON, ROY ARTHUR, government official; b. Ashland, Wis., Dec. 8, 1938; s. Elof Herman and Beatrice Lorraine (Dolezal) O.; m. Elisabeth Rigge Behrens, June 24, 1967; children—Heather Elisabeth, Peter Roy. B.S., Northwestern U., 1960. Lic. real estate salesman, Ill. Writer, editor Chgo. Am., 1956-68; pres. Roy Olson Pub. Relations Co., Oak Park, Ill., 1968-70; asst. regional adminstr. SBA, Chgo., 1970—; dir. Am.food Industries, Chgo., Convenant Village Retirement Ctr., Northbrook, Ill., 1975-81, Brandel Care Ctr., Northbrook, 1975-81. Chmn. Northbrook Covenant Ch., 1980-81. Mem. Soc. Profl. Journalists, Art Inst. Chgo. Clubs: City (media com.), Executives, Chgo. Press, Chgo. Headline (past dir. 1964-66), Northwestern (Chgo.). Home: 2015 Prairie St Glenview IL 60025 Office: US Small Bus Adminstrn 230 S Dearborn St Chicago IL 60604

OLSON, RUE EILEEN, librarian; b. Chgo., Nov. 1, 1928; d. Paul H. and Martha M. (Fick) Meyers; student Herzl Coll., 1946-48, Northwestern U., 1948-50, Ill. State U., 1960-64, Middle Mgmt. Inst. Spl. Libraries Assn., 1985-87; m. Richard L. Olson, July 18, 1964; children—Catherine, Karen. Accountant Ill. Farm Supply Co., Chgo., 1948-59; asst. librarian Ill. Agrl. Assn., Bloomington, 1960-66, librarian, 1966-86, dir. library services, 1986—. Mem. area com. Nat. Library Week, 1971, area steering com., 1972; mem. steering com. Illinet/OCLC, 1985-87; mem. adv. council of librarians Grad. Sch. Library Sci. U. Ill., 1976-79; mem. Ill. State Library Adv. Com. for Interlibrary Cooperation, 1979-80; del. Ill. White House Conf. on Library and Info. Services, 1978; coordinator Vita Income Tax Assistance, Bloomington, Ill., 1986—. Mem. Am., Ill., McLean County (pres. 1970-71) Library Assns., Spl. Libraries Assn. (pres. Ill. 1977-78), Ill. OCLC Users Group (treas. 1988—), Internat. Assn. Agrl. Librarians and Documentalists, Am. Soc. Info. Sci., Am. Mgmt. Assn. Lodge: Zonta (pres. 1987-89). Club: Bloomington. Office: Ill Agrl Assn 1701 Towanda Ave Bloomington IL 61701

OLSON, WILLIAM HERBERT, physician, administrator; b. Sioux City, Dec. 3, 1925; s. Victor L. and Leona (Hewitt) O.; m. LuEtta Brunn, Sept. 4, 1949; children—Daniel John, Susan Louise. B.A., Sioux Falls Coll., 1949; M.D., State U. Iowa, 1953. Diplomate Am. Bd. Internal Medicine, Am. Bd. Nuclear Medicine. Resident in internal medicine Seaside Meml. Hosp., Long Beach, Calif., 1954-55, Long Beach VA Hosp., 1955-57; practice medicine specializing in internal medicine, Long Beach, 1958-67; dir. dept. nuclear medicine Long Beach Community Hosp., 1967—, chief of staff, 1985-87; cons. nuclear medicine Long Beach VA Hosp., 1958-72; clin. instr. medicine U. Calif.-Irvine, 1962—. Contbr. articles to profl. jours. Ruling elder Convenant Presbyn. Ch., Orange, Calif., 1981. Served with UASSF, 1944-46. Fellow ACP.; mem. Long Beach Soc. Internal Medicine (pres. 1967). Republican. Home: 4609-8 Via La Paloma Orange CA 92669 Office: Long Beach Community Hosp 1720 Termino Ave Long Beach CA 90804

OLSSON, CARL ALFRED, urologist; b. Boston, Nov. 29, 1938; s. Charles Rudolph and Ruth Marion (Bostrom) O.; m. Mary DeVore, Nov. 4, 1962; children: Ingrid, Leif Eric. Grad., Bowdoin Coll., 1959; M.D., Boston U., 1963. Diplomate Am. Bd. Urology (trustee 1988—). Asst. prof. urology Boston U. Sch. Medicine, 1971-72, assoc. prof., 1972-74, prof., chmn. dept., 1974-80; dir. urology dept. Boston City Hosp., 1974-77; chief urology dept. Boston VA Med. Ctr., 1971-75; urologist-in-chief Univ. Hosp., Boston, 1971-80; John K. Lattimer prof., chmn. dept. urology Coll. Phys. and Surgs., Columbia U., N.Y.C., 1980—; dir. Squier Urol. Clinic, urology service Presbyn. Hosp., N.Y.C.; lectr. surgery Tufts U. Sch. Medicine. Boston Interhosp. Organ Bank, 1976-79; mem. working cadre Nat. Prostate Cancer Project, Nat. Cancer Inst., 1979-84. Editorial bd. Jour. Microsurgery and Prostate; asst. editor: Jour. Urology; contbr. chpts. to books, articles to med. jours. Recipient Disting. Alumnus award Boston U., 1985. Fellow ACS; mem. Am. Urol. Assn. (coordinator continuing med. edn. New Eng. sect. 1977-80, del. research com., Gold Cystoscope award 1979, Grayson-Carroll award 1971, 73), Boston Surg. Soc. (exec. com. 1976-80), Am. Assn. Clin. Urologists, Am. Assn. Genitourinary Surgeons, Clin. Soc. Genitourinary Surgeons, Am. Fertility Soc., AMA, Assn. Acad. Surgery, Am. Soc. Artificial Internal Organs, Am. Soc. Transplant Surgeons, Assn. Med. Colls., Can. Urol. Assn., Transplant Soc., Societe Internationale d'Urologie, Internat. Urodynamics Soc., Mass. Med. Soc., Soc. Govt. Urologists, New Eng. Handicapped Sportsmen's Assn. (exec. com. 1977-81), Soc. Univ. Urologists, Alpha Omega Alpha. Episcopalian. Clubs: U.S. Yacht Racing Union, Yacht Racing Union L.I. Sound, N.Y. Yacht, Cottage Park Yacht, Larchmont Yacht. Home: 18 Elm St Larchmont NY 10538 Office: 630 W 168th St New York NY 10032

OLSSON, CURT OLOF, Finnish supreme court executive; b. Helsinki, Sept. 28, 1919; s. Harry and Elsa Fanny Maria (Castré n) O.; m. Ingrid Persson, July 3, 1943; children—Olof, Ingmar, Ylva. LL.M., U. Law, Helsinki, 1944, LL.D., 1950; LL.D. (hon.), Uppsala U., Sweden, 1984; Dr. Bus. Adminstrn. (hon.), Swedish Sch. Econs., Helsinki, 1984. Asst. prof. law U. Helsinki, 1946-50; prof. comml. law Swedish Sch. Econs., Helsinki, 1951-70, pres., 1958-66; mem. Supreme Ct. Finland, Helsinki, 1970-75, pres., 1975—; chmn. and/or mem. law coms. Govt. of Finland, 1952—. Author books including: Company Law, Contracts, Sales and Judicial Administration; contbr. articles to profl. jours. Mem. Aland Delegation, Finland, 1957-70; chmn. Sigrid Juselius stiftelse, Helsinki, 1981—. Decorated Grand Cross of Finnish White Rose Order, 1980, Grand Cross of Swedish North Star Order, 1982. Mem. Societas Scientiarum Fennica, Finnish Law Assn. (hon.). Lutheran. Home: Granfeltsvagen 8B, 00570 Helsinki Finland Office: Supreme Ct, Pohjoiseplanadi 3, 00170 Helsinki 17 Finland

OLSSON, GUNNAR PAUL, geography educator; b. Eksharad, Sweden, Sept. 11, 1935; s. Paul Efraim and Eva Maria (Melin) O.; m. Birgitta Magnusson, Apr. 24, 1962; children: Ulrika, Ylva. Fil Kand, Uppsala U., 1960, Fil Lic., 1965, Fil Dr, 1968. Fellow Am. Council Learned Socs., Phila., 1963-64; asst. prof. geography U. Mich., Ann Arbor, 1966-67, assoc. prof., 1967-71, prof., 1971-74, collegiate prof., 1974-77; prof. geography Nordplan, Stockholm, 1977—; research assoc. Applied Sci. Research Corp., Bangkok, 1970. Author: Distance and Human Interaction, 1965, Birds in Egg/Eggs in Bird, 1980; editor: Philosophy in Geography, 1977, A Search for Common Ground, 1982; contbr. numerous articles to profl. jours. Mem. Regional Sci. Assn. (v.p. 1973-74), Assn. Am. Geographers (honors award 1984), Sauskapet for Anthropologi o Geografi. Office: Nordplan Skeppsholmen, Box 1658, 111 86 Stockholm Sweden

OLSSON, NILS WILLIAM, former association executive; b. Seattle, June 11, 1909; s. Nils A. and Mathilda (Lejkell) O.; m. Dagmar T. Gavert, June 15, 1940; children: Karna B., Nils G. and Pehr C. (twins). Student, North Park Coll., Chgo., Northwestern U., U. Minn., 1929-34; A.M., U. Chgo., 1938, Ph.D., 1949; Ph.D., U. Uppsala, Sweden, 1968. Admissions counselor, instr. Swedish North Park Coll., 1937-39; asst. Scandinavian U. Chgo., 1939-42, instr., 1945-50, asst. prof., 1950; mem. U.S. diplomatic service, 1950-67; 2d sec., pub. affairs officer Am. legation, Reykjavik, Iceland, 1950-52; attache, pub. affairs officer Am. embassy, Stockholm, Sweden, 1952-55; 1st. sec., consul Am. embassy, 1955-57; pub. affairs adviser Dept. State, 1957-59; chief Am. sponsored schs. abroad, 1959-62; 1st sec. Am. embassy, Oslo, Norway, 1962-64; counselor for polit. affairs Am. embassy, 1964-66; diplomat in residence Ind. U., 1966-67; dir. Am. Swedish Inst., Mpls., 1967-73; exec. dir. Swedish Council of Am., 1973-84. Author: Swedish Passenger Arrivals in New York 1820-1850, 1967, Swedish Passenger Arrivals in U.S. Ports (except New York) 1820-1850, 1979, Tracing Your Swedish Ancestry, 1974; Editor: A Pioneer in Northwest America, 1841-1858, vol. I, 1950, vol. II, 1959; editor, pub.: Swedish American Genealogist, 1981—; editor: A Swedish City Directory of Boston 1881, 1986; contbr. to hist. and ednl. jours. Mem. bd. Evang. Covenant Hist. Commn., Chgo., 1958; asst. naval attache Am. legation, Stockholm, 1943-45. Served from lt. (j.g.) to lt. comdr. USNR, 1942-45. Decorated knight Order Vasa 1st class, knight comdr. Order North Star, Sweden; recipient Swedish Pioneer Centennial medal, 1948; King Carl XVI Gustaf Bicentennial Gold medal; Carl Sandburg medal Swedish Pioneer Hist. Soc., 1982; named Swedish Am. of Year Stockholm, 1969. Fellow Geneal. Soc. (Finland), Geneal. Soc. (Sweden), Am. Soc. Genealogists; mem. Wermländska Sällskapet Stockholm (hon.), Nat. Geneal. Soc., Swedish Pioneer Hist. Soc. (exec. sec. 1949-50, 57-68), Carl Johan Soc. Sweden, Swedish-Am. Hist. Soc. (exec. sec. 1949-50, 57-68, pres. 1986—); fgn. corr. mem. Royal Acad. Belles Lettres, History and Antiquities (Sweden); hon. mem. Pro Fide et Christianismo (Sweden); fgn. mem. Royal Soc. Pub. Manuscripts Dealing with Scandinavian History (Sweden). Clubs: Skylight (Mpls.); Grolier (N.Y.C.); Cosmos (Washington); Explorers (Central Fla.); Univ. (Winter Park, Fla.). Lodge: Rotary. Home: PO Box 2186 662 Granville Dr Winter Park FL 32790

OLSTOWSKI, FRANCISZEK, chemical engineer, educator; b. N.Y.C., Apr. 23, 1927; s. Franciszek and Marguerite (Stewart) O.; A.A., Monmouth Coll., 1950; B.S. in Chem. Engring., Tex. A. and I. U., 1954; m. Rosemary Sole, May 19, 1952; children—Marguerita Antonina, Anna Rosa, Franciszek, Anton, Henryk Alexander. Research and devel. engr. Dow Chem. Co., Freeport, Tex., 1954-56, project leader, 1956-65, sr. research engr., 1965-72, research specialist, 1972-79, research leader, 1979-87; dir. Tech. Cons. Services, Freeport, 1987—. Lectr. phys. scis. elementary and intermediate schs., Freeport, 1961—. Vice chmn. Freeport Traffic Commn., 1974-76, chmn., 1976-79, vice chmn. 1987—. Served with USNR, 1944-46. Fellow Am. Inst. Chemist; mem. Electrochem. Soc. (sec. treas. South Tex. sect. 1963-64, vice chmn. 1964-65, chmn. 1965-67, councillor 1967-70), AAAS, Am. Chem. Soc., N.Y. Acad. Sci. Patentee in synthesis of fluorocarbons, natural graphite products, electrolytic prodn. magnesium metal and polyurethane tech.

OLTMAN, JOHN HAROLD, patent lawyer; b. Grand Rapids, Mich., Nov. 18, 1929; s. Peter Harold and Hazel Evelyn (Kelly) O.; B.S. in Chem. Engring., U. Mich., 1952, J.D., 1957; m. Lita Marilyn Hagen, Aug. 16, 1952; children—David K., Laura G., John K. Admitted to Ill. bar, 1957, Ariz. bar, 1964, Mich. bar, 1965, Fla. bar, 1968; mem. firms Mueller & Aichele (Attys.), Chgo., and Phoenix, 1957-64, Barnes, Kisselle, Raisch & Choate (Attys.), Detroit, 1964-65, Settle, Batchelder & Oltman (Attys.), Detroit, 1965-67, Settle & Oltman (Attys.), Detroit and Ft. Lauderdale, Fla., 1967-72, Oltman and Flynn (Attys.), Ft. Lauderdale, 1972—. Served with USMCR, 1952-54. Mem. ABA, Fla. Bar Assn., Broward County Bar Assn., Am. Patent Law Assn., Patent Law Assn. of So. Fla. (v.p. 1988), Am. Judicature Soc., Fla. Engring. Soc., IEEE, Phi Eta Sigma, Tau Beta Pi. Kiwanian (dir. Ft. Lauderdale Club 1972-74, 77-78, pres. 1983—chmn. Key Club com. 1970-78). Home: 2130 NE 55th St Fort Lauderdale FL 33308 Office: 915 Middle River Dr Fort Lauderdale FL 33304

OLUFOSOYE, TIMOTHY OMOTAYO, archbishop; b. Ondo, Nigeria, Mar. 31, 1918; s. Chief Daniel and Felecia (Akinduro) O.; widowed, 1945; 4 children. Degree in Theology, St. Andrew's Coll., Oyo, Nigeria, 1958; DD, U. B.C., Can.; DD Honoris Causex. Archbishop Ch. Nigeria, Idibañ, 1979—; justice of the peace. Decorated Order of the Officer (Nigeria). Office: POB 3075 Mapo 3 Arigidi St, Bodija Estate, Idibañ Nigeria

OLVER, MICHAEL LYNN, lawyer; b. Seattle, June 22, 1950; s. Manley Deforest and Geraldine (Robinson) O.; m. Wendy Kay Williams, July 6, 1974; children: Erin Marie, Christina Lynne. BA, U. Wash., 1972; JD, Calif. Western Sch. Law, 1976. Bar: Wash. 1976, U.S. Dist. Ct. (we. dist.) Wash. 1977. Assoc. Robbins, Merrick & Kraft, Seattle, 1976-77; sole practice Michael L. Olver, Seattle, 1977-80; ptnr. Merrick & Olver, P.S., Seattle, 1980—. Asst. mng. editor Calif. West. Internat. Law Jour., 1975-76. Lectr. Assumption Cath. Ch., Seattle, 1978—; mem. Full Gospel Businessmen Internat., Seattle, 1984; bd. dirs. trust and investment com. Found. for the Handicapped; chmn. Community Living Program. Mem. Seattle King County Bar Assn. (mem. internat. law sect. 1976—, judiciary and cts. com. 1986, family law sect. 1986), Wash. State Bar Assn. (mem. World Peace Through Law sect. 1980—), Alpha Theta Delta (dir., sec. 1977—). Catholic Evangelical. Home: 5545 33d NE Seattle WA 98105 Office: Merrick & Olver PS 1522 Seattle Tower Seattle WA 98101

OLVERA MARTINEZ, ALFONSO, telecommunications company executive; b. Mexico City, Oct. 28, 1949; s. Alfonso Olvera and Elia (Martinez) De Olvera; m. Pilar Figueras De Olvera, June 16, 1972; children: Alfonso Olvera Figueras, Enrique Olvera Figueras. Diploma in MechE, Inst. Politechnico Nat., Mexico City, 1971; proficiency in English, U. Cambridge, Eng., 1974; diploma in Italian, Dante Alighieri, Mexico City, 1974; diploma in bus. mgmt., Inst. Panam. de Alta Direccion de Empresas, Mexico City, 1977. Cert. mech. engr. Materials mgr. Grup Condumex, Mexico City, 1974-81, ops. mgr., 1981-83; plant mgr. Power Cables div. Condumex, Mexico City, 1983-86; gen. mgr. Salmat div. Condumex, Mexico City, 1983-86; plant mgr. Telecommunications div. Condumex, Mexico City, 1986—; ops. mgmt. prof. U. Anahuac, Mexico City, 1974-86. Mem. Am. Prodn. Inventory Control Soc. (pres. Mexico City chpt. 1979-82, CPIM award 1978), Instituto Tecnologico Y De Estudiossan Juan Del Rio (vocal), Superiores De Monterrey. Office: Condumex, Sor Juana Ines De La Cruz, 344-3PSO, 54000 Tlalnepantla Mexico

OLVING, SVEN, academic administrator; b. Tallinn, Estonia, Sept. 11, 1928; arrived in Sweden, 1944; s. Verner C. and Toni (Laas) O.; m. Eha Engman, Sept. 30, 1950; children: Lennart, Ann, Lena. MSc in elec. Engring., Chalmers U., Gothenburg, Sweden, 1952; DSc in Electronics, Chalmers U., 1959. Electrician SKF, Gothenburg, 1947-48; elec. engr. Electroscandia, Gothenburg, 1948-52; research asst. Chalmers U. Tech., Gothenburg, 1952-59, asst. prof. phys. electronics, 1959-60, prof., 1962—, v.p., 1966-74, pres., 1974—; assoc. prof. Cornell U., Ithaca, N.Y., 1960-62; chmn. bd. dirs. Volvofinans, Gothenburg; bd. dirs. Electrolux, Stockholm, Ericsson, Stockholm, Boliden, Stockholm, Celsius Industries, Gothenburg, Gotabanken, Gothenburg. Bd. dirs. Swedish Bd. Tech. Devel., Stockholm. Fellow Imperial Coll. Sci. and Tech.; mem. IEEE, Royal Acad. Scis., Royal Swedish Acad. Engring. Sics. Lodge: Rotary. Home: Gotabergsgatan 34, S 41134 Gothenburg Sweden Office: Chalmers U Tech, S 41296 Gothenburg Sweden

O'MALLEY, WARD, petroleum geologist; b. N.Y.C., Nov. 2, 1918; arrived in Ireland, 1969; s. Frank Ward O'Malley and Grace (Dalrymple) Mohlman; m. Catherine Holowecki, Nov. 14, 1962. Student, Princeton U., 1936-38; EM, Colo. Sch. Mines, 1942; MS, Stanford U., 1948. Registered profl. engr., Colo.; cert. profl. geologist, surveyor. Mining engr. South Am. Devel. Co., Ecuador, 1945-46; geologist U.S. Geol. Survey, Idaho, 1948, Continental Oil Co., Denver, 1949-51; div. geologist Billings, Mont., 1951-54; mgr. exploration Tidewater Oil, Ankara, Turkey, 1956-60, Iran Pan Am. Oil Co., Tehran, Iran, 1960-66; chief geologist Amoco Internat., Chgo., 1966-69; petroleum geologist Sweden, Turkey and Ireland, 1969—. Hon. treas. Nat. Trust, Tipperary, Ireland, 1975—; mem. com. County Tipperary Agrl. and Indsl. Show, Half Bred Breeders Soc., County Tipperary. Served to capt. C.E. U.S. Army, 1942-45. Fellow Inst. Petroleum; mem. Am. Assn. Petroleum Geologists, Am. Inst. Profl. Geologists, Irish Geol. Soc. Roman Catholic. Clubs: Princeton U.; County Tipperary Lawn Tennis (pres. 1987—). Home and Office: Golden Hills, County Tipperary, Munster Ireland

OMAN, JULIA TREVELYAN, theatrical designer; b. London, July 11, 1930; d. Charles Chichele and Joan (Trevelyan) O.; m. Roy Strong, 1971. Ed., Royal Coll. Art. Designer BBC-TV, 1955-67; designer for theater, opera and ballet, London, N.Y.C., Boston, Vienna, Stockholm and West Germany, 1967—. Designer Mme. Tussand's Hall of Historical Tableaux, 1979; art dir. various films including The Charge of the Light Brigade, 1967, Laughter in the Dark, 1968; prodn. designer film Julius Caesar, 1969; design cons. film Straw Dogs, 1971; dir. Oman Prodns. Ltd.; author: (with B.S. Johnson) Street Children, 1964; (with Roy Strong) Elizabeth R., 1971, Mary Queen of Scots, 1972, The English Year, 1982. Mem. vis. com. dept. edn. and sci. Royal Coll. of Art, 1980. Recipient Silver medal Royal Coll. of Art, Designer of Yr. award, 1967; named Royal scholar; elected Royal Designer for Industry. Address: care London Mgmt, 235-241 Regent St, London W1, England

OMAN, LAFEL EARL, former chief justice New Mexico Supreme Court; b. Price, Utah, May 7, 1912; s. Earl Andrew and Mabel (Larsen) O.; m. Arlie Edna Giles, June 3, 1936; children: Sharon O. Beck, Phyllis O. Bowman, Conrad LaFel, Kester LaFel. J.D., U. Utah, 1936. Bar: Utah bar 1936, N.Mex. 1947. Practiced in Salt Lake City and Helper, Utah, 1937-40; Las Cruces, N.Mex., 1948-66; investigator, examiner CSC, Denver, 1941-43; with office chief atty. VA, Albuquerque, 1946-48; asst. city atty. Las Cruces, 1958-59; city atty. City of Truth or Consequences, N.Mex., 1959-61; judge N.Mex. Ct. Appeals, Santa Fe, 1966-70; justice N.Mex. Supreme Ct., 1971-77, chief justice, 1976-77; spl. master, dist. judge pro tem. in adjudication Suits of Waters of N.Mex. Rivers, 1977—; mem. firm Sutin, Thayer & Browne P.A., 1977-85, Oman & Carmody P.A., 1985-86; ptnr. Oman, Gentry & Yntema, P.A., 1986-87, of counsel, 1987—; mem. N.Mex. Jud. Standards Commn., 1968-70, 71-72, N.Mex. Jud Council, 1972-77, N.Mex. Bd. Bar Examiners; bd. dirs. N.Mex. Continuing Legal Edn., Inc. Bd. dirs. N.Mex. Soc. Crippled Children; active Boy Scouts Am., Girl Scouts U.S.A., Polio Found.; chmn. ofcl. bd. St. John's United Methodist Ch., Santa Fe.; bd. dirs. Vis. Nurse Service, Inc., 1980-84, pres., 1983-84. Served to lt. USNR, 1943-46. Mem. ABA, Utah Bar Assn., N.Mex. Bar Assn., Dona Ana County (N.Mex.) Bar Assn. (pres. 1952-53), 1st Judicial Dist. Bar Assn., N.Mex., Santa Fe hist. socs., Santa Fe Opera Guild, Law-Sci. Acad., Def. Research Inst., Am. Trial Lawyers Assn., Inst. Jud. Adminstrn., Appellate Judges Conf., Nat. Legal Aid and Defender Assn., Am. Judicature Soc. (dir. 1970-74), Phi Alpha Delta. Lodge: Rotary (pres. Las Cruces club 1952-53, Santa Fe club 1976-77). Home: 510 Camino Pinones Santa Fe NM 87501

OMAR, ISA HAJI, plastic surgeon; b. Kuala Trengganu, Malaysia, Dec. 12, 1945; s. Omar Mat Amin and Mariam Abdul Rahman; m. Mariam Abdullah, Aug. 23, 1975; 1 child, Malizah. MBBS, U. Bombay, India, 1971. Resident Gen. Hosp., Kuala Lumpur, Malaysia, 1972-73; lectr. Nat. U. Malaysia, Kuala Lumpur, 1973-80; research fellow in plastic surgery St. Marianna U., Kawasaki, Japan, 1980-82; lectr. Nat. U. Malaysia, Kuala Lumpur, 1982-83; assoc. prof. Nat. U. Malaysia, 1983—, chief dept. plastic surgery, 1982—. Fellow Royal Coll. Surgeons; mem. Malaysian Med. Assn., Coll. Surgeons Malaysia, Malaysian Assn. Plastic Surgeons. Moslem. Office: Dept Surgery, Jalan Baja Muda, 50300 Kuala Lumpur, Selangor Malaysia

O'MARA, THOMAS PATRICK, manufacturing company executive; b. St. Catharine's, Ont., Can., Jan. 17, 1937; s. Joseph Thomas and Rosanna Patricia (Riordan) O'M.; m. Nancy Irene Rosevear, Aug. 10, 1968; children: Patricia Catharine, Tracy Irene, Sara Megan. B.S., Allegheny Coll., 1958; M.S., Carnegie Inst. Tech., 1960. Mktg. analyst U.S. Steel Corp., Pitts., 1960-65; dir. info. systems Screw & Bolt Corp., Pitts., 1965-68; v.p., gen. mgr. Toy div. Samsonite Corp., Denver, 1968-73; regional mgr. Mountain Zone, Hertz Corp., Denver, 1973-75; asst. to chmn. Allen Group, Melville, N.Y., 1975-76; group exec. v.p. fin. and adminstrn. Bell & Howell Co., Chgo., 1976-77; controller Bell & Howell Co., 1977-78, corp. v.p., 1978-85, pres. visual communications, 1978-85; pres., chief operating officer, dir. Bridge Product Inc., Northbrook, Ill., 1985-87; chmn., chief exec. officer Micro Metl Corp., Indpls., 1987—. Served with USAR, 1961-66. Mem. Econs. Club Chgo., Fin. Execs. Inst., Newcomen Soc. U.S., Sigma Alpha Epsilon. Club: Knollwood. Home: 1350 Inverlieth Lake Forest IL 60045 Office: Micro Metl Corp 3419 Roosevelt Ave Indianapolis IN 46210

OMER, EL-FADIL EL-OBEID, medical microbiologist, educator; b. Kamlin, Sudan, Jan. 1, 1944; s. Mohammed El-Obeid Omer and Nafisa Imam Saad; m. Zeineb Omer, July 31, 1970; children: Wifaq, Wala, Faiha, Ola, Mohammed. MBBS, Khartoum (Sudan) U., 1969, D in Medicine, 1984; Diploma in Bacteriology, Manchester (Eng.) U., 1975; Diploma in Venereology, London U., 1976. Med. officer Ministry of Health, Khartoum, 1969-73; research asst. Khartoum U., 1973-76, lectr., 1976-82, assoc. prof., 1982-83; assoc. prof., cons. microbiologist Umm Al-Qura U., Makka, Saudi Arabia, 1983—; lab. dir. Soba U. Hosp., Khartoum, 1976-83. Author: Basic Microbiology, 1986, Medical Microbiology, 1987, Trichomoniasis, 1987, Medical Bacteriology, 1988. Fellow Internat. Coll. Tropical Medicine; mem. Royal Coll. Pathologists, Brit. Soc. Microbiology, British Royal Soc. Medicine, Am. Soc. Microbiology, Am. Assn. Venereal Diseases, African Union Sexual Diseases (v.p. 1983—), Internat. Union Against Venereal Diseases and Treponematoses. Club: Merrikh Sport (Khartoum). Home: PO Box 8189, Amarat, Khartoum Sudan

OMER, HAIM, clinical psychologist, researcher; b. Sao Paulo, Brazil, June 20, 1949; s. Abraham and Sonia (Braun) Kuperman; m. Aliza Lowi, Feb. 2, 1970 (div. Jan. 1978); children: Anat, Jonathan; m. Rina Faraggi, Apr. 16, 1978; children: Michael, Noam. BA, Hebrew U., 1971, MA, 1976, PhD, 1985. Researcher Israel Def. Force, Tel Aviv, 1971-77, Ezrata Nashim Hosp., Jerusalem, 1977-79; clin. psychologist, researcher Hebrew U., Jerusalem, 1980-85; asst. in edn. Harvard U., Cambridge, Mass., 1986-87, clin. psychotherapy, 1987—. Contbr. articles on preterm labor and psychotherapy to profl. jours. Postdoctoral grantee Rothschild Found., 1986, Fulbright Found., 1986. Home: 6 Borochov, Shchunat Hapoalim A, Hod-Hasharon Israel

OMER-COOPER, JOHN DAVID, historian, educator; b. Newcastle-on-Tyne, Northumberland, Eng., Oct. 23, 1931; arrived in New Zealand, 1974; BA in History and Philosophy, Rhodes U., Grahamstown, Republic of South Africa, 1951, BA in Philosophy with honors, 1952, MA in Philosophy, 1957; BA in History, Cambridge (Eng.) U., 1955. From asst. lectr. to sr. lectr. U. Ibadan (formerly U. Coll. Ibadan), Nigeria, 1955-62; prof. history U. Zambia, Lusaka, 1966-73, dean of arts, 1966, dean of edn., 1973; prof. history U. Otago, Dunedin, New Zealand, 1974—; mem. Univ. Council U. Zambia, 1967-73, pro-vice-chancellor, 1970-73. Author: The Zulu Aftermath, 1966; contbg. author: Cambridge History of Africa, vol. 5, 1976, The Making of Modern Africa (2 vols.), 1971, rev. edit., 1986, History of Southern Africa, 1987. Pres. Ecology Action, Otago, 1979-82; active Royal Forest and Bird Protection Soc., Dunedin, New Zealand, 1979—, Hist. Places Trust, Dunedin, 1974—; bd. govs. Taieri High Sch., Dunedin, 1985—. Mem. New Zealand Hist. Assn., New Zealand Inst. Internat. Affairs, African Studies Assn. of Australia and the Pacific (mem. exec. com. 1980-86), Otago Br. of Royal Soc. of New Zealand, Univ. Club (pres. Dunedin chpt. 1983), Univ. Staff Club (pres. 1986—). Office: U Otago, History Dept, Albany St PO Box 56, Dunedin New Zealand

OMHOLT, BRUCE DONALD, product designer, mechanical engineer, consultant; b. Salem, Oreg., Mar. 27, 1943; s. Donald Carl and Violet Mae (Buck) O.; m. Mavis Aronow, Aug. 18, 1963 (div. July 1972); children—Madison, Natalie; m. 2d, Darla Kay Faber, Oct. 27, 1972; 1 son, Cassidy. B.S.M.E., Heald Coll. Engring., San Francisco, 1964. Real estate salesman R. Lea Ward and Assocs., San Francisco, 1962-64; sales engr. Repco Engring., Montebello, Calif., 1964; in various mfg. engring. and mgmt. positions Ford Motor Co., Rawsonville, Saline, Owosso and Ypsilanti, Mich., 1964-75; chief engr. E. F. Hauserman Co., Cleve., 1975-77; dir. design and engring. Am. Seating Co., Grand Rapids, Mich., 1977-80; pres. Trinity Engring., Grand Rapids, Mich., 1980-81, Rohnert Park, Calif., 1981—; 1986 U.S. Patent For Vertical Mitre Machine; cons. mfg. U.S., fgn. patentee carrier rack apparatus, motorcycle improvements, panels.

OMLAND, TOV, physician, medical microbiologist; b. Kviteseid, Telemark, Norway, May 15, 1923; s. Hans Omland and Torbjorg Lid; m. Ellen-Margrethe Soderstrom, Aug. 13, 1949 (dec. Mar. 1981); children—Anne Katerine, Hans Harald. M.D., Oslo U., 1949, specialist med. microbiology, 1959. Med. officer Internat. Tb Campaign, Greece, 1950-51; gen. practice medicine, Norway, 1951-52; med. officer WHO, Egypt and Turkey, 1952-53; trainee internal medicine and surgery Oslo City Hosp., 1954-55; trainee, asst. prof. Oslo U., 1955-63; dir. microbiology State Microbiology Lab., Lillehammer, Norway, 1963-68; dir. Norwegian Def. Microbiology Lab., Oslo, 1968—; bd. dirs. Ellen-Margrethe & Tov Omland's Lab. for Med. Microbiology, Ski, Norway, 1973—; adv. on disarmament biological weapons Ministry of Fgn. Affairs, Norway. Contbr. chpts. books and articles to profl. jours. Served to col. Norwegian Med. Corps, 1978. Recipient prize Schering Corp. U.S.A., 1986. Mem. Norwegian Soc. Microbiology (pres. 1973-75), Norwegian Soc. Pathology, Norwegian Soc. Infectious Diseases, Soc. Gen. Microbiology (U.K.), Am. Soc. Microbiology. Conservative. Lutheran. Club: Oslo Militaere Samfund. Home: Gamlevegen 55, 1400 Ski Norway Office: Norwegian Def Microbiology Lab, Oslo mil/Akershus, Oslo Norway

OMMAYA, AYUB KHAN, neurosurgeon; b. Pakistan, Apr. 14, 1930; came to U.S., 1961, naturalized, 1968; s. Sultan Nadir and Ida (Counil) Khan; children: David, Alexander, Shana, Aisha. M.D., U. Punjab, Pakistan, 1953; M.A., Oxford U., Eng., 1956. Intern Mayo Hosp., Lahore, Pakistan, 1953-54; resident in neurosurgery Radcliffe Infirmary, Oxford, Eng., 1954-61; vis. scientist NIH, Bethesda, Md., 1963-63, assoc. neurosurgeon, 1963-68, head sect. applied research, 1968-74, chief neurosurgery, 1974-79; clin. prof. George Washington U. Med. Sch., 1970; cons. VA, Armed Forces Radiobiology Research Inst.; mem. Inter-Agy. Com. for Protection Human Research Subjects of Fed. Coordinating Council for Sci. Engring. and Tech.; chmn. biomechanics adv. com. Nat. Hwy. Traffic Safety Adminstrn.; inaugural Lewin meml. lectr. U. Cambridge, Eng., 1983. Contbr. articles, book chpts. to profl. lit. Pres. Found. for Fundamental and Applied Neurosci., Bethesda. Recipient J. W. Kirkdaldy prize Oxford U., 1956; recipient Sitara-i-Imtiaz for Achievements in Neurosurgery Govt. Pakistan, 1981; Hunterian prof. Royal Coll. Surgeons, 1968; Rhodes scholar, 1954-60. Mem. So. Neurosci., Am. Assn. Neurol. Surgeons, Research Soc. Neurosurgeons, ASME, Brit. Soc. Neurol. Surgeons, Am. Assn. Pakistani Physicians (pres.), Internat. Brain Research Orgn.; life mem. pan. Am. Med. Assn. Home: 8901 Burning Tree Rd Bethesda MD 20817 Office: 8006 Glenbrook Rd Bethesda MD 20814

OMOANREGHAN, GODWIN IYERE, paper and book industries executive; b. Ewatto Ishan, Bendel State, Nigeria, June 24, 1947; s. Dick and Omorahie Omoanreghan; m. Victoria Okoromi, Dec. 31, 1975; children—Evelyn, Lovell, Eromosele, Osaze, Osaremhen. Diploma in mktg., Trans-World Tutorial Coll., Gt. Brit., 1974. Clk./typist Fed. Ministry of Trade, Lagos, Nigeria, 1969-74; mktg. officer Dastus World Agys. Ltd., Lagos, 1976-77, mktg. mgr., 1977-79; group exec. dir. Bob Jasco & Co., paper and booksellers, Lagos, 1979—. Pub. ednl. mag. and children's books. Pub. relations officer Ewatto Progressive Union, Lagos, 1980—. Mem. Inst. Sales and Mktg. Mgmt. U.K., Nigerian Mktg. Assn. Clubs: Ewatto Social of Nigeria (chmn. bd. trustees 1978—, cert. merit 1983) (Benin); Tusk Club of Nigeria (dir. social matters and publicity 1985) (Lagos). Avocations: reading; television; music. Home: 110 Clegg St, Surulere, Lagos Nigeria Office: Promotes Paper & Book Ind Ltd, PO Box 1989, Surulere, Lagos Nigeria

OMOIELE, MARNA TAMBURA, sociologist, radio station moderator; b. Dayton, Ohio, May 6, 1948; d. Morgan and Mary Louise (Marshall) Revere; children: Nyota Binta Ain Omoiele. BA in Sociology, Wright State U., 1974, postgrad. in liberal arts, 1978-79; MS in Corrections, Xavier U., Cin., 1976. Cert. secondary edn. tchr., Ohio; lic. cosmetologist. Pre-sentence investigator Montgomery County Adult Probation Dept., Dayton, 1973-75; social counselor Hamilton County Adult Parole, Cin., 1975-77; tchr. Huber Heights Sch., Dayton, 1979; mem. exec. bd., treas. West Montgomery County Food Program, Dayton, 1979—; coordinator Northwest Office Neighborhood Affairs City of Dayton, 1983—. Chmn. internat. div. Nat. Council of Negro Women, Va., 1979—; pres. Man-to-Man/Woman-to-Woman, Inc. Adv. Bd., 1986—. Recipient Employee of Yr. award City of Dayton 1981. Mem. Dayton and Montgomery County Black Mgr. Assn., Nat. Assn. Blacks in Criminal Justice (charter), Am. Soc. Criminology, Fedn. of Dayton/N.Y. Bus. and Profl. Women, Inc. (chmn. ways and means 1982-84). Baptist. Home: 334 Kenwood Ave Dayton OH 45405 Office: City of Dayton 702 Salem Ave Dayton OH 45406

O'MORRISON, KEVIN, playwright; b. St. Louis; s. Sean E. and Dori Elizabeth (Adams) O'M.; privately educated; m. Linda Soma, Apr. 30, 1966. Author: (plays) Three Days Before Yesterday, 1965, Requiem, 1969, The Morgan Yard, 1970, The Realist, 1973, A Report to Stockholders, 1975, Ladyhouse Blues, 1975, Dark Ages, 1978, A Party for Lovers (Nat. Play award NRT 1981), 1979, Unfinished Business, 1980-81 (rewritten as a cabaret-opera titled The Old Missouri Jazz 1985, then as The Power Play 1986), The Mutilators, 1988; (TV plays) The House of Paper, 1959, A Sign for Autumn, 1962, And Not a Word More, 1960, Pompeii . . . February 13th, When The Dead Walk, 1988; (radio version) Ladyhouse Blues, 1977; (novel) Something Perfect; actor (film) The Set-Up, 1948, Eugene O'Neill: Journey Toward Genius, 1987, Funny Farm, Lonesome Dove, 1988, in PBS prodn. The Watergate Coverup Trial, 1975, in American Playhouse miniseries Concealed Enemies, 1984; (film plays) Next Time, Dynamite and Honey, rev. 1988; (pop song lyrics) I Need Someone, 1987; vis. prof. U. Mo., Kansas City, 1976; artist-in-residence numerous univs. and colls. Served with USAAF, 1943-45. Creative Artists Public Service fellow, 1975; Nat. Endowment for Arts fellow, 1979-80. Mem. ASCAP, AFTRA, Dramatists Guild, Writers Guild Am., PEN Am. Center, Actors Equity Assn., Amnesty Internat. USA, Screen Actors Guild.

OMURA, YOSHIAKI, physician, educator; b. Tomari, Toyama-ken, Japan, Mar. 28, 1934; came to U.S., 1959, naturalized, 1979; s. Tsunejiro and Minako (Uozu) O.; degree in elec. engring. Nihon U., 1952-54; B.Sc. in Applied Physics, Waseda U., 1957; M.D., Yokohama City U., 1958, postgrad. exptl. physics, 1958; postgrad. Columbia U., 1960-63; Sc.D. (Med.), Coll. Physicians and Surgeons, Columbia U., 1965. Rotating intern Tokyo U. Hosp., 1958, Norwalk (Conn.) Hosp., 1959; research fellow cardiovascular surgery Columbia U., N.Y.C., 1960, resident physician in surgery, Francis Delafield Hosp., Cancer Inst., Columbia U., 1961-65; asst. prof. pharmacology and instr. surgery N.Y. Med. Coll., 1966-72; vis. prof. U. Paris, summers 1973-77; Maitre de recherche, Disting. Fgn. Scientist program of INSERM, Govt. of France, 1977; research cons. orthopedic surgery Columbia U., 1965-66; part-time emergency rm. physician Englewood Hosp., 1965-66; research cons. pharmacology dept. N.Y. Down State Med. Center, SUNY, 1966; cons. Lincoln Hosp. Drug Detoxification Program, 1973-74; chmn. Columbia U. Affiliation and Community Medicine com., Community Bd., Francis Delafield Hosp., 1974-75; vis. research prof. dept. elec. engring., Manhattan Coll., 1962—; chmn. Sci. Div., Children's Art & Sci. Workshops, N.Y.C., 1971—; dir. Med. Research, Heart Disease Research Found., Bklyn., 1972—; adj. prof. dept. pharmacology Chgo. Med. Sch., 1982—; founder, editor-in-chief Acupuncture & Electro-Therapeutics Research Internat. Jour., 1974—; editorial cons. Jour. Electrocardiology, 1980-86, Functional Neurology, 1988—; editorial bd. Alternative Medicine, 1985—; attending physician Dept. Neurosci., L.I. Coll. Hosp., 1980—, New York Pain Center, 1988—; v.p. Internat. Kirlian Research Assn., 1981—; mem. N.Y. State Bd. Medicine, 1984—; mem. alumni council Coll. Phys. and Surg. Columbia U., 1986—. Columbia U. research fellow, 1960; Am. Cancer Soc. Inst. grantee, 1961-63; John Polacek Found. grantee, 1966-72; NIH grantee, 1967-72; Heart Disease Research Found. grantee, 1972—, others. Fellow Internat. Coll. Acupuncture and Electro-Therapeutics (pres. 1980—); mem. N.Y. Cardiol. Soc. (fellow), Am. Coll. Angiology (fellow), Am. Coll. Acupuncture (fellow), N.Y. Acad. Sci., Japan Bi-Digital O-Ring Test Assn. (hon. pres. 1986—), Am. Soc. Artificial Internal Organs, N.Y. Japanese Med. Soc. (pres. 1963-73), others. Author 5 books, also chpts. in books; contbr. over 130 articles to profl. jours. Home: 800 Riverside Dr Apt 8-I New York NY 10032

O'NAN, MARTHA, foreign language educator; b. Shelbyville, Ky., June 28, 1921; d. Samuel Gross and Mary S. (Mays) O'N. B.A., Agnes Scott Coll., 1941; M.A., U. Ky., 1942; Ph.D., Northwestern U., 1952; diploma, U. Paris, 1953; cert. univ. adminstrn., U. Wis., 1977. Instr. Spanish, Pikeville Coll., 1942-44, Jacksonville Coll., 1944-46; asst. prof. Centre Coll., 1946-48; chmn. French Elmhurst Coll., 1951-54; assoc. prof. to chmn. modern langs. Millikin U., 1956-63; assoc. prof., then prof. modern langs. Ohio U., 1964-69, asst. chmn. modern langs., 1964-69; prof. SUNY, Brockport, 1969—; chmn. fgn. langs. SUNY, 1969-77; dir. of overseas program SUNY, Tours, France, 1986; vis. prof. Ind. U., 1987; evaluator Middle States Assn. Colls. and Schs., 1978—; owner Dutch Creek Hereford and Angus cattle. Author: The Role of Mind in Hugo, Faulkner, Beckett and Grass, 1967; gen. editor: Folio, 1970—, Papers on Romance Literary Relations, 1987; co-editor: Romance Literary Studies, 1979, 87; contbr.: French Rev, 1954, 58, Ky. Fgn. Lang. Quar, 1957, Symposium, 1958, Hispania, 1959, Instants: Poems, 1964, Names, 1982, CELFAN, 1983; also numerous book revs.; corr.: Littératures, 1983. Master conservationist Commonwealth of Ky., 1988. French Govt. fellow, 1952-53; SUNY grantee, 1976, 80, 81; Bibliothèque Nationale grantee, 1981; named Col. of Commonwealth of Ky., 1986. Mem. Am. Assn. Tchrs. Spanish and Portuguese, MLA (del. 1976-77), Assn. des Amis d'Andre Gide, Am. Name Soc. (dir. 1983), Commonwealth of Ky. (master conservationist 1988), Eta Sigma Phi, Phi Sigma Iota. Home: Rural Route 1 Box 316 Pleasureville KY 40057

ONARHEIM, LEIF FRODE, food and drink industry executive; b. Oslo, Norway, Aug. 23, 1934; s. Frode M.A. and Lillemor (Host) O.; m. Anne Helene Nygaard, Dec. 19, 1958; children—Anders, Oivin, Ingvild, Halvor. Student U. Ga., 1956; M.B.A., Norwegian Econ. Coll., Bergen, 1960. Mgr. sales Norsk Impregnerings Co., Larvik, Norway, 1960-62; mgmt. cons. Asbjorn Habberstad, Oslo, 1962-69; pres. Nora Sunrose A/S, Oslo, 1970-79; pres. Nora Industrier A/S, Oslo, 1980—; chmn. Helly-Hansen A/S , Norges Hypotekforening; dir. Wilhelm Wilhelmsen Ltd. Oslo, Standard Telefone Kabelfabrik, Oslo, Forenede Forsikring, Trondheim, Norway. Chmn., Fedn. Norwegian Industries, 1981-83. Named Leader of Yr. Farmand, 1987; recipient St. Olav award His Majesty King Olav, 1986; Rotary Student Fund scholar, 1955-56. Lutheran. Avocations: hunting, skiing. Home: Idunnsvei 56, 1370 Asker Norway Office: Nora Industrier A/S, Holbergsg 1, 0306 Oslo Norway

ONATE, SANTIAGO, member of congress, lawyer; b. Mexico City, May 24, 1949; s. Santiago and Clara (Laborde) O.; m. Laura Madrazo, Apr. 4, 1981; children: Lucia, Andrea, Laura. LLB, U. Nat. Autonoma Mex., 1973; postgrad., U. Pavia, Italy, 1973-74; LLM, London Sch. Econs., 1975; JD, U. Wis., 1987. Asst. researcher, inst. legal research U. Nat. Autonoma Mex., Mexico City, 1970-72, prof. law, 1976—; sole practice Mexico City, 1976—; prof. law U. Autonoma Met., Mexico City, 1975-83, Inst. Nat. Ciencias Penales, Mexico City, 1982-85; mem. Congress Mex., 1985-88; mem. Assembly of Reps. Mex. DF, 1988—; cons. legal history various U.S. law firms, Tex., N.Mex., 1976; vis. scholar law sch. U. Wis., Madison, 1981-82. Author: Los Trabajadores Migratorios, 1972, 1982; editor: La Jornada, 1985—; contbr. articles to profl. jours. Fellow Assn. Nat. de Abogados al Servicio del Estado; mem. Law and Soc. Assn., Assn. Latinoamericana de Metodologia de la Enseñanza del Derecho, Inter-Am. Legal Services Assn., Inst. Argentino de Derecho Parlamentario. Mem. Institutional Revolutionary Party. Clubs: Univ. (Mexico City), Assoc. (Dallas). Home: Alfa 235, 04320 Coyoacan Mexico Office: Congreso de la Union, Ave Congreso de la Union, Mexico City Mexico

ONDREJKA, HEINZ LENNART, manufacturing company executive; b. Bukovice, Czecho-Slovakia, Dec. 23, 1930; came to Sweden, 1940; s. Max and Marta (Steckman) O.; m. Mejt Gunborg, Apr. 3, 1958. Econ. and Bus. Adminstrn. degree TBV, Borlange, Sweden, 1966; D.B.A., Buckner U., Fort Worth, 1979. Auditor, Ohrlings Revbyra, Falun, Sweden, 1952-55; office mgr. Caltex Oil Co., Falun, 1955-58; internal auditor Stora Kopparberg AB, Falun, 1958-67; fin. dir. Gema Kem. Fabrik AB, Falun, 1967-72, mng. dir., 1972-75; fin. dir., mem. bd. Melkers Chark Ab, Falun, 1975—; chmn. bd. Brod. Karlssons Slakter AB, Vara, Sweden, 1975—; dir. Wasa Fors bol, Stockholm, Sweden. Author: Internal Auditing, 1962. Served as sgt. Swedish Army, 1952-78. Recipient Internat. Pres.'s award Lions Clubs Internat., 1981, 87. Conservative. Lutheran. Lodge: Lion (dist. gov. 1975-76, chmn. council 1981-82). Home: Ekvagen 33, S79143 Falun Sweden Office: Melkers Chark AB, PO Box 3014, S79103 Falun Sweden

ONDRUS, MILAN FRANCIS, manufacturing company executive; b. Trnava, Czechoslovakia, Aug. 13, 1923; s. Francis and Maria (Uhrovic) O.; m. Marilee Adele Rumpf, July 30, 1955; 1 child, Marina Catherine. JD, U. Bratislava, Czechoslovakia, 1947, postgrad., 1948-49; postgrad., Acad. Internat. Law, The Hague, The Netherlands, 1949, Harvard U. Bus. Sch., 1978. Asst. to dep. prime minister Govt. of Czechoslovakia, 1946-48; radio info. specialist U.S. Dept. State, Washington, 1952-55; polit. commentator Radio Free Europe, N.Y.C., 1955-57; with pub. relations dept. Dow Chem. Co., 1957-58; mgr. pub. relations, advt. Dow Chem. Co., Midland, Mich., 1958-61; gen. mgr. Dow Chem. GmbH, Hamburg, Fed. Republic of Germany, 1961-73; v.p. for Europe, Mid. East and Africa Brunswick Corp., Brussels, 1973-82; corp. regional dir. Europe FMC Corp., Brussels, 1983—; chmn., dir. Kinetics Tech. Internat., Zoetermeer, The Netherlands, 1986—. Decorated Grand Cross of Merit (Fed. Republic of Germany); Order of Leopold II (Belgium). Clubs: Am. Brussels, Assn. Belgo-Américaine, Royal Waterloo Golf (Brussels); St. James (London), Harvard (Brussels). Home: 20 Ave de l'Orée, 1050 Brussels Belgium Office: FMC Europe SA, 523 Ave Louise, 1050 Brussels Belgium

O'NEIL, HERBERT EARL, artificial intelligence, metrology educator, systems analyst; b. Duluth, Minn., Mar. 26, 1944; s. Jack and Maxine (Brown) O'N.; m. Aino Lavarärjäri (div.); children: Tiina, Tanya, Tara; m. Judy Elaine Coleman, Jan. 5, 1984; children: Tiia, Tyriina, Tim. BS, U. Wis., 1971, MA, 1973. Cert. tchr.; Wis., Minn. Electronics technician Litton Communication, Europe and Middle East, 1965-67; tech. engr. DeMarc Cable Corp., Elmwood, Wis., 1971-72; instr. math, sci. Marion (Wis.) Jr. High Sch., 1973-78; curriculum analyst AVCO/E Systems, Saudia Arabia, 1978-79; instr. computer hardware Cray Research, Chippewa, Wis., 1979-80; instr. metrology Hutchinson (Minn.) Vo-Tech, 1980—; artificial intelligence tech. developer Tech. Inst. Hutchinson, 1988—; chief exec. officer Alpha Omega Enterprises, Hutchinson, 1980—; adj. instr. U. Minn., St. Paul, 1981-82; asst. dir., instr. U. Wis., Green Bay, 1976-79. Pres. Hutchinson Edn. Assn., 1982-84, Hutchinson Community Video Network, 1980-82, Marion Edn. Assn., 1975-76. Served with USAF, 1962-65. Named Outstanding Vocational Educator, Minn. Dept. Edn., 1981. Mem. Instrument Soc. Am. (chmn. standards and practice com. 1986—, chmn. honors and awards com. 1985-86, chmn. edn. com. 1984-85, named Outstanding Adv. 1985), Inst. Electrical and Electronics Engrs. (sr.), Nat. Conf. Standard Labs., Metrology Soc. Home: 1201 Lewis Ave Hutchinson MN 55350 Office: Hutchinson Tech Inst 200 Century Ave Hutchinson MN 55350

O'NEIL, ROBERT MARCHANT, university administrator; b. Boston, Oct. 16, 1934; s. Walter George and Isabel Sophia (Marchant) O'N.; m. Karen Elizabeth Elson, June 18, 1967; children—Elizabeth, Peter, David, Benjamin. A.B., Harvard U., 1956, A.M., 1957, LL.B., 1961; LL.D., Beloit Coll., 1985, Ind. U., 1987. Bar: Mass. 1962. Law clk. to justice U.S. Supreme Ct., 1962-63; acting assoc. prof. law U. Calif.-Berkeley, 1963-66, prof., 1966-67, 1969-72; exec. asst. to pres., prof. law SUNY-Buffalo, 1967-69; provost, prof. law U. Cin., 1972-73, exec. v.p., prof. law, 1973-75; v.p., prof. law Ind. U., Bloomington, 1975-80; pres. U. Wis. System, 1980-85; prof. law U. Wis.-Madison, 1980-85; prof. law, pres. U. Va., Charlottesville, 1985—; gen. counsel. AAUP, 1970-72; bd. dirs. James River Corp. Author: Civil Liberties: Case Studies and the Law, 1965; Free Speech: Responsible Communication Under Law, 2d edit., 1972; The Price of Dependency: Civil Liberties in the Welfare State, 1970; No Heroes, No Villians, 1972; The Courts, Government and Higher Education, 1972; Discrimination Against Discrmination, 1976; Handbook of the Law of Public Employment, 1978; Classrooms in the Crossfire, 1981; co-author: A Guide to Debate, 1964, The Judiciary and Vietnam, 1972, Civil Liberties Today, 1974. Trustee, Carnegie Found. Advancement Teaching; bd. dirs. Council on Post-secondary Accreditation, Ednl. Testing Service, Johnson Found. Home: Carr's Hill 1910 Carr's Hill Rd Charlottesville VA 22903 Office: U Va Main Campus Office of Pres Charlottesville VA 22903

O'NEILL, BRIAN JUAN, anthropology educator; b. N.Y.C., Jan. 29, 1950; s. George Caracena and Betty D. (Dross) O'N.; m. Isabel Maria Monteiro Rua Pinto, Sept. 27, 1986. BA cum laude, Columbia Coll., 1972; MA, Essex U., Eng., 1974; PhD, London Sch. Econs., 1982. Research fellow Gulbenkian Inst. Sci., Oeiras, Portugal, 1982-85; asst. prof. in social anthropology Inst. Superior de Ciencias de Trabalho e da Empresa, Lisbon, Portugal, 1984—; v.p. Social Anthropology Ctr., Lisbon, 1986-87, pres., 1988—. Contbr. articles to profl. jours. Fellow Royal Anthropol. Inst.; mem. Am. Anthropol. Assn., N.Y. Acad. Scis. Office: ISCTE, Antropologia Social, Av das Forças Armadas, 1600 Lisboa Portugal

O'NEILL, JOSEPH DEAN, lawyer; b. Bayonne, N.J., June 11, 1940; s. Austin Joseph and Ann (Lynch) O'N.; m. Susan Marie Clancy, Nov. 5, 1941; children—Kimberley Kelly. A.B., Allegheny Coll., Meadville, Pa., 1962; J.D., N.Y. Law Sch., 1967. Bar: N.J. 1968, U.S. Dist. Ct. N.J. 1968, U.S. Supreme Ct. 1974; cert. civil and criminal trial atty. Pres. Joseph D. O'Neill, P.A., Vineland, N.J., 1968—; lectr. trial tactics, personal injury and criminal law. Contbr. articles to legal jours. Pres. Cumberland County Legal Aid Soc., 1974-87; assoc. counsel N.J. Jaycees, 1970-71. Mem. ABA (mem. trial techniques com., products liability com.), N.J. State Bar Assn. (mem. cert. trial attys. sect.), Nat. Assn. Criminal Def. Lawyers (mem. nat. hotline panel of experts in homicide cases, outstanding contbn. award 1978), Assn. Trial Lawyers Am. (pres., N.J. affiliate). Address: 30 W Chestnut Ave PO Box 847 Vineland NJ 08360

O'NEILL, MARY JANE, health agency executive; b. Detroit, Feb. 24, 1923; d. Frank Roger and Kathryn (Rice) Kilcoyne; Ph.B. summa cum laude, U. Detroit, 1944; postgrad. U. Wis., 1949-50; m. Michael James O'Neill, May 31, 1948; children—Michael, Maureen, Kevin, John, Kathryn. Editor, East Side Shopper, Detroit, 1939-45; club editor Detroit Free Press, 1945-48; reporter UP, Milw. and Madison, Wis., 1949; dir. public relations Fairfax-Falls Church (Va.) Community Chest, 1955-60; copy editor Falls Ch. Sun-Echo, 1958-60; free-lance writer, Washington, 1960-63; assoc. editor Med. World News, Washington, 1963-66; dir. public relations Westchester Lighthouse, N.Y. Assn. for Blind, 1967-71; dir. public edn. The Lighthouse, N.Y.C., 1971-73, dir. public relations, 1973-80; exec. dir. Eye-Bank for Sight Restoration, Inc., 1980—. Bd. dirs. N.Y. Regional Transplant Program, 1987—. Mem. Women in Communications (pres. N.Y. chpt. 1980-81), Eye-Bank Assn. Am. (lay adv. bd. 1981-83, dir. 1983-86), Public Relations Soc. Am., Publicity Club, Women Execs. in Pub. Relations (dir. 1982-88, pres. 1986-87), N.Y. Acad. Scis. Club: Cosmopolitan. Office: 210 E 64 St New York NY 10021

O'NEILL, MICHAEL J., English language educator; b. Dublin, Ireland, Mar. 1, 1913; s. Patrick J. and Anne J. (O'Neill) O'N.; m. Bridget Reidy, Nov. 27, 1950. BA, Fordham U., 1937; MA, Dublin U. Coll., 1950, PhD, 1952. Instr. La Salle Acad., N.Y.C., 1939-42; with U.S. Air Corps, North Africa, 1942-46; asst. prof. St. Louis U., 1946-58; chmn. English dept. Bellarmine Coll., Louisville, 1958-62; prof., dir. comtemporary English lit. program U. Ottawa, Can., 1962-82; asst. to dir., archives researcher Abbey Theatre, Dublin, 1950-52. Author: Lennox Robinson, 1964; co-editor: Holloway's Abbey Theatre, 1967, Holloway's Irish Theatre (4 vols.), 1970. Com. Jr. Great Books Program, Louisville, 1959-61. Served with USAAF, 1942-46, ETO. Recipient Royal Soc. Antiquarians of Dublin fellowship, 1950, Research grant Can. Council, Ottawa, 1965, 66. Mem. AAUP, Can. Assn. Univ. Profs., Am. Assn. Univ. Profs., Nat. Council Tchrs. English. Democrat. Roman Catholic. Club: Univ. Coll. Grad. (Dublin). Home: Coolbunnia Cottage, Cheekpoint Co Waterford, Ireland

O'NEILL, PAUL HENRY, aluminum company executive; b. St. Louis, Dec. 4, 1935; s. John Paul and Gaynald Elsie (Irvin) O'N.; m. Nancy Jo Wolfe, Sept. 4, 1955; children—Patricia, Margaret, Julie, Paul Henry. A.B., Fresno State Coll., 1960; Haynes Found. fellow, Claremont Grad. Sch., 1960-61; postgrad., George Washington U., 1962-65; M.P.A., Ind. U., 1966. Site engr. Morrison-Knudsen, Inc., Anchorage, 1955-57; systems analyst VA, Washington, 1961-66; budget examiner Bur. of Budget, Washington, 1967-69; chief human resources program div. U.S. Govt. Office of Mgmt. and Budget, Washington, 1969-70; asst. dir. U.S. Govt. Office of Mgmt. and Budget, 1971-72, assoc. dir., 1973-74, dep. dir., 1975-77; v.p. Internat. Paper Co., N.Y.C., 1977-81, sr. v.p., 1981-85, pres., dir., 1985-87; chmn., chief exec. officer Aluminum Co. Am., Pitts., 1987—, also bd. dirs.; mem. adv. com. Fin. Acctg. Standards Bd., 1982-86; bd. dirs. Nat. Westminster Bank. Chmn. health and welfare com. Fairfax Fedn. Civic Assns., 1967; mem. JFK bd. visitors Harvard U., 1977-82, mem. adv. com, 1982—; bd. dirs. Gerald R. Ford Found., 1981—; mem. Manpower Devel. Research Corp., 1981—, Pres.'s Nat. Commn. on Productivity, 1981-83. Recipient Nat. Inst. Pub. Affairs Career Edn. award, 1965, William A. Jump Meritorious award, 1971; Fellow Nat. Inst. Pub. Affairs, 1966. Methodist. Home: 3 Von Lent Pl Pittsburgh PA 15232 Office: Aluminum Co of Am 1501 Alcoa Bldg Pittsburgh PA 15219

O'NEILL, RICHARD MICHAEL, pediatrician; b. San Francisco, June 11, 1923; s. Richard Michael and Marcella (Woods) O'N.; B.S., U. San Francisco, 1947; postgrad. Gonzaga U., 1943, Northwestern U., 1944; M.D., Creighton U., 1951; postgrad. U. Calif. at San Francisco, 1951-54; m. Nancy Catherine Gorman, June 19, 1948; children—Richard Michael, Kevin, Kerry Ellen, Barry. Intern, San Francisco Gen. Hosp.-U. Calif., 1951-52; sr. resident in pediatrics U. Calif. at San Francisco, 1954; practice medicine, specializing in pediatrics and pediatric allergy, San Jose, Calif., 1954—; pres. Med. staff O'Connor Hosp., San Jose, 1978—; faculty Santa Clara Valley Med. Center, O'Connor Hosp., San Jose, 1954—. Trustee Found. for Med. Care; mem. Task Force on New Age for Pediatrics; bd. dirs. Californians Preventing Violence; editor Santa Clara County Med. Soc. Bull. Served with USN, 1942-46; PTO. Mead Johnson fellow U. Calif. Med. Center, 1952-53. Fellow Am. Acad. Pediatrics (sec. 1954, com. on communications and pub. info., chmn. No. Calif., Chmn. No. Calif. 1981-84), Am. Coll. Allergy; mem. Santa Clara County Med. Soc., AMA, Calif. Med. Assn., Smithsonian Assocs., Am. Med. Writers Assn., Task Force on Children's TV. Democrat. Roman Catholic. Club: San Jose Swim and Racquet. Editor Calif. Pediatrician, 1974-84; contbr. articles in field to med. jours. and texts. Home: 1650 Cabana Dr San Jose CA 95125 Office: 100 O Connor Dr San Jose CA 95128

O'NEILL, THOMAS GABRIEL, finance company executive; b. Dundalk, Louth, Ireland, Dec. 23, 1939; s. Patrick and Kathleen (Forbes) O'Neill; m. Maeve Elizabeth Elliott, Aug. 28, 1972; children: Shane, Ronan, Katie, Brian. Grad. pub. sch., Dundalk. Acct. trainee Malone & Co., Dundalk, 1958-60; audit clk. Stokes Kennedy Crowley div. Peat Marwick Mitchell, Dublin, Ireland, 1960-65; chief acct. A.H. Masser Ltd., Dublin, 1965-70; acct. Bank of Ireland Fin. Ltd., Dublin, 1970-74, mgr. fin. services, 1974-80, dir.; dir. British Credit Trust Ltd., Slough, Eng., 1982—. Fellow Chartered Assn. Cert. Accts., Inst. Dirs.; mem. Inst. Taxation in Ireland (assoc.). Mem. Conservative Party. Roman Catholic. Office: British Credit Trust Ltd, 34 High St, Slough SL1 1ED, England

O'NEILL, WILLIAM ALEXANDER, business executive, chemist; b. Edinburgh, Scotland, July 11, 1925; s. Hugh and Grace (Chapman) O'N.; m. Julia Freeman, July 10, 1945; 1 dau., Juliet Mary. B.Sc. with 1st class honors, U. Glasgow, 1951, Ph.D., 1954. Research assoc. I.C.I. Ltd., Harrogate, Yorks., 1954-64; research mgr. Comml. Plastics, Newcastle, 1964-68; dir. Jupiter Plastics, London, 1968-73; mng. dir. Satellite Extrusions Ltd., Ely, Cambs., 1973—; dir. Press Mouldings, Ltd., 1973—; cons., lectr. in field. Patentee in field. Served with Royal Navy, 1943-47. Fellow Brit. Inst. Mgmt., Inst. Dirs., Plastics Inst. Home: 19 The Bowls, Chigwell, Essex England Office: Satellite Extrusions Ltd, Fordham Rd, Soham, Ely, Cambs CB5 5AJ, England

O'NEILL, WILLIAM A(TCHISON), governor of Connecticut; b. Hartford, Conn., Aug. 11, 1930; m. Natalie. Ed., New Brit. Tchr.'s Coll., U. Hartford. Owner O'Neill's Restaurant, East Hampton, Conn.; mem. Conn. Ho. of Reps., 1966-78, asst. house majority leader, 1971-72, asst. minority leader, 1973-74, house majority leader, chmn. com. on exec. nominations, 1975-76, 77-78; lt. gov. State of Conn., 1979-80, gov., 1980—; past chmn. New Eng. Gov.'s Conf.; mem. Conn. Gov.'s Fin. Adv. Com., 1968-74, East Hampton Democratic Town Com., 1954-80, East Hampton Zoning Bd. Appeals, East Hampton Bd. Fin.; state chmn. Ella Grasso For Gov. Com., 1974; chmn. Conn. Dem. Party, 1975-78, Coalition Northeastern Govs., 1984. Mem. East Hampton Fire Dist. Commn. Served with USAF, 1950-53. Recipient cert. of appreciation Conn. Firefighters Assn., 1972; Am. Legion Dept. Conn. award as outstanding legis. leader, 1974; Man of Yr. award Marine Club, 1979; Disting. Humanitarian award Nat. Jewish Hosp. and Research Center, 1981; Man of Yr. award Elks, 1981; Man of Yr. award United Irish Soc., 1982; Man of Yr. award Conn. High Sch. Coaches Assn., 1982; others. Mem. Nat. Govs. Assn. (com. transp., commerce and communication, com. on energy and environment), C. of C. of East Hampton (pres.), Am. Legion, VFW. Lodges: Elks; Moose. Office: State Capitol Office of Gov Room 202 Hartford CT 06115

O'NEILL, WILLIAM JAMES, JR., corporate executive, investor; b. Cleve., Aug. 28, 1933; s. William James and Dorothy (Kundtz) O'N.; children: Alec M., Sara L., Jessie A., Laura E.; m. Katherine Templeton Coquillette, July 18, 1987; 1 child, Carolyn P. Coquillette. B.S. cum laude, Georgetown U., 1955; J.D., Harvard U., 1958. Bar: Ohio 1958. Gen. counsel Leaseway Transp. Corp. and subs., 1961-67; East coast group head Leaseway Transp. Corp. and subs., Phila., 1967-68; v.p. East Coast group Leaseway Transp. Corp. and subs., 1968-69; sr. v.p. Leaseway Transp. Corp. and subs., Cleve., 1969-74; pres., chief operating officer Leaseway Transp. Corp. and subs., 1974-80, exec. v.p., chief planning officer, 1981-85, spl. projects adviser to chief exec. officer, 1985-86, also dir.; pres. Clanco Mgmt. Corp., Cleve., 1984—, also dir.; chmn. exec. com. Med. Payment Systems, also dir.; pres. Truck Renting and Leasing Assn., Washington, 1980-81, also dir.; founder, chmn Alliance for Simple, Equitable and Rational Truck Taxation, 1983-86, also dir. Trustee Dyke Coll. Corp., Hawken Sch., O'Neill Bros. Found., Univ. Hosps., Bluecoats, W.J. and D.K. O'Neill Found., Cleve. Council Ind. Schs. Served to capt. USAF, 1958-61. Recipient Air Force Commendation medal with oak leaf clusters; named Man of Year Gilmour Acad., 1974. Roman Catholic. Clubs: Chagrin Valley Hunt, Kirkland Country, Union. Office: Suite 123 30195 Chagrin Blvd Cleveland OH 44124

ONG, CHARLES CHEN CHUNG, marketing executive; b. Semarang, Cent. Java, Indonesia; s. Hans Ramana and Vera Saerang; m. Linda Suryadinata, Oct. 27, 1985. BS, Miami U., Ohio, 1976; MS in Mktg., Kensington U., 1979, Phd in Mktg., 1981. Tchr. stats. U. 17 Agustus Semarang, 1976-85, tchr. mktg. mgmt. economy dept., 1976—; tchr. bus. policy Diponegro U. Administrasi Niaga Dept., 1980—; treas. Employers' Assn. Indonesia, Cent. Java, 1982-85, sec., 1985—; advisor Pacific Asian Mgmt. Inst., U. Hawaii Coll. Bus. Adminstrn., 1984—; vice chmn. Recreation Park Orgn. Indonesia, Cent. Java, 1984—; chmn. compartment fgn. relations Kadinda, Cent. Java, 1985—; gen. chmn. Yadora, Sport Fund Found., Cent. Java, 1986—; mktg. trainee battery div. Union Carbide, Jakarta, 1976; mktg. dir. Nyonya Meneer, Semarang, Indonesia, 1976; lectr. Diponegoro U.; freelance writer Suara Merdeka, Berita Buana, Buana Minggu, 1976—. Mem. British Inst. Mgmt., Inst. Mktg. Eng. Lodge: Lions (pres. 1983-86, zone chmn. 1985-87). Office: P T Nyonya Meneer, Jalan Raden Patah 199, Semarang, Central Java Indonesia

ONG, DIONISIO CHUA, oil and gas executive; b. Majayjay, Laguna, Philippines, Oct. 31, 1922; s. Ignacio Antonio and Chua (Hun) Ongchoco; m. Julia Ang, Dec. 1, 1957; children: Evelyn, Oscar, Carlos, Veronica, Regina, Daniel. Student, U. Philippines, 1941. Pres. Overseas Gas Corp., Mandaluyong, Metro Manila, 1946—, Gen. Mercantile Corp., 1959—, Allied Steel Corp., 1960—, Sampaguita Investment and Devel. Corp., Makati, Metro Manila, 1960—, Alco Bus. Corp., Makati, Metro Manila, 1966—, Oceanic Air Products, Quezon City, Philippines, 1965—, Ogasco, Inc., Iloilo and Bacolod, Philippines, 1967—, Filfor Internat. Corp., 1968—; bd. dirs. Consol. Indsl. Gases, Inc., Mandaluyong, Metro Manila, Jacon & Co Services, Inc., Makati. Roman Catholic. Club: Army and Navy, Club of Manila. Home: 511 Buendia Ave Extension, North Forbes Park, Makati, Metro Manila Philippines Office: Alco Bus Corp, 3d F Exec Bldg Ctr, Makati, Metro Manila Philippines

ONG, ENG CHEE, computer company executive; b. Kuala Lumpur, Selangor, Malaysia, July 26, 1944; s. Sng Tuck Ong and Swee Leng Sim; m. Selena Chan; children: Chou Ch'ng, Lee-Yuin. Apprentice Nat. Cash Register, Kuala Lumpur, 1963-69; engr. On-Line Co., Ltd., Kuala Lumpur, 1970-75; dir. engring. Dataprep (M) Co., Ltd., Kuala Lumpur, 1976-80; dir. ops. Unidata Co., Ltd., Kuala Lumpur, 1980—, also bd. dirs.; bd. dirs. Sum Ming SDN BHD, Kuala Lumpur, Unimation SDN BHD, Kuala Lumpur. Chmn. Christian Approach to Rehab. Edn., Selangor, Malaysia, 1980. Home: 55 SS20/18 Damansara Utama, Petaling Jaya, Selangor Malaysia Office: Unidata SDN BHD, 20th Floor, Menara MPPJ, Petaling Jaya, Selangor Malaysia

ONG, THEAN BOK, manufacturing company executive; b. Georgetown, Penang, Malaysia, Dec. 5, 1936; s Eng Beng and Poh Kee (Lim) O.; m. Pang Lian Sim, May 12, 1955; children—Phaik Eong, Seng Huck, Seng Chean, Seng Ban, Seng Choh. Grad., Penang Free Sch., Georgetown, 1946-55; diploma in mgmt. Malaysian Inst. Mgmt. Field engr. Brit. Army, Kluang, Johore, 1957-59, criminal investigator, Singapore, 1959-63; criminal investigator Malaysian Army, Kuala Lumpur, Selangor, 1963-70, detachment comdr., 1970-73; transp. mgr. Holidaymakers Sdn Bhd, Kuala Lumpur, 1973-74; security mgr. Motorola Malaysia Sdn Bnd, Sungei-Way, Selangor, 1974—. Author: Security Procedures Manual, 1979. Contbr. articles to profl. publs. Recipient Gen. Service medal Brit. Army, 1963. Mem. Malaysian Electronic Security Council (vice chmn. 1984, sec. 1984), Malaysian Profl. Security Assn. (pres. 1976-80), Central Zone Security Council (vice chmn. 1984), Malaysian Inst. Personnel Mgmt. (lectr.), Am. Soc. Indsl. Security (cert. protection profl.), Internat. Criminologists, Internat. Chartered Investigators, Malaysian Electronic Security Council (vuce chmn. 1984, sec. 1985, vice chmn. 1987), Malaysian Profl. Security Assn. (v.p. 1987). Club: Selangor Shooting Assn. Lodge: Rosicrucian Order. Avocations: reading; dogs; fishes; gardening; martial arts. Home: 12 Jalan, SS22/33 Damansara Jaya, 47400 Petaling Jaya Selangor Malaysia Office: Motorola Malaysia Sdn Bhd, PO Box 1001, 46960 Petaling Jaya, Jalan Semangat, Selangor Malaysia

ONGARO, MARIO PETER, priest; b. Verona, Italy, Apr. 7, 1926; came to U.S., 1947; s. Giuseppe and Giulia (Bonfante) O. BA, Athenaeum of Ohio, 1951; MA, Xavier U., 1961; MLS, U. Mich., 1964. Ordained priest Roman Cath. Ch., 1951; lic. psychologist, Ohio. Pastoral ministry Pala Indians, San Diego, 1956-58; instr. classics Sacred Heart Sem., Monroe, Mich., 1952-56, instr. philosophy classics, 1961-64; instr. classics Sacred Heart Sem., Cin., 1958-61, sch. counselor, 1964-68; adminstr. Comboni Mission Ctr., Cin., 1968-83; psychologist, educator Casa Comboni, Los Angeles, 1983-87; vice provincial superior Provincial Hdqrs., Cin., 1987—; mem. com. re-writing constitutions Comboni Missionaries, Rome, 1976-79, provincial counselor, 1979-84. Mem. Am. Psychol. Assn., Ohio Psychol. Assn., Am. Orthopsychiat. Assn., Soc. Personality Assessment. Home and Office: 8108 Beechmont Ave Cincinnati OH 45255

ONGMAHUTMONGKOL, THIRACHAI, chemical company executive, management consultant; b. Bangkok, Aug. 24, 1948; s. Ngeg Kim Eng and Lao Thor Lao; m. Vipa P. Ongmahutmongkol, Nov. 17, 1975; children: Chavapas, Pattachee. AS, So. Ill. U., Carbondale, 1969, BS, 1971; MBA, U. East Asia, Taipa, Macau, 1985. Sucessively advt. and promotion exec., plant mgr., import-export mgr. Inch-Cape Group, Bangkok, 1972-75; asst. tech. mgr. F. E. Zuellig Ltd., Bangkok, 1975-77; mktg. mgr. Du Pont Thailand Ltd., Bangkok, 1977-82; regional mgr. Du Pont Asia Pacific Ltd., Hong Kong, 1982-85; gen. mgr. Du Pont China Ltd., Hong Kong, 1985-87; mnging. dir. Du Pont-TOA Co., Ltd., Bangkok, 1987—. Author books and articles. Mem. Thailand Mgmt. Assn., Mktg. Assn. Thailand, Soc. Automotive Engrs., The Diplomatic Speaking Club. Bhuddist. Clubs: Royal Bangkok Sports, Hong Kong Country. Lodge: Rotary. Home: 1 Muban Kanda, Ramkamhaeng 38 Hua Mak, 10240 Bangkok Thailand Office: Du Pont-TOA Co Ltd, 9th Fl Yaoa Bldg, 56 Silom Rd, Bangkok 10500, Thailand

ONIKI, HAJIME, economics educator; b. Tokyo, June 13, 1933; s. Masami and Yoshiko Oniki; m. Mieko Kurihara, June 5, 1966; children—Yumi, Shuntaro. B.A. in Econs., U. Tokyo, 1958, M.A., 1960; Ph.D., Stanford U., 1968. Research assoc. Stanford U., Calif., 1964-65; asst. prof. econs. Tohoku U., Sendai, Japan, 1965-69, Harvard U., Cambridge, Mass., 1969-72; asst. prof. Queen's U., Kingston, Ont., Can., 1972-74, assoc. prof., 1974-79; prof. Osaka U., Japan, 1979—. Ford Found. fellow, 1963-65; Social Sci. Res. Council fellow, 1973-74; recipient Telecommunications Social Sci. award Nippon Telephone and Telegraph Corp., 1984. Mem. Am. Econ. Assn., Econometric Soc. Home: 1-1-12-108 Fujishiro, Suita, Osaka 560, Japan Office: Inst Social and Econ Research, Osaka U, Mihogaoka, Ibaraki Osaka 567, Japan

ONISHI, AKIRA, economics educator, academic administrator; b. Tokyo, Jan. 5, 1929; s. Tatsunosuke and Tomi (Fusegawa) O.; m. Noriko Shimizu, Sept. 27, 1963; children—Kimihiro, Masahiro. B.A. in Econs., Keio U., Tokyo, 1954, M.A. in Econs., 1958, Ph.D. in Econs., 1963. Research officer Inst. Developing Economies, Tokyo, 1963-65; assoc. prof. Chuo U., Tokyo, 1965-67; econ. affairs officer UN Econ. Commn. for Asia and Far East, Bangkok, Thailand, 1967-68; econ. affairs officer ILO, Geneva, 1968-70; chief economist Japan Econ. Research Ctr., Tokyo, 1970-71; prof. econs. Soka U., Tokyo, 1971—, dir. Inst. Applied Econ. Research, 1976—, dean Grad. Sch. Econs., 1978—. Author: Japanese Economy in Global Age, 1974; numerous articles on global econ. modeling, 1977—. Grantee Japan Found., 1958-60, Japan Econ. Research Found., 1974-75, Australia-Japan Found., 1981-82; recipient SGI Culture award, 1985. Fellow Japan Soc. Internat. Econs., Japan Soc. Econ. Policy. Buddhist. Home: 4-9-4 Seijyo, Setagaya-ku, Tokyo 157, Japan Office: Soka U, 1-236 Tangi-cho, Hachiji-shi, Tokyo 192, Japan

ONO, KEINOSUKE, business administration educator; b. Tokyo, Oct. 30, 1940; s. Yoshiaki and Kikuko (Kimori) O.; m. Yoshiko Imaizumi, Oct. 24, 1968; children: Ai, Yumi, Nana. BS, Keio U., 1963, MS, 1965, DEng, 1983. Research asst. Keio U., Tokyo, 1965-71, from asst. prof. to prof. bus. adminstrn., 1984—; vis. prof. Asian Inst. Mgmt., Manila, 1973; cons. Asian Productivity Orgn., Tokyo, 1974—. Author: Management Decision Making in Overseas Production, 1984 (Keiko prize 1984), (with others) The Motor Vehicle Industry in Asia, 1983, The Automobile Industry in Japan, 1988. Mem. Japan Indsl. Mgmt. Assn., Japan Ops. Research Assn., Japan Inst. Indsl. Engrs. Home: 2762 Naracho, Midoriku, Yokohama 227, Japan Office: Keio Bus Sch, 2-1-1 Hiyoshihoncho Kohukuku, Yokohama 223, Japan

ONO, TOSHIYUKI ANTONIO, bridge company executive; b. Chiba, Japan, May 4, 1926; s. Michinosuke and Fumi (Taguchi) O.; B.S. in C.E., U. Tokyo, 1954; postgrad. (Internat. Rd. Fedn. fellow) Purdue U., 1960-61; m. Sumiko Elizabeth Suzuki, May 27, 1958; children—Haruo Francisco, Kazuko Ruchia. Research ofcl. Tech. Research Inst. Civil Engring., Tokyo, 1954-58; dir. Kanto Regional Constrn. Bur., Japan Ministry Constrn. and Rd. Planning, 1958-73, 75-78; dep. gen. dir. Assn. for Internat. Ocean Expo, Okinawa, 1973-75; constrn. cons. Ministry of Constrn., 1978-79; mng. dir. Yokogawa Bridge Works, Ltd., Tokyo, 1979—; cons. Suratani Rd Asian Hwy., Thailand; dep. rep. Japanese Govt., Internat. Ocean Expn. Mem. Japan Soc. Civil Engring., Japan Concrete Inst., Japan Rd Assn. Roman Catholic. Clubs: Totuka Country, President. Office: 4-4-44 Shibaura, Minato-ku, Tokyo 108, Japan

ONRUST, DICK, retail executive; b. Zaandam, The Netherlands, May 31, 1946; s. D. and G. (Groot) O.; married 1965; children: Esther, Sylvia. With SRV-Noord-Holland, Krommenie, The Netherlands, 1967-72, Ahold, Zaandam, The Netherlands, 1972-88; dep. dir. Albert Heijn b.v., Zaandam, 1988—; adj. dir. Ins. voor Sociale Wetenschappen, Stichting voor Reklame en Marketingonderwys, 1972-87. Home: Smient 8, 1721 DG Broek Op Langedijk The Netherlands Office: Albert Heijn BV, Ankersmidplein 2, 1506 CK Zaandam The Netherlands

ONSTOTT, EDWARD IRVIN, research chemist; b. Moreland, Ky., Nov. 12, 1922; s. Carl Ervin and Jennie Lee (Foley) O.; m. Mary Margaret Smith, Feb. 6, 1945; children—Jenifer, Peggy Sue, Nicholas, Joseph. B.S. in Chem. Engring., U. Ill., 1944, M.S. in Chemistry, 1948, Ph.D. in Inorganic Chemistry, 1950. Chem. engr. Firestone Tire & Rubber Co., Paterson, N.J., 1944, 46; research chemist Los Alamos Nat. Lab., 1950—. Patentee in field. Served with C.E., AUS, 1944-46. Fellow AAAS, Am. Inst. Chemists; mem. Am. Chem. Soc., Electrochem. Soc., N.Y. Acad. Scis., Internat. Assn. Hydrogen Energy, Rare Earth Research Confs., Izaak Walton League. Republican. Methodist. Home: 225 Rio Bravo Los Alamos NM 87544 Office: Los Alamos Nat Lab MS G738 Los Alamos NM 87545

ONUIGBO, WILSON IKECHUKU BENIAH, pathologist, researcher; b. Oraifite, Anambra, Nigeria, Apr. 28, 1928; s. Joseph Oranekwu and Margaret Amanna (Imonugo) O.; m. Edith Nneka Odukwe, Sept. 30, 1960; children: Chy, Nwamaka, Unoma, Kenechi, Nwanneka, Obiora, Enuma. ScB, London U., 1954, PhD, 1961; MB, B in chemistry, Glasgow (Scotland) U., 1957, MD, 1979. Med. officer Ministry of Health, Enugu, Nigeria, 1959-62, cons., 1964-70, sr. cons., 1970-75, chief cons., 1975-77; lectr. U. Lagos (Nigeria), 1962-63; vis. prof. U. Nigeria, Enugu, 1977-78, prof., 1985—, dean, 1986—; founder, dir. Med. Found. and Clinic, Enugu, 1979—; hon. cons. Specialist Hosp., Enugu, Teaching hosp., Enugu. Editor jour. Bull. of Enugu Med. Soc., 1985—; contbr. articles to profl. jours., chpts. to books. Councillor Oraifite Town Council; bd. dirs. Oraifite Boys' Secondary Sch., 1975; chmn. Laity Council of Anglican Diocese, Enugu, 1985. Recipient John Reid prize Glasgow U., 1955, Mary Ure prize Glasgow U., 1956, Disting. Alumni award U. Ibadan, Enugu br., 1982; awarded Onowu Chieftaincy, Traditional Ruler of Oraifite, 1978; research fellow U. Glasgow, 1962. Fellow Royal Soc. Medicine, Internat. Coll. Surgeons; mem. Path. Soc. of Gt. Britain and Ireland, Nigerian Cancer Soc., Forensic Sci. Soc. Mem. Anglican Ch. Home: 8 Nsukka Ln, P O Box 1792, Enugu, Anambra Nigeria Office: Med Found and Clinic, 8 Nsukka Ln, Enugu, Anambra Nigeria

ONYONKA, ZACHARY, government official; b. Feb. 28, 1939; s. Godrico Deri and Kerobina (Kebati) O.; married; 6 children. Student, Mosocho Sch., Nyaburu Sch., St. Mary's Sch.; D. in Pub. Service (hon.), Syracuse U., 1981. Lectr. dept econs. U. Coll., Nairobi, Kenya, 1968-69; M.P. Govt. of Kenya, 1969—, minister econ. planning and devel., 1969-70, 79-83, minister of info. and broadcasting, 1970-73, minister of health, 1973-74, minister of edn., 1974-76, minister of housing and social services, 1976-78, minister of fgn. affairs, 1987-88; mem. nat. exec. com. Kenya African Nat. Union; pres. African-Caribbean and Pacific Group of Countries, 1981. Research fellow U. Coll., Nairobi, 1967; recipient Elder Golden Heart medal. Felow Internat. Bankers Assn. Office: Ministry of Fgn Affairs, Nairobi Kenya *

OOSTERBAAN, DINANT THEODOOR LAW, lawyer; b. Amsterdam, The Netherlands, Sept. 4, 1944; s. Dinant P. and Anna A. (Vissink) O.; m. Marie-Anne P. Schouten, Nov. 29, 1969; children: Machteld, Olivier. JD, Erasmus U., Rotterdam, The Netherlands, 1968; M Comparative Jurisprudence, NYU, 1972. Bar: Amsterdam 1981. Atty. Netherland's Ministry Def., The Hague, 1970-71; legal counsel IBM Nederland N.V., Amsterdam, 1971-76, 79-80; atty. IBM Europe S.A., Paris, 1976-77, IBM Corp., Kingston, N.Y., 1977-79; ptnr. Aberson, Sybrandy Attys. at Law, Amsterdam, 1981—; chmn. 1st European Computer/Law Conf., Brussels, 1984; bd. dirs. Infostore Nederland B.V., Nieuwegein. Editor-in-chief Internat. Computer Law Adviser, 1986—; editor Computerrecht, 1984—; mem. internat. adv. bd. Software Protection, 1986—. Mem. Netherlands Bar Assn., Internat. Bar Assn., Netherlands Assn. for Computers and Law (pres. 1986—), Computer Law Assn. (speaker Toronto, Can. 1986), Amsterdam Council on Telecommunications and Info. (bd. dirs. 1987—). Home: Bentveldsweg 148, 2111 EE Aerdenhout The Netherlands Office: Aberson Sybrandy, Johannes Vermeerplein 1, 1071 DV Amsterdam The Netherlands

OOSTERHUIS, HERMAN HENDRIK, diesel engine company executive; b. Amsterdam, Holland, Apr. 1, 1926; s. Folkert and Clasina Elisabeth (Morlang) O.; came to U.S., 1963, naturalized, 1969; degrees in marine engring. Amsterdam Marine Engrs. Coll., 1946, 54; m. Adriana Theresa VanRoey, Mar. 26, 1956; 1 child, Patrick Herman. Engr., Netherlands Navigation Co., Rotterdam, 1946-56, chief engr., 1956-58; supervising engr. Vinke & Co., Rotterdam, 1958-60, asst. to pres., 1960-62; pres., mgr. Power Engring. Inc., New Orleans, 1963-66, Oosterhuis Industries, Inc., Belle Chasse, La., 1966—; dir. Marine Engring. Inc., Marine Financing Corp., Am. Brons Corp. Mem. Soc. Naval Architects and Marine Engrs., Vereniging Technici Scheepvaart Gebied (Netherlands). Club: Propeller (New Orleans). Home: 51 Park Timbers Dr New Orleans LA 70131 Office: 1701 Engineers Rd Belle Chasse LA 70037

OPDEBEECK, HERLINDE, orthodontist, educator; b. Oostende, West-Vlaanderen, Belgium, Mar. 18, 1946; d. Willy and Jacqueline (Fernagut) O.; m. Guy Mannaerts, Aug. 22, 1970; children—Herlinde, Jan, Inge. M.D., K.U. Leuven, Belgium, 1970, D.D.S., 1971, postgrad. in oral surgery, 1976. Postdoctoral fellow U. Tex. Med. Sch., 1975-76. Practice dentistry specializing in orthodontics, Leuven, 1979—; assoc. prof. U. Limburg Dental Sch., Hasselt, Belgium, 1982—. Contbr. articles to profl. jours. NATO fellow, 1975; recipient Belgian-Am. Woman Assn. award Fulbright Found., 1975. Mem. Belgian Profl. Assn. Orthodontics, Am. Assn. Orthodontics, Belgian Assn. Oral Surgeons. Lodge: Soroptimists. Home: Lei 7, B3000 Leuven, Brabant Belgium Office: U Limburg Dental Sch, Universitaire Campus, Diepenbeek, B3610 Hasselt, Limburg Belgium

OPEL, JOHN R., business machines company executive; b. Kansas City, Mo., Jan. 5, 1925; s. Norman J. and Esther (Roberts) O.; m. Julia Carole Stout, Dec. 28, 1953; children: Robert, Nancy, Julia, Mary, John. A.B., Westminster Coll., 1948; M.B.A., U. Chgo., 1949. With IBM Corp., Armonk, N.Y., 1949—, salesman, various mgmt. positions, 1949-66, v.p., 1966-68, mem. mgmt. com., 1967, v.p. corp. finance and planning, 1968-69, sr. v.p. finance and planning, 1969-72, group exec. data processing group, 1972-74, dir., 1972—, pres., 1974-83, chief exec. officer, 1981-86, chmn., 1983-86, chmn. exec. com., 1986—; chmn. Fed. Res. Bank N.Y., N.Y.C., 1986—; bd dirs. Pfizer, Inc., Time Inc., Prudential Ins. Co. Am., Fed. Res. Bank of N.Y. Trustee U. Chgo., Westminster Coll. Served with U.S. Army, 1943-45. Mem. Bus. Council, Council on Fgn. Relations. Office: IBM Corp OLd Orchard Rd Armonk NY 10504 *

OPIE, LIONEL HENRY, educator, researcher; b. Hanover, Cape Town, Republic South Africa, May 6, 1933; s. William Henry and Maria Magdalena (le Roux) O.; m. Carol June Sancroft-Baker, Aug. 16, 1969; children: Jessica June, Amelia Louise. Rhodes scholar, Lincoln Coll., Oxford, Eng., 1957-59. Research fellow Harvard Med. Sch., Boston, 1959-61; lectr. U. Stellenbosch, Republic South Africa, 1961-64; Wellcome fellow dept. biochemistry U. Oxford, 1964-66; fellow dept. biochemistry Imperial Coll. Sci. and Tech., London, 1967-69; lectr., cons. cardiovascular research Dept. Research, Royal Postgrad. Med. Sch., London, 1969-71; sr. lectr. medicine U. Cape Town, 1971-76, assoc. prof., 1976-80, prof. medicine, 1980—, dir. med. research council unit, 1976—. Author: Drugs and the Heart, The Lancet, 1980, The Heart: Physiology, Metabolism, Pharmacology and Therapy, 1984, revised edit., 1986; co-founder Jour. Molecular and Cellular Cardiology, 1980—, Cardiovascular Drugs and Therapy, 1986—; editor: Drugs for the Heart, 1987; co-author: Biochemistry and Pharmacology of the Heart, 1982; co-editor Calcium and the Heart, 1971. Recipient First Prize, Am. Coll. Chest Physicians, 1953; Gold Medal, Lorenzini Found., Italy, 1981. Fellow Royal Coll. Physicians London, Am. Coll. Cardiology; mem. Physiol. Soc. Gt. Britain Internat., Soc. Heart Research (pres. 1976-78). Ch. of Eng. Clubs: Chevalier du Tastevin, Owl. Home: 66-A Dean St, Newlands Republic of South Africa 7700

OPITZ, JOHN MARIUS, pediatrician, clinical geneticist; b. Hamburg, Germany, Aug. 15, 1935; came to U.S., 1950, naturalized, 1957; s. Friedrich and Erica Maria (Quadt) O.; children—Elisabeth, Gabriella, John, Chrisanthi, Felix. B.A., State U. Iowa, 1956, M.D., 1959; D.Sc. (hon.), Mont. State U., 1983; MD (hon.), U. Kiel, Fed. Republic of Germany, 1986. Diplomate Am. Bd. Pediatrics, Am. Bd. Med. Genetics. Intern, State U. Iowa Hosp., 1959-60, resident in pediatrics, 1960-61; resident and chief resident in pediatrics U. Wis. Hosp., Madison, 1961-62; fellow in pediatrics and med. genetics U. Wis., 1962-64, asst. prof. med. genetics and pediatrics, 1964-69, assoc. prof., 1969-72, prof., 1972-79; dir. Wis. Clin. Genetics Ctr., 1974-79; clin. prof. med. genetics and pediatrics U. Wash., Seattle, 1979—; adj. prof. medicine, biology, history and philosophy, vet. research and vet. sci. Mont. State U., Bozeman, 1979—; adj. prof. pediatrics, med. genetics U. Wis., Madison, 1979—; coordinator Shodair Mont. Regional Genetic Services Program, Helena, 1979-82; chmn. dept. med. genetics Shodair Children's Hosp., Helena, 1983—; Farber lectr. Soc. Pediatric Pathology, 1987. Author 12 books; founder, editor-in-chief Am. Jour. Med. Genetics, 1977—; mng. editor European Jour. Pediatrics, 1977-85; contbr. numerous articles on clin. genetics. Mem. German Acad. Scientists Leopoldina, Am. Soc. Human Genetics, Am. Pediatric Soc., Soc. Pediatric Research, Am. Bd. Med. Genetics, Birth Defects Clin. Genetic Soc., Am. Inst. Biol. Scis., Am. Soc. Zoologists, AAAS, Teratology Soc., Genetic Soc. Am., European Soc. Human Genetics, Soc. Study Social Biology, Am. Acad. Pediatrics, German Soc. Pediatrics (corr.), Western Soc. Pediatrics Research, Sigma Xi. Democrat. Roman Catholic. Home: 579 2d St Helena MT 59601 Office: Shodair Children's Hosp 840 Helena Ave Helena MT 59601

OPPEDAHL, PHILLIP EDWARD, computer company executive; b. Renwick, Iowa, Sept. 17, 1935; s. Edward and Isadore Hannah (Gangstead) O.; B.S. in Naval Sci., Navy Postgrad. Sch., 1963, M.S. in Nuclear Physics, 1971; M.S. in Systems Mgmt., U. S.C., 1978; m. Sharon Elaine Ree, Aug. 3, 1957; children—Gary Lynn, Tamra Sue, Sue Ann, Lisa Kay. Commd. ensign U.S. Navy, 1956, advanced through grades to capt., 1977; with Airborne Early Warning Squadron, 1957-59, Anti-Submarine Squadron, 1959-65; asst. navigator USS Coral Sea, 1965-67; basic jet flight instr., 1967-69; student Armed Forces Staff Coll., 1971; test group dir. Def. Nuclear Agy., 1972-74; weapons officer USS Oriskany, 1974-76; program mgr. for armament Naval Air Systems Command, Washington, 1977-79; test dir. Def. Nuclear Agy., Kirtland AFB, N.Mex., 1979-82, dep. comdr. Def. Nuclear Agy., 1982-83; pres., chief exec. officer Computer Horizons Corp., Albuquerque, 1983—. Decorated Disting. Service medal. Mem. Naval Inst., Am. Nuclear Soc., Aircraft Owners and Pilots Assn., Assn. Naval Aviation Navy League. Lutheran. Author: Energy Loss of High Energy Electrons in Beryllium, 1971; Understanding Contractor Motivation and Incentive Contracts, 1977. Home: 13305 Desert Flower Pl NE Albuquerque NM 87111 Office: Computer Land of Albuquerque 2226A Wyoming NE Albuquerque NM 87112

OPPENHEIM, GARRETT, psychotherapist, hypnotherapist; b. N.Y.C., June 7, 1918; s. James and Lucy Oppenheim; Ph.D., Columbia Pacific U., 1981; m. Fae Robin, Feb. 26, 1966 (div. Nov. 6, 1987); m. Gwendolyn Jean Hoffman, Jan. 19, 1988; 1 child, Lyn. Cert. med. psychotherapist; nat. cert. counselor. Editor, Wall St. Jour., 1940-42, N.Y. Herald Tribune, 1942-58, N.Y. Times, 1958-59, Med. Econs., 1959-63; sr. editor Venture mag., 1963-71, Med. Econs., 1971-77; pres., dir. Confide--Personal Counseling Services, Inc., Tappan, N.Y., 1971—; lectr., workshop leader; instr. self-hypnosis and past-life regression White Plains Adult Edn. System, N.Y., 1984—; former instr., bd. dirs. Assn. Past-Life Research and Therapy. Fellow Internat. Council Sex Edn. and Parenthood; mem. Am. Assn. Sex Educators, Counselors and Therapists, N.Y. Milton H. Erickson Soc. Psychotherapy and Hypnosis, Am. Soc. Psychosomatic Dentistry and Medicine, Internat. Platform Assn., Sex Info. and Edn. Council of U.S., Assn. to Advance Ethical Hypnosis, Soc. Sci. Study Sex, Am. Mental Health Counselors Assn., Assn. for Research and Enlightenment, Am. Assn. Counseling and Devel., Harry Benjamin Internat. Gender Dysphoria Assn., Inst. Noetic Scis., Nat. Ataxia Found. (hon. dir.). Author numerous articles in field. Home: Box 56 Tappan NY 10983 Office: 200 Washington St Tappan NY 10983

OPPENHEIM, ROBERT, beauty industry executive; b. N.Y.C., May 21, 1925; s. Hyman and Hannah (Lieberman) O.; BS cum laude, Syracuse U., 1950; m. Ruth Wigler, Feb. 7, 1954; children: Nancy Ellen, David Paul, Howard P. Product sales specialist McKesson & Robbins, Yonkers, N.Y., 1950-55; asst. sales mgr. Clairol, Inc., N.Y.C., 1955-60; dir. marketing Haircolor div. Revlon, Inc., N.Y.C., 1960-68, dir. marketing and sales Salon div., 1968-70; exec. v.p. Milton R. Barrie Co., Inc., 1970-71; mgmt. cons., 1971-76; pub. Beauty Salon Newsletter, N.Y.C., 1971-83; pres. Salon div. Clairol, Inc., N.Y.C., 1988—, chmn. Profl. Products div., 1983-87; pres. Oppenheim Communications, N.Y.C., 1988—; pub. Salon Update, 1987—, The Oppenheim Letter, 1988—, mgmt. cons., 1988—. Served with AUS, 1942-44; ETO. Mem. Nat. Beauty and Barber Assn. (pres. 1984-85), Am. Beauty Assn. (pres. 1985-86). Mason. Home: 241 Sickletown Rd West Nyack NY 10994 Office: 153 E 57th St New York NY 10022

OPPOWA, RUDOLF JOHANN, metal processing executive; b. Munich, Apr. 29, 1928. Student, U. Munich, 1951; M in Polit. Economy, NYU, 1954. Export dir., v.p. BMF, Nuernberg, Fed. Republic of Germany, 1976—. Office: BMF, Sigmundstrasse, 8500 Nuernberg Federal Republic of Germany

OPRE, THOMAS EDWARD, magazine editor, film company executive; b. Evansville, Ind., Nov. 6, 1943; s. William Jennings and Ruth (Strouss) O.; m. Norlin Kay Hartley, June 20, 1965; children—Thomas Andrew, William Hartley. A.B. in Journalism, Ind. U., 1965. Writer sports and outdoors Decatur (Ill.) Herald and Rev., 1965-66; outdoor editor Detroit Free Press, 1966—; field editor Midwest div. Field and Stream mag., 1971-81; editorial dir. Gt. Lakes Sportsman mag., 1972-75; editor-at-large and sports vehicles editor Outdoor Life mag., 1981—; pres. Tom Opre Prodns., 1967—. Author numerous articles in outdoor and travel fields. Recipient James Henshall award Am. Fish Tackle Mfrs. Assn., 1969, Teddy award Internat. Outdoor Travel Film Festival, 1973, Environ. award EPA, 1977, Nat. Writer's award Safari Club Internat., 1977, Deep Woods Writing award OWAA, 1977, Conservation Service award Ducks Unltd., 1977; World Wildlife Found. award, 1981; named to Internat. Fishing Hall of Fame, 1968, Conservation Communicator of Yr., 1985. Mem. Outdoor Writers Assn. Am. (past dir., pres., v.p., chmn. bd.), Assn. Gt. Lakes Outdoor Writers (past dir., chmn. bd., pres., v.p.), Mich. Outdoor Writers Assn. (v.p., pres., chmn. bd. dirs.), Alpha Tau Omega. Home and Office: PO Box 517 Brighton MI 48116 Office: 321 W Lafayette Blvd Detroit MI 48231

OPREA, GHEORGHE, Romanian deputy prime minister; b. Tintea-Baicor, Prahova County, Romania, Apr. 15, 1927; ed. Poly. Inst. Bucharest. Gen. mgr. Ministry of Machine Building Industry, 1957-62, dep. minister, 1962-70; alt. mem. Central Com. Romanian Communist Party, 1965-72, mem. Central Com., 1972—, counselor Central Com., 1970-74, mem. exec. polit. com. from 1974, mem. Standing Bur., from 1974, vice chmn. Supreme Council for Econ. and Social Devel., from 1974, dep. chmn. Council of Ministers, 1974-78; 1st dep. prime minister, 1978—; mem. Grand Nat. Assembly, 1975—, Nat. Council Front of Socialist Democracy and Unity, 1980. Address: Central Committee, Partidul Comunist Roman, Str Academiei 34, Bucharest Romania *

O'QUIGLEY, SEAN, retired physician, consultant; b. Listowel, County Kerry, Ireland, Mar. 12, 1914; s. John Joseph and Ahhie (O'Leary) O'Q.; m. married, Sept. 5, 1945; children: Patrick St. John, Luke Damian, Sorcha Ann. Student, St. Michael's Coll., Listowel, Blackrock Coll., Dublin, Ireland; BChir, BA in Obstetrics, Univ. Coll., Dublin, 1944, Cert. in Pub. Health, 1947. Enlisted Irish Army M.C., 1944; med. officer Irish Air Corps, Gormanstown, Ireland, 1944-47, Baldonnel, Ireland, 1947-53; physician Civil Pilots Med. Bd., Dublin, 1947-60, St. Bricin's Hosp., Dublin, 1953-58; chief med. officer Aer Lingus, Dublin, 1960-81; dep. chief med. officer UN Observation group, Lebanon, 1958; cons. Clery & Co. Ltd., Dublin, Airmotive Ireland Ltd., Rathcoole, Tegral Pipes Ltd., Drogheda, Ireland, Irish Cement Ltd., Platin Drogheda, and Icl Limerick, Kinsealy Farms Ltd.; lectr. aviation med. Univ. Coll., Dublin, 1974-80, Royal Coll. Surgeons, Dublin, 1974-80. Contbr. articles to profl. jours. Recipient UN medal for Services. Fellow Aerospace Med. Assn. (v.p. 1964), Royal Coll. Physicians Ireland (treas. faculty occupational medicine 1974-80, founding fellow faculty occupational medicine 1976); mem. Internat. Acad. Aviation and Space Medicine (v.p. 1978), Airline Med. Dirs. Assn. (pres. 1973-74), European Airlines Med. Dirs. Soc. (pres. 1962-76), Internat. Cong. Aviation and Space Medicine (pres. 1964), Irish Soc. Occupational Medicine (pres. 1970-72), Internat. Air Transport Assn. (vice-chmn. med. adv. com. 1974-76). Home: Cappagh Beg The Hill, Malahide County, Dublin Ireland Office: Airmotive Ireland Ltd, Naas Rd, Rathcoole County Ireland

OR, KUI CHUN, accountant, manufacturing company executive; b. Hong Kong, Nov. 28, 1956; s. Ming Yau Or and Sui Kwan Wong; m. Connie Fu Sui King, Mar. 27, 1982; 1 child, Ka Shun. Diploma, Evening Sch. of Higher Chinese Studies, Hong Kong, 1978, Hong Kong Poly. and Hong Kong Mgmt. Assn., 1987. Acctg. clk. Chen Hsong Machinery Co. Ltd., Hong Kong, 1975-81, acctg. supr., 1981-82, acctg. mgr., 1982—. Author: Adventure Beyond Time and Space, 1985, Stories of the Zodiac, 1987. Home: Flat 406, Block F Luk Yeung Sun Chuen, Tsuen Wan Hong Kong Office: Chen Hsong Machinery Co Ltd, 265-267 Un Chau St G/F, Shamshuipo, Kowloon Hong Kong

ORACHA, CHRISTIAN BARNABAS, beverage company executive; b. Mombasa, Nyanza, Kenya, Dec. 12, 1946; s. Joanes and Rosalia (Aboge) Omolo; m. Mary Ollyv Adhiambo, Sept. 6, 1976; children: Patricia, Maureen, Kezia, Cindy. B in Commerce, Nairobi U., Kenya, 1973; MBA, Iran Cen. for Mgmt. Studies, 1975. Comml. mgr. Van Leer E.A. Ltd., Mombasa, 1975-81; mktg. mgr. Caltex Oil (Kenya) Ltd., Nairobi, 1981-84; gen. mgr. Stationery & Office Supplies Ltd., Nairobi, 1984-86, Umoja Beverages Ltd., Umoja Ventures Ltd., Nairobi, 1987—; chmn., bd. dirs. Hairways Cosmetics Salon Equipment Ltd., Nairobi, 1986—, Kaduro Enterprises Ltd., Nairobi, 1983—. Patron Rambira Primary Sch., Nyanza, Siaya, 1984—; chmn. Siger Secondary Sch., Nyanza, 1985—. Mem. Kenya Inst. Mgmt. Mem. KANU Party. Roman Catholic. Clubs: Nairobi Safari; Mombasa. Home: PO Box 21436, Nairobi Kenya Office: Umoja Beverages Ltd, PO Box 21436, Nairobi Kenya

ORAVECZ, MICHAEL GEORGE, physicist, researcher; b. Akron, Ohio, Jan. 31, 1956; s. John and Miriam Jane (Partsch) O. B. in Physics, U. Chgo., 1978; M. in Physics, SUNY-Stony Brook, 1979. Jr. research asst. Cloud Physics Lab. Dept. Geophysics U. Chgo., 1975-76; Yerkes Obs., Williams Bay, Wis., 1977; teaching asst. physics SUNY-Stony Brook, 1978-79, research asst. quantum electronics group Physics dept., 1979; chief scientist Sonoscan, Inc., Bensenville, Ill., 1981-88; systems engr. KLA Instruments Corp., Santa Clara, Calif., 1988—; internat. speaker Ultrasonic Tech., Toyohashi, Japan. Contbr. articles to profl. jours. Sustainer Inst. for Independent Social Journalism. Mem. Am. Ceramics Soc., Am. Soc. Metals, Am. Soc. Nondestructive Testing, Inst. Elec. and Electronic Engrs., Inc., Am. Soc. for Quality Control, Am. Soc. Mech. Engrs. (mem. tech. com. on biomed. uses of acoustics, 1984-85), NOW. Avocations: computers; classical music. Home: 555 E El Camino Real Apt 119 Sunnyvale CA 94087-1901 Office: KLA Instruments Corp 3530 Bassett St PO Box 58016 MS 3-241 Santa Clara CA 95052

ORBISON, JAMES GRAHAM, civil engineer, educator; b. Cleve., Oct. 27, 1953; s. James Lowell and Olga Andrea (Dianich) O.; m. Nancy Anne Miller, June 11, 1977; children: Ryan Brantly, Eric James. BSCE, Bucknell U., 1975; MEC, Cornell U., 1976, PhD, 1982. Project engr. English Engring. Corp., Williamsport, Pa., 1976-77; lectr. Bucknell U., Lewisburg, Pa., 1977-78, asst. prof. civil engring., 1982-87, assoc. prof. engring., 1987—; reviewer ASME, ASTM, Am. Inst. Steel Construction, Prestressed Concrete Inst, Pa. Dept. Commerce, Harper & Row Pubs; contbr. articles to profl. jours. Mem. ASCE (Linback award for Distinguished Teaching 1988), Pa. Soc. Profl. Engrs. (Engr. of Yr. 1985), Am. Acad. Mechanics, Am. Inst. Steel Constrn., Am. Soc. for Engring. Edn., Am. Concrete Inst., Sigma Xi. Office: Bucknell U Civil Engring Dept Lewisburg PA 17837

ORDA, RUBEN, surgeon; b. Buenos Aires, Argentina, Dec. 22, 1935; s. Moshe and Esther (Oiberman) O.; m. Sara Grossberg, Mar. 12, 1960; children—Ariel, Ruth Miriam. M.D. with honors, Buenos Aires U., 1959; Master in Surgery, Tel-Aviv U., 1975. Resident Fiorito Hosp., Buenos Aires, Argentina, 1959-64; sr. surgeon Rawson Hosp., Buenos Aires, 1964-67, Tel-Aviv Med. Center (Israel), 1968-83; head surgery Assaf Harofe Hosp., Zerifin, Israel, 1983—; clin. and research fellow Westminster Hosp., London, 1976-77; lectr. surgery Buenos Aires U., 1964-67; lectr. anatomy Tel Aviv U., 1967-73; assoc. prof. surgery Tel Aviv U., 1983—; examiner gen. surgery Israel Bd. Examinations, 1983—; mem. adv. com. for surgery Ministry of Health, Israel, 1986—. Sec. gen. of the 9th World Congress of the Collegium Internat. Chirurgiae Digestivae, Jerusalem, Israel, 1986, nat. del., chmn. of the Israeli chpt., 1988—. Grantee Gordon Research Found., 1978; Tel Aviv U., 1978, 80, 81, 82, 85. Fellow Royal Soc. Medicine (Eng.); mem. Societe Internationale de Chirurgie, Collegium Internationale Chirurgiae Digestivae, European Soc. Surg. Research, N.Y. Acad. Scis., Israel Surg. Soc., World Assn. of Hepato-Pancreato-Biliary Surgery. Home: Keren Hayesod 3/27, Ramat Ilan Givat Shmuel 51905, Israel Office: Assaf Harofe Hosp Surgery A, Tel Aviv U, Zerifin Israel

ORDAZ, JORGE GARGALLO, geologist, educator, writer; b. Barcelona, Catalonia, Spain, Aug. 24, 1946; s. Pedro and Laura (Gargallo) O.; m. Ana Maria de Torres Canadell, Oct. 11, 1980; children: Irene, Juan. Degree in geology, U. Barcelona, 1968; PhD in Geology, U. Oviedo, Spain, 1973. Asst. prof. geology, faculty of scis. U. Barcelona, 1970-72; prof. geology U. Oviedo, 1972—. Author: Celebración De La Impostura, 1980, Prima Donna, 1986 (2d place Premio Herralde award 1985); (with J.L. Martinez) Gabinete De Ciencias Asturales, 1981; contbr. articles to profl. jours. Mem. Internat. Soc. Rock Mechs., Hist. Sci. Soc., Spanish Soc. Geology, Petrography Group (econs stone com.), Catalana Inst. Natural Hist. Home: Foncalada 14 6 D, 33002 Oviedo Spain Office: U Oviedo Dept Geology, Arias De Velasco S/n, 33080 Oviedo Spain

ORDMAN, JEANNETTE, artistic director, dancer; b. Germiston, Republic of South Africa; arrived in Israel, 1965; Grad., Damelin Coll., Johannesburg, Republic of South Africa, 1951, Royal Acad. Dance London, Johannesburg. Prin. dancer Johannesburg Festival Ballet, 1957-60; soloist, lead dancer London TV Ballet, 1960-66; dir. rehearsals Batsheva Dance Co., Tel Aviv, 1966; artistic dir. Bat-Dor Studios Dance, Tel Aviv, 1967—, Beer Sheva, Israel, 1975—, Bat-Dor Dance Co., Tel Aviv, 1968—; introduced Royal Acad. Dance London syllabus and Pilates system tng., Israel; mem. jury Internat. Ballet Competition, Jackson, Miss., 1982, vice chmn., 1985; chmn. profl. adv. com. Israel Dance Medicine Ctr., 1985. Recipient 1st prize Guild Loyal Women Bursary, 1948, Ceccheti award Acad. Medicea, Florence, Italy, 1984, Am Yafe Am Ehad award, 1988, numerous others; hand and foot imprinted Nico Malan Theatre, Capetown, Republic of South Africa, 1976. Home: 24 Shamir St, Afeka, Tel Aviv 69693, Israel Office: Bat-Dor Dance Co, 30 Ibn Gvirol St, Tel Aviv 64078, Israel

ORDONEZ, JORGE EZEQUIEL, mining company executive; b. Tulsa, Oct. 22, 1939; s. Georges and Angelina (Cortes) O.; m. Magdalena Del Hoyo, Dec. 9, 1967; children—Jorge Antonio, Ana Alejandra, Xavier Jose. Geol. engr., Nat. U. Mex., Mexico City, 1962; M.S., Stanford U., 1965. Exploration mgr. Grupo Frisco, Mexico City, 1972-75, dir. projects, 1975-79; mng. dir. Minera Real de Angeles, Mexico City, 1979-80; mng. dir. mining Grupo Alfa, Mexico City, 1980-81; pres. Empresas Frisco, Mexico City, 1981—, also dir.; dir. Quimica Fluor, Minera Lampazos. Editor: Minas Mexicanas, vols. 1-3, 1986-87. Contbr. articles to profl. jours. Mem. AIME (pres. Mex. sect.), Geol. Soc. Am., Soc. Econ. Geologists, AAAS, Can. Inst. Mining and Metallurgy, Mex. Assn. Mining-Geol.-Metall. Engrs. (dist. v.p. 1974-75, exec. pres. XI Nat. Conv. 1974-75, XII Nat. Conv. 1976-77), Mex. Mining Chamber (bd. dirs., past pres. non-metallics group, pres. non-ferrous group), Silver Inst. (v.p.). Avocations: tennis; astronomy. Home: Santa Antia 215, Lomas Hipodromo, 53900 Mexico City Mexico Office: Empresas Frisco SA de CV, Jaime Balmes 11-C-500, 11510 Mexico City Mexico

ORDOVER, ABRAHAM PHILIP, legal educator; b. Far Rockaway, N.Y., Jan. 18, 1937; s. Joseph and Bertha (Fromberg) O.; m. Carol M. Ordover, Mar. 23, 1961; children: Andrew Charles, Thomas Edward. BA magna cum laude, Syracuse U., 1958; JD, Yale U., 1961. Bar: N.Y. 1961, U.S. Dist. Ct. (so. and ea. dists.) N.Y., U.S. Ct. Appeals (2d cir.), U.S. Supreme Ct. Assoc. Cahill, Gordon & Reindel, N.Y.C., 1961-71; prof. law Hofstra U., Hempstead, N.Y., 1971-81; L.Q.C. Lamar prof. law Emory U., Atlanta, 1981—; vis. prof. Cornell U., Ithaca, N.Y., 1977; team leader nat. program Nat. Inst. Trial Advocacy, Boulder, Colo., 1980, 82, 84, 86, tchr. program Cambridge, Mass., 1979-84, 88, adv. program Gainesville, Fla., 1978-79, northeast regional dir., 1977-81. team leader SE regional program, 1983; team leader Atlanta Bar Trial Tech. Property, 1981—; lectr. in field. Author: Argument to the Jury, 1982, Problems and Cases in Trial Advocacy, 1983, Advanced Materials in Trial Advocacy, 1988; producer ednl. films; contbr. articles to profl. jours. Bd. dirs. Atlanta Legal Aid Soc., 1984—. Recipient Gumpert award Am. Coll. Trial Lawyers, 1984, 85, Jacobsen award Roscoe Pound Am. Trial Lawyer Found., 1986. Mem. ABA, N.Y. State Bar Assn., Assn. Am. Law Schs. (chmn. litigation sect. 1986), Atlanta Lawyers Club. Office: Emory U Law Sch Atlanta GA 30322

ORDOWER, MYRNA E., insurance broker; b. Chgo., Oct. 8; d. Abe Herman and Gussie (Rubinsky) Berliner; m. Sidney L. Ordower, Mar. 4, 1961; children: Cheryl, Karyn, Steven. Student, U. Ill., Northwestern U. Underwriter, Bergman & Lefkow Ins., Chgo., 1952-61; unit mgr. Near North Ins., Chgo., 1974-82; owner, pres. Myrna Ordower Enterprises, Chgo., 1982—; v.p., stockholder Rockwood Co., 1982—, also bd. dirs. Founder, Women's Exec. Network, Chgo., 1983—; co-founder Corp. Connections, Chgo., 1985. Bd. dirs. Little City Found. for Mentally Retarded Children, Women's bd. Chgo. Urban League; fund raiser Muscular Dystrophy, Chgo.; del. White House Conf. Small Bus., 1986. Recipient Outstanding Leadership proclamation Mayor of Chgo. Eugene Sawyer, 1988. Mem. Nat. Assn. Women Bus. Owners (bd. dirs.), Nat. Assn. Ins. Women. Home: 5502 S Harper Ave Chicago IL 60637 Office: Myrna Ordower Enterprises 20 N Wacker Dr Chicago IL 60606

OREFFICE, PAUL FAUSTO, chemical executive; b. Venice, Italy, Nov. 29, 1927; came to U.S., 1945, naturalized, 1951; s. Max and Elena (Friedenberg) O.; m. Franca Giuseppina Ruffini, May 26, 1956; children: Laura Emma, Andrew T. B.S. in Chem. Engring., Purdue U., 1949. With Dow Chem. Co., various internat. locations, 1953—; assigned to Switzerland, Italy, Brazil and Spain to 1969; pres. Dow Chem. Latin Am., Coral Gables, Fla., 1966-70; corporate fin. v.p. Dow Chem. Co., Midland, Mich., 1970-75, pres. Dow Chem. U.S.A., 1975-78, pres., chief exec. officer, 1978-86, chmn., pres., chief exec. officer, 1986-87, chmn. bd., 1987—; bd. dirs. Morgan Stanley Group Inc., Inc., CIGNA Corp., No. Telecom Ltd., Coca Cola Co. Trustee Am. Enterprise Inst. Served with AUS, 1951-53. Decorated Encomienda del Merito Civil Spain, 1966. Mem. Chem. Mfrs. Assn., Bus. Council, Conf. Bd. Office: The Dow Chem Co 2030 Willard H Dow Ctr Midland MI 48674

O'REILLY, ANTHONY JOHN FRANCIS, food company executive; b. Dublin, Ireland, May 7, 1936; s. John Patrick and Aileen (O'Connor) O'R.; m. Susan Cameron, May 5, 1962; children: Susan, Cameron, Justine, Gavin, Caroline, Tony. Student, Belvedere Coll., Dublin, Univ. Coll., Dublin, Wharton Bus. Sch. Overseas, 1965; B.C.L.; D.C.L. (hon.), Ind. State U.; Ph.D. in Agrl. Mktg, U. Bradford, Eng.; LL.D. (hon.), Wheeling Coll., Trinity Coll., Dublin, Rollins U. Indsl. cons. Weston Evans, 1958-62; personal asst. to chmn. Suttons Ltd., Cork, 1960-62; lectr. dept. applied psychology Univ. Coll., Cork, 1960-62; dir. Robert McCowen & Sons Ltd., Tralee, 1961-62; gen. mgr. An Bord Bainne/Irish Dairy Bd., 1962-66; dir. Agrl. Credit Corp. Ltd., 1965-66, Nitrigin Eireann Teoranta, 1965-66; mng. dir., chief exec. officer Comhlucht Siuicre Eireann Teo. and Erin Foods Ltd., 1966-69; joint mng. dir. Heinz-Erin Ltd., 1967-70; dir. Allied Irish Investment Bank Ltd., 1968-71; mng. dir. H.J. Heinz Co. Ltd., U.K., 1969-71; sr. v.p. N.Am. and Pacific H.J. Heinz Co., 1971-72; exec. v.p., chief operating officer H.J. Heinz Co., Pitts., 1972-73, pres., chief operating officer, 1973-79, pres., chief exec. officer, 1979—, chmn., 1987—; chmn. Atlantic Resources, Dublin, Ind. Newspapers Ltd., Dublin, Fitzwilton Ltd., Dublin, Ireland Fund; ptnr. Cawley Sheerin Wynne and Co., Dublin; chmn. Fitzwilton Ltd., Dublin, Atlantic Resources, Dublin, Ind. Newspapers Ltd., Dublin; bd. dirs. Mobil Oil Corp., Bankers Trust N.Y. Corp., Bankers Trust Co., N.Y., Washington Post Co., London Tablet Found.; bd. trustees U. Pitts.; bd. dirs. and mem. exec. com. Pitts. Opera. Author: Prospect, 1962, Developing Creative Management, 1970, The Conservative Consumer, 1971, Food for Thought, 1972. Bd. govs. Hugh O'Brian Found., Los Angeles; mem. council Rockefeller U., N.Y.C.; bd. dirs. Assocs. Grad. Sch. Bus. Adminstrn. of Harvard U., Cambridge, Mass.; sr. bd. dirs. The Conf. Bd.; trustee U. Pitts., Com. for Econ. Devel.; mem. Nat. Com. Whitney Mus. Am. Art. Fellow Brit. Inst. Mgmt., Royal Soc. Arts; mem. Inst. Dirs., Inc., Law Soc. Ireland (treas.), Grocery Mfrs. Am. (sec., bd. dirs.), Am. Irish Found., Internat. Life Scis. Inst. Nutrition Found. (chmn., chief exec. officer council), Irish Mgmt. Inst. (council), Exec. Council Fgn. Diplomats (bd. dirs.). Clubs: St. Stephens Green, Kildare St., University (Dublin); Annabels, Les Ambassadeurs (London); Union League (N.Y.C.); Duquesne, Allegheny, Pitts. Golf, Fox Chapel Golf (Pitts.); Rolling Rock (Ligonier) (bd. govs.); Lyford Cay (Bahamas). Office: H J Heinz Co 600 Grant St PO Box 57 Pittsburgh PA 15230 also: Mobil Corp 150 E 42d St New York NY 10017

O'REILLY, JAMES CHRISTOPHER, library information director; b. Dublin, Ireland, May 6, 1943; s. Christopher and Teresa (Redmond) O'R; m. Anne Kenny, Apr. 29, 1969; children: Gavin, Emmet. Diploma in Pub. Adminstrn., U. Coll. of Dublin, 1966; Diploma in Info. Studies, Trinity Coll., Dublin, 1974; MA, Queen U., Belfast, No. Ireland, 1985. Clerical officer Coras Iompair Eireann, Dublin, 1961-64; clerical officer Radio Ireland, Dublin, 1964-67, asst. librarian, 1967-70, chief cataloguer, 1970-74, head of library services, 1974—; cons. Coll. of Indsl. Relations, Dublin, 1980—. Contbr. articles, conf. reports to profl. jours. Mem. Inst. of Info. Scientists, Library Assn. of Ireland. Roman Catholic. Home: 15 Clonard Dr, Dundrum, Dublin 16, Ireland Office: Electricity Supply Bd, Lower Fitzwilliam St, Dublin 2, Ireland

O'REILLY, JAMES THOMAS, lawyer, author; b. N.Y.C., Nov. 15, 1947; s. Matthew Richard and Regina (Casey) O'R.; m. Rosann Tagliaferro, Aug. 26, 1972; children: Jean, Ann. BA cum laude, Boston Coll., 1969; JD, U. Va., 1974. Bar: Va. 1974, Ohio, 1974, U.S. Supreme Ct. 1979, U.S. Ct. Appeals (6th cir.) 1980. Atty. Procter & Gamble Co., Cin., 1974-76, counsel, 1976-79, sr. counsel for food, drug and product safety, 1979-85, corp. counsel, 1985—; adj. prof. in adminstrv. law U. Cin., 1980—; cons. Adminstrv. Conf. U.S., 1981-82; arbitrator State Employee Relations Bd.; mem. Ohio Bishops Adv. Council, Mayor's Infrastructure Commn. Author: Federal Information Disclosure, 1977, Food and Drug Administration Regulatory Manual, 1979, Unions' Rights to Company Information, 1980, Federal Regulation of the Chemical Industry, 1980, Administrative Rulemaking, 1983, Ohio Public Employee Collective Bargaining, 1984, Protecting Workplace Secrets, 1985, Emergency Response to Chemical Accidents, 1986, Product Defects and Hazards, 1987, Toxic Torts Strategy Deskbook, 1988; Trade Secrets and SARA, 1988; contbr. articles to profl. jours.; editorial bd. Food and Drug Cosmetic Law Jour. Mem. Hamilton County Dem. Central Com. Served with U.S. Army, 1970-72. Mem. Food and Drug Law Inst., ABA (chmn. com. on food, drug and cosmetic law, com. on consumer product regulation), Fed. Bar Assn., Leadership Cin. Democrat. Roman Catholic. Office: Procter & Gamble Co PO Box 599 Cincinnati OH 45201

O'REILLY, JOHN FRANCIS, gaming commissioner; b. St. Louis, July 23, 1945; s. John Francis and Marie Agnes (Cooney) O'R.; m. Rene E. Lee; children: Molly, Bryan, Erin, Timothy. BS, St. Louis U., 1967, JD cum laude, 1969; MBA cum laude, U. Nev., Las Vegas, 1974. Lic. real estate broker. Auditor, tax acct. Ernst & Whinney, St. Louis, 1966-69; pres. Keefer, O'Reilly & Ferrario, Las Vegas, Nev., 1972—; atty. Nev. Gaming Commn., Las Vegas, 1983—, chmn., 1986—; pres. Nev. Fed. Credit Union, Las Vegas. Editor-in-chief Communique mag., 1985. Alt. mcpl. judge City of Las Vegas, 1975-86; mem. adv. bd. Boulder Dam council Boy Scouts Am., Las Vegas; mem. Nev. Gaming Policy Com., Las Vegas, 1983—; pres. adv. bd. Bishop Gorman High Sch., Las Vegas; mem. Engaged Encounter program of Cath. Ch., Nev. Devel. Authority. Served to capt., mil. judge USAF, 1969-73. Mem. ABA, Mo. Bar Assn., Nev. Bar Assn., St. Louis Bar Assn., Clark County Bar Assn. (pres. 1984), Air Force Assn., So. Nev. Home Builders Asn. (Homer award 1986), Las Vegas C. of C. Democrat. Roman Catholic. Clubs: Variety, Breakfast Exchange, Hualapai (Las Vegas). Lodges: KC, Knights of Malta, Sons of Erin. Office: Keefer O'Reilly & Ferrario 325 S Maryland Pkwy #1 Las Vegas NV 89101

O'REILLY, TERENCE JOHN, lawyer; b. Farnborough, England, Apr. 12, 1945; came to U.S., 1960, naturalized, 1965; s. Arthur Francis and Doris Eileen (Burden) O'R; m. Katharine Van Dyke Wallace, Sept. 26, 1970; children—Tobin Cooper, Matthew Wallace. B.A., Loyola U., 1966; J.D., U. Calif.-Berkeley, 1969. Bar: Calif., 1970. Assoc. Voegelin, Barton, Los Angeles, 1969-70, Walkup, Downing & Sterns, San Francisco, 1970-75; mem. Walkup, Shelby, Bastian, Melodia, Kelly & O'Reilly, San Francisco, 1975-87; prin. Law Offices of Terry O'Reilly, Menlo Park, Calif., 1987—; lectr. Kennedy Law Sch., Moraga, Calif., 1975-76, Continuing Edn. Bar, Berkeley, 1978—, Assn. Trial Lawyers Am., 1970—. Vice pres. No. Calif. Rugby Football, San Francisco, 1975-80, bd. dirs., 1975—. Trustee The Philip Brooks Sch., 1986—. Mem. Am. Bd. Profl. Liability Lawyers, Boalt Hall Alumni (bd. dirs. 1982-85), Assn. San Francisco Trial Lawyers (bd. dirs. 1985—). Roman Catholic. Clubs: Bohemian; Burlingame Country; Menlo Circus.. Office: 2500 Sand Hill Rd Menlo Park CA 94025

OREM, CHARLES ANNISTONE, retired military officer, nuclear engr., marine and hydraulic products co. exec.; b. Bryn Mawr, Pa., Apr. 1, 1929; s. Howard Emery and Elizabeth Clements (Stone) O.; B.S. in Engring., U.S. Naval Acad., 1950; postgrad. George Washington U., 1968-69; M.E.E., U.S. Navy Postgrad. Sch., 1960; m. Gerry Morgan Wellborn, June 15, 1951; children—Nancy Elizabeth, Catherine Stone, Sarah Annistone. Commd. ensign U.S. Navy, 1950, advanced through grades to comdr.; commd. U.S.S. Seawolf, 1957; navigator U.S.S. Abraham Lincoln; exec. officer U.S.S. Thomas Jefferson; comdr. U.S.S. Simon Bolivar, 1965-68; submarine specialist Office of Chief of Naval Ops., 1968-70; ret., 1970; various mgmt. positions Babcock & Wilcox Co., Barberton, Ohio, 1970-77, dir. corp. planning and devel., N.Y.C., 1977-79; exec. v.p. Bird-Johnson Co., Walpole, Mass., 1979-80, pres., chief exec. officer, 1980—; lectr. mgmt. prins. Am. Mgmt. Assn. Bd. dirs. New Eng. Council, U.S. Bus. & Indsl. Council, Bay Bank. Recipient 6 Polaris Patrol award U.S. Navy, 1968; recipient Meritorious Service medal USN, 1970. Mem. IEEE, Soc. Naval Architects and Marine Engrs., Am. Soc. Naval Engrs., Am. Mgmt. Assn., AIAA, Machinery and Allied Products Inst. (mktg. council 1979—), Navy League, Ret. Officers Assn., Sigma Xi (asso.). Republican. Clubs: Wellesley Country, Metropolitan (D.C.), Army-Navy Country. Home: 25 Saddlebrook Rd Sherborn MA 01770 Office: 110 Norfolk St Walpole MA 02081

ORFIELD, GARY ALLAN, political scientist, educator; b. Mpls., Sept. 5, 1941; s. Myron Willard and Melba Berniece (Lindseth) O.; m. Antonia Marie Stoll, May 24, 1963; children: Amy, Sonia, Rosanna. B.A., U. Minn., 1963; M.A., U. Chgo., 1965, Ph.D., 1968. Asst. prof. politics and pub. affairs U. Va., Charlottesville, 1967-69, Princeton U., 1969-73; scholar-in-residence U.S. Civil Rights Commn., Washington, 1972-73; research assoc. Brookings Inst., Washington, 1973-77; asso. prof. U. Ill., Urbana, 1977-80, prof., 1980-81; prof. polit. sci., public policy, and edn. U. Chgo., 1982—; ct.-apptd. expert St. Louis, Los Angeles and San Francisco sch. desegregation cases; chmn. study group on desegregation research Nat. Inst. Edn., 1978-81; bd. dirs. Fund for an Open Society; cons. HUD, Dept. Edn., Dept. Justice, Ford Found.; founder Movement for a New Congress, 1970; mem. commn. on women's employment and related social issues NRC, 1981-85; adj. fellow Joint Ctr. for Polit. Studies, 1982—. Author: Reconstruction of Southern Education: The Schools and the 1964 Civil Rights Act, 1969, Congressional Power: Congress and Social Change, 1975, Must We Bus? Segregated Schools and National Policy, 1978, Toward a Strategy of Urban Integration, 1982, Public School Desegregation in the United States, 1968-80, 1983, (with W. Ricardo Tostado) Latinos in Metropolitan Chicago, 1983, Chicago Study of Access and Choice in Higher Education, 1984, Job Training under the New Federalism: JPTA in the Industrial Heartland, 1985; assoc. editor: Am. Jour. Edn., 1983-87. Danforth fellow; Woodrow Wilson fellow; Falk fellow; Brookings Inst. fellow; grantee Carnegie Found., Ford Found., Twentieth Century Fund, Joyce Found., Spencer Found., MacArthur Found., Woods Trust. Mem. Am. Polit. Sci. Assn., Soc. for Values in Higher Edn. Democrat. Roman Catholic. Office: Dept Political Science Pick Hall U Chicago Chicago IL 60637

ORGAD, BEN ZION, composer; b. Germany, 1926; came to Israel. Ed. Acad. of Music, Jerusalem, Brandeis U.; pvt. instrn. in composition. Supr. musical edn. Israel Ministry Edn. and Culture, Tel-Aviv, 1950—; composer cantatas: The Story of the Spies (UNESCO Koussevitsky prize 1952), Isaiah's Vision; composer orchestral works: Building a King's Stage, Choreographic Sketches, Movements on 'A', Kaleidoscope, Music for Horn and Orchestra, Ballad for Orch., Dialogues on the First Scroll; Suffering for Redemption (mezzo-soprano, choir and orchestra); Out of the Dust (soloist and instruments); Ballada (for violin); Taksim (for harp); Monologue (for viola); numerous works for soloists and orchestra, piano pieces. Recipient numerous awards for compositions. Mem. Israel Composers' League (chmn.). Home: 14 Bloch St, Tel Aviv Israel *

ORGAIN, BENJAMIN DARBY, lawyer; b. Bastrop, Tex., Dec. 26, 1909; s. William Edmund and May (Bolinger) O.; m. Martha Chastain Avery, Apr. 16, 1977; children: Lucy Allen Orgain White, Benjamin Darby. Student, South Park Coll., Beaumont, Tex., 1926-27; B.A., LL.B., U. Tex., 1933; LL.M., Harvard U., 1934. Bar: Tex. bar 1933. Since practiced in Beaumont; of counsel firm Orgain, Bell & Tucker.; Dir. Gulf States Utilities Co., 1963-75, adv. dir., 1975-80. Chmn. Jefferson County Democratic Com., 1940-42; Vice chmn. devel. bd. U. Tex., 1966-68, mem., 1963—; trustee U. Tex. Law Sch. Found.; assoc. mem. bd. visitors U. Tex. Cancer Found.; mem. Chancellor's Council U. Tex. Served to lt. comdr. USNR, 1942-46. Decorated Commendation ribbon. Fellow Am. Bar Found.; mem. Am., Tex., Jefferson County bar assns., Tex. Ornithol. Soc. (pres. 1979-81), Beaumont C. of C., Friar Soc., Phi Delta Phi, Kappa Sigma. Methodist. Clubs: Rotary, Beaumont, Beaumont Country; Headliners (Austin); Piping Rock (Locust Valley, N.Y.). Home: 1970 Shady Lane Beaumont TX 77706 Office: 470 Orleans 4th Floor Beaumont TX 77701

ORIO, OSCAR ANGEL, chemistry educator; b. Buenos Aires, Argentina, June 1, 1927; s. Angel and Marí a Angé lica (Mangiante) O.; m. Gladys Edith Veiga, July 8, 1961; children—Marí a Julia, Maximiliano Oscar. Chem. Technician, Industrial Otto Krause, Buenos Aires, 1945; Lic. in Chemistry, U. La Plata, 1952, D. Chemistry, 1955. Asst., U. La Plata (Argentina), 1954-55; research chief, govt. oil fields, Florencio Varela, Argentina, 1955-58; prof. Nat. U. Có rdoba (Argentina), 1958-80, dean of chemistry faculty, 1971-73; prof. organic chemistry Nat. U. Tech., Có rdoba, 1980—, head fuels research group, 1980—; mem. Nat. Com. for Catalysis. Recipient Biennial award for outstanding tech. contbn. Union Carbide Argentina, 1982. Mem. Assn. Quimica Argentina, Assn. de Investigadores en Ingenieri a Quimica y Quimica Aplicada, Assn. Argentina de Investigadores en Quimica Organicè , Sociedad Argentina de Enseñanza de la Ingeniera, Internat. Union for Pure and Applied Chemistry. Roman Catholic. Office: Universidad Tecnológica Nacional, Casilla de Corre 36, 5016 Córdoba Argentina

ORKAND, DONALD SAUL, management consultant; b. N.Y.C., Mar. 2, 1936; s. Harold and Sylvia (Wagner) O.; B.S. summa cum laude, N.Y.U., 1956, M.B.A., 1957, Ph.D., 1963; children—Dara Sue, Katarina Day. Statistician, Western Electric Co., N.Y.C., 1956-58; group v.p. Ops. Research, Inc., Silver Spring, Md., 1960-69; pres. Ops. Research Industries, Ltd., Ottawa, Ont., Can., 1968-69; pres., chief exec. officer The Orkand Corp., Silver Spring, 1970—. Served with Ordnance Corps, U.S. Army, 1958-60. Mem. Am. Econs. Assn., Am. Statis. Assn., Ops. Research Soc. Am. Contbr. articles to profl. jours. Home: 5225 Pooks Hill Rd 204-N Bethesda MD 20814 Office: 8484 Georgia Ave Silver Spring MD 20910

ORKIN, LAZARUS ALLERTON, physician; b. N.Y.C., Feb. 2, 1910; s. John and Anne (Davidow) O.; B.S., N.Y.U., 1930, M.S., 1931, M.D., 1935; m. Sylvia M. Hollard, May 30, 1941; children—Fredrick, Stuart. Intern Bellevue Hosp., N.Y.C., 1935-37, asst. resident in ob-gyn 1937-38, resident in urology, 1940-42; resident in urology Royal Victoria Hosp., Montreal, Que., Can., 1938-40; pvt. practice, N.Y.C., 1942-64; cons. urologist Beekman Downtown; dir. urology Beth Israel Hosp., 1964-78, dir. urology emeritus, cons. urologist, 1978—; clin. prof. urology Mt. Sinai Sch. Medicine, N.Y.C., 1970-78, emeritus, 1978—; cons. urologist Peninsula Gen. Hosp., Far Rockaway Hosp., N.Y., Gracie Sq. Hosp., Cath. Med. Center Bklyn.; sci. advisor to bd. trustees, v.p., chmn. sci. advisors Nat. Parkinson Inst., Inc., founder, 1986; founder Miami Sch. Medicine, 1984. Diplomate Am. Bd. Urology. Fellow Internat. Fertility Assn., Am. Soc. Study Sterility, ACS, Am. Geriatrics Soc., Am. Trauma Soc. (founding), Am. Assn. Surgery Trauma, Acad. Medicine N.Y., Pan Pacific Surg. Assn.; mem. Am., Can. urol. assns., N.Y. Urol. Soc., AMA, Pan Am. Med. Assn., Phi Beta Kappa, Sigma Xi, Alpha Omega Alpha. Club: Town (N.Y.C.). Author: Surgery of Trauma of the Ureter, 1962; Genito Urinary Trauma in Lawyer's Medical Cyclopedia, 1963; Trauma to the Ureter Its Pathogenesis and Management, Textbook, 1964; Urinary Tract Infections; asso. editor Trauma; contbg. editor Trauma to Bladder, Ureter, and Kidney (Davis Obstetrics and Gynecology), Aggiornamenti in ostetricae ginecologia; editor Nat. Parkinson Report.

ORKIN, MARTIN RONALD, literature educator; b. Johannesburg, Transvaal, Republic of South Africa, June 13, 1942; s. Morris and Jenny (Tudin) O.; m. Joan Katzenellenbogen, Mar. 29, 1970; children: Chloe Meave, Mikhail Benedict. BA, Witwatersrand U., Johannesburg, 1965; BA with honors, U. London, 1969, PhD, 1980. Tchr. King David High Sch., Johannesburg, 1969-70; lectr. U. Natal, Durban, Republic of South Africa, 1971-73; lectr. Witwatersrand U., 1975-82, sr. lectr., 1982-87, prof., 1988—; vis. prof. English, Tel-Aviv U., 1987-88. Author: Shakespeare Against Apartheid, 1987; editor: The English Acad. Rev., 1979-87; mem. editorial com. Ravan Press, 1984-86; contbr. articles to profl. publs. Mem. exec. council English Acad. South Africa, 1982—; convener adjudicators Olive Schreiner Prize for Drama Bd., 1984. Jewish. Office: Witwatersrand U, Dept English, 1 Jan Smuts Ave, Johannesburg 2050, Republic of South Africa

ORLAND, FRANK J., historiographer, oral microbiologist, educator; b. Little Falls, N.Y., Jan. 23, 1917; s. Michael and Rose (Dorner) O.; m. Phyllis Therese Mrazek, May 8, 1943; children—Frank R., Carl P., June R., Ralph M. A.A., U. Chgo., 1937, S.M., 1945, Ph.D., 1949; B.S., U. Ill., 1939, D.D.S., 1941. Diplomate: Am. Bd. Microbiology. With U. Chgo., 1941—; intern U. Chgo. (Zoller Meml. Dental Clinic), 1941-42, Zoller fellow, asst. in dental surgery, 1942-49, instr., asst. prof., asso. prof., prof. dental surgery, 1949—, instr., asst. prof., asso. prof. microbiology, 1950-58; research asso. (prof.) 1958-64; attending dentist Country Home for Convalescent Children, 1942-45; dir. W.G. Zoller Meml. Dental Clinic of U. Chgo., 1954-66; spl. cons. Nat. Inst. Dental Research of NIH, Bethesda, Md.; mem. panel on dental drugs The Nat. Formulary. Author: The First Fifty-Year History of the International Association for Dental Research, 1974; Editor: Journal Dental Research, 1958-69; past chmn. dental adv. bd.: Med. Heritage Soc; editor, contbr.: Microbiology in Clinical Dentistry; Contbr. articles to profl. jours.; editor Centennial brochure Loyola U. Sch. Dentistry, 1983. Past chmn. adv. council Forest Park (Ill.) Bd. Edn.; mem. Forest Park Citizens Com. for Better Schs.; past pres. Garfield Sch. P.T.A., 1953-55; chairperson heritage com. Bicentennial Commn. of Forest Park, 1983-85; editor Chronicles of Forest Park, 1976-86. Recipient Research Essay award Chgo. Dental Soc., 1955. Fellow Inst. Medicine Chgo. (chmn. com. publ. communications), Am. Acad. Microbiology, AAAS, Am. Coll. Dentists, Internat. Coll. Dentists; mem. Internat. Assn. Dental Research (pres. 1971-72, past councilor Chgo. sect., past chmn. program com., past chmn. com. on history), ADA (past chmn. council dental therapeutics), AAUP, Am. Assn. Dental Schs. (past chmn. conf. oral microbiology past chmn. com. on advanced edn.), Am. Assn. Dental Editors (hon. mention, William Gies Editorial award 1968), Ill. State Dental Soc. (chmn. com. on history), Fedn. Dentaire Internat. (Commn. on Research), Am. Acad. History Dentistry (past pres.), Hist. Soc. Forest Park (pres.), Soc. Med. History Chgo. (past pres.), Sigma Xi, Gamma Alpha. (pres. Chgo. chpt.). Club: Chgo. Literary. Home: 521 Jackson Blvd Forest Park IL 60130 Office: U Chgo Med Ctr 5841 Maryland Ave Box 418 Chicago IL 60637

ORLEANS, NEIL JEFFREY, lawyer; b. N.Y.C., June 7, 1948; s. Fred Allan and Shirley (Kovner) O.; m. Joan Elizabeth Painter, Aug. 10, 1974; children: David Anthony, Kimberly Ann. BA with high honors, U. Tex., Austin, 1969, JD with honors, 1971. Bar: Tex. 1972, U.S. Ct. Mil. Appeals, 1972, U.S. Ct. Appeals (5th cir.) 1981, U.S. Dist. Ct. (no. dist.) Tex. 1978, U.S. Dist. Ct. (we. dist.) Tex. 1981, U.S. Dist. Ct. (ea. dist.) Tex. 1983. Assoc. Eldridge, Goggans, Dallas, 1976-78, Baldwin & Assocs., Dallas, 1978-79; ptnr. Wise, Stuhl, Andrea, Orleans and Morris, Dallas, 1979-87, Goins, UnderKofler, Crawford & Langdon, Dallas, 1988—. Contbr. to Tex. Law Rev., 1970. Ruling elder North Park Presbyn. Ch., Dallas, 1980-82. Served to capt. JAGC, USAF, 1972-76. Recipient Am. Jurisprudence award, 1969. Mem. ABA, Tex. Bar Assn., Dallas Bar Assn., Dallas Bankruptcy Bar Assn., Dallas Hist. Preservation Soc., Phi Beta Kappa. Republican. Clubs: Oakridge (Garland); Towne (Dallas). Office: Goins UnderKofler Crawford & Langdon 3300 Thanksgiving Tower Dallas TX 75201

ORLEBEKE, WILLIAM RONALD, lawyer; b. El Paso, Tex., Jan. 5, 1933; s. William Ronald and Frances Claire (Cook) O.; m. Barbara Raye Pike, Aug. 29, 1954; children—Michelle, Julene, David. B.A., Willamette U., 1956; M.A., Kans. U., 1957; J.D., Willamette U., 1966. Bar: Calif. 1966, U.S. Dist. Ct. (no. dist.) Calif. 1967, U.S. Ct. Appeals (9th cir.) 1967. Assoc. Eliassen & Postel, San Francisco, 1966-69; ptnr. Coll, Levy & Orlebeke, Concord, Calif., 1969-77, Orlebeke & Hutchings, Concord, 1977-86, Orlebeke, Hutchings & Pinkerton, 1986-88, Orlebeke & Hutchings, 1988—; hearing officer Contra Costa County, Calif., 1981—; arbitrator Contra Costa County Superior Ct., 1977—, U.S. Dist. Ct. No. Calif., 1978—; judge pro tem Mt. Diablo Mcpl. Ct., 1973-77. Alumni bd. dirs. Willamette U., 1978-81, trustee, 1980-81; scholarship chmn. Concord Elks, 1977-79; del. Joint U.S/China Internat. Trade Law Conf., Beijing, Peoples Republic of China, 1987. Served with USMCR, 1952-59. Sr. scholar, Willamette U., 1955-56; Woodrow Wilson fellow, Kans. U., 1956-57; U.S. Bur. Nat. Affairs fellow, 1966, others. Mem. SAR. Republican. Lodges: Order Ea. Star, Masons, Shriners, Elks, Rotary (charter pres. Clayton Valley/Concord Sunrise chpt.). Office: 3330 Clayton Rd Suite F Concord CA 94519

ORLOV, VLADIMIR PAVLOVICH, Soviet government official; b. 1921. Grad., Ivanono Textile Inst., USSR, 1942. Mem. Communist Party Soviet Union, 1948—; dep. to USSR Supreme Soviet, 1966—; 1st sec. Kuibyshev Oblast com. Communist Party Soviet Union, 1967-79; 1st dep. chair Russian Soviet Federative Socialist Republic Council Ministers, 1979-85; pres. Presidium Supreme Soviet Russian Soviet Federative Socialist Republic, Moscow, 1985—; vice chmn. Presidium Supreme Soviet USSR, Moscow, 1985—. Decorated Order of Lenin (twice). Address: Supreme Soviet RSFSR, Moscow USSR *

ORLOWSKI, STANISLAW TADEUSZ, architect; b. Skarzysko, Poland, Sept. 24, 1920; s. Tadeusz and Irena (Malawczyk) O.; m. Krystyna Joanna Przyborowska, July 23, 1949; children—Alexandra Maria Izabela, Irena Krystyna, Helena Victoria. Reader in econs., Leicester U., Eng., 1945-46, Diploma Architecture, 1951; M.Sc. in Architecture with hons., Univ. London, 1954. Architect Ont. Dept. Pub. Works, 1952-55, Page & Steel, Architects, Toronto, 1955-57; Allward & Gouinlock, Toronto, 1965-67; area architect Pub. Works of Can., Toronto, 1957-65; chief research architect Ont. Ministry of Edn., 1967-73, assoc. chief architect, 1980-85, chief architect, 1985; chief architect Ont. Ministry of Colls. and Univs., 1973-80; cons. on ednl. facility design, 1968—; vis. prof., lectr. various internat. Univs. and profl. orgns., 1967—; lectr. Ont. Inst. Studies & Edn., 1967—. Researcher, editor planning and design studies. Contbr. articles to Can., Brit. and Italian jours. World v.p. Polish Girl Guides and Boy Scouts Assn., 1970—; 1st v.p. Polish-Can. Congress, 1980-86, pres. 1986—; chmn. World Polonia Coordinator Council, 1986—; mem. Royal Canadian Legion. Served to lt. Polish

Army, NATOUSA, 1941-45. Decorated Polish and British mil. medals, 1945; Field Marshal Alexander scholar, U.K., 1945. Fellow Royal Archtl. Inst. of Can.; mem. Royal Inst. Brit. Architects, Polish Engrs. Assn. Can., Internat. Union Architects (ednl. facilities com. UNESCO 1975-80), Polish Engrs. (nat. pres. 1967-70), AIA (architecture for edn. com. 1983-86), Internat. Energy Commn. (council ednl. facilities planners 1979-86), Polish Inst. Arts and Scis., Royal Can. Mil. Inst. Roman Catholic. Club: Empire. Home: 42 Braeside Rd, Toronto, M4 Canada M4N 1X7

ORMEROD, STEPHEN JAMES, ecology educator; b. Burnley, Lancashire, Eng., Jan. 24, 1958; s. Mathew Henry and Marjorie (Crossley) O. BSc in Life Scis., Huddersfield Poly., 1980; MSc in Applied Biology, U. Wales, Cardiff, 1981, PhD in Applied Biology, 1986. Sr. ecologist, head acid waters unit Inst. Sci. and Tech. U. Wales, 1984—; mem. United Kingdom Acid Waters Review Group, 1986—; dir. numerous ecol. project groups. Nat. Environment Research Council grantee, Swindon, Eng., 1980, 81-84; Winston Churchill Meml. Trust fellow, London, 1987. Mem. British Ecol. Soc., Ecol. Soc. Am., British Ornithol. Union, Freshwater Biol. Assn., British Trust Ornithology. Home: 38 Bryn Gwili Rd, Pontarddulais, Dyfed Wales Office: U Cardiff, PO Box 13, Cardiff CF1 3XF, Wales

ORMESSON, JEAN D' (JEAN D'ORMESSON), author, journalist; b. France, June, 1925; s. Marquis d' Ormesson; m. Francoise Beghin, 1962; 1 dau. Ed. Ecole Normale Superieure. Dep. sec.-gen. Internat. Council for Philosophy and Humanistic Studies, UNESCO, 1950-71, sec.-gen., 1971; mem. staff various govt. ministers, 1958-66; dep. editor Diogenes internat. jour., 1952-72, mem. mng. com., 1972—; mem. editorial com. Editions Gallimard, 1972-74; editor-in-chief, columnist Le Figaro, 1972-77. Author: L'amour est un plaisir, 1956; Du cote de chez Jean, 1959; Un amour pour rien, 1960; Au revoir et merci, 1966; Les illusions de la mer, 1968; La gloire de l'empire, 1971 (Grand Prix du Roman, Acad. Francaise 1971); Au plaisir de Dieu, 1974; Le vagabond qui passe sous une ombrelle trouee, 1978; Dieu, sa vie, son oeuvre, 1981; Mon dernier reve sera pour vous, 1982; Jean qui grogne et Jean qui rit, 1984; Le vent du soir, 1985; Tous les hommes sont fous, 1986; contbr. numerous articles to mags. Mem. Control Commn. of Cinema, 1962-69, Le Bonhuer à San Miniato, 1982. Mem. Acad. Francaise. Office: 10 Ave du Parc-Saint-James, 92200 Neuilly-sur-Seine France

ORMOND, LEONEE, English literature educator; b. Kingston-on-Thames, England, Aug. 27, 1940; m. Richard Louis Ormond, May 11, 1963; children: Augustus Jasper, Marcus Conrad. BA, Oxford U., 1962; MA, Birmingham U., 1965. Asst. lectr. in English City of Birmingham (Eng.) Coll. Edn., 1963-65; lectr. in English King's Coll., London, 1965-85, sr. lectr., 1985—. Author: (biographies) George Du Maurier, 1969, Lord Leighton (with Richard Ormond), 1974, J.M. Barrie, 1987. Mem. Ch. of Eng. Club: Women's U. (London). Office: U London Kings Coll, Strand, London WC2, England

ORN, TORSTEN, Swedish ambassador; b. Stockholm, Mar. 27, 1933; s. Wilhelm and Carin (Nordstedt) O.; m. Philippa Wistrand, May 6, 1964. M. Polit. Sci., Upsala U., 1956. Third sec. Swedish Fgn. Service, Stockholm, 1956-58, Rome, 1958-60, 2d sec., New Delhi, 1960-61, head sect., Stockholm, 1962-66, first sec. U.N., N.Y.C., 1966-70, dir., Stockholm, 1970-74, minister, Moscow, 1974-78, chargé d'affaires, New Delhi, 1978-79, ambassador Tel Aviv, 1979-83, Moscow, 1983-86, under sec. polit. affairs, Stockholm, 1987—; chmn. Swedish Fgn. Service Entrance Commn., 1983-87. Contbr. articles to profl. jours. Sr. assoc. mem. St. Antony's Coll., Oxford, 1979; officer Al Merito della Repubblica Italiana; Royal Order No. Star (Sweden). Mem. Royal Swedish Acad. Mil. Sci. Lutheran. Club: Travellers (Stockholm). Avocations: history; travel. Office: Ministry Fgn Affairs, PO Box 16121, 103 23 Stockholm Sweden

ORONA, ERNEST JOSEPH, real estate and construction company executive; b. Belen, N.Mex., Oct. 5, 1942; s. Joseph B. and Melinda (Sanchez) O.; B.A. in Latin Am. Affairs and Spanish, U. N.Mex., 1968; m. Margaret M. Guinan, Aug. 22, 1964; children—Mary Melinda, Marie-Jeanne. Vol. community devel. Peace Corps, Colombia, S. Am., 1962-64; instr. Peace Corps tng. U. Mo., Kansas City, summer 1964, Baylor U., Waco, Tex., summer 1965, also U. Ariz., N.Mex. State U., Las Cruces, 1966, U. N.Mex., Albuquerque, 1966; exec. dir. Mid-Rio Grande Community Action Project, Los Lunas, N.Mex., 1965-66; community devel. cons. Center for Community Action Services, Albuquerque, 1967-68; project dir. Peace Corps Tng. Center, San Diego State U., Escondido, Calif., 1968-70; propr., developer GO Realty and Constrn. Co., Albuquerque, 1970—; pres. La Zarzuela de Alburquerque; pres. Benchmark Real Estate InvestmentInc. Mem. Albuquerque Sister Cities. Mem. Nat. Bd. Realtors, Albuquerque Bd. Realtors, Albuquerque C. of C., Albuquerque Com. on Fgn. Relations. Roman Catholic. Home: 908 Sierra Dr SE Albuquerque NM 87108 Office: 10601 Lomas NE Suite 112 Albuquerque NM 87112

O'RORKE, JAMES FRANCIS, JR., lawyer; b. N.Y.C., Dec. 4, 1936; s. James Francis and Helen (Weber) O'R.; m. Carla Phelps, Aug. 6, 1964. A.B., Princeton U., 1958; J.D., Yale U., 1961. Bar: N.Y. 1962. Assoc. Davies, Hardy & Schenck, 1962-69; ptnr. Davies, Hardy, Ives & Lawther, 1969-72, Skadden, Arps, Slate, Meagher & Flom, N.Y.C., 1972—; dir. Clinipad Corp., E.B. Meyrowitz, Inc. Trustee Mus. Am. Indian-Heye Found., 1977-80. Mem. ABA, N.Y. State Bar Assn., Assn. Bar City N.Y., Am. Coll. Real Estate Lawyers. Club: City Midday (N.Y.C.). Office: Skadden Arps Slate Meagher & Flom 919 3d Ave New York NY 10022

OROSEL, GERHARD OSKAR, economics educator; b. Vienna, Austria, July 31, 1946; s. Egon Walter and Auguste (Studnicka) O.; m. Renate Taubenbeck, July 30, 1971 (div. 1979); children: Christian, Stefan. JD, U. Vienna, 1970, Habilitation in Econ. Theory, 1974. Asst. Inst. Advanced Studies, Vienna, 1971; asst. dept. econs. U. Vienna, 1971-74, prof. econs., 1977—; wissenschaftlicher rat and prof. econs. U. Bonn, Fed. Republic Germany, 1974-77; vis. scholar NYU, 1984, U. Calif., San Diego, 1987-88. Mem. com. Social and Med. Relief for Palestinians, Vienna, 1985—, Amnesty Internat., 1975. Mem. Am. Econs. Assn., Theoretischer Ausschuss des Vereins für Socialpolitik, Nationalökonomische Gesellschaft, European Econ. Assn. Home: Weimarerstr 7/20, A-1180 Vienna Austria Office: U Vienna Dept Econs, Liechtensteinstrasse 13, A-1090 Vienna Austria

O'ROURKE, JAMES TIERNAN, art museum director; b. Langdon, N.D., July 20, 1933; s. Joseph M. and Mildred G. (Gustafson) O'R.; B.A., Concordia Coll., Moorhead, Minn., 1956. Founder, 1960, since dir. Rourke Gallery, Moorhead; instr. painting and design Moorhead State U., 1965-66; instr. art history N.D. State U., 1969; exec. dir., bd. dirs. Plains Art Mus., Moorhead, 1975-87; v.p. Wahpeton (N.D.) Art Gallery, 1972-76; adv. panel Minn. Arts Bd., 1977-82; mem. Moorhead Mayor's Art Adv. Panel, 1974-79; one-man shows include Fergus Falls (Minn.) Gallery, 1979, Dacotah Prairie Mus., Aberdeen, S.D., 1980, 2d Crossing Gallery, Valley City, N.D., 1980, The Saint Paul (Minn.) Gallery, 1987, Second Crossing Gallery, Valley City, N. Dak., 1987, Jamestown (N. Dak.) Arts Ctr., 1987, Mind's Eye Gallery, Dickinson, N. Dak., 1987, Elan Gallery, Bismarck, N. Dak., 1988, Minot (N. Dak.) Art Gallery, 1988. Served with AUS, 1957-60. Recipient Bismarck (N.D.) art citation award, 1969, N.D. State Arts Council Achievement award 1980. Mem. Am. Assn. Museums, Plains Archtl. Heritage Found. (v.p., dir.). Home: 316 S 5th St Moorhead MN 56560 Office: 523 S 4th St Moorhead MN 56560

ORR, SIR DAVID ALEXANDER, corporate executive; b. Dublin, Ireland, May 10, 1922; s. Adrian William Fielder and Grace (nee Robinson) O.; m. Phoebe Rosaleen Davis, 1949; 3 children. LLB, Trinity Coll., Dublin, 1946, LLD (hon.), 1978. MC and bar 1945. With various Unilever Cos., 1948-82, Lever Bros. Co., N.Y., 1963, pres., 1965-67; dir. Unilever Ltd., 1967-82, chmn., 1974-82; chmn. Leverhulme Trust, 1982—; exec. chmn. Inchcape PLC, 1983-86, dep. chmn., 1986—; dir. Shell Transport & Trading Co., 1982—, Rio Tinto-Zinc Corp. PLC, 1981—, Bank of Ireland, Dublin; chmn. Brit. Council, 1985—. Pres. Liverpool Sch. Tropical Medicine, 1981—; gov. LSE, 1980—. Served with Royal Engrs., 1941-46. Decorated comdr. Order of Orange Nassau, 1979; created knight, 1977. Fellow Royal Soc. Arts. Club: Athenaeum. Avocations: golf, rugby, travel. Home: 81 Lyall Mews, London SW1, England Address: Farm House, Shackleford Surrey, England

ORR, DAVID IVAN, private investigator; b. N.Y.C., May 16, 1947; s. Ivan and Norma Rose (Steele) O.; m. Gayke Sandra Smith, Aug. 23, 1972 (div. Aug. 1974); 1 child, Danillie C.; m. Barbara Jean Crowder, May 16, 1985; 1 child, David, Jr. Grad., Merchant Marine Acad., 1963; degree in law enforcement, Detroit Police Acad., 1967; grad., Secret Service Sch. for Mcpl. Police, 1970; BA in Personnel Mgmt., Wayne State U., 1976. Lic. pvt. investigator, legal asst. Police officer City of Detroit, 1967-79; gen. mgr. Profl.'s Unlimited, Inc., Detroit, 1979—. Recipient Medal of Valor City of Detroit, 1974. Mem. Detective and Police Officers Assn., Retired Police and Firefighters Assn. Office: Profls Unlimited Inc 21630 W 6 Mile Detroit MI 48219

ORR, KAY A., governor of Nebraska; b. Burlington, Iowa, Jan. 2, 1939; d. Ralph Robert and Sadie Lucille (Skoglund) Stark; m. William Dayton Orr, Sept. 26, 1957; children: John William, Suzanne. Student, U. Iowa, 1956-57. Exec. asst. to Gov. Charles Thone, Lincoln, Nebr., 1979-81; treas. State of Nebr., Lincoln, 1981-86; gov. elect. 1986; governor State of Nebr., Lincoln, 1987—. Co-chmn. Thone for Gov. Com., 1977-78; del., mem. platform com. Rep. Nat. Conv., 1976, 80, 84, co-chmn. 1984; trustee Hastings (Nebr.) Coll., 1985—; appointed to USDA Users Adv. Bd. 1985, Pres.'s Adv. Com. for Arts John F. Kennedy Performing Arts Ctr., 1985; chmn. Nat. Rep. Platform Commn., 1988—; appointed Nat. Adv. Council on Rural Devel., 1988. Named Outstanding Young Rep. Woman in Nebr., 1969. *

ORR, ROBERT DUNKERSON, governor of Indiana; b. Ann Arbor, Mich., Nov. 17, 1917; s. Samuel Lowry and Louise (Dunkerson) O.; m. Joanne Wallace, Dec. 16, 1944; children: Robert Dunkerson, Susan Orr Jones, Marjorie R. Orr Hail. A.B., Yale U., 1940; postgrad., Harvard Bus. Sch., 1940-42; hon. degrees, Ind. State U., 1973, Hanover Coll., 1974, Butler U., 1977, U. Evansville, 1985, Ind. U., 1986; hon., Tri-State U., 1986, Purdue U., 1987. Officer, dir. Orr Iron Co., 1946-60, Sign Crafters, Inc., 1957-74, Hahn, Inc., 1957-69, Indian Industries, Inc., 1962-73; mem. Ind. Senate, 1968-72; lt. gov. Ind., 1973-80; gov. 1980—; dir. Nat. Passenger Rail Co. (Amtrack), 1981—. Leader Fgn. Ops. Adminstrn. evaluation team to, Vietnam, 1954; Pres. Buffalo Trace council Boy Scouts Am., 1957-58; v.p. Evansville's Future, Inc., 1958-62; Chmn. Vanderburgh County Republican Com., 1965-71; alternate del. Rep. Nat. Conv., 1956, 76, del. 1984; Trustee Hanover Coll., Willard Library, Evansville YMCA, 1950-70. Served to maj. AUS, 1942-46. Decorated Legion of Merit. Mem. Scroll and Key Soc., Delta Kappa Epsilon. Presbyn. (elder, trustee, deacon). Clubs: Rotary, Meridian Hills, Columbia. Office: Office of Gov State Capitol Indianapolis IN 46204 *

ORR, ROBERT VERNON, school business administrator; b. Pasadena, Calif., Sept. 12, 1949; s. George Vernon and Joan (Peak) O.; m. Cynthia Ann Darling, July 5, 1986; 1 child, Kaitlyn Joanne. BA with honors, Colorado Coll., 1971; MA, Calif. State U., Northridge, 1980; MBA, U. So. Calif., 1982. CPA, Md. Counselor Windward Sch., Santa Monica, Calif., 1975-78, dir., 1977-78; ptnr. Orr Enterprises, Santa Monica, 1978-80; spl. asst. U.S. Senate Budget Com., Washington, 1981; legis. asst. Sen. Rudy Boschwitz, Washington, 1982-85; bus. mgr. Poly. Sch., Pasadena, 1986—. Mem. Am. Inst. CPA's, Pi Gamma Mu, Beta Gamma Sigma, Beta Alpha Psi. Republican. Club: Grand Lake (Colo.) Yacht. Office: Poly Sch 1030 E California Blvd Pasadena CA 91106

ORR, WILLIAM HAROLD, product development manager; b. Buffalo, Nov. 3, 1930; s. William Joseph and Margaret Gertrude (Morrow) O.; m. Donola Yvonne Burcham, June 23, 1984; children by previous marriage—William Goehrig, Barron Joseph, Elise Morrow, Wade Frank. B.Engring. Physics, Cornell U., 1953, Ph.D., 1962; M.S., Cath. U., 1957. Instr., U.S. Naval Acad., Annapolis, Md., 1955-57; research asst. Cornell U., Ithaca, N.Y., 1958-61; mem. tech. staff Bell Labs., Murray Hill, N.J., 1962-65, supr. IC devel. group, Allentown, Pa., 1966-70, head process capability dept., Indpls., 1970-73, head telephone tech. dept., 1974-83; head advanced products dept. AT&T Bell Labs., Indpls., 1984—; mem. microelectronics com. Ind. Corp. for Sci. & Tech., Indpls., 1983—; indsl. adv. com. Ind. U./ Purdue U., Ft. Wayne, 1982-85; program com. Electronics Components Conf., 1976-82; trustee Fedn. Materials Socs., Washington, 1974-77, sec.-treas., 1977. Author: (chpt.) Thin Film Technology, 1968, Physical Design of Electronic Systems, 1971, Active Inductorless Filters, 1971. Mem. editorial bd. IEEE Spectrum, 1972. Contbr. articles to profl. jours. Patentee in field. Pres., Hamilton Centers Youth Service Bur., Noblesville, Ind., 1977-79, bd. dirs., 1973-79, 82-85, treas., 1983-85; mem. Carmel Clay Curriculum Adv. Com., Ind., 1979-82; vol. Marion County Juvenile Ct., Indpls., 1972-73; deacon Orchard Park Presbyn. Ch., Carmel, 1972-74, elder, 1975—, session, 1975-77, 84-86, clk., 1977; mem. Dean's adv. com. Purdue U. Sch. Sci., Indpls., 1985—. Served with USN, 1953-57. Recipient outstanding contbn. award Hamilton Ctrs., 1985, ann. service award, 1987; NROTC fellow, 1949-53; John McMullen fellow, 1957-58. Mem. IEEE Consumer Electronics Soc., IEEE Communications Soc., IEEE Components, Hybrids and Mfg. Tech. Soc. (sec. 1977), Sigma Xi, Kappa Sigma, Phi Kappa Phi. Current work: Design and development of consumer electronics products including pub. telephone systems. Subspecialties: Microelectronics; Materials (engineering). Home: 1114 Ridge Rd Carmel IN 46032

ORRJE, OLLE, civil engineer; b. Kristianstad, Skåne, Sweden, Apr. 7, 1937; s. Alfred and Svea (Holmberg) O.; m. Stina Jacobsson, Dec. 1, 1962; children: Henrik, Carl Fredrik, Peter, Jacob. Degree in Civil Engring., Royal Inst. Tech., Stockholm, 1965, D in Tech., 1968. Research engr. Swedish Geotech. Inst., Stockholm, 1965-69; research asst. Royal Inst. Tech., Stockholm, 1965-69; head dept. geotech. engring. Alfred Orrje AB, Stockholm, 1969—, dir., 1977—. Recipient Swedish Louis Armstrong award, 1981. Mem. Swedish Soc. Civil Engrs., Swedish Soc. Cons. Engrs., Swedish Geotech. Soc., Soc. Swedish Engring. Geology, Swedish Union of Writers. Home: Brötvägen 39, S16139 Bromma Sweden Office: Alfred Orrje AB, Krukmakargatan 42, Box 17138, S10462 Stockholm Sweden

ORSBON, RICHARD ANTHONY, lawyer; b. North Wilkesboro, N.C., Sept. 23, 1947; s. Richard Chapman and Ruby Estelle (Wyatt) O.; m. Susan Cowan Shivers, June 13, 1970; children: Sarah Hollingsworth, Wyatt Benjamin, David Allison. BA disting. mil. grad. ROTC, Davidson Coll., 1969; JD, Vanderbilt U., 1972; honor grad. Officers Basic Course, U.S. Army, 1972. Bar: N.C. 1972, U.S. Dist. Ct. (we. dist.) N.C., 1972; cert. in estate planning and probate law; cert. specialist in probate and fiduciary law. Assoc. Kennedy, Covington, Lobdell & Hickman, Charlotte, N.C., 1972-75; assoc. Parker, Poe et. al., Charlotte, 1975-77, ptnr. 1978—. Assoc. editor, contbr. Vanderbilt Law Review, 1971-72. Pres. ECO, Inc., Charlotte, 1982—; bd. dirs. Charlotte United Way, 1983—; mem. planning bd. Queens Coll. Estate Planning Day, 1978—; active Myers Park United Methodist Ch.; mem. YMCA basketball com., Dem. precinct chmn., 1980-86; mem. Dem. state exec. com., 1980; bd. dirs. law explorer program Boy Scouts Am., Charlotte, 1976-78; bd. vis. Johnson C. Smith Univ., 1986—. Served to 1st lt. U.S. Army, 1972-73. Named Outstanding Vol., Charlotte Observer/ United Way, 1984; Patrick Wilson Merit scholar Vanderbilt U. Law Sch., 1969-72. Mem. ABA (real property probate sect.), N.C. State Bar (cert. specialist estate planning and probate, 1987), N.C. Bar Assn. (probate and fiduciary law sect., author, speaker 1987—), N.C. Bar Assn. Coll. of Advocacy, Mecklenburg County Bar Assn. (law day com., vol. lawyers program, bd. dirs.), Deans Assn. of Vanderbilt U. Law Sch. (bd. dirs.), Davidson Coll. Alumni Assn. (bd. dirs. 1983, class alumni sec. 1986—), Charlotte Estate Planning Council, ECO Inc. (pres. 1983—, bd. dirs. 1982—), Omicron Delta Kappa. Club: Foxcroft Swim and Racquet (pres. 1986-87, bd. dirs. 1985-88). Home: 2819 Rothwood Dr Charlotte NC 28211 Office: Parker Poe Thompson et al 2600 Charlotte Plaza Charlotte NC 28244

ORSELLO, GIAN PIERO, radio/TV executive, educator; b. Modena, Italy, Nov. 3, 1927. Degree in law and philosophy; diploma Faculty of Polit. Sci., Paris; student Inst. Pub. Law, Madrid, Faculty Law, Strasburgh. Lawyer, atty. at law and publicist; pres. Italian Legis. Studies, 1970; v.p. Italian RAI-TV, Rome, 1975—; prof. Rome U. Contbr. articles to profl. jours. Vice-pres. Italian Council, European Movement, Italian Commn. of Fed. European Movement; mem. directive com. Inst. Internat. Affairs; sec. gen. Italian Centre for European Studies. Decorated Knight of Grand Cross for Merit of Italian Republic; recipient Gold medal Ministry of Edn. Mem. Italian Assn. Ednl. Progress. Office: RAI-TV, Via Mazzini 14, 1-00195 Rome Italy *

ORTEGA SAAVEDRA, (JOSE) DANIEL, Nicaraguan president; b. Chontales, Nicaragua, 1945. Student law Central Am. U. Joined Sandinista Nat. Liberation Front (FSLN), 1962—; supr. student movement, founder newspaper El Estudiante, apptd. Nat. Directorate, FSLN, 1965, captured by secret police, imprisoned, 1967-74, liberated, 1974, leader ops., 1974-79, mem. Junta Nat. Reconstrn., 1979; elected pres. of Nicaragua, 1984—. Office: Office of Pres, Managua Nicaragua *

ORTEGO, JOHN HARVEL, economist; b. Opelousas, La., Nov. 24, 1942; s. Adner Paul and Ellen Jane (Ardoin) O.; m. Karen Elizabeth LaHaye, July 15, 1967; children: Heidi Elizabeth, Joshua Garrett. BS in Chem. Engring., La. State U., 1964; MBA in Mgmt. Sci., St. Louis U., 1969; postgrad. in econs., 1977—. Chem. engr. Tech. Service dept. J.F. Queeny Plant Organic Chems. div. Monsanto Co., St. Louis, 1964-68, supt. fin. and ops. analysis, corp. engring. dept., 1968-76, mgr. planning and info. internat. div., 1977-78; dir. inflation planner service Chase Econometrics, Bala Cynwyd, Pa., 1978-83, sr. dir. gen. industry services, 1983; pres. MicroEconometrics, editor Commodity Cost Planning Letter, 1983-85; asst. prof. econs. and fin. West Chester State U., Penn., 1984-85; v.p., sr. economist Key Corp., Albany, N.Y., 1985—; lectr. St. Louis U., 1976-77; mem. econ. adv. bd. N.Y. State Assembly Ways and Means Com. Contbg. author Handbook of Economic and Financial Measures, 1984. Mem. Nat. Assn. Bus. Economists, N.Y. State Bankers Assn. (econ. adv. bd. 1985—), N.Y. State Assembly Ways and Means Com. (econ. adv. bd.). Home: 25 Traditional Ln Loudonville NY 12211-1703 Office: 60 State St Albany NY 12207

ORTEL, SIEGFRIED EMIL, medical microbiologist, researcher; b. Bahn, Germany, Mar. 16, 1916; s. Emil Karl and Erna Martha (Loewke) O.; m. Ingrid Brandt, Mar. 16, 1959; children—Christian, Astrid, Claudia, Petra, Birgit, Dietmar, Sieghard. Abitur Oberschule, Pyritz, 1936; D.Sci. Medicine, U. Greitswald, 1944. Prof. sci. medicine, dir. Inst. for Med. Microbiology and Epidemiology, U. Halle/S, German Dem. Republic, 1958-81, head reference lab. for listeriosis, 1981—. Home: Schwuchtstr 1d, 4020 Halle PF 692, German Democratic Republic Office: Univ Halle/S, Med Sect, Leninallee 6, 4020 Halle/S German Democratic Republic

ÖRTENGREN, JOHN, marketing and financial consultant; b. Stockholm, Sept. 27, 1931; s. Helmer and Amparo Maria Del Carmen (Carreras) Ö; B.B.A., Stockholm Grad. Sch. Advt., 1954; M.B.A., Syracuse U., 1955, Ph.D., 1961; m. Lena Cedrenius, Apr. 13, 1957; children—Henrik, Anders, Torsten. Pub. relations cons. Dr. Axel Wenner-Gren, 1954-55; mktg. dir. Young & Rubicam, Stockholm, 1955-62; pres., prin. owner AB Marknadsforskning, Sollentuna, Sweden, 1962—, Marknadsföring AB John Örtengren, Sollentuna, 1972—; chmn. Sibe Group Cos., 1975—, Sams-företagen AB, 1981—; dir. AB Femco, Dantherm Trading AB, LBC Tureberg AB; head instr. advt. Grad. Sch. Advt., Stockholm, 1956-60. Served to capt. Swedish Antiaircraft Corps, 1964-67. Mem. Assn. Market Researchers in Sweden, European Mktg. Assn., European Soc. for Opinion and Mktg. Research, Swedish Mktg. Research Inst. Assn., Swedish Mktg. Fedn. (auditor, 1984), Alumni Assn. Grad. Sch. Advt. (chmn. 1962-67), Internat. Advt. Assn. (chmn. Stockholm chpt. 1967-71), Swedish Forum for Market Econs. (chmn. 1981—), Swedish Soc. Hist. Certs. (chmn. 1986—). Clubs: Rotary (past pres., Paul Harris fellow, Sollentuna-Tureberg chpt.). Author: Market and Consumer Legislation in Sweden, 1977, 2d edit., 1980; co-author: Management 83/84. Home: Alvagen 17B, 19143 Sollentuna Sweden Office: PO Box 4, 19121 Sollentuna Sweden

ORTHWEIN, WILLIAM COE, mechanical engineer; b. Toledo, Ohio, Jan. 27, 1924; s. William Edward and Millie Minerva (Coe) O.; m. Helen Virginia Poindexter, Feb; children—Karla Frances, Adele Diana, Maria Theresa. B.S., M.I.T., 1946; M.S., U. Mich., 1957, Ph.D., 1959. Registered profl. engr., Ill., Ind., Ky. Aerophysicist Gen. Dynamics Co., Ft. Worth, 1951-52; research asso. U. Mich., 1952-59; adv. engr. IBM Corp., Owego, N.Y., 1959-61; dir. computer centers U. Okla., Norman, 1961-63; research scientist Ames Lab., NASA, Moffett Field, Calif., 1963-65; mem. faculty So. Ill. U., Carbondale, 1965—; prof. engring. So. Ill. U., 1967—; cons. in field. Author: Clutches and Brakes, 1986; papers, revs., books in field. Pres. Jackson County (Ill.) Taxpayers Assn., 1976. Served with AUS, 1943-46. Mem. ASME (Outstanding Service award 1972), Am. Gear Mfrs. Assn., Am. Acad. Mechanics, Soc. Automotive Engrs., Ill. Soc. Profl. Engrs. (chmn. salary and employment com. 1974, chmn. ad hoc com. continuing edn. 1975), Nat. Rifle Assn., Aircraft Owners and Pilots Assn., Sigma Xi. Mormon. Home: PO Box 3332 Carbondale IL 62902 Office: So Ill Univ Carbondale IL 62901

ORTIZ, ARTHUR LOUIS, banker; b. Taos, N.M., Sept. 27, 1928; s. E.B. and Ofelia (Santistevan) O.; children—Jane, Lisa, Susan, Ardyth, Todd. B.A., U. Wis., 1951; B.F.T., Am. Grad. Sch. Internat. Mgmt., 1955. Mktg. mgr. Quaker Oats, Colombia, S.Am., 1956-59, gen. mgr., Venezuela, 1959-63; gen. mgr. Yucca Builders Supply, Taos, N.Mex., 1964-66; state planning dir. State of N.Mex., Santa Fe, 1966-68, personnel dir., 1970-72; adminstrv. asst. U.S. Dept. Commerce, Washington, 1968-70; pres., chief exec. officer Centinel Bank, Taos, N.Mex., 1972-77; commr. banking State of N.Mex., Santa Fe, 1977-81; pres., chief exec. officer Western Bank, Santa Fe, 1981—. Treas. N.Mex. Student Loan Guarantee Bd., 1981-83; bd. dirs. Conf. of State Bank Suprs., 1979-81; ex officio mem. N.Mex. Mortgage Fin. Authority, 1977-81, others. Served with U.S. Army, 1946-48. Mem. N.Mex. Bankers Assn. (pres. 1983-84), Conf. State Bank Suprs. (dist. 4 chmn. 1980-81). Republican. Roman Catholic. Home: 260 Camino de la Sierra Santa Fe NM 87501 Office: Western Bank 600 San Mateo Santa Fe NM 87501

ORTIZ, RAFAEL MONTAÑEZ, computer, laser, video and performance artist, art educator; b. Bklyn., Jan. 30, 1934; s. Joseph H. and Eusabia (Velazquez) O. BS, Pratt Inst., 1964, MFA, 1964; MEd, Columbia U., 1974, EdD, 1982. Instr. grad. art faculty Columbia U. Tchrs. Coll., N.Y.C., 1967; instr. art NYU, N.Y.C., 1968; adj. prof. art Hostos Coll., N.Y.C., 1970, Fordham U., N.Y.C., 1971, C. W. Post Coll., L.I., N.Y., 1971; adj. prof. art Livingston Coll., Rutgers U., New Brunswick, N.J., 1971, assoc. prof. art, 1972, grad. and undergrad. faculty Mason Gross Sch. Arts. Numerous one-man performances including: Piano Destruction Concert, BBC, London, 1966, Mother Father, Mercury Theater, London, 1966, Paper Bag and Piano Destruction Concert, Fordham U., N.Y.C., 1967, Ecce Homo Gallery, N.Y.C., 1967, Theater Ritual, Temple U. physio-psycho-alchemey, San Francisco Art Inst., 1982, physio-psycho-alchemy, UCLA, 1985, physio-psycho-alchemy, Twin Palms Gallery, San Francisco, 1985, physio-psycho-alchemy, Gwent, Wales, Eng., 1986; physio-pscho-alchemy, Museo Del Barrio, N.Y.C., 1988; group shows include Whitney Mus. Am. Art, N.Y.C., 1965, The Object Transformed, sculpture, Mus. Modern Art, N.Y.C., 1966; Participated in Internat. Destruction in Art Symposium, London, 1966, Finch Coll. Mus. Art Destruction in Art Symposium Sculpture, 1968 Ancient Roots New Visions, sculpture, Palacio de Mineria, Mexico City, 1980, Rutgers Computer Art Group, Walters Gallery, Rutgers U., 1982, computer animation , Paul Robeson Gallery, Rutgers U., 1983, Computer Art, The Salem Syndrome, Tamasulo Gallery, N.J., 1985, Computer Graphics and Sound, Computer-Laser-Video, Bonnefanten Mus., Maastricht, Holland, 1986, Computer-Laser-Video, De-Haag, Fed. Republic Germany, 1986, Computer-Laser-Video Bridge Game, Mülheim Mus., Fed. Republic Germany, 1986, Computer-Laser Video, Berlin Film Festival, 1987, Computer-Laser Video The Kitchen, Techno-Bop 87, N.Y.C.; numerous one man exhbns. including Retrospective, sculpture, performance, Computer-Laser-Video, Museo del Barrio, N.Y.C, 1988, Computer--Laser-video, Gwent, Wales, Eng., 1986; drawings, Columbia U., N.Y.C., 1975, sculpture, Fordham U., N.Y.C., 1967. Represented in permanent collections; Computer-Laser-Video, Ludwig Mus., Cologne, Fed. Republic Germany, 1988, Computer-Laser-Video, Mus. Modern Art, Brussels, 1987, Computer-Laser-Video, Friedricheshof Mus., Zurndorf, Austria, 1986, Computer-Laser-Video, Everson Mus., Syracuse, N.Y., 1985, Computer-Laser-Video, Museo Del Barrio, 1985; sculpture, Feather Pyramids, Museo del Barrio, 1982, sculpture, Disassembled Sofa, Everson Mus., Syracuse, N.Y.,1972, sculpture, Disassembled Upholstered Chair, Chrysler Mus., Va., 1965, sculpture, Shoe Construct-Destruct, Menil Mus., Houston, 1965, sculpture, Disassembled Sofa, Whitney Mus. Am. Ar, 1964, sculpture, Destroyed Mattress, Mus. Modern Art, 1963. Mem. Mus. Computer Art (founder, pres. 1984), Hispanic Assn. Higher Edn., N.J., Art Educators N.J., Coll. Art Assn., Assn. Research and Enlightenment. Office: Rutgers Univ Visual Arts Dept 125 New St New Brunswick NJ 08903

ORTIZ MENA, ANTONIO, retired banker; b. Parral, Chihuahua, Mexico, 1912. Grad., Sch. Law, Nat. Autonomous U. Mexico; postgrad., Sch. Fine Arts and Philosophy, Sch. Econs.; Dr. h.c, U. Guadalajara, Mex. Chief legal counsel, then departmental rep. Mixed Agrarian Commn., Dept. Fed. Dist., Govt. Mexico, 1932-38; dir. Property Nationalization Service; then chief legal counsel Office of Atty. Gen., 1940-45; 1st dir. gen. professions Ministry Pub. Edn., 1945-46; dep. dir. gen., trust rep., then chmn. Banco Nacional de Obras y Servicios Públicos, 1947-52; chmn., chief exec. officer Mexican Social Security Inst., 1952-58; chmn. Permanent Inter-Am. Social Security Com., 1955-59; sec. fin. and pub. credit Govt. Mexico, 1958-70; pres. Inter-Am. Devel. Bank, Washington, 1971-87; Mem. Polit. Def. Com. of Am. Continent, World War II; cons. Mexican del. Inter-Am. Conf. to Consider Problems of War and Peace, Chapultepec, Mex., 1945; gov. for Mex. IMF, World Bank, Internat. Devel. Assn., Internat. Finance Corp., 1959-70; founding Mexican gov. Inter-Am. Devel. Bank, 1960-70, chmn. bd. govs., 1966-67; Mexico rep. Inter-Am. Econ. and Social Council at Ministerial Level, 1961-70, pres., 1962-63; chmn. bd. dirs. Nacional Financiera, Altos Hornos de Mex., Compañia Mexicana de Luz y Fuerza Motriz, Compañia Nacional de Subsistencias Populares, Industria Petroquimica Nacional, Guanos y Fertilizantes de Mex.; vice chmn. bd. dirs. Petroleos Mexicanos, Ferrocarriles Nacionales de Mex. Author: El Desarrollo Estabilizador, 1969, Finanzas Públicas de Mexico, 1969, Development in Latin-America, 1971-75, 76-80. Decorated grand cross Order of Crown of Belgium; grand officer Legion of Honor; grand cross Nat. Order of Merit France; grand cross Order of Merit Fed. Republic Germany; Order of Flag with Banner Yugoslavia; grand cross Nat. Order of So. Cross Brazil; grand cross Order Orange-Nassau Netherlands; grand cross Order of Merit Bernardo O'Higgins Chile; others. Mem. Mexican Hwy. Assn. (life), AIM (council of presidents). Clubs: Metropolitan (Washington); Bretton Woods (Md.).

ORTLIP, PAUL DANIEL, artist; b. Englewood, N.J., May 21, 1926; s. Henry Willard and Aimee (Eschner) O.; m. Mary Louise Krueger, Dec., 1980; children from previous marriage: Carol, Kathleen, Sharon (dec.), Danielle, Michelle. Diploma, Houghton Acad., 1944; student, Art Students League, 1947-49; diploma, Acad. la Grande Chaumiere, Paris, 1950. Tchr. Fairleigh Dickinson U., Teaneck, N.J., 1956-68; artist in residence, curator Fairleigh Dickinson U., Rutherford, N.J., 1968-72; official USN artist on assignment, Cuban missile crisis, Fla., 1963, Gemini 5 Recovery, Atlantic Ocean, 1965, Vietnam, 1967, Apollo 12 recovery, Pacific Ocean, 1969, Apollo 17 recovery, Pacific Ocean, 1972, Internat. Naval Rev., N.Y. harbor, 1976, USCG Sta., Key West, Fla., 1985; mem. USN Art Coop. and Liason Com. Exhbns. include Salonde L'Art Libre, Paris, 1950, Nat. Acad. Design, 1952, Allied Artists of Am., N.Y.C., Acad. Sci., Rundell Gallery, Rochester, N.Y., Monclair Art Mus., Hist. Mus. Lima, Ohio, Butler Art Inst., Youngstown, Ohio, Fine Arts Gallery, San Diego, State Capitol Bldg., Sacramento, Calif., Capitol Mus., Olympia, Wash., Mus. Gt. Plains, Lawton, Okla., Witte Meml. Mus., San Antonio, Nimitz Meml. Mus., Fredericksberg, Tex., Pentagon Collection of Fine Arts, James Hunt Barker Galleries, Palm Beach, Fla., Nantucket, Mass. N.Y.C., Smithsonian Inst., Gallerie Vollem Breuse, Biarritz, France, Galerie Mouffe, Paris, Guggenheim Gallery, London, Wickersham Gallery, N.Y.C., Soc. Illustrators, N.Y.C.; retrospective exhbn. Bergen Community Mus., Paramus, N.J. 1970; represented permanent collections Houghton (N.Y.) Coll., Portrait Meml. J.F. Kennedy Library, Fairleigh-Dickinson U., Nat. Air and Space Mus., Smithsonian Inst., Intrepid Sea-Air Space Mus., N.Y.C., Hist. Mural Visitors Ctr., Palisades Interstate Pk., Ft. Lee, N.J., Vets. Med. Ctr., East Orange, N.J., USN Exhbn. Ctr., Washington Navy Yard, Am. Coll. Clin. Pharmacology, N.Y.C., N.J. U. Dentistry & Medicine, Newark, Bergen County Ct. House, Kackensack, N.J., Dickinson Coll., Carlisle, Pa., George Washingtogn Meml Pk., Paramus, N.J., Marietta (Ohio) Coll., Mcpl. Bldg., Ft. Lee, N.J. Served to sgt. U.S. Army, 1944-47, ETO, Korea. Recipient 1st prize Am. Artists Profl. League State Exhibit N.J. chpt., Paramus, 1960, 1st prize U.S. Armed Forces Exhibit Far East, Seoul, Korea, Tokyo, 1946, Franklin Williams award, Salmagundi Club, N.Y., 1967, Outstanding Achievement award for oil painting, USN, 1968, Artist of Yr. award, Hudson Artists, Jersey City (N.J.) Mus., 1970, Statue of Victory World Culture prize, Academia Italia, Parma, 1982; Am. Portrait Soc. artists fellow, USCG Art Program fellow. Mem. Allied Artists Am. (art coop. and liaison com. with USN), Nat. Soc. Mural Painters, Bergen County Artists Guild (pres. 1960-62), Art Students League N.Y. (life), Navy League U.S., VFW. Clubs: Salmagundi (N.Y.C.) (art chmn. 1979-81); Boca Raton (Fla.). Home: 588 Summit Ave Hackensack NJ 07601 Office: care The Curzon Gallery 501 E Camino Real Boca Raton FL 33432

ORTNER, REINHOLD, educator; b. Neukirchen St. Christoph, Germany, Nov. 26, 1930; s. Joseph and Barbara (Stiefler) O.; dipl. psychologe U. Wurzburg, 1959, Dr.Phil., 1963; m. Arngard Glier, Aug. 23, 1958; children—Ulrich, Cordula, Alexandra, Michaela, Carolina. Primary sch. tchr., 1954-64; univ. asst. U. Bamberg, 1964-66, tchr., 1966-72, ordinary prof. primary edn., 1972—. Author: Das Sprachlabor im Leseunterricht, 1971; Audiovisuelle Medien, 1972; Lernbehinderungen und Lernstö rungen bei Grundschulkindern, 1977; In die Tiefen der Seele, 1976; Kind-Schule-Gesundheit, 1979; Erziehung aus christlicher Verantwortung, 1980; Die Berge werden erleben, 1982; Du und dein Leben, 1984; Was weisst du von dir, 1986; Gott in deinem Leben, 1988; also numerous essays on religion and primary edn. Roman Catholic. Home: 5 Birkenstrasse, D8608 Memmelsdorf Federal Republic of Germany Office: 3 Markusplatz, D8600 Bamberg Federal Republic of Germany

ORTOLI, FRANCOIS-XAVIER, economist; b. Feb. 16, 1925. Ed. Hanoi Faculty of Law and Ecole Nationale d'Administration; hon. degree, Oxford U., Athens (Greece) U. Insp. fins. French Govt., 1948-51, tech. advisor to the Office of Minister of Econ. Affairs and Info., 1951-53, tech. advisor to the Office of Minister of Fins., 1954-55, asst. dir. to Sec. of State for Econ. Affairs, 1955-57; sec.-gen. Franco-Italian Com. of EEC, 1955-57; head comml. politics service Sec. of State for Econ. Affairs, 1957-58; dir.-gen. Internal Market Div. of the EEC, 1958-61; sec.-gen. Inter-Ministerial Com. for Questions of European Econ. Cooperation, Paris, 1961-62; dir. Cabinet of Prime Minister France 1962-66, Commr.-Gen. of the Plan, 1966-67; Minister of Works France, 1967-68, Minister of Edn., 1968, Minister of Fin., 1968-69, Minister of Indsl. and Scientific Devel., 1969-72; pres. Com. of European Communities, 1973-76; v.p. for Econ. and Monetary Affairs Govt. of France, 1977-84; pres., exec. dir. TOTAL Co. Française Des Petroles, 1984—; bd. dirs. Philips NV; adv. dir. Unilever Corp., 1985—; pres. Coll. of Europe. Decorated Légion d'Honneur, Croix de Guerre, Médaille Militaire, Médaille de la Résistance, numerous others. Home: 18 rue de Bourgogne, 75007 Paris France *

ORWOLL, GREGG S. K., lawyer; b. Austin, Minn., Mar. 23, 1926; s. Gilbert M. and Kleonora (Kleven) O.; m. Laverne M. Flentie, Sept. 15, 1951; children—Kimball G., Kent A., Vikki A., Tristen A., Erik G. B.S., Northwestern U., 1950; J.D., U. Minn., 1953. Bar: Minn. 1953, U.S. Supreme Ct. 1973. Assoc. Dorsey, Owen, Marquart, Windhorst and West, Mpls., 1953-59; ptnr. Dorsey, Owen, Marquart, Windhorst and West, 1959-60; assoc. counsel Mayo Clinic, Rochester, Minn., 1960-63; gen. counsel Mayo Clinic, 1963-87, sr. legal counsel, 1987—; gen counsel, dir. Rochester Airport Co., 1962-84, sec., 1962-81, v.p., 1981-84; gen. counsel Mayo Med. Services, Ltd., 1972—; bd. dirs., sec., gen. counsel Mayo Med. Found. for Med., Edn. and Research, 1984—; gen. counsel Mid-Am. Orthopedic Soc., 1982—, Minn. Orthopedic Soc., 1985—; asst. sec. Mayo Found., Rochester, 1972-76, 82-86 , sec., 1976-82, 86—; dir. Travelure Motel Corp., 1968-86, sec., 1972-83, 86, v.p., 1983-86; adj. prof. William Mitchell Coll. Law, St. Paul, 1978-84. Contbr. articles and chpts. to legal and medico-legal publs.; bd. editors HealthScan, 1984—; editorial bd. Minn. Law Rev., 1952-53. Trustee Minn. Council on Founds., 1977-82, Mayo Found., 1982-86, William Mitchell Coll. Law, 1982—; pres. Rochester Council Chs., 1968-69; mem. bd. advisers Rochester YWCA, 1966-72; bd. dirs. Rochester Med. Ctr. Ministry, Inc., 1975-81; bd. dirs. Zumbro Luth. Ch., 1962-64, 77-79, pres., 1964-65; bd. dirs. Rochester YMCA, 1966-70; trustee Courage Found., 1974-80, YMCA-YWCA Bldg. Corp., 1966-73 ; bd. visitors U. Minn. Law Sch., 1974-76, 1985—. Served with USAAF, 1944-45. Mem. Am. Acad. Hosp. Attys., Minn. Soc. Hosp. Attys. (dir. 1981-86), Minn. State Bar Assn. (chmn. legal med. com. 1977-81), ABA, Olmsted County Bar Assn. (v.p. 1977-78, pres. 1978-79), Rochester C. of C., AMA (affiliate), U. Minn. Law Alumni Assn. (bd. dirs. 1973-76, 85—), Phi Delta Theta, Phi Delta Phi. Republican. Club: Rochester University (pres. 1977). Office: Mayo Clinic 200 1st St SW Rochester MN 55905

ORY, CHARLES NATHAN, lawyer; b. Atlanta, Mar 25, 1946; s. Marvin Gilbert and Esther Rose (Levine) O.; m. Carolyn Susan Pruett, June 21, 1976; children: Jebidiah Marlowe, Brett Elizabeth. BA in Econs., George Washington U., 1968; JD, U. Tex.-Austin, 1972. Bar: Tex. 1972, U.S. Dist. Ct. (no. dist.) Tex. 1982, U.S. Dist. Ct. (ea. dist.) Wash. 1981, U.S. Ct. Appeals (5th cir.) 1982; U.S. Dist. Ct. (we. dist.) Tex. 1987. Trial atty. Dept. Justice, Washington, 1973-82; spl. asst. to U.S. Atty., Spokane, 1981; asst. U.S. atty. Dept. Justice, Dallas, 1982-86; dir. litigation, Palmer & Palmer, 1986—; EEO investigator Exec. Offices of U.S. Attys., Dept. Justice, Washington, 1984-86. Co-founder and mng. editor Am. Jour. Criminal Law, 1971-72. Bd. dirs. Munger Place Hist. Homeowners Assn., Dallas, 1984-86; mem. Clean Dallas East, Inc., 1984-85. Recipient Spl. Achievement award U.S. Dept. Justice civil rights div., 1979, Atty. Gen.'s Spl. Achievement award U.S. Dept. Justice, 1986. Home: 5020 Junius St Dallas TX 75214 Office: Palmer & Palmer PC 1510 One Main Pl Dallas TX 75250

ORZAC, EDWARD SEYMOUR, otolaryngologist; b. N.Y.C., Jan. 11, 1917; s. Philip Edward Orzac and Gertrude (Wachtler) Orzac Cohen; m. Beatrice Fleiss, July 18, 1948; children—Carolyn, Virginia, Elizabeth. B., U. N.C., 1936; M., U. Va., 1937, M.D., 1941; B.A. in History, Adelphi U., 1974; M.A. in Asian Studies, St. John's U., 1978. Diplomate Am. Bd. Otolaryngology. Intern Wilkes Barre Gen. Hosp., Pa., 1941-42; resident Morisania City Hosp., N.Y., 1945-46, 47-48, NYU-Bellevue Grad. Sch. Medicine, 1946-47; practice medicine specializing in otolaryngology, Valley Stream, N.Y., 1948-81; med. dir. Franklin Gen. Hosp., Valley Stream, 1973—; cons. otolaryngologist Nassau County Med. Ctr., 1983—; founder, dir. Gertrude Wachtler Cohen Hearing, Vertigo and Speech Ctr., Valley Stream, 1974—; asst. prof. clin. surgery SUNY-Stony Brook Med. Sch., 1971—; ann. vis. prof. Kasturba Med. Coll., Manipal Karnataka, India, 1975-82; adj. prof. speech and hearing Adelphi U., 1979—; assoc. adj. prof. hearing and speech, St. John's U. Contbr. articles to profl. jours. Chmn. United Jewish Appeal, Franklin Gen. Hosp. and South Nassau Communities Hosp., 1974; chmn. Israel Bond Drive, Franklin Gen. Hosp., 1965-72, co-chmn., Nassau County, 1976; chmn. Nassau Physicians and Dentists div. United Jewish Appeal, 1978-79. Served to maj. U.S. Army, 1942-45. Hon. fellow Acad. Gen. Edn., Kasturba Med. Coll., Manipal, Karnataka, 1979. Fellow Nassau Surg. Soc., Am. Acad. Ophthalmology and Otolaryngology, Am. Plastic Surgeons, Nassau Acad. Medicine, Am. Acad. Med. Dirs.; mem. Am. Coll. Emergency Physicians, Am. Coll. Physician Execs., Nassau County Soc. Otolaryngology (pres. 1959-60), Phi Alpha Theta. Home: 221 Albon Rd Hewlett Harbor NY 11557 Office: Franklin Gen Hosp 900 Franklin Ave Valley Stream NY 11582

ORZECHOWSKI, MARIAN ODON, former minister of foreign affairs of Poland, historian; b. Radom, Poland, Oct. 24, 1931. Grad. State A. Zhdanow U., Leningrad, 1955; Dr. Humanities, Wroclaw U., 1961, Dr. Habilitatis, 1964. Tchr. Wroclaw U., 1955-85, asst., 1955-61, lectr., 1961-65, asst. prof., 1965-71, extraordinary prof., 1971-77, dir. Inst. Polit. Scis., 1969-72, rector, 1972-75, ordinary prof., 1977-85; minister of fgn. affairs, Poland, 1985-88; mem. Central Commn. for Acad. Appointments of Prime Minister, 1976-79; mem. Youth Orgn. of Workers' Univ. Soc., 1947-48, Polish Youth Union, 1948-55; mem. Polish United Workers' Party, 1952—, mem. central com., 1981—, sec. Central Com., 1981-83, alt. mem. Polit. Bur. Central Com., 1983-86, mem., 1986—; rector Acad. Social Scis. attached to Central Com., 1984-85; sec.-gen. Provisional Nat. Council of Patriotic Movement for Nat. Rebirth Patriotyczny Ruch Odrodzenia Narodowego, 1982-83; sec. Gen. Nat. Council, 1983-84. Author: Narodowa Demokracja na Gornym Slasku do 1919 r, 1965, Wojciech Korfanty. Biografia polityczna, 1975, Rewolucja. Socjalizm. Tradycje, 1978, Maxa Webera teoria polityki, 1982, others. Recipient Knight's Cross of Order of Polonia Restituta, medal Nat. Edn. Commn., Comdr's Cross Order Polonia Restituta. Office: Ministry Fgn Affairs, Warsaw Poland *

OSAKA, NAOYUKI, psychologist; b. Kyoto, Japan, Dec. 16, 1946; s. Ryoji and Ritsuko O.; m. Mariko Yamamoto, Dec. 25, 1977. BA, Kyoto U. Edn., 1971; MA, Kyoto U., 1973, PhD, 1979. Research assoc. dept. psychology U. Kyoto, 1976-77, assoc. prof. psychology, 1987—; asst. prof. Otemon-Gakuin U., Osaka, Japan, 1977-80, assoc. prof., 1981-86. Author: Psychophysical Analysis of Peripheral Vision, 1973, Computer Communication, 1973, Computer Control, 1973. Recipient Hashimoto prize Japanese Ergonomic Soc., 1986; Japan Soc. for the Promotion of Sci.-Deutscher Akademischer Austauschdienst fellow, Japan Soc. for the Promotion of Sci.-Nat. Eye Inst. fellow. Mem. Japanese Psychol. Assn., Psychonomic Soc., Assn. Research in Vision and Ophhalmology, Brit. Applied Vision Assn., Optical Soc. Am. Home: 1-14-72 Nishitakenosato-cho, Oharano Nishikyoku, Kyoto 610-11, Japan Office: Kyoto U, Dept Psychology Faculty Letters, Kyoto 606, Japan

OSAKWE, CHRISTOPHER, legal educator; b. Lagos, Nigeria, May 8, 1942; came to U.S. 1970, naturalized 1979; s. Simon and Hannah (Morgan) O.; m. Maria Elena Amador, Aug. 19, 1982. LL.B., Moscow State U., 1966, LL.M., 1967, Ph.D., 1970; J.S.D., U. Ill., 1974. Prof. law Tulane U. Sch. Law, New Orleans, 1972-81, 1986—, Eason-Weinmann prof. comparative law, dir. Eason-Weinmann Ctr. for Comparative Law, 1981-86; vis. prof. U. Pa., 1978, U. Mich., 1981, Washington and Lee U., 1986; vis. fellow St. Anthony's Coll., Oxford U., Eng., 1980, Christ Church Coll., Oxford U., 1988-89; cons. U.S. Dept. Commerce, 1980-85. Author: The Participation of the Soviet Union in Universal International Organizations, 1972, The Foundations of Soviet Law, 1981; (with others) Comparative Legal Traditions in a Nutshell, 1982, Comparative Legal Traditions—Text, Materials and Cases, 1985; editor Am. Jour. Comparative Law, 1978-86, Am. Jour. Legal Edn., 1983-85. Carnegie doctoral fellow Hague Acad. Internat. Law, 1969; Russian research fellow Harvard U., 1972; USSR sr. research exchange fellow, 1982, reserach fellow Kennan Inst. for Advanced Russian Studies, 1988. Mem. ABA, Am. Law Inst., Am. Soc. Internat. Law, COIF. Republican. Roman Catholic. Home: 339 Audubon Blvd New Orleans LA 70125 Office: Tulane U Sch Law 6801 Freret St New Orleans LA 70118

OSBORN, CHARLES EDGAR, business executive; b. Toronto, Ont., Can., Oct. 5, 1934; s. John Henry and Esme Emily (Saunders) O.; m. Lillian Ann Meredith, May 15, 1954; children: John Charles, Tracey Deanne, Donna May Esme, Lesley Meredith, Paige Emily. Student in engring., math., Ryerson Coll., Toronto, 1952-53; student in human relations, U. Waterloo, Ont., 1968-69; student in mgmt., Conestoga Coll., Doon, Ont., 1970. Wind tunnel model builder Roe Aircraft, Malton, Ont., 1950-60; layout inspector Babcock-Wilcox, Cambridge, Ont., 1960-63; gen. foreman Wean Can. Ltd., Cambridge, 1963-71; sales mgr. Hall Smith Co., Burlington, Ont., 1971-77; sales mgr. Wean Can. Ltd., Cambridge, 1977-80, mgr. mfg., 1980-84, v.p., gen. mgr., 1984—; bd. dirs. Can. Mfrs. Assn. Grand Valley chpt., Kitchener, Ont., Machinery and Equipment Mfrs. Assn. of Can. Custom Machinery Div., Toronto, Wean Can. Ltd., Heavy Steel Mill Equipment Mech. Stamping Presses. Bd. dirs. Cambridge Indsl. Tng. Commn., 1979—, mem. adv. com. Conestoga Coll, 1980-82. Mem. C. of C. Conservative. Anglican. Club: Galt Country. Office: Wean Can Ltd, 100 Savage Dr, Cambridge, ON Canada N1R 5V6

OSBORN, GLENN RICHARD, audio engineer; b. Los Angeles, Oct. 25, 1928; s. Glenn Litts and Nellie (Hoffman) O.; BS in Audio Engring., U. Hollywood, 1949; m. Joye Elise Hughes, Feb. 15, 1963 (div. 1984); children—Eric William, John Howard; m. Jean B. Linderman, Feb. 14, 1988. Head transmission engr., 1352 Motion Picture Squadron, Hollywood, 1953-60; head sound dept. Sandia Corp., Albuquerque, 1960-65; supr. sound dept. A-V Service Corp., Seabrook, Tex., 1965-80; owner G.R. Osborn & Co., Audio Engrs., Seabrook, 1975-80, supr. sound dept., Mede Service Corp., 1980—, pres., CEO, Travel Services, Inc., 1987—. Served with AUS, 1950-52. Mem. Audio Engring. Soc., Acoustical Soc. Am., Soc. Motion Picture and TV Engrs. Office: Travel Services Inc PO Box 59834 Houston TX 77258-8934

OSBORN, LESLIE ANDREWARTHA, psychiatrist; b. Warrnambool, Victoria, Australia, Aug. 10, 1906; came to U.S., 1931, naturalized, 1938; s. Andrew Rule and Annie (Delbridge) O.; m. Dora Wright, June 12, 1931 (dec.); children: Anne L. Osborn Krueger Henderson, June E.; m. Gwen F. Arnold, Aug. 13, 1960 (dec. Mar. 12, 1976); m. Corinne H. Kirchmaier, June 7, 1985. Student, Wesley Coll., Melbourne, 1920-23; M.B., B.S., Melbourne Med. Sch., 1929; M.D., U. Buffalo, 1945. Diplomate: Am. Bd. Psychiatry and Neurology, 1944. Intern Melbourne Gen. Hosp., 1930-31; postgrad. Post Grad. Hosp., N.Y.C., 1934; in chest diseases Trudeau Sch. Tb, Saranac Lake, 1937; in neurology and psychiatry Columbia U., 1940; gen. practice medicine, physician Endicott-Johnson Med. Dept., Binghamton, N.Y., 1932-38; asst. physician Willard (N.Y.) State Hosp., 1938-41; psychiatrist Meyer Meml. Hosp.; assoc. psychiatry U. Buffalo, 1941-45; attending psychiatrist, dir. psychiatry Edward J. Meyer Meml. Hosp., psychiat. service, 1946-49; prof. psychiatry U. Buffalo Sch. Medicine, 1946, acting dir. dept. psychiatry, 1946-49, head dept., 1949-50; dir. Wis. Psychiat. Inst.; prof. psychiatry U. Wis. Med. Sch., 1950-60; dir. div. mental hygiene Wis. Dept. Pub. Welfare, 1950-60; dir. Walworth County Family Counseling Center, 1960; prof. psychiatry dept. neurology and psychiatry U. Nebr., 1960-66; dir. Swanson Clinic for Multiply Handicapped Children, Nebr. Psychiat. Inst., Omaha, 1960-64; med. dir. Winnebago County Mental Health Clinic, Rockford, Ill., 1966; dir. Mental Health Services, Tompkins County, 1967-68; pvt. practice psychiatry Seneca Falls, N.Y., 1968-74, Scottsdale, Ariz., 1974—. Author: Psychiatry and Medicine, 1952, Prognosis, A Guide to the Study and Practice of Clinical Medicine, 1966, Foundation Learning and Innumeracy, 1977, King of the Hill: Chess for Children, 1981, Preventing War: A Doctor's Trilogy (Vol. I, The Insanity of War, Vol. II, Education--Or Catastrophe, Vol. III, Freedom or Frustration). Fellow Am. Psychiat. Assn. (life); mem. Société de Médecine de Paris (corr.). Presbyterian. Address: 5158 N 83d St Scottsdale AZ 85253

OSBORN, MALCOLM EVERETT, lawyer, educator; b. Bangor, Maine, Apr. 29, 1928; s. Lester Everett and Helen (Clark) O.; m. Claire Anne Franks, Aug. 30, 1953; children—Beverly, Lester, Malcolm, Ernest. B.A., U. Maine, 1952; postgrad. Harvard U. 1952-54; J.D. Boston U. 1956, LL.M., 1961. Bar: Maine 1956, Mass. 1956, U.S. Dist. Ct. 1961, U.S. Tax Ct. 1961, U.S. Claims 1961, N.C. 1965, U.S. Supreme Ct. 1979, U.S. Ct. Appeals (4th cir.) 1980. Tax counsel State Mut. Life Assurance Co., Worcester, Mass., 1956-64; v.p., gen. tax counsel Integon Corp. and other group cos., Winston-Salem, N.C., 1964-81; ptnr. House, Blanco & Osborn, Winston-Salem, 1981—, v.p., gen. counsel, dir. Settlers Life Ins. Co., Bristol, Va., 1984—; lectr. The Booke Seminars, Life Ins. Co., 1985-87; adj. prof. Wake Forest U. Sch. Law, Winston-Salem, 1974-82; Disting. guest lectr. Ga. State U., 1965; guest lectr. N.Y.U. Ann. Inst. Fed. Taxation, 1966, 68, 75, 80. Trustee N.C. Council Econ. Edn., 1968-76; bd. dirs. Christian Fellowship Home, 1972-80; co-founder Bereaved Parents Group Winston-Salem, 1978—. Mem. ABA (chmn. com. ins. cos. of taxation sect. 1980-82; chmn. subcom. on continuing legal edn. and publs. 1982—), Am. Bus. Law Assn. (mem. com. fed. taxation 1968—, chmn. 1972-75), Assn. Life Ins. Counsel (com. on co. tax, tax sect. 1965—), N.C. Bar Assn. (com. taxation 1973-78), Fed. Bar Assn. (taxation com. 1973—), Internat. Bar Assn. (com. on taxes of bus. law sect. 1973—), AAUP. Club: Masons (Lincoln, Maine). Com. editor The Tax Lawyer, ABA, 1974-76; author numerous articles in field. Office: 215 Executive Park Blvd Winston-Salem NC 27103

OSBORN, MARVIN GRIFFING, JR., university consultant; b. Baton Rouge, Sept. 7, 1922; s. Marvin Griffing and Mamie (Hester) O.; m. Sarah Fleming, Aug. 3, 1945; children: Jane Fleming, Charles Porter. B.A., La. State U., 1942, M.A., 1946; LL.D., St. Xavier Coll., 1971; D.Hum., Phillips U., 1977. Pub. relations counsel La. State U., 1945-47, acting dir. bur. pub. service, 1947; asso. prof., chmn. dept. journalism and dir. pub. relations Howard Coll. (now Frank Samford U.), 1947-49; dir. pub. relations, lectr. journalism Miss. State Coll. (now Miss. State U.), 1949-53; dir. information Washington U., 1953-58, pub. relations adviser, 1955-58, dir. Devel. Funds, 1958-61; cons. coll. and univ. adminstrn. 1961—, including Drake, Duke, Phillips, Tampa, Tex. Christian univs., Atlantic Christian Coll., Bethany (W.Va.), Eckerd, Loretto Heights, St. Xavier, Tenn. Wesleyan, Webster, Hendrix, Mercy (Detroit), Bethel (Tenn.), McMurry, St. Scholastica, Coker Coll., Christian Ch. Found., Nat. Meth. Found. Christian Higher Edn., Lexington Theol. Sem., Memphis Theol. Sem., Nat. Benevolent Assn. Christian Ch., Sisters of Loretto; interim pres. St. Xavier Coll., 1968-69; mem. planning com. Conf. Advancement Understanding and Support of Higher Edn., White Sulphur Springs, W.Va., 1958; mem. exec. com. program and arrangements com. Gen. Assembly Christian Ch., 1977, 87-89. Bd. dirs. St. Louis Heart Assn., 1969-75; trustee Nat. City Christian Ch. Corp., 1981-85; bd. dirs. Fla. Christian Ctr., 1986—. Served from lt. to capt., 28th Inf. Div. AUS, 1942-45. Mem. Am. Coll. Pub. Relations Assn. (v.p. dists. 1951-52, v.p. membership 1952-53, sec.-treas. 1953-55, pres. 1959-60), Sigma Chi, Sigma Delta Chi, Omicron Delta Kappa. Mem. Christian Ch. (dir., exec. com., sec. Bd. Higher Edn. 1973-77). Home: 600 Manatee Ave Apt 107 Holmes Beach FL 34217 also: PO Box 27 Glenville NC 28736

OSBORNE, MICHAEL JOHN, classical studies educator; b. Eastbourne, Sussex, Eng., Jan. 25, 1942; s. Samuel and Olive May (Shove) O.; m. Dawn Maxine Brindle, Feb. 23, 1978. BA in Lit. Humaniores, U. Oxford, Eng., 1965, MA in Lit. Humaniores, 1967; PhD en Lettren, Katholieke U., Leuven, Belgium, 1977. Lectr. in classics U. Bristol, Eng., 1965-66; lectr. in classics U. Lancaster, Eng., 1966-78, sr. lectr. in classics, 1978-82; prof. of classical studies U. Melbourne, Australia, 1983—; dep. dean Faculty Arts, Univ. Melbourne, 1985-86. Author: Naturalization in Athens (4 vols.), 1981-83. Named Laureate Belgium Royal Acad., Brussels, 1980. Fellow Australian Acad. Humanities; mem. Inst. Advanced Study. Office: U Melbourne, Dept Classical Studies, Parkville, Victoria 3052, Australia

OSBORNE, STANLEY DE JONGH, investment banker; b. San Jose, Costa Rica, Mar. 27, 1905; m. Elizabeth Ide, Oct. 28, 1929 (dec. Sept. 1984); children: Mary Ide (Mrs. John Witherbee), Richard de Jongh, Cynthia Adams (Mrs. Richard M. Hoskin). Student, Phillips Acad., Andover, Mass., 1918-22; A.B. cum laude, Harvard, 1926, postgrad. bus. sch., 1926-27. Dir. publicity Harvard Athletic Assn., 1927-28; with Old Colony Corp., Boston, 1928-29; asst. to pres. Atlantic Coast Fisheries Co., 1929-30, treas., 1930-36, 39-43, sec., 1932-42, v.p., 1936-43; spl. asst. to rubber dir. Washington, 1942-43; v.p. Eastern Airlines, Inc., 1944-50; financial v.p. Mathieson Chem. Corp., Balt., 1950-54; exec. v.p. Olin Mathieson Chem. Corp., 1954-57, pres., chmn. dir., 1957-64; gen. partner Lazard Freres & Co., 1963-69, ltd. partner, 1970—; chmn. Pvt. Investment Corp. for Asia, Singapore, 1980-85. Spl. adviser to Pres. John F. Kennedy, 1963-64; mem. Pres.'s Adv. Com. Supersonic Transport, 1964-67; spl. cons. to adminstr. NASA, 1966-68; Bd. govs. Soc. N.Y. Hosp.-Cornell Med. Center, N.Y.C., pres., 1975-80, chmn., 1980-85, hon. chmn., 1986—. Episcopalian. Clubs: Harvard (N.Y.C.), Brook (N.Y.C.), River (N.Y.C.); Buck's (London, Eng.). Home: 1 East End Ave New York NY 10021 also: Greensboro VT 05841 Office: Lazard Freres & Co 1 Rockefeller Plaza New York NY 10020

OSBURG, PETER H(EIN), electrotechnical manufacturing company executive; b. Dortmund, Germany, Oct. 17, 1938; s. K. Willy and Else E.A. (Groening) O.; m. Brigitte R.B. Pietsch, Dec. 6, 1962; children: Hubertus, Sonja, Markus. Ing. KFM, Akademie d. Führungskräfte, Bad Harzburg, W.Ger., 1962. Chief clk. AEG, Dortmund, 1956-59, head dept., Kiel, W.Ger., 1959-62; sales mgr. C.A. Weidmueller, Detmold, W.Ger., 1962-67; mng. dir. Gustav Hensel KG, Lennestadt, W.Ger., 1967—. Office: Gustav Hensel KG, Gustav Hensel Strasse 6, D-5940 Lennestadt Federal Republic of Germany

OSCARSSON, GOSTA VALENTIN, venture capital executive; b. Boras, Sweden, Oct. 9, 1944; s. Ivan G. and Signe L. (Johansson) O.; m. Eva B. Larsson, Aug. 5, 1973; children—Hanna, Nils. M.B.A., Gothenburg Sch. Econs., 1970. Asst. Astra-Meditec AB, Gothenburg, Sweden, 1970-72; exec. v.p. Astra Nutrition AB, Gothenburg, 1972-74; project mgr. Swedish Investment Bank AB, Stockholm, 1974-79, v.p., 1979-83; pres. Four Seasons Venture Capital AB, Stockholm, 1983—. Home: Bergviksvagen 7, S161 38 Bromma Sweden Office: Four Seasons Venture Capital AB, Sveavagen 17, S111 57 Stockholm Sweden

OSDENE, THOMAS STEFAN, tobacco company executive, chemist; b. Prague, Czechoslovakia, Dec. 10, 1927; came to U.S., 1955; m. Philippa P. Joss, Aug. 5, 1955 (div. July 1978); children—Clare S., Joanna A.; m. Candace H. Ostergard, Aug. 25, 1979; 1 child, Stefan R.H. B.Sc. with 1st class honors Birbeck Coll., U. London, 1951, Ph.D. in organic chemistry Inst. Cancer Research, 1955. Mgr. chem. and biochem. research Philip Morris USA, Richmond, Va., 1967-69, dir. research, 1969-81, dir. research and extramural studies, 1981-84, dir. sci. and tech., 1984—; mem. sci. com. Coop. Ctr. Sci. Research Relative to Tobacco, Paris, 1976-80, v.p. com.,

1984—, pres. smoke study group, 1985—; pres. sci. commn. CORESTA, 1986. Contbr. articles and book chpts. to sci. lit.; patentee in field. Bd. dirs. Four Services Bd., social work, Richmond, 1980-82, Richmond Community High Sch., 1983—. Mem. Am. Chem. Soc., N.Y. Acad. Scis., Royal Soc. Chemistry, Royal Philatelic Soc., Sigma Xi. Episcopalian. Clubs: Commonwealth, Bull and Bear (Richmond). Home: 1608 Hanover Ave Richmond VA 23220 Office: Philip Morris USA Ops Ctr PO Box 26603 2001 E Walmsley Blvd Richmond VA 23261

OSGOOD, FRANK WILLIAM, urban and economic planner; b. Williamston, Mich., Sept. 3, 1931; s. Earle Victor and Blanche Mae (Eberly) O.; children: Ann Marie, Frank William Jr. BS, Mich. State U., 1953; M in City Planning, Ga. Inst. Tech., 1960. Prin. planner Tulsa Met. Area Plnning Commn., 1958-60; sr. assoc. Hammer & Co. Assocs., Washington, 1960-64; econ. cons. Marvin Springer & Assocs., Dallas, 1964-65; sr. assoc. Gladstone Assocs., Washington, 1965-67; prof. urban planning Iowa State U., Ames, 1967-73; pres. Frank Osgood Assoc./Osgood Urban Research, Dallas, 1973-84; dir. mktg. studies MPSI Americas Inc., Tulsa, 1984-85, Comarc Systems/Roulac & Co., San Francisco, 1985-86; pres. Osgood Urban Research, Millbrae, Calif., 1986—; adj. prof. U. Tulsa, 1974-76; lectr. U. Tex., Dallas, 1979, 83. Author: Control Land Uses Near Airports, 1960, Planning Small Business, 1967, Continuous Renewal Cities, 1970; contbr. articles to profl. jours. Chmn. awards Cub Scouts Am., Ames, 1971-73; deacon Calvary Presbyn. Ch., San Francisco, 1987. Served to 1st lt. USAF, 1954-56. Recipient Community Leaders and Noteworthy Americans award 1976. Mem. Am. Planning Assn. (peninsula liason, No. Calif. sect., Calif. chpt., 1987, dir. N.Cen. Tex. sect., Tex. chpt., 1983), Am. Inst. Planners (v.p. Okla. chpt. 1975-77), Okla. Soc. Planning Cons. (sec.-treas. 1976-79), Urban Land Inst. Republican. Presbyterian. Club: Le Club. Home and Office: 12 Elder Ave Millbrae CA 94030

O'SHEA, BRIAN, consulting psychiatrist; b. Clonmel, County Tipperary, Ireland, May 16, 1949. MB BCh BAO, U. Coll. Dublin, 1974. Intern James Connolly Hosp., Dublin, 1975; sr. house officer Royal Victoria Eye and Ear Hosp., Dublin, 1976, St. Columcille's Hosp., Dublin, 1976-77; sr. house officer, registrar Jervis St. Hosp., Dublin, 1977-79; registrar Mater Hosp., Dublin, 1979-80; registrar Ea. Health Bd., Dublin, 1980-83, cons., 1983-85, chmn., 1988—; cons. County Wicklow, Ireland, 1985—; clin. lectr. U. Coll. Dublin, 1981—; tutor Royal Coll. Surgeons, 1981-86; advisor Huntington's Disease Assn., 1985—; chmn. Cons. Psychiatrists Med. Bd., 1988—. Author: Essays in Psychiatry, Vol. 1, 1985, (with J. Falvey) A Textbook of Psychological Medicine for the Irish Student, 1985, 2d edit., 1988, Essays in Psychiatry, Vol. 2, 1988; contbr. numerous articles to med. jours. Fellow Royal Acad. Medicine Ireland (mem. council, pres. psychiat. sect. 1988—); mem. Royal Coll. Psychiatrists (tutor 1985—). Roman Catholic. Home: 5 Crofton Ct Crofton Ave, Dunlaoghaire County, Dublin Ireland Office: Newcastle Hosp, Ea Health Bd, Greystones County, Wicklow Ireland

O'SHEA, JOHN, lawyer, accountant; b. N.Y.C., May 3, 1928; s. William and Margaret (Heffron) O'S.; BS, NYU, 1952; LLM, 1966; JD, St. John's U., 1955; m. Mary Ward, May 25, 1963. Admitted to N.Y. State bar, 1955, U.S. Supreme Ct. bar, 1964; mem. audit staff Haskins & Sells, 1955-58, Lopez, Edwards Co., 1958, S.D. Leidesdorf & Co., 1958; tax specialist J.K. Lasser & Co., 1958-65; tax. supr. Ernst & Ernst, 1965-68, Hurdman & Cranstoun, 1968-72; tax mgr. Louis Sternbach & Co., 1972-74, Sperduto, Priskie Co., 1974, George F. Sheehan & Co., 1947-77, Price, Waterhouse & Co., 1977-80, Kaufman, Nachbar & Co., 1980-83, Faculty Bank, Found. Acctg. Edn.; sole practice tax atty., acct. John O'Shea & Co., 1984—; lectr. in field. Candidate for Democratic nomination U.S. Ho. of Reps. from 3d N.Y. dist., 1982. Served with USMC, 1946-48. CPA, N.Y. State. Mem. New York County Lawyers Assn., Am. Inst. CPAs, N.Y. State Soc. CPAs, Am. Assn. Atty.-CPAs. Roman Catholic. Club: Strathmore-Vanderbilt Country. Contbr. articles to profl. jours. Home: 305 Mill Spring Rd Manhasset NY 11030

OSHIMA, NAGISA, film director; b. Kyoto, Japan, 1932; student Kyoto U.; m. Akiko Koyama. With Shochiku Co., 1954-59; owner film co., 1959—; dir. films including: Ai To Kibo No Machi (A Town of Love and Hope), 1959, Taiyo No Hakaba (The Sun's Burial), 1960, Nihon No Yoru To Kiri (night and Fog in Japan), 1960, Shiiku (The Catch), 1961, Amakusa Shiro Tokisada (The Rebel), 1962, Yunbogi No Nikki (Yunbogi's Diary), 1965, Ninja Bugeicho (Bandof Ninja), 1967, Muri Shinju Nihon No Natsu (Japanese Summer: Double Suicide), 1967, Koshikei (Death By Hanging), 1968, Shinjuku Dorobo Nikke (Diary of a Shinjuku Thief), 1968, Shonen (Boy), 1970, Tokyo Senso Sengo Hiwa, 1970, Gishiki (The Ceremony), 1971, Natsu No Imooto (Dear Summer Sister), 1972, Ai no corrida (In The Realm of Senses, 1976, Ai no Borei (Empire of Passion), 1978, Merry Christmas Mr. Lawrence, 1982, Max mon Amorr, 1986; dir. documentaries: Daitoa senso (The Pacific War), 1968, Mo taku-to to bunkadai-kakumei (Mao Tse-tung & the Cultural Revolution), 1969; dir. TV series: Asia no akebono (The Dawn of Asia), 1964-65. Address: Oshima Prodns, 2-15-7 Akasaka, Minato-ku, Tokyo Japan

OSIAS, RICHARD ALLEN, international financier and investor, real estate investment executive; b. N.Y.C., Nov. 13, 1938; s. Harry L. and Leah (Schenk) O.; m. Judy D. Bradford, Oct. 26, 1985; children: A. Kimberly, Alexandra Elizabeth. Student, Columbia U., 1951-63. Founder, chmn., chief exec. officer Osias Orgn., Inc., N.Y.C., also Ft. Lauderdale, Fla., St. Clair, Mich., San Juan, P.R., 1953—. Prin. works include city devel., residential and apt. units, complete residential housing communities, shopping centers, country clubs, golf courses, hotel chains, comprehensive housing communities. Mem. North Lauderdale City Council, 1967—, vice mayor, 1968—, police commr., 1967—; mem. Gold Circle, Atlanta Ballet; benefactor Atlanta Symphony Soc.; patron High Mus. Art, Alliance Theatre Co.; active Boys Clubs Broward County, Tower council Pine Crest Prep. Sch., Ft. Lauderdale. Served with USAF, 1953. Recipient Am. House award Am. Home mag., 1962, Westinghouse award, 1968; named Builder of Yr. Sunshine State Info. Bur. and Sunshine State Sr. Citizen, 1967-69; profiles on network TV, and in internat. and nat. media. Mem. Ft. Lauderdale Better Bus. Bur., Offshore Power Boat Racing Assn., Fraternal Order Police Assn. (pres.), Fla. C. of C., Margate C. of C., Ft. Lauderdale C. of C., Soc. Founders of U. Miami, Tower Council and Columns Soc. Pinecrest. Clubs: Bankers Top of First (San Juan); Quarter Deck (Galveston, Tex.); Boca Raton Yacht and Country (Fla.); Maunalua Bay (Honolulu); Tryall Golf and Country; Bankers (Miami, Fla.); Top of the Home (Puerto Rico); Service Plus (France); Offshore Power Boat Racing Assoc. (U.S.A.); Smithsonian Instn. (D.C.). Office: 5353 Hillsboro Rd Nashville TN 37215 also: Kimberly Plantations Sparta GA 31087

OSKEY, D. BETH, banker; b. Red Wing, Minn., Dec. 23, 1921; d. Alvin E. and Effie D. (Thompson) Feldman; student U. Wis., River Falls, 1939-41; B.A., Met. State U., Minn., 1975; grad. degree in banking, U. Wis., 1973, postgrad. in banking, 1977; student in interior decorating LaSalle Extension U., Chgo., 1970; m. Warren B. Oskey, Sept. 27, 1941; children—Jo Cheryl, Warren A., Peter (dec.), Jeffrey L. Officer, Hiawatha Nat. Bank, Hager City, Wis., 1959—, cashier, 1978-79, pres., 1979, chmn. bd., 1984—, exec. v.p., dir., sec. bd. dirs., 1959—, sec., mem. discount com.; with First Nat. Bank of Glenwood, Glenwood City, Wis., 1965— pres., exec. v.p., 1979—, dir., sec. bd., 1965—, chmn. bd., 1984—, sec., mem. discount com.; speaker on women in banking. Banking com. Vo-Tech Sch., Red Wing, Minn.; former officer civic orgns. Mem. Ind. Bankers Am., Wis. Bankers Assn., Am. Bankers Assn., Gen. Fedn. Women's Clubs Internat., Inc. (bd. dirs.). Republican. Lutheran. Club: Minn. Fedn. Women's Clubs (v.p. 1983—, pres. dist. III 1978—, pres. elect 1986-88, pres. 1988—). Home: 1022 Hallstrom Dr Red Wing MN 55066 also: 1561 Leisure World Mesa AZ 85206 Office: Hiawatha Nat Bank Hager City WI 54014

OSKIN, DAVID WILLIAM, paper company human resources executive; b. Clairton, Pa., Aug. 30, 1942; s. David L. and M. Catherine (Nicodemus) O.; m. JoEllen Rosss, Sept. 5, 1964; 1 child, David W., Jr. B.A., Pa. Mil. Coll., 1964. Dir. employee relations Davol, Inc., Cranston, R.I., 1975-76, dir. U.K. ops., 1976-77, v.p. ops., 1977-79; dir. compensation and benefits Internat. Paper Co., N.Y.C., 1979-81, v.p. human resources, 1981-88, sr. v.p., 1988— . Mem. Fgn. Policy Com., N.Y.C., 1984-85; mem. adv. bd. U. Ill.-Chgo., 1984—; mem. Bus. Roundtable-Employee Relations Com., Washington, 1984—. Served to capt. U.S. Army, 1964-65, Vietnam. Republican. Methodist. Avocations: sailing; tennis. Home: 12 Father Peters Ln New Canaan CT 06840

OSLER, GORDON PETER, utility company executive; b. Winnipeg, Man., Can., June 19, 1922; s. Hugh Farquarson and Kathleen (Harty) O.; m. Nancy A. Riley, Aug. 20, 1948; children: Sanford L., Susan Osler Matthews, Gillian (Mrs. Michel Fortier). Student, Queen's U., Kingston, Ont., Can., 1940-41. Pres. Osler, Hammond & Nanton Ltd., Winnipeg, 1952-64; pres. UNAS Investments Ltd., Toronto, Ont., Can., 1964-72; chmn. Slater Steel Industries, Toronto, Ont., Can., 1972-86, N.Am. Life Assurance Co., Hamilton, Ont., 1986—, TransCan. Pipelines, Toronto, 1983—; dir. Toronto-Dominion Bank, Toronto, Household Internat., Prospect Heights, Ill., Maclean Hunter Ltd., Toronto, IPSCO Inc., Regina, Sask., MICC Investments Ltd., Toronto, Co-Steel Inc., Toronto. Bd. dirs. Can. Hearing Soc., 1983—. Served to lt. Can. Army, 1942-45; ETO. Clubs: Toronto, York (Toronto); Everglades (Palm Beach, Fla.). Home: 112 Dunvegan Rd, Toronto, ON Canada M4V 2R1 Office: TransCan Pipelines, 36th Floor Commerce Ct W, PO Box 54, Toronto, ON Canada M5L 1C2

OSMAN, ABDILLAHI SAID, ambassador; b. Berbera, Somali Democratic Republic, July 7, 1939. LLB, Hull U., England, 1962; postgrad., Longon, 1966-67. Bar: Somali, 1965. Sec., legal counsellor Office of Prime Minister, Somali, 1964-65; dir. legal dept. Ministry Justice and Religious Affairs, Somali, 1965-68; dir. gen. Ministry Justice, Religious Affairs and Labour, Somali, 1968-71; sr. legal adviser to Pres. of Republic Somali, 1971-76; ambassador plenipotentiary, permanent rep. Somalia UNOffice, Spl. Agys., Geneva, 1976-84; permanent rep. of Somalia UN Indsl. Devel. Orgn., Vienna, Austria, 1981-84; ambassador extraordinary UN, N.Y.C., 1984—. Office: Somali Mission UN 50 E 30 St New York NY 10021-0236

OSNOS, DAVID MARVIN, lawyer; b. Detroit, Jan. 10, 1932; s. Max and Florence (Pollock) O.; m. Glenna DeWitt, Aug. 10, 1956; children—Matthew, Alison. A.B. summa cum laude, Harvard U., 1953, J.D. cum laude, 1956. Bar: D.C. 1956. Assoc. Arent, Fox, Kintner, Plotkin & Kahn, Washington, 1956-61, ptnr., 1962—, chmn. exec. com., 1978—; dir. EastPark Realty Trust, Jackson, Miss., VSE Corp., Alexandria, Va., Washington Real Estate Investment Trust, Bethesda, Md., Capital Centre, Landover, Md., Washington Bullets Basketball Club, Landover, Washington Capitals Hockey Club, Landover. Trustee Mt. St. Mary's Coll., Emmitsburg, Md., 1981—; bd. dirs. Greater Washington Jewish Community Found., Rockville, Md., Jewish Community Ctr. Greater Washington, 1964-75. Office: Arent Fox Kintner Plotkin & Kahn 1050 Connecticut Ave NW Washington DC 20036

OSOL, ARTHUR, chemist, former college president; b. Riga, Latvia, Dec. 1, 1905; came to U.S., 1906, naturalized, 1915; s. Peter and Caroline (Irbit) O.; m. Amelia Virginia Lebo, Dec. 28, 1928 (dec. Aug. 1981). Ph.G., Phila. Coll. Pharmacy and Sci., 1925, B.S. in Chemistry, 1928; M.S. in Chemistry, U. Pa., 1931, Ph.D., 1933; LL.D., Eastern Bapt. Coll., 1964; Sc.D., Thomas Jefferson U., 1971. With Phila. Coll. Pharmacy and Sci., 1928—, instr., 1930-33, asst. prof., 1933-34, assoc. prof., 1934-37, prof., 1937-75, prof. emeritus, 1975—, dir. chem. labs., 1937-43, dir. chem. dept., 1943-63, dean sci., 1959-63, pres., 1963-75, pres. emeritus, 1975—; prescription editor Am. Druggist Mag., N.Y.C., 1933-45; editorial cons. Blakiston-McGraw-Hill, N.Y.C., 1944-73; dir. Univ. City Sci. Center Corp.; pres. West Phila. Corp.; chmn. com. phys. chemistry Nat. Conf. Pharm. Research, 1934-41; collaborating research worker League of Nations Health Com. (investigating methods of analysis of opium and coca), 1933-37; mem. sci. adv. com. Smaller War Plants Corp., World War II; mem. U.S. Pharmacopeia rev. com., 1950-70; chief chem. br. Phila. Tech. Def. Div. Assoc. editor: United States Dispensatory 22d edit., 1937, supplement, 1940; co-editor (with Horatio C. Wood, Jr. 23d edit.), 1943, supplement, 1944, editor-in-chief 24th to 27th edits., 1947-73; chmn. editorial bd.: Remington's Pharm. Scis., 14th edit., 1970, 15th edit., 1975, 16th edit., 1980; co-editor: Blakiston's New Gould Med. Dictionary, 1949, 2d edit., 1956, 3d edit., 1972, Blakiston's Illustrated Pocket Med. Dictionary, 1952, 2d edit., 1960, 3d edit., 1973, A Sesquicentennial of Service (of Phila. Coll. Pharmacy and Sci.), 1971; contbr. to sci. jours. Trustee, Chapel of Four Chaplains. Recipient Procter gold medal for disting. service in pub. welfare Phila. Drug Exchange, 1975, Griffith Alumni Sci. award Phila. Coll. Pharmacy and Sci., 1987. Fellow Am. Inst. Chemists, AAAS; mem. Am. Chem. Soc. (chmn. Phila. sect. 1943-44, councilor, dir.), Am. Electrochem. Soc. (chmn. Phila. sect. 1949-51), Am. Pharm. Assn. (pres. Phila. sect. 1939-40), Franklin Inst., Am. Acad. Polit. and Social Sci., N.Y. Acad. Scis., Phila. Sci. Council (dir.), Sigma Xi, Phi Delta Chi, Rho Chi. Republican. Presbyterian. Clubs: Rotary (dir. Phila.), Metachemical. Home: 128 Colwyn Ln Bala-Cynwyd PA 19004 Office: Phila Coll Pharmacy and Sci 43d St and Kingsessing Mall Philadelphia PA 19104

OSOSAMI, OLAYIDE THEOPHILUS, pharmacist; b. Owu, Epe, Lagos, Nigeria, Feb. 5, 1932; s. Caleb Ogunpehin and Alice Bodin (Aiyere) O.; m. Adeola Olujimi Israel, Sept. 29, 1959; children: Oluwole, Olabode, Bolaji, Folarin, Oladipo. Diploma, Sch. Pharmacy, Lagos, 1955. Registered pharmacist, Nigeria. Sr. pharmacist Fed. Ministry Health, Lagos, 1955-60; supt. pharmacist Major & Co. Nigeria Ltd., Lagos, 1960-61; mng. dir. Drug Houses Nigeria Ltd., Lagos, 1961—; bd. dirs. Galenika Nigeria Ltd. Fellow Pharm. Soc. Nigeria (chmn. 1973-76, pres. 1979-82). Home: 80 Adeniran Ogunsanya St, Suru-Lere, Lagos Nigeria Office: Drug Houses Nigeria Ltd, PO Box 482, Yaba Nigeria

OSTAPUK, DAVID R., lawyer; b. Tucson, July 12, 1948; s. John M. and Beverly A. (Armstrong) O.; m. Sandra H. Ewing, Jan. 31, 1981; children: Monica, Benjamin. BA, U. Ariz., 1970, JD, 1973. Bar: Ariz. 1973, U.S. Dist. Ct. Ariz. 1973, U.S. Supreme Ct. 1978. Dep. county atty. Pima County, Tucson, 1973-76; ptnr. Wolfe & Ostapuk, Chartered, Tucson, 1976—; lectr. State Bar Ariz., 1986; judge pro tempore domestic relations div. Pima County Superior Ct., Tucson, 1986—. Bd. dirs. So. Ariz. Legal Aid Soc., 1977-78; legal advisor Kino Learning Ctr., Tucson, 1982; bd. dirs. Las Primeras Lomas, 1982-83. Fellow Ariz. Bar Found., Am. Acad. Matrimonial Lawyers; mem. ABA, Ariz. State Bar (lectr., treas. family law sect. 1980-81). Democrat. Roman Catholic. Club: Old Pueblo (Tucson). Home: 5545 N Entrada Quince Tucson AZ 85718 Office: Wolfe & Ostapuk Chartered 160 N Stone Ave 3d Floor Tucson AZ 85701

OSTAR, ALLAN WILLIAM, association executive; b. East Orange, N.J., Sept. 4, 1924; s. William and Rose (Mirmow) O.; m. Roberta Hutchison, Sept. 10, 1949; children: Karen, Rebecca, John. Cert. engring., U. Denver, 1943; B.A., Pa. State U., 1948; postgrad., U. Wis., 1949-55; LL.D., U. No. Colo., 1968, Eastern Ky. U., 1972, Whittier Coll., 1973; L.H.D., U. Maine, 1975; D.Letters, Central Mich. U., 1975; D.P.S., Bowling Green State U., 1975, R.I. Coll., 1983; D.Higher Edn., Morehead State U., 1977; L.H.D., Appalachian State U., 1977, No. Mich. U., 1978, Dickinson State Coll., N.D., 1979, Towson State U., 1980, Salem State Coll., 1980, Mont. Coll. Mineral Sci. and Tech., 1983, Ball State U., 1984; LL.D., U. Alaska, 1978, Ill. State U., 1983, Western Mich. U., 1984; D. Polit. Sci., Kyung Hee U., Korea, 1984; L.H.D., Fitchburg State Coll., 1986, Bridgwater State Coll., 1988, No. State Coll., 1988, Harris-Stowe State Coll., 1988; LCD, Edinboro U. Pa., 1987. Dir. nat. pub. relations U.S. Nat. Student Assn., 1948-49; exec. asst. Commonwealth Fund, N.Y.C., 1952-53; asst. to dean extension div. U. Wis., 1949-52, dir. office communications services, 1954-58; dir. Joint Office Instnl. Research, Nat. Assn. State Univs. and Land Grant Colls., Washington, 1958-65; pres. Am. Assn. State Colls. and Univs., Washington, 1965—; mem. Nat. Commn. to Assess Vets. Edn. Policy; bd. adv. commrs. Edn. Commn. of States, 1985—; mem. nat. adv. bd. Inst. for Mgmt. of Lifelong Edn., Harvard U.; mem. secretariat Am. Council on Edn., 1965—; mem. Labor-Higher Edn. Council; mem. adv. council U. Md. Inst. for Research in Higher and Adult Edn.; exec. commr. High Commn. for Peace. Co-author: Colleges and Universities for Change, 1987; gcontbr. chpts. in books. Chmn. bd. dirs. Consortium for Internat. Cooperation in Higher Edn., 1986; bd. dirs. Com. for Improvement of Higher Edn. in the Ams., 1980; pres. Am. Energy Week II, 1982-86. Served with AUS, 1943-46. Decorated Bronze Star; Recipient Centennial award for disguished service to edn. U. Akron, 1970; Fogelsanger award Shippensburg (Pa.) State Coll., 1974; World Peace Through Edn. medal Internat. Assn. U. Pres., 1975; Disting. Achievement award U. So. Colo., 1979, Chancellor's award U. Wis., 1985; Alumni fellow Pa. State U., 1975; Chancellor's medal CUNY, 1986. Mem. Internat. Assn. Univ. Pres., Md. PTA (life), Sigma Delta Chi. Unitarian-Universalist. Home: 2014 O St NW Washington DC 20036 Office: 1 Dupont Circle Washington DC 20036

OSTBERG, HENRY DEAN, company executive; b. Bocholt, Germany, July 21, 1928; s. Fred and Lotte (Hertz) O.; m. Sydelle Burns, Dec. 13, 1987; stepchildren: Elysa Bari, Brent Adam, Ross Jay; came to U.S., 1939, naturalized, 1945; LL.B., N.Y. Law Sch., 1950; M.B.A., Ohio State U., 1953, Ph.D., 1957; divorced; 1 son, Neal. Pres., H.D. Ostberg Assos., N.Y.C., 1950—; chmn. bd. Admar Research Co., Inc., N.Y.C., 1960; dir. Self-Instructional Devel. Corp., Amherst Group, Porter Industries, Inc.; pres. Eastman Enterprises, Inc.; assoc. prof. mktg. N.Y. U., 1954-63. Trustee Ostberg Found. Served to capt. USAF, 1950-53. Mem. Inst. Mgmt. Scis., Am. Mktg. Assn.. Am. Assn. for Pub. Opinion Research. Jewish. Contbr. articles to profl. jours. Home: 278 Fountain Rd Englewood NJ 07631 Office: Admar Research Inc 304 Park Ave S New York NY 10010

OSTENDORF, FREDERICK OTTO, real estate executive, former county official; b. Milw., May 24, 1913; s. Frederick and Emily (Smith) O.; A.A., Glendale Coll., 1933; B.A., UCLA, 1937; M.A. in Sociology, U. So. Calif., 1949, cert. in real estate, 1954; m. Beryl Louverne Bell, May 29, 1941; children—Frederick Otto, Margaret Ann. With Los Angeles County Probation Dept., 1939-73, cons. juvenile delinquency, 1948-51, adult investigator, 1951-61, hearing officer juvenile traffic Superior Ct., 1961-63, adult supervision officer, 1964-73; owner Ostendorf Properties, LaCanada, Calif., 1959—. Cub scout commr. Boy Scouts Am., La Canada, 1952-54. Served to lt. USNR, 1942-46; lt. comdr. Res. ret. Named Outstanding Older Am., La Canada City Council-Los Angeles County Bd. Suprs., 1980. Mem. Crescenta-Canada Art Assn. (past pres.), Naval Res. Assn. (charter mem.; past pres. Rose Bowl chpt.), Alpha Kappa Delta. Clubs: Toastmasters (pres. 1967, 75, 87, Disting. Toastmaster award 1980), Descanso Garden Guild (docent La Canada 1973-79, lectr. 1975, tour dir. 1978-79), Leisure (pres. 1980-81). Author: The Art of Retirement, 1980. Home: 1084 Inverness Dr Flintridge CA 91011

OSTER, MARTIN WILLIAM, oncologist; b. N.Y.C., Apr. 9, 1947; s. Joseph A. and Bella O.; B.A. summa cum laude, Columbia U., 1967, M.D., 1971; m. Karen A. Strauss, May 18, 1975; children—Bonnie Felice, Michelle Rae, Nancy Meredith. Intern, resident in medicine Mass. Gen. Hosp., Boston, 1971-73; clin. assoc. div. of cancer treatment Nat. Cancer Inst., Bethesda, Md., 1973-76; asst. prof. medicine Columbia Coll. Physicians and Surgeons, 1976-86, assoc. prof. clin. medicine, 1986—, asst. prof. medicine Cancer Research Center, Columbia U., 1976-86, assoc. prof. medicine, 1986—; asst. attending physician Columbia-Presbyn. Med. Center, N.Y.C., 1976-86, assoc. attending physician, 1986—. Served with USPHS, 1973-76. Recipient Physician Recognition awards AMA, 1976-78, 79-81, 82-84; Am. Cancer Soc. jr. faculty clin. fellow, 1976-79; diplomate Am. Bd. Internal Medicine and subsplty. med. oncology. Fellow ACP; mem. Am. Assn. Cancer Research, N.Y. Cancer Soc., Am. Soc. Clin. Oncology, N.Y. Met. Breast Cancer Group, Phi Beta Kappa, Alpha Omega Alpha. Home: 5 Birch Grove Dr Armonk NY 10504 Office: 161 Fort Washington Ave New York NY 10032

OSTERGARD, PAUL MICHAEL, foundation executive; b. Akron, Ohio, Apr. 1, 1939; s. Paul and Janette Beryl (Laube) O.; m. Elizabeth K. McCombs, Jan. 1965 (div. Nov. 1971). A.B. magna cum laude, Case-Western Res. U., 1961; J.D., U. Mich., 1964; M.P.A., Harvard U., 1969; student, U. Madrid, Spain, 1959-60. Bar: Ohio 1964. Atty. U.S. Steel Corp., 1967-69; gen. atty. Trans World Airlines, Inc., 1969-71; sec., counsel Pa. Co., 1971-74; v.p. adminstrn., sec., counsel Buckeye Pipe Line Co., 1972-74; dir. Pullman Co.; v.p., dir. Clearfield Bituminous Coal Corp., Penn Towers, Inc., 1971-74; pub. affairs exec. Gen. Electric Co., Fairfield, Conn., 1974-77, 78-84; pres. Gen. Electric Found., 1984—; dir. Diebold Group, 1977. Served to capt. USAF, 1965-68, Vietnam. Decorated Bronze Star; Legion of Merit Vietnam).; Univ. scholar, 1957-61; Littauer fellow, 1968-69. Mem. ABA, N.Y. State, Ohio bar assns., Phi Beta Kappa, Omicron Delta Kappa. Episcopalian. Clubs: Harvard, Atrium (N.Y.C.). Home: 106 S Compo Rd Westport CT 06880 Office: Gen Electric Found 3135 Easton Turnpike E2C Fairfield CT 06431

OSTERLAND, MARTIN, sociology educator; b. Köthen, Germany, Feb. 22, 1937. Abitur, Propädeuticum, Wilhelmshaven, Fed. Republic Germany, 1961; PhD in Sociology, U. Göttingen, Fed. Republic Germany, 1969. Asst. prof. U. Göttingen, 1969-71; dir. Sociol. Research Inst., Göttingen, 1971-78; prof. sociology U. Bremen, Fed. Republic Germany, 1978—; chmn. Research Inst. Work and Industry, Bremen, 1982-87. Author: Film Und Gesellschaftsbilder, 1971, Lebens-und Arbeitssituat, 1973, Drehbank zum Computer, 1974, others; contbr. articles to profl. jours. Various grants. Office: U Bremen, Universitätsallee, Bremen 28 Federal Republic of Germany

OSTERMAN, PETER ERIK, company executive; b. Sydney, New South Wales, Australia, Dec. 18, 1956; s. John Frederick and Madeleine Georgina (Hamelin) O. B in Commerce, Concordia U., Montreal, Can., 1978; Diploma in Pub. Acctg., Mcgill U., Montreal, 1980. Chartered acct. Auditor Coopers & Lybrand, Montreal, 1978-81, Geneva, 1981-83; fin. controller, treas. Ares-Serono Pharms. Co., Geneva, 1983-86; asst. to chmn. Cartier Monde, Geneva, 1986-88; fin. controller, treas. Piaget, Baume and Mercier, Geneva, 1988—; fin. cons. Stinger Sports Co., Montreal, 1980-82, Feelfree Rafting Holidays, Impst, Austria, 1984-85. Mem. Internat. Assn. Students in Sci., Econs. and Bus. Club: Concordia Outdoors/Ski (Montreal) (pres. 1976-78). Home: 28 rue du Grand Bureau, 1227 Geneva Switzerland

OSTFELD, ALEXANDER MARION, advertising agency executive; b. St. Louis, Feb. 13, 1932; s. Simon and Margaret (Fishmann) O.; B.S., Washington U., St. Louis, 1953; postgrad. St. Louis U., 1953-56. Mktg. mgr. lighting div. Emerson Electric Co., St. Louis, 1955-59; dir. research and media Frank Block Assos., St. Louis, 1959-61; research and media supr. Compton Advt., Chgo., 1961-65; media and mktg. supr. Leo Burnett Advt., Chgo., 1965-68; dir. mktg. and account planning, v.p. McCann-Erickson, Chgo., 1968-72, Kenyon & Eckhardt, Chgo., 1972; dir. Canadian and internat. ops. A. Eicoff & Co., Chgo.; owner Alex Ostfeld Co. Advt. and Mktg., Woodbridge, Conn. Cons. Am. Assn. Advt. Agys., Yale/New Haven Sci. Park. Mem. Am. Mktg. Assn. (sec. St. Louis 1956-57), Internat. Platform Assn., Broadcast Advt. Club, Am. Research Found. Clubs: Chgo. Exec., Woodbridge Hunt (Conn.). Home: 4 Ledge Rd Woodbridge CT 06525 Office: 6 Ledge Rd Woodbridge CT 06525

ÖSTLUND, HANS ERIK, higher education executive; b. Härnösand, Sweden, Dec. 11, 1925; s. Hans and Esther (Kallin) O.; m. Gerd Hallén, June 27, 1953; 1 child, Häkan. MA, U. Uppsala (Sweden), 1953, PhD, 1959. Tchr. Upper Secondary Sch., Uppsala, 1954-60; lectr. Sch. of Edn., Malmö, Sweden, 1960-62; counselor Ministry of Edn., Stockholm, 1962-64, 70-74, dep. undersec., 1974-83; chief exec. Regional Bd. Higher Edn., Umeå, Sweden, 1983—; head dept. Nat. Bd. Edn., Stockholm, 1964-70; chmn. Com. for Internat. Tech. Assistance, Stockholm, 1975-79, Archive for Sound and Moving Pictures, Stockholm, 1984—. Author numerous books and articles in field of edn. Chmn. Social Dem. Student Orgn., Malmö, 1960-62; sec. Social Dem. Party, Sollentuna, 1973-76; mem. Local Bd. Planning, Sollentuna, 1972-79; vice chmn. Local Bd. of Schs., Sollentuna, 1979-80. Home: Disavagen 10, 19162 Sollentuna Sweden

OSTRACH, MICHAEL SHERWOOD, lawyer, business executive; b. Providence, Nov. 7, 1951; s. Morris Louis and Marion Molly Ostrach. AB magna cum laude, Brown U., 1973; JD, Stanford U., 1976. Bar: N.Y. 1977, Calif. 1977, U.S. Dist. Ct. (so. and ea. dists.) N.Y. 1977. Assoc. Debevoise & Plimpton, N.Y.C., 1976-78, Pillsbury, Madison & Sutro, San Francisco, 1978-81; v.p., gen. counsel Cetus Corp., Emeryville, Calif., 1981-86, sr. v.p. legal affairs and gen. counsel, 1986—. Bd. editors Stanford Law Rev., 1976. Mem. ABA, Phi Beta Kappa. Office: Cetus Corp 1400 53d St Emeryville CA 94608

OSTRANDER, ROBERT EDWIN, UN interregional advisor; b. Pitts., June 30, 1931; s. Robert Jesse and Elizabeth Raymond (Comstock) O.; m. Margaret Valentina Servello, Dec. 21, 1958; children—Robert Glen, Roseanne. B.A., Cornell U., 1952. Cert. petroleum geologist; registered geol. scientist. Area reservoir engr. Mene Grande Oil Co., San Tome, Venezuela, 1956-61;

dist. engr. Oasis Oil Co. of Libya, Tripoli, 1962-67; chief engr. Occidental Oil of Libya, Tripoli, 1967-71; div. head Iranian Oil Consortium, Ahwaz, Iran, 1972-75; mgr. ops. Ultramar Co. Ltd., Mt. Kisco, N.Y., 1975-81; v.p. engring. Weeks Petroleum Ltd., Westport, Conn., 1982-85; mng. dir. Reomag Inc., South Salem, N.Y., 1980—; tech. expert World Bank, Washington, 1981—; cons. UN Secretariat, 1985—; advisor to govts. of China, India, others in Asia, Africa, Middle East; guest lectr. Asian univs., internat. seminars. Contbr. articles to profl. jours. Sec. Rep. Com. Town of Lewisboro ; mem. Rep. Com. Westchester County; pres., dir. Oakridge Condominium Assn., Vista, N.Y. Served to 1st lt. U.S. Army, 1953-55. Mem. Am. Assn. Petroleum Geologists, Assn. Profl. Geol. Scientists, Soc. Petroleum Engrs., Petroleum Exploration Soc. N.Y. Home: 159 Stone Meadow South Salem NY 10590 Office: UN Dept Tech Cooperation for Devel Natural Resources & Energy Room DC1-894 44th St & 1st Ave New York NY 10017

OSTREM, GUNNAR MULDRUP, glaciologist; b. Oslo, Mar. 25, 1922; s. Sigurd and Alfhild (Paulsen) O.; m. Britta Louise Nystrom, June 30, 1952; children—Hans Peter, Anne Christine, Eva Louise, Karin Johanne. B.A., U. Oslo, 1948, M.A., 1954; Fil. lic., U. Stockholm, 1961, Fil. Dr., 1965. Lectr. various high schs. and colls., Koping and Tranas, Sweden, 1950-58; asst. prof. U. Stockholm, 1958-62, assoc. prof., 1966-81, prof., chmn. dept. phys. geography, 1981-83; chief glaciology div. Fed. Dept. Mines and Tech., Services, Ottawa, Ont., 1965-66; chief glaciologist Norwegian Water Resources and Electric Bd., Oslo, 1983—. Editor Geografiska Annaler Jour., 1976—. Contbr. articles to profl. jours. Recipient Hans Egede medal, 1982; fellow Norwegian Geophy. Soc.; mem. Internat. Glaciological Soc., Swedish Geog. Soc., European Assn. Remote Sensing Labs. (treas. 1976-85), Can. Remote Sensing Soc. Home: Otto Ruges Vei 25A, N-1345 Osteras Norway Office: Norwegian Water Resources and Energy Adminstrn, PO Box 5091-Mj, Oslo 3 Norway

OSTROWER, FAYGA PERLA, artist, educator; b. Lodz, Poland, Sept. 14, 1920; d. Froim K. and Frimet K. (Tepper) Krakowski; m. Heinz Ostrower, May 10, 1941; children—Carl Robert, Anna Leonor. Grad. Fundacao Getulio Vargas, Rio de Janeiro, 1946. Exhibiting artist, 1949—; tchr. Mus. Modern Art, Rio de Janeiro, 1954-71; lectr. Fed. U. Minas Gerais, Belo Horizonte, 1966, 71, Fed. U. Bahia, 1971, Fed. U. Rio Grande do Sul, Porto Alegre, 1971, Fed. U. Parana, Curityba, 1972; John Hay Whitney lectr. Spellman Coll., Atlanta, 1964; bd. dirs. Internat. Council Internat. Ctr. for Integrative Studies, N.Y.C., 1979; counsellor Inst. Goethe, Rio de Janeiro, 1980, Mus. Modern Art, 1981; counsellor State Council of Culture, Rio de Janeiro, 1987; pres. Soc. Brasil de Educacao atraves da Arte, Rio de Janeiro, 1986; postgrad. tchr. art edn. and print-making U. Rio de Janeiro, 1982—; v.p. Brazilian sector Internat. Assn. Artists, 1963-66; mem. jury Nat. Show Fine Arts, Rio de Janeiro, 1957-58, Biennial Sao Paulo, 1959, Nat. Show Ministry Transp., Rio de Janeiro, 1970; Brazilian del. to Internat. Congress Art, Brasilia, 1958, N.Y.C., 1963, Internat. Congress Art Edn., London, 1965. Author: Creativity and Creative Processes, 1977, 1978, 6th edit., 1987; Universos da Arte, 1983, 4th edit., 1987. Decorated Chevalier Order Rio Branco; named hon. citizen Rio de Janeiro, 1985; recipient grand nat. award IV Biennial Sao Paul, 1957; grand internat. award prints XXIX Biennial Venice, 1958; grand award Buenos Aires, 1960; prize Interam. Biennial, Caracas, Venezuela, 1967; prize II Internat. Exhbn. Graphic Arts, Florence, Italy, 1970, grand award artistic creativity Rio de Janeiro, 1968; Hilton prize, 1981; Cultural Personality of Yr. award Union Brazilian Writers, 1982; Artistic Personality award Sao Paul Critics, 1983; Best Show of Yr. award Brazilian Critics' Assn., Rio de Janeiro, 1984. Fellow Internat. Assn. Plastic Arts, Assn. Brazilian Assn. Plastic Arts Profls. (v.p. 1963-66), Brazilian Writers Assn.; hon. mem. Accademia Delle Arte del Disegno, Florence.

OSUMI, MASATO, utility company executive; b. Osaka, Japan, Aug. 20, 1942; s. Masahiro and Sachiko Osumi; m. Masako Nakajima, Apr. 21, 1968; children: Masanori, Koji, Yuko. BS, Yokohama Nat. U., 1966; MS, NYU, 1971; D in Engring., Kyoto U., 1978. Chief researcher research ctr. Sanyo Elec. Co., Hirakata, Osaka, 1981-85, mgr., 1985-87, mgr. control and system research ctr., 1987—. Contbr. articles to profl. jours. Mem. Japanese Soc. Mech. Engrs. (bd. dirs. 1986-87), Japanese Soc. Precision Engrs. Home: 3-33 Takiimotomachi, Moriguchi Osaka 570, Japan Office: Sanyo Elec Co Ltd, 1-18-13 Hashiridani, Hirakata Osaka 573, Japan

OSUNDE, JOHN IRIOWEN, trading company executive; b. Benin City, Nigeria, Sept. 28, 1939; s. Peter Oduwa and Ayanon Evbima (Ovbiogbe) O.; LL.B., Blackstone Sch. Law, 1967, D.D. (hon.), Christ Sch. Theology, 1975, m. Victoria King, Dec. 28; children—Patrick, Paul. Edn. officer, Benin City, 1956-57, Nigerian Civil Service, 1958-61; mem. UN Peace Mission to Congo Republic, 1961-62; pres. Manson Overseas Trade Corp., Lagos, 1976—. Rehab. coordinator Nigeria Civil War, 1969-70; founder, 1970, since pres. Gen. Internat. Helpless Children Soc. Recipient Nigerian Ind. medal, 1960, UN God medal, 1962. Mem. Internat. Trade Orgn., Chambers Inst. Mgmt., Internat. Fundamental Human Rights Assn. Democrat. Clubs: African Golf (pres.), Masons (Lagos). Author poems. Home: 62 Lawanson Rd, Surulere, Lagos Nigeria Office: 45 Tejuosho St, PO Box 1485, Surulere, Lagos Nigeria

OSVALD, PER HAKAN, lawyer; b. Stockholm, Aug. 28, 1928; s. Gunnar Sixten and Margit (Stenbeck) O.; m. Maj Astrid Soderman, Oct. 10, 1953; children—Hakan, Ulla, Erik. LLB, Uppsala U., 1952. Law clk. Vadsbo County Ct., Mariestad, Sweden, 1953-55; lawyer Advokatfirman Lagerlof, Stockholm, 1955-78, ptnr., 1963-78; ptnr. Carl Swartling Advokatbyra, Stockholm, 1978—; dir. Wallenius Lines, Stockholm, 1970—, chmn., 1970-80; dir. Marabou, Vargön Alloys; chmn. bd. Swedish subs. Texaco Inc., Nokia, St. Gobain, Osram and Merck & Co. Mem. Swedish Bar Assn. (bd. dirs. 1975-82), The Stock Market Panel. Home: Kommendorsgatan 8H, 114 48 Stockholm Sweden Office: Carl Swartling Advokatbyra, PO Box 1650, 111 86 Stockholm Sweden

OSWAL, VASANT HANSRAJ, otolaryngologist; b. Poona, India, Sept. 13, 1934; came to Eng., 1963, naturalized, 1968; s. Hansraj Ramchandra and Shribai Hansraj (Fulfagar) O.; m. Nirmala Bhandari, May 15, 1962; 1 child, Neena Vasant. MB, BS, B.J. Med. Coll., Poona, 1960; D.O.R.L., Coll. Physicians and Surgeons, Bombay, 1961; MS in Otolaryngology, Grand Med. Coll., Bombay, 1963. Registrar in ear, nose and throat Dundee Royal Infirmary, Dundee, 1964-66; sr. registrar in ear, nose and throat Coventry and Warwickshire Hosp., Coventry, Eng., 1967-70; cons. ear, nose and throat surgeon South Cleveland Dist., Middlesbrough, Cleveland, Eng., 1970—; chmn. vocation tng. No. Region, U. Newcastle, Newcastle Upon Tyne, 1982—; chmn. 1st Brit. CO2 Laser Conf. in Ear, Nose and Throat, 1983. Editor: CO2 Laser in Otolaryngology and Head and Neck Surgery, 1988. Fellow Royal Coll. Surgeons (Edinburgh), Royal Soc. Medicine, Royal Coll. Surgeons (London); mem. North of Eng. Otolaryngol. Soc. (council 1981), Assn. Otolaryngology India (life mem., hon. sec. 1975), Brit. Laser Soc., Eye, Ear, Nose and Throat Cogwheel (sec. 1984—). Avocations: gardening, bonsai, culinary interests, walking. Office: 8 Longbeck Rd, Marske by Sea, Cleveland TS11 6EZ, England

OSWALD, IAN, psychiatrist, researcher; b. London, Aug. 4, 1929; s. John Stevenson Lawson and Lily (Hawkins) O.; m. Joan Thomsett, Aug. 8, 1951 (div. Mar. 1982); children: Andrew John, Sally, Malcolm, James; m. Kirstine Adam, Apr. 15, 1982. BA, Cambridge (Eng.) U., 1950, MB, BChir, 1954, MD, 1958; DSc, Edinburgh (Scotland) U., 1963. Lectr. psychiatry Edinburgh U., 1959-65, sr. lectr., 1968-77, prof., 1977—; prof. U. Western Australia, 1965-67; pres. European Sleep Research Soc., 1980-84. Author: Sleeping and Waking, 1962, Sleep, 1966, Get a Better Night's Sleep, 1983. Served with Royal Air Force, 1955-57. Beit research fellow, 1957-59. Fellow Royal Coll. Psychiatrists. Social Democrat. Home: 41 St Ronan's Terr, Innerleithen EH44 6RB, Scotland Office: Edinburgh U, Morningside Park, Edinburgh EH10 5HF, Scotland

OSWALD, WILLIAM JACK, financial investor; b. Chgo., Feb. 10, 1927; s. Jeho and Maria Jeanette (Van Calcar) O.; student Ill. Inst. Tech., 1943-44, U. Wis., 1944-45; B.S., Barry Coll., 1978, MBA, Barry U., 1986; m. Delores Jean Kipple, Dec. 6, 1958; 1 son, William Randolph. Pres. Star Corps., Chgo., 1953-74, chmn. bd., 1964-74; pres. Interam. Car Rental, Inc., 1976-81, Am. Autolet Corp., 1977-81; chmn. bd. Capital & Devel. Control Corp., Ft. Lauderdale, Fla., 1975—; pres. Star Nat., Inc.; pres. Williams Investment Realty, Inc., 1984—; chmn. Advanced Computeronics, Inc., 1984—; dir. Ostar, Inc., Williams & Co. Inc. Served with USAAF, 1945-46. Cert. employment cons. Am. Inst. Employment Counseling. Home: 6662 Boca del Mar Dr Boca Raton FL 33433 Office: 1515 N Federal Hwy Boca Raton FL 33432

OTA, AKIRA, small business owner; b. Hagi, Yamaguchi, Japan, July 8, 1933; s. Kanemitsu and Kumayo (Suizu) O.; m. Chieko Mogi, May 12, 1961; children: Takashi, Kazumi. Chmn. Fujitsu-kiden Labor Union, Tokyo, 1961-63, cons., 1963-66; pres. Clever Industry Corp., Tokyo, 1986—. Mem. Japan Skin Esthetic Assn. Home: 2-9-1 Masugata, Tama Devision, Kawasaki, Kanagawa 214, Japan Office: Clever Industry Corp, 3-6-17 Osaki, Shinagawa, Tokyo 141, Japan

OTAIBA, MANA SAID AL- (MANI IBN SAID AL- UTAYBA), government official, economist; b. Abu Dhabi, May 15, 1946; married; 5 children. B.Sc. in Econs., Baghdad U., 1969; M.Sc., Cairo U., 1974; Ph.D., 1976. Head Petroleum Dept., Abu Dhabi, 1969; minister of petroleum and industry, 1972-73, minister of petroleum and mineral resources, 1973-79; minister of petroleum and natural resources, 1979—; chmn. bd. Abu Dhabi Nat. Oil Co.; mem. Abu Dhabi Planning Bd.; pres. Dept. Petroleum, Minerals and Industry; pres. OPEC, 1980. Author: Abu Dhabi Planning Board, Economy of Abu Dhabi, Organization of the Petroleum Exporting Countries and the Oil Industry, Interest and Recreations. Address: Ministry of Petroleum and, Mineral Resources, PO Box 59, Abu Dhabi United Arab Emirates *

OTESTEANU, MARIUS-EMIL, electronics engineer, educator; b. Timisoara, Romania, Feb. 18, 1954; s. Emil and Liana-Ivone (Vidrighin) O.; m. Erica Selaru, Apr. 26, 1980; 1 child, Calin-Remus. Diploma Engr. in Electronics, Poly. Inst., Romania, 1978, D.Engr. in Electronics, 1983. Project leader Elec. Measurment Equipment Co., Timisoara, 1978-82, researcher, 1982-83; asst. prof. Poly. Inst., Timisoara, 1982-87, prof., 1987—; researcher Pasteur Inst., Bucharest, Romania, 1983-87. Contbr. articles to profl. jours. Patentee watthour meter automatic testing. Communist. Orthodox. Avocation: photography, windsurfing. Home: bd Salajan 11-13, B-16, 1900 Timisoara Romania Office: Poly Inst, str Parvan 2, 1900 Timisoara Romania

OTHMER, DONALD FREDERICK, chemical engineer, educator; b. Omaha, May 11, 1904; s. Frederick George and Fredericka Darling (Snyder) O.; m. Mildred Jane Topp, Nov. 18, 1950. Student, Ill. Inst. Tech., Chgo., 1921-23; B.S., U. Nebr., 1924, D.Eng. (hon.), 1962; M.S., U. Mich., 1925, Ph.D., 1927; D.Eng. (hon.), Poly. U., Bklyn., 1977, N.J. Inst. Tech., 1978. Registered profl. engr., N.Y., N.J., Ohio, Pa. Devel. engr. Eastman Kodak Co. and Tenn. Eastman Corp., 1927-31; prof. Poly. U., Bklyn., 1933; disting. prof. Poly. U., 1961—, sec. grad. faculty, 1948-58; head dept. chem. engring. 1937-61; hon. prof. U. Conception, Chile, 1951; cons. chem. engr., licensor of process patents to numerous cos., govtl. depts., and countries, 1931—; developer program for chem. industry of Burma, 1951-54; cons. UN, UNIDO, WHO, Dept. Energy, Office Saline Water of U.S. Dept. Interior, Chem. Corps. and Ordnance Dept. U.S. Army, USN, WPB, Dept. State, HEW, Nat. Materials Advisory Bd., NRC Sci. Adv. Bd., U.S. Army Munitions Command; mem. Panel Energy Advisers to Congress, also other U.S. and fgn. govt. depts.; sr. gas officer Bklyn. Citizens Def. Corps.; lectr. Am. Swiss Found. Sci. Relations, 1950, Chem. Inst. Can., 1944-52, Am. Chem. Soc., U.S. Army War Coll., 1964, Shri RAM Inst., India, 1980, Royal Mil. Coll. Can., 1981; plenary lectr. Peoples Republic of China; hon. del. Engring. Congresses, Japan, 1983; plenary lectr., hon. del. Fed. Republic of Germany, Greece, Mex., Czechoslovakia, Yugoslavia, Poland, P.R., France, Can., Argentina, India, Turkey, Spain, Rumania, Kuwait, Iran, Iraq, Algeria, China, United Arab Emirates. Contbr. over 350 articles on chem. engring., chem. mfg., synthetic fuels and thermodynamics to tech. jours.; co-founder/co-editor: Kirk-Othmer Ency. Chem. Tech., 17 vols, 1947-60, 24 vols., 2d edit., 1963-71, 26 vols., 3d edit., 1976-84, Spanish edit., 16 vols., 1960-66; editor: Fluidization, 1956; co-author: Fluidization and Fluid Particle Systems, 1960; mem. adv. bd.: Perry's Chem. Engr.'s Handbook; tech. editor: UN Report, Technology of Water Desalination, 1964. Bd. regents L.I. Coll. Hosp., bd. dirs. numerous ednl. and philanthropic instns., engring. and indsl. corps. Recipient Golden Jubilee award, Ill. Inst. Tech., 1975, Profl. Achievement award, Ill. Inst. Tech., 1978; named to Hall of Fame, Ill. Inst. Tech., 1981. Fellow AAAS, Am. Inst. Cons. Engrs., Am. Inst. Chemists (Honor Scroll 1970, Chem. Pioneer award 1977), ASME (hon. life, chmn. chem. processes div. 1948-49), N.Y. Acad. Scis. (hon. life, chmn. engring. sect. 1972-73), Instn. Chem. Engrs. (London) (hon. life), Am. Inst. Chem. Engrs. (Tyler award 1958, chmn. N.Y. sect. 1944, dir. 1956-59); mem. Am. Chem. Soc. (council 1945-47, E.V. Murphree-Exxon award 1978, hon. life mem.), Soc. Chem. Industry (Perkin medal 1978), Am. Soc. Engring. Edn. (Barber Coleman award 1958), Engrs. Joint Council (dir. 1957-59), Societe de Chimie Industrielle (pres. 1973-74), Chemurgic Council (dir.), Japan Soc. Chem. Engrs., Assn. Cons. Chemists and Chem. Engrs. (award of Merit 1975), Newcomen Soc., Am. Arbitration Assn. (panel mem. or sole arbitrator numerous cases), Sigma Xi (citation disting. research 1983), Tau Beta Pi, Phi Lambda Upsilon, Iota Alpha, Alpha Chi Sigma, Lambda Chi Alpha; hon. life mem. Deutsche Gesellschaft für Cheme. Apparatewesen. Clubs: Norwegian (Bklyn.), Chemists (N.Y.C.) (pres. 1974-75), Rembrandt (Bklyn.). Home: 140 Columbia Heights Brooklyn NY 11201 Office: 333 Jay St Brooklyn NY 11201

OTOKPA, AUGUSTINE EMMANUEL OGABA, JR., research scientist, consultant; b. Agila town, Izote, Nigeria, Sept. 8, 1945; s. Otokpa and Ochanya (Obande) Okpekwu; m. Grace Onefeli, Jan. 3, 1969; children—Evelyn, Christabel, Loretta, Paul, Isaac, Jocelyn (dec.). A.B., Tenn. Christian Coll., 1974; M.B.A., Western Colo. U., 1978; S.J.D., Heed U., Fla., 1984; Ph.D. in Bus. Adminstrn. and Mgmt., Columbia Pacific U., 1982; cert. Am. Inst. Mgmt., 1974; cert. Assn. Cost and Exec. Accts., London, 1980; cert. and diploma Inst. Mktg., London, 1982; cert. fundamental and applied econs. Henry George Sch. of Social Sci., N.Y.C., 1968; cultural doctorate in parapsychology World U., Tucson, 1980. Pres., BRMC, Kano, Nigeria, 1976-81; dir. BIMS, Mangalore, India, 1981-84; personnel dir. DMB Internat., Belgium, from 1973; cons. prof. Faculty Accts. Pakistan, 1981-86; chair doctoral com. Asian Research Ctr., UNIDO, 1983-86; chair council econ. affairs World U., Tucson, 1982; faculty adviser N.Am. Regional Coll., Ariz., 1984. Corr., Interavia Air Letter, Geneva, 1981-86. Author: Scientific Evidence of the Proof of Immortality of the Human Soul, 1982; The Truth about Parapsychology in Ultimate Reality and Meaning, 1982; also articles; assoc. rev. editor Leadership & Orgn. Devel. Jour., 1980-86. Dep. mem. gen. assembly Internat. Parliament Safety and Peace. Fellow Inter-Univ. Seminar on Armed Forces and Soc., Coll. Preceptors (cert.) (London); mem. Internat. Inst. Adminstrv. Scis. (Belgium), Am. Soc. Inernat. Law, Am. Arbitration Assn. (internat. panel), Irish Mgmt. Inst. (cert.; council 1982); AFRICA: Council of Reprographics Execs. and Orgn. Planning Mgmt. Assn. (v.p. 1979-86), Acad. Mgmt., Acad. Internat. Bus., Am. Cons. League (cert.), Young Pres. Orgn., Internat. Council Psychologists, Assn. Behavior Analysis (area resource person 1982-86), Thomas Jefferson Research Ctr. (assoc.), Am. Mgmt. Assn., Nat. Mil. Intelligence Assn., Aviation-Space Writers Assn., Internat. Assn. Religion and Parapsychology (Japan). Emergency World Council in The Hague, Inst. Jud. Adminstrn., Fed. Jud. Ctr., Comml. Law League Am., Inst. of Sci. and Tech. Communicators (Eng.), Internat. Indsl. Relations Assn. (Geneva), Geneva Consultants Registry Ltd. (U.S.), Ctr. for Devel. of Industries, Acad. Cert. Adminstrv. Mgrs., Internat. Peace Research Assn., Internat. Registry of Orgn. Devel. Profls., Nat. Council Tchrs. of English, Speech Communication Assn., Dignity of Man Found. (African rep. 1973-86), Internat. Assn. Chiefs of Police (assoc.). Roman Catholic. Club: London (Topeka). Avocations: writing; travel; photography; correspondence; music. Home: 54B Airport Rd, PO Box 117-2384, Kano Nigeria Office: BRMC, PO Box 117-2384, Kano Nigeria

O'TOOLE, EDWARD THOMAS, JR., microbiologist, educator; b. Frederick, Md., July 7, 1933; s. Edward Thomas and Margaret Russelle (Dorsey) O'T.; B.S., U. Md., 1958; postgrad. Balt. Med. Campus, 1959-66, Loyola Coll., 1960; Sc.M., Johns Hopkins Sch. Hygiene and Public Health, 1971; Ph.D., Union Grad. Sch., 1977; m. Edith Helen Stimson, Apr. 19, 1958; children—Shirley Hope, Edward Thomas III, Eugene Stanley. Tchr., dept. chmn., audio-visual coordinator Baltimore County Bd. Edn., Towson, Md., 1958-60; chief microbiologist St. Joseph Hosp., Balt., 1960-64; cons. microbiology and cytopathology Hosp. for Women Md., Balt., 1964-65; microbiologist Becton, Dickinson & Co., Cockeysville, Md., 1964-65, chief microbiologist Biol. Safety and Control Labs., 1965-68; dir. sterility services and clin. lab. Huntingdon Research Center, Inc., Balt., 1968-72; tchr. biology, health and social scis. Balt. City Bd. Edn., 1972—; microbiologist FDA, 1978-86; sr. partner firm E squared plus 3, Glyndon, Md., 1969—; cons. sterility services and clin. lab., also microbial limits. Vol. instr. cardiopulmonary resuscition and firearms safety. Served with AUS, 1956-58. Registered pathogenic microbiologist, specialist microbiologist Nat. Registry. Mem. Am., Md. socs. med. technologists, Am. Soc. Clin. Pathologists, Am. Soc. Cytology, AAAS, Am. Inst. Biol. Scis., Am. Soc. Microbiology (sec.-treas. Md. br. 1969-74, spl. chmn. clin. meeting 1970, mem. archives com. 1974-80), Inst. Food Tech. Roman Catholic. Address: PO Box 303 Riderwood MD 21139

O'TOOLE, PETER, actor; b. County Galway, Ireland, Aug. 2, 1932; s. Patrick Joseph and Constance (Ferguson) O'T.; m. Sian Phillips, 1959 (div.); children: Kate, Pat; m. Karen Brown, 1983 (div.); 1 child, Lorcan. Student, Royal Acad. Dramatic Arts. Actor Bristol Old Vic Co., 1955-58; London stage debut in Major Barbara, 1956; other stage appearances include Present Laughter, The Apple Cart, 1986, Pygmalion, 1987; films include Kidnapped, 1960, The Day They Robbed the Bank of England, 1960, Savage Innocents, 1961, Lawrence of Arabia, 1962, Becket, 1964, Lord Jim, 1965, What's New, Pussycat?, 1965, How to Steal a Million, 1966, The Bible... in the Beginning, 1966, The Night of the Generals, 1967, Great Catherine, 1968, The Lion in Winter, 1968, Goodbye Mr. Chips, 1969, Murphy's War, 1971, Under Milk Wood, 1971, Brotherly Love, The Ruling Class, 1972, Man of LaMancha, 1972, Rosebud, 1975, Man Friday, 1975, Foxtrot, 1976, Coup d'Etat, 1977, Zulu Dawn, 1978, Power Play, 1978, Caligula, 1979, Stuntman, 1980, The Antagonists, 1981, My Favorite Year, 1981, Supergirl, 1984, Creator, 1985, Club Paradise, 1985, The Last Emperor, 1987; appeared in: Rogue Male, BBC-TV, 1976, Strumpet City, RTE-TV, 1979; TV mini-series Masada, 1981, Svengali, 1982; TV film Kim, 1984. Office: care William Morris Agy Inc 1350 Avenue of Americas New York NY 10019 also: care Veerline Ltd, 54 Baker St, London W1M 1DJ England *

O'TOOLE, RICHARD HENRY, European community official; b. Galway, Ireland, Apr. 26, 1947; m. Maria Helena Lee; children: Conor, Sinead, Fiona. BS with honours, Univ. Coll., Galway, 1969, MS with 1st class honours, 1972. Pres. Unions Students in Ireland, Dublin, 1969-71; 1st sec. Dept. Fgn. Affairs, Dublin, 1972-76; spl. asst. to exec. dir. Internat. Energy Agy., Orgn. for European Cooperation and Devel., Paris, 1976-79; European correspondent Polit. div. Dept. Fgn. Affairs, Dublin, 1979-82; dep. permanent rep. Irish mission Dept. Fgn. Affairs, Geneva, 1979-85; chef de cabinet Sutherland Commn. European Communities, Brussels, 1985—. Office: Commn European Communities, rue de la Loi 200, 1049 Brussels Belgium

OTOSHI, TOM YASUO, electrical engineer; b. Seattle, Sept. 4, 1931; s. Jitsuo and Shina Otoshi; B.S.E.E., U. Wash., 1954, M.S.E.E., 1957; m. Haruko Shirley Yumiba, Oct. 13, 1963; children—John, Kathryn. With Hughes Aircraft Co., Culver City, Calif., 1956-61; mem. tech. staff Jet Propulsion Lab., Calif. Inst. Tech., Pasadena, 1961—; cons. Recipient NASA New Tech. awards. Mem. I Cantori and The Early Music Ensemble of Los Angeles. Mem. IEEE (sr.), Sigma Xi. Contbr. articles to profl. jours. Patentee in field. Home: 3551 Henrietta St La Crescenta CA 91214 Office: Jet Propulsion Lab 4800 Oak Grove Dr Pasadena CA 91109

OTOSHI, YUTAKA, electronics executive; b. Oct. 12, 1916; m. Michiko Otoshi. Grad., Waseda U., 1937. Founder, pres. Tokyo Koki; with TDK Electronics Co., Ltd., Tokyo, 1952—, mng. dir., from 1974, now v.p. Home: 9-3 Tamagawa Denenchofu, 2-chome Setagaya-ku, Tokyo 158, Japan *

OTS, LENNART, office systems company executive; b. Valjala, Saaremaa, Estonia, Feb. 7, 1933; came to Sweden, 1944; s. Juhan and Hilda Anette (Poldemaa) Ots; m. Mai-Britt Viola Johansson, Oct. 31, 1959; children—Helena Christina, Jan Christer. Marketing economist, Inst. Higher Mktg., Gothenburg, 1977. Musician orchs., Gothenburg, 1954-57; clk. Freon-Kyl Bil & Truck Co., Gothenburg, 1957-59; salesman, sales mgr. Singer Co., Husqvarna, Gothenburg, 1959-69; rep. systems Remington Rand Co., Gothenburg, 1969-72; rep. Esselte System, Gothenburg, 1972-78; owner, mgr. System-Lots AB, Angered, 1978—. Composer popular music, poet. Condr. Estonian Ch. Choir, Gothenburg, 1957-58. Mem. Swedish Music Composers Assn. Lutheran. Club: L/S Gothia (Gothenburg). Home and Office: Briljantgatan 88, 421 49 V Frolunda Sweden

OTSUKA, EIJI, chemical company executive, researcher; b. Iizuka, Fukuoka-ken, Japan, Sept. 16, 1919; s. Yosaku and Makino (Nomiyama) O.; m. Sayoko Ogata, Nov. 29, 1946; children: Hideaki, Sachiko. B, Tokyo U., 1941, PhD, 1960. Dir. Mitsui Toatsu Chems., Tokyo, 1966-83, exec. v.p., 1981-83, exec. adv., 1983—; lectr. Hokkaido U., Sapporo, Japan, 1962-77, Kyushu U., Fukuoka, Japan, 1963-81. Author: Reaction System, Part I,II, 1974; Separation System, Part I,II, 1976. Patentee in field. Served to lt. Navy, 1942-45. Recipient Tech. Merit award Japanese Govt. 1959; Purple Ribbon medal Japanese Govt. 1969; Okochi medal Okochi Meml. Found. 1975. Mem. Am. Chem. Soc., Am. Inst. Chem. Engrs., Chem. Soc. Japan (v.p. 1980-81, tech. devel. award 1974), Soc. Chem. Engrs. Japan (hon. mem., v.p. 1981). Buddhist. Lodge: Myoho Temple. Avocations: gardening, liquor collection. Home: 241-48 Fukaya-cho, Totsuka-Ku, Yokohama Japan

OTT, EMILE CUTRER, lawyer; b. New Orleans, Jan. 18, 1932; s. John Jacob and Kathryn Bingham (Percy) O.; m. Jewell Vegas, June 11, 1960; children—Emile Cutrer, Paul Vegas, Kathryn Ruth. BA, U. Miss., 1954, LLB, 1959. Bar: Miss. 1959. Trial atty. NLRB, New Orleans, 1959-66; atty. Auther Sullivan, Jackson, Miss., 1966-69; mem. Fuselier Ott McKee & Walker, P.A., Jackson, Miss., 1969—. Served to 1st lt. USAF, 1954-57. Mem. ABA, Def. Lawyers Assn. Home: 2315 Irving Pl Jackson MS 39211 Office: 2100 Deposit Guaranty Plaza Jackson MS 39201

OTT, GILBERT RUSSELL, JR., lawyer; b. Bklyn., Apr. 15, 1943; s. Gilbert Russell, Sr. and Bettina Rose (Ferrel) O.; m. Lisa S. Weatherford, Apr. 12, 1986; 1 child, Gilbert R. III. BA, Yale U., 1965; JD, Columbia U., 1969, MBA, 1969. Admitted to N.Y. State bar, 1970; assoc. firm Chadbourne, Parke, Whiteside & Wolff, N.Y.C., 1969-72, LeBoeuf, Lamb, Leiby & MacRae, N.Y.C., 1972-78; asso. gen. counsel, asst. sec. Kidder, Peabody & Co., Inc., N.Y.C., 1978—, asst. v.p., 1978-79, v.p., 1979-86, mng. dir., 1986—; v.p. Webster Cash Res. Fund, Inc., 1980—, gen. counsel, sec., 1982—, bd. dirs., 1985—; v.p., gen. counsel, sec. Kidder, Peabody Premium Account Fund, 1982—, trustee, 1985—; v.p., gen. counsel, sec. Kidder, Peabody Govt. Money Fund, Inc., 1983—; dir., 1985—. Mem. Assn. Bar City N.Y. Clubs: Piping Rock, Down Town, University (N.Y.C.). Home: 260 Highwood Circle Oyster Bay NY 11771-3205 Office: 20 Exchange Pl New York NY 10005

OTT, HARRY, diplomat; b. Chemnitz, Germany, Oct. 15, 1933; m. Anita Ott, 1962; children: Tamara, Gerald. Student, Karl-Marx U., Leipzig, German Dem. Republic; grad., State Inst. Internat. Relations, Moscow. Dep. head internat. relations dept. Cen. Com. Socialist Unity Party of Germany, Berlin, 1959-74; ambassador to the USSR 1974-81; dep. minister fgn. affairs, permanent rep. UN, 1982—; bd. dirs. Inst. for East-West Security Studies, N.Y.C. Contbr. articles to profl. jours. Mem. Cen. Auditing Commn. Socialist Unity Party of Germany, Berlin, 1971-76, cen. com., 1976—. Recipient Nat. Order of Merit (Gold) award, Star of Internat. Friendship Order award. Home: 245 E 40th St Apt 32-E New York NY 10016 Office: Permanent Mission of German Democratic Republic to the UN 58 Park Ave New York NY 10016

OTT, WAYNE ROBERT, environmental engineer; b. San Mateo, Calif., Feb. 2, 1940; s. Florian Funstan and Evelyn Virginia (Smith) O.; m. Patricia Faustina Bertuzzi, June 28, 1967 (div. 1983). BA, Claremont McKenna Coll., 1962; BSEE, Stanford U., 1963, MS, 1965, MA, 1966, PhD, 1971. Commd. lt. USPHS, 1966, advanced to comdr., 1982; chief lab. ops. br. U.S. EPA, Washington, 1971-73, sr. systems analyst, 1973-79, sr. research engr., 1981-84, chief air toxics and radiation monitoring research staff, 1984—; vis. scientist dept. stats. Stanford (Calif.) U., 1979-81. Author: Environmental Indices: Theory and Practice, 1976, Statistical Models for the Environmental Sciences; contbr. articles to profl. jours. Decorated Commendation medal. Mem. Am. Statis. Assn., Am. Soc. for Quality Control, Air Pollution Control Assn., Phi Beta Kappa, Sigma Xi, Tau Beta Pi, Kappa Mu Epsilon. Democrat. Clubs: Theater, Jazz, Sierra. Avocations: hiking, photography, model trains, jazz recording. Developer nationally uniform air pollution index, first human exposure activity pattern models. Home: 1003 N Terrill St Alexandria VA 22304 Office: US EPA 401 M St SW Washington DC 20460

OTTER, PIETER WIEGER, lecturer; b. Rotterdam, Zuid-Holland, Netherlands, Aug. 23, 1946; s. Wieger and Katharina (Oosterhof) Otter Klok. M.S. in Quantitative Econs., State U. Groningen, 1971. Asst., Inst. Econ. Research, State U. Groningen, 1968-71, reader, Econometric Inst., 1971-77, lectr., 1977—. Author: Dynamic Feature Space Modelling, 1983; contbr. articles to profl. jours. Rep. Amnesty Internat., Groningen, 1969. U. Groningen grantee, 1981; I.I.A.S.A. grantee, 1983. Mem. Systemsgroup Holland, Werkgemeenschap Econometrie. Club: Theatre Group Roden. Home: Uiterburen 47, 9636 EC Zuidbroek Groningen The Netherlands Office: State U Groningen, Econ Inst, PO Box 800, 9700 AV Groningen The Netherlands

OTTERSTAD, RAGNAR, electronics executive; b. Oslo, Jan. 31, 1937; came to Denmark, 1981; s. Kaare and Marie (Wilhelmsen) O.; m. Vibeke Trolle Andersen, 1968; children—Paal, Mia Susanne, Eva Pernille. Examen Artium, Vahl, Oslo, 1956; Kandidateksamen, Oslo Inst. Bus. Adminstrn., 1961. Radio officer Mcht. Marine, Oslo, 1958-59; sales adminstr. Margarincentralen, Oslo, 1962-64; sales mgr. Gustav A. Ring a/s, Oslo, 1964-70, mktg. mgr., 1970-79; mktg. mgr. Lehmkuhl Elektronikk a/s, Oslo, 1979-81; mng. dir. Phelps Dodge Communications Co., Hillerod, Denmark, 1981-82; mng. dir., pres. M E C a/s, Ballerup, Denmark, 1982—; dir. Multicover A/S, 1987—, EB Scanword a/s, Virum, Denmark. Council mem. Norwegian Radio Relay League, Oslo, 1958-66, v.p., 1966-68. Served with Royal Norwegian Signals, 1956-58. Mem. Polyteknisk Forening, Dansk Civilokonomforening. Home: Vejdammen 5, 2840 Holte Denmark

OTTESEN, STEINAR, engineering company executive; b. Oslo, Mar. 21, 1944; s. Ole Birger and Elsa (Jensen) O.; m. Astri Larsen; 1 child, Lars Martin. MBA, BBA, Norwegian U. Commerce and Bus. Adminstrn., Bergen, Norway, 1967. Cons. computer dept. U. Bergen, 1969-70; cons. IKO Software Service A/S, Oslo, 1970-74; sr. cons. Kongsberg-Ikoss Cons. A/S, Oslo, 1974-76; fin. mgr. Kongsberg Engring. A/S, Asker, Norway, 1976-82, systems mgr., 1982-84; fin. mgr. Dyno Engring. A/S, Baerum, Norway, 1984-88; adminstrv. mgr. Kvaerner Subsea Contracting A/S, Baerum, 1988—. Served in Norwegian Navy, 1968-69. Mem. Norwegian Assn. MBA Candidates. Office: Kvaerner Subsea Contracting A/S, PO Box 290, Lysarer, N1324 Baerum Norway

OTTING, FREDERICK PAUL, manufacturing executive; b. Milw., Mar. 4, 1916; s. Fred E. and Hilda (Felber) O.; m. Juel Papenthien, June 18, 1938; m. 2d, Margaret Steffenhagen, Sept. 2, 1978; children—Robyn M., Derf N. Student Marquette U., U. Wis.-Milw. Plant supr. Western Leather Co., Milw., 1939-48; v.p. Racine Glove Co., Rio, Wis., 1948-79; pres. Gaskets Inc., Rio, 1961—. Mem. exec. com. Nat. Safety Council. Mem. Nat. Welding Supply Assn., Am. Welding Soc., Am. Soc. Safety Engrs., Internat. Platform Assn. Republican. Presbyterian. Clubs: Marco Island Country, Marco Island Yacht; Madison; Masons, Shriners. Office: Gaskets Inc 100 Hy 16 W Rio WI 53960

OTTMANN, HENNING, educator; b. Vienna, Austria, Mar. 9, 1944; s. Theodor and Johanna (Schwarz) O.; m. Fanika Goricki, Feb. 26, 1947; 1 child, Christian. MA, U. Munich, 1970, PhD, 1974, D in Philosophy and Polit. Theory, habilitation, 1984. Asst. prof. U. Munich, 1972-86; prof. U. Augsburg, Fed. Republic Germany, 1986-87, U. Basel, Switzerland, 1987—; mng. editor Zeitschrift für Politik, Munich, 1983—. Contbr. articles to prof. jours. Roman Catholic. Home: Bündtenweg 77, CH4102 Binningen Switzerland Office: U of Basel Philosophy Sem, Am Nadelberg 6/8, CH4051 Basel Switzerland

OTTO, GILBERT FRED, zoologist, educator; b. Chgo., Dec. 16, 1901; s. Martin and Fredericka Christina (Rose) O.; A.B., Kalamazoo Coll., 1926; M.S., Kans. State U., 1927; Sc.D., Johns Hopkins U., 1929; m. Loudale Simmons, Dec. 20, 1932; children—Sandra Otto Abbott, Frederick Simmons. Instr. Johns Hopkins U., Balt., 1929-31, asst. prof., 1931-42, assoc. prof., 1942-53, asst. dean Sch. of Pub. Health, 1940-47; dir. Parasitology Lab. of Med. Clinics, Johns Hopkins Hosp., Balt., 1946-53; mgr. Parasitology Research Div., Abbott Labs., North Chicago, Ill., 1953-61, dir. of agrl. and vet. research, 1961-66; prof. zoology U. Md., College Park, 1966-72, adj. prof., lectr., 1972-80, lectr. med. entomology Sch. of Hygiene and Pub. Health Johns Hopkins U., 1980-88, sr. research assoc., 1980—; cons. Naval Med. Research Inst., 1948-54; mem. sci. adv. bd. biology dept. U. Notre Dame, 1958-67; vis. prof. U. Mich. Biol. Sta., summers 1946-53; cons. NIH, 1945-50, WHO, 1952-75, FDA, 1941, 77-81; cons. mosquito-borne disease Nat. Acad. Sci., 1983-86; sec. gen. 2d Internat. Congress Parasitology, 1970. Chief judge High Sch. Sci. Fairs, Prince Georges County (Md.), 1967-70; trustee B.H. Ransom Meml. Trustee Fund, 1936—, chmn. bd., 1956-73. Named Disting. Alumnus, Kalamazoo Coll., 1951; Disting. Editor of Yr., Council Biology Editors, 1986. Fellow AAAS, Royal Soc. Tropical Medicine and Hygiene; mem. Ill. Mosquito Control Assn. (pres. 1960-61; hon. life), Am. Soc. Tropical Medicine, AVMA (hon. life), World Assn. Advancement Vet. Parasitology, Am. Soc. Parasitologists (treas. 1937-41, 44, v.p. 1955, pres. 1957; hon. life), Helminthological Soc. Washington (pres. 1936, editor 1952-66; hon. life), Am. Micros. Soc., Am. Heartworm Soc. (hon. life mem.; sec.-treas. 1974-77, asst. editor 1974, editor 1977—, pres. 1977-80), Council Biol. Editors (Meritorious award 1986). Contbr. numerous articles on parasitology to sci. jours; contbr. chpts. to med. and vet. texts. Developer treatment for heartworm in dogs. Home: 10506 Greenacres Dr Silver Spring MD 20903 Office: Zoology Dept U Md College Park MD 20742

OTTO, INGOLF HELGI ELFRIED, institute fellow; b. Duesseldorf, Fed. Republic of Germany, May 7, 1920; s. Frederick C. and Josephine (Zisenis) O.; m. Carlyle Miller, 1943 (div. 1960); children—George Vincent Edward, Richard Arthur Frederick. A.B., U. Cin., 1941; M.A., George Washington U., 1950, Ph.D., 1959. CPCU. Assoc. prof. fin. NYU, N.Y.C., 1960-62; prof. fin. U. Nuevo Leon, Monterrey, Mexico, 1962-65, U. So. Miss., Hattiesburg, 1965-67, U. So. Ala., Mobile, 1967-81; sr. fellow Inst. Banking and Fin., Mexico City, 1981—. Contbr. articles on fin. to profl. jours. Served to col. U.S. Army, 1941-46. Decorated Legion of Merit, Meritorious Service medal, Purple Heart. Mem. Am. Econ. Assn., N.Am. Econ. and Fin. Assn.

OTTO-RIEKE, GERD, editor, writer; b. Schlagsdorf, Federal Republic Germany, Mar. 3, 1950; m. Heide Rieke, Diplom-Volkswirt, Hamburg U., Federal Republic Germany, 1977. Chmn. Junge Presse Schleswig-Holstein, Kiel, Federal Republic Germany, 1968-73; vice chmn. Deutsche Jugendpresse e.V., Bonn, Federal Republic Germany, 1969-73; editor-in-chief Deutscher Verkehrs-Verlag GmbH, Hamburg, 1981-85; editor-in-chief touristik aktuell and Der Fremdenverkehr, Jaeger Verlag GmbH, Darmstadt, Fed. Republic Germany, 1986-87; editor-in-chief Check-In, Verlag Industriemagazin, Muenchen, 1987—. Author: Der Formalitaeten-Wegweiser, 1982, Der Grosse Hobby-ynd Erlebnis-Urlaubsfuehrer, 1986. Mem. Hamburger Journalisten-Verband. Club: Luftfahrt Presse. Home: Wrangelstrasse 28, D2000 Hamburg 20 Federal Republic of Germany Other: Knorrstrasse 10, D8000 Muenchen 40 Federal Republic of Germany Office: Verlag Industriemagazin, Ingolstaedter Strasse 22, D8000 Muencheh 45 Federal Republic of Germany

OTTOSSON, (PER AXEL) RUNE, mechanical engineer; b. Jonkoping, Sweden, Sept. 30, 1919; s. Axel Gideon and Agnes Emelia (Jonsson) O.; m. Greta Willners, Oct. 8, 1942; children: Göran, Thomas. Degree in Engring., Boras U., Sweden, 1942. Lic. engr. Chief engr. Varnamo (Sweden) Maskinaktiebolag, 1942-46, Varnamo Wellpappfabrik, 1946-51; tech. mgr. AB Gustaf Kahr, Nybro, Sweden, 1951-60; pres. Kahrs Maskiner AB, Nybro, 1960-84; chief cons. Ikea Engring. Co., Nybro, 1984-87; chmn. bd. Intorg AB, Nybro, 1984—; bd. dirs. Hjaltevadshus AB, Textec AB. Bd. dirs. Com. Promotion Trade Sweden-East Europe, Stockholm, 1965—, Com. Swedish Project Export, Stockholm, 1982—. Lodge: Rotary. Office: Intorg AB, Tallgolsgatan 4, 38200 Nybro, Kalmar Sweden

OTTUNGA, MAURICE CARDINAL, archbishop of Nairobi; b. Chebukwa, Kenya, Jan. 1923; son of tribal chief. Ordained priest Roman Catholic Ch., 1950; formerly tchr. Kisumu Maj. Sem.; attaché apostolic del. Mombasa, 1953-56; titular bishop of Tacape, also aux. Kisumu, 1957; bishop of Kisii, 1969-69; titular archbishop of Bomarzo, also coadjutor of Nairobi, 1969-71; archbishop of Baitobi, Nairobi, 1971—; elevated to Sacred Coll. of Cardinals, 1973; titular ch. St. Gregory Barbarigo; mil. vicar of Kenya, 1981; primate of Kenya, 1983—; mem. Congregation of Sacraments and Divine Worship, Congregation of Religious and Secular Insts., Commn. Revision Code of Canon Law. Address: PO Box 14231, Nairobi Kenya *

OTTURI, HECTOR ALFREDO, wool trading company executive; b. Buenos Aires, Mar. 29, 1952; s. Antonio Alfredo and Nelida (Solari) O.; m. Graciela Adriana Orfano, May 20, 1978; children—Estefania, Leandro Alfredo. M.Adminstrn., Econs. Coll., State U. Buenos Aires, 1976. Export mgr. asst. Lahusen y Cia Ltda., Buenos Aires, 1976-77, export mgr., 1977-81, fin. mgr., 1982—; mem. exec. com., 1982-87; mem. exec. com. Thormac S.A., 1982—, Nortoorf SA, 1982—, Tiendas y Almacenes, 1982—, Lahusen SA, 1982—, Frigorifico Hughes, 1985-86; chmn. bd. dirs. Cardoclor Industrias Quimicas S.A.; cons. commodities markets, pvt. corps., Buenos Aires, 1983—. Mem. Consejo Profesional de Ciecncias Economicas de Argentina, Internat. Airline Passenger Soc., Nat. Geog. Soc. Roman Catholic. Avocation: tennis. Home: Virrey Loreto 1733, 1426 Buenos Aires Argentina Office: Lahusen y Cia ltda, Lima 187, 1073 Buenos Aires Argentina

OTUNGA, MAURICE CARDINAL, cardinal Roman Catholic Church; b. Chebukwa, Kenya, Jan. 23, 1957. ordained 1950. Consecrated titular bishop Tacape, 1957; bishop Kisii, 1961; titular archbishop Bomarzo, 1969; archbishop Nairobi, Kenya, 1971—; proclaimed cardinal 1973, primate Kenya, 1983—, dir. castrense Kenya. Address: Cardinal's Residence, PO Box 14231, Nairobi Kenya *

OU, FONG-LIEH, civil engineer; b. Chung-Hua, Taiwan, Sept. 8, 1940; came to U.S., 1967, naturalized, 1978; s. Ja and Mee (Wu) O.; m. Julie Chen, Sept. 5, 1967; children—King, Harris. B.S., Chung-Yang U., Taiwan, 1964; M.S., Pa. State U., 1970; Ph.D., U. Utah, 1980. Registered profl. engr., D.C. Lectr., U. Chinese Culture, Taipei, Taiwan, 1966-67; transp. planner Pa. Dept. Transp., Harrisburg, 1968; planning analyst Pa. State Planning Bd., Harrisburg, 1969-75; research asst. Pa. Transp. Inst., State College, 1975-77; civil engr. Salt Lake Internat. Airport, 1978-80, U.S. Dept. Agr., Washington, 1980—; cons. Govt. Taiwan, Trans Systems, Vienna, Va., Allstar Engring., Washington. Contbr. articles to profl. jours. Mem. ASCE, Western Regional Sci. Assn., Sigma Xi. Home: 3333 Happy Heart Ln Annandale VA 22003 Office: US Dept Agr PO Box 96090 Washington DC 20013

OUDERKIRK, MASON JAMES, lawyer; b. Des Moines, Feb. 1, 1953; s. Mason George and Florence Astor (Lowe) O.; m. Kari Aune Hormel, May 28, 1983; 1 child, Mason Christopher. BA, Drake U., 1975, JD, 1978. Bar: Iowa 1978, U.S. Dist. Ct. (so. dist.) Iowa 1978; lic. real estate broker. Assoc. M.G. Ouderkirk Law Office, Indianola, Iowa, 1978-79; ptnr. Ouderkirk Law Firm, Indianola, 1979—; pres. Landmark Real Estate, Ltd., 1978—; mem. Vol. Lawyers Project, 1987—. Mem. Indianola Police Retirement Bd., 1984—. Mem. ABA, Iowa Bar Assn., Warren County Bar Assn. (sec., treas. 1985-87), 5th Jud. Dist. Bar Assn. Episcopalian. Home: 307 W Madison Pl Indianola IA 50125 Office: Ouderkirk Law Firm 110 S Howard Box 156 Indianola IA 50125

OUELLETTE, JANE LEE YOUNG, biology educator; b. Charlotte, N.C., Dec. 29, 1929; d. James Thomas and Nancy Isabel (Yarbrough) Young; m. Armand Roland Ouellette, Aug. 3, 1951 (dec. Oct. 1984); children—Elizabeth Anne, James Young, Emily Jane, Frances Lee. B.A., Winthrop Coll., 1950; M.A., Oberlin Coll., 1952; postgrad. Coll. Medicine, Baylor U., 1974, U. Tex.-Houston, 1976-83, Tex. Woman's U., 1980-82. Lic. tchr., Tex. Tchr. Maria Regina High Sch., Hartsdale, N.Y., 1969-70, Spring Ind. Sch. System, Tex., 1972-78; coordinator biology program, instr., North Harris County Coll., Houston, 1979—. Mem. Internat. Assn. for Study of Pain, Internat. Pain Found., N.Y. Acad. Sci., AAAS, Internat. Chronobiol. Soc., People to People Internat. Democrat. Home: 1619 Big Horn St Houston TX 77090 Office: North Harris County Coll 2700 W Thorne Dr Houston TX 77073

OUGHTON, JAMES HENRY, JR., business executive, farmer; b. Chgo., May 14, 1913; s. James H. and Barbara (Corbett) O.; student Dartmouth Coll., 1931-35; m. Jane Boyce, Jan. 23, 1940; children: Diana (dec.), Carol Oughton Biondi, Pamela Oughton Armstrong, Deborah Oughton Callahan. Pres., dir. L.E. Keeley Co., Dwight, Ill., 1936—, Nev. Corp.; past adminstr. The Keeley Inst., Dwight, 1938-66; dir. 1st Nat. Bank of Dwight, Ill., 1939-88. Valley Investment Co.; farmer, farm mgr., livestock feeder, Ill.; sec., dir. Dwight Indsl. Assn.; past mem. Ill. Ho. of Reps. Co-chmn. 1st Indsl. Conf. on Alcoholism, 1948; chmn. Midwest Seminar on Alcoholism for Pastors, 1957, 58, 59, 60; chmn. adv. bd. Ill. Dept. Corrections; chmn. Gov.'s Task Force on Mental Health Adminstrn., 1971-72; mem. adv. bd. Ill. Dept. Mental Health; dir., mem. exec. bd. W.D. Boyce council Boy Scouts Am.; del. 31st Internat. Congress on Alcoholism and Drug Dependence, Bangkok, 1975; mem. Internat. Council on Alcohol and Addictions, Lausanne, Switzerland, 1977; mem. Ill. Trade and Investment Mission to Japan and Korea, 1985; mem. adv. council Small Bus., Fed. Reserve Bank Chgo., 1985-86. Served as lt. (j.g.) USNR, 1944-46; PTO. Republican. Episcopalian. Clubs: Univ., Union League (Chgo.). Address: 103 W South St Dwight IL 60420

OUKU, ROBERT JOHN, politician; b. Kusumu, Kenya, Mar. 31, 1932; s. Erasto and Susanah Seda Ouku; m. Christabel Akumu Odolla, 1965; 5 children. Grad., Siriba Coll., Haile Sellassie I U., Makarere U. Tchr. 1952-55; with Ministry of African Affairs, Kisii Dist., 1955-58; asst. sec. Fgn. Affairs Dept. Office of the Prime Minister, 1962-63, sr. asst. sec., 1963; permanent sec. Ministry of Fgn. Affairs, 1963-64, Ministry of Works, 1965-69; E. African Minister for Fin. and Adminstrn. Kenya Govt., 1969-70, minister for Common Market and Econ. Affairs, 1970-77, minister of econ. planning and community affairs, 1978-79, minister of fgn. affairs, 1979-83, minister of planning and nat. devel., 1985-87, minister of industry, 1987, minister of fgn. affairs and internat. cooperation, 1988—; pres. African Assn. for Pub. Adminstrn. and Mgmt., 1971-74; mem. E. African Legis. Assembly, ILO. Contbr. articles to profl. jours.; co-author university textbook on mgmt. Fellow Kenya Inst. Mgmt. Office: Ministry of Fgn Affairs, PO Box 48935, Nairobi Kenya *

OUNJIAN, MARILYN J., employment and training company executive; b. Harrisburg, Pa., Oct. 24, 1947; d. Stanley Wolf and Rebecca (Darrow) Freeman; m. Irving Henry Schwartz, Aug. 24, 1974 (dec. May 1975); 1 child, Jennifer; m. George Edward Ounjian, July 31, 1982; children: Jonathan, Kori. Student, U. Md. Pres. Today's People, Phila., 1973-81; chmn., founder, chief exec. officer The Career Inst., Phila., 1981—; pres., chief exec. officer Careers USA, Phila., 1981—. Mem. Rep. Senatorial Inner Circle. Mem. Cen. City Proprietors Assn., Nat. Assn. Female Execs. Inc., Nat. Assn. Women Bus. Owners, Greater Phila. C. of C., Pa. C. of C., Assn. Venture Founders. Club: Gov.'s Del. Office: Careers USA 1825 JF Kennedy Blvd Philadelphia PA 19103

OUSSANI, JAMES JOHN, stapling company executive; b. Bklyn., Jan. 3, 1920; s. John Thomas and Clara (Tager) O.; B.M.E., Pratt Inst., 1938-42; m. Lorraine G. Tutundgy, Apr. 25, 1954; children—James J., Gregory P., Rita C. Dir. research, mfg. Supertronic Co., N.Y.C., 1943-46; sr. partner Perl-Oussani Machine Mfg. Co., N.Y.C., 1946-49; founder The Staplex Co., Bklyn., 1949, pres., 1949—; exec. dir. Lourdes Realty Corp.; dir. Junios Corp., Gregrita Realty Corp.; producer air sampling equipment for radioactive fallout AEC, 1951—. Mem. Bur. Research Air Pollution Control, Pres.'s Council on Youth Opportunity, Cardinal's Com. for Edn.; trustee Ch. of Virgin Mary; founder, bd. dirs. Oussani Found.; mem. cardinal's com. of laity, bishop's com. of laity; mem. council St. John's U.; mem. Coll. of Boca Raton Aux. Recipient Blue Ribbon Mining award, Sch. Mgmt. award, Aerospace Pride Achievement award. Mem. Adminstrv. Mgmt. Soc., Office Adminstrn. Assn., Nat. Stationery and Office Equipment Assn., Office Exces. Assn., Nat. Office Machine Mfg. Assn., Nat. Office Machine Dealers Assn., Nat. Office Products Assn., Bus. Equipment Mfrs. Assn., Our Lady Perpetual Help Holy Name Soc., Knights of Holy Sepulchre, Knights of St. Gregory. Clubs: Knights of Malta; Rotary, Salaam (N.Y.C.); Mahopac Golf (Lake Mahopac, N.Y.); Boca Raton Hotel. Inventor automatic electric stapling machine. Patentee in field. Office: 777 5th Ave Brooklyn NY 11232

OUTLER, ALBERT COOK, clergyman, educator; b. Thomasville, Ga., Nov. 17, 1908; s. John Morgan and Gertrude Flint (Dewberry) O.; A.B., Wofford Coll., 1928, D.D., 1952; B.D., Emory U., 1933, Litt.D. (hon.), 1968; Ph.D., Yale U., 1938; D.D., Kalamazoo Coll., 1962; L.H.D. (hon.), Lycoming Coll., 1964, Ohio Wesleyan U., 1967, Duke U., 1974; LL.D. (hon.), U. Notre Dame, 1966; D.S.T. (hon.), Gen. Theol. Sem., 1967; D.H.L. (hon.), Loyola U., New Orleans, 1978, Cath. U. Am., 1979; m. Carlotta Grace Smith, Dec. 18, 1931; children—Frances Gertrude, David Stevens. Ordained to ministry Meth. Ch.; pastor, Baxley, Ga., 1928-30, Pineview, Ga., 1930-32, Gordon, Ga., 1932-34, Macon, 1934-35; instr. theology Duke U., 1938-39, asst. prof., 1939-41, asso. prof., 1941-45; asso. prof. Yale U., 1945-48, Dwight prof. theology, 1948-51; prof. theology So. Meth. U., Dallas, 1951-80, prof. emeritus, 1980—, chmn. grad. council of humanities, 1960-63; research prof. religion Tex. Wesleyan Coll., 1983-85. Del. Meth. Ch. 3d World Council on Faith and Order, Lund, Sweden, 1952; chmn. Am. sect. FOC Theol. Commn. on Tradition; Meth. del. to 3d Assembly World Council Chs., New Delhi, 1961; vice chmn. 4th World Council on Faith and Order, Montreal, 1963; del.-observer 2d Vatican Council, 1962-65; vis. sr. fellow, Council Humanities, Princeton U., 1956-57; hon. fellow Wesley Coll., Sydney, Australia, 1980. Fellow Am. Acad. Arts and Sci.; mem. Am. Soc. Ch. History (pres. 1963-64), World Council Chs., Am. Theol. Soc. (pres. 1960, sec. 1960-62), Acad. of Tex., Nat. Council Religion Higher Edn., Am. Cath. Hist. Assn. (pres. 1972-73), Duodecim, Phi Beta Kappa. Club: Elizabethan. Author: A Christian Context for Counseling, 1946; Colleges, Faculties and Religion, 1949; Psychotherapy and the Christian Message, 1954; The Confessions and Enchiridion of St. Augustine, 1955; The Christian Tradition and the Unity We Seek, 1957; John Wesley, 1964; Who Trusts in God, 1968; John Wesley, Sermons, I-IV; contbr. articles to profl. jours.Recipient Pax Christi award Benedictine Order, 1987. Home: Asbury Towers 1533 Fourth Ave W Bradenton FL 34205

OUTRAM, JERRY ROOPNARINE, research scientist, scientific consultant, researcher; b. Guyana, S. Am., Aug. 16, 1953; arrived Eng., 1962; s. Umrao Patrick and Kamaldai (Ragnauth) O.; m. Eileen McCarroll, Jan. 9, 1981. B. Sc. with honors, Kingston Poly. (Eng.), 1976; Ph.D., D.I.C., Imperial (London) Coll., 1979. Post doctoral fellow U. Mo., Columbia, 1979-81, asst. research prof., 1981-82; cons., analytical research scientist Pollock and Pool Sci. Cons., Reading, Eng., 1982-85; sect. head environ. chemistry dept. Rhone Poulenc Agriculture, Ongar, Essex, Eng., 1985—. Contbr. articles to profl. jours. Research fellow Sci. Research Council, 1976-77, Cancer Research Council, 1977. Mem. Am. Chem. Soc., Sigma Xi. Liberal. Ch. England. Club: Surrey Cricket (Young Profl., 1969-72).

OUVRIEU, JEAN-BERNARD, diplomat; b. Creil, France, Mar. 13, 1939; s. Ouvrieu René and Franchet Renée; m. Arabella Cruse, July 16, 1968; children: Christophe, Lorraine, Constance. Student, Inst. d'Etudes Politiques, Paris, Ecole des Hautes Etudes Commerciales, Paris, Ecole Nat. d'Administration, Paris. Various govt. positions Paris, 1966-75; counsellor Ambassade de France en Irak, Bagdad, 1975-77, Ambassade de France aux U.S., Washington, 1977-79; staff Ministries of Affairs, Paris, 1979-80; various govt. positions Paris, 1980-85; ambassador Ambassadeur de France en Corée, Seoul, 1985-87; dir. econ. and fin. affairs Ministry Fgn. Affairs, Paris, 1987—. Office: Ministry of Fgn Affairs, 37 Quai d'Orsay, 75007 Paris France

OUYANG, CHAOHO, pharmacology educator; b. Paiho, Taiwan, May 27, 1919; s. Chunwei and Yuechu (Wang) O.; m. Shiuhong Hong, May 22, 1945; children—Chunghua, Chungling, Chungmei, Chungching. B.M., Taihoku Imperial U., Taipei, 1945; M.D., Kyoto U., 1958. Instr., Nat. Taiwan U., Taipei, 1953-56, assoc. prof., 1956-61, prof., 1961—, chmn. dept. pharmacology, 1972-78, chmn. Pharmacol. Inst., 1972-78. Contbr. more than 80 articles to profl. jours.; reviewer internat. jours., 1982. Recipient Acad. award Ministry of Edn., Republic of China, 1976. Mem. Academia Sinica (Republic of China), Internat. Soc. Toxinology (mem. editorial council 1982), Chinese Pharmacol. Soc. (mem. standing com. 1982), Internat. Soc. Hematology, Chinese Physiol. Soc., Chinese Biochem. Soc., Hematol. Soc. Republic of China, Formosan Med. Assn., Chinese Toxicol. Soc. Office: Nat Taiwan U Coll Medicine, No 1 Jen-Ai Rd, First Sect, Dept Pharmacology, Taipei Republic of China

OVENDALE, RITCHIE, political science educator; b. Pretoria, South Africa, Mar. 28, 1944; s. Richard and Jean Rainnie (Christie) O. MA, Natal U., Pietermaritzburg, Republic South Africa, 1965, McMaster U., Hamilton, Ont., Can., 1966; PhD, Oxford U., 1972, MA, 1977. Lectr. Univ. Coll. Wales, Aberystwyth, 1968-84, sr. lectr., 1984-85, reader, 1985—; vis. research scholar Am. Council Learned Socs., U. Va., 1979; vis. research fellow Australian Nat. U., Canberra, 1984. Author: 'Appeasement' and the English Speaking World, 1975, The Origins of the Arab-Israeli Wars, 1984, The Foreign Policy of the British Labour Governments, 1985, The English Speaking Alliance, 1985. Brit. Acad. grantee, 1979, 84. Fellow Royal Hist. Soc. Anglican. Home: 41 Maesceinion, Waun Fawr, Aberystwyth SY23 3QQ, Wales Office: Univ Coll Wales, Dept Internat Politics, Aberystwyth SY23 3QQ, Wales

OVERDUIN, HENK, museum deputy director; b. Leiden, The Netherlands, May 1, 1943; s. Machiel and Jo (Zweegman) O.; m. Ria Matze, June 27, 1967. Grad. sociology of art, U. Leiden, 1969. Asst. curator modern art Frans Halsmuseum, Haarlem, The Netherlands, 1970-72, head dept. edn., 1972-75; head dept. edn. Haags Gemeentemuseum, The Hague, The Netherlands, 1975-82, dep. dir., 1982—; chmn. Dutch Mus. Assn., Amsterdam, 1983—. Contbr. articles on mus. policy to profl. jours.; also catalogues. Mem. Internat. Council Mus. Home: Stephenson Straat 43, 1561 XR The Hague The Netherlands Office: Haags Gemeentemuseum, Stadhouderslaan 41, 2517 HV The Hague The Netherlands

ÖVERGAARD, GERD IRIS, English educator; b. Gudmundra, Sweden, Feb. 4, 1930; d. Bengt Isedor and Elin Erika (Gerdin) Wernblom; m. Sven W. Övergaard, Dec. 3, 1950 (div. 1967); children: Gunnar Erik, Bengt Harald. Candidate in philosophy, Uppsala U., Sweden, 1952, M in Philosophy, 1954, Licentiate in Philosophy, 1970; MA, U. So. Calif., 1958. High sch. tchr. Umea, Sweden, 1954-57; supr. Tchrs.' Tng. Coll., Uppsala, 1964-65, lectr., 1965-83; assoc. prof. Uppsala U., 1983—. Author (textbook): Text and Tapes, 1973; co-author: (textbook) Modern Engelska, 1975, Outlook, 1979; co-editor: (textbook) Short Fictions, 1986. Univ. grantee Swedish-Am. Found., 1957-58, State of Sweden, 1948-51; fellow Norrlands Nation Uppsala U., 1950-51. Mem. Lärarna i Moderna Sprak, Linguistic Soc. Am. Club: Lidingö Golf (Stockholm). Lodge: Soroptimist Internat. (pres. Uppsala 1968-70). Home: Artillerigat 28C, S-11451 Stockholm Sweden Office: Uppsala U, Kyrkogardsgat 10, S-75120 Uppsala Sweden

OVERMAN, DEAN LEE, lawyer, investor, author, real estate developer; b. Harvey, Ill., Oct. 9, 1943; s. Harold Levon and Violet Claire (True) O.; m. Linda Jane Olsen, Sept. 6, 1969; children: Elisabeth True, Christiana Hart. BA, Hope Coll., 1965; student, Princeton (N.J.) Sem., 1965-66; JD, U. Calif., Berkeley, 1969; postgrad. in bus., U. Chgo., 1974, U. Calif. Bar: Ill. 1969, D.C. 1977. Assoc. to ptnr. D'Ancona, Pflaum et al., Chgo., 1970-75; white house fellow Washington, 1975-76; assoc. dir. Domestic Council The White House, Washington, 1976-77; sr. ptnr. Winston-Strawn, Washington, 1977—; cons. The White House; spl. counsel to Gov. James Thompson, Springfield, Ill.; adj. faculty in secured financing U. Va. Law Sch., Charlottesville; vice chmn. J.F. Forstmann Co. Author: Toward a National Policy on State and Local Government Finance, 1976, Effective Writing Tecniques, 1980, (with others) Financing Equipment, 1973, Sales and Financing Under the Revised UCC, 1975; monthly newspaper column Chgo. Daily Law Bull.; contbr. articles to profl. jours. Commencement speaker Hope Coll., Holland, Mich., 1978. Mem. ABA, Ill. Bar Assn., D.C. Bar Assn., Chgo. Bar Assn. Office: Winston & Strawn 2550 M St NW Suite 500 Washington DC 20037

OVERTON, GEORGE WASHINGTON, lawyer; b. Hinsdale, Ill., Jan. 25, 1918; s. George Washington and Florence Mary (Darlington) O.; m. Jane Vincent Harper, Sept. 1, 1941; children—Samuel Harper, Peter Darlington,

Ann Vincent. A.B., Harvard U., 1940; J.D., U. Chgo., 1946. Bar: Ill. 1947. Counsel Wildman, Harrold, Allen & Dixon, Chgo. Bd. dirs. Open Lands Project, 1961—, pres., 1978-81; bd. dirs. Upper Ill. Valley Assn., 1981—, chmn., 1981-84; mem. com. on profl. responsibility of Ill. Supreme Ct., 1986—. Mem. ABA (mem. com. on counsel responsibility 1985—), Ill. Bar Assn., Chgo. Bar Assn. (bd. mgrs. 1981-83), Assn. Bar City N.Y. Home: 5648 Dorchester Ave Chicago IL 60637 Office: 1 IBM Plaza Chicago IL 60611

OVERTON, KENNETH, human resources consultant; b. Port Arthur, Tex., Nov. 15, 1908; s. Ellis Andrew and Myrtle Amelia (Morgan) O.; Asso. Sci. in Econs., U. Houston, 1946; student U. Mo., Peabody Coll., Baylor U., Sam Houston U., U. Tex.; m. Mary Lou Johnson, July 17, 1932; 1 dau., Carey O. Randall. Tchr. phys. edn. Port Arthur (Tex.) Pub. Schs., 1928-32; supr. indsl. relations mgmt. and oil ops. Texaco Inc., Port Arthur, 1933-50; supt. Central/Western Arabia mgmt. Arabian Am. Oil Co. (Aramco), Saudi Arabia, 1951-63; exec. cons. to Jean Paul Getty, Getty Oil Co., Kuwait, 1963-65; project admin. Wilbros-Shell, Oman, 1966-67; sr. cost engr. Pipeline Technologists, Inc., Houston/Alaska, 1967-75; resources cons., Saudi Arabia, Houston, 1977, EG&G, Saudi Arabia and Far East, Houston, Rockville, Arlington, 1976—; condr. econs. and agrl. Middle East Seminars for doctoral grads. at Tex. A&M U., 1968; round table participant Middle East-Far East forums for high schs., Tex., La., Va., Md., Saudi Arabia, 1960, 81-85. Author manuals; contributing advisor: Oil and War. Mem. Am. Petroleum Inst. Clubs: Port Arthur Country, Air Force Officers (hon.), Press. Home: 5131 N 15th ST Arlington VA 22205

OVSYSHCHER, ILYA AARON, cardiologist; b. Gomel, USSR, May 30, 1936; came to Israel, 1973; s. Aaron S. and Helen J. (Doith) O.; m. Lili Markow, May 13, 1964; children—Masha, Raya. M.D., 2d Med. Inst., Leningrad, USSR, 1960; Ph.D., Med. Sch., Leningrad-Kaunas, 1971. Cert. in cardiology. Intern and resident in cardiology Hosp. Kostroma, Pskov, Leningrad, 1960-69; head cardiac unit Sestroretsk Hosp., Leningrad, 1969-72; sr. cardiologist Soroka Med. Ctr., BeerSheba, Israel, 1973-81, dir. ECG and Pacemaker Labs., 1981—; assoc. prof. Ben Gurion U., 1982—. Contbr. articles to profl. jours. Mem. Israel Heart Soc., N.Y. Acad. Scis. Office: Soroka Med Ctr Cardiology, PO Box 151, BeerSheba 84101, Israel

OWEN, DAVID ANTHONY LLEWELLYN, member of parliament, physician; b. Plymouth, U.K., July 2, 1938; s. John William Morris and Mary (Llewellyn) Owen; m. Deborah Schabert, 1968; 3 children. Educated Bradfield Coll., Sidney Sussex Coll., Cambridge U., St. Thomas' Hosp. Mem. med. staff St. Thomas' Hosp., 1962-64, neurological and psychiatric registrar, 1964-66, research fellow med. unit, 1966-68; M.P., Sutton div. of Plymouth, 1966-74, Devonport div., 1974—; parliamentary sec. to Minister of Def., Adminstrn., 1967; under-sec. of state for def., Royal Navy, 1968-70; opposition def. spokesman, 1970-72; under-sec. of state Dept. Health and Social Security, 1974, Minister of State, 1974-76; sec. of state for Fgn. and Commonwealth Affairs, 1977-79; opposition spokesman for energy, 1979-80; chmn. Decision Tech. Internat., 1970-72; mem. Ind. Commn. on Disarmament and Security Issues, 1980—, Ind. Commn. on Internat. Humanitarian Issues, 1983—. Co-founder Social Democratic Party, 1981, leader, 1983-87, 88. Author: The Politics of Defense, 1972; In Sickness and in Health—The Politics of Medicine, 1976; Human Rights, 1978; Face the Future, 1981; A Future That Will Work, 1984; A United Kingdom, 1986, Our NHS, 1988; contbr. numerous articles to med. jours. Gov. Charing Cross Hosp., 1966-68; patron Disablement Income Group, 1968—; chmn. S.W. Regional Sports Council, 1967-71; co-founder Social Democratic Party, 1981, mem. nat. com., 1982—, leader 1983-87, 88—.

OWEN, GORDON PETER, local government officer, trust company director/secretary; b. London, England, June 28, 1953; s. William and Lucy Theodosia (Adams) O.; m. Janice Joel, Sept. 12, 1981; 1 child, Matthew David Peter. Prin., Messrs. G. Owen & Co., London, 1972—, Messrs. Rent-A-Bar Service, 1981—; chmn. Newham Youth Leaders' Assn., London, 1979-85, vice-chmn., 1978-79, exec. officer 1987—; dir., sec., trustee, founder Newham Youth Trust Ltd., London, 1983-85, chmn., 1976-79; now exec. officer, cons., developer, fundraiser, founder Newham Youth Lodge Hostel Project, 1967-69; Regional Health Authority appointee Newham Community Health Council, 1982-85. Brit. Council grantee, 1983. Fellow Inst. Dirs.; mem. Internat. Mgmt. Assn., Brit. Inst. Mgmt., Newham Youth Leaders Assn., Nat. Assn. Youth Clubs, Nat. Youth Bur., Newham Conf. Vol. Youth Orgns., London Union of Youth Clubs (chmn., coordinator 1980-85), Newham Vol. Agys. Council (children and young peoples steering com. 1981-83), Newham C. of C., Inst. Conf. Execs., Nat. Camping and Caravaning Club, Nat. Lic. Victuallers Assn., British Apple Systems Users Group, Nat. Assn. Youth Clubs. Mem. Church of England (mem. devel. com. St. Bartholomew's Ch. and Centre 1976-83, sec., mem. council, 1977, mem. council Parish East Ham Parochial Council, London 1977-85, sec. St. Bartholomew's Dist. Ch. Council, 1977—, mem. Newham Deanery Synod, London 1980-81, 82-84), The Carnival Guild. Home: 23 Beverley Rd, East Ham, London E6 3LH, England Office: PO Box 45, London E6 3LR, England

OWEN, HERBERT RODNEY, data processing executive; b. Bremerton, Wash., Oct. 10, 1935; s. Herbert Harry Owen and Maude Winona (Byington) Garner; children: Jeffrey Rod, Perry Jay. BSCE, Walla Walla Coll., 1962; BS in Phys. Scis., Wash. State U., 1973; M in Internat. Mgmt., Am. Grad. Sch. Internat. Mgmt., 1974. ADP intern Mgmt. Engring. Tng. Agy., Rock Island, Ill., 1963-64; ADP dir. Naval Sta., Keflavik, Iceland, 1968-70; ADP project mgr. Naval Ships System Command, Bremerton, 1970-74; supr. systems analyst Naval Supply Depot, Subic Bay, Philippines, 1975-79; ADP coordinator Far East Engring. Dist., Seoul, Republic of Korea, 1981-83; ADP security officer Trident Tng. Facility, Bangor, Wash., 1979-81, 83-85; ADP dir. Commdr. Fleet Activities, Okinawa, Japan, 1985—. Bus. mgr. Northwest Chess Mag. Mem. U.S. Chess Fedn. (sr. tournament dir.), Wash. Chess Fedn. (bd. dirs.), Am. Bowling Assn. (regional pres.). Republican. Clubs: Flying (Keflavik), Toastmasters. Office: Navy Air Facility Kadena ADP Commdr Fleet Activities Okinawa Seattle WA 98770-1150

OWEN, JOHN WYN, health care executive; b. Bangor, N. Wales, May 15, 1942; s. Idwal Wyn and Myfi (Hughes) O.; m. Elizabeth Ann MacFarlane, Apr. 1, 1967; children—Sian Wyn, Dafydd Wyn. B.A. St. Johns Coll. Cambridge, 1964; student Hosp. Adminstrv. Staff Coll., London, 1964-66; M.A., U. Cambridge, 1968; diploma in Hosp. Adminstrn., Inst. Health Service Adminstrs., London, 1968. Hosp. sec., Glantawe H.M.C., Swansea, 1967-70; sr. tng. officer Welsh Hosp. Bd., Cardiff, 1968-70; divisional adminstr., Univ. Hosp.-Wales, Cardiff, 1970-72; asst. clk. St. Thomas' Hosp., London, 1972-74, adminstr., 1974-79; exec. dir. United Med. Enterprises, London, 1979-85; dir. Allied Med. Group, London, 1979-85, Brit. Nursing Cooperations, London, 1979-85, AMG Healthcare Canada, Edmonton, 1982-85, Allied Shanning, London, 1983-85; dir. Welsh Office of Nat. Health Service, Cardiff, 1985—; chmn. Welsh Health Common Services Authority, 1985—. Author: publs. on hosp. planning. Trustee REFRESH, St. Thomas', Lambeth, London, 1976-78, The Florence Nightingale Mus. Trust, St. Thomas' Hosp., London, 1983—; sec. Standing Com. on Tching., Nat. Assn. Health Authorities, Birmingham, 1976-79; organist, United Reformed Ch., Fleet, Hampshire, 1975-85, United Free Ch., Cowbridge, 1985—. Travel fellow King Edward's Hosp. Fund, London, 1968, vis. fellow Am. Univ. Programs Health Adminstrn., U.S., 1971, Sch. Health Adminstrn., U. New South Wales, Australia, 1979. Fellow Royal Geog. Soc.; assoc. Inst. Health Service Adminstrs.; mem. Royal Inst. Pub. Adminstrn. Clubs: Johnian Soc. (Cambridge); Atheneum (London). Home: 3 Newton Farm, Newton near Cowbridge CF7 7RZ, Wales Office: Nat Health Services, Welsh Office, Cardiff CF1 3NQ, Wales

OWEN, LARRY GENE, university educator, electronic consultant; b. Pine Bluff, Ark., Oct. 2, 1932; s. Cecil Earl and Helen Marie (Jacks) O.; m. Ruth Myra Newton, Sept. 3, 1953; children—Deborah, Patricia, Larry Jr., Shea. BS in Physics and Math., U. So. Miss., 1967; MS in Ops. Mgmt., U. Ark., 1987. Enlisted in U.S. Air Force, 1951, advanced through ranks to m. sgt., 1968; electronic technician, 1951-61; communications supt., 1961-71, retired, 1971; tchr. math. and physics Southwestern Tech. Inst., Camden, Ark., 1971-72, tchr. electronics, 1972-75; dean tech. engring. So. Ark. U. Tech., Camden, 1975—. Mem. Instrumentation Soc. Am. (sr.); Am. Assn. Physics Tchrs., Am. Tech. Edn. Assn., Am. Vocat. Assn. Baptist. Home: 306 Lakeside Ave Camden AR 71701 Office: So Ark U Tech Camden AR 71701

OWEN, ROBERT HUBERT, lawyer, realtor; b. Birmingham, Ala., Aug. 3, 1928; s. Robert Clay and Mattie Lou (Hubert) O.; m. Mary Dane Hicks, Mar. 14, 1954; children: Mary Kathryn, Robert Hubert. B.S., U. Ala., 1950; J.D., Birmingham Sch. Law, 1956. Bar: Ala. 1957, Ga. 1965. Methods and procedures analyst, supr. Ala. Power Co., Birmingham, 1952-58; assoc. Martin, Vogtle, Balch & Bingham, Birmingham, 1958-63; asst. sec. So. Services, Atlanta, 1963-69; sec. Southern Co., Atlanta, 1969-71; sec., asst. treas. Southern Co., 1971-77; exec. v.p., sec., gen. counsel, dir. Proverbs 31 Corp., Marietta, Ga., 1978-81; pvt. practice law Marietta, 1978-85; v.p., gen. counsel Hubert Properties, 1985-86; now realtor Metro Brokers, Atlanta. Atlanta area rep. Inst. Basic Youth Conflicts, 1970-80. Served to maj. USAF, 1951-52, 61-62. Mem. Jasons, Delta Chi, Omicron Delta Kappa, Beta Gamma Sigma, Delta Sigma Pi, Phi Eta Sigma. Baptist. Home: 6590 Bridgewood Valley Rd NW Atlanta GA 30328 Office: 750 Hammond Dr Bldg One Atlanta GA 30328

OWEN, THOMAS LLEWELLYN, senior investment exec.; b. Patchogue, N.Y., June 24, 1928; s. Griffith Robert and Jeanette Roberts (Hatfield) O.; A.B. in Econs., Coll. William and Mary, 1951; postgrad. Columbia U., 1952, N.Y. Inst. Fin., 1960-62; M.B.A., N.Y. U., 1966. Exec. trainee Shell Oil Co., N.Y.C. and Indpls., 1951-59, supr., 1958-59; petroleum and chem. investment analyst Paine, Webber, Jackson & Curtis, N.Y.C., 1959-62; sr. oil investment analyst DuPont Investment Interests, Wilmington, Del., N.Y.C., 1962-66, asst. dir. research, 1964-66; v.p., sr. investment officer, mem. policy, investment coms. Nat. Securities and Research Corp., N.Y.C., 1966-75; sr. investment exec., v.p., portfolio mgr. F. Eberstadt & Co. and Eberstadt Asset Mgmt., Inc., N.Y.C., 1975—, mem. policy com., 1979—, also dir. portfolio rev. com. Mem. N.Y. Soc. Security Analysts, Oil Analysts Group N.Y., Am. Econ. Assn., Investment Assn. N.Y., Am. Petroleum Inst., Nat. Assn. Petroleum Investment Analysts, Internat. Assn. Energy Economists. Contbr. chpt. "Oil and Gas Industries" to Financial Analysts Handbook, 1975. Home: 251 E 32d St New York NY 10016 Office: Eberstadt Asset Mgmt Inc 61 Broadway New York NY 10006

OWENS, GARY, radio-TV performer, author; b. Mitchell, S.D., May 10; s. Bernard Joseph and Vennetta Florence (Clark); m. Arleta Lee Markell, June 26; children: Scott Michael, Christopher Dana. Student (Speech scholar), Dakota Wesleyan U., Mitchell; student, Mpls. Art Inst. With KMPC, Los Angeles, 1962-82; with KPRZ, Los Angeles, 1982—; with KFI, Los Angeles, 1986—; pres. The Foonman & Sons, Inc.; radio host Gary Owens Music Weekend, Lorimar Telepictures, 1987—; v.p., nat. creative dir. Gannett Broadcasting, 1985—. Radio performer, 1955—; nat. creative dir., Golden West Broadcasters, 1981-82; syndicated radio show The G.O. Spl. Report, 1969—; host: world-wide syndicated show Soundtrack of the 60's, 1981—, Biff Owens Sports Exclusive, 1981—; USA Today, Mut. Broadcasting System, 1982—; performer, writer: world-wide syndicated show Sesame St, 1969—, Electric Co, 1969—, Dirkniblick (Mathnet) CTW, 1988; numerous animated cartoons including Dyno-Mutt, ABC-TV, 1975—, Roger Ramjet, 1965—, Space Ghost, 1968, Perils of Penelope Pitstop, 1970, Square One, 1987, also over 1400 animated cartoons including Godzilla's Power Hour, 1979, Space Heroes, 1981, Mighty Orbots, 1984, World's Greatest Adventures, 1986; appeared: in films The Love Bug, 1968, Prisoner of Second Ave., 1975, Hysterical, 1982, Nat. Lampoon's European Vacation, 1985, others; performer: Rowan and Martin's Laugh-in, 1968-73; TV host: Gong Show, ABC-TV, 1976—, Monty Pythons Flying Circus, 1975—; regular performer: TV Games People Play, 1980-81, Breakaway, 1983—; author: Elephants, Grapes and Pickles, 1963; 12 printings The Gary Owens What To Do While You're Holding the Phone Book, rev, 1973, A Gary Owens Chrestomathy, 1980; author: (screenplay) Three Caraway Seeds and an Agent's Heart, 1979; columnist: (screenplay) Radio and Records newspaper, 1978—, Hollywood Citizen-News, 1965-67, Hollywood mag., 1983—, The Daily News, 1981—; rec. artist (screenplay), MGM, ABC, Epic, Warner Bros., RCA, Reprise, Decca. Chmn. Multiple Sclerosis dr. Los Angeles, 1972; chmn., grand marshall So. Calif. Diabetes Dr., 1974—; mayor City of Encino, Calif., 1972—; bd. govs. Grammy awards, 1968—, Emmy awards, 1972; adv. bd. Pasadena (Calif.) City Coll., 1969—, Sugar Ray Robinson Youth Found., 1971—; mem. nat. miracle com. Juvenile Diabetes Found., 1981—, nat. com. for Carousel Ball Children's Diabetes Found. Denver; radio adv. bd. U. So. Calif., 1980—; hon. chmn. Goodwill Industries Sporting Goods Dr., 1986, chmn. 1986 campaign.; bd. dirs. D-Fy (anti-drug org.), D.A.R.E. (drug education program) Los Angeles Police Dept., 1986. Named outstanding radio personality in U.S., 1965-79, top Radio Personality in World, Internat. Radio Forum, Toronto, 1977, Man of Yr. All-Cities Employees Assn., City of Los Angeles, 1968, Top Radio Broadcaster, Nat. Assn. Broadcasters, 1986, Radio Man of Yr. Nat. Assn. Broadcasters, 1986; recipient Distinguished Service award Hollywood Jaycees, 1966, David award, 1978, Hollywood Hall of Fame award, 1980, Am. award Cypress Coll., 1981, Carbon Mike award Pacific Broadcasters, 1987, 5 Grammy nominations, Emmy award for More Dinosaurs, 1986; Star on Hollywood Walk of Fame, 1981; honored by U.S. Dept. Treasury, 1985. Hon. mem. No. Calif. Cartoonists Assn.; mem. Cartoonists and Artists Profl. Soc. Office: 610 S Ardmore Los Angeles CA 90005

OWENS, GARY MITCHELL, family physician; b. Salisbury, Md., July 31, 1949; s. Avery Donovan and Elizabeth (Mitchell) O.; B.A., U. Pa., 1971; M.D., Thomas Jefferson U., 1975; m. Kristy Margaret Terrock, July 1, 1978; children: Aaron David, Scott Christopher, Stefanie Erin. Resident in family medicine Wilmington (Del.) Med. Center, 1975-78, chief resident, 1978, teaching assoc. dept. family medicine, 1978—; practice medicine specializing in family practice, Wilmington, 1978—; teaching assoc. dept. family medicine St. Francis Hosp., Wilmington, 1978—; med. dir. Phoenix Steel Co., 1980-87; med. dir. HMO of Delaware Valley, Delaware Plan, 1985—, assoc. med. dir. Quality Assurance, 1987—; cons. NorAm. Chem. Co., 1984—. Diplomate Am. Bd. Family Practice. Fellow Am. Acad. Family Physicians; mem. AMA, Med. Soc. Del. (congress of del. 1986-87), New Castle County Med. Soc., Del. Acad. Family Physicians (pres. 1984), Am. Occupational Med. Assn., Alpha Omega Alpha. Roman Catholic. Home: 76 Carter Way Glen Mills PA 19342 Office: 2700 Silverside Rd Wilmington DE 19810

OWENS, JOSEPH HERRON, lawyer, association executive; b. Winnsboro, S.C., Sept. 30, 1937; s. Joseph Herron and Eva (Nicholson) O. B.A., Univ. S.C., 1960, J.D., 1963; postgrad. Georgetown U. Law Ctr., 1965. Bar: S.C. Trust atty. C&S Nat. Bank, Atlanta, 1964-65; atty. U.S. Dept. Labor, Washington, 1965-66; asst. to U.S. Senator R.C. Byrd, Washington, 1966-73; exec. dir. Council State Rehab. Adminstrs., Washington, 1973—; mem. adj. faculty U. San Francisco, 1975—. Bd. dirs. Nat. Industries for Severely Disabled, 1974-77, St. John's Sch. for Spl. Children, Washington, 1980, Met. YMCA, Washington, 1971; exec. com. Pres.'s Com. on Employment of Handicapped, Washington, 1973—. Served with USAF, 1963-64. Mem. Nat. Rehab. Assn. (President's award 1980), Council for Exceptional Children, Nat. Rehab. Adminstrn. Assn., Assn. U.S. Senate Adminstrv. Assts. and Exec. Secs.

OWENS, RICHARD GEORGE, mental health administrator; b. Clinton, Iowa, June 1, 1946; s. Murray Riley and Margaret McBain (Owens) O.; BA, Hope Coll., 1968, tchr. cert., 1970; MA, Mich. State U., 1979, PhD, Mich. State U., 1987; m. Susan Elizabeth Sentman, June 15, 1968; 1 child, Joshua Morgan. Designer, draftsman Stone Container Corp., Chgo., 1968-69; chmn. art dept. Covert (Mich.) public schs., 1970-73; staff writer, art cons. United Educators, Inc., Lake Bluff, Ill., 1972-74; client supr. work activity center Allegan County Com. Mental Health Services, Allegan, Mich., 1974-75, supr. sheltered workshop, 1975-76; prodn. supr. Celebration Candle, Hart, Mich., 1976-77; direct care worker Alternative Services, Inc., Livonia, Mich., 1978-79, home mgr., 1979-80, Lansing area adminstr., 1980-84, tng. dir., 1984-87, chmn. ad hoc com. on staff tng. and devel., 1981-87; exec. dir. Making Things Work, Inc. 1987—; bd. dirs. Life Ctr., Inc., 1984—, Human Potential, Inc., 1985—; instr. adult edn. Pres., Saugatuck Renaissance Guild, 1974-75. Mem. Assn. Supervision and Curriculum Devel., State Wide Care Assn., East Lansing Arts Workshop. Presbyterian. Author: Ceramics As A Career, 1973; Kohoutek and the Queen, 1974. Home: 16400 Upton Rd #246 East Lansing MI 48823 Office: 15694 N East St Ste 7 Lansing MI 48906

OWNBY, PAUL DARRELL, ceramic engineer, educator; b. Salt Lake City, Nov. 9, 1935; s. Paul William and Isabel Hope (Pearson) O.; B.S., U. Utah, 1961; M.S. (Kaiser Aluminum & Chem. Co. fellow), Mo. Sch. Mines and Metallurgy, 1962; Ph.D. (Kennecott Copper fellow), Ohio State U., 1967; m. Nina Rose Mugleston, Aug. 31, 1961; children—Melissa, Heather, Kirsten, Shannon, Paul William, Evan Darrell, Martha. Research ceramist Battelle Meml. Inst., Columbus, Ohio, 1963-68; asst. prof. U. Mo., Rolla, 1968, assoc. prof., 1969-74, prof. ceramic engring., 1974—; chmn., chief exec. officer MRD Corp., 1984—; vis. scientist Max Planck Institut fur Werkstoff Wissenschaften, Stuttgart, Germany, 1974-75, 79; dir. Rinco, Inc., Rolla, Mo., 1972-77; cons. Battelle Meml. Inst., Columbus, 1968-70, Dynasil Corp. Am., 1969-74, 79-82, Eagle Picher Industries, Inc., 1968—, McDonnell Douglas Astronautics Co., 1974-76, Monsanto Co., 1979—, A.P. Green Refractories Co., 1979-80, Aspen Research, 1987, Digital Controls Inc., 1987—, Terratek, 1987—. Neighborhood commr. Central Ohio dist. Boy Scouts Am., 1966-67, instl. rep., 1970, 73-74, troop com., 1961-62, 70-74, chmn., 1973, instl. head, 1979-83, scoutmaster 1987—. Battelle Meml. Inst. fellow, 1973; recipient ASTM and ASM Hot Isostatic Pressing Hist. Landmark award Battelle Meml. Inst., 1985. Mem. Am. Ceramic Soc., Materials Research Soc., Ceramic Edn. Council, Keramos (outstanding Tchr. award 1985), Sigma Xi. Republican. Mem. Ch. Jesus Christ of Latter-day Saints. Inventor in field. Home: 8 Burgher Dr Rolla MO 65401 Office: U Mo Rolla MO 65401

OWONA, JOSEPH, political science educator; b. Akom, Cameroon, Jan. 23, 1945; s. Mathias Nguini Fouda and Elisabeth Ntsama; m. Emilierno Ngo Basse, 1969 (div. 1976); children: Nguini, Basse Francis; m. Oumou Waya Guindo, 1977; children: Joseph Wladiuni, Fuda Antin, Nfagne Felicite, Biudzi Toluas Boris. Lic. en droit, U. Yaounde, Cameroon; DES in Droit Public, U. Paris, 1969, DES in Polit. Sci., 1970, D of Polit. Sci. Asst. prof. U. Paris, 1970-72; head e. Office: Institut des Relations Internat, du Cameroon, BP 1637, Yaounde Cameroon

OWSLEY, WILLIAM CLINTON, JR., radiologist; b. Austin, Tex., Oct. 6, 1923; s. William Clinton and Lois (Lamar) O.; B.A., U. Tex., 1944; M.D., U. Pa., 1946; m. Betty Pinckard, 1949; 2 children. Intern, Hermann Hosp., Houston, 1946-47; resident Hosp. of U. Pa., Phila., 1949-52; instr. radiology U. Pa., 1950-52; practice medicine specializing in radiology, Houston, 1952—; mem. staff Hermann Hosp., Twelve Oaks Hosp., Bellville Hosp., St. Elizabeth Hosp., Brazos Valley Hosp.; assoc. clin. prof. radiology U. Tex. Served with USNR, 1947-48. Diplomate Am. Bd. Radiology. Fellow Am. Coll. Radiology, Am. Roentgen Ray Soc., Radiol. Soc. N.Am., Interam. Coll. Radiology, AMA. Republican. Baptist. Office: 214 Hermann Profl Bldg Houston TX 77030

OWUSU-ANSAH, TWUM, mathematics educator; b. Kumasi, Ghana, July 23, 1935; s. Kofi and Emma Twumwaa (Assoku) O.-A.; m. Faustina Forson, Jan. 6, 1966; children: Kwame Osei, Amma Twumwaa, Kwadwo Asare Ntim. BS (Lond.) Math., U. Ghana, Accra, 1960; MS, U. Alta., Edmonton, Can., 1968; PhD in Math., U. Toronto, Ont., Can., 1972. Math. tchr. St. Augustine's Coll., Cape Coast, Ghana, 1960-63; lectr. math. U. Sci. and Tech., Kumasi, 1963-74, sr. lectr., 1974-78, assoc. prof. math., 1978-84; prof. math. , 1984—; prof. math U. Ghana, Legon, part-time 1984-86. Editor: Proc. 2d Internat. Symposium on Functional Analysis and Its Applications, 1979; mem. editorial bd. Afrika Mathematika, Brazzaville, Congo, 1978—. Contbr. articles to profl. jours. and books. Govt. of Ghana scholar, 1957-60; Commonwealth scholar Govt. of Can., 1966-68; fellow U. Toronto, 1969-71. Mem. Am. Math. Soc., Can. Math. Soc., African Math. Union (exec. com. 1976-86), Governing Council of CSIR Ghana, African Network of Sci. and Tech. Instns. (vice chmn. 1985—). Anglican. Club: Sr. Staff (U. Sci. and Tech.). Avocations: music; reading; volleyball; cycling; swimming. Office: U Sci and Tech, Dept Math, Kumasi Ghana

OXNARD, CHARLES ERNEST, anatomist, anthropologist, educator; b. Durham, Eng., Sept. 9, 1933; arrived in Australia, 1987; s. Charles and Frances Ann (Golightly) O.; m. Eleanor Mary Arthur, Feb. 2, 1959; children: Hugh Charles Neville, David Charles Guy. B.Sci. with 1st class honors, U. Birmingham, Eng., 1955, M.B., Ch.B. in Medicine, 1958, Ph.D., 1962, D.Sc., 1975. Med. intern Queen Elizabeth Hosp., Birmingham, 1958-59; research fellow U. Birmingham, 1959-62, lectr., 1962-65, sr. lectr., 1965-66, court govs., 1958-66; assoc. prof. anatomy, anthropology and evolutionary biology U. Chgo., 1966-70, prof., 1970-78, gov. biology collegiate div., 1970-78, dean coll., 1973-77; dean grad. sch. U. So. Calif., Los Angeles, 1978-83; univ. research prof. biology and anatomy U. So. Calif., 1978-83, univ. prof., prof. anatomy and cell biology, prof. biol. scis., 1983-87; prof. anatomy and human biology, head dept. of anatomy and human biology U. Western Australia, 1987—; research assoc. Field Mus. Natural History, Chgo., 1967—; overseas assoc. U. Birmingham, 1968—; Lo Yuk Tong lectr. U. Hong Kong, 1973, hon. prof., 1978—, Chan Shu Tzu lectr., 1980, Octagan lectr. U. Western Australia, 1987, Latta lectr. U. Nebr., Omaha, 1987; research assoc. Los Angeles County Natural History Mus., 1984—, George C. Page Mus., Los Angeles, 1986—. Author: Form and Pattern in Human Evolution, 1973, Uniqueness and Diversity in Human Evolution, 1975, Human Fossils: The New Revolution, 1977, The Order of Man, 1983, Humans, Apes and Chinese Fossils, 1985, Fossils, Teeth and Sex, 1987, Animal Anatomies and Lifestyles, 1988; mem. editorial bd. Annals of Human Biology; cons. editor: Am. Jour. Primatology; contbr. articles to anat. and anthrop. jours. Recipient Book award Hong Kong Council, 1984, S.T. Chan Silver Medal, Univ. of Hong Kong, 1980; grantee USPHS, 1960-71, 74—, NSF, 1971—. Fellow N.Y. Acad. Sci., AAAS, So. Calif. Acad. Sci. (bd. dirs. 1985); Mem. Chgo. Acad. Soc. (hon. life), Australasian Soc. for Human Biology (pres.), Soc. for Study Human Biology (treas. 1962-66), Sigma Xi (pres. chpt., nat. lectr. 1987—), Phi Beta Kappa (pres. chpt.), Phi Kappa Phi (pres. chpt., Book award 1984). Office: U Western Australia, Nedlands WA 6009, Australia

OZ, AMOS, author; b. Jerusalem, Israel, 1939; m. Nily Zuckerman; children—Fania, Galia, Daniel. B.A., Hebrew U. Jerusalem; M.A., Oxford U. (vis. fellow 1969-70). Mem. Kibbutz Hulda, Israel, 1957—; author-in-residence Hebrew U. Jerusalem, 1975; author: Where the Jackals Howl, 1965; Somewhere Else, 1966; My Michael, 1968; Unto Death, 1971; Touch the Water, Touch the Wind, 1973; The Hill of Evil Counsel, 1976; Soumchi, 1978; Under the Blazing Light, 1979; A Perfect Peace, 1982; In the Land of Israel, 1983; A Black Box, 1987; contbr. articles to profl. jours. Recipient Holon prize for Lit., 1966; B'nai B'rith Annual Lit. award, 1972; Brenner prize, 1977; Bialik prize, 1986; Am. Israel Cultural Found. fellow. Mem. I.T.I., Internat. PEN Assn. Address: 17 Nof St, Arad Israel

OZAL, TURGUT, Turkish prime minister; b. Malatya, Turkey, 1927; s. Mehmet Siddik and Hafize Ozal; MSEE, Tech. U., Istanbul, Turkey, 1950; m. Semra Yeginmen; children: Ahmet, Zeynep Gonenc, Efe. With Elec. Survey Adminstrn., asst. to gen. dir.; spl. tech. adv. to prime minister Govt. of Turkey, 1965-67; undersec. State Planning Orgn., 1967-71, undersec. to prime minister, 1979-80, dep. prime minister, 1980-83, prime minister, 1983—; minister of state, from 1980; spl. projects advisor, sr. economist World Bank, 1971-83; leader Anatavan Partisi (Motherland Party). Office: Basbakanlik, Bakanliklar, Office of Prime Minister, Ankara Turkey *

OZAWA, SAKIHITO, secretary general of political party; b. Kofu, Japan, May 31, 1954; s. Takashi and Yoshino (Koike) O.; m. Toshiko Kikushima, Sept. 15, 1981; children: Kei, Yuh. Student in law, U. Tokyo, 1974-78. Banker dept. fgn. exchange Bank of Tokyo, 1983; sec.-gen. Forum for a Fair Soc. Japan's Liberal Dem. Party, Tokyo, 1983—. Buddhist. Office: Forum for a Liberal Society, Shuwa TBR Bldg 806, 10-2 Nagata-cho 2-chome Chiyoda-ku Tokyo 100, Japan

OZAWA, SEIJI, conductor, musical director; b. Shenyang, People's Republic of China, Sept. 1, 1935; s. Kaisaku and Sakura Ozawa; m. Vera Motoki-Ilyin; children: Seira, Yukiyoshi. Student, Toho Sch. Music, Tokyo, Japan, 1953-59; studies with, Hideo Saito, Eugene Bigot, Herbert Von Karajan, Leonard Bernstein; student at the invitation of Charles Munch, Tanglewood, 1959. Music dir. Boston Symphony Orch., 1973—. One of three asst. condrs., N.Y. Philharm., 1961-62 season, music dir. Ravinia Festival, 1964-68, music dir. Toronto Symphony Orch., 1965-69, San Francisco Symphony Orch., 1970-76, appointed artistic advisor Tanglewood Festival, 1970, condr. Boston Symphony Orch. Evening at Symphony (Emmy award);

music advisor Boston Symphony Orch., 1972-73; guest condr. major orchs. Recipient 1st prize Internat. Competion Orch. Condrs., 1959, Koussevitzky prize Tanglewood Music Ctr., 1960; conducting fellow Tanglewood Music Ctr., summer 1959. Home: via Giardini 941, 41040 Saliceta, Modena Italy Office: Boston Symphony Orch 301 Massachusetts Ave Boston MA 02115

OZAWA, YASUTOMO, nuclear scientist, educator; b. Hokkaido, Japan, Aug. 24, 1919; s. Torao and Nobu Ozawa; M.Sc. in Engring., Hokkaido U., 1942; D.Sc. (Brit. Council scholar 1952-54), Imperial Coll., London U., 1953; m. Yoko Shima, Nov. 2, 1946; 1 child, Tomohisa. Asst. prof., then prof. Research Inst. Applied Electricity, Hokkaido U., 1945—, prof. nuclear engring., 1959—; prof. Kyoto U., 1976-78; dir. Direct Energy Conversion Research Inst., 1978, dean Faculty Engring., 1981—; chmn. dept. elec. engring. Hokkaido Inst. Tech., 1984—; pres. Hakkaido Automotive Engring. Coll., 1985—; vice chmn. internat. liaison group on magnto hydro-dynamic elec. power generation, chmn. internat. orgNIZING COM. UNESCO, 1985—; mem. adv. com. Japanese Nuclear Regulatory Commn., 1979—. Recipient Prof. Shimizu's prize, 1942, Imperial Silver Watch, 1942. Mem. Atomic Energy Soc. Japan (v.p. 1978), Brit. Council Scholar's Assn. (pres. Hokkaido 1977—). Author books, papers in field. Home: West 27 North 1st, Sapporo 064, Japan Office: West 8, North 13, Sapporo 060, Japan

OZKAN, GUNER, physician, surgeon; b. Izmir, Turkey, Feb. 18, 1945; came to U.S., 1975; s. Ismail and Raziye (Tekin) O.; m. Gunay Karasu, Aug. 14, 1970; children—Ozgur Ismail, Zeynep Ozlem. M.D., Ege Universitesi, Izmir, 1968; specialist in physiology Ataturk U., Erzurum, Turkey, 1970. Diplomate Am. Bd. Surgery. Intern Washington Hosp. Ctr., 1975-76, resident, 1976-80; asst. prof. Ataturk U., 1968-73; staff surgeon VA Med. Ctr., Grand Island, Nebr., 1981—. Research grantee Turkish Sci. and Tech. Found., 1967-70; recipient Achievement award Upjohn Co., 1980. Islam. Avocation: swimming. Home: 1709 S Doreen St Grand Island NE 68801 Office: VA Med Ctr 2201 N Broadwell Grand Island NE 68801

ÖZKAN, HIKMET, diplomat; b. Mersin, Turkey, Apr. 10, 1924; s. Sakir and Fatma Özkan; m. Yasemin Özkan, Apr. 4, 1985. Licence, Faculty Polit. Scis., Ankara, Turkey, 1947. 3d sec. Ministry of Fgn. Affairs, Ankara, 1948-51, head section, 1957-59, dir. gen., 1971-75, dep. undersec., 1981-84; consul Consulate Gen. Turkey, Tabriz, Iran, 1951-57; counsellor Embassy of Turkey, Athens, Greece, 1959-64; consul gen. Stuttgart, Fed. Republic Germany, 1966-71; ambassador to Libya, Tripoli, 1975-78, Yugoslavia, Belgrade, 1978-81, German Dem. Republic, Berlin, 1984—. Home: Stavanger Str No 16, 1071 Berlin German Democratic Republic Office: Turkish Embassy, Schadow Str 6, 1080 Berlin German Democratic Republic

OZOLS, SANDRA LEE, lawyer; b. Casper, Wyo., June 24, 1957; d. Virgil Carr and Doris Louise (Conklin) McC.; m. Ojars Herberts Ozols, Sept. 2, 1978 (div.); children: Michael Ojars, Sara Ann, Brian Christopher. BA with distinction, U. Colo., 1978; JD magna cum laude, Boston U., 1982. Bar: Colo. 1982, U.S. Dist. Ct. Colo. 1985. Assoc. Cohen, Brame and Smith, Denver, 1983-84, Parcel, Meyer, Schwartz, Ruttum and Mauro, Denver, 1984-85, Mayer, Brown and Platt, Denver, 1985-87; region counsel Gen. Electric Capital Corp., Englewood, Colo., 1987—. Mem. Denver Bar Assn., Colo. Bar Assn., Phi Beta Kappa, Phi Delta Phi. Republican. Mem. Ch. of Christ. Home: 8086 S Willow Ct Englewood CO 80112 Office: Gen Electric Capital Corp 7409 S Alton Court #208 Englewood CO 80112

OZYAMAN, ISMAIL YAMAN, psychiatrist; b. Izmir, Turkey, May 22, 1929; came to U.S., 1962, naturalized, 1973; s. Halit and Feride O.; M.D., U. Ankara, 1955; m. Guler Basaran, Apr. 1, 1955; children—Emre Ak, Ege Roskow, Kenan. Diplomate Turkish Bd. Urology, Am. Bd. Psychiatry and Neurology; cert. mental health administr. Resident, U. Ankara Faculty of Medicine Urology Clinic, 1955-59; intern, Regina (Sask., Can.) Gen. Hosp., 1960-61, Grey Nuns' Hosp., Regina, 1961-62; resident St. Lawrence Psychiat. Center, Ogdensburg, N.Y., 1962-63; resident Harlem Valley Psychiat. Center, Wingdale, N.Y., 1963-64; resident Hudson River Psychiat. Center, Poughkeepsie, N.Y., 1967-68, chief service, 1970-84, also chmn. forensic and pharmacy coms.; urologist U. Ankara Faculty of Medicine, 1958; chief urology dept. Corlu Mil. Hosp., Turkey, 1959-60; chief urology service S.S. Yenisehir Hosp., Turkey, 1965-66; cons. Castlepoint (N.Y.) VA Hosp., 1977—; physicians' advisor Adirondack-Hudson-Mohawk Med. Peer Rev. Orgn.; cons. Greenhaven Correctional Facility, Stormville, N.Y., 1980—; med. dir. Harlem Valley Psychiatric Ctr., Wingdale, 1984—; cons. psychiatrist supreme and county cts., Dutchess County, N.Y., 1969—. Served with Turkish Army, 1959-60. Diplomate Am. Bd. Psychiatry and Neurology, Turkish Bd. Urology. Home: 3 Wallnut Hill Rd Poughkeepsie NY 12603 Office: Box 27 PO 330 Wingdale NY 12594

PABARCIUS, ALGIS, investment executive; b. Telsiai, Lithuania, May 1, 1932; came to U.S., 1950, naturalized, 1956; s. Vacius and Brone (Ziuryte) P.; B.S., U. Ill., 1955; M.S., Ill. Inst. Tech., 1958, Ph.D., 1964; postgrad. Technische Hochschule Muenchen, Germany, 1962; m. Eleanor A. Rakovic, Aug. 18, 1956; children—Nina, Lisa, Algis. Engr., Esso Research & Engring. Co., Linden, N.J., 1955-56; instr. U. Ill., Chgo., 1956-59, asst. prof., 1959-64; partner Zubkus, Zemaitis & Assocs., Architects and Engrs., Chgo., Washington, 1959-67; v.p. Garden Hotels Investment Co. and Whitecliff Corp., Lanham, Md., 1967-75; pres. Aras Investment Corp., 1975-79, Colony Funding Corp., Washington, 1979—. Registered profl. engr. Ill., D.C.; structural engr. Ill.; Danforth Found. grantee, 1960-61; NSF faculty fellow, 1961-62. Mem. ASCE, Sigma Xi, Tau Beta Pi, Sigma Tau, Chi Epsilon, Phi Kappa Phi. Home: 3251 Prospect St NW Washington DC 20007 Office: 3062 M St NW Washington DC 20007

PACE, LEONARD, retired management consultant; b. Torrington, Conn., Oct. 24, 1924; s. Anthony and Maria G. P.; m. Maureen Therese Murphy, Sept. 15, 1956; children: Leonard Anthony, Susan Maria, Daniel Graham, Thomas William, Mary Macaire, Cathleen Anne. Student, Syracuse U., 1943; B.S.M.E., U. Conn., 1949; postgrad., N.Y. U., 1951-52, Wayne U., 1955. Cert. mgmt. cons. With GAF, 1949-57, asst. to div. controller, 1954-57; with Deloitte Haskins and Sells, N.Y.C., 1957—, head N.Y. mgmt. adv. services, 1965-67, head Eastern region, 1967-76, nat. dir. mgmt. adv. services, 1976-85. Served as officer, pilot USAAF, 1943-45. Mem. Am. Mgmt. Assn., Inst. Mgmt. Cons. (dir., chmn. profl. standards com.). Clubs: Baltusrol Golf, Union League, Circumnavigators. Home: 35 Little Wolf Rd Summit NJ 07901 Office: Deloitte Haskins & Sells 111 Madison Ave Morristown NJ 07960

PACE, STANLEY CARTER, aeronautical engineer; b. Waterview, Ky., Sept. 14, 1921; s. Stanley Dan and Pearl Eagle (Carter) P.; m. Elaine Marilyn Cutchall, Aug. 21, 1945; children: Stanley Dan, Lawrence Timothy, Richard Yost. Student, U. Ky., 1939-40; B.S., U.S. Mil. Acad., 1943; M.S. in Aero. Engring., Calif. Inst. Tech., 1949; LLD (hon.), Maryville Coll., 1987. Commd. 2d lt. USAAF, 1943, advanced through grades to col., 1953; pilot, flight leader B-24 Group, 15th Air Force 1943-44; chief power plant br., procurement div. Hdqrs. Air Materiel Command Wright-Patterson AFB, Ohio, 1945-48; assignments, procurement div. Hdqrs. Air Materiel Command 1949-53, dep. chief prodn. Hdqrs. Air Materiel Command, 1952-53, resigned, 1954; with TRW, Inc., Cleve., 1954-85, successively sales mgr., asst. mgr., mgr. West Coast plant; mgr. jet div. Tapco plant, Cleve.; asst. mgr. Tapco group, 1954-58, v.p., gen. mgr., 1958-65, exec. v.p. co., 1965-77, pres., 1977-85, vice chmn., 1985, dir., 1965-85; vice chmn., dir. Gen. Dynamics Corp., St. Louis, 1985, chmn., chief exec. officer, 1985—, also bd. dirs.; dir. Consol. Natural Gas Co. Head United Way drive, Cleve., 1984; former council commr., pres. Great Cleve. Council Boy Scouts Am.; former trustee Nat. Jr. Achievement, Denison U., Judson Park; former chmn. Greater Cleve. Roundtable, Cleve. Found. Distbn. Com., Nat. Assn. Mfrs.; trustee Washington U. Decorated Air medal with oak leaf clusters. Mem. AIAA, Soc. Automotive Engrs., Delta Tau Delta. Clubs: Union, Pepper Pike, Eldorado, Rolling Rock, Log Cabin, St. Louis, St. Louis Country. Home: 2 Chatfield Rd Saint Louis MO 63141 Office: Gen Dynamics Corp Pierre Laclede Ctr Saint Louis MO 63105

PACEA, ION, painter; b. Salonica, Greece, Sept. 7, 1924; s. Dumitru and Ecaterina (Girtu) P.; m. Lucrezia Hagi; children—Liliana, Constantin. BA Bucharest Fine Arts Coll., 1949. Exhbns. in Romania, U.S.A., U.S.S.R., Fed. Republic Germany, German Dem. Republic, France, Eng., Italy, Israel, Greece, Poland, Czechoslovakia, Hungary, Bulgaria, Albania, Turkey, Yugoslavia, Tokyo, Venice, Sao Paulo; represented in pub. collections Collections of Aachem, Mannheim, Fed. Republic Germany, Szczecin, Poland, Sofia and Plovdiv, Bulgaria, Bucharest, Sibiu, Constanta, Romania; pvt. collections in Rome, Turin, Milan, Venice, N.Y.C., Munich, Paris, Chartres, France, Memphis, Toronto, Linköping, Stockholm, Tokyo, Sofia, Oberhauser, Siegen, N.Y.C., Washington. Recipient Romanian Acad. award, 1963, Trionfo 81 award, Rome. Mem. Romanian Fine Arts Union (sec., v.p., Acad. award 1963, Great Prize 1965). Office: 42 N Iorga, Bucharest Romania 1

PACH, JÁNOS, mathematician, researcher; b. Budapest, Hungary, May 3, 1954; s. Zsigmond Pal and Clara (Sos) P.; m. Anna Jemnitz, July 11, 1985. MA in Math., Eötvos U., Budapest, 1977, PhD in Math., 1980. Research asst. Math. Inst. Hungarian Acad. Scis., Budapest, 1977-80, research assoc., 1980-85, sr. research fellow, 1986—; research fellow Univ. Coll. London, 1981-82; vis. scientist McGill U., Montreal, Can., 1984, NYU Courant Inst., N.Y.C., 1986, 88; vis. asst. prof. SUNY, Stony Brook, 1985-86. Author: (with W.O.J. Moser) Research Problems in Discrete Geometry, 1985; editor Discrete and Computer Geometry, 1987—; contbr. articles on graph theory, combinatorics, convexity, discrete and computational geometry to profl. jours. Recipient Order of Higher Edn. Council Ministers Hungary, 1978, Gold Ring Pres. of Hungary, 1983, Young Researcher's award Hungarian Acad Scis., 1984. Mem. J. Bolyai Math. Soc. (editor Combinatorica 1981—, Grunwald medal 1982). Home: Nemetvolgyi ut 72/C, H-1124 Budapest Hungary Office: Hungarian Acad Scis Math Inst, Realtanoda u13-15, H-1053 Budapest Hungary

PACH, ZSIGMOND PAL, historian, educator; b. Oct. 4, 1919; s. Lipot and Rozsa (Weisz) P.; m. Klara Edit Sos, 1945; 2 children. Student, Budapest U. of Arts and Scis.; D. (hon.), Tartu U., 1982. Tchr. high sch. 1943-48; reader Budapest U. of Econs., 1948-52, prof. econ. history, 1952—, rector, 1963-67; dep. dir. Hungarian Acad. Sci. Inst. History, 1949-56, dir., 1967-85. Author: Gazdasagtortenet-a feudalizmus hanyatlasaig (Economic History up to the decline of Feudalism, 1947; Az eredeti tokefelhalmozas Magyarorszagon (Previous accumulation of capital in Hungary), 1952; A foldesuri gazdasag porosz-utas fejlodese Oroszorszagban a 19 sz masodik feleben (Development of the Prussian type manorial economy in Russia in the second part of the 19th century), 1958; Nyugateuropai es magyarorszagi agrarfejlodes a 15-17 sz-ban (West European and Hungarian Development of Agrarian Relations in the 15th to 17th centuries), 1963; Die ungarische Agrarentwicklung im 16-17 Jahrhundert, 1964; Problemi razvitiya vengerskoy marxistskoy istoricheskoy nauki, 1966; A nemzetkozi kereskedelmi utvonalak 15-17 sz-i athelyezodesenek kerdesehez (On the shifting of internat. trade routes in the 15th to 17th centuries), 1968; The Role of East Central Europe in International Trade: 16th and 17th Centuries, 1970; Le commerce du Levant et la Hongrie au Moyen Age, 1976; Tortenetszemlelet es tortenettudomany (History and Its View), 1978; The Transylvanian Route of Levant Trade at the Turn of the 15th and 16th Centuries, 1980; East Central Europe and World Trade at the Dawn of Modern Times, 1982; Business Mentality and Hungarian National Character, 1985; Történelem és nemzettudat (History and National Consciousness), 1987; mem. editorial bd. Jahrbuch fur Wirtschaftsgeschichte, Berlin, 1960—, The Economic History Rev., 1966-75. Mem. Hungarian Acad. Sci. (v.p. 1976-85, editor in chief Acta Historica), Istituto Internat. di Storia Economica, Internat. Econ. History Assn. (pres. 1978-82, hon. pres. 1982—), USSR Acad. Scis. (fgn. mem.), Bulgarian Acad. Scis. (fgn. mem.). Office: Nemetvolgyi ut 72/C, H-1124 Budapest Hungary

PACHE, BERNARD, engineering company executive; b. Sallanches, France, Oct. 13, 1934; s. Joseph and Sabine (Minjoz) P.; m. Yvette Vitaly, 1959; 3 children. Ed. Ecole Poly. de Paris, Ecole des Mines. Mining engr. 1957-63, asst. to Dir. of Mines, 1963-65, tech. advisor to Minister of Industry, 1965-67, Chief Mining Engr., 1967; asst to dir. uranium and nuclear activity dept., then dir. of mines div. of nuclear branch Pechiney-Ugine Kuhlmann, 1969-73; chmn. Compagnie Générale d'Electrolyse du Palais, 1972-76; dir. indsl. policy Pechiney-Ugine Kuhlmann Group, 1979-83; dep. dir. Co. Pechiney, 1983-84, mng. dir., 1984-86, hon. pres., 1986—; dir.-gen. Charbonnages de France, Paris, 1986—; gen. mgr. Soc. des Electrodes et Refractaires Savoie, 1972-73, Soc. Cefilac, 1973-74; bd. dirs., mng. dir. Soc. Française d'Electrometallurgie, 1974-79. Decorated Chevalier Legion d'Honneur. Office: Charbonnages de France, 9 avenue Percier, 75008 Paris France *

PACHECO, HUMBERTO, JR., lawyer; b. San José, Costa Rica, Jan. 10, 1940; s. Humberto and Julia (Alpizar) P.; gen. cert. in edn., Oxford (Eng.) U., 1958; legal degree U. Costa Rica, 1964; M.C.L., U. Miami (Fla.), 1971; postgrad. Harvard U. Law Sch., 1972, 76; m. Cynthia Ortiz, Mar. 7, 1975. Admitted to bar, 1965; mem. firm Pacheco Coto Law Offices, San José, 1959—, sr. ptnr., 1964—; legal adviser to pres. Costa Rica, also to sec. state fgn. affairs, 1970-78; dir. ITT de Costa Rica, S.A., Internat. Fin. Adv. Corp. Mem. Internat., Inter-Am., Costa Rican bar assns., Internat. Fiscal Assn., Am. C. of C. Costa Rica. Clubs: Baur Au Lac (Zurich); Palm Bay (Miami); Union, Country, Colon (Costa Rica). Contbr. articles to profl. jours. Office: PO Box 6610, San José Costa Rica

PACHELEQUE, CALISTO, historian; b. Nampula, Mozambique, May 5, 1957; s. Rodrigues Mauazio Metote P. Lic., U. Eduardo Mondlane, Mozambique, 1985. Asst. documentalist Ctr. African Studies Eduardo Mondlane U., Maputo, Mozambique, 1983-87; documentalist Ctr. African Studies Eduardo Mondlane U., Maputo, 1985—. Office: Ctr African Studies, U Eduardo Mondlane, SP1993 Maputo Mozambique

PACHETTI, RENATO MATTEO, TV company executive; b. Massa Carrara, Italy, Aug. 26, 1925; s. Ulderico and Angela (Ariani) P.; came to U.S., 1970; grad. in Pharm. Chemistry, U. Modena (Italy), 1950; m. Diane Finney, Dec. 29, 1965; children—Alex, Nicholas, Edward. Fgn. news editor RAI-Radio-TV Italiana, Rome, 1955-60; corr. RAI UN, N.Y.C., 1960-62; dir. radio programs RAI, Rome, 1963-69; pres. RAI Corp., N.Y.C., 1970—. Decorated grand officer Order Merit Republic of Italy. Mem. Fgn. Press Assn. (pres. 1972-73), Internat. Council TV Arts and Scis. (chmn. bd. 1978), Am.-Italy Soc. (v.p. 1976), Gruppo Esponenti Italiani (pres. 1977). Clubs: Met., Mid-Atlantic. Home: 525 Park Ave New York NY 10021 Office: 1350 Ave of Americas New York NY 10019

PACIFIC, JOSEPH NICHOLAS, JR., educator; b. Honolulu, Oct. 27, 1950; s. Joseph Nicholas Sr. and Christine Mary (Mondelli) P.; m. Paulette Kay Miller, July 7, 1975. BA in Math., BS in Biology, BSEE, Gonzaga U., 1974; MMSc in Clin. Microbiology, Emory U., 1978. Cert. tchr., Hawaii, Wash. Research specialist Ctr. Disease Control, Atlanta, 1978-82; supr. Joe Pacific Shoe Repair, Honolulu, 1983; lab. technician Mont. State U., Bozeman, 1984; sci. tchr. Hawaii Preparatory Acad., Kamuela, 1985-87; unit mgr. Hawaii Med. Service Assn., Honolulu, 1987—. Mem. Nat. Registry Microbiologists, Sigma Xi, Pi Mu Epsilon, Phi Sigma, Kappa Delta Pi, Alpha Sigma Nu. Home: 2013 Kaola Way Honolulu HI 96813 Office: Hawaii Med Service Assn Utilization Rev Dept 818 Keeaumoku St Honolulu HI 96814

PACINO, FRANK GEORGE, physician; b. Los Angeles, Sept. 4, 1930; s. Frank G. and Alicia (Rodriquez) P. M.D., Calif. Coll. Medicine, 1962; M.P.H., Loma Linda U., 1970. Intern Glendale Community Hosp., Calif., 1961-62; venereal disease physician Los Angeles County Dept. Health, 1963-64, asst. chief div. venereal disease, 1964-66; dist. health officer San Antonio Dept. Health, 1966-72, Harbor Health Dist., 1972—; practice medicine specializing in public health San Pedro, Calif., 1972—; med. dir. South Coast Alcohol Program, 1972—. Served with AUS, 1954-56. Recipient cert. of appreciation Los Angeles County Health Dept., 1966; commendation Los Angeles County Bd. Suprs., 1975. Mem. Physicians Assn. Los Angeles County (pres. 1972-73, 81-82, Physician Recognition award 1972), Am. Assn. Public Health Physicians (pres. 1975-76, pres. Calif. chpt. 1977-78, 81-82), So. Calif. Public Health Assn. (chmn. fins.), Public Health Physicians Assn. (pres. 1970-71), Calif. Med. Assn., AMA (Physician Recognition award 1969, 72, 73-76), Los Angeles Med. Assn., Phi Chi. Office: 122 W 8th St San Pedro CA 90731

PACK, PHOEBE KATHERINE FINLEY, civic worker; b. Portland, Oreg., Feb. 2, 1907; d. William Lovell and Irene (Barnhart) Finley; student U. Calif., Berkeley, 1926-27; B.A., U. Oreg., 1930; m. Arthur Newton Pack, June 11, 1936; children: Charles Lathrop, Phoebe Irene. Layman referee Pima County Juvenile Ct., Tucson, 1958-71; mem. pres.'s council Menninger Found., Topeka; mem. Alcoholism Council So. Ariz., 1960—; bd. dirs. Kress Nursing Sch., Tucson, 1957-67, Pima County Assn. for Mental Health, 1958—, Ariz. Assn. for Mental Health, Phoenix, 1963—, U. Ariz. Found., Casa de los Niños Crisis Nursery; co-founder Ariz.-Sonora Desert Mus., Tucson, 1975—, Ghost Ranch Found., N.Mex.; bd. dirs. St. Mary's Hosp., Tucson, Tucson Urban League, Tucson YMCA Youth Found. Mem. Mt. Vernon Ladies Assn. Union (state vice regent, 1962-84),Mt. Vernon One Hundred (founder), Nature Conservancy (life), Alpha Phi. Home: Villa Compana Apt 415 6653 E Carondelet Dr Tucson AZ 85710

PACKARD, JOHN MALLORY, physician; b. Saranac Lake, N.Y., Sept. 25, 1920; s. Edward Newman and Mary Bissell (Betts) P.; m. Ann Maurine Schoonover, June 15, 1944; children: Michael David, John Mallory, Ann Maurine, Mary Betts, Charles Edward, Kris Asvananda, Frank Schoonover, Charlotte Mellen. B.A., Yale U., 1942; M.D., Harvard U., 1945. Diplomate Am. Bd. Internal Medicine. Intern Presbyn. Hosp., N.Y.C., 1945-46; resident in internal medicine Peter Bent Brigham Hosp., Boston, 1948-49; practice medicine specializing in internal medicine and cardiology Pensacola, Fla., 1954-68; prof. medicine, asso. dean Med. Sch. U. Ala., Birmingham, 1968-76; exec. dir. Ala. Regional Med. Program, Birmingham, 1968-73; corp. v.p. med. edn. Bapt. Med. Centers, Birmingham, 1976—. Contbr. articles to med. jours. Served with USN, 1946-54. Fellow ACP, Am. Coll. Cardiology, Council Clin. Cardiology; mem. Jefferson County Med. Soc., Med. Assn. Ala., AMA, Am. Soc. Internal Medicine, Ala. Soc. Internal Medicine (pres. 1981-82), Alpha Omega Alpha. Democrat. Episcopalian. Office: 3201 4th Ave S Birmingham AL 35222

PACKARD, VANCE OAKLEY, writer; b. Granville Summit, Pa., May 22, 1914; s. Philip Joseph and Mabel (Case) P.; m. Mamie Virginia Mathews, Nov. 25, 1938; children: Vance Philip, Randall Mathews, Cynthia Ann. B.A., Pa. State U., 1936; M.S., Columbia U., 1937; Litt.D., Monmouth Coll., 1975. Reporter Centre Daily Times, State College, Pa., 1936; columnist Boston Record, 1937-38; writer, editor Asso. Press Feature Service, 1938-42; editor, staff writer Am. mag., 1942-56; staff writer Collier's mag., 1956; lectr. reporting, mag. writing Columbia, 1941-44, N.Y.U., 1945-57; guest lectr. several hundred colls. and univs., U.S. and 18 other countries. Author: Animal IQ, 1950, The Hidden Persuaders, 1957, The Status Seekers, 1959, The Waste Makers, 1960, The Pyramid Climbers, 1962, The Naked Society, 1964, The Sexual Wilderness, 1968, A Nation of Strangers, 1972, The People Shapers, 1977 (Notable Book of 1977, ALA), Our Endangered Children, 1983. Mem. planning commn., New Canaan, Conn., 1954-56; pres. Chappaquiddick Island Assn., 1977-78; mem. nat. bd. Nat. Book Com.; Trustee Silvermine Coll. Art. Recipient Distinguished Alumni award Pa. State U., 1961; Outstanding Alumni award Grad. Sch. Journalism, Columbia, 1963. Mem. Soc. Mag. Writers (pres. 1961); mem. Am. Sociol. Assn., Authors' Guild, Am. Acad. Polit. and Social Sci., Population Resource Ctr. (bd. dirs.). Home: 87 Mill Rd New Canaan CT 06840

PACKER, BERNARD JULES, labor association executive; b. Phila., July 7, 1934; s. Samuel and Eve (Devine) P.; children: Tatiana Consuelo, Jessica Lisa. BA, UCLA, 1958. Merchant seaman Scandinavian Vessels, 1958-60; contract interpreter U.S. State Dept., Washington, 1960-68; interpreter, prof. Am. Inst. Free Labor Devel., Front Royal, Va., 1968-78; program dir. Am. Inst. Free Labor Devel., Lima, Peru, 1978-83, Tegucigalpa, Honduras, 1983-84, San Salvador, El Salvador, 1984-85, Bogata, Columbia, 1985-87. Author: Caro, 1975 (book of month club alt. selection, 1975), The Second Death of Samuel Auer, 1979, The Sons of Saintly Women, 1981. Served with USAF, 1952-53. Office: Am Inst Free Labor Devel 1015 20th St NW Washington DC 20036

PACKER, KERRY FRANCIS BULLMORE, publishing company executive; b. Sydney, Australia, Dec. 17, 1937; s. Frank and Lady P.; m. Roslyn Weedon, 1963; 2 children. Student Cranbrook Sch., Geelong Ch. of Eng. Grammar Sch. Chmn. Consol. Press Holdings Ltd. 1974—; chmn. Australian Consol. Press Ltd., 1974—; dir. Muswellbrook Energy & Minerals Ltd. promoter World Series Cricket, Australia, 1978-79; came to agreement with Australian Cricket Bd. in organizing and televising Test Series, Australia, 1979-80. Office: Australian Consol Press Ltd, 54 Park St, Sydney, New South Wales 2000, Australia

PACKO, JOSEPH JOHN, industrialist; b. Toledo, Mar. 9, 1925; s. Joseph Steve and Mary (Toth) P.; student thermodynamics engring. John Carroll U., U. N.C., 1943-44; B.S. in Physics, Math., Bus. Adminstrn., Fin., Bowling Green State U., 1948; postgrad. in nuclear chemistry Toledo U., 1950; D.Sc. in Comml. Sci., Southeastern Mass. U., 1969; m. Bette Throne, July 10, 1948; children—Jo Anne, Mark. With Packo Industries, Ft. Lauderdale, Fla., 1953—; pres. J.J. Packo Mortgage Corp., 1954-69; pres. Packo Enterprises, 1955—, S. Fla. Asphalt Co., 1956-65; pres., chmn. Am. Dynamics Internat., Inc. 1967-73, Packo Internat., 1978—; chmn. bd., chief exec. officer Cryo-Chem Internat. Inc., 1982—. Mem. Trade Mission, West Berlin, 1965; adv. panel Dept. Army, 1974-78. Bd. dirs. Fla. chpt. Nat. Soc. Prevention Blindness, Holy Cross Hosp., Nova U. Alumnae Assn., A.R.C. Served with USNR, 1943-45. Mem. Opera Guild Ft. Lauderdale, Young Presidents Orgn. (vice-chmn., sec.-treas. Fla. chpt.), Am. Mgmt. Assn., AAAS, Symphony Soc., Asphalt Inst., Nat. Bd. Realtors, Nat. Mortgage Bankers Assn., Nat. Bituminous Assn., Bowling Green U. Alumni, Southeastern Mass. U. Alumni, Navy League, Sigma Xi. Clubs: Lago Mar Country, Capitol Hill; Onion Creek Country (Austin, Tex.). Patentee in field. Home: 119 Colonial Dr Saint Simons Island GA 31522

PACKWOOD, BOB, senator; b. Portland, Oreg., Sept. 11, 1932; s. Frederick William and Gladys (Taft) P.; m. Georgie Ann Oberteuffer, Nov. 25, 1964; children: William Henderson, Shyla. A.B., Willamette U., 1954; LL.B., NYU, 1957; LL.B. (hon.), Yeshiva U., 1982, Gallaudet Coll., 1983. Chmn. Multnomah County Rep. Cen. Com., 1960-62; mem. Oreg. Legislature, 1963-69; U.S. senator from Oreg. 1969—, chmn. fin. com., mem. commerce, sci. and transp. com., 1985-87. Mem. Internat. Working Group of Parliamentarians on Population and Devel., 1977; mem. Pres.'s Commn. on Population Growth and the Am. Future, 1972; chmn. Nat. Rep. Senatorial Com., 1977-78, 81-82; bd. dirs. NYU, 1970; bd. overseers Lewis and Clark Coll., Portland, 1966. Named One of Three Outstanding Young Men of Oreg., 1967; Portland's Jr. 1st Citizen, 1966; Oreg. Speaker of Yr., 1968; recipient Arthur T. Vanderbilt award NYU Sch. Law, 1970; Anti-Defamation League Brotherhood award, 1971; Torch of Liberty award B'nai B'rith, 1971; Richard L. Neuberger award Oreg. Environ. Council, 1972; Conservation award Omaha Woodmen Life Ins. Soc., 1974; Monongahela Forestry Leadership award, 1976; Solar Man of Yr., Solar Energy Industries Assn., 1980; Guardian of Small Bus. award Nat. Fedn. Ind. Bus., 1980; Forester of Yr., Western Forest Industries Assn., 1980; Am. Israel Friendship award B'nai Zion, 1982; Grover C. Cobb award Nat. Assn. Broadcasters, 1982; Religious Freedom award Religious Coalition for Abortion Rights, 1983; 22d Ann. Conv. award Oreg. State Bldg. and Constrn. Trade Council, 1983, United Cerebral Palsy Humanitarian award, 1984, Am. Heart Assn. Pub. Affairs award, 1985, Margaret Sanger award Planned Parenthood Assn., 1985, "Worth his Wheat in Gold award Gen. Mills for leadership on tax reform, 1986, Am. Assn. Homes for the Aging for Outstanding Service in cause of elderly, 1987, NARAL award for congrl. leadership, 1987, numerous others. Mem. Oreg., D.C. bar assns., Beta Theta Pi. Office: 259 Russell Senate Bldg Washington DC 20510

PACKWOOD, CYRIL OUTERBRIDGE, librarian; b. Paget, Bermuda, Nov. 22, 1930; s. Cyril Alexander and Gladys (Outerbridge) P.; m. Dorothy C. Cunningham, Nov. 15, 1958; 1 child, Cheryl A. BA in History with honors, Fisk U., 1953; MSLS, Case Western Res. U., 1954; MA, CUNY, 1972. Lic. librarian, N.Y. Supr. librarian N.Y. Pub. Library, N.Y.C., 1957—; chief librarian Borough of Manhattan Community Coll., N.Y.C., 1985; head librarian Bermuda Library, Bermuda, 1985—. Author: Chained on the Rock, 1975, Biography Detour: Bermuda Destination, 1977. Served with U.S. Army, 1955-57. Mem. ALA, Can. Library Assn., Assn. Caribbean U. Research and Instnl. Libraries, Assn. Caribbean Historians, Beta Phi Mu. A.M.E. Home: PO Box HM 762, Hamilton HMCX, Bermuda Office: Bermuda Library, 13 Queen St, Hamilton HM11, Bermuda

PADBERG, MANFRED WILHELM, mathematics educator, researcher; b. Bottrop, North-Rhine, Westphalia, Fed. Republic Germany, Oct. 10, 1941;

came to U.S., 1968; s. Fritz Georg and Franziska (Grosse-Wilde) P.; m. Brigitte Anna Trager, July 7, 1967 (div. 1980); children—Britta, Marc Oliver. Diploma in mathematics Westfalische Wilhelms U., 1967; M.S. in Industrial Adminstrn., Carnegie-Mellon U., 1971, Ph.D., 1971. Scientific asst. Universitat, Mannheim, Fed. Republic Germany, 1967-68; research fellow IIM, Berlin, 1971-74; assoc. prof. NYU, N.Y.C., 1974-78, prof. ops. research, 1978—; vis. prof. Bonn (Fed. Republic Germany) U., 1974, IBM Research, Yorktown Heights, N.Y., 1975-76, Westfälische Wilhelms U., Münster, Fed. Republic Germany, 1978, Inst. Nat. de Recherche en Informatique et d'Automatique, Rocquencourt, France, 1980-81, Univ. Cath. de Louvain, Belgium, 1981-82, Centro Nat. di Riccerche Roma, 1982, U. Scientifique et Med. de Grenoble, France, 1984, SUNY, Stony Brook, 1987, Cen. Nat. de la Recherche Sci., Paris, 1988, others; cons. in field. Editor: Combinatorial Optimization, 1980; contbr. numerous articles to profl. jours. Mem. Ops. Research Soc. (Lanchester prize 1983), Math. Programming Soc. (G.B. Dantzig prize 1985). Avocation: traveling. Office: NYU Washington Sq New York NY 10003

PADEN, CAROLYN EILEEN BELKNAP, dietitian; b. Takoma Park, Md., Dec. 10, 1953; d. Donald Julius and Lydian Allyne (Plyer) Belknap; m. Raymond Louis Paden, Dec. 29, 1985. BS in Home Econs. cum laude, Southern Coll., 1977; MS in Nutrition, Loma Linda (Calif.) U., 1983. Registered dietitian. Dietitic tech. Loma Linda U. Med. Ctr., 1978-82, nutritional support dietitian, 1982-84; clin. dietitian Mercy Meml. Med. Ctr., St. Joseph, Mich., 1984-86, chief clin. dietitian, 1986—; instr. dietetics Andrews U., Berrien Springs, Mich., 1986—; researcher nutritional status of hospitalized patients Mercy Meml. Med. Ctr., St. Joseph, 1986, 87; cons. nutritional support various Berrien County hosps., 1984—. Mem. Am. Dietetic Assn., Am. Soc. Parenteral and Enteral Nutrition. Adventist. Home: 195 Knott Rd Niles MI 49120 Office: Mercy Meml Med Ctr 1234 Napier Ave Saint Joseph MI 49085

PĀDHI, BIBHU PRASAD, English literature educator; b. Cuttack, India, Jan. 16, 1951; s. Nilāchal and Padma (Rath) P.; m. Minākshi Rath, Mar. 7, 1976; children: Buddhāditya, Silāditya. BA, Ravenshaw Coll., Cuttack, India, 1969, MA, 1971. Lectr. English Regional Coll. Edn., Bhubaneshwar, India, 1972-74; sr. lectr. English Ravenshaw Coll., Cuttack, India, 1974—. Author: (poems) Going to the Temple, 1988; D.H. Lawrence: Modes of Fictional Style, 1988; contbr. poems to Indian, Can., Am., Brit., Swiss, Australian and New Zealand mags. Mem. MLA, D.H. Lawrence Soc. N. Am., Indian Assn. English Studies, Indian Assn. for Am. Studies. Home: College Sq, Cuttack 753 003, India Office: Ravenshaw Coll Dept English, College Sq, Cuttack 753 003, India

PADILLA, FELIPE LIM, public health physician; b. Santa Rosa, Nueva Ecija, Philippines, Sept. 22, 1930; s. Numeriano Padilla and Patrocinio Lim; m. Anita Hidalgo, Dec. 26, 1958 (dec. Aug. 1983); children: Teresita, Fraulein; m. Julia Vallarta, Oct. 20, 1984. MD, U. Santo Tomas, 1956. Mcpl. health officer Dept. of Health, Munoz, Nueva Ecija, 1957—. Recipient cert. of Merit Province of Nueva Ecija, 1973, 75, Regional Health Office #3, 1981, 82; named Outstanding Rural Health Physician Govt. of Philippines, 1982, Govt. Physician of Yr. Province of Nueva Ecija, 1971. Mem. Philippine Med. Assn., Nueva Ecija Med. Soc. (plaque of Merit 1976, cert. of Merit 1981). Roman Catholic. Home: San Sebastian St, Munoz Nueva Ecija Philippines

PADILLA, TIBURCIO MENDEZ, physician; b. Argao, Cebu, Philippines, July 13, 1908; s. Wenceslao Kintanar Padilla and Claudia Mendez; m. Concesa Montecillo; children: Rosario, Ernesto, Osbaldo, Merle, Cristino, Marietta, Aida, Mercedita, Carmelita, Francisco, Milagros, Lorenzo, Jane. MD, U. St. Tomas, Manila, 1937. Diplomate Family Medicine. med. referee The Philippine Am. Life Ins. Co., Manila, 1960-80, med. ins. examiner, 1980—. Decorated Papal Knight of St. Gregory the Great Pope John Paul II, 1979; family named Model Filipino Family World Family Inst., 1984. Fellow Philippine Acad. Family Physicians; mem. Philippine Acad. Family Physician (pres. 1975-76), Cebu Med. Soc. (Most Outstanding Physician 1980), Philippine Med. Assn. Roman Catholic. Lodge: KC (Past Faithful Navigator, Past Dist. Dep., Master of 4th degree 1986-88). Home: 32-E Arlington Pond St, Cebu City 6000, Philippines

PAGANI, ALBERT LOUIS, aerospace system engineer; b. Jersey City, Feb. 19, 1936; s. Alexander C. and Anne (Salvati) P.; m. Beverly Cameron, Feb. 23, 1971; children: Penelope, Deborah, Michael. BSEE, U.S. Naval Acad., 1957; MBA, So. Ill. U., 1971. Commd. 2d lt. USAF, 1957, advanced through grades to col., 1978; navigator USAF, Lake Charles, La., 1957-63; pilot USAF, McGuire AFB, N.J., 1963-65; command pilot USAF, Anchorage, Alaska, 1965-68; mgr. airlift USAF, Saigon, Socialist Republic of Vietnam, 1968-69; chief spl. missions USAF, Scott AFB, Ill., 1969-74; commd. tactical airlift group USAF Europe, Mildenhall, Eng., 1974-76; dep. comdr. Rhein Main Air Base USAF Europe, Frankfurt, Fed. Republic Germany, 1976-78; chief airlift mgmt. USAF Military Airlift Command, Scott AFB, Ill., 1978-81, dir. tech. plans and concepts, 1981, dir. command and control, 1982-85; ret. 1985; mem. sr. staff C3I systems Lockheed Missile and Space Co., Sunnyvale, Calif., 1985—. V.p. Cath. Ch. Council, Mildenhall, 1974, pres., 1975. Decorated Legion of Merit, Bronze Star, Air medal, Vietnam Cross of Gallantry. Mem. Nat. Def. Transp. Assn., Soc. Logistics Engrs., Air Force Assn., Armed Forces Communication and Electronics Assn., Air Lift Assn., Daedalions, Mensa. Home: 41090 Driscoll Terr Fremont CA 94539 Office: Lockheed Missile and Space Co Advanced Programs 69-90 1111 Lockheed Way Sunnyvale CA 94539

PAGE, DENNIS, coal industry scientist; b. Darjeeling, India, Aug. 2, 1932; arrived in U.K., 1934; s. Arthur and Doris Harriet (Dixon) P.; m. Mary Bernadette Leonard, June 10, 1957; children: Carol, Julie, Geraldine, Denise, Christopher. Grad. Royal Inst. of Chemistry, Rutherford Coll. Tech., Newcastle Upon Tyne, 1957; M in Philosophy, Sunderland Poly, 1972. mem. tech. com. Brit. Standards Inst., London, 1980—; adviser radiation protection Brit. Coal, London, 1986—. Asst. analyst Nat. Coal Bd., Durham County, Eng., 1949-60; research asst. Nat. Coal Bd., Newcastle upon Tyne, 1964-77, head investigations, 1977-82; hdqrs. scientist Nat. Coal Bd., Harrow, Eng., 1982-87; research asst. Imperial Chem. Industries, Billingham, Eng., 1961-64; sr. scientist Brit. Coal, Burton on Trent, Eng., 1987—. Patentee in field; contbr. articles to profl. jours. Fellow Royal Soc. Chemistry. Roman Catholic. Office: Brit Coal Sci Control, Ashby Rd Bretby, Burton on Trent Staffordshire DE15 0QD, England

PAGE, ELLIS BATTEN, behavioral scientist, educator; b. San Diego, Apr. 29, 1924; s. Frank Homer and Dorothy (Batten) P.; m. Elizabeth Latimer Thaxton, June 21, 1952; children: Ellis Batten (Tim), Elizabeth Page Sigman, Richard Leighton. A.B., Pomona Coll., 1947; M.A., San Diego State U., 1955; Ed.D., UCLA, 1958; postdoctoral (NSF fellow), U. Mich., 1959; postdoctoral (fellow), MIT, 1966-67. Tchr. secondary schs. Calif., 1952-56; mem. psychology dept. San Diego City Coll., 1957-58; dir. guidance and testing Eastern Mich. U., 1958-60; dean Coll. Edn., prof. edn. and psychology Tex. Woman's U., 1960-62, dir. Bur. Edn1. Research, 1962-70; prof. ednl. psychology U. Conn., 1962-79; prof. ednl. psychology and research Duke U., 1979—; vis. prof. U. Wis., 1960, 62, Stanford U., 1964, Harvard U., 1968-69, Universidad Javeriana, Bogotá, 1975; leader Ford Found. research adv. team Venezuelan Ministry Edn., Caracas, 1969-70; vis. prof. Spanish Ministry Edn., 1972, 80, 82-85; research cons. U.S. Office Edn., USN, San Diego, Nat. Inst. Edn., Bur. Edn. Handicapped; chmn. nat. planning com. Nat. Center Edn. Stats.; adviser Brazilian Ministry Edn., 1973, 80; chief Ministerial Commn. Edn., Bermuda, 1983-85; mem. adv. council for edn. stats. U.S. Dept. Edn., 1987—. Author, editor in field. Served to capt. USMCR, 1943-46. Recipient Disting. Alumnus award San Diego State U., 1980. Fellow AAAS (life), Am. Psychol. Assn. (pres. ednl. psychology 1976-77), Nat. Conf. Research English, Philosophy Edn. Soc.; mem. Am. Ednl. Research Assn. (pres. 1979-80), Am. Personnel and Guidance Assn. (life), Nat. Council Measurements in Edn., Am. Statis. Assn. (officer N.C. chpt.), Behavior Genetics Assn., Assn. Computational Linguistics, N.C. Assn. Research Edn. (Disting. Research award 1981, pres. 1984-85), Rhetoric Soc. Am. (dir.), Psychometric Soc., Sociedad Española de Pedagogia (hon.), Sigma Xi, Phi Kappa Phi, Phi Gamma Delta, Psi Chi, Kappa Delta Pi, Phi Delta Kappa (life; service key). Anglican. Home: 110 Oakstone Dr Chapel Hill NC 27514 Office: 213 W Duke Bldg Duke U Durham NC 27708

PAGE, GENEVIEVE, actress; b. Paris, Dec. 13, 1927; d. Jacques Bonjean and Germaine Lipmann; m. Jean-Claude Bujard, 1959; 2 children. Student Lycee Racine, Paris, Sorbonne, Paris, Conservatoire nat. d'art dramatique. Prin. actress in the Comedie Francaise and Jean-Louis Barrault Co.; appeared in many famous classical and tragic stage roles; numerous film appearance include: Ce siecle a cinquante ans, Pas de pitie pour les femmes, Fanfan la tulipe, Lettre ouverte, Plaisirs de Paris, Nuits andalouses, L'etrange desir de M. Bard, Cherchez la femme, L'homme sans passe, Foreign Intrigue, The Silken Affair, Michael Strogoff, Un amour de posche, Song Without End, Le bal des adieux, El Cid, Les egarements, Le jour et l'heure, L'honorable correspondence, Youngblood Hawke, Le majordome, Les corsaires, l'or et le plomb, Trois chambres a Manhattan, Grand Prix, Belle de jour, Mayerling, A Talent for Loving, The Private Life of Sherlock Holmes, Les Gemeaux, Decembre, Buffet Froid. Recipient Chevalier du Merite sportif. *

PAGE, JOHN IRWIN, Bible college president; b. Ft. Scott, Kans., Oct. 2, 1930; s. John Ellis and Ava Leona (Brown) P.; m. Virginia Maxine Witt, Aug. 1, 1951; children—Brenda, Carma, Courtney, Jonathan. B.A., Kans. City Coll. and Bible Sch., 1952; M.S., Pitts. State U., 1955, Ed.S., 1969; Ph.D. Kans. State U., 1987. Pastor Ch. of God (Holiness), Stockton, Mo., 1952-58, Ft. Scott, Kans., 1959-80; prin. Ft. Scott Christian Heights Sch., 1954-80; mgr. Ironquill Estates, Ft. Scott, 1975-80; pres. Kansas City Coll. and Bible Sch., Overland Park, 1980—; v.p. Witt Engring., Inc., El Dorado Springs, Mo., 1968-80, Plainview Farms, Inc., Ft. Scott, 1974—; pres. Bourbon County Police Chaplaincy, Ft. Scott, 1965-80. Pres. Multi-County 4-C, Ft. Scott, 1970; bd. dirs. Human Relations Com., Ft. Scott, 1971; precinct worker Republican Party, Bourbon County, 1963. Named Outstanding Alumnus, Ft. Scott Community Coll., 1980, Hon. Police Col. Bourbon County Police Chaplaincy, 1965. Mem. Phi Delta Kappa (Continuous Service award 1985), Overland Park C. of C. Avocations: hunting, golf, sports. Home: 5301 W 83d St Prairie Village KS 66208 Office: Kansas City Coll and Bible Sch 7401 Metcalf St Overland Park KS 66204

PAGE, LINDA KAY, state official; b. Wadsworth, Ohio, Oct. 4, 1943; s. Frederick Meredith and Martha Irene (Vance) P. Student Franklin U., 1970-75, Sch. Banking, Ohio U., 1976-77; cert. Nat. Personnel Sch., U. Md.-Am. Bankers Assn., 1981; grad. banking program U. Wis.-Madison, 1982-84. Asst. v.p., gen. mgr. Bancohio Corp., Columbus, Ohio, 1975-78, v.p., dist. mgr., 1979-80, v.p., mgr. employee relations, 1980-81, v.p., div. mgr., 1982-83; commr. of banks State of Ohio, Columbus, 1983-87, dir. Commerce, 1988—; guest speaker, lectr. various banking groups. Bd. dirs. Clark County Mental Health Bd., Springfield, Ohio, 1982-83, Springfield Met. Housing, 1982-83; bd. advisers Orgn. Indsl. Standards, Springfield, 1982-83; trustee League Against Child Abuse, 1986—; treas. Ohio Housing Fin. Agy., 1988. Recipient Leadership Columbus award Sta. WTVN and Columbus Leadership Program, 1975, 82, Outstanding Service award Clark County Mental Health Bd., 1983. Mem. Nat. Assn. Bank Women (pres. 1980-81), Bus. and Profl. Women's Club, LWV, Conf. State Bank Suprs. (bd. dirs. 1984-85), dist. chmn. 1984-85), Ohio Bankers Assn. (bd. dirs. 1982-83). Democrat. Lodge: Zonta. Avocations: tennis; animal protection; matchbook collecting, reading, golf. Home: 1330 Erickson Ave Columbus OH 43227 Office: Dept Commerce Div of Banks 2 Natiowide Plaza Columbus OH 43215

PAGE, PHILIP RONALD, chemist; b. Rochford, Essex, Eng., Feb. 21, 1951; s. Arthur Leonard and Joyce Jean (MacFarlane) P.; m. Penny Alison Gambrill, Apr. 8, 1978; children—Sarah Dawn, Karen Louise. B.S., Victoria U. of Manchester (Eng.), 1972, M.S., 1973, Ph.D., 1975. Mgmt. trainee T.B.A. Indsl. Products Ltd., Rochdale, Eng., 1975-76, tech. rep., 1976-77, asst. market devel. mgr., 1977-78; asst. research dir. Hovione-Sociedade Quimica Lda., Loures, Portugal, 1978-80, research dir., 1980-84, exec. and tech. dir., 1984—. Patentee in field. Mem. Royal Soc. Chemistry. Mem. Ch. of Eng.

PAGE, ROBERT HENRY, engineering educator, researcher; b. Phila., Nov. 5, 1927; s. Ernest Fraser and Marguerite (MacFarl) P.; m. Lola Marie Griffin, Nov. 12, 1948; children: Lola Linda, Patricia Jean, William Ernest, Nancy Lee, Martin Fraser. BS in Mech. Engring, Ohio U., 1949; MS, U. Ill., 1951, PhD, 1955. Instr., research assoc. U. Ill., 1949-55; research engr. fluid dynamics Esso Research & Engring. Co., 1955-57; vis. lectr. Stevens Inst. Tech., 1956-57, dir. fluid dynamics lab., prof. mech. engring., 1957-61; prof. mech. engring., chmn. dept. mech., indsl. and aerospace engring. Rutgers-The State U., 1961-76, prof., research cons., 1976-79; dean engring. Tex. A&M U., 1979-83, Forsyth prof., 1983—; spl. research base pressure and heat transfer, wake flow and flow separation. Author papers in field. Served with AUS, 1945-47, PTO. Recipient Western Electric Fund award for excellence in engring. edn. Am. Soc. Engring Edn., 1968; Lindback Found. award for distinguished teaching, 1969; Disting. Alumnus award U. Ill., 1971; Disting. Service award, 1973; Life Quality Engring. award, 1974, James Harry Potter Gold medal, 1983, Ohio U. medal, 1983; named hon. prof. Ruhr U., Buchum, W. Ger., 1984. Fellow ASME, Am. Astronautical Soc. (chmn. Nat. Space Engring. Com. 1969-70, 72-76), AAAS, Am. Soc. Engring. Edn.; assoc. fellow Am. Inst. Aeros. and Astronautics; mem. Am. Phys. Soc. Home: 1905 Comal Circle College Station TX 77840

PAGE, SALLY JACQUELYN, university official; b. Saginaw, Mich., July, 1943; d. William Henry and Doris Effie (Knippel) P.; B.A., U. Iowa, 1965; M.B.A., So. Ill. U., 1973. Copy editor, C.V. Mosby Co., St. Louis, 1965-69; edit. cons. Edit. Assos., Edwardsville, Ill., 1969-70; research adminstr. So. Ill. U., 1970-74, asst. to pres., affirmative action officer, 1974-77; civil rights officer U. N.D., Grand Forks, 1977—, lectr. mgmt., 1978—; polit. commentator Sta. KFJM, Nat. Public Radio affiliate, 1981—. Contbr. to profl. jours. Chairperson N.D. Equal Opportunity Affirmative Action Officers, 1987-88; pres., Pine to Prairie council Girl Scouts U.S.A., 1980-85 ; mem. employment com. Ill. Commn. on Status of Women, 1976-77; mem. Bicentennial Com. Edwardsville, 1976, Bikeway Task Force Edwardsville, 1975-77; mem. Civil Service Rev. Task Force, Grand Forks, 1982, civil service commr., 83, chmn., 1984, 86. Mem. AAUW (dir. Ill. 1975-77), Coll. and Univ. Personnel Assn. (research and publs. bd. 1982-84) Am. Assn. Affirmative Action, Soc. Research Adminstrs., M.B.A. Assn. Republican. Presbyterian. Home: 3121 Cherry St Grand Forks ND 58201 Office: Univ ND Grand Forks ND 58202

PAGEL, DEBORAH JOANNE, health physicist, biologist; b. Chgo., Apr. 25, 1955; d. Raymond Frank and Amelia Emelda (Suchecki) Heppeler; m. Richard Arlin Pagel, Aug. 4, 1979. B.S. in Biology, Elmhurst Coll., 1981. Sr. health physics technician Argonne Nat. Lab. (Ill.), 1977-81; gen. health physicist Commonwealth Edison Dresden Nuclear Sta., Morris, Ill., 1981-85; lead health physicist Prodn. Tng. Ctr., Commonwealth Edison, Wilmington, Ill., 1985-86, health physics supr., 1986—. Contbr. articles to profl. jours. Fund solicitor Crusade of Mercy/United Fund, 1981—. Mem. Nat. Health Physics Soc., Am. Nuclear Soc., Nat. Am. Nuclear Soc., Assn. Women in Sci., Argonne Lab. Equal Opportunity Assn. Republican. Roman Catholic. Office: Commonwealth Edison PTC RR 2 Box 120 Essex Rd Wilmington IL 60481

PAGES, ROBERT CHARLES HENRI, surgeon; b. Alexandrette, Syria, June 18, 1931; s. Louis Guillaume Emile and Marcelle Yvonne Henriette (Leroy) P.; m. Marie Geneviève Guiroy, Nov. 23, 1967; children: Marie-Laure, Béatrice, Antoine, Véronique. M.D., U. Paris, 1962. Asst. embryology U. Paris Faculté de Médecine, 1962-66, clinic chief pediatric surgery, 1968-70; surgeon St. Denis Hosp., part-time 1964— ; practice medicine specializing in surgery, Paris, 1965—; expert in surgery, pediatric surgery Appeals Ct., Paris, 1971—, Adminstrv. Tribunal, Paris, 1984-85, nat. expert, 1985—. Contbr. articles to profl. jours. Mem. French Soc. Infant Surgery, Brit. Assn. Pediatric Surgeons. Avocation: sailing. Home and Office: 22 rue Beaujon, 75008 Paris France

PAGET, ALLEN MAXWELL, investment company executive; b. Karuizawa, Nagano Prefecture, Japan, Sept. 12, 1919 (parents Am. citizens); s. Allen Maxwell and Mary (Baum) P.; m. Dorothy A. Lord, Dec. 22, 1941. BSBA, Lehigh U., 1941. With C. L. Emmert & Co., 1955-58; with Waddell & Reed, Inc., 1958-68, investment mgr., distbr. united group of mutual funds, 1958-68, regional mgr., resident v.p., Harrisburg, Pa., 1961-68; v.p. Mark Securities, Inc., Camp Hill, Pa., 1968—; chmn. bd. dirs., pres., treas. Penn-Ben, Inc., 1969-83; chmn. bd. dirs., pres., treas. Paget-San Enterprises, Inc. (Benihana of Tokyo), 1973-83; gen. ptnr. Penn-Ben Ltd. Partnership, 1983—; v.p. Gamma Lambda Corp., 1973-78. Served to comdr. Supply Corps, USN, 1941-55, capt. Res., ret. 1972. Named Eagle Scout, Boy Scouts Am., 1936. Mem. Am. Philatelic Soc. (life), Navy League U.S., Res. Officers Assn. (pres. Central Pa. chpt. 1972-73), Mil. Order World Wars (comdr. Central Pa. chpt. 1979-82, comdr. Region III 1982-88, staff officer 1988—), The Retired Officers Assn., Internat. Assn. FShrine Assm/in. Counselors (charter), Navy Supply Corps Sch. Alumni Assn. (founding mem.), Mid Atlantic Shrine Clowns Assn., Internat. Shrine Clown Assn., Harrisburg and West Shore Area C. of C., Nat. Sojourners (1st v.p. Cen. Pa. chpt. No. 76, 1987, pres. 1988—), Heros of '76, Brown Key Soc., Lambda Mu Sigma (hon., founder), Pi Kappa Alpha (treas.), Alpha Phi Omega, Pi Delta Epsilon. Clubs: Cen. Pa. Lehigh Alumni (pres. 1966); Cen. Pa. Execs. (bd. dirs. 1985-88); Antique and Classic Car Unit(founder). Lodges: Rotary (bd. dirs.), Masons (master 1968, lodge treas. 1984—), K.T., Shriners (potentate Zembo temple 197)8, pres. Pa. Shrine Assn. 1978-79, v.p. Mid Atlantic A. 1980-82, pres. 1982-83, Shrine Clowns of Zembo Temple, all Shrine clubs), Tall Cedars Lebanon, Legion of Honor (organizer 1974), Grand Sword Bearer of Grand Lodge Pa., 1988. Home: Keiseian 308 Lamp Post Ln Pine Brook Camp Hill PA 17011

PAGET, JOHN ARTHUR, mechanical engineer; b. Ft. Frances, Ont., Can., Sept. 15, 1922; s. John and Ethel (Bishop) P.; B.Applied Sci., Toronto, 1946; m. Vicenta Herrera Nunez, Dec. 16, 1963; children—Cynthia Ellen, Kevin Arthur, Keith William. Chief draftsman Gutta Percha & Rubber, Ltd., Toronto, Ont., 1946-49; chief draftsman Viceroy Mfg. Co., Toronto, 1949-52; supr., design engr. C.D. Howe Co. Ltd., Montreal, Que., Can., 1952-58, sr. design engr. Combustion Engring., Montreal, 1958-59; sr. staff engr. Gen. Atomic, Inc., La Jolla, 1959-81. Mem. ASME, Am. Inst. Plant Engrs., Soc. Mfg. Engrs., Profl. Engrs. Ont., Soc. for History Tech., Inst. Mech. Engrs., Soc. Am. Mil. Engrs., Newcomen Soc., Brit. Nuclear Energy Soc. Patentee in field. Home: 3183 Magellan St San Diego CA 92154 Office: PO Box 427 Nestor CA 92053

PAGNAMENTA, PETER JOHN, television producer; b. Oxford, Eng., Apr. 12, 1941; s. Frank and Daphne P.; m. Sybil Healy, 1969; children: Zoe, Robin. MA, Cambridge U., Eng., 1963. Script writer BBC TV, London, 1965-66, producer (series) "24 Hours", 1966-69; producer BBC TV, N.Y.C., 1969-71; editor "24 Hours" BBC TV, London, 1971-72, editor "Midweek", 1972-75, editor "Panorama", 1975-77, head current affairs Thames TV, 1977-81, exec. producer Documentary Dept., 1981-85, head Current Affairs Dept., 1985-87. Author: (with Richard Overy) All Our Working Lives, 1985. Office: BBC Television, Kensington House Richmond Way, London W14, England

PAGNI, PATRICK ROBERT, banker; b. Nimes, Gard, France, July 15, 1949; arrived in Hong Kong, 1984; s. Robert Joseph and Eliane Louise (Sanouiller) P.; m. Viviane Guyot, Oct. 2, 1978. MS, Paris IX Dauphine, France, 1972; MBA, Harvard, 1974. V.p. Societe Generale, N.Y.C., 1979-80; regional mgr. Societe Generale, Los Angeles, 1981-84; gen. mgr. Societe Generale, Hong Kong, 1984—; dep. chmn. Sogen Asia Ltd., Hong Kong. Club: Royal Hong Kong Jockey. Home: 7 Magazine Gap Rd, Hong Kong Hong Kong Office: Societe Generale, The Landmark II Pedder St, Hong Kong Hong Kong

PAIEWONSKY, MICHAEL ALBERT, editor, publisher; b. N.Y.C., Sept. 28, 1939; s. Isidor and Charlotte (Kaufman) P.; m. Annemarie Lamb Jensen, Sept. 1, 1960 (div. 1967); children: Erik Justus, Paul Ivar, Maline; m. Jeanette Nancy McDonald, Aug. 10, 1975 (div. 1983); m. Maria Gabriella Santoro, Oct. 12, 1983. Student, U. Chgo., 1957-60, U. Edinburgh, Scotland, 1967. Bd., mgr. A.H. Riise Inc., St. Thomas, V.I., 1962-75, cons., 1975—; editor, pub. Mapes Monde Ltd., Rome, 1986—; v.p., bd. dirs. Charles Bellow & Co., St. Thomas, 1964-76; cons. I.P. Assocs. Inc., St. Thomas, 1982—; pres., bd. dirs. Framnor Inc., La Guard Freinet, France, 1971-75; del. Pacific Devel. Conf., Hawaii, 1981, Caribbean Devel. Conf., Miami, Fla., 1980-82. Editor: Slavery to Mass Tourism, 1987; contbr. articles to profl. jours.; producer, writer, announcer (radio program) Small Talk, 1976-82. Mem. V.I. Bd. Edn., 1976-78; senator V.I. Senate, 1976-82; del. Nat. Dem. Conv., 1976, 78, 80, V.I. Constl. Conv., 1979. Mem. Nat. Assn. Bd. Edn., Nat. Assn. State Bd. Edn., Nat. Assn. State Legislators, V.I. C. of C., V.I. Archeology Soc. (trustee 1975-87). Jewish. Home: Hassel Island 8 Saint Thomas VI 00801 Office: Mapes Monde Ltd, P Montevecchio 6, 00186 Rome Italy

PAIKEDAY, THOMAS M(ANUEL), lexicographer, consultant; b. Kerala, India, Oct. 11, 1926; came to U.S., 1962, Can., 1964; s. Manuel Thomas and Anna (Poovelickal) P.; m. Mary Kurien Kizhakethottam, Jan. 4, 1967; children—Anthony, Anne-Marie. L.Ph., Coll. of the Jesuits, Shembaganur, India, 1955; B.A. with 1st class honors, Madras Christian Coll., Tambaram, India, 1958; M.A., U. Madras, India, 1960; postgrad. Boston Coll., Chestnut Hill, Mass., 1962-63, U. Mich., Ann Arbor, 1963-64. Lectr. English, St. Joseph's Coll., Tiruchy, Madras, 1958-59, Ramjas Coll., Delhi, India, 1960-61; copy editor The Statesman, New Delhi, India, 1961-62; asst. lexicographer W.J. Gage Ltd., Toronto, Ont., Can., 1964-66; editor Ont. Ministry of Edn., Toronto, 1966-67; head lexicography div. Holt, Rinehart & Winston, Toronto, 1967-73; chief lexicographer Paikeday Pub. Inc., Mississauga, Ont., 1973—; cons. Collier-Macmillan Can., Toronto, 1980-81; Can. advisor Collins Publishers, Glasgow, Scotland, 1981-82; assoc. Applied Linguistics Research Working Group, York U., Toronto, 1984—. Chief editor: Winston Interm. Dictionary, 1969; Compact Dictionary of Canadian English, 1970; Winston Canadian Dictionary, elem. edit., 1975; New York Times Everyday Dictionary, 1982. Author: The Native Speaker is Dead!, 1985; contbr. articles to profl. jours. Mem. The Authors Guild, European Assn. Lexicography, Dictionary Soc. N.Am. (pubs. com. 1983—), MLA, Tchrs. of English to Speakers of Other Langs., Can. Council Tchrs. of English, Am. Dialect Soc., Am. Name Soc., Assn. Computing and Humanities, Assn. Lit. and Linguistic Computing. Roman Catholic. Avocations: computer applications in lexicography; tennis; swimming. Home: 1776 Chalkdene Grove, Mississauga, ON Canada L4W 2C3 Office: Paikeday Pub Inc, 1776 Chalkdene Grove, Mississauga, ON Canada L4W 2C3

PAINE, STEPHEN WILLIAM, retired college president; b. Grand Rapids, Mich., Oct. 28, 1908; s. Stephen Hugh and Mary Wilfrieda (Fischer) P.; m. Helen Lucile Paul, Aug. 17, 1934; children: Marjorie (dec.), Carolyn Esther, Miriam Ruth, Stephen William, Kathryn Elizabeth. A.B., Wheaton (Ill.) Coll., 1930, LL.D., 1939; A.M., U. Ill., 1931, Ph.D., 1933; L.H.D., Houghton Coll., 1976. Instr. classics Houghton (N.Y.) Coll., 1933-34, prof. Greek, 1934-72, dean of Coll., 1934-37, pres. coll., 1937-72, now emeritus; Mem. bd. adminstrn. Wesleyan Church, 1935-68, 72-80; mem. bd. adminstrn. Nat. Assn. Evangelicals, 1942—, pres., 1948-49; mem. commn. of Christian higher edn. Assn. Am. Colls., 1955-58. Author: Toward the Mark-Studies in Philippians, 1953, Studies in the Book of James, 1955, The Christian and the Movies, 1957, Beginning Greek, 1960, 1961; mem. transl. com.: New Internat. Version Bible; contbr.: Wesleyan Advocate, United Evangel. Action. Trustee Asbury Theol. Sem., 1965-78, Houghton Coll., 1972-80, United Wesleyan Coll., 1974-80. Mem. Evangel. Theol. Soc. (pres. 1967), Classical Assn. Atlantic States, Gideons Internat., Phi Beta Kappa, Wheaton Coll. Honor Soc., Pi Kappa Delta. Address: 7 Circle Dr Houghton NY 14744

PAINTER, JOHN HOYT, electrical engineer; b. Winfield, Kans., Mar. 27, 1934; s. John Paul and Marjorie Marietta (Slack) P.; m. Joy Lou Vaughan, June 7, 1955; children—John Mark, Paul Burton, William Vaughan, Joy Lynn. B.S., U. Ill., Urbana, 1961; Gen. Electric Found. fellow, M.S., 1962; Ph.D., So. Meth. U., 1972; postgrad., Coll. William and Mary, 1967-69. Communications engr. NASA Manned Spacecraft Center, Houston, 1962-65; sr. engr. Motorola Govt. Electronics div., Scottsdale, Ariz., 1965-67; research engr. NASA Langley Research Center, Hampton, Va., 1967-74; asso. prof. elec. engring. Tex. A&M U., College Station, 1974-79, prof., 1979—; pres. ALTAIR Corp. cons., College Station, 1980—. Served with USAF, 1953-58. Recipient Recognition cert. NASA, 1975. Mem. IEEE (sr.). Club: Masons. Home: 1119 Merry Oaks St College Station TX 77840 Office: Tex A&M U Dept Elec Engring College Station TX 77843

PAINTER, MARY ELLA, editor; b. Tulsa, July 15, 1920; d. Ernest Balf Parker and Maggie Mae (Renaud) P.; B.A., Oklahoma City U., 1943; postgrad. Columbia U., 1944; m. Charles J. Yarbrough, Apr. 7, 1946; children—Kirby John, Kevin Lee. Editorial asst., feature writer Office War Info., 1943-46; feature writer, news editor Dept. State, 1946-53; with USIA, Washington, 1953-78, editor USIA World, 1967-78; with U.S. Internat. Communication Agy., 1978-80, editor USICA World, 1978-80; with Food Policy Center, Washington, 1981-84, mng. editor Food Policy Center News/ Views, 1981—; assoc. editor Food Monitor, 1981-83, 87—; editor, 1986—. World Hunger Yr., N.Y.C., 1981—; editor USIAAA Newsletter, Washington, 1980—, Reston (Va.) Interfaith Newsletter, 1982—. Recipient Meritorious Service award USIA, 1964, Spl. Commendation, 1974; Dir.'s award for Outstanding Creativity, U.S. Internat. Communication Agy., 1980. Mem. Women's Action Orgn., NOW, Assn. Am. Fgn. Service Women, Am. Fgn. Service Assn. Democrat. Baptist. Home: 12232 Quorn Ln Reston VA 22091 Office: World Hunger Yr 261 W 35th St New York NY 10001-1906

PAINTING, JOHN HARRISON, transport contracting company executive; b. Bulawayo, Zimbabwe, Feb. 25, 1945; s. John William Charles and Elma Maria (Schafer) P.; m. Elaine Jean Dickson, July 3, 1971; children—Barry John, David Gavin. Ed. pvt. sch. Clk. Nat. Rys., Bulawayo, 1963-68; acct. N. Stipinovich, Bulawayo, 1970-72; personal asst. to mng. dir. Ward's Transport Co., Bulawayo, 1972-78; mng. dir. Fox & Bookless Pvt. Ltd., Bulawayo, 1978—. Vice chmn. C.B.C. Old Boys Union, Bulawayo, 1985. Served to 2d. lt. Rhodesian Army, 1971-80. Club: Byo Country (sec.-treas. 1979) (Bulawayo). Home: 5 Fortunes Gate Rd, Mats, Bulawayo Zimbabwe Office: Fox & Bookless Pvt Ltd, 5 Bellevue Rd, Belmont, Bulawayo Zimbabwe

PAIROA EPPLE, RENÉ, aviation consultant; b. Santiago, Chile, Oct. 29, 1917; s. Amador Pairoa Trujillo and Grete Epple Schwenchke P.; student Law Sch., U. Católica de Chile, 1936-37, U. Chile Law Sch., 1938-41; comml. pilot, Purdue Aero. Corp., W. Lafayette, Ind., 1945; m. Carmen Correa Silva, May 9, 1969; children: José Antonio, Carolina, Mathias, Rosario; children by previous marriage: Patricia, René, Hernán, María Eliana, Andrea. Regional ops. chief Lan Chile Airlines, 1947; founder, dir. Lyonair Airline, Chile, 1949-51, Cinta Airlines, Chile, 1951-58; co-founder, 1954, since dir. Linea Aérea Alas Agrícolas; founder Ladeco Airlines, 1958; founder, pres., dir. Helicopservices Chile Ltd., 1960-78; founder, 1959, since exec. dir. Aerotech, cons. and mfrs. rep.; nat. dir. tourism, Chile, 1965-66; del. tourism of Chile, U.S., 1967-68. Served with Chilean Army, 1938. Clubs: Union, Estadio Espanol. Home: 388 Alcántara, Casilla 3830, Santiago Chile Office: 194 Hernando de Aguirre, Casilla 3830 Santiago Chile

PAISLEY, IAN RICHARD KYLE, clergyman, political activist; b. Apr. 6, 1926; s. J. Kyle and Isabella P.; ed. South Wales Bible Coll., Ref. Presbyn. Theol. Coll., Belfast, No. Ireland; D.D. (hon.), Bob Jones U., Greenville, S.C., 1966; m. Eileen E. Cassells, 1956; 5 children. Ordained to ministry Free Presbyn. Ch., 1946; minister Martyrs Meml. Free Presbyn. Ch., Belfast, from 1946; moderator Free Presbyn. Ch. of Ulster, from 1951; pub. Protestant Telegraph, from 1966; M.P. for North Antrim, Westminster, from 1970; M.P. for Bannside, County Antrim, North Ireland Parliament, 1970-72, leader of opposition, 1972, chmn. public accounts com., 1972; mem. No. Ireland Assembly, 1973-74; mem. European Parliament, from 1979; mem. Constl. Conv., 1975-76; co-chmn. World Congress of Fundamentalists, 1978; leader Democratic Unionist Party, 1971—. Fellow Royal Geog. Soc.; mem. Internat. Cultural Soc. Korea. Author: History of the 1859 Revival, 1959; Christian Foundations, 1960; Ravenhill Pulpit, Vol. I, 1966, Vol. II, 1967; Exposition of the Epistle to the Romans, 1968; Billy Graham and the Church of Rome, 1970; The Massacre of Saint Bartholomew, 1972; Paisley, the Man and his Message, 1976; America's Debt to Ulster, 1976; The Life of Dr. James Kidd, 1982; Those Flaming Tenants, 1983; editor: The Revivalist, 1950. Address: The Parsonage, 17 Cyprus Ave, Belfast BT5 5NT, Northern Ireland

PAISS, DORIS BELL, educational and psychological consultant, lecturer, educator; b. Phila., Nov. 19, 1929; d. Simon and Sarah (Freedman) Cohen; m. Lee Paiss, July 26, 1953; children—Jana, Michael. B.F.A., Barnard Coll., 1954; postgrad. Los Angeles City Coll., 1962-63; M.A., Columbia U., 1963, Ph.D. in Philosophy of Ancient Civilizations, 1976, degree in Geriatrics in Abnormal Psychology, 1978. Active Jewish education, 1963-86; ednl. dir. M.D. Hoffman Regional Hebrew High Sch., Phila., 1973-83; coordinator Daroff Campus of Sr. Adult Studies, Raymond and Miriam Klein br. Jewish Community Ctr., Phila., 1982-85, mem. faculty Daroff Campus Adult Studies, 1978-85; cons. Life Care and Retirement, 1985-88; designing support and ednl. programs for stress related memory loss; lectr. on stress, memory, time mgmt., devel. human potential, Phila., 1976-87, guest lectr. Columbia U., U. Wis., U. Calif.-Santa Barbara, Oberlin Coll., Rochester Inst. Tech., Rutgers U., U. Tampa, Coalition for Jewish Edn., writers' confs., community service orgns., indsl. seminars; mem. faculty Inst. Awareness, 1980-83, Satinsky Inst. for Blind, 1980-85; free-lance writer and producer comml., indsl. and ednl. films, 1950-70. Recipient numerous awards. Mem. Nat. Assn. Female Execs., Am. Film Inst. Democrat. Jewish. Avocations: research on memory; show music.

PAK SONG-CHOL, vice president of North Korea; b. Kiongsan Province, South Korea, Sept. 21, 1913; student Soviet Mil. Coll., 1948-50; In emigration in China, 1921-45; activist Anti-Japanese Movement, from 1931; mem. Kim Il Sen's partisan units, Manchuria; dep. comdr. marine forces Korean War; Korean ambassador to Bulgaria, 1945; dep. minister fgn. affairs, head fgn. dept. Korean Workers Party; minster fgn. affairs, 1959-70; dep. prime minister, 1966-70; dep. chmn. Council of Ministers, chmn. Com. of Service to the People, 1970-76; prime minister People's Republic of Korea, 1976-77, V.P., 1977—. Address: Office of Vice Pres, Pyongyang Democratic Republic of Korea *

PAL, LENARD, physicist; b. Gyoma, Hungary, Nov. 7, 1925; s. Imre and Erzsebet (Varga) P.; m. Angela Danoci, 1963; 1 dau. Student Budapest U., Moscow U. Dept. head Ctr. Research Inst. for Physics, Budapest, 1953-56, dep. dir., 1956-69, dir., 1970-71, dir. gen., 1975-77; prof. nuclear physics Eotvos Lorand U. Budapest, 1961-77; pres. State Office Tech. Devel., 1978-80, 84-85, Nat. Atomic Energy Commn., 1978-80, 84-85; mem. Sci. Policy com. Council of Ministers, 1978-85; sec. Central Com. of the Hungarian Socialist Worker's Party, 1985—. Contbr. articles to profl. jours. Recipient Gold medal Order Labour, 1956, 68; Kossuth prize, 1962; Meml. medal 25th Anniversary of the Liberation, 1970; Kurcsatov Memory medal, USSR, 1970; Gold medal Hungarian Acad. Scis., 1975; Red Banner Order of Labor, USSR, 1975; medal Eotvos Lorand Phys. Soc., 1976; Red Banner Order of Work, 1985. Mem. Hungarian Acad. Sci. (gen. sec. 1980-84, pres. Intercosmos Council 1980-84), Acad. Scis. USSR, Acad. Sci. German Democratic Republic, Acad. Scis. Czechoslovakia. Office: Széchenyi rkp 19, H-1358 Budapest V Hungary

PALACIO, SISTER ROSE ABELLANA, physician, nun; b. Tagbilaran City, Visayas, Philippines, Nov. 25, 1935; d. Jose Amadora and Bonifacia (Abellana) P. MD, U. Santo Tomas, Manila, 1960. Joined Sisters of Mercy, Roman Cath. Ch. Intern Kenmore Mercy Hosp., Buffalo, 1963-64; resident in anesthesia Millard Fillmore Hosp., Buffalo, 1964-65, 68-69, fellow in anesthesiology, 1969-70; dir. Mercy Mobile Clinic, Lanao, Philippines, 1971—; chief physician Philippine Tuberculosis Soc., 1975-78; med. dir. Mercy Community Clinic, Iligan City, Philippines, 1977-78, adminstr., 1979—; mem. Sisters of Mercy, Buffalo, 1965-68; mem. council Sisters of Mercy, Iligan City, 1982-85, vicar, 1985—. Mem. Philippine Med. Assn. (Outstanding Physician in Community Service award 1987), Philippine Women's Med. Assn. (pres. Lanao chpt. 1975-76, Outstanding Woman Physician in Community Service award 1972-73), Philippine Hosp. Assn. (pres. Lanao chpt. 1984-85), Philippine Soc. Anesthesiologists. Home: Mercy Community Clinic, Kamague, Iligan City 8801, Philippines Office: Religious Sisters of Mercy, Kamague, Iligan City 8801, Philippines

PALADE, GEORGE EMIL, cell biologist, educator; b. Jassy, Romania, Nov. 19, 1912; came to U.S., 1946, naturalized, 1952; s. Emil and Constanta (Cantemir) P.; m. Irina Malaxa, June 12, 1941 (dec. 1969); children—Georgia Teodora, Philip Theodore; m. Marilyn G. Farquhar, 1970. Bachelor, Hasdeu Lyceum, Buzau, Romania; M.D., U. Bucharest, Romania. Instr., asst. prof., then asso. prof. anatomy Sch. Medicine, U. Bucharest, 1935-45; vis. investigator, asst. asso., prof. cell biology Rockefeller U., 1946-73; prof. cell biology Yale U., New Haven, 1973-83; sr. research scientist Yale U., 1983—; correlated biochem. and morphological analysis cell structures. Author sci. papers. Recipient Albert Lasker Basic Research award, 1966, Gairdner Spl. award, 1967, Horwitz prize, 1970, Nobel prize in Physiology or Medicine, 1974, Nat. Medal Sci., 1986. Fellow Am. Acad. Arts and Scis.; mem. Nat. Acad. Sci., Pontifical Acad. Sci., Royal Soc. (London), Leopoldina Acad. (Halle), Romanian Acad., Royal Belgian Acad. Medicine. Office: Yale U Sch Medicine Cell Biology Dept 333 Cedar St New Haven CT 06510

PALÁDI-KOVÁCS, ATTILA, anthropologist, educator; b. Ozd, Hungary, Sept. 14, 1940; s. Jozsef and Anna (Talpas) P-K.; m. Csilla Lendvai; children: Adam, Gergely. Lic. tchr. Geography and History, Kossuth U., Hungary, 1963, Phil. Dr., 1965. Museologist Dobó Mus., Eger, Hungary, 1963-64, Déri Mus., Debrecen, Hungary, 1965-68; research fellow Ethnographical Inst. Hungarian Acad. Scis., Budapest, Hungary, 1969-80, dep. dir., 1978-80, dir., 1986—; assoc. prof. Eötvös U., Budapest, Hungary, 1981-84, prof., head of chair, 1985—. Author: La Bergerie des Paloczes Orientaux, 1965, Die Wiesenwirtschaft der Ung Bauern, 1979, The Barkóság and Its People, 1982; editor: Traditionelle Transportmethoden in Ostmitteleuropa, 1981. Mem. Hungarian Soc. Ethnography, Ethnology and Folklore (gen. sec. 1982—, Jankó prize,1970, Györffy medal 1987), Internat. Union of Anthrop. and Ethnological Scis. (IUAES) exec. com., 1988—. Mem. Hungarian Socialist Workers party. Home: Szechenyiu 1, H1054 Budapest Hungary Office: Ethnographical Inst MTA, PO Box 29, H1250 Budapest Hungary

PALANCA, TERILYN, information management consultant; b. Chicago Heights, Ill., Aug. 15, 1957; d. Raymond Anthony and Barbara Jean (Schweizer) P. BA, Coll. William and Mary, 1979; MBA, Rutgers U., 1983. Chief auditor, mgr. Williamsburg Hilton, Va., 1979-81; corp. auditor RCA Corp., Princeton, N.J., 1982-83; EDP cons. Price Waterhouse & Co., N.Y.C., 1983-84; data base adminstr. Chubb & Son, Inc., Warren, N.J., 1984-85; cons., tech. mgr. Applied Data Research, Inc., Princeton, N.J., 1985-88, industry cons., Oracle Corp., Iselin, N.J., 1988—. Mem. Assn. of Inst. for Cert. Computer Profls. (cert. in data processing), Am. Mgmt. Assn., Nat. Assn. Female Execs. Republican. Avocations: Masterwork Chorus, pianist, literature, hiking, animal aid. Office: Oracle Corp 120 Wood Ave South Suite 401 Iselin NJ 08830

PALASINSKI, MAREK LESZEK, mathematician; b. Cracow, Poland, Apr. 25, 1950; s. Leszek and Danuta (Karpina) P.; m. Katarzyna Monika Wrobel, Jan., 8, 1983; children: Magdalena, Joanna. MSc, Jagiellonian U., Cracow, 1972; PhD, Lomonosow U., Moscow, 1977. Lectr. Jagiellonian U., 1972-74; postgrad. Lomonosow Moscow State U., 1974-77; asst. prof. Jagiellonian U., 1978—. Contbr. several articles to profl. jours.; reviewer Zentralblatt für Mathematik, 1981, Math. Revs., 1982. Mem. Am. Math. Soc. (translator 1983), Polskie Towarzystwo Matematyczne. Roman Catholic. Home: Koniewa 5 B/132, 30-150 Cracow Poland Office: Jagiellonian U Math Inst, Reymonta 4, 30-059 Cracow Poland

PALAVIDIS, EMMANUEL (MANOS), advertising executive; b. Alexandria, Arab Republic of Egypt, Apr. 4, 1953; came to Greece, 1957; s. Dimitrios Palavidis and Erifili Maria (Tavridakis) Makris; m. Julie Chapman, May 21, 1975 (div. 1981); m. Maria Foscolos May 21, 1982; 1 child, Paola. BA in Typographic Design, London Coll. Printing, 1974. Designer Kinneir-Culvert-Tuhill Ltd., London, 1974-75, King & Wetheral Ltd., London, 1975-76; mng. dir. Chapman/Palavidis Ltd., Athens, Greece, 1976—. Contbr. articles to mags. Mem. Greek Union Advt., Ind. Advt. Assn. Greek Orthodox. Club: OH (London). Home: 36 Athinon St, 166 75 Glyfada Greece Office: Chapman/Palavidis Ltd, Appolon Tower, 64 L Riankour St, 115 23 Athens Greece

PALAZZINI, PIETRO CARDINAL, cardinal; b. Piobbico, Italy, May 19, 1912; s. Giovanni and Luigia (Conti) P.; grad. Seminario Regionale Marchigiano, 1932; Th.D., U. Lateranense, 1937, J.C.L., 1942. Ordained priest Roman Catholic Ch., 1934; asst. Major Roman Sem., 1942-45; vice rector Pontifical Roman Sem. Juridical Studies, 1945-49; undersec. Vatican Dicastery Religious, 1956-58; sec. Vatican Dicastery for Clergy, 1958-73; created archbishop, 1962, cardinal, 1973; prefect of Sacred Congregation for Causes of Saints, 1980; prof. moral theology and canon law Ponticial Lateran U., 1945-56. Recipient Gold medal Italian Ministry Public Edn. Mem. Theol. Roman Acad., Marian Internat. Acad., Acad. Internat. S. Tommaso, Raffaello Acad., Tiberina delle Scienze di Ferrara, Sistina, Card. Bessarione Acad. Author works on moral theology, canon law, articles. Address: 83 Proba, Petronia, Rome Italy

PALERMO, JOSEPH, educator; b. Trenton, N.J., Sept. 9, 1917; s. Joseph Robert and Margaret (Zoda) P.; m. Eileen Viola Wilcox, Apr. 4, 1943; children: Margaret Ann, Eleanor (Mrs. Francis A. Roxby), Richard Alan. A.B. (William J. Bickett Meml. scholar), Temple U., 1940; A.M. (Herbert Montgomery Bergen fellow), Princeton U., 1948, Ph.D., 1950; postgrad., Poitiers, France, 1960. Asst. editor Merriam-Webster Dictionaries, 1940-43; instr. Mass. div. Univ. Extension, 1941-45, Temple U., Phila., 1945-51, U. Conn., Storrs, 1951-52; asst. prof. U. Conn., 1952-57, asso. prof., 1957-61, prof., 1961-72; now emeritus, chmn. Grad. Admissions Com. for Mediaeval Studies, 1969-72; prof. Va. Poly. Inst. and State U., Blacksburg, 1974-86, prof. emeritus, 1986; head dept. fgn. langs. Va. Poly. Inst. and State U., 1974-75; Vis. lectr. Ecole Libre des Hautes Etudes, N.Y., 1961-64; vis. prof. U. Laval, Que., summers 1962, 63; vis. lectr. Nat. Def. Edn. Act Summer Inst. French, U. Mass., 1963; vis. prof. Ecole Française, Middlebury Coll., summers 1966-68; vis. prof. French Yale, 1968; vis. prof. linguistics U. Palermo, Italy, 1973-74. Author: Le Roman de Cassidorus, 2 vols, 1963, 64, Le Roman d'Hector et Hercules, 1972, Le Nouveau Gargantua, 1982; Contbr. articles to profl. jours. Princeton Grad. scholar in modern langs., 1946; Am. Philos. Soc. grantee, 1954, 60, 65, 82; Belgian-Am. Ednl. Found. fellow, 1958; Am. Council Learned Socs. grantee, 1962, 63, 65, 67; U. Conn. Research Council grantee, 1968, 69, 70, 72; Va. Tech. Ednl. Found. grantee, 1982. Mem. Mediaeval Acad. Am., Modern Lang. Assn. Am., Am. Assn. Tchrs. French, Am. Assn. Tchrs. Italian, Société de Linguistique Romane, Société Internationale Arthurienne, Société des Professeurs Français en Amérique, Assn. Internationale de Littérature Comparée, Assn. Déf. de la Langue Française, Fédn. Internationale des Langues et Littératures Modernes, Alliance Française des Monts de Virginie (founder 1973, pres. 1973-74). Home: 5588 Shady Brook Ct Sarasota FL 34243

PALERMO, REGINO VALENZONA, JR., gynecologist, obstetrician; b. Baybay, Leyte, Philippines, Oct. 21, 1935; s. Regino Poliquit Sr. and Lourdes Medina (Valenzona) P.; m. Lydia de los Reyes Pantig, Jan. 4, 1963; children: Regino P. III, Regino P. IV. BS, U. Philippines, Diliman, Quezon City, 1957; MD, U. Philippines, Manila, 1962. Intern MacNeal Meml. Hosp., Berwyn, Ill., 1962-63, resident ob/gyn and family medicine, 1963-67; examiner Philippine-Am. Life Ins. Co., Manila, 1968-77; hosp. dir. Farmers Med. Ctr., Ormoc Sugarcane Planters Assn., 1978-86; obstetrician/gynecologist, cons. Western Leyte Provincial Hosp., Baybay, 1986—; sch. physician Franciscan Coll. Immaculate Conception, Baybay, 1974-77; participant Reproductive Biology Ctr., Manila, 1976, Echo Seminar on Reproductive Health of the 1980's, Cebu, Philippines, 1985; mem. candidate group ACS, 1967-68; cons. Tinley Park (Ill.) State Hosp., 1967, Ormoc Dist. Hosp., 1982—. Councilor Mcpl. Council Baybay, 1972-79, Barangay head, zone 5 leader, 1972-81; exec. chmn. Baybay Town Feast Celebration, 1973; mem. Community Chests and Councils Philippines, Manila, 1975; pres. Baybay High Sch. Alumni Assn., 1978-79. Recipient cert. of appreciation Town of Baybay, 1974, 82, cert. of appreciation Barangay Zone 10 Council, 1979, Outstanding Community Service award Phillipines Pres.'s Regional Office for Devel., 1976, Dedicated Profl. Assistance award Kiwanis Club of Ormoc, 1979, cert. of appreciation Baybay High Sch. Alumni Assn., 1980. Fellow Internat. Coll. Surgeons, Philippine Coll. Surgeons, Philippine Ob/gyn Soc. (dir. region VIII 1983—, cert. of appreciation 1983, 84, 86, 87); mem. Philippine Med. Assn. (ofcl. del. 1974-75, Most Outstanding Physician 1986), Philippine Med. Assn. in Chgo., Ormoc City Med. Soc. (pres. 1976, cert. of appreciation 1971-72, 75, Most Outstanding Mem. 1976, cert. of merit 1977), U. Philippines Med. Alumni Soc. (life), Mu Sigma Phi. Roman Catholic. Home and Office: C Arellano, Baybay, Leyte 6521, Philippines

PALEY, WILLIAM S., broadcasting executive; b. Chgo., Sept. 28, 1901; s. Samuel and Goldie (Drell) P.; m. Dorothy Hart Hearst, May 11, 1932; children: Jeffrey, Hilary; m. Barbara Cushing Mortimer, July 28, 1947; children: William Cushing, Kate Cushing. Grad., Western Mil. Acad., Alton, Ill., 1918; student, U. Chgo., 1918-19; B.S., U. Pa., 1922; LL.D., Adelphi U., 1957, Bates Coll., 1963, U. Pa., 1968, Columbia U., 1975, Brown U., 1975, Pratt Inst., 1977, Dartmouth Coll., 1979; L.H.D., Ithaca Coll., 1978, U. So. Calif., 1985, Rutgers U., 1986, L.I. U., Southampton, 1987. Vice-pres., sec. Congress Cigar Co., Phila., 1922-28; pres. CBS, Inc., N.Y.C., 1928-46, chmn. bd., 1946-83, founder chmn., 1983-86, acting chmn., 1986-87, chmn., 1987—, also dir.; ptnr. Whitcom Investment Co., 1982—; founder, bd. dirs. Genetics Inst., 1980—, Thinking Machines Corp., 1983—; co-chmn. Internat. Herald Tribune, 1983—. Trustee Mus. Modern Art, from 1937, pres., 1968-72, chmn., 1972-85, chmn. emeritus, 1985—; life trustee Columbia U., 1950-73, trustee emeritus, 1973—, bd. dirs. W. Averell Harriman Inst. for Advanced Study of Soviet Union, Columbia U.; mem. Com. for White House Conf. on Edn., 1954-56; chmn. Pres.'s Materials Policy Commn. which produced report "Resources for Freedom, 1951-52; mem. exec. com. Resources for the Future, 1952-69, chmn., 1966-69, hon. bd. dirs., from 1969; chmn. N.Y.C. Task Force on Urban Design which prepared the report The Threatened City, 1967, Urban Design Council City N.Y., 1968-71; pres., dir. William S. Paley Found., Greenpark Found., Inc.; trustee North Shore Univ., Hosp., 1949-73, co-chmn. bd. trustees, 1954-73; founding mem. Bedford-Stuyvesant D and S Corp., dir., 1967-72; founder, chmn. bd. Mus. of Broadcasting, from 1976; mem. Commn. on Critical Choices for Am., 1973-77, Commn. for Cultural Affairs, N.Y.C., 1975-78; life trustee Fedn. Jewish Philanthropies of N.Y. Served as col. AUS, World War II; dep. chief psychol. warfare div. SHAEF; dep. chief info. control div. USGCC. Decorated Legion of Merit; Medal for Merit; officer Legion of Honor France; Croix de Guerre with Palm France; comdr. Order of Merit Italy; assoc. comdr. Order of St. John of Jerusalem; recipient Gold Achievement medal Poor Richard Club; Keynote award Nat. Assn. Broadcasters; George Foster Peabody award citation, 1958, 1961; spl. award Broadcast Pioneers; award Concert Artist Guild, 1965; Skowhegan Gertrude Vanderbilt Whitney award; gold medal award Nat. Planning Assn., David Sarnoff award U. Ariz., 1979, gold medallion Soc. of Family of Man, 1982, Joseph Wharton award Wharton Sch. Club N.Y., 1983, Life Achievement award TV Guide, 1984, award Ctr. for Communications, 1985; co-recipient Walter Cronkite award Ariz. State U., 1984; Medallion of Honor City of N.Y.; First Amendment Freedoms award Anti-Defamation League B'nai B'rith; Robert Eunson Distinguished Service award Assn. Press Broadcasters; named to Jr. Achievement Nat. Bus. Hall of Fame, 1984. Mem. Council Fgn. Relations, France Am. Soc., Acad. Polit. Scis., Nat. Inst. Social Scis., Royal Soc. Arts (fellow). Clubs: River, Century Assn; The Metropolitan (Washington); Turf and Field, Nat. Golf, Meadowbrook; Economic (N.Y.); Lyford Cay (Nassau); Bucks (London). Office: CBS Inc 51 W 52d St New York NY 10019

PALIN, DAVID JOHN, management consultant; b. London, May 22, 1931; s. John Clarence and Jessie Grace (Butler) P.; m. Lydia Maria Hatvany, Aug. 4, 1957 (div. 1962); children: Jessica, Carlos; m. Ella Agneta Eidman, Jan. 9, 1970; children: Isabella, Adam. BA in Law and Theology, Cambridge U., 1953, MA, 1957, LLB in Internat. Law, 1958. Personnel officer OEEC (later called OECD), Paris, 1958-64; dep. chief personnel OECD, Paris, 1964-68, spl. advisor, 1968-70; chmn. Euromktg. Co., London, 1970-73; researcher, cons. Scandinavian Inst. for Adminstrv. Research, Stockholm, 1973-78; researcher Food and Agrl. Orgn. of UN, Rome, 1978-79; project mgr. Bangledesh Forestry Dept., Chittagong, 1979-81; researcher, cons. Societal and Orgnl. Research Ltd., Guernsey, Channel Isles, Eng., 1981-85; chmn. Societal and Orgnl. Research Ltd., Isle of Man, 1985—; bd. dirs. Markham Research Services Ltd., London, Banner Internat. Mgmt., S.A., Luxembourg. Author: Management of Development Forestry, 1981; editor Two Cities Gazette, London and Westminster, 1970-74; contbr. numerous articles to profl. jours. Chmn. bd. dirs. Two Cities Com. for Europe, London, 1971-74. Fellow Brit. Inst. Mgmt.; mem. Royal Commonwealth Soc. Conservative. Anglican. Club: Pitt (Cambridge). Lodge: Anglo-Saxons (Master 1968-70). Address: Swedforest Cons, Box 154, Danderyd Sweden Office: Societal & Orgnl Research Ltd, Examiner Bldg, Hill St, Douglas Isle of Man

PALIN, MICHAEL EDWARD, writer, actor; b. May 5, 1943; s. Edward and Mary Palin; m. Helen M. Gibbons, 1966; 3 children. BA, U. Oxford, Eng. Actor, writer: (TV shows) Monty Pythons's Flying Circus, 1969-74, Ripping Yarns, 1976-80; (films) And Now for Something Completely different, 1970, Monty Python and the Holy Grail, 1974, Monty Python's Life of Brian, 1978, Time Bandits, 1980, Monty Python's The Meaning of Life, 1982; actor: (TV shows) Three Men in a Boat, 1975; (films) Jabberwocky, 1976, A Private Function, 1984, Brazil, 1985; actor, writer and co-producer: The Missionary, 1982; author: Monty Python's Big Red Book, 1970, Monty Python's Brand New Bok, 1973, Dr. Fegg's Encyclopaedia of All World Knowledge, 1984, Limericks, 1985; (children's books) Small Harry and the Toothache Pills, 1981, The Mirrorstone, 1986, The Cyril Stories, 1986. Club: Turf. Office: 6 Cambridge Gate, London NW1 4JR, England *

PALKA, ZBIGNIEW JANUSZ, mathematics educator; b. Poznan, Poland, May 8, 1951; s. Czeslaw and Stanislawa (Piaseczna) P.; m. Halina Larus, Sept. 11, 1976; 1 child, Ewa. MA, A. Mickiewicz U., Poznan, 1974; PhD, A. Michkiewicz U., Poznan, 1980. Mem. faculty A. Mickiewicz U., Poznan, 1974—, assoc. prof. math., 1988—; postdoctoral fellow U. Fla., Gainesville, 1981-82; vis. asst. prof. St. John's U., N.Y.C., 1982-83, Baruch Coll.-CUNY, N.Y.C., 1986-87. Author: Asymptomatic Properties of Random Graphs, 1988; editor: Random Graphs '85, 1987; contbr. articles to profl. jours. Matsumae Internat. Found. fellow, Tokyo, 1986; grantee Rockefeller U., N.Y.C., 1988. Mem. Polish Math. Soc., Am. Math. Soc., Bernoulli Soc. Home: Os B Chrobrego 7D/101, 60-683 Poznan Poland Office: A Mickiewicz U, Matejki 48/49, 60-769 Poznan Poland

PALLANGYO, EPHATA PARMENA, agricultural ecomonist; b. Arusha, Tanzania, June 13, 1941; s. Parmena Lemanga and Eliavinga (Veria) P.; m. Eliamani Saulo Ayo; children: Avinga, Anande, Akunda. Diploma in Agrl. Sci., Lincoln U. Coll., New Zealand, 1965; BSc in Agrl. Econ., U. Manitoba, Canada, 1970; MSc in Agrl. Econ., U. Guelph, Canada, 1972; postgrad. diploma in mgmt. and research, Internat. Mktg. Inst. Harvard U., 1976. Agrl. trg. officer Ministry of Agrl., Vet., Forestry and Fisheries, Daressalaam, Tanzania, 1965-66; head sect. planning Ministry of Agrl., Vet., Forestry and Fisheries, Darea Salaam, 1972-74; agrl. economist Can. Dept. of Agrl., Regina, 1970; mktg. dir. Liv. Dev. Authority, Darea Salaam, 1974-78; project officer Commonwealth Secretariat, London, 1978-79; sr. regional econ. advisor UN Econ. Commn. for Africa, Addis Ababa, Ethiopia, 1979-82; sr. planning economist UN Econ. Commn. for Africa/FAO Agrl. div., Addis Ababa, 1983-84, policy and planning chief, 1984—; cons. UN Econ. Commn. for Africa/FAO, on study of causes of rural poverty in Ethiopoa, Mozambique, Senegal, Zambia, 1983—; external examiner UN of Addis Ababa, 1986—; mem. U.N. of Daressalaam (Agrl. Econ. Research Coordination Com. 1972-74). Author: Survey of Agricultural Technology (recipient cash prize), 1983; contbr. articles to profl. jours. Mem. Daressalaam Planning Comn., 1972-74. Recipient Commonwealth Scolarship New Zealand Govt., 1963-65, Canadian Govt., 1966-72, U.S. Agy. for Internat. Devel. Fellowship U.S. Govt., 1976. Mem. Am. Agrl. Econ. Assn., Can. Agrl. Econ. Soc., Stanford Food Research Inst., Royal Commonwealth Soc., The Economist. Lutheran. Office: UN Nations ECA FAO div, PO Box 3005, Addis Ababa Ethiopa

PALLASCH, B. MICHAEL, lawyer; b. Chgo., Mar. 30, 1933; s. Bernhard Michael and Magdalena Helena (Fixari) P.; m. Josephine Catherine O'Leary, Aug. 15, 1981. B.S.S., Georgetown U., 1954; J.D., Harvard U., 1957; postgrad., John Marshall Law Sch., 1974. Bar: Ill. 1957, U.S. Dist. Ct. (no. dist.) Ill. 1958, U.S. Tax Ct. 1961, U.S. Ct. Claims 1961, U.S. Ct. Appeals (7th cir.) 1962. Assoc. Winston & Strawn, Chgo., 1958-66; resident mgr. br. office Winston & Strawn, Paris, 1963-65; ptnr. Winston & Strawn, Chgo., 1966-70, sr. capital ptnr., 1971—; dir., corp. sec. Tanis Inc., Calumet, Mich., 1972—, Greenbank Engring. Corp., Dover, Del., 1976—, C.B.P. Engring. Corp., Chgo., 1976—, Chgo. Cutting Services Corp., 1977—; corp. sec. Arthur Andersen Assocs. Inc., Chgo., 1976—, L'hotel de France of Ill. Inc., Chgo., 1980-85; dir. Bosch Devel. Co., Longview, Tex., Lor Inc., Houghton, Mich., Rana Inc., Madison, Wis., Woodlak Co., Houghton. Bd. dirs. Martin D'Arcy Mus. Medieval and Renaissance Art, Chgo., 1975—; bd. dirs. Katherine M. Bosch Found., 1978—; asst. sec. Hundred Club of Cook County, Chgo., 1966-73, bd. dirs., sec., 1974—. Served with USAFR, 1957-63. Recipient Outstanding Woodland Mgmt. Forestry award Monroe County (Wis.) Soil and Water Conservation Dist., 1975; recipient Youth Mayor of

Chgo. award, 1950. Mem. Ill. Bar Assn. (tax lectr. 1961), Advocates Soc., Field Mus. Natural History (life mem.), Max McGraw Wildlife Found., Chgo. Br. The English Speaking Union. Roman Catholic. Clubs: Travellers (Paris); Saddle and Cycle (Chgo.). Home: 3000 N Sheridan Rd Chicago IL 60657 Office: Winston & Strawn 1 First Nat Plaza Suite 5000 Chicago IL 60603

PALLASCH, MAGDALENA HELENA (MRS. BERNHARD MICHAEL PALLASCH), artist; b. Chgo., Sept. 6, 1908; d. Frank and Anna (Meier) Fixari; student Chgo. Acad. Fine Arts, 1922-26, Am. Acad. Fine Arts, 1926-30, U. Chgo., 1960, Art Inst. Chgo.; pvt. study with Joseph Allworthy, 1935-38; hon. doctorate, 1985; m. Bernhard Pallasch, Nov. 26, 1931 (dec. Nov. 1977); children—Bernhard Michael, Diana Pallasch Miller. Contbr. two murals and ten life size figures for Century of Progress Exhbn., Chgo., 1933-34; free-lance portrait artist, subjects include Cardinal Cody, Chgo., 1958—; represented in permanent collections Loyola U., Chgo., Barat Coll., Lake Forest, Ill., Internat. Coll. Surgeons, Chgo., Med. Library, Columbus Hosp. Mem. Presentation Ball Aux.; mem. President's Club, Loyola U., also mem. women's bd. Recipient first award for still life Arts Club, N.Y.C., 1960; First award Nat. League Am. Pen Women, 1972; 1st place and best of show State Exhibit, Springfield, Ill., 1973; 1st award Chgo. Woman's Club, 1978; hon. mention for portrait Italian Cultural Ctr.; hon. alumna award Loyola U., Chgo.; award of excellence for portrait of author Gail Brook Burket, Wheaton Hist. Mus., 1987; Gold Medal of Honor for disting. lifelong achievements, 1987. Mem. Nat. League Am. Pen Women (v.p. Chgo. br. 1966-68, art chmn. 1978-80, Margaret Dingle Meml. award 1979), Mcpl. Art League Chgo., Nat. Soc. Arts and Letters (art chmn. chgo. chpt. 1982—), Friends of Austria, Friends of D'Arcy Gallery of Medieval and Renaissance Art. Clubs: Ill. Cath. Women (gov. 1979—), Cuneo Meml. Hosp. Aux. (dir.), Fidelitas (dir.). Home and Home and Studio: 723 Junior Terr Chicago IL 60613

PALLASCH, THOMAS J., periodontist, pharmacologist, educator; b. Milw., June 15, 1936; s. Joseph John and Stella (Zavis) P.; D.D.S., Marquette U., 1960; M.S. in Pharmacology, certificate in periodontics, U. Wash., 1967; m. Christine Peterson, May 14, 1977; children—Brian, Jennifer, Robert. Rotating dental intern U.S. Navy, 1960-61; asso. prof. pharmacology and periodontics, chmn. dept. pharmacology Sch. Dentistry, U. So. Calif., Los Angeles, 1967—, chmn. dept. periodontics, 1981-83, dir. oral biology grad. program, 1968-77, dir. pain and anxiety control program, 1972-76; pvt. practice periodontics Burbank, Calif., 1968—. Served with USN, 1960-64. Fellow Am. Coll. Dentists, Pierre Fauchard Acad.; mem. Am. Dental Assn., Am. Assn. Dental Schs., Am. Coll. Dentists, AAAS, Delta Sigma Delta (dep. supreme grand master (1968-71), Omicron Kappa Epsilon. Author: Clinical Drug Therapy in Dental Practice, 1973; Synopsis of Pharmacology for Students in Dentistry, 1974; Pharmacology for Dental Students and Practitioners, 1980; editor, pub. Dental Drug Service Newsletter; contbg. editor Dentist's Med. Digest, 1986—. Expert witness on dental malpractice, 1970—. Home: 1411 W Olive Ave Burbank CA 91506 Office: 1411 W Olive Ave Burbank CA 91506

PALLAYEV, GAIBNAZAR PALLAYEVICH, Soviet government official; b. Tadzhik, Soviet Socialist Republic. Mem. Cen. Com. Tadzhik Communist Party, 1961—; chmn. of Tadzhik Republican Assn. for Agrl. Tech., Tadzhikselkhoztekhnika, 1973-77; 1st sec. of Kurgan-Tiube Oblast Com. Tadzhik Communist Party, from 1977, dep. chmn. USSR Supreme Soviet Presidium, 1984—. Address: Supreme Soviet Presidium, Office of Deputy Chmn, Moscow USSR *

PALMA, DOLORES PATRICIA, urban planner, consultant, lecturer, author; b. Bklyn., Jan. 20, 1951; d. Anthony Michael Resse and Eleanor Dorothea (Palma) Graffeo; m. Doyle G. Hyett, Apr. 12, 1986. BA, CUNY, Bklyn., 1972; M of Urban Planning, U. Mich., 1974. Student intern Mich. Mcpl. League, Ann Arbor, 1973-74; park planner Metro Bd. Parks and Recreation, Nashville, 1975; preservation planner Metro. Hist. Commn., Nashville, 1976; sr. community planner Metro Planning Commn., Nashville, 1977-79; exec. dir. Metro Hist. Zoning Commn., Nashville, 1980-82; asst. dir. Mid-Atlantic Regional Office, Nat. Trust for Hist. Preservation, Washington, 1983, dir. Office of Neighborhood Conservation, 1984, project dir. Urban Demonstration Program Nat. Main St. Ctr., 1984-87; pres. Hyett-Palma Inc. 1985—, Hyett-Palma Publs. 1988—; del. Nat. Assn. Neighborhoods Platform Conv., 1979; cons. in field. Neighborhood Reinvestment Council, Nashville, 1978, mayoral appointee Neighborhood Housing Services, Nashville, 1979-82; dir. Restore the U.S. Capitol Campaign, 1983. Author: Salaries, Wages and Fringe Benefits in Michigan Cities and Villages, 1973; Nashville: Conserving a Heritage, 1977; Neighborhood Commercial Buildings: A Survey and Analysis of Metropolitan Nashville, 1983; Business Enhancement for Downtown Poughkeepsie, N.Y., 1987; Future Directions for Seward, Alaska, 1987; Action Agenda for Gay Street, Knoxville, 1987; Agenda for Economic Enhancement of Haymarket Lincoln, Nebraska, 1987; Management of Downtown Palmer, Alaska, 1988; Successful Business Recruitment Strategies in the U.S., 1988, Business Clustering: How to Leverage Sales, 1988, Strategic Thinking for Commercial District Enhancement: A Video Script for the National League of Cities, 1988, Business Plans for Business Districts, 1988; project dir.: A Market and Design Study for the Broadway National Register Historic District, 1982; author studies, pamphlet, articles; contbr. newsletters; editor Edgefield News, Nashville, 1979-80. Publicity dir. Hist. Edgefield, Inc., 1979; hon. mem. Tenn. State Legislature, 1980. Woodlawn scholar Nat. Trust for Hist. Preservation, 1976; named one of Outstanding Young Women of Am., 1985. Office: PO Box 65881 Washington DC 20035

PALMA, NICHOLAS JAMES, lawyer; b. Newark, Oct. 28, 1953; s. James Thomas and Venice Maria (Dibenedetto) P.; m. Mary Jo Cugliari, Sept. 1, 1973; children—Nicholas J., Valerie Michele, James Michael. B.S. cum laude, William Paterson U., 1975; J.D., Seton Hall U., 1979. Bar: N.J. 1979, U.S. Dist. Ct. N.J. 1979, U.S. Ct. Appeals (3d cir.) 1985, N.Y. 1986; cert. firearms expert, Hudson County, N.J. Investigator N.J. Pub. Defender's Office, Essex Region, Newark, 1974-75; investigator Hudson County Prosecutor's Office, Jersey City, 1975-79, asst. prosecutor, 1979-81; ptnr. A.J. Fusco, Jr., P.A., Passaic, N.J., 1981—. Recipient Commendation, Dade County Sheriff, Fla., 1976. Mem. Passaic County Bar Assn., N.J. State Bar Assn. Roman Catholic. Home: 221 Cedar St Cedar Grove NJ 07009 Office: A J Fusco Jr PA 40 Passaic Ave PO Box 838 Passaic NJ 07055

PALMAS, JACQUES, physician, general practitioner; b. Bordeaux, France, Dec. 16, 1947; s. Armand and Jeannine (Bruzac) P.; m. Catherine Serres, Jan. 1985. B, Montesquieu Coll., Le Mans, France, 1964; MD, U. Angers, 1975. Gen. practice medicine Le Mans, 1975—. Mem. Medecin d'Urgence Assn. (founding 1984, treas. 1984—). Roman Catholic. Office: Cabinet Med Ambroise Pare, 128 rue Ambroise Pare, 7200 Le Mans France

PALME, RUDOLF, historian; b. Berlin, Mar. 19, 1942; arrived in Austria, 1946; s. Rudolf Leo and Theresia (Huber) P.; m. Waltrad Comploy; 1 child, Rudolf Johannes. PhD, U. Vienna, Austria, 1969; diploma, Inst. für österreichische Geschichtsforschung, Vienna, 1971. Univ. asst. Inst. für Rechtesgeschichte, Innsbruck, Austria, 1971-87, prof. history, 1987—; mem. Internat. Commn. for History of Representative and Parliamentary Insts., 1987—, Commn. Internat. d'historie du sel, 1987—. Author: Die landesherrlichen Salinenrechte und Salzbergrechte, 1974, Das Messingwerk in Pflach, 1976, Rechtsgeschichte, Wirtschaftsgeschichte und Sozialgeschichte der inneralpinen Salzwerke bis zu deren Monopolisierung, 1983. Recipient Theodor-Körner prize Theodor-Körner-Siftung, Vienna, 1978. Mem. Innsbrucker Gesellschaft zur Pflege der Geisteswissenschaften, Gesellschaft Sozialgeschichte und Wirtschaftsgeschichte. Roman Catholic. Club: Professorenverband (Innsbruck). Office: Inst für Rechtesgeschichte, Innrain 52, 6020 Innsbruck Austria

PALMER, EDWARD B., educational administrator; b. Williamsburg, Va., July 26, 1928; s. Louis and Amelia P.; A.B. in Sociology, Va. State Coll., 1962; M.S., CCNY, 1967; postgrad. Columbia U., 1975—; m. Edith E. Maginley, July 30, 1960; children—Karen Allison, Brian Edward. Technician, Pacific Tel. & Tel. Co., Los Angeles, 1955-58; dormitory supr., counselor Youth House, Bronx, N.Y., 1958-60; tchr., counselor N.Y.C. Bd. Edn., 1960-68; lectr., asst. higher edn. officer City U. N.Y., 1968-70; assoc. regional dir. Coll. Entrance Exam. Bd., N.Y.C., 1970-83; dir. acad. services Coll. Bd. Middle States Regional Office, Phila., 1983—; faculty mem. summer inst. on coll. placement, admissions and fin. aid Coll. Bd./U.N.C., Chapel Hill; mem. adv. com. on tchr. edn. and certification N.Y. State Bd. Regents; mem. coll. scholarship com. United Fedn. Tchrs., 1972—; cons. Dept. Def., 1980. Area dir. Operation Crossroads Africa (West Africa), 1969; bd. dirs. Logos Drug Rehab. Center, N.Y.C., 1972-74; bd. dirs., mem. subcom. on edn. Urban League Bergen County (N.J.). Served with U.S. Army, 1950-53; ETO. Mem. Am. Assn. for Counseling and Devel., N.Y. State Fin. Aid Adminstrs. Assn., N.Y. State Assn. for Counseling and Devel. (exec. com. Ahead div.), Nat. Assn. for Curriculum and Devel., Nat. Assn. Fgn. Student Advisors. Democrat. Home: 522 Kings Croft Cherry Hill NJ 08034 Office: 3440 Market St Philadelphia PA 19104

PALMER, EMMA, business education instructor; b. Kilmichael, Miss., Jan. 30, 1950; d. Joe Arnold and Mattie Eiland; m. John Albert Palmer, Aug. 21, 1970; children: Ashur, John II, Joe Alvin. BS in Bus. Edn., Rust Coll., 1970; MEd in Edn., 1972. Tchr. Milw. Pub. Schs., 1970-71; lead tchr. Midwest Success Tng., Milw., 1971-72; social sci. tchr. Milw. Area Tech. Coll., 1972—. Mem. Office Tech. Assn. (v.p. 1985—), Internat. Soc. Wang Users, Soc. Office Automation Profls., Bus. and Profl. Women (v.p. 1985-86), Milw. County Zool. Soc. Democrat. Methodist. Home: 4740 N 19th St Milwaukee WI 53209 Office: Milw Area Tech Coll 1015 N 6th St Milwaukee WI 53203

PALMER, FRANK ROBERT, linguist, educator; b. Westleigh, Gloucestershire, Eng., Apr. 9, 1922; s. George Samuel and Gertrude Lilian (Newman) P.; m. Jean Elisabeth Moore, June 18, 1948; children: Peter Frank, Robert George, Jane Margaret, Andrew Mark, Ruth Elisabeth May. Student, U. Oxford, Eng., 1941-42, 45-48; MA, Merton Coll., Oxford, 1949. Lectr. linguistics Sch. Oriental and African Studies U. London, 1950-60; prof. linguistics U. Coll. North Wales, Bangor, 1960-65; prof. linguistic sci. U. Reading, Eng., 1965-87; dean Faculty Letters Social Scis. U. Reading, 1969-72. Author: The Morphology of the Tigre Noun, 1962, A Linguistic Study of the English Verb, 1965, Grammar, 1970, The English Verb, 1974, 2d. edit., 1987, Semantics, 1976, 2d edit. 1981, Modality and the English Modals, 1979, Mood and Modality, 1986; editor: Selected Papers of J.R. Firth (1951-58), 1968, Prosodic Analysis, 1970; editor Jour. Linguistics. Served to lt. Royal British Army, 1942-45, Africa. Fellow Brit. Acad. (mem. council 1980-83); mem. Philol. Soc., Linguistic Soc. Am. (profl. 1971), LInguistics Assn. G.B. (chmn. 1965-68). Home: Whitethorns Roundabout Ln, Winnersh, Wokingham, Berkshire RG11 5AD, England

PALMER, GEOFFREY, deputy prime minister New Zealand, lawyer; b. Nelson, N.Z., Apr. 21, 1942; m. Margaret Eleanor Hinchcliff; children: Matthew, Rebekah. B.A. in Polit. Sci., Victoria U., 1964, LL.B., 1965; J.D. cum laude, U. Chgo., 1967. Solicitor, Wellington, N.Z., 1964-66; lectr. polit. sci. Victoria U., 1968; prof. law U. Iowa and U. Va., 1969-73; prin. asst. Australian Nat. Com. of Inquiry on Rehab. and Compensation, 1973; prof. English and N.Z. law Victoria U., 1974-79; vis. fellow Wolfson Coll., Oxford U., 1978; vis. prof. U. Iowa, 1977; cons. Australian Govt., 1974-75; adv. govts. Sri Lanka and Cyprus, 1979-80; M.P. for Christchurch Central, 1979—, now dep. prime minister, atty.-gen., minister for the environ., minister of justice, former leader of house and minister in charge GPO. Mem. Privy Council, 1986—. Author books and articles in field. Office: Office of Atty Gen, Wellington New Zealand

PALMER, JERRY RICHARD, lawyer; b. Jefferson City, Mo., Aug. 22, 1940; s. Noble Edison and Harriet Jane (McCall) P.; m. Ann Leffler, Aug. 20, 1965; children—Christopher Paul, Andrea Leffler. B.A., U. Kans., 1962, J.D., 1966. Bar: Kans. 1966. Ptnr. Fisher, Patterson, Sayler & Smith, Topeka, 1966-70; assoc. Fisher & Benfer, 1971-74; sole practice, 1975-77; ptnr. Stumbo, Palmer et al., 1978-80; pres. Jerry R. Palmer P.A., 1980-85; pres. Palmer, Marquardt & Snyder P.A., 1986—. Fellow Am. Coll. Trial Lawyers; mem. Assn. Trial Lawyers Am. (bd. govs. 1982-85), Kans. Trial Lawyers Assn. (pres. 1977), Nat. Bd. Trial Advocacy, Am. Law Inst. Democrat. Episcopalian. Advocations: skiing; sailing; photography. Home: 305 Greenwood Topeka KS 66606 Office: 112 SW 6th St Suite 102 Topeka KS 66603

PALMER, PATRICIA ANN TEXTER, English language educator; b. Detroit, June 10, 1932; d. Elmer Clinton and Helen (Rotchford) Texter; m. David Jean Palmer, June 4, 1955. B.A., U. Mich., 1953; M.Ed., Nat. Coll. Edn., 1958; M.A., Calif. State U.-San Francisco, 1966; postgrad. Stanford U., 1968, Calif. State Coll.-Hayward, 1968-69. Chmn. speech dept. Grosse Pointe Univ. Sch. (Mich.), 1953-55; tchr. South Margerita Sch., Panama, 1955-56, Kipling Sch., Deerfield, Ill., 1955-56; grade level chmn. Rio San Gabriel Sch., Downey, Calif., 1957-59; tchr. newswriting and devel. reading Roosevelt High Sch., Honolulu, 1959-62; tchr. English, speech and newswriting El Camino High Sch., South San Francisco, 1962-68; chmn. English as 2d lang. dept. South San Francisco Unified Sch. Dist., 1968-81; dir. English as 2d lang. Inst., Millbrae, Calif., 1978—; adj. faculty New Coll. Calif., 1981—; Calif. master tchr. English as 2d lang. Calif. Council Adult Edn., 1979-82; cons. in field. Recipient Concours de Francais Prix, 1947; Jeanette M. Liggett Meml. award for excellence in history, 1949. Mem. Internat. Platform Assn., Calif. Assn. Tchrs. English to Speakers Other Langs., TESOL, Nat. Assn. for Fgn. Student Affairs, Computer Using Educators, AAUW, U. Mich. Alumnae Assn., Nat. Coll. Edn. Alumnae Assn., Ninety Nines (chmn. Golden West chpt.), Chi Omega, Zeta Phi Eta. Club: Peninsula Lioness (pres.). Home: 2917 Franciscan Ct San Carlos CA 94070 Office: 450 Chadbourne Ave Millbrae CA 94030

PALMER, PHILIP ISHAM, JR., lawyer; b. Dallas, June 25, 1929; s. Philip I. and Charlene (Bolen) P.; m. Eleanor Hutson, Mar. 7, 1951; children—Stephen Edward, Michael Bolen. B.B.A., So. Methodist U., 1952; LL.B., U. Tex., 1957. Bar: Tex. 1957. Since practiced in Dallas; ptnr. Palmer & Palmer P.C. (and predecessor firms), 1957—; chmn. bd. Carolina Mfg. Corp., 1973—, pres., 1969-73; chmn. bd. Commonwealth Nat. Bank, 1967-69; pres. Pennyrich Corp., 1969-72. Co-author: Texas Creditors Rights; Contbr. articles to profl. jours. Vice consul Republic Costa Rica, 1973—; bd. dirs. Shepherd's Care, 1987—. Mem. Am. Bar Assn., Am. Judicature Soc. Club: City. Home: 6757 Lake Fair Circle Dallas TX 75214 Office: Palmer & Palmer PC 1510 One Main Pl Dallas TX 75202

PALMER, RANDALL PARHAM, III, lawyer, army officer; b. Birmingham, Ala., Dec. 10, 1944; s. Randall Parham, Jr. and Minnie Palmer; m. Cheryl Ann Jean, Feb. 14, 1970; children—Randall Parham, Brandy Elizabeth. B.A., Langston U., 1968; J.D., Okla. City U., 1976; grad. legal program Judge Adv. Gen.'s Sch., Charlottesville, Va., 1982. Bar: Tex. 1976, U.S. Tax Ct. 1979, U.S. Supreme Ct. 1985. Enlisted U.S. Army, 1969, advanced through grades to maj., 1981; counsel Spl. Rev. Bd., Hdqrs. Dept. Army, Washington, 1979-81; acting clk. of ct., chief spl. actions Army Ct. Mil. Rev., Washington, 1979-81; chief criminal law div. 2d Inf. Div., Korea, 1982; dep. comdr. U.S. Armed Forces Claims Service, Korea, 1983; service sch. instr., Fort Sam Houston, Tex., 1983—; grad. faculty Baylor U., Waco, Tex., Tulane U., New Orleans, Tex. Wesleyan Coll., Fort Worth, 1984; pres. Global Imports, San Antonio. Bd. dirs. United Negro Coll. Fund., San Antonio, 1978-79, Langston U. Devel. Found. (legal counsel 1985—); mem. Carver Devel. Bd., 1988—; pres. Okla. Intercollegiate Student Assn., 1967-68. Decorated Bronze Star, Meritorious Service medal; recipient Leadership award Okla. Intercollegiate Student Assn. Mem. Nat. Bar Assn. (vice chmn. govt. lawyers div. 1984—), State Bar Tex., Assn. Trial Lawyers Am., ABA, Internat. Legal Soc. Korea, San Antonio Black Lawyers Assn. (sec. 1988—), Alpha Phi Alpha (v.p. 1985—, bd. dirs.), Phi Alpha Delta. Lodge: Masons. Office: Global Imports PO Box 8151 San Antonio TX 78208

PALMER, RICHARD WARE, lawyer; b. Boston, Oct. 20, 1919; s. Geroge Ware and Ruth French (Judkins) P.; m. Nancy Fernald Shaw, July 8, 1950; children: Richard Ware Jr., John Wentworth, Anne Fernald. A.B., Harvard U., 1942, J.D., 1948. Bar: N.Y. State 1950, Pa. 1959. Sec., dir. N. Am. Mfg. Co., Natick, Mass., 1946-48; assoc. firm Burlingham, Veeder, Clark & Hupper, Burlingham, Hupper & Kennedy, N.Y.C., 1949-57; ptnr. firm Rawle & Henderson, Phila., 1958-79, firm Palmer, Biezup & Henderson, 1979—; sec., dir. Underwater Technics, Inc., Camden, N.J., 1967-85; adv. on admiralty law to U.S. del. Inter-Govtl. Maritime Consultative Orgn., London, 1967; mem. U.S. Shipping Coordinating Com., Washington legal sub com., 1967—; adv. admiralty law to U.S. del. 6th working session UN Conf. on Internat. Shipping Legis., Geneva, 1974; U.S. del. 30th-33d internat. confs. Comité Maritime International. Mem. permanent adv. bd. Tulane Admiralty Law Inst., Tulane U. Law Sch., New Orleans.; trustee Seamen's Ch. Inst., Phila., 1967—, pres., 1972-84; bd. dirs. Haverford (Pa.) Civic Assn., 1972-85, pres., 1976-79; Consul for Denmark in, State of Pa. Served to lt. comdr. USNR, 1942-46. Fellow World Acad. Art and Sci. (treas. 1986—); Mem. Am. Bar Assn. (chmn. standing com. on admiralty and maritime law 1978-79, mem. 1973-79), N.Y.C. Bar Assn., Phila. Bar Assn., Am. Judicature Soc., Maritime Law Assn. (chmn. limitation liability com. 1977-83, 2d v.p. 1984-86, 1st v.p. 1986-88, pres. 1988—), Assn. Average Adjusters U.S.A. and Gt. Brit., Port of Phila. Maritime Soc. Republican. Episcopalian. Clubs: Union League, Rittenhouse, Downtown (Phila.); Merion (Pa.) Cricket; India House, Whitehall Lunch (N.Y.C.); Harvard (N.Y.C., Phila. and Boston) (v.p., mem. exec. com. 1983-86). Home: 318 Grays Ln Haverford PA 19041 Office: Public Ledger Bldg Philadelphia PA 19106

PALMER, ROBERT TOWNE, lawyer; b. Chgo., May 25, 1947; s. Adrian Bernhardt and Gladys (Towne) P.; BA, Colgate U., 1969; JD, U. Notre Dame, 1974; m. Ann Therese Darin, Nov. 9, 1974; children: Justin Darin, Christian Darin. Bar: Ill. 1974, D.C. 1978, U.S. Supreme Ct. 1978. Law clk. Hon. Walter V. Schaefer, Ill. Supreme Ct., 1974-75; assoc. McDermott, Will & Emery, Chgo., 1975-81, ptnr., 1982-86; ptnr. Chadwell & Kayser, Ltd., 1987—; mem. adj. faculty Chgo. Kent Law Sch., 1975-77, Loyola U., 1976-78; mem. adv. com. Fed. Home Loan Mortgage Corp., 1988—. Mem. ABA, Ill. State Bar Assn., Chgo. Bar Assn., D.C. Bar Assn., Internat. Assn. Def. Counsel, Lambda Alpha. Republican. Episcopalian. Clubs: Chicago, Univerwity (Chgo.); Dairymen's. Contbr. articles to legal jours. and textbooks. Office: Chadwell & Kayser Ltd 8500 Sears Tower Chicago IL 60606-6592

PALMER, R(OBIE MARCUS HOOKER) MARK, diplomat; b. Ann Arbor, Mich., July 14, 1941; s. Robie Ellis and Katherine (Hooker) P.; m. Sushma Palmer. BA, Yale U., 1963. Copy asst. N.Y. Times, N.Y.C., 1963; asst. to producer WNDT-TV, N.Y.C., 1963-64; entered U.S. Fgn. Service 1964; third sec. U.S. Embassy, New Delhi, India, 1964-66; internat. relations officer NATO affiars, Dept State, Washington, 1966-68; second sec. U.S. Embassy, Moscow, 1968-71; prin. speechwriter Sec. of State Rogers, Kissinger, Washington, 1971-75; counselor for polit. affairs U.S. Embassy, Belgrade, Yugoslavia, 1975-78; dir. office disarmament and control of arms Bur. of Polit.-Mil. Affairs Dept. State, Washington, 1978-81, dep. to undersec. for polit. affairs, 1981-82, dep. asst. sec. state for European affairs, 1982-86; ambassador U.S. Embassy, Budapest, Hungary, 1986—. Author: speeches for five Secs. of State and three Pres.'s. Recipient Superior Honor award Dept. State, 1980, Presdl. Meritorious Service award, award, 1984. Mem. Council Fgn. Relations, Am. Fgn. Service Assn., Phi Beta Kappa. Episcopalian.

PALMER, RONALD DEWAYNE FAISAL, diplomat; b. Uniontown, Pa., May 22, 1932; s. Wilbur Fortune and Ethel Danya (Roberts); m. Tengku Intan Badariah Abubakar; children: Derek Ronald, Alyson Cecily. BA, Howard U., 1954; MA in Internat. Studies, Johns Hopkins U., 1957. Vice ambassador to Indonesia, Denmark, Malaysia, The Philippines, prior to 1976; ambassador to Togo, 1976-78; dep. dir. gen. Fgn. Service State Dept., 1978-81; ambassador to Malaysia Kuala Lumpur, 1981-83; sr. scholar, mem. adv. bd. Ctr. Strategic and Internat. Studies, Washington, 1983-86; ambassador to Mauritius Port Louis, 1986—; mem. com. on yr. 2000 Sch. Advanced Studies, Washington. Author: Building Cooperation - 20 Years of ASEAN, 1987. Decorated Order of Mono Pres. of Togo, 1978, Most Hon. Order of Johar Sultan of Johor Bahru, Mali, 1984; recipient Sr. Fgn. Service Performance award State Dept., 1985. Mem. Am. Fgn. Service Assn., Council on Fgn. Relations. Office: American Embassy, John F Kennedy Ave, Port Louis Mauritius also: care State Dept 2201 C St NW Washington DC 20520

PALMER, RUDOLPH MARTIN, JR., lawyer; b. Washington, Feb. 22, 1944; s. Rudolph Martin and Mossie (Ely) P.; m. Shirley Kay Bloss, Aug. 24, 1969; children—Marty, Andrew, Kathryn, Ruth, Kathleen. B.S., U. Md., 1967; J.D., U. Balt., 1970; postgrad. Nat. Coll. Advocacy, Harvard U., 1983. Bar: Md. 1974, U.S. Ct. Appeals (D.C. cir.) 1974, U.S. Supreme Ct. 1977, U.S. Dist. Ct. Md. 1978. Sole practice, Hagerstown, Md., 1974—. Author: A Symphony of the Preborn, 1984; (with others) Modern Trials-The Second, 1982. Fellow Melvin M. Belli Soc.; mem. Assn. Trial Lawyers Am., ABA, Md. Trial Lawyers Assn., Md. Bar Assn. Republican. Presbyterian. Lodge: Kiwanis.

PALMER, SAMUEL COPELAND, III, lawyer; b. Phila., June 9, 1934; s. Samuel Copeland Jr. and Vivian Gertrude (Plumb) P.; m. Janet Louis Schroeder, June 8, 1957; children: Samuel C. IV, Sarah Anne, Bryan Douglas. Grad., Harvard Sch., Los Angeles, 1952; student, Yale U., 1953; A.B., Stanford U., 1955; J.D., Loyola U., 1958. Bar: Calif. 1959, U.S. Dist. Ct. (cen., ea. and so. dists. Calif.) 1959, U.S. Ct. Appeals (9th cir.) 1970, U.S. Supreme Ct. 1971. Dep. city atty. Los Angeles, 1959-60; assoc. firm Pollock & Deutz, Los Angeles, 1960-63; ptnr. firm Pollock & Palmer, Los Angeles, 1963-70, Palmer & Bartenetti, Los Angeles, 1970-81, Samuel C. Palmer III, P.C., 1981-85, Thomas, Snell, Jamison, Russell & Asperger, 1986—. Trustee Western Center Law and Poverty; bd. dirs. Big Bros. and Sisters, Fresno; pres., bd. dirs. Poverello House, 1981—. Mem. Am. Bar Assn., State Bar Calif. (disciplinary subcom., bar examiners subcom.), Am. Bd. Trial Advocates, Delta Upsilon, Phi Delta Phi, Chancery Club. Clubs: Calif., San Joaquin Country, Downtown, Sierra Racquet. Home: 7166 N Dewey Ave Fresno CA 93711 Office: 2445 Capitol St Fresno CA 93721

PALMER, STUART HUNTER, educational administrator, sociology educator; b. N.Y.C., Apr. 29, 1924; s. Herman G. and Beatrice (Hunter) P.; m. Anne Barbara Scarborough, June 22, 1946; 1 dau., Catherine. B.A., Yale U., 1949, M.A., 1951, Ph.D., 1955. Asst. to dean Yale Coll., New Haven, 1949-51; instr. sociology New Haven Coll., 1949-51, 53-55; faculty U. N.H., Durham, 1955—; prof. U. N.H., 1964—, chmn. dept. sociology and anthropology, 1964-69, 79-82, dean Coll. Liberal Arts, 1982—; disting. vis. prof. SUNY, Albany, 1970-71; vis. behavioral scientist N.H. Div. Mental Health; vis. prof. U. Sussex, Eng., 1976, U. Ga., 1977; cons. U.S. Office Edn., USPHS, U.S. Office Delinquency and Youth Devel., Dept. Justice; mem. adv. com. for sociology Com. on Internat. Exchange of Persons; mem. exec. com. N.H. Gov.'s Commn. on Crime and Delinquency; co-chmn. Internat. Symposium on Univs. in Twenty-First Century; co-chmn. 2d Internat. Conf. on Stress Research. Author: Understanding Other People, 1955, A Study of Murder, 1960, (with Brian R. Kay) The Challenge of Supervision, 1961, Deviance and Conformity, 1970, (with Arnold S. Linsky) Rebellion and Retreat, 1972, The Violent Society, 1972, The Prevention of Crime, 1973, (with John A. Humphrey) Deviant Behavior, 1980, Role Stress, 1981; also articles. Chmn. bd. trustees Daniel Webster Coll., New Eng. Aero. Inst. Served to lt. AC AUS, 1942-45; Served to lt. AC USAF, 1951-53. Decorated Air medal with 3 oak leaf clusters; Henry Page fellow, 1953-55. Mem. Am. Sociol. Assn., Eastern Sociol. Soc., Internat. Sociol. Soc., Internat. Soc. Criminology, Internat. Soc. Forecasters, Am. Assn. Colls., Council for Liberal Learning, Am. Assn. Higher Edn., Council Colls. Arts and Scis., Nat. Assn. State Univs. and Land-Grant Colls., AAAS, Am. Acad. Polit. and Social Scis., N.Y. Acad. Scis., Am. Assn. Suicidology, Soc. Cross-Cultural Research, Am. Soc. Criminology, Assn. Gov. Bds. Univs. and Colls., Phi Beta Kappa (hon.), Sigma Xi, Alpha Kappa Delta. Home: Riverview Dr Durham NH 03824 Office: U NH Coll Liberal Arts Murkland Hall Durham NH 03824

PALSSON, THORSTEINN, prime minister of Iceland; b. Oct. 29, 1947; m. Ingibjorg Rafnar; 3 children. Grad., Comml. Coll.; LLD, U. Iceland, 1974. Journalist Morgunbladid; editor Visir newspaper, 1975—; dir. Confedn. Icelandic Employers, 1979; M.P. Iceland, 1983—; chmn. Independence Party, 1983; minister fin. Iceland, Reykjavik, 1985-87, prime minister, 1987—. Address: Office Prime Minister, Reykjavik Iceland *

PÁLSSON, TRYGGVI, banker; b. Reykjavik, Iceland, Feb. 28, 1949; parents: Páll Ágeir and Bjoerg (Ásgeirsdóttir) Tryggvason; m. Rannveig Gunnarsdóttir, Oct. 3, 1970; children: Gunnar Páll, Sólveig Lisa. Candidate econs., U. Iceland, Reykdljavik, 1974; MS in Econs., London Sch. Econs., 1975. Chief economist Landsbanki Islands, Reykjavik, 1976-84, exec. dir.,

1984-88; mng. dir. Iceland Bank Commerce, Reykjavik, 1988—; bd. dirs. Icelandic Securities Exchange, Reykjavik, Iceland Investment Corp., Eurocard Iceland; lectr. U. Iceland, 1977-86. Contbr. articles to profl. jours. Mem. Icelandic Mgmt. Soc. (bd. dirs. 1980-82), Soc. Icelandic Economists and Bus. Adminstrs. (bd. dirs. 1978-79, pres. 1980-82). Lutheran. Home: Kjartansgata 8, 105 Reykjavik Iceland Office: Verzlunarbanki Íslands, Bankastraeti 5, 101 Reykjavik Iceland

PALUMBO, JOHN CHRISTOPHER, educator; b. Bklyn., Feb. 23, 1931; s. John Joseph and Lucy Agnes (Ranelli) P.; B.B.A., St. John's U., N.Y., 1954, M.A., 1966, Ph.D., 1972; postgrad. U.S. Army Lang. Sch., 1956-57; m. Seiko Murakami, Aug. 20, 1959; children—Joseph Michael, Matthew Aloysius, Robert John. Routeman, N.Y. Times, 1948-52, N.Y. Daily News, 1953-55; tchr. N.Y.C. Bd. Edn., 1960—, tchr. 1st Japanese lang. program, 1983-84, asst. dir., coordinator acad. programs Asian Inst. St. John's U., 1987—, chaperone N.Y.C.-Tokyo high sch. student exchange program, coach baseball Port Richard High Sch. Dir. baseball Stapleton Athletic Club, 1969-72; chaperone N.Y.C.-Tokyo high sch. exchange program. Served with U.S. Army, 1955-58. NDEA fellow, 1962-63; Fulbright-Hays grantee, Japan, 1967, 86. Mem. Asian Soc., Assn. Asian Studies, Am. Assn. Tchrs. Chinese, Japan Soc., Archaeol. Soc. Am. Democrat. Roman Catholic. Club: Italian of Staten Island (dir.). Author: Konoe, Fumimaro's Efforts for Peace, 1937-1941, 1972. Home: 960 Annadale Rd Staten Island NY 10312 Office: Saint Johns U Asian Inst Utopia and Grand Central Pkwys Jamaica NY 11439

PALUZZI, JEANNE GERRITSEN, public relations counselor; b. Zeeland, Mich., Sept. 18, 1934; d. Gerrit John and Mary (Staal) Gerritsen; student Calvin Coll., Grand Rapids, Mich., 1952-53, Wayne State U., 1970-76; m. Rocco Paluzzi, Apr. 7, 1956 (div. Apr. 8, 1971); children: Jeanna Marie, Nicholas, Paul, Karen Adele. Asst. to dir. public affairs Smith Hinchman & Grylls, Inc., Detroit, 1972-73; co-mgr. public relations Albert Kahn Asso., Detroit, 1973-74; owner Jeanne Paluzzi & Co., Detroit, 1974-76; public relations exec. Young & Rubicam, Inc., Detroit, 1976-79; pres. JGP Pub. Relations, Inc., Detroit, 1979-84; pres. JGP Mktg. Group Internat., Inc., 1984—; former mem. Livonia Indsl. Devel. Commns. Bd. dirs. Met. Detroit YWCA; mem. Wayne 2d Dist. Republican Exec. Com., 1981-83; bd. dirs. Mich. Rep. Women's Task Force, 1982-83; mem. nat. adv. council SBA, 1982—; del. White House Conf. on Small Bus., 1986. Recipient Demmy award United Found., 1977; SBA Women in Bus. Adv. of Yr., Mich. award, 1981; Vanguard award Detroit Women in Communications Inc., 1984, Heather award, 1988. Mem. Pub. Relations Soc. Am. (accredited), Internat. Pub. Relations Assn., Women In Communications (program chmn. nat. conv. 1978, chmn. fin. com. 1977-78, 1st v.p. Detroit chpt. 1978-79, v.p. chpt. public relations 1980-82), Nat. Assn. Women Bus. Owners (v.p. pub. relations Mich. chpt. 1980-82, pres. 1982, nat. pub. relations chmn. 1983-84, nat. sec. 1984-85, Mich. Pioneering Spirit award, 1988), Small Bus. Assn. Mich. (bd. dirs. 1983-88 , v.p. fed. regislation 1984-85, v.p. polit. action 1985-87, 1st v.p. 1987-88), Livonia C. of C. (dir. 1980-83, bus. and econ. devel. council, Athena award 1988), Greater Detroit C. of C., World Trade Club of Detroit. Clubs: Detroit Press, Women's Econ. of Detroit, Economic of Detroit. Home: 17315 Rougeway St Livonia MI 48152 Office: 34935 Schoolcraft Suite 206 Livonia MI 01317

PAMINTUAN, SHIRLEY GERALDE, physician; b. Sorsogon, Philippines, Dec. 27, 1948; d. Diogenes Garote Garalde and Justiniana Galendez Perez; adopted d. Georgia Dougan; m. Daniel Pamintuan, Nov. 23, 1971; children: Erniel Alvin, Johnny, Daniel, Shierdan. BA, Philippines Union Coll., Caloocan, 1970; MD, Manila Cen. U., Caloocan, 1975. Intern Med. City Hosp., Mandaluyong Manila, 1975-76; practicum Irosin Emergency Hosp., Sorsogon, 1977; public health physician Manila Health Dept., 1979; coll. physician Philippine Union Coll., Silang Cavite, 1980—. Mem. Philippine Med. Assn. Seventh Day Adventist. Office: Philippine Union Coll, Puting Kahoy, Silang Cavite 3120, Philippines

PAMPLIN, ROBERT BOISSEAU, JR., agricultural company executive, minister, writer; b. Augusta, Ga., Sept. 3, 1941; s. Robert Boisseau and Mary Katherine (Reese) P.; m. Marilyn Joan Hooper; children: Amy Louise, Anne Boisseau. Student in bus. adminstrn. Va. Poly. Inst., 1960-62; BSBA, Lewis and Clark Coll., 1964, BS in Acctg., 1965, BS in Econs., 1966; MBA, U. Portland, 1968, MEd, 1975, LLD (hon.), 1972; MCL, Western Conservative Bapt. Sem., 1978, DMin, 1982; PhD, Calif. Coast U.; cert. in wholesale mgmt. Ohio State U., 1970; cert. in labor mgmt., U. Portland, 1972; cert. in advanced mgmt., U. Hawaii, 1975; DD (hon.), Judson Baptist Coll., 1984; DBA (hon.), Marquis Giuseppe Scicluna Internat. U. Found., 1986; LittD (hon.), Va. Tech. Inst. and State U., 1987, LHD (hon.), Warner Pacific Coll., 1988. Pres. R. B. Pamplin Corp., Portland, Oreg., 1964—; chmn. bd. Columbia Empire Farms, Inc., Lake Oswego, Oreg., 1976—; pres. Twelve Oaks Farms, Inc., Lake Oswego, 1977—; dir. Mt. Vernon Mill Inc.; lectr. bus. adminstrn. Lewis and Clark Coll., 1968-69; adj. asst. prof. bus. adminstrn., U. Portland, 1973-76; pastor Christ Community Ch., Lake Oswego, Oreg. lectr. in bus. adminstrn. and economics, U. Costa Rica, 1968, Va. Tech. Found., 1986, dir. R.B. Pamplin Corp., Ross Island Sand & Gravel Co. Author: Everything is Just Great, 1985, The Gift, 1986, Another Virginian: A Study of the Life and Beliefs of Robert Boisseau Pamplin, 1986, (with others): A Portrait of Colorado, 1976, Three in One, 1974, The Storybook Primer on Managing, 1974; editor: Oreg. Mus. Sci. and Industry Press, 1973, trustee, 1971, 74—; editor: Portrait of Oregon, 1973, (with others): Oregon Underfoot, 1975. Mem. Nat. Adv. Council on Vocat. Edn., 1975—; mem. Western Interstate Comm. for Higher Edn., 1981-84; co-chmn. Va. Tech. $50 million Campaign for Excellence, 1984-87, Va. Tech. Found., 1986—, Albert Einstein Acad. Bronze medal, 1986, Va. 0 Oreg. State Scholarship Commn., 1974—, chmn., 1976-78; mem. Portland dist. adv. council SBA, 1973-77; mem. Rewards Review Com., City Portland, 1973-78, chmn., 1973-78; mem. bd. regents U. Portland, 1971-79, chmn. bd., 1975-79, regent emeritus, 1979—; trustee Lewis and Clark Coll., 1980-84, 85, Oreg. Epis. Schs., 1979. Named disting. alumnus, Lewis and Clark Coll., 1974; recipient Air Force ROTC Disting. Service award, USAF, 1974, Albert Einstein Acad. Bronze medal, 1986; Va. Tech Coll. of Bus. Adminstrn. renamed R.B. Pamplin Coll. of Bus. Adminstrn. in his honor. Mem. Acad. Mgmt., Delta Epsilon Sigma, Beta Gamma Sigma, Sigma Phi Epsilon. Republican. Episcopalian. Clubs: Waverley Country, Arlington, Multnomah Athletic, Capitol Hill. Lodge: Rotary.

PAN, FOO, biochemistry educator; b. Sungyang, Chekiang, China, Feb. 23, 1925; s. Sze-Kuen and Ho-Ding (Yeh) P.; m. Shien-Feng Yeh, Mar. 30, 1954; 1 son, Tsung-Yu. B.S., Nat. Def. Med. Ctr., Taipei, Taiwan, 1951; M.S., U. Iowa, 1959; Ph.D., U. Calif.-San Francisco, 1965. Teaching asst. Nat. Def. Med. Ctr., Taipei, 1951-54, instr., 1955-61, asst. prof. biochemistry, 1961-68, prof., 1968—, chmn. dept., 1977-84; investigator in biochemistry Vets. Gen. Hosp., Taipei, 1965-83. Author textbook on biochemistry, 1979; editor Jour. of Chinese Biochem. Soc., 1972—; contbr. numerous articles to sci. jours. Mem. Chinese Chem. Soc., Chinese Pharm. Assn., Chinese Biochem. Soc., Chinese Physiol. Soc. Home: 44-1 Alley 25, Ln 24, Roosevelt Rd, Sect 4, Taipei 107, Republic of China Office: Nat Def Med Ctr Dept Biochem, PO Box 8244, Taipei 107, Republic of China

PAN, HUO-PING, chemist; b. Foochow, China, Feb. 13, 1921; s. Bai-ming and Won-ching (Chen) Pan; B.S. in Chemistry, Nat. S.W. Assoc. U., China, 1946; Ph.D. in Food Sci., U. Ill., 1954; m. Chiou-Wen Sha, Feb. 26, 1955; 1 son, Peno. Staff mem. div. indsl. research MIT, 1954-55, div. sponsored research, 1955-57, research assoc., 1957-58; asst. biochemist agrl. expt. sta. U. Fla., Gainesville, 1958-63, asst. research prof. Coll. Engring., 1963-64; research biochemist to research chemist Patuxent Wildlife Research Center, U.S. Fish and Wildlife Service, U.S. Dept. Interior, Gainesville, 1964-77; research chemist Denver Wildlife Research Cntr., 1977-86; asst. dir. nat. monitoring and residue analysis lab. Animal and Plant Health Inspection Service, USDA, Gulfport, Miss., 1986—. Recipient Outstanding Publ. award Denver Wildlife Research Cntr., 1981; Spl. Achievement award U.S. Fish and Wildlife Service, 1981. Mem. Am. Chem. Soc., Am. Inst. Biol. Scis., AAAS, Internat. Soc. for Study of Xenobiotics (charter), Sigma Xi, Phi Tau Sigma. Democrat. Patentee chromatography developing chamber. Contbr. articles to profl. jours. Home: 291 Venetian Gardens Gulfport MS 39501 Office: 3505 25th Ave Gulfport MS 39505

PAN, LORETTA REN-QIU, retired educator; b. Changchow, China, Oct. 1, 1917, came to U.S., 1951, naturalized, 1965; d. Ke-jun and Mei-ying (Xue) P.; B.A. in English Lit., Ginling Coll., 1940; cert. English Lit., Mt. Holyoke Coll., 1952. Instr. English, Nanking U., 1940-41; instr. English and Chinese, St. Mary's Girls Sch., Shanghai, 1941-44; instr. English, Ginling Coll., 1944-45; sr. translator info. dept. Brit. Embassy, Shanghai, 1945-48; Chinese editor U.S. Consulate Gen., Hong Kong, 1949-51; researcher, editorial asst. modern China project Columbia U., 1955-60, lectr. Chinese, 1960-67, sr. lectr., 1968-87. Methodist. Contbr. to various profl. publs. Home: 600 W 111th St New York NY 10025

PANAGIOTOPOULOS, PANAGIOTIS DIONYSIOS, mechanical engineering educator; b. Thessaloniki, Greece, Jan. 1, 1950; s. Dionysios and Kalliopi Panagiotopoulos. Diplom. Ingenieur, Aristotle U., 1972, Dr. Ingenieur, 1974; dozent habilitation Tech. U. Aachen, 1977. Head research group Tech. U. Aachen, Fed. Republic Germany, 1977-78, privatdozent (research), 1977-81, hon. prof., 1981—; full prof., dir. Inst. Steel Structures, Aristotle U., Thessaloniki, 1978—; vis. prof. U. Hamburg, Fed. Republic Germany, 1981; vis. prof. PUC Rio de Janeiro, 1986; Fulbright scholar MIT, Cambridge, Mass., 1984. Author: Inequality Problems in Mechanics and Applications, 1985. Contbr. numerous articles on convex and nonconvex energy functions to profl. jours. Recipient award for grad. students Tech. Chamber Greece, 1971, 72; Alexander von Humbolt fellow, 1974-77, sr. fellow, 1978. Mem. Soc. Indsl. Applied Math., ASCE, Math. Programming SoCo, Internat. Soc. for Computational Mechanics, Gesellschaft fur Angewandte Math. Mechanik. Office: Aristotle U, Thessaloniki Greece Other: Tech U Aachen, Aachen 51 Federal Republic of Germany

PANARETOS, JOHN, mathematics and statistics educator; b. Kythera, Lianianika, Greece, Feb. 23, 1948; s. Victor and Fotini (Kominu) P.; m. Evdokia Xekalaki; 1 child, Victor. First degree, U. Athens, 1972; MSc, U. Sheffield, Eng., 1974; PhD, U. Bradford, Eng., 1977. Lectr. U. Dublin, Ireland, 1979-80; asst. prof. U. Mo., Columbia, U.S, 1980-82; assoc. prof. U. Iowa, Iowa City, U.S., 1982-83, U. Crete, Iraklio, Greece, 1983-84; assoc. prof. div. applied math., Sch. Engring. U. Patras, Greece, 1984—, assoc. dean sch. engring., 1986-87; vice-rector U. Patras, 1988—; chmn. div. applied math. U. Patras, 1986-87; sec.-treas. Ministry Edn. and Religious Affairs, Greece. Contbr. articles to profl. jours. Active Sci. Counsil of Greek Parliament, 1987—. Mem. Am. Statis. Assn., Inst. Math. Statistics, Bernoulli Soc. for Probability and Math. Statistics, Greek Math. Soc., Greek Statis. Inst., Scientific Council Greek Parliament. Home: 18 Spetson St, 153 42 A Paraskevi, Athens Greece Office: U Patras Sch Engring, PO Box 1325, 26110 Patras Greece

PANCERO, JACK BLOCHER, restaurant executive; b. Cin., Dec. 27, 1923; s. Howard and Hazel Mae (Blocher) P.; student, Ohio State U., 1941-44; m. Loraine Fielman, Aug. 4, 1944; children—Gregg Edward, Vicki Lee. Ptnr., Howard Pancero & Co., Cin., 1948-66; stockbroker Gradison & Co., Cin., 1966-70; real estate asso. Parchman & Oyler, Cin., 1970-72; v.p. Gregg Pancero, Inc., Kings Mills, Ohio, 1972—. Methodist. Clubs: Western Hills Country, Cincinnati, Engrs. Table, Pelican Bay, Bonita Bay Country, Vineyard Country. Lodges: Masons, Shriners. Home: Pelican Bay 806 Rue de Ville Naples FL 33963 Office: Kings Island Columbia Rd Kings Mills OH 45034

PANDA, DURGA PRASAD, engineer, researcher; b. Berhampur, Orissa, India, Oct. 11, 1945; came to U.S., 1969; naturalized, 1982; s. Maheswar and Sundarmani (Panda) P.; m. Fern Alane Lloyd, July 10, 1976; children—Robin Dev, Nina Anjali. B.S.E.E., Regional Engring. Coll., Rourkela, Orissa, India, 1968; M.S.E.E., Iowa State U., 1971; Ph.D. E.E., Purdue U., 1976. Elec. engr. Utkal Machinery Ltd. Kansbahal, Orissa, India, 1968-69; research engr. Purdue U., West Lafayette, Ind., 1971-72; faculty research assoc. U. Md., College Park, 1976-77; sr.-sr. prin. research scientist Honeywell Systems and Research Ctr., Mpls., 1977-81, staff research scientist, 1981-82, sect. chief, signal and image processing scis., 1982-87, mgr., 1987—. Contbr. articles to profl. jours. Bd. dirs. Internat. Ctr., West Lafayette, 1974-76; v.p. India Students Assn., West Lafayette, 1973. Govt. Coll. Merit Scholarship award, Govt. of India, 1963-68; recipient achievement awards (5) Honeywell, 1979-83. Mem. IEEE (reviewer), IEEE Computer Soc. (speaker 1984), Data Processing Mgmt. Assn. (speaker 1985), Advanced Target Recognizer Working Group (co-chmn. artificial intelligence com. 1984—), Soc. of Photo-Optical Instructing Engrs. (panelist application of artificial intelligence, 1985—), Am. Def. Preparedness Assn., Assn. for Unmanned Vehicle Systems, Soc. of Photo-Optical and Instrumentation Engrs., Orissa Soc. of Ams., Inc., Tau Beta Pi, Phi Kappa Phi. Current work: Research and development management in the areas of artificial intelligence, pattern recognition, machine vision, and high speed architecture leading to real time robot vision system for automated manufacturing, autonomous vehicle, and optical inspection systems. Subspecialties: Artificial intelligence; Computer engineering; Graphics, image processing, and pattern recognition. Home: 1698 17th Ave NW New Brighton MN 55112

PANDAY, BASDEO, government official; b. Prince's Town, Trinidad and Tobago, May 25, 1933; s. Sookchand and Kissoondaye (Ajodha) P.; m. Norma Mohammed (div. 1981); 1 child, Niala; m.Oma Ramkisson; children: Niala, Mickela, Nicola, Vastala. Barrister-at-Law degree, Lincoln's Inn, London, 1962; BS in Econs., U. London, 1965. Leader opposition Ho. Reps., Port of Spain, Trinidad and Tobago, 1976-86; minister external affairs Govt. Trinidad and Tobago, Port of Spain, 1986-88; sole practice, San Fernando, Trinidad and Tobago, 1965-86; pres.-gen. All Trinidad Sugar and Gen. Workers Trade Union, Couva, 1973-87. Polit. leader United Labour Front, Trinidad and Tobago, 1976-85; dep. polit. leader Nat. Alliance for Reconstrn., 1985—. Mem. Commonwealth Parliamentary Assn. (exec. mem. Trinidad and Tobago br.). Hindu. Home: 1A Bryansgate Phillipine, San Fernando Trinidad and Tobago Office: Ministry External Affairs, Queen's Park W, Port of Spain Trinidad and Tobago

PANDJI, WISAKSANA, plastics company executive; b. Bandung, Indonesia, June 27, 1925; s. Phan Jam Soe and Phan Tan Po Lan; m. Trijuani Pandji, Aug. 28, 1946; children: Shintawati, Santoso, Sally, Stephen, Charles K. (dec.). MBA, U. 17 August, Jakarta. Pres. Mulia Knitting Factory, Jakarta, 1955-68, Prakarsa Plastic Co., Jakarta, 1963-68, Tjahaja Mulia, Jakarta, 1963-72; chmn. Hoechst Cilegon, Jakarta, 1982—, Pioneer Kimia Agung, Jakarta, 1976—; pres., dir., founder Pioneer Plastics Ltd., Jakarta, 1954—, Vitafoam Indonesia, Jakarta, 1976—, The New Asia Industry Coy., Jakarta, 1969—; chmn., founder Siliwangi Knitting Factory, Jakarta, 1955—. Dist. gov. Lions club Internat., Jakarta, 1982, 83; trustee Trisakti U., Jakarta, 1979—; founder, vice chmn. Bank Mata (Eye Bank) Jakarta, 1968—; founder, gen. chmn. yayasan Pandji Sejahtera, Jakarta, 1975—. Recipient Jakarta gov. award as one of 10 Best Entrepreneurs, 1977, Presdl. award Lions Club Internat., 1982-83, Econ. Devel. award H.E. Pres. Republic Indonesia, 1983. Mem. Asosiasi Industri Plastik Indonesia (chmn., founder 1977-81, hon. chmn. 1981—; appreciation award 1982), Federasi Industri Plastik Indonesia (chmn., founder 1981-84), Asean Fedn. Plastic Industries (chmn., founder 1982-84, hon. chmn. 1984—), Indonesian Packaging Fedn. Office: Pioneer Plastics Ltd, Bandengan Utara 43, Jakarta Utara 14440, Indonesia

PANDURO, SVEND, engineering executive; b. Frederickshavn, Denmark, May 21, 1941; s. Charles and Marie (Vodde) P.; m. Sigrid Moller, Aug. 4, 1965; children: Stig, Sverre. BS in Math., Kathedral Sch., Aarhus, Denmark, 1960; MS, Danish Engring. Acad., Copenhagen, 1964. Engr. Christiani-Nielsen A/S, Sao Paulo, Brazil, 1965-67; v.p. Copenhagen, 1982—; engr. Kaiser Engrs., Oakland, Calif., 1968-71; project mgr. ITT-Sheraton, Boston and Paris, 1971-74; pres. Panprodan ApS, Copenhagen, 1974-79, 80-82; v.p. Total Enterprises, Princeton, N.J., 1979-80; dir. gen. Kurt Thorsen France S.A., Paris, 1988—; chmn. bd. SP Klimatest ApS, Copenhagen, 1981—, Protectors A/S, Copenhagen, 1985—, Pandak Investment A/S, Copenhagen, 1985—. Mem. ASHRAE, Ing. Sci. France, Danish Engrs. Assn. Home: Sveigaardsvej 7, 2900 Hellerup Denmark Office: Kurt Thorsen France SA, Ave des Champs Elysees 142, Paris France

PANDYA, RAMESH DEVSHANKER, bank executive, consultant; b. Anand, Gujarat, India, July 30, 1933; s. Devshanker N. and Savita D. Pandya; m. Anjani R., Feb. 21. 1970; children: Tejas, Nikhil. Diploma in banking, Maharaja Sahayajirao U. Baroda (Gujarat), 1956; M in Commerce, Maharaja Sayajirao U. Baroda (Gujarat), 1958; LLB, M.S. U. Baroda (Gujarat), 1964. From banking tutor to banking prof. Maharaja Sahayajirao U. Baroda, 1956-71; prin. Bank of Baroda, Ahmedabad, 1971-74; gen. sec. Indo-Am. C. of C., Bombay, 1974-76; mgmt. cons. Indo-Am. C. of C., 1976-78, chief sec., 1978—; mem. Senate and Acad. Council M.S. U. Baroda, 1964-70; pres. M.S. U. Union, 1968-70; dir. Internat. Banking Summer Sch., New Delhi, 1988. Editor Jour. Nat. Inst. Bank Mgmt., Indian Inst. Bankers. Mem. World U. Service, New Delhi, 1964-70. Fellow Chartered Inst. Bankers (London) (internat. counsellor), Indian Inst. Bankers (Bombay); mem. World U. Service. Lodge: Rotary. Home: 11 Dial Mahal Cuffe Parade, Bombay, Maharashtr 400 005, India Office: Indian Inst Bankers, Cuffe Parade, Bombay 400 005, India

PANE, REMIGIO UGO, Romance languages educator; b. Scigliano, Italy, Feb. 5, 1912; s. Michele Antonio and Carmela (Gigliotti) P.; m. Philomena Pascale, Apr. 13, 1941 (dec. Aug. 1959); children: Michael A., Elissa A.; m. Josephine R. Bruno, Aug. 15, 1964. B.A., Rutgers U., 1938, M.A., 1939; student, Middlebury Spanish Sch., Italian Sch., summers 1937-38, Columbia U., 1939-41. From instr. to assoc. prof. Romance langs. Rutgers U., 1939-57, prof., 1957-81, chmn. dept., 1952-71; dir., founder Rutgers Jr. Year in Italy, 1971-73; assoc. dean Rutgers Coll., 1977-80, prof. emeritus, 1981—; State coordinator Am. Assn. Tchrs. Spanish and Portuguese, also Am. Assn. Tchrs. Italian, 1958; chmn. Northeast Conf. Teaching Fgn. Langs., 1960; chmn. examining com. Italian achievement test Coll. Entrance Exam. Bd., 1964-71; mem. selection com. Center 20th Century Studies, U. Wis.-Milw., 1970-71; v.p. Nat. Fedn. Modern Lang. Tchrs. Assns., 1969, pres., 1970, exec. council, 1976-87; mem. nat. scholarship com. Internat. Ladies Garment Workers Union, 1964—, Middlesex County Cultural and Heritage Commn., 1984—; dir. NDEA Fgn. Lang. Inst., Rutgers U., summers, 1963, 64, 65, 66, 67; cons. fgn. langs. U.S. Office Edn.; chmn. evaluating bd. Italian program Def. Lang. Inst. Author: English Translations from the Spanish, 1484-1943; A Bibliography, 1944, (with J.G. Fucilla) Ann. Bibliography of Italian Lang. and Lit, 1961-70; editor: Italian Americans in the Professions, 1983; Asst. editor: Modern Lang. Jour, 1965-71; Contbr. to: The Literatures of the World in Translation, 1970; Contbr. articles to profl. jours. Mem. Italian contbrn. sect. nat. com. U.S.A. Bicentennial; mem. Italian heritage com. 41st Internat. Eucharistic Congress. Decorated Lateran Cross Vatican, 1954, Commendatore, 1955, Grande Ufficiale, 1970, dell'Ordine della Stella della Solidarietà Italiana (Italy), 1976, Sovereign Order St. John of Jerusalem Knights Malta; named Man of Year Columbus Civic League, Trenton, 1962, Man of Year Italian Am. Club, North Brunswick, N.J., 1963; recipient award Leonardo da Vinci Soc., Ft. Lee, N.J., 1966, Presdl. plaque Am. Inst. Italian Culture, 1970; Fulbright fellow, 1970. Mem. MLA (life), Am. Assn. Tchrs. Italian (pres. 1968-72, exec. council 1976—, life mem., hon. life pres.), Am. Assn. Tchrs. Spanish and Portuguese (life), Am. Council Teaching Fgn. Langs., AAUP, N.J. Modern Lang. Tchrs. Assn. (pres. 1962-64, award 1979), Am. Italian Hist. Assn. (exec. council 1978—, coordinator nat. conf. 1979). Home: 69 Lincoln Ave Highland Park NJ 08904 Office: Rutgers U New Brunswick NJ 08903

PANEC, WILLIAM JOSEPH, lawyer; b. Pawnee City, Nebr., June 22, 1937; s. Albert and Thelma I. (Sebring) P.; m. Carolyn R. McVitty, Aug. 17, 1963. B.S., U. Nebr., 1962, J.D., 1965. Bar: Nebr. 1965, U.S. Dist. Ct. Nebr. 1965. Sole practice, Fairbury, Nebr., 1965—; county judge Jefferson County, Nebr., 1965-70; mem. Nebr. Jud. Qualifications Commn., 1968-70; chmn. Region XIV Crime Commn., 1968-71; cons., 1971-79; cons. for regions VIII, IX, XIV Regional Jail Study, 1972; profl. instr. Nebr. Law Enforcement Adv. Council, 1972; county atty. Jefferson County, 1973-75; village atty. Diller, Nebr., 1975—; atty. Fairbury Airport Authority, 1981—. Bd. dirs. Housing Authority, Fairbury, 1979—, chmn., 1983; bd. dirs. Legal Services of S.E. Nebr., 1984; chmn. Law Day, Jefferson County, 1972, 73. Served with U.S. Army, 1955-56. Mem. Nebr. Assn. Trial Attys., Assn. Trial Lawyers Am., Am. Judicature Soc., Nebr. County Judges Assn. (v.p., pres.), Jefferson County Bar Assn., Internat. Footprinters Assn., U. Nebr. Alumni Assn., Delta Theta Phi. Methodist (trustee), Clubs: Elks, Masons. Author: Probate Procedures and the Uniform Probate Code, 1969; organizer Nebr. Jud. Reform, 1969.

PANFILOV, GLEB, film director; b. Sverdlovsk, USSR, 1933. Grad. in Chem. Engring., Sverdlovsk Poly. Inst.; studied directing at Mosfilm Studios, USSR. Films include Yevgeniy Gabrilovich' No Ford in the Fire, 1968 (Grand Prix Locarno Festival 1969), Début, 1970, The Theme, 1981. Office: Lenfilm, Kirovsky Prospekt, Leningrad USSR *

PANG, HERBERT GEORGE, ophthalmologist; b. Honolulu, Dec. 23, 1922; s. See Hung and Hong Jim (Chuu) P.; student St. Louis Coll., 1941; B.S., Northwestern U., 1944, M.D., 1947; m. Dorothea Lopez, Dec. 27, 1953. Intern Queen's Hosp., Honolulu, 1947-48; postgraduate course ophthalmology N.Y.U., Med. Sch., 1948-49; resident ophthalmology Jersey City Med. Center, 1949-50, Manhattan Eye, Ear, & Throat Hosp., N.Y.C., 1950-52; practice medicine specializing in ophthalmology, Honolulu, 1952-54, 56—; mem. staffs Kuakini Hosp., Children's Hosp., Castle Meml. Hosp., Queen's Hosp., St. Francis Hosp.; asst. clin. prof. ophthalmology U. Hawaii Sch. Medicine, 1966-73, now asso. clin. prof. Cons. Bur. Crippled Children, 1952-73, Kapiolani Maternity Hosp., 1952-73, Leahi Tb. Hosp., 1952-62. Served to capt. M.C., AUS, 1954-56, Diplomate Am. Bd. Ophthalmology. Mem. AMA, Am. Acad. Ophthalmology and Otolaryngology, Assn. for Research Ophthalmology, ACS, Hawaii Med. Soc. (gov. med. practice com. 1958-62, chmn. med. speakers com. 1957-58), Hawaii Eye, Ear, Nose and Throat Soc. (pres. 1960), Pacific Coast Oto-Ophthalmological Soc., Pan Am. Assn. Ophthalmology. Mason (Shriner). Clubs: Eye Study Club (pres. 1972—)(N.Y.C.). Home: 346 Lewers Rd Honolulu HI 96815 Office: Pang Eye Ear Nose Throat Clinic 1374 Nuuanu Ave Honolulu HI 96817

PANG, JOSHUA KEUN-UK, trade co. exec.; b. Chinnampo, Korea, Sept. 17, 1924; s. Ne-Too and Soon-Hei (Kim) P.; came to U.S., 1951, naturalized, 1968; B.S., Roosevelt U., 1959; m. He-Young Yoon, May 30, 1963; children—Ruth, Pauline, Grace. Chemist, Realemon Co. Am., Chgo., 1957-61; chief-chemist chem. div. Bell & Gossett Co., Chgo., 1961-63, Fatty Acid Inc., div. Ziegler Chem. & Mineral Corp., Chgo., 1963-64; sr. chemist-supr. Gen. Mills Chems. Inc., Kankakee, Ill., 1964-70; pres., owner UJU Industries Inc., Broadview, Ill., 1971—, also dir. Bd. dirs. Dist. 92, Lindop Sch., Broadview, 1976-87; chmn. Proviso Area Sch. Bd. Assn., Proviso Twp., Cook County, Ill., 1976-77; bd. dirs. Korean Am. Community Services, Chgo., 1979-80; mem. governing bd. Proviso Area Exceptional Children, Spl. Edn. Joint Agreement, 1981-84, 85-87; alumni bd. govs. Roosevelt U., 1983—. Mem. Am. Chem. Soc., Am. Inst. Parliamentarians (region 2 treas. 1979-81, region 2 gov. 1981-82), Internat. Platform Assn., Ill. Sch. Bd. Assn., Chgo. Area Parliamentarians, Parliamentary Leaders in Action (pres. 1980-81), Nat. Speakers Assn. (dir. Ill. chpt. 1981-82, nat. parliamentarian 1982-84, 2d v.p. chpt. 1983-84). Club: Toastmasters (dist. gov. 1969-1970), DADS Assn. U. Ill. (chmn. Cook County 1985-87, bd. dirs. 1987—). Home: 2532 S 9th Ave Broadview IL 60153-4804 Office: PO Box 6351 Broadview IL 60153-6351

PANGERAPAN, BOB GEORGE, import-export and freight forwarding companies executive; b. Manado, Indonesia, Jan. 24, 1938; s. Timothius Simon T. Pangerapan and Welhelmina P. Lumingkewas; m. Ivonne Poluan, Nov. 29, 1962; children—Irene, Shirley, Debbie, Daisy. Ed. Faculty Econs., Indonesia U., Jakarta, 1961; PhD in Comml. and Indsl. Econ., WP U., 1988., . Cert. internat. trade lectr. Ministry Trade Republic Indonesia. Import mgr. trading co., Jakarta, 1958-59; br. mgr. shipping co., Jakarta and Surabaya, 1959-63; pres., dir. import export Co., Jakarta, 1964—; ops. dir. stevedoring and transp. co., Jakarta, 1975-80; pres., dir. internat. freight-forwarding co., Jakarta, 1980—, PT. Roda Pelita Angkasa Internat. Freight Forwarding, Jakarta, 1980—, PT. Opedamy Ltd., Jakarta, 1980—, PT. Royal Perintis Abadi Corp., Jakarta, 1981—; chmn. PT. Pettor Indoversco, Jakarta, 1981—; pres. Indonesian Contract Bridge Jakarta, 1986. Sponsor, treas. Bohusami Found., Jakarta, 1983—; sponsor, v.p. Maesa Sport Assn., Jakarta, 1983—; sponsor, advisor student sport activities of various univs., Indonesia, 1979—, Jakarta Capital City Labour Found., 1980—. Sponsor, officer, team mgr. local, nat. and internat. contract bridge orgns., 1978—. Winner more than 20 1st prize cups in bridge competitions, numerous other prizes and certs. Mem. Indonesian Freight Forwarders Assn. (cert.)(chmn. bd. dirs. 1987), Internat. Freight Forwarders Assn., Indonesian C. of C. and Industry, Indonesian Custom Brokerage and Warehousing Assn., Indonesian Contract Bridge Assn. (v.p. 1986). Roman Catholic. Clubs: Frequent Bus. Travellers (Hong Kong); Hilton Exec. (Indonesia); Six Continents (U.S.A.).

Lodge: Kawanua (mem. bd. 1973—). Avocations: playing bridge; hunting; reading. Home: Jln Layur 39, East Jakarta 13220, Indonesia

PANI, MARIO, architect, planner; b. Mexico City, Mar. 29, 1911; s. Arturo and Dolores (Darqui) P.; m. Margarita Linaae, Oct. 30, 1933; children—Margara, Mario, Eugenia, Enrique, Federico, Knut. Grad., Ecole des Beaux Arts, Paris, 1934. Chmn. bd. Mario Pani, Arquitecto y Asociados S.A., Mexico City, 1964—, Deplan S.A., Mexico City, 1970—. Prin. archtl. works include 15 master plans cities in Mexico, master plan and campus U. Mexico, 1950. Fellow AIA (hon.); mem. Academia Nacional de Arquitectura (pres. 1978), Soc. de Arquitectos Mexicano (dir.), Colegio Arquitectos Mexico (dir. 1948-50). Clubs: Industrial Mexico; Acapulco Yacht (commodore 1955-78). Home: Paseo de las Palmas 725, Mexico City Mexico Office: Paseo de la Reforma 369-1, 6500 Mexico City 5 Mexico *

PANICCIA, MARIO DOMENIC, architect; b. Torrice, Italy, May 13, 1948; s. Sebastiano and Clara (Mancini) P.; B.Arch., Cooper Union, 1972. With William F. Griffin & Assocs., Milford, Conn., summers 1968-72; designer Raffone, Elovitz & Fischer, Architects & Engrs., Bridgeport, Conn., 1972-75; prin. Paniccia Assocs., Architects & Planners, Bridgeport, 1975-86, Paniccia Architects and Engrs. Inc., 1987—. Nat. Council Archtl. Registration Bds.; registered architect, Conn., N.Y., Tex., Minn., N.J., Idaho, S.C., Ala., W.Va., Ga., Tenn., Ind., Mich., Mo., Fla., La., Md., Ma., N.C., Ohio, Pa., Iowa. Commr. Monroe Conservation & Water Resources and Inland Wetland Commn. Mem. Conn. Soc. Architects (dir. 1979-80, commr. chpt. affairs 1979, commr. community affairs 1980, commr. profl. practice, 1985-86), Bridgeport Assn. Architects (dir. 1979, v.p. 1980, 83, pres. 1981), AIA (nat. housing com. 1988-89, commr. conservation com. 1980—), Nat. Trust Hist. Preservation, Inst. Urban Design, Bridgeport C. of C. Roman Catholic. Clubs: Elks (Fairfield, Conn.); K.C. (3d deg.); Exchange (Monroe, Conn.). Home: 25 Easton Rd Monroe CT 06468 Office: 4270 Main St Bridgeport CT 06606

PANIKER, K. AYYAPPA, English language educator, poet; b. Kavalam, Kerala, India, Sept. 12, 1930; s. E. Narayanan and M. (Meenakshiamma) Namudiri; m. R. Sreeparvathy, Dec. 9, 1961; children: Meera Devi, Meenakumari. BA with honors, Travancore U., Trivandrum, Kerala, 1951; MA, Kerala U., 1959; AM, PhD, Ind. U., 1971. Lectr. CMS Coll., Kottayam, India, 1951-52, Univ. Coll., Trivandrum, 1952-65; lectr. Kerala U., 1965-73, reader, 1973-80, prof., 1980—; dean Faculty of Arts, 1985—; nat. lectr. Univ. Grants Commn., New Delhi, 1984-85. Author: (poetry) Ayyappa Panikerude Kritical, 1974 (award 1975), Ayyappa Panikerude Kritical II, 1982 (Nat. Acad. Letters award 1984), Selected Poems, 1984; (criticism) Ayyappa Panikerude Lekhanangal, 1981 (Kerala Acad. award 1984). Exec. chmn. CVR Pillai Nat. Found, 1986—; adv. bd. Sahitya Akademi, 1982—. Recipient Kalyanikrishnamenon award Writers Coop. Soc., 1977, SPCS award Writers Coop. Soc., 1978; Fulbright fellow, 1969-70; ACLS grantee, 1981-82; scholar-in-residence Am. Studies Research Ctr., 1986-87. Home: 111 Gandhi Nagar, Trivandrum 695 014, India Office: Keralu U, Cantonment, Trivandrum 695 034, India

PANIKKAR, KOTHA KANTHIMATHY, physician; b. Alor Setar, Kedah, Malaysia, Jan. 4, 1931; d. K.N. Govinda and J. Chellamma (Pillai) Pillai; m. Radhakrishnan Narayana Panikkar, July 1, 1960; children: Krishna Kumar, Apsara. MBBS, Adelaide Sch. Medicine, 1958; student, John's Hopkins U., 1977, diploma in reproductive medicine, 1985; diploma in psycho-sexual medicine, U. London, 1986. Houseman Royal Adelaide Hosp., 1959-60; med. officer Ministry of Health, Malaysia, 1960-61; with Ministry of Def., Taiping, Malaysia, 1961-66; gen. practice medicine Kedah Clinic, Alor Star, West Malaysia, 1966—; med. cons. Internat. Women's Health Coalition, N.Y.C., 1980—, also mem. faculty, 1985—. Bd. dirs. St. Nicholas Convent, Alor Star, 1974—, Sekolah Menengah Sultanah Asma, Alor Star, 1975—. Served with Malaysian Med. Corps., 1961-66. Recipient Ahli Mangku Negara, King of Malaysia, 1977, Pingat Jasa Kebaktian, Sultan of Kedah, 1977, Bintang Kebaktian Masyarakat, Sultan of Kedah, 1985. Mem. Internat. Med. Women's Assn., Kedah Family Planning Assn. (chmn. 1973—), Malaysian Med. Assn., Fedn. Family Planning Assns. Malaysia, Gen. Practitioners Assn. (vice chmn.), Sultan Abdur Hamid Old Collegians' Assn. Hindu. Club: Royal Kedah, Penang. Office: Kedah Klinik, 3A Ialan TA Halim, Alor Star 05100, Malaysia

PANITZ, LAWRENCE, physician; b. Bklyn., Apr. 30, 1928; s. Max and Gussie (Gorenstein) P.; B.A., NYU, 1962, M.D., 1966; m. Adrienne Ruth Luke, June 20, 1965; children—Jennifer, Michael. Intern, St. Joseph's Hosp., Syracuse, N.Y., 1966-67; practice gen. medicine, Elmsford, N.Y., 1967—, Hawthorne, N.Y., 1968—; mem. staff St. Agnes Hosp., White Plains, Phelps Meml. Hosp., North Tarrytown, N.Y., Westchester County Med. Ctr., Valhalla, N.Y., Dobbs Ferry Hosp.; dep. dir. dept. family practice Phelps Meml. Hosp.; dir. Elmsford Med. Ctr.; police surgeon, Tarrytown, Elmsford, Town of Greenburgh; med. dir. Margaret Chapman Sch. for Exceptional Child, Hawthorne; physician Westchester County Correctional Health Dept., Valhalla, sch. physician, Elmsford, N.Y. Served with U.S. Army, 1946-48; lt. col. M.C. USAR (ret.). Diplomate Am. Bd. Family Practice. Fellow Am. Acad. of Family Physicians, AMA, Med. Soc. of the State of N.Y., Westchester County Med. Soc., Westchester Acad. of Medicine. Jewish. Clubs: Shriners, Masons. Home: 49 Roundabend Rd Tarrytown NY 10591 Office: 132 S Central Ave Elmsford NY 10523 Other: 5 Bradhurst Ave Hawthorne NY 10532

PANITZ, LAWRENCE HERBERT, lawyer; b. N.Y.C., Feb. 3, 1941; s. Abraham Alexander and Anita Rosyln (Zuckerberg) P.; m. Karin Blaschke, May 27, 1965. AB, Princeton U., 1962; JD, Columbia U., 1965. Bar: N.Y. 1965. Assoc., Wolf, Haldenstein, Adler, Freeman & Herz, N.Y.C., 1965-69; asst. chief fgn. counsel W.R. Grace & Co., N.Y.C., 1969-74; v.p., chief internat. counsel Revlon, Inc., N.Y.C., 1974-84; exec. v.p., chief adminstrv. officer ICN Pharms., Inc., Costa Mesa, Calif., 1985-87; ptnr. Myerson & Kuhn, N.Y.C., 1987—; arbitrator Am. Arbitration Assn., 1966—. Founder Park Ave. Malls Planting Project, 1984; patron Met. Opera, N.Y.C., 1987. Princeton U. fellow, 1961. Mem. Assn. Bar City N.Y. Republican. Club: Explorers (N.Y.C.). Home: 710 Park Ave New York NY 10021 Office: Myerson & Kuhn 237 Park Ave New York NY 10017

PANKEY, GEORGE EDWARD, former educator; b. Charlotte Court House, Va., Dec. 2, 1903; s. John Wesley and Cora Smith (Daniel) P.; B.A., U. Richmond, 1926; M.A., U. N.C., 1927; m. Annabel Atkinson, Mar. 6, 1931; 1 son, George Atkinson. Mem. faculty Ogden Coll. and Western Ky. State Tchrs. Coll., 1927-28, La. Poly. Inst., 1928-43; with land dept. Gulf Oil Corp., 1944-46; currently in research work. Mem. Huguenot Soc., S.A.R., Sons Am. Colonists, Sigma Tau Delta. Baptist. Mason. Author: John Pankey of Manakin Town, Virginia, and His Descendants, Vol. I, 1969, Vol. II, 1972, Vol. III, 1981; co-author: Five Thousand Useful Words, 1936; former editor La. Tech. Digest. Address: Box 84 Ruston LA 71270

PANKEY, GEORGE STEPHEN, dentist; b. Durham, N.C., Dec. 3, 1922; s. Edwin Wilburn and Julia (Bender) P.; A.B., U. N.C., 1948; D.D.S., Emory U., 1954; m. Christina R. Curry, Jan. 17, 1959 (div. Feb. 1967); children: Julia Gay, Crista Merry; m. 2d, Diane Joy Flaim, Oct. 14, 1967 (dec. Sept. 3, 1982); adopted children: Laura Jean, Julia Ann, George Stephen; m. Christa N. Atwell, June 23, 1988. Practice dentistry, Winter Garden, Fla., 1954-58, North Miami Beach, Fla., 1958-59, St. Cloud, Fla., 1959—; dir. Fla. United Investment, Inc. Served with U.S. Army, 1943-46; ETO. Mem. Am. Dental Assn., Fla. State, Central Dist. dental socs., V.F.W., St. Cloud C. of C. (pres. 1961-62), Sigma Chi. Republican. Episcopalian. Mason (worshipful master 1965, Shriner), Rotarian (pres. 1962-63). Home: Reflections on the River Sebastian FL 32958 Office: 4301 Neptune Rd Saint Cloud FL 32769

PANKIN, JAYSON DARRYL, entrepreneur, biotechnologist, venture capitalist; b. Newark, N.J., June 2, 1957; s. Harvey A. and Edythe R. (Simons) P. BBA in Acctg., George Washington U., 1979, MBA in Internat. Bus., 1980. Chmn., pres. PolyCell, Inc., Detroit, 1983—; pres. Growth Funding Ltd., Detroit, 1983—, also bd. dirs.; v.p. Venture Funding Ltd., Detroit, 1983—, also bd. dirs.; treas., v.p. U. Sci. Ptnrs., Inc., Detroit, 1984-85; pres., sec. Quest Blood Substitute, Detroit, 1986—, also bd. dirs.; bd. dirs. Quest Biotech., Inc., Quest Am., Inc. Home: 200 Riverfront Park Dr Suite #20-J Detroit MI 48226 Office: Venture Funding Ltd 321 Fisher Bldg Detroit MI 48202

PAŃKÓW, WLODZIMIERZ, sociologist; b. Lvow, Poland, May 11, 1946; s. Julian and Maria (Bojarska) P.; m. Grażyna Kaczor, may 18, 1967; children: Sylvia, Marcin, Maciej. MA, U. Warsaw, 1969; PhD, Polish Acad. Scis., 1976. Asst. Inst. Commerce, Poland, 1970-72; specialist Computer's Research Ctr., Poland, 1972-74; adj. instr. orgn. and mgmt. Polish Acad. Sci., 1974-76, Inst. Philosophy and Sociology, 1976-86; assoc. researcher Inst. Research on Contemporary Sites, France, 1986; comml. agt. Coop. UNICUM, Warsaw, 1988—; mem. research team on Solidarity, U. Warsaw, 1981; chief research team Internat. Labor Office, Switzerland, 1981. Coauthor: Organizational Structure and..., 1980; author: Verao Polones, 1980, 2d edit., 1983, On the Sources of Organizational Order, 1988; contbr. articles to profl. jours. Cons. to Solidarity, Masovian Region, Poland, 1981. Fellow Authors Assn.; mem. Polish Sociol. Assn. (bd. 1981-83, 87—). Roman Catholic. Home: Kraszewskiego 4 m 59, Brwinow 403980, Poland

PANNELL, CHRISTOPHER JOHN MASTERMAN, mechanical engineer; b. Middlesex, Eng., Apr. 1, 1938; s. Eustace Joe and Gladys Betty (Thorne) P.; cert. mech. and marine engring. Royal Naval Engring. Coll., 1958; postgrad. Bath Tech. Sch., 1959-60; m. Philomena Mary Wohlfahrt, Apr. 19, 1965; children—Anne, Bernard, Michael, Bridget, Martin, Marita, Julia, Stephen, Barbara, Therese, Dominic. Design engr. Stothert & Pitt Ltd., Bath, 1958-60; application engr. Pannell Plant Ltd., Plymouth, 1960-63, dir., 1978—; with Coates & Co. Ltd., Australia, 1963-73, state mgr. New South Wales, 1967-73; exec. chmn. Pannell Holdings Pty. Ltd., Wyong, Australia, 1973-83; dir. Pannell Plant Engrs. Pty. Ltd., Isivend Pty. Ltd., Hirepool Pty. Ltd., CP Systems Pty. Ltd. Grantee, Australian Indsl. Design and Research Authority, 1974—, pres. Am. Bus. Machines, 1988 ; recipient Australian Design award Indsl. Design Council of Australia, 1981, 84; Prince Philip prize for indsl. design in Australia, 1981; Australian Steel award BHP Ltd., 1981. Mem. Inst. Plant Engrs. (London). Roman Catholic (lay minister). Author: An Illustrated History of Supercompaction. Inventor hydrostatic and mech. devices. Office: PO Box 1, Berkeley Vale, New South Wales 2259, Australia

PANNILL, WILLIAM PRESLEY, lawyer; b. Houston, Mar. 5, 1940; s. Fitzhugh H. and Mary Ellen (Goodrum) P.; m. Deborah Detering, May 9, 1966 (div. Nov. 1986); children: Shelley, Katherine, Elizabeth. BA, Rice U., 1962; MS, Columbia U., 1963; JD, U. Tex., 1970. Bar: Tex. 1970, U.S. Supreme Ct. 1975, U.S. Ct. Appeals (5th cir.) 1973, U.S. Ct. Appeals (D.C. cir.) 1974, U.S. Ct. Appeals (10th cir.) 1980, U.S. Ct. Appeals (11th cir.) 1981, U.S. Dist. Ct. (so. dist.) Tex. 1975. Assoc. Vinson, Elkins, Searls & Connally, 1970-71; staff asst. Sec. of Treasury, Washington, 1971-72; assoc. Vinson, Elkins, Searls, Connally & Smith, 1972-75; sole practice, 1975-76; ptnr. Pannill and Hooper, Houston, 1977-80; bd. dirs. Reynolds, Allen, Cook, Pannill & Hooper, Inc., Houston, 1980-82; ptnr. Pannill and Reynolds, Houston, 1982-85; sole practice, Houston, 1985—; assoc. editor Litigation Jour. of the Sect. of Litigation, ABA, 1979-81, exec. editor, 1981-82, editor-in-chief, 1982-84, dir. publs., 1984-86; lectr. Southwestern Legal Found., 1980, others. Chmn., Legal Found. Am., 1981-82, bd. dirs., 1983—. Served with USMCR, 1963-64. Mem. ABA (council litigation sect. 1986—), Fed. Energy Bar Assn., Houston Bar Assn., Tex. Bar Assn. Episcopalian. Club: Houston. Contbr. articles to profl. jours. Office: 909 Fannin St Suite 1600 Two Houston Ctr Houston TX 77010-1007

PANOFF, MICHEL JEAN, anthropologist, educator; b. Paris, July 19, 1931; s. Vincent and Louise (Vaidis) P.; m. Brigitte Jacqueline Duval, Feb. 15, 1975; children: Jerome, Gregoire; 1 child from previous marriage, Mathilde. Diploma, Hautes Etudes Commerciales, Paris, 1954, Centre Formation aux Recherches Ethnologiques, Paris, 1956; D of Ethnology, U. Sorbonne, Paris, 1964. Trainee Centre Nat. Recherche Scientifique, Paris, 1960-61, head research, 1963-67, dir. research, 1982—, apptd. mem. sci. bd., appts. com., 1979-86; researcher Office Recherche Scientifique et Technique Outre-Mer, French Polynesia, 1961-63; sr. research fellow Australian Nat. U., Canberra, 1967-70. Author: L'Ethnologue Etson Ombre, 1968, La Terre Et L'Organisation Sociale, 1970; editor: L'Acces au Terrain Outre-Mer, 1986; contbr. numerous articles to profl. jours. Mem. exec. bd. Esprit Assn., Paris, 1970-75. Mem. Assn. Francaise Anthropologues (v.p. 1980-83), Soc. Océanistes (sec. gen. 1983). Roman Catholic. Home: 14 Blvd Anatole-France, 92190 Meudon France Office: Centre Nat Recherche Scientifique, 15 Quai Anatole-France, 75700 Paris France

PANOPIO, FELIPE BRUAL, military officer, physician; b. Aplaya, Philippines, Mar. 27, 1931; s. Eliseo Madlangbayan Panopio and Maria (Umali) Brual; m. Alice Macarandang Carandang, Dec. 30, 1957; children: Maria Teresa, Maria Fe, Felipe Jr., Bari Nicolas, Mary Rose. AA, U. Philippines, Quezon City, 1951; MD, Manila Cen. U., 1957; postgrad. in neuroOpsychiatry, V. Luna Gen. Hosp., 1961; postgrad. in neurology, Walter Reed Gen. Hosp. and Army Med. Ctr., Washington, 1967; MHA, U. Philippines, Manila, 1980. Cert. physician; diplomate in mil. medicine, neuropsychiat. screener Armed Forces Philippines, 1959. Joined M.C. Armed Forces Philippines, 1959, advanced through grades to col., 1976; dep. exec. officer Office of Chief Surgeon Army, Ft. Bonifacio, Makati, 1972-74; comdg. officer Army Sta. Hosp., Camp Eldridge, Los Banos, 1977-79, Camp Lapu-Lapu, Cebu City, 1980-81, Army Gen. Hosp., Makati, Rizal, 1981-84; exec. officer V. Luna Gen. Hosp., 1985-86; chief surgeon constabulary Office of Surgeon Gen., Camp Crame, Quezon City, 1986-87; chief med. corps div. Office Surgeon Gen., Armed Forces Philippines, 1988; chmn. Med. Service Selection Bd. A, Quezon City, 1986-87. Active PAMS Inc., Quezon City, 1961—, U.P. Vanguard, Inc., PASIG, Rizal, 1984—; officer-in-charge Philippine Civic Action Group-Vietnam, 1968-69. Decorated Mil. Merit medal, Long Service medal with star, Feb. 1986 Revolution medal (Philippines); Ministry Health medal (Republic Vietnam). Fellow Philippine Assn. Mil. Surgeons (medal 1981, ex-officio bd. mem. 1986-87); mem. U. Philippines Hosp. Adminstrn. Soc., Armed Forces Philippines Med. Soc. (advisor 1986-87), Assn. Mil. Surgeons U.S. (hon. mem.; medal 1986; internat. del. 1986). Home: 5 Liverpool St, Merville Park, Paranaque Metro, 1700 Manila Philippines Office: Camp Gen Emilio Aquinaldo, Quezon City, 1110 Metropolitan Manila Philippines

PANOU, GEORGES, educator; b. Athens, Feb. 14, 1934; s. Basile and Maria (Tsisi) P.; Civil Mining Engr., U. Brussels, 1958, D. Applied Scis., 1964; m. Luigia Cimotti, Jan. 24, 1959; children—Diane, Anne-Marie, Isabelle. Prof., dir. mining dept. U. Brussels 1974—. Mem. Academia Royale des Sciences d'Outre-Mer Belgium. Home: 213 Ave Louise, 1050 Brussels Belgium

PANSINO, SALVATORE ROCCO, electrical engineer, physicist, lecturer, management consultant; b. Monongahela, Pa., Apr. 15, 1935; s. Rocco Fred and Theresa Vee (Malena) P.; m. Vivian Sue Nahar, Apr. 26, 1958; children—Cynthia Claire, Vivian Diana, Sondra Sue, Nancy Elaine. B.S. in Engring., Carnegie Inst. Tech., 1957; M.S., Franklin and Marshall Coll., 1961; postgrad. U. Pitts., 1961-63; Ph.D., Carnegie-Mellon U., 1968; LL.B., LaSalle U., 1976. Microwave engr. Bendix Corp., York, Pa., 1957-61; research asst. U. Pitts., 1961-63; project engr. Carnegie-Mellon U., 1963-68; electronics instr. Forbes Trail Tech. Sch., Monroeville, Pa., 1963; project mgr., electronics group leader, planning staff Babcock & Wilcox Alliance Research Center, Ohio, 1967-81 ; instr. Mt. Union Coll., 1980; instr. Youngstown State U., 1980-81, prof., 1981—, chmn. dept. elec. engring., 1984—. Republican nominee for Ohio State Senate, 1982. NSF grantee, 1963-67; recipient human relations award Dale Carnegie; Explorer Scouts award, 1969; Disting. service award Jaycees. Mem. IEEE (sect. chmn. NE Ohio and NW Pa.), U.S. Tennis Assn., Sigma Pi Sigma. Clubs: Toastmasters (pres., v.p. publicity, chmn. bd., area gov., div. gov. 1983, Gov. of Yr. award 1984, Toastmaster of Yr., Disting. Toastmaster), Babcock & Wilcox Employees (pres., chmn. bd., trustee). Home: 2480 Crestview Ave Alliance OH 44601 Office: Youngstown State U Youngstown OH 44555

PANT, SHRI KRISHNA CHANDRA, Indian government official; b. Bhowali, Utiar Pradesh, India, Aug. 10, 1931; s. Shri Govind Ballabh P.; m. Ila Pant, June 20, 1957; 2 sons. Student, St. Joseph's Coll., Lucknow U. Mem. Lok Sabha, Nainital, India, 1962-77, 78—; minister fin. India, New Delhi, 1967-69, minister steel and heavy engring., 1969-70, minister home affairs, head dept. electronics, 1970-73, head dept. sci. and indsl. research, 1970-71, head dept. sci. and tech., 1971, head dept. atomic energy, 1971-73, minister irrigation and power, 1973-74, minister energy, 1974-77, 79-80, minister edn., 1984-85, minister steel and mines, 1985-87, minister def., 1987—. Mem. Inst. Constitutional and Parliamentary Studies (founder), Inst. Engrs. (life). Club: Dehli Gymkhana. Office: Ministry Def, New Delhi India *

PANTING, SIDNEY JOSE, bank economist; b. San Pedro Sula, Honduras, Dec. 21, 1951; s. Sidney and Maria Ernestina (Paz) P.; m. Edna Maribel Crespo, Mar. 22, 1975; children—Edna Angelina, Sandra Janet. Bachiller, LaSalle Inst., 1969; Grad. Economist, U. Honduras, 1974; M.B.A., Inst. Cent. Am. Adminstrn. Empresas, Nicaragua, 1977. Mgr., Diario Tiempo, San Pedro Sula, Honduras, 1971-72; head dept. math. U. Honduras, Curn, 1973-75, prof., 1973—; vice dir., 1981—; exec. Banco Sogerin, San Pedro Sula, 1977—, planning mktg. mgr., 1982-86, gen. mgr., 1986—, also dir.; dir. Sermeco, San Pedro Sula, 1979—, Super-Tiendas Prisa, San Pedro Sula, 1983; sec. Orgn. Alipo Polit. Party, San Pedro Sula, 1983; council mem. Regional Com. INCAE, San Pedro Sula, 1983; council mem. Honduran Banking Assn., San Pedro Sula., 1982—. Author: The Process of Decision Making, 1984; Strategic Planning, Text and Cases. Named Most Outstanding Grad. Cabelleros de Suyapa, Honduras, 1969; recipient Premio Ramon Rosa Municipalidad de San Pedro Sula, 1969. Mem. Colegio Hondureno de Economistas. Mem. Alipo-Liberal Party. Roman Catholic.

PANTON, VERNER, architect; b. Gamtofte, Fyn, Denmark, Feb. 13, 1926; arrived in Switzerland, 1963; s. Henry and Ellen (Koch-Hansen) P.; m. Marianne Pherson, July 17, 1964; 1 child, Carin. Degree in bldg. constrn., Odense (Denmark) Tech. Sch., 1947; MArch, Royal Acad. Arts, Copenhagen, 1951. Owner, architect, designer Verner Panton AG, Basel, Switzerland, 1964—; vis. prof. indsl. design Hochschule für Gestaltung, Offenbach, Fed. Republic of Germany, 1984. Fellow Royal Soc. Arts; mem. Acad. Arkitecktforening, Danske Arkitekters Landsforbund, Indsl. Designers Denmark, Schweizerischer Werkbund. Home and Office: Kohlenberggasse 21, 4051 Basel Switzerland

PANUFNIK, ANDRZEJ, composer, conductor; b. Warsaw, Poland, Sept. 24, 1914; d. Tomasz and Matylda (Thonnes) P.; m. Camilla Jessel, 1963; 2 children. Ed. Warsaw State Conservatory and the State Acad. Music (with Felix Weingartner), Vienna; R.A.M. (hon.), 1984; D.Phil. (hon.), 1985. Condr. Cracow Philharm. Orch., 1945-46; dir. Warwaw Phil. Orch., 1946-47; v.p. Polish Composers' Union, 1948-54; vice chmn. Internat. Music Council of UNESCO, 1950-53; settled in Eng., 1954, naturalized, 1961; mus. dir. City of Birmingham Symphony Orch., 1957-59; vis. condr. leading European and S. Am. orchs., 1947—; mainly composer 1959. Compositions include: Piano Trio, 1934, Five Polish Peasant Songs, 1940, Tragic Overture, 1942, Nocturne, 1947, Lullaby, 1947, Twelve Miniature Studies, 1947, Sinfonia Rustica, 1948, Hommage á Chopin, 1949, Old Polish Suite, 1950, Concerto in Modo Antico, 1951, Heroic Overture, 1952, Rhapsody, 1956, Sinfonia Elegiaca, 1957, Polonia - Suite 1959, Concerto for Piano and Orch., 1962, Landscape, 1962, Sinfonia Sacra, 1963, Two Lyric Pieces, 1963, Song to the Virgin Mary, 1964, Autumn Music, 1965, Katyn Epitaph, 1966, Jagiellonian Triptych, 1966, Reflections for Piano, 1968, The Universal Prayer, 1968-69, Thames Pageant, 1969, Concerto for Violin and Strings, 1971, Triangles, 1972, Winter Solstice, 1972, Sinfonia Concertante, 1973, Sinfonia di Sfere, 1974-75, String Quartet, 1976, Dreamscape, 1976, Sinfonia Mistica, 1977, Metasinfonia, 1978, Concerto Festivo, 1979, Concertino, 1980, String Quartet No. 2, 1980. Paean for Queen Elizabeth, 1980, Sinfonia Votiva, 1981, A Procession for Peace, 1982, Arbor Cosmica, 1983, Pentasonata, 1984, Bassoon Concerto, 1985, Symphony No. 9, 1986, String Sextet, 1987. Ballet Music: Elegy, 1967, Cain and Abel, 1968, Miss Julie, 1970, Homage to Chopin, 1980, Adieu, 1980, Polonia, 1980, Dances of the Golden Hall, 1980. Recipient 1st prize, Chopin Competition, 1949; Banner of Labour 1st class, 1949; State prizewinner, 1951, 52; Pre-Olympic Competition 1st prize, 1952; 1st prize for mus. composition Prince Rainier III of Monaco, 1963, Sibelius Centenary medal, 1965, Knight of Mark Twain, U.S., 1966, Prix de Prince Pierre de Monaco, 1983. Address: Riverside House, Twickenham, Middlesex TW1 3DJ, England

PANZER, BALDUR M., Slavic philology university professor; b. Pestlin, Germany, Apr. 29, 1934; s. Friedrich and Erika (Lorenz) P.; m. Ilse Wahler, Oct. 9, 1964; children: Regina, Astrid, Wolfgang. Staatsexamen, U. Hamburg, 1959; PhD in philosophy, U. Munchen, 1961, Habilitation, 1966. Universitätsdozent U. Munchen, West Germany, 1966-72; prof. U. Munchen, 1972-74, prof. Slavic philology, 1974—; dir. Slavic Inst., Heidelberg, West Germany, 1977—, dean Neuphilologl. Fakultat, Heidelberg, 1977-79. Author: Verbalaspekt, 1963, Sla. Konditional, 1967, Stukt. Russ., 1975, Genet. Aufbaud Russ, 1978. Mem. Soc. Linguistica Europaea, Verband d. Hochschullehrer f. Slavistik, Verein Niederdt Sprachforschung. Office: Slavisches Institut, Schulgasse 6, D6909 Heidelberg Federal Republic of Germany

PANZERA, CARL, ceramist, researcher; b. Acquaviva, Isernia, Italy, Aug. 11, 1945; came to U.S., 1954, naturalized, 1960; s. Paolino and Belinda (Petrocelli) P.; m. Connie Tummillo, June 15, 1968; children—Paul. B.S., Rutgers U., 1968, postgrad. 1981—; M.S., Rensselaer Poly. Inst., 1971; M.B.A., U. Conn., 1975. Registered profl. engr., N.J. Research asst. P&W Aircraft, Middletown, Conn., 1968-72; research assoc. Brunswick Corp., Milford, Conn., 1972-77; sr. engr. Xaloy, Inc., New Brunswick, N.J., 1977-79, Airco Research, Murray Hill, N.J., 1979-81; mgr. ceramic research and devel. J&J Dental, East Windsor, N.J., 1981—. Editor Trends and Techniques mag., 1984-85. Patentee in field. Contbr. articles to profl. jours. Bd. dirs. Little League, Hillsborogh, N.J., 1981-82, mgr., 1979-83. Mem. Am. Ceramics Soc., N.J. Ceramic Assn., Am. Soc. Metals, Cromwell Jayees (named Jaycee of Quarter, 1973), Keramos, Tau Beta Pi. Republican. Roman Catholic. Current work: Aesthetics of dental porcelain; advanced dental material. Subspecialties: Ceramics; Dental materials. Home: 7 Huntsman Ln Belle Mead NJ 08502

PAOLINI, SHIRLEY JOAN, university dean, humanities educator; b. Cleve.; d. James Francis and Ann Dorothy (Jurist) Burke; m. Maurizio Paolini; children: Kenneth, Marco, Angela, Laura. BA, Mt. St. Mary's Coll., 1954; postgrad. U. Lausanne, Switzerland, 1954-55; MA, Calif. State U.-Fullerton, 1966; PhD, U. Calif.-Irvine, 1973. Asst. dir. edn. Nat. Systems Corp., Newport Beach, Calif., 1971-73; dir. planning Chaminade U., Honolulu, 1975-78; asst. prof. English, asst. specialist U. Hawaii, Manoa, 1977-78; art reach dir. Anchorage Arts Council, Anchorage, 1978-79; asst. dean acad. affairs Alaska Pacific U., Anchorage, 1979-80, dean continuing edn., 1980-82, dean univ. affairs, 1982-83, dean spl. programs, 1983-85; cons. Hawaii State Govts., Honolulu, 1977-78, Alaska Ednl. Agys., 1979—; chmn. dir. of humanities chmn.; dean sch. arts and scis.; dean sch. arts and scis. Barry U., Miami Shores Fla., 1988—. Author: Confessions of Sin and Love, 1982. Editor: North American School of Conservation, 1971-73, Studies in Interdisciplinarity, 1987—. Contbr. articles to various publs. Recipient French Govt. award, Los Angeles Consulate, 1954, Faculty Research award Alaska Pacific U., 1987; Swiss Govt. fellow U. Lausanne, 1954-55. Mem. Am. Comparative Lit. Assn., MLA, Internat. Comparative Lit. Assn., Council for Adult and Exptl. Learning (co-mgr. Alaska region, 1985-87), Philol. Assn. Pacific Coast, Am. Assn. Italian Studies and Australian Studies, World Affairs Council (Anchorage chpt.). Democrat. Roman Catholic. Clubs: La Mirada Womens (v.p. 1965-66) (Calif.). Office: Barry U Sch Arts & Scis 11300 NE 2d Ave Miami Shores FL 33161

PAOLINO, RICHARD FRANCIS, manufacturing company executive; b. Fall River, Mass., Feb. 16, 1945; s. Emelio and Sylvia (Fasciani) P.; m. Elizabeth Jane Maloney, Sept. 9, 1973; children: Christopher Matthew, Kathryn Elizabeth. AB in Engring. Sci., Dartmouth Coll., 1967; MBA in Mktg. and Fin., U. Chgo., 1973. Plant engr. Polaroid Corp., Cambridge, Mass., 1967; from salesman to asst. br. mgr., Fed. Products Corp., Chgo., 1967-74; area mgr., nat. accounts mgr., Husky Injection Molding Systems, Chgo. and Toronto, Can., 1974-76; v.p. mktg. Quality Measurement Systems Inc., Penfield, N.Y., 1976-78; dir. mktg. Automation and Measurement div. Bendix Corp., Dayton, Ohio, 1978-82; gen. mgr. Boice div. MTI, Latham, N.Y., 1982-85; v.p., gen. mgr. coordinate Measuring Systems Div., Brown & Sharpe Mfg. Co., North Kingstown, R.I., 1985—; condr. seminars, lectr. in field. Served with USMCR, 1967-69. Mem. Soc. Mfg. Engrs. (past chmn. quality assurance tech. council), Am. Soc. Quality Control. Address: 16 Quincy Adams Rd Barrington RI 02806

PAOLOZZI, EDUARDO LUIGI, sculptor; b. Leigh, Scotland, Mar. 7, 1924; s. Rudolfo and Carmella P.; m. Freda Elliot, 1951; 3 children. Student Edinburgh Coll. of Art, Slade Sch. Fine Art, Oxford and London; D. (hon.) Royal Coll. Art, London; D.Litt (hon.), U. Glasgow, 1980. Exhbns. Mayor Gallery, London, 1947, 48, 49; tchr. textile design Ctr. Sch. Art and Design, 1949-55; lectr. in sculpture St. Martin's Sch. Art, 1955-58; vis. prof. Hochschule fur Bildende Kunste, Hamburg, 1960-62; vis. lectr. U. Calif., Berkeley, 1968; lectr. in ceramics Royal Coll. Art, 1968—; prof. ceramics Fachhochschule, Koln, 1976-81; prof. sculpture Akad der Bildenen Kunste, Munich, W.Ger., 1981—; prof. master class Internat. Summer Acad., Salzburg, 1982; one man shows: Hanover Gallery, London, 1958, 67, Betty Parsons Gallery, N.Y.C., 1960, 62, Robert Fraser Gallery, London, 1964, 66, Mus. Modern Art, N.Y.C., 1964, Pace Gallery, N.Y.C., 1966, 67, Stedelijk Mus., Amsterdam, 1968, Tate Gallery, London, 1971, Victoria and Albert Mus., 1977, Nationalgalerie, Berlin retrospective, 1975, Crawford Ctr., Edinburgh, 1979, Kolnischer Kunstverein, Cologne, 1979, Westfaliser Kunstverein, 1980, Mus. for Kunst and Gewerbe, Hamburg, 1982, Aedes Gallery, 1983, New Metropole Arts Ctr., 1984, Ivan Daugherty Gallery, Sydney, Australia, 1985, Mus. of Mankind, 1986, others; group shows include: Venice Biennale, 1952, 60, Sao Paulo Biennale, 1957, 63, New Images of Man Mus. of Modern Art, N.Y.C., 1959, 2d, 3d and 4th Internat. Biennial Exhbns. of Prints Mus. Modern Art, Tokyo, 1960, 62, 64, Brit. Art Today (travelling exhbn. tour U.S.A.), 1962, 7th Internat. Art Exhbn., Tokyo, 1963, Neue Realisten und Pop Art, Akad. der Kunste, Berlin, 1964, Premier Bienniale Exhbn., Cracow, 1966, Sculpture from Twenty Nations, Guggenheim Mus., N.Y.C., 1967, Pop Art Redefined, Hayward Gallery, London, 1969, Expo 70, Osaka 1970, Hayward Ann. Arts Council Exhbn., 1977, Jubilee Exhbn. of Brit. Sculpture, Dovecot Studios, 1980, Nat. Gallery of Scotland, 1980, 20th Century Brit. Sculpture, London, 1981, West-Kunst, Cologen, 1981, Innovations in Contemporary Printmaking, Oxford, 1982, Museo Mcpl. of Madrid, 1983; permanent collections include Tate Gallery, Contemporary Art Soc., Mus. Modern Art. Recipient Brit. Critics prize, 1953, Copley Found. award, 1956, Bright Found. award, 1960, Blair prize 64th Ann. Am. Exhbn., Chgo., 1961, 1st prize for sculpture, Carnegie Internat. Exhbn., Pitts., 1967; Saltire Soc. award, 1981; grand prix d'honneur 15th Internat. Print Biennale, Ljubljana, 1983. Office: Akademie der Bildenen Kunste, Akademiestrasse 2, 8000 Munich 2 Federal Republic of Germany also: 107 Dovehouse St, London SW3, England *

PAPA, ANTHONY EMIL, retired army officer; b. Williamstown, N.J., Mar. 31, 1914; s. Gabriel and Mamie (Rizzo) P.; m. Dorothea Louise Gibson, Oct. 3, 1942. Grad., Mil. Police Advanced Sch., 1954; student, U. Pitts., 1955. Commd. 2d lt. U.S. Army, 1940; dir. personnel Mil. Police Corps, Washington, 1943-45; advisor, chief of staff U.S. Mil. Mission w/ Imperial Iranian Gendarmerie, Tehran, Iran, 1945-48; comdg. officer 504th MP Bn., 1954-55; advanced through grades to col. U.S. Army, 1955; asst. chief of staff G-1, I-Corps, Korea, 1955-56; provost marshal thence asst. chief of staff G-1, Fifth U.S. Army, Chgo., 1959-61; dep. provost marshal gen. 1964-66, ret., 1966; v.p. Guardsmark, Inc., Memphis, 1968-69; chmn. spl. projects Guardsmark, Inc., 1977-78; U.S. marshal for D.C. Washington, 1970-73. Decorated Legion of Merit with oak leaf cluster, Army Commendation medal with 3 oak leaf clusters; Iranian medal of merit; Iranian medal of honor. Mem. Internat. Assn. Chiefs of Police (life). Home: 7100 34th St S Apt 904 Saint Petersburg FL 33711

PAPADAKIS, MARI, rental company executive; b. Houston, June 15, 1942; d. George Paul and Sophia (Kestikides) Panagos; m. James T. Papadakis; children—Thomas James, Lainie. Student U. Houston, 1960-62. Exec. com. Alley Theatre, Houston, 1982-83, adv. com., 1985-86; bd. dirs. Juvenile Diabetes, Houston, 1979, 88; pres. March Dimes, Houston, 1983-84, exec. com., 1985-88; pres. Unique Rentals Inc., Houston, 1985—, James Coney Island Catering Co., 1988—; v.p., dir. Pro Houston, 1985—. Co-chmn. Sesquicentennial Celebration, Houston, 1986. Named Pacesetter of Yr., Cancer Assistance League, 1986; one of Ten Best Dressed Women, 1985. Mem. Hellenic League Tex. Republican. Greek Orthodox. Avocations: tennis, dancing, modeling, reading, decorating.

PAPADIMITRIOU, DIMITRI BASIL, economist, college administrator; b. Salonica, Greece, June 9, 1946; came to U.S., 1965, naturalized, 1974; s. Basil John and Ellen (Tacas) P.; BA, Columbia U., 1970; PhD, New Sch. Social Research, 1974; m. Viki Fokas, Aug. 26, 1967; children—Jennifer E., Elizabeth R. Vice pres., asst. sec. ITT Life Ins. Co. N.Y., N.Y.C., 1970-73; exec. v.p., sec., treas. William Penn Life Ins. Co. N.Y., N.Y.C., 1973-78, also dir.; exec. v.p., provost Bard Coll., 1978—, exec. dir. Bard Coll. Ctr., Jerome Levy Econs. Inst., 1980—; adj. lectr. econs. New Sch. Social Research, 1975-76; prof. Bard Coll., 1978—; fellow Ctr. for Advanced Econ. Studies, 1983; dir. William Penn Life Ins. Co. N.Y.; pres. and bd. dirs. Catskill Ballet Theatre, Hudsonia, Inc., mem. adv. com.; bd. overseers Simon's Rock of Bard Coll.; bd. govs. Jerome Levy Econs. Inst., 1986—. Bd. dirs. Dutchess County Council for Arts. Mem. Am. Econ. Assn., Royal Econ. Soc., Am. Fin. Assn., Atlantic Econ. Soc., Econ. Sci. Chamber of Greece. Home and Office: Bard Coll Annandale-on-Hudson NY 12504

PAPADOPOULO, EMILE NICHOLAS, paint company executive; b. Istanbul, Turkey, June 30, 1925; s. Nicolas C. and Phedra A. (Gheorghiadou) P.; B.S., Coll. St. Michel, Istanbul, 1943; B.Sc. in Mech. Engring., Robert Coll., Istanbul, 1948; m. Alice Radovitch, Nov. 4, 1951. Tech. interpreter U.S. Forces in Turkey, 1950-54; mng. dir. Turk-Avis Ltd., Istanbul, 1954-56; propr. Gen. Nr. East Survey, trade co., Istanbul, 1956-74; tech. exec. Oksan Ltd., paints and varnishes, Izmir, 1970-74; founder, 1974, since owner Chromet Inc., paint and varnishes, Iraklion, Crete, Greece; hon. consul for Norway in Crete/Greece, 1976—. Served with Signals Res., Turkish Army, 1949-50. Recipient Gold medal, London, 1976, Luxembourg, 1977, Silver medal, Paris, 1979. Mem. chambers commerce and industry Istanbul, Iraklion. Mem. Eastern Roman Ch. Lodges: Rotary, Ariadne. Home: Platia Agh Dimitriou 24, Iraklion, Crete Greece Office: Agh Dimitrou Square & Vironos, Iraklion, Crete Greece

PAPADOPOULOS, ATHANASE, mathematician, researcher; b. Jan. 14, 1957; s. Dimitri and Marie-Claudine (Zaza) P.; m. Marie-Pascale Hautefeuille; children: Helene, Dimitri, Marie-Claudine. M in Math., U. Paris XI, 1979, D in Math., 1981; Ingenieer, Ecole Cen. De Paris, 1981. Asst. U. Paris XI, 1983-84; mem. Inst. for Advanced Study, Princeton, N.J., 1984-85; head in charge of research Ctr. Nat. Recherche Scientifique U. Strasbourg, France, 1985—. Contbr. articles to pofl. jours. Mem. Am Math. Soc. Office: U Strasbourg, 7 Rue René Descartes, 67084 Strasbourg France

PAPADOPOULOS, DIMITRIOS (DIMITRIOS I), archbishop Eastern Orthodox Church; b. Istanbul, Sept. 8, 1914; D.Theol., Sch. of Haiki, Heybeliada-Istanbul, 1937. Ordained deacon of the Eastern Orthodox Ch., 1937, priest, 1942, bishop, 1964. Sec., preacher, Edessa, Greece, 1937-38; deacon, priest, preacher, Ferikoy, Istanbul, 1939-45; priest Orthodox Community, Tehran, Iran, 1945-50; head priest Orthodox Community, Ferikoy, 1950-64; bishop of Elaia, Aux. Bishop of Patriarach Athenagoras, Istanbul; bishop, Kurtulus, Istanbul, 1964-72, Met. of Imvros and Tenedos, 1972; elected to Holy and Sacred Synod; Archbishop of Constantinople, New Rome and Ecumenical Patriarch, under the name Dimitrios I, 1972—. Address: Rum Ortodoks Patrikhanesi, H Fener, Istanbul Turkey *

PAPADOPOULOS, GEORGE, electronics executive; b. Philippi, Kavala, Greece, July 23, 1946; s. John and Kaliopi (Papadima) P.; m. Ageliki Sarantopoulou; 1 child, John. Diploma, Isle of Ely Coll., Wisbeach, Eng., 1967; grad., U. Thessaloniki, 1969, U. Athens, Greece, 1979. Researcher Inst. Agrl. Research, Chania-Krete, 1971; quality control employee Fix Brewery SA, Athens, 1972, quality control mgr., 1973, prodn. mgr., 1974; plant mgr. L'Air Liquide Hellas SA, Athens, 1974-79, med. div. mgr., 1979-84; founder, chief exec. officer ABC Systems and Software SA, Athens, 1984—. Mem. Greek Bus. Adminstrn. Assn., Computer Sci. Inst. of Greek Bus. Adminstrn. Assn. Office: ABC Systems and Software SA, 44 Syngrou Ave, 11742 Athens Greece

PAPADOPOULOS, GREGORY MICHAEL, computer scientist; b. Oakland, Calif., Apr. 30, 1958; s. Michael Nicholas and Imogen (Sherman) P.; m. Elizabeth Ann Woellner, Nov. 26, 1982; 1 child, Michael Gregory. B.A. in Systems Sci., U. Calif.-San Diego, 1979; S.M. in Computer Sci., MIT, 1983, postgrad., 1983—. Programmer Scripps Inst. Oceanography, La Jolla, Calif., 1977-79; devel. engr. Hewlett-Packard, Inc., San Diego, 1979-81; sr. research scientist Honeywell, Inc., Mpls., 1981-84; pvt. practice cons., Cambridge, Mass., 1984-85; co-founder, chief tech. officer A.I. Architects, Inc., Cambridge, 1985—; research fellow Charles Stark Draper Labs., Cambridge, 1981-83. Contbr. articles to profl. jours. Pres. Meml. chpt. Am. Field Service, Houston, 1975-76. Recipient Spl. distinction award Nat. Forensic League, 1976; U. Calif. Regents scholar, 1978. Mem. AAAS, Phi Beta Kappa, Sigma Xi. Republican. Avocations: bicycle touring; soccer, diving. Home: 30 Howard St Arlington MA 02174 Office: MIT Lab for Computer Sci 545 Technology Sq Cambridge MA 02139

PAPALEO, LOUIS ANTHONY, accountant; b. N.Y.C., Sept. 15, 1953; s. Domenico Vincent and Antoinette (Pica) P.; m. Kathy Maehlenbrock, June 23, 1971; children: Leigh, Domenic, Adriana. BS in Acctg., Iona Coll., 1975, MBA, 1986. Staff acct. Papaleo & Co., New Rochelle, N.Y., 1975-80, v.p., 1980-84, pres., 1984—. Chmn. Downtown Businessman's and Merchants Assn., New Rochelle, 1984. Mem. Nat. Acctg. Assn., N.Y. State Acct. Assn., Nat. Soc. Public Accts. Republican. Roman Catholic. Lodge: Masons. Office: 557 Main St New Rochelle NY 10801

PAPALIA, DIANE ELLEN, human development educator; b. Englewood, N.J., Apr. 26, 1947; d. Edward Peter and Madeline (Borrin) P.; m. Jonathan Finlay, June 19, 1976; 1 child, Anna Victoria Finlay. A.B., Vassar Coll., 1968; M.S., W.Va. U., 1970, Ph.D. (NSF fellow), 1971. Asst. prof. child and family studies U. Wis., Madison, 1971-75; assoc. prof. U. Wis., 1975-78, prof., 1978—, coordinator child and family studies, 1977-79; adj. prof. psychology in pediatrics U. Pa. Sch. Medicine, 1987. Author: (with Sally W. Olds) A Child's World: Infancy through Adolescence, 1975,, 4th edit., 1987, Human Development, 1978, 3d edit., 1986, Psychology, 1985, 2d. edit. 1988; contbr. articles to profl. jours. Am. Council on Edn. fellow, 1979-80; U. Wis. grantee. Fellow Gerontol. Soc.; mem. Am. Psychol. Assn., Soc. Research in Child Devel., Nat. Council Family Relations, Psi Chi.

PAPAMARCOS, JOHN, editor; b. N.Y.C., Dec. 30, 1920; s. Demetri and Alma Cecelia (Nicolaysen) P.; m. Barbara Ann Johnson, Jan. 19, 1952; children—John S., Andrew A., Paula C., Mark S. B.E.E., Cooper Union Coll., 1941; M. in Mech. Engring., U. Del., 1951; M.E.E., Poly. Inst. Bklyn., 1953. Registered profl. engr., N.Y. Lectr. elec. engring. CCNY, 1948-52; instr. elect. engring. Poly. Inst. Bklyn., 1952-55; plant betterment engr. Ebasco Internat., N.Y.C., 1957-58; assoc. editor-mgr. editor Power Engring., Barrington, Ill., 1960-74, editor, 1974-86, cons. editor, 1986—. Contbr. articles to profl. jours. Com. mem. Barrington Area United Dr., 1974-75, v.p., 1975-76, pres., 1976-77. Mem. IEEE, ASME (exec. com. fuels div. 1974-78, chmn. exec. com. 1977-78, nat. nominating com. 1984-85, council on engring. com. on appointment, 1986—), Am. Soc. Engring. Edn. Lodge: Kiwanis (pres. 1973-74). Current work: All 12000 categories (energy science and technology). Subspecialties: Coal; Fuels and sources. Home: 212 Coolidge Ave Barrington IL 60010

PAPANDREOU, ANDREAS GEORGE, prime minister of Greece; b. Chios, Greece, Feb. 5, 1919; s. George and Sophia (Mineiko) P.; MA in Econs., Harvard U., 1942, PhD in Econs., 1943; m. 2d, Margaret Chant, 1951; 4 children. Teaching fellow and tutor Harvard U., 1942-43, instr., 1943-44, 46-47; assoc. prof. econs. U. Minn., 1947-50; assoc. prof. Northwestern U., 1950-51; prof. U. Minn., 1951-55; prof. U. Calif., Berkeley, 1955-63, chmn. dept. econs., 1956-59; prof. econs. U. Stockholm, 1968-69, York U., 1969-74, dir. research York-Kenya Project, 1969-74; minister to the prime minister Govt. of Greece, 1964; minister of Coordination, 1964-65; dep. Greek Parliament, 1964-67; chmn. Panhellenic Liberation Movement, 1968; pres. Panhellenic Socialist Movement, 1974; dep. Greek Parliament and leader Main Opposition Party, 1977-81; prime minister of Greece, 1981-85, re-elected, 1985—, also minister nat. def.; econ. adv. Bank of Greece, 1961-62; dir. Ctr. of Econ. Research, Athens, 1961-64. Fulbright fellow, 1959-60; Guggenheim fellow, 1959-60; Wicksell lectr., Stockholm, 1966; Benjamin Fairless lectr. Carnegie-Mellon U., 1969; Edmund Burk Bicentenary lectr. Trinity Coll., Dublin, 1970; Woodward lectr. U. B.C.; 1973. Author: (with others) An Introduction to Social Science: Personality, Work, Community, 1953, rev. edits., 1957, 61; (with J.T. Wheeler) Competition and its Regulation, 1954; Economics as a Science, 1958; A Strategy for Greek Economic Development, 1962; Fundamentals of Model Construction in Macroeconomics, 1962; Introduction to Macroeconomic Models, 1965; Democracy and National Renaissance, 1966; Toward a Totalitarian World?, 1969; Man's Freedom, 1970; Greece to the Greeks, 1976; Democracy at Gunpoint: The Greek Front, 1970; Paternalistic Capitalism, 1972; Project Selection for National Plans, 1974; (with U. Zohar) The Impact Approach to Project Selection, 1974; Imperialism and Economic Development, 1975; Transition to Socialism, 1977; Toward a Socialist Society, 1977; contbr. chpts. to books; contbr. articles to profl. jours. Office: Office of the Prime Minister, Odos Zalokosta 10, Athens Greece

PAPANDREOU, GEORGE ANDREAS, parliamentarian; b. St. Paul, June 16, 1952; s. Andreas George and Margaret (Chant) P.; divorced; 1 child, Andreas. Student, Stockholm U., 1972-73; BA in Sociology, Amherst Coll., 1975; MS in Sociology and Devel., London Sch. Econs., 1977. Parliamentarian Govt. of Greece, Athens, 1981—, minister edn. and religious affairs, 1988—; undersec. for cultural affairs Greek Parliament, Athens, 1985-87; chmn. parliamentary com. on edn.; vice chmn. multi-partisan parliamentary com. for free radio. Active cen. com. Panhellenic Socialist Movement, Greece, 1984—, mem. exec. com., 1987, sec. agrl. coops., mem. internat. relations com., dep. sec. orgnl. com.; govt. coordinator for the Athens candidacy for the 1996 Olympic Games, 1988. Recipient award for promotion of journalism for the establishment of Free Radio in Greece, Botsis Found. Mem. Found. Mediterranean Studies (mem. research teams), Found. Research and Self-Edn. Mem. Panhellenic Socialist Movement. Office: 14 Patission St, 10677 Athens Greece

PAPANTONIS, ANTONY, wine company executive; b. Athens, Greece, June 17, 1950; s. Dimostenes Papantonis and Katerine Dousias. BBA, Hamilton Coll., Mason City, Iowa, 1974. Gen. mgr. Inachos S.A., Athens, Greece, 1975—; dir. Edok-Eter-Mandilas, Nigeria, Thalis S.A., Saudi Arabia, Overseas Engr. and Gen. Contractor, Libya. Served in the Greek Army, 1970-72. Office: Inachos SA, 95 Alexandras Ave, 11474 Athens Greece

PAPAPANAGIOTOU, JOHN, microbiologist; b. Patras, Greece, Sept. 14, 1921; s. Constantinos and Maria (Moutoussis) P.; MB, U. Athens, 1947, MD, 1956; m. Clea Countouris, Apr. 28, 1957; children: Constantinos, Maria. Dir. microbiol. lab. Seamens Chest Hosp., Melissia, Athens, 1955-65, I.K.A. Gen. Hosp., Penteli, Athens, 1965-67; prof. microbiology Med. Sch., U. Thessaloniki (Greece), 1967—, dean Med. Sch., 1976-77; trustee AHEPA Gen. Hosp., 1975-82, Inst. Pasteur, Athens, 1976-83. Served with Greek Army, 1948-50, 51-53. Decorated D.S.M.; WHO fellow, London, 1954; Greek State scholar, Denmark, 1958-59. Mem. Med. Soc. Thessaloniki (pres. 1975-77), Microbiol. Soc. Thessaloniki (pres. 1982), Greek Soc. Microbiology (v.p. 1966), Soc. Med. Studies, Soc. Gen. Microbiology Gt. Brit., Soc. Applied Bacteriology, N.Y. Acad. Scis. Greek Orthodox. Author: Medical Microbiology and Immunology, 2 vols., 1976; contbr. articles to profl. jours. Home: 5 Mitropolitou Iossif, 54622 Thessaloniki Greece Office: U Thessaloniki, Med Sch Dept Microbiology, 54006 Thessaloniki Greece

PAPAS, PAUL NICHOLAS, II, insurance company executive; b. Boston, Feb. 15, 1951; s. Nicholas M. and Bessie P.; divorced; children from previous marriage : Erica M., Paul Nicholas, III, Margaret M. BS in Criminal Justice, Northeastern U., 1976, MA in Finance, 1977; postgrad., Mass. Mil. Acad., 1978; JD, Thomas Jefferson Coll. Law, 1984. With Centre Assocs., Dedham, Mass., 1970—, owner, 1971—; founder Paul N. Papas II Ins. Agy., Dedham, 1974—; owner, mgr. Bay State Appraisers and Investigators, Dedham, 1976—; onwer, mgr. Concept Leasing, Dedham, 1977—; owner, mgr. Capital Investment Adv. Services, Dedham, 1975—; founder Capital Return Co., Dedham, 1975, Unltd. Concept Ads, Dedham, 1977, Athens Am. Bank, 1983. Founder Alpha and Omega Legal Research; mem. Dedham Charter Commn., 1976; founder, bd. dirs. Christians for Justice, 1984—, Nat. Child Drug Abuse Awareness Program and Day, 1984—; chmn. Dedham Rep. Town Com., 1973-76; trustee Ch. of the Annunciation, Greek Orthodox Ch., Boston, 1977, ex-POW. Named Rep. of Yr., Young Rep. Club, 1973. Mem. Nat. Assn. Life Underwriters, Nat. Assn. Fire Investigators, Dedham C. of C. Lodge: Masons.

PAPAZISSIS, MICHAEL GEORGE, lawyer; b Serres, Macedonia, Greece, Jan. 2, 1935; s. George and Zoe (Katsaridou) P.; m. Athena Vogassari, Oct. 25, 1959; children—Byron, Joan, Georgia, Natalie. LL.B., U. Thessaloniki (Greece), 1961, Postgrad. Diploma Law, 1967; LL.M., U. Montreal, 1968. Bar: Thessaloniki 1965, Athens 1980, Supreme Ct. Athens 1969. Practice, Athens, Greece, 1980—; legal advisor Citibank N.Y., Thessaloniki, Greece, 1969-80, Credit Commercial de France, Athens, 1981-82, B.I.A.O. of Paris, Athens, 1982-85, Bank of Macedonia and Thrace, 1984—. Ford Found. scholar, U. Montreal, 1968-69, medal Youth for Understanding, Student Exchange Program, Ann Arbor, Mich., 1974. Mem. Youth for Understanding Student Exchange Program (nat. chmn. Hellenic com. 1970—). Greek Orthodox. Home: 83 Naiadon St, Paleo Faliro, Athens Greece Office: Law Office, 17 Voulis St, 10563 Athens Greece

PAPE, BARBARA HARRIS, lawyer; b. Casper, Wyo., Aug. 12, 1936; d. Herbert Garfield and Leah Jean (Case) Harris; m. William Martin Pape, June 28, 1969; children: Kyri Dannan, Kirsten Tara. AA in Theatre, Stephens Coll., 1956; BJ, BA, U. Mo., 1960, MA, 1966, BS in Edn., 1968, PhD, JD, 1980. Bar: Mo. 1981, U.S. Dist. Ct. (we. dist.) Mo. 1981, U.S. Supreme Ct., 1986. Mem. faculty U. Mo., Columbia, 1966-74; daily TV show hostess Triton Prodns., Inc., Columbia, 1973-76; realtor Tara Realty, Columbia, 1977-81; sole practice, Columbia, 1981-82; ptnr. Cronan, Robinson, Lampton & Pape, Columbia, 1982-85, Barbara Harris Pape & Assocs, P.C., Columbia, 1986—. Assoc. editor Litigation mag., 1983-85; contbr. articles to mags. Bd. dirs. Columbia Resource Ctr., Inc., 1981—; pres. adv. bd. YWCA, YMCA, Columbia, 1977-78; pres. bd. trustees Coll. Arts and Scis. U. Mo., Columbia, 1986-88; alumni bd. dirs. Stephens Coll., 1977-80. Recipient Roscoe Anderson award. Mem. ABA, Mo. Bar Assn., Boone County Bar Assn., Am. Assn. Trial Lawyers (vice chairperson publs. 1985-87, chairperson 1987—, pub. bd. Everyday Law 1988—, faculty Nat. Coll. Advocacy), Mo. Assn. Trial Lawyers, Mo. Criminal Def. Lawyers, Internat. Order Barristers, U. Mo. Alumni Orgn. (bd. dirs. 1986—), Kappa Tau Alpha, Delta Theta Phi. Democrat. Home: 3301 Westcreek Circle Columbia MO 65201 Office: 16 N 8th St Columbia MO 65201

PAPE, EVA JANINA, art consultant, museum curator; b. Poland, Dec. 24; came to U.S., 1962, naturalized, 19; d. Wojciech and Stefanie Pelczar; m. Walter F. Pape, Feb. 18, 1965 (div. 1985). B.A., Arts Sch., Lodz, Poland, 1960; student U. Ann Arbor, 1963. Curator New Eng. Art Ctr. for Contemporary Art, Bklyn. and Conn., 1982; producer, organizer numerous art shows, 1966—; founder art studio Westbeth for Kosciuszko Found., N.Y.C., 1971. Collaborator: Mother & Child, 1975. Subject of numerous articles in mags., jours., newsletters, newspapers, others. Organizer numerous donations to mus. by Polish and Am. artists, 1970-88. Cons. editor N.Y. Arts Jour., 1981-84. Designer sculpture belt Inst. Contemporary Arts, Boston, 1973, backgammon jewelry Cartier; conceived Buffalo Rock, largest sculpture park in world done by one person, 1985; organized Polish 19th Century shows in N.Y.C., Chgo., Washington., 1986. Organizer, active mem. Waldemar Cancer Research Ctr. for Mental Health, Easter Seals; 1969 hon. chmn. Kosciuszko Found. Ball. Named hon. citizen of New Orleans, 1967; recipient CBWA medal Polish Art Exhibit corp., 1980, Gold medal for promoting Polish culture Polish Ministry of Culture , 1985. Home and Office: 235 E 57th St New York NY 10022

PAPEN, FRANK O'BRIEN, banker, former state senator; b. Dec. 2, 1909; m. Julia Stevenson; 1 dau., Michele Papen-Daniel. Dir. First Nat. Bank Dona Ana County, Las Cruces, N.Mex., 1957-60, exec. v.p., 1957-60, pres., 1960-71, chmn. bd. dirs., chief exec. officer, 1971-82, 88—, pres., chmn. bd. dirs., 1982-87; mem. Ho. of reps. State of N.Mex., 1957-58, senator, 1969-84; vice-chmn. 12 regional adv. com. on banking practices and policies, 1965-66; mem. adv. com. on fed. legis., 1966; mem. N.Mex. State Investment Council, 1963-67; mem. N.Mex. Dept. Devel. Adv. Council, 1967-68; mem. steering com. Edn. Commn. States; mem. Albuquerque dist. adv. council SBA; pres. N.Mex. State U. Pres. Assocs. Mem. N.M. Ho. of Reps., 1957-58 (chmn. legis. fin. com. and legis. sch. study com.), N.M. State Senate, 1969-84. Recipient Citizen of Yr. award N.Mex. Assn. Realtors, 1966, Branding Iron award N.Mex. State U., 1977, The Pres.'s award for Service N.Mex. State U., 1983, Regent's medal N.Mex. State U., 1985. Mem. Am. Bankers Assn. (savs. bond chmn. N.Mex. 1964-66), N.Mex. Bankers Assn. (pres., mem. exec. com. 1965-66), Las Cruces C. of C. (past pres.). Democrat. Lodges: Kiwanis, KC. Office: PO Box FNB Las Cruces NM 88004

PAPENFUSE, EDWARD CARL, JR., archivist, state official; b. Toledo, Oct. 15, 1943; m. Sallie Fisher; children—Eric, David. B.A. in Polit. Sci., Am. U., 1965; M.A. in History, U. Colo., 1967; Ph.D., Johns Hopkins U., 1973. Assoc. editor Am. Hist. Rev., Washington, 1970-73; asst. archivist Md. Hall of Records, Annapolis, 1973-75, archivist, 1975—, commr. land patents, 1975—. Author: In Pursuit of Profit: The Annapolis Merchants in the Era of the American Revolution, 1975; (with others) Directory of Maryland Legislators, 1635-1789, 1974; (with others) Maryland: A New Guide to the Old Line State, 1976; The Hammond-Harwood House Atlas of Historical Maps of Maryland, 1608-1908, 1982; also articles and revs. Mem. Nat. Hist. Publs. and Records Commn.; mem. Johns Hopkins U. Med. Archives. NEH grantee; recipient Disting. Service award to State Govt. Nat. Gov.'s Assn., 1985, Marylander of Yr. award Md. Colonial Soc., 1985. Fellow Soc. Am. Archivists, Md. Hist. Soc., Am. Assn. State and Local History, Am. Hist. Bd. Home: 206 Oakdale Rd Baltimore MD 21210 Office: Md State Archives 350 Rowe Blvd Annapolis MD 21401

PAPOUIN, GÉRARD, cardiologist; b. Le Pas, Mayenne, France, Feb. 19, 1947; arrived in Tahiti, 1980; s. Theo and Simone (Tourrier) P.; m. Rauzy Micheline, Dec. 23, 1969; children: Vaea, Jean-Christophe, Maïre. MD, U. Angers, France, 1973, cert. in cardiology, 1978, cert. in sports medicine, 1979. Asst. of medicine Papeete Hosp., Tahiti, 1980-83, chief div. cardiology, 1983—. Contbr. articles to profl. jours. Mem. Asian Pacific Soc. Cardiology, South Pacific Internat. Cardiology Cong. (pres. organizing com. 1987). Home: PK 13 Mahina, Tahiti French Polynesia Office: ctr Hosp Territorial, Box 1640, Papeete, Tahiti French Polynesia

PAPOULIAS, KAROLOS, Greek government official; b. Ioannina, Greece, 1929; married; 3 daughters. Student, U. Athens, U. Munich, U. Cologne. M.P. Greece, 1977, 81, 85, dep. minister fgn. affairs, 1981-85, minister fgn. affairs, 1985—. Contbr. articles to profl. jours. Office: Ministry Fgn Affairs, Athens Greece *

PAPP, LASZLO GEORGE, architect; b. Debrecen, Hungary, Apr. 28, 1929; came to U.S., 1956; m. Judith Liptak, Apr. 12, 1952; children: Andrea, Laszlo-Mark (dec. 1978). Archtl. Engr., Poly. U. Budapest, 1955; M.Arch., Pratt Inst., 1960. Designer Harrison & Abramovitz, Architects, N.Y.C., 1958-63; ptnr. Whiteside & Papp, Architects, White Plains, N.Y., 1963-67; pres. Papp Architects, P.C., White Plains, Conn., 1967—. Mem. Pres.'s Adv. Com. on Pvt. Sector Initiatives; mem. adv. com. Westchester Community Coll., 1971, Iona Coll., New Rochelle, N.Y., 1982—, Norwalk State Tech. Coll., 1983—; bd. dirs. Clearview Sch., 1985—. Fellow AIA (regional dir. 1983-85); mem. Internat. Union Architects (rep. Habitat com. 1986—), N.Y. State Assn. Architects (v.p. 1977-80, pres. 1981), Am.-Hungarian Engrs. Assn. (dir. 1978-86), Hungarian Univ. Assn. (pres. 1958-60), White Plains C. of C. (dir. 1968-71, vice chmn. bd. for area devel. 1983—). Home: 1197 Valley Rd New Canaan CT 06840 Office: Papp Architects PC 7-11 S Broadway White Plains NY 10601

PAPPALARDO, SALVATORE CARDINAL, cardinal, archbishop of Palermo; b. Villafranca, Sicula, Sicily, Sept. 23, 1918. Ordained priest Roman Catholic Ch., 1941; entered diplomatic secretariat of state, 1947; titular archbishop of Miletus, 1966; pro-nuncio in Indonesia, 1966-69; pres. Pontifical Ecclesiastical Acad., 1969-70; archbishop of Palermo, 1970—; elevated to Sacred Coll. of Cardinals, 1973; titular ch. St. Mary Odigitria of the Sicilians; mem. Congregation of Oriental Chs., Congregation of Clergy. Address: Arcivescovado via Mateo, Bonello 2, 90134 Palermo Italy

PAPPAS, DAVID CHRISTOPHER, lawyer; b. Kenosha, Wis., Mar. 18, 1936; s. Theros and Marion Lucille (Piperas) P.; m. Laurie Jean Lacaskey,

Nov. 26, 1956 (div. 1969); children—Christopher David, Andrea Lynn; m. Nancy Marie Pratt, June 11, 1983. B.S., U. Wis., 1959, S.J.D., 1961. Bar: Wis. 1961, U.S. Dist. Ct. (ea. and we. dists.) Wis. 1965, U.S. Supreme Ct. 1971. Asst. corp. counsel Racine County, Wis., 1961; atty., adviser U.S. Dept. Labor, Washington, 1961-62; staff atty. U.S. Commn. Civil Rights, Washington, 1962-63; asst. city atty. City of Madison, Wis., 1963-65; sole practice, Madison, 1965—. Chmn. Madison Mayor's Citizen Adv. Com., 1964-65; pres. Wis. Cup Assn., Madison, 1965; co-chmn. 2d Congl. Dist. Humphrey for Pres., Madison, 1972. Recipient commendation for Supreme Ct. work Madison City Council, 1965, commendation resolution City of Madison, 1965. Mem. Wis. Bar Assn., Dane County Bar Assn., Wis. Acad. Trial Lawyers, Assn. Trial Lawyers Am., Gt. Lakes Hist. Soc. Republican. Clubs: Madison; South Shore Yacht (Milw.). Home: Strawberry Hill Deerfield WI 53531 Office: Suite 212 James Wilson Plaza 131 W Wilson St Madison WI 53703

PAPPAS, EDWARD HARVEY, lawyer; b. Midland, Mich., Nov. 24, 1947; s. Charles and Sydell (Sheinberg) P.; m. Laurie Weston, Aug. 6, 1972; children—Gregory Alan, Steven Michael. B.B.A., U. Mich., 1969, J.D., 1973. Bar: Mich. 1973, U.S. Dist. Ct. (ea. dist.) Mich. 1973, U.S. Dist. Ct. (we. dist.) Mich. 1980, U.S. Ct. Appeals (6th cir.) 1983, U.S. Supreme Ct. 1983. Ptnr. firm Dickinson, Wright, Moon, Van Dusen & Freeman, Bloomfield Hills and Detroit, Mich., 1973—; mediator Oakland County Cir. Ct., Pontiac, Mich., 1983—; hearing panelist Mich. Atty. Discipline Bd., Detroit, 1987—. Trustee Oakland Community Coll., Mich., 1982-86, 87-88, Oakland-Livingston Legal Aid, 1982—, v.p., 1982-85, pres., 1985-87; trustee adv. bd. Mich. Regional Anti-Defamation League of B'nai Brith, Detroit, 1983—; mem. nat. and community relations agy. div. Jewish Welfare Fedn.; planning commr., Village of Franklin, Mich. Mem. State Bar Mich. (co-chmn. nat. moot ct. competition com. 1974, 76, com. on legal aid., com. on atty. grievances), Oakland County Bar Assn. (vice-chmn. continuing legal edn. com., chmn. continuing legal edn. com. 1985-86, editor Laches monthly mag.), ABA, Am. Judicature Soc., Mich. Def. Trial Lawyers, Def. Research and Trial Lawyers Assn., (com. practice and procedure), B'nai B'rith Barristers. Home: 32223 Scenic Ln Franklin MI 48025 Office: PO Box 509 Dickinson Wright Moon Van Dusen & Freeman 525 N Woodward Ave Bloomfield Hills MI 48013

PAPPAS, GEORGE FRANK, lawyer; b. Washington, Oct. 5, 1950; s. Frank George and Lora Marie (Stauber) P.; m. Susan Elizabeth Bradshaw, Apr. 25, 1980; 1 child, Christine Bradshaw Pappas. B.A., U. Md., 1972, J.D., 1975. Bar: Md. 1976, U.S. Dist. Ct. Md. 1976, U.S. Ct. Appeals (4th cir.) 1976, U.S. Ct. Appeals (D.C. cir.) 1984, U.S. Supreme Ct. 1984, U.S. Dist. Ct. (D.C. cir.) 1986. Assoc. H. Russell Smouse, Balt., 1976-81; assoc. Melnicove, Kaufman, Wiener & Smouse, Balt., 1981-83, ptnr. 1983-88; ptnr. Venable, Baetjer and Howard, Balt., 1988—; lectr. Wash. Coll. Law, Am. U., Washington, 1980-84; mem. moot ct. bd., 1974-75. Founding editor-in-chief Internat. Trade Law Jour., 1974-75. Served to 1st lt. USAF, 1972-76. Mem. Nat. Assn. R.R. Trial Counsel, Md. Bar Assn. (chmn. internat. coml. law sect., 1980-81), ABA, Omicron Delta Kappa, Phi Kappa Phi, Phi Beta Kappa. Republican. Greek Orthodox. Club: L'Hirondelle. Home: 7916 Ruxway Rd Ruxton MD 21204 Office: Venable Baetjer and Howard 1800 Mercantile Bank and Trust Bldg 2 Hopkins Plaza Baltimore MD 21201

PAPPAS, MIKE J., restauranteur, former mayor; b. Canea, Crete, Greece, July 5, 1934; s. James M. and Katherine (Tornazakis) P.; B.S., B.A., U. Denver, 1956; m. Joy Ann Walker, Aug. 27, 1962; 1 dau., Anne Marie. Jr. acct. Arthur Young and Co., 1956-57; city clk. City of Raton (N.Mex.), 1957-58; pres. Sweet Shop, Inc., Raton, 1958—; pres. Joy's, Inc.; city commr. City of Raton, 1977-83, mayor, 1978-83. Mem. Raton C. of C., Beta Alpha Psi, Sigma Chi. Clubs: Masons, Shriners, Elks. Patentee; contbr. articles to trade publs. Office: 1201 S Second St Raton NM 87740

PAPSONOVÁ, MÁRIA LUKUSOVÁ, philosopher, educator; b. Prešov, Czechoslovakia, Nov. 6, 1946; d. Ján and Margita (Gilaková) Lukuš; m. Jozef Papson (div. 1984); children: Erika, Zuzana. Cert. sch. tchr., Faculty of Arts, Prešov, 1970, PhD, 1979; CSc, Bratislava, Czechoslovakia, 1981. Tchr. grammar sch., Spisská Stará Ves, Czechoslovakia, 1970-71; asst. lectr. linguistics Faculty of Arts, Presov, 1971—. Mem. Modern Philologists Circle ot Slovak Acad. Scis. Office: PJ Safarik U Faculty Philosophy, Gottwaldova 1 VSA, 080 78 Presov Czechoslovakia

PAQUE, CLAUDE, pediatrician, physiologist; b. Paris, Dec. 7, 1916; s. André and Suzanne (Debrie) P.; ed. Ecole Alsacienne, Paris, 1929-34; M.D., U. Paris, 1945; m. Laurence de Castelbajac, Aug. 31, 1960; children: Frederic, Laure, Blandine; children by previous marriage: Isabelle, Claire. Externe, Hôpitaux de Paris; resident Hôpital Vaugirard, Paris, 1942, Hopital Bicêtre, Paris, 1943, Hopital Laënnec, Paris, 1944; sci. explorations (human ecology and physiology), Tafilalt, 1958, Western Sahara (UNESCO, 1961, Inst. Scientifique Chérifien, 1964); Current Anthropology asso., 1977; participant Salt Symposium, Philadelphia, 1979; practice medicine specializing in pediatrics, Rabat, Morocco, 1945-53; chief pediatrics Avicenne Hosp., Rabat, 1954-61. Served with Med. Corps French Army, 1938-40, 45. Recipient Bronze and Silver medals French Acad. Medicine, 1965-75, Med. prize French Minister of Environment, 1981. Mem. French Assn. Pediatrics. Lutheran. Club: Royal Golf Dar es Salam. Author: Sodium Deficiency in Infant Malnutrition, 1958; Oral Therapy for Infant Cholera, 1968; How to Interpret an Infant Diarrhea, 1968; A Model for Salt Intake, 1980; Infant Salt Taboos in Morocco, 1984. Home and Office: 15 Baghdad, Rabat Morocco

PARADICE, SAMMY IRWIN, real estate investor; b. Beaumont, Tex., May 26, 1952; s. Alfred E. and Timmia E. (Holder) P. Student, Lamar U., 1970, Okla. State U., 1970, U. Tulsa, 1971. Lic. real estate broker, Tex. Page U.S. House of Reps., Washington, 1969-70; owner Southwestern Mktg. Systems, Beaumont, 1972-75; owner, mgr. First Realty, Sam Paradice & Assocs., Vidor, Tex., 1976—. Author: (books) Arab Money Hotline, 1985, Real Estate Counterattack, 1984, (cassette study course) How To Be A Business Tycoon. Methodist. Club: Toastmasters. Office: 935 N Main Vidor TX 77662

PARADIES, HASKO HENRICH, educator; b. Bremen, Germany, Feb. 18, 1940; s. Henry J. and Erna (Poppinga) P.; m. Gundrun K. Patzelt, June 28, 1973; children—Gesa-Kundry, Jan-Henry, Felix-Benjamin. Diploma chem., M.D., U. Munster, 1966, Ph.D. in Medicine, 1967, postgrad., 1970; Ph.D. in Chemistry, U. Uppsala, 1969; postgrad. King's Coll., 1969-71, MIT, 1971-72, PhD in Biochem. (hon.), Royal Crown Spain, 1986. Research assoc. U. Munster, 1966; postdoctoral fellow King's Coll., 1969-71, Boston, 1971-72; research assoc. Max Planck Inst., Berlin, 1971; prof. biochemistry Free U. Berlin, 1974-82, chmn. dept. chemistry and biochemistry, 1974-77, chmn. dept. plant physiology and cell biology, 1980-82; guest and vis. prof. chemistry Cornell U., Ithaca, N.Y., 1977-79; dir. research and devel. Medici-Corp., Ltd., 1984-86, dir. 1986— ; adj. prof. chemistry U. Mo.-Rolla, 1985; sr. lectr. tech. chemistry dept. engring. U. Hagen, 1985-86; guest prof. Biotech. and Physical Chem. Märkische Hochschule Iserlohn, 1987-88, Chaired Prof., 1988—. Author 3 books. Contbr. articles to profl. jours. Recipient Albert Einstein Internat. Acad. Found. Bronze Medal for Peace, III class. Deutsche Forschungsgem fellow, 1967-71, grantee, 1974-79, grantee, colloid and surface sci., 1982; Umweltbundesant grantee, 1979, 82, grantee Internat. Copper Research Assn., 1987. Mem. Am. Chem. Soc., N.Y. Acad. Scis., Gesellschaft Deutscher Chemiker, Gesellschaft Deutsche Naturforscher und Arzte. Club: Stadler (Ithaca). Home: 38 Kuhloweg, 5860 Iserlohn Federal Republic of Germany Office: Märkische Hochschule, Frauenstuhlweg 37, D 5860 Iserlohn Federal Republic of Germany

PARADISGARTEN, HYMIE CHARLES, physician, radiologist; b. Keetmanshoop, Namibia, Dec. 25, 1917; s. Abraham Reuben and Ida (Schneider) P.; m. Mildred Fivelowitz, Dec. 27, 1942; children—Avrim, Ivan, Steven, Samuel. M.B.Ch.B., U. CapeTown (South Africa), 1942, D.M.R., 1945. Houseman, Rondebosch Cottage Hosp., Cape Town, 1943; radiologist Pretoria Gen. Hosp. (South Africa), 1947-48; pvt. practice medicine, specializing in radiology, Pretoria, 1948-52, Windhoek, South-West Africa, 1952-77; radiologist State Hosps., Windhoek, part-time 1960-79, cons. radiology, head dept. radiology, 1979-80; sr. radiologist Tygerberg Hosp., Cape Town, 1980-83; advisor radiol. services South-West Africa Adminstrn., 1965; now life mem. Med. Assn. of South Africa and Coll. Medicine, South Africa. Pres. Windhoek Hebrew Congregation, 1960-62, 74-76, 79-80, hon. life v.p., 1980—; v.p. Mus. Soc. South-West Africa; mem. Mcpl. Town Council, Windhoek, 1958-61, chmn. traffic control, fire and ambulance com., 1958-61; past asst. commr. South-West Africa div. Boy Scouts Assn., chmn. local assn., Windhoek, chmn. group com., chmn. bldg. com.; chmn. bldg. com. Girl Guides Assn., Windhoek; chmn. Windhoek br. Road Safety Orgn. South-West Africa, 1960-61; chmn. parent-tchrs. com. Centaurus High Sch., Windhoek; chmn. Windhoek Civil Def. Orgn.; mem. com. Windhoek Pub. Library. Mem. Med. Assn. South Africa (hon. sec. South-West Africa br. 1953-58, pres. South-West Africa br. 1958-59, mem. fed. council, life mem. 1983—), Scientific Soc. South-West Africa. Club: Stadium Bowling (Capetown). Lodge: Lions (pres. 1975) (Windhoek). Address: #403 La Rochelle Beach Rd, Sea Point, Cape Town 8001, Republic of South Africa

PARAMESHVARA, VISHVANATHAPURA, internist, cardiologist; b. May 8, 1930; s. Narasimha Bhatta and Parvathi Hande; m. Nalini Rao, Mar. 8, 1962; children—Ashok, Aparna, Ashvin. M.B.B.S., Mysore Med. Coll., U. Mysore (India), 1957. Asst. surgeon Mysore Med. Coll, India, 1958-59; med. registrar Gen. Hosp., Birmingham, 1964-65; asst. prof. gen. medicine Bangalore Med. Coll., India, 1966-71; pvt. practice medicine as cons. physician and cardiologist, Bangalore, 1971—; med. referee Life Ins. Corp. India; ofcl. cons. physician and cardiologist for various Indian cos.; chmn. Sharada Dhanvantari Hosp., Sringeri, India, 1979—; chmn. Sri Abhinava Vidyatheertha Swamigal Sci. Research Acad., Sringeri, 1979—; trustee Med. Edn. and Research Trust, Bangalore, 1980—, sec., 1980—; trustee Dr. V. Parameshvara Charitable Trust, Bangalore, 1980—; bd. dirs. Clin. Research Lab., Bangalore; organised, conducted various mass med. and cardiac check-up camps, Bangalore and Karnataka State, 1965; speaker in field. Author: Medical Emergencies in General Practice, 1970. Editor: Jour. Mysore Med. Assn., 1967-77; founder, editor: Indian Med. Assn. Bangalore br. News Bull., 1979-80, IMA Focus, 1982—; mem. editorial bd.: Indian Hart Jour., 1976-77. Fellow Am. Coll. Cardiology, Am. Coll. Chest Physicians, Internat. Coll. Angiology, Indian Soc. Electrocardiology, All India Inst. Diabetes, Internat. Med. Scis. Acad., Royal Coll. Physicians London, Internat. Coll. Nutrition, Assn. Physicians of India (founder), Indian Med. Assn. (pres. 1985-86), Indian Med. Assn. of Med. Specialities (chmn. 1986—); mem. Brit. Med. Assn., Assn. Physicians India (mem. governing council 1981-83, v.p. 1986—), Indian Med. Assn. (pres. 1985-86; Mysore br. Dr. Govinda Setty Meml. orator 1981), Assn. History Medicine, Cardiological Soc. India, Soc. Nuclear Medicine, Indian Assn. Occupational Health (Silver Jubilee Commemoration award 1980), Asthma Research Soc. (founder sec. Bangalore 1975). Clubs: Bangalore Turf, Century, Bangalore Golf (Bangalore). Lodge: Lions (founder pres.). Home: 54 Kumarakrupa Rd, Bangalore 560 001, India Office: 45 Race Course Rd, Bangalore 650 001, India

PARAMES VARAN, KANDIAH, railway finance executive; b. Kuala Lumpur, Malaysia, June 26, 1940; s. S. Kandiah and M. Sinnamah Parames Varan; m. Vijayalet Chumi, Jan. 19, 1975; 1 child, Vijay Ananda. Student, Chartered Inst. Transport, London, 1959-62, Fellow Permanent Way Instn., London. Asst. traffic supt. Port Authority Port Klana, Malaysia; acct. Malayan Ry., Malaysia, 1969-76, sr. acct., 1976-81, dep. dir., 1981—; mem. cen. com. Internat. Coop. Alliance, Geneva; pres. Ry. Coop., Malaysia, 1967-84; v.p. Coop. Union of Malaysia, 1986—; bd. dirs. Coop. Cen. Ry., Malaysia. Served with Malaysian Army, 1976-79. Recipient Gold medal Coop. Union of Malaysia, 1972. Mem. Chartered Inst. Transport London, Am. Mgmt. Assn. Hindu. Home: 45 Jalan Damansara, 50780 Kuala Lumpur Malaysia Office: Malayan Ry Hdqtrs, Jalan Sultan Hishamuddin, PO Box 12528, 50621 Kuala Lumpur Malaysia

PARAMHANS, SWAMI ATMANANDA, mathematician, researcher; b. Paraspur, Gonda, Uttar Pradesh, India, July 31, 1941; s. Ambika Datt and Raj Devi Pandey. PhD in Neology, Varanaseya Sanskrit U., Varanasi, India, 1969; MS in Math., Jabalpur U., India, 1971; PhD in Math., Banaras Hindu U., Varanasi, 1977, U.G. Diploma in French, 1978. Pool scientist Council Sci. and Indsl. Research, New Delhi, 1981-84; vis. mem. Mehta Research Inst. Math. and Math. Physics, Allahabad, India, 1984; fellow Indian Inst. Advanced Study, Shimla, India, 1984-87; research assoc. U. Grants Commn. New Dehli, 1987-88, research scientist, 1988—. Author: Knowledge in Vedic Philosophies, 1982 (Spl. award Uttar Pradesh Sanskrit Acad. 1984); also research papers on modern algebra, history of math., neology. Mem. Am. Math. Soc. (reviewer 1980—), Indian Math. Soc. (life), Allahabad Math. Soc. (life), Nat. Acad. Scis. India (life), Acad. Progress of Math. (Varanasi, life), Parmar Inst. Math Scis. (life). Hindu. Avocation: yoga. Home: B 1/148 1 KA, Assi, Varanasi Uttar Pradesh 221 005, India Office: Banaras Hindu U, Dept Math, Faculty Sci, Varanasi Uttar Pradesh 221 005, India

PARAN, MARK LLOYD, lawyer; b. Cleve., Feb. 1, 1953; s. Edward Walter and Margaret Gertrude (Ebert) P. AB cum laude in Sociology, Harvard U., 1977, JD, 1980. Bar: Ill. 1980, Mass. 1986. Assoc. Wilson & McIlvaine, Chgo., 1980-83, Lurie Sklar & Simon, Ltd., Chgo., 1983-85, Sullivan & Worcester, Boston, 1985—. Mem. ABA, Mass. Bar Assn. Avocations: tornado hunting, observation of severe thunderstorms, photography. Home: 84 Gainsborough St #106W Boston MA 02115 Office: Sullivan & Worcester One Post Office Sq Boston MA 02109

PARAS, RENATO LARDIZABAL, manufacturing executive; b. Manila, June 25, 1926; s. Conrado and Concepcion Ocampo (Lardizabal) P.; m. Aurea Gutierrez; children—Lourdes, Joanna, Conrado, Bernadette, Teresa, Aureo. BS in Commerce, Far Eastern U., 1949; MS in Acctg., Columbia U., 1952. CPA, Philippines. Jr. exec. trainee Procter & Gamble Philippines Mfg. Corp., Manila, 1950, mgr. cost acctg., 1950-51, mgr. gen. acctg., 1953-57, asst. treas., 1957-62, treas., 1962-66, dir. fin., 1966-83, dir. corp. planning, 1984-87; on spl. assignment Asia Pacific div., 1987, Europe div. Richardson Vicks, 1988; fin. mgr. Procter and Gamble, Taiwan, 1988—; dir. Bathala Mktg. (Ziebart) Philippines, Manila, Mut. Books Philippines, Manila, Union Bank Philippines; trustee IBM Retirement Fund, Manila, 1980—, Insular Life Assurance Co. Bd. visitors Armed Forces Retirement Systems Quezon City, Philippines, 1981-82; mem. council advisors Philippine Christian U., 1984—. Outstanding Alumnus in Commerce and Industry, Far Eastern U., 1974. Mem. Fin. Execs. Inst. of Philippines (pres. 1980), Acctg. Standards Council (vice chmn. 1981—), Internat. Fedn. Accts. (mgmt. actg. network), Internat. Assn. Fin. Execs. (planning com. 1981-83, 83-85), Philippines Inst. CPA (bd. dirs., Outstanding CPA in Mgmt. 1972, Outstanding CPA in Community Services 1981). Roman Catholic. Clubs: Makati Sports (pres. 1980-81), Manila Polo (bd. dirs., treas. 1986-87). Lodge: Rotary (pres. 1987—, pres. found. 1980-81, dist. chmn. internat. youth exchange dist. 380, 1979-80), Makati. Home: 16 Encarnacion St, Magallanes Village, Makati, Manila Philippines Office: Procter & Gamble Philippine Inc 777 Paseo de Roxa, Makati, Manila Philippines

PARASCOS, EDWARD THEMISTOCLES, utilities executive; b. N.Y.C., Oct. 20, 1931; s. Christos and Nina (Demitrovich) P.; B.S. in Mech. Engring., CCNY, 1956, M.S. in Mech. Engring., 1958; postgrad. ops. research N.Y.U., 1964; m. Jenny Morris, July 14, 1978; children—Jennifer Melissa, Edward Themistocles. Design engr. Ford Instrument, 1957-61; reliability engring. supr. Kearfott div. Gen. Precision Inc., 1961-63; staff cons. Am. Power Jet, 1963-64; reliability mgr. Perkin Elmer Corp., 1964-66; dir. system effectiveness CBS Labs., Stamford, Conn., 1966-72; pres. Dipar Cons. Services Ltd., East Elmhurst, N.Y., Lapa Trading Corp.; gen. mgr. power generation services Consol. Edison Co., N.Y.C., 1972—; pres., chmn. bd. RAM Cons. Assocs.; pres. , 1968-70; vice chmn. Reliability Div., 1968-72; chmn. 1st Reliability Engring. Conf. Electric Power Industry, 1974, also 4th conf.; lectr. in field. Registered profl. engr., Calif. Fellow Am. Soc. Quality Control (vice chmn. 1968-70, sr. mem.); mem. Am. Mgmt. Assn., ASME, Am. Statis. Assn., Inst. Environ. Scis., Soc. Reliabilty Engrs., Edison Engring. Soc. Home: 30-02 83d St Jackson Heights NY 11370 Office: 4 Irving Pl New York NY 10003

PARASKAKIS, MICHAEL EMANUEL, insurance company executive; b. Crete, Greece, Apr. 18, 1930; s. Emanuel and Calliopi (Hatzakis) P.; m. Georgia-Maria Etta Zoides, June 4, 1960; 1 child, Emanuel. Diploma, Athens Sch. Econ. and Comml. Scis., 1955. Internat. purchase agreements Ministry Agr., Athens, 1951-56; personnel asst. Mobil Oil Greece, Athens, 1958-62; mng. prin. Legal and Gen. Assurance Soc., Agy. for Greece, 1962—; mng. dir. Pegasus Ins. Co., Athens, 1974-82, chmn., mng. dir., 1983—; elector Ins. Hall of Fame, Ohio State U., 1978—; mem. Internat. Ins. Seminars, U. Ala., 1978—; dir. Horizon Ins. Co., Athens, 1970-83; vice chmn. bd. Ras Hellas S.A., 1986—; chmn. Greek Insurers European Com., Athens, 1983—. Contbr. articles to profl. jours. Served to cpl. Greek Army, 1953-54. Mem. Assn. Ins. Cos. (chmn. 1977-81, bd. mem. 1981—), Brit. Hellenic Chamber, Athens (hon.), Internat. (green card) Motor Insurers Bureau (chmn. 1986—). Greek Orthodox. Home: 21 Lykavittou St, 10672 Athens Greece Office: Pegasus Ins Co, 5 Stadiou St, 10562 Athens Greece

PARDOS, FRANCOISE, management consultant; b. Aix en Provence, France, Jan. 2, 1932; s. Leo and Denyse (Bernard) P.; m. Gabriel Jacques, Feb. 16, 1958. Grad., Inst. d'Etudes Politiques, Paris, 1955; MA in Econs., U. Calif., Berkeley, 1956; D in Econ. Sci., U. Paris, 1957. Econ. asst. Kaiser Aluminum & Chem., Oakland, Calif., 1962-63; sr. researcher SEMA, Paris, 1963-64; cons. dir. Pardos Mktg., Bures Orgeval, France, 1964—. Fellow Soc. Plastics Engring.; mem. European Chem. Market Research Association, Soc. Francaise Ingenieurs Plasticiens (pres. 1978-79). Roman Catholic. Home and Office: Beau-Voir, 78630 Bures Orgeval France

PARECATTIL, JOSEPH CARDINAL, retired archbishop; b. Kidangoor, India, Apr. 1, 1912; s. Ittyra and Eliswa (Ittyra) P.; Licentiate in Philosophy, Papal Sem., Kandy, 1936, Th.D., 1941; postgrad. Sacred Heart Coll., Thevara, 1945; B.A., Madras U., 1947; D.D., Windham U., 1970. Ordained priest Roman Cath. Ch., 1939; parish priest, 1941-47; editor Sathyadeepam weekly, 1947-53; aux. bishop, 1953; adminstr. Apostolic, 1956; archbishop of Ernakulam, from 1956, now emeritus; elevated to Sacred Coll. of Cardinals, 1969. Mem. Pontifical Commns., consultor to Sacred Oriental Congregation, 1963, mem., 1968; chmn. Oriental Canon Law Codification Com., 1972; mem. Secretariat for Christian Unity, 1970; v.p. Cath. Bishops Conf. of India, 1966, pres., 1972; chancellor Pontifical Inst., Alwaye, 1972; pres. Syro-Malabar Bishops' Conf.; chancellor Dharmaram Pontifical Inst. Theology and Philosophy, Bangalore. Founder univ. colls., maj. hosps., ednl. trusts, housing projects, irrigation project, tech. insts. and indsl. concerns. Address: Archbishops House, PB 2580, Cochin Kerala 682031, India *

PARENTE, ROBERT BRUCE, electrical engineer; b. N.Y.C., Sept. 10, 1936; s. Almerico Elmer and Royda (Boyd) P.; B.S. in Elec. Engring., MIT, 1959, M.S. in Engring., 1959, E.E., 1961, Ph.D., 1966; m. Rozalinda Thelma Saturnio, May 28, 1977; children—Jennifer Dee, Jessica Dale, Jacquelyn Dawn. Instr. elec. engring. Mass. Inst. Tech., Cambridge, 1959-65; asst. prof. engring. UCLA, 1965-70; mgr. electric power systems System Devel. Corp., Santa Monica, Calif., 1970-72, dir. planning, 1973-75, dep. dir. energy devel., 1975-76; sr. cons. Theodore Barry & Assos., Los Angeles, 1976-78; propr. Parente & Assocs., mgmt. cons., 1978—; expert witness before utility commns. Res. lt. sheriff Los Angeles County Sheriff's Dept., 1970—. Registered profl. engr., Calif. Mem. IEEE, Inst. Mgmt. Scis., Ops. Research Soc. Am., Sigma Xi, Tau Beta Pi, Eta Kappa Nu, Hex-Alpha, Theta Chi. Author: Electric Power Pools, 1983; contbr. articles to profl. jours. Patentee in field. Office: PO Box 241987 Los Angeles CA 90024

PARENTE, WILLIAM JOSEPH, political science educator; b. Chgo., July 7, 1937; s. Salvatore S. and Genevieve (Rooney) P.; m. Diane Alpern, Nov. 30, 1963; children: Elizabeth, Margaret, William Joseph, Caroline, Rebecca, Catherine, Abigail, Christopher, Natalya. A.B. cum laude, Xavier U., Ohio, 1961; Ph.D. (Woodrow Wilson fellow, Woodrow Wilson dissertation fellow), Georgetown U., 1970. Woodrow Wilson intern Wilberforce (Ohio) U., 1965-66; asst. prof., chmn. polit. sci. dept. Antioch Coll., 1966-69, assoc. dean faculty, 1969-70; dean Coll. Arts and Scis., U. Scranton, Pa., 1970-85; assoc. prof. polit. sci. Coll. Arts and Scis., U. Scranton, 1970-73, prof., 1973—; Fulbright scholar Chulalongkorn U., Bangkok, Thailand, 1985-86, Inst. for Policy Studies, Washington, 1986-87; mem. nat. Fulbright screening com. for East Asia, mem. adv. com. Inst. Internat. Edn.; cons. on world affairs to Peace Corps. Author articles in field. Fellow Inst. Acad. Deans, 1971; Fellow Inst. Ednl. Mgmt., Harvard Bus. Sch., 1972; Scholar-Diplomat Program, State Dept., 1970, 73; Fulbright fellow Korea, 1974, Indonesia, 1978, Germany, 1980, Thailand, 1985-86; fellow Nat. Endowment Humanities Seminar U. Va., 1976, Harvard U., 1985, Columbia U., 1988. Fellow Union Experimenting Colls. and Univs., Inst. for Policy Studies, Soc. for Religion in Higher Edn.; mem. Am. Polit. Sci. Assn., Assn. Jesuit Colls. and Univs. (chmn. conf. on internat. edn. 1981-85), Alpha Sigma Nu (nat. sec.-treas. 1979-82, nat. pres. 1983-85), Pi Sigma Alpha, Eta Sigma Phi, Alpha Sigma Lambda, Tau Kappa Alpha, Phi Alpha Theta. Roman Catholic. Office: Univ Scranton Scranton PA 18510

PARERA, JOSE MIGUEL, chemistry educator, researcher; b. Santa Fe, Argentina, Sept. 29, 1930; s. Jose Francisco and Francisca (Rekers) P.; m. Nora Suana Figoli, Aug. 18, 1972; children: Mariana, Cecilia. Degree in Chem. Engring. Facultad de Ingenieria Quimca, 1958. Scholar, Consejo Nacional de Investigaciones Cientificas y Tenicas, Argentina, 1958-59, Imperial Coll. Sci. and Tech., London U., 1959-60; asst. prof. chem. engring. Universidad Nacional del Litoral, 1960-61, prof., 1961—, head dept. indsl. chemistry, 1965-74, dir. research inst. on catalysis and petrochemistry, 1974—, pres. Research Council, 1976. Fellow Consejo Nacional de Investigaciones Cientificas y Tecnicas, Orgn. de Estados Americanos, 1965; recipient award for work in petrochemistry, Asociacion Quimica Argentina Fabricaciones Militares, 1978. Mem. Am. Inst. Chem. Engring., Am. Chem. Soc., Soc. Iberoamericana de Catalisis (founder, pres. 1970-72, 78-80), Inst. Petroquimica Argentino (founder, mem. council), Soc. Argentina de Investigadores en Ciencia de la Ingenieria Quimica y Quimica Aplicada (founder, mem. council), Sociedad Cientifica (local council), Assn. Quimica Argentina (local rep.), Asociacion Argentina de Ingenieros Quimicos, Instituto Argentino del Petroleo. Roman Catholic. Contbr. articles on chem. engring., petrochemistry and edn. to profl. jours. Home: 3500 Francia, 3000 Santa Fe Argentina Office: 2654 Santiago del Estero, 3000 Santa Fe Argentina

PARGETER, RONALD ALBERT, chemical company executive; b. London, Oct. 3, 1919; s. Albert Henry and Lily Nelly Pargeter; m. Iva Patricia Stones, Sept. 15, 1978; 4 children. Gen. mgr. Bryce Roberts Co. Ltd., 1946-50; mktg. dir. KK Chems. Ltd., 1950-74; dir. Federated Chem. Holdings Ltd., 1974-76, chief exec., 1977-78; chmn. Rapadex Ltd.; dir. Brit. Tar Products PLC, Chemrite Internat. (Pty) Ltd., Sutcliffe Speakman PLC. Served as officer RAF, 1939-45. Mem. Fedn. Européene du Commerce Chimique (past pres.), Brit. Chem. Traders and Dyestuffs Assn. (pres.), Soc. Chemistry and Industry, Inst. Dirs. Mem. Ch. of England. Clubs: RAF, Cricketers, Dulwich Lodge, Freeman of City of London. Home: Mill Hill, Mill Ln, Rodmell Near Lewes, East Sussex BN7 3HS, England

PARIENTE, RENÉ GUILLAUME, physician, educator; b. La Marsa, France, Sept. 1, 1929; s. Jules and Vera (Guttieres) P.; M.D., U. Paris, 1962, Sc.B., 1959; m. Dominique Savary, Dec. 26, 1971; children: Pierre, David, Benjamin. Prof. medicine U. Paris, 1966—, head dept. i tensive care and chest disease; bd. dirs. Inst. Nat. du Recherche Med. Mem. Soc. Française de Cardiologie, Soc. de Pathologie Respiratoire, Soc. de la Tuberculose, Soc. Française de Microscopie Electronique, Am. Soc. Chest Physicians, N.Y. Acad. Sci. Home: 12 rue de la Neva, 75008 Paris France Office: 100 G LeClerc Hospitol, Beaujon, Clichy France

PARIKH, ASHOK, economics educator; b. Ahmedabad, India, Nov. 24, 1936; s. Kanchanlal and Champaben (Mehta) P.; m. Daksha (Mehta) Feb. 3, 1963; 1 child, Ami. B.Com., H.L. Commerce Coll., 1957; M.Com., R.A. Podar Coll., 1959; M.Sc. in Econs., London Sch. Econs., 1962. Lectr. commerce Sardar Patel U., Anand, India, 1959-60; research assoc. Inst. Econ. Growth, Delhi, India, 1963-65; reader in econs. Gokhale Inst. Politics, Poona, Maharashtra, India, 1965-66; lectr. econs. U.Sussex, Brighton, Eng., 1966-68; vis. prof. Columbia U., N.Y.C., summers 1967-69; research economist IMF, Washington, 1969-70; lectr. econs. U. East Anglia, Norwich, Eng., 1968-69, 70-71, reader, 1971-80, prof., 1980—. Contbr. articles to profl. jours. Fellow Royal Statis. Soc.; mem. Econometric Soc., Royal Econ. Soc., Am. Econ. Assn. Home: 3 Cringleford Chase, Norwich NR4 7RS,

England Office: U East Anglia, Sch Econ and Social Studies, Norwich NR4 7TJ, England

PARIS, COUNT OF, (Prince Henri Robert Ferdinand Marie Louis-Philippe d'Orleans) head House of France; b. Nouvion-en-Thierache, France, July 5, 1908; s. Jean d'Orleans, Duke of Guise and Princess Isabelle d'Orleans (Isabelle de France); ed. U. Louvain; m. Princess Isabelle d'Orleans et Bragance, Apr. 8, 1931; children: Isabelle (Countess Frederic Carl de Schoenborn-Buchheim), Henri (Count of Mortain), Helene (Countess Evrard de Limburg-Stirum), Francois (Duc d'Orleans; dec.); Anne (Princess Carlos de Bourbon), Diane (Duchess of Wurtemberg), Michel (Comte d'Evreux), Jacques (Duc d'Orleans), Claude (Madame la Cagnina), Chantal (Baronne Francois-Xavier de Sambucy de Sorgue), Thibaut (dec.). Lived in exile, 1926-50; chief House of France (House of Bourbons), 1940—; returned to France, 1950; founder periodical Le Courrier Royal, 1934-40, Bull. Mensuel, 1948-67. Author: Frenchmen, Among Ourselves, 1947; Mémoires d'Exil et de Combats; Lettre aux Français, L'Avenir Dure Longtemps. Address: Fondation Condé, BP 203-60501 Chantilly Cedex France

PARIS, STEVEN MARK, software engineer; b. Boston, May 26, 1956; s. Julius Louis and Frances (Keleishik) P. BS, Rensselaer Poly. Inst., 1978; MS, Boston U., 1980, postgrad., 1980-84. Sr. software engr. Prime Computer Inc., Framingham, Mass., 1978-82; sr. analyst Computervision Corp., Bedford, Mass., 1982-84, prin. engr. Lotus Devel., Inc., Cambridge, Mass., 1984—. Lt. Mass. Civil Def. Recipient Boston Sci. Fair 1st prize, 1973, 74; State of Mass. Sci. Fair 3d prize, 1973; 2d prize, 1974. Mem. Assn. for Computing Machinery, IEEE, Boston Computer Soc., Planetary Soc. Jewish. Home: 27 Colwell Ave Brighton MA 02135 Office: 161 1st St Cambridge MA 02142

PARISEAU, JEAN-BAPTISTE, historian, career officer; b. Montreal, Can., Nov. 3, 1924; s. Adelard Pariseau and Alda Cote; m. Therese Maisonneuvé, Sept. 1, 1948; children: Jacques, Jocelyne, Suzanne, Robert, Michel. BA, U. Ottawa, 1963, MA in History, 1973; D es L in History, U. Paul Valery III, Montpellier, France, 1981. Commd. lt. Loyal Edmonton (Can.) Regiment, 1951; transferred to Princesss Patricia's Can. Light Infantry, 1952; advanced through grades to maj. 1965; assigned to Germany, Congo, Cyprus; historian Can. Armed Forces, Ottawa, Ont., 1968-73; sr. historian Directorate History, Ottawa, 1974—; founding mem. bibliography com. Internat. Mil. History Com., 1982—; gen. sec., pres. Can. Commn. Mil. History, 1983—. Author: (poems) Albertaines Images, 1972, (short stories) Les contes de mon patelin, 1985; editor, author: French-Canadians and Bilingualism in the Canadian Armed Forces, 1987; translator Songs of a Sourdough (Robert Service), 1973. Sec. Consol. Sch. Dist. 66, Donnelly, Alta., Can., 1948-51. Served with Royal Can. Air Force, 1943-44; served to sgt. Can. Army, 1944-46. Mem. Can. Hist. Assn., Inst. Histoire francaise en Amerique, Societe Histoire Genealogie Ottawa (v.p. 1985—). Roman Catholic. Home: 1668 Grasmere Crescent, Ottawa, ON Canada K1V 7T9 Office: Directorate History, Nat Def Hdqrs, Ottawa, ON Canada K1A OK2

PARISH, H(AYWARD) CARROLL, JR., educator, business executive; b. Pasadena, Calif., Feb. 13, 1920; s. Hayward Carroll and Gertrude I. (Riggs) P. AB, UCLA 1949, MA, 1950, PhD, 1958. Los Angeles County youth commr., 1938-42, pres. commn., 1938; asst. prof. naval sci. U. Calif., 1946-47, 52-53, assoc. prof., 1954, asst. dean, 1957-62, assoc. dean, 1962-71, dean, 1966-71; provost, trustee Miller Community Coll., 1971-79; adj. prof. polit. sci. U. La Verne, 1976-85; pres. Environ. Design Assocs., 1982—; pres. Kapa Co., 1969—; attaché Calif. State legislature, 1947; Fulbright research fellow Waseda U. Tokyo, 1958-59; engaged in property mgmt.; lectr. Asiatic Studies, U. So. Calif., 1961; collaborator Inst. Internat. Relations, Aoyama Gakuin U., Tokyo, 1960-64. Mem. scholarship adv. com. Calif. State Scholarship and Loan Commn., 1964-71; cons. U.S. Office Edn., 1969-71; cons. Time-Life Books Inc. Sec. citizens ind. vice investigating com. which initiated successful recall against corrupt Los Angeles adminstrn., 1938; mem. exec. com. Los Angeles Co. Coordinating Councils, 1939-41. Served in USNR, World War II, Korea; capt., 1964; comdg. officer Naval Res. Officers Sch., 1965-68. Twice decorated for combat service Pacific area; for valor at Okinawa when ship was hit by Kamikaze plane; for meritorious service as flag-sec. to comdr. assault transport div. Decorated Order Golden Merit, Japanese Red Cross, 1970, Japan's Order of Rising Sun, 1984; knight grand officer Order St. John The Bapt. Am.; knight comdr. Hospitaller Order St. John of Jerusalem; knight grand cross Mil. and Hospitaller Order St. Lazarus of Jerusalem; knight Order of Merit; knight of honor Venerable Order of Rose of Lippe; Manorial Soc. Great Britain (Life). Fellow Institut International des Arts et des Lettres (life), AAAS, Augustan Soc.; mem. Am. Legion (mem. Nat. Security Commn. 1950-53, life), Am. Polit. Sci. Assn., Founders and Patriots Am. (gov. gen. 1978-81), Soc. Colonial Wars, S.R., Internat. Polit. Sci. Assn., Assn. Asian Studies (chmn. Pacific Coast regional conf. 1967), Am. Coll. Personnel Assn. (chmn. commn.), Assn. Ind. Colls. and Schs. (com. chmn.), Coll. Scholarship Service, Com. on Fgn. Students, Navy League (life), Asia Soc., Am. Siam Soc. (pres.), Siam Soc. (life), Nat. (pres. 1971, distinguished service award 1971), Western (pres. 1970, distinguished achievement award 1971) assns. student financial aid adminstrs., Associated Japan Am. Socs. U.S. (v.p. 1979-81), Japan Am. Soc. So. Calif. (hon. officer), Phi Eta Sigma, Alpha Mu Gamma, Pi Sigma Alpha, Pi Gamma Mu (chancellor Western region, hon. trustee 1984-87, vice chancellor 1984— , nat. honor Key 1973). Episcopalian. Clubs: Jonathan (Los Angeles); Internat. House of Japan (Tokyo), UCLA Faculty Center. Author: Canada and the United Nations, 1950. Co-author: Thailand Bibliography, 1958. Contbr. articles on internat., Far East, S.E. Asian Affairs to profl. jours. Home: 633 24th St Santa Monica CA 90402

PARISH, MARGARET CECILE (PEGGY), writer; b. Manning, S.C., July 14, 1927; d. Herman Stanley and Margaret Cecile (Rogers) P. B.A., U. S.C., 1948. Tchr. schs. in Ky., Okla. and N.Y., 1948-67; lectr. colls. and univs., tchr. workshops. Author books for juveniles, 1961—, latest being Mind Your Manners, 1978, Be Ready at Eight, 1979, Amelia Bedelia Helps Out, 1979, Beginning Mobiles, 1979, Amelia Bedelia and the Baby, 1981, No More Monsters for Me, 1981 (Recipient Garden State Children's Book award 1974, 80, Palmetto Writers Juvenile award 1977), Mr. Adam's Mistake, 1982, The Cats' Burglar, 1983, Amelia Bedelia Goes Camping, 1985, The Ghosts of Cougar Island, 1986, Merry Christmas Amelia Bedelia, 1986, Amelia Bedelia's Family Album, 1988, Scruffy, 1988, Good Hunting Blue Sky, 1988. Recipient Milner award City of Atlanta, 1984, Keystone State Children's Book award State of Pa., 1986, Garden State Children's Book award N.J., 1988. Mem. Author Guild Am., Delta Kappa Gamma.

PARISI, MARIO NESTOR, medical educator; b. Buenos Aires, Oct. 1, 1939; arrived in France, 1977; s. Jose and Angela Maria (Petrone) P.; m. Margarita Freedman, 1966; children: Eric, Muriel. MD, U. Buenos Aires, 1962, PhD in Medicine, 1971. Adj. prof. biophysics U. Buenos Aires, 1973-76; research dir. Ctr. Nat. Recherche Sci., Paris, 1977-86; career investigator Consejo Nacional de Investigaciones Cientificas y Tecnicas, Buenos Aires, 1986—; prof. Dept. Physiology, Faculty Medicine, 1986—; vis. prof. dept. physiology Faculty Medicine, Sao Paulo, Brazil, 1976; vis. assoc. prof. Mt. Sinai Sch. Medicine, N.Y.C., 1975, 78. Fellow Guggenheim Found., 1976. Office: Dept Physiology Faculty Medicine, Buenos Aires Argentina

PARISSE, MICHEL JEAN, historian, educator; b. Void, Meuse, France, May 1, 1936; s. Emile and Léonie (Chauvet) P.; m. Claude Brassens; children: Christophe, Jerome, Matthieu. Grad., U. Nancy, France, 1962. Prof. U. Nancy, 1965-85; dir. Mission Historique Française, Göttingen, Federal Republic of Germany, 1985—. Author: Noblesse et Chevalerie en Lorraine Médiévale, 1982, Les Nonnes au Moyen Age, 1983, La Tapisserie de Bayeux, 1983. Roman Catholic. Office: Mission Historique, Francaise, Hermann-Fogge Weg 12, D3400 Gottingen Federal Republic of Germany

PARÍZKOVÁ, JANA, physiologist; b. Prague, Czechoslovakia, May 9, 1931; d. Jan Blahoslav and Vlasta (Dufková) Capek; M.D., Charles U., Prague, 1956; Ph.D., Czechoslovak Acad. Scis., 1960, Dr.Sc., 1977; m. Jiri Parizek, Jan. 25, 1958. Sr. research officer Inst. Research in Phys. Edn., Charles U., 1956—; mem. research com. Internat. Council Sport and Phys. Edn., UNESCO, 1963—. Recipient P.N. Baker prize Internat. Council Sport and Phys. Edn., 1977. Mem. Internat. Union Nutritional Scis. (chmn. com. on nutrition and phys. performance). Author: (monograph) Body Fat and Physical Fitness, 1974 (also English, Japanese and Portuguese edits.); editor monographs; contbr. over 330 articles to sci. publs. Home: 32 Myslikova, 12000 Prague 2 12000, Czechoslovakia Office: 450 Ujezd, 11800 Prague 1 Czechoslovakia

PARK, CHAN HYUNG, cell biologist, physician; b. Seoul, Korea, Aug. 16, 1936; s. Chung Suh and Yoon Sook Yuh; m. Mary Hyungrok Kim, Apr. 16, 1966; 1 son, Christopher Myungwoo. M.D., Seoul Nat. U., 1962, M.S., 1964; Ph.D., U. Toronto, Ont., Can., 1972. Diplomate: Am. Bd. Internal Medicine with subplty. of med. oncology. Asst. prof. U. Kans. Med. Center, 1974-80, assoc. prof., 1980-86, prof., 1986—. Transl. novel from German to Korean. Mem. editorial bd. Jour. Nutrition, Growth and Cancer. Contbr. articles to biomed. and sci. jours. Recipient research career devel. award USPHS, NIH, 1979-84. Mem. ACP (fellow), Am. Assn. Cancer Research, Am. Soc. Clin. Oncology, Am. Soc. Hematology, Internat. Soc. Exptl. Hematology, Cell Kinetics Soc., Am. Fedn. Clin. Research, Soc. for Analytical Cytology Internat. Assn. for Vitamin and Nutritional Oncology. Home: 9137 Grandview Dr Overland Park KS 66212 Office: 39th and Rainbow Blvd Kansas City KS 66103

PARK, DONG HWA, neurobiologist, educator; b. Seoul, Mar. 3, 1937; U.S., 1963, naturalized, 1976; s. Chi Ho and Ok Nam (Shin) P.; m. Min Jung, Sept. 9, 1967; children—Henry, Bernard. B.S. in Chemistry, Seoul Nat. U., 1961; M.S. in Biochemistry, Brigham Young U., 1968, Ph.D., 1970. Nat. Vitamin Found. postdoctoral fellow Columbia U.-St. Luke's Hosp. Ctr., N.Y.C., 1970-72; asst. scientist NYU, N.Y.C., 1972-75; instr. neurobiology Cornell U. Med. Coll., N.Y.C., 1975-78, asst. prof., 1978-84, assoc. research prof., 1984—. Contbr. articles to sci. jours. Mem. AAAS, Am. Chem. Soc., Am. Soc. for Neurochemistry, Soc. for Neurosci. Baptist. Research on neurotransmitter synthesizing enzymes, purification, characterization, prodn. of antibodies to above enzymes and immunochem. studies. Home: 50-21 59th Pl Woodside NY 11377 Office: 785 Mamaroneck Ave White Plains NY 10605

PARK, EDWARD CAHILL, JR., physicist; b. Wollaston, Mass., Nov. 26, 1923; s. Edward Cahill and Fentress (Kerlin) P.; m. Helen Therese O'Boyle, July 28, 1951. AB, Harvard U., 1947; postgrad., Amherst Coll., 1947-49; PhD, U. Birmingham, Eng., 1956. Instr. Amherst (Mass.) Coll., 1954-55; mem. staff Lincoln Lab., Lexington, Mass., 1955-57, Arthur D. Little, Inc., Cambridge, Mass., 1957-60; group leader electronic systems Arthur D. Little, Inc., Santa Monica, Calif., 1960-64; sr. staff engr., head laser system sect. Hughes Aircraft Co., Culver City, Calif., 1964-68; sr. scientist Hughes Aircraft Co., El Segundo, Calif., 1986-88; mgr. electric optical systems sect. Litton Guidance and Control Systems, Woodland Hills, Calif., 1968-70; sr. phys. scientist The Rand Corp., Santa Monica, 1970-72; sr. scientist R&D Assocs., Marina Del Rey, Calif., 1972-1986, cons., 1986—. Contbr. articles to profl. jours.; patentee in field. Served to 1st lt. USAAF, 1943-46. Grantee Dept. Indsl. and Sci. Research, 1953. Fellow Explorers Club (sec. So. Calif. chpt. 1978-79); mem. IEEE, Optical Soc. Am., Armed Forces Communications and Electronics Assn., Assn. Old Crows, Sigma Xi. Democrat. Clubs: 20-Ghost (Eng.), Harvard (So. Calif.). Home and Office: 932 Ocean Front Santa Monica CA 90403

PARK, FRANK GEORGE STEPHEN, data processing executive; b. Aberdeen, Scotland, Sept. 15, 1948; s. Frank Scot and Janet Abernethey (Stephen) P.; m. Rita Eddie, Dec. 26, 1969; children: Alison, Stephen. MA, Aberdeen U., 1969. From programmer to sr. programmer So. Gas, Southampton, Eng., 1969-72; cons. computing Altergo Ltd., London, 1972-76, no. region mgr., 1976-79, U.K. service mgr., 1979-83, bus. systems mgr. Data Logic div., 1983-84; dir. mktg. Bluebird Software Ltd., London, 1984—; bd. dirs. Cairnmain Ltd., London. Editor Inflight newsletter, 1985—. Mem. Conservative Party. Mem. Ch. Scotland. Home: 2 Burston Dr, Park St, Saint Albans, Herts AL2 2HR, England Office: Bluebird Software Ltd, Old Bushey Ct High St, Bushey, Hertshire WD2 3DB, England

PARK, HONG-SUH, mathematics educator; b. Daegu, Korea, Dec. 30, 1931; s. Sung-Ryol and Wye-Bong (Whang) P.; m. Nam-Ho Hong; children: Chan-Gun, Myin-Gyung, Sun-Yeung. Bachelor's degree, Kyungpook U., Daegu, 1959, master's degree, 1961, DSci, 1974. Instr. Kyungpook U., Daegu, 1961-64; asst. prof. Chung-Gu Tech. Coll., Daegu, 1964-68; asst. prof. math. Yeungnam U., Gyongsan, Korea, 1968-73, assoc. prof., 1973-78, prof., 1978—. Reviewer Am. Math. Revs., 1969—. Mem. Korean Math. Soc., Japan Math. Soc., Tensor Soc., Am. Math. Soc. Home: 878-79 Bong-Duk Dong, Daegu 705-022, Republic of Korea Office: Yeungnam U, Gyongsan 713-800, Republic of Korea

PARK, JON KEITH, dentist, educator; b. Wichita, Kans., May 26, 1938; s. William Ray and Eleanor Jeanette (Cunningham) P.; D.D.S., U. Mo., 1964; B.A., Wichita State U., 1969; M.S. in Dental Hygiene Edn., U. Mo., 1971; M.S. in Oral Pathology, U. Md., 1982; cert. in dental radiology U. Pa. Sch. Dental Medicine, 1982. Gen. practice dentistry, Wichita, 1964-67; chmn. dept. dental hygiene Wichita State U., 1967-72; assoc. prof. oral diagnosis, coordinator dental radiology Balt. Coll. Dental Surgery, U. Md., 1972—; program dir. U. Md. dental externship, 1974-77; lectr. Essex Community Coll., Harford County Community Coll.; cons. in radiology VA Hosp.; mem. Md. State Radiation Control Adv. Bd., 1981—. Mem. bd. dirs. Univ. One Residents' Assn., 1975—. Recipient U. Md. Media Achievement award, 1977, 78; diplomate Am. Bd. Oral and Maxillo-facial Radiology. Fellow Am. Acad. Dental Radiology; mem. Am., Md. dental assns., Balt. City Dental Soc. (ad hoc com. radiation safety), Am. Acad. Oral Pathology, Orgn. Tchrs. Oral Diagnosis, Am. Theater Organ Soc., Kans. Dental Hygienists Assn. (hon.), Balt. Music Club, Am. Acad. Dental Radiology (editorial bd.), Am. Assn. Dental Schs., Internat. Assn. Dental and Maxillofacial Radiology, Balt. Opera Guild, Engring. Soc. Balt., Met. Opera Guild, Balt. Symphony Orch. Assn., Ute Pass Community Assn., Omicron Kappa Upsilon, Psi Omega. Episcopalian. Patentee pivotal design dental chair. Club: University of U. Md.

PARK, KWANG-WON, anesthesiologist, educator; b. Kyungi-Do, Republic of Korea, Feb. 10, 1929; s. Yong-Sam Park and He-Shu Yang; m. Soon Kim, June 7, 1963; children: Sang-Yoo, So-Yun, Sang-Don. MD, Severance Med. Coll., Seoul, Korea, 1951; DMS, Yonsei U., Seoul, Republic of Korea, 1967. Resident in anesthesia Vanderbilt U. Hosp., 1958-59; instr. anesthesia Yonsei U. Coll. Medicine, Seoul, 1963-72, prof. anesthesia, 1972—. Co-author: (with others) Textbook of Anesthesiology, 1987. Mem. Korean Soc. Anesthesiologists (pres. 1969-70, 84-85), Korean Soc. Critical Care Medicine (pres. 1982-83). Office: Yonsei Univ Coll Medicine, Dept Anesthesiology, CPO Box 8044 Seoul Republic of Korea

PARK, LEE CRANDALL, psychiatrist; b. Washington, July 15, 1926; s. Lee I. and Alice (Crandall) P. Grad. Putney Preparatory Sch., Vt.; B.S. in Zoology, Yale, 1948; M.D., Johns Hopkins, 1952; m. Barbara Anne Merrick, July 1, 1953; children—Thomas Joseph, Jeffrey Rawson; m. Mary Woodfill Banerjee, Apr. 27, 1985. Intern medicine Johns Hopkins Hosp., Osler Clinic, Balt., 1952-53; resident psychiatry USN Hosp., Oakland, Calif., 1954, Henry Phipps Psychiat. Clinic, Johns Hopkins Hosp., 1955-59; asst. psychiatrist out patient dept. Johns Hopkins Hosp., 1955-59, staff psychiatrist, 1959—, staff dept. medicine, 1970—, dir. psychiat. outpatient services and community psychiatry program, 1972-74, asst. dir. clin. services (psychiatry), 1973-74, deptl. council (psychiatry), 1974-76; fellow psychiatry Johns Hopkins U., 1955-59, faculty in psychiatry, 1959—, assoc. prof., 1971—, physician charge psychiat. services student health service, 1961-66, sr. psychiat. cons., 1966-73; vis. psychiatrist Balt. City Hosp., 1960-61; co-prin., prin. investigator NIMH Psychopharmacology Research Br. Outpatient Study of Drug-Set Interaction, 1960-68, co-dir. (with Eugene Meyer) Time-Limited Psychotherapy Research Grant, 1969-73; pvt. practice psychiatry, 1964—; cons. Met. Balt. Assn. Mental Health, 1961-63, Bur. Disability Ins., Social Security Adminstrn., 1964-81; attending staff Seton Psychiat. Inst., 1966-73, exec. bd., 1970-73; staff Sheppard and Enoch Pratt Hosp., 1974—. Served to lt. M.C., USNR, 1953-55, div. psychiatrist 1st Marine Div., Korea, staff psychiatrist USN Hosp., Camp Pendelton, Calif., 1954-55. Diplomate Nat. Bd. Med. Examiners, Am. Bd. Psychiatry and Neurology. Fellow Am. Psychiat. Assn. (mem. assembly 1983—), AAAS; mem. Md. Psychiat. Soc. (pres. 1978-79), Am. Psychosomatic Soc., AMA, Am., Md. socs. adolescent psychiatry, Soc. Psychotherapy Research, N.Y. Acad. Scis., Md. Interdisciplinary Council Children and Adolescents (treas.), Med. and Chirurg. Faculty Md., Balt. City, Baltimore County med. socs., Johns Hopkins Med. and Surg. Assn., AAUP, Md. Assn. Pvt. Practicing Psychiatrists, Am. Coll. Neuropsychopharmacology, SAR, Phi Beta Pi. Clubs: Johns Hopkins (Balt.); Metropolitan (Washington); Farmington Country (Charlottesville, Va.); Chevy Chase (Md.) Country. Research includes controlled studies of interrationships of psychotherapy and psychopharmacotherapy, time ltd. psychotherapy, borderline and narcissistic conditions, ethical considerations in clin. research. Contbr. articles to profl. jours. and books. Home: 308 Tunbridge Rd Baltimore MD 21212 Office: 1205 York Rd Lutherville MD 21093

PARK, MERLE FLORENCE, British ballerina; b. Salisbury, Rhodesia, Oct. 8, 1937; d. P.J. Park; m. James Monahan, 1965 (div. 1970); 1 son; m. 2d, Sidney Bloch, 1971; 1 son. Grad. Elmhurst Ballet Sch. and Royal Ballet Sch. Joined Royal Ballet, 1954; first solo role, 1955; opened own ballet school, 1977; dir. Royal Ballet Sch., 1983—; repertoire includes: Facade, Coppelia, Sleeping Beauty, La Fille Mal Gardee, Giselle, Les Sylphides, The Dream, Romeo and Juliet, Triad, The Nutcracker, La Bayadere, Cinderella, Shadow Play, Anastasia, Swan Lake, The Firebird, Walk to the Paradise Garden, Dances at a Gathering, Shadow, Don Quixote, Deux Pigeons, Serenade, Scene de Ballet, Wedding Bouquet, Les Rendevous, Mirror Walkers, Symphonic Variations, Daphnis and Chloe, Serenade, In the Night, Laurentia, Mamzelle Angot, Manon, Apolo, Flower Festival, Le Corsaire, The Moor's Pavane, Aureole, Elite Syncopations, Lulu, The Taming of the Shrew, Mayerling, Birthday Offering, La Fin du Jour, Adieu, Isadora, Raymonda, others. Office: 21 Millers Ct, Chiswick Mall, Chiswick, London W4 2PF, England *

PARK, QUE TE, optical industry executive; b. Pohang City, Republic of Korea, Dec. 5, 1946; came to U.S., 1981; s. In K. and K.R. (Yang) P.; m. Jung J. Kim, June 2, 1974; children: Chang S., June S., Nina S. BA, Hankuk U. Fgn. Studies, Republic of Korea, 1973, MBA, 1981; exec. program, Northwestern U. Kellogg Grad. Sch. Bus., 1984. Pres. Sambo Optical Co., Ltd., Masan, Republic of Korea, 1977-78; exec. dir. Tongkook Corp., Seoul, Republic of Korea, 1978-81; pres. Tongkook Am., Inc., Elk Grove Village, Ill., 1982-86, Samyang Optical, Inc., Elk Grove Village, 1986—. Mem. Northwest Internat. Traders Club. Mem. Assembly of God. Club: Greater O'Hare (Ill.). Office: Samyang Optical Inc 1157 Pagni Dr Elk Grove Village IL 60007

PARK, THOMAS JAMES, JR., educator; b. Wilkes-Barre, Pa., July 8, 1927; s. Thomas James and Ruth Elizabeth (Good) P.; B.S. in Edn., State Tchrs. Coll., Millersville, Pa., 1950; M.S. in Guidance, U. Scranton, 1958; m. Bertha Line Arnold, July 1, 1951; 1 son, Thomas James. Tchr. indsl. arts, Bladensburg, Md., 1952-54, Grand Army Republic High Sch., 1954-58, Meyers High Schs., Wilkes-Barre, 1958—; middle states evaluator of high schs. Camping dir. Boy Scouts Am., bd. dirs. Penn Mt. council, also camp insp., past scoutmaster, mem. exec. bd.; nat. camp. insp. northeast region; scoutmaster Nat. Jamboree for Penn Mt. council, 1973, chmn., 1981, 85; commr. Wilkes Barre area Boy Scouts Am.; chmn. bd. trustees, moderator 1st Baptist Ch., Wilkes-Barre. Served with USN, 1945-46, 1951-52. Recipient Silver Beaver award Boy Scouts Am., 1979, Silver Cross, 1980; Commr. Arrowhead Honor, 1986. Mem. Wilkes-Barre Edn. Assn. (past pres.), Pa. Edn. Assn., NEA, Indsl. Arts Assn., Am. Vocat. Assn., Pa. Indsl. Arts Assn., Pa. Vocat. Assn. Lodge: Masons.

PARK, WEE HYUN, medical educator; b. Taegu, Korea, Mar. 1, 1945; s. Sang-Ho and Duk-Sang (lee) P.; m. Jung-Hee Suh, Aug. 23, 1972; 1 child, Soo-Young. MB, Kyungpook Nat. U., Taegu, 1969; MMedicine, Kyungpook Nat. U., 1972, PhD, 1976. Diplomate Korean Bd. Internal Medicine. Intern the resident Kyungpook Nat. U. Hosp., 1969-74; dep. chmn. dept. internal medicine Fatima Hosp., Japan, 1974-76; instr. Sch. Medicine Kyungpook Nat. U., 1976-79, from asst. to assoc. prof., 1979-88, prof., 1988—, chief div. cardiology, 1983—. Author: Hypertension, 1986. French Govt. scholar, 1980-81. Mem. Korean Med. Assn., Korean Assn. Internal Medicine (councilor 1983—), Korean Soc. Cardiology (councilor 1976—). Roman Catholic. Home: 7 Dong 1108Ho Chung-un, Apt 111-1, Daebong Dong Taegu 700, Japan Office: Kyungpook U Hosp Dept Medicine, 52 Samduk-Dong, Taegu 700, Japan

PARK, WILLIAM LAIRD, agricultural economics educator, consultant; b. Idaho Falls, Idaho, Mar. 29, 1931; s. William D. and Ardella (Laird) P.; m. Ann Payne, Aug. 7, 1953; children—Leslie, David W., Wayne I., Andrea, John L. B.S., Utah State U., 1957, M.S., 1958; Ph.D., Cornell U., 1963. Dep. chief coop. relations N.Y./N.J. Milk Marketing Adminstrn., N.Y.C., 1958-65; assoc. prof. agrl. econs. Rutgers U., New Brunswick, N.J., 1965-68, chmn. dept. agrl. econs. and mktg., 1970-77; sr. agrl. economist Devel. and Resources Corp., Sacramento, 1969-70; chmn. dept. agrl. econs. Brigham Young U., Provo, 1977-83, prof., 1983—; pres. Ag-Econ Research Assocs., Orem, Utah, 1978—; bd. dirs. N.E. Agrl. Econs. Council, 1972-77; cons. agr., agribus. Author: Estimating Demand and Price Structures by Residual Analysis 1970; author numerous bulls., reports on dairy econs., feasibility analysis, internat. econ. devel.; contbr. articles to profl. jours. Served to cpl. U.S. Army, 1953-55. Mem. Western Agrl. Econs. Assn., Am. Agrl. Econs. Assn., Sigma Xi, Phi Kappa Phi. Republican. Mormon. Home: 1051 E 600 N Orem UT 84057 Office: Brigham Young U Assoc Dean Agr 302 WIDB Provo UT 84602

PARK, YONG CHOL, surgeon, educator; b. Seoul, Republic of Korea, Jan. 28, 1929; s. Pil Byong Park and Yoo Soon Yeom; m. Jeong Ran Shin, July 28, 1959; 1 child, Kyong A. MD, Yonsei U., Seoul, 1951; PhD, Korea U., Seoul, 1965; postgrad. in mgmt., Seoul U., 1981; postgrad. in adminstrn., Yonsei U., Seoul, 1983. Mem. surg. staff Republic Korea Army and Mobile Hosp., Seoul, 1951-55; resident in surgery Med. Coll. Va. Hosp., Richmond, 1955-61; prof., chmn. dept. surgery Ewha U. Hosp., Seoul, 1962-75, Kyong Hee U. Hosp., Seoul, 1975-80; dir., dean surg. staff Railroad Hosp, Nursing Coll., Seoul, 1980-85; clin. prof. surgery Yonsei U., Seoul, 1982—; clin. prof. Kyong Hee U., Seoul, 1986-88, Soonchon Hyang Med. Coll., Seoul, 1981-88. Author: (with others) Principle of Surgery, 1975, Textbook of Modern Surgery, 1987. Fellow ACS, Internat. Coll. Surgeons, Korean Coll. Surgeons; mem. Korean Surg. Soc. (pres. 1984-85), Seoul Drs. Assn. (hons. award 1973), Korean Med. Assn. (hons. award 1979), Korean Med. Soc. Transp. (pres. 1981-88), Fedn. Med. Ins. Socs. (madicam claims review com. 1986—). Home: 812-16 Yeog Sam Dong, Seoul Kang Nam Ku Republic of Korea

PARK, YOON-KEE, dermatologist, educator; b. Dae Jun, Chung-Nam, Korea, July 26, 1944; s. Pyoung O and Hi Ja (Kim) P.; m. Kyung Sook Shin; children: Sun-Min, Jim-Mo, Yonsei. MD, Yonsei U., Seoul, Republic of Korea, 1969, PhD, 1977. Asst. prof. Yonsei U., 1979-84, assoc. prof., 1984-87; chief dept. dermatology Yonsei U. Yong Dong Severance Hosp., Seoul, 1986—; prof. Yonsei U., Seoul, 1988—. Editor: Korean Jour. Dermatology, 1982. Fellow Am. Acad. Dermatology (non-resident); mem. Korean Dermatological Assn. (treas. 1985), Seoul Med. Soc. (acad. affairs 1988—). Office: Yonsei U Coll Medicine, Dept Dermatology, 120 Seoul Republic of Korea

PARKER, ARCHIE DAVID, JR., state official; b. West Monroe, La., Aug. 23, 1929; s. Archie David and Ethel (Crowell) P.; B.A., Northeast La. U., 1956, M.A., 1969; student U. Ark., 1951-53; certificate social work La. State U., 1959, M.S.W., 1974, PhD Oxford U., 1984-85; m. Gene Clair Rife; children—Daniel, Mark, Barbara. Probation officer, Monroe, La., 1959-62; dist. supr. probation Monroe dist. State of La., 1962-70, correctional instn. supt., Baker, La., 1970-75; asst. dir. for adult corrections La. Dept. Corrections, 1975-76, asst. sec. corrections, 1976-82, asst. prof. sch. social work La. State U., 1982-84, pvt. practice social work, 1986—, pres. Parker-Bergeron Distbg. Co., Monroe, 1963-66. Northeast La. U. dir. Students for Morrison, Barnham for Gov., 1955. Served to lt. col. AUS, 1945-48, 53-58. Recipient Northeast La. Alumni Assn. President's Service award, 1969; named Optimist of Yr., Greater Monroe chpt., 1970. Mem. Nat. Assn. Social Workers, Nat. Council on Crime and Delinquency, Nat. Assn. Correctional Supts., DAV, Ret. Officers Assn., La. Council Criminal Justice (pres. 1979), Northeast La. U. Alumni Assn. (1st v.p. 1967-68). Episcopalian. Mason (Shriner). Optimist (state bldg. chmn. 1972, pres. Tigertown chpt. 1973). Home: 432 Kennilworth Pkwy Baton Rouge LA 70808 Office: State Capitol PO Box 44304 Baton Rouge LA 70804

PARKER, CHARLES EDWARD, lawyer; b. Santa Ana, Calif., Sept. 9, 1927; s. George Ainsworth and Dorothy P.; m. Marilyn Esther Perrin, June 23, 1956; children—Mary, Catherine, Helen, George. Student, Santa Ana Coll., U. So. Calif.; J.D., S.W. U.-La. Bar: Calif. 1958, U.S. Dist. Ct. (cen. dist.) Calif. 1958, U.S. Supreme Ct. 1969, D.C. 1971, U.S. Dist. Ct. (no. and so. dists.) Calif. 1981. Prof. law Western State U., Fullerton, Calif., 1973-81; spl. counsel Tidelands, First Am. Title Co., 1980-82; dir. First Am. Fin. Corp., 1981-82. Served to sgt. U.S. Army, 1951-53. Mem. ABA (com. improvement land records, sect. real property), Orange County Bar Assn., Calif. Bar Assn., D.C. Bar Assn. Club: Santa Ana Kiwanis. Lodge: Elks (Santa Ana). Contbr. articles in field to profl. jours. Office: 18101 Charter Rd Villa Park CA 92667

PARKER, CHARLES WALTER, JR., consultant, retired equipment company executive; b. nr. Ahoskie, N.C., Nov. 22, 1922; s. Charles Walter and Minnie Louise (Williamson) P.; m. Sophie Nash Riddick, Nov. 26, 1949; children: Mary Parker Hutto, Caroline Parker Robertson, Charles Walter III, Thomas Williamson. B.S. in Elec. Engring., Va. Mil. Inst., 1947; Dr. Engring. (hon.), Milw. Sch. Engring., 1980. With Allis-Chalmers Corp., 1947-87; dist. mgr. Allis-Chalmers Corp., Richmond, Va., 1955-57, Phila., 1957-58; dir. sales promotion industries group Allis-Chalmers Corp., Milw., 1958-61; gen. mktg. mgr. new products Allis-Chalmers Corp., 1961-62, mgr. mktg. services, 1962-66, v.p. mktg. and public relations services, 1966-70, v.p., dep. group exec., 1970-72, staff group exec. communications and public affairs, 1972-87, ret., 1987; prin. Charles Parker & Assocs., Ltd., Milw., 1987—; founding mem. World Mktg. Contact Group, London.; dir. Wis. Heritage Corp., Internat. Gen. Ins. Corp. Gen. chmn. United Fund Greater Milw. Area, 1975; trustee Boy Scouts Am. Trust Fund., Milw.; bd. dirs. Jr. Achievement; pres. bd. trustees Univ. Sch. Milw., 1978-80; trustee Carroll Coll., Waukesha, Wis.; bd. dirs. Milw. Children's Hosp.; exec. bd. dirs. YMCA Greater Milw.; bd. regents Milw. Sch. Engring.; mem. Greater Milw. Com.; chmn. bd. dirs. Milw. Found., 1987—. Served to capt. AUS, 1943-46, ETO. Decorated Bronze Star. Mem. Wis. C. of C. (pres. 1974-76), NAM (dir.), IEEE (asso.), Sales and Mktg. Execs. Internat. (pres., chief exec. officer 1974, 75, Eduardo Rihan Internat. Mktg. Exec. of Year award 1979), Wis. Mfrs. and Commerce Assn. (mem. exec. com.), Pi Sigma Epsilon (pres. 1976-77, trustee nat. edn. found. 1980—), Kappa Alpha. Home: 2907 E Linnwood Ave Milwaukee WI 53211 Office: PO Box 512 Milwaukee WI 53201

PARKER, COLLIN DAVID, financial executive; b. Hastings, Sussex, Eng., June 29, 1935; s. Frederick Charles and Elsie Mary (Marchant) P.; m. Eileen Joan Smart, Sept. 23, 1959 (dec. Apr. 1972); children—David Nicholas, Andrew Michael; m. 2d Brigid Maria Kelly, May 10, 1975. Student Hastings Grammar Sch., 1946-51. Chartered acct. Fin. exec. RMC Group PLC, Feltham, Eng., 1960-71, fin. dir., 1971-77; fin. dir. Abdul Latif Jameel Establishment, Jeddah, Saudi Arabia, 1977-80; investment mgr. Jameel S.A.M. Monte-Carlo, Monaco, 1980-83; dir. Global Natural Resources Inc., Houston. Fellow Inst. Chartered Accts. in Eng. and Wales. Mem. Ch. of Eng.

PARKER, DANIEL LOUIS, lawyer; b. Smithfield, N.C., Sept. 2, 1924; s. James Daniel and Agnes Augusta (Toussaint) P.; m. Mae Comer Osborne, Aug. 2, 1958. A.B., U.N.C., 1947, LL.B., 1950. Bar: N.C. 1950. With escrow sect. mortgage loan dept. Pilot Life Ins. Co., Greensboro, N.C., 1950-53, with trust dept. N.C. Nat. Bank, Greensboro, 1953-62; investment counsel Pilot Life Ins. Co., 1962-71, counsel 71-77, 2nd v.p., 1977-84; 2nd v.p., asst. gen. counsel Jefferson Standard Life Ins. Co. (now Jefferson-Pilot Life Ins. Co.), Greensboro, 1984—. Served with U.S. Army, 1944-46. Mem. N.C. Bar Assn., Assn. Life Ins. Counsel, Greensboro Bar Assn., Greensboro Jr. C. of C., Phi Beta Kappa. Republican. Roman Catholic. Home: 308 W Greenway S Greensboro NC 27403 Office: Jefferson-Pilot Life Ins Co 101 N Elm St Greensboro NC 27401

PARKER, EDWARD INGRAHAM, manufacturing company executive; b. Worcester, Mass., Apr. 15, 1925; s. Charles Conrad and Winifred Rose (Ingraham) P.; B.S. in Aero. Engring., Purdue U., 1946; m. Shirley Fryer Clark, Oct. 2, 1948. Aerodynamics engr. Chance Vought Aircraft, Dallas, 1946-49, Kaman Aircraft, Bloomfield, Conn., 1949-52; ptnr. Parker & McPherson Ins. Agy., Worcester, Mass., 1952-66; pvt. practice engring. cons., Holden, Mass., 1966—; pres., treas. Detectrol, Inc., Holden, 1976—; sr. product designer Parker Mfg. Inc., Worcester, 1984—. Corporator, Friendly House of Worcester, 1953-66, Worcester Sci. Center, 1973—, Goddard Home for Aged Men, Worcester, 1982. Mem. Am. Soc. Quality Control. Republican. Congregationalist. Clubs: Trout Unltd., Kiwanis, New England Fly Tyers, Masons, Scottish Rite. Patentee non-destructive quality tester, broken needle detector, electromech. games. Home: 34 Oak Ridge Rd Holden MA 01520 Office: 10 Bearfoot Rd Northboro MA 01532

PARKER, HAROLD TALBOT, educator; b. Cin., Dec. 26, 1907; s. Samuel Chester and Lucile (Jones) P.; m. Louise Salley, July 9, 1980. Ph.B., U. Chgo., 1928, Ph.D., 1934; postgrad., Cornell U., 1929-30. Mem. faculty Duke U., Durham, N.C., 1939—, assoc. prof., 1950-57, prof. history, 1957-77, emeritus, 1977—; adj. prof. U. Ala., Huntsville, 1978-81; faculty U. N.C., Chapel Hill, 1984. Author: The Cult of Antiquity and the French Revolutionaries, 1937, Three Napoleonic Battles, 1944, 83, (with Marvin Brown) Major Themes in Modern European History, 3 vols., 1974, Bureau of Commerce in 1781, 1979; editor: (with Richard Herr) Ideas in History, 1965, Problems in European History, 1979, (with Georg Iggers) International Handbook of Historical Studies, 1979, Theory and Social History, 1980, (with L.S. Parker) Proc. Consortium of Revolutionary Europe, 1981, 84, 85, 86; assoc. editor Historical Dictionary of Napoleonic France, 1985; also articles. Served with USAAF, 1942-45. Mem. French Hist. Studies (pres. 1957), AAUP (pres. Duke U. chpt. 1960), Phi Beta Kappa (pres. Duke chpt. 1961). Episcopalian. Home: 2211 Arrington Street Durham NC 27707

PARKER, HENRY GRIFFITH, III, insurance executive; b. Plainfield, N.J., Oct. 27, 1926; s. Henry Griffith and Ruth Martin (Van Auken) P.; m. Audrey Lansing Turner, May 11, 1957; children: Henry Griffith, IV, Elizabeth Wright. AB, Princeton U., 1948; postgrad., U. Pa. Sch. Law. With Chubb & Son, Inc., 1949—, v.p., 1968-70, sr. v.p., dir., 1971—, mng. dir., 1986—; v.p. Fed. Ins. Co., 1968-73, sr. v.p., 1973—; v.p. Vigilant Ins. Co., 1966—, mgr. internat. div., 1967-84; bd. dirs. La Federal Compania de Seguros S.A., Bogota, Colombia, Eberhard Faber, Inc.; chmn. adv. bd. Bolivar Compania de Seguros, Ecuador, bd. dirs. La Federacion Compania de Seguros, Caracas, Venezuela; mem. industry sector adv. com. on services U.S. Dept. Commerce, Washington; bd. dirs. Nat. Fgn. Trade Council, chmn. declarations com., 1974-81, chmn. ins. com., 1976-81; chmn. internat. policy com. U.S. C. of C., 1970-73; chmn. U.S. del. XII-XIII-XX-XXI Hemispheric Ins. Conf., Chile, 1969, Paraguay, 1971, 87, Panama, 1985; chmn. Internat. Ins. Adv. Council, Washington, 1970-73, 85-88; mem. N.J. Commn. on Internat. Trade, 1986—. Contbr. articles to profl. jours. Chmn. bd. Overlook Hosp., Summit, N.J., 1973-80; trustee Drew U., Madison, 1974—; bd. dirs. Nat. Assn. Prevent Blindness, N.J. Dist. Export Council. Served as lt. (j.g.) USNR, 1944-46. Recipient Internat. Ins. award U.S. C. of C., 1981, Disting. Service award Internat. Ins. Council, 1988. Mem. Psi Upsilon. Republican. Episcopalian. Clubs: Downtown Assn. (N.Y.C.), Princeton (N.Y.C.), River (N.Y.C.); Devon Yacht, Morris County (N.J.) Golf, Morristown Field. Home: 38 East Ln Madison NJ 07940 Office: 15 Mountain View Rd PO Box 1615 Warren NJ 07061

PARKER, JACK ROYAL, engineering company executive; b. N.Y.C., Apr. 25, 1919; s. Harry and Clara (Saxe) P.; m. Selma Blossom, Dec. 8, 1946; children: Leslie Janet, Andrew Charles. Student, Bklyn. Poly. Inst., 1943; D.Sc. (hon.), Pacific Internat. U., 1956. Instr. Indsl. Tng. Inst., 1938-39; engr. Brewster Aero Corp., 1939-40; pres. Am. Drafting Co., 1940; design engr., plan div. Navy Dept., 1941-44; also supr. instr. N.Y. Drafting Inst.; instr. Gasoline Handling Sch., also Inert Gas Sch., U.S.N.T.S., Newport, R.I., 1944-46; cons. Todd Shipyards Corp., 1947-54; tech. adviser to pres. Rollins Coll., 1949-50; v.p. Wattpar Corp., 1947-54; pres. Parco Co. Can. Ltd., 1951-55; pres., dir., chief project mgr. Royalpar Industries, Inc., N.Y.C., 1947-75; chmn. Med. Engrs. Ltd., Nassau, Bahamas, 1957-60; pres. Parco Chem. Systems, Inc., 1965-69; pres., dir. Parco Internat., Inc., 1965-69; pres. Guyana Oil Refining Ltd., S.A., 1966-69, Refineria Peruana del Sur S.A., 1965-68; v.p., dir., founder Refinadora Costarricense de Petreoleo, S.A., 1963-73; pres. Oleoducto Trans Costa Rica, 1970-73, Trans Costa Rica Pipeline Operating Co., 1970-73, Due Diligence, Inc., 1985—; gen. mgr. Kellex power services Pullman Kellogg Co., 1975-77; past pres., sec., dir. Vernitron Corp., Amsterdam Fund, European securities Pub. Co.; Cons., Dominican Republic, 1964, Republic Costa Rica, 1964-65; Cons. Malta Indsl. Devel. Study Co. Ltd., 1965-67, Hambros Bank Ltd., London, 1967-68, Stone & Webster Engring. Corp., Boston, 1957-75, Hambro Am. Bank & Trust Co., N.Y.C., 1968-70; pres. J. Royal Parker Assos., Inc., 1975—, pres. Due Diligence, Inc., 1985—; Internat. Mfg. Centers, Inc., 1977-81, Delaware Valley Fgn. Trade Zone, Inc., 1977-80, Brown & Root (Delaware Valley) Inc., 1980-84 ; chmn. Summa Engring. Ltd., 1985-86; lectr. One World Club, Cornell U., 1963; chmn. project fin. panel Global Energy Forum '84. Author: Gasoline Systems, 1945; also articles; developer Due Diligence process for project fin. analysis. Mem. adv. bd. Drafting Ednl. Adv. Commn. N.Y.C. Bd. Edn., 1968; founder museum U.S. Mcht. Marine Acad., 1977 (Disting. Service award 1987); pres. Am. Mcht. Marine Mus. Found., U.S. Mcht. Marine Acad., Kings Point, N.Y., 1981-87, pres. emeritus 1987—; Trustee Coll. Adv. Sci., Canaan, N.H. Decorated knight Order St. John of Jersusalem.; recipient Humanitarian award Fairleigh Dickinson U., 1974, Disting. Service award U.S. Merchant Marine Acad. Alumni Found., 1987. Fellow A.A.A.S.; mem. Inst. Engring. Designers (London), Am. Petroleum Inst., Soc. Am. Mil. Engrs., Presidents Assn., Am. Mgmt. Assn., Am. Inst. Chem. Engrs., Am. Inst. Dsgn. and Drafting. Republican. Clubs: Masons; Marco Polo (N.Y.C.); Royal Automobile (London). Home: 106 The Mews Haddonfield NJ 08033 Office: 1100 Kings Hwy N Cherry Hill NJ 08034

PARKER, JAMES JOHN, electrical engineering administrator; b. Oak Park, Ill., June 16, 1947; s. John J. and Marjorie (Grohmann) P.; m. Mary P. Nash, Oct. 21, 1972; children: Elizabeth Ann, John James, Patricia Mary. BS in Elec. Engring., Marquette U., 1971; BSBA, Elmhurst Coll., 1981; MBA, U. Chgo., 1987. Student engr. Motorola Consumer Products, Franklin Park, Ill., 1968-70, engring. assoc., 1972-74; co-op engr. Warwick Electronics, Niles, Ill., 1971-72; sr. engr. research and devel. Quasar Electronics, Inc., Franklin Park, 1974-76; sr. project engr. Motorola Data Products, Carol Stream, Ill., 1976-79; sr. project engr. Zenith Electronics Co., Glenview, Ill., 1979-82, market research mgr., 1982-85, sect. mgr., 1985—; part-time faculty Wright Jr. Coll., Chgo., 1975-80. Editorial adv. bd. Electronic Products Mag., 1976-77. Adviser Jr. Achievement, Chgo., 72-78. Mem. IEEE Midcon. (vice-chmn. pub. relations, 1979, chmn. spec. exhibits, 1981, vice-chmn. spec. exhibits, 1983), Delta Mu Delta. Home: 421 Berkley Ave Elmhurst IL 60126 Office: Zenith Electronics Corp 1000 Milwaukee Ave Glenview IL 60025

PARKER, JEFFREY BERRYMAN, data processing specialist; b. Detroit, Jan. 6, 1950; s. Benjamin L. and Jean Hart (Woodard) P.; m. Charlotte J. King, May 24, 1980. B.in Continuing Studies, U. Nebr.-Omaha, 1983. Cert. systems profl. Sr. programmer Foremost Ins. Co., Grand Rapids, Mich., 1978-81; project leader Mut. of Omaha, 1981-84; dept. mgr. ALR Systems & Software, Omaha, 1984—. Served with USAF, 1970-78. Fellow Life Office Mgmt. Assn.; mem. Assn. Systems Mgmt. (chpt. sec. 1983-85, spl. publs. chmn. 1985-88). Republican. Mem. Christian Ch. Avocations: strategic simulations; cooking; wine making; stained glass; bookbinding. Office: ALR Systems 234 S 108th Ave Suite 7 Omaha NE 68154

PARKER, JOHN OSMYN, management consultant; b. Denver, May 31, 1919; s. George Lindsey and Marie (Bloedorn) P.; B.S. in Bus., U. Colo., 1942; m. Judith Fehr, July 20, 1942; children—Craig Steven, John Fehr, Diane, Newton Lindsey. Jr. indsl. engr. U.S. Steel Corp., Gary, Ind., 1942-43; mgr. personnel research Trans World Airlines, Kansas City, Mo., 1945-55; mgmt. cons. Douglas Williams Assos., N.Y.C., 1955-56; dir. personnel Central Hudson Gas & Electric Corp., Poughkeepsie, N.Y., 1956-69, United Hosp., Port Chester, N.Y., 1969-78; v.p. human resources Mountainside Hosp., Montclair, N.J., 1978-83; mgmt. cons.; instr. mgmt. Rutgers U., Ocean County Coll. Chmn. budget div., bd. dirs. United Way, Dutchess County, N.Y., 1963-69; adv. bd. Montclair Salvation Army; pres. Fellowship Club, Presbyn. Ch., 1985; mem. Philharmonic Garden State Chorus. Served with U.S. Army, 1943-45; ETO. Mem. Am. Soc. Personnel Adminstrn. (research awards com. 1958—, accredited exec. in personnel), Am. Soc. Tng. Dirs., Am. Mgmt. Assn., DAV (commander 1988—). Phi Kappa Psi. Republican. Presbyterian. Club: Rotary (dir. Rye, N.Y. 1975-78, pres. 1977-78; dir. Montclair 1978-83, dir. Central Ocean, Toms River, N.J. 1985-88). Home: 10 Morningside Drive Toms River NJ 08755

PARKER, JOHN WILLIAM, pathology educator, investigator; b. Clifton, Ariz., Jan. 5, 1931; s. Vilas William and Helen E. (Coughlin) P.; m. Barbara A. Atkinson, June 8, 1957; children: Ann Elizabeth, Joy Noelle, John David, Heidi Susan. BS, U. Ariz., 1953; MD, Harvard U., 1957. Diplomate Am. Bd. Pathology. Clin. instr. pathology U. Calif. Sch. Medicine, San Francisco, 1962-64; asst. prof. U. So. Calif. Sch. Medicine, Los Angeles, 1964-68, assoc. prof., 1968-75, prof., 1975—, co-chmn. dept. Pathology, 1985—; assoc. dean sci. affairs U. So. Calif., 1987—; co-chmn. 15th Internat. Leucocyte Culture Conf., Asilomar, Calif., 1982; chmn. 2nd Internat. Lymphoma Conf., Athens, Greece, 1981. Founding editor (jour.) Hematological Oncology, 1982—; assoc. editor Jour. Clin. Lab. Analysis, 1985—; co-editor: Intercellular Communication in Leucocyte Function, 1983; contbr. over 150 articles to profl. jours., chpts. to books. Named sr. oncology fellow Am. Cancer Soc., U. So. Calif. Sch. Medicine, 1964-69, Nat. Cancer Inst. vis. fellow Walter and Eliza Hall Inst. for Med. Research, Melbourne, Australia, 1972-73. Fellow Coll. Am. Pathologists, Am. Soc. Clin. Pathologists, Royal Soc. Medicine; mem. Am. Assn. Pathologists, Am. Soc. Hematology, Internat. Acad. Pathology, Am. Assn. Clin. Scientists, Phi Beta Kappa, Phi Kappa Phi. Republican. Office: U So Calif Sch Medicine KAM 506 Dean's Office 1975 Zonal Ave Los Angeles CA 90033

PARKER, JOSEPHUS DERWARD, corporation executive; b. Elm City, N.C., Nov. 16, 1906; s. Josephus and Elizabeth (Edwards) P.; A.B., U. of South, 1928; postgrad. Tulane U., 1928-29, U. N.C., 1929-30, Wake Forest Med. Coll., 1930-31; m. Mary Wright, Jan. 15, 1934 (dec. Dec. 1937); children—Mary Wright (Mrs. Mallory A. Pittman, Jr.), Josephus Derward; m. 2d, Helen Hodges Hackney, Jan. 24, 1940; children—Thomas Hackney, Alton Person, Derward Hodges, Sarah Helen Parker. Founder, chmn. bd. J.D. Parker & Sons, Inc., Elm City, 1955—, Parker Tree Farms, Inc., 1956—; founder, pres. Invader, Inc., 1961-63; pres. dir. Brady Lumber Co., Inc., 1957-62; v.p., dir. Atlantic Limestone, Inc., Elm City, 1970—; owner, operator Parker Airport, Eagle Springs, N.C., 1940-62. Served to capt. USAF, 1944-47. Episcopalian. Clubs: Moose, Lions; Wilson (N.C.) Country. Address: PO Box 905 Elm City NC 27822

PARKER, MARGERY ELEANOR, sales representative; b. Scranton, Pa., Sept. 24, 1946; d. Roswell James and Margery Elizabeth (Thomas) Parker; B.S. in Med. Tech., Temple U., 1968. Research technologist Temple U. Sch. Medicine, Phila., 1968-76; instr. Coulter Electronics, Islamorada, Fla., 1976-77; sales rep. Curtin Matheson Sci., Allentown, Pa., 1977-80, Calbiochem-Behring Corp., Allentown, 1980-83, Rupp and Bowman, 1983-84, The Jobst Inst., 1984-85, NTRON Internat. Sales Co., Inc., 1986—. Mem. Am. Soc. Clin. Pathologists, Allentown Art Mus. Assn., Cetronia Ambulance Corps. Republican. Presbyterian.

PARKER, PAUL KENNETH, environmental studies educator; b. Wolfville, N.S., Can., Mar. 27, 1957; arrived in Eng., 1987; s. Kenneth Lorne and Florence Emily (Paine) P.; m. Margaret Ann Grocke, Dec. 29, 1984. BA, BS, Mt. Allison U., N.B., Can., 1979; MA, Australian Nat. U., Canberra, 1982, grad. diploma in internat. law, 1986. Research asst. Mt. Allison U., N.B., Can., 1978; program asst. Cath. Relief Services, Thailand, 1980; cons. Singleton Shire Council, New South Wales, Australia, 1982; researcher Australian Nat. U., Canberra, 1982-84, postdoctoral fellow, 1985-87; asst. dir. research and stats. Dept. Local Govt. and Adminstrv. Services, Canberra, 1984-85; lectr. Centre for Energy Studies, London, 1987—, Internat. Resources Programme, London Sch. Econs., 1987—; convener Rainforest Info. and Research Group, Canberra, 1985-87; contbr. World Conservation Strategy Conf., Ottawa, Can., 1986; contract researcher Regional Devel. and Local Govt., Canberra, 1986, Australia-Japan Research Centre, Canberra, 1988. Contbr. numerous articles to profl. jours. Recipient Young Scientist Travel award Australian and New Zealand Assn. for Advancement of Sci., 1984, Can. Airlines Internat. Can. Studies award Assn. Can. Studies, 1987. Mem. Internat. Assn. Energy Economists, Inst. Brit. Geographers, Environ. Law Assn. Home: 14 Byron Ct, 26 Mecklenburgh Sq, London WCIN 2AF, England Office: London Sch Econs, S504, Houghton St, London WC2A 2AE, England

PARKER, RICHARD ANTHONY, Egyptologist; b. Chgo., Dec. 10, 1905; s. Thomas Frank and Emma Ursula (Heldman) P.; m. Gladys Anne Burns, Feb. 10, 1934; children: Michael (dec.), Beatrice Ann. A.B., Dartmouth Coll., 1930; Ph.D., U. Chgo., 1938. Research asst. Oriental Inst., U. Chgo., 1938-42, research assoc., 1942-46, asst. prof. of Egyptology, 1946-48; Wilbour prof. Egyptology Brown U., 1948-72, prof. emeritus, 1972—; epigrapher, epigraphic and archtl. survey Luxor, Egypt, 1938-40; asst. field dir., epigraphic and archtl. survey 1946-47, field dir., 1947-49; Trustee Am. Research Center Egypt, 1948-74; mem. vis. com. dept. Middle Eastern civilizations Harvard, 1950-61, dept. Egyptian art Boston Mus. Fine Arts, 1950—. Author: (with Harold H. Nelson and others) Medinet Habu IV. Festival Scenes of Rameses III, 1940, Babylonian Chronology 626 B.C.-A.D. 45, 1942, (with Waldo H. Dubberstein) Babylonian Chronology 626 B.C.-A.D. 45, 1942, 46, rev. edit. 626 B.C.-A.D. 75, 1956, The Calendars of Ancient Egypt, 1950, (with G. R. Hughes and others) The Bubastite Portal, 1953, Medinet Habu V: The Temple Proper, Part I, 1957, Medinet Habu VI: The Temple Proper, Part II, 1963, A Vienna Demotic Papyrus on Eclipse and Lunar-Omina, 1959, (with O. Neugebauer) Egyptian Astronomical Texts I: The Early Decans, 1960, Egyptian Astronomical Texts II: The Ramesside Star Clocks, 1964, Egyptian Astronomical Texts III: Decans, Planets, Constellations and Zodiacs, 1969, A Saite Oracle Papyrus from Thebes, 1962, Demotic Mathematical Papyri, 1972, (with J. Leclant and J.C. Goyon) The Edifice of Taharqa by the Sacred Lake of Karnak, 1979. Corr. fellow Brit. Acad.; mem. Oriental Soc., Egypt Exploration Soc., Société Française d'Egyptologie, Deutsches Archaologisches Institut, Phi Beta Kappa, Theta Chi. Roman Catholic. Home: 91 Larch St Providence RI 02906

PARKER, ROBERT MICHAEL, teratologist, toxicologist, anatomy educator; b. San Diego, Aug. 31, 1946; s. Thomas Jackson Parker and Sue Ellen (Randall) Muka; stepson Joseph Abbott Muka, Jr.; m. Karen May Green, Jan. 29, 1972; children—Jenifer May, Alexis Diane. B.S., San Diego State Coll., 1970; M.S., U. Calif.-Davis, 1975, Ph.D., 1980. Staff research assoc. Calif. Primate Research Ctr., Davis, 1976-80, postgrad. researcher, 1980-81; lectr. in biol. sci., Calif. State U., Sacramento, 1978; guest lectr. in embryology, Sch. Medicine U. Calif., Davis, 1980; lectr. in biology, Calif. State Coll., San Bernardino, 1982-84; asst. prof. anatomy Coll. Osteo. Medicine of the Pacific, Pomona, Calif., 1981-85; perinatal biologist, Pathology Assocs., Inc., Nat. Ctr. for Toxicol. Research, Jefferson, Ark., 1985—. Contbr. articles to profl. jours. Mem. Republican Presdl. Task Force, Washington, 1983-86, U.S. Senatorial Club, 1983-86, Jefferson County Rep. Cen. Com., 1985-86, coach Girls softball, 1985-88; mem. sci. com. Southeast Ark. Arts and Sci. Ctr., 1985-86. Mem. Teratology Soc., Am. Assn. Anatomists, AAAS, Sigma Phi Epsilon (alumni bd. 1975-78). Roman Catholic. Club: Toastmasters. Office: Pathology Assocs Inc Nat Ctr Toxicol Research PO Box 26 Jefferson AR 72079

PARKER, THEODORE CLIFFORD, electronics engineer; b. Dallas, Oreg., Sept. 25, 1929; s. Theodore Clifford and Virginia Bernice (Rumsey) P.; B.S.E.E. magna cum laude, U. So. Calif., 1960; m. Jannet Ruby Barnes, Nov. 28, 1970; children—Sally Odette, Peggy Claudette. Vice pres. engring. Telemetrics, Inc., Gardena, Calif., 1963-65; chief info. systems Northrop-Nortronics, Anaheim, Calif., 1966-70; pres. AVTEL Corp., Covina, Calif., 1970-74, Aragon, Inc., Sunnyvale, Calif., 1975-78; v.p. Teledyne McCormick Selph, Hollister, Calif., 1978-82; sr. staff engr. FMC Corp., San Jose, Calif., 1982-85; pres. Power One Switching Products, Camarillo, Calif., 1985-86; pres. Condor D.C. Power Supplies, Inc., 1987-88, pres. Intelligence Power Tech. Inc., Camarillo, 1988—. Mem. IEEE (chmn. autotestcon '87), Am. Prodn. and Inventory Control Soc., Am. Def. Preparedness Assn., Armed Forces Communications and Electronics Assn., Nat. Rifle Assn. (life), Tau Beta Pi, Eta Kappa Nu. Home: 1290 Saturn Ave Camarillo CA 93010 Office: 2311 Statham Pkwy Oxnard CA 93033

PARKHILL, HAROLD LOYAL, artist; b. Fresno, Ohio, Feb. 16, 1928; s. Jesse Blair and Ella (Buser) P.; m. Rosalee Lavonne Croup, Aug. 5, 1950 (div. Nov. 1969); children: Lorie Cathrine, Scott Thomas, Cynthia Anne, Carrie Sue. Grad. high sch., Keene, Ohio, 1947. Farmer Fresno, 1947-52, 1964-80; bus driver Western Greyhound Lines, Calif, Ariz., N.Mex. and Tex., 1952-61; dispatcher Ea. Greyhound Lines, Cin., 1963; artist Coshocton, Ohio, 1980—. Represented in permanent collections Zanesville Art Ctr. Mem. Coshocton Art Guild; former trustee Coshocton Pomerene Fine Art Ctr. Served with USNR, 1945-46, PTO. Recipient numerous best of show awards in oil and watercolor art. Mem. Internat. Platform Assn., VFW, Am. Legion. Republican. Methodist. Lodges: Elks, Moose. Home: PO Box 85 Coshocton OH 43812

PARKINSON, CECIL EDWARD, secretary of state for energy; b. England, Sept. 1, 1931; s. Sidney P.; m. Ann Mary Jarvis, 1957; 3 daus. Grad., Royal Lancaster Grammar Sch.; BA, Emmanuel Coll., Cambridge, 1955, MA, 1961. Mgmt. trainee Metal Box Co., 1955; with West, Wake, Price, chartered accts., 1956, ptnr., 1961-71; founder Parkinson Hart Securities Ltd, 1967; dir. of several cos. 1965-79, 1984—; constituency chmn. Hemel Hempstead Conservative Assn.; chmn. Herts. 100 Cub, 1968-69; PPS to minister for aerospace and shipping 1972-74, asst. govt. whip, 1974, opposition whip, 1974-76, opposition spokesman on trade, 1976-79; minister for trade Dept. of Trade, 1979-81; paymaster gen. 1981-83; chancellor Duchy of Lancaster, 1982-83; sec. of state for trade and industry 1983, sec. of state for energy, 1987—; chmn. Conservative Party, 1981-83; sec., Conservative Party Fin. Com., 1971-72; chmn. Anglo-Swiss Party Group, 1979-82; pres. Anglo-Polish Conservative Soc., 1986—. Ran for combined Oxford and Cambridge team against Am. Univs., 1954; ran for Cambridge against Oxford, 1954, 55. Clubs: Carlton; Hawks (Cambridge). Address: House of Commons, SW1A 0AA London England *

PARKINSON, JAMES THOMAS, III, investment consultant; b. Richmond, Va., July 10, 1940; s. James Thomas and Elizabeth (Hopkins) P.; m. Molly O Owens, June 16, 1962; children: James Thomas, Glenn Walser. BA, U. Va., 1962; MBA, U. Pa., 1964. Trainee Chem. Bank, N.Y.C., 1964-66; assoc., corp. fin. dept. Blyth & Co., Inc., N.Y.C., 1968-69; v.p., corp. fin. dept. Clark Dodge & Co., Inc., N.Y.C., 1969-74; pvt. practice investment mgmt., N.Y.C., 1974-85, 87—; v.p. Pleasantville Advisors, Inc., N.Y.C., 1986-87; bd. dirs. Thetford Corp., Ann Arbor, Mich.; bd. mgrs. Am. Bible Soc., N.Y.C.; instr. corp. fin. Ind. U., 1966-68. Sr. warden Ch. of Holy Trinity, N.Y.C., 1978-79; trustee Cancer Care Inc., Nat. Cancer Care Found. Inc. Served with AUS, 1966-68. Republican. Episcopalian. Clubs: Univ., Ch. (N.Y.C.); Va. Country (Richmond). Office: 575 Madison Ave Suite 1006 New York NY 10022

PARKINSON, PHILIP WILLIAM, financial controller; b. Brussels, Aug. 22, 1956; arrived in France, 1985; s. Guy and Monique (Stainforth) P.; m. Veronique Alenson, Mar. 24, 1984. BBA, Brussels U., 1982. Mgmt. cons. Metra Proudfoot Internat., Brussels, 1982-84, installation project mgr., 1984-85; sr. cons. F.A.E. Conseil, Paris, 1985-86; fin. controller Jouveinal Labs., Paris, 1987—. Home: 8 Ave des Cerennes, 91940 Les Ulis France Office: Jouveinal Labs, 1 Rue des Moissons, 94263 Fresnes France

PARKINSON, THOMAS IGNATIUS, JR., lawyer; b. N.Y.C., Jan. 27, 1914; s. Thomas I. and Georgia (Weed) P.; A.B., Harvard U., 1934; LL.B., U. Pa., 1937; m. Geralda E. Moore, Sept. 23, 1937; children—Thomas Ignatius III, Geoffrey Moore, Cynthia Moore. Admitted to N.Y. bar, 1938, since practiced in N.Y.C.; assoc. Milbank, Tweed, Hope & Hadley, 1937-47, partner, 1947-56; pres. Mar Ltd., 1951—; pres. Breecom Corp., 1972-80, chmn. bd., 1980—; dir., exec. com. Pine St. Fund, Inc., N.Y.C., 1949-83, Trustee State Communities Aid Assn., 1949-83; dir. Fgn. Policy Assn., 1949-53; bd. dirs., exec. com. Milbank Meml. Fund, 1948-84. Mem. Am. Bar Assn., Assn. Bar City N.Y., Pilgrims U.S.A., Brit. War Relief Soc. (officer), Met. Unit Found., Phi Beta Kappa. Clubs: Down Town Assn., Knickerbocker, Union. Office: 780 Third Ave 25th Floor New York NY 10017

PARKINSON-BATES, ROBIN SIMON, banker; b. Redruth, Cornwall, Eng., Oct. 18, 1948; s. Frank and Mary Doreen (Simmons) Parkinson-Bates; m. Diana Claire Sumpter; children: Simon Andrew, Nicholas Anthony, Edward Alexander. Internat. bank exec. Hong Kong and Shanghai Banking Corp., U.K., Hong Kong, Japan, United Arab Emirates, Australia, 1967—.

Office: Hong Kong Bank of Australia, 1 Queens Rd Central, Hong Kong Hong Kong

PARKS, ALBERT LAURISTON, lawyer; b. Providence, July 18, 1935; s. Albert Lauriston and Dorothy Isabel (Arnold) P.; m. Martha Ann Anderson, Jan. 12, 1961; children: Amy Woodward, George Webster, Reed Anderson. BA, Kent State U., 1958; JD, U. Chgo., 1961. Bar: R.I. 1962, U.S. Dist. R.I. 1963, U.S. Ct. Appeals (1st cir.) 1966, U.S. Supreme Ct. 1980. Assoc. Hanson, Curran & Parks, Providence, 1961-65, ptnr., 1966—; town solicitor, North Kingstown, R.I., 1978-80. Fellow Am. Coll. Trial Lawyers; mem. ABA, R.I. Bar Assn., Maritime Law Assn., Assn. of Ins. Attys., Squantum Assn. Republican. Episcopalian. Clubs: Saunderstown (R.I.) Yacht. Lodge: Masons. Home: Hammond Hill Saunderstown RI 02814 Office: Turks Head Bldg Suite 1210 Providence RI 02903

PARKS, ARLENE GARVERICH, ceramist, artist, sculptor, educator; b. Harrisburg, Pa., May 18, 1930; d. Charles and Thelma (Stambaugh) Garverich; student Wilson Coll., 1948-50; B.S., Johns Hopkins U., 1952; B.F.A, Md. Inst. Art, 1952; postgrad. Towson State U., 1974-75, Johns Hopkins U., 1952; M.F.A. in Ceramics, Antioch Coll., Columbia, Md., 1982; m. H. Emslie Parks, June 14, 1952; children—Douglas Wayne, Cinda Lee, Donna Lynn. Tchr. art, Catonsville (Md.) High Sch., 1952-53; elementary art adviser Md., 1953-54; adviser to occupational therapist Summitt Nursing Home, Bd. Edn. Baltimore County, 1969-70; tchr. ceramics, adult edn., Baltimore County, 1959-64, 68-82; tchr. pottery Coll. Bahamas, Abaco Island, 1981—. Two-person show Visual Arts Ctr., Columbia, Md., 1982; exhibited in group shows Lyric Theatre, Balt., 1983-84, Hanover (Pa.) Art League, 1982, Harford County Community Coll., 1983, Essex Community Coll., Baltimore County, 1983-86. Adviser, Girl Scouts, 4H; edn. chmn. Baltimore County Hosp. Aux., 1970-72. Recipient grand award Middle Atlantic Ceramics Assn., 1973, 1st prize Md. Biennial of Crafts. Nat. League Am. Pen Women, 1973, award of merit Md. Art Biennial, 1983. Mem. Alumnae Assn. Johns Hopkins U., Alumnae Assn. Md. Inst., Nat. League Am. Pen Women (2d v.p. Carroll br. 1978, pres. 1982-84), Md. Art League, Rehobeth Art League, Chesapeake Potters Assn. Episcopalian. Home: 3144 Granite Rd Woodstock MD 21163 Other: Marsh Harbor, Abaco Bahamas

PARKS, FLOYD MASON, accounting firm consultant; b. Phila., Dec. 9, 1952; s. Kenneth Earl and Twila Elene (Tomlin) P.; m. Melanie Ann Leonard, Feb. 17, 1979. AAS in Data Processing with distinction, U. So. Colo., 1976, BBA with distinction, 1978; MBA, U. Utah, 1982. Cert. systems profl.; cert. info. systems auditor. Dir. residence hall U. So. Colo., Pueblo, 1978; dir. student family housing U. Utah, Salt Lake City, 1978-79, staff specialist, 1979-82; mgr. Deloitte Haskins & Sells, Denver, 1982—. Rep. precinct chmn., Salt Lake City, 1981-82. Served with USNR, 1971-79, USAR, 1979-82, Vietnam. Mem. Am. Mgmt. Assn., Assn. MBA Execs., Internat. Platform Assn., Mensa. Baptist. Office: Deloitte Haskins & Sells 1560 Broadway Suite 1800 Denver CO 80202

PARKS, JANET ELAINE, pharmacist; b. Watertown, S.D., Oct. 20, 1946; d. Dale O. and Della E. (Horn) P. B.S., S.D. State U., 1970; M.B.A., U. Minn., 1981. Registered pharmacist, Minn., Iowa, Wis. Staff pharmacist St. Luke's Hosp., Duluth, Minn., 1970-81; fin. cons. Parks & Parks, Marshall, Minn., 1981-82; pharmacy cons. J. Parks, Mason City, Iowa, 1982-85; night pharmacist St. Joseph Mercy Hosp., Mason City, 1982-85; dir. pharmacy Tomah Meml. Hosp., Wis., 1985-86; pharmacy cons. Tomah Care Ctr., 1985-86; mgr. pharmacy computer ops. St. Nicholas Hosp., Sheboygan, Wis., 1986—; fin. cons. Methodist chs. Mem. AAUW, Am. Soc. Hosp. Pharmacists (region sec. 1975), Nat. Assn. Future Women (photographer 1984), Nat. Assn. Female Execs., Phi Kappa Phi, Rho Chi. Methodist. Avocations: nature photography; needlecraft; cross-country skiing; bicycling; personal computers. Home: 1628 N 28th St Sheboygan WI 53081 Office: St Nicholas Hosp Sheboygan WI 53081

PARKS, LLOYD LEE, oil company executive; b. Kiefer, Okla., Dec. 9, 1929; s. Homer Harrison and Avis Pearl (Motes) P.; m. Mary Ellen Scott, Aug. 20, 1948; children: Connie Jo, Karyn Ann, Rebecca Lee. Student, Okla. State U., 1948-50, Tulsa U., 1950-51, Harvard U. Bus. Sch., 1965. Acct. Deep Rock Oil Corp., 1951-54; chief acct. Blackwell Oil & Gas Co., Tulsa, 1954-60; sec. treas. Blackwell Oil & Gas Co., 1960-62; v.p., controller Amax Petroleum Corp., Houston, 1962-67; pres. Amax Petroleum Corp., 1968—; v.p. Amax, Inc., 1975—; dir. First Interstate Bank, Meml. Br. Served with AUS, 1946-48, 50-51. Mem. Ind. Petroleum Assn. Am. (dir.), Am. Petroleum Inst. Republican. Club: Lakeside Country. Office: 1300 W Belt S Houston TX 77042

PARKS, MARY IRENE, bookseller, antiques dealer; b. Asheboro, N.C., Apr. 19, 1919; d. Carl Clifton and Revella Rose (Strickland) Rollins; m. Albert Lee Parks, July 3, 1938; children—Albert Lee, Jr. (dec.), Rachel Yvonne White, Teresa Diana Cooper, Candace Susan Kirk, James Michael, Cynthia Revella Whitley. Bookseller Grandpa's House, Troy, N.C., 1963—. Baptist. Office: Grandpa's House Hwy 27 Rt 3 Box 292 Troy NC 27371

PARKS, MICHAEL, journalist; b. Detroit, Nov. 17, 1943; s. Robert James and Rosalind (Smith) P.; m. Linda Katherine Durocher, Dec. 26, 1964; children: Danielle Anne, Christopher, Matthew. AB, U. Windsor, Ont., Can., 1965. Reporter Detroit News, 1962-65; corr. Time-Life News Service, N.Y.C., 1965-66; asst. city editor Suffolk Sun, Long Island, N.Y., 1966-68; polit. reporter, foreign corr. The Balt. Sun, Saigon, Singapore, Moscow, Cairo, Hong Kong, Peking, 1968-80; foreign corr. Los Angeles Times, Los Angeles, Peking, Johannesburg, Moscow, 1980—. Recipient Pulitzer Prize, 1987. Club: Foreign Corr. (Hong Kong). Home: Sadova-Samotechnaya 12/24, Kv 37, Moscow USSR Office: Los Angeles Times Times Mirror Sq Los Angeles CA 90053

PARKS, RICHARD DEE, theater director; b. Omaha, Aug. 29, 1938; s. Charles and Josephine Marie-Rose P. B.A., San Jose State U., 1961; M.A., U. Wash., 1963; postgrad. Stanford U. Tchr. San Jose State U., 1964-65; tchr. oral interpretation Stanford U., 1965-66; tchr. San Jose State U., 1966-71, B.F.A. program U. Wash., 1971-72; dir. theatre San Jose State U., 1972-79, coordinator performance area, 1979—, coordinator auditions, 1975—, chmn. performance area, coordinator M.F.A. performance degree program, 1983—; exchange prof. Ventura Coll., spring 1982; exec. dir. Actors Symposium of Hollywood; actor, dir., producer; sr. producer Star Weekend projects NBC, 1978—; cons. profl. and community theatre orgns.; interim coordinator theatre arts grad. program, 1977-78; producer, dir., dialects coach San Jose Civic Light Opera; research cons. Ednl. Films of Hollywood; cons. Monterey Peninsula's 4th St. Playhouse; cons., dir. Gen. Electric Sales Conf., Pajaro Dunes, 1983, Lockheed Missles and Space Co., 1987—; mem. adv. council sta. KRON-TV, San Francisco. Winner New Play Directing award Am. Coll. Theatre Festival Region I, 1975. Mem. Calif. Ednl. Theatre Assn. (exec. sec.-treas. 1978-80), AAUP, Calif. Assn. Am. Conservatory Theatre, Am. Coll. Theatre Festival, Am. Film Inst., Dramatists Guild, Authors League Am., Women's History Resources, Nat. Women's History Project. Episcopalian. Clubs: Brit. Am., San Jose Players. Author: How to Overcome Stage Fright, 1978; American Drama Anthology, 1979; (plays) Charley Parkhurst Rides Again!, 1978, Wild West Women, 1980, Ken Kesey's Further Inquiry, 1980; (book) Career Preparation for the TV-Film Actor, 1981; (play) stage adaptation of Tandem Prodns. Facts of Life, 1982; (teaching supplement) Calendar of American Theatre History, 1982; The Role of Myth in Understanding Amber in the Ancient World, 1983; (textbook) Oral Expression, 1985, 2d. rev. edit., 1986. Office: San Jose State U Theater Arts Dept San Jose CA 95192

PARKS, SUZANNE LOWRY, psychiatric nurse, educator; b. Columbus, Ohio, Feb. 29, 1936; d. Frank Carson and Mabel (Brown) Lowry Morris; BS, Emory U., 1958; MS, U. Md., 1959; postgrad. U. Hawaii, 1983-85, Columbia Pacific U., 1981-83, 86—; children: Jennifer, Kristin, Greg. Asst. prof. psychiat. nursing U. Va., 1959-61, U. N.C., Chapel Hill, 1961-63, grad. faculty, 1975-81; asst. prof., dir. div. psychiat. nursing Duke U., 1964-67; clin. instr. psychiatry Sch. Medicine, Emory U., Atlanta, 1968-71; asst. prof., nursing coordinator Appalachian Area Nursing Inservice project Clemson (S.C.) U., 1973-75; clin. staff Northside Mental Health Center, 1975-81; dir. staff devel. Hawaii State Hosp., Kaneohe, 1981-83; nurse Lainolu Retirement Center, Wakakii, 1983-85; asst. prof. Hawaii Loa Coll., Kaneohe, 1985-88; nurse Chem. Dependancy sect., Charter Winds Hosp., Athens, Ga., 1988—; owner Suzanne's Selections 1988—. Mem. Am.-Hawaii nurses assns., Am. Guild of Hypnotherapists, Assn. Research and Enlightenment, Friends and Families of Schizophrenics, Mental Health Assn. Home: care Fred or Sally Westmoreland Route #1 P O Box 470 Clermont GA 30527

PARLINDUNGAN, BADURAMAN DORPI, engineering and construction executive; b. Bandung, West Java, Indonesia, Sept. 1, 1952; s. Manggaradja Onggang and Supadminah (Tjokronegoro) P.; m. Amaryllis Irina, Jan. 22, 1956; 1 child, Nonggol Suti Darapati. BA, Coll. of Ins., N.Y.C., 1973; MBA, NYU, 1975. Mgmt. trainee Philip Morris Internat., Inc., N.Y.C., 1976; personal accident mgr. Am. Internat. Assurance, Jakarta, Indonesia, 1977; asst. dir. fin. P.T. Kiagoos, Jakarta, 1978; asst. dir. underwriting P.T. Asuransi Timur Jauh, Jakarta, 1978; exec. dir. P.T. Pelita Wijaya Kerta, Jakarta, 1978-82; co. sec. P.T. Inti Karya Persada Tehnik, Jakarta, 1982-83, gen. coordinator, 1983-85, asst. dir. services, 1986—; bd. dirs., cons. P.T. Prima Bencana, Jakarta, 1982—, P.T. Bina Analisindo Semesta, Jakarta, 1984-87, P.T. Sumber Cipta Lestari, 1985—. Mem. Indonesian Weightlifting and Bodybuilding Fedn. (gen. sec. 1986), Asian Bodybuilding Fedn. (rules com. 1986). Home: Jl Lebak Bulus II/58, Cilandak Jakarta, Indonesia 12430 Office: PT Inti Karya Persada Tehnik, Jl Bendungan Hilir Raya #50, Jakarta Indonesia

PARMER, DAN GERALD, veterinarian; b. Wetumpka, Ala., July 3, 1926; s. James Lonnie and Virginia Gertrude (Guy) P.; student Los Angeles City Coll., 1945-46; D.V.M., Auburn U., 1950; m. Donna Louise Kesler, June 7, 1980; 1 son, Dan Gerald; 1 dau. by previous marriage, Linda Leigh. Gen. practice vet. medicine, Galveston, Tex., 1950-54, Chgo., 59—; vet. in charge Chgo. Commn. Animal Care and Control, 1974—; chmn. Ill. Impaired Vets. Com.; tchr. Highlands U., 1959. Served with USNR, 1943-45, PTO; served as staff vet. and 2d and 5th Air Force vet. chief USAF, 1954-59. Decorated 9 Battle Stars; recipient Vet. Appreciation award U. Ill., 1971, Commendation, Chgo. Commn. Animal Care and Control, 1987. Mem. Ill. Vet. Medicine Assn. (chmn. civil def. and package disaster hosps. 1968-71, Pres.' award 1986), Chgo. Vet. Medicine Assn. (bd. govs. 1969-72, 74-13, pres. 1982), South Chgo. Vet. Medicine Assn. (pres. 1965-66), Am. Animal Hosp. Assn. (dir.), AVMA (nat. com. for impaired vets.), Ill. Acad. Vet. Practice, Nat. Assn. of Professions, Am. Assn. Zoo Vets., Am. Assn. Zool. Parks and Aquariums, VFW. Democrat. Clubs: Midlothian Country, Valley Internat. Country. Lodges: Masons, Shriners, Kiwanis. Discoverer Bartonellosis in cattle in N.Am. and Western Hemisphere, 1951; co-developer bite-size high altitude in-flight feeding program USAF, 1954-56. Address: 4350 W Ford City Dr Apt 402 Chicago IL 60652

PARMLEY, LOREN FRANCIS, JR., medical educator; b. El Paso, Tex., Sept. 19, 1921; s. Loren Francis and Hope (Bartholomew) P.; m. Dorothy Louise Turner, Apr. 4, 1942; children—Richard Turner, Robert James, Kathryn Louise. B.A., U. Va., 1941, M.D., 1943. Diplomate Am. Bd. Internal Medicine, Am. Bd. Internal Medicine-Cardiovascular Disease. Commd. 1st lt. U.S. Army, 1944; advanced through grades to col. 1968; intern Med. Coll. Va., 1944; resident in internal medicine Brooke Gen. Hosp., San Antonio, 1948-49, U. Wis. Gen. Hosp., Madison, 1949-51; asst. prof. mil. med. sci. Med. Coll. U. Wis., Madison, 1949-51; asst. attache (med.) U.S. Embassy, New Delhi, 1953-55; fellow in cardiovascular disease Water Reed Gen. Hosp., Washington, 1956-57; chief medicine and cardiology Letterman Gen. Hosp., San Francisco, 1958-63; med. and cardiology cons. U.S. Army Europe, Heidelberg, Germany, 1963-64; chief medicine Walter Reed Gen. Hosp., Washington, 1965-68; prof. medicine, asst. dean Med. U. S.C., Spartanburg, 1968-75; dir. med. edn. Spartanburg Gen. Hosp., Spartanburg, 1968-75; prof. medicine U. South Ala., Mobile, 1975-87, chief div. cardiology, 1980-87, prof. emeritus medicine, 1988—; lectr. medicine U. Calif.-San Francisco, 1959-63; clin. assoc. prof. medicine Georgetown U., Washington, 1967-68; clin. prof. medicine Med. Coll. Ga., Augusta, 1969-75; cons. internal medicine Surgeon Gen. U.S. Army, Washington, 1966-68. Contbg. author: The Heart, 1966, 70, 74, 78 Cardiac Diagnosis and Treatment, 1976, 80, The Heart in Industry, 1970, 60. Recipient Gold award sci. exhibit Am. Soc. Clin. Pathologists and Coll. Am. Pathologists, 1959; Certificate of Achievement in cardio-vascular disease Surgeon Gen. U.S.A., Washington, 1962; Bronze Medallion Meritorious Service, Am. Heart Assn., S.C., Columbia, 1969, 73; decorated Legion of Merit. Fellow Coll. Cardiology (gov. U.S. Army, 1967, gov. S.C. 1969-73), ACP, Am. Heart Assn. (council clin. cardiology), Am. Coll. Chest Physicians; mem. Soc. Med. Cons. Armed Forces. Republican. Episcopalian. Home: 5862 Falls Church Rd Mobile AL 36608 Office: U South Ala Coll Medicine Dept Medicine 2451 Fillingim St Mastin Bldg Mobile AL 36617

PARMLEY, ROBERT JAMES, lawyer, consultant; b. Madison, Wis., Oct. 23, 1950; s. Loren Francis and Dorothy Louise (Turner) P.; m. Debra Paliszewski, Dec. 23, 1982; 1 child, Michelle Hope. B.A., U. Va., 1972; J.D., U. S.C., 1975. Bar: S.C. 1975, Tex. 1976, U.S. Dist. Ct. (so. dist.) Tex. 1976, U.S. Tax Ct. 1976, U.S. Ct. Appeals (5th cir.) 1978, U.S. Dist. Ct. (we. and no. dists.) Tex. 1980, U.S. Supreme Ct. 1980. Staff atty., VISTA vol., Tex. Rural Legal Aid, Inc., Alice, 1975-76, mng. atty., Kingsville, 1976-79, sr. staff atty., Kerrville, 1979-81; cons. atty.; sole practice, Kerrville, 1981—. Mem. State Bar Tex., State Bar S.C., Kerr County Bar Assn. Episcopalian. Office: 222 Sidney Baker S Suite 615 Kerrville TX 78028

PARODI, ALAIN ANDRÉ ALEXANDRE, advertising company executive; b. Paris, Nov. 2, 1943; s. Andre Alexandre and Helene Simone (Niclot) P.; m. Mylene Tong; children: Maxime, Thomas. Ingenieur, Ecole Cen., Paris, 1968; licence, Scis. Economiques, Paris, 1970. Cons. Sema, Paris, 1970-72; mgr. research and devel. Interdeco, Paris, 1972-82; chief exec. Idemedia., Neuilly-sur-Seine, France, 1982—; v.p. Credome, Neuilly-sur-Seine, 1984—; mem. council Inst. Recherches, Paris, 1985—; prof. Ecole Superieure Commerce, Reims, 1984—, celsa, Neuilly-sur-Seine, 1985—, Ecole Superieure Publicite, Paris, 1983—. Home: 82 Blvd Raymond-Poincare, 92380 Garches France Office: Idemia, Credome 41 rue Ybry, 92200 Neuilly sur Seine France

PARODI, LUIS, vice president Ecuador. V.p. Ecuador, Quito, 1988—. Address: Office Vice Pres, Quito Ecuador *

PARODI, MARCEL, public administrator; b. Paris, Aug. 5, 1916; s. Hippolyte and Aimee (Lombard) P.; LL.D., Lycée Buffon; diploma Ecole Libre des Sciences Politiques, 1937; Docteur en droit, 1941; m. Raymonde Cantrainne, Mar. 25, 1941; children: Paul Cecile. Civil adminstr. then insp. Industry and Commerce, Ministry Industry, Commerce and Handicrafts, 1952; reporter GATT internat. conf., 1953, Second Modernization and Supply Plan, 1953-54; head dept. Fin. and Regional Econ. Expansion, 1954-60; tech. adv. Ministry deptl. staff, 1958, 63-66; head French del. Intergovtl. Conf. for Conversion of Regions affected by Coal Mine Closings, Luxembourg, 1960; insp. gen. Industry and Commerce, 1963; head Dept. Gen. Affairs, 1967-70; dir. chambers of Commerce, Industry, Handicrafts and Indsl. Property, 1967-70; dir. Gen. Adminstrn., Budget and Claims, 1970-77; pres. Coal Imports Tech. Assn., 1977-84, Agy. for Studies and Further Tng. in Trades and Crafts, 1980—; numerous career related activities including adminstr. pension plan for engrs. and exec. staff; prof. Inst. Applied Law. Served in French Army, 1938-40. Recipient Croix de guerre (2), medaille des blessé s militaires; officer, Légion d'Honneur, comdr. Merite Nat., officer Merite Comml. et Industriel. Roman Catholic. Author various articles in field. Home: 29 Jasmin, 75016 Paris France Office: 21 Mathurin Régnier, Paris France

PAROLA, PIER LUIGI, industrial executive; b. Rome, June 26, 1936; s. Mario and Ilde (Gambetti) P.; m. Elena Pajan, Jan. 18, 1975. Degree in elec. engring., U. Genova, Italy, 1964. Tech. cons. Genova, 1960-65; design engr. div. engring. U.S. Army, Livorno, Italy, 1965; mgr. design engring. R.F. Generators Lab., Fiar Electronic div. CGE S.p.A., Milan, Italy, 1965-67, mgr. advanced def. program mktg., 1971-74, mgr. TCL program sector, 1974-76, mgr. def. system ops., 1976-78; mgr. electronic div. Ducati S.p.A., Zanussi Group, Bologna, Italy, 1978-80; comml. dir. TLC div. AEG-Telekunken Italiana S.p.A., Milan, 1980-82; gen. mgr. Compagnia Generale di Elettricità, S.p.A., Milan, 1982—. Patentee in field. Named Knight of Order of Knights Holy Sepulcre Jerusalem, 1986. Home: via Giotto 3, 20145 Milan Italy

PARONT, GEORGE JOHN, clergyman, institute administrator; b. Flushing, N.Y., Feb. 28, 1943; s. George Henry and Harriet Ann (Warner) P. BA in Scholastic Philosophy, Sacred Theology, St. Mary's U., 1967, MA in Sacred Theology, 1968; postgrad. St. John's U., 1971; cert. human resources devel., Cornell U., 1985. Ordained priest Roman Cath. Ch., 1977; awarded canonical mission Archdiocese San Antonio, 1967. Chmn. dept. sci. Cath. Youth Orgn., Diocese Bklyn, Cresthaven, N.Y., 1959-71; instr. theology Incarnate Word Acad., San Antonio, 1967-68; tchr. Holy Cross High Sch., San Antonio, 1968-69; asst. pastor St. Gregory's Ch., Ronkonkoma, N.Y., 1977-78; pastor St. John the Evangelist Ch., Brookhaven, N.Y., 1978—; dir. Inst. Roman Cath. Studies, Brookhaven, 1978—; mem. nat. adv. bd. Am. Christian Coll., Tulsa, 1973. Author: Experiments in Electricity, 1962, Experiments in Light, 1962, The Invalidity of the Thuc Consecrations, 1988; editor: The Armorer, 1972-74, The Guardsman, 1972-74; contbr. articles to profl. jours. Sustaining mem. Rep. Nat. Com., 1974—; treas. local 253 AFL-CIO AFSCME, 1971-75, pres. CSEA local 1000-253, 1980—; mem. labor mgmt. coms. N.Y. State Gov's. Office Employee Relations, 1987-88. Served with N.Y.G., 1971-83. Mem. Found. for Christian Theology, Queens Inst. Anthropology, Archaeol. Inst. Am., Am. Bible Soc., Epsilon Delta Chi. Republican. Lodge: K.C. Avocations: biblical archaeology, numismatics, public speaking.

PARR, ALBERT F. W., systems scientist; b. Tauberbischofsheim, Germany, Jan. 9, 1923; s. Ferdinand Franz and Hildegard Marie (Hessler) P.; came to U.S., 1926, naturalized, 1932; B.S. in Electronics, CUNY, 1943; certificate display engring. Harvard U., 1944; M.S., Mass. Inst. Tech., 1951; certificate space optics U. Calif. at Los Angeles, 1962; certificate ednl. tech., U. Calif. at Berkeley, 1974; certificate in advanced radiation physics U. Conn., 1986; m. Dorothy Adele Hennesey, June 12, 1948; children—Stephen Joseph, Virginia Katherine, Andrew Albert, William Raymond. Project engr. Instrumentation Lab., Mass. Inst. Tech., Cambridge, 1946-52; program mgr. combined systems Gen. Precision Lab., Pleasantville, N.Y., 1952-55; head systems dept. Norden div. United Techs. Co., Norwalk, Conn., 1955-58; dir., v.p., mgr. engring. Powertronics, Inc., New Rochelle, N.Y., 1958-61; div. mgr. control instrument prodn., mktg. mgr. Farrand Optical Co., Valhalla, N.Y., 1961-85; sr. systems mgr. Norden Systems, United Techs. Co., Norwalk, Conn., 1985—. Served from 2d. lt. to 1st. lt., tech. intelligence, U.S. Army, 1943-46; ETO. Mem. Instrument Soc. Am., IEEE, Soc. Motion Picture and TV Engrs., Assn. Edn. and Communication Tech. div. NEA, Sigma Xi. K.C. Patentee in field. Home: Beech Pl Pine Knolls Valhalla NY 10595 Office: Norden Systems Norden Pl Norwalk CT 06856

PARR, DORIS ANN, financial institution executive, consultant; b. Fergus Falls, Minn., July 10, 1933; d. Henry Fritzolf and Esther Marie (Ahlgren) Peterson; m. Mark Hoffman, 1949 (div. 1960); children: Cynthia Lee Davis, David Alan; m. Harold R. Parr, 1961 (div. 1974). Student Am. Savs. and Loan Inst., 1965-66, Pioneer Nat. Title Ins. Co., 1969, Menlo Coll., 1975. Comml. loan officer Savbank Service Corp., Seattle, 1975-77; exec. v.p., mgr. Sound Savs. & Loan, Seattle, 1976-78; v.p. Queen City Savs. & Loan, Seattle, 1978-82; v.p., mgr. State Savs. & Loan Assn., Dallas, 1983-84; pres. Nat. Real Estate Mortgage Services Inc., Dallas, 1984—; instr. real estate law San Francisco City Coll., 1975. Recipient 1st Pl. Speech trophy Am. Savs. & Loan Inst., 1964. Mem. Assn. Profl. Mortgage Women (program chmn. Seattle chpt. 1969-70, program chmn. San Jose chpt. 1973-74, pres. 1975-76, Woman of Yr. 1979), U.S. Savs. and Loan League (consumer affairs and secondary market com.), Nat. Assn. Females Execs., Fed. Home Loan Bank Bd. (maj. comml. loan underwriter). Organized and managed 1st U.S. minority savs. and loan assn. Home: 5767 Caruth Haven Ln Dallas TX 75206

PARR, EUGENE QUINCY, orthopaedic surgeon; b. Erlanger, Ky., Aug. 4, 1925; s. Benjamin Franklin and Sallie Frances (Wright) P.; m. Joan Lykins, June 9, 1951; children—Eugene Quincy Jr., Jeffrey Wright, Valerie. Student Berea Coll., Ky., 1944-45, 46-48; M.D., U. Louisville, 1952; fellow Mayo Grad. Sch. Medicine, 1956-60. Diplomate Am. Bd. Orthopaedic Surgery. Intern Baroness Erlanger Hosp., Chattanooga, 1952-53; resident in orthopaedic surgery Mayo Clinic, Rochester, Minn., 1956-60; practice medicine specializing in orthopaedic surgery, Lexington, Ky., since 1960—; adminstrv. trustee Central Baptist Hosp., Lexington, 1975-84. Trustee Berea Coll., 1966-72. Fellow Am. Acad. Orthopaedic Surgeons; mem. Doctors Mayo Soc. (founding), Orthopaedic Research and Ednl. Found., Lexington Orthopaedic Soc. (pres. 1964-66), Ky. Orthopaedic Soc. (pres. 1986), Phi Kappa Phi. Avocation: thoroughbred horse breeding and development. Home: Foxtale Farm 1825 Keene Rd Nicholasville KY 40356 Office: 2368 Nicholasville Rd Lexington KY 40503

PARR, JACK RAMSEY, judge; b. Dallas, May 10, 1926; s. Richard Arnold and Mary Lillian (Ramsey) P.; m. Martha Suttle, July 2, 1955; children—Richard Arnold II, Beverly Ann, Geoffrey Alan. B.A., U. Okla., 1949, L.L.B., 1950, J.D., 1970; grad. Nat. Jud. Coll., 1966, Am. Acad. Jud. Edn., 1979, JAG Sch., U.S. Army, 1981. Cert. mil. judge. Bar: Okla. 1950, U.S. Ct. Mil. Appeals 1955, U.S. Supreme Ct. 1955. Sole practice, Edmond, Okla., 1953-58; asst. U.S. atty. Western Dist. Okla., 1958-65; judge 7th Jud. Dist. Okla., 1965—, presiding judge, 1980; vice presiding judge appellate div. Court on the Judiciary; chmn. Okla. Supreme Ct. Commn. Uniform Civil Jury Instrns.; mem. Uniform Criminal Jury Instrn. Commn.; asso. prof. law Oklahoma City U., 1966-67. Served to capt. JAGC, USNR, 1944-46, 51-53; Korea; mem. Naval Res. Trial Judiciary Unit 107, 1980-85. Mem. Okla. Bar Assn. (Outstanding Com. Service award 1969), Oklahoma County Bar Assn. (cert. of merit 1971, Outstanding Service award 1977-78), ABA, Jud. Conf. Okla., Am. Judicature Soc., Navy-Marine Res. Lawyers Assn., Judge Advs. Assn. U.S., Am. Legion, Mil. Order World Wars, Res. Officers Assn. U.S., Ret. Officers Assn., Naval Res. Assn., Delta Theta Phi. Clubs: Masons, Elks. Home: 2601 NW 55th Pl Oklahoma City OK 73112 Office: 706 County Courthouse 321 Park Ave Oklahoma City OK 73102-3603

PARR, JOHN BRIAN, economist, educator; b. Epsom, England, Mar. 18, 1941; s. Jack Maynard and Lilian May (Ball) P.; m. Pamela Jean Harkins, Dec. 11, 1964; children: Sheila Jean, Anne Fiona. BS in Econs., U. London, 1962; PhD, U. Wash., 1967; MA, U. Pa., 1973. Instr. U. Wash., Seattle, 1966; asst. prof. U. Pa., Phila., 1967-72, assoc. prof. regional sci., 1972-75; lectr. U. Glasgow, Scotland, 1975-77, sr. lectr., 1977-80, reader, 1980—, mem. bd. mgmt. Urban Studies jour., 1981—; instr. Advanced Studies Insts., NATO, Fed. Republic of Germany, The Netherlands, 1972, 78, 81; lectr. Polish Acad. Scis., Warsaw, 1977. Author: (with N. Alao) Christaller Central Place Structures, 1977, (with B. Berry) Market Centers and Retail Location, 1988; editor: (with R. Funck) The Analysis of Regional Structure, 1978, (with D. Maclennan) Regional Policy: Past Experience and New Directions, 1979; assoc. editor: Regional Sci. Research Inst. Jour., 1978—; contbr. articles to profl. jours. Mem. com. Scottish War on Want, Glasgow, 1978-85. Recipient Spl. Visitor award Brit. Council, 1986. Mem. Internat. Regional Sci. Assn. (editor jour. 1968-75, councillor 1978-79, v.p. 1979-80), Brit. Regional Sci. Assn. (chmn. 1981-85), Royal Econ. Soc., Scottish Econ. Soc., Inst. Brit. Geographers. Home: 8 Queen's Gardens, Glasgow G12 9DG, Scotland Office: U Glasgow, Dept Social and Econ Research, Glasgow G12 8RT, Scotland

PARR, ROYSE MILTON, lawyer; b. Elk City, Okla., Sept. 11, 1935; s. Clinton Riley and Ruth Caroline (Royse) P.; m. Sheila Ann Harshaw, May 28, 1960; children: Clint Howard, Reagan Royse. B.S., Okla. State U., 1958; J.D., U. Tulsa, 1964. Bar: Okla. 1964. Research scout Jersey Prodn. Research Co., Tulsa, 1960-64; atty. Sun Oil Co., 1964-70, White Shield Corp., 1970-71; sec., atty., asst. gen. counsel MAPCO, Inc., Tulsa, 1971—; lectr. Southwestern Legal Found., 1977. Vice chmn. Tulsa County Election Bd., 1973—; pres. Ret. Sr. Vol. Program, 1982-83. Served to 1st lt. U.S. Army, 1958-60; capt. Res. 1960-63. Mem. Am. Bar Assn., ASME, Soc. Petroleum Engrs., Okla. Bar Assn., Tulsa County Bar Assn., Am. Soc. Corp. Secs. (pres. Okla. chpt. 1983-84), Phi Delta Phi. Republican. Methodist. Clubs: Oaks Country, Kiwanis (Tulsa). Office: Mapco Inc 1800 S Baltimore Ave Tulsa OK 74119

PARRA-MEJIA, TULIO E., surgeon; b. Pamplona, Colombia, Aug. 27, 1950; s. Jose D. and Florentina (Mejia) P. B.S., Colegio Carmelitano, Pamplona, 1968; M.D., U. Nacional de Colombia, Bogota, 1976. Cert. cardiovascular and thoracic surgeon Colombia. Intern and resident U. Nacional, Bogota, 1979-82; surgeon Hosp. Regional, Villavicencio, Colombia, 1982-83, chmn. dept. surgery, Duitama, Colombia, 1983-84; mem. dept. thoracic and cardiovascular surgery Hosp. Militar Central, Bogota, 1985—; dir. intern program Villavicencio, 1982-83. Contbr. articles to profl. jours. Mem.

Sociedad Colombiana de Cirugia, Asociacion de Antiguos Alumnos de Medicina U. Nacional, Soc. Internationale de Chirurgie, Sociedad Colombiana de Cardiologia, N.Y. Acad. Scis. Home: Apartado Aereo, 42813 Bogota Colombia

PARREIRA, HELIO CORREA, chemist; b. Rio de Janeiro, Brazil, July 12, 1926, came to U.S., 1960, s. Francisco Correa and Maria Faria Parreira; m. Dulcinea M. Moreira, Feb. 1, 1953; children—Rogerio M., Regina M. B.S. in Chemistry, U. Brazil, Rio de Janeiro, 1949, tchrs. diploma, 1950; Ph.D., U. Cambridge, 1958. Asst. prof. U. Rio de Janeiro, 1950-52; phys. chemist Brazilian Atomic Commn., 1958-67, research assoc. Columbia U., N.Y.C., 1960-62, dir. instrn. in chemistry Joint Program for Tech. Edn., 1960-64, asst. prof., 1963-65; group leader and prin. scientist Inmont Corp., Clifton, N.J., 1965-69; asst. dir. research Johnson & Johnson, Brazil, 1969-70, exec. dir. research, 1970-72, sr. research assoc., New Brunswick, N.J., 1972-84, sr. scientist, 1984—. Contbr. articles to profl. jours. Contbg. editor Chemistry A to Z, 1964. Brit. Council scholar Rio de Janeiro, 1954; Oliver Gatty Scholar U. Cambridge, 1956-58. Mem. Am. Chem. Soc., Sigma Xi. Current work: Electrokinetics; surface phenomena in general; transcutaneous drug delivery. Subspecialties: Surface chemistry; Physical chemistry.

PARRIS, PAUL MARTIN, sales executive; b. Nottingham, Eng., Oct. 9, 1951; s. Peter Albert and Audrey (Hatto) P.; m. Angela Mary Downs; children: Ruth Elizabeth, David Sinclair. Higher Nat. Cert. in civil engring., Trent Poly., Nottingham, 1974. Officer cadet B.P. Tanker Co. Ltd., London, 1969-71; design technician Nottingham City Engrs., 1971-73; engr. traffic Nottingham County Council, 1973-79; sales exec. Mills Assocs. Ltd., Monmouth, Wales, 1979-84; sales exec. Peterborough Software (U.K.) Ltd., Eng., 1984-88, sales mgr. IBM products, 1988—; Chmn. Nottingham Round Table, 1983-84. Mem. Conservative Party. Home: 15 East End, Langtoft, Peterborough PE6 9LP, England

PARRISH, FRANK JENNINGS, frozen foods company executive; b. Manassas, Va., Dec. 29, 1923; s. Edgar Goodloe and Alverda (Jennings) P.; m. Lorene Lomax, Feb. 11, 1944 (div. Apr. 1984); children: Edgar Lee, Julia Lorene; m. Mary Jane Biser, Aug. 25, 1984. Student, Va. Poly. Inst., 1942-43. Pres. Manassas Frozen Foods, Inc., 1946—; pres., mgr. Certified Food Buyers Service, Inc., 1953—; pres. First Nat. Acceptance Co., 1966—; v.p. Manassas Ice & Fuel Co. Mem. bus. adminstrn. adv. com. No. Va. Community Coll. Served to maj. USAAF, 1943-46, CBI; ret. brig. gen. Res. comdr. 909th TAC Airlift Group 1969-73; moblzn. asst. DCS plans and ops. Hdqrs. USAF, 1973-79. Decorated Legion of Merit, Air medal. Mem. Nat. Inst. Locker and Freezer Provisioners Am. (past pres., Industry Leadership award 1968), Va. Frozen Foods Assn. (past pres., dir.), Hump Pilots Assn., Va. Assn. Meat Packers (pres. 1986—), Am. Heat Assn. (chmn. bd. North Va. council 1987-88). Methodist (chmn. bd. trustees 1958-66). Lodges: Kiwanis, Moose. Home: 9107 Park Ave Manassas VA 22110 Office: 9414 Main St Manassas VA 22110

PARRISH, GEORGE R(ODERICK), architectural specifications writer; b. Litchfield, Minn., Apr. 19, 1943; s. Clarence Lestor and Georgia Jane (Fitze) P.; m. Donna Jean Sjogren, June 11, 1966; children: Catherine Jeneen, Robert Thomas, Michelle Marie. Student, U. Minn., 1962-63, Winona State Coll., 1964-66, Roosevelt U., 1982. Cert. constrn. specifier. Archtl. draftsman Setter Leach & Lindstrom, Inc., Mpls., 1966-68, Armstrong, Schlichting, Torseth & Skold, Inc., Mpls., 1968-72; chief specifications writer and archtl. draftsman Chapman Desai Sakata, Inc., Honolulu, 1972-88, sr. assoc., 1983-88; prin. specifications cons. G. Parrish Services, Kailua, Hawaii, 1981—; guest speaker U. Hawaii Sch. Architecture; guest instr. Earle M. Alexander, Ltd. Author/editor (computer program package) Office Cost Control System, 1982, 4th rev. edit., 1984. Mem. New Eng. Hist. Geol. Soc., Internat. Platform Assn., Constrn. Specifications Inst. (v.p. Honolulu chpt. 1985-86, pres. 1986-87, Certificate of Appreciation for Ednl. Service 1979, Certificate of Appreciation 1980, 1981, Pres'. Cert. Appretiation, 1987). Roman Catholic. Home and Office: 647 N Kainalu Dr Kailua HI 96734

PARRISH, OVERTON BURGIN, JR., pharmaceutical corporation executive; b. Cin., May 26, 1933; s. Overton Burgin and Geneva Opal (Shinn) P. B.S., Lawrence U., 1955; M.B.A., U. Chgo., 1959. With Pfizer Internat., 1959-74; pharm. salesman Pfizer Internat., Chgo., 1959-62; asst. mktg. product mgr. Pfizer Internat., N.Y.C., 1962-63; product mgr. Pfizer Internat., 1964-66, group product mgr., 1966-67, mktg. mgr., 1967-68, v.p. mktg., 1969-70, v.p., dir. ops., 1970-71, exec. v.p. domestic pharm. div., 1971-72, exec. v.p., dir. internat. div., 1972-74; pres., chief operating officer G.D. Searle Internat., Skokie, Ill., 1974-75; pres., chief exec. officer G.D. Searle Internat., 1975-77; pres. Worldwide Pharm./Consumer Products Group, 1977-86; pres., chief exec. officer Phoenix Health Care, 1987—. Author: The Future Pharmaceutical Marketing; International Drug Pricing, 1971. Trustee Mktg. Sci. Inst.; trustee Food and Drug Law Inst., 1979—, Lawrence U., 1983—. Served to 1st lt. USAF, 1955-57. Mem. Am. Mktg. Assn., Am. Mgmt. Assn., Beta Gamma Sigma, Phi Kappa Tau. Home: 505 N Lake Shore Dr Chicago IL 60611 Office: Phoenix Health Care 980 N Michigan Ave Chicago IL 60611

PARRISH-HARRA, CAROL WILLIAMS, clergywoman, author, lectr.; b. Nettleton, Ark., Jan. 21, 1935; d. Claremce Elmer and Corinne (Parrott) Williams; m. Charles Clayton Harra, Dec. 2, 1975. Accounts control mgr. Caledesi Nat. Bank, Dunedin, Fla., 1963-66; analysis coordinator Capital Formation Counselor Co., Clearwater, Fla., 1966-71; ordained Spiritual Center St. Petersburg (Fla.), 1971; asso. minister Temple of Living God, St. Petersburg, 1971-75; pres. Fla. Humanistic Inst., St. Petersburg, 1974-75; dir. Villa Serena Spiritual Community, Sarasota, 1976-81; pres. Light of Christ Community Ch., Tahlequah, Okla., 1981—; mem. faculty Internat. Coll. Nat. Health Scis., 1977-82; moderator, speaker Sarasota chpt., NCCJ, 1979-81; workshop leader, lectr. retreats Spiritual Frontiers Fellowship; trustee Nat. Council Community Chs., 1980-84; trustee, Internat. Assn. Near Death Studies, regional trustee Internat. Council of Community Chs. Mem. Am. Bus. Women's Assn., NOW. Democrat. Author: New Age Handbook on Death and Dying, 1982; Messengers of Hope, 1983, The Aquarian Rosary, 1988; contbr. articles to religious jours. Address: PO Box 1274 Tahlequah OK 74465

PARRY, ALBERT, educator, writer, lecturer; b. Rostov on-the-Don, Russia, Feb. 24, 1901; came to U.S., 1921, naturalized, 1926; s. Joseph and Elizabeth (Blass) P.; m. Louise Emily Goodman, Oct. 25, 1941 (div. 1971); children—James Donald, Thomas Hugh. Student, Columbia U., 1925-26; A.B., U. Chgo., 1935, Ph.D., 1938. Newspaper and mag. free-lance writer 1921-37; editor Consol. Book Pubs., Inc., Chgo., 1937-41; asst. div. social scis. U. Chgo., 1939; research dir. radio broadcasts Chgo. Sun, 1941-42; information officer OSS, Washington, 1942-45; exec. bd. Chgo. Council Fgn. Relations, 1943-47; asso. prof. polit. sci. Northwestern U., 1946-47; prof. Russian civilization and lang., chmn. dept. Russian studies Colgate U., 1947-69; dir. Russian Area and Lang. Insts., 1961-66; prof. emeritus; prof. Russian civlization and lang., chmn. Slavic studies Case Western Res. U., 1969-71; program cons. Radio Free Europe, N.Y.C., 1950-52; vis. lectr., cons. U.S. Army War Coll., 1958-72; cons. Spl. Ops. Research Office, Dept. Army, 1960; vis. lectr. Inter-Am. Def. Coll., 1962-68; vis. scholar Radio Liberty, Munich, 1967-68; Exec. officer Com. to Defend Am. by Aiding Allies, 1940-41, Fight for Freedom Com., 1941. Author: Garrets and Pretenders, a history of bohemianism in America, 1933, rev. edit., 1960, Tattoo, 1933, Whistler's Father, 1939, Riddle of the Reich, (with Wythe Williams), 1941, Russian Cavalcade, a military record, 1944, Korea, an annotated bibliography of Russian publications, (with John T. Dorosh and Elizabeth G. Dorosh), 1950, Russia's Rockets and Missiles, 1960, The New Class Divided, Science and Technology Versus Communism, 1966, America Learns Russian, 1967, The Russian Scientist, 1973, Twentieth-Century Russian Literature, (with Harry T. Moore), 1974, Terrorism: From Robespierre to Arafat, 1976; Full Steam Ahead! The Life of Peter Demens, Founder of St. Petersburg, Florida, 1987; column Soviet Affairs in Missiles and Rockets mag, 1957-63; contbr. to Some Historians of Modern Europe, 1942; translator Building Lenin's Russia (Liberman), 1945, The Moscow Puzzles (Kordemsky) 1972; translator, editor Peter Kapitsa on Life and Science, 1968; frequent contbr. to profl. and popular jours. Grantee Am. Council Learned Socs., 1961; Grantee U.S. Office Edn.; Grantee Modern Lang. Assn., 1965-66. Mem. Am. Assn. Tchrs. Slavic and East European Langs. (nat. pres. 1961), Phi Beta Kappa. Address: 6919 Place de la Paix South Pasadena FL 33707

PARRY, JEYMO, psychiatrist; b. La Trinite, Manche, Normandy, France, Oct. 7, 1936; s. Raymond Parry and Mary Laisne; m. Boissieres Boissieres, Aug. 4, 1979; children: Sophia, Cecilia, William, John. PhD, Faculty of Medicine, Paris, 1968. Intern Dijon, France, 1965-68; resident Marcel Riviere Inst., Paris, 1968-70; cons. Hosp. St. Dizier, France, 1972-74, Hosp. Bayeux, France, 1974-76, Hosp. Saintes, France, 1978. Served to lt. French Navy, 1964-65. Mem. French Psychiatrist Assn. Roman Catholic. Home: 9 Quai des Roches, 17100 Saintes Charente 17 France Office: CATAS, 8 Boiffiers St, 17100 Saintes Charente France

PARRY, RANDINE ELIZABETH, psychologist; b. Hartford, Conn., Sept. 6, 1947; d. William Brown and Mary Elizabeth (Caton) P.; m. Stanley A. Cruwys; children—Robert W. Parry-Cruwys, Brendon C. Parry-Cruwys. A.B., Mt. Holyoke Coll., 1968; Ph.D. (USPHS fellow, 1968-72), U. Chgo., 1977. Staff psychologist behavior analysis research lab., dept. psychiatry, U. Chgo., 1971-74, dir. fluency clinic, 1974-77; dir. psychology Walter Fernald State Sch., Waltham, Mass., 1977-80, chief psychologist, 1980—; lic. psychologist SE Counseling Assocs., Norwood, Mass., 1980-82; vis. asst. prof. Northeastern U., Boston, 1977-80; cons. Human Resource Inst. of Franklin, Mass., 1979-81. Contbr. papers to profl. confs. Active NOW, 1974—, chmn. ERA com., Chgo. chpt., 1974-77; mem. Women's Polit. Caucus, 1977—, ACLU, 1978—, Nat. Abortion Rights Action League, 1977—, Friends of Family Planning, 1981—, Belmont Day Sch. Parents Assn., 1984—, Friends of Sturbridge Village, 1981—, N.E. Aquarium, Mus. Fine Arts, Mus. Sci., Boston, 1979—; bd. dirs. Waverley Oaks Child Devel. Center, 1984-86. Mem. Am. Psychol. Assn., Eastern Psychol. Assn., New Eng. Psychol. Assn., Mass. Psychol. Assn., Assn. for Applied Behavior Analysis, Assn. for Advancement of Behavior Therapy, Assn. for Advancement of Psychology, Assn. for Women in Psychology, Boston Behavior Therapy Interest Group. Home: 15 Cherry Oca Ln Framingham MA 01701 Office: Walter Fernald State Sch Dept Psychology 200 Trapelo Rd Waltham MA 02154

PARRY, RAWDON MOIRA CROZIER, advertising executive; b. Phila., Apr. 16, 1949; s. Richard and Nesta Irene (Crozier) P.; m. Emily Loughran Foley, Sept. 30, 1978; children: Thomas Rawdon, Richard Coleman, William Loughran. BA, Harvard U., 1971; MBA, U. Pa., 1974. Asst. to pub. Oil Daily, N.Y.C., 1974-76; asst. to acct. exec. Tatham-Laird and Kudner Advt., Chgo., 1976-77, acct. exec., 1977-80, acct. supr., 1980-83, mgmt. supr., 1983-86, sr. ptnr., 1986—. Chief crusader United Way Crusade of Mercy, Chgo., 1986; nation chief YMCA Indian Guides, Evanston, Ill., 1986; mem. aux. bd. Art Inst. Chgo. Mem. Chgo. Advt. Club. Republican. Episcopalian.

PARRY, ROBERT WALTER, chemistry educator; b. Ogden, Utah, Oct. 1, 1917; s. Walter and Jeanette (Petterson) P.; BS, Utah State Agr. Coll., 1940; MS, Cornell U., 1942; PhD, U. Ill., 1946; D.Sc. (hon.), Utah State U., 1985; m. Marjorie J. Nelson, July 6, 1945; children—Robert Bryce, Mark Nelson. Research asst. NDRC Munitions Devel. Lab., U. Ill. at Urbana, 1943-45, teaching fellow 1943-46; mem. faculty U. Mich., 1946-69, prof. chemistry, 1958-69; Distinguished prof. chemistry U. Utah, 1969—; indsl. cons., 1952—. Chmn. com. teaching chemistry Internat. Union Pure and Applied Chemistry 1968-74. Recipient Mfg. Chemists award for coll. teaching, 1972, Sr. U.S. Scientist award Alexander Von Humboldt-Stiftung (W. Ger.), 1980, First Govs. Medal of Sci. State Utah, 1987. Mem. Am. Chem. Soc. (Utah award Utah Sect. 1978, dir., past chmn. inorganic div. and div. chem. edn. award for distinguished service to inorganic chemistry 1965, for chem. edn., 1977, dir. 1973-82, bd. editors jour. 1969-80, pres.-elect 1981-82, pres. 1982-83), Internat. Union Pure and Applied Chemistry (chmn. U.S. nat. com.), AAAS, Sigma Xi. Founding editor Inorganic Chemistry, 1960-63. Research, pubs. on some structural problems of inorganic chemistry, and incorporation results into theoretical models chemistry, phosphorus, boron and fluorine chemistry. Office: U Utah Dept Chemistry Salt Lake City UT 84112

PARSONS, GAIL, accountant; b. Salt Lake City, Mar. 12, 1946; d. Paul Eugene and Virginia (Jarvis) P.; B.S. in Acctg., U. Utah, 1969; m. Carl Andersen Heyes, July 25, 1975. CPA, Utah. Staff acct. Hansen, Barnett & Maxwell, C.P.A.'s, Salt Lake City, 1969-75; controller Timberhaus Ski Shops, Inc., Park City and Snowbird, Utah, 1975-76; pvt. practice as cert. public accountant, Salt Lake City, 1976—. Mem. Am. Inst. CPA's, Utah Am. Woman's Soc. CPA's, Utah Assn. CPA's, Am. Woman's Soc. CPA's. Home and Office: 5641 Oakdale Dr Salt Lake City UT 84121

PARSONS, LEONA MAE, health services administrator; b. Newark, Ohio, Sept. 13, 1932; d. Enos Andrew and Emma Mae (Simmers) Chew; RN, Andrews U., 1960; BS in Nursing, So. Missionary Coll., 1980; MBA, Rollins Coll., 1986; m. David J. Parsons, June 14, 1953; children—Davona Joy, Cynthia Carol, David J. Operating room supr. Bongo Hosp., Angola, Africa, 1961-68; dir. nurses Bongo Mission Hosp., Angola, 1968-75; nurse in charge refugee camps S. African Govt., Windhoek, S.W. Africa, 1975-76; matron, dir. nurses Windhoek (S.W. Africa) State Hosp., 1976-79; asst. v.p. Fla. Hosp., Orlando, 1980-87; v.p. patient services, Hays Meml. Hosp., San Marcos, Tex., 1987—. Mem. adv. bd. Seminole Community Coll., 1981-87; adv. com. Seminole Community Coll. co-op., Seminole County Child Abuse Prevention. Mem. Assn. Seventh-day Adventist Nurses (bd. dirs. 1981-87), Nat. League Nurses, Fla. League Nurses, Fla. Nurses Assn., Coalition Childbirth Educators (bd. dirs.), Fla. Hosp. Assn., Fla. Orgn. Nurse Execs., Nat. Perinatal Assn., Fla. Perinatal Assn., Loma Linda Med. Soc. Aux., Fla. Med. Soc. Aux., Am. Orgn. Nurse Execs., Tex. Orgn. Nurse Execs., Tex. Nurses Assn., Am. Soc. Psychoprophylaxis in Obstetrics, Fla. Soc. Hosp. Nursing Service Adminstrs., Nat. Assn. Female Execs., S. African Nurses Assn., Orange County Med. Soc. Aux. (bd. dirs.), Am. Med. Assn. Aux., Rollins Coll. Alumni (bd. dirs.)

PARTHENIOS, head of religious order; b. Port-Said, Egypt, Nov. 30, 1919; s. Minas Coinidis and Heleni Lahanas. Degree in theology, Theol. Sch. Halki Constantinople, Istanbul, 1939. Ordained to ministry Greek Orthodox Ch. as deacon, 1939, as priest, 1948. Chief sec., patriarchiel vicar Greek Orthodox Ch., Alexandria, Egypt, 1954-58; bishop Met. of Carthage, Tripoli-Libya-Tunis and Casablanca, 1958-87; patriarch Greek Orthodox Patriarchiate, Cairo and Alexandria, 1987—; rep. World Council Churches; mem. coms. for dialogues Roman Cath.-Mid. East Council Churches. Home: Rue El Attuine 104, PO Box 2006, Alexandria Arab Republic of Egypt

PARTINEN, MARKKU MIKAEL, neurologist; b. Helsinki, Finland, Dec. 4, 1948; s. Vaino and Kerttu Elisabeth (Havunen) P.; m. Ritva Anneli Koponen, Oct. 27, 1984; 1 child, Vaino Eemil. MD, Faculty Medicine, Montpellier, France, 1975; DSc in Medicine, Epidemiology, Faculty Medicine, Helsinki, 1982. Gen practitioner Health Care Ctr., Leppavirta, Finland, 1975-76; asst. physician Clinic Neurophysiology and Medicine, Helsinki, 1975-78; resident in neurology U. Helsinki, 1978-82, asst. dept. pub. health sci., 1980-81, asst. prof. neurology, 1981-83, dir. sleep disorders unit, dept. neurology, 1983-84, staff neurologist, 1987—; dir. Ullanlinna Sleep Disorders Clinic and Research Ctr., Helsinki, 1984—; sr. researcher epidemiology, Inst. Occupational Health, Helsinki, 1983-85; research fellow Sleep Disorders Ctr., Stanford, Calif., 1985-86; vis. lectr. Coll. Nurses, Helsinki, 1979-83; docent U. Helsinki, 1987. Spl. editor Annales Clin. Research (Sleep), 1985; editorial adv. bd. Jour. Sleep, 1986—. Served to sub lt. medicine, Finnish Armed Forces, 1976-77. Sleep and Heart Found. fellow Cardiovascular Research Finland, 1980, internat. research fellow Fogarty Internat. Pub. Health Service-NIH, Stanford, Calif., 1985-86; grantee Paavo Nurmi Found., 1983-84, Miina Sillanpaa Found., 1983-87. Mem. Finnish Neurol. Soc., Finnish Brain Research Soc., Scandinavian Sleep Research Soc. (exec. bd. 1982—, pres. 1988—), European Sleep Research Soc. (sci. com. 1986—), Sleep Research Soc. U.S., Finnish Sleep Research Soc. (pres. 1988—). Evangelist Lutheran. Home: Maistraatinkatu 2 D 27, SF 00240 Helsinki Finland Office: U Helsinki, Dept Neurology Haartmaninkatu 4, SF 00290 Helsinki Finland

PARTNER, PETER DAVID, writer, journalist, educator; b. Little Heath, Herts, Eng., July 15, 1924; s. David and Bertha E. (Partridge) P.; m. Leila May Fadil, Oct. 24, 1953; children: David Michael, Simon Christopher, Sumaya Mary. BA, Oxford U., Eng., 1950, MA, DPhil, 1955. Asst. master Winchester Coll., 1955-86; mem. Inst. Advanced Study Princeton U., N.J., 1976-77. Author: Papal State under Martin V, 1958, Lands of St. Peter, 1972, Renaissance Rome, 1976, Murdered Magicians, 1981, Arab Voices, 1988. Served to lt. Royal Naval Res., 1943-46. Fellow Soc. Antiquaries of London; mem. Soc. Italian Studies. Club: Athenaeum (London). Home: 17 Clausentum Rd, Winchester SO23 9QE, England

PARTON, JAMES, historian; b. Newburyport, Mass., Dec. 10, 1912; s. Hugo and Agnes (Leach) P.; m. Jane Audra Bourne, Dec. 9, 1950 (dec. 1962); children: James III, Dana, Sara. A.B., Harvard U., 1934. Asst. E.L. Bernays, N.Y.C., 1934-35; aviation editor Time Mag., 1935-36, bus. and financial editor, 1937-39, asst. gen. mgr., 1940, bus. mgr. air express edit., 1941; promotion mgr. Time-Life Internat., 1945; editorial dir. Pacific Coast news burs. Time, Inc., 1947; editor and pub. Los Angeles Ind., 1948-49; cons. U.S. Dept. State, 1949; promotion dir. N.Y. Herald Tribune, 1950; asst. to pres., chmn. Herald Tribune Forum and dir. N.Y. Herald Tribune, Inc., 1951-53; v.p., treas. Thorndike, Jensen & Parton, Inc., 1953-57; founder, pres. Am. Heritage Pub. Co., Inc., 1954-70; pres. Ency. Brit. Ednl. Corp., Chgo., 1970-72; chmn. exec. com. Ency. Brit. Ednl. Corp., 1973; pres. James Parton & Co., N.Y.C., 1973-81, Parton Enterprises, Inc., 1981-84; dir. planning study Custom House Inst., N.Y.C., 1973; chmn. Nat. Advt. Rev. Bd., 1974-76; asst. librarian for pub. edn. Library of Congress, 1976-77; chmn. exec. com. Hist. Times, Inc., 1979-81; chmn. U.S. Army com. which produced ofcl. Eighth Air Force book Target-Germany, 1943. Author: "Air Force Spoken Here", General Ira Eaker and the Command of the Air, 1986. Editor, pub. Impact, The Army Air Forces Confidential Picture History of World War II, 8 vols, 1980. Trustee Loomis Inst., 1952—, pres., 1964-66, chmn., 1967-70; trustee USAF Hist. Found. Commd. 2d lt. in USAAF, 1942; and advanced through grades to lt. col. 1944. Decorated Legion of Merit, Bronze Star, European Theater ribbon with 4 battle stars. Clubs: Harvard (N.Y.C.), Century (N.Y.C.); Army and Navy (Washington). Home: PO Box 796 Hanover NH 03755

PARTRIDGE, JOHN ALBERT, architect; b. London, Aug. 26, 1924; s. George and Gladys P.; m. Doris Foreman, 1953; 2 children—. Student Poly. Sch. Architecture, London. With housing architects dept. London County Council, 1951-59; sr. and founding ptnr. Howell, Killick, Partridge & Amis, 1959—; external examiner in architecture U. Bath, 1975-78, Thames Poly., 1978-86, U. Cambridge, 1979-81, U. Manchester, 1982—, South Bank Poly., London, 1981-87. Archtl. works include: Wolfson Rayne and Gatehouse Bldg, St. Anne's Coll., Oxford, New Hall and Common Room, St. Antony's Coll., Oxford, Wells Hall, U. Reading, Middlesex Poly. Coll. Art, Cat Hill, Medway Magistrates Ct., The Albany, Deptford, Hall of Justice, Trinidad and Tobago; contbr. articles to profl. jours. Mem. RIBA (v.p. 1977-79, hon. librarian 1977-81, chmn. archtl. research steering com. 1978—), Concrete Soc. (v.p. 1979-81). Office: Cudham Ct, Cudham near Sevenoaks, Kent TN14 7QF, England *

PARTSCH, KARL JOSEF H., legal educator; b. Freiburg, Germany, June 24, 1914; s. Josef and Ilse E. (Roesler) P.; m. Juliane Bernhardt; 1 child, Susanna. D, U. Freiburg, 1937; assessor, Cologne Ct. Appeals, 1948. Legal adviser bank/machine factory, Berlin, Cologne and Ulm, Germany, 1938-41; constl. analyst Deutscher Städtetag, Cologne, 1948-50; asst. legal adviser Auswäiges Amt, Bonn, Fed. Republic Germany, 1950-54; consul Fed. Republic Germany Naples, Italy, 1955-57; prof. law U. Kiel, Fed. Republic Germany, 1957-60, U. Mainz, Fed. Republic Germany, 1960-66; prof. law U. Bonn, 1966-79, prof. emeritus, 1979—; lectr. law U. Bonn, 1953-57, rector, 1968-69; mem., reporter com. on elimination racial discrimination UN, 1970—; mem. com. on human rights UNESCO, Paris, 1981—. Author: Europ Menschenrechte, 1966, Zoologische Station Neapel, 1980; co-author: Victims of Armed Conflicts, 1982; contbr. articles to profl. jours. Bd. dirs. German Civil Liberties Union, Cologne, 1949-54. Recipient Great Cross Merit, Pres. Fed. Republic Germany, 1984, Peace medal Sec. Gen. UN, 1984. Mem. Deutsche Staatsrechtslehrer, Gesellschaft Für Völkerrecht, Am. Soc. Internat. Law, German Assn. UN. Home: Frankenstrasse 10, D6507 Ingelheim/Rhein Federal Republic of Germany

PARTUM, ANDRZEJ, writer; b. Warsaw, Poland, Dec. 16, 1938; came to Denmark, 1984; s. Henryk and Maria (Mikiewicz) P.; m. Ewa Partum, Feb. 15, 1969; 1 child, Pia. Grad., Music Conservatoire, Warsaw, 1958; D in Art, Music Conservatoire, 1962. Founder Partum Sch. of Positive Nihilism of Art, Copenhagen, 1986—; dir. Office of Poetry and Gallery, PRO/LA, 1971-82; lectr. art theory U. Warsaw, 1972-80. Author: Frequency from the Description, 1961, Osypka woli, 1969, Oxygene of Resources, 1970, Invention of the New Direction in Art-The Art PRO/LA, 1971, The Art PRO/LA, 1973, Rules of the Monidic Art, 1973, Avantgarde Silence, 1975. Roman Catholic. Home: 6/36 Podchorazych, Warsaw Poland Office: Partum Sch Positive, Nihilism of Art, PO Box 2642, 2100 Copenhagen Denmark

PASCO, RICHARD EDWARD, actor; b. Barnes, Eng., July 18, 1926; s. Cecil George and Phyllis (Widdison) P.; m. Greta Watson, 1956 (div. 1964); m. 2d, Barbara Leigh-Junt, 1967; 1 son. Student Colet Ct. and King's Coll. Sch., Wimbledon, Ctr. Sch. Speech and Drama, Bklyn. Acad. Music. First appearance on stage Q Theatre, 1943; actor Old Vic Co., 1950-52, Birmingham Repertory Co., 1952-55; played Fortinbras in Hamlet (Moscow and London), 1955; actor English Stage Co., 1957, played in The Member of the Wedding, Look Back in Anger, The Entertainer, Man from Bellac and The Chairs; roles include: The Entertainer, N.Y.C., 1958, Look Bank in Anger, Moscow, 1959, Teresa of Avila (Dublin Theatre Festival and Vaudeville), 1961, Henry V, Love's Labour's Lost (Bristol Old Vic, Old Vic and tour to Europe), 1964; Hamlet, Bristol Old Vic, 1965, Measure for Measure, Peer Gynt, Man and Superman, Hamlet, 1966; toured U.S. and Europe 1967; joined Royal Shakespeare Co., 1969, roles include: Polixenes in the Winter's Tale, Proteus in The Two Gentlemen of Verona, Buckingham in Henry VIII, 1969, Major Barbara, Richard II, Duchess of Malfi, 1971, Becket in Murder in the Cathedral, Medraut in the Island of the Mighty, 1972, Richard and Bolingbroke in Richard II, 1973-74; The Marrying of Ann Leete, 1975, Jack Tanner in Man and Superman, 1977, Trigorin in The Seagull, 1978, Timon in Timon of Athens, 1980, Clarence in Richard III, 1980, The Forest, 1981, La Ronde, 1982, Six Characters in Search of an Author, 1987, Fathers and Sons, 1987; tours with Royal Shakespeare Co. to Japan, Australia, 1970, Japan, 1972; assoc. artist of Royal Shakespeare Co., Nat. Theatre, 1987—; TV appearances include: Henry Irving, The Three Musketeers, Savages, As You Like It, Julius Caesar, British in Love, Trouble with Gregory, Philby, The House Boy, Number 10-Disraeli, The Plot to Murder Lloyd George, Sorrell and Son, Let's Run Away to Africa, Pythons on the Mountain, Drummonds (2 series); films include: Room at the Top, Yesterday's Enemy, Rasputin, Watcher in the Woods, Wagner, Arch of Triumph, Lady Jane; many recs. of poetry and plays, most recently The Complete Sonnets of Shakespeare, and with Sir John Gielgud and Barbara Leigh-Hunt, A Selection from the Psalms. Recipient C.B.E. (Queen's New Year's Honours, 1977). Office: care Michael Whitehall Ltd, 125 Gloucester Rd, London SW7 4TE England Other: MacNaughton Lowe Represent Ltd, 194 Old Brompton Rd, London SW5 OAS England

PASCOE, JEROME KAY, marketing executive; b. Winnipeg, Man., Can., Dec. 27, 1938; arrived in Belgium, 1977; s. Benjamin Harvey and Betty Constance (Elston) P.; m. Larissa Aisenshtat; children: Jeffrey Ben, Michael Conrad. BA, U. N.D., 1963; BFT, Am. Grad. Sch. Internat. Mgmt., 1965. Regional coordinator Union Carbide Internat., N.Y.C., 1965-68; sr. sales engr. Firestone Internat. Co., Akron, Ohio, 1968-73; sales mgr. Europe Firestone Indsl. Products Co., London, 1973-77; sales dir. Europe Firestone Steel Products Co., Brussels, 1977-81; zone mgr. north cen. states Akron, 1981-83; dir. European sales Teledyne Monarch, Brussels, 1983—. Club: International Chateau Ste. Anne (Brussels). Lodge: Chevalier Ramsay. Home: Av Louis Huysmans 87, 1050 Brussels Belgium Office: Teledyne Belgium SA, 181 Ch De La Hulpe, 1170 Brussels Belgium

PASEK, MICHAEL ANTHONY, computer technologist; b. Duluth, Minn., Sept. 5, 1951; s. Antone William and Helene (Tunsky) P.; m. Robin Carol Solem, Nov. 1, 1986. Grad. coll. operator, bd. pensions, Luth. Ch. in Am., 1973-75; corp. mgr. Microtex Corp., Cloquet, Minn., 1975-79; v.p. internat. ops. Microtex Corp., Mpls., 1979-81, pres., 1981—; systems programmer NCR Comten, Inc., 1977-80, supr./sr. systems programmer, network software devel., 1980-83, chief software engr. switching software devel., 1984-85, lead software engr. switching software devel., 1985-87, cons. software engr. switching softward devel., 1987—; mem. Data Communications Adv. Panel. Mem. Am. Philatelic Soc. Home: 9741 Foley Blvd NW Coon Rapids MN 55433 Office: 2700 N Snelling Roseville MN 55113

PASHA, MANSOOR, sales executive; b. Kanpur, U.P., India, June 19, 1943; arrived in Pakistan, 1950; parents; Iftikhar Ahmed Saghar and Rafiq Bano; m. Rehana Mansoor, Aug. 13, 1966; children: Mohammad Ali, Uzma, Ashar Ali. BA, U. Karachi (Pakistan), 1970. Office mgr. M/S Hydrosealers, Karachi, 1969-73; services coordinator M/S Arab Construct Ltd., Abu Dhabi, United Arab Emirates, 1974-75; mgr. sales M/S Emirates Specialties Co., Abu Dhabi, 1975—. Mem. Inst. Profl. Mgrs. Moslem. Home: PO Box 5245, Abu Dhabi United Arab Emirates Office: Emirates Specialties Co, PO Box 6564, Abu Dhabi United Arab Emirates

PASQUALI, JOHN, financial officer; b. Weehawken, N.J., June 1, 1931; s. Giovanni Battista and Angela (Sommariva) P.; m. Rosetta E. Osellame, Feb. 5, 1955; children—Elizabeth, Mark. B.S. in Acctg., St. Peter's Coll., 1953; M.B.A. in Taxation, NYU, 1963. C.P.A., N.J., N.Y. Sr. tax specialist Price Waterhouse & Co., N.Y.C., 1955-63; sr. v.p. and treas. Young & Rubicam, Inc., N.Y.C., 1963-76; v.p. fin. various advt. agys., N.Y.C., 1976-80; controller Campaign '80, Inc. (advt. agy. Reagan-Bush Com.), 1980-81; controller N.Y. Football Giants, Inc., East Rutherford, N.J., 1981—. Served with U.S. Army, 1953-55. Mem. Am. Inst. C.P.A.s, N.J. Soc. C.P.A.s. Republican. Roman Catholic. Club: Order of Alhambra Zamora. Home: 461 9th St Palisades Park NJ 07650 Office: NY Football Giants Inc Giants Stadium East Rutherford NJ 07073

PASQUALUCCI, FAUSTO, aerospace engineer, consultant; b. Rome, Italy, May 9, 1943; came to U.S., 1977; s. Francesco and Luigia (Renzi) P.; m. Virginia L. Norlund, May 10, 1986. MSc in Electronics Engring., U. of the Witwatersrand, Johannesburg, Republic of South Africa, 1972, PhD in Electronics Engring., 1977. Registered profl. engr., Calif., Fla., Colo. Chief research officer Council Sci. and Indsl. Research Nat. Inst. Telecommunications Research, Johannesburg, 1967-77; vis. scientist Rosenstiel Sch. Marine and Atmospheric Sci. U. Miami, Coral Gables, Fla., 1973-74; postdoctoral research assoc. NRC, Washington, D.C., 1978; research assoc. Coop. Inst. Research in Environ. Scis. U. Colo., Boulder, 1978-80; project mgr. radar meteorology dept. Environ. Research and Wave Propagation labs., divs. of NOAA, Boulder, 1980-84; also cons. Environ. Research and Wave Propogation labs., divs. of NOAA, Boulder; dept. mgr. microwave products div. Hughes Aircraft Co., Torrance, Calif., 1984—; session leader polarization techniques workshop, Miami, Fla., 1980. Contbr. sci. articles to profl. jours. Kans. Fgn. Student scholar Inst. Internat. Edn., 1965. Mem. Am. Meteorol. Soc., IEEE, Am. Geophys. Union, AAAS, N.Y. Acad. Scis., Amici d'Italia (pres. 1983-84). Home: 6407 Ridgebyrne Ct Rancho Palos Verdes CA 90274 Office: Hughes Aircraft Co 3100 Fujita St 245/1420 Torrance CA 90505

PASQUARELLI, JOSEPH J., real estate, engineering and construction executive; b. N.Y.C., Mar. 5, 1927; s. Joseph and Helen (Casabona) P.; B.C.E. cum laude, Manhattan Coll., 1949; m. JoAnne Brienza, June 20, 1964; children—Ronald, Richard, June, Joy. Engr., Madigan-Hyland, N.Y.C. and Burns & Roe Inc., N.Y.C., 1949-56; sr. engr., asst. to exec. dir. Office of Sch. Bldgs., N.Y.C. Bd. Edn., 1956-67; dir. design and constrn. mgmt. City U. N.Y., 1967-72; dir. constrn. mgmt. Morse/Diesel Inc., N.Y.C., 1972-76; dir. projects and proposals Burns & Roe Indsl. Services Corp., Oradell, N.J., 1976-80, dir. facilities and infrastructure, 1980-86; dir. constrn. Xerox Realty Corp., Stamford, Ct., 1986—; instr. Mechs. Inst., N.Y.C. Community Coll. Applied Arts, Sci., 1955-58. Chmn. United Fund R. for Morse/Diesel Inc., 1973-75; mem. Cardinal's Com. of Laity for Roman Catholic Charities of N.Y.C., 1967-77; mem. North Caldwell (N.J.) Skating Pond Com. Served with U.S. Army, 1944-46. Licensed profl. engr., N.Y., N.J. Fellow ASCE; mem. N.Y. Bldg. Congress (past gov., chmn. legis. com.), Nat. Soc. Profl. Engrs., Mcpl. Engrs., Am. Arbitration Assn. (panel of arbitrators), Chi Epsilon. Club: Essex Fells Country. Contbr. articles to profl. jours. Home: 38 Oak Pl North Caldwell NJ 07006 Office: 800 Long Ridge Rd Stamford CT 06904

PASS, CAROLYN JOAN, dermatologist; b. Balt., May 14, 1941; d. Isidore Earl and Rhea (Koplowitz) P.; B.S., U. Md., 1962, M.D., 1966; m. Richard Malcolm Susel, June 23, 1963; children—Steven, Gary. Rotating intern USPHS Hosp., Balt., 1966-67; med. resident St. Agnes Hosp., Balt., 1967-68; dermatology resident and fellow U. Md. Sch. Medicine Hosps., 1968-71; pvt. practice specializing in dermatology, Balt. and Ellicott City, Md., 1971—; mem. staff James Lawrence Kernan, St. Agnes, South Baltimore Gen.; vol. dermatology clinics U. Md., St. Agnes hosps.; asst. clin. prof. dermatology U. Md. Sch. Medicine, 1978—; mem. exec. com. adv. bd. Nat. Program in Dermatology, 1975. Diplomate Am. Bd. Dermatology. Mem. AMA, Med. and Chirurgical Faculty Md., Balt. City Med. Soc. (del. 1974), Am. Women's Med. Assn., Am. Acad. Dermatology (award exhibit 1970), Soc. Investigative Dermatology, Md. Dermatology Soc. (sec.-treas. 1974-76, pres. 1976-77), Soc. Contemporary Medicine and Surgery, U. Md. Sch. Medicine Alumnae Assn. (bd. dirs. 1987—). Jewish. Clubs: Suburban Country (Balt.); Country Garden. Gourmet. Home: Timberlane 8410 Park Hts Ave Pikesville MD 21208 Office: Pine Heights Med Center Suite 301 1001 Pine Heights Ave Baltimore MD 21229

PASSANO, E. MAGRUDER, JR., printing/publishing executive; b. Balt., Oct. 2, 1942; s. Edward M. and Mildred P. (Nelson) P.; m. Helen C. Marikle, Sept. 4, 1971; children—Catherine, Tammy, Sarah. B.S., Johns Hopkins U., 1967, M.L.A., 1969. With Waverly Press, Inc., Balt., 1965—, salesman, 1970-73, v.p., 1973-75, v.p. adminstrn., sec., 1975—. Pres., Passano Found., Balt., 1982—, Am. Lung Assn. Md., 1982-84; mem. exec. com. Vol. Council for Equal Opportunity, Balt., 1978—; pres. (CHA) Combined Health Agys., Balt., 1985—; pres. 12:30 Club Balt., 1981-83; mem. exec. com. Balt. City Life Museums, 1982—, v.p. 1987—; mem. adv. council Johns Hopkins U. Sch. Continuing Studies, 1984—, exec. chair alumni chpt., 1986—; mem. Md. Gov.'s Commn. on High Blood Pressure and Related Cardiovascular Risk Factors; bd. govs. Md. New Directions, Inc., 1987—. Served with USN, 1963-65. Recipient Prince Hall Bicentennial award Masons, 1975; citations Mayor of Balt., 1976, City of Balt., 1977, Vol. of Yr. award for outstanding service to CICHA, 1984-85, Presdl. award for outstanding service to Am. Lung Assn. Md., 1985, Disting. Service award Soc. Profl. Journalists, 1987. Mem. Purchasing Mgmt. Assn. Md. (chmn. com. 1968-70), Balt. Jaycees (v.p. 1974-76, internat. senator 1975), Greater Balt. Minority Purchasing Council (Service award 1978), Soc. Colonial Wars (chpt. lt. gov.), Johns Hopkins U. Alumni Assn. (pres. Balt. 1984-86, Univ. Heritage award 1987). Democrat. Episcopalian. Home: 3925 Linkwood Rd Baltimore MD 21210 Office: Waverly Press 1314 N Guilford Ave Baltimore MD 21202

PASSINIEMI, PENTTI JUHANI, chemical engineer; b. Kauhava, Finland, Mar. 13, 1949; s. Antti and Eeva Rakel (Pelkkikangas) P.; m. Ritva Eila I. Laitinen, Dec. 30, 1973; 1 child, Antti Mikko J. M.S. in Chem. Engring., Tech. U. Helsinki, 1973; Dr. Tech., 1982. Asst. Tech. U., Helsinki, 1974-77, asst. lectr., 1980-81, assoc. prof., 1982; assoc. prof. Tech. U. Lappeenranta, Finland, 1977-79; researcher Neste Ltd., Kulloo, Finland, 1983-86, sr. research assoc. in electrochemistry, 1986—. Contbr. articles to profl. jours. Neste Found. Finnish Cultural Found. scholar, 1975-77. Fellow Finnish Chem. Soc. (governor 1986—), Reps. of Finnish Chem. Soc. (steering group teaching sect. 1981-83). Lutheran. Avocations: ornithology; cross country skiing; music; philosophy of sciences. Home: Aurapolku 1 B, 00750 Helsinki Finland Office: Neste Ltd Research Ctr, 06850 Kulloo Finland

PASSMORE, JOHN MURRAH, JR., physician; b. Columbus, Ga., June 2, 1947; s. John Murrah and June (Mabrey) P.; m. Donna Olney, June 21, 1969; children—Starr, Dawn, Skye, Grant. BS, Davidson Coll., 1969; MD, Vanderbilt U., 1973. Diplomate Am. Bd. Internal Medicine, Am. Bd. Emergency Medicine, Am. Bd. Cardiovascular Diseases. Resident in internal medicine Ind. U. Med. Ctr., 1973-76, fellow in endocrinology, 1976-77; chief emergency services Decatur Hosp., Greensburg, Ind., 1977-81, chief intensive care, 1982-84; fellow in critical care U. Pitts., 1981-82; fellow in cardiology U. Tex., Houston, 1984-86; pres. Questar, Inc., Indpls., 1976—, JPSA, Inc., Indpls., 1979-84, Optima, Inc., Indpls., 1977-84, Greensburg Med. Assocs. P.C., 1977-84; clin. faculty, cons. in Cardiology, S.W. Meml. Hosp., Houston, 1986—, chmn. interdisciplinary com., critical care com., 1986—; clin. asst., prof. U. Tex. Med. Sch., Houston, 1987—; dir. critical care symposium Nat. TMA, 1988; lectr. in field. Author: Endocrine Aspects of Critical Care, 1985, Cardiopulmonary Critical Care, 1986; contbr. articles to profl. jours. Recipient Best Prof. award U. Tex. Med. Sch., 1987-88. Fellow Am. Coll. Emergency Physicians; mem. Soc. Critical Care Medicine, Internat. Brotherhood of Magicians, Mensa. Methodist. Avocations: handball, racquetball tournaments, piano music composition, performing magic, writing science fiction novel, screenplay with musical score. Home: 110 Mayfair Ct Sugarland TX 77478 Office: 7777 Southwest Freeway Suite 420 Houston TX 77055

PASSWATER, RICHARD ALBERT, biochemist, author; b. Wilmington, Del., Oct. 13, 1937; s. Stanley Leroy and Mabel Rosetta (King) P.; BS, U. Del., 1959; PhD, Bernadean U., 1976; m. Barbara Sarah Gayhart, June 2, 1964; children: Richard Alan, Michael Eric. Supr. instrumental analysis lab. Allied Chem. Corp., Marcus Hook, Pa., 1959-64; tech. services rep. F & M Sci. Corp., Avondale, Pa., 1965; dir. applications lab. Am. Instrument Co., Silver Spring, Md., 1965-77; dir. Am. Gen. Enterprises, Minn.; daily broadcaster Sta. WMCA, N.Y.C., 1980—; former daily broadcaster Sta. WRNG, Atlanta, 1982-85; research dir. Solgar Nutritional Research Ctr., 1979—; chmn. Worcester County Emergency Planning Com.; pres. Subaqueous Exploration and Archeology Ltd.; Bd. dirs. Sci. Documentation Ctr., Dunfermline, Eng.; chief Ocean Pines Vol. Fire Dept., 1984—; Emergency Med. Tech.; adviser Nat. Inst. Nutrition Edn.; past adv. bd. Stephen Decatur High Sch., Worcester County Dept. Edn. Recipient Citizen of Yr. award Ocean Pines, Md., 1987. Fellow Internat. Acad. Preventive Medicine, Am. Inst. Chemists; mem. Am. Chem. Soc., Gerontology Soc., Am. Geriatric Soc., Am. Aging Assn., Soc. Applied Spectroscopy, Internat. Found. Preventive Medicine (v.p.), Internat. Union Pure and Applied Chemistry, Royal Soc. Chemistry (London), Internat. Acad. Holistic Health and Medicine, ASTM, Capital Chem. Soc., AAAS, Nutrition Today Soc., Am. Acad. Applied Health Scis. (pres., dir.), Internat. Found. Preventive Medicine (v.p., dir.), Inst. Nutritional Research, Internat. Platform Assn., N.Y. Acad. Scis., Pi Kappa Alpha. Author: Guide to Fluorescense Literature, vol. 1., 1967, vol. 2, 1970, vol. 3, 1974; Supernutrition: Megavitamin Revolution, 1975, paperback edit., 1976; Cancer: Nutritional Therapies, 1978; Super Calorie and Carbohydrate Counter, 1978; Supernutrition for Healthy Hearts, 1977, paperback, 1978; The Easy No-Flab Diet, 1979; Selenium as Food and Medicine, 1980; The Slendernow Diet, 1982; (with E. Cranton) Trace Elements, Hair Analysis and Your Health, 1983 Editor Fluorescence News, 1966-77, Jour. Applied Health Scis., 1982-83. editorial bd. Nutritional Perspectives, 1978-86, The Body Forum, 1979-80, Jour. Holistic Medicine, 1981—, VIM Newsletter, 1979—; contbr. over 200 health articles to mags.; co-editor booklet series Your Good Health; sci. adv. and columnist Whole Foods Mag. Patentee in field. Office: 4 Manklin Ct Berlin MD 21811

PASTINEN, ILKKA OLAVI, diplomat; b. Turku, Finland, Mar. 17, 1928; s. Martti Mikael and Ilmi Saga (Karlström); married, 1950; children: Kristiina Eva Marie, Johanna Eva Helena. M in Polit. Sci., Abo Akademi, Turku, Finland, 1950; Student, Inst. d'Etudes Poliques, Paris, Inst. Internat. des Scis. et Recherches Diplomatiques, Paris. Diplomat Finnish Foreign Service, 1952-55, Stockholm, 1955-57; diplomat Permanent Finnish Mission to UN, 1957-60; diplomat Finnish Foriegn Service, Beijing, 1962-64, London, 1966-69; Ambassador and Diplomatic Rep. Finland to UN Finnish Foriegn Service, 1969-71, special rep. of sec. gen. UN, 1971-75, ambassador and permanent rep. to UN, 1977-83; ambassador to court of St. James' Finnish Foriegn Service, London, 1983—. Recipient: Knight Comdr. St. Michael and St. George Queen Elizabeth II, 1972, Knight Comdr. White Rose Finland pres. Finland, 1986. Clubs: Athenaeum, Travellers', Swinley Forest Golf (London). Office: Embassy of Finland, 38 Chesham Pl, London SW1X 8HW England

PASTOR, STEPHEN DANIEL, chemistry educator, researcher; b. New Brunswick, N.J., Feb. 15, 1947; s. Stephen and Irene (Bors) P.; m. Joan Ordemann, Apr. 3, 1971 (div. 1979); 1 child, Melanie; m. Joanne Behrens, July 13, 1985. BA in Chemistry, Rutgers U., 1969, MS in Chemistry, 1978, PhD in Chemistry, 1983. Chemist Nat. Starch and Chem. Corp., Bridgewater, N.J., 1972-79; research group leader CIBA-Geigy Corp., Ardsley, N.Y., 1979-84, research mgr., 1985-87; group leader Cen. Research Labs. CIBA-GEIGY AG, Basel, Switzerland, 1987—; asst. adj. prof. PACE U., Pleasantville, N.Y., 1984—; mechanistic organic chemistry; conformation of large-membered heterocycles. Contbr. articles to profl. jours. 31 patentees in field. Served to 1st lt. U.S. Army, 1969-71, Vietnam. Mem. Am. Chem. Soc., N.Y. Acad. Sci., Sigma Xi. Current work: Organophosphorus and organosulfur chemistry, ornaometallic chemistry, asymmetric synthesis, homogeneous catalysis. Home: Neuensteiner Strasse 27, Postfach, CH-4053 Basel Switzerland Office: CIBA-Geigy Corp AG Cen Research Lab, R-1060-2-30 Postfach, CH-4002 Basel Switzerland

PATAKI, GÁBOR ISTVÁN, art historian; b. Fejēr, Hungary, Nov. 10, 1955; s. István and Ilona (Vēgh) P.; m. Judit Mazányi, Aug. 28, 1986. Grad., ELTE U., Budapest, 1980; PhD, ELTE U., 1985. Scholar Art History Research Group, Hungary Acad. Sci., Budapest, 1980-83, sci. researcher, 1983—; lectr. Trade Union Coll., Budapest, 1983-85, ELTE U., Budapest, 1984—. Author: (with others) History of Hungarain Art, 1985, Lajos Kassák, 1987; contbr. articles to profl. jours. Mem. Studio of Young Artists Hungary, Soc. Archeol. and Art History, Smohay Found., Assn. of Hungarian Fine Artists. Roman Catholic. Home: Zenta u 5, 1111 Budapest Hungary Office: Art History Research Group of, Hungarian Acad Sci, Uri u 52, 1014 Budapest Hungary

PATAKI-SCHWEIZER, KERRY JOSEF, behavioral scientist, medical anthropologist; b. Peekskill, N.Y., Nov. 1, 1935; s. John Josef and Helen Ida (Schweizer) Pataki; S.B., U. Chgo., 1960; M.A., U. Wash., Seattle, 1965, Ph.D., 1968; m. Lalitha Shirin Harben, Nov. 16, 1973; children—Nicholas Josef, Kiran Sarah. Asst. prof. anthropology and humanities Reed Coll., Portland, Oreg., 1967-69; research asso. Inst. Behavioral Sci., vis. lectr. U. Colo., 1970; asst. research anthropologist U. Calif., San Francisco, 1971-73, research asso. dept. epidemiology and internat. health, 1979—; sr. lectr. community medicine U. Papua New Guinea, 1974-82, assoc. prof. behavioral sci. and med. anthropology, 1983—; guest prof. Max-Planck-Institut, Fed. Republic of Germany, 1987-88; cons. WHO, Papua New Guinea Dept. Health. Served with AUS, 1955-56. Woodrow Wilson fellow, 1961; NIMH fellow, 1965-66; recipient French Govt. award for translation, 1960. Fellow Am. Anthrop. Assn., Internat. Coll. Psychosomatic Medicine, Royal Anthrop. Soc., Soc. Applied Athropology, World Assn. Social Psychiatry; mem. Am. Assn. Acad. Psychiatry. Malaysian Soc. Parasitology and Tropical Medicine, Papua New Guinea Med. Soc., Soc. Med. Anthropology, Soc. Psychol. Anthropology. Clubs: S. Pacific Aero, Royal Port Moresby Yacht, Returned Servicemen's League. Author: A New Guinea Landscape: Community, Space and Time of the Eastern Highlands, 1980; also articles. Home: Port Moresby Papua New Guinea Office: U Calif Dept of Epidemiology San Francisco CA 94143

PATANE, GIUSEPPE, conductor; b. Napoli, Italy, Jan. 1, 1932; s. Franco and Giulia (Caravaglios) P.; m. Rita Saponaro, May 7, 1958 (div.); children: Francesca, Paola. Student, Naples Conservatory. Debuts include Teatro San Carlo, Milan; permanent dir. Landestheater, Linz, Austria, 1961-62, Deutsche Oper Berlin, 1962-72; numerous opera and orchestral recordings: Targa d'Oro, Brescia, Italy, 1970, Bacchetta d'Oro, Parma, Italy, 1973, Grand Prix de Disque, Paris; conducted at La Scala, Milan, Rome, Palermo, Turin, Trieste, Bologna, Verona, Met. Opera, Chgo. Lyric Opera, San Francisco Opera, Cleve. Orch., Vienna State Opera, Paris Opera; prin. guest condr. Budapest Philharmonic; condr. Berlin Philharmonic, Vienna Philharmonic, Slovak Philharmonic. Office: Immeuble Michelangelo, 7 avenue Des Papalins, Apt 32, Monte Carlo Monaco *

PATARLAGEANU, RADU CONTANTIN, surgeon, consultant; b. Bucharest, Romania, Aug. 3, 1925; came to Germany, 1973; m. Constantin and Elena (Nestorescu) P.; m. Nora-Gerta Heidel, Aug. 16, 1952; children—Edda Antonia, Nora Joan. M.D., Faculty Medicine, Bucharest, Romania, 1949, D.Medicine, 1957, Traumatology, 1968, Resident surgeon State Hosp. 1, Brasov, Romania, 1949-55, cons. surgeon, 1955-57; cons. surgeon State Hosp., Budesti, Romania, 1962-64; chief surgeon State Hosp., Fierbinti, Urziceni, 1964-73; sr. surgeon Country Hosp., Sigmaringen, W.Ger., 1973-74; practice medicine specializing in surgery, Muhleim, W.Ger., 1974—; cons. medicine Shacko, Wieser, Lawton, Oswald Leibinger, Fridingen, Muhleim, Tuttlingen, Kolbingen, W.Ger., 1976—. Contbr. articles to profl. jours. Chmn. Christian Democratic Union, 1983-85. Served as sgt. Med. Service, 1944. Polit. prisoner Law Ct. Bucharest, State Security Prison Malmaison, 1957-58. Mem. Medecins Union, U.S. Strategic Inst., Inst. Francais des Relations Internationales. Orthodox. Club: German-Am. (Stuttgart). Avocations: polit. economy studies; U.S. history; English grammar. Home: Kitzenbuhlstrasse 7, 7202 Muhlheim/Donau, 7202 Baden-Wurttemberg Federal Republic of Germany

PATE, JOHN GILLIS, JR., consultant, accounting educator; b. Chattanooga, Jan. 27, 1928; s. John Gillis Pate and Iona Estelle (Bowman) Pate Ketchman; m. Daphne Mae Davis, Feb. 8, 1946; children—John Gillis III, Daphne Iona, Donna Gay. Student U. Tampa, 1947-48; A.A. with highest honors, U. Fla., 1950; B.S. cum laude, Fla. State U., 1953, M.S., 1958; Ph.D., Columbia U., 1968. Mgr. Grocery Concession, Albany, Ga., 1944-45, Variety Store, Panama City, Fla., 1946-47; asst. to CPA Standard Brands, Inc., Birmingham, Ala., 1951-53, acctg. supervising trainee, Birmingham, Ala., 1953-54; grad. asst. Fla. State U., Tallahassee, 1957-58; asst. to CPA, Pensacola, Fla., 1956-58; pub. acct., Pensacola, 1958; asst. prof. U. Ga., Athens, 1958-60; lectr. Columbia U., N.Y.C., 1961-64; asst. prof. Bernard M. Baruch Coll. of CUNY, 1963-69; prof. acctg. U. Tex.-El Paso, 1969-85, U. S.C., Spartanburg, 1988—; cons., resource person Personnel Dept. City of El Paso, 1981—. Author: Accounting Trends and Techniques, 1967-88; Index C.P.A. Exams and Unofficial Answers, 1974-81; co-author: Index to Accounting and Auditing Services, 1971; contbr. articles to ann. profl. publs. Tither, Coronado Bapt. Ch., El Paso, 1969-86; cons. Alderman of El Paso, 1982. Served as lt. j.g. USN, 1955-56. Columbia U. fellow, 1960; Earhart Found. fellow, 1960; Am. Acctg. Assn. fellow, 1960; recipient Haskins and Sells award, 1960; Ford Found. fellow, 1961-62. Mem. Am. Inst. C.P.A.s (cons.), Am. Acctg. Assn., Nat. Assn. Accts., Inst. Cost Analysts (cert. office automation profl.),Beta Alpha Psi, Beta Alpha Chi. Republican. Clubs: Lancer's; Anthony Rod and Gun. Lodges: Moose, Masons, Shriners. Home and Office: 264 Northwind Dr El Paso TX 79912

PATE, LARRY EUGENE, scholar, researcher, consultant; b. Dayton, Ohio, Jan. 27, 1945; s. Leslie Edgar and Mildred Georgia (Miller) P.; m. Pamela May Paton, Jan. 20, 1969; 1 son, Benjamin David; m. Kathryn Anne Clyde, July 9, 1979; children—Anna Kathryn, Lesley Elizabeth. B.A. summa cum laude (Honors scholar), U. Calif.-Irvine, 1971, M.S., 1973; Ph.D., U. Ill., 1979. Research asst. U. Calif. System, 1972-73; engr. schedules analyst McDonnell Douglas Astronautics, 1972-73; research/teaching asst. U. Ill., Urbana, 1973-75; vis. asst. prof. mgmt. U. Nebr., Lincoln, 1975-77, U. Wis., Madison, 1977-78; vis. assoc. prof. orgnl. behavior U. So. Calif., Los Angeles, summer 1981, vis. assoc. prof. Inst. Safety and Systems Mgmt., summer 1982; asst. prof. orgn. and adminstrn. Sch. Bus., U. Kans., Lawrence, 1978-81, assoc. prof. organizational behavior, 1981-88; vis. scholar U. Queensland, Australia, 1986-8 vis. assoc. prof., Grad. Sch. Bus. Admnstrn., U. So. Calif., 1988—;. YMCA Soccer coach, Kansas City, 1981-82. Guest editor Jour. Mgmt. Devel., 1988; editor Jour. Orgnl. Change Mgmt., 1988—. Served to capt. U.S. Army, 1965-70; Vietnam. Decorated Bronze Star, Air medal, Purple Heart, Vietnamese Cross of Gallantry. Mem. Acad. Mgmt. (program com. 1979-87), Organizational Devel. Inst. (chmn. membership com. 1985—; chmn. com. to select O.D. profl. of yr. 1985—; bd. advisors 1986—; assoc. editor jour. 1986—), AAAS, Am. Inst. Decision Sci. (program com. 1979-88), Am. Psychol. Assn., Brit. Psychol. Soc., Soc. Psychol. Study Social Issues, Internat. Assn. Applied Psychology. Contbr. numerous articles to profl. jours.; mem. editorial bd. Jour. Mgmt., 1983-84; mem. editorial rev. bd.J. Mgmt. Devel., 1987—; bd. advisors Faculty Scholar, U. Kans., 1981-83. Office: Grad Sch Bus Adminstrn Univ So Calif Los Angeles CA 90089-1421

PATEL, ANIL S., biomedical engineer, researcher; b. Baroda, India, June 28, 1939; came to U.S. 1961; s. Shankerbhai S. and Gangaben T. Patel; children—Ravi, Sunil. B.S., U. Baroda, India, 1960; M.S., Purdue U., 1963; Ph.D., Northwestern U., 1966. Sr. research scientist Baxter Travenol Labs. Inc., Morton Grove, Ill., 1968-74; chief scientist Cavitron Corp., N.Y.C., 1974-79; chief scientist and mgr. advanced products research Cooper Vision Systems div. Cooper Vision Inc. (formerly Cavitron Corp.), Irvine, Calif., 1979-83, Cooper Vision Inc. div., Bellevue, Wash., 1983-86, dir. advanced product research, chief scientist, Cooper Vision CILCO div. The Cooper Cos., Inc., Bellevue, 1986—. Contbr. articles to profl. jours.; patentee in field. Organizer Highland Park (Ill.) Chess Club, 1970-74, White Plains Chess Club, N.Y., 1974-77. NIH postdoctoral fellow Northwestern U., 1966-67; recipient free passage from India to U.S., Ministry Sci. and Cultural Affairs of Govt. India, 1961. Fellow Am. Soc. Laser Medicine and Surgery (founder); mem. Assn. Advancement Med. Instrumentation (chmn. infrared warmers and incubators standards com. 1978-80, pulmonary function devices-spirometer standards subcom. 1978-80), Assn. Research in Vision and Ophthalmology, Inc., Internat. Soc. Refractive Keratoplasty, AAAS, IEEE, Soc. Biomaterials, Sigma Xi. Home: 104 NE 62d St Seattle WA 98115

PATEL, GEV JAMSHED, real estate manager; b. Bandra, Maharshtra, India, Aug. 7, 1944; came to United Arab Emirates, Nov. 10, 1974; s. Jamshed Shapurji and Maneck (Patel) P.; m. Florence Gev. D'Souza; children: Xerses, Darius. BN, Gamadia Techical Inst., Bombay, India; student, Gulf Computer Services-Tng. Ctr., Sharjah, United Arab Emigrates. Rep. Belgenur Corp., Bombay, 1962-64, J.K. Bus. Machines Ltd., Bombay, 1964-65; ptnr. Bahadur S. Patel and Co., Bombay, 1965-73; mgr. commercial Mody Aviation, Bombay, 1973-74; dep. mgr. Cementco, Sharjah, United Arab Emirates, 1974-75; gen. mgr. Euro-Arab Investments Ltd./Property Mgmt. Services, Sharjah, 1975-83, Arabian Estates Mgmt. Est., Sharjah, 1983—, Arabian Propinvest J.V., Sharjah, 1983—. Warden Civil Defense, Greater Bombay, 1971; commr. deeds for State of Fla., 1984. Mem. Estate Afts. Assn. India (life), Indian Assn. Sharjah (life), Inst. Profl. Mgrs., Internat. Real Estate Fedn., Bombay Rifle. Zoroastrian-Parsee. Office: Arabian Estate Mgmt Est, PO Box 1602, Sharjah United Arab Emirates

PATEL, INDRAPRASAD GORDHANBHAI, college director; b. Baroda, India, Nov. 11, 1924; s. Gordhanbhai and Kashiben Patel; m. Alaknanda Dasgupta, 1958; 1 child, Rehana. BA with honors, Bombay U., 1944; BA, Cambridge (Eng.) U., 1946, PhD, 1949; DLitt (hon.), Sardar Patel U. Prof. econs., prin Maharaja Sayajirao U., Baroda, 1949-50; spl. sec. Ministry of Fin., India, 1968-69, sec., 1970-72; dep. adminstr. UN Devel. Programme, 1972-77; gov. Res. Bank of India, 1977-82; dir. Indian Inst. of Mgmt., Ahmedabad, 1982-84, London Sch. Econs., 1984—. Author: Essays in Economics Policy and Ecoomic Growth, 1987. Hon. fellow King's Coll., Cambridge, 1986. Mem. Overseas Devel. Inst. (council), Royal Econ. Soc. (council), Group of Thirty, Wider (bd. dirs.). Club: Athenaeum (London). Office: London Sch Econs and Polit Sci, Office of Dir, Houghton St, London WC2A 2AE, England

PATEL, JERAM, painter, graphic designer; b. June 20, 1930. Student Sir J.J. Sch. Art, Bombay, Central Sch. Arts and Crafts, London. Reader in applied arts M.S. U., Baroda (now Vadodara), India, 1960-61, 66—; reader in visual design Sch. Architecture, Ahmedabad, 1961-62; dep. dir. All India Handloom Bd., 1963-66; mem. Group 1890 (avant-garde group of Indian artists), Lalit Kala Akademi; one man shows: London, 1959, New Delhi, 1960, 62-65, Calcutta, 1966, Tokyo Biennale, 1957-63, Sao Paulo Biennale, 1963; represented in permanent collections: Nat. Gallery of Modern Art, New Delhi, Art Soc. of India, Bombay, Sir J.J. Inst. Applied Art, Bombay; numerous pvt. collections. Recipient Lalit Kala Akademi Nat. awards, 1957, 64; Bombay State award, 1957; Silver medal Bombay Art Soc., 1961; Gold medal Rajkot Exhbn. Office: M S University, Faculty of Fine Arts, Vadodara 2 India *

PATEL, THAKORBHAI KHODABHAI, consulting physician; b. Karamsad, Gujarat, India, Dec. 4, 1934; s. Khodabhai Jhaverbhai and Kashiben Khodabhai P.; m. Kalpana Kanubhai, May 23, 1967; children: Sheena, Parth. MBBS, Bombay U., 1959; MRCP, Glasgow, 1965. Hon. asst. prof. medicine NHL Med. Coll., Ahmeddabad, Gujaret, India, 1966-68; hon. asst. prof. medicine B.J. Med. Coll., Ahmeddabad, 1969-77, hon. prof., dir. inst. cardiology, 1977—; med. specialist Oil and Natural Gas Commn., Ahmedabad, 1977—, Employees State Ins. Scheme, Ahmedabad, 1971—; hon. med. advisor Space Applications Ctr., Ahmedabad, 1984—. Contbr.

articles to profl. jours. Mem. Royal Coll. Physicians. Home: A-3 Nikita Apts, Usmanpura, Ahmedabad Gujarat 380 013, India Office: B-2 Medicaire, B/H MJ Library, Ellisbridge, Ahmedabad, Gujarat 380 013, India

PATERIA, ANIL KUMAR, sociology educator; b. Bilaspur, Madhya Pradesh, India, Mar. 30, 1946; s. Parmanand and Uma Godavaribai (Choube) P.; m. Varlaxmi Naidu, Nov. 23, 1981. BS, Govt. Sci. Coll., Raipur, Madhya Pradesh, 1967; MA in Sociology, Ravishankar U., Raipur, 1969; postgrad., Ravishankar U., 1983-85. Lectr. Ravishankar U., 1969—; presenter papers VII Internat. Human Sci. Research Conf., Seattle, 1988. Author: Manan Phir Prayas, 1980, Modern Commentators of Veda, 1985; contbr. articles to profl. jours., internat. confs. Founder, producer, dir. Theatrical Group-Agragami-Prayas Natya Samiti, Raipur, 1962-74. Fellow Indian Social Sci. Acad.; mem. Indian Sociol. Soc. (life), Madhya Pradesh Sociol. Soc. Home: 24/248 Shankar, Chowk Nayapara, Raipur Madhya Pradesh 492 001, India Office: Ravishankar U, Dept Sociology, Raipur Madhya Pradesh 492 010, India

PATERIA, VARLAXMI, sociology educator; b. Waltaire, Andhra-Pradesh, India, May 22, 1947; d. Konkpudi Ramarao and Narsayyamma Naidu; m. Anil Kumar Pateria, Nov. 23, 1981. BA, Govt. Girls Coll., Raipur, Madhya Pradesh, India, 1966; MA in Sociology, Ravishanker U., Raipur, 1968, PhD, 1974. Research fellow Ravishankar U., 1968-72, research asst., lectr., 1972-80, lectr., 1980—; vis. tchr. Govt. Employment Bur., Raipur, 1978—, Mahya Pradesh Council Child Welfare, Raipur, 1986—; contbr. research papers to 7th Internat. Human Sci. Reserch Conf., Seattle, 1988. Contbr. articles to profl. jours. Active Andhra Assn., Raipur, 1972—. Fellow Indian Social Sci. Acad.; mem. Indian Assn. Women's Studies. Home: 24/248 Shankar, Chowk Nayapara, Raipur 492 001, India Office: Ravishankar U, Dept Sociology, Raipur 492 010, India

PATERNU, BORIS, history of Slovene literature educator; b. Predgrad, Yugoslavia, June 5, 1926; s. Karl and Pavla (Triplat) P.; m. Breda Macek Paternu, Aug. 5, 1955; children—Marko, Uros. Diploma, Arts Faculty, Ljubljana, Yugoslavia, 1951, Ph.D., 1960. Asst., Arts Faculty, Ljubljana, 1951-60, asst. prof., 1960-66, assoc. prof., 1966-72, prof. history of Slovene lit., 1972—; mem. Internat. Com. Slavists Bd. for Poetics and Stylistics, 1973—. Author: Slovenska proza do moderne, 1957; Slovenska literarna kritika pred Levstikom, 1960; Pogledi na slovensko knjizevnost I, II, 1974; France Preseren in njegovo pesnisko delo I, II (award 1981), 1976, 77. Mem. Nat. Com. for Research Work, Ljubljana, 1975-79; mem. Exec. com. Research Community of Slovenia, Ljubljana, 1975-78. Recipient Boris Kidric award Research Community Slovenia, Ljubljana, 1981; Zupancic award City of Ljubljana, 1981, Medal of Honor, Order of Work with a Silver Wreath, Order of Merit with a Silver Wreath, Order of Work with a Red Flag. Mem. Slavonic Soc., Slovene Acad. Scis. and Arts, Chair for History of Slovene Lit. (head. 1963). Home: Linhartova 22, 61000 Ljubljana Yugoslavia Office: Filozofska fakulteta, Askerceva 12, Ljubljana Yugoslavia

PATERSON, ALAN LEONARD TUKE, mathematics educator; b. Dunfermline, Scotland, Mar. 8, 1944; s. William and Isabella (MacMaster) P.; m. Christina Mackie Anderson, Sept. 20, 1969; children: Mark, Lydia, Stephen. BS, U. Edinburgh, Scotland, 1966, MS, 1967, PhD, 1969. Prof. U. Aberdeen, Scotland, 1969—, U. Western Ont., Can.da, 1984, U. B.C., Can.da, 1985. Author: Amenability, 1988. Mem. Edinburgh Math. Soc., London Math Soc., Am. Math Soc. Home: 2 Primrosehill Gardens, Aberdeen AB2 2EQ, Scotland Office: Univ Aberdeen, Edward Wright Bldg, Dunbar St, Aberdeen AB9 2TY, Scotland

PATERSON, GRAHAM LINDSAY, mining engineer; b. Adelaide, South Australia, Aug. 20, 1934; s. Owen Thomas and Gladys Maud (Whyte) P.; diploma civil engring., Brit. Inst. Engring. Tech., 1958; m. Cynthia Margaret Saunders, Sept. 22, 1959; children—Alisdair Graham, Stuart Thomas. Programmetric engr., articled surveyor S.Australian Land Dept., 1951-54; mine surveyor Eldorado (T.C.) Ltd., 1954-55; photogrammetrist Australian Petroleum Ltd., 1955-57; exploration surveyor Geosurveys Australia Ltd., 1957-59; chief surveyor, devel. engr. Rompin Mining Ltd., Malaya, 1960-63; mng. dir. AERO Service (NG) Ltd., also Qasco (NG) Pty. Ltd., 1964-69; owner G.L. Paterson Cons. Service, Indonesia, 1969-73; chief surveyor Bougainville Copper Ltd., 1973-75; mine planning engr., chief surveyor Telfer project Newmont Pty. Ltd., 1975-81; mine controller New Guinea Goldfields Ltd. Wau N.G., 1981-82, mine mgr. Gt. No. Mining Corp., Herberton, Queensland, Australia, 1982-83; gen. mgr. Plenty River Mining Co. (N.T.) Ltd., Jervois Range, No. Ter., Australia, 1983-84; mine mgr. Cape Flattery Silica Mines, North Queensland, 1984-85; gen. mgr. North Flinders Mines Ltd. Granites Gold Mine Project, No. Terr., 1986-87; ops. mgr. Consol. Rutilt, Ltd., North Stradbroke Island, Queensland, 1987—; founding pres. Photogrammetric Soc. Papua New Guinea, 1968. sec. Redcliffe br. Liberal Party, 1975. Fellow Am. Congress Surveying and Mapping; life mem. Photogrammetric Soc. London; mem. Soc. Mining Engrs., ASCE, Can. Inst. Surveying. Clubs: Mountaineering Assn. (life) (London); Handicapper Papua Yacht (officer). Author aerial indexes of Indonesia, W.Iran. Home: 13 Logan St, Atherton Queensland 4883, Australia Office: PO Dunwich, North Stradbroke Island Queensland, Australia

PATHAK, VIJAY DAMODAR, mathematics educator; b. Baroda, Gujarat, India, Dec. 26, 1944; s. Damodar Dattatrya and Shakuntala Pathak; m. Shubhangi Vijay Bharati Gajanan, May 12, 1969; children: Manish, Nandini. BS, Maharaja Sayajirao U., Baroda, 1964, MS, 1966; PhD, S.P. U., 1981. Research asst. Tata Inst. Fundamental Research, Bombay, Maharashtra, 1966-67; asst. lectr. faculty tech. and engring. Maharaja Sayajirao U., 1967-71, lectr. math., 1971-81, reader applied math., 1981-87, prof., 1987—; lectr. internat. conf. Warsaw (Poland) U., 1985. Author numerous research papers. Mem. Akhil Bharatiya Vidyarthi Parishad, 1967. Fellow Indo-U.S. Commn. on Edn. and Culture, U. Calif., Santa Barbara, 1978-79. Mem. Am. Math. Soc., Indian Math. Soc. (life), Bd. Studies in Applied Math. Hindu-Brahmin. Home: Vitthal Mandir, Radhakrishnas Pole, Palace Rd Baroda, Gujarat 390 001, India Office: MS U Dept Applied Math, Faculty Tech and Engring Baroda, Gujarat 390 001, India

PATHY, JAGANATH, social anthropologist, educator; b. Berhampur, India, June 13, 1948; s. Bhagaban and Kamala P.; m. Suguna Paul, Oct. 10, 1978; children: Suma, Sumit. BSc, Berhampur U., 1969; MSc, Saugar U., 1972; M in Philosophy, Jawaharlal Nehru U., 1974, PhD, 1977. Lectr. Sambalpur U., Orissa, India, 1976-79; reader in sociology, social anthropology S. Gujarat (India) U., 1979—; mem. study group New Delhi Planning Commn., 1985—. Author: Tribal Peasantry; contbr. articles and book revs. to various publs. Grantee U. Grants Commn., New Delhi, 1983-86. Mem. Nat. Integration Council (exec. mem. 1971-73, S. Gurat U. Tchrs. Assn. (pres. 1983-84), Indian Sociol. Soc. (mng. com. 1986—), Ethnographic and Folk Culture Soc. (life mem.), Indian Acad. Social Scis. (life mem.), Regional Sci. Assn. India, Third World Network Malaysia. Home: B2 Lectr Quars S Gujarat U Surat, South Gujarat 395 007, India Office: Dept Sociology S Gujarat U, Udhna Magdalla Rd Surat, Gujarat 395 007, India

PATINKIN, DON, educator, economist; b. Chgo., Jan. 8, 1922; s. Albert and Sadie Brezinsky P.; m. Deborah Trossman, 1945; 4 children. Student U. Chgo. Research asst. Cowles Com. for Econ. Research, 1946-47, research assoc., 1947-48; asst. prof. econs. U. Chgo., 1947-48; assoc. prof. econs. U. Ill., 1948-49; lectr. in econs. Hebrew U. of Jerusalem, 1949, assoc. prof., 1952, prof., 1957—, rector, 1982-85, pres., 1983-86; dir. research Maurice Falk Inst. for Econ. Research in Israel, 1956-72. Author: Money, Interest and Prices: An Integration of Monetary and Value Theory, 1956, 65; The Israel Economy: the First Decade, 1959; Studies in Monetary Economics, 1972; Keynes Monetary Thought: A Study of Its Development 1976; Essays On and In the Chicago Tradition, 1981; Anticipations of the General Theory? and other Essays on Keynes, 1982; editor: (with J.C. Leith) Keynes, Cambridge and the General Theory: The Process of Criticism and Discussion Connected with the Development of the General Theory, 1977. Recipient Rothschild prize, 1959; Israel prize, 1970. Mem. Econometric Soc. (pres. 1974), Israel Econ. Assn. (pres. 1976), Am. Econ. Assn. (hon. mem.), Israel Acad. Scis. and Humanities, Am. Acad. Arts and Scis., British Acad. Office: Hebrew U of Jerusalem, Israel Acad of Scis and, Humanities, PO Box 4040, Jerusalem 91040, Israel

PATKAR, VIVEK NARAYAN, operations researcher; b. Bombay, India, Oct. 25, 1953; parents: Narayan Ganesh and Kamal Narayan P. BS, U. Delhi, India, 1972; MS, U. Delhi, 1974, PhD, 1979. Research scholar dept. operatinal research U. Delhi, India, 1976-78; research assoc. Nat. Inst. Bank Mgmt., Bombay, India, 1978-79; ops. research specialist Bombay Met. Region Devel. Authority, 1979—. Mem. council adivsers Times of Sci. and Tech. India mag.; contbr. papers to various jours. Research fellow Univ. Grants Commn., Delhi, 1976; grantee Brit. Council, London, 1982. Mem. Operational Research Soc. India, Regional Sci. Assn. India, Pure and Applied Math. Scis., Indian Water Works Assn. (recipient pub. paper award, 1986-87), Indian Inst. Pub. Adminstrn., World Conf. Transport Research Soc. USA. Home: F 3/2 Sector 7 Vashi, Bombay Maharashtra 400 703, India Office: Bombay Met Region Devel Authority, Griha Nirman Bhavan, Bandra (E) Bombay 400 051, India

PATMAN, PHILIP FRANKLIN, lawyer; b. Atlanta, Tex., Nov. 1, 1937; s. Elmer Franklin and Helen Lee (Miller) P.; m. Katherine Sellers, July 1, 1967; children—Philip Franklin, Katherine Lee. B.A., U. Tex., 1959, LL.B., 1964; M.A., Princeton U., 1962. Bar: Tex. 1964, U.S. Dist. Ct. (we. dist.) Tex. 1975, U.S. Dist. Ct. (so. dist.) Tex. 1971, U.S. Supreme Ct. 1970. Atty. office of legal adviser Dept. State, Washington, 1964-67; dep. dir. office internat. affairs HUD, Washington, 1967-69; sole practice, Austin, Tex., 1969—. Ofcl. rep. of Gov. Tex. to Interstate Oil Compact Commn., 1973-83, 87—. Woodrow Wilson fellow 1959. Mem. ABA, Tex. Bar Assn., Tex. Ind. Producers and Royalty Owners Assn., Tex. Law Review Assn., Phi Beta Kappa, Phi Delta Phi. Democrat. Episcopalian. Clubs: Austin, Citadel, Westwood Country, Princeton (N.Y.C.). Contbr. articles to legal jours. Office: Perry-Brooks Bldg Suite 312 Austin TX 78701

PATMODIHARDJO, SOEROSO, bank executive; b. Jombang, East Java, Indonesia, Mar. 20, 1918; s. Moenasir Patmodihardjo and Soemari Marsodihardjo; m. Sri Poerwati Soeroso, June 17, 1940 (dec. Nov. 1984); children: Wahono, Damaiati, Boediono, Setiono, Setiati, Wahjoeno, Rahardjo; m. Ida Badilla Soeroso, June 21, 1985. LLB, Shihokanri U., Jakarta, Indonesia, 1944; BBA, Indonesian Acad. Commerce, Jakarta, Indonesia, 1953. Clk. Primary Ct., Nganjuk, Indonesia, 1942-44; pub. prosecutor Dept. Justice, Bandung, Yogya, Tulungagung, Indonesia, 1944-50; with Escomptobank N.V., Jakarta, Indonesia, 1950-56; procurist Escomptobank N.V., Jakarta, Indonesia and Amsterdam, Netherlands, 1956-58; asst. mng. dir. Escomptobank N.V. Bank Dagang Negara, Jakarta, Indonesia, 1958-60; pres., dir. P.T. Sucointra, Surabaya, Indonesia, 1962-77, P.T. Inimexintra, Surabaya, Indonesia, 1972-77, Excelsior N.V., Surabaya, Indonesia, 1962-77, P.T. Bank Rama, Jakarta, Indonesia, 1977—; chmn. P.T. Priscolin, 1977—, P.T. Sucointra, 1977—, P.T. Inimexintra, 1977—, Excelsior N.V., 1977—; mem. supervisory bd. Olie Fabriek Olvado, Surabaya, 1958-59, Technish Bur. Vena, Surabaya, 1958-59, Stroohoedenveem, Surabaya, 1958-59, Tjandi, Pandji & Tanjungsari Suiker Fabr, Surabaya, 1958-59. Chmn. Indonesian Socialist Party, 1948-58; mem. exec. bd. local ho. of reps., 1947-50. Mem. Bankers Club. Lodge: Rotary (pres. Surabaya chpt. 1960-61, pres. Jakarta chpt. 1979-80). Home: Balitung II - 12, Kebayoran 12110, Indonesia Office: PT Bank Rama, 3 Jalan Thamrin, Jakarta Indonesia

PATON, BORIS EVGENIJEVICH, metallurgist; b. Kiev, USSR, Nov. 27, 1918; m. Olga Borisovna Milovanova, 1948; 1 child. Ed., Kiev Poly. Inst. Corr. mem. Ukranian S.S.R. Acad. Scis., 1951-58, mem., 1958, pres., 1962—, dir. E.O. Paton Electric Welding Inst., 1953—; mem. USSR Acad. Scis., 1962—; mem. Presidium, 1963—; chmn. Coordination Council on Welding in USSR, 1958—; chmn. coordination bd. CMEA, 1972—; chmn. USSR Nat. Com. on Welding. Author numerous books, articles in field. Mem. editorial bd., editor-in-chief numerous sci. and tech. jours. Patentee in field. Mem. CPSU, 1952—, mem. central com., 1966; mem. central com. of Ukraine, 1960—; dep. USSR Supreme Soviet, 1962—; vice chmn. Union USSR Supreme Soviet, 1959—. Recipient State Prize, 1950, Lenin prize, 1957, Gold Medal Hammer and Sickle of Hero of Socialist Labour, 1969, 78, numerous other Gold medals; named to Order of Lenin, Order of October Revolution, 1984, Order of Red Banner of Labour, 1943; named Honoured Scientist of Ukranian S.S.R., 1968, Honoured Inventor of USSR, 1983. Mem. Acad. Scis. of Bulgaria, (fgn. mem.), Acad. Scis. of Czechoslovakia (fgn. mem.), Royal Swedish Acad. Engring. Sci. (fgn. mem.). Avocation: tennis. Address: E O Paton Electric Welding Inst, 11 Bozhenko St, Kiev 5 USSR

PATON, DAVID, ophthalmologist, educator; b. Balt., Aug. 16, 1930; s. Richard Townley and Helen (Meserve) P.; m. Diane Johnston, Mar. 9, 1985; 1 child from previous marriage, D. Townley. B.A., Princeton U., 1952, D.Sci. (hon.), 1985; M.D., Johns Hopkins U., 1956; D.Sci., (hon.), Bridgeport U., 1984. Diplomate Am. Bd. Ophthalmology. Intern, Cornell Med. Sch.-N.Y. Hosp., 1956-57; research fellow in ophthalmology NIH, Bethesda, Md., 1957-59; resident Wilmer Inst., Johns Hopkins Sch. Medicine, Balt., 1959-64, assoc. prof. ophthalmology Wilmer Inst., asst. prof. Johns Hopkins Sch. Medicine, 1964-71; prof., chmn. dept. ophthalmology Baylor Coll. Medicine, Houston, 1971-82; med. dir. King Khaled Eye Specialist Hosp., Riyadh, Saudi Arabia, 1982-84; chmn., chief med. officer OcuSystems, Inc., Greenwich, Conn., 1985-87, prof. clin. ophthalmology Cornell U. Coll. Medicine, 1986—; chmn., program dir. dept. ophthalmolgy Cath. Med. Ctr. of Bklyn. and Queens, 1986—; founder Project ORBIS, Inc., N.Y.C., 1971, med. dir. 1971-87. Author books. Contbr. articles to profl. jours. Recipient Royal Decoration 3d Order, Royal Decoration 2d Order (Jordan), Pres.'s Citizen medal, 1987, Legion of Honor (France); Markle scholar in acad. medicine, 1967-72. Fellow Am. Acad. Ophthalmology (sec. continuing edn. 1977-82, 1st v.p. 1982; Honor award 1975), ACS (bd. govs. substitute 1972-73), mem. Am. Bd. Ophthalmology (chmn. 1982), AAUP in Ophthalmology (trustee 1978-81), Md. Ophthalmol. Soc. (pres. 1969-70), Pan Am. Assn. Ophthalmology (council 1973—), numerous other med. soc. memberships. Home: 120 East End Ave 18B New York NY 10028 Office: St Joseph's Hosp Eye Care Ctr 158-40 79th Ave Flushing NY 11366

PATON, LENNOX MCLEAN, lawyer; b. Kuala lumpur, Malaysia, Mar. 19, 1928; s. Robert and Morag (McLean) P.; m. Cheryl Lee Williams, Oct. 17, 1959 (dec. Dec. 22, 1977); 1 child, Michael Lennox; m. Lydie Sheelah Milne, Mar. 25, 1978 (div. Mar. 1985); 1 child, Charles Robert Matthew. BA, Cambridge U., Eng., 1951, LLB, 1952, MA, 1953. Bar: Singapore 1955, Malaysia 1957, Bahamas, 1967, Eng. Supreme Ct. 1954. Assoc. Donaldson and Burkinshaw, Singapore, 1954-57, Linklaters and Paines, London, 1957-58, Higgs and Johnson, Nassau, Bahamas, 1958-68; dir. Slater, Walker and Withers Ltd., Nassau, 1968-71; prin. Lennox Paton & Co., 1971-72; ptnr. Paton Toothe and Co., Nassau, 1973-74, Paton, Alexiou and Co., Nassau, 1974-79, Toothe, Paton and Co., Nassau, 1980-86; prin. Lennox M. Paton Co., Nassau, 1986—. Served to 2d lt. Royal Engrs., 1946-49. Mem. Law Soc. of Eng. and Wales, Bahamas Bar Assn. Office: Claughton House Charlotte St, PO Box N4875, Nassau The Bahamas

PATON, WILLIAM DRUMMOND MACDONALD, pharmacologist, educator; b. May 5, 1917; s. William Paton and Grace Mackenzie P.; scholar New Coll., Oxford U., hon. fellow, 1980; BA with 1st class honors, Univ. Coll., 1958, MA, 1948, DM, 1953; BM, BC., Oxford U., 1942; DSc (hon.), London U., 1985, Edinburgh U., 1986; m. Phoebe Margaret Rooke, 1942. Demonstrator in physiology Oxford U., 1938-39; Goldsmid exhbn. UCH Med. Sch., 1939; editor UCH Mag., 1941; house physician UCH Med. Unit, 1942; pathologist King Edward VII Sanatorium, 1943-44; mem. sci. staff Nat. Inst. Med. Research, 1944-52; reader in pharmacology Univ. Coll. and UCH Med. Sch., 1952-54; prof. pharmacology RCS, 1954-59; prof. pharmacology Oxford U., 1959-84; emeritus fellow Balliol Coll.; dir. Wellcome Inst. History of Medicine, 1984-87; del. Clarendon Press, 1967-72; hon. lectr. St. Mary's Hosp. Md. Sch., 1950; vis. lectr. Swedish univs., 1953, Brussels, 1956; delivered Robert Campbell oration, 1957, Clover lectr., 1958; Bertram Louis Abrahams lectr. RCP, 1962; Ivison Macadam lectr. RCSE, 1973; Osler lectr. RCP, 1978. Rhodes trustee, 1968-87; Wellcome trustee, 1978-87. Knighted, 1979; decorated comdr. Order Brit. Empire; recipient Fellowes Gold medal, 1941, Bengue Meml. prize, 1952, Cameron prize, 1956, Gairdner Found. award, 1959, Gold medal Soc. Apothecaries, 1976. Fellow Royal Coll. Physicians, Royal Soc., RSA, FFARCS. Mem. Pharmacol. Soc. (chmn. editorial bd, 1969-74), Physiol. Soc. (hon. sec. 1951-57, chmn. 1985), Brit. Toxicol. Soc. (chmn. 1982-83), Inst. Study of Drug Dependence, Inst. Animal Technicians (pres. 1969-75), Research Def. Soc. (chmn., Paget lectr. 1978, Boyd medal 1987); hon. mem. Société Francaise d'Allergie, Australian Acad. Forensic Sci.; corr. mem. German Pharmacol. Soc. Address: 13 Staverton Rd, Oxford OX2 6XH, England Office: care Royal Soc, 6 Carlton House Terr, London SW1Y 6AG, England

PATRA, AMIT LAL, mechanical engineer; b. Jamshedpur, India, July 18, 1947; came to U.S., 1971, naturalized, 1977; m. Ananta Lal and Prabhas Bala (Pathak) P.; B.S., Calcutta U., 1968; M.S., N.C. State U., Raleigh, 1976, Ph.D., 1979; m. Shuva Rani Pyne, July 22, 1977; children—Cithara Susan, Amark Sumit. Design engr. Structural Form Products, 1972-73; project engr. Reeves Bros., 1973-74; teaching asst. N.C. State U., 1974-79; research asst. Becton and Dickinson Co., 1977-79; phys. scientist EPA, 1979-80; phys. scientist Northrop Services Inc., Research Triangle Park, N.C., 1980—; adj. asst. prof. N.C. State U., 1979—; cons. in field. Sec., India Assn. Raleigh, 1974-75. Mem. ASME, AAAS, Bio-Med. Engrs. Soc., N.C. Acad. Scis., Sigma Xi, Pi Mu Epsilon. Hindu. Contbr. articles to profl. jours. Home: 105 Muscadine Ct Durham NC 27703

PATRICK, GEORGE MILTON, dentist; b. Accoville, W.Va., Sept. 27, 1920; s. Milton Michael and Martha Mary (Mullins) P.; m. Shirley Ann Rutherford, Mar. 22, 1952 (div. June 1966); 1 child, Geoffrey Milton (dec.); m. Jane Lee Austin, Oct. 1, 1971; stepchildren: Anthony Duke Spencer, T.L.C. Hughes. BS, Capital U., 1950; DDS, Ohio State U., 1955; postgrad., U. N.C., 1972. Gen. practice dentistry Columbus, Ohio, 1956-67; dir. mktg. and research Kirkman Labs., Portland, Oreg., 1968; gen. practice dentistry specializing in orthodontics Columbus, 1968; pub. health dentist Ohio Dept. Health, Bowling Green, Ohio, 1968-80; practice dentistry specializing in pedodontics 1980-82; pvt. practice computer cons. Columbus, 1982-87, mgmt. cons., 1987—. Production mgr. Vaud-Vilities, Columbus, 1979-86; singer First Community Ch., Columbus, 1972-86, opera singer Columbus Chorus, 1984-86. Served to 2d lt. U.S. Army, 1942-46, ETO. Decorated Bronze Star, Purple Heart with Oak Leaf Cluster. Mem. ADA, Ohio Dental Assn., Columbus Dental Soc. (chmn. children's dental health week), Columbus Council World Affairs, Pub. Relations Soc. (membership com. 1986), Career Execs. of Columbus (pres. 1987—). Home: 2511 Onandaga Dr Columbus OH 43221 Office: 2400 Corporate Exchange Dr Columbus OH 43229

PATRICK, JAMES DUVALL, JR., lawyer; b. Griffin, Ga., Dec. 28, 1947; s. James Duvall and Marion Wilson (Ragsdale) P.; m. Carol Crosby, June 13, 1970 (div. 1985). BS in Indsl. Mgmt., Ga. Inst. Tech., 1970; JD, U. Ga., 1973. Bar: Ga. 1973, U.S. Dist. Ct. (mid. dist.) Ga. 1973, U.S. Dist. Ct. (so. dist.) Ga. 1983, U.S. Ct. Appeals (5th cir.) 1974, U.S. Supreme Ct., U.S. Ct. Appeals (11th Cir.) 1981, U.S. Tax Ct. 1985. Assoc. Cartledge, Cartledge & Posey, Columbus, Ga., 1973-74; ptnr. Falkenstrom, Hawkins & Patrick, Columbus, 1975, Falkenstrom & Patrick, Columbus, 1975-77; sole practice, Columbus, 1977—; instr. bus. law Chattahoochee Valley Community Coll., Phenix City, Ala., 1975-77; instr. paralegal course Columbus Coll., 1979, 84; del. U.S./China Joint Session on Trade, Investment, and Econ. Law, Beijing, 1987. Mem. Hist. Columbus Found., Mayor's Com. for the Handicapped, 1987-88; local organizer, worker Joe Frank Harris for Gov. Campaign, Columbus, 1982; bd. dirs. Columbus Symphony Orchestra, 1988. Mem. State Bar Ga., Ga. Assn. Criminal Def. Lawyers (bd. dirs., v.p.), ABA, Assn. Trial Lawyers Am., Ga. Trial Lawyers Assn., Columbus Young Lawyers Club, Columbus Lawyers Club, Columbus Kappa Alpha Alumni Assn. (sec.), Phi Delta Phi, Kappa Alpha. Methodist. Clubs: Civitan (bd. dirs. 1975-77), Country of Columbus, Georgian (Atlanta), Buckhead. Office: 831 2d Ave Columbus GA 31902

PATRICK, JOHN, playwright; b. Louisville, May 17, 1905; s. John Francis and Myrtle (Osborne) Goggan; student pvt. schs., Holy Cross Coll., New Orleans, St. Edwards Coll., Austin, Tex., St. Mary's Sem., LaPorte Tex.; D.F.A. (hon.), Baldwin-Wallace Coll., 1972; D.F.A. (hon.), Canisius Coll., 1982; summer student Harvard U., Columbia U. Radio writer NBC, San Francisco, 1933-36; first play Hell Freeze Over appeared N.Y.C., 1936; freelance writer, Hollywood, 1936-38; C., 1936; freelance writer, Hollywood, 1936-38; recent plays include The Hasty Heart, 1945, Story of Mary Surratt, 1947, Curious Savage, 1950, Lo and Behold, 1951, Teahouse of the August Moon, 1953, Good as Gold, 1957, Everbody Loves Opal, 1961, Everbody's Girl, 1967, Scandal Point, 1968, Love Is a Time of Day, 1969, Barrel Full of Pennies, 1970, (mus.) Lovely Ladies, Kind Gentlemen, 1971, Opal Is a Diamond, 1971, Macbeth Did It, 1972, The Dancing Mice, 1972, The Savage Dilemma, 1972, Anybody Out There?, 1972, A Bad Year for Tomatoes, 1974, Sex on the Sixth Floor, 1974, Love Nest for Three, 1974, Noah's Animals, 1975, Enigma, 1975, Roman Conquest, 1975, Opal's Husband, 1975, Divorce Anyone? , 1976, Suicide Anyone'9 , 1976, People!, 1977, Magenta Moth, 1978, That's Not My Mother, 1978, That's Not My Father, 1978, Girls of the Garden Club, 1979, Opal's Million Dollar Duck, 1979, The Indictments, 1980, Cheating Cheaters, 1985, The Reluctant Rogue, 1986, The Gay Deciever, 1987, The Green Monkey, 1987; TV play The Small Miracle, 1972; wrote scripts for motion pictures, including Enchantment, President's Lady, Three Coins in the Fountain, 1954, Love is a Many Splendored Thing, 1955, High Society, 1956, Teahouse of August Moon, 1956, Les Girls (Royal Command Performance, London), 1957, Some Came Running, 1958, The World of Suzie Wong, 1960, Gigot, 1961, Main Attraction, 1962, Shoes of the Fisherman, 1968. Served as capt. with Am. Field Service, India, Burma, 1942-44. Received Pulitzer prize, 1954, N.Y. Drama Critics award, 1954, Perry award, Donaldson award, Aegis Theater Club award for play Teahouse of the August Moon, 1954, Fgn. Corr. award, 1957; award for best Am. musical (for Les Girls), Screen Writers Guild, 1957, William Inge award for Lifetime achievement in the Theater, presented by the Gov. of Kans., 1986. Home: Fortuna Mill Estate Box 2386 Saint Thomas VI 00801

PATRICK, JOHN JOSEPH, education educator; b. East Chicago, Ind., Apr. 14, 1935; s. John W. and Elizabeth (Lazar) P.; m. Patricia Grant, Aug. 17, 1963; children—Rebecca, Barbara. A.B., Dartmouth Coll., 1957; Ed.D., Ind. U., 1969. Social studies tchr. Roosevelt High Sch., East Chicago, 1957-62; social studies tchr. Lab. High Sch., U. Chgo., 1962-65; research assoc. Sch. Edn., Ind. U., Bloomington, 1965-69, asst. prof., 1969-74, assoc. prof., 1974-77, prof. edn., 1977—, dir. social studies devel. ctr., 1986—, dir. ERIC clearinghouse for social studies, social sci. edn., 1986—; bd. dirs. Biol. Scis. Curriculum Study, 1980-83; ednl. cons. Author: Progress of the Afro-American, 1968, The Young Voter, 1974; (with L. Ehman, Howard Mehlinger) Toward Effective Instruction in Secondary Social Studies, 1974, Lessons on the Northwest Ordinance, 1987; (with R. Remy) Civics for Americans, 1980, rev. edit. 1986; (with Mehlinger) American Political Behavior, 1972, rev. edit. 1980, (with C. Keller) Lessons on The Federalist Papers, 1987; America Past and Present, 1983; (with Carol Berkin) History of the American Nation, 1984, rev. edit. 1987; Lessons on the Constitution, 1985. Bd. dirs. Law in Am. Soc. Found., 1984-88, Social Sci. Edn. Consortium, 1984—; mem. Gov.'s Task Force on Citizenship Edn., Ind., 1982-87; active Ind. Commn. on Bicentennial of U.S. Constitution. Mem. Nat. Council Social Studies, Assn. Supervision and Curriculum Devel., Social Sci. Edn. Consortium (v.p. 1985-87), Council for Basic Edn., Soc. History Edn., Am. Polit. Sci. Assn., Am. Hist. Assn., Phi Delta Kappa. Home: 1209 E University St Bloomington IN 47401 Office: Ind U 2805 E 10th St Bloomington IN 47405

PATTANAIK, PRASANTA KUMAR, economist, educator; b. Cuttack, Orissa, India, Apr. 5, 1943; s. Kshetramohan and Krisnapriya (Mohanty) P.; m. Geeta Mohanty, June 11, 1968; 1 child, Swaha. B.A. with honors, Utkal U., Orissa, 1963; M.A., U. Delhi, India, 1965, Ph.D., 1968. Asst. prof. econs. Harvard U., 1968-70; research fellow Nuffield Coll., Oxford, Eng., 1970-71; vis. fellow U. Delhi, 1971-72, reader in econs., 1972-73, prof., 1973-75; prof. LaTrobe U., Bundoora, Victoria, Australia, 1975-77, So. Methodist U., Dallas, 1977-78; prof. math. econs. U. Birmingham, Eng., 1978—. Author: Voting and Collective Choice, 1971; Strategy and Group Choice, 1978; also numerous articles, chpts. Co-editor: Social Choice and Welfare, 1983; assoc. editor Jour. Econ. Theory, 1975—; mng. editor Social Choice and Welfare, 1984—. Fellow Econometric Soc. Avocation: literature. Office: U Birmingham, Dept Econs, Birmingham B15 2TT, England

PATTEN, BEBE HARRISON, clergywoman; b. Waverly, Tenn., Sept. 3, 1913; d. Newton Felix and Mattie Priscilla (Whitson) Harrison; m. Carl Thomas Patten, Oct. 23, 1935; children: Priscilla Carla and Bebe Rebecca (twins), Carl Thomas. D.D., McKinley-Roosevelt Coll., 1941; D.Litt., Temple Hall Coll. and Sem., 1943. Ordained to ministry Ministerial Assn. of Evangelism, 1935; evangelist in various cities of U.S. 1933-50; founder, pres.

Christian Evang. Chs. Am., Inc., Oakland, Calif., 1944—, Patten Acad. Christian Edn., Oakland, 1944—, Patten Bible Coll., Oakland, 1945-83; chancellor Patten Coll., Oakland, 1983—; founder, pastor Christian Cathedral of Oakland, 1950—; held pvt. interviews with David Ben-Gurion, 1972, Menachim Begin, 1977. Founder, condr.: radio program The Shepherd Hour, 1934—; daily TV, 1976—, nationwide telecast, 1979—; Author: Give Me Back My Soul, 1973; Editor: Trumpet Call, 1953—; composer 20 gospel and religious songs, 1945—. Exec. bd. Bar-Ilan U. Assn., Israel; mem. Am.-Israel Pub. Affairs Com., Washington, 1983. Recipient numerous awards including medallion Ministry of Religious Affairs, Israel, 1969; medal Govt. Press Office, Jerusalem, 1971; Christian honoree of yr. Jewish Nat. Fund of No. Calif., 1975; Hidden Heroine award San Francisco Bay council Girl Scouts U.S.A., 1976; Ben-Gurion medallion Ben-Gurion Research Inst., 1977; Resolution of Commendation, Calif. Senate Rules Com., 1978; hon. fellow Bar-Ilan U., 1981; Dr. Bebe Patten Social Action chair established Bar-Ilan U. Mem. Am. Assn. for Higher Edn., Religious Edn. Assn., Am. Acad. Religion and Soc. Bibl. Lit., Zionist Orgn. Am., Am. Assn. Pres. of Ind. Colls. and Univs., Am. Jewish Hist. Soc. Office: 2433 Coolidge Ave Oakland CA 94601

PATTEN, BENTON PENROD, artist, educator; b. Elberta, Utah, Jan. 3, 1934; s. Carl Alva and Vera (Penrod) P.; m. Karol June Payne, Jan. 15, 1959; children—Craig Payne, Lori Michelle, Kendal David. B.S., Brigham Young U., 1960, M.A., 1963; postgrad. Bklyn. Mus. Art Sch., 1963-65; Ed.D., Ill. State U., 1974. Asst. prof. Tex. Women's U., Denton, 1974-75, Pan Am. U., Edinburg, Tex., 1977, N.Mex. Highlands U., Las Vegas, 1977-78; instr. art dept. U. Utah, Salt Lake City, 1979-82; prof. graphic design Utah Tech. Coll., Salt Lake City, 1981-86; vis. artist Bountiful-Davis Artcenter, Utah, 1984—; gallery dir. Tex. Women's U., N.Mex. Highlands U., Salt Lake Community Coll.; artist-in-residence Utah Arts Council, Salt Lake City, 1981-82. One man shows include Weber State Coll., Ogden, Utah, 1967, Ill. State U., Normal, 1972, 73, Tex. Women's U., Denton, 1974, Ricks Coll., Rexburg, Idaho, 1979; exhibited in group shows at Utah Rotunda, Salt Lake City, 1969, North Shore Art League, Winnetka, Ill., 1974, Mail Art Exhibit, Utrecht, Holland, 1977, Bountiful Art Ctr., Utah, 1984, 85, Springville Salon, 1986, Nat. Acad. Art and Design, 1986, Utah Portraiture Christmas exhibit Springville Mus., 1986, Salt Lake Community Coll., 1983-86; represented in permanent collections Brigham Young U., Ill. State U., N.Mex. Highlands U., also pvt. collections. Max Beckmann Meml. scholar Bklyn. Mus. Art Sch., 1963-65, Monitor scholar Pratt Graphic Art Ctr., N.Y.C., 1964; Springville Salon, 1986; Nat. Acad. Art and Design, 1986, recipient Storefront Renewal Program award McClean County Assn. Commerce and Industry, Normal, Ill., 1972-73. Mem. Coll. Art. Assn., NEA. Republican. Mormon. Address: 548 Woodland Hills Dr Bountiful UT 84010

PATTEN, CHARLES ANTHONY, management consultant; b. Allentown, Pa., May 12, 1920; s. Charles Henerie and Mae (Doyle) P.; m. Kathleen Marie Breene, Jan. 6, 1951; children: Charles Anthony Jr., Amy Elizabeth, Nancy Kathleen. B.S.M.E., Lehigh U., 1942. With Joy Mfg. Co., 1947-63, works mgr., 1956-63; v.p. mfg. White Motor Corp., 1963-68, Colt Industries, 1968-69; With Dravo Corp., Pitts., 1942-47, 69-85; gen. mgr. engring. works div. Dravo Corp., 1970-71, corp. v.p., gen. mgr. engring. works div., 1971-75, corp. group v.p., chief exec. officer Dravo Mfg. Group, 1975-81, corp. sr. v.p., mem. corp. policy com., chief exec. officer Dravo Mfg. Group, 1981-83, corp. sr. v.p., asst. to pres. and chief exec. officer, mem. exec. com., 1984-85; pres. C.A. Patten Enterprises, 1985—; bd. dirs., v.p. Dravo (Can.) Ltd., 1975-85; dir., pres. Dravo-Okura Co. Ltd., 1974-79; dir. Dravo Mfg. (Can.) Ltd., 1975-83, Tru Weld Grating Inc., 1983-85; v.p. Dravo Internat., Inc., 1974-85. Trustee Ohio Valley Gen. Hosp., McKees Rocks, Pa., 1975-82, Marietta (Ohio) Coll., 1979—; bd. dirs. Vocat. Rehab. Center of Allegheny County, 1972-79, Jr. Achievement of S.W. Pa., 1975-80. Mem. Am. Mgmt. Assn., ASME, Am. Waterways Operators, Am. Waterways Shipyard Com., Water Resources Congress, Neville Island Mfrs. Assn. (pres. 1975-85), Nat. Mgmt. Assn. (exec. com. 1972-85). Republican. Roman Catholic. Clubs: Duquesne, Shannopin. Home and Office: 2304 Clearvue Rd Pittsburgh PA 15237

PATTEN, FLORENCE WOODWORTH, cytotechnologist, educator; b. Albany, Oreg., Jan. 27, 1935; d. Marshall Melvin and Grace Janet (Chalmers) Woodworth; m. Stanley Fletcher Patten, Jr., Oct. 20, 1979. B.S., U. Oreg., 1957, postgrad., 1958, 59. Chief cytotechnologist U. Wash., Seattle, 1959-65; cytology supr. U. Oreg. Med. Sch., Portland, 1966-70; chief cytotechnologist and ednl. coordinator U. Rochester (N.Y.) Med. Center, 1970-80, asst. prof. pathology, 1977-80, clin. asst. prof. pathology and sr. tech. assoc. obstetrics/gynecology, 1980-83, asst. prof. ob-gyn, 1983—; mem. faculty-tutorials in clin. cytology Internat. Acad. Cytology and U. Chgo., 1971—. Recipient Internat. Acad. Cytology Cytotechnologist award, 1977; Am. Soc. Cytology Cytotechnologist of the Yr. award 1979, Cert. of Merit, 1980. Mem. Am. Soc. Cytology, Am. Soc. Clin. Pathologists, Internat. Acad. Cytology, Am. Soc. Cytotechnology (nat. pres. 1981-82), Phi Beta Kappa, Alpha Chi Omega. Club: P.E.O. Editor, The Cytotechnologist Bull., 1973-80; asst. editor Acta Cytologica, 1982—. Cert. Scuba diver Nat. Assn. Scuba Diving Schs. also: PO Box 668 601 Elmwood Ave Rochester NY 14642

PATTERSON, ANDY JAMES, educator, composer; b. Gordon, Tex., Feb. 20, 1929; s. Andrew Ebenezer and Ida Kate (Fulferi) P.; B.A. in Music, Tex. Christian U., 1948, Mus.M., 1951; Mus.D., Fla. State U., 1969; m. Beverly Jane Shaw, Jan. 25, 1963; children—Andy James, Michael, Philip. Adminstrv. asst. to dean fine arts, instr. music Tex. Christian U., Ft. Worth, 1948-51, 53-56; grad. asst. music Fla. State U., Tallahassee, 1956-58; asst. prof. music Fla. A&M U., 1967-68; asst. prof. music Ga. Tchrs. Coll., Statesboro, 1958-59; mem. faculty Hardin-Simmons U., Abilene, Tex., 1959—, assoc. prof. music, 1959-69, prof., 1969—, chmn. dept. theory and composition, 1959—, acting dean Sch. Music, 1981, also chmn. grad. studies in music. Ruling elder First Central Presbyterian Ch., Abilene. Served with AUS, 1951-53. Andy J. Patterson award named in his honor Theta Lambda chpt. Phi Mu Alpha-Sinfonia at Hardin-Simmons U.; recipient 1st place award orchestral composition Tex. Composers League Competition Contest, 1969; teaching award Cullen Found., 1980, research and creativity award, 1984; meet the Composer/Tex. grantee Tex. Composers Forum/Kaleidasound Orch., 1986. Mem. Am. Soc. U. Composers, Am. Music Center, Inc., AAUP (chpt. pres. 1964-66), Nat. Assn. Coll. Wind and Percussion Instrs., Southeastern Composers League, Pi Kappa Lambda, Phi Mu Alpha-Sinfonia (province gov. 1962-66; Orpheus award Theta Lambda chpt. 1979). Composer large works for orch., sonatas, songs and choral works, piano and organ works, concerti for various instruments, others; 151 compositions printed in 30 vols. in Smith Music Library; compositions performed in U.S., Can., Eng., France, Austria, Germany, USSR, Australia; 2 compositions listed with Shakespeare Music Soc., Victoria, B.C., Can. Home: 1642 Swenson St Abilene TX 79603

PATTERSON, DAWN MARIE, educator, consultant; b. Gloversville, N.Y., July 30; d. Robert Morris and Dora Margaret (Perham) P.; m. Robert Henry Hollenbeck, Aug. 3, 1958 (div. 1976); children: Adrienne Lyn, Nathaniel Conrad. BS in Edn., SUNY, Geneseo, 1962; MA, Mich. State U., 1973, PhD, 1977; postgrad., U. So. Calif. and Inst. Ednl. Leadership. Librarian Brighton (N.Y.) Cen. Schs., 1962-67; asst. to regional dir. Mich. State U. Ctr., Bloomfield Hills, 1973-74; grad. asst. Mich. State U., East Lansing, 1975-77; cons. Mich. Efficiency Task Force, 1977; asst. dean Coll. Continuing Edn., U. So. Calif., Los Angeles, 1978-84; dean continuing edn. Calif. State U., Los Angeles, 1985—; pres. Co-Pro Assocs. Mem. Air Univ. Bd. Visitors, 1986—, Commn. on Extended Edn. Calif. State U. Calif., 1988—; Hist. Soc., Los Angeles Town Hall, Los Angeles World Affairs Council. Dora Louden scholar, 1958-61; Langworthy fellow, 1961-62; Edn. Professions Devel. fellow, 1974-75; Ednl. Leadership Policy fellow, 1982-83. Mem. AAUW (pres. Pasadena br. 1985-86), Am. Assn. Adult and Continuing Edn. (charter), Nat. Univ. Continuing Edn. Assn., Calif. Coll. and Mil. Educators Assn. (pres.), Los Angeles Airport Area Edn. Industry Assn. (pres. 1984), Kappa Delta Pi, Phi Delta Kappa. Republican. Unitarian. Club: Fine Arts of Pasadena. Lodge: Zonta. Office: 5151 State University Dr Los Angeles CA 90032

PATTERSON, DONALD ROSS, lawyer; b. Overton, Tex., Sept. 9, 1939; s. Sam Ashley and Marguerite (Robinson) P.; m. Peggy Ann Schulte, May 1, 1965; children—D. Ross, Jerome Ashley, Gretchen Anne. B.S., Tex. Tech U., 1961; J.D., U. Tex., 1964; LL.M., So. Meth. U., 1972. Bar: Tex. 1964, U.S. Ct. Claims 1970, U.S. Ct. Customs and Patent Appeals 1970, U.S. Ct. Mil. Appeals 1970, U.S. Supreme Ct. 1970, U.S. Dist. Ct. (ea. dist.) Tex. 1982. Commd. lt. (j.g.) U.S. Navy, 1964, advanced through grades to lt. comdr., 1969; asst. officer in charge Naval Petroleum Res., Bakersfield, Calif., 1970-72; staff judge adv., Kenitra, Morocco, 1972-76; officer in charge Naval Legal Service Office, Whidbey Island, Washington, 1976-79; head Mil. Justice Div., Subic Bay, Philippines, 1979-81; ret., 1982; sole practice law, Tyler, Tex., 1982—; instr. U. Md., 1975, Chapman Coll., 1977-79, U. LaVerne, 1980-81. Mem. Tex. Bar Assn., Smith County Bar Assn., Am. Immigration Lawyers Assn., Phi Delta Phi. Republican. Baptist. Club: Toastmasters (Tyler) (past pres.). Lodges: Masons, Rotary, Shriners. Home: 703 Wellington St Tyler TX 75703 Office: 777 S Broadway Suite 106 Tyler TX 75701

PATTERSON, GERTRUDE, English literature educator; b. Ballymena, No. Ireland, Sept. 26, 1938; d. Vincent Clarence and Grace (Hilton) P.; m. Peter C.W. Frost, Mar. 26, 1980. M.A., Trinity Coll., U. Dublin, Ireland, 1960, M.Litt., 1967, Ph.D., 1986. Tchr., Cambridge House, Ballymena, 1960-65; lectr. in English lit. Stranmillis Coll., Belfast, No. Ireland, 1967-78, prin. lectr., 1975—, dean women students, 1986—. Author: T.S. Eliot: Poems in the Making, 1971; cons. editor Yeats Eliot Jour.; contbr. chpt. to book, articles to profl. publs. Mem. Ch. of Ireland. Home: 10 Thornhill Malone, Belfast BT9 6SS, Northern Ireland Office: Stranmillis Coll, Stranmillis Rd, Belfast County, Antrim Northern Ireland

PATTERSON, HARLAN RAY, finance educator; b. Camden, Ohio, June 27, 1931; s. Ernest Newton and Beulah Irene (Hedrick) P.; m. Carol Lee Reighard, Aug. 31, 1970; children by previous marriage: Kristan Lee, Elizabeth Jane; children: Leslie, Nolan Gene. BS, Miami U., Oxford, Ohio, 1953, MBA, 1959; PhD, Mich. State U., 1963. Asst. prof. fin. U. Ill., Champaign-Urbana, 1962-66; mem. faculty Ohio U., Athens, 1966—; prof. fin. Ohio U., 1977—; vis. prof., fellow Chgo. Merc. Exchange, 1971; fin. cons., researcher projects for industry. Contbr. articles to acad. and profl. jours. Chmn. City of Athens Adv. Bd., 1972-77; state chmn. scholarship com. for Ohio Rainbow Girls, 1975-87. Served as commd. officer USN, 1953-56. Won competitive appointment U.S. Naval Acad., 1950. Stonier fellow, 1961; Found. Econ. Edn. fellow, 1965, 67, 69, 71; Chgo. Bd. Trade summer intern, 1983. Mem. Phi Beta Kappa, Beta Gamma Sigma, Phi Eta Sigma, Omicron Delta Epsilon, Pi Kappa Alpha, Alpha Kappa Psi, Delta Sigma Pi. Republican. Lodges: Masons (32 deg.), Shriners, Order of Eastern Star. Home: 17 La Mar Dr Athens OH 45701

PATTERSON, JERRY GENE, banker; b. Syracuse, Kans., Sept. 21, 1943; s. Eugene Taylor and Linda (Weiman) P.; m. Norma Jean Boor; children—Craig, Christine, Clay, Kathryn. B.A. in Sociology, Fort Hays U., 1965; grad. Colo. Sch. Banking, U. Colo., 1976. Registered Kans. Real Estate Broker, Dist. scouts exec. Boy Scouts Am., Junction City, Kans., 1965-67; exec. sec. Milford Lake Assn., Junction City, 1967-69; gen. mgr. Flag Stop Camp Inns, Inc., Belleville, Kans., 1969-70; v.p. Farmers & Mcht. State Bank, Wakefield, Kans., 1970-80, pres. 1980—; pres. Wakefield Bancshares, Inc., 1985—, Big Lakes Certified Devel. Co., Inc., 1983-84, v.p., 1986-87, also bd. dirs.; mem. State Banking Bd. of Kans., 1987—. Author: Kansas Travel Guide, 1970; nat. travel guide Campgrounds Unlimited, 1970-74. Bd. dirs. Big Lakes Regional Planning Com., Manhattan, Kans., 1974-83; sec. Kans. Landscape Arboretum, Wakefield, 1976—; chmn. Wakefield Pride Program, 1971-74; v.p. Wakefield Area Devel. Corp., 1979—; sec.-treas. Emergency Med. Services Council, 1978—; scoutmaster Coronado Area council Boy Scouts Am., 1975-85, Kans. Anthrop. Assn. Recipient St. George award Nat. Boy Scout Council and Catholic Ch., 1983, Dist. of Merit award, Pawnee District Boy Scouts Am.; appointed State Banking Bd., 1987—. Mem. Kans. Bankers Assn. (bd. dirs. 1985-86, consumer credit com. 1986-87, state banking bd. 1987—), Flint Hills Bankers Assn. (v.p. 1986-87, pres. 1987—), Profl. Ins. Agts. Assn. Republican. Roman Catholic. Lodge: Lions (pres. Wakefield Kans.). Home: 105 7th Street Wakefield KS 67487 Office: Farmers & Mchts State Bank PO Box 278 Wakefield KS 67487

PATTERSON, LAWRENCE THOMAS, publishing executive; b. Cin., Aug. 8, 1937; s. Lawrence Thomas Sr. and Helen Adelaid (Wintering) P.; m. Diessla Stauffer, Aug. 8, 1967 (div. 1979); m. Barbara Broden, May 11, 1980; children: Blake Shannon, Kimberly Helen. BS cum laude, Miami U., Oxford, Ohio, 1957; postgrad., U. Pa., 1957; MBA, U. Mich., 1959. Sec.-treas. P-G Products Inc., Cin., 1959-61, Arrington Van Pelt Mgr., Cin., 1960-61; founder, pres. Patterson Internat. Corp., Cin., 1964-75; founder, pres., treas. Am. Youth Mktg. Corp., Cin., 1964-75; founder, pres. Patterson Fin. Services, Cin., 1975—, Swiss Fin. Services, Cin., 1982—; founder, pres. Ctr. Fin. Freedom, Cin., 1975—; founder Silver Dollar Polit. Action Com., Cin., 1982—. Author: Swiss Real Estate and How to Retire in Switzerland, 1977; pub.: Freedom Fighter Index, 1975, Conspiracy Theory Catalog, 1975; (newsletter) Monthly Lesson in Criminal Politics, 1975. Life mem. Com. to Restore the Constitution, Ft. Collins, Colo., 1975—, Commn. Monetary Research and Edn. Served to capt. USAF, 1961-62. Mem. Am. Numismatic Assn. (life), Am. Assn. State and Local History, Am. Security Council, Newsletter Assn. Am. (bd. dirs. 1976), Phi Beta Kappa, Phi Beta Sigma, Delta SIgma Pi. Lutheran. Club: Queen City (Cin.). Home: 2295 Grandin Rd Cincinnati OH 45208 Office: Patterson Strategy Fin Services 105 W Fourth St Suite 633 Cincinnati OH 45202

PATTERSON, PEGGY PRACHT, science laboratory financial administrator; b. Oakland, Calif., Dec. 23, 1947; d. Loren Eugene and Frankie Ethelene (DuPree) P.; m. Michael William Patterson, Dec. 10, 1983 (annulment July 1985); 1 child, John Thomas Yeandle; m. James Charles Schlieper, Sept. 12, 1987. BA in Music, Calif. State U., Hayward, 1970, postgrad. in Bus., 1979-81. Computer operator Haskins & Sells CPA, San Francisco, 1974-75; staff asst. to dir. Lawrence Berkeley (Calif.) Lab., 1976-86; fin. adminstr. for directorate Lawrence Berkeley Lab., 1986—. Mem. Nat. Notary Assn. Republican. Baptist. Home: 15267 Central Ave San Leandroy CA 94578 Office: Lawrence Berkeley Lab 1 Cyclotron Rd Berkeley CA 94720

PATTERSON, ROBERT ARTHUR, physician, health care consultant, retired health care company executive, retired air force officer; b. Palestine, Ill., Sept. 3, 1915; s. Robert Bruce and Nera (McColpin) P.; m. Judith Scheirer, May 15, 1961; children: Mary Kay, Elaine Alice Mills, Robert Arthur II, Victoria Patterson Goodrum. Student, U. Ill., 1933-35; M.D., U. Louisville, 1939. Diplomate: aerospace medicine Am. Bd. Preventive Medicine. Intern Detroit Receiving Hosp., 1939-40; joined Mich. N.G., 1940; commd. USAAF, 1946; advanced through grades to lt. gen. USAF, 1972; rated chief flight surgeon and command pilot; assigned U.S. and ETO, 1940-45; assigned U.S., Spain, Japan, Philippines, 1945-63; dep. dir. plans and hospitalization Office Surgeon Gen., USAF, Washington, 1963-65; dir. plans and hospitalization Office Surgeon Gen., USAF, 1965-68; surgeon Hdqrs. USAFE, Lindsey Air Sta., Germany, 1968-71, Hdqrs. SAC, Offutt AFB, 1971-72; surgeon gen. USAF, 1972-75, ret., 1975; health care cons. Arlington, Va., 1975; sr. v.p. sci. affairs Baxter Travenol Labs., Inc., Deerfield, Ill., 1976-86, health care cons., 1987—; bd. dirs. Gorgas Inst. of Tropical Medicine. Bd. dirs. Gorgas Inst. of Tropical Diseases. Decorated D.S.M. with oak leaf cluster, Legion of Merit with oak leaf cluster, Air Force Commendation medal; recipient citation of honor Air Force Assn., citation of distinction Fed. Hosp. Execs., citation of distinction Am. Hosp. Assn. Fellow Am. Coll. Preventive Medicine, Aerospace Medicine Assn., Am. Coll. Physician Execs. (founder); mem. Assn. Mil. Surgeons (pres. 1972), AMA, Am. Acad. Med. Dirs., Air Force Assn., Ret. Officers Assn., Soc. Mil. Cons. to Armed Forces, Soc. Armed Forces Med. Labs. Scientists, Internat. Anesthesia Research Soc., NIH Alumni, U. Ill. Alumni Assn., Aircraft Owners and Pilots Assn., Order Daedalians, Assn. for Advancement of Med. Instrumentation, Exptl. Aircraft Assn., Chgo. Council on Fgn. Affairs, Deutsch Kurzhaar Verband, N.A. Versatile Hunting Dog Assn., Uniformed Services U. Health Scis. Alumni Assn., Air Safety Found. Clubs: Mid-America (Chgo.); Exmoor Country (Highland Park, Ill.); Bull Valley Hunt (Woodstock, Ill.); Yacht and Country, Sunshine Gun, Yacht (Stuart, Fla.). Home: 2645 Crestwood Ln Riverwoods Deerfield IL 60015 Office: Baxter Travenol Labs One Baxter Pkwy Deerfield IL 60015

PATTERSON, ROBERT BRUCE, JR., lawyer; b. Bklyn., Aug. 29, 1946; s. Robert Bruce and Marian (Mitchell) P.; m. Catherine M. Lenz, June 27, 1982. B.A. in Polit. Sci. with distinction, Pa. State U., 1968; J.D. cum laude, Northwestern U., 1971. Bar: Ill. 1971, U.S. Dist. Ct. (no. dist.) Ill. 1971, U.S. Ct. Appeals (7th cir.) 1973, U.S. Supreme Ct. 1978, U.S. Ct. Appeals (8th cir.) 1980. Assoc. Louis G. Davidson & Assocs., Ltd., Chgo., 1971-82; ptnr. Drumke & Patterson, Ltd., Chgo., 1982—; lectr. in field. Served to capt. U.S. Army, 1972; with Army N.G., 1972-77. Russell Sage Found. scholar, 1968-71. Mem. Chgo. Bar Assn., Ill. State Bar Assn., ABA, Ill. Trial Lawyers Assn., Assn. Trial Lawyers Am., Appellate Lawyers Assn., Phi Beta Kappa. Club: Penn State of Chgo. (pres. 1976-77). Contbr. articles to legal jours. Office: 221 N LaSalle St Suite 1050 Chicago IL 60601

PATTERSON, ROGER LEWIS, psychologist; b. Opelika, Ala., Oct. 30, 1939; s. Homer Lee and Ruby (White) P.; B.A., Auburn U., 1963, M.S., 1965; Ph.D., Fla. State U., 1971; m. Martiza Nunez de Gracia, Dec. 21, 1967; children—Anne Marie, Richard Allen. Clin. research unit Camarillo (Calif.) State Hosp., 1969-72; psychologist Mental Health Center of Escambia County, Pensacola, Fla., 1972-73; psychologist, dir. day treatment U. Ala. and Montgomery Police Dept., 1974-75; mem. faculty Fla. Mental Health Inst., Tampa, 1975-84, prof., 1979-84, dir. gerontology program, 1977-84; adj. asso. prof. dept. psychology U. So. Fla., clin. asso. prof. dept. psychiatry Coll. Medicine, assoc. project dir. Suncoast Gerontology Center, 1980-84; dir. geriatric psychosocial rehab. program VA Med. Ctr., Tuskegee, Ala., 1984-86; coordinator day treatment program VA Outpatient Clinic, Daytona Beach, Fla., 1986—. Served with U.S. Army, 1961-62. Mem. Am. Psychol. Assn., Southeastern Psychol. Assn., Assn. Advancement Behavior Therapy, Fla. Assn. Applied Behavior Analysis, Behavior Therapy and Research Soc. (clin. fellow). Author, editor books; contbr. chpts. to books, articles to profl. jours. Office: VA Outpatient Clinic 1900 Mason Ave Daytona Beach FL 32017

PATTERSON, ROSALYN VICTORIA MITCHELL, biologist, educator; b. Madison, Ga., Mar. 25, 1939; d. Walter Melvin and Hazeltine Virginia (Jones) Mitchell; B.A., Spelman Coll., 1958; M.S., Atlanta U., 1960; Ph.D. Univ. fellow, Emory U., 1967; children—Hazelyn Mamette, Joseph William II, Rosman Victor Melvin. Instr. to prof. biology Spelman Coll., 1960-70; So. Fellowship Funds postdoctoral fellow Ga. Inst. Tech., 1969-70; staff specialist to commr., cons. Bur. Reclamation, Dept. of Interior, Washington, 1970-71; coordinator nat. environ. edn. devel. program Nat. Park Service, Dept. of Interior, 1971-72; NIH postdoctoral fellow exptl. cytology br. NIH and Bur. Biologics, FDA, Bethesda, Md., 1972-73; assoc. prof. biology Ga. State U., 1974-76; prof., chmn. dept. biology Atlanta U., 1977-86; prof. biology Spelman Coll., 1986-87; dir. research careers office, adj. prof. biology Morehouse Coll., Atlanta, 1988—; cons. Dept. Interior, 1970-71. NRC postdoctoral fellow Ctrs. for Disease Control, Atlanta, 1983-84; NIH fellow Ctrs. for Disease Control and Ga. State U., 1984-85. Mem. AAAS, Am. Soc. Cell Biology, Soc. Devel. Biology, Tissue Culture, Assn., Sigma Xi, Phi Sigma, Baptist. Research on mammalian chromosomes in cell culture. Home: 109 Burre Ln SW Atlanta GA 30331 Office: 830 Westview Dr SW Atlanta GA 30314

PATTIE, ANNE HUTCHISON, clinical psychologist; b. Glasgow, Scotland, Mar. 7, 1934; d. Matthew Robertson and Muriel Carrington (Wilson) Sproul; m. J.A. Allan Pattie, Aug. 7, 1956; children: Steven, Graham, Douglas, Caroline. MA with honors, U. Edinburgh, Scotland, 1955; MSc, U. Durham, Eng., 1975; PhD, U. York, Eng., 1980. Ednl. psychologist Local Edn. Authority, Norwich, Eng., 1956-58; psychotherapist Local Health Authority, Stevenage, Eng., 1961-66; clin. psychologist Area Health Authority, N. Yorkshire, Eng., 1966-82; dist. clin. psychologist York Health Authority, York, Eng., 1982—; mem. Health Adv. Service, 1985. Co-author: Clifton Assessment Procedures for the Elderly, 1979. Yorkshire Regional Health Authority grantee, 1978, 86. Mem. Brit. Psychol. Soc. (chmn. div. clin. psychology, 1986), Trent Regional Health Authority Panel of Inquiry (1986-88). Home: 22 The Vale, Skelton, York Y03 6YH, England Office: Clin Psychology Services, Clifton Hosp, York England

PATTIN, ADRIAAN JULIEN, philosophy educator, researcher; b. Hasselt, Limburg, Belgium, June 17, 1914; s. Emile Corneille Pattin and Anna Joanna Decoster. Ph.D., U. Louvain (Belgium), 1952; M.A., U. Ottawa (Ont., Can.), 1953. Joined Oblate Fathers, Roman Catholic Ch., 1935; prof. philosophy U. Ottawa, 1953-67, Centre of Ecclesiastical Studies, Louvain, Belgium, 1967—; asst. Nat. Research Dept. Scis., Brussels, 1966-80. Author: De verhouding tussen zijn en wezenheid en de transcendentale relatie in de 2e helft der XIIIe eeuw, 1955; Le Liber de causis, 1966; Simplicius. Commentaire sur les catégories d'Aristote. Traduction de Guillaume de Moerbeke, vol. 1, 1971, vol. 2, 1975; Repertorium Commentariorum Medii Aevi in Aristotelem Latinorum quae in Bibliothecis Belgicis Asservantur, 1978; Pour l'histoire du sens agent. La controverse entre Barthélemy de Bruges et Jean de Jandun, 1988; researcher in mediaeval philosophy. Chaplain, Belgian Army, 1950-68, chaplain emeritus, 1968. Decorated knight Crown of Belgium; named Laureate, Royal Acad., Brussels, 1954; fellow De Wulf-Mansion Centre U Louvain, 1966-83. Home: Kanunnik De Deckerstraat 27, B2800 Mechelen Antwerp, Belgium

PATTISHALL, BEVERLY WYCKLIFFE, lawyer; b. Atlanta, May 23, 1916; s. Leon Jackson and Margaret Simkins (Woodfin) P.; children by previous marriage: Margaret Ann Arthur, Leslie Hansen, Beverly Wyckliffe, Paige Terhune Pattishall Watt, Woodfin Underwood; m. Dorothy Daniels Mashek, June 24, 1977. BS, Northwestern U., 1938; JD, U. Va., 1941. Bar: Ill. 1941, D.C. 1971. Practiced in Chgo., 1946—; now ptnr. Pattishall, McAuliffe & Hofstetter and predecessor firms, Chgo.; dir. Juvenile Protective Assn. Chgo., 1946-79, pres., 1961-63, hon. dir., 1979—; dir. Vol. Interagy. Assn., 1975-78, sec., 1977-78; U.S. del. Diplomatic Confs. on Internat. Trademark Registration Treaty, Geneva, Vienna, 1970-73, Diplomatic Conf. on Revision of Paris Conv., Nairobi, 1981; mem. U.S. del. Geneva Conf. on Indsl. Property and Consumer Protection, 1978; adj. prof. trademark, trade identity and unfair trade practices law Northwestern U. Sch. Law, Chgo. Author: (with Hilliard) Trademarks, Trade Identity and Unfair Trade Practices, 1974, Unfair Competition and Unfair Trade Practices, 1985, Trademarks, 1987; contbr. articles to profl. jours. Served to lt. comdr. USNR, World War II, ETO, PTO; comdr. Res. ret. Fellow Am. Coll. Trial Lawyers (bd. regents 1979-83); mem. Internat. Patent and Trademark Assn. (pres. 1955-57, exec. com. 1955—), Assn. Internationale Pour La Protection De La Propriete Industrielle (mem. of hon.), ABA (chmn. sect. patent, trademark and copyright Law 1963-64), Ill. Bar Assn., Chgo. Bar Assn., D.C. Bar Assn., Chgo. Bar Found. (dir. 1977-83), U.S. Trademark Assn. (dir. 1963-65), Phi Kappa Psi. Clubs: Legal (Chgo.), Law (Chgo.) (pres. 1982-83), Econ. (Chgo.), Mid-Day, Univ. (Chgo.), Mid-America (Chgo.), Selden Soc. London (Ill. rep.), Chikaming Country (Lakeside, Mich.). Home: 2244 Lincoln Park W Chicago IL 60614 Office: Pattishall McAuliffe & Hofstetter 33 W Monroe St Chicago IL 60603

PATTISON, DAVID HARRY, aerospace company executive; b. Newark, Eng., May 26, 1939; s. Leslie and Audrey May (Healey) P.; m. Gerlinde Anna Maria Federspiel, Oct. 12, 1963; children: Christian David, Nicola. Cert. aircraft engr. Corp. regional exec. Latin Am. and Caribbean Brit. Aerospace PLC, London, Rio de Janeiro. Office: British Aerospace PLC, 11 Strand, London WC2N 5JT, England

PATTON, AUDLEY EVERETT, retired business executive; b. Eve, Mo., Nov. 9, 1898; s. Charles Audley and Letitia Virginia (Earhart) P.; B.S. in Indsl. Adminstrn., U. Ill., 1921, M.S. in Bus. Orgn. and Operation, 1922, Ph.D. in Econs., 1924; m. Mabel Dickie Gunnison, Aug. 5, 1930 (dec. Feb. 1976); 1 dau., Julie Ann Patton Watson; m. 2d, Mary Ritchie Key, June 24, 1977. Auditor, Mfg. Dealers Corp., Cambridge, Mass., 1921; instr. econs. public utilities U. Ill., Champaign-Urbana, 1924-25, asst. prof. econs. Coll. Commerce and Bus. Adminstrn., 1925-26; asst. to pres. Chgo. Rapid Transit Co., Chgo. South Shore & South Bend R.R. Co., Chgo. North Shore & Milw. R.R. Co., Chgo. Aurora & Elgin R.R. Co., 1926; asst. to pres. Public Service Co. No. Ill., Chgo., 1926-43, sec., 1928-52, asst. treas., 1928-44, v.p., 1943-53; v.p., dir. No. Ill. Gas Co., Aurora, 1953-54; v.p. Commonwealth Edison Co., Chgo., 1952-63, ret., 1963; asst. to pres. Presbyn-St. Luke's Hosp., Chgo., 1963-65; former v.p., dir. Big Muddy Coal Co.; past dir. Gt. Lakes Broadcasting Co., Chgo., Chgo. & Ill. Midland Ry. Co., Allied Mills, Inc., Chgo., Am. Gage & Machine Co., Elgin, Ill., HMW Industries, Inc., Stamford, Conn. Treas., Katherine Kreigh Meml. Home for Children, Libertyville, Ill., 1929-36; mem. adv. com. on pub. utilities U. Ill., 1937-40, mem. gen. adv. com., 1943-46. Bd. dirs. Am. Cancer Soc. Ill. div., 1948-76, pres., 1957-59, chmn. bd., 1959-62, mem. fin. com., 1970-76; bd. dirs. Civic Fedn. Chgo., 1945-63, v.p., 1954-63; bd. dirs. South Side Planning Bd. Chgo., 1950-58; bd. dirs., mem. exec. com. Ill. C. of C., 1957-61; trustee Kemper Hall Sch. for Girls, Kenosha, Wis., 1929-37, Highland Park (Ill.) Hosp., 1946-51, Christine and Alfred Sonntag Found. for Cancer Research, 1965-81. Recipient Am. Cancer Soc. medal, 1951. Mem. U. Ill. Found., U.S. Men's (dir. 1958-62, v.p. 1960-65), Midwest (dir. 1956-60) curling assns., OX5 Aviation Pioneers (life mem.), Beta Gamma Sigma, Phi Eta, Delta Sigma Pi, Phi Kappa Phi, Delta Chi. Episcopalian. Clubs: Tower (Chgo.); Chgo. Curling (pres. 1956-57) (Northbrook, Ill.). Contbr. articles to profl. jours. Home and Office: 14782 Canterbury Tustin CA 92680

PATTON, DANIEL CRAIG, business executive; b. Ft. Wayne, Ind., Feb. 7, 1952; s. Lynn James and Phyllis Ilene (Brown) P.; B.S., Ind. U., 1974; M.S., St. Francis Coll., 1982; m. Linda Lorell Montoney, Sept. 10, 1982. Plant acct. Weatherhead Corp., Antwerp, Ohio, 1974-77; plant acct. United Technologies-Essex-MWI div., Ft. Wayne, Ind., 1977-79, div. acctg. supr., 1979-80, supr. gen. acctg., 1980-81, acctg. systems specialist, 1981-82, controller U.S. Samica Corp. div. United Technologies, Ft. Wayne, Ind., 1982-83, MWI inventory control and insulation acctg. mgr., 1984-86, sr. internal auditor, 1986—. Bd. dirs. Essex Credit Union, 1979-82, 85-86, supervisory com., chmn. audit, 1980-81, treas., legis. dir., 1986; mem. fin. com. Vt. Rev. Bd., 1982. Mem. Ind. U. Alumni Assn., Allen County Hist. Soc., Ft. Wayne Fine Arts Found., Ft. Wayne Zool. Soc., N.E. Ind. P.C. Users Group. Republican. Presbyterian. Home: 8518 Bull Rapids Rd Woodburn IN 46797 Office: 1601 Wall St Fort Wayne IN 46804

PATTON, HAROLD PRESTON, art consultant; b. Calgary, Alta., Can., Nov. 9, 1929; s. William Lawrence and Ida Wilhelmina (Mackie) P.; m. Eleanor Isabella Smith, Sept. 25, 1953; children: Fiona Marri Margaret, Isabelle Carol Ann. Student, Vancouver Art Sch., B.C., Can., 1945-50, Banff (Alta.) Sch. Fine Art, 1948. Asst. dir. Calgary Allied Art Cen., 1950; dir. Vincent Price Fine Art Gallery, Chgo., 1966-69, London Arts, Detroit, 1970-71; fine art cons. H. Patton Internat., U.S. and Can., 1971—; resident art cons. Kmart Corp., Troy, Mich., 1970-83; mem. Presdl. Com. on Fine Arts, 1974; lectr. various colls. and univs.; cons. S.S. Kresge World Internat. Hdqrs., Troy, Mich., Smith Hinchman & Grylles, Detroit, A. Kahn & Assocs., Detroit, City Nat. Bank, Detroit, Nat. Bank Detroit, Coast Claims Service Ltd., Victoria, B.C., Art Gallery Victoria, Northumberland Art Gallery, Coburg, Ont., Can.; cons. D.C. Woolley Q.C., Harris Stein, Chris Yaneff Internat. Gallery, McDowell Gallery, Juliane Galleries, Aetna Ins., Art Gallery Ont., all Toronto, Ont. Author: Correspondence with a Sculptor, Nicholas Hornyansky, 1987; columnist various Can. newspapers, 1961-65; music editor Chicagoland Omnibus, 1967-70; music critic Birmingham Eccentric, 1970-75; music reviewer Impressario mag.; set designer Theatre Can., 1959-62, Alta. Soc. Artists, Calgary, 1960-65; artist Vancouver Art Gallery, 1950, Calgary Allied Arts Centre, Alta., 1953; executed murals (3) Canneto Soc. Inc., Toronto. Recipient Jean Martinon U.S. Music Critic's award, 1967-68. Mem. Can. Mozart Soc. (founder). Home: 525 A Mt Pleasant Rd, Toronto, ON Canada M4S 2M4

PATTON, JAMES RICHARD, JR., lawyer; b. Durham, N.C., Oct. 27, 1928; s. James Ralph and Bertha (Moye) P.; m. Mary Margot Maughan, Dec. 29, 1950; children: James Macon, Lindsay Fairfield. A.B. cum laude, U. N.C., 1948; postgrad., Yale U., 1948; J.D., Harvard U., 1951. Bar: D.C. bar 1951, U.S. Supreme Ct. 1963. Attache of Embassy; spl. asst. to Am. ambassador to, Indochina, 1952-54; with Office Nat. Estimates, Washington, 1954-55; atty. Covington & Burling, Washington, 1956-61; sr. partner firm Patton, Boggs & Blow, Washington, 1962—; Lectr. internat. law Cornell Law Sch., 1963-64, U.S. Army Command and Gen. Staff Coll., 1967-68; Mem. Nat. Security Forum, U.S. Air War Coll., 1965, Nat. Strategy Seminar, U.S. Army War Coll., 1967-70, Global Strategy Discussions, U.S. Naval War Coll., 1968, Def. Orientation Conf., 1972; mem. Com. of 100 on Fed. City, Washington; mem. adv. council on nat. security and internat. affairs Nat. Republican Com., 1977-81; bd. dirs. Madeira Sch., Greenway, Va., 1975-81, Lawyers Com. for Civil Rights Under Law, Washington, Legal Aid Soc. Washington; mem. Industry Policy Adv. Com. for Trade Policy Matters, 1984-87; councillor of Atlantic Council of U.S., 1987—; mem. visiting com. Ackland Art Mus. U. N.C., 1987—. Served with U.S. Army, 1954-55. Mem. ABA (past com. chmn.), Inter-Am. Bar Assn. (past del.), Internat. Law Assn., Am. Soc. Internat. Law (treas., exec. council), Washington Inst. Fgn. Affairs, Phi Beta Kappa Assocs., Alpha Epsilon Delta. Clubs: Metropolitan (Washington); Brook (N.Y.C.); Pacific (Honolulu).

PATTON, JOHN M.S., internist; b. Kingston, Ont., Can., Mar. 27, 1941; s. John M.S. Patton and Mary Robertson (Teskey) Freeman; m. Susan Diane Hughes; children: Katherine S., Jessica C., John A.E. MD, Queen's U., Kingston, 1966; M in Philosophy, London U., 1971. Intern Vancouver (B.C.) Gen. Hosp., 1966-67; resident Vancouver Gen. Hosp., St. Paul's Hosp., 1967-68; commonwealth med. scholar Middlesex Hosp., Hammersmith Hosp., London, 1968-71; resident St. Paul's Hosp., Vancouver, 1971-72, Montreal (Can.) Gen. Hosp., 1972-73; instr. medicine McGill U., Montreal, 1972-73; cons. physician King Edward VII Hosp., Paget, Bermuda, 1973—; chmn. div. of medicine King Edward VII Hosp., 1979-82, 88—. Fellow Ryal Coll. Physicians and Surgeons (Can.), Am. Coll. Physicians; mem. Royal Coll. Physicians (U.K.), Bermuda Med. Soc. (pres. 1984-86), Council for Professions Supplying to Medicine (chmn. 1975—). Presbyterian. Office: Bermuda Med Soc, care King Edward VII Meml Hosp, Paget Bermuda

PATTON, JOSEPH DONALD, JR., management consultant; b. Washington, Pa., Jan. 4, 1938; s. Joseph Donald and Priscilla Ann (Johnson) P.; BS in Phys. Scis. and Math. Edn., Pa. State U., 1959; MBA in Mktg., U. Rochester (N.Y.), 1970; m. Susan Oertel, June 3, 1967; children: Jennifer Ann, Joseph Donald, III. Tchr., Aschaffenburg (W.Ger.) Am. Sch., 1963-64; with Xerox Corp., Rochester, 1964-75, mgr. field engring., 1973-75; pres. Patton Cons., Inc., Rochester, 1975—; mem. adj. faculty Rochester Inst. Tech., SUNY, Geneseo. Served as capt. U.S. Army, 1959-63. Registered profl. quality engr., Calif.; cert. profl. logistician; cert. quality engr., cert. reliability engr.; cert. service exec. Fellow Am. Soc. Quality Control (reliability and maintainability tech. award 1982), Soc. Logistics Engrs. (Sole Armitage medal 1980, 82); sr. mem. Instrument Soc. Am.; mem. Assn. Field Service Mgrs. (publs. award 1981), IEEE, Nat. Assn. Service Mgrs., Am. Prodn. and Inventory Control Soc., Soc. Reliability Engrs. Republican. Presbyterian. Author 5 texts in field; contbr. over 100 articles to profl. jours. Office: 3699 W Henrietta Rd Rochester NY 14623

PATURIS, E(MMANUEL) MICHAEL, lawyer; b. Akron, Ohio, July 12, 1933; s. Michael George and Sophia G. (Manos) P.; m. Mary Ann, Feb. 28, 1965; 1 child, Sophia G. BS in Bus., U. N.C., 1954, JD with honors, 1959, postgrad., 1959-60. Bar: N.C. 1959, D.C. 1969, Va. 1973; CPA, N.C. With acctg. firms, Charlotte and Wilmington, N.C., 1960-63; assoc. Poyner, Geraghty, Hartsfield & Townsend, Raleigh, N.C., 1963-64; atty. Chief Counsel's Office, IRS, Richmond, Va. and Washington, 1964-69; ptnr. Reasoner, Davis & Vinson, Washington, 1969-78; sole practice, Alexandria, Va., 1978—; instr. bus. law, econs. and acctg. Bd. editors U. N.C. Law Rev. Served with U.S. Army, 1954-56. Recipient Block award U. N.C. Law Sch. Mem. ABA, D.C. Bar Assn., Va. Bar Assn., Am. Assn. Attys.-CPAs (past pres. Potomac chpt.), Phi Beta Kappa, Beta Gamma Sigma. Republican. Greek Orthodox. Club: Washington Golf and Country (Arlington, Va.). Lodge: Rotary. Home: 431 N Lee St Alexandria VA 22314-2350 Office: 431 N Lee St Alexandria VA 22314

PATZER, FRANZ JOHANN ANTON, library official; b. Vienna, Austria, Aug. 18, 1924; s. Franz and Hedwig (Prochaska) P.; PhD, U. Vienna, 1950, Mag.phil., 1972, EMed., 1982; m. Gertraude Alscher, Oct. 20, 1951; children: Harald, Ursula, Barbara. Prof. Viennese High Schs. for History and Geography, 1950-51; with Viennese Travel Agency, 1952, Austrian Union of Local Authorities, 1953; dep. for culture, edn. and sport City of Vienna, 1954-56; sec. vice mayor, Vienna, 1956-73; dir. Viennese City and County Library, 1974—. Served with signal corps German Army, 1942-45. Recipient Hofrat, 1976, Silb. Abz of SPO, 1975, Silb.Abz of BSA, 1978, other honors. Nö Skomtk, 1984, oö SEZ, 1985, WrGEZ, 1986. Mem. Austrian Red Cross, Austrian Motor Assn., Austrian Children Village Assn., Vereinigung Osterreichischer Bibliothekare. Author: Pioniere im Wiener Rathaus, 1953; Der Wiener Gemeinderat 1918-1934, 1961; Bis die Schuesse fielen, 1964; Die Wiener Stadt-und Landes-bibliothek, 1976; Streiflichter zur Wiener Kummunalpolitik, 1978; Die Tagebücher des Matthias Perth, 1979; Wiener Kongresstagebú ch 1814-1815, 1981; contbr. articles to profl. jours. Home: 29 Muhlsangergasse, A-1110 Vienna Austria Office: MA 9 Rathaus, A-1082 Vienna Austria

PATZKE, JOHN CHARLES, lawyer; b. Milw., Mar. 23, 1954; s. Clifford C. and Valerie S. (Duenow) P.; m. Mary T. Silver, Oct. 2, 1982. B.A. magna cum laude, Marquette U., 1976; J.D., U. Wis., 1979. Bar: Wis. 1979, U.S. Dist. Ct. (ea. dist.) Wis. 1979, U.S. Ct. Appeals (7th cir.) 1980, U.S. Dist. Ct. (ea. dist.) Tex. 1982; U.S. Dist Ct. (we. dist.) Wis., 1984. Law clk. Melli, Shiels, Walker & Pease, Madison, Wis., 1977, Wis. Employment Relations Commn., 1978, NLRB, Milw., 1979; from assoc. to ptnr. Brigden & Petajan, Milw., 1979—. Author (mag.) Milw. Lawyer, 1985, Communications and the Law, 1986; Bus. Age Mag., 1986, 87, 88; Women in Bus. Mag., 1987. Mem. adv. bd. of editors Mid-West Labor and Employment Law Jours., 1983—. Mem. ABA, Milw. Young Lawyers Assn. (com. chmn.), Milw. Bar Assn., Wis. Bar Assn., Am. Soc. Personnel Adminstrn., Personnel and Indsl. Relations Assn. Wis., Alpha Sigma Nu, Pi Sigma Alpha. Lutheran. Home: 8143 W Winston Way Franklin WI 53132 Office: Brigden & Petajan 600 E Mason St Milwaukee WI 53202

PAUER, JIRÍ, national theatre official, educator, composer; b. Libusin, Czechoslovakia, Feb. 22, 1919; s. Josef and Anna P.; m. Zora Pauerová-Seflová, 1944; 1 son, Jiri. Grad. Pedagogical Sch., Kladno, Czechoslovakia, Acad. Arts, Prague, Czechoslovakia, Conservatory, Prague. Tchr. various schs., Czechoslovakia, 1939-45; mgr. Music Agy., Prague, 1945; dep. chief Ministry of Edn., Prague; dep. mgr. Czechoslovac Radio, Prague; mgr. Czechoslovak Philharmony, Prague, 1957-79; gen. mgr. Nat. Theatre, Prague, 1979—; prof. Acad. Arts, 1956—; composer 85 opus pieces. Decorated Order of Labour Pres. Czechoslovakia, Nat. Artist; Artist of Merit Govt. Czechoslovakia. Mem. Czechoslovak Composers Union, Czech Composers and Concert Artists Union. Home: Pomnenkova 46, 10600 Prague 10 Czechoslovakia Office: Nat Theatre, Divadelni 2, PO Box 865, Prague 1 Czechoslovakia

PAUGH, THOMAS FRANCIS, magazine editor, writer, photographer; b. Newark, Mar. 15, 1929; s. George Ruel and Gladys (Organ) P; m. Martha Anne Freeze, Apr. 10, 1954; children—Jennifer Paugh Kopp, Lawrence David. B.A., Colgate U., 1952. Photographer, reporter Ridgewood News, N.J., 1954-55; reporter Bergen Record, Hackensack, N.J., 1955-56; assoc. editor Sports Afield, N.Y.C., 1957-62, managing editor, 1962-67; field editor Sports Afield, Miami, Fla., 1967-76; regional editor Outdoor Life, Miami, 1977-78; editor in chief Sports Afield, N.Y.C., 1978—; editor in chief S.A. Spl. Pubs., N.Y.C., 1978—. Columnist: Sports Afield, 1967-76; contbr. articles to profl. jours. Served to 1st lt., USAF, 1952-54. Mem. Am. Soc. Mag. Editors, Outdoor Writers of Am., Soc. of Illustrators. Office: Sports Afield 250 W 55th St New York NY 10019

PAUGH, WILLARD STANLEY, JR., printing company executive; b. Marinette, Wis., Aug. 8, 1930; s. Willard Stanley and Norma Minnie (Peth) P.; m. Delores Jean King, Sept. 5, 1953; children—Debra L. Paugh Glodowski, Robert S., Thomas W. Student U. Wash., 1949-50; BS, U. Wis., 1956. With R. R. Donnelley & Sons Co., Crawfordsville, Ind., Chgo. and Willard, Ohio, 1956-86 , indsl. engr., supr., prodn. control mgr., mfg. supt., group supt., 1956-74, group research and devel. mgmt., Crawfordsville, 1976-86 ; cons. to Her Majesty's Bur., Teheran, Iran, 1974-75. Served with USN, 1948-52. Mem. Am. Mgmt. Assn., Am. Inst. Indsl. Engrs., Book Mfrs. Inst. Republican. Lutheran. Developer automated adhesive mfg. system for protein base and hydroexpansivity theory for cellulose fibre materials. Home: 2430 Mary St Marinette WI 54143

PAUL, ALIDA RUTH, arts and crafts educator; b. San Antonio, May 30, 1953; d. Richard Irving and Anne Louise (Holman) Paul. B.S. in Edn., Southwest Tex. State U., 1975; M.Ed., U. Houston, 1984. Cert. tchr., Tex. Tchr. art and crafts Houston Ind. Sch. Dist., 1975—. Mem. Am. Assn. Counseling and Devel., Tex. Assn. Counseling and Devel. Republican. Episcopalian. Home: 17727 Wolfhollow St Houston TX 77084

PAUL, CARLOS LAMAS, association executive; b. Santiago, Chile, Sept. 20, 1932; s. Roberto and Maria (Lamas) P.; m. Gloria Fresno, Nov. 27, 1954; children: Carlos, Roberto, Luis Hernan, Magdelena, Cristian. JD, Cath. U. Chile, Santiago, 1954. Gen. mgr. Diario el Sur S.A., Santiago, 1958—; chmn. bd. dirs. Nat. Press Assn., Santiago, 1984—; legal advisor Evans y Cia, Santiago, 1975—. Mem. Lawyers Assn. Roman Catholic. Clubs: La Union (Santiago). Lodge: Lions. Home: 2269 La Higuera, Santiago Chile Office: Diario el Sur SA, 1009 Catedral of 306, 39 Santiago Chile

PAUL, DAVID LEWIS, real estate developer, financial executive; b. N.Y.C., May 1, 1939; s. Isadore and Ruth (Goldstein) P.; m. Sandra Rosenzweig; children: David J., Michael M., Deanna M. Student, Wharton Sch. Bus., U. Pa.; MBA, Columbia U., 1965, JD, 1969. Developer Hawthorne Towers, Montclair, N.J., 1967, Colony House, Lakewood, N.J., 1968, Pequannock (N.J.) Shopping Plaza, 1969, Townhouse of Amherst, Mass., 1971; developer Brandywine Village, Amherst, 1972, Shrewsbury, Mass., 1973; developer Regency Hyatt House, Sarasota, Fla., 1974, Tall Oaks Village, Weymouth, Mass., 1975, Somerset Village, Ft. Lauderdale, Fla., 1977, Am. Furniture Mart, Chgo., 1979; chmn., chief exec. officer CenTrust Savs. Bank, 1983—, CenTrust Trust (formerly Westport Co.), 1983—; bd. dirs. CenTrust Mortgage Corp., Calvin Klein Industries, Weintraub Entertainment Group. Author: The effect of the AFL-CIO Merger on Centralization, 1961, Progressive Architecture, 1967. Mem. policy adv. bd. Ctr. for Real Estate and Urban Econs. U. Calif. Berkeley; bd. dirs. St. Thomas U. Sch. of Law, Pub. Health Trust, Jackson Meml. Hosp., Miami; trustee NCCJ, Miami, Nat. Found. for Advancement of Arts; chmn. New World Symphony; mem. steering com. Greater Miami Jewish Fedn.; bd. dirs., former governing mem. Lincoln Ctr. Repertory Theatre; bd. govs. Philharmonic Orch. of Fla. Clubs: Standard, Mid-America (Chgo.); City Club, Brickell, Fisher Island (Miami); Ocean Reef, Key Largo and Cat Cay, Chubb Cay, Viscayans.

PAUL, GABRIEL (GABE PAUL), former professional baseball club executive; b. Rochester, N.Y., Jan. 4, 1910; s. Morris and Celia (Snyder) P.; m. Mary Frances Copps, Apr. 17, 1939; children: Gabriel, Warren, Michael, Jennie Lou, Henry. Ed. pub. schs., Rochester. Reporter Rochester Democrat and Chronicle, 1926-28; publicity mgr., ticket mgr. Rochester Baseball Club, 1928-34, traveling sec., dir., 1934-36; publicity dir. Cin. Reds Baseball Club, 1937, traveling sec., 1938-50, asst. to pres., 1948-49, v.p., 1949-60, gen. mgr., 1951-60, v.p., 1949-60; v.p., gen. mgr. Houston Astros Baseball Club, 1960-61; gen. mgr. Cleve. Indians Baseball Club, 1961-63, pres., treas., 1963-72, pres., 1978-84; pres. N.Y. Yankees, 1973-77. Dir. or trustee various charitable instns. Served with inf. AUS, 1943-45. Named Major League Exec. of Yr. Sporting News, 1956, 74, Sports Exec. of Yr. Gen. Sports Time, 1956, Baseball Exec. of Yr. Sporting News, 1974, Exec. of Yr., Braves 400 Club, 1974, Baseball Exec. Yr., Milw. Baseball Writers, 1976, Major League Exec. of Yr. U.P., 1976; recipient J. Lewis Comiskey Meml. award Chgo. chpt. Baseball Writers Assn. Am., 1961, Judge Emil Fuchs Meml. award Boston chpt., 1967, Bill Slocum award N.Y. chpt., 1975, Sports Torch of Learning award, 1976; named to Ohio Baseball Hall of Fame, 1980. Clubs: Palma Ceia Country (Tampa, Fla.). Office: 3601 Swann Ave Tampa FL 33609

PAUL, GRACE, retired medical technologist, author; b. Liberal, Kans., Mar. 12, 1908; d. David and Myrtle Helen (Brewer) P.; student Tulsa U., 1930-36, Auburn U., 1948, Columbia U., 1949-51. Med. technologist St. Johns Hosp., Tulsa, 1930-36, VA Hosp., Wadsworth, Kans., 1947-48; plant quarantine insp. U.S. Dept. Agr., N.Y.C., 1948-51; claims examiner Social Security Adminstrn., Balt., 1956-71; market research interviewer Response Analysis, Princeton, N.J., 1973-76. Vol. worker United Way of Temple (Tex.), 1974-84, Cultural Activities Center, Youth Services Bur., Ret. Sr. Vol. Program; active CAC Humanities Council of Temple, 1972-86. Served with WAC, 1944-46. Recipient Jefferson award for Central Tex., 1983; named Outstanding Vol. in Temple Chs., 1985. Mem. Am. Soc. Med. Technologists, Entomol. Soc. Am., Internat. Platform Assn. Presbyn. Club: Business and Professional Women's. Author: Your Future in Medical Technology, 1962; A Short Course in Skilled Supervision, 1965; contbr. to Environ. Engr.'s Handbook, vol. III, 1975. Home: 18 Carlton Rd Hutchinson KS 67502

PAUL, HERBERT MORTON, lawyer, accountant, taxation educator; b. N.Y.C.; s. Julius and Gussie Paul; married; children—Leslie Beth, Andrea Lynn. BBA, Baruch Coll.; MBA, NYU, LLM; JD, Harvard U. Ptnr. Touche Ross & Co., N.Y.C., 1957-82; assoc. dir.-tax Touche Ross & Co., dir. fin counseling; mng. ptnr. Herbert Paul, P.C., N.Y.C., 1982—; dir. N.Y. Estate Planning Council; prof. taxation, trustee NYU. Author: Ordinary and Necessary Expenses; editor: Taxation of Banks; adv. tax editor The Practical Accountant; mem. adv. bd. Financial and Estate Planning, Tax Shelter Insider, Financial Planning Strategist, Tax Shelter Litigation Report; bd. dirs. Partnership Strategist, The Business Strategist; cons. Professional Practice Management Mag.; mem. panel The Hot Line; advisor The Partnership Letter, The Wealth Formula; cons. The Insider's Report for Physicians; mem. tax bd. Business Profit Digest; cons. editor physician's Tax Advisor; bd. fin. cons. Tax Strategies for Physicians; tax and bus. advisor Prentice Hall. Mem. bd. overseers Grad. Sch. Bus., NYU; mem. com. on trusts and estates Rockefeller U.; trustee Alvin Ailey Am. Dance Theatre, Associated Y's of N.Y.; bd. dirs. Alumni Fedn. of NYU; co-chmn. accts. div. Fedn. Philantropies. Served with U.S. Army, 1954-56. Mem. Inst. Fed. Taxation (adv. com. chmn.), Internat. Inst. on Tax and Bus. Planning (adv. bd.), Assn. of Bar of City of N.Y., NYU Tax Soc. (pres., chmn. com. on tax shelters), Bur. Nat. Affairs-Tax Mgmt. (adv. com. on exec. compensation), Am. Inst. CPAs (com. on corp. taxation), Tax Study Group, ABA (tax sect.), N.Y. County Lawyer's Assn., N.Y. State Soc. CPAs (chmn. tax div. com. on fed. taxation, gen. tax com., furtherance com., com. on relations with IRS, bd. dirs.), Nat. Assn. Accts., Assn. of Bar of City of N.Y., Accts. Club of Am., Pension Club, Nat. Assn. Estate Planners (bd. dirs.), N.Y. C. of C. (tax com.), Grad. Soc. Bus. of NYU Alumni Assn. (pres.), Pres. Council (NYU). Clubs: Wall St., City Athletic (N.Y.C.); Middle Bay (Oceanside, N.Y.). Office: 805 3d Ave New York NY 10022

PAUL, HERMAN LOUIS, JR., valve manufacturing company executive; b. N.Y.C., Dec. 30, 1912; s. Herman Louis and Louise Emilie (Markert) P.; student Duke, 1931-32, Lehigh U., 1932-33; m. Janath Powers; children—Robert E., Charles Thomas, Herman Louis III. Power plant engr. Paul's Machine Shop, N.Y.C., 1935-43; pres., chief engr. Paul's Machine Shop, N.Y.C., 1943-48; v.p., chief engr. Paul Valve Corp., East Orange, N.J., 1948-54; pres., chief engr. P-K Industries, Inc., North Arlington, N.J., 1954-59; v.p., dir. research Gen. Kinetics, Englewood, N.J., 1959-62; engring. cons., N.Y.C., 1962-65; v.p., dir. Hydromatics, Inc., Bloomfield, N.J., 1965-67; with P.J. Hydraulics, Inc., Myerstown, Pa., 1967—, pres., chief engr., 1968-80, dir. and stockholder, 1980-81; pres. Flomega Industries, Inc., Cornwall, Pa., 1982—; cons. to Metal Industries Devel. Center, Taiwan, 1979; engring. cons. valves and complimentary equipment, 1980—; valve cons. Continental Disc Corp., Kansas City, Mo., 1980—. Vice chmn. Nat. UN Day Com., 1977, 78, 79, 80. Mem. ASME, Instrument Soc. Am., Am. Soc. Naval Engrs., Internat. Platform Assn., Nat. Contract Mgmt. Assn., AAAS, The Navy League, The Naval Inst. Club: Heidelberg Country (Bernville, Pa.), Quentin (Pa.) Riding. Patentee in field. Home: 370 Dogwood Ln RD 5 Lebanon PA 17042

PAUL, JAMES ROBERT, energy company executive; b. Wichita, Kans., Sept. 10, 1934; s. Harold Robert and Zona Belle (Marlatt) P.; B.S., Wichita State U., 1956; m. Julia Ann Haigh, Aug. 14, 1955; children: John Robert, Jeffrey James, Julie Renee. With Boeing Co., Wichita, 1956-67; mgmt. cons. Peat, Marwick, Mitchell & Co., Houston, 1967-70; v.p. fin. and adminstrn. Robertson Distbn. Systems, Inc., Houston, 1970-73; treas. Colo. Interstate Gas Co., Colorado Springs, 1973-74; treas. The Coastal Corp., Houston, 1974-75, v.p. fin., 1975-78, sr. v.p. fin., 1978-81, chief fin. officer, from 1981, sr. exec. v.p., from 1981, now pres., chief operating officer, dir. Mem. Am. Petroleum Inst., Fin. Execs. Inst. Republican. Methodist. Office: Coastal Corp 9 Greenway Plaza E Houston TX 77046 *

PAUL, PHILIP FRANKLIN, JR., management consultant; b. Chgo., Feb. 1, 1941; s. Philip Franklin and Dorothy (Hite) P.; m. Anne Catherine Rush, June 12, 1960; children—James Franklin, Philip Franklin III, Patricia Joy. BS in Indsl. Mgmt., U. So. Calif., 1963; grad. exec. program, Dartmouth Coll., 1976. Pres., Communications Equipment Co., Beverly Hills, Calif., 1960-63; supr. communications engring. Autonetics div. N.Am. Rockwell, 1963-66; mgr. field mktg. Honeywell Info. Systems, 1966-70, dir. product and strategic planning, 1970-74, dir. systems mgmt. and engring., 1974-78; mgmt. cons. to electronics industry, Sudbury, Mass., 1979-86; sr. v.p. ops. Adelie Corp., 1986-88; dir. bus. devel. Computer Task Group, Waltham, Mass., 1988—; mem. faculty Northeastern U., 1974-79, Boston U. Sch. of Pub. Health, 1981—. Author: Management Systems for Planning, 1975, Executive Decision Systems, 1982. Mem. IEEE (past chmn. communications group).

PAUL, ROBERT, lawyer; b. N.Y.C., Nov. 22, 1931; s. Gregory and Sonia (Rijock) P.; m. Christa Holz, Apr. 6, 1975; 1 child, Gina. BA, NYU, 1953; JD, Columbia U., 1959. Bar: Fla. 1958, N.Y. 1959. Ptnr. Paul, Landy, Beiley & Harper, P.A., Miami, 1964—; counsel Republic Nat. Bank Miami, 1967—. Past pres. Fla. Philharm., Inc., 1978-79; trustee U. Miami. Mem. ABA, N.Y. Bar Assn., Fla. Bar Assn., Inter-Am. Bar Assn., French-Am. C. of C. of Miami (pres. 1986-87). Home: 700 Alhambra Circle Coral Gables FL 33134 Office: Paul Landy Beiley & Harper PA 200 SE 1st St Miami FL 33131

PAUL, ROBERT ARTHUR, steel company executive; b. N.Y.C., Oct. 28, 1937; s. Isadore and Ruth (Goldstein) P.; m. Donna Rae Berkman, July 29, 1962; children: Laurence Edward, Stephen Eric, Karen Rachel. A.B., Cornell U., 1959; J.D., Harvard U., 1962, M.B.A., 1964. With Ampco-Pitts. Corp. (formerly Screw & Bolt Corp. Am.), 1964—, v.p., 1969-71, exec. v.p., 1972-79, pres., 1979—, treas., 1973—, dir., 1969—; v.p., asst. sec., asst. treas., dir. Parkersburg Steel Corp., Louis Berkman Co., Follansbee Steel Corp., Louis Berkman Realty Co.; dir. 1st Nat. Bank of Washington, Pa., Union Nat. Corp., U.S. Biochem. Corp.; gen. partner Romar Trading Co.; Instr. Grad. Sch. Indsl. Adminstrn., Carnegie Mellon U., 1966-69; trustee Montefiore Hosp., pres. bd. 1982-85. Trustee H.L. and Louis Berkman Found.; trustee, treas. Ampco-Pitts. Found. Mem. Am., Mass. bar assns., Soc. Security Analysts. Republican. Jewish. Clubs: Harvard (Boston and N.Y.C.); Concordia (Pitts.) , Harvard-Yale-Princeton (Pitts.), Pitts. Athletic (Pitts.), Duquesne (Pitts.). Office: AMPCO-Pittsburgh Corp 600 Grant St Pittsburgh PA 15219

PAUL, ROBERT URQUHART, airline executive; b. Melbourne, Victoria, Australia, Apr. 24, 1923; s. Robert and Isobell Margaret (Urquhart) P.; m. Katherine Cornelia, Nov. 29, 1947; children: Anthony Robert, Russell Urquhart, Robin Bruce, Gael Katherine, Brett Ian. Cert., Hurlstone Agrl. Coll., Australia, 1939. Jackeroo New South Wales Land Agy. Sheep and Cattle Sta., Australia, 1939-40; supr. engr. Burns Philip Ships, New Hebrides Islands, 1946-48; capt. ind. ships New Hebrides Islands, 1949-53, planter, trader, 1951-80; founder, chmn. New Hebrides Airways (now known as Air Melanesiae), 1960—; chmn. Flight West Airlines, Queensland, Australia, 1987—. Councillor New Hebrides Adv. Council, 1957-75. Served with Australian Army, 1941-44, Royal Australian Air Force, 1944-45. Named to Order Brit. Empire, Queen Elizabeth II, London, 1969; recipient New Hebrides Medal of Honor Vila 1980. Mem. Returned Soldier League (pres., trustee 1982-86, hon. life mem.). Lodge: Discovery. Home: Golf Course Rd, Mount Tamborine Queensland 4272, Australia

PAULEY, RICHARD HEIM, real estate counselor; b. Cleve., Dec. 14, 1932; s. Kenneth H. and Romaine (Heim) P.; m. Jan E. Minnick, Oct. 26, 1957; children—Tyler Kent, Elysa Pauley Del Guercio. B.A. in Polit. Sci., Stanford U., 1954; postgrad. U. So. Calif. Sch. Law, 1956-57. Lic. pvt. pilot. Sr. cons. Coldwell Banker & Co., Newport Beach, Calif., 1963-77; owner Richard H. Pauley Co., Investment Realtors, Newport Beach, Beverly Hills and Tustin, Calif., 1977—; sr. mktg. exec. The Seeley Co., Irvine, Calif., 1986—. Bd. dirs. Orange Coast YMCA, 1973-78. Served to capt. USAFR, 1965. Recipient cert. of appreciation City of Newport Beach, 1975-76; Disting. Service award Rehab. Inst. Orange County, 1973. Mem. Am. Soc. Real Estate Counselors, Internat. Real Estate Fedn., Calif. Assn. Realtors, Nat. Assn. Realtors, SAR, Beta Theta Pi, Phi Delta Phi; Stanford Club of Orange County (past pres.). Republican. Club: Center (Costa Mesa, Calif.). Home:

22 Morning Sun Irvine CA 92715 Office: 100 Pauley Bldg 17371 Irvine Blvd Suite 100 Tustin CA 92680 Office: One Park Plaza Suite 100 Irvine CA 92714-5910

PAULIN, ANDREJ, metallurgical engineer, educator; b. Ljubljana, Yugoslavia, Sept. 22, 1939; s. Robert and Marija (Pintar) P.; diploma engr. U. Ljubljana, 1962; diploma Imperial Coll. Sci. and Tech., London, 1967, Ph.D., 1968, DSc in Metallurgy (honoris causa) Marguis Guiseppe Scieluna Internat. U. Found., Del., 1988; m. Slavka Levec, Jan. 9, 1971; children—Maja, Irena. Research asst. Inst. Metallurgy, Ljubljana, 1962-63; tchr. asst. dept. mining and metallurgy U. Ljubljana, 1964-71, reader, 1971-77, asso. prof., 1977-82, prof., 1982—, head metall. div., 1973-76, dep. head dept. geology, mining and metallurgy, 1983-85, mem. exec. council Faculty for Natural Scis. & Tech., 1973-76; mem. Internat Com. for Study of Bauxites, Alumina and Aluminum, 1977—; mem. exec. council Research Council of Slovenia for Geology, Mining and Metallurgy, 1978-80, mem. presidium, 1981-83; organizer 3d Yugoslav Symposium on Aluminum, Sibenik, 1978, 4th Yugoslav Internat. Symposium on Aluminum, Titograd, 1982, 5th symposium, Mostar, 1986; pres. com. for tech. terminology at Slovenian Acad. of Sci. and Arts, 1987—. Mem. Instn. of Mining and Metallurgy (Great Britain, fellow 1988—), Union Slovenian Mining and Metall. Engrs. (v.p. 1973—, recipient award 1973, 83, exec. com.), Union Yugoslav Mining and Metall. Engrs. (exec. com. 1978-80, award 1979). Editor metallurgy Ency. Slovenia, 1975—, Tech. Ency. (Zagreb), 1979—; author numerous works in field of extractive metallurgy of lead, aluminum, copper, zinc, mercury, silver and gold. Home: 2 b V dolini, 61113 Ljubljana Yugoslavia Office: 20 Askerceva, Ljubljana 61000,, Yugoslavia

PAULING, LINUS CARL, chemistry educator; b. Portland, Oreg., Feb. 28, 1901; s. Herman Henry William and Lucy Isabelle (Darling) P.; m. Ava Helen Miller, June 17, 1923 (dec. Dec. 7, 1981); children: Linus Carl, Peter Jeffress, Linda Helen, Edward Crellin. B.S., Oreg. State Coll., Corvallis, 1922, Sc.D. (hon.), 1933; Ph.D., Calif. Inst. Tech., 1925; Sc.D. (hon.), U. Chgo., 1941, Princeton, 1946, U. Cambridge, U. London, Yale, 1947, Oxford, 1948, Bklyn. Poly. Inst., 1955, Humboldt U., 1959, U. Melbourne, 1964, U. Delhi, Adelphi U., 1967, Marquette U. Sch. Medicine, 1969; L.H.D., Tampa, 1950; U.J.D., U. N.B., 1950; LL.D., Reed Coll., 1959; Dr. h.c., Jagiellonian U., Montpellier (France), 1964; D.F.A., Chouinard Art Inst., 1958; also others. Teaching fellow Calif. Inst. Tech., 1922-25, research fellow, 1925-27, asst. prof., 1927-29, assoc. prof., 1929-31, prof. chemistry, 1931-64; chmn. div. chem. and chem. engring., dir. Calif. Inst. Tech. (Gates and Crellin Labs. of Chemistry), 1936-58, mem. exec. com., bd. trustees, 1945-48; research prof. (Center for Study Dem. Instns.), 1963-67; prof. chemistry U. Calif. at San Diego, 1967-69, Stanford, 1969-74; pres. Linus Pauling Inst. Sci. and Medicine, 1973-75, 78—, research prof., 1973—; George Eastman prof. Oxford U., 1948; lectr. chemistry several univs. Author several books, 1930—, including How to Live Longer and Feel Better, 1986. Contbr. articles to profl. jours. Fellow Balliol Coll., 1948; Fellow NRC, 1925-26; Fellow John S. Guggenheim Meml. Found., 1926-27; Recipient numerous awards in field of chemistry, including; U.S. Presdl. Medal for Merit, 1948, Nobel prize in chemistry, 1954, Nobel Peace prize, 1962, Internat. Lenin Peace prize, 1972, U.S. Nat. Medal of Sci., 1974, Fermat medal, Paul Sabatier medal, Pasteur medal, medal with laurel wreath of Internat. Grotius Found., 1957, Lomonosov medal, 1978, U.S. Nat. Acad. Sci. medal in Chem. Scis., 1979, Priestley medal Am. Chem. Soc., 1984, award for chemistry Arthur M. Sackler Found., 1984, Chem. Edn. award Am. Chem. Soc., 1987. Hon., corr., fgn. mem. numerous assns. and orgns. Home: Salmon Creek 15 Big Sur CA 93920 Office: Linus Pauling Inst Sci and Medicine 440 Page Mill Rd Palo Alto CA 94306

PAULS, THOMAS ALBERT, astrophysicist, educator; b. Paterson, N.J., Jan. 17, 1944; s. Albert and Alyson (Blackshaw) P.; m. Eleanor Pelta, Nov. 1987. A.B., Gettysburg Coll., 1965; M.S., W.Va. U., 1967; M.A., Ind. U., 1970; Ph.D., N.Mex. State U., 1974. Staff scientist Max Planck Inst. for Radio Astronomy, Bonn, W.Ger., 1972-79; asst. prof. physics U. Cologne, West Germany, 1979-86; staff Naval Research Lab., Washington, 1986—. Contbr. articles to profl. jours. Grantee German Sci. Found., U. Cologne, 1981-84. Fellow Internat. Astron. Union, Am. Astron. Soc., Royal Astron. Soc.; mem. AAAS, N.Y. Acad. Sci. Office: Code 4130 Naval Research Lab Washington DC 20375

PAULSEN, POVL, aircraft company executive; b. Skamby, Denmark, Dec. 18, 1931; s. Martinus and Eva (Hansen) P.; m. Jytte Margrethe Ringsted Pedersen, Feb. 16, 1957; children—Steen Ringsted, Jane Ringsted, Christian Ringsted. B.S. in Engring., Odense Teknikum, Denmark, 1958. Engr., Birch & Krogboe, Odense, 1958-59, J.H. Quitzau, Sonderborg, Denmark, 1959-62, Fiome A/S, Frederikssund, Denmark, 1963-64; v.p., gen. mgr. Per Udsen Co., Grenaa, Denmark, 1964-82; pres. Per Udsen Co. Aircraft Industry A/S, Grenaa, 1982—; mem. com. Def. Command, Vedbaek, Denmark, 1980-83. Mem. Fedn. Danish Industries, Assn. Europeenne des Constructeurs de Materiel Aerospati (indsl. and tech. commn., airframe sectoral group, bd. dirs.), Assn. Danish Mfrs. Aero Equipment (pres.). Home: Sommerlyst 16, 8500 Grenaa Denmark Office: Per Udsen Co Aircraft Industry AS, Fabrikvej 1, 8500 Grenaa Denmark

PAULSON, ALAN CHARLES, editor; b. Milw., Dec. 1, 1947; s. Robert C. and Dorothy (Lohneis) P.; B.S., U. Wis., 1970; M.S., U. Alaska, 1973. Instr. biology Kodiak Community Coll., Alaska, 1974-75; fisheries biologist Alaska Dept. Fish and Game, Kodiak, 1973-75; instr. biology U. Alaska, Fairbanks, 1975, research biologist Inst. Marine Sci., 1975-76; editor Inst. Water Resources, 1978-86, Inst. No. Engring., 1986—; freelance writer, Fairbanks, 1975—; comml. hot air balloon pilot, Fairbanks, 1981—, profl. diver, 1964—, freelance photographer, 1974—. Contbr. articles photographs on natural history, biology, art, panoramic photography, no. engring., silenced and automatic weapons, aviation to profl. jours. and popular mags. Recipient Fejes book writing award, journalism dept. U. Alaska, 1984; named Alaska Writer of Yr. in Natural Resources, Alaska N.W. Publ. Co., 1977; Mem. Internat. Assn. Panoramic Photographers, Nat. Press Photographers Assn., AAAS, Am. Soc. Ichthyologists and Herpetologists, Balloon Fedn. Am. Home: 1349 Chena Ridge Rd Fairbanks AK 99709 Office: U Alaska Inst No Engring Fairbanks AK 99775-1760

PAULSON, MOSES, physician; b. Balt., May 2, 1897; s. David and Deborah (Bogatsky) P.; m. Helen Golden, June 9, 1926. B.S., U. Md., 1917, M.D., 1921. House physician Sinai Hosp., Balt., 1921-22; chief gastroenterology Sinai Hosp., 1946-64, attending physician, 1964—; resident physician St. Agnes Hosp., 1922-23; in charge night accident service Emergency Hosp., Washington, 1923-24; resident Children's Hosp., Washington, 1923-24; gen. practice Balt., 1924-26; full-time research in digestive diseases (gastro-enterology) Johns Hopkins U., 1926-29, part time, 1929—, asst. in medicine, 1927-28, instr., 1928-33, assoc., 1933-46, asst. prof. medicine, 1946-55, assoc. prof., 1955-84, assoc. prof. emeritus, 1984—; physician Johns Hopkins Hosp., 1930-84, hon. physician, 1984—; cons. gastroenterology Diagnostic Clinic, 1934-55; cons. pvt.-out-patient services Johns Hopkins Hosp., 1946-68, Regional Office VA, 1950; cons. gastroenterology Perry Point (Md.) VA Hosp.; practice internal medicine, specializing in gastroenterology 1930-84; hon. vis. physician Ch. Home and Infirmary, Mercy, St. Agnes, Sinai hosps., Greater Balt. Med. Center.; Cons. Council on Drugs, A.M.A., 1958-70. Author: Gastroenterlogic Medicine, 1969; Editorial bd.: Am. Jour. Digestive Diseases, 1934-50, Gastroenterology, 1940-55; Contbr. numerous articles to med. publs. Served as hosp. apprentice 1st class USNR, 1917-21. Professorship of Gastroenterology named in honor of Moses and Helen Paulson Johns Hopkins U., 1983. Fellow A.C.P., Am. Coll. Gastroenterology; mem. Am. Soc. Gastrointestinal Endoscopy, A.A.A.S., A.M.A., Am. Soc. Microbiology, So. Med. Assn., Am. Gastro-Enterol. Assn., Am. Soc. for Research in Psychosomatic Problems, Med. and Chirurgical Faculty Md., Phi Delta Epsilon. Clubs: Johns Hopkins, Masons. Home: Roland Park Pl 830 W 40th St Baltimore MD 21211 Office: Johns Hopkins Hosp Baltimore MD 21205

PAULU, BURTON, retired media educator; b. Pewaukee, Wis., June 25, 1910; s. Emanuel Marion and Sarah Marie (Murphy) P.; m. Frances Tuttle Brown, June 29, 1942; children—Sarah Leith, Nancy Jean, Thomas Scott. BA cum laude, U. Minn., 1931, BS, 1932, MA, 1934, postgrad., 1934-38; PhD, NYU, 1949. Mgr. Sta. KUOM, U. Minn., Mpls., 1938-57, prof., dir. radio and TV, 1957-72, prof., dir. media resources, 1972-78, ret. lectr. Sch. Journalism and Dept. of Speech, 1951-78; vis. prof. U. So. Calif., 1958, Los Angeles State Coll., 1961; assoc. dir. study of new ednl. media in Kennedy Cultural Ctr., Washington, 1949-52; sr. Fulbright lectr. faculty of journalism Moscow State U., USSR, 1980-81, 86-87; lectr. U.S. Info. Agy., Spain and Fed. Republic Germany, 1983. Author: A Radio and Television Bibliography, 1952; Lincoln Lodge Seminar on Educational Television Proceedings, 1953; British Broadcasting: Radio and Television in the United Kingdom, 1956; British Broadcasting in Transition, 1961; Radio and Television Broadcasting on the European Continent, 1967; Radio and Television Broadcasting in Eastern Europe, 1974; Television and Radio Broadcasting in the United Kingdom, 1981. Served with U.S. Office of War Info., 1944-45. Grantee Rockefeller Found., 1942, Ford Found., 1958-59, 64-65, 70, 78, U. Minn., 1965-73; Fulbright scholar, 1953-54; recipient Citation of Radio and TV Broadcasting on European Continent, Nat. Journalism Soc., 1967, Pioneering award Internat. Broadcasting Soc. of Netherlands, 1968, Broadcast Preceptor award San Francisco State U., 1968, 82. Mem. Minn. Fulbright Alumni Assn. (bd. dirs. 1985-88), U. Minn. Retirees Assn. (bd. dirs, pres.), AAUP, Phi Beta Kappa, Phi Kappa Phi, Phi Delta Kappa, Kappa Delta Pi, Phi Alpha Theta, Sigma Delta Chi. Democrat. Congregationalist. Avocations: photography, travel, reading, music. Home: 5005 Wentworth Ave Minneapolis MN 55419

PAULU, FRANCES BROWN, international center administrator; b. Hastings, Minn., June 22, 1920; d. Thomas Andrew and Florence Ida (Tuttle) Brown; m. Burton Paulu, June 29, 1942; children: Sarah Leith Paulu Boittin, Nancy Jean Paulu Hyde, Thomas Scott. BA magna cum laude, U. Minn., 1940, postgrad. sch. social work, 1942-44. Case worker Family Welfare Assn. Mpls., 1943-45; interviewer Community Health and Welfare Council, Mpls., 1963; sch. social worker Project Head Start, Mpls., 1966; program dir. Minn. Internat. Ctr., Mpls., 1970-72, exec. dir., 1972—; mem. tourism adv. com. City of Mpls., 1976-83; mem. adv. council Minn. World Trade Ctr., 1984-86. Pres. UN Rally, 1970-72; chmn. Mpls. Charter Commn., 1972-74; bd. dirs. Urban Coalition of Mpls., 1967-70; dir. Minn. World Trade Week, 1977-81; participant Intercultural Communication Project, Japan, 1974; mem. mgmt. team Minn. Awareness Project, 1982—. DeWitt Jennings Payne scholar, 1939-40; recipient Nat. People to People Disting. Membership award, 1987. Mem. Nat. Council for Internat. Visitors (officer and/or exec. com. mem. 1975-81, leader fact-finding team North Africa, Middle East, India 1978), Nat. Assn. for Fgn. Student Affairs, People to People Internat., LWV (pres. Mpls. 1967-69), UN Assn. Minn. (adv. council 1979—), Mpls.-St. Paul Com. on Fgn. Relations, Phi Beta Kappa, Alpha Omicron Pi, Lambda Alpha Psi. Home: 5005 Wentworth Ave Minneapolis MN 55419 Office: Minn Internat Center 711 East River Rd Minneapolis MN 55455

PAULUS, JOHN DOUGLAS, writer, editor, public relations executive; b. Canton, Ohio, July 6, 1917; s. James and Helen (Pateas) P.; B.A., U. Pitts., 1936; postgrad. Georgetown U., Washington; m. Mildred Hankey, Dec. 4, 1937. Sports editor Washington Post, 1936-40; editorial exec. Pitts. Press, 1940-45; promotion dir., assoc. pub. Bklyn. Eagle, 1945-47; sr. account exec., Ketchum Inc., 1947-51; dir. public relations and advt. Jones & Laughlin Steel Corp., Pitts., 1951-57; dir. public relations Firestone Tire & Rubber Co., 1957-58; pres. Hankey Paulus & Co., public relations, fund raising, advt.; lectr. editing, public relations U. Pitts., 1945-53; v.p. public relations Allegheny Ludlum Steel Corp., 1958-70; v.p. public relations and public affairs Allegheny Ludlum Industries, Inc., 1971-80; v.p. public relations and public affairs Allegheny Internat., Inc., 1980-86; sr. cons. Marigus/Catanzano P.R., 1986—; book editor Pitts. Press, 1945-66, Am. Metal Market, daily newspaper, 1960-70; editor-in-chief Mid-Continent Feature Syndicate, 1953—; mng. partner Adelphi Assocs., internat. public relations cons., 1980—. Cons., Task Force on Water Resources and Power, 2d Hoover Commn., 1953-55. Trustee Mercy Hosp., Pitts., Point Park Coll., Pitts., Seton Hill Coll., Greensburg, Pa.; bd. dirs. Duquesne U., ARC, Pitts. Ballet Theatre. Mem. Internat. Iron and Steel Inst. (com. on public affairs and public relations 1968—, chmn. com. 1971—), Am. Iron and Steel Inst. (sr. v.p. 1970-71), NAM (public relations council 1977), Assn. Nat. Advertisers, European Public Relations Roundtable (Geneva), Internat. Public Relations Assn. (Geneva), Sigma Delta Chi, Omicron Delta Kappa. Episcopalian. Clubs: Duquesne, Univ., Press. Author: Pittsburgh in Music, 1949; Our Dollar in Danger, 1961; For Whom the (Steel) Bell Tolls, 1962; Rome Wasn't Bilked in a Day, 1963; House Organs—Sour Notes and Lullabies, 1966; Carrying Kumquats to Khartoum, 1972; The Curious Case of the Busted Back, 1973; Toward Economic Chaos-Via Majority Vote, 1973; Of Sheiks and Shahs and Commissars, 1974; Canada, Mexico, U.S.—A Common Market, 1978; Don't Shoot the Trombone Player, 1979; The Social Irresponsibility of Business in America, 1979; Will the Real Ayatollah Please Stand Up?, 1980; Can We Better the Bitter Society?, 1981; Can We Engineer Our Way Out of the Crisis of Costs?, 1982; Reindustrialization—Revitalizing Industrial Society, 1983; Updating an Old Aphorism—Nothing Ventured, Nothing Changed, 1984; For the Business of America—Congressional Politics are Obsolete, 1985; Three Horns of America's Economic Dilemma: Tax Reform, Trade, the Deficit, 1986, Economic Armageddon 1987 and the Casino Society, 1987. Home: 826 N Meadowcroft Ave Pittsburgh PA 15216 Office: 3 PPG Pl Pittsburgh PA 15222 Other: 76 Rue De Grunewald GD, 1647 Luxembourg Federal Republic of Germany Other: Allegheny Internat Inc, Oberrather Strasse 2, 4000 Dusseldorf 30 Federal Republic of Germany Other: Heiterwanger Weg 4A, 1000 Berlin 45 Federal Republic of Germany

PAUMGARTNER, GUSTAV, hepatologist, educator; b. Neumarkt, Styria, Austria, Nov. 23, 1933; s. Gustav and Grete (Egghart) P.; grad. Bundesrealgymnasium, Graz, Austria; student Princeton U.; MD, U. Vienna, 1960; m. Dagmar List, June 24, 1963. Fellow pharmacology U. Vienna, 1961-63; resident internal medicine U. Vienna Hosp., 1963-65, 66-71; fellow medicine N.J. Coll. Medicine, 1965-66; assoc. dir. dept. clin. pharmacology U. Berne (Switzerland), 1974-79; prof. medicine, chmn. dept. Medicine II, U. Munich (Germany), 1979—; sec. European Assn. Study of Liver, 1971-73; mem. com. for nomenclature and diagnostic criteria Internat. Assn. Study Liver, 1974—. Author: The Liver, Quantitative Aspects of Structure and Function, 1973; also articles. Home: 13 Tassilostrasse, D8032 Graefelfing Federal Republic of Germany Office: Med Klinik II, Klinikum Grosshadern, D8000 Munich 70 Federal Republic of Germany

PAUPINI, GIUSEPPE CARDINAL, cardinal; b. Mondavio, Italy, Feb. 25, 1907. Ordained priest Roman Catholic Ch., 1930; titular archbishop of Sebastopolis in Abasgia, 1956; served in Vatican Diplomatic Corps, 1956-69; internuncio to Iran, 1956-57; nuncio to Guatemala and El Salvador, 1958-58, to Colombia, 1959-69; elevated cardinal, 1969; titular ch. All Saints Ch.; major penitentiary, 1973; mem. Congregation of Causes of Saints, Commn. State of Vatican City. Address: Via Aristofane 41, Rome Italy *

PAVALON, EUGENE IRVING, lawyer; b. Chgo., Jan. 5, 1933; m. Lois M. Frenzel, Jan. 15, 1961; children—Betsy, Bruce, Lynn. B.S.L., Northwestern U., 1954, J.D., 1956. Bar: Ill. 1956. Sr. ptnr. Asher, Pavalon, Gittler and Greenfield, Ltd., Chgo., 1970—; lectr., mem. faculty various law schs. Former mem. state bd. dirs. Ind. Voters Ill. Served to capt., USAF, 1956-59. Fellow Am. Coll. Trial Lawyers, Internat. Soc. Barristers, Internat. Acad. Trial Lawyers; mem. ABA, Chgo. Bar Assn. (bd. mgrs. 1978-79), Ill. Bar Assn., Ill. Trial Lawyers Assn. (pres. 1980-81), Assn. Trial Lawyers Am. (parlimentarian 1983-84, sec. 1984-85, v.p. 1985-86, pres. elect 1986-87, pres. 1987-88), Am. Bd. of Profl. Liability Attys. (Diplomat). Club: Chgo. Athletic Assn., Standard. Author: Human Rights and Health Care Law, 1980; contbr. articles to profl. jours., chpts. in books. Home: 1540 N Lake Shore Dr Chicago IL 60611 Office: 2 N LaSalle Dr Chicago IL 60602

PAVAN, PIETRO CARDINAL, cardinal Roman Catholic Church; b. Treviso, Italy, Aug. 30, 1903. ordained 1928. Proclaimed cardinal 1985; deacon San Francesco da Paola ai Monti. Address: Via della Maglina 1240, Ponte Galeria, 00050 Rome Italy *

PAVAROTTI, LUCIANO, lyric tenor; b. Modena, Italy, Oct. 12, 1935; s. Fernando and Adele (Venturi) P.; m. Adua Veroni, Sept. 30, 1961; children—Lorenza, Cristina, Giuliana. Diploma magistrale, Istituto Magistrale Carlo Sigonio, 1955; studies with, Arrigo Pola, Ettore Campogalliani. Formerly tchr. elem. schs.; salesman ins. Debut as Rodolfo in La Bohème, Reggio Emilia, Italy, 1961; roles include Edgardo in debut Lucia di Lammermoor, Amsterdam, 1963, the Duke in debut Rigoletto, Carpi, 1961, Rodolfo in La Bohème, Covent Garden, 1963, Tonio in debut The Daughter of The Regiment, Covent Garden, 1966, appeared in Lucia di Lammermoor, Australia, 1965, Am. debut, Miami, Fla., 1965; numerous European performances including La Scala, Milan, Italy, Vienna Staatsoper, Paris, Hamburg, San Francisco Opera, 1967, debut, Met. Opera, N.Y.C., 1968; appeared in Daughter of Regiment, Met. Opera, 1971, Elisir d'Amore, Met. Opera, 1973, La Boheme, Chgo. Opera, 1973, La Favorita, San Francisco Opera, 1973, Il Trovatore, San Francisco Opera, 1975, Bellini I Puritani, Met. Opera, 1976, numerous internat. performances, concert series of Am. and European cities, including Carnegie Hall, 1973; appeared in film Yes, Giorgio, 1983; rec. artist on Winner Concorso Internationale, Reggio Emilia, 1961. Recipient Grammy award, 1981. Office: care Herbert Breslin 119 W 57th St New York NY 10019

PAVELKA, ELAINE BLANCHE, mathematics educator; b. Chgo.; d. Frank Joseph and Mildred Bohumila (Seidl) P.; B.A., M.S., Northwestern U.; Ph.D., U. Ill. With Northwestern U. Aerial Measurements Lab., Evanston, Ill.; tchr. Leyden Community High Sch., Franklin Park, Ill.; prof. math. Morton Coll., Cicero, Ill.; speaker 3d Internat. Congress Math. Edn., Karlsruhe, Germany, 1976. Recipient sci. talent award Westinghouse Elec. Co. Mem. Am. Edn. Research Assn., Am. Math. Assn. 2-Year Colls., Am. Math. Soc., Assn. Women in Math., Can. Soc. History and Philosophy of Math., Ill. Council Tchr. of Math., Ill. Math. Assn. Community Colls., Math. Assn. Am., Math. Action Group, Ga. Center Study and Teaching and Learning Math., Nat. Council Tchrs. of Math., Sch. Sci. and Math. Assn., Soc. Indsl. and Applied Math., Northwestern U. Alumni Assn., U. Ill. Alumni Assn., Am. Mensa Ltd., Intertel, Sigma Delta Epsilon, Pi Mu Epsilon. Home: PO Box 7312 Westchester IL 60153 Office: Morton Coll 3801 S Central Ave Cicero IL 60650

PAVLIS, ERRICOS CONSTANTINOS, geodesist, scientist, consultant; b. Chios, Chios Island, Greece, Oct. 5, 1953; s. Constantinos Markos and Anna Kalliopi (Bolla) P.; m. Despina Erricos Bartsakoulia, Aug. 18, 1976; children—Daphne, Constantine, Theodore. Dipl. Ing., Nat. Tech. U., Athens, 1975; M.S. in Geodetic Sci., Ohio State U., 1979, Ph.D. in Geodetic Sci., 1983. Registered surveyor and rural engr., Athens, 1975. Engring. apprentice for pvt. cos., Athens, 1972-73; research asst. Nat. Tech. U., 1975-76; research assoc. Ohio State U., Columbus, 1977-83; research scientist Deutsches Goedatisches Forschungs-institut, Munich, Fed. Republic Germany, 1983-85; project cons., 1983-85; sr. analyst EGG/WASC, Inc., Lanham, Md., 1985—; co-investigator CDProject, NASA, Columbus, 1979-83, 85—, team scientist TOPEX project, 1985—; co-investigator for ESA's POPSAT/ERS, Munich, 1983-84; Merit co-investigator, DGFi/I.Abt., Munich, 1984-85; mem. spl. study group IAG/IUGG, Munich, 1984—. Contbr. articles to sci. jours. Wild-Heerbrugg Geodetic fellow Am. Congress on Surveying and Mapping, 1980. Mem. Am. Geophys. Union, Smithsonian Assocs., Nat. Geog. Soc., Ohio State U. Alumni Assn. Greek Orthodox. Avocations: philately; photography; airplane model building; science books and record collecting. Home: 1112 Cavendish Dr Silver Spring MD 20904 Office: EGG/Washington Analytical Services Ctr Inc 5000 Philadelphia Way Lanham MD 20706

PAVLOV, SERGEI PAVLOVICH, diplomat; b. Rzhev, Kalinin, USSR, Jan. 19, 1929; Pavel Petrovich and Valentina Nilolaevna P.; m. Natalia Alexeyevna; children: Lioudmila, Pavel. Cert., Moscow Inst. Phys. Culture. With Moscow City Komsomol Com., 1956-68; sec. Komsomol Cen. Com., 1958-59, 1st sec., 1959-68; chmn. USSR Com. for Sports and Phys. Culture, 1968-83; ambassador to Mongolia USSR, 1983-85; ambassador to Burma USSR, Rangoon, 1985—. Author books in field; contbr. articles to profl. jours. Mem. cen. com. Communist Pty. Soviet Union, 1961-71, mem. cen. auditing com., 1971-86; chmn. Cen. Council SPorts Socs., 1968; dep. to USSR Supreme Soviet, 1962-70;. Office: Embassy of USSR, 38 Newlyn Rd, Rangoon Burma

PAVLOVIC, PREDRAG, radiation oncologist, educator; b. Bijeljina, Yugoslavia, Mar. 20, 1930; s. Mato and Ana (Job) P.; m. Janja Sikic, Aug. 9, 1958; children—Ira, Ivan. MD, U. Zagreb, 1954; speciality diploma of radiotherapy, Univ. Hosp. Zagreb, 1959; PhD, U. Zagreb, 1968. Asst. on spec. Univ. Hosp. Zagreb, 1956, 59; fgn. asst. Inst. Gustave Roussy, Paris, 1957, Hol Radium Inst., Manchester, Eng., 1958; asst. prof. Sch. Medicine, Rijeka, Yugoslavia, 1969-74, assoc. prof., 1974-76, prof., 1976—, head dept. radiotherapy, 1960-68, dir. Inst. Radiotherapy and Oncology, U. Hosp. Ctr. Rijeka, 1968-88. Contbr. articles to profl. jours. Adv. council Sch. Medicine Rijeka, 1979, U. Rijeka, 1981; health com. Municipality of Rijeka, 1982. Recipient medal Municipality of Rijeka, 1970; U. Rijeka grantee, 1982. Mem. Cancer Soc. Croatia (pres. 1982), Oncol. Soc. Yugoslavia. Roman Catholic. Home: Bulevar oslobodenja 17, 51000 Rijeka Yugoslavia Office: Hosp Ctr Rijeka, Borisa Kidrica 42, Rijeka Yugoslavia

PAVLOWITCH, STEVAN K., historian; b. Belgrade, Yugoslavia, Sept. 7, 1933; s. Kosta St. and Mara (Dyoukitch) P.; m. France Raffray, 1967; 1 child, Kosta. Licence ès Lettres in History, Sorbonne U., Paris, 1956; BA with honors in History, U. London, 1956, MA in History, 1959. Author: Anglo-Russian Rivalry in Serbia, 1961, Yugoslavia, 1971, Bijou d'Art, 1978, Unconventional Perceptions of Yugoslavia, 1940-45, 1985, The Improbable Survivor, Yugoslavia: 1918-88, 1988. Fellow Royal Hist. Soc. Office: Univ of Southampton, Southampton S09 5NH, England

PAVY, BERNARD MARIE, plastic surgeon, pediatric surgeon; b. Versailles, France, Feb. 13, 1938; s. Jacques Francois and Elisabeth Marie (Roussille) P.; m. Nicole de Lussigny, Feb. 19, 1962 (div. 1964); 1 child, Veronique; m. Daniele Emilie Accart, Dec. 4, 1965; children—Agnes, Marie Odile, Stephan, Delphine. Intern Hosp. de Paris, 1965-69; chef de clinique Faculty Medicine, Paris, 1970-75; practice medicine specializing in plastic and reconstructive surgery, pediatric surgery, Paris, 1972—; staff Hosp. St. Vincent de Paul; prof. College de Chirurgie Plastique Reconstructive et Esthetique, Paris, 1980—. Author: Techniques of Pediatric Surgery, 1979. Contbr. numerous articles on plastic and reconstructive surgery for children to profl. publs. Mem. French Soc. Pediatric Surgery, French Soc. Plastic and Reconstructive Surgery (bd. dirs. 1976—), French Coll. Plastic and Reconstructive Surgery (teaching mem. 1980—), Am. Cleft Palate Assn. Club: Racing (Paris). Avocation: tennis. Office: Hosp St Vincent de Paul, 74 Ave Denfer, Rochereau Paris France

PAWELEC, WILLIAM JOHN, ret. electronics co. exec.; b. Hammond, Ind., Feb. 15, 1917; s. John and Julia (Durnas) P.; B.S. in Acctg., Ind. U., 1939; m. Alice E. Brown, May 30, 1941 (dec. Dec. 1970); children—William John, Betty Jane Pawelec Conover; m. 2d, June A. Shepard, Nov. 27, 1976 (div. June 1980). Statistician, Ind. State Bd. Accounts, 1939-41; with RCA, 1941—, mgr. acctg. and budgets internat. div., 1957-61, controller internat. div., 1961-68, corp. mgr. internat. fin. ops. and controls, 1968-75, mgr. corp. acctg., 1975-77, dir. internat. acctg., 1977-81, ret., 1981; controller RCA Internat., Ltd., Electron Ins. Co., 1977, RCA Credit Corp., 1979; ret., 1981. Active, Westfield United Fund, 1967—. Mem. Nat. Assn. Accts. (past nat. v.p.), Watchung Power Squadron, N.J. State C. of C., Commerce and Industry Assn. N.Y., Stuart Cameron McLeod Soc., Ind. U. Alumni Assn. (pres. N.J. chpt.), Beta Gamma Sigma, Sigma Epsilon Theta. Club: Echo Lake Country. Home: 86 New England Ave Summit NJ 07901

PAWLOWSKI, LUCJAN, chemist, educator; b. Poland, 1946; MS, Maria Curie-Sklodowska U., Lublin, 1969; ScD, Poly. Inst. Wroclaw, 1976, habilitation, 1980; m. Krystyna Kostrzewska, 1967; 1 son, Artur. Asst., Inst. Chemistry, Maria-Curia Sklodowska U., 1969-72, sr. asst., 1972-76, asst. prof. chemistry, 1976-80, assoc. prof., 1980-87, prof., 1987—, head water and wastewater treatment research group, 1977-84; head dept. environ. chemistry and tech. Poly. Inst. Lublin, 1984-86; head dept. water and wastewater tech. Tech. U. Lublin; cons. Biprowod of Ministry Polish Chem. Industry, 1974-81. Recipient awards Ministry Higher Edn., Sci. and Techniques, 1977, 80; Silver Cross of Merit, 1979; Paul Sabatier medal (France), 1983; Cath. U. Leuven medal, 1985; named Young Master of Technique for patents, 1974. Mem. Internat. Water Resources Assn., Polish Chem. Soc., Polish Engring. Soc. (2 awards 1976, award 79), Polish Acad. Sci. (environ. engring. com. 1974—, san. engring. 1975—, com. on man and biosphere 1975—), Polish Com. for IAWPRC (pres. 1987—), Internat. Com. Chemistry for Protection of Environment. Co-author: Nowa Technika, Vol. 7, 1977, Vol. 9, 1978, Vol. 15, 1982; Ion Exchange for Pollution Control, 1979; (with B. Bolto) Wastewater Treatment by Ion Exchange, 1986; editor: Physicochemical Methods for Water and Wastewater Treatment, 1980, 82; co-editor Reactive Polymers Jour., 1980, 82, Environ. Protection Engring. Jour., 1985—, Environ. Internat. Jour., 1986—; Nuclear and Chem. Waste Mgmt. Jour., 1986—; (with Verdier and Lacy) Chemistry for the Protection of the Environment, 1984; (with Alaerts and Lacy) Chemistry for Protection of the Environment, 1986. Author sci. articles; abstractor Chem. Abstracts; patentee in field. Home: 72 Goscinna Str, 20 532 Lublin Poland Office: Tech U of Lublin, Dept Water and Wastewater Tech, 40 Nadbystrzyca St, 20 618 Lublin Poland

PAWLOWSKI, ZBIGNIEW STANISLAW, parasitologist; b. Poznan, Poland, July 29, 1926; s. Stanislaw and Ewa Wanda (Kaminska) P.; MD, U. Poznan, 1951, specialist in internal medicine, 1958, specialist in parasitology, 1959; diploma tropical medicine and hygiene, Liverpool (Eng.) Sch. Tropical Medicine, 1964; m. Eugenia Grzankowska, Sept. 3, 1952; children: Magdalena, Jan. Mem. faculty Med. Acad., Poznan, 1967—, prof. med. scis., 1977—, chief clinic parasitic and tropical diseases, 1970-79, 87—, dir. Inst. Microbiology and Infectious Diseases, 1978-79; expert WHO, 1973-78; cons. Ministry Health, 1974-79; mem. staff Parasitic Disease Program, WHO, Geneva, 1979-86; sec.-gen. Internat. Commn. Trichinellosis, 1972-76, pres., 1976-80; pres. Council European Schs. and Insts. Tropical Medicine, 1978. Mem. Polish Parasitol. Soc. (pres. 1973-76), Polish Soc. Infectionists and Epidemiologists (v.p. 1975-78), European Fedn. Parasitologists (v.p. 1973-80), Royal Soc. Tropical Medicine, Brit. Soc. Parasitologists; hon. mem. Am. Vet. Epidemiol. Soc. Author, editor papers and profl. jours. in field. Home: Ul Asnyka 3, 60-832 Poznan Poland Office: Clinic Parasitic and Tropical, Diseases, Acad Medicine, Ul Przybyszewskiego, 60-355 Poznan Poland

PAWSEY, MAXWELL JOHN, civil engineer; b. Coburg, Victoria, Australia, Dec. 16, 1930; s. Raymond John and Agnes Madge (Butler) P.; m. Lorna May Vine, Nov. 24, 1956; children—Karen Ann, Barry John, Kim Susan, Nicole Debra. Assoc. in Civil Engring., Swinburne Tech. Coll., 1956. Engring. asst. City of Moorabbin, Victoria, Australia, 1952-54; engr., works engr. City of Preston, Victoria, 1954-61; dep. city engr., city engr. City of Coburg, 1961-63, 66-73; dep. shire engr. Shire of Doncaster and Templestowe, Victoria, 1963-66; dep. city mgr., city engr. City of Berwick, Victoria, 1973—. Author numerous presentations. Contbr. articles to profl. jours. Mem. numerous mcpl. coms. on engring. Mem. Primary Sch. Council, Pascoe Vale South, 1972-73; found. chmn. Batman Automotive Coll. Council, 1972-74; mem., treas. Hallam High Sch. Council, 1974—; mem. edn. dept.'s planning com. to establish Berwick High Sch., 1976-79; pres. Rosebud and Dist. Life Saving Club, 1970-77; del. State Council Royal Lifesaving Soc. Victoria br., 1971-73; del. Port Phillip Safety Council, 1980—; vestryman, church warden Ch. of Eng., Coburg and Berwick. Recipient recognition badge Royal Life Saving Soc., 1978, Service award Southeastern Beaches Assn., 1980; Cedric Tuxen medal Local Govt. Engring., 1986; Found. for Tech. Advancement of Local Govt. Engring. in Victoria fellow, 1977. Fellow Local Govt. Engrs. Assn. (pres. 1975-76, group sec. 1979—), Instn. of Engrs. Australia (chmn. civil br. Victoria 1983-84); mem. Assn. Profl. Engrs., Australian Inst. Mgmt. (assoc.), Australian Inst. Bldg. Surveyors, Melbourne Univ. Bus. Sch. Assn. Lodges: Rotary (numerous offices; dist. extension com. 1985—), Masons (master 1972-73). Avocations: photography; art; tennis; golf. Office: City of Berwick, Princes Hwy Narre Warren, Berwick Victoria 3806, Australia

PAXTON, ALICE ADAMS, artist, interior architect and designer; b. Hagerstown, Md., May 19, 1914; d. William Albert and Josephine (Adams) Rosenberger; m. James Love Paxton Jr., June 26, 1942 (div.); 1 child, William Allen III. Student, Peabody Inst. Music, Balt., 1937-38; grad., Parson's Sch. Design, N.Y., 1940; studies with J. Laurie Wallace, 1944-46; studies with Augustus Dunbier, 1947-48, Sylvia Curtis, 1949, Milton Wolsky, 1950, Frank Sapousek, 1951. Free-lance work archtl. renderings and interior design, N.Y., 1937-40; interior designer, designer spl. furnishings, muralist Orchard and Wilhelm, Omaha, 1940-42; tchr. art classes Alice Paxton Studio, Omaha, 1957-64; tchr. mech. drawing, archtl. rendering and mech. perspective Parson's Sch. Design, N.Y., 1937-40. Designer (interior) Chapel Boys' Town, Nebr., 1942; one-woman show of archtl. renderings Washington County Mus. Fine Arts, Hagerstown, 1944; exhibited group shows at Joslyn Mus., Omaha, 1943-44, Ann. Exhbn. Cumberland Valley Artists, Hagerstown, 1945; represented in permanent collections at No. Natural Gas Co. Bldg., Omaha, Swanson Found., Omaha; also pvt. collections; vol. designer, decorator: recreation room Omaha Blood Bank, ARC, 1943, recreation room Creighton U., 1943, lounge psychiat. ward Lincoln (Nebr.) Army Hosp., 1944; planner, color coordinator Children's Hosp., Omaha, 1947, painted murals, 1948, decorated dental room, 1950; designed Candy Stripers' uniforms; painted and decorated straw elephant bag presented to Mrs. Richard Nixon, 1960; contbr. articles and photographs to Popular Home mag., 1958. Co-chair camp and hosp. coms. ARC, 1943-45, mem. county com. to select and send gifts to servicemen, 1943-46; mem. Ak-Sar-Ben Ball Com., Omaha, 1946-48, Nat. Mus. Women in the Arts, The Md. Hist. Soc.; judge select Easter Seal design, Joslyn Mus., 1946; mem. council Girl Scouts U.S., Omaha, 1943-47; spl. drs. chmn. Jr. League, Omaha, 1947-48, chair Jr. League Red Cross fund dr., 1947-48; bd. dirs., vol. worker Creche, Omaha, 1954-56; mem. Omaha Jr. League; chmn. Jr. League Community Chest Fund Dr., 1948-50; co-chair Infantile Paralysis Appeal, 1944; numerous vol. profl. activities for civic orgns., hosps., clubs, chs., community playhouse, and for establishing wildlife sanctuary. Recipient three teaching scholarships Parson's Sch. Design, 1937-40, presdl. citation ARC activities, 1946, 1st prize Ann. Midwest Show Joslyn Mus., 1943. Mem. Associated Artists Omaha (charter), Am. Security Council (nat. adv. bd.), Internat. Platform Assn., U.S. Hist. Soc., Nat. Mus. Women in Arts (charter), Md. Hist. Soc. Republican. Episcopalian. Club: Fountain Head Country. Home: 300 Meadowbrook Rd Hagerstown MD 21740

PAXTON, HARRY THEODORE, editor, writer; b. N.Y.C., May 5, 1915; s. Henry Cook and Elsa Louise (Weston) P.; m. Olwyn Neil Adamson, June 12, 1937; children—Vicky Paxton Smith, Jean L. Paxton Silveira. B.A., Haverford Coll., 1936. Mem. editorial staff Main Line Daily Times, Ardmore, Pa., 1937, Germantown (Pa.) Courier, 1938-39, Tide mag., N.Y.C., 1940-42; editorial staff Saturday Evening Post, 1942-44, 46-62, sports editor, 1949-62; polit. speechwriter for Nelson Rockefeller, Senator Kenneth Keating, 1963-64; editorial staff Hosp. Physician, Oradell, N.J., 1965-70, Med. Econs., Oradell, 1970-86, freelance writer, 1986—. Author: The Whiz Kids, 1950; This Life I've Led: The Autobiography of Babe Didrikson Zaharias, 1955; Casey at the Bat - The Life Story of Casey Stengel, 1962; editor anthology Sport U.S.A., 1961. Served with AUS, 1944-46. Recipient Neal award Am. Bus. Press, 1975, 82, Mert certs., 1974, 78, 85. Home and Office: 246 Calle Cuervo San Clemente CA 92672-2436

PAXTON, JOHN VAN MIDDLESWORTH, marketing research executive; b. Jersey City, Jan. 4, 1938; s. John Joseph and Helen (VanMiddlesworth) P.; m. Karlene Reinhardt, Apr. 20, 1963; children—Lucinda, Kristin, A.B., Hamilton Coll., 1959; M.B.A., NYU, 1967. Assoc. research dir. Campbell Ewald Advt., N.Y.C., 1967-68; v.p., research dir. Ted Bates Advt., N.Y.C., 1968-80, John F Murray Advt., N.Y.C., 1980-82; exec. v.p. Schrader Research & Rating Service, Cranbury, N.J., 1982—. Vice pres. amateur dramatic group The Villagers, Middlebush, N.J., 1960-63. Mem. Am. Mktg. Assn. Republican. Home: 4 Jefferson Ct Princeton NJ 08540 Office: Schrader Research & Rating Service South River Rd Cranbury NJ 08512

PAYNE, ALFRED OSWALD, research scientist, mechanical engineer; b. Colombo, Ceylon, Jan. 4, 1919; s. Charles W. and Ada (Knight) P.; m. Myra Isabel Hiddlestone, Aug. 24, 1943; children—Michael Charles. B.Eng.Sc., U. Tasmania, 1941; B.Mech.E., U. Melbourne, 1952, M.E., 1962; D.Sc., Columbia U., 1964. Chartered engr., Australia. Instr. fire control instruments, A.I.F., 1942-43, lt. elec./mech. engr., 1943-45; research officer structures div. A.R.L., Melbourne, 1946-54, sr. research scientist, 1954-62, prin. research scientist, 1965-75, sr. prin. research scientist, head life aircraft structures, 1975-80, sr. research fellow R.M.I.T., Melbourne, 1980—; research fellow Columbia U., N.Y.C., 1962-64; Australian rep. def. sci. service negotiations with Eng., U.S., France, and Switzerland. Contbr. 28 articles to profl. jours. Fed. councillor, Australian Profl. Engrs. Assn., 1972-80. Decorated M.B.E., 1974. Fellow Instn. Engrs., Royal Aeron. Soc.; mem. ASME, Australian Inst. Def. Sci. Home: 18 Withers St, East Ivanhoe, Victoria 3079 Australia

PAYNE, ANTHONY EDWARD, composer; b. London, Aug. 2, 1936; s. Edward Alexander and Muriel Margaret (Stroud) P.; m. Jane Muriel Manning, Sept. 25, 1966. BA with honors, Durham U., Eng., 1961. Freelance journalist, musicologist, lectr. London, 1961-72, freelance composer, 1973—; chmn. Macnaghten Concerts, London, 1967-69. Composer of over 30 concert works; author musical analyses Schoenberg, 1968, The Music of Frank Bridge, 1984. Com. mem. Myra Hess Trust, London, 1985—, Mendlessohn/Boise Scholarship Com., London, 1987—. Recipient Radcliffe Trust award, 1975. Mem. Soc. Promotion of New Music (chmn.). Home: 2 Wilton Sq, London N1 3DL, England Address: care J&W Chester, 7-9 Eagle Ct, London EC1M 5QD, England

PAYNE, BARBARA CASTEEL, lawyer; b. Houston, Jan. 23, 1940; d. Bryon Wharton Casteel and Sydell Louise (Sterling) Dodson; m. Thomas Nelson Payne, Oct. 5, 1957; children—Gary Allen, Melanie Rhea, Dina Dae, Deidre Dee. B.A. summa cum laude in Psychology, U. Bridgeport (Conn.), 1979; J.D., Hofstra U., 1981. Bar: Conn. 1983, U.S. Tax Ct., U.S. Dist. Ct. Conn. Sole practice, Wilton, Conn., 1983-84, Stamford, Conn., 1986—; atty. ITT, Tempe, Ariz., 1984-85; assoc. Law Offices of David Wallman, 1985-86; sole practice, 1986—; legis. cons., Phoenix, 1984. Dana scholar, 1979. Mem. ABA, Conn. Attys. Title Ins. Co., Assn. Trial Lawyers Am., Conn. Bar Assn. (lawyers and community sect.), Stamford/Darien Bar Assn. (chmn. lawyers community com.). Club: Toastmasters (ednl. v.p.). Democrat. Congregationalist. Home: 35 W Brother Dr Greenwich CT 06830 Office: 733 Summer St Stamford CT 06901

PAYNE, BETTIE SELDEN WATFORD, health association executive; b. Texas City, Tex., June 20, 1948; d. Wilbur Horsley and Bettie Selden (Friedell) Watford; m. John Howard Payne, III, Jan. 24, 1970 (div. 1981). B.J., U. Tex., 1970. Pub. relations dir. Lyndon B. Johnson Sch. Pub. Affairs, U. Tex., Austin 1971-72; pub. info. officer Area II Regional Med. Program, U. Calif. Med. Sch., Davis, 1972-73, acting info. officer Med. Sch., 1973-74; congl. staff asst. Washington, 1975-76; dir. pub. relations Nat. Soc. Med. Research, Washington, 1976-79; dir. office communications and pub. affairs Group Health Assn., Inc., Washington, 1979-83; radio/TV relations specialist ARC, 1984; mgr. communications and info. services Nat. Mental Health Assn., 1985-86, health care communications advisor, 1986-87; dir. corporate communications Am. Psych Mgmt., Inc., 1987—. Mem. Alpha Omicron Pi. Democrat. Episcopalian.

PAYNE, FRED J., physician; b. Grand Forks, N.D., Oct. 14, 1922; s. Fred J. and Olive (Johnson) P.; m. Dorothy J. Peck, Dec. 20, 1948; children: Chris Ann Paybe Graebner, Roy S., William F., Thomas A. Student U. N.D., 1940-42; BS, U. Pitts., 1948, MD, 1949; MPH, U. Calif., Berkeley, 1958. Diplomate Am. Bd. Preventive Medicine. Intern, St. Joseph's Hosp., Pitts., 1949-50; resident Charity Hosp., New Orleans, 1952-53; med. epidemiologist Center Disease Control, Atlanta, 1953-60; prof. tropical medicine La. State U. Med. Center, New Orleans, 1961-66; dir. La. State U. Internat. Ctr. for Med. Research and Tng., San Jose, Costa Rica, 1963-66; exec. sec. 3d Nat. Conf. on Pub. Health Tng., Washington, 1966-67; epidemiologist Nat. Nutrition Survey, Bethesda, Md., 1967-68; chief public health professions br. NIH, Bethesda, 1971-74, med. officer, sr. research epidemiologist Nat. Inst. Allergy and Infectious Diseases, 1974-78; asst. health dir. Fairfax County (Va.) Health Dept., 1978—, dir. HIV case mgmt. program, 1988—, AIDS case mgmnt. program, 1988—; clin. prof. La. State U., 1966—; cons. NIH, 1979—; leader WHO diarrheal disease adv. team, 1960. Served with AUS, 1942-46, 49-52. Decorated Combat Medic Badge. Fellow Am. Coll. Preventive Medicine, Am. Coll. Epidemiology; mem. Am. Public Health Assn., AMA, Am. Soc. Microbiology, AAAS, Internat. Epidemiology Assn., Soc. Epidemiologic Research, USPHS Commd. Officers Assn., Sigma Xi. Contbr. articles to profl. jours. Home: 2945 Fort Lee St Herndon VA 22070 Office: 10777 Main St Fairfax VA 22030

PAYNE, KENNETH EUGENE, lawyer; b. Kansas City, Kans., Jan. 12, 1936; s. Felton T. and Irene Elizabeth (Snyder) P.; m. Deidre Lee Hood, Aug. 11, 1957; children—Steven Scott, Kendra Ann. B.S., U. Kans., 1959; J.D., Am. U., 1965. Bar: Mo. 1965, D.C. 1967. Assoc., Irons, Birch, Swindler & Mckie, Washington, 1966-69, Irons, Stockman, Sears & Santorelli, 1969-71; asst. gen. counsel U.S. Dept. Commerce, Washington, 1971-73; ptnr. Finnegan, Henderson, Farabow, Garrett & Dunner, Washington, 1973—; del. Inter-Am. Commn. on Sci. and Tech. Transfer, U.S. Dept. State; cons. UN Indsl. Devel. Orgn.; lectr. Practicing Law Inst., Licensing Law and Bus. Inst. Served to capt. U.S. Army, 1960-68. Mem. Licensing Execs. Soc. Internat. (treas. 1986-87, pres.-elect 1988), Licensing Execs. Soc. U.S. and Can. (pres.-elect 1982-83, pres. 1983-84), ABA, Am. Patent Law Assn., Assn. Trial Lawyers Am. Republican. Methodist. Contbr. articles to profl. jours. Home: 3107 N Peary St Arlington VA 22207 Office: Finnegan Henderson Farabow et al 1775 K St NW Suite 600 Washington DC 20006

PAYNE, LESLIE JULIAN, lawyer; b. N.Y.C., Aug. 1, 1945; s. Harry Leslie and Kathryn Louise (Bobel) P.; m. Johanna Ariadne van Nispen, Dec. 28, 1972; children—Chris, Alexander, Theodore, William. B.S. in M.E., Worcester Poly. Inst. (Mass.), 1967; J.D., Catholic U. Am., 1971; LL.M., Georgetown U., 1976. Bar: D.C. 1973, Ill. 1974. Patent examiner U.S. Patent & Trademark Office, Washington, 1967-73; patent atty. Cushman, Darby & Cushman, Washington, 1973-74; patent atty. Pennie & Edmonds, Arlington, Va., 1974-78; patent atty. Polaroid Corp., Cambridge, Mass., 1978—. Author chpt. to book. Mem. ABA, Boston Patent Law Assn. (chmn. pub. relations and activities com. 1981), Am. Intellectual Property Assn. (chmn. subcom. licensing of genetic material 1981-85, univ. industry licensing subcom., 1986—, edn. com. 1986—). Democrat. Roman Catholic. Office: Polaroid Corp 549 Technology Sq Cambridge MA 02139

PAYNE, WILLIAM TAYLOR, JR., word processing and technical publications consultant; b. Bradshaw, W.Va., Mar. 15, 1930; s. William Taylor and Clara Mae (Horn) P.; m. Joan M. Reinhardt, Mar. 11, 1954; children: Susan C., William Taylor III, Karen L. Student various USAF tech. courses, 1948-49, 51-52, Keio U., 1949, Sch. Electronics, Balt., 1953, Comml. Radio Inst., Balt., 1954-55. Publs. engr. Westinghouse Electric Corp., Balt., 1953-56, Collins Radio Co., Cedar Rapids, Iowa, 1956-58; supr. tech. publs. Gen. Dynamics Corp., Rochester, N.Y., 1958-60; supr. engring. writing Curtiss Wright Corp., East Patterson, N.J., 1960-61; mgr. tech. publs. ACF Industries, Riverdale, Md., 1961-65; services mgr. tech. publs. Bechtel Power Corp., Gaithersburg, Md., 1965-77. Contbr. articles to profl. jours. Served with USAF, 1947-52, Japan. Mem. Internat. Word Processing Assn., Research Inst. Am., Internat. Assn. Tech. Communication for Co. Communicators, Nat. Assn. Govt. Communicators, Soc. Tech. Communication. Address: PO Box 486 Lanham MD 20706

PAYNE, WINFIELD SCOTT, national security policy research executive; b. Denver, Jan. 20, 1917; s. Winfield Scott and Mildred (Hulse) P.; AB, U. Colo., 1939, MA (grad. scholar), 1941; postgrad. (fellow) Syracuse U., 1942; MPA, Harvard U., 1947, Ph.D., 1955; m. Barbara P. Reid, Nov. 18, 1945; children—Judith Lynn, Patricia Lee. Economist, Bur. Budget, Washington, 1945-46; staff Inter-Univ. Case Program, Washington, 1948-50; indsl. analyst Pres.'s Materials Policy Commn., Washington, 1950-52; project leader Ops. Research Office, Johns Hopkins U., Bethesda, Md., 1952-63; sr. research staff, panel dir. Inst. for Def. Analyses, Arlington, Va., 1963-72; asst. to pres. System Planning Corp., Arlington, 1972-86; cons. 1986—; assoc. prof., lectr. George Washington U., Washington, 1963-65; cons. Def. Advanced Research Project Agy., 1972-76; guest lectr., various univs. Mem. Cabin John (Md.) Fire Bd., 1955-65; bd. dirs. Providence Club, Inc., 1976-77. Served with USMC, 1942. Littauer fellow, 1946-48. Mem. AAAS, Am. Polit. Sci. Assn., Am. Econ. Assn., U.S. Strategic Inst., Phi Gamma Delta, Pi Gamma Mu. Club: Cosmos. Contbr. articles to profl. jours.; contbr.: Public Administration and Policy Development: A Case Book, 1951. Home: 209 Providence Rd Annapolis MD 21401 Office: 1500 Wilson Blvd c/o SPC Arlington VA 22209

PAYTON, CHRISTOPHER CHARLES, oil service company executive; b. London, June 24, 1957; s. Albert Alexander and Ermine (Brown) P.; m. Fiona Lilias Fraser, Sept. 3, 1984. MA in Engring., Cambridge U., Eng., 1978. Field engr. Dresser Atlas, Bremen, Fed. Republic Germany, 1978-81, tech. mgr., 1981-82; tech. mgr. Aberdeen, Scotland, 1982-84; area tech. mgr. Dresser Atlas Worldwide, London, 1984-85; gen. mgr. Dresser Atlas, Abu Dhabi, United Arab Emirates, 1985-87; mgr. U.K. Atlas Wireline Services, Aberdeen, 1987—. Mem. Soc. Profl. Well Log Analysts, Soc. Petroleum Engrs. Conservative. Club: Aberdeen Petroleum. Office: Atlas Wireline Services, Wellheads Crescent, Aberdeen AB2 OGA, Scotland

PAYTON-PROUD, ROBERT DONALD, broadcasting executive; b. Cleve., Nov. 1, 1949; s. Lloyd Donald and Eleanore Matilda (Cihon) P.; grad. Cleve. Inst. Broadcasting, 1968; m. K. Diane Siler, Feb. 17, 1979; 1 child, James Siler Owen. Dir. programming Sta. WGCL, Cleve., 1972-74; program mgr. Sta. WRBR, South Bend, Ind., 1974-75; ops. mgr. Sta. XEROK, Juarez, Chihuahua, Mex., 1975-77; program mgr. Sta. WZZP, Cleve., 1977-78; gen. mgr. Sta. KELP, El Paso, 1978-82; gen. sales mgr. Sta. KAMZ, El Paso, 1982-85; gen. mgr. KAMA/KAMZ Radio, El Paso, 1985-87; gen. mgr. Fiouciary Broadcasting Co., 1987—. Bd. dirs. Ashtabula County (Ohio) March of Dimes, 1969-72. Mem. Am. Heart Assn. (bd. dirs., chmn. communications), El Paso Assn. Radio Stas. (past pres.), El Paso C. of C., Advt. Fedn. El Paso, Nat. Assn. Broadcasters, Media Softball Assn. El Paso. Home: 735 Tepic El Paso TX 79912 Office: 4180 N Mesa El Paso TX 79902

PAZ, OCTAVIO, Mexican diplomat, writer; b. Mar. 31, 1914; ed. U. Mex. Founder, dir., editor several Mexican lit. revs. including Barandal, 1931, Taller, 1939, El Hijo Prodigo, 1943; Guggenheim fellow, U.S.A., 1944; former sec. Mexican embassy, Paris; charge d'affairs to Japan, 1951; posted to sec. external affairs; ambassador to India, 1962-68; Simon Bolivar prof. Latin Am. studies, fellow Churchill Coll., Cambridge, Eng., 1970; Charles Eliot Norton prof. poetry Harvard U., 1971-72; now dir. Revista Vuelta, Mexico City. Recipient Internat. Poetry Grand Prix, 1963; Jerusalem prize, 1977; Grand Golden Eagle Internat. Festival, Paris, 1979; T.S. Eliot award for Creative Writing, Ingersoll Found., 1987. Mem. AAAL (hon.). Author: (poetry) Luna Silvestre, 1933; Raiz del Hombre, 1937; Entre la Piedra y la Flor, 1940; A la Orilla del Mundo, 1942; Libertad bajo Palabra, 1949; Piedra de Sol, 1957; La Estacion Violenta, 1958; Selected Poems, 1935-57, 1963; Configurations, 1958-69, 1973; (prose) El Laberinto de la Soledad, 1950; Aguila o Sole, 1951; El Arco y la Lira, 1956; Las Peras del Olmo, 1957; Labyrinth of Solitude, 1961; Posdata, 1971; Claude Levi-Strauss: An Introduction, 1972; Alternating Current, 1972; Bow and the Lyre, 1974; The Siren and the Seashell, 1976; Marcel Duchamp, 1978, Appearance Stripped Bare, 1981, One Earth, Four or Five Worlds, 1985, others. Home: care Revista Vuelta, Leonardo Da Vinci 17, Mexico City 03910, Mexico *

PAZ ESTENSSORO, VICTOR, president Republic of Bolivia; b. Tarija, Bolivia, Oct. 2, 1907; s. Domingo Paz Rojas and Carla Estenssoro de Paz; m. Carmela Cerruto Calderón, 1936; children: Miría, Ramiro; m. Teresa Cortéz Velasco; children: Patricia, Moira, Silvia. Grad., Faculty of Law, Universidad Mayor de San Andrés, La Paz, Bolivia. Founder, leader Nat. Revolutionary Movement in Bolivia from 1942, nat. dep., 1938-39, 40-43, nat. senator, 1944-46, sec. Nat. Office of Fin. Stats., La Paz, fin. ofcl. Permament Fiscal Commn., La Paz, 1930-32, comptroller Gen. of Republic, La Paz, 1932; atty. Credit Union of the Workers, La Paz, 1936, undersec. Ministry of Fin., La Paz, 1936-37, minister of econs., La Paz, 1942, minister of fin., La Paz, 1944-46, pres. Republic of Bolivia, 1952-56, 60-64, 85—; ambassador of Netherlands to U.K., Amsterdam, 1956-59; pres. Banco Minero de Bolivia, La Paz, 1939; corr. Revista de Económica Continental de México, Buenos Aires, 1947; project dir. Compania Fabril Financiera de Buenos Aires, 1948-49; functionary Fábrica de Hilados de Lana Lanasur, Montevideo, Uruguay, 1950-51; prof. history of econ. process Universidad de San Andrés, La Paz, 1939-46; prof. introduction to planning and theories of econ. devel. Universidad Nacional de Ingeniería, Lima, Peru, 1966-70; prof. comtemporary history of S.Am., UCLA, 1977, U. N.Mex., Albuquerque, 1978; sole practice law, 1938-46. Contbr. articles to profl. jours. Recipient numerous awards and decorations from Peru, Colombia, Ecuador, Yugoslavia, Panamá , Guatemala, France, Brazil, Venezuela, Federal Republic of Germany, Uruguay, Egypt, Malta, Argentina, Eng. Office: Office of Pres of Republic, La Paz Bolivia *

PAZI, MARGARITA, literature educator; b. Altstadt, Czechoslovakia, Apr. 16, 1926; arrived in Israel, 1945; d. Siegmund and Marie (Lowy) Gutmann; m. Moshe Pazi (dec. 1984). Grad., London U., 1959, BA with honors, 1966; diploma in French, Sorbonne U., 1962; PhD summa cum laude, U. Wurzburg, Fed. Republic Germany, 1969; hon. prof., Julius-Maximilian U., Wurzburg, 1986. Mem. faculty Tel Aviv U., 1966—, lectr. lit., 1972—; sr. lectr. symposia in Israel, Austria, U.S., Fed. Republic Germany and Poland, 1978—; vis. prof. numerous ednl. instns., U.S. and Fed. Republic Germany, 1983—. Author, co-author books about Jewish writers, 1970—; contbr. numerous essays to Internat. lit. jours. Mem. Fedn. Israeli Writers Writing in German, Israel Writers Assn., PEN Israel, PEN Internat. Home: 21 Sharett St, Tel Aviv 62092, Israel Office: Tel Aviv U, Ramat Aviv, Tel Aviv Israel

PAZIK, GEORGE JAMES, editor, pub.; b. Milw., Apr. 7, 1921; s. Richard Francis and Josephine (Bartos-Bucek) P.; B.S., U. Wis., 1944; m. Bernice Emily Thiele, June 19, 1943; children—Marjorie Anne, Carol Sue. Mgr., Pazik's Delicatessen, Milw., 1946-54; owner Kitchens by Pazik, Milw., 1952-59; exec. dir. Upper 3d St Comml. Assn., Milw., 1959-64; exec. v.p., founder Northtown Planning and Devel. Council, Milw., 1964-74; editor, pub. Fishing Facts mag., Menomonee Falls, Wis., 1970—. Chmn. Milwaukee County Expressway and Transp. Commn., 1971-74; chmn. Wis. state com. of U.S. Commn. on Civil Rights, 1970-72. Served with U.S. Army, 1944-46. Recipient Human Relations award Milw. Council B'nai B'rith, 1968. Mem. Outdoor Writers Assn. Am., AAAS, Sierra Club, Wilderness Soc. Lutheran. Home: 8549 N Servife Dr Unit 204 Milwaukee WI 53223 Office: N84 W13660 Leon Rd Menomonee Falls WI 53051

PAZ SOLDÁN, MIGUEL MATEO, financial/tax planner; b. Lima, Peru, Feb. 11, 1945; came to U.S., 1968; s. Fernando and Elsa Ricardina (Estrada) P.; m. Harriet Sue Skousen; children: Michelle, Monica, Miguel Jr., Manuel, Marcy, Marc, Marcella, Melinda, Melissa, Myra. BS in Chemistry and Microbiology, Ariz. State U., 1980; M of Internat. Mgmt., Am. Grad. Sch. Internat. Mgmt., Glendale, Ariz., 1982. Chemist Motorola Inc., Phoenix, 1980-82; fin. planning, adminstrv. mgr. Motorola Inc., Mesa, Ariz., 1984-85; process engineer Motorola Inc., Mesa, 1983-84, 85-86; mgr. fin. and tax planning M.P.S. Acctg. and Tax Services, Chandler, Ariz., 1986—. Cubmaster Boy Scouts Am., Chandler, Ariz., 1980—. Mem. Electrochem. Soc., Am. Chem. Soc., Internat. Platform Assn. Republican. Mormon. Home: 22231 S 118th St Chandler AZ 85249 Office: MPS Acctg and Tax Services 22231 S 118th St Chandler AZ 85249

PAZZAGLINI, MARIO PETER, JR., psychologist; b. Endicott, N.Y., Mar. 9, 1940; s. Mario and Dina Julia (Albertini) P.; B.A., SUNY, Binghamton, 1961; M.A., George Washington U., 1965; Ph.D., U. Del., 1969. Staff psychologist Del. State Hosp., 1968-72, co-dir. adolescent program, 1972-77; with Bur. of Alcoholism and Drug Abuse State of Del., 1970-83; pvt. practice psychotherapy, Newark, Del., 1973—; mem. staff St. Francis Hosp., Wilmington, Del., 1977—; adj. asst. prof. psychology U. Del., 1972—; clin. instr. Jefferson Med. Sch.; cons. street drug research. HEW grantee, 1971, 1972. Mem. AAAS, Am. Psychol. Assn., N.Y. Inst. Gestalt Therapy, N.Y. Acad Scis., Sigma Xi. Democrat. Roman Catholic. Research in imagery and ancient use of symbols; also pioneer in-residence adolescent psychiat. treatment, drug treatment for State of Del. Office: 523 Capitol Trail Newark DE 19711

PEABODY, ALBERT R., military officer; b. Keeseville, N.Y., Jan. 28, 1937; s. Harry O. and Marie (Hacker) P.; m. Mary Joan Ryan; children: Albert R. Jr., Barbara A., Robert J. BSBA, Empire State Coll., 1978; MBA, Monmouth (N.J.) Coll., 1982. Pres. Peabody's Refinishing Service, Schenectady, N.Y., 1954-63; adminstrv. asst. USNG, Albany, N.Y., 1963-79; commd. lt. col. U.S. Army, 1979, advanced through grades to col., 1985; stationed U.S. Army, Fort Dix, N.J., 1979-83, Rheinberg, Fed. Republic Germany, 1983-85; stationed Allied Powers Europe Supreme Hdqrs., Casteau, Belgium, 1985—. Mem. Hist. Soc. Schenectady, 1960. Mem. N.G. Assn. U.S., Militia Assn. N.Y., Assn. U.S. Army. Roman Catholic. Home: 110 Rue de la Haute Folie, 7401 Naast Belgium Office: US Army Element Shape OPS CRB Land APO New York NY 09055

PEACE, MIRIAM SISKIN, cytotechnologist, lawyer; b. Winnipeg, Man., Can., Feb. 13, 1931; d. David L. and Rissa (Ghitter) Siskin; cert. Sch. of Cytology, Med. Coll. of Ga., 1951; L.L.B., John Marshall Sch. Law, 1972; children—Brian Smiley, Carl Smiley, Janice Smiley Hazlehurst, Vickie Smiley

Sholes, Rissa Peace. Cytologist Med. Coll. of Ga., Augusta, 1951-52, Grady Hosp., Atlanta, 1956-57; supr. St. Joseph's Infirmary, Atlanta, 1957-62, Peace Labs., Atlanta, 1962-69; cytotechnologist Peachtree Lab., Atlanta, 1969-86; supr. Piedmont Hosp., Atlanta, 1979—; admitted to Ga. bar, 1973; individual practice law, Atlanta, 1974-75. Precinct co-chmn. Andrew Young campaign for Congress, 1970, 72. Mem. Am. Soc. Clin. Pathologists (registered cytotechnologist, charter mem.), Am. Soc. for Cytotechnology, State Bar of Ga. Democrat. Jewish. Home: 4717 Roswell St NE Apt D7 Atlanta GA 30342 Office: 1968 Peachtree Rd NW Atlanta GA 30309

PEACE, RICHARD ARTHUR, language educator; b. Burley-in-Wharfedale, Yorkshire, Eng., Feb. 22, 1933; s. Herman and Dorothy (Wall) P.; m. Shirley Mary Virginia Wright, Oct. 18, 1960; children: Mary Virginia, Catherine Elizabeth. MA with honors, Oxford (Eng.) U., 1957, BLitt., 1962. Lectr.-in-charge Russian Bristol (Eng.) U., 1963-75, prof. Russian, 1984—; prof. Hull (Eng.) U., 1975-84. Author: Dostoyevsky: An Examination of Major Works, 1971, The Enigma of Gogol, 1981, Chekhov: A Study of Major Plays, 1983. Mem. Brit. Univs. Assn. Slavists (pres. 1978-80). Home: 5 Wellesley Ave, Beverley High Rd, Hull, Humberside HU6 7LN, England Office: Bristol U, Dept Russian Studies, 17 Woodland Rd, Bristol, Avon B58 1TE, England

PEACOCK, MARKHAM LOVICK, JR., English educator; b. Shaw, Miss., Sept. 19, 1903; s. Markham Lovick and Mary (Patton) P.; m. Dora Greenlaw, Dec. 29, 1928. Grad., Webb Sch., 1921; B.A., Washington and Lee U., 1924, M.A., 1926; Ph.D., Johns Hopkins, 1942. Mem. faculty Va. Polytech. Inst., 1926—, prof. English, 1945—, chmn. dept., 1960-66. Author: The Critical Opinions of William Wordsworth, 1949, also critical, ednl. and lit. articles. Mem. Am. Assn. U. Profs., Nat. Council of Tchrs. English, Modern Lang. Assn., Internat. Fedn. of Modern Langs. and Lits., Modern Humanities Research Assn., Acad. Polit. Sci., N.E.A., Guild of Scholars, Omicron Delta Kappa, Lambda Chi Alpha, Sigma Upsilon, Phi Kappa Phi, Gold Triangle. Episcopalian. Clubs: Shenandoah; Tudor and Stuart (Balt.), Johns Hopkins (Balt.); Princeton. Home: 801 Draper Rd Blacksburg VA 24060

PEACOCKE, ARTHUR ROBERT, physical biochemist, theologian; b. Watford, Eng., Nov. 29, 1924; s. Arthur Charles and Rose Elizabeth (Lilly) P.; m. Rosemary Winifred Mann, 1948; 2 children. BA in Chemistry, BSc, Oxford U., 1946, MA, DPhil, 1948, DSc, 1962, DD, 1982; DipTh, U. Birmingham, 1960, BD, 1971; ScD, Cambridge U., 1973; ScD (hon.), Depauw U., 1983. Ordained priest Ch. of Eng., 1971. Univ. lectr. biochemistry Oxford U., 1959-73; dean, fellow Clare Coll., Cambridge, 1973-84; lectr. various univs., 1951-83; prof. Judeo-Christian studies Tulane U., 1984. Author: numerous books including, Creation and the World of Science, 1979, The Physical Chemistry of Biological Organization, 1983, God and the New Biology, 1986; editor: Monographs in Physical Biochemistry, 1968-83, The Sciences and Theology in the Twentieth Century, 1982, Reductionism in Academic Disciplines, 1985; mem. editorial bd. Biochem. Jour., 1966-71, Biopolymers, 1966-71, Zygon, 1973—; contbr. articles to sci. and theol. jours. Chmn. Sci. and Religion Forum, 1972-78, v.p., 1981—; v.p. Inst. Religion in Age of Sci., U.S., 1984-87; warden Soc. Ordained Sientists, 1987—. Recipient Lecomte du Nuoy prize, 1973. Mem. Brit. Biophys. Soc. (meetings sec., sec., chmn. 1965-69). Home: 55 St John St, Oxford OX1 2LQ, England Office: Oxford U, St Cross Coll, Oxford OX1 3LZ, England

PEAKS, MARY JANE (MRS. ROBERT MALCOLM POLK), orthodontist; b. N.Y.C., Aug. 19, 1916; d. Archibald Garfield and Emilie Henrietta (Stauderman) Peaks; D.D.S., U. Pa., 1939; orthodontic cert. Columbia U., 1974; cert. interior design N.Y. U., 1977; m. Robert Malcolm Polk, Sept. 29, 1942; children: Robert, Mary Moneen Polk Duhé, Eileen. Individual practice dentistry specializing in orthodontics, N.Y.C., 1939-52, Garden City, N.Y., 1950—. Fellow Royal Soc. Health; mem. N.Y. Acad. Scis., ADA, ASCAP, Am. Assn. Orthodontists, N.Y. Soc. Orthodontists, N.Y. Assn. Professions, Soroptimist Internat., Am. Guild Authors and Composers. Composer: I Told A Lie, 1954. Home: 152 W 11th St New York NY 10011 Office: 520 Franklin Ave Garden City NY 11530

PEALE, NORMAN VINCENT, clergyman; b. Bowersville, Ohio, May 31, 1898; s. Charles Clifford and Anna (DeLaney) P.; m. Ruth Stafford, June 20, 1930; children: Margaret (Mrs. Paul F. Everett), John, Elizabeth (Mrs. John M. Allen). AB, Ohio Wesleyan U., 1920, DD, 1936; STB, Boston U., 1924, AM, 1924, DD (hon.), 1986; DD, Syracuse U., 1931, Duke U., 1938, Cen. Coll., 1964; LHD (hon.), Lafayette Coll., 1952, U. Cin., 1968, Wm. Jewell Coll., 1952; LLD (hon.), Hope Coll., 1962, Brigham Young U., 1967, Pepperdine U., 1979; STD, Millikin U., 1958; LittD, Iowa Wesleyan U., 1958, Ea. Ky. State Coll., 1964, Jefferson Med. Coll., 1955; LHD (hon.), Northwestern U., 1984, Pace U., 1984, Milw. Sch. Engring., 1985, St. John's U., 1985, Marymount Manhattan, 1985; DD (hon.), Boston U., 1986, Mt. Union Coll., 1988. Ordained to ministry M.E. Ch., 1922; pastor Berkeley, R.I., 1922-24, Kings Hwy. Ch., Bklyn., 1924-27, Univ. Ch., Syracuse, N.Y., 1927-32, Marble Collegiate Ref. Ch., N.Y.C., 1932-84; co-editor, co-publisher (with Mrs. Peale) Guideposts (an inspirational mag.). Author: A Guide to Confident Living, 1948, The Power of Positive Thinking, 1952, The Coming of the King, 1956, Stay Alive All Your Life, 1957, The Amazing Results of Positive Thinking, 1959, The Tough-Minded Optimist, 1962, Adventures in the Holy Land, 1963, Sin, Sex and Self-control, 1965, Jesus of Nazareth, 1966, The Healing of Sorrow, 1966, Enthusiasm Makes the Difference, 1967, Bible Stories, 1973, You Can If You Think You Can, 1974, The Positive Principle Today, 1976, The Positive Power of Jesus Christ, 1980, Treasury of Joy and Enthusiasm, 1981, Positive Imaging, 1981, The True Joy of Positive Living, 1984; Have a Great Day, 1985; Why Some Positive Thinkers Get Powerful Results, 1986; Power of the Plus Factor, 1987; co-author: (with Ken Blanchard) The Power of Ethical Management, 1988; co-author: chpt. in Am's. 12 Master Salesmen; writer for various secular and religious periodicals; Tech. adviser representing Protestant Ch. in filming of motion picture: motion picture One Man's Way, based on biography, 1963; film What It Takes To Be A Real Salesman. Trustee Ohio Wesleyan U., Central Coll.; mem. exec. com. Presbyn. Ministers Fund for Life Ins.; mem. Mid-Century White House Conf. on Children and Youth, Pres.'s Commn. for Observance 25th Anniversary UN; pres. Protestant Council City N.Y., 1965-69, Ref. Church in Am., 1969-70; lectr. pub. affairs, personal effectiveness; Chaplain Am. Legion, Kings County, N.Y., 1925-27. Recipient numerous awards including: Freedom Found. award, 1952, 55, 59, 73, 74; Horatio Alger award, 1952; Am. Edn. award, 1955; Gov. Service award for Ohio, 1955; Nat. Salvation Army award, 1956; Disting. Salesman's award N.Y. Sales Execs., 1957; Salvation Army award, 1957; Internat. Human Relations award Dale Carnegie Club Internat., 1958; Clergyman of Year award Religious Heritage Am., 1964; Paul Harris Fellow award Rotary Internat., 1972; Disting. Patriot award Sons of Revolution, N.Y. State, 1973; Order of Aaron and Hur Chaplains Corps U.S. Army, 1975; Christopher Columbus award, 1976; All-Time Gt. Ohioan award, 1976; Soc. for Family of Man award, 1981; Disting. Achievement award Ohio Wesleyan U., 1983; Religion in Media Gold Angel award, 1984; Presdl. Medal of Freedom, 1984; 2d Ann. Family Weekly Nat. Treasure award, 1984; Disting. Am. award Sales and Mktg. Execs. Internat., 1985; Theodore Roosevelt Disting. Service award, 1985; World Freedom award Shanghai Tiffin Club, 1985; Napolean Hill Fedn. Gold medal for Literary Achievement, 1985; St. George Assn. Golden Rule award, 1985; Old Hero award NFL, 1987; Adele Rogers St. John Round Table award, 1987; Communicator of the Yr. award Sales and Mktg. Exec. Internat., Little Rock, 1987; Disting. Achievement award Am. Aging, 1987, Grand Cross award Supreme Council, Mother Council of World of 33d and last degree Masons, 1987, Magellan award Circumnavigators Club, 1987; Van Rensselaer Gold medal Masonic Temple Cin. Mem. Am. Found. Religion and Psychiatry (pres.), Ohio Soc. N.Y. (pres. 1952-55), Episcopal Actors Guild, Am. Authors Guild, S.A.R., Alpha Delta, Phi Gamma Delta. Republican. Clubs: Metropolitan, Union League, Lotos. Lodges: Rotary, Masons (past grand prelate), Shriners, K.T.

PEARCE, TOM FINLEY, finance planning company executive; b. Victoria, Tex., Nov. 4, 1941; s. Hailds Robert and Sue Finley Pearce; m. Janet Ann, Mar. 21, 1981; children: Grep, Jennifer. BBA in Acctg., North Tex. State U., 1965. Project mgr. Vought Corp., Dallas, 1970-77, mgr. applications, 1974-77; systems cons. Arco Oil & Gas Co., Dallas, 1977-81, dir. fin., 1981-86; pres. Pearce Capital Mgmt., 1986—. Pres. Plano (Tex.) Homeowners Assn., 1985-86. Recipient Outstanding Achievement award Vought Corp., 1972, Exceptional Contbn. award Arco Oil & Gas Co., 1986. Mem. Am. Mgmt. Assn., Data Processing Mgmt. Assn., Dallas Tennis Assn. (bd. dirs. 1977-78), Los Rios Tennis Assn. (bd. dirs. 1983-84). Home: 2600 Skipwith Plano TX 75023

PEARINCOTT, JOSEPH VERGHESE, educator, physiologist; b. Travancore, India, May 26, 1929; s. George F. and Elizabeth (Kottakaram) P.; B.Sc., Travancore U., 1949; M.Sc., Aligarh U., 1951; Ph.D., Fordham U., 1959; m. Michaeleen Ferrara, May 1, 1958; 1 son, George Joseph. Came to U.S., 1952, naturalized, 1959. Instr. biology Fordham U., N.Y.C., 1952-56; postdoctoral fellow Columbia Coll. Physicians and Surgeons, N.Y.C., 1959-61; research asso., dept. physiology and pharmacology N.Y. Med. Coll., N.Y.C., 1961-62; asst. prof. biology Northeastern U., Boston, 1962-68, asso. prof. biology, 1968—. Mem. N.Y. Acad. Scis., AAAS, Am. Soc. Zoologists, Entomol. Soc. Am., AAUP, Sigma Xi. Home: 61 Webb St Lexington MA 02173 Office: 360 Huntington Ave Boston MA 02115

PEARLMAN, PETER STEVEN, lawyer; b. Orange, N.J., June 11, 1946; s. Jack Kitchener and Tiela Josephine (Fine) P.; m. Joan Perlmutter, June 19, 1969; children—Heather, Christopher, Megan. B.A., U. Ill., 1967; J.D., Seton Hall U., 1970. Bar: N.J. 1970, U.S. Dist. Ct. N.J. 1970, U.S. Tax Ct. 1973, U.S. Supreme Ct. 1974, U.S. Ct. Appeals (2d cir.) 1981, U.S. Ct. Appeals (3d cir.) 1983, U.S. Ct. Appeals (7th cir.) 1985. Assoc. Cohn & Lifland, Esquires, Saddle Brook, N.J., 1970-72, ptnr., 1972—; lectr. Nat. Inst. Trial Advocacy, 1988—; mem. panel arbitrators Am. Arbitration Assn.; lectr. for Inst. Continuing Legal Edn. for State of N.J.; panel mem. for med. malpractice panel hearing N.J. Supreme Ct. Trustee, Temple B'Nai Or, 1981-82. Mem. ABA, N.J. Bar Assn., Assn. Trial Lawyers Am. Home: 9 Harvey Dr Short Hills NJ 07078 Office: Cohn & Lifland Park 80 Plaza West One Saddle Brook NJ 07662

PEARNE, NICHOLAS KENNETH, electronics company executive; b. Guilford, Eng., Feb. 5, 1949; s. Francis Edward and Theodora Bickern (Neal) P.; m. Clare McNamara, Dec. 5, 1980; children: William, Rupert, Chloe. BSc with honors, Manchester U., 1970, MBA, 1977. Cert. patent atty., U.K. Tech. asst. Marks & Clark, London, 1970-75; bus. analyst, acct. Jersey, Channel Islands, 1975-77; ptnr., mktg. dir. BPA Technology and Mgmt., Dorking, Eng., 1977—; cons. IPC, Chgo., 1979—. Contbr. articles to profl. publs. Fellow Inst. of Dirs.; mem. B.O.K.S. (chmn. Morris Minor Rescue Ltd.). Home: Barn Farm, Clayhidon Devon EX15 3TU, England Office: BPA Technology and Mgmt Abinger House, Church St, Dorking, Surrey RH4 1DF, England

PEARSON, CHARLES THOMAS, JR., lawyer; b. Fayetteville, Ark., Oct. 14, 1929; s. Charles Thomas and Doris (Pinkerton) P.; m. Alice Ann Paddock, Mar. 7, 1952; children: Linda Sue, John Paddock. B.S., U. Ark., 1953, J.D., 1954; postgrad., U.S. Naval Postgrad. Sch., 1959; A.M., Boston U., 1963. Bar: Ark. bar 1954. Practice in Fayetteville, 1963—; dir., officer N.W. Communications, Inc., Dixieland Devel., Inc., Jonlin Investments, Inc., World Wide Travel Service, Inc., Okliana Farms, Inc., N.W. Ark. Land & Devel., Inc., Garden Plaza Inns, Inc., Word Data, Inc., M.P.C. Farms, Inc., Fayetteville Enterprises, Inc., NWA Devel. Co., Delta Comm, Inc.; dir., organizer N.W. Nat. Bank. Adviser Explorer Scouts, 1968—; past pres. Washington County Draft Bd.; past pres. bd. Salvation Army. Served to comdr. Judge Adv. Gen. Corps USNR, 1955-63. Mem. Am., Ark., Washington County bar assns., Judge Advs. Assn., N.W. Ark. Ret. Officers Assn. (past pres.), Methodist Men (past pres.), U. Ark. Alumni Assn. (dir.), Sigma Chi (past pres. N.W. Ark. alumni, past chmn. house corp.), Alpha Kappa Psi, Phi Eta Sigma, Delta Theta Phi. Republican. Methodist. Clubs: Mason (32 deg., K.T., Shriner), Moose, Elk, Lion, Metropolitan. Office: 36 E Center St Fayetteville AR 72701

PEARSON, DONALD STUART, emeritus mathematics and engineering educator; b. Cleve., Feb. 19, 1905; s. David Browne and Dorothy Mathilda (Oehlhoff) P.; m. Doris Marion White, Apr. 1, 1985. B.S., Case Western Res. U., 1929, M.S., 1933; Ph.D., St. Andrews U., 1958, LL.D., 1968; Ed.D. (hon.), Phila. Coll., 1973. Registered profl. engr., surveyor, Ariz., Ohio, Pa. chartered engr., London. Prof., chmn. elec. engring. dept. Ohio No. U., 1938-43; design engr. Westinghouse Electric Corp., 1944-45; mem. grad. faculty Mich. State U., 1945-49; mem. grad. faculty Pa. State U., 1949-65, research supr., 1957, emeritus prof., 1965—; prof. math. Lorain County Community Coll., 1965-76, chmn. dept. math., 1971; voluntary prof. Ariz. State U., 1980-85; alumni ednl. adviser Case Western Res. U., 1972—; adviser Engring. Coll. Mag. Associated, 1964; examiner Ohio State Bd. Profl. Engrs., 1939-53; founder OHIOMATYC, U. Cin., 1972; research project supr. Boeing, 1957. Author: Creative Image, 1959, Creativeness for Engineers, 4th edit, 1961, Basic Energy Converters, 1962, Reflections, 1981, Meaning of Time, 1982, Living Today, 1983, The Great Spirit, 1987; contbr. articles profl. jours.; regional editor: MATYC jour., 1970-75. Mem. Environ. Protection Bd., Olmsted Falls, Ohio, 1972-75; charter mem. Engrs. Found. Ohio, Columbus, 1970. Recipient Army-Navy E award, 1944, Lee Gold medal research award, 1958, cert. Nat. Council Engring. Examiners, 1970, Community Leader of Am. award, 1972, Outstanding Educator of Am. award, 1973, citation 88th Congress Invention and Patent System, Library of Congress, 1964, LCCC cert. of recognition, 1975; fellow Ohio No. U., 1957; fellow St. Andrews Res., 1958. Fellow Instn. Elec. Engrs. (London) (life), Royal Soc. Arts (London), Intercontinental Biog. Soc., Am. Soc. Engring. Edn. (life; br. chmn. 1949), Worldwide Acad. of Scholars (life); mem. IEEE (life sr. mem., br. counselor, chmn. Central Pa. sect. 1953), AAUP (emeritus mem.), Ohio Ret. Tchrs. Assn. (life), Math. Assn. Am., Planetary Soc., Newcomen Soc., Franklin Inst., Ohio Soc. Profl. Engrs., AAAS, Amateur Yacht Research Soc. (London), Lloyds Register Am. Yachts, Sun City Engrs., Tau Beta Pi (eminent mem.; founder, pres. Sun City alumnus chpt. 1981-83), Eta Kappa Nu (life, benefactor), Phi Delta Kappa, Pi Mu Epsilon (hon.), Theta Chi, Ariz. State Poetry Soc. Clubs: Masons, Shriners, Kiwanis (dir. 1940), Bay View Boat (life mem.), Sun City Scots, Amateur Radio, University, Statesman's. Home: 1665 Berkshire Ave Winter Park FL 32789

PEARSON, GARY DEAN, dentist; b. Rockford, Ill., Dec. 25, 1952; s. Miles Addison and Pauline (Hammond) P.; m. Marcea Lou Schlenske, Dec. 4, 1981; 1 child, Grant Addison. BS cum laude, Rockford Coll., 1974; DDS, U. Ill., Chgo., 1978. Pvt. practice dentistry Rockton, Ill., 1978—. Recipient Gen. Assembly Scholarship, State of Ill., 1977. Mem. Am. Dental Assn., Ill. State Dental Soc., Winnebago County Dental Soc., U. Ill. Alumni Assn., Rockton C. of C., Phi Theta Kappa. Lutheran. Club: Rockford Coll. Alumni. Home: 295 Rockton Rd Roscoe IL 61073 Office: 213 W Main St Rockton IL 61072

PEARSON, JOHN, mechanical engineer; b. Leyburn, Yorkshire, U.K., Apr. 24, 1923; came to U.S., 1930, naturalized, 1944; s. William and Nellie Pearson; m. Ruth Ann Billhardt, July 10, 1944; children—John, Armin, Roger. B.S.M.E., Northwestern U., 1949, M.S., 1951. Registered profl. engr., Calif. Research engr. Naval Ordnance Test Sta., China Lake, Calif., 1951-55, head warhead research br., 1955-58, head solid dynamics bd., 1958-59, head detonation physics group, 1959-67; head detonation physics div. Naval Weapons Ctr., China Lake, Calif., 1967-83, sr. research scientist, 1983—; cons., lectr. in field; founding mem. adv. bd. Ctr. for High Energy Forming, U. Denver; mem. bd. examiners Sambalpur U., India, 1982-83. Author: Explosive Working of Metals, 1963; Behavior of Metals Under Impulsive Loads, 1954. Contbr. articles to profl. publs. Patentee impulsive loading, explosives applications. Charter mem. Sr. Exec. Service U.S., 1979. Served with C.E., U.S. Army, 1943-46. Recipient L.T.E. Thompson medal, 1965, William B. McLean medal, 1979, Superior Civilian Service medal U.S. Navy, 1984, Haskell G. Wilson award, 1985, cert. of recognition Sec. Navy, 1975, Merit award Dept. Navy, 1979, cert. of commendation Sec. Navy, 1981. Fellow ASME; mem. Am. Soc. Metals, Am. Phys. Soc., N.Y. Acad. Scis., AIME, NSPE, Fed. Exec. League, Sigma Xi, Tau Beta Pi, Pi Tau Sigma, Triangle. Home and Office: 858 N Primavera Rd PO Box 1390 Ridgecrest CA 93555

PEARSON, NELS KENNETH, retired manufacturing executive; b. Algonquin, Ill., May 2, 1918; s. Nels Pehr and Anna (Fyre) P.; student pub. schs.; m. Louise Mary Houston Lenox, June 28, 1941; children—Lorine Marie Pearson Walters, Karla Jean. Assembler, Oak Mfg. Co., Crystal Lake, Ill., 1936-38, machine operator, assembly line foreman, 1938-43, apprentice tool and die maker, 1946-50; co-founder, pres. Wauconda Tool & Engring. Co., Inc., Algonquin, 1950-86; owner, founder Kar-Lor Enterprises, 1987—; co-founder, treas. Kenmode Tool & Engring. Co., Inc., Algonquin, 1960-72. Mem. McHenry County Edn. and Tng. Com., 1961-86, treas., 1961-86. Served with AUS, 1943-46. Mem. Am. Soc. Tool and Mfg. Engrs. Clubs: Moose, Antique Auto, Classic Car, Vet. Motor Car, Horseless Carriage. Home: 125 Dole Ave Crystal Lake IL 60014 Office: Huntley Rd Algonquin IL 60102

PEARSON, NORMAN, planning consultant, writer; b. Stanley, County Durham, Eng., Oct. 24, 1928; arrived in Can., 1954. Joseph and Mary (Pearson) P., m. Gerda Maria Josefine Reidl, July 25, 1972. BA with honors in Town and Country Planning, U. Durham (Eng.), 1951; PhD in Land Economy, Internat. Inst. Advanced Studies, 1979; MBA, Pacific Western U., Colo., 1980, DBA, 1982; PhD In Mgmt. Calif. U. for Advanced Studies, 1986—; m. Gerda Maria Josefine Riedl, July 25, 1972. Cons. to Stanley Urban Dist. Council, U.K., 1946-47; planning asst. Accrington Town Plan and Bedford County Planning Survey, U. Durham Planning Team, 1947-49; planning asst. to Allen and Mattocks, cons. planners and landscape designers, Newcastle upon Tyne, U.K., 1949-51; adminstrv. asst. Scottish Div., Nat. Coal Bd., Scotland, 1951-52; planning asst. London County Council, U.K., 1953-54; planner Central Mortgage and Housing Corp., Ottawa, Ont., Can., 1954-55; planning analyst City of Toronto Planning Bd., 1955-56; dir. of planning Hamilton Wentworth Planning Area Bd., Hamilton, Ont., Can., 1956-59; dir. planning for Burlington (Ont.) and Suburban Area Planning Bd., 1959-62, also commr. planning, 1959-62; pres. Tanfield Enterprises Ltd., London, Ont., Can., 1962—, Norman Pearson & Assocs. Ltd., Can., 1962—, Internat. Planning Mgmt. Cons.; cons. in urban, rural and regional planning, 1962—; life mem. U.S. Com. for Monetary Research and Edn., 1976—; spl. lectr. in planning McMaster U., Hamilton, 1956-64, Waterloo (Ont.) Luth. U., 1961-63; asst. prof. geography and planning U. Waterloo (Ont.), 1963-67; assoc. prof. geography U. Guelph (Ont.), 1967-72, chmn., dir. Ctr. for Resource Devel.; prof. polit. sci. U. Western Ont., London, 1972-77; adj. prof. of ecological planning and land econs. Internat. Inst. for Advanced Studies, Clayton, Mo., 1980—; core faculty Doctoral Program in Mgmt. Walden U., Mpls., 1986—; mem. bd. regents Calif. U. for Advanced Studies, Petaluma, 1987; mem. Social Scis., Econ. and Legal Aspects Com. of Research Adv. Bd. Internat. Joint Commn., 1972-76; cons. to City of Waterloo, 1973-76, Province of Ont., 1969-70; adviser to Georgian Bay Regional Devel. Council, 1968-72; real estate appraiser, province of Ont., 1976—; pres., chmn. bd. govs. Pacific Western U., Canada, 1983-84; with faculty adminstn./mgmt. dept., PhD program Walden U., Mpls., 1985—. Pres. Unitarian Ch. of Hamilton, 1960-61. Served with RAF, 1951-53. Knight of Grace, Sovereign Order St. John of Jerusalem. Fellow Royal Town Planning Inst. (Bronze medal award 1957), Royal Econ. Soc.; mem. Internat. Soc. City and Regional Planners, Am., Canadian insts. planners, Canadian Polit. Sci. Assn. L'Association Internationale des Ingenieurs et des Docteurs ès Sciences Appliquées à l'Industrie. Clubs: Empire; Ontario; University (London). Author: (with others) An Inventory of Joint Programmes and Agreements Affecting Canada's Renewable Resources, 1964. Editor, co-author (with others) Regional and Resource Planning in Canada, 1963, rev. edit., 1970; editor (with others) The Pollution Reader, 1968. Contbr. numerous articles on town planning to profl. jours. and chpts. in field to books. Office: PO Box 5362, Station A, London, ON Canada N6A 4L6

PEARSON, PAUL BROWN, nutritionist, educator; b. Oakley, Utah, Nov. 28, 1905; s. Levi and Ada (Brown) P.; m. Emma Snow, June 20, 1933; children—Paula (Mrs. Raymond Soller), Marilyn (Mrs. Walter Johnson). B.S., Brigham Young U., 1928; M.S. (Walsh fellow), Mont. State U., 1930; Ph.D. (fellow), U. Wis., 1937. Asst. prof. Mont. State U., 1930-31; research assoc. U. Calif., 1932-35; prof. A&M Coll. Tex., 1937, disting. prof., 1941, dean grad. sch., head dept. biochemistry and nutrition, 1947; chief biology AEC, 1949-58, cons., 1958-70; prof. Johns Hopkins U., 1951-58; with program in sci. and engring. Ford Found., 1958-63; pres., sci. dir. Nutrition Found., 1963-72; chmn. dept. nutrition Drexel U., 1972-73; prof. dept. family and community medicine and dept. nutrition and food sci. U. Ariz., Tucson, 1974—; chief dept. nutrition U. Autónoma de Guadalajara, Mexico, 1974-84; Collaborator Bur. Animal Industry.; Del. 6th Internat. Zootechnic Congress, Copenhagen, 1952, 2d Internat. Biochem. Congress, Paris, 1952, U.S.-Japan Conf. on Radiobiology, Tokyo, 1954; World Conf. Peaceful Uses Atomic Energy, Geneva, 1955, Internat. Symposium on Biochemistry of Sulphur, Roscoff, France, 1956; mem. exec. com. div. biol. and agrl. NRC, 1950-52. Author bulls., NRC, numerous sci. publs. on nutrition and biochemistry. Liaison Food and Nutrition Bd.; program com. Internat. Congress on Nutrition, 1960; cons. Pres.'s Sci. Adv. Com., Nat. Agr. Research Adv. Com., 1952-58; chmn. adv. com. P.R. Nuclear Center, 1962-73; adv. com. McCollum-Pratt Inst.; trustee Food Drug Law Inst., 1967-85, Nutrition Found., 1972-74; Del. White House Conf. Internat. Cooperation, 1965, White House Conf. on Food, Nutrition and Health, 1969. Fellow AAAS, Soc. for Animal Sci., Am. Inst. Nutrition; mem. Biochem. Soc. London, Am. Chem. Soc., Brit. Nutrition Soc., Soc. Biol. Chemists, El Coligeo de Medicos Cirujanos de Jalisco. Clubs: Lochinvar, Cosmos. Home: 5925 E 3d St Tucson AZ 85711 Office: Agrl Scis Bldg U Ariz Tucson AZ 85721 also: U Autonoma Guadalajara, Faculty Medicine, Apdo Postal 1-440, Guadalajara Jalisco, Mexico

PEARSON, PAUL RODNEY, clinical psychologist; b. Sheffield, Eng., Jan. 6, 1944; s. William Ernest and Phyllis (Hampshire) P.; m. Rachel Richards, Aug. 16, 1986. BA with honors in Psychology, Sheffield U., 1965. Clin. psychologist Fairmile Hosp., Berkshire, Eng., 1970-71, Blackpool, 1971-78, Derbyshire, 1978-86; clin. psychologist West Suffolk Hosp., Bury St. Edmunds, Eng., 1986—. Contbr. articles to profl. jours. Mem. Brit. Psychol. Soc., Internat. Soc. Study Individual Differences, European Assn. Personality Psychology. Club: Cartoonists Gt. Britain. Office: West Suffolk Hosp Psychology Dept, Hardwick Ln, Bury Saint Edmunds, Suffolk IP33 2QZ, England

PEARSON, WILLIAM ROWLAND, nuclear engineer; b. New Bedford, Mass., Sept. 30, 1923; s. Rowland and Nellie (Hilton) P.; B.S., Northeastern U., 1953; postgrad. U. Ohio, 1960; m. Arlene Cole Loveys, June 14, 1953; children—Denise, Robert, Rowland, Nancy. Engr., Goodyear Atomic Corp., Portsmouth, Ohio, 1953-63, Cabot Titania Corp., Ashtabula, Ohio, 1963-64; supr. United Nuclear, Wood River, R.I., 1964-72; sr. engr. Nuclear Materials and Equipment Co., Apollo, Pa., 1972-74; engr. U.S. Nuclear Regulatory Commn., Rockville, Md., 1974—. Served with USNR, 1942-45. Decorated Air medal. Mem. Am. Nuclear Soc., Am. Inst. Chem. Engrs. (chmn. 1966-67), AAAS. Republican. Baptist. Clubs: Masons, Elks. Home: 19108 Dowden Circle Poolesville MD 20837 Office: Chem Engring Br Office Nuclear Regulatory Research Nuclear Regulatory Commn Washington DC 20555

PEARSON-HANDEL, CARREN, direct marketing consultant, writer; b. Hampton, Iowa, Feb. 6, 1945; d. Carl William and Vona Irene (Snyder) Pearson; m. William Keating Handel, Oct. 29, 1972 (div. 1984); m. Edwin Russell Heaton, July 31, 1986. B.A., Long Beach State Coll., 1966. Asst. to gen. mgr. Triad Corp., Glendale, Calif., 1967-70; asst. v.p. Direct Mktg. Corp. Am., Los Angeles, 1970-81; internat. creative dir. Direct Mktg. Internat., Los Angeles, 1970-81; sr. ptnr., co-owner Heaton, Rheinfrank & Handel, Sydney, Australia, 1981—; guest lectr. confs. and seminars. Contbr. articles to various mags. Bd. dirs., v.p. Direct Mktg. Club So. Calif., Los Angeles, 1973-80, pres., 1981. Named Outstanding Women in Bus., YWCA, Los Angeles, 1979. Mem. Soc. Women Writers Australia, Australian Direct Mktg. Assn., Gemmological Assn. New South Wales. Avocations: painting; creative writing; gourmet cooking; reading. Office: Heaton Rheinfrank & Handel Pty, 148B Wycombe Rd, Neutral Bay, Sydney, New South Wales 2089, Australia

PEASLEE, CHARLOTTE HOFFMAN, writer, cons., editor; b. N.Y.C., July 13, 1931; d. Edmund Witherbee and Emily (Delafield) Peaslee; student Radcliffe Coll., 1949-52; B.J., U. Mo., 1958. Reporter, Paterson (N.J.) Morning Call, 1958; editorial asst. Electronic and Appliance Specialist, N.Y.C., 1958-60, Palmerton Pub. Co., N.Y.C., 1960-61; asst. editor in charge prodn. Sci. Digest, Hearst Mag. div., N.Y.C., 1961-64; writer Consol. Edison Co., N.Y.C., 1964-69; tech. editor Nat. Elec. Mfrs. Assn., N.Y.C., 1969-70; free-lance writer, copy editor, 1970-71; mng. editor Lady's Circle mag. Lopez Publs., N.Y.C., 1971-75; free-lance writer, editor, cons. Spl. Projects by

Charlotte Peaslee, 1976—. Mem. Women in Communications, NOW (N.Y. exec. v.p. 1972, dir. 1973), N.Y. Assn. Women Bus. Owners, Women's Econ. Round Table, Publicity Club N.Y., Kappa Tau Alpha, Kappa Alpha Mu. Club: Overseas Press (N.Y.C.). Home: 165 E 72d St New York NY 10021

PEAT, ANDREW BRIAN, insurance broker; b. Bexle Heath, Kent, Eng., Dec. 18, 1952; came to W. Germany, 1977; s. Norman Frank Richard and Dorothy Agnes (Neale) P.; m. Jillian Lancaster Smith, June 30, 1973; children—James St. John, Abigail Clare. Gen. Eng. Cert., Nat. Diploma, Huntingdon Tech. Coll., Cambridgeshire. Negotiator Ekins Dilley & Handley, St. Ives, Cambs, Eng., 1971-72; branch mgr. David Williams Hudson, Huntingdon, Cambs, 1972-75; co. dir. Woolly & Harris, St. Neots, Cambs, 1975-77; co. dir., ptnr. D.N. Slater Assoc., W. Germany, 1977-80; mng. dir., prin. Andrew Peat Fin. Cons., Monchengladbach, W. Germany, 1980—, Andrew Peat Fin. Cons. (UK) Ltd. Radio commentator on fin. topics. Trainee civil service, London, 1969-71; mem. Young Conservatives, St. Ives-Cambs, 1971; Round Table St. Neots-Cambs, 1976; British German Trade Council, W. Germany, Frankfurt, 1981. Mem. Nat. Assn. Estate Agents, Property Cons. Soc., Ins. Brokers Registration Council, British C. of C. Germany, Conservatives Abroad (northrheinwestphalia region). Fellow Corp. of Ins. and Financial Advisers, Conservatives Abroad (Nordrheinwestphalia region). Mem. Ch. of Eng. Club: British Businessmans (Dusseldorf) (sec. 1981—). Office: Andrew Peat Finance Cons, 52 Roermonderstrasse, Monchengladbach 4050, Federal Republic of Germany

PEAVY, HOMER LOUIS, JR., real estate executive, accountant; b. Okmulgee, Okla., Sept. 4, 1924; s. Homer Louis and Hattie Lee (Walker) P.; children: Homer Martin, Daryl Mark. Student Kent State U., 1944-49; grad. Hammel-Actual Coll., 1962. Sales supr. Kirby Sales, Akron, Ohio, 1948-49; sales mgr. Williams-Kirby Co., Detroit, 1949-50; area distributor Peavy-Kirby Co., Phila., 1953-54; salesman James L. Peavy Realty Co., Akron, 1954-65; owner Homer Louis Peavy, Jr., Real Estate Broker, Akron, 1965—; pvt. practice acctg., Akron, 1962—; fin. aid officer Buckeye Coll., Akron, 1982. Author: Watt Watts, 1969; poet: Magic of the Muse, 1978, P.S. I Love You, 1982; contbr. poetry to Am. Poetry Anthology, 1983, New Worlds Unlimited, 1984, Treasures of the Precious Moments, 1985, Our World's Most Cherished Poems, 1985; songs: Sh...Sh, Sheree, Sheree, 1976, In Akron O, 1979; teleplay: Revenge, 1980. Bd. dirs. Internat. Elvis Gold Soc., 1978—; charter mem. Statue of Liberty-Ellis Island Found., 1984, Nat. Mus. of Women in Arts, 1986; mem. Nat. Trust for Hist. Preservation. Recipient Am. Film Inst. Cert. Recognition, 1982, Award of Merit cert. World of Poetry 10th ann. contest, 1985, Golden Poet award World of Poetry, 1985, 87, 88. Mem. Ohioana Library Assn., Internat. Black Writers Conf., Acad. Am. Poets, Manuscript Club Akron, Internat. Platform Assn., Kent State U. Alumni Assn. Democrat. Home and Office: 1160 Cadillac Blvd Akron OH 44320

PECCATI, LORENZO ACHILLE, mathematics and finance educator; b. Sabbioneta, Mantua, Italy, Feb. 26, 1944; s. Giovanni Alfredo and Franceschina (Filippi) P.; m. Alba Zerbini (div.); 1 child, Giovanni. Laurea, U. Bocconi, Milan, 1967. Asst. prof. U. Parma, Italy, 1970-80; prof. U. Turin, Italy, 1980-82, 85—, U. Milan, 1982-85, U. Bocconi, 1986—; cons. in field. Author: Mathematics for Economic Analysis, 1980; editor: (with others) Rivista di Mat., 1982-86. Mem. Am. Math. Assn., Unione Mat. Italiana, Associazione Per La Mat. Applicata Alle Sci. Econ. E Sociali (gen. sec. 1982-86, v.p. 1987—). Office: U Torino Fac Econ Comm, Piazza Arbarello 8, 10122 Torino Italy

PECCI BLUNT, FERDINAND, securities company executive; b. Brides les Bains, France, Aug. 1, 1921; s. Cecil Charles and Anna Laetitia (Pecci) P.B.; m. Joan Russell, 1948 (div. 1950); m. Donatella Perotti Kraft, 1984. BA in Internat. Law and Internat. Relations, Harvard U., 1943. Trainee Lazard Freres 7 Co., N.Y.C., 1946-48; film producer U.S. and Italian TV, Rome, 1959-58; mgr. Bache & Co., Rome, 1959-76; v.p., acting mgr. Bache Securities Co., Monte Carlo, Monaco and N.Y.C., 1976—. Served to 1st lt. military intelligence U.S. Army, 1943-46. Decorated knight Crown of Italy, comdr. Italian Republic, comdr. S. Maurizio and Lazzaro. Clubs: Circolo degli Scacchi (Rome); Corviglia Ski (St. Moritz, Switzerland) (life mem.). Home: Piazzi Aracoeli 300186, Rome Italy Office: Prudential-Bache Securities Inc, Sporting d'Hiver, Place du Casino, Monte Carlo Monaco

PECHACEK, FRANK WARREN, JR., lawyer; b. Winona, Minn., May 1, 1944; s. Frank Warren and Gladys (Bjoraker) P.; m. Beth E. Horn, June 4, 1966; children—Jill Ellan, Holly Jo, Frank Warren III. Student Iowa State U., 1963-64; B.A. with honors, U. No. Iowa, 1966; J.D. with honors, U. Iowa, 1969. Bar: Iowa 1969, Nebr. 1983, U.S. Dist. Ct. (so. dist.) Iowa 1969, U.S. Dist. Ct. (no. dist.) Iowa 1970, U.S. Ct. Appeals (8th cir.) 1970, U.S. Ct. Claims 1980, U.S. Tax Ct. 1982. Assoc. Smith, Peterson, Beckman & Willson, Council Bluffs, Iowa, 1969-72, ptnr., 1973—; lectr. Iowa State U., Ames, 1973—; mem. Iowa Supreme Ct. Commn. on Continuing Legal Edn., Des Moines, 1975-82. Contbr. articles to profl. jour. Chmn. Garner Twp. Republican Party, Council Bluffs, 1978—; co-founder, bd. dirs. Pottawattamie County Taxpayers Assn., Council Bluffs, 1979—, pres. 1979-80; bd. dirs. St. John's Luth. Ch., Council Bluffs, 1979-83; co-founder, bd. dirs., pres. Southwest Iowa Ednl. Found., Inc., Council Bluffs, 1984—, pres. 1986—. Mem. Internat. Assn. Assessing Officers, ABA, Nat. Assn. Rev. Appraisers and Mortgage Underwriters (sr. mem., cert. rev. appraiser, cert.), Nat. Assn. Real Estate Appraisers, Nebr. Bar Assn., Iowa Bar Assn. Club: Kiwanis (bd. dirs. 1977-83) (Council Bluffs). Home: 17 Vista Ln Council Bluffs IA 51501 Office: Smith Peterson Beckman & Willson 370 Midlands Mall PO Box 249 Council Bluffs IA 51502

PECH-PÉTEL, CHRISTIANE, anesthetist, physician; b. Toulouse, Haute Garonne, France, June 21, 1930; d. Raoul Pétel and Hermine Bacalerie; m. Jean-Pierre Pech, July 27, 1963; children: Jean-Hugues, Catherine. MD, Med. U., Toulouse, 1960. Cert. anesthetist, reanimator. Non-resident med. asst. Hospitalier Univ. Ctr., Toulouse, 1955-60, attache, 1962-71, hospitalier practicioner, 1971—; anesthetist attache Handicapped Childrens' Ctr., Ramonville-St. Agne, France, 1963—. Author reports in field. Mem. French Anesthesia-Analgesia-Reanimation Soc. (nat. correspondent 1969-80, Titular Anesthetist 1980—). Roman Catholic. Office: Hospitalier Regional Ctr, Place Docteur Baylac, 31300 Toulouse France

PECK, CURTISS STEVEN, management consultant; b. Kenosha, Wis., May 3, 1947; s. Curtiss Wesley and Frances Helen (Kowalkowski) P.; m. Susan Carol Kostritza, Nov. 3, 1975; children: Stephanie Jean, Curtiss Wesley II, Stacey Marie. BS, U. Wis., Milw., 1976, MS, 1980, PhD candidate, 1987. Investigator, police officer Greendale (Wis.) Police Dept., 1971-80; cons. NCTI, Milw., 1980-83, pres., 1983—; instr. Cardinal Stritch Coll., Milw., 1982—; advisor Booth-Wright, Inc., Boulder, Colo., 1983-87; cons. Howard & Assocs., Chgo., 1985—, Mgmt. Resources Assn., Brookfield, 1985—; coordinator Trainer's Roundtable Inst. Fin. Edn., 1985—; mem. adv. com. Milw. Area Tech. Coll., 1988—. Bd. dirs. Multiple Sclerosis Soc., Milw., 1983—, pres. 1985, 86; coordinator Assn. Adult Educators, Milw., 1984; advisor Goodwill Industries, Milw., 1985, 86. Served with USAF, 1966-70, USANG, 1970-80. Mem. Nat. Organizational Devel. Network, Chgo. Organizational Devel. Network, Am. Soc. for Personnel Adminstrn., Personnel and Indsl. Relations Assn., Organizational Devel. Inst. (cert.). Lutheran. Home: S68 W17924 East Dr Muskego WI 53150 Office: NCTI 15350 W National Ave New Berlin WI 53151-9990

PECK, DWIGHT CLARK, librarian; b. Teaneck, N.J., Jan. 4, 1945; arrived in Switzerland, 1977.; s. Dwight Clark and Alice (Wynkoop) P.; m. Elizabeth Greed, May 3, 1965 (div. 1984); children: Alison Beth, Deirdre Joy; m. Elizabeth Jane Wilson; 1 child, Marlowe Tyson. BA in Philosophy and English, U. Kans., 1967; MA in English Lit., Ohio U., 1971, PhD in Renaissance Studies, 1972; MLS, U. R.I., 1977. Asst. prof. English Okla. Baptist U., Shawnee, 1972-75; head librarian Am. Coll. Switzerland, Leysin, 1977—, academic dean, 1978-81. Author: Leicesters Commonwealth, 1985; contbr. articles to profl. jours. Home: Chalet Pollux, CH-1854 Leysin Vaud, Switzerland Office: Am Coll Switzerland, CH-1854 Leysin Vaud, Switzerland

PECK, GREGORY, actor; b. La Jolla, Calif., Apr. 5, 1916; m. Veronique Passani; 5 children. Ed., U. Calif., Neighborhood Playhouse Sch. Dramatics. Mem. Nat. Council on Arts, 1965—. Actor: (plays) including Sons and Soldiers, (films) including: Keys of the Kingdom, 1945, Valley of Decision, 1945, Spellbound, 1945, The Yearling, 1946, Duel in the Sun, 1947, The Macomber Affair, 1947, Gentlemen's Agreement, 1947, The Paradine Case, Yellow Sky, The Great Sinner, 1948, Twelve O'Clock High, 1949, The Gunfighter, 1950, Captain Horatio Hornblower, 1951, Only the Valiant, 1951, David and Bathsheba, 1951, Snows of Kilamanjaro, 1952, Roman Holiday, 1953, Night People, Man With a Million, Purple Plains, Moby Dick, 1954, Man in the Grey Flannel Suit, 1956, The Designing Woman, 1956, The Bravados, 1958, Pork Chop Hill, 1959, Beloved Infidel, 1959, On The Beach, 1959, Guns of Navarone, 1961, To Kill a Mockingbird (Acad. award as best actor 1962), Cape Fear, 1962, How the West Was Won, 1963, Captain Newman, M.D, 1963, Behold a Pale Horse, 1964, Mirage, 1965, Arabesque, 1966, Mackenna's Gold, 1967, The Chairman, 1968, The Stalking Moon, 1968, Marooned, 1969, I Walk the Line, 1970, Shootout, 1971, Billy Two-Hats, 1972, Amazing Grace and Chuck, 1987; co-producer, star: (films) The Big Country, 1958; producer, star: (films) The Omen, 1976, MacArthur, 1977, The Boys from Brazil, 1978, The Sea Wolves, 1981, The Scarlet and Black, 1983, (TV miniseries) The Blue and the Gray, 1982; rec.: (audio cassette) The New Testament, 1985-86. Nat. chmn. Am. Cancer Soc., 1966. Recipient Presdl. medal of freedom, Jean Hersholt Humanitarian award, 1968. Mem. Acad. Motion Picture Arts and Scis. (gov.; pres. 1967-70), Am. Film Inst. (founding chmn. bd. trustees 1967-69). *

PECK, STEPHEN D., publishing company executive; b. Lincoln, Nebr., Apr. 14, 1945; s. Harold and Rosalie (Pollock) P.; m. Gayle Marcia Serabin, May 14, 1972; children: Lisa Michelle, Lauren Rachel. BBA, U. Cin., 1968. Acct. Peat Marwick Mitchell & Co., Cin., 1968-70; sr. acct. Price Waterhouse & Co., Washington, 1970-72; sr. auditor Macke Co., Cheverly, Md., 1972-73; controller Rossmore Leisure World, Silver Spring, Md., 1973-75, Stanley Martin Communities, Silver Spring, 1975-77; sr. v.p. The Viguerie Co., Falls Church, Va., 1977-86; sr. v.p., chief fin. officer Phillips Pub. Inc., Potomac, Md., 1986—; dir. The Viguerie Co. Inventor in field. Bd. dirs. Adat Shalom Synagogue, Montgomery Village, Md., 1986, sch. bd., 1986; active PTA, Stedwick Elem. Sch., 1985-86. Mem. Newsletter Assn. Republican. Jewish. Home: 10004 Desoto Ct Montgomery Village MD 20879 Office: Phillips Pub Inc 7811 Montrose Rd Potomac MD 20854

PECK, WILLIAM ARNO, physician; b. New Britain, Conn., Sept. 28, 1933; s. Bernard Carl and Molla (Nair) P.; m. Patricia Hearn, July 10, 1982; children by previous marriage—Catherine, Edward Pershall, David Nathaniel. A.B., Harvard U., 1955; M.D., U. Rochester, N.Y., 1960. Intern, then resident in internal medicine Barnes Hosp., St. Louis, 1960-62; fellow in metabolism Washington U. Sch. Medicine, St. Louis, 1963; mem. faculty U. Rochester Med. Sch., 1965-76, prof. medicine and biochemistry, 1973-76, head div. endocrinology and metabolism, 1969-76; John E. and Adaline Simon prof. medicine, co-chmn. dept. medicine Washington U. Sch. Medicine, St. Louis, 1976—; physician in chief Jewish Hosp., St. Louis, 1976—; chmn. endocrinology and metabolism adv. com. FDA, 1976-78; chmn. gen. medicine study sect. NIH, 1979-81; chmn. Gordon Conf. Chemistry, Physiology and Structure of Bones and Teeth, 1977; chmn. Consensus Devel. Conf. on Osteoporosis, NIH, 1984; co-chmn. Workshop on Future Directions in Osteoporosis, NIH, 1987; chmn. Spl. Topic Conf. on Osteoporosis, U.S. FDA, 1987. Editor Bone and Min. Research Annuals, 1982-88; contbr. med. jours. Pres. Nat. Osteoporosis Found., 1985—. Served as med. officer USPHS, 1963-65. Recipient Mosby Book award Alpha Omega Alpha, 1960, Doran J. Stephens award U. Rochester Sch. Medicine, 1960, Lederle Med. Faculty award, 1967, NIH Career Program award, 1970-75. Fellow A.C.P.; mem. Am. Soc. Biol. Chemists, Am. Physiol. Soc., Am. Soc. Clin. Investigation, Am. Fedn. Clin. Research, Am. Diabetes Assn., Am. Soc. Bone and Mineral Research (pres. 1983-84; editor annuals 1982-88), Assn. Am. Physicians, Endocrine Soc., Orthopedic Research Soc., Nat. Inst. Arthritis, Musculoskeletal and Skin Diseases (adv. council 1986—), Sigma Xi, Alpha Omega Alpha. Home: 912 Cabernet Town & Country MO 63017 Office: Washington U Sch Med and Jewish Hospitol Saint Louis MO 63110

PECKER, JEAN-CLAUDE, astronomer, educator, author; b. Reims, Marne, France, May 10, 1923; s. Victor Noel and Nelly Catherine (Herrmann) P.; m. Charlotte Wimel, Sept. 14, 1947 (div. 1964); children: Martine Kemeny, Daniel, Laure; m. Anne-Marie A. Vormser, Dec. 14, 1974. Student Lycée de Bordeaux, U. Grenoble and Paris (Sorbonne), Agrégr. des Scis. Physiques, Ecole Normale Supérieure, Paris, 1946; Dr.Scis., Centre Nat. de la Recherche Scientifique (C.N.R.S.), Paris, 1950. Research asst. C.N.R.S., 1946-52; assoc. prof. U. Clermont-Ferrand, 1952-55; assoc. astronomer Paris Obs., 1955-62, astronomer, 1962-65; dir. Nice Obs., 1962-69; prof. Coll. de France, Paris, 1962-88; dir. Inst. Astrophysics, Paris, 1972-78; sec. gen. Astron. Internat. Union, Nice, 1964-67; chmn. Nat. Com. for Sci. and Tech. Culture, 1985-87; chmn. adv. com. Mus. LaVillette, Paris, 1983-85. Author: (with P. Couderc and E. Schatzman) L'astronomie au jour le jour, 1954; (with E. Schatzman) Astrophysique gé nérale, 1959; Le ciel, 1959; L'astronomie expérimentale, 1969; Les laboratoires spatiaux, 1969; Papa, dis-moi: L'astronomie, qu'est-ce que c'est?, 1971; editor L'astronomie nouvelle, 1971, Clefs pour l'Astronomie, 1981, Sous l'Etoile Soleil, 1984, Astronomie Flammarion, 1985. Sec.-gen. Human Rights Com., Acad. Scis., Paris, 1978. Served with French Army, 1944-45; France. Decorated comdr. Palmes acadé miques; officer Lé gion d'honneur; officer Ordre Nat. du Mé rite, 1979; recipient prix Forthuny, Inst. de France, mé daille d'Argent, C.N.R.S., 1956; mé daille Janssen, Astron. Soc. France, 1967; prix Jean Perrin, Soc. Franç aise de Physique, 1973; others. Mem. Acad. Scis. (Paris), Acad. Scis. (Brussels), European Acad. Scis., Fine Arts and Humanities, Internat. Acad. Humanism, Acad. Europaea. Club: Société Philomathique (Paris). Office: College de France, 11 Pl Marcelin Berthelot, 75005 Paris France

PEDEN, GEORGE CAMERON, academic educator; b. Dundee, Scotland, Feb. 16, 1943; s. Robert George Cameron and Margaret Scott (Thomson) P.; m. Alison Mary White, Sept. 26, 1981; children: Alexander, Robert, William. MA, Dundee U., 1972; DPhil, Oxford U., Eng., 1976. Research fellow Inst. Hist. Research, London, 1975; tutorial asst. Dundee U., 1975-76; temporary lectr. Leeds U., 1976-77; lectr. Bristol U., 1977-87, reader, 1987—. Author: British Rearmament and the Treasury 1932-1939, 1979; contbr. Brit. Acad. Research Reader, 1987—. Scottish Nat. Party. Presbyterian. Office: U Bristol Sch History, 13-15 Woodland Rd, Bristol BS8 1TB, England

PEDERSEN, CHARLES J., chemist; b. Fusan, Republic of Korea, Oct. 3, 1904; came to U.S., 1922; naturalized, 1953; widowed; 2 children. MS, MIT, 1927. Research chemist E.I. du Pont de Nemours and Co., Wilmington, Del., 1927-69. Recipient Nobel Prize in Chemistry, 1987. Home: 57 Market St Salem NJ 08079 *

PEDERSEN, GUNNAR SVERRE, oil company executive; b. Trondheim, Norway, Aug. 29, 1916; s. Sverre and Edith Gretchen (Borseth) P.; m. Joan Catherine Johnson, Sept. 29, 1945 (dec. 1984). Degree in Civil Engring., Tech. U., Trondheim, 1939. Civil engr. bridge office Norway Rd. Dept., 1939-40; enlisted Norwegian Mil., 1940, advanced through grades to lt. col., 1981; mil. dist. engr. Norwegian Corps Engrs., Trondelag dist., 1945-81; ret. Norwegian Corps Engrs., 1981; exec. v.p. Norsk Polar Navigasjon A/S, Ny Aalesund, Norway, 1958—; also chmn. bd. Norsk Polar Navigasjon A/S, Ny Aalesund; bd. dirs. K/S/A/s Norsk Svalbardolje, Oslo, Norsk Vikingolje A/A, Trondheim; chmn. bd. Geopol. Inc., Anchorage, 1975-86. Editor: Svalbardveg I and II, 1959. Pres. Trondheim Officers Soc., 1961-62. Recipient Order Grand-Ducal de la Couronne de Chene, 1981. Fellow ASCE; mem. Norwegian Soc. Civil Engrs., Norwegian Petroleum Soc., Norwegian Poly. Soc., Arctic Inst. N.Am., Shipping, Hunting and Fishing Soc. Mem. Norwegian State Ch. Office: Norsk Polar Navigasjon A/S, PO Box 576, Sandvika N-1301, Norway

PEDERSEN, JORGEN GERVIN, corporation executive, marketing consultant; b. Copenhagen, Aug. 1, 1938; s. Charles and Oda (Gervin) P. Engr., Tech. High Sch., Copenhagen, 1962; Economist H.D., Econ. High Sch., Copenhagen, 1970. Mng. dir. Tattersall, 1967-70; chmn. Group 4 A/S, 1970-78; mng. dir. Group 4 Internat. A/S, Copenhagen, 1978-85, IBI ApS, 1985—. Contbr. articles to newspapers. Served to lt., Danish Army, 1962-64. Clubs: Royal Danish Yacht, Royal Automobile (London). Home: Frederiksgade 5, DK 1625 Copenhagen K Denmark Office: IBI ApS, DK 1022 Copenhagen Denmark

PEDERSEN, SVEND ERIK, publishing company executive; b. Bogense, Denmark, Oct. 5, 1942; s. Chr Pedersen; m. Jutta Larsen, Aug. 14, 1965. Journalist, Aktuelt, Copenhagen, 1964-66; sub-editor Sabroe Pub. Co., Copenhagen, 1966-70, editor in chief, 1970-77; owner, mgr. Specialbladsforlaget, Hellerup, Copenhagen, 1977—. Mem. Internat. Advt. Assn. (pres.). Home: Nyhavn 14, 1051 Copenhagen Denmark Office: Specialbladsforlaget, Hellerupvej 66, 2900 Hellerup Denmark

PEDERSEN, THOMAS AUGUST, lawyer; b. Ribe, Denmark, Aug. 26, 1908; s. Peder and Marie (Hahn) P.; m. Inez Smitherman, Apr. 28, 1940; children: Thomas Douglas, William Randolph. A.B., U. Mich., 1932, J.D., 1934. Bar: Tenn. 1935, U.S. Supreme Ct. 1938, other fed. ct. bars 1938. Since practiced in Knoxville; law clk. TVA, 1935, jr. atty., 1936-39, assoc. atty., 1939, atty., 1940, sr. atty., 1941-48, prin. atty., 1948-53, asst. gen. counsel, 1953-69, solicitor, 1969-71; Lawyer del., life mem. U.S. Jud. Conf.; cons. U. Tenn. Mem. exec. bd., dist. chmn. Gt. Smokey Mountain council Boy Scouts Am., 1959. Served to capt. C.E. AUS, 1942-46. Fellow Am. Coll. Trial Lawyers; mem. Fed., Tenn., Knoxville bar assns., Am. Judicature Soc., Supreme Ct. Hist. Soc., East Tenn. Hist. Soc., Internat. Platform Assn., Order Ky. Cols. Clubs: Nat. Lawyers (Washington); Knoxville Execs. (Knoxville), Holston Hills Country (Knoxville), U. Tenn. Faculty (Knoxville); Rotary. Home: 5801 Marilyn Dr Knoxville TN 37914

PEDERSEN, THOR, government official; b. Sollerod, Denmark, June 14, 1945; s. Laurits Pedersen. Grad. polit. sci., Copenhagen U., 1971. Mem. local council City of Helsinge, Denmark, then mayor; then mem. Folketing, Denmark, 1985; minister of housing Govt. of Denmark, 1986-87, minister of liaison, 1987—. Office: Ministry of Interior, Copenhagen Denmark *

PEDERSEN, WESLEY NIELS, public relations and public affairs executive; b. South Sioux City, Nebr., July 10, 1922; s. Peter Westergaard and Marie Gertrude (Sorensen) P.; m. Angela Kathryn Vavra, Oct. 17, 1948; 1 son, Eric Wesley. Student, Tri-State Coll., Sioux City, Iowa, 1940-41; B.A. summa cum laude, Upper Iowa U.; postgrad., George Washington U., 1958-59. Editor, writer Sioux City Jour., 1941-50; corr. N.Y. Times, Life, Time, Fortune, 1948-50; editor Dept. State, 1950-53; fgn. service officer Dept. State, Hong Kong, 1960-63; fgn. affairs columnist, roving corr., counselor summit meetings and fgn. ministers confs. USIA, 1953-60, chief, worldwide spl. publs. and graphics programs, 1963-69; chief Office Spl. Projects, Washington, 1969-78, Office Spl. Projects, Internat. Communication Agy., 1978-79; v.p. Fraser Assocs., pub. relations, Washington, 1979-80; dir. communications and pub. relations Public Affairs Council, Washington, 1980—; lectr. creative communications Upper Iowa U., 1975; chmn., Europe, Ambassadorial Internat. Affairs Seminar, Fgn. Service Inst., 1975; lectr. internat. public relations Pub. Relations Inst., Am. U., 1976; lectr. bus. and mgmt. div. N.Y. U., 1976, 77, 78; cons. pub. relations, editorial and design; del. founding sessions 1st Amendment Congress, Phila. and Williamsburg, Va., 1980, exec. com., 1980. Columnist: Public Relations Jour., 1980-85; author: Legacy of a President, 1964, American Heroes of Asian Wars, 1969; co-author: Effective Government Public Affairs, 1981; editor: Escape At Midnight and Other Stories (Pearl S. Buck), 1962, Exodus From China (Harry Redl), 1962, Education in China (K.E. Priestley), 1962, The Peasant and the Communes (Henry Lethbridge), 1962, China's Men of Letters (K.E. Priestley), 1963, Children of China (Pearl S. Buck and Margaret Wylie), 1963, Macao (Richard Hughes), 1963, The Americans and the Arts (Howard Taubman), 1969, The Dance in America (Agnes de Mille), 1969, Getting the Most from Grassroots Public Affairs Programs, 1980, Cost-Effective Management for Today's Public Affairs, 1987, Making Community Relations Pay Off: Tools and Strategies, 1988, Public Affairs Rev. mag, 1980-86, Impact, newsletter on nat. and internat. pub. affairs, 1980—, Perspectives on Managing International Public Affairs, 1980—; contbr. to: The Commissar, 1972, Political Action for Business, 1981, Informing the People: A Public Affairs Handbook, 1981, The Practice of Public Relations, 1984; mem. editorial bd.: Public Relations Quar, 1975—, Fgn. Service Jour., 1975-81; contbr. articles to profl. jours. Founding chmn. bd. dirs. Nat. Inst. for Govt. Public Info. Research, Am. U., 1977-80. Served with USAAF, 1943-46. Recipient 2 awards A.P. Mng. Editors Assn., Iowa, 1949, Meritorious Service award USIA, 1963, 1st prizes Fed. Editors Assn., 1970, 74-75, 1st prizes Soc. Tech. Communication, 1974, 75-76, Gold award Internat. Newsletter Conf., 1982, Silver award, 1985, Eddi award for design excellence Editor's Workshop, 1983, Gold Circle award for outstanding communications, Am. Soc. Assn. Execs., 1983-87; named Most Outstanding Info. Ofcl. in Exec. Br. Govt. Govt. Info. Orgn., 1975, named Ky. Col. and Adm. Nebr. Navy, 1984. Mem. Am. Fgn. Service Assn., Internat. Assn. Bus. Communicators (vice chmn. govt. relations com. 1976-77, chmn. nat. capital dist. conf. 1977, dir. Washington chpt. 1977-78, Communicator of Yr. Washington chpt. 1978, various awards 1973, 76-78, 84), Nat. Assn. Govt. Communicators (pres. 1978-79, Communicator of Yr. 1977, Disting. Service award 1978), Pub. Relations Soc. Am. (mem. Counselor's Acad. 1980—, chmn. 1st Amendment task force 1980-81, co-recipient Thoth award 1980, co-recipient award 1981). Episcopalian. Clubs: Fgn. Service, Nat. Press (Washington); Overseas Press (N.Y.C.). Home: 5214 Sangamore Rd Bethesda MD 20816 Office: Public Affairs Council 1255 23rd St NW Suite 750 Washington DC 20037

PEDERSON, WILLIAM DAVID, political scientist, educator; b. Eugene, Oreg., Mar. 17, 1946; s. Jon Moritz and Rose Marie (Ryan) P. BS in Polit. Sci., U. Oreg., 1967, MA in Polit. Sci., 1972, PhD in Polit. Sci., 1979. Teaching asst. polit. sci. dept. U. Oreg., Eugene, 1975-77; instr. govt. dept. Lamar U., Beaumont, Tex., 1977-79; asst. prof. polit. sci. dept. Westminster Coll., Fulton, Mo., 1979-80; asst. prof., head polit. sci. and pre-law Yankton Coll. U. S.D., 1980-81; assoc. prof., dir. Am. studies polit. sci. dept. La. State U., Shreveport, 1981—; program analyst NIH, Bethesda, Md., summer 1973; assoc. prof. jr. state program Am. U., Washington, summer 1984; research assoc. Russian and East European Ctr. U. Ill., Urbana, summers 1982-88; . Author: The Rating Game in American Politics, 1987; editor: The Barbarian Presidency, 1988; co-editor: Grassroots Constitutionalism, 1988; contbr. articles to profl. jours. Mem. Mayor's Comm. on the Bicentennial U.S. Constn., 1987; active Barnwell Ctr., Shreveport, 1984, Am. Rose Soc., Shreveport, 1982. Served with U.S. Army, 1968-70. Recipient training award NIH 1973; Outstanding Prof. award Westminster Coll. 1980, La. State U., 1984; La. State U. grantee 1982, La. Endowment for Humanities grantee, 1987; fellow NEH, 1981-85. Fellow Am. Polit. Sci. Assn., Am. Judicature Soc.; mem. Ctr. Study Presidency, Internat. Soc. Polit. Psychology, Am. Studies Assn. Office: La State U Dept Polit Sci One University Pl Shreveport LA 71115-2399

PEDOUSSAUT, YVES, hospital executive; b. Montpellier, France, July 17, 1946; s. Roger and Odette (Liautaud) P.; m. Marie-France Rulquin, Oct. 21, 1972; 1 child, Cyril. Diploma in law studies, U. Nice (France), 1968; Diploma in superior studies of law, U. Grenoble (France), 1971. Asst. U. Grenoble Hosp. Ctr., 1971-72; dir. adjoint Trousseau Hosp., Paris, 1973-76, Lariboisiere Hosp., Paris, 1977-80; chef de service Direction Med. Affairs, Paris, 1981-85; dir. Lariboisiere Hosp., 1985—. Home: 2 Rue Ambroise Pare, 75010 Paris France Office: Groupe Hospitalier Lariboisiere, 2 Rue Ambroise Pare, 75010 Paris France

PEELEN, FRED GEUCHIEN, hotel executive; b. The Hague, Netherlands, Aug. 28, 1941; s. Gerrit Jacob and Margriet (Veldkamp) P. B.A., Sch. Hotel Adminstrn., 1962; postgrad. Cornell U., 1963-64; Program Mgmt. Devel., Harvard U., 1972. Gen. mgr. various Inter-Continental Hotels, 1964-73, dir. eastern Europe, Hamburg, W.Ger., 1973-75, v.p. of Germany, Frankfurt, 1978-81, v.p., gen. mgr., N.Y.C., 1981-82, regional v.p., 1983—. Bd. dirs. N.Y.C. Conv. and Visitors Bur., 1982—; bd. govd., dir. Olympic Tower-N.Y.C. Mem. Cornell Soc. Hotelmen, N.Y.C. Hotel Assn. (dir. 1982—), Chaine des Rotisseurs, Ordre des Coteaux. Clubs: Netherland (bd. dirs.)(N.Y.), Harvard, Doubles. Home: 153 Transylvania Rd Woodbury CT 06798 Office: Inter-Continental Hotels 111 E 48th St New York NY 10017

PEELER, JOSEPH DAVID, retired lawyer; b. Nashville, Sept. 29, 1895; s. Joseph David and Virginia (McCue) P.; m. Elizabeth F. Boggess, Apr. 27, 1927; children—Stuart Thorne, Joyce Woodson. A.B., U. Ala., 1915; LL.B.

cum laude, Harvard, 1920. Bar: Ky. 1920, Calif. 1929. Practiced law in Louisville, 1920-29, Los Angeles, 1929-87; mem. firm Musick, Peeler & Garrett. Bd. fellows Claremont U. Center.; Mem. U.S.A. teams Internat. Tuna Tournament, 1939, 47, 48, 55. Served as capt. A.C. U.S. Army, World War I; lt. col. USAAF, World War II. Mem. Am., Calif. State, Los Angeles bar assns., Phi Beta Kappa, Delta Kappa Epsilon. Republican. Conglist. Clubs: California, Tuna (past pres.), Los Angeles (past pres.), Wilshire Country. Home: 131 N June St Los Angeles CA 90004 Office: One Wilshire Building Los Angeles CA 90017

PEELER, WILLIAM JAMES, lawyer; b. Highland Park, Mich., Nov. 27, 1927; s. Herb and Beulah (Wells) P.; m. Nancy Jean Bradley, Dec. 26, 1949; children: Nannette Peeler Goddard, Jeana Peeler Hosch, Jacqueline Peeler Fuqua. LLB, Cumberland U., 1952. Bar: Tenn. 1952. Ptnr. Porch, Peeler, Williams, Thomason & Bradley, Waverly, Tenn., 1952—; gen. counsel, bd. dirs. Sovran Bank, Waverly, 1968—, New Life Found., Burns, Tenn., 1983—. Mem. Tenn. Ho. of Reps., 1959-63; majority leader Tenn. Senate, 1967-75; trustee Cumberland U., Lebanon, Tenn., 1985—. Fellow Am. Coll. Trial Lawyers, Tenn. Bar Found.; mem. Am. Judicature Soc., ABA, Tenn. Bar Assn., Humphreys County Bar Assn. Democrat. Mem. Ch. of Christ. Clubs: Cumberland, City, Capitol (Nashville); Jefferson (Louisville). Lodges: Elks, Masons. Home: Little Richland Creek Rd Waverly TN 37185 Office: Porch Peeler Williams Thomason & Bradley 102 S Court Sq Waverly TN 37185

PEERTHUM, SATTEEANUND, ambassador; b. Mauritius, Mar. 15, 1941; s. Chandraduth and Hurbansia (Rajpalsingh) P.; m. Dulary Ramesar, Mar. 9, 1967; children: Sandhya, Zoya, Satyendra. MA with hons., People's Friendship U., Moscow, 1970, PhD in Internat. Relations, 1973. Tchr. Ministry of Edn., Mauritius, 1960-65; sr. research fellow Inst. Oriental Studies of Acad. of Sci. of USSR, Moscow, 1973-74; journalist Le Militant, Port Louis, Mauritius, 1974-78; mem. parliament, minister of labor Govt. of Mauritius, 1982-83; adminstr. Sugar Industry Devel. Fund, Port Louis, 1984-87; ambassador to UN, 1987—. Co-author: Toward Collective Security in Asia, 1973. Mem. Cen. Com. Movement Militant Mauritian, 1977-82; founding mem. Movement Socialiste Militant, Mauritius, 1983. Address: Mauritius Mission to UN 211 E 43d St New York NY 10013

PEET, RICHARD CLAYTON, lawyer, consultant; b. N.Y.C., Aug. 24, 1928; s. Charles Francis and Florence L. (Isaacs) P.; m. Barbara Jean McClure, Mar. 17, 1956 (div. July, 1988); children: Victoria Clementine, Alexandra Constance, Elizabeth Erica, Clarissa Barbara. JD, Tulane U., 1953. Bar: La. 1955, D.C. 1955. Law clk. firm Melvin M. Belli, San Francisco, 1954; with The Calif. Co., Standard Oil of Calif., 1955; atty. appellate sect. Lands div. Dept. Justice, Washington, 1956; asst. to dep. gen. counsel Dept. Commerce, 1957; with Republican policy com. U.S. Senate, 1958; office minority leader William F. Knowland, 1958; asso. counsel anti-trust subcom. House Judiciary Com., 1959-62; asso. minority counsel House Pub. Works Com., 1969-74; pres. Citizens for Hwy. Safety, 1978-84; practiced in Washington, 1962-68; prin. Richard Clayton Peet & Assos., 1972—; partner Anderson, Pendleton, McMahon, Peet & Donovan, 1977-80, Anderson, Peet & Co., 1980-84; pres., dir. Lincoln Research Center, 1965-72; v.p. Oil East Corp., 1978-83. Author: Goals for a Constructive Opposition, 1966; contbg. editor: Jour. Def. and Diplomacy, 1983-86; composer: song Stand Up For America, 1971 (George Washington medal Freedom's Found. 1971). Chmn. bd. Workshop Library on World Humor. Served with U.S. Army, 1946-47; Served with USAFR, 1950-55. Mem. Phi Delta Phi, Pi Kappa Alpha. Club: Cosmos. Home: PO Box 971 McLean VA 22101

PEI, DINGYI, mathematician; b. Zhangdian, People's Republic of China, Aug. 8, 1941; s. Shouheng Pei and Yunhua Tang; m. Keming Gao, May 12, 1970; children: Baicheng, Baikang. BD, U. Sci. and Tech. of China, Beijing, 1964, PhD, 1968. Technician Taching Oil Field, 1968-77; asst. prof. Inst. of Applied Math. Academia Sinica, Beijing, 1978-82, assoc. prof., 1982-86, prof. grad. sch., 1986—. Contbr. articles to profl. jours.; reviewer Math. Review, 1985—, Zentralblatt fur Mathematik, Berlin, 1985—. Mem. Am. Math. Soc. Office: Dept Mathematics, PO Box 3908, Beijing Peoples Republic of China

PEI, IEOH MING, architect; b. Canton, China, Apr. 26, 1917; came to U.S., 1935, naturalized, 1954; s. Tsu Yee Pei and Lien Kwun Chwong; m. Eileen Loo, June 20, 1942; children: T'ing Chung, Chien Chung, Li Chung, Liane. B.Arch., Mass. Inst. Tech., 1940; M.Arch., Harvard, 1946; D.F.A., U. Pa., 1970, Rensselaer Polytech. Inst., 1978, Carnegie Mellon U., 1980, U. Mass., 1980, Brown U., 1982, NYU, 1983; LL.D., Chinese U., Hong Kong, 1970; L.H.D., Columbia U., 1980, U. Colo., 1982, U. Rochester, 1982. Practice architecture Boston, N.Y.C., Los Angeles, 1939-42; asst. prof. Harvard Grad. Sch. Design, 1945-48; dir. archtl. div. Webb & Knapp, Inc., 1948-55; with I.M. Pei & Partners (formerly I.M. Pei & Assos.), N.Y.C., 1955—. Prin. projects include, Mile High Center, Denver, Nat. Center Atmospheric Research, Boulder, Colo., Dallas City Hall, John Fitzgerald Kennedy Library, Boston Mass., Canadian Imperial Bank of Commerce Complex, Toronto, Oversea-Chinese Banking Corp. Centre, Singapore, Grave for Robert F. Kennedy, Arlington Nat. Cemetery, Dreyfus Chemistry Bldg. at Mass. Inst. Tech., East-West Center U. Hawaii, Honolulu, Mellon Art Center, Choate Sch., Wallingford, Conn., Univ. Plaza, N.Y. U., TWA Domestic Terminal John Fitzgerald Kennedy Internat. Airport, N.Y.C., Johnson Mus. Art at Cornell U., Ithaca, N.Y., Washington Sq. East, Phila., Everson Mus. Art, Syracuse, N.Y., Nat. Gallery Art, East Bldg., Washington, Wilmington Tower, Raffles City, Singapore, master plan, Columbia U., Bedford Stuyvesant Super Block, Bklyn., West Wing Mus. Fine Arts, Boston, others, planning projects, S.W. Washington Redevel. Plan, Dallas Symphony Hall, Govt. Center Redevel. Plan, Boston, MIT Arts and Media Ctr., Oklahoma City Downtown Redevel. Plan, N.Y. Conv. and Exhbn. Center, Fragrant Hill Hotel, Beijing, China, Texas Commerce Tower, Houston. Mem. Nat. Def. Research Com., Princeton, N.J., 1943-45, Nat. Council Humanities, 1966-70, Nat. Council on Arts, 1980—. Mass. Inst. Tech. traveling fellowship, 1940; Wheelwright fellow Harvard, 1951; Thomas Jefferson Meml. Medal for Architecture, 1976; gold medal for architecture Am. Acad. Arts and Letters, 1979; La Grande Medaille D'or L', 1981; Nat. Arts Club Gold Medal of Honor, 1981; Mayor's Award of Honor for Art and Culture N.Y.C., 1981; La Grande Medaille D'or L'Académie d'Architecture, 1981; Pritzker Architecture prize, 1983; Medal of French Legion of Honor, 1987. Fellow A.I.A. (Medal of Honor N.Y. chpt. 1963, Gold Medal 1979); hon. fellow ASID; mem. Nat. Inst. Arts and Letters (Arnold Brunner award 1961), Am. Acad. Arts and Scis., Am. Acad. and Inst. Arts and Letters (chancellor 1978-80), Royal Inst. Brit. Architects, N.A.D., Urban Design Council. Office: I M Pei & Ptnrs 600 Madison Ave New York NY 10022 *

PELAVIN, SOL HERBERT, educational research company executive; b. Detroit, Dec. 16, 1941; s. Norman J. and Alice A. (Levinson) P.; m. Diane Christine Blakemore, Aug. 14, 1966; children—Shayna Beth, Adam Blake. BA in Math., U. Chgo., 1965, MAT in Math., 1969; MS in Stats., Stanford U., 1974, PhD candidate in mathematical models of edn. research, 1975. Tchr. pub. schs., 1965-70. Teaching research asst. Stanford (Calif.) U., 1972-74; cons. Rand Corp., Santa Monica, Calif., 1975; policy analyst SRI Internat., Menlo Park, Calif., 1975-78; exec. officer NTS Research Corp., Durham, N.C., 1978-82; pres. Pelavin Assocs., Inc., Washington, 1982—; expert witness to U.S. Congress, 1977, 79, Cabinet briefing, 1983; cons. Frank, Bernstein, Conway and Goldman, Balt., 1980-81; dir. Ednl. Analysis Ctr., Washington, 1982-85. Contbr. articles to profl. jours. NSF fellow U. Chgo., 1968-69; Cuneo fellow Stanford U., 1973. Mem. AAAS, Am. Ednl. Research Assn., Am. Psychol. Assn., Nat. Council Measurement in Edn. Democrat. Jewish. Office: Pelavin Assocs Inc 1300 19th St NW Suite 500 Washington DC 20036

PELCZAR, ANDRZEJ MARIA, educator; b. Gdansk, Poland, Apr. 12, 1937; s. Marian Wiktor and Maria Klara (Trnka) P.; m. Janina Felicja Fajczak, Feb. 6, 1961; children: Maria, Anna. MSc, Jagiellonian U., Krakow, Poland, 1959, PhD, 1964, DSc, 1971. Asst. Acad. Mining and Metalurgy, Krakow, 1960-61, Jagiellonian U. Inst. of Math., Krakow, 1961-64; prof. Jagiflonian U. Inst. of Math., Krakow, 1980—, asst. prof., 1964-71; asst. associé faculté des scis. d'orsay U. Paris, 1967-68; assoc. prof. dept. math. Ahmadu Bello U., Zaria, Nigeria, 1978-81; dir. inst. math. Jagiellonian U., Krakow, 1981-84, 1987—, v.p., 1984-87; assoc. prof. Jagiellonian U., Krakow, 19671-80. Contbr. articles to profl. jours. Mem. Polish Math. Soc. (pres., Zaremba award, 1972), Am. Math. Soc. Roman Catholic. Office: U Jagiellonian, Instutut Matematyki, Reymonta 4, 30 054 Crakow Poland

PELCZAR, OTTO, electrical engineer; b. Vienna, Austria, Aug. 9, 1934; moved to Australia, 1950; s. Joseph Franz and Brigitte (Von Witkowski) P.; m. Amy Margueritte Ludovici, May 9, 1959; children—Suzanne Patricia, Vicki Josephine, Michelle Amy, Paul Daniel. Diploma Elec. Engring., Perth Tech. Coll., W. Australia, 1967; B.Applied Sci., Inst. Tech., Perth, 1978; M.B.A., U. Western Australia, Perth, 1982. Labourer, welder Roads Bd., Maylands, 1950-56; chief draughtsman Westate Elec. Ind., Perth, 1956-70; dist. engr. Pub. Works Dept., 1970-72; comdg. officer Her Majesty's Australian Ship Acute, 1973-78; engr. Pub. Works Dept., Perth, 1972-85; lectr. Tech. Coll., Subiaco, 1979—; mng. dir. Opex Pty. Ltd., W. Perth, 1982—; elec. engr. Dept. Marine and Harbours, Fremantle, 1985—. Convener, West Coast Secession Movement, Perth, 1981; nominee W. Australian Parliament, 1983. Served to comdr. Royal Australian Naval Res., 1956—. Australian Commonwealth scholar, 1967. Fellow Inst. Engrs.; mem. Royal United Services Inst. (v.p. 1983—), Inst. Draughtsmen, Royal Australian Inst. Pub. Adminstrn., Australian Inst. Internat. Affairs. Club: Old Austria (life mem.). Lodge: Rotary (program dir. 1984—). Avocations: chess; tennis; yachting. Home: 230 Oceanic Dr, City Beach 6015 Australia Office: Dept Marine and Harbours, 1 Essex St, Fremantle 6160, Australia

PELGER-JENSEN, JUNE ROSE MARY, foundation administrator; b. Kearny, N.J., May 23, 1928; arrived in The Netherlands, 1959:; d. James and Charlotte (Smith) Jensen; m. Alfred Pelger, June 20, 1959. BA, Colby Coll., 1950; MS, N.Y.U., 1952. Tech. asst. Bell Telephone Labs., Murray Hill, N.J., 1950-54; asst. prof. math. Poly. Inst. Bklyn., 1954-59; treas. Internat. Electronics, Havelte, The Netherlands, 1961—, Betty McDonald Found., Amsterdam, The Netherlands, 1966—; bd. dirs. Het Electron Found., Amsterdam, 1985—; mem. com. Audio Video and Electronics Exhibition, Amsterdam, 1985—. Bd. dirs. Havelte Library, 1976—, Community Ctr., 1985—. Mem. Math. Assn. Am. Home: Boskampbrugweg 9, 7971CL Havelte The Netherlands

PELISSIER, EDOUARD-PIERRE, surgeon; b. Bastia, Corse, France, Sept. 1, 1937; s. Jean-Baptiste and Francoise (Geronimi) P.; m. Sylvie Geoffroy-Emmanuelli, Feb. 9, 1967; children—Emmanuelle, Pierre, Francois, Anne-Catherine. M.D., U. Paris, 1968. Ancien interne des Hopitaux de Paris, 1963-67; attache cons. Centre Hospitalier Universitaire de Besancon, France, 1975; surgeon Clinique St. Vincent, Besancon, 1968—; sec. Conseil de l'Ordre des Medecins, Doubs, France, 1980-83. Contbr. articles to med. revs. Served with French Marine Corps, 1961-63. Mem. Academie de Chirurgie (assoc.), Collegium Internationale Chirurgiae Digestivae, Société Nationale Francaise de Gastro-Enterologie (assoc.). Office: Clinique St Vincent, 24 rue des deux Princesses, 25000 Besancon France

PELISSON, GERARD FERDINAND, hotels and restaurtants company executive; b. Lyon, France, Feb. 9, 1932; s. Jules and Jeanne Gaymard; m. Suzanne Arnoux, Mar. 8, 1956. Engr., Ecole Centrale, Paris, 1955; student Harvard Bus. Sch., 1959-60; M.S. in Indsl. Mgmt., MIT, 1960. Engr. Compagnie Géné rale d'Organisation, Paris, 1958-61; engr. exec. Centre Français Recherche Opérationnelle, Paris, 1961-62; exec. IBM Europe, Paris, 1963-71; co-chmn., chief exec. officer ACCOR, Paris, 1971—; dir. SPHERE, Evry, France, 1974—. Decorated chevalier de l'Ordre National du Mérite, Legion d'honneur, French State, 1984. Avocations: golf, skiing. Home: 1 Rue Gambetta, 77780 Bourron-Marlotte France Office: ACCOR, 2 Rue de la Mare Neuve, 91021 Evry France

PELL, CLAIBORNE, U.S. senator; b. N.Y.C., Nov. 22, 1918; s. Herbert Claiborne and Matilda (Bigelow) P.; m. Nuala O'Donnell, Dec. 1944; children: Herbert Claiborne III, Christopher T. Hartford, Nuala Dallas Yates, Julia L.W. Student, St. George's Sch., Newport, R.I.; A.B. cum laude, Princeton U., 1940; A.M., Columbia U., 1946; 33 hon. degrees. Enlisted USCGR, 1941; served as seaman, ensign N. Atlantic sea duty, Africa, Italy; hospitalized to U.S., 1944; instr. Navy Sch. Mil. Govt., Princeton, 1944-45; capt. USCGR; ret.; on loan to State Dept. at San Francisco Conf., 1945, State Dept., 1945-46, U.S. embassy, Czechoslovakia, 1946-47; established consulate gen. Bratislava, Czechoslovakia, 1947-48; vice consul Genoa, Italy, 1949; assigned State Dept., 1950-52; v.p., dir. Internat. Rescue Com.; senator from R.I., 1961—; U.S. del. Internat. Maritime Consultative Orgn., London, 1959, 25th Gen. Assembly, 1970. Author: Megalopolis Unbound, 1966, (with Harold L. Goodwin) Challenge of the Seven Seas, 1966, Power and Policy, 1972. Hon. bd. dirs. World Affairs Council R.I.; trustee St. George's Sch.; trustee emeritus Brown U.; Cons. Democratic Nat. Com., 1953-60; exec. asst. to chmn. R.I. State Dem. Com., 1952-54; chmn. R.I. Dem. Fund drive, 1952, Dem. nat. registration, chmn., 1956, co-chmn., 1962; chief delegation tally clk. Dem. Nat. Conv., 1956, 60, 64, 68. Decorated knight Crown of Italy, grand cross Order of Merit Italy; Red Cross of Merit Portugal; Legion of Honor France; comdr. Order of Phoenix Greece; grand cross Order of Merit Liechtenstein; Grand Cross Order of Christ Portugal, Order of Henry the Navigator, Portugal; grand cross Order of N. Star Sweden; Grand Cross of Merit Knights of Malta; Caritas Elizabeth medal Cardinal Franz Koenig; Grand decoration of honor in silver with sash Austria; grand officer of merit Luxembourg; Gold medal of St. Barnabas (Cyprus); recipient Pres.'s Fellow award R.I. Sch. Design. Mem. Soc. Cin. Episcopalian. Clubs: Hope (Providence); Knickerbocker (N.Y.C.), Racquet and Tennis (N.Y.C.), Brook (N.Y.C.); Metropolitan (Washington); Travellers (Paris); Reading Room (Newport); White's (London). Office: 335 Russell Senate Bldg Washington DC 20510 *

PELL, ERNEST EUGENE, broadcasting executive; b. Paducah, Ky., Mar. 15, 1937; s. Ernest Joseph and Edna Marie (Stewart) P.; m. Linda Winthrop, July 17, 1959 (div. May 1985); children: Anne Frances, Jennifer Susan; m. Linda Ann Holwick, June 15, 1985. BA in English, Harvard U., 1959; MS in Journalism, Boston U., 1962. Anchorman WBZ-TV, Boston, 1963-67, WBZ-TV, WCVB-TV, Boston, 1975-77; polit. corr. Westinghouse Broadcasting Co., Washington, 1967-69; dir. fgn. news Westinghouse Broadcasting Co., London, Eng., 1969-74; fgn. corr. NBC News, Moscow, 1977-80; Washington corr. NBC News, 1980-82; dep. dir. Voice of Am., Washington, 1983-84, dir., 1984-85; pres. Radio Free Europe/Radio Liberty, Munich, Fed. Republic Germany, 1985—. Served to lt. (j.g.) USNR, 1959-62. Nieman fellow Harvard U., 1974-75, Vis. fellow, 1977; recipient Best Fgn. Reporting award Overseas Press Club, 1974, Outstanding Alumnus award Boston U., 1981. Republican. Home: Maurerkircher St 75, 8000 Munich 81 Federal Republic of Germany Office: Radio Free Europe/Radio Liberty 1201 Connecticut Ave NW Washington DC 20036

PELLEGRINI, UMBERTO, electronics engineer, educator; b. Rome, Aug. 31, 1930; s. Leopoldo and Walterina (Biancucci) P.; m. Anna Sabatini, Aug. 4, 1955; children: Paolo, Laura, Alessandra. PhD in Physics, U., Rome, 1953, Libero Docente, 1959. Electronic researcher State U., Rome, 1953-60; prof. electronics State U., Milan, 1960—; gen. mgr. Laben-Laboratori Elettronici, Milan, 1960-69, Montedel, Milan, 1969-73; corp. mgr. Olivetti, Ivrea, Italy, 1973-80; chmn. Carlo Gavazzi Controls, Milan, 1980-84; vice chmn. Carlo Gavazzi, Milan, 1985—; chmn. Officine Galileo, Florence, Italy, 1985-87; founder Tecnetra, Milan, 1980—; chmn. Federazione Associazioni Scientifiche e Tecniche, Milan, 1974-80. Author 5 tech. books on electronics and info., 50 sci. articles; mem. editorial bd. Associazione Elettrotecnica Italiana-Alta frequenza Rev., 1970—; 7 patents in electronic circuits. Chmn. Found. for Sci. and Tech. Edn., Milan, 1974-80. Recipient Cert. Appreciation U.S. Embassy in Italy and U.S. Trade Ctr. in Milan. Fellow IEEE; mem. Associazione Nazionale per L'Automazione (chmn. 1969-73, editor Automation Rev. 1980—). Lodge: Rotary (pres. 1988—). Home: Residenza La Sorgente 941, Milan 2-MI 20090, Italy Office: Physics Inst State U, Via Celoria 16, Milan 20133, Italy

PELLETIER, ALCID MILTON, psychologist; b. Bridgeport, Conn., Aug. 27, 1926; s. Alcid L. and Mary Jane (Auger) P.; children: Paulette, Alcid Milton, Lionel, Debra, Jon, Jacques, Angelique. AA, Graceland Coll., 1951; BA in Psychology, U. Mo., Kansas City, 1971; MA in Psychology, Western Mich. U., 1972, EdD, 1975. Ordained to ministry, Reorganized Ch.of Jesus Christ of Latter Day Saints, 1951. Assigned to transfers, Ont., Can., Ill., Pa., Mo., Mich., 1951-72; chief forensic psychology, Kent County Jail, Grand Rapids, Mich., 1972-74; asst. to med. dir., clin. coordinator, chief psychologist, chief admissions officer, Kent Oaks Hosp., Grand Rapids, 1974-78; adminstr. Mich. Med. Weight Control Clinics, Grand Rapids, Lansing, Kalamazoo, 1978; owner, pres. Ctr. for Human Potential, P.C., Grand Rapids, 1978—; pvt. practice psychology, Grand Rapids; cons. Family Services Assn., Grand Rapids, 1972-74; instr. Calhoun County Juvenile Ct., 1974-77, Grand Valley State Colls., 1975, Western Mich. U., 1974; instr. nursing Butterworth Gen. Hosp., 1974; instr. New Clinic for Women, 1974, 77-78; condr. workshops for Mich. Supreme Ct., annually 1973-78, probate cts., Mich. Dept. Social Services, 1977, 78. Mem. sheriff's adv. com., 1976-78; mem. Human Devel. Assn., Mt. Vernon, Ill., 1959, Kent County Mental Health Assn., Mich. Soc. for Mental Health. Served with U.S. Army, 1945-46. Recipient certificate of appreciation for profl. services Western Mich. U., 1974; lic. psychologist, Mich., also certified rehab. counselor. Mem. Am., Mich. psychol. assns., Am., Mich. personnel and guidance assns., Assn. Counselor Edn. and Supervision, Am. Rehab. Counselors Assn., Mich., Am. socs. clin. hypnosis, Insts. Religion and Health. Republican. Contbr. articles to profl. jours., speeches to confs. in fields of use of hypnosis as treatment. Home and Office: 555 Maynard NW Grand Rapids MI 49504

PELLETIER, CLAUDE HENRI, biomedical engineer; b. Riviere-Ouelle, Can., Que., Dec. 15, 1941; s. Lucien Pelletier and Ernestine Michaud. Immatriculation sr., Coll. Universitaire U. Sherbrooke, 1961; B.Sc.A., U. Sherbrooke, 1966; M.Sc.A., Ecole Poly technique, U. Montreal, 1972. Project engr. Alcan, Alma, Can., 1966-69; mgr. computer ctr. in physiology dept. faculty medicine U. Montreal, 1972-73; biomed. engr. Sacre-Coeur Hosp., Montreal, 1973-75; chief engr. biomed. engring. dept. Montreal Heart Inst., 1975—; lectr. faculty of medicine U. Montreal, 1972-74, research asst. faculty of medicine, 1973-75; cons. Montreal Heart Inst., 1975—. Contbr. articles to profl. jours. Mem. Order of Engrs. Que., IEEE, Assn. Advancement Med. Instrumentation, Assn. Des Physiciens Et Ingenieurs Biomedicaux Du Que. Roman Catholic. Avocations: swimming; tennis. Home: 5732 Plantagenet, Montreal, PQ Canada H3S 2K3

PELLETREAU, ROBERT HALSEY, diplomat; b. Patchogue, N.Y., July 9, 1935; s. Robert H. and Mary (Pigeon) P.; m. Pamela Day, Dec. 17, 1966; children: Katherine Day, Erica Pigeon, Elizabeth Anne. B.A., Yale U., 1957; LL.B., Harvard U., 1961. Bar: N.Y. 1961. Assoc. firm Chadbourne, Parke, Whiteside & Wolfe, N.Y.C., 1961-62; joined U.S. Fgn. Service, 1962; service in Morocco, Mauritania, Lebanon, Algeria, Jordan and Syria; ambassador to Bahrain 1979-80, dep. asst. sec. def., 1980-81, 85-87, dep. asst. sec. state, 1983-85, ambassador to Tunisia, 1987—. Served with USNR, 1957-58. Mem. Am. Fgn. Service Assn., Middle East Inst. Office: US Ambassador to Tunisia care Dept State Washington DC 20520-6360

PELLINO, CHARLES EDWARD, JR., lawyer; b. Chgo., May 2, 1943; s. Charles Edward Sr. and Ella (Didomendico) P.; m. Melinda Poorman, Aug. 20, 1966; children: Charles, Tracy, William. BA, Drake U., 1965; JD, U. Wis., 1968. Bar: Wis. 1968, U.S. Dist. Ct. (we. dist.) Wis. 1972, U.S. Tax Ct. 1984, U.S. Dist. Ct. (ea. dist.) Wis. 1985, U.S. Ct. Appeals (7th cir.) 1985, U.S. Supreme Ct. 1985. Assoc. McAndrews, Fritschler & Huggett, Madison, Wis., 1968-70; ptnr. Fritschler, Ross, Pellino & Protzman, Madison, 1970-73, Fritschler, Pellino & Assocs., Madison, 1973-76, Fritschler, Pellino, Schrank & Rosen, Madison, 1976-88, Fritschler, Pellino, Rosen and Mowris, Madison, 1988—; bd. dirs. Frontier Econ. Devel. Corp., N.Y.C. Contbr. articles to profl. jours. Mem. ABA, Wis. Bar Assn., Nat. Assn. Criminal Def. Lawyers, Wis. Acad. Trial Lawyers, Wis. Assn. Criminal Def. Lawyers (sec.-elect 1987—). Office: Fritschler Pellino Rosen & Mowris 131 W Wilson Suite 601 Madison WI 53703

PELS, DONALD ARTHUR, broadcasting company executive; b. New Rochelle, N.Y., Jan. 23, 1928; s. Herbert and Alice Miriam (Brady) P.; m. Josette Jeanne Bernard, Feb. 11, 1965; children: Juliette, Valerie, Laurence. BS, U. Pa., 1948; JD, NYU, 1953. CPA. With Filene's Dept. Store, Boston, 1948-49, Arthur Young & Co., N.Y.C., 1953-56; bus. mgr. Sta. WABC-TV, N.Y.C., 1956-59; exec. v.p., dir. Capital Cities Communications, N.Y.C., 1959-69; chmn., pres. LIN Broadcasting Corp., N.Y.C., 1969—. Trustee Barnard Coll.; bd. dirs. U.S. Trust, Philharm. Symphony Soc. N.Y. Club: Univ. (N.Y.C.). Home: 10 Gracie Sq New York NY 10028 Office: Lin Broadcasting Corp 1370 Avenue of the Americas New York NY 10019

PELTASON, JACK WALTER, university chancellor; b. St. Louis, Aug. 29, 1923; s. Walter B. and Emma (Hartman) P.; m. Suzanne Toll, Dec. 21,1946; children: Nancy Hartman, Timothy Walter H., Jill K. B.A., U. Mo., 1943, M.A., 1944, LL.D. (hon.), 1978; A.M., Princeton U., 1946, Ph.D., 1947; LL.D. (hon.), U. Md., 1979, Ill. Coll., 1979, Gannon U., 1980, U. Maine, 1980, Union Coll., 1981, Moorehead (N.D.) State U., 1980; L.H.D. (hon.), 1980, Ohio State U., 1980, Mont. Coll. Mineral Scis. and Tech., 1982, Buena Vista Coll., 1982, Assumption Coll., 1983, Chapman Coll., 1986. Asst. prof. Smith Coll., Mass., 1947-51; asst. prof. polit. sci. U. Ill., Urbana, 1951-52, assoc. prof., 1953-59, dean Coll. Liberal Arts and Scis., 1960-64, chancellor, 1967-77; vice chancellor acad. affairs U. Calif., Irvine, 1964-67, chancellor, 1984—; pres. Am. Council Edn., Washington, 1977-84; Cons. Mass. Little Hoover Commn., 1950. Author: The Missouri Plan for the Selection of Judges, 1947, Understanding the Constitution, 11th edit, 1988, Federal Courts in the Political Process, 1957, (with James M. Burns) Government by the People, 13th edit, 1987, Fifty-eight Lonely Men, 1961, also articles, revs. Recipient James Madison medal Princeton U., 1982. Fellow Am. Acad. Arts and Scis.; mem. Am. Polit. Sci. Assn. (council 1952-54), Phi Beta Kappa, Phi Kappa Phi, Omicron Delta Kappa, Alpha Phi Omega, Beta Gamma Sigma. Home: 6 Gibbs Ct Irvine CA 92715 Office: Univ of Calif Irvine Campus Dr Office of the Chancellor Irvine CA 92717

PELTIER, PHILIPPE, diplomat; b. Tarbes, France, June 27, 1937; s. Raymond and Marie (Brossard) P.; m. Denise Ginestet, Feb. 1, 1959; children: Marianne, Marc. Degree, Ecole Nat. D'Administrn., Paris, 1964; degree in Internat. Affairs, Harvard U., 1976. Diplomat French Ministry of Fgn. Affairs, Paris, 1964-66, head budget service, 1979-81; counsellor French Mission to European Communities, Brussels, 1966-75; head internat. service French Ministry Sci. Research, Paris, 1979-1981; dir. de cabinet French Ministry European Affairs, Paris, 1981-84; ambassador to Norway Oslo, 1985—. Served to lt French Cavalry, 1960-62, Algeria. Recipient Legion D'Honneur Chevalier, French Military Cross; named to nat. orders of Portugal, Cameroons, Gabon. Home and Office: Embassy of France, 69 Drammensveien, Oslo Norway 0271

PELTON, WILLIAM HARVEY, geophysicist; b. New Westminister, B.C., Can., July 21, 1946; came to U.S.; s. Ralph Charles and Ethel Lilly (Moe) P.; BS in Engring. Physics, U.B.C., 1969; Ph.D., U. Utah, 1977. Geophysicist, McPhar Geophysics, Toronto, Ont., Can., 1969-71; v.p., gen. mgr. McPhar Philippines, Manila, 1971-73; v.p. Phoenix Geophysics, Toronto, 1977-85, pres., Denver, 1982-85; founder, pres. Phoenix Geosci., Denver, 1987— ; mem. trade mission to Peking, 1972; cons. UN Devel. Program, India, 1978, 80; dir. spectral ip research program for 11 mining cos., 1978-81; dir. hydrocarbon research for 14 oil cos., 1981. Recipient Best Paper award Geophysics Mag., 1978. Mem. Soc. Exploration Geophysicists (award 1977). European Assn. Exploration Geophysicists, Can. Inst. Mining and Metallurgy, AIME. Developer spectral induced polarization method and equipment, 1979; supr. design of magnetotelluric equipment, 1981. Home: 1625 Larimer St #1005 Denver CO 80202 Office: Phoenix Geosci Inc 555 17th St #2570 Denver CO 80202

PELTONEN, KEIJO KALERVO, light manufacturing executive; b. Lahti, Finland, May 18, 1939; s. Lauri Valdemar and Impi Irene (Lahti) P.; m. Raija-Leena Fagerholm; children: Pia-Irene, Laura-Johanna (div. 1981); m. Raijaliisa Rytinki; 1 child, Juha-Pekka. Student, U. Helsinki, Finland, 1960-64, Helsinki Flight Acad., 1964. Cert. comml. pilot. V.p. Hämeen Kalustaja, Lahti, 1971-82; export mgr. Finnbo Oy, Lahti, 1982-83; pres. Expoline Oy, Lahti, 1983—; mng. dir. Valtti Kaluste, Helsinki, 1962-76, Finnmeb Oy, Lahti, 1971-73; pres. Lahti-Air Oy, 1980-85, Akvor, Helsinki, 1969—; mgr. mktg. Obaid Trading Establishment, Riyadh, Saudi Arabia, 1985-86. Served to capt. Finnish mil. Mem. Finnish Furniture Exporters Assn. (bd. dirs. 1970-74). Mem. Kokoomus Party. Club: Lc Laune. Lodge: KK 54. Home: Huvilatie, 16500 Herrala Finland Office: Expoline Oy, Vuorikatu 35, 15100 Lahti Finland

PELZER, CHARLES FRANCIS, geneticist, biology educator, researcher; b. Detroit, June 5, 1935; s. Francis Joseph and Edna Dorothy (Ladach) P.; m. Veronica Ann Killeen, July 7, 1972; 1 child, Mary Elizabeth. BS in Biology, U. Detroit, 1957; PhD in Human Genetics, U. Mich., 1965. Postdoctoral fellow Wabash Coll., Crawfordsville, Ind., 1965-66; instr. U. Detroit, 1966-68; asst. prof. Saginaw Valley State U., University Center, Mich., 1969-74, assoc. prof., 1974-79, prof., 1979—; research assoc. Mich. State U., East Lansing, 1976-77; research fellow Henry Ford Hosp., Detroit, 1982-83; v.p. Saginaw Valley Retinitis Pigmentosa Found., Mich., 1979-81; vis. scientist Am. Inst. Biol. Scis., Washington, 1975-78; grant reviewer U.S. Dept. Edn., Washington, 1984-87. Contbr. articles to profl. jours. Recipient Alumni award Saginaw Valley State U. Alumni Assn., 1971; grantee Ford Hosp. Found., 1983, Mich. State U., 1977, Saginaw Valley State U. Found., 1979-82, 83-85, 86—, Kettering Found., 1965-66, Kellogg Found., 1961, NIH, 1961-64, Monsanto Co. research grant, 1987. Fellow Human Biology Council; mem. Am. Soc. Human Genetics, Genetics Soc. Am., N.Y. Acad. Sci., Electrophorisis Soc., Nat. Assn. Biology Tchrs. (dir. for Mich. Outstanding Tchrs. award), others. Home: 4900 Schneider Saginaw Twp MI 48603 Office: Saginaw Valley State U Dept Biology SI53 University Center MI 48710

PEMBERTON, JOHN MAXWELL, microbial geneticist; b. Melbourne, Victoria, Australia, Dec. 23, 1944; s. Mathew Carew and Jean Elizabeth Pemberton; m. Margaret Elizabeth Jones, Dec. 5, 1969; children—Nicholas John, Amy Louise. B.Agrl. Sci., Melbourne U., 1967; Ph.D., Monash U., 1971; grad. diploma in ednl. adminstrn. Darling Downs Inst. for Advanced Edn., 1982. Postdoctoral research molecular biologist dept. molecular biology and virology U. Calif.-Berkeley, 1971-73; research fellow Sch. Biol. Scis., Flinders U. (South Australia), 1973-74; lectr. dept. microbiology U. Queensland, St. Lucia, 1974-80, sr. lectr., 1980-86; assoc. prof., 1986—. Mem. Australian Soc. Microbiology, Am. Soc. Microbiology. Roman Catholic. Discoverer first pesticide degrading plasmids; prod. first genetic map of a photosynthetic bacterium using plasmid mediated chromosome transfer. Home: 142 Burbong, Brisbane 4069, Australia Office: U Queensland, Dept Microbiology, Saint Lucia 4067, Australia

PEMSLER, J(OSEPH) PAUL, research, development and consultant company executive; b. N.Y.C., July 9, 1929; s. Samuel and Anna P.; B.S., N.Y.U., 1949, Ph.D., 1954; m. Suzanne Aaronson, Feb. 14, 1954; children—Seth, Clifford, Warren. Head, spectroscopy lab. Goodyear Atomic Corp., Portsmouth, Ohio, 1953-56; group leader chem. metallurgy Nuclear Metals, Inc., Concord, Mass., 1956-62; mgr. exploratory research Kennecott Copper, Lexington, Mass., 1962-77; dir. new tech. EIC Corp., Newton, Mass., 1977-78; pres. Castle Tech., Woburn, Mass., 1978—. Fellow Am. Inst. Chemists; mem. Internat. Soc. Electrochemistry, Am. Chem. Soc., AIME, Electrochem. Soc., Sigma Xi. Contbr. articles to profl. jours.; patentee in field. Home: 6 Castle Rd Lexington MA 02173 Office: 262 W Cummings Park Woburn MA 01801

PENA, RICHARD, lawyer; b. San Antonio, Feb. 13, 1948; s. Merced and Rebecca (Trejo) P.; m. Carolyn Sarah Malley, May 25, 1979; 1 stepchild, Jason Charles Schubert. BA, U. Tex., 1970, JD, 1976. Bar: Tex. 1976, Colo. 1986. ptnr. Law Offices of Pena & Jones, Austin, 1976—; instr. bus. law St. Edwards U., Austin, 1983, Austin Community Coll., 1981-82; broker Tex. Real Estate Commn., 1980—. Sports editor, Austin Light newspaper, 1982. Bd. dirs. Ctr. for Battered Women, Austin, 1979-82, Austin Assn. Retarded Citizens, 1980-82; chmn. Austin Travis County Mental Health/Mental Retardation Pub. Responsibility Comm., 1979-84; chmn. pvt. facilities monitoring com. Austin Assn. Retarded Citizens, 1981. Named One of Outstanding Young Men Am., Jaycees, 1982. Mem. Travis County Bar Assn. (trustee lawyer referral service 1984-85, bd. dirs. 1986—, sec. 1988-89), Capitol Area Mexican Am. Lawyers (pres. 1985), Legal Aid Soc. Cen. Tex. (bd. dirs. 1984), Travis County Bar Assn. (bd. dirs. 1986, lawyer referral service com.), Austin Young Lawyers Assn., Tex. Trial Lawyers Assn., State Bar Tex. (fed. judiciary appointments com. 1984), Austin C. of C. (leadership Austin 1985-86), Brotherhood Vietnam Vets. Democrat. Home: 312 Golf Crest Austin TX 78734 Office: Pena & Jones 901 Mopac Suite 325 Barton Oaks Plaza Two Austin TX 78743

PEÑAHERRERA, BLASCO MANUEL, former vice president of the Republic of Ecuador, journalist; b. Quito, Ecuador, Feb. 22, 1934. J.D., Universidad Central, 1963; married; 3 children. Editorial mem., columnist VISTAZO mag., 1963 83; various govt. positions, 1952 79; vice minister edn., councilman City of Quito, minister govt., pres. planning bd.; dir. Andean Corp. of Fostering; alt. nat. dep., 1979-84; v.p. Republic of Ecuador, 1984-88. Mem. Partido Liberal Radical Ecuatoriano, 1954—, nat. dir., 1983-85. Mem. Casa de la Cultura Ecuatoriana, Ateneo Ecuatoriano, Sociedad Jurídica Literaria, Nat. Confederation de Periodistas. Office: Oficina del Vice Presidente, Quito Ecuador *

PEÑASALES, SERGIO VILLAR, architect, landscape architect; b. Iloilo City, The Philippines, June 10, 1935; s. Silvestre Pabale and Consuelo (Villar) P.; m. Virginia Jocson, May 21, 1966; children: Carlo J., Oscar J. BArch, U. Santo Tomas, Manila, 1957; M in Landscape Architecture, U. Calif., Berkeley, 1963. Registered architect, landscape architect. Draftsman Angel E. Nakpil, Architect-City Planner, Manila, 1956-60; designer Royston, Hanamoto, Mayes & Beck, San Francisco, 1962-64; prin. S.V. Peñasales, Architect and Landscape Architect, Iloilo City; instr. architecture U. Iloilo, 1966-71; vis. lectr. various colls. and Univs., Philippines, 1966—; cons. Iloilo City Planning and Devel. Bd., 1966-81, mem. taskforce on environ. planning, 1987; cons. Iloilo Garden Club, 1981-83; examiner Landscape Architecture Profl. Regulation Bd., Manila, 1982-86; architecture researcher Visayan studies U. Philippines Visayas, 1986—. Contbr. articles to profl. publs. Trustee Iloilo Cultural and Research Found., 1971—; chmn. ecology com. Gov.'s Citizens Adv. Council, Iloilo, 1987. Recipient Alma Mater award Iloilo Sch. Arts and Trades, 1975. Fellow United Architects of Philippines (pres. Iloilo chpt. 1981-83); mem. Internat. Fedn. Landscape Architects (Philippine del. ea. region 1978), Philippine Inst. Architects (corp.), Philippine Assn. Landscape Architects (charter), Chamber Real Estate and Builders Assn. (bd. dirs. Iloilo chpt. 1981), Cultural Planners Assn. Philippines, Iloilo Integrated Accredited Profl. Assns. (v.p. 1987), Iloilo Soc. Arts (trustee 1982—), U. Calif. Alumni Assn., U. Santo Tomas Alumni Assn. (award for environ. devel. 1983). Home and Office: 249 Luna St, La Paz, Iloilo City 5000, Philippines

PENBERTHY, STANLEY JOSIAH, JR., publisher; b. Des Moines, Sept. 3, 1921; s. Stanley Josiah and Beatrice Ann (Voith) P.; student Drake U., Des Moines, 1940-43; m. Dorothea Oehmke, July 7, 1945; 1 son, Robert Bruce. Engaged in broadcasting, 1941-56; freelance radio, TV, motion picture actor, narrator, 1956—; v.p. Fed. I-D Equipment Corp., Dearborn, Mich., 1956-62; pres. Publishers, Inc., Detroit, 1976—. Bd. dirs. Sleeping Bear Dunes Citizens Council, Traverse City, Mich., 1970-75; pres. Heritage Village Condominum Assn.; trustee Detroit Masonic Temple Assn; mem. Founders Soc. Detroit Inst. Arts. Mem. Adcraft Club Detroit, Detroit Execs. Assn. (dir.), Screen Actors Guild, AFTRA (past dir.), Am. Film Inst., Detroit Producers Assn., Broadcast Pioneers, Alpha Tau Omega (past alumni pres.). Congregationalist. Lodge: Masons (33 deg.). Author, producer, narrator nat. radio series These Were Our Presidents, 1975, Mich. Sesquintennial hist. articles. Home: 35560 Heritage Ln Farmington MI 48024 Office: 500 Temple Ave Detroit MI 48201

PENDERECKI, KRZYSZTOF, composer, conductor; b. Debica, Poland, Nov. 23, 1933; s. Tadeusz and Zofia P.; m. Elzbieta Solecka; children: Lukasz, Dominique. Grad., State Acad. Music, Krakow, 1958; student, Arthur Malawski and Stanislaw Wiechowicz; Dr. honoris causa, U. Rochester, St. Olaf Coll., Northfield, Minn., Cath U., Leuven, Belgium, U. Bordeaux, France. Prof. composition Krakow State Sch. Music, 1959-65, Folkwang Hochschule für Musik, Essen, Fed. Republic Germany, 1966-68; composer-in-residence Sch. Music, Yale U., alternate years; guest condr. London Symphony Orch., Polish Radio Orch., Berlin Philharm. Orch. Composer: Psalms of David for chorus and percussion, 1958, Emanations for 2 string orchs., 1959, Strophes for soprano, narrator and 10 instruments, 1959, Dimensions of time and silence, 1959-60, Anaklasis, 1959-60, Threnody for the Victims of Hiroshima, 1960, Psalmus for tape, 1961, Polymorphia, 1961; Fluorescences, 1962, Stabat Mater, 1962, Canon, 1962, Sonata for cello and orch., 1964, St. Luke Passion, 1965-66, De Natura Sonoris I, 1966, Dies Irae, 1967, Capriccio for violin and orch., 1967, Capriccio for cello Solo, 1968; opera The Devils of Loudun, 1968-69; Utrenja for double chorus, soloists and orch., 1969-71, Actions for jazz ensemble, 1971, Partita for harpsichord, 4 solo instruments and orch., 1971-72, Cello Concerto, 1971-72; for double chorus, soloists and orchestra Ecloga VIII for 6 male voices, 1972; Symphony 1, 1972-73, Canticum Canticorum Salomonis for 16 voices and chamber orch., 1970-73, Magnificat, 1973-74, When Jacob Awoke for orch., 1974, Violin Concerto, 1976-77, Paradise Lost (rappresentazione), 1976-78, (Christmas) Symphony No. 2, 1980, Te Deum, 1979-80, Lacrimosa, 1980, Agnus Dei for a cappella chorus, 1981, Cello Concerto, 1982, Requiem, 1983, Concerto per Viola, 1983, Polish Requiem, 1983-84 also other works. Recipient 1st prize for Strophes Polish Composers Assn., 1959, UNESCO award, Fitelberg prize and Polish Ministry Culture award all for Threnody, 1960, Krakow composition prize for Canon, 1961, grand prize State N. Rhine-Westphalia for St. Luke Passion, 1966, Pax prize Poland, 1966, Jurzykowski prize Polish Inst. Arts and Scis., 1966, Sibelius award, 1967, Prix d'Italia, 1967-68, Polish 1st Class State award, 1968, Gottfried von Herder prize, 1977, prix Arthur Honegger, 1978, Sibelius prize Wihouri Found., 1983, Wolf Found. prize, 1987, 3 Grammy awards; grantee several founds., govts., insts. Mem. Royal Acad. Mus. London (hon.), Accademia Nazionale di Santa Cecilia (Roma) (hon.), Royal Swedish Acad. Music, Akademie der Kuenste West Berlin (extraordinary mem.), Akademie der Kuenste E. Ger. (corr.), Academia Nacional de Bellas Artes (Buenos Aires) (corr.). Home: ul Cisorva 22, 30229 Cracow Poland Office: care ICM Artists 40 W 57th St New York NY 10019 also: Panstwowa Wyzsza Szkola Muzyczna, ul Bohaterow Stalingradu 3, 31-038 Cracow Poland *

PENDLETON, ELMER D., JR., military officer; b. Kansas City, Mo., June 26, 1927; s. Elmer Dean and Martha Lucille (Friess) P.; m. Anne Bittner, Sept. 10, 1971; children: V. Allison Lange, John K. Lange, Christian D. Pendleton. BS, U.S. Mil. Acad., West Point, 1951; MS, George Washington U., Washington, 1969. Pvt. U.S. Army, 1944-47, commd. 2d lt., 1951, advanced through grades to maj. gen., ret., 1986; platoon leader 11th airborne div., Fort Campbell, Ky., 1951-52; co. commdr. 7th infantry div., Korea, 1952-53, 82d airborne div., Fort Bragg, N.C., 1954-56; instr. Ranger Sch., Eglin AFB, Fla., 1957-58; aide to comdg. gen. Teheran, Iran, 1958; staff officer 3d inf. (Old Guard), Washington, 1958-59, Dept. of Army, Washington, 1960-63; bn. comdr. 24th inf. div., Berlin, Fed. Republic Germany, 1964-65; sector advisor Can Tho, Vietnam, 1965-66; bn. comdr. 1st inf. div., Vietnam, 1966-68; brigade comdr. 1st inf. div. and II field force, G-3, Vietnam, 1969-70; corps G-3 XVIII airborne corps, Fort Bragg, N.C., 1971-74; dep. chief of staff and chief of staff XVIII airborne corps, 1974-75; comdr. 1st corps Support Command, Fort Bragg, N.C., 1975-78, 19th Support Command, Taegu, Korea, 1978-80; logistics officer U.S. Readiness Command, MacDill AFB, Fla., 1980-81; ops. officer U.S. Readiness Command, 1981-82; chief Joint U.S. Mil. Mission for Aid to Turkey, Ankara, 1982-86; cons. Washington, 1986—; bd. dirs. Am. Friends Turkey. Decorated Silver Star with 3 oak leaf clusters, Legion of Merit with 2 oak leaf clusters, D.F.C. with 2 oak leaf clusters, Bronze Star with 8 oak leaf clusters and V device, Combat Infantry Badge 2d award, Air medal, Purple Heart, Def. D.S.M., D.S.M., others. Club: Army-Navy (Washington). Office: 3028 Knoll Dr Falls Church VA 22042

PENDLETON, OTHNIEL ALSOP, fund raiser, clergyman; b. Washington, Aug. 22, 1911; s. Othniel Alsop and Ingeborg (Berg) P.; m. Flordora Mellquist, May 15, 1935; children: John, James (dec.), Thomas, Ann, Susan. AB, Union Coll., Schenectady, N.Y., 1933; BD, Eastern Bapt. Theol. Sem., 1936; MA, U. Pa., 1936, PhD, 1945; postgrad., Columbia U., 1937-38. Ordained to ministry Bapt. Ch., 1936. Pastor chs. Jersey City, 1935-39, Phila., 1939-43; dean Sioux Falls Coll., S.D., 1943-45; fund raiser Am. Bapt. Ch., N.Y.C., 1945-47; fund-raiser Mass. Bapt. Ch., Boston, 1947-54; fund-raiser Seattle, Chgo., Boston, Washington, N.Y.C. and Paris, France, 1955-64, Westwood, Mass., 1971-84; staff mem. Marts & Lundy, Inc., N.Y.C., 1964-71; lectr. Andover-Newton Sem., Newton, Mass., 1958, Boston U. Sch. Theology, 1958, Harvard U., Cambridge, Mass., 1977-84. Author: New Techniques for Church Fund Raising, 1955, Fund Raising: A Guide to Non-Profit Organizations, 1981; contbr. articles in field to profl. jours. Address: 529 Berkeley Ave Claremont CA 91711

PENDLETON, SYDNEY HARRISON, nurse researcher, writer; b. Pitts., Dec. 28, 1939; d. Dudley Digges and Mary Sutherland (Harrison) P.; student Wellesley Coll., 1956-58; diploma Episcopal Hosp. Sch. Nursing, Phila., 1961; B.S.N., U. Pa., 1963; M.Ed., Tchrs. Coll., Columbia U., 1971, Ed.D. (USPHS spl. predoctoral fellow), 1975; adopted children—Jennifer Page, Elizabeth Stockton, Beverly Sutherland. Staff nurse Bryn Mawr Hosp., 1961-62; asst. instr. Sch. Nursing, Hosp. U. Pa., 1962-64; instr. Women's Med. Coll. Hosp. Sch. Nursing, 1965-66; pvt. duty nurse, 1966-76; asso. prof. nursing, area coordinator adult health and illness grad. program La. State U., 1976-78; asso. prof., clin. coordinator rehab. nursing U. Ala., Birmingham, 1978-83; assoc. prof. Sch. Nursing, U. Mo.-Kansas City, 1983-87; nursing cons. and writer, Prairie Village, Kans., 1987—. Bd. dirs. Village de L'est Improvement Assn., New Orleans, 1977-78; founding mem. bd. dirs. and treas. Ala. Friends of Adoption, 1979-81. N.Y. State Regents fellow, 1968-69; USPHS trainee, 1963, 66-68. Fellow Am. Anthrop. Assn., Soc. Applied Anthropology; mem. Am. Nurses Assn., Am. Med. Writers Assn., Nat. Writers Union, The Author's League, Internat. Womes Writing Guild, Council Nurse Researchers, Nat. League Nursing, Nurses Coalition for Action in Politics, NOW, Nat. Women's Polit. Caucus, Kappa Delta Pi, Phi Delta Kappa, Pi Lambda Theta. Episcopalian. Author: (with others) Guia Para Investigaciones sobre el Dessarrollo de la Enfermeria en America Latina, 1974; contbr. articles to profl. publs. Home: 3112 W 73d St Prairie Village KS 66208

PENDLETON, THELMA BROWN, physical therapist, health service administrator; b. Rome, Ga., Jan. 30, 1911; d. John O. and Alma (Ingram) Brown; diploma Provident Hosp. Sch. Nursing, 1931; cert. Loyola U., 1942, Northwestern U., 1946; m. George W. Pendleton, Mar. 2, 1946; 1 son, George William. Pediatric nurse Rosenwald Found., Chgo., 1931-32; staff nurse Vis. Nurse Assn., Chgo., 1932-45; chief phys. therapy Provident Hosp., Chgo., 1946-55; phys. therapy cons. Parents Assn., Inc., Chgo., 1956-60; cons. United Cerebral Palsy of Greater Chgo.'s Pipers Portal Schs., 1961-63, dir., 1963-64; dir. phys. therapy services LaRabida Children's Hosp. and Research Center, Chgo., 1964-75; mem. nat. com. Joint Orthopedic Nursing Adv. Services, 1947-55; clin. supr., instr. programs in phys. therapy Northwestern U. Med. Sch., Chgo., 1947-55, 64-75; cons. United Cerebral Palsy, 1970-75; lectr. Japanese service com. on Cerebral Palsy, 1970; mem. Ill. Phys. Therapy Exam. Com., 1952-62. Recipient cert. of commendation CSC Cook County (Ill.), 1961, Citation of Merit, Wands Cerebral Palsy Unit, 1961. Mem. Am., Ill. phys. therapy assns., Provident Hosp. Nurses Alumni Assn. Democrat. Clubs: Tu-Fours Bolivia. Author: Low Budget Gourmet, 1977; (booklet) Patient Positioning, 1981; contbr. articles on phys. therapy to profl. jours.; contbr. to Am. Poetry Anthology. Address: 2631 S Indiana Ave Chicago IL 60616

PENEDO, LUIS FILIPE DO CRUZEIRO GONCALVES, computer company executive; b. Lisbon, Portugal, Nov. 16, 1941; s. Joao Baptista and Rosa Maria (Cruzeiro) P.; m. Lidia Graca, Apr. 25, 1974; 1 child, Tania Cristina. Diploma in Engring., Tech. U. Lisbon, 1968. Project mgr. telecommunications TAP Air Portugal, Lisbon, 1968-69, div. tech. mgr., 1969-71; from sales rep. to account mgr. IBM Corp., Lisbon, 1971-85, br. mgr., 1986, telecommunications sales mgr., 1987—. Mem. Portuguese Computer Soc. (pres. 1975-77, 83-85), Portuguese Soc. a Programming Language (founding), Internat. Fedn. for Info. Processing (trustee 1983—, chmn. developing countries support com. 1986—), Inst. Gen. Semantics. Home: Urbanizacao da Portela, Lote 1-3-Dio, 2685 Sacavem Portugal

PENG, LIANG-CHUAN, mechanical engineer; b. Taiwan, Feb. 6, 1936; came to U.S., 1965, naturalized, 1973; s. Mu-Sui and Wang-Su (Yang) P.; diploma Taipei Inst. Tech., 1960; M.S., Kans. State U., 1967; m. Wen-Fong Kao, Nov. 18, 1962; children—Tsen-Loong, Tsen-Hsin, Lina, Linda. Project engr. Taiwan Power Co., 1960-65; asst. engr. Carlson & Sweatt, N.Y.C., 1966-67; asst. engr. Pioneer Engrs., Chgo., 1967-68; mech. engr. Bechtel, San Francisco, 1969-71; sr. specialist Nuclear Services Co., San Jose, Calif., 1971-75; sr. engr. Brown & Root, Houston, 1975; stress engr. Foster Wheeler, Houston, 1976; staff engr. AAA Technologists, Houston, 1977; prin. engr. M.W. Kellogg, Houston, 1978-82; pres., owner Peng Engring., Houston, 1982—; instr. U. Houston. Chmn., South Bay Area Formosan Assn., 1974, No. Calif. Formosan Fedn., 1975. Registered profl. engr., Tex., Calif. Mem. ASME, Nat. Soc. Profl. Engrs. Confucian. Home: 3010 Manila Ln Houston TX 77043

PENG ZHEN, government official; b. Quwo, Shanxi Province, People's Republic of China, 1902; m. Zhang Jieping. Sec. Beijing Municipality Communist Party, from 1949; mayor Beijing, 1951-66; vice-chmn., sec.-gen. Standing Com. Nat. People's Congress, from 1954; vice-chmn. Chinese People's Polit. Consultative Conf., from 1954; dep. for Beijing Municipality to 5th Nat. People's Congress, 1979, vice-chmn. then acting sec.-gen. Standing Com., 1979; mem. Chinese Communist Party Cen. Com. and Politburo, from 1979; permanent chmn. 4th session 5th Nat. People's Congress, 1981; mem. Presidium, 12th Congress Chinese Communist Party, 1982; chmn. 6th Nat. People's Congress, from 1983. Address: Nat Peoples Congress, Chmn Standing Com, Beijing Peoples Republic of China *

PENINGTON, DAVID GEOFFREY, university administrator; b. Australia, Feb. 4, 1930; s. Geoffrey Alfred and Marjorie Doris (Fricke) P.; m. Audrey Mary Grumitt, Apr. 14, 1956 (div.); children: Anne Catherine, Michael Geoffrey, Anthony John, Elizabeth Clare; m. Sonay Hussein, Sept. 29, 1984. BA, Oxford U., 1953, B of Surgery and Medicine, 1955, MA, 1957, MD, 1959. Staff physician London Hosp., 1963-67; 1st asst. prof. medicine U. Melbourne, Australia, 1968-70; prof., chmn. dept. U. Melbourne, 1970-87, dean Faculty Medicine, 1978-87, univ. vice-chancellor, 1988—; staff physician St. Vincent's Hosp., Melbourne, 1970-87; vis. research fellow Wolfson Coll.-Oxford U., 1975-76; chmn. bd. social studies U. Melbourne, 1970-75; lectr. Med. Coll. of London Hosp., 1957-60; founding chmn. North Richmond Family Care Ctr., 1973-75. Editor: De Gruchy's Clinical Hematology in Medical Practice, 4th edit., 1978; contbr. chpts. to med. texts; author papers in field. Mem. mng. bd. Walter and Eliza Hall Inst. for Med. Research, 1978-87, Melbourne Cancer Inst., 1978-87; chmn. Australian Red Cross Nat. Blood Transfusion Com., 1976-83, mem. Nat. Council, 1976-83, chmn. Nepal transfusion devel. project, 197-8-83. Fellow Royal London Coll. Physicians, Royal Australasian Coll. Physicians; mem. Med. Research Soc. of U.K., Australian Soc. Med. Research, Royal Soc. Medicine, Med. Soc. London, Australian Med. Assn., Brit. Soc. Hematology, Hematology Soc. Australia (past pres.), Australian Univs. Clin. Profs. Assn. Club: Melbourne. Office: U Melbourne, Office of the Vice Chancellor, Melbourne 3052, Australia

PENKAVA, ROBERT RAY, radiologist, educator; b. Virginia, Nebr., Jan. 30, 1942; s. Joseph Everet and Velta Mae (Oviatt) P.; m. Kathryn Bennett Secrest, Apr. 6, 1973; children: Ashley Secrest, J. Carson Bennett. AB BS, Peru State Coll., Nebr., 1963; MD, U. Nebr., Omaha, 1967. Intern Lincoln Gen. Hosp., Nebr., 1967-68; resident Menorah Med. Cen., Kansas City, 1968-71; chief resident Menorah Med. Ctr., Kansas City, 1970-71; adj. faculty U. Mo., Kansas City, 1970-71; staff radiologist Ireland Army Hosp., Ft. Knox, Ky., 1971-72, chief, dept. radiology & nuclear med., 1972-73; staff radiologist Deaconess Hosp., Evansville, Ind., 1973—; mem. faculty U. So. Ind., Evansville, 1973—; assoc. faculty Ind. U. Coll. Med., Bloomington, 1973—; med. dir. Sch. Radiol. Tech. U. So. Ind., Evansville, 1978—; chmn. So. Ind. Health Systems, 1980-83; pres. Vanderburgh Country Med. Soc. Service Bur., 1979—, mem. roentgen soc. liaison com. Ind. Bd. Health, 1968—. Author numerous articles on med. ultrasound, nuclear med., angiography, and computed tomography. Chmn. profl. div. United Way of So. Ind., 1983; bd. dirs. S.W. Ind. Pub. Broadcasting, 1978-84, S.W. Ind. PSRO, 1982. Served to maj. U.S. Army, 1971-73. Named Sci. Tchr. of Year, Lewis & Clark Jr. High Sch., 1963. Mem. Evansville Med. Radiol. Assn. (treas. 1987—), Tri-State Radiology Assn. (pres.), Vanderburgh County Med. Soc. (pres.), Am. Coll. Radiology, Radiol. Soc. N.Am., Am. Roentgen Ray Soc., Am. Inst. Ultrasound in Medicine, AMA. Office: 611 Harriet St Evansville IN 47710

PENLAND, JOHN THOMAS, business executive; b. Guntersville, Ala., Mar. 31, 1930; s. James B. and Kathleen (Bolding) P.; m. Carolyn Joyce White, May 30, 1961; children—Jeffrey K., Mark A., Michael J. B.A., George Washington U., 1957. Vice pres., dir. Rouse, Brewer, Becker & Bryant, Inc., Washington, 1957-63; staff mem. SEC, Washington, 1963-67; pres., dir. INA Trading Corp., Phila., 1968-69; v.p. INA Security Corp., Phila., 1967-69; v.p. Shareholders Mgmt. Co., Los Angeles, 1969, sr. v.p., 1970, exec. v.p., 1970-73, pres., 1973-75; also dir.; founding pres. Shareholders Investor Service Corp., Los Angeles, 1970-75; also dir.; v.p., dir. Shareholders Mktg. Corp., Los Angeles, 1969-75; v.p. Shareholders Capital Corp., Los Angeles, 1972-73; v.p., dir. several mut. funds managed by Shareholders Mgmt. Co., 1970-75; pres., chmn., chief exec. officer HMO Internat., Los Angeles, 1975; pres., dir. Coastal Ins. Co., Los Angeles, 1975; founder, pres., chmn. bd. Pendlar Corp., Atlanta, 1977—; chmn., pres. CompuComp Corp., Atlanta, 1977-81; pres., chmn. Fran Stef Corp., N.Y.C., 1983—, Engineered Products Corp., Dandridge, Tenn., 1983—; founder, pres., chmn. Am. Accessories, Atlanta, 1983—; pres., chmn. United Am. Products Corp., Dandridge, 1983—; chmn. Einson Freeman & Detroy Corp., Fair Lawn, N.J., 1978-83. Served with AUS, 1948-55. Republican. Episcopalian. Home: PO Box 549 Social Circle GA 30279 Office: 708 Hwy 11N Social Circle GA 30279

PENNANT-REA, RUPERT LASCELLES, editor, economist; b. Harare, Zimbabwe, Jan. 23, 1948; came to Britain, 1966; s. Peter Athelwold and Pauline Elizabeth (Creasy) Pennant-Rea; m. Louise Greer, Oct. 3, 1970 (div. 1976); m. Jane Trevelyan Hamilton, Aug. 18, 1979 (div. 1986); children—Emily Trevelyan, Rory Marcus; m. Helen Jay, June 24, 1986; 1 child, Edward Peter. B.A. with honors, Trinity Coll., Dublin, 1970; M.A., U. Manchester, 1972. Economist, Confedn. Irish Industry, Dublin, 1970-71, Gen. and Mcpl. Workers Union, Eng., 1972-73, Bank of Eng., 1973-77; journalist The Economist, London, 1977—, editor, 1986—. Author: Gold Foil, 1979; The Pocket Economist, 1983; The Economist Economics, 1986. Recipient Wincott prize for fin. journalism Wincott Found., London, 1984. Mem. Ch. of Eng. Clubs: Marylebone Cricket, Reform (London). Avocations: music; tennis. Office: The Economist, 25 St James's St, London SW1, England

PENNELL, WILLIAM BROOKE, lawyer; b. Mineral Ridge, Ohio, Oct. 28, 1935; s. George Albert and Katherine Nancy (McMeen) P. AB, Harvard U., 1957; LLB cum laude, U. Pa., 1961; m. Peggy Polsky, June 17, 1958; children: Katherine, Thomas Brooke. Bar: N.Y. 1963, U.S. Dist. Ct. (so. dist.) N.Y. 1964, U.S. Dist. Ct. (ea. dist.) N.Y. 1964, U.S. Ct. Appeals (2d cir.) 1966, U.S. Ct. Claims 1966, U.S. Tax Ct. 1967, U.S. Supreme Ct. 1967. Clk. U.S. Dist. Ct., (so. dist.) N.Y., N.Y.C., 1961-62; assoc. Shearman & Sterling, N.Y.C., 1962-71, ptnr., 1971—. Recent case editor U. Pa. Law Rev., 1960-61. Bd. govs. Bklyn. Heights Assn., 1964-74, pres., 1969-71; chmn. bd. Willoughby House Settlement, 1972—. Served with U.S. Army, 1957. Fellow Salzburg Seminar Am. Studies, 1965. Mem. Fed. Bar Council, ABA, N.Y. State Bar Assn., Assn. Bar City N.Y. Club: Rembrandt. Office: Shearman & Sterling 153 E 53rd St New York NY 10022 also: Shearman & Sterling 599 Lexington Ave at 53rd St New York NY 10022

PENNER, STANFORD SOLOMON, educator; b. Unna, Germany, July 5, 1921; came to U.S., 1936, naturalized, 1943; s. Heinrich and Regina (Saal) P.; m. Beverly Preston, Dec. 28, 1942; children: Merilynn Jean, Robert Clark. B.S., Union Coll., 1942; M.S., U. Wis., 1943, Ph.D., 1946; Dr. rer. nat. (hon.), Technische Hochschule Aachen, W. Ger., 1981. Research asso. Allegany Ballistics Lab., Cumberland, Md., 1944-45; research scientist Standard Oil Devel. Co., Esso Labs., Linden, N.J., 1946; sr. research engr. Jet Propulsion Lab., Pasadena, Calif., 1947-50; mem. faculty Calif. Inst. Tech., 1950-63, prof. div. engring., jet propulsion, 1957-63; dir. research engring. div. Inst. Def. Analyses, Washington, 1962-64; prof. engring. physics, chmn. dept. aerospace and mech. engring. U. Calif. at San Diego, 1964-68, vice chancellor for acad. affairs, 1968-69, dir. Inst. for Pure and Applied Phys. Scis., 1968-71, dir. Energy Ctr., 1973—; pres. Energy Research Found.; dir. Ogden Corp., Optodyne Corp.; U.S. mem. adv. group aero. research and devel. NATO, 1952-68, chmn. combustion and propulsion panel, 1958-60; mem. adv. com. engring. scis. USAF-Office Sci. Research, 1961-65; mem. subcom. combustion NACA, 1954-58; research adv. com. air-breathing engines NASA, 1962-64; mem. coms. on gas dynamics and edn. Internat. Acad. Astronautics, 1969-80; mem. coms. NRC; cons. to govt., univs. and industry, 1953—; chmn. NRC/U.S. com. Internat. Inst. Applied

Systems Analysis, 1978-81; nat. Sigma Xi lectr., 1977-79; spl. guest Internat. Coal Sci. Confs., 1983, 85; Baetjer speaker Princeton U., 1985. Author: Chemical Reactions in Flow Systems, 1955, Chemistry Problems in Jet Propulsion, 1957, Quantitative Molecular Spectroscopy and Gas Emissivities, 1959, Chemical Rocket Propulsion and Combustion Research, 1962, Thermodynamics, 1968, Radiation and Reentry, 1968; sr. author: Energy, Vol. I (Demands, Resources, Impact, Technology and Policy), 1974, 81, Energy, Vol. II (Non-nuclear Energy Technologies), 1975, 77, 84, Energy, Vol. III (Nuclear Energy and Energy Policies), 1976; Editor: Chemistry of Propellants, 1960, Advanced Propulsion Techniques, 1961; Detonations and Two-Phase Flow, 1962, Combustion and Propulsion, 1963, Advances in Tactical Rocket Propulsion, 1968, In Situ Shale Oil Recovery, 1975, New Sources of Oil and Gas, 1982, Coal Combustion and Applications, 1984, Advanced Fuel Cells, 1986, Coal Gasification: DIrect Applications and Syntheses of Chemicals and Fuels, 1987 ; assoc. editor Jour. Chem. Physics, 1953-56; editor Jour. Quantitative Spectroscopy and Radiative Transfer, 1960—, Jour. Def. Research, 1963-67, Energy, The Internat. Jour, 1975—. Recipient spl. awards People-to-People Program, spl. awards NATO, pub. service award U. Calif. San Diego; N. Manson medal Internat. Colloquia on Gasdynamics of Explosions and Reactive Systems.; Internat. Columbus award Internat. Inst. Communications, Genoa, Italy; Guggenheim fellow, 1971-72. Fellow Am. Phys. Soc., Optical Soc. Am., AAAS, N.Y. Acad. Scis., AIAA (dir. 1964-66, past chmn. com., G. Edward Pendray award 1975, Thermophysics award 1983, Energy Systems award 1983), Am. Acad. Arts and Scis.; mem. Nat. Acad. Engring., Internat. Acad. Astronautics, Am. Chem. Soc., Combustion Inst., Sigma Xi. Home: 5912 Ave Chamnez La Jolla CA 92037 Office: U Calif San Diego CA 92093

PENNER, VERNON DUBOIS, diplomat; b. N.Y.C., Oct. 20, 1939; s. Vernon DuBois and Edna Anna Johanna (Burhenn) P.; m. Dorothy Anne Skripak, July 6, 1963; children—Alexandra Suzanne, Robert DuBois. Student, Deep Springs Coll., 1957-60; B.A., Union Coll., Schenectady, 1962; M.P.A., Syracuse U., 1963. Joined Fgn. Service, Dept. State, 1963; vice consul, 2d sec. Kobe, Japan, 1963-72, Warsaw, Poland, 1963-72, Zurich, Switzerland, 1963-72; prin. officer Oporto, Portugal, 1975-77, Salzburg, Austria, 1978-79; consul Am. consulate gen., Frankfurt, Fed. Republic Germany, 1980-83; dep. asst. sec. state for overseas citizens services Dept. State, Washington, 1983-84, dep. asst. sec. state Visa Office, 1985-86; U.S. Ambassador to the Republic of Cape Verde Praia, 1986—. recipient Superior Honor award Dept. State, 1983; Woodrow Wilson fellow Princeton U., 1979-80. Mem. Am. Fgn. Service Assn. also: Dept State Praia Washington DC 20520

PENNEY, CHARLES RAND, lawyer, civic worker; b. Buffalo, July 26, 1923; s. Charles Patterson and Gretchen (R) P. B.A., Yale U., 1945; J.D., U. Va., 1951. Bar: Md. 1952, N.Y. 1958, U.S. Supreme Ct. 1958. Law sec. to U.S. Dist. Ct. Judge W.C. Coleman, Balt., 1951-52; dir. devel. office Children's Hosp., Buffalo, 1952-54; sales mgr. Amherst Mfg. Corp., Williamsville, N.Y., 1954-56, also; Delevan Electronics Corp., East Aurora, N.Y.; mem. firm Penney & Penney, Buffalo, 1958-61; practiced in Niagara County, N.Y., 1961—. Mem. Lockport Meml. Hosp. Served to 2d lt. AUS, 1943-46. Recipient disting. service to culture award SUNY-Potsdam Coll. Arts and Scis., 1983. Mem. Albright-Knox Art Gallery Buffalo (life), Buffalo Mus. Sci. (life), Buffalo and Erie County Hist. Soc. (life), Niagara County Hist. Soc. (life), Old Ft. Niagara (life), Buffalo Soc. Artists (hon. trustee), Hist. Lockport (life), Landmark Soc. of Western N.Y., Nat. Trust Hist. Preservation, Am. Ceramic Circle, Rochester Mus. and Sci. Center, Historic Lewiston (life), Friends of U. Rochester Libraries (life); mem. Meml. Art Gallery U. Rochester (dir.'s circle, hon. bd. mgrs.), Smithsonian Instn., Rochester Hist. Soc.; Mus. Am. Folk Art; mem. Whitney Mus. Am. Art, Am. Craft Council, Cleve. Artists Found., Am. Fedn. Arts, Archives Am. Art, Margaret Woodbury Strong Mus. (charter), Met. Mus. Art, Mus. Modern Art, Mark Twain Soc. (hon.), U. Rochester's Pres.'s Soc. (hon.), U. Iowa's Pres.'s Club (hon.), Internat. Mus. Photography, George Eastman House, Va. Law Found., Roland Gibson Art Gallery, SUNY Coll. of Arts and Sci., Visual Studies Workshop of Rochester, Genesee Country Mus., numerous other art assns. and museums, Am. Assn. Ret. Persons, Ctr. African Studies, Nat. Geog. Soc. (life), Chi Psi, Phi Alpha Delta. Clubs: Automobile (Lockport); Zwicker Aquatic, Niagara County Antiques (hon.); Rochester Art (hon. life), Plaza Athletic (Rochester). Address: 538 Bewley Bldg Lockport NY 14094

PENNIMAN, HOWARD RAE, political scientist; b. Steger, Ill., Jan. 30, 1916; s. Rae Ernest and Alethea (Bates) P.; m. Morgia Anderson, Dec. 30, 1940; children: Barbara, Ruth, William, Catherine, Matthew. A.B., La. State U., 1936, M.A., 1938; Ph.D., U. Minn., 1941. Social Sci. Research Council pre-doctoral field fellow 1940-41; instr. polit. sci. U. Ala., 1941-42; instr. dept. govt. Yale U., 1942-45, asst. prof., 1945-48; staff CIA, 1948-49; external research staff, asst. chief Dept. State, 1949-52, chief external research staff, 1953-55; staff Psychol. Strategy Bd., 1952-53; chief overseas book div. USIA, 1955-57; prof. govt. Georgetown U., 1957-83, head dept. govt., 1959-63; resident scholar Am. Enterprise Inst., 1971—; columnist, America, 1958-64, Fulbright research grant, France, 1964-65; cons. Congl. fellowship program Am. Polit. Sci. Assn., 1959; cons. to team observers on presdl. elections in, Vietnam, 1967; election cons. ABC, 1968—; mem. Presdl. observer teams, El Salvador, 1982, 84, Guatemala, 1985, 88, Philippines, 1986. Author: Sait's American Parties and Elections, rev. edit, 1952, The American Political Process, 1962, Elections in South Vietnam, 1973; Editor: John Locke on Politics and Education, 1947, Britain at the Polls, 1974, 80, France at the Polls, 1975, 78, 81, 86, Canada at the Polls, 1975, 79, 80, 84, Australia at the Polls, 1977, 80, Italy at the Polls, 1978, 81, Ireland at the Polls, 1978, 81, 82, 87, Israel at the Polls, 1977, 81, Switzerland at the Polls, 1979, New Zealand at the Polls, 1980, Greece at the Polls, 1981, Spain at the Polls, 1977, 79, 82; contbr. articles to profl. jours. Del. Md. Constl. Conv., 1967-68, chmn. com. on style; co-chmn. Montgomery County Com. on Drug Abuse, 1969-70; trustee Montgomery Coll., 1971-80. With AUS, 1945-46. Mem. Am. Polit. Sci. Assn. (pres. D.C. chpt. 1958-59), Internat. Polit. Sci. Assn., Phi Beta Kappa, Pi Gamma Mu, Pi Sigma Alpha (nat. pres. 1966, nat. dir. 1975—, Nat. Capital Area Polit. Sci. Assn. award, 1988), Sigma Delta Chi. Episcopalian. Home: 6019 Neilwood Dr Rockville MD 20852 Office: Am Enterprise Inst 1150 17th St Washington DC 20036

PENNISTEN, JOHN WILLIAM, actuary, computer scientist; b. Buffalo, Jan. 25, 1939; s. George William and Lucy Josephine (Gates) P. A.B. with hons. in math. and chem., Hamilton Coll., 1960; NSF fellow in math. Harvard U., 1960-61; postgrad. U.S. Army Lang. Sch., 1962-63; MS in Computer Sci. with hons., N.Y. Inst. Tech., 1987; cert. Taxation, NYU, 1982; cert. in Profl. Banking Am. Inst. of Banking of Am. Bankers Assn., 1988. Actuarial asst. New Eng. Mut. Life Ins. Co., Boston, 1965-66; asst. actuary Mass. Gen. Life Ins. Co., Boston, 1966-68; actuarial assoc. John Hancock Mut. Life Ins. Co., Boston, 1968-71; asst. actuary George B. Buck Cons. Actuaries, Inc., N.Y.C., 1971-75, Martin E. Segal Co., N.Y.C., 1975-80; actuary Laiken Siegel & Co., N.Y.C., 1980; cons. Bklyn., 1981—; timesharing and database analyst Chem. Bank N.Y.C. banklink corp. cash mgmt. div. 1983-85; programmer analyst Empire Blue Cross and Blue Shield, N.Y.C., 1986—; enrolled actuary U.S. Fed. Pension Legis. Bklyn., 1976—. Contbr. articles to profl. jours. Served with U.S. Army, 1961-64. Mem. AAAS, Soc. Actuaries (fellow), Am. Acad. Actuaries, Practising Law Inst., Am. Mgmt. Assn., Assn. Computing Machinery, IEEE Computer Soc., Am. Assn. Artificial Intelligence, Linguistic Soc. Am., Assn. Computational Linguistics, Am. Math. Soc., Math. Assn. Am., Nat. Model R.R. Assn. (life), Nat. Ry. Hist. Soc., Ry. and Locomotive Hist. Soc. (life), N.Y.C. Opera Guild, Met. Opera Guild, Am. Friends of Covent Garden, Harvard Gra. Soc., Am. Legion, Phi Beta Kappa, others. Address: 135 Willow St Brooklyn NY 11201

PENNOCK, DONALD WILLIAM, mechanical engineer; b. Ludlow, Ky., Aug. 8, 1915; s. Donald and Melvin (Evans) P.; B.S. in M.E., U. Ky., 1940, M.E., 1948; m. Vivian C. Kern, Aug. 11, 1951; 1 son, Douglas. Stationary engring., constrn. and maintenance Schenley Corp., 1935-39; mech. equipment design engr. mech. lab. U. of Ky., 1939; exptl. test engr. Wright Aero. Corp., Paterson, N.J., 1940, 1941, investigative and adv. engr. to personnel div., 1941-43; indsl. engr. Eastern Aircraft, div. Gen. Motors, Linden, N.J., 1943-45; factory engr. Carrier Corp., Syracuse, N.Y., 1945-58, sr. facilities engr., 1958-60, corporate material handling engr., 1960-63, mgr. facilities engring. dept., 1963-66, mgr. archtl. engring., 1966-68, mgr. facilities engring. dept., 1968-78. Staff, Indsl. Mgmt. Center, 1962, midwest work course U. Kan., 1959-67. Mem. munitions bd. SHIAC, 1950-52; trustee Primitive Hall Found., 1985—. Elected to Exec. and Profl. Hall of Fame, 1966. Registered profl. engr., Ky., N.J., D.C. Fellow Soc. Advancement Mgmt. (life mem., nat. v.p. material handling div. 1953-54); mem. ASME, Am. Material Handling Soc. (dir. 1950-57, chmn. bd., pres. 1950-52), Am. Soc. Mil. Engrs., Nat. Soc. Profl. Engrs., Am. Mgmt. Assn. (men. packaging council 1950-55, life mem. planning council), Nat. Material Handling Conf. (exec. com. 1951), Found. N.Am. Wild Sheep (life), Internat. Platform Assn., Tau Beta Pi. Protestant. Mng. editor Materials Handling Engring. (mag. sect.), 1949-50; mem. editorial adv. bd. Modern Materials Handling (mag.), 1949-52. Contbr. articles to tech. jours. Contbg., cons. editor: Materials Handling Handbook, 1958. Home: 24 Pebble Hill Rd De Witt NY 13214

PENNOCK, JAMES ROLAND, political scientist, educator; b. Chatham, Pa., Feb. 4, 1906; s. James Levis and Alice Rakestraw (Carter) P.; m. Helen B. Sharpless, Jan. 24, 1931; children: Joan Pennock Barnard, Judith Carter Pennock Lilley. Student, London Sch. Econs., 1925-26; B.A., Swarthmore Coll., 1927; M.A., Harvard U., 1928, Ph.D., 1932. Instr. polit. sci. Swarthmore (Pa.) Coll., 1929-32, asst. prof., 1932-41, asso. prof., 1941-45, prof., 1946-62, Richter prof., 1962-76, Richter prof. emeritus, 1976—, chmn. dept., 1941-70, acting chmn., 1974-75; vis. prof. Columbia U., 1950; vis. lectr. Harvard U., 1953; lectr. U. Pa., 1976-77; vis. prof. U. Calif., San Diego, 1978; Hill disting. vis. prof. U. Minn., 1979. Author: Administration and the Rule of Law, 1951, Liberal Democracy: Its Merits and Prospects, 1950, (with others) Democracy in the Mid-Twentieth Century: Problems and Prospects, (with David G. Smith) Political Science: An Introduction, 1964, Democratic Political Theory, 1979; editor: Self-Government in Modernizing Nations, 1964, NOMOS (yearbook Am. Soc. Polit. and Legal Philosophy), 1965-86, Equality, 1967, Representation, 1968, Voluntary Associations, 1969, Political and Legal Obligation, 1970, Privacy, 1971, Coercion, 1972, The Limits of Law, 1974, Participation in Politics, 1975, Human Nature in Politics, 1976, Due Process, 1977, Anarchism, 1978, Constitutionalism, 1979, Compromise in Ethics, Law, and Politics, 1979, Property, 1980, Human Rights, 1981, Ethics, Economics, and the Law, 1982, Liberal Democracy, 1983, Marxism, 1983, Criminal Justice, 1985, Justification, 1986, Authority Revisited, 1987; mem. editorial bd.: Am. Polit. Sci. Rev, 1964-68, 73-76; contbr. articles to profl. jours. Adminstrv. specialist U.S. Social Security Bd., 1936-37; prin. divisional asst. Office Fgn. Relief, Dept. State, 1943; panel chmn. Regional War Labor Bd., 1943-44; chmn. com. on fellowships polit. theory and legal philosophy Social Sci. Research Council, 1954-64, bd. dirs., 1960-66; trustee Primitive Hall Found., 1973—, pres., 1984-86. Guggenheim fellow, 1954-55. Mem. Am. Polit. Sci. Assn. (council 1954-55, v.p. 1963-64), Am. Soc. Polit. and Legal Philosophy (pres. 1969-70), Phi Beta Kappa. Mem. Soc. Friends. Office: Swarthmore College Swarthmore PA 19081

PENNY, LINDA LEA, social work administrator; b. Big Spring, Tex., Aug. 6, 1943; d. Charlie Nichol and Bonnie Wayne (Tartt) Farrar; 1 child, Larry Lee II. B in Social Work, Tex. Woman's U., 1975, MA in Sociology, 1977; diploma Inst. for English Speaking Students, Internat. Grad. Sch., U. Stockholm, 1978. Cert. social worker. Coordinator human resources Catholic Charities, Fort Worth, 1975-76; program specialist Tex. Dept. Human Resources, Austin, 1977; program specialist/ombudsman Tex. Gov.'s Com. on Aging, Austin, 1978-80; project dir., tng. dir. Ctr. for Pub. Interest, Dallas, 1980-82; dir. social work dept. Presbyn. Hosp., Dallas, 1982-84, Meml. Hosp., Cleburne, Tex., 1984-86; coordinator Johnson County Health Dept. Indigent Health Program, Cleburne, 1986—; pvt. cons./trainer, Cleburne, 1980—; ptnr., cons. Gormet Basket, Cleburne, 1985-86. Bd. dirs. Johnson County Family Crisis Ctr., Cleburne, 1985-86; allocations com. Johnson County United Way, Cleburne, 1985-86. Samuel E. Ziegler Found. fellow, Dallas, 1976-77. Mem. Tex. Soc. Hosp. Social Work Dirs., Am. Bus. Women's Assn., Nat. Assn. Female Execs., Assn. Ind. Real Estate Owners, Am. Mensa. Democrat. Lutheran. Avocations: real estate investments; refinishing antiques; collecting glassware. Home: 1305 N Wood St Cleburne TX 76031 Office: Johnson County Health Dept PO Drawer E Cleburne TX 76031

PENNY, NICHOLAS BEAVER, museum curator; b. London, Dec. 21, 1949; s. Joseph Noel and Anges Celia (Roberts) P.; m. Anne Philomel Udy; children: Caroline Emil, Elizabeth Joan. BA, St. Catharines Coll., Cambridge, Mass.; MA, Courtauld Inst., London; PhD, Courtauld Inst. Leverhulme fellow Cambridge U., 1973-75; lectr. history of art dept. U. Manchester, 1975-82; sr. research fellow King's Coll., Cambridge, 1982-84; keeper dept. Western art Ashmolean Mus., Oxford, Eng., 1984—; Slade prof. U. Oxford, 1980-81. Author: Church Monuments in Romantic England, 1977; co-author: Taste and The Antique, 1981, Raphael, 1983; editor exh. catalog and book, Reynolds, 1984. Home: Balliol Coll, Oxford England Office: Ashmolean Mus, Beaumont St, Oxford England

PENROSE, GILBERT QUAY, financial planning company executive; b. Robinson, Pa., Sept. 8, 1938; s. Albert Snyder and Olive Jeanette (Boring) P.; m. Anna Mae Riffle, Aug. 22, 1959; children: Kim Denise, Kevin Lee, Kara Lynn. BS in Chem. Engring., Pa. State U., 1960. Registered investment advisor SEC. Registered rep. Investors Diversified Services, 1969-70, div. mgr., Huntington, W.Va., 1972-73, Miami, 1973-76; mgr. South Fla. region Westam. Fin. Corp., Miami Lakes, 1976—; pres. Gilbert Penrose & Assocs., Inc., Miami, 1976—; pres., chmn. bd. dirs. Three K Investments, Inc., Swank Mgmt. Co., Inc., G & K Constrn. Co., Inc., West Fla. Mgmt. Co. Inc., Penrose Internat., Inc., Western Pa. Mgmt. Co., Inc., New Dimension Constrn. Co., Inc., New Dimension Mgmt. Co., Inc., New Expectations Realty Co., Inc., New Expectations Mortgage Co., Inc., Multi-State Mgmt. co., Inc. Chmn. bd. dirs. Miami Lakes Civic Assn., 1975-76. Mem. Internat. Assn. Fin. Planners, Assn. Cert. Fin. Planners. Home: 17531 SW 68th Ct Fort Lauderdale FL 33331 Office: 1 SW Flamingo Dr Suite 307 Pembroke Pines FL 33027

PENROSE, ROGER, mathematics educator; b. Colchester, Essex, England, Aug. 8, 1931; s. Lionel Sharples; m. Joan Isabel Wedge (marriage dissolved 1981); three children. BS in Math., U. London; PhD, St. John's Coll., Cambridge, London, 1975. Asst. lectr. math. Bedford Coll., London, 1956-57; research fellow St. John's Coll., Cambridge, 1957-60; NATO research fellow Princeton U. and Syracuse U., 1959-61; research assoc. King's Coll., London, 1961-63; vis. assoc. prof. U. Tex., Austin, 1963-64, reader, 1964-66, prof. applied math., 1966-73; Lovett prof. Rice U., Houston, 1983-87; Rouse Ball prof. math. U. Oxford, 1987—; vis prof. Yeshiva U., Princeton U., Cornell U., 1966-67, 69. Author: Techniques of Differential Topology in Relativity, 1973; (with W. Rindler) Spinors and Space-time, vol. 1, 1984, vol. 2, 1986; contbr. many articles in sci. jours. Recipient Adams Prize Cambridge U., 1966-67, Dannie Heineman Prize Am. Phys. Soc. and Am. Inst. Physics, 1971, Eddington Medal RAS, 1975, Royal Medal Royal Soc., 1985. Mem. London Math. Soc., Cambridge Philos. Soc., Inst. for Math. and its Applications, Internat. Soc. for Gen. Relativity and Gravitation. Office: Oxford U, Math Inst, 24-29 St Giles, Oxford OX1 3LB, England *

PENSE, ALAN WIGGINS, metallurgical engineer; b. Sharon, Conn., Feb. 3, 1934; s. Arthur Wilton and May Beatrice (Wiggins) P.; m. Muriel Drews Taylor, June 28, 1958; children—Daniel Alan, Steven Taylor, Christine Muriel. B.Metall. Engring., Cornell U., 1957; M.S., Lehigh U., 1959, Ph.D., 1962. Research asst. Lehigh U., Bethlehem, Pa., 1957-59, instr., 1960-62, asst. prof., 1962-65, asso. prof., 1965-71, prof., 1971—, chmn. dept. metallurgy and materials engring., 1977-83, assoc. dean Coll. Engring. and Applied Scis., 1984-88, acting dean, 1988—; assoc. dir. advanced tech. for large structural systems, Nation Sci. Found. Ctr.cons. adv. com. on reactor safeguards NRC, 1965-86. Author: (with R.M. Brick and R.B. Gordon) Structure and Properties of Engineering Materials, 4th edit, 1978; also articles. Recipient Robinson award Lehigh U., 1965, Stabler award, 1972; Danforth fellow, 1974—. Mem. Am. Soc. Metals, Internat. Inst. Welding, Am. Welding Soc. (William Spraragan award 1963, Adams membership award 1966, Jennings award 1970, Adams lectr. 1980, William Hobart medal 1982, hon. membership award 1986), ASTM, Am. Soc. Engring. Edn. (Western Elec. award 1968). Republican. Evang. Congregationalist (pres. bd. trustees Evang. Sch. Theology). Home: 2227 West Blvd Bethlehem PA 18017 Office: Lehigh U Packard Lab 19 Bethlehem PA 18015

PENSINGER, JOHN LYNN, lawyer; b. Hagerstown, Md., June 5, 1949; s. Linford Snider and Marguerite Joan (McNeal) P.; m. Eileen Sue Howard, Nov. 7, 1972. BA, U.Md., 1971; J.D., U. Balt., 1976, LL.M. George Washington U., 1987. Bar: Md. 1976, D.C. 1977, U.S. Ct. Claims 1977, U.S. Tax Ct. 1977, U.S. Dist. Ct. Md. 1978, U.S. Dist. Ct. D.C. 1978, U.S. Ct. Appeals (4th cir.) 1978, U.S. Ct. Mil. Appeals 1978, U.S. Ct. Appeals (D.C. cir.) 1978, U.S. Customs Ct. 1979, U.S. Supreme Ct. 1980, U.S. Ct. Internat. Trade 1981, U.S. Ct. Appeals (fed. cir.) 1982, U.S. Ct. Appeals (5th cir.) 1986. Mgr., E.M. Willis & Sons, Washington, 1977-79; sole practice, Rockville, Md., 1978-79; atty. Amalgamated Casualty Ins. Co., Washington, 1979-86; asst. gen. counsel Legal Services Corp., Washington, 1986—. Mem. ABA, Md. Bar Assn., Am. Soc. Internat. Law, Fed. Bar Assn. Roman Catholic. Home: 11716 Galt Ave Wheaton MD 20902

PENSION-SMITH, MATTHEW OMOLOLU, investment company executive; b. Lagos, Nigeria, Oct. 28, 1945; s. Edwin Olowolaiyemo and Victoria Olajumoke (Odunsi) Pension-S.; m. Comfort Iyabosola-Olabisi Banjo, Apr. 20, 1981 (div. March 1988). Mng. dir. Mattops Holdings (W.A.) Ltd., Nigeria, 1973-80, chmn., 1980—; chmn. MaJ Animal and Drug Supply Corp., Ibadan, Nigeria, 1977—, Corn Products Nigeria Ltd.; chmn., mng. dir. Alole Panko (Nigeria) Ltd., 1980—; dir. John Enterprises, Korobiowu Enterprises; chmn. Panko Communications Co. Nigeria Ltd. Served to capt. Nigerian Army, 1964-73. Fellow Inst. Dirs., Brit. Inst. Mgmt., Inst. Indsl. Mgrs., Inst. Prodn. Control, Inst. Mfg., Inst. Materials and Handling, Inst. of Mgmt. Anglican. Home and Office: P O Box 29448, Secretariat P O, Ibadan Nigeria

PENSLER, THOMAS, marketing professional; b. Benediktbeuern, Fed. Republic Germany, July 8, 1952; s. Adolf and Hilde (Starsetzky) P.; m. Anne Graf; children: Alexandra, Vera. Diploma, U. Augsburg, Fed. Republic Germany, 1977. Market researcher Daimler-Benz, Fed. Republic Germany, 1978-81; market researcher SKW, Fed. Republic Germany, 1981-87, mktg. mgr., 1987—. Office: SKW Trostberg AG, Box 1262, D-8223 Trostberg Federal Republic of Germany

PENTTILÄ, TIMO JUSSI, architectural educator; b. Tampere, Finland, Mar. 16, 1931. MArch., U. Tech., Helsinki, 1956. Designer various archtl. firms, Helsinki, 1953-56, Aarne Ervi Archtl. Office, Helsinki, 1957-59; chmn. bd. dirs. Timo Penttilä, Heikki Saarela, Kari Lind, Architects, Ltd., Helsinki, 1976—; prof. architecture Akademie der Bildenden Künste, Vienna, Austria, 1980—; asst. lectr. U. Tech., Helsinki, 1959-60; vis. prof. U. Calif., Berkeley, 1968-69. Pres. Mus. Finnish Architecture, Helsinki, 1976-80, bd. dirs., 1970-80. Decorated knight 1st class Order of the Lion (Finland); recipient Republic of Finland State Architecture award, 1976, Pub. Bldgs. award Union of Finnish Towns, 1984. Mem. Assn. Finnish Architects (vice chmn. 1968), Finnish Acad. Tech. Scis., CHamber Architects and Engrs. in Austria. Office: Nervanderinkatu, 5 D 44, 00100 Helsinki Finland

PENZIAS, ARNO ALLAN, astrophysicist, research scientist; b. Munich, Germany, Apr. 26, 1933; came to U.S., 1940, naturalized, 1946; s. Karl and Justine (Eisenreich) P.; m. Anne Pearl Barras, Nov. 25, 1954; children: David Simon, Mindy Gail, Laurie Ruth. BS in Physics, CCNY, 1954; MA in Physics, Columbia U., 1958, PhD in Physics, 1962; LHD, William Paterson Coll., 1987; Dr. honoris causa, Observatoire de Paris, 1976; ScD (hon.), Rutgers U., 1979, Wilkes Coll., 1979, CCNY, 1979, Yeshiva U., 1979, Bar Ilan U., 1983, Monmouth Coll., 1984, Technion-Israel Inst. Tech., 1986, U. Pitts., 1986, Ball State U., 1986, Kean Coll., 1986, Ohio State U., 1988, Iona Coll., 1988. Mem. tech. staff Bell Labs., Holmdel, N.J., 1961-72, head radiophysics research dept., 1972-76; dir. radio research lab. Bell Labs., 1976-79, exec. dir. research, communications scis. div., 1979-81, v.p. research, 1981—; adj. prof. earth and scis. SUNY, Stony Brook, 1974-84; lectr. dept. astrophys. scis. Princeton U., 1967-72, vis. prof., 1972-85; research assoc. Harvard Coll. Obs., 1968-80; Edison lectr. U.S. Naval Research Lab., 1979, Kompfner lectr. Stanford U., 1979, Gamow lectr. U. Colo., 1980, Jansky lectr. Nat. Radio Astronomy Obs., 1983; mem. astronomy adv. panel NSF, 1978-79, mem. indsl. panel on sci. and tech., 1982—; affiliate Max-Planck-Inst. für Radioastronomie, 1978-85, chmn. Fachbeirat, 1981-83; lectr. Michelson Meml., 1985, Grade Adams Tanner, 1987; disting. lectr. NSF, 1987. Mem. editorial bd. Ann. Rev. Astronomy and Astrophysics, 1974-78; mem. editorial bd. AT&T Bell Labs. Tech. Jour., 1978-84, chmn., 1981-84; assoc. editor Astrophys. Jour, 1978-82; contbr. over 80 articles to tech. jours.; patentee in field. Trustee William Paterson Coll., 1974-85, Trenton (N.J.) State Coll., 1977-79; mem. bd. overseers U. Pa. Sch. Engring. and Applied Sci., 1983-86; mem. vis. com. Calif. Inst. Tech., 1977-79; mem. Com. Concerned Scientists, 1975—, vice chmn., 1976—; mem. adv. bd. Union of Councils for Soviet Jews, 1983—. Served to lt. Signal Corps U.S. Army, 1954-56. Recipient Nobel prize for physics, 1978, Herschel medal Royal Astron. Soc., 1977, Townsend Harris medal CCNY, 1979, Newman award CCNY, 1983, Joseph Handleman prize, 1983, Grad. Faculties Alumni award Columbia U., 1984, Achievment in Sci. award Big Bros., Inc., N.Y.C., 1985. mem. Am. Acad. Arts and Scis., Am. Astron. Soc., Am. Phys. Soc., Nat. Acad. Scis. (Henry Draper medal 1977), Internat. Astron. Union. Republican. Jewish.

PEPER, CHRISTIAN BAIRD, lawyer; b. St. Louis, Dec. 5, 1910; s. Clarence F. and Christine (Baird) P.; m. Ethel C. Kingsland, June 5, 1935; children—Catherine K. (Mrs. Kenneth B. Larson), Anne C. (Mrs. John M. Perkins), Christian B. A.B. cum laude, Harvard, 1932; LL.B., Washington U., 1935; LL.M. (Sterling fellow), Yale, 1937. Bar: Mo. bar 1934. Since practiced in St. Louis; of counsel Peper, Martin, Jensen, Maichel & Hetlage.; Lectr. various subjects Washington U. Law Sch., St. Louis, 1943-61; partner A.G. Edwards & Sons, 1945-67; pres. St. Charles Gas Corp., 1953-72; dir. St. Louis Steel Casting Inc., Hydraulic Press Brick Co.; pres. Tricor Drilling Co. Editor: An Historian's Conscience: The Correspondence of Arnold J. Toynbee and Columba Cary-Elwes, 1986. Contbr. articles to profl. jours. Mem. vis. com. Harvard Div. Sch., 1964-70; counsel St. Louis Art Mus.; bd. dirs. Chatham House Found. Mem. Am., Mo., St. Louis bar assns., Order of Coif, Phi Delta Phi. Roman Catholic. Clubs: Noonday, University, Harvard (St. Louis); East India (London). Home: 1454 Mason Rd Saint Louis MO 63131 Office: 720 Olive St Saint Louis MO 63101

PEPEU, GIANCARLO, pharmacologist, educator; b. Milan, Mar. 29, 1930; s. Francesco and Edvige (d'Anna) P.; m. Ileana Marconcini. MD, Florence U., 1954. Research fellow U. Florence, Italy, 1954-58, assoc. prof., 1965-68, prof. pharmacology, 1974—; research fellow Yale U., New Haven, 1958-60; asst. prof. U. Sassari, Italy, 1961-62, U. Pisa, Italy, 1962-65; prof., chmn. dept. U. Cagliari, Italy, 1968-74; cons. Italian Ministry Health, Rome, 1971-87. Author: Handbook of Pharmacology, 1983, 2d edit., 1986; editor: Receptors for Neurotransmitters, 1980, Cholinergic Mechanisms, 1981; contbr. over 100 sci. papers to profl. publs. Mem. Italian Soc. Pharmacology, Brit. Pharmacol. Soc., European Neurochemistry Soc. (councillor 1985—), Internat. Coll. Neuropsychopharmacology (councillor 1976-81), Soc. Neurosci. Home: Carducci 20, 50121 Florence Italy Office: Dept Pharmacology, Florence U, Viale Morgagni 65, 50134 Florence Italy

PEPINE, CARL JOHN, physician, educator; b. Pitts., June 8, 1941; s. Charles John and Elizabeth (Hovan) P.; m. Lynn Divers, Aug. 3, 1963; children—Mary Lynn, Anne, Elizabeth. B.S., U. Pitts., 1962; M.D., N.J. Coll. Medicine, 1966. Intern Allegheny Gen. Hosp., U. Pitts., 1966-67; resident in internal medicine Jefferson Med. Coll. Hosp., Phila., 1967-68, naval med. ctr., 1968-69, fellow in physiology and cardiovascular disease, 1969-71; asst. prof. medicine Jefferson Med. Coll., Phila., 1971-74; asst. prof. medicine U. Fla., Gainesville, 1974-75, assoc. prof., 1975-79, prof., 1979—, assoc. dir. div. cardiovascular medicine, 1982—; dir. cardiology catheterization lab. Shands Hosp., U. Fla., Gainesville, 1974-86; chief cardiology VA Regional Med. Ctr., Gainesville, 1979—. Mem. editorial bd. Internat. Jour. Cardiology, Am. Jour. Cardiology, Jour. Am. Coll. Cardiology, Cardiac Catherization, Cardiovascular Diagnosis; contbr. articles to profl. jours.; developer catheters to measure blood flow and heart circulation. Served to comdr. USN, 1968-74. Grantee Dept. of Def., 1971-74, VA, 1975—, Am. Heart Assn., 1977—, NHLBI, 1985—. Fellow Am. Coll. Cardiology (gov. for Fla. 1984-87, chmn. bd. govs. 1986-87, bd. trustees 1985-87, pres. Fla. Chpt. 1986-87), Am. Heart Assn. (council on clin. cardiology and on circulation, bronze award 1983), Am. Fedn. Clin. Research, Soc. Cardiac Angiography, Am. Soc. Clin. Investigation; mem. N.Y. Acad. Scis., AAAS, Pi Kappa Alpha, Alpha Omega Alpha. Research on dynamics of coronary circulation, effects of coronary artery spasm and stenosis, silent myocardial ischemia, effects of lasers on blood vessels, calcium antagunists. Office: U Fla 1400 SW Archer Rd Box J-277 Gainesville FL 32610

PEPPER, CURTIS BILL, author; b. Huntington, W.Va., Aug. 30, 1920; s. Curtis Gordon and Edwina Neihl (Sheppard) P.; student U. Ill., 1937-39, U. Florence, Italy, 1947-49; m. Beverly Stoll, Oct. 11, 1949; children: Jorie Graham, John Randolph. Free-lance writer, TV, films, 1949-55; reporter UP, Rome, 1955-57, CBS, 1957-58; bur. chief Newsweek, Rome, 1958-68; free-lance writer, author, N.Y.C., 1968—. Author: The Pope's Back Yard, 1966; An Artist and the Pope (Book of Month Club), 1968; (with Christiaan Barnard) One Life (Lit. Guild), 1969; Marco (Book of Month Club alt.), 1977; Kidnapped! 17 Days of Terror, 1978; We the Victors, 1984. Served to major U.S. Army, 1943-47, ETO. Decorated bronze star, Knight of New Europe. Mem. Authors Guild, Century Assn. Clubs: Overseas Press, City Athletic (N.Y.C.). Avocations: tennis, swimming. Office: Julian Bach Lit Agy 747 3d Ave New York NY 10017 Also: Torre Olivola Torre Gentile, 06059 Todi Perugia Italy

PEPPER, DAVID M., physicist, educator, author, inventor; b. Los Angeles, Mar. 9, 1949; s. Harold and Edith (Kleinplatz) P. BS in Physics summa cum laude, UCLA, 1971; MS in Applied Physics, Calif. Inst. Tech., 1974, PhD in Applied Physics, 1980. Mem. tech. staff Hughes Research Labs., Malibu, Calif., 1973-87, sr. staff physicist, 1987—; adj. prof. math. and physics Pepperdine U., Malibu, 1981—. Co-author: Optical Phase Conjugation, 1983, Laser Handbook Vol. 4, 1985; guest editor Soc. Photo-Optical Engring. Instrumentation Jour. 1982 (Rudolf Kingslake award 1982), IEEE Jour. Quantum Electronics, 1988-89; contbr. numerous articles to profl. tech. jours. and periodicals including Scientific American; patentee in field. Mem. Sons and Daughters of 1939 Club, 2d Generation of Martyrs Meml., Mus. Holocaust. NSF trainee Calif. Inst. Tech., 1971; Howard Hughes fellow Hughes Aircraft Co., 1973-80; recipient Hughes Research Labs Publ. of Yr., 1986. Mem. Am. Phys. Soc. , Optical Soc. Am., IEEE (guest editor Jour. Quantum Electronics 1988—), Sigma Xi (v.p. 1986-87, chpt. pres. 1987-88), Sigma Pi Sigma. Jewish. Office: Hughes Research Labs RL 65 3011 Malibu Canyon Rd Malibu CA 90265

PEPPER, JOHN ENNIS, JR., consumer products company executive; b. Pottsville, Pa., Aug. 2, 1938; s. John Ennis Sr. and Irma Elizabeth (O'Connor) P.; m. Frances Graham Garber, Sept. 9, 1967; children: John, David, Douglas, Susan. BA, Yale U., 1960. With Procter & Gamble Co., Cin., 1963—, gen. mgr. Italian subs., 1974-77; v.p., gen. mgr. div. packaged soap and detergent Proctor & Gamble Co., Cin., 1977-80, group v.p., 1980-84, exec. v.p., 1984-86, pres., 1986—, also dir. Trustee Cin. Symphony Orch., Cin. Med. Inst.; group chmn. Cin. United Appeal Campaign, 1980; bd. trustees Xavier U., 1985—. Served to lt. USN, 1960-63. Mem. Nat. Alliance Businessmen (chmn. communication com.), Soap and Detergent Assn. (bd. dirs.). Office: Procter & Gamble Co 1 Procter & Gamble Plaza Cincinnati OH 45202 *

PEPPER, JOHN ROY, oil and gas executive; b. Denver, Feb. 24, 1937; s. Wesley Wayne and Lucille (Stith) P.; m. Sallie K. Force, Dec. 13, 1958 (div. July 1970); m. Judithea Lawrence, Sept. 24, 1977; stepchildren: Sarah Douglas, Kenneth R. Douglas. BSBA, U. Denver, 1961; postgrad., UCLA, 1962, U. Denver, 1965. Analyst Texaco, Inc., Los Angeles, 1962-63; landman Texaco, Inc., Bakersfield, Calif., 1963-65; prin. John Pepper, Landman, Denver, 1965-75; owner, operator John R. Pepper Oil & Gas Co., Denver, 1975—; bd. dirs. Trans-Telecom, Miami, Fla.; cons. Organizer Friends of Bob Crider campaign, Denver, 1985. Mem. Ind. Petroleum Assn. Mountain States, Ind. Petroleum Assn. of Ams. (pub. lands com. 1968-74), Denver Assn. Petroleum Landmen. Republican. Lutheran. Clubs: Kenosha Trout (Park County, Colo.) (chmn. first aid and fish procurement coms. 1974-82); Denver, Rump (Denver). Home: 6161 S Forest Ct Littleton CO 80121 Office: John R Pepper Oil & Gas Co 1800 Glenarm Pl Denver CO 80202

PEPPIATT, NICHOLAS ANTHONY, product designer; b. London, Mar. 29, 1947; s. Henri Camil and Phyllis Elizabeth (Ponsford) P.; m. Christine Gillian Wright, May 22, 1971; children: Andrew James, Jennifer Karen. BSc, U. Bristol, Eng., 1968; PhD, U. Bristol, 1974. Grad. trainee Rolls-Royce Ltd., Derby, Eng., 1968-70, preliminary designer, 1970-71; research assoc. U. Bristol, 1974-77; research engr. Wilkinson Match Research Div., Slough, Eng., 1977-79; sect. leader product devel. Wilkinson Sword Ltd., London, 1979-82; product design mgr. Hallite Seals Internat., London, 1982-87, tech. mgr., 1987—. Contbr. articles to profl. jours; patentee in field. Mem. Instn. Mech. Engrs. Home: 52 Mt Pleasant Close, Lightwater GU18 5TR, England Office: Hallite Seals Internat, Oldfield Rd, Hampton TW12 2HT, England

PERAHIA, MURRAY, pianist, conductor; b. N.Y.C., Apr. 19, 1947; s. David and Flora P.; m. Naomi Shohet Ninetti, 1980; 2 children. MS, Mannes Coll. Music; student, Jeannette Haien, Arthur Balsam, Mieczyslaw Horszowski. Appeared with Berlin Philharm., Chgo. Symphony Orch., English Chamber Orch., Boston Symphony Orch., N.Y. Philharm., Cleve. Orch., Los Angeles Philharm., Phila. Orch., others; performed with Budapest, Guarneri and Galimir string quartets; frequent performer, artistic dir.: Aldeburgh Festival, from 1983; past participant: Marlboro Music Festival; recital tours in U.S., Can., Europe and Japan; recs. for CBS Masterworks; 1st Am. to record the Complete Mozart Concertos as condr. with English Chamber Orch. Recipient Kosciusko Chopin prize, 1965, Avery Fisher prize, 1975, over 10 maj. rec. awards. Office: care Frank Salomon Assocs 201 W 54th St Suite 4C New York NY 10019 also: care Harold Holt Ltd, 31 Sinclair Rd, London W14 0NS, England *

PERALTA, SOTERO ANTONIO, accountant; b. Moca, Espaillat, Dominican Republic, Sept. 6, 1941; s. Pedro Antonio and Dolores Aniberca (Ferreira) P.; m. Evarista Tuma; children: Eva Orietta, Sotero Elias. Degree in acctg. and auditing, U. Autónoma de Santo Domingo, Domincan Republic, 1968. Mgr. Salvador Ortiz & Assocs., S.A., Santo Domingo, 1968-70; specialist in budgeting and acctg. Agy. for Internat. Devel., Santo Domingo, 1970-72; exec. ptnr. Sotero Peralta & Assocs., Santo Domingo, 1973—; sr. prin. Horwath & Horwath, S.A., Santo Domingo, 1986—, mem. exec. council; instr. fin. adminstrn., hotel acctg. U. Santo Domingo, UNAPEC; speaker in field. Co-author: Hotel Accounting, 1987. Pres. Latin Am. Regional Internat., 1982-84. Mem. Interam. Assn. Accts., Dominican Republic Inst. CPA's (pres. 1980-82). Club: Arroyo Hondo (Santa Domingo). Office: Sotero Peralta & Assocs, Av Winston Churchill No 71, Santo Domingo Dominican Republic

PERBECK, LEIF GUSTAV, surgeon, educator; b. July 28, 1944; s. Hans Gustav and Anna-Lisa (Dahlin) P.; m. Eva Brigitta Klackenberg, June 7, 1969; children—Henrik, Helene, Richard. D., Karolinska Inst. Med. Sch., Stockholm, 1972. Diplomate Swedish Bd. Surgery, 1977. Intern and resident in surgery St. Eriks Hosp., Stockholm, 1972-77; post resident staff Serafimer Hosp., Stockholm, 1977-80; surgeon Huddinge U. Hosp., Stockholm, 1980—. Author: Fluorescein Flowmetry, 1985; Carrier Mediated Substance, 1985; (jour.) Clinical Physiology, 1985. Served with Swedish Armed Forces. Mem. Swedish Soc. Medicine, European Soc. Microcirculation, Internat. Soc. Biorheology. Avocations: tennis; downhill skiing; sports car racing. Home: Vilansvag 14, 182 35 Danderyd, Stockholm Sweden Office: Kirurgkliniken Huddinge sjukhus, 141 86 Huddinge, Stockholm Sweden

PERCHER, PHILIPPE MARIE LOYS, gynecologist, obstetrician; b. Le Grand-Lucé, France, July 24, 1935; s. Gérard and Madeleine (Boivin) P.; m. Bernadette Gouesse; children: Benoît, Valérie, Vincent. DM, Faculty Medicine Paris, 1962. Intern Hosp. Puteaux, France, 1959-62; asst. ob/gyn. Ctr. Hospitalier Géneral de Montbéliard, France, 1963-75; head maternity hosp. Ctr. Hospitalier Géneral de Montbeiland, France, 1975—. Home: 36 Ave Wilson, 25200 Montbéliard France Office: Cen Hosp Gen André Boulloche, 25200 Montbéliard France

PERCHIK, BENJAMIN IVAN, operations research analyst; b. Passaic, N.J., May 3, 1941; s. Morris and Frances (Antman) P.; m. Ellen Mae Colwell, Aug. 25, 1963; children—Joel, Dawn. B.A., Rutgers U., 1964; postgrad. N.Y. Inst. Tech., 1964-65. Quality control E.R. Squibb Corp., New Brunswick, N.J., 1964-67; edn. specialist Signal Sch., Ft. Monmouth, N.J., 1967-74; edn. specialist Armor Sch., Ft. Knox, Ky., 1974-75, ops. research analyst, 1975-78; ops. research analyst HQ TRADOC, Ft. Monroe, Va., 1978-80; ops. research analyst Army Materiel Command, Alexandria, Va., 1980—, chmn. supervisory com. credit union, 1985—; cons. Delta Force, Carlisle Barracks, Pa., 1982-84, Internat. Policy Inst., 1983-85, World Future Soc., 1982—; nat. coordinator Mensa Investment SIG, 1983—; coordinator econ. forecasting group Met. Washington Mensa, 1983—; chmn. security com. Watergate at Landmark, 1985-88. Author: ADP Program and Repair, 1972; writer, editor, pub. newsletter Speculation and Investments, 1983—. Chmn. credit com. Devel. and Readiness Command, 1982-85. Mem. Inst. Mgmt. Scis., Internat. Platform Assn., Ops. Research Soc. Am. Club: Old Dominion Boat. Home: HQ US Army Europe, Rohrbacher Str #73, 6900 Heidelberg W Germany Office: 5001 Eisenhower Ave Alexandria VA 22333 also: PSC Box 195 Apo NY 09063

PERCY, RODNEY ALGERNON, circuit judge; b. Alnmouth, Eng., May 15, 1924; s. Hugh James and Gertrude (Mitchell) P.; m. Mary Allen Benbow, Mar. 27, 1948; children—Shian, Duncan Charles and Wendy Sara (twins), Suzanne. B.A. (honors), Oxford U., 1948, M.A., 1951; Barrister, Middle Temple, 1950; Barrister, Lincoln's Inn 1986; Chambers practice from Newcastle-Upon-Tyne, 1950-79; circuit judge North East Circuit, Eng., 1979—; dep. coroner North Northumberland, 1957-75; asst. recorder Sheffield Quarter Sessions, 1964; dep. chmn. County of Durham Quarter Sessions, 1966-71; recorder of Crown Ct., 1972-79. Pres. Tyneside Marriage Guidance Council, 1983-88; founder, mem. Conciliation Service for Northumberland and Tyneside, 1982—. Served as lt. Royal Corps of Signals, 1942-46; Burma, India, Malaya, Java. Editor: Charlesworth on Negligence, 1962 (4th edit.); 1971 (5th edit.), 1977 (6th edit.); Charlesworth and Percy on Negligence, 1983 (7th edit.). Home: Brookside, Lesbury Alnwick, Northumberland NE66 3AT, England

PEREIRA, ARISTIDES MARIA, president of Cape Verde; b. Boa Vista, Cape Verde, Nov. 17, 1923; student Liceu Gil Eanes, Cape Verde; m. Carlina Fortes; 1 son, 2 daus. Formerly head Telecommunications Services, Bissau, Portuguese Guinea (now Guinea-Bissau); co-founder Partido Africano da Ind. da Guiné e Cabo Verde (PAIGC), 1956; mem. polit. bur., central com. PAIGC, 1956-70; exile in Republic Guinea, 1960; asst. sec. gen. PAIGC, 1964-73, sec. gen., 1973-80, mem. council of war, 1965-80, mem. permament com. of exec. com. for struggle, 1966-70; pres. Republic Cape Verde, 1975-80, re-elected 1981; co-founder Partido Africano Ind. de Cabo Verde (PAICV), 1981; elected sec. gen. PAICV, 1981; re-elected pres. Republic Cape Verde, 1986. Address: Presidencia da Republica, Cidade de Praia Republic of Cape Verde

PEREIRA, AZAMOR TENŌRIO, economist, electronics company executive, management consultant; b. Belém, Brazil, Feb. 10, 1927; s. Andrē and Vitalina (Tenōrio) P.; m. Oswaldina Bastos, Oct. 16, 1947; children: Dillian, Azamor, Alexandre, Lidian. M in Econs., Consellio Regional de Economistas-Profissionais, São Paulo, Brazil, 1961; MBA, U. San Francisco, 1968. Founder, pres. Maestro Internat. Industries, Rochester, N.Y., 1968-74; founder, gen. mgr. Tektronix Industria e Comērcio, Ltda., São Paulo, 1976-81; founder, gen. dir. ATP/HI Tek Electronica, Ltda., São Paulo, 1981—; founder, cons. Econ. Prestação de Serviços Ltda., São Paulo, 1980—. Recipient Civilian Honorable Service award U.S. Air Transport Command, 1946. Fellow Nat. Council Profl. Economists. Club: Tennis (Alphaville, Sã Paulo). Home: Al Equador 557, Alphaville Barueri, 06400 São Paulo Brazil Office: ATP/HI Tek Electonica, Ltda., Al Amazonas 422, 06400 Alphaville Barueri Brazil

PEREIRA, SIR (HERBERT) CHARLES, agricultural scientist; b. London, May 12, 1913; s. Herbert John and Maud Edith (Machin) P.; B.Sc., U. London, 1934, Ph.D., 1940, D.Sc., 1961; D.Sc. (hon.), U. Cranfield, 1976; m. Irene Beatrice Sloan, 1941; children—David, Julie, Martin, Nigel. Head physics div., then dep. dir. E. African Agrl. and Forestry Research Orgn., 1952-61; dir. Agrl. Research Council Central Africa, 1961-67, East Malling Research Sta., Maidstone, Kent, Eng., 1969-72; chief scientist Ministry Agr., Fisheries and Food, 1972-77; cons. tropical agrl. and hydrol. research, 1978—; chmn. sci. adv. panel Commonwealth Devel. Corp., 1979—; mem. Tech. Adv. Com. to World Bank Cons. Group Internat. Agrl. Research, 1971-76. Served to maj. Brit. Army, 1939-46. Created knight bachelor, 1977; recipient Haile Selassie prize, 1966; award Rhodesian Nat. Farmers Union, 1967. Fellow Royal Soc., Royal Agrl. Soc. Eng., Inst. Biology; comp. mem. Instn. Civil Engrs. Mem. Ch. of Eng. Clubs: Atheneum, Alpine, Harare. Author: Land Use and Water Resources, 1973; Policy and Practice in Management of Tropical Watersheds, 1988; also papers on landuse, soil physics, forest hydrology. Office: Peartrees Teston Maidstone, Kent ME18 5AD, England

PEREIRA, ROSARIO JERVIS, economic consultant; b. Lisbon, Portugal, May 1, 1960; s. Antonio Jervis and Manuela (Capueho) Paulo P. Degree in Bus. Adminstrn., Catholic U., Lisbon, 1983. Sec. gen. ANCRIF, Lisbon, 1983—; sec. gen. ANAPO, Lisbon, 1986—; econ. adviser ANCAVE, Lisbon, 1986—. Author: Implications of EEC on the Portuguese Poultry Market, 1983. Home: R Francisco Hetrass 42 I-D, 1300 Lisbon Portugal Office: ANCRIF, R Alexandre Herculano 51 8, 1200 Lisbon Portugal

PEREL, JONATHAN SETH, real estate executive; b. Richmond, Va., Jan. 24, 1950; s. Milton and Ruth Z. Perel; m. Anne Marie Schalcher, Nov. 22, 1986; 1 child, Carolyn Anne. BA, Princeton U., 1971. Founder, chmn., pres. Gen. Services Corp., Richmond, 1971—, Triangle Communities, Durham, N.C., 1978—, HMK Corp., Richmond, 1983—. Mem. exec. com. Center Leadership of Nat. Football Found. and Hall of Fame, 1970-78; founder, chmn., pres. Found. Student Communication, 1967-71, bd. dirs., 1967—; trustee The Collegiate Schs., 1988—. Founder, chmn., editor-in-chief Bus. Today, 1967-71. Served with USAR, 1970-76. Mem. Nat. Apt. Assn., Nat. Assn. Home Builders, Home Builders Va., Richmond Apt. Council, Princeton Assn. Va. (bd. dirs. 1986—). Clubs: Princeton (N.Y.C.); Cannon. Office: PO Box 8984 Richmond VA 23225

PERELMAN, LEON JOSEPH, paper manufacturing executive, university president; b. Phila., Aug. 28, 1911; s. Morris and Jennie (Davis) P.; m. Beverly Waxman, Jan. 27, 1945 (div. Apr. 1960); children: Cynthia, David. B.A., LaSalle Coll., 1933, LL.D., 1978; postgrad., U. Pa. Law Sch., 1933-35; L.H.D. (hon.), Dropsie U., 1976. Ptnr., Am. Paper Products Co. (later Am. Paper Products Inc.), Phila., 1935-42; pres. Am. Paper Products Co. (later Am. Paper Products Inc.), 1943—, Am. Cone & Tube Co. Inc., 1953—, United Ammunition Container Inc., 1961—, Ajax Paper Tube Co., 1962—; vice chmn. bd. Belmont Industries, 1963—; pres. Dropsie U., 1978—. Author: Perelman Antique Toy Mus., 1972. Fin. chmn. Valley Forge council Boy Scouts Am., 1968; founder, bd. dirs. Perelman Antique Toy Mus., Phila., 1969; pres. West Park Hosp., 1975-78, 81—; trustee La Salle U., Balch Inst. Ethnic Studies. Served to 1st lt. USAAF, 1942-45. Recipient citation Jewish Theol. Sem., 1965; Beth Jacob award, 1966; award Pop Warner Little Scholars Inc., 1972; Cyrus Adler award Jewish Theol. Sem., 1976. Mem. AAUP, Jewish Publ. Soc. Am. (treas. 1983), Franklin Inst., Am. Assn. Mus. Republican. Jewish. Clubs: Union League (Phila.); Masons, Shriners. Office: 2113-41 E Rush St Philadelphia PA 19134

PERES, SHIMON, Israeli government official, politician; b. Poland, 1923; immigrated to Palestine, 1934; s. Isaac and Sarah Persky; ed. Harvard U.; m. Sonia Gelman; children: Zvia, Jonathan, Nechemia. Sec., Working Youth Movement, 1943; mem. Mapai Secretariat, 1947; dir. gen. ministry def., 1953-59; mem. Knesset, 1959—; dep. minister def., 1959-65; founder mem., sec.-gen. Rafi Party, 1965, mem. Labour Party after merger, 1968, chmn., 1977—; minister for econ. dept. in administered areas and for immigrant absorption, 1969-70, minister of transport and communications, 1970-74, minister of info., 1974, minister of def., 1974-77, acting prime minister, 1977; leader of opposition, 1977-84, minister interior and religious affairs, 1984-85, prime minister, 1984-86, vice prime minister, minister fgn. affairs, 1986—; chmn. Yad Ben-Gurion. Decorated officer Legion of Honor, 1959. Author: The Next Phase, 1965, David's Sling, 1970, Tomorrow is Now, 1978, From These Men, 1979; also articles. Office: Israel Labour Party, PO Box 3263, 63571 Tel Aviv Israel *

PEREZ, DAGOR, electronic engineer; b. Santiago, Chile, Jan. 19, 1945; s. Javier and Daphne (Giles) P. Electronic Engring. Degree, U. Tecnica del Estado, 1977. Prof. U. Santiago de Chile, 1971-83, chief X-ray Diffraction Lab., 1973-77, chief Instrumental Electronics Lab., 1977-80, chief Instrumentation Electronic Devel. Ctr., 1980—; audio cons., Santiago, 1971—; indsl. electronics cons., 1976—; tech. mgr. Pioneer, Santiago, 1977-80. Mem. IEEE. Patentee in field. Contbr. papers to sci. jours. Office: U de Santiago de Chile, Matucana 28D Casilla 5659, Correo 2 Santiago Chile

PEREZ, EDUARDO RAMON, financial director; b. Guatemala, Nov. 18, 1949; arrived in Colombia, 1987; s. Eduardo and Juanita Perez; m. Marina Angelica Calito, Apr. 10, 1976; children: Gabriela Juanita, Ana Lucia, Marina Alejandra. BA in Bus. Adminstrn., Rafael Landivar U., Guatemala, 1967-73. Budget supr. Colgate Palmolive (C.A.) S.A., Guatemala, 1973-75, mgr. acctg., 1975-77, sub controller, 1977-79; controller Colgate Palmolive (D.R.) Inc., Santo Domingo, 1979-87; dir. fin. Colgate Palmolive Co., Cali, Colombia, 1987—. Mem. Assn. Economists, Pub. Accts and Bus. Adminstrs. Roman Catholic. Lodge: Rotary. Home: Carrera 3 Oeste No 7-43, Cali Colombia Office: Colgate Palmolive Co, Apartado Aereo 2324, Cali Colombia

PEREZ-CASTILLO, JOSE GABRIEL, truck company executive; b. Puerto-Lope, Granada, Spain, May 1, 1937; s. Jose Perez Perez and Encarnacion Castillo Galvez; m. Magdalena de la Coba, Nov. 15, 1968; children: Vilma, Sira, Zaira. D in Engring., U. Madrid, 1960, Diploma in Math and Physics, 1971. With tech. services dept. I.S.A., Seville, Spain, 1960-63; quality dir. Empresa Nat. de Autocamiones, Madrid, 1963-81; with engine engring. dept. Empresa Nat. de Autocamiones, Barcelona, 1981-82; plant mgr. Empresa Nat. de Autocamiones, Madrid, 1982-84; engring. v.p. Empresa Nat. de Autocamiones, Barcelona, 1984-86; v.p. quality Empresa Nat. de Autocamiones, Madrid, 1986—; chmn. I.S.O., 1970—; prof. Escuela de Orgn. Indsl., Madrid, 1986. Mem. Soc. Automotive Engrs., Assn. Española para el Control de la Calidad. Home: Brescia 1, 28028 Madrid Spain Office: ENASA, Avda Aragon 402, Madrid Spain

PEREZ-COMAS, ADOLFO, physician; b. Mayaguez, P.R., Nov. 27, 1941; s. Adolfo and Alma Luz (Comas-Lugo) Perez-Sosa; B.S., U. P.R., 1961; M.D., U. Barcelona (Spain), 1967, Ph.D., 1975; m. Maria del Rosario Fraticelli, Mar. 30, 1985; children—Adolfo, Alberto. Intern, San Juan City Hosp., 1968, fellow in endocrinology, 1970-72; resident in pediatrics San Juan City Hosp., P.R. Med. Center, Rio Piedras, 1969-70; practice medicine specializing in endocrinology and med. genetics, Mayaguez, P.R., 1972—; asst. prof. physiology and biochemistry Sch. Medicine, U. Barcelona, 1963-67; dir. pediatric endocrinology and med. genetics sect. Mayaguez Med. Center, 1972—, sec. of faculty, 1972-73, chief of staff, 1975-79; vis. prof. U. Salamanca (Spain), 1981-84; lectr. physiology U. P.R., Mayaguez, 1973—, assoc. prof. pediatrics, 1974—. Counselor, Growth Hormone Fund, Inc., 1974; advisor to Senate of P.R., 1980—. Named Citizen of Year, Mayaguez, 1974, Most Disting. Young Man in Fields of Sci. and Medicine, Rio Piedras Jaycees, 1974. Fellow Superior Council Sci. Investigations (hon.) (Spain); mem. Am. Acad. Pediatrics (sci. ann. award 1968), Am. Soc. Human Genetics, Am. Soc. Andrology, Internat. Diabetes Fedn., Fedn. Latinoam. de Assns. de Lucha Contra la Diabetes (exec. council) (Venezuela), Am. Diabetes Assn., Latinam. Assn. Diabetes (dir., v.p. 1980-84), Diabetes Assn. Caribbean (chmn.-elect 1987—), AAAS, N.Y. Acad. Sci., Am. Med. Writers Assn., Soc. Nuclear Medicine P.R., Western Dist. Med. Soc. (dir. med. edn.), Govtl. Physicians Assn. P.R. (pres. 1979—), Iberoam. Med. Assn. (Madrid) (v.p. 1980—), Craniofacial Genetics Assn. N.Am., P.R. Med. Assn., Endocrine Soc., Dominican Republic Acad. Sci. (hon.), Peru Diabetic Assn. (hon.), Ecuador Diabetic Assn. (hon.), Caribbean Diabetes Assn. (pres. elect), Nu Sigma Beta. Mormon. Contbr. articles on research in endocrinology, diabetes and med. genetics to med. jours. Home: Manuel Rodriguez Serra #79 Condado Santurce PR 00907 Office: 22 N Dr Basora Mayaguez PR 00708 Other: Condominio Ada Ligia 1452 Ashford Ave Suite 310 Condado-Santurce PR 00708 also: PO Box 20 Mayaguez PR 00709-0020

PEREZ-CRUET, JORGE, psychiatrist,' psychopharmacologist; b. Santurce, P.R., Oct. 15, 1931; s. Jose Maria Perez-Vicente and Emilia Cruet-Burgos; m. Anyes Heimendinger, Oct. 4, 1958; children—Antonio, Mikie, Graciela, Isabela. B.S. magna cum laude, U. P.R., 1953, M.D., 1957; diploma psychiatry McGill U., Montreal, Que., Can., 1976. Diplomate Am. Bd. Psychiatry and Neurology, Nat. Bd. Med. Examiners; lic. Can. Council Med Examiners. Rotating intern Michael Reese Hosp., Chgo., 1957-58; fellow in psychiatry Johns Hopkins U. Med. Sch., 1958-60, instr., then asst. prof. psychiatry, 1962-73; lab. neurophysiologist Walter Reed Army Inst. Research, Washington, 1960-62, cons., 1963-68; research asso. lab. chem. pharmacology, also research asso. adult psychiatry br. and lab. clin. sci. NIMH, Bethesda, Md., 1969-73; psychiatry resident diploma course in psychiatry McGill U. Sch. Medicine, Montreal Gen. Hosp., 1973-76, Montreal Children's Hosp., 1975; prof. psychiatry U. Mo.-Mo. Inst. Psychiatry, St. Louis, 1976-78; chief psychiatry service San Juan (P.R.) VA Hosp., also prof. psychiatry U. P.R. Med. Sch., 1978—; spl. adviser on mental health P.R. Senate, P.R. sec. health; spl. cons. NASA, 1965-69. Served to capt. M.C., USAR, 1960-62. Recipient Coronas award, 1957, Ruiz-Arnau award, 1957, Diaz-Garcia award, 1957, Geigy award, 1975, 76, AMA Recognition award, 1971, 76, 81, Horner's award, 1975, 76, Pavlovian award, 1978. Fellow Interam. Coll. Physicians and Surgeons, Royal Coll. Physicians and Surgeons (Can.); mem. AMA, Am. Psychiat. Assn., Am. Physiol. Soc., N.Y. Acad. Scis., Pavlovian Soc., Am. Fedn. Clin. Research, Can. Psychiat. Assn., Am. Soc. Clin. Pharmacology and Therapeutics, Soc. Neurosci., Internat. Soc. Research Aggression, Nat. Assn. VA Chiefs Psychiatry, P.R. Med. Assn. Roman Catholic. Home: PO Box 1797 Guaynabo PR 00657 Office: Chief Psychiatry Service 116 A PO Box 4867 VA Med Ctr San Juan PR 00936

PEREZ DE CUELLAR, JAVIER, Peruvian diplomat, United Nations secretary general; b. Jan. 19, 1920; ed. Cath. U., Lima, Peru; LL.D., U. Nice (France); hon. degrees: Jagiellonian U., Poland, 1983, Charles U., Czechoslovakia, 1983, Sofia (Bulgaria) U., 1984, U. Nacional Mayor de San Marcos, Peru, 1984, Free U. Brussels, 1984, Carleton U., Ottawa, 1985, Sorbonne, Paris, 1985, U. Leiden, Netherlands, 1988; m. Marcela Temple; 2 children. Joined Peruvian Fgn. Ministry, 1940, diplomatic service, 1944; diplomatic posts in France, Eng., Brazil, 1945-61; dir. legal dept., adminstrn., protocol and polit. affairs Ministry Fgn. Affairs, 1961-64; ambassador to Switzerland, 1964-66; sec. gen. Fgn. Office, 1966-69; ambassador to USSR and Poland, 1969-71; permanent rep. to UN, 1971-75, rep. to Security Council, 1973-74; spl. rep. of UN Sec.-Gen. in Cyprus, 1975-77; ambassador to Venezuela, 1978-81; under sec.-gen. for spl. polit. affairs UN, 1979-81, personal rep. UN Sec. Gen. on Afghanistan, 1980-82; UN sec. gen., 1982—; former prof. diplomatic law Academia Diplomatica del Peru; prof. internat. relations Academia de Guerra Aérea del Peru. Mem. Peruvian Soc. Internat. Law, Sección Peruana de la Comisión Internacional de Juristas, Interam. Inst. Juridical Internat. Studies. Recipient several nat. and fgn. decorations. Author: Manual de Derecho Diplomatico, 1964. Address: PO Box 20 Grand Central New York NY 10017

PÉREZ DE VARGAS LUQUE, ALBERTO IGNACIO, biomathematics educator; b. Algeciras, Andalucia, Cadiz, Spain, Aug. 26, 1942; s. Ignacio Perez de Vargas Mena and Isabel Luque Matias; m. Maria Cristina Martinez Calvo, Dec. 30, 1967; children: Maria Cristina, Isabel Maria, Alberto Ignacio. MS, U. Madrid, 1966, PhD, 1973; diplomé és scis., U. Geneva, 1972. Asst. in math. U. Madrid, 1966-69, asst. prof. math., 1974-75; asst. in math. U. Geneva, 1969-74; prof. biomath. U. Alcala, Madrid, 1975-82, U. Complutense Madrid, 1982—. Author: Elementos de Biomatemáticas, 1977, Fundamentos de Biomatemáticas, 1984; contbr. articles to profl. jours. Office: U Complutense de Madrid, Faculty Biologia, Ciudad Universitaria, 28040 Madrid Spain

PEREZ ESQUIVEL, ADOLFO, human rights activist; b. 1931; grad. Nat. Sch. Fine Arts, Buenos Aires and La Plata, Argentina, 1956; m. Amanda E., 1956; 3 children. Sculptor, prof. art Manuel Belgrano Nat. Sch. Fine Arts, Buenos Aires, 1956—; founder Servico Paz y Justica, 1971, sec. gen., 1974—; joines Oouddian (Militant Noviolence) group, 1974; founder mag. Paz y Justice,; imprisoned for peace activites, 1977-78. Recipient Pope John XXIII award Pax Christi, 1977; Nobel prize for peace, 1980. Author: Christ in a Poncho: Testimonials of the Nonviolent Struggles in Latin America, 1983. Address: care Servicio Paz y Justica, Carre Mexico 479, 1097 Buenos Aires Argentina *

PEREZ-LAZO, PEDRO FRANCISCO, textile company executive; b. Milan, Italy, Nov. 19, 1934; s. Mario Perez-Pisanty and Adelina Lazo-Marti; m. Reselia Nunez, Jan. 25, 1958; children—Mario, Pedro Luis, Maria Elisa, Maria Antonia, Maria Eugenia. Cert. textile engr. Phila. Coll. Textiles and Sci., 1956. Pres. La Industrial Metropolitana C.A., Caracas, Venezuela, 1956-62, C.A. Silka, Caracas, 1962—. Bd. dirs. Fondo Desarrollo Algodonero, Caracas, 1982—, Hosp. Prtopedico Infantil, Caracas, 1978—. Recipient Medal of Distinction, Jose Felix Rivas, Caracas, 1973; named hon. citizen City of New Orleans, 1976. Mem. Assn. Textil Venezolana (bd. dirs. 1982—), Internat. Fellowship Flying Rotarians, Internat. Pilot Assn. U.S.A., Assn. Nacional de Pilotos. Roman Catholic. Clubs: Valle Arriba Golf (Caracas); Playa Azul (Naiguata, Venezuela). Lodge: Rotary. Avocation: aviation. Office: CA Silka, Apartado 1788, Caracas 1010A, Venezuela

PEREZ SANCHEZ, ALFONSO EMILIO, museum director; b. Cartagena, Murcia, Spain, June 16, 1935; s. Alfonso Perez Bernardez and Delores Bolea. PhD in Art History, U. Madrid, 1978. Subdir. Prado Mus., Madrid, 1971-81, dir., 1983—; vice-rector of univ. extension services U. Madrid, 1978-82, prof. Art History, 1978—. Author: Pintura Italiana del Siglo XVII en España, 1965, Pintura Madrileña del Primer Tercio del Siglo XVII, 1969, Pintura Tolendana de la Primera Mitad del Siglo XVII, 1973, A Corpus of Spanish Drawings, 1975. Decorated Comdr. Order of Merit, Comdr. Order of St. Olav, Comdr. Order of Isabel la Cath., Comdr. Nordstjärneorden Govt. Sweden, Officer Order of Arts and Letters Govt. France, Grand Duchy of Louxembourg. Home: Alberto Aguilera 68, Madrid Spain Office: Museo del Prado, Paseo del Prado s/n, 28014 Madrid Spain

PERGAM, ALBERT STEVEN, lawyer; b. N.Y.C., Dec. 23, 1938; s. Irving and Gertrude (Newman) P.; m. Natalie J. Chaliff, Aug. 14, 1965; children—Ilana N., Elizabeth A. B.A. summa cum laude, Yale U., 1960; postgrad., St. John's Coll., Cambridge, Eng., 1960-61; LL.B. magna cum laude, Harvard U., 1964. Bar: N.Y. 1965. Law clk. to judge U.S. Ct. Appeals (2d cir.), 1964-65; spl. asst., asst. atty. gen. civil rights div. U.S. Dept. Justice, Washington, 1965-66; assoc. firm Cleary, Gottlieb, Steen & Hamilton, N.Y.C., 1966-72; ptnr. Cleary, Gottlieb, Steen & Hamilton, 1973—; resident ptnr Cleary, Gottlieb, Steen & Hamilton, London, 1980-84. Contbr. chpt. on Eurobonds to International Capital Markets and Securities Regulation, 1983; author: Legal Dimensions of Eurobond Financing, So. Meth. U. Inst. on Internat. Finance, 1988; editorial advisor and contbr. Internat. Fin. Law Review. Henry fellow, 1960-61. Mem. ABA, Internat. Bar Assn., N.Y. State Bar Assn., Assn. Bar City N.Y., Phi Beta Kappa. Clubs: Elihu, Elizabethan (New Haven); Yale (assoc. fellow) (N.Y.C.); Branford Coll. (assoc. fellow); United Oxford and Cambridge (London). Office: Cleary Gottlieb Steen & Hamilton 1 State St Plaza New York NY 10004

PERICOLI, TULLIO, artist; b. Colli del Tronto (Ascoli Piceno), Marche, Italy, Oct. 2, 1936. Works exhibited in group shows at Inst. di Storia dell'Arte, U. Parma, Italy, 1972, U. Degli Studi Urbino, Italy, 1978, Padiglione d'Arte Contemporanea, Italy, 1985, Galerie Bartsch & Chariau, Munich, 1985, Wilhelm Busch Mus., Hannover, Fed. Republic Germany, 1988; collaborating artist for La Repubblica newspaper, L'Indice mag., L'Espresso mag. Home and Studio: Via Pestalozza 4, 20131 Milan Italy

PERIER, FRANCOIS (FRANCOIS PILLU), actor; b. Paris, Nov. 10, 1919; m. Jacqueline Porel, 1941; 3 children—m. 2d, Marie Daems, 1949; m. 3d, Colette Boutouland, 1961. Student Conservatoire Nat. d'Art Dramatique, Paris. Co-dir., Theatre de la Michodiere, Paris, 1951-65; appeared in numerous plays including: Les jours heureux, Les J 3, Les mains sales, Bobosse, Le ciel de lit, Gog et Magog, La preuve par quatre, Le Diable et le Bon Dieu, Ne reveillez pas Martame, Le tube, Equus, Coup de chapeau, Amadeus; films include: Premier bal, 1941, Lettres d'amour, 1942, Un revenant, Le silence est d'or, 1946, Orphee, 1949, Les evades, 1954, Gervaise, 1955, Le Notti di Cabiria, 1956, Bobosse, 1958, Le testament d'Orphee, 1960, L'amant de cinq jours, 1961, La visita, 1963, Les enfants du palais (TV), 1967, Z, 1968, Le cercle rouge, 1970, Max et les ferrailleurs, 1971, Juste avant la nuit, 1971, L'attentat, 1972, Antoine et Sebastien, 1973, Stavisky, Sarah (TV), 1974, Dr. Francoise Gailland, 1975, Police Python, 1976, Mazarin (TV), 1978, La raison d'etat, 1978, La guerre des polices, 1979, Le bar du Telephone, 1980. Decorated Comdr. Ordre des Arts et Lettres; recipient British Film Acad. award, 1956, Victoria du Cinema Francais, 1957, Medaille George Melies, 1976, Grand Prix nat. du Theatre, 1977. Office: care Artmedia, 10 ave George V, 75008 Paris France

PERISSIN, ALDO ARRIGO, scientific instruments company executive; b. Monfalcone, Italy, July 18, 1938; s. Giulio and Angela (Pelizzari) P.; m. Sara Giulini Neri, Oct. 1, 1983; children from previous marriage: Robert, Barbara. Student, Leeds U., 1960-61. Mktg. specialist Varian Assocs., Zug, Switzerland, 1962-63; resident rep. Quickfit & Quarts Ltd., Stone, Stafordshire, Eng., 1963-67; project mgr. U.O.P., London, 1967-68; gen. mgr. Packard Instruments, Inc., Milan, 1968-77, Extracorporeal, Milan, 1977-78; mng. dir. Beckman Instruments, Milan, 1978—; pres. Supelco Italy, Milan, 1978-85, pres. high tech., 1985—; pres. Sensormedics Italy, Milan, 1984. Home: 34 Via M Melloni, 20100 Milan Italy Office: Sensormedics Italia Srl, Via Mameli, 20129 Milan 10 Italy

PERKEL, DAVID N., micro computer exec.; b. Jersey City, June 5, 1946; s. Morris Milton and Dorothy Haspel (Mann) P.; m. Donna Marie Rzigalinski, Nov. 21, 1967; 1 son, Daniel Arron. B.S. in Acctg., St. Peter's Coll., 1968; postgrad., N.Y.U., 1968-69. Mgr. acctg. Bali Bra, Jersey City, 1968-72; controller Littman Dist., Highland Park, N.J., 1972-76; pres. Select Temps., Metuchen, N.J., 1976—; v.p. Prodigy Systems, Iselin, N.J., 1978-82; pres. Select Solutions, Colonia, N.J., 1982—. Contbr. articles to magazines, profl. jours. Republican. Jewish. Home: PO Box 126 Colonia NJ 07067

PERKIN, THOMAS JOHN, college administrator; b. Flint, Mich., July 11, 1948; s. John Woolcock and Mary Annie (Jenkins) P.; m. Linda Ellen Putt, Jan. 9, 1971; children—Joel Thomas, Lindsey Marie. B.S. in Edn., Central Mich. U., 1971, M.A., 1983. Tchr. Morrice Area Schs., Mich., 1971-74; asst. gen. mgr. Standard Lumber Co., Owosso, Mich., 1976-80; asst. mgr. Pine Lumber Co., Owosso, 1981-84; asst. to dean Baker Jr. Coll., Owosso, 1984-86, asst. to v.p. academics, 1986-87, dean academics, 1987-88, v.p. academics, 1988—. Chairperson citizens com. on vocat. edn. Corunna Schs., Mich., 1983-86; mem. Council for Deaf, Owosso, 1984-86; counselor Congregational Ch., Perry, Mich., 1983—, chairperson bd. trustees, 1987—. Mem. Am. Assn. Counseling and Devel., Am. Coll. Personnel Assn., Assn. Counselor Edn. and Supervision, Mich. Personnel Guidance Assn., Goodfellows (pres. Owosso chpt. 1986-88), Assn. for Supervision and Curriculum Devel. Lodge: Kiwanis (Shiawassee-Owosso) (pres. 1987-88). Avocations: reading; skiing; swimming; fishing; camping. Office: Baker Jr Coll 1020 S Washington Owosso MI 48867

PERKINS, DONALD W., lawyer; b. Boston, Oct. 2, 1933; s. Eustace Judson and Ruth (Walker) P.; m. Laures Terry, June 19, 1955; children—Donald W. Jr., David J., Terry. A.B. summa cum laude with honors in Econs., Tufts U., 1955; J.D., Harvard U., 1961. Bar: Maine 1961, Mass. 1961, U.S. Dist. Ct. Maine 1961, U.S. Ct. Appeals (1st cir.) 1979, U.S. Supreme Ct. 1980. Law clk. to judge U.S. Dist. Ct. Maine, Portland, 1961-62; ptnr. Pierce, Atwood, Scribner, Allen, Smith & Lancaster, Portland, 1965—. Mem. Gov.'s Task Force on Forest Taxation, 1971-72, Gov.'s Task Force on Indian Claims, 1977-78, Speaker's Select Com. on Workmen's Compensation, 1983-84. Served to capt. USMC, 1955-62. Mem. ABA, Assn. Trial Lawyers Am., Maine State Bar Assn., Cumberland County Bar Assn., Phi Beta Kappa. Home: 136 Oakhurst Rd Cape Elizabeth ME 04107 Office: 1 Monument Sq Portland ME 04101

PERKINS, EDWARD J., U.S. ambassador to Republic of South Africa; b. Sterlington, La., June 8, 1928; m. Lucy Liu; 2 children. Student, U. Calif., Lewis and Clark Coll.; B.A., U. Md., 1967; M.P.A., U. So. Calif., 1972, D.P.A., 1978; studied French, Fgn. Service Inst., 1983. Chief of personnel Army and Air Force Exchange Service, Taipei, Taiwan, 1958-62; dep. chief Army and Air Force Exchange Service, Okinawa, Japan, 1962-64, chief personnel and adminstrn., 1964-66; asst. gen. services officer Far East bur. AID, 1967-69, mgmt. analyst, 1969-70; asst. dir. for mgmt. U.S. Ops. Mission to Thailand, 1970-72; staff asst. Office of Dir. Gen. Fgn. Service, 1972, personnel officer, 1972-74; adminstrv. officer Bur. Near Eastern and South Asian Affairs, 1974-75; mgmt. analysis officer Office Mgmt. Ops., Dept. State, 1975-78; counselor for polit. affairs Accra, Ghana, 1978-81; dep. chief of mission Monrovia, Liberia, 1981-83; dir. Office of West African Affairs, Bur. African Affairs, Dept. State, 1983-85; U.S. ambassador to Liberia 1985-86, U.S. ambassador to South Africa, 1986—. also: Am Embassy, Thibault House, 225 Pretorius St, Pretoria Republic of South Africa *

PERKINS, ESTHER ROBERTA, literary agent; b. Elkton, Md., May 10, 1927; d. Clarence Roberts and Esther Crouch (Terrell) P.; student West Chester State Tchrs. Coll., 1945-47, U. Del. Acct., E. I. duPont de Nemours & Co., Inc., Wilmington, Del., 1947-65; records specialist U. Del., 1966-78; partner Holly Press, Hockessin, Del., 1977-83; owner Esther R. Perkins Lit. Agy., Childs, Md., 1979—; author's agt. Mem. Cecil County Arts Council. Mem. Authors Guild, Nat. Assn. Female Execs., Nat. Writer's Club, DAR, Romance Writers of Am. Republican. Methodist. Author: Backroading Through Cecil County Maryland, 1978; Things I Wish I'd Said, 1979; Canal Town, Historic Chesapeake City, Maryland, 1983. Home and Office: PO Box 48 Childs MD 21916

PERKINS, EUGENE ORAL, lawyer, oil company executive, rancher; b. Washington, Ind., July 2, 1923; s. Charles R. and Gladys (Billings) P.; m. Delores S. Student DePaul U., 1941-42; B.S. in Elec. Engring., U. Iowa, 1946; J.D., U. Colo., 1949. Bar: Colo. 1949. Sole practice, Colorado Springs, 1949-68, 85—; sr. ptnr. Perkins, Goodbee & Martin, Colorado Springs, 1968-85; pres. Perkins Oil Co. Served with U.S. Army. Mem. ABA, Colo. Bar Assn., El Paso County Bar Assn., Colo. Cattlemen's Assn. Oriental Ceramic Soc., Am. Quarter Horse Assn., Am. Gelbvieh Assn., Tau Beta Pi, Phi Alpha Delta. Republican. Clubs: Garden of Gods, El Paso, Broadmoor Golf, Balboa. Author booklets on fin. and Chinese art; contbr. articles on fin., horses, racing and Chinese ceramic art to mags., jours. Home: 1900 Mesa Ave Colorado Springs CO 80906 Office: 925 Arcturus Dr Colorado Springs CO 80906

PERKINS, FLOYD JERRY, theology educator; b. Bertha, Minn., May 9, 1924; s. Ray Lester and Nancy Emily (Kelley) P.; m. Mary Elizabeth Owen, Sept. 21, 1947 (dec. June 1982); children: Douglas Jerry, David Floyd, Sheryl Pauline; m. Phyllis Geneva Hartley, July 14, 1984. AB, BTh, N.W. Nazarene Coll., 1949; MA, U. Mo., 1952; MDiv, Nazarene Theol. Sem., 1952; PhD, U. Witwatersrand, Johannesburg, South Africa, 1974. Ordained to Christian ministry, 1951. Pres. South African Nazarene Theol. Sem., Florida Transvaal, Africa, 1955-67; pres. Nazarene Bible Sem., Lourenzo Marques, Mozambique, 1967-73, Campinas, Brazil, 1974-76; prof. missions N.W. Nazarene Coll., Nampa, Idaho, 1976; prof. theology Nazarene Bible Coll., Colorado Springs, Colo., 1976—; chmn., founder com. higher theol. edn. Ch. of Nazarene in Africa, 1967-74; sec. All African Nazarene Mission Exec., 1967-74; ofcl. Christian Council Mozambique, 1952-74. Author: A History of the Christian Church in Swaziland, 1974. Served with USN, 1944-46. Mem. Am. Schs. Oriental Research, Am. Soc. Missiology, Assn. Evan. Missions Profs. Republican. Home: 1529 Lyle Dr Colorado Springs CO 80915 Office: Nazarene Bible Coll 122 Chapman Dr Colorado Springs CO 80935

PERKINS, JAMES FRANCIS, physicist; b. Hillsdale, Tenn., Jan. 3, 1924; s. Jim D. and Laura Pervis (Goad) P.; A.B., Vanderbilt U., 1948, M.A., 1949; Ph.D., 1953; m. Ida Virginia Phillips, Nov. 23, 1949; 1 son, James F. Sr. engr. Convair, Fort Worth, Tex., 1953-54; scientist Lockheed Aircraft, Marietta, Ga., 1954-61; physicist Army Missile Command Redstone Arsenal, Huntsville, Ala., 1961-77; cons. physicist, 1977—. Served with USAAF, 1943-46. AEC fellow, 1951-52. Mem. Am. Phys. Soc., Sigma Xi. Contbr. articles to profl. jours. Home and Office: 102 Mountainwood Dr Huntsville AL 35801

PERKINS, JAMES SECOR, industrial engineer, production management consultant; b. Oak Park, Ill., Mar. 16, 1911; s. Augustus Thompson and Emily Charlotte (Secor) P.; student engring. Cornell U., 1930-31; BS in Bus. Adminstrn., Northwestern U., 1939; m. Helen Dorchak, May 29, 1958 (dec.); children—Diane Lea Kulik, Sandra Lea Merin; m. Kathryn M. Moss, Jan. 2, 1984. Indsl. engr. Bauer & Black Co., Chgo., 1934-35; cons. in plant layout Berger div. of Republic Steel Corp., Canton, Ohio, 1936; cons. cost accountant Barco Mfg. Co., Chgo., 1936; cons. indsl. engring. Belmont Radio Corp., Chgo., 1936; indsl. engr. Western Electric Co., Chgo., 1935-46; chief indsl. engr. Ball Bros. Co., Muncie, Ind., 1946-48; plant supt. Courier-Citizen Co., Chgo., 1948-52; v.p. mfg. Wallace Bus. Forms Corp., Chgo., 1952-60; gen. mgr. Rec. & Statis. Corp., Danville, Ill., 1960-63; dir. prodn. mgmt. Printing Industries Am., Inc., Arlington, Va., 1963-71; pres. mgmt. cons. Perkins Assocs., Bethesda, Md., 1971-77, Savannah, Ga., 1977—; instr. prodn. mgmt. Northwestern U., Evanston, 1941; instr. indsl. engring. night sch. Ill. Inst. Tech., Chgo., 1941-46. Recipient Excellence in Indsl. Engring. Chgo. Coll. Indsl. Engring., 1946. Mem. ASME, Am. Inst. Indsl. Engrs. (Graphic Arts award 1980), Soc. Advancement Mgmt. (Gilbreth Gold medal award 1945), Graphic Arts Assn. Execs., Assn. Graphic Arts Cons. (pres. 1983, hon. life 1987—), Printing Assn. Ga., Sigma Chi. Clubs: Marshwood/Landings Golf and Country (Savannah); Cornell (dir. 1964-65). Author: The Original Films of Frank B. Gilbreth, 1969 (film); contbr. numerous articles on mgmt. to printing trade mags. Address: 3 Middleton Rd The Landings on Skidaway Island Savannah GA 31411

PERKINS, KENNETH, writer, retired army officer; b. Newhaven, Sussex, Eng., Aug. 15, 1926; s. George Samuel and Arabella (Wise) P.; m. Anne Theresa Barry, Oct. 15, 1949 (div. 1984); children: Maureen, Jane, Nicola; m. Celia Sandys (granddaughter of Sir Winston Churchill), July 24, 1985; children: Alexander, Sophie. Student, Lewes County Sch., 1939-43, Oxford U., 1944, Staff Coll., Pakistan, 1958, Royal Coll. Def. Studies, London, 1973. Commd. officer Royal Artillery, 1946, advanced through grades to maj. gen., 1974; service includes aviation in Korean War and Malayian Emergency, instr. Staff Coll. Camberly, 1965-66, comdr. 1st Regiment Royal Horse Arty., 1967-69, 24th Inf. Brigade, 1971-72, on loan to Sultan Qaboos to command the Omani Armed Forces during the Dhofar War, 1975-77, asst. chief Def. Staff, 1978-79, dir. Mil. Assistance, London, 1980-81; def. advisor Brit. Aerospace Dynamics Group, 1982-84, head Middle East mkgt., 1984-87; internat. lectr. in war studies. Author: Weapons and Warfare, 1987, A Fortunate Soldier, 1988; exhibited in Royal Acad.; contbr. articles to profl. jours. Decorated D.F.C.; mem. Brits. Empire, Companion of the Bath; decorated Order of Oman; Hashemite Order of Independence; Selangor Disting. Conduct Medal. Club: Army and Navy. Home: Coombe Head, Bampton, Devon RG16 9LB, England

PERKINS, MARVIN EARL, psychiatrist, educator; b. Moberly, Mo., June 1, 1920; s. Marvin Earl and Nannie Mae (Walden) P.; A.B., Albion Coll., 1942; M.D., Harvard U., 1946; M.P.H. (USPHS fellow), Johns Hopkins U., 1956; L.H.D., Albion Coll., 1968; grad. U.S. Army Command and Gen. Staff Coll., 1966, U.S. Army War Coll., 1972; m. Mary MacDonald, May 24, 1943 (div.); children—Keith, Sandra, Cynthia, Marvin, Mary, Irene; m. 2d, Sharon Johnstone, May 20, 1978; 1 dau., Sharon. Intern, Henry Ford Hosp., Detroit, 1946-47; post surgeon, hosp. comdg. officer Fort Eustis, Va., 1948; resident physician psychiatry Walter Reed Army Hosp., Washington, 1949-52; chief psychiatry br., psychiatry and neurology cons. div. Office U.S. Army Surgeon Gen., Washington, 1952-53, chief records rev. br., 1953-55; chief psychiat. services div. D.C. Dept. Public Health, 1955-58, chief bur. mental health, 1959-60; dir. N.Y.C. Community Mental Health Bd., 1960-68, commr. mental health services, 1961-68; lectr. Johns Hopkins U., Balt., 1960-65; adj. prof. Columbia U., 1961-67; prof. psychiatry Mt. Sinai Sch. Medicine of CUNY, 1967-72; clin. prof. psychiatry Coll. Physicians and Surgeons, Columbia U., 1972-77; prof. psychiatry N.Y. Coll. Medicine, 1977-78, U. Va., 1978—; dir. psychiatry Beth Israel Medical Center, N.Y.C., 1967-72, dir. Morris J. Bernstein Inst., 1968-72; dir. Community Mental Health Services Westchester County, 1972-77; dir. psychiatry Westchester County Med. Center, 1977-78; med. dir. Mental Health Services of Roanoke Valley, 1978-82, Catawba Hosp., 1988—; med. dir. Roanoke Valley Psychiat. Center, 1980-82, pres. med. staff, 1985-86. Served with AUS, 1943-46; col. M.C. Res. ret. Diplomate in psychiatry Am. Bd. Psychiatry and Neurology; certified mental hosp. adminstr. Am. Psychiat. Assn. Fellow Am. Psychiat. Assn. (life), N.Y. Acad. Medicine; mem. AMA, Group Advancement Psychiatry, Roanoke Acad. Medicine, Nat. Geneal. Soc., New Eng. Hist. Geneal. Soc., N.Y. Psychiat. Soc., Neuropsychiat. Soc. Va., Med. Soc. Va., State Hist. Soc. Mo. (life), N.Y. Hist. Soc., Res. Officers Assn. (life), N.Y. Geneal and Biog. Soc. Home: Rt 2 Box 444 Fincastle VA 24090

PERKINS, NANCY JANE, industrial designer; b. Phila., Nov. 5, 1949; d. Gordon Osborne and Martha Elizabeth (Keichline) P.; student Ohio U., 1967-68; BFA in Indsl. Design, U. Ill., Champaign, 1972. Indsl. designer Peterson Bednar Assos., Evanston, Ill., 1972-74, Deschamps Mills Assos., Bartlett, Ill., 1974-75; dir. graphic design Cameo Container Corp., Chgo., 1975-76; indsl. design cons. Sears Roebuck & Co., Chgo., 1977-88; cons. indsl. design, 1988—; founder Perkins Design Ltd., indsl. design cons. co., 1979—; adj. prof. grad. design Seminar U. Ill. at Chgo., 1982, 88, instr. undergrad. design, 1984, 1988; adj. prof. Ill. Inst. Tech., 1987; instr. Inst. Design Ill. Inst. of Tech., Chgo., 1987; juror Annual Design Rev. Industrial Design mag., 1986; keynote speaker Soc. Automotive Engrs., 1980, Women in Design, 1982, 84, Meadow Club, 1983, U. Ill. Disting. Alumni Lecture Series, 1983, Human Factors Soc. Interface '85, 1985. Contbr. articles to profl. jours.; profiled in Industrial Design mag., 1986. Co-leader Cadette troop DuPage County council Girl Scouts U.S.A., 1978-79. Recipient Outstanding Alumni award U. Ill. Alumni Jour., 1981. Mem. Indsl. Designers Soc. Am. (treas. Chgo. chpt. 1977-79, vice chmn. 1979-80, chmn. 1981, dist. membership 1982, ann. conf. com. 1983, publs. com. 1985-86, dir. at large 1987—). Patentee marine, automotive and consumer products. Home and Office: 1111 N Dearborn #606 Chicago IL 60610

PERKINS, WILLIAM H., JR., finance company executive; b. Rushville, Ill., Aug. 4, 1921; s. William H. and Sarah Elizabeth (Logsdon) P.; m. Eileen Nelson, Jan. 14, 1949; 1 child, Gary Douglas. Ed., Ill. Coll. Pres. Howlett-Perkins Assos., Chgo.; mem. Ill. AEC, 1963-84, sec., 1970-84; mem. adv. bd. Nat. Armed Forces Mus., Smithsonian Instn., 1964-82. Sgt.-at-arms Democratic Nat. Conv., 1952, 56, del.-at-large, 1964, 68, 72; spl. asst. to chmn. Dem. Nat. Com., 1960; mem. Presdl. Inaugural Com., 1961, 65, 69, 73. Served with U.S. Army, 1944-46. Mem. Health Ins. Assn. Am., Ill. Ins. Fedn. (pres. 1965-84), Ill. C. of C. (chmn. legis. com. 1971), Chgo. Assn. Commerce and Industry (legis. com.), Internat. Platform Assn. Methodist. Clubs: Sangamo (Springfield, Ill.); Riverside Golf. Lodges: Masons, Shriners. Home: 52 N Cowley Rd Riverside IL 60546 Office: 7222 Cermak Rd Suite 701 North Riverside IL 60546

PERKINSON, DIANA AGNES ZOUZELKA, rug import company executive; b. Prostejov, Czechoslovakia, June 27, 1943; came to U.S., 1962; d. John Charles and Agnes Diana (Sincl) Zouzelka; m. David Francis Perkinson, Mar. 6, 1965; children—Dana Leissa, David. B.A., U. Lausanne (Switzerland), 1960; M.A., U. Madrid, 1961; M.B.A., Case Western Res. U., 1963; cert. internat. mktg. Oxford (Eng.) U., 1962. Assoc. Allen Hartman & Schreiber, Cleve., 1963-64; interpreter Tower Internat. Inc., Cleve., 1964-66; pres. Oriental Rug Importers Ltd., Cleve., 1979—; treas. Oriental Rug Designers, Inc., Cleve., 1980—; sec., treas. Oriental Rug Cons., Inc., Cleve., 1980—; chmn. Foxworthy's Inc. subs. Oriental Rug Importers Ft. Myers, Naples, Sanibel, Fla.; dir. Beckwith & Assocs., Inc., Cleve., Dix-Bur Investments, Ltd. Trustee, Cleve. Ballet, 1979, exec. com., 1981; mem. Cleve. Mayor's Adv. Com.; trustee Diabetes Assn. Greater Cleve.; chmn. grantsmanship Jr. League of Cleve., 1982; mem. mem. Cleve. Found.-Women in Philanthropy, 1982; trustee Diabetes Assn. Greater Cleve. Mem. Women Bus. Owners Assn., Oriental Rug Retailers Am. (dir. 1983). Republican. Roman Catholic. Clubs: Cleve. Racquet, Recreation League (Cleve.). Home: Ravencrest 14681 County Line Rd Cleveland OH 44022 also: Stratford at Pelican Bay Crayton Rd Naples FL 33940 Office: Oriental Rug Importers Ltd Inc 23533 Mercantile Rd Beachwood OH 44122

PERKOVIC, ROBERT BRANKO, international consultant; b. Belgrade, Yugoslavia, Aug. 27, 1925; came to U.S., 1958, naturalized, 1961; s. Slavoljub and Ruza (Pantelic) P.; m. Jacquelyn Lee Lipscomb, Dec. 14, 1957; children: Bonnie Kathryn, Jennifer Lee. M.S. in Econs, U. Belgrade, 1954; B.F.T., Am. Grad. Sch. Internat. Mgmt., 1960; grad. Stanford exec. program, Stanford U., 1970. Auditor Gen. Foods Corp., White Plains, N.Y., 1960-62; controller Gen. Foods Corp., Mexico City, 1962-64; dir. planning Monsanto Co., Barcelona, Spain, 1964-67; dir. fin. Monsanto Co., Europe, Brussels, 1967-70; dir. fin. planning-internat. Monsanto Co., St. Louis, 1970-71; asst. treas. Monsanto Co., 1971-72, Brussels, 1972-74; corp. treas. Fiat-Allis Inc. & BV, Deerfield, Ill., 1974-78; v.p., treas. TRW Inc., Cleve., 1978-88; pres. RBP Internat. Cons., Cleve., 1988—; bd. dirs. Trenwick Group Inc., Westport, Conn.; mem. World Bus. Adv. Council Am. Grad. Sch. Internat. Mgmt., Phoenix. Active Cleve. Commn. on Fgn. Relations. Served with Yugoslavian Army, 1944-47. Mem. Fin. Execs. Inst. Clubs: Cleve. Treas. (bd. dirs., pres.); Park East Racquet (Beachwood, Ohio). Office: RBP Internat Cons 26 Pepper Creek Cleveland OH 44124

PERKS, BARBARA ANN MARCUS, psychologist; b. Wilson, Pa., July 1, 1937; d. Alfred M. and Lillian (Reibman) Marcus; B.S., Pa. State U., 1959; M.A., Columbia U., 1963; cert. in ednl. psychology Oxford (Eng.) U., 1965; postgrad. U. Oreg., U.S. Internat. U.; Ed.D., U. B.C., 1984; m. Anthony Manning Perks, Sept. 9, 1963. Tchr. gifted Hamden (Conn.) Sch. Dist., 1959-62; reading cons. Oxfordshire County, Littlemore, Eng., 1964-65; sch. psychologist Vancouver (B.C., Can.) Sch. Bd., 1972-76; supr. student tchrs. U. B.C., Vancouver, 1977-78, cons. Research Center, 1978-79, ednl. psychologist, child and family unit child psychiatry Health Scis. Centre Hosp., 1979-81, lectr., 1977—; instr. psychology Langara Coll., 1985; pvt. practice counseling and teaching, Vancouver, 1984—, counseling and sch. psychology, Burnaby, B.C., 1985—. Recipient Can. Daus. League award; Provincial Council of B.C. award, 1981, U. B.C. awards, 1980; Jonathan Rogers award, 1984; Univ. fellow, Dr. MacKenzie Am. Alumni scholar U. B.C., 1976; U. B.C. summer scholar, 1982; cert. psychologist, B.C. Mem. Am. Psychol. Assn., B.C. Psychol. Assn., Assn. Humanistic Psychology, Nat. Assn. Sch. Psychology, Am. Ednl. Research, N.Am. Soc. Adlerian Psychology, Am. Orthopsychiat. Assn., Mortar Bd., Pi Sigma Alpha, Pi Lambda Theta, Kappa Delta Pi. Clubs: Figure Skating (Vancouver, B.C., New Haven, Conn., Allentown, Pa.). Author research papers. Home: 4570 Glenwood Ave, North Vancouver, BC Canada V7R 4G5

PERLAKI, IVAN, organizational psychologist, researcher; b. Bratislava, Slovakia, Czechoslovakia, Apr. 3, 1940; s. Andrej and Alzbeta (Wertheimer) P.; m. Jaroslava Ciran, Sept. 12, 1968; children: Ivan, Daniela. MS, Slovak Tech. U., Bratislava, 1962; PhD in Psychology, Czechoslovakia Acad. Scis, Prague, 1976. R and D worker Priemstav, Bratislava, 1963-66; staff worker Office of Slovak Nat. Council for Food Industry, Bratislava, 1966-67; researcher Czechoslovak Research Inst. of Labour and Social Affairs, Bratislava, 1967-77; sr. researcher, dept. head Inst. of Mgmt., Bratislava, 1978; assoc. prof. psychology Slovak Tech. U., Bratislava, 1978—; external lectr. Dept. Psychology Comenius U., Bratislava, 1975-86; mgmt. devel. cons. different insts. and orgns., Czechoslovakia, 1986—. Recipient Silver Medal for Socialist Edn. Socialist Union of Youth, Bratislava, 1982, Gold Medal, 1985, 86. Mem. Sci. and Methodical Council for Edn. and Psychology, Profl. Group for Psychology in Mgmt., Slovak Psychol. Assn. Home: Royova 22, 831 01 Bratislava Czechoslovakia Office: Slovak Tech U, Pionierska 15, 831 02 Bratislava Czechoslovakia

PERLIS, HOWARD WILLIAM, computer consultant; b. Paterson, N.J., June 20, 1941; s. Leo and Betty Francis (Gantz) P.; B.A., Adelphi U., 1969; Ph.D., U. Ala., 1978; m. Loretta J. Stodel, Dec. 26, 1965; children—Jonathan Andrew, Melissa Amy. Research asst. Albert Einstein Coll. Medicine, N.Y.C., 1965-67; project engr. MIRU, U. Ala. Med. Center, Birmingham, 1967-70, mgr. obstetrics computer center, 1970-79, asst. prof. biophysics dept. ob-gyn, 1979-84; office automation cons., 1984—; pres. Compu-Train, Inc. (tng. and custom software), Pelham, Ala., 1984—; instr. Sch. Bus., U. Ala., Birmingham, 1979-86. Recipient cert. of Merit, Central Assn. Obstetricians and Gynecologists. Mem. So. Repub. Exchange. Home and Office: 2621 Chandalar Ln Pelham AL 35124

PERLMAN, ITZHAK, violinist; b. Tel Aviv, Aug. 31, 1945; s. Chaim and Shoshana P.; m. Toby Lynn Friedlander, 1967; 5 children. Student, Tel Aviv Acad. Music, Juilliard Sch., Meadowmount Sch. Music. Appeared with, N.Y. Philharm., Cleve. Orch., Phila. Orch., Nat. Symphony Orch., most orchs. in, U.S., with, Berlin Philharm., English Chamber Orch., London Symphony, London Philharm., Royal Philharm., BBC Orch., Vienna Philharm, Concertgebouw; participant numerous music festivals, including, Ravinia Festival, Berkshire Music Festival, Aspen Music Festival, Israel Festival, Wolf Trap Summer Festival, recital tours, U.S., Can., S.Am., Europe, Israel, Australia, Far East; recorded for, Angel, London, RCA Victor, DG, CBS records. (Recipient Leventritt prize 1964). Recipient

Grammy awards, 1977, 78, 80-82, 87. Address: care IMG Artists 22 E 71st St New York NY 10021 *

PERLMAN, LAWRENCE, business executive, lawyer; b. St. Paul, Apr. 8, 1938; s. Irving and Ruth (Mirsky) P.; m. Medora Scoll, June 18, 1961; children: David, Sara. B.A., Carleton Coll., 1960; J.D., Harvard U., 1963. Bar: Minn. 1963. Law. clk. for fed. judge 1963; partner firm Fredrikson, Byron, Colborn, Bisbee, Hansen & Perlman, Mpls., 1964-75; gen. counsel, exec. v.p. U.S. pacing ops. Medtronic, Inc., Mpls., 1975-78; sr. partner firm Oppenheimer, Wolff and Donnelly, Mpls., 1978-80; sec., gen. counsel, v.p. corp. services Control Data Corp., Mpls., 1980-83; pres., chief operating officer, dir. Comml. Credit Co., 1984-85; pres. Data Storage Products Group, 1985—, exec. v.p., 1986—; bd. dirs. Am. Hoist & Derrick Co., Control Data Corp., Bio-Medicus Corp., Inter-Regional Fin. Group, Inc., The Computer Network and Tech. Corp.; adj. prof. Law Sch., U. Minn., 1974-76, 79-80. Chmn. Mpls. Municipal Fin. Commn., 1978-79; bd. dirs. Walker Art Center, Minn. Orchestral Assn.; trustee Carleton Coll; chmn. bd. visitors U. Minn. Law Sch., 1978-80. Mem. Phi Beta Kappa. Club: Mpls. Home: 2366 W Lake of the Isles Pkwy Minneapolis MN 55405 Office: Control Data Corp 8100 34th Ave S Minneapolis MN 55420

PERLMUTTER, JACK, artist, lithographer; b. N.Y.C., Jan. 23, 1920; s. Morris and Rebecca (Schiffman) P.; m. Norma Mazo, Dec. 24, 1942; children: Judith Faye, Ellen. Staff Dickey Gallery, D.C. Tchrs. Coll., 1951-68, dir., 1962-68, now prof. art; chmn. printmaking dept. Corcoran Gallery Sch. Art, 1960-82, now prof. art; Fulbright research prof. painting and printmaking Tokyo U. Arts, 1959-60; art cons. Pres.'s Com. to Hire Handicapped. Artist-in-residence, Gibbs Art Gallery, Charleston, S.C., 1974—, NASA artist for, 1st Saturn V moon rocket, Apollo 6, Apollo 16, Orbiter Columbia (space shuttle), Voyager II; Contbg. editor: Art Voices South, 1979-80, Art Voices, 1980-82; numerous one-man shows, U.S. and Tokyo, including, Nat. Acad. Scis., 1981, Arts Club Washington, 1981, Annapolis, Md., 1982; exhibited nat. shows, U.S., Switzerland, Yugoslavia, traveling exhibits, Europe, S.Am., Can., works in. permanent collections, Bklyn. Mus., Cin. Mus. Art, Carnegie Inst. Art, Corcoran Gallery Art, Library Congress, Met. Mus. Art, N.Y.C., Nat. Gallery Art, Washington, Phila. Mus. Art, Walker Gallery, Mpls., Nat. Mus. Modern Art, Tokyo, others. Fellow Internat. Inst. Arts and Letters; mem. Soc. Am. Graphic Artists. Club: Cosmos (Washington). Studio: 2511 Cliffbourne Pl NW Washington DC 20009

PERLMUTTER, JEROME HERBERT, communications specialist; b. N.Y.C., Oct. 17, 1924; s. Morris and Rebecca (Shiffman) P.; m. Evelyn Lea Friedman, Sept. 19, 1948; children: Diane Muriel, Sandra Pauline, Bruce Steven. A.B. cum laude, George Washington U., 1949; M.A., Am. U., 1957. Chief editor service, prodn. editor N.E.A., Washington, 1949-50; editor in chief Jour. AAHPER, Washington, 1950-51; editor Rural Elec. News, REA, USDA, Washington, 1951-53; publ. writer Agrl. Research Service, 1953-56; chief, editor br. Office Info., 1956-60; sec. Outlook and Situation Bd.; chief econ. reports Econ. Research Service, 1960-62; chief div. pub. and reprodn. services U.S. Dept. State, Washington, 1962-79; pres. Perlmutter Assocs., 1979—; writing cons. CSC, 1956, World Bank, 1967—; communication cons. European Investment Bank, Canadian., Inter-Am. Devel. Bank, Internat. Monetary Fund; faculty U. Md. Agr. Grad. Sch., also Fgn. Service Inst.; pub. cons. White House Conf. on Children and Youth, 1971. Author: A Practical Guide to Effective Writing, 1965; Contbr. articles profl. jours. Coordinator fed. graphics Nat. Endowment for Arts, 1972-79, graphic designer, conv. of maj. polit. party, 1980. Served with USNR, 1943-46. Recipient award U.S. Jr. C. of C., 1963. Mem. Am. Assn. Agr. Coll. Editors, Assn. Editorial Bus. (dir.), Fed. Editors Assn., Am. Farm Econ. Assn., Soc. Tech. Communication (dir.), Phi Beta Kappa, Sigma Delta Chi, Phi Eta Sigma, Artus. Home: 513 E Indian Spring Dr Silver Spring MD 20901

PERLOFF, ROBERT, psychologist, educator; b. Phila., Feb. 3, 1921; s. Myer and Elizabeth (Sherman) P.; m. Evelyn Potechin, Sept. 22, 1946; children: Richard Mark, Linda Sue, Judith Kay. A.B., Temple U., 1949; M.A., Ohio State U., 1949, Ph.D., 1951; D.Sc. (hon.), Oreg. Grad. Sch. Profl. Psychology, 1984; D.Litt. (hon.), Calif. Sch. Profl. Psychology, 1985. Diplomate: Am. Bd. Profl. Psychology. Instr. edn. Antioch Coll., 1950-51; with personnel research br. Dept. Army, 1951-55, chief statis. research and cons. unit., 1953-55; dir. research and devel. Sci. Research Assos., Inc., Chgo., 1955-59; vis. lectr. Chgo. Tchrs. Coll., 1953-56; mem. faculty Purdue U., 1959-69, prof. psychology, 1964-69; field assessment officer univ. Peace Corps Chile III project, 1962; prof. bus. adminstrn. and psychology U. Pitts. Joseph M. Katz Grad. Sch. Bus., 1969—; dir. research programs U. Pitts. Grad. Sch. Bus., 1969-77; dir. Consumer Panel, 1980-83; bd. dirs. Book Center.; cons. in field, 1959—; adv. com. assessment exptl. manpower research and devel. labs. Nat. Acad. Scis., 1972-74; mem. research rev. com. NIMH, 1976-80, Stress and Families research project, 1976-79. Contbr. articles to profl. jours., Editor: Indsl. Psychologist, 1963-65, Evaluator Intervention: Pros and Cons; book rev. editor: Personnel Psychology, 1952-55; co-editor: Values, Ethics and Standards sourebook, 1979, Improving Evaluations; bd. cons. editors: Jour. Applied Psychology; bd. advs.: Archives History Am. Psychology, Psychol. Service Pitts., Recorded Psychol. Jours.; guest editor: Am. Psychologist, May 1972, Education and Urban Society, 1977, Profl. Psychology, 1977. Bd. dirs., v.p. Sr. Citizens Service Corp., Calif. Sch. Profl. Psychology, 1985—; chmn. nat. adv. com. Inst. Govt. and Pub. Affairs, U. Ill., 1986—. Served with U.S. Army, World War II, PTO. Decorated Bronze Star. Fellow AAAS, Am. Psychol. Assn. (mem.-at-large exec. com. div. consumer psychology 1964-67, 70—, pres. div. 1967-68, mem. council reps. 1965-68, 72-74, chmn. sci. affairs com., div. consumer psychology 1968—, edn. and tng. bd. 1969-72, chmn. finance com., treas., dir. 1974-82, chmn. investment com. 1977-82, pres., 1985, author column Standard Deviations in jour.), Eastern Psychol. Assn. (pres. 1980-81, dir. 1977-80); mem. Internat. Assn. Applied Psychology, Pa. Psychol. Assn. (Disting. Service award 1985), Assn. for Consumer Research (chmn. 1970-71), Am. Psychol. Found. (v.p. 1988), Am. Evaluation Assn. (pres. 1977-78), Sigma Xi, Beta Gamma Sigma, Psi Chi. Home: 815 Saint James St Pittsburgh PA 15232

PERNA, ALBERT FREDRIC, podiatrist, educator; b. Concord, Mass., Dec. 30, 1915; s. Joseph and Rachel (Mangone) P.; D.Podiatric Medicine, Temple U., 1946; Ed.M., Framingham State U., 1965; m. Elizabeth Annie Dugas, Apr. 18, 1942; children—Susan Elizabeth, John Joseph. Gen. practice podiatry, Waltham, Mass., 1946—; staff podiatrist Waltham Hosp., 1946-88; prof. anatomy and physiology, also philosophy Bay State Jr. Coll., 1966-77; prof. philosophy Fitchburg (Mass.) State Coll., 1968-77. First aid instr. ARC, Waltham, 1959-75; mem. Waltham Sch. Bd., 22 yrs., vice chmn., 1957, 58, 75, 82, 84, 87; past bd. dirs. Waltham Boys Club; past chmn. YMCA, Cancer Fund, Heart Fund, Cerebral Palsy Fund; parade marshal Waltham Bicentennial, 1976. Served with AUS, 1941-42, as combat glider pilot USAAF, 1942-45, Mass. Air N.G., 1945-66; Korea; lt. col. Res. ret. Awarded D.S.C. (U.S.); 13 U.S. medals; Orange Lanyard and Erasmus medal (Netherlands); recipient City Keys, Mobile, Ala. Mem. Am. Philos. Assn., Acad. Podiatry (pres. 1967-69), Soaring Soc. Am., Mass. N.G. Alumni Assn., Nat. World War II Glider Pilot Assn., Am. Legion, VFW, Mil. Order World Wars, Air Force Assn., Res. Officers Assn. Roman Catholic. Club: Waltham Rotary (pres. 1957-58). Author: The Glider Gladiators, 1970; Glider Warfare Diary, 1978; editor The Glider Rag, summer 1942; Glider Gazette, fall 1942; footnote editor Mass. Chiropody Soc. jours., 1947-51. Home: 26 Lincoln Terr Waltham MA 02154

PERNOT-MASSON, ANNE-CATHERINE, psychiatrist; b. Paris, May 29, 1955; d. Jean-Marc and Catherine (Raichlen) Pernot; m. Henry Masson, June 21, 1985. MD, U. Paris, 1980. Research fellow UCLA, 1979, Harvard Med. Sch., Boston, 1979-80; resident in child psychiatry Paris, 1980-84, practice medicine specializing in child psychiatry, 1984—; cons. pediatric dept., Paris, 1985—; dr. on mountaineering expeditions Nepal, 1981, Pakistan, 1984. Contbr. articles to profl. jours. Recipient Silver Medal of Theses Paris U., 1980. Fellow French Soc. Children and Adolescent Psychiatry. Calvinist. Office: 30 rue de Liege, 75008 Paris France

PEROTTI, ROSE NORMA, lawyer; b. St. Louis, Aug. 10, 1930; d. Joseph and Dorothy Mary (Roleski) Perotti. B.A., Fontbonne Coll., St. Louis, 1952; J.D., St. Louis U., 1957. Bar: Mo. 1958. Trademark atty. Sutherland, Polster & Taylor, St. Louis, 1958-63, Sutherland Law Office, 1964-70; trademark atty. Monsanto Co., St. Louis, 1971-85, sr. trademark atty., 1985—. Honored with dedication of faculty office in her name, St. Louis U. Sch. Law, 1980. Mem. Mo. Bar Assn., Bar Assn. Met. St. Louis, ABA, Am. Judicature Soc., Smithsonian Assocs., Friends St. Louis Art Museum, Mo. Bot. Garden. Office: Monsanto Co 800 N Lindbergh Blvd Saint Louis MO 63167

PERPICH, RUDY GEORGE, governor Minnesota; b. Carson Lake, Minn., June 27, 1928; s. Anton and Mary (Vukelich) P.; m. Delores Helen Simic, Sept. 4, 1954; children: Ruby George, Mary Susan. A.A., Hibbing Jr. Coll., 1950; D.D.S., Marquette U., 1954. Lt. gov. State of Minn., 1971-76, gov., 1977-79, 83—; v.p., exec. cons. Control Data Worldtech, Inc., Mpls., 1979-82. Mem. Hibbing Bd. Edn., Minn., 1956-62; mem. Minn. Senate, 1962-70. Served to sgt. AUS, 1946-47. Mem. Nat. Govs. Assn. Democrat. Roman Catholic. Office: Office of Gov 130 State Capitol Aurora Ave Saint Paul MN 55155 *

PERRETEN, FRANK ARNOLD, eye surgeon; b. Boulder, Colo., Jan. 13, 1927; s. Arnold Ervin and Keene (Nichols) P.; B.A., U. Colo., 1948; M.D., U. Pa., 1952; m. Marilyn Ann Peterson, June 26, 1953; 1 son, Michael Peterson. Intern, St. Lukes Hosp., Denver, 1952, Denver Gen. Hosp., 1953; resident postgrad. Mass. Eye and Ear Infirmary of Harvard, 1957; practice medicine, specializing in ophthalmology, Winston-Salem, N.C., 1957-60, Denver, 1960—; mem. staff Children's, St. Joseph's, St. Luke's, Mercy, Presbyn., Luth. hosps.; cons. Brighton (Colo.) Community Hosp.; assoc. prof. U. Colo., 1961—; dir. N.C. Eye Bank, 1957-60. Bd. dirs. Collegiate Sch. of Denver, Goodwill Industries. Served with USNR, 1944-46. Diplomate Am. Bd. Ophthalmology. Fellow Am. Acad. Ophthalmology and Otolaryngology; mem. AMA, N.C., S.C. eye, ear, nose and throat socs., Colo. Ophthalmology Soc., Colo., Denver County med. socs., Colo. Soc. to Prevent Blindness (bd. dirs.), N.Y. Acad. Sci., Newcomen Soc., U. Colo. Alumni (bd. dirs.), Delta Tau Delta Alumni (pres.). Clubs: Denver, Cherry Hills Country (Denver). Lodge: Lions (bd. dirs.). Contbr. Pediatric Ophthalmology. Home: 60 S Birch St Denver CO 80222 Office: 1801 High St Denver CO 80218

PERRETTE, JEAN RENE, banker; b. Dinan, France, May 24, 1931; s. Rene Jean and Marie Cecile (Ollivier) P.; came to U.S., 1961; HEC Bus. Sch. Paris, 1953; LL.D., U. Paris, 1955; Ph.D. in Econs., 1959; m. Virginia Moore Schott, Sept. 8, 1962; children—Virginie-Alvine, Clarisse, Jean-Briac, Julien-Yannick. Asst. to gen. mgmt. Worms CMC, Paris, 1959-61, U.S. rep. N.Y.C., 1961-65; U.S. rep. Banque Worms, N.Y.C., 1965-86 ; pres. Worms & Co. Inc. and Permal Mgmt. Services, Inc., U.S. reps. Messrs. Worms & Cie., Paris, other European cos., N.Y.C., 1965-86, Services, Inc.; dir. several cos.; cons. French pub. group, 1967-71. Served with French Navy, 1956-59. Mem. HEC Bus. Sch. U.S. Alumni Assn. (pres. 1975-76), French C. of C. in U.S. (exec. com. 1975-82). Club: Union (N.Y.C.). Home: 14 E 90th St New York NY 10128 Office: 900 3d Ave New York NY 10022

PERRIG, WALTER JOSEF, psychologist, researcher; b. Ried Brig, Switzerland, Jan. 24, 1951; s. Julius and Pauline (Meyenberg) P.; Pasqualina Maria Chiello; children: Wolfgang, Roman. Lic., U. Fribourg, Switzerland, 1976; PhD, U. Fribourg, 1980; Habilitation, U. Basel, Switzerland, 1986. Sci. asst. U. Fribourg, Switzerland, 1976-79, U. Basel, Switzerland, 1979-82; prof. psychology U. Basel, 1987—; vis. fellow U. Colo., Boulder, 1982-84, Brown U., Providence, R.I., 1984, U. Saarlandes, 1985-86. Author: Wissensstrukturen und Informationsaufnahme, 1982, Vorstellungen und Gedächtnis, 1988. Grantee Swiss Nat. Sci. Found., 1980, 86, fellow, 1982. Mem. Swiss Psychol. Assn. (mem. exec. bd. 1987—), Swiss Assn. Behavioral Therapy (exec. bd. 1979-81). Home: Löwenbergstr 30, 4059 Basel Switzerland Office: Univ Basel, Dept Psychology, Bernoullistr 14, 4056 Basel Switzerland

PERRIN, BILL, diplomat; b. Feb. 18, 1938; married; 1 child. Grad., Okla. State U. Produce clk. Safeway Foods, 1958-59; co-owner Perrin Real Estate in Covington, 1959-60; co-mgr. Humpty Dumpty Supermarkey, 1963-66; sales rep. Kraft Foods, 1963-66; co-owner Perrin Internat. Corp., Brownsvillw, Tex., 1966-69; with sales dept. Lever Bros., 1971-72; co-owner FGC Corp., Bronsville, 1972-74, Dollar Rent-a-Car RGV, Bronsville, 1977-81; dir. in Belize 1983-84, dir. for the Ea. Carribean, 1984-85; regional dir. for Africa Peace Corps, 1985-77; U.S. ambassador to Cyprus 1988—. Office: Dept of State US Ambassador to Cyprus Washington DC 20520 *

PERRIN, ELLEN HAYS, retired university dean; b. Buckhannon, W.Va.; d. Charles Gilbert and Geraldine Sexton (Hays) P.; B.S. in Music Edn., Duquesne U., 1946; M.Edn., U. Pitts., 1952, Ph.D., 1974. Tchr. music West Mifflin (Pa.) Dist. Schs., 1947-61, counselor, 1961-64; dean women Slippery Rock (Pa.) U., 1965-70, asst. to v.p. for student affairs, 1970-72, dir. counseling and career services, 1972-74, assoc. prof. counseling and ednl. psychology, 1980-85, dean students, 1974-85; mem. supts. adv. com. West Mifflin Dist. Schs., 1955-60. Mem. steering com. Pitts. Fgn. Affairs Forum, 1959-60; mem. com. on edn. Pa. Gov.'s Commn. on Status of Women, 1965-66; mem. Pitts. Bicentennial Assembly, 1958-59. Mem. NEA, Pa. Edn. Assn. (pres. West Mifflin br. 1962-64, exec. com. west region 1963-64, v.p. assn. ind. sch. dists. Allegheny County 1963-64), AAUW (pres. Pitts. br. 1958-62, Pa. div. chmn. status of women 1962-63, chmn. cultural interests 1963-64, area rep. for edn. 1964-66, chmn. edn. projects for state div., chmn. topic of study 1967-69, fellowship award named in her honor 1970), Nat. (parliamentarian 1975-76, 77-78, nat. treas. 1981-83), Pa. (parliamentarian 1969-72, 2d v.p. 1972-74, legis. chmn. 1976-78, pres. 1979-81), Western Pa. (sec. 1970-71) assns. women deans, adminstrs. and counselors, DAR (conservation chmn. local chpt. 1959-62, chpt. chaplain 1963-65), Nat. Soc. U.S. Daus. of 1812 (state registrar 1987—), Nat. soc. Dames of Ct. of Honor (organizing state pres. 1985—), Hereditary Order of First families of Mass. (charter mem. 1985), Nat. Soc. Daus. Colonial Wars (state registrar 1985—), Daus. Am. Colonists, Nat. Soc. Women Descs. of Ancient and Hon. Arty. Co., (state pres. 1985—), Colonial Dames XVII Century (bylaws chmn. local chpt. 1978-80, parliamentarian chpt. 1980-82, state corr. sec. 1981-83, 1st v.p. chpt. 1983-85, chpt. pres. 1985-87, state pres. 1985-87, nat. parliamentarian gen. 1985—), Descendant Most Noble Order of Knights of the Garter, Colonial Order of the Crown, Magna Charta Dames, United Daus. of the Confed., Nat. Soc. Descendants of Early Quakers, Descendants of Founders of Hartford, Nat. Soc. New Eng. Women (parlimentarian gen. 1987—), Nat., Pa. (membership chmn. 1972) assns. student personnel adminstrs., Doctoral Assn. U. Pitts., Phi Delta Kappa. Presbyterian. Clubs: South Hills Coll. (Pitts.); Pitts. Coll.; Woman's Club Mt. Lebanon; Zonta Internat. (organizing pres. Slippery Rock-New Wilmington-Grove City area 1980-81, parliamentarian dist. IV 1974-76); Order Eastern Star (Grove City, Pa.). Home and Office: 140 Longue Vue Dr Mt Lebanon Pittsburgh PA 15228

PERRIN, SARAH ANN, lawyer; b. Neoga, Ill., Dec. 13, 1904; d. James Lee and Bertha Frances (Baker) Figenbaum; LL.B., George Washington U., 1941, J.D., 1964; m. James Frank Perrin, Dec. 24, 1926. Bar: D.C. 1942. Assoc. atty. Mabel Walker Willebrandt, law office, Washington, 1941-42; atty. various fed. housing agys., 1942-69, asst. gen. counsel FHA, Washington, 1959-60, asst. gen. counsel HUD, Washington, 1960-69; sec. Nat. Housing Conf., Washington, 1970-80; research cons. housing and urban devel., Palmyra, Va., 1970-76 ; acting sec. Nat. Housing Research Council, Washington, 1973-80; bd. dirs. Nat. Housing Conf., 1972—. Trustee Found. for Coop. Housing, 1975-80 ; mem. Blue Ridge Presbytery Div. Mission, Presbyterian Ch., 1979-80. Mem. Am. Bar Assn., Fed. Bar Assn., Women's Bar Assn. D.C. (pres. 1959-60), Nat. Assn. Women Lawyers, George Washington Law Assn., Charlottesville Area Women's Bar Assn., Fluvanna County Bar Assn., Phi Alpha Delta (internat. pres. 1955-57), Fluvanna County Hist. Soc. (pres. 1973-75, exec. com. 1985—). Lodge: Order Eastern Star. Home: Solitude Plantation Palmyra VA 22963

PERRONE, VINCENZO, banker; b. Naples, Italy, July 24, 1927; s. Antonio and Maria Anna (Navarra) P.; m. Dora Castrignano, Sept. 3, 1955; children—Anna, Fiorella. Dr.Law, Naples U., 1950. Clk., Banca D'America E D'Italia, Naples, 1944, central mgr., 1965-76; gen. mgr. and chief exec. officer Credito Artigiano Spa, Milan, 1977—; chmn. exec. com. Italfortune, 1977—; dir. Instituto Centrale B.B., 1977—, GEFIN, 1977-86, C.B.I.-Factor, 1979—. Contbr. articles to profl. jours. Decorated grand officer Ordine al Merito Della Repubblica Italiana, Labour Star. Mem. Jr. Chamber (nat. pres. 1962-63). Partito Liberale Italiano. Roman Catholic. Club: Rotary. Home: via Tortona 68, Milan Italy Office: Credito Artigiano SpA, Piazza San Fedele 4, 20121 Milan Italy

PERRY, CHRISTOPHER RICHARD, chemical engineer; b. Southsea, Hampshire, Eng., Jan. 13, 1932; s. Claude Bernard and Evelyn Lily (Casewell) P.; m. Bernadette Marie McCartan, Apr. 20, 1960; children: Gabrielle, Bernard, Damian, Bronagh. BS with honors, U. Birmingham, Eng., 1954. Chartered chem. engr. Plant supr. Monsanto Chems. Ltd., Newport, Eng., 1956-60, project supt., 1964-65; sr. chem. engr. Monsanto Chem. Co., St. Louis, 1960-62, Monsanto Chems. Ltd., Fawley, Eng., 1963-64; project mgr. Monsanto Internat. Engring. Co., London, 1965-70; mgr. distbn. Monsanto Europe SA, Brussels, 1970-72, mgr. materials supply planning, 1972-84, mgr. product acceptability, 1984—; user project mgr. European Computerized Inventory System, 1983, Translation of Safety Data Sheets By Computer, 1985. Served to lt. comdr. Royal Naval Res., 1954-70. Fellow Instn. Chem. Engrs. U.K. (treas. European br. 1972-86). Clubs: Commodore, Balt. Sailing (Ireland); Brussels Badminton. Home: Rue Vallee Bailly 61, 1420 Braine L'alleud Belgium Office: Monsanto Europe SA, Ave Tervuren 270, 1150 Brussels Belgium

PERRY, CYNTHIA SHEPARD, diplomat; b. Terre Haute, Ind., Nov. 11, 1928; d. George William and Flossie (Phillips) N.; m. James O. Shepard, Nov. 2, 1946 (div. June 1970); children: Donna Ross, James O. Jr., Milo Kent, Mark; m. James O. Perry Sr., Mar. 20, 1971; children: Paula Lucille, James O. Jr. BS in Polit. Sci., Ind. State U., 1967, DCL (hon.), 1987; EdD, U. Mass., 1972; LLD (hon.), U. Md., 1984. Sec. Nichols Investment Corp., Terre Haute, 1956-61; ednl. rep. Ohio region IBM Corp., Terre Haute, 1962-68; dir. tchrs. corps U. Mass., Amherst, 1968-71; assoc. prof. edn. Tex. So. U., Houston, 1971-74, dean internat. student affairs, 1978-82; cons., lectr., U. Nairobi U.S. Peace Corps, Kenya, 1974-76; staff devel. officer UN Econ. Com. for Africa, Addis Ababa, Ethiopia, 1976-78; chief edn. and human resources div. Agy. for Internat. Devel., Washington, 1982-86; U.S. ambassador to Sierra Leone, Freetown, 1986—. Contbr. articles to profl. jours. Recipient Disting. Alumni award U. Mass., 1981, Ind. State U., 1987. Mem. Nat. Bus. and Profl. Women, Internat. Council for Ednl. Devel. (bd. dirs. 1984—), Altrusan Soc. (bd. dirs. 1981-82), Delta Sigma Theta (pres. 1982-83). Republican. Office: Am Embassy/Freetown Dept of State 2201 C St NW Washington DC 20520

PERRY, DALE LYNN, chemist; b. Greenville, Tex., May 12, 1947; s. Francis Leon and Violet (Inabinette) P. BS, Midwestern U., 1969; MS, Lamar U., 1972; PhD, U. Houston, 1974. NSF fellow dept. chemistry Rice U., Houston, 1976-77; Miller Research fellow dept. chemistry U. Calif.-Berkeley, 1977-79; prin. investigator inorganic and surface chemistry Lawrence Berkeley Lab. U. Calif., 1979—, sr. scientist, 1987—. Contbr. articles to profl. jours. Recipient Sigma Xi Nat. Research award U. Houston, 1974. Mem. Am. Chem. Soc., Soc. Applied Spectroscopy, Coblentz Soc., Materials Research Soc. Sigma Xi. Office: Lawrence Berkeley Lab U Calif Mail Stop 70A-1115 Berkeley CA 94720

PERRY, EVELYN REIS, sound communications company executive, consultant; b. N.Y.C., Mar. 9; d. Lou L. and Bertl (Wolf) Reis; m. Charles G. Perry III, Jan. 7, 1968; children—Charles G. IV, David Reis. B.A., Univ. Wis., 1963; student Am. Acad. Dramatic Arts, 1958-59, Univ. N.Mex., 1963-64. Lic. real estate broker, N.C. Vol. ETV project Peace Corps, 1963-65; program officer-radio/tv Peace Corps, Washington, 1965-68; dir. Vols. in Service to Am. (VISTA), Raleigh, N.C., 1977-80; exec. dir. CETA Program for Displaced Homemakers, Raleigh, 1980-81; cons. exec. dir. to Recycle Raleigh for Food and Fuel, Theater in the Park, 1981-83, Artspace, Inc., Raleigh, 1983-84; pres., gen. mgr. Carolina Sound Communications, MUZAK, Charleston, S.C., 1984—; pub. relations account exec. various cos., Washington, Syracuse, N.Y., 1969-71; cons. pub. relations and orgn. Olympic Organizing Com., Mexico City, 1968; cons. pub. relations, fundraising, arts mgmt. pub. speaking, Ill., Pa., N.C., 1971-77; organizational and pub. speaking cons. Perry & Assocs., Raleigh, 1980—. Mem. adv. bd. Gov.'s Office Citizen Affairs, Raleigh, 1981-85; mem. Involvement Council of Wake County, N.C., Raleigh, 1981-84; mem. Adv. Council to Vols. in Service to Am., Raleigh, 1980-84; mem. Pres.'s adv. bd. Peace Corps, Washington, 1980-82; v.p., bd. dirs. Voluntary Action Center, Raleigh, 1980-84, bd. dirs., Charleston, 1988—; sec. bd. dirs. Temple Kahil Kadosh Beth Elohim, 1987—. Mem. N.C. Council of Women's Orgns. (pres., v.p. 1982-84), Charleston Hotel and Motel Assn., N.C. Assn. Vol. Adminstrs. (bd. dirs. 1980-84), Internat. Planned Music Assn. (bd. dirs. 1986—, newsletter editor), Nat. Assn. Female Execs., Nat. Fedn. Ind. Businesses (mem. adv. bd. 1987—), Internat. Platform Assn., Charleston Assn. Female Execs. Office: Carolina Sound Communications Inc 1023 Wappoo Rd Suite B-27 Charleston SC 29407

PERRY, GEORGE WILLIAMSON, lawyer; b. Cleve., Dec. 4, 1926; s. George William and Melda Patricia (Arther-Holt) P. B.A. in Econs., Yale U., 1949; J.D., U. Va., 1953. Bar: Ohio 1953, D.C. 1958, U.S. Supreme Ct. 1958, U.S. Ct. Appeals (D.C. cir.) 1959. Atty. U.S. Dept. Justice, Washington, 1954-56; atty. assoc. counsel Com. on Interstate Fgn. Commerce, U.S. Ho. of Reps., Washington, 1960-65; atty., advisor ICC, Washington, 1965-68; assoc. dir. devel. Yale U., New Haven, 1968-70; dir. tax research Pan Am. World Airways, N.Y.C., 1973-75; hearing officer Indsl. Commn. Ohio, Cleve., 1978-81; sole practice, Cleve., 1981—. Served with U.S. Army, 1945-46. Mem. D.C. Bar Assn., Soc. of Cincinnati in State of Conn., Phi Delta Phi. Episcopalian. Office: 1801 E 12th St Cleveland OH 44114

PERRY, HAROLD TYNER, dentist, educator; b. Bismarck, N.D., Jan. 26, 1926; s. Harold Tyner and Isabel (McGillis) P.; m. Mary Lynn Moss, 1952; children: Harold Tyner III, Dana Lynn. Student, Bismarck Jr. Coll., 1946-47, U. N.D., 1948; DDS, Northwestern U., 1952, PhD in Physiology, 1961. USPHS research fellow 1952-56; practice dentistry Elgin, Ill., 1956—; faculty Northwestern U. Dental Sch., 1954—, prof., chmn. dept. orthodontics, 1961—; research asso. Mooseheart (Ill.) Hosp.; guest lectr. U. Nebr.; dental cons. Middle East sect. WHO.; Dir. Union Nat. Bank & Trust Co., Elgin; cons. VA.; specialist cons. N.E. Regional Dental Bds. (NERB), 1987—. Editorial chmn. Jour. Craniomandibular Disorders, Facial/Oral Pain, 1986—. Bd. dirs. Fox Valley council Boy Scouts Am., Elgin YMCA, Found. Ill. Archeology, 1980—, Max McGraw Wildlife Found., 1979—, CAA; bd. govs. United Community Fund, Elgin. Served with inf. AUS, 1944-46, ETO. Decorated Bronze Star medal, Combat Inf. badge, Croix de Guerre; named Young Man of Year Elgin Jr. C. of C., 1961; recipient Award of Merit Northwestern U., 1974. Fellow Internat., Am. Colls. Dentists, Inst. Medicine Chgo.; mem. ADA, Am. Assn. Orthodonists, AAAS, Soc. Paulista de Orthodontia (hon.), South African Soc. Orthodontists (hon.), Sigma Xi, Alpha Tau Omega, Delta Sigma Delta, Omicron Kappa Upsilon. Methodist. Home: 413 N Alfred St Elgin IL 60120 Office: 100 E Chicago St Elgin IL 60120

PERRY, JESSE LAURENCE, JR., investment manager, financier; b. Nashville, Oct. 15, 1919; s. Jesse Laurence and Mamie Lucretia (White) P.; m. Susan Taylor White, Nov. 5, 1949 (dec. Mar. 1972); children—Robert Laurence, Judith Foulds; m. 2d Sarah Kinkead Stockell, Apr. 6, 1974. B.A. magna cum laude, Vanderbilt U., 1941; M.B.A., Harvard U., 1943; postgrad. in edn. retarded children George Peabody Coll., summer 1953. Treas., J.L. Perry Co., Nashville, 1947-48; v.p., 1949-54, pres., 1954-73, also dir.; pres., chmn. bd. Perry Enterprises, Nashville, 1973-80, Naples, 1980. 1st So. Savs. & Loan, Inc., 1973-80; pres. PortersField, Inc., Nashville, 1973-80, The Jelpee Co., Naples, Fla. Pres., Police Assistance League, 1973-74; hon. col., Staff Gov. Tenn., 1962-74; 1st v.p. Tenn. Assn. for Retarded Children, 1954-62; mem. Tenn. Mental Retardation Adv. Council, 1966-72; bd. advisers Salvation Army, 1958-72; founder, sec. Tenn. Bot. Garden and Fine Arts Ctr., 1958—; chmn. 5th dist. Republican Exec. Com., 1950-54; vice chmn. Tenn. Rep. Exec. Com., 1950-54; Middle Tenn. Campaign mgr., 1956, 60, 66; state mgr. Pub. Service Com. Campaign, 1964; mem. spl. com. on urban devel. Rep. Nat. Exec. Com., 1962; del. Rep. Nat. Exec. Com., 1960, vice chmn. Tenn. del., 1960, alt. del., 1968; dist. mem. Rep. State Exec. Com., 1954-75; state chmn. Rep. Capitol Club, 1971-73; state Rep. committeeman, 1956-74; bd. govs. U. South, Sewanee Acad., 1968-74. Served to capt. AUS, 1943-46. Decorated knight Hospitaller Order St. John Jerusalem, chevalier Ordo Constantini Magni knight (comdr.) Order Temple of Jerusalem. Mem.

Episc. Churchmen Tenn. (v.p. 1956), Am. Ch. Union (v.p. 1958), SAR (chpt. pres. 1977-79), U.S. C. of C., Nat. Office Mgmt. Assn. (pres. Nashville chpt. 1958-59), Am. Legion, English Speaking Union, Magna Charta Barons, Baronial Order Magna Charta, Gen. Soc. Colonial Wars, Ams. of Royal Descent, Plantagenet Soc., Order Crown Charlemagne, Phi Beta Kappa, Omicron Delta Gamma, Pi Kappa Alpha. Clubs: Nashville Exchange, Nashville Sewanee, Nashville City, Capitol Hill (Washington), Naples Harvard, Royal Poinciana Golf (Naples). Home: Colonial Club 1275 Gulf Shore Blvd N Naples FL 33940 Office: PO Box 915 Naples FL 33939

PERRY, KENNETH WALTER, integrated oil company executive; b. Shamrock, Tex., Feb. 24, 1932; s. Charles Bowman and Sunshine Virginia (Grady) P.; m. Mary Dean Sudderth, Aug. 28, 1953; children: Mary Martha Perry Mitchell, Kathryn Virginia Perry Foster. BS in Mech. Engring., U. Okla., 1954. Sales engr. Mid-Continent Oil Well Supply Co., 1954-55; with Cosden Oil & Chem. Co., Big Spring, Tex., from 1957, jr. engr., 1957-59, project engr., 1959-60, chem. salesman, 1960-64, chem. products mgr., 1964-65, mktg. mgr., then v.p. mktg., 1965-69, v.p. chems., 1969-72, sr. v.p., 1972-76, pres., from 1976; group v.p. Am. Petrofina, Inc. (now Fina Oil and Chem. Co.), Dallas, 1976-85, sr. v.p., from 1985, now pres., chief exec. officer, dir.; bd. dirs. Fina Oil and Chem. Co., Dallas, 1984—; vice chmn. bd. dirs. United Commerce Bank, Highland Village, Tex., 1987—. Mem. bd. govs. Dallas Symphony Orch., 1987—; bd. dirs. Dallas Council World Affairs, 1980; mem. engring com. U. Okla. Aerospace, Nuclear, 1982; bd. dirs. Colo. Mcpl. Water Dist., 1972. Served to 1st lt. USASC, 1955-57. Mem. Am. Petroleum Inst. (bd. dirs. 1986—); Nat. Petroleum Council; Nat. Petroleum Refiners Assn. (chmn. petrochemical com. 1984-87); Ctr. Strategic and Internat. Studies; 25-yr. clubs, Petroleum Industry, Petrochemical Industry. Clubs: Northwood, Petroleum, Energy (Dallas). Office: Petrofina Inc PO Box 2159 Dallas TX 75221

PERRY, LEE ROWAN, lawyer; b. Chgo., Sept. 23, 1933; s. Watson Bishop and Helen (Rowan) P.; m. Barbara Ashcraft Mitchell, July 2, 1955; children: Christopher, Constance, Geoffrey. B.A., U. Ariz., 1955, LL.B., 1961. Bar: Ariz. 1961. Since practiced in Phoenix; clk. Udall & Udall, Tucson, 1960-61; mem. firm Carson, Messinger, Elliott, Laughlin & Ragan, 1961—. Mem. law rev. staff, U. Ariz., 1959-61. Mem. bd. edn. Paradise Valley Elementary and High Sch. Dists., Phoenix, 1964-68, pres., 1968; treas. troop Boy Scouts Am., 1970-72; mem. Ariz. adv. bd. Girl Scouts U.S.A., 1972-74, mem. nominating bd., 1978-79; bd. dirs. Florence Crittenton Services Ariz., 1967-72, pres., 1970-72; bd. dirs. U. Ariz. Alumni, Phoenix, 1968-72, pres., 1969-70; bd. dirs. Family Service Phoenix, 1974-75; bd. dirs. Travelers Aid Assn. Am., 1985-88; bd. dirs. Vol. Bur. Maricopa County, 1975-81, 83-86, pres., 1984-85; bd. dirs. Ariz. div. Am. Cancer Soc., 1978-80, Florence Crittenton div. Child Welfare League Am., 1976-81; bd. dirs. Crisis Nursery for Prevention of Child Abuse, 1978-81, pres., 1978-80. Served to 1st lt. USAF, 1955-58. Mem. State Bar Ariz. (conv. chmn. 1972), Am., Maricopa County bar assns., Phi Delta Phi, Phi Delta Theta (pres. 1954). Republican (precinct capt. 1970, chmn. Reps. for Senator De Concini 1976, 82, 88, precinct committeeman 1983-84). Episcopalian (sr. warden 1968-72). Clubs: Rotary (dir. 1971-77, pres. 1975-76), Plaza, Ariz. Office: United Bank Tower PO Box 33907 Phoenix AZ 85067

PERRY, PETER PATRICK, management consultant; b. Sydney, New South Wales, Australia, Dec. 2, 1932; s. Percy Patrick and Myrtle Veronica (McDonald) P.; m. Deirdra Elizabeth Quirk, Dec. 26, 1955; children: Michael, Diane, Mark, James, Andrew, David, Katherine. BS in Chem. Engring. with honors, U. New South Wales, Sydney, 1954. Prodn. supt. I.C.I., Sydney, 1956, Firestone (Hardie), Sydney, 1956-62; mgr. mfg. service Hyster, Sydney, 1962-65; group mgr. P.A. Mgmt. Cons., Sydney, 1965-77; chmn., mng. dir. MSL Australia, Sydney, 1977—. Fellow Australian Inst. Mgmt., Australian Inst. Dirs.; mem. Inst. Mgmt. Cons. in Australia (pres. Coll. Prins. 1984-87), Jaycees Internat. (Australian pres. 1963, world treas. 1966). Roman Catholic. Clubs: Australian, Concord Golf. Lodges: Rotary. Office: MSL Australia, 5/20 Loftus St, Sydney New South Wales 2000, Australia

PERRY, RACHEL, cosmetics company executive; b. Bklyn., June 28; d. Samuel and Rose (Podell) Solat; m. Jon Mayer, 1978 (div. 1982). Student, Los Angeles City Coll., UCLA. Pvt. practice skincare cons. Beverly Hills, Calif., 1971—; pres., owner Rachel Perry Inc., Chatsworth and Beverly Hills, 1974—; cons. in field. Author: Reverse The Aging Process of Your Face, 1982; composer: Blue Lights in The Basement (Gold Record award Atlantic Records) 1981; songwriter recordings for Melba Moore, Nancy Wilson, Vicki Carr, and Roberta Flack, 1974-85; created award-winning packaging devel. Lip Lover Display, 1983. Active doner Green Peace Animal Protection Soc., Washington, 1982—. Mem. Nat. and Nutritional Foods Assn., Nat. Assn. Recording Arts and Scis. (singer, songwriter 1972—), ASCAP. Democrat. Jewish. Office: 9111 Mason Ave Chatsworth CA 91311

PERRY, RUSSELL H., lawyer, consultant; b. Cornell, Ill., Nov. 8, 1908; s. Walter O. and Mabel (Hilton) P.; m. Phoebe Sherwood, June 2, 1956. Student, N.Y. U., 1937; J.D. cum laude, Bklyn. Law Sch., 1940; D.C.L., Atlanta Law Sch., 1973; hon. doctor Civil Law, Dallas Bapt. U. Northwood Inst., 1986. Bar: N.Y. bar 1941, Tex. bar 1963. Clk. Chgo. Fire & Marine Ins. Co., 1925-32; underwriter Republic Ins. Co., N.Y.C., 1934-38; charge Republic Ins. Co. (Eastern dept. underwriting), 1939-42, asst. to v.p., 1942-43; spl. agt. L.I., Westchester, 1943-44; mgr. L.I. (Eastern dept.), 1945-47, resident sec., 1947-49, v.p., 1949-59, exec. v.p., 1959-61; pres., chief exec. officer, dir. Republic Financial Services, Inc., Republic Ins. Co. Group, 1961-71, chmn. bd., pres., chief exec. officer, 1971-72, chmn. bd., chief exec. officer, 1972-84, chmn. bd., 1985-Apr. 87; ptnr. Rubinstein & Perry, 1987—; mem. found. community adv. bd. KERA-TV, Dallas; dir. Taca, Inc., Dallas; alt. bd. dirs. USA Cafes, Inc., Dallas, Ins. Information Inst., Celtic Internat. Ins. Co., Navigators Ins. Co.; adv. dir. Met. Fin. Savs. & Loan Assn.; chmn., chief exec. officer Union Bank & Trust Co. Mem. exec. com. Assn. Tex. Fire-Casualty Cos.; mem. adv. council Airline Passengers Assn.; bd. dirs., past chmn. Tex. Good Rds. Transp. Assn.; mem. Dallas Bapt. Coll. Devel. Bd.; bd. dirs. Tex. Soc. to Prevent Blindness.; mem., former chmn., nat. adv. bd. Salvation Army Adv. Bd., Dallas; chmn. emeritus Dallas Council on World Affairs; adv. dir. Am. Cancer Soc.; bd. dirs. Tex. Research League; Nat. Devel. Council mem. Big Bros./Big Sisters Am., Hon. bd. govs. Citizen's Choice, Washington; dir. Tex. Assn. Taxpayers, Nat. Legal Center for Public Interest, Washington; past chmn. Landmark Legal Found., Kansas City, Mo.; pres. Trinity Improvement Assn.; dir., past pres. Tex. Bur. Econ. Understanding; past chmn. Bus.-Industry Polit. Action Com.; chmn. Nat. Ctr. For Policy Analysis. Recipient G. Mabry Seay award Dallas Assn. Ins. Agts., 1970; Headliner of Year award Press Club of Dallas, 1975; Person of Vision award Tex. Soc. Prevention of Blindness, 1977; Linz award for Dallas civic service, 1978; Torch of Liberty award Anti-Defamation League, 1979; Horatio Alger award, 1981; others. Mem. U.S. C. of C. (mem. public affairs com.), E. Tex. C. of C. (dir., past chmn.), N.Y. C. of C., Am. Ins. Assn. (alternate dir.), La. Ins. Adv. Assn. (exec. com.), Philonomic Soc., Am., N.Y. bar assns., State Bar Tex., Newcomen Soc. N.Am., Delta Theta Phi. Clubs: New York University, Insurance, Dallas Petroleum, Dallas Country, Dallas Knife and Fork (dir., mem. exec. com.), Rock Creek Barbecue, Austin. Lodge: Rotary. Home: 2817 Park Bridge Ct Dallas TX 75219 Office: Rubinstein & Perry 500 N Akard Suite 3230 Dallas TX 75201

PERRY, THAD PUZYREWSKI, consulting company executive; b. Chgo., Jan. 30, 1927; s. Joseph Kul and Catherine (Druszcz) Puzyrewski; m. Loretta Elizabeth Corky, Feb. 11, 1950; children: Conrad Joseph, Zosia Rebecca Blair. BS, Aero. U., 1947; LLB, Blackstone Sch. Law, 1957; grad., Indsl. Coll. Armed Forces, 1968; MBA, Xavier U., Cin., 1971; JD, Blackstone Sch. Law, 1981; PhD, Calif. Coast U., 1988. Designer, test dir. aircraft div. Globe, Joliet (Ill.), Point Mugu (Calif.), 1947-51; program mgr. USAF, Dayton, Ohio, 1951-58, sci. advisor on missiles, 1958-72; tech. dir. USN, Point Mugu, 1972-82; v.p. Macroman, Inc., Somis, Calif., 1982—, also bd. dirs.; cons. Sci. Applications Internat., Thousand Oaks, Calif., 1982-86; state advisor U.S. Congl. Adv. Bd., 1982—; sci. advisor to Air Force sec. E. Zuckert, 1965. Sr. exec. to Pres. Jimmy Carter, 1979, sec. of Navy Middendorf, 1975, sec. of Navy Hidalgo, 1980. Recipient Top Hat award Camarillo (Calif.) Bus. and Profl. Women, 1974, Centennial Citation of Merit award Polish Nat. Alliance, Chgo., 1982, cert. Merit Rep. Presdl. Task Force, Washington, 1986; named Boss of Yr., Nat. Secs. Assn., Oxnard, Calif., 1974. Mem. Naval Aviation Exec. Assn., Inst. Aero. Sci., Polish Nat. Alliance. Republican. Roman Catholic. Home: 5345 Bradley Rd Somis CA 93066

PERSHING, DIANA KAY, financial investment executive; b. Battle Creek, Mich., Jan. 17, 1943; d. James Harry and Frances Virginia (Garrett) Prill; m. Robert Geroge Pershing, Sept. 16, 1961; children: Carolyn Frances, Robert James Lester. Student, Kent (Ohio) State U., 1967. Real estate sec. Village Realty, Glen Ellyn, Ill., 1975-76, rep. real estate, 1976-77; real estate sales Crown Realty, Glen Ellyn, 1977-79; corp. sec. Teltend Inc., St. Charles, Ill., 1979-88, also bd. dirs.; pres. DKP Prodns. Inc., Villa Park, Ill., 1985—, also bd. dirs. Mem. Nat. Assn. Female Execs., Nat. Acad. Rec. Arts and Scis., Nat. Assn. Ind. Record Distbrs. Office: DKP Prodns 739 N Harvard Villa Park IL 60181

PERSSON, RONNY ANDERS, accountant, historian; b. Helsingborg, Skane, Sweden, Nov. 19, 1945; s. Oscar Valfrid and Ellen Valborg Persson; m. Eva Gunilla Lindqvist, Oct. 5, 1968; children—Mikael, Thomas, Annika. Economy, Nicolai, 1971. Chief acct. Byggprodukter, Helsingborg, 1970-73, Bilakarna, Helsingborg, 1973-80, Bjuvs Congregation, Bjuv, Sweden, 1980—; founder, mgr. R.P. Company Service, Bjuv, 1981-85, R.P. Trading, Bjuv, 1985—. Sector pres. World Union Protection Life; founder Internat. Peace, Economy and Ecology, Bjuv, 1982. Environ. Party. Avocations: reading; sports. Home and Office: Liljegatan 7, S267 00 Bjuv Sweden

PERSSON, S AKE I, food company executive; b. Vaxjo, Sweden, July 14, 1924; s. Gottfrid and A. A. Lisa (Johansson) P.; m. Ingegerd Cato, July 9, 1949 (div. Jan. 1976); children: Birgitta, Elisabeth, Bjorn Ake; m. Dorrit Anna Karin Ogle, Nov. 5, 1977. Student, Malmö Bus. Sch., 1944. Chief acct. AB Insulator, Malmö, Swedeb, 1947-48, Skand Chuckfabriken, Tyringe, Sweden, 1948-49; fin. controller, mktg. dir. Helsingborgs Fryshus ab (Frigoscandia), Sweden, 1950-54; mng. dir. Samford AB, Stockholm, 1960-80; exec. dir. NCS Sinpore PTD Ltd., Stockholm, 1981-88; farmer Sjobacka gard AB, Strangnas, 1970-88; dir. Eurofood Singapore Pte Ltd., 1981, AB Svenska Aggprodukter, 1980, Skandinaviska Enskilda Banken Strangnas, 1980. Served to capt. Swedish Army, 1947-71. Mem. Tonga Maritime Projects (chmn. 1982—), Fontanen Restauranter AB (chmn. 1981—), AB Lango (chmn. 1982-87), Swedish Energi Invest Nyköping, AFAB Electronic AB (chmn. 1986—), Candtherm, Montreal Can. (chmn. 1986-88), Bege Fisk Strangnas (chmn. 1987—). Lodge: Rotary (Strangnas). Home: Sjobacka Gard, 152 00 Strangnas Sweden

PERSSON, SVEN HELMER, oil and chemical company executive; b. Karlstad, Sweden, May 29, 1918; s. Karl Helmer and Helena Matilda (Jansson) P.; m. Elisabeth Louise Christine Frieda Otten, July 27, 1941; children—Hans Helmer, Ulf Christer. B.A., Uppsala U., 1938; B.S. in Chem. Engring., Royal Inst. Tech., 1940, M.S. in Chem. Engring., 1955; D. h.c., (hon.), Chalmers Inst. Tech., 1974. Registered chem. engr., Sweden. Devel. engr. Uddeholm AB, Skoghall, Sweden, 1946-49; refinery mgr. Koppartrans Olje AB, Gothenburg, Sweden, 1949-55; gen. mgr. chem. div. Uddeholm AB, Skoghall, 1955-60; plant mgr. Esso Chem. AB, Stenungsund, Sweden, 1961-67; gen. mgr. elastomers div. Essochem SA, Brussels, 1968-71; chief exec. Esso Chem. Norden, Stockholm, 1972-74; Axel Johnson Group, Stockholm, 1974-81; dir. Berol Kemi AB, Stenungsund, Beroxo AB, Stenungsund. Inventor chlorine dioxide, chloroacetic acid. Adviser, Higher Technical Edn., Stockholm and Gothenburg, 1965—. Mem. Am. Chem. Soc., Royal Acad. Engring. Soc. (chmn. com. 1972—). Lutheran. Lodge: Rotary (sec. 1958-60). Avocations: sailing; skiing; golf. Home: Schuetzenstr 17a, 4970 Bad Oeynhausen Federal Republic of Germany Office: Berol Kemi AB, PO Box 851, 444 01 Stockholm Sweden

PERSSON, WALTER HELGE, church official; b. Göteborg, Sweden, May 8, 1928; s. Helge and Elisabeth Persson; m. Maj Gunnel; children: Anders, Pergunnar, Tomas, Jonas. MEd, Göteborg Folkskolesem, 1950; postgrad. in theology, Lidingö Sem., Sweden, 1953; diploma, Colonial Sch., Brussels, 1954; DD (hon.), North Park Sem. and Coll., 1984. Sch. insp. Swedish Missions, The Congo, 1955-58, high sch. dir., 1958-60; edn. sec. Mission Covenant Ch., Sweden, 1961-75, sec. world missions, 1976-83, pres., 1983—; bd. mgrs. World Council Christian Edn., 1967-72; mem. edn. unit World Council Chs., 1972-80; mem. area com. World Alliance Reformed Chs., 1987—; gen. sec. Internat. Fedn. Free Evang. Chs., 1971-86, pres., 1987—. Office: Mission Covenant Ch4, Tegnérgatan 8, PO Box 6302, S-11381 Stockholm Sweden

PERSSON-TANIMURA, INGA KERSTIN, economist, educator; b. Kristianstad, Skåne, Sweden, Sept. 14, 1945; d. Gösta V. and Hedvig A. (Hedberg) Persson; m. Richard M. Tanimura, Jan. 15, 1975; children: Emily, Philip. MS in polit. sci., Lund (Sweden) U., 1968, PhD in Econs., 1980. Instr. econs. Lund U., 1968-75, assoc. prof., 1984—, docent, 1987; asst. prof. Gothenburg (Sweden) U., 1975-80; researcher Swedish Inst. for Social Research, Stockholm, 1981-84, Swedish Social Sci. Research Council, Lund, 1986—; sec. Del. for Labor Market Policy Research, Stockholm, 1976-85. Author: Studier kring arbets marknad och information, 1980; editor: Kvinnan i ekonomin, 1983; author, editor various books; contbr. articles to profl. jours. Mem. steering group Study of Power and Democracy in Sweden, Uppsala, 1985—. Mem. Am. Econ. Assn., Nationalekon Föreningen, European Econ. Assn. Office: Lund U Dept Econs, Box 7082, S 22007 Lund Sweden

PERTICONE, FRANCESCO, cardiologist, educator; b. Savelli, Italy, Sept. 15, 1949; s. Giuseppe and Emilia Maria (Frontera) P.; m. Lucia Cocchia, Dec. 14, 1978. MD, U. Napoli, 1975, degree in cardiology, 1978. Attending physician Napoli U., Italy, 1974-76; CNR research assoc. Naples U., Itlay, 1976-78; asst. prof. medicine Naples U., 1979-84; vice chmn. dept. medicine Reggio Calabria U., Italy, 1985—; cons. in surgery, 1986—, lectr. in oncology, 1985. Mem. European Soc. Cardiology, Am. Soc. Magnesium Research. Home: Via Nicola Lombardi 9, 88100 Catanzaro Italy Office: Policlinico Materdomini, Via T Campanella, 88100 Catanzaro Italy

PERTSCH, CHRISTOPHER FREDERICK, JR., trading company executive; b. N.Y.C., July 26, 1926; s. Christopher Frederick and Clara Frances (Tesar) P.; B.S., Cornell U., 1949; m. Aida Medina Moreno, Aug. 11, 1951; children—Aida Marie Pertsch Talty, Katherine Anne Pertsch McCrath, Christopher Frederick, III. Trainee, Internat. Basic Economy Corp., 1949-50; with Venezuelan Basic Economy Corp., 1950-54; owner Rio Chico Farm & Equipment Co., Ithaca, N.Y., 1955-66; asst. to pres. Cisneros Group Venezuela, 1969; cons. Dunlap & Assocs., 1966-68, World Cons., Inc., 1963-73; pres. Furatena Ltda., Bogota, Colombia, 1973—, Internacional Furatena Ltda., 1973—, Tipicana Ltda., 1974—, Galerias Tipicol Ltda., 1974—; owner Representaciones Fred Pertsch III, Cartagena, Colombia; dir. Furatena de Venezuela, S.R.L.; mem. businessmen's adv. com. to Am. ambassador, Colombia, 1980, mem. men's liaison com. Dir. Peace Corps, Venezuela, 1966-68. Mem. Colombian Am. C. of C. (Bogota and Cartagena de Indias chpts.), Colombian Venezuelan C. of C., Am. Soc. Bogota (dir. 1977-85, pres. 1982-83). Club: Executive (Cartagena de Indias). Office: Calle 69 #9-78 Bogota, Colombia

PERTSCHUK, LOUIS PHILIP, pathologist; b. London, July 4, 1925; s. Isaac M. and Rose P.; m. Andrea Roberts, June 28, 1985; children: Eric, Shawn, Brandy. A.B., NYU, 1946; D.O., Phila. Coll. Osteo. Medicine, 1950. Diplomate: Am. Bd. Pathology. Instr. Downstate Med. Ctr., SUNY-Bklyn., 1974-75, asst. prof., 1975-79, assoc. prof., 1979-86, prof., 1986—; cons. Corning (N.Y.) Glass Works, 1982—, Zeus Sci. Co., 1982—, Abbott Labs., 1982—. Editor: Localization of Putative Steroid Receptors, 1985. Served with U.S. Army, 1943-46. NCI/NIH grantee, 1979, 82, 85. Fellow Coll. Am. Pathologists, Am. Soc. Clin. Pathologists; mem. Am. Assn. Pathologists, AAAS, Internat. Acad. Pathology, N.Y. Acad. Sci. Current Work: Identification of steroid hormone binding sites in human neoplasms by histochemical and immunohistological techniques. Subspecialty: Pathology (medicine). Home: Bridlepath House New Hempstead NY 10977

PERTWEE, JON, actor; b. London, July 7, 1919; s. Roland and Avice (Schö lz) P.; m. Ingeborg Rhö esa, Aug. 13, 1960; children—Dariel, Sean. Diploma Royal Acad. Dramatic Art, 1937. Appearances on London stage include Touch It Light, 1963, There's A Girl in My Soup (also Broadway), 1967, A Funny Thing Happened on the Way to the Forum, 1966, Irene, 1976-77, The Bedwinner, 1974, Oh Clarence, 1973; radio series The Navy Lark, 1959-75; TV series Whodunnit, 1974-78, Dr. Who, 1971-74, Worzel Gummidge, 1979-80, 87-88. Served with Brit. Navy, 1939-45. Recipient award Aegis Theatre N.Y., 1968; Best Actor on I.T.V. award Variety Club Gt. Britain, 1981. Conservative. Mem. Ch. of Eng. Clubs: Eccentric (London); Grand Order Water Rats.

PERUTZ, MAX FERDINAND, molecular biologist; b. May 19, 1914; s. Hugo and Adele Perutz; ed. U. Vienna; Ph.D., U. Cambridge, 1940; m. Gisela Peiser, 1942; 1 son, 1 dau. Dir. Med. Research Council Unit for Molecular Biology, 1947-62; chmn. European Molecular Biology Orgn., 1963-69; reader Davy Faraday Research Lab., 1954-68, Fullerian prof. physiology, 1973-79; chmn. Med. Research Council Lab. Molecular Biology, 1962-79; Decorated comdr. Order Brit. Empire, Companion of Honor; Order of Merit, Orden für Wissenschaft und Kunst, Austria, Order Pour le Mérite, Fed. Republic Germany; recipient Nobel prize for chemistry, 1962. Fellow Royal Soc. (Royal medal 1971, Copley medal, 1979); mem. Royal Soc. Edinburgh, Am. Acad. Arts and Scis. (hon.), Austrian Acad. Scis. (corr.), Am. Philos. Soc. (fgn.), Nat. Acad. Scis. (fgn. asso.), Royal Netherlands Acad. (fgn.), French Acad. Scis., Bavarian Acad. Scis., Nat. Acad. Scis. of Rome (fgn.), Accademia dei Lincei (Rome) (fgn.), Pontifical Acad. Scis. Author: Proteins and Nucleic Acids, Structure and Function, 1962, Is Science Necessary and Other Essays, 1988. Office: MRC Lab Molecular Biology, Cambridge CB2 2QH, England

PERUZZO, ALBERT LOUIS, actuary, accountant; b. Chgo., Dec. 27, 1951; s. Anthony L. and Annette (Gentile) P. BS in Math., No. Ill. U., 1973, BS in Accountancy, 1974, MBA, 1975. CPA, Ill. Auditor Deloitte, Haskins & Sells, CPA's, Chgo., 1976-79; mgr. valuation compliance CNA Ins., Chgo., 1979—. Treas., bd. dirs. Dignity/Chgo., 1982-84; dep. vol. Voter's Registrar Bd. Elections, Chgo., 1984—. Recipient Ill. Silver medal Nat. Hon. Mention, 1975. Mem. Am. Acad. Actuaries, Soc. Actuaries (assoc.), Am. Inst. CPA's, Ill. CPA Soc. Democrat. Roman Catholic.

PERVEZ, IMTIAZ AHMAD, bank official; b. Srinagar, Kashmir, India, Aug. 1, 1940; d. Sheikh Ghulam Mohamed and Bilquis (Khanum) Ahmed; m. Ghazala Pervez, Mar. 15, 1969; children: Usman, Khadija, Sadia. BA, Punjab U., Lahore, Pakistan, 1962. With Nat. Bank of Pakistan, Lahore, 1958-83, mgr. brs., 1968-73; head credit, mgr. securities Nat. Bank of Pakistan, London, 1973-74; asst. v.p. Nat. Bank of Pakistan, Scotland, 1974-81, v.p., 1982-83; co. mgr. Faysal Islamic Bank of Bahrain, Manama, 1983-84; dep. gen. mgr., chief operating officer Massrah Faysal Al-Islami, Manama, Bahrain, 1984—. Mem. U.K.-Pakistan C. of C. (sec. 1982-83). Home: 8 Delmon Garden Area 517, Rd 1728, Saar Manama Office: Faysal Islamic Bank of Bahrain, King Faysal Rd, Manama Bahrain

PERZANOWSKI, JERZY WACLAW, philosopher, logician; b. Aix-Les-Bains, Savoie, France, Apr. 23, 1943; arrived in Poland, 1946; s. Adam Ryszard and Helena (Kosiba) P.; m. Alina Krystyna Kania, Dec. 31, 1974; 1 child, Jerzy Michal. MA in Philosophy and Math., Jagiellonian U., Cracow, Poland, 1968, PhD, 1973. Asst. Jagiellonian U., 1965-73, reader, 1974—. Author: Ontological Enquiry, 1987; editor, co-author Essays on Logic and Philosophy, 1987; contbr. articles to, editor profl. jours. Mem. Polish Philos. Assn. (pres. Epistemology and Methodology sects., 1983—). Roman Catholic. Home: Krakusow la/43, 30-092 Cracow Poland Office: Jagiellonian, U Dept Logic, Grodzka 52, 31-042 Cracow Poland

PESCH, LEROY ALLEN, physician, educator, health and hospital consultant, business executive; b. Mt. Pleasant, Iowa, June 22, 1931; s. Herbert Lindsey and Mary Clarissa (Tyner) P.; children from previous marriage: Christopher Allen, Brian Lindsey, Daniel Ethan; m. Donna J. Stone, Dec. 28, 1975 (dec. Feb. 1985); stepchildren: Christopher Scott Kneifel, Linda Suzanne Kneifel; m. Gerri Ann Cotton, Sept. 27, 1986; 1 child, Tyner Ford. Student, State U. Iowa, 1948-49, Iowa State U., 1950-52; MD cum laude, Washington U., St. Louis, 1956. Intern Barnes Hosp., St. Louis, 1956-57; research assoc. NIH, Bethesda, Md., 1957-59; asst. resident medicine Grace-New Haven Hosp., New Haven, 1959-60; clin. fellow Yale Med. Sch., New Haven, 1960-61; instr. medicine Yale Med. Sch., 1961-62, asst. prof. medicine, 1962-63, asst. dir. liver study unit, 1961-63; assoc. physician Grace-New Haven Hosp., 1961-62; assoc. prof. medicine Rutgers U., New Brunswick, N.J., 1963-64; prof. Rutgers U., 1964-66, chmn. dept. medicine, 1965-66; assoc. dean, prof. medicine Stanford Sch. Medicine, 1966-68; mem. gen. medicine study sect. NIH, 1965-70, chmn., 1969-70; dean, dir. univ. hosps. SUNY, Buffalo, 1968-71; spl. cons. to sec. for health HEW, 1970—; prof. div. biol. scis. and medicine U. Chgo., 1972-77; prof. pathology Northwestern U., 1977-79; health and hosp. cons.; pres. Concept Group, Inc., Chgo., 1976-77, L.A. Pesch Assocs., Inc., Chgo., 1977-81; chief exec. officer Pesch and Co., 1984—; chmn., chief exec. officer Health Resources Corp. Am., 1981-84; chmn. bd. dirs. Republic Health Corp., 1985—. Contbr. articles on internal medicine to profl. jours. Bd. dirs. Buffalo Med. Found., 1969-72, Health Orgn., Western N.Y., 1968-71, Joffrey Ballet, N.Y.C., 1980—; trustee Michael Reese Hosp. and Med. Center, Chgo., 1971-76, pres., chief exec. officer, 1971-77; mem. exec. bd. Auditorium Theatre Council, Chgo.; trustee W. Clement and Jessie V. Stone Found.; mem. adv. com. Congressional Awards; pres. Pesch Family Found. Served with USPHS, 1957-59. Mem. Am. Assn. Study of Liver Diseases, Am. Fedn. Clin. Research, Am. Soc. Biol. Chemists, AAAS, Sigma Xi, Alpha Omega Alpha. Clubs: Buffalo, Standard, Internat. Quadrangle, Mid-Am, Capitol Hill, Acapulco Yacht, Chicago Yacht. Home: Box 12 Sun Valley ID 83353 Office: 207 Westminster Lake Forest IL 60045 also: Republic Health Corp 14951 Dallas Pkwy Dallas TX 75240

PESHKIN, SAMUEL DAVID, lawyer; b. Des Moines, Oct. 6, 1925; s. Louis and Mary (Grund) P.; m. Shirley R. Isenberg, Aug. 17, 1947; children—Lawrence Allen, Linda Ann. B.A., State U. Iowa, 1948, J.D., 1951. Bar: Iowa bar 1951. Since practiced in Des Moines; partner firm Bridges & Peshkin, 1953-66, Peshkin & Robinson, 1966—; Mem. Iowa Bd. Law Examiners, 1970—. Bd. dirs. State U. Iowa Found., 1957—, Old Gold Devel. Fund, 1956—, Sch. Religion U. Iowa, 1966—. Fellow Am. Bar Found., Internat. Soc. Barristers; mem. ABA (chmn. standing com. membership 1959—, ho. of dels. 1968—, bd. govs. 1973—), Iowa Bar Assn. (bd. govs. 1958—, pres. jr. bar sect. 1958-59, award of merit 1974), Inter-Am. Bar Assn., Internat. Bar Assn., Am. Judicature Soc., State U. Iowa Alumni Assn. (dir., pres. 1957). Home: 505 36th St Apt 302 Des Moines IA 50312 Office: 1010 Fleming Bldg Des Moines IA 50309

PESKO, ZOLTAN, conductor; b. Budapest, Hungary, Feb. 15, 1937; student Liszt Ferenc Acad. Music, Budapest, Accademia di S. Cecilia, Rome. Collaborator, Hungarian Radio-TV, Budapest, 1960-64; condr. Deutsche Oper, W. Berlin, 1966-73; prin. condr. Teatro Comunale, Bologna, Italy, 1974-76; chief condr. Teatro La Fenice, Venice, 1976-77; prin. condr. Symphony Orch. RAI, Milan, 1978-83; guest condr. maj. European orchs., 1983—; prof. Theater Acad., Budapest, 1960-64, Hochschule Musik, W. Berlin, 1969-73. Address: Resia via Manzoni 31, 20121 Milan Italy

PESONEN, JORI EINO, paper machine manufacturing company executive; b. Tampere, Finland, Aug. 21, 1925; s. Niilo Kustaa and Hilma Maria (Uusivirta) P.; m. Riitta Kyllikki Marttinen, Apr. 18, 1957; children—J. Walter, Jussi Heikki, Eeva Maria Elina. M.Sc., U. Tech., Helsinki, Finland, 1951. Mfg. and research engr. Hallsta Pappersbruk, Hallstavik, Sweden, 1951-52, Anglo-Nfld. Devel. Co. and Anglo-Can. Pulp and Paper Mills, Can., 1953-54; mfg. engr. United Paper Mills, Kaipola, Finland, 1954-58; tech. mgr. Cartiere del Timavo, Italy, 1958-60; tech. mgr. Kajaani Oy, Finland, 1960-70, mill mgr., 1970-74; gen. mgr. Valmet Oy, Jyvaskyla, Finland, 1975-80, corp. v.p., 1980-86; pres., chief exec. officer Valmet Paper Machinery Inc., Helsinki, 1987—; chmn. bd. Valmet-Ahlström Inc., Karhula, Finland, Valmet-KMW AB, Karlstad, Sweden, Valmet-KMW Inc., Charlotte, N.C.; bd. dirs. Valmet Corp., Helsinki, Ateliers de Constructions Allimand, Rives, France. Served with inf., Finnish Army, 1943-44. Mem. Finnish Paper Engrs. Assn. (chmn. 1974-76), TAPPI, Can. Pulp and Paper Assn. Lutheran. Lodge: Rotary. Home: Pietarinkatu 3 A 10, 00140 Helsinki Finland Office: Valmet Paper Machinery Inc, PO Box 132, SF 00131 Helsinki Finland

PESSES, PAUL D., real estate and investment management company executive; b. Davenport, Iowa, Oct. 4, 1955; s. Marvin and Elaine (Katz) P.; m.

Kim Meisel, Aug. 19, 1978. BA in Econs. summa cum laude, Ohio State U., 1977; MBA, Harvard U., 1980. Bus. analyst engineered products group Cabot Corp., Boston, 1979-80; v.p., treas., dir. Metcoa, Inc., Solon, Ohio, 1980-82, Columbia Alloys Co., Twinsburg, Ohio, 1980-82; adminstrv. mgr. splty. metals and alloys Ashland Chem. Co. div. Ashland Oil, Inc., Cleve., 1983; pres. Stonestreet Mgmt. Co., Beachwood, Ohio, 1983—, also dir. Trustee Cleve. com. UNICEF; vol. Cleve. Playhouse, Kidney Found. Ohio, United Way campaign; big bro., trustee Big Bros.; treas. Pesses Charitable Found. Mem. Phi Eta Sigma, Phi Kappa Phi. Clubs: Northeast Yacht., Harvard Bus. Sch. (officer) (Cleve.), Oakwood Country.

PESSI, YRJÖ, chemical company executive; b. Kaukola, Finland, Aug. 30, 1926; Urho and Hilma (Kinnunen) P.; m. Liisa Nokka, 1950; children: Pirkko, Urho-Pekka (dec.), Marja, Jyrki, Piija, Petri. MS in Agri. and Forestry, U. Helsinki, 1951, D of Agri. and Forestry, 1956. Dir. Frost Reserach Sta., 1951-57; mng. dir. Peat Cultivation Soc., 1957-64; dir. Leteensuo Experimental Sta., 1957-64; research mgr. Rikkihappo Oy (Kemira Oy), 1964-71, asst. mgr., 1972-73; mng. dir. Kemira Oy, 1975-78, pres., chief exec. officer, 1978—; dir., prof. Agrl. Research Ctr., 1973-74; bd. dirs. Econ. Info. Bur., Confedn. Finnish Industries, Finnish Employers Gen. Group, Research Inst. Finnish Economy (supporting com.); mem. supervisory bd. Kansallis-Osake-Pankki, Indsl. Mut. Ins. Co., World Wide Fund for Nature, Finnish Cultural Found.; mem. Finnish Acad. Tech. Scis., 1978—, adv. bd. Helsinki U. Tech., 1979—, chmn. 1984—, commn. Supporting Found. Helsinki Sch. Econs., 1983—; chmn. Delegation of Finnish Inst. Export, 1983—. Contbr. 100 articles to sci. jours. Chmn. cen. bd. Finnish Child Welfare Assn., 1984; mem. supervisory bd. Finnish Cultural Found., 1985—. Mem. Finnish Chem. Industry Fedn. (bd. dirs., chmn. sci. adv. bd. 1984—), Peat Cultivation Soc. (chmn. bd. dirs.), Found. Research Higher Edn. and Sci. Policy (council mem.), Internat. Fertilizer Industry Assn. (council mem.), Internat. Peat Soc. (council mem., pres. council 1985—, chmn. Finnish Nat. com. 1985—). Office: Kemira Oy, Malminkatu 30, 00101 Helsinki, Uusimaa Finland

PESTANA, ANGEL, biochemist; b. Ubeda, Jaen, Spain, June 18, 1938; s. Angel and Pilar (Vargas) P.; m. Sacramento Marti; children: Rosa, Marcia. MD, U. Valencia, Spain, 1965; PhD, U. Valencia, 1967. Asst. prof. U. Valencia, 1965-67; postdoctoral fellow Centro Investigaciones Biologias, Madrid, 1967-70; research assoc. McArdie Lab. Cancer Research Inst., Madison, Wis., 1973-74; career investigator Spanish Research Council, Madrid, 1973—; bd. dirs. Inst. Investigaciones Biomedicas, Madrid, 1985—. Contbr. articles to profl. jours. Fellow NIH, 1971-73. Mem. Spanish Soc. Biochemistry, Spanish Soc. Cell Biology, Spanish Soc. Cancer Research. Office: Inst Investigaciones Biomedicas, Arzobispo Morcilla 4, 28029 Madrid Spain

PETER, JACQUES, gynecologist, obstetrician, surgeon; b. Limoges, France, Aug. 24, 1950; s. Gay Peter; widower; children: Christine, Philippe, Eric. MD, U. Limoges, 1976. Intern, resident Limoges, 1976-80, asst. chief clinic, 1980-83; practice medicine specializing in gynecology and obstetrics Chatellerault, France, 1982—. Author: Revision accelerée en gynecologie, 1981, Dossiers de l'infirmière Physiologie, 1984. Home: General Reibel, 86100 Chatellerault France Office: Clinique Ste Anne Abbe Lalanne, 86100 Chatellerault France

PETER, LILY, plantation operator, writer; b. Marvell, Ark.; d. William Oliver and Florence (Mowbrey) P. B.S., Memphis State U., 1927; M.A., Vanderbilt U., 1938; postgrad. U. Chgo., 1930, Columbia U., 1935-36; L.H.D., Moravian Coll., Bethlehem, Pa., 1965, Hendrix Coll., Conway, Ark., 1983; LL.D., U. Ark., 1975. Owner, operator plantations, Marvell and Ratio, Ark.; writer poetry, feature articles pub. in S.W. Quar., Delta Rev., Cyclo Flame, Etude, Am. Weave, others; mem. staff S.W. Writers Conf., Corpus Christi, Tex., 1954—, sponsor Ark. Writers' Conf. Chmn., Poetry Day in Ark., 1953—; chmn., sponsor music Ark. Territorial Sesquicentennial, 1969. Author: The Green Linen of Summer, 1964; The Great Riding, 1966; The Sea Dream of the Mississippi, 1973; In the Beginning, 1983. Bd. dirs. Ark. Arts Festival, Little Rock, Grand Prairie Festival Arts; chmn. bd. Phillips County Community Center, 1969-73; hon. trustee Moravian Music Found. Recipient Moramus award Friends of Moravian Music, 1964, Disting. Alumni award Vanderbilt U., 1964, Gov.'s award as Ark. Conservationist of Year, Ark. Wildlife Fedn., 1975, Whooping Crane award Nat. Wildlife Fedn., 1976; named Poet Laureate Ark., 1971, Democrat Woman of Year, 1971, 1st Citizen of Phillips County, Phillips County C. of C., 1985, Most Disting. Woman of Ark., Ark. C. of C., 1985. Mem. DAR, (hon. state regent), Nat. League Am. Pen Women, Ark. Authors and Composers Soc., Poets' Roundtable Ark., poetry socs. of Tenn., Tex., Ga., Met. Opera Assn., So. Cotton Ginners Assn. (dir. 1971—), Big Creek Protective Assn. (chmn. 1974—), Sigma Alpha Iota (hon.). Democrat. Episcopalian. Clubs: Pacaha (Helena, Ark.); Woman's City (Little Rock). Home: Route 2 Box 69 Marvell AR 72366

PETER, PHILLIPS SMITH, electrical products executive, lawyer; b. Washington, Jan. 24, 1932; s. Edward Compston and Anita Phillips (Smith) P.; m. Jania Jayne Hutchins, Apr. 8, 1961; children: Phillips Smith Peter Jr., Jania Jayne Hutchins. B.A., U. Va., 1954, J.D., 1959. Bar: Calif. 1959. Assoc. McCutchen, Doyle, Brown, Enerson, San Francisco, 1959-63; with Gen. Electric Co. (and subs.), various locations, 1963—; v.p. corp. bus. devel. Gen. Electric Co. (and subs.), 1973-76; v.p. Gen. Electric Co. (and subs.), Washington, 1976-79; v.p. corp. govtl. relations Gen. Electric Co. (and subs.), 1980—; bd. dirs. Inst. for Research on Econs. of Taxation. Mem. editorial bd. Va. Law Rev., 1957-59. Trustee Howard U.; v.p. Federal City Council, Washington, 1979-85. Served with Transp. Corps, U.S. Army, 1954-56. Mem. Calif. Bar Assn., Order of Coif, Omicron Delta Kappa. Episcopalian. Clubs: Wee Burn (Darien); Eastern Yacht (Marblehead, Mass.); Farmington Country (Charlottesville, Va.); Ponte Vedra (Fla.); Lago Mar (Ft. Lauderdale, Fla.); Racquet (Miami Beach, Fla.); Landmark (Stamford, Conn.); Congl. Country (Bethesda, Md.); Georgetown, Chevy Chase, Pisces, F Street (Washington); Coral Beach and Tennis (Bermuda); John's Island (Vero Beach, Fla.); Carlton (bd. dirs.). Home: 10805 Tara Rd Potomac MD 20854 also: 1000 Beach Rd John's Island Vero Beach FL Office: 1331 Pennsylvania Ave Washington DC 20004

PETERMAN, MARJANA, food products executive; b. Ljubljana, Slovenija, Yugoslavia, Jan. 24, 1946; came to Can., 1971; d. Joseph and Angela (Marinc) S.; m. Branko Franc Peterman. BSc., U. Ljubljana (Yugoslavia), 1969. Plant mgr. Ault, Ottawa, Can., 1980-85; mgr. quality control Beatrice Foods, inc., Barrie, Can., 1985-86; dir. quality assurance Beatrice Foods, inc., Toronto, 1986—. Mem. Can. Inst. of Food, Sci., and Tech. (dir. 1984-86), Internat. Assn. Mill, Food and Environ. Sanitarians Inc. Office: Beatrice Foods Inc, 295 The West Mall, Toronto, ON Canada M9C 4Z4

PETERMANN, GOTZ EIKE, mathematics educator, researcher; b. Berlin, Aug. 24, 1941; came to Sweden, 1945; s. Erwin Karl Eduard and Selma Alwine Ida (Dunker) P.; m. Gunlog Birgitta Bjorkhem, May 17, 1970; children—Veronica, Ingemar, Waldemar, Ingmarie, Elisabeth, Johannes. Fil. Kand., U. Stockholm, 1963, Fil. Mag./Fil. Lic., 1970; Fil. Dr., Royal Inst. Tech., Stockholm, 1974. Asst., lectr. U. Stockholm, 1962-73; lectr. math. Royal Inst. Tech., Stockholm, 1973—. Author: Konvexitet och Optimering, 1973; Analytiska och Numeriska Metoder, 1981. Contbr. articles to profl. jours. Mem. Swedish Math. Soc. (treas. 1975-78), Am. Math. Soc. Avocations: music; reading. Home: Satravagen 1A, S184 52 Osterskar Sweden Office: Royl Inst Tech, S100 44 Stockholm Sweden

PETERS, CAROL BEATTIE TAYLOR (MRS. FRANK ALBERT PETERS), mathematician; b. Washington, May 10, 1932; d. Edwin Lucius and Lois (Beattie) Taylor; B.S., U. Md., 1954, M.A., 1958; m. Frank Albert Peters, Feb. 26, 1955; children—Thomas, June, Erick, Victor. Group mgr. Tech. Operations, Inc., Arlington, Va., 1957-62, sr. staff scientist, 1964-66; supervisory analyst Datatrol Corp., Silver Spring, Md., 1962; project dir. Computer Concept, Inc., Silver Spring, 1963-64; mem. tech. staff, then mem. sr. staff Informatics Inc., Bethesda, Md., 1966-70, mgr. systems projects, 1970-71, tech. dir., 1971-76; sr. tech. dir. Ocean Data Systems, Inc., Rockville, Md., 1976-83; dir. Informatics Gen. Co., 1983—. Mem. Assn. Computing Machinery, IEEE Computer Group. Home: 12321 Glen Mill Rd Potomac MD 20854 Office: 6011 Executive Blvd Rockville MD 20852

PETERS, CHARLES WILLIAM, research and development company manager; b. Pierceton, Ind., Dec. 9, 1927; s. Charles Frederick and Zelda May (Line) P.; A.B., Ind. U., 1950; postgrad. U. Md., 1952-58; m. Katharine Louise Schuman, May 29, 1953; 1 dau., Susan Kay; m. 2d, Patricia Ann Miles, Jan. 2, 1981; children—Bruce Miles Merkle, Leslie Ann Merkle Sanaie, Philip Frank Merkle, William Macneil Merkle. Supervisory research physicist Naval Research Lab., Washington, 1950-71; physicist EPA, Washington, 1971-76; mgr. advanced systems Consol. Controls Corp., Springfield, Va., 1976 . Served with U.S. Army, 1945-47. Mem. Am. Phys. Soc., IEEE, AAAS. Home: 12034 Willowood Dr Woodbridge VA 22192 Office: PO Box 726 Springfield VA 22150

PETERS, DAVID LOUIS, food company executive; b. Mt. Pleasant, Pa., Oct. 12, 1945; s. William O. and Mary (Maciupa) P.; m. Barbara J. Kelanic, Oct. 18, 1968; children: Marian, Michael. BA, California (Pa.) State U., 1971; MA, Cen. Mich. U., 1977. Area mgr. Hormel Co., Austin, Minn., 1971-76; v.p. sales Holsum Co., Waukesha, Wis., 1976-80; v.p. sales and mktg. PVO Internat., St. Louis, 1981; sr. v.p. Doskocil Foods Group, Jefferson, Wis., 1982—. Pres. Time-Out, Inc., 1983-85. Served with USMC, 1963-67. Mem. Am. Mgmt. Assn., Am. Legion. Republican. Mem. Ch. Brethren. Club: Kettle Moraine Soccer (pres. 1987—). Home: 632 Wakefield Downs Wales WI 53183 Office: Doskocil Foods Group 1 Rock River Rd Jefferson WI 53549

PETERS, DOUGLAS CAMERON, mining engineer, geologist; b. Pitts., June 19, 1955; s. Donald Cameron and Twila (Bingel) P. BS in Earth and Planetary Sci., U. Pitts., 1977; MS in Geology, Colo. Sch. Mines, 1981, MS in Mining Engring., 1983. Technician, inspector Engring. Mechanics Inc., Pitts., 1973-77. Research asst. Potential Gas Agy., Golden, Colo., 1977-78; geologist U.S. Geol. Survey, Denver, 1978-80; cons. Climax Molybdenum Co., Golden, 1981-82; cons., Golden, 1982-84; mining engr., prin. investigator U.S. Bur. Mines, Denver, 1984—; bur. rep. to Geosat Com., 1984—; program chmn. Geotech Conf., Denver, 1984-88. Author: Physical Modeling of Draw of Broken Rock in Caving, 1984, Bur. Mines Articles and Reports; editor COGS Computer Contbns., 1986—. Contbr. articles to profl. jours. Mem. Computer Oriented Geol. Soc. (charter, com. chmn. 1983—, pres. 1985, dir. 1986), Geol. Soc. Am., Rocky Mountain Assn. Geologists, Soc. Mining Engrs. (jr. mem.), Am. Assn. Petroleum Geologists (com. mem. 1984—), Am. Soc. Photogrammetry and Remote Sensing, Nat. Space Soc., Colo. Mining Assn., Pitts. Geol. Soc. Republican. Office: US Bur Mines Denver Fed Ctr Box 25086 Bldg 20 Denver CO 80225

PETERS, JOHN BASIL, electronic company executive; b. Vancouver, B.C., Can., Nov. 3, 1952; s. James John and Una Lois (Timms) P. Tech. diplomas with hon., B.C.I.T., Burnaby, B.C., 1973; BSEE with hon., U. B.C., 1977, PhDEE, 1982. Registered profl. engr., B.C. Chmn., chief exec. officer Nexus Engring. Corp., Burnaby, 1982—; research and devel. cons. RMS Indsl. Controls, Port Coquitlan, B.C., 1980-82, Channel One Video, Vancouver, 1979-81; project coordinator U. B.C. Electric Vehicle Project, Vancouver, 1974-77; bd. dirs. Infostat Telecommunications Inc.; adj. prof. Engring. Simon Fraser U., Burnaby, 1986—. Bd. govs. U. B.C., Vancouver, 1976-79. Recipient Alumni Achievement award B.C. Inst. Tech., 1986; named B.C. Hydro and Power Authority scholar, 1973, Sherwood Lett Meml. scholar, 1977-79, Hector J. MacLeod scholar, IEEE, 1971-81, Nat. Scis. and Engring. Research Council scholar, 1977-81, C.A. and J.C.A. Banks Found. scholar, 1974-77. Mem. Assn. Profl. Engrs. of the Province of B.C. (prize 1977), Young Presidents Orgn., Sci. Council B.C. (electonics and communications com. 1987—, post-doctoral fellow, 1982-84).

PETERS, MERCEDES, psychoanalyst; b. N.Y.C.; B.S., L.I. U., 1945; postgrad. Columbia U., 1944-45; M.S., U. Conn., 1953; tng. in psychotherapy Am. Inst. Psychotherapy and Psychoanalysis, 1960-70; grad. Postgrad. Center Mental Health; postgrad. Union U. Grad. Sch., 1987—. Social worker various agys., pub. instns., 1945-63; staff affiliate, sr. psychotherapist Community Guidance Service, 1960-75; affiliate Postgrad. Center for Mental Health, 1974-76; pvt. practice psychotherapy, Bklyn., 1961—. Certified psychoanalyst Am. Examining Bd. Psychoanalysis; certified mental health cons. Fellow Am. Orthopsychiat. Assn.; mem. Nat. Assn. Social Workers, LWV, NAACP, Brooklyn Heights Mus. Soc. Office: 142 Joralemon Brooklyn NY 11201

PETERS, RALPH EDGAR, banker; b. Harrisburg, Pa., Feb. 20, 1923; s. George Edward and Rebecca Flavia (Michener) P.; m. Roberta Jane Shafer, June 12, 1948; children—Sheila Jane, Gail Marie, Ralph Edgar, Bret Edward. Student in acctg. Wharton Sch., U. Pa., 1942; B.A. in Bus. Adminstrn., Pa. State U., 1948. From payroll supr. to asst. budget supr. Pa. State U., 1948-52; chief acct., personnel officer Haller, Raymond & Brown, State College, Pa., 1952-54; from controller to v.p. adminstrn. Benatec Assocs., Inc. (formerly Berger Assocs., Inc.), Camp Hill, Pa., from 1954, nowchief exec. officer; dir. CCNB Bank, New Cumberland, Pa., 1972—. Chmn. bd. advisors Pa. State U., Harrisburg, 1979-84; chmn. bd. dirs. Holy Spirit Hosp., Camp Hill, 1982—; past pres. Tri-County United Way, Harrisburg, from 1978; chmn. Pvt. Industry Council, Harrisburg, 1982-87. Served with U.S. Army, 1943-45; ETO. Recipient Community Service award Salvation Army, 1980; Disting. Alumnus award Pa. State U., 1980; Disting. Pennsylvanian award Greater Phila. C. of C., 1981. Mem. Pa. C. of C. (dir., transp. com. chmn. 1972-87), Harrisburg Area C. of C. (pres., chmn. 1979-83), Americans for Competitive Enterprise System (pres. 1981-83), Pa. Jaycees (pres. 1955-56, nat. v.p. 1956-57), Delta Sigma Pi. Lutheran. Lodges: Lions, Masons. Office: Benatec Assocs Inc 101 Erford Rd Camp Hill PA 17011

PETERS, RAYMOND ROBERT, banker; b. Concord, Calif., Sept. 14, 1942; s. Robert V. and Pegi M. (Carr) P.; m. Nancy Choy; children: Angel, Ray, Matthew. BBA, U. Oreg., 1964. Head customer securities Bank of Am., San Francisco, 1969-71, Eurocurrency and fgn. exchange mgr., London, 1971-72, San Francisco, 1972-76, sr. v.p., head offshore funds, 1976-85, sr. v.p. head treasury, 1985—; mem. fgn. exchange com. N.Y. Fed. Res. Bank, 1978-87, chmn., 1984-85; mem. Chgo. Merc. Exchange, 1987—; exec. v.p. Bank Am. Corp., 1987—; mem. Chgo. Bd. Trade, 1987—; cons. on fgn. currency, offshore banking matters U.S. Fed. Res., fgn. central banks. Served to lt. USN, 1964-68. Office: Bank of Am Treasury Div 555 California St Suite 3170 San Francisco CA 94104

PETERSEN, A. LEE, lawyer; b. Murray, Utah, June 6, 1930; s. Franklin H. and Myrtle (Jensen) P.; m. Cynthia Z. Dalley, Mar. 4, 1961 (div. Sept. 1974); children—Kirsten Marie, Jared Franklin, Eric John, Adam Lewis, Mark Haydn, Amanda Simone. A.B., Brigham Young U., 1955; J.D., NYU, 1959. Bar: Utah 1960. Law clk., assoc. Monroe J. Paxman, Provo, Utah 1959-60; assoc. Thacher, Proffit, Priser, Crawley & Wood, N.Y.C., 1960-62; sole practice, Fillmore, Utah, 1962-68; asst. U.S. atty. Dist. Alaska, 1968-75; mem. Gregg, Fraties, Petersen, Page & Baxter, 1975-77, Fraties & Petersen, 1977-78; sole practice, Anchorage, 1978-84 ; of counsel Cummings & Routh, P.C., 1984-86; prin. Law Offices of A. Lee Petersen, P.C., 1987—; atty. fin. center br. 1st Nat. Bank, Ketchikan, Alaska, 1976-78; atty. Flowell Electric Assn., 1962-68; city atty. Fillmore, 1964-68, Whittier, Alaska, 1976-77; pres., dir. INI Builders, Inc., 1984—. Republican party legis. dist. chmn., 1965-68, voting dist. chmn., 1966-68; bd. dirs. Fillmore Indsl. Found., 1966-68. Mem. So. Utah Bar Assn. (pres. elect 1967), Fed. Bar Assn., Utah Bar Assn., Assn. Trial Lawyers Am., Alaska Bar Assn., ABA, N.Y. State Bar, Fillmore C. of C. (past dir., sec.). Office: 720 M St Suite 200 Anchorage AK 99501

PETERSEN, DONALD E(UGENE), automobile company executive; b. Pipestone, Minn., Sept. 4, 1926; s. William L. and Mae (Pederson) P.; m. Jo Anne Leonard, Sept. 12, 1948; children: Leslie Carolyn, Donald Leonard. BSME, U. Wash., 1946; MBA, Stanford U., 1949; DSc (hon.), U. Detroit, 1986; LHD (hon.), Art Ctr. Coll., Pasadena, 1986. With Ford Motor Co., Dearborn, 1949—, v.p. car planning and research, 1969-71, v.p. truck ops., 1971-75, exec. v.p. diversified products ops., 1975-76, exec. v.p. internat. automotive ops., 1977-80, pres., 1980-85, chmn. bd. dirs., chief exec. officer, 1985—, also bd. dirs. Trustee Cranbrook Inst. Sci., Bloomfield, Mich., 1973—, Citizens Research Council of Mich., Safety Council for S.E. Mich., Detroit Inst. Arts, Mich. Cancer Found., Corp. Found. for Aid to Edn., TARGET; mem. adv. bd. U. Wash. Grad. Sch. Bus. Adminstrn.; bd. overseers Oreg. Health Sci. Univ.; mem. New Detroit, Inc., Detroit Renaissance, Inc.; bd. dirs. Hewlett-Packard Co., Dow Jones & Co., Inc., Detroit Strategic Planning Project, Mich. Commn. Sch. Fin. Served with USMC, 1946-47, 51-52. Recipient Disting. Alumnus award U. Wash., 1981, Arbuckle award Stanford U. Bus. Sch. Alumni Assn., 1985, 1st Am. Achievement award Brookgreen Gardens, 1986, Bus. Statesman award Harvard Bus Sch. Club Detroit, Good Neighbor award U.S. Mex. C. of C., Man of Yr. award Motor Trend Mag., 1987, Nat. Humanitarian award Nat. Jewish Ctr. Immunology and Respiratory Medicine. Mem. The Bus. Council, Bus. Roundtable (mem. policy com., mem. U.S.-Japan bus. council, mem. adv. com. for trade negotiations, mem. emergency com. for Am. trad), Bus.-Higher Edn. Forum, Soc. Automotive Engrs., Engring. Soc. Detroit, Mensa, Motor Vehicle Mfrs. Assn., Phi Beta Kappa, Sigma Xi, Tau Beta Pi. Episcopalian. Clubs: Detroit, Bloomfield Hills Country, Bloomfield Open Hunt, Ostego Ski, Detroit Economic. Office: Ford Motor Co The American Rd Dearborn MI 48121

PETERSEN, FLEMMING BRÖCHNER, banker; b. Aarhus, Denmark, Feb. 18, 1944; s. S.A. Bröchner and Ragnhild (Blicher) P.; m. Dorthe Terkildsen, Nov. 25, 1967; children: Christel, Malene. Grad., Niels Brock Handelseksamen, Copenhagen, 1967; examined exporter, Merkonomskolen, Copenhagen, 1969. Apprentice Korn & Foderstof Kompagniet, Aarhus, 1960-63; sec. Törsleff, Copenhagen, 1967-68; export mgr. Scandrug A/S, Havdrup, Denmark, 1969-74; comml. officer Danish Ministry of Trade, Tripoli, Libya, 1974-76, Edinburgh, Scotland, 1976-77; comml. counsellor Danish Ministry Fgn. Affairs, Budapest, Hungary, 1977-81; chief rep. Danish SUgar Factories, Moscow, 1982-86; area mgr. Privatbanken A/s, Copenhagen, 1986—. Mem. Round Table, Edinburgh, 1976-77. Served as sgt. Danish mil., 1963-65. Home: Ravnevej 21, 2970 Horsholm Denmark

PETERSEN, GEORGE THOMAS, management consultant; b. Hummelstown, Pa., Oct. 3, 1916; s. Hjalmar Hjelm and Emma Romaine (Spangler) P.; B.S. in Aero. Engring., U. Mich., 1938; advanced mgmt. program Harvard U., 1959; D. Engring. (hon.), Tex. A&M U., 1972; D.Sc. (hon.), London Inst., 1973; m. Opal Janett Herberg, Dec. 11, 1941; children—Karen, Barbara, Teressa. Commd. 2d lt., U.S. Army, 1941, advanced through grades to col., 1953; ret., 1961; dir. research Continental Motors, Detroit, 1961-69; gen. ops. mgr. transp. systems Ford Motor Co., Dearborn, Mich., 1969-76; v.p. engring. Rayco Creative Services, Royal Oak, Mich., 1976-77; v.p. Corp. Fin. Assos., Phoenix, 1977-78; pres. George T. Petersen Assos., Inc., Sun City, Ariz., 1977—; exec. v.p., cons. Bernard Haldane Assos.; cons. tank design Israeli, Brit. and German armies. Decorated Bronze Star with 3 oak leaf clusters, Legion of Merit with 2 oak leaf clusters (U.S.), Order Brit. Empire, Croix de Guerre (France), cert. career counselor; registered profl. engr., Mich., Ariz. Mem. Am. Mgmt. Assn., Mil. Order World Wars, Am. Def. Preparedness Assn., Assn. U.S. Army, Nat. Security Assn. (dir., past chpt. pres.), Phi Delta Theta. Republican. Lutheran. Clubs: Lakes (Sun City); Biltmore Country (Phoenix); Wabeek Country (Bloomfield Hills, Mich.). Developer tanks, night vision devices, variable compression ratio diesel engine, Ford automated transit system. Home: 16025 Aqua Fria Dr Sun City AZ 85351 Office: 3225 N Central St Suite 1220 Phoenix AZ 85012

PETERSEN, NORMAN WILLIAM, naval officer, engineer; b. Highland Park, Ill., Aug. 26, 1933; s. Jens Edlef and Marie (Wenderling) P.; m. Ann Nevin, Aug. 24, 1956; children: Richard Nevin, Robert William, Thomas Marshall, Anita, David Arthur. BEE, U. N.Mex., 1956; MEE with distinction, Naval Postgrad. Sch., Monterey, Calif., 1962; postgrad., Harvard Bus. Sch., 1982. Registered profl. engr., Mass., Calif. Shops engr. Naval Station, Key West, Fla., 1956-59; personnel dir. Bur. Yards and Docks, Washington, 1959-60; pub. works officer Fleet Anti-Air Warfare Ctr., Dam Neck, Va., 1962-64; engring. coordinator Southwest div. Naval Facilities Engring. Command, San Diego, 1964-66; exec. officer Amphibious Constrn. Battalion 1, San Diego, 1966-67; force civil engr. Comdr. Naval Air Force Pacific, San Diego, 1967-70; pub. works officer Naval Air Sta. Miramar, San Diego, 1970-73; exec. officer Pub. Works Ctr., Great Lakes, Ill., 1973-75; comdg. officer Navy Civil Engring. Research Lab., Port Hueneme, Calif., 1975-78, Pub. Works Ctr. San Francisco Bay Area, Oakland, Calif., 1978-80; comptroller, programs dir. Naval Facilities Engring. Command, Washington, 1980-84; pub. works officer Pacific Missile Test Ctr., Point Mugu, Calif., 1984-86; deputy assoc. dir. for plant engring. Lawrence Livermore (Calif.) Nat. Lab., 1986—. Contbr. articles to profl. jours. Bd. dirs. CBC Fed. Credit Union, Port Hueneme, 1984-86, Ventura County United Way, Oxnard, Calif., 1976-78, strategic planning com., Camarillo, Calif., 1984-86; guest mem. Ventura County Assn. Govts., 1984-86. Decorated (twice) Legion of Merit; Gallantry Cross (Republic Vietnam). Mem. Am. Soc. Mil. Comptrollers, Soc. Am. Mil. Engrs., Assn. Phys. Plant Adminstrs. (affiliate), Navy League, Oxnard Gem and Mineral Soc. (2d v.p.), Sigma Xi, Lambda Chi Alpha. Office: Lawrence Livermore Nat Lab PO Box 5506 L-657 Livermore CA 94550

PETERSEN, WILLIAM JOHN, writer, educator; b. Dubuque, Iowa, Jan. 30, 1901; s. Charles Lewis and Bertha Louise (Helm) P.; m. Bessie Josephine Rasmus, Sept. 25, 1937. B.A., U. Dubuque, 1926; M.A., U. Iowa, 1927, Ph.D., 1930; LL.D., Iowa Wesleyan Coll., 1958. Grad asst., fellow U. Iowa, 1926-30, instr. history, 1930-36, lectr. history, 1936—, asso. prof., 1948-69; research asso. State Hist. Soc. Iowa, 1930-47, supt., 1947-72; hist. lectr. Am. Sch. Wild Life, summers 1932, 36-40, Drake U. Tours, summers 1933, 34; prof. history Washington U., St. Louis, summers 1940, 41, 65, Iowa Wesleyan Coll., summers 1962, 63. Author: (with Edith Rule) True Tales of Iowa, 1932, Two Hundred Topics in Iowa History, 1932, Steamboating on the Upper Mississippi, 1937, rev. edit., 1968, Iowa: The Rivers of Her Valleys, 1941, A Reference Guide to Iowa History, 1942, Iowa History Reference Guide, 1952, The Story of Iowa, 2 vols, 1952, Mississippi River Panorama: Henry Lewis Great National Work, 1979, Towboating on the Mississippi, 1979; Editor: (John Plumbe, Jr.) Sketches of Iowa and Wisconsin, 1948, (Isaac Galland) Galland's Iowa Emigrant, 1950, (John B. Newhall) A Glimpse of Iowa in 1846, 1957; author-editor: (John B. Newhall) The Pageant of the Press, 1962, The Annals of Iowa-1863, Illustrated Historical Atlas of the State of Iowa in 1875, (A.T. Andreas), 1970; contbr. to profl. mags. Bd. dirs. Alvord Meml. Commn., 1940; mem. Iowa Centennial Com., 1946; chmn. Johnson County Red Cross War Fund, 1945. Recipient Iowa Library Assn. award for best contbn. to Am. lit. by an Iowan, 1937. Mem. Am. Hist. Assn., So. Hist. Assn., Miss. Valley Hist. Assn. (editorial bd. 1953-56), Soc. Am. Archivists, Am. Acad. Polit. and Social Sci., Minn., Kans. hist. socs., State Hist. Soc. Iowa, Phi Kappa Delta, Pi Gamma Mu, Zeta Sigma Pi, Delta Upsilon. Republican. Presbyn. Clubs: Mason (32 deg.), Iowa Author (pres. 1940-42); Propeller (Quad City); Westerners (Chgo.), Cliff Dwellers (Chgo.), Caxton (Chgo.); Research (Iowa City) (sec.-treas. 1944-46), Triangle (Iowa City), S.P.C.S. Rotary (Iowa City), C. of C. (Iowa City). Home: 329 Ellis Ave Iowa City IA 52240

PETERSMEYER, JOHN CLINTON, architect; b. Regina, Sask., Can., Sept. 10, 1945; s. Karl Clifford and Dora Irene (Bourne) P.; m. N. Jane Simpkins, May 7, 1966; children—Brooke D., J. Croft. B.Arch., U. Man., Winnipeg, 1969. Registered architect, Mng. prin. GBR Architects, Winnipeg, 1969—, prin.-in-charge design mgmt., 1973—. Chmn. Man. Bd. Referees Unemployment Ins. Commn., Winnipeg, 1973-85. Mem. Royal Archtl. Inst. Can., Man. Assn. Architects (pres. 1983), Ont. Assn. Architects. Liberal. Presbyterian. Club: Winnipeg Winter. Avocations: graphic design, curling. Home: 103 Fulham Ave, Winnipeg, MB Canada R3n 0G5 Office: GBR Architects, 1314 Ellice Ave, Winnipeg, MB Canada

PETERSON, ARTHUR MAURICE, franchising company executive; b. Centerville, S.D., Oct. 16, 1934; s. Arthur M. and Mursedus G. (Sorenson) P.; m. Carol L. Sigueido, May 27, 1957; children—Curt, Bryan, Kristin. With retail mgmt. and supervision Genesco, 1952-69; mdse. mgr. Kampgrounds of Am., Billings, Mont., 1969-72, v.p., 1972-76, sr. v.p., 1976-78, exec. v.p., chief operating officer, 1978-80, pres., chief exec. officer, 1980—. Bd. dirs. Yellowstone Art Mus., Billings, 1976—; regent Pacific Luth. U.; v.p. Forward Billings, 1983—; dir. Am. Recreation Coalition. Served with U.S. Army, 1957-59. Republican. Club: Yellowstone Country (Billings). Lodge: Rotary. Office: Kampgrounds of Am Box 30558 Billings MT 59114

PETERSON, BRUCE O., educational administrator; b. Wis., May 20, 1939; s. Torger and Opal Peterson; B.A., Northland Coll., 1961; M.A., N.Mex. State U., 1965, Ph.D., 1968; children—Nathan, Matthew, Andrea, Chris. Asst. exec. sec. Bd. Ednl. Fin., Santa Fe, 1969-74; v.p., dean. gen. studies Stockton State Coll., Pomona, N.J., 1974-77; assoc. dean, assoc. prof. Nat.

Tech. Inst. for the Deaf Rochester Inst. Tech., Rochester, N.Y., 1977—. Mem. Am. Assn. for Higher Edn., Am. Deafness and Rehab. Assn., Am. Ednl. Research Assn., Am. Vocat. Assn., Alexander Graham Bell Assn., Assn. for Moral Edn., Assn. Supervision and Curriculum Devel., Conf. of Execs. of Am. Schs. for the Deaf, Conv. Am. Instrs. for the Deaf, Council for Basic Edn., Nat. Assn. Student Personnel Adminstrs., N.Y. State Assn. Jr. Colls., Soc. for Coll. and Univ. Planning, World Future Soc., Phi Delta Kappa. Contbr. articles to profl. publs., papers to profl. confs. Office: 1 Lomb Meml Dr Rochester NY 14623

PETERSON, CHARLES HAYES, trading company executive; b. St. Louis, May 8, 1938; s. Edmund Herbert and Dorothy Marie (Brennan) P.; m. Auli Irene Ahonen, Nov. 28, 1981; children: Mika, Charles, Michael, Katja. BS, U.S. Naval Acad., 1960; MBA, Stanford U., 1971, JD, 1974. Bar: Calif. Commd. ensign USN, 1956, advanced through grades to capt., resigned, 1969; with USNR, 1969—; counsel Gen. Electric, San Jose, Calif., 1973-79; div. counsel Syracuse, N.Y., 1980-83; v.p. COGEMA, Inc., Washington, 1983-87; pres., chief exec. officer Nuexco Internat. Corp., Denver, 1987—. Mem. fin. com. bd. trustees Stanford U., Calif., 1981, student fin. mgr. Assn. Students Stanford U., 1981; trustee Cazenovia Coll., N.Y., 1983. Recipient Meritorious Service medal State of Calif., 1986. Mem. Calif. Bar Assn. Lutheran. Home: 9951 Stoneglen Trail Littleton CO 80124 Office: Nuexco Internat Corp 1515 Arapahoe St Suite 900 Denver CO 80202

PETERSON, CYNTHIA JANE KITTSON, building materials company executive; b. Prosser, Wash., Nov. 24, 1948; d. Augustan and Myrna Ann (Nickisch) Kittson; AA with honors in Bus. Adminstrn., Columbia Basin Coll., 1975; postgrad. Wash. State U., 1975-77, Central Wash. State U., 1976-77; m. George Charles Peterson, Jan. 13, 1968. Receptionist, St. Luke's Hosp., Marquette, Mich., 1969; dep. treas. Kittitas County Treas.'s Office, Ellensburg, Wash., 1971-73; exec. sec. Frank B. Hall Ins. Co., Portland, Oreg., 1973-74; treas./controller Kennewick (Wash.) Indsl. & Elec. Supply, Inc., 1974—. Bd. dirs. Kennewick-Pasco Community Concert Assn., 1976, vol. membership dr., 1975—; dir. A Woman's Place Shelter; dir., treas. Tri-Cities Planned Parenthood; bd. dirs. Consumer Credit Counseling Service; dir. Carondelet Psychiat. Care Ctr.; dir. Tri-City Indsl. Devel. Council (bd. dirs. econ. devel. com.), Kennewick; vice chmn. Pub. TV Auction Cabinet, 1987, 88; chmn. Tri-Cities Legis. Council, 1987-88; mem. Wash. State Commn. to Tri-Cities Diversification Bd., 1988—; bd. dirs. United Way of Benton-Franklin Counties, 1988—. Recipient Outstanding Leadership award Columbia Basin Coll., 1975, Kennewick BPW Woman of Achievement award, 1986. Mem. Soc. Cert. Consumer Credit Execs., Internat. Credit Assn. (pres. Dist. 10, 1988—, pres. Tri-Cities chpt. 1982-83, conf. chmn. 1982, Credit Individual of Yr. 1982, Herb Barnes Disting. Service award 1985), Wash. State Credit Assn. (legis. liaison, pres. 1986-87), Credit Women-Internat. (pres. Tri-Cities chpt. 1979-80; chpt. Credit Woman of Yr. 1982), Internat. Credit Assn. (Disting Service award 1985). Club: Soroptimist Internat. Home: 4905 W 7th Ave Kennewick WA 99336 Office: 113 E Columbia Dr Kennewick WA 99336

PETERSON, DONALD ROBERT, magazine editor, vintage automobile consultant; b. Sandstone, Minn., Apr. 1, 1929; s. Martin Theodore and Margaret Mildred (Dezell) P.; m. Lois Taylor, Dec. 31, 1951 (div. 1975); children: Wyatt A., Winston B., Whitney C. (dec.), Westley D., Webster E.; m. Edie Tannenbaum, Aug. 31, 1975; 1 child, Ryan Kerry. Student, U. Minn., 1947-50; B.S., Gustavus Adolphus Coll., 1952. Asst. underwriter Prudential Ins. Co. Am., Mpls., 1953-64; chief health underwriter North Central Life, St. Paul, 1964-66; pres. 1st State Bank Murdock, Minn., 1967-73, EDON, Inc., Roswell, Ga., 1974—; editor Car Collector mag., Atlanta, 1977—; v.p., dir. Classic Pub. Inc., Atlanta, 1979—. Councilman, City of Murdock, 1968-72, mayor, 1972-74; del. State Republican Conv., 1970-72; treas. Swift County Rep. Com., 1970-73. Served with U.S. Navy, 1946-47. Recipient citation for disting. service Classic Car Club Am., 1965. Mem. Internat. Soc. Philos. Enquiry, Atlanta Press Club, Intertel, Mensa (pres. Ga. chpt. 1976-78), Swift County Bankers Assn. (pres. 1970-73), Soc. Automotive Historians, Milestone Car Soc., Classic Car Club Am. (chpt. pres. 1959, 60, 63). Republican. Clubs: Antique Automobile, Veteran Motor Car Am, Packard. Home: 1400 Lake Ridge Ct Roswell GA 30076 Office: 8601 Dunwoody Pl Suite 144 Atlanta GA 30350

PETERSON, HARRY EDWARD, packaging company executive; b. Chgo., Aug. 13, 1921; s. Palmer and Florence (Skedd) P.; student Ill. Inst. Tech., 1939; B.S. in Chemistry, DePaul U., 1943; m. Elaine Meyer, May 26, 1944; children—Pamela Elaine Jewell, Liane Marie, Kevin Edward, Daryl Megan Britton, Neil Evan. Chemist research dept. Continental Can. Co., Chgo., 1937-47, sect. chief indsl. products, 1941-47; founder Continental Filling Corp., 1947, v.p. gen. mgr., 1947-53, pres., 1953-55, dir., 1947-55; chmn. bd. Peterson-Puritan, Inc. (formerly Peterson Filling & Packaging Co.), Danville, Ill., 1955-80; pres., dir. Hepco, Inc., 1981—; dir. First Midwest Bank, Danville, (formerly Bank of Danville), Transnational Market Devel. Mem. Sci. Manpower Conservation Com., 1950-59; conservation com. WPB, World War II. Mem. adv. bd. St. Elizabeth Hosp., Danville, 1954—, pres., 1955; bd. dirs. United Hosp. Fund, Inc. of Danville; mem. Danville Econ. Devel., 1982—. Mem. Am. Chem. Soc., Soc. Cosmetic Chemists, Chem. Spltys. Mfg. Assn. (chmn. aerosol div. 1948-51, gov. 1952-53, pres. 1957, gov. 1958-61), Ill., Danville chambers commerce. Clubs: Danville Country (dir.), Elks. Home and Office: 1511 N Vermilion St Danville IL 61832

PETERSON, JEANNIE ELLEN, association executive; b. Traverse City, Mich., Feb. 18, 1940; d. Paulus E. Peterson and Ellen Rebecca (Glommen) Peterson Johnson; B.S. in Journalism, Northwestern U.-Ill., 1962, M.S. in Journalism, 1963. Freelance travel writer, Europer, 1963-67, 70-71; advt. writer McCann-Erickson, San Francisco, 1968-69; asst. editor Ambio, Internat. Environ. Jour., Royal Swedish Acad. Scis., Stockholm, 1972-77, editor-in-chief, 1978-81; dep. chief info. and external relations UN Population Fund, N.Y.C., 1981-85, sr. info. policy officer, 1985-86, dep. rep., sr. adviser population, Manila, 1986—; dir. pub. info. Ctr. Consequences of Nuclear War, Washington, 1984; mem. adv. com. U.S. Nat. Acad. Scis. Inst. Medicine Cont. Med. Implications of Nuclear War, 1985. Editor: The Aftermath: The Human and Ecological Consequences of Nuclear War, 1983. Recipient awards San Francisco Advt. Art Dirs. Club Show, 1968, Los Angeles Advt. Art Dirs. Club Show, 1968, Am. Advt. Fedn. Competition, 1969. Mem. Sci. Journalism (chmn. organizing com. 1980), Club of Rome. Home: 333 E 49th St Apt 10-L New York NY 10017 Office: UNDP UNFPA Manila Pouch United Nations New York NY 10017

PETERSON, KENNETH ALLEN, SR., superintendant of schools; b. Hammond, Ind., Jan. 20, 1939; s. Chester E. and Bertha (Hornby) P.; B.Ed. cum laude, Chgo. State U., 1963; M.S., Purdue U., 1970; NSF grantee U. Iowa, 1964-65; postgrad. U. Ill., 1977-81; Vanderbilt U.; m. Marilyn M. Musson, Jan. 3, 1961; children—Kimberly, Kari, Kenneth Allen. Tchr., Markham (Ill.) Sch. Dist. 144, 1961-67; prin. Brookwood Sch., Glenwood (Ill.) Sch. Dist. 1967, 1967-77, prin. Hickory Bend Sch., 1977-78, dir. spl. edn., 1978-80, asst. supt. schs., 1981-83, supt schs., 1983—; mem. No. Ill. Planning Commn. for Gifted Edn. Chmn. Steger (Ill.) Bicentennial Commn., 1976; vice chmn. Ashkum dist. Boy Scouts Am., 1981-83, lodge advisor, exec. bd., Vigil honor mem. Order of Arrow Calumet council Boy Scouts Am.; program com. South Cook County council Girl Scouts U.S.A., 1971-73, 80-81, mem. fin. com., 1981-86, also bd. dirs.; mem. Steger Community Devel. Commn. Recipient Order of Arrow Service nat. founders award, Silver Beaver award, Dist. award of merit Boy Scouts Am. Mem. Council Exceptional Children, Assn. Supervision and Curriculum Devel., P.T.A. (life), Am. Assn. Sch. Adminstrs., Kappa Delta Pi. Republican. Lutheran. Home: 3208 Phillips Ave Steger IL 60475 Office: 201 Glenwood Dyer Rd Glenwood IL 60425

PETERSON, LOWELL, cinematographer; b. Los Angeles, Feb. 1, 1950; s. Lowell Stanley and Catherine Linda (Hess) P.; m. Deanna Rae Terry, Aug. 2, 1981. Student, Yale U., 1968-69; BA in Theater Arts, UCLA, 1973. Camera operator Hollywood, Calif., 1973-83, Hollywood, 1983—. Asst. cinematographer various prodns. including Blind Ambition, 1979, Hawaii Five-O, 1979-80, White Shadow, 1980-81, Lou Grant, 1981-82, Two of a Kind, 1982, Remington Steele, 1982-83, Something About Amelia, 1983; camera operator various prodns. including Newhart, 1983, Scarecrow and Mrs. King, 1983-85, Children in the Crossfire, 1984, Stranded, 1986, Knots Landing, 1986-87, Star Trek: The Next Generation, 1987—, Like Father Like Son, 1987; contbr. articles to Film Comment, 1974, International Photographer, 1984—. Mem. Soc. Motion Picture and TV Engrs., Internat. Photographers Guild, Los Angeles Music Ctr. Opera Assn., Friends of UCLA Film Archive, U.S. Chess Fedn. Home and Office: 3815 Ventura Canyon Ave Sherman Oaks CA 91423

PETERSON, MELVIN NORMAN ADOLPH, marine geologist, academic administrator, educator, researcher; b. Evanston, Ill., May 27, 1929; s. Frederick Gothard Walter and Norma Alberta (Johnson) P.; m. Margaret Stewart Forbes, June 14, 1958; children—Katrina Elizabeth, John Frederick Forbes, Bruce Norman Adolph, Valerie Anne. B.S., Northwestern U., 1951, M.S., 1956; Ph.D., Harvard U., 1960. Registered profl. geologist, Calif. Asst. research geologist U. Calif.-San Diego, Scripps Instn. Oceanography, La Jolla, 1960-63, asst. prof., 1963-66, assoc. prof., 1966-71, acad. adminstr. V-VII marine geology program, 1971-87, chief scientist deep sea drilling project, 1967-72, program dir. deep sea drilling project, 1973-87. Program dir. series: Initial Reports of the Deep Sea Drilling Project, 1969-87; chief scientist Nat. Oceanic and Atmospheric Adminstrn., 1988—. Mem. sch. bd. Del Mar Union Elem. Schs., Calif., 1965-77, pres., 1975-77. Served to lt. (j.g.) USN, 1951-54, Korea. Recipient Blue Pencil award Fed. Editors Assn., 1969, spl. commendation Marine tech. Soc., 1970. Fellow Geol. Soc. Am.; mem. Pacific Research Found. (founder, pres. bd. dirs.). Republican. Presbyterian. Home: 1221 Umatilla Rd Del Mar CA 92014 Office: Office of the Chief Scientist Nat Oceanic and Atmospheric Adminstrn Herbert C Hoover Bldg Room 5808 15th & Constitution Ave Washington DC 20230

PETERSON, OSCAR EMMANUEL, pianist; b. Montreal, Que., Can., Aug. 15, 1925. LL.D. (hon.), Carleton U., 1973; D.Mus. (hon.), Berklee Coll. Music, Boston, 1984; studied classical music. Began music career on weekly radio show, then with Johny Holmes Orchestra, Can., 1944-49; appeared with Jazz at the Philharmonic, Carnegie Hall, 1949; toured the U.S. and Europe, 1950—; leader trio with Ray Brown, Irving Ashby, later Barney Kessel, Herb Ellis, Ed Thigpen, Sam Jones, Louie Hayes, concert appearances with Ella Fitzgerald, Eng., Scotland, 1955; appeared Stratford (Ont.) Shakespeare Festival, Newport Jazz Festival; recorded and performed solo piano works, 1972—; toured USSR, 1974, recordings with Billie Holiday, Fred Astaire, Benny Carter, Count Basie, Roy Eldridge, Lester Young, Ella Fitzgerald, Joe Pass, Orsted Pederson, Dizzy Gillespie, Harry Edison, Clark Terry ; author: Jazz Exercises and Pieces: Oscar Peterson New Piano Solos. Recipient award for piano Down Beat mag. 1950-54, 60-63, 65, 83, critics poll 1953; award Metronome mag., 1953-54; Grammy award 1974, 75, 77; 10-time jazz poll winner Playboy mag., named number one (piano) Jazz and Pop, Readers Poll 1968, 85. Service medal Order of Can., 1973, as a companion. Address: 2421 Hammond Rd, Mississauga, ON Canada L5K 1T3

PETERSON, RICHARD ALLEN, furniture design and manufacturing company executive; b. Chgo., July 29, 1955; s. Lawrence William and Marian (Malmquist) P.; m. Patricia Anne McLaughlin, Dec. 21, 1980; children: Christopher, Michael. B.A., So. Ill. U., 1980. Owner, mgr. Rick Peterson Design, Murphysboro, Ill., 1979-81; pres. Peterson Design Ltd., 1981—. Mem. Indsl. Designers of Am., Inst. of Bus. Designers (allied), Hayward C. of C. Republican. Methodist. Avocation: boating. Office: Peterson Design Furniture Inc 30962 San Benito Ct Hayward CA 94544

PETERSON, RICHARD CARSON, financial management company executive, healthcare consultant; b. Wilmington, N.C., Sept. 15, 1953; s. Graham Howard and Lillie Truman (Johnson) P.; m. Karen Zurn, Feb. 14, 1982. B.A. in Econs., Duke U., 1975, M.H.A. (Equitable Assurance Soc. U.S. Scholar), 1977. Adminstrv. resident The Duke Endowment, Charlotte, N.C., 1977; adminstrv. asst. N.C. Baptist Hosps., Inc., Winston-Salem, N.C., 1977-78;ptnr. mgmt. info. cons. div. Arthur Andersen & Co., St. Louis, 1978—. Mem. Am. Coll. Healthcare Execs., Healthcare Fin. Mgmt. Assn., Hosp. Mgmt. System Soc., Duke U. Alumni Assn. Republican. Episcopalian. Home: 14645 Brittania Dr Chesterfield MO 63017 Office: Arthur Andersen & Co 1010 Market St Saint Louis MO 63101

PETERSON, ROBERT AUSTIN, mower manufacturing company executive; b. Sioux City, Iowa, July 5, 1925; s. Austen W. and Marie (Mueller) P.; m. Carol May Hudy, May 19, 1925; children: Roberta, Richard, Thomas, Bruce. B.S., U. Minn., 1946, B.B.A., 1947. Credit mgr. New Holland Machine div. Sperry Rand Corp., Mpls., 1952-61; credit mgr. Toro Co., Mpls., 1961-68; treas. Toro Co., 1968-70, v.p. and treas. of internat. fin., 1970-83; v.p. fin., pres. Toro Credit Co., 1983—; bd. dirs. State Bond & Mortgage Co., State Bond Ins. Co., New Ulm, Tesco, South Miami, Fla., Duke Equipment Co., Sacramento, Toro Australia. Chmn. Prior Lake Spring Lake Watershed Dist., 1970-80; Chmn., mem. bd. dirs. Prior Lake Bd. Edn., 1965-71; chmn. Scott County Republican Party, 1969-70; Bd. dirs. Scott Carver Mental Health Center, 1969-73, Minn. Watershed Assn., 1972-76. Served to ensign USNR, 1943-46. Mem. Fin. Execs. Inst. Clubs: Prior Lake Yacht (bd. dirs.); Decathlon Athletic (Mpls.); St. Petersburg Yacht. Home: 14956 Pixie Point Circle SE Prior Lake MN 55372 Office: The Toro Co 8111 Lyndale Ave S Minneapolis MN 55420

PETERSON, ROBERT L., meat processing executive; b. Nebr., July 14, 1932; married; children: Mark R., Susan P. Ed., U. Nebr., 1951. With Wilson & Co., Jim Boyle Order Buying Co.; cattle buyer R&C Packing Co., 1956-61; cattle buyer, plant mgr., v.p. carcass prodn. Iowa Beef Processors, 1961-69; exec. v.p. ops. Spencer Foods, 1969-71; founder, pres., chmn., chief exec. officer Madison (Nebr.) Foods, 1971-76; group v.p. carcass div. Iowa Beef Processors, Inc. (name now IBP, Inc.) div. Occidental Petroleum Corp., Dakota City, Nebr., 1976-77, pres., chief operating officer, 1977-80, chief exec. officer, 1980-81, co-chmn. bd. dirs., 1981-82, chmn., chief exec. officer, dir., 1982—; exec. v.p., dir. Occidental Petroleum Corp., Los Angeles, 1982-87. Served with Q.M.C. U.S. Army, 1952-54. Club: Sioux City (Iowa) Country. Office: IBP Inc Box 515 Dakota City NE 68731 *

PETERSON, THERISIA LEE, commercial real estate broker; b. Pasadena, Calif., Oct. 19, 1941; d. Nathan Davis and Bonny May (Williams) Whitman; m. Harold Kenneth Peterson, Oct. 14, 1973 (div. Mar. 1980); 1 dau. Lauren Elizabeth. BS in Econs., U. Nev., 1964; MA in Neuro-Linguistics, U. San Francisco. Purchaser Nev. Dept. Motor Vehicles, Carson City, 1960-67; job devel. and placement specialist Nev. Dept. Human Resources, Carson City, 1967-70; bus. mgr. Nev. League Cities, Carson City, 1970-73; office mgr. econs. dept. U. Nev., Reno, 1973-75; owner T&P Investments, Reno, 1975—; from sales assoc. to prtnr. Lucini & Assocs., Reno, 1977-83, cons. real estate investments, 1978—; comml. div. mgr., cons. Keystone Realty, Reno, 1983-85; broker, owner Comml. Investment, 1985—; real estate brokerage and cons.; instr. Realty 500, Reno, 1980-83. Chmn. Nev. affiliate Am. Heart Assn., 1982-84, pres. No. Div., 1980-82, sec. No. Div., 1979-80, SW region rep. Nev. affiliate, 1984-86; subcom. chmn. Easter Seals, 1981—, Am. Lung Assn., 1985—; bd. dirs. Community Runaway and Youth Services, v.p. 1986—. Recipient Devoted Service award Am. Heart Assn., 1983, Ann. Million Dollar Club awards, 1978—. Mem. Realtors Nat. Mktg. Inst. (cert. Comml. Investment Mem. 1981—, grader, mem. other coms., governing counsellor 1985—), Nat. Assn. Realtors, Nev. Assn. Realtors (Grad. Realtors Inst., 1979, Omega Tau Rho award 1984), Real Estate Securities and Syndications, Internat. Real Estate Fedn., Reno Bd. Realtors. Republican. Lutheran. Club: Toastmasters (cert., Bronze award 1988 Lodge: Soroptomist (dir. 1979-81). Avocations: skiing, water skiing, hiking and camping, reading, piano. Home: 959 Nixon Ave Reno NV 89509 Office: 401 Ryland St Suite #300 Reno NV 89502

PETERSON, WALLACE CARROLL, SR., economics educator; b. Omaha, Mar. 28, 1921; s. Fred Nels and Grace (Brown) P.; m. Eunice V. Peterson, Aug. 16, 1944 (dec. Nov. 24, 1985); children: Wallace Carroll Jr., Shelley Lorraine. Student, U. Omaha, 1939-40, U. Mo., 1940-42; BA in Econs. and European History, U. Nebr., 1947, MA in Econs. and European History, 1948, PhD in Econs. and European History, 1953; postgrad., Handelshochschule, St. Gallen, Switzerland, 1948-49, U. Minn., 1951, London Sch. Econs. and Polit. Sci., 1952. Reporter Lincoln (Nebr.) Jour., 1946; instr. econs. U. Nebr., Lincoln, 1951-54, asst. prof., 1954-57, assoc. prof., 1957-61, prof., 1962—, chmn. dept. econs., 1965-75, George Holmes prof. econs., 1966—, v.p. faculty senate, 1972-73, pres. faculty senate, 1973-74; S.J. Hall disting. vis. prof. U. Nev., Las Vegas, 1983-84. Author: Income, Employment and Economic Growth, 6th edit, 1988, The Welfare State in France, 1960, Elements of Economics, 1973, Our Overloaded Economy: Inflation, Unemployment, and the Crisis in American Capitalism, 1981; editor: Nebr. Jour. Econs. and Bus., 1970-80; mem. editorial bd. Jour. Post Keynesian Econs; author bi-weekly newspaper column Money in Am. (Champion Media awards); contbr. articles to profl. jours. Mem. Nebr. Dem. Cen. Com., 1968-74, vice chmn., chmn. Nebr. Polit. Accountability and Disclosure Commn., 1977-80. Served to capt. USAAF, 1942-46. Recipient Outstanding Prof. award U. Nebr. at Lincoln, 1973-74, Outstanding Research and Creative Activity award U. Nebr., 1981, Burlington-No. Outstanding Tchr.-Scholar award U. Nebr., 1986; faculty research fellow U. Nebr., 1954, 59, 63, Fulbright fellow, 1957-58, 64-65; Mid-Am. State Univs. honor scholar, 1982-83. Mem. Assn. for Evolutionary Econs. (pres. 1976), AAUP (pres. Nebr. 1963-64, nat. council), Am. Econs. Assn., Midwest Econs. Assn. (pres. 1968-69), Mo. Valley Econ. Assn. (pres.-elect 1989), Assn. Social Econs., AAAS, Fedn. Am. Scientists, Common Cause, ACLU, UN Assn. U.S.A. (state pres.), Nebr. Council Econ. Edn. (chmn. 1976-77). Home: 4549 South St Lincoln NE 68506 Office: U Nebr Dept Econs 338 CBA Lincoln NE 68588-0489

PETERSON, WILLIAM FRANK, physician, administrator; b. Newark, Sept. 28, 1922; s. Edgar Charles and Margaret Benedict (Heyn) P.; m. Margaret Henderson Lee, June 28, 1946 (div. 1978); children: Margaret Lee, Edward Charles; m. 2d, Mary Ann Estelle McGrath, Nov. 29, 1980. Student, Cornell U., 1940-43; MD, N.Y. Med. Coll., 1946. Commd. lt. U.S. Air Force, 1946, advanced through grades to col., 1963; med. officer U.S. Air Force, 1946-70; chmn. dept. ob-gyn Washington Hosp. Ctr. 1970—; dir. Women's Clinic. Washington, 1971—, Ob-Gyn Ultrasound Lab., Washington, 1974—. Contbr. articles to profl. jours. Chmn., Maternal Mortality Com., 1981—. Decorated Legion of Merit, 1960, 70; Cert. Achievement, Office Surgeon Gen., USAF, 1967. Fellow Am. Coll. Ob-Gyn, ACS, Nat. Bd. Med. Examiners (diplomate), Washington Gynecol. Soc. (exec. council 1980-85). Republican. Episcopalian. Home: 50 Stonegate Dr Colesville MD 20904 Office: Washington Hosp Ctr 110 Irving St NW Washington DC 20010

PETERSON, WILLIAM PALMER, computer software company president; b. Urbana, Ill., Sept. 19, 1953; s. Robert Lenus and Evelyn Cortelyou (Fry) P. BA in Econs., Vassar Coll., 1976. Ptnr. Valhalla Marketers, Seattle, 1976-80; pres. RadioCom, N.Y.C., 1980—. Office: RadioCom 335 E 70th St New York NY 10021

PETHICK, CHRISTOPHER JOHN, physicist; b. Horsham, Sussex, Eng., Feb. 22, 1942; s. Richard Hope and Norah Betty (Hill) P. BA, Magdalen Coll., Oxford (Eng.) U., 1962, PhD, 1965. Fellow Magdalen Coll., Oxford U., 1965-70; research assoc. U. Ill., Urbana, 1966-68, research asst. prof., 1968-69, assoc. prof. physics, 1970-73, prof. physics, 1973—; prof. physics Nordita, Copenhagen, 1975—. A.P. Sloan research fellow, 1970-72. Fellow Am. Phys. Soc.; mem. Am. Astron. Soc., European Phys. Soc. Office: U Ill Dept Physics 1110 W Green St Urbana IL 61801 also: Nordita, Blegdamsvej 17, DK-2100 Copenhagen Denmark

PETIT, JACQUES, surgeon; b. Albert, Somme, France, Aug. 10, 1946; s. Louis and Claire (Penet) P.; m. Jacqueline Lech, Sept. 27, 1969; children: François, Thomas. Grad., Lille U., Nord, France, 1969, Amiens U., Somme, 1971. Asst. Amiens Hosp., 1974-79; urologist Univ. Hosp., Amiens, 1976, prof. surgery, 1979—, oncologist, 1987—. Served as med. officer with French Army, 1971-72. Home: 80 Delpech St, 80000 Amiens, Somme France Office: CHU Hopital Sud, 80000 Amiens Somme, France

PETIT, PARKER HOLMES, healthcare corporation executive; b. Decatur, Ga., Aug. 4, 1939; s. James Percival and Ethel (Holmes) P.; m. Sally Knight Simpson, Dec. 1, 1985; children: William Wright, Patricia Monique, Meredith Katherine. BS in Mech. Engring., Ga. Inst. Tech., 1962, MS in Engring. Mechanics, 1964; MBA, Ga. State U., 1973. Engr. Gen. Dynamics Corp., Fort Worth, Tex., 1966-67; engring. project mgr. Lockheed-Ga. Co., Marietta, 1967-71; pres., founder, chief exec. officer Healthdyne, Inc., Marietta, 1971—; dir. Atlantic S.E. Airlines, Atlanta, 1983—, CytRx Corp., Atlanta, 1985—. Author: Primer on Composite Materials, 1968; patentee in field. Chmn. bd. dirs. Sudden Infant Death Syndrome Inst., Atlanta, 1983—; active nat. adv. council Emory U. Med. Sch., Council fellows for the Emory, Ga. Tech. Biomed. Tech. Research Ctr. Served to 1st lt. U.S. Army, 1964-66. Recipient Humanitarian award La Societe Francaise De Bienfaisance, 1981; Internat. Bus. fellow , 1986. Mem. Health Industry Mfrs. Assn., Cobb County C. of C. (bd. dirs. 1980-82), Pi Kappa Phi. Republican. Presbyterian. Office: Healthdyne Inc 1850 Parkway Pl Marietta GA 30067

PETIT, PIERRE, composer; b. Poitiers, France, Apr. 21, 1922; s. Roger and Yvonne (Bouchet) P.; m. 3d, Liliane Fiaux, 1974; 5 children from previous marriages. Student Lycee Louis-le-Grand, Universite de Paris a la Sorbonne, Conservatoire de Paris. Head of course Conservatoire de Paris, 1950; dir. light music Office de Radiodiffusion et TV Francaise, 1960-64, dir. musical prodns., 1964-70, chamber music, 1970—; producer Radio-TV luxembourgeoise (R.T.L.), 1980; dir.-gen. Ecole Normale de Musique de Paris, 1963; music critic, Figaro; mem. Gov. Council Conservatoire de Paris. Compositions include: Suite for four cellos, 1945, Zadig (ballet), 1948, Cine-Bijou (ballet), 1952, Feu rouge, feu vert, 1954, Concerto for piano and orch., 1956, Concerto for organ and orch., 1960, Furia Italiana, 1960, Concerto for two guitars and orch., 1965; publs. include: Verdi, 1957, Ravel, 1970. Decorated Chevalier Legion d'honneur, Officer des arts et Lettres, Order nationale du Merit, Officier de l'Ordre du Cedre du Liban; Premier Grand Prix de Rome, 1946. Office: 114 Bis Blvd Malesherbes, 75017 Paris France *

PETIT, ROLAND, dancer, choreographer; b. Villemomble, France, Jan. 13, 1924; s. Edmond and Victoria (Repetto) P.; student Paris Opera Ballet Sch.; m. Zizi Jeanmaire, 1954; 1 son. Premier danseur Paris Opera, 1940-44; founder Les Vendredis de la Danse, 1944, Les Ballets de Champs-Elysees, 1945, Les Ballets de Paris, 1948; dir. Paris Opera Ballet, 1970; founder Les Ballets de Marseilles; works include: Le Rossignol et la Rose, Le Jeune Homme et la Mort, Les Demoiseiles de la Nuit, Deuil en Vingtquatre Heures, Le Loup, Cyrano de Bergerac, Camen, Les Forains, La Belle au Bois Dormant, Hans Christian Andersen, Folies Bergères, L'Eloge de la Folie, Paradise Lost, Pelleas et Melisande, Les Intermittences du Coeur, 1974, La Symphone Fantastique, 1975, Die Fledermaus, 1980; appeared in films, Hollywood, 1950-52. Decorated chevalier Légion d'Honneur des Arts et des Lettres, Grand prix nat. des arts et des lettres, 1979. Office: Ballet Nad de Marseille, Roland Petit, 1 place Auguste-Carli, 13001 Marseilles France *

PETITFRERE, CLAUDE YVES, historian; b. Calais, Pas-de-Calais, France, May 12, 1936; s. Marc and Lydie (Gauquié) P.; m. Christiane Péron; children: Isabelle, Bertrand. Licence, Faculté des Lettres, Tououse, 1957; agrégation, Paris, 1960; Doctorat d'Etat, U. de Mirail, Toulouse, 1977. Prof. Lycée Blaise Pascal, Clermont-Ferrand, France, 1960-64, Lycée Gay-Lussac, Limoges, France, 1964-66; censeur Lycée David d'Angers, Angers, France, 1966-67; asst. puis maître Faculté des Lettres, Toulouse, France, 1967-71; chargé de recherche au CNRS, Angers, France, 1971-74; maître-asst. U. François Rabelais, Tours, France, 1974-79, prof., 1979—. Author: Le Général Dupuy 1792-98, 1962, Les Vendéens d'Anjou, 1981, La Vendée et les Vendéens, 1981, Les Bleus d'Anjou, 1985, L'Oeil du Maître, 1986. Mem. Commn. d'Histoire de la Révolution française (v.p. 1986—), Commn. Internat. d'Histoire de la Révolution française. Home: 14 rue du Lude, 37300 Joué-lès-Tours France Office: Univ François Rabelais, 3 rue des Tanneurs, 37000 Tours France

PETNEL, JOSEPH ANTHONY CESARE, inventor; b. Rome, June 2, 1894; s. Francisco and Matilda (Formato) P.; came to U.S., 1900, naturalized, 1905; student public schs., night classes Ford Motor Co., Western Electric Co., Russell Sage Coll., 1925-32; m. Elsa C. Bartels, May 26, 1917; 1 dau., Daphne E. Petnel Westcott. Began as newsboy, 1905; apprentice mechanic, 1910; chauffeur, taxi bus. owner, 1918-20; with Ford Motor Co., 1925-29, Western Electric Co., 1929-32, dir., 1960; founder, pres. Telephone Dial Finger-Wheel Corp., N.Y.C., 1932; electrician Watervliet Arsenal, 1940-43, recipient award Merit, 1942; atty. pro se Western Electric AT&T merger, 1967; pres. Independent Inventor's Corp. Mem. Internat. Platform Assn., Masonic Vet. Assn. Elk. Patentee in U.S., Gt. Britain, Can.; patents include automobile accessories; metal tape, radiator shutter and cap, auto signal system, electric switches, gauge stencils, armament prodn. improvement, phonograph eccentric, telephone dials, dust shields, silent dial pawl, improved fingerwheels, outside lettering, three-way lamp, other communications and lighting equipment. Home: 598 3d Ave Troy NY 12182

PETRAITIS, KAREL COLETTE, lawyer; b. Chgo., Apr. 4, 1945; d. Ferdinand John and Dolores (Karroll) P.; B.A., U. Md., 1967, postgrad., 1967-68; J.D., George Washington U., 1971. Bar: Md. 1972, U.S. Supreme Ct. 1977. Law clk. Prince George's County Office of Law (Md.), 1971-72, atty., 1972-80; real estate agt. Harloff & Perkins, Riverdale, Md., 1978-82; individual practice law, College Park, Md., 1980—. Youth coordinator Agnew for Gov., 1966, Mathias for Senate, 1968, Beall for Senate, 1970; nat. committeewoman Md. Young Republicans, 1971-79, dir., 1979-81, legal counsel, 1972-79. Recipient cert. appreciation Prince George County Circuit Ct., 1979; cert. public service Prince George County, 1980; pres. Friends of Md. Summer Inst. for Creative and Performing Arts, 1983-86. Mem. Md. Bar Assn., Prince George County Bar Assn., AAUW, College Park Bd. Trade, past pres., v.p., treas., dir. Elizabeth Seton Alumni Assn., George Washington Law Alumni Assn. (dir. 1979-81, sec. 1982-84, pres. Md. chpt. 1985-87), U. Md. Alumni Assn. (pres. young alumni 1978-80, pres. Prince George's 1986-88). Roman Catholic. Home: 7307 Radcliffe Dr College Park MD 20740 Office: 4321 Hartwick Rd L201 College Park MD 20740

PETRI, ENRICO LODOVICO, accounting and taxation educator; b. N.Y.C., Dec. 9, 1929; s. Ludwig and Jean (Mascari) P.; m. Marion Joy Rogers; children—Robert, Jane, Victor. B.Sc., NYU, 1953, M.B.A., 1956, Ph.D., 1971. C.P.A., N.Y. Assoc. prof. acctg. Ferris State Coll., Big Rapids, Mich., 1965-66; prof. acctg. SUNY-Albany, 1966—, dir. acctg. programs, 1981-83, chmn. faculty, 1985—, dir. continuing profl. devel. course in taxation, 1982-84; adj. prof. Rensselaer Poly. Inst., 1975, Union Coll., 1978; cons. in field. Author, editor: (with others) Management Engineering and Research, 1969; Taxation of Earnings and Profits, 1973; Taxation of Accumulated Earnings, 1973. Contbr. articles to acad. and profl. jours. Manuscript reviewer Acctg. Rev. Jour., 1979—. SUNY/Touche Ross grantee, 1984—; Ford Found. fellow, 1963-65; named Outstanding Grad. Prof., Sch. Bus., SUNY-Albany, 1984, 85, Disting. Lectr., SUNY-Albany, 1981, 82. Fellow Sci. Inst. Pub. Info; mem. Am. Acctg. Assn., Am. Tax Assn., Nat. Assn. Accts. Am. Assn. Internat. Accts., (manuscript com. Albany chpt. 1971-80), Fin. Execs. Inst. (chmn. profl. devel. com. 1979-85, chmn. acctg. and law 1986—). Avocations: chess; skiing; bodybuilding; opera; oil painting. Listed among top 10 of most published authors in leading acad. jours. from 1965-85. Office: SUNY 1400 Washington Ave Albany NY 12222

PETRICIOLI ITURBIDE, GUSTAVO, government official; b. Mexico City, Aug. 19, 1928; m. María Luisa Castellón Cervantes. Student, Mex. Techol. Autonomous Inst., 1947-51; MS in Econs., Yale U., 1956. With Instl. Revolutionary Party, 1952—; chief tech. office, aide to gen. dir., advisor to chmn., chmn., dep. dir. Bank of Mex., 1948-67; dir. financing studies Ministry of Fin., 1967-70, undersec. income, 1970-74; pres. Nat. Commn. of Stock, 1976-82; dep. gen. dir. Multibanca Comermex, 1982; now sec. fin. and pub. credit Ministry Fin. and Pub. Credit, Mexico City; prof. econs. numerous univs. Office: Dept Fin & Pub Credit, Palacio Nacional, 1 Patio Mariano, 06066 Mexico City Mexico *

PETRIE, KEITH JAMES, psychologist; b. Hamilton, New Zealand, June 6, 1957; s. Eric Charlton and Isobel Mary (Mill) P.; m. Catherine Ann Ferguson, Jan. 4, 1985; 1 child, Jack Hugh. BA, Massey U., Palmerston North, New Zealand, 1978, PhD, 1984, diploma in clin. psychology, 1985; MA, Calif. State U., Los Angeles, 1981. Social worker Tokoroa (New Zealand) Hosp., 1979-80; sr. tutor Massey U., 1980-83; clin. psychologist Waikato Hosp., Hamilton, 1983-87, sr. clin. psychologist, 1987—. Contbr. articles to profl. jours. Office: PO Box 58, Hamilton 2000, New Zealand

PETRIZZELLI, GAETANO JOHN, product research director; b. Udine, Italy, Aug. 8, 1929; came to France, 1965; s. Pasquale Attilio and Teresa (Rumignani) P.; m. Renate Erna Mederer, Aug. 9,1962. BChemE, U. Rome, 1953. Plant engr. Shell Oil Co., Cardon, Venezuela, 1953-58; research and devel. lab chief Procter & Gamble, Amtimano, Venezuela, 1958-60; plant mgr. Corn Products Internat., Valencia, Spain, 1960-65, Strasburg, France, 1965-67; research and devel. dir. Corn Products Internat., Clamart, France, 1967—. Author: (with others) Food, Man and Society, 1975, La qualité des Produits Alimentaires, 1985; patentee in field. Mem. Europe Dessert Mixes Mfg. Assn. (pres. 1986—), Internat. Assn. Soup and Broth Mfg., Assn. Fabricants Desserts an Entremets, Assn. Fabricants Product Dietitiques. Home: 1 Allée Du Bois de Graville, 91190 Gil/Yvette France Office: Corn Products Europe-SPM, 379 Ave du Gen De Gaulle, 92142 Clamart France

PETRONE, WILLIAM FRANCIS, physician, microbiologist, corporate executive; b. Bklyn., Sept. 12, 1949; s. Arthur Carmen and Helen (Kenny) P.; B.A., U. Conn., 1972; M.S., U. Mass., 1974; Ph.D., U. R.I., 1978; M.D., U. South Ala., 1984; m. Kathleen Anne Baron, Aug. 25, 1979; children—William Gaetano, Katherine Bridget, Jason Daniel. Research asso. Coll. Medicine, U. South Ala., Mobile, 1978-80; resident in pediatrics Orlando (Fla.) Regional Med. Ctr., 1984-85, W.Va. U. Med. Ctr., 1985-87; emergency room pshysician Mercy Hosp., Springfield, Ma., 1987; pres. Med. Simulation Software. Mem. AAAS, AMA, Am. Med. Student Assn., N.Y. Acad. Scis., Sigma Xi. Roman Catholic. Contbr. articles on inflamation and white blood cell function to sci. jours.

PETRONI, ROBERTO, banker; b. Florence, Italy, July 13, 1948; s. Carlo and Lara (Del Brutto) P.; m. Patrizia Perfetto, Sept. 11, 1976; 1 dau., Francesca. Student Dartmouth Coll., Hanover, N.H., 1968-69; B.B.A. with high honors, U. Florence, 1972. With Banca Nazionale del Lavoro, 1972—, served in various bank brs., 1972-78, officer in charge legal office, 1981—. Fulbright scholar, 1968-69. Mem. Alpine Club, World Wildlife Fund, Kulturgemeinschaft Mitteleuropa. Home: 2 Via San Marino, 50126 Florence Italy Office: Banca Nazionale del Lavoro, Via Bettino 2, 50047 Prato Italy

PETROVIC, SVETOZAR, literature educator; b. Karlovac, Yugoslavia, June 28, 1931; s. Branko and Vera (Gjacic) P.; m. Radmila Gikic; 1 child from previous marriage, Ranko. BA, U. Zagreb, 1956, PhD, 1966. Lectr., asst. prof. U. Zagreb, Yugoslavia, 1959-70; from assoc. prof. to prof. U. Novi Sad, Yugoslavia, 1970-77; prof. comparative lit. U. Belgrade, Yugoslavia, 1977—; vis. prof. U. Chgo., 1965-69, 71, 75, 81; coordinator Colloquia Litteraria, Novi Sad, 1982—. Author: Criticism and the Work of Art, 1963 (award City of Zagreb 1964), The Problem of Sonnet in Early Croatian Literature, 1968, The Nature of Criticism, 1972 (award Republic of Croatia 1973), Form and Meaning, 1986 (Best Book of Criticism award 1986). Mem. Vojvodina Acad. Arts and Scis. Home: Fruskogorska 25, Stan 12, YU-21000 Novi Sad Yugoslavia Office: Filoloski Fakultet U Belgrade, Studentski Trg 3, YU-11000 Belgrade Yugoslavia

PETRUZZI, CHRISTOPHER ROBERT, business educator, consultant; b. Peoria, Ill., July 28, 1951; s. Benjamin Robert and Mary Katherine (Urban) P.; m. Therese Michele Vaughan, Aug. 21, 1982 (div.1987). B.A., Wabash Coll., 1972; M.B.A., U. Chgo., 1974; Ph.D., U. Southern Calif., 1983. Lectr. bus. U. Wis., Milw., 1975-77; cons. H.C. Wainwright, Boston, 1978-79; lectr. U. Southern Calif., 1978-81; prof. bus. U. Pa., Phila., 1981-84; prof. acctg. NYU, 1984—; dir. Health Hut, Inc., Los Angeles; pres. ECON, N.Y.C., 1987—. Earhart fellow, 1972-73; U. Chgo. fellow, 1974-76. Libertarian. Home: 2 Washington Sq Village New York NY 10012 Office: NYU Merrill Hall 100 Trinity Pl New York NY 10007

PETTERSEN, KJELL WILL, stock broker; b. Oslo, Norway, June 19, 1927; came to U.S., 1946, naturalized, 1957; s. Jens Will and Ragna O. (Wickstrom) P.; m. Marilyn Ann Stevens, Aug. 16, 1952; children: Thomas W., Maureen, Kevin W., Maryann, Kathleen. Student, Zion Theol. Sch., 1945-49, N.Y. Inst. Finance, 1955-56. Mgr. A.M. Kidder & Co., N.Y.C., 1954-64; sr. v.p., sec., dir. Halle & Stieglitz, Fillor Bullard Co., Inc., 1964-73; sr. v.p., dir. mktg. Parrish Securities, Inc., N.Y.C., 1973-74; cons. Loeb, Rhoades & Co., N.Y.C., 1974-79; sr. v.p., div. dir. Prudential Bache Securities,, N.Y.C., 1979—; dir. Ski for Light Inc., Mpls., Creative Arts Rehab. Ctr. Inc., N.Y.C.; Allied mem. N.Y. Stock Exchange, Am. Stock Exchange, Chgo. Bd. Trade.; Dir. Norwegian affairs N.Y. World Fair, 1964-65. Democratic candidate N.Y. State Assembly, Nassau County, 1962. Served with U.S. Army, 1949-53. Mem. N.Y. C. of C., Security Industry Assn., Nat. Assn. Security Dealers, Scandinavian Found., Bankers Club of Am., Norwegian-Am. C. of C. (dir.). Club: Norwegian (N.Y.C.). Home: The Excelsior 140 Prospect Ave Hackensack NJ 07601 also: 420 N Collier Blvd Marco Island FL 33937 Office: 100 Gold St Bache Plaza New York NY 10292

PETTERSEN, TOR ARVE, graphic designer; b. Trondheim, Norway, Jan. 24, 1940; arrived in Eng., 1962; s. Odd and Cally Agathe (Andersen) P.; m. Joan Lilian Rooke, May 10, 1969; children: Nicholas Tor, Joanna. Diploma in Design, London Coll. of Printing, 1965. Trainee artist Ekko Reklamebyra, Trondheim, 1956-59; art dir. asst. Alfsen & Becker A.S., Oslo, 1961-62; designer Caps Design, Ltd., London, 1965-66; designer, ptnr. Pettersen & Ptnrs., Ltd. (name formerly Lock Pettersen Ltd.), London, 1966—. Home: 20 Castle Rd, Weybridge England Office: Lock Pettersen Ltd, 56 Greek St, London W1V 5LR England

PETTERSON, DONALD K., foreign service officer, ambassador; b. Huntington Park, Calif., Nov. 17, 1930; s. Walter H. and Muriel Frances (McIntyre) P.; m. Julieta Rovirosa Argudin, Aug. 26, 1961; children: Susan, Julie, John, Brian. Student, San Luis Obispo Jr. Coll., 1952-53; B.A., U. Calif., Santa Barbara, 1956, M.A., 1960; postgrad., UCLA, 1959-60, Stanford U., 1967-68. Personnel analyst State of Calif., 1958-59; teaching asst. UCLA, 1959-60; commd. fgn. service office Dept. State, 1960; consul Am. embassy, Mexico City, 1961-62; vice consul Am. embassy, Zanzibar, 1963-64; prin. officer Am. embassy, 1964-65; polit. officer Lagos, 1966-67; served in personnel office Dept. State, Washington, 1968-70; dep. chief of mission Freetown, Sierra Leone, 1970-72; polit. counselor Pretoria, 1972-75; mem. policy planning staff Dept. State, Washington, 1975-77; dir. Office So. African Affairs Dept. State, 1977-78, dep. asst. sec. of state, 1978; U.S. ambassador to Somalia 1978-82; vis. disting. scholar UCLA, 1983-84; dep. dir. office Mgmt. Ops., Dept. State, Washington, 1984-86; Am. ambassador to Tanzania Washington, 1986—. Served with USN, 1948-52. Recipient Superior Honor award Dept. State, 1964, 71, Order of the Somali Star award; named Alumnus of Yr. U. Calif., Santa Barbara, 1965. Home: 3395 S Niguera No 7 San Luis Obispo CA 93401 Office: Dar Es Salaam' Dept of State Washington DC 20520

PETTERSON, WILHELMUS JOHANNES ANTONIUS, semiconductor company executive; b. Rotterdam, The Netherlands, Oct. 19, 1932; s. Hendrikus Johannes Marinus and Cornelia Maria (Wyzenbroek) P.; m. Agnes Anna van der Jeuyd; children: Frank Ronald, Marjolein Helena, Hanneke Maria. Grad. engr., High Tech. Sch., Amsterdam, 1962. Research and devel. engr. testing and installation van de Graaff partical acceleration High Voltage Engring., Amersfoort, The Netherlands, 1962-70; mktg. and sales exec. Advanced Semiconductor Materials, Bilthoven, The Netherlands, 1970—; cons. assembly semiconductors, The Netherlands, 1978—. Served to lt. Dutch Air Force, 1952-54. Roman Catholic. Home: Breeland 8, 3828 VA Hoogland The Netherlands

PETTERSSON, KARL HENRIK, bank executive, author; b. Linkoping, Sweden, Sept. 13, 1937; s. Timar and Saga Pettersson; m. Ulla Lind (div. 1970); m. Anita Klintsell, July 10, 1974; children: Carina, Andreas. Masters in Econs., Stock U., 1963; PhD, Royal Inst. Tech., 1966; postgrad., Stanford U., 1966-67. Asst. to chief exec. officer Sundsvallsbanken, Sundsvall, Sweden, 1967-70; dept. head Ministry of Industry, Stockholm, 1970-75, undersec., 1975-77; gen. mgr., chief exec. officer Lanssparbanken, Goteborg, Sweden, 1977-82, Forsta Sparbanken, Goteborg, 1982—. Author: Reap the Whirlwind, 1974, Exit Welfare State ?, 1987. Office: Forsta Sparbanken, S-404 80 Gothenburg Sweden

PETTERSSON, LARS KARL JOHAN, art historian; b. Ruovesi, Finland, Aug. 12, 1918; s. Johan Walfrid and Elin Alina (Kraftenberg) P.; M.A., U. Helsinki, 1941, Ph.D., 1951; m. Helvi Hokkanen, 1941; children: Eero, Marjatta Pettersson Nielsen. Intendant, Mus. Suomenlinna (Finland), 1944-45, 49-51, Hist. Dept. Archaeol. Com., Finland, 1945-49; prof. art history U. Helsinki, 1951-81. Mem. restoration com. Turku Castle, 1949-61; mem. restoration com. Hämeenlinna Castle, 1956-87, chmn. 1971-87; mem. restoration com. Olavinlinna Castle, 1961-75; mem. Finland State Fine Arts Com., 1953-56, chmn., 1955-56; chmn. bd. Finnish Art Acad., 1955-57; rep. Finnish Archtl. Mus., 1956-82. Served to lt., Finnish Army, 1940-45. Recipient E.J. Nyströms prize Societas Scientiarum Fennica. Mem. Ehrensvärd-Assn. (sec. 1945-52, mem. honor 1977), Finnish Archaeol. Assn. (chmn. 1968-73), Finnish Archtl. Soc., Finnish State Price of Bldg. and Planning Soc. Author: Äänisniemen kirkollinen puuarkkitehtuuri, 1950; Die kirchliche Holzbaukunst auf der Halbinsel Zaoneže in Russisch-Karelien (diss.), 1950; Hämeen linna ja Hämeen keskiaikaiset kirkot (Hämeen historia I), 1955; Utajärven kirkko ja tapuli, 1962; Suomenlinna arkkitehtuurin muistomerkkinä , 1968; Hailuodon palanut puukirkko ja sen maalaukset, 1971; Haapaveden kirkot (Haapaveden kirja), 1973; Kaksikymmentäneljäkulmaisen ristikirkon syntyongelmia, 1978; Kyrkor och klockstarlar i svenska Österbotten (Soenska Österbottens historia V), 1985, Temprum Saloense, 1987. Home: Purjetuulenkuja 8, 00850 Helsinki Finland

PETTEY, DIX HAYES, mathematics educator; b. Salt Lake City, Mar. 16, 1941; s. Leo Melvin and Kathleen (Hayes) P. B.S., U. Utah, 1965, Ph.D., 1968. Asst. prof. to prof. U. Mo., Columbia, 1968—; vis. prof. U.S. Mil. Acad., 1984; sr. scientist Presearch, Inc., summer 1985. Contbr. articles to profl. jours. Mem. Math. Assn. Am., Soc. Indsl. and Applied Math., Ops. Research Soc. Am., Mormon. Current Work: Reliability of communications networks; military applications; computer memory systems; P-minimal and P-closed topological spaces. Subspecialty: Operations research (mathematics).

PETTIBONE, PETER JOHN, lawyer; b. Schenectady, N.Y., Dec. 11, 1939; s. George Howard and Caryl Grey (Ketchum) P.; m. Jean Kellogg, Apr. 23, 1966; children: Stephen, Victoria. AB summa cum laude, Princeton U., 1961; JD, Harvard U., 1964; LLM, NYU, 1971. Bar: Pa. 1965, D.C. 1965, N.Y. 1968, U.S. Supreme Ct. 1974. Assoc. Cravath, Swaine & Moore, N.Y.C., 1967-74, Lord Day & Lord, Barrett Smith, N.Y.C., 1974-76; ptnr. Lord Day & Lord, Barrett Smith, N.Y.C. and Washington, 1976—; bd. dirs., vice chmn. N.Y. State Facilities Devel. Corp., N.Y.C., 1983—. Trustee Civitas, N.Y.C., 1984—. Served to capt. U.S. Army, 1965-67. Mem. ABA, Assn. of Bar of City of N.Y., U.S.- USSR Trade and Econ. Council, Inc., (U.S. co-chmn. legal com. 1980—). Episcopalian. Clubs: Anglers (N.Y.C.), Shelter Island (N.Y.) Yacht, Soc. of Cin. Home: 1158 Fifth Ave New York NY 10029 Office: Lord Day & Lord Barrett Smith 25 Broadway New York NY 10004 also: 1201 Pennsylvania Ave NW Washington DC 20004

PETTIT, HENRY JEWETT, JR., editor, emeritus English language educator; b. Olean, N.Y., Dec. 8, 1906; s. Henry Jewett and Anne Benson (Edwards) P.; student Bucknell U., 1924-25; B.A., Cornell U., 1932, Ph.D., 1938; M.A., U. Oreg., 1934; m. Mary Madelyn Mack, July 18, 1927 (dec.); 1 dau., Judith Walsh; m. 2d, Gertrude Stockton Eckhardt, Apr. 9, 1977. Instr. English, U. Tulsa, 1934-36, Cornell U., Ithaca, N.Y., 1936-38, Yale, 1938-39; asst. prof. English, Beloit (Wis.) Coll., 1939-40; from assoc. prof. to prof. English, U. Colo., Boulder, 1940-72, prof. emeritus, 1972—, hon. keeper of rare books Norlin Library, 1950-62; vis. prof. U. Vt., summer 1958. Served with USNR, 1942-45. Recipient U. Colo. Faculty fellowships, 1948, 54, 60, 66, 69; Am. Philos. Soc. grantee, 1960, 66, 69; Am. Council Learned Socs. grantee, 1963. Mem. Modern Humanities Research Assn. (nat. sec. 1958-63), MLA (exec. sec. Rocky Mountain chpt. 1966-70), AAAS, Naval Res. Assn. Democrat. Clubs: Town and Gown (Boulder); Univ. (Denver). Author: A Bibliography of Young's Night-Thoughts, 1954; A Collection of English Prose, 1660-1800, 1962; The Correspondence of Edward Young 1683-1765, 1971; Annual Bibliography of English Language and Literature, 1942-52; A Dictionary of Literary Terms, 1951; The Authentic Mother Goose, 1960; mem. editorial bd. Western Humanities Rev., 1950-85, Colo. Quar., 1957-77; English Language Notes, 1963-74. Home: 1333 King Ave Boulder CO 80302

PETTIT, HORACE, allergist, consultant; b. Jan. 28, 1903; s. Horace and Katherine (Howell) P.; B.S., Harvard Coll., 1927; M.D., 1931; m. Millicent Lewis, Nov. 22, 1924; children—Emily Connery, Horace (dec.), Deborah Myers, Norman; m. Jane Mann Hiatt, May 13, 1950; 1 adopted dau., Barbara Mann Ralph. Intern, Bryn Mawr Hosp., 1933-34; asst. instr., instr., assoc. bacteriology U. Pa. Sch. Medicine, 1932-39, instr. medicine, 1939-53; pvt. practice allergy, 1940-42, 1947-75; cons. in allergy Bryn Mawr Hosp.; cons. allergist Bryn Mawr Coll. Served from maj. to lt. col. AUS, 1942-46. Fellow Coll. Physicians of Phila.; mem. Am. Acad. Allergy, Am. Soc. Microbiology, Phila. County, Pa. med. socs., AMA, Phila. Allergy Soc. (pres. 1958-59), United World Federalists (mem. nat. exec. council 10 years), St. Andrew's Soc. Phila. Unitarian. Clubs: Harvard (Phila.); Merion Cricket (Haverford, Pa.); Camden (Maine) Yacht. Home and Office: 123 Kennedy Ln Bryn Mawr PA 19010

PETTIT, PHILIP NOEL, philosopher, educator; b. Ballinasloe, Ireland, Dec. 20, 1945; arrived in Australia, 1983; s. Michael Antony and Bridget Christina (Molony) P.; m. Eileen Theresa McNally, July 1, 1978; children: Rory Conor, Owen Patrick. BA with honors, Nat. Univ. Ireland, Dublin, 1966, MA with honors, 1967; PhD, Queen's U., Belfast, Ireland, 1970. Lectr. Queen's U., 1967-68, University Coll., Dublin, 1968-72, Univ. Coll., Dublin, 1975-77; research fellow U. Cambridge, Eng., 1972-75; prof. philosophy U. Bradford, Eng., 1977-83; professorial fellow Inst. Advanced Studies Australian Nat. U., Canberra, 1983—. Author: The Concept of Structuralism, 1977, Judging Justice, 1980; co-author: Semantics and Social Science, 1981. Fellow Acad. Social Scis. Australia. Home: 46 Southwell St, Weetangera 2614, Australia Office: Australian Nat U, PO Box 4, Research Sch Social Scis, Canberra 2600, Australia

PETTITE, WILLIAM CLINTON, pub. affairs cons.; b. Reno, Nev.; s. Sidney Clinton and Wilma (Stibal) P.; m. Charlotte Denise Fryer; children—Patrick Keane, William Ellis, Joseph Clinton. Owner, Market Lake Citizen & Clark County Enterprise Newspapers, Roberts, Idaho, 1959-70, pub., 1959-61; publicity dir. Golden Days World Boxing Champs, Reno, 1970; public affairs cons., Fair Oaks, Calif., 1966—. County probate judge, Idaho, 1959-61; acting County coroner, 1960-61; sec., trustee Fair Oaks Cemetery Dist., 1963-72; dir. Fair Oaks Water Dist., 1964-72, v.p., 1967-68, pres., 1968-70; dir., v.p. San Juan Community Services Dist., 1962-66, 68-72; exec. sec. Calif. Bd. Landscape Architects, 1976-77. Cons. Senate-Assembly Joint Audit Com. Calif. Legislature, 1971-73; exec. officer Occupational Safety and Health Appeals Bd., 1981-82; mem. regulatory rev. commn. Calif. FabricCare Bd., 1981-82; mem. Sacramento County Grand Jury, 1981-82, cons. bd. supvs. Sacramento County, 1985-86. Election campaign coordinator for E.S. Wright, majority leader Idaho Senate, 1968, Henry Dworshak, U.S. Senator, 1960, Hamer Budge, U.S. Rep., 1960, Charles C. Gossett, former Gov. Idaho, 1959-74; asst. sgt. at arms Rep. Nat. Conv., 1956; chmn. Rep. County Central Com., 1959-61; del. Rep. State Conv., 1960. Chmn. Idaho County Centennial Commn., 1959-61. Recipient Idaho Centennial award, 1968, 69. Mem. Assn. Sacramento County Water Dists. (dir. 1967-72, pres. 1970-72), Nat. Council Juvenile Ct. Judges (com. 1959-61). Author: Memories of Market Lake, Vol. I, 1965; A History of Southeastern Idaho, Vol. II, 1977, Vol. III, 1983; contbr. articles to newspapers, profl. jours. Home: PO Box 2127 Fair Oaks CA 95628 Office: 2631 K St Sacramento CA 95816

PETTY, GUY JAMES, designer, scenic engineer, theatrical consultant; b. Pueblo, Colo., Sept. 8, 1951; s. Walter Lee and Anna Elizabeth (Kilsay) P.; m. Carla Rene Hord, Oct. 6, 1972. BS, U. So. Colo., 1973; postgrad., U. Wyo., 1973-75. Art dir., theater mgr. Lincoln Plaza, Oklahoma City, 1975-76; art dir. Design Concepts, Las Vegas, Nev., 1976-79; freelance art dir. The Design Table, Las Vegas, 1979-83, freelance art dir., producer, 1985—; art dir. Las Vegas Scenery Studios, 1983-85; cons. design Safari's, Las Vegas, Mitsui Greenland, Fukuoka, Japan, Maritz Communications, St. Louis; art dir. Englebert Humperdinck, Hollywood, Calif. Prin. works include: (concert tour) stage design Michael Jackson World Tour, 1979; (stage show) scenic design Mikado 20th anniversary, Tokyo, 1984, A Caesars Palace Christmas Show, Crystal Palace Hotel & Casino, Nassau, Bahamas, 1988; designs for John Denver, Loretta Lynn, Beach Boys, Gatlin Bros., Lou Rawls, Kenny Rogers, Robert Guillaume, Babby Vinton, Supertramp, Mills Brothers, Della Reese shows; (ice stage show) scenic design New Fujiya Grand Opening, Atami, Japan, 1986; (trade show) exhibit design include Shell Oil Co., 1986, Mobil Oil Conv., Nat. Benefit Life, Deltona, Rodeo Am., Gulf State Toyota; scenic design local chpt. Muscular Dystrophy Assn., Las Vegas, 1983-85, United Cerebral Palsy, 1984; produced and directed 1987 Toyota Can. New Car Show, Am. Super Dream, Fugiya Hotel; projects include The Floorplan Library offering floorplan specifications for all Las Vegas theaters and conv. facilities. Recipient scholarship U. So. Colo., 1970-73, Best Show Design award Am. Water Exhibit, Las Vegas, 1984. Mem. Internat. Assn. Theatrical Stage Employees (Local 720). Home and Office: The Design Table 241 N Crestline Dr Las Vegas NV 89107

PETTY, OLIVE SCOTT, geophysical engineer; b. Olive, Tex., Apr. 15, 1895; s. Van Alvin and Mary Cordelia (Dabney) P.; m. Mary Edwina Harris, July 19, 1921; 1 son, Scott. Student Ga. Inst. Tech., 1913-14; BS in Civil Engring., U. Tex., 1917, CE, 1920. Registered profl. engr., Tex. Adj. prof. civil engring. U. Tex., 1920-23; structural engr. R.O. Jameson, Dallas, 1923-25; pres. Petty Geophys. Engring. Co., Petty Labs., Inc., San Antonio, 1925-52, chmn. bd., 1952-73; chmn. bd. Petty Geophys. Engring. Co. de Mex. S.A. de C.V., 1950-73; partner Petty Ranch Co., 1968—; ranching, oil, timber and investment interests, 1937—. Author: Seismic Reflections, Recollections of the Formative Years of the Geophysical Exploration Industry, 1976; A Journey to Pleasant Hill, The Civil War Letters of Capt. E. P. Petty, C.S.A., 1982; patentee geophys. methods, instruments, equipment, including electrostatic seismograph detector in op. on the moon and on Mars and now NASA's standard for space exploration. Benefactor, San Antonio Symphony Soc., McNay Art Mus.; mem. exec. com., founding mem. chancellor's council U. Tex. System, Austin, also founding mem., hon. life mem. Geology Found.; adv. council U. Tex., Austin. Served as lt. Engrs., U.S. Army, 1917-18; AEF in France. Hon. adm. Tex. Navy; recipient Disting. Grad. award U. Tex. Coll. Engring., Austin, 1962; Tex. Acad. Sci. (hon. life), N.Y. Acad. Sci.; mem. ASCE (hon. life), AIME (Legion of Honor), Am. Assn. Petroleum Geologists, AAAS (50-yr. mem.), Am. Petroleum Inst., Nat. Soc. Profl. Engrs. (life), Am. Geophys. Union, Houston Geophys. Soc., San Antonio Geophys. Soc., South Tex. Geol. Soc., Soc. Petroleum Engrs. (Legion of Honor), Am. Assn. Petroleum Geologists (life), Soc. Am. Mil. Engrs. (life), Soc. Exptl. Geophysicists (founding mem.; hon. life), Soc. 1st Inf. Div. (founding), Tex. Soc. Profl. Engrs., Explorers Club (life), Mil. Profl. Engrs. in Pvt. Practice, Wisdom Soc., Am. Geol. Inst. (Centurian Club), Am. Assn. Petroleum Geologists Trustee Assn. (life), Chi Epsilon (hon. life), Theta Xi, Tau Beta Pi. Baptist. Clubs: San Antonio Country, Argyle, St. Anthony, Girard. Home: 101 E Kings Hwy San Antonio TX 78212 Office: 711 Navarro St Antonio TX 78205

PETTY, RONALD FRANKLIN, public relations executive; b. Trenton, Mar. 17, 1947; s. Warren Herman Lee and Geraldine Frances (Roberts) P.; m. Cynthia Ann Hoover, Sept. 16, 1967 (div. 1987); children: Scott Eric, Christopher Lee. BA in Advt., Syracuse U., 1969, BA in Econs., 1972. Asst. sales promotion mgr. Cambridge Filter Corp., Liverpool, N.Y., 1969-72; advt. mgr. Am. Challenger, Fulton, N.Y., 1972, mgr. communications, 1973; advt./pub. relations account exec. Barlow/Johnson Advt., Fayetteville and Latham, N.Y., 1973-75; advt./pub. relations account exec. Nowak-Voss Advt., Syracuse, N.Y., 1975-77, dir. pub. relations, 1976-77; pub. relations dir. U.S Pioneer Electronics Corp., Moonachie, N.J., 1977-81, gen. mgr. communications, 1981-82; dir. communications Pioneer Video, Inc., 1982-84; dir. mktg. services SONY Broadcast Products Co., 1984-86; dir. mktg. broadcast and profl. audio products SONY Communications Products Co., 1986-87; dir. corp. communications SONY Corp. of Am., 1987—; pub. relations cons. to artist Peter Max; cons. in field. Mem. com. for redistricting, Liverpool (N.Y.) Sch. Bd., 1976; mem. Rockaway Boro Citizens Adv. Com., 1981-82, mem. planning bd., 1982-85, chmn. planning bd., 1983, councilman, 1983-87, chmn. ordinance com., 1984-85, chmn. personnel com., 1986-87, mem. pub. safety com., 1984, 86, 87, mem. pub. works com., 1985; del. N.J. State Dem. Conv., 1983; mem. Rockaway Boro Shade Tree Commn., 1983-84; benefactor, patron Met. Opera Assn., 1981-84; sustaining mem. Republican Nat. Com., 1980-83, 86. Recipient citation for community service United Way of Central N.Y., 1976; dir. Project-of-the-Yr. award, Syracuse Jr. C. of C., 1977. Mem. Assn. of Indsl. Advertisers, Public Relations Soc. Am., Electronic Industry Assn. (chmn. show adv. com. 1982). Contbr. articles to profl. jours. Office: Sony Dr Park Ridge NJ 07656

PETTY, TRAVIS HUBERT, pipeline company executive; b. Clarksville, Tex., July 31, 1928; s. Joseph H. and Kathleen (Mauldin) P.; m. Berenice Wieland, Feb. 10, 1948; children: Brian, Paul, David, Kevin, Sean, Karen, Michael. Student, U. Tex., 1945-46. With El Paso (Tex.) Natural Gas Co., from 1946, asst. controller, 1961-65, controller, 1965-69, v.p., 1969-73, dir., 1971—, exec. v.p., 1973-76, pres., 1976-78, chmn., 1978-85; dir. The El Paso Co., 1974—, exec. v.p., 1974-78, vice-chmn., 1978-79, chmn., 1979—, pres., 1980—; vice chmn. Burlington No., Inc. (parent co.), Seattle, 1983—; dir. Tex. Commerce Bank, El Paso, Burlington No. Inc., Tex. Commerce Bancshares. Mem. Am. Gas Assn., Pacific Coast Gas Assn. (past chmn.), Interstate Natural Gas Assn. (dir.), So. Gas Assn., past chmn. adv. council). Office: The El Paso Co PO Box 1492 El Paso TX 79978 also: Burlington No Inc 999 3rd Ave Seattle WA 98104 *

PETZAL, DAVID ELIAS, editor, writer; b. N.Y.C., Oct. 21, 1941; s. Henry and Aline Born (Bixer) P.; m. Arlene Ann Taylor, May 29, 1974. B.A., Colgate U., 1963. Editor Maco Publs., N.Y.C., 1964-69; mng. editor Davis Publs., N.Y.C., 1969-70; features editor Hearst Publs., N.Y.C., 1970-72; mng. editor CBS Publs., N.Y.C., 1972-79, editor, 1979-83, exec. editor, 1983-87; exec. editor Times-Mirror Mags., N.Y.C., 1987—. Author: The .22 Rifle, 1972; editor: The Experts Book of the Shooting Sports, 1972, The Experts Book of Upland Game and Waterfowl Hunting, 1975, The Experts Book of Big-Game Hunting in North America, 1976. Home: PO Box 219 Bedford NY 10506 Office: Times Mirror Mags 380 Madison Ave New York NY 10017

PETZEL, FLORENCE ELOISE, educator; b. Crosbyton, Tex., Apr. 1, 1911; d. William D. and A. Eloise (Punchard) P.; Ph.B., U. Chgo., 1931, A.M., 1934; Ph.D., U. Minn., 1954. Instr., Judson Coll., 1936-38; vis. instr. Tex. State Coll. for Women, 1937; asst. prof. textiles Ohio State U., 1938-48; asso. prof. U. Ala., 1950-54; prof. Oreg. State U., 1954-61, 67-75, 77, prof. emeritus, 1975—, dept. head, 1954-61, 67-75; prof., div. head U. Tex., 1961-63; prof. Tex. Tech U., 1963-67; vis. prof. Wash. State U., 1967. Effie I. Raitt fellow, 1949-50. Mem. Seattle Art Mus., Oreg. Art Mus., Textile Mus., Met. Opera Guild, San Francisco Opera Assn., Portland Opera Assn. Sigma Xi, Phi Kappa Phi, Omicron Nu, Iota Sigma Pi, Sigma Delta Epsilon. Author Textiles of Ancient Mesopotamia, Persia and Egypt, 1987; contbr. articles to profl. jours. Home: 730 NW 35th St Corvallis OR 97330

PETZOLD, HORST WILLY, aviation research executive; b. Leipzig, German Dem. Republic, Feb. 21, 1923; came to U.S., 1962; m. Margarete Gertrud Reher, Jan. 20, 1948; 1 child, Gunnar Horst. Student, numerous flying schs., German Dem. Republic, Indsl. Engring. Sch., German Dem. Republic. Pres. World Import, Canada, 1955-60; cons. Canada, U.S., 1962—, writer, 1955—; gen. mgr. Kasper Aircraft, Seattle, 1971-81; pres. Aviation Research, Seattle, 1962—. Contbr. articles to profl. jours. Adv. mem. Rep. Party, Washington. Served with German Air Force, 1939-45. Numerous decorations, awards, citations. Mem. Am. Security Council, German Am. Nat. Congress, Aviation Space Writers Assn. Home and Office: 3935 SW Elmgrove Seattle WA 98136

PEUGEOT, ROLAND, automobile company executive; b. Mar. 20, 1926; ed. Lycees Janson-de-Sailly and St. Louis Paris, Harvard. Pres., Peugeot Freres, 1959—; v.p. gen. mgr. Peugeot S.A., 1964—, pres. bd. surveillance, 1972—; v.p. bd. dirs. Automobiles Peugeot, 1965—, v.p. bd. surveillance, 1973—; bd. surveillance S.K.F., co. for mech. applications; adminstr. Chambre Syndicale des Constructeurs d'Automobiles. Address: 170 ave Victor-Hugo, 75116 Paris France *

PEW, GEORGE THOMPSON, JR., investment banker; b. Bryn Mawr, Pa., Mar. 25, 1942; s. George Thompson and Constance (Clarke) P.; student Yale U., 1965, U. Pa., 1971; m. Sandra Kennedy, Oct. 23, 1982; children: George Thompson III, Alexis Clarke, Jameson E. Delk. Mgmt. trainee Sun Co., Phila., 1963-64; registered rep. N.Y. Stock Exchange, Butcher & Singer Inc., Phila., 1971-84; chief exec. officer, pres. Nat. Ry. Mgmt. Corp., Villanova, Pa., 1979—; cons. in field; dir. Naramco, Villanova, The Glenmede Fund, Inc.; prin. Phila. Investment Banking Co.; dir. Crusader Savs. & Loan.Mem. govt. and founds. com. United Way of Phila., 1973-75; dir. Phila. Charity Ball, 1976—; v.p., bd. dirs., exec. com. Opera Co. Phila. Served with U.S. Army, 1966-69. Mem. Assn. of MBA Execs. Republican. Episcopalian. Clubs: Union League, Racquet, Rittenhouse, Merion (Pa.) Cricket, The Courts, Bay Head Yacht, Corinthian Yacht, St. Elmo, Radnor Hunt. Office: 1 Aldwyn Center Villanova PA 19085

PEWITT, JAMES DUDLEY, academic administrator; b. Franklin, Tenn., July 28, 1930; s. James Isaac and Eleanor (Dudley) P.; m. Betty Louise Hightower, Oct. 31, 1952; children: Ransom D., James P., Thomas E. Student, Vanderbilt U., 1948-51; MBA, MS, U. So. Calif., 1964, D in Bus. Adminstrn., 1967. Commd. lt. USAF, 1952, advanced through grades to col., 1969; spl. asst. for econ. analysis Office of Sec. of Air Force, 1967; exec. to asst. sec. Air Force for Fin. Mgmt.; asst. Da Nang Air Base, Vietnam, 1972; dep. comdr. for ops. Vietnam, 1972, vice comdr. Gunfighters, 1972; chief linebacker ops. Staff of Dir. of Ops., Vietnam, 1972; dir. mgmt. analysis USAF, 1973, ret., 1973; dir. grad. sch. bus., asst. to v.p. for fiscal affairs U. Ala., Birmingham, 1973-74, asst. v.p. ops. and planning, 1974-77, v.p. adminstrn., 1977-84, chmn. faculty athletic com., 1984—, sr. v.p. adminstrn., 1984—; bd. dirs. Birmingham Cable Communications, Allied Products Co. Mem. Birmingham Airport Authority, 1986—; mem. Fgn. Relations Com., Birmingham, 1975-87, Operation New Birmingham, 1978-80, Downtown Action Com., 1980-81, ; mem. exec. bd. Boy Scouts Am., Birmingham, 1979-81; div. chmn. United Way, 1976-78, 87, sect. chmn., 1979-86; spl. gifts chmn. State of Ala. Heart Assn., 1980-81, chmn. Jefferson-Shelby County Heart Fund Drive, 1981-82, bd. dirs., 1982-85, 86—, state devel. chmn., 1985-86; bd. stewards Canterbury Meth. Ch., 1977-80, 82-85; faculty rep. Sun Belt Conf., 1983—; trustee Birmingham Symphony Assn., 1978-83; bd. dirs. Birmingham area chpt. ARC, 1978-81; bd. dirs. All Am. Bowl, 1981-87, exec. com., 1985-86; bd. dirs. Met. Devel. Bd., 1980-83, 84-87, v.p., 1981-82, exec. com., 1984, 2d vice chmn., 1986, 87; bd. dirs. YMCA, 1979-83; bd. dirs. Positive Maturity, 1980. Decorated D.F.C. with 3 oak leaf clusters, Bronze Star, Legion of Merit with 2 oak leaf clusters, Air medal with 11 v-devices, 10 other awards and fgn. decorations. Mem. Am. Mgmt. Assn., Assn. Ala. Coll. Adminstrs., Coll. and Univ. Personnel Adminstr., Nat. Assn. Coll. and Univ. Bus. Officers, Soc. for Coll. and Univ. Planning, So. Growth Policy Bd. (assoc.), Birmingham C. of C. (bd. dirs. 1977-84, pres. 1983, chmn. 1984, exec. com. 1980-84, policy com. 1982-87, v.p. research and resource devel. 1977-79, 1st v.p. 1981, nominating com. 1982-87), Phi Kappa Phi, Beta Gamma Sigma, Sigma Xi, Omicron Delta Kappa, Kappa Alpha, Order of Daedalians. Clubs: Birmingham Country; Shoal Creek Country; Willow Point Golf and Country (Alex City); Army-Navy Country (Washington); Relay House. Lodge: Kiwanis. Office: Univ of Ala at Birmingham University Station Birmingham AL 35294

PEYRAUBE, ALAIN, sinologist, linguist; b. Bordeaux, France, Nov. 22, 1944; s. Fernand Flavien and Angele Marie (Lupiet) P.; m. Elisabeth Françoise Maitre, Aug. 31, 1973; children: Marie, Zoe. BA in Chinese and Linguistics, U. Bordeaux, France, 1968, MA in Chinese, 1970; PhD in Chinese Linguistics, U. Paris, 1976, State Doctorate, 1984. Research fellow Nat. Ctr. Sci. Research, Paris, 1975-84, dir. of research, 1985—; chargé of Confs., Ecole des Hautes en Scis. Sociales, Paris, 1981. Author: 3 Chinese Linguistics books; contbr. over 50 articles to profl. jours.; editor Cahiers de Linguistique Asie Orientale, 1977—. Mem. Asian Soc., European Assn. of Sinologie, Assn. Francaise d'etudes Chinoises. Home: 5 Rue Paulin Mery, 75013 Paris France Office: Ecole des Hautes Etudes, en Scis Sociales, 54 Blvd Raspail, 75006 Paris France

PEYTON, WILLIAM MAUPIN, business executive, educator; b. Richmond, Ky., Jan. 5, 1932; s. Russell Page and Amanda Thomas (Bogie) P.; m. Margaret Christine Dahl, Sept. 8, 1956; children: Michael William, Stephen Todd, John Patrick. B.S. in Bus. Adminstrn., UCLA, 1957; M.B.A. in Fin., U. So. Calif., 1967; postgrad., Harvard U., 1980. Office mgr., cost acct. Ralphs Grocery Co., Los Angeles, 1957-62; cost acctg. supr. Lockheed Air Terminal, Burbank, Calif., 1962-69; chief acctg. supr. Lockheed Air Terminal, Burbank, Calif, 1969-72, treas., 1972-80, exec. v.p., 1980-86, also dir.; treas. Lockheed Air Terminal, Panama City, 1976—; pres. Peyco, Inc., Burbank, 1986—; asst. prof. Glendale (Calif.) Coll., 1969—. Served with USAF, 1951-55. Mem. Nat. Assn. Accts. (dir. 1963). Republican. Episcopalian. Home: 41 Conejo Circle Palm Desert CA 92260 Office: Peyco Inc 321 E Alameda Inc Burbank CA 91502

PEZZELLA, JERRY JAMES, JR., investment and real estate corporation executive; b. Chesapeake, Va., Sept. 30, 1937; s. Jerry James Sr. and Mabel (Aydlett) P.; m. Carolyn Blades; children: James M., Stanley J., Julie M. BS, U. Richmond, 1963; MBA, U. Pa., 1964. Asst. v.p. Va. Nat. Bank div. Sovran Bank, Norfolk, 1964-68; chmn. bd., pres. First Am. Investment Corp., First Ga. Investment Corp., Atlanta, 1968-74; v.p. Great Am. Investment Corp., Atlanta, 1974-78; sr. v.p. Equity Fin. & Mgmt. Co., Chgo., 1978—; pres., chmn. bd. First Capital Fin. Corp., Chgo., 1983-85; pres. Great Am. Credit Corp., Chgo., 1983—; bd. dirs. Great Am. Mgmt. and Investment, Inc., Chgo., Zell-Merrill Lynch Real Estate Opportunity Ptnrs., Chgo. Club: River, Metropolitan (Chgo.). Office: Equity Fin and Mgmt Co Chicago IL 30342

PEZZINO, PAOLO, historian, educator; b. Pescara, Italy, Aug. 7, 1948; s. Alberto and Tonina (Martelli) P.; m. Maria Grazia Ruggeri, June 27, 1971; children: Francesco, Giulia. Degree in letters and philosophy, U. Degli Studi, Pisa, Italy, 1970. Fellow Fondazione Luigi Einaudi, Torino, Italy, 1971-72, Inst. Modern Contemporary History, Pisa, 1975-78; prof. Scuola Media Stagio Stagi, Pietrasanta, Italy, 1973-74; tchr. humanities U. Degli Studi, 1979-84, assoc. prof., 1985—. Author: La Riforma Agraria in Calabria, 1977; contbr. articles to profl. jours. Home: Via Corte Capanni, Tr 1 N 31, 55100 Lucca Italy Office: Dipartimento Storia Moderna Contemp, Piazza Torricelli, 3 B, 56100 Pisa Italy

PFEFFER, LEO, lawyer, educator; b. Hungary, Dec. 25, 1910; came to U.S., 1912, naturalized, 1917; s. Alter Saul and Hani (Yaeger) P.; m. Freda Plotkin, Sept. 18, 1937; children—Alan Israel, Susan Beth. B.S.S., CCNY, 1930; J.D., NYU, 1933; L.H.D. (h.c.), Hebrew Union Coll.-Jewish Inst. Religion, 1979, Long Island U., 1988. Bar: N.Y. 1933. Practice in N.Y.C., 1933—, pvt. tchr. law, 1933-45; lectr. New Sch., 1954-58, Mt. Holyoke Coll., 1958-60; David W. Petergorsky prof. constl. law Yeshivah U., 1962-63; gen. counsel Am. Jewish Congress, 1958-64, spl. counsel, 1964-85; prof. polit. sci. L.I. U., 1964-80, adj. prof., 1981—, chmn. dept., 1964-79; Vis. prof. constl. law Rutgers U., 1965; frequent radio and TV appearances, 1954—. Author: Church, State and Freedom, 1953, rev. edit., 1967, The Liberties of an American, 1956, Creeds in Competition, 1958, (with Anson Phelps Stokes) Church and State in the United States, 1964, This Honorable Court, 1965, God, Caesar and the Constitution, 1975, Religious Freedom, 1977; Religion, State and the Burger Court, 1984; editorial bd.: Jour. Ch. and State, 1958—, Judaism, 1964—; contbr. to various books, encys.; honored by Religion and State: Essays in Honor of Leo Pfeffer, 1985. Pres. Lawyers Constl. Def. Com., 1964-66, counsel, 1967-82, emeritus counsel, 1982—; cons. counsel Religious Coalition for Abortion Rights, 1976—; adv. com. Nat. Project Ctr. for Film and the Humanities, 1974—; mem. religious liberty com. Nat. Council Chs. of Christ in U.S.A.; mem. nat. legal affairs com. Anti-Defamation League B'nai B'rith, 1986—; mem. nat. adv. bd. Ams. for Religious Liberty, 1986—. Recipient Religious Freedom award Ams. United for Separation Ch. and State, 1955, citation contbns. to civil rights Minn. Jewish Community Council, 1962, Thomas Jefferson Religious Freedom award Unitarian-Universalist Ch. N.Y., 1967, Bklyn. Civil Liberties award, 1968, citation for contbns. to pub. edn. Horace Mann League, 1972, Lawyers Constl. Def. Com., 1972, award Com. for Pub. Edn. and Religious Liberty, 1972, Townsend Harris medal CCNY, 1974, Rabbi Maurice N. Eisendrath Meml. award Union of Am. Hebrew Congregations, 1977, George Brussel Meml. award Stephen Wise Free Synagogue, 1978, Trustee award for Scholarly Achievement L.I. U., 1978, Ams. United Fund award, 1979, Am. Jewish Congress award, 1980, cert. of merit Council Jewish Fedns., 1984, award of recognition Nat. Jewish Community Relations Adv. Com., 1987, Humanist of Yr. award Am. Humanist Assn., 1988. Fellow Jewish Acad. Arts and Scis.; Mem. Am. Jewish Congress, Am. Acad. Religion, Am. Acad. Polit. and Social Scis., AAUP (pres. L.I. U. chpt. 1967-68), Jewish Peace Fellowship (exec. com. 1969—, counsel 1979—), ACLU (cons., cooperating atty.), Soc. Sci. Study Religion, NYU Law Rev. Alumni Assn. (pres. 1964-66), Am. Judicature Soc., Am. Polit. Sci. Assn., Am. Arbitration Assn. (panel arbitrators), Nat. Assn. Intergroup Relations Ofcls., Horace Mann League U.S. (gen. counsel), Am. Soc. for Legal History, Com. for Pub. Edn. and Religious Liberty (founder 1967, gen. counsel 1967-82, Counsel Emeritus award 1982—), Nat. Coalition Pub. Edn. and Religious liberty (founder 1967, gen. counsel 1967-82, counsel exec. 1982—). Home: 29 Ridge Terr Central Valley NY 10917

PFLUG, GUENTHER, library director; b. Oberhausen, Fed. Republic Germany, Apr. 20, 1923; s. Richard and Annemarie (Winzer) P.; m. Irmgard Hoefken, June 12, 1953. PhD, U. Bonn, Fed. Republic Germany, 1950; degree in math and philosophy, Cologne U., Fed. Republic Germany, 1953; PhD (hon.), U. Bochum, Fed. Republic Germany, 1967, U. Frankfurt, Fed. Republic Germany, 1978. Referendar Library Sch., Cologne, Fed. Republic Germany, 1953-55; bibliotheksrat/oberbibliotheksrat U. Library, Cologne, 1955-62; bibliotheks direktor U. Library, Bochum, Fed. Republic Germany, 1963-74; dir. Hochschul bibliothek szentrum, Cologne, 1974-76; dir. gen. Deutsche Bibliothek, Frankfurt, Fed. Republic Germany, 1976—. Author: Henri Bergson, 1959, Die Bibliothek im Umbruch, 1984; editor: (jour.) Zeitschrift für Bibliothekswesen und Bibliographie, (ency.) Lexikon für das gesamte Buchwesen. Mem. Gesellschaft fur deutsche Sorache (pres. 1981—), Arbeitskreis selbstandiger Kulturinst. (pres. 1985—), Goethe Inst., UNESCO Commn. Lodge: Rotary (Frankfurt). Office: Deutsche Bibliothek, Zeppelinallee 4-8, 6000 Frankfurt Federal Republic of Germany

PFNISTER, ALLAN OREL, educator; b. Mason, Ill., July 23, 1925; s. Ardon Orel and Rose Margaret (Sandtner) P.; m. Helen Edith Klobes, Dec. 18, 1948; children: Alicia Ann, Jonathan Karl, Susan Elaine. A.B. summa cum laude, Augustana Coll., 1945; M.Div. summa cum laude, Augustana Theol. Sem., 1949; A.M. with honors, U. Chgo., 1951, Ph.D., 1955; LL.D. (hon.), U. Denver, 1978. Instr. in religion Augustana Coll., 1946-47; instr. in philosophy and German Luther Coll., Wahoo, Nebr., 1949-52; dean Luther Coll., 1953-54; research asst., univ. fellow U. Chgo., 1952-53, instr., 1954-57, asst. prof., 1957-58; dir. research joint bds. parish edn. Lutheran Ch. Am., 1958-59; vis. asso. prof. U. Mich., 1959-62, asso. prof., 1962-63; dean Coll. Liberal Arts, prof. philosophy Wittenberg (Ohio) U., 1963-67, provost, prof., 1967-69, acting pres., 1968-69; prof. higher edn. U. Denver, 1969-77, 78—, exec. vice chancellor and acting chancellor, 1977-78, vice chancellor acad. affairs, 1984-87, assoc. provost, 1988—; dir. study fgn. study programs Fedn. Regional Accrediting Commns. Higher Edn., 1970-72; cons. in field; bd. dirs. Nat. Ctr. for Higher Edn. Mgmt. Systems Mgmt. Services; bd. trustees Capital U., Ohio, 1983, vice chmn. bd. trustees, 1987—. Author: Teaching Adults, 1967, Trends in Higher Education, 1975, Planning for Higher Education, 1976; contbr. numerous articles on higher edn. to profl. jours. Bd. visitors Air Force Inst. Tech., 1978-83, chmn. bd. visitors, 1981-83. Recipient Outstanding Achievement Alumni award Augustana Coll., 1963. Mem. AAAS, Am. Acad. Polit. and Social Sci., Am. Studies Assn., N.Y. Acad. Scis., Am. Assn. Higher Edn., Assn. for Study Higher Edn., Comparative and Internat. Edn. Soc., Blue Key, Phi Beta Kappa (alumnus mem.), Phi Delta Kappa. Democrat. Home: 7231 W Linvale Pl Denver CO 80227 Office: GCB 136 U Denver Denver CO 80208

PFORZHEIMER, CARL HOWARD, JR., investment banker; b. N.Y.C., July 17, 1907; s. Carl H. and Lily Maud (Oppenheimer) P.; m. Carol Jerome Koehler, Sept. 1, 1931; children: Nancy (Mrs. Edgar D. Aronson), Carl Howard III. AB, Harvard U., 1928, MBA, 1930; HHD, Capital U., Columbus, 1969; DCS, Pace U., N.Y.C., 1959. Faculty Centre de Preparation aux Affaires, Paris, 1930; banking apprentice France, Germany, Eng., 1930-32; sr. partner investment banking firm Carl H. Pforzheimer & Co., N.Y.C., 1934—; pres., dir. Petroleum & Trading Corp. Bd. dirs. Central Park South, Inc.; bd. dirs. Nat. Acad. Sch. Execs.; Mem. N.Y. State Bd. Regents, 1958-78, vice chancellor, 1975-78, emeritus, 1978—; chmn. Nat. Conf. on Govt., 1979-81; treas. Citizens Forum on Self Govt., Nat. Mcpl. League, 1958-75, pres., 1975-78, chmn. council, 1982-86, hon. life bd. dirs.; pres. Carl and Lily Pforzheimer Found.; treas. Neustadter Found., 1950-58; mem. research libraries com. N.Y. Pub. Library, 15 yrs.; mem. exec. com. Nat. Council on Ednl. Research, 1973-80; rep. to Edn. Commn. of States, 1971-74; past pres. Nat. Assn. State Bds. Edn.; vis. com. Harvard U. Grad. Sch. Edn., Univ. Library; mem. N.Y. State Commn. on Campus Unrest, 1969-73, Nat. Reading Council, 1969-74; trustee Mt. Sinai Med. Ctr., 1936-86, hon. trustee, 1986—; former mem. bd. dirs. Econ. Devel. Corp., N.Y.C.; hon. trustee Horace Mann Sch., Boys Club of N.Y.; mem. council Rockefeller U. Served as col. War Dept. Gen. Staff, AUS, World War II; expert cons. to sec. war 1947. Decorated Legion of Merit, Medalile de la Reconaissance (France); recipient Harvard U. medal; named Officer, Legion of Honor. Mem. N.Y. Chamber Commerce and Industry (past bd. dirs.), Keats-Shelley Assn. (pres. 1969-87, hon. pres.), Am. Assn. Community and Jr. Colls. (past dir.), Harvard U. Alumni Assn. (past pres., now hon. dir.), Signet Soc. (hon. fellow). Clubs: Union Interalliée (Paris); Century Assn., City Midday, Harvard, Grolier (N.Y.C.); Harvard, Union Boat (Boston); Army and Navy (Washington); Piper's Landing, Harbor Ridge, Sailfish Point (Stuart, Fla.). Office: Room 3030 70 Pine St New York NY 10270

PFORZHEIMER, HARRY, JR., oil consultant; b. Manila, Nov. 19, 1915; s. Harry and Mary Ann (Horan) P.; B.S. in Chem. Engring., Purdue U., 1938; postgrad. Case Inst. Tech., Law Sch., George Washington U., Case Western Res. U.; m. Jean Lois Barnard, June 2, 1945; children—Harry, Thomas. with Standard Oil Co. (Ohio), various locations, 1938-80, pres. White River Shale Oil Corp., 1974-76, v.p. Sohio Natural Resources Co., 1971-80, program dir. Paraho oil shale demonstration, Grand Junction, 1974-80; pres., chmn. bd., chief exec. officer Paraho Devel. Corp., 1980-82, sr. mgmt. advisor and dir., 1982-85, cons., 1985—; pres. Harry Pforzheimer Jr. and Assocs., 1983—; dir. IntraWest Bank Grand Junction; adj. prof. chem. engring. Cleve. State U. Contbr. articles to tech. and trade jours. Mem. planning adv. bd. St. Mary's Hosp. and Med. Ctr.; bd. dirs. Colo. Sch. Mines Research Inst.; chmn. Wayne N. Aspinall Found. Mem. Am. Inst. Chem. Engrs. (chmn. Cleve. 1955, gen. chmn. internat. meeting, Cleve. 1961), Am. Petroleum Inst., Am. Mining Congress, Colo. Mining Assn., Rocky Mountain Oil and Gas Assn., Denver Petroleum Club, Purdue Alumni Assn., Sigma Alpha Epsilon. Clubs: Army and Navy (Washington), Bookcliff Country, Rio Verde Country. Summer Home: 2700 G Rd #1-C Grand Junction CO 81506 Winter Home: 25604 Abajo Dr Rio Verde AZ 85255 Office: 743 Horizon Ct Grand Junction CO 81506

PFOTENHAUER, HELMUT, German studies educator; b. Nuremberg, Bavaria, Fed. Republic Germany, Aug. 3, 1946; s. Hermann and Babette (Zimmermann) P.; m. Margot Schödel, May 29, 1969; 1 child, Bettina. PhD, U. Erlangen, 1974, Habilitation, 1982. Asst. U. Erlangen, Bavaria, 1974-84; Heisenberg scholarship Deutsche Forschungsgemeinschaft, 1984-87; prof. German Institut für Deutsche Philolgie, U. Würzburg, Fed. Republic Germany, 1987—; guest prof. Univs. Wurzburg, Munich, Vienna, 1982-86. Author: Benjamin, 1975, Nietzsche, 1985, Autobiography, Anthropology 18th and 19th Century, 1987. Mem. Nat. Orgn. Germanists, Internat. Orgn. Germanists. Office: Institut für Deutsche Philolgie, U Würzburg, 8520 Würzberg Federal Republic of Germany

PFOUTS, RALPH WILLIAM, economist, consultant; b. Atchison, Kans., Sept. 9, 1920; s. Ralph Ulysses and Alice (Oldham) P.; m. Jane Hoyer, Jan. 31, 1945 (dec. Nov. 1982); children: James William, Susan Jane (Mrs. Osher Portman), Thomas Robert (dec.), Elizabeth Ann (Mrs. Charles Klenowski); m. Lois Bateson, Dec. 21, 1984. B.A., U. Kans., 1942, M.A., 1947; Ph.D., U. N.C., 1952. Research asst., instr. econs. U. Kans., Lawrence, 1946-47; instr. U. N.C., Chapel Hill, 1947-50, lectr. econs., 1950-52, assoc. prof., 1952-58, prof., 1958-87, chmn. grad. studies dept. econs. Sch. Bus. Adminstrn., 1957-62, chmn. dept. econs. Sch. Bus. Adminstrn., 1962-68; cons. econs. Pacific Grove, Calif., 1987—; vis. prof. U. Leeds, 1983; vis. research scholar Internat. Inst. for Applied Systems Analysis, 1983. Author: Elementary Economics-A Mathematical Approach, 1972; editor: So. Econ. Jour, 1955-75; editor, contbr.: Techniques of Urban Economic Analysis, 1960, Essays in Economics and Econometrics, 1960; editorial bd.: Metroeconomica, 1961-80, Atlantic Econ. Jour, 1973—; contbr. articles to profl. jours. Served as deck officer USNR, 1943-46. Social Sci. Research Council fellow U. Cambridge, 1953-54; Ford Found. Faculty Research fellow, 1962-63. Mem. AAAS, Am. Statis. Assn., N.C. Statis. Assn. (past pres.), Am. Econ. Assn., So. Econ. Assn. (past pres.), Atlantic Econ. Soc. (v.p. 1973-76, pres. 1977-78), Population Assn. Am., Econometric Soc., Phi Beta Kappa, Pi Sigma Alpha, Alpha Kappa Psi, Omicron Delta Epsilon.

PFUND, EDWARD THEODORE, JR., electronics co. exec.; b. Methuen, Mass., Dec. 10, 1923; s. Edward Theodore and Mary Elizabeth (Banning) P.; B.S. magna cum laude, Tufts Coll., 1950; postgrad U. So. Calif., 1950, Columbia U., 1953, U. Calif., Los Angeles, 1956, 58; m. Marga Emmi Andre, Nov. 10, 1954 (div. 1978); children—Angela M., Gloria I., Edward Theodore III; m. Ann Lorenne Dille, Jan. 10, 1988. Radio engr., WLAW, Lawrence-Boston, 1942-50; fgn. service staff officer Voice of Am., Tangier, Munich, 1950-54; project. engr. Crusade for Freedom, Munich, Ger., 1955; project mgr., materials specialist United Electrodynamics Inc., Pasadena, Calif., 1956-59; cons. H.I. Thompson Fiber Glass Co., Los Angeles, Andrew Corp., Chgo., 1959, Satellite Broadcast Assocs., Encino, Calif., 1982; teaching staff Pasadena City Coll. (Calif.), 1959; dir. engring., chief engr. Electronics Specialty Co., Los Angeles and Thomaston, Conn., 1959-61; with Hughes Aircraft Co., various locations, 1955, 61—, mgr. Middle East programs, also Far East, Latin Am. and African market devel., Los Angeles, 1971—, dir. internat. programs devel., Hughes Communications Internat., 1985—. Served with AUS, 1942-46. Mem. Phi Beta Kappa, Am. Inst. Aeros. and Astronautics, Sigma Pi Sigma. Contbr. articles to profl. jours. Home: 25 Silver Saddle Ln Rolling Hills Estates CA 90274 Office: PO Box 92919 Airport Station Los Angeles CA 90009

PHADKE, BHALCHANDRA BALVANT, mathematician, educator; b. Sangli, Maharashtra, India, Jan. 17, 1944; s. Balvant Ramchandra and Malati (Kamal) P. BA, Parashurambhau Coll., Poona, India, 1964; MA, U. Poona, 1966; PhD, U. So. Calif., 1970. Fellow U. Toronto, Can., 1970-72; lectr. math. Flinders U. South Australia, Bedfon Park, 1972-76; sr. lectr. Flinders U. South Australia, Bedford Park, 1976—. Author: (with H. Busemann) Spaces With Distinguished Geodesics, 1987. Mem. Indian Math. Soc. Hindu. Home: 75 Yarmouth St, Brighton 5048, Australia Office: The Flinders U South Australia, Bedford Park South Australia 5042, Australia

PHALON, PHILIP ANTHONY, marketing executive; b. Paterson, N.J., Apr. 18, 1929; s. John J. and Agnes (Maher) P.; m. Anna M. Moran. B.S., Boston Coll., 1950. Vice-pres. internat. Whittaker Corp., Los Angeles, 1972-73; v.p. internat. affairs Raytheon Co., Lexington, Mass., 1973-83; sr. v.p. corp. mktg. Raytheon Co., 1983—; dir. New Japan Radio Co., Tokyo. Bd. dirs. World Affairs Council Boston, Emerson Hosp., Concord, Mass., 1981—. Served with U.S. Army, 1950-53. Roman Catholic. Office: Raytheon Co 141 Spring St Lexington MA 02173

PHAM, KINH DINH, electrical engineer, educator, administrator; b. Saigon, Republic of Vietnam, Oct. 6, 1956; came to U.S., 1974; s. Nhuong D. and Phuong T. (Tran) P.; m. Ngan-Lien T. Nguyen, May 27, 1985. BS with honors, Portland State U., 1979; MSEE, U. Portland, 1982. Registered profl. engr., Oreg., Calif. Elec. engr. Irvington-Moore, Tigard, Oreg., 1979-80; elec. engr. Elcon Assocs., Inc., Beaverton, Oreg., 1980-87, sr. elec. engr., assoc. ptnr., 1987—; adj. prof. Portland (Oreg.) Community Coll., 1982—. Contbr. articles to profl. jours. Recipient Cert. Appreciation Am. Pub. Transit Assn. and Transit Industry, 1987. Mem. IEEE. Buddhist. Office: Elcon Assocs Inc 12670 NW Barnes Rd Portland OR 97229

PHAM, QUANG HUU, state official, engineer; b. Thanh Hoa, Viet Nam, Dec. 24, 1942; s. Ba Van and Oanh Thi (Le) P.; came to U.S., 1975; B.S. in C.E., U. Saigon, 1966; M.S. in C.E., U. Okla., 1971; m. Thanh Thi, Apr. 15, 1969; children—Tuyet, Tuan. Asst. chief bur. City of Saigon (Viet Nam), 1966-67, chief bur., 1969-70, asst. chief dept., 1972-75; instr. Engring. Sch. Corps. of Engrs., Viet Nam, 1967-68; dist. engr. Okla. State Health Dept., Oklahoma City, 1975-80, dir. public water supply engring., 1980-82, dir., chief engr. permits and compliance, 1982—; lectr. U. Saigon, 1974-75; chmn. Okla. com. to revise and update constrn. standards for public water supply facilities, 1981. Vice pres. Vietnamese Buddhist Assn. Okla. Recipient awards City of Saigon, 1972-75; AID scholar, 1971-72. Registered profl. engr., Okla. Water Pollution Control Assn., Sao Viet Athletic Assn. (pres.). Buddhist. Author: Proposal for Improving the Solid Waste System Management of Saigon City, 1971. Home: 6913 Greenway Dr Oklahoma City OK 73132 Office: NE 10th and Stonewall Sts Oklahoma City OK 73105

PHAM, TUAN DINH, mathematical statistician; b. Hanoi, Vietnam, Feb. 10, 1945; came to France, 1964; s. Hien Gia and Nang Thi (Nguyen) P.; m. Kung Thi-My Nguten, Aug. 5, 1979; children: Laura Kim Loan, Cecil Kim Chi. BSc in Applied Math, U. Grenoble, France, 1967; BSc in Math and Computer Sci., U. Grenoble, 1968, MA in Statistics, 1970, PhD in Statistics, 1975. Jr. researcher Nat. Ctr. Sci. Research, St. Martin d'Heres, France, 1969-75; researcher Nat. Ctr. Sci. Research, St. Martin d'Heres, 1975-78, 80-84, sr. researcher, 1984—; prof. Ind. U. 1979-80. Contbr. articles to profl. jours. Mem. Soc. Applied and Indsl. Math., Am. Math. Soc., Brit. Biomed. Info. Soc. Home: 31 rue Pascal, 38100 Grenoble France Office: Nat Ctr Sci Research BP 68, Lab TIM3, 38402 Grenoble France

PHAM VAN DONG, former chairman Council of Ministers of Socialist Republic of Vietnam; b. Quang Ngai Province, Vietnam, Mar. 1, 1906. Collaborator with Ho Chi Minh; underground Communist worker, from 1925; imprisoned by French authorities for 7 years, released, 1936; a founder of Viet Minh, 1941; mem. Vietnam Workers' Party, 1951—; prime minister Democratic Republic of Vietnam, 1954-76; chmn. Council of Ministers (prime minister) Socialist Republic Vietnam, 1976-87; adviser to Cen. Com., 1986—; minister of fgn. affairs, 1954-61. Address: Office of Chmn, Council of Ministers, Hanoi Socialist Republic of Vietnam *

PHANG (FANGS), JAIK-HUI FRANCIS, electronic publishing company executive; b. Singapore, July 16, 1949; s. Yar-Shen Philips Phang and Mary (Cheng) Toh; m. Pheck-Sim-Theresa Teo, Jan. 8, 1951; 1 child, Lian-Jin George Fang. BEE, U. Singapore, 1974. Registered profl. engr., Singapore. Data communications mgr. Singapore Telecommunications Authority, 1977-80; regional mgr. Siemen's Databit Inc., N.Y.C., 1980-82; gen. mgr./dir. Telecoms Systems Group Inc., N.J., 1982-83; mng. dir., telecommunications cons. Lynx-Pontine Inc., Calif., 1983-85; sr. exec. Integrated Info. Pte. Ltd., Singapore, 1985—; internat. telecommunications cons. Lynx-Pontine Assocs. Inc., 1982—. Population censorship officer Govt. of Singapore, 1970. Served to lt. Singapore Army, 1974-77. Mem. IEEE (sr.), Brit. Computer Soc. (assoc.), Inst. Mktg. (U.K.) (assoc.). Roman Catholic. Home: 801 Upper Serangoon Rd, #06-02, Singapore 1953, Singapore Office: Integrated Info Pte Ltd, Nol Bldg, 456 Alexander Rd, Singapore 0511, Singapore

PHARES, ALAIN JOSEPH, physicist, educator; b. Beirut, Apr. 20, 1942; came to U.S., 1975, naturalized, 1982; s. Joseph Michel and Renee Cecile (Doummar) P.; m. Claude Tawa, July 27, 1968; children—Caroline, Denis, Pascal. B.S. in Engring., St. Joseph U., 1964; Docteur-es-Sciences, U. Paris, 1971; Ph.D., Harvard U., 1973. Research fellow Nat. Council Sci. Research, Lebanon, 1973-75; assoc. prof. Lebanese U., 1973-75; research fellow Internat. Centre Theoretical Physics, Trieste, Italy, 1974, Harvard U., 1975-76; vis. asst. prof. U. Mont., 1976-77; asst. prof. physics Villanova U., Pa., 1977-79, assoc. prof., 1979-82, prof., 1982—, chmn. dept., 1981—, dir. secondary sch. sci., 1981—. Contbr. articles to profl. jours. IAEA fellow, 1974; Villanova Research grantee, 1978; French Govt. fellow, 1964-66; recipient Outstanding Faculty Research award Villanova U., 1986. Mem. Am. Phys. Soc., Internat. Assn. Math. and Computers in Simulation, Sigma Xi. Office: Villanova U Dept Physics Villanova PA 19085

PHELAN, JAMES BERNARD, insurance company executive; b. Akron, Ohio, Sept. 28, 1941; s. Bernard W. and Waneta (Magoteaux) P.; B.A., Kent State U., 1963; married; children—Todd W., Brent J. C.P.C.U.; C.L.U., C.I.C., C.P.I.A. Ins. agt. Phelan Ins. Agy., Inc., Versailles, Ohio, 1962-72; v.p. Midwestern Ins. Group, Cin., 1972-76; pres. Ins. Mktg. Assos., Versailles, 1976—; pres. Continental Nat. Indemity Co., Cin., 1988—. tchr. CLU program, Cin.; bd. dirs. ACORD Corp. Pres. Versailles Devel. Assn., 1969-70. Chmn. Versailles Poultry Days Festival, 1970, exec. dir., 1970, 71. Mem. Profl. Ins. Agts. of Ohio (dir. 1978-81; pres. 1984-85), Ind. Ins. Agts. Assn. of Ohio, Profl. Ins. Agts. of Am. (vice chmn. automation com.), Ind. Ins. Agts. Assn. Am., Western Ohio Trucking Assn., Soc. Chartered Life Underwriters, Soc. Chartered Property and Casualty Underwriters, So. Cert. Ins. Counselors, Nat. ARC/AMS Users Group (treas. 1988—, pres. 1985-86, bd. dirs.). Republican. Roman Catholic. Clubs: Elks, K.C., Eagles, Rotary (pres. 1971-72). Home: 11720 Conover Versailles OH 45380 Office: 9624 Conti-Columbus Rd Cincinnati OH 45243

PHELAN, JOHN DENSMORE, insurance executive, consultant; b. Kalamazoo, Aug. 31, 1914; s. John and Ida (Densmore) P.; m. Isabel McLaughlin, July 31, 1937; children—John Walter, William Paul, Daniel Joseph. BA magna cum laude, Carleton Coll., 1935. With Hardware Mut. Ins. Co. (name now Sentry Ins. Co.), Stevens Point, Wis., 1936-45; with Am. States Ins. Co., Indpls., 1945—, pres., 1963-76, chmn., 1976-79, also dir. numerous subs.; chmn. Phelan Ins. Inc., Columbus, Ind.; bd. govs. Internat. Ins. Seminars. Author: Business Interruption Primer, 1949, also later edits.; contbr. articles to profl. jours. Past pres. Marion County Assn. Mental Health; chmn. CPCU-Harry J. Loman Found.; adv. bd. ins. dept. Ball State U. Sch. Bus.; trustee Longboat Island (Fla.) Chapel. Mem. CPCU Soc. (past nat pres.), CLU Soc., Ind. State C. of C. (past dir.), Am. Bonanza Soc. (past officer and dir.), Phi Beta Kappa. Presbyterian. Clubs: Indpls. Athletic, Woodland Country (Indpls.); El Conquistador Country (Bradenton, Fla.). Home: 307 Woodland Ln Carmel IN 46032 Winter Home: 6460 Mourning Dove Dr Apt #205 Bradenton FL 34210

PHELAN, PHYLLIS WHITE, psychologist; b. Harrisonburg, Va., Aug. 12, 1951; d. Shirley Lewis and Jean Elwood (Driver) White; m. Kenneth Edward Phelan, May 21, 1983. BA with honors, Coll. William and Mary, 1973, MA, 1977; PhD, U. Minn., 1984. Lic. cons. psychologist. Intern Ramsey Mental Health Ctr., St. Paul, 1983-84; psychologist Mental Health Clinics of Minn. P.A., St. Paul, 1983-84, Harley Clinics, Mpls., 1983-84; psychologist, dir. eating disorders program Primary Health Care, Bloomington, Minn., 1984-87; pvt. practice psychology St. Paul, 1987—; exec. dir. Eating Disorders Inst. for Edn. and Research, St. Paul, 1987—; instr. Continuing Edn. program, U. Minn., 1983-84, clin. asst. prof. dept. psychiatry, 1986—. Contbr. articles to profl. jours. Coll. of William and Mary scholar, 1975-77; U. Minn. fellow 1981, 82-83. Mem. Am. Psychol. Assn., Minn. Psychol. Assn., Minn. Psychologists in Pvt. Practice, Minn. Women Psychologists. Home: 942 Summit Ave Saint Paul MN 55114 Office: 570 Asbury St Saint Paul MN 55105

PHELAN, WILLIAM FRANCIS, educational consultant; b. Pompey, N.Y., Jan. 19, 1906; s. John and Catherine (Kinney) P.; B.A., Niagara U., 1928, M.A., 1934; postgrad. Buffalo State Tchrs. Coll., summer 1936, Buffalo U. Sch. Edn., 1936-40; Ed.D., Tchrs. Coll., Columbia U., 1949; m. Hilda Clements, June 26, 1929; children—Margaret Jane (Mrs. Daniel J. O'Connell), Elizabeth Ann (Mrs. Richard Amari). Tchr., coach, asst. prin. Lewiston (N.Y.) Public Schs., 1928-34; supervising prin. North Collins (N.Y.) Public Schs., 1934-43; supt. Depew (N.Y.) Public Schs., 1943-57; dist. prin. North Babylon (N.Y.) Public Schs., 1957-62; dist. supt. schs. 2d supr. dist. Suffolk County, Patchogue, N.Y., 1962-74; ednl. cons., 1974-80; pres. William F. Phelan & Assocs., Ednl. Cons. Services, Brightwaters, N.Y., 1980—; vis. prof. Buffalo State Tchrs. Coll. Grad. Sch., 1948-50, Buffalo U. Grad. Schs., summers 1950, 57, Niagara U. Grad. Sch., 1950-57; vis. instr. St. John's U., 1958-62; ednl. cons. N.Y. State Fedn. Womens' Clubs, 1952-54; mem. L.I. Citizens Com. on Sch. Finance, 1959-62, pres., 1960, v.p., 1960-62; v.p. L.I. Ednl. Leadership Conf., 1963-64; adv. bd. Erie County Vocat. and Ednl. Extension Bd., 1954-57; mem. N.Y. State Congress Sch. Dist. Adminstr. Orgns., 1971-74, pres., 1972-73. Chmn. adv. bd. Family Service Soc. Buffalo and Erie County, 1956-57, bd. dirs., 1956-57; mem. L.I. Regional Mental Health Planning Com.; pres. Lancaster Town Planning Comm., 1954-55; bd. dirs. Depew Boys' Club, Inc., 1945-55, Community Chest Buffalo and Erie County, 1945-55, Suffolk County Mental Health Assn., 1963—; mem. Commr.'s Adv. Council Sch. Suprs., 1968-73, Suffolk County Econ. Opportunity Commn., 1964-67; mem. Suffolk County Interdept. Welfare Adv. Commn. Mem. N.Y. State Assn. Sch. Dist. Adminstrs. (chmn.; legis. com. 1964-67), N.Y. State Council Sch. Supts. (chmn. legis. com. 1968-71, v.p. 1970-71, pres. 1971-72, Disting. Service award 1974), Am. Assn. Sch. Adminstrs. (Disting. Service award 1978). Club: Rotary (1st pres. Eden-N. Collins, N.Y. 1940-41). Home: 45 Orchard Dr Brightwaters NY 11718

PHELPS, FLORA L(OUISE) LEWIS, editor, anthropologist, photographer; b. San Francisco, July 28, 1917; d. George Chase and Louise (Manning) Lewis; student U. Mich. AB cum laude, Byrn Mawr Coll., 1938; AM, Columbia U., 1954; m. C(lement) Russell Phelps, Jan. 15, 1944; children—Andrew Russell, Carol Lewis, Gail Bransford. Acting dean Cape Cod Inst. Music, East Brewster, Mass., summer 1940; assoc. social analyst sci., U.S. Govt., 1942-44; co-adj. staff instr. anthropology Univ. Coll., Rutgers U., 1954-55; mem. editorial bd. Américas mag. OAS, Washington, 1960—, sr. editor, 1963-71, editor English edit., 1971-74, mng. editor, 1974-82, contbg. editor, 1982—; N.J. vice chmn. Ams. Dem. Action, 1950; mem. Dem. County Com. N.J., 1948-49. Mem. AAAS, Am. Anthrop. Assn., Anthrop. Soc. Washington, Latin Am. Studies Assn., Soc. for Am. Archaeology, Soc. Woman Geographers. Author articles in fields of anthropology, art, architecture, edn., travel; contbr. Latin Am. newspapers. Home and Office: 3618 Albemarle St NW Washington DC 20008

PHIBBS, CLIFFORD MATTHEW, surgeon, educator; b. Bemidji, Minn., Feb. 20, 1930; s. Clifford Matthew and Dorothy Jean (Wright) P.; m. Patricia Jean Palmer, June 27, 1953; children—Wayne Robert, Marc Stuart, Nancy Louise. B.S., Wash. State U., 1952; M.D., U. Wash., 1955; M.S., U. Minn., 1960. Diplomate Am. Bd. Surgery. Intern Ancker Hosp., St. Paul, 1955-56; resident in surgery U. Minn. Hosps., 1956-60; practice medicine specializing in surgery Oxboro Clinic, Mpls., 1962—, pres., 1985—; mem. staff St. Barnabas Hosp., Children's Hosp. Ctr., Northwestern-Abbott Hosp., Fairview-Southdale Hosp., 1965—, chief of surgery, 1970-71, chmn. intensive care unit, 1973-76; clin. asst. prof. U. Minn., Mpls., 1975-78, clin. assoc. prof. surgery, 1978—. Contbr. articles to med. jours. Bd. dirs. Bloomington Bd. Edn., Minn., 1974—, treas., 1976, sec., 1977-78, chmn., 1981-83; mem. adv. com. jr. coll. study City of Bloomington, 1964-66, mem. community facilities com., 1966-67, advisor youth study commn., 1966-68; vice chmn. bd. Hillcrest Meth. Ch., 1970-71; mem. Bloomington Adv. and Research Council, 1969-71; bd. dirs. Bloomington Symphony Orch., 1976—, Wash. State U. Found.; dir. bd. mgmt. Minnesota Valley YMCA, 1970-75; bd. govs. Mpls. Met. YMCA, 1970—; pres. Oxboro Clinics, 1985—. Served to capt. M.C., U.S. Army, 1960-62. Mem. AMA (Physician's Recognition awards 1969, 73—), Assn. Surg. Edn., Royal Soc. Medicine, Am. Coll. Sports Medicine, Minn. Med. Assn., Minn. Surg. Soc., Mpls. Surg. Soc., Hennepin County Med. Soc., Pan-Pacific Surg. Assn., ACS, Jaycees, Bloomington C. of C. (chmn. bd. 1984, chmn. 1985-86). Home: 9613 Upton Rd S Minneapolis MN 55431 Office: 9820 Lyndale Ave S Minneapolis MN 55420

PHILBERT, GEORGES MARIE VICTOR, physicist, educator; b. Paris, Jan. 5, 1922; s. Victor Marie and Georgette (Dufaux) P.; Licencie es Sciences, Sorbonne, 1942, Diplome d'Etudes Superieures de Physique, 1944; D. Science, 1953; 1 dau., Dominique-Chantal. Research physicist Kaiser Wilhelm Inst. Physics, Hechingen (Germany), 1945-51, nuclear physics lab., College de France, Paris, 1951-58; asso. prof. dept. nuclear physics U. Lyon, 1958-63, prof., 1963—. Recipient Ordre des palmes academiques. Mem. French Soc. Physics. Research, numerous publs. on electrodynamics of supracondrs., mass spectrometry, high energy exptl. and theoretical research. Office: Université Cl Bernard, 43 Blvd du 11 Novembre 1918, 69621 Villeurbanne France

PHILIP, A. G. DAVIS, astronomer, writer; b. N.Y.C., Jan. 9, 1929; s. Van Ness and Lillian (Davis) P.; m. Kristina Drobavicius, Apr. 25, 1964; 1 dau., Kristina Elizabeth Elanor. B.S., Union Coll., 1951; M.S., N.Mex. State U., 1959; Ph.D., Case Inst. Tech., 1964. Tchr. physics, math. and chemistry Brooks Sch., 1954-59; instr. Case Inst. Tech., 1962-64; asst. prof. astronomy U. N.Mex., 1964-66; asst. prof. astronomy SUNY-Albany, 1966-67, assoc. prof., 1967-76, mem. exec. com. Arts and Scis. Council, 1975-76; prof. astronomy Union Coll., Schenectady, 1976—, astronomer Dudley Obs., 1967-81, Frank L. Fullam chair astronomy, 1980-81, editor Dudley Obs. Reports, 1977-81; astronomer Van Vleck Obs., Weslayan U., 1982—, editor contbns. of VVObs., 1982—; vis. prof. Yale U., 1972, 73, La. State U., 1973, 76, 86, Acad. Scis. Lithuania, USSR, 1973, 76, 79, 86 Stellar Data Ctr., Strasbourg, France, 1978, 79, 80, 82, 85, 86; dir., sec.-treas. N.Y. Astron. Corp.; pres., treas. L. Davis Press, Inc., 1982—, Inst. Space Observations, 1986—; trustee Fund Astrophys. Research, 1985—. Exhibited: 2d Ann. Photography Regional, Albany, 1980; author: (with M. Cullen and R.E. White) UBV Color-Magnitude Diagrams of Galactic Globular Clusters, 1976; editor: The Evolution of Population II Stars, 1972, (with D.S. Hayes) Multicolor Photometry and the Theoretical HR Diagram, 1975, (with M.F. Mc Carthy) Galactic Structure in the Direction of the Galactic Polar Caps, 1977, (with D. H. DeVorkin In Memory of Henry Norris Russell, 1977, (with Hayes) The HR Diagram, 1978, Problems in Calibration of Multicolor Systems, 1979, (with M.F. McCarthy and G.V. Coyne) Spectral Classification of the Future, 1979, X-Ray Symposium, 1981, (with Hayes) Astrophysical Parameters for Globular Clusters, 1981, (with A.R. Upgren) The Nearby Stars and the Stellar Luminosity Function, 1983, (with Hayes and L. Pasinetti) Calibration of Fundamental Stellar Quantities, 1985, (with D.W. Latham) Stellar Radial Velocities, Horizontal-Branch and UV-Bright Stars, 1985, Spectroscopic and Photometric Classification of Population II Star, 1986, (with J. Grindley) IAU Symposium No. 126, Globular Cluster Systems in Galaxies, 1987, (with Hayes and Liebert) IAU Colloquium No. 95, The Second Conference on Faint Blue Stars, (with Hayes and Adelman) New Directions in Spectrophotometry, 1988, Calibration of Stellar Ages, 1988. Contbr. chpts. to books, articles to profl. jours. Served with AUS, 1951-53. Yale U. vis. fellow, 1976; research grantee Research Corp., NSF, NASA, Nat. Research Lab., Nat. Acad. Scis. Fellow Royal Astron. Soc., AAAS; mem. Am. Phys. Soc., Am. Astron. Soc. (Harlow Shaply lectr. 1973-85, auditor 1977, 79-85), Internat. Astron. Union (chmn., sec. various comms. and commns., pres. commn. 30 1982-85), N.Y. Acad. Scis., Astron. Soc. Pacific, Astron. Soc. N.Y. (sec.-treas. 1969—, editor newsletter 1974—), Sigma Xi. Home: 1125 Oxford Pl Schenectady NY 12308 Office: Union Coll Physics Dept Schenectady NY 12308

PHILIP, JOHN ROBERT, physicist, mathematician; b. Ballarat, Australia, Jan. 18, 1927; s. Percival Norman and Ruth (Osborne) P.; m. Frances Julia Long, Apr. 30, 1949; children: Peregrine, Julian, Candida. BCE, U. Melbourne, Victoria, Australia, 1946, DSc, 1960, DEng (hon.), 1983. Research asst. U. Melbourne, 1947; engr. Queensland Irrigation Commn., Brisbane, 1948-51; mem. research staff Commonwealth Sci. and Indsl. Research Orgn., Canberra, Australia, 1951—, sr. prin. research scientist, 1961-63, chief research scientist and asst. chief div. plant industry,, 1963-71, assoc. mem. exec., 1978, dir. inst. phys. scis., 1980-83, chief div. environ. mechanics, 1971-80, 83—; vis. prof., fellow Cambridge (Eng.) U., 1954-55, 61-62, Calif. Inst. Tech., 1957-58, U. Ill., 1958, 61, Harvard U., 1966-67, U. Fla., 1969, Cornell U., 1979, numerous others. Contbr. numerous articles to profl. jours. Coordinator Sci. Task Force of Royal Commn. on Australian Govt. Adminstrn., 1975. Nuffield Found. fellow, 1961-62; Vinton-Hayes fellow, 1972. Fellow Australian Acad. Sci. (sec. biology 1974-78, Lyle medal 1981), Royal Soc. London, Am. Geophys. Union (Horton award 1957, Horton medal 1982), Royal Meterol. Soc., Australian and New Zealand Assn. (pres. physic sect., math., sect.). Home: 42 Vasey Crescent, Campbell 2601, Australia Office: Commonwealth Sci & Indsl Research Orgn, GPO Box 821, Canberra 2601, Australia

PHILIP, PRINCE (DUKE OF EDINBURGH), Earl of Merioneth, Baron Greenwich; b. Corfu, June 10, 1921; s. Prince Andrew of Greece and Denmark and Princess Alice (d. Marquess of Milford Haven); ed. Germany, Scotland and Eng.; hon. degrees: LL.D., U. Wales, 1949, U. London, 1951, U. Edinburgh, 1951, U. Cambridge, 1952, U. Karachi, 1959, Royal U. Malta, 1964, UCLA, 1966; D.C.L., U. Durham, 1951, Oxford U.; D.Sc., Delhi U., 1959, Reading U., 1960, U. Salford, 1967, U. Southampton, 1967, U. Victoria (B.C., Can.), 1969; hon. degree Engring., U. Lima (Peru), 1962; m. Princess Elizabeth Alexandra Mary (now Queen Elizabeth II), Nov. 20, 1947; children—Charles Philip Arthur George, Anne Elizabeth Alice Louise, Andrew Albert Christian Edward, Edward Antony Richard Louis. Became naturalized British subject, Feb. 1947, adopting surname Mountbatten; created Baron Greenwich, County of London, Earl of Merioneth and Duke of Edinburgh, with title of His Royal Highness, 1947; created knight Most Noble Order of Garter, 1947, knight Most Ancient and Most Noble Order of Thistle, 1952; grand master and first or prin. knight Order Brit. Empire, 1953; prince of U.K. of Gt. Britain and No. Ireland, 1957; mem. Order of Merit, 1968. Became personal a.d.c. to King George VI, 1948, Privy councillor, 1951, col.-in-chief Army Cadet Force, 1952, air commodore-in-chief Air Tng. Corps, 1952, adm. of fleet, 1953, field marshall, 1953, marshall RAF, 1953, capt. gen. Royal Marines, 1953, extra master Merchant Navy, 1954, Privy councillor of Can., 1957, col. Grenadier Guards, 1975; chancellor U. Cambridge, 1976—; life gov. King's Coll., London; vis. Churchill Coll., Cambridge. Officer in Brit. Navy; with Mediterranean Fleet and Brit. Pacific Fleet, 1939-45. Decorated grand cross Order of Redeemer, Order of St. George and St. Constantine, 1st class, grand cross Order of George I, grand cross Order of Phoenix (Greece); Knight Order of Elephant (Denmark); grand cross Order of St. Olaf (Norway); Order of Seraphim (Sweden); grand cross Legion d'Honneur (France); grand cross Order Netherlands Lion; grand cross Order of San Martin (Argentina); grand cordon Order of Leopold (Belgium); grand cross Order of the Condor (Bolivia); grand cordon Supreme Order of Chrysantheum (Japan); grand band Order Star of Africa (Liberia), numerous others; granted freedoms London, Greenwich, Edinburgh, Belfast, Cardiff, Glasgow, Melbourne, also others; mentioned in despatches. Mem. and former officer or current officer numerous orgns., assns., also clubs, yachting assns., and learned socs. Author: Seabirds in Southern Waters, 1962; Selected Speeches. Address: Buckingham Palace, London SW 1 England *

PHILIPPE, JEAN CLAUDE, engineer, economic consultant; b. Avignon, France, Sept. 10, 1948; s. Paul Emile and Marie (Plaindoux) P.; 1 child, Adrienne Philippe. BA, U. Provence, France, 1972; postgrad, UCLA, 1981; PhD in Econs., U. Aix-Marseille, France, 1978. Lectr. U. Tech., Port Harcourt, Nigeria, 1974-77; researcher U. Aix-Marseille, Aix in Provence, France, 1977-80, Sch. Architecture and Planning UCLA, 1980-81; research engr. Ministry of Nat. Edn., Paris, France, 1981—. Author: Crise Industrie et Regions; contbr. articles to profl. jours. Recipient Ernest Mercier Comite du Rayonnement Francais, Paris, 1980, Research award Ministry of Fgn. Affairs, Paris, 1979. Mem. Assn. Evolutionary Econs., Regional Studies Assn., Canadian Regional Sci. Assn., Royal African Soc., Assn. Sci. Regionale Francaise. Home: La Bastide Forte 2, Route du Tholonet, Aix en Provence FRANCE F-13100 Office: C E R, 23 cours Gambetta, Aix en Provence 13627, Aix en Provence FRANCE F-13100

PHILIPPOU, ANDREAS NICOLAOU, Cyprus Minister of Education; b. Nicosia, Cyprus, July 15, 1944; s. Nicolaos and Maria Georgiou (Protopapa) P.; m. Athina Roustani, Dec. 29, 1984; children: Margarita, Melina. BS in Math., U. Athens, 1967, MS, 1970; PhD in Stats., U. Wis., 1972. Asst. prof. math. U. Tex., El Paso, 1972-74; 2d chaired prof. applied math. U. Patras, Greece, 1974-82; prof. U. Patras, 1982—; vice-rector of the Univ. 1983-86, chmn. dept. math., 1984-86, Minister of Education of the Republic of Cyprus, 1986—; asst. prof. Am. U., Beirut, Lebanon, 1978-79, assoc. prof., 1979-80; cons. Beirut U., 1979-80; v.p. Hellenic Aerospace Industry, Athens, 1981-82. Editor: Fibonacci Numbers and Their Applications, 1986, Applications of Fibonacci Numbers, 1988; contbr. numerous articles, revs. to profl. jours. Founder, pres. Greek Am. Community of El Paso, 1974; v.p. 1st World Congress of Cypriot Scientists Abroad, 1978. Served with Greek Army, 1964. Fulbright traveling fellow, 1967-68, 74. Mem. Am. Statis. Assn., Fibonacci Assn. (co-chair 1st, 2d and 3d Internat. Confs.), Greek Math. Soc., Math. Assn. Am., Inst. Math. Stats. Home: Govt House Z-50, Patras Greece Office: Ministry of Edn, Nicosia Cyprus

PHILLIPS, ALAN BRANSBY, advertising specialist; b. Hatfield, Hertfordshire, Eng., June 7, 1947; s. David Henry and Lilian (Hertzberg) P.; m. Bernice Janet Winter, Apr. 8, 1973; children: Julia Lynne, Claire Hayley, Wendy Helen. Media buyer Lintas Ltd., London, 1966-68; media group head Sharp's Advt. Ltd., London, 1966-70; media mgr. Gerald Green Assocs. Ltd., London, 1970-72; dep. media dir. Osborne Advt. Ltd., London, 1972-74; dir. Media Mktg. Consultancy Group Ltd., London, 1974-76; media dir., chmn. bd. dirs. Phillips Russell PLC, London, 1976—; bd. dirs. Cen. Media Unit Ltd., London, Stephens Advt. Service Ltd., London, Magpie Research Ltd., London. Contbr. articles to profl. jours. Mem. Inst. of Mktg., Inst. Practitioners in Advt., British Inst. Mgmt. Office: Phillips Russell PLC, 58 Wardour St, London W1V 3HN, England

PHILLIPS, ASA EMORY, JR., lawyer; b. Washington, Dec. 7, 1911; s. Asa Emory and Virginia N. (Boyd) P.; m. Anne Wight, 1956; children: Asa Emory III, Anne Crocker (mrs. Henry McFarlan Ogilby). AB cum laude, Harvard Coll., 1934; JD, Harvard U., 1938. Bar: Mass. 1939, D.C. 1938, Maine 1953, U.S. Supreme Ct. 1944. Sr. partner firm Asa E. Phillips, Jr., Boston, 1952—; dep. head atty. Compliance div. War Prodn. Bd., Washington, 1942-44; asst. to sec. state and vice pres. U.S., 1945-47. Vice chmn. lawyers div. Greater Boston Community Fund, 1948-50; dist. dir. Federal St. dist., 1947; chmn. Heart Fund for Brookline, 1958-60; chmn. adv. com. Gov. of Commonwealth U.S.S. Mass. Relics, 1965; chmn. com. of mgmt. YMCA, Charlestown, Mass., 1969-71; sec.-treas. Friends of Chamber Music, Inc., 1954-64; chmn. Gov.'s Prayer Breakfast, 1978; mem. council Freedom Trail Found., 1977—; mem. advisory bd. Salvation Army Greater Boston, 1977—; bd. dirs. Youth Found., Inc., N.Y.C.; founder, pres. bd. trustees Thomas W. Sidwell Meml. Scholarship, Mrs. Asa E. Phillips Meml. Fund; founder, chmn. bd. trustees Charles Francis Adams Meml. Trophy; trustee Mass. Trustees of Internat. Com. of YMCA for Army and Navy Work, Inc.; corporator Brookline Savs. Bank; mem. overseers com. to visit mil. depts. Harvard U., 1960-66. Served as ensign USN, World War II. Decorated knight Order St. Lazarus; recipient Meritorious Pub. Service citation Sec. Navy, 1960. Mem. ABA (moderator weekly radio broadcasts), Boston Bar Assn., Friends Sch. Alumni Assn. (past pres.), Greater Boston C. of C., Navy League of U.S. (nat. v.p. 1962-68, pres. 1958-77, 1st v.p. Boston council 1977—, nat. chmn. Navy Day 1965-68, mem. nat. exec. com. 1962-68), Soc. Colonial Wars (treas. 1957-60, gov. Mass. 1963-65, nat. gov. gen. 1969-72), Order Founders and Patriots Am. (gov. Mass. Soc. 1964—, gov. gen. Gen. Ct. 1972-78), Soc. of Lees of Va. (past nat. v.p.), Huguenot Soc. Mass. (pres. 1966-68, counselor 1985—), Mass. Com. of Patriotic Socs. (founder, chmn. 1962—), Soc. of Cin., Roger Williams Family Assn., Soc. Descs. of Colonial Clergy, Order of Lafayette (nat. dir. 1966—, pres. gen. 1974—), U.S. Flag Found., Inc. (counselor), SAR (pres. Mass. Soc. 1975-77, Patriot medal 1977, chmn. Ann. Congress 1975, trustee 1977-83, chmn. state pres.' caucus Nat. Soc. 1976-78, nat. trustee 1977-79, historian gen. 1978-80, v.p. gen. 1980-82, Minuteman medal 1981, parliamentarian 1983—), S.R. (pres. Mass. 1974—, regional gen. v.p. 1977-78), New Eng. Historic Geneal. Soc., Sovereign Mil. Order, Nat. Smoke, Fire and Burn Inst., Inc. (co-founder, pres. 1973—), Charitable Irish Soc. (pres. 1985-86, dir. 1986—), Friends of Ft. Washington, Inc. (sec., treas. 1985—). Clubs: Country (Brookline); Union, Eastern Yacht, Harvard, Marblehead Soc. (Boston); Essex Inst. (Salem); St. Nicholas Soc., Colonial Order of Acorn, N.Y. Yacht, Univ., Met., Chevy Chase (Washington); Bar Harbor, Bar Harbor Yacht; Seal Harbor Yacht, Harbor (Seal Harbor); Ends of the Earth. Lodge: Rotary (dir. Boston club 1975-82, pres. 1979-80). Home: Seawold Ogunquit ME 03907 also: Hilltop 90 Sargent Rd Brookline MA 02146 Office: 53 State St 14th Floor Boston MA 02109

PHILLIPS, BESSIE GERTRUDE WRIGHT, mathematics educator; b. Erie, Pa.; d. Charles Clayton and Mary Gertrude (Allen) Wright; m. Stephen Phillips, Oct. 2, 1942 (dec. Jan. 1971); children—Jane Appleton, Margaret Duncan (Mrs. Robert Cummings), Ann Willard (Mrs. Kevin Waters). A.B., Fla. State Coll. Women, Tallahassee, 1930; M.A., Mount Holyoke Coll., 1933. Sec. internat. hdqrs. World YMCA, Geneva, Switzerland, 1933-34; math. tchr. Washington Sem., Pa., 1930-32; acad. head, math tchr. Milw.-Downer Sem., Wis., 1934-37; trustee New Eng. Coll., Henniker, N.H., 1952-61, Orme Sch., Mayer, Ariz. 1962—, Peabody Mus., Salem, Mass., 1971—; bd. advisers Council for Advancement Small Colls., Washington, 1959-69; vis. com. for edn. Peabody Mus., 1983—; ednl. cons. in field. Bd. dirs. Salem Female Charitable Soc., 1943—, Mack Indsl. Sch., Salem, 1943—. Mem. Nat. Soc. Colonial Dames, Bostonian Soc., Cum Laude Soc. Republican. Presbyterian. Clubs: Chilton, Union, Eastern Yacht. Home: 30 Chestnut St Salem MA 01970

PHILLIPS, CARLTON VERNON, banker; b. Dartmouth, Mass., July 19, 1924; s. Robert Henry and Helen Estelle P.; A.B. in Econs., Brown U., 1957; grad. U.S. Army Command and Staff Coll., 1972, U.S. Air Force War Coll., 1976; M.A. in Mgmt., St. Mary's Coll. of Calif., 1979; m. Gladys Marie Lynch, Apr. 23, 1949; children—Carlton Vernon, John, Maura, Sally, Sheila, Regina, Nathan. Resident mgr. Mitchum Jones & Templeton, Phoenix, 1966-70, Quinn and Co., Phoenix, 1970-71; sr. v.p., pres. Continental Am. Securities, Inc., 1971-84; chmn. and chief exec. officer Century Pacific Corp., 1984-88; dir. Ad Tech Microwave, First Cen. Bank of Ariz., States West Airline. Served with U.S. Army, 1942-54, served to col. AUS. Decorated D.F.C., Air Medal with 3 oak leaf clusters. Republican. Roman Catholic. Clubs: Brown U. (Ariz. chpt., Phoenix), U.S. Army Assn. (Scottsdale), KC

(Scottsdale). Home: 5112 N Wilkinson Rd Paradise Valley AZ 85253 Office: 3200 E Camelback Phoenix AZ 85018

PHILLIPS, DAVID COLIN, chemist; b. Rhosllanerchrugog, Wales, Sept. 6, 1940; came to U.S., 1968; s. John and Sarah Elizabeth (Dodd) P.; m. Irfonwy Lloyd Thomas, Sept. 21, 1968; children: Tudor Joseph Colin, Gareth John Gwilym. B.Sc., U. Wales, 1965, Ph.D. in Phys. Chemistry, 1968. Chemist Shell Chem. Co., Eng., 1962-63, Monsanto Chems. Ltd., Ruabon, Wales, 1963-64; sr. scientist Westinghouse Research Labs., Pitts., 1968-76; mgr. chem. reaction dynamics Westinghouse Research Labs., 1976-79, mgr. chem. physics, 1979-83, mgr. phys. chemistry research, 1983-85; mem. faculty U. Wales, 1965-68. Author. Recipient Indsl. Research-100 award Indsl. Research Mag., 1976. Mem. Royal Inst. Chemistry, Am. Chem. Soc. Address: Greenbank Church St, Rhosllanerchrugog, Wrexham CLWYD, LL14 2BP, England

PHILLIPS, ELIZABETH LOUISE (BETTY LOU), author; b. Cleve.; d. Michael N. and Elizabeth D. (Materna) Suvak; m. John S. Phillips, Jan. 27, 1963 (div. Jan. 1981); children—Bruce, Bryce, Brian; m. 2d, John D.C. Roach, Aug. 28, 1982. B.S., Syracuse U., 1960; postgrad. in English, Case Western Res. U., 1963-64. Cert. elem. and spl. edn. tchr., N.Y. Tchr. pub. schs., Shaker Heights, Ohio, 1960-66; sportswriter Cleve. Press, 1976-77; spl. features editor Pro Quarterback Mag., N.Y.C., 1976-79; freelance writer specializing in books for young people, 1976—. Author: Chris Evert: First Lady of Tennis, 1977; Picture Story of Dorothy Hamill (ALA Booklist selection), 1978; American Quarter Horse, 1979; Earl Campbell: Houston Oiler Superstar, 1979; Picture Story of Nancy Lopez, (ALA Notable book), 1980; Go! Fight! Win! The NCA Guide for Cheerleaders (ALA Booklist), 1981; Something for Nothing, 1981; Brush Up on Your Hair (ALA Booklist), 1981; Texas ... The Lone Star State, 1987, Who Needs Friends? We All Do!, 1989; also contbr. articles to young adult and sports mags. Mem. Soc. Children's Book Writers, Delta Delta Delta. Republican. Roman Catholic. Home: 4 Random Rd Englewood CO 80110

PHILLIPS, ELWOOD HUDSON, bookstore executive, real estate executive; b. Ludlow, Ky., May 30, 1914; s. Clarence Bell and Hallie Josephine (Hudson) P.; m. Edna Mae Johnson, May 20, 1934; children—Janet Carolyn, Martha Lee. Student U. Cin., 1933, Anderson Coll., 1952-54. Foreman, supt. sales, service mgr., packaging engr. Container Corp. Am., Cin. and Rock Island, Ill., 1932-47; owner, mgr. Phillips Book Store, Springfield, Ohio, 1947—; mgr. bookstore Anderson Coll., Ind., 1950-68; owner, mgr. Phillips Real Estate, Anderson, 1956—. Pres. Madison County (Ind.) Hist. Soc., 1985-87, chmn. bd. dirs. 1988; v.p. Anderson East Side Community Club, 1987-88, pres. 1988—. Mem. Nat. Bd. Realtors, Ind. Assn. Realtors, Am. Booksellers Assn., Anderson Bd. Realtors, Christian Booksellers Assn. Democrat. Mem. Ch. of God. Avocation: geneology. Home: 807 Nursery Rd Anderson IN 46012 Office: Phillips Book Store 32 E Washington St Springfield OH 45502

PHILLIPS, GENEVA FICKER, editor; b. Staunton, Ill., Aug. 1, 1920; d. Arthur Edwin and Lillian Agnes (Woods) Ficker; m. James Emerson Phillips, Jr., June 6, 1955 (dec. 1979). B.S. in Journalism, U. Ill., 1942; M.A. in English Lit., UCLA, 1953. Copy desk Chgo. Jour. Commerce, 1942-43; editorial asst. patents Radio Research Lab., Harvard U., Cambridge, Mass., 1943-45; asst. editor adminstrv. publs. U. Ill., Urbana, 1946-47; editorial asst. Quar. of Film, Radio and TV, UCLA, 1952-53; mng. editor The Works of John Dryden, Dept. English, UCLA, 1964—. Bd. dirs. Univ. Religious Conf., Los Angeles, 1979—. UCLA teaching fellow, 1950-53, grad. fellow 1954-55. Mem. Assn. Acad. Women UCLA, Friends of Huntington Library, Friends of UCLA Library, Renaissance Soc. So. Calif., Samuel Johnson Soc. of So. Calif., Assocs. of U. Calif. Press., Conf. Christianity and Lit., Soc. Mayflower Descs. Lutheran. Home: 213 First Anita Dr Los Angeles CA 90049 Office: UCLA Dept English 2225 Rolfe Hall Los Angeles CA 90024

PHILLIPS, HENRY WELDON, mechanical engineer, consultant; b. Evington, Va., Oct. 24, 1917; s. Laurence and Violet Moreau (Anthony) P.; B.S.M.E., U. Va., 1940; m. Lillian Grace Steele, May 22, 1943; 2 children. With G.E. Aeronautics & Ordnance Systems Div., 1940-46; with AMF Inc., Buffalo, 1946-48; Knolls Atomic Power Lab., Gen. Electric Co., Schenectady, 1948-51; chief gen. staff engr. uranium enrichment F.H. McGraw & Co., Paducah, Ky., 1951-53; ops. mgr. U.S. Air Force Ballistic Missile Early Warning System, RCA Corp., Moorestown, N.J., later mgr. spl. computer systems, N.Y.C., 1953-67; with Raytheon Co., Lexington, Mass., 1968-70; project mgr. Stone & Webster Engring. Corp., Boston, 1970-74; with United Engrs. & Constructors, Inc., Phila., 1974-77, constrn. mgr., nuclear power plants, Richland, Wash., 1974-77; program leader power projects Wash. Public Power Supply System, Richland, 1977-82; profl. staff U.S. Nuclear Regulatory Commn., Washington, 1982-87 ; owner Henry Phillips & Assos., consultants. Recipient Nat. Soc. Profl. Engrs. Pres.'s award, 1965, spl. achievement award U.S. Nuclear Regulatory Commn., 1987; registered profl. engr., N.Y., Mass., N.J., Va., Wash. Mem. ASME, Nat. Soc. Profl. Engrs. (pres. chpt. 1964-65), Tau Beta Pi. Episcopalian. Contbr. articles to profl. jours.; patentee in field. Home and Office: 318 Spring St Richland WA 99352

PHILLIPS, JAMES ALLEN, clergyman; b. Monahans, Tex., Aug. 21, 1952; s. James Allen and Margeret (Webb) P.; divorced; 1 child, Amber Mashea. Assoc. in Bibl. Studies, Nazarene Bible Coll., Colorado Springs, Colo., 1980; student U. Colo., 1981. Ordained to ministry Ind. Holiness Ch., 1985. Registered evangelist Ch. of Nazarene, Colorado Springs, 1979-81; assoc. pastor Trinity Ch. of Nazarene, Abilene, Tex., 1982-83, Moore Ch. of Nazarene, Okla., 1984; founder. dir. S.O.L.O. Sch. Ministry, Moore, 1985; founder, dir. Bet-Limud Biblical Inst., Moore, 1986—; dir. edn. Bet Ami, Oklahoma City, 1987—; ednl. dir. Congregation Bet Ami, 1987—. Mem. Simon Wiesenthal Ctr., Internat. Christian Embassy Jerusalem. Served with USN, 1971-77. Mem. Am. Assn. Counseling and Devel., Wesleyan Theol. Soc., Union of Councils for Soviet Jews, Simon Wiesenthal Ctr. Avocations: technical rock climbing; ice climbing; mountaineering. Home: 616 S W 8th St Moore OK 73160 Office: 3629 NW 19th St Oklahoma City OK 73107

PHILLIPS, JAMES D., diplomat; b. Peoria, Ill., Feb. 23, 1933; s. James D. and Ehila (Hardy) P.; m. Rosemary Leeds, Mar. 30, 1957 (div. Dec. 1981); children—Michael, Madolyn, Catherine; m. Lucie Gallistel, Jan. 7, 1984; stepchildren—Charles, David. B.A., Wichita State U., 1956, M.A., 1957; cert., U. Vienna, Austria, 1956; postgrad., Cornell U., 1958-61. Joined fgn. service Dept. State, 1961; served at Am. embassy Paris, before 1975; Am Consulate Zaire, before 1975; Dept. State Washington, before 1975; dep. chief of mission Am. Embassy, Luxembourg, 1975-78; charge d'affaires Am. Embassy, Banjul, The Gambia, 1978-80; staff Nat. War Coll., Washington, 1980-81; office dir. Dept. State, Washington, 1981-84; consul gen. Am. Consulate, Casablanca, Morocco, 1984-86; U.S. Ambassador to Burundi Bujumbura, 1986—. Contbr. articles to Fgn. Service Jour. Served to cpl. U.S. Army, 1953-55. Home and Office: US Ambassador's Office Dept of State Bujumbura Washington DC 20520

PHILLIPS, JOHN P(AUL), physician; b. Danville, Ark., Oct. 14, 1932; s. Brewer William Ashley and Wave Audrey (Page) P.; A.B. cum laude, Hendrix Coll., 1953; M.D., U. Tenn., 1956; m. June Helen Dunbar, Dec. 14, 1963; children—Todd Eustace, Timothy John Colin, Tyler William Ashley. Intern, Charity Hosp. La., New Orleans, 1957; resident in surgery U. Tenn. Hosps., 1958; resident in neurol. surgery U. Tenn. Med. Units, 1958-62; practice medicine, specializing in neurol. surgery, Salinas, Calif., 1962—; chief of staff, chief of surgery Salinas Valley Meml. Hosp.; mem. staffs Community Hosp. Monterey Peninsula, U. Calif. Hosp., San Francisco; asst. clin. prof. U. Calif., 1962—. Commd. Ky. col. Diplomate Am. Bd. Neurol. Surgeons. Mem. ACS, Internat. Coll. Surgery, Harvey Cushing Soc., Congress Neurol. Surgery, Western Neurosurg. Assn., AMA, San Francisco Neurol. Soc., Pan Pacific Surg. Assn., Alpha Omega Alpha, Phi Chi, Alpha Chi. Home: 6 Mesa del Sol Salinas CA 93901 Office: 220 San Jose St Salinas CA 93901

PHILLIPS, JULIA MILLER, film producer; b. N.Y.C., Apr. 7, 1944; d. Adolph and Tanya Miller; m. Michael Phillips (div.); 1 dau., Kate Elizabeth. B.A., Mt. Holyoke Coll., 1965. Former prodn. asst. McCall's Mag.; later advt. copywriter MacMillan Publs.; editorial asst. Ladies Home Journal, 1965-69; later asso. editor; East Coast story editor Paramount Pictures, N.Y.C., 1969; head Mirisch Prodns., N.Y., 1970; creative exec. First Artists Prodns., N.Y.C., 1971; founded (with Tony Bill and Michael Phillips) Bill/Phillips Prodns., 1971; founder, producer Ruthless Prodns., Los Angeles, 1971—. Films include Steelyard Blues, 1972, The Sting, 1973 (Acad. award for best picture of yr.), Taxi Driver, 1976 (Palme d'or for best picture), The Big Bus, 1976, Close Encounters of the Third Kind, 1977, (co-producer) The Beat, 1988; dir. The Estate of Billy Buckner, for Women Dirs. Workshop, Am. Film Inst., 1974. Recipient Katherine McFarland Short Story award, 1964. Mem. Acad. Motion Picture Arts and Scis., Writers Guild, Phi Beta Kappa. Office: care Writers Guild 8955 Beverly Blvd Los Angeles CA 90048

PHILLIPS, LARRY EDWARD, lawyer; b. Pitts., July 5, 1942; s. Jack F. and Jean H. (Houghtelin) P.; m. Karla Ann Hennings, June 5, 1976; 1 son, Andrew H.; 1 stepson, John W. Dean IV. B.A., Hamilton Coll., 1964; J.D., U. Mich., 1967. Bars: Pa. 1967, U.S. Dist. Ct. (we. dist.) Pa. 1967, U.S. Tax Ct. 1969. Assoc. Buchanan, Ingersoll, Rodewald, Kyle & Buerger, P.C. (now Buchanan Ingersoll P.C.), Pitts., 1967-73, mem., 1973—. Bd. dirs. Psychol. Service of Pitts., 1972—, pres., 1985-87. Mem. Am. Coll. Tax Counsel, Tax Mgmt. Inc. (adv. bd.), Pitts. Tax Club, ABA (sect. taxation, com. corp. stockholder relationships and sect. real property, probate and trust law), Allegheny County Bar Assn., Pa. Bar Assn. Republican. Presbyterian. Clubs: Duquesne, St. Clair County. Contbr. articles to profl. jours. Address: 57th Floor 600 Grant St Pittsburgh PA 15219

PHILLIPS, LEO HAROLD, JR., lawyer; b. Detroit, Jan. 10, 1945; s. Leo Harold and Martha C. (Oberg) P.; m. Patricia Margaret Halcomb, Sept. 3, 1983. BA summa cum laude, Hillsdale Coll., 1967; MA, U. Mich., 1968; JD cum laude, 1973; LLM magna cum laude, Free Univ. of Brussels, 1974. Bar: Mich. 1974, N.Y. 1975, U.S. Supreme Ct. 1977, D.C. 1979. Fgn. lectr. Pusan Nat. U. (Korea), 1969-70; assoc. Alexander & Green, N.Y.C., 1974-77; counsel Overseas Pvt. Investment Corp., Washington, 1977-80, sr. counsel, 1980-82, asst. gen. counsel, 1982-85; asst. gen. counsel Manor Care, Inc., Silver Spring, Md., 1985—; vol. Peace Corps, Pusan, 1968-71; mem. program for sr. mgrs. in govt. Harvard U., Cambridge, Mass., 1982. Contbr. articles to legal jours. Chmn. legal affairs com. Essex Condominium Assn., Washington, 1979-81; deacon Chevy Chase Presbyn. Ch., Washington, 1984-87, moderator, 1985-87, supt. ch. sch., 1987—, elder, trustee, pres., 1988—. Recipient Alumni Achievement award Hillsdale Coll., 1981; Meritorious Honor award Overseas Pvt. Investment Corp., 1981, Superior Achievement award, 1984. Mem. ABA (internat. fin. transactions com., vice chmn. com. internat. ins. law), Am. Soc. Internat. Law (Jessup Internat. Law moot ct. judge semi-final rounds 1978-83), Internat. Law Assn. (Am. br.; com. sec. 1982), D.C. Bar, N.Y. State Bar Assn., Royal Asiatic Soc. (Korea br.), State Bar Mich., Washington Fgn. Law Soc. (sec.-treas. 1980-81, bd. dirs., program coordinator 1981-82, v.p. 1982-83, pres.-elect 1983-84, pres. 1984-85), Washington Internat. Trade Assn. (bd. dirs. 1984-87), Assn. Bar City N.Y., Hillsdale Coll. Alumni Assn. (co-chmn. Washington area 1977—). Club: University (N.Y.C.). Home: 4740 Connecticut Ave NW Apt 702 Washington DC 20008 Office: Manor Care Inc 10750 Columbia Pike Silver Spring MD 20901

PHILLIPS, MARK ANTHONY PETER, farmer; b. Tetbury, Eng., Sept. 22, 1948; s. Peter W.G. and Anne (Tiarks) P.; m. Princess Anne, Nov. 14, 1973; children—Peter Mark Andrew, Zara Anne Elizabeth. Ed. Marlborough Coll., 1963-66, Sandhurst; student Royal Agrl. Coll., Cirencester, 1978-79. Joined 1st Queen's Dragoon Guards, 1969; regimental duty, 1969-74 co. instr. Royal Mil. Acad. Sandhurst, 1974-77; army tng. directorate, 1977-78; personal aide de camp to Queen, 1974—. Mem. U.K. World Champion equestrian team, 1970, European Champion team, 1971, Olympic Gold medallist team, Munich, 1972. Chmn. Gloucestershire Assn. Youth Clubs, Everyman Theatre, Liveryman Farriers Co., Farmers Co.; hon. yeoman Saddlers' Co.; freeman Loriners Co., City of London; v.p. Minchinhampton Cricket Club. Mem. Royal Caledonian Hunt, Hunters Improvement and Nat. Light Horse Soc. (life), Royal Agrl. Soc., Gloucestershire Trust Nature Conservation, Dressage Group Horse Trials Group, Melton Hunt Club, Brit. Field Sports, Beaufort Hunt. *

PHILLIPS, MARTIN EDWARD, sales and marketing executive; b. Solihull, West Midlands, Eng., Feb. 14, 1946; m. Fiona Hamilton Pollock, Apr. 1970. BSc, Rubgy Coll. Advanced Tech., Warwickshire, Eng., 1969. Chartered engr. Gen. sales mgr. Philips, Ltd., Stevenage, Hertfordshire, Eng., 1974-80; export sales mgr. G.E.C., Ltd., Slough, Bucks, Eng., 1980-84; sales and mktg. dir. KDG Instruments, Ltd., Crawley, West Sussex, Eng., 1984—; pres. KDG Houdec SA, Paris, 1984—; bd. dirs. KDG Instruments Propriety, Ltd., Sydney, Australia. Mem. Inst. Elec. Engrs. Mem. Conservative Party. Office: KDG Holdings Ltd, Cropmton Way, Crawley, West Sussex RH10 24Z, England

PHILLIPS, MERVYN JOHN, bank executive; b. Sydney, Australia, Apr. 1, 1930; m. Moya Bleazard, 1956; 2 children. AM, U. Sydney, 1987. With Commonwealth Bank Australia, 1946-60; with Res. Bank Australia, 1960—, mgr. PNG, 1962-64, asst. mgr. PNG div., 1965-70, mgr., 1972-73, asst. sec., 1970-72, chief mgr. internat. dept., 1976-79, chief mgr. securities markets dept., 1980-82, chief mgr. fin. markets group, 1983-85, adviser, 1982-85, chief adminstrv. officer, 1985-87, dep. gov., dep. chmn., 1987—; mem. PNG Currency Converson Commn., 1965-66, adv. com. New South Wales Credit Union, 1968-72, Govt. Coms. PNG Banking, 1971-73, Off-Shore Banking in Australia, 1984. Office: Reserve Bank of Australia, 65 Martin Pl, GPO Box 3947, Sydney NSW 2001, Australia

PHILLIPS, PHILIP KAY, stained glass manufacturing and retail company executive; b. Kansas City, Mo., Jan. 3, 1933; s. Ernest Lloyd and Mildred Blanche (Moser) P.; B.A., Bob Jones U., Greenville, S.C., 1958; postgrad. Central Mo. State U., 1977-78, 81-83; m. Constance Diana Lucas, June 12, 1955; children—John Allen, David Lee, Stephen Philip, Daniel Paul, Joy Christine. Ordained minister Baptist Ch., 1959; pastor Mt. Moriah Baptist Ch., Clarksburg, Mo. 1958-59; security officer Mo. Dept. Corrections, Jefferson City, Mo., 1959-64; field mgr. office Darby Corp. and Piping Contractors Inc., Kansas City, Kans., 1965-72, safety and security dir. Darby Corp. and Leavenworth Steel Inc., Kansas City, 1972-84; with Stained Glass Creations, North Kansas City, Mo., 1984—. Mem. planning com. Kans. Gov.'s Indsl. Safety and Health Conf., 1977-78, chmn. mfg. sect., 1978. Mem. Nat. Safety Mgmt. Soc., Am. Soc. Safety Engrs. (chpt. exec. com. 1980-81, treas. chpt. 1981-82, sec. chpt. 1982-83, 2d v.p. chpt. 1983-84, 1st v.p. 1984-85, chpt. pres. 1985-86), Kans. Safety Assn. (v.p., mem. exec. com. 1979-80), North Kansas City Mchts. Assn. (pres. 1986—). Home: 3205 NE 66th St Gladstone MO 64119 Office: Stained Glass Creations 316 Armour Rd North Kansas City MO 64116

PHILLIPS, ROBERT JAMES, manufacturing company executive; b. Mart, Tex., Aug. 25, 1922; s. William B. and Katie (Barrow) P.; B.S. in Chem. Engring., U. Tex., 1948; m. Mary Jo Bass, Dec. 27, 1944; children—Andrew Bass, Robert James II. Chem. engr. Humble Oil & Refining Co., Baytown, Tex., 1948-52; editorial dir. Gulf Pub. Co., Houston, 1952-53; with Howe-Baker Engrs., Inc., Tyler, Tex., 1955-70, v.p., 1955-60, pres., 1960-69, chmn. bd., 1970, dir., 1957-70; pres. Internat. Technovation, Inc., 1970-71; pres. Amtech, Inc., 1971-77, chmn. bd., 1971-77; chmn. bd. Philco Industries, Inc., 1977-83; pres. R.J. Phillips Co., Tyler, 1977—; dir. Ark. Best Corp., Republic Bank Tyler. Bd. dirs. United Community Fund, 1962, Salvation Army, 1964. Served to capt. USAAF, World War II. Mem. Am. Chem. Soc., Tex. Soc. Profl. Engrs., Am. Inst. Chem. Engrs., East African Wild Life Soc., Methodist (chmn. ofcl. bd.). Lodge: Masons (32 deg.). Clubs: Shikar-Safari, Houston, Willow Brook Country. Home: 2107 Parkway Pl Tyler TX 75701 Office: PO Box 6515 Tyler TX 75711

PHILLIPS, ROBERT QUAIFE, commodity executive; b. Sarnia, Ont., Can., July 10, 1925; s. William Edward and Emily (Homer) P.; m. Lorna Jean Torgeson, Nov. 16, 1949; children: Robin Lee Phillips Patterson, Kathleen Ann Phillips Goodwin, Robert Quaife, Laurie Jean. BSA, Ont. Agrl. Coll., U. Toronto, 1947. Registered profl. agrologist. Sales rep. Can. Industries, Toronto and Winnipeg, 1947-55; advt. and sales promotion mgr. Chipman Ltd., Hamilton, Ont., 1955-57; sales mgr. Chipman Ltd., Montreal, 1957-60; pres., chief exec. officer Agr. Chem. Ltd., Toronto, 1960-67; regional gen. mgr. Agrico-Chem.-Conoco, Memphis, 1968-70; nat. acct. exec. Tampa, Fla., 1970-72; v.p. mktg. Phosphate Rock Export Assocs., Tampa, 1972-78; pres., chief exec. officer Cansulex Ltd., Vancouver, 1978—; chmn. Tampa World Trade Council, 1976-78; pres. Can.-China Trade Council, Toronto, 1980—; dir., mem. exec. com. Sulphur Inst., Washington, 1983. Mem. Republican Nat. Com., 1977; dir. adv. com. Vancouver Community Coll., 1982. Named Hon. Order Ky. Cols. Mem. B.C. Inst. Agrologists, Agrl. Inst. Can., Can. Exporters Assn. (vice chmn., dir. 1964). Episcopalian-Anglican. Clubs: Royal Vancouver Yacht (Vancouver), Shaughnessy Golf & Country (Vancouver), Vancouver Club (Vancouver); Ducks Unlimited (dir., vice-chmn. internat. com.); Calgary Petroleum (Alta.). Home: 6340 Cedarhurst St, Vancouver, BC Canada V6N 1J1 Office: Cansulex Ltd, World Trade Ctr, 760-999 Canada Pl, Vancouver, BC Canada V6C 3E1

PHILLIPS, SIAN, actress; b. Bettws, Wales; d. D. and Sally P.; m. Peter O'Toole, 1960 (div. 1979); 2 children; m. 2d, Robin Sachs, 1979. Student U. Wales, Art Council Bursary, 1955. Appeared with BBC Radio Wales, 1940s, BBC TV, 1950s; newsreader, announcer, mem. Repertory Co. BBC, 1953-55; toured for Welsh Arts Council with Nat. Theatre Co., 1953-55; London stage appearances: Hedda Gabler, 1959, Ondine and The Dutchess of Malfi, 1960-61, The Lizard on the Rock, 1961, Gentle Jack, Maxibules and the Night of the Iguana, 1964, Ride a Cock Horse, 1965, Man and Superman, Man of Destiny, 1966, The Burglar, 1967, Epitaph for George Dillon, 1972, A Nightingale in Bloomsburg Square, 1973, The Gay Lord Quex, 1975, Spinechiller, 1978, You Never Can Tell, 1979, Lyric, 1979, Hammersmith, 1979, Pal Joey, 1980, Half Moon and Albery Theatres, 1980, 81, Dear Liar, 1982, Major Barbara, 1983, Peg Phoenix, 1984, Thursday's Ladies, 1987, Apollo, 1987; films include: Becket, 1963, Goodbye Mr. Chips (Critics Circle award, N.Y. Critics award, Famous Seven Critics award 1969), Laughter in the Dark, 1968, Murphy's War, 1970, Under Milk Wood, 1971, The Clash of the Titans, 1979; TV appearances include: Shoulder to Shoulder, 1974, How Green was my Valley (BAFTA award), 1975, I, Claudius (Royal TV Soc. award, BAFTA award 1978), 1976, The Oresteia of Aeschylus, 1978, Crime and Punishment, 1979, Tinker, Tailor, Soldier, Spy, 1979, Sean O'Casey, 1980, Churchill: The Wilderness Years, 1981, How Many Miles to Babylon, 1982, Smiley's People, 1982; author: Sian Phillips' Needlepoint, 1987. Office: care Saraband Ltd, 265 Liverpool Rd, Barnsbury N1 1HS, England *

PHILLIPS, THOMAS L., corporate executive; b. Istanbul, Turkey, May 2, 1924. BSEE, Va. Poly. Inst., 1947, MSEE, 1948; hon. doctorates, Stonehill Coll., 1968, Northeastern U., 1968, Lowell U., 1970, Gordon Coll., 1970, Boston Coll., 1974, Babson Coll., 1981, Suffolk U., 1986. With Raytheon Co., Lexington, Mass., 1948—, exec. v.p., 1961-64, chief operating officer, 1964-68, pres., 1964-75, chief exec. officer, 1968—, chmn. bd., 1975—; bd. dirs. John Hancock Mut. Life Ins. Co., State St. Investment Corp., Knight-Ridder, Inc. Trustee Gordon Coll., Northeastern U.; mem. corp. Joslin Diabetes Ctr., Mus. Sci., Boston. Recipient Meritorious Pub. Service award for work in Sparrow III missile system, U.S. Navy, 1958. Mem. Nat. Acad. Engring., Bus. Council, Bus. Roundtable. Office: Raytheon Co 141 Spring St Lexington MA 02173

PHILLIPS, THOMAS PORTER, lawyer; b. Los Angeles, Dec. 25, 1940; s. Thomas P. and Patricia (Tucker) P. B.A. in Econs, Pomona Coll., 1962; J.D., Hastings Coll. Law, U. Calif., 1965. Bar: Calif. 1966. Since practiced in Los Angeles; asso. firm Meserve, Mumper & Hughes, 1965-70; prin., dir., head litigation dept. Rodi, Pollock, Pettker, Galbraith & Phillips (Law Corp.), 1970—, pres., 1979-80, treas., chief fin. officer, 1980—; arbitrator Am. Arbitration Assn., 1975—; lectr. U. Calif. Continuing Edn. of Bar, 1976; judge pro tem Los Angeles Mcpl. Ct., 1977-79; mem. bench and bar council Los Angeles Superior Ct., 1976-77, mem. spl. com. to prepare civil trial manual, 1975-76, arbitrator, 1983-85; lectr. Pepperdine U. Sch. Law, Los Angeles Coll. Trial Advocacy; spl. hearing officer Los Angeles Community Coll. Dist., 1975-78; cons. Calif. State Jud. Council, 1980; cons. on one justice system, lt. gov. Calif., 1981—. Author: How to Survive the Insurance/Product Liability Crisis, 1986. Bd. dirs., pres. San Marino (Calif.) Men's Republican Club; bd. dirs. Pasadena (Calif.) Lincoln Club; bd. dirs., v.p. Lan Jordan Inst. Counseling Psychotherapy, 1973—; bd. dirs. Pasadena Child Guidance Clinic, 1975-79, v.p., 1977-79; reader Braille Inst., 1984—. Mem. State Bar Calif., Am., Los Angeles County (sec. 1973-75, vice chmn. 1975-76, chmn. 1976-77, mem. bd. exec. com. trial lawyers sect. 1973—, founding mem., vice-chmn. appellate cts. com. 1977-79, lawyer referral service com. 1978-81) bar assns., Assn. Bus. Trial Lawyers, Los Angeles Trial Lawyers Assn. Office: Suite 1600 611 W 6th St Los Angeles CA 90017

PHILLIPS, WALTER MILLS, III, psychologist, educator; b. N.Y.C., Sept. 29, 1947; s. Walter Mills and Grace Mary (Mullen) P.; B.S., Fordham U., 1970; M.A., U. S.D., 1973, Ph.D., 1975; m. Anne Marie Boyle, July 3, 1971; children: Jonathan, Elizabeth. Adolescent resident counselor Hawthorne (N.Y.) Cedar Knolls Sch., 1970-71; NIMH tng. fellow, 1971-75; clin. psychology intern Inst. of Living, Hartford, Conn., 1974-75, clin. staff psychologist, 1975-79, sr. staff psychologist, 1979-82, asst. dir. dept. clin. psychology, 1980-82, dir. clin. psychology tng., 1980-82; co-dir. outpatient psychiatry U. Conn., Farmington, 1982-88 ; asst. prof. psychiatry, dir. psychiatry evaluation service U. Conn. Health Ctr., 1982-88 ; pvt. practice psychotherapy, Hartford, 1976—, dir. Anxiey Research and Treatment Ctr., 1985-88 ; unit chief adolescent/young adulty service Di. Psychiatry Waterbury Hosp. Health Ctr., 1988—; asst. clin. prof. psychiatry Sch. Medicine Yale U., New Haven, Conn., 1988—. Licensed clin. psychologist, Conn. Mem. Am., Conn. (council of dirs., chmn. ins. com.). Psychol. Assns., Soc. Psychotherapy Research, Soc. Personality Assessment, Sigma Xi. Contbr. articles to profl. jours. Home: 82 Cider Brook Rd Avon CT 06001 Office: Waterbury Hosp Health Ctr Dept Psychiatry Waterbury CT 06721

PHILLIPS, WALTER RAY, lawyer, educator; b. Democrat, N.C., Mar. 19, 1932; s. Walter Yancey and Bonnie (Wilson) P.; m. Patricia Ann Jones, Aug. 28, 1954; children: Bonnie Ann, Rebecca Lee. A.B., U. N.C., 1954; LL.B., Emory U., 1957, LL.M., 1962, J.D., 1970; postgrad., Yale U., 1965-66. Bar: Ga. 1957, Fla. 1958, U.S. Supreme Ct. 1962, Tex. 1969. With firm Jones, Adams, Paine & Foster, West Palm Beach, Fla., 1957-58; law clk. to chief judge U.S. Dist. Ct., Atlanta, 1958-59; with firm Powell, Goldstein, Frazer & Murphy, Atlanta, 1959-60; bankruptcy judge U.S. Cts., Atlanta, 1960-64; prof. law U. N.D., 1964-65; teaching fellow Yale U., 1965-66; prof. law Fla. State U., 1966-68, Tex. Tech. U., Lubbock, 1968-71; Disting. vis. prof. law Baylor U., 1971; atty. Commn. on Bankruptcy Laws of U.S., Washington, 1971-72; dep. dir., adminstrv. officer 1972-73; prof. Sch. Law, U. Ga., 1973—, asso. dean, 1975-83, acting dean, 1976, Joseph Henry Lumpkin prof., 1977—, also dir. univ's self. study, 1978; Chapman disting. vis. prof. law U. Tulsa, 1985-86; reporter Gov.'s Legislation for Ga., 1973; v.p., dir. Killearn Estates, Inc. Author: Florida Law and Practice, 1960, Encyclopedia of Georgia Law, 1962, Seminar for Newly Appointed Referees in Bankruptcy, 1964, Damages: Cases and Materials, 1967, (with James William Moore) Debtors' and Creditors' Rights, Cases and Material, 1966, 5th edit., 1979, The Law of Debtor Relief, 1969, 2d edit., 1972, supplement, 1975, (with James William Moore) Rule 6, Moore's Federal Practice, 1969, Adjustment of Debts for Individuals, 1979, 2d edit., 1981, supplement 1982, 84, 85, Liquidation Under the Bankruptcy Code, 3d edit, 1988, Cases and Materials on Corporate Reorganization, 1983, 3d edit., 1986, 4th edit, 1988, Family Farmer and Adjustment of Individual Debts, 1987, supplement, 1988. Bd. dirs. Lubbock Day Nurseries, 1969, pres., 1970-71; trustee Joseph Henry Lumpkin Found., Inst. Continuing Legal Edn. Served with USAF, 1950. Mem. ABA (consumer bankruptcy com. 1973—, chmn. 1986—), Fed. Bar Assn., Fla. Bar Assn., Tex. Bar Assn., Western Circuit Bar Assn., Ga. Bar Assn. (vice chmn. publs. com. 1977—, com. on profl. responsibility 1983—), Am. Judicature Soc., Am. Trial Lawyers Assn., Phi Alpha Delta (chief tribune). Baptist. Lodge: Rotary. Home: 310 Red Fox Run Athens GA 30605

PHILLIPS, WILLIAM AULT, pediatric dentist; b. Louisville, June 28, 1946; s. Clyde Custer, II, and Geraldine (Ault) P.; m. Karen Walters, June 28, 1969; children—Taylor Brett, Hayden Reign. D.M.D., U. Ky., 1971; M.S.D., Boston U., 1973. Diplomate Am. Acad. Pediatric Dentistry; chmn. Am. Bd. Pediatric Dentistry. Pvt. practice pediatric dentistry, Louisville, 1973—; clin. instr. U. Louisville, 1973-78. Trustee Council Retarded Citizens, 1978-81; dir. Community Coordinated Child Care, 1980—. Fellow Am. Acad. Pediatric Dentistry, Am. Soc. Dentistry for Children, Acad. of Gen. Dentistry, Pierre Fauchard Acad. Republican. Presbyterian. Clubs: Louisville Boat (sec., treas.), Hobie Cat Fleet. Home: 208 Totem Rd Louisville KY 40207 Office: 1001 Dupont Sq N Louisville KY 40207

PHILLIPS, WILLIAM CHARLES, T'ai Chi and karate instructor; b. N.Y.C., Jan. 28, 1947; s. Ned Richardson and Ruth Phillips. A.A., S.I. Community Coll., 1966; B.A., Bklyn. Coll., 1968; M.S., St. Johns U., 1979; studied T'ai Chi under Grand Master Ch'eng Man Ching, 1970-75. Chief instr. Patience T'ai Chi Assn., Bklyn., pres., chief instr., 1982—; instr. T'ai Chi and Self Defense, Sheepshead Bay High Sch. Adult Edn., 1975-77, Kingsborough Community Coll., div. continuing edn., 1977-80; adj. instr. T'ai Chi Kingsborough Community Coll. CUNY, 1987—; lectr. Whole Life Expo, N.Y.C., 1983, 84, T'ai Chi Ch'uan Soc., Rutgers, N.J., 1983, Mind Devel. Assn., St. Louis, 1980, Festival of Yoga and Sci., Columbus, Ohio, 1980; demonstrator Oriental World of Martial Arts in Felt Forum, N.Y.C., 1977; designer T'ai Chi program for blind in conjunction with Kings Bay, Bklyn.; coordinator 1st ann Holistic Weekend, Ellenville, N.Y., 1987—. Author/narrator tape, video demonstrator T'ai Chi Meditative Exercise, 1984. Mem. Manhattan Beach Community Group, Bklyn., 1974—; spl. advisor to pres. Am. Karate Council, 1970-82, pres. council, 1984—; karate cons. 61st Precinct Youth Council, 1984—, Glenwood Houses recreation program, summer 1986; mem. N.Y. State Senator Donald Halperins Com. on Youth; mem. N.Y. Martial Arts Theater Group, 1985—. Office: Patience T'ai Chi Assn 2620 E 18th St Brooklyn NY 11235

PHILLIPSON, DAVID WALTER, archaeologist, museum curator; b. Appletreewick, Yorkshire, England, Oct. 17, 1942; s. Herbert and Mildred (Atkinson) P.; m. Laurel Lofgren, June 26, 1967; children: Arthur Veric, Tacye Elizabeth. BA, Gonville and Caius Coll., Cambridge, Eng., 1964; PhD, U. Cambridge, 1978. Dir. Nat. Monument Commn., Livingstone, Zambia, 1964-72; asst. dir. Brit. Inst. Eastern Africa, Nairobi, Kenya, 1972-78; keeper Glasgow City Mus., Scotland, 1979-81; curator U. Mus. Archaeology and Anthropology, Cambridge, Eng., 1981—; hon. sec. Brit. Inst. Eastern Africa., London, 1986—; dir. studies in archaeology Gonville and Caius Coll., 1981. Editor Jour. African Archeol. Review, 1986—. Chmn. Madingley Sch. Trust, Cambridge, 1983-85. Fellow Gonville and Caius Coll., 1988. Fellow Soc. antiquaries London (treas. 1981—), Royal Geog. Soc. Home: Elm Cottage, Madingley CB3 8AD, England Office: U Mus Archaeology Anthropology, Downing St, Cambridge CB2 3DZ, England

PHILLIS, YANNIS ANASTASIOS, engineering educator, poet; b. Nafplion, Greece, Mar. 3, 1950; came to U.S., 1976; s. Anastasios and Philippia (Arabos) P.; m. Nili Boren, 1979; children—Anastasia, Philip. Diploma, Nat. Polytechnic, Athens, 1973; M.S., UCLA, 1978, Engr., 1979, Ph.D., 1980. Research asst. UCLA, 1977-78, teaching assoc., 1978-80; asst. prof. engring. dept. Boston U., 1980-86; assoc. prof. engring. Tech. U., Crete, Chania, Greece, 1986—. Author: Starting in Nafplion, 1975 (Ministry of Culture and Scis. award 1976); Arctic Zone, 1976; The Last Gasp of Planet Earth, 1984; Zarathustra and the Five Vespers, 1985 (Best Book award 1986). Recipient Harry Kurnitz Lit. award UCLA, 1979 and 1980. Served to 2d lt. Greek Army, 1973-75. Mem. IEEE (sr.), Sigma Xi, Tau Beta Pi. Avocations: poetry; cooking; classical guitar. Home: Assini, Naflpion Greece Office: Tech U Crete, Prodn Systems Dept, Chania Greece

PHILLON, NICHOLAS, manufacturing company executive; b. Villia, Greece, Apr. 3, 1934; arrived in Fed. Republic Germany 1975; s. Alciviades and Anastasia (Consta) P. BSEE, La. Poly. U., 1959, MSEE, 1961; postgrad., San Francisco State U., 1966-68. Applications engr. Fairchild Semicondr. Co., San Rafael, Calif., 1961-62, mgr. applications lab., 1962-63; product engr. Fairchild Semicondr. Co., Mountain View, Calif., indsl. applications engr., 1964-65, product mktg. engr., 1965-66, sr. product mktg. engr., 1966-72; European product mktg. mgr. Fairchild Semicondr. Co., Wiesbaden, Fed. Republic Germany, 1975-76; So. European product mktg. mgr. all semicondr. components Fairchild Semicondr. Co., Milan, 1976-82; European product mktg. mgr. digital integrated circuits Fairchild Semicondr. Co., Wasserburg, Fed. Republic Germany, 1982-85, European product mktg. mgr. memory and high speed logic products, 1985-87; export mktg. mgr. Metellotechnica Electra, Athens, 1973-75. La. Poly U. scholar, 1960-61. Mem. IEEE. Democrat. Greek Orthodox. Home: Am Anger 18, 8090 Babensham Federal Republic of Germany

PHILP, FRANCIS HIGGINSON, banker; b. N.Y.C., Aug. 21, 1930; s. Leonard Jerome and Louise Genevieve (Fellows) P.; A.B. cum laude, Princeton, 1952; postgrad. Harvard Law Sch., 1952-54, 56-58. Asso. law firm Dunnington, Bartholow & Miller, 1958-59, Dominick & Dominick, 1960-63 (both N.Y.C.); asst. treas. Empire Trust Co. (merged into Bank N.Y. 1967), N.Y.C., 1963-66, asst. v.p., 1968-72; v.p. Fiduciary Trust Co. N.Y., N.Y.C., 1972—. Trustee N.Y. Infirmary-Beekman Downtown Hosp., Big Bros. N.Y., Clarion Music Soc., Council Arts Westchester, Clear Pool Camp, Carmel, N.Y., Princeton Library, N.Y.C.; pres. bd. trustees Fund for Blind; mem. Alumni Council, Phillips Exeter Acad. Mem. N.Y. Soc. Security Analysts, SAR, SR, Soc. Colonial Wars, Pilgrims of U.S. Republican. Episcopalian. Clubs: Union, Brook, Down Town Assn. (N.Y.C.); Larchmont (N.Y.) Yacht. Home: 25 Rocky Rd Larchmont NY 10538 Office: Fiduciary Trust Co NY 94th Floor 2 World Trade Ctr New York NY 10048

PHINIZY, ROBERT BURCHALL, electronics exec.; b. Ben Hill, Ga., June 30, 1926; B.S., U. Ariz., 1951; postgrad. U. So. Calif., 1952-55, UCLA, 1956-62; children—Robert B., William, David. Pres., LB Products, Santa Monica, Calif., 1954-68, IMC Magnetics Western, South Gate, Calif., 1968-69, Am. Electronics, Fullerton, Calif., 1969-71; gen. mgr. electronics div. Eaton Co., Anaheim, Calif., 1971-82; pres., chief exec. officer Genisco Tech. Corp., Compton, Calif., 1982—; chmn. bd., chief exec. officer Genisco Computers Corp., Costa Mesa, Calif., 1982-86; chmn., chief exec. officerTrans Tech. Alliances, Calif., 1986— . Bd. dirs. U. Calif., Dominguez Hills; mem. Los Angeles Town Hall; bd. chmn. Calif. State U. Found., 1986. Served to capt. USN, 1943-47, USNR, 47—. Fellow Coll. Engrs. Los Angeles; mem. IEEE, Communication and Computers Indsl. Assn. Electronics Assn. Calif. (treas. 1986). Democrat. Contbr. articles to tech. jours.; patentee in field. Home: PO Box 151 Yorba Linda CA 92686 Office: 3365 E Miraloma Ave Anaheim CA 92806

PHIPPS, JOHN TOM, lawyer; b. Chgo., Sept. 20, 1937; s. J. Oliver and Jean C. (Kirkwood) P.; m. Dorothy B. Barth, Aug. 19, 1961; children: Anne Marie, John B., Karen Louise. BA, DePauw U., 1959; JD, U. Ill., 1965. Bar: Ill. 1965, U.S. Dist. Ct. (cen. dist.) Ill. 1966. Practice, Champaign, Ill., 1965—; spl. prosecutor Champaign County, Ill., 1968; bd. dirs. Champaign County Legal Assistance Found., 1966-73, pres., 1971-73; incorporator Land of Lincoln Legal Assistance Found., 1973, bd. dirs., 1972—, chmn., 1981—. Bd. dirs. Clark-Lindsey Village, 1969-80, pres. 1973-75. Served as lt. USAF, 1959-62. Decorated Air Force Commendation medal. Mem. Champaign County Bar Assn. (bd. govs. 1972-74, v.p. 1973-74), ABA (gen. practice sect., vice-chmn. solo and small firms com. 1985—, chmn. 1987—), Ill. Bar Assn. (mem. corp. and securities law sect. council 1976-78, chmn. mgmt. and econs. of practice of law sect. council 1980-82, family law sect. 1985—), Assn. Trial Lawyers of Am., Ill. Trial Lawyers Assn. Contbr. articles to profl. jours. and continuing legal edn. books. Office: 44 Main St PO Box 1866 Champaign IL 61820

PHIRI, ALICE NAKONYANI, personnel administrator; b. Blantyre, Malawi, Feb. 23, 1960; d. Edison Sidon and Esnat Nyekanyeka Thomas-Konyani; m. John Anthony Phiri; children: Natasha Fedora, Andrew Lombani. B in Social Sci., U. Malawi, Zomba, 1976-80. Pensions officer Old Mut. Soc., Blantyre, 1980-83, personnel officer, 1983-87; mgr. personnel adminstrn. Oilcom of Malawi, Blantyre, 1987—. Mem. Inst. Personnel Mgmt., Magzeentha Promotions, Alexander Hamilton Inst. Presbyterian. Home: care Oilcom (1978) Ltd, P O Box 469, Blantyre Malawi Office: Oil Co of Malawi, Independence Dr, Blantyre Malawi

PHIRI, MARK KATSONGA, chief executive; b. Blantyre, Malawi, July 29, 1951; s. Chester Katsonga Phiri and Alice (Sebastian) Zimpita; m. Agnes Wedson Kaunda, Aug. 27, 1983; children: Heather, Yolanda. Diploma in bus. adminstrn., Universal Coll., Harare, Zimbabwe, 1976-77; diploma in export mgmt., Helsinki Sch. Econs., 1983; diploma in gen. mgmt., Research Inst. Mgmt. Scis., Delft, The Netherlands, 1987. Civil servant Malawi Govt., Blantyre, 1971-75; salesman Southern Bottlers Ltd., Blantyre, 1975; area sales mgr. Lever Bros. Ltd., Blantyre, 1977-80; gen. mgr. Mfg. Industries Ltd., Blantyre, 1981-82; founder, mng. dir. Candlex Ltd., Blantyre, 1983—; bd. dirs., founder Kamp Products (PVT) Ltd., Harare. Fellow Inst. Prodn. Control; mem. British Inst. Mgmt., Inst. Sales and Mktg. Mgmt, Internat. Air Passengers Assn., Frequent Bus. Travellers Assn. Clubs: Blantyre Sports. Home: PO Box 782, Blantyre Malawi Office: Candlex Ltd, PO Box 80140, Maselema, Blantyre 8, Malawi

PHLEGAR, DONALD VAUGHN, communications executive; b. Roanoke, Va., Dec. 20, 1933; s. Eugene Vaughn and Syble Estine (Ware) P.; m. Barbara Ann Carley, June 10, 1956; children: Linda Dianne, Cynthia Joyce. BA, Wake Forest U., 1954; M of Theology, So. Bapt. Seminary, 1958; student, Monterey Inst. Fgn. Studies, 1961, Union Lang. Sch., Bangkok, 1968-70. Rep. So. Bapt. Gen. Conv. Calif., various cities, 1958-67; mgr. Pattaya (Thailand) Conf. Ctr., 1972-78; dir. Bapt. Mass Communications, Bangkok, 1988—; mgr. Pattaya (Thailand) Conf. Ctr., 1987-88. Producer TV programs: Refreshing Life, 1978-82, Greatest Song, 1984, 85, Christmas Gifts, 1986; film Forgiving Love, 1984; Concert for Eagles, Singapore, 1987. Club: Fgn. Corr. Thailand (Bangkok). Office: Bapt Mass Communications, PO Box 832, Bangkok Thailand 10501

PHO, ROBERT W.H., orthopedic surgery educator; b. Apr. 30, 1940; 3 children. MBBChir, U. Sydney, 1966. Head univ. dept. orthopedic surgery Singapore Gen. Hosp.; head of hand surgery unit Singapore Ministry Health; prof. orthopedic surgery Nat. U. Singapore. Fellow Royal Coll. Surgeons, Brit. Orthopaedic Assn., Brit. Soc. Hand Surgery, Am. Soc. for Hand Surgery (hon.), Internat. Reconstructive Microsurgery Soc. Clubs: Tanglin, Singapore Island, Country.

PHOCAS, GEORGE JOHN, international lawyer, business executive; b. N.Y.C., Dec. 1, 1927; m. Katrin Gorny, Feb. 26, 1966; 1 child, George Alexander. A.B., U. Chgo., 1950, J.D., 1953. Bar: N.Y. 1955, U.S. Supreme Ct. 1962. Assoc. Sullivan & Cromwell, N.Y.C., 1953-56; counsel Creole Petroleum Corp., Caracas, Venezuela, 1956-60; internat. negotiator Standard Oil Co. N.J. (Exxon), 1960-63; sr. ptnr. Casey, Lane & Mittendorf, London, 1963-72, counsel, 1972—; exec. v.p. Occidental Petroleumm Corp., Los Angeles, 1972-74; adv., U.S. del. UN, ECAFE, Teheran, 1963. Trustee Assn. Naval Aviation, Washington, Owl's Head Aviation Mus., Maine; mem. vis. bd. U. Chgo. Law Sch.; bd. visitors U. Chgo. Law Sch. Served to capt. U.S. Army, 1945-47. Mem. Law Soc. London, Brit. Inst. Comparative Law, Am. Soc. Internat. Law, ABA, Assn. Bar City N.Y. Clubs: Boodles (London); Metropolitan (N.Y.C.); Sleepy Hollow. Home: 28 Aubrey Walk, London England W8 also: 5020 Goodridge Ave Riverdale NY 10471

PHOUMI VONGVICHIT, government official. Acting pres., vice chmn. Govt. of Laos, 1986—. Office: Office of Acting Pres, Vientiane Laos *

PHYLACTOU, CHRIS PINDAR, industrial development company executive; b. Limassol, Cyprus, Oct. 26, 1930; s. Pindar C. and Kroustallo (Skyrianides) P.; m. Eugenia Papadopoulos, May 14, 1956 (dec. Aug. 1985); 1 child, Maria-Christina. B.A., Trinity Coll., U. Cambridge, 1953, M.A., 1956. Dir. Cyprus Cold Stores Ltd., Nicosia, Cyprus, 1955-74, Textiles Mfg. Co., Ltd., Nicosia, 1956-74, Indsl. Devel. Services, Tehran, Iran, 1975-78; mng. dir. Moorgate Merchants Ltd., London, 1980-85, chmn., 1985—; v.p. Granite Holdings, Inc. (div. Del. Corp.), 1982—; cons. Granite Indsl. Devel. and Services, Atlanta, 1981—. Fellow Inst. Dirs., Inst. Chartered Secs. Conservative. Greek Orthodox. Avocations: reading; swimming; antique collecting; motoring; travelling. Home: 55 Brompton Sq, London SW3 2AG, England Office: Moorgate Merchants Ltd, 27 Throgmorton St, London EC2, 2AN., England

PIASKOWSKI, JERZY JOZEF, metallurgist; b. Zawiercie, Silesia, Poland, Aug. 5, 1922; s. Mieczyslaw and Waclawa (Pasierbinska) P.; m. Helena Ciepierska; children: Jerzy, Jan. MA in Engring., Acad. Mines, Krakow, Poland, 1948; MA in Physics, Jagiellonian U., Krakow, Poland, 1952; D in Tech. Sci., Silesian Poly. Sch., Gliwice, Poland, 1960, D in Habilitation, 1963. Chief malleable cast iron team Foundry Research Inst., Kraków, Poland, 1947-55; chief phys. labor Cast Foundry Research Inst., Kraków, Poland, 1955-73, chief malleable and ductile cast irons team, 1973-82, chief dept. metals exams., 1982—; asst. prof. 1974-87, prof. 1987—; bd. dirs. Sci. Council of Foundry Research Inst. Author: (with A. Jankowski) Ductile Iron, 1957, 74, On the Damascene steel, 1974; author Technology of Early Objects of Art Casting, 1982; contbr. articles to profl. jours. Active Sci. Council of Inst. History Sci., Edn., and Tech., Kraków. Decorated Gold Cross of Merit Govt. of Poland, 1956; Knight of Cross Polania Restituta, 1962. Mem. Tech. Assn. Polish Foundrymen, Bibliophiles' Soc. (pres. Kraków br. 1969-84). Home: Ul Zywiecka 40/12, 30-427 Crakow Poland Office: Foundry Research Inst, Ul Zakopianska 73, 30-418 Crakow Poland

PIAZZA, DUANE EUGENE, biomedical researcher; b. San Jose, Calif., June 5, 1954; s. Salvador Richard and Mary Bernice (Mirassou) P.; m Debra J. Coath, Dec. 19, 1987. BS in Biology, U. San Francisco, 1976; MA in Biology, San Francisco State U., 1986. Staff research assoc. I U. Calif., San Francisco, 1975-81; sr. research technician XOMA Corp., San Francisco, 1981-82; biologist II Syntex USA Inc., Palo Alto, Calif., 1982-85; pres., cons. Ryte For You, Oakland, Calif., 1985—; research assoc. I Cetus Corp., Emeryville, Calif., 1986—. CPR instr. ARC, San Francisco, 1980-86; instr., First Aid sta. vol., Santa Cruz, Calif., 1985-86; First Aid sta. vol. disaster action team ARC, Oakland, 1986—; branch chmn. disaster action team ARC, 1987-88. Mem. AAAS, N.Y. Acad. Scis., Astron. Soc. Pacific. Republican. Roman Catholic. Home: 3755 Emerson Way Apt E Oakland CA 94610 Office: Cetus Corp 1400 53d St Emeryville CA 94608

PICACHY, LAWRENCE TREVOR CARDINAL, archbishop of Calcutta; b. Darjeeling, India, Aug. 7, 1916; s. Edwin and May (McCue) P.; ed. St. Joseph's Coll. Ordained to ministry Roman Cath. Ch.; rector, headmaster St. Xavier's Coll., Calcutta, India, 1954-60; bishop of Jamshedpur, India, 1962-69; archbishop of Calcutta, India, 1969—; v.p. Cath. Bishop's Conf. of India, 1972-76, pres., 1976-81; cardinal Sacred Consistory of Pope Paul VI, 1976—. Club: Rotary. Address: Archbishops House, 32 Park St, Calcutta 700 016 India *

PICARD, HANS RUDOLF, education educator; b. Düsseldorf, Nordrhein, Fed. Republic of Germany, July 29, 1928; s. Rudolf and Elisabeth (Schneider) P.; m. Monelle Barbier, Sept. 27, 1955; children: Emmanuel, Stephan. Staasexamen, U. Heidelberg, Fed. Republic of Germany, 1954, PhD, 1959; habilitation, U. Bonn, Fed. Republic of Germany, 1976. Tchr. high sch. and coll. Düsseldorf, 1956-59; dir. Goethe Inst., Barcelona, Spain, 1959-67; student prof. U. Bonn., 1967-76; prof. lit. criticism U. Konstanz, Fed. Republic of Germany, 1976—. Author: The Epistolary Novel, 1971, Autobiography in France, 1978, Poetry and Religion, 1984, Narration in Literary Tradition, 1987. Mem. Assn. Internacional Hispanistas, Deutscher Hispanisten Verband, Deutscher Romanisten Verband. Home: Werner-Sombart St 14, D7750 Konstanz Federal Republic of Germany Office: U Konstanz, Postfach 5560, D7750 Konstanz Federal Republic of Germany

PICARD, JEAN, physician; b. Garnat, England, Aug. 8, 1931; m. July 27, 1959; 1 child, Alain. Med. studies, Med. Faculté Lyon, France; MD, Med. Faculté Paris. Practice medicine Moulins, France; lectr. Free Faculté Medicine, Paris. Contbr. articles to sci. jours. Served as capt. French mil. forces. Mem. Internat. Soc. Bio-Elecronics (1st pres. research group Environment-Health). Home: 90 Rue des Tanneries, 03000 Moulins France Office: 38 Rue de Villars, 03000 Moulins France

PICARD, LAURENT, management educator, administrator, consultant; b. Quebec, Que., Can., Oct. 27, 1927; s. Edouard and Alice (Gingras) P.; m. Therese Picard; children: Andre, Marc, Robert, Denys, Jean-Louis. BA, Laval U., Quebec, 1947, BS, 1954; DBA, Harvard U., 1964. Prof. U. Montreal, Que., Can., 1962-68, dir. bus. adminstrn. dept., 1964-68; exec. v.p. Can. Broadcasting Corp., Ottawa, Ont., 1968-72, pres., chief exec. officer, 1972-75; joint prof. McGill U. and U. Montreal, 1977-78; dean faculty mgmt. McGill U., Montreal, 1978-86, prof., 1986—; mem. Royal Commn. on Newspapers, Royal Commn. on Econ. Union and Devel. Prospects for Can.; conciliation commr. Maritime Employers Assn., Port of Montreal; bd. dirs. Astral Bellevue Pathe, Lombard-Odier Trust Co., Cablevision Ltd., Jean Coutu Group, Télémetropole, Inc., Farmico, Canagex Placements, Inc., Videotron, Fondation des diplomés de Polytechnique; cons. to industry; guest speaker internat. meetings. Contbr. articles to profl. jours. Chmn. Nat. Book Festival, 1978-79; chmn. jury Prix Gerin Lajoie, Ministry Cultural Affairs, 1982. Decorated companion Order of Can., 1977. Mem. Commonwealth Broadcasting Assn. (1st pres.). Home: 5602 Wilderton Ave, Montreal, PQ Canada H3T 1R9 Office: McGill U Faculty Mgmt, 845 Sherbrooke St W, Montreal, PQ Canada H3A 2T5 *

PICARD, THOMAS JOSEPH, JR., manufacturers representative; b. Boston, Dec. 7, 1933; s. Thomas Joseph and Bertha Mildred (Brightman) P.; B.S. in Mech. Engring., U. Mass., 1959; M.B.A., Rollins Coll., 1985; m. Renee E. Coulmas, Aug. 20, 1977; children by previous marriage: T. Gerald, Pamela P. Mfg. engr. Gen. Electric Co., 1959-60; application and sales engr. Masoneilan Div., McGraw Edison Co., 1960-65; v.p. M.D. Duncan & Assocs., Inc., Orlando, Fla., 1965-74, pres., 1974—. Pres., Brookshire Sch. PTA, Winter Park, Fla., 1969-71, Glenridge Jr. High Sch. PTA, Winter Park, 1972-73; v.p. Winter Park Little League, 1968; mem. Orange County Republican Exec. Com., 1973. Served with AUS, 1953-55. Named Exec. of Month, Orlando Area, Sta. WDBO, June 1977; profl. tennis umpire. Mem. Instrument Soc. Am. (sr.; chmn. 1980, dist. v.p. 1981-83, nominating com., chmn. dist. honors and awards com. 1987—, mem. nat. edn. com., profl. cert. com., parliamentarian 1984-86, dir. edn. dept. 1985—), U.S. Tennis Assn. Conglist. Clubs: Rotary Orange County East (charter mem., pres. 1972-73), Masons.

PICAZO, EUGENIO ACEVEDO, physician, consultant, medical educator; b. Manila, May 30, 1938; s. Leopoldo and Pilar Acevedo (Albar) P.; m. Maria Cristina Aberasturi Lopez, Nov. 21, 1969; children: Cristine, Ana, Leopoldo, Cesar, Rosario. MD, U. Philippines, 1962. Diplomate Philippine Bd. Internal Medicine, Philippine Bd. Gastroenterology; lic. physician, Calif. Resident in medicine Mt. Sinai-Elmhurst City Hosp., N.Y.C., 1963-66; resident in gastroenterology Lahey Clin., Boston, 1966-67; cons. U. Philippines-Philippine Gen. Hosp. Med. Ctr., Manila, 1968-73; lectr. in gastroenterology M.C.U. Coll. Medicine, Manila, 1973; cons. Hosp. ng Manila, 1976; chmn. dept. medicine and intensive care Makati (Philippines) Med. Ctr.; chmn. dept. medicine Coll. Medicine of City Manila; pres. med. staff orgn. Hosp. ng Maynila; cons. Cardinal Santos Hosp. Editor-in chief U. Philippines Alumni Yearbook, 1987; contbr. articles to med. jours. and newspapers. Entrance scholar U. Philippines Coll. Medicine, scholar in gastroentestinal endoscopy Nat. Cancer Ctr., Tokyo, 1975. Mem. Philippine Soc. Gastroenterology (pres. 1982-84), Philippine Soc. Gastrointestinal Endoscopy (sec. 1980-82), Philippine Coll. Physicians, Philippine Med. Assn., Manila Med. Soc., U. Philippines Alumni Soc. (v.p., chmn. 1986-87). Lodge: Rotary (pres. 1988-89). Home: 22 Arthur North Greenhills, San Juan Philippines Office: Makati Med Ctr Suite 215, 2 Amorsolo, Makati Philippines

PICCARD, JACQUES ERNEST JEAN, scientist; b. Brussels, Belgium, July 28, 1922; s. Auguste and Marianne (Denis) P.; m. Marie-Claude Maillard, 1953; 3 children. Student U. Geneva, Inst. Universitaire de Hautes Etudes Internationales, Geneva; D.Sc. (hon.), Am. Internat. Coll., Hofstra U. Asst. prof. econs. U. Geneva, 1946-48; cons. scientist to several Am. orgns. for deep sea research; collaborated with Prof. Auguste Piccard in constrn. of bathyscaph Trieste; has made more than 100 dives in Mediterranean and Pacific oceans, one to 35,800 feet (deepest ever dive), 1960; chief scientist research submarine Ben Franklin for the Grumman-Piccard Gulf Stream Drift Mission, 1969; built research submersible F.A.-FOREI, 1978; vis. prof. oceanic engring. Stevens Inst. Tech., Hoboken, N.J. Decorated Croix de guerre (France); Officier Ordre de Leopold (Belgium); recipient U.S. Disting. Pub. Service award, 1960.

PICCENNA, CARLO, research administrator; b. Naples, Italy, May 12, 1945; s. Antonio and Ketty (Flugy) d'Aspermont; m. Angela Calcagno, July 2, 1969; children: Marika, Miriam. Student, Italian Naval Acad., Livorno, 1964-65. Commd. lt. Italian Navy, 1965, advanced through grades to lt. comdr., 1986, ret., 1986; pilot Algero, Italy, 1966-68; lt. antisubmarine pilot Catania, Italy, 1969; chmn. Downs Syndrome Ctr., Catania, 1986—; psychol. selector Italian Navy, 1975-86; consejero Assn. Latin Am. Sindrome de Down, 1987—. Editor test for handicapped children, 1986. Mem. European Down Syndrome Assn. (pres. 1987—). Home: Manzoni 40, 95100 Catania, Sicily Italy Office: Downs Syndrome Ctr, Gramsc 11, 95030 Gravina, Sicily Italy

PICCHI, MARIO, author, journalist, translator; b. Leghorn, Livorno, Italy, Mar. 6, 1927; s. Osvaldo and Maria (Delagramaticas) P.; B.A., U. Rome, 1948; M.A., U. Bari, 1969; m. Domenica Recchia, Oct. 2, 1954; children—Stefano, Alessandro, Michele. Editor, La Fiera Letteraria, Rome, 1949-54; cultural editor, info. specialist USIS, Rome, 1954-70; mem. editorial staff L'Espresso Weekly, Rome, 1970-87 . Recipient award for Short Story, Premio Il Ceppo, 1965; award for novel Premio Asti D'Appello, 1965. Author: Roma di giorno, 1960; Il muro torto, 1964; Storia di una notte, 1968; Ritratto di famiglia, 1974; Parlare ai figli, 1984; Storie di casa Leopardi, 1986. Home: 7 Piazza Madama, 00186 Rome Italy Office: 18 via Lancellotti, 00186 Rome Italy

PICCINALI, JEAN PIERRE, neuropsychologist; b. Lyon, France, July 1, 1940; married; children: Fabrice, Thomas, Jean Guillaume. MD, 1968. Practive medicine specializing in neuropsychiatry Vienne, France; attaché cons. in field. Roman Catholic. Office: 6 Place St Pierre, 38200 Vienne France

PICCINNI, PAOLO, mathematics educator; b. Roma, Feb. 20, 1952; s. Francesco and Delia (Danzi) P. Laurea, U. Rome, 1976; MS, U. Ill., 1984. Researcher U. Rome, 1981-87; assoc. prof. U. Salerno, Italy, 1987—; vis. research scholar Mich. State U., East Lansing, 1984. Contbr. articles to scientific jours. Mem. Unione Matematica Italiano, Am. Math. Soc. Home: Via O Gentiloni 41, 00139 Roma Italy Office: U Salerno, Dept Math, 84100 Salerno Italy

PICCOLI, MICHEL, actor; b. Paris, Dec. 27, 1925; s. Henri P.; m. Juliette Greco, 1966; m. 2d, Ludivine Clerc, 1978; 1 son. Student Coll. d'Annel, Coll. Ste. Barbe, Paris. Mgr., Theatre de Babylone; joined Madeleine Renaud and Jean-Louis Barrault Theatre Co.; appeared in Phedre at the Theatre Nationale Populaire; films include: Le point du jour, 1946, Parfum de la dame in noire, 1949, French Cancan, 1955, The Witches of Salem, 1956, Le mepris, 1963, Diary of a Chambermaid, 1964, De l'amour, 1965, Lady L, 1965, La curee, 1965, Les demoiselles de Rochefort, 1967, Belle de jour, 1967, Dillinger is Dead, 1968, The Milky Way, 1969, Topaz, 1969, The Discreet Charm of the Bourgeoisie, 1972, Themroc, 1972, Blowout, 1973, The Infernal Trio, 1974, Le fantome de la liberte, 1974, La faille, 1975, Leonar, 1975, Sept morts sur ordonnance, 1976, La derniere femme, 1976, Savage State, 1978, Le divorcement, 1979, Le saut dans le vide, 1979, Le mors aux dents, 1979, La citta delle donne, 1980, Salto nel Vuoto, 1980, La Passante du Sans-Souci, 1983. Author: Dialogues egoistes, 1976. Named Best Actor for Salto nel Vuoto, Cannes Film Festival, 1980. *

PICHERAL, JEAN FRANCOIS, radiologist; b. Montpellier, France, Feb. 26, 1934; s. Emil and Edith (Mahistre) P.; m. Marie Picheral, Nov. 16, 1967; children: Fille, Garcon. MD, U. Medicine, Montpellier, 1961. Intern Ctr. Hosp. U. de Montpellier, 1952-59; ancien intern Hosp. Aix en Provence, France, 1962-66, staff appointment, 1962—, radiologist dept. medicine, 1966. Counsellor Municipal et di Adjoint Mairie Aix en Provence, 1971-78, Regional Provence Cote d'Azur, 1984—, gen. Bouche du Rhone, 1979—. Decorated Croix Valeur Militaire, 1962; Mmmedaille d'or Jeuneese et Sport. Socialiste. Club: 41. Lodge: Rotary. Office: 1 Forbin Place, 13100 Aix en Provence France

PICILLO, LAURA MARIA, wine and distilled spirits company executive; b. Kearny, N.J., Apr. 25, 1957; d. Louis and June E. (Aromando) Picillo; divorced. Student N.J. Inst. Tech., 1977; BS in Acctg., Montclair State Coll., 1980. Gas station auditor Amerada Hess Corp., Woodbridge, N.J., 1980, corp. staff auditor, 1981-82; auditor Joseph E. Seagram Sons, N.Y.C., 1982-83, audit supr., 1983, mgr. adminstrn., 1983-86, budget mgr. MIS, 1986, mgr. capital resource devel., 1987—; sales rep. Schlott Realtors, Matawan, N.J. Mem. Nat. Assn. Female Execs., N.J. Bd. Realtors. Democrat. Roman Catholic. Office: Joseph E Seagram & Sons Inc 800 3d Ave New York NY 10022

PICK, JAMES BLOCK, university administrator; b. Chgo., July 29, 1943; s. Grant Julius and Helen (Block) P.; B.A., Northwestern U., 1966; M.S. in Edn., No. Ill. U., 1969; Ph.D., U. Calif., Irvine, 1974, C.D.P., 1980. C.S.P., 1985, C.C.P., 1986. Asst. research statistician, lectr. Grad. Sch. Mgmt. U. Calif., Riverside, 1975-84, dir. computing, adj. lectr., 1984—, mem. Univ. Commons Bd., 1982-86; cons. U.S. Census Bur. Internat. Div., 1978. Trustee Newport Harbor Art Mus., 1981-87, 88—, chmn. permanent collection com., 1987-88. Mem. Assn. Computing Machinery, Assn. Systems Mgmt. (profl., pres. Orange County chpt. 1978-79, sec.-treas. Div. 22 regional council 1979-80, vice chmn. 1980-81, chmn. 1981-82), AAAS, Am. Statis. Assn., Population Assn. Am., Internat. Union for Sci. Study of Population, Soc. Info. Mgmt. Clubs: Balboa Bay (Newport Beach); Standard (Chgo.). Author: Computer Systems in Business, 1986; co-author: (with Edgar W. Butler) Geothermal Energy Development: Problems and Prospects in the Imperial Valley, California, 1982; condr. research in info. systems, environ. studies; contbr. sci. articles to publs. in field. Home: 1833 Galatea Terr Corona del Mar CA 92625 Office: Grad Sch Mgmt U Calif Riverside CA 92521

PICK, OTTO, educator, journalist; b. Prague, Czechoslovakia, Mar. 4, 1925, came to United Kingdom, 1939; s. Hugo and Heda (Gerstl) P.; m. Zdenka Hajek, Apr. 8, 1948; children—Georgina, Joan, Thomas Michael. Dr. law, Charles U., Prague, 1948; B.A. with honors in Modern History, Queen's Coll., Oxford U., Eng., 1950. Interpreter Am. embassy, Prague, 1946-48; editor B.B.C., 1950-58; prof. U. Surrey, Guildford, Eng., 1971-83, dean human studies, 1976-79, pro vice chancellor, 1981-83; emeritus prof., 1983—; vis. prof. Munich U., 1987—, Boston U., 1987—; prof. Johns Hopkins Bologna Ctr., 1986—; dir. Atlantic Info. Centre Tchrs., London, 1966-76; vis. fellow Internat. Inst. Strategic Studies, 1981. Co-author: Collective Security, 1974; contbr. to Soviet Union and Third World, 1980, Reagan's Leadership and the Atlantic Alliance, 1986, Clash in the North, 1988; also articles. Sec.-gen. Council Afro-Brit. Relations, London, 1961-66, Atlantic Assn. Young Politicians, London and Paris, 1963-68; treas. Standing Conf. Atlantic Orgns., London, 1972—; chmn. fgn. affairs com. Liberal Party U.K., 1973-79; active current affairs com. English Speaking Union, London, 1978-83. Rockefeller research fellow London Sch Econs., 1958-61. Mem. Com. Atlantic Studies (chmn. 1969-72), Royal Inst. Internat. Affairs, Internat. Inst. Strategic Studies. Clubs: American (London); English Speaking (Munich). Avocations: skiing; mountain-walking; opera. Home: Kunzweg 21, 8000 Munich 60 Federal Republic of Germany Office: Boston U USMCA-Munich APO New York NY 09407

PICK, ROBERT YEHUDA, orthopedic surgeon, consultant; b. Haifa, Israel, Dec. 24, 1945; came to U.S., 1957; s. Andre B. and Hanna (Gross) P.; m. Roni L. Kestenbaum, Sept. 25, 1977; children: Benjamin A., Joseph E., Jennifer L., Abigail I. BA, B in Hebrew Lit., Yeshiva U., 1967; MD, Albert Einstein Coll. Med., 1971; MPH, Harvard U., 1979. Diplomate Nat. Bd. Med. Examiners, Am. Bd. Orthopaedic Surgery. Intern Brookdale Hosp., Bklyn., 1971-72; resident in orthopedic surgery Albert Einstein-Bronx (N.Y.) Mcpl. Hosp. Ctr., 1972-74; resident in orthopedic surgery USPHS Hosp., Staten Island, N.Y., 1974-75, asst. chief orthopedic surgery, 1975-77; asst. chief orthopedic surgery USPHS Hosp., Boston, 1977-78; fellow orthopedic trauma Boston City Hosp., 1979-80, assoc. dir. orthopedic surgery, 1980-84, dir. pediatric orthopedics, 1981-83; practice medicine specializing in orthopedic surgery Chestnut Hill, Mass., 1984—; instr. orthopedic surgery Boston U., 1980-82, asst. prof., 1982—; adj. asst. prof. health scis. and orthopedics Touro Coll., N.Y.C., 1976-78; dir. spinal screening program Dept. Health and Hosps., Boston, 1979-82; dist. med. advisor U.S. Dept. Labor, Boston, 1984—; cons. Boston Retirement Bd., 1983-84, New Eng. Telephone, Boston, 1985—, Commonwealth of Mass. Pub. Employee Retirement Adminstrn., Boston, 1985—. Contbr. articles on med. issues to profl. jours. Trustee Young Israel Jackson Heights, Queens, N.Y., 1969-76, pres., 1976-77; sec. Young Israel Brookline, Mass., 1978-79. Served to lt. comdr. USPHS, 1975-78. Fellow Am. Acad. Orthopedic Surgeons; mem. Am. Physicians Fellowship for Medicine in Israel (trustee 1975—, exec. com. 1976—, asst. treas. 1987—, Man of Yr. award 1977), Nat. Inst. Occupational Safety and Health (traineeship 1978-79), Mensa. Office: 25 Boylston St Chestnut Hill MA 02167

PICKARD, JAN ALBERTUS JACOBUS, investment company executive; b. Piketberg, Republic of South Africa, Dec. 25, 1927; s. Jan Albertus Jacobus and Alida Wilhelmina (Wiese) P.; m. Ingrid Corneilia Dönges, Nov. 26, 1954; children: Maria Teresa, Jan A.J., Karin Louise, Thea Ebenelle. BS in Agriculture, U. Stellenbosch, 1952. Chmn. Picardi Investments Ltd., Cape Town, Republic of South Africa, 1965—, Picardi Holdings Ltd., Cape Town, 1976—, Picardi Properties Ltd., Cape Town, 1976—, Union Wine Ltd., Wellington, 1976—. Exec. mem. Pres.'s Council, Cape Town, 1981-87. Recipient Tinie Louw award Afrikaanse Handels Inst., Pretoria, Republic of South Africa, 1980, Mktg. award of Yr. Inst. Mktg. Mgmt., 1981, Order Meritorious Service Gold award State Pres., 1988. Mem. Nationalist Party. Dutch Reformed Ch. Clubs: Western Province Rugby Football Union (pres. 1981—), Hamiltons Rugby Football. Home: Hillwood Ave, Bishopscourt, Cape Town 7700, Republic of South Africa Office: Picardi Investments Ltd, 1372 Picbel Parkade, Strand St Box 1134, Cape Town 8000, Republic of South Africa

PICKENS, ALEXANDER LEGRAND, educator; b. Waco, Tex., Aug. 31, 1921; s. Alex LeGrand and Elma L. (Johnson) P.; m. Frances M. Jenkins, Aug. 20, 1955. B.A., So. Methodist U., 1950; M.A., North Tex. State U., Denton, 1952; Ed.D., Columbia U., 1959. Tchr. art public schs. Dallas, 1950-53, Elizabeth, N.J., 1953-54; mem. faculty U. Mich. Coll. Architecture and Design, 1954-59, U. Ga., Athens, 1959-62, U. Hawaii Coll. Edn., Honolulu, 1962—; prof. edn. U. Hawaii Coll. Edn., 1968—, dir. coll. devel., 1984—, chmn. doctoral studies curriculum instrn., 1984—; dir. children's classes Ft. Worth Children's Museum, 1951-53; head art Nat. Music Camp, Interlochen, Mich., summers 1957-58, U. Oreg., Portland, summers 1959-60, 62; cons. youth art activities Foremost Dairies, 1964-74; cons. art films United World Films, 1970-75; art edn. cons. Honolulu Paper Co., 1970-76, Kamehameha Sch., Bishop Estate, 1978—. Exhibited ceramics, Wichita Internat. Exhbn., Syracuse (N.Y.) Nat. Exhbn., St. Louis Mus., Dallas Mus., San Antonio Mus., Detroit Art Inst., Hawaii Craftsmen, also others; editorial bd.: Arts and Activities mag, 1955-82; editor: U. Hawaii Ednl. Perspectives, 1964—; contbr. articles to profl. jours. Mem. adult com. Dallas County chpt. Jr. ARC, 1951-53; exec. com. Dallas Crafts Guild, 1950-53; v.p., publicity chmn. U. Ga. Community Concert Assn., 1960-62. Served with USAAF, 1942-44. Recipient award merit Tex. State Fair, 1957; All Am. award Ednl. Press Assn. Am., 1968, 70, 72, 75, 79. Mem. Internat. Soc. Edn., NEA, Nat. Art Edn. Assn., AAUP, Phi Delta Kappa, Kappa Delta Pi. Address: 1471 Kalaepohaku St Honolulu HI 96816

PICKERING, AVAJANE, specialized education facility executive; b. New Castle, Ind., Nov. 5, 1951; d. George Willard and Elsie Jean (Wicker) P. BA, Purdue U., 1974; MS in Spl. Edn., U. Utah, 1983, postgrad., 1985—. Tchr. Granite Community Edn., Salt Lake City, 1974-79; tchr. coordinator Salt Lake City Schs., 1975-85; co-dir., owner Specialized Ednl. Programming Service, Inc., Salt Lake City, 1976—; adj. instr. U. Utah, Salt Lake City, 1985—. Rep. del. Utah State Conv., also county conv.; vol. tour guide, hostess Temple Square, Ch. Jesus Christ of Latter-Day Saints, 1983—. Mem. Council for Exceptional Children, Assn. Children and Adults with Learning Disabilities, Delta Kappa Gamma. Home: 1595 S 2100 E Salt Lake City UT 84108 Office: 2022 S 2100 E Suite 201 Salt Lake City UT 84108

PICKERING, ROBERT EASTON, writer, translator; b. Carlisle, Cumberland, Eng., Feb. 12, 1934; s. Edward and Janet (Easton) P. Degree in Modern Langs., Oxford U., Eng., 1958. Author: Himself Again, 1966, In Transit, 1968, The Word Game, 1982. Address: 07150 Lagorce France

PICKERING, ROBERT HARVEY, financial consultant; b. N.Y.C., May 12, 1937; s. Harvey Pickering and Rose S. (Sekeres) Stohr; children: Shari, Sally, Katherine; m. Nell H. Hartwick, June 30, 1984; stepchildren, Terri, Jerry. BS, Northwestern U., 1959. CLU. V.p. John M. Shannon & Assoc., Inc., Chgo., 1964-72; pres. Robert H. Pickering & Assoc. Ltd., Denver, 1972—; radio show commentator Money Talks Sta. KNUS-AM, Denver, 1981-84, Sta. KOA-AM, Denver, 1986—. Contbr. articles to profl. jours.; inventor anchor bolt. Mem. Sch. Bd., Deerfield, Ill., Arapahoe County (Colo.) Retirement Bd., 1980—, vice chmn., 1986—; treas. Suburban Community Service Council, Englewood, Colo., 1978, chmn. 1979-81. Served with USAR, 1960-66. Recipient Service award Regional Social Security Adminstrn., 1985. Mem. Nat. Assn. Life Underwriters, Internat. Assn. Fin. Planners, Denver Assn. Life Underwriters, Rocky Mountan Chpt. Fin. Planners, Nat. Assn. Securities Dealers. Republican. Episcopalian. Clubs: Columbine Country (Littleton, Colo.); Ocean Reef (Key Largo, Fla.). Office: Robert H Pickering Assocs Ltd 3773 Cherry Creek Dr N Suite 1000 Denver CO 80209

PICKERING, THOMAS REEVE, diplomat; b. Orange, N.J., Nov. 5, 1931; s. Hamilton R. and Sarah C. (Chasteney) P.; m. Alice J. Stover, Nov. 24, 1955; children: Timothy R., Margaret S. A.B., Bowdoin Coll., 1953; M.A., Fletcher Sch. Law and Diplomacy, 1954, U. Melbourne, Australia, 1956. Joined U.S. Fgn. Service, 1959; fgn. affairs officer ACDA, 1961; polit. adviser U.S. del. 18 Nation Disarmament Conf., Geneva, 1962-64; consul Zanzibar, 1965-67; counselor of embassy, dep. chief mission Am. embassy, Dar es Salaam, Tanzania, 1967-69; dep. dir. Bur. Politico-Mil. Affairs, State Dept., 1969-73; spl. asst. to Sec. of State; exec. sec. Dept. State, 1973-74; ambassador to Jordan, Amman, 1974-78; asst. sec. for Bur. Oceans, Internat. Environ. and Sci. Affairs, Washington, 1978-81; ambassador to Nigeria Lagos, 1981-83; ambassador to El Salvador San Salvador, 1983-85; ambassador to Israel 1985—. Served to lt. comdr. USNR, 1956-59. Mem. Council Fgn. Relations, Internat. Inst. Strategic Studies, Phi Beta Kappa. Office: Am Embassy Tel Aviv APO New York NY 09672-0001

PICKETT, GEORGE BIBB, JR., retired military officer; b. Montgomery, Ala., Mar. 20, 1918; s. George B. and Marie (Dow) P.; B.S., U.S. Mil. Acad., 1941; student Nat. War Coll., 1959-60; m. Beryl Arlene Robinson, Dec. 27, 1941; children—Barbara Pickett Harrell, James, Kathleen, Thomas; m. 2d, Rachel Copeland Peeples, July 1981. Commd. 2d lt. U.S. Army, 1941, advanced through grades to maj. gen., 1966; instr. Inf. Sch., Fort Benning, Ga., 1947-50, instr. Armed Forces Staff Coll., Norfolk, Va., 1956-59; comdg. officer 2d Armored Cav. Regt., 1961-63; chief of staff Combat Devel. Command, 1963-66; comdg. gen. 2d inf. div., Korea, 1966-67; ret., 1973; field rep. Nat. Rifle Assn., 1973-85. Decorated Purple Heart with oak leaf cluster, D.S.M. with two oak leaf clusters, Bronze Star with two oak leaf clusters and V device, Silver Star, Legion of Merit with two oak leaf clusters, Commendation medal with two oak leaf clusters. Mem. SAR (pres. Ala. Soc. 1984), Old South Hist. Assn., Ala. Assn. Engrs. and Land Surveyors, Am. Legion, VFW. Episcopalian. Club: Kiwanis (chmn. 1974—). Author: (with others) Joint and Combined Staff Officers Manual, 1959; contbr. articles on mil. affairs to profl. jours. Home: 3525 Flowers Dr Montgomery AL 36109 Office: PO Box 4 Montgomery AL 36101

PICKFORD, JOHN ASTON, professor water and waste engineering, consultant; b. London, Dec. 28, 1924; s. Aston Charles and Gladys Ethel (May) P.; m. Daphne Annie Ransom, Sept. 27, 1947; children: Robert Aston, William John, Ian Charles Pickford Helen Sheard. BS, London U., 1943, MS in Engring., 1963. Registered profl. engr., Eng. Asst. engr. Borough Sutton & Cheam, Surrey, Eng., 1947-49, Borough Southall, Middlesex, Eng., 1949-50; sr. asst. engr. Borough Gravesend, Kent, Eng., 1950-54; town engr. Sekondi-Takoradi Mcpl. Council, Ghana, West Africa, 1954-60; lectr. Loughborough Coll. Tech., Leicestershire, Eng., 1960-63; sr. lectr. Loughborough U. Tech., Leicestershire, 1963-84, prof., 1984—; cons. Overseas Devel. Adminstrn., Uganda, India, Nigeria, 1977—, UNICEF, Pakistan, Ghana, 1978-87, Howard Humphries & Ptnrs., Tanzania, Malaysia, 1981—, The World Bank, India, 1984—. Author: Analysis of Surge, 1968; editor in chief: Developing World Water, vols. 1-3, 1985-87; contbr. articles to profl. jours. Served with Brit. Army, 1943-47. Named Officer Order Brit. Empire, 1984. Fellow Instn. Civil Engrs., Instn. Water and Environ. Mgmt. (hon.); mem. Instn. Pub. Health Engrs. (pres. 1981-82, 87). Methodist. Office: U Tech Water Engring Devel Ctr, Loughborough LE11 3TV, England

PIDGEON, JOHN ANDERSON, headmaster; b. Lawrence, Mass., Dec. 20, 1924; s. Alfred H. and Nora (Regan) P.; children: John Anderson, Regan S., Kelly; m. Barbara Hafer, May 1986. Grad., Hebron Acad., 1943; B.A., Bowdoin Coll., 1949; Ed.D., Bethany Coll., 1973; D.Litt., Washington and Jefferson Coll., 1979. Instr. Latin, adminstrv. asst. to headmaster Deerfield Acad., 1949-57; headmaster Kiskiminetas Springs Sch., Saltsburg, Pa., 1957—; dir. Saltsburg Savs. & Trust. Served as ensign USNR, 1943-46. Mem. New Eng. Swimming Coaches Assn. (pres. 1956-57), Cum Laude Soc., Delta Upsilon. Home: Kiskiminetas Springs School Saltsburg PA 15681

PIEDRA, ALBERTO MARTÍNEZ, diplomat; b. Havana, Cuba, Jan. 29, 1926; came to U.S., 1959; s. Francisco and Conchita (Piedra) Martinez-Gomez; m. Edita Enriquez Piedra, June 26, 1955; children—Alberto, Javier, Pedro, Edita, Conchita. LL.D., U. Havana, Cuba, 1951; Ph.D. in Polit. Economy, U. Madrid, Spain, 1957; Ph.D. in Econ., Georgetown U., Washington, 1962; LLD (hon.), St. Thomas U., 1986. Instr. Spanish Georgetown U., Washington, 1956; prof. econ. Universidad de Santo Tomaás de Villanueva, Havana, Cuba, 1958-59; tech. asst. dept. econ. devel. Nat. Econ. Council, Havana, Cuba, 1958-59; dir. gen. exports and imports Ministry of Commerce, Havana, Cuba, 1959; staff economist dept. polit. affairs OAS, Washington, 1960-62; lectr. Washington Internat. Ctr., 1963; dir. Latin Am. Inst. Catholic U., Washington, 1965-82, chmn. dept. econ., 1967-74, ordinary prof. econ., 1980; dep. rep. OAS-Dept. of State, Washington, 1982-84; sr. policy adv. Bur. Inter-Am. Affairs, 1982-84; ambassador to Guatemala U.S. Dept. State, Guatemala, 1984-87; area advisor 42d UN Gen. Assembly, 1987; alt. rep. to Conf. of the Human Rights Commn., Geneva, 1988—; cons. and lectr. in field. Contbr. chpts. to books, articles to profl. jours. Mem., Fgn. Policy Discussion Group. Decorated Knight of the Order of Malta; Knight of Justice of the Constantinean Order; Knight of the Order of Illescas, Spain; Knight of Corpus Christi of Toledo; Asociacion de Hidalgos a Fuero de Espana. Mem. Georgetown Alumni Assn., Blue Key Honor Soc., Sigma Beta Kappa. Republican. Clubs: Kenwood Country (Bethesda); Internat., Army and Navy (Washington). Lodge: Rotary. Office: UN Ctr for Human Rights, Palcis des Nations, Room S-3660, CH-1211 Geneva 10 Switzerland *

PIEGL, LESLIE, electronic software company executive; b. Komlo, Hungary, Feb. 21, 1955; s. Janos and Anna (Volcsanyi) P.; m. Agnes Kortvelyesi, Aug. 7, 1979; 1 child, Martin. MS, Eotvos U., Budapest, Hungary, 1979, PhD, 1982; grad., Inst. of Math., Southen-on-Sea, Eng., 1983, British Computer Soc., London, 1985. Asst. prof. Tech. U., Budapest, 1979-84, prof. math., 1984-87; cons. CAD/MATH, Milford, Ohio, 1987—. Fellow Alexander von Humboldt Found., Braunschweig, Federal Republic Germany, 1985-87. Mem. N.Y. Acad. Scis., Am. Math. Soc., Can. Math. Soc., London Math. Soc., Soc. for Indsl. and Applied Math., IEEE, Assn. for Computing Machinery, The British Computer Soc., The Inst. Math. and its Applications, Eurographics Assn. Office: CAD/MATH PO Box 458288 Cincinnati OH 45245

PIEL, GERARD, editor, publisher; b. Woodmere, L.I., N.Y., Mar. 1, 1915; s. William F.J. and Loretto (Scott) P.; m. Mary Tapp Bird, Feb. 4, 1938; children: Jonathan Bird, Samuel Bird (dec.); m. Eleanor Virden Jackson, June 24, 1955; child, Eleanor Jackson. A.B. magna cum laude, Harvard U., 1937; D.Sc., Lawrence Coll., 1956, Colby Coll., 1960; U. B.C., Brandeis U., 1965, Lebanon Valley Coll., 1977, L.I. U., 1978, Bard Coll., 1979, CUNY, 1979, U. Mo., 1985, Blackburn Coll., 1985; Litt.D., Rutgers U., 1961, Bates Coll., 1974; L.H.D., Columbia, 1962, Williams Coll., 1966, Rush U., 1979, Hahnemann Med. Coll., 1981, Mt. Sinai Med. Sch., 1985; LL.D., Tuskegee Inst., 1963, U. Bridgeport, 1964, Bklyn. Poly. Inst., 1965, Carnegie-Mellon U., 1968, Lowell U., 1986; Dr. (honoris causa), Moscow State (Lomonosov) U., 1985. Sci. editor Life mag., 1938-44; asst. to pres. Henry J. Kaiser Co. (and assoc. cos.), 1945-46; organizer (with Dennis Flanagan, Donald H. Miller, Jr.), pres. Sci. Am., Inc., 1946-84, chmn., 1984-87, chmn. emeritus, 1987—; pub. mag. Sci. Am., 1947-84. Translated editions: Le Scienze, 1968, Saiensu, 1971, Investigacion y Ciencia, 1976, Pour la Science, 1977, Spektrum der Wissenschaft, 1978, KeXue, 1979, V Mire Nauki, 1983, Tudomany, 1985, Majallat Al Oloom, 1986; Author: Science in the Cause of Man, 1961, The Acceleration of History, 1972. Chmn. Commn. Delivery Personal Health Services City N.Y., 1967-68; trustee Am. Mus. Nat. History, Radcliffe Coll., 1962-80, Phillips Acad., N.Y. Bot. Garden, Henry J. Kaiser Family Found., Mayo Found., René Dubos Ctr.; trustee emeritus Found. for Child Devel.; bd. overseers Harvard U., 1966-68, 73-79. Recipient George Polk award, 1961, Kalinga prize, 1962, Bradford Washburn award, 1966, Arches of Sci. award, 1969; Rosenberger medal U. Chgo., 1973, A.I. Djavakhishvili medal U. Tbilisi, 1985; named Pub. of Yr. Mag. Pubs. Assn., 1980. Fellow Am. Acad. Arts and Scis., AAAS (pres. 1985, chmn. 1986); mem. Council Fgn. Relations, Am. Philos. Soc., Nat. Acad. Scis. Inst. Medicine, Phi Beta Kappa, Sigma Xi. Clubs: Harvard, Century, Cosmos (Washington), Somerset (Boston). Office: care Sci Am Inc 41 Madison Ave New York NY 10010

PIENAAR, LOUIS ALEXANDER, government official; b. Stellenbosch, Republic of South Africa, June 23, 1926; s. Jaocbus Alexander and Eleanora Angelique (Stiglingh) P.; m. Isabel Maud van Niekerk, Dec. 11, 1954; children: Jacobus Francois, Isabel Maud, Willie Van Niekerk. BA in Law, U. Stellenbosch, 1945; LLB, U. South Africa, Pretoria, 1952. Mcpl. employee Municipalities of Brakpan, Vereniging and George, Republic of South Africa, 1946-52; atty. at law Bellville, Republic of South Africa, 1954-75; mem. parliament Republic of South Africa, Cape Town, 1970-75; ambassador to France Republic of South Africa, Paris, 1975-79; mem. Pres.'s Council Republic of South Africa, Cape Town, 1981-85; adminstr. gen. S.W. Africa territory Govt. Republic of South Africa, Windhoek, Namibia, 1985—; advocate Cape Town, 1980-85. Mem. provincial council Cape of Good Hope, Cape Town, 1966-70. Decorated Grand Officer Nat. Order of Merit (France). Mem. Nat. party. Mem. Dutch Reformed Ch. Club: Here Sewentien (Cape Town). Home: SWA-House, Leutweinstreet, Windhoek Namibia Office: Office Adminstr Gen, Goring St, Windhoek 9000, Namibia

PIEPER, ERNST, metal processing company executive; b. Germany, Dec. 20, 1928; m. Marianne; children—Joachim, Anne. Diploma U. Cologne, 1954. With Klöckner-Werke AG, Duisburg, Germany, 1954-62, Fed. Office of Trade and Industrie, Frankfurt, 1962-64; undersec. Fed. Ministry of Economy, Bonn., 1964-73; dep. sec. Fed. Ministry Fin., Bonn, 1974-77; vice chmn. mng. bd. Salzgitter AG, Germany, 1977-79, chmn. mng. bd., 1979—. Recipient GroBes Bundesverdienstkreuz, award Fed. Republic of Germany, GroBes Verdienstkreuz des Niedersächsischen Verdienstordens. Office: Salzgitter AG, PO Box 41 11 29, D-3320 Salzgitter 41 Federal Republic of Germany

PIEPER, PATRICIA R., artist, photographer; b. Paterson, N.J., Jan. 28, 1923; d. Francis William and Barbara Margareth (Ludwig) Farabaugh; student Baron von Palm, 1937-39, Deal (N.J.) Conservatory, summers 1939, 40, Utah State U., 1950-52; m. George F. Pieper, July 1, 1941 (dec. May 3, 1981); 1 dau., Patricia Lynn. One-woman shows: Charles Russell Mus., Great Falls, Mont., 1955, Fisher Gallery, Washington, 1966, Tampa City Library, 1977, 78, 79, 80, 81, 83, 84, Center Place Art Ctr., Brandon, Fla., 1985; exhibited in group shows: Davidson Art Gallery, Middletown, Conn., 1968, Helena (Mont.) Hist. Mus., 1955, Dept. Commerce Alaska Statehood Show, 1959, Joslyn Mus., Omaha, 1961, Denver Mus. Natural History, 1955, St. Joseph's Hosp. Gallery, 1980, 82, 84-86; represented in pvt. collections. Pres. Bell Lake Assn., 1976-78, 79. Winner photog. competition Gen. Telephone Co. of Fla., 1979; recipient Outstanding Service award Bell Lake Assn., 1987; photography winner in top 100 out of 8,000 Nat. Wildlife Fedn. competition, 1986. Mem. Pasco County (Fla.) Water Adv. Council, 1978—, chmn., 1979-82, 83-84, 86-88; gov.'s appointee to S.W. Fla. Water Mgmt. Dist., Hillsborough River Basin Bd., 1981-82, 84-87, vice chair, 1987; active Save Our Rivers program, 1982-84, 85-86, chmn., 1986; pres. Bell Lake Assn., 1986, 87; adv. bd. Tampa YMCA, 1979-80. Mem. Nat. League Am. Pen Women (v.p. Tampa 1976-78, Woman of Yr. award 1977-78), Tampa Art Mus., Retired Officer's Wives Assn., Land O' Lakes C. of C. (dir. 1981-82, outstanding service award 1980), Fla. Geneal. Soc., West State Archaeol. Soc.; distaff mem. Retired Officer's Assn., MacDill AFB, 1982—. Clubs: Lutz, Land O' Lakes Women's. Home and Studio: PO Box 15 Land O' Lakes FL 34639

PIÉRART, MARCEL AIME, classics educator; b. Tertre, Belgium, Oct. 25, 1945; emigrated to Switzerland, 1976; s. Pol Joseph and Gabrielle Josephine (Smal) P.; m. Christiane Thonnard, May 8, 1969; children: Isabelle, Geneviève, Dominique, Anne. Licence en Philologie Classique, Université de Liège (Belgium), 1967, Agrégé Enseignement Secondaire Supérieur, 1968, Docteur en Philosophie et Lettres, 1972. Research worker Fonds National Belge de la Recherche Scientifique, Liège, 1968-72; mem. Ecole Francaise, Athens, Greece, 1972-76; prof. classics (Latin and Greek), U. Fribourg, Switzerland, 1976—, vice rector, 1983-87, dean faculty letters, 1982-83. Author: Platon et la Cité grecque, 1975; also learned papers. Mem. editorial com. Les Etudes Classiques. Recipient prix de l'Academie Royale de Belgique, 1973. Mem. Assn. Suisse des Professeurs D'Université (pres. 1984-86, v.p. 1986-88), Assn. Suisse pour l'Etude de l'Antiquité (treas. 1982-86, pres. 1986—). Home: Es Agges 28, Avry sur Matran, CH1754 Fribourg Switzerland Office: Université de Fribourg, 190 rue Pierre-Aeby, CH1700 Fribourg Switzerland

PIERCE, CHESTER MIDDLEBROOK, psychiatrist, educator; b. Glen Cove, N.Y., Mar. 4, 1927; s. Samuel Riley and Hettie Elenor (Armstrong) P.; m. Jocelyn Patricia Blanchet, June 15, 1949; children: Diane Blanchet, Deirdre Anona. A.B., Harvard U., 1948, M.D., 1952; Sc.D. (hon.), Westfield Coll., 1977, Tufts U., 1984. Instr. psychiatry U. Cin., 1957-60; asst. prof. psychiatry U. Okla., 1960-62, prof., 1965-69; prof. edn. and psychiatry Harvard U., 1969—; pres. Am. Bd. Psychiatry and Neurology, 1977-78; mem. Polar Research Bd.; cons. USAF. Author publs. on sleep disturbances, media, polar medicine, sports medicine, racism; mem. editorial bds. Advisor Children's TV Workshop; chmn. Child Devel. Asso. Consortium; bd. dirs. Action Children's TV., Boston Children's Mus. Served with M.C. USNR, 1953-55. Fellow Royal Australian and N.Z. Coll. Psychiatrists (hon.); mem. Inst. Medicine, Black Psychiatrists Am. (chmn.), Am. Orthopsychiat. Assn. (pres. 1983-84). Democrat. Home: 17 Prince St Jamaica Plain MA 02130

PIERCE, DELILA FRANCES, judge; b. St. Cloud, Minn., Jan. 21, 1934; d. Lawrence August and Alvina Elizabeth (Hechtel) Pierskalla. BS, U. Minn., 1957, JD cum laude, 1958. Bar: Minn. 1958. Assoc. Robert L. Ehlers, St. Paul, Minn., 1958-59; ptnr. Mitchell & Pierce, Mpls., 1959-65; sole practice, Mpls., 1966-73; referee Family Ct., Dist. Ct., Hennepin County, Minn., Mpls., 1973-74; judge Hennepin County Mcpl. Ct., Mpls., 1974-83, Dist. Ct. Minn. (4th jud. dist.), 1983—; mem. adv. bd. Genesis II, Mpls., 1975-76. Fellow Am. Acad. Matrimonial Lawyers; mem. Am. Judges Assn., Nat. Assn. Women Judges, ABA, Am. Judicature Soc., Minn. State Bar Assn., Hennepin County Bar Assn., Minn. Dist. Judges Assn., Minnesota County Judges Assn. (bd. dirs. 1984-87), Hennepin Hist. Soc., Mpls. Soc. Fine Arts. Office: Dist Ct Minn 4th Dist Hennepin County Govt Ctr Minneapolis MN 55487

PIERCE, DONALD FAY, lawyer; b. Bexley, Miss., Aug. 28, 1930; s. Percy O. and Lavada S. (Stringfellow) P.; m. Norma Faye Scribner, June 5, 1954; children—Kathryn Pierce Peake, D. F., John S., Jeff G. B.S., U. Ala., 1956, J.D., 1958. Bar: Ala. 1958, U.S. Ct. Appeals (5th cir.) 1958, U.S. Dist. Ct. (no. and so. dists.) Ala. 1958, U.S. Ct. Appeals (11th cir.) 1982. Law clk. to presiding judge U.S. Dist. Ct. (so. dist.) Ala., 1958-59; ptnr. Hand, Arendall, Bedsole, Greaves & Johnston, Mobile, Ala., 1964—. Trustee, UMS Prep. Sch., 1980—. Served to 1st lt. U.S. Army, 1951-53. Mem. Ala. Def. Lawyers Assn. (past pres.), Fedn. Ins. Counsel, Am. Acad. Hosp. Attys., Internat. Assn. Def. Counsel, Assn. Ins. Attys., Ins. Counsel Trial Acad. (dir. 1983, 84), Def. Research Inst. (pres. 1987, chmn. 1988). Baptist. Contbr. articles to profl. jours. Home: 4452 Winnie Way Mobile AL 36608 Office: PO Box 123 Mobile AL 36601

PIERCE, FRANCIS CASIMIR, civil engineer; b. Warren, R.I., May 19, 1924; s. Frank J. and Eva (Soltys) Pierce; student U. Conn., 1943-44; B.S., U. R.I., 1948; M.S., Harvard U., 1950; postgrad. Northeastern U., 1951-52; m. Helen Lynette Steinouer, Apr. 24, 1954; children—Paul F., Kenneth J., Nancy L., Karen H., Charles E. Instr. civil engring. U. R.I., Kingston, 1948-49, U. Conn., Storrs, 1950-51; design engr. Praeger-Maguire & Ole Singstad, Boston, 1951-52; chief found. engr. C.A. Maguire & Assocs., Providence, 1952-59, assoc., 1959-69, v.p., 1969-72; sr. v.p. C.E. Maguire, Inc., 1972-76, officer-in-charge Honolulu office, 1976-78, exec. v.p., corp. dir. ops., 1975-87; gen. mgr. East Atlantic Casualty Co., Ltd., 1987—; also dir.; pres. Magma, Inc., tech. ops. service co., 1984—; lectr. found. engring. U. R.I., 1968-69, trustee, 1987—; mem. U.S. com. Internat. Commn. on Large Dams. Vice chmn. Planning Bd. East Providence, R.I., 1960-73; bd. dirs. R.I. Civic

Chorale and Orch., 1986—. Served with AUS, 1942-46. Mem. ASCE (chpt. past pres., dir.), R.I. Soc. Profl. Engrs. (nat. dir., engr. of year award 1973), Am. Soc. Engring. Edn., Soc. Am. Mil. Engrs., ASTM, Soc. Marine Engrs. and Naval Architects, Am. Soc. Planning Ofcls., Harvard Soc. Engrs., Scientists, Providence Engrs. Soc., R.I. Soc. Planning Agys. (past pres.). Contbr. articles to profl. jours. Recipient USCG Meritorious Pub. Service award, 1987. Home: 156 Barney St Rumford RI 02916 Office: One Davol Sq Providence RI 02903

PIERCE, JAMES FRANKLIN, data systems consultant; b. Seaford, N.Y., Aug. 24, 1950; s. James Franklin and Marion April (Augustine) P.; m. Kit Lan Lee, July 4, 1980; 1 child, James Franklin. AAS, Olympic Coll., 1970; BSBA, U. Phoenix, 1984; BS, SUNY, 1984; MBA, U. Phoenix, 1986. Cert. systems profl. Cons. GTE-Informatics Co., N.Y.C., 1974-75, Frito-Lay Co., Dallas, 1976-77, Occidental Petroleum Co., Houston, 1977-78, Lockheed Missiles & Space Co., Sunnyvale, Calif., 1978-79; cons., owner Intel Corp., San Jose, Calif., 1979—. Mem. Republican Task Force. Mem. Assn. Systems Mgmt., ACM. Home and Office: 32807 Orick St Union City CA 94587

PIERCE, JOHN ROBERT, lawyer; b. Boston, Nov. 3, 1949; s. Irving Russell and Mary Elizabeth (Powers) P. BA, Harvard U., 1971; JD, Boston Coll., 1982. Bar: Mass. 1982, U.S. Dist. Ct. Mass. 1983. Assoc. Widett, Slater & Goldman P.C., Boston, 1982-83; sole practice Boston, 1983—. Articles editor Boston Coll. Law Rev., 1981-82. Mem. ABA, Mass. Bar Assn., Boston Bar Assn., Norfolk County Bar Assn., Assn. Trial Lawyers Am., New England Hist. Soc., Mass. Soc. Mayflower Descendants. Roman Catholic. Clubs: Old Colony Harvard (southeast Mass.) (exec. com. 1984-87, pres. 1987—); Harvard (Boston). Office: 11 Beacon St Boston MA 02108

PIERCE, JOSEPH REED, III, marketing executive; b. McPherson, Kans., Mar. 21, 1942; s. Joseph Reed, Jr. and Maxine Lahoma (Burnside) P.; B.A., U. Kans., 1964, M.B.A., 1966. Project mgr. Boeing Co., Seattle, 1966-70; systems rep. Honeywell, Inc., San Francisco, 1970-71; systems analyst P.I.E., Oakland, Calif., 1972; project mgr. Crown Zellerbach Co., San Francisco, 1972-75; systems planner Fibreboard Co., San Francisco, 1975-76; dist. mgr. Cutler Williams Co., San Francisco, 1976-78; dir. bus. devel. San Francisco Cons. Group, 1978-80; product mktg. mgr. Mathematica, San Francisco, 1980-85; account exec. Security Pacific Computer Solutions, San Francisco, 1986—; instr. computer studies San Francisco Community Coll., Coll. of Marin. Mem. San Francisco Citizens Adv. Bd. Mental Health Services, 1976. Sumerfield grantee, 1965. Mem. Am. Mktg. Assn., Assn. Systems Mgrs. (chmn. tech. seminars com. 1980-81, chmn. membership 1981-82, bd. dirs. 1983-84), Psy Chi, Phi Alpha Theta. Clubs: Commonwealth of Calif., Hold Your Horses. Author: The Little Restaurants of San Francisco, 1973. Home: 1544 Union St San Francisco CA 94123 Office: PO Box 26216 San Francisco CA 94126

PIERCE, RALPH, consulting engineer; b. Chgo., Apr. 14, 1926; s. Charles and Fay (Reznik) P.; B.E.E., Northwestern U., 1946; m. Adrian H. Rosengard, Sept. 3, 1978; children—Marc Fredrick, Deborah Ann, Elizabeth Allison. Test engr. Am. Elec. Heater Co., Detroit, 1946-47; sr. asso. engr. Detroit Edison Co., 1947-52; sec., chief utility engr. George Wagschal Assos., Detroit, 1952-58; sr. partner Pierce, Yee & Assos., Engrs., Detroit, 1958-73; mng. partner Harley Ellington Pierce Yee & Assos., 1973-86, pres., 1986—; mem. Dept. Commerce Mission to Yugoslavia. Served to ensign USNR, 1944-46; comdr. Res. ret. Registered profl. engr., Mich., Ind., Ill., Ohio, Ky., N.Y., Washington, Mo., Fla., Can., Calif., Colo., N.Mex. Mem. Nat. Council Engring. Examiners, Nat. Soc. Profl. Engrs., Engring. Soc. Detroit, IEEE, Soc. Coll. and Univ. Planners, Illuminating Engring. Soc., Mich. Soc. Architects (asso.). Home: 31825 Lakeside Dr Apt 22 Farmington Hils MI 48018 Office: 26913 Northwesten Hwy Suite 200 Southfield MI 48034

PIERCE, ROBERT L., petroleum company executive. Pres., dir. Nova Corp. of Alberta, Calgary, Can. Office: Nova an Alberta Corp, 801 7th Ave SW, Calgary, AB Canada T2P 2N6 *

PIERCE, ROBERT RAYMOND, materials engineer, consultant; b. Helena, Mont., Feb. 17, 1914; s. Raymond Everett and Daisy Mae (Brown) P.; m. Stella Florence Kankos, June 12, 1938; children—Keith R., Patricia L., Diana L. B.S. in Chem. Engring., Oreg. State U., 1937. Process supr. Pennwalt Corp., Portland, Oreg., 1941-45, asst. tech. service mgr., Tacoma, 1945-47, gen. mgr., Phila., 1947-58, Natrona, Pa., 1958-65, tech. mgr., Phila., 1965-78, sr. tech. cons., Phila., 1978-80; self-employed cons., also Ohio State U., 1980—; pres. Pierce Cormat Services, Inc. Contbr. articles to prof. jours. Patentee in field. Vice chmn. Phila. Air Pollution Control Bd., Phila., 1969-79, chmn. Ad Hoc #1, 1974-79; Ky. Colonel, Louisville 1975—; mem. People to People del. on corrosion, People's Republic China, 1986. Recipient Phila. award City of Phila., 1973, Resolution award, City of Phila., 1979. Mem. Am. Inst. of Chem. Engrs., Nat. Assn. of Corrosion Engr., Internat. Com. for Industrial Chimneys (recipient best paper award Dusseldorf, Germany 1970), Am. Ceramic Soc., Nat. Inst. of Ceramic Engrs. Lutheran. Current work: Engineering of coatings; engineering of brickwork; stress analyses of coatings; stress analyses of brickwork; corrosion of non-metallic materials; design of polymeric concrete; design of chimney linings. Subspecialties: Corrosion; Materials.

PIERCE, SAMUEL RILEY, JR., lawyer, government official; b. Glen Cove, L.I., N.Y., Sept. 8, 1922; s. Samuel R. and Hettie E. (Armstrong) P.; m. Barbara Penn Wright, Apr. 1, 1948; 1 dau., Victoria Wright. A.B. with honors, Cornell U., 1947, J.D., 1949; postgrad. (Ford Found. fellow), Yale Law Sch., 1957-58; LL.M. in Taxation, NYU, 1952, LL.D., 1972; various other hon. degrees including LL.D., L.H.D., D.C.L., Litt.D. Bar: N.Y. 1949, Supreme Ct. 1956. Asst. dist. atty. County N.Y., 1949-53; asst. U.S. atty. So. Dist. N.Y. 1953-55; asst. to under sec. Dept. Labor, Washington, 1955-56; asso. counsel, counsel Jud. Subcom. on Antitrust, U.S. Ho. Reps., 1956-57; pvt. practice law 1957-59, 61-70, 73-81; sec. Housing and Urban Devel., 1981—; faculty N.Y. U. Sch. Law, 1958-70; guest speaker colls., univs.; judge N.Y. Ct. Gen. Sessions, 1959-61; gen. counsel, head legal div. U.S. Treasury, Washington, 1970-73; Cons. Fund Internat. Social and Econ. Edn., 1961-67; chmn. impartial disciplinary rev. bd. N.Y.C. Transit System, 1968-81; Chmn. N.Y. State Minimum Wage Bd. Hotel Industry, 1961; mem. N.Y. State Banking Bd., 1961-70, N.Y.C. Bd. Edn., 1961, Adminstrv. Conf. U.S., 1968-70, Battery Park City Corp. Authority, 1968-70, N.Y.C. Spl. Commn. Inquiry into Energy Failures, 1977; mem. nat. adv. com. comptroller of currency, 1975-80; adv. group commr. IRS, 1974-76; mem. Nat. Wiretapping Commn., 1973-76; Dir. N.Y. 1964-65 World's Fair Corp.; former Dir. Prudential Ins. Co., U.S. Industries, Inc., Internat. Paper Co., Gen. Electric Co., Rand Corp., 1st Nat. Boston Corp., 1st Nat. Bank of Boston, Pub. Service Electric and Gas Co.; gov. Am. Stock Exchange, 1977-80. Contbr. articles to profl. jours. Trustee Inst. Civil Justice, Mt. Holyoke Coll., 1965-75, Hampton Inst., Inst. Internat. Edn., Cornell U., Howard U., 1976-81; bd. dirs. Tax Found. U.S. del. Conf. on Coops., Georgetown, Brit. Guiana, 1956; mem. panel symposium Mil.-Indsl. Conf. on Atomic Energy, Chgo., 1956; fraternal del. All-African People's Conf., Accra, Ghana, 1958; mem. Nat. Def. Exec. Res., 1957-70; mem. nat. exec. bd. Boy Scouts Am., 1969-75; mem. N.Y.C. U.S.O. Com., 1959-61; mem. panel arbitrators Am. Arbitration Assn. and Fed. Mediation and Conciliation Service, 1957—; Bd. dirs. Louis T. Wright Meml. Fund, Inc., Nat. Parkinson Found., Inc., 1959-61; sec., dir. YMCA Greater N.Y., 1960-70; Mem. N.Y. State Republican Campaign Hdqrs. Staff, 1952, 58; gov. N.Y. Young Rep. Club, 1951-53. Served with AUS, 1943-46; as 1st lt. J.A.G.C. Res., 1950-52. Recipient N.Y.C. Jr. C. of C. Ann. Distinguished Service award, 1958, Alexander Hamilton award Treasury Dept., 1973. Fellow Am. Coll. Trial Lawyers; mem. Cornell Assn. Class Secs., Telluride Assn. Alumni, Cornell U. Amumni Assn. N.Y.C. (gov.), C.I.D. Agts. Assn. (gov.), Am. Bar Assn., Assn. N.Y.C. Bar, N.Y. County Lawyers Assn., Inst. Jud. Adminstrn., Phi Beta Kappa, Phi Kappa Phi, Alpha Phi Alpha, Alpha Phi Omega. Methodist (former mem. commn. on interjurisdictional relations United Meth. Ch.). Office: HUD 451 7th St SW Washington DC 20410 *

PIERCE, SHELBY CRAWFORD, oil co. exec.; b. Port Arthur, Tex., May 26, 1932; s. William Shelby and Iris Mae (Smith) P.; B.S.E.E., Lamar State Coll. Tech., Beaumont, Tex., 1956; student M.I.T. Program for Sr. Execs., 1980; m. Marguerite Ann Grado, Apr. 2, 1954; children—Cynthia Dawn, Melissa Carol. With Amoco Oil Co., 1956—, zone supr., gen. foreman, maintenance, 1961-67, operating supt., 1967-69, coordinator results mgmt., Texas City (Tex.) refinery, 1969-72, dir. results mgmt., corp. hdqrs., Chgo., 1972-75, ops. mgr. refinery, Whiting, Ind., 1975-77, asst. refinery mgr., 1977-79, dir. crude replacement program, Chgo., 1979-81, mgr. refining and transp. engring., 1981—. Fin. chmn. Bay Area council Boy Scouts Am., 1974; dir. JETS (Jr. Engring. Tech. Soc.); chmn. bd., chmn. fin. com. Methodist Ch., 1967-72. Mem. Am. Inst. Chem. engrs. (chmn. engring. constrn. contracting div.), N.W. Ind. Bus. Roundtable (chmn. exec. com.), Sigma Tau. Republican. Home: 18840 Loomis Ave Homewood IL 60430 Office: 200 E Randolph Dr Chicago IL 60601

PIERCE, VERLON LANE, pharmacist, store proprietor; b. Greensburg, Ky., July 13, 1949; s. Ogle Lee and Aleene (Hall) P.; m. Brenda Mildred Russell, May 20, 1973; children—Amanda Lee, Daniel Russell. B.S. in Math. and Chemistry, Western Ky. U., 1972; B.S. in Pharmacy, U. Ky., 1975. Relief pharmacist Shugart & Willis Drug Store, Franklin, Ky., 1975-78; staff pharmacist Franklin Simpson Meml. Hosp., Franklin, 1976-79; owner, pres. pharmacist Medicine Shoppe, Bowling Green, Ky., 1978—; pres. Westland Drug Inc., Bowling Green, 1984—; sec. 21st Investment Group, Bowling Green, 1984—. Recipient Franny award Internat. Franchise Assn., 1980; Hall of Fame bust Medicine Shoppe, St. Louis, 1983. Mem. 4th Dist. Pharmacy Group (pres. 1983-84), Ky. Pharmacy Assn. Democrat. Baptist. Avocations: golf; swimming. Home: Route 6 Box 507 Franklin KY 42134 Office: Medicine Shoppe 816 US 31 W Bowling Green KY 42101

PIERCY, NIGEL FRANCIS, management educator; b. Hounslow, Eng., Jan. 13, 1949; s. Gilbert and Helena Gladys (Sargent) P.; m. Patricia Jean Barber (div. 1983); 1 child, Niall Christopher; m. Stephanie Monica Burges. BA in Commerce with honors, Heriot Watt U., 1972; MA, Durham U., 1980; PhD, U. Wales, 1985. Mgr. Tesco Stores Ltd., Cambridge, Eng., 1967-68; lectr. Newcastle Poly., 1972-74, sr. lectr., 1977-81; mktg. planner Amersham Internat., Eng., 1974-77; lectr. bus. sch. U. Wales, Cardiff, 1981-83, sr. lectr., 1983-86, reader, 1986-88, prof., 1988—; mgmt. cons., 1981—. Author 7 books, numerous academic papers. Fellow U.K. Inst. Mktg; mem. Mktg. Edn. Group U.K., Am. Acad. Mktg. Sci. Home: 9 The Green, Radyr, Cardiff South Glamorgan CF4 8BR, England Office: Cardiff Bus Sch, Colum Dr, Cardiff Wales CF1 3EU, England

PIERGIOVANNI, FABIO, management science educator; b. Perugia, Italy, Aug. 14, 1946; s. Luigi and Anna (Binucci) P.; m. Maud Tampellini; children: Marta, Anna, Elisabetta, Paolo. Degree in Stats., Pub. Univ., Rome, 1972; MBA, Inst. Adriano Olivetti, Ancona, Italy, 1977. With Assn. Indsl. Perugia, 1974-76, Coop. Assn., 1978; pvt. practice cons. Perugia, 1978-79; mng. dir. Progetto Terziario SpA, Spoleto, Italy, 1979—; tchr. mgmt. courses, 1984—. Served with Italian army, 1972-73. Mem. Italian Tng. Assn., Italian Assn. Work Studies. Roman Catholic. Home: Corso Bersaglieri 23, 06100 Perugia Italy

PIERPONT, ROBERT, fund-raising executive, consultant; b. Somers Point, N.J., Jan. 27, 1932; s. Robert E. and Elise D. (White) P.; m. Marion J. Welde, Oct. 11, 1958; children: Linda J., Nancy L., Robert W., Richard F. B.S. in Bus. Adminstrn, Pa. Mil. Coll., 1954; postgrad. Inst. Ednl. Mgmt, Harvard Grad. Sch. Bus. Adminstrn., 1970. Comml. sales rep. Atlantic City (N.J.) Electric Co., 1956-58; asst. dir. devel. Widener Coll. (formerly Pa. Mil. Coll.) Chester, 1958-61, asst. to pres., 1961-62, dir. devel., 1962-68, v.p. for devel., 1968-70; sr. cons. v.p and dir. Brakeley, John Price Jones, Inc., N.Y.C., 1970-79; v.p. devel. Mt. Sinai Med. Center, N.Y.C., 1979-85; ptnr. Pierpont Assocs., 1986—; guest faculty mem. Big 10 Fund Raisers Inst., Mackinac Island, Mich., 1971; mem. adv. com. on application of standards Philanthropic Adv. Service, Council of Better Bus. Burs., Washington, 1978-81. Mem. bishops adv. com. on stewardship Diocese of Pa., 1968-69; vestryman Trinity Episcopal Ch., Swarthmore, 1970-72; pres. Wall Street Mus., 1983-84; trustee Putnam Valley Free Library, 1986—. Served to 1st lt. inf. U.S. Army, 1954-56. Mem. Nat. Soc. Fund Raising Execs. (dir.-at-large 1970-78, pres. found. 1977-79, chmn. bd. 1979-82, chmn. cert. bd. 1982-87), Nat. Council for Culture and Art (chmn. bd. 1980-84). Office: The Stone House Route 9 P O Box 222 Garrison NY 10524

PIERRE, MARIE-JOSEPH, patristics educator; b. Argentan, Normandy, France, Nov. 12, 1945; arrived in Israel, 1977; s. Louis and Brigitte (Lepetit) P. Lic. philosophy, 1971; ThD, Cath. Inst., Paris, 1985; Dr. Sci. of Religions, Sorbonne U., Paris, 1985. Prof. patristics Ecole Biblique & Archeologique francaise, Jerusalem, 1983—. Author: (with J. Rousée) Catalogue de la bibliotheque de l' ecole biblique, 1983—, Aphraate Le Sage Persan, Les Exposés Paris, 1988. Mem. Assn. pour l'étude de la litterature apocryphe chétienne. Home: Prophets St 38, Jerusalem Israel

PIERRE-BENOIST DE VAUBUZIN, JEAN, consultant, international trade specialist; b. N.Y.C., July 22, 1947; s. Yves Maurice and Madeleine (Maillet) P.; m. Matilde Eugenia Pefaur Fernández, Sept. 8, 1973; children—Angélique Madeleine, Jean-Louis Réginald, Paul-Michel Théodore. B.A., Am. U., 1973, M.A., 1982. Owner, cons., mgr. PBM Enterprises, Vienna, Va., 1970—; analyst C.W.W., Inc., Alexandria, Va., 1977-80, staff economist U.S. Dept. Agr., Washington, 1980-82; internat. trade analyst U.S. Internat. Trade Commn., 1982—; v.p., dir. mktg. intelligence Latin Am. Cons., Inc., 1984-85; with PBM Enterprises, Vienna, Va., 1970—. Contbr. articles to profl. jours. Project leader and sec. 4-H, 1985-88; scoutmaster, mem. com. French Speaking Scouts of Washington, 1975—; eucharistic minister 3d Order of Preachers, mem. council French-speaking Parish of Washington, 1984-87. Served with USAF, 1964-68, Vietnam. Mem. Am. Econ. Assn., Soc. for Internat. Devel., Vols. in Tech. Assistance, Nat. Rifle Assn. Republican. Roman Catholic. Avocations: fishing; hunting; photography; archery; mountaineering. Home: 103 Elmar Dr SE Vienna VA 22180 Office: PBM Enterprises 103 Elmar Dr SE Vienna VA 22180

PIERSANTE, DENISE, marketing executive; b. Detroit, Jan. 9, 1954; d. Joseph Lawrence and Virginia (Grunwald) P.; m. Wilfred Lewis Was II, June 7, 1975 (div. 1981). BA in Communications, Mich. State U., 1978. Tchr. Northwestern Ohio Community Action Commn., Defiance, 1979-80, counselor, 1980-82, job developer, 1982-83; job developer Pvt. Industry Council, Defiance, 1983, job developer coordinator, 1983-84, dir. pub. relations and job devel., 1984-86; market master North Market, Columbus, Ohio, 1986-87; dir. mktg. Richard S. Zimmerman Jr., Columbus, 1987—; cons. Small Bus. Mgmt., Archbold, Ohio, 1985-87; promotion dir. Miss N.W. Ohio Pageant, Defiance, 1985-87; promotion dir. Gallery Jazz Series, 1988, organizer, Prism Awards Competition, 1987; scholarship auction, 1988; pub. relations coordinator Defiance County Social Service Agys., 1981-86; author of various grants. Editor Job Tng. Partnership Act newsletter, 1984-86, (newsletter) North Market Soc., 1986-87. Defiance County Social Service Agys. newsletter, 1981-86; Value/Style Community News, 1987—. Organizer Auglaize River Race, Defiance, 1985. Nat. Merit scholar, 1972; recipient Am. Legion Citizenship award, 1969, 72. Mem. Pub. Relations Soc. Am., Nat. Assn. Female Execs., Am. Mktg. Assn., Jaycees (Jaycee of Month 1985). Club: Bus. and Profl. Women (Defiance); Corps de Ballet (Columbus): Conductors (Columbus); Operation Operatics (Columbus). Home: 2363 Meadow Village Dr Worthington OH 43085 Office: 100 S 3d St Suite 414 Columbus OH 43215

PIERSON, RICHARD NORRIS, JR., medical educator; b. N.Y.C., Sept. 22, 1929; s. Richard Norris and Dorothy (Stewart) P.; m. Alice Roberts, Aug. 26, 1974; children by previous marriage—Richard N., Olivia Tiffany, Alexandra de Forest, Cordelia S.C.; stepchildren—Alice W. Dunn, Eric C.W. Dunn. B.A., Princeton U., 1951; M.D., Columbia U., 1955. Diplomate Am. Bd. Internal Medicine, Am. Bd. Nuclear Medicine. Resident St. Luke's Roosevelt Hosp., N.Y.C., 1955-61, assoc. dir., 1961-65, dir. div. nuclear medicine, 1965—, attending physician, 1975—; prof. clin. medicine Columbia U., 1980—; dir. medicine Hackensack Hosp., 1973-74; staff assoc. Brookhaven Nat. Lab., 1970—; research scholar Lawrence Radiation Lab., Berkeley, Calif., 1970-71. Editor: Quantitative Radiocardiography, 1975. Contbr. articles to profl. jours. Bd. dirs. Englewood Health Dept., N.J., 1966-74; warden St. Paul's Ch., 1980-82, bd. dirs. Blue Cross/Blue Shield Empire, N.Y., 1978—. Served as lt. USNR, 1956-58. NIH grantee, 1973-76, 86—; John A. Hartford Found. grantee, 1967-70. Fellow N.Y. Acad. Medicine, ACP; mem. N.Y. County Med. Soc. (pres. 1978-79), N.Y. County Health Service Rev. Orgn. (chmn. 1980-82), Am. Bur. Med. Advancement in China (pres. 1979-87), Am. Med. Rev. Research Ctr. (pres. 1985—), Alliance for Continuing Med. Edn. (pres. 1987—), Soc. Nuclear Medicine (greater N.Y. area pres. 1982-83). Clubs: Century, Englewood Field. Home: 94 Beech Rd Englewood NJ 07631 Office: Saint Lukes Roosevelt Hosp Ctr 425 W 113th St New York NY 10025

PIETERSE, HENDRIK JOHANNES CHRISTOFFEL, theologian, educator; b. Brits, Republic South Africa, June 11, 1936; s. Barend Jacobus and Magdalena (Van Greunen) P.; m. Louisa Maria DeBruyn, Apr. 8, 1961; children: Louise, Barend Jacobus. BA, U. Pretoria, 1958, BDiv, 1961; Dth, U. Stellenbosch, 1978. Ordained to ministry, Dutch Reformed Ch., 1962. Pastor Dutch Reformed Ch., Shabani, Zimbabwe, 1962-66, Pretoria, Republic South Africa, 1965-72, Johannesburg, Republic South Africa, 1973-75; lectr. U. Pretoria, 1976-79; prof. practical theology U. South Africa, Pretoria, 1980—; chmn. Marriage Council South Africa, 1968-73; sec. Nationwide Cong. on Ch. in the 80s in South Africa, 1982. Author: Huweliks Pastoraat, 1977, God's Work for Today, 1980, Communicative Preaching, 1987; contbr. articles to jours. Recipient Pro Arte medal, U. Pretoria, 1980. Mem. Inst. Contextual Theology, Co. Practical Theology (v.p. 1981—), Arbeitsgemeinshaft für Homiletick, Internat. Biog. Assn. Office: Practical Theology U, South Africa Muckleneukrand, Pretoria 0001, Republic of South Africa

PIETILA, REIMA FRANS ILMARI, architect; b. Turku, Finland, Aug. 25, 1923; s. Frans Viktor and Ida Maria (Lehtinen) P.; m. Raili Inkeri Marjatta Paatelainen, 1961; 1 child. Student Inst. Tech. Ptnr., Reima Pietila & Raili Paatelainen, Architects, Helsinki, 1974—; State prof. of arts, 1971-74; prof. architecture U. Oulu (Finland), 1973-78. Archtl. works: Finnish Pavilion at Brussels World Fair, 1958, Kaleva Ch., Tampere, Finland, 1966, Students Activity Ctr., Dipoli, Congress Centre, Otaniemi, 1966, Hervanta Cultural Ctr., Tampere, 1979, Sief Palace Area Bldgs., Kuwait, 1981, Suvituuli Housing, Tapiola, 1981-82, Council of Ministers, 1982, Ministry of Fgn. Affairs, 1982, Lieksa Ch., East Finland, 1982, Tampere Main Library, 1983, Finnish Embassy, New Delhi, 1983. Decorated Chevalier Ordre de la Couronne (Belgium), 1958; Knight Order of Finnish Lion, 1967; recipient Tapiola medal for Town Planning Services, 1981; Prince Eugene medal (Sweden), 1981. Fellow AIA (hon.); mem. Royal Acad. Liberal Arts (Sweden), Assn. Finnish Architects (vice chmn. 1959-60, mem. governing body 1969-70). Office: Laivurinrinne 1A5, 00120 Helsinki 12 Finland *

PIETRANGELI, CARLO, archeologist, museum director; b. Rome, Italy, Oct. 20, 1912; s. Antonio Giuseppe and Maria (Antonelli) P.; grad. history of art and archeology, U. Rome, 1934; m. Laetitia Angeli Nieri Mongalli, Feb. 20, 1943; children: Maria Laura, Giovanni, Filippo, Giuseppe. Insp. antiquities and fine art City of Rome, 1938, supt. mus., monuments and archaeol. excavations, 1973-77; dir. gen. The Vatic Mus., 1978—; adj. prof. U. Rome, 1955. Decorate Medaglia D'Oro Benemeriti Scuola Cultura ed Arte, 1962; officer Legion of Honor (France); comdr. Ordine Stella Polare (Sweden); comdr. Ordine Dannebrog (Denmark); Knight of Order of Malta; gr. uff. S. Gregorio Magno (Vatican). Mem. Istituto Italiano dei Castelli-Sezione Lazio (v.p.), Consulta dell' Istituto Storico e di Cultura dell'Arma del Genio, Pontificia Accademia Romana di Archeologia (pres. 1974), Accademico di S. Luca, Galleria Accademica (supt.), Accademico Corrispondente della Real Accademia de Bellas Arts de San Fernando, Ordinario dell'Istituto di Studi Romani, Socio effettivo della Societa Romana di Storia Patria, Socio Ordinario dell'Istutito Archeologico Germanico, Pontificia Accademie dei Virtuosi al Pantheon; hon. mem. Brit. Acad. at Rome; corr. mem. l'Arcadia, Oesterreichische Ehrenkreuz fü r Wissenschaft und Kunst 1 klasse (Austria), Accademico Spoletino, Tuscolano. Author: La famiglia di Augusto, 1938; Spoletium, 1939; Ocriculum, 1943; Scavi e scoperte di antichita sotto il pontificato di Pio VI, 1943, 2d edit., 1958; Museo Barracco, 1973; Musei Capitolini, 1951; Mevania, 1953; Palazzo Braschi, 1958; Villa Paolina, 1961; Museo Napoleonico, 3d edit., 1966; Guide Rionali di Roma, 1967-81; Otricoli, 1978; I musei Vaticani: cinque secoli di storia, 1985, Palazzo Scierra, 1986; contbr. to Enciclopedie Italiana, Enciclopedia Cattolica, Enciclopedie dell'Arte Antica, Britannica, others; contbr. articles to periodicals and profl. publs. Home: 83 Via in Caterina, 00186 Rome Italy Office: The Vatican Museums, Vatican City Vatican

PIETROVITO, GUY ROY, lawyer; b. Columbia, S.C., Mar. 25, 1954; s. Jeremiah and Bess (Nahigian) P.; m. Janet Mary Giles, May 12, 1984; 1 child, Timothy Guy. BA, Coll. William & Mary, 1976; JD cum laude, Capital U., 1981; LLM in Taxation, Georgetown U., 1982. Bar: Va. 1981, D.C. 1983, U.S. Dist. Ct. D.C. 1984, U.S. Dist. Ct. (ea. dist.) Va. 1985, U.S. Ct. Appeals (4th cir.) 1985. Gen. mgr. Metro Paper Co. Inc., Washington, 1976-78, assoc. Pompan & Murray, Washington, 1982-83, Pompan & Assocs., Alexandria, Va., 1983-84; ptnr. Murray & Pietrovito, Fairfax, Va., 1985-87; atty.-advisor U.S. Gen. Acctg. Office, Washington, 1987—. Editor Capital U. Law Rev., 1979-81. Bd. dirs. St. Stephen's Sch. Alumni Assn., Alexandria, 1982—. Mem. ABA, Fed. Bar Assn., Order of Curia, Order of White Jacket. Episcopalian. Home: 6018 Crown Royal Circle Alexandria VA 22310 Office: US Gen Acctg Office 441 G St NW Washington DC 20548

PIETROWSKI, ROBERT FRANK, JR., lawyer; b. Pasadena, Calif., Feb. 7, 1945; s. Robert Frank Sr. and Annabelle (Johnson) P.; m. Barbara Holly Himel, June 25, 1966; children: Robert Frank III, Michael Scott. BS in Petroleum Engring., Stanford U., 1970; JD, U. Va., 1973. Bar: D.C. 1974, U.S. Supreme Ct. 1978. Assoc. Law Offices of Northcutt Ely, Washington, 1973-77, ptnr., 1977-84; ptnr. Bracewell & Patterson, Washington, Houston, London, 1984—; chief counsel to Govt. Rep. of Guinea in Guinea-Bissau case, The Hague, 1984-85; arbitrator S.P.P. vs. Egypt case, 1984—; mem. U.S. Panel of Arbitrators, 1988—; bd. dirs. Environ. Chems., Inc., Chgo., 1982—. Contbr. articles to profl. jours. Served to 1st lt. U.S. Army, 1966-69. Fellow Am. Bar Found.; mem. ABA, Am. Soc. Internat. Law, Internat. Bar Assn., Internat. Law Assn., Union Internationale Des Avocats, Sigma Chi. Republican. Episcopalian. Clubs: Metropolitan, Cosmos (Washington); Farmington Country (Charlottesville, Va.); Guards Polo (Windsor, Eng.). Office: Bracewell & Patterson 2000 K St NW Suite 500 Washington DC 20006

PIETRUSKA-MADEJ, ELZBIETA, philosopher, educator; b. Lwów, Poland, June 7, 1938; d. Stanislaw and Maria (Ochocka) Pietruska; m. Kazimierz Madej, June 1, 1935. MSc in Phys. Chem., Maria Curie-Sklodowska U., 1962; MA in Philosophy, Warsaw U., 1969, PhD, 1971, Habilitated Doctor, 1981. Adj. dept. philosophy Warsaw U., Poland, 1972-82, docent, 1983—. Author: The Methodological Problems of theScientific Revolution in Chemistry, 1975, The Search for the Laws of the Growth of Science, 1980; co-author, co-editor: The Relationships between the Theories and the Growth of Science, 1978; mem. editorial bd. Philos. Study, 1985; contbr. articles on philosophy, methodology and history of sci. to profl. jours. Mem. Polish Philos. Soc. (gen. sec. 1986—). Office: Warsaw U Dept Philosophy, Krakowskie Przedmiescie 3, 00-063 Warsaw Poland

PIETRZYNSKI, GRZEGORZ JERZY, chemistry educator; b. Opole, Poland, Aug. 22, 1959; s. Grzegorz Boleskaw and Jadwiga (Wolak) P.; m. Krystyna Ludwik, Mar. 27, 1982; children: Pawel, Magdalena. Grad., Wroclaw U., Poland, 1983. Chemist Pedagogical U., Opole, 1983-85, asst. lectr., 1985—. Contbr. articles to profl. jours. Office: Inst Chem WSP, Oleska 48, 45-052 Opole Poland

PIETSCHMANN, HERBERT VICTOR, physicist, educator; b. Vienna, Austria, Aug. 9, 1936; s. Victor and Margarete (Keldorfer) P.; m. Edeltraud Sicka, Mar. 3, 1960; children: Werner, Dieter, Brigitte. Ph.D., U. Vienna, 1960, Habilitation, 1966; Docent Tech. U., Sweden, 1966. Prom. sub auspiciis (hon.) U. Vienna, 1961. Fellow CERN, Geneva, Switzerland, 1960-61; research U. Vienna, 1961-64, U. Va., U.S., 1964-65; docent Tech. U., Göteborg, Sweden, 1966; vis. prof. Bonn U., 1967-68; prof. physics U. Vienna, 1968—; cons. Research Ctr. Seibersdorf, 1970—; dir. Inst. High En. Phys. Austrian Acad. Sci., 1972-75; vis. prof. NORDITA, Göteborg, 1975; Austrian del. CERN Council, 1972-75. Author: Formulae and Results in Weak Int., 1974; D. Ende d. naturwissensch Zeitalters, 1980; Weak Int.-Formulae, Results, and Derivations, 1983; D. Welt d. Wir uns Schaffen, 1984, Electroweak Interactions, 1988. Recipient Eotvos medal Hungarian Phys. Soc., 1976. Mem. Austrian Phys. Soc., European Phys. Soc., Gesellschaft Deutsche Naturforscher u. Arzte, Soc. Social Responsibility of Sci., Humboldt Gesellschaft, Hungarian Phys. Soc. (hon.). Roman Catholic. Home: Arbeiterg 13/18, A1050 Vienna Austria Office: Inst Theoretical Physics, Boltzmanng, A1090 Vienna Austria

PIGGOTT, HARRY, orthopedic surgeon, researcher; b. Kilburn, Derbyshire, Eng., Dec. 16, 1925; s. John Henry and Elizabeth (Barnett) P.; m. Doreen Emily House, Oct. 9, 1948; children—Susanna, Charles. M.B., B.Chir., Cambridge U., 1948; M.A., Cambridge U., 1949. Resident St. Thomas Hosp., London, 1948-49, Royal Nat. Orthopedic Hosp., London, 1956-59; sr. registrar Middlesex Hosp., London, 1960-63; cons. orthopedic surgeon Royal Orthopedic Hosp., Birmingham and Birmingham Children's Hosp., Eng., 1963—; hon. cons. orthopedic surgeon Midland Centre for Neurosurgery, Birmingham, 1965—; clin. lectr. in surgery, Birmingham U., 1963—. Contbr. articles to profl. jours., chpt. to books. Served to capt. M.C., Brit. Army, 1949-51, North Africa. Fellow Brit. Orthopedic Assn., Royal Coll. Surgeons, Hellenic Orthopedic Assn. (hon.), European Spinal Deformity Soc., Brit. Orthopedic Research Soc., Internat. Coll. Surgeons, Societe Internat. de Chirurgie, Orthopedique et Tramatique; mem. Brit. Scoliosis Soc. (pres. 1985—), Naughton Dunn Club (pres. 1982-84). Mem. Ch. of England. Clubs: Oxford and Cambridge (London). Avocations: opera; Shakespeare. Home: White House, Icknield St, Beoley, Worcestershire B98 9AP, England Office: 7 Chad Rd, Edgbaston, Birmingham B15 3EN, England

PIGLOWSKI, JEAN, physician; b. Ouveillan, Aude, France, Nov. 17, 1943; s. Henri and Jeanne (Cahuzac) P.; m. Marie Laure Anselme-Martin, July 5, 1972; children: Hervé, Odile. MD, U. Montpellier, France, 1972, PhD, 1973. Clin. asst. Univ. Hosp., Montpellier, 1972-78; med. inspector French Ministry of Health, Paris, Montpellier, 1978—. Inventor in field. Fellow French Soc. Allergology, European Acad. Allergology, Internat. Fedn. Med. Elecs. Home: 72 ave d'Assas, 34000 Montpellier, Herault France Office: Ministere de la Sante, Drass du Languedoc Roussillon, 386 Ave Antigone, 34000 Montpellier, Herault France

PIHERA, LAWRENCE JAMES, advertising agency executive, writer; b. Cleve., Jan. 9, 1933; s. Charles and Dorothy P.; student U. Hawaii, Cooper Sch. Art, Cleve. Inst. Art; m. Patricia Dunn, Aug. 22, 1955; children—Lauren, Scott. Advt. mgr. Johnson Rubber Co. and subs., 1957-58; creative dir. Mansfield Advt. (Ohio), 1958-60, G. W. Young Public Relations, Dayton, 1960-70; pres. Pihera Advt. Assos., Inc., Centerville, Ohio, 1970—; pub. relations counsel City of Trotwood, 1982-86, Madison Twp., 1984-86; mktg. counsel Muir Pub., 1984-86, Newport/Cocke County, Tenn., 1985-86; mem. adv. bd. Carlton Systems Group, 1987; publicity dir. Indpls. 500 Racing Team; lectr. in field; cons. environ. design. Founder Trotwood Rail Mus.; bd. dirs. Centerville Fine Arts Commn. Served with USN. Commd. col., Gov. Tenn., 1987; recipient 1st Place Advt. Writing, 1970, 71, 74, 76, 77, 78. Mem. Soc. Bus. Cons., Art Center Dayton, Centerville C. of C. (bd. (dirs.). Author: Making of a Winner, 1972; (juvenile fiction) Wee Wams Wander, 1985; Living in Style in a Log Home, 1985, Confederation Moves Into U.S. Market, 1986, Tropical Plants in Restaurants, 1986, A Dream Come True, 1987, Will Your First Home Be Built of Logs?, 1987, Interior Plantscapes in Retirement Centers, 1987; editor: McCall Spirit, 1970, The Heritage Report, 1983—, FEG Stamping Newsletter, 1987—, Yesteryear Newsletter, Horticultural Mgmt. Report, Lincoln Log News; architecture critic Instl. Mgmt. mag.; producer, writer (film) The Log Experience, 1985; contbr. articles to profl. jours. Clubs: Dayton Advt., Am. Business (bd. dirs.), Dayton Exec.'s.

PIIRAINEN, ILPO TAPANI, educator; b. Kiihtelysvaara, Finland, Nov. 15, 1941; arrived in Fed. Repub. Germany, 1972.; s. Eemil and Irja Augusta (Honkasalo) P.; m. Elisabeth Martha Dörrie, Sept. 28, 1967; children: Ilpo Heikki, Anne Elisabeth, Martti Tapani. MA, U. Helsinki, Finland, 1965, Licenciate of Philosophy, 1967, PhD, 1969. Docent U. Jyväskylä, Jyväskylä, Finland, 1970-72; researcher Acad. of Finland, Helsinki, 1970-72; prof. Pedagogical Coll., Münster, Fed. Repub. Germany, 1972-80, U. Münster, 1980—; hon. prof. U. Bochum, Bochum, Fed. Repub. Germany, 1980—. Author: Stadtrechtsbuch Sillein, 1972, Stadtrecht Kremnica, 1983, Stadtrecht Banská Štiavnica, 1986. Lodge: Rotary. Home: Dumte 32, D4430 Steinfurt-Borghorst Federal Republic of Germany Office: Univ Münster, Schlossplatz 2, D4400 Münster Federal Republic of Germany

PILARD, PATRICK, homeopathologist, accupuncturist; b. Saint Benoit, Brittany, France, Oct. 20, 1947; s. Pilard and DeTonquedec; m. Brigitte Sandere, Mar. 10, 1973; children: Solena, Helori. MD, Faculty Medecine, Nantes, France, 1975. Homeopathic diplomate, France. Resident Chu, Nantes; homeopathologist Centr Homeopathology France, Paris, 1977-78; acupuncturist OEDA, Paris, 1978-80, Group Hotel Dieu, D'Borsarello, 1981-84; parisitologist Faculty Medecine, Nantes, 1980-82, biologist, 1982-84, physician sports medicine, 1984—. Author: Le Draineage, 1987, L'Homeopathie, 1987, Les Energies, 1987, L'Insommnie, 1987, Les Troubles Du Sormeil, 1987. Mem. Fedn. Internat. Socs. Homeopaths (pres. 1984), Inst. Acupuncture France (pres. 1980). Home: 10 R des epinettes, 44880 Sautron France

PILCHER, JAMES BROWNIE, lawyer; b. Shreveport, La., May 19, 1929; s. James Reece and Martha Mae (Brown) P.; m. Maxine Pettit, Jan. 23, 1951; children: Lydia, Martha, Bradley. BA, La. State U., 1952; JD, John Marshall Law Sch., 1955; postgrad. Emory U., 1957. Bar: Ga. 1955. Legal aide to Speaker of Ho. of Reps., 1961-64; assoc. city atty. City of Atlanta, 1964-69; sole practice, Atlanta, 1969—. Exec. committeeman Dem. Exec. Com. of Fulton County, Ga., 1974-86; bd. dirs. Whitehead Boys Club. Mem. State Bar Ga. (vice chmn. gen. practice and trial sect. 1985—, chmn. criminal law sect. 1986-87), Ga. Assn. Criminal Def. Lawyers (pres. 1980-82), Ga. Trial Lawyers (mem. exec. com. 1980—), Ga. Claimants Attys. Assn. (pres. 1983-84), Nat. Assn. Criminal Def. Lawyers (bd. dirs. 1980-85), Ga. Inst. Trial Advocacy (bd. dirs. 1986—), South Fulton Bar Assn. (pres. 1987—). Baptist. Club: Kiwanis (Peachtree, Atlanta pres. 1983-84). Home: 434 Brentwood Dr NE Atlanta GA 30305 Office: 3355 Lenox Rd NE Atlanta GA 30324

PILCHIK, ELY EMANUEL, rabbi, author; b. Russia, June 12, 1913; came to U.S., 1920, naturalized, 1920; s. Abraham and Rebecca (Lipovitch) P.; m. Ruth Schuchat, Nov. 20, 1941 (dec. 1977); children: Susan Pilchik Rosenbaum, Judith Pilchik Zucker; m. Harriet Krichman Perlmutter, June, 1981. A.B., U. Cin., 1935; M.Hebrew Lit., Hebrew Union Coll., 1936, D.D., 1964. Ordained rabbi 1939; founder, dir. Hillel Found. at U. Md., 1939-40; asst. rabbi Har Sinai Temple, Balt., 1940-41; rabbi Temple Israel, Tulsa, 1942-47, Temple B'nai Jeshurun, Short Hills, N.J., 1947-81; prof. Jewish Thought Upsala Coll., 1969—; pres. Jewish Book Council Am., 1957-58. Author: books, including Hillel, 1951, From the Beginning, 1956, Judaism Outside the Holy Land, 1964, Jeshurun Essays, 1967, A Psalm of David, 1967, Talmud Thought, 1983, Midrash Memoir, 1984, Touches of Einstein, 1987, Luzzatto on Loving Kindness, 1987; author: play Toby, 1968; lyricist 6 cantatas; contbr. articles to profl. and gen. jours. Bd. dirs. Newark Mus.; mem. ethics com. N.J. Bar Assn. Served as chaplain USNR, 1944-46. Mem. N.J. Bd. Rabbis (pres. 1955-57), Central Conf. Am. Rabbis (pres. 1977-79). Office: 1025 S Orange Ave Short Hills NJ 07078

PILET, PAUL-EMILE, biologist; b. Lausanne, Switzerland, July 26, 1927; s. William and Berthe (Lemat) P.; Bachelor, Master, Ph.D., U. Lausanne; Docteur honoris causa, U. Toulouse (France), 1966, U. Geneva, 1976, U. Besançon (France), 1985; m. Suzanne Gervaix, Aug. 15, 1962; 1 son, François. Staff, Bordeaux (France) U., Calif. Inst. Tech., Pasadena, London U., Sorbonne, Paris, Leicester Polytechnic; mem. faculty U. Lausanne, prof. plant biology and physiology, 1958—, dir. Inst. Plant Biology, 1966—; assoc. prof. Sorbonne, Paris, 1967—; vis. prof. Leicester Polytechnic, 1980—; founding pres., mem. com. Swiss Soc. Plant Physiology. Mem. Swiss Acad. Sci. (past pres.), Internat. Assn. Plant Physiologists (council, past gen. sec.), Royal Acad. Sci. Belgique (assoc.), Doct. h. causa, Toulouse, 1966, Geneve, 1976, Besançon, 1985. Author: Les Phytohormones de croissance, 1961; La cellule, 3d edit., 1968; L'Energie végétale, 2d edit., 1967; Les Mouvements des Végétaux, 2d edit., 1968; Catabolisme auxinique, 1968; Les parois cellulaires, 1971; Plant Growth Regulation, 1977, Physiological Properties of Plant Protoplasts, 1985; also numerous original papers; dir. Dialectica; editorial bd. various internat. jours. Analysis of plant cell growth; research on biochem. and biophys. processes related to cell extension and protoplast differenciation, hormone metabolism, transport and balance, physiology and biochemistry of growth inhibitors, gravity effect on plant cells, methodology of biol. sci. epistemology. Home: 13 Ave Reymondin, 1009 Pully Switzerland Office: Batiment de Biologie de l'Université, Campus de Dorigny, 1015 Lausanne Switzerland

PILGER, PAUL FRED, oil company executive; b. Detroit, Oct. 22, 1945; s. Fred George and Virginia Lois (Churchill) P.; B.S. in Mech. Engring., Oreg. State U., 1967; M.S., MIT, 1974. Engr., Bell Telephone Labs., Indpls., 1966; mech. engr. Global Assos., Kwajalein Missile Range, Marshall Islands, 1970-73; permanent staff mem. Energy Lab., Mass. Inst. Tech., Cambridge, 1974-75; engr., supr. Aramco, Ras Tanura, Saudi Arabia, 1975-79, engring. adv., 1979-81; boiler cons. Yanbu Gas Plant, Ghazlan Power Plant, 1978-81; mgr. San Ardo cogeneration project Texaco Co. (Calif.), 1981-86; exec. dir. SOBEL cogeneration Corp., joint venture between Texaco and So. Calif. Edison Co., 1986=87. Served with USAF, 1968-69. Alcoa scholar Oreg. State U., 1965, 66; NSF grantee MIT, 1967. Mem. Nat. Mgmt. Assn. (charter mem. Kwajalein chpt. 1972-73), Soc. Am. Mil. Engrs., Soc. Petroleum Engrs., Sigma Xi. Home: PO Box 1704 Paso Robles CA 93447 Office: Texaco PO Box 1767 Paso Robles CA 93447

PILIKIAN, HOVHANNESS I., dramatist, theatre and film director; m. Gail Rademacher; 3 children. Grad. dir.'s course Royal Acad. Dramatic Art, 1967; B.A. in English Lit., U. Munich, 1963; MA in Social Anthropology, U. London, 1987. Producer Electra, Greenwich Theatre, London, 1971, Medea, Yvonne Arnaud Theatre, 1971, Oedipus Tyrannus, Chichester Festival, London, 1974, Die Raüber, Roundhouse Theatre, London, 1975, King Lear, Nat. Theatre Iceland, 1977, Phèdre, Nat. Theatre Yugoslavia, 1971; creator (1st all-black actors theatre co. in Eng. and Europe) Cervantes Players; (film) Mary Wilson & New Supremes, 1985; author: My Hamlet, 1961; 1915 An Armenian Symphony and Other Poems, 1980; Armenian Cinema, A Source Book, 1981; Kaloo Yertal (transl. Beckett's Come and Go), 1982; Flower of Japanese Theatre, 1984; Aspects of Armenian History (Ancient and Modern), 1986; contbr. to Ency. Brit.; numerous others. Vis. prof. Yerevan U. Spl. award for Contribution to Theatre Art, Armenian SSR Ministry of Culture, 1986. U. Munich fellow. Fellow Royal Anthrop. Inst. Great Britian and Ireland, Dirs.' Guild Great Britain. Address: 8 Elm Park Rd, Finchley, London N3 1EB, England

PILKINGTON, LIONEL ALEXANDER BETHUNE, business executive; b. Jan. 7, 1920; s. L. G. and Mrs. L. G. Pilkington; ed. Cambridge U.; D.Tech. (hon.), U. Loughborough, 1968; D.Eng. (hon.), U. Liverpool, 1971; LL.D. (hon.), U. Bristol, 1979; D.Sc. (hon.), U. London, 1979. m. Patricia Nicholls Elliott, 1945 (d. 1977); 2 children; m. Kathleen Haynes, 1978. With Pilkington Bros. Ltd., St. Helens, 1947—, prodn. mgr. and asst. works mgr., Doncaster, 1949-51, head office, 1952, sub-dir., 1953, exec. dir., 1955-85, dep. chmn., 1971-73, chmn., 1973-80, pres., 1985—. dep. chmn. Chloride Group Ltd., 1979—; dir. Brit. Petroleum Co. Mem. Central Adv. Council Sci. and Tech., 1970—, Sci. Research Council, 1972—, Brit. Rys. Bd., 1973-76; mem. ct. govs. Adminstrv. Staff Coll., 1973—; pro-chancellor Lancaster U., 1980—; bd. dirs. Wellcome Found. Ltd. Served with Brit. Armed Forces, 1939-46. Recipient Toledo Glass and Ceramic award, 1963; Mullard medal Royal Soc., 1968; John Scott medal, 1969; Wilhelm Exner medal, 1970; hon. fellow Imperial Coll., 1974; decorated knight Order Brit. Empire. Fellow Royal Soc., Brit. Inst. Mgmt. Address: Goldrill Cottage, Patterdale, near Penrith, Cumbria England also: 76 Eaton Pl, Flat 2, London SWIX 8AU, England *

PILLAR, CHARLES LITTLEFIELD, mining consultant; b. Denver, May 25, 1911; s. Charles and Alice May (Littlefield) P.; m. Elizabeth Reed Broadhead, Sept. 10, 1932 (div. May 1939); m. 2d Gwendola Elizabeth Lotz, Sept. 16, 1939; children—Ann, Catherine, Pamela. Engr. mines, Colo. Sch. Mines, 1935. Registered profl. engr., B.C., Ariz. Various positions in field, 1935-75; mine cons. Pillar, Lowell & Assocs., Tucson, Ariz., 1976-83; cons. Bechtel Corp., San Francisco, 1976-79, Fluor Corp., Redwood City, Calif., 1979—; mem. Colo. Sch. Mines Research Inst., Golden, 1975—; dir. Internat. Geosystems Corp., Vancouver, B.C. Contbr. articles to profl. jours. Served to capt. USAF, 1942-45. Mem. AIME (William Saunders Gold Medal award, Disting. mem. award), Can. Inst. Mining and Metallurgy, Profl. Engrs. B.C. Republican. Episcopalian. Club: U.S. Senatorial, Vancouver, Tucson Nat. Country. Home: 9460 N Camino Del Plata Tucson AZ 85741 Office: Mining Cons 5115 N Oracle Rd Tucson AZ 85704

PILLAR, SIR WILLIAM (THOMAS), navy officer; b. Feb. 24, 1924; s. William and Lily Pillar; m. Ursula Ransley, 1946; 4 children. Grad., Blundells Sch., Tiverton, Eng. Commd. Royal Navy, 1942; with HMS Illustrious, 1946-48; staff Royal Navy Engring. Coll., 1948-51, capt., 1973-75; with HMS Alert, 1951-53, HM Dockyard, Gibraltar, 1954-57, HMS Corunna, 1957-59; base engr. officer HMS Lochinvar, 1959-61; staff of comdr.-in-chief SASA, Cape Town, 1961-64, HMS Tiger, 1964-65; staff of dir. of naval officer 1965-67; naval ship prodn. overseer Scotland and No. Ireland, 1967-69, Imperial Def. Coll., 1970; asst. dir. DG Ships, 1971-73; port adm. Rosyth, 1976-77; asst. chief of fleet support 1977-79, chief of fleet support (mem. admiralty bd. of def. council), 1979-81; comdr. Royal Coll. Def. Studies, 1982-83; lt.-gov., comdr.-in-chief Jersey Islands, 1985—; comdr. RNSA, 1980-83; mem. council RUSI, 1984-87; mgr. dir. Engring. Mgmt. Div. Bd., Inst. Mech. Engring., 1984—. Decorated GBE, 1983, KCB, 1980. Mem. RN Modern Pentathlon Assn. (pres. 1978-83), Royal Naval Sailing Assn. Clubs: Army and Navy, Royal Yacht Squadron. Office: Government House, Jersey Channel Islands *

PILLIOD, CHARLES J., JR., diplomat; b. Cuyohoga Falls, Ohio, Oct. 20, 1918; m. Nancy J. Conley; 7 children. Student, Muskingum Coll., 1937-38, Kent State U., 1941. With Goodyear Tire and Rubber Co., Akron, Ohio, 1945-87, sales staff export div., 1945-47; v.p., gen. mgr. Panama, 1947-51; sales mgr. Peru, 1951-54, Columbia, 1954-56; mng. dir. Brasil, 1956-63; sales dir., mng. dir. Great Britain, 1963-70; pres. Goodyear Internat. Corp., 1970-72; chmn., chief exec. officer Goodyear Corp., 1974-83, cons., also bd. dirs., 1983-87; ambassador to Mexico, 1987—. Served with USAF, 1942-45. Office: Embassy of Mexico care State Dept 2201 C St NW Washington DC 20520 *

PILOUS, BETTY SCHEIBEL, nurse; b. Cleve., July 30, 1948; d. Raymond W. and Dorothy E. (Groth) S.; m. Lee Alan Pilous, Sept. 11, 1970; 1 child. Diploma in nursing Huron Rd. Hosp., Cleve., 1970. RN, Ohio; student St. Joseph's Coll.; cert. med.-surg. nurse, nursing adminstr. Nurse Huron Rd. Hosp., Cleve., 1970-71, Hillcrest Hosp., Cleve., 1974-77; head nurse, relief supr. Oak Park Hosp., Oakwood, Ohio, 1977-81; head nurse med.-surg. Bedford Hosp., Ohio, 1981-87; dir. med.-surg. nursing Meridia Euclid Hosp., Euclid, Ohio; instr. ARC, Am. Heart Assn.; mem. nursing standatds com. Community Hosp. of Bedford. Mem. health and safety com. Twinsburg Schs., Ohio, 1984—, mem. curriculum com., 1981-83; chairperson standards com. Community Hosp. of Bedford; counselor jr. high youth 1st Congl. Ch., Twinsburg. Mem. Ohio Hosp. Assn., Nat. League Nursing, Southeast Cleve. Mid Mgrs. Networking Group. Lodge: Order Eastern Star. Avocations: aerobics, hiking. Office: Euclid Hosp 18901 N Lake Shore Blvd Euclid OH 44143

PILUN-OWAD, CHAIYUT, financial and securities company executive; b. Nakornratchasima, Thailand, Jan. 1, 1949; s. Bugyong and Teing P.-O.; m. Orawan Lophansri; children: On-Anong, On-Naromol, Chaichat, Chaivichit. BBA in Acctg., Thammasat U., Bangkok, 1971; MBA in Mgmt., NYU, 1974, PhD in Fin. and Econs., 1977. CPA, Thailand. V.p. corp. fin. and planning dept. Asia Credit Ltd., Bangkok, 1977-78; exec. v.p. Union Asia Fin. Ltd., Bangkok, 1979-86, pres., 1987—; researcher customs dept. Ministry Fin., Bangkok, 1977-78; lectr. fin. Thammasat U., Nat. Inst. Devel. Adminstrn., Bangkok, 1977-81. Mem. Assn. Fin. Cos. in Thailand (bd. dirs.), Assn. Mems. Securities Exchange in Thailand (bd. dirs.). Clubs: Heritage, Royal Bangkok Sport. Home: 204 25 Pasuk Village, Bangkok 10250, Thailand Office: Union Asia Fin Ltd, 132 Silom Rd, Bangkok 10500, Thailand

PIMENTEL, ENRIQUE, physician, educator; b. Caracas, Venezuela, Apr. 7, 1928; s. Enrique and Paulina (Malaussena) Pimentel-Parilli; m. Emmy Gehrenbeck, Nov. 22, 1952; children: Luis (dec.), Gonzalo, Javier (dec.), Ana, Beatriz, Ignacio. MD, Central U., Madrid, 1953. Endocrinologist Mil. Hosp., Caracas, 1955-77; prof. Cen. U., Caracas, 1953—; dir. Inst. Exptl. Medicine, Caracas, 1977-80, Nat. Ctr. Genetics, Caracas, 1978—. Editor, founder Critical Revs. in Oncogenesis jour.; contbr. numerous articles to profl. jours. and books. Recipient Grosse Verdienstkreunz, German Govt., 1976, Orden J.M. Vargas, Cen. U., 1979, Nat. Award Sci., Nat. Council Sci., Caracas, 1982, Orden Andres Bello Venezuelan Govt., 1983, Orden del Libertador, 1987. Mem. Venezuelan Nat. Acad. Medicine, Humboldt Cultural Assn., Ibero-Am. Diabetes Fedn. (pres. sci. com.), Internat. Acad. Tumor Marker Oncology (v.p.), Assn. Clin. Scientists (U.S.), Am. Assn. Cancer Research. Office: Centro Nacional de Genetica, Apartado Postal 50587, Caracas 1050-A, Venezuela

PINA MARTINS, JOSÉ V. DE, renaissance historian, educator; b. Penalva de Alva, Alva, Portugal, Jan. 18, 1920; s. Antõnio V. Abrantes and Maria Olímpia (Faria de Pina) de Abrantes Martins; m. Primola Vingiano, Feb. 15, 1954; 1 child, Eva Maria. M, U. Coimbra, Portugal, 1948; D, U. Paris, 1974. Lectr. in Portugese U. Rome, 1949-55, U. Poitiers, France, 1955-62; asst. prof. U. Lisbon, Portugal, 1962-72, prof., 1983—; assoc. prof. Ecole des Hautes Etudes U. Paris, 1974-83; dir. Portugese Cultural Ctr., Paris, 1972-83, dept. edn. C. Gulbenkian Found., Lisbon, 1983—. Author: Cultura Portuguesa, 1971, Tratado de Confissiom, 1971, also editor, Sá de Miranda, 1972, Humanismo e Erasmismo, 1973, Cultura Italiana, 1974, Camões e il Rinascimento Italiano, 1975, Jean Pic de la Mirandole: Un Portrait Inconnu de l'Humaniste. Une Édition Très Rare de ses Conclusiones, 1976, Erasmo na Biblioteca Nacional, 1987, also editor, Humanisme et Renaissance de l'Italie au Portugal, 1988. Recipient Golden Cultural medal Italian Dept. Fgn. Affairs, 1964; named to Order of Santiago Pres. Portugal, 1983. Mem. Acad. das Sci. de Lisboa (dir. library 1985—), Acad. Portuguesa da Historia (hon.). Office: Fundacao C Gulbenkian, Ave de Berna 45 A, 1000 Lisbon Portugal

PINATEL, CHRISTIANE MADELEINE, archaeologist, researcher; b. Peyrehorade, Landes, France, Apr. 14, 1935; d. Henri Xavier Germaine Gilberte (Brehier Emile) P. Diploma in archaeology, Ecole du Louvre, Paris, 1962. Cert. interpreter (English), guide Ministry of Culture. Curator assistant Musée des Beaux-Arts, Rouen, France, 1963-65; cert. research assoc. Nat. Ctr. for Sci. Research: Greek Dept. Louvre Museum, Paris, 1965-82, Museum of Ancient Monuments, Versailles, France, 1970-82; archaeol. research specialist, ingénieur Nat. Ctr. for Archaeol. Research: Louvre Museum, 1983-87, Charbonneaux Data Processing Ctr., Paris, 1985-87, Museum of Ancient Monuments, 1983-87; archaeol. guide various agys., 1962-83. Contbr. articles to profl. jours. Scholar Georges Jamati Assn., Greece, 1958, London Internat. Seminar, 1960; grantee nat. museums and ctrs. for archaeol. research, Greece, Italy, England, Germany, others, 1970-82. Mem. Internat. Council of Museums, French Soc. Classical Archaeology, Nat. Soc. French Antiquarians. Roman Catholic. Club: Racing de France (Paris). Home: 45 Rue Boileau, 75016 Paris France Office: Louvre Mus Greek Dept, 32 Quai du Louvre, 75001 Paris France

PINDERA, JERZY TADEUSZ, mechanical and aeronautical engineer; b. Czchow, Poland, Dec. 4, 1914; immigrated to Can., 1965, naturalized, 1975; s. Jan Stanislaw and Natalia Lucia (Knapik) P.; m. Aleksandra-Anna Szal, Oct. 29, 1949; children: Marek Jerzy, Maciej Zenon. BS in Mech. Engring, Tech. U., Warsaw, 1936; MS in Aero. Engring, Tech. U., Warsaw and Lodz, 1947; D in Applied Scis., Polish Acad. Scis., 1959; DS in Applied Mechanics, Tech. U., Cracow, 1962. Registered profl. engr., Ont. Asst. Lot Polish Airlines, Warsaw, 1947; head lab. Aero. Inst., Warsaw, 1947-52, Inst. Metallography, Warsaw, 1952-54; dep. prof., head lab. Polish Acad. Scis., 1954-59; head lab. Bldg. Research Inst., Warsaw, 1959-62; vis. prof. mechanics Mich. State U., East Lansing, 1963-65; prof. mechanics U. Waterloo (Ont. Can.), 1965-83, adj. prof., 1983-86, prof. emeritus, 1987—; pres. J.T. Pindera & Sons Engring. Services, Inc., Waterloo, 1980—; chmn. Internat. Symposium Exptl. Mechanics, U. Waterloo, 1972, dir. Inst. for Exptl. Mechanics, 1983-86; chmn. 10th Can. Fracture Conf., 1983; hon. adv. prof. Chongging (Sichuan, China) U., 1988—; hon. chmn. Internat. Conf. on Advanced Exptl. Mechanics, U. Tianjin, People's Republic of China, 1988; vis. prof. in France and Fed. Republic Germany; cons. in field. Mem. editorial adv. bd. Mechanics Research Communications, 1974—; mem. bd. editors Theoretical and Applied Fracture Mechanics, 1984—; patentee in field; contbr. tech. books, articles and chpts. in books. Served with Polish Army, 1939. Fellow Soc. Exptl. Mechanics (M.M. Frocht award 1978); mem. Canadian Soc. Mech. Engring. (chmn. exptl. mechanics group-research and devel. div.), Gesellschaft Angewandte Mathematik und Mechanik, N.Y. Acad. Scis., Soc. Engring. Sci., ASME, Soc. Française des Mécaniciens, Assn. Profl. Engrs. Ont. Home: 310 Grant Crescent, Waterloo, ON Canada N2K 2A2 Office: U Waterloo Dept Civil Engring, 200 University Ave, Waterloo, ON Canada N2L 3G1

PINDLING, LYNDEN OSCAR, prime minister and minister finance of The Bahamas; b. Nassau, Bahamas, Mar. 22, 1930; s. Arnold Franklin and Viola (Bain) P.; LLB, London U., 1952; barrister-at-law, Middle Temple, 1953; LLD (hon.), Howard, 1972; LHD (hon.), U. Miami, 1977; LLD (hon.) Bethune-Cookman Coll., 1978, Fisk U., 1979; m. Marguerite McKenzie, May 5, 1956; children: Lynden Obafemi, Leslie, Michelle, Monique. Admitted to Eng. and Bahamas bar, 1953; mem. Parliament for So. Dist., New Providence, 1956-62, So. Central Dist., 1962-67, Kemp's Bay, Andros constituency, 1967—; Parliamentary leader Progressive Liberal Party, 1956—; mem. several dels. to former Colonial Office, 1956-66; mem. Constl. Conf., 1963; leader of opposition, 1964-66; mem. del's. spl. com. 24, UN, 1965; premier, minister tourism and devel., 1967-69; leader Bahamian del. Constl. Conf., London, 1968; prime minister Commonwealth of The Bahamas, 1969—, minister econ. affairs, 1969-82, from 1984, minister of def., 1983-84; minister of fin., 1984—; leader Independence Conf., London, 1972; privy councillor, 1976; chmn. Fgn. Investment Bd. Office: Office of Prime Minister, Rawson Sq, Nassau The Bahamas *

PINE, CHARLES JOSEPH, clinical psychologist, health services administrator; b. Excelsior Springs, Mo., July 13, 1951; s. Charles E. and LaVern (Upton) P.; m. Mary Day, Dec. 30, 1979; children: Charles Andrew, Joseph Scott, Carolyn Marie. BA in Psychology, U. Redlands, 1973; MA, Calif. State U.-Los Angeles, 1975; PhD, U. Wash., 1979; postdoctoral UCLA, 1980-81. Lic. psychologist, Calif. Psychology technician Seattle Indian Health Bd., USPHS Hosp., 1977-78; psychology intern VA Outpatient Clinic, Los Angeles, 1978-79; instr. psychology Okla. State U., 1979-80, asst. prof., 1980; asst. prof. psychology and native Am. studies program Wash. State U., 1981-82; dir. behavioral health services Riverside-San Bernardino County Indian Health Inc., Banning, Calif., 1982-84; clin. psychologist, clin. co-dir. Inland Empire Behavioral Assocs., Colton, Calif., 1982-84; clin. psychologist VA Med. Ctr., Long Beach, Calif., 1984-85; clin. psychologist, psychology coordinator Psychiatry div. VA Med. Ctr., Sepulveda, Calif., 1985—; clin. dir. Traumatic Stress Treatment Ctr., Thousand Oaks, Calif., 1985—; asst. clin. prof. UCLA Sch. Medicine, 1985—, Fuller Grad. Sch. Psychology, Pasadena, Calif., 1985—; mem. Los Angeles County Am. Indian Mental Health task force, 1987—. Editorial cons. White Cloud Jour., 1982-85; cons. Dept. Health and Human Services, USPHS, NIMH, 1980. Vol. worker Variety Boys Clubs Am., 1973-75; coach Rialto Jr. All-Am. Football League, 1974, Conejo Youth Flag Football Assn., Conejo Valley Little League. U. Wash. Inst. Indian Studies grantee, 1975-76, UCLA Inst. Am. Cultures grantee, 1981-82; fellow Menninger Found. Mem. Am. Psychol. Assn. (chair task force on service delivery to ethnic minority populations bd. ethnic minority affairs 1988—, bd. ethnic minority affairs 1985-87), Soc. Indian Psychologists (pres. 1981-83), Western Psychol. Assn., AAAS, Calif. State Psychol. Assn., N.Y. Acad. Sci., Soc. for Psychol. Study Ethnic Minority Issues (exec. com. 1987-88), Sigma Alpha Epsilon. Republican. Baptist. Contbr. psychol. articles to profl. lit. Home: 2379 Sirius St Thousand Oaks CA 91360 Office: VA Med Ctr Psychology Service 116B 16111 Plummer St Sepulveda CA 91343

PINEAU, MICHEL JEAN PIERRE, physician; b. Bordeaux, France, Feb. 12, 1928; s. Georges Henry and Marie Jeanne (Lescarret) P.; m. Sept. 25, 1954 (div. 1968); 1 child, Axel. CES, Medicine du Travail, France, 1954; Faculte' de Medicine, Paris U., 1955. Diplomate French Bd. Family Practice. Gen. practice medicine Le Vesinet, France, 1959—. Roman Catholic. Office: 24 rue Mal Foch, 78110 Le Vesinet France

PINEDA, MAURICIO HERNAN, reproductive physiologist, educator; b. Santiago, Chile, Oct. 17, 1930; came to U.S., 1970, naturalized, 1982; s. Teofilo Pineda-Garcia and Bertila Pinto-Bouvret; m. Rosa A. Gomez, July 26, 1956; children—Anamaria, George H., Monserrat. D.V.M., U. Chile,

1955; M.S., Colo. State U., 1965, Ph.D., 1968. Prof. Coll. Vet. Medicine, Austral U. Chile, Valdivia, 1958-63, prof., head animal reprodn. lab., 1968-70; postdoctoral trainee U. Wis., Madison, 1970-72; postdoctoral fellow Colo. State U., Ft. Collins, 1972-74, research assoc., 1972-78; assoc. prof. physiology, dept. physiology and pharmacology Coll. Vet. Medicine, Iowa State U., Ames, 1979-84, prof., 1984—. Contbr. chpts. to books, articles to profl. jours. Recipient Best Student award U. Chile Coll. Vet. Medicine, 1954; Rockefeller Found. scholar, 1963; Morris Animal Found. fellow, 1974. Mem. Chilean Vet. Med. Assn. (Disting. Services award 1987), Soc. for Study of Fertility (Eng.), Sigma Xi, Beta Beta Beta, Phi Kappa Phi. Office: Dept Physiology and Pharmacology Vet Med Iowa State U Ames IA 50011

PINEDA, VINSON BAGTAS, dermatologist, researcher, consultant; b. Manila, July 13, 1936; s. Atanacio Alincastre and Felicisima (Bagtas) P.; m. Maria Aurora Dee; children: Joseph Arnold, Maria Rachel Verone, Maria Angela. MD, U. of East, Manila, 1964. Fellow in dermatology China Med. Bd. U. Philippines Gen. Hosp. Med. Ctr., Manila, 1967-69; fellow in dermatopathology NYU Med. Ctr., 1980; pres. Dermclin., Inc., Manila, 1976—; asst. prof. dermatology sect. UERM Meml. Med. Ctr., Manila, 1977—; pres. Dermatology Inst. Found. of Philippines, Manila, 1981—; chief researcher Internat. Skin and Hair Ctr., Inc., Manila, 1986—. Entrance scholar U. Philippines, 1954. Fellow Am. Acad. Dermatology, Philippine Soc. Aesthetic Medicine (diplomate); mem. Am. Soc. Dermatol. Surgery, Internat. Soc. Tropical Surgery, Internat. Soc. Dermatopathology, Internat. Soc. Dermatol. Surgery (advisor 1986-87), Manila Med. Soc. (pres. 1982-83). Lodge: Lions. Home: 26 Oliva St Valle Verde IV, Pasig, Metro Manila Philippines Office: Dermclinic Inc, care Capitol Med Ctr Bldg III, Quezon Ave cor sct, Magbanue, Quezon City Philippines

PINES, NED LEWIS, insurance company executive; b. Malden, Mass., Dec. 10, 1905; s. Joseph and Dora (Goldes) P.; m. Jacquelyn Sangor, Aug. 29, 1938 (div. 1959); children: Judith Ann (Mrs. Judith P. Bernard), Susan Jane; m. Maxine Firestone, Nov. 19, 1967. Student, Columbia U., 1923-24. Pres. Pines Publs., Inc., 1928-61; pres. Popular Library, Inc., 1942-66, chmn., 1966-68; chmn. bd., dir. mem. finance and exec. coms. Eastern Life Ins. Co. N.Y., 1949-71; cons. U.S. Life Corp., N.Y.C., 1971-76; Mem. coordinating com. Columbia U. Inst. Research, 1945-47. Contbr. articles on Paris restaurants to Avenue Mag., 1985-86. Bd. dirs. Jewish Guild for Blind, 1950-73; life trustee Fedn. Jewish Philanthropies N.Y., 1968; mem. nat. judging com. Boys' Clubs Am.; adv. com. Commentary mag., 1970—; bd. dirs. Merce Cunningham Dance Found., 1970-74, Am. Friends of Israel Mus., Jerusalem, 1976—; Founder United Jewish Appeal, 1940. Recipient U.S. Treasury award, 1945; award Bur. Intercultural Edn., 1949; Nat. Mass Media award Thomas Alva Edison Found., Inc., 1956; gold medallion and certificate Boys' Clubs Am., 1956. Clubs: Harmonie (N.Y.C.); Noyac Golf (Sag Harbor, N.Y.); Southampton (N.Y.) Golf; American (Paris). Office: 355 Lexington Ave New York NY 10017

PINES, WAYNE LLOYD, public relations counselor; b. Washington, Dec. 31, 1943; s. Jerome Martin and Ethel (Schnall) P.; B.A., Rutgers U., 1965; postgrad. George Washington U., 1969-71; m. Nancy Freitag, Apr. 16, 1966; children—Noah Morris, Jesse Mireth. Reporter, city editor Middletown (N.Y.) Times Herald-Record, 1965-68; copy editor Reuters News, 1968-69; asso. editor FDC Reports, Washington, 1969-72; chief Consumer Edn. and Info., FDA, also editor FDA Consumer, 1972-74; exec. editor Product Safety Letter and Devices and Diagnostics Letter, Washington, 1974-75; dep. asst. commr. for pub. affairs, chief press relations FDA, Rockville, Md., 1975-78, assoc. commr. public affairs, 1978-82; adj. prof. Washington Public Affairs Center, U. So. Calif., 1980-81; instr. N.Y.U. Sch. Continuing Edn., 1982-84; spl. asst. to dir. NIMH, 1982-83; sr. v.p., sr. counselor Burson-Marsteller, 1983-87 ; exec. v.p., 1987—; instr. Profl. Devel. Inst., 1983-85; columnist Med. Advt. News. Contbr. numerous articles in field to profl. jours. Home: 5821 Nevada Ave NW Washington DC 20015 Office: 1850 M St NW Washington DC 20036

PINGKIAN, ORLANDO YABO, mechanical engineer; b. Lopez-Jaena, Misamis Occidental, Philippines, Oct. 24, 1944; s. Pantaleon O. and Agripina (Yabo) P.; m. Exequiela Rafanan, Oct. 15, 1969; children: Maharlika, H. Frances, Orlando, Jr., Joseph Kit, Faela Nina. BSME, Cebu Inst. Tech., Philippines, 1965; BMP in Managerial Processes and Practices (hon.), Asian Inst. Mgmt., 1981. Cert. mech. engr. Sales rep. NCR Philippines, Inc., Cebu City, 1965-66; tech. cons. Stella Maris Machineries, Zamboanga City, Philippines, 1967; sales engr., supr., br. mgr. Honiron Philippines, Inc., Iligan City and Bacolod City, 1967-76; br. mgr., then regional mgr. AG&P Co. Manila, Inc., Cebu City, 1977—, mem. group mgmt. com., 1985—; cons. EXOR Philippines Bus. Resources, Mandaue City, 1981—; mem. Japan-Taiwan Overseas Study Mission, 1987. Pres. Jr. Achievement Cebu, 1983-85. Recipient Boss of Yr. award Philippines Assn. Secs., 1983, Outstanding Alumnus award Cebu Inst. Tech., 1985; Philippines/APO scholar ENERCON seminar, Japan and Taiwan, 1985. Mem. Philippines Soc. Mech. Engrs. (regional dir. 1985, host chmn. nat. conv. 1984, Presdl. award 1984), Cebu Chamber of Commerce and Industry. Lodge: Rotary (pres. Cebu West club, 1988-89). Roman Catholic. Avocation: physical fitness through sports. Home: Greenview Subdiv, Pagsabungan Rd, Mandaue City, Cebu Philippines Office: AG&P Co Manila Inc, 156 Hwy, Mandaue City, Cebu 6014, Philippines

PINGS, ANTHONY CLAUDE, architect; b. Fresno, Calif., Dec. 16, 1951; s. Clarence Hubert and Mary (Murray) P.; m. Carole Clements, June 25, 1983. AA, Fresno City Coll., 1972; BArch, Calif. Poly. State U., San Luis Obispo, 1976. Lic. architect, Calif.; cert. Nat. Council Archtl. Registration Bds. Architect Aubrey Moore Jr., Fresno, 1976-81; architect, prin. Anthony C. Pings, AIA, Fresno, 1981-83, 86—, Pings-Taylor Assocs., Fresno, 1983-85. Prin. works include Gollaher Profl. Office (Masonry Merit award 1985, Best Office Bldg. award 1986), Fresno Imaging Ctr. (Best Institutional Project award 1986, Nat. Healthcare award Modern Health Care mag. 1986), Orthopedic Facility (award of honor Masonry Inst. 1987, award of merit San Joaquin chpt. AIA 1987). Mem. Calif. Indsl. Tech. Edn. Consortium Calif. State Dept. Edn., 1983, 84. Mem. AIA (bd. dirs. Calif. chpt. 1983-84, v.p. San Joaquin chpt. 1982, pres. 1983, Calif. Council evaluation team 1983, team leader Coalinga Emergency Design Assistance team). Democrat. Home: 4350 N Safford Ave Fresno CA 93704 Office: 1640 W Shaw Suite 107 Fresno CA 93711

PINGS, CORNELIUS JOHN, university official; b. Conrad, Mont., Mar. 15, 1929; s. Cornelius John and Marjorie (O'Loughlin) P.; m. Marjorie Anna Cheney, June 25, 1960; children: John, Anne, Mary. B.S., Calif. Inst. Tech., 1951, M.S., 1952, Ph.D., 1955. Inst. chem. engring. Stanford U., 1955-56, asst. prof., 1956-59; assoc. prof. chem. engring. Calif. Inst. Tech., 1959-64, prof., 1964-81, exec. officer chem. engring., 1969-73, vice-provost, dean grad. studies, 1970-81; provost, sr. v.p. acad. affairs U. So. Calif., 1981—; mem., dir. Nat. Commn. on Research, 1978-80; bd. mgmt. Council on Govtl. Relations, 1980-83; bd. dirs. Pacific Horizon Funds Los Angeles; pres. Assn. Grad. Schs., 1977-78; pres.-elect Western Coll. Assn., 1987-88; mem. sci. engring and pub. policy com. NAS, 1987—. Contbr. articles to tech. jours. Mem., chmn. bd. trustees Mayfield Sr. Sch. Bd., 1979-85; mem. Pasadena Redevel. Agy., 1968-81, chmn., 1974-81; bd dirs. Huntington Meml. Hosp., Pasadena, Los Angeles Central City Assn. Recipient City of Pasadena Arthur Nobel medal, 1981. Fellow Am. Inst. Chem. Engrs.; mem. Am. Soc. Engring. Edn., Nat. Acad. Engring. Roman Catholic. Clubs: California, Twilight, Bohemian. Home: 393 S Sierra Bonita Ave Pasadena CA 91106 Office: U So Calif Office of Provost University Park Los Angeles CA 90089-4019

PINHEIRO, JOÀO DE DEUS, Portugese government official, engineer, educator; b. 1945. MS, U. Birmingham, Eng., PhD. With U. Minho; former sec. state for higher edn. VIII Constitutional Govt., Portugal; former minister edn. IX Constitutional Govt., Portugal; mem. Parliament Portugal; minister edn. and culture X Constitutional Govt.; minister fgn. affairs Portugal, Lisbon, 1987—. Contbr. articles to profl. jours. Address: Ministry Fgn Affairs, Lisbon Portugal *

PINHEIRO, ROBERTO PETTI, cinema, TV and video director; b. Rio de Janeiro, Apr. 23, 1956; s. Mauricio Menezes and Therezinha (Petti) P.; m. Rosa Maria N. Rodrigues Alves, Nov. 10, 1985. BS in Cinema, Univ. Fed. Fluminense, Niteroi, Brazil, 1977-81. Producer various TV Broadcasting Stas., Sao Paulo (Brazil) and Rio de Janeiro, 1982-85; prodn. mgr. Regina Filmes, Rio de Janeiro, 1985-86; prodn. gen. coordinator TV Manchete, Rio de Janeiro, 1986; dir./editor TV Educativa and Cen. de Video-Tape, Rio de Janeiro, 1987; dir. Bem-Te-Vi Producoes Artisticas, Rio de Janeiro, 1985—; instr. video prodn. Univ. Santa Ursula, Rio de Janeiro, 1988—. Contbr. articles to profl. jours. Mem. Sindicato Dos Artistas e Tecnicos Do Estado Do Rio de Janeiro. Home: Ladeira de Santa Teresa, 117 Casa 1, 20241 Rio de Janeiro Brazil Office: Bem-Te-Vi Producoes Artisticas, Av Churchill 97 Gr 306/308, 20020 Rio de Janeiro Brazil

PINKE, JUDITH ANN, state official; b. Ft. Snelling, Minn., Oct. 16, 1944; d. August Henry and Dorothy E. (Bartelt) Hinrichs; m. Kurt G.O. Pinke, June 29, 1974. B.A. cum laude, St. Olaf Coll., 1966; postgrad. Kennedy Sch. Govt., Harvard U., 1980. Supr., tchr. Mpls. Pub. Schs., 1966-71; writer/editor U. Minn., Mpls., 1971-72; counselor Secretarial Placement, Edina, Minn., 1972-73; asst. to commr. Minn. Dept. Labor and Industry, St. Paul, 1973-76; mgr. info. resources Minn. Dept. Adminstrn., St. Paul, 1976-77; asst. commr. for fin. and adminstrn. Minn. Dept. Transp., St. Paul, 1977-85; dir. met. systems dept. Met. Council Twin Cities Area, 1985-87; asst. commr. InterTechnologies Group Minn. Dept. Adminstrn., St. Paul, 1987—; reader advanced placement exams. Ednl. Testing Service, Princeton, N.J., 1968-71; curriculum planner, instr. Exec. Devel. Inst. Hamline U., 1986—; Producer televideo conf. presentation The Productive Office, 1984. Mem. Minn. Info. Policy Council 1979-85 chmn., 1982-85. Mem. Women in State Employment (co-founder 1976), Minn. Ctr. Women in Govt. (adv. bd., exec. com. 1985—, chmn. long range planning and evaluation com., 1985-86, chmn. alliances com., 1987—), Loft, Women's Transp. Seminar, Women Execs. in Govt. (Nat. Leadership Council, chair spl. membership task force), Horizon 100, LWV. Office: State Minn, Dept Adminstrn Room 200 Adminstrn Bldg Saint Paul MN 55155

PINKERT, DOROTHY MINNA, chemist; b. N.Y.C., June 2, 1921; d. Harry Pinkert and Frieda Dorothy (Pinkert) Klein. A.B., Bklyn. Coll., 1944; M.S., Bklyn. Poly. Inst., 1952. Creep lab. technician Am. Brakeshoe Co., Mahwah, N.J., 1942-44; research and quality control chemist Reed and Carnrick, Jersey City, 1944-48; chief quality control chemist Gold Leaf Pharmacal Co., New Rochelle, N.Y., 1948-56; research chemist Internat. Salt Co., Watkins Glen, N.Y. and N.Y.C., 1957-61; sr. asso. drug regulatory affairs Hoffmann-LaRoche Inc., Nutley, N.J., 1962-83. Mem. Poly. Inst. N.Y. Alumni Assn. (life dir.), Am. Chem. Soc., Am. Inst. Chemists, AAAS, Am. Soc. Quality Control, N.Y. Acad. Scis. Republican.

PINKERTON, ROBERT BRUCE, mechanical engineer; b. Detroit, Feb. 10, 1941; s. George Fulwell and Janet Lois (Hedke) P.; student MIT, 1959-61; m. Barbara Ann Bandfield, Aug. 13, 1966; 1 child, Robert Brent. BS in Mech. Engring., Detroit Inst. Tech., 1965; MAE, Chrysler Inst. Engring., 1967; JD, Wayne State U., 1976. From mech. engr. to emissions and fuel economy planning specialist Chrysler Engring. Office, Chrysler Corp., Highland Park, Mich., 1967-80; dir. engring. Replacement div. TRW, Inc., Cleve., 1980-83, v.p. engring. TRW Automotive Aftermarket Group, 1983-86; v.p. engring. and research Blackstone Corp., Jamestown, N.Y., 1986—; mem. Mich. Adv. Com. on Vehicle Inspection and Maintenance, 1979-80; trustee Nat. Automotive Tech. Edn. Found.; pres. Chautauqa Co. Fund for Arts. Mem. Soc. Automotive Engrs. (chmn maintenance div.). Presbyterian. Clubs: Moon Brook Country, Chautauqua Lake Yacht. Home: 5 Ridgley Terr Jamestown NY 14701

PINKHAM, ELEANOR HUMPHREY, university librarian; b. Chgo., May 7, 1926; d. Edward Lemuel and Grace Eleanor (Cushing) Humphrey; AB, Kalamazoo Coll., 1948; MS in Library Sci. (Alice Louise LeFevre scholar), Western Mich. U., 1967; m. James Hansen Pinkham, July 10, 1948; children—Laurie Sue, Carol Lynn. Pub. services librarian Kalamazoo Coll., 1967-68, asst. librarian, 1969-70, library dir., 1971—; vis. lectr. Western Mich. U. Sch. Librarianship, 1970-84; mem. adv. bd., 1977-81, also adv. bd. Inst. Cistercian Studies Library, 1975-80. Mem. ALA (chair coll. library sect. 1988-89), ACRL (chmn. coll. library sect. 1988—), AAUP, Mich. Library Assn. (pres. 1983-84, chmn. acad. div. 1977-78), Mich. Library Consortium (exec. council 1974-82, chmn. 1977-78, Mich. Librarian of Yr 1986), OCLC Users Council, Beta Phi Mu. Home: 2519 Glenwood Dr Kalamazoo MI 49008 Office: 1200 Academy St Kalamazoo MI 49007

PINKSTON, CALDER FINNEY, lawyer; b. Macon, Ga., Jan. 26, 1957; s. Frank Chapman and Lucille Park (Finney) P.; m. Mary Anne Shouppe, July 28, 1979; 1 child, Alexander Webb. BA, Mercer U., 1978, JD, 1981. Bar: Ga. 1981, U.S. Dist. Ct. (mid. dist.) Ga. 1982, U.S. Ct. Appeals (11th cir.) 1982, U.S. Supreme Ct. 1985. Ptnr. Pinkston & Pinkston, Macon, 1981—; judge protempore civil ct. Bibb County, Macon, 1982—. Mem. fund raising com. Am. Heart Assn., 1984-86; mem. corp. fund com. United Way, 1985; grad. Leadership Macon, 1985, program chmn., 1986, vice chmn. bd. dirs., 1987—; bd. dirs. Macon-Bibb County Humane Soc., 1982—, pres., 1988; bd. dirs. Harriett Tubman Hist. and Cultural Mus., 1985—, Macon Arts Alliance, Goodwill Industries, Inc., 1988, Hay House, 1986—, vice chmn., 1987, chmn., 1988; bd. dirs., mem. exec. com. Ga. Trust for Hist. Preservation, 1987—. Named one of Outstanding Young Men Am., 1985. Mem. ABA, Ga. Bar Assn. (real property sect.), Macon Bar Assn., Assn. Trial Lawyers Am., Ga. Trial Lawyers Assn., Am. Fin. Services Assn., Macon-Bibb C. ov C. (local govt. com.), Phi Eta Sigma. Democrat. Baptist. Club: Civitan (Macon) (bd. dirs. 1986—). Home: 5347 Yorktown Rd Macon GA 31210 Office: Pinkston & Pinkston 165 1st St Macon GA 31201

PINNELL, GARY RAY, lawyer; b. San Antonio, Oct. 2, 1951; s. Raymond A., Jr., and Mary Ruth (Waller) P. B.B.A., U. Tex.-Austin, 1973, postgrad., 1976-77; J.D., St. Mary's U., San Antonio, 1976. Bar: Tex. 1976, U.S. Supreme Ct. 1982, U.S. Ct. Appeals (all cirs.), U.S. Tax Ct. 1976, U.S. Ct. Claims 1977, U.S. Ct. Customs and Patent Appeals 1978. Sole practice, Austin, Tex., 1976-77, San Antonio, 1977—; legis. asst. to Rep. Danny E. Hill, 1977; instr. U. Tex.-Austin, 1976-77. Bd. govs. Soc. Colonial Wars, Tex., 1978—, gov., 1987-88. Decorated officer Order St. John, Queen Elizabeth II, 1977, comdr., 1985; officer Order Polonia Restituta (Poland), 1982, comdr. with star, 1984, grand cross, 1986; knight Teutonic Order (Vatican), 1979, Order Constantine St. George, Italy, 1979, numerous others. Mem. Internat. Bar Assn., State Bar Tex., Mexican Acad. Internat. Law, Tex. Soc. S.R., Tex. Soc. SAR, Omicron Delta Kappa, Delta Sigma Pi, Phi Alpha Delta. Republican. Roman Catholic. Club: St. John's (London). Contbr. articles legal jours. Home: 7500 Callaghan Rd Apt 234 San Antonio TX 78229 Office: La Quinta Plaza 10010 San Pedro Suite 540 San Antonio TX 78216

PINNELL, WILLIAM GEORGE, university administrator; b. Clarksburg, W.Va., Sept. 6, 1922; s. George Mason and Anna (Wagner) P.; m. Dorothy Elizabeth Graham, June 25, 1946; 1 child, Georgia Pinnell Stowe. A.B., W.Va. U., 1950, M.A., 1952; D.B.A., Ind. U., 1954. Asst. dean Ind. U. Sch. Bus., Bloomington, 1954-56; asso. dean, then acting dean Ind. U. Sch. Bus., 1956-63, dean, 1963-71, univ. v.p., treas., 1971-74, exec. v.p., 1974-88; pres. Ind. U. Found., 1983-88; dir. Kroger Co., Pub. Service Co. Ind., Consolidated Products, Inc. Author: An Analysis of the Economic Base of Evansville; co-author: Case Study of a Depressed Area; contbr. articles to profl. jours. Bd. dirs. Ind. U. Found. Served to lt. (j.g.) USNR, 1942-47. Mem. Am. Econ. Assn., Am. Fin. Assn., Internat. Bus. Edn. Assn., Regional Sci. Assn., Midwest Econ. Assn., Midest Bus. Adminstrn. Assn., Beta Gamma Sigma, Beta Alpha Psi, Sigma Iota Epsilon, Alpha Kappa Psi, Pi Alpha Alpha. Methodist. Address: 2700 Pine Lane-Bittner Woods Bloomington IN 47401

PINNEY, EDWARD LOWELL, JR., physician, educator; b. Gauley Bridge, W.Va., Nov. 11, 1925; s. Edward Lowell and May (Vencill) P.; A.B., Princeton U., 1949; B.S., W.Va. Med. Sch., 1947; M.D., Washington U., St. Louis, 1949; m. Arline Claire Caldwell, Aug. 2, 1957 (div. May 1980); children—David Edward, Diane Arline, Michael Leslie. Intern, St. Louis City Hosp., 1949-50; resident Bklyn. State Hosp., 1952-54, sr. psychiatrist, 1954-55; practice medicine specializing in psychiatry, Bklyn., 1955-68; mem. staff St. John's Episcopal Hosp., 1956-68, Meth. Hosp., 1956-67, Bklyn. Cumberland, Gracie Square hosps., Beekman Downtown Hosp., N.Y.C., 1968-78; partner, med. dir. Bklyn. Med. Assos. Psychiatry and Neurology, 1958-64; psychiat. cons., dir. Mental Hygiene Clin. Cumberland Hosp. div., Bklyn.-Cumberland Med. Center, 1964-68, attending psychiatrist, 1968-76, psychiat. cons., 1976-82; psychiat. cons. Bklyn. Eye and Ear Hosp., 1967-76; attending psychiatrist Manhattan Eye, Ear and Throat Hosp., 1976-82; clin. instr. SUNY, Down State Med. Center, 1958-68; clin. asst. prof. psychiatry Cornell U. Med. Coll., 1968-71, clin. asso. prof., 1971-78; clin. asso. prof. N.Y. U., 1978-82, U. Tex., San Antonio, 1982, 1984-87; physician health service L.I. U., 1962-82; psychiat. cons. Bd. Edn. N.Y.C.; dir. psychiatry N.Y.C. Dept. Correction, 1979-80; co-dir. tng. program in group psychotherapy N.Y. U. Postgrad. Med. Sch., 1979-82; psychiat. cons. VA Hosp. Bklyn., 1972-82; med. dir. Austin-Travis County (Tex.) Mental Health/Mental Retardation Center, 1982-83; mem. faculty dept. psychiatry U. Tex. Med. Br., Galveston, 1983-84; dir. residency tng. program Austin State Hosp., 1984—; lectr. in psychiatry Psychotechnol. Inst. Japan, Tokyo, 1987, Group Approach Inst., Hiroshima, Japan, 1987. Bd. mgrs. Bklyn. Central YMCA, 1964-68; chmn. profl. adv. com. Archeus Found., N.Y.C., 1968—, pres., 1975-76; mem. profl. adv. com. Epilepsy Soc. for Social Service, 1970-82. Served as lt., M.C., USNR, 1950-52. Fellow Am. Psychiat. Assn., Am. Soc. Psychoanalytic Physicians (pres. 1973-74), Am. Group Psychotherapy Assn.; mem. Schilder Soc., AMA, Kings County, N.Y. County med. socs., N.Y. Soc. Clin. Psychiatry, Assoc. Physicians L.I., Pan Am. Med. Assn., Assn. Mil. Surgeons U.S., Med. Soc. N.Y. State (chmn. sect. psychiatry 1976-77, alt. del. 1978), Eastern Psychiat. Research Assn. (sec.-treas.), Assn. Research Nervous and Mental Diseases, AAAS, N.Y. State Hosps. Med. Alumni Assn. (pres. 1968-72), Phi Beta Pi. Club: N.Y. Athletic. Author: A First Group Psychotherapy Book, 1970; A Glossary for Group and Family Therapy, 1982; contbr. articles to profl. jours.; assoc. editor The Bull. Area II dist. brs. Am. Psychiat. Assn. Home: 8403A Cima Oak Ln PO Box 49680 Austin TX 78765 Office: Austin State Hosp 4110 Guadalupe Austin TX 78751 also: 4200 Marathon Blvd Austin TX 78756

PINNOW, ARNO LEE, quality assurance executive; b. Milw., July 21, 1941; s. Roy Lee and Lila Viola (Uphoff) P.; m. Leta Sheila Williams, Dec. 28, 1963; children—Christopher Gene, Marjorie Lee. B.S. in Chem. Engring., Ill. Inst. Tech., 1964. Registered profl. engr., Ill. Mgr. systems and tng. Amp-vial project Abbott Labs., North Chicago, Ill., 1971-72, mfg. quality mgr. Hosp. div., Rocky Mount, N.C., 1972-74, sect. mgr. quality audits, North Chicago, 1974-77, ops. mgr. quality evaluation, 1977-82; dir. quality assurance Hollister, Inc., Libertyville, Ill., 1981-85; mgr. quality engring. Advanced Cardiovascular Systems subs. Eli Lilly & Co., Temecula, Calif., 1985—; cons. in field, Gurnee, Ill., 1984-85. Patentee in field. Judge Sci. Fair Gurnee Schs., 1968-70; leader Boy Scouts Am., 1959-77; mem. ch. council Lutheran Chs., Waukegan, Ill., 1971-73, Rocky Mount, 1971-73; mem. Citizens Adv. Bd. Warren Twp. High Sch., Gurnee, 1979-81. Mem. Nat. Soc. Profl. Engrs. Calif. Soc. Profl. Engrs., Am. Soc. Quality Control, Am. Prodn. and Inventory Control Soc., Regulatory Affairs Profl. Soc., Am. Inst. Chem. Engrs., Marquetry Soc. Am., Woodworkers Assn. N.Am., Pi Kappa Phi, Alpha Phi Omega. Lutheran. Avocations: woodworking, stained glass, construction, locksmithing, landscaping. Home: 1619 Ranchwood Ln Fallbrook CA 92028-4358

PINO, LITA VAZQUEZ, marketing consultant; b. Havana, Cuba, Jan. 1, 1951; came to U.S., 1960; d. Eugenio A. and Maria Teresa (Garcia-Montes) Vazquez; m. J. Pino, 1969 (div. 1981); children—George, Lianne. B.B.A. with honors, U. Miami, 1972, postgrad., 1980. Project specialist U. Miami (Fla.), Coral Gables, 1977-80; coordinator copywriting Cons. Pharm. Advt., Key Biscayne, Fla., 1980-81; mng. cons. M.E.T.A., Pub. Relations Cons., Miami, Fla., 1981-82; mktg. project mgr. Paramount Internat. Coin Corp., Miami, 1982-83; mktg. mgr. Interval Internat., South Miami, 1983-84; with Mgmt. Consultants of South Fla., 1984—. Mem. Am. Mktg. Assn., Nat. Assn. Female Execs., Am. Mgmt. Assn. Republican. Roman Catholic. Office: Mgmt Cons South Fla 9951 SW 108th St Miami FL 33176

PINOCHET UGARTE, AUGUSTO, president of Republic of Chile; b. Valparaiso, Chile, Nov. 25, 1915; s. Augusto and Avelina P.; ed. Mil. Acad. Sch. Infantry; m. Maria Lucia Hiriart Rodriguez; children: Inez Lucia, Augusto Osvaldo, Maria Veronica, Marco Antonio, Jaqueline Marie. Joined Chilean Army, 1933, advanced to brig. gen., 1969, gen., 1973; instr. Acad. War, 1954, dep. dir., 1964; instr. Acad. of War, Ecuador, 1956-59; comdr.-in-chief, 1973-80; led coup to depose Pres. Salvador Allende, 1973; pres. Governing Council Chile, 1973-74; pres. Chile, 1974—, elected pres., 1981. Decorated Mil. Star, Grand Mil. Merit Cross, High Command Hon. Officer (Ecuador), Abdon Calderon Parra medal (Ecuador); Order Mil. Merit (Colombia); Grand Cross Mil. Merit (Spain). Roman Catholic. Author several publs. Office: Office of Pres. Santiago Chile *

PINSCHOF, THOMAS, flutist; b. Vienna, Austria, Feb. 14, 1948; s. Karl and Susanne (Leitmaier) P. Grad. diploma Conservatorium of Vienna, 1972; postgrad. Hochschule für Musik, Freiburg, W.Ger., 1972-75, Ind. U., 1975-76. First pub. appearance, Brahmssaal Wien, 1965; appeared at Tanglewood Festival, U.S.A., 1969; mem. Vienna Symphony Orch., 1971-72; founder ENSEMBLE I, Internat. Chamber Group, 1971; artist-in-residence Victorian Coll. of Arts, Melbourne, Australia, 1976—, lectr., 1979—, head woodwind dept., 1983—; rec. and concert artist. Contbr. articles to music publs. and editions of music. Inventor of Pinschofon, a new type of bass-flute, first presented at the Internat. Frankfurt Fair, 1971. Bd. dirs. Carl Ludwig Pinschof Found. Recipient 2d prize Internat. Flute competition Severino Gazzelloni, 1975; Koussewitzky scholar, Tanglewood, 1969, Austrian Govt. scholar, 1971, 72; Alban-Berg Found. grantee, 1971; Australia Council Music Bd. grantee, 1983. Mem. Gewerkschaft für Kunst und freie Berufe (Austrian Musicians Union), ACT Flute Soc. (pres.), Verein der Freunde des ENSEMBLE I (chmn.), Victorian Flute Guild (hon.), Mercedes Benz Club of Victoria. Office: PO Box 326, Blackburn, Victoria 3130, Australia

PINSKY, STEVEN MICHAEL, radiologist, educator; b. Milw., Feb. 2, 1942; s. Leo Donald and Louise Miriam (Faldberg) P.; m. Sue Brona Rosenzweig, June 12, 1966; children—Mark Burton, Lisa Rachel. BS, U. Wis., 1964; MD, Loyola U., Chgo., 1967. Resident in radiology and nuclear medicine U. Chgo., 1968-70, chief resident in diagnostic radiology, 1970-71, asst. prof., 1973-77, then assoc. prof. radiology and medicine, 1977-84, prof., 1984—; dir. nuclear medicine Michael Reese Med. Center, Chgo., 1973-87, vice chmn. radiology, 1984-87, chmn. radiology, 1987—, v.p. med. staff, 1986-87, pres., 1988, trustee, 1984-86; dir. nuclear medicine tech. program Triton Coll., River Grove, Ill., 1974—. Contbr. chpts. to books, articles to med. jours. Served to maj., M.C., U.S. Army, 1971-73. Am. Cancer Soc. research fellow, 1969-70. Fellow Am. Coll. Nuclear Physicians (Ill. del., treas. 1982-84), Am. Coll. Radiology (alt. councilor 1986-87); mem. Soc. Nuclear Medicine (trustee 1979-87, pres. central chpt. 1980-81). Home: 1821 Lawrence Ln Highland Park IL 60035 Office: Michael Reese Hosp and Med Ctr Lake Shore Dr at 31st Chicago IL 60616

PINSON, MARGUERITE LORETTA, ednl. cons.; b. Willard, N.Mex., May 25, 1912; d. Ephriam Eastlan and Lucy Ethlyn (Angle) Berry; B.S. in Edn., Ark. State Coll., Conway, 1948; M.S., U. Ark., Fayetteville, 1951; children—Ralph Young, Sue Young Wilson. Tchr., Little Rock Schs., 1943-53; tchr. Anaheim (Calif.) Elem. Sch., 1953-57; dir. elem. edn. Chapman Coll., Orange, Calif., 1957-59; cons. Orange County (Calif.) Dept. Edn., Santa Ana, 1959-77; program rev. cons. Calif. State Dept. Edn., 1977-82; mem. adv. panel Nat. Affiliation for Literacy Advance, 1980—. Mem. NEA, Calif. Tchrs. Assn., Fgn. Lang. Assn., Phi Theta Kappa, Alpha Chi, Kappa Delta Pi, Delta Kappa Gamma. Democrat. Methodist. Home: 2744 Lorenzo Ave Costa Mesa CA 92626

PINSUVANA, ADUL, fertilizer company executive; b. Bangkok, Sept. 18, 1938; s. La-Erb and Udom P.; m. Malulee Kunjara, Mar. 16, 1962; children: Lalida, Argard, Aswin, Anond. SB in Aero. Engring., MIT, 1959; MSc in Mech. Engring., Ariz. State U., 1965. Research analyst Joint Thai-U.S. Mil. Research and Devel. Ctr., Bangkok, 1968-69; tech. services mgr. Air Siam Air Co. Ltd., Bangkok, 1970-76; asst. v.p. mgmt. services, adminstrv. officer The Asean Secretariat, Jakarta, Indonesia, 1977-79; gen. affairs dir. P.T. Asean Aceh Fertilizer, Jakarta, 1980-84, comml. dir., 1985—. Served as capt. Royal Thai Air Force, 1959-68. Club: Am. Univ. Alumni Assn. (Bangkok) (sec.-gen. 1966-76). Home: 72 Jalan Kartanegara, Kebayoran Baru, Jakarta Indonesia Office: PT Asean Aceh Fertilizer, 59 Jalan Sisingamangaraja, Kebayoran Baru, Jakarta Indonesia

PINTAT SOLANS, JOSEP, government official; b. Sant Julià de Lòria, Andorra, Jan. 21, 1925; married. Conseller gen. MI Consell Gen. de les

Valls, Sant Julià de Lòria, Andorra, 1960-63; consol maj. Community of Sant Julià de Lòria, 1968-69, conseller de community, 1970-71, 1982-84; conseller gen. MI Consell Gen. de les Valls, Andorra, 1984-88; head of govt. Govt. of Andorra, 1986-88. Office: Office of Pres of Govt, Andorra La Vella Principality of Andorra

PINTER, HAROLD, playwright; b. London, Oct. 10, 1930; s. Hyman and Frances (Mann) P.; m. Vivien Merchant, Sept. 14, 1956 (div. 1980); 1 son, Daniel; m. Antonia Fraser, Nov. 1980. Student, Brit. schs.; D.Litt. (hon.), U. Reading, 1970, U. Glasgow, 1974, U. East Anglia, 1970, Brown U., 1982, U. Birmingham, 1979, U. Stirling, 1979, U. Hull, 1986. Actor in repertory theatres, 1949-57; dir. plays and films, 1970-83; assoc. dir. Nat. Theatre, 1973-83; author: (plays) Dumb Waiter, 1957, Slight Ache, The Room, The Birthday Party, 1958, The Hothouse, 1958, A Night Out, The Caretaker, 1959, Night School, The Dwarfs, 1960, A Slight Ache and the Dumb Waiter, 1961, The Collection, 1961, The Lover, 1962 (Italia prize 1963), Tea Party, 1963, The Homecoming, 1964, The Dwarfs and Eight Revue Sketches, 1965, The Basement, 1966, Landscape, 1968, Silence, 1969, Night, 1969, Old Times, 1971, Monologue, 1972, No Man's Land, 1975, Betrayal, 1979, Family Voices, 1981, Old Times, Other Places, 1984, One for the Road, 1984, Mountain Language, 1988; (screenplays) The Caretaker, 1962, The Servant, 1962, The Pumpkin Eater, The Quiller Memorandum, 1966, Accident, 1967, The Go-Between, 1969, Langrishe Go Down, 1970, A la Recherche du Temps Perdu, 1972, The Last Tycoon, 1974, The French Lieutenant's Woman, 1981, Turtle Diary, 1986; (TV plays) A Night Out, Night School, The Lover, Tea Party, The Basement; (anthology) Collected Poems and Prose, 1986; (book) One for the Road, 1985. Recipient Shakespeare prize, Hamburg, W. Ger. 1970, Austrian prize lit. 1973, Pirandello prize 1980, Commonwealth award, 1981, Donatello prize, 1982; decorated comdr. Order Brit. Empire. Address: care Judy Dalsch Assocs Ltd, 83 E Bourne Mews, London W2 6LQ, England

PINTI, MARIO, journalist; b. Rome, May 16, 1920; s. Orazio and Erina (Adanti) P.; m. Magda Brandolini, July 12, 1951; children: Alessandra Flavia, Daniele Luigi. Student U. Rome, 1939-45. Cert. journalist, Italy. Editor-in-chief Ali Weekly mag., Milan, Italy, 1943-45, Notiziario Quotidiano Scientifico, Rome, 1956-73, Prospettive Americane, Rome, 1975-77; N.W. corr. CBC, Vancouver, B.C., 1953-54; prin. editor USIA, Rome, 1955-77; press and info. officer NRC, Rome, 1977-82; sr. editor JP-4 Aerospace Yearbook, Florence, Italy, 1983—; war corr. Il Secolo-Sera, Milan, 1944-45; anchorman Sci. Hour Sta. Rai-TV, 1st Radio Network, Rome, 1982; contbr. Sci. Horizons TV series, 1966-72, Scienza é Vita, 1965-70; contbg. editor Mondo Occidentale, Rome, 1956-73, Civilta delle Macchine, Rome, 1964-80, Americana, Rome, 1973-78, Media 2000, Rome, 1983—. Author: Ency. of Tech., 1951; Atom: a Promise, 1962; co-author: Satelliti, 1984. Editor: Missiles and Rockets A to Z, 1962. Recipient Commendable Service award USIA, 1956, Meritorious Honor award, 1968. Fellow Italian Union Aerospace Journalists; Italian Union Sci. Journalists (v.p. 1979-84).

PINTO, MORAGODAGE CHRISTOPHER WALTER, international official, international law consultant. lecturer; b. Colombo, Sri Lanka, Nov. 17, 1931; s. Moragodage Walter Leopold and Judith Beatrice (Blazé)P.; m. Neiliya Jayawardena, Jan. 20, 1960 (div. 1973); children: Asoka Milinda Moragoda, Ruvani Chandrika Moragoda; m. Ilse Roswitha Dobernig, Oc. 26, 1974 (div. May 1987). LLB, U. Sri Lanka, 1955; LLM, Cambridge U., 1957, Diploma in Internat. Law, 1958. Bar: Inner Temple, London, Supreme Ct. Sri Lanka. Legal officer Internat. Atomic Energy Agy., Vienna, Austria, 1960-62; atty. legal dept. World Bank, Washington, 1963-67; head legal and treaties div. Ministry Fgn. Affairs, Colombo, 1967-79; ambassador to Fed. Republic of Germany, Austria Bonn, 1976-80; ambassador UN Conf. on the Law of the Sea, Geneva, 1980-81; sec.-gen. Iran-U.S. Claims Tribunal, The Hague, The Netherlands, 1982—; lectr. Bandaranaike Inst. Internat. Affairs, Colombo, Inst. Social Studies, The Hague, World Maritime U., Malmo, Sweden; mem. UN Gen. Assembly 6th com. UN N.Y., 1967-80; mem., delegation chmn. UN Conf. on the Law of the Sea and other confs., 1967-81; mem. UN Internat Law Com, 1973-81, chmn., 1980. Contbr. articles to profl. jours. Office: Iran-US Claims Tribunal, Parkweg 13, 2585 JH The Hague The Netherlands

PINTO BALSEMAO, FRANCISCO JOSÉ PEREIRA, Portuguese political leader, lawyer, journalist; b. 1937. Editor-in-chief rev. Mais Alto, 1962-63; sec. to mng. bd. Diario Popular, later mgr., until 1971; founder weekly Expresso, 1973. Founder (with others) Social Democratic Party (formerly Popular Dem. Party), 1974, chmn. internat. relations com., mem. polit. com. of party, party leader, 1980—; v.p. Constituent Assembly, 1975, opposition spokesman on fgn. affairs, 1977; mem. Assembly of Republic, 1979, 80-85; minister without portfolio, also dep. prize minister, 1980; prime minister Portugal, 1981-83; vis. prof. U. Lisbon, Portugal. Address: Care Sojornal, Rua Duque de Palmela 37-2, 1200 Lisbon Portugal

PINTO DA COSTA, MANUEL, president Sao Tomé and Principe; b. Aug. 5, 1937. Founder Movement for Liberation and Principe, 1972, sec. gen., 1972-75; pres. Sao Tomé and Principe, 1975—; minister. agr., land reform and def., 1975-78, labor and social security, 1977-78, terr. adminstrn., 1978—; prime minister, from 1978; comdr.-in-chief armed forces, former minister of def. and nat. security. Address: Office of Pres, CP 38 Sao Tomé Sao Tome and Principe *

PINTOR-RAMOS, ANTONIO, philosopher, educator; b. El Pino, Galicia, Spain, Mar. 2, 1947; s. Ramón Pintor and Hortensia Ramos Míguez; m. Socorro González Gardón, Oct. 20, 1973. PhD, U. Pontificia, Salamanca, Spain, 1973. Fellow philosophy U. Pontificia, Salamanca, 1975-80, chmn. philosophy, 1980—, decano (heath), 1983—. Author: Humanismo de M. Scheler, 1978, Deismo de Rousseau, 1982, Génesis de Zubiri, 1983; researcher, sec. Jour. Cuadernos Salmantinos de Filos; contbr. articles to profl. jours. Mem. Sem. X. Zubiri, Philosophy Soc. Castile-Leon. Roman Catholic.

PIONTEK, HEINZ, author; b. Kreuzburg, Silesia, Nov. 15, 1925; m. Gisela Dallmann, 1951. Student Theologisch-Philosophische Hochschule, Dillingen, W.Ger. Author: Die Furt (poems), 1952, Die Rauchfahne (poems), 1953, Vor Augen (stories), 1955, Wassermarken (poems), 1957, Buchstaf-Zauberstab (essays), 1959, Aus meines Herzens Grunde (anthology), 1959, John Keats: Poems, 1960, Weisser Panther (radio play), 1962, Mit einer Kranichfeder (Poetry), 1962, Kastanien aus dem Feuer (Stories), 1963, Windrichtungen, 1963, Neue deutsche Erzahlgedichte (anthology), 1964, Klartext (Poetry), 1966, Die mittleren Jahre (novel), 1967, Liebeserklarungen (essays), 1969, Manner, die Gedichte machen, 1970, Die Erzahlungen, 1971, Tot oder lebendig (poems), 1971, Helle Tage anderswo, 1973, Gesammelte Gedichte, 1974, Dichterleben (novel), 1976, Wintertage-Sommernachte (short stories), 1977, Juttas Neffe (novel), 1979, Was mich nicht loslasst (poetry), 1981, Die Munchner Romane, 1981, Zeit meines Lebens, 1984, Werke in sechs Bänden, 1985, Helldunkel, 1987, Fruh im September (collected poems), 1982; editor: ensemble, 1969-79, Deutsche Gedichte seit, 1960, 72, Lieb', Leid und Zeit und Ewigkeit, 1981, Münchner Edition, 1980-86, Jeder Satz ein Menschengesicht, 1987. Recipient Berlin prize for Literature, 1957, Andreas Gryphius prize, Esslingen, 1957, Rom prize, Villa Massimo, 1960; Munchner Literature prize, 1967; Eichendorff prize, 1971, Tukan prize, 1971, Literature prize des Kulturkreises im BDI, 1974; Georg-Buchner prize, 1976; Werner-Egk prize, 1981, Oberschlesischer Kultur prize, 1983. Mem. Bavarian Acad. Fine Arts, Central PEN of Federal Republic Germany.

PIOVANELLI, SILVANO CARDINAL, cardinal Roman Catholic Church; b. Feb. 21, 1924. ordained 1947. Consecrated bishop Titular Ch. Tubune, Mauritania, 1982; archbishop Florence, Italy, 1983—; proclaimed cardinal 1985. Address: Arcivescovado, Piazza S Giovanni 3, 50129 Florence Italy *

PIOW, TEH HONG, bank executive; b. Singapore, People's Republic of China, Mar. 14, 1930; s. Teh Chong Ngee; m. Tay Sock Noy, Feb. 8, 1956; children: Teh Li Hua, Teh Lee Pang, Teh Li Shian. Grad., Anglo-Chinese Sch., Singapore, 1950; BS, Pacific Western U., 1981, MBA, 1982, LLD (honoris causa), 1984; PhD in Fin., Clayton U., 1985. With Overseas-Chinese Banking Corp. Ltd., Singapore, 1950-59; with Malayan Banking Berhad, Kuala Lumpur, 1960-62, mgr., 1962; area mgr. Malayan Banking Berhad, Selangor, 1964, gen. mgr., 1964-66; mem. sr. credit seminar Chase Manhattan Bank, N.Y.C., 1962; dir., chief exec. officer Pub. Bank Berhad and Pub. Fin. Berhad, Kuala Lumpur, Malaysia, 1966—, chmn., 1978—; chmn. Tong Meng Industries Group Ltd., Singapore, Pub. Securities Group Ltd., Singapore, London & Pacific Ins. Co. Berhad Group, Malaysia and Singapore; exec. chmn. Pub. Bank Berhad Malaysia Group; chmn., mng. dir. Pub. Internat. Investment Ltd., Hong Kong. Fellow Assn. Bus. Execs. U.K., Brit. Inst. Mgmt., Institut Bank Malaysia, Inst. Adminstrv. Accts. (Malaysia Dist. Soc. and U.K. chpt.), Inst. Adminstrv. Mgmt., Inst. Bus. Adminstrn. Austria, Inst. Commerce, Inst. Credit Mgmt., Inst. Dirs. U.K., Malaysian Inst. Mktg., Malaysian Econ. Assn., Malaysian Inst. Mgmt. Address: Pub Bank Berhad-Bangunan Pub Bank, 6 Jalan Sultan Sulaiman, 50000 Kuala Lumpur Malaysia

PIPER, ALAN EDWARD, corporate communications specialist; b. Romford, Essex, Eng., Feb. 17, 1942; s. Edward Charles and Irene Vera (Coppins) P.; m. Mary Elizabeth Porter-Roe, Apr. 3, 1965; children: Mark Alan, David John, Steven Richard James. Student, Clarke's Coll., Romford, 1958-60. Editorial asst. Aero. Mag., London, 1960-62, Aviation & Space Mag., London, 1962-63; pub. relations officer Brit. Aircraft Corp., Eng., 1963-74, various corps., Eng., 1974-78; press officer Brit. Airports Authority, London, 1978; press and pub. relations mgr. Brit. Caledonian Airways, Gatwick Airport, 1979-84; medi relations mgr. Brit. Aerospace Plc, Weybridge, Eng., 1984—. Mem. Royal Aero. Soc. Mem. Church of England. Home: 25 Croft Rd, Ringwood, Hampshire BH24 1TA, England Office: Brit Aerospace Plc, 11 Strand, London WC2N 5JT, England

PIPER, SIR DAVID TOWRY, museum director, author; b. London, July 21, 1918; s. S.H. and Mary P.; m. Anne Richmond, 1945; 4 children. Student Clifton Coll., St. Catharine's Coll., Cambridge. Asst. keeper Nat. Portrait Gallery, London, 1946-64, dir. 1964-67; Slade prof. fine art Oxford U., 1966-67; dir. Fitzwilliam Mus., Cambridge, Eng., 1967-73, Ashmolean Mus., Oxford, Eng., 1973-85; Clark lectr. Cambridge U., 1977-78; fellow Worcester Coll. Oxford, 1973-85; mem. Royal Fine Art com. Author: The English Face, 1957, Catalogue of 17th Century Portraits in the National Portrait Gallery, 1963; Companion Guide to London, 1964, Painting in England, 1500-1880, 1965, Shades, 1970, London (World Cultural Guide series), 1971, The Treasures of Oxford, 1977, Kings and Queens of England and Scotland, 1980; novels (as Peter Towry) include: It's Warm Inside, 1953, Trial By Battle, 1959; editor: Enjoying Paintings, 1964, The Genius of British Painting, 1975. Served with Indian Army, 1940-45; Japanese POW, 1942-45. Office: Overford Farm, Wytham, Oxford OX2 8QN, England *

PIPER, LLOYD LLEWELLYN, II, service industry executive; b. Wareham, Mass., Apr. 28, 1944; s. Lloyd Llewellyn and Mary Elizabeth (Brown) P.; B.S.E.E., Tex. A&M U., 1966; M.S. in Indsl. Engring., U. Houston, 1973; m. Jane Melonie Scruggs, Apr. 30, 1965; 1 son, Michael Wayne. With Houston Lighting & Power Co., 1965-74; project engring. mgr. Dow Chem. Engring. & Constrn. Services, Houston, 1974-78; project mgr. Ortloff Corp., Houston, 1978, mgr. engring., 1979-80, v.p., 1980-83; pres., chief exec. officer Plantech Engrs. & Constructors, Inc. subs. Dillingham Constrn. Corp., Houston, 1983-86; pres. The Delta Plantech Co., Houston, 1985-86; dir. on-site tech. devel. Chem. Waste Mgmt., Inc., Oak Brook, Ill., 1986—; bd. dirs. Harris County Water Control and Improvement Dist., 1973-83, pres., 1973-83; trustee Ponderosa Joint Powers Agy. Harris County, 1977-83, pres., 1977-83. Recipient Disting. Service award Engrs. Council Houston, 1970; Outstanding Service award Houston sect. IEEE, 1974, Tex. Young Engr. of Yr., 1976, Nat. Young Engr. of Yr., 1976; registered profl. engr., Tex. Mem. Nat. Soc. Profl. Engrs. (chpt. pres. 1978, nat. chmn. engrs. in industry div. 1977, nat. v.p. 1977, chmn. nat. polit. action com. 1980-83), IEEE, Project Mgmt. Inst., Phi Kappa Phi. Roman Catholic. Contbr. articles to profl. jours. Home: 1226 Indian Trail Hinsdale IL 60521 Office: Chem Waste Mgmt Inc 3001 Butterfield Rd Oak Brook IL 60521

PIPITONE, PHYLLIS L., psychologist, educator, author; b. Chgo.; m. S. Joseph Pipitone, Aug. 28, 1948 (dec.); children: Guy, Daniel, Paul; m. Thomas A. Cox, Jan. 3, 1980. Student Chgo. Conservatory Music, 1941-44, Peabody Conservatory Music, 1945, Chgo. Tchrs. Coll., 1946-47, So. Meth. U., 1951-52; MA, U. Akron (Ohio), 1967; PhD, Kent (Ohio) State U., 1974. With B.S. & H. Advt. Agy., Chgo., 1941-43; instr. piano and theory Music Acad. Chgo.; psychologist, instr. U. Akron and Kent State U., 1970-79; pvt. practice psychology, Akron, 1967—; lectr. in field in U.S and abroad. Served with WAC, AUS, 1944-46. NIMH grantee, 1974, HEW Child Devel. fellow, 1974. Mem. Am. Psychol. Assn., Nat. Assn. Sch. Psychologists, Mensa, Council Exceptional Children, Am. Hypnosis Soc., Kent Psi Research Group, Study/Dreams (assoc.), Am. Soc. Psychical Research. Clubs: Tuesday Musical, Weathervane Theatre Women's Bd., Akron Women's City, Wadsworth Women's. Home: 224 Pheasant Run Wadsworth OH 44281

PIPKIN, JAMES HAROLD, JR., lawyer; b. Houston, Jan. 3, 1939; s. James Harold and Zenda Marie (Lewis) P. BA, Princeton U., 1960; JD, Harvard U., 1963; Diploma in Law, Oxford (Eng.) U., 1965. Bar: D.C. 1964, U.S. Supreme Ct. 1969, D.C. Ct. Appeals, 1972. Law ck. to assoc. justice U.S. Supreme Ct., Washington, 1963-64; assoc. Steptoe and Johnson, Washington, 1965-70, ptnr., 1971—; counsel Friends of Music, Smithsonian Inst., Washington, 1984-88; mem. Nat. Arbitration Panel, 1983—. Co-author: The English Country House: A Grand Tour, 1985, The Country House Garden: A Grand Tour, 1987; contbr. photographs and articles to mags. including: House & Garden, Smithsonian mag., The Mag. Antiques, Art and Antiques, Archtl. Digest, Am. Illustrated. Mem. ABA, D.C. Bar Assn. Club: Metropolitan (Washington). Home: 8405 Burdette Rd Bethesda MD 20817 Office: Steptoe & Johnson 1330 Connecticut Ave NW Washington DC 20036

PIRES, PEDRO VERONA RODRIGUES, prime minister Republic of Cape Verde; b. Ilha do Fogo, Portugal, Apr. 29, 1934; s. Luis Rodrigues Pires and Maria Fidalga Lopes Pires; m. Adélcia Maria da Luz Lima Barreto Pires; 2 children. Educated Licee Gil Eanes de São Vicente, Faculty of Sci., Lisbon U., Portugal. Joined Partido Africano da Independência do Guiné e Cabo Verde (PAIGC), 1961; mem. PAIGC dels., 1961-63; involved in preparation for liberation of Cape Verde, 1963-65; mem. Central Com. of PAIGC, 1965—, of Council of War, from 1967; mem. Commn. Permanente do Comité Executive da Luta (CEL), 1970—; adminstr. liberated areas So. Guinea-Bissau, 1971-73; pres. Nat. Com. PAIGC for Cape Verde, 1973; apptd. asst. state commr. in 1st govt. of Republic of Guinea-Bissau, 1973-74; negotiator independence agreements of Cape Verde and Guinea-Bissau, 1974; dep. Nat. Popular Assn. of Cape Verde, 1975—; prime minister of Cape Verde, 1975—, mem. permanent commn. of Struggle Exec. Com., 1977, also vice-sec. gen. PAICV. Decorated medal of Amilcar Cabral, Great Cross of Mil. Order of Christ, Portugal, 1985. Address: Office of Prime Minister, Cidade de Praia Republic of Cape Verde

PIRKLE, GEORGE EMORY, television writer, producer; b. Atlanta, Sept. 3, 1947; s. George Washington and Glanna Adeline (Palmer) P.; m. Karen Leigh Horn, Oct. 20, 1973; 1 child, Charity Caroline. Student North Ga. Coll., 1965-66; BA in Journalism, U. Ga., 1969, MA, 1971. Radio announcer, sportscaster for various radio stas., North Ga. area, 1968-70; TV producer, dir. Instructional Resources Ctr., Athens, Ga., 1969-70; info. officer, Southeastern Signal Sch., U.S. Army, 1971; prodn./dir. Motion Picture Service, Continental Army Command and Signal Corps TV Div., 1972-73; pub. info. officer Ga. Dept. Revenue, Atlanta, 1973-78; coordinator TV prodn. services So. Co. Services, Inc., Birmingham, Ala., 1978—; exec. v.p. Mgmt. and Human Devel. Assocs., Inc., Birmingham, 1984-86; producer Prodn. Works, Birmingham, 1984—; actor for various radio and TV commercials, corp. TV programs, radio dramas, stage plays, 1968—. Editor monthly newsletter Ga. Revenews, 1973-78; writer, producer, exec. producer more than 500 corp. and pub. service TV and film programs. Recipient So. Superlative outstanding employee award, So. Co. Services, 1986. Mem. communications com. Birmingham Area Council Boy Scouts Am., 1983-85; Master of ceremonies gov.'s vet. awards presentation World Peace Luncheon, Birmingham, 1981, 82, 84; exec. producer videotape for Birmingham Film Council, 1985; producer, dir. Highway in Crisis, 1986; writer, producer, dir. campaign film Birmingham Area United Way, 1986, 87; writer, producer, narrator, 1987 campaign film; bd. dirs. Birminham Internat. Ednl. Film Festival, 1987—; chmn. Sadie award com., student video competition dir.; comml. acting instr. elan/Casablanças Modeling/Career Ctr., 1988; sponsor Am. Film Inst.; mem. Ga. Hist. Soc., contbr. mem. Ctr. for Environl. Edn. Served to 1st lt. U.S. Army, 1971-73. Recipient various awards. Mem. Internat. TV Assn. (charter pres. Birmingham chpt. 1984-85, pres. pro tem 1984, editor newsletter Freeze Frame) , So. Electric System Visual Communications Subcom. (founding). Republican. Baptist. Avocations: photography, music, genealogy, computers, archaeology. Home: 2313 Countryridge Dr Birmingham AL 35243 Office: So Co Services Inc PO Box 2625 Birmingham AL 35202

PIRNAY, PAUL MARTIN, personnel management consultant, time study analyst; b. Liege, Belgium, Feb. 2, 1928; s. Louis and Berthe (Hanlet) P.; m. Claire Delcroix, July 5, 1956; children: Marie-Noelle, Anne-Claire, Elizabeth. Bachelors, U. Louvain, Belgium, 1968. Journalist Le Courrier Wallon et Fair Play, Liege, 1946; chemist Esperance Longdoz, Liege, 1946-48; editor Editions Jocistes, Brussels, 1948-52; civil servant Belgian State Co., Brussels, 1952-53; personnel mgr. La Vesdre Group, Brussels, 1963-78, Franki, Liege, 1978-88, Human Engring., Limal, Belgium, 1988—; assoc. prof. Ecole Pratigue des Etudes Commls., Brussels; lectr. Ecole Cent. des Arts et Metiers, Brussels, 1976—. Contbr. articles to profl. jours. Decorated Chevalier, Order of the Crown, 1978. Home and Office: Avenue de la Bourse 15, B1350 Limal Belgium

PIRONIO, EDUARDO CARDINAL, Argentinian ecclesiastic; b. Buenos Aires, Argentina, Dec. 3, 1920; ed. Diocesan Sem. La Plata, Pontifical U. Angelicum, Rome. Ordained priest Roman Catholic Ch., 1943; prof. maj. Diocesan Sem. Mercedes; rector Sem. Metropolitano Buenos Aires Sem. Buenos Aires-Villa Devoto; vicar gen. of Mercedes; dean Faculty of Theology, Cath. U. Argentina; aux. bishop of La Plata, 1964; sec.-gen. CELAM, 1968-71, pres., 1971-75; 1971-75; bishop of Mar del Plata, 1975; pro-prefect Sacred Congregation for Religious and Secular Insts., 1975; cardinal prefect SCRIS, 1976—, mem. Pontifical Council for Laity (pres. 1984—). Participant in synods of bishops, 1967, 69, 71, 74, 78, 80; dir. retreats for priests, men religious, women religious; dir. retreat for Pope Paul and Roman Curia, 1974. Office: Piazza del S Uffizzio 11, 00193 Rome Italy *

PIRS, JOZE KARL, engineer, educator; b. Trbovlje, SR Slovenia, Oct. 22, 1925; s. Josip and Maria (Rezun) P.; diploma in engring., U. Ljubljana, 1951, D in Tech. Scis., 1960; m. Fides Pellegrini, Jan. 31, 1956; 1 child, Fredi. Head metall. lab. Torpedo Factory of Diesel Engines, Rijeka, Croatia, 1951-60; asst. prof. mech. engring. U. Zagreb, 1960-66, asso. prof., 1966-71; vis. prof. UCLA, 1975-76; prof. Tech. Faculty Rijeka, Sveuciliste u Rijeci, Yugoslavia, 1972—. Recipient award for sci. work City of Rijeka, 1968; Nikola Tesla award for sci. work Socialist Rep. Croatia, 1974; medal Stanislaw Staszic U., Cracow, 1979. Mem. Internat. Metallographic Soc. (dir. 1970-75), Assn. Yugoslav Engrs. and Technicians (Beograd), Verein Deutscher Eisenhuttenleute (Dusseldorf), Deutsche Gesellschaft fur Metallkunde (Stuttgart), Internat. Metallographic Soc. (Columbus), Yugoslav Soc. Nondestructive Testing Materials, Yugoslav Soc. Electron Microscopy (Zagreb), ABIRA (Raleigh, life). Roman Catholic. Editorial bd. Metallography, 1969—. Home: 5 Nikole Cara, 51000 Rijeka Yugoslavia Office: 58 Narodnog Ustanka, 51000 Rijeka Yugoslavia

PISACANO, NICHOLAS JOSEPH, physician, educator; b. Phila., June 6, 1924; s. Joseph Harry and Rafaella (Saquella) P.; m. Virginia Leigh Burleson; children: Toni Ann, Nicki Rae, Dean Alan, Don Arlie, Lorie Sue. B.A., Western Md. Coll., 1947; M.D., Hahnemann Med. Coll., 1951; D.Sc. (hon.), Western Md. Coll., 1980. Intern Stamford (Conn.) Hosp., 1951-52, resident, 1952-53; gen. practice medicine South Royalton, Vt., 1953-55, Phila., 1955-62; asst. prof. medicine Med. Sch., U. Ky., Lexington, 1962-65; asso. prof. Med. Sch., U. Ky., 1965—, asso. prof. biology, 1966—, dir. continuing med. edn., 1962-66; asst. dean Coll. Arts and Scis., 1966; asst. v.p. Med. Center, 1968—, prof., chmn. dept. allied health edn. and research, 1971—; exec. dir., sec. Am. Bd. Family Practice, 1969—; med. dir. Phila. div. Am. Cancer Soc., 1958-62. Pres. Ky. Mental Health Assn., 1977—; trustee U. Ky., 1987. Served with U.S. Army, 1943-46. Recipient Most Popular Prof. award, 1965; Distinguished Teaching award U. Ky., 1967; Spl. Recognition plaque Student Am. Med. Assn., 1967; Spokewheel award, 1968; Spl. Recognition for Family Practice Edn. Ky. Acad. Family Physicians; Max Cheplove M.D. award N.Y. Acad. Family Physicians, 1975; U. Ky. fellow, 1975; Outstanding Alumnus of Yr. award Hahnemann Med. Sch., 1979. Mem. Pan Am., So., Ky. med. assns., Am. Acad. Family Physicians (Thomas Johnston award 1977, John G. Walsh award 1987), Can. Coll. Family Physicians (hon., W. Victor Johnson orator 1977), AAAS, N.Y. Acad. Scis., Assn. Am. Med. Colls., Soc. Health and Human Values. Home: 2228 Young Dr Lexington KY 40505

PISANI, ANTHONY MICHAEL, architect; b. Watertown, Mass., May 18, 1943; s. Anthony Joseph and Josephine Ann (Tortorella) P.; diploma Mus. Sch., 1966; B.F.A., Tufts U., 1966; M.Arch., Harvard U., 1971; m. Emilia D'Agostino, Aug. 27, 1967; children—Emilia-Bianca, Giancarlo. Project architect Kallmann & McKinell, Architects, Boston, 1971-73, Charles G. Hilgenhurst & Assos., Boston, 1973-74, Desmond & Lord, Architects, Boston, 1974-77; pres. Anthony M. Pisani & Assos., Architects, Boston, 1978—; instr. design Boston Archtl. Center, 1971-74; vice- chmn. Boston Landmarks Commn., 1987—. Registered architect, Mass., Calif., Maine, Mich., N.Y., N.H., Tex., Vt. Mem. AIA, Boston Soc. Architects, Constrn. Specifications Inst., Urban Land Inst., Nat. Council Archtl. Registration Bds., Soc. Archtl. Historians. Major works in Eastern U.S., Ireland, Can., Mex., P.R.; author several articles. Home: 65 East India Row Boston MA 02110 Office: 374 Congress St Boston MA 02210

PISELLI, MAURO, contract company executive; b. Perugia, Pg-Umbria, Italy, Nov. 18, 1941; s. Roberto and Piera (Brachini) P.; m. Pia Maria Ferrando, Aug. 6, 1942; children: Alessandro, Elena Maria. Student, U. Trieste, 1967; grad. in Journalism, Geneva U., Switzerland, 1972. Inspector Torino Ins., Udine, Italy, 1964-67; legal adv. E.C.C., Brussels, Belgium, 1968-69; purchase mgr. Red Cross, Geneva, 1970-72; mng. dir. Friulmicrotron SPA, Udine, 1973-77, Cor Be Spa, Udine, 1985-86; ins. broker Brokers Medolanum, Udine, 1977-81; export mgr. Cordovado Spa, Udine, 1982-84; exec. dir. Edilvil-Nuova Edilvil Group, Verona, Italy, 1986—. Served as soldier Italy Cavalry, 1962-64. Roman Catholic. Home: Piazza S Biagio 11/5, I 33050 Lestizza Udine Italy Office: Edilvil Nuova Edilvil Group, Via Nino Bixio 1010, Villafranca Verona Italy

PISKACEK, VLADIMIR RICHARD, psychiatrist; b. Pilsen, Czechoslovakia, Apr. 13, 1929; came to U.S., 1958, naturalized, 1964; s. Frank and Ludmila (Drchkovka) P. MD, Charles IV U., Prague, Czechoslovakia, 1956. Intern Coney Island Hosp., N.Y.C., 1958-59; resident Bellevue Hosp., N.Y.C., 1962-65, Mt. Sinai Hosp., N.Y.C., 1965-66, Psychiat. Inst., Columbia U., N.Y.C., 1967-68; practice medicine specializing in psychiatry Manhasset, N.Y., 1971—; mem. staff North Shore Univ. Hosp.; instr. psychiatry Columbia U. Med. Sch., 1968-73; asst. dir. Madeline Borg Child Guidance Clinic, N.Y.C., 1969-71; med. dir. Nassau Ctr. for Developmentally Disabled, 1978—; clin. asst. prof. psychiatry Cornell U. Med. Coll., 1978—. Author: (with M. Golub) Psychiatric and Social Work Problems of Children of Interracial Marriages, 1973; Deja Vu in Tibet, 1982; book Bender Gestalt Performance in Children of Papua, New Guinea, 1983. Recipient award Congresso Panamericano de Hipnologia e Medicina Psicosomatica, Rio de Janeiro, Brazil, 1978. Mem. AMA (Physician's Recognition award), Am. Psychiat. Assn. Home: 1641 3d Ave New York NY 10028 Office: 444 Community Dr Manhasset NY 11030

PISNEY, RAYMOND FRANK, management consultant, writer; b. Lime Springs, Iowa, June 2, 1940; s. Frank A. and Cora H. P. BA, Loras Coll., 1963; postgrad., Cath. U. Am., 1963; MA, U. Del., 1965. Asst. for adminstrn. and research Mt. Vernon, Va., 1965-69; historic sites adminstr. N.C. Archives and Hist. Dept., Raleigh, 1969; asst. adminstr. div. historic sites and museums N.C. Dept. Art, Culture and History, Raleigh, 1969-72; exec. dir. Woodrow Wilson Birthplace Found., Staunton, Va., 1973-78; dir. Mo. Hist. Soc., St. Louis, 1978-87; freelance mgmt. cons., writer Alexandria, Va., 1987—; pres. Va. History and Museums Fedn., 1977-78; pres. Mo. Museums Assos., 1982-84. Author: Historical Markers: A Bibliography, 1977, Historic Markers: Planning Local Programs, 1978, A Preview to Historical Marking, 1976, Old Buildings: New Resources for Work and Play, 1976; editor: Virginians Remember Woodrow Wilson, 1978, Woodrow Wilson in Retrospect, 1978, Woodrow Wilson: Idealism and Realty, 1977, Historic Preservation and Public Policy in Virginia, 1978. Hagley fellow U. Del., 1963-65;

Seminar for Hist. Adminstrs. fellow, 1965. Mem. Am. Assn. Museums, Nat. Trust Historic Preservation U.S., Am. Assn. State and local History, Can. Museums Assn., Brit. Museums Assn., Internat. Council Monuments and Sites, Internat. Council Museums, Phi Alpha Theta. Roman Catholic.

PISSARIDES, CHRISTOPHER ANTONIOU, economics educator; b. Nicosia, Cyprus, Feb. 20, 1948; came to U.K., 1965; s. Antonios and Evdokia (Georgiadou) P.; m. Francesca Cassano, July 24, 1986; 1 child, Antony Giulio. B.A. in Econs., U. Essex, Colchester, Eng., 1970, M.A. in Econs., 1971; Ph.D. in Econs., London Sch. Econs., 1974. Research economist Central Bank Cyprus, Nicosia, 1974; lectr. in econs. U. Southampton, Eng., 1974-75; lectr. London Sch. Econs., 1976-82, reader, 1982-86, prof., 1986—; research dir. Centre for Labour Econs., London, 1985—. Author: Labour Market Adjustment, 1976. Editor jour. Economica, 1980-83. Mem. Editorial bd. Rev. Econ. Studies, 1983—. Contbr. articles to profl. publs. Grantee Econ. and Soc. Research Council, 1980—, Dept. Employment, 1980—. Mem. Royal Econ. Soc., Am. Econs. Assn., Soc. Econ. Analysis, Ecomonetric Soc. Greek Orthodox. Home: 1-B Claremeont Rd, London N6 5DA, England Office: London Sch Economics, Houghton St, London WC2A 2AE, England

PISTOR, CHARLES HERMAN, JR., banker; b. St. Louis, Aug. 26, 1930; s. Charles Herman and Virginia (Brown) P.; m. Regina Prikryl, Sept. 20, 1952; children: Lori Ellen, Charles Herman III, Jeffrey Glenn. BBA, U. Tex., 1952; MBA, Harvard U., 1956, So. Meth. U., 1961. Chmn., chief exec. officer First RepublicBank Dallas, 1980-88, also bd. dirs.; chief exec. officer Northpark Nat. Bank, Dallas, 1988—, also chmn. bd. dirs.; bd. dirs. Am. Brands, AMR, Centex Corp. Trustee So. Meth. U., Dallas; elder Presbyn. Ch. Served to lt. USNR, 1952-54. Mem. Am. Bankers Assn. (pres., bd. dirs.). Club: Dallas Country. Home: 4200 Belclaire Dallas TX 75205 Office: Northpark Nat Bank PO Box 12206 Dallas TX 75225

PITBLADO, JOHN M., retired manufacturing company executive; b. Mpls., Jan. 25, 1918; s. James M. and Jennie S. (Bark) P.; m. Jeanne F. Oistad, Jan. 21, 1942; children—James M., Judy Pitblado Skoglund. B.S. in Chem. Engring., U. Minn., 1940. Chem. engr. U.S. Steel South Works, Chgo., 1940-41; chem. engr. Mobil Oil Co., Milw., 1941-43; with 3M Co., 1946-81, gen. sales and mktg. mgr. coated abrasives and related products div., 1966-68, gen. mgr. bldg. service and cleaning products div., 1968-70, div. v.p., 1970-75, group v.p., 1975-79, pres. U.S. ops., 1979-81; dir. Jostens, Inc. Served with USNR, 1943-46. Home: 47090 Amir Dr Palm Desert CA 92260

PITT, BERTRAM, cardiologist, consultant; b. Kew Gardens, N.Y., Apr. 27, 1932; s. David and Shirley (Blum) P., m. Elaine Liberstein, Aug. 10, 1962; children—Geoffrey, Jessica, Jillian. BA, Cornell U., 1953; MD, U. Basel, Switzerland, 1959. Diplomate Am. Bd. Internal Medicine, Am. Bd. Cardiology. Intern Beth Israel Hosp., N.Y.C., 1959-60; resident Beth Israel Hosp., Boston, 1960-63; fellow in cardiology Johns Hopkins U., Balt., 1966-67; from instr. to prof. Johns Hopkins U., 1967-77; prof. medicine, dir. div. cardiology U. Mich., Ann Arbor, 1977—; pres. Cardiovascular Research Cons. Inc., Ann Arbor, 1980—. Author: Atlas of Cardiovascular Nuclear Medicine, 1977; editor: Cardiovascular Nuclear Medicine, 1974. Served to capt. U.S. Army, 1963-65. Mem. Am. Coll. Cardiology, Am. Soc. Clin. Investigation, Assn. Am. Physicians, Am. Physiol. Soc., Am. Heart Assn., Am. Coll. Physicians, Assn. Univ. Cardiology, Am. Coll. Chest Physicians, Royal Soc. Mich., Royal Soc. Medicine. Jewish. Home: 24 E Ridgeway Ann Arbor MI 48104 Office: Univ Hosp 1405 E Ann St Ann Arbor MI 48109

PITT, BRICE MASTERMAN, psychiatrist, educator; b. Wallington, Surrey, Eng., Dec. 10, 1931; s. Norman Ernest and Emily Margery (Crawford) P.; m. Jeanne Mary Hyde, Aug. 11, 1956 (div. 1979); children—Gareth, Caroline, Tristram, Rosalind; m. Susan Margaret Chapman, Aug. 30, 1982 (div. 1986). M.B.B.S., Guys Hosp. London, 1955; M.D., U. London, 1966. Resident, Springfield Hosp., London, 1960-62; sr. resident, research asst. London Hosp., 1962-66; cons. psychiatrist Claybury Hosp., Essex, Eng., 1966-69, London Hosp., 1971-84, St. Bartholomews Hosp., London, 1984-86; sr. lectr. St. Bartholomews Med. Coll., 1984-86; hon. cons. psychiatrist Royal Hosp. Chelsea, 1978-86; prof. psychiatry of old age St. Mary's Hosp. Med. Sch. and Royal Postgrad. Med. Sch., London, 1986—; chmn. Sect. Psychiatry Old Age Royal Coll. Psychiatrists, Eng., 1987—. Author: Psychogeriatrics, 1974; Feelings About Childbirth, 1979; Mid-Life Crisis, 1981; contbr. articles to profl. jours.; editor Dementia, 1987. Mem. bd. visitors Pentonville Prison, 1971; mem. Central Council Edn and Tng. Social Workers, London, 1980. Served as maj. Brit. Army, 1956-68. Fellow Royal Coll. Psychiatrists (ct. electors 1981-84, 1st sec., sect. psychiatry for old age 1972-75), Royal Soc. Medicine London. Club: Tavistock Repertory Co. Avocations: acting; walking. Home: 8 Palmers Hill, Epping, Essex CM16 6SG, England Office: St Charles Hospital, Ladbrok Grove, Dept Psychiatry of Old Age, London W10 6DZ, England

PITT, GAVIN ALEXANDER, management consultant; b. Berkeley, Calif., Aug. 4, 1915; s. David Alexander and Maude Elizabeth (Hanna) P.; m. Eleanore Whiting, Sept. 2, 1939; children: Gavin Alexander, Gaele Whiting, Judson Hamilton. AB, Brown U., 1938; MEd, Johns Hopkins U., 1959. Asst. dean Brown U., Providence, 1938-42; mgr. exec. tng. Macy's, N.Y.C., 1942-43; dir. personnel Hazeltine Electronics Corp., N.Y.C., 1943-45; asst. indsl. adminstr. AMF, Inc., N.Y.C., 1945-49; assoc. Booz, Allen & Hamilton, N.Y.C., 1949-55; dir. personnel services Gen. Dynamics Corp., N.Y.C., 1955-57; v.p. Johns Hopkins U. and Hosp., Balt., 1957-60; pres. Presbyn.-St. Lukes Hosp., Chgo., 1960-63; pvt. practice cons. 1963-66, 70-74; pres. St. John's Mil. Acad., Delafield, Wis., 1966-70; adminstrv. officer Antioch Coll., Yellow Springs, Ohio, 1974-79; devel. officer Wright State U., Dayton, Ohio, 1981-86; pres. Gavin Pitt Assocs., Inc., Chgo. and Dayton, 1986—; lectr. CUNY, 1948-57; exec. dir. Inst. Medicine of Chgo., 1963-66; bd. dirs. Balt. Life Ins. Co. Author: The Twenty Minute Lifetime, 1959. Sec., bd. dirs. Am. Assn. Gifted Children, N.Y.C, 1985-86, v.p. Chgo. area council Boy Scouts Am., 1961-66; trustee Latin Sch. Chgo., 1962-64; bd. corporators The Peddie Sch., Hightstown, N.J. Mem. Am. Mgmt. Assn. (personnel div. adv. council), Assn. Military Schs. and Colls., Nat. Council Chs. (gen. personnel com.), Brown U. Alumni Assn. (Brown Bear Disting. Alumnus 1961), Omicron Delta Kappa, Newcomen Soc. Club: Dayton Racquet, Engineers; Saddle and Cycle (Chgo.). Office: 625 N Michigan Ave Chicago IL 60611

PITT, GEORGE, lawyer; b. Chgo., July 21, 1938; s. Cornelius George and Anastasia (Geocaris) P.; m. Barbara Lynn Goodrich, Dec. 21, 1963; children: Elizabeth Nanette, Margaret Leigh. BA, Northwestern U., 1960, JD, 1963. Bar: Ill. 1963. Assoc. Chapman and Cutler, Chgo., 1963-67; ptnr. Borge and Pitt, and predecessor, 1968-87; ptnr. Katten Muchin & Zavis, Chgo., 1987—. Served to 1st lt. AUS, 1964. Mem. ABA, Ill. State Bar Assn., Chgo. Bar Assn., Phi Delta Phi, Phi Gamma Delta. Home: 600 N McClurg Ct Chicago IL 60611 Office: 525 W Monroe St Suite 1600 Chicago IL 60606

PITTASCH, FRANK, anesthesiologist; b. Dessau, Anhalt, German Dem. Republic, Aug. 24, 1950; s. Edmund and Christel Anne Luise (Laux) P. BS, E.M. Arndt Coll., Bonn, Fed. Republic Germany, 1970; MS, Pedagogische Hochschule, Bonn, 1974; MD, Friedrich Wilhelm Univ., Bonn, 1982. Tchr. Heine (Fed. Republic Germany) High Sch., 1974-75; anesthesiologist St. Elisabeth Hosp., Bonn, 1982-85, Evang. Hosp., Bonn-Bad Godesberg, Fed. Republic Germany, 1985-87, St. Marien Hosp., Bonn, 1987—. Author: The Human Kidney, 1974, The Mendel Rules, 1975, EIA and RIA to Measure the CEA, 1982. Clubs: Rheinischer Verein fuer Deukmals-und Laudespflege, Bonner Heimet und Geschichts-Verein. Home: Sebastianstrasse 81, 5300 Bonn Federal Republic of Germany Office: St Marien Hosp, Robert Koch Strasse 1, 5300 Bonn Federal Republic of Germany

PITTMAN, DAVID JOSHUA, sociology educator, researcher, consultant; b. Rocky Mount, N.C., Sept. 18, 1927; s. Jay Washington and Laura Frances (Edwards) P. B.A., U. N.C., 1949, M.A., 1950; postgrad., Columbia U., 1953; Ph.D., U. Chgo., 1956. Cert. sociologist. Asst. prof. sociology Washington U., St. Louis, 1958-60, assoc. prof., 1960-64, prof., 1964—, chmn. dept. sociology, 1976-86, dir. Social Sci. Inst., 1963-76; cons. Jellinek Clinic, Amsterdam, The Netherlands, 1965-68, HEW, Washington, 1967-73, U.S. Brewers Assn., Washington, 1977-85, Wine Inst., 1985—; mem. sci. adv. com. Distilled Spirits Council, Washington, 1976-86; field ed., Social Sciences, J. Stud. Alcoh., 1985—. Author: Revolving Door: A Study of Chronic Police Case Inebriates, 1958, The Drug Scene in Great Britain, 1967, Primary Prevention of Alcoholism, 1980; editor: Alcoholism, 1967. Pres. N. Am. Assn. Alcoholism Programs, Washington, 1965-67; chmn. 28th Internat. Congress on Alcohol and Alcoholism, Washington, 1968, Mo. Adv. Council on Alcoholism and Drug Abuse, Jefferson City, 1972-75, 1987—; mem. Mo. Mental Health Commn., Jefferson City, 1975-78. Served to cpl. USAF, 1946-48. Recipient Page One Civic award St. Louis Newspaper Guild, 1967, Bronze Key, St. Louis Council on Alcoholism, 1976, Silver Key, Nat. Council on Alcoholism, N.Y.C., 1978; spl. fellow NIMH, 1966. Fellow Am. Sociol. Soc.; mem. Soc. Study Social Problems (chmn. alcoholism com. 1957-59), Internat. Council on Alcohol and Addictions (exec. com. 1968-84). Episcopalian. Office: Sociology Dept Washington Univ Box 1113 Saint Louis MO 63130

PITTMAN, GEORGE HENRY, JR., airport executive, former air force officer; b. Falkland, N.C., Mar. 16, 1920; s. George Henry and Daisy Pauline (Carman) P.; m. Anne Lamoreaux Crawford, June 12, 1941 (div. 1960); children: Theresa Anne, George Henry; m. Christine Halbhuber, Nov. 1, 1960; 1 child, Gabriele Antonia. Student The Citadel; BS, U.S. Mil. Acad., 1941; grad. Air U., 1950; postgrad. various schs. Commd. 2d lt. U.S. Army, 1941, advanced through grades to col. USAF, 1961; pilot Air Navigation Sch., Kelly Field, Tex., 1942; test pilot Air Depot, Duncan Field, Tex., 1942-43; chief insp. maintenance div. San Antonio Air Service Command, Kelly Field, 1943-44; comdr. 5th Floating Air Depot, Tex. and Ala., 1944; base ops. officer, Tinker Field, Okla., 1944; maintenance chief Air Service Ctr., Tinian Island, 1944-45; chief maintenance 20th Air Force, Guam, 1946-67; chief plans Mil. Air Transp. Service, Calif. wing and Mass. div., 1948-50, air transport wing ops., Mass., 1951; comdr. and ops. officer for air resupply and communications, Idaho and Philippines, 1951-54; div. chief, exec. U.S. Air Force Directorate for Flight Safety Research, Calif., 1954-58; comdr., tactical missile squadron and dep. comdr. materiel 38th Tactical Missile Wing, W.Ger., 1958-63; dep. comdr. material, 1st Fighter Wing, Mich., 1963-66; electronics maintenance chief Aerospace Def. Command, 1966-67; ret., 1968; dep. and asst. dir. aviation Melbourne (Fla.) Regional Airport, 1968—; active pilot; guest lectr. Fla. Inst. Tech., also various aviation groups; participant in seminars; farm operator, Falkland. Mem. tech. adv. com. Met. Planning Orgn.; former program chmn. Port Malabar Civic Assn.; mem. Melbourne Area Devel. Council; past mem. Palm Bay Mayor's Adv. Named to Hon. Order of Ky. Cols. Mem. Continuing Fla. Aviation System Planning Process (steering com.), Fla. Airport Mgrs. Assn., Palm Bay Area C. of C. (dir. 1974-76), Air Force Assn., Space Coast West Point Soc., Nat. Pilots Assn. (disting. pilot), Aircraft Owners and Pilots Assn., Melbourne Comets (past pres.), Quiet Birdman. Democrat. Lutheran. Lodges: Masons (comdr. Southeastern Shrine Flying Fezzes Assn., 1984-85, 87-88, various other flying groups), Order of Daedalians, Shriners (past pres. Greater Melbourne, 1973), Jesters (past bd. dirs.). Home: 1490 Country Club Dr NE Palm Bay FL 32905 Office: 1050 S Joe Walker Rd Suite 220 Melbourne FL 32901

PITTMAN, JAMES ALLEN, JR., physician; b. Orlando, Fla., Apr. 12, 1927; s. James Allen and Jean C. (Garretson) P.; m. Constance Ming-Chung Shen, Feb. 19, 1955; children—James Clinton, John Merrill. B.S., Davidson Coll., 1948, D.Sc. (hon.); M.D., Harvard, 1952; D.Sc. (hon.), U. Ala. at Birmingham. Intern, asst. resident medicine Mass. Gen. Hosp., Boston, 1952-54; teaching fellow medicine Harvard, 1953-54; clin. asso. NIH, Bethesda, Md., 1954-56; instr. medicine George Washington U., 1955-56; chief resident U. Ala. Med. Ctr., Birmingham, 1956-58, instr. medicine, 1956-59, asst. prof., 1959-62, assoc. prof., 1962-64, prof. medicine, 1964—, dir. endocrinology and metabolism div., 1962-71, co-chmn. dept. medicine, 1969-71, also assoc. prof., physiology and biophysics, 1966—, prof. medicine, 1964—; dean U. Ala. Med. Ctr. (Sch. Medicine), 1973—; asst. chief med. dir. research and edn. in medicine U.S. VA, 1971-73; prof. medicine Georgetown U. Med. Sch., Washington, 1971-73; mem. endocrinology study sect. NIH, 1963-67; mem. pharmacology, endcrinology fellowships rev. coms., 1967-68; chmn. Liaison Com. Grad. Med. Edn., 1976; mem. Grad. Med. Edn. Nat. Adv. Com., 1977-78, U.S. Dept. Health and Human Services Council on Grad. Med. Edn., 1986. Author: Diagnosis and Treatment of Thyroid Diseases, 1963; Contbr. articles in field to profl. jours. Fellow ACP (life); mem. Assn. Am. Physicians, Endocrine Soc., Am. Thyroid Assn., N.Y. Acad. Scis. (life), Soc. Nuclear Medicine, Am. Diabetes Assn., Am. Chem. Soc., Wilson Ornithol. Club (life), Am. Ornithologists Union, Am. Fedn. Clin. Research (pres. So. sect., mem. nat. council 1962-66), So. Soc. Clin. Investigation, Harvard U. Med. Alumni Assn. (pres. 1986-88, mem. com. on grad. med. evaluation 1987—), Phi Beta Kappa, Alpha Omega Alpha, Omicron Delta Kappa. Office: U Ala School of Medicine Office of Dean Birmingham AL 35294

PITTOCK WESSON, JOAN HORNBY, English language and literature educator; b. Featherstone, Yorkshire, Eng., May 1, 1930; d. George Hornby Mould and Dorothy Muriel Skelhorne Poyner; m. Malcolm John Whittle Pittock, Aug. 22, 1955 (div. Aug. 1973); 1 son, Murray George Hornby; m. 2d, Harry Chamberlain Wesson, July 19, 1974 (dec. July 1983). BA in English Lang. and Lit. with 1st class honors, U. Manchester, 1951, MA, 1952, PhD, 1960. Lectr., Workers' Ednl. Assn., Cumberland and Cheshire, Eng., 1956-63, Alsager Tng. Coll., Cheshire, 1962-63; lectr. English lang. and lit. U. Aberdeen (Scotland), 1964-77, sr. lectr., 1978—; vis. research fellow Magdalen Coll., Oxford U., 1986; convener cultural history group, degree organiser, U. Aberdeen, 1986—. Author: The Ascendancy of Taste, 1973. Editor: Joseph Warton, 'Odes on Various Subjects', 1977; Rowley and Chatterton in the Shades (George Hardinge), 1978; editor: (with J.J. Carter) Aberdeen and The Englightenment, 1987. Founder, editor, mem. editorial bd. Brit. Jour. for 18th Century Studies, 1978—. 18th Century Studies. Contbr. articles and revs. to lit. jours. Founder-mem. Bertrand Russell's Com. 100. Grantee Brit. Acad., 1982, Carnegie Trust, 1983; fellow Edinburgh U. Inst. Advanced Studies in Humanities, 1984-86. Mem. Brit. Soc. for 18th Century Studies (exec. com. 1974-88, pres. 1980-82), Internat. Soc. for 18th Century Studies (Brit. del. exec. com. 1980-84), MLA, Assn. for Scottish Lit. Studies. Conservative. Mem. Ch. of England. Office: Taylor Bldg, Dept English, Old Aberdeen AB9 2UB, Scotland

PITTS, BEN ELLIS, media specialist, educator; b. Pennington Gap, Va., Sept. 20, 1931; s. Ellis R. and Mary Kelly P.; B.S., Lincoln Meml. U., 1954; M.Ed., U. Ga., 1970, Ed.S., 1971, Ed.D., 1973; M.Div., Emory U., 1974. Tchr., prin. Lee County (Va.) Public Schs., 1950-54; ordained to ministry, United Meth. Ch., 1959; minister chs., 1955-67; media specialist Gwinnett County (Ga.) Public Schs., 1968-73; media specialist Rockdale County (Ga.) Public Schs., 1973-74; coordinator learning resource center Tenn. Tech. U., Cookeville, 1974-79; assoc. prof. library/media Delta State U., Cleveland, Miss., 1979-81; media specialist South Ga. Coll., Douglas, 1981—, dir. library services, 1983—; cons. Upper Cumberland Regional Library System, Tenn. Mem. Phi Kappa Phi, Kappa Delta Pi, Pi Delta Kappa. Club: Masons. Contbr. articles to profl. jours. Home: Box 1604 Douglas GA 31533 Office: South Ga Coll Douglas GA 31533

PITTS, MARGARET JANE, chemist; b. Spokane, Wash., Aug. 10, 1923; d. Herbert Ryder and Gladys (Burchett) P. BS in Chemistry, Wash. State U., 1946. Chemist, Electrometall. Co., Spokane, 1943-44, div. indsl. research Wash. State U., Pullman, 1945-46, Haynes Stellite Co., Kokomo, Ind., 1946-51, Pacific NW Alloys, Spokane, 1951-53, Pitts. Testing Labs., Portland, 1954-56, Boeing Co., Seattle, 1956-60, U. Wash., Seattle, 1960-63, Comml. Chems., Inc., Seattle, 1964-65, Puget Sound Naval Shipyard, Bremerton, Wash., 1966-77, Naval Undersea Warfare Engring. Station, Keyport, Wash., 1977-86. Mem. Am. Chem. Soc., ASTM, AAUW, Federally Employed Women, Bus. and Profl. Women, Iota Sigma Pi, Alpha Delta Pi. Home: 2100 3rd Ave #1601 Seattle WA 98121-2303

PIVIN, LAURENT HENRY, banker; b. Mannheim, Fed. Republic Germany, June 30, 1950; s. Jean L. Pivin and Marie-Henriette Portail; m. Benedicte M. Dubois; children: Alexander J.P., Edward S.F. BA, U. Pa., 1971, MBA, 1973. Analyst Leperco de Neuflize, N.Y.C., 1973; analyst, fund mgr. Chase Manhattan Bank, Paris, 1973-75; v.p. Citicorp-Merchant Bank, Paris, N.Y.C., Miami, Luxembourg, 1975-85; mgr. rep. office Hentsch & Cie, Geneva, 1985-87; v.p. Ban Indosvez, Geneva, Switzerland, 1987—. Mem. Conservative Party. Clubs: Racquet and Tennis, Jeu de Paume, Paris Wharton. Home: 370 Park Ave #127 New York NY 10022 Office: Banque Indosvez, 4 Quai Gen Guisan, 1204 Geneva Switzerland

PIXLEY, JOHN SHERMAN, SR., research company executive; b. Detroit, Aug. 24, 1929; s. Rex Arthur and Louise (Sherman) P.; B.A., U. Va., 1951; postgrad. Pa. State U., 1958-59; m. Peggy Marie Payne, Oct. 16, 1949; children—John Sherman, Steven, Lou Ann. Asst. cashier Old Dominion Bank, Arlington, Va., 1953-56; tech. dir. John I. Thompson & Co., research and engring. firm, Bellefonte, Pa., 1956-65; co-founder, exec. v.p. Potomac Research Inc., Alexandria, Va., 1965-80; v.p. Gov. Sevs. Div. Electronic Data Systems, 1980-81; co-founder, pres. Potomac Research Inc. Inc., Alexandria, Va., 1981—. Owner Edgeworth Farm, Orlean, Va. Mem. Fairfax County Republican Com., Annandale, Va., 1964-72; mem. fin. com. for U.S. Rep. Joel T. Broyhill, Republican, Va., 1970-72. Served to 1st lt. AUS 1952-53; maj. Res. ret. Decorated Army Commendation medal. Mem. IEEE, Am. Radio Relay League, Sleepy Hollow Woods Civic Assn. (v.p., pres. 1969-71). Episcopalian. Club: Quantico (Va.) Flying (charter mem.). Home: 3711 Sleepy Hollow Rd Falls Church VA 22041 Office: Potomac Research Inc 6121 Lincolnia Rd Alexandria VA 22312

PIZA, ARTHUR LUIZ, painter; b. Brazil, Jan. 13, 1928; came to France, 1951; one-man exhbns.: Brazil, Germany, Yugoslavia, U.S., France, Switzerland, Sweden, Spain, Belgium, Italy; represented in permanent mus. and pvt. collections. Recipient Purchase prize, 1953; Nat. prize for Prints Sao Paulo Biennale, 1959; prizes at biennales at Ljubljana, 1961, Santiago, 1966, Venice, 1966, Grenchen triennale, 1961, biennales of Norway and Mex., 1980. Address: 16 rue Dauphine, 75006 Paris France

PIZANO-MALLARINO, CARLOS, manufacturing executive; b. Bogotá, Colombia, Sept. 29, 1953; s. Bernardo and Olga (Mallarino) Pizano; m. Camila Obregon, July 28, 1979. BS, MIT, 1974, MS, 1976. Cert. mech. engr. Asst. to pres. Avianca, Bogotá, 1976-78; fin. v.p. Pizano SA, Bogotá, 1978-81, v.p. ops., 1981-85; pres. Sinclair SA, Bogotá, 1986—; bd. dirs. Electromanufacturas SA, Bogotá, Mineros de Antioquia SA, Bogotá, Fiducor SA, Bogotá, Colpatria SA, Bogotá. Mem. Pi Tau Sigma, Tau Beta Pi. Mem. Conservative Party. Roman Catholic. Club: Jockey. Office: Sinclair SA, Calle 21 #42c-47, Bogota Colombia

PIZER, IRWIN HOWARD, medical librarian; b. Wellington, N.Z., Oct. 16, 1934; s. Harry and Cecelia (Cohen) P. B.S., Antioch Coll., Yellow Springs, Ohio, 1957; M.S., Columbia U., 1960. Librarian, assoc. prof. medical history Upstate Med. Ctr., SUNY, Syracuse, 1964-69, dir. biomed. communication network, 1966-70; assoc. dir. libraries SUNY, Buffalo, 1969-71; univ. librarian health scis., prof. library adminstrn. U. Ill. at Chgo., 1971—; dir. Region 3 Regional Med. Library, Nat. Library Medicine, 1980—; chmn. BRS User Adv. Bd., 1977-78, 82-83; mem. Biomed. Communication Network, 1981—, chmn., 1982-83; chmn. 5th Internat. Congress on Med. Librarianship, Tokyo, 1981-85, 6th Congress, New Delhi, 1985—; peer reviewer U.S. Dept. Edn. Office Edn. Research and Improvement, 1987—. Author articles in field, chpts. in books.; Editorial bd. INSPEL-Internat. Jour. Spl. Libraries, 1981-85. Bd. dirs. Ranch Triangle Conservation Assn., Chgo., 1971-74, pres., 1973; bd. dirs. Lincoln Park Conservation Assn., 1972-73. Mem. ALA, Med. Library Assn. (bd. dirs. 1975-78, chmn. nat. program com. 1986—, editor Bull. Med. Library Assn. 1988—, Murray Gottlieb prize 1964, Ida and George Eliot prize 1966, Janet Doe lectr. 1984, Archives award 1985, Pres.'s award 1986, Frank Bradway Rogers Info. Advancement award 1987), Internat. Fedn. Library Assns. and Instns. (chmn. sect. biol. and med. scis. libraries 1977-83, sec. 1983-85, standing com. 1983-87, chmn. div. spl. libraries 1981-85, mem. profl. bd. 1981-87, chmn. 1985-87, mem. exec. bd. 1985-87, mem. program mgmt. com. 1985-87, chmn. 51st council theme com. chmn. conf. program coms., mem. standing com. sect. on conservation 1987—), Spl. Libraries Assn., AAUP, Upstate N.Y.-Ont. Med. Library Assn. (hon.), Health Sci. Librarians Ill., Soc. of Scholarly Pub., Sigma Xi. Home: 1875 N Fremont St Chicago IL 60614 Office: 1750 W Polk St Chicago IL 60612

PIZZOCARO, MASSIMO CESARE, finance company executive; b. Pavia, Lombardia, Italy, July 9, 1957; s. Alberto Giulio and Ada Olga (Gandini) P. PhD, U. Pavia, 1983; cert., SUNY, Buffalo, 1985. Auditor Coopers and Lybrand, Milan, Italy, 1984-86; electronic data processing auditor Coopers and Lybrand, Milan, 1986-87; gen. mgr. Consulenze Finanziarie S.r.l., Pavia, 1987—. Served with Italian Army, 1978. Club: Mediterranee. Home: Via Della Rocchetta 12, 27100 Pavia Italy Office: Comsulemze Fimamziarie SrL, Via Menocchio 1, Pavia 27100, Italy

PLAKOSH, PAUL, JR., psychologist; b. Pitts., May 17, 1949; s. Paul and Leonora (Durso) P.; B.S. summa cum laude, U. Pitts., 1973; M.A., U. Iowa, 1976; Ph.D., Palo Alto Sch. Profl. Psychology, 1978. Research psychologist Langley Porter Inst., U. Calif., San Francisco, 1978-81; exec. dir. Franklin Clinic, San Francisco, 1981—. Mem. Am. Psychol. Assn., Internat. Neuropsychol. Soc., AAAS. Address: 291 Broderick St San Francisco CA 94117

PLANEL, HUBERT, biology educator; b. Paris, Mar. 27, 1923; s. Planel Georges and Jublot (Germaine) P.; m. Plantie Christiane, 1953; children: Didier, Michele, Marc. MD, Toulouse U., 1951, D. in Sci., 1958. Prof. biology, dir. research group biology Med. Sch. Toulouse U., 1970—. Author: brochure A Survey of Space Biology and Space Medicine. Recipient Chevalier de l'Ordre Nat. Du Merite award. Mem. Internat. Astronautical Fedn. (com. bioastronautics). Club: Capitole. Lodge: Lions. Home: 25 rue Ozenne, 61-526064 Toulouse France Office: Med Sch, 37 Allees J Guesde, 61-252123 Toulouse France

PLANT, GORDON TERENCE, neurologist; b. Harrogate, Eng., July 4, 1952; s. Thomas Edmund and Sheila May (Atkinson) P.; m. Marilyn Jane Dirkin, Apr. 29, 1978; children: Eleanor Margaret, Emma Louise. BA, Cambridge U., Eng., 1974, MB, BChir, 1977, MD, 1987. House physician St. Thomas' Hosp., London, 1977-78; sr. house physician Westminster Hosp., London, 1978-80; registrar Addenbrooke's Hosp., Cambridge, Eng., 1980-83; research assoc. physiol. lab. Cambridge U., 1983-86; registrar in neurology Nat. Hosp. for Nervous Diseases, London, 1986-87; sr. regsistrar in neurology Nat. Hosp. for Nervous Diseases, Univ. Coll. and Maida Vale Hosps., London, 1987—. Editor: Optic Neuritis, 1986; contbr. numerous articles to profl. jours. Scholar Downing Coll., 1974; named exhibitioner St. Thomas' Hosp., 1975. Mem. Royal Coll. Physicians (cert.). Mem. Labour Party. Office: Med Sch, Maida Vale Hosp, London W9 1TL, England

PLANTEVIN, JEAN-PAUL ALBERT, corporate executive; b. Bourg, France, June 24, 1935; s. Albert Louis and Colette (Laurent) P.; m. Lucy Mee; 1 child, Jean-Philippe. Grad. ngring., ENS Aeronautique, Paris, 1952; MSc, Stanford U., 1958; postgrad., Stanford Bus. Sch., 1972. Sales dir. Aerospatiale, France and Far East, 1961-69; sales dir., v.p. sales Airbus Industries, Paris, 1969-70; v.p. planning SCAC, Paris, 1970-76; v.p. Ereusotloire, Paris, 1976-83; pres., chmn. Ziegler SA, Paris, 1983-86; chmn., chief exec. officer Trefilunion, Paris, 1986-87; chief exec. officer Fives Cail Babcock, Montrevil, France, 1987—; chmn. French Mgmt. Assn., 1982-86; assoc. prof. HEC Bus. Sch., Paris, 1986—. Contbr. articles to profl. jours. Served to 1st lt. French Army, 1958-61. Mem. Chamber Syndicate Trefileries (v.p. 1987). Home: 22 Rue Emeriau, 75015 Paris France Office: Fives Cail Babcock, 38 rue de la Republique, 93100 Montrevil France

PLANTROU, ERIC, physician; b. Rouen, France, July 6, 1952; s. Pierre and Denise (Canet) P.; m. Catherine Daragon, May 31, 1982; children: Morgane, Astrid. MD, U. Rouen, 1980. Gen. practice medicine various 3d world nations, 1981-83, Pont de L'Arche, France, 1984—. Author: Bubonic Plague in Rouen (1368-1669), 1980. Served with French armed forces, 1979-80. Recipient annual prize Acad. Letters, 1980. Fellow Dr. Without Frontier. Home and Office: 14 Rue Blin, 27340 Pont de L'Arche France

PLAS, JANE, corporate secretary, adminstration director; b. Leek, Groningen, The Netherlands, Dec. 30, 1932; arrived in Can., 1953; d. Cornelius Jacob Plas and Agnes Janke Postma. Diploma, U. Toronto, Ont., Can., 1961; BA in French, U. Western Ont., 1971. Teaching master secretarial sci. dept. St. Lawrence Coll. Applied Arts Tech., Brockville, Ont., 1971-73; mgr. adminstrn., corp. sec. Canpotex Limited, Toronto, 1973-85; dir. adminstrn., corp. sec. Canpotex Limited, Saskatoon, Sask., Can., 1985—; sec. Canpotex

Shipping Services Ltd., Canpotex (Asia) Ltd., Canpotex Bulk Terminals Ltd. Bd. dirs. Jr. Achievement, Saskatoon. Fellow Inst. Chartered Secs. Adminstrs. Presbyterian. Home: #801, 430 - 5th Ave, Saskatoon, SK Canada S7K 6Z2 Office: Canpotex Ltd, #400, 111 - 2d Ave So, Saskatoon, SK Canada S7K 1K6

PLATNICO, EDMUND ROY, systems analyst; b. Mpls., Jan. 6, 1930; s. Raymond Platnico; m. Alice Mae Johnson, Jan. 7, 1950; children—Valerie Lynn Platnico Foster, John Edmund. Student U. Calif.-Berkeley. Research analyst Bank of Am., San Francisco, 1957-71; cons., Dublin, Calif., 1971-73; instr. City of San Lorenzo, Calif., 1973-78; instr. Ray Ctr., U. Alaska-Juneau, 1979—; systems analyst Alaska Div. Vocat. Rehab., Juneau, 1978—. Served with USMC, 1948-57, Korea. Mem. Data Processing Mgmt. Assn. Jewish. Home: 8601 Marilyn Ave Juneau AK 99801 Office: Alaska Div Vocat Rehab Dept Correcitons MS 2000 Juneau AK 99801

PLATT, JEROME JOSEPH, psychologist, educator; b. N.Y.C., May 3, 1941; s. Benjamin and Rose (Weissman) P.; m. Arleen Kay Adair, Jan. 20, 1964; 1 son, Gregory. A.B., U. Mo., 1961; M.S., U. Ga., 1965, Ph.D. (NASA predoctoral trainee), 1967. Clin. research psychologist, sr. instr. in psychiatry Hahnemann Med. Coll. and Hosp., 1968-71, asst. prof. mental health scis., 1971-73, assoc. prof., 1973-77, prof., 1977-86, assoc. dir. grad. edn. in psychology, 1977—; dir. research Hahnemann mental health services at Phila. prisons, 1978-81, prof. dir. div. research, 1981-86; prof. psychiatry, dir. Ctr. Excellence in Addiction Treatment Research U. Medicine and Dentistry of N.J. Sch. of Osteopathic Medicine, Camden, N.J., 1986—, asst. dean for clin. research, 1987-88, acting assoc. dean for research, 1988—; adj. prof. psychiatry and human behavior Jefferson Med. Coll., 1984—; rep. U.S. Dept. State/Fed. Republic Germany workshop on drug abuse treatment, 1985; cons. in field; chair organizing program coms. Dutch/Am. Conf. on Effectiveness of Drug Abuse Treatment, 1987; peer rev. com. Nat. Inst. Drug Abuse, 1984—. Author several books including Heroin Addiction: Theory, Research, and Treatment, 1977, 2d edit., 1986, German lang. edit., 1982, The Psychological Consultant, 1979, Heroin Addiction: Treatment and AIDS (2d vol.), 1988, The Effectiveness of Drug Abuse Treatment, 1988; contbr. numerous articles to profl. jours., chpts. to books. Bd. dirs. Burlington County chpt. Am. Cancer Soc., 1976-79; mem. Mayor's Commn. on Health in the 80s City of Phila., 1982. Nat. Inst. Drug Abuse grantee, 1978—; NIH grantee, 1968-70; clin. fellow Behavior Therapy and Research Soc.; clin. fellow Temple U. Sch. Medicine, 1978-80. Fellow Pa. Psychol. Assn., Am. Coll. Forensic Psychology, Am. Psychol. Assn.; mem. N.J. Psychol. Assn., Eastern Psychol. Assn., AAAS, So. Soc. Philosophy and Psychology Sigma Xi. Office: U Medicine & Dentistry of NJ Sch Osteopathic Medicine 401 Haddon Ave Camden NJ 08103

PLATT, JOSEPH BELNAP, wildlife advisor; b. Ogden, Utah, Aug. 2, 1946; s. James Le Grand and Jean (Belnap) P.; m. Paula Bunker, Oct. 6, 1971; children—Catharine Jean, Andrew Bunker, Eric Alkhalifa, Sarah Elisabeth. B.S., Utah State U., 1970; M.S., Brigham Young U., 1973; Ph.D., Cornell U., 1976. Founder 1st falcon breeding project in Middle East, 1978; developer 1st Arabian wildlife preserve, 1980; ruling family rep. in internat. conservation, Awali, Bahrain, 1977-82; ruling family rep. in conservation, Dubai, United Arab Emirates, 1982—; founder Dubai Wildlife Research Centre, 1982; bd. dirs. Peregrine Fund (U.S.A.); chmn. ICBP falconry group; CIC chmn. Houbarba group. Editor 4 books on wildlife in United Arab Emirates. Vol. worker Mormon Ch., N.Z., 1966-67. Mem. Am. Ornithologists Union, Cooper Ornithol. Union, Nat. Wildlife Fedn., Raptor Research Found., Wildlife Soc., N. Am. Falconer's Assn., Fondation Internationale Pour la Sauvegarde du Gibier, Sigma Xi. Reviewer for editors Jour. Wildlife Mgmt., Condor and Middle East pubs.; contbr. sci. articles to profl. lit. Office: PO Box 11626, Dubai United Arab Emirates

PLATT, LESLIE A., lawyer; b. Bronx, N.Y., Aug. 7, 1944; s. Harold and Ann (Bienstock) P.; m. Marcia Ellin Berman, Aug. 10, 1969; 1 son, Bill Lawrence. B.A., George Washington U., 1966; J.D., N.Y.U., 1969. Bar: N.Y. 1970, U.S. Dist. Ct. D.C. 1972. Atty. advisor Office Gen. Counsel, HUD, Washington, D.C., 1971-72, legis. atty., 1972-75, asst. gen. counsel for legis. services, 1975-78, assoc. gen. counsel for legis., 1978-80; dep. gen. counsel-legal counsel HEW (HHS 1980), Office Gen. Counsel, Washington, 1980-81, legal counsel and staff dir. White House Agent Orange working group, 1980-81; ptnr. Coan, Couture, Lyons & Moorhead, Washington, D.C., 1981-85, law offices Leslie A. Platt, Washington, 1986—. Patentee in field. Co-chmn. community adv. bd. Fairfax Hosp. Assn. Cameron Glen Facility; chair steering com. Reston/Herndon Bus.-High Schs. partnership. Recipient Disting. Service award HUD, 1978. Mem. ABA, Fed. Bar Assn., Am. Jud. Soc., Fed. Sr. Exec. Service (charter). Home: 11616 Newbridge Ct Reston VA 22091 Office: 2000 L St NW Suite 200 Washington DC 20036

PLATT, NICHOLAS, foreign service officer, ambassador; b. N.Y.C., Mar. 10, 1936; s. Geoffrey and Helen (Choate) P.; m. Sheila Maynard, June 28, 1957; children: Adam, Oliver, Nicholas. B.A. cum laude, Harvard U., 1957; M.A., Johns Hopkins U., 1959. Commd. fgn. service officer Dept. State, 1959; vice consul Windsor, Ont., Can., 1959-61; Chinese lang. trainee 1962-63; polit. officer consulate gen. Hong Kong, 1964-68; chief Asian Communist areas div. Bur. Intelligence and Research, Dept. State, Washington, 1969, chief North Asia div., 1970, dept. dir. Exec. Secretariat staff, 1971, dir. staff, 1972-73; chief polit. sect. U.S. Liaison Office, Peking, China, 1973-74; 1st sec. Am. embassy, Tokyo, 1974-77; dir. Office of Japanese Affairs, Dept. State, 1977-78; mem. staff Nat. Security Council, White House, 1978-79; dep. asst. sec. for internat. security affairs Dept. Def., 1980-81; dep. asst. sec. for internat. orgn. affairs Dept. State, 1981-82; ambassador to Zambia Lusaka, 1982-84; exec. sec., spl. asst. to sec. state Dept. State, 1985-87; ambassador to Philippines Manila, 1987—. Recipient Meritorious award exemplary achievement pub. adminstrn. William A. Jump Found., 1973, Disting. Civilian Service medal Dept. Def., 1981, Presdl. Merit award, 1985, Disting. Honor award U.S. Dept. State, 1987. Mem. N.Y. Council Fgn. Relations. Clubs: Metropolitan (Washington); Century (N.Y.C.). Home: APO San Francisco CA 96528

PLATTHY, JENO, cultural association executive; b. Dunapataj, Hungary, Aug. 13, 1920; s. Joseph K. and Maria (Dobor) P.; m. Carol Louise Abell, Sept. 25, 1976. Diploma, Peter Pazmany U., Budapest, Hungary, 1942; PhD, Ferencz J. U., Kolozsvar, Hungary, 1944; M.S., Cath. U., 1965; PhD (hon.), Yangmingshan U., Taiwan, 1975; DLitt (hon.), U. Libre Asie, Philippines, 1977, Kasetsart U., Bangkok, 1988. Lectr. various univs. 1956-59; sec. Internat. Inst. Boston, 1959-62; adminstrv. asst. Trustees of Harvard U., Washington, 1962-85; exec. dir. Fedn. Internat. Poetry Assns., UNESCO, 1976—; pub. New Muses Quar., 1976—. Author: Winter Tunes, 1974, Ch'u Yüan, His Life and Works, 1975; Springtide, 1976, (opera) Bamboo, Collected Poems, 1981, The Poems of Jesus, 1982, Holiness in a Worldly Garment, 1984, Ut Pictures Poeta, 1984, European Odes, 1985, The Mythical Poets of Greece, 1985, Book of Dithyrambs, 1986, Asian Elegies, 1987, Space Eclogues, 1988, Cosmograms, 1988, Nova Comoedia, 1988, Bartók: A Critical Biography, 1988, numerous others, translations; editor-in-chief Monumenta Classica Perennia, 1967-84. Named poet laureate 2d World Congress of Poets, 1973; recipient Confucius award Chinese Poetry Soc., 1974. Mem. Internat. Soc. Lit., PEN, Die Literarische Union, ASCAP, Internat. Poetry Soc., Melbourne Shakespeare Soc., 3d Internat. Congress Poets (pres. 1976, poet laureate 1976). Office: Fedn Internat Poetry Assns UNESCO PO Box 579 Santa Claus IN 47579

PLATZACK, JAN CHRISTER GEORG, linguist, educator; b. Lund, Sweden, Nov. 18, 1943; s. Georg and Sally (Borén) P.; m. Lena Birgitta Ekberg, Oct. 4, 1986; 1 child, Sara Johanna. PhD, U. Lund, 1974. Prof. Swedish U. Stockholm, 1982-86; prof. Scandinavian langs. U. Lund, 1987—; head dept. Scandinavian langs. U. Lund, 1986—. Author: Språket och läsbarheten, 1974, The Semantic Interpretation of Aspect and Aktionsarten, 1979; editor: Arkiv För Nordisk Filologi, 1987; editorial bd. Norsk Lingvistisk Tidskrift, Linguistik Aktuell; contbr. articles to profl. jours. Mem. Generative Linguists of Old World, Vetenskapssocieteten i Lund, Filologiska Sällskapet i Lund. Home: Plåtslagarevägen 7, 22230 Lund Sweden Office: Inst för Nordiska Språk, Helgonabacken 14, 22362 Lund Sweden

PLAUT, MARTIN EDWARD, physician, author; b. Leipzig, Germany, Feb. 19, 1937; came to U.S., 1939, naturalized, 1946; s. Otto L. and Hannah (Lowenstein) P.; m. Sharon Evert, Sept. 10, 1965; children—Benjamin Bogart, Anne, Susan. A.B., Brown U., 1958; M.D., Tufts U., 1962. Intern Buffalo Gen. Hosp., 1962-63; resident Buffalo Gen. Hosp. and; New Eng. Med. Center, Boston; fellow infectious diseases New Eng. Med. Center, 1964-67; practice medicine, specializing in infectious diseases; asst. prof. medicine SUNY, Buffalo, 1967-72; asso. prof. medicine SUNY, 1972-79, prof. medicine, 1980—; asso. chief medicine Sisters of Charity Hosp., Buffalo, 1981—. Author: Doctor's Guide to You and Your Colon, 1982; contbr. articles to profl. jours.; author novels (pseudonym Paul Marttin), Heartsblood, 1970, Cocoa Blades, 1972; pseudonym Harrison Hopkins: Grand Rounds, 1974. Fellow ACP, Infectious Disease Soc. Am. Clubs: Ft. Erie (Ont.); Turf. Home: 135 Parkwood Dr Snyder NY 14226

PLAYER, GARY JIM, professional golfer; b. Johannesburg, South Africa, Nov. 1, 1935; s. Francis Harry Audley and Muriel (Ferguson) P; m. Vivienne Verwey, 1955; children: Jennifer, Marc, Wayne, Michele, Theresa, Amanda. Ed., King Edward Sch., Johannesburg. Profl. golfer 1953—; joined PGA, 1957—; winner East Rand Open, Republic of South Africa, 1955-56, Egyptian Matchplay, 1955, South African Open, 1956, 60, 65-69, 72, 75-77, 79, 81, Dunlop Tournament, Eng., 1956, Ampol Tournament, Australia, 1956, 58, 61, Australian PGA, 1957, Coughs Harbour Tournament, Australia, 1957-58, Natal Open, South Africa, 1958-60, 62, 66, 68, Ky. Derby Open, 1958, Australian Open, 1958, 62-63, 65, 69-70, 74, Transvaal Open, South Africa, 1959, 60, 62, 63, 66, South African PGA, 1959-60, 69, 79, 82, Western Province Open, South Africa, 1959-60, 68, 71-72, Dunlop Masters, South Africa, 1959-60, 63-64, 67, 71-74, 76-77, Brit. Open, 1959, 68, 74, Victoria Open, Australia, 1959, Masters Tournament, U.S., 1961, 74, 78, Lucky Internat. Open, U.S., 1961, Sunshine Open, U.S., 1961, Yomiuri Open, Japan, 1961, PGA Championship, U.S., 1962, 72, Sponsored 5000, South Africa, 1963, Liquid Air Tournament, South Africa, 1963; winner Richelieu Grand Prix, Capetown, 1963, Johannesburg, 1963; winner San Diego Open, 1963, Pensacola Open, 1964, 500 Festival Open, U.S., 1964, U.S. Open (1st foreigner to win in 45 yrs.), 1965, Piccadilly World Match Play, Eng., 1965, 66, 68, 71, 73, NTL Challenge Cup, Can., 1965, World Series of Golf, U.S., 1965, 68, 72, World Cup Internat., 1965, Australian Wills Masters, 1968, 69, Tournament of Champions, U.S., 1969, 78, Greater Greensboro Open, 1970, Dunlop Internat., Australia, 1970, Gen. Motors Open, South Africa, 1971, 73, 74, 75, 76, Jacksonville Open, 1971, Nat. Airlines Open, U.S., 1971, New Orleans Open, 1972, Japan Airlines Open, 1972, Brazilian Open, 1972, 74, So. Open, U.S., 1973, Rand Internat. Open, South Africa, 1974, Gen. Motors Internat. Classic, South Africa, 1974, Memphis Classic, 1974, Ibergolf Tournament, Spain, 1974, La Manga Tournament, Spain, 1974, Gen. Motors Classic, 1975, ICL Transvaal, South Africa, 1977, World Cup Individual, Philippines, 1977, Houston Open, 1978, Kronenbrau Masters, South Africa, 1979, Sun City, S. Am., 1979, Trophee Boigny, Ivory Coast, 1980, Chilean Open, S. Am., 1980, Australian Tooth Gold Coast Classic, 1981, Johnnie Walker Trophy, Spain, 1984, Quadel Srs. Classic, 1985, PGA Srs. Championship, 1986, Northville Srs., 1987, Sr. Tournament, 1987, U.S. Sr. Open, 1987. Named Christian Athlete of Yr. So. Bapt. Conv., 1967; Richardson award Golf Writers Assn. Am., 1975; named to World Golf Hall of Fame. Office: care Internat Mgmt Group 1 Erieview Plaza Cleveland OH 44114 also: care Mark McCormack Agy, 14 Fitzhardinge St, London W1H 9PL, England *

PLAYER, THELMA B., librarian; b. Owosso, Mich.; d. Walter B. and Grace (Willoughby) Player; B.A., Western Mich. U., 1954. Reference asst. USAF Aero. Chart & Info. Center, Washington, 1954-57; reference librarian U.S. Navy Hydrographic Office, Suitland, Md., 1957-58; asst. librarian, 1958-59; tech. library br. head U.S. Navy Spl. Project Office, Washington, 1959-68, Strategic Systems Project Office, 1969-76. Mem. Spl. Libraries Assn., D.C. Library Assn., AAUW, Canterbury Cathedral Trust in Am., Nat. Geneal. Soc., Internat. Soc. Brit. Genealogy and Family History, Ohio Geneal. Soc., Royal Oak Found., Daus. of Union Vets. of Civil War, Friends Folger Library. Episcopalian. Home: 730 24th St NW #320 Washington DC 20037

PLAZA, ANGEL GUTIERREZ, antique dealer, interior designer; b. Madrid, Apr. 29, 1936; s. Domingo Gutierrez Blanco and Justa Plaza De Gutierrez. MD, U. Complutense, Madrid, 1960; student, U. Calif., Berkeley, 1978. Physician Parke Davis España, Madrid, 1961-62; physician Sanidad Militar, Canary Islands, 1962-63, antiquarian, 1963—, interior designer, 1963—; artistic cons. Eulen, S.A., Madrid, 1963—; also cons. other Spanish socs.; expert collector Napolitan Gouaches; collaborator on restoration of Spanish bldgs. of nat. interest. 1974—. Contbr. articles to mags. Recipient Premio Escaparatismo award Soc. Escaparatismo e Interior, Granada, 1970. Mem. Soc. Española de Anticuarios. Office: Zana, Doctor Esquerdo 20, 28028 Madrid Spain

PLAZA, HECTOR HUGO, chemical company executive, consultant; b. Guayaquil, Ecuador, Jan. 8, 1950; s. Hector Hugo and Ana Rebeca (Saavedra) P.; m. Blanca Beatriz Subia, Aug. 5, 1977; children: Marissa Beatriz, Hector Hugo, Alejandra Maria. BS in Indsl. Engring., U. Guayaquil, 1976; MBA, Inst. Tech. de Monterrey, Mexico, 1978. Planning dept. asst. Fabrica de Papel "La Reforma", Guayaquil, 1973-75; maintenance engr. Fabrica de Papel "La Reforma", Babahoyo, 1975-76, plant mgr., 1976-77; fin. mgr. Poliquimicos del Ecuador, Guayaquil, 1979-80, gen. mgr., 1980—; bd. dirs. Consejo Empresarial Andino, Guayaquil, Fedn. de Exportadores, Quito. Pres. Nucleo de Ejecutivos, Guayaquil, 1986-88. Recipient Al Merito Industrial award Ministro de Indutrias del Ecuador, 1987. Mem. Am. Mgmt. Assn., Colegio de Ingenieros Industriales (bd. dirs. 1984-85), Assn. Ejecutivos de Ventas (bd. dirs. 1986-87). Roman Catholic. Clubs: Nacional, Liga Deportiva Estudiantil (Guayaquil). Lodge: Rotary (v.p. Guayaquil club 1987-88). Home: Manzana A-10, Villa 6 Puerto Azul, Guayaquil Ecuador Office: Poliquimicos del Ecuador SA, PO Box 214 (U), Guayaquil Ecuador

PLECHKO, VLADIMIR YAKOVLEVICH, ambassador; b. 1934. Jr. diplomat Consulate Gen. USSR, Bratislava, 1958-60; diplomat Embassy of the USSR, Czechoslovakia, 1960-63, 1969-71, Eng., 1967-69; diplomat Ministry of Fgn. Affairs, Moscow, 1963-67, 1971-79, head consular directorate, 1985-87; consul gen. Consulate Gen. of the USSR, N.Y.C., 1979-80; dep. rep. USSR Permanent Mission at UN, N.Y.C., 1980-85; ambassador to Malta St. Julians, 1987—. Office: Embassy of USSR, Makik Flats The Gardens, Saint Julians Malta

PLEMING, LAURA CHALKER, educator; b. Sheridan, Wyo., May 25, 1913; d. Sidney Thomas and Florence Theresa (Woodbury) Chalker; B.A., Long Beach State Coll. (now Calif. State U., Long Beach), 1953, M.A. in Speech and Drama, 1954; postgrad. U. So. Calif., 1960-63; Rel.D., Sch. Theology, Claremont, Calif., 1968; m. Edward Kibbler Pleming, Aug. 25, 1938; children—Edward Kibbler, Rowena Pleming Chamberlin, Sidney Thomas. Profl. Bible tchr., 1953—; lectr. Calif. State U., Long Beach, 1960-66, U. So. Calif., 1963-65; Bible scholar for teaching Scriptures Program, First Ch. of Christ Scientist, Boston, 1970-75; free-lance Bible lectr., tchr., resource person for adult seminars, 1954—; active in summer teaching for young people, 1963-68, 86-87; tchr. adult edn. Principia Coll., summers 1969-71; tour lectr. to Middle East, yearly, 1974—; mem. archaeol. team, Negev, Israel. Mem. Am. Acad. Religion, AAUP, Soc. Biblical Lit. and Exegesis, Am. Schs. Oriental Research, Inst. Mediterranean Studies, Religious Edn. Assn., Internat. Congress Septuagint and Cognate Studies, Internat. Platform Assn., Phi Beta, Zeta Tau Alpha, Gamma Theta Upsilon. Republican. Christian Scientist. Author: Triumph of Job, 1979; editor Bibleletter Rev., 1968, 76, 81, 8-84.

PLENER, AAGE, commercial communications and design consultant; b. Copenhagen, Aug. 12, 1930; s. Jens Lauritz and Ann-Johanne (Pedersen) P.; m. Jeanne Cilius (dec.); 1 child, Michael Cilius Boorn; m. Vibeke Sanders, Mar. 21, 1987. Free-lance designer 1952-54; asst. advt. mgr. Scandinavian-Am. Nylon-Hosiery Co., 1954-55; visualizer A/S Lintas Ltd., 1955-56, free-lance designer, cons., art dir., 1956-62; art dir. Bern-Hansen & Egeberg Advt. Agy. AS (now Young & Rubicam Copenhagen, Internat.), 1962-67, Bernhansen Advt. Agy. AS, 1967-69; creative dir. Univas Reklame A/S (div. Univas Internat. and Needham, Harpers and Steers Inc.), 1970-73; sr. account exec. Egeberg & Co. A/S (now SSC & B, Lintas), 1973; owner, operator Aage Plener, Communication & Design Cons. Inc., Charlottenlund, Denmark, 1973—; rep. in Europe for Walter Dorwin Teague Assocs. Inc., 1985—. Represented in exhbns.: Arts, Crafts and Indsl. Design Exhbn., Copenhagen and Oslo (Norway), 1953, Designers Exhbn., Copenhagen, 1954, Scandinavian Designers, Oslo, 1957, Internat. Typography Design, N.Y.C., 1958, Typomundus 20, N.Y.C., 1965, Art Dirs. Club of N.Y., 48th ann. show, N.Y.C., 1968, Communication Graphics, N.Y.C., 1968; posters collected in permanent exhbn. Mus. Applied Art, Copenhagen; sponsor collection of graphic books Denmark Graphic Mus., Odense; contbr. internat. publis. including Modern Publicity (London), Graphics Ann. (Zurich), Lettering at Work (London), Internat. Packaging Graphics (Zurich), Internat. Poster Ann. (Zurich), Photo Graphics (Zurich), Ency. Danish Arts and Crafts; contbr. articles on creative problems and other topics in field to communications to mags. and jours. Recipient Cert. of Merit Internat. Ctr. for Typographic Arts, N.Y.C, 1965, Cert. of Excellence Am. Inst. Graphic Arts, 1968, Award of Distinctive Merit and Cert. of Merit Art Dirs. Club of N.Y., 1968. Mem. Arts Club London, Danish Mktg. Assn. Club: Am. (Copenhagen). Home and Office: 156 Strandvejen, DK-2920 Charlottenlund Denmark

PLESS, JORGEN EMIL, plastic surgery consultant; b. Copenhagen, Denmark, Apr. 13, 1934; s. Villy Emanuel and Gerda Frederikke (Bork) P.; m. Eva Festersen, May 21, 1961; children—Thomas, Torsten. M.D., Copenhagen U., 1960; D.D.S., Copenhagen Dental Sch., 1969. Intern Sundby Hosp., 1960-61, Odense U. Hosp., Denmark, 1961; intern Svendborg Hosp., 1961-62, resident, 1963, asst. registrar surg. dept., 1962-65; registrar Rigshospital Copenhagen, 1965-67, 70-71; registrar Finsen Instituttet, Copenhagen, 1969-70, sr. registrar, 1971-73; sr. registrar Odense U. Hosp. 1973-76, cons. plastic surgery dept., 1976—, vice chmn. med. com., 1982-85, chmn. med. com., 1985—; com. mem. Inst. Exptl. Surgery, Copenhagen, 1970-73. Contbr. articles to profl. jours. Mem. Danish Soc. Plastic and Reconstructive Surgery (pres. 1986—), Danish Soc. Head and Neck Oncology (sec. 1974-85), Danish Soc. Microsurgery (pres. 1974-88), Scandinavian Assn. Plastic Surgeons (pres. 1986-88). Lodge: Rotary (Paul Harris fellow 1988). Home: Liljevej 4, DK5700 Svendborg Denmark Office: Odense U Hosp, Sdr Blvd, 5000 Odense Denmark

PLETSCHER, THOMAS, lawyer; b. Switzerland, July 29, 1954; s. Carl Heinrich and Anna Martha (Horber) P.; m. Ina Manser, 1982; children: Ralph Alain, Marco Andreas. JD, U. Zurich, Switzerland, 1979. Asst. Arthur Andersen A.G., Zurich, 1979-80; sec. to the bd. Handels Bank Natwest, Zurich, 1980-83; legal counsel Metaucol Ltd./Fibaco Group, Lausanne, Switzerland, 1983-85; sec. gen. Swiss Office for Trade Promotion, Zurich, 1986-88; mem. mgmt. com. Swiss Assn. for Commerce and Industry, Zurich, 1988—. Served to capt. artilery Swiss armed forces, 1974. Mem. Swiss Corp. Lawyer's Assn., Jaycees Internat. (Zurich bd. dirs. 1984-85, sec. 1987, pres. 1988), Internat. Advt. Assn. (Swiss chpt. bd. dirs. 1988—). Office: Swiss Assn Commerce and Industry, Borsenstrasse 26, CH-8001 Zurich Switzerland

PLEZBERT, MICHAEL JOSEPH, marriage and family counselor; b. Chgo., July 1, 1934, s. Michael and Regina (De Cristopher) P.; B.S., Evangel Coll., 1969; M.S. in Guidance and Counseling, Southwestern Mo. State U., 1972; postgard. U. Calif., Santa Cruz, 1973-75, Heed U., Hollywood, Fla.; Ph.D. in Psychology, Columbia Pacific U., 1982; m. Janice Sherrill Pietrini, Feb. 13, 1965; 1 son, Michael Paul. Tchr. spl. edn. Spokane (Mo.) Sch. Dist., 1969-70; psychologist, counselor Family Service Assn., Watsonville, Calif., 1970-72; adult instr. hosp. adminstrn. and psychology Santa Cruz Dept. Edn., 1972-75; pres. Inst. Personal and Family Communications, Springfield, Mo., 1975—, Esse Pubs., Springfield, 1987—; dir. Alternatives Counseling Ctr., Springfield, Mo.; marriage, family and child guidance counselor and cons.; public speaker. Mem. Mo. Gov.'s Com. on Employment of Handicapped. Served with AUS, 1956-64. Mem. Greene County Mental Health Assn., Nat. Autistic Soc., Nat. Council Family Relations, Nat. Assn. Social Workers, Am. Personnel and Guidance Assn. Mem. Assemblies of God Ch. Club: Lions. Author: A Dynamic Approach to Counseling, 1983; The Courage to Love, 1984, Courage: The Road to Love (A Christian Approach to Emotional Healing), 1987.

PLICHTA, THOMAS FRANCIS, real estate executive, b. Wyandotte, Mich., Apr. 10, 1952; s. Frank R. and Wanda (Latta) P.; m. Marlene Kovacs, June 14, 1975; children—Brandon Travis, Thomas Francis Jr., Drew Robert. B.A. with honors, Mich. State U., 1974; M.B.A., Wayne State U., 1978. C.P.A., Mich., Tex. Mgr. Deloitte Haskins & Sells, Inc., Detroit, 1974-79; v.p., treas. Condo Marine Properties, Detroit, 1980-81, Paul Bosco & Sons, Dallas, 1982; exec. v.p., chief operating officer, chief fin. officer Barge Assocs., Inc., Dallas, 1982-85, also dir.; pres. Assoc. Prime Equities, Inc., Dallas, 1984-85; pres. Prime Devel., Inc., Dallas, 1985—; vice chmn. dir. Med. Bldg. Corp., Dallas, 1985-86. Recipient Disting. Advisor of Yr. award Jr. Achievement Assn. Southeastern Mich., 1977. Mem. Am. Inst. C.P.A.s, Mich. Assn. C.P.A.s, Tex. Soc. C.P.A.s, Beta Alpha Psi. Roman Catholic. Home: 170 Highview Dr Lewisville TX 75067 Office: Prime Devel Inc PO Box 1713 Lewisville TX 75067

PLIMPTON, PAULINE AMES, civic worker; b. N. Easton, Mass., Oct. 22, 1901; d. Oakes and Blanche Ames; B.A., Smith Coll., 1922; m. Francis T.P. Plimpton, June 4, 1926; children: George Ames, Francis T.P., Oakes Ames, Sarah Gay. Pres., House of Industry, 1940-48; bd. dirs. Inst. World Affairs, 1940-74, Pub. Edn. Assn., 1933-44; chmn. United Campaign Fund for Planned Parenthood of Manhattan and Bronx, 1946-49; chmn. Planned Parenthood Fedn. Am. campaign, 1959-60, bd. dirs. 1959-67, 70-73; chmn. United Campaign, 1964; bd. dirs. Planned Parenthood of N.Y.C., 1965-74; rep. Western Hemisphere region Internat. Planned Parenthood Fedn., 1970-73; fund raiser Ladies' Aux. Philharm. Symphony Soc. N.Y., N.Y. Legal Aid Soc., ARC; mem. adv. council Friends of the Columbia Libraries, 1986-89. Recipient Planned Parenthood award for devoted service, 1969, Republican. Unitarian. Clubs: Cosmopolitan, River (N.Y.C.); Ausable (Adirondacks). Contbg. author, editor, compiler Orchids at Christmas, 1975, The Ancestry of Blanche Butler Ames and Adelbert Ames, 1977, Oakes Ames: Jottings of a Harvard Botanist, 1979, The Plimpton Papers: Law and Diplomacy, 1985, A Window on Our World: More Plimpton Papers, 1988. Home: 131 E 66th St New York NY 10021 also: 168 Chichester Rd West Hills Huntington NY 11743

PLIMPTON, ROBERT JAMES, international marketing executive, consultant; b. Callicoon, N.Y., May 8, 1938; came to Switzerland, 1970; s. James Horace and Vera Ann (Lickel) P.; m. Franziska Stefania Hefti, Jan. 13, 1968; 1 child, Andreas Robert; m. Lease Anderson, Sept. 5, 1957 (div. Mar. 1966); children: Katherine B., Karen L., Kristian J. BEE, Rensselaer Poly Inst., 1959; MBA, Washington U., St. Louis, 1970. Project mgr. High Voltage Engring., Burlington, Mass., 1963-67; regional sales mgr. High Voltage Engring., St. Louis, 1967-70; European sales mgr. High Voltage Engring., Zurich, Switzerland, 1970-72; cons. Risch, Switzerland, 1972-77; gen. mgr. Cat Pumps AG, Zug, Switzerland, 1977—; cons. Gen. Ionex Corp., Peabody, Mass., 1972-75, Indsl. Coils, Inc., Peabody, 1972-77, Cat Pumps AG, Zug, 1977. Served to capt. USAF, 1960-63. Mem. Swiss-Am. C. of C. Club: Swiss Aero (Golden Proficiency award 1982). Home: Rebhalde 20, CH-6340 Baar Switzerland Office: Cat Pumps AG, CH-6300 Zug Switzerland

PLIMPTON-HEFTI, FRANZISKA STEFANIA, child psychologist, educator; b. Pecel, Hungary, Oct. 9, 1938; d. Paul and Marta (Von Bodnar) Hefti; m. Robert James Plimpton, Jan. 13, 1968; 1 child, Andreas Robert. Tchrs. Cert., Kantonales Oberseminar, Zurich, 1960; MS in Edn., SUNY, Oswego, 1961; PhD, Washington U., St. Louis, 1970. Cert. tchr., Zurich, N.Y. Research asst. Social Sci. Inst. Washington U., St. Louis, 1968-70; pvt. practice child psychology Zurich, 1970—; cons., lectr. in psychology. Co-author: Enhancing Motivation, 1976, Motivation in der Klasse, 1976. Salzburg Seminar in Am. Studies fellow, 1965; HEW nat. fellow, 1968-70, research grantee, 1969. Mem. Kappa Delta Pi. Home: Rebhalde 20, CH-6340 Baar Switzerland

PLOEM, JOHAN SEBASTIAAN, medical educator, physician; b. Sawah Loento, Sumatra, Indonesia, Aug. 25, 1927; came to The Netherlands, 1929; s. Victor Herman and Cornelia (de Hoog) P.; m. Johanna Jacoba Zaaijer, June 13, 1964; children: Corette, Carolijn. MD, U. Utrecht (The Netherlands), 1951; MPH cum laude, Harvard U., 1954; PhD, U. Amsterdam, 1967. Scientist, Honig Corp., Koog a/d Zaan, The Netherlands, 1956-59, Ciba Corp., Basel, Switzerland, 1960-61; sr. scientist U. Amsterdam (The Netherlands), 1961-70; sr. scientist U. Leiden (The Netherlands), 1970-80, prof. cell biology, 1980—; vis. research prof. U. Miami, 1978-81; vis. lectr. Monash U., Melbourne, Australia, 1978; prelectorship U. Dundee (Scotland), 1983; vis. prof. Academia Sinica, Beijing, China, 1983; vis. prof. Free U., Brussels, 1985; cons. in field. Inventor Epi-illuminator for fluorescence microscopy, 1967, reflection contrast microscopy, 1975. Papanicolaou Cancer Research Inst. fellow, Miami, 1977; recipient C. E. Alken Found. award, Bern, Switzerland, 1982. Fellow Royal Microscopical Soc. (councillor 1977-80, pres. 1986—); mem. Soc. Analytical Cytology (councilor 1979-82), Dutch Soc. Cytology (councilor 1979-83), Internat. Acad. Cytology (com. on cytology automation 1980—). Home: President Kennedylaan 256, 2343 GX Oegstgeest The Netherlands

PLOTKA, RICHARD F., lawyer; b. Utica, N.Y., Sept. 5, 1935; s. Maxim Jay and Marian (LaPoten) P.; children: Richard Mark, Jeffrey Jay. AB, Hamilton Coll., 1956; LLB, Harvard U., 1959. Bar: N.Y. 1959, U.S. Dist. Ct. (so. and ea. dists.) N.Y. 1962; U.S. Ct. Appeals (2d cir.) 1962, U.S. Supreme Ct. 1963, Fla. 1981. Assoc. Alfred S. Koffler, Islip, N.Y., 1959-60; sole practice, Bay Shore, N.Y., 1961-63; ptnr. Koffler, Flower & Plotka, Islip, 1963-69, Flower & Plotka, Bay Shore, 1969—. Mem. legal com., adv. bd. Good Samaritan Hosp., West Islip, N.Y., 1978-85, mem. planning com., 1982-85; bd. dirs. Suffolk Hearing and Speech Ctr., Bay Shore, 1974—, L.I. Charities Found., Bay Shore, 1974—; mem. Fire Island Adv. Commn., Islip, 1969-79, chmn., 1973-79. Fellow Am. Acad. Matrimonial Lawyers; mem. Suffolk County Bar Assn. (chmn. civil rights com. 1968-69, chmn. med.-legal com. 1970-75, bd. dirs. 1975-78), N.Y. State Bar Assn. (family law com. 1980), Suffolk County Criminal Bar (v.p. 1969), N.Y. State Trial Lawyers Assn. Clubs: Southward Ho, Bay Shore Yacht, Le Club (N.Y.). Home: PO Box P-663 Bay Shore NY 11706 Office: Flower & Plotka 120 4th Ave Bay Shore NY 11706

PLOTKIN, SAMUEL, county official, financial consultant; b. Bklyn., Mar. 16, 1911; s. Benjamin and Dora (Dron) P.; m. Betty Steinberg, Mar. 17, 1934; children—Marc Hugh, Diane Faith. B.B.A., St. John's U., 1933. Pres. Kimberley Girl Coats, N.Y.C., 1938-49; ptnr. Kinsley Coats, N.Y.C., 1949-59, Smartshire, Inc., N.Y.C., 1959-77; pub. administr. Surrogates Ct. County of Kings, 1978—; cons. Job Devel. Authority, N.Y. State, 1978—; sec., dir. Indsl. Devel. Authority, N.Y.C., 1975—. Chmn., assoc. bd. dirs. Brookdale Hosp. Med. Ctr., Bklyn., 1958—, v.p. bd. trustees, 1978—; pres. Bklyn. Sch. Special Edn. for Children, 1978-86; treas. bd. dirs. Bklyn Soc. Prevention Cruelty to Children, 1979—; chmn. bd. dirs. Bklyn. PAL, 1985—; mem. bd. trustees PAL Orgn., N.Y., 1987—; mem. St. John's U. Council, Queens, N.Y., 1982—.Recipient Prime Minister's award State of Israel, 1966; Leadership award Yeshiva U., 1970; Man of Yr. award Brookdale Hosp., 1981, Bklyn. Sch., 1975. Mem. N.Y. State Assn. Pub. Adminstrs. (treas. 1981-87, pres. elect 1987—). Lodge: B'nai B'rith (Century Club 1983—, pres. Congregation Israel of Midwood 1970-72). Office: Public Adminstr 360 Adams St Brooklyn NY 11201

PLOTNICK, CHARLES KEITH, lawyer, educator, author; b. Phila., Apr. 8, 1931; s. Benjamin and Gertrude (Jacobson) P.; m. Diane M. Needle, June 27, 1954; children—Steven L., Amy B. BS, Temple U., 1953; LLB, U. Pa., 1956. Bar: Pa. 1957. Sole practice, Phila., 1957-62; field atty. Office Chief Atty., VA, Phila., 1962-68; ptnr. Miller & Plotnick Norristown, Pa., 1968-73, Hurowitz & Plotnick, King of Prussia, Pa., 1973-83; prin. Charles K. Plotnick, P.C., 1983—; agt., div. mgr. Prudential Ins. Co., 1957-62; lectr. estate planning Grad. Sch. Bus. Adminstrn., now adj. prof. Recipient N.Y. Times award, 1952. Mem. ABA, Pa. Bar Assn., Montgomery County Bar Assn. (chmn. Law Day 1968-78, dir. 1974-77), Montgomery County Estate Planning Council (pres. 1973-74), Nat. Assn. Estate Planning Councils (co-chmn. nat. meeting 1973, regional v.p. 1974-80), C.L.U. Author: Die Rich, 1983, Get Rich, Stay Rich, 1984, Keeping Your Money, 1987, The Executor's Manual, 1986; contbr. articles on estate planning to profl. jours. Office: Breyer Office Park York and Township Line Elkins Park PA 19117

PLOWRIGHT, JOAN ANNE, actress; b. Brigg, Lancashire, Eng., Oct. 28, 1929; d. William and Daisy (Burton) P.; m. Roger Gage, 1953 (div.); m. 2d, Sir Laurence (now Lord) Olivier, 1961; 3 children. Student Old Vic Theatre Sch. Mem. Old Vic Co., toured South Africa, 1952-53; 1st leading role in The Country Wife, London, 1956; mem. English Stage Co., 1956; at Nat. Theatre, 1963-74; plays include: The Chairs, 1957, The Entertainer, 1958, Major Barbara and Roots, 1959, A Taste of Honey, 1960, Uncle Vanya, 1962, 63, 64, St. Joan, 1963, Hobson's Choice, 1964, The Master Builder, 1965, Much Ado About Nothing, 1967, Tartuffe, 1967, Three Sisters, 1967, 69 (film 1969), The Advertisement, 1968, 69, Love's Labour's Lost, 1968, 69, The Merchant of Venice, 1970, 71-72, Rules of the Game, 1971-72, Woman Killed with Kindness, 1971-72, Taming of the Shrew, 1972, Doctor's Dilemma, 1972, Rosmersholm, 1973, Saturday Sunday Monday 1973, Eden's End, 1974, The Sea Gull, 1975, The Bed Before Yesterday, 1975, Filumena, 1977, Enjoy, 1980, Who's Afraid of Virginia Woolf?, 1981, Cavell, 1982, The Cherry Orchard, 1983; The Way of the World, 1985, The House of Bernada Alba, 1986-87; films: Equus, 1976, Richard Wagner, 1982, Britannia Hospital, 1981, Brimstone and Treacle, 1982, Revolution, 1983, The Dressmaker, 1987, Drowning By Numbers, 1987; TV films: Merchant of Venice, 1973, Daphne Laureola, 1977, Saturday Sunday Monday, 1977, The Importance of Being Earnest, 1986, The Birthday Party, 1986. Recipient Tony award for Best Actress for A Taste of Honey, 1960; Evening Standard award Best Actress for St. Joan, 1964; Variety Club award for The Bed Before Yesterday, 1976; Best Actress award for Filumena, Soc. West End Theatre, 1978. Office: care LOP Ltd, 33-34 Chancery Ln, London WC2A 1EN, England

PLOYART, JOHN WILLIAM, marketing executive; b. Vancouver, B.C., Can., Oct. 29, 1930; s. Claude Halliday and Deborah Olina (Paulson) P.; m. Helen Marilyn Lamb, July 2, 1954 (div. 1971); children: Shelley Diane, Linda Christine, John Bruce; m. Nancy Ann Biggs, July 24, 1980. B of Commerce, U. B.C., Vancouver, 1952. Sales rep. Davis & Geck div. of Cyanamid Can., Inc., Calgary, Alta., Can., 1958-65; sales mgr. Davis & Geck div. of Cyanamid Can., Inc., Winnipeg, Man., Can., 1965-75; product mgr. Davis & Geck div. of Cyanamid Can., Inc., Montreal, Que., Can., 1975-76; mktg. mgr. Davis & Geck div. of Cyanamid Can., Inc., Montreal, Que., 1976-84; dept. mgr. Davis & Geck div. of Cyanamid Can., Inc., Toronto, Ont., Can., 1984-87; divisional mgr. Davis & Geck div. of Cyanamid Can., Inc., Toronto, Ont., 1987—. Mem. Canadian Fund Advancement Gen. Surgery (bd. dirs. 1985—), Canadian Assn. Mfrs. Med. Devices, Toronto Bd. Trade. Home: 22 Deanbank Dr, Thornhill, ON Canada L3T 1Z3 Office: Davis & Geck div Cyanamid Can Inc, 88 McNabb St, Markham, ON Canada L3R 6E6

PLUMBRIDGE, ROBIN ALLEN, mining company executive; b. Republic South Africa, Apr. 6, 1935; s. Charles Owen and Marjorie Aileen (Bevan) P.; m. Celia Anne Millar, Nov. 18, 1959; twin sons. Grad., St. Andrew's Coll., Republic South Africa; MA, Oxford (Eng.) U. Statistician Goldfields of S. Africa Ltd., 1957-62, asst. mgr., 1962-65, mgr., 1965-69, exec. dir., 1969-74, dep. chair, 1974-80, chair, 1980—, also chair mining house; chair Driefontein Consolidated Ltd., Gold Fields Mining and Devel. Ltd., Gold Fields S. Africa Holdings Ltd., Vellefontein Tin Mining Co. Ltd., Waterval (Rustenburg) Platinum Mining Co. Ltd., West Driefontein Gold Mining Co., Ltd.; bd. dirs. Black Mountain Mineral Devel. Co. (Pvt.) Ltd., Consolidated Gold Fields PLC, Deelkraal Gold Mining Co. Ltd., Kloof Gold Mining Co. Ltd., O'Okiep Copper Co. Ltd., Devel. Bank of S.A., Newmont Mining Corp., Std. Bank Investment Corp. Ltd., Tsumeb Corp. Ltd. Trustee S.A. Found., S.A. Nature Found.; mem. Council for Sci. and Indsl. Research St. Andrew's Coll.; bd. govs. Rhodes U.; mem. Econ. Adv. Council State Pres. Decorated for Meritorious Service, S. African govt., 1982. Mem. Witwatersrand Agr. Soc. (life v.p.). Club: Rand. Office: W Driefontein Gold Mining Co, 75 Fox St, Johannesburg Republic of South Africa *

PLUMIDAKIS, NICK KONSTANTINOS, electronic engineer; b. Chania, Greece, Dec. 17, 1951; s. Konstantinos and Joan (Mamalaki) P.; m. div.; children—Joan-Aphrodite, Mary. Student in telecommunications, Atom, Greece, 1971-75. Electronic engr. OTE, Athens, 1974—. Asst. editor SV News, 1983. Mem. Radio Amateur Assn. Greece, No. Calif. DX Found. Home: 92 Galatsiu Ave, 111 46 Athens Greece Office: OTE, G Palama 3, 111 10 Athens Greece

PLUMMER, (ARTHUR) CHRISTOPHER (ORME), actor; b. Toronto, Ont., Can., Dec. 13, 1929; s. John and Isabella Mary (Abbott) P.; m. Tammy Grimes (div.); 1 child, Amanda; m. Particia Audrew Lewis, May 4, 1962 (div.); m. Elaine Taylor. Ed. pub. and pvt. schs., Can.; pupil, Iris Warren, C. Herbertcasari. Stage debut in The Rivals with Can. Repertory Theatre, 1950; Broadway debut in Starcross Story, 1954; London debut in Becket, 1961; leading actor Am. Shakespeare Theeatre, Stratford, Conn., 1955, Royal Shakespeare Co., London and Stratford, Avon, Eng., 1961-62, Stratford (Ont.) Shakespeare Festival, 1956, 57, 58, 60, 62, 67, Nat. Theatre Co., London; radio roles include Shakespeare, Canada; plays include Home is the Hero, 1954, Twelfth Night, 1954, 70-71, Dark is Light Enough, The Lark, Julius Caesar, The Tempest, 1955, Henry VI, 1956, Hamlet, 1957, Winter's Tale, 1958, Much Ado About Nothing, 1958, J.B., 1958, King John, 1960, Romeo and Juliet, 1960, Richard III, 1961, Arturo Ui, 1963, The Royal Hunt of the Sun, 1965, Antony and Cleopatra, 1967, Danton's Death, 1971, Amphitryon 38, 1971; (musicals) Cyrano, 1973, The Good Doctor, 1973, Love and Master Will, 1975; Othello, 1982, Macbeth, 1988; made TV debut 1953; TV prodns. include Little Moon of Alban, Johnny Belinda, 1958, Cyrano de Bergerac, 1962, Oedipus Rex, After the Fall, 1974, The Doll's House, The Prince and the Pauper, Prisoner of Zenda, Hamlet at Elsinore, BBC, 1964, Time Remembered, Capt. Brassbound's Conversion, The Shadow Box, 1981, The Thorn Birds, 1983, Little Gloria—Happy at Last, A Hazard of Hearts, 1987, Crossings; star TV series The Moneychangers, 1977; made film debut in 1957; films include Stage Struck, 1957, Wind Across the Everglades, 1958, The Fall of the Roman Empire, 1963, Inside Daisy Clover, 1965, Sound of Music, 1965, Triple Cross, 1967, Nobody Runs Forever, 1969, The Battle of Britain, 1969, The Royal Hunt of the Sun, 1969, Lock up your Daughters, 1969, The Phyx, 1970, Waterloo, 1971, The Man Who Would Be King, 1975, The Return of the Pink Panther, 1975, Conduct Unbecoming, 1975, International Velvet, 1978, Murder By Decree, 1979, Starcrash, 1979, The Silent Partner, 1979, Hanover Street, 1979, Somewhere in Time, 1980, Eye witness, 1981, The Disappearance, 1981, The Amateur, 1982, Dreamscape, 1984, Ordeal by Innocence, 1984, Lily in Love, 1985, The Bosse's Wife, 1986, Souvenir, 1987, Dragnet, 1987. Decorated companion Order of Can., 1968; recipient Theatre World award, 1955, Evening Standard award, 1961, Delia Austrian medal, 1973, 2 Drama Desk awards, 1973, 82, Antoinette Perry award, 1974, Emmy award Nat. Acad. TV Arts and Scis., 1977, Genie award, Can., 1980, Golden Badge of Honor, Austria, 1982, Maple Leaf award Nat. Acad. Arts and Letters. Mem. Theatre's Hall of Fame. *

PLUMMER, JACK MOORE, psychologist; b. Galveston, Tex., Apr. 19, 1940; s. Jack Moore and Sarah Carroll (Cochran) P.; B.A., St. Mary's U., 1962; M.S., Trinity U., 1968; Ph.D., Tex. Tech. U., 1969; A.A.S., Garland County Community Coll., 1978; m. Rose Marie Taylor, July 22, 1960; children—Cynthia Marie, Edward Moore, Elizabeth Anne, Sarah Lorraine, Jack Moore. Psychologist Okla. rehab. div. Okla. State Reformatory, Granite, 1968-69; dir. tng. Ark. Rehab. Research and Tng. Center, Hot Springs, 1970-71; pvt. practice psychology, Hot Springs, 1971—; exec. dir. Plummer Assocs. for Consultation and Tng., 1982—; dir. Ark. Behavioral Services Clinic, 1983—; exec. officer Tng. Inst. for Edn. in Security, 1983—; psychol. cons. to Rehab. Services, Dept. Correction, Probation and Parole Div., also to physicians, attys., cts., law enforcement agys.; instr. Garland County Community Coll., Hot Springs, 1973—; continuing edn. instr. nursing degree program Coll. St. Francis, Joliet, Ill., 1979—; cons. Parents Without Partners. Mem. bd. L.P.N. nurse program Ouachita Vocat.-Tech. Sch., Hot Springs, 1979—. Fellow Ark. Psychol. Assn.; mem. Nat. Rehab. Assn., Nat. Rehab. Counseling Assn., Am. Psychol. Assn., Ark. Psychol. Assn. (chmn. fellow status rev. com. 1980, 81, chmn. profl. standards rev. com. 1982, 83), Hot Springs Psychol. Assn. (pres. 1979, 80), Internat. Soc. for Study Symbols. Democrat. Roman Catholic. Elk, Lion. Contbr. articles to profl. jours., chpt. in Handbook of Measurement and Evaluation in Rehabilitation. Mailing Address: 207 Hagen Hot Springs AR 71913

PLUMMER, KENNETH ALEXANDER, communications executive; b. Chgo., Mar. 24, 1928; s. Alexander Oliver and Estella Marie (Koziol) P.; m. Marie M. Ricci, Oct. 10, 1943; children: Pamela, Diane, Kenneth, Stacy. Student North Cen. Coll., 1940-41, The Citadel, 1941-42, Far Eastern U. (Philippines), 1946-48. Commd. 2d lt. U.S. Army, 1943, advanced through grades to col., 1966, ret., 1973; dir. Ancilla Domini Health Services, Inc., Des Plaines, Ill., 1973-82; dir. Oak Park Hosp. (Ill.), 1982—; chmn. Vets. Adv. Commn. City of Chgo., 1986-87; chmn. Village Oak Park Bd. Health; cons. Cambodian Refugee Program for Cath. Relief Services; moderator, instr. Air War Coll. Non-Resident Program; installed med. relief teams in Cambodian refugee camps; spl. parade cons. Girl Scouts Chgo.; mem. govt. affairs com. Chgo. Assn. Commerce and Industry, 1976-79, Atty. Gen. Ill. Veterans Advocacy Com. Decorated Bronze Star, Combat Infantry badge, Meritorious Service medal, Army Commendation medal; recipient Assn. of U.S. Army citation, 1961, Res. Officers Assn. award, 1964, Cath. Relief Service award, 1980; Ancilla Domini Sisters award, 1980. Mem. Mil. Order World Wars (comdr. 1962-63), Hosp. Pub. Relations Soc., Chgo. Council on Fgn. Relations, Assn. U.S. Army, Ret. Officers Assn. Roman Catholic. Home: 415 N Elmwood St Oak Park IL 60302 Office: Oak Park Hosp Ctr 715 Lake St Suite 519 Oak Park IL 60301

PLUMMER, ROGER SHERMAN, JR., oil company executive, consultant; b. Portland, Oreg., Aug. 4, 1922; s. Roger Sherman and Ruth (Barlow) P.; m. Lois Virginia Ross, Aug. 15, 1960; 1 dau., Pamela Ruth Martin. B.A., U. Tex., 1948, M.A. in Geology, 1949. Geologist, Socony Mobil Oil Co., Caracas, Venezuela, 1949-53; chief subsurface geologist Internat. Petroleum Colombia, Bogota, 1952-56; exploration mgr. Libyan Am. Oil Co., Benghazi, Libya, 1956-58, gen. mgr., 1958-60, v.p., gen. mgr., Benghazi, 1961-64; v.p., dir. Grace Petroleum Corp., Benghazi, 1965-66, exec. v.p., dir. Grace Petroleum Corp., Grace Oil Corp. (Italy). Rome, 1966-68; pres., chief exec. officer, dir. Champlin Petroleum Co., Fort Worth, 1968-75, cons., 1975-77; internat. petroleum cons., 1978—; teaching fellow U. Tex., 1948-49, mem. Geology Found.; instr. Southwestern U., 1948-49; dir. Continental Nat. Bank of Fort Worth. Served to 1st lt. USAAF, 1942-46. Mem. Am. Assn. Petroleum Geologists, AIME Tex. Mid-Continent Oil and Gas Assn., Am. Petroleum Inst. (dir.), Am. Inst. Profl. Geologists, Fort Worth C. of C. (dir.), Explorers Club, Phi Beta Kappa, Sigma Xi, Sigma Gamma Epsilon. Republican. Methodist. Clubs: Fort Worth Petroleum; Plaza (Tyler, Tex.); Sulphur Springs Country. Home: 405 Vonda Dr Sulphur Springs TX 75482

PLUMMER, WILLIAM FRANCIS, real estate executive; b. Worcester, Mass., Feb. 7, 1934; s. William Nelson and Mary Mildred (Foley) P.; m. JoAnne Johnson, July 16, 1955 (div. June, 1970); children: Karen Michelle, Michael David; m. Claire Fitzpatrick, Oct. 16, 1981. Student, Alexander Hamilton Inst., 1955-58, LaSalle U., 1968-70. Dir. mktg. and sales Landex Corp., Las Vegas, Nev., 1971-74, Spanish Trails Resorts, Las Vegas, 1974-78, Holiday Trails, Inc., Scottsdale, Ariz., 1978-80, Western Sun Corp., El Paso, Tex., 1980-85; dir. mktg. Real Vest, Inc., Tulsa, 1985-86; pres., chief exec. officer Bill Plummer & Assocs., Las Vegas, 1971—; exec. v.p. Integrated Fin. Group, Las Vegas, 1986—; dir. sales and mktg. Red Apple Inn and Country Club, Heber Springs, Ark., 1987—; gen. mgr. RPM Market Research Div., Memphis, 1987—; cons. Coronado State Bank, El Paso, 1983-85, Mail Mart, Dallas, 1979—, Pend Orielle Shores Resort, Hope, Idaho, 1985, Great Outdoor Am. Adventure, Seattle, 1980, Landex Corp., Las Vegas, Nev. Author: Passport to Independence, 1979, Passport to Excitement, 1981, Passport to Paradise, 1982. Served to sgt. USMC, 1951-54, Korea. Mem. Internat. Boxing Hall of Fame (exec. com. 1979-86), Nat. Film Soc. (adv. bd. 1982-86), Am. Legion, VFW. Republican. Roman Catholic. Clubs: Santiago Yacht and Country (Manzanillo, Mexico), Outrigger Canoe (Oahu, Hawaii). Lodge: Elks.

PLUNKETT, JOSEPH CHARLES, electrical engineering educator; b. Centerville, Tenn., Dec. 3, 1933; s. Harold D. and Lorraine (Lewis) P. B.S., Middle Tenn. State U., 1964; B.S.E.E., U. Tenn., 1966; M.S.E.E., Ga. Inst. Tech., 1973; Ph.D., Tex. A&M U., 1978. Registered profl. engr., Mass. Devel. engr. Martin Marietta Co., Orlando, Fla., 1966-69; research engr. Raytheon Co., Wayland, Mass., 1969-71, IIT Research Inst., Annapolis, Md., 1971-72, Tex. A&M U., College Station, 1974-77; assoc. prof. elec. engring. Calif. State U.-Fresno, 1977-80, prof., 1980—, chmn. dept., 1980-84; cons. Author numerous articles in field. Served to capt. Ordnance Corps USAR, 1958-66. Mem. IEEE, Nat. Soc. Profl. Engrs., N.Y. Acad. Scis., Sigma Xi, Eta Kappa Nu. Republican. Mem. Ch. of Christ. Office: Calif State U Fresno CA 93740

PNIAKOWSKI, ANDREW FRANK, structural engineer; b. Grodno, Poland, Aug. 18, 1930; s. Josef Leon and Janina (Kodzynski) P.; Diploma Engr., Politechnika Warszawska, 1952; m. Margaret M. Czajkowski, Aug. 15, 1957; 1 dau., Mary. Bridge design and field engr. Govt. of Poland, Ministry of R.R., Warsaw, 1952-57; bridge design engr. Dept. Hwys., of Ont. (Can.), Toronto, 1958-66; sr. structural engr. Sverdrup & Parcel Assos. Inc., Boston, 1967-71; prin. structural engr. Louis Berger & Assos. Inc., Wellesley, Mass., 1972—; cons. engr. in transp., pub. bldgs., others. Registered profl. engr., Ont., Mass., Maine, N.H. Mem. Assn. Profl. Engrs. of Province Ont., Nat. Soc. Profl. Engrs. Roman Catholic. Office: 20 William St Wellesley MA 02181

PO, CLAUDE, corporate professional; b. Paris, Mar. 31, 1934; s. Jacques Joseph and Luce Eliane (Darcy) P.; m. Noelle Barbe; children: Jaques-Olivier, Guillaume, Jean-Damien. Grad., Naval Acad., 1956, cert. submarine engring., 1961; degree in Econs., Coll. Scis. Sociales Econs., Paris, 1967. Naval officer with the French Navy, 1957; ret. 1969; sr. v.p. Banque Union Europeenne, Paris, 1969-83; chief exec. officer Frantour, 1983—. Roman catholic. Home: 85 Bd Pasteur, Paris France 75015 Office: Frantour, 66 Rue De Monceau, Paris France 75008

POAGE, GEORGE RICHARD, historian, retired educator; b. Gallatin, Mo., July 25, 1914; s. George Naylor and Linda Lane (Doolin) P.; student Harvard U., 1932-33; B.A. summa cum laude, U. No. Iowa, 1951; M.A., U. Iowa, 1952, Ph.D., 1954; m. Patricia Ann Lowe, May 20, 1946; 1 dau., Susan Kathleen. Cryptanalist, War Dept., Washington, 1941-42; instr. history, U. Iowa, 1952-53, univ. fellow, 1953-54, vis. prof. German history, 1966-67; asst. prof. history U. No. Iowa, 1954-59, assoc. prof., 1959-65, prof., 1965-83, prof. emeritus, 1983—; chmn. exec. council Coll. Behavioral Scis., 1967-72, chmn. univ. faculty, 1972-74; dir. Iowa High Sch. Model UN, 1965-83; bd. dirs. Iowa div. UN Assn., 1965—, Council on Internat. Relations and UN Affairs, 1967-73, UN Assn. of U.S.A., 1973-80, nat. council, 1980—; chmn. Gov. Iowa's Com. on UN, 1976-79. Served with Signal Corps, U.S. Army, 1942-45; MTO. Decorated Silver Battle Star; recipient citation for outstanding service Gov. Iowa, 1975; Roswell Garst Meml. award UN Assn., 1979. Mem. Am. Hist. Assn., Conf. Group for Central European History, AAUP (pres. U. No. Iowa chpt. 1957). Democrat. Presbyterian. Club: Masons. Home: 1421 W 18th St Cedar Falls IA 50613

POCHAT, GÖTZ, art historian, educator; b. Gotha, German Dem. Republic, Nov. 28, 1940; s. Karl August and Märta (Beskow) P.; m. Mareike Woellert; children: Madeleine, Christine. PhD, U. Stockholm, 1968, DrPhil, 1973, lic. in comparative lit., 1974. Docent U. Stockholm, 1974-80; prof. art history Rheinisch-Westfälische Tech. Hochschule Aachen, Fed. Republic of Germany, 1981-87; prof. Art History Inst., Graz (Austria) U., 1987—. Author: Der Exotismus, 1970, Figur und Landschaft, 1973 (award 1974), Der Symbolbegriff, 1983, Geschichute der Ästhetik und Kunst Theorie, 1986. Lerici Found. grantee, Rome, 1965, 70, Beskowska, Stockholm, 1974; Tatti fellow, Harward U., Florence, 1975. Mem. German Art History Assn., Austrian Art History Assn. Office: U Graz Art History Inst, University Platz 3, 8010 Graz Austria

POCRASS, RICHARD DALE, management consultant; b. Meadville, Pa., Mar. 7, 1940; s. Irving F. and Roslyn (Sperber) P.; m. Rena Levy, Feb. 3, 1968; children—Michael B., S. Douglas. B.S. in Math., U. Pitts., 1962; M.B.A. in Fin., 1964. EDP sales mgr. NCR Corp., Pitts., 1962-67, retail mktg. mgr., Los Angeles, 1972-74; v.p., dir. Nanoseconds Systems, Fairfield, Conn., 1967-69, dir. 1968-72; v.p. gen. mgr. Hart Jewelry Co., Warren, Ohio, 1969-71, dir. 1981—; mktg. mgr. Data Source Corp subs. Hercules, Inc., El Segundo, 1974-75; pres. Webster-Pocrass & O'Neil (name changed to Pocrass Assocs. 1981), Los Angeles, 1976—, Health Tech. Inc. Pub., author: The Recruitment Letter; author (with Maronde) Drug Abuse Study for Hoffman LaRoche, 1980. Bd. dirs. West Valley Little League. Mem. Los Angeles Speakers Bur., Am. Soc. Personnel Adminstrs., Woodland Hills C. of C., Am. Mktg. Assn., Bank Mktg. Assn., Retail Controllers Assn., Calif. Exec. Recruiters Assn., Personnel and Indsl. Relation Assn., Internat. Platform Assn., Personnel and Indsl. Relations Assn. Republican. Jewish. Lodge: Rotary. Home: 18815 Paseo Nuevo Dr Tarzana CA 91356 Office: 16760 Stagg St #218 Van Nuys CA 91406

PODBOY, JOHN WATTS, clinical psychologist; b. York, Pa., Sept. 27, 1943; s. August John and Harriett Virginia (Watts) P.; m. Carolyn Sue Baughman, Feb. 6, 1972; 1 son, Matthew John. B.A., Dickinson Coll., 1966; M.S., San Diego State Coll., 1971; Ph.D., U. Ariz., 1973. Dir., Vets. Counseling Center, U. Ariz., Tucson, 1972-73; project dir. San Mateo County (Calif.) Human Relations Dept., Redwood City, 1974; staff psychologist Sonoma State Hosp., Eldridge, Calif., 1975-81; cons. clin. psychologist Comprehensive Care Corp., Newport Beach, Calif., 1974-75, Sonoma County (Calif.) Probation Dept., 1976—; asst. prof. Sonoma State U., 1977-81; dir. Sonoma Diagnostic and Remedial Center, 1979-82. Chmn. San Mateo County Diabetes Assn., 1975. Served to USNR, 1966-69. Fellow Am. Coll. Forensic Psychology, Am. Bd. Med. Psychotherapists (fellow); mem. Am. Psychol. Assn., Western Psychol. Assn., Redwood Psychol. Assn. (pres. 1983), Nat. Council Alcoholism, Nat. Rehab. Assn. Home: PO Box 488 Kenwood CA 95452

PODDAR, RAMENDRA KUMAR, biophysics educator, scientist; b. Sagarkandi, Bangladesh, Nov. 9, 1930; s. Brojendra Kumar and Sushila Bala Poddar, m. Jharna Sarkar, Mar. 9, 1955; children: Mallika, Tapan, Pinaki. BS with hon., Calcutta U., India, 1950, MS in Physics, 1952, PhD, 1957. Biophysicist U. Calif., Berkeley, 1958-60; research fellow Purdue U., La Fayette, Ind., 1960-61; sci. adviser Internat. Atomic Energy Authority, Mali, 1962; lecturer and reader Saha Inst. Nuclear Physics, Calcutta, India, 1963-68; assoc. prof. Saha Inst. Nuclear Physics, Calcutta, 1968-73; research fellow Calif. Inst. Tech., Pasadena, 1970; prof. biophysics Calcutta U., 1973—; pro vice chancellor Calcutta U., 1977-79, vice chancellor, 1979-83. Contbr. articles to profl. jours. Mem. Parliament India, 1985—; chmn. Inst. Wetland Mgmt. and Ecological Design, Calcutta, 1986—, Indain Sch. Social Scis., Calcutta. Recipient Adhar Chandra medal, Calcutta U., 1946, Gold medal, Scottish Ch. Coll., Calcutta, 1950. Mem. Indain Biophysics Soc., Sci. and Tech. Com. Home: AA 10/7 Deshbandhu Nagar, Calcutta 700 059, India Office: U Coll Sci, 92 APC Rd, Calcutta India 700009

PODGORNY, GEORGE, emergency physician; b. Tehran, Iran, Mar. 17, 1934; s. Emanuel and Helen (Parsian) P.; came to U.S., 1954, naturalized, 1973; B.S., Maryville Coll., 1958; postgrad. Bowman Gray Sch. Medicine, 1958; M.D., Wake Forest U., 1962; m. Ernestine Koury, Oct. 20, 1962; children—Adele, Emanuel II, George, Gregory. Intern in surgery N.C. Bapt. Hosp., Winston-Salem, 1962-63, chief resident in gen. surgery, 1966-67, in cardiothoracic surgery, 1967-69; sr. med. examiner Forsyth County, N.C., 1972—; dir. dept. emergency medicine Forsyth Meml. Hosp., Winston-Salem, 1974-80; sec.-treas. Forsyth Emergency Services, Winston-Salem, 1970-80; clin. prof. emergency medicine East Carolina U. Sch. Medicine, Greenville, 1984—. Dir., Emergency Med. Services Project Region II of N.C., 1975—; chmn. bd. trustees Emergency Medicine Found.; chmn. residency rev. com. emergency medicine Accreditation Council Grad. Med. Edn.; founder Western Piedmont Emergency Med. Services Council, 1973; mem. N.C. Emergency Med. Services Adv. Council, 1976-81; assoc. prof. clin. surgery Bowman Gray Sch. Medicine, Wake Forest U., Winston-Salem, 1979—. Bd. dirs. Piedmont Health Systems Agy., 1975-84; trustee Forsyth County Hosp., Authority, 1974-75; bd. dirs. N.C. Health Coordinating Council, 1975-82, Medic Alert Found. Internat. Fellow Internat. Coll. Surgeons, Internat. Coll. Angiology, Royal Soc. Health (Gt. Britain), Southeastern Surg. Congress; mem. Am. Coll. Emergency Physicians (charter; pres. 1978-79), AMA, (chmn. council of sect. emergency medicine 1982—), Am. Bd. Emergency Medicine (pres. 1976-81). Contbr. articles to profl. publs. on trauma, snake bite and history of medicine; editorial bd. Annals of Emergency Medicine, Med. Meetings. Office: 2115 Georgia Ave Winston-Salem NC 27104 also: One American Plaza Suite 805 Evanston IL 60201

POEGER, SUGIRI, pediatrician, educator; b. Indramayu, Indonesia, Jan. 17, 1911; m. Siti Zubaidah, Dec. 26, 1939; children: Ospari Amzafi, Sugiri Pradana, Uwati Sugiri. Grad., Faculty Geneeskunde Batavia, Jakarta, 1940; D of Specialization, Perguruan Tinggi Ketabiban, Jakarta, 1949. Resident pediatric dept. Faculty Medicine, Jakarta, 1940-41; gen. practitioner and head service Talang Padang Estate, Tanjung Karang, Lampung, South Sumatra, 1941-42; pres. dept. pediatrics Inst. Higher Edn., Jakarta, 1942-46; dir. Gen. Hosp., Purwakarta, West Java, Indonesia, 1946-50, Hasan Sadikin Hosp., Bandung, 1950-75; reader, chmn. dept. pediatrics Padjadjaran U., Bandung, 1960; dean Sch. Medicine Padjadjaran U., 1969-70, prof. pediatrics emeritus, 1976—, chmn. bd. med. curriculum, 1972-73; pvt. practice medicine specializing in pediatrics Bandung, 1950—; prof. pediatrics, chmn. dept. pediatrics Hassan Sadikin Gen. Hosp., Padjadjaran U., 1965-76; prof. Pediatrics postgrad. tng. in oral surgery, Padjadjaran U., 1972-74; invited participant Conf. on Med. Ethics and Doctors' Oaths Ministry of Health, Jakarta, 1969, Nat. Consultation of Med. Ethics, 1982; chmn. com. on accreditation Dept. Pediatrics, Faculties of Med., Sumatra Pediatric Tng. Ctr., 1973. Contbg. editor Pediatrica Indonesia, 1968-76; contbr. articles to profl. jours. Mem. Nat. Council on Tb, Ministry of Health, Jakarta, 1958; chief Indonesian del. WHO Seminar on Malnutrition, Hyderabad, India, 1963, invited speaker pediatric edn. Internat. Pediatric Assn., Mexico City, 1968; participant WHO Conf. on Pediatric and Ob. Edn., Jakarta, 1969, WHO Conf. on Family Planning and Nat. Devel., Internat. Planned Parenthood Fedn., Bandung, 1969; chmn. Com. Teaching Hosp., Bandung, 1970-75. Recipient Karyalancana Karya Satya award Pres. Republic Indonesia, 1978, numerous certs.of merit from nat. and regional med. orgns. Mem. Indonesian Med. Assn. (sr. disting. mem. 1984), Indonesian Pediatric Assn. (chmn. West Java chpt. 1968-76), Med. Assn. Bandung (chmn. com. med. ethics 1979-80), Indonesian Heart Found. (adv. bd. West Java chpt.). Home and Office: Naripan 53, Bandung, West Java 40112, Indonesia

POEHNER, GEORGE RICHARD, lawyer; b. Bakersfield, Calif., Oct. 11, 1938; s. George Edwin and Kathryn Elaine (Ray) P.; m. Charlotte Catherine Lindsay, Jan. 28, 1961; children—Laura Louise, Lisa Lynn. B.A., U. Calif.-Berkeley, 1965, J.D., 1968. Bar: D.C. 1969, U.S. Ct. Appeals (D.C. cir.) 1969, U.S. Ct. Appeals (5th and 9th cirs.) 1971, U.S. Ct. Appeals (4th and 10th cirs.) 1972, U.S. Supreme Ct. 1972, U.S. Ct. Appeals (2d cir.) 1974, Tex. 1976, U.S. Ct. Appeals (11th cir.) 1981. Assoc., Covington & Burling, Washington, 1968-75; ptnr. Coke & Coke, Dallas, 1976-82, Moore & Peterson, 1982—. Mem. ABA (antitrust, adminstrv. law, litigation sects.), State Bar Tex. (antitrust, litigation sects.), Dallas Bar Assn. (antitrust sect.), Am. Law Inst. Democrat. Roman Catholic. Home: 1132 Edith Circle Richardson TX 75080 Office: Moore & Peterson 2800 First City Center Dallas TX 75201

POFF, WILLIAM BEVERLY, lawyer; b. Montgomery County, Va., Aug. 23, 1932; s. John William and Pansy Louise (Booze) P.; m. Magdalen Andrews, Dec. 28, 1957. B.S., Va. Tech. U., 1952; LL.B., Washington and Lee U., 1955. Bar: Va. 1955, U.S. Supreme Ct. 1958. Assoc. Woods, Rogers, & Hazlegrove, Roanoke, Va., 1959-62, ptnr., 1963—; mem. adv. com. on rules of ct. Va. Supreme Ct., 1983—. Mem. Va. State Bd. Edn., 1971-76; chmn. Roanoke Valley Bicentennial Commn., 1973-77; state rep. Sister Cities Internat., 1973-80; pres. Roanoke Sister Cities, 1965-75. Served to 1st lt. JAGC, U.S. Army, 1956-59. Named Outstanding Young Man, Roanoke Jaycees, 1969; One of Five Outstanding Young Men, Va. Jaycees, 1969. Mem. Va. State Bar (pres. 1981-82, del. to ABA Ho. of Dels. 1984-87), Va. Trial Lawyers Assn. (pres. 1971-72), Va. Assn. Def. Attys. (v.p. 1975-79), Internat. Acad. Trial Lawyers, Am. Coll. Trial Lawyers, Internat. Soc. Barristers, ABA (bd. govs. 1987—), Internat. Assn. Ins. Counsel. Republican. Clubs: Bull and Bear (Richmond, Va.); Jefferson (Roanoke). Home: 2231 Woodcliff Rd SE Roanoke VA 24014 Office: 105 Franklin Rd SW PO Box 720 Roanoke VA 24004

POFFENBERGER, THOMAS, psychologist; b. Pitts., Aug. 9, 1921; s. Millard C. and Rebecca R. (Siviter) P.; B.A., Mich. State U., 1948, M.A., 1949, Ed.D. in Counseling Psychology, 1954; m. Shirley Briggs, Aug. 30, 1947; 1 child, Mark. Advanced fellow Merrill Palmer Inst., Detroit, 1949-50; asso. prof. and specialist family relations agrl. extension service Oreg. State U., Corvallis, 1951-53; asso. prof. family sociology U. Calif., Davis, 1953-61; vis. prof. child devel. U. Baroda, India, 1961-65; cons. family planning Ford Found., New Delhi, India, 1965-68; sr. specialist East-West Center, Honolulu, 1968-69; prof. edn. and population planning U. Mich. Sch. Public Health, Ann Arbor, 1969-84, prof. emeritus, 1984—, dir. program in population planning, 1977-79; pvt. practice (part-time) clin. psychology, Oreg., 1951-53, Calif., 1961-65. Served with USN, 1942-46. Cert. psychologist, Calif. Fellow AAAS, Am. Psychol. Assn., Soc. for Applied Anthropology. Contbr. articles on psychology and population to profl. jours. Home: 1206 Caribou Pl Davis CA 95616

POGU, MARC MARCEL, mathematics educator; b. Rennes, France, Dec. 2, 1946; s. Laurent and Aglaé (Hery) P.; m. Eliane Madeleine, Jan. 31, 1968; 1 child, Franck. Masters degree, U. Rennes, 1970, PhD, 1973, Doctorate, 1983. Technician Lab. Computation, Rennes, 1971; lectr. Nat. Inst. Applied Scis., Rennes, 1972-85; prof. Ecole Nationali Supeérieure de Méanique, Nantes, 1986—; mgr. young researchers U. Rennes Math. Lab., 1978-87. Author: Finite Element Programming, 1987; contbr. articles to profl. jours. Served to lt. French Arty., 1973-74. Recipient Testimony of Gratification, Gen. Officer HEIM, Rennes, 1979. Office: Ecole Nationale Suprérieure, de Mécanique, 1 Rue de la Noe, 44300 Nantes France

POGUE, FORREST CARLISLE, retired historian; b. Eddyville, Ky., Sept. 17, 1912; s. Forrest Carlisle and Frances (Carter) P.; m. Christine Brown, Sept. 4, 1954. AB, Murray (Ky.) State Coll., 1931, LLD, 1970; MA, U. Ky., 1932, LittD, 1983; PhD, Clark U., 1939, LHD, 1975; LittD, Washington and Lee U., 1970. Instr. history Western Ky. State Coll., 1933; from instr. to assoc. prof. Murray State Coll., 1933-42, prof., 1954-56; with Office Chief Mil. History, U.S. Dept. Army, 1946-52; ops. research analyst Johns Hopkins U., U.S. Army Hdqrs., Heidelberg, Fed. Republic of Germany, 1952-54; dir. George C. Marshall Research Ctr., Lexington, Va., 1956-64, George C. Marshall Research Library, Lexington, Va., 1964-74; exec. dir. George C. Marshall Research Found., Arlington, 1965-74; Harmon Meml. lectr. U.S. Air Acad., 1968; disting. Bicentennial lectr. U.S. Mil. Acad., 1974; disting. vis. prof. Va. Mil. Inst., 1972; professorial lectr. George Washington U.; past chmn. Am. Com. on History 2d World War; former mem. adv. groups U.S. Army, USAF and Navy Hist. Office; chmn. adv. com. Senate Hist. Office; mem. adv. bd. Former Mems. Congress, Ky. Bicentennial Oral History Commn.; mem. adv. com. on Eisenhower papers, Marine Hist. Found.; adj. fellow Woodrow Wilson Internat. Ctr. Scholars, 1974-77; mem. Hist. Found., Centennial Adv. Com. on the History of the Eisenhower Era; life trustee, mem. adv. com., bd. dirs. Dwight D. Eisenhower Inst. Hist. Research, Nat. Mus. Am. History, Smithsonian Inst., 1974-84; trustee Marine Corps Hist. Found. Author: The Supreme Command, 1954, George C. Marshall: Education of a General, Vol. 1, 1963, Ordeal and Hope, 1939-42, Vol. 2, 1966, Organizer of Victory, 1943-45, Vol. 3, 1973, Vol. 4, 1987, Statesman, 1945-59, (with others) The Meaning of Yalta, 1956; contbr. to books including Command Decisions, 1960, Total War and Cold War, 1962, D Day: The Normandy Invasion in Retrospect, 1970, America's Continuing Revolution, 1975, The War Lords, 1976, Bicentennial History of the United States, 1976; contbg. editor: Guide to American Foreign Relations Since 1700, 1983. Trustee Harry S. Truman Inst. of Truman Library; mem. adv. com. Nat. Hist. Soc. Served with U.S. Army, 1942-45, ETO. Decorated Bronz Star, Croix de Guerre, France; recipient Disting. Alumni Centennial award U. Ky., 1965, Samuel Eliot Morison award Am. Mil. Inst., 1988; U. Paris Inst. des Hautes Etudes Internationales Am. Exchange fellow, 1937-38. Fellow U.S. Army History Research Collection (hon., past adv. group), Am. Mil. Inst. (past pres.); mem. Oral History Assn. (past pres.), U.S. Commn. on Mil. History (trustee), Am. Hist. Assn., So. Hist. Assn., Orgn. Am. Historians, Soc. Am. Historians (Francis Parkoran medal 1988), NEA (life), English Speaking Union, Am. Legion, Murray State U. Alumni Assn. (past pres.). Democrat. Presbyterian. Club: Cosmos. Address: 1111 Army-Navy Dr Arlington VA 22202

POGUE, LLOYD WELCH, lawyer; b. Grant, Iowa, Oct. 21, 1899; s. Leander Welch and Myrtle Viola (Casey) P.; m. Mary Ellen Edgerton, Sept. 8, 1926; children: Richard Welch, William Lloyd, John Marshall. A.B., U. Nebr., 1924; LL.B., U. Mich., 1926; S.J.D., Harvard Law Sch., 1927. Bar: Mass., N.Y., D.C., Ohio, U.S. Supreme Ct. bars. Asso. Ropes, Gray, Boyden and Perkins, 1927-33; partner firm Searle, James and Crawford, N.Y.C., 1933-38; asst. gen. counsel CAA (now CAB), 1938-39, gen. counsel, through 1941, chmn. bd., 1942-46; mem. firm Jones, Day, Reavis & Pogue, Washington, to 1981. Mem. U.S. dels. Chgo. Internat. Civil Aviation Conf., 1944, Bermuda United Kingdom-U.S. Conf., 1946; vice-chmn. Interim Assembly PICAO, 1946; del. 1st Assembly ICAO, 1947. Served with AUS, 1918. Fellow Am. Helicopter Soc.; Benjamin Franklin fellow Royal Soc. Arts. Hon. mem. Nat. Inst. Aeronautic Scis.; mem. New Eng. Hist. Geneal. Soc. (trustee). Clubs: Metropolitan, University; Wings (N.Y.C.); Bohemian (San Francisco). Lodge: Masons. Home: 5204 Kenwood Ave Chevy Chase MD 20815 Office: Metropolitan Sq 655 15th St NW Washington DC 20005

POGUE, THOMAS FRANKLIN, economics educator, consultant; b. Roswell, N.Mex., Dec. 28, 1935; s. Talmadge Franklin and Lela (Cox) P.; m. Colette Marie LaFortune, June 3, 1961; children—Michael Frederick, Robert Franklin. B.S., N.Mex. State U., 1957; M.S., Okla. State U., 1962; Ph.D., Yale U., 1968. Asst. prof. econs. U. Iowa, Iowa City, 1965-69, assoc. prof., 1970-75, prof., 1975—, chmn. dept., 1983-84; vis. prof. Tex. Tech. U., Lubbock, 1975-76, U. Adelaide, Australia, 1985. Author: Government and Economic Choice, 1978. Contbr. articles to profl. jours. Author, researcher Gov.'s Tax Study, State of Iowa, Des Moines, 1967, Minn. Tax Study Commn., St. Paul, 1984, Iowa Econ. Devel. Policy Study, 1986-87, Iowa Econ. Devel. Plan, Des Moines, 1987. Served to capt. USAF, 1957-60. Grantee Nat. Inst. Justice, Washington, 1978-79, Consumers Research Group, Washington, 1970, HUD, 1970. Mem. Am. Econ. Assn., Nat. Tax Assn. Democrat. Presbyterian. Avocation: tennis. Home: 3 Wellesley Way Iowa City IA 52240 Office: U Iowa Phillips Hall Dept Econs Iowa City IA 52242

POHJOLAINEN, SEPPO ANTERO, technology educator; b. Helsinki, Finland, Jan. 27, 1948; s. Leevi and Eila Annikki (Kortelainen) P.; m. Eeva Kaisa Tuorila, Mar. 15, 1973; children: Veera, Jussi. MsC, Tampere (Finland) U. Tech., 1974, lic. tech., 1978, D in Tech., 1980. Asst. Tampere U. Tech., 1972-80, acting assoc. prof, 1986—; research fellow Acad. Finland, 1980-86. Contbr. articles to profl. jours. Mem. Soc. Indsl. and Applies Math., Am. Math. Soc., IEEE. Club: Hikiliikkujat (Tampere). Home: Nuolialantie 22, 33900 Tampere Finland Office: Tampere U Tech, PO Box 527, SF 33101 Tampere Finland

POHL, GAIL PIERCE, trade association executive, editor; b. Stigler, Okla., Nov. 18, 1938; s. William James and Kathleen Louise (McConnell) Pierce; m. Lee W. Pohl, July 7, 1962; 1 dau., Leslie Kathleen. B.A. in Journalism, U. Okla., 1960. Statehouse reporter Okla. Bus. News, Oklahoma City, 1960-66, news editor, 1966-72; editor Jour. Am. Ins., Chgo., 1973-77; pub. relations assoc. Alliance of Am. Insurers, Chgo., 1972, dir. publs., 1977-78, dir. policy communications, 1978-79; exec. dir. Self-Service Storage Assn., Eureka Springs, Ark., 1981—. Contbr. articles and news stories to various publs. Pres., Parent's Orgn., 1st Montessori Sch. Atlanta, 1980-81, trustee, 1980-81. Recipient 1st place award for Jour. Am. Ins. mag. Nat. Mut. Ins. Communicators, 1977, Mag. Honor award, 1978; 1st prize for news story Chgo. Assn. Bus. Communicators, 1978, honor award for feature article, 1978. Mem. Chgo. Ins. Women (bd. dirs. 1978-79), Women in Communications, Inc., Bus. and Profl. Women (pres. 1985—), bd. dirs. Eureka Springs chpt.), Am. Soc. Assn. Execs. Clubs: Beaver Lake Sailing (Ark.). Home: 270 Spring St Eureka Springs AR 72632 Office: Self-Service Storage Assn PO Box 110 16 First St Eureka Springs AR 72632

PÖHL, KARL OTTO, banker; b. Hannover, Germany, Dec. 1, 1929; m. Ulrike Pesch; 4 children: student U. Gottingen, 1952-55; hon. degrees Ruhr U., Tel-Aviv U., Georgetown U., Md. U.; m. Ulrike Pesch; 4 children. Div. chief, Ifo, Inst. Econ. Research, Munich, Germany, 1955-60; econ. journalist, Bonn, 1961-67; mem. bd. Fed. Assn. German Banks, Cologne, 1968-70; div. chief Fed. Ministry Econs., Bonn, 1970-71; dept. chief Fed. Chancellery, 1971-72; state sec. Fed. Ministry Finance, 1972-77; deputy gov. Deutsche Bundesbank, Frankfurt, 1977-79, pres., chmn. central bank council, 1980—; chmn. Group of 10, central bank govs., 1980—. Decorated Grosses Verdienstkreuz mit Stern und Schulterband des Verdienstordens der Bundesrepublik Deutschland. Office: Deutsche Bundesbank, 14 Wilhelm Epstein Strasse, 6000 Frankfurt Federal Republic of Germany

POHLE, KLAUS, manufacturing company executive; b. Potsdam, Fed. Republic Germany, Nov. 3, 1937; s. Walter H. O. and Alice E. (Lingenberg) P.; m. Carmen Mendez Alvarado, Dec. 8, 1964; children: Veronica, Alexandra, Johannes. LLB, U. Munich, 1960; LLM, Harvard U., 1963; JD, U. Frankfurt, Fed. Republic Germany, 1966. Various positions BASF Group, U.S., Spain and Brazil, 1966-75; group treas. BASF, Ludwigshafen, Fed. Republic Germany, 1975-80; exec. mng. dir. Schering, Berlin, Fed. Republic Germany, 1981—; prof. bus. adminstrn. Tech. U., Berlin, 1986—. Vice chmn. Friends Berlin Opera, 1982; bd. dirs. Friends Berlin Tech. U., 1986. Lodge: Rotary. Home: Menzelstr 15, D1000 Berlin 33 Federal Republic of Germany Office: Schering AG, Muellerstr 170-178, D1000 Berlin 65 Federal Republic of Germany

POHOLE, FRANK ANTHONY, artist; b. Trieste, Italy, Sept. 8, 1920; came to U.S., 1962, naturalized, 1967; s. Franc Florian and Amalija Polonia (Makovec) P.; student Trappist Monastery Sem., Banja Luka, Yugoslavia, 1934-37, Comml. U. Ljubljana, 1937-40, Ljubljana U., 1940-41; degree in scis., U. Buenos Aires, 1962; m. Maria Filippa Falchi, Nov. 11, 1947; 1 son, Francisco Mario. Painter; one man shows include: Asociacion Estimulo de Bellas Artes, Buenos Aires, 1954-62, Galeria Libertad, Buenos Aires, 1953-62, Galeria Renoir, Buenos Aires, 1953-62, Minerva Art Gallery, N.Y.C., 1977-79; exhibited in group shows Ligoa Duncan Gallery, N.Y.C., 1977-79, Bklyn. Mus. Community Gallery, 1978, N.Y. Artists Equity Assn., 1979, Bklyn. Coll. Alumni Assn., 1980. Served with AUS, 1943-46. Recipient various awards for painting. Mem. N.Y./Artists Equity Assn., Inc., Internat. Soc. Artists, Soc. N.Am. Artists, World Art Services, AAAS, Am. Mus. Natural History Assocs., Smithsonian Assocs., Inter-Am. Soc., Internat. Platform Assn., Ctr. for Inter-Am. Relations, N.Y. Acad. Scis. Roman Catholic. Home: 753 39th St Brooklyn NY 11232

POIDEVIN, RAYMOND, history educator; b. Bennwihr, France, June 8, 1928; s. Edmond Poidevin and Marie Wagner; children: Anne-Marie, Elisabeth. Degree in superior studies, Sorbonne Université, Paris, 1951; doctorat ès lettres. Tchr. Lycée Fromentin, La Rochelle, France, 1954-57, Lycée Bartholdi, Colmar, France, 1957-61; chercheur Ctr. Nat. Recherche Sci., Paris, 1961-64; assistant Strasbourg (France) U., 1964-67; prof. history Metz Université, 1967-80; doyen Faculté des Lettres, Metz, 1968-70; dir. Ctr. Relations Internat., Metz, 1971-80, Strasbourg, 1980—, Centre d'Études Germaniques, Strasbourg, 1986—. Author: Les Relations Économiques entre la France et l'Allemagne 1898-1914, 1969 (Prix Strasbourg 1970, Prix Académie Science Morales et Politiques 1970), L'Allemagne de Guillaume II à Hindenbourg 1900-1933, 1972, L'Allemagne et le Monde au XX Siècle, 1983, Robert Schuman, Homme d'État, 1986; co-author: Les Relations Franco-Allemandes 1815-1975, 1977; editor: Histoire des Débuts de la Construction Européenne 1948-1950, 1986. Named chevalier Ordre National du Mérite, France, 1976; officier Palmes Académiques, France, 1985; recipient I Klasse Bundesverdientstkreuz Bundesrepublik Deutschland, 1980. Mem. Inst. Histoire des Relations Internat., Groupe de Liaison des Historiens, Commn. Archives Diplomatiques, Com. Français des Scis.Historiques, Revue D'Allemagne (dir. 1986—). Office: Institut Hautes Etudes Europeennes, Rue des Ecrivains N 8, 67081 Strasbourg France

POINDEXTER, JOHN BRUCE, venture capitalist; b. Houston, Oct. 7, 1944; s. George Emerson and Rose Ellen (McDowell) P.; B.S.B.A. with honors, U. Ark., 1966; M.B.A., N.Y. U., 1971, Ph.D. in Econs. and Fin., 1976. Assoc., Salomon Bros., N.Y.C., 1971-72; v.p. Lombard, Nelson & McKenna, N.Y.C., 1972-76; v.p., registered prin. Dominick & Dominick, Inc., N.Y.C., 1973-76; sr. v.p. Smith Barney Venture Corp., N.Y.C., 1976-83; gen. partner First Century Partnership, N.Y.C., 1980-83; mng. partner KD/P Equities, ptnr. Kellner, DiLeo & Co., N.Y.C., 1983-85; mng. ptnr., J.B. Poindexter and Co., 1985—; chmn. bd. dirs. Carolina Steel Corp., EFP Corp., Nat. Steel Service Ctr., Leer, Inc.; adj. assoc. prof. L.I. U. Served to capt. U.S. Army, 1966-70; Vietnam. Decorated Silver Star, Bronze Star (2), Purple Heart (2), Air medal, others. Mem. Beta Gamma Sigma, Alpha Kappa Psi. Club: Metropolitan. Home: 1111 Hermann Dr Houston TX 77004 also: 1100 Lousiana Houston TX 77002

POINDEXTER, VERNON STEPHENSON, artist, illustrator; b. Roanoke, Va., Nov. 28, 1918; s. Henry Nelson and Lillian (Staples) P.; m. Ollie Henry Poindexter, Sept. 13, 1947. Student Va. State Coll., 1938, Art Students League N.Y., 1945-48. Advt. specialist Gen. Electric Co., Washington, 1956-78; court room sketch artist Jet Mag., 1978; sketch artist Metromedia News Chanel 5 TV, Washington, 1981; free lance illustrator, N.Y., 1948—, Infantry Jour. mag., Washington, 1950-52, Combat Forces mag., Washington, 1950-52. Exhibited in group shows Library of Congress, 1946, Brookland Mus., 1947, ACA Gallery, N.Y.C., 1947, Phila. Print Club, 1947, Met. Mus., 1953; represented in permanent collection Howard U. Scoutmaster Nat. Capitol council Boy Scouts Am., 1952-58; past adjutant Am. Legion, Washington, 1953-85; trustee Lincoln Temple Congl. Ch., Washington, 1972-78. Served with U.S. Army, 1942-45. Recipient numerous awards Gen. Electric Co., 1956-78, Outstanding Service award Lincoln Temple United Ch. of Christ, Washington, 1981, Meritorious Service award Am. Legion, 1954, Lincoln Douglas Humanities award N.Am. Theatre Group, 1984, Internat. Cultural diploma of honor, 1987, Medal of Honor Am. Biog. Inst., 1987. Mem. Nat. Trust for Hist. Preservation, Confederation of Chivalry (commdr.), NRA, Smithsonian Instn., Internat. Platform Assn. Democrat. Club: Braxton Village Mens. Lodge: Masons. Avocations: fishing; hunting; swimming; painting. Home: 1826 Porter Ave Suitland MD 20746

POINSETTE, DONALD EUGENE, business executive, value management consultant; b. Fort Wayne, Ind., Aug. 17, 1914; s. Eugene Joseph and Julia Anna (Wyss) P.; student Purdue U., 1934, Ind. U., 1935-37, 64; m. Anne Katherine Farrell, Apr. 15, 1939; children—Donald J., Eugene J., Leo J., Sharon Poinsette Smith, Irene Poinsette Snyder, Cynthia Poinsette West, Maryanne Poinsette Stohler, Philip J. With Gen. Electric Corp., RCA, Stewart Warner Corp., 1937-39; metall. research and field sales cons. P.R. Mallory Corp., 1939-49; dist. sales mgr. Derringer Metall. Corp., Chgo., 1949-50; plant engr. Cornell-Dubilier Electric Corp., Indpls., 1950-53; with Jenn-Air Corp., Indpls., 1953-74, purchasing dir., 1953-71, mgr. value engring. and quality control, 1969-74; bus. mgmt. cons. Mays and Assocs., Indpls., 1974-76; Recipient Testimonial Golden Anniversary award Purdue U., 1987; named to U.S. Finder's List, Nat. Engrs. Register, 1956. Pres., Marian Coll. Parents Club, Indpls., 1969-70; com. mem. Boy Scouts Am. Nat trustee Xavier U., 1972-73, Dad's Club, Cin. Mem. Nat. Assn. Purchasing Mgmt., Indpls. Purchasing Mgmt. Assn., Soc. Am. Value Engrs. (certified value specialist; sec.-treas. Central Ind. chpt. 1972-73), Soc. Ret. Execs. Indpls., Ind. U., Purdue U. alumni assns., Columbian (pres. 1972-73), Triad choral groups, Internat. Platform Assn., Tau Kappa Epsilon. Club: K.C. (4 deg.). Home: 5760 Susan Dr E Indianapolis IN 46250

POIS, JOSEPH, lawyer, educator; b. N.Y.C., Dec. 25, 1905; s. Adolph and Augusta (Lesser) P.; m. Rose Tomarkin, June 24, 1928 (dec. May 1981); children: Richard Adolph (dec.), Robert August, Marc Howard.; m. Ruth Livingston, Nov. 27, 1983 (div. 1984). A.B., U. Wis., 1926; M.A., U. Chgo., 1927, Ph.D., 1929; J.D., Chgo.-Kent Coll. Law, 1934. Bar: Ill. 1934, Pa. 1978. Staff mem. J.L. Jacobs & Co., Chgo., 1929-35; jr. partner J.L. Jacobs & Co., 1946-47; gen. field supr. Pub. Adminstrn. Service, Chgo., 1935-38; chief adminstrv. studies sect. U.S. Bur. Old Age and Survivors Ins., 1938-39; chief adminstrv. and fiscal reorgn. sect. U.S. Bur. Budget Exec. Office of Pres., 1939-42; dir. finance State of Ill., 1951-53; counsel, asst. to pres., v.p., treas., dir. Signode Corp., 1947-61; prof. U. Pitts., 1961-76, emeritus, 1976—, chmn. dept. pub. adminstrn., 1961-71, asso. dean, 1973-75; dir. Vision Service Plan of Pa., 1984-85; cons. ECA, 1948, Dept. State, 1949, 62-65, U.S. Dept. Def., 1954, Brookings Instn., 1962-63, AID, 1965, Indian Inst. Pub. Adminstrn., 1972, Commn. on Operation Senate, 1976, Pitts. Citizens' Task Force on Refuse Disposal, 1976-78; mem. cons. panel Comptroller Gen. of U.S., 1967-75. Author: The School Board Crisis: a Chicago Case Study, 1964, Financial Administration in the Michigan State Government, 1938, Kentucky Handbook of Financial Administration, 1937, Public Personnel Administration in the City of Cincinnati, 1936, (with Edward M. Martin and Lyman S. Moore) The Merit System in Illinois, 1935, Watchdog on the Potomac, 1979; contbg. author: the New Political Economy, 1975, Eric Louis Kohler, Accounting's Man of Principles, 1979, State Audit-Developments in Public Accountability, 1981; contbr. articles to profl. jours. Mem. Chgo. Bd. Edn., 1956-61; pres. Chgo. Met. Housing and Planning Council, 1956-57, Immigrants Service League, Chgo., 1960-61; dir. Pitts. Council Pub. Edn., 1965-67; mem. citizens bd. U. Chgo., 1958-78; mem. Pitts. Bd. Pub. Edn., 1973-76; bd. dirs. Pitts. Center for Arts, 1977-85, World Federalist Assn. Pitts., 1984—, Pitts. dist. Zionist Orgn. Am., 1979-81, mem. Hunger Action Coalition, Pitts., 1985-86 ; mem. Allegheny County Bd. Assistance, chmn. 1981-87. Served from comdr. to capt. USCGR, 1942-46. Decorated Navy Commendation medal; recipient alumni citation for pub. service U. Chgo., 1960; award for pub. service U.S. Gen. Accounting Office, 1971. Mem. Am. Acad. Polit. and Social Sci., Am. Accounting Assn., Am., Chgo., Fed., Pa., Allegheny County bar assns., Am. Polit. Sci. Assn., Am. Soc. Pub. Adminstrn.(award for pub. service Pitts. Area chpt., 1985), Center Study Presidency, Govt. Fin. Officers Assn. (bd. govs. Western Pa. chpt.), Fin. Execs. Inst., Nat. Assn. Accountants, Royal Inst. Pub. Adminstrn. (Britain), Phi Beta Kappa, Pi Lambda Phi, Phi Delta Phi. Clubs: Army and Navy (Washington); U. Chgo. Alumni (Pitts.) (pres. 1981-84). Home: 825 Morewood Ave Pittsburgh PA 15213

POITOUT, DOMINIQUE GILBERT M., orthopedic surgeon, educator; b. Paris, Dec. 1, 1946; s. Pierre Augustin M. and Helene Marie J. (Baudrais) P.; m. Anne Marie S. Gros, Apr. 4, 1972; children: Pierre-Brice R., Jean-Roch D., Marie-Elodie A. D Medicine, U. Paris, 1973; M Human Biology, U. Marseille, 1976. Extern hosp. Paris, 1967-70; intern hosp. Marseille, France, 1971-76; asst. in anatomy 1973-76, chief of clinic, 1976-82; prof. orthopedic surgery U. Hosp. Ctr., 1982—, chief of service, 1986—; dir. diploma program orthopedic biomechanics, 1984—, Nat. Diploma d'Etudes Approfondies de Scis. Chirrurgicales, 1986—; organizer confs. Author: Locomotor System Allografts, 1986, Orthopedic Biomechanic, 1987; contbr. articles, papers to numerous profl. jours. Councillor of the Townhall of Marseille, 1983; v.p. of the commn. of Social Action of the Townhall of Marseille, 1983; pres. Perspectives for Health Futures in France, 1984; mem. Council for France Future, Paris, 1985. Recipient High French Com. for Civil Def., 1985. Mem. European Soc. Biomechanics, European Soc. Biomaterials, French Soc. Orthopedic Surgery, French Coll. Orthopedic Sugeons, Inter. Soc. Orthopedic Surgery. Roman Catholic. Club: Chevalier du Tastevin. Lodge: Lions. Home: 122 Rue du Cdt Rolland Le Valencay, 13008 Marseilles France Office: Centre Hosp U, Nord Chemin des Bourrely, 13015 Marseilles France

POKA, GABOR, architect; b. Mainburg, Bavaria, Germany, Mar. 3, 1945; came to Paraguay, 1949; s. Kalman Eduardo and Piroska (Szabo) P.; m. Ana Maria Gaona, Apr. 30, 1970; children—Gabor Martin, Gisela Maria, Geza Matyas. Student Horticulture Soc. Paraguay, 1968, U. Arch., Asuncion, 1969, U. Engring. Asuncion, 1969, Inst. Tech., Asuncion, 1981. Registered architect, Paraguay, 1970. Designer, Estudio Poka, Asuncion, 1967-69, mgr. constrn., 1969-71, mng. dir., 1971—; mgr., dir. Master SRL Constrn. Co., Asuncion, 1978—; dir., Solar Savs. bank, Asuncion, Fenix Ins. Co., Asuncion. Pres., Program Christian Solidarity, disaster resettlements, 1983-84. Mem. Constrn. Chamber Asuncion (v.p. 1975-77), Paraguayan Assn. Architects (treas. 1976-78), Bldg. Soc. Asuncion. Roman Catholic. Clubs: Centenario (Ascuncion); Nautico (San Bernardino). Lodge: Apadem. Avocations: swimming; football. Home: Sargneto Gauto 736, Asuncion Paraguay Office: Estudio Poka, Ayala Velaquez 660, Asuncion Paraguay

POKHREL, GOKUL PRASAD, journalist, media consultant; b. Dhankuta, Kosi, Nepal, Dec. 15, 1937; s. Chhabi Lal and Balmaya P.; m. Ranjana Pokhrel, Dec. 4, 1965; children: Suzanne, Roshan, Anup. BA, Patna U., India, 1958; MA in English, Tribhuwan U., Kathmandu, Nepal, 1960, BL, 1962; cert. in journalism, Editorial Studies Ctr., Cardiff, Eng.; cert., U. Strausburg, France. Sr. tchr. Dhankuta (Nepal) High Sch., 1956-58; dep. editor RSS Nat. News Agy., Kathmandu, 1962, chief editor, 1963-65; assoc. editor The Rising Nepal newspaper, Kathmandu, 1966-71; features editor Gorkhapatra Daily newspaper, Kathmandu, 1971-80, chief editor, 1980-84, cons. editor, 1984—. Author: Search for Peace, 1981; researcher (report) Working Conditions of Nepalese Journalists, 1986. Mem. Nepal Press Inst. (founder, sec. 1984); Nepal Sci. Writers Assn. (convenor, founder 1987), Royal Nepal Acad. Sci. and Tech. (bd. dirs. 1985—). Home: GA 2, 264, Battisputali, Kathmandu 1, Nepal Office: Gorkhapatra, Dharma Path, Kathmandu Nepal

POKOTILOW, MANNY D., lawyer; b. Paterson, N.J., June 26, 1938; s. Samuel Morris and Ruth (Fuchs) P.; children by previous marriage: Mali,

Mona, Charyse, Andrew. BEE, Newark Coll. Engring., 1960; LLB, Am. U., 1964. Bar: Pa. Examiner U.S. Patent Office, Washington, 1960-64; ptnr. Caesar, Rivise, Bernstein, Cohen & Pokotilow Ltd., Phila., 1965—; lectr., expert witness on protection of computer software, patents, trademarks, trade secrets and copyrights; faculty Temple U. Sch. Law, 1985—. Vol. Support Ctr. for Child Advocates, Phila., 1979—; dir., organizer Phila. Bar-Diabetes 10k Race, Phila., 1980—, Packard Press Road Run Grand Prix, 1986. Recipient Superior Performance award U.S. Patent Office, 1964. Mem. ABA (chmn. proprietary rights in software com.), Assn. Trial Lawyers Am., Phila. Bar Assn. (bd. govs. 1982-84, chmn. sports and recreation com. 1977—), Phila. Patent Law Assn. (bd. govs. 1982-84, chmn. fed. practice and procedure com. 1983—), Phila. Trial Lawyers (chmn. fed. cts. com. 1986—), Lawyers Club Phila. (bd. govs. 1984—), IEEE, Pa. Trial Lawyers, Tau Epsilon Rho (vice chancellor Phila. grad. chpt. 1986-88, chancellor 1988—). Office: Caesar Rivise Bernstein et al 21 S 12th St Philadelphia PA 19107

POLAN, NANCY MOORE, artist; b. Newark, Ohio; d. William Tracy and Francis (Flesher) Moore; A.B., Marshall U., 1936; m. Lincoln Milton Polan, Mar. 28, 1934; children—Charles Edwin, William Joseph Marion. One-man shows Charleston Art Gallery, 1961, 67, 73, Greenbrier, 1963, Huntington Galleries, 1963, 66, 71, N.Y. World's Fair, 1965, W.Va. U., 1966, Carroll Reese Mus., 1967; exhibited in group shows Am. Watercolor Soc., Allied Artists of Am., Nat. Arts Club, 1968-74, 76-77, 86, 87, Pa. Acad. Fine Arts, Opening of Creative Arts Center W.Va. U., 1969, Internat. Platform Assn. Art Exhibit, 1968-69, 72, 73, 74, 79, 85, 86. Allied Artists W.Va., 1968-69, 86, Joan Miro Graphic Exhbn., Barcelona, Spain, 1970, XXI Exhibit Contemporary Art, La Scala, Florence, Italy, 1971, Rassegna Internazionale d'Arte Grafica, Siena, Italy, 1973, 79, 82, Opening of Parkersburg (W.Va.) Art Center, 1975, Internat. Platform Assn. Ann. Exhbn., 1979, others. Hon. v.p. Centro Studi e Scambi Internazionale, Rome, Italy, 1977; life mem. Huntington (W.Va.) Mus. Art. Recipient Acad. of Italy with Gold medal, 1979; recipient Norton Meml. award 3d Nat. Jury Show Am. Art, Chautauqua, N.Y., 1960; Purchase prize, Jurors award, Watercolor award Huntington Galleries, 1960, 61; Nat. Arts Club for watercolor, 1969; Gold medal Masters of Modern Art exhbn., La Scala Gallery, Florence, 1975, gold medal Accademia Italia, 1984, 1986, diploma Internat. Com. for World Culture and Arts, 1987, many others. Mem. DAR, Allied Artists W.Va., Internat. Platform Assn. (3d award-painting in ann. art exhbn. 1977), Allied Artists Am. (asso.), Huntington Mus. Fine Arts, Tri-State Arts Assn. (Equal Merit award 1978), Sunrise Found., Pen and Brush (Grumbacher golden palette mem.; Grumbacher award 1978), Am. Watercolor Soc. (asso.), Am. Fedn. Arts, Nat. Arts Club, Leonardo da Vinci Acad. (Rome), Accademia Italia, Sigma Kappa. Episcopalian. Clubs: Vero Beach Arts (Fla.), Riomar Bay Yacht; Guyan Golf and Country (Huntington). Address: 2 Prospect Dr Huntington WV 25701 Other: 2106 Club Dr Vero Beach FL 32963

POLANIS, MARK FLORIAN, banker; b. Milw., Jan. 11, 1944; s. Henry Anthony and Adele Rose (Czarnecki) P.; m. Gloria Jean Grebe, Feb. 16, 1963; children: Laura J., James A., Henry C., Julie D., Rex A. BS in Acctg., Marquette U., 1965, MA in Econs., 1973. CPA, Wis., Ill.; chartered bank auditor. Audit mgr. 1st Wis. Bankshares, Milw., 1965-69; sr. corp. auditor Montgomery Ward, Inc., Chgo., 1969-72; gen. auditor Lake View Trust & Savs. Bank, Chgo., 1972-76; v.p., dir. Bank Adminstrn. Inst., Rolling Meadows, Ill., 1976-81; sr. v.p. audit Pan Am. Banks, Inc., Miami, Fla., 1981-85; sr. v.p., audit dir. NCNB Corp., Charlotte, N.C., 1986—; mem. cons. bd. bank publs. Am. Acctg. Assn., 1981-88. Author: Audit Organization and Practice in Banks Over $50 Million, 1977, (with others) Statement of Principles and Standards for Internal Auditing in the Banking Industry, Internal Auditing in the Banking Industry, 3 vols., 1977; editor books in field. Mem. Am. Inst. CPAs (task force on EDP fraud 1979-81), Bank Adminstrn. Inst. (task force on audit standards 1976-77), Inst. Internal Auditors, Beta Alpha Psi, Beta Gamma Sigma. Republican. Roman Catholic. Office: NCNB Corp One NCNB Plaza T05-1 Charlotte NC 28255

POLANSKI, KAZIMIERZ CZESLAW, linguist, educator; b. Brzozdowce, Poland, Apr. 6, 1929; s. Julian and Emilia (Sliwak) P.; m. Maria Tokarz, 1956; children: Jaroslaw, Andrzej. MA, Yaguellonian U., Poland, 1955; PhD, Yaguellonian U., 1961, D Habil., 1967. Asst. Polish Acad. Scis., Krakow, 1956-58, adj., 1958-67; docent U. Poznan, Poland, 1967-73; prof. linguistics U. Silesia, Katowice, Poland, 1973—; vis. prof. Yale U., New Haven, 1969-70, 80, 86. Editor in chief Bull. de la Soc. Polonaise de Linguistique, 1986—. Mem. Polish Linguistic Soc., Polish Linguistic Com. Home: Sikorek 7, 40-537 Katowice Poland Office: U Silesia, ul Bando 10, 41-200 Sosnowiec Poland

POLANSKI, ROMAN, film director, writer, actor; b. Paris, Aug. 18, 1933; s. Ryszard and Bule (Katz-Przedborska) P.; m. Barbara Lass (div.); m. Sharon Tate (dec.). Ed., Art Sch., Cracow, State Film Coll., Lodz. Appeared in children's radio show The Merry Gang, stage prodn. Son of the Regiment; dir. films Two Men and a Wardrobe, 1958, When Angels Fall, 1958, Le Gros et le Maigre, 1960, Knife in the Water, 1962 (Venice Film Festival award), The Mammals, 1963 (Tours Film Festival award), Repulsion, 1965 (Berlin Film Festival award), Cul-de-Sac, 1966 (Berlin Film Festival award), The Vampire Killers, 1967, Rosemary's Baby, 1968, Macbeth, 1971, What?, 1972, Chinatown, 1974 (Best dir. award, Soc. Film and TV Arts, Prix Raoul-Levy, 1975), The Tenant, 1976, Tess, 1980, Pirates, 1986, Frantic (also co-writer), 1988; actor: on stage The Metamorphosis, 1988; in films A Generation, The End of the Night, See You Tomorrow, The Innocent Sorcerers, Two Men and a Wardrobe, The Vampire Killers, What?, Chinatown, The Tennant, Pirate; star, dir.: play Amadeus, Warsaw, 1981; dir. operas Lulu (Spoleto Festival), 1974, Rigoletto, 1976; author (autobiography): Roman, 1984. Address: care Bureau Georges Beaume, 3 quai Malaquais, 75006 Paris France also: care Carlin Levy & Co 265 N Robertson Blvd Beverly Hills CA 90211 *

POLANSKY, SOL, diplomat; b. Newark, Nov. 7, 1926; married; 1 child. BA, U. Calif., Berkeley, 1950; postgrad., Columbia U., 1950-52, Fgn. Service Inst., 1958-59, Nat. War Coll., 1972-73. Translator Am. Embassy, Moscow, 1952, asst. agrl. attaché, 1952-55, chief external affairs, 1966-71; dep. prin. officer U.S. Consulate, Poland, 1960-62; multi lateral affairs officer Soviet Desk of State Dept., Washington, 1962-66; dep. chief Office Cultural Presentations, Washington, 1971-72; dep. dir. exchanges Soviet Desk of State Dept., Washington, 1973-76; dep. chief mission East Berlin, 1976-79; dep. chief mission Am. Embassy, Vienna, Austria, 1979-81, interin chargé d'affaires, 1981-83; vice chmn. Strategic Arms Reduction Talks Del., Washington, 1983-85; dep. chmn. U.S. Del. Conf. on Security and Cooperation in Europe, Washington, 1985-86; ambassador to Bulgaria Washington, 1987—. Office: US Ambassador to Bulgaria care Dept of State Washington DC 20520 *

POLANYI, JOHN CHARLES, chemist, educator; b. Jan. 23, 1929; m. Anne Ferrar Davidson, 1958; 2 children. B.Sc., Manchester (Eng.) U., 1949, M.Sc., 1950, Ph.D., 1952, D.Sc., 1964; D.Sc. (hon.), U. Waterloo, 1970, Meml. U., 1976, McMaster U., 1977, Carleton U., 1981, Harvard U., 1982, Rensselaer U., 1984, Brock U., 1984, Lethbridge U., 1987, Victoria U., 1987, Ottawa U., 1987, Sherbrooke U., 1987, Laval U., 1987; LLD (hon.), Trent U., 1977, Dalhousie U., 1983, St. Francis-Xavier U., 1987. Mem. faculty dept. chemistry U. Toronto, Ont., Can., 1956—; prof. U. Toronto, 1962—, Univ. prof., from 1974; William D. Harkins lectr. U. Chgo., 1970; Reilly lectr. U. Notre Dame, 1970; Purves lectr. McGill U., 1971; F.J. Toole lectr. U. N.B., 1974; Philips lectr. Haverford Coll., 1974; Kistiakowsky lectr. Harvard U., 1975; Camille and Henry Dreyfus lectr. U. Kans., 1975; J.W.T. Spinks lectr. U. Sask., Can., 1976; Laird lectr. U. Western Ont., 1976; CIL Disting. lectr. Simon Fraser U., 1977; Gucker lectr. Ind. U., 1977; Jacob Bronowski meml. lectr. U. Toronto, 1978; Hutchinson lectr. U. Rochester, N.Y., 1979; Priestley lectr. Pa. State U., 1980; Barré lectr. U. Montreal, 1982; Sherman Fairchild disting. scholar Calif. Inst. Tech., 1982; Chute lectr. Dalhousie U., 1983, Redman lectr. McMaster U., 1983, Wiegand lectr. U. Toronto, 1984, Edward U. Condon lectr. U. Colo., 1984, John A. Allan lectr. U. Alta., 1984, John E. Willard lectr. U. Wis., 1984, Owen Holmes lectr. U. Lethbridge, 1985, Walker-Ames prof. U. Wash., 1986, John W. Cowper disting. vis. lectr. U. Buffalo, SUNY, 1986, vis. prof. chemistry Tex. A&M U., 1986, Disting. Vis. speaker U. Calgary, 1987, Morino lectr. U. Japan, 1987, J.T. Wilson lectr. Ontario Sci. Ctr., 1987, Welsh lectr. U. Toronto, 1987, Spiers Meml. lectr. Faraday div. Royal Soc. Chemistry, 1987, Polanyi lectr. Internat. Union Pure & Applied Chemistry, 1988. Co-editor: (with F.G. Griffiths) The Dangers of Nuclear War, 1979; contbr. articles to jours., mags., newspapers; producer: film Concepts in Reaction Dynamics, 1970. Decorated officer Order of Can., companion Order of Can.; recipient Marlow medal Faraday Soc., 1962; Centenary medal Chem. Soc. Gt. Brit., 1965; with N. Bartlett Steacie prize, 1965; Mack award and lectureship Ohio State U., 1969; Noranda award Chem. Inst. Can., 1967; award Brit. Chem. Soc., 1971; Mack award and lectureship Ohio State U., 1969; medal Chem. Inst. Can., 1976; Henry Marshall Tory medal Royal Soc. Can., 1977; Nobel Prize in chemistry, 1986; Sloan Found. fellow, 1959-63; Guggenheim fellow, 1979-80; Remsen award and lectureship Am. Chem. Soc., 1978. Mem. Nat. Acad. Scis. U.S. (fgn.), Am. Acad. Arts and Sci.(hon. fgn.), Sci. Adv. Bd. Max Plank Inst. for Quantum Optics, German, Pontifical Acad. Scis., Rome, Nat. Adv. Bd. on Sci. and Tech., Can. Pugwash Com. (founding mem.), Can. Com. Scis. and Scholars (founding mem.), Royal Soc. Can. Com. on Scholarly Freedom (founding mem.), Am. Acad. Arts Scis. Com. on Internat. Security Studies, Can. Ctr. for Arms Control and Disarmament (bd. dirs.); fellow Royal Soc. Can., Royal Soc. London; companion of the Order of Can. Office: U Toronto Dept of Chemistry, 80 St George St, Toronto, ON Canada M5S 1A1 *

POLAREK, LOUISE, nurse; b. Chgo., July 19, 1927; d. Ernest William and Jonnie May (Hall) Bremer; m. Daniel Richard Hopkins, June 9, 1945 (div. 1965); children—Patricia Lynn, Daniel Mark; m. Robert Stanley Polarek, Aug. 6, 1966. Student portrait coloring, Chgo. Sch. Photography, 1946; student Selan's Beauty Sch., Chgo., 1971; diploma Chgo. Bd. Edn., 1981; diploma in Nursing, Triton Coll., 1981. Med. receptionist Rush Presbyn. St. Lukes Hosp., Chgo., 1964-66; med. sec. K.D. Kittleson, Chgo., 1971-73, Frederick J. Szymanski, Chgo., 1966-70, 1973-79; nurse MacNeal Meml. Hosp., Berwyn, Ill., 1981-82; charge nurse Pine Manor Nursing Center, Palos Hills, Ill., 1982-85; nurse West Side VA Hosp., Chgo., 1985-87, Jerry L. Pettis Meml. VA Hosp., Loma Linda, Calif., 1987—. Recipient Scholastic Honor award Chgo. Bd. Edn., 1981. Home: 10850 Miami Bloomington CA 92316

POLASCIK, MARY ANN, ophthalmologist; b. Elkhorn, W.Va., Dec. 28, 1940; d. Michael and Elizabeth (Halko) Polascik; B.A., Rutgers U., 1967; M.D., Pritzker Sch. Medicine, 1971; m. Joseph Elie, Oct. 2, 1973; 1 dau., Laura Elizabeth Polascik. Jr. pharmacologist Ciba Pharm. Co., Summit, N.J., 1961-67; intern Billings Hosp., Chgo., 1971-72; resident in ophthalmology U. Chgo. Hosp., 1972-75; practice medicine specializing in ophthalmology, Dixon, Ill., 1975—; pres. McNichols Clinic, Ltd.; cons. ophthalmology, Dixon Devel. Ctr.; mem. staff Katherine Shaw Bethea Hosp., Dixon, Dixon Developmental Ctr. Hosp. Bd. dirs. Sinissippi Mental Health Ctr., 1978-82; bd. med. dirs. Winnebago Ctr. for Blind. Mem. AMA, Ill. Med. Soc., Ill. Assn. Ophthalmology, Am. Assn. Ophthalmology, Alpha Sigma Lambda. Roman Catholic. Clubs: Galena Territory, Dixon Country. Office: 120 S Hennepin Ave Dixon IL 61021

POLASKI, WILLIAM ALBERT, regional health and welfare agency executive, former state official; b. Donora, Pa., Mar. 5, 1911; s. John Anthony and Anna (Vargo) P.; m. Jane Louise Allison, Dec. 31, 1940; children—Amy Jane Polaski Spernak, Sally Ann Polaski Kemp, William Allison, Daniel Allison. Student Pitts. Sch. Accountancy (now Robert Morris Coll.), 1931-33. Owner, mgr. Polaski News Store, Monongahela, Pa., 1935-68; dir. Pa. Bur. Elections, Harrisburg, 1962-63; chief clk. to Washington County Commrs. (Pa.), 1964-65; dir. Pa. Bur. Weights and Measures, Harrisburg, 1966-69; dir. Pa. Bur. Pub. Assistance Audits, Harrisburg, 1969-74; ret., 1977; treas. Monongahela Valley Health and Welfare Authority, Monessen, Pa., 1979—; mem. exec. bd. Nat. Conf. Weights and Measures, Washington, 1968-69; pres. N.E. region U.S. Dirs. Weight and Measures, 1968; pres. Redevel. Authority of Monongahela, 1974-78. Mem. city council City of Monongahela, 1949-51, mayor, 1952-56; chmn. Monongahela Democratic Party, 1957-62; mem. parish council Transfiguration Ch., Monongahela; Pa. League Cities (bd. dirs.); apptd. mem. Pa. Intra-Govtl. Long-Term Council, 1988. Served to master sgt. U.S. Army, 1943-46; ETO. Recipient Disting. Service medal Am. Legion Dept. Pa., 1948; named Outstanding Alumnus, Ringgold High Sch., 1985. Mem. Am. Assn. Ret. Persons (vice-chmn. Pa. state legis. com.), Am. Legion (past comdr.), VFW. Roman Catholic. Lodge: K.C. (past grand knight). Home: 1362 4th St Monongahela PA 15063

POLEN, DAVID MARTIN, financial executive; b. Bklyn., July 31, 1943; s. Sol and Estelle (Kimmel) P.; m. Rosa Polen; children: Carra, Solomon. BA, Bklyn. Coll., 1965. With Walston & Co., N.Y.C., 1967-70, Oppenheimer & Co., N.Y.C., 1971-72, Hornblower & Weeks, N.Y.C., 1972-73, Goldberg Polen & Co., N.Y.C., 1973-79; owner, pres., chmn. bd. Polen Capital Mgmt. Corp., N.Y.C., 1979—. Served with USMC, 1967-72. Cert. fin. planner; registered fin. prin. Mem: Internat. Assn. Fin. Planners (dir. N.Y.C. chpt. 1978-82). Jewish. Clubs: Lone Star Boat. Home: 500 E 77th St New York NY 10162 Office: 100 Wall St 29th Floor New York NY 10005

POLESKIE, STEPHEN FRANCIS, artist, educator; b. Pringle, Pa., June 3, 1938; s. Stephen Francis and Antoinette Elizabeth (Chludzinski) P.; m. Jeanne Mackin, 1979. B.S., Wilkes Coll., 1959; postgrad., New Sch. for Social Research, 1961. Owner Chiron Press, N.Y.C., 1961-68; instr. Sch. Visual Arts, N.Y.C., 1968; prof. art Cornell U., Ithaca, N.Y., 1969—; vis. critic Pratt Graphic Arts Center, N.Y.C., 1965-68; vis. artist Colgate U., Hamilton, N.Y., 1973, USSR, 1979; vis. artist Escuela de Bellas Artes, Honduras, 1980; vis. prof. U. Calif., Berkeley, 1976. One-man shows include Louis K. Meisel Gallery, N.Y.C., 1978-80, Galerie Kupinski, Stuttgart, Germany, 1979, Palace of Culture and Sci., Warsaw, Poland, 1979, Sky Art Presentation, MIT, 1981, Am. Ctr., Belgrade, 1981, William and Mary Coll., 1983, McPherson Art Gallery, Victoria, B.C., Can., 1984, Studio D'Ars, Milan, 1985, Gallery Flaviana, Locarno, Switzerland, 1985, Galleria Schneider, Rome, 1987, Mus. Sztuki Lodz, Poland, 1987, Alternative Mus., Lido di Spina, Italy, 1987, Galerie Klaus Lea, Munich, 1987, Patricia Carega Gallery, Washington, 1988; works represented in collections at Met. Mus., N.Y.C., Mus. Modern Art, N.Y.C., Victoria and Albert Mus., London, Whitney Mus., N.Y.C., Walker Art Center, Mpls., Tate Gallery, London, Fort Worth Art Center, Nat. Collection, Washington, others. Am. Fedn. of Arts grantee, 1965; Carnegie Found. grantee, 1967; Nat. Endowment for Arts grantee, 1973; N.Y. State Council on Arts grantee, 1973; Creative Artists Public Service Program grantee, 1978; Best Found. grantee, 1985. Mem. Exptl. Aircraft Assn., Aircraft Owners and Pilots Assn., Polish Acad. Sci. and Art, Internat. Aerobatic Club. Home: 306 Stone Quarry Rd Ithaca NY 14850 Office: Cornell U Tjaden Hall Ithaca NY 14853

POLETTI, UGO CARDINAL, Italian ecclesiastic; b. Omegna, Italy, Apr. 19, 1914. Ordained priest Roman Catholic Ch., 1938. Served in various diocesan offices, Novara, Italy; consecrated titular bishop of Medeli and aux. of Novara, 1958; pres. Pontificial Mission Aid Soc. for Italy, 1964-67; archbishop of Spoleto, 1967-69; titular archbishop of Cittanova, from 1969; served as 2d vice-regent of Rome, 1969-72; pro-vicar gen. of Rome, 1972; elevated to cardinal, 1973; vicar gen. of Rome, 1973—; now pres. Bishops' Conf.; archpriest Patriarchal Lateran Archbasilica, from 1973; grand chancellor Lateran U. Mem. Congregations of Clergy, Sacraments and Divine Worship, Oriental Chs., Religious and Secular Insts., Council for Laity. Address: Vicariato di Roma, Piazza San Giovanni, Laterano 6, 00184 Rome Italy *

POLEVOY, NANCY TALLY, lawyer, social worker; b. N.Y.C., May 27, 1944; d. Charles H. and Bernice M. (Gang) Tally; m. Martin D. Polevoy, Mar. 19, 1967; children: Jason Tally, John Gerald. Student, Mt. Holyoke Coll., 1962-64; BA, Barnard Coll., 1966; MS in Social Work, Columbia U., 1968, JD, 1986. Bar: N.Y. 1987. Caseworker unmarried mothers' service Louise Wise Services, N.Y.C., 1967, caseworker adoption dept., 1969-71; caseworker Youth Consultation Service, N.Y.C., 1968-69; asst. research scientist, psychiat. social worker dept. child psychiatry NYU Med. Ctr., N.Y.C., 1973-81; adv. ct. apptd. spl. advs. Manhattan Family Ct., N.Y.C., 1981-82; matrimonial assoc. Ballon, Stoll & Itzler, 1987, Herzfeld & Rubin, P.C., 1987—; cons. social work, 1981-86. Contbr. articles on early infantile autism to profl. jours. Recipient French Govt. prize, 1963. Mem. Assn. of City of N.Y. Bar Assn., N.Y. State Bar Assn., Nat. Assn. Social Workers, Acad. Cert. Social Workers, Alumni Assn. Columbia U. Sch. Social Work. Home: 1155 Park Ave New York NY 10128 Office: Herzfeld & Rubin 40 Wall St New York NY 10005

POLICANO, JOSEPH DANIEL, public relations executive; b. Bklyn., Dec. 15, 1933; s. Angelo Marie and Marie Ann (Galardi) P.; m. Kathleen Inez Larregui, June 22, 1957; children—Christopher Dante, Lisa Bernadette, Matthew Joseph. B.A., Bklyn. Coll.; postgrad., N.Y. U., New Sch. Corr. Wall St. Jour., 1955-57; sr. assoc. editor, bur. chief Washington; sr. asso. editor, bur. chief Central Feature News, Inc., 1957-61; pub. relations dir. M.J. Jacobs, Inc., 1961; pres. Joseph D. Policano, Inc., 1961-70, Policano/Pace, Inc., N.Y.C., 1968-70; chmn. bd. Policano/Rothholz, Inc., N.Y.C., 1970-77; pres. Policano, Inc., N.Y.C., 1977—; dir. Auto-Europe, Inc., Med. Features, Inc. Author: Martin Monti, GI Traitor, 1962, Franz Kafka Lived in Prague, 1964, Leos Janacek, His Life and Music, 1965. Pres. Kennedy King Democratic Club, 1969-71; commr. Mayor's Commn. for Protocol, N.Y.C.; bd. advisers Mcpl. Broadcasting System; bd. dirs. Queens Child Guidance Ctr. Served with AUS, 1954-55. Recipient Columbus award Fedn. Italian-Am. Dem. Orgns., 1974. Mem. Am. Med. Writers Assn., N.Y. Acad. Sci., Am. Acad. Polit. and Social Sci., ACLU. Roman Catholic. Clubs: Nat. Arts, Overseas Press; Union League (N.Y.C.).

POLIC-BOBIC, MIRJANA, educator; b. Perusic, Yugoslavia, Oct. 7, 1951; d. Ilija and Vida (Krekovic) Polic; m. Slobodan Bobic, July 3, 1982; children: Vida, Katarina. BA, Faculty Philosophy, Zagreb, Yugoslavia, 1974, MA, 1981. Tchr. English Sch. Fgn. Lang., Zagreb, 1977, Spanish Ctr. Fgn. Langs., Zagreb, 1978; teaching asst. Latin Am. lit. Faculty of Philosophy, Zagreb, 1979, asst. prof. Latin Am. lit., 1980—; collaborator, editor Gen. Ency. of Yugoslav Lexicographical Inst., 1985-86. Author/editor: History of Latin American Literature, 1987; contbr. articles to profl. jours. Grantee Sec. of Exterior Relations, Mex., 1975, 76, consejo Superor de Investigaciones, Madrid, 1978, Ministry of Culture, Spain, 1983-84. Mem. Assn. Internat. de Hispanistas. Home: Medvedgradska 36, 41000 Zagreb Yugoslavia Office: Faculty of Philosophy, Dure Salaja 3, 41000 Zagreb Yugoslavia

POLING, HAROLD ARTHUR, automobile company executive; b. Troy, Mich., Oct. 14, 1925; s. Plesant Arthur and Laura Elizabeth (Thompson) P.; m. Marian Sarita Lee, 1957; children—Pamela Lee, Kathryn Lyn, Douglas Lee. BA, Monmouth (Ill.) Coll., 1949; MBA, Ind. U., 1951; LHD (hon.), Monmouth Coll., 1981, Hofstra U., 1986. With Ford Motor Co., Dearborn, Mich., 1951-59, 60—, asst. controller transmissions and chasis div., 1964-66, controller transmission and chasis div., 1966-67, controller engine and foundry div., 1967-69; controller product devel. group Ford Motor Co., 1969-72; v.p. finance Ford of Europe, 1972-75; pres. Ford of Europe, Inc., Brentwood, Eng., 1975-77; chmn. bd. Ford of Europe, Inc., from 1977; exec. v.p. Ford Motor Co., Dearborn, Mich., 1979, exec. v.p. N.Am. automotive ops., 1980-85, mem. office of chief exec., 1985, pres., 1985-87, chief operating officer, 1985—, vice chmn., 1987—, also dir.; bd. dirs. NCR Corp. bd. dirs. The Monmouth (Ill.) Coll. Senate; mem. dean's adv. Council Ind. U. Sch. Bus., chmn. univ. ann. giving program; chmn. Nat. 4-H Council; bd. visitors Sch. Econs. and Mgmt. Oakland U., Mich., Grad. Sch. Bus. U. Pitts., chmn. annual giving program; conf. bd., v.p. Boys and Girls Club Southeast Mich.; conf. bd. Bus.-Higher Edn. Forum, U.S. Korea Bus. Council. Served with USNR, 1943-45. Recipient Disting. Service Citation award Automotive Hall Fame, 1986, Leadership award Engring. Soc. Detroit, 1986. Mem. The Bus.-Higher Edn. Forum, U.S. Korea Bus. Council. Clubs: Renaissance (Detroit); Birmingham (Mich.); Athletic; Bloomfield Hills (Mich.); Golf, Masons. Office: Ford Motor Co The American Rd Room 118 Dearborn MI 48121

POLING, RICHARD DUANE, lawyer; b. Parkersburg, W.Va., Nov. 4, 1955; s. W. Duane and Willadene (Riggs) P.; m. Debra Ann Holstein, Feb. 23, 1985. AB magna cum laude, W.Va. U., 1978, JD, 1981. Bar: W.Va. 1981, U.S. Dist. Ct. (no. and so. dists.) W.Va. 1981, U.S. Dist. Ct. Idaho 1983, U.S. Ct. Appeals (9th cir.) 1983, U.S. Ct. Appeals (4th cir.) 1984, N.C. 1986, U.S. Dist. Ct. (we. dist.) N.C. 1988, U.S. Dist. Ct. (mid. dist.) N.C. 1988. Assoc. Wilson, Frame & Poling, Morgantown, W.Va., 1981-82, Preiser & Wilson, Charleston, W.Va., 1982-85; ptnr. Karney & Poling, Charlotte, N.C., 1985—; adj. prof. law W.Va. U., Morgantown, 1981-82. Mem. Advocates for a Safer Vaccine, 1984—, Dissatisfied Parents Together, Vienna, Va., 1985—; mem. adminstrv. bd. Myers Park United Meth. Ch., 1987—, United Way Legal Adv. com., 1987—; mem. nat. council W.Va. U. Coll. Law, 1988—. Named Outstanding Adv., Allegheny County Acad. Trial Lawyers, 1981, One of Outstanding Young Men Am., 1981. Mem. ABA (law and medicine com.), Assn. Trial Lawyers Am. (chmn. young lawyers sect. 1987-88, exec. com. D.P.T. litigation sect. 1986—), N.C. Bar Assn. (health law com. 1987—), W.Va. State Bar (com. on law and medicine 1985 86), Va. Trial Lawyers Assn., W.Va. Trial Lawyers Assn. (pub. relations com.), N.C. Acad. Trial Lawyers (victims rights com., legis. com.), Am. Soc. Law and Medicine, Phi Beta Kappa, Phi Kappa Phi, Phi Delta Phi, Pi Sigma Alpha (past pres.). Democrat. Methodist. Home: 1911 S Wendover Rd Charlotte NC 28211 Office: Karney & Poling 1208 S Tryon St Charlotte NC 28202

POLINSZKY, KÁROLY, engineering educator; b. Budapest, Hungary, Mar. 19, 1922; s. Gyula Polinszky and Róza Morbitzer; married, 1946; children: Tibor, Gábor, András. MSChemE, Tech. U. Budapest, 1944, PhDChemE, 1948; Dr. honoris causa, Tech. U., Leningrad, USSR, 1967. Asst. prof. Tech. U. Budapest, 1944-49, prof., 1980—, pres. tech., 1980-87; dean Tech. U. Veszprém, Hungary, 1949-61, pres., 1961-63; dep. minister edn. Ministry of Edn., Budapest, 1963-74, minister of edn., 1974-80; research prof. Research Inst. for Tech. Chemistry, Veszprém, 1987—. Presdl. mem. Hungarian Nat. Front, Budapest, 1978. Recipient Kossuth award Council of Ministers, 1961, Apáczai-Csere award Minister of Edn., 1987. Mem. Tech. Union (presdl. mem.), Hungarian Acad. Sci. (presdl. mem., academician 1964), Alumin Assn. Tech. U. Budapest (presdl. mem.). Home: Nagyajtai 4/b, 1026 Budapest Hungary Office: Technical Univ, XI Budafoki 8, 1521 Budapest Hungary

POLISI, JOSEPH W(ILLIAM), college administrator; b. N.Y.C., Dec. 30, 1947; s. William Charles and Pauline (Kaplan) P.; m. Elizabeth Marlow. BA in Polit. Sci., U. Conn., 1969; MA in Internat. Relations, Tufts U., 1970, MusM, 1973, M of Mus. Arts, 1975; DMA, Yale U., 1980; DHL (hon.), Ursinus Coll., Collegetown, Pa., 1986. Exec. officer Yale Sch. of Music, New Haven, 1976-80; dean of faculty Manhattan Sch. of Music, N.Y.C., 1980-83; dean Coll. Conservatory of Music U. Cin., 1983-84; pres. The Juilliard Sch., N.Y.C., 1984—. Performances as bassonist throughout the U.S.; contbr. articles to various publs. in U.S. and France. Office: The Juilliard Sch Office of Pres Lincoln Ctr New York NY 10023 *

POLITI, BETH KUKKONEN, publishing services company executive; b. Englewood, N.J., Sept. 18, 1949; d. Andrew and Beatrice G. (Druskin) Kukkonen; BS in Mktg., Miami U., Oxford, Ohio, 1971; m. Joseph Politi, Oct. 21, 1982; children: Andrew, Joseph. Media buyer Schwab, Beatty & Porter, Inc., 1971-72; media planner Adler, Schwartz & Connes, 1972-73; media buyer/planner Schwab Beatty div. Marstellar, 1973-74; dir. insert advt. Benjamin Co., Inc., Elmsford, N.Y., 1975-78, prodn. mgr., 1978-80, v.p., client services, 1980-83, editorial supr., 1979-83, assoc. pub. various books, 1981-83; v.p. Bergen County Profl. Services, Ft. Lee, N.J., 1983—. Home: 11 Alpine Ct Ridgefield Park NJ 07660

POLIVCHAK, PHILIP MICHAEL, trade association executive; b. Mpls.; s. Michael and Ilona (Berta) P. Dir. dept. manpower devel. and tng. Nat. Assn. Home Builders, Washington, 1967-81, staff v.p., 1981-83; pres. Home Builders Inst., Washington, 1983—. Participant White House Conf. on Corrections, 1971; mem. Pres.'s Jobs for Vets. Nat. Com., 1972; mem. Pres.'s Com. for Prisoners of War, 1973; co-chmn. Job Corps at Work Competition, Dept. Labor, 1981; sponsor: Builders Examine the Many Faces Homelessness, Nat. Symposium, 1988. Mem. Nat. Assn. Home Builders (v.p. 1967-83), U.S. C. of C. (edn., employment and tng. com. 1985—). Contbg. editor: Builder, 1967—; producer film: Build a Better Life, 1977. Home: 1721 P St NW Washington DC 20036 Other: 8 Bridge Rd Middlesex Beach DE Office: Home Builders Inst 15th St and M Sts NW Washington DC 20005

POLLACK, MARY LOUISE, hotel executive; b. Phila., Nov. 15, 1949; d. Edward Latshaw and Mary Louise (Dempsey) Gruber; m. Stephen J. Pollack, May 15, 1977 (div. 1981). BA in English, Duke U., 1971; postgrad. Hotel Sch., Cornell U. Cert. tchr., Pa. Travel agt. G & O Travel, N.Y.C., 1977-80; sales mgr. Halloran House, N.Y.C., 1980-81; regional dir. Halloran Hotels, N.Y.C., 1981-83, nat. dir. sales, 1983-84; assoc. dir. mktg. Treadway Hotels and Resorts, Saddle Brook, N.J., 1984-85, dir. mktg., 1985-86, v.p.

mktg., 1986-87, also bd. dirs.; dir sales, mktg. Eastern region Prime Mgmt., Fairfield, N.J., 1987—; dir. Somerset Hotels, N.J., Treadway Inns Corp. Mem. Hotel Sales Mgrs. Assn. Internat., U.S. Tour Operators Assn., Am. Bus Assn., Meeting Planners Internat., Nat. Passenger Traffic Assn. (hotel com. 1986), Am. Soc. Travel Agts., Travel Industry Assn. Am. (planning com. 1983-84), Nat. Tour Assn. (conv. com. 1982-84, membership com. 1984, cert. com. 1986, mktg. com. 1987), Pa. Travel Council (program chmn. for 1st Gov.'s Conf. on Travel 1983, mem. mktg. com. 1983).

POLLAND, REBECCA ROBBINS, foundation executive; b. Phila., Jan. 11, 1922; d. Louis Aron Jonah and Edith Frances (Kapnek) Robbins; B.A., Bryn Mawr Coll., 1942; M.A., U. Calif., Berkeley, 1957, Ph.D., 1971; m. Harry L. Polland, July 14, 1946 (div. 1979); children—Louise, Margaret, Jonathan. Analyst, cons., commisson mem., local and nat. govt., 1942-82; cons. U.S. Dept. Agr., 1977; lectr. Polit. sci. Sacramento State U., 1975-76; asst. prof. Sonoma State U. (Calif.), 1976-78; asst. prof. Rutgers U., Camden, N.J., 1978-86. Chmn. bd. Frogmore Tobacco Estates Ltd., Zimbabwe; Presdl. appointee Bd. Internat. Food and Agrl. Devel., 1979-82. Exec. trustee J.F. Kapnek Charitable Trust, Phila., 1980—, also pres. 1988— ; mem. Berkeley City Commn. on Recreation and Parks, 1970-75; v.p.; mem. White House Conf. Food, Nutrition, Health, 1969, World Food Conf., Rome, 1974. Mem. Am. Polit. Sci. Assn., AAUP, Am. Soc. Public Adminstrn., Am. Soc. Tropical Medicine and Hygiene, Assn. Dirs. Internat. Agrl. Programs Assn. Women in Devel. (founding). Contbr. articles to profl. jours. Home: 220 Locust St Apt 30A Philadelphia PA 19106 Office: 204-205 Cecil House, 95 Stanley Ave, Harare Zimbabwe

POLLARD, DAVID EDWARD, editor; b. Columbus, Ohio, Oct. 7, 1927; s. James Edward and Marjorie Olive (Pearson) P.; m. Ilse Knack, Dec. 24, 1960; children—Walter Thomas, Marcus Andreas, Michael David, Christopher James. B.S., Ohio State U., 1950; postgrad. in cotton econs, Memphis State U., 1967. With Columbus Citizen, 1943-50; with Army Times Pub. Co., 1952-60; mng. editor U.S. Coast Guard Mag., Washington, 1956-57; asso. editor Am. Weekend, Washington, also Frankfurt, Ger., 1957-60; info. specialist Air Forces Europe Exchange, Wiesbaden, Ger., 1961-63; reporter Comml. Appeal, Memphis, 1963-66; fin. writer Comml. Appeal, 1967-68; news-desk editor U.S. News & World Report, Washington, 1968-76; chief news desk U.S. News & World Report, 1976—. Served with USMC, 1945-46, 51-52. Mem. White House Corrs. Assn., Sigma Delta Chi, Alpha Delta Sigma, Alpha Tau Omega. Roman Catholic. Office: 2400 N St NW Washington DC 20037

POLLARD, JOSEPH AUGUSTINE, retail marketing executive; b. N.Y.C., June 22, 1924; s. Joseph Michael and Mary Theresa (Sheerin) P.; m. Helen Frances O'Neill, Jan. 18, 1947 (dec.); children: Christopher (dec.), Kenneth, Eugene, Daniel, Theresa, Michael; m. 2d, Lee Sharon Rivkins, Jan. 1, 1981. Student Pratt Inst., 1946-50. Advt. mgr. Boston Store, Utica, N.Y., 1951-53; sales promotion dir. Interstate Stores, N.Y., 1954-60, 67-70; v.p. sales Community Discount Stores, Chgo., 1960-63; dir. sales S. Klein, N.Y., 1964-66; v.p. advt. and pub. relations Peoples Drug Stores, Alexandria, Va., 1970—. Trustee D.C. div. Am. Cancer Soc., pres. 1985-86; pres. Modern Retailers Ill., 1962. Served with USAF, 1943-46, 50-51. Recipient Am. Advt. Fedn. Silver medal award, 1982, St. George's medal Am. Cancer Soc., 1984. Mem. Advt. Club Met. Washington (pres. 1975-76). Club: Country of Fairfax (Va.). Home: 5848 Kara Pl Burke VA 22015 Office: Peoples Drug Stores Inc 6315 Bren Mar Dr Alexandria VA 22312

POLLARD, KATHARINE MILLER, business organization executive; b. Norfolk, Va., Dec. 8, 1943; d. William Roland and Katharine (Byrd) Miller; children: John Garland Pollard IV, K.C. Pollard. AA, St. Mary's Coll., Raleigh, N.C., 1963; BA, Old Dominion U., 1972. Asst. dir. Inst. Scottish Studies Old Dominion U., Norfolk, 1982-85; program dir. Va. World Trade Ctr., Norfolk, 1985-86; dir. Va. Internat. Visitor's Assn; mem. econ. devel. com. Virginia Beach Tommorrow, Tidewater Scottish Festival, Inc.; asst. dir. Hampton Roads C. of C. Editor Internat. Network Directory of Greater Hampton Roads, 1987. Founder Lynn Haven Clean Waters Assn., Virginia Beach, Virginia Beach chpt. Soc. Prevention Cruelty to Animals; past pres. St. Mary's Coll. Alumnae Assn.; chmn. Internat. Scottish Festival of Art, Music and Drama, Norfolk, 1981 (filmed by BBC-TV, BBC radio); bd. dirs. Brit. Isles Festival, Norfolk; active Virginia Beach Sister Cities Bd. Grantee Univ. Edinburgh summer study, 1979. Fellow Soc. Antiquaries of Scotland; mem. The Hist. Assn., Scottish History Soc., Hampton Roads Fgn. Commerce Club, Colonial Dames Am. (life), Garden Club Va. Avocations: sailing, gardening, travel. Home: Quail Trail 1929 Lynn Cove Ln Virginia Beach VA 23454 Office: Hampton Roads C of C 4512 Virginia Beach Blvd Virginia Beach VA 23462

POLLARD, MICHAEL ROSS, lawyer, health policy researcher and consultant; b. Flint, Mich., Apr. 14, 1947; s. Gail Winton Pollard and Evelyn Georgeanna (LeMire) Goplen; m. Penelope Brigham, Aug. 22, 1970. AB in Polit. Sci., U. Mich., 1969; JD, Harvard U., 1972, MPH, 1974. Bar: Mass. 1972, D.C. 1975. Profl. assoc. for program devel. Nat. Acad. Scis. Inst. Medicine, Washington, 1974-77, dir. law and ethics div., 1977-78; atty. advisor Office of Policy Planning, FTC, Washington, 1978-81, asst. dir. Bur. Consumer Protection, 1981-83; dir. Office of Policy Analysis, Pharm. Mfrs. Assn., Washington, 1983-88; exec. dir. Am. Pharm. Inst., Washington, 1988—; counsel Michaels & Wishner P.C., Washington, 1988—; cons. Nat. Ctr. for Health Services Research, Rockville, Md., 1975-80, Office Tech. Assessment U.S. Congress, 1984—. Contbr. articles to profl. jours. James B. Angell scholar U. Mich., 1967, 68, 69. Mem. ABA, Phi Beta Kappa, Pi Sigma Alpha. Democrat. Club: Harvard (Washington). Home: 7300 Maple Ave Chevy Chase MD 20815 Office: Am Pharm Inst 2215 Constitution Ave NW Washington DC 20037

POLLARD, WILLIAM SHERMAN, JR., civil engineer, educator; b. Oak Grove, La., Jan. 1, 1925; s. William Sherman and Carrie Lois (Hornor) P.; m. Gloria Louise Ponder, June 29, 1946; children: William Sherman, III, Katherine Lynn. B.S. in Civil Engring, Purdue U., 1946, M.S., 1948. Instr. civil engring. Purdue U., 1948-49; instr. U. Ill., 1949-51, assoc. prof., 1951-55; with Harland Bartholomew & Assos., St. Louis, 1955-71; assoc. partner, chief civil engr. Harland Bartholomew & Assos., 1956-58; partner Harland Bartholomew & Assos., Memphis, 1958-71; head ops. Harland Bartholomew & Assos., 1958-60; head Harland Bartholomew & Assos. (Memphis office), 1960-71; pres. William S. Pollard Cons. (Ins.), Memphis, 1971-81; prof. civil engring. U. Colo., Denver, 1981—; adj. prof. urban planning Memphis State U., 1973-81; dir. Ctr. Urban Transp. Studies, U. Colo.; chmn. WKNO-TV, Memphis. Served with USMC, 1942-46. Named Distinguished Engring. Alumnus Purdue U., 1969. Fellow Am. Cons. Engrs. Council, ASCE (state of the art award 1970), Inst. Transp. Engrs.; mem. Am. Rd. Builders Assn., Cons. Engrs. Memphis, Nat. Assn. Environ. Profls., Nat. Soc. Profl. Engrs., Soc. Am. Mil. Engrs., Urban Land Inst., Transp. Research Bd., Navy League, Lambda Alpha. Presbyterian. Clubs: Engrs, Summit. Lodge: Rotary (pres. 1979-80). Office: U Colo 1200 Larimer St Campus Box 113 Denver CO 80204-5300

POLLEDO, CÉSAR ALBERTO, construction company executive; b. Buenos Aires, Aug. 25, 1925; s. César Manuel and Sara (Solari) P.; m. María Irene de Elía, Dec. 10, 1951; children: María, César, Sara, Marcela, Ana, Antonio. BCE, Colegio Nacional Buenos Aires, 1944. Pres., gen. mgr., engr. Polledo S.A.I.C.yF., Buenos Aires, 1950—; v.p. Calera Avellaneda, Buenos Aires; bd. dirs. La Constrn. S.A. Co. Argentina de Seguros, Buenos Aires, Camara Argentina de la Constrn., Capital Federal, Argentina. Clubs: Jockey (Buenos Aires); Mar Del Plata Golf. Office: Polledo SAICyF, Venezuela 925, 1095 Buenos Aires Argentina

POLLEY, TERRY LEE, lawyer; b. Long Beach, Calif., June 2, 1947; s. Frederick F. and Geraldine E. (Davis) P.; m. Patricia Yamanoha, Aug. 4, 1973; children: Todd, Matthew. AB, UCLA, 1970; JD, Coll. William and Mary, 1973. Bar: Calif. 1973, U.S. Tax Ct. 1974, U.S. Supreme Ct. 1987. Assoc. Loeb & Loeb, Los Angeles, 1973-78; ptnr. Ajalat & Polley, Los Angeles, 1978—; lectr. taxation law U. So. Calif. Author (with Charles R. Ajalat) California's Water's Edge Legislation, 1987; contbr. articles to profl. jours, legal jours.; editorial bd. William and Mary Law Rev. Mem. sch. bd. Greater Long Beach Christian Schs.; elder Grace Brethren Ch., Long Beach. Mem. ABA (sate and local tax com.), Calif. Bar Assn. (steering com., property, sales and local tax com. taxation sect.), Los Angeles County Bar Assn. (chmn. and exec. com. taxation sect., chmn. state and local tax com. taxation sect.), Omicron Delta Epsilon. Democrat. Office: Ajalat & Polley 643 S Olive St Suite 200 Los Angeles CA 90014

POLLIO, RALPH THOMAS, editor, publisher; b. Bronx, N.Y., Nov. 1, 1948; s. Thomas and Dolores (Miccioli) P.; m. Rita Lucia Napolitano, Sept. 29, 1974; 1 child, Christopher. BCE, Manhattan Coll., 1978; postgrad., Columbia U. Editor, pub. Ea. Basketball Publs., Franklin Square, N.Y., 1975—. Founder, owner High School News, 1984, EB News, 1981, Ea. Basketball Mag. Served to sgt. U.S. Army N.G., 1969-74. Mem. U.S. Basketball Writers Assn. (1st Place award for best mag. feature 1984), ASCE, Soc. Profl. Journalists, Internat. Platform Assn., Internat. Soc. Philos. Enquiry, World Lit. Acad., Nat. Notary Assn., Magazine Publishers Assn., Am. Soc. Magazine Editors, Mensa, and numerous other high IQ socs., Psi Chi. Roman Catholic. Clubs: N.Y. Road Runners (N.Y.C.), Dix Hills Runners. Avocations: running, listening to jazz, gourmet cooking, reading, films. Home: 7 May Court West Hempstead NY 11552 Office: Ea Basketball Publs 4 New Hyde Park Rd Franklin Square NY 11010

POLLMANN, HORST, information systems specialist; b. Duisburg, Fed. Republic Germany, Nov. 20, 1938; s. Friedrich Ernst and Maria (Straeten) P.; m. Meinert Baerbel, Feb. 7, 1964; children: Dirk, Ralf. BEE, Tech. U., Aachen, Fed. Republic Germay, 1963; PhD in Electronic Engring., Tech. U. Aachen, 1971. Research engr. AEG-Telefunken, Ulm, Fed. Republic of Germany, 1964-71; devel. dept. head Thyssen Industrie AG Henschel, Kassel, Fed. Republic of Germany, 1971-80, devel. dir., 1980—. Lodge: Rotary. Home: Am Hilgenberg 61, 3500 Kassel Federal Republic of Germany Office: Thyssen Industrie AG Henschel, Henschelplatz 1, 3500 Kassel Federal Republic of Germany

POLLOCK, JACK PADEN, biology and dental educator, consultant, freelance writer, retired army officer; b. Columbus, Miss., May 12, 1920; s. Samuel Lafayette and Pauline Elizabeth (Pollock) O'Neal; m. Anne Olamae Silbernagel, Aug. 25, 1945; children—Poli A., Elizabeth D. Student, Gulf Coast Mil. Acad., 1936-38, Tulane U., 1938-41; B.S., Southeastern La. U., 1942; D.D.S. cum laude, Loyola U., New Orleans, 1945; diploma, Army War Coll., 1965, Indsl. Coll. Armed Forces, 1966; hon. degree, Baylor U., 1974. Asst. prof., Loyola U., New Orleans, 1945-46, prof., 1977-86, U.S.A. Command and Gen. Staff Coll., 1968, prof., 1977-86; commd. 1st lt. U.S. Army, 1946, advanced through the grades to brigadier gen., 1972; career officer U.S. Army, 1946-77; dental advisor to Sec. of Defense, 1970-73; cons. Surgeon Gen. U.S. Army, Washington, 1981-84; U. rank and tenure com. Loyola U., New Orleans, 1982-85. Author: International Communism: Its Future Prospects, 1965. Contbr. articles to profl. jours. Active in Nat. Council Boy Scouts Am., South Ctl. Region 1973—, Nat. Exploring Com., 1973—. USAR, 1942-46. Decorated D.S.M., Legion of Merit with oak leaf cluster, Bronze Star with one oak leaf cluster, Master Paracutist badges (U.S. and foreign); recipient Silver Beaver award, Boy Scouts of Am., numerous other military awards and honors. Fellow Am. Coll. Dentistry (life), Internat. Coll. Dentistry; mem. Am. Dental Assn., La. Dental Assn., New Orleans Dental Assn., Am. Coll. Dentists, Internat. Coll. Dentists, Fedn. Dentaire Internationale, Assn. Mil. Surgeons of U.S. (life), Pierre Fauchard Acad., C. Victor Vignes Odontological Soc., Am. Assn. Dental Schs., NRA (life), Assoc. U.S. Army (life), Military Order of World Wars (life), Retired Officers Assoc. (life) , Disabled Am. Vets. (life), Delta Sigma Delta, Kappa Sigma, Phi Kappa, Omicron Kappa Upsilon. Clubs: Army and Navy (Washington), Univ. (San Antonio). Avocations: gardening; writing; travel; conservation. Home: 118 Bayberry Dr Covington LA 70433 Office: PO Box 1423 Mandeville LA 70470

POLLOCK, JOHN PHLEGER, lawyer; b. Sacramento, Apr. 28, 1920; s. George Gordon and Irma (Phleger) P.; m. Juanita Irene Gossman, Oct. 26, 1945; children: Linda Pollock Harrison, Madeline Pollock Chiotti, John, Gordon. A.B., Stanford U., 1942; J.D., Harvard U., 1948. Bar: Calif. 1949, U.S. Supreme Ct. 1954. Partner Musick, Peeler & Garrett, Los Angeles, 1953-60, Pollock, Williams & Berwanger, Los Angeles, 1960-80, Rodi, Pollock, Pettker, Galbraith & Phillips, Los Angeles, 1980—. Contbr. articles to profl. publs. Active Boy Scouts Am.; former trustee Pitzer Coll., Claremont, Calif., 1968-76; trustee Fletcher Jones Found., Good Hope Med. Found., Pacific Legal Found. Served with AUS, 1942-45. Fellow Am. Coll. Trial Lawyers; mem. ABA, Los Angeles County Bar Assn. (trustee 1964-66), Am. Judicature Soc. Home: 30602 Paseo del Valle Laguna Niguel CA 92677 Office: 611 W 6th St Los Angeles CA 90017

POLON, LINDA BETH, educator, writer, illustrator; b. Balt., Oct. 7, 1943; d. Harold Bernard and Edith Judith Wolff; m. Marty I. Polon, Dec. 18, 1966 (div. Aug. 1983); m. Robert Dorsey, Apr. 13, 1986 (Nov. 6, 1986). B.A. in History, UCLA, 1966. Elem. tchr. Los Angeles Bd. Edn., 1967—; writer-illustrator Scott Foresman Pub. Co., Glenview, Ill., 1979—, Frank Schaffer Pub. Co., Torrance, Calif., 1981-82, Learning Works, Santa Barbara, Calif., 1981-82; editorial reviewer Prentice Hall Pub. Co., Santa Monica, Calif., 1982-83. Author: (juvenile books) Creative Teaching Games, 1974; Teaching Games for Fun, 1976; Making Kids Click, 1979; Write up a Storm, 1979; Stir Up a Story, 1981; Paragraph Production, 1981; Using Words Correctly, 3d-4th grades, 1981, 5th-6th grades, 1981; Whole Earth Holiday Book, 1983; Writing Whirlwind, 1986; Magic Story Starters, 1987. Mem. Soc. Children's Book Writers. Democrat. Home: 1515 Manning Ave Apt 3 Los Angeles CA 90024 Office: Los Angeles Bd of Edn 980 S Hobart Blvd Los Angeles CA 90006

POLON, MARTIN ISHIAH, science and technology consultant; b. Chgo., May 18, 1942; s. Solomon I. and Bernice V. Polon; m. Janine Petit, Feb. 11, 1984. BA, UCLA, 1964, MA in TV, 1968, postgrad., 1970. Dir. audio-visual services UCLA, 1970-80; founder Computer Merchandising and Software Merchandising Mags., 1980-83; prin. Polon Research Internat., Boston, 1983—; lectr. U. Lowell, Mass.; assoc. prof. U. Colo., Denver; forecaster of consumer acceptance of high tech. Spkr. various conventions and profl. orgns.; v.p., mem. bd. review Audio Engring. Soc. Jour.; contbr. over 200 articles to mags. and profl. jours., including: Video Mag., Audio Mag. and Billboard, Sight and Sound (U.K.), Studio Sound (U.K.), One to One (U.K.), Broadcast Systems Engring. (U.K.). Mem. Audio Engring. Soc. (gov., chmn. edn. com. 1985—, govs. award for service in edn.), Soc. Motion Picture and TV Engrs. (participating mem. com. on audio), Soc. Profl. Audio Recording Studios, Assn. Profl. Rec. Studios (U.K.), Japan Soc. Boston, Sapphire Audio Group, U.S. Naval Inst. Democrat. Jewish.

POL POT, Democratic Kampuchean politician; b. Prek Sbauv, Kompong Svay, Kompong Thom (Kampuchea), May 19, 1926. Student of electricity, Kampuchea and Paris. Joined anti-French colonialists, 1953; after Geneva Agreement in 1954 carried out militant underground activities, then joined marquis, 1963; dep. sec., then sec. Communist Party of Kampuchea, 1963-81; prime minister Democratic Kampuchea, 1976-79; left govt., 1979; comdr. nat. army and guerillas fighting Vietnamese forces occupying Kampuchea, 1978-85; ret., 1985. Address: Permanent Mission of Democratic Kampuchea to UN 747 3d Ave, 8th Floor New York NY 10017 *

POLSON, GORDON FAIRLIE, architect; b. Stevenston, Ayrshire, Scotland, Aug. 2, 1929; came to Can., 1954; s. John Sutherland Gordon and Elizabeth McDonald (Hamilton) P.; m. Mary Constance Campbell, Oct. 23, 1954; children—Carolyn Anne, Alasdair Leslie, Valerie Christine, Irene Constance. B.Arch., U. Strathclyde, Glasgow, Scotland, 1954. Registered architect. Archtl. asst. Sam Bunton & Assocs., Architects and Town Planners, Glasgow, 1947-50; Noad & Wallace FFRIBA, Architects, Glasgow, 1950-51, Burgh Surveyors Office, Clydebank, Scotland, 1953, 54; project architect Page & Steele Architects, Toronto, Ont., Can., 1954-55; project architect, designer Pentland Baker & Polson Architects, Toronto, 1955-64, ptnr. in-charge-design, 1964-70; archtl. mgr. Bank of Montreal, 1970-75; ptnr. Dominik Polson Thompson Laframboise Mallette Architects and Engrs., Cornwall, Ont., 1975-81; corp. archtl. advisor Petro Can. Inc., Calgary, Alta., 1981-85, facilities mgr., Eastern Can., 1985-88; devel. mgr. Comml. Devel. div. Royal Le Page Real Estate, 1988—. Mem. exec. council Que. council Boy Scouts Can., 1971-76; mem. adv. vocat. com. Dawson Coll., 1971-76. Bellahouston travelling scholar, Italy, 1952, John Keppie scholar, 1954; Mem. Royal Inst. Brit. Architects (Silver medal 1954), Royal Archtl. Inst. Can., Ont. Assn. Architects, Order of Architects in Que., Alta. Assn. Architects. Clubs: Royal Can. Yacht (Toronto); Pointe Claire Yacht (Montreal). Presbyterian. Avocations: architecture; sailing; painting. Home: 9 Billy Joel Crescent, Markham, ON Canada L3P 3C4

POLUKHINA, VALENTINA PLATONOVNA, Russian studies educator; b. Uriup, USSR, June 18, 1936; d. Platon Yevseevich and Pelageya (Innonkentyevna) Borisova; divorced. Student, Pedagogical Coll., Mariinsk, USSR, 1954; BA, Tula (USSR) State U., 1959; MA, Moscow State U., 1972; PhD, Keele U., Newcastle, Eng., 1985. Tchr. Russian Kayakent (USSR) High. Sch., 1959-61; lectr. Russian Friendship U., Moscow, 1962-68, 72-73; lang. asst. U. Keele, 1973-76, lectr. Russian studies, 1976—. Contbr. articles to profl. jours. Brit. Acad. grantee, 1979, 87. Mem. British Univs. Assn. Slavists. Russian Orthodox. Office: U Keele, Dept Modern Lang, Newcastle ST5 5BG, England

POLUNIN, NICHOLAS, environmentalist, author, editor; b. Checkendon, Oxfordshire, Eng., June 26, 1909; s. Vladimir and Elizabeth Violet (Hart) P.; m. Helen Lovat Fraser, 1939 (dec.); 1 son, Michael; m. Helen Eugenie Campbell, Jan. 3, 1948; children: April Xenia, Nicholas V. C., Douglas H. H. Open scholar, Christ Church, U. Oxford, 1932, BA (1st class honors), MA, 1935, PhD, 1935, DSc, 1942; MS, Yale U., 1934. Participant or leader numerous sci. expdns., 1930-65, primarily in arctic regions, including Spitsbergen, Greenland; curator, tutor, demonstrator, lectr. various instns., especially Oxford U., 1933-47; vis. prof. botany McGill U., 1946-47, Macdonald prof. botany, 1947-52; Guggenheim fellow, research fellow Harvard U., 1950-53; also fgn. research asso., USAF botanical Ice-island research project dir., lectr. plant sci. Yale, also biology Brandeis U., 1953-55; prof. plant ecology and taxonomy, head dept. botany, dir. U. Herbarium and Botanic Garden, Baghdad, Iraq, 1955-58; guest prof. U. Geneva, 1959-61, 75-76; adviser establishment, founding prof. botany, dean faculty sci. U. Ife, Nigeria, 1962-66; founding editor plant sci. monographs and world crops books 1954-78, Biol. Conservation, 1967-74, Environ. Conservation, 1974—; chmn. internat. steering com., editor proc. Internat. Conf. Environ. Future, Finland, 1971; chmn. internat. steering com., editor proc. sec. gen., 2d conf. Internat. Conf. Environ. Future, Iceland, 1977; 3d conf. Internat. Conf. Environ. Future, Scotland, 1987; pres. Found. for Environ. Conservation, 1975—; participant Internat. Bot. Congresses, Stockholm, 1950, Paris, 1954, Edinburgh, 1964, Seattle, 1969, Leningrad, 1975, Sydney, 1981; councillor (pres.) World Council for the Biosphere, 1984—. Author: Russian Waters, 1931, The Isle of Auks, 1932, Botany of the Canadian Eastern Arctic, 3 vols., 1940-48, Arctic Unfolding, 1949, Circumpolar Arctic Flora, 1959, Introduction to Plant Geography, 1960 (various fgn. edits), Eléments de Géographie botanique, 1967; editor: The Environmental Future, 1972, Growth Without Ecodisasters?, 1980, Ecosystem Theory and Application, 1986, Environ. Monographs and Symposia, 1979—; founding chmn. edit. bd. Cambridge Studies in Environmental Policy, 1984—; contbr. to various jours. Decorated comdr. Order Brit. Empire, 1975; recipient undergrad., grad. student scholarships, fellowships, research associateships Yale U., 1933-34, Harvard U., 1936-37; Rolleston Meml. prize, 1938; D.S.I.R. spl. investigator, 1938; Leverhulme Research award, 1941; sr. research fellow New Coll., Oxford; Arctic Inst. N.A. research fellow, 1946-47; Guggenheim fellow, 1950-52; recipient Ford Found. award Scandinavia, USSR, 1966-67, Marie-Victorin medal Can., 1957, Indian Ramdeo medal, 1986, Internat. Sasakawa Environ. prize, 1987, USSR Vernadsky medal. Fellow Royal Geog. Soc., Royal Hort. Soc., Linnean Soc. London, AAAS, Arctic Inst. N.A., Insona; mem. Internat. Soc. for Environ. Edn. (life), Torrey Bot. Club (life), Bot. Soc. Am. (life), N.Am. Assn. for Environ. Edn. (life), Asian Soc. Environ. Protection (life), various fgn. and nat. profl. and sci. socs. Clubs: Harvard (N.Y.C.) (life); Canadian Field Naturalists (Ottawa); Reform (London) (life). Address: Found for Environ Conservation, 7 Chemin Taverney, 1218 Grand-Saconnex, Geneva Switzerland

POLZIN, JOHN THEODORE, lawyer; b. Rock Island, Ill., Dec. 23, 1919; s. Max August and Charlotte Barbara (Trenkenschuh) P.; m. Helen Louise Hosford, Nov. 27, 1969. A.B., U. Ill., 1941, J.D., 1943. Bar: Ill. 1943. Sole practice, Galva, Ill., 1946-55, Chgo., 1975—; city atty., Galva, 1950-54; assoc. Langner, Parry, Card & Langner, Chgo., 1955-75; lectr. Ill. Inst. for Continuing Legal Edn., 1978. Served to lt. USNR, 1943-46. Mem. ABA, Ill. State Bar Assn. (chmn. patent, trademark and copyright law sect. 1981-82), Patent Law Assn. Chgo. (chmn. fgn. trademark com. 1972, 74). Republican. Home: 1503 Oak Ave Evanston IL 60201 Office: 122 S Michigan Ave Suite 1452 Chicago IL 60603

POMEROY, BENJAMIN SHERWOOD, veterinary medicine educator; b. St. Paul, Apr. 24, 1911; s. Benjamin A. and Florence A. (Sherwood) P.; D.V.M., Iowa State U., 1933; M.S., Cornell U., 1934; Ph.D., U. Minn., 1944; m. L. Margaret Lyon, June 25, 1938; children—Benjamin A., Sherwood R., Catherine A., Margaret D. Diagnostician, U. Minn., 1934-38, faculty, 1938-81, prof., 1948-81, prof. emeritus, 1981—, head dept. vet. microbiology and pub. health, 1953-73, assoc. dean, 1970-74, acting dean, 1979-80. Mem. adv. com. FDA; cons. animal scis. div. and animal health div., meat insp. service, animal health service USDA. Republican precinct officer, 1958-60, chmn., 1960-61; chmn. Ramsey County (Minn.) Rep. Com., 1961-65, 4th Congl. Dist., 1961-63, 67-69; mem. Minn. Rep. Central Com., 1961-71; del. Minn. Rep. Conv., 1960-71, Rep. Nat. Conv., 1964. Named Veterinarian of Year in Minn., 1970; recipient Eminent Citizen award St. Anthony Park Legion Post and Aux., 1955, Alumni Merit award, 1975, Stange award, 1977, Disting. Achievement citation, 1981 (all Iowa State U.); named to Am. Poultry Hall Fame, 1977. Fellow Poultry Sci. Assn.; mem. Nat. Turkey Fedn. (life; Research award 1950), Tex. Poultry Assn. (life), Minn. Turkey Growers Assn. (life), Soc. Exptl. Biology and Medicine, Am. Assn. Avian Pathologists (life), Am. Coll. Vet. Microbiologists, Am. Acad. Microbiology, Am. Soc. Microbiology, AVMA (council research 1961-73, Pub. Service award 1980), Minn. Vet. Med. Assn. (sec.-treas. 1950-75, pres. 1978-79, Disting. Service award 1980), Sigma Xi, Phi Kappa Phi, Alpha Gamma Rho, Phi Zeta, Gamma Sigma Delta. Presbyterian (elder). Co-author: Diseases and Parasites of Poultry, 1958; contbg. author: Diseases of Poultry, 1972, 78, 84. Home: 1443 Raymond Ave Saint Paul MN 55108

POMEROY, ROBERT WATSON, III, consultant; b. N.Y.C., May 22, 1935; s. Robert W. and Estelle C. (Bassett) P.; B.A., Stanford U., 1958; postgrad. Am. U. of Beirut, 1958-59; m. Jane Graham Adams Ramsay, Feb. 11, 1960; children—Janet Fraser, Seth Bassett. Sales mgr. Fin. Services, Overseas Brokerage Services, Beirut, 1958-60; exec. asst. to gen. mgr. Internat. Basic Economy Corp., Brazil, 1961-64; dir. Arbor Acres, S.A., Indusquima S.A., Sao Paulo, Brazil, 1961-64; fin. analyst Inter-Am. Devel. Bank, Washington, 1965-73; advisor Inter-Am. Devel. Bank, Washington, 1973-87; chmn. Washington area Bus. Resource Group, Nat. Coordinating Com. for Promotion History, 1977-80; mem. founding steering com., treas., dir. Nat. Council on Public History, 1979-83; cons. Pres.'s Commn. on Fgn. Lang. and Internat. Studies, 1979; founding dir. The Maine Consortium, 1981; adv. bd. dept. history Ariz. State U., 1981—; founding dir. Nat. Ctr. for Study of History, sec.-treas., 1984—; bd. advisors MTSU Ctr. for Hist. Preservation, 1985—; cons. to programs in public history and internat. studies. Served with Signal Corps, U.S. Army, 1954-56. Mem. Am. Hist. Assn., Orgn. Am. Historians (com. on public history 1982-83), Newcomen Soc. N.Am. Author: Educating Historians for Business; A Guide for Departments of History; Careers for Graduates in History; Careers in Information Management; mem. nat. bd. editors Public Historian, 1980—; editorial policy bd. Office, Technology and People, 1981—; editor (with David F. Trask) The Craft of Public History. Contbr. articles to profl. jours. Home and Office: RR #1 Box 679 Cornish ME 04020

POMPEIANO, OTTAVIO, physiologist, educator; b. Faenza, Italy, Sept. 29, 1927; s. Antonio and Maria (Padula) P.; m. Stefi Möller, Sept. 13, 1960; children: Maria, Maria Cristina, Lucia, Antonio. MD Bologna (Italy) U., 1950. Docent physiology Bologna U., 1958; asst. prof. physiology Bologna U. and U. Pisa, 1954-66; prof. physiology Med. Sch., Pisa U., 1966—, dir. inst. physiology, 1981-83; acting prof. physiology Rome U., 1962-63; vis. prof. dept. physiology Göteborg U. (Sweden), 1964; prof. neurophysiology Scuola Normale Superiore, Pisa, 1968—; Rockefeller Found. research fellow Anat. Inst., Oslo U., 1956-57; research fellow Nobel Inst. Neurophysiology, Karolinska Inst., Stockholm, 1958-59; Henderson Trust lectr., Edinburgh, Scotland, 1961; Moruzzi lectr., Liège, Belgium, 1981; Tarbox Disting. Neuroscientist lectr., Lubbock, Tex., 1982; vis. prof. Wash. State U., Pullman, 1985. NIH grantee, 1961—; recipient Vittorio Emanuele II prize, 1950; E. Cavazza prize Bologna U., 1950; A. Feltrinelli prize for medicine

Accademia dei Lincei, Rome, 1974; R. Barany Gold medal, Uppsala U., 1983; P. Caliceti Gold medal Bologna U., 1984. Mem. European Neurosci. Assn., N.Y. Acad. Scis., Academia Rodinensis, Internat. Postural and Gait Research, s., European Soc. Sleep Research, Italian Physiol. Soc., Am. Neurosci. Soc., Barany Soc., Collegium ORLAS, Internat. Brain Research Orgn. (central council 1976-86). Author: (with A. Brodal and F. Walberg) The Vestibular Nuclei and Their Connections, Anatomy and Functional Correlations; (with A. Brodal) Basic Aspects of Central Vestibular Mechanisms; (with R. Granit) Reflex Control of Posture and Locomotion; (with C. Ajmone Marsan) Brain Mechanisms of Perceptual Awareness and Purposeful Behavior; (with J.H.J. Allum) Vestibulospinal Control of Posture and Movement; editor: Archives Italiennes de Biologie, Pflügers Archiv, European Jour. Physiology. Discovered inhibition of motoneurons during sleep, mechanisms of sensorymotor integration during sleep; developed problems of central and reflex control of posture and movements, and brain integration of neck and labyrinth inputs; discovered mechanisms of gain regulation of vestibulospinal and cervicospinal reflexes; described (with A. Brodal) somatotopical organization of efferent projections from cerebellum, lateral vestibular nucleus and red nucleus. Home: 46 SS 12, 56010 Rigoli, Pisa Italy Office: 31 Via S Zeno, 56100 Pisa Italy

POMPIAN, RICHARD OWEN, communications company executive, educator; b. Chgo., July 17, 1935; s. Bertram Edwin and Molly Mavis (Pumpian) P.; AB, cert. in Journalism, U. Mich., 1958, Intern cert. in Advt., 1961; MBA in Mktg. with distinction, NYU, 1965, cert. in pub. and graphics, 1966, cert. in TV, 1967, cert. in computer systems, 1970; postgrad. in bus. communication U. Tex.-Austin, 1982—; m. Rita Lillian Beyers, Dec. 20, 1970 (div. Jan. 1984). Copywriter, Dancer-Fitzgerald-Sample, Inc., N.Y.C., 1960-68; self-employed advt. cons., N.Y.C., 1968-69; advt. agt., prin. ProSell Communications Co. (now Pompian Advt., Inc.), N.Y.C., 1970-74, pres., 1974-84; editor Northeast Gazette, 1976-80; partner The Pompians, Tng. Cons., 1977—; dir. Pompian Pools, Inc., Detroit, 1965-76; lectr. advanced writing course Pace U., N.Y.C., 1974-75; adj. asst. prof. communication arts St. John's U., N.Y.C., 1979-80, asst. prof., 1980-85; adj. lectr. journalism Fordham U., N.Y.C., 1979-80; adj. lectr. communication arts Marymount Manhattan Coll., N.Y.C., 1979-80; lectr. in advtg. U. Tex., Austin, 1987-88. Served to 1st lt. arty. AUS, 1958-60. Nat. Endowment for Arts grantee, 1978. Mem. Soc. Profl. Journalists, Assn. for Bus. Communication, Nat. Acad. TV Arts and Scis., AAAS, N.Y. Acad. Scis., Soc. Gen. Systems Research, U. Mich. Alumni Assn., N.Y. U. Alumni Assn., Delta Sigma Phi, Phi Kappa Phi. Club: NYU. Author: Advertising: A First Book, 1970; Writing for Professionals, 1981; editor: The Rhythm Book (Peter Phillips), 1971. Home: 4313 Charlemagne Ct Austin TX 78727

PONCE, GONZALO MANUEL, banker; b. Caracas, Venezuela, July 10, 1955; s. Gonzalo and Libia (Salazar) Ponce Lugo; children: Andres G., Simon G. Degree in engring., U. Simon Bolivar, Caracas, 1979; M in Organizational Devel., U. Simón Bolivar, Caracas, 1987. Trainee Irving Trust Co., N.Y.C., 1979-80, Union Chelsea Nat. Bank, N.Y.C., 1980-81; systems analyst Banco Mercantil, Caracas, 1981-83, systems coordinator, 1983-85, dept. mgr., 1985-86, div. mgr., 1986-87; gen. mgr. Prococima, C.A., Caracas, 1987—. Office: Prococima CA, PO Box 789, Caracas 1011, Venezuela

PONCES DE CARVALHO, JOÃO DE DEUS RAMOS, film director, director of photography; b. Lisbon, Portugal, Mar. 17, 1957; s. Fernando de Melo Vieira and Maria da Luz Deus (Ramos) P.; m. Maria Lopes Cravo, Dec. 20, 1976 (div. 1986); children: João, Miguel. MA in History, Classic U., Lisbon, 1981. Freelance photographer Portugal, 1974-79, film dir., 1979—. Dir. films Moinhos Velhos, 1979, Portex 79, 1979, João De Deus, 1980, The Child and the Kindergarten, 1982, A Data E O Feito, 1982, The Portuguese Forest, 1983, Dialogue, 1984, Lives in Danger series, 1984-85, Eccentric, 1985, Cape Verde, 1988, Romance of a Music, 1988; dir. and dir. photography Animals of Portugal, 1987. Home: Av Visconde Valmor 76-2D, P-1000 Lisbon Portugal

PONDER, CATHERINE, clergywoman; b. Hartsville, S.C., Feb. 14, 1927; d. Roy Charles and Kathleen (Parrish) Cook; student U. N.C. Extension, 1946, Worth Bus. Coll., 1948; BS in Edn., Unity Ministerial Sch., 1956; 1 son by previous marriage, Richard. Ordained to ministry, Unity Sch. Christianity, 1958; minister Unity Ch., Birmingham, Ala., 1956-61; founder, minister Unity Ch., Austin, Tex., 1961-69, San Antonio, 1969-73, Palm Desert, Calif., 1973—. Mem. Assn. Unity Chs., Inc. (hon. DD 1976), Internat. New Thought Alliance, Internat. Platform Assn. Clubs: Bermuda Dunes Country, Racquet (Palm Springs, Calif.); Los Angeles. Author: The Dynamic Laws of Prosperity, 1962; The Prosperity Secret of the Ages, 1964; The Dynamic Laws of Healing, 1966; The Healing Secret of the Ages, 1967; Pray and Grow Rich, 1968; The Millionaires of Genesis, 1976; The Millionaire Moses, 1977; The Millionaire Joshua, 1978; The Millionaire from Nazareth, 1979, The Secret of Unlimited Prosperity, 1981; Open Your Mind to Receive, 1983; Dare to Prosper!, The Prospering Power of Prayer, 1983; The Prospering Power of Love, 1984; Open Your Mind to Prosperity, 1984, The Dynamic Laws of Prayer, 1987. Office: 73-669 Hwy 111 Palm Desert CA 92260

PONDER, JAMES ALTON, clergyman, evangelist; b. Ft. Worth, Jan. 20, 1933; s. Leo A. and Mae Adele (Blair) P.; B.A., Baylor U., 1954; M.Ed., Southwestern Bapt. Theol. Sem., 1965; m. Joyce Marie Hutchison, Sept. 1, 1953; children—Keli, Ken. Ordained to ministry Baptist Ch., 1953; pastor Calvary Bapt. Ch., Corsicana, Tex., 1953-57, First Bapt. Ch., Highlands, Tex., 1957-62, Ridglea West Bapt. Ch., Ft. Worth, 1963-66, First Bapt. Ch., Carmi, Ill., 1966-67; dir. evangelism Ill. Bapt. State Conv., 1968-70, Fla. Bapt. Conv., 1970-81; pres. Jim Ponder Ministries, Inc., 1981—; dir. Inst. World Evangelism div. Jim Ponder Ministries; preacher Crossroads radio program; fgn. mission bd. evangelist in various countries of Asia, Central Am., Middle East, 1960—; project dir. Korea Major Cities Evangelization Project, 1978-80; evangelist ch. revivals, area crusades and evangelism confs., 1951—; mem. faculty Billy Graham Schs. Evangelism, 1970—; co-founder Ch. Growth Inst. Fla., 1976; co-dir. Ch. Growth Crusades, 1978-79; founder, dir. Inst. World Evangelism (I-Owe), 1987—; pres. Conf. Fla. Baptist Evangelists, 1986-87; sports announcer Sta. KIYS, Waco, Tex., 1950-54. Bd. dirs. N. Fla. chpt. Leukemia Soc. Am. Mem. Internat. Platform Assn., Fellowship Christian Athletes, Smithsonian Instn., N. Am. Soc. Church Growth, Acad. Evangelism in Edn., Acad. Evangelism Profs. Democrat. Club: Kiwanis. Author: The Devotional Life, 1970; Evangelism Men...Motivating Laymen to Witness, 1975; Evangelism Men...Proclaiming the Doctrines of Salvation, 1976; Evangelism Men...Preaching for Decision, 1979; author, video tchr. Becoming a Witness; contbr. articles to religious publs.; speaker in field. Home: 2280 Shepard Apt 304 Jacksonville FL 32211 Office: PO Box 8881 Jacksonville FL 32239

PONGRATZ, OLAF HEINZ, business executive; b. Berlin, Oct. 29, 1937; s. Heinz and Adolfine (Mlakar) P.; BA in Journalism, U. Munich (W. Ger.), 1962; D.Polit. Sci., U. Bradford Pasadena; Dr. h.c., U. Tucson, Ariz., 1983; m. Maria Gabriela Roger, Feb. 28, 1970; 1 son, Gilbert Marcell. Journalist, then chief editor Styrian comml. newspaper Steirische Wirtschaft, Graz, Austria, 1964-67; consul gen. of Costa Rica for provincies of Styria and Carinthia, Austria, 1970-72; v.p. Centro Larga Vida, San Jose, Euroimpex SA, San Jose; owner Foto-Video-Kino Pongratz, Graz, wholesale, export, and retail photograph equipment; pres. Pongratz Trans Trade, Ltd., Graz, Miami, Budapest; bd. dirs. Minimundus Ltd., Reagenfurt. Mem. bd. Austrian com. to Council of Europe; v.p. Styrian Br. Save the Children. Decorated Cross of Comdr., French Lazarus Order; Cross of Comar. of Brazilian São Paulo Apostolo Order; Carolus medal (gold and bronze, Carolus Cross); Royal Scots Medal of Merit; cert. photog. expert. Mem. Austrian-Tunisian Soc. (mem. bd.). Clubs: Cariari, Union (San Jose); Shooting, Austria-Inst. (Graz). Address: 6 Opernring, Graz Austria

PONIATOWSKI, MICHEL CASIMIR, French deputy to European Parliament, author; b. Paris, May 16, 1922; s. Prince Charles-Casimir and Princess Anne (Caraman-Chimay) P.; law degree, U. Paris; higher cert. Cambridge U.; diploma Nat. Coll. Adminstrn.; m. Gilberte de Chavagnac, Feb. 18, 1946; children—Ladislas, Isabelle, Axel, Bruno. Civil adminstr. Ministry of Fin., 1948; prin. pvt. sec. to dir. fin., Morocco, 1949-52; 1st French dep. European Union of Payments, 1954; tech. counsellor in Pres.'s Cabinet, 1955; fin. attache, Washington, 1956-57; fin. and econ. counsellor French embassy, Morocco, 1958-62; sub-dir. Ministry of Fin., minister of fin., 1962-63; dir. ins. Ministry Fins. and Econ. Affairs, 1963; dep. of Val d'Oise, also sec.-gen. Nat. Fedn. Ind. Republicans, 1967-73; mayor of Isle-Adam, Val d'Oise, 1971—; minister of public health and social security, 1973-74; minister of state, minister of interior, 1974-77; itinerant ambassador, 1977-81; dep. to European Parliament, 1979—, pres. Commn. for Devel. and Cooperation, 1979—; pres. Commn. for Fgn. Affairs, U.D.F.; pres. Inst. Polit. Prospect, pres. Commn. Energy Research and Tech. of European Parliament, 1984. Decorated knight Legion of Honor, others. Author: The Future of Underdeveloped Nations, 1954; History of Russia, America and Alaska, 1958; Talleyrand in the United States, 1967; The Choices of Hope, 1970; Cards on the Table, 1972; The Jagellons, 1973; Handling Change, 1975; Cadoudal, Moreau, Pichegru, 1977; The Future Is Written Nowhere, 1978; Louis Philippe et Louis XVIII, 1980; History Is Free, 1982; Talleyrand and the Directoire 1796-1800, 19982 (Prix Gobert 1983); Garnerin, the First Parachutist of History, 1983; Open Letter to the President of the Republic, 1983; Europe or Death, 1984; Socialism in the French Mode, 1985, New Technologies, 1986, Talleyrand and the Consulate, 1986, Talleyrand et l'ancienne France, 1988. Office: Parlement Europeen, Centre Europeen, BP1601 Plateau de Kirchberg Luxembourg

PONKA, LAWRENCE JOHN, manufacturing planning administrator; b. Detroit, Sept. 1, 1949; s. Maximillian John and Leona May (Knobloch) P.; m. Nancy Kathleen McNamara, Feb. 20, 1988. A.A., Macomb County Community Coll., 1974; B.S. in Indsl. Mgmt., Lawrence Inst. Tech., 1978; M.A. in Indsl. Mgmt., Central Mich. U., 1983. Engr.'s asst. Army Tank Automotive Command, 1967-68; with Sperry & Hutchinson Co., Southfield, Mich., 1973, Chrysler Corp., Detroit, 1973; with Gen. Motors Corp., Warren, Mich., 1973-82, engring. systems coordinator engring. staff, 1976-82, current product engring. until 1982; mfg. engr. Buick-Oldsmobile-Cadillac Group, Gen. Motors Assembly Div.-Orion Pontiac, Mich., 1982-84, sr. analyst advanced vehicle engring. Chevrolet-Pontiac-Can. group Engring. Ctr., Warren, 1985-86; mfg. planning adminstr. Detroit-Hamtramck Assembly Ctr., Cadillac Motor Car Co., Allanté, 1986—. cons. internal; mfg. planning administr./human resource advisor. Served with USAF, 1968-72, Vietnam. Decorated Air Force Commendation medal. Mem. Soc. Automotive Engrs., Engring. Soc. Detroit, Am. Legion, Vietnam, Japan, Okinawa DAV. Roman Catholic. Home: PO Box 732 Plymouth MI 48170-0732 Office: Gen Motors Corp 2500 E General Motors Blvd Detroit MI 48211-2002

PONNAIAH, LIONEL FRANCIS WIGNARAJAH, management consultant; b. Colombo, Sri Lanka, Feb. 23, 1933; s. Clement Basil and Agnes Lily (Gnanam) P.; m. Rajini Therese Emmanuel, Apr. 18, 1975; stepchildren—Diane Peter, Suren Peter, Arunesh Peter. B.Sc. Econs., London U., 1958. Clk., Ceylon & Fgn. Trades Ltd., Colombo, Sri Lanka, from 1952, Shell Co. of Ceylon Ltd., from 1963; cons. Assoc. Mgmt. Services Ltd., Colombo, 1964-80; group gen mgr. V.T.V. Group of Cos., Colombo, 1981—; cons. in field. Author: All-in-One Planning and Accounting System, Programmed Instruction Course in Planning and Accounting for Small Business Entrepreneurs. Contbr. articles to profl. jours. Treas. Sri Lanka Inst. Mktg., 1973-76. Fellow Chartered Inst. Mgmt. Accts., Inst. Cost and Mgmt. Accts. U.K.; mem. Am. Mgmt. Assn., VITA (U.S.), Sri Lanka Inst. Mktg., Sri Lanka Mgmt. Assn., Sri Lanka Assn. for the Advancement of Sci., Sri Lanka Economists Assn. Roman Catholic. Club: Royal Colombo Golf. Lodge: Tri Ratna. Home: 86 College St, Colombo Sri Lanka Office: VTV Group of Cos, 267 Sea St, Colombo 11 Sri Lanka

PONS, BERNARD, politician, physician; b. Béziers, France, July 18, 1926; s. Claude and Veronique (Vogel) P.; M.D., Faculté de Medecine, Montpellier; m. Josette Cros, 1952; 5 daus. Gen. practice medicine, Cahors, France, 1952-67; elected dep. for Lot, Nat. Assembly, 1967, for Essonne, 1978; sec. state Ministry of Agr., Govt. of France, 1969-73; conseiller general Canton of Carjac, 1967-78; mcpl. councillor City of Souillac, 1971-77; regional councillor City of Ile-de-France, 1978-81; deputy for Paris, 1981, 88—; Paris twp. counsellor, 1983; mem. Rassemblement pour la Republique (gen. sec. 1979-84); minister, Ministry Overseas Dept. & Territories, 1986-88; pres. Groupe RPR (polit. party), 1988—. Office: Assemblee Nationale, 126, rue de l'Université, 75007 Paris France

PONS IRAZAZABAL, FELIX, Spanish governement official; b. Palma De Mallorca, Spain, Sept. 14, 1942; s. Felix Pons Marques and Maria Josefa Irazazabal; m. Carmen Aguirre Ferrer, Mar. 23, 1968; children: Felix Pons Aguirre, Maria Jose Pons Aguirre, Celia Pons Aguirre. Atty. 1965—; prof. Sch. Social Aid, Palma De Mallorca, 1965-70; prof. polit. law Facultad de Derecho, Palma De Mallorca, 1972-74, prof. adminstrv. law, 1974-77; rep. Legis. Assembly, 1977-79, rep. in 1st legislature, 1979-82; sec. gen. Socialist Fedn. Balear, Spain, 1982-85, pres., 1985—; minister territorial adminstrn. Spain, 1985-86; pres. Congress Deps., Madrid, 1986—, v.p. commn. economy, mem. econ., justice, presuppositions and order commns., 1986—. Mem. Spanish Socialist Worker's Party. Roman Catholic. Address: Congress of Deputies, c/ Floridablanco s/n, 28014 Madrid Spain *

PONT, RAMON AMENOS, vegetable oil company executive; b. Tarrega, Spain, Apr. 1, 1937; s. Jose Creus and Carmen Foix (Amenos) P.; m. Reyes Tintore Viladomiu, June 5, 1962; children—Jose Ma, Ma Del Mar, Cristina, Enrique. Prof. Mercantil, Altos Estudios Mercantiles, Barcelona, 1960; Engr. Indsl. Tech., Escuela Engring. Tecnicos Industriales, Barcelona, 1960. Mgr., Industrias Pont, S.A., Tarrega, Spain, 1962—. Mem. Assn. Internat. des Etudiants en S. Econs. et Comerciales (internat. pres. 1960), Jr. Chamber (nat. pres. 1972-73, senator 1972). Home: Avenida Trepat 32, Tarrega Spain

PONTI, CARLO, film producer; b. Milan, Italy, Dec. 11, 1913; s. Leone and Maria (Zardone) P.; Law Degree, U. Milan, 1934; m. Sophia Loren, Apr. 9, 1966; children: Carlo, Edoardo; children by previous marriage: Guendalina, Alex. Engaged in legal practice, Milan, 1935-38; film producer, 1938—; prodns. include Roma Citta' Aperta (N.Y. Critics prize 1947), 1945, To Live in Peace, 1945, Attila, 1953, Ulysses, 1953, La Strada (Acad. Motion Picture Arts and Scis. award 1956), 1954, War and Peace, 1955, Two Women, 1960, Boccaccio '70, 1961, Yesterday, Today, Tomorrow (Motion Picture Acad. Arts and Scis. award 1964), 1963, Marriage, Italian Style, 1964, Casanova '70, 1964, Operation Crossbow, 1964, Lady L, 1965, Dr. Zhivago, 1965, 25th Hour, 1966, Blow Up (Palmares award Cannes Film Festival 1967), 1966, The Girl and the General, 1966, More Than a Miracle, 1966, Ghosts, Italian Style, 1967, Smashing Time, 1967, Diamonds for Breakfast, 1967, Best House in London, 1968, A Place for Lovers, 1968, Zabriskie Point, 1969, Sunflowers, 1970, The Priest's Wife, 1970, Love Stress, 1971, Lady Liberty, 1971, White Sister, 1972, Pisciotta Case, 1972, What?, 1972, Dear Parents, 1972, Carnal Violence, 1972, Dirty Weekend, 1972, Massacre in Rome, 1972, Flesh for Frankenstein, 1973, Blood for Dracula, 1973, Revolt of the City, 1973, Hercules V. Karate, 1973, Virility, 1973, Carnal Cousins, 1973, The Passenger, 1973, Run, Run, Joe, 1973, The Voyage, 1973, Verdict, 1974, Blood Money, 1974, Mastodoons, 1974, La Poliziotta, 1974, Poopsie, 1974, Cipolla Colt, 1974, Babysitter, 1975, The Devil and The Schoolteacher, 1975, The Boss and The Worker, 1975, The Cassandra Crossing, 1977, A Special Day, 1977, The Naked Sun, 1979; producer TV film The Fortunate Pilgrim, 1987. Decorated officer de l'Ordre des Arts et des Lettres, Ministère de Affaires Culturelles of Paris; named Champion Producer, Motion Picture Herald N.Y.-Fame Annual, 1967; recipient Gt. Film Maker award Internat. Film Importers and Distbrs. Am. Inc., 1969. Address: Bürgenstock, Nidwalden Switzerland other: 32 Ave Georges V, Paris 8e France other: 1 Piazza d'Ara Coeli, I-00186 Rome Italy *

PONZI, FRANK JOSEPH, art historian, author; b. New Castle, Pa., May 18, 1929; s. Attilio and Josephine (Largo) P.; m. Gudrún Tómasdóttir, July 7, 1956; children: Tómas, Margrét. BA, CCNY, 1951; MA, Oxford U., Eng., 1956. Conservator, film maker Solomon R. Guggenheim Mus., N.Y.C., 1956-58, 60-61; tech. dir. Screen Gems (Columbia Pictures), N.Y.C., 1961; conservator, artist Nat. Mus. Iceland, Reykjavik, Iceland, 1959-60; curator Mcpl. Art Mus., Reykjavik, 1971-73; art advisor Reykjavik and Kópavogur, 1971-73, 1980—; freelance writer, art cons. Almenna Bókafélagid Publs., Reykjavik, Europe, USA, 1987—; museum design advisor, conservator Kópavogur City Mus., Iceland, 1980—, Icelandic Parliament, Reykjavik, 1987—. Author: 18th Century Iceland, 1983, Finnur Jónsson (Artist Before his Time), 1985, 19th Century Iceland, 1986, Perugino's Albizi Fresco, 1987. Chmn. Fulbright Bd. Dirs., Reykjavik, 1964—; organizer, dir. various exhibitions Nordic House, Reykjavik, 1979, 80. Art Students League scholar N.Y.C., 1947; grantee Icelandic Sci. Found., Reykjavik, 1985, 86. Home: Brennholt, Mosfellssveit Iceland

PONZILLO, STEPHEN JOSEPH, III, educational administrator; b. Balt., Jan. 16, 1947; s. Stephen Joseph and Patricia Rosemary (Harrison) P.; B.S., Towson State U., 1969, M.Ed., 1972; postgrad. Loyola Coll. Balt., 1973, Morgan State U., 1974-75, Johns Hopkins U., 1974, U. Md., 1975—; m. Marie Ione Petts, Apr. 7, 1974; children—Marie Kathleen, Holly Anne. Tchr. social studies Sparrow Point High Sch., Baltimore County Bd. Edn. (Md.), 1969-77; tchr. Dundalk Sr. High Sch., 1977-85, asst. prin., 1977-85; prin. Gen. John Stricker Middle Sch., 1985—. Mem., co-founder Heritage Com. Sparrows Point, 1974-77; active United Way; chmn. Md. KT Ednl. Found. Named an outstanding young educator Dundalk Jaycees (Md.), 1973. Mem. Tchrs. Assn. Baltimore County, Md. Tchrs. Assn., NEA, Nat., Md. assns. secondary sch. prins., Secondary Sch. Adminstrs. Assn. Baltimore County (past exec. bd.), Nat. Hist. Soc., Am. Hist. Assn. Democrat. Methodist. Lodges: DeMolay, Masons (past grand master Md. Cryptic Masons), Shriners. Home: Marsteph Hall 4 Norgate Ct Hunt Valley MD 21030 Office: Gen John Stricker Mid Sch 7855 Trappe Rd Dundalk MD 21222

POOL, MARY JANE, design and marketing consultant, editor; b. La Plata, Mo.; d. Earl Lee Pool and Dorothy (Matthews) Evans. Grad., St. de Chantal Acad., 1942; B.A. with honors in Art, Drury Coll., 1946. Mem. staff Vogue mag., N.Y.C., 1946-68; assoc. merchandising editor Vogue mag., 1948-57, promotion dir., 1958-66, exec. editor, 1966-68; editor-in-chief House and Garden mag., 1970-80; Mem. com. of friends of environ. design collections Cooper-Hewitt Mus. of Smithsonian Instn.; mem. industry adv. council, dept. interior design Fashion Inst. Tech.; past bd. govs. Fashion Group, Inc., N.Y.C.; bd. govs. Decorative Arts Trust. Co-author: The Angel Tree, 1984. Editor: 20th Century Decorating, Architecture, Gardens, Billy Baldwin Decorates, 26 Easy Little Gardens. Mem. bus. com. N.Y. Zool. Soc., 1979-86; trustee Drury Coll., 1971—; bd. dirs. Isabel O'Neil Found., 1978—. Recipient Vogue Prix de Paris, 1946; award Nat. Soc. Interior Designers.; Disting. Alumni award Drury Coll., 1961. Mem. Am. Soc. Mag. Editors, Decorative Arts Soc., Women's Forum. Address: 1001 Park Ave New York NY 10028

POOL, PATRICK LAURENCE, print company executive; b. London, May 31, 1947; s. Laurence John and Gertrude Amy (Archer) P.; m. Janice Sharon Cohen, May 1971; children: Rebecca, Kevin, Trevor. BSc, Girton Coll., Cambridge, Eng., 1969. Grad. trainee Wiggins Teape, London, 1970-71; envelope gum researcher John Dickinson, London, 1971-75; dir. James Pool & Sons Ltd., London, 1975—; bd. dirs. Simon Dodds Advt., London, Shires Brewery, Borsetshire. Author: Envelopoe, Gum and Research Manual, 1973. Chmn. Ambridge Parish Council, Borsetshire, 1985, Paper Spoilers Fedn., 1986. Served to capt. British mil., 1980—. Fellow Inst. Dirs., Resin and Paper Mfrs. Soc. (chmn. 1975); mem. Retired Jewish Sailors Soc. SDP. Clubs: Army and Navy (London), Kennel; Grey Gables Country (Borsetshire) (bd. dirs. 1984—). Lodge: Masons. Home: The Instn Priestlands, Letchmore Heath WD2 8EW, England Office: James Pool and Sons Ltd, 1-3 North Rd, London N7 9HD, England

POOLE, JAMES EDWIN, business executive; b. Toledo, May 23, 1924; s. Alfred Edwin and Margaret (Brown) P.; student Ohio Wesleyan U., 1946; B.B.A., Western Res. U., 1949; m. Judy M. Holder, May 24, 1978; children—Carol Christine, James Edwin. Asst. to chief engr. Pickands Mather & Co., Cleve., 1949-54; v.p. sales and mktg. Huron Portland Cement Co., Detroit, 1955-65; v.p. mktg., dir. Medusa Portland Cement Co., Cleve., 1965-70, exec. v.p., 1970, pres., 1970-72; v.p., dir. Cement Transit Co., Manitowoc Portland Cement Co. (Wis.), 1970-72; v.p. Medusa Products Co. Can., Ltd., 1970-72; pres., chmn. bd., chief exec. officer Marquette Co. (formerly Marquette Cement Mfg. Co.), Chgo., 1972-74, Nashville, 1974—; pres. Natural Resources Group, Gulf Western Industries, Inc., 1977-83; pres., chief operating officer Service Mdse. chief exec. officer McDowell Enterprises, Inc., Nashville, 1984—, Lynwood Enterprises, Inc., Nashville; dir. 3d Nat. Bank, Nashville. Bd. dirs. St. Thomas Hosp. Devel. Found. Served with USMC, 1943-46. Mem. Nashville C. of C. (dir.), Delta Tau Delta. Episcopalian. Clubs: Belle Meade Country (Nashville); Sailfish Point (Stuart, Fla.). Home: 303 Lynnwood Blvd Nashville TN 37205 Office: Lynwood Enterprises 210 Wilson Pike Circle Brentwood TN 37027

POOLE, JOHN BAYARD, broadcasting executive, lawyer; b. Chgo., May 17, 1912; s. John Eugene and Edna (Carpenter) P.; m. Evelyn Singer, Apr. 10, 1979; 1 child, Leah Kathleen. Student, U. Chgo., 1929-32; LL.B., Detroit Coll. Law, 1936, J.D., 1968. Bar: Mich. 1936. Partner Poole, Littell & Sutherland, Detroit, 1936-76; of counsel Butzel, Long, Gust, Klein & VanZile, 1976-79, 84; chmn. exec. com. Capital Cities Communications, 1960-64; chmn. Poole Broadcasting Co. (WJRT-TV), Flint, Mich., WPRI-TV, Providence, WTEN-TV, Albany, N.Y.; sec., v.p., dir. Storer Broadcasting Co., Detroit, 1945-55; dir. Knight Ridder Newspapers, Inc., 1978-84, Mich. Nat. Bank of Detroit, 1964-82, dir. Mich. Nat. Corp., 1972-82. Pres., chmn., trustee William Beaumont Hosp., 1960-84; trustee U. Chgo., 1974—, Cranbrook Ednl. Community, 1976-79. Fellow Am. Bar Found.; mem. ABA, Detroit Bar Assn., Mich. Bar Assns., Am. Judicature Soc. Episcopalian (vestryman 1959-62). Clubs: Bloomfield Hills Country (bd. govs., pres.); Indian Creek Country, Surf (Miami). Home: 45 Scenic Oaks Dr North Bloomfield Hills MI 48013 also: 8 Indian Creek Island Miami Beach FL 33154 Office: 1700 N Woodward Ave Bloomfield Hills MI 48013

POOLE, MILLICENT ELEANOR, education educator; b. Ingham, Queensland, Australia, Jan. 29, 1940. Cert. in edn., Kelvin Grove (Australia) Tchrs.' Coll., 1960; BA, U. Queensland, 1963, BEd, 1967; MA with honors, U. New Eng., Australia, 1970; PhD, La Trobe U., Australia, 1973. Tchr. Hughenden (Australia) State High Top Sch., Queensland, 1960, Ingham State High Sch., 1961-63, Te Awamutu Coll., New Zealand, 1964-65; writer, research officer, lectr. Queensland Health Edn. Council, 1966-67; research asst. student counseling unit U. New Eng., Armidale, New South Wales, Australia, 1967-69; sr. tutor Centre For Urban Edn., La Trobe U., Bundoora, Victoria, Australia, 1970, lectr., 1971-72, sr. lectr., 1973-76; assoc. prof. Sch. Edn., Macquarie U., North Ryde, New South Wales, Australia, 1977-81, 82-86, intersch. fellow Sch. Behavioural Scis.,; prof. Faculty of Edn., Monash U., Clayton, Victoria, Australia, 1987—; mem. BEd adv. com. State Coll. Edn., Melbourne, Australia, 1979—; mem. field of study rev. com. Bd. Tchr. Edn., Queensland, 1983-88, ministerial working party, 1984-85; mem. evaluation team to advise on new arrangements for assessment of Victorian Cert. Edn., Victorian Ministry Edn., 1988—. Author: Social Class and Language Utilization at the Tertiary Level, 1976, The Developing Child, 1980, Creativity Across the Curriculum, 1980, School Leavers in Australia, 1981, Youth: Expectations and Transitions, 1983; (with J. Anderson and B. Durston) Efficient Reading: A Practical Guide, 1969, Thesis and Assignment Writing, 1970; (with others) Study Methods: A Practical Guide, 1969, Under 5 in Australia, 1973, Before School Begins: A Book of Readings on Australian Children, 1975; editor: (with P. R. de Lacey) Mosaic or Melting Pot: Cultural Evolution in Australia, 1979; (with P. R. de Lacey and B. Randhawa) Culture and Life Possibilities: Australia in Transition, 1985; assoc. editor Victorian region Australian Jour. Edn., 1973-77, adv. editor, 1980-85, editor, 1985—; contbr. articles to profl. jours. Recipient Mackenzie traveling lectureship, 1982; fellow, U. Calif.-Berkeley, 1973-74, U. Oreg., 1979, Harvard U., 1983, U. Melbourne, 1985; grantee Myer Found., 1970, Australian Research Grant Council, 1971, 72-74, Ednl. Research and Devel. Com., 1974-76, Ednl. Research and Devel. Com./Macquarie U. Research Grant, 1979-83, Australian Research Grant Scheme, 1984-87, 87—. Mem. Australia Council for Ednl. Research (nat. adv. com. 1979-83, 84—, council 1982-85, exec. mem. 1984—, chairperson adv. com. social context of edn. div. 1985—). Home: 63 Male St, Brighton, Victoria 3186, Australia Office: Monash U, Wellington Rd, Clayton, Victoria 3186, Australia

POOLE, PATRICK HENRY, psychologist, educator; b. Columbus, Kans., Oct. 18, 1932; s. William Harvey and Dorothy Ann (Hicks) P.; Student U. Kans., A.B., U. Tulsa, 1955; M.S., Pittsburg State U.-Kans., 1962; postgrad. San Francisco State U., 1964, San Jose State U., 1964, Stanford U., 1965, UCLA, 1966; Ph.D., U. So. Calif., 1976. Lic. marriage, family, and child counselor. Floor mgr. J.C. Penney Co., Tulsa, 1954-55; with Eagle-Picher Co., various locations, 1955-60; asst. to dean men Pittsburg State U., Kans., 1960, asst. instr. psychology, 1961; instr. spl. edn. elem. sch., Derby, Kans.,

1962-63; instr. Wyandotte High Sch., Kansas City, Kans., 1963-64, Kansas City (Kans.) Jr. Coll., 1963-64; test officer Monterey (Calif.) Peninsula Coll., 1964-66; asst. prof. edn. Calif. State U., Fresno, 1966-68, student affairs officer, coordinator group counseling program, 1968-83; mem. faculty Calif. Sch. Profl. Psychology, Fresno, 1978-83; pvt. practice as marriage, family and child counselor, Calif., 1976-82; staff psychologist, coordinator of services to students with disabilities, Counseling Ctr., Fairleigh Dickinson U., Teaneck, N.J., 1983—; cons. A. & D. Life Edn. Center, Denver, 1978-82. Founder, owner, mng. dir. The Harbor Far from the Sea, 1971-82, The Harbor Far From the Sea Co., 1980-82, The Harbor Mus. Art, 1980-82, The Harbor Midyear Cultural and Performing Arts Festival, 1980-82. Bd. dirs. Fresno Dance Repertory Assn., pres., 1972-73; bd. dirs. baritone soloist Fresno Community Chorus. Member of Schola Cantorem, General Theological Seminary, NYC, 1984-85; sec. leader, baritone voice Collegiate Chorale, N.Y.C., 1984—. Lic. counseling psychologist, Mass., N.J., S.C., Monterey Peninsula Counseling and Guidance Assn. (v.p. 1964-66), pres. profl. and adminstrv. senate FDU, Teaneck, N.J. American Psychological Association, Division 17, Met. Coll. Mental Health Assn. N.Y.C. (bd. dirs. 1987—, pres.-elect 1988—), Internat. Platform Assn., SAR (Fresno chpt. sec. 1973-75), County and City of Fresno C. of C. (cultural arts com. Somerset chpt., Phila.) Magna Charta Barons, Psi Chi, Phi Delta Kappa, Phi Mu Alpha, Pi Delta Epsilon, Delta Epsilon, Sigma Chi (life mem., founder Zeta Iota chpt.). Composer Missa Brevis performed by Monterey Peninsula Coll. Chorus, 1965, Coventry Chorale, Tulsa, 1987. Extensive travel throughout C. Am., S. Am., Europe, Eng., N. Am., Middle East and Asia, 1955—. Home: 496A Hudson Suite G12 New York NY 10014 Office: Fairleigh Dickinson U Counseling Center Teaneck NJ 07666

POOLEY, JAMES HENRY ANDERSON, lawyer, author; b. Dayton, Ohio, Oct. 4, 1948; s. Howard Carl and Daisy Frances (Lindsley) P.; children by previous marriage: Jefferson Douglas, Christopher James; m. Laura Jean Anderson, Oct. 13, 1984; 1 child, Catherine Lindsley. BA, Lafayette Coll., 1970; JD, Columbia U., 1973. Bar: Calif. 1973, U.S. Dist. Ct. (no. dist.) Calif. 1973, U.S. Ct. Appeals (9th cir.) 1974, U.S. Supreme Ct. 1977, U.S. Dist. Ct. (cen. dist.) Calif. 1978. Assoc. Wilson, Mosher & Sonsini, Palo Alto, Calif., 1973-78; ptnr. Mosher, Pooley & Sullivan, Palo Alto, 1978—; lectr. Practicing Law Inst., N.Y.C., 1983, 85-86, Santa Clara U. Sch. Law, 1985—. Author: Trade Secrets, 1982, Protecting Technology, 1983, Trying the High Technology Case, 1984, The Executive's Guide to Protecting Proprietary Business Information and Trade Secrets, 1987; contbr. articles to profl. jours.; editor-in-chief Trade Secret Law Reporter, 1984-85; bd. advisors Santa Clara Computer and High Tech. Law Jour., 1984—. Arbitrator, judge pro tem Santa Clara County Superior Ct., San Jose, 1979—. Mem. ABA, Computer Law Assn., Assn. Bus. Trial Lawyers, Am. Electronics Assn. (chmn. lawyers' com. 1981-82). Republican. Methodist. Office: Mosher Pooley & Sullivan 525 University Ave Palo Alto CA 94301

POOLEY, ROGER FRANCIS, literary critic; b. Watford, Eng., June 19, 1947; s. Francis Richard and Daisy (Felstead) P. BA, Cambridge U., Eng., 1969, PhD, 1977. Lectr. English U. Coll. Swansea, Eng., 1972-73, U. Keele, Staffordshire, Eng., 1973—; exchange prof. U. Tulsa, 1983. Editor: The Green Knight: Selected Works of George Gascoigne, 1980; co-editor: The Lord of the Journey: A Reader in Christian Spirituality, 1986. Mem. Soc. Renaissance Studies. Methodist. Home: 57 Greatbatch Ave, Penkhull, Stoke-on-Trent ST4 7BY, England Office: U Keele Dept English, Keele ST5 5BG, England

POORVU, WILLIAM JAMES, educator, real estate investment executive; b. Boston, Apr. 10, 1935; s. Sumner L. and May C. Poorvu; B.A. Yale U., 1956; M.B.A. Harvard U., 1958; m. Lia Gelin, June 9, 1957; children—Alison, Jonathan. Officer, dir. Boston Broadcasters, Inc., 1963-83 ; lectr. Harvard Bus. Sch., 1973-81, adj. prof., 1981—; chmn. The Baupost Group Inc.; trustee, dir. Mass. Fin. Services Group Mut. Funds; dir. Sonesta Internat. Corp.; trustee Trammell Crow Real Estate Investors, 1985—, Conn. Gen. Mortgage and Realty Investments Inc., 1980-81; cons. Bank of Boston Pooled Real Estate Investment Fund, 1971—. Treas., vice chmn. bd. trustees Boston Symphony Orchestra, 1984—; trustee, bd. govs. New Eng. Med. Ctr.; trustee Gardner Mus. Recipient Cert. of Merit, HUD, 1968. Contbr. articles to profl. publs. Office: Harvard U Grad Sch Bus Morgan Hall 237 Boston MA 02163

POOS, JACQUES FRANCOIS, vice president of the Govt. of Luxembourg; b. Luxembourg, June 3, 1935; s. Adolphe and Catherine (Weimerskirch) P.; m. Monique Lorang, July 3, 1969; children: Daniel, Yasmine, Xavier. Dipl. fin. d et sec., Athenee, Luxembourg, 1954; Lic. ès Sc. Ec. et Commn. H.E.C., Switzerland, 1958; Dipl. Sup. Ec. Comparée, U. Internat., Luxembourg, 1960; Docteur ès Sciences Comm. et Ec., U. Lausanne, Switzerland, 1961. Seconded to Ministry of Nat. Economy, 1959-62, mem. Research at Nat. Statis. Office (STATEC), 1962-64; mng. dir. Imprimerie Coopérative and newspaper Tageblatt, 1964-76; minister of fin. Luxembourg, 1976-79, vice pres. of govt., minister for fgn. affairs, external trade and coop., minister of economy, minister of treasury, 1984—; mng. dir. Banque Continentale de Luxembourg S.A., 1980-82, Banque PARIBAS, Luxembourg S.A., 1982-84; Author: Le Luxembourg dans le Marché Commun, 1961; Le Modèle Luxembourgeois, 1977; other publs. in field. City counsellor of Esch/Alzette, 1969-76; mem. of Parliament, 1974-76, head of the Socialist Workers Party Group in Parliament, 1975-76, chmn. Parliament's Commn. for Budget and Fin., 1975-76. Vice pres. Socialist Workers Party Group in Parliament (Commn. for Fgn. Affairs, Commn. for Budget and Fin. 1979—); mem. mng. bd. Socialist Workers Party, 1976—, v.p., 1982—. Office: Ministry of Fgn Affairs, 5 rue Notre-Dame, 2240 Luxembourg Luxembourg

POP, EMIL, research chemist; b. Tirgu Mures, Romania, Aug. 12, 1939; came to U.S., 1983; s. Victor and Rosalia (Graf) P.; m. Elena Petrina Petri, Apr. 28, 1964; 1 child, Andreea Christina. BS, Babes-Bolyai U., Cluj., Romania, 1961; PhD, Inst. Chemistry, Cluj. and Supreme Council of Romanian Acad. Sci., 1973. Chemist Chem. Pharm. Research Inst., Cluj-Napoca, Romania, 1962-65, researcher, 1965-78, sr. researcher, group leader, compartment leader, 1978-83; researcher Rugjer Boskovic Inst., Zagreb, Yugoslavia, 1971-72; postdoctoral research assoc. U. Fla., Gainesville, 1983-86; sr. research scientist Pharmatec, Inc., Alachua, Fla., 1986-87, group leader, 1987—. Contbr. articles to profl. jours.; inventor in field. Recipient Romanian Acad. award for chemistry. Fellow Am. Inst. Chemists; mem. Am. Chem. Soc., AAAS, Am. Assn. Pharm. Scientists, Internat. Union Pure and Applied Chemistry, N.Y. Acad. Scis. Greek Catholic. Current work: Design and synthesis of pharmaceutical compounds in particular brain chemical drug delivery systems; M.O. calculations. Home: 810 SW 51st Way Gainesville FL 32607

POPE, DAVID E., geologist, micropaleontologist; b. Forrest City, Ark., Dec. 20, 1920; s. Jesse Ellis and Mary Ruth (Remley) P.; m. Dorothy Angeline Salario, June 8, 1947 (dec. Jan. 1982); children—David Brian, Mark Alan. BS, La. State U., 1947, MS, 1948; grad. U.S. Army Command and Gen. Staff Coll., 1967. Cert. petroleum geologist. Paleontologist, Union Producing Co., Houston, 1948-49, New Orleans, 1949-55, dist. paleontologist, New Orleans, 1955-63, Lafayette, La., 1963-67; cons., Lafayette, La., 1967-75; sr. research geologist La. Geol. Survey, Baton Rouge, 1975—; lectr. La. State U., 1979, 80, N.E. La. U., 1983. Mem. nat. adv. bd. Am. Security Council, 1983—; bd. dirs. La. State U. Mus. Geosci. Assocs., 1980—, pres. 1981-82, 1987—. Served to capt. U.S. Army, 1942-46, to lt. col. USAR, 1945-70. Contbr. articles to profl. jours. Decorated Silver Star medal with oak leaf cluster, Purple Heart, Combat Inf. badge. Mem. Am. Assn. Petroleum Geologists (ho. of dels. 1981—), Am. Inst. Profl. Geologists, Soc. Econ. Paleontologists and Mineralogists (pres. Gulf Coast sect. 1959-60, hon. life mem. 1987), New Orleans Geol. Soc. (v.p. 1959-60, 1962-63), Lafayette Geol. Soc., Baton Rouge Geol. Soc. (pres. 1980-81), Gulf Coast Assn. Geol. Socs. (exec. com. 1980-87, historian 1984—, pres. 1985-86), Res. Officers Assn. (life), Mil. Order World Wars, La. State U. Sch. Geology Alumni Assn. (pres. 1958-59, 84-85), La. Petroleum Council. Home: 299 Roselawn Blvd Lafayette LA 70503 Office: La Geol Survey Univ Sta PO Box G Baton Rouge LA 70893

POPE, LEAVITT JOSEPH, broadcast company executive; b. Boston, Apr. 2, 1924; s. Joseph and Charlotte (Leavitt) P.; m. Martha Pascale, Nov. 20, 1948; children—Joseph, Daniel, Patricia, Elizabeth, Nancy, Maria, Joan, Christopher, Virginia, Matthew, Charles. B.S., Mass. Inst. Tech., 1947. Adminstrv. asst. N.Y. Daily News, N.Y.C., 1947-51; asst. to gen. mgr. Sta. WPIX-TV, N.Y.C., 1951-56; v.p. ops. Sta. WPIX-TV, 1956-72, Sta. WPIX-FM, N.Y.C., 1956-72; sec. WPIX, Inc., N.Y.C., 1958-75; exec. v.p. WPIX, Inc., 1972-75, pres., chief exec. officer, 1975—, also dir.; sec., exec. v.p. Conn. Broadcasting Co., Bridgeport, 1967-75, pres., chief exec. officer, dir., 1975-87; dir. N.Y. Daily News, 1975-78, Tribune Co., 1978-81. Mem. N.Y. State Regents Ednl. TV Adv. Council, 1958; bd. govs. Daytop Village, 1972—; trustee Catholic Communications Found., St. Thomas Aquinas Coll., 1968-75, Cardinal Cooke Hosp., 1979—; dir. Archdiosese N.Y. Instructional TV com. 1976—. Served with Signal Corps U.S. Army, 1942-46. Mem. Assn. Ind. TV Stas. (pres. 1976-78, bd. dirs.), ASME, Internat. Radio and TV Soc., Nat. Assn. Broadcasters (bd. dirs. 1986—), N.Y. State Broadcasters Assn. (pres. 1976-77), Sigma Nu. Clubs: Univ. (N.Y.C.); Internat. (Washington); Knight of Malta. Home: 173 Dorchester Rd Scarsdale NY 10583 Office: 220 E 42d St New York NY 10017

POPE, MAX LYNDELL, pub. utility ofcl.; b. Clinton, N.C., Nov. 5, 1932; s. William Walter and Maggie (Honeycutt) P.; B.A., Idaho State Coll., 1962; grad. U.S. Army Command and Gen. Staff Coll., 1977, Security Manpower Program, Indsl. Coll. Armed Forces, 1980; m. Sarah Jane Norris, Dec. 10, 1954. City mgr. City of Rangely (Colo.), 1963-66, City of Seaside (Oreg.), 1966-69, City of Pasco (Wash.), 1969-70; city adminstr. City of Coeur d'Alene (Idaho), 1971-72; planner State of Idaho, Boise, 1972-75; city adminstr. City of Woodburn (Oreg.), 1975-85; gen. mgr. Woodinville Water Dist., Wash., 1986—. Ordained elder Presbyn. Ch., 1958, elder, Woodburn, 1976—. Served with U.S. Army, 1953-56, 70-71. Recipient Distinguished Service award Rangely Jaycees, 1964. Mem. Internat. City Mgmt. Assn., Am. Soc. Public Adminstrn., Am. Public Works Assn., Internat. Union Local Authorities, Civil Affairs Assn., Res. Officers Assn., Woodinville C. of C., Woodburn C. of C. Clubs: Rotary, Gowen Field Officers, Elks. Home: 14206 NE 181st Pl Suite L203 Woodinville WA 98072 Office: 17238 Woodinville-Duvall Rd Woodinville WA 98072

POPE-HENNESSY, JOHN WYNDHAM, art historian; b. London, Dec. 13, 1913; s. L.H.R. and Dame Una (Birch) P.-H. Ed., Downside Sch., Balliol Coll., Oxford (Eng.) U.; LL.D. (hon.), U. Aberdeen, 1972. Mem. staff Victoria and Albert Museum, 1938-73, keeper dept. architecture and sculpture, 1954-66, dir., sec., 1967-73; dir. Brit. Mus., 1974-76; consultative chmn. dept. European Paintings Met. Mus. Art, 1977-86; prof. art Inst. of Fine Arts, NYU, 1977—; Slade prof. fine art Oxford U., 1956-57, Cambridge (Eng.) U., 1964-65; Robert Sterling Clark prof. art Williams Coll., Williamstown, Mass., 1961-62; mem. Arts Council, Eng., 1968-76, Ancient Monuments Bd. for Eng., 1969-72; dir. Royal Opera House, 1971-76; hon. bd. dirs. Royal Coll. Art, London, 1973—; adv. bd. dirs. Met. Opera House, 1979-86. Author: Giovanni di Paolo, 1937, Sassetta, 1939, Sienese Quattrocento Painting, 1947, A Sienese Codex of the Divine Comedy, 1947, The Drawings of Domenichino at Windsor Castle, 1948, A Lecture on Nicholas Hilliard, 1949, Paolo Uccello, 1950, rev. edit., 1969, Fra Angelico, 1952, rev. edit., 1974, Italian Gothic Sculpture, 1955, 3rd rev. edit., 1985, Italian Renaissance Sculpture, 1958, 3rd rev. edit., 1985, Italian High Renaissance and Baroque Sculpture, 1963, 3rd rev. edit., 1985, Catalogue of Italian Sculpture in the Victoria and Albert Museum, 1964, Renaissance Bronzes in The Kress Collection, 1965, The Portrait in the Renaissance, 1967, Essays on Italian Sculpture, 1968, The Frick Collection, Sculpture, 1970, Raphael, 1970, (with others) Westminster Abbey, 1972, Luca della Robbia (Mitchell prize 1981), 1980, The Study and Criticism of Italian Sculpture, 1981, Benvenuto Cellini, 1985, The Robert Lehman Collection, I: Italian Paintings, 1987. Decorated comdr. Brit. Empire; created knight, 1971; named Grand Officer, Republic of Italy, 1988, hon. citizen City of Siena, 1982, hon. fellow Baillol Coll., Oxford U., Pierpont Morgan Library, N.Y.; recipient Serena medal Brit. Acad. Italian Studies, 1961, medal NYU, 1965, Torch of Learning award Hebrew U., Jerusalem, 1977, Mangia d'Oro, 1982, award Art Dealers Assn. Am., 1984. Fellow Brit. Acad., Soc. Antiquaries, Royal Soc. Lit.; mem. Am. Acad. Arts and Scis., Am. Philos. Soc. (fgn.), Accademia Senese degli Intronati (corr.), Bayerische Akademie der Wissenschaften (corr.), Accademia del Disegno (hon. accademician), Accademia Clementina, Bologna, Ateneo Veneto. Address: 28 via de' Bardi, 50125 Florence Italy

POPESCU, DORIN MIHAIL, mathematics researcher; b. Buzău, Romania, Mar. 21, 1947; s. Ion and Mihailina (Levitki) P. M in Algebra, Faculty of Math., Bucharest, Romania, 1969, PhD, 1974. Asst. Faculty of Math., Bucharest, 1969-79; sr. researcher Nat. Inst .for Sci. and Tech. Creation, Bucharest, 1979—. Contbr. articles to profl. jours. Recipient citation Romanian Acad., 1979; NSF grantee, 1980-81. Mem. Am. Math. Soc., Romanian Math. Soc. Home: GH Missail 17, 78226 Bucharest Romania Office: INCREST, Bd Pacii 220, 79622 Bucharest Romania

POPHAM, WILLIAM LEE, investment company executive; b. Washington, July 17, 1950; s. James Edward Popham and Jeanne (Minear) Popham Baker; m. Peggy Crook, Oct. 11, 1968 (div. Apr. 1987); children: William Lee, Erik, Laura. AB, Duke U., 1971; JD, U. Miami, Fla., 1976. Bar: Fla. 1978; CPA, Fla., 1972. Ptnr. Peat Marwick Main & Co., Miami, 1971-83; pres. First Atlantic Capital Corp., Miami, 1983-85; chmn., pres. Caesar Creek Holdings Inc., Miami, 1985—, Adm. Fin. Corp., Miami, 1987—; bd. dirs. Cruise Am. Inc. formerly known as Am. Land Cruisers Inc., Miami, Jeanne Baker Realty Inc., Miami, Haven Fed. Savs. and Loan Assn., Winter Haven, Fla. Editor: Tax Research, 1976. Mem. exec. bd., v.p. S. Fla. Council Boy Scouts Am., 1977—; active U. Miami Citizens Bd., 1985—; bd. dirs. Goodwill Industries of S. Fla. Inc., Miami, 1982—, Vizcayan Found. Bd. Inc., 1985—. Recipient Silver Beaver award Boy Scouts Am., 1983; named an Outstanding Young Man of Am., U.S. Jaycees, 1983. Mem. ABA, Fla. Bar Assn., Am. Inst. CPA's, Fla. Inst. CPA's, Exec. Assn. Greater Miami, Duke U. Alumni Assn. (nat. bd. dirs. 1981-85), Miami Duke Alumni (pres. 1977-84), Vizcayans. Republican. Presbyterian. Clubs: University (Miami) (social chmn. 1980-83), Coral Reef Yacht (Miami) (fin. com. chmn. 1986—). Home: 1000 Venetian Way #1204 Miami FL 33139 Office: Caesar Creek Holdings Inc 600 Brickell Ave #600 Miami FL 33131

POPLAWSKI, PAUL EDWIN, psychotherapist; b. Phila., Aug. 22, 1949; s. Edwin Joseph and Ellen Catherine (Jones) P.; BA in Psychology, U. Del., 1972; M in Human Services, Lincoln U., 1978; postgrad. Temple U. Clin. superintendent and psychotherapist Bur. Alcoholism and Drug Abuse, Newark, Del., 1971-75, dir. Newark Counseling Ctr., 1975-76, dir. training and edn., 1979—, cons., 1987—, dir. mental health tng., 1985—, coordinating state troubled employees program, 1983—, dir. outpatient care, Wilmington, Del., 1976-79; co-founder Nat. Training Network, 1982, Psychology of Music Research, 1984; pvt. practice psychotherapy, Newark, Del., 1976—. Composer numerous musical compositions. Advisor, Lincoln U. Masters Program, (Pa.), 1981-83; cons. City of Newark (Del.), 1983-84; trainer Del. Council on Alcoholism, Wilmington, Del., 1983; advisor Resources Ctr. for Performing Arts, Wilmington, 1984. Nat. Inst. Alcohol Abuse and Alcoholism, 1979-82, Nat. Institute Drug Abuse grantee, 1979-83. Mem. Am. Soc. Training and Devel., World Future Soc., Global Futures Network, Networking Inst., N.Y. Inst. for Gesalt Therapy. Roman Catholic. Home: 72 Welsh Tract Rd #110 Newark DE 19713 Office: Bur Alcoholism and Drug Abuse 1901 N DuPont Highway New Castle DE 19711

POPOVIC, NENAD DUSHAN, economics educator; b. Srem, Mitrovica, Serbia, Yugoslavia, June 17, 1909; came to U.S., 1961, naturalized, 1972; s. Dushan L. and Angelina S. (Yovanovic) P.; LL.B., U. Belgrade; m. Tatyana V. Popovic, Mar. 23, 1948; children—Deyan, Gina, Sanya. Research asst. Yugoslavian Nat. Bank, 1930-37, Chartered Agrarian Bank, 1938-41; dir. Yugoslav War Reparation Bd., 1945-46; v.p. Planning Commn. of Serbia, 1947-49; v.p. Econ. Council of Serbia, 1949-50; exec. dir. IMF, Washington, 1950-52; alt. exec. dir. World Bank, 1953; vice gov. Yugoslav Nat. Bank, 1953-55; asst. state sec. for fgn. trade, 1956-59; plenipotentiary minister Yugoslavian fgn. affairs, 1955-56, 59-61; prof. Syracuse (N.Y.) U., 1961-75, prof. emeritus, 1976—. Author: Foreign Exchange Controls in Yugoslavia, 1936; Statistics and Accounting in National Economy, 1949; National Economic Planning, 1949; International Financial Organizations, 1964, 66; Yugoslavia: The New Class in Crisis, 1968. Home: 319 Wedgewood Terr Dewitt NY 13214 Office: Syracuse U, Dept Econs 206 Maxwell Syracuse NY 13210

POPOVIC, VESNA, industrial design educator; b. Belgrade, Yugoslavia, June 2, 1943; came to Australia, 1981; s. Pavle and Zorica (Bojovic) P. Grad. Engr. Arch., U. Belgrade, 1966; M of Indsl. Design, U. Ill., 1976. Indsl. designer Industry Agrl. Equipment Zmaj., Belgrade, 1967-74, chief designer, 1976-81; editor news sect. Indsl. Design Mag., Belgrade, 1970-81; indsl. design educator in charge program Queensland Inst. Tech., Brisbane, Australia, 1981—. Designer combine harvester, first aid emergency unit, integrated work sta.; contbr. articles to profl. jours. U. Ill. fellow, Urbana-Champaign, 1973; Fulbright travel grantee Yugoslav-Am. Commn., Belgrade, 1974; recipient October Saloon award, Belgrade, 1976. Mem. Indsl. Design Inst. (Ulupus award 1973), Design Inst. Australia, Ergonomics Soc. Australia, Design Research Soc., Human Factors Soc. Office: Queensland Inst Tech, Faculty Built Environ, 2 George St, Brisbane Queensland 4001, Australia

POPPEL, SETH RAPHAEL, business executive; b. Bklyn., Mar. 17, 1944; s. Frank M. and Fritzi R. (Axenzow) P.; B.S. magna cum laude, L.I. U., 1965; M.B.A., Columbia U., 1967; m. Danine Vokt, Jan. 5, 1974; children—Clarysa, Jared, Stacy. Asst. prof. L.I. U., Greenvale, N.Y., 1967-68; v.p. Synergistic Systems Corp., N.Y.C., 1968-77; v.p., dir. corp. planning Chase Manhattan Corp., N.Y.C., 1977—; owner harness horses Seth Poppel Stables, 1983—. E.I. DuPont fellow, 1965-67, Downie Muir fellow, 1965-66; recipient Claire F. Adler award in math., 1964-65. Mem. Am. Statis. Assn., Ops. Research Soc. Am., Inst. Mgmt. Sci., Nat. Assn. Bus. Economy, N.Am. Soc. Corp. Planning, U.S. Trotting Assn., Beta Gamma Sigma, Psi Chi, Omega Epsilon. Home: 38 Range Dr Merrick NY 11566 Office: 1 Chase Manhattan Plaza New York NY 10081

POPPER, KARL (RAIMUND), author; b. Vienna, Austria, July 28, 1902; s. Simon Siegmund Carl and Jenny (Schiff) P.; m. Josefine Anna Henninger, Apr. 11, 1930 (dec. Nov. 1985). PhD, U. Vienna, 1928; DLit, U. London, 1948; LLD (hon.), U. Chgo., 1962, U. Denver, 1966; LittD (hon.), U. Warwick, Eng., 1971, U. Canterbury, N.Z., 1973; DLitt (hon.), City U. London, 1976, Salford (Eng.) U., 1976, Oxford, 1982; Dr. (hon.), U. Mannheim (Fed. Republic of Germany), 1978; Dr. rer. nat. (hon.), U. Vienna, 1978; DLitt (hon.), U. Guelph, Can., 1978; Dr. rer. pol. (hon.), U. Frankfurt, Can., 1979; PhD (hon.), U. Salzburg, Austria, 1979; LittD, U. Cambridge, Eng., 1980, U. Oxford, Eng., 1982; DSc (hon.), Gustavus Adolphus Coll., St. Peter, Minn., 1982, U. London, 1986. Sr. lectr. U. N.Z., 1937-45; reader, then prof. logic and sci. method U. London, 1949-69, emeritus, 1969—; William James lectr. Harvard U., 1950; Compton Meml. lectr. Washington U., St. Louis, 1965; Henry Broadhead Meml. lectr. U. Christchurch, N.Z., 1973; Herbert Spencer lectr. Oxford U., 1961, 73; Shearman Meml. lectr. U. London, 1961; Romanes lectr. Oxford U., 1972; Darwin lectr., Cambridge U.; fellow Ctr. Advanced Studies, Stanford U., 1956-57, Inst. Advanced Studies, Canberra, Australia, 1962, Vienna, 1964; vis. prof. univs. in U.S., Australia; hon. fellow Darwin Coll., Cambridge, 1980; hon. research fellow dept. history and philosophy of sci. Chelsea Coll., U. London, 1982. Created knight, 1965; decorated insignia Order of Companions of Honor; recipient prize City of Vienna, 1965, Sonning prize U. Copenhagen, 1973, Lippincott award Am. Polit. Sci. Assn., 1976, Grand Decoration of Honour in gold, Austria, 1976, Dr. Karl Renner prize, Vienna, 1977, Dr. Leopold Lucas prize U. Tubingen, 1981, Grand Cross with star. Fellow Royal Soc., Brit. Acad., London Sch. Econs. (hon.), Darwin Coll. Cambridge U. (hon.); mem. l'Inst. de France; mem. Am. Acad. Arts and Scis. (fgn. hon.), Internat. Acad. Philosophy Sci. (titulaer), Acad. Royale de Belgique (assoc.), Royal Soc. N.Z. (hon.), Acad. Internat. d'Histoire des Scis. (hon.), Deutsche Akadamie für Sprache und Dichtung (hon.), Acad. Europeéne des Sciences, des Arts et des Lettres, Soc. Straniero dellé Accad. Nazionale dei Lincei, Austrian Acad. Sci. (hon.), Phi Beta Kappa (Harvard U. chpt.). Author: Logik der Forschung, 8th edit., 1984, The Open Society and Its Enemies, 14th edit., 1983, The Poverty of Historicism, 9th edit., 1976, The Logic of Scientific Discovery, 9th edit., 1977, Conjectures and Refutations, 9th edit., 1984, Objective Knowledge, 7th edit., 1984, Unended Quest: An Intellectual Autobiography, 5th edit., 1980, Realism and the Aim of Science, 1983, The Open Universe, 1982, Quantum Theory and the Schism in Physics; co-author: The Self and Its Brain, 1977. Office: care London Sch of Econs, Houghton St, Aldwych, London WC2A 2AE, England

POPPING, ROEL, educator; b. Beilen, Drente, The Netherlands, Oct. 24, 1948; s. Aaldert and Henrica (Sikkenga) P.; m. Mária Szanyi, Sept. 6, 1977; children: Attila, Gergely. MD, U. Groningen, 1978, PhD, 1983. Researcher Gradap-Project, Groningen, 1978-79; asst. prof. methodology of social scis. U. Groningen, 1979—. Author Overeenstemmingsmaten Voor Nominale Data, 1983. Office: U Groningen, Oude Boteringe Straat 23, Groningen 9712GC, The Netherlands

POPRICK, MARY ANN, psychologist; b. Chgo., June 25, 1939; d. Michael and Mary (Mihalcik) Poprick; B.A., De Paul U., 1960, M.A., 1964; Ph.D., Loyola U., Chgo., 1968. Intern in psychology Elgin (Ill.) State Hosp., 1961-62; staff psychologist, 1962; staff psychologist Ill. State Tng. Sch. for Girls, Geneva, 1962-63, Mt. Sinai Hosp., Chgo., 1963-64; lectr. psychology Loyola U. at Chgo., 1964-67; asst. prof. Lewis U., Lockport, 1967-70, assoc. prof., 1970-75, chmn. dept., 1968-72 (on leave 1972-73); postdoctoral intern in clin. psychology Ill. State Psychiat. Inst., Chgo., 1972-73; pvt. clin. practice David Psychiat. Clinic, Ltd., South Holland Ill., 1973-87; pvt. practice, South Holland, Ill., 1987—; assoc. sci. staff Riveredge Hosp., Forest Park, Ill., 1975-76; mem. sci. staff dept. psychiatry Christ Hosp., Oak Lawn, Ill., 1983—. Co-chmn. commn. on personal growth and devel. Congregation of 3d Order St. Francis of Mary Immaculate, Joliet, 1970-71; clin. resource person Cath. Archdiocese of Chgo., 1977-88 . Mem. Am. Psychol. Assn. (rep. from Ill. 1985-88), Calif., Ill. (sec.-treas. acad. sect. 1975-77, mem. student devel. com. 1975-77, chmn. acad. sect. 1977-78, 78-79, mem. program com. 1977-78, sec. 1979-81, pres.-elect 1981-82, pres. 1982-83, past pres. 1983-84, chmn. program com. 1981-82, awards com. 1983-86), Midwestern psychol. assn., Soc. for Sci. Study Religion, AAAS, Chgo. Assn. Psychoanalytical Psychology, Kappa Gamma Pi, Psi Chi (sec. 1964-65, pres. 1965-66). Home: 547 Marquette Ave Calumet City IL 60409 Office: 16284 Prince Dr South Holland IL 60473

PORCELLI, BRUNO, Italian language educator; b. Rome, June 27, 1932; s. Giacomo and Vera (Angeloro) P.; m. Gabriella Panichi, Oct. 7, 1963; children: Andrea, Francesco. D in Lit., U. Pisa, Italy, 1954; PhD, U. Rome, 1971. Asst. lectr. lang. faculty U. Pisa, 1957-70, lectr., 1970-82, assoc. prof., 1982-87, prof., 1987—. Author: Novellieri Italiani, 1969, Studi Sulla Divina Commedia, 1970, La Novella Del Cinquecento, 1973, Gozzano, 1974, Momenti dell'Antinaturalismo, 1975, Le Misure Della Fabbrica, 1980, I Romanzi della Mia Terra di Moretti, 1983, Dante Maggiore E Boccaccio Minore, 1987. Home: Viale Delle Piagge 13, 56100 Pisa Italy Office: Pisa U Lang Faculty, Via Santa Maria 44, 56100 Pisa Italy

PORTE, JEAN, mathematician, statistician; b. Toulouse, France, Oct. 16, 1916; s. Gabriel and Jeanne (Chedozeau) P.; M. Zoe Poudevigne, July 6, 1968. M.A. in Philosophy, Toulouse, 1941; Sc.D. in Math., Paris, 1965. Statistician, French Inst. Stats., Paris, 1947-65; prof. Nat. U. Zaire Lubumbashi, 1965-75, U. Sci. of Algiers, 1976-84. Author: Nomenclature des Categories Socio-professionnelles, 1954; Recherches sur les Systems Formels, 1965. Served with French Armed Forces, 1940. Mem. Am. Math. Soc., Société Mathématique de France, Com. for Sci. Investigation of Claims of Paranormal. Home: 1 Villa Ornano, 75018 Paris France

PORTEOUS, TIMOTHY, art school administrator; b. Montreal, Que., Can., Aug. 31, 1933; s. John Geoffrey and Cora Ann (Kennedy) P.; m. Wendy Elizabeth Farris, June 28, 1968 (div. Dec. 1986); 1 child, Vanessa Bell; m. Beatrice Donald, Feb. 7, 1987; 1 child, Nicholas William. B.A., McGill U., Montréal, 1954, B.C.L., 1957; postgrad., Université de Montréal, 1957-58, Université de Paris Inst. de Droit Comparé, 1958-59; LLD, Trent (Ont.) U., 1986. Bar: Called to Que. bar 1958. Assoc. firm Bourgeois, Doheny, Day & Mackenzie, Montreal, 1958-66; exec. asst. to Minister of Industry of Can., Ottawa, Ont., 1966-68; spl. asst. to Prime Minister, Ottawa, 1968-73, exec. asst., 1970-73; assoc. dir. Can. Council, Ottawa, 1973-82, dir., 1982-85; assoc. dir. Can. Ctr. for Architecture, Montreal, 1986-88; pres. Ont. Coll. Art, 1988—. Co-author, assoc. producer: My Fur Lady, 1957-58. Bd. dirs Les Grands Ballets Candiens, Montréal, 1987—. Mem. Composers-Authors-Publs. Assn. Can., Can. Mus. Assn., Can. Conf. of the Arts, Assn. Cultural Execs. (bd. dirs.). Office: Ont Coll Art, 100 McCaul St, Toronto, ON Canada M5T 1W1

PORTER, ANDREW BRIAN, writer; b. Cape Town, South Africa, Aug. 26, 1928; came to U.S., 1972; s. Andrew Ferdinand and Vera Sybil (Bloxham) P.; B.A., M.A., Univ. Coll., Oxford, Eng., 1952. Music critic Fin. Times, London, 1950-74; music critic New Yorker, N.Y.C., 1972—; mem. music panel Arts Council of Great Britain, 1962-74; mem. music adv. panel Brit. Council, 1966-74; vis. fellow All Souls Coll., Oxford, 1973-74; Bloch prof. U. Calif., Berkeley, 1981. Mem. Royal Musical Assn., Am. Acad. Arts and Scis., Am. Musicology Soc., Donizetti Soc. (v.p.), Am. Music Center, ASCAP, Am. Inst. for Verdi Studies. Author: A Musical Season, 1974; Wagner's Ring, 1976; Music of Three Seasons, 1978; Music of Three More Seasons, 1981; Wagner's Tristan and Isolde, 1981; Verdi's Macbeth: A Sourcebook, 1984, Musical Events: A Chronicle, 1980-83, 87; editor: Musical Times, 1960-67; editorial bd. Grove Dictionary of Music and Musicians. Office: The New Yorker 25 W 43d St New York NY 10023

PORTER, DARWIN FRED, writer; b. Greensboro, N.C., Sept. 13, 1937; s. Numie Rowan and Hazel Lee (Phillips) P. B.A., U. Miami, 1959. Bur. chief Miami Herald, 1959-60; v.p. Haggart Assocs., N.Y.C., 1961-64; editor, author Arthur Frommer Inc., N.Y.C., 1964-67, Frommer/Pasmantier Pub. Corp., N.Y.C., 1967-86, Prentice Hall Press, N.Y.C., 1987—. Author: Frommer Travel Guides to Eng., 1964, Frommer Travel Guides to Spain, 1966, Frommer Travel Guides to Scandinavia, 1967, Frommer Travel to Los Angeles, 1969, Frommer Travel Guide to London, 1970, Frommer Travel Guide to Lisbon/Madrid, 1972, Frommer Travel Guide to Paris, 1972, Frommer Travel Guide To Morocco, 1974, Frommer Travel Guide to Rome, 1974, Frommer Travel Guide to Portugal, 1968, Frommer Travel Guide to England, 1969, Frommer Travel Guide to Italy, 1969, Frommer Travel Guide to Germany, 1970, Frommer Travel Guide to France, 1970, Frommer Travel Guide to Caribbean, Bermuda, the Bahamas, 1980, Frommer Travel Guide To Switzerland, 1984, Frommer Travel Guide to Austria and Hungary, 1984; Frommer Travel Guide to Bermuda and the Bahamas, 1985; Frommer Travel Guide to Scotland and Wales, 1985; novel Butterflies in Heat, 1976, Marika, 1977, Venus, 1982. Recipient Silver award Internat. Film and TV Festival N.Y., 1977. Mem. Soc. Am. Travel Writers, Smithsonian Assocs., Sigma Delta Chi. Home: 75 St Marks Pl Staten Island NY 10301

PORTER, ERIC (RICHARD), actor; b. London, Eng., Apr. 8, 1928; s. Richard John and Phoebe Elizabeth (Spall) P.; ed. Wimbledon Tech. Coll. First profl. appearance Shakespeare Meml. Theatre Co., Arts, Cambridge, Eng.; 1945; 1st appearance in London stage travelling repertory co. St. Joan, King's Hammersmith, 1946; with Birmingham Repertory Theatre, 1948-50; under contract H.M. Tennant, Ltd., 1951-54; appeared in plays The Silver Box, 1951, The Three Sisters, 1951, Thor, With Angels, 1951, Noah, 1951, The Same Sky, 1952, Under the Sycamore Tree, 1952; with Lyric, Hammersmith, 1953, Bristol Old Vic Co., 1954, 55-56, Old Vic Co., 1954-55; Romanoff and Juliet, Piccadilly, 1956, A Man of Distinction, Edinburgh Festival and Princes, 1957; Time and Again, 1957, The Visit, N.Y.C., 1958; Coast of Coromandel, 1959; Rosmersholm, Royal Ct., 1959, Comedy, 1965; under contract Royal Shakespeare Co., 1960-65; Government Inspector, Aldwych, 1966; Stratford Season, 1968; U.S. tour Dr. Faustus, 1969; My Little Boy . . . My Big Girl, Fortune, 1969; The Protagonist, Brighton, 1971; Peter Pan, London Coliseum, 1971; Twelfth Night, St. George's Elizabethan Theatre, 1976 (films) The Fall of the Roman Empire, 1964, The Pumpkin Eater, 1964, The Heroes of Telemark, 1965, Kaleidoscope, 1966, The Lost Continent, 1968. Hands of the Ripper, 1971, Nicholas and Alexandra, 1971, Anthony and Cleopatra, 1972. Hitler, the Last 10 Days, 1973, The Day of the Jackal, 1973, The Belstone Fox, 1973, Callan, 1974, Hennessy, 1975, The 39 Steps, 1978, Little Lord Fauntleroy, 1980, also appeared on TV including The Forsyte Saga, BBC (Best Actor award Guild TV producers and Dirs. 1967), The Jewel in the Crown, 1984, Sherlock Holmes, 1984, Oliver Twist, 1985. Recipient Drama award as best actor of 1959. Club: Buckstone. Address: care Duncan Heath Assocs, 162 Wardour St, London W1, England *

PORTER, SIR GEORGE, chemist, educator; b. Stainforth, Yorkshire, Eng., Dec. 6, 1920; s. John Smith and Alice Ann (Roebuck) P.; B.Sc., U. Leeds (Eng.), 1941; M.A., Ph.D., Cambridge (Eng.) U., 1949, Sc.D., 1959; D.Sc. (hon), U. Utah, 1968, Sheffield U., 1968, U. East Anglia, U. Surrey, U. Durham, 1970, U. Leicester, U. Leeds, U. Heriot-Watt, City U., 1971, U. Manchester, U. St. Andrews, London U., 1972, Kent U., 1973, Oxford U., 1974, DSc. (hon.) U. Hull, 1980, Inst. Quimico de Sarria, Barcelona, U. Pa., U. Coimbra, Portugal, Open U., 1984, U. Philippines, 1985, U. Notre Dame, 1986, U. Bristol, 1986, U. Reading, 1986, U. Loughborough, 1987; m. Stella Jean Brooke, Aug. 12, 1949; children: John B., Andrew C. G. Asst. research dir. phys. chemistry Cambridge U., 1952-54; asst. dir. Brit. Rayon Research, 1954-55; prof. phys. chemistry U. Sheffield (Eng.), 1955-63, Firth prof., head Dept. Chemistry, 1963-66; dir., Fullerian prof. chemistry Royal Instn., 1966—; pres. The Royal Soc., 1985—; prof. photochemistry Imperial Coll., London; vis. prof. chemistry Univ. Coll. London; hon. fellow Emmanuel Coll., Cambridge; hon. prof. phys. chemistry U. Kent; Richard Dimbleby lectr., 1988, John P. McGovern lectr., 1988. Trustee Bristol Exploratory, 1986—; pres. London Internat. Youth Sci. Fortnight, 1987, 88. Served with Royal Navy, 1941-45. Recipient (with M. Eigen and R. G. W. Norrish) Nobel prize in chemistry, 1967; Kalinga prize, 1977; created knight, 1972. Fellow Royal Soc. (Davy medal 1971, Rumford medal 1978), Royal Inst. Chemistry, Royal Scottish Soc. of Arts, Royal Soc. of Edinburgh; mem. Chem. Soc. (pres. 1970-72, pres. Faraday div. 1973-74, Faraday medal 1979, 80, Longstaff medal 1981), Sci. Research Council (Brit.) (council, sci. bd. 1976-80), Comite Internat. de. Photobiologie (pres. 1968-72), N.Y. (hon.), Göttingen (corr.), Pontifical acads. scis., Nat. Acad. Scis. (fgn. assoc. Washington), La Real Academia de Ciencias (Madrid; fgn. corr.), Am. Acad. Arts and Scis. (fgn. hon.), Nat. Assn. Gifted Children (pres. 1975-80). Author: Chemistry for the Modern World, 1962; author BBC TV series Laws of Disorder, 1965; Time Machines, 1969-70; Natural History of a Sunbeam, 1976. Editor: Progress in Reaction Kinetics. Contbr. to profl. jours. Research on fast chem. reactions, photochemistry, photosynthesis. Office: Office of Pres, The Royal Soc, 6 Carlton House Terr, London SW14 5AG, England

PORTER, JAMES ROBERT, member of the House of Representatives; b. Adelaide, Australia, Feb. 19, 1950; s. Janes Frederick Brooke and Patricia Constance (Smeaton) P.; m. Amanda Jane Gray, Mar. 15, 1980; children: Edwina, Stephanie, Victoria. LLB, U. Adelaide, 1973, BE, 1978. Mem. Ho. of Rep. Barker, South Australia, 1975—; shadow minister aboriginal affairs Ministry Fgn. Affairs, 1983-84, shadow minister for health, 1984-87, shadow minister family and community services, 1987, shadow minister housing and pub. aadminstrn., 1987—. Mem. Liberal Party. Home: 12 College St, College Park 5069, Australia

PORTER, JOHN ISSAC, lawyer; b. Camden, N.J., Apr. 8, 1949; s. Elwood and Mary Elizabeth (Pitts) P.; m. Linda Joyce McMillan, June 7, 1975; children: Tiffany, John, Joseph, Jeffrey. BS, Rutgers U., 1971, JD, 1979; MBA, Temple U., 1975. Bar: Pa. 1979, N.J. 1979, U.S. Dist. Ct. N.J. 1979, U.S. Dist. Ct (ea. dist.) Pa. 1982, U.S. Supreme Ct. 1983, U.S. Tax Ct. 1985, U.S. Ct. Appeals (3d cir.) 1985. Sales rep. Union Carbide Corp., Cherry Hill, N.J., 1972-73; fin. analyst Ford Motor Co., Dearborn, Mich., 1973-75; fin. research assoc. The Conf. Bd., N.Y.C., 1975-76; atty. Comptroller of the Currency, Washington, 1979-80; assoc. Porter & Jones, East Orange, N.J., 1980-83; sr. atty. Essex-Newark Legal Services, Newark, 1983-84; assoc. counsel Newark Bd. of Edn., 1984-86, Beneficial Mgmt. Corp., Peapack, N.J., 1986—; v.p. Bethany Bapt. Fed. Credit Union, Newark, 1985—; trustee Essex-Newark Legal Services. Mem. N.J. Black Rep. Counsel, Newark, 1979. Named one of Outstanding Young Men in Am., U.S. Jaycees, 1979, 81. Mem. Am. Corp. Counsel Assn., ABA (architects and engrs. liability subcom.), N.J. Bar Assn., Salem County Bar Assn., Assn. Trial Lawyers Am., Assn. of Fed. Bar, Nat. Bankers Assn., N.J. Rep. Lawyers, Nat. Sch. Bds. Assn., NAACP, Phi Alpha Delta. Baptist. Home: 92 Sanford St East Orange NJ 07018

PORTER, JOHN WESTON, guidance counselor, administrator; b. Fostoria, Ohio, Dec. 26, 1939; s. William Thomas and Ida Elizabeth (Carter) P.; student U. Cin., 1958; B.A., Heidelberg Coll., 1961; M.A. in Community Psychology, U. D.C., 1973, M.A. in Counseling, 1975; postgrad. Antioch Coll., 1974, Frostburg (Md.) State Coll., 1970, George Washington U., 1968; cert. Nat. Bd. Cert. Counselors. Claims rep. Social Security Admnstrn., Cleve. and Akron, Ohio, 1961-62; office mgr. Phoenix Cos., Washington and Los Angeles, 1966-70; researcher, grad. student Frostburg State Coll., U. D.C., 1970-73; edn. and career devel. specialist D.C. Public Schs., 1973-79, career edn. unit, 1979-83, Career Assessment Ctr., 1983-85, asst. dir. guidance and counseling, 1985—; mem. community adv. council Washington Hosp. Ctr., 1987—. Vice chmn. adv. council Group Health Assn., Washington 1977-79, 81-83. Served from ensign to lt., USN, 1962-66. Recipient awards Ohio Acad. of Sci., 1954-57, Cleve. Plain Dealer Operation Demonstrate, 1956, service award Heidleberg Coll. Publs., 1961, recognition certs. D.C. Assn. Career Devel., 1975, 1976, D.C. City Council, 1982; recipient recognition award Outstanding Contbn. to Guidance and Counseling 1987. Mem. D.C. Assn. Counseling and Devel. (sec. 1977—, treas. 1975-77, exec. bd., 1975-80, pres. 1979-80; Mem. of Yr. 1980, Outstanding Leadership award 1980), Assn. Counseling and Devel. (chmn. govt. relations North Atlantic region 1980-81, cert. for outstanding contbn. in govt. relations 1982, Recognition award 1987), Am. Sch. Counselors Assn. (career guidance com., leadership recognition cert. 1987), D.C. Career Devel. Assn. (trustee), Nat. Assn. Career Devel. (del.), Nat. Assn. Career Devel. (assembly del. 1984), D.C. Sch. Counselors Assn., D.C. Vocat. Guidance Assn. (treas., exec. com. 1983—), Ret. Officers Assn. Episcopalian. Home: 1700 Harvard St NW Washington DC 20009

PORTER, SIR LESLIE, business executive; b. July 10, 1920; s. Henry Alfred and Jane Porter; m. Shirley Cohen, 1949; 2 children. Student, Holloway County Sch., Eng.; PhD in Bus. Mgmt. (hon.), Tel Aviv U., 1973. Joined J. Porter and Co., 1938, mng. dir., 1955; dir. Tesco Stores (Holdings) Ltd., 1959, asst. mng. dir., 1964, dep. chmn., 1970, dep. chmn., mng. dir., 1972-73, chmn., 1973-85; pres. Tesco plc, 1985—; mem. Lloyd's, 1964—. V.p. Age Concern Eng.; mem. court Cranfield Inst. Tech., 1977—; chmn. bd. govs., Tel Aviv U.; gov. Hong Kong Baptist Coll.; chmn. Sports Aid Found., 1985—. Served with Brit. mil., 1939-46. Mem. Nat. Playing Fields Assn. (v.p.), Inst. Grocery Distbn. (pres. 1977-80). Clubs: Royal Automobile, City Livery, Dyrham Park County (Barnet, Herts), Coombe Hill Golf (Kingston Hill, Surrey), Frilford Heath Golf (Abingdon). Office: Tesco plc, Tesco House, Delawar Rd, Chestnut England *

PORTER, MICHAEL PELL, lawyer; b. Indpls., Mar. 31, 1940; s. Harold Troxel and Mildred Maxine (Pell) P.; m. Alliene Laura Jenkins, Sept. 23, 1967 (div.); 1 child, Genevieve Natalie; m. Janet Kay Smith Hayes, Feb. 13, 1983. Student, DePauw U., 1957-58; BA, Tulane U., 1961, LLB, 1963. Bar: La. 1963, U.S. Ct. Mil. Appeals 1964, N.Y. 1969, Hawaii 1971. Clk., U.S. Ct. Appeals (5th cir.), New Orleans, 1963; assoc. Sullivan & Cromwell, N.Y.C., 1968-71; assoc. Cades Schutte Fleming & Wright, Honolulu, 1971-74, ptnr., 1975—; mem. deans council Tulane Law Sch., 1981-88; dep. vice chancellor Episcopal Diocese Hawaii, 1980—, chancellor designate, 1988; chancellor Episcopal Ch., Micronesia, 1988—. Bd. dirs. Jr. Achievement Hawaii, Inc., 1974-84, Inst. Human Services, Inc., 1980-88. Served with JAGC, U.S. Army, 1963-66, Vietnam. Tulane U. fellow, 1981. Mem. ABA, Assn. Bar City N.Y., Hawaii State Bar Assn., Friends of U. Hawaii Law Sch. Republican. Episcopalian. Club: Pacific (Honolulu). Office: Cades Schutte Fleming & Wright 1000 Bishop St Honolulu HI 96813

PORTER, RAYMOND EARL, international marketing executive, consultant; b. Ft. Worth, Aug. 25, 1926; s. Edward Kinney and Eula Mable (Barton) P.; m. Mae Gwendolyn Westbrook, June 17, 1944 (dec. 1967); children—Rama Jean Porter Jordan, Gwendolyn Ann Porter Reed; m. Florinda Grace Humphrey, Nov. 17, 1977. B.S. in Mech. Engring., U. Tex.-Austin, 1947; B.A. in Bus., Tex. Christian U., 1953. Chief engr. heat transfer div. Cobell Industries, Inc., Ft. Worth, 1953, gen. mgr., 1954; pres. Mathes-Porter Engring. Co., Ft. Worth, 1955-61; S.W. mfrs. rep. York div. Borg-Warner Corp., Ft. Worth, 1961-69; v.p. mktg. and sales Pitts Industries Inc., Electro-Lock and Surfaces Inc. Divs., Dallas, 1970-77; mktg. mgr. Condensers Inc., Jacksonville, Tex., 1977-78; chief exec. officer Profl. Mktg. Co. Am. (PROMARK), Ft. Worth, 1979—. Mem. Petroleum Engrs., ASHRAE, AAAS, Internat. Mobile Air Conditioning Assn. Republican. Methodist. Lodges: Masons, Shriners. Contbr. articles, designs in field; patentee clutch pulley measuring device; founder Sam Houston Inst. Tech. Inc., a Tex. Corp., Ft. Worth, 1986. Office: PO Box 18768 North Richland Hills TX 76118

PORTER, ROBERT, medical researcher, educator; b. Port Augusta, Australia, Sept. 10, 1932; s. William John and Amy (Tottman) P.; m. Anne Dorothy Steell, July 29, 1961; 4 children. B of Med. Sci., Adelaide (Australia) U., 1954, DSc, 1974; BA with honors, U. Oxford, Eng., 1956, MA, BM, BCh, 1959, MD, 1969. House physician, surgeon Radcliffe Infirmary, Oxford, 1959-60; lectr. lab. physiology U. Oxford, 1960-67; vis. scientist, Radcliffe traveling fellow in med. sci. Brain Research Inst., UCLA, 1963-64; ofcl. fellow, med. tutor St. Catherine's Coll., U. Oxford, 1963-67; prof. physiology Monash U., Clayton, Australia, 1967-80; dir. John Curtin Sch. Med. Research, Canberra, Australia, 1980—; bd. dirs. Anutech, Canberra, Australian Biomed. Corp., Melbourne. Author: (with C.G. Phillips) Corticospinal Neurons- Their Role in Movement, 1977. Rhodes scholar South Australia and Lincoln Coll., U. Oxford, 1954. Fellow Australian Acad. Sci., Royal Australian Coll. Physicians. Home: #7/130 Shackleton Circt, Mawson, Australian Capital Territory 2607, Australia Office: John Curtin Sch Med Research, GPO Box 334, Canberra 2601, Australia

PORTER, ROBERT CHAMBERLAIN, lawyer, investment adviser; b. Pitts., Feb. 13, 1912; s. Horace C. and Helen (Dana) P.; m. Elizabeth Pattison Watkins, Feb. 28, 1941; children: Robert Chamberlain, Marion Dana. A.B., Bowdoin Coll., 1934; LL.B., U. Pa., 1939, L.L.D., 1985. Bar: N.Y. 1939. With Bankers Trust Co. N.Y.C., 1934-36; asso. Cravath, Swaine & Moore, 1939-42, 1945-50; v.p. Chem. Bank & Trust Co., N.Y.C., 1950-51; sec., counsel, dir. Pfizer Inc., Bklyn., 1951-56; gen. partner F. Eberstadt & Co., 1956-62, Shearson, Hammill & Co., 1962-65, F. Eberstadt & Co., 1965-69; pres. F. Eberstadt & Co., Inc., 1969-77, chmn., 1977-78, also dir.; chmn. Eberstadt Fund Mgmt., Inc., 1979-84; pres., then chmn. Chem. Fund, Inc., 1966-87; bd. dirs. Alliance Fund; bd. overseers Bowdoin Coll., 1975-87, Pres. bd., 1983-85; trustee Drew U., 1978-84; bd. govs. Investment Co. Inst., 1976-80. Served as lt. comdr. USNR, 1942-45. Mem. Am. Bar Assn. Clubs: University, Economic, N.Y. Yacht (N.Y.); Baltusrol Golf (N.J.), Lost Tree Golf (Fla.); Brunswick Golf (Maine). Home: 12184 Seaward Dr E North Palm Beach FL 33408

PORTER, RUSSELL MACKINLAY, lawyer; b. Paris, July 31, 1924; s. Russell Hobbins and Anne (MacKinlay) P.; m. Paula Viala, July 16, 1958; 1 child, Caroline Anne. LLB, Tulane U., 1950; Doctorate, U. Paris, 1953. Bar: La. 1953, U.S. Supreme Ct. 1953. Ptnr. Porter & Porter, Paris, 1950-66, Porter & Dunham, Paris, 1966—; bd. dirs. Titan Trust Services, Jersey, Eng., Craigmount Gilt Fund, Jersey. Pres. Pershing Hall Found., Paris, 1965—, Lafayette Escadrille Meml. Found., Paris, 1976—, Mona Bismarck Found., N.Y.C., Paris, 1980—; sec. bd. trustees Am. Coll. in Paris, 1970—. Decorated Legion of Honor, Croix de Guerre (France), Polonia Restituta (Polish Govt. in Exile). Mem. La. Bar Assn., Assn. Juristes Etrangers, Res. Officers Assn. Am. (pres. Paris chpt.). Clubs: RAF (London); Union Interallie (Paris). Home: 47 Ave General Dubail, 78100 Saint Germain en Laye France Office: Porter & Dunham, 261 rue St Honore, 75001 Paris France

PORTER, WAYNE RANDOLPH, physician; b. Washington, Jan. 10, 1948; s. James Randolph and Betty Rose (Burgess) P.; B.S., MIT, 1970; M.D., Duke U., 1973. Intern, U. Miami Affiliated Hosps., 1973-74, resident in internal medicine U. Miami Sch. Medicine (Fla.), 1973-76, resident in dermatology, 1976-78, clin. instr., then asst. prof. dermatology, 1978-85, assoc. prof., 1985—; practice medicine specializing in dermatology, North Miami Beach, 1978—; mem. staff U. Miami-Jackson Meml. Hosp., North Miami Med. Ctr., Parkway Regional Med. Ctr., Biscayne Med. Ctr. Diplomate Am. Bd. Internal Medicine, Am. Bd. Dermatology. Mem. med. adv. bd. Dade-Broward chpt. Lupus Found. Am. Fellow Internat. Soc. for Dermatologic Surgery, Am. Acad. Dermatology, Am. Assn. Dermatologic Surgeons; mem. AMA, Dade County Med. Assn., Fla. Med. Assn., Fla. Dermatology Soc., Miami Dermatol. Soc., So. Med. Assn., ACP, Internat. Soc. Pediatric Dermatology, Miami Dermatol. Soc. (pres.). Club: Kiwanis. Home: 3600 Curtis Ln Coconut Grove FL 33133 Office: 909 North Miami Beach Blvd North Miami Beach FL 33162

PORTER, WILLIAM GLOVER, JR., lawyer; b. Columbus, Ohio, Nov. 4, 1923; s. William Glover and Anne (Searight) P.; m. Eve Breslin Peterson, Jan. 12, 1946; children—Cynthia Porter Brown, Marcia Porter Hill. Student Dartmouth Coll., 1941-43, U. Calif.-Berkeley, 1946; L.L.B., Ohio State U., 1949. Bar: Ohio, 1949, U.S. Dist. Ct. (so. and ea. dists.) Ohio 1956, U.S. Dist. Ct. (D.C. dist.) 1982, U.S. Ct. Appeals (D.C. cir.) 1978, U.S. Supreme Ct. 1977. Assoc. Porter, Stanley, Treffinger & Platt, Columbus, Ohio, 1949-56; ptnr. Porter, Wright, Morris & Arthur, Columbus, 1956-81, sr. resident ptnr., Washington, 1981-83, of counsel 1984—. Mem. D.C. Mayor's Internat. Adv. Council, 1983—, Internat. Com. of the Greater Washington Bd. Trade, 1981—; mem. Washington Chamber Orch., 1982—, pres., 1985—. Served to lt. (j.g.) USNR, 1943-45. Fellow Columbus Bar Assn. Found. (charter); mem. ABA, D.C. Bar Assn., Fed. Energy Bar Assn., Ohio State Bar Assn. (chmn. special com. on pub. utilities 1963-70), Edison Elec. Inst. (legal com. 1961-79), Ohio Elec. Utility Inst. (legal com. 1955-79). Republican. Episcopalian. Clubs: Dartmouth (N.Y.C.); Columbia Country (Chevy Chase, Md.), Rocky Fork Hunt and Country (Columbus). Avocations: cabinet making, photography, bird watching, tennis. Office: Porter Wright Morris & Arthur 1233 20th St NW Washington DC 20036

PORTMAN, GLENN ARTHUR, lawyer; b. Cleve., Dec. 26, 1949; s. Alvin B. and Lenore (Marsh) P.; m. Katherine Seaborn, Aug. 3, 1974 (div. 1984); m. Susan Newell, Jan. 3, 1987. B.A. in History, Case Western Res. U., 1968; J.D., So. Meth. U., 1975. Bar: Tex. 1975, U.S. Dist. Ct. (no. dist.) Tex. 1975, U.S. Dist. Ct. (so. dist.) Tex. 1983. Assoc. Johnson, Bromberg & Leeds, Dallas, 1975-80, ptnr., 1980—. Asst. editor-in-chief: Southwestern Law Jour., 1974-75; contbr. articles to profl. jours. Mem. ABA, Dallas Bar Assn., So. Meth. U. Law Alumni Assn. (council bd. dirs., v.p. 1980-86, chmn. admissions com.). Republican. Methodist. Clubs: 500 Inc., Assemblage. Home: 9503 Winding Ridge Dr Dallas TX 75238 Office: Johnson Bromberg & Leeds 2600 Lincoln Plaza 500 N Akard St Dallas TX 75201

PORTNOFF, COLLICE HENRY, English language educator emeritus; b. San Luis Obispo, Calif., Dec. 9, 1898; d. James H. and Kate E. (Wilson) Henry; m. George E. Portnoff, Aug. 16, 1931; 1 dau., Lisa (Mrs. James Crehan). A.B., U. Calif.-Berkeley, 1921, M.A., 1922; Ph.D., Stanford U., 1927; Carter Meml. fellow, also fellow acad. Am. Acad. in, Rome, 1927-30, M.A., 1930. Instr. Belmont (Calif.) Mil. Acad., 1922-23; teaching asst. Stanford, 1923-27; instr. Ariz. State Coll., Flagstaff, 1930-41; cryptanalyst U.S. Signal Corps, Washington, 1942; translator Allied Mil. Govt., Washington, 1942-43; prof. English Ariz. State U., Tempe, 1945-69; prof. emeritus Ariz. State U., 1969—, chmn. dept., acting head div. lang. and lit., 1957-58, chmn. English dept., 1957-64; Dir. pageant Miracle of the Roses, Scottsdale, Ariz., 1960, gen. chmn., 1961. Author: (play) (with Samuel R. Golding) Naked Came I, 1957; ofcl. translator: Gregorio and Maria Martinez Sierra, 1947—; editor: (with Stanley Milstein)The History of Otology (Adam Politzer); contbg. editor The Ariz. Republic, Phoenix; co-translator (book rev.): The Cursillo Movement (from Spanish); book reviewer Scottsdale Daily Progress, 1978—. Bd. dirs. Phoenix Chamber Music Soc., Valley Shakespeare Theatre; mem. adv. council Greater Phoenix chpt. UNA-USA. Recipient medal for achievement in drama Nat. Soc. Arts and Letters; Distinguished Tchr. award Ariz. State U. Alumni Assn. Mem. AAUP, Ariz. Coll. Assn., Soc. Gen. Semantics, Nat. Soc. Arts and Letters, Washington, Nat. Council Tchrs. English, Conf. Coll. Communication and Composition, Centro Studié E Scambi Internazionali (v.p.), Bus. and Profl. Womens Club Tempe, Cath. Bus. Assn., Am. Translators Assn., Alumni Assn. Am. Acad. in Rome, Rocky Mountain Modern Lang. Assn. (pres. 1964), Pi Sigma, Sigma Delta Pi, Alpha Lambda Delta, Gamma Phi Beta, Phi Kappa Phi. Clubs: Faculty, Women's Faculty (Ariz. State U.); Dinner (Scottsdale), Paradise Valley Country (Scottsdale). Home: 6310 Quail Run Rd Paradise Valley AZ 85253 Office: English Dept Ariz State U Tempe AZ 85287

PORTOCARRERO, JOSE MANUEL, manufacturing company executive; b. Porto, Portugal, Dec. 8, 1947; s. Jose and Maria Fernanda (Fernandes) P. BS in Engring., U. Paul Pastur, Tournai, Belgium, 1971. Product devel. mgr. Textil Manuel Goncalves, Porto, 1973-79; mfg. cons. Interposto Comml. E Indsl. Do Norte, Porto, 1980—; mng. dir. Empresa Fabril Do Norte SA, Porto, 1985—, Heltex, Porto, 1987; Contbr. articles to profl. jours. Mem. Am. Mgmt. Assn., Assn. Portuguesa de jestac e Engenharia Indsl. Roman Catholic. Office: Efanor SA, Av Senhora Da Hora, 4457 Matosinhos Portugal

PORUS, VLADIMIR N., philosopher; b. Osch, Russia, Sept. 19, 1943; s. Natan A. and Bronislava (Ostanovskaya) P.; m. Galina Tarasova, Jan. 30, 1953; children: Dmitriy, Mery. PhD, Moscow State U., 1974. Soldier Voroschilovgrad, 1960-62, 62-65; researcher Inst. of Philosophy, Moscow, 1973—. Contbr. articles to profl. jours. Mem. Communist Party. Home: 140056, DzerjinskyTomilinscaya 13/11, USSR Office: Acad of Sci, Inst of Philosophy, Moscow V 71, USSR

POSADA-ANGEL, JUAN CARLOS, trading company executive; b. Bogotá,Colombia, July 8, 1951; s. Gabriel and Rosa (Angel) Posada; m. Maria Isabel Henao, Dec. 16, 1977; children: Alexandra, Juan Carlos. B., Lycee Français, Bogotá, 1969; LL.D., Colegio Mayor del Rosario, Bogotá, 1976; M. Tax Law, Adean Group, U. Los Andes, Bogotá, 1977. Asst. pres. Unitexa S.A., Bogotá, 1969-72, Coltegrupo S.A., Bogotá, 1969-72; sec. gen. Los Tres Elefantes S.A., Bogotá, 1973-75, comml. mgr., 1975-82; v.p. fin. and adminstrn. Seguros la Andina S.A., Bogotá, 1983-87; pres. Inversiones Posada-Angel, Promotora Angel, Promotora Angel Posada, Hepo Ltd., Impex Inc., Petromat Ltda., Hydrocarbons Trading Services Ltda; dir. Alejandro Angel & Cia S.A. Clubs: Gun, Jockey, Country, San Andrés Golf, Am. Tennis (Bogotá). Home: Cl 70 N 6-76 PH, Apto 101, PO Box 76072, Bogota 2 Colombia Office: Hepo Ltda, Calle 72 No 1-10, A A PO Box 76072, Pi S04 DE2 Bogotá Colombia

POSADAS, MARTIN POSADAS, medical educator, physician, business executive; b. San Carlos, Pangasinan, Philippines, Nov. 11, 1921; m. Rosalina Quebral, Feb. 14, 1950; 1 child, Marili (Mrs. Angelo Juan). B.A., U. Philippines; M.D., U. Santo Tomas, Philippines; career exec. cert. Devel. Acad. Philippines. Gen. practice medicine; pres., founder Virgen Milagrosa Med. Ctr., Virgen Milagrosa Inst. Medicine Found. Inc., Virgen Milagrosa Ednl. Instns. Inc., St. Dominic High Sch., San Luis High Sch., Virgen Milagrosa Child Learning Ctr., Virgen Milagrosa Special Sci. High Sch.; pres., proprietor Plaza View Hotel, San Carlos Press & Publisher, Palaris Radio Broadcasting System; pres., founder Virgen Milagrosa Trading & Devel. Co. Author: Pangasinan-English Dictionary, Pharmacology, Microbiology. Past pres. Boy Scout Council; chmn. Posadas Clan Found.; founder-pres. Binalatongan Hist. and Cultural Soc., Western Civic League; past pres. San Carlos Parish Council, archdiocese council; bd dirs. Assn. Pvt. Schs., Colls. and Univs.; past bd. dirs. Assn. Philippine Med. Colls. and Univs. Named Most Outstanding Physician, Philippine Med. Assn., Most Outstanding Educator, San Carlos City Govt., Pioneer in Countryside Devel., San Carlos City Govt., Most Outstanding Alumnus U. Santo Tomas; recipient Papal award Pro-Eclesia Pontificae, Vatican, Lay Christian Apostolate award. Mem. Pangasinan Med. Soc. (past pres.), Philippine Hosp. Assn. (past v.p.), San Carlos Medicare Council (past chmn.), Filipino Assn. Med. Educators (treas.), San Carlos City C. of C. and Industry, Posadas Clan of the Philippines (pres.), N.Y. Acad. Scientist, Jaycees (past pres., v.p. Luzon). Club: Archdiocesan Catholic Action (Pangasinan) (pres. 1980). Lodges: K.C. (4th degree, faithful navigator , grand knight, dist. deputy), Rotary (past pres., past sec.). Avocation: golf. Home: Taloy Dist, San Carlos City, Pangasinan 0740, Philippines Office: Virgen Milagrosa Complex, Taloy, Pangasinah, San Carlos City 0740, Philippines

POSAMENTIER, ALFRED STEVEN, mathematics educator; b. N.Y.C., Oct. 18, 1942; s. Ernest and Alice (Pisk) P.; m. Noreen Renee Woller, Sept. 17, 1967; children—Lisa Joan, David Richard. A.B., Hunter Coll., 1964; M.A., CCNY, 1966; postgrad., Yeshiva U., N.Y.C., 1967-69; Ph.D., Fordham U., 1973. Tchr. math Theodore Roosevelt High Sch., Bronx, 1964-70; asst. prof. math. edn. CCNY, N.Y.C., 1970-76, assoc. prof., 1977-80, prof., 1981—, dept. chmn. dept. secondary and continuing edn., 1974-80, chmn., 1980-86; assoc. dean Sch. Edn. CCNY, 1986—, dir. select program in sci. and engring., 1978—; dir. CCNY, U.K., iniatives program dir., 1983—, dir. sci. lectr. program, 1981—; dir. Ctr. for Sci. and Maths. Edn. CCNY, 1986—; supr. math. and sci. Mamaroneck High Sch., N.Y., 1976-79; project dir. Math Proficiency Workship, Ossining, N.Y., 1976-79, NSF math. devel. program for secondary sch. tchrs. math., 1978-82, N.Y.C., Profl. Preparation of Math. and Sci. Tchrs., 1978-79; cons. Inst. Ednl. Devel. N.Y.C., 1970-73,

Croft Ednl. Services, New London, 1971, Design and Evaluation, 1973, N.Y.C. Bd. Edn., 1973-75, N.Y.C. Bd. Edn. Office of Evaluation, 1974-80, N.Y.C. Bd. Edn. Examiners, 1979—, Ossining Bd. Edn., 1975-83, numerous others; coordinator NSF N.E. Resource Ctr. Sci. and Engring., 1981—, lectr. various convs. and meetings; vis. prof. U. Vienna, Austria, 1985, 87, 88. Author: Geometric Constructions, 1973, Geometry, Its Elements and Structure, 1972, rev. edit., 1977, Challenging Problems in Geometry, 2 vols, 1970, Challenging Problems in Algebra, 2 vols., 1970, A Study Guide for the Scholastic Aptitude Test in Math., 1969, rev. edit., 1983, Excursions in Advanced Euclidean Geometry, 1980, 2d edit., 1984, Teaching Secondary School Mathematics: Techniques and Enrichment Units, 1981, 2d edit., 1986, Uncommon Problems for Common Topics in Algebra, 1981, Unusual Problems for Usual Topics in Algebra, 1981, Using Computers in Mathematics, 1983, 2d edit., 1986, Math Motivators: Investigations in Pre-Algebra, 1982, Math Motivators: Investigations in Geometry, 1982, Math Motivators: Investigations in Algebra, 1983, Using Computers: Programming and Problem Solving, 1984, 2d edit., Advanced Geometric Constructions, 1988, Challenging Problems in Algebra, 1988, Challenging Problems in Geometry, 1988; contbr. numerous articles to profl. jours. Trustee Demarest Bd. Edn., 1977-80. Mem. Math. Assn. Am., Sch. Sci. and Math. Assn., Nat. Council Tchrs. Math., (reviewer new publs., referee articles Math. Tchr. Jour.), Assn. Tchrs. Math. N.Y.C. (exec. bd. 1966-67, referee articles assn. jour.), Assn. Tchrs. of Math. of N.Y. State, Assn. Tchrs. Math. N.J. (editorial bd. N.J. Math. Tchr. Jour. 1981-84), Nat. Council of Suprs. of Maths. Home: 32 Drury Ln Demarest NJ 07627 Office: City Coll CUNY New York NY 10031

POSEY, GLENNIS BAILEY, educator; b. Arab, Ala., July 19, 1936; d. Loyd Marion and Iva Irene (Maze) Bailey; m. Donald S. Posey, May 27, 1957; 1 child, Donald Loyd. B.S., Florence State U., 1957, M.A., 1962. Tchr. Lauderdale Bd. Edn., Florence, Ala., 1957-58, Winston County Bd. Edn., Double Springs, Ala., 1959—, chmn. bus. dept., 1973—; adviser Future Bus. Leaders Am., Ala., 1957—. Mem. Double Springs Library Bd., 1960-68, Double Springs Recreation Bd., 1978-84. Mem. Ala. Vocat. Assn. (v.p. 1985-86; named Outstanding Bus. Edn. Tchr. 1983, Outstanding Vocat. Tchr. Ala. 1983), Tenn. Valley Bus. Tchrs. Assn., NEA, Data Processing Mgmt. Assn., Delta Pi Epsilon, Alpha Delta Kappa. Republican. Mem. Ch. of Christ. Club: Double Springs Study. Avocations: tole painting; crocheting. Home: PO Box 244 Double Springs AL 35553 Office: Winston County Vocat Ctr PO Box 146 Double Springs AL 35553

POSNER, BEN, former public broadcasting executive, educator; b. Tucson, Aug. 12, 1914; s. Phillip and Rose (Tsibula) P.; B.S. in Bus. Adminstrn. cum laude, U. Ariz., 1936; M.A. in Govt., George Washington U., 1942; Ph.D., Am. U. 1962; m. Selma E. Sheftelman, July 30, 1940; children—Richard Daniel, David Barnett. With U.S. Govt. burs., 1937-72, asst. dir. for adminstrn. USIA, 1963-72; v.p., treas. Corp. for Pub. Broadcasting, Washington, 1973-78; spl. lectr. Royal-McBee Co., 1941-63; professorial lectr. George Washington U., 1962-78; adj. prof. Coll. of V.I., 1979—; exec. dir. Pres.'s Study Commn. on Internat. Radio Broadcasting, 1973. Pres. Hebrew Congregation of St. Thomas. Served to 1st lt. AUS, 1943-46; PTO. Recipient Disting. Service award USIA, 1961; Rockefeller Pub. Service award, 1970. Mem. Am. Soc. Pub. Adminstrn., Fed. Govt. Accts. Assn. Author articles in field. Home: PO Box 9296 Saint Thomas VI 00801 Office: U of VI Saint Thomas VI 00802

POSNER, ROLAND, linguist, educator; b. Prague, Bohemia, June 30, 1942; s. Herbert and Elisabeth (Schindler) P.; m. Marlene Landsch; children: Britta, Astrid, Ingmar. Diploma, U. Bonn, 1967; PhD, Tech. U., West Berlin, 1972; D in Habilitation, Tech. U., Berlin, 1973. Prof. linguistics, chmn. dept. linguistics and semiotics Tech. U. Berlin, 1975—, dir. Inst. for Linguistics, 1975-80; vis. prof. Hamburg U., 1973, U. Montreal, 1977, Pontifícia Cath. U. São Paulo, Brazil, 1985; prof. summer insts., Salzburg, Austria 1977, Tunis, 1979, Toronto, Ont., Can., 1982, Estoril, Portugal, 1983, Mysore, India, 1984. Editor: Zeichenprozesse, 1977, Die Welt als Zeichen, 1981, Nach-Chomskysche Linguistik, 1985, Iconicity, 1986, A World of Signs, 1987, Semiotik und Wissenschaftstheorie, 1988, Semiotics and the Arts, 1988, (jour.) Zeitschrift für Semiotik, 1979—, (book series) Foundations of Communication, 1973—, Approaches to Semiotics, 1978—, Problems in Semiotics, 1983—; author: Theorie des Kommentierens, 1972, 80, Rational Discourse and Poetic Communication, 1982; mem. editorial bd.: Research in Text Theory, 1979—, Encyclopedic Dictionary Semiotics, 1980-86, Recherches Sémiotiques, 1982—, Poetics Today, 1983—, Bochum Publs. in Evolutionary Cultural Semiotics, 1985—, Semiotics Handbook, 1986—, Encyclopedia del Diseño, 1986—, Eutopias, 1986—, Lenguaje y Ciencias, 1986—, Utrecht Publs. in General and Comparative Lit., 1988—. Research grantee Deutsche Forschungsgemeinschaft, 1976-79, 80-82, Tech. U. Berlin, 1985—, Volkswagen Found., 1987—; Netherlands Inst. for Advanced Study in Humanities and Social Scis. fellow, 1986-87. Mem. Internat. Semiotics Inst. (exec. bd. 1988—), Internat. Assn. for Semiotic Studies (v.p. 1984—), German Assn. for Semiotic Studies (founder, 1st pres.), Semiotisches Kolloquium Berlin (bd. dirs. 1975—), Internat. Comparative Lit. Assn. (com. on literary theory), Akademio Internacia de la Sciencoj, Internat. Soc. for Research in Emotion. Home: Suedwestkorso 19, D1000 Berlin 33 Federal Republic of Germany Office: Technische Universitaet, Ernst-Reuter-Platz 7, D1000 Berlin 10 Federal Republic of Germany

POSNER, ROY EDWARD, finance executive; b. Chgo., Aug. 24, 1933; s. Lew and Julia (Cvetan) P.; m. Donna Lea Williams, June 9, 1956; children: Karen Lee, Sheryl Lynn. Student, U. Ill., 1951-53, Internat. Accountants Soc., 1956-59, Loyola U., Chgo., 1959; grad., Advanced Mgmt. Program, Harvard U., 1976. CPA, Ill. Public accountant Frank W. Dibble Co., Chgo., 1956-61; supr. Harris, Kerr, Forster & Co. (C.P.A.s), Chgo., 1961-66; with Loews Corp., N.Y.C., 1966—; v.p. fin. services, chief fin. officer Loews Corp., 1973-86, sr. v.p., chief fin. officer, 1986—; bd. dirs. Bulova Italy S.P.A., Milan, Bulova Systems and Instruments Corp., N.Y.C., Loews Hotels Monaco S.A.M., Monte Carlo, Monaco, Loews Internat. Services S.A., Switzerland; G F Corp., Youngstown, Ohio. Mem. editorial com.: Uniform System of Accounting for Hotels, 7th edit. Pres. No. Regional Valley High Sch. Music Parents Assn., 1978-79; trustee Loews Found., N.Y.C. Served with U.S. Army, 1953-55. Mem. Am. Inst. CPA's, Fin. Execs. Inst., Ins. Acctg. and Stats. Assn., Internat. Hospitality Accountants Assn., Am. Hotel and Motel Assn., Ill. Soc. CPAs, N.Y. State Soc. CPAs (chmn. com. on hotel restaurant and club acctg. 1980-82), Tri-County Golf Assn. (treas. 1985-88, v.p. 1988—), Delta Tau Delta. Clubs: Alpine Country. (bd. govs. 1982—), Alpine Country (exec. com. 1982—, pres. 1988—). Home: 273 Whitman St Haworth NJ 07641 Office: 667 Madison Ave New York NY 10021-8087

POSNETT, NORMAN WILLIAM, science librarian, researcher; b. Wakefield, Yorks, Eng., Nov. 25, 1937; s. Norman and Mary Ethel (Moon) P.; m. Joan Veronica Luckock; children: David William, Susan Jane. BS in Zoology, U. London, 1967. Full study mem. Sci. Info. for the Tropics Overseas Devel. Adminstrn., London, 1978-80; head publs. info. and library unit Land Resources Devel. Ctr., Surbiton, Eng., 1981—; bd. dirs. Info. for Internat. Devel., Hyderabad, India, 1985; com. mem. U.K. Focus Agrl. Info., London, 1980-81, Agrl. Libraries and Info. Services Southeastern U.K., 1982. Author numerous book revs., invited conf. papers; compiler over 10 sci. bibliographies; contbr. articles to profl. jours. Bd. govs. St. Matthew's Sch., Surbiton, 1982; active Civil Service Orgn. London. Fellow Zool. Soc. London; mem. Inst. Biology (chartered), Inst. Info. Scis. (various past offices), Tropical Agriculture Assn., Internat. Assn. Agrl. Librarians and Documentarists (com. mem. 1985—). Mem. Church of England. Home: 24 Hamilton Ave, Tolworth-Surbiton Surrey, England KT6 7PN Office: Land Resources Devel Ctr, Tolworth Tower, Surbiton Surrey, England KT6 7DY

POSPISIL, RADOMIR BEDRICH, museum director; b. Prerov, Czechoslovakia, Apr. 8, 1938; s. Radomir Frantisek and Marie Ludmila Pospisil; m. Jaroslava Linhartova, Dec. 6, 1969; children: Eva, Ludmila, Radomir. M.Sc. in Econs., Sch. of Econs., Prague, 1963; B.A., Acad. Film Art, Prague, 1964; D.Sc., Acad. Sci., Prague, 1977; Ph.D., Palacky U., Czechoslovakia, 1982. Dir., Czechoslovak Presse Agy., Prague, 1963-64; dir. Internat. Orgn. Journalists, Prague, 1965-75; head scientific research Acad. Scis., Council of Indsl. Design, Prague, 1975-79; dir. gen. Nat. Muzeum of Czech Lit., Prague, 1979—; mem. ICOM, Paris, 1979—; scientific mem. Nat. Forschungs und Gedenkstatten der Deutsche Klasische Literatur, 1980—; State Mux. Literature, Moscow, Mickiewicz Mus., Warsaw, Petofi Irodalmi Mus., Budapest, Matica Slovenska Martin. Author numerous books; contbr. to mags. and profl. jours.; sculptor; poet. Mem. Czechoslovak-Soviet Friendship Soc., 1957—. Recipient Gold medal, IOJ, Prague, 1969, IEMA, Warsaw, 1971; State award for bldg. society, Prague, 1984. Mem. Soc. Czech Bibliophy, Soc. Writers and Poets, Numis. Soc., Writers Trade Union, Union of Arts. Mem. Communist Party. Clubs: Tenis (Prague), Kinologic. Office: Muzeum of Czech Literature, Strahovske nam 132, 11838 Prague 1 Czechoslovakia

POSPISZYL, KAZIMIERZ, psychologist, educator, researcher; b. Busk, Poland, Mar. 22, 1938; s. Marian and Agnieszka (Naspinka) P.; m. Anna Kawulok, Dec. 6, 1966 (div. 1973); 1 child, Marcin; m. Irena Klebczyk, July 26, 1983. MS, U. Gdansk, Poland, 1963; PhD, U. Krakow, Poland, 1967, Habilitation, 1974. Researcher Silesian Sci. Inst., Katowice, Poland, 1967-72; asst. prof. State Inst. Spl. Edn., Warsaw, Poland, 1972-82, dean, 1975-78; prof. Maria Curie Sklodowska U., Lublin, 1983—, dir. inst. psychology, 1983—. Author 10 books most recent being: The Psychology of the Majadjusted Child, 1980, 2d edit., 1982, 3 edit., 1985, The Psychopathy, 1985, Tristan and Don Juan: The Patters of Man's Love in European Culture, 1986; contbr. numerous articles to profl. jours. Mem. Internat. Soc. for Study of Behavioral Devel., Internat. Soc. for the Study of Individual Differences. Home: Fundamentowa 44 m 5, 04-057 Warsaw Poland Office: Inst Psychology, Plac Litewski 5, 20-080 Lublin Poland

POSSATI, MARIO, electronic gauge company executive; b. Cordoba, Argentina, Apr. 7, 1922; s. Pompeo and Rosa (Badini) P.; B.S. in Mech. Engring., Bologna U., 1946; m. Manfredi Gabriella, June 4, 1947; children—Stefano, Marco, Edoardo, Alberto. Tech. mgr. Officine Maccaferri, Bologna, Italy, 1946-48; gen. mgr. Baschieri & Pellagri, 1949-52; founder MARPOSS, Bologna, 1952, chmn., chief exec. officer, 1952—. Served with Italian Air Force, 1943. Mem. Profl. Engrs. Assn. Italy, Soc. Mfg. Engrs., Cavaliere del Lavoro. Office: Marposs SpA, Via Saliceto 13 Bentivoglio, 40010 Bologna Italy

POST, ALAN, economist, artist; b. Alhambra, Calif., Sept. 17, 1914; s. Edwin R. and Edna (Stickney) P.; m. Helen E. Wills, Nov. 21, 1940; 1 son, David Wills. A.B., Occidental Coll., 1938; student Chouinard Inst. Art, 1938; M.A., Princeton, 1940; LL.D., Golden Gate U., 1972, Occidental Coll., 1974, Claremont Grad. Sch., 1978. In banking bus., 1933-36; instr. econs. Occidental Coll., 1940-42; asst. prof. Am. U., 1943; economist Dept. State, 1944-45; research dir. Utah Found., 1945-46; chief economist, adminstrv. analyst State of Calif., 1946-50, state legis. analyst, 1950-77; cons. to commn. studying higher edn. Wells Commn., N.Y.; cons. Milton Eisenhower Com. Higher Edn. and State, 1964; mem. Nat. Com. Support of Public Schs., 1967; mem. nat. adv. panel Nat. Center Higher Edn. Mgmt. Systems, 1971-72; chmn. Calif. Gov.'s Commn. on Govt. Reform, 1978—; mem. faculty U. So. Calif. Grad. Sch. Public Adminstrn., 1978—; Regents' prof. U. Calif., Davis, 1983, vis. prof., 1984; spl. cons. Touche Ross and Co., 1977-87; cons., interim exec. dir. Calif. Commn. for Rev. of Master Plan for Higher Edn., 1985, vis. prof. U. Calif., Davis, 1984-85.; mem. adv. bd. Cali. Tomorrow nat. shows and one-man shows; dir. Crocker Art Gallery Assn., pres., 1966-67; dir. IMMUDX Inc. Bd. dirs. People to People Council; bd. dirs. U. Calif. Art Mus., 1984—, trustee, 1986—; mem. adv. com. on future ops. Council State Govts., 1965; bd. mgrs., pres. YMCA; bd. dirs. Sacramento Civic Ballet Assn.; trustee Calif. Coll. Arts and Crafts, 1982—; chmn. Calif. State Task Force on Water Future, 1981-82, Sacramento Regional Found.; bd. dirs. Calif. Mus., pres., 1976-77, mem adv. bd. Calif. Tomorrow, 1984—, Policy Analysis for Calif. Edn., 1985—, Senate Adv. Commn. on Control of Cost of State Govt., 1986—. Served with USNR, 1943-44. Mem. Council State Govts. (research adv. com. 1966-—), Nat. Legis. Service Conf. (exec. com. 1956-57), Nat. Acad. Public Adminstrn., Phi Beta Kappa, Kappa Sigma. Home: 1900 Rockwood Dr Sacramento CA 95864

POSTLER, ERMIN JOSEPH, audio engineer; b. Prague, Czechoslovakia, Aug. 13, 1942; s. Ladislav and Ermina (Pokorná) P.; m. Blanka P. Postler (div. 1979); 1 child, Richard P.; m. Maria Pavla Zákora. Diploma engring., Czech High Tech. Sch., Prague, 1965. Audio engr. sound dept. Ceskoslovenská Televize (CST), Prague, 1966-78, chief sound dept., 1978-80, researcher tech. devel. dept., 1980-83, audio expert concept and tech. dept., 1983—. Contbr. articles to profl. jours. Mem. Sci. and Tech. Cons. CST. Office: Ceskoslovenska televize, Jindrisska 16, 111 50 Prague Czechoslovakia

POSTMAN, ROBERT DEREK, mathematics educator; b. Kearny, N.J. July 13, 1941; s. Benjamin and Edith (Maw) P.; m. Elizabeth Ann Del Corso, Aug. 14, 1965; children—Chad, Blaire, Ryan. B.A., Kean Coll., 1966; M.A., Columbia U. Tchrs. Coll., 1967, Ed.D., 1971. Faculty Hunter Coll., N.Y.C., 1970-76, Tchrs. Coll. Columbia U., N.Y.C., 1977-81; prof. math. and edn. Mercy Coll., Westchester County, N.Y., 1976—, chair dept., 1978—; grad. coordinator L.I. U., Westchester County, 1979—; math. cons. to sch. dists. and state edn. depts.; cons. to Psychol. Corp. for Devel. of the Calif. Achievement Test; presented numerous workshops and lectures at local and nat. meetings of orgns. Author: Mathematics on the Geoboard, 1974; Intermediate Mathematics, 1980; (series) Growth in Mathematics, 1980, 82; (series) Computer Programming, 1983; Collegiate Reading, 1985; (series) Mathematics Unlimited, 1986, High School Mathematics (2 volumes), 1988; also computer programs, filmstrips; contbr. articles to profl. jours. Mem. Closter Bd. Edn., N.J., 1973-79; del. N.J. Sch. Bds. Assn., 1974-77; coach, organizer Closter Recreation Commn., 1973—; coach Closter Comets Soccer Team, 1984—. Served with USAF, 1959-63. NDEA fellow, 1966-70. Mem. Nat. Council Tchrs. of Math., Soc. Applied Learning Tech., N.Y. Acad. Scis., Assn. Tchr. Educators (exec. bd.), Kappa Delta Pi, Phi Delta Kappa. Roman Catholic. Home: 33 Julia St Closter NJ 07624 Office: Mercy Coll 555 Broadway Dobbs Ferry NY 10522

POTÁC, SVATOPLUK, deputy premier Socialist Republic of Czechoslovakia; b. Tupec, Czechoslovakia, Mar. 24, 1925; grad. Prague Sch. Econs.; m. Miloslava Krpatová; 2 children. With Státní banka ceskoslovenská, Prague, 1952—, dir., 1964—, dep. gen. mgr., 1964-69, chmn. bd., gen. mgr., 1969-71, pres., 1971-81; chmn. State Planning Commn., 1981—; mem. Central Com. of Communist Party of Czechoslovakia, 1981—; mem. Parliament of Czechoslovakia, 1981—, now dep. premier Czechoslovakia; CSSR rep. in planning com. COMECON; chmn. Econ. Research Council of CSSR, from 1983. Decorated Order Republic, Order Labor, Decoration Merits for Reconstrn. Author articles in field. Office: Office Deputy Premier, Prague Czechoslovakia

POTASH, MARLIN SUE, psychologist; b. Paterson, N.J., Oct. 23, 1951; d. Monroe and Perle (Cohen) P.; B.S. magna cum laude, Tufts U., 1973; M.Ed., Boston U., 1975, Ed.D., 1977; m. Frederick H. Fruitman, Nov. 21, 1981; children: Laura Potash Fruitman, Hilary Potash Fruitman. Research assoc. Center for Study of Edn., Yale U., 1976; vis. lectr. Tufts U., 1975-76; instr. Emmanuel Coll., 1975-79; dir. clin. services, resocialization treatment coordinator Columbus Nursing Home, East Boston, 1975-76; asst. prof. behavioral sci., dept. public health and community dentistry Boston U. Sch. Grad. Dentistry, 1977-81, asst. clin. prof., 1981-85; pvt. practice psychotherapy, orgnl. cons., 1979—; asso. Levinson Inst., Cambridge, Mass., 1980-83; instr. Radcliffe Coll. Seminars, 1983-85; psychol. cons. Middlesex Probate Ct., Cambridge, 1980-87; instr. Lesley Coll., 1982-84; supr. grad. internship program in pastoral counseling Danielsen Counseling Ctr., Boston, 1979-80. Co-Author: Cold Feet: Why Men Don't Commit; contbr. chpt. to books, articles to profl. jours. Trustee, Boston Ballet Soc., 1981-82; assoc. commr. Mass. Gov.'s Commn. on Status of Women, 1981-82; commr. Human Relations/Youth Resources Commn. of Brookline (Mass.), 1982-84. Fellow Mass. Psychol. Assn. (bd. profl. affairs 1979-82); mem. Am. Psychol. Assn., Am. Orthopsychiat. Assn., Acad. Family Psychology, Fin. Women's Assn., Am. Assn. Marriage and Family Therapists. Home: 1133 Park Ave New York NY 10128

POTEL, JOAQUIN, surgery educator, surgeon; b. Caldas de Reyes, Galicia, Spain, Feb. 20, 1937; s. Jose and Ana (Lesquereux) P.; m. Maria Jose Fernandez-Cervera, Sept. 15, 1937; children—Joaquin, Jose, Marta. MD, Med. Sch. Santiago de Compostela, 1960, PhD, 1966. Diplomate in gen. surgery. Resident surgery U. Hosp. Santiago Compostela, 1960-65; asst. prof. Med. Sch. Santiago Compostela, 1966-71, assoc. prof., 1971-77; prof. surgery U. and Med. Sch. Santiago Compostela, 1977; head surg. service U. Hosp. Santiago Compostela, 1973; vis. scientist U. Wash., Seattle, 1967; vice-dean Med. Sch. Santiago Compostela, 1979-82, dean, 1982-84. Author: Infecciones de la herida operatoria, 1982; co-author: Patologia Quizurgica, 1986. Postgrad. grantee Univ., 1960, research grantee Puente Castro Found., 1963, Edn. Dept., 1965, Juan March Found., 1967. Fellow Internat. Soc. Surgery, Internat. Coll. Surgeons, Collegium Internat. Chirurgiae Digestivae, Asociacion Espanola de Cirujanos, Sociedad Espanola Patologia Digestiva, Sociedad Espanola Coloproctologia. Home: Av Feanes 5, Santiago de Compostela Galicia Spain Office: Hosp Gen de Galicia, Galeras, Santiago de Compostela Spain

POTENTE, EUGENE, JR., interior designer; b. Kenosha. Wis., July 24, 1921; s. Eugene and Suzanne Marie (Schmit) P.; Ph.B., Marquette U., 1943; postgrad. Stanford U., 1943, N.Y. Sch. Interior Design, 1947; m. Joan Cioffe, Jan. 29, 1946; children—Eugene J., Peter Michael, John Francis, Suzanne Marie. Founder, pres. Studios of Potente, Inc., Kenosha, Wis., 1949—; pres., founder Archtl. Services Assos., Kenosha, 1978—, Bus. Leasing Services of Wis. Inc., 1978—; past nat. pres. Inter-Faith Forum on Religion, Art and Architecture; vice chmn. State Capitol and Exec. Residence Bd., 1981-88. Sec., Kenosha Symphony Assn., 1968-74. Bd. dirs. Ctr. for Religion and the Arts, Wesley Theol. Sem., Washington, 1983-84. Served with AUS, 1943-46. Mem. Am. Soc. Interior Designers (treas., pres. Wis. 1985—, chmn. nat. pub. service 1986), Inst. Bus. Designers, Sigma Delta Chi. Roman Catholic. Lodge: Elks. Home: 8609 2d Ave Kenosha WI 53140 Office: 914 60th St Kenosha WI 53140

POTHAST, HENRY LYNN, school social worker; b. Marshalltown, Iowa, Apr. 2, 1952; s. Lester Raymond and Annie (Dunham) P.; student Marshalltown Community Coll., 1970-71; B.A., U. Iowa, 1974, M.S.W., 1981; postgrad. U. No. Iowa, 1977-78, Iowa State U., 1983-88; m. June Dubberke, Feb. 14, 1976; children—Emily Ann, Laura Rachael. Youth services worker Iowa Tng. Sch. for Boys, Eldora, 1974-75, youth counselor I, 1975-78, youth counselor II, 1978-79, instr. high sch. equivalency, 1975-77; social worker Area Edn. Agy. 6, Eldora, 1981—. Mem. Nat. Assn. Social Workers, Acad. Cert. Social Workers, Iowa Sch. Social Workers' Assn., Phi Beta Kappa, Phi Kappa Phi, Omicron Nu. Club: DeMolay (orator 1969-70). Home: Rt 1 Box 512 Hubbard IA 50122 Office: Area Edn Agy 6 Eldora IA 50627

POTHIER, JACQUES, language professional; b. Grenoble, France, Aug. 21, 1954; s. Rene and Jeanine (Durix) P. BA, U. Lyon, France, 1974; MA, U. Paris, 1976, postgrad., 1977—. Student tchr. Ecole Normale Supérieure de l'E.T., Cachan, France, 1974-79; French lang. asst. U. Strathclyde, Glasgow, Scotland, 1975-76; tchr. English French Lycée, Madrid, 1980-82, Lycée Verneuil sur Avre, Normandy, France, 1982-87; lectr. U. Paris VII, 1983-84, 86—; tchr. English Coll. Condorcet, Paris, 1987—. Contbr. articles to profl. jours. Fulbright research grants with U. Va., U. Miss., U. Tex., 1982. Mem. Assn. Francaise d'Etudes Américaines, European Assn. Am. Studies. Home: 26 Rue Auguste Comte, 92170 Vanves France

POTIER, GHISLAIN FRANCOIS, neurological rehabilitation physician; b. Amboise, France, Sept. 23, 1938; s. Alfred Alexandre and Antoinette (Vandeville) P.; m. Marie Laure Senie, Oct. 23, 1969; children: Camille, Romain, Justine, Clemence. MD U. Paris, 1967. External physician Paris Hosps., 1962-67; med. asst. Pub. Hosp., Aincourt, France, 1975-84; chief med. officer Pub. Hosp., Aincourt, 1984—; nat. expert Supreme Ct. Justice, Aincourt, 1986—. Served with Health Corps French Navy, 1965-67, lt. col. res. Roman Catholic. Home: 9 Rue Capitaine Rouveure, 27200 Vernon France Office: Public Hosp, 95510 Aincourt France

POTIER, JEAN CLAUDE, physician, educator; b. Caen, Calvados, France, Aug. 16, 1936; s. Rene and Marie Therese (Julienne) P.; m. Annick Desmet, Jan. 9, 1965; children: Severin, Jerome, Benoit. Extern Paris, 1958-62; intern Paris area, 1962-63, Paris, 1965-69; resident in cardiology Caen, 1969-74, aggregate prof., 1974—; med. asst. in cardiology unit, Caen, 1974-80; med. chief coronary care unit, Caen, 1980—; prof. Med. U., Caen, 1981. Contbr. articles to sci. jours. Served with French army, 1965. Laureate Nat. Acad. Medicine, 1969, 71. Mem. French Soc. Cardiology. Roman Catholic. Home: 3 Charlemagne, 14000 Caen France Office: CHU Sec Cardiology, Coteren Acre, Caen France 14040

PÖTSCHER, BENEDIKT MARIA, mathematician; b. Vienna, Austria, Nov. 27, 1955; s. Walter August and Georgine (Dobias) P. PhD, U. Vienna, 1979. Asst. prof. U. Tech., Vienna, 1979-85, universitätsdozent, 1985—; vis. research scientist Yale U., New Haven, 1986-87; lectr. U. Klagenfurt, Austria, 1981—; vis. assoc. prof. U. Md. Co-editor spl. issue Applied Math. and Computation: Modelling Problems in Econometrics, 1986; assoc. editor Econometric Theory, 1988—; contbr. articles to profl. jours. Research grantee Austrian Ministry of Sci., Vienna, 1979; Max Kade fellow Max Kade Found., N.Y.C., 1986. Mem. Am. Math. Soc., Am. Statis. Soc., Austrian Statis. Soc. Office: Univ of Technology, Argentinierstrasse 8, A-1040 Vienna Austria

POTTER, ANTHONY NICHOLAS, JR., security company executive, consultant; b. N.Y.C., Jan. 6, 1942; s. Anthony Nicholas Sr. and Alta Lorene (Downing) P.; m. Patricia Anne Tlumac, Apr. 4, 1964 (div. Oct. 1981); children: Merika Elizabeth, Victoria Hope Nora; m. Cheryl Kay Dittman, Oct. 15, 1983. AA, Westchester Community Coll., 1970; BS in Criminal Justice, U. Cin., 1975. Cert. protection profl., security trainer. Chief police Tampa Internat. Airport, Fla., 1970-73; prin. cons. Booz, Allen & Hamilton, Cin., 1973-75; chief police City of Danville, Ill., 1976-78; police commr. City of York, Pa., 1978-80; v.p. Omni Internat. Security, Atlanta, 1980-83; exec. dir. Internat. Assn. Shopping Ctr. Security, Atlanta, 1981—; cons. shopping ctr. developers, operators, retailers; faculty mem. Internat. Council Shopping Ctr. Mgmt. Insts., 1970-85; expert witness security matters fed. and state cts. Author: Shopping Center Security, 1976, Recommended Security Practices for Shopping Centers, 1987; contbr. articles to profl. jours. Various positions local, council, regional, nat. Boy Scouts Am., 1950—. Served to sgt. USMC, 1959-65. Recipient Disting. Service award Internat. Security Conf. 1970; Merit award Security World Mag., 1972. Mem. Met. Atlanta Crime Commn., Internat. Assn. Chiefs Police (pvt. security com. 1978-85), Internat. Assn. Profl. Security Cons. (bd. dirs. 1988—), Am. Soc. Indsl. Security (chmn. St. Petersburg chapt. 1970-71, chmn. nat. transp. security com. 1971-74, regional v.p. region VI 1975-76, com. standards and codes 1977-80, chmn. legis. com. 1986-87, pvt. security services council 1988—), ABA (assoc.), Am. Acad. Forensic Scis. (elected mem. 1987), Nat. Acad. Police Specialists (v.p. 1988—), Internat. Assn. Profl. Security Cons. (bd. dirs. 1988—). Republican. Lutheran. Avocations: model railroading, gun collecting, scuba diving. Home: 2493 Willow Wood Ct NE Atlanta GA 30345 Office: Internat Assn Shopping Ctr Security 2830 Clearview Pl NE Suite 300 Atlanta GA 30340

POTTER, RICHARD CLIFFORD, international lawyer; b. Providence, Nov. 25, 1946; s. Peter Rex Potter and Helen Louise (McDevitt) St. Onge; m. Anne Algie, Mar. 22, 1975; children: Catherine Anne, David Henry. BA, U. N.C., 1968; JD cum laude, Ind. U., 1973. Bar: Ill. 1973, U.S. Dist. Ct. (no. dist.) Ill. 1973, U.S. Ct. Appeals (8th cir.) 1975, U.S. Ct. Appeals (3d cir.) 1978, U.S. Ct. Appeals (4th and 5th cirs.) 1979, U.S. Ct. Appeals (9th cir.) 1980, U.S. Supreme Ct. 1979. Assoc. Kirkland & Ellis, Chgo., 1973-75; atty. and ptnr. Bell, Boyd & Lloyd, Chgo., 1975—; lobbyist Boise Cascade Corp., Washington, 1981-84. Assoc. editor, exec. officer Ind. Law Jour., 1972-73; author various publs. Bd. dirs. Northbrook (Ill.) Park Dist. adv. council, 1982. Mem. ABA (co-chair litigation subcom. on FTC, vice chmn. internat. law and practice com. on internat. aspects litigation, chmn. internat. law and pracitce subcom. on settlement and ADR), Internat. Bar Assn. (Midwest regional dir. com. R), Legal Club Chgo., Law Club Chgo., Asia-Pacific Lawyers Assn., Japan-Am. Soc. Am., Am. Arbitration Assn. Club: University (Chgo.). Home: 2134 Butternut Ln Northbrook IL 60062 Office: Bell Boyd & Lloyd 70 W Madison Chicago IL 60602

POTTER, ROBERT ELLIS, librarian; b. Knoxville, Tenn., Mar. 16, 1937; s. Pollye Jack and Violet Belle (Walker) P.; B.S.J., U. Tenn., 1961; M.S. in L.S., U. Tenn., 1978; postgrad. U. So. Calif., 1963-64, U. South Fla., 1981, Miami U., Oxford, Ohio, 1983; m. Rosemary Byrd Lee, Dec. 28, 1963; children—Robert Ellis II and Kenyon David (twins). Student asst. U. Tenn. Libraries, 1959-61; copyreader The Knoxville News-Sentinel, 1961-62; library asst. U. Tenn. Libraries, 1962-63; library aide Los Angeles County Library

System, El Monte, Calif., 1963-65; reference librarian, bus. and sci. collection City of Hialeah Library div. Hialeah John F. Kennedy Library (Fla.), 1966-73, head librarian bus., sci. and tech. dept., 1973-80; head tech. services, circulation Dunedin (Fla.) Public Library, 1980-83; dir. circulation 1983-85, dir. tech. services, 1983—. Counselor, Trail Blazer's Camps, Inc., N.Y.C., 1958; chaplain's asst. U.S. Army Res., 1959-64; cubmaster Boy Scouts Am., 1976-77, 83-84, asst. cubmaster, 1984-88, asst. Webeloes leader, 1977-78, committeeman, 1978-80, advancement chmn., 1980-86, mem. publicity com. West Central Fla. council, 1983-86, chmn. post 468 com., 1986, publicity chmn. fall encampment Central Fla. Council, 1986; 1st v.p. Clearwater High Sch. Parent Tchr. Student Assn., 1984-85, treas., 1985-86; scouting coordinator United Meth. Ch., 1984—; mem. stewardship com. St. Paul United Meth. Ch., 1983—. Served with AUS, 1959. Mem. Am. Pub. Libray Assn., Southeastern Pub. Library Assn. (mem. nominating com., acting sec. resources and tech. services sect. 1984), Fla. Pub. Library Assn. (chmn. tech. services caucus 1986-87, chmn. pub. relations caucus 1987-88, editor newsletter 1987—), Fla. Library Assn. (charter, by-laws and manual coms. 1988—), Dade County Pub. Library Assn. (pres. 1970-71, historian 1976-77, archivist 1975), Pinellas County Pub. Librarian's Assn. (sec. 1982-83, mem.-at-large 1983-84, v.p., pres. elect 1984-85, pres. 1985-86, editor newsletter 1985-86), Hialeah Library Div. Staff Assn. (pres. 1974-75, sec. 1976, 80), Tampa Bay Library Consortium (sunline data base com. 1987—), U. Tenn. Century Club, U. Tenn. Nat. Alumni Assn. (bd. govs. Greater Miami chpt., v.p. 1973-74, pres. 1975-77), Maryville Coll. Alumni Assn. (sec.-treas. Fla. chpt. 1982-85), Toastmasters Internat. (adminstrv. v.p. Dunedin 1983, ednl. v.p. 1983-84, sergeant-at-arms 1984-85, pres. 1985-86 , editor weekly bull. 1983-84), Sigma Delta Chi. Mem. United Ch. of Christ (treas. 1974-77, pres., 1977, chmn. ch. council 1977, mem. mission council Dade-Monroe counties). Author various library publs. Editor newsletter Dade County Library Assn., 1970-75, bull. SORT, ALA, 1971-74, The Wind Word newsletters, 1982-83; contbr. articles to profl. jours. Office: 223 Douglas Ave Dunedin FL 34698

POTTER, ROBERT JOSEPH, technical and business executive; b. N.Y.C., Oct. 29, 1932; s. Mack and Ida (Bernstein) P.; m. Natalie Joan Silverstein, Sept. 9, 1956; children: Diane Gail, Suzanne Lee, David Craig. B.S. cum laude (Kroner scholar), Lafayette Coll., 1954; M.A. in Physics, U. Rochester, 1957, Ph.D. in Optics, 1960. Cons. ANPA Research Inst., AEC Brookhaven Nat. Lab., RCA Labs., U.S. Naval Research Labs., 1952-60; mgr. optical physics and optical pattern recognition IBM Thomas J. Watson Research Center, Yorktown Heights, N.Y., 1960-65; assoc. dir. Applied Research Lab., Xerox Corp., Rochester, N.Y., 1965-67; v.p. advanced engring. Xerox Corp., 1967-68, v.p. devel. and engring., 1968-69; v.p., gen. mgr. Spl. Products and Systems div. Xerox Corp., Stamford, Conn. and Pasadena, Calif., 1969-71; v.p. info. tech. group Xerox Corp., Rochester, 1971-73; v.p. info. tech. group Xerox Corp., Dallas, 1973-75, pres. Office Systems div., 1975-78; sr. v.p., chief tech. officer Internat. Harvester Co., Chgo., 1978-82; with R.J. Potter & Co., 1983-84; group v.p. integrated office systems No. Telecom Inc., Richardson, Tex., 1985-87; pres., chief exec. officer Datapoint Corp., San Antonio, 1987—; dir. Molex Inc. Contbr. articles to profl. jours. Bd. dirs. So. Meth. U. Found. Sci. and Tech.; trustee Ill. Inst. Tech. Recipient IBM Outstanding Tech. Contbn. award, 1964, Disting. Achievement award Soc. Mfg. Engrs., 1981. Fellow Optical Soc. Am., Am. Phys. Soc.; mem. Soc. Automotive Engrs., Phi Beta Kappa, Sigma Xi. Office: Datapoint Corp 9725 Datapoint Dr S01 San Antonio TX 78284

POTTER, ROBERT LAWRENCE, communications company executive; b. Buffalo, July 27, 1943; s. William Ervin and Mildred Katharine (Poppenberg) P.; B.S. summa cum laude in Elec. Engring. (N.Y. State scholar), SUNY, Buffalo, 1964; S.M. in Elec. Engring., MIT, 1965; m. Louise Marie Hayek, Feb. 3, 1968; children—Amy Katherine, Eric Rudolph, Rebecca Louise. In electronic switching devel. Bell Telephone Labs., Naperville, Ill. and Holmdel, N.J., 1964-69, operator systems design, 1969-77; asst. mgr. exchange systems design AT&T, Parsippany, N.J., 1977-79, supr. product devel., public services mktg., 1979-80, operator systems planning Bell Telephone Labs., Naperville, Ill., 1980-84, head remote digital switching devel. AT&T Bell Labs., 1984-85, 5ESS Switch Software applications dept., 1986—. Named Student Engr. of Yr., Erie County chpt. N.Y. State Soc. Profl. Engrs. Mem. IEEE (sr.), AAAS, Assn. Computing Machinery, U.S. Power Squadrons (sr.), Sigma Xi, Tau Beta Pi, Phi Eta Sigma. Republican. Baptist. Patentee telephone circuitry and systems; author tech. articles and papers. Home: 843 E Gartner Rd Naperville IL 60540 Office: AT&T Bell Labs 200 Park Plaza Naperville IL 60566

POTTER, TANYA JEAN, lawyer; b. Washington, Oct. 30, 1956; d. John Francis and Tanya Agnes (Kristof) P. BA, Georgetown U., 1978, JD, 1981. Bar: D.C. 1982, U.S. Ct. Appeals (D.C. cir.), U.S. Ct. Appeals (fed. cir.), U.S. Dist. Ct. (D.C. dist.), U.S. Ct. Internat. Trade. Assoc. Ragan and Mason, Washington, 1981—; mediator D.C. Superior Ct., 1986—. Author: Practicing Before the Federal Maritime Commission, 1986, supplement, 1988. Mem. exec. council Washington Opera Jr. Com., 1983-88, chmn. com. 1988; bd. trustees The Washington Opera, 1988—; mem. internat. com. ARC, Washington, 1986—; auction chmn. Young Friends of ARC, Washington, 1985-86; mem. benefit com. Vincent T. Lombardi Cancer Ctr., Washington, 1985—; del. Georgetown U. Nat. Law Alumni Bd. Dirs., 1986-88. Recipient Community Service Recognition award ARC, Washington, 1986. Mem. ABA, Bar Assn. of D.C. (exec. council ad law sect. 1985—, moderator adminstrv. law symposium 1986-88). Roman Catholic. Clubs: Pisces, Georgetown U. Met. (bd. govs. 1986-87) (Washington). Office: Ragan and Mason 900 17th St NW Washington DC 20006

POTTIER, BERNARD MARC, diplomat; b. Vernon, Eure, France, July 11, 1942; s. Henry Eugene and Odette Danielle (Dulac) P. BS, U. Law, 1963; diploma, Inst. Polit. Studies, Paris, 1963, Nat. Sch. Adminstrn., 1969, Nat. Sch. Oriental Langs., 1970. Press attaché Embassy of Laos, 1966-67; adminstrv. officer French Ministry Industry, Paris, 1969-71; 1st sec. Embassy Indonesia, 1971-73; personal advisor to minister for French overseas territories 1976-77; resident commr. New Hebrides, 1978-79; 1st counselor Embassy of Cameroon, 1979-82; head Francophone Affairs Dept., 1982-87; dir. dept. communications French Ministry Fgn. Affairs, Paris, 1987—; tchr. Nat. Sch. Adminstrn., 1974-75; govt. controller New Caledonian Electricity Co., 1976-79. Decorated Nat. Order Merit, 1979. Mem. Internat. Richelieu Circle Paris (sec.-gen.). Home: 19 Rue des Moines, 75017 Paris France

POTTS, BERNARD, lawyer; b. Balt., Aug. 22, 1915; s. Phillip Louis and Anna (Novey) P.; A.B.A., Balt. Coll. Commerce, 1936; LL.B., Eastern U., Balt., 1949; J.D., U. Balt., 1950; m. Frieda Hochman, 1949; children—Phillip Louis, Neal Allen, Bryan H., Andrea Maria. Tax cons., Balt., 1936-49; admitted to Md. bar, 1950, since practiced in Balt.; partner firm Potts & Potts, 1975—, sr. counsel, 1975—. Founder, counsel Gamber Community Vol. Fire Co., 1968; founder, pres. Mary Dopkin's Children's Fund, 1950-60; founder, v.p. Boys Town Homes Md., 1965-80; founder, chmn. Accident and Prevention Bur. Md., 1965-75; pres. Safety First Club Md., 1966-68; bd. dirs. NCCJ-Md. Conf. Social Concern, 1976-80; mem. Md. bd. NCCJ, 1976-80; co-founder, co-chmn. Greater Balt. Mental Health Council, 1980; founder E. Balt. Children's Fund, Council Ind. Self-Help, Police Community Relations Councils, Crime Prevention Bur. Md. Served with AUS, 1943. Recipient cert. police community relations Mich. Police Inst., 1961, Disting. Citizens award Office Gov. Md., 1971, Presdl. citation Balt. City Council, 1977, Outstanding Alumnus award Mt. Vernon Law Sch., Eastern U., 1970, Wheel Master's award Metro Civic Assn., 1963; numerous awards B'nai B'rith, Safety First Club Md. Mem. Am. Bar Assn., Fed. Bar Assn., Am. Trial Lawyers Assn., Balt. Bar Assn., Met. Civic Assn. Balt. (v.p. 1968-80), Humanitarian Assn. Md. (v.p.), Jewish War Vets. (past post comdr.). Democrat. Clubs: Masons, B'nai B'rith (past pres. Balt. 1965, internat. commr. community services 1972—, sec. CVS exec. commn.). Home: 3206 Midfield Rd Baltimore MD 21208 Office: Suite 1207 Court Sq Bldg Baltimore MD 21202

POTTS, GERALD NEAL, manufacturing company executive; b. Franklin, N.C., Apr. 10, 1933; s. Joseph Thomas and Virgie (Bryant) P.; m. Ann Eliza Underwood, Dec. 21, 1956; children: Catherine, Thomas, Alice. B.S., U. N.C., 1954; grad., Advanced Mgmt. Program, Harvard, 1973. With Vulcan Mold & Iron Co., Chgo., 1957-59; sales engr. Vulcan Mold & Iron Co., 1959-62; gen. sales mgr. Vulcan Mold & Iron Co., Latrobe, Pa., 1963-65; v.p. sales Vulcan Mold & Iron Co., 1965-68; v.p. Vulcan, Inc., Latrobe, 1968-72; exec. v.p. Vulcan, Inc., 1972-73, pres., 1973-85, chief exec. officer, 1977-85, chmn., 1981-85; with Eastern Group Hdqrs. Teledyne Inc., Latrobe, Pa., 1985-86; group exec. Teledyne Inc., 1986—; Active Young Pres.'s Orgn., 1973-83. Bd. dirs. Latrobe Area Hosp., 1967—, chmn., 1985-88; trustee Greater Latrobe Community Chest, 1970-87, pres., 1978-79; adv. bd. U. Pitts. at Greensburg, 1974-80; trustee Seton Hill Coll., Greensburg, 1978-80. Served with AUS, 1954-56. Mem. Am. Iron and Steel Inst., AIME, Chi Phi. Clubs: Masons (32 deg.), Shriners; Laurel Valley Golf (Ligonier, Pa.), Rolling Rock (Ligonier, Pa.); Duquesne (Pitts.). Office: PO Box 151 Latrobe PA 15650

POTTS, RAMSAY DOUGLAS, lawyer, aviator; b. Memphis, Oct. 24, 1916; s. Ramsay Douglas and Ann Clifton (VanDyke) P.; m. Veronica Hamilton Raynor, Dec. 22, 1945; children: Ramsay Douglas, David Hamilton, Lesley Ann, Lindsay Veronica. B.S., U. N.C., 1941; LL.B., Harvard U., 1948. Bar: Tenn. 1948, D.C. 1954, U.S. Supreme Ct. 1957. Commd. 2d lt. USAAF, 1941, advanced through grades to maj. gen. Res., 1961; various combat and operational assignments (8th Air Force and Air Force Res.), 1942-60; chmn. Air Force Res. Policy Com., 1967-68; practice of law Washington, 1955—; spl. asst. to chmn. Nat. Security Resources Bd., 1951; pres. Ind. Mil. Air Transport Assn., 1952-55; ptnr. Shaw, Pittman, Potts & Trowbridge, 1956—; dir. Emerson Electric Co. Contbr. articles to profl. jours. Mem. State Council Higher Edn. for Va., 1968-71; Trustee Air Force Hist. Found., pres., 1971-75; pres. Washington Area Tennis Patrons Found. Decorated D.S.C., other combat decorations. Mem. Am., D.C. bar assns., Phi Beta Kappa. Clubs: City Tavern (Washington), Metropolitan (Washington); Harvard (N.Y.C.); Army Navy Country (Arlington, Va.); Internat. Lawn Tennis Clubs of U.S., Gt. Brit., India. Home: 2818 N 27th St Arlington VA 22207 Office: 2300 N St NW Washington DC 20037

POUGET, GÉRARD MARCEL RENÉ, orthopedic surgeon; b. Paris, July 9, 1938; s. Louis Jean Nicolas and Marcelle Madeleine (Thiel) P.; m. Jacqueline Jeanne Garnier, May 30, 1960 (div. Oct. 1982); children: Sophie, Jerome, Carole; m. Michele Courtiau, Apr. 13, 1985. MD, U. Paris, 1971. Extern various hosps., Paris, 1960-65, intern, 1966-71; asst. in anatomy Faculté de Medecine, Paris, 1966-69; asst. clin. chief various hosps., Paris, 1971-74; practice medicine specializing in orthopedic surgery Clinique Chirurgicale de l'Archette, Olivet, France, 1974—. Contbr. articles to profl. jours. Recipient Laureat de la Faculté de Medicine Paris. Mem. French Orthopedic Soc., Internat. Orthopedic Soc. Home: Les Blancs Bouleaux, 45160 Ardon, Olivet France Office: Clinique de l'Archette, 504 Ave du Loiret, 45160 Olivet, Orleans France

POUGET, RÉGIS, psychiatrist, educator; b. St. Pons, France, Dec. 10, 1930; s. René and Fernande (Esteve) P.; m. Mireille Coste, Dec. 21, 1955; 1 child, Marie. MD. Dept. chief Hosp. Ctr., Vannes, France, 1957-58, Privas, France, 1960-64; dir. Hosp. Ctr., Uzes, France, 1965-73; prof. psychiatry Med. U., Montpellier, France, 1974—; expert Ct. Justice, Montpellier, 1961—; cons. French Nat. Railways, Montpellier, 1975—, Post, Telegraph and Telephone, Montpellier, 1977—. Author: Precis of Psychiatry, 1980, Dangerousness, 1987; contbr. over 250 articles to sci. jours. Pres. Psychol. Functional Read., Montpellier, 1974. Served as col. with Army Health Service, 1986—. Decorated Chevalier de l'Ordre Nat. du Merite, Officier des Palmes Acad. Mem. Soc. Psychol. Medicine, Soc. Legal Medicine, Mediterranean Soc. of Psychiatry, French Colombiere Soc. Psychiatry (pres. 1981), Reserve Officers of Army Heatlh Service (pres. 1986). Roman Catholic. Lodge: Rotary (pres. 1980-81). Home: 1600 Route de Mende, 34980 Montferrier-Sur-Lez France Office: Hôpital de la Colombiere, 39 Ave Charles Flahault, 34059 Montpellier France

POUILLOT, JEAN PIERRE, psychiatrist; b. Paris, May 13, 1929; s. Henri and Nadeleine Pouillot; m. Colette Vercel (div. 1975); children: Roger-Pierre, Catherine, Marie-Francoise; m. Nicole Bourdarie, 1977; 1 child, Frederic. MD, U. Paris, 1958. Attache de consultation Univ. Hosp. Pitie Salpetriere, Paris, 1977-86, Hosp. Boucicaut, Paris, 1982-85; cons. neuropsychiatry Centre de Forcilles, Seine et Marne, France, 1985—. Mem. Conseil Regional Ordre de Medicine, Council Regional d'Ile de France. Home and Office: Rue Pascal #11, 75005 Paris France

POUL, FRANKLIN, lawyer; b. Phila., Nov. 6, 1924; s. Boris and Anna P.; m. Shirley Weissman, June 26, 1949; children—Leslie R., Alan M., Laurie J. Student, U. Pa., 1942-43, Haverford Coll., 1943-44; LL.B. cum laude, U. Pa., 1946. Bar: Pa. bar 1949, U.S. Supreme Ct 1955. Asso. firm Gray, Anderson, Schaffer & Rome, Phila., 1948-56, Wolf, Block, Schorr and Solis-Cohen, Phila., 1956-60; partner Wolf, Block, Schorr and Solis-Cohen, 1960—. Bd. dirs. ACLU, Phila., 1955—, pres., 1975-76. Served with AUS, 1943-46. Mem. Am. Law Inst., Am. Bar Assn., Order of Coif. Office: 12th Fl Packard Bldg Philadelphia PA 19102

POULET, CHRISTINE BLANCHE, physician; b. Lille, Nord, France, Nov. 30, 1949; d. Michel and Mireille (Marsy) P.; 1 child, Willy Francois. MD, U. Lille, 1979. Asst. Calmette Hosp., Lille, 1977-79; practice medicine specializing in mesotherapy Lille, 1980—. Roman Catholic. Office: Consulting Room, Residence Aurelia III, 59110 La Madeleine, Nord France

POULIOT, ASSUNTA GALLUCCI, business school owner and director; b. West Warwick, R.I., Aug. 14, 1937; d. Michael and Angelina (DeCesare) G.; Gallucci; m. Joseph F. Pouliot, July 4, 1961; children—Brenda, Mark, Jill, Michele. B.S., U. R.I., 1959, M.S., 1971. Bus. tchr. Cranston High Sch., R.I., 1959-61; bus. dept. chmn. Chariho Regional High Sch., Wood River Junction, R.I., 1961-73; instr. U. R.I., Kingston, 1973-78; founder, dir. Ocean State Bus. Inst., Wakefield, R.I., 1977—; dir. Fleet Nat. Bank, 1985—; bd. mgrs. Bank of New Eng., 1984-85; speaker in field. Pres. St. Francis Women's Club, Wakefield, 1975; sec. St. Francis Parish Council, Wakefield, 1980; mem. Econ. Devel. Commn., Wakefield, 1981-85; mem. South County Hosp. Corp., Wakefield, 1978—; fin. dir. Bus. and Profl. Women's Club, Wakefield, 1982-84. Mem. R.I. Bus. Edn. Assn. (newsletter editor 1979-81), New Eng. Bus. Coll. Assn. (sec. 1984-86, pres. 1985-87), R.I. Assn. Career and Tech. Schs. (treas., bd. dirs. 1979-86), Eastern Bus. Edn. Assn. (conf. leader), Nat. Bus. Edn. Assn. (conf. leader), Assn. Ind. Colls. and Schs. (conv. speaker, pub. relations com., govt. relations com.), R.I. Women's Golf Assn. (exec. bd., tournament co-chmn.), Phi Kappa Phi, Delta Pi Epsilon (pres., newsletter editor). Roman Catholic. Club: Point Judith Country. Avocations: golf; gardening. Home: 137 Kenyon Ave Wakefield RI 02879 Office: Ocean State Bus Inst 1 High St PO Box 377 Wakefield RI 02880

POULOS, GEORGE, African Languages educator; b. Johannesburg, Republic of South Africa, Feb. 9, 1949; s. Athos and Cleo (Varsamopoulos) P. BA, U. Witwatersrand, 1970, BA with honors, 1971, MA, 1976; PhD, Rhodes U., 1982. Jr. lectr. African langs. U. Witwatersrand, Johannesburg, 1971-75, asst. lectr., 1975-77; sr. lectr. African langs. U. South Africa, Pretoria, 1980-83, assoc. prof., 1983-85, prof., 1985—; neurolinguistic researcher, 1987—. Author: Venda: A Select Bibliography, 1981, Issues in Zulu Relativization, 1982, A Grammar of the Venda Language, 1987; contbr. articles to profl. jours. Raikes scholar U. Witwatersrand, 1971; Inst. for Study of Man Africa research grantee, 1972. Greek Orthodox. Home: 62 Van Deventer Rd, Verwoerdburg 0157, Republic of South Africa Office: U South Africa, PO Box 392, Pretoria 0001, Republic of South Africa

POULOS, MICHAEL JAMES, insurance company executive; b. Glens Falls, N.Y., Feb. 13, 1931; s. James A. and Mary P.; m. Mary Kay Poulos; children: Denise, Peter. BA, Colgate U., 1953; MBA, N.Y. U., 1963. With sales and mgmt. depts. U.S. Life Ins. Co., N.Y.C., 1958-70; asst. v.p. Calif.-Western States Life Ins. Co., Sacramento, 1970-75, v.p. adminstrn., 1975-79; pres., chief exec. officer, dir. Am. Gen. Corp., Houston, 1979—, pres., chief operation officer, mem. of exec. , fin. coms. , dir., 1981—. Mem. Sam Houston Area council Boy Scouts Am. Mem. Am. Soc. C.L.U.s, Nat. Assn. Life Underwriters, Houston Assn. Life Underwriters, Life Office Mgmt. Assn., Am. Mgmt. Assn., Beta Gamma Sigma, Delta Sigma Pi. Greek Orthodox. Clubs: Heritage, University. Office: Am Gen Corp 2929 Allen Pkwy Houston TX 77019

POUMADERE, MARC PIERRE, psychologist; b. France, July 22, 1951; m. Claire Marina Mays. Masters degree, U. Paris IX, 1974, diplôme d'etudes approfondies, 1976, doctorate degree, 1978; post MBA, U. Oregon, 1977. Teaching asst. psychology dept. U. Oregon, Eugene, 1976-77; research fellow lab. psychol. and social relations Harvard U., Cambridge, 1979-81; prof. Ecole Superieure de Commerce, Paris, 1983-87; program dir. Inst. Symlog, Cachan, France, 1982—; sci. adv. Nat. Edn., France, 1983—; cons. nuclear power plants Electricité de France 1984—. Contbr. articles to profl. jours.; mem. editorial bd. Internat. Jour. Small Group Research, Ariz., 1985—. Fullbright fellow, 1976-77, research grantee French Govt., 1976-77. Mem. Am. Psychol. Assn., Soc. Risk Analysis. Club: Harvard of France, Garbure, Gagner (Paris). Office: Inst Symlog, BP 125, 94230 Cachan France

POUNCEY, PETER RICHARD, college president, classics educator; b. Tsingtao, Shantung, China, Oct. 1, 1937; came to U.S., 1964; s. Cecil Alan and Eugenie Marde (Lintilhac) P.; m. Bethanne McNally, June 25, 1966; 1 son, Christian; m. Susan Rieger, Mar. 21, 1973; 1 dau., Margaret. Lic. Phil., Heythrop Coll., Eng., 1960; B.A., Oxford U., Eng., 1964, M.A., 1967; Ph.D., Columbia U., 1969; AM (hon.), Amherst Coll., 1985; LLD (hon.), Williams Coll., 1985; LHD (hon.), Doshisha U., 1987. Instr. classics Fordham U., Bronx, N.Y., 1964-67; asst. prof. Columbia U., N.Y.C., 1969-71, dean Columbia Coll., 1972-76, assoc. prof., 1977-83, prof. classics, 1983-84; pres. Amherst Coll., Mass., 1984—; cons. classical lit. Columbia Ency., 1970-73; trustee Columbia Univ. Press, 1972-75. Author: The Necessities of War: A Study of Thucydides' Pessimism, 1980 (Lionel Trilling award 1981). Trustee Brit.-Am. Edn. Found., N.Y.C., 1971-75. Recipient Great Tchr. award Soc. Columbia Grads., 1983. Mem. Am. Philol. Assn., Phi Beta Kappa. Office: Amherst Coll Office of Pres Amherst MA 01002 *

POUND, ANDREA, psychologist; b. London, July 3, 1935; d. Arthur and Lucy May (Woodcock) Skegg; m. David Charles Pound, Nov. 9, 1957 (div. 1974); children: Andrew, Nicholas, Catherine. BSc in Psychology, U. London, 1971, M in Clin. Psychology, 1974. Lectr. Inst. Psychiatry U. London, 1973-75; sr. psychologist Tavistock Clinic, London, 1975-78, prin. psychologist, 1980-84; sr. psychologist St. George's Hosp., London, 1978-80; dist. psychologist The London Hosp., 1984—; researcher S. London Under-Fives project Inst. Psychiatry, 1980—. Contbr. articles to profl. jours. Com. mem. Nat. Assn. Mental Health, Tower Hamlets, London, 1985—; chmn. New Parent-Infant Network, Tower Hamlets, 1987. Inst. Psychiatry Med. Research Council grantee, 1980, Dept. Health and Social Security grantee, 1985. Mem. British Psychology Soc., Assn. Child Psychology and Psychiatry (hon. sec. 1983—). Mem. Labour Party. Mem. Ch. of Eng. Home: 41 Kelly St, London NW1 8PG, England Office: The London Hosp, Whitechapel High St, London E1 1BB, England

POUNGUI, ANGE-EDOUARD, prime minister of People's Republic of Congo; b. Mouyondzi, People's Republic of Congo, Jan. 4, 1942; s. Casimir and Agnes Moungondo; married; 8 children. Student Centre d'Enseignement Superieur, Brazzaville, People's Republic of Congo, law sch., 1969. Legal rep. Bank of Central African States, 1973-76, asst. dir., 1976-79; dir. gen. Congolese Comml. Bank, 1979-84; minister of fin. People's Republic of Congo, Brazzaville, 1971-73, minister of planning, 1973, prime minister, 1984—; v.p. State Council, 1972-73; fin. counsel to head of state, 1979—; mem. Nat. Council for Revolution, 1968, mem. directorate, 1969; gov. for People's Republic of Congo at IMF and African Devel. Bank, 1971-73; adminstr. Bank for Devel. of Central African States, 1976—; pres. Nat. Com. for Cellulose. Mem. polit. bur. Parti Congolais du Travail, 1969-75, 84—, mem. central com., 1969—. Mem. Fedn. of Profl. Assns. of Banks of Bank of Central African States (pres. 1982—), Profl. Assn. of Banks of Congo (pres. 1984). Office: Office of Prime Minister, Brazzaville People's Republic of Congo *

POUNTAIN, ERIC JOHN, construction company executive; b. Cannock, Staffordshire, U.K., Aug. 5, 1933; s. Horace and Elsie Pountain; student public schs., W. Midlands; m. Joan Patricia Sutton, June 21, 1960; children—Ian, Louise. Joint prin. F. Maitland Selwyn & Co., 1956-64; founder Midland & Gen. Devels., 1964-69; chief exec. John McLean & Sons, Ltd. (now subs. of Tarmac PLC), 1969—13 ; chmn. Housing & Properties div. Tarmac, Wolverhampton, W. Midlands, Eng., dep. chmn., chief exec.; chmn. Tarmac PLC, 1983—; bd. dirs. Glynwed Internat., Midland Bank; dep. chmn. James Beattie PLC, 1985-87, chmn., 1987—, also bd. dirs. Trustee, Ironbridge Gorge Mus.; mem. council Burton upon Trent Grad. Med. Centre. Fellow Soc. Valuers and Acutioneers; companion British Inst. Mgmt.; mem. Brit. Inst. Dirs. Mem. Ch. of England. Home: Edial House, Edial, Lichfield Staffordshire, England Office: Tarmac PLC, PO Box 8, Ettingshall, Wolverhampton West Midlands WV4 6JP, England *

POUPARD, PAUL CARDINAL, cardinal Roman Catholic Church; b. Aug. 30, 1930. ordained 1954. Titular bishop Usula 1979, archbishop, 1980, proclaimed cardinal, 1985; deacon Saint Eugenio. Address: Piazza San Calisto 16, 00153 Rome Italy *

POVEY, THOMAS GEORGE, office systems co. exec.; b. Norristown, Pa., Dec. 27, 1920; s. Thomas and Blanche (Groff) P.; B.S., Temple U., 1948; m. Bettina O. Houghton, June 2, 1945; children—Bettina C., Denise E. With Sperry Remington div. Sperry Rand Corp., Phila., also Newark, N.Y.C., 1948-76, eastern regional gen. sales mgr., 1960-63, nat. gen. sales mgr., N.Y.C., 1966-67, dir. mktg., Marietta, Ohio, 1968-71, v.p. mktg., 1972-73, v.p. fed. govt. mktg., Washington, 1973-76; pres. Remco Bus. Systems, Inc., Washington, 1976—; lectr. Newark High Sch., 1954-56, Belleville (N.J.) High Sch., 1956-58, Fairleigh Dickinson Coll., Paterson, N.J., 1957-58, Pace Coll., N.Y.C., 1965—, Georgetown U., 1974, ednl. TV, N.Y.C., 1965—. Dir. Community Fund, Essex Fells, N.J., 1967. Served as 1st lt. with USAF, 1942-45. Decorated Air medal; named Remington Dartnell Salesman of Yr., 1950. Mem. Internat. Platform Assn., Smithsonian Assos., Internat. Systems Dealer Assn. (dir. 1977-78), Office Systems Equipment Coop. (pres. 1978-80), Pi Delta Epsilon (pres. 1948). Republican. Methodist. Home: 227 Cape St John Rd Annapolis MD 21401 Office: 8000 Parston Dr Forestville MD 20747

POWELL, ANTHONY DYMOKE, writer; b. London, Dec. 21, 1905; s. P.L.W. and Maud (Wells-Dymoke) P.; M.A., Balliol Coll., Oxford U., 1926, D.Litt., 1980; D.Litt., U. Sussex, 1971, Leicester, Kent, 1976, U. Bristol, 1982; m. Lady Violet Pakenham, Dec. 1, 1934; children—Tristram Roger Dymoke, John Marmion Anthony. Trustee Nat. Portrait Gallery, 1962-76. Served to maj. Brit. Army, 1939-45. Decorated Order White Lion (Czechoslovakia); Order Leopold II (Belgium); Oaken Crown, Croix de Guerre (Luxembourg); comdr. Brit. Empire. Fellow MLA (hon.); mem. Am. Acad. Arts and Letters (hon.). Club: Travellers (London). Author: novels) Afternoon Men, 1931; Venusberg, 1932; From A View to A Death, 1933; Agents and Patients, 1937; What's Become of Waring, 1939; John Aubrey and His Friends, 1948; Selected Writings of Aubrey, 1949; in Music of Time series; A Question of Upbringing, 1951; A Buyer's Market, 1952; The Acceptance World, 1955; At Lady Molly's (James Tait Black Meml. prize), 1957; Casanova's Chinese Restaurant, 1960; The Kindly Ones, 1962; The Valley of Bones, 1964; The Soldier's Art, 1966; The Military Philosophers, 1968; Books Do Furnish a Room, 1971; Temporary Kings, 1973; Hearing Secret Harmonies (W.H. Smith prize), 1975; The Album to Music of Time, 1987, The Fisher King, 1986; (plays) The Garden God, The Rest I'll Whistle, 1971; (memoirs) To Keep the Ball Rolling) Vol. I—Infants of The Spring, 1976, Vol. II—Messengers of Day, 1978; Vol. III, Faces in My Time, 1980; Vol. IV, The Strangers All Are Gone, 1982; (novella) O, How The Wheel Becomes It!, 1983, The Album of Anthony Powell's Music of Time, 1987, Companion of Honour, 1988.

POWELL, CAROL CHRISTINE, restaurant owner; b. Seattle, Feb. 15, 1941; d. Benjamin Olaf and Lois Carol (Smith) Michel; m. William Fred Roth, Apr. 8, 1961 (div. Dec. 1972); children: Christine Roth, Fred Roth, Traci Roth; m. George Benjamin Powell, Dec. 22, 1972; children: Kathy Powell Rank, George Powell Jr. Grad., Franklin High Sch., Seattle, 1959. Dishwasher Happy Chef, Cherokee, Iowa, 1978; dishwasher, waitress Randall's Cafe, Cherokee, 1978-79, mgr., 1979-82; owner, operator The Food Broker Restaurant, Cherokee, 1983—. Mem. adv. com. Cherokee Sch. Mem. Assn. Consumer Preferred Bus., Cherokee C. of C. Democrat. Home: 320 N 6th St Cherokee IA 51012 Office: The Food Broker Restaurant Hwy 59 S Cherokee IA 51012

POWELL, DIANA KEARNY, lawyer, poet; b. Washington, Apr. 15, 1910; d. William Glasgow and Alice Van Voorhees (Joline) P.; LL.B., Columbus U., 1940, LL.M., 1942; A.A., George Washington U., 1945; postgrad. Law

Sch. Georgetown U., 1957. Admitted to D.C. bar, 1940, U.S. Supreme Ct. bar, 1959; practice law, Washington; contbr. poetry to various mags., 1930—; poetry recitations. Precinct chmn. Republican Party, 1965-68, co-chmn., 1972-75; mem. various campaign coms.; sec. Sodality Holy Name Soc. of St. Matthew's Cathedral, 1978-81, chmn. workshop com., 1975-81, 83-86, pres., 1981-83; mem. Republican Presdl. Task Force, 1982. Recipient various local and nat. poetry awards Nat. League Am. Pen Women; cert. of appreciation Anchor Mental Health Assn., 1975. Mem. ABA, Nat. Assn. Women Lawyers, Internat. Platform Assn, Saintpaulia Internat. Roman Catholic. Author: Selected Poems, 1986. Assoc. editor: Washington Vistas, 1953.

POWELL, DON RICHARD, psychologist; b. Bklyn., Aug. 14, 1950; s. Robert B. and Yvette (Steinmetz) P.; m. Nancy Talberg, July 18, 1976; children—Jordan Scott, Brett Ryan. B.A., U. Mich., 1971, Ph.D. cum laude, 1978. Instr. psychology dept. U. Mich., Ann Arbor, 1971-76; sr. staff psychologist Inst. for Behavior Change, Ann Arbor, Mich., 1977-78; v.p. Smoke Stoppers, Inc., Ann Arbor, 1978-79; regional dir. div. health promotion services Am. Health Found., Southfield, Mich., 1979-83; pres. Am. Inst. Preventive Medicine, 1983—; ; Commentator TV health news series, For Your Health, 1983; TV and radio talk show guest; cons. to pvt. industries and U.S. govt. Author column Your Patient and Cancer. Recipient Healthy Am. Fitness Leader award U.S. Jaycees and President's Council on Phys. Fitness and Sports, 1983, Gov.'s Phys. Fitness and Health award for State of Mich., 1982. Mem. Am. Psychol. Assn., Am. Public Health Assn., Midwest Psychol. Assn., Am. Inst. for Prev. medicine (pres. 1983—). Home: 3154 Shadydale Ln West Bloomfield MI 48033 Office: 19111 W 10 Mile Rd Suite 101 Southfield MI 48075

POWELL, ERNESTINE BREISCH, retired lawyer; b. Moundsville, W.Va., Feb. 16, 1906; d. Ernest Elmer and Belle (Wallace) Breisch; student Dayton YMCA Law Sch., 1929; m. Roger K. Powell, Nov. 15, 1935; children—R. Keith (dec.), Diane L.D., Bruce W. Admitted to Ohio bar, 1929; tax analyst tax dept. Wall, Cassell & Groneweg, Dayton, Ohio, 1929-31; practiced law, 1931-40; gen. counsel for Dayton Jobbers and Mfrs. Assn., 1931-41; mem. firm Powell, Powell & Powell, Columbus, Ohio, 1944-86, ret. Ohio chmn. Nat. Woman's Party, Washington, 1950-51, nat. chmn., 1953, hon. nat. chmn. Pres. vol. activities com. Columbus State Sch., 1960-61, mem. bd. trustees, 1957-59. Mem. Nat. Assn. Women Lawyers, Am., Ohio, Columbus bar assns., Nat. Soc. Arts and Letters (pres. Columbus chpt. 1963-64), Nat. Lawyers Club (charter mem.), Nat. Mus. Women in Arts (charter mem.). Co-author: Tax Ideas, 1955; Estate Tax Techniques, 1956—. Editor-in-chief: Women Lawyers Jour., 1943-45. Office: 1382 Neil Ave PO Box 8010 Columbus OH 43201

POWELL, IVOR BLAKE, filmmaker; b. Northwood, Middlesex, Eng., Mar. 14, 1943; s. Ivor and Winifred (Venus) P.; m. Marion Louise Fisher, 1967; children: Blake, Sam. Student, St. Paul's Sch., London, 1959. Asst. stage mgr. H.M. Tennents Co., London, 1959-61; floor asst. BBC, London, 1963-64; asst. dir. for spl. effects for film 2001: A Space Odyssey; location mgr. The Adventurers, 1968; assoc. producer Memory of Justice, 1973, The Duellists, 1977; line producer Alien, 1979, Blade Runner, 1981; producer U.K. Comms. Co., Barrie Joll Assn., 1981—. Mem. Brit. Writers Union, Brit. Acad. Film and TV. Home: 6 Glamorgan Rd, Hampton Wick, Surrey KT1 4HP, England Office: Barrie Joll Assocs, 58 Frith St, London W1V 5TA, England

POWELL, JAMES BOBBITT, biomedical laboratories executive, pathologist; b. Burlington, N.C., Aug. 28, 1938; s. Thomas Edward and Sophia (Sharpe) P.; m. Pamela Oughton, Sept. 12, 1969 (div. Sept. 1979); 1 child, Daphne Oughton; m. Anne Ellington, Oct. 20, 1984; children: James Bobbitt (dec.), John Banks. B.A., Va. Mil. Inst., 1960; M.D., Duke U., 1964. Diplomate Am. Bd. Pathology. Intern, Duke U. Med. Ctr., Durham, N.C., 1964-65; resident Cornell Med. Ctr., N.Y.C., 1965-67, Englewood Hosp., N.J., 1967-69; founder Roche Biomed. Labs., Burlington, 1969—, pres., 1969—; dir. Carolina Biol. Supply Co., Burlington, First South Bank, Burlington, N.C. Trust Co., Greensboro. Contbr. articles to sci. publs. Trustee Elon Coll. (N.C.), 1981—; bd. overseers Duke U. Comprehensive Health Ctr.; dir. Twin Lakes Retirement Ctr., Alamance Homeless Shelter. Served as maj. M.C., U.S. Army, 1969-72. Fellow Am. Soc. Clin. Pathologists, Coll. Am. Pathologists; mem. AMA, Young Pres. Orgn. Republican. Club: Alamance Country (Burlington). Home: 2307 York Rd Burlington NC 27215 Office: Biomed Reference Labs Inc 430 Spring St Burlington NC 27215

POWELL, LARSON MERRILL, investment advisory service executive; b. Pittsfield, Mass., Mar. 8, 1932; s. Harry LeRoy and Elsie Madeline (Larson) P.; A.B., Harvard U., 1954; student Columbia U. Law Sch., 1957-59; m. Anne C. Millett, Dec. 8, 1956; children—Larson Merrill, Anne Coleman, Miles Sloan. News editor, reporter Boston Daily Globe, 1954, 56-57; security analyst Moody's Investors Service, N.Y.C., 1959-62, regional mgr., 1964-67, v.p., 1967-68; pres. instl. investment mgmt. div. Anchor Corp., Elizabeth, N.J., 1968-70; pres. Res. Research, Ltd., N.Y.C., 1971—, Powell Publs. Corp., N.Y.C., 1980—. Bd. mgrs. W.Side br. YMCA of Greater N.Y., 1970-79, mem.-at-large citywide bd., 1976-79; chmn. men's com. Am. Mus. Natural History, 1970-72; mem. Boro of Manhattan Community Planning Bd. 7, 1966-69; bd. dirs. Children's Home of Portland, 1986—, Sweetser Children's Home, 1988—, Episcopal Camp and Conf. Center, 1978-80. Served with AUS, 1954-56. Fellow Fin. Analysts Fedn.; mem. Internat. Soc. Fin. Analysts, N.Y. Soc. Security Analysts, N.Y. Newsletter Pubs. Assn. Episcopalian. Club: Harvard (N.Y.C.); Cumberland (Portland, Maine). Editor, pub. Powell Monetary Analyst, 1971—, Powell Gold Industry Guide and Internat. Mining Anlayst, 1976—, Powell Alert, 1980-88. Home: 413 Blackstrap Rd Falmouth ME 04105 Office: PO Box 4135 Station A Portland ME 04101

POWELL, LOUISA ROSE, psychologist; b. Highland Park, Mich., Oct. 10, 1942; d. Albert and Mildred Loraine (Bos) Feldman; B.S., Roosevelt U., 1966; M.S., U. Chgo., 1969, Ph.D., 1973; m. Philip Melancthon Powell, Dec. 29, 1962; children—David, Aaron, Robert. Intern in psychology VA Hosp., Newington, Conn., 1973-75; instr. So. Conn. State Coll., New Haven, 1975-76; psychologist Austin (Tex.) Evaluation Ctr., 1979-80, 81-82; dep. dir. gen. clin. services Austin Child Guidance and Evaluation Ctr., 1982-86; sch. psychologist San Rafael (Calif.) Schs., 1980-81; instr. S.W. Tex. State U., San Marcos, 1978-79; adj. prof. dept. psychology U. Tex., Austin, 1984—, clin. coordinator learning abilities Child-Family Practicum Ctr., 1986-87; pvt. practice psychology. Chmn. Cub Scouts Pack No. 54, 1977-78; v.p. pub. affairs Austin Alliance for Mentally Ill, 1987-88; mem. Nat. Alliance for Mentally Ill, Tex. Alliance for Mentally Ill; bd. dirs. Capital Area Mental Health Ctr., 1985-86; cellist Austin Community Orch. Lic. psychologist, health services provider, Tex. Fellow Am. Orthopsychiat. Assn.; mem. Am. Psychol. Assn., Southwestern Psychol. Assn., Tex. Psychol. Assn., Capital Area Psychol. Assn. (sec. 1985, 86), Am. Assn. Marital and Family Therapy, Soc. Research in Child Devel., Central Tex. Assn. Gifted Children (co-v.p. 1984-85), Am. Group Psychotherapy Assn. (assoc.). Democrat. Home: 3910 Edgerock Dr Austin TX 78731 Office: 3724 Jefferson St Suite 209 Austin TX 78731

POWELL, MELANIE JANE, economics educator; b. Essex, Eng., Apr. 26, 1957; d. Ronald Frank Powell and Joyce Kathleen (Ringrose) Powell Duckitt. BA in Econs. with honors, Kingston Poly., 1982; MSC in Econs., London U., 1984. Reporter Westminster Press, London, 1976-79; lectr. Kingston Poly., Surrey, Eng., 1982-84, Leeds (Eng.) Poly., 1987—; research fellow U. York, Eng., 1984-87; vis. researcher U. York, 1987—; rep. Collaborating Ctr. Regional Office Europe on addiction policy WHO, 1985—; mem. adv. com. Women's Nat. Commn. Addiction Working Group, London, 1987. Author: Economics of Alcohol Policy, 1988; contbr. articles to profl. publs. Mem. Health Economists Study Group U.K. Home: 89 Heslington Rd, York, Yorkshire YO1 5AX, England Office: Leeds Poly Dept Econs and Pub Policy, 43 Woodhouse Ln, Leeds LS2 8BW, England

POWELL, SIR (ARNOLD JOSEPH) PHILIP, architect; b. Bedford, Eng., Mar. 15, 1921; s. Arnold and Winnifred (Walker) P.; m. Philippa Powell, Jan. 17, 1953; children—Dido, Ben. A.A. Diploma, Sch. Architecture, Epsom Coll. Ptnr. Powell Moya & Ptnrs., London, 1946—. Works include: Churchill Gardens flats, Westminster, 1948-62, Skylon for Festival of Britain, 1951, Chichester Theater, 1962, Brit. Pavilion, Expo70, Osaka, Japan, 1970, Mayfield Sch., Putney, 1955, Plumstead Manor Sch. Woolwich, 1970, dining romms at Bath Acad. Art, Corsham, 1970, Eton Coll., 1974, Mus. of London, 1977, Queen Elizabeth II Conf. Ctr., 1986; extensions Brasenose Coll., Oxford, 1961, Corpus Christi Coll., Oxford, 1969, many others. Mem. Royal Fin Art Commn., London, 1969—; trustee Soane Mus., London. Decorated officer Order Brit. Empire, Companion of Honour; recipient Royal Gold medal Royal Inst. Brit. Architects, 1974. Mem. Royal Acad. Arts (trustee and treas.). Office: Powell Moya & Ptnrs Architects, 21 Upper Cheyne Row, London SW3, England

POWELL, RAMON JESSE, lawyer, government official; b. Macon, Mo., Mar. 1, 1935; s. Robert Evan and Blanche Odella (Dry) P.; A.B. in Econs. with distinction, U. Mo., 1957; postgrad. (Fulbright scholar) U. Brussels, 1957-58; J.D., Harvard U., 1965. Admitted to D.C. bar, 1966, Va. bar, 1975, U.S. Supreme Ct. bar, 1975; atty., advisor Office Gen. Counsel, Office Chief Engrs., Dept. Army, 1965-70; gen. counsel U.S. Water Resources Council, Washington, 1970-74, 80-82; asst. counsel for interagy. relations Office of Chief Counsel, Office of Chief of Engrs., Dept. Army, Washington, 1982-87, asst. chief counsel for legal services policy and programs, 1987—; sole practice law, Washington, 1975-76; pres., gen. counsel Leman Powell Assos., Inc., Alexandria, Va., 1976-80. Served as officer USAF, 1958-62. Mem. ABA, Fed. Bar Assn., D.C. Unified Bar, Bar Assn. D.C., Va. State Bar, Phi Beta Kappa, Omicron Delta Kappa, Delta Sigma Rho, Beta Theta Pi. Club: Nat. Lawyers. Office: 20 Massachusetts Ave NW Washington DC 20314

POWELL, RICHARD PITTS, writer; b. Phila., Nov. 28, 1908; s. Richard Percival and Lida Catherine (Pitts) P.; m. Marian Carleton Roberts, Sept. 6, 1932 (dec. Nov. 1979); children: Stephen Barnes, Dorothy Louise; m. Margaret M. Cooper, 1980. Grad., Episcopal Acad., 1926; A.B., Princeton, 1930. Reporter Phila. Evening Ledger, 1930-40; with N.W. Ayer & Son, Phila., 1940-58; mem. pub. relations dept. N.W. Ayer & Son, 1940-42, charge info. services, 1949-58, v.p., 1951-58. Author: mystery books Don't Catch Me, 1943, All Over but the Shooting, 1944, Lay That Pistol Down, 1945, Shoot If You Must, 1946, And Hope to Die, 1947, Shark River, 1950, Shell Game, 1950, A Shot in the Dark, 1952, Say It with Bullets, 1953, False Colors, 1955; novels The Philadelphian, 1957, Pioneer, Go Home, 1959, The Soldier, 1960, I Take This Land, 1963, Daily and Sunday, 1965, Don Quixote, U.S.A, 1966, Tickets to the Devil, 1968, Whom the Gods Would Destroy, 1970, Florida: A Picture Tour, 1972; novel under pen name Jeremy Kirk The Build-Up Boys, 1951; Contbr. short stories, articles, serials to mags. Served as lt. col. AUS, 1942-46; chief news censor 1945, S.W. Pacific Theatre. Home: 1201 Carlene Ave Fort Myers FL 33901

POWELL, WILLIAM ARNOLD, JR., banker; b. Verbena, Ala., July 7, 1929; s. William Arnold and Sarah Frances (Baxter) P.; m. Barbara Ann O'Donnell, June 16, 1956; children: William Arnold III, Barbara Ann, Susan Frances, Patricia Baxter. BSBA, U. Ala., 1953; grad., La. State U. Sch. Banking of South, 1966. With Am. South Bank, N.A., Birmingham, Ala., 1953—, asst. v.p., 1966, v.p., 1967, v.p., br. supr., 1968-72, sr. v.p., br. supr., 1972-73, exec. v.p., 1973-79, pres., 1979-83, vice chmn. bd., 1983—, also bd. dirs.; pres First Nat. Bank Birmingham, 1983—, also bd. dirs.; pres. AmSouth Bancorp., 1979—; bd. dirs. AmSouth Mortgage Co., Inc., AmSouth Bancorp. Bd. dirs. Am. Cancer Soc., Birmingham Better Bus. Bur.; pres. Sch. Banking of South; trustee, chmn. Ala. Ind. Colls.; bd. visitors, U. Ala.; bd. dirs., sec.-treas. Warrior-Tombigbee Devel. Assn., Met. Arts Council, Sch. Fine Arts Found., Discovery Place, Brookwood Med. Ctr.-AMI, Big Brothers/Big Sisters of Greater Birmingham; campaign chmn. United Way, 1987. Served to lt. AUS, 1954-56. Mem. Birmingham Area C. of C. (pres., bd. dirs.), Birmingham Hist. Soc. (bd. dirs.). Clubs: The Club, Downtown, Mountain Brook, Riverchase Country, Birmingham Country, Green Valley Country (Birmingham). Lodge: Kiwanis (Birmingham) (past pres.). Home: 3309 Thornton Dr Birmingham AL 35226 Office: Am South Bank NA 5th Ave & 20th St PO Box 11007 Birmingham AL 35288

POWELL-BROWN, ANN, educator, publicist; b. Boonville, Mo., Mar. 19, 1947; d. Edward Marsh and Ethel M. (Benton) Powell; m. Richard Lee Brown, Dec. 29, 1978. BS, Cen. Mo. State U., 1969, MSE, 1975; postgrad. U. Mo., Kansas City. Tchr. Gulfport and Biloxi (Miss.) Schs., 1969-70; mem. adj. staff Providence Coll., Taichung, Taiwan, 1971-72; mem. reading and learning disabilities staff, Kansas City (Mo.) Sch. Dist., 1973-78, mem. learning disabilities identification team, 1978-79, mem. spl. edn. placement com., 1979-83; co-owner Am. Media Enterprises, 1983—; learning disabilities cons., 1984—; v.p., bd. dirs. Nat. Tutoring Inst., 1976; adj. faculty Ottawa Coll., 1980, instr. English as 2d lang., 1976-77; adj. faculty U. Mo., Kansas City, 1981; bi-weekly columnist Kansas City Bus. Jour., 1985-86; speaker various orgns. Mem. public affairs com. Jewish Community Center, 1978; v.p. Com. for Indochinese Devel., 1977; mem. edn. council Episcopal Diocese Western Mo., 1977; mem. selection com. Paul Harris Fellowship; founder, bd. dirs. Friends of St. Mary's; mem. profl. adv. bd. Oak Park Home Health Care, 1983; mem. Kansas City Jazz Festival Com., 1983; active Kansas City Riverfront Devel. Task Force., 1987; mem. adv. com. CASE Program, 1988; sub-com. chmn. IRA State Conf. Mem. Council Exceptional Children, Assn. Children with Learning Disabilities, Internat. Reading Assn. (state publicity com. 1983), Nat. Reading Council, Quality Edn. Coalition, Doctoral Student Spl. Interest Group, Gt. Alkali Plainsmen, St. David's Welsh Soc., Eggs and Issues Breakfast, Kansas City Blues Soc., Phi Delta Kappa. Democrat. Episcopalian. Home and Office: Am Media Enterprises 501 Knickerbocker Pl Kansas City MO 64111

POWER, BENJAMIN JOHN, food company executive; b. Dublin, Apr. 26, 1942; s. Robert and Maureen (Byrne) P.; m. Aida Merville Lawler, Oct. 1, 1963; children: Eleanor, Garrett. Grad. commerce, City of London Coll., Eng., 1966. Cert. sec. inc. acct. Accounts mgr. B.W. Credit Corp. Ltd., London, 1960-65; fin. controller Tyzack & Ptnrs. Ltd., London, 1965-67; company sec. De Beers/Anglo Am. Corp. Ltd., Shannon, Ireland, 1967-71; dir. W & R Jacob PLC, Dublin, 1971—; dir. Albany Office Supplies Ltd., Dublin. Author: Accounting Law for Limited Companies, 1987, Irish Company law, 1984; editor Employment Legislation, 1978. Mem. com. Irish Govts. Indsl. Costs Group, Dublin, 1984. Fellow Inst. of Chartered Secs. and Adminstrs. (world pres. 1987), Inst. of Dirs. (mem. com. Irish region 1984—); mem. Soc. of Comml. Accts. (assoc.), EEC Assn. for Biscuit, Chocolate and Sugar Confectionery Industries (pres. Paris 1982), Food Industries Assn. (head Irish del. Brussels conf. 1981). Roman Catholic. Clubs: Stephens Green, Fitzwilliam (Dublin). Office: W & R Jacob PLC, Belgard Rd, Dublin 24, Ireland

POWER, JOEL R., public relations executive; b. Berwyn, Ill., Sept. 7, 1939; s. J. Ralph and Lois M. (Lindsey) P.; B.A. in English, No. Ill. U., 1963; m. Sharon Mary Newman, June 17, 1961; children—Andrew Baird, Mary Joel. Writer, mgr. Sears, Roebuck and others, Washington, 1965-70; dir. pub. info. McKendree Coll., Lebanon, Ill., 1970-71; pub. relations supr. Standard Oil Co. Ind., Chgo., Atlanta, New Orleans, 1971-76; pres. Powerline, Inc., Grand Rapids, Mich., 1977-79, also associated with E.F. Hutton & Co., Keller-Crescent Co., J.I. Scott Co.; mgr. corp. relations Mitchell Energy & Devel. Corp., Houston, 1980-86; cons. ind. communications various advt. and pub. relations agys.; chmn. public info. COST Atlantic and Clean Atlantic Assos., 1976; nat. publicity chmn. Agr. Day, 1979, 80; lectr. various colls. and univs. 1970—. Served with U.S. Army, 1963-65. Pullman Found. scholar, 1963; cert. N.Y. Stock Exchange, Nat. Assn. Securities Dealers. Mem. Nat. Investor Relations Inst. (award of excellence 1981), Fin. Analysts Fedn. (corp. reporting award 1981), Internat. Assn. Bus. Communicators (gold quill award 1982, 84), Pub. Relations Soc. Am. (silver anvil award 1972, 76), Alpha Tau Omega. Contbr. articles to profl. publs.

POWER, MICHAEL JOHN, psychologist; b. London, Aug. 10, 1954; s. John Joseph and Mary Ellen (Golden) P.; m. Lorna Ann Champion, Aug. 31, 1985. BSc in Psychology, U. Coll., 1976; PhD, Sussex U., 1981; MSc in Psychology, Birmingham U., 1982. Clin. psychologist Guy's Hosp., London, 1982-84; research psychologist Med. Research Council, London, 1984—; tutor Open U., Milton Keynes, Eng., 1983—, S.E. Thames Regional Health Authority, 1984—. Author: (with others) Social Cognitive Theory of Depression, 1986, 87, The SOS Scale, 1988; asst. editor Holistic Medicine, London, 1985—; contbr. articles to profl. jours., 1983. Assoc. fellow, mem. Brit. Psychol. Soc., Inst. Psychiatry (honorary lectr. 1987). Club: Pentax (London). Office: MRC Social Psychiatry Unit, De Crespigny Park, London SE5 8AF, England

POWER, NOEL PLUNKETT, judge; b. Dec. 4, 1929; s. John Joseph and Hilda Power; m. Irma Maroya; 3 children. Student, Downlands Coll., 1948-50; BA, LLB, U. Queensland. Magistrate Hong Kong, 1965-76; pres. Lands Tribunal, Hong Kong, 1976-79; judge High Court Hong Kong, 1979-87, judge of appeal, 1987—; editor Lands Tribunal Law Reports, 1976-79. Clubs: Hong Kong; Queensland (Brisbane, Australia). Home: 76-G Peak Rd, Hong Kong Hong Kong

POWER, RICHARD JOHN DIXON, software company executive; b. London, Mar. 6, 1948; arrived in Italy, 1978; s. Basil Dixon and Lorna Mary (Edwards) P.; m. Maria Felicita Dal Martello, Nov. 20, 1976; 1 child, Katherine. BA in Psychology with honors, U. Sheffield, Eng., 1970; PhD, U. Edinburgh, Scotland, 1974. Research fellow U. Sussex, Eng., 1975-78; lettore in English lang. U. Padua, Italy, 1979-86; tech. dir. Artificial Intelligence Software SPA, Rovigo, Rome and Milan, Italy, 1986—. Contbr. over 15 articles to profl. jours. Home: Via S Biagio 45, 35100 Padua Italy Office: Artificial Intelligence Software SPA, Viale Della Pace 9, 45100 Rovigo Italy

POWER, STEPHEN CHARLES, mathematician, educator; b. Dunfermline, Fife, Scotland, June 20, 1951; s. John Charles and Alice Flora (Black) P.; m. Jane Elizabeth Pleming, Sept. 23, 1971 (div. May 1976); 1 child, Rebecca; m. Ann Elizabeth Davidson, Oct. 2, 1976; children: Daniel, Anna. BS, Imperial Coll., U. London, 1973; PhD, U. Edinburgh, 1976, DSc, 1988. Postdoctoral fellow Dalhousie U., N.S., 1976-78; Bateman instr. Calif. Inst. Tech., Pasadena, 1978-79; lectr. math. U. Lancaster, Eng., 1979—; vis. prof. Mich. State U., East Lansing, 1982-83, Houston U., 1986, U. Ala., 1987, U. Waterloo, Ont., 1987. Author: Hankel Operators on Hilbert Space, 1982; editor: Operators and Function Theory, 1985. Grantee Fulbright Commn., N.A.T.O., Sci. and Engring Research Council. Mem. London Math. Soc., Am. Math. Soc. Office: Dept Math, U Lancaster, LA1 4YL Lancaster England

POWERS, ANTHONY WILLIAM, JR., data processing executive; b. Indpls., Sept. 18, 1946; s. Anthony William and Rosalie P.; BSIM, Purdue U., 1968; postgrad. U. Chgo., 1968-69; children: Timothy, Katharine. Applications analyst Control Data Corp., 1968-69; cons. staff, mgr. Arthur Andersen & Co., 1969-76; v.p. No. Trust Co., 1976-79; sr. v.p. Nat. Sharedata, Schaumburg, Ill., 1979-81; pres. Micro Book, Inc., Schaumburg, 1982-85; Am. Data Tech., 1982-85, Am. Data Tech., 1982-85; sr. v.p., gen. mgr. MTech Midwest, 1985—. Active Boy Scouts Am. Mem. Ill. St. Bank Data Processing Com. Republican. Roman Catholic. Author: Bank Calc. Home: 773 Whalom Ln Schaumburg IL 60195 Office: MTech Midwest 443 N Wabash Chicago IL 60611

POWERS, BRUCE RAYMOND, college administrator; b. Bklyn., Dec. 10, 1927; s. George Osborne and Gertrude Joan (Bangs) P.; student U. Conn., 1947-49; A.B., Brown U., 1951, M.A., (tuition scholar 61-62), 1965; postgrad. U. Pa., 1961; m. Dolores Anne Dawson, July 25, 1969; children—Christopher, Patricia. Announcer/engr. Sta. WNLC, New London, Conn., 1946-47; tng. officer CIA, Dept. Def., 1951-55; TV sales/service rep. NBC, 1955; TV news writer and reporter Movietone News, United Press Assns., Inc., 1955-56; asst. to pres. Gotham-Vladimir Advt., Inc., 1956-57; asst. account exec. D'Arcy Advt. Co., 1957-58; asst. campaign dir. Community Counselling Services, Inc., 1958-59; fund-raising campaign dir. Tamblyn & Brown, Inc., 1959-60; instr. Brown U., Providence, 1963-65, Ryerson Poly. Inst., Toronto, 1966, Nazareth Coll., Rochester, N.Y., 1966-67; asst. prof. English and communication studies Niagara U., Lewiston, N.Y., 1967-86, assoc. prof., 1986—, chmn. permanent curriculum com. English dept., 1970-71, dir. Film Repertory Center, 1971—, dir. communication studies program, 1973-87; research asso. Center Culture and Tech., U. Toronto, 1977-81. Served with USNR, 1945-46; PTO. Recipient Carpenter prize in elocution, Brown U., 1951. Mem. MLA, Broadcast Edn. Assn., Soc. Cinema Studies, Am. Soc. Journalism Sch. Adminstrs., Assn. for Edn. in Journalism and Mass Communication, Internat. Exptl. Film Soc. (founding pres. 1971-73), Western N.Y. Audio-Visual Assn., N.Y. Coll. English Assn., Phi Beta Kappa. Roman Catholic. Editor, The Film Study Guide, 1973-74. Home: 915 Sun Valley Dr North Tonawanda NY 14120 Office: Niagara U Lewiston NY 14109

POWERS, ELEANOR MAY, recreational vehicle company executive; b. Langley, B.C., Can., July 28, 1928; d. Frederick William and Ellen Mary (MacAuley) Jones; m. Frank Clayton Powers, Dec. 11, 1959; 1 child, Clayton Scott. With B.C. Telephone Co., Langley, 1943-63; flying instr. Skyway Air Services Ltd., Langley, 1950-59; exec. Claynor Enterprises Ltd., Langley, 1967—. Mem. Recreation Dealers Assn. B.C. (sec. 1976-77, treas. 1982-84, v.p. 1984-85, pres. 1985-86), Recreation Vehicle Dealers Assn. Can. (treas. 1984-85, v.p. 1985-86, pres. 1986-87), Recreation Vehicle Dealers Assn. U.S. (dir. 1987—). Office: Claynor Enterprises Ltd, 4053-208th St, Langley, BC Canada V3A 2H3

POWERS, MARK GREGORY, consultant, lawyer; b. Galveston, Tex., Aug. 14, 1948; s. Robert Kenneth and Ann Joan (Brugliera) P.; m. Kim M. Walker, Aug. 21, 1971; children: Jason Robert, Erin Alison. BBA in Acctg., Georgetown U., 1970; MBA, Gonzaga U., 1972, JD, 1974; CLU, Am. Coll., Bryn Mawr, Pa., 1975, Chartered Fin. Cons., 1982. Bar: Wash. 1974. Prin. Profl. Services Group, Spokane, Wash., 1970-82; sr. v.p. Nat. Assocs., Inc., Spokane, 1982—. Coach, Spokane Youth Soccer, 1982—; pres. Spokane Indoor Soccer Ctr., 1986—. Mem. Wash. State Bar Assn., Nat. Assn. Life Underwriters, Am. Soc. CLU's (pres. 1980-81). Clubs: Spokane; Green Bluff Polo (Mead, Wash.). Home: Rt 3 Box 207 Chattaroy WA 99003 Office: National Assocs Inc NW-W 600 Riverside Spokane WA 99201

POWERS, RONALD GEORGE, management consultant; b. N.Y.C., July 9, 1934; s. Lee Whitney and R. Anne Powers; m. Elizabeth Braislin McClellan, July 24, 1980. Pres., Ronald Powers, Inc., Winter Park, Fla. and Westport, Conn., 1971; adviser to chief execs. of banks, corps. and govts. on strategic mgmt. issues, 1971—. Trustee Trinity Sch., Fla. Symphony Orch. Mem. Interlachen C. of C. Republican. Episcopalian. Club: La Coquille (Palm Beach, Fla.), Winter Park Racquet. Home: 561 Virginia Dr Winter Park FL 32789 Office: PO Box 2174 Winter Park FL 32790

POWNALL, THOMAS GILMORE, aerospace and technology manufacturing executive; b. Cumberland, Md., Jan. 20, 1922; m. Marilyn Cunnick, June 7, 1946. B.S. in Elec. Engring, U.S. Naval Acad., 1946. With Martin Marietta Corp., Bethesda, Md., 1963—, v.p. aerospace, 1963-69, pres. aerospace, 1969-76, dir., 1971—, corp. exec.v.p., 1976-77, corp. pres., chief operating officer, 1977-82, chief exec. officer, 1982-88, chmn., 1983—; dir. Sundstrand Corp., The Mellon Stuart Co., Geico Corp. Served USN. *

POŽÁR, LADISLAV, psychologist, educator; b. Znojmo, Czechoslovakia, May 26, 1931; s. František and Ružena (Kravalová) P.; m. Magdalena Alexandrova Guseva, June 22, 1957; children: Svetlana, Elena. Grad. in Edn., Psychology, U. Leningrad, USSR, 1957; PhD, Comenius U., Bratislava, Czechoslovakia, 1968, Candidate Psychol. Scis., 1968. Asst. in psychology Faculty of Arts, Bratislava, 1957-66, 67-70; with Research Inst. Child Psychology and Pathopsychology, Bratislava, 1966-67, mem., 1976—; head dept. pathopsychology, social pathology Faculty of Edn., Trnava, Czechoslovakia, 1970—, vice dean, 1972-86, dean, 1986-87; mem. research council Pub. Ctr. of Psychodiagnostic and Ednl. Tests, Bratislava, 1976—. Author: Patopsychologia zrakovo chybnynch, 1972; author, editor: Patopsychologia postihnutého dietata I, 1984, II, 1987, Patopsychologia, 1975; contbr. articles to profl. jours.; mem. editorial com. Jour. Child Psychology and Patopsychology, 1974—, Jour. Studia Psychologica, 1976—, Bull. Psychodiagnostika v socialistickych krajinách, 1976—. Recipient Silver medal for Socialistic Edn. Dist. Com. Socialistic Union of Youth, Bratislava, 1982; named Meritorious Worker Bratislava Ministry of Edn., 1981. Mem. Slovak Lit. Found. (registered translator). Office: Pedagogicka Fakulta, UK Moskovska 3, 813 34 Bratislava Czechoslovakia

PRADE, GERD, electronic company engineer; b. Reichenberg, Austria, Feb. 4, 1928; s. Franz and Aloisia (Fritsch) P.; m. Elfriede Stiepani, July 18, 1953.

Engr., Tech. Sch., Vienna, Austria, 1951. Technician, Schrack Electronic Ag, Vienna, 1946-51, tech. engr., 1951-60, prin. engr., 1960-65, chief engr., 1965—. Contbr. articles to profl. publs. Patentee in field. Mem. Austrian Electronic Com. Home: Jacquing Strasse 37, A 1030 Vienna Austria Office: Schrack Electronic Ag, Pottendorferstrasse 25-27, A 1121 Vienna Austria

PRADHAN, BISHWA, diplomat; b. Nepal, Jan. 10, 1936; s. Jagat Lal and Tulsi Maya Shrestha; m. Durga Devi, 1955; children: Rita, Bhushan, Bhuwan, Rebecca, Bhupendra. MA in Polit. Sci., U. Poona, India, 1958. Joined fgn. service, Nepal, 1959; dep. chief mission Royal Nepalese Embassy, Washington, 1968-70; chief protocol to His Majesty's Govt. of Nepal, 1970-74, joint sec. Ministry Fgn. Affairs, 1977-79, spl. sec., 1979-83, fgn. sec., 1983-86; Nepalese ambassador to Egypt, 1974-77, to U.S., Washington, 1986-88; chmn. for Nepalese side Nepal-China Boundary Commn., 1977-80. Author: Panchayat Democracy in Nepal, 1962, Foreign Policy and Diplomacy, 1963, King Mahendra and Nepal Foreign Policy, 1970, Nepal: A Peace Zone, 1982, Nepal in the Context of the Changing Situation in South Asia. Decorated TP 2d class, Nepal, 1978, GDB 1st class, 1984, also by Egypt, France, Spain, Yugoslavia, Thailand. Hindu. Office: Royal Nepalese Embassy 2131 Leroy Pl NW Washington DC 20008 also: Royal Nepal Airlines Corp, RNAC Bldg, Kanti Path, Kathmandu Nepal

PRADO, JUAN GUILLERMO OCARANZA, historian and writer; b. La Sereno, El Qui, Chile, Mar. 7, 1951; s. Guillermo and Mireya Prado; m. Ximena Blanco, May 26, 1952; children: Cristian, Juan Guillermo, Ximena, Felipe. Pub. employee Congress Library, Santiago, Chile, 1976-81; advisor Sec. Office of Govt., Santiago, 1981-82, chief of cabinet, 1983-84; nat. sec. Sec. Office Cultural Relations, Santiago, 1984-86; writer free lance, Santiago, 1986—; tchr. Met. U., Santiago, 1987—; ptnr. Folklore Researcher Assn., Cordobo, Argentina, 1981—. Author: Fiestas y Santuarios Marianos en Chile, 1980, Síntesis Historica del Foklore en Chile, 1982, Sectas Juveniles en Chile, 1984 (best book yr., 1984), La Tirana, 1986 (centenary book, 1986); editor: El Mercurio, 1978-82, La Nagōn, 1986—, La Tercera, 1986—, Chile Today, 1986—. Recipient Espuelo de Plata Nat. Fedn. Cueca, 1984, Mascara de Oro Syndicate Actors, 1985, Lircay Badge Lircay Inst. History, 1985, Godoy Cruz Badge Godoy Cruz Municipality, 1984. Mem. PanAm. Inst. Geography and History, Medicine Compare Assn., Hist. and Archeology Soc. San Felipe, Genealogic Investigation Inst., Pen Club Internat. (dir. 1984—); fellow Chilean Soc. History and Geography. Office: Congress Library, Compañia 1175, Santiago, Met Region Santiago Chile

PRAEFCKE, KLAUS WILHELM, chemistry educator, researcher; b. Ostseebad Wustrow, Mecklenburg, Germany, Jan. 3, 1933. Diploma Tech. U. Berlin, 1961, Ph.D., 1963, Habilitation, 1970. Privatdozent, Tech. U. Berlin, 1970-71, asst. prof., 1970, prof. chemistry, 1971—. Contbr. articles to profl. jours. Patentee in field. Home: Kranzallee 62, D1000 Berlin 19 Federal Republic of Germany Office: Tech U, Str des 17 Juni 135, D1000 Berlin 12 Federal Republic of Germany

PRAEGER, DONALD LEWIS, ophthalmologist; b. Poughkeepsie, N.Y., Aug. 25, 1933; s. M. Fred and Isabel (Abramsky) P.; B.S., Union Coll., 1955; M.D., N.Y. Med. Coll., 1959; postgrad. U. Pa., 1960; divorced; children—Jennifer, Frederick, Denton Cooley. Intern, Albany (N.Y.) Med. Center, 1959-60; resident in ophthalmic surgery Wills Eye Hosp., Pa., 1961-63; practice medicine specializing in ophthalmology, Poughkeepsie, 1964—, N.Y.C., 1980—; attending ophthalmic surgeon St. Francis Hosp., Poughkeepsie, 1970—, dir. ophthalmology, 1969-72; attending ophthalmic surgeon Vassar Bros. Hosp., Poughkeepsie, 1968-83; former dir. cataract surg. service N.Y. Med. Coll.-Westchester County Med. Center, Valhalla, 1977-81, assoc. clin. prof. ophthalmology, 1978—, attending ophthalmic surgeon, 1977-80; asso. attending opthalmic surgeon Cabrini Med. Center, 1981—; assoc. attending surgeon Med. Arts Hosp., 1986; assoc. clin. prof. N.Y. Med. Coll., 1978—; cons. in field; surgeon dir. N.Y. Intraocular Lens Seminar Inc., 1974—; mem. adv. com. ophthalmology Catholic Charities N.Y., 1975—; guest TV surgeon in U.S. cities, also London, Paris, Rome, The Netherlands, Brazil, Japan, Dublin, Waterford, Ireland, Kingston, Jamaica; instr. cataract surgery Found. for Ophthalmic Edn., Santa Monica, Calif., 1974; cons. Wassaic (N.Y.) Developmental Center, Sharon (Conn.) Hosp.; cons. ophthalmic surgeon Charing Cross Hosp., U. London, 1977, Wellington Hosp., Wellington Found., London, 1981. Diplomate Nat. Bd. Med. Examiners, Am. Bd. Ophthalmology (asso. examiner 1974-76). Fellow Am. Soc. Geriatrics, Mil. Soc. Ophthalmologists, Am. Acad. Ophthalmology, Ophthalmic Sox. U.K., Ophthalmic Soc. Republic France, Am. Acad. Facial and Reconstructive Plastic Surgery, ACS, Barraquer Inst. (Spain), W. Ger. and Irish Ophthal. Soc., Coll. Physicians Phila., Westchester Acad. Medicine, N.Y. Shamrock-Emerald Soc. (hon.); mem. Internat. Coll. Surgeons (splty. chmn. ophthalmology 1970-74), Soc. Contemporary Ophthalmology (bd. govs.), Internat. Assn. Ocular Surgeons (bd. govs.), Pan-Am. Assn. Ophthalmology, Contact Lens Soc. Am., U. Pa. Alumni Ophthalmologic Assn., Internat. Intraocular Implant Soc., Am. Intra-Ocular Implant Soc. (founding mem., mem. sci. adv. bd. 1978-80), Internat. Phaco Emulsification Cataract Methodology Soc. (dir. 1975, sci. adv. bd. 1979), N.Y. State Ophthalmologic Soc., N.Y. Soc. Clin. Ophthalmology (med. adv. bd. project ORBIS), N.Y. State Athletic Commn. (boxing panel mem. 1987). Recipient Am. Coll. Eye Surgeons award, Tex., 1988, Medal award Azar Found., New Orleans, 1982. Author med. textbooks on cataract and lens implant surgery; mem. editorial bd. Annals Ophthalmology; holder patents in field; contbr. chpts. to texts, articles to profl. jours. Club: Friars. Office: 944 Park Ave New York NY 10028 also: 12 Davis Ave Poughkeepsie NY 12603

PRAGER, EDWARD, social work educator; b. Bklyn., Jan. 20, 1939; arrived in Israel, 1967; s. Morris A. and Gertrude (Fishman) P.; m. Miriam Halbreich, June 16, 1963; children: Amiel Ram, Shira. BS, Columbia U., 1961, MSW, 1966; PhD, Case Western Res. U., 1980. Cert. social worker, N.Y. Retirement counselor Community Service Soc., N.Y.C., 1965-67; ptnr., founder Multimedia Ednl. Services, Israel, 1971-74; dir. psychiat. research Hill House Rehab., Cleve., 1976-80; lectr. social work Bob Shapell Sch. Social Work Tel Aviv U., 1980-86, sr. lectr., 1986—; cons. research and program devel. in family care of aged, 1983—, program devel. Mobile Video Ctr., Israel, 1986—; dir. devel. aging programs Beit Berl Coll., Israel, 1986—;. Mem. editorial com. Comprehensive Gerontology, Denmark, 1986—; contbr. articles to profl. jours. Mem. wind ensemble City of Kfar Sava, Israel. Community Services Soc. scholarship, N.Y.C., 1966; NIMH grantee, 1974-75, Ohio Mental Health Dept. research grantee, 1977, 78, 79. Mem. Internat. Assn. Gerontology, Israel Gerontol. Soc. (mem. adv. bd.), Israel Assn. Social Workers, Assn. for Anthropology and Gerontology, Nat. Com. Gerontology in Social Work Edn. Home: Herzl St 56, Kfar Sava 44213, Israel Office: Tel Aviv U, Bob Shapell Sch Social Work, Ramat Aviv 69978, Israel

PRAK, NIELS LUNING, architectural educator; b. Eindhoven, The Netherlands, Aug. 8, 1926; s. Jacob Luning and Tjetske (Veenstra) P.; m. Elisabeth De Waha Baillonville, May 8, 1954; children: Maarten, Agnes, Katrien, Edith. BArch, Delft Inst. Tech., The Netherlands, 1951. Pvt. practice architecture Flushing and Rotterdam, The Netherlands, 1955-70; prof. Basic Design Delft (Netherlands) Tech. U., 1963-87. Author: The Language of Architecture, 1968, The Visual Perception of the Built Environment, 1977, Architects: The Noted and the Ignored, 1984. Home: Larixlaan 193, 3053 LB Rotterdam The Netherlands Office: Delft Tech U, PO Box 5043, 2600 GA Delft The Netherlands

PRANATA, RICHARD BUDI, tire cord manufacturing company manager; b. Jakarta, Indonesia, Sept. 5, 1940; s. Leo Aditya Pranata and Turiana Pranadjaja; m. Sunny Trina Sistyawati, Dec. 19, 1971; children: Grace Cynthia Cecilia, Caroline Claudia, Angela Clara. MD, Yarsi Sch. Medicine, Jakarta, 1969. Lab. asst. Dowell Schlumberger (Ea.) Inc., Jakarta, 1972-75; sales mgr. NV. PD. Pamitran, Jakarta, 1975-76, E. Merck Chem. Div., Jakarta, 1976-80; mktg. mgr. PT. Eka Warna Kimia, Jakarta, 1980-84, PT. Branta Mulia, Jakarta, 1985—. Mem. Am. Chem. Soc. Office: PT Branta Mulia, Jl Jend Sudirman Kav 70-71, Jakarta 12910, Indonesia

PRATHER, WILLIAM CHALMERS, lawyer, writer; b. Toledo, Ill., Feb. 20, 1921; s. Hollie Cartmill and Effie Fern (Deppen) P. B.A., U. Ill., 1942, J.D., 1947. Bar: Ill. 1947, U.S. Supreme Ct. 1978. Asst. dean U. Ill., 1942-43; atty. First Nat. Bank of Chgo., 1947-51; asst. gen. counsel U.S. Savs. and Loan League, Chgo., 1951-59; gen. counsel U.S. League of Savs. Instns., Chgo., 1959-82, gen. counsel emeritus, 1982—; sole practice, Cumberland County, Ill., 1981—. sem. lectr. in law, banking. Served to lt. Armed Forces, 1943-45. Decorated Bronze Star. Mem. ABA, Internat. Bar Assn., Fed Bar Assn., Ill. Bar. Assn., Chgo. Bar Assn., Union Internat. des Avocats, Nat. Lawyers Club Washington, Phi Delta Phi. Clubs: Cosmos, University, Mattoon Golf and Country, Exeter & County (Eng.); Phi Gamma Delta. Editor: The Legal Bulletin, 1951-81, The Federal Guide, 1954-81; author: Savings Accounts, 1981; contbr. articles to publs. Home: Applewood Farm Box 157 Toledo IL 62468 Office: US League of Savs 111 E Wacker Dr Chicago IL 60601 Office: 738 Courthouse Square Toledo IL 62468

PRATT, ALAN JOHN, business and marketing consultant; b. Eng., July 21, 1927; s. Alan Reginald and Ellen Gwendoline (Roff) P.; B.A. in Engring., Watford Coll., 1948; M.B.A., Calif. Western U., 1974, Ph.D., D.B.A., 1976; m. Asako Tsuneyoshi, May 1, 1961. Surveyor, Air Registration Bd., Gt. Britain and Hong Kong, 1957-63; pres. Eutectic of Japan, Tokyo, 1963-66; group v.p. Alexander Industries, 1966-69; mgr. Far East, Digital Equipment Corp., Japan, 1969-72; dir. for Japan, Gen. Instrument Corp., 1972-75; exec. v.p. Klingelnberg Japan Ltd., Tokyo, 1975-79; mng. ptnr. Alan J. Pratt and Assocs., Kailua-Kona, Hawaii, 1979—; v.p. Kosei, Inc., 1979—; pres. Astra-Pacific Internat. Inc., Kailua-Kona; assoc. sr. cons. Adams-Boston Cons. Co., Tokyo, 1964-68; guest lectr. Japan-Am. Inst. Mgmt. Sci., Honolulu. pres. Kona Coffee Festival, 1984-86, Crime Stoppers West Hawaii, 1984-85. Served with RAF, 1942-46. Mem. Soc. Lic. Engrs., Am. Mgmt. Assn., Inst. Quality Engrs., Soc. Mfg. Engrs., Am. C. of C. in Japan (chmn. programs com. 1972-74), Royal Aero. Soc. Gt. Britain, Brit. Inst. Mgmt., Brit. Mgmt. Assn., Kona Coast C. of C. (chmn. programs and communications com. 1980, pres. 1981-82, chmn. Japan-Asia-Australia tourist and trade relations com. 1983-86), C. of C. of Hawaii (dir.). Roman Catholic. Clubs: American, Vivi Athletic (Tokyo); Masons (Hong Kong), South Kona Aloha Lions. Home: PO Box 5186 Kailua-Kona HI 96745 Office: PO Box AP Kailua-Kona HI 96745

PRATT, ALICE REYNOLDS, retired educational administrator; b. Marietta, Ohio, Oct. 5, 1922; d. Thurman J. and Vera L. (Holdren) Reynolds. BA, U. Okla., 1943. Reporter, high sch. tchr., 1944-50; asst. dir. Houston office Inst. Internat. Edn., 1952-58, dir. office, 1958-87, v.p., 1976-87, ret. 1987. Founding bd. govs. Houston Forum; mem. Houston Com. Fgn. Relations; bd. dirs. Houston World Trade Assn., former v.p.; founding mem. Japan Am. Soc. Houston; v.p., bd. dirs., founding mem. Korea-Houston Soc., 1983—; founding mem. Houston-Taipei Soc., Stavanger Sister City Assn.; past nat. bd. dirs. Sister Cities Internat., Nat. Council Internat. Visitors. Decorated Palmes Academiques (France), 1966; Order of Merit (Fed. Republic Germany), 1972; knight Order of Leopold II (Belgium), 1973; named Woman of Yr., Houston Bus. and Profl. Women, 1958; recipient Matrix award Theta Sigma Phi, 1961; Nat. Carnation award Gamma Phi Beta, 1976. Republican. Episcopalian.

PRATT, EDMUND T., JR., pharmaceutical company executive; b. Savannah, Ga., Feb. 22, 1927; s. Edmund T. and Rose (Miller) P.; m. Jeanette Louise Carneale, Feb. 10, 1951; children: Randolf Ryland, Keith Taylor. B.S. in Elec. Engring. magna cum laude, Duke U., 1947; M.B.A., U. Pa., 1949; hon. degrees, L.I. U., Marymount Manhattan Coll., Poly. U. of N.Y., St. Francis Coll. With IBM Corp., 1949-51, 54-57, asst. to exec. v.p., 1956-57; with IBM World Trade Corp., 1957-62, controller, 1958-62; asst. sec. financial mgmt. Dept. Army, 1962-64; controller Pfizer Inc., N.Y.C., 1964-67; v.p. operations internat. subsidiaries Pfizer Inc., 1967-69, chmn. bd., pres. internat. subsidiaries, 1969-71, exec. v.p., 1970-71, pres., 1971-72, chmn., chief exec. officer, 1972—, also chmn. exec. com., bd. dirs.; dir. Chase Manhattan Corp., Internat. Paper Co., Gen. Motors Corp.; trustee Com. for Econ. Devel.; trustee Am. Enterprise Inst. Bd. dirs. N.Y.C. Partnership; mem. N.Y. State Bus. Adv. Council; chmn. Emergency Com. for Am. Trade; trustee Duke U.; bd. overseers Wharton Sch. Commerce and Finance.; mem. Adv. Com. on Trade Negotiations; chmn. Nat. Indsl. Adv. Council for Opportunities Industrialization Ctrs. of Am. Served to lt. (j.g.) USNR, 1952-54. Mem. Bus. Roundtable (mem. policy com.), N.Y. Chamber Commerce and Industry (dir.), Bus. Council (chmn.), Phi Beta Kappa. Office: Pfizer Inc 235 E 42nd St New York NY 10017

PRATT, GEORGE JANES, JR., psychologist, consultant; b. Mpls., May 3, 1948; s. George Janes and Sally Elvina (Hanson) P., BA cum laude, U. Minn., 1970, MA, 1973; PhD with spl. commendation for overall excellence, Calif. Sch. Profl. Psychology, San Diego, 1976; 1 dau., Whitney Beth. Psychology trainee Ctr. for Behavior Modification, Mpls., 1971-72, U. Minn. Student Counseling Bur., 1972-73; predoctoral clin. psychology intern San Bernardino County (Calif.) Mental Health Services, 1973-74, San Diego County Mental Health Services, 1974-76; affiliate staff San Luis Rey Hosp., 1977-78; postdoctoral clin. psychology intern Mesa Vista Hosp., San Diego, Calif., 1976; clin. psychologist, dir. Psychology and Cons. Assocs. of San Diego, 1976—; chmn. Psychology and Cons. Assocs. Press, 1977—; bd. dirs. Optimax, Inc., 1985—; pres. George Pratt Ph.D., Psychol. Corp., 1979—; chmn. Pratt, Korn & Assocs., Inc., 1984—; founder La Jolla Profl. Workshops, 1977; clin. psychologist El Camino Psychology Ctr., San Clemente, Calif., 1977-78; grad. teaching asst. U. Minn. Psychology and Family Studies div., 1971; teaching assoc. U. Minn. Psychology and Family Studies div., Mpls., 1972-73; instr. U. Minn. Extension div., Mpls., 1971-73; faculty Calif. Sch. Profl. Psychology, 1974-83, San Diego Evening Coll., 1975-77, Nat. U., 1978-79, Chapman Coll., 1978, San Diego State U., 1979-80; vis. prof. Pepperdine U., Los Angeles, 1976-80; cons. U. Calif. at San Diego Med. Sch., 1976—, also instr. univ., 1978—, Facial Pain Clinic at U. Calif. San Diego Med. Ctr., 1983—; psychology chmn. Workshops in Clin. Hypnosis, 1980-84; cons. Calif. Health Dept., 1974, Naval Regional Med. Ctr., 1978-82, ABC-TV; also speaker. Mem. South Bay Youth Services Com., San Diego, 1976-80. Served with USAR, 1970-76. Licensed and cert. psychologist, Calif. Fellow Am. Soc. Clin. Hypnosis; mem. Am. Psychol. Assn., Calif. Psychol. Assn., Internat. Soc. Hypnosis, San Diego Psychology Law Soc. (exec. com.), Am. Assn. Sex Educators, Counselors and Therapists (cert.), San Diego Soc. Sex Therapy and Edn. (past pres.), San Diego Soc. Clin. Hypnosis (past pres.), Acad. San Diego Psychologists, Soc. Clin. and Exptl. Hypnosis., U. Minn. Alumni Assn., Nat. Speakers Assn., Beta Theta Pi. Republican. Lutheran. Author: HyperPerformance; A Clinical Hypnosis Primer; Sensory/Progressive Relaxation; Effective Stress Management; Clinical Hypnosis: Techniques and Applications; contbr. chpts. to various books. Office: Scripps Hosp Med Bldg 9834 Genesee Ave Suite 321 La Jolla CA 92037

PRATT, JOHN EDWARD, law educator, lawyer; b. Key West, Fla., June 29, 1945; s. Lloyd Edward and Marilyn June (Havercamp) P.; m. Sharon Louise Brown, Aug. 31, 1968; 1 child, Randolph Winfield. B.A., So. Meth. U., 1967, J.D., 1974. Bar: Tex. 1974, U.S. Dist. Ct. (no. dist.) Tex. 1975. Ptnr. Schuerenberg, Grimes & Pratt, Mesquite, Tex., 1974-77; asst. city atty. City of Dallas, 1978-80; mem. faculty Cedar Valley Coll., Lancaster, Tex., 1981—. Pres. Friends of Mesquite Pub. Library, Tex., 1975-77; chmn. United Way Fund Drive, Mesquite, 1975; del. Dem. State Conv., Houston, 1988; alt. del. Dem. State Conv., Houston, 1984; pres. Ponderosa Estates Homeowners Assn., 1986—; v.p. Pirrung PTA, 1987—. Served to lt. USNR, 1967-71. Mem. Am. Bus. Law Assn., Internat. Platform Assn., State Bar Tex., Tex. Jr. Coll. Tchrs. Assn., Cedar Valley Coll. Faculty Assn. (pres. 1983-85). Democrat. Mem. Christian Ch. Home: 1001 Villa Siete Mesquite TX 75181 Office: Cedar Valley Coll 3030 N Dallas Ave Lancaster TX 75134

PRATT, MARGARET WADE, information science executive; b. Kansas City, Mo., Apr. 5, 1925; d. Walter Wesley and Leone (Smith) P.; B.A., Washburn U., 1945; postgrad. in law Southwestern U. Dir. maternal and child health studies George Washington U., Washington, 1962-73; dir. maternal and child health studies project Minn. Systems Research, Inc., Washington, 1974-75; pres., project dir. Info. Sciences Research Inst., Vienna, Va., 1976—. Mem. Am. Public Health Assn., Assn. MCH Programs.

PRATT, ROSALIE REBOLLO, harpist, educator; b. N.Y.C., Dec. 4, 1933; d. Antonio Ernesto and Eleanor Gertrude (Gibney) Rebollo; Mus.B., Manhattanville Coll., 1954; Mus.M., Pius XII Inst. Fine Arts, Florence, Italy, 1955; Ed.D., Columbia U., 1976; m. George H. Mortimer, Esquire, Apr. 22, 1987; children—Francesca Christina Pratt Ferguson, Alessandra Maria Pratt Jones. Prin. harpist N.J. Symphony Orch., 1963-65; soloist Mozart Haydn Festival, Avery Fisher Hall, N.Y.C., 1968; tchr. music public schs., Bloomfield and Montclair, N.J., 1962-73; mem. faculty Montclair State Coll., 1973-79; prof. Brigham Young U., Provo, Utah, 1985-87, coordinator grad. studies dept. music, 1987—; coordinator grad. studies dept. music. Fulbright grantee, 1979; Myron Taylor scholar, 1954. Mem. Am. Harp Soc. (Outstanding Service award 1973), AAUP (co-chmn. legis. relations com. N.J. 1978-79), Internat. Assn. of Music for the Handicapped (co-founder, exec. dir., jour. editor), Coll. Music Soc., Music Educators Nat. Conf., Phi Kappa Phi, Sigma Alpha Iota. Co-author: Elementary Music for All Learners, 1980; contbr. articles to Music Educators Jour., Am. Harp Jour., others. Editor procs. 2d, 3d and 4th Internat. Symposia Music Edn. for Handicapped, 1981, 83, 85. Office: Brigham Young U Harris Fine Arts Ctr Provo UT 84602

PRATT, VAUGHAN RONALD, computer engineering educator; b. Melbourne, Australia, Apr. 12, 1944; s. Ronald Victor and Marjorie (Mirams) P.; m. Margot Frances Koster, Feb. 2, 1969; children: Jennifer Katherine, Jacqueline Andrea. BSc with honors, Sydney U., Australia, 1967, MSc, 1970; PhD, Stanford U., 1972. From asst. to assoc. prof. MIT, Cambridge, 1972-82; head of research Sun Microsystems Inc., Mountain View, Calif., 1983-85; prof. Stanford (Calif.) U., 1981—; pres. Triangle Concepts Inc., Palo Alto, Calif., 1988—. Author: Shellsort and Sorting Networks, 1979. Mem. Assn. for Computing Machinery, Assn. for Symbolic Logic. Office: Stanford U Dept Computer Sci Stanford CA 94305

PRAWER, SIEGBERT SALOMON, author, Germanic language and literature eductor; b. Feb. 15, 1925; s. Marcus and Eleonora P.; m. Helga Alive Schaefer, 1949; 4 children (1 dec.). M.A., Litt.D., Cambridge U.; M.A., Litt.D., Oxford U., U. Birmingham, Ph.D.; Dr.Phil. honoris causa, U. Cologne. Adelaide Stoll resident student Christ's Coll., Cambridge U. (Eng.), 1947-48; asst. lectr. lectr., then sr. lectr. U. Birmingham (Eng.), 1948-63; prof. German, Westfield Coll., London U., 1964-69; Taylor prof. German lang. and lit. Oxford U. (Eng.), 1969-86, Taylor prof. emeritus, 1986—; vis. prof. CCNY, 1956-57, U. Chgo., 1963-64, Harvard U., 1968, Hamburg U., 1969, U. Calif., Irvine, 1975, Otago U. (N.Z.), 1976, U. Pitts., 1977, Australian Nat. U., Canberra, 1980, Brandeis U., 1981-82; hon. dir. London U. Inst. of Germanic Studies, 1967-69. Author: German Lyric Poetry, 1952; Mörike und seiner Leser, 1960; Heine's Buch der Lieder: A Critical Study, 1960; Heine: The Tragic Satirist, 1962; The Penguin Book of Lieder, 1964; The Uncanny in Literature (inaugural lecture), 1965; Heine's Shakespeare, A Study in Contexts (inaugural lecture), 1970; Comparative Literary Studies: An Introduction, 1973; Karl Marx and World Literature, 1976; Caligari's Children: The Film as Tale of Terror, 1980; Heine's Jewish Comedy: A Study of His Portraits of Jews and Judaism, 1983; editor: (with R. H. Thomas and L. W. Forster) Essays in German Language, Culture and Society, 1969; The Romantic Period in Germany, 1970; Seventeen Modern German Poets, 1971; Frankenstein's Island: England and the English in the Writings of Heinrich Heine, 1986; contbr. numerous articles on German, English and comparative lit. to profl. jours.; co-editor Oxford Germanic Studies, 1971-75, Anglica Germanica, 1973-79. Recipient Goethe medal, 1973, Isaac Deutscher Meml. prize, 1977; Friedrich Gundolf prize German Acad., 1986; resident fellow Knox Coll., Dunedin, N.Z., 1976; fellow Queen's Coll., Oxford U., 1969—. Fellow Brit. Acad., London U. Inst. Germanic Studies (hon.); mem. Modern Lang. Assn. Am. (hon.). Address: The Queen's Coll, Oxford OX 7EY, England

PREATE, ERNEST D., lawyer; b. Pescopagano, Italy, Jan. 10, 1909; s. Dominick J. and Theresa B. (Manzo) P.; m. Anne R. Smith, Feb. 11, 1939; children—Ernest D., Donald L., Robert A., Carlon. A.B., Columbia U., 1927; J.D., U. Pa., 1934; L.H.D. (hon.), U. Scranton, 1969. Bar: Pa. 1934, U.S. ct. apls. (3d cir.) 1957. Ptnr. Levy, Mattes, Preate & McNulty, Scranton, Pa., 1958-66, Levy & Preate, Scranton, 1966—; dir., gen. csl. Scranton Lackawanna Indsl. Bldg. Co., Lackawanna Indsl. Fund Enterprises, 1982; chmn. Pocono N.E. Devel. Fund, 1984; dir. First Eastern Bank. Pres., dir. Econ. Devel. Council N.E. Pa. 1977, MetroAction, Inc., 1981; mem. adv. bd., csl. U. Scranton, 1981; trustee Scranton Prep. Sch., 1982; chmn. bd. dirs. Scranton State Gen. Hosp., 1969; bd. dirs., gen. csl. Pa. Devel. Credit Corp., 1963—; chmn. Gov.'s Trial Ct. Nominating Commn., 1986-87 Named Disting. Pennsylvanian, William Penn Soc., 1980. Mem. ABA, Pa. Bar Assn., Am. Judicature Soc., Lackawanna County Bar Assn., Community Assn. Inst., Scranton C. of C. (dir.). Republican. Roman Catholic. Clubs: Scranton Country, Scranton. Co-author: Pennsylvania Industrial Development Authority Law, 1956. Contbr. articles to profl. jours. Home: 216 E Morton St Old Forge PA 18518 Office: 507 Linden St Suite 400 Scranton PA 18503

PREBAY, MICHEL A., industrial engineer; b. Poitiers, France, Mar. 28, 1935; s. Yves L. and Madeleine M. (Jourda) P. m. Marie Christine Lucquet, Dec. 2, 1967; children: Marie Astrid, Alban. Registered profl. engr., France. Indsl. engr. Procter & Gamble, Paris and Brussels, 1963-77; with manpower planning Fiat-Iveco, Turin, Italy, 1978-81; indsl. engr. BSN Groupe Worldwide, Paris, 1981-88; dir. human resources planning and control Aerospatiale, Paris, 1988—. Served to lt. French Calvary, 1959-62. Office: Aerospatiale, 37 Bd de Montmorency, 75781 Paris Cedex 16 France

PRECUPANU, ANCA-MARIA COSTINESCU, educator; b. Iasi, Romania, Sept. 21, 1940; d. Nicolae and Margareta (Petrovanu) C.; m. Theodor Precupanu, July 30, 1967. Faculty of Math., Iasi, 1962, D in Math., 1971. Asst. prof. U. Iasi, 1962-68, maitre conf., 1968-79, prof., 1979—. Author: Real Functions and Measure Theory, 1972, Mathematical Analysis-Real Functions, 1976, Problems in Analysis, 1976, Mathematical Analysis, 1987; contbr. articles to profl. jours. Named a Distinguished Prof. Ministerul Educatiei Si Invatamintului, 1984. Mem. Roumanian Math. Soc., Am. Math. Soc. Mem. Communist Party. Office: U Al I Cuza Sem Math, 23 August, 6600 Iasi Romania

PRELOG, VLADIMIR, chemist; b. Sarajevo, Yugoslavia, July 23, 1906; s. Milan and Mara (Cettolo) P.; Ing.chem., Inst. Tech. Sch. Chemistry, Prague, Czechoslovakia, 1928, Dr., 1929; Dr.h.c., U. Zagreb (Yugoslavia), 1954, U. Liverpool (Eng.), U. Paris, 1963, Cambridge U., 1969, U. Brussels, 1969, U. Manchester, 1971, Inst. Quim. Sarria, Barcelona, 1978, Weizmann Inst., Rehovot, 1985; m. Kamila Vitek, Oct. 31, 1933; 1 son, Jan. Chemist, Lab. G.J. Driza, Prague, 1929-35; docent U. Zagreb, 1935-40, asso. prof., 1940-41; mem. faculty Swiss Fed. Inst. Tech., Zurich, 1942—, prof. chemistry, 1950—, head Lab. Organic Chemistry, 1957-65; ret., 1976; dir. CIBA Geigy Ltd., Basel, Switzerland, 1963-78. Recipient Werner medal, 1945; Stas medal, 1962; medal of honour Rice U., 1962; Marcel Benoist award, 1965; A.W. Hofmann medal, 1968; Davy medal, 1968; Roger Adams prize, 1969; Nobel prize for chemistry, 1975; Paracelsus medal, 1976. Fellow Royal Soc., 1962; mem. Am. Acad. Arts and Scis. (hon.), Nat. Acad. Scis. (fgn. assoc.), Acad. dei Lincei (Rome) (fgn.), Leopoldina, Halle/Saale, Acad. Scis. USSR (fgn.), Royal Irish Acad. (hon.), Royal Danish Acad. Scis. (hon.), Acad. Pharm. Scis. (hon.), Am. Philos. Soc., Acad. Scis. (Paris) (fgn. mem.), Pontificia Acad. Sci., Rome. Research, numerous publs. on constn. and stereochemistry alkaloids, antibiotics, enzymes, other natural compounds, alicyclic chemistry, chem. topology. Office: Eidgenossische Techn Hochschule, Universitatsstrasse 16, 8092 Zurich Switzerland

PREMADASA, RANASINGHE, prime minister Democratic Socialist Republic of Sri Lanka; b. June 23, 1924; ed. Lorenz Coll., St. Joseph Coll., Colombo, Sri Lanka; m. Hema Wickrematunga, 1964; 2 children. Mem. Mcpl. Council, Colombo, from 1950, dep. mayor, 1955; 3d mem. Colombo Central Constituency, Ho. of Reps., 1960-65, 2d mem., 1965-70, 1st mem., 1970-77; parliamentary sec. to minister local govt., 1965; chief whip Govt. Parliamentary Group, 1965; parliamentary sec. to minister info. and broadcasting, also to minister local govt., 1966; minister of local govt., 1968-70; chief whip Opposition Parliamentary Group, 1970-77; dep. leader United Nat. Party, from 1976; minister local govt., housing and constrn., leader Nat. State Assembly, from 1977; prime minister of Sri Lanka, 1978—, minister of hwys., 1981—, minister of emergency civil adminstrn., 1984—, del. Buddha Sangayana, Burma, 1955, to China and Soviet Union, 1959, to Commonwealth Parliamentary Conf., Canberra, Australia, 1970. Author numerous books in Sinhala. Address: Office of Prime Minister, 58 Sir Ernest de Silva, Mawatha, Colombo 7 Sri Lanka

PREM NATH, architect, interior designer; b. Lyalpur, Pakistan, June 6, 1941; arrived in India, 1947; parents Balkrishan and Lajwanti; m. Priti Nath; children: Gesu, Pronit, Parinita, Pankaj. Diploma architecture, Sir J.J. Sch. Architecture, Bombay, 1965. Pres. Prem Nath and Assocs., Bombay, 1966—. Named Outstanding Young Architect, Jaycees, 1982. Fellow Indian Inst. Architects, Constrn. Surveyors Inst. U.K.; mem. Internat. Inst. U.S.A. (sr. cert. valuer), Am. Soc. Interior Designers (assoc.), Indian Inst. Interior Designers (pres.). Home: 35 Union Park, Bombay 400 052, India Office: Prem Nath and Assocs, 4 Merewether Rd, Bombay 400 039, India

PREM TINSULANONDA, former Thai prime minister; b. Songkhla Province, Aug. 26, 1920; ed. Suan Kularb High Sch., Bangkok, Chulachomklao Royal Mil. Acad. Began mil. career as sub-lt., 1941; co. and bn. comdr. courses U.S. Army Cav. Sch., Ft. Knox, Ky.; comdr. Cav. Hdqrs., 1968; royal a-d-c, 1969, 75; dep. comdr. in chief, then comdr. in chief 2d Army, 1973-77; asst. comdr. in chief Thai Army, 1977, comdr. in chief, 1978—; dep. minister of interior, 1977-79; prime minister of Thailand, 1980-88, minister of def., from 1980. Decorated Ramathipbodi Order (Thailand). Office: Office of Prime Minister, Govt House, Luke Luang Rd, Bangkok 2 Thailand *

PRENDERGAST, JOHN PATRICK, accounting company executive; b. Jersey City, Dec. 13, 1927; s. William James and Hannah (Conmy) P.; m. Peg Prendergast, Dec. 27, 1952; children—Kevin, William, Mary Kay, Brian, Sheila; m. Margaret Teresa McGrath. A.B., Fordham U., 1950; M.B.A., NYU, 1957. Ptnr., cons. Arthur Young & Co., N.Y.C., 1961-63, mng. assoc., 1963-66; prin. Arthur Young, N.Y.C., 1966-68, ptnr., 1968—. Track and field ofcl. Olympic Games, Los Angeles, 1984; mem. adv. council Fordham U., Pace U., N.C. Central U., Durham, 1985. Served to lt. USN, 1950-53, Korea; capt. USNR (ret.). Roman Catholic. Clubs: Fordham (pres. 1970-75) (N.Y.C.); Spiked Shoe. Home: 167 Godwin Ave Wyckoff NJ 07481 Office: Arthur Young 277 Park Ave New York NY 10172

PRENDERGAST, MARVA CYRBEA, insurance company executive; b. Port-of-Spain, Trinidad and Tobago, Sept. 25, 1935; arrived in Jamaica, 1957; d. Wilston Oliver and Winnifred (Hall) L.; m. Wilfred Norman Prendergast, June 21, 1956; children: Karen Andrea, David Anthony, Andrew Arthur. BA in History and Modern Langs., Univ. W.I., Kingston, Jamaica, 1962, BA in Edn., 1963. Grad. tchr. modern langs. St. Mary's High Sch., Jamaica, 1966-72, The Queen's Sch., Jamaica, 1972-79; bilingual sec. Internat. Bauxite Assn., Jamaica, 1981-82; exec. sec. The Ins. Co. W.I. Ltd., Jamaica, 1983-86, tng. officer, 1986—. Orgn. Am. States fellowship, 1974. Mem. Ins. Inst. Jamaica, Jamaica Inst. Tng. and Devel., Bus. and Profl. Women's Club. Clubs: St. Andrew. Office: Ins Co WI Ltd, 2 St Lucia Ave, PO Box 306, Kingston 5 Jamaica

PRENTICE, EUGENE MILES, III, lawyer; b. Glen Ridge, N.J., Aug. 27, 1942; s. Eugene Miles and Anna Margaret (Kiernan) P.; m. Katharine Kirby Culbertson, Sept. 18, 1976; children: Eugene Miles IV, Jessie Kirby. BA, Washington and Jefferson Coll., 1964; JD, U. Mich., 1967. Bar: N.Y. 1973, U.S. Dist. Ct. (so. dist.) N.Y. 1973, U.S. Dist. Ct. (ea. dist.) N.Y. 1974, U.S. Ct. Appeals (2d cir.) 1974. Mgmt. trainee Morgan Guaranty Trust, N.Y.C., 1967-68, 71-73; assoc. White & Case, N.Y.C., 1973-78; assoc. Windels, Marx et al, N.Y.C., 1978-80, ptnr., 1980-84; ptnr. Brown & Wood, N.Y.C., 1984—; bd. dirs. various corps. Trustee Vt. Law Sch., South Royalton, 1984—, Washington and Jefferson Coll., Pa., 1985—. Served to capt. U.S. Army, 1968-70. Mem. ABA, Assn. of Bar of City of N.Y. Republican. Clubs: Links, Union League, N.Y. Athletic Club (N.Y.C.), Spring Lake Bath & Tennis. Home: 34 W 95th St New York NY 10025 Office: Brown & Wood One World Trade Ctr New York NY 10048

PRENTIS, MALCOLM DAVID, historian, educator; b. Brisbane, Australia, June 27, 1948; s. Noel and Claire Florence (Cornelius) P.; m. Marion Anne Bird, Jan. 7, 1972. BA with honors, U. Sydney, 1970; MA with honors, Macquarie U., 1973, PhD, 1980. Lectr. Cath. Coll. Edn., Sydney, 1975—. Author: A Study in Black and White, 1975, 2d edit., 1988, The Scots in Australia, 1983, The Scottish in Australia, 1987; editor: Warringah History Series, 1988; contbr. articles to profl. jours. Mem. Australian Hist. Assn., Scottish Ch. Hist. Soc.; v.p. Ch. Records and Hist. Soc., 1980—, mem. Warringah Shire Council Bicentennial com., New South Wales, 1984-88. Fellow Royal Hist. Soc., Soc. Antiquaries Scotland. Office: Cath Coll Edn Sydney, PO Box 968, North Sydney 2059, Australia

PRESCOD, LENNARD PHILIP, banker; b. Port of Spain, Trinidad and Tobago, May 31, 1947; s. Kenwick and Eileen (Corbin) P.; m. Kimlyn Pearl, Sept. 6, 1971; children: Kamaria, Kwese, Kurleigh, Nikita, Carson, Garvin, Andreé. BS in Acctg., U. W.I., St. Augustine, 1971; ACCA, Poly. of North London, 1973; MS in Acctg. and Fin., U. London, 1978. Post primary tchr. Minstry of Edn., Port of Spain, 1965-68; productivity advisor Mgmt. Devel. Ctr., Port of Spain, 1974-77; fin. comptroller Nat. Comml. Bank of Trinidad and Tobago, Port of Spain, 1979-83, corp. mgr. fin. adminstrn., 1983—; lectr. U. W.I. St. Augustine Campus, Port of Spain, 1978-83; chmn. bd. dirs. Lake Asphalt of Trinidad and Tobago, 1984-85. Mem. Nat. Productivity Council, Trinidad, 1982-84. Recipient scholarship in acctg. Govt. Trinidad and Tobago, 1971-73; fellow in acctg. UN Devel. Program, 1977-78. Fellow Chartered Assn. Cert. Accts. (FCCA award 1983), Brit. Inst. Mgmt. (FBIM award 1983); mem. European Acctg. Assn., Inst. Chartered Accts. Trinidad and Tobago. Roman Catholic. Home: #81 Alyce Glen, Petit Valley, Port of Spain Trinidad and Tobago Office: Nat Comml Bank of Trinidad, and Tobago, 50 St Vincent St, Port of Spain Trinidad and Tobago

PRESCOTT, LAWRENCE MALCOLM, medical and health writer; b. Boston, July 31, 1934; s. Benjamin and Lillian (Stein) P.; BA, Harvard U., 1957; MSc, George Washington U., 1959, PhD, 1966; m. Ellen Gay Kober, Feb. 19, 1961 (dec. Sept. 1981); children: Jennifer Maya, Adam Barrett; m. Sharon Lynn Kirshen, May 16, 1982; children: Gary Leon Kirshen, Marc Paul Kirshen. Nat. Acad. Scis. postdoctoral fellow U.S. Army Research, Ft. Detrick, Md., 1965-66; microbiologist/scientist WHO, India, 1967-70, Indonesia, 1970-72, Thailand, 1972-78; cons. health to internat. orgns., San Diego, 1978—; author mans. and contbr. articles in diarrheal diseases and lab. scis. to profl. jours., 1965-81; contbr. numerous articles, stories, poems to mags., newspapers, including Living in Thailand, Jack and Jill, Strawberry, Bangkok Times, Sprint, 1977-81; mng. editor Caduceus, 1981-82; pub., editor Teenage Scene, 1982-83; pres. Prescott Pub. Co., 1982-83; med. writer Anesthesiology News, Cardio, Jour. AMA, Med. Post, Health, Health and Care, Genetic Engring. News, Diagnostic Imaging, Med. Tribune, Am. Family Physician, Med. Week, ACP Observer, Dermatology Times, Urology Times, Ophthalmalogy Times, Drug Therapy, Cardivascular News, Med. Tribune, Select Australian Dr. Weekly, others, 1982—; author: Curry Every Sunday, 1984. Home and Office: 11307 Florindo Rd San Diego CA 92127

PRESL, JIŘÍ, gynecologist, obstetrician; b. Strážov, Czechoslovakia, Sept. 15, 1926; s. Václav and Jaroslava (Denková) P.; m. Věra Herejková, Mar. 3, 1952; children: Jiří, Martin. MD, Charles U., Prague, Czechoslovakia, 1950, DSc, 1968; PhD, Czechoslovak Acad. Scis., Prague, 1958. Research worker Inst. for Care Mother and Child, Prague, 1954-68, chief research worker, 1968—, head div. gynecology, 1966—, substitute dir., 1984—; assoc. prof. Charles U., 1987; mem. dept. ob-gyn Inst. for Postgrad. Edn. in Medicine and Pharmacy, Prague, 1979—. Author, co-author 5 Czech books, 1 English book; contbr. numerous articles to profl. jours. Mem. Czechoslovak and Czech Soc. for Gynecology and Obstetrics (hon., award 1964, 71, 75, 80, 85, J.E. Purkyně medal 1986). Home: Nábřeží K Marxe 394, 147 00 Prague 4, Podolí Czechoslovakia Office: Inst for Care of Mother and Child, Nábřeží K Marxe 157, 147 10 Prague Czechoslovakia

PRESS, FRANK, educator, geophysicist; b. Bklyn., Dec. 4, 1924; s. Solomon and Dora (Steinholz) P.; m. Billie Kallick, June 9, 1946; children: William Henry, Paula Evelyn. B.S., CCNY, 1944, LL.D. (hon.), 1972; M.A., Columbia U., 1946, Ph.D., 1949; D.Sc. (hon.), 23 univs. Research asso. Columbia, 1946-49, instr. geology, 1949-51, asst. prof. geology, 1951-52, asso. prof., 1952-55; prof. geophysics Cal. Inst. Tech., 1955-65, dir. seismol. lab., 1957-65; prof. geophysics, chmn. dept. earth and planetary scis. Mass. Inst. Tech., 1965-77; sci. advisor to Pres., dir. Office Sci. and Tech. Policy, Washington, 1977-80; Inst. prof. M.I.T., 1981; pres. Nat. Acad. Scis., 1981—; mem. Pres.'s Sci. Adv. Com., 1961-64; mem. Baker and Ramo Pres.'s Sci. Adv. Com., 1974-76; mem. Nat. Sci. Bd., 1970—; mem. lunar and planetary missions bd. NASA; participant bilateral scis. agreement with Peoples Republic of China and USSR; mem. U.S. delegation to Nuclear Test Ban Negotiations, Geneva and Moscow. Author: (with M. Ewing, W.S. Jardetzky) Propagation of Elastic Waves in Layered Media, 1957, (with R. Siever) Earth, 1986; also over 160 publs.; co-editor: (with R. Siever) Physics and Chemistry of the Earth, 1957—. Recipient Columbia medal for excellence, 1960, pub. service award U.S. Dept. Interior, 1972, gold medal Royal Astron. Soc., 1972, pub. service medal NASA, 1973; named as most influential scientist in Am., U.S. News and World Report, 1982, 84, 85. Mem. Am. Acad. Arts and Scis., Geol. Soc. Am. (councilor), Am. Geophys. Union (pres. 1973), Soc. Exploration Geophysicists, Seismol. Soc. Am. (pres. 1963), AAUP, Nat. Acad. Scis. (councilor), Am. Philos. Soc., French Acad. Scis., Royal Soc. (UK), Nat. Acad. Pub. Adminstrn., Phi Beta Kappa. Office: Nat Acad Scis 2101 Constitution Ave Washington DC 20418

PRESSEL, PAMELA FAYE, health care administrator; b. Storm Lake, Iowa, Aug. 8, 1945; d. Merle Claude and Vera Maude (Van Buskirk) Pressel; m. N. Goeddel, Feb. 4, 1966 (div. June 1983); children: Sarah Elizabeth, Heather Lorien. BS in Bus. Adminstrn., U. Phoenix, 1984. Sec., Vis. Nurse Service, Denver, 1967-71, acctg. clk., 1977-78; acct. Rx Home Health, Wheat Ridge, Colo., 1978-80; adminstr. Ptnrs. Extended Care, Lakewood, Colo., 1981—; asst. adminstr. Ptnrs. Home Health, Lakewood, 1981-83, adminstrv./v.p., 1983-86; v.p., treas. Health Care Ptnrs., Nashville, 1983—; br. mgr. Total Pharm. Care, Inc., 1987—. Author: You Can Get Well at Home, 1986. Chair, Denver Sch. Bilingual Com., 1976-77; del. Colo. Democratic Conv., 1976; mem. Alameda Music Boosters, Lakewood, 1986—, Alameda PTSA, 1986—. Mem. Am. Fedn. Home Health Agys. (regional dir. 1983-85), Am. Soc. Profl. and Exec. Women, Exec. and Profl. Women's Council, Denver C. of C., Lakewood C. of C. Democrat. Methodist. Avocations: photography. Home: 6215 W 1st Ave Lakewood CO 80226 Office: 2505 W 2d Ave Suite 12 Denver CO 80219

PRESSER, STEPHEN LEE, insurance and investment counselor; b. Blytheville, Ark., Feb. 19, 1944; s. Broadus Lee and Mary Iola (Pyland) P.; divorced; children—Stephanie Diane, Todd Stephen. AA, Sch. of Ozarks, 1964; BS, U. Ark., 1967. CLU. Ins. and investment counselor Equitable Fin. Services Inc., Atlanta, 1971—. Served with U.S. Army, 1967-70. Decorated Bronze Star with oak leak cluster, Purple Heart; Mem. Nat. Assn. Life Underwriters, Ga. Dist. Builder's Club (chmn. 1987-88), Atlanta Assn. Life Underwriters, Am. Soc. CLU's, Million Dollar Roundtable, U. Ark. Alumni Assn. Met. Atlanta (bd. dirs. 1985-87, pres. 1988). Republican. Lodge: Kiwanis (bd. dirs., Outstanding Kiwanian 1985, 86, 87). Avocations: jogging, nautilus, racquetball. Home and Office: 1988 Bramblewood Dr NE Atlanta GA 30329

PRESSLER, LARRY, U.S. senator; b. Humboldt, S.D., Mar. 29, 1942; s. Antone Lewis and Loretta Geneive (Claussen) P.; m. Harriet Dent, 1982. B.A., U. S.D., 1964; diploma (Rhodes scholar), Oxford U., Eng., 1965; M.A., Kennedy Sch. Govt., Harvard U., 1971; J.D., Harvard U., 1971. Mem. 94th-95th Congresses from 1st S.D. Dist.; mem. U.S. Senate from S.D., 1979—; U.S. del. Inter-Parliamentary Union for 97th Congress.; mem. commerce, sci. and transp. com., fgn. relations com., spl. com. on aging, small bus. com., chmn. subcom. of commerce and tourism. All-Am. del. 4-H agrl. fair, Cairo, 1961. Served to 1st lt. AUS, 1966-68, Vietnam. Recipient Nat. 4-H Citizenship award, 1962, Report to the Pres. 4-H award, 1962. Mem. Am. Assn. Rhodes Scholars, VFW, ABA Phi Beta Kappa. Office: 411 Russell Senate Bldg Washington DC 20510 *

PRESSLEY, JOYCE CAROLYN, clinical research analyst; b. Edneyville, N.C., Jan. 11, 1953; d. Merrimon Lewis and Barbara Lee (Gilliam) P. A.B. in Chemistry, Psychology, U. N.C., 1975; M.P.H. in Health Adminstrn., U. S.C., 1980. Asst. dir. emergency med. service Centralina Council of Govts., Charlotte, N.C., 1976-78; dir. emergency med. services Area IV EMS Program, Research Triangle, N.C., 1980-81; clin. research analyst Duke U., Durham, N.C., 1981—; bd. dirs. Carolina Cinema Corp.; mem. Triangle Cultural Arts Com. Author abstracts; contbr. articles to profl. jours. Docent bd. dirs. N.C. Mus. Art, Raleigh, 1984-85, chmn. library com.; del. N.C. Rep. Party, Chapel Hill, 1976-78. Acad. trainee HEW, 1978-80. Mem. Am. Heart Assn., S.C. Student Pub. Health Assn. (pres. 1978-79), Triangle Cultural Arts Com., N.C. Art Soc., Duke Faculty Club, LWV. Club: Duke Mgmt. Avocations: tennis, art. Home: 1016 Minerva Ave Durham NC 27701 Office: Duke U Box 3860 Durham NC 27710

PRESSOUYRE, LEON, medieval archeology educator, consultant; b. Bayonne, France, Jan. 27, 1935; s. Ferdinand Pierre and Jeanne Marie (Diharce) P.; m. Sylvia Paule Capitaine, July 29, 1961 (dec. 1987). Licence d'Histoire, Universite de Bordeaux, 1960, Licence d'Archeologie, 1960; Agrégation d'Histoire, Universite de Paris, 1963; Doctorat es Lettres, Universite de Strasbourg, 1979. Mem. Ecole francaise d'archeologie, Rome, 1964-66; attache Centre National de la Recherche Scientifique, Paris, 1967-70, maître de recherche, 1973-80; mem. Inst. for Advanced Study, Princeton, N.J., 1971-72; prof. medieval archeology U. Paris, 1980—, chmn. dept. Art and Archaeology, 1987—; Focillon fellow Yale U., 1967-68; vis. prof. U. Mich., Ann Arbor, 1979; chmn. medieval sect. Centre National de la Recherche Scientifique, 1980-82; permanent expert Internat. Council Monuments and Sites, Paris, 1980—. Author: Le cloître de Notre-Dame-en-Vaux (French, English, German edits.), 1981; editorial com.: Archeologie medievale, Bulletin archéologique, Bulletin monumental, Monuments historiques, Revue de l'art, Arte Medievale; contbr. articles in field to publs. Regional del. for culture Comité Economique et Social, Chalons, 1979-83. Served to lt. French Armed Forces, 1960-62. Decorated Chevalier des Arts et Lettres, Republic of France, 1970, Chevalier du Merite National, 1978, Officier du Merite National, 1987; recipient Great Cross Brasilia Order of Merit, 1988, Prix Houllevigne, Institut de France, 1957, Prix Lefevre-Pontalis, Societe francaise d'archeologie, 1977. Mem. Societe nationale des antiquaires de France, Commission superieure des monuments historiques, Commission nationale de l'inventaire, Comite des travaux historiques et scientifiques. Roman Catholic. Office: Institut d'Art et d'Archeologie, 3 rue Michelet, 75006 Paris France

PRESTEL, ALEXANDER, mathematics educator; b. Berchtesgaden, Fed. Republic of Germany, Jan. 17, 1941; s. Friedrich and Maria (Brandl) P.; m. Rita Forster, Feb. 16, 1968. Degree, U. Münster, 1966, U. Bonn, 1972. Sci. counselor U. Bonn, 1972-75; prof. U. Konstanz, Fed. Republic of Germany, 1975—. Home: Hoheneggstrasse 13, 7750 Konstanz Federal Republic of Germany Office: Univ Konstanz, 7750 Konstanz Federal Republic of Germany

PRESTEL, BERNHARD MARC, consultancy company executive; b. Freiburg, Fed. Republic Germany, Aug. 1, 1944; s. Ernst and Lisa (Maurer) P.; m. Barbara Schwoerer, Apr. 11, 1970; children: Victor, Wonee, Ben. D in Law and EDP, U. Freiburg, 1971. Asst. U. Frankfurt, Fed. Republic Germany, 1969-71; cons., sci. advisor Team Consult ag, Zurich and Geneva, Switzerland, Brussels, 1971—; pres. Team Consult Belgium. Home: Jagerhausleweg 21, D7800 Freiburg Federal Republic of Germany Office: TC Team Consult, 196 Ave de Tervuren, B1150 Brussels Belgium

PRESTIA, MICHAEL ANTHONY, accounting exec.; b. S.I., N.Y., Oct. 6, 1931; s. Anthony and Antoinette (Folino) P.; M.B.A., N.Y. U., 1956; B.A., 1953; m. Nancy Ferrandino, July 4, 1959 (div. May 1970); 1 son, Anthony. Sr. accountant Gluckman & Schacht, C.P.A.'s, N.Y.C., 1953-60; chief financial officer Franklin Broadcasting Co., N.Y.C., 1960-63; chief accountant asst. to bus. officer, sec. Cooper Union for Advancement Sci. and Art, N.Y.C., 1963-66; bus. officer Inst. Pub. Adminstrn., N.Y.C., 1966-71, controller, 1971-78, treas., 1978—. Cons. taxation and tax planning, 1959—. Served with AUS, 1953-55. C.P.A., N.Y. Mem. Am. Inst. C.P.A.'s, N.Y. State Soc. C.P.A.'s. Home: 53-06 Francis Lewis Blvd Bayside NY 11364 Office: 1457 Broadway New York NY 10036

PRESTON, ANDREW JOSEPH, pharmacist, drug co. exec.; b. Bklyn., Apr. 19, 1922; s. Charles A. and Josephine (Rizzutto) Pumo; B.Sc., St. John U., 1943; m. Martha Jeanne Happ, Oct. 10, 1953; children—Andrew Joseph, Charles Richard, Carolyn Louise, Frank Arthur, Joanne Marie, Barbara Jeanne. Mgr. Press Club, Bklyn. Nat. League Baseball Club, 1941-42; purchasing agt. Drug and Pharm. div. Intrassind, Inc., 1947; chief pharmacist Hendershot Pharmacy, Newton, N.J., 1949; agt. Bur. of Narcotics, U.S. Treasury Dept., 1948-49; with Preston Drug & Surg. Co., Boonton, N.J., 1949-86; chief exec. officer Preston Pharmaceuticals, Inc., Butler, N.J., 1970-80, pres. Preston Cons., Inc., Kinnelon, N.J., 1987—; commr. N.J. State Bd. Pharmacy, 1970-72, pres., 1973; organizer State of N.J. Drug Abuse Speakers Program, 1970-76; lectr. drug abuse and narcotic addiction various community orgns., 1968-78; mem. adv. bd. Nat. Community Bank, Boonton, N.J., 1973. Chmn. bldg. fund com. Riverside Hosp., Boonton, 1963; mem. Morris County (N.J.) Republican Fin. Com., 1972—, Pres. Ronald Reagan N.J. Re-Election Adv. Bd., 1984, exec. com. Gov. Tom Kean Annual Ball, 1985—; chmn. Pharmacists of N.J. for election of President Ford, 1976, Pharmacists for Gov. Tom Kean, 1981-84, N.J. Pharmacists for Reagan/Bush '84; mem. exec. com. Morris County Overall Econ. Devel. Com., 1976-82; chmn. Pharmacists for Fenwick, 1982; v.p. Kinnelon Republican Club, 1980. Served to lt. (j.g.), USN, 1943-46; PTO. Recipient Bowl Hygeia award Robbins Co., 1969, E.R. Squibb President's award, 1968, N.J. Pharm. Square Club award, 1969. Mem. Am. Pharm. Assn., N.J. Pharm. Assn. (mem. econs. com. 1960-65, pres. 1967-68, Oscar Singer Meml. award 1987), Nat. Assn. of Retail Druggists, Internat. Narcotic Enforcement Officers Assn., N.J. Narcotic Enforcement Officers Assn., Pharmacists Guild Am. (pres. N.Y. div. 1946-47), Pharmacists Guild of N.J., N.J. Public Health Assn., Morris County Pharm. Assn., Morris-Sussex Pharmacists Soc., Am. Legion, St. John's Alumni Assn. Roman Catholic. Clubs: Elks, K.C., Smoke Rise. Contbr. editorials to profl. jours. Home: 568A Pepperidge Tree Ln Kinnelon NJ 07405 Office: Preston Cons Inc 568A Pepperidge Tree Lane Kinnelon NJ 07405

PRESTON, BRUCE MARSHALL, lawyer, educator; b. Trinidad, Colo., Feb. 24, 1949; s. Marshall Caldwell and Juanita (Killgore) P.; m. Mariannina Erra, Aug. 10, 1974; children: Charles Marshall, Robert Arthur. BS summa cum laude, Ariz. State U., 1971; MA, U. Ariz., 1972, JD, 1975. Bar: Ariz. 1975, U.S. Ct. Appeals (9th cir.) 1976, U.S. Ct. Claims 1983, U.S. Tax Ct. 1983, U.S. Supreme Ct. 1983; cert. fin. planner. Atty. Maricopa County Office of Pub. Defender, Phoenix, 1975-84; ptnr. Simonsen & Preston, Phoenix, 1985-86, Simonsen, Preston, Sargeant & Arbetman, Phoenix, 1986; atty. office of atty. gen. State of Ariz., 1987—; judge pro tem Mcpl. Ct., Phoenix, 1984-86; licensee in sales Ariz. Dept. Real Estate, Phoenix, 1981-87; adj. faculty Phoenix Coll. for Fin. Planning, Denver, 1984—, Maricopa County Community Coll. Dist., Phoenix, 1985-87, Ariz. State U. Coll. of Bus., Tempe, 1986-87, Ottawa U., Phoenix, 1986. Chmn. com., treas., pres. bd. dirs Kachina Country Day Sch., 1982—. Named one of Outstanding Young Men in Am., 1984, 85. Mem. ABA, Ariz. Bar Assn. (cert. specialist criminal law 1982-84), Inst. of Cert. Fin. Planning, Internat. Assn. Fin. Planners, Ariz. State U. Coll. of Liberal Arts Alumni Assn. (chmn. com. 1978-80, 87—). Clubs: Economics (Tempe); Variety (Phoenix). Home: 7247 Black Rock Trail Paradise Valley AZ 85253 Office: Office of Atty Gen 1275 W Washington St Phoenix AZ 85007

PRESTON, CAROL ANNE, academic dean; b. Lithgow, Australia, Oct. 26, 1948; d. Arthur and Wynifred (Smith) Stone; m. Alfred Neil Preston, July 1, 1967; children: Tamara Lee, Adam Steve. BA, U. Wollongong, 1981, PhD, 1986. Supr. Wollongong Crisis Ctr., Australia, 1979-80; research asst. U. Wollongong, Australia, 1981-84, tutor, 1985, research officer, 1986; acad. dean Inst. Contemporary Ch. Leadership, Wollongong, Australia, 1987—. Contbr. articles to profl. jours. Recipient Postgrad. Research award Dept. Edn. Govt. of Syndey, Australia, 1982-86, Australian Psychol. Soc. prize, 1981. Mem. Religious Research Assn., Australian Assn. for Study Religions, Soc. for Sci. Study of Religion. Mem. Ch. of Christ. Home: 115 Mt Keira Rd, West Wollongong 2500, Australia Office: Wollongong City Ch Christ, 3 Regent St, Wollongong 2500, Australia

PRESTON, CHARLES BRIAN, orthodontist, school administrator; b. Johannesburg, South Africa, Nov. 19, 1937; s. David Charles and Mary (Meerkotter) P.; m. Joy Pretorius, Jan. 1, 1966; 1 child, Bridgette. B.D.S., Witwatersrand Sch. Dentistry, 1961, diploma orthodontics, 1973, M.Dent., 1974, Ph.D. Lectr. dentistry Sch. Dentistry, Johannesburg, 1967-73, lectr. orthodontics, 1973-77, acting head dept. orthodontics, 1977-79, prof., head dept. orthodontics, 1979-84, dep. dean, 1983, 84, 85, 86; dean and dir. Oral and Dental Teaching Hosp. U. of the Witwatersrand, 1988. Contbr. articles to profl. jours. Active South African Council Alcoholism; life mem. Operation Wild Flower. Recipient Middleton-Shaw award Dental Assn. of South Africa, 1987; grantee Research, Edn. and Devel. Fund, 1979-80, Med. Research Council, 1979-82; Elida Gibbs research fellow Dental Assn. South Africa, 1980. Mem. South African Soc. Orthodontists (exec. bd.), European Orthodontic Soc., Am. Assn. Orthodontists, Internat. Assn., Dental Research, Aircraft Owners and Pilots Assn. Methodist. Clubs: Univ. Flying (chmn. 1980-81), Emmarentia Sailing, Lions. Office: U Witwatersrand, 1 Jan Smuts Ave, Johannesburg 2001, Republic of South Africa

PRESTON, CHARLES GEORGE, lawyer, lecturer; b. Fairbanks, Alaska, Nov. 11, 1940; s. Charles William and Gudveig Nicoline (Hoem) P.; m. Hilde Delphine van Stappen, Mar. 12, 1970; children—Charles William, Stephanie Delphine, Christina Nicoline. B.A., U. Wash., 1964, M.P.A., 1968; J.D., Columbia U., 1971. Bar: Wash. 1971, D.C. 1981, U.S. Dist. Ct. D.C. 1981, U.S. Dist. Ct. (we. dist.) Wash. 1971, U.S. Ct. Appeals (9th cir.) 1972, U.S. Ct. Appeals (4th cir.) 1979, U.S. Ct. Appeals (5th cir., D.C. cir.) 1978, U.S. Ct. Appeals (2d cir.) 1980, U.S. Ct. Appeals (11th cir.) 1983, U.S. Supreme Ct. 1977, U.S. Ct. Claims 1982, U.S. Ct. Appeals (fed. cir.) 1982, Va. 1987, U.S. Ct. Appeals (3d adn 6th cirs.) 1987. Assoc. Jones, Grey, Bayley & Olson, Seattle, 1971-72; atty. and asst. csl. for litigation Officer of Solicitor, U.S. Dept. Labor, Seattle, 1972-76, Washington, 1976-81; atty. Air Line Pilots Assn., Washington, 1981-82; mng. ptnr. MacNabb, Preston & Waxman, Washington, 1981-86, Preston & Preston, Great Falls, Va., 1986— . Lectr. seminars. Mem. ABA, Wash. State Bar, D.C. Bar, Tng. Law Inst. (pres. 1985—). Office: 9912-A Georgetown Pike PO Box 820 Great Falls VA 22066-2504

PRESTON, KENDALL, JR., electro-optical engineer; b. Boston, Oct. 22, 1927; s. Kendall and Dorothy Fletcher (Allen) P.; m. Sarah Malcolm Stewart, Aug. 23, 1952; 1 dau., Louise. Grad., Milton Acad., 1945; B.A. cum laude, Harvard U., 1950, M.S., 1952. Mem. tech. staff Bell Telephone Labs., Murray Hills, N.J., 1952-60; sr. staff scientist Perkin-Elmer Corp., Norwalk, Conn., 1961-74; prof. elec. engring. and bioengring. Carnegie-Mellon U., Pitts., 1974—; prof. radiation engring. Grad. Sch. Public Health, U. Pitts., 1977—; gen. mgr., chief engr. Kensal Cons., 1980—; pres. Pathology Imaging Corp., 1986—; chmn. Internat. Optical Computing Conf., Zurich, Switzerland, 1974, conf. automatic cytology Engring. Found., N.Y.C., 1971-72, conf. Coherent Radiation Systems, 1973, conf. Comparative Productivity of Non-invasive Techniques for Med. Diagnosis, 1976; U.S. chmn. U.S.-Japan Seminar on Digital Processing of Biomed. Images, Pasadena, Calif., 1975; faculty NATO Advanced Study Inst. on Digital Image Processing and Analysis, Bonas, France, 1976; mem. Tech. Audit Bd., Inc., N.Y.C., 1976—. Author: Coherent Optical Computers, 1972, Kogeretnye Optiches; in Russian, 1974; editor: (with Dr. Onoe) Digital Processing of Biomedical Images, 1976, (with Drs. Ayers, Johnson and Taylor) Medical Imaging Techniques: A Comparison, 1979, (with Drs. Onoe and Rosenfeld) Real-Time Medical Image Processing, 1980, Real-Time/Parallel Computing, 1981; (with Dr. Duff) Modern Cellular Automata, 1984; editor: (with Drs. Duff, Levialdi, Uhr) Evaluation of Multicomputers for Image Processing, 1986; asso. editor: Pattern Recognition; editorial adviser: Biocharacterist, Analytical and Quantitative Cytology; mem. editorial com.: Pattern Analysis and Machine Intelligence; contbr. articles to profl. jours. Chmn. Ecclesia, YMCA, Summit, N.J., 1958-60; chmn. health services industry com. Automation Research Council, Am. Automatic Control Council, N.J., 1973-76; mem. NSF Fact Finding Team on Egyptian Scientific Instrumentation, 1974-75. Served with arty. AUS, 1946-47. Fellow IEEE (chmn. Conn. PTGEC 1966-67); mem. AAAS, Biol. Engring. Soc. Gt. Britain, Biomed. Engring. Soc. (charter), Harvard Engrs. and Scientists (pres. students 1952), N.Y. Acad. Sci., Cum Laude Soc. Clubs: D.U, Hasty Pudding Inst. 1770, Harvard of Western Pa; Country (Brookline, Mass.); Lake (Dublin, N.H.); Hillsboro (Pompano Beach, Fla.); Lawn (New Haven); Capitol Hill (Washington). Office: Carnegie Mellon U Dept Elec and Computer Engring Schenley Park Pittsburgh PA 15213

PRESTON, LEWIS THOMPSON, banker; b. N.Y.C., Aug. 5, 1926; s. Lewis Thompson and Priscilla (Baldwin) P.; m. Gladys Pulitzer, Apr. 17, 1959; children: Linda Pulitzer Bartlett, Victoria Maria Bartlett, Lucile Baldwin, Lewis Thompson, Priscilla Munn, Electra. Grad., Harvard U.,

1951. With J.P. Morgan & Co. (merged with Guaranty Trust Co., named Morgan Guaranty Trust Co. 1959), N.Y.C., 1951—; vice chmn. bd., dir. J. P. Morgan & Co. and Morgan Guaranty Trust Co., N.Y.C., 1976-78, mem. corporate office, mem. exec. com., 1976—; pres. J.P. Morgan and Morgan Guaranty Trust Co., N.Y.C., 1978-80; chmn. bd. J. P. Morgan and Morgan Guaranty Trust Co., N.Y.C., 1980—, chmn. exec. com., chief exec. officer; bd. dirs. Fed. Res. Bank of N.Y. Trustee NYU. Served with USMC, 1944-46. Mem. The Pilgrims, Council Fgn. Relations (dir.), Assn. Res. City Bankers. Republican. Episcopalian. Clubs: The Brook (N.Y.C.), The River (N.Y.C.); Bedford Golf and Tennis. Office: J P Morgan & Co Inc 23 Wall St New York NY 10015 *

PRESTON, LOYCE ELAINE, educator; b. Texarkana, Ark., Feb. 25, 1929; d. Harvey Martin and Florence (Whitlock) P.; student Texarkana Jr. Coll., 1946-47; B.S., Henderson State Tchrs. Coll., 1950; certificate in social work La. State U., 1952; M.S.W., Columbia U., 1956. Tchr. pub. schs., Dierks, Ark., 1950-51; child welfare worker Ark. Dept. Public Welfare, Clark and Hot Spring counties, 1951-56, child welfare cons., 1956-58; casework dir. Ruth Sch. Girls, Burien, Wash., 1958-60; asst. prof. spl. edn. La. Poly. Inst., Ruston, 1960-63; asst. prof. Northwestern State Coll., Shreveport, La., 1963-73; asst. prof. La. State U., Shreveport, 1973-79; ret., 1979. Chpt. sec. La. Assn. Mental Health, 1965-67, Gov's. adv. council, 1967-70; mem. Mayor's Com. for Community Improvement, 1972-76. Mem. AAUW (dir. Shreveport br. 1963-69), Acad. Cert. Social Workers, Nat. Assn. Social Workers (del. 1964-65, pres. North La. chpt., state-wide com. 1968-69), La Conf. Social Welfare, La. Fedn. Council Exceptional Children (pres. 1970-71), La. Tchrs. Assn. Home: 9609 Hillsboro Dr Shreveport LA 71118

PRESTWICH, MICHAEL CHARLES, historian, educator; b. Oxford, Eng., Jan. 30, 1943; s. John Oswald and Menna (Roberts) P.; m. Margaret Joan Daniel; children: Robin James, Christopher Michael, Kate Elizabeth. BA, Oxford U., England, 1964, DPhil, 1968. Research lectr. Oxford U., 1965-69; lectr. U. St. Andrew's, Fife, Scotland, 1969-79; reader history U. Durham, Eng., 1979-86, prof., 1986—. Author: War, Politics and Finance under Edward I, 1972, The Three Edwards, 1980, Edward I, 1988; editor: Documents Illustrating the Crisis of 1297-98, 1980. Fellow Royal Hist. Soc., Soc. Antiquaries; mem. Surtees Soc. (v.p. 1987—). Office: U Durham, 43/46 N Bailey St, Durham DH1 3EX, England

PRESTWOOD, ALVIN TENNYSON, lawyer; b. Roeton, Ala., June 18, 1929; s. Garret Felix and Jimmie (Payne) P.; m. Sue Burleson Lee, Nov. 27, 1974; children: Ann Celeste Prestwood Waller, Alison Bennett, Cynthia Joyce Lee Koplos, William Alvin Lee, Garret Courtney. B.S., U. Ala., 1951, LL.B., 1956, J.D., 1970. Bar: Ala. 1956, U.S. Supreme Ct. 1972, U.S. Ct. Appeals (6th and 11th cirs.) 1981. Law clk. Supreme Ct. Ala., 1956-57; asst. atty. gen. Ala., 1957-59; commr. Ala. Dept. Pensions and Security, 1959-63; pvt. practice Montgomery, Ala., 1963-65, 77-82; partner Volz, Capouano, Wampold, Prestwood & Sansone, 1965-77, Prestwood & Rosser, 1982-85, Capouano, Wampold, Prestwood & Sansone, 1986—; Chmn. Gov.'s Com. on White House Conf. on Aging, 1961; mem. adv. com. Dept. Health, Edn. and Welfare, 1962; sec. Nat. Council State Pub. Welfare Adminstrs., 1962. Editorial bd.: Ala. Law Rev, 1955-56; Contbr. articles to profl. jours. Pres. Morningview Sch. P.T.A., 1970; chmn. Am. Nursing Home Assn. Legal Com., 1972; bd. dirs. Montgomery Bapt. Hosp., 1958-65; chmn. bd. mgmt. East Montgomery YMCA, 1969. Served to 1st lt., inf. AUS, 1951-53. Decorated Combat Inf. Badge.; Recipient Sigma Delta Kappa Scholastic Achievement award U. Ala. Sch. Law, 1956, Law Day Moot Ct. award U. Ala. Sch. Law, 1956. Mem. ABA, Ala. Bar Assn. (chmn. adminstrv. law sect. 1972, 78, 83), Fed. Bar Assn., Montgomery County Bar Assn. (chmn. exec. com. 1971), Farrah Order Jurisprudence, Eleventh Circuit Jud. Conf., Kappa Sigma, Phi Alpha Delta. Club: Exchange Greater Montgomery (pres. 1971). Home: 1431 Magnolia Curve Montgomery AL 36106 Office: 350 Adams Ave Montgomery AL 36104

PREUSS, ROGER E(MIL), artist; b. Waterville, Minn., Jan. 29, 1922; s. Emil W. and Edna (Rosenau) P.; m. MarDee Ann Germundson, Dec. 31, 1954 (dec. Mar. 1981). Student, Mankato Comml. Coll., Mpls. Sch. Art. instr. seminar Mpls. Coll. Art and Design, Mpls. Inst. Arts Speakers Bur.; former judge ann. Goodyear Nat. Conservation Awards Program. Painter of nature art; one-man shows include: St. Paul Fine Art Galleries, 1959, Albert Lea Art Center, 1963, Hist. Soc. Mont., Helena, 1964, Bicentennial exhbn., Le Sueur County Hist. Soc. Mus., Elysian, Minn., 1976, Merrill's Gallery of Fine Art, Taos, N.Mex., 1980; exhbns. include: Midwest Wildlife Conf. Exhbn., Kerr's Beverly Hills, Calif., 1947, Joslyn Meml. Mus., Omaha, 1948, Minn. Centennial, 1949, Federated Chaparral Authors, 1951, Nat. Wildlife Art, 1951, 52, N.Am. Wildlife Art, 1952, Ducks Unltd. Waterfowl exhibit, 1953, 54, St. Paul Winter Carnival, 1954, St. Paul Gallery Art Mart, 1954, Salmagundi Club, 1968, Animal Artists, Grand Cen. Art Galleries, N.Y.C., 1972, Holy Land Conservation Fund, N.Y.C., 1976, Faribault Art Ctr., 1981, Wildlife Artists of the World Exhbn., Bend, Oreg., 1984; represented in permanent collections: Demarest Meml. Mus., Hackensack, N.J., Smithsonian Instn., N.Y. Jour. Commerce, Mont. Hist. Soc., Inland Bird Banding Assn., Minn. Capitol Bldg., Mont. State U., Wildlife Am. Collection, LeSueur Hist. Soc., Voyageurs Nat. Park Interpretive Ctr., Roger Preuss Art Collection, Lucky 11 VFW Post, Mpls., Nat. Wildlife Fedn. Collection, Minn. Ceremonial House, U.S. Wildlife Service Fed. Bldg., Fort Snelling, Minn., Crater Lake Nat. Park Visitors Ctr., VA Hosp., Mpls., Luxton Collection, Banff, Alta., Can., Inst. Contemporary Arts London, Mont. Capitol Bldg., People of Century-Goldblatt Collection, Lyons, Ill., Stark Mus., Orange, Tex., others, numerous galleries and pvt. collections; designer: Fed. Duck Stamp, U.S. Dept. Interior, 1949, Commemorative Centennial Pheasant Stamp, 1981, Gold Waterfowl medallion Franklin Mint, 1983, Gold Stamp medallion Wildlife Mint, 1983; panelist: Sportsman's Roundtable, WTCN-TV, Mpls., from 1953; author: Is Wildlife Art Recognized Fine Art?, 1986; contbr.: Christmas Echos, 1955, Wing Shooting, Trap & Skeet, 1955, Along the Trout Stream, 1979; contbr. Art Impressions mag., Can., Wildlife Art, U.S.; also illustrations and articles in Nat. Wildlife, others.; assoc. editor: Out-of-Doors mag.; compiler and artist: Outdoor Horizons, 1957, Twilight over the Wilderness, 1972, 60 limited edition prints Wildlife of America, from 1970; contbr. paintings and text Minnesota Today; creator paintings and text Preuss Wildlife Calendar; inventor: paintings and text Wildlife Am. Calendar; featured artist Art West, 1980-84, Wildlife Art; featured in film Your BFA- Care and Maintenance. Del. Nat. Wildlife Conf.; bd. dirs. Voyageurs Nat. Park Assn., Deep-Portage Conservation Found., from 1977, Wetlands for Wildlife U.S.A.; active Wildlife Am.; co-organizer, v.p., bd. dirs. Minn. Conservation Fedn., 1952-54; trustee Liberty Bell Edn. Found.; hon. life mem. Faribault Art Ctr., Waseca Arts Council. Served with USNR, World War II. Recipient Stamp Design award U.S. Fish and Wildlife Service, 1949, Minn. Outdoor award, 1956, Patron of Conservation award, 1956, award for contbns. to conservation Minn. Statehood Centennial Commn., 1958, 1st award Am. Indsl. Devel. Council, citation of merit V.F.W., Award of Merit Mil. Order Cootie, 1963, Merit award Minn. Waterfowl Assn., 1976, Silver medal Nat. S.A.R., 1978, Services to Arts and Environment award Faribault Art Ctr., 1981; named Wildlife Conservationist of Yr., Sears Found.-Nat. Wildlife Fedn. Program, 1966, Am. Bicentennial Wildlife Artist, Am. Heritage Assn., 1976; hon. mem. Ont. Chippewa Nation of Can., 1957; named Knight of Mark Twain for contbns. to Am. art Mark Twain Soc., 1978; named to Water, Woods and Wildlife Hall of Fame, named Dean of Wildfowl Artists, 1981, Hon. Ky. Col.; recipient Honor degree U.S. Vets. Venison Program, 1980. Fellow Internat. Inst. Arts (life), Soc. Animal Artists (emeritus), N.Am. Mycol. Assn.; mem. Nat. Audubon Soc., Internat. Sci. Info. Service, Nat. Wildlife Fedn. (nat. wildlife week chmn. Minn.), Minn. Ducks Unltd. (bd. dirs.), Minn. Artists Assn. (v.p., bd. dirs. 1953-59), Soc. Artists and Art Dirs., Outdoor Writers Am., Am. Artists Profl. League (emeritus), Mpls. Soc., Fine Arts, Wildlife Soc., Zool. Soc., Minn. Mycol. Soc. (pres. emeritus, hon. life mem.), Le Sueur County Hist. Soc. (hon. life mem.), Minn. Conservation Fedn. (hon. life), Wildlife Artists World (charter mem., internat. v.p. 1986—, chmn. fine arts bd.), The Prairie Chicken Soc. (patron), The Sharp-tailed Grouse Soc. (patron). Clubs: Beaverbrook (hon. life), Minn. Press (Mpls.); Explorers (N.Y.C.). Studio: 2224 Grand Ave Minneapolis MN 55405 Office: care Wildlife of America PO Box 556-A Minneapolis MN 55458

PREUSS, RONALD STEPHEN, lawyer, educator; b. Flint, Mich., Dec. 1, 1935; s. Edward Joseph and Harriette Beckwith (Pease) P.; 1 child, William Stephen. AB, U. Mo., 1958, MA, 1963; JD, St. Louis U., 1973; postdoctoral, Worchester Coll., Oxford, Eng., 1979, U. Calif., Berkeley, 1979, U. Paris, 1984. Bar: Mo. 1973, U.S. Dist. Ct. (ea. and we. dists.) Mo. 1973, U.S. Tax Ct. 1979. From instr. to assoc. prof. English St. Louis Jr. Coll. Dist., 1965—; ptnr. Anderson & Preuss, Clayton, Mo., 1973—. Author: Laudamus Te, 1962, The St. Louis Gourmet. 1979, 86, English Elegies, 1983, Melville: A Psychic Biography, 1984, Theater I, 1987, Letting Go, 1988; editor St. Louis Gourmet, Newsletter, 1981—; co-editor Criterion mag. 1961-62; columnist Capital Courier newspaper 1962-64. Mem. ABA, Mo. Bar Assn., St. Louis County Bar Assn., Phi Alpha Delta (John L. SUllivan chpt. vice justice 1971-72, justice 1972-73). Club: Clayton. Home: 32 Conway Cove Chesterfield MO 63017 Office: Anderson & Preuss 230 South Bemiston Suite 410 Clayton MO 63105

PREVIN, ANDRE, composer, conductor; b. Berlin, Germany, Apr. 6, 1929; came to U.S., 1938, naturalized, 1943; s. Jack and Charlotte (Epstein) P.; m. Mia Farrow, Sept. 10, 1970 (div. 1979); children: Matthew and Sascha (twins), Fletcher, Lark, Daisy, Soon-Yi.; m. Heather Hales, Jan. 1982; 1 son, Lukas. Student, Berlin Conservatory, Paris Conservatory; privately with, Pierre Monteux, Mario Castelnuovo-Tedesco. mem. faculty Guildhall Sch., London, Royal Acad. Music., Berkshire Music Ctr. Rec. artist classical music, for RCA, EMI, Phillips, Telarc, 1946—; composer chamber music, Cello Concerto, Guitar Concerto, piano music, serenades for violin, brass quintet, song cycle on poems by Philip Larkin Every Good Boy Deserves Favour, Principals, Reflections, Piano Concerto, 2d Cello Concerto, Triplet for Brass Ensemble, film scores, 1950-59; condr.-in-chief Houston Symphony, 1967-69; prin. condr. London Symphony Orch., 1968-79, Royal Philharmonic Orch., Eng., 1985—; guest condr. maj. symphon orchs. and festivals in U.S. and Europe including: Covent Garden Opera, festivals in Salzburg, Edinburgh, Flanders, Vienna, Osaka, Prague, Berlin, Bergen; music director South Bank Music Festival, London, 1972-74, Pitts. Symphony, 1976-84, Los Angeles Philharmonic, 1984—; author: Music Face to Face, 1971, Orchestra, 1979. Served with AUS, 1950-51. awards Nat. Grammophone Soc. Mem. Acad. Motion Picture Arts and Scis., Dramatists Guild, Brit. Composers Guild, Nat. Composers and Condrs. League. Club: Garrick. Office: care Los Angeles Philharm 135 North Grand Los Angeles CA 90012 also: care Harrison/Parrott Ltd, 12 Penzance Pl, London W11 4PA, England *

PREVOST, EDWARD JAMES, brewing company executive; b. Baie Comeau, Que., Can., May 26, 1941; s. Omer and Jeanne (Ouellet) P.; m. Anna Marie Murphy, June 20, 1964; children: Marc, Louise, Eric. Luc. BA in History with honors, Loyola Coll., Montreal, Que., 1962; MBA, U. Western Ont., London, 1964. Cert. Advt. Agy. Practitioner. Account exec. J. Walter Thompson Co. Ltd., Montreal, 1964-66; successively account exec., account supr., group mgr. and v.p. Cockfield Brown & Co. Ltd., Montreal, 1966-69; gen. mgr. CJRP Radio, Quebec City, 1969-71; exec. v.p., chief operating officer Mut. Broadcasting Ltd., 1971-72, pres., chief operating officer, 1973; chmn. bd. Stephens and Towndrow Co. Ltd., Toronto, 1973-74; exec. v.p. Civitas Corp. Ltd., Montreal, 1973-74, pres., chief exec. officer, 1974-82, also chmn. bd. operating cos., 1974-82; pres., chief exec. officer La Brasserie O'Keefe Ltée, Montreal, 1983—; sr. v.p. Carling O'Keefe Breweries Can. Ltd., 1983—; bd. dirs. BBM Bur. Broadcasting Measurement, 1971-78; mem. Montreal Bd. Trade. Gov. Can. Advt. Found., 1982; chmn. Telefilm Can., 1983-86; bd. dirs. U. Western Ont., NCMRD, 1986; v.p. bd. dirs. Loyola High Sch. Found. (Concordia), 1987; pres. ann. campaign Provincial March of Dimes, 1978 ; bd. dirs. Que. chpt. Canadian Council Christians and Jews; chmn. Montreal Heart Inst. Research Fund, 1979-81, exec. com. 1981-86; hon. patron Telethon of Stars, 1982. Mem. Bd. L'Assn. des Brasseurs du Que. (chmn. 1984-86), Montreal C. of C. (dir. 1980, co-pres. cinematographic com. 1980-81), Province Que., Can., chambers commerce, Canadian Assn. Broadcasters (dir. 1975, vice chmn. radio 1976-77, chmn. 1978-79, past chmn., mem. exec. com. 1980-81), Inter-Am. Assn. Broadcasters Uruguay (sec., past treas), Young Pres. Orgn. (chmn. Que. chpt. 1987), Inst. Canadian Advt., Que. Diabetes Assn., Chambre de Commerce Belge et Luxembourgeoise, Am. Mktg. Assn. (pres. Quebec City chpt. 1970), Assn. des MBA du Que. (chmn. 1985-86),. Clubs: St.-Denis (Montreal), Western Bus. Sch. (Montreal) (founding pres. 1972), Royal Montreal Golf. Office: La Brasserie O'Keefe Ltée, 990 Rue Notre Dame W, Montreal, PQ Canada H3C 1K2 also: Carling O'Keefe Breweries, of Canada Ltd, 4100 Yonge St, North York, ON Canada M2P 2C4

PREWOZNIK, JEROME FRANK, lawyer; b. Detroit, July 15, 1934; s. Frank Joseph and Loretta Ann (Parzych) P.; m. Marilyn Johnson, 1970; 1 son, Frank Joseph II. AB cum laude, U. Detroit, 1955; JD with distinction, U. Mich., 1958. Bar: Calif. 1959. Practice law Calif., 1960—. Bd. dirs. Calif. Econ. Devel. Corp., 1984—; mem. nat. com. U. Mich. Law Sch. Fund, 1969-72, 82-83; mem. com. visitors U. Mich. Law Sch., 1972-75. Served with U.S. Army, 1958-60. Mem. ABA (bus. law sect., law and acctg. com. 1980-88, chmn. auditing standards subcom. 1981-86, fed regulation of securities com., proxy solicitations and tender offers subcom. 1978-88), State Bar Calif. (bus. law sect., exec. com. 1983-86, corp. governance and takeovers com. 1985 87, corps. com. 1980-83), Los Angeles County Bar Assn., Order of Coif. Republican. Home: 431 Georgina Ave Santa Monica CA 90402 Office: 100 Wilshire Blvd Santa Monica CA 90401-1100

PREYSZ, LOUIS ROBERT FONSS, III, management consultant, educator; b. Quantico, Va., Aug. 1, 1944; s. Louis Robert Fonss, Jr., and Lucille (Parks) P.; BA, U. Wis., Madison, 1968; MBA, U. Utah, Salt Lake City, 1973; grad. Stonier Grad. Sch. Banking, Rutgers U., 1983, The Command and Gen. Staff and Coll., Ft. Leavenworth, Kans., 1986; m. Claudia Ann Karpowitz, Sept. 9, 1967; children—Louis Robert Fonss IV, Christine Elizabeth, Michael Anthony, Laura Ann, Daniel Timothy. Teaching and research asst. U. Utah, 1972-73; mktg. and personnel officer Security 1st Nat. Bank of Sheboyan (Wis.), 1973-76; mktg. dir. 1st Nat. Bank Rock Island (Ill.), 1976-77; asst. v.p., mktg. sales mgr. 1st Nat. Bank Birmingham (Ala.), 1977-78; v.p., mktg. mgr. Sun 1st Nat. Bank Orlando (Fla.), 1978-80; pres. Preysz Assocs. (Fla.), 1980—; asst. prof. mgmt. and banking Flagler Coll., St. Augustine, Fla., 1982—; mem. part-time faculty U. Wis., 1973-76, Fla. Inst. Tech., 1976-77, St. Ambrose Coll., Davenport, Iowa, 1976-77, U. Cen. Fla., 1979-81, Columbia Coll. (Mo.), 1981-82; mem. Tng. and Profl. Devel. Council, Bank Mktg. Assn., 1976-78, chmn., 1978; mem. mktg. and pub. relations com. Wis. Bankers Assn., 1975; v.p. Ala. Automated Clearing House Assn., 1978; mem. Wis. Automated Clearing House Assn., 1975-76. Mem. Rep. Presdl. Task Force, Rep. Nat. Com.; bd. dirs. Cath. Charities Bur. Inc., 1988—. Served to capt. U.S. Army, 1968-72; officer Fla. Army N.G. Mem. Soc. Advancement Mgmt. (internat. v.p., bd. dirs. 1984—), U. Wis. Alumni Assn., U. Utah Alumni Assn., Nat. Geog. Soc., N.G. Officers Assn., Phi Gamma Delta. Republican. Roman Catholic. Clubs: St. Augustine Officers, Anastasia Athletic. Lodge: Rotary. Author: How to Introduce a New Service, 1976; Energy Efficiency Programs and Lending Practices for Florida's Financial Institutions, 1980; Credit Union Marketing, 1981, An Effective Management Structure for Multi-Bank Holding Companies, 1983; contbg. editor: Target Market, an Instructional Approach to Bank Cross Selling of Services, New Accounts Training Manual, 1977; Tested Techniques in Bank Marketing, 1977; contbr. articles to mags. Home: 42 Southwind Circle Saint Augustine FL 32084 Office: PO Box 1027 Saint Augustine FL 32085

PRIBOR, HUGO CASIMER, physician; b. Detroit, June 12, 1928; s. Benjamin Harrison and Wanda Frances (Mioskowski) P.; m. Judith Eleanor Smith, Dec. 22, 1955; children—Jeffrey D., Elizabeth F., Kathryn A. B.S., St. Mary's Coll., 1949; M.S., St. Louis U., 1951, Ph.D., 1954, M.D., 1955. Diplomate: Am. Bd. Pathology. Intern Providence Hosp., Detroit, 1955-56; resident pathologic anatomy and clin. pathology NIH, Bethesda, Md., 1956-59; field investigator gastric cytology research project Nat. Cancer Inst., Bowman-Gray Sch. Medicine, Winston-Salem, N.C., 1959-60; assoc. pathologist, dir. clin. lab. Bon Secours Hosp., Grosse Pointe, Mich., 1960-63; pathologist, dir. labs. Samaritan Hosp. Assn., East Side Gen. Hosp., Detroit, 1963-64, Anderson Meml. Hosp., Mt. Clemens, Mich., 1963-64; cons. pathologist Middlesex County Med. Examiners Office, New Brunswick, N.J., 1964-73; dir. dept. labs., chief pathologist, sr. attending physician Perth Amboy (N.J.) Gen. Hosp., 1964-73; chmn., chief exec. officer Ctr. Lab. Medicine, Inc., Metuchen, N.J., 1968-77; v.p. med. affairs Damon Corp., Med. Services Group, 1977-78; exec. med. dir. MDS Health Group, Inc., Red Bank, N.J., 1978-80; med. dir. Internat. Clin. Labs., Inc., Nashville; physician Assoc. Pathologists (P.C.), Nashville, 1981—; research assoc. dept. pathology St. Louis U. Sch. Medicine, 1954-55; instr. pathology Bowman-Gray Sch. Medicine, Winston-Salem, N.C., 1959-60; asst. prof. chemistry U. Detroit, 1961-64; instr. pathology Wayne State U. Sch. Medicine, Detroit, 1962-64; clin. assoc. prof. dept. pathology Rutgers Med. Sch., Rutgers, The State U., New Brunswick, N.J., 1966-68; cons. Health Facilities Planning and Constrn. Service, USPHS, HEW, Rockville, Md., 1970-71; prof. biomed. engrng. Coll. Engring., Rutgers, The State U., New Brunswick, N.J., 1971-75, 80—; chmn. bd. trustees St. Mary's Coll., Winona, Minn., 1972-74, chmn. fin. com., 1971-72; clin. prof. pathology Vanderbilt U. Sch. Medicine, Nashville, 1981—. Author: (with G. Morrell and G. H. Scherr) Drug Monitoring and Pharmacokinetic Data, 1980; contbr. articles in field to profl. jours. Fellow Am. Soc. Clin. Pathologists (Silver award 1968); mem. AMA (physicians recognition award 1969, 74), Am. Assn. Exptl. Pathology, Coll. Am. Pathologists (chmn. subcom. 1974-78), Internat. Acad. Pathology, Pan Am. Med. Assn. (life), Assn. Advancement Med. Instrumentation, N.J. State Med. Soc., Acad. Medicine N.J. (chmn. clin. pathology sect. 1965-67), N.J. Soc. Pathologists (exec. com. 1965-67), Sigma Xi. Republican. Roman Catholic. Home: 200 Olive Br Rd Nashville TN 37205

PRICE, CAROL-ANN, academic administrator; b. West Orange, N.J., Apr. 10, 1936; d. Clifford Harold and Helen Anna (Hollum) Minier; m. Thomas J. Price, Sr., Apr. 17, 1955; children: Thomas J. Jr., Robert Alan. BA in Bus. Adminstrn., Bellevue Coll., 1975; postgrad. in bus. Creighton U., 1982-83; MBA, U. Neb., 1986. Cert. Coll. Bus. Mgmt., Nat. Assn. Coll. and U. Bus. Officers. Bus. mgr. Nebr. Coll. Bus., Omaha, 1975-79; controller Bellevue Coll., Nebr., 1979-80, bus. mgr., 1980-81, seminar speaker, panelist, 1982—; mgr. adminstrv. services Land Bank Nat. Data Processing Ctr., Omaha, 1981-84, dir. mgmt. services, 1984-86; bus. mgr., corp. sec. Coll. St. Mary, Omaha, 1986—. Coordinator USAF Family Services Orgn., Madrid, Spain, 1958-63; bd. dirs. Am. Kindergarten, Madrid, 1963; team leader United Way Midlands, Omaha, 1973-74, account exec. 1986; active Bellevue Coll. alumni fund raiser, 1982-85; chmn. bd. dirs. San. Improvement Dist. #5, 1985—. Mem. Adminstrv. Mgmt. Soc. Internat. (local pres. 1980-81, area asst. dir. 1982-83, internat. bd. dirs. 1983-85, internat. v.p. 1985-87. pres. elect 1987-88, internat. pres. 1988—, Merit Scroll award 1982, Diamond Merit award 1984, Diplomat award 1986, Ambassador award 1987, cert. adminstrv. mgr.). Republican. Episcopalian. Club: Bay Hills Golf (bd. dirs. 1985—) (Plattsmouth, Nebr.). Avocations: opera, symphony, theatre, travel, golf. Home: Rural Rt 2 Buccaneer Bay Plattsmouth NE 68048 Office: Coll St Mary 1901 S 72 St Omaha NE 68124

PRICE, CHARLES H., II, ambassador; b. Kansas City, Mo., Apr. 1, 1931; s. Charles Harry and Virginia (Ogden) P.; m. Carol Ann Swanson, Jan. 10, 1969; children: Caroline Lee, Melissa Marie, Charles H., C. B., Pickette. Student, U. Mo., 1951-53; LHD (hon.), Westminster Coll., 1984; LLD (honoris causa), U. Mo., 1988. Chmn. bd., dir. Price Candy Co., Kansas City, 1969-81, Am. Bancorp., Kansas City, 1973-81; chmn., chief exec. officer Am. Bank & Trust Co., Kansas City, 1973-81; chmn. bd., dir. Am. Mortgage Co., Kansas City, 1973-81; dir. Earle M. Jorgensen & Co., Los Angeles, Ameribanc, St. Joseph, Mo.; Am. ambassador to Belgium Brussels, 1981-83; Am. ambassador to U.K. London, 1983—; Vice chmn., mem. exec. com. Midwest Research Inst., Kansas City, 1978-81. Trustee U. Mo.-Kansas City; bd. dirs. Civic Council of Greater Kansas City, 1979-80, St. Luke's Hosp., Kansas City, 1970-81; trustee Sunset Hill Sch., 1970-81; mem. Heart Inst. Com., Kansas City; mem. oversight com. Solar Energy Research Inst., Golden, Colo. Served with USAF, 1953-55. Hon. fellowship Regent's Coll., London, 1986; recipient William Booth award Salvation Army, 1985, World Citizen of Yr. award Mayor of Kansas City, 1985, Trustee Citation award Midwest Research Inst., 1987. Mem. Young Pres. Orgn., Internat. Inst. Strategic Studies, World Bus. Council., Am. Royal Assn. (bd. govs.). Republican. Episcopalian. Clubs: Eldorado Country (Palm Springs, Calif.); Castle Pines Country (Denver); Kansas City Country, River, Carriage, Kansas City, Racquet (Kansas City, Mo.); Sunningdale, Swinley Forest Golf (London). Office: American Embassy, 24/31 Grosvenor Sq, London W1A 1AE, England

PRICE, DAVID GEOFFREY, geography educator; b. Cockermouth, Cumberland, Eng., July 6, 1931; s. Philip Richard and Amy (Hill) P.; m. Patricia Moir, Sept. 7, 1955; 1 child, Helen Ceridwen. BA in Geography with honors, U. Bristol, Eng., 1952, MA, 1960; PhD, London Sch. Econs., 1967. Cert. tchr., Eng. Tchr. Secondary Tech. Sch., Brighton, Sussex, Eng., 1956-60; lectr. Coll. Tech. and Art, High Wycombe, Bucks, Eng., 1960-65, Polytech. Cen., London, 1965—. Co-author: Changing Geography of Service Sector, 1988; contbr. articles to profl. jours. Served to lt. RAF, 1953-56. Recipient Research award Leverhulme Found., Dartmoor, Eng. 1977; grantee Internat. Geographical Union, 1981. Fellow Royal Geographical Soc.; mem. Inst. Brit. Geographers, Geographical Assn., Prehistoric Soc. Methodist. Home: 339 Desborough Ave, High Wycombe Bucks HP11 2TH, England

PRICE, EARL LAWRENCE, banker; b. Laramie, Wyo., Feb. 25, 1946; s. Earl Raymond and Bella (Williams) P.; student U. Wyo., 1963-67; 1 dau., Julia Elizabeth. Pres., Price Motors, Laramie, 1968-70; pres. Real Estate Investment, Laramie, 1972-76; ind. cons. internat. finance, Zurich, Switzerland, 1972-76; mng. partner Price & Co., Chgo., 1976-83; mng. ptnr., chmn. Newcomb Securities Co., Inc., 1978-82; mng. ptnr. E.L. Price Bank (Uninc.), Galveston, Tex., Imprint Editions, N.Y. 1979-87, Internat. Software Data Base Corp., 1979-87; pres. E.L. Brice Bank Capital Corp. Mem. NASD. Episcopalian. Office: 212 Kempner Galveston TX 77550

PRICE, EDGAR HILLEARY, JR., business consultant; b. Jacksonville, Fla., Jan. 1, 1918; s. Edgar Hilleary and Mary Williams (Phillips) P.; m. Elise Ingram, June 24, 1947; 1 son, Jerald Steven. Student, U. Fla., 1937-38. Mgr. comml. flower farm 1945-49, Fla. Gladiolus Growers Assn., 1949-55; exec. v.p. Tropicana Products, Inc., Bradenton, Fla., 1955-73, dir. div. govt. and industry regulations, to 1979; dir.; exec. v.p. Indsl. Glass Co., Inc., Bradenton, 1963-73; pres., chmn. bd. Price Co., Inc., Bradenton, cons., 1973—; dir. Fla. Power and Light Group, Inc., Fla. Power and Light Co.; past chmn. Fla. Citrus Commn., Fla. Gov.'s Freeze Damage Survey Team, Spl. Commn. for Study Abolition Death Penalty; bd. dirs. Fla. Fair Assn., Fla. Citrus Expn., Fla. Fruit and Vegetable Assn.; past chmn. Joint Citrus Legis. Com.; past mem. Fla. Plant Bd., Fla. Bd. Control, Fla. Legis. Council; exec. com. Growers and Shippers League Fla., Fla. Agrl. Council, Spl. Health Agrl. Research and Edn.; past pres., chmn. bd. Fla. Hort. Soc. Past chmn., commr. census 12th Jud. Circuit; mem. Gov. Fla. Com. Rehab. Handicapped, Fla. Commn. on Ethics, Presdl. Inaugural Fin. Com., 1977, Eastern 5th Circuit U.S. Jud. Nominating Commn., 1977—, Fla. Senate from 36th Dist., 1958-66; past chmn. Manatee County Bd. Sch. Dist. Trustees, Local Housing Authority Bradenton, Bradenton Sub-Standard Housing Bd., Bradenton Charter Adv. Com.; del. Democratic Nat. Conv., 1960, dist. del., 1964; past trustee, mem. exec. com. Stetson U.; trustee Aurora Found. Served to 1st lt. USAAF, 1941-45. Named Boss of Yr., Nat. Secs. Assn., 1959, Man of Yr. for Fla. Agr., Progressive Farmer mag., 1961; recipient Merit award Am. Flag Assn., 1962, Merit award Gamma Sigma Delta, 1965; Leadership award Fla. Agrl. Extension Service, 1963; Outstanding Senator award Fla. Radio Broadcasters, 1965; Allen Morris award as most valuable mem. Fla. Legislature, 1965; Most Valuable Mem. Fla. Senate award St. Petersburg Times, 1965; Brotherhood award Sarasota chpt. NCCJ, 1966; Disting. Citizen award Manatee County, 1970; Disting. Alumnus award U. Fla., 1972; Service to Mankind award Sertoma Internat., 1976; Goodwill Disting. Citizen award, 1979. Mem. Manatee C. of C. (past pres.), Fla. C. of C. (dir. emeritus and past pres.), Fla. Hort. Soc. (past pres., chmn. bd.), Fla. Flower Assn., Blue Key (hon.), Omicron Delta Kappa (hon.), Sigma Alpha Epsilon. Baptist (deacon 1953—). Club: Kiwanis (pres. 1955). Home: 3009 Riverview Blvd Bradenton FL 34205 Office: PO Box 9270 Bradenton FL 34206

PRICE, FRANK, motion picture and television company executive; b. Decatur, Ill., May 17, 1930; s. William F. and Winifred A. (Moran) P.; m. Katherine Huggins, May 15, 1965; children: Stephen, David, Roy, Frank. Student, Mich. State U., 1949-51. V.p., dir. MCA, Inc., 1976-78; pres. Columbia Pictures Prodn., 1978-79; chmn., chief exec. officer Columbia Pictures, 1979-84, also bd. dirs.; chmn. MCA Motion Picture Group, 1984-86; chmn., chief exec. officer Price Entertainment Inc., 1987—; dir. Columbia Pictures Industries, Inc. Writer, story editor, CBS-TV, N.Y.C., 1951-53, Columbia Pictures, Hollywood, Calif., 1953-57, NBC-TV, 1957-58, Hollywood, producer, writer, ZIV-TV, 1958, Universal Television, Universal City, Calif., 1959-64, v.p., 1964-71, sr. v.p., 1971-73, exec. v.p. in charge of production, 1973-74, pres., 1974-78. Served with USN, 1948-49. Mem. Writers Guild Am., West. Office: Price Entertainment Inc Columbia Plaza E Burbank CA 91505

PRICE, HOLLISTER ANNE CAWEIN, airline project administrator, interior design consultant; b. Memphis, Feb. 11, 1954; d. Madison Albert Cawein and Billie Jeanne (Roberts) Stewart; m. James H. Price, Jr., Oct. 21, 1978 (div. 1985). BA in Journalism Memphis State U., 1988. Office mgr. Bruce Motor Co., Memphis, 1975-76; br. mgr. Central States Agy., Memphis, 1976-78; facility coordinator Fed. Express Corp., Memphis, 1978-86, corp. interior designer, project mgr., 1986—; design cons. Smart Shoppes, Inc., Hardy and Trumann, Ark., 1985-86; Fed. Express dept. coordinator interior design student interns Memphis State U. Dept. leader Ch. Sch. Edn. Program, Central Ch., 1984-85; mem. Arts Services League for Greater Memphis Area, 1986—; active Very Spl. Arts Council for Handicapped, Memphis, 1987—. Mem. Nat. Assn. Female Execs., Delta Gamma Alumnae. Republican. Episcopalian. Club: Duration (Memphis). Avocations: scuba diving, horseback riding, biking, antique collecting. Office: Fed Express Corp Dept 1870 PO Box 727 Memphis TN 38194

PRICE, JAMES MELFORD, physician; b. Onalaska, Wis., Apr. 3, 1921; s. Carl Robert and Hazel (Halderson) P.; B.S. in Agr., U. Wis., 1943, M.S. in Biochemistry, 1944, Ph.D. in Physiology, 1949, M.D., 1951; m. Ethelyn Doreen Lee, Oct. 23, 1943; children—Alta Lee, Jean Marie, Veda Michele. Intern, Cin. Gen. Hosp., 1951-52; mem. faculty U. Wis. Med. Sch., 1952—, prof. clin. oncology, 1959—, Am. Cancer Soc.-Charles S. Hayden Found. prof. surgery in cancer research, 1957—; on leave as dir. exptl. therapy Abbott Labs., 1967—, v.p. exptl. therapy, 1968, v.p. corp. research and exptl. therapy, 1971—, v.p. corp. sci. devel., 1976-78; v.p. med. affairs Norwich-Eaton Pharms., 1978—, v.p. internat. R&D, 1980-82; pres. RADAC Group, Inc., 1982—, Biogest Products, Inc., 1984—; mem. metabolism study sect. NIH 1959-62, pathology B study sect., 1964-68; sci. adv. com. PMA Found.; chmn. research adv. com. Ill. Dept. Mental Health; sci. com. Nat. Bladder Cancer program; mem. Drug Research Bd. Nat. Acad. Scis./NRC. Bd. dirs. Grandview Coll., Des Moines, 1977-78. Served with USNR, 1944-45. Diplomate Am. Bd. Clin. Nutrition. Fellow Am. Coll. Nutrition, Royal Soc. Medicine; mem. Am. Soc. Pharmacology and Exptl. Therapeutics, Am. Assn. Cancer Research, Am. Cancer Soc. (com. etiology 1957-61), Pharm. Mfrs. Assn. (chmn. research and devel. sect. 1974-75), Am. Soc. Biol. Chemists, Am. Inst. Nutrition, Am. Soc. Clin. Nutrition, Research Dirs. Assn. Chgo., Soc. Exptl. Biology and Medicine, Soc. Toxicology. Spl. research trytophan metabolism, metabolism vitamin B complex, chem. carcinogenesis; research and devel. pharm., diagnostic and consumer products; licensing and bus. devel. Home: PO Box 308 Norwich NY 13815

PRICE, JOHN ALEY, lawyer; b. Maryville, Mo., Oct. 7, 1947; s. Donald Leroy and Julia Catherine (Aley) P.; m. Julie Ann Seipel, Aug. 16, 1969; children—Theodore John, Joseph Andrew. B.S., N.W. Mo. State U., 1969; J.D., U. Kans., 1972. Bar: Kans. 1972, U.S. Dist. Ct. Kans. 1972, U.S. Ct. Appeals (10th cir.) 1972, Tex. 1984, U.S. Ct. Appeals (5th cir.) 1984, U.S. Supreme Ct., 1987. Law clk. U.S. Dist. Ct. Kans., Wichita, 1972-74; assoc., then ptnr. firm Weeks, Thomas and Lysaught, Kansas City, Kans., 1974-82; ptnr. firm Winstead, McGuire, Sechrest & Minick, Dallas, 1982—; spl. prosecutor Leavenworth County Dist. Atty., 1970-71, Sedgwick County Dist. Atty., Wichita, Kans., 1971-72. Editor mag. Academic Analyst, 1968-69; assoc. editor U. Kans. Law Rev., 1971-72; author legal publs. Co-dir. Douglas County Legal Aid Soc., Lawrence, Kans., 1971-72; co-pres. Northwood Hills PTA, Dallas, 1984. Mem. ABA, Kans. Bar Assn. (mem. task force for penal reform; Pres.'s Outstanding Service award 1981), Tex. Bar Assn., Blue Key, Order of Coif, Phi Delta Phi, Sigma Tau Gamma (v.p. 1968-69). Democrat. Roman Catholic. Office: Winstead McGuire Sechrest & Minick 5400 Renaissance Tower 1201 Elm St Dallas TX 75270

PRICE, LEONTYNE, concert and opera singer; b. Laurel, Miss., Feb. 10, 1927; d. James A. and Kate (Baker) P.; m. William Warfield, Aug. 31, 1952 (div. 1973). B.A., Central State Coll., Wilberforce, Ohio, 1949, D.Mus., 1968; student, Juilliard Sch. Music, 1949-52; pupil, Florence Page Kimball; L.H.D., Dartmouth Coll., 1962, Fordham U., 1969, Yale U., 1979; Mus.D., Howard U., 1962; Dr. Humanities, Rust Coll., 1968. Profl. opera debut in 4 Saints in 3 Acts, 1952; appeared as Bess in Porgy and Bess, Vienna, Berlin, Paris, London, under auspices U.S. State Dept., also N.Y.C. and U.S. tour, 1952-54; recitalist, soloist with symphonies, U.S., Can., Australia, Europe, 1954—; appeared concerts in India, 1956, 64; soloist, Hollywood Bowl, 1955-59, 66, Berlin Festival, 1960; role as Mme. Lidoine in Dialogues des Carmelites, San Francisco Opera, 1957; opera singer, NBC-TV, 1955-58, 60, 62, 64, San Francisco Opera Co., 1957-59, 60-61, 63, 65, 67, 68, 71, as Aida at La Scala, Milan, 1957, Vienna Staatsoper, 1958, 59-60, 61, Berlin Opera, 1964, Rome Opera, 1966, Paris Opera, 1968, recital, Brussels Internat. Fair, auspices State Dept., 1958, Verona Opera Arena, 1958-59, recitals in Yugoslavia for, State Dept., 1958; rec. artist, RCA-Victor, 1958—, appeared Covent Garden, London, 1958-59, 70, Chgo. Lyric Theatre, 1959, 60, 65, Oakland (Calif.) Symphony, 1980, soloist, Salzburg Festival, 1959-63, Tetro alla Scala, Milano, 1960-61, 63, 67, appeared Met. Opera, N.Y.C., 1961-62, 64, 66, 75, 76; since resident mem., until 1985; soloist, Salzburg Festival, 1950, 60, debut, Teatre Dell'Opera, Rome, 1967, Teatro Colon, Buenos Aires, Argentina, 1969, Hamburg Opera, 1970. Hon. bd. dirs. Campfire Girls; hon. vice-chmn. U.S. com. UNESCO; co-chmn. Rust Coll. Upward Thrust Campaign; trustee Internat. House. Decorated Order at Ment Italy; recipient merit award for role of Tosca in NBC-TV Opera; Mademoiselle mag., 1955; 20 Grammy awards for classical vocal recs. Nat. Acad. Rec. Arts and Scis.; citation YWCA, 1961; Spirit of Achievement award Albert Einstein Coll. Medicine, 1962; Presdl. medal of freedom, 1964; Springarn medal NAACP, 1965; Schwann Catalog award, 1968; Nat. Medal of Arts, 1985; named Musician of Year, Mus. Am. mag., 1961; others. Fellow Am. Acad. Arts and Sci.; mem. AFTRA, Am. Guild Mus. Artists, Actors Equity Assn., Sigma Alpha Iota, Delta Sigma Theta. Address: Attention Melly Walters care Columbia Artists Mgmt Inc 165 W 57th St New York NY 10019 also: 1133 Broadway New York NY 10010 *

PRICE, LUCILE BRICKNER BROWN, civic worker; b. Decorah, Iowa, May 31, 1902; d. Sidney Eugene and Cora (Drake) Brickner; B.S., Iowa State U., 1925; M.A., Northwestern U., 1940; m. Maynard Wilson Brown, July 2, 1928 (dec. Apr. 1937); m. 2d, Charles Edward Price, Jan. 14, 1961 (dec. Dec. 1983). Asst. dean women Kans. State U., Manhattan, 1925-28; mem. bd. student personnel adminstrn. Northwestern U., 1937-41; personnel research Sears Roebuck & Co., Chgo., 1941-42, overseas club dir. ARC, Eng., Africa, Italy, 1942-45; dir. Child Edn. Found., N.Y.C., 1946-56. Participant 1st and 2d Iowa Humanists Summer Symposiums, 1974, 75. Del. Mid Century White House Conf. on Children and Youth, 1950; mem. com. on program and research of Children's Internat. summer villages, 1952-53; mem. bd. N.E. Iowa Mental Health Ctr., 1959-62, pres. bd., 1960-61; mem. Iowa State Extension Adv. Com., 1973-75; project chmn. Decorah Hist. Dist. (listed Nat. Register Historic Places); trustee Porter House Mus., Decorah, 1966-78, emeritus bd. dirs., 1982—; participant N. Cen. Regional Workshop Am. Assn. State and Local History, Mpls., 1975, Midwest Workshop Hist. Preservation and Conservation, Iowa State U., 1976, 77; mem. Winneshiek County (Iowa) Civil Service Commn., 1978-87; rep. Class of 1940 Northwestern U. Sch. Edn. and Social Policy, 1986—. Recipient Alumni Merit award Iowa State U., 1975, Extension award Iowa State U., 1988. Mem. Am. Coll. Personnel Assn., (life), Am. Overseas Assn. (nat. bd.; life), AAUW (life mem., mem. bd. Decorah; recipient Named Gift award 1977), Nat. Assn. Mental Health (del. nat. conf. 1958), Norwegian-Am. Mus. (life, Vesterheim fellow), Winneshiek County Hist. Soc. (life, cert. of appreciation 1984), DAR, Pi Lambda Theta, Chi Omega. Designer, builder house for retirement living. Home: 508 W Broadway Decorah IA 52101

PRICE, MARK MICHAEL, building development consultant; b. Cleve., Jan. 20, 1920; s. Mark Michael and Sarah Ann (Moran) P.; ed. U. Detroit, 1940, Cleve. Coll., 1946; m. Ellen Elizabeth Hafford, June 3, 1948; children—Marilyn Michelle, Pamela Susan. Founder Desk Tops, Inc., Cleve., 1950, Vistron Door Corp., Cleve., 1962; pres., chief exec. officer Bldg. Devel. Counsel Inc., Washington; founder Desk Tops Inc., Vistron Door Corp. Mem. Cleve. Mayor's Bus. Men's Civic Com., 1977-78. Mem. Soc. Mktg. Profls. Democrat. Roman Catholic. Clubs: Army-Navy, Nat. Press, Capital Hill (Washington), University, Capitol. Office: Bldg Devel Counsel Internat Suite 400 Internat Sq Bldg 1825 I St NW Washington DC 20006

PRICE, ROBERT EDMUNDS, civil engineer; b. Lyndhurst, N.J., Jan. 8, 1926; s. William Evans and Charlotte Ann (Dyson) P.; B.S. in Civil Engring., Dartmouth Coll., 1946; M.S., Princeton U. 1947; m. Margaret Akerman Menard, June 28, 1947; children—Robert Edmunds, Alexander Menard. Mgr., P&S Standard Vacuum Oil Co., N.Y., London and Sumatra, 1947-55; project engr. Metcalf & Eddy, Cons. Engrs., Boston, 1956-59; structural engr. Lummis Co., Cons. Engrs., Newark, 1960-61; mgr. engring. materials Interpace Corp., Wharton, N.J., 1961-78; pres. Openaka Corp., Denville, N.J., 1979—; cons. cement and concrete design and constrn. Mem. Denville Bd. Health, 1963-66, chmn., 1966; mem. Denville Bd. Adjustment, 1966-69. Served with USNR, 1943-46. Registered profl. engr., N.J., Md. Fellow Am. Concrete Inst. (dir. 1981-84); mem. ASTM (chmn. subcom. spl. cements 1976-84), Nat. Assn. Corrosion Engrs. Episcopalian. Home: Lake Openaka Denville NJ 07834 Office: Openaka Corp 565 Openaki Rd Denville NJ 07834

PRICE, ROBERT MCCOLLUM, computer company executive; b. New Bern, N.C., Sept. 26, 1930. B.S. in Math. magna cum laude, Duke U., 1952; M.S. in Applied Math., Ga. Inst. Tech., 1958. Research engr. Gen. Dynamics div. Convair, San Diego, 1954-56; research mathematician Ga. Inst. Tech., 1956-58; mathematician Standard Oil of Calif., San Francisco, 1958-61; with Control Data Corp., Mpls., 1961—, pres. systems and services, 1973-75, pres. systems, services and mktg., 1975-77; pres. Computer Co., Control Data Corp., Mpls., 1977-80; pres., chief operating officer Control Data Corp., Mpls., 1980-86, chmn., pres., chief exec. officer, 1986—, also dir. Office: Control Data Corp 8100 34th Ave S Minneapolis MN 55420 *

PRICE, SAMUEL MAURICE, broadcast engineer; b. N.Y.C., June 10, 1953; s. Bernard and Rose (Federman) P.; m. Verena Belinda Sieber, July 22, 1983; children: Andrea, Eva Natascha. BA, Emerson Coll., 1975. Operator's lic. Asst. video tape editor Dolphin Prodns., N.Y.C., 1975-76; chief video tape editor Image West, Hollywood, Calif., 1976-81; mgr. prodn. Telecentro Canal 10, Guayaquil, Ecuador, 1981-83; chief engr. Conauto, Guayaquil, 1983—; cons. Assn. Ecuatoriana de Ags. de Publ., Guayaquil, 1987—. Mem. Soc. Motion Picture and TV Engrs., Ecuadorian Assn. of Film and TV Prodn. Companies (honor tribunal, 1st speaker 1987). Democrat. Jewish. Club: Apple Macintosh de Guayaquil (v.p. 1987—). Home: Ave 3d #11 Urdesa Norte, Guayaquil Guayas, Ecuador Office: Conauto, Tomas Martinez 102, Guayaquil Guayas, Ecuador

PRICE, WILLIAM CHARLES, geologist, geophysics researcher; b. Fort Worth, Aug. 26, 1930; s. Jesse B. and Eula Kathrine (Weems) P.; m. Helen JoAnn, Nov. 30, 1952; children—Darrell Dean, Dwayne Douglas. B.S. in Geology, U. Tex., 1958. Electro/mech. engr. Martin-Marietta Corp., Denver, 1960-64; systems engr., geologist Lockheed Aircraft Co., Marietta, Ga., 1964-70; engring. geologist Dept. Main Rds., Sydney, Australia, 1970-74; geologist Geotechnics, Austin, Tex., 1974-78; geologist Bur. Solid Waste Mgmt. Tex. Dept. Health, Austin, 1978-80, program chief hydrology and geotech. Bur. Radiation Control, 1980—. Author tech. guide Use of Earth Resistivity in Solid Waste Mgmt., 1980, Use of Earth Restivity in Subsoils Evaluations and Leachate Monitoring of Near Surface Waste Burial Sites, 1987; patentee in field; developer simplified technique for performing earth resistivity sounding Named Price Array, 1985. Served with USAF, 1950-54. Mem. Austin Geol. Soc., Am. Inst. Profl. Geologists (cert.), Geol. Soc. Am., Assn. Engring. Geology. Republican. Current work: Evaluating the impacts on the hydrological environment associated with the construction, operation and closure of uranium recovery facilities, mining by-product waste, low level radioactive waste disposal facilities; promoting the use of earth resistivity in site characterization and vadose zone monitoring of waste disposal facilities. Home: 8909 Briardale Dr Austin TX 78758

PRICHARD, EDGAR ALLEN, lawyer; b. Brockton, Mont., Mar. 6, 1920; s. Clifford B. and Helen (Ouwersloat) P.; m. Nancy M. McCandlish, Apr. 7, 1945; children: Helen Montague (Mrs. Thomas C. Foster), Robert Walton, Thomas Morgan. Student, U. Tulsa, 1937-39, U. Okla., 1940-41; LL.B., U. Va., 1948. Bar: Va. 1947. Ptnr. Boothe, Prichard & Dudley, Fairfax, Va., 1948-87, McGuire, Woods, Battle & Boothe, Fairfax, 1987—; dir. George Mason Bank. Mem. gen. bd. Nat. Council Chs., 1966-72; counsel Va. Councils Chs., 1955—, Councilman, Fairfax, 1953-64, mayor, 1964-68; chmn. Fairfax Democratic Com., 1962-64, 69-72; mem. Va. Bd. Elections, 1970-75; pres. Lynch Found., 1981-82; chmn. Trinity Episcopal Sch. Ministry; bd. dirs. George Mason U. Found., pres. bd. dirs., 1972; bd. visitors George Mason U., 1982—. Served to 1st lt. OSS AUS, 1942-45. Fellow ABA; mem. Va. Bar Assn., Fairfax Bar Assn. (pres. 1959), Va. State Bar (v.p. 1969), Am. Law Inst., Diosesan Missionary Soc. (pres. 1986—), Urban Land Inst., 4th Cir. Jud. Conf. Episcopalian (lay reader, warden). Home: 3820 Chain Bridge Rd Fairfax VA 22030 Office: 4103 Chain Bridge Rd Fairfax VA 22030

PRICHARD, JOHN FRANKLIN, dentist; b. Lancaster, Tex., Apr. 16, 1907; s. John Allen and Lillie (Hood) P.; DDS, Baylor U., 1928; m. Edna Crabtree, Nov. 6, 1928; 1 dau., Catherine Prichard Kaplan. Diplomate Am. Bd. Periodontology (vice chmn. bd. dirs. 1970-76). Pvt. practice dentistry, Lamesa, Tex., 1928-30, Ft. Worth, 1930—; sr. cons. periodontal dept. U. Wash., Seattle, 1950—; vis. lectr. periodontal dept. U. Pa., Phila., 1946—; bd. dirs. Dental Services Corp., 1967-74. Trustee Baylor U. Coll. Dentistry, 1985—. Recipient Outstanding Alumnus award Baylor U. Coll. Dentistry, 1978. Named Disting. Practitioner Nat. Acads. of Practice, 1987; fellow Tex. Dental Assn., Am. Acad. Periodontology (lectr. continuing edn. courses), Am. Coll. Dentists, Am. Med. Writers Assn., S.W. Soc. periodontology (John F. Prichard ann. research prize established 1985); mem. Am. Soc. Periodontists (pres. 1964-65), Am. Acad. Oral Roentgenology, Internat. Assn. Dental Research, Southwestern Soc. Dental Medicine (pres. 1940-41), Ft. Worth Dist. Dental Soc. (pres. 1942), Delta Sigma Delta, Omicron Kappa Upsilon. Baptist (deacon 1936-70). Author: Diagnosis and Treatment of Periodontal Disease, 1979, others; editorial cons. Internat. Jour. Periodontics and Restorative Dentistry, Dorland's Med. Dictionary, 27th edit.; contbr. articles to profl. jours. Home: 5662 Westover Ct Fort Worth TX 76107 Office: 3833 Camp Bowie Blvd Fort Worth TX 76107

PRIDE, KENNETH RODNEY, lawyer, consultant; b. Los Angeles, Dec. 31, 1953; s. James Allen and Mable Louise (Jones) P.; divorced; children: Kenneth Rodney II, Jason Alexander. AA, Los Angeles Harbor Coll., 1975; BA, U. So. Calif., 1977; JD, Loyola U., Los Angeles, 1982; MBA, Pepperdine U., 1988. House counsel Mark Industries, Long Beach, Calif., 1982—; chmn. Am. Equipment Ins. Ltd., Cayman Islands; bd. dirs. Mark Credit Corp, Powered Mobile Platforms Corp, Mark Comml. Fin. Corp, Mark Industries Corp.; cons. Golden West Risk Mgmt. Inc., Los Angeles, 1986—. Author: The Cook Book for Men, 1986. Active Los Angeles County Cen. Com., 1974-79, State Cen. Com., Calif., 1975-78; asst. scout master Boy Scouts Am. Served with USAF, 1971-73. Recipient Outstanding Community Service Resolution Calif. State Legis., 1975. Mem. Farm and Indsl. Equipment Inst. (legal and legis. com. 1983—). Roman Catholic. Home: 6520 Selma Ave Hollywood CA 90028 Office: 4204 Palos Verdes Dr Rancho Palos Verdes CA 90274

PRIEST, ROBERT GEORGE, psychiatrist, educator, author; b. London, Sept. 28, 1933; s. James George and Phoebe (Logan) Young P.; m. Marilyn Baker, June 24, 1955; children—Ian N.R., Roderick J.D. M.B., B.S., U. London, 1956, M.D., 1970. Lectr. U. Edinburgh, Scotland, 1964-67; exchange lectr. U. Chgo., 1966-67; sr. lectr. St. George's Hosp. Med. Sch., London, 1967-73; prof. St. Mary's Hosp. Med. Sch., London, 1973—; chmn. dept. psychiatry, 1973—; cons. Nat. Health Service Gt. Britain, 1967—; prof. psychiatry U. London, 1973—; chmn. bd. studies in medicine, U. London, 1987—. Author: Insanity, 1977, Anxiety and Depression, 1983; co-author: Handbook of Psychiatry, 1986. Contbr. articles to profl. jours, chpts. to books. Served to maj. Brit. Army, 1957-60. Recipient A. E. Bennett award Soc. Biol. Psychiatry, 1965, Doris Odlum Prize, Brit. Med. Assn., London, 1968, Gutheil von Domarus award Assn. for Advancement of Psychotherapy, 1970. Fellow Royal Coll. Psychiatrists Eng. (registrar 1983-88); mem. Internat. Coll. Psychomatic Medicine (sec. 1981-85, v.p. 1985-87), Soc. Psychosomatic Research (pres. 1980-81), World Psychiat. Assn. (mem. central com. 1984—), Brit. Med. Assn. (chmn. mental health group 1982-84), Central Com. for Hosp. Med. Services (chmn. psychiat. subcom. 1983-87). Avocations: squash; tennis; swimming; foreign langs. Office: St Mary's Hospitol, Acad Dept Psychiatry, Praed St, London W2 1NY, England

PRIEUR, JEAN LUC, physician; b. France, Aug. 3, 1953; s. Jacques and Marie Therese (Noblesse) P.; m. Marie Christine Damecour; children: Julien, Valentin. MD, U. Rouen, 1980. Gen. practice medicine Offranville, France, 1982—. Home: Colmesnil, 76550 Offranville France Office: 16 rue Gustave Flaubert, 76550 Offranville France

PRIGMORE, CHARLES SAMUEL, social sciences educator; b. Lodge, Tenn., Mar. 21, 1919; s. Charles H. and Mary Lou (Raulston) P.; m. Shirley Melaine Buuck, June 7, 1947; 1 son, Philip Brand. A.B., U. Chattanooga, 1939; M.S., U. Wis., 1947, Ph.D., 1961; extension grad., Air War Coll., 1967, Indsl. Coll. Armed Forces, 1972. Social caseworker Children's Service Soc., Milw., 1947-48; social worker Wis. Sch. Boys, Waukesha, 1948-51; supr. tng. Wis. Bur. Probation and Parole, Madison, 1951-56; supt. Tenn. Vocat. Tng. Sch. for Boys, Nashville, 1956-59; assoc. prof. La. State U., 1959-64; ednl. cons. Council Social Work Edn., N.Y., 1962-64; exec. dir. Joint Commn. Correctional Manpower and Tng., Washington, 1964-67; prof. Sch. Social Work, U. Ala., 1967-84, prof. emeritus, 1984—, chmn. com. on Korean relationships; Fulbright lectr., Iran, 1972-73; vis. lectr. U. Sydney, 1976; cons. Iranian Ministry Health and Welfare, 1976-78; frequent lectr., workshop leader. Author: Textbook on Social Problems, 1971, Social Work in Iran Since the White Revolution, 1976, Social Welfare Policy Analysis and Formulation, 1979, 2d edit., 1986; editor 2 books; contbr. articles to profl. jours. Chmn. Ala. Citizens Environ. Action, 1971-72, Tuscaloosa Council Environ. Quality, 1970-72; pres. Ala. Conservancy, 1969-72; mem. Ala. State Citizens Advisory Bd. Health and Environ. Protection, 1972-73; chmn. pub. safety com. Community Devel. Action Group, Tuscaloosa, 1974; adv. com. for former prisoners of War VA, 1981-83; chmn. Prisoner of War Bd., State of Ala., 1984—; state comdr. Am. Ex-Prisoners of War, Ala., 1985-86, legis. officer, 1985—; gov.'s liaison U.S. Holocaust Meml. Council, 1983—; mem. Ala. Bd. Vets. Affairs, 1986—, Ala. Bicentennial Commn. on Constn., 1987—; bd. dirs. Community Services Programs of West Ala., 1985—. Served to 2d lt. USAAF, 1940-45, lt. col. Res., ret., prisoner of war, Germany 1944-45. Decorated Air medal with oak leaf cluster; recipient Conservation award Woodmen of the World, 1971; Fulbright research fellow Norway, 1979-80. Fellow Am. Sociol. Assn., Royal Soc. Health; mem. Acad. Cert. Social Workers, Nat. Council Crime and Delinquency, Tuscaloosa C. of C., Tuscaloosa Civitan Club, Alpha Kappa Delta, Beta Beta Beta. Clubs: Tuscaloosa Country, Capitol Hill. Home: 923 Overlook Rd N Tuscaloosa AL 35406 Office: Box 1935 University AL 35486

PRIGOGINE, ILYA, physics educator; b. Moscow, Jan. 25, 1917; s. Roman and Julie (Wichmann) P.; m. Marina Prokopowicz, Feb. 25, 1961; children: Yves, Pascal. Ph.D., Free U. Brussels, 1942; hon. degrees, U. Newcastle (Eng.), 1966, U. Poitiers (France), 1966, U. Chgo., 1969, U. Bordeaux (France), 1972, U. de Liege, Belgium, 1977, U. Uppsala, Sweden, 1977, U de Droit, D'Economie et des Sciences, d'Aix-Marseille, France, 1979, U. Georgetown, 1980, U. Cracovie, Poland, 1981, U. Rio de Janeiro, 1981, Stevens Inst. Tech., 1981, Heriot-Watt U., Scotland, 1985, l'Universidad Nacional de Educacion a Distancia, Madrid, 1985, U. Francois Rabelais de Tours, 1986, U. Nankin, People's Republic of China, 1986, U. Peking, People's Republic of China, 1986. Prof. U. Brussels, 1947—; dir. Internat. Insts. Physics and Chemistry, Solvay, Belgium, 1959—; dir. Ilya Prigogine Ctr. for studies in statis. mechanics and thermodynamics U. Tex., Austin, 1967—; dir. social scis. l'Ecole des Hautes Etudes, France, 1987. Author: (with R. Defay) Traite de Thermodynamique, conformement aux methodes de Gibbs et de Donder, 1944, 50, Etude Thermodynamique des Phenomenes Irreversibles, 1947, Introduction to Thermodynamics of Irreversible Processes, 1962, (with A. Bellemans, V. Mathot) The Molecular Theory of Solutions, 1957, Statistical Mechanics of Irreversible Processes, 1962, (with others) Non Equilibrium Thermodynamics, Variational Techniques and Stability, 1966, (with R. Herman) Kinetic Theory of Vehicular Traffic, 1971, (with R. Glansdorff) Thermodynamic Theory of Structure, Stability and Fluctuations, 1971, (with G. Nicolis) Self-Organization in Nonequilibrium Systems, 1977, From Being to Becoming-Time and Complexity in Physical Sciences, 1979, French, German, Japanese, Russian, Chinese and Italian edits., (with I. Stengers), Order Out of Chaos, 1983, La Nouvelle Alliance, Les Métamorphoses de la Science, 1979, German, English, Italian, Spanish, Serbo-Croatian, Romanian, Swedish, Dutch, Danish, Russian, Japanese, Chinese and Portugese edits., (with G. Nicolis) Die Erforschung des Komplexen, 1987. Chmn. rector's adv. com. United Nations Univ. Recipient Prix Francqui, 1955; Prix Solvay, 1965; Nobel prize in chemistry, 1977; Honda prize, 1983; medal Assn. Advancement of Sci., France, 1975; Rumford gold medal Royal Soc. London, 1976; Karcher medal Am. Crystallographic Assn., 1978; Descartes medal U. Paris, 1979; Prix Umberto Biancamano, 1987, others. Mem. Royal Acad. Belgium, Am. Acad. Sci., Royal Soc. Scis. Uppsala (Sweden), Nat. Acad. Scis. U.S.A. (fgn. assoc.), Soc. Royale des Scis. Liège Belgium (corr.), Acad. Gottingen Ger., Deutscher Akademie der Naturforscher Leopoldina (medaille Cothenius 1975), Osterreichische Akademie der Wissenschaften (corr.), Chem. Soc. Poland (hon.), Internat. Soc. Gen. Systems Research (pres. 1987), Royal Soc. Chemistry of Belgium (hon.), others. Address: 67 Ave Fond' Roy, 1180 Brussels Belgium Office: U Tex Ilya Prigogine Ctr for Studies Stat Mechanics & Thermodynamics Austin TX 78712

PRIMATESTA, RAUL FRANCISCO CARDINAL, archbishop of Córdoba (Argentina); b. Capilla del Señor, Argentina, Apr. 14, 1919. Ordained priest Roman Catholic Ch., 1942; formerly tchr. minor and maj. seminaries, La Plata; titular bishop of Tanais, also aux. of La Plata, 1957; bishop of San Rafael, 1961-65; archbishop of Córdoba, 1965—; elevated to Sacred Coll. Cardinals, 1973; titular ch., St. Mary of Sorrowful Virgin; mem. Congregation of Bishops, Congregation of Religious and Secular Insts., Congregation Sacraments and Divine Worship, Commn. Revision Code Canon Law. Address: Hipolito Yrigoyen 98, 500 Córdoba Argentina *

PRIMICH, THEODORE, sheet metal company executive; b. Manassas, Va., May 28, 1915; s. John and Mary (Zudock) P.; grad. high sch.; m. Katherine Pollak, Jan. 30, 1938; children—Geraldine Mary (Mrs. John R. Pigott), Katherine Jean (Mrs. Tom Workman). Vice pres. G.W. Berkheimer Co., Gary, Ind., 1936—; pres. Gary Steel Products Corp., 1945—; v.p. Primich Warehouses; pres. Primich Engineered Products. Mem. Air Distbn. Inst., Ind. Mfrs. Assn., Nat., Ind., Gary chambers commerce, NAM, Midwest Indsl. Mgmt. Assn., N.Am. Heating and Air Conditioning Assn. Clubs: Gary Country, Lions. Patentee in field. Home: 1937 W 61st Pl Merrillville IN 46410 Office: 2700 E 5th Ave Gary IN 46402

PRIMO, MARIE NASH, shopping centers official; b. Clarksburg, W.Va., Dec. 10, 1928; d. Frank and Josephine (DiMaria) Nash; student pub. schs. Clarksburg; m. Joseph C. Primo, Sept. 27, 1953; 1 dau., Joan E. Sec., Nat. Bank Detroit, 1945-46; exec. sec. Cutting Tool Mfrs. Assn., Detroit, 1946-50; adminstrv. asst. Irwin I. Cohn atty., Detroit, 1950-84; mgr. Bloomfield (Mich.) Shopping Plaza, 1959—; North Hill Center, Rochester Hills, Mich., 1957—; Drayton Plains Shopping Center (Mich.), 1958-84; South Allen Shopping Center, Allen Park, Mich., 1953-77, Huron-Tel Corner, Pontiac, Mich., 1977—; officer, dir., numerous privately held corps. Mem. steering com., treas. Univ. Liggett Antiques Show, 1971-76, advisory com., 1977-80; mem. parents' com. Wellesley Coll., 1979-1981. Mem. Founders Soc. Detroit Inst. Arts, Women's Econ. Club, Mich. Humane Soc., Detroit Sci. Center, Detroit Zool. Soc., Smithsonian Assos., Hist. Soc. Mich., Grosse Pointe War Meml. Assn., Grosse Pointe Pub. Library Assn., Mich. Opera Theatre Guild. Roman Catholic. Home: 1341 N Renaud Rd Grosse Pointe Woods MI 48236 Office: 1631 1st National Bldg Detroit MI 48226

PRIMORATZ, IGOR, philosopher, educator; b. Moscow, Oct. 6, 1945; s. Rudolf and Rachel (Deutsch) P. BA, U. Belgrade, Yugoslavia, 1970, PhD, 1980. Teaching asst. U. Belgrade, 1970-80, asst. prof., 1980-83; vis. lectr. Hebrew U., Jerusalem, 1982-83, sr. lectr., 1983—. Author: Banquos Geist, 1986, Justifying Legal Punishment, 1989; contbr. articles to profl. jours. Mem. Am. Philos. Assn., Royal Inst. Philosophy, Soc. Applied Philosophy, Kant-Gesellschaft, Societas Ethica. Office: Hebrew U, Dept Philosophy, Jerusalem Israel

PRIMPS, WILLIAM GUTHRIE, lawyer; b. Ossining, N.Y., Sept. 8, 1949; s. Richard Byrd and Mary Elizabeth (Guthrie) P.; m. Sophia Elizabeth Beutel, Aug. 25, 1973; children: Emily Ann, Elizabeth Armstrong. BA, Yale U., 1971; JD, Harvard U., 1974. Bar: N.Y., 1975. Assoc. LeBoeuf, Lamb, Leiby & MacRae, N.Y.C., 1974-82; ptnr. LeBoeuf, Lamb & MacRae,

N.Y.C., 1983—; mem. counsel Bd. Zoning Appeals, Bronxville. Mem. class council Yale U., New Haven, 1986—; bd. dirs. Community Fund Bronxville Tuckahoe, Eastchester Inc., Bronxville, N.Y., 1986—; mem. legal counsel Zoning Bd. Appeals, Bronxville. Mem. ABA, N.Y. State Bar Assn. Republican. Mem. Reformed Ch. Am. Clubs: Yale (N.Y.C.), Bronxville Field. Office: LeBoeuf Lamb Leiby & MacRae 520 Madison Ave New York NY 10022 Home: 71 Summit Ave Bronxville NY 10708

PRINCE, FRANCES ANNE KIELY, civic worker; b. Toledo, Dec. 20, 1923; d. John Thomas and Frances (Pusteoska) Kiely; student U. Louisville, 1947-49; A.B., Berea Coll., 1951; postgrad. Kent Sch. Social Work, 1951, Creighton U., 1969; M.P.A., U. Nebr., Omaha, 1978; m. Richard Edward Prince, Jr., Aug. 17, 1951; children—Anne, Richard III. Instr. flower arranging Western Wyo. Jr. Coll., 1965, 66; editor Nebr. Garden News, 1983—. Chmn., Lone Troop council Girl Scouts U.S.A., 1954-57, trainer leaders, 1954-68, mem. state camping com., 1959-61, bd. dirs. Wyo. state council, 1966-69; chmn. Community Improvement, Green River, Wyo., 1959, 63-65, Wyo. Fedn. Women's Clubs State Library Services, 1966-69, U.S. Constitution Bicentennial Commn. Nebr. 1987—, Omaha Commn. on the Bicentennial 1987—; mem. Wyo. State Adv. Bd. on Library Inter-Co-op., 1965-69, Nat. sub com. Commn. on the Bicentennial of the U.S. constitution; bd. mem. Sweetwater County Library System, 1962—, pres. bd., 1967-68; adv. council Sch. Dist. 66, 1970—; bd. dirs. Opera Angels, 1971, fund raising chmn., 1971-72, v.p., 1974—; bd. dirs. Morning Musicale, 1971—; bazaar com. Children's Hosp., 1970-75; docent Joslyn Art Mus., 1970—; mem. Nebr. Forestry Adv. Bd., 1976—; citizens adv. bd. Met. Area Planning Agy., 1979—; mem. Nebr. Tree-Planting Commn., 1980—;Recipient Library Service award Sweetwater County Library, 1968; Girl Scout Services award, 1967; Conservation award U.S. Forest Service, 1981; Plant Two Trees award, 1981; Nat. Arbor Day award, 1982; Pres. award Nat. council of State Garden Clubs, 1986. Mem. AAUW, New Neighbors League (dir. 1969-71), Ikebana Internat., Symphony Guild, Omaha Playhouse Guild, ALA, Nebr. Library Assn., Omaha Council Garden Clubs (1st v.p. 1972, pres. 1973-75, mem. nat. council 1979—), Internat. Platform Assn., Nat. Trust for Hist. Preservation, Nebr. Flower Show Judges Council, Nat. Council State Garden Clubs (chmn. arboriculture 1985—), Nebr. Fedn. Garden Clubs (pres. 1978-81). Mem. United Ch. of Christ. Clubs: Intermountain (dir. 1963-69), Garden (dir. 1970-72, pres. 1972-75). Author poetry. Editor Nebr. Garden News, 1983—. Home: 8909 Broadmoor Dr Omaha NE 68114

PRINCE, HELEN DODSON, astronomy educator, solar consultant; b. Balt., Dec. 31, 1905; d. Henry Clay and Helen Falls (Walter) Dodson; m. Edmond Lafayette Prince (dec.), Oct. 24, 1956. A.B., Goucher Coll., 1927, Sc.D. (hon.), 1952; M.A., U. Mich., 1932, Ph.D., 1933. Asst. prof. Wellesley Coll., 1933-45; mem. staff radiation lab. MIT, 1943-45; prof. astronomy Goucher Coll., 1945-50; mem. faculty U. Mich., 1947-76, prof. astronomy, 1957-76, prof. emeritus, 1976—; assoc. dir. McMath-Hulbert Obs., 1962-76; solar cons. Applied Physics Lab. Johns Hopkins U., 1979-85. Contbr. articles to profl. jours. Recipient Disting. Faculty Achievement award U. Mich., 1975. Mem. Am. Astron. Soc. (Annie Jump Cannon prize 1954), Internat. Astron. Union, Am. Geophys. Union, Phi Beta Kappa. Episcopalian. Home: 4800 Fillmore Ave Apt 820 Alexandria VA 22311

PRINCE, JULIUS S., retired foreign service officer, physician; b. Yonkers, N.Y., July 21, 1911; s. Julius and Clara B. (Rich) P.; m. Eleanora Molloy, July 6, 1943; children: Thomas Marc, Tod Ainslee, Richard M. Johnson. B.A., Yale U., 1932; M.D., Columbia U., 1938, M.P.H., 1948; Dr.P.H., Harvard, 1957. Intern Sinai Hosp., Balt., 1939-40; asst. resident medicine N.Y. U. div. Goldwater Meml. Hosp., 1941-42; dist. health officer N.Y. State Dept. Health, Jamestown, 1948-58; chief pub. health div. USAID, Ethiopia, 1958-67; prin. investigator demonstration and evaluation project AID, 1959-67; chief Africa div. Population and Humanitarian Affairs, Population Office, AID, Washington, 1967-73; dir. Africa Regional Population Office, Accra, Ghana, 1973-74; chief health, population and nutrition projects U.S. AID/Ghana, Accra, 1974-76; cons. internat. health Pacific Cons., Inc., 1978-82, Am. Pub. Health Assn., 1977-78, RONCO Inc., 1982; pub. health specialist/sr. health advisor One Am., Inc., 1982—; pub. health nutrition specialist Internat. Sci. and Tech. Inst. Inc., 1985—. Served from lt. to maj. M.C. Royal Canadian Army, 1942-46. Recipient Letter of Commendation, Adj. Gen. Can. Army, 1946, Superior honor award AID, 1968, Letter of Commendation, 1977. Fellow Am. Pub. Health Assn., N.Y. State Pub. Health Assn. (pres. 1957), Am. Coll. Preventive Medicine, Royal Soc. Health, Am. Soc. Applied Anthropology; mem. AMA, Pan. Am. Med. Assn., Am. Assn. World Health (v.p.), Internat. Union Sci. Study Population, AAAS, Internat. Health Soc. (pres. 1979), Internat. Soc. on Hypertension in Blacks, Population Assn. Am., Soc. Internat. Devel., Washington Acad. Scis., N.Y. Acad. Scis., World Med. Assn., Soc. Prospective Medicine. Home: 7103 Pinehurst Pkwy Chevy Chase MD 20815 Office: Internat Sci and Tech Inst Inc 1601 N Kent St Arlington VA 22209

PRINCE, LESLIE PETER, social psychologist, designer; b. Nottingham, Eng., July 29, 1952; s. Kenneth Leslie Joseph and Mary Patricia (Taplin) P.; m. Alison Claire De Reybekill, July 26, 1980; children: Martha Dorothy, Thomas Calum. Diploma in graphic design, Loughborough (Eng.) Coll., 1972; BA in Psychology and Philosophy with honors, Warwick U., Coventry, Eng., 1983; postgrad., Aston U., Birmingham, Eng., 1983—. Sr. group visualizer Scott Brailsford & Assocs., Nottingham, 1972-76, 79-80; studio mgr. Boswell Publicity, Nottingham, 1973; mgr. creative services Fine Fare Art & Print, Nottingham, 1976-79; tchr. calligraphy Birmingham Adult Edn., 1980-84, 87; tutor Aston U., 1983-86; vis. lectr. Bournville Coll., Birmingham, 1983-84, Warwick U., 1986—; art dir. Partizan Press, Essex, Eng., 1983—; design cons. Cienfuegos Press, Orkney, Scotland, 1977-84. Author: Introduction to Calligraphy, 1982; founding editor, mem. editorial bd.: Doctoral Working Paper Series; contbr. articles and papers in field. Mem. Brit. Psychol. Soc., Aristotelian Soc., Brit. Soc. for Philosphy of Sci., Warwick U. Psychology Soc. (sec., v.p. 1981-83), Eng. Civil War Soc., Soc. Lithographic Artists, Designers, Engravers and Process Workers (br. com. 1978-79). Home: 149 Gillot Rd, Edgbaston, Birmingham B16 0ET, England Office: Aston U, Gosta Green, Birmingham B4 7ET, England

PRINCE, THOMAS RICHARD, accountant, educator; b. New Albany, Miss., Dec. 7, 1934; s. James Thompson and C. and Florence (Howell) P.; m. Eleanor Carol Polkoff, July 14, 1962; children—Thomas Andrew, John Michael, Adrienne Carol. B.S., Miss. State U., 1956, M.S., 1957; Ph.D. in Accountancy, U. Ill., 1962. C.P.A., Ill. Instr. U. Ill., 1960-62; mem. faculty Northwestern U., 1962—, prof. acctg. and info. systems, 1969—; chmn. dept. accounting and info. systems Northwestern U. (Grad. Sch. Mgmt.), 1968-75; cons. in field; dir. Applied Research Systems, Inc. Author: Extension of the Boundaries of Accounting Theory, 1962, Information Systems for Management Planning and Control, 3d edit, 1975. Served to 1st lt. AUS, 1957-60. Mem. Am. Accounting Assn., Am. Inst. C.P.A.s, Am. Econ. Assn., Inst. Mgmt. Scis., Fin. Execs. Inst., AAAS, Ill. Soc. C.P.A.s, Nat. Assn. Accts., Alpha Tau Omega, Phi Kappa Phi, Omicron Delta Kappa, Delta Sigma Pi, Beta Alpha Psi. Congregationalist (treas. 1984). Home: 303 Richmond Rd Kenilworth IL 60043 Office: Northwestern U Leverone Hall Evanston IL 60208

PRINCE, WARREN VICTOR, mechanical engineer; b. Kansas City, Mo., May 21, 1911; s. Charles William and Bertha (Lybarger) P.; student engring. Baker U., 1930-34; m. Edna Skinner Scott, Aug. 31, 1975; children—Charlotte E. Prince Smith, Leslie Warren (dec.), Charles Allan, Charlene Diane Prince Tercovich. Design engr. Hoover Co., North Canton, Ohio, 1934-39; tool and machine design Thompson Products, Inc., Cleve., 1939-41; devel. engr. The Acrotorque Co., 1941-42; asst. chief devel. engr. The Weatherhead Co., 1942-45; pres. Prince Indsl. Plastics Corp., 1945-46; cons. engr., mech., plastics and plant prodn. problems, Kansas City and Los Angeles, 1946-50; project engr. Aerojet Gen. Corp., 1950-64; chief engr. Deposilube Mfg. Co., 1964-65; cons., 1965-66; sr. mech. engr. Avery Label Co., 1966-68; sr. project engr. machine design projects AMF, Inc., 1969-72; mech. cons. engr. as machine and product design specialist, 1972-80; pres. Contour Spltys., Inc., 1980-85; v.p. mech. engring. HEP Inc., 1985—; evening instr. Mt. San Antonio Coll., 1954—. Registered mech. engr., Calif. Received Soc. Plastics Engrs. 1948 Nat. award for establishing basic laws of plastic molding process. Mem. Soc. Plastics Engrs., Soc. Plastics Industry, Soc. Mfg. Engrs., Kappa Sigma. Presbyterian. Lodges: Masons, Shriners, Rotary. Contbr. articles to profl. jours. Patentee in field. Office: 838 N West St Anaheim CA 92801

PRINCE, WILLIAM TALIAFERRO, lawyer; b. Norfolk, Va., Oct. 3, 1929; s. James Edward and Helen Marie (Taliaferro) P.; m. Anne Carroll Hannegan, Apr. 12, 1958; children: Sarah Carroll Prince Pishko, Emily Taliaferro, William Taliaferro, John Hannegan, Anne Martineau, Robert Harrison. Student, Coll. William and Mary, Norfolk, 1947-48, 49-50; A.B., Williamsburg, 1955, B.C.L., 1957, M.L.T., 1959. Bar: Va. bar 1957. Lectr. acctg. Coll. William and Mary, 1955-57; lectr. law Marshall-Wythe Sch. Law, 1957-59; assoc. firm Williams, Worrell, Kelly & Greer, Norfolk, Va., 1959-63; partner Williams, Worrell, Kelly & Greer, 1963—; pres. Am. Inn of Ct. XXVII, 1987—. Bd. editors: The Virginia Lawyer, A Basic Practice Handbook, 1966. Bd. dirs. Madonna Home, Inc., Soc. Alumni of Coll. William and Mary, 1985-88. Served with U.S. Army, 1948-49, 50-52. Fellow Am. Coll. Trial Lawyers, Am. Bar Found., Va. Law Found.; mem. ABA (House of dels. 1984—), Am. Judicature Soc. (bd. dirs. 1984-88), Va. State Bar (council 1973-77, exec. com. 1975-80, pres. 1978-79), Va. Bar Assn., ABA, Am. Counsel Assn., Nat. Assn. R.R. Trial Counsel, Va. Assn. Def. Attys., Norfolk and Portsmouth Bar Assn. Roman Catholic. Clubs: Harbor, Mallory Country (Norfolk): Lodge: Elks (Norfolk). Home: 1227 Graydon Ave Norfolk VA 23507 Office: 600 Crestar Bldg Norfolk VA 23510

PRINEAS, RONALD JAMES, epidemiologist, public health educator; b. Junee, New South Wales, Australia, Sept. 19, 1937; came to U.S., 1973; s. Peter John and Nancy (MacDonald) P.; m. Julienne Swynny, Apr. 21, 1961; children—Matthew Leigh, Anna Mary, John Paul, Miranda Jane. M.B.B.S., U. Sydney, Australia, 1960; Ph.D., U. London, 1969. Med. house officer Prince Henry Hosp., Sydney, 1961; sr. med. house officer Royal Perth Hosp., Australia, 1962; registrar in medicine Royal Glasgow Infirmary, Scotland, 1963-64; research fellow London Sch. Hygiene and Tropical Medicine, 1964-67, lectr., 1967-68; asst. in medicine U. Melbourne, Australia, 1968-72; prof. epidemiology U. Minn., Mpls., 1973-88, prof. medicine, 1974-88; prof., chair epidemiology U Miami, Fla., 1988—; cons. WHO, Geneva, 1976—, Nat. Heart Lung and Blood Inst., 1976—; prin. investigator Nat. Health Lung and Blood Inst., 1973—. Author books, including; Blood Pressure Sounds; Their Measurement and Meaning, 1978; The Minnesota Code Manual of Electrocardiographic Findings, 1982; also numerous articles. Recipient numerous cardiovascular disease research grants and contracts. Mem. Minn. affiliate Am. Heart Assn., Mpls., 1973—, chmn. adv. groups, 1975—. Fellow Royal Coll. Physicians Edinburgh, Am. Coll. Cardiology, Am. Pub. Health Assn., Soc. Epidemiologic Research, Am. Heart Assn. Council on Epidemiology, Internat. Soc. Hypertension, Council on Human Biology, Internat. Soc. Cardiology, Soc. Controlled Clin. Trials, Am. Coll. Epidemiology, Am. Soc. Epidemiology, Internat. Soc. Human Biology; mem. Royal Coll. Physicians London. Avocations: reading; raising a family. Office: U. Miami Sch Medicine Dept Epidemiology and Public Health (R-669) P O Box 016069 Miami FL 33101

PRINGLE, ROBERT MAXWELL, diplomat; b. N.Y.C., Nov. 12, 1936; s. Henry Fowles and Helena Huntington (Smith) P.; m. Barbara Ann Cade, Sept. 26, 1964; children: James Maxwell, Anne Elizabeth. BA, Harvard U., 1958; PhD, Cornell U., 1967. Dir. econ. policy staff Bur. African Affairs Dept. State, 1981-83; dep. chief mission Ouagadougou, Burkina Faso, 1983-85, Port Moresby, Papua New Guinea, 1985-87; ambassador to Mali 1987—. Author: Rajahs and Rebels: The Ibans of Sarawak under Brooke Rule, 1970, Indonesia and the Philippines: American Interests in Island Southeast Asia, 1980. Mem. Assn. Asian Studies. Home and Office: Dept State Bamako Embassy Washington DC 20520-2050 *

PRIOR, JAMES MICHAEL LEATHES (RIGHT HON. LORD PRIOR), utilities executive; b. Norwich, Oct. 11, 1927; s. C.B.L. and A.S.M. P.; m. Jane P. Gifford, 1945; 4 children. Ed. Charterhouse and Pembroke Coll., Cambridge. M.P. for Lowestoft, 1959-83, for Waveney, 1983-87, ; parliamentary pvt. sec. to Pres. of Bd. of Trade, 1963, to Minister of Power, 1963-64, to Rt. Hon. Edward Heath, 1965-70; vice chmn. Conservative Party, 1965, 72-74; Minister of Agr., Fisheries and Food, 1970-72, Lord Pres. of Council, 1972-74, Conservative spokesman on Employment, 1974-79; Sec. of State for Employment, 1979-81, for No. Ireland, 1981-84; chmn. GEC, 1984—; dir. Barclays PLC, 1984—, J. Sainsbury PLC, 1984—, United Biscuits, 1974-79, 84—. Home: 36 Morpeth Mansions, London SW1, England Office: The Gen Electric Co PLC, 1 Stanhope Gate, London W1A 1EH, England

PRITCHARD, JOHN (MICHAEL), conductor; b. London, Feb. 5, 1921. Music dir. Royal Liverpool Philharm. Orch., 1957-63, London Philharm., 1962-66, Glyndebourne Festival Opera, 1969-77; chief condr. Cologne Opera, 1979-81, BBC Symphony Orch., 1982—; joint music dir. Théâtre Royal de la Monnaie, Brussels, 1981—; music dir. San Francisco Opera, 1986—. Office: San Francisco Opera Opera House San Francisco CA 94102 *

PRITCHETT, ANNA MARIE WHITE, fashion consultant, pianist; b. Vienna, Ga., Feb. 10, 1941; d. James Edward White and Vivia Trippe (Waters) White-McDuffie; m. Carl Blair Pritchett, Jr., May 2, 1959 (div. 1965); children: Carl Blair III, Laura White. Student Perry Bus. Sch., Albany, Ga., 1966-68, U. Ga., Athens, 1974; student Alliance Theatre Sch., Atlanta, 1984—; grad. Columbia Sch. Broadcasting, 1985. Asst. to curator Swan House, Atlanta Hist. Soc., 1981-84; fashion cons. The Clothes Bin, Atlanta, 1984-87, Play it Again, Atlanta, 1984—; pianist, network television performances include: Bob Crosby Show, 1955, Art Linkletter Show, 1955; classical pianist Bids for Broadway, WMAZ-TV, Macon, Ga., 1955-57; participant USA Honors Tour on television stas. in major cities, 1955. Contbr. articles to mags. Newsletter editor St. Patrick's Ch., Albany, Ga., 1968-70; asst. publicity chmn. Atlanta Met. Opera, 1979-81. Mem. Jr. League Atlanta (chmn. juvenile justice com. 1975, rep. to Council for Children, 1974-76), Nat. Council on Crime and Delinquency, Republican Senatorial Inner Circle, Successful Singles Internat., Nat. Trust for Hist. Preservation, Ga. Trust for Hist. Preservation. Episcopalian. Address: 20 Springlake Pl NW Atlanta GA 30318

PRITCHETT, LOUIS ALEXANDER, consumer products executive; b. Memphis, Nov. 5, 1931; s. Joseph Zeniford and Thelma Gertrude (Tipton) P.; m. Barbara Burnette, Dec. 19, 1954; children—Bradley Louis, Robert Joseph. B.S., Memphis State U. 1953. Sales rep. Procter and Gamble Co., Cin., 1953-55, unit mgr., 1955-61, dist mgr., 1961-64; div. mgr. Procter and Gamble Co., 1965-70, sales mgr., 1971-81; pres., gen. mgr. Procter and Gamble Co., Philippines, 1981-85; v.p. sales Procter and Gamble Co., 1985—. Bd. dirs. Dan Beard council Boy Scouts Am., 1985, 2d Harvest. Served with U.S. Army, 1956-57. Mem. Soap and Detergent Assn. Philippines (pres. 1984-85). Republican. Methodist. Clubs: Manila Polo, Baquio (Philippines); Queen City (Cin.). Home: 8325 Kroger Farm Rd Cincinnati OH 45243 Office: Procter & Gamble Co One Procter & Gamble Plaza Cincinnati OH 45202

PRITCHETT, SIR VICTOR SAWDON, author; b. Ipswich, Eng., Dec. 16, 1900; s. Sawdon and Beatrice (Martin) P.; m. Dorothy Roberts, Oct. 2, 1936; children: Josephine, Oliver. Ed., Alleyn's Sch., Dulwich; D.Litt. (hon.), Leeds U., 1973, Columbia U., 1978, U. Sussex, 1980, Harvard U., 1985. Free-lance journalist France, Ireland, Spain and U.S., 1921-28; lit. critic New Statesman, London, 1928-78; dir. New Statesman, 1951-78; Christian Gauss lectr. Princeton U., 1953; Beckman prof. U. Calif., Berkeley, 1960; writer-in-residence Smith Coll., 1966-71; Zisskind prof. Brandeis U., Waltham, Mass., 1969; vis. prof. Sch. Fine Arts, Columbia U., 1972; Clark lectr. Cambridge (Eng.) U., 1969, Vanderbilt U., 1981. Author: Marching Spain, 1928, Clare Drummer, 1929, The Spanish Virgin, 1930, Elopement into Exile, 1932, Nothing Like Leather, 1935, You Make Your Own Life, 1938, It May Never Happen, 1945, The Living Novel, 1949, Mr. Beluncle, 1951, The Spanish Temper, 1954, Books in General, 1962, In My Good Books, 1953, The Working Novelist, 1965, When My Girl Comes Home, 1961, Dead Man Leading, 1949, The Key to My Heart, 1963, London Perceived, 1962, The Offensive Traveller, 1964, New York Proclaimed, 1965, (with Elizabeth Bowen and Graham Greene) Why Do I Write?, 1948, Dublin: A Portrait, 1967, A Cab at the Door, 1967, Blind Love, 1970, Meredith's English Comedy, 1970, Midnight Oil, 1971, Balzac, 1973, The Camberwell Beauty, 1974, The Gentle Barbarian: Turgenev: Selected Stories, 1978, The Myth Makers, 1979, On the Edge of the Cliff, 1980, The Tale Bearers (essays), 1980, Collected Stories, 1981, More Collected Stories, 1983, The Turn of the Year, 1984, The Oxford Book of Short Stories, 1981, Man of Letters (essays), 1986, Chekhov, 1987; contbr. stories to leading mags. Decorated comdr. Order Brit. Empire; created knight; recipient Royal Soc. Lit. award, 1969, 87. Mem. Soc. Authors (pres. 1978). Clubs: Savile (London), Beefsteak (London). Address: 12 Regents Park Terr, London NW1, England *

PRIYATNA, ABDURRASYID, legal educator, research center executive; b. Bandung, Indonesia, Dec. 5, 1929; s. Abdurrasyid and Raratnasari; m. Arena Sitti Zoubeidah Ida Zuraida, June 19, 1957; children: Maya, Sara, Sari, Mounty, Prisya. LLM, U. Jakarta, 1955; LLD, U. Bandung, 1972. Dep. atty. gen. Office Atty. Gen., Jakarta, Indonesia, 1966-70; prof. law U. Padjadjaran, Bandung, 1973—; chmn. Air and Space Law Research Ctr., 1971—; asst. to coordinating minister for politics and security, 1987—; legal advisor Indonesian Air Force, 1973—, Nat. Space Inst., 1974, Dept. Justice, 1976, Indonesian Dept. Tourism, Post and Telecommunications, 1976—; vice chmn. Indonesian del. UN Com. on the Peaceful Uses of Outer Space, 1975—; chmn. Joint Com. on Air Law The Netherlands-Indonesia, 1987—; mem. panel legal experts INTELSAT, 1976, Indonesian Nat. Arbitration Bd., 1977, World Bank, 1979, Internat. Civil Aviation Orgn., 1981. Author: State's Sovereignty in Air Space, 1972, Introduction to Space Law, 1977, Space Law, 1986. Served to 1st lt. inf. Indonesian Army, 1945-51. Mem. Internat. Inst. Space Law (bd. dirs. 1979—, award 1979), Internat. Acad. Astronautics (diploma 1981, 87). Moslem. Home: 15 Jalan, Banyumas, Jakarta, Pusat 10310, Indonesia Office: Air and Space Law Research Ctr, 12 Gatot Subroto Case Bldg, 7th Floor, R6 Jakarta Indonesia

PROBSTEIN, RONALD FILMORE, engineering educator; b. N.Y.C., Mar. 11, 1928; s. Sidney and Sally (Rosenstein) P.; m. Irene Weindling, July 30, 1950; 1 son, Sidney. B.M.E., NYU, 1948; M.S.E., Princeton U., 1950, A.M., 1951, Ph.D., 1952; A.M. (hon.), Brown U., 1957. Research asst. physics N.Y. U., 1946-48, instr. engring. mechanics, 1947-48; research asst. dept. aero. engring. Princeton U., 1948-52, research assoc., 1952-53, asst. prof., 1953-54; asst. prof. divs. engring., applied math. Brown U., 1954-55, assoc. prof., 1955-59, prof., 1959-62; prof. mech. engring. M.I.T., 1962—; disting. prof. engring. U. Utah, 1973; sr. partner Water Purification Assos., Cambridge, 1974-82; chmn. bd. Water Gen. Corp., Cambridge, 1982-83; sr. corp. tech. advisor Foster-Miller, Inc., 1983—; commr. commn. on engring. and tech. systems NRC, 1980-83. Author: Hypersonic Flow Theory, 1959, Hypersonic Flow, Inviscid Flows, 1966, Water in Synthetic Fuel Production, 1978, Synthetic Fuels, 1982, Physicochemical Hydrodynamics, 1988; editor: Introduction to Hypersonic Flow, 1961, Physics of Shock Waves, 1966, Jour. PhysicoChem. Hydrodynamics, 1987—; contbr. articles to profl. jours. Guggenheim fellow, 1960-61. Fellow Am. Acad. Arts and Scis. (councilor 1975-79), Am. Phys. Soc., AIAA, AAAS; mem. Internat. Acad. Astronautics, Nat. Acad. Engring., ASME (Freeman award 1971), Am. Inst. Chem. Engrs. Home: 5 Seaver St Brookline MA 02146 Office: 77 Massachusetts Ave Cambridge MA 02139

PROCOS, DIMITRI, urban and rural planning educator; b. Athens, Greece, Sept. 14, 1940; came to Can., 1967, naturalized, 1973; s. Patroclos and Maria (Buhler) P.; m. Marcia DeV., Carlyn, Jan. 27, 1967 (div. 1981); children—Alexis, Nicolas. Student Brandeis U., 1960-62; B.Arch., MIT, 1966; M.Arch., Pratt Inst., 1967. Urban planner Mcpl. Planning Cons., Toronto, Ont., Can., 1967-69; assoc. prof. faculty architecture, head dept. urban and rural planning, Tech. U. Nova Scotia, Halifax, 1969—; prin. D. Procos Cons., 1975—; vis. fellow Dalhousie U., 1975; vis. researcher Athens Ctr. Ekistics, Athens, Greece, 1978; vis. prof. U. Paris/Sorbonne, 1984-85. Author: Mixed Land Use, 1976. Contbr. articles to profl. jours. Mem. editorial bd. Plan Can., Can. Inst. Planners, 1983—. Mem. Royal Archtl. Inst. Can., N.S. Assn. Architects, Can. Inst. Planners, Atlantic Planners Inst. Avocation: photography. Home: 6834 Quinpool Rd, Halifax, NS Canada B3L 1C4 Office: Tech U Nova Scotia, POB 1000, Halifax, NS Canada B3J 2X4

PROCTOR, JOHN HOWARD, industrial and organizational psychologist; b. Bronx, N.Y., June 3, 1931; s. John Carol and Carolyn Elizabeth (Slade) P.; B.S., Davidson Coll., 1953; M.S., Purdue U., 1954, Ph.D., 1958; m. Karen Jane Boyer Crye, Apr. 21, 1984; children—Donna Lynn, Susan Carol, John Christopher, James Alexander. Cons. Humble Oil & Refining Co., 1957-58; dir. tng. and personnel research Bleached Bd. div. W Va. Pulp and Paper Co., 1958-60; mem. tech. staff Mitre Corp., 1960-64; sr. project dir. Data Dynamics Inc., 1964-66; gen. mgr. Eastern ops. Mellonics div. Litton Systems Inc., Ft. Walton Beach, Fla., 1966-70; pres. Data Solutions Corp., Vienna, Va., 1970-85, also chmn. bd.; v.p. advanced programs B-K Dynamics, Inc., Rockville, Md. Mem. adv. com. on rights and responsibilities of women HEW, 1976; mem. Nat. Def. Exec. Res.; del. White House Conf. on Aging, 1982; sec. gen. elect World Acad. Art and Sci., 1987. Served with AUS, 1954-56. Diplomate Am. Bd. Profl. Psychology. Fellow World Acad. Art and Sci.; mem. AAAS, Am. Psychol. Assn., Soc. Gen. Systems Research, Soc. Engring. Psychologists, Sigma Xi. Author: (with W.M. Thornton) Training: A Handbook for Line Managers, 1961; editor: (with Lorenz K.Y. Ng) Management of Pain and Stress, 1985; contbr. to Strategies for Public Health: Promoting Health and Preventing Disease, 1982; contbr. articles to profl. jours. Club: River Bend Golf and Country (pres. 1986-88). Lodge: Masons (32 degree). Home: 308 East St NE Vienna VA 22180 Office: B-K Dynamics Inc 3204 Monroe St Rockville MD 20850

PROCTOR, TERRELL WILLIAM, lawyer, art gallery owner; b. Austin, Tex., Aug. 4, 1934; s. William Owen and Arlene G. (Holdeman) P.; m. Joan Farrar, Dec. 20, 1958 (div.); children—Douglas, David, Donna Proctor Kester, Diana. B.S. in Bus. Adminstrn., Tulsa U., 1957, postgrad., 1958; J.D., South Tex. Coll. Law, Houston, 1963. Bar: Tex. 1963, U.S. Dist. Ct. (so. dist.) Tex., U.S. Ct. Appeals (5th cir.) 1965. Pres., owner San Jacinto Gallery, also Proctor Supply, Houston, 1967—; master 246th Dist. Ct. of Harris County (Tex.), 1984; mcpl. judge, Jacinto City, Tex., 1967-71, 73-74, city sec., 1967; city atty., Lomax, Tex., 1968-70; dean Proctor's Acad. Fine Arts, 1977—; prin. T.W. Proctor & Assocs., attys., Houston. Appeared in theater prodns, several TV films and TV commls. Mem. Democratic Exec. Com., Houston, 1968-70; del. Dem. State Conv., 1981; mem. Rep. Nat. Conv., 1982, 86; Rep. candidate for U.S. Ct. Appeals (14th cir.); pres. N.E. Houston C. of C., 1970-72, Northshore Area Art League, 1980-81; bd. dirs. Baytown Art League, 1981-82, 82-83, Watercolor Art Soc., Houston, 1981. Served with USAF, 1952-60. Mem. Tex. Bar Assn., Houston Bar Assn., North Channel Bar Assn. (sec.-treas.), Greater Northshore Area Bar Assn. (sec.-treas. 1967-81), North Harris County Bar Assn. (pres. 1982, sec.-treas. 1988—), Assn. Trial Lawyers Am., Am. Judicature Soc. Methodist (past trustee). Winner writing contests, 1963, 77. Address: 630 Uvalde Houston TX 77015

PROCTOR, WILLIAM ZINSMASTER, lawyer; b. Des Moines, Nov. 30, 1902; s. Frank and Louise (Zinsmaster) P.; m. Alice S. Bowles, Nov. 24, 1944; children: David J. W., Mary Martha. Student, Drake U., 1920; J.D., U. Mich., 1925. Bar: Iowa 1925. Assoc. Bradshaw, Schenk & Fowler, 1925-35; ptnr. Bradshaw, Fowler, Proctor & Fairgrave, Des Moines, 1935—; dir., gen. counsel emeritus Employers Mut. Casualty Co., Employers Modern Life Co., Emcasco Ins. Co., EMC Ins. Group Inc., Dakota Fire Ins. Co., Bismarck, N.D., Am. Liberty Ins. Co., Birmingham, Ala., Union Mut. Ins. Co. Providence; dir. emeritus Norwest Des Moines N.A. Pres. Des Moines Community Chest, 1956, Des Moines United Community Services, 1957; mem. bd. SSS, 1942-55, Iowa appeal bd., 1955-67; Pres. Des Moines Roadside Settlement, 1950-53; trustee Hawley Welfare Found., 1968—, chmn., 1974-86; chmn. bd. trustees Preston Ednl. Trust, 1952—. Mem. ABA, Iowa Bar Assn., Polk County Bar Assn. (pres. 1945), Internat. Bar Assn., Inter-Am. Bar Assn., Am. Judicature Soc., Assn. Bar City N.Y., Fedn. Ins. Counsel. Clubs: Mason (Shriner, Jester), Wakonda, Des Moines (pres. 1953); University (Chgo.). Home: 3401 Lincoln Pl Dr Des Moines IA 50312 Office: Bradshaw Fowler Proctor & Fairgrave Des Moines Bldg Des Moines IA 50307

PRODANIUK, ROLAND GEORGE, engineer; b. St. Paul, Alta., Can., Feb. 2, 1947; s. John and Sophie (Sorochan) P.; m. Evelyn Lillie Alexandra Boisvert, Mar. 6, 1972; children—Zane Anatole, Prosper John, Melodie Vera Lee. Assoc. in Archtl. and Engring. Tech., No. Alta. Inst. Tech., Edmonton, 1965-67; B.Sc. in Engring., U. Alta., Edmonton, 1968, M.B.A. in Bus. Adminstrn. and Commerce, 1970; Doctor of Engring. (hon.), U. Lisbon, 1982. Registered profl. engr., Alta. Mem. engring. staff Can. Engring. Surveys Ltd., Edmonton, summer 1966; archtl. engring. staff Tri-Eng Services Ltd., Edmonton, summer 1967, John Dragon and Assocs. Ltd., Edmonton, summer 1968, Plishka-Eichhorn & Assocs. Ltd., Edmonton, summer 1968; dir., co-chmn. investment com. U-12 Investments, Ltd., Edmonton, 1977-85; pres. Plishka, Prodaniuk, Woods, Assocs. Ltd., Edmonton, 1969—; prime cons. cultural ctrs. and religious insts., 1969—; tech. adv. Govt. India, Ministry Energy, Dept. Non-Conventional Energy Sources, New Delhi, 1985—; participant in bilateral tech. exchange State Sci. and Tech. Commn. People's Republic of China, 1984; contbr. to Discovery Digest series Access Ednl. TV Network, 1986-87. Author of monographs, nomograms, and computer programs on archtl., engring., and sci. topics; patentee in field, Edmonton Exhbn. Assn. award 1984. Founding. dir. Ukrainian-Can. Archives and Mus. Alta., Edmonton, 1972—; exec. dir Ukrainian Drama and Opera Soc. of Edmonton, 1985—; fund raiser Edmonton Sch. for Autistic Children, 1977-81; supporter Can. Orgn. Small Bus., Markham, Ont., Can., 1981—; computer instr. Assn. for Bright Children, Edmonton, 1982-84. Recipient award of merit Ukrainian-Can. Archives and Mus. Alta., 1983. Mem. Britannica Soc., Can. Fed. Independent Bus., East Edmonton Bus. Assn., Better Bus. Bur., Solar Energy Soc. Can. Inc., Internat. Solar Energy Soc., Italian Cultural Soc. (hon.), Sikh Cultural Soc. (hon.). Lodge: Rotary (cultural dir. 1982—). Avocations: multiculturalistic and family activities; chess; cycling; billiards. Home: 3405-106 Ave, Edmonton, AB Canada Office: Plishka Prodaniuk, Woods Assocs Ltd, 12634 Ft Trail, Edmonton, AB Canada T5C 3C1

PRODI, ROMANO, economist, educator; b. Scandiano, Reggio Emilia, Italy, Aug. 9, 1939; married; 2 children. Degree in econs. and commerce, Cath. U. Milan, Italy, 1961. Prof. indsl. econs. and policy Dept. Polit. Sci. U. Bologna; dir. Ctr. for Econ. and Indsl. Policy; pres. sci. com. Nomisma, Bologna, 1978-79; minister for industry Govt. of Italy, 1978; pres. Inst. Indusl. Reconstrn., 1982; mem. Council for Italo-Am. Relations, 1983—. Editor mag. Energia and Industria. Home: Via Gerusalemme 7, I-40125 Bologna Italy *

PROEMPER, HERBERT, banker; b. Aachen, Germany, Feb. 14, 1931; s. Josef and Thea (Nicoll) P.; m. Sigrid Schrader, May 16, 1958; children:Claudia, Silke, Ingvild, Heike. Grad. Couvengymnasium, Aachen, 1951. Br. mgr. Deutsche Bank, Juelich, Münster and Bielefeld, 1968-77; speaker bd. dirs. Aachener Bank, Aachen, 1977—; mem. supervisory bd. Einhard Verlag, Aachen, 1980—. Office: Aachener Bank eG, Theaterstrasse 5, D5100 Aachen Federal Republic of Germany

PROESCHER, WARD HORNBLOWER, entrepreneur, writer, public speaker; b. Cary, N.C., Aug. 31, 1935; s. Andrew Jay and Gladys (Jones) P.; m. Susan Dittmar, May 1, 1971; children; Tobin Dittmar, Morgan Boehm. BS in Indsl. Relations, U. N.C., 1958. Personnel supr. Campbell Soup Co., Modesto, Calif., 1960-62; sales mgr. U.S. Audio & Copy Corp., San Francisco, 1962-65; stockbroker Hornblower & Weeks-Hemphill, Noyes, San Francisco, 1966-73; founder, pres. Hornblower Yachts, Inc., Berkeley, Calif., 1973-80; prin., chmn. Hornblower, Upson, Monfils & Proeschcer, Pleasant Hill, Calif., 1985; pres. Sea Ventures, Inc., Fla., 1975—; founder Commodore Cruises, Oakland, Calif., 1986—; founder, pres. Data Tab Inc., Castro Valley, Calif., 1982. Author: Secrets of Success-Techniques for Building Greater Personal Effectiveness; founder, host (TV show) How Now Mr. Dow?, The Ward Proescher Forum, 1968-72; pub. Montgomery Street Opinion, 1968-70; founder seminars Secrets of Success. Bd. dirs. Andrew and Gladys Proescher Ednl./Vocat. Loan Fund, 1975—. Served with USN, 1958-60. Mem. Internat. Platform Assn., Nat. Speakers Assn., Bay Area Speakers Service (v.p. 1986—). Clubs: Little Venice Yacht (Stockton, Calif.) (fleet capt. 1984); Campbell Soup Mgmt. (Modesto) (pres. 1961-62). Home: 3266 Elvia St Lafayette CA 94549 Office: 91 Gregory Ln Suite 7 Pleasant Hill CA 94523

PROHOSKY, DONALD E., social worker; b. Omaha, Feb. 25, 1930; s. Joseph Prohosky and Anna Mae (Drost) Taylor; m. Holly Idelle Ringsby, Aug. 28, 1964 (dec. May 1973); 1 child, Kathleen Kay Feeken. BS, Regis Coll., 1952; MSW, Ariz. State U., 1985. Chem. dependency therapist Camelback Hosp. Inc., Phoenix, 1983—; social worker VA Med. Ctr., Phoenix, 1984—; counselor, educator City of Phoenix DWI Ctr., 1984-85; mem. Research Soc. Process-Oriented Psychology, Zurich. Mem. Nat. Assn. Social Workers, Ariz. Bd. Cert. Alcoholism Counselors, Nat. Assn. Alcoholism and Drug Abuse Counselors, Phoenix Friends Carl Jung. Democrat. Roman Catholic. Home: PO Box 15072 Phoenix AZ 85060 Office: VA Med Ctr 7th St and Indian Sch Rd Phoenix AZ 85012

PROKHOROV, ALEKSANDR MIKHAILOVICH, radiophysicist; b. Atherton, Australia, July 11, 1916; grad. Leningrad State U., 1939; postgrad. Physics Inst. USSR Acad. Scis., 1939-41, 44-46. Joined Communist Party Soviet Union, 1950; mem. staff Lebedev Physics Inst., USSR Acad. Scis., 1954-72, head of Lab., 1972-83, vice dir., 1983—, also bd. dirs., academician-sec. gen physics and astronomy dept., 1971—; chmn. Nat. Commn. Soviet Physicists; author standard works on laser. Served with Soviet Army, 1941-43. Decorated Hero of Socialist Labor; recipient Lenin prize, 1959; Nobel prize, 1964; Lomonosov medal Soviet Acad. Scis., 1987. Mem. Am. Acad. Sci. and Art. Address: Dept Gen Physics and Astronomy, USSR Acad Scis, Leninsky prospect 14, Moscow USSR

PROKOPEC, MIROSLAV, anthropologist; b. Prague, Czechoslovakia, Aug. 6, 1923; s. František Prokopec and Marie (Pálová) Prokopcová; m. Marie Tesašová, July 20, 1965; 1 child, Hana. Student in athropology, U. Coll. London, 1947-48; MA, Charles U., Prague, 1950, PhD, 1957, DSc, 1969. Asst. dept. anthropology Charles U., 1950-54, educator pedagogical faculty, 1960-62, 87—; sci. worker Inst. Hygiene and Epidemiology, Prague, 1954-69, leading scientist, 1969—; vis. curator South Australian Mus., Adelaide, 1974-75, 82; external lectr. human biology House of Youth, Prague, 1973—, pedagogical faculty Charles U., Prague, 1987—. Author: Tracing Man's Evolution, 1956, Antropologie, 1967, Physical and Mental Development of the Present Generation of Our Children, 1969 (Best Book of Yr. 1969), (mus. exhibition) Descent of Man and Life and Work of Dr. A. Hrdlička, 1959, 69, 88; mem. editorial bd. Annals Human Biology, 1973—. Dr. A. Hrdlička medal City of Humpolic, Czechoslovakia, 1959; Moravian Mus. research fellow, 1969; grantee Indian Statis. Inst., 1964, Wenner-Gren Found. for Anthrop. Research, 1965, 68, 73, Australian Inst. for Aboriginal Research, 1974-75, Smithsonian Instn., 1983. Mem. European Anthrop. Assn.. (council mem. 1982—), Internat. Assn. for Human Auxology (exec. com. 1979—), Czechoslovak Anthrop. Assn. (founder), Soc. for Study Human Biology. Home: Narcisova 2850, 10600 Prague 10 Czechoslovakia Office: Inst Hygiene and Epidemiology, šrobárova 48, 10042 Prague 10 Czechoslovakia

PROMDHEP, ARUN, air force officer; b. Samut-Prakan, Thailand; Dec. 4, 1927; s. Kam and Phye (Kardprom) P.; m. Chuanpit Promdhep; children—Medha, Phatcha, Peraporn, Adisorn. B.S. in Aero. Engring., Royal Mil. Acad., Bangkok, Thailand, 1950. Commd. officer Royal Thai Air Force, 1950, advanced through grades to air chief marshal, 1981; chief of air staff, Bangkok, 1981-83; dep. supreme comdr. Royal Thai Armed Force (Supreme Command Hdqrs.), Bangkok, 1983—; mem. long term planning com. Thai Airways Internat. Ltd., Bangkok, 1981—; lectr. in field. Contbg. author Air Force News. Senator Nat. Assembly, Bangkok, 1977—; mem. exec. bd. dirs. Nat. Research Council, Thailand, Bangkok, 1985—. Decorated Knight Grand Cordon of Most Exalted Order of the White Elephant, 1981, Night Grand Cordon of the Most Noble Order of Crown of Thailand, 1983. Buddhist. Avocations: reading; special seminar participations. Office: Office of Permanent Sec, Ministry of Def, Sanam Chai Rd, Bangkok 10200, Thailand

PROMPICHAI, PRAKONG, real estate executive, accounting consultant; b. Dansai, Thailand, Mar. 18, 1938; s. Thung and Linla (Saensobha) P.; m. Thongkam Khluikaew, Nov. 6, 1959; children—Montri, Ratchani, Chedsada, Parameth. Diploma in Acctg., LaSalle Extension U., 1971; advanced cert. in acct., Coll. of Pub. Accts., Bangkok; B.S. in English, Villa Wina Inst., 1967. Chief acct. Mason (Thailand) Co., Ltd., Bangkok, 1973-76; chief acct. Bara, Windsor & Co., Ltd., Bangkok, 1977-80, dep. mng. dir., 1981-84; exec. dir. Bara Chem. Co., Ltd., Dangkok, 1982-84; exec. sec., 1985—; acctg. mgr. Strongman Co., Ltd., Bangkok, 1984-85; mgr. Uah Land Devel. Co., Ltd., Bangkok, 1985—; dir. Toyota Car Rental and Leasing Co., Bangkok, 1981-84. Bara Icee Co., Ltd., 1983—. Club: LaSalle Alumni (life). Office: Bara Windsor & Co Ltd, PO Box 22, Bangkok Thailand

PROSPERI, ADRIANO, historian, educator; b. Lazzeretto, Florence, Italy, Aug. 21, 1939; s. Lorenzo Maggino and Marina Giuseppina (Giacomelli) P.; m. Anna Corsi; children: Valentina, Marilena, Margherita. MA, Sch. Normale, Pisa, Italy, 1963. Asst. prof. history U. Bologna, Italy, 1968-75, prof., 1975-86; prof. history U. Pisa, 1986—. Author: (books) Evangelismo e Controriforma, 1968; (with C. Ginzburg) Giochi di Pazienza, 1975. Home: via Sancasciani 13, 56100 Pisa Italy Office: Dept di Storia U Pisa, Piazza Torricelli 2A, 56100 Pisa Italy

PROSSER, JOHN MARTIN, architect, architectural educator, university dean, urban design consultant; b. Wichita, Kans., Dec. 28, 1932; s. Francis Ware and Harriet Corinne (Osborne) P.; m. Judith Adams, Aug. 28, 1954 (dec. 1982); children—Thomas, Anne, Edward; m. Karen Ann Cleary, Dec. 30, 1983; children—Timothy, Jennifer. B.Arch., U. Kans., 1955; M.Arch., Carnegie Mellon U., 1961. Registered architect, Kans., Colo. Architect, Robinson and Hissem, Wichita, 1954-56, Guirey, Srnka, and Arnold, Phoenix, 1961-62, James Sudler Assocs., Denver, 1962-68; ptnr., architect Nuzum, Prosser and Vetter, Boulder, 1969-73; from asst. prof. to prof. U. Colo., Boulder, U. Colo.-Denver, 1968—, acting dean, 1980-84, dean, 1984; dir. urban design U. Colo.-Denver, 1972-85; cons. John M. Prosser Assoc., Boulder and Denver, 1974—; vis. prof. urban design Oxford Poly. U., Eng., 1979; vis. Critic Carnegie Mellon U., U. N.Mex., U. Ariz., Colo. Coll., Ft. Lewis Coll. Author, narrator PBS TV documentary Cities Are For Kids Too, 1984. Prin. works include (with others) hist. redesign Mus. Western Art, Denver (design honor 1984), Villa Italia, Lakewood, Colo., Mt. Carbon Community Ctr., Lakewood, Republic Bldg. parking facility, Denver, Auraria Higher Edn. Ctr., Colo., Auto World, Fiarfield, Calif., Motor World, Colorado Springs Colo. Bd. dirs. Balarat Outdoor Edn. Assn., Denver, 1978-86, Cranmer Park Hilltop Assn., Denver, 1974—, Cherry Creek Found., Denver, 1981—; chmn. design rev. bd. Univs. Colo., Boulder, Denver and Colorado Springs, 1980—; mem. archtl. control com. Denver Tech. Ctr., 1984—; planning cons. Denver Trans Global Airport Expansion Project. Served to capt., as pilot USAF, 1956-59. Co-recipient 2d place nat. award Am. Soc. Interior Designers, 1984, honor award Colo. Soc. Architects, 1984. Mem. AIA (v.p. Denver chpt. 1979-80, pres. 1983, v.p. Colo. chpt. 1972-73, treas. 1974-75, sec. Western Mountain region 1984-86, treas. Colo. Central chpt. 1977-78). Republican. Club: Denver Country (bd. dirs. 1984—, pres. 1986-87). Lodge: Rotary. Home: 324 Ash St Denver CO 80220 Office: U Colo 1200 Larimer St Denver CO 80204

PROSSER, RICHARD DEANE, energy economist; b. London, Dec. 23, 1936; s. Jack Ames and Margaret (Herbert) P. BA, U. Oxford, Eng., 1961; MSc, U. London, 1965, PhD, 1971. Exec. engr. P.O. Research Sta., London, 1961-65; research asst. U. London Imperial Coll., 1965-70; cons. physicist UN Food and Agriculture Orgn., Rome, 1971-74; lectr. U. Stirling, Scotland, 1974-75; economist Cen. Electricity Generating Bd., London, 1978—. Contbr. articles to profl. jours. Served with Brit. Army, 1956-58. Mem. Internat. Assn. Energy Economists. Anglican. Home: 16 Elaine Ct, 123 Haverstock Hill, London NW3 4RT, England Office: Cen Electricity, Generating Bd, 15 Newgate St, London EC1A 7AU, England

PROST, ALAIN MARIE PASCAL, race car driver; b. Lorette, France, Feb. 24, 1955; s. André and Marie-Rose (Karatchian) P.; m. Anne-Marie Prost; 1 child, Nicolas. Student, Coll. Sainte-Marie, Saint Chamond, France. Race car driver 1973—. Grand Prize Winner, Las Vegas and Argentina, 1981, Belgium, Gt. Britain, France and Austria, 1983; winner Brazilian Grand Prix, 1982, 84, 85, 87, Brazilian and Monaco Formula One Grand Prix, 1988. Office: care Fedn des Sports Automobiles, 116 et 136 rue de Longchamp, 75116 Paris France *

PROTOPAPAS, DIMITRIOS, electrical engineer; b. Apiranthos, Naxos, Greece, Dec. 13, 1939; came to U.S., 1970; s. Antonios and Maria Petrou (Bardanis) P.; m. Helen Michalopoulos, June 1, 1967; children—Alexander, Anthony. B.Sc., U. Athens, 1962, Dipl. Radio-Elec. Engring., 1963; M.A.Sc., U. Toronto, 1968; Ph.D. in Elec. Engring, Poly. Inst. N.Y., 1980. Design engr. Honeywell Corp., Scarboro, Ont., Can., 1969-70; sr. design engr. Gould Inc., Cleve., 1970-72; sr. project engr. Cambridge Memories, Inc., Bedford, Mass., 1972-75; mgr. Technicon Corp., Tarrytown, N.Y., 1976-78; mgr. ITT Advanced Tech. Ctr., Shelton, Conn., 1978-87; adj. prof. Poly. Inst. N.Y., 1980—; adv. engr. Timeplex, Inc., Woodcliff Lake, N.J., 1987—. Author: Microcomputer Hardware Design, 1988. Contbr. articles to tech. jours. Mem. IEEE (sr. mem.), AAAS, Assn. Computing Machinery, Assn. Profl. Engrs. Subspecialties: Computer architecture; Computer engineering. Current work: Design of microprocessor-based systems; computer architecture; multiprocessing systems, modeling and analysis of computer systems; computer communication networks. Home: 65 Cloverdale Ave Huntington CT 06484 Office: 530 Chestnut Ridge Rd Woodcliff Lake NJ 07675

PROUDFOOT, PETER REGINALD, architect; b. Sydney, Australia, Nov. 27, 1936; s. John Edric and Adele Ruvé (Bowden) P.; m. Helen Colleen Baker, Feb. 3, 1968; children: Ann Leila, Emma May. BArch, U. Sydney, 1960; MArch. U. Pa., 1967; PhD, U. New S. Wales, 1974. Registered architect, Australia. Design architect Office New S. Wales Govt. Architect, Sydney, 1960-63; supervising architect Richard Sheppard, Robson and Ptnrs., London, 1964-65; architect Louis I. Kahn, Phila., 1966; lectr., then sr. lectr. U. New S. Wales, Sydney, 1968, subject master in communication, 1968-79, dir. archtl. history, 1979—; cons. Nat. Inst. Dramatic Art, 1970-73, Nat. Estate Div. Australian Govt., 1973-74, Commn. of Inquiry into Maritime Industry, 1976, Australian Devel. Corp., 1981—. Contb. articles to profl. jours. Dept. Edn. Commonwealth scholar, 1954-60; recipient Rome prize in architecture, 1965. Mem. Royal Australian Inst. Architects (assoc.), Royal Australian Hist. Soc., Assn. Maritime Historians, Soc. Rome Scholars, Soc. Archtl. Historians (pres. Australia and New Zealand 1985—). Mem. Ch. of Eng. Home: 1 Ontario Ave, 2069 Roseville Australia Office: Univ New South Wales, PO Box 1, Kensington, 2033 Sydney Australia

PROUT, CARL WESLEY, history educator; b. Bakersfield, Calif., Apr. 19, 1941; s. George Hecla and Ruth (King) P. BA, U. Calif., Santa Barbara, 1964, MA, 1965; postgrad., U. Tenn., Knoxville, 1968-71, Am. U., Cairo, 1974, U. So. Calif., 1981, Ain Shams U., Cairo, 1981. Instr. history Santa Barbara Coll., 1965-66, U. Tenn., Knoxville, 1968-71; instr. Orange Coast Coll., Costa Mesa, 1966-68, asst. prof., 1971-73, assoc. prof., 1973-75, prof., 1975—; treas. Willmore Corp., 1980-81, sec., 1984-85, v.p., 1985-86, pres., chmn., 1988—, also bd. dirs.; pres. Marina Bay Cleaners, Inc., 1987—; group facilitator Coastview Meml. Hosp., Long Beach, 1986—. Research and publs. in field. Mem. Long Beach Beautification Assn.; pres., chmn. bd. Alamitos Heights Improvement Assn., 1979-80, bd. dirs., 1980-82; co-chmn. Ban Ugly Light Bulbs, 1978; mem. East Long Beach Joint Council, 1979-80, Local Coastal Planning Adv. Com., 1979-80. Recipient Salgo Outstanding Tchr. award, 1974-76. Mem. Am. Hist. Assn., Sigma Nu. Clubs: Atlantic Alano, Meml. West Alumni. Office: Orange Coast Coll 2701 Fairview Rd Costa Mesa CA 92626

PROVATAS, FOTIS, public official; b. Athens, Greece, June 7, 1943; s. Harilaos and Marietta (Emmanoïlidi) P.; m. Fotini Tomaï, Mar. 8, 1975 (div. 1984); 1 child, Marietta. MS, Nat. Poly. U., Athens, 1972. Vice-chmn. Athens Gas Authority, 1979-86, Vipetva S.A. Constrn. Mgmt. Co., Athens, 1985—; chmn. bd. dirs. Gevi S.A. Georgovimichaniki Pierias, Methoni, Greece, 1987—; gen. sec. Ctr. Greek Pub. Enterprises, Athens, 1987—; ind. cons. engring. Athens, 1972—. Mcpl. councilor Athens, 1978-83; vice-mayor of Athens, 1984-86; mem. cen. com. Greek Left Party. Mem. Greek Union Civil Engrs. (gen. sec. 1977-78), Tech. Chamber of Greece. Mem. Greek Left Party. Greek Orthodox. Home: 3 M Botsari St, 152 33 Halandri Athens Greece

PROVENCHER RYDER, FRANCES NORMA, public relations executive; b. Exeter, N.H., Apr. 22, 1947; d. Roger Arthur and Josette Marguerite (Camus) Provencher; m. Benjamin C. Ryder, Apr. 12, 1969 (div. Mar. 1979); 1 child, Tiffany Nicholas. BA, U. N.H., 1969. Clk. typist, editorial asst. U.S. Embassy, Moscow, 1964-65; asst. editor Durham (N.H.) Advertiser, 1965-69; assoc. editor Kaman Aerospace Corp., Bloomfield, Conn., 1970-71; publs. editor The Hartford Ins. Group (Conn.), 1974-76; pub. relations cons. Fran Ryder Assocs., Farmington, Conn., 1976-78; pub. relations account exec. Shailer Davioff Rogers, Inc., Fairfield, Conn., 1978-80; sr. account exec. Creamer Dickson Basford, Inc., Hartford, Conn., 1980-83; account group mgr., account exec. Spiro & Assocs., Phila., 1983-84, v.p., assoc. pub. relations dir., 1984-85; sr. v.p. pub. relations LSGE Advt. Inc., Avon, Conn., 1985-87; v.p. corp. communications Wondriska Assocs., Farmington, Conn., 1987—. Translator: The Cogito in Edmund Husserl's Phenomenology, 1969. Founder, The Art Guild, 1975; bd. dirs. Parent's Assn., Hartford Sch. Ballet, 1982-83, U. Conn. Found., 1986—. Recipient Gold Quill awards Internat. Assn. Bus. Communicators, 1974. Mem. Pub. Relations Soc. Am. (accredited; bd. dirs. 1980-88, mem. Counselors Acad. 1982—, assembly del. 1987-88, spl. commendation 1985). Republican. Congregationalist. Home and Office: 1712 Hunting Ridge Rd Raleigh NC 27615

PROVORNY, FREDERICK ALAN, lawyer; b. Bklyn., Sept. 7, 1946; s. Daniel and Anna (Wurm) P.; m. Nancy Ileene Wilkins, Nov. 21, 1971; children—Michelle C., Cheryl A., Lisa T., Robert D. B.S. summa cum laude, NYU, 1966; J.D. magna cum laude, Columbia U., 1969. Bar: N.Y. 1970, U.S. Supreme Ct. 1973, D.C. 1975, Mo. 1977, Md. 1987; C.P.A., Md., Mo. Law clk. to Judge Harold R. Medina, U.S. Ct. Appeals (2d cir.), N.Y.C., 1969-70; asst. prof. law Syracuse U., 1970-72; assoc. Debevoise, Plimpton, Lyons & Gates, N.Y.C., 1972-75; lectr. Bklyn. Law Sch., Bklyn., 1973-74; assoc. Cole & Groner P.C., Washington, 1975-76; with Monsanto Co., St. Louis, 1976-86, asst. co. counsel, 1978-86; sole practice, Washington, 1986-87, 88—; ptnr. Keller & Heckman, 1987-88; pres. Sci. and Tech. Assocs., Inc., 1986—. Trustee, Christian Woman's Benevolent Assn. Youth Home, 1979-83. Mem. ABA, Am. Law Inst., Fed. Bar Assn., Assn. Bar City N.Y., Bar Assn. Met. St. Louis (treas. Young Lawyers Sect. 1980-81), Am. Arbitration Assn. (panel comml. arbitrators), Beta Gamma Sigma. Jewish. Clubs: Philo-Mt. Sinai Lodge No. 968, Masons. Contbr. articles to profl. jours. Home: 11803 Kemp Mill Rd Silver Spring MD 20902 Office: Keller & Heckman 818 Connecticut Ave NW Suite 1010 Washington DC 20006

PROVVIDENZA, MICHELE, cardiologist; b. Rome, Nov. 15, 1953; s. Antonino and Anna (Longo) P.; m. Annamaria Veronesi, June 6, 1981; 1 child, Giulo. MD, U. Perugia, 1979, D in Cardiology, 1983; D in Sport Medicine, U. Rome, 1986. Intern Inst. Med. Semiotica U. Perugia, Italy, 1972-74; intern Inst. Morbid Anatomy U. Perugia, 1974-78, resident in cardiology, 1980-81; resident in cardiology Mil. Hosp. S. Giuliana, 1981-82; asst. cardiologist Hosp. Calai, Gualdo Tadino, Italy, 1982-83, registrar in cardiology, 1985—; resident med. officer Italian Hosp., London, 1983. Pres. Mil. Health Service Assn., Perugia, 1983. Mem. Royal Coll. Medicine, Italian Soc. Cardiology, Italian Soc.Internal Medicine, Italian Soc. Sport Medicine, Italian Fedn. Sport Medicine. Home: Via C Battisti n 11, 06083 Bastia Umbra Italy

PROXMIRE, WILLIAM, U.S. senator; b. Lake Forest, Ill., Nov. 11, 1915; s. Theodore Stanley and Adele (Flanigan) P.; m. Ellen Hodges. Grad., Hill Sch., 1934; B.A., Yale, 1938; M.B.A., Harvard, 1940, M.P.A. in Pub. Adminstrn, 1948. Pres. Artcraft Press, Waterloo, Wis., 1953-57; U.S. senator from Wis., 1957—, Nominee gov., 1952, 54, 56; assemblyman Wis. Legislature, 1951. Author: The Fleecing of America. Democrat. Office: US Senate 530 Dirksen Senate Bldg Washington DC 20510 *

PROYE, CHARLES ANDRE, surgeon, educator; b. Lille, Nord, France, Oct. 16, 1938; s. Charles Georges and Antoinette Marie (Baillieul) P.; m. Annie Elmire Deltombe, March 31, 1962; children: Laurence, Morgane, Marina. MD, U. Lille, France, 1962. Extern Lille Hosp., 1957-60, intern, 1960-66, attending surgeon, 1966-70, assoc. prof. surgery, 1970-84, prof., 1984—; editorial bd. Annales de Chirurgie, Paris, 1977—; mem. Academie de Chirurgie, Paris, 1980—; vice dean Lille Med. Sch., 1977-81. Author: Endocrine Tumors Pancreas, 1985, contbr. (book) Surgical Endocrinology, 1988; contbr. over 300 articles to sci. jours. Served with French mil., 1963-64. Mem. Internat. Soc. Surgery, Internat. Coll. Digestive Surgery, French Assn. Surgery, BRitish Assn. Endocrine Surgery, Internat. Assn. Endocrine Surgery. Home: Calmette, 59152 Gruson, Nord France Office: Lille Univ Hosp, Verdun Pl, 59037 Lille, Nord France

PRUDDEN, JOHN FLETCHER, surgeon; b. Fostoria, Ohio, Feb. 4, 1920; s. Meryl Ashley and Sallie Wells (Gibson) P.; B.S. cum laude, Harvard U., 1942, M.D., 1945; Med. Sc.D., Columbia Coll. Physicians and Surgeons, 1950; m. Ruth Carla Williamson, Jan. 22, 1955; children—Peter, Pamela, Elaine, John Fletcher, Sarah Milford, James Nelson. Intern, Bellevue Hosp., N.Y.C., 1945-46; resident Roosevelt Hosp., N.Y.C., 1947-49, Peter Bent Brigham Hosp., Boston, 1950-51, Pondville Cancer Hosp., Walpole, Mass., 1951-52; instr. Columbia Coll. Physicians and Surgeons, 1954-62, asst. prof., 1962-67, asso. prof. surgery, 1967-76; asso. atending surgeon Presbyn. Hosp., N.Y.C., 1967-76; attending surgeon Delafield Hosp., N.Y.C., 1966-76, Nyack (N.Y.) Hosp., 1976-84, Drs. Hosp., N.Y.C., 1976—, Roosevelt Hosp., N.Y.C., 1977-81; cons. surgery Harlem Hosp., N.Y.C., 1964-76, N.Y. Rehab. Hosp., Haverstraw, N.Y., 1967-81; chmn., sci. dir., chief exec. officer Lescarden, Inc., N.Y.C., 1981—; dir. Barinco, Inc., Blooming Grove, N.Y., 1978-82, Trustee Nyack (N.Y.) Hosp., 1974-80. Served to capt. AUS, 1952-54. Mem. N.Y. Surg. Soc., Soc. for Exptl. Biology and Medicine, Harvey Soc., Soc. for Alimentary Tract Surgery, N.Y. Acad. Scis., ACS, AAAS, AMA, Am. Geriatrics Assn., Am. Chem. Soc., N.Y. State, N.Y. County med. socs., Pan Pacific Surg. Assn., AAUP, Whipple Soc. Clubs: Mid-Ocean (Bermuda); Fishers Island Country, Univ. (N.Y.C.); Hay Harbor. Contbr. articles to profl. jours. Home: 97 Lyon Ridge Rd Katonah NY 10536 Office: Lescarden Inc 790 Madison Ave Suite 601 New York NY 10021

PRUSSIA, LELAND SPENCER, banker; b. San Jose, Calif., 1929; s. Leland Spencer and Doris E. (Fowler) P.; m. Vivian Blom; children: Leslie, Alan L., Gregory. BA in Econs., Stanford U., 1951, MA in Econs., 1956; grad. Advanced Mgmt. Program, Harvard U., 1970; D in Econ. (hon.), U. San Francsico, 1984. Research economist Bank of Am. Nat. Trust & Savs. Assn., San Francisco, 1956-62, with bank investments securities div., 1962-65, v.p. investment portfolio activities, 1965-71, sr. v.p. investment securities div., 1971-74; exec. v.p., chief fin. officer Bank of Am. Nat. Trust & Savs. Assn., BankAm. Corp., San Francisco, 1974-78, 84-86, exec. officer World Banking div., 1979-81; chmn. bd. BankAm. Corp., San Francisco, 1981-87, ret., 1987; adv. dir. Gen. Motors-Hughes Electronics Corp.; bd. dirs. Calif. Econ. Devel. Corp., chmn. Pacific Rim Task Force; bd. dirs. Dimensional Corp. Fin., Inc.; prin. Diversified Corp. Loans, Inc.; mem. Calif. Senate Commn. on Corp. Governance, Shareholders Rights, Securities Transactions; lectr. in econs., U. San Francsico, 1957-65. Author: The Changing World of Banking: Bank Investment Portfolio Management. Trustee U. San Diego, Neighborhood Housing Services Am.; bd. dirs. Council for Basic Edn., U. San Francisco, U. Calif. Santa Barbara Found., Com. For Responsible Fed. Budget, St. Francis Found. of St. Francis Meml. Hosp.; adv. council J.L. Kellogg Grad. Sch. Mgmt. Northwestern U., San Francisco State U. Sch. Bus.; chmn. bd. Calif. Nature Conservancy, gov. nat. orgn.; mem. San Francisco Bay Area Leadership Task Force, Bus. Com. for Arts; adv. bd. Holy Family Day Home. Mem. Am. Econ. Assn., Western Econ. Assn., Am. Fin. Assn., Securities Industry Assn. (former Calif. region chmn., former dir. gov. bd.), Security Analysts of San Francisco, Stanford Assocs., Am. Polit. Found. (bd. dirs.). Clubs: Commonwealth of Calif., San Francisco Bond, Bankers San Francisco, Merchants Exchange, Pacific-Union, Bohemian. Office: Bank of Am Ctr Suite 4740 PO Box 37000 San Francisco CA 94137 *

PRYCE, (GEORGE) TERRY, food products company executive; b. Mar. 26, 1934; s. Edwin and Hilda Florence (Price) P.; m. Thurza Elizabeth Tatham, 1957; 3 children. Student, Nat. Coll. Food Tech. Dir. various food cos. THF Group, 1965-70; asst. mgr. dir. Dalgety (U.K.) Ltd., 1970, mng. dir., 1971, chmn., 1978—; bd. dirs. Dalgety Ltd., 1972—, mng. dir., 1978-81, chief exec., 1981—; chmn. Dalgety Spillers Ltd., 1980—; bd. dirs. H.P. Bulmer Holdings, 1984—; chmn. bd. of food studies, Reading U., 1986—. Gov. Nat. Coll. Food Tech., 1981—. Office: Dalgety plc, 19 Hanover Sq, London W1, England *

PRYOR, DAVID HAMPTON, U.S. senator; b. Camden, Ark., Aug. 29, 1934; s. Edgar and Susan (Newton) P.; m. Barbara Lunsford, Nov. 27, 1957; children—David, Mark, Scott. B.A. in Polit. Sci, U. Ark., 1957, LL.B.,

1961. Bar: Ark. 1964. Practiced in Camden; mem. firm Pryor and Barnes; founder, pub. Ouachita Citizen newspaper, Camden, 1957-60; mem. Ark. Ho. of Reps., 1961-65, 89th-92d Congresses from 4th Dist., Ark.; gov. of Ark., Ark., 1974-79; senator from Ark., 1979—. Office: 264 Russell Senate Bldg Washington DC 20510

PRYOR, HUBERT, editor, writer; b. Buenos Aires, Argentina, Mar. 18, 1916; (parents Am. citizens); s. John W. and Hilda A. (Cowes) P.; m. Ellen M. Ach, 1940 (div. 1959); children: Alan, Gerald, David. Grad., St. George's Coll., Argentina, 1932; student, U. London, Eng., 1934-36. Corr. in S.Am. for United Press, 1937-39; pub. relations rep. Pan Am. Airways in Buenos Aires, 1939-40; reporter N.Y. Herald Tribune, 1940-41; writer, dir. short-wave newsroom CBS, 1941-46; asst. mng. editor Knickerbocker Weekly, 1946-47; sr. editor Look mag., 1947-62; creative supr. Wilson, Haight & Welch (advt.), 1962-63; editor Science Digest, 1963-67; mng. editor Med. World News, 1967; editor NRTA Jour. Modern Maturity, 1967-82; editorial dir. Dynamic Years, 1977-82; publs. coordinator Modern Maturity, Dynamic Years, 1982-84; editorial cons., writer 1985—. Served to lt. USNR, 1943-46. Mem. Am. Soc. Mag. Editors. Address: 3501 S Ocean Blvd Palm Beach FL 33480

PRYOR, RICHARD WALTER, telecommunications executive, retired air force officer; b. Poplar Bluff, Mo., Nov. 6, 1932; s. Walter V. and Mary (Clifford) P.; m. Barbara LeCompte, Feb. 19, 1955; children: Richard, Susan Davis, Robert, William. B in Gen. Studies, U. Nebr., Omaha, 1972; MA, Webster Coll., St. Louis, 1975; grad., U. No. Colo., 1975. Commd. 2d lt. USAF, 1953, advanced through grades to maj. gen., 1982, ret., 1982, instr. Acad., DVMT engr. space and missile systems, chief of staff Communication Services; mgr. worldwide def. communication system Def. Communications Agy., 1980-81; pres. ITT World Communications, N.Y.C., 1982-84, ITT Indsl. Transmission Co., N.Y.C.; sr. v.p. engring. ops. ITT Communication Services GP; pres., gen. mgr. ITT Christian Rovsing-Copenhagen DK, 1984-86; chmn. Christian-Rovsing Inc., Tulsa; exec. Electric Data Systems, 1986—; bd. dirs. Automotive Satellite TV Network, Westcott Communications, TDS (Spain); exec. v.p. Communications Corp. Contbr. articles to tech. publs. Assoc. dir. Boy Soucts Am., N.Y.C., 1983. Recipient Cert. of Appreciation Okla. Mental Health Assn., 1979, Kansas City Lions Club, 1974. Mem. Armed Forces Communications and Electronics Assn. (pres. N.Y.C. 1983, nat. dir.), Air Force Assn., Oklahoma City Soc. Profl. Engrs., Phi Alpha Theta. Republican. Roman Catholic. Clubs: Bolling AFB Officers; Canoe Brook Country (Short Hills, N.J.); Army-Navy (Washington). Home: 7802 Mason Dells Dallas TX 75230 Office: Electronic Data Systems Corp 7171 Forest Ln Dallas TX 75230

PRYOR, SHEPHERD GREEN, III, lawyer; b. Fitzgerald, Ga., June 27, 1919; s. Shepherd Green Jr. and Jeffie (Persons) P.; m. Lenora Louise Standifer, May 17, 1941 (dec.); m. Ellen Wilder, July 13, 1984; children from previous marriage: Sandra Pryor Clarkson, Shepherd Green IV, Robert Stephen, Patty Pryor Smith (dec.), Alan Persons, Susan Lenora Pryor Day . BSAE, Ga. Inst. Tech., 1947; JD, Woodrow Wilson Coll. Law, Atlanta, 1974. Bar: Ga. 1974, U.S. Dist. Ct. (no. dist.) Ga. 1974, U.S. Ct. Appeals (5th cir.) 1974, U.S. Ct. Appeals (11th cir.) 1982, U.S. Supreme Ct. 1977; registered profl. engr. Ga., comml. pilot. engr. Hartford Accident and Indemnity Co., 1947-56, nuclear engr. Lockheed Ga. Co., 1956-64, research and tech. rep., 1964-87, real estate salesman Cole Realty Co. and Valient Properties, 1955-74, Sole practice of law, Atlanta, 1974—. Past pres. Loring Heights Civic Assn.; past mem. Sandy Springs Civic Assn. Devenwood Br., Trustee Masonic Children's Home of Ga. Served to capt. U.S. Army, 1942-45, USAFR, 1942-55. Mem. Ga. Bar Assn., Mensa, Intertel, Soc. Automotive Engrs., Assn. Old Crows, Sigma Delta Kappa, Pi Kappa Phi, Kappa Kappa Psi. Republican. Methodist. Lodges: Masons, Shriners Address: 135 Spalding Dr Atlanta GA 30328

PRYOR, WILLIAM LEE, humanities educator; b. Lakeland, Fla., Oct. 29, 1926; s. Dahl and Lottie Mae (Merchant) P.; A.B., Fla. So. Coll., 1949; M.A., Fla. State U., 1950, Ph.D., 1959; postgrad. U. N.C., 1952-53; pvt. art study with Florence Wilde; pvt. voice study with Colin O'More and Anna Kaskas. Asst. prof. English, dir. drama Bridgewater Coll., 1950-52; vis. instr. English Fla. So. Coll., MacDill Army Air Base, summer 1951; grad. teaching fellow humanities Fla. State U., 1953-55, 57-58; instr. English, U. Houston, University Park, 1955-59, asst. prof., 1959-62, assoc. prof., 1962-71, prof., 1971—; assoc. editor Forum, 1967, editor, 1967-82; vis. instr. English, Tex. So. U., 1961-63; vis. instr. humanities, govt. U. Tex. Dental Br., Houston, 1962-63; lectr. The Women's Inst., Houston, 1967-72; lectr. humanities series Jewish Community Center, 1972-73; originator, moderator weekly television and radio program The Arts in Houston on KUHT-TV and KUHF-FM, 1956-57, 58-63; performed in operas: as Sir Edgar in Der Junge Lord (Henze), Houston Grand Opera Assn., 1967, the title role in Aella (Chatterton), Am. premiere, U. Houston, 1970. Bd. dirs. Houston Shakespeare Soc., 1964-67; bd. dirs., program annotator Houston Chamber Orch. Soc., 1964-76 ; narrator Houston Symphony Orch., Houston Summer Symphony Orch., Houston Chamber Orch., U. Houston Symphony Orch., St. Stephen's Music Festival Symphony Orch., Ind.; narrator world premier of The Bells (Jerry McCathern), 1969, U. Houston Symphony Orch., 1969, Am. premier Symphony No. Seven, Antartica (Vaughn-Williams), Houston Symphony Orch., 1967, L'Históire du Soldat (Stravinski), U. Houston Symphony Orch., 1957, Am. premier Babar the Elephant (Poulenc-Françaix), 1967, Houston Chamber Orch., 1979, Voice of God in opera Noye's Fludde (Britten), St. Stephen's Music Festival, 1981; bd. dirs., program annotator Music Guild, Houston, 1960-67, v.p., 1963-67, adv. bd. 1967-70; bd. dirs. Contemporary Music Soc., Houston, 1958-63; mem.-at-large bd. dirs. Houston Grand Opera Guild, 1966-67; mem. repertory com. Houston Grand Opera Assn. 1967-70; bd. dirs. Houston Grand Opera, 1970-75, adv. bd., 1978-79; mem. cultural adv. com. Jewish Community Center, 1960-66; bd. dirs. Houston Friends Pub. Library, 1962-67, 73-75, 1st v.p., 1963-67; adv. mem. cultural affairs com. Houston C. of C., 1972-75; adv. bd. dirs. The Wilhelm Schöle, 1980—, Buffalo Bayou Support Com., 1985-87. Recipient Master Teaching award Coll. Humanities and Fine Arts U. Houston, 1980. Mem. Coll. English Assn., Modern Langs. Assn. L'Alliance Francaise, English-Speaking Union, Alumni Assn. Fla. So. Coll., Fla. State U., Am. Assn. U. Profs., S. Central Modern Lang. Assn., Conf. Editors Learned Jours., Coll. Conf. Tchrs. English, Am. Studies Assn., Phi Beta (patron), Phi Mu Alpha Sinfonia, Alpha Psi Omega, Pi Kappa Alpha, Sigma Tau Delta, Tau Kappa Alpha, Phi Kappa Phi. Episcopalian. Contbg. author: National Poetry Anthology, 1952; Panorama das Literaturas das Americas, 4 vols., 1958-60; contbr. articles to scholarly jours. Club: Caledonian (London). Home: 2625 Arbuckle St Houston TX 77005 Office: 3801 Cullen Blvd Houston TX 77004

PRZYBYLOWICZ, CAROLYN LYON, controller, personnel administrator; b. Clare, Mich., Jan. 18, 1947; d. Aaron Eugene and Alice Marie (Fall) Prout; m. Stanley George Lyon, July 13, 1968 (dec. May 1971); children: Lori Anne Lyon, Jamie Lynn Lyon; m. Dennis Karl Hunt, Jan. 1975 (div. Nov. 1977); 1 child, Julie Marie Hunt Przybylowicz; m. Arthur Roy Przybylowicz, Nov. 3, 1979. Cert. acctg., Lansing Bus. U., 1965. Bank teller Citizens Bank & Trust, Rosebush, Mich., 1965-68; bookkeeper, sec. Doyle & Smith P.C., Lansing, Mich., 1968-74; legal sec. Foster, Swift, Collins & Coey P.C., Lansing, 1974-79; mgr. office ARC, Lansing, 1979-81; controller, personnel adminstr. Mich. Protection & Advocacy Service, Lansing, 1981-88; bus. adminstr. White, Beekman, Przybylowicz, Schneider & Baird, P.C., Okemos, Mich., 1988—. Vol. bookkeeper Citizens Alliance to Uphold Spl. Edn., Lansing, 1977-79; coordinator bingo IHM Sch., Lansing, 1979-80; mem. St. Casimir Christian Service, Lansing, 1981-84, chairperson, 1983-84; bd. dirs. Immaculate Heart of Mary Sch., Lansing, 1977-80. Democrat. Roman Catholic. Office: White Beekman Przybylowicz Schneider & Baird PC 2214 University Park Dr Suite 200 Okemos MI 48864

PSOMIADES, PAUL, insurance company executive; b. Piraeus, Greece, July 26, 1939; s. Daniel Psomiades and Olga Siowakides; m. Maria Tsiricos, Nov. 5, 1972; children: Olga, Daniel. BA in Polit. Sci., Pantios Polit. Sci. Sch., Athens, Greece, 1963. Agt. Am. Life Ins. Co., Athens, 1967-69; unit mgr. Interam. Life Ins. Co., Athens, 1970-77; sales mgr. Aspis-Pronia Life Ins. Co., Athens, 1978-82, pres., chief exec. officer, 1982—. Served as sgt. Greek Paratroopers, 1964-66. Mem. Union Ins. Cos. (mem. life com. 1986—). Home and Office: 4 Othonos St, 10557 Athens Greece

PUAPUA, TOMASI, Tuvalu prime minister; m. 1971; 3 children. Student U. Otago, N.Z. Prime minister, minister for local govt., minister for fgn. affairs Tuvalu, Funafuti, 1981—. Office: Office of Prime Minister, Fongafale Tuvalu *

PUCCI, EMILLO (MARCHESE DI BARSENTO), fashion designer; b. Naples, Italy, Nov. 20, 1914; s. Orazio and Augusta (Pavoncelli) Pucci; student U. Milan (Italy), 1933-35, U. Ga., 1935-36; M.A. in Social Scis., Reed Coll., Portland, Oreg., 1937; Dr. Polit. Sci., U. Florence (Italy), 1941; m. Cristina Nannini, Feb. 7, 1959; children: Alessandro, Laudomia. Pilot-lt. col. Italian Air Force, 1941-52; fashion creator, pres. Casa di Alta Moda Emilio Pucci, Ltd., Florence, 1951—; pres. Antico Satificlo Florentino, 1958, Emilio Pucci Parfums, Paris, Emilio Pucci Ltd., N.Y.C.; prod. collections for fashion show in Florence, Jan. and July 1950; with other fashion designers showed collection Italian fashions in Russia, 1958. Mem. Italian Parliament for Florence, 1963-72; counsellor Florence City Council, 1964—. Recipient Neiman Marcus Fashion award, 1954, Burdines Sunshine award, 1955, Sports Illustrated Sporting Look Designers award, 1961; medallion Harper's Bazaar. Mem. Associazone Proprieta' Edilizia (pres.), Società Fiorentina per le Corse dei Cavalli (horse racing assn.), (pres.), Società di San Giovanni Battista (pres.), Società di San Giovanni di Dio (pres.), Italian Pvt. Sector Initiative, Italian Styling Assn. (hon. pres.), Cavaliere del Lavoro (hon. pres.). Clubs: Circolo Unione de Golf, Rotary, Tennis, Florence; Circolo della Caccia (Rome); Eagle Ski (Gstaad, Switzerland); Corviglia (St. Moritz). Address: Palazzo Pucci, via del Pucci 6, Florence Italy

PUCHNER, PETER ENDRE, electronics engineer; b. Port Augusta, Australia, Feb. 19, 1952; s. Endre Carl and AnneMarie Irene (Sorgel) P. Registered engr., Australia. TV technician Australian Broadcasting Commn., Tasmania, 1971-76; audio-visual mgr. Contact TV Electronics, Tasmania, 1976-80; freelance producer Australia, 1978-85; research and devel. mgr. Mach. Systems, Melbourne, Australia, 1984-87; dir., engr. Electronic Visual Displays, Tasmania, 1980-86; dir. engring. Infomate Holdings Pty. Ltd., Tasmania, 1985—; cons. in field. Mem. Inst. Radio and Electronic Engrs. Home: Hall St, 7101 Ridgeway Australia Office: Puchner Electronics P/L, 165 Harrington St, 7000 Hobart Australia

PUCKETT, JAMES MANUEL, JR., genealogist; b. Oakman, Ga., Dec. 8, 1916; s. James Manuel and Alma (Willkie) P.; student West Ga. Coll., Emory U.; m. Robbie Horton, Sept. 13, 1944; 1 son, James William (dec.). Retail mcht., 1937-42; with Treasury Dept., 1944-53; public acct., 1955-60; feature writer Ga. Geneal. Soc. quar., 1965-75; genealogist, lectr., 1965—. Mayor of Oakman, 1940-42. Served with USNR, 1942-44. Mem. SAR, Sons Confederate Vets., Order Stars and Bars (Ga. comdr. 1966-70), Nat. Hist. Soc., So. Hist. Soc., Ga. Hist. Soc., Orgn. Am. Historians, Ctr. for Study of the Presidency, Internat. Platform Assn., Am. Coll. of Genealogists, Ga. Geneal. Soc., Nat. Geneal. Soc. Home: 1563 Runnymeade NE Atlanta GA 30319 Office: 240 Peachtree St NE Suite 10-J-10 Atlanta GA 30303

PUELLO, ANTONIO, JR., first secretary of the embassy; b. Colon, Panama, July 12, 1951; s. Antonio and Bartola (Solis) P.; m. Maria Eva Vargas, Mar. 22, 1980; 1 child, Lituania Rosario. B of Internat. Relations, Nat. U., Panama, 1975. Prof. help Panama U., 1974-76, asst. prof., 1976-77, prof., 1977-78; advisor fgn. affairs Ministry Fgn. Affairs, 1979; 3d sec. Panama Enbassy in La Paz (Bolivia), 1980, charge d'affaires, 1981; 1st sec. of embassy Panama Embassy in Tel Aviv, 1982—; mem. XII Meeting of the Nuclear Energy, Bolivia, 1981, econ. evaluation FAO UN, Bolivia, 1981; vice dir. Ctr. of Ops. Fgn. Affairs Ministry, 1988. Contbr. articles to profl. jours. Polit. advisor Student Assn., 1974; pres. Diplomatic Assn., La Paz, 1981. Dem. Revolutionary Party. Roman Catholic. Home: PO Box 21260, Tel Aviv 61210, Israel

PUENTE, JOSE GARZA, safety coordinator; b. Cuero, Tex., Mar. 19, 1949; s. Roque Leos and Juanita Vela (Garza) P.; m. Francisca Rodriguez Estrada, Sept. 7, 1969; 1 son, Anthony Burk. B.A., W. Tex. State U., Canyon, 1972; postgrad. U. Ariz.-Tucson, 1980; grad. U.S. Army transp. courses, 1972, 78. Cert. U.S. Council Accreditation in Occupational Hearing; cert. Audiometric Technicians of Am. Indsl. Hygiene Assn. Asst. gen. mgr. Am. Transit Corp., Tucson, 1972-75; pub. transp. supt. City of Tucson, 1975-77; asst. safety coordinator, Tucson, 1977-81; safety coordinator Mesa, Ariz., 1981—; owner La Paz Gospel Supplies & Gift shop, Tucson, 1979-80. Mem. Tucson Child Care Assn., 1973-74; mem. Citizen Task Force, Sunnyside sch. bd., 1977; co-founder Ray Morales Aid Fund, 1980. Serving as maj. USAR, 1971—. Fellow Advanced Mgmt. Seminar Urban Mass Transp. Adminstrn., Northeastern U., Boston, 1976-77; recipient Excellence award Ariz-Safety Assn., 1984. Mem. Am. Soc. Safety Engrs. (Safety Profl. of Yr. 1984), Mexican Am. Govtl. Employees (charter mem. Tucson), Res. Officers Assn., Ariz. Safety Engrs., Internat. Platform Assn. Assn. Democrat. Baptist. Clubs: Internat. Order DeMolay (charter), Dobson Ranch Lions, Mesa Bowling League, Toastmasters. Home: 2253 S Estrella Mesa AZ 85202 Office: 648 N Mesa Dr Mesa AZ 85201

PUFFER, RICHARD JUDSON, college chancellor; b. Chgo., Aug. 20, 1931; s. Noble Judson and Lillian Katherine (Olson) P.; m. Alison Foster Cope, June 28, 1952; children—Lynn, Mark, Andrew. Ph.B., Ill. Wesleyan U., 1953; M.S. in Edn, Ill. State U., 1962; Ph.D. (Univ. scholar), 1965-66; Ph.D. Roy Clark Meml. scholar, Northwestern U., 1967. Asst. plant supt. J.A. Olson Co., Winona, Miss., 1957-59; tchr. Leroy Community Unit Dist. (Ill.), 1959-60; tchr., prin. Community Unit, Dist. 7, Lexington, Ill., 1960-62; asst. county supt. schs. Cook County, Ill., 1962-65; dean arts and scis. Kirkwood Community Coll., Cedar Rapids, Iowa, 1967-69; v.p. Black Hawk Coll., Moline, Ill., 1969-77; pres. Black Hawk Coll., 1977-82, chancellor, 1982-87; dir. W. Central Ill. Ednl. TV Corp., Springfield, Ill., 1977—; cons. examiner North Central Assn., 1978—. Editor: Cook County Ednl. Digest, 1962-65. Bd. dirs. Cedar Rapids Symphony, 1967-69, United Way of Rock Island and Scott Counties, Ill., 1978-80; sec. treas. Ill. Ednl. Retirement Ctrs., 1987—; vice-chmn. Illini Hosp. Bd., 1988—; bd. dirs. Illowa Council Boy Scouts Am., 1979-83, v.p., 1981-83. Served with Supply Corps USNR, 1953-57. Mem. Ill. Council Pub. Community Coll. Pres., Green Medallion, Blue Key, Pi Gamma Mu, Phi Delta Kappa. Clubs: Rotary (East Moline, Ill.) (pres. 1975-76); Masons. Home and Office: 1119 20th Ave East Moline IL 61244

PUGEL, ROBERT JOSEPH, publisher, English educator; b. Pueblo, Colo., Aug. 15, 1941; s. Joseph E. and Margaret E. (Jachetta) P.; A.A., U. So. Colo., 1959; B.A., Western State Coll. Colo., 1961, M.A., 1965; postgrad. (Univ. internat. fellow) U. London, 1968, U. Denver, 1967-69; m. E. Elke Williamson, June 29, 1968. Asst prof. English, U. So. Colo., 1965-67; teaching fellow U. Denver, 1967-69; prof. English, Met. State Coll., 1969-86; pres., owner Pugel Ranch, Pueblo, Colo., 1986—; founder, pub. Scribes mag., Denver, 1975—; poetry judge; Can./U.S.A. grantee McMaster U., Hamilton, Ont., Can., 1975; Rocky Mountain advisor Brit. Univs., 1970—; owner, operator Pugel Ranch, Pueblo, Colo. Mem. Colo. Dem. Central Com., 1970-81; chmn. Colo. Dem. House Dist. 39, 1974-80; del. Colo. Gov.'s Conf. on Aging, 1980. Recipient award for outstanding community service Public Relations Soc. Am., 1978; named Outstanding Contbr. to Colo. Sr. Community, 1978, 79, 80. Mem. Nat. Council Tchrs. English, Internat. Assn. Bus. Communicators, Pub. Relations Soc. Am., Congress Colo. Communicators, Am. Poetry Soc., NEA, AAUP, English-Speaking Union (internat. bd. govs. 1970-81, 1st v.p. 1974—, chmn. scholarship com. 1975—, organizer, condr. Conoco (Colo.) speech forum, Nat. Writers Club (featured poet 1978 Conf.), St. Andrew's Soc., Denver Zoo, Denver Art Mus., Denver Mus. Natural History, PEN, Colo. Poetry Soc., Poetry Soc. Am., Inst. Internat. Edn., Greenpeace, Sierra Club, Nat. Wildlife Fedn., Fund for Animals, Sr. Support Service (bd. dirs.). Roman Catholic. Club: Racquet World. Editor, pub.: (poems) Chrysalis Seed, 1986; lit. mags. Paradigm Shift, Reality and Other Illusions, Turquoise Windows; founder, pub. Metrosphere, 1983—. Contbr. fiction, articles and poetry to various nat., region and local mags. and newspapers. Home: 7239 E Euclid Dr Englewood CO 80111 Office: Pugel Ranch 125 S Pugel Dr Pueblo CO 81004

PUGH, HELEN PEDERSEN, realtor; b. San Francisco, Feb. 17, 1934; d. Christian Edward and Gladys Phoebe Zumwalt Pedersen; m. Howard Brooks Pugh, Sr., Oct. 11, 1974; children—Catherine Collier, Stephen Leach, Matthew Leach, Virginia Schmitt. AA, U. Calif.-Berkeley, 1953. Pvt. sec. to exec. dir. Rep. party, Phoenix, 1972, Henderson Realty, Phoenix, 1973; sta. mgr. Mobil Oil Co., Phoenix, 1973-74; realtor, Russ Lyon Realty, Scottsdale, Ariz., 1978—. Vol. coordinator William Baker for Congress, Phoenix, 1972; vol. Phoenix Meml. Hosp., Scottsdale Hosp. North Devel. Com.; master tchr. Presbyn. Ch., youth leader; troop leader Cactus-Pine council Girl Scouts U.S.A., 1960-74; asst. den leader Roosevelt Council Boy Scouts Am.; instr. Jr. Achievement; v.p. Planned Parenthood Aux., Family Service Agy. Aux.;bd. dirs. Phoenix Symphony Aux., Phoenix Art Mus.; deacon Presbyn. Ch. Mem. Scottsdale Bd. Realtors, Scottsdale Comml. Bd., Phoenix Comml. Bd. (Multiple Listing Service Forms Com. award 1981), Internat. Real Estate Fedn. (Ariz. chpt. bd. dirs.), Farm and Land Inst., Valley of Sun Real Estate Exchangers, LWV, Scottsdale C. of C. (ambassador), U. Calif. Alumni Assn. (Ariz. chpt. pres.), Scottsdale Rep. Forum, Cactus Wren Rep. Women, Palo Verde Rep. Women, Delta Zeta. Clubs: Toastmasters (past pres., youth leader, gov. area 7, disting.). Lodge: Soroptimists. Home: 7463 E Raintree Ct Scottsdale AZ 85258 Office: 7150 E Lincoln Dr Scottsdale AZ 85253

PUGH, RICHARD CRAWFORD, lawyer; b. Phila., Apr. 28, 1929; s. William and Myrtle (Crawford) P.; m. Nanette Bannen, Feb. 27, 1954; children—Richard Crawford, Andrew Lembert, Catherine Elizabeth. A.B. summa cum laude, Dartmouth Coll., 1951; B.A. in Jurisprudence (Rhodes scholar), Oxford (Eng.) U., 1953; LL.B., Columbia U., 1958. Bar: N.Y. bar 1958. Asso. firm Cleary, Gottlieb, Steen & Hamilton, N.Y.C., 1958-61; partner Cleary, Gottlieb, Steen & Hamilton, 1969—; mem. faculty Law Sch. Columbia, 1961—, prof., 1964-69, adj. prof., 1969—; lectr. Columbia-Amsterdam-Leyden (Netherlands) summer program Am. law, 1963, 79; dep. asst. atty. gen. tax div. U.S. Dept. Justice, 1966-68; Cons. fiscal and financial br. UN Secretariat, 1962, 64. Editor: Columbia Law Rev, 1957-58; editor: (with W. Friedmann) Legal Aspects of Foreign Investment, 1959, (with others) International Law, 1987, The Study of Federal Tax Law, 1988. Served with USNR, 1954-56. Mem. ABA, Am. Bar Found., Am. Law Inst., Am. Coll. Tax Counsel, N.Y. State Bar Assn., Bar Assn. City N.Y. (chmn. internat. law com. 1984-86), Am. Soc. Internat. Law, Council Fgn. Relations, Internat. Fiscal Assn. (pres. U.S. br. 1978-79). Home: 68 Otter Rock Dr Greenwich CT 06830 Office: Cleary Gottlieb Steen & Hamilton 1 State St Plaza New York NY 10004

PUGH, ROBERT L., U.S. ambassador to Mauritania; b. Clinton, Pa., Oct. 27, 1931; m. Bonnie Barnes Coverley; children—Malcolm R., Anne C. B.A., U. Wash., 1954; postgrad., Fgn. Service Inst., 1961, 63-64, 84-85. Joined Fgn. Service, Dept. State, 1961; internat. economist Dept. State, 1961-63; polit./mil. officer Ankara, Turkey, 1964-67; prin. officer Am. Consulate, Isfahan, Iran, 1967-69; polit. officer Office Turkish Affairs, Bur. Near Eastern and South Asian Affairs, Dept. State, 1969-72; polit./mil. officer Athens, Greece, 1972-76; congl. relations officer Dept. State, 1976-77; polit. adviser CINCUSNAVEUR, London, 1977-79; dep. dir. Office So. European Affairs, Bur. European Affairs, 1979-81; personnel placement officer Bur. Personnel, Dept. State, 1981-82; dep. chief of mission Beirut, 1982-84; U.S. ambassador to Mauritania 1985—. Served as officer USMC, 1954-61. Office: US Ambassador to Mauritania care US State Dept Washington DC 20520 also: Am Embassy, BP 222, Nouakchott Mauritania *

PUGH, SANDRA (SASS) KAY, construction and plastic and metal engraving company executive; b. Aberdeen, S.D., June 3, 1950; d. John D. and Ellabeth A. (DeYoung) P. Student Black Hills State Coll., 1968-72. Cert. electrician, S.D. Apprentice electrician Pugh Elec. Construction, Miller, S.D., 1974-81, mgr., journeyman electrician, 1981-86, elec. contractor 1986—, owner, 1984-86. Contbr. poetry to West River Verses volume. Chmn. Hand County Teen Crippled Children, 1967-68; mem. Miller Civic and Commerce, 1983-87, Cen. Plains Arts Council, 1984-86. Recipient Gov.'s award in Photography S.D. State Fair, 1970. Club: Jobs Daughters (state officer 1965). Avocations: photography, collecting bottle openers and cork screws, leather and engraving work. Home: 620 1/2 W 4th St Miller SD 57362

PUGH, WILLIAM WALLACE, lawyer; b. Flushing, N.Y., Sept. 13, 1941; s. Wallace Raymond and Martha (Greenewald) P.; m. Joyce Curry, Dec. 17, 1977; children: James Thomas, Kristin Anne, Katherine Elizabeth. BS in Physics, Bucknell U., 1963; MS in Ops. Research, NYU, 1966; JD, Cath. U., 1972. Bar: D.C. 1973, U.S. Dist. Ct. D.C. 1976, U.S. Ct. Appeals (D.C. cir.) 1977, U.S. Supreme Ct. 1977, U.S. Ct. Appeals (5th cir.). Electronics engr. Grumman Aircraft Engring. Corp., Beth Page, N.Y., 1964-65; mem. tech. staff TRW Systems Group, McLean, Va., 1966-69; advertising examiner FTC, Washington, 1970-72; assoc. Keller & Heckman, Washington, 1972-75; gen. counsel Nat. Motor Freight Traffic Assn., Alexandria, Va., 1975—. Mem. ABA, D.C. Bar Assn., Fed. Bar Assn., Transp. Lawyer Assn., Assn. Transp. Law Practitioners, Delta Theta Phi. Home: 3404 Kimberly Dr Falls Church VA 22042 Office: Nat Motor Freight Traffic Assn 2200 Mill Rd Alexandria VA 22314

PUGSLEY, ALFRED GRENVILE, civil engineer; b. May, 1903; s. H.W. Pugsley; attended London U.; D.Sc. (hon.), Belfast, 1965, Cranfield, 1978, Birmingham, 1982; D.Univ. (hon.), Surrey, 1968; m. Kathleen M. Warner, 1928 (dec. 1974). Civil engring. apprentice Royal Arsenal, Woolwich, Eng., 1923-26; tech. officer Royal Airship Works, Cardington, 1926-31; mem. sci. and tech. staff Royal Aircraft Establishment, Farnborough, Eng., 1931-45, head dept. structural and mech. engring., 1941-45; prof. civil engring. U. Bristol (Eng.), 1944-68, now emeritus prof., prof. vice-chancellor, 1961-64; vis. lectr. on aircraft structures Imperial Coll., London, 1938-40; chmn. Aero. Research Council, 1952-57; mem. Adv. Council on Sci. Policy, 1956-69; mem. Tribunal of Inquiry on Ronan Point, 1968; mem. various sci. and profl. instn., coms.; pres. Inst. Structural Engrs., 1957-58; a v.p. ICE, 1971-73. Decorated Order Brit. Empire; knight bachelor; recipient Structural Engrs. Gold medal, 1968, Civil Engrs. Ewing Gold medal, 1979. Fellow Royal Soc., RAeS (hon.)., ICE (hon.), U. Bristol (hon.). Author: The Theory of Suspension Bridges, 1957, 2d edit., 1968; The Safety of Structures, 1966; editor, contbr. The Works of Isambard Kingdom Brunel, 1976; numerous reports and memoranda of Aero. Research Council; contbr. articles, revs. to profl. publs. Office: care Royal Soc, 6 Calton House Terr, London SW1 England

PUHVEL, MARTIN, English language and literature educator, philologist, folklorist; b. Tallinn, Estonia, Dec. 9, 1933; came to Can., 1949, naturalized, 1959; s. Karl and Meta Elisabeth (Pärn) P.; m. Kersti Arvo, Nov. 2, 1963; children: Toomas Karl, Kristian Arthur. B.A., McGill U., Montreal, Que., Can., 1953, M.A., 1954; Ph.D., Harvard U., 1958. Lectr. McGill U., 1957-59, asst. prof. English, 1959-64, assoc. prof., 1964-80, prof., 1980—; cons. Can. Council, Ottawa, Ont., 1969-78. Author: Beowulf and Celtic Tradition, 1979; also lit., philol. and folkloristic articles and essays. Mem. MLA, Medieval Acad. Am., PEN Internat. (Can. and Estonian Ctrs.), Assn. Advancement Baltic Studies, Estonian Central Council Can. (v.p.). Lutheran. Avocations: hunting; fishing; tennis. Home: 32 Sunshine Dr, Dollard des Ormeaux, PQ Canada H9B 1G4 Office: McGill U, Dept English, 853 Sherbrooke St W, Montreal, PQ Canada H3A 2T6

PULFER, JAMES DOUGLAS, physical chemistry educator; b. Weyburn, Sask., Can., Aug. 27, 1943; s. Maxwell Beverly and Veronica Francis (Myers) P.; m. Margaret Hilary Diana Brooke, Mar. 6, 1971; children: Mark Douglas, Rachel Barbara. BA cum laude, U. Sask., 1964, BA with honors in Chemistry, 1965, MSc in Theoretical Chemistry, 1968; PhD in Applied Math. and Theoretical Chemistry, McGill U., 1975. Lay missionary United Ch. of Can., Jamaica, 1967-69; chemistry programmer Knox Coll., Jamaica, 1969-70, researcher, 1967-70; chemistry lectr. Lester B. Pearson Coll. of Pacific, Victoria, B.C., 1975-77; chemistry lectr. U. Botswana and Swaziland, Kwaluseni, 1977-79, research team leader, 1977-79; selection com. rep. for Pearson Coll. in Swaziland, United World Colls., 1977-79; lectr. in math. Brandon U., Man., Can., 1979-81; sr. lectr. in chemistry Nat. U. of Lesotho, Roma, 1981-86; researcher Warwick U., 1987; lectr. in Chemistry U. Papua New Guinea, Port Moresby, 1988—. Contbr. poetry, articles to profl. jours. Recipient T. Sterry Hunt prize U. McGill U., 1971, 72; McConnell Meml. fellow, 1972-74; Can. NRC grantee, 1971-72; Can. Kokak Co. scholar, 1965, Cave and Co. scholar, 1962. Avocations: golf; investment clubs. Home: care Mrs V Pulfer, 603 Maple Dr, Weyburn, SK Canada S4H 1A5 Office: U PNG, Chem Dept, Box 320, Port Moresby Papua New Guinea

PULFER, LESLIE LOUIS, state official; b. Elgin, Iowa, Jan. 22, 1932; s. John and Ida (Fischer) P.; A.A., Iowa State U., 1966; B.B.A., Ill. State U., 1971; m. Wilma Wettstein, July 18, 1954; children—Jeffrey, Kathleen, Eldon, Doris. With Rath Packing, Waterloo, Iowa, 1951-52, Borden Milk Co., Pekin, Ill., 1956-59, Standard Brands, Inc., Pekin, 1959-71; ops. mgr. Soldwedel All Star Dairy, Canton, Ill., 1972; asst. adminstr. Bur. Animal Health Ill. Dept. Agr., Springfield, 1972—; pres. New World Sweeteners, Eureka, Ill., 1979—; cons. Standards Brands, 1959-71, Malt Products Co., 1972-78; field project supr. State of Ill., 1983. Advisor, Jr. Achievement, Pekin Ill., 1959-64; pres. Boys Club of Pekin, 1969-71; v.p. bd. dirs. Jr. Achievement, 1963-71; pres. Shade Youth Camp, 1975-79, Pekin Leaders of Youth, 1963-65. Served with USMC, 1951-52. Recipient Herbert Hoover award, 1974; Bronze Keystone award Boys' Clubs Am., 1978; named Man of Distinction, Am. Legion, 1965, others. Mem. NAIC (pres., founder Ill. regional council), Inst. Food Tech., Iowa Dairy Industry Club, Tazewell County Farm Bur., Am. Mgmt. Assn., Inst. Internal Auditors, Am. Legion (comdr. 1964). Republican. Apostolic Christian Ch. Clubs: Pekin Celestial Investment (pres. 1981—), Iowa State Alumni, Ill. State Alumni, Giraffe (charter). Patentee in field. Home: 1504 S 7th St Pekin IL 61554 Office: State Fairgrounds Springfield IL 62706

PULIAFITO, CARMEN ANTHONY, ophthalmologist, laser researcher; b. Buffalo, Jan. 5, 1951; s. Dominic F. and Marie A. (Nigro) P.; m. Janet H. Pine, May 19, 1979. AB cum laude, Harvard Coll., 1973, MD magna cum laude, 1978. Diplomate Am. Bd. Ophthalmology. Resident Mass. Eye and Ear Infirmary, Boston, 1979-82, retina fellow, 1982-83; instr. Harvard Med. Sch., Boston, 1983-85, asst. prof., 1985—; vis. scientist MIT Regional Laser Ctr., Cambridge, 1982, asst. prof. health scis. and tech. program, 1987—; mem. staff Mass. Eye and Ear Infirmary, Boston, 1983; bd. dirs. Morse Laser Ctr. Mass. Eye and Ear Infirmary, 1986—. Author (with D. Albert) Foundations of Ophthalmic Pathology, 1979; (with R. Steinert) Principles and Practice of Ophthalmic YAG Laser Surgery, 1984; editor-in-chief jour. Lasers in Surgery and Medicine, 1987—; contbr. 40 sci. articles to profl. jours. Fellow Am. Acad. Ophthalmology, 1983. Roman Catholic. Home: 236 Glen Rd Weston MA 02193 Office: Harvard Med Sch Mass Eye and Ear Infirmary 243 Charles St Boston MA 02114

PULLEN, GEOFFREY PETER, psychiatrist; b. Brighton, England, Dec. 23, 1945; s. Peter Cecil and Daphne Doreen (Shorter) P.; m. Indra Singh, June 10, 1967; children: Katherine Emily Indra, Robert Geoffrey Peter. BA, Cambridge U., Eng., 1968, MA, 1971, MB, 1972, BChir, 1971; Diploma in Psychol. Medicine, Conjoint Bd., London, 1975. Neurosurg. house officer Middlesex Hosp., London, 1971-72; house physician Kettering Hosp., Northamptonshire, Eng., 1972; psychiat. sr. house officer Shenley Hosp., London, 1972-73; registrar Middlesex Hosp., London, 1974, Ealing Child Guidance Clinic, London, 1975; sr. registrar Fulbourn Hosp., Cambridge, Eng., 1975-79; cons. psychiatrist Dept. Rehab. and Community Care, Oxford, Eng., 1980—; tutor higher psychiat. tng. Oxford Regional Health Authority, 1979-87; regional adviser rehab. Royal Coll. Psychiatrists, 1987—. Contbr. articles to profl. jours. Mem. Assn. Therapeutic Communities (conf. organizer 1980-86), Brit. Psychol. Soc., Royal Coll. Psychiatrists. Home: Fairlight House, Brightwell cum Sotwell, Oxfordshire OX10 ORU, England Office: Littlemore Hosp, Oxford England

PULLING, NATHANIEL H(OSLER), mechanical engineer, educator; b. Boston, Jan. 10, 1920; s. Howard Edward and Mildred Hosler P.; A.B., Brown U., 1942; Ph.D., Harvard U., 1951; m. Lillian E. Donnelly, Sept. 9, 1955. Chief optics subsect. U.S. Naval Bur. Ordnance, 1945-46; research fellow Harvard U., 1950-52; devel. engr. Gen. Electric Co., Lynn, Mass., 1953-61, product and bus. planner, 1962-66; project dir. automotive safety Liberty Mut. Ins. Co., Hopkinton, Mass., 1967—; adj. prof. mech. engring. Worcester (Mass.) Poly. Inst., 1973—. Served to lt. comdr. USNR, 1942-46. Registered profl. engr., Mass. Mem. ASME, Soc. Automotive Engrs., Transp. Research Bd., Am. Assn. Automotive Medicine, Profl. Photographers Am., Photog. Resource Center (Boston), Cape Mus. Fine Arts, Human Factors Soc., Creative Arts Ctr. Cape Mus. Fine Arts, Photog. Soc. Am. Episcopalian. Club: Boston Camera. Lodge: Rotary. Contbr. articles to profl. jours.; patentee in field. Home: 11 Manito Rd PO Box 608 East Orleans MA 02643

PULS, RICHARD JOHN, physician, educator; b. Ft. Worth, July 14, 1925; s. George and Ada (Reinhardt) P.; m. Mary Janina Rentschler, June 11, 1950; children: Alan R., Gloria R., Larry E. BA, U. Tex., 1947; MD, Washington U., St. Louis, 1950; postgrad. So. Meth. U., 1962-68, U. Tex.-Dallas, 1970-75. Diplomate Am. Bd. Internal Medicine; lic. investment advisor. Intern, Wesley Meml. Hosp., Chgo., 1950-51; resident Univ. Hosp., Columbus, Ohio, 1951-53, Parkland Hosp., Dallas, 1953-54; practice medicine specializing in internal medicine, Dallas, 1954—; med. dir. Procter & Gamble Mfg. Co., 1958—, Northhaven Nursing Home, Dallas, 1976-82; clin. asst. prof. medicine U. Tex. Health Sci. Ctr., Dallas, 1977—; physician advisor Tex. Med. Found., 1985—. Bd. dirs. Dallas All Sports Assn., 1975—. Served with USNR, 1942-44, 46-50. Mem. ACP, Am. Soc. Internal Medicine, AMA, Tex. Med. Assn. (alt. del. 1982-86, del. 1986—), Dallas County Med. Soc., Dallas Internist Club. Republican. Presbyterian (elder 1980-82). Contbr. articles to profl. jours. Home: 6849 Greenwich Ln Dallas TX 75230 Office: 8215 Westchester St Suite 327 Dallas TX 75225

PULVERMACHER, LOUIS C., lawyer; b. N.Y.C., May 10, 1928; s. Joseph and Lucille Lottie (Meyer) P.; grad. Horace Mann Sch., 1945; A.B., Franklin and Marshall Coll., 1948; J.D., U. Pa., 1951; m. Jo Kuchai, May 17, 1974; children—Lewis, Andrew, Stanley, Robin. Admitted to N.Y. bar, 1955; partner law firm Port & Pulvermacher, N.Y.C., 1956-68; sole practice law Louis C. Pulvermacher P.C., 1968—. Served with USNR, 1951-54. Mem. Found. Fed. Bar Council (pres.), Fed. Bar Council (chmn. bd. dirs.), ABA (co-chmn. econs. law), N.Y. State Bar Assn. Jewish. Office: 598 Madison Ave New York NY 10022

PUN, PATTLE PAK TOE, microbiologist, educator; b. Hong Kong, Sept. 30, 1946; s. Sak-Chi and Ngan-Chu (Kwan) P.; m. Gwen Yam Qun, Aug. 22, 1970; children: Patrick Hank, Benjamin Tim. B.S. in Chemistry with high honors and distinction, San Diego State U., 1969; M.A. in Biology, SUNY-Buffalo, 1972, Ph.D., 1974; M.A. in Theology, Wheaton Coll., 1985. Resident assoc. div. biol. and med. research Argonne Nat. Lab., Ill., 1974-76; vis. microbiologist U. Ill. Med. Ctr., Chgo., 1980-81, No. Ill. U., DeKalb, 1985, 86, 87, 88; vis. scientist Am. Critical Care Inc., 1984; prof. biology Wheaton Coll., Ill., 1973—. Author: Evolution: Nature and Scripture in Conflict? , 1982; contbr. articles to profl. jours. Research Corp. grantee, 1975, 76, 79, 80, 82, 83; NSF grantee, 1985, 86, 87, 88. Fellow Am. Sci. Affiliation; mem. Am. Soc. Microbiology, N.Y. Acad. Sci. Mem. Chinese Bible Ch. Oak Park. Subspecialties: Microbiology; Genetics and genetic engineering (biology). Current work: Cloning of the morphogenesis genes of Bacillus megaterium and its genetic and biochemical analysis. Office: Dept Biology Wheaton Coll Wheaton IL 60187

PUNDT, RICHARD ARTHUR, lawyer, inventor; b. Iowa City, Iowa, Apr. 18, 1944; s. Arthur Herman and Johanna Celeste (Pasterik) P.; B.A., State U. Iowa, 1966; J.D., Drake U., 1969; m. Joyce Kay Schoenfelder, Dec. 1, 1968; children—Vincent Arthur, Jennifer Johanna, Heather Ann. Temporary claims dep. Iowa Employment Security Commn., 1968-69; admitted to Iowa bar, 1969; staff atty. Polk County Legal Aid, Office Econ. Opportunity, 1969-71; spl. agt. FBI, 1969-71; prin. Richard A. Pundt Law Office; dir. Cedar Rapids Profl. Football Corp., 1972-73, pres., 1972-73. Exec. dir. Iowans for Rockefeller, 1968; exec. dir. Polk County Republican Com. 1968-69; mem. Linn County Rep. Central Com., 1972-78; chmn. Linn County Rep. party, 1977-78; asst. atty. Linn County, 1972-76. Mem. Am., Iowa, Linn County bar assns., Metro Athletic Assn. (dir. 1976—). Roman Catholic. Club: Sertoma. Home: 711 Grant Wood Dr SE Cedar Rapids IA 52403-2922

PUNGOR, ERNO, chemist, educator; b. Vasszecseny, Hungary, Oct. 30, 1923; s. Jozsef and Franciska (Faller) P.; diploma of chemistry Pazmany Peter U., Budapest, 1948; Dr.h.c., Tech. U. Vienna, 1983; m. Elisabeth Lang, Oct. 26, 1950; children: Erno, Andras, Katalin; m. Tünde Horváth, Sept. 8, 1984. Asst. prof. Inst. Inorganic and Analytic Chemistry, Eotvos Lorand U., Budapest, 1948-51, reader, 1951-53, assoc. prof., 1953-62; prof. Inst. Analytical Chemistry, U. of Chem. Industry, Veszprem, 1962-70; prof. Inst. for Gen. and Analytical Chemistry, Tech. U. Budapest, 1970—; mem. nat. environ. com. Com. for Nat. Tech. Devel. of Hungary; redwood lectr. English Soc. for Analytic chemistry, 1979. Recipient 3d Robert Boyle gold medal in analytical chemistry, 1986, Talanta Gold medal, 1986. Mem. Internat. Union Pure and Applied Chemistry, Fedn. European Chem. Socs. (chmn. working group of European analysts), Hungarian Chem. Soc. (head analytical group), Hungarian Acad. Sci. (head analytical div.), Czechoslovakian Acad. Scis. (hon. mem. chemistry div.), Austrian Analytical and Microanalytical Soc. (hon.), Finnish Chem. Soc. (corr.), Japanese Analytical Chem. Soc. (hon.). Author: Oscillometry and Conductometry, 1965; Flame Photometry, Theory, 1967. Mem. editorial bd. Acta Chimica Hungarica, 1967—, Periodica Polytech., 1972, Mikrochimica Acta, 1964, Kemiai Kozlemenyek, 1970, Talanta, 1968, Analyst, 1970, Analitica Chimica Acta, 1966, Analytical Letters, 1967, Bull. des Soc. Chimiques Belges, 1974, Bunseki Kegaku, 1981. Mem. adv. bd. Analytical Chemistry, 1985-88. Contbr. over 300 articles to profl. jours. Home: 4 Meredek, 1112 Budapest Hungary Office: Tech U Budapest, 1 Gellert ter, 1111 Budapest Hungary

PURCELL, DALE, institute executive, educator; b. Baxley, Ga., Oct. 20, 1919; s. John Groce and Agnes (Moody) P.; m. Edna Jean Rowell, Aug. 2, 1944; children: David Scott, Steven Dale, Pamela Jean; m. Mary Louise G. Gerlinger, Aug. 26, 1962; stepchildren: Amelia Allerton, Jon Allerton. B.A., U. Redlands, 1948, M.A., 1949; postgrad., Northwestern U., 1951-52; LL.D., Lindenwood Colls., 1974. Topographer U.S. E.D., 1939; U.S. counter-intelligence agt. 1940-42; asso. prof. Ottawa U., 1953-54, asst. to pres., 1954-58; gen. sec. Earlham Coll., 1958-61; dir. devel. U. So. Fla., 1961-63; exec. dir. Cancer Research Center, Columbia, Mo., 1963-65; pres. Dale Purcell Assocs., Inc., 1965—, Westminster Coll., Fulton, Mo., 1973-76; dir. plans and resources Am. Sports Medicine Inst., Birmingham, 1987—; cons. Hughston Sports Medicine Found., Columbus, Ga., Berry Coll., Mt. Berry, Ga., Hope Coll., Holland, Mich., William Woods Coll., Fulton, Mo., Eureka (Ill.) Coll., Brescia Coll., Owensboro, Ky., Cranbrook Instns., Bloomfield Hills, Mich., Penrose Hosp., Colorado Springs, Colo., Northwestern Coll., Orange City, Iowa, Centro Médico Docente, Caracas, Venezuela, Wayland Acad., Beaver Dam, Wis., Central Coll., Pella, Iowa, U. Stirling, Scotland, U. Ottawa, Ont., Can., Washington & Lee U., Taylor U., Upland, Ind., Menninger Clinic, Topeka, Ill. Wesleyan U., Bloomington, Cox Med. Center, Springfield, Mo., Nat. Council Family Relations, Mpls., Albert Schweitzer Center, Great Barrington, Mass., Stephens Coll., Columbia, Mo., Hist. Savannah Found., Ga., 1965-86; cons. Hughston Sports Medicine Found., Columbus, Ga., Berry Coll., Mt. Berry, Ga., Hope Coll., Holland, Mich., William Woods Coll., Fulton, Mo., Eureka (Ill.) Coll., Brescia Coll., Owensboro, Ky., Cranbrook Insts., Bloomfield Hills, Mich., Penrose Hosp., Colorado Springs, Colo., Northwestern Coll., Orange City, Iowa, Centro Medico Docente, Caracas, Venezuela, Wayland Acad., Beaver Dam, Wis., Cen. Coll., Pella, Iowa, U. Stirling, Scotland, U. Ottawa, Ont., Can., Washington & Lee U., Taylor U., Upland, Ind., Menninger Clinic, Topeka, Kans., Ill. Wesleyan U., Blommington, Cox Med. Ctr., Springfield, Mo., Nat. Council Family Relations, Mpls., Albert Schweitzer Ctr., Great Barrington, Mass., Stephens Coll., Columbia, Mo., Hist. Savannah Found., Ga. Served to capt. USMCR, 1942-46, 52-53. Decorated D.F.C., Air medal with 4 gold stars, Bronze Star, Purple Heart; recipient Disting. Achievement award Berry Coll., 1974, medal Pres. of China, medal Pres. of Korea. Mem. Pi Kappa Delta. Presbyn. (elder 1964—). Clubs: Saugahatchee (Auburn), St. Louis (Clayton), Univ. (St. Louis and N.Y.C.). Address: 2408 Heritage Dr Opelika AL 36801 also: 120 Belden St Falls Village CT 06031

PURCELL, EDWARD MILLS, physics educator; b. Taylorville, Ill., Aug. 30, 1912; s. Edward A. and Mary Elizabeth (Mills) P.; m. Beth C. Busser, Jan. 22, 1937; children: Dennis W., Frank B. B.S. in Elec. Engring, Purdue U., 1933, D. Engring. (hon.), 1953; Internat. Exchange student, Technische Hochschule, Karlsruhe, Germany, 1933-34; A.M., Harvard U., 1935, Ph.D., 1938. Instr. physics Harvard U., 1938-40, asso. prof., 1946-49, prof. physics, 1949-58, Donner prof. sci., 1958-60, Gerhard Gade Univ. prof., 1960-80, emeritus, 1980—; sr. fellow Soc. of Fellows, 1949-71; group leader Radiation Lab., MIT, 1941-45. Contbg. author: Radiation Lab. series, 1949, Berkeley Physics Course, 1965; contbr. sci. papers on nuclear magnetism, radio astronomy, astrophysics, biophysics. Mem. Pres.'s Sci. Advisory Com., 1957-60, 62-65. Co-winner Nobel prize in Physics, 1952; recipient Oersted medal Am. Assn. Physics Tchrs., 1968, Nat. Medal of Sci., 1980, Harvard medal, 1986. Mem. Am. Philos. Soc., Nat. Acad. Sci., Phys. Soc., Am. Acad. Arts and Scis. Office: Harvard Univ Dept of Physics Cambridge MA 02138

PURCELL, GEORGE RICHARD, artist, postal employee; b. Clayton, N.Y., May 4, 1921; s. George Thomas and Katherine Eileen (Eagan) P.; B.S., Niagara (N.Y.) U., 1947; postgrad. Syracuse (N.Y.) U., 1952-53, 55-56; m. Mary Sutter, Apr. 3, 1961. With Eagan Real Estate, Syracuse, 1948-49; claims interviewer N.Y. State Div. Unemployment Ins., 1949-50, 52; with U.S. Postal Service, Syracuse, 1957—, cert. classifier of mails, 1975-77, with registry dept., 1977—; tutor philosophy, 1971—; exhibited in Central N.Y. Art Open, 1981, Drake Gallery, Fayetteville, N.Y., 1982, Assoc. Artists Gallery, Syracuse, 1983, Fayetteville Art Festival, 1984, Recreation Generation Art Exhibit, 1982—, DeWitt (N.Y.) Library, 1986—. Founder, pres. Syracuse chpt. Cath. Med. Mission Bd., 1973-76, rep., 1976—; mem. Cath. Near-East Welfare Assn., Book Mission Prgram. Served with U.S. Army, 1943-46. N.Y. State War Service scholar, 1955. Fellow Internat. Biog. Assn. (life); mem. Am. Cath. Philos. Soc. (assoc.), Am. Biog. Inst. (life assoc., research bd. advisors nat. div.), Internat. Soc. Neoplatonic Studies. Roman Catholic. Home: 1 Gregory Pkwy Syracuse NY 13214

PURCELL, STEVEN RICHARD, international management consultant, engineer, economist; b. N.Y.C., Mar. 1, 1927; s. Jacob Louis and Bertha Purcell. B.Mech. and Indsl. Engring., NYU, 1950; M.S. in Indsl. Engring., Columbia U., 1951; Ed.M., Harvard U., 1968. Registered profl. engr., Can. Lectr. engring. NYU Coll. Engring., N.Y.C., 1948-50; gen. mgr. Dapol Plastics Co., Inc., Boston, 1956-58; gen. div. mgr. Am. Cyanamid Co., Sanford, Maine, 1958-61; sr. prin. Purcell & Assocs., mgmt. cons., N.Y.C., 1961-66; prof., div. chmn. Bristol Coll., Fall River, Mass., 1966-68; assoc. dean grad. faculty adminstrv. studies York U., Toronto, Ont., Can., 1969-71; chief economist Dept. Manpower and Immigration, Ottawa, Ont., Can., 1970-71; cons. Treasury Bd., Ottawa, Ont., Can., 1971-72; dir. urban and environ. policy Ministry of State for Urban Affairs Internat. Activities, Ottawa, Ont., Can., 1973-74; mem. com. on challenges of modern soc. NATO, Ottawa, Ont., Can., 1973-74; mem. sci., econ. policy com. OECD, UN, Ottawa, Ont., Can., 1973-74; prof. Grad. Sch. Bus. Adminstrn. and Econs., Algonquin Coll., Ottawa, Ont., Can., 1974-76; advisor, cons. House of Commons, 1976-77; sr. prin. Purcell & Assocs., Washington, 1977-80; exec. dir. nat. coastal zone mgmt. adv. com. U.S. Dept. Commerce, NOAA, Washington, 1980-81; pres. Purcell & Assocs., internat. mgmt. counsel, Washington, 1981—; professorial lectr. Northeastern U. Grad. Sch. Bus. Adminstrn., Boston, 1953-56, U. Toronto, 1968-69, George Washington U. Grad. Sch. Bus. Adminstrn., Washington, 1979; vis. prof. Rensselaer Poly. Inst. Advanced Mgmt. Program, 1967, U. Ottawa Grad. Sch. Bus. Adminstrn., 1971-74; lectr. Council for Internat. Progress in Mgmt., N.Y.C., 1960, Royal Bank Can. Mgmt. Assn., Toronto, Ont., 1970; corp. appointment cons. Harvard U., Cambridge, Mass., 1967-68; cons. Govt. Venezuela, 1967-68, Can. Inst. Bankers, Toronto, 1969-70; internat. sr. adviser NASA, 1985-86, mem. nat. adv. bd. Ctr. for Nat. Policy; dir. Rental Resource Corp., 1986—. Contbr. articles on indsl. orgn., sci. policy and fin. to profl. jours. Served to lt. AC, USNR, 1943-46. Mem. UN Assn., Soc. for Advancement of Mgmt. (pres. 1949-50, leadership award 1950), Tau Beta Pi, Alpha Pi Mu (v.p. 1949-50). Clubs: Columbia U. (Washington) (trustee 1982-84, chmn., sr. trustee 1984-85); Harvard. Home and Office: 12904 Old Chapel Pl Bowie MD 20715

PURCHASE, FLOYD STACEY, transit company executive; b. Newark, Oct. 14, 1928; s. Floyd Stacey and Mae Lucinda (Gilpin) P.; student Drakes Bus. Coll., 1949, Rutgers U., 1950; cert. expert accident investigation Dept. Transp.; m. Joan J. Jackson, Aug. 28, 1953 (div.), m. Ruth Reed Oct. 6, 1984; children—Barbara Ann, Christine. Div. claims mgr. Public Service Coordinated Transport, Maplewood, N.J., 1948-70; dir. safety Transport of N.J., Maplewood, 1970-72, dir. safety, tng. and employment EEO and pensions, 1972-80; dir. operational tng. and safety N.J. Transit, Maplewood, 1980—; tchr. Middlesex Coll., U. Ind., U.S. Dept. Transp. Safety Inst.; cons. in field. Bd. dirs. Alexian Bros. Hosp. Found., Elizabeth, N.J., 1968-70. Served to capt. Signal Corps, U.S. Army, 1948-69. Recipient United Way Community Service award, 1981; N.J. Soc. Prevention of Blindness cert. of appreciation. Mem. Am. Soc. Safety Engrs. (past pres.), Internat. Hazard Control Mgrs. Assn. Republican. Contbr. articles to profl. jours. Home: Apt 106 Sumner Ave W Roselle Park NJ 07204 Office: 180 Boyden Ave Maplewood NJ 07040

PURDY, WILLIAM MARSHALL, consulting services company executive, mechanical engineer; b. Fall River, Mass., Aug. 23, 1940; s. William Marshall and Irma Josephine (Hofling) P.; m. Caroline Bascom, Sept. 2, 1967; children: Steven J., Rachel. BMechE, Southeastern Mass. U., 1964; MBA, Harvard U., 1975. Systems engr. Naval Sea Systems Command, Washington, 1964-68, project engr. nuclear submersible NR-1, 1968-70, non-nuclear design engr., mgr. Los Angeles class nuclear submarine, 1970-73; European programs mgr. Submarine Signal div. Ratheon Corp., Portsmouth, R.I., 1975-77; v.p., gen. mgr. def. div. Am. Mgmt. Systems, Inc., Arlington, Va., 1977—; chmn. bd. AMS Tech. Systems, Inc., Arlington, 1984—. Club: Megansett Yacht (bd. dirs. 1985—). Home: 2804 N Harrison St Arlington VA 22207 Office: Amer Mgmt Systems Inc 1777 N Kent St Arlington VA 22209

PURI, AJIT S., physician, health service administrator; b. Patiala, Punjab, India, Feb. 17, 1941; s. Dewan K.S. and Sushila Devi P.; m. Alka Kapoor, Feb. 8, 1972; 1 son, J.S. Puri. M.B.B.S., Govt. Med. Coll., Patiala, 1964, M.D., 1972, postgrad. tng. in allergy and immunology U. Delhi, 1975. Sr. research fellow Govt. Med. Coll., Patiala, 1966-67; intern Govt. R.H. Patiala, 1964-65, house physician, 1965-66; research officer in medicine Govt. Med. Coll., 1967-72; practice medicine specializing in immunology vascular medicine, allergy and neurology, Patiala; asst. dir., head medicine dept. and labs. Central Research Inst., Patiala, 1972-76; head Univ. Health Ctr. Punjabi U., Patiala, 1976-83, chief med. officer, 1983—; vis. mem. faculty Gen. Hosp., Newcastle U., Eng., 1982. Author: Warning Signals of Diseases, 1977; For Diabetics-A Manual, 1979; Hypertension-A Silent Killer, 1978; contbr. articles to profl. jours. Fellow Internat. Coll. Angiology, Indian Coll. Alergy and Applied Immunology; mem. Indian Med. Assn. (hon. gen. sec. 1974-75), Assn. Physicians of India, Indian Assn. Sports Medicine, Geriatric Soc. of India (founder-mem.) Lodge: Lions (hon. joint sec. 1972-73). Home: Puri Rd, Patiala 147 001, India

PURI, RAJENDRA KUMAR, business and tax consultant; b. Hoshiarpur, Punjab, India, Dec. 22, 1932; came to U.S., 1965, naturalized, 1969; s. Harbans Lal and Satya Vati (Jerath) P.; children—Neena, Veena, Ram. BS, Agra U., 1952; diploma in Russian Lang. and Lit., U. Delhi, 1958; BA, U. Wash., 1968, MBA, 1969; MS in Taxation, Golden Gate U., 1982. Customs officer Govt. of India, New Delhi, 1955-60; asst. treas. Merc. Bank Ltd., New Delhi, 1960-65; mem. staff Peat, Marwick, Mitchell & Co., C.P.A.s, Seattle, 1969-70; state exminer State of Wash., 1970-72, asst. supervising state examiner, 1972-74, supervising state examiner, 1974-77; sr. internal auditor Lockheed Missiles and Space Co., Sunnyvale, Calif., 1977-79, sci. programming analyst, 1979-80, data processing specialist, 1980-84, sci. programming specialist, 1984-88. Del., Wash. State Rep. Conv., 1976, Snohomish County Rep. Conv., 1976; spl. advisor U.S. Congl. Adv. Bd., 1982-83. Mem. Am. Inst. CPA's. Home: 2608 Hunlac Cove Round Rock TX 78681

PURI, SHAMLAL, news agency executive, editor; b. Nangli, India, July 4, 1951; arrived in Eng., 1975; s. Hussan Chand and Lajya (Devi) P.; m. Manjula Puri, Apr. 26, 1979; 1 child, Samir. BA with honors, Punjab U., Chandigarh, 1973. Corr. Tanzania Standard Newspapers, 1973-75; asst. editor India Weekly, London, 1975-77; sr. editor World Times, London, 1977-79; dir. Harambee, London, 1980-87; mng. editor Newslink Africa, London, 1983—; mng. dir. Newslink Africa Ltd., London, 1984—; bd. dirs. Harambee P.R. Assocs., London. Author: The Twilight, 1976, Best of Matatu, 1987, Press in East Africa, 1988; contbr. articles to profl. jours. Mem. Tanganyika African Nat. Union, Kigoma, 1970. Mem. Nat. Union Journalists, Pan African Orgn. Writers and Journalists. Mem. Revolutionary Party of Tanzania. Hindu. Office: Newslink Africa Ltd, 76 Shoe Ln, Fleet St, London Internat Press Centre, Suite 411, London EC4A 3JB, England

PURIS, MARTIN FORD, advertising agency executive; b. Chgo., Feb. 22, 1939; s. Martin and Virginia Lee (Farmer) P.; m. Beverly M. Bokerman, May 25, 1964; children—Kimberly Mayo, Jason Patterson. DePauw U., 1961. With Campbell-Ewald Co., N.Y.C., 1962-64; with Young & Rubicam, Inc., N.Y.C., 1964-66; v.p. Carl Ally, Inc., N.Y.C., 1966-74; pres., chief exec. officer Ammirati & Puris, Inc., N.Y.C., 1974—, co-chmn., chief exec. officer, 1986—; bd. dirs. The Upward Fund Inc., The Boase Massimi Pollitt Partnership, Ltd. Mem. Am. Assn. Advt. Agys., Inc. (gov.). Recipient awards Art Dirs. Club N.Y., Copy Club N.Y., Cannes Film Festival. Democrat. Roman Catholic. Clubs: Larchmont Yacht, N.Y. Yacht, Nantucket Yacht. also: Nantucket MA 02554 Office: Ammirati & Puris Inc 100 Fifth Ave New York NY 10011

PURSEL, HAROLD MAX, SR., mining engineer, civil engineer, architectural engineer.; b. Fruita, Colo., Sept. 15, 1921; s. Harold Maurice and Viola Pearl (Wagner) P.; B.S. in Civil Engring., U. Wyo., 1950; m. Virginia Anna Brady, May 6, 1950; children—Harold Max, Leo William, Dawn Allen, Helen Virginia, Viola Ruth. Asst. univ. architect U. Wyo., 1948-50; with Sharrock & Pursel, Contractors, 1951-55; owner Max Pursel, Earthwork Constrn., 1955-59; project engr. Farson (Wyo.) Irrigation Project, 1960-61; owner Wyo. Builders Service, Casper, 1962-66; head dept. home improvement Gamble Stores, Rawlins, Wyo., 1967; resident work instr. Casper (Wyo.) Job Corps Conservation Center, 1968; P.M. coordinator Lucky Mc Uranium Mine, Riverton, Wyo., 1969-80; constrn. insp. U.S. Bur. Reclamation, 1983—; cons. freelance heavy and light constrn., 1984—. Served with U.S. Army, 1942-45. Mem. Nat. Rifle Assn., Internat. Platform Assn., Mensa. Lodges: Eagles, Masons, Shriners. Exptl. research with log, timber and frame constrn. in conjunction with residential applications. Home: PO Box 572 Riverton WY 82501

PURSELL, JULIE CROW, corporate communications administrator, media consultant, journalist; b. Nashville, Feb. 26, 1936; d. William Russell and Eleanor Farrell (Weber) Crow; m. William Whitney Pursell, Apr. 26, 1965; children—Ellen Pursell Spicer, Margaret, Laura, Bill, 1 stepchild, Sharon. Student Vanderbilt U., 1953-55, Peabody Coll., 1958-60, U. Tenn., 1961-62. Reporter, feature writer, The Tennessean, Nashville, 1958-65; freelance writer, Nashville, 1965-73; art-home editor Nashville Banner, 1973-80; asst. to mayor City of Nashville, 1980-84; asst. to chmn. Earl Swensson Assocs., Nashville, 1984-86; dir. corp. communications, Yearwood Johnson Stanton & Crabtree, Inc., 1986—. Editor: Symphony Guild newsletter, 1966-68; contbg. writer, editorial bd. Tenn. Architect mag., 1985—; contbg. writer, Nashville! mag. Dir. publicity Vietnam Veterans Day Salute, Nashville, 1981; mem. adv. bd. Nashville Pub. TV, 1981—; dir. publicity Metro Courthouse Day, Nashville, 1982, Historic Belmont Assn., 1988; mem. adv. bd. Belmont Coll. Dept. Communications Arts, Nashville, 1983—; co-dir. grand opening Riverfront Park, Nashville, 1983. Mem. Nashville C. of C. (mem. cultural affairs com. 1984-86), Pub. Relations Soc. Am. (bd. dirs. 1984, 86), Tenn. State Mus. Assn. Inc., AIA (affiliate mem.), Assn. for Preservation of Tenn. Antiquities, Kappa Delta. Roman Catholic. Clubs: Exchange of Nashville; Savage of London (affiliate). Avocations: art; historic preservation; urban planning; travel; history. Home: 895 S Curtiswood Ln Nashville TN 37204 Office: Earl Swensson Assocs Inc 2100 W End Ave Nashville TN 37203

PURUGANAN, HONORIO MADAMBA, general practioner; b. Dingras, Ilocos Norte, Philippines, Aug. 6, 1924; s. Honorio S. Puruganan and Victoria (Antero) Madamba; m. Eva Resultan, Jan. 2, 1957; children: George, Victoria Gay, Dominic, Hubert. AA, U. Santo Tomas, Manila, 1948, Dr. in Medicine, 1953. Practice gen. medicine Quezon City, Philippines, 1953-55, Dingras, 1956-66; rural health physician Dept. Health, Marcos, Ilocos Norte, 1967-76; mcpl. health officer Dept. Health, Dingras, 1976-86; clinic physician Ilocos Norte Electric Coop., Dingras, 1982—; coordinator Mpcl. Rural Services, Dingras, 1977-79, Primary Health Care Com., Dingras, 1981-86; mem. Mcpl. Nutrition Com., Dingras, 1976-82; pres. Farmers Coop. Mktg., Dingras, 1958-62; chmn. bd. dirs. Dingras Water Dist., 1987—; conducted clinics and various programs in Ilocos Norte, 1957—. Mem. Mcpl. Devel. Council, Dingras, 1977-82, Mcpl. Sports Devel., Dingras, 1978-82, Dingras Council Elders, 1979-81; active United Way Philippines Inc.; elected councilor Barangay Madamba Council, Dingras, 1956-58, Dingras Mcpl. Council, 1964-66; pres. St. Joseph Inst. PTA, Dingras, 1978-

79; gen. dir. Town Fiesta Directorate, Marcos, 1970, Dingras, 1981. Served to 1st lt. Philippines Guerillas, 1941-45. Recipient Parish award Diocese Laoag, 1958, Cert. Appreciation Rotary Club, 1974, Plaque and Trophy Provincial Nutrition Com., 1978, Cert. Recognition Boy Scouts Philippines, 1981. Mem. Philippine Med. Assn., Ilocos Norte Med. Soc. (past pres. 1983-84, v.p. 1977-79, Recognition award 1986), Vets. Fedn. Philippines, YMCA (life corp.), Assn. Mcpl. Health Officers Philippines (pres. Ilocos Norte chpt. 1981-86, Merit award 1972), U. Santo Tomas Class 1953 Assn. (Distinction award 1973). Roman Catholic. Lodges: KC, Kiwanis. Home: Brgy Madamba, Dingras, Ilocos Norte Philippines Office: Ilocos Norte Electric Coop, Dingras, Ilocos Norte Philippines

PURVIS, JOHN ANDERSON, lawyer; b. Greeley, Colo., Aug. 31, 1942; s. Virgil J. and Emma Lou (Anderson) P.; m. Charlotte Johnson, Apr. 3, 1976; 1 child, Whitney; children by previous marriage—Jennifer, Matt. B.A. cum laude, Harvard U., 1965; J.D., U. Colo., 1968. Bar: Colo. 1968, U.S. Dist. Ct. Colo. 1968, U.S. Ct. Appeals (10th cir.) 1978, U.S. Ct. Claims, 1980. Dep. dist. atty. Boulder, Colo., 1968-69; asst. dir. and dir. legal aid U. Colo. Sch. Law, 1969; assoc. Williams, Taussig & Trine, Boulder, 1969; head Boulder office Colo. Pub. Defender System, 1970-72; assoc. and ptnr. Hutchinson, Black, Hill, Buchanan & Cook, Boulder, 1972-85; ptnr. Buchanan, Gray, Purvis and Schuetze, 1985—; acting Colo. State Pub. Defender, 1978; adj. prof. law U. Colo., 1981, 84-88 , others; lectr. in field. Chmn., Colo. Pub. Defender Commn., 1979—; mem. nominating commn. Colo. Supreme Ct., 1984—; chmn. Boulder County Criminal Justice Com., 1975-81, Boulder County Manpower Council, 1977-78. Recipient Ames award Harvard U., 1964; Outstanding Young Lawyer award Colo. Bar Assn., 1978. Mem. Internat. Soc. Barristers, Colo. Bar Assn., Boulder County Bar Assn., Colo. Trial Lawyers Assn., Am. Trial Lawyers Assn., Trial Lawyers for Pub. Justice. Democrat. Address: 1050 Walnut St Suite 501 Boulder CO 80302

PUSCHKARSKI, THEODOR PETER, design company executive, consultant; b. Vienna, Austria, Oct. 10, 1946; s. Anton and Eleonore (Matys) P.; m. Evelyn Baar, Dec. 9, 1969 (div. 1976); 1 child, Peter; m. jSabine Wegener, Mar. 15, 1977. Architect, Tech. U. Vienna, 1969-74, B.A., 1970. Designer, Vienna, 1964-69, Giffels & Rossetti, Detroit, 1968, Hans Hollein, Puschkarski GMBH, Vienna, 1969; exec. mgr. Klem System Internat., Vienna, 1972—. Patentee in field. Recipient Collection of Indsl. Design award Mus. Modern Art, 1970; Austrian State award Ministry Commerce, 1980, 87. Mem. Austrian Design Inst., First Austrian Bank, Inst. Tech. Conservative Party Austria. Roman Catholic. Club: Wiener Park (Vienna). Avocations: tennis, archery, skiing alpine, Japanese art, arms and armor. Home: Florianigasse St Maria, A3034 Anzbach Austria Office: Puschkarski GmBH, Auhofstrasse 170, A1130 Vienna Austria

PUSEY, MICHAEL REGINALD, sociologist, educator; b. Guilford, Eng., June 26, 1939; s. Alec Jabez Butchers and Suzanne Marie Denise (Fauconnet) P.; m. Vivienne Ruth Kay; children: Cara Jane, Lisa Ellen. Diploma, U. Paris, 1960; BA, U. Melbourne, Australia, 1965; MEd, Harvard U., 1969, EdD, 1972. Tchr. Hobart Matriculation Coll., Tasmania, Australia, 1965-68; cons. Tasmanian Edn. Dept., Hobart, 1972-74; research fellow Australian Nat. U., Canberra, 1974-78; cons. Australian Schs. Commn., Canberra, 1974-78; sr. lectr. U. New South Wales, Sydney, 1978-88, assoc. prof., 1988—; cons. in field. Author: Dynamics of Bureaucracy, 1976, Jürgen Habermas, 1987; editor: Control and Knowledge, 1978. Mem. Australian Schs. Commn., Nat. Innovation Com., Canberra, 1974-78; chmn. Australian Capital Territory Innovation Com., Canberra, 1974-87. Recipient Danta Alighieri Soc. award, 1969, research award Australian Research Grants Com., 1985; Harvard scholar, 1970-71, English Speaking Union grantee, 1969. Mem. Sociology Assn. Australia and N.Z. Club: Harvard (Sydney). Home: 13 Winburn Ave, Kingsford 2032, Australia Office: U New South Wales, PO Box 1, Kensington 2032, Australia

PUSHKAREV, BORIS S., research director, writer; b. Prague, Czechoslovakia, Oct. 22, 1929; came to U.S., 1949, naturalized, 1954; s. Sergei G. and Julie T. (Popov) P.; B.Arch., Yale U., 1954, M.C.P., 1957; m. Iraida Vandellos Legky, Oct. 20, 1973; Instr. city planning Yale U., New Haven, 1957-61; chief planner Regional Plan Assn., N.Y.C., 1961-69, v.p. research, 1969—; adj. assoc. prof. N.Y.U., 1967-79; chmn. Russian Research Found. for Study of Alternatives to Soviet Policy, 1981—. Recipient Nat. Book award (with C. Tunnard), 1964. Mem. Am. Assn. for Advancement of Slavic Studies, editorial bd. POSSEV, Frankfurt, Germany. Russian Orthodox. Author: (with Christopher Tunnard) Man-Made America, 1963; (with Jeffrey Zupan) Urban Space for Pedestrians, 1975, Public Transportation and Land Use Policy, 1977; Urban Rail in America, 1982; contbr. articles to profl. jours. Home: 300 Winston Dr Cliffside Park NJ 07010 Office: 1040 Ave of Americas New York NY 10018

PUTERBAUGH, KATHRYN ELIZABETH, retired corporate executive; b. Denver, Mar. 5, 1924; d. Fredric John and Cora (Zoph) P.; B.A., U. Colo., 1945. Acct., F.J. Puterbaugh & Co., Denver, 1946-49; sec. to Herbert Bayer, artist, designer, 1950-51; acct. Himel's, New Orleans, 1951-53; asst. controller Berol Pen Co., 1953-54; office mgr., controller Garratt-Callahan Co., Millbrae, Calif., 1955-65, corp. treas., 1966-85, also dir. Mem. com. for dedication Millbrae library, 1961; mem. steering com. People-to-People Program, Millbrae, 1962; historian Millbrae Sister City Program, 1962-63; mem. Belmont-San Carlos Human Relations Com., 1968-70; active various community fund drives; judge Bank Am. Youth Achievement Awards, 1973. Mem. Calif. Republicans. LWV. Episcopalian. Clubs: Ski (Bear Valley, Calif.). Lodge: Soroptimist Millbrae-San Bruno (pres. 1965-66, various regional offices, coms.). Home: Box 1429 San Carlos CA 94070

PUTLITZ, UWE, architect; b. Johannesburg, Transvaal, Republic South Africa, Aug. 28, 1950; parents: Walter and Charlotte P. BArch, U. Witwatersrand, Johannesburg, 1975, MS in Bldg., 1985. Architect SABC, Johannesburg, 1976-78; mktg. mgr. Everite, Johannesburg, 1978-79; project mgr. Britz & Scholes, Johannesburg, 1979-81; sr. prin. architect, project mgr. South African Broadcasting Corp., Johannesburg, 1981-87; assoc. MLH & Ptnrs., Johannesburg, 1987—. Author: Brief Formulation in Public Utilities, 1985. Chmn. Carols By Candelight, Johannesburg, 1980, Round Table, Johannesburg, 1981. Mem. Inst. South African Architects, Royal Inst. British Architects, Assn. Arbitrators, Fire Protection Assn., Assn. Facilities Mgmt., Endangered Wildlife Trust (fund raising com.ü. Lutheran. Home: 106-S Ave, Melville, Johannesburg 2092, Republic of South Africa Office: MLH & Partners, PO Box 9188, Johannesburg 2000, Republic of South Africa

PUTMAN-CRAMER, DANIEL GERHARD HENRI, management consultant; b. Velp, The Netherlands, Aug. 26, 1948; s. Adolph H. and Ada (Hugenholtz) P.C.; m. Patricia France Vanriemsdyk, 1984; 1 child, Barbara. MBA, U. Rotterdam, The Netherlands, 1973; LLM, U. Lieden, The Netherlands, 1977. Mgmt. cons. KLM Royal Dutch Airlines, Amsterdam, The Netherlands, 1977-82; mgr. sta. affairs Schiphol Airport, Amsterdam, 1982-87; sr. cons. info. mgmt. M8I/Ptnrs. B.V., Amersfoort, The Netherlands, 1987—. Mem. Dutch Order Mgmt. Cons. Club: Round Table (Amsterdam). Home: Keizersgracht, 327 Amsterdam The Netherlands Office: M8I/Ptnrs BV, PO Box 1179, 3800 BD Amersfoort The Netherlands

PUTNAM, ALLAN RAY, association executive; b. Melrose, Mass., July 16, 1920; s. Carl Eugene and Alice (Atwood); B.S. in Econs., U. Pa., 1942; m. Marion S. Witmer, Aug. 8, 1942; children—Judith H. (Mrs. Martin Kaliski), Robert W., Victoria, Christian. Mem. exec. staff Am. Electroplaters Soc., 1946-49; asst. exec. sec., pub. mag. Tool Engr., Am. Soc. Tool and Mfg. Engrs., 1949-59; mng. dir. Am. Soc. Metals, Metals Park, Ohio, 1959-84, sr. mng. dir., 1983-85; sec.-gen. World Materials Congress, 1986—; pres. Nat. Assn. Exhibit Mgrs., 1955, Council Engring. and Sci. Soc. Execs., 1958; mgr. Am. Soc. Metals Found. Edn. and Research, 1963-85. Bd. govs. Cape Cod Conservatory of Music and Arts. Served to capt. USAAF, 1942-46. Mem. Am. Soc. Assn. Execs. (past dir.), Cleve. Conv. and Visitors Bur. (past dir.), Pres.'s Assn., Am. Mgmt. Assn., Metal Properties Council (past dir.), Franklin Inst., Internat., Am., S.E. Asia iron and steel insts., Metals Soc. (London) (hon.), ASTM, Am. Assn. Cost Engrs., Associacao Brasileira de Metais, Italian Soc. of Metallurgy, Chinese Soc. Metals, German Soc. Metals, Australasian Inst. Metals, Am. Nuclear Soc., Cleve. Soc. Assn. Execs., Soc. Automotive Engrs., Soc. Mfg. Engrs., AAAS, Cyrogenic Soc., Soc. for Advancement Materials and Process Engring., Am. Soc. for Engring. Edn., Iron and Steel Inst. Japan (hon.), Nat. Sci. Tchrs. Assn. (life), Metall. Soc., Greater Cleve. Growth Assn., Buckeye Trail Assn. Clubs: Country (Pepper Pike, Ohio); Cleve. Athletic; Appalachian Mountain; Horseshoe Trail; University (Washington); Orleans Yacht. Home: 17 Pride's Path PO Box 1130 Orleans MA 02653 Office: ASM Internat Metals Park OH 44073

PÜTSEP, ERVIN PEETER, hospital architect; b. Võru, Estonia, Apr. 18, 1921; came to Sweden, 1944; s. Karl Immanuel and Adèle (Korrol) P.; m. Liidia Voolaid, Aug. 1, 1946; children: Peeter Ervin, Ann Piret. B.Arch., Royal Inst. Tech., Stockholm, 1950, M.Tech., 1954; D.Tech., Inst. Tech., Lund, Sweden, 1968. Architect, Central Bd. Hosp. Planning, Stockholm, 1954-59; dir. planning Second Teaching Hosp., Stockholm, 1959-61, Karolinska Teaching Hosp., Stockholm, 1961-63; pvt. practice, Stockholm, 1963-86; asst. prof. Nordic Sch. Pub. Health, Gothenburg, Sweden, 1984. Author: Planning of Surgical Centres, 1968, 73; Modern Hospital, 1979; prin. archtl. works include Råcksta Hosp., Stockholm, 1970, Sundsvall Hosp., 1975. British Council fellow U.K., 1956; WHO fellow, U.S., Can., Mexico, 1958. Fellow AIA (hon.). Lutheran.

PUTTFARKEN, THOMAS, art history educator; b. Hamburg, Fed. Republic Germany, Dec. 19, 1943; s. Franz Ferdinand and Traut Dorothea (Bruhn) P.; m. Herma Zimmer, Dec. 19, 1969 (div. 1981); children: Nathalie, Malte Ian; m. Elspeth Crichton Stuart, Oct. 10, 1981. PhD, U. Hamburg, 1969. Lectr. dept. art history U. Hamburg, 1971-74; sr. lectr. dept. art history and theory U. Essex, Eng., 1974-78, chmn., 1974-77, reader, 1978-84, dean of students, 1978-81, dean sch. comparative studies, 1984-86, prof., 1984—, pro vice chancellor social, 1987—. Author: Roger de Piles' Theory of Art, 1985; contbr. articles to profl. jours. Office: U Essex, Wivenhoe Park, Colchester CO4 3SQ, England

PUTTNAM, DAVID TERENCE, British film producer; b. London, Feb. 25, 1941; s. Leonard Arthur and Marie Beatrix Puttnam; m. Patricia Mary Jones, 1961; two children. With advt. firms, 1958-66; photographer, 1966-68; film producer, 1968—. Chmn., Columbia Pictures, New York, 1986-87. Producer films including That'll Be the Day, 1971, Mahler, 1973, Swastica, 1974, Bugsy Malone, 1975, The Duellists (Spl. Jury prize Cannes 1977), 1977, Midnight Express, 1977, Chariots of Fire (three BAFTA awards including Best Film award 1981), Local Hero, 1982, The Killing Fields, 1984, Cal, 1984, Forever Young, 1984, The Frog Prince, 1985, Mr. Love, 1986, Knights and Emeralds, 1986, The Mission, 1986. Bd. dirs. Nat. Film Fin. Corp.; gov. Nat. Film and TV Sch. Recipient four Acad. Awards, Michael Balcon award for Outstanding Contbn. Brit. Film Industry, BAFTA, 1982. Address: 11/15 Queen's Gate Pl Mews, London SW7 5BG, England

PUVEREL, ROLAND MARIE PIERRE, civil engineer; b. Istanbul, Turkey, July 23, 1913; s. Charles Alfred and Marie (Clemenschitsch) P.; m. Suzanne Herve, Aug. 19, 1952. Bachelorship, 1931; student, Civil Service Sch., 1947. Civil engr. French Ministry Def., 1942—; founder, pres. Internat. Confedn. Pub. Services Officers, 1955—, pres. of honor, 1977; rep. ILO Confs., 1962—. Editorialist La Voix des Cadres Fonctionnaires. Mem. Econ. Council France, 1951-54. Served with French Army, 1934-35, 38-42. Decorated Cross of Combat, Golden medal of Labour. Mem. Gen. Fedn. Sr. Officers (pres. 1952—), Sr. Civil Servants Soc. (exec. bd.), Nat. and Local Govt. Officers Assn. U.K. (hon.). Home: 133 Leon Maurice Nordmann, 75013 Paris France also: La Dragonniere, 16 ave Paul Doumer, 06190 Roquebrune Cap Martin France

PUZO, MARIO, author; b. N.Y.C., Oct. 15, 1920; married; children: Anthony, Joey, Dorothy, Virginia, Eugene. Ed., Columbia U., New Sch. for Social Research. Lit. reviewer various mags, former civil service employee, former editor Male mag. Author: The Dark Arena, 1955, The Fortunate Pilgrim, 1965, The Runaway Summer of Davie Shaw, 1966, The Godfather, 1969, The Godfather Papers and Other Confessions, 1972, Inside Las Vegas, 1977, Fools Die, 1979, The Sicilian, 1984; film screenplays The Godfather, 1972, The Godfather, Part II, 1974, Earthquake, 1974, Superman, 1979, Superman II, 1980. Recipient Acad. awards for best screenplay with Francis Ford Coppola The Godfather, 1972, The Godfather, Part II, 1974. Address: care CP Putnam and Sons 200 Madison Ave New York NY 10016 *

PYKE, THOMAS NICHOLAS, JR., government science and engineering administrator; b. Washington, July 16, 1942; s. Thomas Nicholas and Pauline Marie (Pingitore) P.; m. Carol June Renville, June 22, 1968; children—Christopher Renville, Alexander Nicholas. B.S., Carnegie Inst. Tech., 1964; M.S.E., U. Pa., 1965. Electronic engr. Nat. Bur. Standards, Gaithersburg, Md., 1964-69, chief computer networking sect., 1969-75, chief computer systems engring. div., 1975-79, dir. ctr. for computer systems engring., 1979-81, dir. ctr. programming sci. and tech., 1981-86; asst. adminstr. for satellite and info. services NOAA, Washington, 1986—; organizer profl. computer confs., 1970—; mem. Presdl. Adv. Com. on Networking Structure and Function, 1980; program chmn. Interagy. com. on Info. Resources Mgmt., 1983-84, bd. dirs., 1984-87, vice chmn. 1986-87; speaker in field. Editorial bd. Computer Networks Jour., 1976-86; contbr. articles to profl. jours. Bd. dirs. Glebe Commons Assn., Arlington, Va., 1976-79, v.p., 1977-79; chmn. Student Congress, Carnegie Inst. Tech., 1963-64; mem. Task Force on Computers in Schs., Arlington, 1982-85; pres. PTA, Arlington, 1983-84. Recipient Silver medal Dept. Commerce, 1973, award for exemplary achievement in pub. adminstrn. William A. Jump Found., 1975, 76; Westinghouse scholar Carnegie Inst. Tech., Pitts., 1960-64; Ford Found. fellow U. Pa., Phila., 1964-66. Fellow Washington Acad. Scis. (Engring. Sci. award 1974); mem. Am. Fedn. Info. Processing Socs. (bd. dirs. 1974-76), IEEE (sr. mem.), Computer Soc. of IEEE (bd. govs. 1971-73, 75-77, vice chmn. tech. com. on personal computing 1982-86, chmn. 1986-87), AAAS, Assn. Computing Machinery, Sigma Xi, Eta Kappa Nu, Omicron Delta Kappa, Pi Kappa Alpha (chpt. v.p. 1963-64). Episcopalian. Office: NOAA Nat Environ Satellite Data and Info Service Washington DC 20233

PYLE, GERALD FREDRIC, medical geographer, educator; b. Akron, Ohio, Dec. 22, 1937; s. Russell Roy and Ruth (Martin) P.; m. Carole Wood, Aug. 29, 1959; children—Eric, Frances. BA, Kent State U., 1963; MA, U. Chgo., 1968, PhD, 1970. Cartographer, Rand McNally, Chgo., 1962-64; research geographer Ency. Britannica, Chgo., 1964-65; cartographer U. Chgo., 1965-70; asst. to full prof. U. Akron, Ohio, 1970-80; prof. geography and earth sci. U. N.C., Charlotte, 1980—; vis. fellow Macquarie U., Sydney, Australia, 1988; research dir. Center for Urban Studies, Akron, 1973-80; tech. dir. Akron Area Census File, 1974-80. Author: Heart Disease, Cancer and Stroke in Chicago, 1971; Spatial Dynamics of Crime, 1974; Applied Medical Geography, 1979; Diffusion of Influenza: Patterns and Paradigms, 1986. Sr. editor Med. Geography, Social Sci. and Medicine, 1977-84. Grantee Ill. Regional Med., 1969, Law Enforcement Adminstrn. Agy., 1972, 74, NSF, 1979, 82, Nat. Geog. Soc., 1988. Fellow Ohio Acad. Sci.; mem. Assn. Am. Geographers, Nat. Council Geog. Edn. Democrat. Anglican. Current work: Continued research in spatial diffusion of infectious diseases and the location of health care delivery facilities. Subspecialty: Urban geography.

PYLE, LUTHER ARNOLD, lawyer; b. Pontotoc County, Miss., Dec. 5, 1912; s. Thomas Luther and Lillie Dean (Reynolds) P.; m. Elizabeth McWillie Browne, Aug. 9, 1941; children—William A., Robert Bradford, Ben Cameron. LL.B., Cumberland U., 1936, J.D., 1960. Bar: Miss. 1936, D.C. 1974, U.S. Dist. Ct. (no. dist.) Miss. 1936, U.S. Dist. Ct. (so. dist.) Miss. 1946, U.S. Ct. Apls. (5th cir.) 1946, U.S. Ct. Appeals (11th cir.) 1981, U.S. Supreme Ct. 1959. Sole practice, New Albany, Miss., 1936-42; pros. atty. Union County, Miss., 1940-42; assoc. Cameron & Wills, Jackson, Miss., 1946-52; chancellor 5th chancery ct. dist. Miss., 1952-58; ptnr. Watkins, Pyle, Ludlam, Winter & Stennis, Jackson, 1958-80; ptnr. Barnett, Alagia & Pyle, Jackson, 1981-83; sr. ptnr. Pyle, Dreher, Mills & Woods, 1983—; participant World Law Conf., Manila, 1977, Madrid, 1979; bd. dirs. Miss. Bar Commn., 1959-63. Mem. exec. bd. Andrew Jackson council Boy Scouts Am., 1946; bd. govs. Jackson Little Theatre, 1964-67; pres. Jackson Jr. C. of C., 1949; chmn. downtown div. United Givers, Mental Health Assn. Served to lt. col. JAG Corps, U.S. Army, 1942-46. Recipient Silver Beaver award Boy Scouts Am. Fellow Miss. Bar Found.; mem. Fed. Bar Assn., ABA (chmn. continuing legal edn. 1958-74), Am. Judicature Soc. (dir.), Hinds County Bar Assn., Miss. Bar Assn. (chmn. jud. adminstrn. com. 1966-70), U.S. Supreme Ct. Hist. Soc., U.S. C. of C., Jackson C. of C. (dir. 1960-63), Miss. Dept. Res. Officers Assn. (pres. 1950), Am. Legion (past comdr.). Episcopalian. Clubs: University (dir. 1972—), Jackson Country, Annandale Golf. Contbr. articles to profl. jours. Home: 1803 E Northside Dr Jackson MS 39211 Office: Pyle Dreher Mills & Woods 111 E Capitol St Suite 390 Jackson MS 39201

PYLE, RAYMOND JAMES, JR., advertising executive; b. Oak Park, Ill., Jan. 15, 1932; s. Raymond James and Bessie Inez (Osborn) P.; student U. Wis., 1951-56, U. Notre Dame, 1968; student mgmt. U. South Fla., 1972; m. Mabel Lee Freeman, June 28, 1952; children—Dale, David, Steven, Carol Lynn. Sales rep. London Wholesale Hardware, 1957-58; sales rep. Martin Outdoor Advt., 1958-65, gen. mgr., 1965-66, v.p., 1966-69, pres., 1969-76; Fla. regional mgr., v.p. Foster & Kleiser div. Metromedia, Tampa, Fla., 1976-82, sr. v.p., 1982-86, v p., gen. mgr., Patrick Media Group, 1986—; bd. fellows, counselor U. Tampa, 1970-77. bd. dirs. Town and Country Med. Ctr., Hall of Fame Bowl Assn., Gulf Ridge Council Boy Scouts of Am. Mem. Outdoor Advt. Assn. Fla. (pres.; Disting. Service award 1981). Inst. Outdoor Advt. S.E. U.S.A. (treas.), Tampa Advt. Fedn. (past pres.; Advt. Man of Year 1969, Silver Medal award 1979-80), Sales and Mktg. Execs. Tampa (past pres. 1970, Sales and Mktg. Exec. Top Mgmt. award 1982, Man of the Year, 1970), Pi Sigma Epsilon. Democrat. Baptist. Clubs: Centre, Rotary (Tampa); Feather Sound Golf and Tennis; Masons. Home: 1206 S Suffolk Dr Tampa FL 33629 Office: 5555 Ulmerton Rd Clearwater FL 34620

PYLE, ROBERT NOBLE, public relations executive; b. Wilmington, Del., Oct. 23, 1926; s. Joseph Lybr and LaVerne Ruth (Noble) P.; m. Claire Thoron; children: Robert Noble Jr., Mark C., Nicholas A., Sarah L. B.A., Dickinson Coll., 1948; postgrad., Wharton Sch., U. Pa., 1949, U. Minn. Pres. Robert N. Pyle & Assos., Inc., Wilmington, 1949-52; adminstrv. asst. to U.S. Congress, Washington, 1952-63; bus. and polit. cons. and lobbyist Robert N. Pyle & Assoc., Washington, 1970—; pres. Ind. Bakers Assn., 1981—; dir. Barlow Corp., Small Bus. Legis. Council; mem. commodity adv. group USDA. Contbr. numerous articles to profl. jours.; reporter covering Nurnburg Trials, Paris Peace Conf. for, Stars & Stripes, Europe, 1946. Part-time field man Republican Nat. Congl. Com., 1959-74; Selective Service Bd. Served with U.S. Army, 1945-46, ETO. Presbyterian. Clubs: City Tavern, Nat. Press, Commodity, Dublin Lake. Home: 1343 27th St NW Washington DC 20007 Office: 3222 N St NW Suite 32 Washington DC 20007

PYM, BARON (FRANCIS LESLIE), British legislator; b. Abergavenny, Wales, Feb. 13, 1922; s. Leslie Ruthven and Iris Rosalind (Orde) P.; attended Magdalene Coll., Cambridge (Eng.) U.; m. Valerie Fortune Daglish, 1949; 4 children. Mem. Liverpool (Eng.) Univ. Council, 1949-53, Herefordshire County (Eng.) Council, 1958-61; M.P. for Cambridgeshire, 1961-83, Cambridgeshire S.E., 1983-87, opposition dep. chief whip, 1967-70, govt. chief whip and parliamentary sec. to Treasury, 1970-73, sec. of state for No. Ireland, 1973-74, opposition spokesman for agr., 1974-76, for House of Commons affairs and devolution, 1976-78, for fgn. and commonwealth affairs, 1978-79, sec. of state for def., 1979-81, lord pres. of council, leader of House of Commons, 1981-82, chancellor of Duchy of Lancaster and paymaster gen., from 1981, sec. of state for fgn. and commonwealth affairs, 1982-83; pres. Atlantic Treaty Assn., 1985-88; chmn. English-Speaking Union of the Commonwealth, 1987—. Author The Politics of Consent, 1984. Hon. fellow Magdalene Coll. Served with 9th Queen's Royal Lancers, 1942-46; North Africa, Italy. Office: House of Lords, Westminster, London SW1 England

PYOKARI, MAURI KULLERVO, geography educator; b. Johannes, Finland, Jan. 11, 1936; s. Otto and Hilja Josefina (Hyvonen) P.; m. Maire Hellevi Saastamoinen, Aug. 10, 1968; 1 child, Heikki. M.S., U. Turku, 1967, Lic. Philosophy, 1973, Ph.D., 1979. Sr. tchr. high sch., Rovaniemi, Finland, 1968-72, Turku, Finland, 1972—; researcher U. Turku, 1974, asst., 1975-76, docent in geography, 1982—; mem. working group on dynamics of shoreline erosion Internat. Geog. Union, 1976, commn. on coastal environment, 1979, 84. Author: Mixed Sand and Gravel Shores in the SW Finnish Archipelago, 1973. Editor jour. Publs. Inst. Geog. Univ. Turkuensis, 1976. Contbr. articles to profl. jours. Lectr. Worker's Ednl. Inst., Turku, 1975—. Grantee Finnish Nat. Research Council, Helsinki, 1976, Finnish Cultural Found., Helsinki, 1978, Found. of Univ. Turku, 1988, Finnish Cultural Found., 1979. Fellow Geog. Soc. Finland, Geog. Soc. Turku (bd. 1976-77, 81-82), Astron. Soc. Lutheran. Avocations: nature; travelling. Home: Kuikankatu 7 AS 6, 20760 Piispanristi Finland Office: U Turku, Dept Geography, 20500 Turku Finland

PYSELL, PAUL EDWARD, lawyer; b. Covington, Va., Jan. 20, 1944; s. Charles Glenn and Carrie (Helper) P.; children—Paula Kaye, James Paul; m. Mary Frances Lane, Mar. 1, 1981; 1 child, Paul Edward II. B.A., U. Va., 1971; J.D. cum laude, Washington and Lee U., 1974; student Judge Adv. Gen. Sch., 1975. Bar: Va. 1974, U.S. Dist. Ct. (we. dist.) Va. 1974, U.S. Ct. Mil. Appeals 1975, U.S. Ct. Appeals (4th cir.) 1978, U.S. Supreme Ct. 1986. Lawyer, dir. Legal Aid Soc., Lynchburg, Va., 1974-75; ptnr. Black, Menk, Pysell, Noland & Powers, Staunton, Va., 1978-87; pvt. practice law, 1987—; asst. commonwealth atty. for City of Staunton, 1987—. Mem. Hist. Stanton Found., Woodrow Wilson Birthplace Found.; bd. dirs. Staunton-Augusta Mental Health Assn., 1983—; campaign chmn. United Way Staunton-West Augusta, 1984—, pres., 1987—; fin. com. chmn. Christ United Meth. Ch., 1985—. Served to capt. U.S. Army, 1975-78, with Res. Decorated Meritorius Service medal. Mem. ABA, Va. State Bar, Assn. Trial Lawyers Am., N.G. Assn., Izaak Walton League, Phi Beta Kappa. Club: Parents without partners (legal adviser 1981-83). Lodges: Lions, Moose, Elks. Home: 480 Mountain View Dr Staunton VA 24401 Office: PO Box 933 Staunton VA 24401

PYTTE, AGNAR, university president, theoretical physicist; b. Kongsberg, Norway, Dec. 23, 1932; came to U.S., 1949, naturalized, 1965; s. Ole and Edith (Christiansen) P.; m. Anah Currie Loeb, June 18, 1955; children: Anders H., Anthony M., Alyson C. A.B., Princeton U., 1953; A.M., Harvard U., 1954, Ph.D., 1958. Mem. faculty Dartmouth Coll., 1958-87, prof. physics, 1967-87, chmn. dept. physics and astronomy, 1971-75, assoc. dean faculty, 1975-78, dean grad. studies, 1975-78, provost, 1982-87; pres. Case Western Res. U., Cleve., 1987—; mem. Project Matterhorn, Princeton, 1959-60; bd. dirs. Goodyear Tire & Rubber Co., 1988—. Author: (with R.W. Christy) Structure of Matter, 1965. Bd. dirs. Sherman Fairchild Found. Inc., 1987—. NSF faculty fellow U. Brussels, 1966-67; Plasma Physics Lab., Princeton, 1978-79. Mem. Am. Phys. Soc., Phi Beta Kappa, Sigma Xi. Office: Case Western Res U Office of Pres Cleveland OH 44106

QABOOS BIN SAID, His Majesty Sultan of Oman; b. Salalah, Oman, Nov. 18, 1940; s. Said Bin Taimur; ed. privately in U.K., Royal Mil. Acad., Sandhurst; m. Mar. 23, 1976. Succeeded father as sultan of Oman, 1970—, also prime minister, minister of def., minister of fin., minister of fgn. affairs. Avocations: horseback riding, history, music, political science. Address: Office of Prime Minister, The Palace, Muscat Oman *

QADDAFI, MUAMMAR MUHAMMED, See GADHAFI, MUAMMAR MUHAMMED

QADIR, CHAUDRY ABDUL, philosopher, educator, researcher, writer; b. Jullander, Bharat, Nov. 5, 1909; s. Mahbub Alam and Attar Bibi Q.; m. Majida Begum, Apr. 24, 1927; children: Sarwar, Muzaffar, Ashraf, Jamila, Imtiaz, Shakila, Ijaz, Rukhsana, Sajjad. BA with honors, Murray Coll., Sialkot, Pakistan, 1930; MA, Govt. Coll., Lahore, Pakistan, 1932; B of Teaching, Cen. Tng. Coll., Lahore, 1934; DLitt, U. Panjab, Lahore, 1977. Lectr. Govt. Coll., various locations, Pakistan, 1934-52; sr. lectr. Govt. Coll., Lahore, 1952-63; prof., prin. Govt. Evaluators Coll., Lyallpur, Pakistan, 1963-64; Iqbal prof., head dept. philosophy U. of the Panjab, 1964-70, vis. prof. dept. philosophy, 1973—; vis. prof. Ulema Acad., Lahore, 1971-72, Civil Services Acad., Lahore, 1972, Fin. Services Acad., Lahore, 1972; subject specialist West Pakistna Urdu Acad., Lahore, 1972-79; mem. exec. com. West Pakistan Urdu Acad., 1964—, sec.-gen., 1987—; sr. fellow, chmn. several curriculm coms. Univ. Grants Commn. Commn., Islamabad, Pakistan, 1977-79.; convenor bd. studies Univ. of Punjab, 1965-80, Bd. of Intermediate and Secondary Edn., Lahore, 1987—; regional dir., cons. internat. adv. body World Univ., U.S.A., 1973-75; bd. dirs. Mashal (pub. co.), Lahore. Author: (in Urdu) Ethics, 1961, Psychology of Adjustment, 1969, Psychology, 4th edit., 1972, Technical Terms of Applied Psychology, 1972, Industrial Psychology, 1973, Social Psychology, 1973, Sociology, 1974, Developmental Psychology, 1973, Military Psychology, 1975, Sociological

Thinkers, 1976, Industrial Sociology, 1977, Human Ecology, 1981, Criminology, 1979, Scientific Method, 1980, Child Psychology, 1980, Sociology of Populations, 1981, Change and Theories of Change, 19981, Philosophy Today and Its Schools, 1981, Robert Malthus and His Teachings, 1984, History of Science, 1985, (in English) Logical Positivism, 1965, The World of Philosophy, 1963, Islamic Philosphy of Life and its Significance, Quest for Truth, 1985, Science and Philosophy in the Islamic World, 1987; editor-in-chief Pakistan Philos. Jour., 1977—; editor research jour. U. Panjab, 1965-70; contbr. 60 articles in English, 15 in Urdu to profl. jours. Sec. Soc. Prevention Cruelty Animals, 1973; hon. cons. Fountain House (half-way house for mental patients), Lahore; v.p. Children Aid Soc., 1974. Recipient Iqbal Gold medal Govt. Pakistan, 1977, Golden Ring and monetary award for 50 yrs. of teaching Ch. of Pakistan, Diocese of Lahore, 1987, numerous others. Mem. Pakistan Philos. Congress (pres. 1977—, Golden Pin award 1985, Festchrift award 1987), Internat. Islamic Philos. Assn. (pres. 1984—), Pakistan Assn. Inter-Religious Dialogue (pres. 1984—), Metaphys. Soc. (pres. 1970-86). Home: 62 Shah Jamal, Lahore Pakistan Office: U of the Panjab, New Campus, Lahore Pakistan *Died Dec. 2, 1987.*

QASIM, SAYED ZAHOOR, government agency official; b. Allahabad, Uttar Pradesh, India, Dec. 31, 1926; s. Syed Zamir Qasim and Fakhra Begum; m. Birjees Zahoor; children: Yasmin Mohiuddin, Seeme, Sabin Siddiqui. PhD, U. Wales, 1956, DSc, 1968; MSc in Zoology, Aligarh Muslim U., Uttar Pradesh; DSc with honors, Andhra U. Waltair, Andhra Pradesh, 1982. Dir. Nat. Inst. Oceanography, Goa, India, 1964-81; sec. Dept. Environment Govt. India, New Delhi, 1981-82, sec. Dept. Ocean Devel., 1982—. Editor numerous jours.; mem. editorial bd. several profl. jours.; contbr. more than 175 articles to profl. jours. Recipient Padma Shri award Pres. of India, 1974, Rafi Ahmed Kidwai Meml. prize I.C.A.R., 1975, Padma Rhushan award Pres. of India, 1982; hon. prof. Madurai-Kamaraj U. Aligarh Muslim. Mem. Nat. Acad. Scis. (pres. 1983-85), Soc. Offshore Engring and Underwater Tech. (pres.), Indian Nat. Sci. Acad. (v.p. 1984-86), Marine Biol. Assn. U.K. (life), Marine Biol. Assn. India (life). Clubs: Golf, Gymkhana (New Delhi). Home: AB-10 Pandara Rd, New Delhi, Pin 110 003, India Office: Nat Acad of Scis, 5 Lajpatrai Rd, Allahabad 211 002, India

QAZI, KHIZIR HAYAT A., civil engineer; b. Ratodero, Larkana, Sindh, Pakistan, Apr. 12, 1945; s. Abdul Hayee A. and Raziya Abdul Hayee Qzai; m. Khursheed Khizir, Aug. 29, 1965; children—Waheeda Khizir, Fahmeeda Khizir, Tahmena Khizir, Sanjeeoa Khizir, Sikandar Aftab Khizir. Debates and fine arts Govt. Coll. Larkana, 1962-64; Sind U. Engring. Coll., Jamshoro, 1964-68. B.E. in Civil Engring., Sind U., Jamshoro, 1968; diploma in fine arts, Bd. Intermidiate Drawing Grade Examinations, Hyderabad, 1958; M.I.E., Inst. of Engrs. Pakistan, Karachi, 1979. Registered profl. engr., Lectr. Sind U. Engring. Coll., Jamshoro, 1969-70, N.E.D. Gov't. Engring. Coll., Karachi, 1970-73; asst. engr. P.I.D.C., Karachi, 1973-75; project engr. N.F.C. (Paksaudi Fertilizer Ltd.), Lahore, 1975-81; exec. engr. Mehran U. of Engring. & Tech., Jamshoro, 1981—; prin. Sikandar Art Gallery, Nawabshah. Author: Engineering Drawing, 1973, (with M.I. Baloch) Engineering Drawing, 1979. Recipient Cash Prize & Certificate, Gov. of Sindh, Karachi, 1984, Gold Medal, Sindh Grad. Assn. Pakistan, Karachi, 1985. Mem. Inst. Engrs. Clubs: Officer's (Mirpur Mathelo, Nawabshah). Home: Al-Manzar Ratodero, Dist Larkana Sindh Pakistan Office: Mehran U of Engring & Tech, Nawabsha Sindh Pakistan Office: Sikandar Art Gallery, PO Box 96, Nawabshah Sindh Pakistan

QAZILBASH, ALI ASGHAR, physician; b. Peshawar, Pakistan, Mar. 8, 1932; d. Sardar Mahammad Rafi and Mubarik (Sultan) Q.; m. Naz Ashgar, July 14, 1968; children: Fatima Asghar, Asma Asghar. M Medicine and Sci., King Edward Coll., Lahore, Pakistan, 1955. Rotating jobs in depts. medicine, surgery, respiratory dieseases, anesthesia Lady Reading Tchg. Hosp., Peshawar, 1955-58, registrar medicine, 1958-62; registrar respiratory diseases, medicine Castle Hill Hosp., Hull, Eng., 1963-65; registrar St. Nicholas Hosp., London, 1965-66; registrar medicine Hackney Hosp., London, 1965-66; cons. physician Sargodha/Mardan Hosp., Pakistan, 1967-72, Khoms Hosp., Libya, 1972-75; asst. prof. medicine Khyber Med. COll., Peshawar, 1976-80; assoc. prof. medicine Khyber Med. Coll., Peshawar, 1980—; cons. physician Khyber Tchg. Hosp., Peshawar, 1977—, Khyber Teaching Hosp., 1988; prof. Kyhber Med. Coll., 1988. Contbr. articles to profl. jours. Fellow Royal Coll. Medicine, Royal Coll. Physicians; mem. Pakistan Med. Assn., Pakistan Cardiac Soc., Family Physicians Assn. Club: Peshawar. Home: 1-A Railway Rd University, Peshawar Pakistan Office: Khyber Teaching Hosp, Jamrud Road University, Peshawar Pakistan

QAZILBASH, IMTIAZ ALI, engineering company executive, consultant; b. Peshawar, North West Frontier, Pakistan, July 15, 1934; s. Nawazish Ali and Jahan Ara (Samdani Khan) Q.; m. Rubina Satti, Dec. 20, 1964; children—Zulfiqar Ali, Haider Ali, Zainab. Intermediate cert., Islamia Coll., Peshawar, Pakistan, 1951; gen. cert. edn. advanced level Coll. Tech., Northampton, U.K., 1952; diploma in French lang. Geneva U., 1953; B.Sc. in Engring., Imperial Coll. Sci. and Tech., London, 1957; Assoc., City and Guilds of London Inst., 1957. Registered profl. engr., Pakistan. Engr. N.Z. Power Co. Nord Sjaeland Elektricitet og Sporveje Aktieselskab, Copenhagen, 1957; telefoningenior Copenhagen Telephone Co., Kopenhavns Telefon Aktieselskab, Copenhagen, 1957-58; telecomm engr. Pakistan Indsl. Devel. Corp., Karachi, 1958-59; asst. dir. telecommunications Water and Power Devel. Authority, Lahore, Pakistan, 1959-64, dir. telecommunications, 1964-74; mng. dir., pres. Engrs. Internat., Lahore, Peshawar, 1975—; expert to study com. on communications Internat. Conf. on Large High Tension Electric Systems CIGRE, Paris, 1974—; expert roster UN, N.Y.C., 1970—; leader engrs. select com. West Pakistan Gov.'s Panel on Water and Power Devel. Authority Reorgn., Lahore, 1969-70; mem. Pakistan delegation Internat. Conf. on Large High Tension Electric Systems CIGRE, Paris, 1970, 74, 76; chmn. session Conf. on Implementation of Adminstrn. Reforms, Lahore, 1974-75; convenor com. on orgn. and adminstrn. Nat. Conf. on Acceleration of Devel. Process, Lahore, 1974; mem. energy panel Nat. Sci. Policy Group Islamabad, 1974-75; mem., organizer Nat. Seminar on Role of Hydroelectric Resources in Pakistan's Devel., Lahore, 1975; mem. selection com. U. Engring. and Tech., Lahore, 1969—; cons. Pakistan Adminstrv. Staff Coll., Lahore, 1972-74. Contbr. articles to profl. jours. Founder mem., central council mem. Fedn. Engring. Assns. Pakistan, Lahore, 1969—; v.p. Service of Elec. Engrs. Assn., Lahore, 1969-71; convenor ann. conv. Instn. Engrs., Dacca, 1970. Fellow Instn. Engrs. Pakistan (exec. council, vice-chmn. elec. sect. 1986—); mem. Pakistan Engring. Congress (council 1970-72, 76), IEEE, Instn. Elec. Engrs. U.K., Clubs: Lahore Gymkhana; Peshawar; Punjab (Lahore); Golf (Peshawar). Avocations: books; music; ballet; golf; trout fishing; shooting; flying. Home: 9 Mulberry Rd, University Town, Peshawar Pakistan Office: Engrs Internat Pakistan Pltd, 9 Mulberry Rd, University Town, Peshawar Pakistan

QIAN QICHEN, government official; b. 1928. Student, Cen. Youth League Sch., USSR, after 1954. Active Communist Party and Youth League activities, 1940's; 2d sec. Chinese Embassy, USSR, after 1955; dep. head fgn. affairs dept. Higher Edn. Ministry, after 1955; counsellor Chinese Embassy, USSR, after1972; ambassador to Guinea after 1972; head info. dept. Ministry of Fgn. Affairs, after 1972; vice-fgn. minister 1982-88, fgn. minister, 1988—. Office: Ministry of Fgn Affairs, Beijing Peoples Republic of China *

QIAO SHI, Chinese Communist Party official; b. Dinghai County, Zhejiang Province, China, 1924. Joined Chinese Communist Party, 1940, dep. dir. internat. liaison dept. Central Com., 1978-82, dir. internat. liaison dept. Cen. Com., 1982-83, mem. 12th Cen. Com., 1982—, alt. mem. Secretariat Cen. Com., 1982-85, mem. Secretariat and Politburo, 1985—, mem. Standing Com., 1987—; vice premier State Council, until 1988; sec. Afro-Asian Solidarity Com., Cultural Revolution, from 1965. Office: Chinese Communist Party, Beijing People's Republic of China *

QIN, ZENGFU, mathematics educator; b. Shanghai, Dec. 16, 1937; s. Qin Zhigan and Xi Teng; m. Yu Yunmin, Oct. 1, 1960 (dec. Mar. 1982); 1 child, Yongqing; m. Zhu Liping, May 7, 1984; 1 child, Yongdan. Math. grad., Fudan U., 1960. Prof. of math. Fudan U., Shanghai, 1960—. Co-author: Mathematical Analysis, Vol. I., II, 1982. Home: Guo-Nian Rd, Ln 135 Number 10 Room 101, Shanghai Peoples Republic of China Office: Math Dept, Fudan U, Shanghai Peoples Republic of China

QIN JIWEI, government official; b. Qiliping, Hubei, People's Republic of China, 1914; m. Tang Xianmei. Student, Anti-Japan Mil. and Polit. Acad., 1937-38. Comdr. South Yunan Mil. Dist., 1950, Yunan Mil. Dist., 1954-58; promoted to lt. gen. 1955; mem. Nat. Defense Council, 1965-1966; mem. Central Com. Chinese Communist Party, 1973—; People's Liberation Army dep. 5th Nat. Party Congress, 1978-83, mem. Presidium, 3d-5th sessions, 1980, 81, 82; alt. mem. Politburo, Chinese Communist Party 12th Cen. Com., 1982—; minister nat. defense 1988—; state councilor State Council, 1988—. Address: Office State Council, Beijing Peoples Republic of China *

QUAAL, WARD LOUIS, broadcasting executive; b. Ishpeming, Mich., Apr. 7, 1919; s. Sigfred Emil and Alma Charlotte (Larson) Q.; m. Dorothy J. Graham, Mar. 9, 1944; children—Graham Ward, Jennifer Anne. A.B., U. Mich., 1941; LL.D. (hon.), Mundelein Coll., 1962, No. Mich. U., 1967; D.Pub. Service, Elmhurst Coll., 1967; D.H.L. (hon.), Lincoln Coll., 1968, DePaul U., 1974. Announcer-writer Sta. WBEO (now sta. WDMJ), Marquette, Mich., 1936-37; announcer, writer, producer Sta. WJR, Detroit, 1937-41; spl. events announcer-producer WGN, Chgo., 1941-42, asst. to gen. mgr., 1945-49; exec. dir. Clear Channel Broadcasting Service, Washington, 1949-52, pres., chief exec. officer, 1964-74; pres. Crosley Broadcasting Corp., Cin., 1952-56, asst. gen. mgr., 1953, v.p., gen. mgr., 1953-56; v.p., gen. mgr., mem. bd. WGN Inc., Chgo., 1956-61; exec. v.p., then pres. WGN Continental Broadcasting Co., Chgo., 1961-74; pres. Ward L. Quaal Co., 1974—; former dir. Tribune Co.; dir., mem. exec. com. U.S. Satellite Broadcasting Corp., 1982—; co-founder, bd. dirs. Universal Resources, Inc., 1966-86; bd. dirs. Christine Valmy Inc.; chmn. exec. com., dir. WLW Radio Inc., Cin., 1975-81; mem. adv. com. on advanced TV sytems FCC, 1988. Author: (with others) Broadcast Management, 1968, 3d rev. edit., 1989; co-producer (Broadway play) Teddy and Alice, 1988. Mem., Hoover Commn. Exec. Br. Task Force, 1949-59; mem. U.S.-Japan Cultural Exchange Commn., 1960-70; mem. Pres.'s Council Phys. Fitness and Sports, 1983—; bd. dirs. Farm Found., 1963-73, MacCormac Jr. Coll., Chgo., 1974-80; bd. trustees Hollywood (Calif.) Mus., 1964-78; chmn. exec. com. Council for TV Devel., 1969-72; mem. bus. adv. council Chgo. Urban League, 1964-74; bd. dirs. Broadcasters Found., Internat. Radio and TV Found., Sears Roebuck Found., 1970-73; trustee Mundelein Coll., 1962-72, Hillsdale Coll., 1966-72. Served as lt. USNR, 1942-45. Recipient Disting. Bd. Gov.'s award Nat. Acad. TV Arts and Scis., 1966, 87, Disting. Alumnus award U. Mich., 1967; award Freedoms Found., Valley Forge, 1966, 68, 70; Loyola U. Key, 1970; Advt. Man of Yr., Gold medallion, Chgo. Advt. Club, 1968; Advt. Club Man of Yr., 1973; Disting. Service award Nat. Assn. Broadcasters, 1973; Communicator of Yr., Jewish United Fund, 1969; Ill. Broadcaster of Yr. award, 1973, Press Vet. of Yr. award, 1973; Communications award of distinction Brandeis U., 1973; first recipient Sterling Medal, Barren Found., 1985; 1st person named to Better Bus. Bur. Hall of Fame, Council of Better Bus. Burs. Inc., 1975; named Radio Man of Yr. Am. Coll. Radio, Arts, Crafts & Scis., 1961, Laureate in Order of Lincoln, Lincoln Acad. Ill., 1965. Mem. Nat. Assn. Broadcasters (bd. dirs. 1952-56), Broadcast Music Inc. (bd. dirs. 1953-70), Assn. Maximum Service Telecasters Inc. (bd. dirs. 1952-72), Broadcast Pioneers (pres., bd. dirs. 1962-73), Broadcast Pioneers Library (pres. 1981-84), Broadcast Pioneers Ednl. Fund Inc., Am. Advt. Fedn. (ethics com.), Delta Tau Delta (Disting. Service chpt.), Nat. Acad. TV Arts and Scis. (bd. govs. 1966, 87). Clubs: Mid-America; Exmoor Country (Chgo.); Marco Polo (N.Y.C.); Kenwood Golf and Country; Internat. (Washington); Lakeside Golf (North Hollywood, Calif.); Boulders Golf (Carefree, Ariz.). Home: 711 Oak Winnetka IL 60093 Office: Ward L Quaal Co 401 N Michigan Ave Suite 3140 Chicago IL 60611

QUACKENBUSH, KEITH DAVID, oil company data processing executive; b. Kansas City, Mo., July 3, 1936; s. Bert David and Helen Elizabeth (Keith) Q.; m. Barbara Mae Lord, Aug. 31, 1957 (div. Feb. 1968); children—Keith David, Susan Diane, Laura Jean; m. 2d, Carol Ann Cannon, May 16, 1968; children—Anne Elizabeth, Jayne Kathleen, Wade Lee. B.S., U. Ill., 1958. Systems engr. IBM Corp., Phila., 1961-65; mktg. rep., Washington, 1965-67, systems engring. mgr., St. Louis, 1967-69; exec. Nat. Info. Systems, Valley Forge, Pa., 1969-72, Champlin Petroleum, Ft. Worth, 1972-75; exec. Occidental Petroleum Corp., Houston, 1975-78; dir. MIS-Europe/Africa Occidental Internat. Oil, Inc., London, 1978—. Pres., bd. dirs. Antwerp Internat. Sch. (Belgium), 1980-83; pres. Am. Club Antwerp, 1982; pres., chmn. Am. Protestant Ch., Antwerp, 1982; solicitor United Fund Belgium, Brussels, 1979-83; v.p. Am. Belgian Assn., 1980-83; dir. Am. Sch., Aberdeen, 1985—, chmn. bd. dirs., 1986—. Served to 1st lt. U.S. Army, 1959-61. Mem. Am. Petroleum Inst. (mem. com. on drilling and prodn. 1973-74, subcom. on systems and computation 1973-75). Republican. Episcopalian. Home: 15 Culter Den, Peterculter, Aberdeen AB1 OWA, Scotland

QUADRI, FAZLE RAB, lawyer, government official; b. Dacca, Pakistan, Aug. 5, 1948; came to U.S., 1967; s. Gholam Moula and Jehan (Ara) Q.; children: Ryan F., Tania M. AA, Western Wyo. Coll., 1969; BA, Calif. State U., 1972; JD, Western State U., 1978. Bar: Calif. 1981. Sr. adminstrv. analyst San Bernardino County, Calif., 1978-82, acting legis. adv., 1982, sr. legis. analyst, 1982—, acting pub. defender, 1984; local gov. rep. State Hazardous Waste Mgmt. Council, Sacramento, Calif., 1982-84; chmn's. rep. County Projects Selection Coms., San Bernardino, 1983—; county rep. S. Coast Air Quality Mgmt. Dist., El Monte, Calif, 1983-87. Advisor Mcpl. Adv. Councils, San Bernardino, 1984-87; mem. Law Library Bd. Trustees, 1984-85. Named one of Outstanding Young Men of Am., Montgomery, Ala., 1981-82; recipient Presdl. Achievement award Rep. Nat. Com., Washington, 1984. Mem. Calif. Bar Assn., Acad. Polit. Sci.; Calif. State U. Alumni Assn. (bd. dirs. 1985-86), County Suprs. Assn. of Calif. (bd. liaison). Republican. Islamic. Lodges: Kiwanis, Masons, Shriners. Home: 535 E Mariposa Dr Redlands CA 92373 Office: County San Bernardino Bd Suprs 385 N Arrowhead 5th floor San Bernardino CA 92415

QUAINTON, ANTHONY CECIL EDEN, diplomat; b. Seattle, Apr. 4, 1934; s. Cecil Eden and Marjorie Josephine (Oates) Q.; m. Susan Long, Aug. 7, 1958; children: Katherine, Eden, Elizabeth. B.A., Princeton U., 1955; B.Litt., Oxford (Eng.) U., 1958. Research fellow St. Antony's Coll., Oxford, 1958-59; with Fgn. Service, State Dept., 1959—; vice consul Sydney, Australia, 1960-62; Urdu lang. trainee 1962-63; 2d sec., econ. officer Am. embassy, Karachi, Pakistan, 1963-64, Rawalpindi, Pakistan, 1964-66; 2d sec., polit. officer Am. embassy, New Delhi, 1966-69; sr. polit. officer for India Dept. State, Washington, 1969-72; 1st sec. Am. embassy, Paris, 1972-73; counselor, dep. chief mission Am. embassy, Kathmandu, Nepal, 1973-76; ambassador to Central African Empire, Bangui, 1976-78, Nicaragua, Managua, 1982-84, Kuwait, 1984-87; dir. Office for Combatting Terrorism, Dept. State, Washington, 1978-81; dep. insp. gen. Dept. State, 1987—. English Speaking Union fellow, 1951-52; Marshall scholar, 1955-58; recipient Rivkin award, 1972, Herter award, 1984. Mem. Am. Fgn. Service Assn., Phi Beta Kappa. Home: 3424 Porter St NW Washington DC 20016 Office: Dept of State 2201 C St NW Washington DC 20520

QUALLS, CORETHIA, archaeologist; b. Sparta, Tenn., Jan. 17, 1948; d. Malcolm Talmadge and Lucille (Jackson) Qualls. BA, Marlboro Coll., 1970; MPhil, Columbia U., 1980, PhD, 1981. Exec. curator Mus. of Archaeology of Staten Island, 1981; asst. prof. St. John's U., S.I., 1981-82; cons. curator Queens Mus., N.Y., 1982-83; cons. curator Kuwait Nat. Mus., 1984-86; curatorial advisor for archaeology, Bahrain Nat. Mus., 1987—; archaeologist Columbia U., 1970-74, NYU Inst. Fine Arts, 1972-73, 84, Johns Hopkins U., 1974, Fulbright prof. archaeology, 1985-86. Dir. excavations Hamad Town, Bahrain, 1985-86. Editor: Seals of the Marcopoli Collection, vol. 1, 1984; contbr. articles to profl. jours. Columbia U. fellow, 1970-74; Am. Schs. Oriental Research fellow, 1973-74. Mem. Am. Inst. Archaeology, Am. Oriental Soc., Am. Schs. Oriental Research, Inst. Nautical Archaeology, Brit. Sch. Archaeol. in Iraq, Oriental Club of N.Y.C., Egypt Exploration Soc., Am. Soc. Profl. and Exec. Women, Nat. Assn. Bus. and Profl. Women, Nat. Assn. Female Execs. Roman Catholic.

QUALLS, ROBERT L., banker, former state official; b. Burnsville, Miss., Nov. 6, 1933; s. Wes E. and Letha (Parker) Q.; m. Carolyn Morgan, Feb. 10, 1979; 1 dau., Stephanie Elizabeth. BS, Miss. State U., 1954, MS, 1958; PhD, La. State U., 1962; LLD, Whitworth Coll., 1974; DBA (honoris causa), U. of the Ozarks, 1984. Prof., chmn. div. econs. and bus. Belhaven Coll., Jackson, Miss., 1962-66; asst. to pres. Belhaven Coll., 1965-66; asst. prof. finance Miss. State U., State College, 1967-69, adj. prof., 1969-73; sr. v.p., chmn. venture com. Bank of Miss., Tupelo, 1969-73; v.p. Wesleyan Coll., Macon, Ga., 1974; pres. U. of the Ozarks, Clarksville, Ark., 1974-79; mem. cabinet Bill Clinton Gov. of Ark., 1979-80; exec. v.p. Worthen Bank & Trust Co., N.A., 1980-85; sr. v.p. First Ark. Bankstock Corp. (name changed to Worthen Banking Corp.), 1980-85; pres., dir. First Bank Fin. Services, Inc., 1980-85, Advt. Assocs., Inc., 1980-85; chmn., chief exec. officer, dir. 1st Nat. Bank of Harrison affiliate Worthen Banking Corp., 1985—; bd. dirs. First Nat. Bank, Mena, Bank Montgomery County, Baldor Electric Co.; cons. Unifirst Savs. & Loan Assn., Jackson, 1963-68, dir. mktg., 1968-69; mktg. cons. Ill. Central Industries, Chgo., 1964; mem. faculty, thesis examiner Stonier Grad. Sch. Banking, Rutgers U., 1973-86; mem. faculty Miss. Sch. Banking, U. Miss., 1973-78; course coordinator Sch. Banking of the South, La. State U., 1978-88, Banking Sch., Duke U., 1977; lectr. Southwestern Sch. Banking, So. Meth. U., 1983; adj. prof. bus. adminstrn. U. Central Ark., 1985-86. Author: Entrepreneurial Wit and Wisdom, 1986; co-author: Strategic Planning for Colleges and Universities: A Systems Approach to Planning and Resource Allocation, 1979; mem. editorial adv. bd.: Bank Mktg. Mag., 1984-86. Chmn. community service and continuing edn. com. Tupelo Community Devel. Found., 1972-73; mem. Miss. 4-H adv. council, 1969; active Boy Scouts Am.; mem. Lee County Democratic Exec. Com., 1973-74; trustee Wal-Mart Found., 1975-79; trustee, mem. exec. com. U. of Ozarks, 1982—; mem. Pres.'s Roundtable U. Central Ark., 1982-87; mem. exec. com. Coll. Bus. Adv. Bd. U. Ark.-Little Rock, 1980-85. Served to lt. AUS, 1954-56. Found. for Econ. Edn. fellow, 1964; Ford Found. faculty research fellow Vanderbilt U., 1963-64; recipient Pillar of Progress award Johnson County, 1977. Mem. Am. Bankers Assn. (mktg. planning and research com. 1972-73), Am. Mgmt. Assn. (pres.'s assn.), Bus. and Profl. Group of Am. (dir. 1969), Ark. Council Ind. Colls. and Univs. (chmn. 1978-79), Newcomen Soc., Johnson County C. of C. (pres. 1977), Blue Key, Omicron Delta Kappa, Delta Sigma Pi, Sigma Phi Epsilon (citation 1977). Presbyn. Clubs: Masons (32 deg.), Clarksville Rotary (pres. 1979). Office: 1st Nat Bank Bldg Harrison AR 72601

QUAN, LYNDA MARYE, clinical social worker; b. New Orleans, July 9, 1945; d. William Evans and Mary (Hom) Q.; BA, U. Colo., 1966; MA, U. Mo., 1971, MSW, 1975. Diplomate Nat. Register Clin. Social Workers. Mem. Peace Corps, Brazil, 1967-69; grad. teaching asst. U. Mo., Columbia, 1969-71; substitute tchr. Columbia Public Schs., 1971; psychiat. social worker Fulton (Mo.) State Hosp., 1971-76; dep. juvenile officer St. Louis County Juvenile Ct., 1975; with Farmington (Mo.) State Hosp., 1976—, supr. psychiat. social work, 1981—; cons., speaker in field. Pres., bd. dirs. Homeless Young Mothers Network. Mem. Nat. Assn. Social Workers (chmn. nominations and leadership Mo. chpt. 1981-82, 87—, unit chmn. 1982-84, sec. Mo. state chpt. 1984-85), Acad. Cert. Social Workers (del. assembly 1981, 84), Bus. and Profl. Women, Women's Sports Found., U. Mo. Alumni Assn. (life). Home: 609 Hillsboro Rd Farmington MO 63640 Office: SE Mo Mental Health Ctr Farmington MO 63640

QUANT, MARY, fashion and cosmetics company executive, designer; b. London, Feb. 11, 1934; d. Jack and Mildred (Jones) Q.; m. Alexander Plunket Greene, 1957; 1 son. Ed. Goldsmiths Coll. Art, London. Began career in Chelsea, London, 1954; dir. Mary Quant Group of Cos., 1955—; mem. Design Council, 1971—; mem. U.K.-U.S.A. Bicentennial Liaison Com., 1973—; mem. adv. council Victoria and Albert Mus., 1976-78. Retrospective exhbn. of 60's fashion: London Mus., 1974. Decorated Order Brit. Empire; recipient Internat. Fashion award Sunday Times; Rex award (U.S.); Piavolo d'Oro (Italy); named Royal Designer for Industry. Fellow Soc. Indsl. Artists and Designers (Ann. Design medal). Office: Mary Quant Ltd, 3 Ives St, London SW3 England *

QUARLES, HOLLACE ELLEN HENKEL, businesswoman; b. Cleve., June 4, 1945; d. Charles Edward and Betty Jane (Bowman) Henkel; B.A., U. Ky., 1967; M.L.S., U. Pitts., 1968; m. Frederick Hundley Quarles III, Apr. 12, 1969; children—Ashley Louise, Ellen Michelle. Mem. faculty, dir. computer systems Med. Sch. Library U. Va., Charlottesville, 1968-70; pres. Eastern Mdse. Corp., Charlottesville, 1970-74; owner Holly's Glass Studio, 1975-85, Henkel-Quarles Glass Studio, 1986-88; dir. pub. relations MooneyMite Aircraft Corp., Charlottesville, 1969—; pres. Commonwealth Capital Corp., Charlottesville, 1978—; Reference Librarian Claude Moore Health Scis. Library, 1985; audio tape librarian Trinity Presbyn. Ch., 1984—. Librarian, asst. to pres. Christian Aid Mission, 1986-88; organizer Va. Skyline Girl Scout of Am. Council, 1984-87. Malloch scholar Med. Library Assn., 1967. Mem. Nat. Assn. Women Bus. Owners, U. Ky. Alumni Assn. Presbyterian.

QUARLES, STEVEN PRINCETON, lawyer; b. Kansas City, Mo., May 9, 1942; s. Samuel Princeton and Marianna (Platt) Q.; m. Suzanne Margaret-Mary Cleary, June 2, 1970. AB, Princeton U., 1964; JD, Yale U., 1968. Bar: N.Y. 1980, D.C. 1981. Counsel Senate Com. Energy and Natural Resources, Washington, 1971-78; dir. office coal leasing U.S. Dept. Interior, Washington, 1978-79, dep. under sec., 1979-81; ptnr. Nossaman, Guthner, Knox & Elliott, Washington, 1981-83, Crowell & Moring, Washington, 1983—. Chmn. Sugarloaf Citizens Assn., Dickerson, Md., 1977-81, Md. Hazardous Waste Facilities Siting Bd., Annapolis, 1985-87; mem. Md. Sewage Sludge Mgmt. Commn., Annapolis, 1984; mem. Montgomery County Solid Waste Adv. Com., Rockville, Md., 1980-85. Fulbright scholar India, 1964-65. Mem. ABA (pub. lands and land use com. natural resources sect.), N.Y. State Bar Assn., D.C. Bar Assn., Nat. Acad. Scis. (energy and mineral resources bd. 1985—, abandoned mine lands com. 1985-86). Democrat. Episcopalian. Home: Some Day Soon Farm 14001 Mattie Haines Rd Mount Airy MD 21771 Office: Crowell & Moring 1001 Pennsylvania Ave NW Washington DC 20004

QUARLES, WILLIAM DANIEL, lawyer; b. Balt., Jan. 16, 1948; s. William Daniel and Mabel (West) Q.; m. Deborah Ann Grant, Oct. 7, 1969 (div. Aug. 1976); 1 child, Eloise. BS, U. Md., 1976; JD, Cath. U., 1979. Bar: D.C. 1979, U.S. Dist. Ct. Md. 1980, U.S. Ct. Appeals (4th cir.) 1980, U.S. Supreme Ct. 1988. Law clk. to presiding judge U.S. Dist. Ct. Md., Balt., 1979-81; assoc. Finley Kumble, Washington, 1981-82; asst. U.S. atty. U.S. Dept. Justice, Balt., 1982-86; ptnr. Venable, Baetjer, Howard & Civiletti, Washington, 1986—; Permanent mem. U.S. 4th Cir. Jud. Conf., Richmond, Va., 1986—. Coordinator Presdl. Regional Task Force on Organized Crime and Drug Law Enforcement, 1984-85. Mem. ABA, Serjeants Inn. Home: 2440 Virginia Ave NW D704 Washington DC 20037 Office: 1301 Pennsylvania Ave NW Suite 1200 Washington DC 20004

QUASHA, WILLIAM HOWARD, lawyer; b. N.Y.C., May 19, 1912; B.S. in Mech. Engring., N.Y. U., 1933, M.A., 1935; LL.B., St. John's U., 1936; m. Phyllis Grant, Apr. 17, 1946; children: Wayne Grant, Alan Grant, Jill. Admitted to N.Y. bar, 1936, Philippine bar, 1945, U.S. Supreme Ct. bar, 1947; practiced in N.Y.C., 1936-42, Manila, Philippines, 1946—; sr. partner Quasha, Asperilla, Ancheta, Peña, and Nolasco; dir. Marcopper Mining Corp., Manila. Faculty, N.Y. U., 1933-35, Santo Tomas U., Manila, 1946-48; vis. asso. prof. L.I. U., summer 1966; lectr. Harvard Law Sch., summer 1976, U. Philippines Coll. Law, 1979. Mem. nat. exec. bd. Boy Scouts Philippines, 1955-74, mem. exec. bd. Manila council, 1949-74, v.p., treas., 1964-74, hon. life pres., 1970; v.p., legal counsel Acacia Mut. Aid Soc., Inc., Manila, 1963—; mem. exec. bd. Far East council Boy Scouts Am., 1973—, mem. nat. exec. bd., 1977—; pres., chmn. bd. trustees St. Luke's Med. Ctr., Manila, 1975—; trustee Jose P. Laurel Meml. Found.; chmn. Republicans Abroad Com., Philippines, 1979-84, chmn. Asia-Pacific region, 1985-86, chmn. adv. com. 1987—. Served with AUS, 1942-46; PTO; lt. col. Res. Decorated Bronze Star with oak leaf cluster, Philippine Legion of Honor (officer rank); recipient Silver Tamaraw, Boy Scouts Philippines, 1959, Silver Fir Tree Br., Boy Scouts Austria, 1960; Distinguished Eagle Scout award Boy Scouts Am., 1970, Silver Buffalo award, 1974. Spl. award and citation City of Manila, 1970; tribute of appreciation U.S. Dept. State, 1983; Conrado Benitez Heritage award Philippine Women's U., 1983. Mem. Am., Fed. bar assns., Integrated Bar of Philippines, Law Asia, Internat. Bar Assn., Am. Soc. Internat. Law, Am. C. of C. of Philippines, Philippine Hist. Soc., Navy League U.S. (judge adv., chartermem.), Am. Assn. Philippines, Propeller Club U.S. (past pres., charter mem. Manila chpt.), Philippine Constn. Assn. (life), Philippine Soc. Internat. Law, Ramon Magsaysay Meml. Soc., Knights of Rizal (knight comdr.), Nat. Sojourners (pres. 1959), Am. Legion (dept. comdr. 1954-55), Manila Jr. C. of C. (asso., v.p. 1949), Internat. C. of C. (gov. Philippine council 1964—). Episcopalian (sr. warden, chancellor). Mason (33 deg., grand master 1962-63, Chevalier of Legion of

Honor Supreme Council of Order De Molay 1986), regent, trustee Cathedral St. John the Divine, N.Y., 1988—, Shriner, Elk (bd. dirs. palsy project 1954-69, chmn. 1963-65), Rotarian (past dir. Manila). Clubs: Nat. Lawyers' (Washington); Am. Nat. (Sydney, Australia); Creek (L.I.); University (N.Y.); Army and Navy, Manila Polo, Valle Verde Country; others. Author: (with Rensis Likert) Revised Minnesota Paper Form Board Test. Home: 22 Molave Pl, Makati Metro, Manila Philippines Office: Don Pablo Bldg, 114 Amorsolo St, Legaspi Village, Metro Manila Philippines

QUASIM, MOHAMMED, psychiatrist, educator; b. Hazro, Punjab, Pakistan, Oct. 29, 1932; came to Britain, 1959; s. Yusuf and Mariam (Khan) Q.; m. Maxine Skinner, June 23, 1962; children—Isma, Tara. Pre-med. student Sind Muslim, Karachi, Pakistan, 1950-52; M.B., B.S., Dow Med. U., Karachi, 1957. Cons. psychiatrist West Midlands Regional Health Authority, Birmingham, Eng., 1971—; postgrad. clin. tutor in psychiatry Birmingham U., 1973—. Fellow Royal Coll. Psychiatrists, Royal Coll. Physicians. Muslim. Avocation: archeology. Home: 239 Lutterworth Rd, Nuneaton Warwickshire CV11 6PX, England Office: St Matthews Hospitol, Burntwood near Walsall England

QUATTLEBAUM, WALTER EMMETT, JR., telephone co. exec.; b. Midville, Ga., Dec. 22, 1922; s. Walter Emmett and Eva (Bagley) Q.; student Murrey Vocational Sch., Charleston, S.C., 1941, U. Hawaii, 1943; m. Dorothy Evelyn Clewis, Oct. 19, 1946; children—Walter Emmett III, Amalia Ann. Former owner Fla. Telephone Exchange, Sneads, Cottondale, Grand Ridge, Bonifay, Westville, and Seagrove Beach, Quattlebaum Telephone Supply Co., Quattlebaum Investments, also Spanish Trail Motel, Bonifay, Fla.; v.p., dir. Seminole Telephone Co., Donalsonville, Ga.; now investment analyst Quattlebaum Investments and others. City councilman, Sneads, 1950-52, pres. City Council, 1953. Served with AUS, 1944-46. Mem. Fla. Telephone Assn., Telephone Pioneers Am. Methodist. Office: Bonifay FL 32425

QUAYLE, ANTHONY (JOHN ANTHONY), theatre director, actor; b. Ainsdale, Lancashire, Eng., Sept. 7, 1913; s. Arthur and Esther Overton; ed. Rugby, Royal Acad. Dramatic Art; m. Hermione Hannan (div.); m. 2d, Dorothy Hyson, 1947; children—Rosanna, Jenny, Christopher. First appeared as straight man to a comic in vaudeville; stage appearance O Theatre, 1931; joined Old Vic Co., 1932; first stage appearance, N.Y.C., 1936; dir., actor, producer numerous films and plays in Eng., also ran Stratford-on-Avon theatre, 1948-56; producer Harvey, London, 1948, dir., 1975; on stage in Henry VIII, 1949; Henry IV, 1950; Volpone, 1952; Titus Andronicus, 1955; View from the Bridge, 1956; Galileo, 1967; Sleuth, 1970; The Idiot, 1970; The Headhunters, 1974; You Turn Somersaults, 1977; Hobson's Choice, 1982; toured England in King Lear, 1980; dir., co-star The Firstborn, 1958; motion pictures Saraband for Dead Lovers, 1949; Hamlet, 1950; Woman in a Dressing Gown, 1957; Pursuit of Graf Spee, 1958; Ice Cold in Alex, 1958; Guns of Navarone, 1961; Lawrence of Arabia, 1962; Fall of the Roman Empire, 1964; Operation Crowbow, 1965; A Study in Terror; Anne of the Thousand Days; Q.B. VIII; Bequest to the Nation; The Tamarind Seed; 21 Hours at Munich, 1976; The Eagle Has Landed, 1977; Murder by Decree, 1978; Dial M for Murder; dir. Tiger at the Gates, 1968; actor, dir. Clarence Brown Co., Tenn., from 1975; numerous radio and TV appearances including Q.B. VII, Moses, 1974, Great Expectations, 1974, Benjamin Franklin, 1974, David and Saul, 1975, Ice Age, Henry IV, Masada, The Manions of America, The Tempest, King Lear, Oedipus at Colonus; producer, dir. Caesar and Cleopatra NBC; producer The Idiot, 1970; dir. plays Harvey, 1975, Rip Van Winkle, 1975, The Old Country, 1978, The Rules of the Game, 1982. Author: Eight Hours from England, 1945; On Such a Night, 1947.

QUAYLE, DAN, U.S. senator; b. Indpls., Feb. 4, 1947; s. James C. and Corinne (Pulliam) Q.; m. Marilyn Tucker, Nov. 18, 1972; children—Tucker Danforth, Benjamin Eugene, Mary Corinne. BS in Polit. Sci., DePauw U., Greencastle, Ind., 1969; JD, Ind. U., 1974. Bar: Ind. bar 1974. Ct. reporter, pressman Huntington (Ind.) Herald-Press, 1965-69, asso. pub., gen. mgr., 1974-76; mem. consumer protection div. Office Atty. Gen., State of Ind., 1970-71; adminstrv. asst. to gov. Ind. 1971-73; dir. Ind. Inheritance Tax Div., 1973-74; mem. 95th-96th Congresses, 4th Dist. Ind., U.S. Senate from Ind., 1981—; tchr. bus. law Huntington Coll., 1975. Republican nominee for Vice Pres. U.S., 1988. Mem. Huntington Bar Assn., Hoosier State Press Assn., Huntington C. of C. Republican. Club: Rotary. Office: 524 Hart Senate Bldg Washington DC 20510 *

QUEEN, BARRY LLOYD, lawyer, real estate executive; b. Springfield, Mass., Feb. 7, 1942; s. Sidney E. and Dinah Queen; B.S., St. Lawrence U., 1963; LL.B., Western New England Coll., 1969; m. Norine M. Cohen, June 22, 1963; children—Heidi, Dara. Real Estate analyst Mass. Mut. Life Co., Springfield, 1964-69; mortgage officer Schostak Bros., Detroit, 1969-71; v.p. Citizens Mortgage Corp., Detroit, 1971-75; v.p. Rainbow Devel., also Bella Vista Devel., Buffalo, 1975-77; pres. Mut. Investment Group, Boston, 1977-84; v.p. Mut. Bank, Boston, 1977-84; gen. partner Mabell Assocs., Boston, 1978—; mem. firm Warner & Stackpole, 1984—; pres. Univ. Fin. Services Corp., 1985-88, pres. First Am. Service Corp., 1988—; lectr. in field. Mem. Nat. Assn. Mut. Banks, Am. Bar Assn., Mass. Bar Assn. Home: 958 Salem End Rd Framingham MA 01701 Office: 181 Wells Ave Newton MA 02159

QUEEN, DANIEL, acoustical engineer, consultant; b. Boston, Feb. 15, 1934; s. Simon and Ida (Droker) Q.; 1 child, Aaron Jacob. Student U. Chgo., 1951-54. Quality control mgr. Magnacord, Inc., Chgo., 1955-57; project engr. Revere Camera Co., Chgo., 1957-62; dir. engring. for Amplivox products Perma Power Co., Chgo., 1962-70; prin. engr. Daniel Queen Assocs., Chgo., 1970—, pres. Daniel Queen Labs., Inc., 1980—; chmn. Am. Nat. Standards Subcom. PH7-6, mem. com. PH-7; mem. standards com. P8-5 Electronic Industries Assn. Contbr. editor Sound and Communications, 1973—; patentee in field; contbr. papers to profl. jours., also articles to trade and popular jours.; editorial bd. Jour. Audio Engring. Soc., 1978—. Fellow Audio Engring. Soc. (standards mgr., chmn. tech. council), mem. IEEE (sr.), Am. Nat. Standards Inst. (sec. com. S4 on audio engring.), Acoustical Soc. Am. (chmn. Chgo. regional chpt. 1976-78, mem. engring. acoustics com.), Midwest Acoustics Conf. (pres. 1971-72), Chgo. Acoustical and Audio Group (pres. 1969-70), Assn. Ednl. Communications and Tech., Soc. Motion Picture and TV Engrs. (audio rec. and reprodn. com.), ASTM, AAAS, Am. Pub. Health Assn., Nat. Council Acoustical Cons., Catgut Acoustic Soc. Home and Office: 222 W 23d St New York NY 10011

QUEENAN, JOHN THOMAS, obstetrician, gynecologist, educator; b. Aurora, Ill., June 4, 1933; s. John William and Alice Margaret (Thomas) Q.; B.S. cum laude, U. Notre Dame, 1954; M.D., Cornell U., 1958; m. Carrie Ethel Neher, June 15, 1957; children—John Thomas, Carrie Lynne. Intern, Bellevue Hosp., N.Y.C., 1958-59; resident N.Y. Hosp., 1959-62; instr. Cornell U., 1962-65, clin. asst. prof. ob-gyn, 1965-70, asso. prof., 1970-72; prof. ob-gyn, chmn. dept. ob-gyn U. Louisville, 1972-80; prof., chmn. dept. ob-gyn Georgetown U., 1980—, obstetrician and gynecologist-in-chief Georgetown U. Hosp., 1980—; chief ob-gyn Norton-Children's Hosps., Louisville, Louisville Gen. Hosp.; spl. adv. ob-gyn devices panel FDA, 1978—. Bd. dirs. ARC, Greenwich, Conn., 1970-72. Diplomate Am. Bd. Ob-Gyn. Fellow Am. Gynec. and Obstet. Soc.; mem. Am. Coll. Obstetricians and Gynecologists, ACS, Am. Fertility Soc., Nat. Perinatal Assn. (pres. 1976-78), So. Perinatal Assn. (pres. 1975), Royal Soc. Medicine, Alpha Omega Alpha. Clubs: Round Hill (Greenwich); River Valley (Louisville); Cosmos (Washington); Chevey Chase (Md.). Author: Modern Management of the Rh Problem, 1977; Management of High Risk Pregnancy, 1980, 2d edit., 1985; A New Life, 1980, 2d edit., 1986, (with Kimberly K. Leslie) Preconceptions, 1988; editor: (with John C. Hobbins) Protocols for High Risk Pregnancies, 1987; editor-in-chief Contemporary Ob-Gyn, 1973—. Home: 3257 N St NW Washington DC 20007 Office: Georgetown U Hosp 3800 Reservoir Rd Washington DC 20007

QUEFFÉLEC, ANNE, pianist; b. Paris, Jan. 17, 1948; d. Henri and Yvonne Q.; m. Luc Dehaene, Oct. 5, 1983; 1 child Gaspard. Baccalaureat of Philosophy, Paris, 1965. Toured Europe, Asia, N.Am.; 18 recordings 1970-88. Recipient 1st prize award Munich Internat. Piano Competition, 1968, finalist and prize winner Internat. Piano Competition, Leeds, Eng., 1969. Roman Catholic. Address: 15 ave Corneille, 78600 Maisons-Lafitte France

QUEIROZ, TOME DE BARROS, business executive; b. Sintra, Portugal, May, 1926; s. Carlos Barros and Alda Farria (Barros) Q.; student public schs.; m. Maria Luiza de Barros, June 21, 1952; children—Carlos Tome, Adriana Maria. Opera singer, 1945-65; several recs.; gen. mgr., owner Publirama, Lisbon, 1960—, Editorial Eva, Lisbon, 1975—; chmn. Red Portuguesa, Lisbon, 1972—; dir., owner Placard, Lisbon, 1967—, Estudios Sete, Lisbon, 1979—; owner Radio Ribatedo, Santarem, Portugal, 1972—; dir. Publiedil. Bd. dirs. Siarte, nat. entertainers union, 1976. Mem. European Fedn. Outdoor Advt. (vice chmn.), Internat. Advt. Assn., Port Assn. Outdoor Advt. (chmn.). Club: Sporting. Home: 11 Rua D Cristovao da Gama, 1400 Lisbon Portugal Office: 5 Rua de Emenda S-1, 1200 Lisbon Portugal

QUEISSER, HANS JOACHIM, physicist; b. Berlin, July 6, 1931; s. Herbert W. and Hanni (Kaufmann) Q.; Ph.D., U. Goettingen, 1958; m. Ingeborg K. Scheven, Aug. 23, 1962; children—Monika, Andreas, Joachim. Sr. scientist Shockley Transistor Corp., Palo Alto, Calif., 1959-63; vis. prof. U. Frankfurt/Main (W. Ger.), 1963-64; mem. tech. staff Bell Telephone Labs., Murray Hill, N.J., 1964-66; prof. physics U. Frankfurt/Main, 1966-71; dir. Max Planck Inst. Solid State Research, Stuttgart, 1971—; dir. Wacker Chemitronic, 1969-83, Robert Bosch Co., Heidelberg Instruments Inc., Sci. Am., N.Y.; curator Found. Volkswagenwerk, 1977-87; senator Max Planck Soc., 1975-87; hon. prof. U. Stuttgart, 1974—. Recipient Outstanding Achievement award USAF, 1963. Mem. German Phys. Soc. (pres. 1975-77), Am. Phys. Soc. Author, editor, patentee in field. Home: 21D Knappenweg, D7000 Stuttgart 80 Federal Republic of Germany Office: 1 Heisenberg Strasse, D7000 Stuttgart 80 Federal Republic of Germany

QUEK, SWEE-SAN SUSAN, cardiologist, consultant; b. Singapore, July 9, 1949; d. Kiok Lee and Puay Eng (Tan) Q.; m. Boon-Keng Tay, Aug. 10, 1974; children: Darren Keng-Jin Tay, Sherilyn Keng-Lin Tay, Stacie Keng-Min Tay. MBBS, U. Singapore, 1973, M of Internal Medicine, 1977, degree in medicine, 1982. House officer Singapore Gen. Hosp. div. Ministry of Health, 1973-74, med. officer, 1974-77, registrar cardiology, 1977-81, sr. registrar cardiology, 1981-85, cons. cardiologist, 1985—. Vol. doctor Ling Kwang Home for the Aged, Singapore, 1982—. Mem. Singapore Cardiac Soc. (sec. 1988—). Presbyterian. Home: 14 Dunsfold Dr, 1335 Singapore Office: Singapore Gen Hosp, Ministry of Health, Outram Rd 0316 Singapore

QUELLMALZ, HENRY, printing company executive; b. Balt., May 18, 1915; s. Frederick and Edith Margaret (Shaw) Q.; BA with high honors, Princeton U., 1937; m. Marion Agar Lynch, Aug. 2, 1940; children—Lynn Quellmalz Johnson, Susan Quellmalz Mastan, Jane Quellmalz Carey. Pres. Princeton Advt. Agy., 1936-37; dir. personnel, Macy's Men's Store, 1938-40; asst. mgr. Fowlers Dept. Store, Glens Falls, N.Y., 1940-41; personnel dir. U.S. Army postexchanges, Ft. Meade, Md., 1941-44; with Boyd Printing Co., Albany, N.Y., 1944—, pres., 1952-84, chmn. bd., 1984—; v.p. Q Corp. U.S. agt. for WHO publs., 1965—; adv. bd. First Am. Bank N.Y., 1984-86; dir. Bankers Trust Co. Albany 1965-84. Campaign chmn. ARC, Albany, 1956, 57; bd. govs. Doane Stuart Sch., Albany, 1977-79, treas. bd., 1977-78; vice chmn. Family Service Assn. Am. Salute to Families, 1979—, Nat. UN Day com., 1980-82; mem. adv. bd. Ind. Coll. Fund of N.Y., 1971—; bd. dirs. Am. Assn. World Health, 1977-82, Combined Health Appeal of Capitol Dist., Inc., 1984, Camelot Home for Boys, 1975; mem. adv. bd. Ind. Coll. Fund of N.Y., Inc., 1971; trustee St. Peter's Hosp. Found., Albany, 1982—, asst. sec., 1987—. Served with AUS, 1943. Recipient Pres.'s award Am. Assn. Mental Deficiency, 1976; 25 Yrs. Service award N.Y. State Bar Assn., 1983, 34 Yrs. Service Award Am. Sociol. Assn., 1985. Mem. Albany Area C. of C., Printing Industry Am. Assn. of East Cen. N.Y., (pres. 1958). Democrat. Episcopalian. Clubs: Princeton (N.Y.C.); Fort Orange, Hudson River. Home: 1 Park Hill Dr Apt 6 Menands NY 12204 Office: 49 Sheridan Ave Albany NY 12210

QUEMADA, CONRADO VARGAS, JR., surgeon, clergyman; b. Bago, Negros Occidental, Phillipines, Sept. 28, 1927; s. Conrada Jimenez and Cristeta Magkilat (Vargas) Q.; m. Eva Pelayo Ignacio, June 14, 1952; children: Evelyn Christela, Linda Faith. AA in Pre-Med., Silliman U., 1948; MD, Manila Cen. U., 1953. Ordained minister of Gospel, 1962. Intern Meth. Hosp. Cen. Ill., Peoria, 1954, resident in gen. practice, 1955, resident in gen. surgery, 1955-56; resident in gen. surgery Emanuel Hosp., Portland, Oreg., 1956-60, preceptorship in plastic and reconstructive surgery, 1959-60; dir., med. missionary Philippine Gospel Assn., 1963—; resident minister Philippine Gospel Ch., Cagayan de Oro City, Philippines, 1963-79; med. dir. Philippine Gospel Assn. Med.-Sugery Clinic, Cagayan de Oro City, 1964-80; pvt. practice gen. medicine Cagayan de Oro City, 1963—. Lodge: Masons (chaplin Cagayan de Oro chpt. 1969-79). Home: PO Box 1023, Cebu City 6000, Philippines Office: PO Box 157, Cagayan de Oro 9000, Philippines

QUENNELL, PETER, author; b. Bickley, Kent, Eng., Mar. 9, 1905; s. C. H. B. and M. Quennell. Ed. Balliol Coll., Oxford U. Former prof. English lit. Tokyo Bunrika Daigaku. Author: Baudelaire and the Symbolists; A Superficial Journey; Byron: The Years of Fame, Byron in Italy, 1941; Caroline of England, Four Portraits, 1945; Ruskin: The Portrait of a Prophet, 1952; Spring in Sicily, The Singular Preference, Hogarth's Progress, 1954; The Sign of the Fish, 1960; Shakespeare: The Poet and His Background, 1963; Alexander Pope: the Education of Genius, 1968; Romantic England, 1970; Casanova in London, 1971; Samuel Johnson, his Friends and Enemies, 1972; The Marble Foot, 1976; The Wanton Chase, 1980; Customs and Characters: Contemporary Portraits, 1982; editor: Aspects of 17th Century Verse; (transl.) Memoirs of the Comte de Gramont; Letters of Madame le Lieven; Memoirs of William Hickey; Byron; A Self Portrait (1798-1824); Mayhew's London Labour and the London Poor, 3 vols.; Marcel Proust: 1871-1922, 1971; Genius in the Drawing Room; Vladimir Nabakov, his Life, his Work, his World, 1979; A Lonely Business: A Self Portrait of James Pope-Hennessy, 1981; editor Cornhill Mag., 1944-51, History Today, 1951-79. Decorated Order Brit. Empire. Address: 26 Cheyne Row, London SW3 England *

QUEZADA-DIAMONDSTEIN, MARIA DEL SOCORRO, political scientist; b. Loma Linda, Calif., Sept. 16, 1949; d. Jose Ramiro Quezada M. and Margarita Medrano de Quezada; m. Bert M. Diamondstein, Aug. 11, 1978; 1 child, Socorro Mayuko. Teaching degree, Instituto Pedagogico de Chihuahua (Mex.), 1967; BA, U. Tex., Austin, 1970; postgrad., Sorbonne, Paris, 1971, Sophia U., Tokyo, 1973; MA in Polit. Sci., U. Tex., El Paso, 1977; postgrad. U. Chgo., 1979—. Coordinator, lectr. workshops in social scis. and humanities Centro de Estudios Generales, Chihuahua, 1971-72; import-export supr. Admiral Corp. Am., Ciudad Juarez, Mex., 1974-75; instr. polit. sci. U. Tex., El Paso, 1975-78, El Paso Community Coll., 1978; asst. survey dir. III, Nat. Opinion Research Ctr., U. Chgo., 1979-82; producer/account exec. Ted Hearne Assocs., 1982-83; v.p. mktg. and communications Americas, Inc., 1983-84; dir. mktg. Emery Advt., 1985-86; sr. assoc. pres. Incomar & Assocs., El Paso, 1986—; condr. workshops; asst. to pres. U. Autonoma de Chihuahua, 1971-72; prodn.-mktg. researcher Duraplay de Parral, 1973-74; mem. nat. Chicano research network Inst. Social Research, U. Mich., 1980—. Mem. Chgo. Council Fine Arts. Recipient prize for oil painting Banco Comercial Mexicano Ann. Art Exhbn., 1968; U. Calif., San Diego grantee, 1978. Mem. Latin Am. Studies Assn., Pi Sigma Alpha. Roman Catholic.

QUIBRIA, MUHAMMAD GHULAM, economist; b. Dhamura, Bangladesh, Jan. 16, 1949; s. Arshad and Amina A.; m. Syeda H. Rahman, June 16, 1972; children: Naureen, Nasreen. BA with honors, U. Dhaka, Bangladesh, 1969, MA in Econs., 1970; MA in Econs., Princeton U., 1975, PhD in Econs., 1978. Lectr. in econs. U. Dhaka, 1972-73, asst. prof., 1977-78, assoc. prof., 1978-82; vis. fellow Nuffield Coll., Oxford, Eng., 1982-83; vis. prof. Boston U., 1983-84; research assoc. Ctr. Asian Devel. Studies, Boston, 1983-84; research economist Asian Devel. Bank, Manila, 1984—; cons. Ford Found., Dhaka, 1978, 82, Agrl. Devel. Council Dhaka, 1979, UN FAO, Rome, 1984. Contbr. research papers to econs. jours. Ford Found. fellow, Princeton U., 1973-77, Commonwealth Found. fellow, Oxford U., 1982-83, Fulbright fellow, Boston U., 1983-84. Mem. Am. Econs. Assn., Royal Econ. Soc., Econometric Soc., European Econ. Assn., Can. Econ. Assn. Office: Asian Devel Bank, PO Box 789, Manila Philippines

QUICK, JACK BEAVER, club executive, tax consultant; b. Biloxi, Miss., Oct. 31, 1947; s. Murdoch Alexander and Ethel Christine (Martin) Q. B.S. in Acctg., N.E. La. U., 1971; postgrad. U. So. Calif., 1975-76; AAS in Hotel, Restaurant and Instl. Mgmt., No. Va. Community Coll., 1986. Asst. for systems mgmt. Office of Sec. of Def., Washington, 1977-79; pres. Northeastern Food Corp., Columbia, Md., 1979-80; v.p. Bojangles of Washington, Inc., Washington, 1980-83; adminstrv. asst. The University Club, Washington, 1983-85, gen. mgr., 1985—; tax cons. Profl. Tax Service, Alexandria, Va., 1974—. Served to capt. U.S. Army, 1971-79. Mem. Internat. Food Service Execs. Assn. (1st v.p. 1983, Key award 1983), Club Mgrs. Assn. Am. (chmn. govt. affairs Nat. Capital chpt. 1988—, Wine Soc. Idea Fair award 1988), Nat. Restaurant Assn., Restaurant Assn. Met. Washington (bd. dirs., chmn. mem. com., 1987-88), Am. Soc. Assn. Execs., Knights of the Vine, Delta Sigma Pi (life mem., sr. v.p. 1970-71). Republican. Lutheran. Clubs: Half-Fast Social (Alexandria, Va.) (pres. 1983—), Swan Point Yacht and Country, Mercedes Benz (1st place in class Starfest 88 Concours). Avocations: classic cars; swimming; tennis; jogging. Home: 5902 Mount Eagle Dr Suite 1101 Alexandria VA 22303 Office: The University Club 11135 16th St NW Washington DC 20036

QUIGLEY, BEHNAZ ZOLGHADR, educator, consultant; b. Tehran, Iran, Nov. 17, 1944; came to U.S., 1968, naturalized, 1978; d. Hamid and Behjat (Shoaibi) Zolghadr; m. Herbert Gerald Quigley, Aug. 24, 1968; children: Narda, Paran. Diploma in Edn., Tchrs. Tng. Coll., Tehran, 1964; BA, U. Tehran, 1968; MBA, U. D.C., 1975; PhD, U. Md., 1987. Tchr. secondary sch. Ministry of Edn., Tehran, 1964-68; instr. in bus. Strayer Coll., U. D.C. Washington, Prince George's Community Coll., Md., U. Md., College Park, 1975-87; asst. prof. bus. adminstrn. Mt. Vernon Coll., Washington, 1977-88, assoc. prof., 1983—, chmn. dept. bus. adminstrn., 1978—; aide to chief economist Iranian Econ. Mission, 1974; freelance cons. World Trade Assocs., Distbn. Systems, co-owner, freelance cons. Univ. Systems Assocs., Inst. Curriculum Devel., Mid. East Inst., 1975-80. Author several books; co-editor: Management Systems: Contemporary Perspectives; contbr. articles to profl. jours. Faculty devel. grantee Mt. Vernon Coll., Mid. East Inst. Mem. Nat. Assn. Female Execs. (bd. dirs. Washington area chpt.), Assn. MBA Execs., Am. Acctg. Assn., Acad. Mgmt., Am. Soc. for Pub. Adminstrn., U. D.C. Alumni Assn., U. Md. Alumni Assn. Democrat. Home: 5 Canfield Ct Potomac MD 20854 Office: 2100 Foxhall Rd Washington DC 20007

QUIMBY, GEORGE IRVING, anthropologist, former museum director; b. Grand Rapids, Mich., May 4, 1913; s. George Irving and Ethelwyn (Sweet) Q.; m. Helen M. Ziehm, Oct. 13, 1940; children: Sedna H., G. Edward, John E., Robert W. B.A., U. Mich., 1936, M.A., 1937, grad. fellow, 1937-38; postgrad., U. Chgo., 1938-39. State supr. Fed. Archaeol. Project in La., 1939-41; dir. Muskegon (Mich.) Mus., 1941-42; asst. curator N.Am. archaeology and ethnology Field Mus. Natural History, 1942-43, curator exhibits, anthropology, 1943-54, curator N.Am. archeology and ethnology, 1954-65, research assoc. in N. Am. archaeology and ethnology, 1965—; curator anthropology Thomas Burke Meml. Wash. State Mus.; prof. anthropology U. Wash., 1965-83, emeritus prof., 1983—, mus. dir., 1968-83, emeritus dir., 1983—; lectr. U. Chgo., 1947-65, Northwestern U., 1949-53; Fulbright vis. prof., U. Oslo, Norway, 1952; archaeol. expdns. and field work, Mich., 1935, 37, 42, 56-63, Wis., 1936, Hudson's Bay, 1939, La., 1940-41, N.Mex., 1947, Lake Superior, 1956-61. Author: Aleutian Islanders, 1944, (with J. A. Ford) The Tchefuncte Culture, an Early Occupation of the Lower Mississippi Valley, 1945, (with P. S. Martin, D. Collier) Indians Before Columbus, 1947, Indian Life in the Upper Great Lakes, 1960, Indian Culture and European Grade Goods, 1966; producer documentary film (with Bill Holm) In the Land of the War Canoes, 1973; Edward S. Curtis in the Land of the War Canoes: A Pioneer Cinematographer in the Pacific Northwest, 1980; Contbr. articles to profl. jours. Honored by festschrift U. Mich. Mus. Anthropology, 1983. Fellow AAAS, Am. Anthrop. Assn.; mem. Soc. Am. Archaeology (pres. 1958, 50th Anniversary award 1983), Am. Soc. Ethnohistory, Wis. Archeol. Soc., Soc. Historical Archeology (council 1971-74, 75-78, J.C. Harrington medal 1986), Assn. Sci. Mus. Dirs. (pres. 1973—), Arctic Inst. N.Am., Am. Assn. Museums (council 1971-74), Sigma Xi, Phi Sigma, Chi Gamma Phi, Zeta Psi. Home: 6001 52d Ave NE Seattle WA 98115 Office: Thomas Burke Meml Wash State Mus U Washington Seattle WA 98195

QUIMLAT, MARQUEZ DOMINGO, editor; b. Morong, Philippines, Sept. 14, 1928; s. Dionisio Quimlat and Silvina Marquez; m. Filomena S. Quimlat; children Gerardo, Reynaldo. Student, Far Eastern U., Manila, 1948-52, Lyceum of the philippines, Manila, 1953-56. Reporter The Evening News, Manila, 1951-52; reporter, deskman Philippine News Service, Manila, 1953-72; polit. reporter Taliba Manila Times Pub. Co, 1957-72; mng. editor Balita, Manila, 1972-73, editor-in-chief, 1973—; feature writer Interco Press, Inc., Manila, 1986—. Author series Journey to Redland, 1967, 23 Days in China, 1976. Mem. Manila Overseas Club. Roman Catholic. Clubs: Nat. Press Philippines, Manila Overseas. Home: 40 Dexter St, project 8, Quezon City Manila Office: Liwayway Pub Inc, 2249 Pasong Tamo, Makati Philippines

QUINLAN, MICHAEL ROBERT, fast food franchise company executive; b. Chgo., Dec. 9, 1944; s. Robert Joseph and Kathryn (Koerner) Q.; m. Marilyn DeLashmutt, Apr. 23, 1966; children: Kevin, Michael. BS, Loyola U., Chgo., 1967, MBA, 1970. With McDonald's Corp., Oak Brook, Ill., 1966—, v.p., 1974-76, sr. v.p., 1976-78, exec. v.p., 1978-79, chief ops. officer, 1979-80, pres. McDonald's U.S.A., 1980-82, pres., 1982—, chief operating officer, 1982—, chief exec. officer, 1987—, dir. Republican. Roman Catholic. Clubs: Butterfield Country, Oakbrook Handball-Racquetball. Home: 720 Midwest Corp Oak Brook IL 60515 Office: McDonald's Corp 1 McDonald's Plaza Oak Brook IL 60521 *

QUINN, ANTHONY RUDOLPH OAXACA, actor, writer, artist; b. Chihuahua, Mexico, Apr. 21, 1915; naturalized, 1947; s. Frank and Nellie (Oaxaca) Q.; m. Katherine de Mille, Oct. 2, 1937 (div.); children: Christina, Kathleen, Duncan, Valentina; m. Iolanda Addolori, Jan. 1966; children: Francesco, Daniele, Lorenzo. Student pub. schs. Actor in plays including Clean Beds, 1936, Gentleman from Athens, 1947, Street Car Named Desire, Let Me Hear the Melody, Beckett, 1961, Tchin-Tchin, 1963, Zorba, 1983-86; has appeared in 175 motion pictures including Guadalcanal Diary, 1943, Buffalo Bill, 1944, Irish Eyes are Smiling, 1944, China Sky, 1945, Back to Bataan, 1945, Where Do We Go From Here?, 1945, Tycoon, 1947, The Brave Bulls, 1951, Mask of the Avenger, 1951, World in his Arm, 1952, Against all Flags, 1952, Viva Zapata (Acad. award 1952), Ride Vaquero, 1953, City Beneath the Sea, 1953, Seminole, 1953, Blowing Wild, 1953, East of Sumatra, 1953, Long Wait, 1954, Magnificent Matador, 1955, Ulysses, 1955, Naked Street, 1955, Seven Cities of Gold, 1955, Lust for Life, (Acad. award best supporting actor 1956), La Strada, 1954, Man from Del Rio, 1956, Wild the Wind, 1957, Attila the Hun, 1958, The Wild Party, 1956, The Ride Back, 1957, The Hunchback of Notre Dame, 1957, The River's Edge, 1957, Hot Spell, 1958, Heller with a Gun, Savage Innocents, 1959, The Black Orchid, 1958, Last Train From Gun Hill, 1958, Warlock, 1959, Heller in Pink Tights, 1960, Portrait in Black, 1960, Guns of Navarrone, 1961, Becket, 1961, Barabbas, 1962, Lawrence of Arabia, 1962, Requiem for a Heavyweight, 1963, The Visit, 1963, Behold a Pale Horse, 1964, Zorba the Greek, 1964, High Wind in Jamaica, 1965, Guns for San Sebastian, 1968, The Shoes of the Fisherman, 1968, The Secret of Santa Vittoria, 1969, A Dream of Kings, 1969, Flap, 1970, A Walk in Spring Rain, 1970, R.P.M., 1970, The City, 1971, Jesus of Nazareth, 1971, Across 110th Street, 1972, Arruza, Deaf Smith and Johnny Ears, 1973, The Don Is Dead, 1973, Mohammed Messenger of God, 1977, Caravans, 1978, The Children of Sanchez, 1978, The Greek Tycoon, 1978, The Inheritance, 1978, The Passage, 1979, Lion of the Desert, 1981, High Roll, 1981, Valentina, 1984, The Salamander, 1984, Treasure Island, 1986, Stradivarius, 1987; appeared in TV prodns. of The Life of Christ, Onassis: The Richest Man in the World, 1988; script writer: Metro-Goldwyn-Mayer prodn. The Farm; author: The Original Sin, 1972; artist 8 major exhbns. oil paintings, sculptures and serigraphs Hawaii, 1982 and 87, San Francisco, 1983, N.Y.C., 1984, San Antonio, 1984, Houston, 1984, Washington, 1985, Beverly Hills, Calif., 1986. Address: care McCartt Oreck Barrett 402 E 90th St New York NY 10128

QUINN, CHRISTINE AGNES, radiologist; b. Cleve., Sept. 23, 1946; d. Paul Leo and Estelle Christine Q.; B.A., Marquette U., 1967; M.D., Med. Coll. Pa., 1971; m. Paul C. Janicki, July 11, 1970; children—Sarah Christine, Megan Alexandra. Intern, St. Luke's Hosp., Cleve., 1971-72; resident in diagnostic radiology Cleve. Clinic Found., 1972-75, radiologist, 1975-81; radiologist Marymount Hosp., Cleve., 1981—. Diplomate Am. Bd. Radiology. Mem. Radiol. Soc. N. Am., Am. Coll. Radiology, Soc. Nuclear

Medicine, Ohio Med. Soc., Cuyahoga County Med. Soc., AMA. Contbr. to CRC Handbook Series, Vol. II, 1977; contbr. articles to profl. jours. Home: 2781 Sherbrooke Rd Shaker Heights OH 44122 Office: 12300 McCracken Rd Cleveland OH 44125

QUINN, EDWARD JAMES, banker; b. N.Y.C., Apr. 2, 1911; s. Edward M. and Mary M. (Schneider) Q.; m. Marie A. Stafford, Apr. 22, 1939 (dec. 1972); children—Mary Ann Brown, James E., Patrick M., Sheila G.; m. Margaret B. O'Neill, Nov. 4, 1982. Student, Hofstra Coll., 1946-52; grad., Am. Inst. Banking, 1932-39, Grad. Sch. Banking at Rutgers, 1955-57. Messenger J.S. Bache & Co., N.Y.C., 1926-27; bookkeeper Nassau-Suffolk Bond & Mortgage Guaranty Co., Mineola, N.Y., 1928; sr. v.p. European-Am. Bank & Trust Co., 1928—. Chmn. investment com. United Fund L.I., 1968-71; treas. Nassau County Boy Scouts Am., 1936-39, Nassau County March Dimes, 1947-48, Nassau County Easter Seal Appeal, 1948-55, Suffolk County Cancer Soc., 1955-57, Union Free Sch. Dist. 22, Farmingdale, 1948-57; mem. U.S. Savs. Bond Com., Nassau County, 1952-65; bd. regents Royal Arcanum, 1938-39, grand committeeman, 1940-41; Mem. Bd. Appeals Village Farmingdale, 1941-56. Served with Med. Detachment AUS, 1943-46. 1st Sgt. Army Commendation ribbon, 1986. Mem. Mcpl. Forum N.Y., Mcpl. Finance Officers Assn. U.S., L.I. Bankers Assn. (chmn. check clearing com. 1955, legis. com. 1965-71), Nat. Assn. Accts., Am. Legion. Clubs: St. George's Golf and Country (Stony Brook, N.Y.); Southward Ho Country (Brightwaters, N.Y.); Atlantis (Fla.) Country. Home: 383 West Hills Rd Huntington NY 11743 Home: 130 Driftwood Terr Atlantis FL 33462 Office: 383 W Hills Rd Huntington NY 11743

QUINN, FRANCIS XAVIER, labor arbitrator-mediator, writer, lecturer; b. Dunmore, Pa., June 9, 1932; s. Frank T. and Alice B. (Maher) Q.; m. Marlene S. Quinn; children: Kimberly, Catherine, Cameron. AB, Fordham U., 1956, MA, 1958; STB, Woodstock Coll., 1964; MSIR, Loyola U., Chgo., 1966; PhD in Indsl. Relations, Calif. Western U., 1976. Assoc. dir. St. Joseph's Coll. Inst. Indsl. Relations, Phila., 1966-7; Manpower fellow Temple U., 1969-71, spl. asst. to dean Sch. Bus. Adminstrn., 1972-78; arbitrator Fed. Mediation and Conciliation Service, Nat. Mediation Bd., Am. Arbitration Assn., Pa. Dept. Labor and Industry, N.J. Pub. Employment Relations Commn., Okla. Pub. Employment Relations Commn.; apptd. to Ry. Emergency Bd., 1975, to Fgn. Service Grievance Bd., 1976, 78, 81. Named Tchr. of Yr., Freedom Found., 1959; recipient Human Relations award City of Phila., 1971, others. Mem. Nat. Acad. Arbitrators (gov.), Indsl. Relations Research Assn., Assn. for Social Econs. (exec. council), Soc. for Dispute Resolution, Am. Arbitration Assn. (arbitrator), Internat. Soc. Labor Law and Social Security, Internat. Ombudsman Inst. Democrat. Author: The Ethical Aftermath of Automation, Ethics and Advertising, Population Ethics, The Evolving Role of Women in the World of Work, Developing Community Responsibility. Editor: The Ethical Aftermath Series, 1962-89; contbr. articles to profl. jours. Home: 230 Hazel Blvd Tulsa OK 74114

QUINN, JULIA PROVINCE, civic worker; b. Franklin, Ind., Feb. 23; d. Oran Arnold and Lillian (Ditmars) Province; B.A., Franklin Coll., 1937; M.S., Smith Coll. Sch. Social Work, 1939; m. Robert William Quinn, Jan. 21, 1942; children: Robert Sean, Judith Ditmars. Caseworker, student supr. Community Service Soc., N.Y.C., 1939-44; caseworker community research Family Service Soc., New Haven, 1946; social worker in research, dept. preventive medicine Yale U. Sch. Medicine, New Haven, 1946-49; research asst. dept. preventive medicine Vanderbilt U. Sch. Medicine, Nashville, 1969-70. Bd. dirs. Tenn. Bot. Gardens and Fine Arts Center, 1976-81, Friends of J. F. Kennedy Center, 1976-81, Family and Children's Service, Nashville, 1977-83, Friends of Cheekwood, 1966-81, Nashville Symphony Assn., 1978-85, Tenn. Performing Arts Found., 1979—; active Friends of the Tenn. Performing Arts Ctr., 1985—, charter mem., 1986—; bd. dirs. Nashville Opera Assn., 1983—, chmn. pub. relations, 1985—, Nashville Opera Guild (charter mem., bd. dirs. 1987); chmn. pub. relations Friends of Cheekwood, 1966-68, 72-74, 76-78, Tenn. Performing Arts Found., 1978-85, Family and Children's Service, 1978-83; mem. adv. bd. Vanderbilt Center for Fertility and Reproductive Research, 1981-85; charter mem., bd. dirs. Nashville Opera Guild, 1987—. Recipient Nashville Vol. Activist award Cain-Sloan and Germaine Monteil, 1979. Mem. Nat. Assn. Social Workers, Acad. Cert. Social Workers, Ladies Hermitage Assn., Vanderbilt Med. Center Aux., Nashville Opera Assn. Guild, Nashville Area C. of C. (cultural affairs com. 1979-85). Democrat. Presbyterian. Clubs: Smith Coll., Centennial (Nashville); Vanderbilt Garden, Vanderbilt Woman's. Contbr. articles to social work and med. jours. Home: 508 Park Center Dr Nashville TN 37205

QUINN, LUCY DIANA, accountant; b. Richmond, Va., Feb. 9, 1933; d. Lewis Hopkins and Mary Caperton (Horsley) Renshaw. Student, Harvard U., 1950-52; BS, Am. U., 1972. CPA, Md. With U.S. State Dept., Washington, 1963-64, consular officer, 1964-74; budget and fiscal officer Am. Embassy Kinshasa, Zaire, 1974-76, Am. Embassy Damascus, Syria, 1976-80; budget officer State Dept., Washington, 1980-86; budget and mgmt. officer Am. Embassy Riyadh, Saudi Arabia, 1986—. Mem. Am. Inst. CPAs, D.C. Inst. CPAs, U.S. Employees Recreation Assn. (v.p. 1986-87). Democrat. Episcopalian.

QUINN, ROBERT WILLIAM, physician, educator; b. Eureka, Calif., July 22, 1912; s. William James and Norma Irene (McLean) Q.; student Stanford U., 1930-33; M.D., C.M., McGill U., 1938; m. Julia Rebecca Province, Jan. 21, 1942; children—Robert Sean Province, Judith D. Rotating intern Alameda County Hosp., Oakland, Calif., 1938-39; postgrad. tng. internal medicine U. Calif. Hosp., San Francisco, 1939-41, research fellow internal medicine, 1940-41; postgrad. tng. internal medicine Presbyn. Hosp., N.Y.C., 1941-42; research fellow Yale U., 1946- 47, instr. preventive medicine, 1947-49; assoc. prof. preventive medicine and student health U. Wis., 1949-52; prof., head dept. preventive medicine and public health Vanderbilt U., 1952-80; dir. venereal disease control Met. Nashville Health Dept. Bd. dir. Planned Parenthood Assn. Nashville; adv. com. Family Planning Tenn. and Nashville. Served as capt. M.C., USNR, 1942-46. Diplomate Am. Bd. Preventive Medicine. Mem. Am. Acad. Preventive Medicine, Infectious Diseases Soc. Am., Middle Tenn. Heart Assn. (pres. 1957), Assn. Am. Med. Colls., Nashville Acad. Medicine, Assn. Tchrs. Preventive Medicine, Am. Public Health Assn., Am. Epidemiol. Soc., Am. Venereal Disease Assn., Physicians for Social Responsibility (pres. Greater Nashville chpt.). Club: Belle Meade Country. Author med. articles. Home: 508 Park Center Dr Nashville TN 37205

QUINONES AMÉZQUITA, MARIO RAFAEL, former Guatemala government official, lawyer, educator; b. June 4, 1933; s. Hector and Elisa Quinones; m. Yolanda De Quinones, 1963; 2 sons, 2 daughters. Student, U. San Carlos, Guatemala, U. Rio Grande do Sul, Brazil. Ptnr. Viteri, Falla, Quinones, Umana, Orellana & Caceres, 1959—; prof. law Rafael Landivar U., Guatemala, 1962—, dean dept. legal and social scis., 1974-82; v.p. Landivar U., Guatemala, 1978-82, pres., 1982; permanent rep. to UN 1982-84; minister fgn. affairs Guatemala, Guatemala City, 1986-87. Home: 6A Calle 5-47, Zona 9, Guatemala City Guatemala *

QUINOT, RAYMOND, writer, educator; b. Brussels, Etterbeek, Belgium, Feb. 12, 1920; s. Edgard and Juliette (Degalant) Q; m. Suzanne Cambron, Sept. 3, 1952. Dir. Adminstrn. of Teaching, Brussels, 1946-80; bd. dirs. Les Etoiles; adminstr. Charles Plisnier Found. Author 42 books, coll. anthologies. Adminstr. Internat. Biennial Poetry of Liége. Recipient Max Rose prize for Lit., Interfrance prizes for essay and poetry, Davaine award Acad. Française, Ville de Bruxelles award, Rime d'Or Acad. Disque de Poésie, Paris. Mem. Literary Young (pres.), Internat. Pen Club (sec.), Assn. Belgian Writers (adminstr.), Royal Assn. Walloon Writers (adminstr.). Office: Internat PEN Club-French, Speaking Br, 76 ave 11 Novembre, Bte 7, 1040 Brussels Belgium

QUIRK, RANDOLPH, British Academy president, consultant; b. Isle of Man, U.K., July 12, 1920; s. Thomas and Amy Randolph (Simcocks) Q.; m. Gabriele Stein. B.A., U. London, 1947, M.A., 1949, Ph.D., 1951, D.Litt., 1961; hon. doctorate Lund U., 1976, Uppsala U., 1977, U. Paris, 1979, U. Liège, 1980, U. Nijmegen, 1983, U. Leicester, 1983, U. Reading, 1983, U. Salford, 1984, U. Bath, 1985, U. Newcastle, 1985, U. Durham, 1986, U. Essex, 1986, Open U., 1986, U. Glasgow, 1988. Postdoctoral fellow Yale U., 1951-52; prof. English, Durham U., 1954-60, London U., 1960-81; vice chancellor London U., 1981-85; Lee Kuan Yew fellow Nat. U. Singapore, 1985-86; pres. British Acad., 1985—, Coll. Speech Therapists, 1987—; chmn. Brit. Govt. Inquiry into Speech Therapy Service, 1969-72, chmn. adv. com. Brit. Library, 1984—, Hornby Ednl. Trust, 1979—; trustee Am. Sch. in London, 1986—, Wolfson Found., 1987—. Author numerous books. Decorated comdr. Order Brit. Empire, 1976, knight, 1984. Fellow Brit. Acad., Royal Belgian Acad. Scis., Royal Swedish Acad.; mem. Linguistic Soc. Am., Philol. Soc. U.K. Club: Athenaeum. Home: Univ Coll, Gower St, London WC1, England Office: British Acadamy, 20-21 Cornwall Terr, London NW1 4QP, England

QUITO, EMERITA SANTOS, educator; b. Pampanga, Philippines, Sept. 11, 1929; d. Pablo and Rosario (Santos) Q. PhB, U. Santo Tomas, Manila, 1946-49, MA in Philosophy, 1950-57; PhD, U. Fribourg, Switzerland, 1958-65. Chmn. philosophy dept. De La Salle U., Manila, 1971—, dean grad. sch., 1978-80. Author: La Notion de Liberté Participee dans la Philosophie de Louis Lavelle, 1965, A New Concept of Philosophy, 1967, Four Essays in the Philosophy of History, 1979. Vice chmn. Nat. Movement for Free Elections, 1986. Decorated Ordre de Palmes Academiques (France); named Most Outstanding Educator, Metrobank, 1985. Mem. Philippine Acad. Philos. Research (founder, first pres. 1985—), Philippine-French Assn. (pres. 1986-87). Office: De La Salle U, 2401 Taft Ave, Manila Philippines

QUITTMEYER, CHARLES LOREAUX, business educator; b. Peekskill, N.Y., Dec. 23, 1917; s. Ernest Martin and Edith Grace (Loreaux) Q.; m. Maureen J. Rankin, June 2, 1956; children: Peter Charles, David Rankin, Andrew Robert, Jane Loreaux. A.B., Coll. William and Mary, 1940; M.B.A., Harvard U., 1947; Ph.D. (fellow), Columbia U., 1955. Bus. and govt. positions 1941-42, 47-48; asst. prof. bus. adminstrn. Coll. William and Mary, Williamsburg, Va., 1948-54; prof., head dept. Coll. William and Mary, 1962-68; dean Coll. William and Mary (Sch. Bus. Adminstrn.), 1968-83; Floyd Dewey Gottwald prof. bus. Coll. William and Mary, 1982-88, emeritus, 1988—; lectr., asst. prof. mktg. U. Buffalo, 1954-57; research assoc., asso. prof. commerce U. Va., 1957-61; sr. scientist Tech. Ops., Inc., 1961-62; dir., adv. bd. First & Mchts. Nat. Bank, Peninsula, 1972-83; dir., treas., exec. com. Williamsburg Landing, Inc. Contbr. to: Ency. Brit; author papers in field. Bd. suprs. James City County, 1969-71, chmn., 1971; Mem. Peninsula Airport Commn., 1971-81, sec., 1973-81. Served to capt., F.A. and M.I. AUS, 1942-46. Recipient William and Mary Alumni medallion, 1976. Mem. Acad. Mgmt., Am. Econ. Assn., So. Bus. Adminstrn. Assn. (pres. 1976-77), Soc. of Alumni Coll. William and Mary (dir. 1984—), Phi Beta Kappa, Beta Gamma Sigma. Episcopalian. Club: Harvard of Virginia. Home: 210 Kingswood Dr Williamsburg VA 23185

QURAISHI, ALI AKHTAR, civil engineering educator; b. Kushtia, Bangladesh, May 8, 1936; moved to Saudi-Arabia, 1967; s. Shamsul and Jamila (Khatun) Haque; m. Rowshan Ara Sufyani, Apr. 16, 1965; children—Faria, Uzma, Sadeq. Matriculation, Nabakumar Inst., Dhaka (Bangladesh), 1952; Intermediate Sci., Dhaka Coll., 1954; B.Sc. in Engring., Dhaka U. (Bangladesh), 1958; M.S. in Civil Engring., Tex. A&M U., 1961; Ph.D. in Civil Engring., Colo. State U., Ft. Collins, 1964. Lectr., Ahsanullah Engring. Coll., Dhaka, 1958-59; research asst., engr. Colo. State U., 1961-64; asst. prof. U. Engring. and Tech., Dhaka, 1964-67; from asst. to prof. civil engring. King Saud U., Riyadh, Saudi Arabia, 1967—; cons. in field. Contbr. articles to profl. jours. Exec. mem. Pakistan Internat. Sch., Riyadh, 1970; adviser Banladeshi Sch., 1977. Merit scholar, Govt. East Pakistan, 1952-58; AID scholar Govt. U.S.A., 1959-61; Research awards King Saud U., 1978-83. Fellow ASCE; mem. Internat. Assn. Hydraulic Research, Internat. Water Resources Assn., Pakistani Assn. (exec. mem. 1960, 63). Muslim. Avocations: playing bridge; traveling. Home and Office: King Saud U, Coll of Engring, PO Box 800, Riyadh 11421, Saudi Arabia

QURAISHI, MOHAMMED SAYEED, health scientist, administrator; b. Jodhpur, India, June 23, 1924; came to U.S., 1946, naturalized, 1973; s. Mohammed Latif and Akhtar Jahan Q.; m. Akhtar Imtiaz, Nov. 12, 1953; children—Rana, Naveed, Sabah. B.Sc., St. John's Coll., 1942; M.Sc., Aligarh Muslim U., 1944; Ph.D., U. Mass., 1948. Sr. mem. UN, WHO Team to Bangladesh, 1949-51; entomologist Malaria Inst. Pakistan, 1951-55; sr. research officer Pakistan Council Sci. and Indsl. Research, 1955-60; sr. sci. officer Pakistan AEC, 1960-64; assoc. prof. entomology U. Man., 1964-66; assoc. prof. entomology N.D. State U., Fargo, 1966-70, prof., 1970-74; chief scientist biology N.Y. State Sci. Service, Albany, 1974-75; entomologist, toxicologist, chief pest control and consultation sect. NIH, Bethesda, Md., 1976-84; health scientist adminstr., exec. sec. microbiology and infectious disease research com. Nat. Inst Allergy and Infectious Diseases, Bethesda, Md., 1984—; sr. scientist Central Treaty Orgn., Inst. Nuclear Sci., Tehran, Iran, 1960-64; program mgr. interdepartmental contract Project THEMIS, Dept. Def., 1968-74. Author: Biochemical Insect Control: Its Impact on Economy, Environment and Natural Selection, 1977; mem. editorial bd. Jour. Environ. Toxicology and Chemistry, 1981; author numerous sci. papers. Chmn. NIH Asian-Am. Cultural Assn., 1980-81. Mem. Am. Chem. Soc., Soc. Environ. Toxicology and Chemistry. (mem. publs. com. in charge spl. publs. 1982—), Sigma Xi, Phi Kappa Phi. Home: 19813 Cochrane Way Gaithersburg MD 20879 Office: Room 706 Westwood Bldg Bethesda MD 20892

QURASHI, MAZHAR MAHMOOD, physicist; b. Gujranwala, Pakistan, Oct. 8, 1925; s. Ferozud Din and Rashida Begum Q.; B.A. with honors, Punjab U., 1942, B.Sc. with honors, 1943, M.Sc. in Physics, 1944; Ph.D. in Crystal Structure Analysis, Manchester (Eng.) U., 1949, D.Sc. (hon.), 1962; m. Khalida Adiba, Nov. 16, 1958; 9 children. Mem. staff Pakistan Council Sci. and Indsl. Research, 1950-63, 68-71, 73-76, 83-85; chief scientist Ministry Def., 1963-68; dir. Inst. Physics, Islamabad U., 1972-73; dir. gen. Appropriate Tech. Devel. Orgn., Ministry Sci. and Tech., Islamabad, 1976-81; dir. studies Nat. Sci. Council, Islamabad, 1981-83; mem. faculty Karachi U., 1953-63. Postdoctoral fellow NRC Can., 1950-51, vis. scientist, 1961-62. Fellow Inst. Physics London, Pakistan Acad. Scis. (assoc. sec. gen. 1972-84, sec. gen. 1988—, Physics Open medal 1972); life mem. Pakistan Assn. Advancement Sci. (pres. physics sect. 1971-72); life mem. Sci. Soc. Pakistan (pres. 1968-69, exec. com. 1969—). Muslim. Author monographs, papers in field; editor profl. jours. Home: 34 32d St F-7/1, Islamabad Pakistan Office: Editor Pakistan Acad, 5 Constitution Ave, Islamabad Pakistan

QURESHI, MOHAMED NAWAZ, hotel executive; b. Rawalpindi, Pakistan, May 21, 1952; s. Ghulam Rasool and Sahib (Jan) Q.; m. Shamim Nawaz, Nov. 21, 1978; 1 child, Hina. BA, U. of Punjab, Lahore, Pakistan, 1971; studied creative mktg., mktg. mgmt., Cornell U., summer 1984. Mgmt. trainee Hotel Intercontinental, Ralwalpindi, Pakistan, 1973-74; acct. Carlton Hotel, Sharjah, United Arab Emirates, 1975-76; night club mgr. S.S.H. Bon Vivant Flotel, Dubai, United Arab Emirates, 1976-78; accounts receivable supr., acting credit supr. Hilton Internat. Dubai, 1978; credit mgr. Hyatt Regency, Dubai, 1980, sales mgr., 1983, asst. dir. sales, 1984, asst. dir. sales worldwide sales office, 1985-86; with The Oceanic Hotel, Khor Fakkan Sharjah, United Arab Emirates, 1986—; acting gen. mgr. The Oceanic Hotel, Khor Fakkan Sharjah, 1987-88, gen. mgr., 1988—. Office: The Oceanic Hotel, PO Box 10444, Khor Fakkan Sharjah, United Arab Emirates

QURESHI, MOHAMMAD AKRAM, physician; b. Sialkot-1, Punjab, Pakistan, Mar. 5, 1935; s. Rehmat Ullah Qazi and Begum Amna; m. Naeema Akram, Dec. 4, 1965; children: Humera, Hammad, Sumaira, Umair. B in Medicine and BS, King Edward Med. Coll., Lahore, Pakistan, 1958. Practice family medicine Pakistan, 1986—; mem. Com. to Solve Problems Faced by Med. Profession in Punjab. Sec. Tb Assn., Sialkot, 1972-76; founder, chmn. City Edn. Bd., Sialkot. Mem. Pakistan Med. Assn. (pres. 1981-86, joint sec. 1978-80). Home: Dar-Ul-Rehmat, Norgate St Cantt Rd, Sialkot-1, Punjab Pakistan Office: Clinic Dr Mohammad Qureshi, Maharaja Rd, Sialkot-1, Punjab Pakistan

QURESHI, MOHAMMED JAMIL, college official, consultant; b. Jagadhri, Panjab, India, Mar. 29, 1939; came to U.S., 1971; s. Mohammad Ibrahim and Fatima (Bibi) Q.; m. Saeeda Farhat, Apr. 13, 1975; children—Khalid Jamil, Naz Jamil. B.S. U. Panjab, 1962, D.L.S., 1964; M.A., U. Karachi, Pakistan, 1966; M.L.S., U. Toronto, Ont., Can., 1968; Ed.D., U. No. Colo., 1978. Audit clerk, fin. advisor, chief accounts officer Pakistan Western Rys., Lahore, 1960-63; lectr. Forward Coll., Lahore, 1963-65; librarian Panjab U. Library, 1964-65; bookmobile librarian Cape Breton Regional Library, Sydney, N.S., Can., 1966-67; adult services librarian North York Pub. Libraries, Toronto, 1968-69; asst. librarian, asst. dir. learning resources ctr. Red River Community Coll., Winnnipeg., Man., Can., 1969-72; dir. learning resources ctr. State Community Coll., East St. Louis, Ill., 1971-72, dean learning resource services, 1972-73; dir. learning resources ctr. Pikes Peak Community Coll., Colorado Springs, Colo., 1974-80, assoc. dean, 1980-83, v.p. student services, 1981-87, v.p. adminstrv. services, 1987—; mem. library formula com. State of Colo., 1976-82; mem. instrn./instructional support/student services subcom., centralization/decentralization com. Colo. Bd. Community Colls. and Occupational Edn., 1982-83, chmn. instructional support com., mem. student services com., mem. credential rev. com. for vocat. guidance specialist and job devel. specialist, 1982-84, chmn. state adv. com. for student personnel services, 1983-85; vice chmn. ednl. accountability com., chmn. vocat. edn. sub-com. Sch. Dist. 11, Colorado Springs, 1982—. Author: Book Selection Aids for the Community College Staff, 1970; Cataloging and Classification Use and Trends in Canadian Community College Libraries (survey), 1971; compiler (with Master Rasheeduddin) bibliography on 1st prime minister of Pakistan, Nawabzada Liaqat Ali Khan, 1966; mem. Urban League Colorado Springs, 1974—; mem. planning com. Plains and Peaks Regional Library System, Colorado Springs, 1975-76, pres. governing bd., 1977-78; chmn. edn. com. Colorado Springs br. NAACP, 1979-83, bd. dirs., 1979-85. Grad. library fellow U. Toronto, 1967-68; grad. acad. scholar U. No. Colo., 1971-72. Mem. ALA, Assn. Ednl Communications and Tech., Community Coll. Assn. Instrn. and Tech., Colo. Library Assn. (chmn. coll. and univ. action subcom. 1976-77, mem. legis. com. 1977-78, budget com. 1978-79), Assn. Colo. Community Coll. Learning Resources Ctrs. (v.p. 1977-78, pres. 1978-79), Colo. Ednl. Media Assn., Nat. Assn. Student Personnel Adminstrs., Kappa Delta Pi. Home: 2855 Villa Loma Dr Colorado Springs CO 80917 Office: Pikes Peak Community Coll 5675 S Academy Blvd Colorado Springs CO 80906

RAAB, HARRY FREDERICK, JR., physicist; b. Johnstown, Pa., May 9, 1926; s. Harry Frederick and Marjorie Eleanor (Stiff) R.; m. Phebe Ann Duerr, June 16, 1951; children—Constance Diane, Harry Frederick, Cynthia Ann Raab Morgenthaler. Student Navy Electronics Tech. Sch., 1944-45; SB and SM E.E., MIT, 1951; postgrad. Oak Ridge Sch. Reactor Tech., 1954-55. Reactor control engr. Bettis Atomic Power Lab. Westinghouse Electric Corp., West Mifflin, 1951-54, mgr. surface ship physics, 1955-62, mgr. light water breeder reactor physics, 1962-72; chief physicist Navy Nuclear Propulsion Directorate, Washington, 1972—. Patentee light water breeder reactor. Lay reader Episc. Ch. of the Good Shepherd, Burke, Va., 1957—, Sunday Sch. tchr., 1957-72, stewardship chmn., 1979-82, 84 sr. warden, 1983, 85, mem. stewardship com. Diocese of Va., 1983—. Served with USNR, 1944-46, PTO. Fellow Am. Nuclear Soc.; mem. Internat. Platform Assn., Sigma Xi, Tau Beta Pi, Eta Kappa Nu. Republican. Lodge: Masons. Home: 8202 Ector Ct Annandale VA 22003 Office: Naval Sea Systems Command Code 08A Washington DC 20039

RAAB, IRA JERRY, lawyer; b. N.Y.C., June 20, 1935; s. Benjamin and Fannie (Kirschner) R.; divorced; children: Michael, Shelley; m. Katie Rachel McKeever, June 30, 1979; children—Julie, Jennifer, Joseph. BBA, CCNY, 1955; JD, Bklyn. Law Sch., 1957; MPA, NYU, 1959, postgrad., 1961; MS in Pub. Adminstrn., L.I. U., 1961; postgrad., Adelphi U., 1981—. Bar: N.Y. 1958, U.S. Dist. Ct. (so. and ea. dists.) N.Y. 1960, U.S. Supreme Ct. 1967, U.S. Tax Ct. 1976, U.S. Ct. Appeals (2d cir.) 1977. Sole practice, Woodmere, N.Y., 1958-87, sr. ptnr. Raab & Raab, 1988— ; agt. Westchester County Soc. Prevention of Cruelty to Children, White Plains, N.Y., 1958; counsel Dept. Correction, City of N.Y., 1959, trial commr., 1976; staff counsel SBA, N.Y.C., 1961-63; asst. corp. counsel Tort Div., City of N.Y., 1963-70; counsel Investigation Com. on Willowbrook State Sch., Boro Hall, S.I., N.Y., 1970; gen. counsel Richmond County Soc. Prevention of Cruelty to Children, Boro Hall, 1970-81; pro bono counsel N.Y.C. Patrolmen's Benevolent Assn., 1974-81; rep. to UN from Internat. Criminal Ct., 1977-78; arbitrator Small Claims Ct., N.Y.C., 1970—, L.I. Better Bus. Bur., 1976—, Nassau County Dist. Ct., 1978—; hearing officer, 1982—; spl. master N.Y. Supreme Ct., 1977—; lectr. community and ednl. orgns.; instr. paralegal course Lawrence Sch. Dist., N.Y., 1982-84. Chmn. Businessmen's Luncheon Club, Wall St. Synagogue, 1968-79; sec. Community Mediation Ctr., Suffolk County, 1978-80, exec. v.p., 1980-81; vice chmn. Woodmere Incorporation Com., 1980-81; mem. adv. bd. Nassau Expressway Com., 1979-80; bd. dirs. Woodmere Mchts. Assn., 1979-80, v.p., 1979-83, chmn. 1984—; Candidate for dist. judge, Nassau County, 1987, 88. Recipient Consumer Protection award FTC, 1974, 76, 79, Recognition award Pres. Ronald Reagan, 1986, Man of Yr. award L.I. Council of Chambers, 1987; Mem. Am. Judges Assn. (nat. treas. 1978-82, exec. com. 1978-84, 86—, gov. dist. II 1974-78, 82-83 , chmn. civil ct. ops. com. 1975-76, chmn. ednl. film com. 1974-77, editorial bd. Court Rev. mag. 1975-79, 82-86, chmn. speakers' bur. com. 1976-77, chmn. legis. com. 1983—, William H. Burnett award 1983), Am. Judges Found. (pres. 1977-79, chmn. bd. trustees 1979-83, treas. 1974-75, 76-77, trustee 83—), Assn. Arbitrators of Civil Ct. City N.Y. (past pres.), ABA (chmn. cts. and community com. 1987—), N.Y. State Bar Assn. (sec. dist. city town and villages torts com), Nassau County Lawyers Assn., Nassau County Bar Assn. (mem. criminal cts. com., matrimonial and family ct. com., ct. com., ethics com.), Profl. Group Legal Service Assn. (past pres.), Internat. Assn Jewish Lawyers and Jurists (com. to draft Internat. Bill of Rights of Privacy 1982, council 1981—, bd. govs. 1984—), Am. Arbitration Assn. (arbitrator 1975—, adv. bd. community dispute ctr. 1979-81). Democrat. Hebrew. Lodge: K.P. Address: 375 Westwood Rd Woodmere NY 11598

RAAB, WALTER FERDINAND, manufacturing company executive; Phila., Nov. 25, 1924; s. BSE, U. Pa., 1945; m. Bernice M. Jacobs, 1952; children: Laurie Ann Kucher, Wendy Louise Robbins, Mandy Margaret. With Coopers Lybrand Co., 1945-53; with AMP Inc., Harrisburg, Pa., 1953—, treas., 1968-71, v.p., treas., 1971-75, v.p., treas., dir., 1975-79, v.p., chief fin. officer, 1979-81, vice chmn., chief fin. officer, 1981, chmn. bd., chief exec. officer, 1982—; dir. The West Co., Harris Corp., Dauphin Deposit Trust Co., Air Products and Chems., Inc. Bd. dirs. Holy Spirit Hosp.; trustee, Harrisburg Area YMCA. Mem. Elec. Mfrs. Club (bd. govs.), Pa. Bus. Roundtable, Machinery and Allied Products Ins. (exec. com.). Office: AMP Inc PO Box 3608 Harrisburg PA 17105

RAACH, FREDERICK RAYMOND, business executive; b. Kokomo, Ind., Sept. 12, 1914; s. Elery Earl and Sadie C. (Carney) R.; m. Ruth Mildred Aurada, Sept. 7, 1940; children: Frederick Ellward, Sally Ruth. B.A., Case Western Reserve U., 1940; postgrad., NYU, 1941; Ph.D., Bloomfield Coll., 1972. Engr., plant controller, plant asst. gen. mgr. lamp dept. Gen. Electric Co., 1938-42; exec. Cleve. Pneumatic Tool Co., 1942-44; partner Robert Heller & Assocs., Inc. (mgmt. cons.), Cleve., 1945-59; v.p. RCA, N.Y.C., 1960-61; v.p., dir. Robert Heller & Assocs., Inc., Cleve., 1961-63; v.p. finance and adminstrn. UNIVAC-Sperry Rand Corp., N.Y.C., 1963; v.p., gen. mgr. UNIVAC-Sperry Rand Corp., 1964-66; sr. v.p. Wallace-Murray Corp., N.Y.C., 1966-68; exec. v.p., dir. Wallace-Murray Corp., 1968-69, pres., chief exec. officer, 1969-73; pres. Fred R. Raach Assos., Inc., 1973—; dir. Interstate Brands Corp., Kansas City. Trustee Council for Technol. Devel.-Machinery and Allied Products Inst., 1969-74; bd. dirs. Nat. Council on Crime and Delinquency, 1970-75. Mem. A.I.M., Am. Mgmt. Assn., Bus. Equipment Mfrs. Assn. (chmn., dir. 1966), Mfrs. Assn. Greater Phila. (dir.), Newcomen Soc., Beta Alpha Psi. Republican. Presbyn. Clubs: University (N.Y.C.); Turtle Creek Country (Tequesta, Fla.); Yacht of Stone Harbor (N.J.); Wildcat Cliffs Country (Highlands, N.C.). Home: 58 Turtle Creek Dr Tequesta FL 33469

RAAFLAUB, VERNON ARTHUR, religious educator; b. Magnetawan, Ont., Can., Apr. 30, 1938; s. Arthur Frederick and Olga Elizabeth (Hoerner) R. Diploma in electronics, Radio Electronics TV Schs., North Bay, Ont., 1959; diploma in theology, Concordia Theol. Sem., Springfield, Ill., 1965, BTh, 1972; MDiv, Concordia Theol. Sem., Ft. Wayne, Ind., 1987; postgrad., Wilfrid Laurier U., Waterloo, Ont., 1974-75; MA in Adminstrn., Briercrest Bible Coll., Caronport, Sask., 1985. Ordained minister Luth. Ch., 1965. Pastor Nipawin (Sask.) Choiceland Luth. Parish, 1965-76; instr. Can. Luth. Bible Inst., Camrose, Alta., 1976-77, acad. dean, instr., 1977-85, prof. Old Testament studies, acad. dean, 1985—; Counsellor Luth. Ch. Mo. Synod, Carrot River Cir., 1971-75. Co-editor: The Creation Alternative, 1970; contbr. numerous articles to profl. jours. Chmn. Easter Seal Campaign, Nipawin; mem. Can. council World Mission Prayer League, 1980-85; bd. dirs. Concordia Coll., Edmonton, Alta., 1975-78. Grantee Luth. Ch. Can.,

Zion Found., 1975. Mem. Am. Schs. Oriental Research, Near East Archeol. Soc., Am. Sci. Affiliation (assoc.), Creation Research Soc. (assoc.), Assn. Psychol. Type (gen. mgr.), Histadruth Ivrith Am. Lodge: Rotary (pres. Nipawin chpt. 1972-73, bd. dirs. 1968-71). Office: Can Luth Bible Inst, 4837 52A St, Camrose, AB Canada T4V 1W5

RAAHAVE, DENNIS, general surgeon, researcher, surgical educator; b. Copenhagen, Denmark, Sept. 20, 1938; s. Hans Christian and Vera Marie (Jacobsen) Raahave-Petersen; m. Kate Schneider Jorgensen, Mar. 21, 1964; children—Jane, Christian, Claus, Dorte. M.D., U. Copenhagen, 1965, Ph.D., 1979. Intern Glostrup Hosp., Copenhagen, 1965-69; resident Rigshospitalet, Copenhagen, 1969-71, sr. resident St. Josephs Hosp., Copenhagen, 1975-77, chief resident Bispebjerg Hosp., Copenhagen, 1977—; assoc. prof. University Copenhagen, 1980—; educator Danish Surg. Soc., 1973—; lectr. surgery U. Copenhagen, 1977—, lectr. microbiology, 1977—; vis. prof. U. Calif.-San Francisco, 1985, Harvard U., Cambridge, Mass., 1987. Author: Bacterial Densities in Operation Wounds, 1979. Contbr. articles to profl. jours. Served to lt. Army, 1967-68. Mem. Danish Med. Assn., Danish Surg. Soc., Surg. Infection Soc. Avocations: badminton, cycling. Office: Surgical Infection Lab, Anemonevej 24, 2970 Horsholm Denmark

RAAK, YVON, water agency executive; b. Hautmont, France, July 6, 1953; s. Leon and Marcelle (Latour) R.; m. Marie Claire Miaux, May 21, 1977; 1 child, Anne Claire. Diploma in Engring., Ecole Polytech., 1977, Sch. Mines, 1980. Registered profl. engr., France. Div. head Regional Office for Industry and Research, Douai, France, 1980-83; dir. Artois-Picardy Water Agy., Douai, 1983—; prof. econs. Sch. for Industry Techniques and Mines, 1980-83. Author: Machines A Soigner, 1981. V.p. French Com. for Water Pollution Research and Control. Lodge: Rotary. Home: 293 Quai Devigne, 59500 Douai France Office: Artois Picardy Water Agy, 764 Blvd Lahure, 59500 Douai France

RAAS, JOHANNES REGINALD, distilling company executive; b. Bandung, Java, May 3, 1929; s. Johannes and Regina (Florentine (van Teyn) R.; m. Mary Chaldea Green, Nov. 26, 1957; children—Maria Barbara, Patrick Anthony. Process engr., S.V.S.I., Amsterdam, 1952; Mech. Engr., L.O.I., Leiden, Holland, 1956; A.M.P., Harvard Bus. Sch., 1966. Process engr. Caroni (Tate & Lyle), Trinidad, 1953-56; mech. engr. Wisco (Tate & Lyle), Jamaica, 1957-58; chief engr. Hampden Estates, Jamaica, 1959, factory mgr., 1960; tech. mgr. H.H. Pott Mfg. Co., Flensburg, Germany, 1961-70; tech. dir. Asbach & Co., Ruedesheim, Germany, 1971-87, mng. dir. and pres. Y.G. Monnet Cognac, France, 1987— . Mem. Netherlands Inst. Profl. Engrs. (chem.), Netherlands Inst. Profl. Engrs. (mech.), Harvard Alumni Assn. Club: Harvard Bus. Sch. (Rhein; sec. 1976—). Home: Schlossheide 18, 6222 Geisenheim 2 Federal Republic of Germany Office: Asbach & Co, AM Rottland 2-10, 6220 Ruedesheim Federal Republic of Germany

RABAGO, RAMON HERNANDO, JR., physician; b. Cotabato, Philippines, July 9, 1940; s. Ramon Hernando and Rosario (de Castro) R.; m. Perla Kimpo, Dec. 28, 1963; children: Bernadette, Madelline, Ramon III, John Andrew. MD, U. of the East, Quezon City, Philippines, 1967. Adj. resident physician Cotabato Regional Hosp., 1968-69, jr. resident physician dept. medicine, 1969-70, resident physician dept. surgery, 1970-72, sr. resident physician dept. eye, ear, nose and throat, 1972-74, sr. resident physician dept. Ob-gyn, 1976-83; practice medicine specializing in family medicine Cotabato City, 1983—. Contbg. columnist on drug abuse local weekly newspaper The Mindanao Cross, 1981-82. Mem. com. of region 12 Drug Abuse Rehab. Ctr., Cotabato City, 1981; sustaining mem. charitable orgn. Kapwa Ko, Mahal Ko Found., Quezon City, 1982-87. Mem. Cotabato City Med. Soc. (pres. 1981-82, Most Outstanding Physician award 1984), Philippine Acupuncture Assn., Philippine Acad. Family Physicians (founding pres. Cotabato City chpt. 1981-83), Philippine Assn. for Study of Surg. Sterilization, Philippine Assn. Gynecol. Endoscopy and Microsurgery, Philippine Sci. Acupuncture Assn., Philippine Med. Assn. (bd. govs. 1986-89), Philippine Combat Karate Judo Assn. Roman Catholic. Lodge: Rotary. Home: 149 Mabini St, Cotabato City Mindanao 9301, Philippines

RABB, BRUCE, lawyer; b. Cambridge, Mass., Oct. 4, 1941; s. Maxwell M. and Ruth (Cryden) R.; m. Harriet Rachel Schaffer, Jan. 4, 1970; children: Alexander Charles, Katherine Anne. A.B., Harvard U., 1962; C.E.P., Institut d'Etudes Politiques, Paris, 1963; LL.B., Columbia U., 1966. Bar: N.Y. 1966. Clk. to Judge John Minor Wisdom, U.S. 5th Circuit Ct. Appeals, 1966-67; assoc. firm Stroock & Stroock & Lavan, N.Y.C., 1967-68, 71-75; ptnr. Stroock & Stroock & Lavan, 1976—; staff asst. to Pres. U.S., 1969-70; bd. dirs. Internat. League Human Rights, 1971—; vice chmn., bd. dirs. Lawyers Com. Human Rights, 1977—; pub. mem. Adminstrv. Conf. of U.S., 1982-86, spl. counsel, 1986—; mem. adv. panel internat. human rights trial observer project ABA, 1987—. Bd. dirs. Citizens Union of N.Y., 1981-87, Ams. Watch, 1982—, Helsinki Watch, 1985—, Fund for Free Expression, 1987—, Am. Friends of Alliance Israelite Universelle, 1987—; mem. internat adv. com. Internat. Parliamentary Group for Human Rights in the Soviet Union, 1984—, exec. com. Human Rights Watch, 1987—; sec. Lehrman Inst., 1978—. Mem. Assn. Bar City N.Y., ABA, Am. Law Inst. Clubs: Harvard (N.Y.C.); Met. (Washington). Office: Stroock & Stroock & Lavan 7 Hanover Sq New York NY 10004

RABB, MAXWELL M., lawyer, diplomat; b. Boston, Sept. 28, 1910; s. Solomon and Rose (Kostick) R.; m. Ruth Criedenberg, Nov. 2, 1939; children: Bruce, Sheila Rabb Weidenfeld, Emily Rabb Maltby, Priscilla Rabb Haskins. A.B., Harvard U., 1932, LL.B., 1935; LL.D., Wilberforce U., 1957, Mt. St. Mary's Coll., 1983. Bar: Mass. 1935, N.Y. 1958. Mem. firm Rabb & Rabb, Boston, 1935-37; adminstrv. asst. to U.S. Senator H.C. Lodge, Mass., 1937-43; adminstrv. asst. U.S. Senator Sinclair Weeks, Mass., 1944; legal and legis. cons. Sec. Navy Forestal, 1946; practice law Boston, 1946-51; cons. U.S. Senate Rules Com., 1952; presdl. asst. Sec. to Cabinet, 1953-58; partner Stroock, Stroock & Lavan, N.Y.C., 1958—; ambassador to Italy, 1981—. Exec. asst. campaign mgr. Eisenhower presdl. campaign, 1951-52; del. Republican Nat. Conv., 1952, 56, 76, 80; mem. exec. com. U.S. Commn. for UNESCO, 1959-60; Mem. exec. com. Council on Fgn. Relations, 1978—; chmn. U.S. del. UNESCO conf., Paris, 1958; pres. Congregation Emanu-El, N.Y.C., 1973-81; mem. bd. advisors John F. Kennedy Sch. Govt., Harvard U.; trustee Cardinal Cooke's Inner City Scholarship Fund; bd. mgrs. Seamens Ch. Inst.; mem. presdl. adv. panel on South Asian Relief assistance, 1971; mem. panel conciliations World Bank Internat. Centre for Settlement of Investment Disputes, 1967-73, U.S. rep., 1974-77; mem. Presdl. Commn. on Income Maintenance Programs, 1968-69. Served as lt. amphibious corps USNR, 1944-46. Decorated Commendation Ribbon, commendatore Order of Merit, 1958, cavaliere Order of Merit (Italy), 1982. Mem. ABA, Am. Law Inst. Clubs: Harvard (N.Y.C.), Harmonie (N.Y.C.); Army and Navy (Washington), Metropolitan (Washington); Circolo della Caccia (Rome). Home: Wilson Hill Rd Colrain MA 01340 Office: US Embassy, Via Veneto 119/A, Rome Italy 00187 *

RABE, RICHARD FRANK, dentist, lawyer; b. Crystal Lake, Iowa, May 19, 1919; s. Otto Henry and Agnes Marie (Juhl) R.; m. Barbara Jean McNeal, Mar. 15, 1946; children—Richard Frank, Mary Elizabeth, Kathleen Ann, Michelle. A.A., Waldorf Coll., 1938; D.D.S., U. Iowa, 1942; J.D., Drake U., 1952. Bar: Iowa 1952. Practice dentistry, Des Moines, 1946—; sole practice law, Des Moines, 1952—; cons. M.F. Patterson Dental Supply Co., 1956-61, Nat. Bd. Dental Examiners, 1955-60; chmn. Iowa Bd. Dental Examiners, 1962-63, Iowa Bd. Nursing Home Examiners, 1980-84; lectr. dental assns. throughout U.S., Contbr. articles to profl. jours. Fellow Am. Coll. Dentists; mem. ADA (Vice chmn. council on legis. 1977-78), Am. Acad. Dental Practice Adminstrn., Iowa Dental Study Club (past pres.), Iowa Dental Assn. (pres. 1972, trustee 1960-71), ABA, Iowa Bar Assn., Des Moines Dist. Dental Soc. (past pres.), Milw. Dental Research Group, Central Regional Dental Testing Agy., Am. Inst. Parliamentarians., Psi Omega, Delta Theta Phi. Episcopalian. Clubs: Des Moines Golf and Country. Lodge: Masons, Shriners. Avocations: sailing; flying. Home: 5709 N Waterbury Rd Des Moines IA 50312 Office: 5709 N Waterbury Rd Des Moines IA 50312

RABIN, YITZHAK, minister of defense of Israel; b. Jerusalem, Mar. 1, 1922; s. Nehemia and Rosa (Cohen) R.; m. Lea Schlossberg, Aug. 23, 1948; children: Dalia, Yuval. Student, Kadoorie Agrl. Sch., Kfar Tabor, 1936-40; grad. Staff Coll., Eng., 1953; Ph.D. (hon.), Hebrew U., Jerusalem, 1967, Dropsie Coll., Phila., 1968, Brandeis U., 1968, Yeshiva U., N.Y.C., 1968, Coll. Jewish Studies, Chgo., 1969. Mem. Israel delegation at Rhodes Armistice Negotations, 1949; head tactical ops. Hdqrs., 1950-53; head tng. dept. Israel Def. Force, 1954-56, comdg. officer Northern Command, 1956-59, head manpower br., 1959-60, dep. chief of staff and head Gen. Starr br., 1960-64, chief of staff, 1964-68; ambassador of Israel to U.S., Washington, 1968-73; mem. Knesset, 1974—; minister of labor, 1974; leader Labor Party, 1974-77; prime minister Israel, 1974-77; minister of communications, 1974-75, minister of def., 1984—. Author: The Rabin Memoirs, 1979. Address: Ministry of Defense, Jerusalem Israel *

RABOCH, JAN, sexologist, educator; b. Praha, Czechoslovakia, Aug. 25, 1917; s. Josef and Rozalie (Vitkovcová) R.; m. Miloslava Říhová, Sept. 30, 1947; children: Pavel, Jiří. MD, Charles U., Praha, 1947, DSc, 1965. Diplomate Czechoslovakian Bd. Medicine. Asst. prof. Charles U., 1947-64, assoc. prof., 1964-73, prof., head sexological inst., 1973—. Author over 350 books and articles; mem. editorial bd. Sexualmedizin, 1971, Archives of Sexual Behavior, 1971, Cahiers de Sexologie Clinique, 1974, Jour. Sex and Marital Therapy, 1974. Dep. City of Prague, Czechoslovakia, 1971-76. Recipient Award of Merit, Soc. for Sci. Study of Sex, 1976. Mem. Internat. Acad. Sex Research (pres. 1976-77), Czechoslovakian Sexological Soc. (chmn. 1971-87), Polish Med. Soc. (hon.), Czechoslovakian Med. Soc. (hon.), East German Dermatol. Soc. (hon.). Club: Lokomotiva (Praha). Office: Sexological Inst, Karlovo náměstí 32, 120 00 Prague 2, Czechoslovakia

RABON, WILLIAM JAMES, JR., architect; b. Marion, S.C., Feb. 7, 1931; s. William James and Beatrice (Baker) R.; B.S. in Arch., Clemson (S.C.) Coll., 1951; B.Arch., N.C. State Coll., 1955; M.Arch., MIT, 1956. Registered architect, Calif., Ky., Md., N.Y., N.C., Ohio, Pa. Designer archtl. firms in N.Y.C. and Birmingham, Mich., 1958-61; designer, asso. John Carl Warnecke and Assos., San Francisco, 1961-63, 64-66, Keyes, Lethbridge and Condon, Washington, 1966-68; prin. archtl. partner A.M. Kinney and William J. Rabon Assocs., Cin., 1968-85; v.p., dir. archtl. design A.M. Kinney, Inc., Cin., 1977-85; v.p., dir. programming services Design Art Corp., 1977-85; assoc. John Portman & Assocs., Atlanta, 1985-88; dir. architectural design and assoc. Robert and Co., Atlanta, 1988—; lectr. U. Calif., Berkeley, 1963-65; asst. prof. archtl. design Cath. U. Am., 1967-68; planning cons. China Nat. Bur. Standards, 1982. Prin. works include Kaiser Tech. Center, Pleasanton, Calif. (Indsl. Research Lab. of Yr. award), 1970; Clermont Nat. Bank, Milford, Ohio, 1971; Pavilion bldg. Children's Hosp. Med. Center, Cin. (AIA design award), 1973; EG&G, Hydrospace, Inc., Rockville, Md. (AIA design award), 1970; Mead Johnson Park, Evansville, Ind. (Indsl. Research Lab. of Yr. hon. mention), 1973; Hamilton County Vocat. Sch., Cin., 1972; hdqrs. lab. EPA, Cin., 1975; Arapahoe Chem. Co. Research Center, Boulder, Colo. (Indsl. Research Lab. of Yr. award 1976; Concrete Reinforced Steel Inst. Nat. Design award), 1976; corporate hdqrs. Ohio River Co., Cin., 1977; Children's Hosp. Therapy Center, Cin. (AIA design award 1978, award of merit Am. Wood Council 1981); VA Hosp. addition, Cin. (ASHRAE award 1980); NALCO Chem. Co. Research Center, Naperville, Ill. (AIA design award 1980, 81), 1980; Proctor & Gamble-Winton Hill Tunnel, Cin. (AIA design award), 1978; Toyota Regional Center, Blue Ash, Ohio (AIA and Ohio Masonry Council combined design award 1981); planning cons. Nat. Bur. Standards, Republic of China, 1982; East-West fleet hdqrs. Complex of Royal Saudi Arabian Navy, 1983, Data Libraries, 1983; corporate hdqrs. The Drackett Co., Cin., 1983; corporate hdqrs. Brown & Williamson, Louisville, 1984, others Served to 1st lt. AUS, 1951-53; Korea. Decorated Silver Star, Bronze Star with V device, Purple Heart with bronze cluster; MIT Grad. Sch. scholar, 1955-56; Fulbright scholar, Italy, 1957-58. Mem. AIA, Nat. Council Archtl. Registration Bds. Office: 225 Peachtree ST NE Atlanta GA 30335

RABUN, JOHN BREWTON, JR., criminal justice agency administrator; b. Augusta, Ga. Nov. 16, 1946; s. John Brewton and Alsie Imor (Bateman) R.; m. Anna Betsy Park, Dec. 27, 1967; children—Kerry Kristin, John Candler. B.A., Mercer U., 1967; postgrad. So. Bapt. Theol. Sem., 1967-70; M.S. in Social Work, U. Louisville, 1971. Cert. social worker, Ky. Exec. dir. Ky. Civil Liberties Union, Louisville, 1971-72; dir. Community Residential Treatment Services, Louisville, 1973-78; program mgr. Field Services, Louisville, 1978-80; program mgr. Exploited and Missing Child Unit, Louisville, 1980-84; dep. dir. Nat. Ctr. for Missing and Exploited Children, Washington, 1984—; mem. Alderman's Task Force on Social Services, Louisville, 1982, Mayor's City Youth Commn., Louisville, 1983-84; trainer and/or cons. to numerous agys. Contbr. articles to criminal justice publs. and books. Named hon. chief of police City of Louisville, 1982; recipient Key to City of Louisville, 1983; Disting. Alumnus award U. Louisville, 1985. Mem. Nat. Assn. Social Workers, Nat. Sheriff's Assn., ACLU, Nat. Council Juvenile and Family Ct. Judges, Internat. Juvenile Officers Assn., Acad. Cert. Social Workers, Internat. Assn. Chiefs of Police. Baptist. Avocations: photography; hunting; fishing. Home: 12711 Nathan Ln Herndon VA 22070 Office: Nat Ctr for Missing and Exploited Children 1835 K St NW Suite 600 Washington DC 20006

RACHLIN, ROBERT, pension and financial planning executive; b. N.Y.C., Feb. 6, 1925; s. I. Jack and Jennie (Bezahler) R.; m. Pearl Sherman, June 27, 1948; children: Jeffrey, Amy, Wendy. BBA, CCNY, 1948; MS in Fin. Services, Am. Coll., 1980. Accountant, Biller & Snyder, N.Y.C., 1948-49; life ins. agt. Equitable Life Assurance Soc., N.Y.C., 1949-51, Conn. Mut. Life Ins. Co., N.Y.C., 1951-60; propr. Corp. Planning Assos., N.Y.C., 1961-75; chmn. bd. Compensation Planning Corp., N.Y.C., 1976-79; pres. Rachlin Pension Adminstrn. Inc., 1979—; pres. Fin. Planning Assocs., Inc., 1983—; ptnr. Rachlin Assocs., Ins. and Exec. Benefit Planning; pres. Asset Allocation Securities, Inc.; adj. asst. prof. income taxation Coll. of Ins., N.Y.C., 1972-81; adj. tchr. income taxation C.W. Post Coll., L.I. U., 1977-79, N.Y. Center Fin. Studies, N.Y.C., 1980-84. Pres. Sleepy Hollow Community Concert Assn., Tarrytown, N.Y., 1960's Served with U.S. Army, 1943-46. Decorated Combat Inf. badge. CLU; chartered fin. cons.; enrolled actuary. Mem. Am. Soc. CLU's, Am. Soc. Pension Actuaries, Am. Acad. Actuaries, Internat. Assn. Fin. Planning.. Home: Gracemere Tarrytown NY 10591 Office: 360 Lexington Ave New York NY 10017

RACKLEY, AUDIE NEAL, editor; b. Oney, Okla., Oct. 11, 1934; s. Emmet Irvin and Jesse Lela (Morrison) R.; m. Willie Mae Holsted, Aug. 26, 1956; children—Leicia Leann, Renee, Audette Marshelle. B.S. in Animal Sci, Okla. State U., 1957. Mgr. Hissom A. and M. Farm, Okla. State U., Sand Springs, 1957; swine herdsman Okla. State U., 1959-61; field rep., advt. salesman Cattleman Mag., Ft. Worth, 1961-67; pub. relations and field rep. Am. Angus Assn., St. Joseph, Mo., 1967-70; dir. advt. Quarter Horse Jour., Amarillo, Tex., 1970-72; editor, mgr. Quarter Horse Jour., 1972—. Served with AUS, 1957-59. Recipient Grad. with distinction award Okla. State U., 1987. Mem. Livestock Publs. Council (bd. dirs. 1983-86, 2d v.p., 1st v.p. 1987), Am. Horse Publs. (1st v.p. 1974-76, pres. 1976—), Soc. Nat. Assn. Publs. (dir. 1978—, sec. 1979, treas. 1980, 2d v.p 1981). Home: Rt 4 Box 58 Amarillo TX 79119 Office: PO Box 32470 Amarillo TX 79120

RACTLIFFE, GEORGE WILLIAM JEREMY, finance company executive; b. Bedford, Eng., Jan. 8, 1936; arrived in Republic of South Africa, 1939.; s. William Charles and Helen Margaret (Forbes) R.; m. Barbara Elizabeth Julia Grenfell (div. Apr. 1979); children: Jo Anne, Toni, Tamzin, Sylvia, Laura, Trilby; m. Gail Evelyn (nee) Maxwell, May 28, 1983; children: Justin, Simon, Dominic, Claudia, Antonia. B in Commerce, Diocesan Coll., Cape Town, 1957. Exec. trainee B.P., Cape Town, Republic of South Africa, 1958-60; exec. dir. Brick & Clay, Cape Town, 1960-76; mng. dir. Cape Gas, Cape Town, 1974-76; fin. dir. Murray & Stewart, Cape Town, 1976-77; exec. dir. Murray & Roberts Holdings Ltd., Johannesburg, Republic of South Africa, 1977-79; joint fin. dir Murray & Roberts Holdings Ltd., Johannesburg, 1979-86, group fin. dir., 1986—; also bd. dirs. Murray & Roberts Holdings Ltd. and 19 others in the Murray & Roberts group of companies. trustee The Murray Trusts, Cape Town, Johannesburg, 1978—. Mem. Internat. Tax Planning Assn. Club: Inanda (Sandton). Office: Murray & Roberts Holdings Ltd, PO Box 1000, Bedfordview Tvl 2008, Republic of South Africa

RADA, ALEXANDER, university official; b. Kvasy, Czechoslovakia, Mar. 28, 1923; s. Frantisek and Anna (Tonnkova) R.; came to U.S., 1954, naturalized, 1959; M.S., U. Tech. Coll. of Prague, 1948; postgrad. Va. Poly. Inst., 1956-59, St. Clara U., 1966-67; Ed.D., U. Pacific, 1975; m. Ingeborg Solveig Blakstad, Aug. 8, 1953; children: Alexander Sverre, Frank Thore, David Harald. Head prodn. planning dept. Mine & Iron Corp., Kolin, Czechoslovakia, 1941-42; mgr. experimenting and testing dept. Avia Aircraft, Prague, 1943-45; sec.-gen. Central Bldg. Office, Prague, 1948; head metal courses dept. Internat. Tech. Sch. of UN, Grafenaschau, W.Ger., 1949-50; works mgr. Igref A/S, Oslo, 1950-51; cons. engr., chief sect. machines Steel Products Ltd., Oslo, 1951-54; chief engr., plant supr. Nelson J. Pepin & Co., Lowell, Mass., 1954-55; sr. project engr., mfg. supt. Celanese Corp. Am., Narrows, Va., 1955-60; mgr. mfg., facilities and maint. FMC Corp., San Jose, Calif., 1960-62; mgr. adminstrn. Sylvania Electronic Systems, Santa Cruz, Calif., 1962-72; asst. to pres., devel. officer Napa (Calif.) Coll., 1972-88; chief exec. officer NAVCO Pacific Devel. Corp., Napa, 1984—; prof. indsl. mgmt. Cabrillo Coll., Aptos, Calif., 1963-72; mgmt. and engring. cons., 1972—. Pres. ARC, Santa Cruz, 1965-72, bd. dirs., pres., Napa, 1977—; mem. Nat. Def. Exec. Res., U.S. Dept. Commerce, Washington, 1966—, chmn. No. Calif. region 9, 1981—; mem. President's Export Council-DEC, San Francisco, 1982—. Recipient Meritorious Service citation ARC, 1972, Etoile Civique l'Ordre de l'Etoile Civique, French Acad., 1985; registered profl. engr., Calif. Mem. Nat., Calif. socs. profl. engrs., Am. Def. Preparedness Assn., Assn. Calif. Community Coll. Adminstrs., World Affairs Council No. Calif., Phi Delta Kappa. Editor-in-chief Our Youth, 1945-48; co-editor (with P. Boulden) Innovative Management Concepts, 1967. Home: 1019 Ross Circle Napa CA 94558 Office: 5 Financial Plaza Suite 120 Napa CA 94558

RADCLIFFE, GERALD EUGENE, judge, lawyer; b. Chillicothe, Ohio, Feb. 19, 1923; s. Maurice Gerald and Mary Ellen (Wills) R.; m. Edythe Kennedy, Aug. 11, 1947; children—Jerilynn K. Radcliffe Ross, Pamela J. Radcliffe Dunn. B.A., Ohio U., 1948; J.D., U. Cin., 1950. Bar: Ohio 1950, U.S. Dist. Ct. 1951, U.S. Supreme Ct. 1957. Sole practice, Chillicothe, 1950-66; asst. pros. atty. Ross County, Ohio, 1966-70; acting mcpl. judge Chillicothe Mcpl. Ct., 1970-72; judge probate, juvenile divs. Ross County Ct., Chillicothe, 1973—; mem. rules adv. com. Ohio Supreme Ct., 1984; mem. Ohio Legis. Oversite com., 1974-81; trustee Ohio Jud. Coll., 1979. Editor Cin. Law Rev., 1949-50. Co-author: Constitutional Law, 1979. Contbr. articles to profl. jours. Project dir. South Central Ohio Regional Juvenile Detention Ctr., 1971-72; co-chmn. Chillicothe United Way Fund Campaign, 1972; mem. Youth Services Adv. Council, 1984. Recipient Outstanding Citizen of Yr. award, Jr. C. of C., 1972, Superior Jud. award Ohio Supreme Ct., 1976-82, Meritorious Service award Probate Ct. Judges Ohio, 1984, Dirs. award Ohio Dept. Youth Services, 1984. Mem. Ohio Juvenile Judges Assn., (pres. 1983-84), Nat. Council Juvenile and Family Ct. Judges (trustee 1982-84), Ohio Jud. Conf. Democrat. Lodges: Kiwanis (lt. gov. 1983-84, Ohio Statehood Achievement award 1979), Masons. Avocation: golf. Home: 5 Edgewood Ct Chillicothe OH 45601 Office: Ross County Juvenile and Probate Ct Corner Paint and Main Sts Chillicothe OH 45601

RADCLIFFE, MARK HUGH JOSEPH, corporate director; b. London, Apr. 22, 1938; s. Hugh J.R.J. and Marie Therese (Pereira) R.; m. Anne Brocklehvrst, Feb. 20, 1963; children: Lucinda Mary, Emily Louise, Camilla Mary. Student, Downside Sch., Eng., 1951-56, Ashridge Coll. Various positions Cape Asbestos Group PLC, London, 1958-68; chief exec. officer Lancer Boss Group, Leighton Buzzard, Eng., 1968-74, Triang Pedigree, Eng., 1974-78; mng. dir. T.I. Metsec Ltd., Birmingham, Eng., 1978-81; dep. chmn., chief exec. officer Crane Packing Ltd., Slough, Eng., 1981—; dir. exec. bd. T.I. Group, London, 1986—, bd. dirs., 1988—; pres., mng. dir. John Crane Internat., London, 1988—. Served to 2d lt. Brit. Army, 1956-58. Mem. Inst. Dirs. Mem. Conservative Party. Roman Catholic. Clubs: Guards and Cavalry, MCC (London). Home: The Malt House, Upton, Andover, Hampshire England Office: TI Group PLC, Crossbow House Liverpool Rd, Slough SL1 49X, England

RADECKI, TADEUSZ, computer and information science educator, researcher; b. Borawe, Poland, Jan. 15, 1950; came to U.S., 1984; s. Stanislaw and Helena (Sutnik) R. M.Sc. in Elec. Engring. Cybernetics, Tech. U. Wroclaw, 1973, Ph.D. in Computer Sci., 1978. Researcher, lectr. Tech. U. Wroclaw, 1973-78, asst. prof., 1978-80; vis. research fellow U. Sheffield, Eng., 1980-81; sr. vis. research fellow U. London, 1982-83; vis. assoc. prof. La. State U., Baton Rouge, 1984-85; vis. assoc. prof. U. Nebr., Lincoln, 1985-87, assoc. prof. computer sci., 1987—; vis. research fellow research and devel. dept. Brit. Library, 1979; sr. vis. research fellow Sci. and Engring. Research Council, Gt. Britain, 1981; vis. scientist U. Regina, Can., 1985; invited lectr. U.K., U.S., Can., Fed. Republic Germany, and Belgium. Contbr. articles to profl. jours. Mem. editorial bd. Info. Processing & Mgmt. jour., 1984—, guest editor spl. issue, 1988; mem. editorial bd. Info. Tech. jour., 1981-85. Mem. Assn. for Computing Machinery, Am. Assn. Artificial Intelligence, Com. on Informetrics/Fédération Internationale de Documentation, EURO Working Group on Fuzzy Sets, Brit. Computer Soc. Info. Retrieval Specialist Group, Tau Beta Pi. Office: U Nebr Dept Computer Sci and Engring Lincoln NE 68588

RADEN, LOUIS, tape and label corporation executive; b. Detroit, June 17, 1929; s. Harry M. and Joan (Morris) R.; m. Mary K. Knowlton, June 18, 1949; children: Louis III, Pamela (Mrs. T.W. Rea III), Jacqueline. BA, Trinity Coll., 1951; postgrad. NYU, 1952. With Time, Inc., 1951-52; with Quaker Chem. Corp., 1952-63, sales mgr., 1957-63; exec. v.p. Gen. Tape & Supply, Inc., Detroit, 1963-68, pres., chmn. bd., 1969—; pres. Mich. Gun Clubs, 1973-77. Fifth reunion chmn. Trinity Coll., 1956, pres. Mich. alumni, 1965-72, sec. Class of 1951, 81-86, pres. 1986—; trustee, v.p. Mich. Diocese Episcopal Ch., 1980-82, mem. urban evaluation com., 1975-78, chmn. urban evaluation com., 1978, chmn. urban affairs com., 1977-79; vice chmn. bd. dirs. Robert H. Whitaker Sch. Theology, 1983-85; founding sponsor World Golf Hall of Fame; mem. Founders Soc. Detroit Inst. Arts. Mem. Nat Rifle Assn. (life), Nat. Skeet Shooting Assn. (life, nat. dir. 1977-79, 5 Man Team World Champion award 1977), Greater Detroit Bd. Commerce, Automotive Industry Action Group, Mich. C. of C., U.S. C. of C., Greater Hartford Jaycees (exec. v.p. 1955-57, Key Man award 1957), Theta Xi (life; Disting. Service award 1957, alumni pres. 1952-57, regional dir. 1954-57). Republican. Clubs: Detroit Golf, Detroit Gun, Katke-Cousins Golf, Black Hawk Indians, Pinehurst Country; Oakland U. Pres.'s, Round Table. Home: 1133 Ivyglen Circle Bloomfield Hills MI 48013 Office: 7451 W Eight Mile Rd Detroit MI 48221

RADER, RALPH TERRANCE, lawyer; b. Clarksburg, W.Va., Dec. 5, 1947; s. Ralph Coolidge and Jeanne (Cover) R.; m. Rebecca Jo Vorderman, Mar. 22, 1969; children—Melissa Michelle, Allison Suzanne. B.S. in Mech. Engring., Va. Poly. Inst., 1970; J.D., Am. U., Washington, 1974. Bar: Va. 1975, U.S. Ct. Customs and Patent Appeals 1977, U.S. Dist. Ct. (ea. dist.) Mich. 1978, Mich. 1979, U.S. Ct. Appeals (6th cir.) 1979, U.S. Dist. Ct. (we. dist.) Mich. 1981, U.S. Ct. Appeals (fed. cir.) 1983. Supervisory patent examiner U.S. Patent Office, Washington, 1970-77; patent atty., ptnr. Cullen, Sloman, Cantor, Grauer, Scott & Rutherford, Detroit, 1977—. Contbr. articles to profl. jours. Mem. adminstrv. bd. First United Methodist Ch., Birmingham, Mich., 1980—. Served with U.S. Army, 1970-76. Recipient Superior Performance award U.S. Patent Office, Washington, 1971-77. Mem. Am. Patent Law Assn., ABA, Mich. Patent Law Assn., Mich. Bar. (mem. governing council patent trademark and copyright law sect. 1981-84), Engring. Soc. Detroit, Tau Beta Pi, Pi Tau Sigma, Phi Kappa Phi. Methodist. Lodge: Masons. Home: 4713 Riverchase Dr Troy MI 48090 Office: Cullen Sloman Cantor Grauer Scott & Rutherford 2400 Penobscot Bldg Detroit MI 48226

RADETZKI, MARIAN, economist, researcher; b. Poland, Dec. 8, 1936. Grad., Stockholm Sch. Econs., 1958; B of Social Anthropology, Stockholm U., 1961, lic. econs., 1969, D of Econs., 1972. Researcher mkrtg. Volvo Co., 1959-60; dir. Coop. Mgmt. Tng. Inst. South and East Asia, New Delhi, India, 1961-66, Swedish Coop. Union and Wholesale Soc., 1961-66; dir. Found. Swedish Coop. Ctr. Stockholm, 1966-68; chief economist Intergovtl. Council Copper Exporting Countries, Paris, 1973-75; researcher Inst. for Internat. Econ. Studies, Stockholm, 1975—; vis. prof. mineral econs. Colo. Sch. Mines, 1986-87; cons. in field. Author: International Commodity Market Arrangements, 1970, Den Ihåliga Välfärden, 1972, Aid and Development, 1973, En Ny Ekonomisk Världsordning?, 1976, Financing Mining Projects in Developing Countries, 1979, Sverige och den Tredje Världen; Industrins Roll i den Internationella Utvecklingen, 1980, (with Stephen A. Zorn) Mineral Processing in Developing Countries, 1980, Uranium, A Strategic Source of Energy, 1981, Sverige Avskärmat, 1981,

State Mineral Enterprises: An Investigation into Their Impact on International Mineral Markets, 1985; contbr. to Dagens Nyheter newspaper, Sweden, 1969-79, Dagens Industri newspaper, Sweden, 1976-86; contbr. articles to profl. jours. Office: Inst for Internat Econ Studies, 10691 Stockholm Sweden

RADFORD, ANTHONY JAMES, physician, medical educator, consultant; b. Melbourne, Victoria, Australia, May 7, 1937; s. Paul and Winifred (Kent Hughes) R.; m. Robin Burnard, Dec. 31, 1960; children: Mark Hughes Burnard, David Paul, Sarah Margaret Radford Wauchope. B in Medicine, B in Surgery, U. Adelaide, 1960; D in Tropical Medicine and Hygiene, Liverpool (Eng.) U., 1965; SM in Epidemiology, Harvard U., 1970. Resident med. officer Queen Elizabeth Hosp., Adelaide, 1961-62, Queen Victoria Maternity Hosp., Adelaide, 1962, Adelaide Children's Hosp., 1962-63; lectr. Papuan Med. Coll., Port Moresby, New Guinea, 1963-70; med. officer Dept. Pub. Health, Kainantu and Saiho, Papua, New Guinea, 1963-67; cons. physician, cons. in pub. health Dept. Pub. Health, Papua, New Guinea, 1966-72; assoc. prof. U. Papua, 1970-72; sr. lectr. Liverpool Sch. Tropical Medicine and U. Liverpool, 1972-75; Found. prof. primary care and community medicine Flinders U. South Australia, Adelaide, 1975—; cons. WHO, UNICEF, World Bank, govts. of U.S., Australia, Papua New Guinea. Author or editor numerous papers on clin. medicine, epidemiology, organization and mgmt. of health services, med. edn. Pres. South Australian Council on Aging, 1984-86. Research grantee various state and fed. instns., 1975—. Fellow Royal Australian Coll. Gen. Practitioners (state faculty bd. 1975-86), Royal Australasian Coll. Physicians, Royal Soc. Tropical Medicine and Hygiene (regional sec. 1975—), Royal Coll. Physicians (Edinburgh and London), Faculty Community Medicine; mem. Internat. Epidemiology Assn., Australasian Epidemiology Assn., Pub. Health Assn. of Australia and New Zealand. Anglican. Office: Flinders U South Australia, Bedford Park, Adelaide, South Australia 5042, Australia

RADFORD, NANCY HELEN, educational researcher; b. Denver, July 10, 1954; d. Robert Peter and Agnes MacLachlan (Orr) Ramer; m. Giles Edward Radford, Sept. 3, 1983; 1 child, Alexander Blair. BA with honors, U. Durham, Eng., 1975. Various nursing positions Eng., 1975-82; research officer U. Surrey, Guildford, Eng., 1984-85, research fellow dept. ednl. studies, 1985-86, 87—. Author: Strategies for Change, 1986; co-author: District Nurse Education Training In U.K., 1985, Direct Entry: A Preparation for Midwifery Practice, 1988. Mem. Church of England. Club: Ewhurst Rifle. Office: U of Surrey, Dept Ednl Studies, Guildford GU2 5XH, England

RADIL, TOMÁS, neurophysiologist, psychologist; b. Bratislava, Czechoslovakia, Nov. 8, 1930; s. Ernest Weiss and Margita Büchlerová; m. Jirina Radilová; children: Gabriela, Michaela, Marketa, Karolina. MD, Charles U., Prague, Czechoslovakia, 1955; postgrad. in physiology, Czechoslovakian Acad. Sci., Prague, 1957-60, Docent in Physiology, 1977. Neurologist Hosp. Komárno, Czechoslovakia, 1955-57; neurophysiologist Czechoslovakian Acad. Scis., 1960—, head sect. neurophysiology, dept. psychophysiology, 1980—; assoc. prof. psychophysiology Charles U., 1967-80, prof. psychology, 1980—. Author 2 books on neurophysiology of sleep, 1967, 79 (Czechoslovakian Med. Soc. award 1979), 3 textbooks on neurophysiology, 1963, 73, 76. Recipient Czechoslovakia State prize, 1978, Czechoslovakian and Polish Acad. Sci. prize, 1979-80, Purkyně Silver medal, 1985. Mem. Czechoslovakian Med. Soc. (Purkyně medal 1986), Internat. Orgn. for Psychophysiology. Office: Czechslovak Acad Scis, Inst Physiology, Videnska 1083, 14000 Prague Czechoslovakia

RADILOVÁ, JIŘINA, psychologist, linguist; b. Prague, Czechoslovakia, July 12, 1930; d. Rudolf and Marie Radil; m. Tomáš Radil; children: Gabriela, Michaela, Markéta, Karolina. Lic., U. Prague, 1955, PhD, 1976; postgrad., Czechoslovakian Acad. Scis., Prague, 1977. Translator, interpreter PIS Prague, 1959-67; asst. instr. Inst. Physiology Czechoslovakia Acad. Scis., Prague, 1968-85; psychophysiologist Lab. Evolutionary Biology-Czechoslovakia Acad. Scis., Prague, 1985—. Author: Reversible Figures, 1983; translator various books from Italian and Spanish, 1953-63. Mem. Czechoslovakia Med. Soc., Soc. for Higher Nervous Activity, Internal Orgn. for Psychophysiology. Home: Praha 2, 72800 Vratislavova 30 Czechoslovakia Office: Czechoslovak Acad Scis, Lab Evolutionary Biology, Víděnská 1083, Prague 4, Czechoslovakia 14000

RADMER, MICHAEL JOHN, lawyer, educator; b. Wisconsin Rapids, Wis., Apr. 28, 1945; s. Donald Richard and Thelma Loretta (Donahue) R.; children from previous marriage: Christina Nicole, Ryan Michael; m. Laurie J. Anshus, Dec. 22, 1983; 1 child, Michael John. B.S., Northwestern U., Evanston, Ill., 1967; J.D., Harvard U., 1970. Bar: Minn. 1970. Assoc. Dorsey & Whitney, Mpls., 1970-75, ptnr., 1976—; lectr. law Hamline U. Law Sch., St. Paul, 1981-84; gen. counsel, rep., sec. 60 federally registered investment cos., Mpls. and St. Paul, 1977—. Contbr. articles to legal jours. Active legal work Hennepin County Legal Advice Clinic, Mpls., 1971—. Mem. ABA, Minn. Bar Assn., Hennepin County Bar Assn. Club: Mpls. Athletic. Home: 4329 E Lake Harriet Pkwy Minneapolis MN 55409 Office: Dorsey & Whitney 2200 First Bank Pl E Minneapolis MN 55402

RADNER, SIDNEY HOLLIS, rug company executive; b. Holyoke, Mass., Dec. 8, 1919; s. William I. Radner; m. Helen Jane Cohen, Dec. 12, 1946; children: William Marc, Richard Scott. Student, Yale U., 1941. Pres. Am. Rug Co., Holyoke, 1946; lectr., cons., investigator crooked gambling, U.S. Armed Forces, FBI, gov. of Canada, various state and mcpl. police vice squads; appearances in BBC film on Houdini as well as various TV shows, including "In Search Of...". Author: Radner on Poker, Radner on Dice, Radner on Roulette and Casino Games, How to Detect Card Sharks; contbr. articles to profl. jours. Past pres. Holyoke C. of C.; co-founder Volleyball Hall of Fame; bd. dirs. Greater Springfield (Mass.) Better Bus. Bur. Served with criminal investigation div. U S. Army, 1942-46. Mem. Soc. Am. Magicians (mem. Occult Investigation Com.), Internat. Brotherhood Magicians, Magic Circle (London); charter mem. Magician's Guild, Magic Collector's Assn., Am. Platform Assn. Jewish. Lodges: Rotary, Masons, Shriners. Home: 1050 Northampton St Holyoke MA 01040 Office: Am Rug 1594 Dwight St Holyoke MA 01040

RADO, PETER THOMAS, lawyer; b. Berlin, Germany, Nov. 12, 1928; came to U.S., 1931, naturalized, 1937; s. Sandor and Emmy (Chrisler) R.; m. Jacqueline Danenberg, Sept. 11, 1977. A.B., Harvard U., 1949, LL.B., 1952, LL.M., 1953. Bar: N.Y. 1952. Assoc., Ide, Haigney & Rado, N.Y.C., 1956-61, ptnr., 1961—. Served as cpl. U.S. Army, 1953-55. Mem. ABA, N.Y. State Bar Assn., Assn. Bar City N.Y., Internat. Bar Assn. Club: Harvard (N.Y.C.). Home: 176 E 71st St New York NY 10021 Office: 41 E 42d St New York NY 10017

RADOMSKI, JACK LONDON, scientist; b. Milw., Dec. 10, 1920; s. Joseph Elwood and Evelyn (Hansen) R.; B.S., U. Wis., 1942; Ph.D., George Washington U., 1950; m. Teresa Pascual, Feb. 19, 1971; children—Mark, Linda, Eric, Janet, Mayte. Chemist, Gen. Aniline & Film Corp., Binghamton, N.Y. 1942-44; pharmacologist FDA, Washington, 1944-52, acting chief acute toxicity br., 1952-53; prof. pharmacology U. Miami, Coral Gables, Fla., 1953-82; pres. Covington Tech. Services, Andalusia, Ala., 1982-88; pvt. practice cons. in toxicology, Hudson, Fla., 1988—; cons. WHO, IARC, Gen. Acctg. Office, EPA, HEW, NIOSH. Contbr. articles to profl. jours. Recipient Spl. award Commr. FDA, 1952; diplomate in gen. toxicology Acad. Toxicol. Scis., 1982. Mem. Am. Soc. Pharmacology and Exptl. Therapeutics, Soc. Toxicology, Am. Assn. Cancer Research, N.Y. Acad. Scis. Home and Office: 6432 Driftwood Dr Hudson FL 34667

RADON, JENIK RICHARD, lawyer; b. Berlin, Germany, Jan. 14, 1946; came to U.S., 1951, naturalized, 1956; s. Louis and Irmgard (Hinz) R.; m. Heidi B. Duerbeck, June 10, 1971; 1 child, Kaara H.D. BA, Columbia Coll., 1967; MCP, U. Calif.-Berkeley, 1971; JD, Stanford U., 1971. Bar: Calif. 1972, N.Y. 1975, U.S. Ct. Appeals (2d cir.) 1975, U.S. Dist. Ct. (so. dist.) N.Y. 1975. Ptnr. Radon & Ishizumi, N.Y.C., Tokyo, Hong Kong, Munich and Bangkok, 1981—; lectr. Polish Acad. Scis., 1980, Tokyo Arbitration Assn., 1983, Japan External Trade Orgn., 1983, 86, Japan Mgmt. Assn., 1983, Japan Inst. Internat. Bus. Law, 1983-84, Va. Ctr. World Trade, 1985, UN Indsl. Devel. Orgn., Warsaw, 1987-88, Wichita World Trade Council, 1987, Inst. Nat. Economy of Poland, 1987, Hungarian Econ. Roundtable, 1987, USSR. Com. on Sci. and Tech. Editor The International Acquisitions Handbook, The Toyo-Kaizai Pub. Co., Tokyo, 1987, editor-in-chief Stanford Jour. Internat. Studies, 1970-71; contbr. articles to German bus. and legal pubs. Active Am. Council on Germany, N.Y.C., 1978—, U.S.-Polish Econ. Council, 1987—; mem. exec. com. Afghanistan Relief Com., N.Y.C., 1980—; mem. bd. dirs. Internat. Med. Services for Health, Washington, 1987—, Internat. Video Inst., N.Y.C., 1988—; seminar participant U.S. Polish Trade Commn., Washington, 1981; mem. bd. dirs. Direct Relief Internat., Santa Barbara, Calif., 1987; mem. bd. dirs. Freedom Medicine, Honolulu, 1987—; advisor UN Indsl. Devel. Orgn., 1988. NSF grantee, 1966; Slavic and E. European Inst. grantee, 1968; HUD fellow, 1968-70. Mem. ABA, German-Am. Law Assn., German Forum, Polish-U.S. Econ. Council, Asia-Pacific Lawyers Assn., Estonian C. of C., W. Palm Beach C. of C. Roman Catholic. Club: Deutscher Verein. Office: Radon & Ishizumi 269 W 71st St New York NY 10023

RADOVANOVIC, ZORAN, epidemiologist; b. Belgrade, Yugoslavia, Apr. 17, 1940; s. Milutin and Danica (Grujic) R.; m. Ruzica Slobodanovic, Oct. 28, 1965; children—Vera, Milutin. M.D., Belgrade Sch. Medicine, 1965, Diploma in Epidemiology, 1973; Diploma in Tropical Pub. Health, London Sch. Hygiene and Tropical Medicine, 1970; D.Sc., U. Belgrade, 1977. Asst. prof. U. Belgrade, 1967-77, assoc. prof., 1977-83, prof. epidemiology, 1983-88, dir. Inst. Epidemiology, 1983-88, sec.-gen. Yugoslav Med. Assn., 1988, prof. epidemiology Kuwait U., 1988—. Co-author, editor: General Epidemiology, 1979; co-author: Epidemiology of Infectious Diseases, 1980. Mem. Royal Soc. Tropical Medicine and Hygiene, Sci. Soc. History of Medicine, Internat. Epidemiol. Assn., Am. Pub. Health Assn., European Assn. for Cancer Research. Home: Sindjeliceva 4/I, 11000 Belgrade Yugoslavia Office: Kuwait U Comm Med Fac Med, PO Box 24923, Sarafat Kuwait

RADUSINOVIC, DIMITRIVE, electrical engineer; b. Titograd, Montenegro, Yugoslavia, Nov. 26, 1943; s. Luka and Milka (Radinovic) R.; married, 1965; children: Vanja, Igor, Sanja. Grad. in elec. engring., Elec. Faculty, Titograd, 1964, 69. Tchr. tech. terms secondary sch., Titograd, 1965-71; positions include technologist, main technologist, prin. tech. and constrn. engr., dir. maintenance and toolmaking, dir. mktg., dir. fgn. commerce IGM Radlje Dakic, Titograd, 1971-87; dir. bus. selling ctr. UNIS Sarajevo, Titograd, 1987—. Decorated Order Silver Wreath (Yugoslavia). Home: Donja Goriea bb, 81000 Titograd Montnegro, Yugoslavia Office: UNIS Sarajevo, Edvarda Kardelja 11-13, 81000 Titograd Montenegro, Yugoslavia

RADZINOWICZ, LEON, criminologist; b. Lodz, Poland, Aug. 15, 1906; LL.D., U. Paris, 1925, U. Geneva, 1927, U. Rome, 1928, U. Cracow (Poland), 1929; M.A., Cambridge U., 1949, LL.D., 1951; LL.D. (hon.), U. Leicester, 1965, U. Edinburgh (Scotland). Fellow Trinity Coll., Cambridge, 1948—; assoc. fellow Silliman Coll., Yale U., 1966—; asst. dir. research Cambridge U., 1946-49, dir. dept. criminal sci., 1949-59, 1st Wolfson prof. criminology, 1959-73, 1st dir. Inst. Criminology, 1960-72; Walter E. Meyer research prof. Yale U. Law Sch., 1962-63; adj. prof. criminal law and criminology Columbia U. Law Sch., 1964-77; Lionel Cohen lectr. Jerusalem U., 1963; disting. vis. prof. Rutgers U., 1968-72, 79-81; vis. prof. sociology U. Pa., 1970-74; vis. prof. U. Va. Law Sch., 1968-69, 70-74, U. Minn. Law Sch., 1979; Disting. vis. prof. criminal justice John Jay Coll., CUNY, 1978-79; disting. vis. prof. law Benjamin N. Cardozo Law Sch., Yeshiva U., N.Y.C., 1978-79; visitor Princeton Inst. Advanced Study, 1975; vis. lectr. numerous univs. Europe, S.Am.; 1st chmn. Criminological Council, Council of Europe, 1963-70; mem. Royal commn. Capital Punishment, 1949-68; mem. Royal Commn. Penal System, 1964-66; cons. mem. Pres. Johnson's Commn. on Violence, 1968-69, mem. Home Office Adv. Council, 1950-74. Created knight, 1970; decorated chevalier Ordre de Leopold (Belgium), 1930; recipient James Barr Ames prize and medal Harvard U. Law Sch., 1950; Coronation medal, 1953; Bruce Smith Sr. award Acad. Criminal Justice Scis., 1976; Sellin-Glueck award Am. Soc. Criminology, 1976; Joseph L. Andrews award Am. Assn. Law Libraries.(with Roger Hood) hon. fgn. mem. Am. Acad. Arts and Scis., Am. Acad. Forensic Scis., Australian Acad. Forensic Scis. Fellow Brit. Acad.; mem. Brit. Acad. Forensic Scis. (1st pres. 1973), Am. Law Inst. (hon.). Club: Athenaeum (London). Author: In Search of Criminology, 1961; Ideology and Crime, 1966; The Dangerous Offender, 1968; History of English Criminal Law, Vol. I-Vol. IV, 1948-68, Vol. V (with Roger Hood), 1986. Editor: Cambridge Studies in Criminology, 52 vols.; (with Marvin Wolfgang) Crime and Justice, 3 vols., 2d edit., 1977; (with Joan King) The Growth of Crime, 1977. Home: Rittenhouse Claridge 2416 Rittenhouse Sq Philadelphia PA 19103 other: Trinity Coll, Cambridge England also: British Acad, 20-21 Cornwall Terr, London NW1 4QP, England

RAE, MATTHEW SANDERSON, JR., lawyer; b. Pitts., Sept. 12, 1922; s. Matthew Sanderson and Olive (Waite) R.; m. Janet Hettman, May 2, 1953; children: Mary-Anna, Margaret, Janet. AB, Duke, 1946, LLB, 1947; postgrad., Stanford U., 1951. Bar: Md. 1948, Calif. 1951. Asst. to dean Duke Sch. Law, Durham, N.C., 1947-48; assoc. Karl F. Steinmann, Balt., 1948-49, Guthrie, Darling & Shattuck, Los Angeles, 1953-54; nat. field rep. Phi Alpha Delta Frat., Los Angeles, 1949-51; research atty. Calif. Supreme Ct., San Francisco, 1951-52; ptnr. Darling, Hall & Rae and predecessor firms, Los Angeles, 1955—; mem. Calif. Commn. Uniform State Laws, 1985—. V.p. Los Angeles County Rep. Assembly, 1959-64; mem. Los Angeles County Rep. Cen. Com., 1960-64, 77—, exec. com., 1977—; vice chmn. 17th Congl. Dist., 1960-62, 28th Congl. Dist., 1962-64; chmn. 46th Assembly Dist., 1962-64, 27th Senatorial Dist., 1977—; mem. Calif. Rep. State Cen. Com., 1966—, exec. com., 1966-67; pres. Calif. Rep. League, 1966-67; trustee Rep. Assocs., 1979—, pres., 1983-85, chmn. bd. dirs., 1985-87. Served to 2d lt. USAAF, World War II. Fellow Am. Coll. Probate Counsel; academician Internat. Acad. Estate and Trust Law (exec. council 1974-78); mem. ABA, Los Angeles County Bar Assn. (chmn. probate and trust law com. 1964-66, chmn. legislation com. 1980-86, chmn. program com. 1981-82, chmn. membership retention com. 1982-83, trustee 1983-85, dir. Bar Found. 1987—), South Bay Bar Assn., State Bar Calif. (chmn. state bar jour. com. 1970-71, chmn. probate com. 1974-75, exec. com. estate planning trust and probate law sect. 1977-83, chmn. legislation com. 1977—, probate law cons. group Calif. Bd. Legal Specialization 1977-88, chmn. conf. dels. resolutions com. 1987, exec. com. conf. dels. 1987—), Lawyers Club of Los Angeles (bd. govs. 1981-87, 1st v.p. 1982-83), Am. Legion (comdr. Allied post 1969-70), Legion Lex (dir. 1964—, pres. 1969-71), Air Force Assn., Aircraft Owners and Pilots Assn., Town Hall (gov. 1970-78, pres. 1975), World Affairs Council, Internat. Platform Assn., Los Angeles Com. on Fgn. Relations, Phi Beta Kappa (councilor Alpha Assn. 1983—, v.p. 1984-86), Omicron Delta Kappa, Phi Alpha Delta (supreme justice 1972-74, elected to Disting. Service chpt. 1978), Sigma Nu. Presbyterian. Clubs: Commonwealth (San Francisco); Chancery, Stock Exchange (Los Angeles). Lodge: Rotary. Home: 600 John St Manhattan Beach CA 90266 Office: Darling Hall & Rae 550 S Flower St 6th Floor Los Angeles CA 90071

RAEBER, JOSEPH G., biologist; b. Benzenschwil, Aargovie, Switzerland, Mar. 19, 1924; m. Gudrun Maria Rita Brachler, Aug. 16, 1936; children: Eva Sylvia, Jutta Karin. Diploma Agronomy, Swiss Fed. Inst. Tech., Zurich, 1948; MS, Iowa State U., Ames, 1951, PhD in Genetics, Plant Breeding, 1953. Tobacco breeder Tobacco Research Bd., Salisbury, Rhodesia, 1953-58, head plant breeding dept., 1958-74; mgr. internat. research and devel. Ciba-Giegy, Ltd., Basle, Switzerland, 1975-86, biotechnology regulaton and patent policy specialist, 1986—. Contbr. articles to profl. jours. and books. Mem. Sci. Commn. Coresta, Paris, France, 1963-70, v.p., 1970-74. Mem. various commissions on regulatory matters on biotech., Gamma Sigma Delta. Democrat. Roman Catholic. Home: 130 Gempenring, CH-4143 Dornach Switzerland Office: Ciba Geigy Ltd, Dept AG 5.4, Postfach, CH-4002 Basle Switzerland

RAES, JAN PAUL, neurolinguist, researcher; b. Mechelen, Belgium, Apr. 2, 1951; s. Frans Hendrik and Jeanne Lodewijk (Van der biesen) R. M.A. in Germanic Philology, U. Brussels, 1973, M.A. in Neurolingistics, 1975. Tchr. phonetics Sch. Film and Theatre, Brussels, 1973-76; researcher Pediatric Hosp., U. Helsinki, Finland, 1978; neurolinguist Academic Hosp. U. Brussels, 1978—, asst., 1982—. Editor: (with Yvan Lebrun) Aspecten van de neurolinguistiek, 1985. Contbr. articles to profl. jours. Served at Royal Mil. Sch., Brussels, 1977-78. Grantee Nationaal Fonds voor Wetenschappelijk Onderzoek, 1980-81, Fondation Van Goethem-Brichant, 1982. Mem. European Assn. Audiophonol. Centres, Internat. Assn. Logopedics and Phoniatrics, Belgian Assn. Neurolinguists (founding mem. 1987, treas.) Office: Academic Hosp Univ Brussels, Laarbeeklaan 101, 1090 Brussels 1090, Belgium

RAFAELI, ADA, entomology educator; b. Tel Aviv, Aug. 17, 1949; d. Zvi and Katia R.; m. Peter Stanley Stern; children: Ronen David, Elisheva Rachel, Hilla. BSc with honors, U. B.C., 1975; PhD, U. London Imperial Coll., 1978. Asst. lectr. dept. entomology Faculty of Agr., Hebrew U., Rehovot, Israel, 1978-81, research assoc. dept. entomology, 1982-83, research scientist, 1982—; lectr. dept entomology, Faculty Agr. Hebrew U., Rehovot, Israel, 1983—; research assoc. dept. hormone research Kimron Vet. Inst., Bet Dagan, Israel, 1981-82. Contbr. articles to profl. jours. Scholar Marshall Found. Royal Coll. Sci., London, 1976, Carlo Campolin U. London, 1976, Israel Nat. Acad. Scis., 1979, U.S. Israel Binat. Agrl. Research and Devel. Fund, 1985. Mem. Internat. Soc. Chem. Ecology, Entomol. Soc. Israel, Soc. Exptl. Biology of Eng. Office: Hebrew U Faculty Agr, Dept Entomology, Rehovot 76100, Israel

RAFFARD, HUBERT CHARLES, insurance company executive; b. Paris, Mar. 31, 1933; s. Henri Paul and Marie Hélène (Ripault) R.; m. Monique Marie de Baudoüin; 1 child, Isabelle. Ecole des Cadres des Affaires Economiques, EDC, Paris, 1955; Capacité en Droit (Faculté de Droit et des Scis. Economiques), Economy and Law U., Paris, 1955; Inst. Com. Internat., Institut de Commerce Internat., Paris, 1960; degree Institut de contrôle de Gestion, IFG, Paris, 1981. Fin. exec. Ateliers et Chantiers de la Seine Maritime, Paris, 1958-64; comml. mgr. Weiller, Angouleme, France, 1965-66; export exec. Compagnie Francaise des Produits Chimiques Shell, Paris, 1966-67, Kodak Pathé, Paris, 1967-74; France coordinator Elysees Export, Paris, 1974-75; internat. mgr. Turquetil, Ivry, France, 1976-82; exec. ASSEDIC, Nanterre, France, 1983—. Author: French Free Zones, 1960, A New Industry Group, 1981; author/editor: (jour.) Verdin Bulletin, 1985. instr. Auxilia, Vanves, France, 1970-80; adminstr. Maison de la Famille, Neuilly, France, 1983-86. Served with French Army, 1956-57. Roman Catholic. Lodge: Grande Loge Nat. Francaise. Home: 37 Rue Pauline Borghèse, 92200 Neuilly-Sur-Seine France Office: Assedic Hauts de Seine, 27 Rue de Sèvres, 92100 Boulogne France

RAFFELSON, MICHAEL, financial executive; b. Bklyn., Jan. 2, 1946; s. Leo and Fay Rebecca (Clumpus) R.; B.B.A., Coll. City N.Y., 1967; M.B.A., CUNY, 1969; m. Eileen Judith Tauber, Mar. 23, 1975; 1 dau., Elyse Lauren. Acct., Am. Metal Climax Inc., N.Y.C., 1967-69; fin. analyst Anaconda Co., N.Y.C., 1971-74; sr. fin. analyst corp. staff Internat. Paper Co., N.Y.C., 1975-76, bus. analyst white papers group, 1976-79, applications coordinator paper and packaging mgmt. systems, 1979-81, mgr. mgmt. services info. systems, 1981-85; mgr. ops. analysis and control info. services The First Boston Corp., N.Y.C., 1986-87, mgr. telecommunications analysis and control 1987-88, asst. v.p. 1988; fin. officer Chase Manhattan Bank, N.Y.C., 1988—; instr. fin. mgmt. edn. program Internat. Paper, 1977. Served with AUS, 1969-71. Mem. Phi Epsilon Pi (pres. chpt. 1966). Office: Chase Manhattan Bank 1 World Trade Center New York NY 10017

RAFFERTY, EDSON HOWARD, lawyer, consultant; b. Newark, N.J., Jan. 7, 1943; s. Martin James and Amber Louise (Leach) R.; m. Sarah Webster, Bartlett, Sept. 18, 1976 (div. 1981); children: Ethan Eric, Heather Knowles. AB in Chemistry, Syracuse U.; BSME; MS in Bio-engring., U. Tex. Grad. Sch. Bio-Med. Scis.; JD, Hamline Law Sch.; MBA, MIT. Bar: Mass., 1982. Chief engr. Artificial Heart Project, VA Hosp., Houston and Syracuse, N.Y., 1966-68; prin. scientist, mgr. Artificial Heart Program Applied Sci. div. Litton Industries, Inc., Mpls., 1968-70; chief operating officer, exec. v.p., chief fin. officer, dir. Bio-Medicus, Inc., Mpls., 1970-78, acting pres., 1970-73; sr. ptnr. Consultus, Inc., Cambridge, Mass., 1978—, sr. ptnr., Attys at Law Rafferty & Polich, Cambridge, 1982—. Over 50 patents in field. Contbr. numerous articles to profl. jours. Legis. dist. Dem. chairperson Mpls., 1970-74; nat. coordinator med. exchange between U.S. and U.S.S.R., Mpls., 1975-79; chmn. corp. fin. Council on U.S./U.S.S.R. Health Care Exchange, Mpls., 1975-79; participant numerous TV spls. on artificial heart, 1968-78. Recipient IR-100 award Indsl. Research Inc., 1972, Bachner award Plastic Industry Trade Org., 1976. Mem. ABA, Mass. Bar Assn., Am. Soc. for Artificial Internal Organs, Assn. Advancement of Med. Instrumentation. Club: Warren Tavern (Charlestown, Mass.) (founder). Office: Rafferty & Polich 1675 Massachusetts Ave Cambridge MA 02138

RAFI, MOHAMMED, goverment official; b. Kabul, Afghanistan, 1944. Student, Kabul Mil. U., Mil. Acad. USSR. Minister pub. works Govt. of Afghanistan, then minister of def.; dep. pres. Revolutionary Council Afghanistan; minister of def. 1986-88, v.p., 1988—; mem. People's Dem. Party Afghanistan, 1973, mem. cen. com. 1978; mem. Politburo, 1981. Decorated Order of the Red Banner. Address: Office of Vice Pres, Kabul Afghanistan *

RAFLA, SAMIR MORCOS, cardiologist, educator; b. Egypt, Aug. 31, 1947; S. Morcos Rafla and A.B. Morcos; m. Mirande Ayad Salib Mikhail, 1981. MB, Alexandria U., Egypt, 1970, diploma in medicine, 1974, MD, 1982, cert. Ednl. Commn. for Fgn. Med. Grads., 1983. Lectr. medicine cardiology unit Alexandria U., 1982-88, assoc. prof. cardiology, 1988—; cons. cardiology Jeddah Med. Ctr., Saudi Arabia, 1985—. Cleve. Clinic Found. research fellow, 1983-84. Fellow Am. Coll. Cardiology (assoc.); mem. N.Am. Soc. Pacing and Electrophysiology, Am. Soc. Echocardiography, Egyptian Soc. Cardiology, Pan African Soc. Cardiology.

RAFTIS, ALKIS, engineering educator; b. Athens, Greece, Oct. 31, 1942; s. Constantine and Fotini (Meziltzoglou) R.; diploma in engring. Nat. Tech. U., Athens, 1966; M.Sociology, U. Paris, 1974, diploma in sociology, 1976, Dr. Mgmt. Sci., 1977, Plant engr. Pfizer Internat., Athens, 1969-70; chief engr. Nigerian Flour Mills, Ltd., Lagos, 1970-72; project mgr. Nigerian Bag Mfg. Co., Lagos, 1972-73; sr. lectr. U. Patras Sch. Engring., Athens, from 1978, now assoc. prof.; vice gov. ETBA Bank, Athens, 1984-86; cons. engr. Author: Management et Démocratie Industrielle, 1979; Work and Management, 1984, Work in Poetry, 1984, Democratic Management, 1985, The World of Greek Dance, 1986; contbr. articles to profl. jours. Served with Signal Corps, Greek Army, 1967-69. Mem. Brit. Inst. Plant Engrs., Brit. Inst. Mech. Engrs., Internat. Orgn. Folk Art, Am. Mgmt. Assn. Internat., Nigerian Soc. Engrs., Tech. Chamber of Greece, Brit. Inst. Mgmt. Club: Doa Statou Dance Ctr. Home: 12 Hadjimichali St, 10558 Athens Greece

RAGAN, SAMUEL TALMADGE, newspaper editor, educator; b. Berea, N.C., Dec. 31, 1915; s. William Samuel and Emma Clare (Long) R.; m. Marjorie Usher, Aug. 19, 1939; children: Nancy, Ann Talmadge. A.B., Atlantic Christian Coll., 1936, Litt.D., 1972; Litt.D., U. N.C., 1987; D.Letters, Meth. Coll., 1980; D.Lit., St. Andrews Coll., 1987. Newspaperman in N.C. and Tex., 1936—; mng. editor, author column Southern Accent in Raleigh (N.C.) News and Observer, 1948-69; exec. editor Raleigh News and Observer, also Raleigh Times, 1957-69; editor, pub. The Pilot, Southern Pines, N.C., 1969—; sec. N.C. Dept. Arts, Culture and History, 1972-73; conductor program, commentator sta. WTVD, Durham, 1969—; spl. lectr. contemporary issues N.C. State U., 1959-68; dir. Writer's Workshop, 1963—; instr. creative writing St. Andrews Coll., 1970—, Sandhills Coll., 1969—; cons. editor St. Andrews Rev., Pembroke Mag. Author: (collected poems) The Tree in the Far Pasture, 1964, To the Water's Edge, 1971, Journey Into Morning, 1981, In the Beginning, 1985; The Democratic Party: Its Aims and Purposes, 1961, The New Day, 1964, Free Press and Fair Trial, 1967, (with Elizabeth S. Ives) Back to Beginnings, 1969, In the Beginning (with Thad Stem Jr.), 1984, A Walk Into April, 1986; Editor: Weymouth Anthology, 1987; Contbg. editor: World Book Ency, 1964—; author articles, poems. Pres. Friends Coll., Inc., N.C. State, 1961-62; mem. N.C. Library Resources Com., N.C. Govt. Reorgn. Commn., 1970—; moderator N.C. Writers Forum of Charlotte, 1963—; Trustee N.C. Sch. Arts, 1963-72; mem. N.C. Adminstrn. of Justice Council, 1964—, chmn., 1980-83; bd. dirs. N.C. Symphony Soc., 1975-79. Served with AUS, 1943-46, PTO. Recipient N.C. Tercentenary Poetry award, 1963, spl. citation for contbns. to journalism Atlantic Christian Coll.; North Caroliniana Soc. award, 1981; Disting. Service medal DAR, 1974; Edward Arnold Young award for poetry, 1965, 72; Morrison award for contbns. to arts in N.C., 1976; N.C. award for achievements in arts, 1979; R. Hunt Parker award for Contributions to Lit., 1987; apptd. poet laureate of N.C., 1982; named to N.C. Journalism Hall of Fame,

1984. Mem. N.C. Lit. Forum (moderator 1956—), N.C. Writers Conf. (chmn. 1962-63), Eastern N.C. Press Assn. (past pres.), N.C. Press Assn. (pres. 1973-74), Asso. Press Mng. Editors Assn. (dir. gen. chmn. continuing studies 1961, sec. 1962, v.p. 1963, pres. 1964), Am. Soc. Newspaper Editors (dir., chmn. freedom of info. com. 1968), Roanoke Island Hist. Soc. (dir.), N.C. News Council (past pres.), N.C. Arts Council (chmn. 1967-72), Am. Newspaper Pubs. Assn., N.C. Lit. and Hist. Assn. (pres. 1977), Sigma Delta Chi. Democrat. Presbyn. Club: Sandhills Kiwanis (Southern Pines); Builders Cup 1985. Home: 255 Hill Rd Southern Pines NC 28387 Office: 145 W Pennsylvania Ave Southern Pines NC 28387

RAGAN, SEABORN BRYANT TIMMONS, former oil company executive; b. Augusta, Ga., Apr. 28, 1929; s. Alexander Timothy and Ela Lucille (Timmons) R.; m. Sandra Glyn Farris, Sept. 5, 1958; children—Seaborn Bryant Timmons, Sandra Leigh. Student Emory U., 1946-49, U. Ga., 1952-53; A.B., Ga. State Coll., 1959. With Gulf Oil Co., various locations, 1957-82, v.p. Korea Oil mktg. ops., Seoul, Korea, 1967-73, dist. mktg. mgr., Phila., 1973-76, project mgr. new products and new bus. devel., mktg. coordination, Houston, 1976-79, dir. market research Gulf Oil U.S., 1979-82; chief exec. officer Ragan and Ragan, Inc., 1983—. Counselor, USO, Korea, 1972-73; mem. alumni exec. com. Salisbury Sch., Conn., 1975-76, S.W. field rep., 1976—. Served with USAR, 1948-60. Mem. SAR, Audubon Soc., Soc. Archtl. Historians, Nat. Trust for Historic Preservation, Nat. Hist. Soc., Nat. Geog. Soc., Smithsonian Assos., Am. Mus. Natural History Assos., Am. Enterprise Inst. for Public Policy Research (assoc.), Nat. Archives Assos., Victorian Soc., Cousteau Soc., Oceanic Soc., Am. Field Service, Internat. Platform Assn., Am. Mktg. Assn., Houston Bd. Realtors. Republican. Episcopalian. Home: 5477 Chamblee-Dunwoody Rd Dunwoody GA 30338

RAGHEB, MAGDI, engineering educator, researcher; b. Nov. 25, 1946; m. Barbara Rose Wesolek, Feb. 16, 1980. MS, U. Wis., 1974, PhD, 1978. Vis. research scientist Brookhaven Nat. Lab., Upton, N.Y., summers 1975, 81; research assoc. Oak Ridge Nat. Lab., summer 1978; research asst. U. Wis.-Madison, 1973-78, postdoctoral assoc., 1979; assoc. prof. nuclear engring. U. Ill., Urbana, 1979—; vis. faculty, interdisciplinary research ctr. Nat. Ctr. for Supercomputing Applications U. Ill., 1986-88, assoc. faculty, 1985-87; vis. faculty Idaha Nat. Engring Lab., 1987. Engring. Distinction fellow, 1965-70. Mem. Am. Nuclear Soc., AAAS, Sci. Research Soc., N.Y. Acad. Scis., AAUP, Sigma Xi. Contbr. articles on engring. to profl. jours. Home: 401 Edgebrook Dr Champaign IL 61820 Office: 223 Nuclear Engring Lab U Ill Urbana IL 61801

RAGHEB, YOUSSEF, historian; b. Cairo, Arab Republic Egypt, June 5, 1941; s. Ali and Omneya (Rida) R. BA, Cairo U., 1963; D of Islamic Studies, U. Paris, 1972. Researcher Ctr. Nat. Recherche Scientifique, Paris, 1975. Author: Marchands d'étoffes, 1982; contbr. articles to profl. jours. Mem. Soc. Asiatique Paris. Home: 105 rue Saint-Denis, 75001 Paris France Office: Ctr Hist Studies, 9 rue Malher, 75004 Paris France

RAGNARSSON, RAGNAR JOHN, company executive; b. Pottsville, Pa., July 30, 1945; s. Ragnar Jon and Anastasia (Gogotz) R.; m. Steinunn Rannveig Magnus, Jan. 1, 1965; children: Ragnhildur, Birgir, Eythor. Comml. pilot Reykjavik, Iceland, 1963-65; salesman Tekkneska Bifreidaumbodid Ltd., Reykjavik, 1965-68, sales mgr., 1969-74; pres., chief exec. officer Jofur Ltd., Kopavogur, Iceland, 1975—; rep. Icelandic-Czech. Trade Commn., 1982-87; mgr. Northrop N-3PB Recovery Project, 1979. Editorial dir. Flug mag., 1982—; contbr. articles to profl. jours. Decorated Knight 1st Class Order of St. Olaf (Norway). Mem. Icelandic Aviation Hist. Soc. (founder, pres. 1981-82, 86—, exec. bd.), Icelandic Automobile Trade Assn. (bd. dirs. 1986—), Iceland Aero Club (v.p. 1984—). Home: Dynskogar 3, 109 Reykjavik Iceland Office: Jofur Ltd, Nybylavegur 2, 2000 Kopavogur Iceland

RAGONE, DAVID VINCENT, former university president; b. N.Y.C., May 16, 1930; s. Armando Frederick and Mary (Napier) R.; m. Katherine H. Spaulding, Dec. 18, 1954; children: Christine M., Peter V. S.B., MIT, 1951, S.M., 1952, Sc.D., 1953. Asst. prof. chem. and metall. engring. U. Mich., Ann Arbor, 1953-57; assoc. prof. U. Mich., 1957-61, prof., 1961-62; asst. dir. John J. Hopkins Lab for Pure and Applied Sci., also chmn. metallurgy dept. Gen. Atomic div. Gen Dynamics, La Jolla, 1962-67; Alcoa prof. metallurgy Carnegie-Mellon U., Pitts., 1967-69; assoc. dean Carnegie-Mellon U. (Sch. Urban and Pub. Affairs), 1969-70; dean Thayer Sch. of Engring., Dartmouth Coll., 1970-72, U. Mich. (Coll. Engring.), 1972-80; pres. Case Western Res. U., Cleve., 1980-87; vis. prof., dept. materials sci. and engring. MIT, Cambridge, Mass., 1987—; trustee Mitre Corp.; bd. dirs. Cabot Corp., Cleve. Cliffs Iron Co., Augat Inc., Sifco Inc. Mem. Nat. Sci. Bd., 1978-84; mem. tech adv. bd. U.S. Dept. Commerce, 1967-75; chmn. adv. com. advanced auto power systems Council on Environ. Quality, 1971-75; Trustee Henry Luce Found. Named Outstanding Young Engr., Engring. Soc. Detroit, 1957. Mem. Sigma Xi, Tau Beta Pi. Clubs: Cosmos (Washington); Union (Cleve.); University (N.Y.C.). Home: 52 Woodcliff Rd Wellesley MA 02181 Office: MIT Dept Materials Sci and Engring Room 13-5030 Cambridge MA 02139

RAGSDALE, CHARLES WILLIAM, electronics engineer, consultant; b. St. Petersberg, Fla., July 24, 1943; s. William Edward and Ida Marie (Chamberlain) R.; m. Barbara Louise Cannard, Nov. 2, 1969; 1 child, Melody. B.S.E.E., U. Fla., 1966; M.S. in Bioengring., U. Wyo., 1972. Design engr. Harry Diamond Labs, Washington, 1966-71; engr. specialist Bourns Life Systems, Riverside, Calif., 1972-75; program mgr. Gulton Electro Optics, Santa Barbara, Calif., 1975-77; mgr. biotronics Engring. Cavitron/Syntel, Irvine, Calif., 1977-79; sr. research specialist, dir. electronics engring. Cordis Dow/Seratronics, Concord, Calif., 1979-83; mgr. electronics engring. Mistogen Equipment Co., Oakland, Calif., 1983-84; v.p. engring., quality assurance Seratronics Inc., Concord, 1984-85; elec. engring. mgr. Bio-Rad Labs., Richmond, Calif., 1985—; free-lance cons. for various firms. Contbr. articles to prof. jours. Church organist in various chs. Bay area. Mem. IEEE. Current works: Development of medical systems in the areas of cardiac monitoring surgical monitoring, respiratory therapy, ophthalmology, dialysis. Subspecialties: Biomedical engineering; Electronics. Office: Bio-Rad Labs 1414 Harbor Way S Richmond CA 94804

RAGSDALE, ROBERT LEE, aviation company executive; b. Yoakum, Tex., Feb. 23, 1916; s. Robert Lee and Ethel Mae (Johnston) R.; m. Pearle Baird, July 7, 1940. Student, Tex. Tech U., 1933-38; C.F.I., Spartan Sch. Aeronautics, 1939. Owner, operator Ragsdale Aerial Service, Las Cruces, Socorro and Silver City, N.Mex., 1940-41, Ragsdale Flying Service, Austin, Tex., 1941-58; pres. Ragsdale Aviation, Inc., Austin, 1958-84, Capitol Aviation, Inc., Dallas, 1958-73; sec., owner Tideland Aviation, Inc., Houston, 1966-70, Gen.-Aero, Inc., San Antonio, 1964-82; chmn. bd., dir. Interfirst Bank N.W., 1980—; pres., dir. 7th and Congress Inc., Austin, 1971-81; dir. Interfirst Bank, Inc., Austin, 1963-87; pres. RA 77, Inc., Driftwood, Tex., 1982—; owner Ragsdale Investments, Inc., Austin, 1984—; mem. Cessna Aircraft Distbr. adv. council, Wichita, Kans., 1966-67. Adv. bd. City of Austin aviation adv. council, 1965-66, Tex. Aeronautics Com., 1962-63; mem. Tex. Hwy. Pub. Works, Austin, Bergstrom Air Force Base and Austin Community Council, 1965—; chancellor Knights of Symphony Soc., Austin, 1975-76; mem. Tex. Motor Vehicle Commn., Austin, 1975-81, chmn., 1980-81; pres. Austin Community Found., 1981-82, bd. govs., founder, 1978-81. Mem. Nat. Aviation Trades Assn., Nat. Pilot Assn., Aviation Hall of Fame, Tex. Pvt. Flyers Assn. (past dir., charter mem.), Nat. Flying Farmers Assn., Tex. Flying Farmers Assn., Confederate Air Force, OX-5 Assn. Tex., Tex. Aviation Dealer Assn., Austin C. of C. (dir. 1963-64, v.p. 1975-76). Clubs: Admirals, University (bd. advisors, founder), Westwood, Headliner (trustee). Lodge: Rotary. Home: 3408 Mountain Top Circle Austin TX 78731

RAHAL, GEORGE MICHEL, electrical and biomedical engineer; b. Damascus, Syria, Aug. 2, 1943; s. Michel J. and Mary A. (Mousleh) R.; B.S. in Elec. Engring., U. Miami (Fla.), 1968, M.S. in Biomed. Engring., 1971; m. Maria Navickas, Aug. 16, 1972 (div.); 1 dau., Nicole; m. Samia Saoma; children: Raymond, Ronald, Michel. Lab. supr. U. Miami Engring. Sch., 1966-68; instr. Broward Community Coll., Miami, 1968-69; dir. Greer Tech. Inst., Chgo., 1972; mgr. tech. devel. Ryder Schs., Miami, 1973-75; v.p. engring. Office Constrn. and Devel., Damascus, 1976-77; founder, pres. electronic and med. div., corp. v.p. Engring. Devel. Orgn., Damascus, 1977—; established the EDCO group (the first med. engring. planning in Syria), 1987; cons. in field. U. Miami fgn. student grantee, 1966-69, fellow, 1969-71, recipient Internat. Student of Yr. award, 1970; Friends of Middle East award, 1969. Mem. IEEE, Am. Cultural Center Damascus. Home: Haffar Bldg, Aleppo St, Kouzbari, Damascus Syria Office: Parlement, Salhieh, Damascus Syria

RAHBAR, ZITA INA, health insurance executive; b. Kaunas, Lithuania, Mar. 15, 1937; came to U.S. 1949; d. Stasys and Ona (Eitkeviciute) Carneckas; m. Vytautas Dudenas, June 20, 1960 (div. 1965); m. 2d, Darius Rahbar, Mar. 26, 1970. B.A. St. Xavier Coll., Chgo., 1957; postgrad. in physiology U. Chgo., 1957-59, M.B.A., 1978. Mng. editor Lyons & Carnahan div. Meredith Corp., Chgo., 1960-68, mgr. program planning, 1968-73; exec. cons. George S. May Co., Chgo., 1973-75; sr. cons. planning Blue Shield Assn., Chgo., 1975-76, dir. corp. planning Blue Shield/Blue Cross Assn., 1976-78, sr. dir. program devel. and implementation, 1978-81, v.p. mktg. Blue Cross Calif., Los Angeles and Oakland, Calif., 1981-87; pres., Creative Mktg. Solutions, 1987—. Bd. dirs. Bethune Ballet, Los Angeles, 1982—; mem. com. Orgn. Women Execs., Los Angeles, 1982—; co-founder Women in Pub., Chgo., 1965; mem. NOW, Town Hall Calif., Chgo. Council Fgn. Relations, World Affairs Council Los Angeles. Fellow U. Chgo., 1957-58. Mem. Am. Mgmt. Assn., Am. Mktg. Assn., AAAS. Republican. Roman Catholic. Home: 912 Blue Spring Dr Westlake Village CA 91361

RAHMAN, M. HABIBUR, legal educator, researcher; b. Baniagati, Bogra, Bangladesh, Dec. 12, 1946; s. M.P. Talukder and Delsor Begum; m. Morjina Khatun Bilkis, Nov. 3, 1972; children: Humairath Hilmi, Niath Mahmud. MSc, U. Dacca, Bangladesh, 1968, LLB, 1969; LLM, U. Rajshahi, Bangladesh, 1979, U. Wales, 1982. Lectr. in law Rajshahi U., 1970-74, from asst. prof. law to assoc. prof., 1974—, chmn. dept. law, 1987—. Author: (research monographs) Delimitation of Maritime Boundaries with Special Reference to the Bangladesh-India Situation, Deep Seabed Mining Under the Law of the Sea Convention 1982 - A Study of the Rights of Developing Countries; contbr. articles on maritime law to legal jours. in Australia, Bangladesh, Hong Kong, India, Pakistan, U.K. and U.S. Office: Rajshahi U, Dept Law, Rajshahi Bangladesh

RAHMAN, MOHAMED HABIBUR, architectural educator; b. Barisal, Bangladesh, Aug. 13, 1945; s. Abdur Rashid Talukder and Jahanara Begum; m. Shamsad Ara Nanni, Dec. 5, 1971; children: Shaily Rahman, Shoumik Rahman, Shanak Rahman. BArch, Bangladesh U. of Engring. and Tech., Dhaka, 1968; M in Philosophy of Architecture, U. Newcastle Upon Tyne, Eng., 1975. Lectr. Bangladesh U. of Engring. and Tech., Dhaka, 1969-72, asst. prof., 1972-77, assoc. prof., 1977-82; assoc. prof. King Faisal U., Dammam, Saudi Arabia, 1982—; cons. Bangladesh Cons. Ltd., Dhaka, 1976-77, Nasim and Assocs., Dhaka, 1979-82; advisor Dexterous Cons., Dhaka, 1977-79. Prin. works include archtl. contbn. to high rise bldg. project, Shilpa Bank, Bangladesh (1st prize), 1978; editor Bidesh newsletter, 1987; contbr. articles to profl. jours. Grantee Animation Film Making, No. Arts, Eng., 1974; recipient Animation Film Script award Habitat, UN Ctr. for Human Settlements, 1980. Mem. Bangladesh Inst. Architects (hon. sec.). Office: King Faisal U, PO Box 2397, Dammam 31451, Saudi Arabia

RAHTZ, PHILIP ARTHUR, archaeologist, writer; b. Bristol, Eng., Mar. 11, 1921; s. Frederick John and Ethel May (Clothier) R.; m. Mary Hewgill Smith, Sept. 14, 1940 (dec. May 1977); children: Philippa, Nicholas, David, Diana, Sebastian; m. Lorna Rosemary Watts, Apr. 7, 1978. MA, U. Bristol, 1964. Lectr. then sr. lectr., reader U. Birmingham, Warwickshire, Eng., 1963-78; prof. archaeology U. York, Yorkshire, Eng., 1978-86; pres. Council British Archaeology, London, 1986—. Author: Ed Rescue Archaeology, 1971, Invitation to Archaeology, 1985. Served to sgt. RAF, 1944-46. Fellow Soc. of Antiquaries; mem. Inst. Field Archaeologists. Home: The Old Sch Harome, Helmsley Y06 4JE, Yorkshire, England

RAI, GURCHARAN SINGH, physician, educator; b. Ludhiana, Punjab, India, July 30, 1947; s. Gurdev Singh and Kartar (Kaur) R.; m. Harsha Bhatia, Nov. 8, 1977; children—Sandeep Gurdev Singh, Gurdeep Singh. M.B., B.S., U. Newcastle, Newcastle-uopn-Tyne, Eng., 1971, M.D., 1978; M.Sc., U. London, 1977. House physician and surgeon Gen. Hosp., Nottingham, Eng., 1971-72; sr. house officer Univ. Hosps., Newcastle-upon-Tyne, 1972-73, registrar, 1974-76, sr. research assoc., 1976-78; sr. registrar Chesterton Hosp., Cambridge, 1978-80; cons. physician Whittington Hosp., London, 1980—; sr. lectr. geriatric medicine Univ. Coll. Hosp. Med. Sch., London, 1980—. Author: Databook on Geriatrics, 1980, Case Presentations in Clinical Geriatric Medicine, 1987; contbr. articles to profl. jours. Fellow Royal Coll. Physicians; mem. Brit. Nuclear Medicine Soc., Brit. Geriatric Soc., Brit. Assn. Services for Elderly, Brit. Med. Assn. Home: 114 Draycott Ave, Kenton Harrow HA3 0BY, England Office: Whittington Hospital, Highgate Hill, London NI9 5NF, England

RAILTON, WILLIAM SCOTT, lawyer; b. Newark, July 30, 1935; s. William Scott and Carolyn Elizabeth (Guiberson) R.; m. Karen Elizabeth Walsh, Mar. 31, 1979; 1 son, William August; children by previous marriage: William Scott, Anne Greenwood. BSEE, U. Wash., 1962; JD with honors, George Washington U., 1965. Bar: D.C. 1966, Md. 1966, U.S. Patent Office 1966. Assoc., then ptnr. Kemon, Palmer & Estabrook, Washington, 1966-70; sr. trial atty. Dept. Labor, Washington, 1970-71, asst. counsel for trial litigation, 1971-72; chief counsel U.S. Occupational Safety and Health Rev. Commn., Washington, 1972-77; acting gen. counsel U.S. Occupational Safety and Health Rev. Commn., 1975-77; ptnr. Reed, Smith, Shaw & McClay, Pitts., 1977—; lectr. George Washington U. Law Sch., 1977-79, seminar chmn. Occupational Safety and Health Act, 1979—; lectr. Practicing Law Inst., 1976-79. Author: (legal handbooks) The Examination System and the Backlog, 1965, The OSHA General Duty Clause, 1977, The OSHA Health Standards, 1977; contbg. author Employee Relations Law Jour., 1978—. Regional chmn. Montgomery County (Md.) Republican Party, 1968-70; pres. Montgomery Sq. Citizens Assn., 1970-71; bd. dirs., pres. Foxvale Farms Homeowners Assn., 1979-82. Served with USMC, 1953-58. Recipient Meritorious Achievement medal Dept. Labor, 1972, Outstanding Service award OSHA Rev. Commn., 1977. Mem. ABA, Md. Bar Assn., Bar Assn. D.C. (vice chmn. young lawyers sect. 1971), Order of Coif, Sigma Phi Epsilon, Phi Delta Phi. Clubs: Oval of U. Wash. (Seattle); River Bend Country (Gt. Falls). Home: 10102 Walker Lake Dr Great Falls VA 22066 other: 8201 Greensboro Dr McLean VA 22102

RAIMOND, JEAN-BERNARD, former French minister of foreign affairs, diplomat; b. Paris, Feb. 6, 1926; s. Henri and Alice (Auberty) R.; m. Monique Chabanel, Oct. 18, 1975; children: Sophie, Catherine. Attache, Nat. Ctr. Scientific Research, France, 1951-53; student Sch. Nat. Adminstrn., France, 1954-56, dept. polit. affairs Central Adminstrn., Ministry Fgn. Affairs, 1956-66, dep. dir. Europe, Ministry Fgn. Affairs, 1967, asst. dir. Cabinet of Ministry, 1967-68, tech. cons. Cabinet of Prime Minister, France, 1968-69, mission charge, then tech. cons. to Sec.-Gen. of the Presidency of the Republic, 1970-73, Minister Plenipotentiary, 1972, ambassador of France to Morocco, 1973-79, dir. N. Africa and The Levant, 1977-78, dir. Cabinet of the Ministry Fgn. Affairs, 1978-79, dir.-gen. of Cultural Relations, Ministry Fgn. Affairs, 1979-81, ambassador of France to Poland, 1982-84, to U.S.S.R., 1985-86, Minister Fgn. Affairs, France, 1986-88. Decorated Legion of Honor, Nat. Order of Merit, Chevalier Ordre des Palmes Academiques, Grand-Cordon du Ouissam-Alaouite, Morocco. Address: 37 Quai d'Orsay, 75007 Paris France *

RAIMONDI, RUGGERO, opera singer; b. Bologna, Italy, Oct. 3, 1941. Studies with, Teresa Pediconi, Rome, Maestro Piervenanzi. Debut as opera singer in La Boheme, Spoleto, Italy, 1964; opera singer in major houses, Europe and U.S.; Met. debut in Ernani, N.Y.C., 1970; favorite roles include Don Giovanni, Philip II, Boris and Don Quichotte; recorded Verdi Requiem, Vespri Siciliani, La Boheme, Aida, Attila, Don Carlos, Macbeth, I Masnadieri, Simon Boccanegra, Don Giovanni, Boris Godunov, Il Pirata, Norma, Tosca, Turandot, Berbiere di Siviglia, Mosé, Nozze di Figaro; appeared in films Don Giovanni (Joseph Lozey), 1978, Six Characters in Search of a Singer (Maurice Bejart), 1983, Carmen (Francesco Rosi), 1986, others. Office: care CAMI 165 W 57th St New York NY 10019 *

RAINBOLT, JOHN VERNON, II, lawyer; b. Cordell, Okla., May 24, 1939; s. John Vernon (Mike) and Mary Alice (Power) R.; m. Janice Glaub, Oct. 2, 1976; children—John Vernon, III, Sara McLain, Charles Joseph. B.A., Okla. U., 1961, LL.B., 1964; postgrad. George Washington U. 1971-73. Bar: Okla. 1964, D.C. 1971, U.S. Supreme Ct. 1971. Legis. counsel, adminstrv. asst. U.S. Rep. Graham Purcell, Washington, 1967-72; counsel agr. com. U.S. Ho. of Reps., Washington, 1972-74, chief counsel, 1975; commr. Commodity Futures Trading Commn., Washington, 1975-78; sole practice, Washington, 1978—; ptnr. Miles & Stockbridge, Washington, 1982-86; advisor agr. policy Tokyo Roundtable White House, 1978-81; mem. Adminstrn. Conf., U.S., 1976-79. Author and draftsman Commodity Futures Trading Commn. Act, 1974; contbr. articles to legal jours. Served to 1st lt. Inf., U.S. Army, 1964-67. Vice chmn. Commodity Futures Trading Commn., 1975-78. Mem. ABA (chmn. subcom. on fgn. markets and traders 1982-85), U.S. Futures Industry Assn. (assoc.). Clubs: Commodity of Washington, Pisces.

RAINE, ADRIAN, psychology educator; b. Darlington, Eng., Jan. 27, 1954; s. Reuben and Anna (Bellezza) R. BA in Exptl. Psychology, U. Oxford, 1977, MA in Psychology, 1982; D Phil in Psychology, York U., Eng., 1982. Sr. psychologist Frankland Prison, Durham, Eng., 1981-84; lectr. dept. psychiatry Nottingham (Eng.) U. Hosp. and Med. Sch., 1984-87; asst. prof. psychology U. So. Calif., Los Angeles, 1987—. Contbr. articles to profl. jours. Mem. Brit. Psychol. Assn., Brit. Psychophysiol. Soc., Internat. Soc. for Study Individual Differences. Office: U So Calif Dept Psychology University Park SGM Bldg Los Angeles CA 90089-1061

RAINES, RONALD BRUCE, accountant; b. Sydney, Australia, Nov. 6, 1929; s. Douglas William and Jean Laurie (Pilcher) R.; m. Helen Janet Cadwallader, Oct. 21, 1977; children: Ronald Douglas, Fenella Jann, Douglas Antony. Diploma Sydney Boys High Sch., 1947. Ptnr. R.A. Irish & Michelmore, Chartered Accts., Sydney, 1955-65; dep. chmn. Alexander Stenhouse Ltd.; chmn. bd. Pastoral & Agrl. Mgmt. Ltd., Australian Elec. Industries Ltd., 1964-68, New South Wales State Dockyard, 1968-77; chmn. Med. Resources Ltd.; dep. chmn. Letona Coop Ltd.; bd. dirs. Penfold Printers Ltd., Stenhouse Securities Ltd., Found. 41, 600 Machinery Australia Pty. Ltd., Australian Canned Fruits Corp., Case Communication Systems Ltd. Mem. Legis. Council New South Wales, 1977-78, Met. (Sydney) Waste Disposal Authority. Fellow Chartered Inst. Accts. Australia, Australian Inst. Mgmt., Inst. Dirs. Clubs: Australian, Royal Sydney Golf, Australian Jockey, Bowral Golf. Home: Point Piper, New South Wales Australia Office: GPO Box 1742, Sydney, New South Wales Australia

RAINFORD, HENRY JAMES, agricultural products executive; b. Mar. 29, 1930; s. Justin Powell and Matilda (Francis) R.; m. Dorothy May Chen Rainford; children: Andrea, Richard, Angella, Henry. Diploma, Kingston Tech. Sch., 1976; LLD (hon.), U. Fla., 1987. Mktg. officer exports div. Jamaican Cocoa Industry Bd., 1954-57, sr. acctg. officer, 1957-61; acct. Jamaica Livestock Assn., Kingston, 1961-63, chief acct., sec., chief exec. officer, 1963-67, mng. dir., chief exec. officer, 1967—; advisor Inter-Am. Confederation Cattlemen, Caracas, Venezuela; mem. Jamaica Agrl. Devel. Found. Research Adv. Council; Justice of the Peace. Recipient gold medal Jamaica Agrl. Soc. Mem. Jamaica Inst. Mgmt. Anglican. Clubs: Kingston Polo, Royal Soc. of Commonwealth (London). Office: Jamaica Livestock Assn, Newport East, PO Box 36 Kingston Jamaica

RAINIER, PRINCE III, (Louis Henri Maxence Bertrand) Sovereign Prince of Monaco; b. Principality of Monaco, May 31, 1923; s. Comte Pierre de Polignac and Princesse Charlotte de Monaco; ed. Summerfields, Hastings, Eng., Le Rosey, Faculte de Montpellier, Ecole des Scis. Politiques de Paris; m. Grace Kelly, Apr. 19, 1956 (dec. 1982); children: Caroline (Mrs. Stefano Casiraghi), Albert Alexandre Louis Pierre, Stephanie Marie Elizabeth. Became hereditary Prince of Monaco, June 2, 1944; delegated by reigning prince to administer affairs of the Principality, Apr. 1949; succeeded his grandfather, Prince Louis, II, May 9, 1949. Founder Red Cross of Monaco, 1948; founder Am. Friends of Monaco, 1952, Prix Prince Rainier, III, de Monaco (annual lit. prize for fgn. writers). Served as lt. and col. French Army, 1944-45; Decorated Grand Master of Ordre de Saint-Charles; Grand Cross of Legion of Honor (France); mem. Ordre des Seraphins (Sweden); Grand Cross of Royal Orr. of Geo. 1st of Greece; Grand Cross of Ordre de Leopold de Belgique: Grand Cross of Ordre de Lion d'Or de Nassau (Netherlands); Grand Cross of Ordre Equestre de Saint-Martin (Republic San Marino); Grand Cross of Ordre du Sauveur de Greece; Grand Master Ordre de la Couronne; Grand Master Ordre des Grimaldi (Monaco); mem. Ordre Militaire Pontificial de l'Esperon d'Or, Grand Cordon Ordre du Merite de la Republique Italienne; Grand Cross Ordre de Mohamed Ali; Grand Cross Ordre de l'Etoile de Karageorgevitch; Croix de Guerre (France, Belgium, Italy); others. Address: Palais, 98000 Princier Monaco

RAINWATER, GILES DEAN, psychologist; b. Snyder, Tex., Dec. 26, 1950; s. Tinsley A. and Edna L. (Hester) R.; BA with honors in Psychology, Tex. Tech U., 1973; MA in Clin. Psychology, Ind. State U., 1975; PhD in Clin. Psychology, U. Oreg., 1978. Intern, U. Wash. Med. Sch., 1977-78; psychologist Melbourne (Fla.) Neurologic, 1978-81; pvt. practice psychology, Melbourne, 1981-87; dir. behaviror med., coordinator out patient trauma Sea Pines Rehab. Hosp., Melbourne, 1987—; chmn. bd. Psychometric Software Inc.; adj. prof. Fla. Inst. Tech. Mem. Am. Psychol. Assn., Biofeedback Soc. Am., Mensa. Republican. Clubs: Imperial Cts., Racquetball. Contbr. articles to profl. jours. Office: PO Box 1677 Melbourne FL 32902-1677

RAIS, MAHMOUD, publishing executive, educator; b. Korba, Tunisia, Mar. 2, 1941; s. Abdelkader Ben Mohamed and Chelbia Bent Mohamed (Rabah) R.; m. Sihem Bent Tahar Landoulsi, July 20, 1979; children: Abdelkader, Nadia, Heykal. Baccalaureat, Lycee Du Bardo, Tunis, Tunisia, 1960; Licence es-Lettres Anglaises, U. Tunis, 1966; MA, Northwestern U., 1967; PhD, Cornell U., 1972. Asst. prof. English dept. U. Tunis, 1972-82, chmn. English dept., 1977-80; editor Statis., Econ. and Social Research and Tng. Ctr. for Islamic Countries, Ankara, Turkey, 1982-84, head of pubs. dept., 1984—. Editor: (books) Training Institutions, 1985, Consultancy Services, 1986; mng. editor : Jour. of Econ. Cooperation, 1982—. Moslem. Office: SESRTCIC, Attar Sok #4, Ankara 06700, Turkey

RAISSIS, GEORGE, shipbroker; b. Beirut, Lebanon, Jan. 2, 1939; arrived Greece, 1965; s. Leonidas and Eleftheria (Carapiperis) R.; m. Melina Fatsiades, Jan. 4, 1969; children—Terry, Tassos, Leonidas. Student Coll. Des Freres, Beirut, Lebanon, 1957. Shipping apprentice L. Raissis Shipping Ag., Beirut, Lebanon, 1959-61, vice-mng. dir., 1964; sales rep. NCR, Saudi Arabia, 1962, Jordan, 1963; mng. dir. Maraship Maritime, Co., Piraeus, Greece, 1965; mng. dir. Maraship (L. Raissis Sons), Piraeus, Greece, 1967-74; pres. Sea Transport Contractors, Piraeus, 1974—, Marachart Shipping Co. Ltd., 1975—. Mem. Greek Shipbrokers Assn. Greek Orthodox. Club: Piraeus Marine, AOK. Home: Raggavi, Kifissia Greece Office: Marachart Shipping Co Ltd, PO Box 80068, 185 10 Piraeus Greece

RAIS YATIM, former Malaysian minister of foreign affairs; b. 1942; m. Datin Masnah Mohamed, 1974; children: Dino, Malini, Danni. LL.B., U. Singapore; Diploma in Psychology, No. Ill. U. Tng. coordinator U.S. Peace Corps, 1964, tchr. Negeri Sembilan, until 1968; mem. United Malays Nat. Orgn. Div., 1970—, Supreme Council, 1978—; parliamentary sec. Ministry of Culture, Youth, and Sports, 1974-78, dep. minister for home affairs, 1978, chief minister Besar of Negri Sembilan state, 1978-82, minister of land and regional devel., 1982-84, minister of info., 1984-86, minister of fgn. affairs, 1976-87. Pres., Nat. Assn. Against Drug Abuse. Author: Faces in the Corridors of Power, 1987. Address: Former Ministry of Fgn Affairs, Kuala Lumpur Malaysia

RAITHEL, FREDERICK J., information system specialist; b. Jefferson City, Mo., Nov. 20, 1949; s. Herbert C. and Mildred (Kemper) R. B.A. in Philosophy, Lincoln U., 1972; M.A. in Library Info. Sci., U. Mo., 1973. Asst. reference librarian Mo. State Library, Jefferson City, 1974; reference librarian Daniel Boone Regional Library, Columbia, Mo., 1974-78; network coordinator Mid-Mo. Library Network, Columbia, 1978-81, head access services U. Mo. Libraries, Columbia, 1981-84, info. system research analyst, dept. agrl. econs. U. Mo., 1984, dir. Mid-Mo. Library Network, Columbia, 1984-87, dir. continuing edn./extension and lectr. Sch. Library and Informational Sci. U. Mo. Columbia, 1987—. chmn. Automation Tech. Com.

of Mo. Libraries Network Bd., 1983-86; pres. U. Mo. Sch. Library Info Sci Alumni Assn., 1977-79; cons. Mem. ALA, Mo. Library Assn. (founder/ organizer computer info. tech. com., sec. 1987-88). Contbr. articles to profl. jours. Home: 501H Columbia Dr Columbia MO 65201 Office: U Mo 104 Stewart Hall Columbia MO 65211

RAITT, DAVID IAN, librarian, information scientist; b. Sulhamstead, Berks, Eng., Nov. 2, 1944; s. David and Aileen (Taylor) R.; m. Brenda Victoria Peachey, Apr. 16, 1966; children: Jocelyne Elizabeth, Matthew Bruce, Belinda Louise, Philip John Edward. A in Library and Info. Sci., North Western Polytech., London, 1967; PhD, Loughborough U., 1984. Chartered librarian. Dep. group librarian Royal Aircraft Establishment, Farnborough, Eng., 1968-69; info. scientist European Space Research Orgn., Paris, 1969-73; customer liaison officer European Space Agy., Frascati, Italy, 1973-79; head library and info. services European Space Agy., Noordwijk, The Netherlands, 1979—. Editor: The Electronic Library, 1983—, Info. Festschrift Series, 1988—; news editor Online Review , 1977—, Elect. and Optical Pub. Review, 1979—. Chmn. adv. com. Internat. Online Info. Meetings, 1983—. Fellow Library Assn., Inst. Info Scientists, Royal Astron. Soc.; mem. Am. Soc. for Info. Sci. (asst. chair Sig. III 1987-88). Home: Frankenslag 179, 2582 HL Den Haag The Netherlands Office: European Space Agy, Postbus 299, 2200 AG Noordwijk The Netherlands

RAJADURAI, NIGEL PUSHPARAJAH, engineer, consultant; b. Colombo, Sri Lanka, Nov. 5, 1950; s. Chelliah Richard and Christobel (Chinniah) R.; m. Lydia Pathmini Chinniah, Nov. 5, 1980. BS, U. Saugar, India, 1973. Sales engr. Asiatic Comml. Agy., Colombo, 1973-81; tech. sales exec. M.S. Hebtaubhoy & Co., Ltd., Colombo, 1981-86; mgr. sales Electro Metallic Industries, Colombo, 1986, dir. sales, 1987—; mng. dir. Ackwell Agys. Pte., Ltd., Singapore; cons. N.L. Power, 1986. Author: Church of the Bible, 1979. Named. Nat. Orator of the Yr. Ceylon Tamil Tchrs. Assn., 1965. Mem. United Nat. Party. Home: 32/1 Pamankade Ln, 06 Colombo Sri Lanka Office: Electro Metallic Industries, 4141/18 K Cyril C Perera Ma, 13 Colombo Sri Lanka

RAJAH, HOOSSAIN GOOLAM MOHYEDEEN, textile company executive, marketing consultant; b. Port Louis, Mauritius; arrived in Eng., 1961.; s. Goolam Mohyedeen Issop and Sarah (Amode) R.; m. Ansan Bibi Ismael; children: Feryal, Najma. BA in Econs with honors, Manchester U., Eng., 1965; cert. in exporting and mktg. Exec. officer Rajah and Co., Port Louis, 1958-61; acct., auditor Chartered Accts., Manchester, 1965-72; mng. dir. Renovex (M/C) Ltd., Manchester, 1972—; mktg. cons. Rahah Bros. & Co., Port Louis, 1972—, Rabroco Internat., Ltd., 1972—; exec. dir. Yorkshire Woolen Worsted Mill Ltd., Manchester, 1987—. Exec. mem. Port Louis Youth Fedn., Mauritius, 1960-61; council mem. Mauritius Youth Council, 1960-61; pres. Manchester U. Student Islamic Soc., 1963-65; trustee Muslim Student Trust, London, 1972—, Islamic Benevolent Assn., Manchester, 1982— (hon. sec. 1980—). Mem. Inst. Mktg., Inst. Export. Office: Renovex M/C Ltd, Lancaster House, 80 Princess St, Manchester M1 6NF, England

RAJAN, AYILLIATH, academic administrator, researcher; b. Cananoore, Kerala, India, Dec. 1, 1937; parents: Kunhikannan Kuppadakkath Nambiar and Meenakshi Amma (Ayilliath) N.; m. Valsala Kizhakkae Valappil; children: Rajiv, Rajesh, Remesh. B Vet. Sci., Madras (India) U., 1959, M Vet. Sci., 1963; PhD, U. Agrl. Scis., Bangalore, India, 1972. Cert. vet. pathologist. Vet. officer Govt. Kerala, Payyannor, India, 1959-63; lectr. Vet. Coll., Trichur, India, 1963-68; assoc. prof. Kerada Agrl. U., Trichur, 1968-78, prof., head. dept., 1978-87, dir. Ctr. Excellence in Pathology, 1987—, mem. acad. council, 1978-81, animal disease project coordinator, 1987. Editor Kerala Jour. Vet Sci., 1978—; contbr. articles to sci. jours. Grantee Govt. of India. Mem. Indian Assn. Vet. Pathologists, Indian Assn. Pathologists and Microbiologists, Indian Vet. Assn. (research article award 1978, 81), Indian Poultry Sci. Assn., Indian Council Med. Research, Indian Council Agrl. Research (panel mem., research grantee), Internat. Goat Assn. Hindu-nair. Lodge: Lions (v.p.). Home: v/201 Block Rd, Ollukkara, Mannuthy, Kerala 680 651, India Office: Vet Coll, Centre Excellence Pathology, Mannuthy, Kerala, Trichur 680 651, India

RAJARATNAM, JESUTHASAN MYLVAGANAM, retired sewing machine company executive, business consultant; b. Point Pedro, No. Sri Lanka, Dec. 23, 1927; s. Ambalavanar Joseph and Mary Rasammah (Subramaniam) Mylvaganam; m. Rajeswary Muttucumaru Dec. 1, 1949; children—Shanthini, Rajakumaran, Rajakanthan, Vathani, Rajarengan. B.S., U. Ceylon, Colombo, Sri Lanka, 1949. Group controller Browns Group, Colombo, 1961-62; controller, fin. mgr. Singer Sewing Machine Co., br. Singer Industries (Ceylon) Ltd., Colombo, 1963-66; chmn., mng. dir., Singer Industries (Ceylon) Ltd., gen. mgr., chief exec. br. Singer Sewing Machine Co., Colombo, 1966-71; controller, ops. mgr. Singer Sewing Machine Co., Singapore, 1972-73; v.p. fin. and acctg. internat. group The Singer Co., N.Y.C., 1973-76, regional v.p. The Singer Co., Stamford, Conn., 1976-85; dir., cons. Biscon Inc., Colombo, Sri Lanka, 1962—; dir. Singer Thailand Ltd., Bangkok, Singer Industreis Thailand Ltd., Bangkok, Indian Sewing Machine Co. Ltd., Bombay, Singer Industries Pakistan Ltd., Karachi, Regnis Pakistan Ltd., Karachi, Singer Industries (Ceylon) Ltd., Colombo, Singer Sri Lanka Ltd., Colombo, Singer Bangladesh Ltd., Dhaka, 1976-85. Fellow Inst. Chartered Accts. Eng. and Wales (hons and 12th cert. of merit 1954), Inst. Chartered Accts. Sri Lanka. Methodist. Club: Colombo Tamil Sangam (v.p. 1960—). Lodge: Rotary (dir. community service 1964-66). Avocations: drama; eastern classical music; econ. and polit. reading; oriental dancing. Home and Office: 109 Wildwood Ave Upper Montclair NJ 07043

RAJARETNAM, EMANUEL KANDIAH, financial executive; b. Jaffna, Sri Lanka, May 7, 1929; came to Zambia, 1976; s. Kandiah Elithamby and Kandiah (Manikam) R.; m. Rita Rajaretnam; children—Antony Terrance, Rajani. B.Sc. in Econs., U. London, 1958. Bursar Poly. Univ. of Malawi, Blantyne, 1967-71; mgr. Cooper and Lybrand, Blantyne, 1972-74; fin. mgr. Blantyne Printing and Pub. Co., 1974-75, Rothmans of Pall Mall (Zambia) Ltd., Lusaka, 1976-87. Fellow Inst. Chartered Accts. (U.K., Australia). Club: Lusaka.

RAJDEV, ASHOKE, manufacturing company executive; b. Calcutta, West Bengal, India, Apr. 18, 1950; arrived in Oman, 1974; s. Pranlal Vithaldas Rajdev and Sushila (Gosalia) R.; m. Priti Ashoke, Mar. 10, 1985; 1 child, Priya Ashoke. BEE, Coll. Engring., Aurangbad, India, 1972; diploma mgmt. course, Small Industries Service Inst., Bombay, 1973. Engring. apprentice Union Carbide, Bombay, 1972-74; sales engr. Philips India Ltd., Bombay, 1974; maintenance engr. Oman Port Services Co., Muscat, 1974-76; elec./mech. div. mgr. Zawawi Trading Co., Muscat, 1976-79; gen. mgr. Oman Mech. Services Co. Ltd., Muscat, 1979—, Gen. Electronics & Trading Co., Muscat, 1981-87, Al Arabi Nails Factory, Muscat, 1986—; bd. dirs. Hilal Mktg. & Services; mem. mgmt. com. Bishara Establishment, Muscat, 1984-85; mem. tender bd. com. Port Services Corp., Muscat, 1984-86; cons. Gen. Electric and Kuljian Corp., Muscat, 1981—. Social Worker Ramkrishnan Mission, Bombay, 1972-74. Mem. Royal Oman Amateur Radio Soc. Office: Oman Mech Services Co Ltd, PO Box 4199, Ruwi Muscat Oman

RAKER, J. RUSSELL, III, academic administrator; b. Phila., Nov. 18, 1941; s. J. Russell Jr. and M. Elmina (Dunkin) R.; m. Carol Barnes, June 14, 1964; children: Jonathan Russell, Timothy Paul. BA cum laude, Alderson-Broaddus Coll., 1963; MA, Columbia U., 1964, diploma, 1968. Cert. fund raising exec., Washington. Dir. devel. Moravian Sem. Girls, Bethlehem, Pa., 1964-66; assoc. dir. devel. Columbia U., N.Y.C., 1966-69, U. Rochester(N.Y.), 1969-71; dir. devel. Hiram (Ohio) Coll., 1971-75; v.p. Ottawa (Kans.) U., 1975-79; assoc. v.p. U. Redlands (Calif.), 1979-81; program dir. Campbell & Co., Chgo., 1981-82; pres. Nebr. Ind. Coll. Found., Omaha, 1982-87; chief exec. officer Kettering Med. Ctr. Found., Dayton, Ohio, 1987—; bd. dirs. Nat. Soc. Fund Raising Execs., Washington. Bd. dirs. Nebr. Women's Commn. Found., Lincoln, 1986—; v.p. Omaha Ballet Bd., 1987—; trustee Ind. Coll. Funds Am., mem. exec. com., 1986—, mem. cert. bd. Internat. Soc. Fund Raising Execs. Recipient Charles L. Foreman Dist. Performance award Ind. Coll. Funds Am., 1987. Mem. Am. Assn. Higher Edn. (life), Am. Assn. Univ. Adminstrs., Nat. Assn. Hosp. Devel., Nat. Soc. Fund Raising Execs. (chpt. pres. 1984-85, Outstanding Prof. 1985, mem. nat. com.), Phi Delta Kappa. Republican. Baptist. Club: Omaha. Home: 8030 Brainard Woods Dr Centerville OH 45458

RAKOCHEVICH, WOOLAY, public mediator, behavioral scientist; b. Belgrade, Yugoslavia, Jan. 10, 1939; came to U.S., 1969; s. Milinko and Zivana (Zujovic) R.; married; 1 child, Beck. PhD in Behavioral Sci., Ljubljana U., Yugaslavia, 1964; postgrad., Columbia U., 1976; PhD, NYU, 1980. Pvt. practice psychology Paradise Valley, Ariz., 1977-85; founder Pub. Mediator Office, Inc., Scottsdale, Ariz., 1981—. Author: How to Become a Public Mediator, 1985; contbr. articles on marriage to profl. jours. Republican. Serbian Orthodox.

RAKOTOARIJAONA, DÉSIRÉ, former prime minister of Democratic Madagascar, army officer; b. 1934; minister of fin., 1975; mem. Supreme Revolutionary Council, 1975—; prime minister, 1977-88; mem. Front National pour la Défense de la Révolution Socialiste Malagache. Address: care Office Prime Minister, Mahazoarivo, Antananarivo Madagascar *

RAKOVER, BERYL BEN DUVID, mathematics and computer science educator, researcher; b. Kishinev, Romania, July 19, 1931; came to U.S., 1980; s. Duvid Boruch Rakover and Tsipora Bentsion (Berdichevsky) Rakover Dubossarsky; m. Rimma Isaac Kronfeld, June 10, 1954; children—David, Anna. MS in Math., Univ. Kishinev, 1955; PhD in Edn. of Math., Acad. Pedagogical Scis., Moscow, 1968. Tchr. math. High Sch. Kishinev, 1953-60; tchr. math. and program in spl. computer sci., 1960-69; assoc. prof. math. Poly. Inst., Kishinev, 1969-79; sci. programmer Xerox Corp., Rochester, N.Y., 1980-81; computer analyst St. Mary Hosp., Rochester, 1981; assoc. prof. St. John Fisher Coll., Rochester, 1981-88, prof., 1988—; presenter papers Internat. Congress Mathematicians, Berkeley, 1986, Budapest, 1988, Interamerican Conf. Guadalajara, 1985, Santo-Domingo, 1987. Author: Elementary Functions, 1971, Solving Different Equations, 1977, Algorithmic Teaching, 1977; also numerous papers; patentee Fatiguability of Math Classes (interim Congress award), 1967. Recipient award Edn. Research, 1961, summer teaching grantee St. John Fisher Coll., 1985. Mem. Math. Assn. Am. Home: 492 Surrey Hill Way Rochester NY 14623 Office: St John Fisher Coll 3690 East Ave Rochester NY 14618

RAKOWSKI, BARBARA ANN, educator; b. Flint, Mich., Jan. 24, 1948; d. Casimir Anthony and Harriet Ann (Craft) R.; BS, Central Mich. U., 1971, MS, 1978. Tchr. langs. and scis. Sts. Peter and Paul Area High Sch., Saginaw, Mich., 1971-79, chmn. dept. fgn. langs., 1974-79; instr. high sch. program field studies Central Mich. U., Beaver Island, Mich., 1973-81; prin., tchr. Beaver Island Community Schs., 1979-84, also career edn. coordinator; chair dept. scis. Sacred Heart Acad., Mt. Pleasant, Mich., 1984—. Mem. Mich. Sci. Tchrs. Assn., Sci. Edn. in Middle Sch. (cadre), Activities to Integrate Math and Sci. (cadre), Project Learning Tree (cadre). Byzantine Catholic Home: 1510 J Portabella Mount Pleasant MI 48858 Office: Sacred Heart Acad 316 E Michigan Mount Pleasant MI 48858

RAKSHIIT, MONOJ, produce company executive; b. Bankura, Bengal, India, Jan. 25, 1952; s. Bibha Nath and Kalyani (Kundu) Rakshit; m. Basudhaa Dasgupta, Dec. 12, 1977; children: Mrinal, Ritesh. B.Comm., Madhav Coll., Gwalior, Madhya Pradesh, India, 1973. Acct. Warner Hindustan Ltd., Bombay, India, 1976-79; fin. controller, co. sec. SD Fine Chem. Pvt. Ltd., Bombay, 1979-80; fin. mgr. Ficom Organics Ltd., Bombay, 1981-82; mgr. fin. and adminstrn. Oman Sun Farms, SAO, Sohar, 1982-86; mgr. mgmt. acctg. Warner Hindustan (div. Parke Davis India Ltd.), Bombay, 1986—. Uttar Pradesh State Edn. Bd. merit scholar Queens Coll. Varanasi, 1966-68. Mem. Inst. Chartered Accts. India, Inst. Co. Secs. India. Avocations: reading; games. Home: 0/10 Nensey Complex, Western Express Hwy Borivli E, Bombay 400 066, India Office: Warner Hindustan, 414/2 Sahas Prabhadevi, Bombay 400 025, India

RALLO, DEBORAH ANN, finance company executive, consultant; b. N.Y.C., Aug. 4, 1958; d. Donald Andrew Mylan and Elizabeth Ann (Ackerman) Welch; m. John Elliott Rallo. Student, UCLA, 1978-80. Free-lance model Paris, Zurich, Geneva, N.Y.C. and Los Angeles, 1976-81; investment adviser Tamerlo Investment Inc., Geneva and Los Angeles, 1981-83; investment mgr. Fed. Fin. and Credit Corp. Ltd., Geneva, 1983-86; fin. cons. Merrill Lynch, Geneva, 1986—; investment dir. ICT Investment Mgmt., Geneva, 1986—; bd. dirs. Frenex Trading Ltd., Ebany Investment Ltd., Fed Property Devel. Ltd., London, Cruse Investment Inc., Geneva. Club: Kensington/Chelsea Womens (London). Home: 1 Chemin de Beau-Soleil, 1026 Geneva Switzerland Office: ICT Investment Mgmt, 5 Route de Chene, 1206 Geneva Switzerland

RALLO, JAMES GILBERT, fleet management company executive; b. Balt., Mar. 1, 1942; s. James Vincent and Thelma Mary (Hannahs) R.; m. Frances Elaine Petro, June 13, 1965; children: James Michael, Robert Francis. BS, U. Md., 1965; postgrad., George Washington U., 1967—. Mktg. trainee Chessie System, Balt., 1965-66; market analyst Bendix Corp., Balt., 1966-68, contract adminstr., N.Y.C., 1968-70; account exec. Peterson, Howell & Heather, Inc., Hunt Valley, Md., 1970-75, regional mgr., 1975-80, v.p. sales, 1980-83, v.p. sales and client relations, 1983-87, sr. v.p. sales and client relations, 1987—. Bd. dirs., mem. fin. com. Towson YMCA, Md., 1981—; coach Cockeysville-Springlake Recreation Council, 1973-82. Mem. Nat. Assn. Fleet Adminstrs. (bd. dirs. 1978-81, affiliate chmn. intercounty chpt. 1980). Club: Optimists (chmn. fundraising com., v.p. Springdale-Cockeysville 1982-84). Avocations: sports car racing, skiing, coaching youth sports, antique cars, reading. Office: Peterson Howell & Heather Inc 11333 McCormick Rd Hunt Valley MD 21031

RALPH, JAMES R., physician; b. Lowell, Mass., Mar. 23, 1933; s. Richard Henry and Alice Claire (Walwood) R.; m. Edith Marquerite Aeschliman, June 7, 1958; children—James R., Lee P., Jon D., David G. BA Middlebury Coll., 1954; MD Yale U., 1959. Diplomate Nat. Bd. Med. Examiners, Am. Bd. Family Practice. Intern, Akron Gen. Med. Ctr., Ohio, 1959-60, resident Akron Gen. Hosp. and Akron Children's Hosp., 1960-61; staff physician Univ. Health Services, U. Mass., Amherst, 1963-72; team physician dept. intercollegiate athletics, U. Mass., 1965—, asst. med. dir. Univ. Health Services, 1971—, coordinator Sports Medicine U. Health Services, 1987—; assoc. family practice community medicine U. Mass. Med. Sch.-Ctr., Worcester, 1980—; attending physician U.S. VA, Florence, Mass., 1964-69; attending staff active Wing Meml. Hosp., Palmer, Mass., 1967-70. Contbr. articles to profl. jours. Bd. dirs. Inter-Faith Housing, Amherst, 1984—, Boston Med. Library, 1985—. Served to capt. USAF, 1961-67. U. Mass. Faculty research grantee, 1967-69. Fellow Am. Acad. Family Physicians; mem. Mass. Acad. Family Physicians (bd. govs. 1980—), Mass. Med. Soc. (exec. bd., bd. dirs. postgrad. med. inst.), Hampshire Dist. Med. Soc. (pres. elect 1984-86, pres. 1986-88), Am. Coll. Sports Medicine, Sigma Xi. Democrat. Roman Catholic. Avocations: tennis; hiking; camping; coin and stamp collecting. Home: 66 Hills Rd Amherst MA 01002 Office: Univ Health Services U Mass Amherst MA 01003

RALPH, JEFFREY JAY, manufacturing executive; b. Glen Cove, N.Y., Apr. 19, 1960; s. Gene and Jane (Mrha) R.; m. Valerie Sue Mullen, Aug. 22, 1987. BBA, Ashland (Ohio) Coll., 1982. Gen. mgr. HRZ Corp., Ontario, 1976-82, The Window Place, Inc., Mansfield, Ohio, 1982—; v.p. Bay World, Inc., Mansfield, Ohio, 1983—, also bd. dirs.; fin. cons. The Window Place, Mansfield, 1983—, chmn. service com., 1985—. Mem. Phi Delta Theta (Brothership award 1982). Republican. Roman Catholic. Home: 335 Marcus Pl Mansfield OH 44903 Office: Bay World Internat 286 Ashland Rd Mansfield OH 44905

RALSTON, CARL CONRAD, construction company executive; b. Owensboro, Ky., Nov. 1, 1927; s. Carl Conrad and Elizabeth Porter (Little) R.; m. Patricia Lucille Beasley, Nov. 12, 1971; children: Pamela Kay, Kelley Michelle. B.A., Ky. Wesleyan Coll., 1956. Chief acct., estimator Mills & Jones Constrn., St. Petersburg, Fla., 1957-60, project mgr., 1960-65, v.p., 1965-79, sr. v.p., 1979—, also dir.; exec. v.p. Fed. Constrn. Co., St. Petersburg, 1982—. Pres. Cross Bayou Little League, Seminole, Fla., 1959-61; treas. Seminole Lakes Civic Assn., 1962-65, pres. 1965-67; bd. dirs. St. Petersburg Gen. Hosp.-Humana, 1981-84, chmn., 1984-85; bd. dirs. At. Anthony's Hosp., 1986—. Served with USAAF, 1944-46, Alaska. Mem. Am. Inst. Constructors, Am. Soc. Profl. Estimators, Constrn. Mgmt. Assn., , Am. Concrete Inst. Democrat. Presbyterian. Clubs: President, Yacht (St. Petersburg); Citrus (Orlando, Fla.); Seminole Lake Country (dir. 1962-66). Lodge: Masons, Elks. Home: 6328 Augusta Blvd Seminole FL 33543 Office: Fed Constrn Co 1355 Snell Isle Blvd NE Saint Petersburg FL 33704

RALSTON, GILBERT ALEXANDER, author, educator; b. Los Angeles, Jan. 5, 1912; s. Alexander Gilbert and Jeanette (Johnston) R.; grad. Pasadena Coll., 1929-32; grad. Am. Acad. Dramatic Arts, 1935; B.C.A., Sierra Nev. Coll., 1972; M.A., Fielding Inst., 1983, D in Psychology, 1987; PhD, Columbia Pacific U., 1986; m. Mary K. Hart, Dec. 20, 1938; children—Michael, David. Actor, stage mgr. theatre prodns. N.Y.C., 1931-35; writer, dir. radio shows NBC, N.Y.C., 1936-38; prodn. supr. Compton Advt., Inc., N.Y.C., West Coast, 1939-42; organizer, mgr. radio dept. Proctor & Gamble, Cin., 1943-47, exec. producer inc. TV div., 1947-50; free lance producer TV films, 1950-55; exec. producer in charge TV drama CBS, 1955, dir. network programs originating in N.Y.C., 1956; producer High Adventure documentaries with Lowell Thomas, 1957; chmn. sch. communication arts Tahoe (Cal.) Paradise Coll., 1968; dean sch. communicative arts Sierra Nevada Coll., Incline Village, Nev., 1960-73, pres., 1973-83, pres. emeritus, 1983—; pres. Ralston Sch. Communicative Arts, Genoa, Nev., 1971—; v.p. Rule of Three Prodns., Los Angeles, 1973—; lectr. Fordham U., City Coll. City U. N.Y., Loyola U. of Los Angeles, St. Mary's Coll. of Calif. Mem. Authors Guild, ASCAP, Western Writers Am., Writers Guild Am., Am. Massage and Therapy Assn. Author: Ben, 1972; (with Richard Newhafer) The Frightful Sin of Cisco Newman, 1972; Dakota Warpath, 1973; Dakota: Red Revenge, 1973; Dakota Cat Trap, 1974; Dakota Murder's Money, 1974; Dakota: Chain Reaction, The Deadly Art, 1975, The Third Circle, 1976, The Tao of Touch, 1983, others. Author screenplays: No Strings Attached, 1962; A Gallery of Six, 1963; A Feast of Jackals, 1963; Cockatrice, 1965; Kona Coast, 1967; Night of the Locust, 1969; Ben, 1971, Third Circle, 1975, Sure, 1975. Author screen adaptations: Willard (by Stephen Gilbert), 1970; Bluebonnet (by Boris Sobelman and Jack H. Robinson), 1971; Dakota Red, 1987. Author scripts for TV sometime under pseudonym Gil Alexander: High Adventure, Naked City, Route 66, Follow the Sun, Bus Stop, The Untouchables, Alcoa Theatre, Ben Casey, Richard Boone Show, 12 O'Clock High, The Name of the Game, Daktari, Laredo, Combat, Big Valley, Gunsmoke, Amos Burke, Slattery's People, Alfred Hitchcock, Star Trek, It Takes a Thief, O'Hara, Cannon, numerous others. Address: PO Box 350 Genoa NV 89411

RAM, RAJA, agricultural educator, researcher; b. Pakhri, India, July 31, 1945; s. Ghansyala Hari and Ghansyala (Kamleshwari) R.; m. Rajeshwari Devi, Feb. 21, 1970; children: Rajeev, Sanjeev, Shivani. BS, Dehradun U., 1964; B in Vet. Sci., Mathura U., 1968, M in Vet. Sci., 1975, PhD, 1982. Vet. surgeon Uttar Pradesh Govt., India, 1968-72, livestock officer, 1973-83; assoc. prof. agr. U. Mathura, 1983—; sci. referee research jour. Punjab Agr. U., Ludhiana, 1986—. Mem. Internat. Symposium Foetal Biology. Hindu. Home and Office: D-19 Veterinary Coll, Anatomy Dept, Mathura, Uttar Pradesh 281001, India

RAMA, CARLOS M., writer, history educator, editor; b. Montevideo, Oct. 26, 1921; s. Manuel Rama and Carolina Facal; m. Judith Dellepiane, 1943; 2 children. Ed. Univ. de la Republica and U. Paris; Ph.D. Journalist, 1940-48, 72—; exec. sec. Uruguayan Bar Assn., 1940-49; prof. universal history in secondary schs., 1944-48; prof. sociology and social research, prof. contemporary history, prof. theory and methodology of history Univ. de la Republica, 1950-72; prof. Latin Am. history Universidad Autonoma de Barcelona (Spain), 1973—. Author: La Historia y la Novela, 1947, 63, 70, 74; Las ideas socialistas en el siglo XIX, 1947, 49, 63, 67, 76; Ensayo de Sociologia Uruguaya, 1956; Teoria de la Historia, 1959, 68, 74, 80; Las clases sociales en el Uruguay, 1960; La Crisis espanola del siglo XX, 1960, 62, 76; Itinerario espanol, 1961, 77; Revolucion social y fascismo en el siglo XX, 1962; Sociologia del Uruguay, 1965, 73; Historia del movimiento obrero y social latinoamericano contemporanee, 1967, 79, 76; Los afrouruguayos, 1967, 68, 69, 70; Garibaldi y el Uruguay, 1968; Uruguay en Crisis, 1969; Sociologia de America Latina, 1970, 77; Chile, mil dias entre la revolucion y el fascismo, 1974; ESpana, cronica entranable 1973-77, 1978; Historia de America Latina, 1978; Fascismo y anarquismo en la Espana contemporanea, 1979; editor Nuestro Tiempo, 1954-56, Gacetilla Austral, 1961-73. Decorated comdr. Order Liberation (Spain), officier des Palmes academiques (France). Mem. PEN Club Latinoamericano en Espana (pres.), Grupo de Estudios Latinoamericanos de Barcelona (sec.-gen.). Address: Monte de Orsa 7, Vallvidrera, 17 Barcelona Spain *

RAMACHANDRAN, GOPALASAMUDRAM NARAYANA, biochemist, crystallographer, mathematical logician; b. Ernakulam, Kerala State, India, Oct. 8, 1922; s. G. R. Narayana Iyer and Lakshmi Ammal; m. Rajalakshmi Sankaran, 1945; 3 children. Ed. Maharaja's Coll., Ernakulam, Indian Inst. Sci., U. Madras, Cambridge U.; Ph.D.; D.Sc. (hon.), Rorkee U., 1978, Indian Inst. Tech., Madras. Lectr. in physics Indian Inst. Sci., 1946-47, asst. prof., 1949-52, prof. biophysics, 1970-77, Inst. prof. math. biology, then of math. philosophy, 1978-84, Albert Einstein prof. math. philosophy Indian Nat. Sci. Acad., Bangalore, 1984—, 1851 Exhbn. scholar U. Cambridge (Eng.), 1947-49; prof. U. Madras (India), 1952-70, head dept. physics, 1952-70, dean Faculty Sci., 1964-67; Fogarty Internat. scholar NIH, Washington, 1977-78; prof. biophysics (part-time) U. Chgo., 1967-79; Disting. Scientist, Ctr. for Cellular and Molecular Biology, Hyderabad, India, 1981-82; mem. Bd. Sci. and Indsl. Research India, 1962-65; mem. Commn. Macromolecular Biophysics, 1969; chmn. Nat. Com. Crystallography, 1963-70; sr. vis. prof. U. Mich., 1965-66. Contbr. articles to profl. publs.; author: Fourier Methods in Crystallography, 1970; Biochemistry of Collagen, 1976; editor: Advanced Method of Crystallography; Aspects of Protein Structure; Treatise on Collagen, 2 vols., 1967; Conformation of Biopolymers, vols. 1 and 2, 1967; Crystallography and Crystal Perfection; editor Current Sci., 1950-58, Jour. Indian Inst. Sci., 1973-77; editorial bd. Jour. Molecular Biology, 1959-66, Biochimica et Biophysica Acta, 1965-72, Indian Jour. Pure and Aplied Physics, 1963—, Indian Jour. Biochemistry and Biophysics, 1970—, Biopolymers, 1973-86, Connective Tissue Research, 1973—, Jour. Biomolecular Structure and Dynamics, 1984—; specialist in optics, crystal physics, x-ray crystallography, biophysics, math. logic. Recipient Bhatnagar Meml. prize, 1961; Watumull prize, 1964; John Arthur Wilson award, 1967; Meghnad Saha medal, 1971; Ramanujan medal, 1972; J.C. Bose award U.G.C., 1974, Bose Inst., 1975; Fogarty medal, 1978; C.V. Raman medal, 1983; R.D. Birla award for med. scis., 1985; Jawaharlal Nehru fellow, 1968-70. Fellow Royal Soc. London, Royal Soc. Arts, Indian Acad. Scis. (council 1953-70, sec. 1956-58, v.p. 1962-64), Nat. Inst. Scis. (now Indian Nat. Sci. Acad.); mem. Internat. Union Pure and Applied Biophysics (council 1969-72), Am. Soc. Biol. Chemists (hon.), Am. Acad. arts and Scis. (hon. fgn.), Afralasian Acad. (Rome) (founding mem.). Home: GITA 10A Main Rd, Mallaswaram West, Bangalore 560055, India Address: CCMB Regional Research Lab Camp, Hyderabad 500009 India *

RAMADAN, SUBHI ABDULMAJEED, civil and sanitary engineer; b. Irbid, Jordan, Oct. 28, 1944; s. Abdulmajeed Subhi Ramadan and Nahida Fakhri Al-Dajani; m. Sawsan Jamiel Al-saadoon; children: Dana, Abdulmajeed, Mohammad. BCE, Al-Hikma Am. U., Baghdad, Irag, 1966; MS in Sanitary Engring., Syracuse (N.Y.) U., 1972. Site engr. Arab Contractors, Irbid, 1966-67, Gen. Engring, Inc. of Helsinki, Finland, Riyadh, Saudi Arabia and Helsinki, 1967-70; projects mgr. Saudi Research and Devel. Corp, Ltd., Jeddah, Saudi Arabia, 1972-75; chief engr. Al-Gubali, Riyadh, 1975-77; gen. mgr. Quartet Corp., Riyadh, 1977-85; div. mgr. Royal Sci. Soc., Amman, Jordan, 1985—. Mem. Engrs. Union Jordon. Moslem. Home: Abdoun St, PO Box 5494, Amman Jordan Office: Royal Sci Soc, Al-Jubaiha, PO Box 925819, Amman Jordan

RAMAHATRA, VICTOR, government official. Prime minister Madagascar, 1988—. Office: Office of the Prime Minister, Antananarivo Madagascar *

RAMAKRISHNAN, VENKATASWAMY, civil engineer, educator; b. Coimbatore, India, Feb. 27, 1929; came to U.S., 1969, naturalized, 1981; s. Venkataswamy and Kondammal (Krishnaswamy) R.; m. Vijayalakshmi Unnava, Nov. 7, 1962; children: Aravind, Anand. B.Engring., U. Madras, 1952, D.S.S., 1953; D.I.C. in Hydropower and Concrete Tech, Imperial Coll., London, 1957; Ph.D., Univ. Coll., U. London, 1960. From lectr. to prof. civil engring., head dept. P.S.G. Coll. Tech., U. Madras, 1952-69; vis. prof. S.D. Sch. Mines and Tech., Rapid City, 1969-70; prof. civil engring. S.D. Sch. Mines and Tech., 1970—, dir. concrete tech. research, 1970-71, head grad. div. structural mechanic and concrete tech., 1971—, program coordinator materials engring. and sci. Ph.D. program, 1985-86; cons., 1955—; Founding mem. PSGR Children's Sch., 1961; founding dir. World Open U.,

1974, v.p., 1980—. Author: Ultimate Strength Design for Structural Concrete, 1969; also over 100 articles. Colombo Plan fellow, 1955-60; recipient Outstanding Prof. award S.D. Sch. Mines and Tech., 1980. Mem. Internat. Assn. Bridge and Structural Engring., ASCE (vice chmn. constrn. div. publs. com. 1974), Am. Concrete Inst. (chmn. subcom. gen. considerations for founds., chmn. com. 214 on evaluation of strength test results, sec.-treas. Dakota chpt. 1974-79, v.p. 1980, pres. 1981), Instn. Hwy. Engrs., Transp. Research Bd. (chmn. com. on mech. properties of concrete), Am. Soc. Engring. Edn., Nat. Soc. Profl. Engrs., Internat. Council Gap-Graded Concrete Research and Application (sec. 1973-78), Sigma Xi (chpt. treas. 1975-78). Address: 1809 Sheridan Lake Rd Rapid City SD 57701

RAMALINGAM, MURUGESAN, electronics engineer; b. Kadathur, India, Oct. 15, 1946; came to Malaysia, 1986; s. Ramalingam Kg and Kamalammal R.; m. P.S. Hemaprabha, Apr. 3, 1977; children: Narayanan, Ravishankar. BS, Presidency Coll., Madras, India, 1971; diploma with honors, Madras Inst. of Tech., 1974. Registered profl. engr., Malaysia. Technician Indians Posts & Telegraph Dept., Madras, 1966-74; asst. engr. J.K. Synthetics Ltd., Kota, India, 1974-75; project engr. Bongaigaon Refinery & Petchem. Co., Assam, India, 1975-80, Ballarpur Industries Ltd., New Delhi, India, 1980-81; instrument engr. Phoenix Pulp & Paper Co., Khon Kaen, Thailand, 1981-82; mgr., instrumentation U.P. State Cement Corp., Dalla, India, 1982-83; plant supt. South India Viscose Ltd., Sirumugai, India, 1983-85; mgr., instrumentation Hindustan Paper Corp., Nagaland, India, 1985-86; area mgr., instrumentation Sabah Forest Industries SDN., BHD., Sipitang, Malaysia, 1986—. Founder, sec. SFI Internat. Sch., Sipitang, 1987. Served with Nat. Cadet Corps and Home Guards, Madras, 1968-71. Recipient Capt. Kalyanaraman prize Presidency Coll., 1970-71, Faculty Best prize Madras Inst. Tech., 1971-74, Nat. Overseas scholarship, Govt. India, 1976, UNDP/IAEA scholarship, Vienna. 1986. Mem. Instn. Engrs., Indian Instn. Plant Engrs., Inst. Standards Engrs., Instn. Measurement & Control, London, Instrument Soc. Am. Home: Plot 5 Street 25, TG Nagar, Nanganallur Madras 60061, India Office: Sabah Forest Industries SDN BHD, WDT 31, 89850 Sipitang, Sabah 89850, Malaysia

RAMAMOORTHY, THENNILAPURAM PARASURAMAIYER, botanist, educator; b. Alleppey, India, Aug. 17, 1945; arrived in Mex., 1980; s. Parasuramaiyer Krishnan Thennilapuram and Subbalakshmi Pitchu Srivaikundam; m. Marguerite Elliott, Sept. 4, 1981. BS, Bangalore (India) U., 1966, MS, 1968; PhD, Washington U., St. Louis, Mo., 1980. Instr. Botany Hassan (India) Govt. Coll., 1968; sci. asst. St. Joseph's Coll., Bangalore, 1969-74, Smithsonian Instn. U.S. Nat. Herbarium, Washington, 1975; investigator titular 'A' Nat. U. Mex. Inst. Biologia, Mexico City, 1980-84; investigator titular 'B' Nat. U. Mex. Inst. Biologia, 1984—; bd. dirs. Conservation Data Base Ctr. Inst. Biologia; mem. editorial bd. Anales Inst. Biologia, Botanica. Contbr. 115 sci. articles to profl. jours. Recipient Smithsonian (Instn.) award, London, 1971; grantee NSF, 1976, Consejo Nat. de Sic. and Tech., Mex., 1984-85, Smithsonian Instn., Washington, 1984. Home: Av El Cantaro 5-6-3, Villa Coapa, 14390 Mexico City Mexico Office: Inst Biologia, Apartado Postal 70-233 UNAM, 04510 Mexico City Mexico

RAMAMURTHY, J. R., librarian, consultant; b. Bharamasagara, Karnataka, India, Dec. 23, 1943; s. Rudrappa Jinka and Krishnamma Rudrappa; m. Savitri, May 9, 1977; children: Malavika, Rajanika, Charulatha. BA, Cen. Coll., Bangalore, 1964, MA, 1973; diploma in library sci., Andhra U., Visakhapatnam, 1967; MLS, Banaras Hindu U., Varanasi, 1971. Asst. librarian Bangalore U., 1968-827; cons. info. ctr. Deccan Herald, Bangalore, 1982—; lectr. Library Sci. Dept., Bangalore U., 1974-81; rapporteurgen. First All India Workshop Journalists, 1987. Contbr. articles to profl. jours. Mem. Amnesty Internat., Bangalore, 1985-87; coordinator Third World Network, Bangalore, 1986-87. Mem. Karnataka Library Assn., Indian Library Assn., Karnataka Union Working Journalists. Club: Press (Bangalore). Home: 260 53rd Cross, IV Block Rajajinagar, Bangalore, Karnataka 560 010, India Office: Deccan Herald, 66 M G Rd, Bangalore, Karnataka 560 001, India

RAMAN, KRISHNAMURTHY SUNDARA, computer science educator, researcher; b. Hassan, Mysore, India, Aug. 23, 1931; s. Krishnamurthy and Meenakshi R.; m. Indira Velpanur Narayan Rao, Sept. 4, 1964; children—Lakshmi, Shankar. B.Sc., U. Mysore, Bangalore, India, 1950; diploma Indian Inst. Sci., Bangalore, 1953, 55; M.S., Ill. Inst. Tech., Chgo., 1958, Ph.D., 1963. Chartered engr., U.K. and Commonwealth Countries. Asst. engr. Bombay Electricy Bd. (India), 1955-56; instr. Ill. Inst. Tech., 1958-63; asst prof. Indian Inst. Tech., Madras, 1963-65, examiner for Ph.D. degrees, 1967-72; mgr. computer adminstrn. Dunlop India, Calcutta, 1965-73; computer cons. Dunlop Industries, Kuala Lumpur, Malaysia, 1973-78; group data processing/info. systems mgr. Sime Darby Berhad, Kuala Lumpur, 1978-84; sr. fellow dept. computer sci. Nat. U. Singapore, 1984—; vis. scholar, hon. fellow U. Minn., 1986. Contbr. articles to profl. jours. Mem. Instn. Elec. Engrs., Eta Kappa Nu, Tau Beta Pi, Sigma Xi. Lodge: Rotary (dir., v.p. 1968-72). Home: 41 XV Cross Rd, Malleswaram, Bangalore 560 003, India Office: Nat U Singapore, Dept Computer Sci, 0511 Kent Ridge Singapore

RAMANNA, RAJA, physicist; b. Bangalore, Karnataka, India, Jan. 28, 1925; s. Bindig Ivavile and Rukhivi R.; m. Malathi Ramanna; children: Nina, Shyah, Nirupa. BS with honors, Madras Christian Coll., India, 1945; PhD, U. London, 1948; DSc (hon.), several univs.; lic., Royal Sch. Music, London. Prof. Tala Inst. Fundamental Research, Bombay, 1948-72; dir. Bhabha Atomic Research Ctr., Bombay, 1972-83; sec., advisor Govt. India, New Delhi, 1983-87, chmn., 1983-87; council chmn. Indian Inst. Sci., Bangalore, 1987—. Author many books in field; contbr. articles to profl. jours. Recipient Bhalnajar award, Padma Vibushau award Govt. India. Fellow Indian Acad. Scis.; Internat. Atomic Energy Agy. (chmn. sci. adv. com. 1983-87). Hindu. Club: Bangalore. Home: 407 Block 2, RT Norgau, Bangalore 560 0032, India Office: Atomic Energy Commission, Chhatrapati Shivaji Maharaj Marg, Bombay 400 039, India

RAMASWAMI, DEVABHAKTUNI, chemical engineer; b. Pedapudi, India, Apr. 4, 1933; came to U.S., 1958, s. Veeriah and Rangamma Devabhaktuni; m. Vijayalakshmi, June 30, 1967; 1 child, Srikrishna. B.Sc., Andhra U., 1953, M.Sc., 1954, D.Sc., 1958; Ph.D., U. Wis., 1961. Research scholar Andhra U., Waltair, India, 1954-56, Indian Inst. Tech., Kharagpur, 1956-57; asst. prof. Benaras Hindu U., Varanasi, India, 1957-58; research asst. U. Wis., Madison, 1958-61; research engr. IBM Corp., San Jose, Calif., 1961-62; chem. engr. Argonne Nat. Lab., Ill., 1962—. Contbr. numerous articles to profl. jours. Patentee in field. Am. Chem. Soc. Disting. and Promising Asian in U.S. award Asia Found., 1960. Fellow Am. Inst. Chem. Engrs. Avocation: photography. Home: PO Box 2969 Westmont IL 60559 Office: Engring Div Argonne National Lab 9700 S Cass St Argonne IL 60439

RAMASWAMY, VISWANATHAN SUBRAMANIAM, chemical company executive; b. Tanjore, India, June 18, 1939; s. Subramaniam Viswanathan and Bageerathi R.; married; 2 children. M in Math., Annamalai U., India, 1959; diploma in mktg. mgmt., Waterloo Luth. U., Can., 1969; PhD, U. Cochin, India, 1983. Asst. mktg. mgr. Fertilisers and Chemicals Travancore Ltd., Cochin, 1965-67, regional mgr., 1967-69, area mgr., 1969-74, mgr. corp. sales, 1974-78, mgr. personnel adminstrn., 1978-80, chief sales mgr., 1980-84, mgmt. devel. mgr., 1984-87, chief sales mgr., 1987—; dir. programs Bharathiya Vidhya Bhavan, Cochin; chmn. MBA examinations, Cochin U. Author: Marketing Management in Indian Environment, 1983, A Study of Marketing of Fertilisers in India. Named Communicator of Yr. Inst. of Mktg. and Mgmt., 1986. Office: Fertilisers and Chems, Travancore Ltd, Udyogamandal P O, Cochin 683 501, India

RAMATI, SHAUL, diplomat, researcher; b. Warsaw, Poland, Jan. 12, 1924; s. Gustav and Pola (Tenenbaum) Rosenberg; m. Esther Dembowski; children: Shlomo David, Pnina. MA in Politics and Econs., Oxford U., 1952. Enlisted Brit. Army, 1943, advanced through grades to capt., 1947, resigned, 1947; enlisted Israeli Def. Forces, 1948, advanced through grades to lt. col., 1959, resigned, 1959; consul for Midwest Israeli Fgn. Service, Chgo., 1959-63; counsellor, Charge d'Affaires Israeli Fgn. Service, Thailand, Cambodia, 1963-64; charge d'affaires Israeli Fgn. Service, Sri Lanka, 1964-66; consul gen. for Midwest U.S. Israeli Fgn. Service, Chgo., 1969-74; ambassador to Japan Israeli Fgn. Service, 1974-77, spl. ambassador, dir. Jewish affairs div., mem. directorate of Ministry of Fgn. Service, 1977-80, ambassador to Brazil, 1980-83, cons. to Minister Sci. and Devel., 1984—; dir. World Orgn. of Jews from Arab Countries, Tel-Aviv, 1986—; lectr. in field. Contbr. articles to major newspapers. Pres. Zionist Group Oxford U. Mem. Jerusalem Inst. for We. Def., Internat. Security Council, Internat. Adv. Bd. Mem. Tehiya Party. Home: 10 Jabotinsky, Jerusalem 92 142, Isreal Office: WOJAC, 118 A Ben-Yehuda, Tel-Aviv 63 401, Israel

RAMAZANI, ROUHOLLAH KAREGAR, government and foreign affairs educator; b. Tehran, Iran, Mar. 21, 1928; came to U.S., 1952, naturalized, 1961; s. Ali Karegar and Khadijeh (Sultani) R.; m. Nesta Shahrokh, Feb. 22, 1952; children: Vaheed, David, Jahan, Sima. LL.M., U. Tehran, 1951; postgrad., U. Ga., 1952; S.J.D., U. Va., 1954. Lectr. fgn. affairs U. Va., Charlottesville, 1954-57; research assoc. Soviet Fgn. Econ. Relations Project U. Va., 1956-59, asst. prof. fgn. affairs, 1957-60, assoc. prof., 1960-64, prof. govt. and fgn. affairs, 1964—, Edward R. Stettinius Jr. prof. govt. and fgn. affairs, 1972, Harry F. Byrd Jr. prof. govt. and fgn. affairs, 1983; Aga Khan vis. prof. Islamic studies Am. U., Beirut, 1967-68; vis. prof. Middle East studies Sch. Advanced Internat. Studies, Johns Hopkins, 1967, 70-71, 72-73, 75, 77, 79; vis. prof. Cambridge (Eng.) U., spring 1975; cons. internat. relations Rockefeller Found.; cons. Inst. Fgn. Policy Analysis, U.S. Dept. State, UN, White House.; Vice pres., trustee Am. Inst. Iranian Studies; cons. Pan Am. Internat. Oil Co., Research Analysis Corp.; bd. govs. Middle East Inst.; Am. participant USIA, 1974, 79, 80, 84, 86. Author: The Middle East and the European Common Market, 1964, The Northern Tier: Iran, Afghanistan and Turkey, 1966, The Foreign Policy of Iran, 1500-1941: A Developing Nation in World Affairs, 1966, The Persian Gulf: Iran's Role, 1972, Iran's Foreign Policy, 1941-1973: A Study of Foreign Policy in Modernizing Nations, 1975, Beyond the Arab-Israeli Settlement: New Directions for U.S. Policy in the Middle East, 1977, The Persian Gulf and the Strait of Hormuz, 1979, Security of Access to Persian Gulf Oil Supplies in the 1980s, 1982, The United States and Iran: The Patterns of Influence, 1982, Revolutionary Iran: Challenge and Response in the Middle East, 1986, paperback edit. with new epilogue on Iranian-American Arms Deal, 1988, The Gulf Cooperation Council: Record and Analysis, 1988; assoc. editor: Jour. South Asian and Middle Eastern Studies; adv. editor: Middle East Jour., Fgn. Policy Report, Levant; contbr.: Soviet Foreign Relations and World Communism, 1965, The Search for World Order, 1971, Concise Ency. of the Middle East, 1973, The Anatomy of Communist Takeovers, 1975, Energy and World Politics, 1975, Iran: Past, Present, and Future, 1976 From June to October: The Middle East Between 1967 and 1973, 1978, Iran in the 1980's, 1978, The Middle East Contemporary Survey, 1967-77, The Middle East Contemporary Survey, 1977-78, World Politics and the Arab-Israeli Conflict, 1979, The Impact of the Iranian Events upon Persian Gulf and United States Security, 1979, The Revolution in Iran: Its Character and Political-Economic Complications, 1979, In Search of Peace, 1980, Comparative Regional Systems, 1980, The Indian Ocean in Global Politics, 1981, Middle East Perspectives, 1981, The Iran Crisis and International Law, 1981, Revolution in Iran: A Reappraisal, 1982, Islam in Foreign Policy, 1983, Arm Disarm for Peace, 1984, The Indian Ocean: Perspectives on A Strategic Arena, 1985, Shi'ism and Social Protest, 1986, The Middle East After the Invasion of Lebanon, 1986. Mem. exec. com. Council on Fgn. Relations, Charlottesville, 1965-67; mem. Citizens for Albemarle, 1972—. Recipient prize for distinguished contbn. Am. Assn. Middle East Studies, 1964; Social Sci. Research Council grantee, 1967; Fulbright research grantee, 1968. Fellow Middle East Studies Assn. N.Am.; mem. Am. Soc. Internat. Law, Am., So. polit. sci. assns., Middle East Inst., Shaybani Soc. Internat. Law (exec. officer), Raven Soc., Phi Beta Kappa. Home: 1140 Mountain Rd Charlottesville VA 22901

RAMDAT MISIER, LACHMIPERSAD F., former president of Suriname; b. Paramaribo, Suriname, Oct. 28, 1926; m. Hilda Doergadei Dewanchand. Lawyer's cert., Suriname Law Sch., 1957; cert. State U. Utrecht, Holland, 1961. Founder, head Free Legal Aid Service, 1952; practice law before Ct. of Justice, 1957-58; investigating magistrate in criminal procs., 1961-63; mem. Ct. of Justice, judge, 1963; tutor Legal Faculty, U. Suriname, 1963-82; v.p. Ct.-Martial in Suriname, 1973, pres., 1980; vice chief justice, 1980, chief justice, 1982; acting pres. Republic of Suriname, Paramaribo, 1982-88; mem. Council for Cultural Cooperation, Netherlands, 1967-75, chmn. Suriname sect.; mem., specialist Commn. of Kingdom for Preparation of Independence of Suriname, 1972; chmn. Suriname Jud. Systems Com., mem. Constl. Commn.; chmn. Found. for Publ. of Suriname Jurisprudence, other ofcl. coms.; del. to internat. confs. Contbr. articles to profl. jours. Co-founder, mem. Found. for Suriname Ency., 1969; mem. com Found. for Nature Preservation in Suriname, Suriname Cultural Centre; gov. Majella Old Age Home. Decorated officer Order of Orange-Nassau (Netherlands); companion Suriname Order of Yellow Star, grand master Suriname Order of Palm-Tree, grand master Suriname Order of Yellow Star. Office: Office of President, Paramaribo Suriname

RAMEL, BENITA SAGA, secretary, silversmith, social artist; b. Washington, July 22, 1928; d. Wilfrid and Greta (Sundberg) Fleisher; m. Claes O.M.O. Ramel, Nov. 25, 1952; children: Stig, Charlotte, Christine, Elisabeth. Student, Royal Acad. Arts, Stockholm, 1948-52. Social sec. Am. Embassy, Stockholm, 1952—. Works exhibited in one-woman silver show Gallery Prisma, Stockholm, 1985; exhibited in group show Konstnarshuset, Stockholm, 1950. Home and Studio: Sagstigen 2, 18147 Lidingo Sweden

RAMEL, HANS, trade association executive; b. Lund, Scania, Sweden, Apr. 26, 1925; s. Otto Bror and Margaretha (Wrangel-von Brehmer) R.; m. Marie Madeleine Douglas, May 28, 1949; children: Otto, Charlotte, Peder. Student Mil. Acad., Stockholm, 1944-47. Chmn. bd. Swedish Sugarbeet Growers Assn., 1971—; bd. mem., working com. Fedn. Swedish Farmers, Stockholm, 1972-87, dep. chmn. bd., 1987—; dep. chmn. bd. Swedish Farmers Meat Marketing Assn., Stockholm, 1974—; chmn. Skanek, Malmoe, 1974—; dep. chmn. bd. Chamber Agr. Malmoehus County, 1976—, Scanian Mortgage Soc., Lund, Sweden, 1984—; chmn. bd. Swedish Agro Projects, Stockholm, 1983—; dir. Skanska Banken, Malmoe, Alfa-Laval Co. Ltd., Stockholm, Swedish Internat. Devel. Authority, 1983-86. Mem. Malmoehus County Adminstrn., Malmoe, 1971-76. Served to capt. Swedish Cav. Res., 1961—. Decorated Knight Order Vasa (Sweden), 1974. Mem. Royal Forestry and Agr. Acad. Lutheran. Home: Oevedskloster, 27500 Sjoebo S-275 94, Sweden

RAMEL, STIG, foundation executive; b. Lund, Sweden, Feb. 24, 1927; s. Malte and Elsa (Nyström) R.; M.A. in Polit. Sci., U. Lund, 1952; m. Ann Marie Wachtmeister, 1953; children: Knut, Henrik, Camilla, Jacqueline. Attache, Dept. Fgn. Affairs, 1953; with Swedish embassy, Paris, 1954-56; del. OECD, Paris, 1956-58; with Swedish embassy, Washington, 1958-60; with Dept. Fgn. Affairs, 1960-66; v.p., later pres., Gen. Swedish Export Assn., 1966-72; exec. dir. Nobel Found., Stockholm, 1972—. Mem. Royal Swedish Acad. Scis. (hon. D). Holder King Charles XVI Gustaf's Gold Medal (12th degree), Comdr. Order Polar Star, St. Olav. Office: Nobel Found, Sturegatan 14 Box 5232, S 102 45 Stockholm Sweden

RAMER, BRUCE, lawyer; b. Teaneck, N.J., Aug. 2, 1933; s. Sidney and Anne S. (Strassman) R.; m. Ann G. Ramer, Feb. 15, 1965; children—Gregg B., Marc K., Neal I. A.B., Princeton U., 1955; J.D., Harvard U., 1958. Bar: Calif. 1963, N.J. 1958. Assoc., Morrison, Lloyd & Griggs, Hackensack, N.J., 1959-60; ptnr. Gang, Tyre, Ramer & Brown, Inc., Los Angeles, 1963—. Exec. dir. Entertainment Law Inst.; bd. of councilors Law Ctr. U. So. Calif.; past pres. Los Angeles chpt., nat. v.p., bd. govs.; chmn. Nat. Affairs Commn. Am. Jewish Com.; trustee Loyola Marymount U.; mem. corp. bd., chmn. discretionary fund distribution com. United Way; bd. of trustees Los Angeles Children's Mus.; v.p. Fraternity of Friends of Los Angeles Music Ctr.; bd. dirs. L.A. Urban League, 1987—; bd. govs. Calif. Community Found. Served to pvt. U.S. Army, 1958-59, 2d lt., 1961-62. Mem. Los Angeles County Bar Assn., ABA, Calif. Bar Assn., Beverly Hills Bar Assn., Los Angeles Copyright Soc. (pres. 1974-75), Calif. Copyright Conf. (pres. 1973-74), Fellows of the Am. Bar Found. Club: Princeton (Los Angeles) (pres. 1975-78). Office: Gang Tyre Ramer & Brown Inc 6400 Sunset Blvd Los Angeles CA 90028

RAMER, LAWRENCE JEROME, corporation executive; b. Bayonne, N.J., July 29, 1928; s. Sidney and Anne (Strassman) R.; m. Ina Lee Brown, June 30, 1957; children: Stephanie Beryl, Susan Meredith, Douglas Strassman. B.A. in Econs, Lafayette Coll., 1950; M.B.A., Harvard U., 1957. Sales rep., then v.p. United Sheet Metal Co., Bayonne, 1953-55; with Am. Cement Corp., 1957-64; v.p. mktg. div. Riverside Cement Co., 1960-62, v.p. mktg. parent co., 1962-64; vice chmn. bd., chief exec. officer Clavier Corp., N.Y.C., 1965-66; exec. v.p., vice chmn. bd. Pacific Western Industries, Los Angeles, 1966-70; pres., chief exec. officer Nat. Portland Cement Co. Fla., 1975—; chmn. bd. Sutro Partners, Inc., Los Angeles, 1977—, Somerset Mgmt. Group, 1975—, Luminall Paints Inc., Los Angeles, 1972—; chmn. bd., chief exec. officer Bruning Paint Co., Balt., 1979—, Pacific Coast Cement Co., Los Angeles, 1979—; bd. dirs. Project Orbis, N.Y.C., The Music Ctr., Los Angeles, Music Ctr. Operating Co., Los Angeles; pres., bd. dirs. Ctr. Theatre Group-Taper/Ahmanson Theatres, Los Angeles. Trustee Lafayette Coll., Easton, Pa.; exec. bd. Am. Jewish Com., Los Angeles. Office: 1800 Century Park E Los Angeles CA 90067

RAMIREZ, SARA DIAZ DE ESPADA, business executive; b. Asunción, Paraguay, May 13, 1926; d. Raul and Maria (Vallverdú de) Diaz de Espada; m. Carlos M. Ramírez Boettner, Sept. 6, 1947; children: Carlos Raúl, Juan Alberto, Javier Martín. PhD, Faculty of Philosophy, Asunción, 1958. Pres. Enterprise Ramírez Díaz de Espada S.A., Asunción, 1980—; dir. Etchegaray y Díaz de Espada S.A., Asunción, 1980—. Contbr. articles to profl. jours. Roman Catholic. Clubs: Centenario, Asunción Tenis. Home: Ave Mcal López #2, PO Box 2329, Asunción Paraguay Office: Ramírez Díaz de Espada SA, Calle Raúl Díaz de Espada, y Curupayty, Asuncion Paraguay

RAMIREZ MERCADO, SERGIO, vice president of Nicaragua; b. Masatepe, Nicaragua, 1942. Grad. in Law with honors, Univ. Leon, 1964. Gen. sec. Confedn. of Central Am. Univs., 1969; founder Central Am. Univ. Pub.; dir. 'Group of Twelve', Sandinista Front, Nicaragua, 1975—, mem. Junta of Govt. of Nat. Reconstrn., Sandinista Assembly, 1979—, now v.p. Republic Nicaragua; co-founder Ventana (lit. movement). Collections of short stories include: Stories, 1963, New Stories, 1969, Central American Story, 1973, 74, Charles Atlas Also Dies, 1977, The Nicaraguan Tale, 1977, author: My Days with the Rector, 1965, Mariano Fiallos, 1972, Sandino's Living Thought, 1975, Did the Blood Frighten You, 1977, Time of Brilliance, 1979, (polit. writings) Toward Golden Dawn, 1983, You Are in Nicaragua, 1987, Castigo Divino, 1988. Office: Office of Vice Pres, Managua Nicaragua *

RAMIREZ-PORTILLA, CARLOS ALFONSO, architect; b. Guatemala, May 18, 1949; s. Carlos Humberto Ramirez Aldana and Estela Portilla Wright; m. Elisa Sinibaldi-Castillo Dalton, Nov. 20, 1976; children: Juan Pablo Jose Antonio, Carlos Adolfo. BArch, U. San Carlos, Guatemala City, 1974; postgrad., U. San Carlos; MBA, U. Francisco Mauroquin, Guatemala City, 1985. Exec. architect Comosa, Guatemala City, 1972-78; pres. C.R.P. Assocs., Guatemala City, 1978—, Showbiz Pizza Place, Guatemala City; dir. Jeff Tours Guatemala. Author: Proyeccion Universiaria Dos Parametros, 1974. Recipient hon. mention Guatemalan Archtl. Mag., 1978, Guatemala C. of C. mem. Interam. Assn., AIA Guatemala. Roman Catholic. Lodge: Rotary. Office: 9 Avenida 4061, Zona 1, Guatemala City Guatemala Also: Ave Reforma 7-62, Zona 9, Guatemala City Guatemala

RAMMOHAN, MEENAKSHI, dietitian; b. Madras, India, May 14, 1943; came to U.S., 1965; d. Kumarappan and Lakshmi (Venkatachalam) Nagappan; m. Alagappa Rammohan Aug. 18, 1962; children—Parvathi, Chidambaram. B.S., U. Madras, 1961, M.S., 1963. Adminstrv. and therapeutic dietitian Bethany Methodist Hosp., Chgo., 1966-68; therapeutic dietitian Passavant Meml. Hosp., Chgo., 1968-72, research dietitian, 1972-73; clin. dietitian Northwestern Meml. Hosp., Chgo., 1973-81, research and renal dietitian, 1981—; cons. dietitian, nursing homes, Chgo., 1968-77; adj. faculty No. Ill. U., DeKalb, 1972—. Mem. Am. Dietetic Assn., Ill. Dietetic Assn., Chgo. Dietetic Assn., Ill. Council Renal Nutrition, Nat. Assn. Research Nurses and Dietitians. Mem. Vivekanandha Vedantha Soc. Author: Vegetarian Wheel, 1979; (with Stone) Fat Chance, 1980. Home: 8417 Autumn Dr Woodridge IL 60517-4505 Office: 303 E Superior St Passavant Pavillion Room 470 Chicago IL 60611

RAMON, SHARON JOSEPHINE, personnel management executive, real estate salesperson; b. Chgo., Nov. 8, 1947; d. Edward Albert and Helen Josephine (Tomaszewski) Mazur; m. Kevin John Ramon, Aug. 4, 1979. BA, U. Ill.-Chicago, 1969. Caseworker, ct. aide Social Service Dept. of Cir. Ct. Cook County, Chgo., 1969-71; investigator aide U.S. Civil Service Commn., Chgo., 1971-72, personnel staffing specialist, 1972-74, personnel mgmt. specialist, 1974-80; mgmt. cons. U.S. Office Personnel Mgmt., Chgo., 1980-82, personnel mgmt. specialist, 1982-83, personnel staffing specialist, 1983-86; salesperson First United Realtors, Barrington, Ill., 1987—. Recipient Certs. of Spl. Achievement, U.S. Office Personnel Mgmt., 1980, Cert. of Appreciation, 1981. Mem. Nat. Assn. Female Execs., AAUW. Roman Catholic. Office: First United Realtors 115 S Hough St Barrington IL 60010

RAMOND, CHARLES KNIGHT, II, financial forecaster, publisher; b. New Orleans, Oct. 9, 1930; s. Charles Knight and Ethel Chamberlain (Bauer) R.; m. Mary Minter Patterson, June 13, 1959; 1 child, Nicholas Bauer. B.S. with honors, Tulane U., 1950; M.S., State U. Iowa, 1952, Ph.D., 1953. Research asso. Human Resources Research Office, Washington, 1953-54; mgr. advt. research E.I. duPont de Nemours & Co., Inc., Wilmington, Del., 1956-59; tech. dir. Advt. Research Found., N.Y.C., 1959-65; assoc. prof. bus. Columbia U., 1965-68, adj. prof., 1968-71; pres. Mktg. Control, Inc., N.Y.C., 1966-79, Predex Corp., N.Y.C., 1974—; chmn. Predex Mgmt. Corp., N.Y.C., 1982—; adj. prof. bus. N.Y. U., 1971-76; chmn. dept. mktg. Rutgers U., 1977-78. Author: The Art of Using Science in Marketing, 1974, Advertising Research: The State of the Art, 1976; Founder, editor: Jour. Advt. Research, 1960-80. Served to 1st lt. AUS, 1954-56. Recipient Marcel Dassault medal for media research, 1970. Fellow Am. Psychol. Assn.; mem. Inst. Mgmt. Scis., Ops. Research Soc. Am., Market Research Council (pres. 1973-74), N.Y. Acad. Scis., Phi Beta Kappa, Omicron Delta Kappa, Kappa Delta Phi, Delta Tau Delta. Clubs: University (N.Y.C.), Coffee House (N.Y.C.). Home: 1170 Fifth Ave New York NY 10029 Office: 3 E 54th St New York NY 10022

RAMOS, ALBERT A., electrical engineer; b. Los Angeles, Feb. 28, 1927; s. Jesus D. and Carmen F. (Fontes) R.; B.S. in Elec. Engring., U. So. Calif., 1950, M.S. in Systems Mgmt., 1972; Ph.D., U.S. Internat. U., 1975; m. Joan C. Pailing, Sept. 23, 1950; children—Albert A., Richard R., James J., Katherine. With guided missile test group Hughes Aircraft Co., 1950-60; with TRW DSG, 1960—, sr. staff engr. Norton AFB, San Bernardino, Calif., 1969—. Served with USNR, 1945-46. Registered profl. engr., Calif. Mem. IEEE, Nat. Soc. Profl. Engrs., Air Force Assn., Mexican-Am. Engring. Soc., Mexican Am. Profl. Mgmt. Assn. (mem. adminstering commn. dept. community services), Sigma Phi Delta, Eta Kappa Nu, Tau Beta Pi. Home: 1457 W Cypress Ave Redlands CA 92373 Office: PO Box 1310 San Bernardino CA 92402

RAMOS, CARMEN BARCELON, pediatrician, public health physician; b. Manila, Feb. 24, 1937; d. Aurelio Jose and Rosario (Barcelon) R. AA, U. Santo Tomas, Manila, 1957, MD, 1962. Diplomate Philippine Med. Bd. Resident in pediatrics Children's Med. Ctr., Quezon City, Philippines, 1963-64; child youth researcher Child And Youth Research Ctr., Quezon City, 1964-67, sr. child-youth reseacher, 1967-80; sr. clinic physician Quezon City Health Dept., 1980—; mgr. Pag-Asa Health Ctr. Quezon City Health Dept., 1980—; chmn. com. continuing med. edn. Quezon City Health Dept. Physicians' Assn., 1987—. Contbr. articles to profl. jours. Chmn. Local Council for the Protection of Children, Pag-Asa, Philippines, Council for the Welfare of Children and Youth, Quezon City. Life mem. Philippine Med. Assn., Philippine Med. Women's Assn., Maternal and Child Health Assn., Quezon City Med. Soc., Philippine Pediatric Soc. Roman Catholic. Home: 1510 Quezon Ave, Quezon City Philippines

RAMOS, FIDEL, Philippines army officer; b. 1928; s. Narciso Ramos; married; 5 daughters. Ed., Nat. U. Manila, U.S. Mil. Acad., West Point, N.Y., U. Ill. Dep. chief staff Philippines Armed Forces, 1981-86, chief staff, 1986—; now sec. nat. def. Philippines, Manila. Decorated Legion of Honour. Address: Ministry Def, Camp Aguinaldo, Quezon City Manila, Philippines *

RAMOS, ROBERTO PRISCO PARAISO, holding company executive; b. Rio de Janeiro, Dec. 21, 1946; s. Celso Ferreira and Maria Helena (Prisco Paraiso) R.; m. Virginia Maria Vasconcellos, Apr. 7, 1973; children: Helena,

Cristina. Grad. in Mech. Engring., U. Fed. Rio De Janeiro, 1971; postgrad., Harvard U., 1981. Planning, cost controller Montreal Engenharia, S.A., Rio De Janeiro, 1972-75, estimation coordinator cost engring. dept., 1975-77, cost engring. officer, 1977-80, sales supt., 1980-83, exec. dir., 1980-86, v.p. fin., 1986-87; chief fin. officer Montreal Empreendimentos Com. Inc., S.A., Rio De Janeiro, 1987—; instr. Funcex-Fundação Comércio Exterior, Rio De Janeiro, 1983-85; speaker in field; bd. dirs. Montreal Informática, Ltd. Mem. Am. Assn. Cost Engrs., Assn. Cost Engrs., Am. Soc. for Metals, Am. C. of C. Clubs: Clube Naval (Rio De Janeiro), Fluminese Football. Home: Rua Faro 54 Apt 903, 22461 Rio de Janeiro Brazil Office: Montreal Empreendimentos Com Ind SA, Rua São José 90 3d Floor, Rio de Janeiro Brazil

RAMOS DE ISLAS, ANA MARIA, artist, educator; b. Mexico City, June 18, 1944; d. Marín Ramos Contreras and Ana María (Palacios) Contreras; m. Jorge Islas Marroquín; children: Ana De Lourdes, Jorge Carlos. Grad. in Art, Nat. Sch. of Bellas Artes, Mexico City, 1979. Art and drawing tchr. Hamilton Sch., Mexico City, 1980—; instr. art various pvt. groups, Mexico City, 1980—. Prin. works include Nature and Life, 1983, 25 Nudes, 1984, Two Themes, 1985, Images and Traditions of Two Countries, 1987. Mem. Soc. Mexicana de Artistas Plasticos, Amigos del Museo de la Acuarela. Lodge: Rotary. Home: Alcazar de Toledo #226, 11020 Mexico City Mexico

RAMOVS, PRIMOZ, composer; b. Ljubljana, Yugoslavia, Mar. 20, 1921; s. Franc and Alba (Zalar) R.; diploma Acad. Music, 1941; m. Stefanija Schubert, Jan. 17, 1955; children: Klemen, Polona, Ales. Librarian, Slovene Acad. Scis. and Arts, Ljubljana, 1945-52, librarian in chief, 1952-87; prof. Conservatory in Ljubljana, 1948-52, 55-64. Served with Naval Inf., 1947. Decorated Order of Work with Golden Wreath; recipient awards Philharmonic Soc., 1944, Festival, 1958, Fund of Preseren, 1962, Yugoslav Radio, 1967, 69, 70, 76, diploma Cop, 1971, Slovene Philharmony, 1978. Mem. Soc. Slovene Composers Ljubljana (v.p. 1967-71), Soc. Slovene Librarians Ljubljana, Slovene Acad. Scis. and Arts (Preseren's prize 1983, medal of honor, 1986), Slovene Alpine Soc., Slovene Lit. Soc. Roman Catholic. Composer: 5 Symphonies, Musiques funèbres, Profils, Symphonic Portrait, Polyptych, Organofonia, 27 Concertos for various instruments with orch., Symphonic Chamber and Instrumental Music (over 250 opuses), 1938—. Home: 18 Kardeljeva, 61000 Ljubljana Yugoslavia

RAMPAL, JEAN-PIERRE LOUIS, flutist; b. Marseilles, France, Jan. 7, 1922; s. Joseph and Andrée (Roggero) R.; m. Françoise-Anne Bacqueyrisse, June 6, 1947; children: Isabelle Rampal Dufour, Jean-Jacques. Student, U. Marseilles. prof. Nat. Conservatory of Music, France; prof. Paris Conservatory, from 1968; editor Internat. Music Co., N.Y.C., 1958—. Flutist throughout world, 1945—; appeared with Vichy Opera, 1947-51, subsequently with Paris Opera; appearances at major internat. festivals. Author: children's book La flûte, 1978. Decorated officier Legion d'Honneur, officier de l'Ordre des Arts et Lettres; recipient Grand Prix du Disque (8), 1954-78; Oscar du Premier Virtuose Français, 1956; Prix Edison, 1969; Prix Leonie Sonning, 1978. Mem. French Musicol. Soc., Assn. Music and Musicians (pres. 1974—). Office: 15 Avenue Mozart, 75016 Paris France *

RAMPHUL, INDURDUTH, bank governor; b. Mauritius, Oct. 10, 1931; m. Taramatee Seedoyal, Sept., 1962; children—Anista Devi Indira, Shaheel Kumar Joy. Diploma in Pub. Adminstrn., U. Exeter, 1964. Asst. sec. Ministry of Fin., Mauritius, 1965-66; mgr. Bank of Mauritius, Port Louis, 1967-69, chief mgr., 1970-72, mng. dir., 1973-81, gov., 1982—. Office: Bank of Mauritius, Sir William Newton St, Port Louis 084164, Mauritius

RAMSAY, GEORGE DANIEL, historian, retired history educator; b. Dublin, Ireland, May 25, 1909; s. Daniel Livingston and Emelie Matilda (Simpson) R.; m. Patricia Emilie St. John Clarke, Sept. 10, 1952; children: Malcolm, Nigel, Rosalind. Grad., Oxford U., Eng., 1931. Fellow, tutor St. Edmund Hall Oxford (Eng.) U., 1937-74, emeritus fellow, 1974—. Author: City of London in International Politics, 1975, The Queen's Merchants, 1986. Served with RAF, 1941-45, PTO. Fellow Royal Hist. Soc. Home: 15 Charlbury Rd, Oxford OX2 6UT, England

RAMSAY, JOHN BARADA, research scientist, educator; b. Phoenix, Dec. 28, 1929; s. John A. and Helen G. Ramsay; m. Barbara Ann Hilsenhoff, Apr. 18, 1953; children—Bryan J., Kathleen L., Carol A., David A. B.S. in Chemistry, Tex. Western U., 1950; Ph.D. in Analytical Chemistry, U. Wis., 1954. Mem. staff Los Alamos Nat. Lab., 1954-70, 73—; assoc. prof. Coll. Petroleum and Minerals, Dhahran, Saudi Arabia, 1970-73; cons. U.S. Navy, USAF, 1980—; adj. prof. U. N.Mex., Los Alamos, 1980-85. Author sci. articles. Recipient award of excellence U.S. Dept. Energy, 1984. Mem. AAAS, N.Mex. Acad. Sci. (pres.-elect 1987), Am. Archeol. Soc. (chpt. pres. 1979), Sigma Xi. Democrat. Home: 6 Erie Ln Los Alamos NM 87544 Office: PO Box 1663 Los Alamos NM 87545

RAMSEY, CLAUDE, foundation executive; b. Ramsey, W.Va., May 25, 1918; s. Melvin G. and Maude (Hawkins) R.; B.S., Morris Harvey Coll., 1938; B.J., U. Mo., 1939; m. Lilien Ernst, June 9, 1945; children—Patrick (dec.), Terry, Perry. Writer, United Press, Kansas City and Denver, 1940-42, bur. chief Houston and Lower Rio Grande Valley, 1945-52; pub. relations counsellor Kostka & Assos., Denver, 1953-55; founder, pres. Pub. Relations Inc., Denver, 1956-64; exec. dir. Morris Animal Found., Denver, 1964—; guest lectr. pub. relations Colo. State U., 1972-79. Mem. City Council, City of Greenwood Village (Colo.), 1973-75; mem. Arapahoe County Republican Exec. Com., 1976-80, 84-85; chmn. Rep. 6th Congl. Dist., 1982—; chmn. Colo. div. Am. Cancer Soc., 1979-81. Served to capt. Signal Corps, U.S. Army, 1941-45. Decorated Bronze Star; recipient award of Excellence, Colo. div. Am. Cancer Soc., 1976; Award of Merit, Am. Animal Hosp. Assn. Mem. Pub. Relations Soc. Am. (past pres. Colo. chpt., mem. nat. bd. 1962-63, Silver Anvil award 1959), Council on Founds., Sigma Delta Chi. Lutheran. Home: 9293 E Arbor Circle Apt C Englewood CO 80111 Office: 45 Inverness Dr E Englewood CO 80112

RAMSEY, INEZ LINN, librarian, educator; b. Martins Ferry, Ohio, Apr. 25, 1938; d. George and Leona (Smith) Linn; m. Jackson Euguene Ramsey, Apr. 22, 1961; children—John Earl, James Leonard. B.A. in Hist. SUNY-Buffalo, 1971; M.L.S., 1972; Ed.D. in Audiovisual Edn., U. Va., 1980. Librarian Iroquois Central High Sch., Elma, N.Y., 1971-73, Lucy Simms Elem. Sch., Harrisonburg, Va., 1973-75; instr. James Madison U., Harrisonburg, 1975-80, asst. prof., 1980-85; assoc. prof. 1985—; mem. Va. State Library Bd., Richmond, 1975-80; cons.; librarian, book reviewer Harrisonburg-Rockingham County Assn. for Retired Citizens. Contr. to Encyclopedia, articles to profl. jours.; author (with Jackson E. Ramsey): Budgeting Basics, Library Planning and Budgeting; project dir. Oral (tape) History Black Community in Harrisonburg, 1977-78; storyteller, puppeteer. Mem. Harrisonburg Republican City Com., 1981-83. Recipient spl. citation for service Va. Readathon Program, Harrisonburg, 1977; research grantee James Madison U., Harrisonburg, 1981. Mem. ALA, Am. Assn. Sch. Librarians, Assn. Edn. Communications, Tech., Children's Lit. Assn., Puppeteers Am., Nat. Assn. Preservation and Perpetuation of Storytelling, Va. Ednl. Media Assn. (sec. 1981-83, citation 1983 pres. 1985-86, Educator of Yr. award 1984-85, Meritorious Service award 1987-88), Phi Beta Kappa (pres. Shenandoah chpt. 1980-81), Children and Young Adults Round Table (exec. bd. 1977-80), Va. Library Assn., Beta Phi Mu. Home: 282 Franklin St Harrisonburg VA 22801 Office: James Madison U Dept Ednl Resources Harrisonburg VA 22807

RAMSEY, JACKSON EUGENE, educator; b. Cin., Dec. 20, 1938; s. Leonard Pershing and Edna Willa (Blakeman) R.; m. Inez Mae Linn, Apr. 22, 1961; children—John Earl, James Leonard. B.S. in Metall. Engring., U. Cin., 1961; M.B.A., SUNY-Buffalo, 1969, Ph.D., 1975. Registered profl. engr., Va., Ohio. Welding engr. Gen. Electric Co., Cin., 1961-62, Westinghouse-Bettis Lab., Pitts., 1962-66; prodn. control mgr. Columbus-McKinnon Corp., Buffalo, 1966-71; asst. prof. mgmt. SUNY, Buffalo, 1971-73; prof. mgmt. James Madison U., Harrisonburg, Va., 1973—; cons. in field. Chmn. Harrisonburg Reps., 1978-86, vice chmn., 1974-78; vice chmn. 6th Dist. Rep. Com., 1984—. Served with USMCR, 1956-62. Named Outstanding Young Scholar Xerox Corp., 1976. Mem. Acad. of Mgmt., Am. Inst. for Decision Scis., Inst. of Mgmt. Sci., Am. Soc. for Metals, Nat. Soc. Profl. Engrs. Republican. Baptist. Author: R D Strategic Decision Criteria, 1986; Handbook for Professional Managers, 1985; Budgeting Basics, 1985; Library Planning and Budgeting, 1986. Contbr. articles to profl. jours. Home: 282 Franklin St Harrisonburg VA 22801 Office: James Madison U Dept Mgmt Harrisonburg VA 22807

RAMSEY, JERRY DWAIN, industrial engineer; b. Tulia, Tex., Nov. 6, 1933; s. Elmer Woodrow and Mila Lou (Culwell) R.; B.S., Tex. A&M U., 1955, M.S., 1960; Ph.D. (NASA trainee 1965-67), Tex. Tech. U., 1967; m. Sue Helen Skelton, Feb. 4, 1956; children—Randall Byron, Randa Sue, Rachel Ruth, Richard Jerry. With Square D Co., Detroit, 1953, Gt. Western Drilling Co., Midland, Tex., 1955, Collins Radio Co., Dallas, 1957-58, Fox & Jacobs Constrn. Co., Dallas, 1959, Sandia Corp., Albuquerque, 1961-65; asst. prof. indsl. engring. Tex. A&M U., 1958-61; adj. prof. U. N.Mex., 1963-65; mem. faculty Tex. Tech U., 1967—, prof. indsl. engring., 1975—, asso. v.p. acad. affairs, 1977—; cons. to govt., 1970—. Bd. dirs. Lubbock Goodwill Industries, 1973-82, SW Lighthouse for the Blind, 1982-88. Served to capt. USAR, 1955-57. Cert. safety exec. NSF summer fellow, 1960; registered profl. engr., N.Mex. Mem. Inst. Indsl. Engrs. (special citation outstanding contbn. to ergonomics 1985), Human Factors Soc., Am. Indsl. Hygiene Assn., Nat. Soc. Profl. Engrs., Am. Soc. Safety Engrs. (Profl. Safety Paper award Tech. Writing Excellence 1987), Nat. Safety Mgmt. Soc., Am. Soc. Engring. Edn., Nat. Safety Council (exec. com. public employees 1974—), Tex. Safety Assn. (dir. 1976—), Sigma Xi, Tau Beta Pi, Phi Kappa Phi, Phi Eta Sigma, Alpha Phi Mu, Alpha Tau Omega. Methodist. Author articles in field, chpts. in books. Home: 6903 Lynnhaven Dr Lubbock TX 79413 Office: Tex Tech U PO Box 4609 Lubbock TX 79409

RAMSEY, JOHN ARTHUR, lawyer; b. San Diego, Apr. 1, 1942; s. Wilbert Lewis and Lillian (Anderson) R.; m. Nikki Ann Ramsey, Feb. 9, 1943; children—John William, Bret Anderson, Heather Nichole. A.B., San Diego State U., 1965; J.D., Calif. Western Sch. Law, 1969. Bar: Colo. 1969, Tex. 1978. Assoc., Henry, Cockrell, Quinn & Creighton, 1969-72; atty. Texaco Inc., 1972-80, asst. to pres. Texaco U.S.A., 1980-81, asst. to div. v.p., Houston, 1981-82, div. atty., Denver, 1982—. Bd. dirs. Selective Service, Englewood, Colo., 1972-76; chmn. council Bethany Lutheran Ch., Englewood, 1976. Mem. ABA (chmn. oil com. sect. natural resource law 1983—). Republican. Editor in chief: Calif. Western Law Rev., 1969. Office: 4601 DTC Blvd Denver CO 80237

RAMSEY, LELAND KEITH, petroleum engineer; b. Topeka, May 31, 1952; s. Keith G. and Darlene (Berndt) R.; m. Kimberly M. Milner, Mar. 31, 1979; children: Jessica Ray, Jeremy Lee. B.S., Kans. State U., 1974. Field engr. Dowell div. Dow Chem. Corp., Rock Springs, Wyo., 1975-78, dist. engr., Williston, N.D., 1978-80, sr. dist. engr., 1980-81; dist. sales supr. Dowell/Schlumberger Inc., Williston, 1981—, field service mgr., 1985— . Mem. Soc. Petroleum Engrs. (chpt. membership chmn. 1982-83, sec.-treas. 1983-84, vice-chmn., 1984-85, chmn. 85-86, scholarship chmn. 1986—), Sooner Oilmen's Club, Am. Assn. Petroleum Geologists, Am. Petroleum Inst., N.D. Geol. Soc. Republican. Baptist. Lodge: Elks. Avocations: golf; racquetball. Home: 618 15th Ave W Williston ND 58801 Office: PO Box 879 Williston ND 58801

RAMSEY, WILLIAM DALE, JR., petroleum company executive; b. Indpls., Apr. 14, 1936; s. William Dale and Laura Jane (Stout) R.; A.B. in Econs. (James Bowdoin scholar), Bowdoin Coll., 1958; m. Mary Alice Ihnet, Aug. 9, 1969; children—Robin, Scott, Kimberly, Jennifer. With Shell Oil Co., 1958—, salesman, Albany, N.Y., 1960, merchandising rep., Milton, N.Y., 1961-63, real estate and mktg. investments rep., Jacksonville, Fla., 1963-65, dist. sales supr., St. Paul, 1965-67, employee relations rep., Chgo., 1967-69, spl. assignment mktg. sfaff-adminstrn., N.Y.C., recruitment mgr., Chgo., 1970-72, sales mgr., Chgo., 1973-75, sales mgr., Detroit, 1975-79, dist. mgr. N.J. and Pa., Newark, 1979-84, Mid-Atlantic dist. mgr. (Md., D.C., Va.) 1984-87, econ. advisor head office, Houston, 1987—; dir. N.Am. Fin. Services, 1971-72; lectr., speaker on energy, radio, TV, appearances, 1972—; guest lectr. on bus. five univs., 1967-72; v.p., dir. Malibu East Corp., 1973-74; mem. Am. Right of Way Assn., 1963-65. Active Chgo. Urban League, 1971-75; mem. program com., bus. adv. council Nat. Republican Congressional Com.; mem. Gov.'s Council on Tourism and Commerce, Minn., 1965-67; mem. Founders Soc., Detroit Inst. Arts, 1978-80; mem. Greater Balt. Com.; bd. dirs. N.J. Symphony Orch. Corp., 1981-85. Served to capt. U.S. Army, 1958-60. Mem. Soc. Environ. Econ. Devel., N.J. Petroleum Council (exec. com. 1979-84 vice chmn. 1982-84), Midwest Coll. Placement Assn., Md. Petroleum Council (exec. com. 1984-87), Va. C. of C., Md. C. of C. Presbyterian. Clubs: Ponte Vedra (Fla.); Bowdoin Alumni (Houston); Morris County (N.J.) Golf; Kingwood (Tex.) Country; Bethesda (Md.) Country. Author: Corp. Recruitment and Employee Relations Organizational Effectiveness Study, 1969.

RAMUNNO, THOMAS PAUL, consultant; b. Chgo., Sept. 13, 1952; s. Anthony Michael and Dolores (Sieibert) R.; B.B.A., U. Ga., 1974, M.B.A., 1978; m. Deborah G. Pauline Benton, Jan. 31, 1976; 1 son, Michael Thomas. Treas., Concept, Inc., Atlanta, 1974-77; product mgr. Johnson-Johnson, Inc., Atlanta, 1978-80; dir. Rollins, Inc., Atlanta, 1979-80; cons. Chase Econometrics, Atlanta, 1980-83; v.p. comml. services, dir. corporate product mgmt./mktg. Union Trust Co. Md., 1983-84; prin., exec. v.p. Mktg. Scis. Group, Inc., Hunt Valley, Md., 1984-85; v.p., dir. Citicorp, Chgo., 1985-86; mgr. fin. instns. cons. Deloitte, Haskins and Sells, Chgo, 1987—; disting. practitioner lectr. U. Ga., 1978-83; cons. in field. Exec. on loan Clarke County United Way, 1974-75. Mem. MBA Alumni U. Ga., U. Ga. Coll. Bus. Alumni (bd. dirs. 1978-83), Beta Gamma Sigma. Home: 242 W Ridge Trail Palatine IL 60067

RAMZAN, FURKAN ALI, naval architect; b. Springlands, Corentyne, Guyana, June 11, 1953; came to Eng., 1968; s. Haji Ramjohn and Zobeida (Walli) R.; m. Bibi Nazifah, June 11, 1978; 1 child, Nadia Aneesa. B.S. in Physics, London U., 1978, Ph.D. in Physics, 1980. Engr. Lloyd's Register, London, 1978-80; mgr. naval architecture Brown & Root (U.K.) Ltd., London, 1980—. Author: Applied Offshore Design, 1982. Mem. Royal Inst. Naval Architects, Under Water Engring. Group (com.), Offshore Engring. Group (com.). Home: 25 Baron Grove, Mitcham, Surrey CR4 4EH, England Office: Brown & Root (UK) Ltd, 125 High St, Colliers Wood, London SW19 2JR, England

RANA, PRABHAKAR SHUMSHERE JUNG BAHADUR, service executive; b. Simha Durbar, Kathmandu, Nepal, Nov. 26, 1935. BA with honors, Patna (India) U., 1959. Personal and purchasing officer Hotel Soaltee, Kathmandu, 1964-65, asst. mgr. gen. adminstrn., 1965-66, gen. mgr., 1966-68; exec. dir. Soaltee Hotel Ltd., Kathmandu, 1968—; bd. dirs. Royal Nepal Shipping corp., Royal Nepal Airlines Corp., Malati Poultries Pvt. Ltd., Himalaya Tea Garden and Farming Pvt., Ltd., Nepal; chmn. Everest Express Tours and Travels Pvt., Ltd., Nepal, Sipradi Trading Co. Pvt., Ltd., Nepal, Surya Tobacco Co. Pvt. Ltd., Gorkha Goodricke Lawrie Pvt. Ltd. Contbr. articles to profl. jours. Founding pres. Nepal Heritage Soc., 1983—; trustee King Mahendra Trust for Nature Conservation, Nepal, 1984—. Recipient Coronation medal Country of Nepal, 1975; decorated Tri Shakti Patta King of Nepal, 1981, Brit. Order Empire, 1986; recipient World Culture preize Centro Studi e Ricerche delle Nazioni Italy, 1985—. Mem. Hotel Assn. Nepal (pres. 1970-77, life pres. 1977—), Nepal Fedn. C. of C. (mem. exec. com. 1971—), Pacific Area Travel Assn. (founding chmn. 1975-84, mem. mktg. authority 1975—, mem. assoc. council 1977—, bd. dirs. proxy com. 1979—, bd. dirs. 1980—), Tourism Promotion Council, Allied Assoc. Council (chmn.-elect 1987—), Internat. Council Asia Soc., Am. Mgmt. Assn., Internat. Mgmt. Assn. Clubs: Royal Nepal (capt., v.p. 1972-73), Six Continents, Marco Polo, Annabelle's, Ladbrokes. Home: 21 Himalayan Hgts, Tahachal Nepal Office: Soaltee Hotel Ltd, Tahachal Nepal

RANA, PRADUMNA BICKRAM, economist; b. Kathmandu, Nepal, June 13, 1947; s. Daulat Bickram Rana; m. Bindu Bickram Rana; 1 child, Abhi Bickram Rana. MA in Math., Econs., Tribhuvan U., Kathmandu, 1970; MA in Econs., Mich. State U., 1973; PhD in Econs., Vanderbilt U., 1979. Lectr. Tribhuvan U., Kathmandu, 1970-83; research fellow Inst. S.E. Asian Studies, Singapore, 1980-83; sr. economist Asian Devel. Bank, Manila, 1983—. Author: Impact of Exchange Rates, 1979, Asian Exchange Rates, 1981; author, editor Asean Stabilization Policies, 1987; contbr. articles to nat. jours. Fulbright Hays scholar, 1973; Vanderbilt fellow, 1978. Mem. Am. Econs. Assn., Philippine Econs. Assn. Office: Asian Devel Bank, PO Box 789, Manila Philippines

RANDALL, CRAIG VAUGHN, military personnel; b. Berkeley, Calif., July 9, 1946; s. Craig A. and Mary Jane (Vaughn) R.; m. Janice Marie Doolin, Dec. 1, 1969; 1 child, Craig. BA, Embry-Riddle U., 1986. Licensed commercial pilot, airplane, helicopter, and instrument. Enlisted U.S. Army, 1973, advanced through ranks to chief warrant officer, 1987; pilot instr. U.S. Army, Wiesbaden, Federal Republic of Germany, 1985—. Artist of military paintings. Mem. Air Force Assn. (life), Army Aviation Assn. Am., Aces Club, Am. Soc. Aviation Artists (charter). Unitarian.

RANDALL, JAMES R., manufacturing company executive; b. 1924; married. BS in Chem. Engring., U. Wis., 1948. Tech. dir. Cargill Inc., 1948-68; v.p. prodn. and engring. Archer-Daniels-Midland Co., Decatur, Ill., 1968-69, exec. v.p., 1969-75, pres., 1975—, also dir. Served with AUS, 1943-46. Office: Archer-Daniels-Midland Co 4666 Faries Pkwy Decatur IL 62525 *

RANDALL, MARION STANTON, motel executive; b. Ogden, Utah; d. Charles Benjamin and Marian (Savyer) Stanton; m. Edmund W. Baker, Aug. 21, 1948 (div. 1976); children—Jeffrey Alan, Roger Edmund, Laurel Terese, Lisa Diane Baker Barbeau and Maureen Louise (dec.) (triplets), Douglas Owen; m. 2d Raymond L. Randall, June 20, 1981. A.B. in Psychology, Marygrove Coll., Detroit, 1943. Adminstrv. sec., sec. to labor mgmt. bd. Ohio Employment Services, Akron, 1943-45; exec. sec. asst. to exec. tech. editor Govt. Labs., Akron, 1945-48; exec. sec.-adminstrv. asst. Eastman Kodak, Chgo., 1948-49; exec. sec. to exec. dir. in-patient psychiatry U. Minn. Hosps., Mpls., 1949-50; exec. sec. in personnel and field support systems Hughes Aircraft, Culver City, Calif., 1950-55; owner, operator Surfside Motel, Port Hueneme, Calif., 1974-84; legal cons. motels. Exec. sec. Minor League Baseball, West Covina, Calif., 1967. Mem. AAUW (editor chpt. bull. 1968-70, chpt. v.p. programs 1971-72), So. Calif. Psychial. Research. Club: Mary and Joseph League (Los Angeles).

RANDALL, RICHARD WILLIAM, optometrist; b. Jamestown, N.Y., Nov. 29, 1931; s. Harry William and Claudia (Thompson) R.; m. Diane Nowak; children—David, Deborah, Douglas, Dawne. OD, Ill. Coll. Optometry, 1963. Optician, House of Vision Inc., Chgo., 1960-63; pvt. practice optometry, Geneseo, N.Y., 1963—; chief optometry sect. No. Livingston Health Ctr., Geneseo, 1974-77, Red Jacket Med. Ctr., Dansville, N.Y., 1975-77; pres. Lad-Nar Realty, Inc.; pres., gen. mgr. Ladco Internat.; exec. dir. Ladco Rental Property, Geneseo Profl. Bldg. (all Geneseo); clin. investigator Bausch & Lomb; lectr. OptiFair East, N.Y.C., 1982, 86, OptiFair West, Calif., 1985; cons. in field. Contbr. articles to profl. jours. Exec. dir. Livingston County (N.Y.) Traffic Safety Bd., 1976-82; bd. dirs. Rochester, N.Y. Safety Council, 1982—; mem. Geneseo Ambulance Squad, N.Y. State Emergency Med. Technicians, 1981-88; bd. dirs. Geneseo Fire Dept., 1982-84; dep. coordinator STOP-DWI Adv. Com., Livingston County, 1982; part-time dep. sheriff Livingston County, 1966-85. Served with USAF, 1951-53, Korea. Recipient scholarship award Am. Bd. Opticianry, 1960, Clin. Optometry award Ill. Coll. Optometry, 1963. Fellow Am. Acad. Optometry; mem. Am. (practice enhancement adv. task force 1982-83), N.Y. State (chmn. master plan com. 1976-78) optometric assns., Optometric Center N.Y., Better Vision Inst., Am. Public Health Assn., Council Sports Vision, Ill. Coll. Optometry (N.Y. State chmn.). Methodist. Contbr. articles to profl. jours. Office: 4384 Lakeville Rd Box 2020 Geneseo NY 14454

RANDALL, ROBERT L., industrial economist; b. Aberdeen, S.D., Dec. 28, 1936; s. Harry Eugene and Juanita Alice (Barstow) R.; MS in Phys. Chemistry, U. Chgo., 1960, MBA, 1963. Market devel. chemist E.I. du Pont de Nemours & Co., Inc., Wilmington, Del., 1963-65; chem. economist Battelle Meml. Inst., Columbus, Ohio, 1965-68; mgr. market and econ. research Kennecott Copper Corp., N.Y.C., 1968-74, economist, 1974-79, dir. new bus. venture devel., 1979-81; pres., mng. dir. R.L. Randall Assocs., Inc., 1981—; economist U.S. Internat. Trade Commn., Washington, 1983—; exec. dir. Rain Forest ReGeneration, 1986—; indsl. panel policy review of effect of regulation on innovation and U.S.-internat. competition U.S. Dept. Commerce, 1980-81. Mem. AAAS, AIME (council econs.), Am. Econ. Assn., Am. Statis. Assn., Am. Chem. Soc., Soc. Mining Engrs., Chemists Club of N.Y.C., Metall. Soc., N.Y. Acad. Scis. Contbr. articles to profl. jours.; contbg. author: Computer Methods for the '80's. Home: 1727 Massachusetts Ave NW Washington DC 20036 Office: 500 E Street SW Washington DC 20436

RANDOLPH, CLYDE CLIFTON, JR., lawyer; b. Elmhurst, Ill., Mar. 11, 1928; s. Clyde Clifton and Madeline (Grady) R.; m. Doris Greene, June 21, 1953 (dec. 1980); children—Rebekah Louise, James Banton; m. Jane Smith, Oct. 8, 1983. LLB, Wake Forest Coll., 1951. Bar: N.C. 1951, U.S. Dist. Ct. (mid. dist.) N.C. 1951, U.S. Ct. Appeals (4th cir.) 1956, U.S. Supreme Ct., 1958. Practice law, Winston-Salem, N.C., 1951—; chmn. Contact Teleministries USA, Inc., Harrisburg, Pa., 1973-78, dir., 1971-80. Pres. Forsyth County Legal Aid Soc., Winston-Salem, 1961; chmn. orgn. com. Contact of Winston-Salem, 1969-70. Served with USAR, 1949-56. Mem. Forsyth County Bar Assn. (pres. 1982-83; Disting. Service award 1977), N.C. State Bar, Assn. Trial Lawyers Am., N.C. Acad. Trial Lawyers. Democrat. Episcopalian. Club: Bermuda Run Golf and Country (Advance, N.C.). Avocations: theology, mil. history. Home: 2650 Merry Oaks Trail Winston-Salem NC 27103 Office: 1100 S Stratford Rd Winston-Salem NC 27114-4487

RANELLI, JOHN RAYMOND, steel products company executive; b. New London, Conn., Sept. 25, 1946; s. Frank Robert and Sue Mary (Bongo) R.; m. Paula Jean Contillo, June 8, 1968; children: Carina, Christina, Jennifer. Student, U. Loyola, Rome, 1966-67; A.B. in History, Coll. Holy Cross, 1968; M.B.A., Dartmouth Coll., 1973. Fin. analyst Gen. Motors Corp., N.Y.C., 1973-74; mgr. fin. adminstrn. No. Telecom, Inc., Nashville, 1975-76; asst. treas. No. Telecom. Inc., Nashville, 1976-77; treas. No. Telecom, Inc., Nashville, 1977-78; asst. controller No. Telecom, Ltd., Montreal, Que., Can., 1978-79; treas. ARA Services Inc., Phila., 1980-81, v.p., treas., sec. to fin. com., dir., mem. retirement com., 1981-83, pres. Aero Enterprises div., 1983-85; chief fin. officer, mem. exec. com. Atcor, Inc., Harvey, Ill., 1985-87; v.p., chief fin. officer Cyclops Industries, Mt. Lebanon, Pa., 1987—. Co-author: Mutual Savings Banking at the Crossroads: Renaissance or Extinction, 1973. Served with submarine force USN, 1968-71. Decorated Nat. Def. medal; Fulbright Scholar, 1968. Mem. Fin. Exec. Inst. Lodges: KC, Folks. Office: Cyclops Industries 650 Washington Rd Pittsburgh PA 15228 Other: ATCOR Inc 16100 S Lathrop Ave Harvey IL 60426

RANFTL, ROBERT MATTHEW, management consulting company executive; b. Milw., May 31, 1925; s. Joseph Sebastian and Leona Elaine (Goetz) R.; m. Marion Smith Goodman, Oct. 12, 1946. BSEE, U. Mich., 1946; postgrad. UCLA, 1953-55. Product engr. Russell Electric Co., Chgo., 1946-47; head engring. dept. Radio Inst. Chgo., 1947-50; sr. project engr. Webster Chgo. Corp., 1950-51, product design engr., 1951-53, head equipment design group, 1953-54, head electronic equipment sect., 1954-55, mgr. product engring. dept., 1955-58, mgr. reliability and quality control, 1958-59, mgr. adminstrn. 1959-61, mgr. product effectiveness lab., 1961-74; corp. dir. engring./design mgmt., 1974-84, corp. dir. managerial productivity Hughes Aircraft Co., Los Angeles, 1984-86; pres. Ranftl Enterprises Inc., Mgmt. Cons., Los Angeles, 1981—; guest lectr. Calif. Inst. Tech., Cornell U., U. Calif.; mem. White House Conf. on Productivity, 1983; mem. human resources productivity task force Dept. of Def., 1985-86. Author: R&D Productivity, 1974, 78; (with others) Productivity: Prospects for Growth, 1981; contbr. articles to profl. jours. Mem. AAAS, AIAA, Am. Soc. Engring. Edn., Am. Soc. Tng. and Devel., IEEE, Inst. Mgmt. Scis., Acad. Mgmt., N.Y. Acad. Scis., U. Mich. Alumni Assn., UCLA Alumni Assn. Office: PO Box 49892 Los Angeles CA 90049

RANGINKAMAN, ASGHAR, import company executive; b. Bombay, Oct. 18, 1946; s. Mohammad Baqer and Ghamar (Kazerani) R.; grad., Siddarth Coll., Bombay, 1968; m. Shanaz, 1968; children—Ali, Zahedeh. Sales comml. clk. Owrang Co. Ltd., Tehran, 1968-70; div. mgr. Mahyar Co. itd., Tehran, 1970-71; office mgr. Shaya Co. Ltd., Tehran, 1971-72, sales mgr. 1972-74; partner, sales dir. Talatom Ltd., Tehran, 1974-77; partner, mng. dir. Volcanic Ltd., Tehran, 1977—; partner, dir. Suprlus Ltd., Sensor Ltd. Office: 48 S J Assadabadi, Tehran Iran

RANGOS, JOHN G., waste management company executive; b. Steubenville, Ohio, July 27, 1929; s. Gust and Anna (Svokas) R.; children:

John G. Jr., Alexander William, Jenica Anne. Attended, Houston Bus. Coll., 1949-50; grad., U.S. Signal and Communications Sch., Ft. Gordon, Ga. Formerly gen. agt. Rockwell Mfg. Co., Pitts.; also formed several cos. and pioneered technol. advances in waste transp. and disposal resources recovery and recycling during 1960; pres., chief exec. officer Chambers Devel. Co., Inc., Pitts., 1971—; pres., chief exec. officer U.S. Services, U.S. Utilities Corp., William H. Martin, Inc. So. Alleghenies Disposal Service Co. Inc., Assocs. Internat. Inc., Chatham Security Services Inc., Palmetto Security Systems, Sec. Bur. Inc.; del. UN of Am. Innovations include converting powerplant boiler ash into a useful product for cinder block material and anti-skid material for hwys.; contbd. to invention of techniques for recycling bituminous by-products, disposing of sewage sludge; co-developer of techniques for disposing liquid indsl. waste; developer of a resource recovery system which converts waste-generated methane into energy. Fundraising chmn. UNICEF; contbr. Children's Hosp., Pitts., United Cerebral Palsy, Muscular Dystrophy, Leukemia Soc.; nat. del. U.S. Olympic Conf.; mem. Truman Library Found.; bd. dirs. Hellenic Coll., Presentation of Christ Diocese, Clergy Liturgy Council. Served with U.S. Army, 1951-54, Korea. Decorated Nat. Def. medal, U.N. medal, Korean Campaign medal; recipient Presdl. Unit citations; elected Archon of Ecumenical Patriarchate Order St. Andrew the Apostle, Greek Orthodox Ch., 1988. Mem. Nat. Dem. Club, Young Dems., Internat. Platform Assn. Clubs: The Allegheny, The Pitts. Press, U. Pitts. Golden Panther, Churchill Valley Country. Lodges: Masons (32nd degree), Shriners (Syria). Home: 78 Locksley Dr Pittsburgh PA 15235 Office: Chambers Devel Co Inc 10700 Frankstown Rd Pittsburgh PA 15235

RANIERI, RUGGERO, historian; b. Perugia, Umbria, Italy, Aug. 21, 1952; s. Uguccione Ranieri Di Sorbello and Maria Maddalena (De Vecchi) Ranieri. Grad., Facolta' Di Lettere e Filosofia, Florence, Italy, 1978. Writer, translator rev. of humanities Il Ponte, Florence, 1977-83; research asst. European U. Inst., Florence, 1985-86; research fellow Vrije U., Amsterdam, The Netherlands, 1987—; lectr. London Sch. Econs., 1987-88. Contbr. articles on 20th Century Italian and European History. Home: Piazza Piccinino 9, 06100 Perugia Italy Office: London Sch Econs, Houghton St, London WC2A 2AE, England

RANK, HUGH ERIC, writer, editor; b. Vienna, Austria, June 17, 1913; arrived in Eng., 1939, naturalized Brit. citizen, 1948; s. Michael Rudolf and Therese (Weiss) Rosenthal; m. Joan Frances Jacobs, Oct. 7, 1948 (dec. Feb. 1962); children: Michael Terence, Hazel Gladys, Carolyn Jean; m. Ellen McCready, Feb. 8, 1965; 1 stepchild, Margaret Hempton. M.A., U. Cambridge, Eng., 1954; Dr.Phil., U. Vienna, 1958. Lectr. St. Mary's Coll., Liverpool, Eng., 1954-61, Lanchester Poly., Coventry, Eng., 1961-65; head dept. modern langs. Tonbridge Sch., Kent, Eng. 1965-70; sr. German master Charterhouse, Godalming, Surrey, Eng., 1970-77, ret., 1977; extramural lectr. Liverpool Poly., Eng., 1955-61, U. Liverpool, 1958-61, U. Surrey, 1972-81; cultural corr. Wiener Zeitung, Vienna, Austrian radio, Vienna, Deutsche Bü hne, Cologne, Federal Republic Germany, Musik & Theater, Zürich, Switzerland; contbr. to BBC radio and TV; mem. press list Royal Acad., Tate Gallery, Arts Council. Editor: Fruhlings Erwachen, 1978; Geschichten aus dem Wiener Wald, 1979; translator dramas: The Life of Confucius, 1958, The Visions of Simone Machard, 1976. Contbr. articles on German drama and lit. to publs. including The Guardian, London Observer. Mem. PEN Eng. (corr. to PEN Internat.), Soc. Authors (Eng.), Assn. Fgn. Journalists (Berlin, Fed. Republic Germany). Avocations: collecting German 1st editions and autographs, theatre, walking. Home: Old Lapscombe, Smithwood Common, Cranleigh, Surrey GU6 8OX, England

RANKIN, KARL LOTT, retired foreign service officer; b. Manitowoc, Wis., Sept. 4, 1898; s. Emmet Woollen and Alberta (Lott) R.; m. Pauline Jordan, Oct. 3, 1925 (dec.); m. Ruth Thompson, Mar. 6, 1978. Grad., Mercerburg Acad., 1916; student, Calif. Inst. Tech., 1917-19, Fed. Polytechnic, Zü rich, 1920-21; C.E., Princeton, 1922; LL.D., Bowdoin Coll., Bates Coll. Constrn. supt. Nr. East Relief, Caucasus, 1922-25; mgr. of real estate devel. co. Linden, N.J., 1925-27; entered U.S. Govt. service 1927; assigned as asst. trade commr. Prague, Czechoslovakia; comml. attaché Prague, 1929, Athens and Tirana, 1932, Brussels and Luxembourg, 1939; comml. attaché, consul Belgrade, 1940; comml. attaché Cairo, 1941; interned by Japanese in Manila before reaching Egypt 1942-43; comml. attaché Cairo, 1944; counselor of embassy for econ. affairs Athens and Belgrade, 1944; chargé d'affaires a.i., Athens 1946; counselor of legation Vienna, 1946-47; counselor of embassy Athens, 1947; chargé d'affaires a.i. 1947-48, apptd. career minister, 1948; consul gen. Canton, 1949, Hong Kong and Macau, 1949; minister and chargé d'affairs Taipei, 1950-53; ambassador to China, 1953-57, to Yugoslavia, 1958-61; ret. 1961. Author: China Assignment, 1964. Hon. trustee Am. Coll. Greece, Athens. Served on active duty USN, 1918; lt. comdr. Res. 1937. Decorated Grand Cordon Order Brilliant Star (China). Mem. ASCE (life), Am.-Hellenic C. of C. (hon. pres.), Phi Kappa Sigma, Dial Lodge (Princeton). Congregationalist. Clubs: Cosmos (Washington); Princeton (N.Y.C.); Burnt Store Country, Isles Yacht (Punta Gorda, Fla.). Home: 1 Colony Point Dr Punta Gorda FL 33950 Office: 1466 Kings Hwy Kennebunkport ME 04046

RANKIN, PEGE BETTY, retired educator; b. Twin Falls, Idaho, July 23, 1919; d. Marion P. and Margaret (Conway) Betty; B.A., U. Calif.-Berkeley, 1941; postgrad. U. Calif.-Berkeley, Calif. State Coll., Savannah State Coll., San Francisco State Coll.; M.Ed., U. San Francisco, 1976; m. Herbert E. Rankin, June 5, 1941; children—Greg Robert, Todd Conway. Tchr. contract bridge San Francisco Bay area, 1950-69; pres., officer Oakland Pub. Schs. (Calif.), 1967—; tchr. journalism Skyline High Sch., Oakland, 1967—; tchr. guide European coll. tours, summers 1970—. Chmn. div. fund Am. Cancer Soc., 1958; organizer, condr. Mental Health Bridge Charity, 1961; mem. Friends of Herrick Hosp., Friends of Berkeley Library, Wall Street Jour., Monterey Aquarium, All Calif., Oakland Mus., San Francisco Commonwealth Club; mem. adv. bd. Invest in America. Named Outstanding Tchr. Journalism, Calif. PTA; Newspaper Fund fellow, 1969. Mem. AAUW, Am. Contract Bridge League, Oakland Press Honor Assn., Women in Communications (scholarship chmn. 1973), Columbia Scholastic Press Assn., Journalism Educators No. Calif. (v.p. 1980), San Francisco Opera Guild (bd. dirs. 1981—), Calif. Acad. Sci., M.H. de Young Meml. Mus., Smithsonian Assocs., Alpha Chi Alpha. Republican. Methodist. Club: Fannie Hill Ski (San Francisco). Home: 752 Cragmont Ave Berkeley CA 94708 Office: 12250 Skyline Blvd Oakland CA 94619

RANKIN, ROBERT ALEXANDER, mathematics educator; b. Garlieston, Wigtownshire, Scotland, Oct. 27, 1915; s. Oliver Shaw and Olivia Theresa (Shaw) Rankin; m. Mary Ferrier Llewellyn, July 25, 1942; children: Susan Mary Llewellyn, Charles Richard Shaw, Fenella Kathleen Clare, Olivia Roberta Mary. BA, U. Cambridge, Eng., 1937, PhD, 1940, MA, 1941, ScD, 1959. Fellow Clare Coll. U. Cambridge, 1939-51, asst. lectr., then lectr., 1945-51; prof. math. Birmingham U., Eng., 1951-54; prof. math. Glasgow U., Scotland, 1954-82, prof. emeritus math., 1982—; clk. of senate Glasgow U., 1971-78, dean of faculties, 1985-88; chmn. Scottish Math. Council, 1967-73. Author: Mathematical Analysis, 1963, The Modular Group, 1969, Modular Forms and Functions, 1977; contbr. articles to profl. jours. Chmn. Clyde Estuary Amenity Council, 1969-81. Recipient Keith prize Royal Soc. Edinburgh, 1964, Sr. Whitehead prize London Math. Soc., 1987; Royal Scottish Acad. Music and Drama fellow, 1982. Fellow Royal Soc. Edinburgh (mem. council 1957-63); mem. London Math. Soc. (v.p. 1966-68), Edinburgh Math. Soc. (pres. 1957-58, 78-79), Math. Assn., Am. Math. Soc., Am. Math. Assn., Scottish Gaelic Texts Soc. (v.p.), Gaelic Soc. Glasgow (hon. pres.). Home: 98 Kelvin Ct, Glasgow G12 OAH, Scotland

RANSOHOFF, PRISCILLA BURNETT, psychologist, educator; b. Pitts., June 16, 1912; d. Levi Herr and Clara Amelia (Brown) Burnett; B.S., U. Pitts., 1941; M.A., Columbia U., 1952, Ed.D., 1954; m. James Hampton Johnston, Aug. 4, 1934; 1 dau., Priscilla Burnett; m. 2d, Nicholas Sigmund Ransohoff, Nov. 27, 1947. Dir. rehab. Monmouth Med. Center, Long Branch, N.J., 1944-54; pres. Cons. Assocs., Inc., Long Branch, 1954-64; v.p. Dale-Elliot Mgmt. Cons., N.Y.C., 1958-60; edn. adviser U.S. Army Electronics Command, Ft. Monmouth, N.J., 1964-78; organizational effectiveness staff officer U.S. Army Communications Materiel Readiness Command, Ft. Monmouth, 1978—; co-adj. prof. Ocean County Community Coll., Toms River, N.J.; co-adj. instr. Monmouth Coll., West Long Branch, N.J., Brookdale Community Coll., Lincroft, N.J. Founder, pres., chmn. bd. Monmouth Rehab. Workshop, Red Bank, N.J., 1954-58; vice chmn. N.J. del. Women's Conf., Houston, 1977. Recipient CECOM Comdr.'s Internat., 1982; Woman of Yr. award Zonta, 1984; cert. practitioner neuro linguistic programming. Mem. Orgn. Devel. Network, Internat. Platform Assn., Federally Employed Women (pres. 1973, 74, chpt. pres. 1984—), Internat. Tng. in Communication Club, Assn. U.S. Army (sec., adv. com. to nat. exec. bd., 3 yrs.), Def. Preparedness Assn., Assn. U.S. Army (sec., drug and alcohol com. Ft. Monmouth chpt., suicide prevention and intervention counicl, human resource com.), Pi Lambda Theta, Kappa Delta Pi, Delta Zeta. Lodges: Zonta Internat. (bd. dirs. Monmouth County chpt.), Order of Eastern Star. Home: 13 River Ave Monmouth Beach NJ 07750 Office: Aviation Research and Devel Activity Fort Monmouth NJ 07703

RANSOM, GRAYCE ANNABLE, emeritus educator; b. La Porte, Ind.; d. Irving H. and Louisa Sabra (Sawin) Annable; B.R.E., McCormick Theol. Sem., 1937; M.A., Lewis and Clark Coll., 1954; B.A., Kalamazoo Coll., 1965; Ph.D., U. So. Calif., 1967; m. John T. Seeley, Mar. 20, 1970; children—Judith Ransom Burney, Kenneth C., Janet. Asst. camp dir., Portland, Oreg., 1947-55; tchr. religious edn., tchr. tng. Portland Council of Chs., 1949-54; tchr. elementary sch., Portland, Los Angeles, 1955-62; asst. prof. Calif. State U., Long Beach, 1963-65; faculty U. So. Calif., Los Angeles, from 1965, prof. curriculum and reading instrn., from 1974, now emeritus, chmn. dept. curriculum and instruction, dir. Campus and NCL Reading Centers, 1967—; cons. Calif. State Dept. Edn., 1966—, various sch. dists. in Calif., 1965—; reading test cons. Ednl. Testing Service, Princeton, N.J., 1971-72; interim dir. parish program Westminster Presbyn. Ch., Portland, 1984-86. Bd. dirs. Footlighters Child Guidance Clinic. Recipient Merit award Calif. State Bd. Edn., 1981. Mem. Internat. (dir.), Calif. (pres. 1976-77, Marcus Foster award for outstanding contbns. to reading 1979), Los Angeles (pres. 1973-74) reading assns., AAUP, Am. Ednl. Research Assn., NEA, Nat. Council Tchrs. English, LWV (pres. Portland 1947-48), Pi Lambda Theta, Phi Delta Kappa (award for research 1982). Presbyterian (elder 1971—). Author: Crackerjacks, 1969; Evaluating Teacher Education Programs in Reading, 1972; Teacher's Guide for Electronic Card-Reading Machines, 1974; The Ransom Reading Program, 1974; Multi Media Kits-Reading, Researching, Reporting in Social Studies, 1975, Science, 1977, Health, 1977; Preparing to Teach Reading, 1978; California Framework for Reading, 1980. Research in computers in early childhood edn. Home: 13775 Old Scholl's Ferry Rd Beaverton OR 97006

RANTANEN, PAAVO ILMARI, Finnish ambassador to U.S.; b. Jyvaskyla, Finland, Feb. 28, 1934; s. Vilho Einar and Jenny Vilhelma (Auer) R.; m. Ritva Mirjam Lehtinen, Feb. 26, 1956; children—Heikki, Virve, Petri. M. in Polit. Sci., U. Helsinki, Finland, 1958. Various positions in Finnish Fgn. Service, 1958-74, ambassador-at-large Ministry for Fgn. Affairs, 1974-76, dir. dept. fgn. trade Ministry Fgn. Affairs, 1976-79, under sec. State for Fgn. Trade, 1979-81, ambassador, permanent rep. Finland to UN, Geneva, 1981-86, ambassador of Finland to U.S., 1986-88; bd. dirs. Finnish Fgn. Trade Assn., Helsinki, 1974-79; bd. dirs. Finnish Export Credit Corp., Helsinki, 1975-79, vice chmn., 1979; v.p., bd. dirs. Nokia Corp., Helsinki, 1988—. Mem. Finnish Defence Coll. Assn., Internat. Mgmt. and Devel. Inst. (diplomatic adv. council 1986—). Avocations: history, music. Home: 3001 Woodland Dr NW Washington DC 20008 Office: Nokia Corp, Mikonkatu, 15 A, 20016 Helsinki Finland

RAO, A. RAMAMOHANA, veterinarian, university dean; b. Mudunuru, India, Nov. 10, 1933. BVSc, Madras U., 1956; MS, U. Ill., 1959; PhD, Royal Vet. Coll., Stockholm, 1971. Asst. lectr. Andhra Pradesh Vet. Coll., 1956-57; asst. research officer Semen Bank, Hyderabad, India, 1959-63; reader Vet. Coll., Tirupati, India, 1964-73, prof., 1973-85, head dept. gynaecology, 1964-85, prin., 1981-83; dean postgrad studies Andhra Pradesh Agrl. U., Rajendranagar, India, 1985—. Mem. Indian Soc. for Study Animal Reprodn. (pres.). Office: Andhra Pradesh Agrl U, Hyderabad 500 030, India

RAO, CHINTAMANI NAGESA RAMACHANDRA, chemist, educator; b. Bangalore, India, June 30, 1934; s. H. Nagesa Rao; m. Indumati Rao, 1960; children—Suchitra, Sanjay-Srinivas. B.S., U. Mysore, 1951, D.Sc., 1961; M.S., Banaras Hindu U., 1953; Ph.D., Purdue U., 1958, D.Sc. (hon.), 1982; D.Sc. (hon.), U. Bordeaux (France), 1983, Banaras U., Venkateswara U., Roorkee U., Manipur U. Lectr., Indian Inst. Sci., Bangalore, 1959-63, prof. chemistry, 1976-84, dir. Inst., 1984—; prof., later sr. prof. Indian Inst. tech., Kanpur, 1963-76, dean R & D, 1969-72; vis. prof. Cambridge U., 1983-84; research chemist U. Calif.-Berkeley, 1958-59; hon. chmn. bd. Hindustan Insecticides Ltd., 1970-75; chmn. sci. adv. com. to prime minister, 1986—. Author: Ultraviolet Visible Spectroscopy, 1960; Chemical Applications of Infra-red Spectroscopy, 1963; Spectroscopy in Inorganic Chemistry, 1970; Modern Aspects of Solid State Chemistry, 1970; Solid State Chemistry, 1974; Educational Technology in Teaching of Chemistry, 1975; Phase Transitions in Solids, 1978, New Directions in Solid State Chemistry, 1986; numerous publs. in field; editorial bd. internat. jours. Recipient Marlow medal Faraday Soc., 1967; Bhatnagar award; 1968; Padma Shri, Pres. India, 1974; Padma Vibhushan, Pres. India, 1985; award for phys. scis. Fedn. Indian C. of C. and Industry, 1977; Sir C.V. Raman award, 1978; Am. Chem. Soc. Centennial fgn. fellow, 1976; Jawaharlal Nehru fellow, 1973-75. Fellow Royal Soc. London, Indian Acad. Scis. (Bose medal 1980), Royal Soc. Chemistry (medal 1981); mem. Internat. Union Pure and Applied Chemistry (pres. 1985-87), Acad. Sci. Yugoslavia (fgn.), Slovenian Acad. Scis. Yugoslavia (fgn.), Third World Acad. Scis. (founder mem.), Internat. Orgn. Chems. for Devel., Indian Nat. Sci. Acad. (pres. 1985-86), Indian Sci. Congress (gen. pres. 1987-88). Office: Indian Inst Sci, Bangalore 560012, India

RAO, DANDAMUDI VISHNUVARDHANA, nuclear medical physicist, educator; b. Maredumaka, India, Apr. 5, 1944; came to U.S., 1968, naturalized, 1979; s. Veeraraghaviah and Sarojini D. (Koneru) R.; m. Sujata L. Rao, Feb. 27, 1967; children—Saroja, Neeraja. MS, U. Mass., 1970, PhD, 1972. Instr. radiology Albert Einstein Coll. Medicine, Bronx, N.Y., 1972-74; asst. prof. radiology U. Medicine and Dentistry, Newark, 1975-78, assoc. prof. radiology, 1978-87, prof., 1987—, dir. health physics, 1974-78, dir. radiation research, 1987—; tech. expert IAEA. Contbr. articles to profl. jours.; Author: Introduction to Physics of Nuclear Medicine, 1977; editor: Physics of Nuclear Medicine: Recent Advances, 1984; Am. Cancer Soc. grantee, 1975-77; Biomed. Research grantee, 1977-78; Nat. Cancer Inst., NIH grantee, 1982—. Mem. Am. Assn. Physicists in Medicine (program dir. summer sch. 1983), N.Y. Acad. Scis., Am. Coll. Med. Physics, NMR Imaging Soc., Soc. Nuclear Medicine. Subspecialties: Nuclear medicine; Imaging technology. Current work: In vivo study of radiation effects in Spermatoponial cells from low energy electrons emitted by nuclear medicine radiopharmaceuticals. Patentee radioactive erbium complexes. Home: 15 Brookfield Dr Basking Ridge NJ 07920 Office: U Medicine and Dentistry of NJ 185 S Orange Ave Newark NJ 07103

RAO, DEVABATHINI VEERA BHADRA, optical engineer; b. Ongole, India, May 16, 1950; s. Subba Rayudu Devabathini and Mahalakshmamma Davuluri; m. Lakshmi Amaraneni, May 4, 1976; 1 child, Subhash Chandra. BSc, Andhra Loyola Coll., 1970; MSc, Andhra U., 1972; PhD in Optics, Regional Engring. Coll., 1979. Research fellow dept. engring, electronics commn. Indian Inst. Sci., Bangalore, 1978-80; scientist, engr. sensor systems div. Indian Space Research Orgn., Bangalore, 1980—. Contbr. papers on optical design, testing and data processing to nat. and internat. publs. Mem. Instrument Soc. India. Home: 278 A KR Reddy Layout, Bangalore 560 017, India Office: Sensor Systems Div Indian Space Research Orgn, Airport Rd, Bangalore 560 017, India

RAO, GANDIKOTA LAKSHMI NARASINGA, mathematics educator; b. Visakhapatnam, India, Nov. 4, 1928; s. Gandikota Baburao and Chatti Sita Raghavendra; m. Maremanda Kamala Devi, Feb. 2, 1952; children: Rama Lakshmi, Raghavendra. BA, M.R. Coll., Vizianagaram, India, 1948, BEd, 1951; MA, Banaras Hindu U., Uttar Pradesh, India, 1958; PhD, Ranchi U., India, 1973. Lectr. Purulia Poly., West Bengal, India, 1959-60, Coop. Coll. Ranchi U., Jamshedpur, Bihar, India, 1960-80; assoc. prof. math. dept. Coop. Coll. Ranchi U., Jamshedpur, Bihar, 1980-85, prof., 1985—; lectr. in field; conf. participant; vis. prof. various univs. in Fed. Republic Germany, 1983-84. Contbr. articles to profl. publs. Grantee Univ. Grants Commn., New Delhi, 1970, 78, Ranchi U., 1975, 78. Mem. Indian Math. Soc., Am. Math. Soc., Indian Sci. Congress Assn., Indian Acad. Math., Math. Parichad (treas. 1971). Home: Old Adityapur Colony, Jamshedpur 831013, India Office: Jamshedpur Coop Coll Circuit, House Area, Jamshedpur 831001, India

RAO, GOPAL UDIAVAR (GENE), banker; b. Bombay; came to U.S., 1960; s. Srinivasa U. and Ratnabai M. Shanbhogue; B.A. with honors, U. Bombay, 1958, M.A. in Econs., 1959; M.B.A., U. Chgo., 1962; m. Theresa M. Schmid, June 17, 1965; children—Ashok G., Sheila Y., Chandani R., Anand A. Research asst. Harvard U., 1962-63; ter. mgr. Alcon Labs., Ft. Worth, 1963-65; ins. programmer Equitable Life Assurance Soc., Des Moines, 1965-66; project leader Dial Fin. Corp., Des Moines, 1967-70; v.p., tech. mgr. Beneficial Mgmt. Corp., Morristown, N.J., 1970-82; v.p. tech. services Chase Manhattan Bank, N.Y.C., 1982—; asso. prof. econs. Drake U., 1966-68. Recipient presdl. awards for excellence in fin. tech. system designs, 1971, 77, 78, 79. Mem. Data Processing Mgmt. Assn., Airlines Control Program Users Group (chmn.), IBM Share and Guide Assn., Nat. Consumers Fin. Assn. (tech. and communication subcom.). Clubs: Arrowhead Tennis, Mt. Freedom Racquet. Author: Elephant Baby, Ency. Britannica, 1962. Office: 1 New York Plaza 16th Floor New York NY 10081

RAO, HARISH GOVINDA, environmental engineering scientist; b. Mysore, Karnataka, India, July 11, 1953; came to U.S., 1977; s. D.R. Govinda Rao and G.K. Rakhama Bai; m. Beena Madhava Rao, Nov. 3, 1985. B in Civil Engring., Bangalore (India) U., 1975; M of Tech. in Civil Engring., Indian Inst. Tech., Kharangpur, 1977; PhD in Civil Engring., Northwestern U., 1981. Teaching, research asst. Northwestern U. Dept. Civil Engring., Evanston, Ill., 1978-80; asst. prof. Civil Engring. U. Miami, Coral Gables, Fla., 1980-81, Old Dominion U., Norfolk, Va., 1981-83; vis. asst. prof. U. Toledo, 1984-85; research fellow, engr. Dept. Indsl. and Systems Engring. Ohio U., Athens, 1986; environ. scientist Ill. Pollution Control Bd., Chgo., 1986—; cons. in field, 1983—. Contbr. articles to Environ. Monitoring and Assessment mag., Computer and Indsl. Engring. mag., ASCE Energy div. jour., ASCE Engring. Mechanics div. jour. Child sponsor World Vision, Guatemala, 1982-84; contbr. Amnesty Internat., 1986—. Indian Inst. Tech. scholar, 1975-77; Brookhaven Nat. Lab. fellow, Upton, N.Y., 1978. Mem. ASCE, Air Pollution Control Assn. (tech. com. 1985—), Water Pollution Control Fedn., Am. Water Works Assn. Office: Ill Pollution Control Bd State of Ill Ctr Suite 11-500 100 W Randolph St Chicago IL 60601

RAO, TADIKONDA LAKSHMI KANTHA, anesthesiologist; b. Rajampet, India, Nov. 23, 1946; s. Atchuta T. and Lakshmi Rao; B.Sc., Govt. Arts Coll., 1963; M.D., Pondicherry Med. Coll., 1971; m. Vyjayanthi Rao, Oct. 9, 1971; children—Usha, Vijay, Madhavi. came to U.S., 1972, naturalized, 1976. Registrar, dept. anesthesiology Pondicherry Med. Coll., India, 1970-72; intern, resident Cook County Hosp., Chgo., 1972-74, assoc. chmn. clin. anesthesia, 1975-77; practice medicine specializing anesthesiology, Chgo., 1976-81; assoc. prof. Loyola U. Med. Ctr., Maywood, Ill., 1978, chmn. dept. anesthesiology. Mem. AMA, Internat. Anesthesia Research Soc., Ill. Med. Assn., Chgo. Med. Soc., Am. Soc. Anesthesiologists, Am. Soc. Regional Anesthesia, Chgo. Soc. Anesthesiologists, Soc. Cardiovascular Anesthesiologists, Ill. Soc. Anesthesiologists Assn. Univ. Anesthetists. Contbr. articles to profl. jours. Home: 1914 Midwest Club Oak Brook IL 60521 Office: 2160 S 1st Ave Maywood IL 60153

RAO, VEDURMUDI RAMAKRISHNA, toxicologist; b. Kakinada, India, Mar. 23, 1937; s. V. Hanumantha and V. Kamala (Bai) R.; B.V.Sc. and A.H., Calcutta U., 1963; M.V.Sc. (jr. fellow Indian Council Agrl. Research 1967-69), Agra U., 1969; Ph.D., Kans. State U., 1975; m. Sudha B. Chandrachud, Aug. 5, 1970; 1 child, Ashutosh. Research asst. Indian Vet. Research Inst., 1964-69; sci. officer Bhabha Atomic Research Centre, Bombay, 1970; grad. research asst. Kans. State U. Coll. Vet. Medicine, 1972-75; head dept. toxicology Haffkine Inst., Bombay, 1976—, asst. dir. inst., 1980—. Fellow Am. Acad. Vet. and Comparative Toxicology; mem. Soc. Toxicology India, Indian Soc. Clin. Pharmacology and Therapeutics, N.Y. Acad. Scis., Assn. Microbiologists of India, Sigma Xi. Home: E 3/2, Sector 1V, CIDCO, Vashi, New Bombay 400 703, India Office: Acharya Donde Marg, Parel, Bombay 400 012, India

RAPAPORT, CHANAN, psychologist; b. Stanislavov, Poland, Sept. 8, 1928; arrived in Israel, 1935; s. Yehoshua and Bronya (Fuer) R.; m. Yehudit Grunwald, May 1, 1957; children: Michal-Ditsa, Shirly-Yiska. BA in Psychology, Hebrew U., Jerusalem, 1952; PhD in Clin. Psychology, NYU, 1963, postdoctoral studies in psychotherapy, 1963-64, 72-73. Sr. clin. psychologist Creedmoor State Hosp., N.Y.C., 1962-63, Mt. Sinai Hosp., N.Y.C., 1963-64; psychotherapist Queens County Neuropsychiat. Ctr., N.Y.C., 1962-64; psychol. advisor, dir. research Israeli Ministry Edn. and Culture, 1965-67; dir. Henrietta Szold Nat. Inst. for Research in Behaviroal Scis., 1965-82; pvt. practice psychotherapy Jerusalem, 1983—; vis. scholar NYU, 1972-73; vis. prof. psychiatry U. Minn., Mpls., 1979-80. Editor, contbg. author: Children and Families in Israel: Some Mental Health Perspectives, 1970, Early Child Care in Israel, 1976, (with A. Levy) Educational Perspectives and Achievements in the Israeli School System, 1978, Arab Youth in Israel, Knowledge and Values in the Social and Political Spheres, 1980, (with Charny) Genocide, The Human Cancer, 1982, Youth Aliyah, The Education of the Culturally Disadvantaged, 1983; mem. editorial bd. Megamot Behavioral Sci. Quar., Israel, 1965-82, Early Child Devel. and Care, Chgo., 1971-81, Social Indicators, Washington, 1973-80. Mem. internal council for comparative research in edn. UNESCO, adv. council on social affairs Prime Minister Israel. Served as comdr. Haganah underground, 1943-48, with Israeli Army, 1948-51. Mem. Israeli Psychol. Assn. (exec. sec.), World Union of Orgns. for Safeguard of Youth, Am. Group Psychotherapy Assn., Internat. Soc. Clin. Exptl. Hypnosis, Internat. Soc. Comprehensive Medicine (charter), Soc. Art and Psychology (bd. dirs.), Israel Soc. Advancement Psychiatry and Behavioral Scis. (bd. dirs.). Home: 21 Shmuel Hanagid St, Jerusalem 94592, Israel Office: 17 Shmuel Hanagid St, Jerusalem 94592, Israel

RAPAPORT, FELIX THEODOSIUS, surgeon, researcher, educator; b. Munich, Fed. Republic Germany, Sept. 27, 1929; s. Max W. and Adelaide (Rathaus) R.; m. Margaret Birsner, Dec. 14, 1969; children: Max, Benjamin, Simon, Michel, Adelaide. A.B., NYU, 1951, M.D., 1954. Diplomate: Am. Bd. Surgery, 1963. Intern Mt. Sinai Hosp., N.Y.C., 1955-56; resident, chief resident NYU Surg. Services, 1958-62, USPHS postdoctoral fellow in pathology, 1956; exec. officer Naval Med. Research Unit No. 1, U. Calif., Berkeley, 1956-58; trainee in allergy and infectious diseases NYU, 1958-61; head, transplantation and immunology div. NYU Surg. Services, 1965-77; dir. research Inst. Reconstrn. and Plastic Surgery, NYU, 1965-77; assoc. prof. surgery NYU Med. Ctr., 1965-70, prof., 1970-77; prof., dep. chmn. dept. surgery, prof. pathology, dir. transplantation service SUNY, Stony Brook, 1977—; attending SUNY (Univ. Hosp.), 1980—; cons. VA Hosp., N.Y.C., 1963-77, Northport, N.Y., 1977—. Editor-in-chief: Transplantation Proceedings, 1968—; assoc. editor: Am. Jour. Kidney Diseases, 1981-86, Am. Jour. Craniofacial Genetics and Developmental Biology, 1980-85; contbr. over 400 articles to profl. jours.; author/editor 12 books on transplantation. Served to lt. comdr. M.C. USNR, 1956-58. Decorated comdr. Order Sci. Merit, chevalier Ordre National du Merite, France, 1970; recipient Gold medal Societe d'Encouragement au Bien, 1979; grand croix Ordre des Palmes Academiques, France, 1981. Mem. Soc. Univ. Surgeons, N.Y. Surg. Soc., Am. Surg. Assn., ACS, Am. Assn. Immunologists, Soc. Exptl. Biology and Medicine, Harvey Soc., Am. Assn. Transplant Surgeons, Am. Assn. Clin. Histocompatibility Testing, Internat. Soc. Exptl. Hematology, Transplantation Soc. (founding sec., v.p., treas., councillor, pres.), Alpha Omega Alpha. Democrat. Jewish. Current Work: Induction of permanent tolerance to major transplantable organs in man; research concerned with effects of total body irradiation and bone marrow transplantation in the production of host unresponsiveness to tissue allografts. Office: SUNY Stony Brook Dept Surgery Health Scis Ctr Stony Brook NY 11794-8192

RAPHAEL, BEVERLEY, psychiatrist, educator; b. Casino, New South Wales, Australia, Oct. 4, 1934; d. Garnet Percy and Isobel (Grieve) R.; divorced; 1 child, Cassandra. MMBS, Sydney (Australia) U., 1957, MD, 1977. Practice medicine specializing in psychiatry 1959-63; psychiat. registrar Royal Prince Alfred Hosp., Camperdown, Australia, 1964-65, clin. asst. psychiatry, 1968-71, hon. asst. psychiatrist, 1971-77; psychiatrist trainee Health Commn., New South Wales, Australia, 1966-67, research psychiatrist, 1973-74; community psychiatrist North Ryde Psychiat. Ctr., New South Wales, Australia, 1968-69; assoc. prof. psychiatry U. Sydney, Repatriation

Gen. Hosp., Concord, New South Wales, 1975-78; dir. psychiat. services Royal Brisbane Hosp., Herston, Australia, 1987—; prof., chairperson dept. psychiatry U. Queensland, 1987—; found. prof. psychiatry U. Newcastle, chmn. research ethics com. 1982-87, Australian Preventive Psychiatry Ctr., 1979-87, Mental Health Service Devel. Group, 1985-87, Community and Prevention Working Group, Psychogeriatrics Working Group, 1985-87, mental health standing com. Nat. Health, Med. Research Council, 1985—; acting chief exec. officer Hunter Mental Health Services, 1985; cons. to govt. Psychiat. Aspects Disaster, 1980—; hon. cons. psychiatry Royal Alfred Hosp., Sydney, 1978—, Royal Newcastle Hosp., 1975-87, Newcastle Mater Miseridordiae Hosp., 1978-87, Wallsend Dist. Hosp., 1978-87; acad. bd. U. Queensland. Contbr. numerous articles to profl. jours.; editorial cons. Australian New Zealand Jour. Psychiatry, New Doctor, 1980-87. New South Wales Inst. Psychiatry research fellow, 1969-72; mem. Order of Australia, 1984. Fellow Royal Australian New Zealand Coll. Psychiatrists (pres. 1983-85, bd. censors 1978-81, disaster com. 1977-85, chmn. steering com. quality assurance 1982-85), Australian Acad. Social Scis., Am. Psychiat. Assn., Royal Coll. Psychiatry; mem. World Psychiat. Assn., World Fedn. Mental Health, Australian Soc. Med. Research, Australian Soc. Psychiat. Research, Australian Nat. Assn. Psychosomatic Ob-gyn., Med. Assn. Prevention War, Assn. Clin. Profs. Australia, Med. Women's Assn., Assn. Univ. Women, Nat. Assn. Loss and Grief. Office: U Queensland Dept Psychiatry, Clin Scis Bldg, Royal Brisbane Hosp, Brisbane Queensland 4029, Australia

RAPHAEL, CHESTER MARTIN, physician; b. Rockaway Beach, N.Y., Oct. 7, 1912; s. Jack and Lena (Schoenfeld) R.; A.B. cum laude, U. Mich., 1933, M.D., 1937; m. Margaret Mary Hubbert, Aug. 15, 1943; children—Maura Ann, Barbara Lynn. Intern, Monmouth Meml. Hosp., Long Branch, N.J., 1937-39; resident physician N.J. State Hosp., Marlboro, N.J., 1939-42, 46-48; practice medicine specializing in psychiatry and orgonomy, Forest Hills, N.Y., 1948—; sec. Wilhelm Reich Found., 1949-54; co-dir. Orgone Energy Clinic, 1949-54. Bd. dirs. Guide Dog Found. for Blind, Friends of Wilhelm Reich Mus. Served with AUS, 1942-46. Fellow Am. Geriatric Soc., Acad. Psychosomatic Medicine; mem. Queens County Med. Soc., AMA, Am. Psychiat. Assn., Am. Assn. Med. Orgonomy, AAAS, Wilhelm Reich Inst. Orgonomic Studies (dir.), Assn. for Advancement Psychotherapy, Tau Delta Phi. Club: University of Michigan (N.Y.C.). Author: (with Helen E. MacDonald) Orgonomic Diagnosis of the Cancer Biopathy, 1952; Wilhelm Reich: Misconstrued-Misesteemed; Some Questions and Answers About Orgone Therapy; asso. editor: Jour. Orgonomic Medicine, 1955-56; editor: (with Mary Higgins) Reich Speaks of Freud, The Cancer Biopathy (Wilhelm Reich); Passion of Youth-An Autobiography (Wilhelm Reich), Early Writings (Wilhelm Reich); The Bion Experiments on The Origin of Life (Wilhelm Reich); Character Analysis (Wilhelm Reich); Genitality (Wilhelm Reich); Bioelectrical Investigation of Sexuality and Anxiety (Wilhelm Reich); Children of the Future (Wilhelm Reich). Home and Office: 69-17 Fleet St Forest Hills NY 11375

RAPIDIS, ALEXANDER DEMETRIUS, maxillofacial surgeon; b. Athens, Greece, Aug. 31, 1948; s. Demetrius Afentoulis and Calliope (Sbrinis) R.; D.D.S. with honors, Athens U., 1973; Ph.D., Athens U., 1983; m. Effie Stergiopoulos, May 8, 1978 (div. 1985); m. Iphigenia Thermidou, Jan. 22, 1986; 1 child. Clin. asst. dept. oral surgery Royal Dental Hosp., London, 1974; dept. oral and maxillofacial surgery London Hosp. Med. Coll., 1975; sr. house surgeon Whipp's Cross Hosp., London, 1976; research fellow dept. oral surgery Queen Mary's Hosp., London, 1977; attending maxillofacial surgeon St. Paul's Accident Hosp., Kifissia, Athens, 1978-81, Laikon Gen. Teaching Hosp. of Athens U., 1981-86; research assoc. dept. oral pathology U. Athens, 1978-86; hon. lectr., research assoc. dept. Maxillofacial Surgery King's Coll., Hosp. U. London, 1986—; hon. cons. maxillofacial surgeon U. Patras, Greece, 1985—. Recipient award Internat. Union Against Cancer, 1977. Mem. Greek Dental Assn., Royal Soc. Medicine London (fellow), Acad. Psychosomatic Medicine (fellow), Internat. Assn. Oral Surgeons (fellow), Internat. Assn. Maxillofacial Surgery. Contbr. articles to profl. jours. Home: 23 Asclipiou, 144 Athens Greece Office: 3 Ravine St, Athens Greece

RAPIER, PASCAL MORAN, chemical engineer; b. Atlanta, Jan. 11, 1914; s. Paul Edward and Mary Claire (Moran) R.; m. Martha Elizabeth Doyle, May 19, 1945; children: Caroline Elizabeth, Paul Doyle, Mollie Claire, John Lawrence, James Andrew. BSChemE, Ga. Inst. Tech., 1939; MS in Theoretical Physics, U. Nev., 1959; postgrad., U. Calif., Berkeley, 1961. Registered profl. engr., Calif., N.J. Plant engr. Archer-Daniels-Midland, Pensacola, Fla., 1940-42; group supr. Dicalite div. Grefco, Los Angeles, 1943-54; process engr. Celatom div. Eagle Picher, Reno, Nev., 1955-57; project mgr., assoc. research engr. U. Calif. Field Sta., Richmond, 1959-62; project mgr. sea water conversion Bechtel Corp., San Francisco, 1962-66; sr. supervising chem. engr. Burns & Roe, Oradell, N.J., 1966-74; cons. engr. Kenite Corp., Scarsdale, N.Y., Rees Blowpipe, Berkeley, 1960-66; sr. cons. engr. Sanderson & Porter, N.Y.C., 1975-77; staff scientist III Lawrence Berkeley Lab., 1977-84; bd. dirs. Newtonian Sci. Found.; v.p. Calif. Rep. Assembly, 1964-65. Contbr. articles to profl jours.; patentee agts. to render non-polar solvents electrically conductive, direct-contact geothermal energy recovery devices. Mem. Am. Inst. Chem. Engrs. Presbyterian. Lodge: Gideons Internat. Home: 3154 Deseret Dr Richmond CA 94803

RAPOPORT, AMNON, psychology educator; b. Affula, Israel, Feb. 6, 1936; s. Meir and Genia (Yudovitch) R.; m. Aviva Kantorovitch, Dec. 24, 1961; 1 child, Meekhal. PhD, U. N.C., 1965. Research asst. prof. U. N.C., Chapel Hill, 1965-66, assoc. prof., 1968-72, prof., 1972-76, 1986—; asst. prof. Hebrew U., Jerusalem, 1966-68, assoc. prof., 1971-72; prof. Haifa U., Israel, 1974—; dean grad. studies Haifa Univ., 1979-81; head Inst. Info. Processing Decision Making, Haifa, 1981—. Author: Structures in the Subjective Lexicon, 1971, Coalition Formation by Sophisticated Players, 1979, Response Models for Detection of Change, 1979, Theories of Coalition Formation, 1984. Recipient Am. Inst. Research award, 1965; Netherlands Inst. Advanced Studies fellow, 1977. Mem. Psychometric Soc., Soc. Math. Psychology. Jewish. Office: Univ NC Dept Psychology Chapel Hill NC 27514

RAPOSO, SUE NORDLUND, television company executive; b. Pierre, S.D., Jan. 14, 1936; d. Raymond Julian and Gertrude Elizabeth (Sandstrom) Nordlund; m. Joseph Guilheme Raposo, Aug. 24, 1958 (div. 1976); children—Joseph Raymond, Nicholas Anthony. A.B., Radcliffe Coll., 1958. Mgr. nat. acquisitions WNET/13, N.Y.C., 1977—; mgr. internat. ops. CBS Cable, N.Y.C., 1982—; dir. cable PBS Network Sales BBC Lionheart TV, N.Y.C., 1985—; judge ACE awards, 1987. Mem. N.Y. Women in Film, Nat. Acad. TV Arts and Scis. (judge 1985-88 Emmys). Democrat. Club: Radcliffe (N.Y.C.). Avocations: arts, travel. Home: 1065 Lexington Ave New York NY 10021 Office: BBC Lionheart TV 630 5th Ave New York NY 10111

RAPP, FRED, virologist; b. Fulda, Germany, Mar. 13, 1929; came to U.S., 1936, naturalized, 1945; s. Albert and Rita (Hain) R.; children: Stanley I., Richard J., Kenneth A. B.S., Bklyn. Coll., 1951; M.S., Albany Med. Coll., Union U., 1956; Ph.D., U. So. Calif., 1958. Diplomate: fellow Am. Acad. Microbiology. Jr. Bacteriologist, div. labs. and research N.Y. State Dept. Health, 1952-55; from teaching asst. to instr. dept. med. microbiology Sch. Medicine, U. So. Calif., 1956-59; cons. supervisory microbiologist Hosp. Spl. Surgery, N.Y.C., 1959-62; also virologist div. pathology Philip D. Wilson Research Found., N.Y.C.; asst. prof. micorbiology and immunology Cornell U. Med. Coll., N.Y.C., 1961-62; assoc. prof. Baylor U. Sch. Medicine, Waco, Tex., 1962-66, prof., 1966-69; prof., chmn. dept. microbiology Pa. State U. Coll. Medicine, University Park, 1969—, Evan Pugh prof. microbiology, 1978—, assoc. provost, dean health affairs, 1973-80, sr. mem. grad. faculty, assoc. dean acad. affairs, research and grad. studies, 1987—; researh career prof. of virology Am. Cancer Soc., 1966-69, prof. virology, 1977—; dir. Coll. Med. Pa. State U. (Specialized Cancer Research Ctr.), 1973-84; mem. delegation on viral oncology, U.S./U.S.S.R. Joint Com. Health Cooperation; chmn., Gordon Research Conf. in Cancer, 1975; virology Task Force, 1976-79; chmn. Atlantic Coast Tumor Virology Group, Nat. Cancer Insts. Health, 1971-77; mem. council for projection and analysis Am. Cancer Soc., 1976-80; chmn. standards and exam. com. on virology Am. Bd. Med. Microbiology, 1977, 80; chmn. subsect. on virology program com. Am. Assn. Cancer Research, 1978-79; mem. adv. council virology div. Internat. Union Microbiol. Socs., 1978-84; referee Macy Faculty Scholar Award Program, 1979-81; mem. programme com. Fifth Internat. Congress for Virology, Strasbourg, France, 1981; mem. basic cancer research group U.S.-France Agreement for Cooperation in Cancer Research, 1980—; mem. organizing com. Internat. Workshop on Herpes viruses, Bologna, Italy, 1980-81, NATO Internat. Advanced Study Inst., Corfu Island, Greece, 1981; mem. Herpes viruses Study Group, 1981-84; mem. Scientific adv. com. Wilmot Fellowship Program, U. Rochester Med. Ctr., 1981—; mem. scientific rev. com. Hubert H. Humphrey Cancer Research Ctr., Boston U., 1981; mem. fin. com. Am. Soc. Virology, 1982—; mem. adv. com. persistent virus-host interactions research program R.J. Reynolds Scientific Bd./Wistar Inst., 1983—; mem. med. adv. bd. Herpes Resource Ctr., Am. Social Health Assn., 1983—; bd. dirs. U.S.-Japan Found. Biomedicine, 1983—; mem. council Soc. Exptl. Biology and Medicine, 1983-87; mem. scientific adv. com. Internat. Assn. Study and Prevention of Virus-Associated Cancers, 1983—; mem. Basil O'Connor Starter Research Adv. Com., 1984—; mem. council for research and clin. investigation awards Am. Cancer Soc., 1984—; mem. recombinant DNA adv. com. NIH, 1984-87; mem. council Am. Soc. Virology, 1984—; mem. outstanding investigator grant rev. com. Nat. Cancer Inst., 1984—; mem. organizing com. Fourth Symposium Sapporo Cancer Seminar, Japan, 1984, Second Internat. Conf. Immunobiology and Prophylaxis of Human Herpes virus Infections, Ft. Lauderdale, Fl., 1984-85, Internat. Congress of Virology, Sendai, Japan, 1984; mem. internat. sci. com. Internat. Meeting on Adv. in Virology, Catania, Italy, 1984-85; mem. adv. bd. Cancer Info., Dissemination and Analysis Ctr. Carcinogenesis and Cancer Biology, 1984—; mem. internat. programme com. 7th Internat. Congress of Virology, Edmonton, Can., 1985-87; councilor div. DNA viruses Am. Soc. Microbiology, 1985-87; mem. adv. com. research on etiology, diagnosis, natural history, prevention and therapy of multiple sclerosis Nat. Multiple Sclerosis Soc., 1985—; mem. sci. adv. bd. Showa U. Research Inst. for Biomedicine in Fla., 1985—. Sect. editor on oncology: Intervirology, 1972-84, assoc. editor, 1978-84, editor-in-chief, 1985—; adv. bd.: Archives Virology, 1976-81; editorial bd. Jour. Immunology, 1966-73, Jour. Virology, 1968—; assoc. editor Cancer Research 1972-79. Recipient 1st CIBA-Geigy Drew award for biomed. research, 1977. Mem. Am. Soc. Microbiology (mem. com. med. microbiology and immunology, bd. pub. scientific affairs, 1979—, chmn. DNA viruses div. 1981-82), Am. Soc. Virology (chmn. fin. com. 1987-88). Home: 2 Laurel Ridge Rd Hershey PA 17033

RAPP, GERALD DUANE, lawyer, manufacturing company executive; b. Berwyn, Nebr., July 19, 1933; s. Kenneth P. and Mildred (Price) R.; m. Jane Carol Thomas, Aug. 14, 1954; children—Gerald Duane Jr., Gregory T., Amy Frances. B.S., U. Mo., 1955; J.D., U. Mich., 1958. Bar: Ohio bar 1959. Practice in Dayton, 1960—; partner Smith & Schnacke, 1963-70; asst. gen. counsel Mead Corp., 1970, v.p. human resources and legal affairs, 1973, v.p., corp. sec., 1975, v.p., gen. counsel, corp. sec., 1976, v.p., gen. counsel, 1979, sr. v.p., gen. counsel, 1981—; chmn. Mead Data Cen., Inc., 1971-73. Sr. editor: U. Mich. Law Review, 1957-58. Past chmn. Oakwood Youth Commn.; past v.p., bd. dirs. Big Bros. Greater Dayton; mem. president's visitors com. U. Mich. Law Sch.; past trustee Urbana Coll.; trustee Ctr. Internat. Mgmt. Studies, Internat. YMCA, Ohio Ctr. Leadership Studies, Robert K. Greenleaf Ctr., Newton Ctr., Mass., Dayton and Montgomery County Pub. Library; mem. bd. visitors Law Sch., U. Dayton; bd. dirs. Miami Valley Regional Small Bus. Incubator, Yellow Springs, Ohio. Served to 1st lt. U.S. Army, 1958-60. Mem. ABA, Ohio Bar Assn., Dayton Bar Assn., Phi Kappa Psi, Phi Delta Phi, Beta Gamma Sigma. Presbyterian. Clubs: Rod and Reel, Moraine Country, Dayton Racquet, Dayton Bicycle, Dayton Lawyers, Ye Buz Fuz; Met. (Washington). Office: Mead Corp Courthouse Plaza NE Dayton OH 45463

RAPP, ROBERT DAVID, lawyer; b. N.Y.C., Mar. 19, 1950; s. Melville Benjamin and Rachel (Marx) R. BA in Econs., U. Tenn., 1973; JD, Antioch U., 1982. Bar: Tex. 1982, U.S. Dist. Ct. (so. dist.) Tex. 1983, U.S. Ct. Appeals (5th cir.) 1983, U.S. Supreme Ct. 1985. Law clk. to presiding judge U.S. Dist. Ct. (so. dist.) Tex., Houston, 1982-83; ptnr. Mandell & Wright, Houston, 1983—; instr. continuing legal edn. Bates Coll. Law, U. Houston, 1986-87. Contbr. articles to law revs. and profl. jours. Mem. ABA, Fed. Bar Assn. (bd. dirs. Houston chpt. 1985-87), Fed. Bar Assn. (lectr. Houston chpt. 1987), Assn. Trial Lawyers Am., Tex. Trial Lawyers Assn., Houston Trial Lawyers Assn. Home: 2634 Yorktown #367 Houston TX 77056 Office: Mandell & Wright 712 Main Suite 1600 Houston TX 77002

RAPPAPORT, YVONNE KINDINGER, educator, lectr.; b. Crestline, Ohio, Feb. 15, 1928; d. Paul Theodore and Florence Iona (Cover) Kindinger; B.S. summa cum laude, Northwestern U., 1949; M.A., Va. Poly. Inst. and State U., 1973, Ph.D., 1980; m. Norman Lewis Rappaport; children—Michael, Laura, Hilary, Stephen, Jocelyn. Personnel officer, then cons. and mgmt. analyst USAF, 1953-63; cons. mgmt. analysis, personnel and public relations, 1963-67; cons. program devel., instr. U. Va., 1967-70, dir. continuing edn. for women, 1970-75, dir. and faculty continuing edn. for adult, 1975—; dir., performer theatre, children's theatre, radio and TV, 1953—; bd. dirs. Coalition Adult Edn. Orgns. U.S., 1979—, sec.-treas., 1981-83, v.p., 1983-84, pres.-elect, 1984-85, pres., 1985-87; U.S. rep. UNESCO conf., 1983; del. Buenos Aires World Assembly, 1985, Helsinki Peace Conf., 1986; cons. in field. Mem. Va. Legis. Adv. Com. Continuing Edn., 1970-71, No. Va. Adv. Com. Ednl. Telecommunications, 1971—; bd. dirs. Home and Sch. Inst., Washington, 1971—; adv. bd. Service League Va., 1976-78. Recipient Meritorious Service award USAF, 1959; Career Devel. award ASTD/TOC, 1980. Mem. Nat. Assn. Women Deans, Adminstrs. and Counselors (S.E. regional coordinator 1973-76), adult edn. assns. U.S. (Nat. Leadership award 1973, 74, 76, 78, 79, 82, 83, 86; v.p. 1978-79; chmn. commn. status women in edn. 1972-74, dir. 1973-83, chmn. council affiliate orgns. 1974-75, chmn. pub. affairs 1975-78, chair program gen. session 1987), Va. (pres. 1971-73; Recognition of Merit award 1971-73), LWV (state dir. 1968-73, nat. public relations com. 1970-75), AAUW, PTA, Am. Personnel and Guidance Assn., Nat. Univ. Extension Assn., Assn. Continuing Higher Edn., World Affairs Council (bd. dirs. 1987—), Am. Bus. Women Assn. (award 1960), Fairfax, Va. C. of C. (mem. edn. com. 1987—), Phi Delta Kappa. Club; Order Eastern Star. Author handbooks and work books, also radio, TV scripts. Home: 3225 Atlanta St Fairfax VA 22030 Office: Sch Continuing Edn Univ Va Charlottesville VA 22903

RAPPAPORT, ZVI HARRY, neurosurgeon; b. Munich, Fed. Rep. Germany, June 25, 1949; arrived in Israel, 1980; s. Aron and Sarah (Silberberg) R.; m. Isabelle Klein, Dec. 19, 1978; children: Yael, Maya, Ron. BA, Columbia Coll., 1969; MD, U. Pa., 1973. Diplomate Am. Bd. Neurol. Surgery. Surg. resident Columbia-Presbyn. Med. Ctr., N.Y., 1973-74; resident in neurosurgery NYU Med. Ctr., 1974-78; fellow in physiol. neurosurgery Westchester County Med. Ctr., Valhalla, N.Y., 1979; sr. neurosurgeon Sheba Med. Ctr., Tel Hashomer, Israel, 1980-83, Hadassah U. Med. Ctr., Jerusalem, 1983—; asst. prof. neurosurgery NYU Med. Sch., 1978-79; sr. lectr. in neurosurgery Hebrew U., Jerusalem, 1985—. Contbr. articles to profl. jours. Served as med. officer Israel Def. Forces, 1985—. Recipient research prize Am. Heart Assn., 1970. Mem. Israel Surg. Soc. Governing Body, Israel Neurosurg. Soc. (sec. 1985-87), World Fedn. Neurosurgery (del. 1985-87), Am. Assn. Neurosurgery (1983—), Congress of Neurol. Surgery, Internat. Assn. for Study of Pain. Jewish. Office: Hadassah U Hosp, Dept of Neurosurgery, Jerusalem 91120, Israel

RAPPARD, JAN FREDERIK HENDRIK VAN, historian, educator; b. Haarlem, The Netherlands, Mar. 15, 1941; s. Willem Arthur and Johanna Elisabeth (Fabius)van R.; married, June 20, 1969; children: Diederik Martijn, Steven Jakob. MA in Clin. Psychology, Free U., Amsterdam, 1969; PhD cum laude, Free U., 1976. With Free U., Amsterdam, 1970—, full prof. history, systems of psychology, 1986—. Author: Psychology as Self-Knowledge: The Development of the Concept of the Mind in German Rationalistic Psychology and Its Relevance Today, 1979; co-author numerous other works in field. Served to 1st lt. The Netherlands Navy, 1961-62. Mem. Internat. Soc. Theoretical Psychology (co-founder 1985, pres. 1987—), Cheiron-Europe (founding pres. 1982-87), Cheiron-N.Am., Am. Psychol. Assn. (fgn. affilate divs. 24 & 26). Office: Free U Dept Psychology, De Boelelaan IIII, 1081 HV Amsterdam The Netherlands

RAPPORT, ROBERT, diagnostic radiologist; b. Havana, Cuba, Sept. 23, 1953; came to U.S., 1961; s. Morris and Suzy (Pearl) R. B.S., U. Fla., 1974; M.D., U. Miami, 1978. Diplomate Nat. Bd. Med. Examiners, Am. Bd. Radiology. Clin. assoc. U. So. Fla. Coll. Medicine, Tampa, 1978-82, chief resident in diagnostic radiology, 1981-82. Mem. Radiol. Soc. N.Am., N.Y. Acad. Scis., AAAS, W. Coast Fla. Radiol. Soc., Fla. Med. Assn., Hillsborough County Med. Assn., Internat. Platform Assn. Jewish. Research in ophthalmoplegia due to spontaneous thrombosis in a patient with bilateral cavernous carotid aneurysms. Home: 3132 W Lambright Ave Unit 906 Tampa FL 33614 Office: Centro Español Hosp Dept Radiology Tampa FL 33614

RASAPUTRA, WARNASENA, banker; b. Matara, Sri Lanka, Sept. 6, 1927; s. Don Nicholas and Jane (Ratnayake) R.; m. Jayanthi Sriya (dec.); 1 child, Jaliya Gajaba; m. Seeta Gopalan, Oct. 28, 1977. BA in Econs. with honors, U. Ceylon, 1950; MA in Econs., U. Wis., 1957, PhD in Econs., 1959. Advisor dept. nat. planning Govt. Sri Lanka, Colombo, 1960-62; dir. econ. research Cen. Bank Sri Lanka, Colombo, 1968-74, asst. to gov., 1974-75, dep. gov., 1975-79, gov., 1979—; alt. exec. dir. for India, Sri Lanka and Bangladesh Internat. Monetary Fund, Washington, 1976-79. Contbr. articles and papers to profl. publs. Fellow Internat. Banker Assn., Soc. for Internat. Devel. (pres. Sri Lanka chpt. 1979—), Sri Lanka Economists Assn. (pres.). Avocations: books, travel, photography. Home: 206 Bauddhaloka Mawatha, Colombo 7 Sri Lanka Office: Cen Bank of Sri Lanka, Janadhipathi Mawatha, Colombo 1 Sri Lanka

RASCH, RUDOLF ALEXANDER, musicologist; b. Borger, Drente, The Netherlands, Dec. 15, 1945; m. Hanneke Provily, June 24, 1981. D of Social Scis., U. Groningen, The Netherlands, 1981; PhD in Musicology, U. Utrecht, The Netherlands, 1985. Research asst. Inst. for Perception, Soesterberg, The Netherlands, 1975-78; lectr. U. Utrecht, 1977—; pub. Diapason Press, Utrecht, 1983—; sec. Huygens-Fokker Found., Haarlem, The Netherlands, 1986—. Author: De Cantiones Natalitiae, 1985; editor: (music edit.) Uitnement Kabinet, 1973-78, Modern Edits. of Early Music, Facsimile Reprints on Musical Tuning and Temperament. Mem. Soc. Dutch Music History (sec. 1981-86), Am. Musicological Soc., Acoustical Soc. Am., Internat. Musicological Soc. Home: Graafschap 27, 3524 TL Utrecht The Netherlands Office: U Utrecht, Kromme Nieuwe Gracht 29, 3512 HD Utrecht The Netherlands

RASE, BEVERLY WILLS BONELLI, school administrator, civic worker; b. Ft. Worth, Mar. 14, 1928; d. Louis Benedict and Venne Armstrong (Wills) Bonelli; m. Howard Frederick Rase, June 12, 1954; children—Carolyn Victoria, Howard Frederick. B.A., Wellesley Coll., 1950. Vol., Ft. Worth Art Assn., 1949; editor West Side Post, Ft. Worth, 1951-53; vol. Ft. Worth Children's Mus., 1952-54; organizer Ft. Worth Wellesley Club, 1954; founding co-chmn. Wellesley Children's Art Show, Austin, Tex., 1955; v.p. U. Tex. Univ. Ladies Club Newcomers, Austin, 1955-56; charter mem. Laguna Gloria Art Guild, Austin, 1955-60; v.p. Laguna Gloria Art Mus., Austin, 1960; pres. Austin Wellesley Club, 1961; founder Eastern Coll. Parents Com., Austin, 1961; pres. Tex. Fine Arts Assn., Austin, 1963-64; dir. Wellesley Fund, Tex. and La., 1964-67; leader Camp Fire Girls of Good Shepherd, 1968-71; area program chmn. Balcones council Camp Fire Girls, Austin, 1969-72; founder, pres. Elisabeth Ney Mus. Guild, 1969; pres. Casis Elem. Sch. PTA, Austin, 1970-71; mem. Altar Guild Episcopal Ch. of Good Shepherd, 1971-73; founder, dir., chmn. bd. trustees Kirby Hall Sch., Austin, 1976—; mem. Symphony League of Austin. Recipient appreciation award Tex. Fine Arts Assn., 1969, Camp Fire Leader award, 1971, Order of the Unicorn appreciation award Kirby Hall Sch., 1979. Mem. Delta Delta Delta. Republican. Author: Tales of a Texas Grandfather, 1957, student and faculty handbooks. Home and Office: 3700 River Rd Austin TX 78703

RASHIDI, ASHFAQ ALI, sales executive; b. Delhi, India, Feb. 22, 1941; arrived in Eng., 1961; s. Abul Hasan and Mohamed (Nisa) R.; m. Cecilia Azzopardi, June 12, 1967; children: Lara, Yasmin. B.Sc., Karachi (Pakistan) U., 1960. Cert. air conditioning engr. Project engr. Univ. Aircool, Ltd., London, 1964-66; tech. controller Hitachi Internat., Ltd., Malta, 1966-67; tech. mgr. Daikin Air Conditioning Corp., Ltd., Malta, 1967-73; sales mgr. Daikin Europe N.V., Ostend, Belgium, 1973-78, asst. dir. sales, 1978-80, dir. sales, 1980—. Mem. Chartered Inst. Bldg. Services, Inst. Refrigeration U.K. Home: Oostende Baan-86, 8240 Gistel Belgium Office: Daikin Europe NV, Zandvoorde Straat-300, 8400 Oostende Belgium

RASHKES, MOSHE, writer; b. Bialystok, Poland, June 16, 1928; s. Arieh Leib and Golda (Haas) R.; grad. Montefiore Coll. Tech., Tel Aviv, 1951; m. Rachel Haimowitch, Nov. 26, 1972; children: Arieh, Gideon. Chmn. War Disabled Vets Orgn., 1950-58; Israel del. Gen. Assemblies of World Vets. Fedn., 1951-58; dir. Ilan Sport Centre for Physically Disabled, Ramat Gan, 1965—. Author: Days of Lead, 1962; Night Hunts Nights, 1966; Collapse, 1975; also plays. Founder, editor War Veteran, 1952. Del., Internat. Writers Guild, Moscow, 1969. Served to lt. Israeli Def. Forces, 1948. Recipient Citation of Valour, 1948. Mem. Internat. Writers Guild (cinema and TV sect., Israeli del. to founding assembly 1966), Israel Screen Play Writers Guild (bd. dirs.), Israel Sports Assn. for Disabled (bd. dirs.). Home: 1 Mizpe Yam St, Hertzliya Israel Office: 123 Rokach St, Ramat Gan Israel

RASHKIND, PAUL MICHAEL, lawyer; b. Jamaica, N.Y., May 21, 1950; s. Murray and Norma (Dorfman) Weinstein; m. Robin Shane, Dec. 20, 1975; children: Adam Charles, Noah Hamilton, Jennifer Elizabeth. AA, Miami-Dade Jr. Coll., 1970; BBA, U. Miami, Coral Gables Fla., 1972, JD, 1975. Bar: Fla. 1975, D.C. 1981, N.Y. 1981, U.S. Dist. Ct. (so. dist.) Fla. 1975, U.S. Ct. Appeals (5th cir.) 1976, U.S. Supreme Ct. 1978, U.S. Dist. Ct. (mid. dist.) Fla. 1979, U.S. Ct. Appeals (2d and 11th cirs.) 1981, U.S. Ct. Appeals (4th and 6th cirs.) 1986, U.S. Dist. Ct. (no. dist.) Fla. 1987; diplomate Nat. Bd. Trial Advocacy-Criminal Law. Asst. state atty. Dade County State Attys. Office, Miami, Fla., 1975-78, chief asst. state atty. in charge of appeals, 1977-78; atty. Sams, Gerstein & Ward, P.A., Miami, 1978-83; ptnr. Bailey, Gerstein, Rashkind & Dresnick, Miami, 1983—; spl. master Ct. Appointment, Miami, 1982-83; arbitrator Dade County Jail Inmates Grievance Program, Miami, 1981—; mem. Fla. Bar Unauthorized Practice of Law Com. C, 11th Jud. Cir., Miami, 1980-84. Contbr. articles on ethics and criminal law to profl. jours. Pres., bd. dirs. Lindgren Homeowners Assn., Miami, Fla., 1981-86. Fellow Am. Bd. Criminal Lawyers (bd. govs. 1980-86; mem. ABA (ethics com. criminal justice sect. 1979—, vice chmn. 1985-87, chmn. 1987—), Fla. Bar Assn. (comn. on Lawyer professionalism 1988—), N.Y. Bar Assn., D.C. Bar Assn., Dade County Bar Assn., Assn. Trial Lawyers Am., Acad. Fla. Trial Lawyers (chmn. criminal law sect. 1985-86, diplomate 1986—), Nat. Assn. Criminal Def. Lawyers, Soc. Bar and Gavel, Iron Arrow, Hon. Order Ky. Cols., Omicron Delta Kappa, Delta Sigma Rho-Tau Kappa Alpha, Pi Sigma Alpha, Phi Rho Pi, Delta Theta Phi. Democrat. Jewish. Office: Bailey Gerstein Rashkind & Dresnick 4770 Biscayne Blvd Suite 950 Miami FL 33137

RASMUSON, ELMER EDWIN, banker, former mayor Anchorage; b. Yakutat, Alaska, Feb. 15, 1909; s. Edward Anton and Jenny (Olson) R.; m. Lile Vivian Bernard, Oct. 27, 1939 (dec. 1960); children: Edward Bernard, Lile Muchmore (Mrs. John Gibbons, Jr.), Judy Ann; m. Col. Mary Louise Milligan, Nov. 4, 1961. B.S. magna cum laude, Harvard U., 1930, A.M., 1935; student, U. Grenoble, 1930; LL.D., U. Alaska, 1970. C.P.A., N.Y., Tex., Alaska. Chief accountant Nat. Investors Corp., N.Y.C., 1933-35; prin. Arthur Andersen & Co., N.Y.C., 1935-43; pres. Nat. Bank of Alaska, 1943-65, chmn. bd., 1966-74, chmn. exec. com., 1975-82, now dir.; mayor City of Anchorage, 1964-67; civilian aide from Alaska to sec. army 1959-67; Swedish consul Alaska, 1955-77; Chmn. Rasmuson Found.; Rep. nominee U.S. Senate from Alaska, 1968; U.S. commr. Internat. N. Pacific Fisheries Commn., 1969-84; mem. Nat. Marine Fisheries Adv. Com., 1974-77, North Pacific Fishery Mgmt. Council, 1976-77, U.S. Arctic Research Commn., 1984—. Mem. City Council Anchorage, 1945, chmn. city planning commn., 1950-53; pres. Alaska council Boy Scouts Am., 1953; sec.-treas. Loussac Found.; regent U. Alaska, 1950-69; trustee King's Lake Camp, Inc., 1944—, Alaska Permanent Fund Corp., 1980-82; bd. dirs. Coast Guard Acad. Found. Decorated knight first class Order of Vasa, comdr. Sweden; recipient silver Antelope award Boy Scouts Am.; outstanding civilian service medal U.S. Army; Alaskan of Year award, 1976. Mem. Pioneers Alaska, Alaska Bankers Assn. (past pres.), Defense Orientation Conf. Assn., NAACP, Alaska Native Brotherhood, Explorers Club, Phi Beta Kappa. Republican. Presbyn. Clubs: Masons, Elks, Anchorage Rotary (past pres.); Harvard (N.Y.C.; Boston); Wash. Athletic (Seattle), Seattle Yacht (Seattle), Rainier (Seattle); Thunderbird Country (Palm Desert, Calif.); Bohemian (San Francisco); Eldorado Country (Indian Wells, Calif.); Boone & Crockett. Address: PO Box 600 Anchorage AK 99510

RASMUSSEN, GORMAN LEONARD, social service administrator; b. Evanston, Ill., Nov. 27, 1931; s. Gorman and Julie (DuRack) R.; m. Lois Bumgarner, Dec. 27, 1958; children—Gorman Leonard, Anne Marie. A.B., Culver Stockton Coll., 1959; M.S.W., U. Mo., 1961. Registered social worker, Alta.; diplomate in clin. social work. Psychiat. social worker U. Mo. Med. Ctr., 1961-62, Grant County Guidance Ctr., Lancaster, Wis., 1962-64, Racine County Mental Health Clinic, Wis., 1964-65; project dir. Gateway House, Racine, 1965-66; dir. casework services Racine Family Service, 1965-68; supr. social worker, dir. dept. med. social work Kitchener-Waterloo Hosp., Ont., Can., 1968-73; field instr. Waterloo Luth. U., 1968-71, lectr. sociology, 1968-69; lectr. social work Conestoga Coll. Applied Arts and Scis., Kitchener, 1970-71; dir. profl. services Family Service of So. Lake County, Highland Park, Ill., 1973-74; dir. dept. social services, asst. prof. social work U. Ky. Coll. Medicine, 1974-76; dir. dept. social services M.D. Anderson Hosp. and Tumor Inst., Houston, 1976-82; mem. health curriculum adv. com. U. Houston, 1976-82; dir. dept. social work Alta. Children's Hosp., Calgary, Can., 1982—; exec. dir. West Iowa Community Mental Health Ctr., Denison, 1981—, mem. adv. council research and demonstration project Lexington-Fayette County Health Dept., 1974-76; treas. Lexington-Fayette County Human Services Council; mem. health task force Ky. State Council, 1975-76; mem. Mo. City Planning Commn., 1979-80; mem. service com. Houston div. Am. Cancer Soc., 1976-82; mem. health care specialization com. Grad. Sch. Social Work, U. Houston, 1979-82; mem. adv. bd. New Age Hospice, Houston, 1978-82; mem. Houston-Galveston Area Council, Area Health Commn., 1980-81; mem. social service adv. com. Mt. Royal Coll., 1984—; mem. Iowa Mental Health Ctr. Assn., Crawford County Pub. Health Adv. Com. (pres.). Nat. Social Work Oncology Group (planning com. nat. inst. 1979-81), Nat. Assn. Social Workers, Tex. Soc. Hosp. Social Work Dirs., Acad. Cert. Social Workers, Soc. Hosp. Social Work Dirs. Am. Hosp. Assn., Can. Assn. Social Work Adminstrs. in Health Facilities (chmn. health advocacy com.), Residential Service Soc. Calgary. Home: 4720 26th Ave, Calgary, AB Canada T3E 0R2 Office: West Iowa Community Mental Health Ctr 147 N 7th Denison IA 51442

RASMUSSEN, HANS EGON, marine company executive; b. Broager, Denmark, Apr. 21, 1977; s. Hans and Magrethe R.; m. Rita Paulsen, Mar. 12, 1977; children: Jeannette, Hans Henrik. BSc, U. Sonderborg, 1974. Sales engr. Sophus Berendsen A/S, Copenhagen, 1974-79, sales mgr., 1979-82; sales mgr. Sperry A/S, Copenhagen, 1982-84; mgr. for Scandinavia Sperry A/S, 1984-85; bd. dirs. Sperry Marine A/S, Copenhagen, 1985—; mng. dir. Sperry Marine GmbH, Hamburg, Fed. Republic Germany, 1986—, chmn. bd. dirs., 1987—; bd. dirs. Sperry Marine A/S, Oslo, Norway. Mem. Engring. Assn. Office: Sperry Marine A/S, Gladsaxe Mollevej 21, 2860 Soeborg Denmark

RASMUSSEN, JULIE SHIMMON, educator, cellist; b. Aberdeen, S.D., June 3, 1940; d. George Barr and Clara (Lange) Shimmon; m. Frederick Robert Rasmussen, Apr. 1, 1961 (div. May 1971). B.Music, Ind. U., 1963; M.Ed., U. Fla., 1967. Cert. tchr., Fla. Coordinator music Bradford County Sch. Bd., Starke, Fla., 1965-68; tchr. Duval County Sch. Bd., Jacksonville, Fla., 1968-69, community edn., 1972-79, program devel., 1979—; master tchr. Clay County Sch. Bd., Orange Park, Fla., 1969-72; facilitator, mem. planning com. Duval County Sch. Bd., Jacksonville, 1985-86. Grant writer in ednl. areas, 1979—. Com. mem. Jacksonville Community Council, Inc., 1973; cellist Jacksonville Symphony, 1963-65; tech. asst. Arts Assembly of Jacksonville, Inc., 1979-82; mem. Cummer Art Gallery, Jacksonville, 1983; bd. dirs. YWCA, 1986; active Resource Devel. Assistance Program Com. for Vol. Jacksonville, 1986. Recipient Little Red Schoolhouse award Fla. Dept. Edn., 1977-78, Sense of Community award Duval County Community Edn., 1979; Internat. String Congress grantee Musician's Union, 1961. Mem. Fla. Ednl. Research Assn., Pi Kappa Lambda, Phi Delta Kappa, Kappa Delta Pi (parliamentarian 1985-86). Democrat. Lutheran. Club: Pilot. Avocations: physical fitness; jogging; swimming; cycling; psychology. Home: 3946 St John's Ave Jacksonville FL 32205 Office: Duval County Sch Bd Adminstrn Bldg 1701 Prudential Dr Jacksonville FL 32207

RASMUSSEN, STUART RICARD, newspaper librarian; b. San Francisco, Nov. 7, 1906; s. Emil Jorgen and Christine (Johnsen) R.; student U. Calif. Extension; m. Nairn Margaret Abbott, June 1, 1940; children—Nairn Christine, Mark Abbott. In library San Francisco Examiner, 1929-37; head librarian San Francisco Call Bull., 1937-59, San Francisco News Call Bulletin, 1959-66; library staff San Francisco Examiner, 1966—, asst. head librarian, 1966-75, acting head librarian, 1975-78, engaged in spl. research for Metro-Goldwyn-Mayer movies, San Francisco Bay area, 1935-—; actor Maxwell Burke Stock Co., Oakland and Berkeley, Calif., 1927-28, Blake, Turner Stock Co., San Francisco area, 1928; dir. children and adult plays San Geronimo Valley Community Centers; sometimes dir. Ross Valley Players Barn Theatre. Pres. Lagunitas Dist. Sch. Bd., 1955-58, San Geronimo Valley Little League, 1961. Mem. Spl. Libraries Assn., Am. Newspaper Guild (charter mem. San Francisco/Oakland chpt.). Democrat. Club: San Francisco Press (life mem.). Author drama revs. for The Peninsulan, 1936; several plays for children, 1955-60. Home: Alta Rd Lagunitas CA 94938 Office: 110 5th St San Francisco CA 94118

RASMUSSEN, THOMAS VAL, JR., lawyer, small business owner; b. Salt Lake City, Aug. 11, 1954; s. Thomas Val and Georgia (Smedley) R.; m. Donita Gubler, Aug. 15, 1978; children: James, Katherine, Kristin. BA magna cum laude, U. Utah, 1978, JD, 1981. Bar: Utah 1981, U.S. Dist. Ct. Utah 1981, U.S. Supreme Ct. 1985. Atty. Salt Lake Legal Defender Assn., Salt Lake City, 1981-83, Utah Power and Light Co., Salt Lake City, 1983—; co-owner, developer Handi Self-Storage, Kaysville, Utah, 1984—; instr. bus. law Brigham Young U., Salt Lake City, 1988—. Adminstrv. editor Jour. Contemporary Law, 1980-81, Jour. Energy Law and Policy, 1980-81. Missionary Ch. of Jesus Christ of Latter-Day Sts., Brazil, 1973-75. Mem. ABA, Utah Bar Assn., Salt Lake County Bar Assn., Phi Eta Sigma, Phi Kappa Phi, Beta Gamma Sigma. Home: 7079 Pine Cone Circle Salt Lake City UT 84121 Office: Utah Power and Light Co 1407 W North Temple Suite 340 Salt Lake City UT 84140

RASOR, CHARLES LEWIS, JR., lawyer; b. Greenwood, S.C., Nov. 9, 1943; s. Charles Lewis Sr. and Mary Elspeth (Stewart) R.; m. Barbara Carlton Brothers, June 6, 1966; m. 2d, Marguerite Chapman Manning, Aug. 19, 1977; children: Charles Lewis III, Clark Stewart, Mary Claytor. Cert. specialist in estate planning and probate law. Student, U.S. Naval Acad., 1962-64; BA cum laude, Furman U., 1966; LLB, U. Va., 1969. Bar: S.C. 1969, U.S. Dist. Ct. S.C. 1969, U.S. Ct. Appeals (4th cir.) 1974. Assoc. Haynsworth, Perry, Bryant, Marion & Johnstone, Greenville, S.C., 1969-75, ptnr., 1975-87; sole practice, 1987—; mem. S.C. State Bar Specialization Adv. Bd. Estate Planning and Probate through 1986; chmn. Greenville Adv. Bd. United Savs. and Loan Assn. Chmn. Meals on Wheels for Sr. Citizens, Inc., Greenville, 1980-82; mem. deferred gifts steering com. Furman U.; mem. planned gifts com. St. Francis Hosp.; bd. dirs. Christ Ch. Endowment Corp. Served with USN, 1962-64. Fellow Am. Coll. Probate Counsel; mem. ABA, S.C. Bar Assn., Greenville County Bar Assn., Greenville Estate Planning Council. Republican. Episcopalian. Clubs: Poinsett, Cotillion (Greenville). Office: 2F Riverside Office Park 880 S Pleasantburg Dr Greenville SC 29607

RASOVSKY, YURI, radio drama producer, director, writer, actor, consultant; b. Chgo., July 29, 1944; s. Samuel Nathan and Clarice Norma (Diamond) Rasof; 1 child, Yuri Piotr Riidl; m. Ginny Boyle, Nov. 5, 1981 (annulled 1982). Mail boy Sta. WBKB-TV, Chgo., 1963-64; drama instr. Chgo. Park Dist., 1968-70; freelance editor, writer, cartoonist, actor, dir., 1969—; founding producer, dir. Nat. Radio Theatre, Chgo., 1973-86; panelist Nat. Endowment Arts, Washington, 1976, Ill. Arts. Council, Chgo., 1983, Chgo. Office Fine Arts, 1984-86, NEH, 1985; cons. Can. Broadcasting Corp., Toronto; spl. asst. to pres. Mus. Broadcast Communications, Chgo., 1987-88; exec. producer radio William Benton Broadcast Project, U. Chgo., 1988—. Author: (radio prodns.) The Amorous Adventures of Don Juan, Dateline 1787, Dracula, An Enemy of The People, Frankenstein, The Odyssey of Homer, A Tale of Two Cities, Three Tales of Edgar Allan Poe, The World of F. Scott Fitzgerald, numerous others, (books) The Publicity Survival Manual for Small Performing Arts Organizations, 1977, WKID, 1988; producer, actor in Magic Circle prodn. Green Julia, 1976 (3 Joseph Jefferson Citations); contbr. articles and revs. to Chicago mag., Stagebill mag., Chgo. Sun-Times, other publs. Served with U.S. Army, 1964-67. Recipient Major Armstrong award, 1975, 76, 79, Ohio State award, 1975, 77, 80, 83, 85, George Foster Peabody Broadcasting award, 1978, 81, Nat. Fedn. Community Broadcasters Program award, 1981, San Francisco State Broadcast Media award, 1982, 85, Grabriel award, 1983, Corp. Pub. Broadcasting Program award, 1983, 85.

RASPAIL, JEAN P. V., writer, diplomat; b. Chemillé, France, July 5, 1925; s. Octave Raspail and Marguerite Chaix; m. Aliette Penet, Feb. 29, 1951; children: Quentin, Marion. Author: Who Remembers Man (Chateaubriand prize 1986), The Lamp of the Saints, 1973, Le Jeu Dyroi, 1976, Septentrion, 1978, Le Roi de Patagonie, 1981, Les Hussard, 1983, Les Yeux D'Irene, 1984, Qui se Souvient des Hommes, 1986. Consul gen. to Patagonia. Home and Office: 32 Ave Matignon, 75008 Paris France

RAS ROMANI, KHALIL HASSAN, pediatric surgeon, medical educator; b. Manama, Bahrain, June 11, 1947; s. Ebrahim Hassan and Fathima (Hassan) Ras R.; m. Salwa al Mahroos, Feb. 12, 1974; 1 child, Amal. MD, Damascus U., Syria, 1972. Sr. house officer, registrar Royal Infirmary Edinburgh, Scotland, 1974-75; registrar Monkaland Hosp., Glasgow, Scotland, 1976-78; sr. registrar Royal Hosp. for Sick Children, Glasgow, 1979-80; chief pediatric surgeon Ministry of Health, Manama, 1980; asst. prof. Arabian Gulf U., Manama, 1986—; cons. Samanya M.C., Manama, 1981-86. Author articles in field. Fellow Royal Coll. Surgeons, Internat. Coll. Surgeons, Internat. Surg. Soc., Am. Soc. Oncology & Hematology, Am. Acad. Sci. Office: Ministry of Health, PO Box 20313, Manama Bahrain

RASSAM, HORMUZD YOUSUF, civil engineer; b. Mosul, Iraq, June 21, 1931; came to U.S., 1958; s. Yousuf Nimrud and Najma Towfiq (Bunney) R.; children—Najma Christine, Yousuf J. Hormuzd. Diploma in Civil Engring., Coll. Engring., Baghdad, Iraq, 1953; M.S.E., U. Mich., 1960; Ph.D., Colo. State U., 1969. Registered profl. engr., Calif., Colo., N.Mex.; registered land surveyor, Colo., N.Mex.; lic. gen. contractor, N.Mex. Civil engr. Iraq Petroleum Co., Iraq and U.K., 1953-58; mem. engring. faculty Ft. Lewis Coll., Durango, Colo., 1962-66; engring. cons., Durango, 1963-68; mem. faculty Colo. Sch. Mines, Golden, 1968-72; pres. TECH, Farmington, N.Mex., 1972—. Contbr. articles to profl. jours. Mem. panel of arbitrators Am. Arbitration Assn. Fellow ASCE; mem. Nat. Soc. Profl. Engrs., ASTM, Council Ednl. Facility Planners Internat., Am. Plannign Assn., Internat. Council for Ednl. Planning, Am. Concil Ind. Labs., Am. Soc. Engring. Edn., Sigma Xi, Chi Epsilon. Democrat. Chaldean Catholic. Lodge: Elks. Home: 1100 Zuni Dr Farmington NM 87401 Office: TECH 333 E Main St Farmington NM 87401

RASSIAS, THEMISTOCLES M., mathematician, educator; b. Pellana, Sparta, Greece, Apr. 2, 1951; s. Michael N. Rassias and Stamatiki Rassia; m. Efrosini-Ourania Contrarou, Dec. 19, 1981; children: Stamatina, Michael. Ph.D., U. Calif.-Berkeley, 1976. Postdoctoral research fellow, dept. math. U. Calif., Berkeley, 1976-77; adj. prof. math. St. Mary's Coll., Minn., 1977-78; research assoc. dept. math. Harvard U., 1980; vis. research prof. math. MIT, 1980; research mathematician Nat. Research Found., Athens, Greece, 1980-83; adj. prof. math. U. LaVerne, Athens, 1983—, chmn. dept. math., 1983—; vis. prof. Inst. Mathematical Physics, U. Torino, Italy, 1988; invited speaker internat. confs. Editor: (with G.M. Rassias) Selected Studies: Physics-Astrophysics, Mathematics, History of Science, 1982; Global Analysis--Analysis on Manifolds, 1983; (with G.M. Rassias) Differential Geometry--Calculus of Variations and their Applications, 1985; Nonlinear Analysis, 1987; Understranding Mathematical Analysis, 1989; editor-at-large Marcel Dekker, Inc., N.Y., 1986—; author: Foundations of Global Nonlinear Analysis, 1986; mem. editorial bd. Internat. Jour. Math. and Math. Scis., 1983—, Facta Universitatis Series: Mathematics and Informatics, 1988—, Jour. of Inst. Math. and Computer Scis. (Math. series), 1988—; reviewer Math. Revs., publ. Am. Math. Soc., Zentralblatt für Mathematik; Contbr. research papers to internat. math. jours. Served with Greek Army, 1978-80. NSF grantee, 1975-76. Mem. N.Y. Acad. Scis., Academia Tibernia of Rome, Am. Math. Soc., French Math. Soc., London Math. Soc., Greek Math. Soc., Australian Math. Soc., Polish Math. Soc. Greek Orthodox. Home: 4 Zagoras St, Paradissos, Amaroussion, 15125 Athens Greece Office: U Laverne, Dept Math, PO Box 51105, Kifissia, 14510 Athens Greece

RATAJCZAK, HENRYK, chemist, educator; b. Kadobno, Sept. 30, 1932; m. Halina Opryszka, 1972; 1 dau. Ed. Tech. U., Wroclaw, Poland, Wroclaw U., U. Wales, U. Salford, Sorbonne, Paris, Centre de Mecanique Ondulatoire Applique e, Paris; M.Sc., Ph.D., D.Sc. Asst. in phys. chemistry U. Wroclaw, 1956-59, sr. asst., 1959-63, adj., 1963-70, docent in chem. physics, 1970-74, extraordinary prof. chemistry, 1975—, head dept. theoretical chemistry and chem. physics, 1969-79, Rector, 1982-84; dep. dir. research Inst. Chemistry, 1970-79, dir., 1979-82; vis. prof. U. Salford, 1975-83, U. Paris, 1977-78. Author: Structural Studies of Some Hydrogen-bonded Ferroelectrics, 1969; Diple Moments of Hydrogen-bonded Complexes and Proton Transfer Effect, 1969; On the Nature of Electron Donor Acceptor Interactions. 1972; Charge Transfer Properties of the Hydrogen Bond, 1972, 73, CNDO/2 Molecular Orbital Calculation of the Dewar Structure of Benzene, 1972, of Pyridine, 1974, of Pyrazine, Pyrimidyne and Pyridazine, 1975; Charge Transfer Theory of Hydrogen Bonds: Relation Between Vibrational Spectra and Energy of Hydrogen Bonds, 1976; Studies on the Lithium Bond, 1976; SCF ab initio Calculations on the Lithium Fluoride-ethylene Complex, 1977; Vibrational Polarized Spectra of Strongly Hydrogen-bonded Systems, 1977; Influence of a.c. Electric Field on IR Spectra of Some Nematic Liquid Crystals with Postive and Negative Dielectric Anisotropy, 1978; Molecular Orbital Calculations for the Glicine and HCI Crystals, 1979; On Some Problems of Molecular Interactions, 1980; Crystal structure of rubidium hydrogen bisdibromoacetate, 1980; Infra-red studies of complexes between carboxylic acids and tertiary amines in argon matrices, 1980; On the non-additivity of the SCF interaction energy in the complex (LiH), 1980; SCF ab initio study of the lithium bonded complexes, 1980; Properities of strong hydrogen-bonded systems, 1980; 13C chemical shifts of phenol derivatives: correlations with electronic structures, 1980; contbr. numerous articles on theory, properties, structure and dynamics of molecular systems to profl. publs.; editor: (with W. J. Orville-Thomas) Molecular Interactions, vols. 1 and 2, 1980; editor for Eastern Europe, Jour. Molecular Structure, Advances in Molecular Relaxation and Interaction Processes; editorial mem. adv. bd. Chem. Physics Letters, 1977—. Decorated knight's cross Order Polonia Restituta; recipient Marie Sklodowska-Curie prize, 1976, Higher Edn. and Tech. prize for research Ministry Sci., 1970, 73, 78. Mem. Polish Acad. Scis. (sci. sec. spectroscopy com. 1969—, dep. chmn. 1979—, corr. mem. 1976—). Office: Wroclaw Univ, Inst Chemistry, ul Joliot-Curie 14, 50-383 Wroclaw Poland *

RATCLIFF, BRUCE EPHLIN, hoist company executive; b. Canton, Ill., Oct. 3, 1941; s. Ralph Anderson and Margaret Hallie (Buck) R.; student Coll. San Mateo, 1960-62, U. Ariz., 1962, U. Calif. at Santa Barbara, 1965; B.A. in Econs., San Francisco State U., 1967. Vice pres. sales Ratcliff Hoist Co., Belmont, Calif., 1967-69, exec. v.p., 1969-75, pres., chief operating officer, 1975—, also dir.; pres., chief exec. officer Ratcliff Co., 1977—. Club: San Francisco Bachelors. Home: 1308 Sunnyslope Belmont CA 94002 Office: 1655 Old County Rd San Carlos CA 94070

RATCLIFFE, PETER JOHN, nephrologist; b. Morecambe, Lancashire, Eng., May 14, 1954; s. William and Alice Margaret (Bibby) R.; m. Fiona Mary MacDougall, Feb. 19, 1983; 1 child, Anna Mary. MA, U. Cambridge, Eng., 1976, MB in Surgery with distinction, 1978, MD, 1986. House officer St. Bartolomew's Hosp., London, 1978-79; sr. house officer Hammersmith Hosp., Brompton Hosp., Nat. Hosp. Nervous Diseases, London, 1979-81; med. registrar Nuffield Dept. Medicine Oxford Hosps., Eng., 1981-83; med. research council fellow Nuffield Dept. Medicine Oxford Hosps., 1983-87; nephrologist, lectr. Nuffield Dept. Medicine John Radcliffe Hosp., Oxford, 1987—. Mem. Royal Coll. Physicians, Renal Assn. Home: Sumnor House 108 Mill St, Kidlington, Oxford England Office: John Radcliffe Hosp. Nuffield Dept Medicine, Oxford England

RATH, FRANCIS STEVEN, lawyer; b. N.Y.C., Oct. 10, 1955; s. Steven and Elizabeth (Chorin) R.; m. Denise Stephania Thompson, Aug. 2, 1980. BA cum laude, Wesleyan U., Middletown, Conn., 1977; JD cum laude, Georgetown U., 1980. Bar: D.C. 1980, U.S. Dist. Ct. D.C. 1981, U.S. Ct. Appeals (D.C. cir.), 1981, U.S. Supreme Ct. 1987, Va. 1988. Atty., advisor Comptroller of the Currency, Washington, 1980-84; assoc. Verner, Liipfert, Bernhard, McPherson & Hand, Washington, 1984-85; founding ptnr. Wolf, Arnold & Monroig, Washington, 1986-88; with Burnham, Connolly, Oesterly & Henry (continuation of practice of Wolf, Arnold & Monroig), Washington, 1988—. Editor: Law and Policy in Internat. Bus. 1979-80. Trustee Dunn Loring (Va.) Vol. Fire Dept., 1986. Mem. ABA, D.C. Bar Assn., Va. Bar Assn. Home: Grey Fox Farm 1051 Kelso Rd Great Falls VA 22066 Office: Burnham Connolly Oesterly and Henry 3050 K St NW Suite 330 Washington DC 20007

RATH, PATRICIA MINK, author, educator; b. Chgo.; d. Dwight L. and Margaret (Strom) Mink; A.B., Oberlin Coll.; M.S. in Merchandising, Simmons Coll.; postgrad. U. Ill., Northwestern U.; m. Philip A. Balsamo Jr., Jan. 13, 1988; 1 son, Eric Clemence. Instr. fashion merchandising Internat. Acad. Merchandising and Design, Ltd., Chgo., 1982—; lecturer fashion merchandising, Chgo. city-wide colls. Bd. dirs. Ill. Found. for Distbv. Edn., Inc. Mem. Am. Mktg. Assn., LWV, Am. Vocat. Assn., Chgo. Council Fgn. Relations. Author: (with Ralph E. Mason) Marketing and Distribution, 1968, 74; (with Mason and Herbert L. Ross) Marketing Practices and Principles, 3d edit., 1980; (with Mason and Stuart Hustead), 4th edit., 1986. Address: 1037 Cherry St Winnetka IL 60093

RATH, R. JOHN, historian, educator; b. St. Francis, Kans., Dec. 12, 1910; s. John and Barbara (Schauer) R.; m. Isabel Jones, June 26, 1937; children: Laurens John (dec.), Donald (dec.), Isabel Ferguson. A.B., U. Kans., 1932; A.M., U. Calif., Berkeley, 1934; Ph.D., Columbia U., 1941. Instr. history U. Ark., 1936-37, summer vis. prof., 1947; pre-doctoral field fellow Social Sci. Research Council in Austria and Italy, 1937-38; head dept. history and polit. sci. Lindenwood Coll., St. Charles, Mo., 1939- 41; assoc. prof. history Miss. State Coll. for Women, 1941-43; chief bur. documentary evidence UNRRA Bur. Documents and Tracing, U.S. Zone of Ger., 1945-46; asst. prof. history U. Ga., 1946-47; assoc. prof. history, assoc. editor Jour. Central European Affairs, U. Colo., 1947-51, vis. prof., summer 1958; prof. history U. Tex., Austin, 1951-63; prof. history, chmn. dept. history and polit. sci. Rice U., 1963-68, Mary Gibbs Jones prof., 1968-80, prof. emeritus, 1980—; prof. history U. Minn., Mpls., 1980-85; vis. prof. U. Wis., 1955, Duke U., 1963; Guggenheim fellow in Italy, 1956-57; mem. hist. commn. Theodor Körner Found., also Leopold Kunshak prize, Vienna, 1971—. Author: The Fall of the Napoleonic Kingdom of Italy, 1941, The Viennese Revolution of 1948, 1957, L'amministrazione austriaca nel Lombardo Veneto, 1814-21, 1959, The Austrian Provisional Regime in Lombardy Venetia, 1969; contbg. author: East Central Europe and the World (edited Stephen Kertesz), 1962; also Ency. Americana; editor: Austrian History Newsletter, 1960-63, Austrian History Yearbook, 1965-82; contbr.: Die Aufloesung des Habsburgerreiches, 1970, Native Fascism in the Successor States, 1971, Beitraege zur Zeitgeschichte, 1976, The Austrian Socialist Experiment, 1985. Mem. Twin Cities Com. Fgn. Relations. Served in AUS, 1943-45. Recipient 1st class Austrian Cross of Honor in arts and scis., 1963. Mem. Am. Hist. Soc. (com. internat. activities 1960-66, exec. com. modern European history sect. 1963-66), So. Hist. Soc. (chmn. European sect. 1961-62, mem. exec. council 1965-68), Soc. Italian Hist. Studies (Sr. Scholar Citation, 1984), Conf. Central European History (mem. nat. exec. bd. 1959-61, vice chmn. 1969, chmn. 1970, mem. com. on Austrian history 1957-68, 70-81, exec. sec. 1957-68), Am. Assn. Study of Hungarian History (chmn. 1978), Southwestern Social Sci. Assn. (pres. 1976-77), Austrian Acad. Sci. (corr.), Deputazione di Storia Patria per le Venezie (corr.), Phi Beta Kappa. Home: 6009 Columbus Ave S Minneapolis MN 55417

RATHBONE, DONALD EARL, college dean; b. Havre, Mont., Jan. 22, 1929; s. Fay Arthur and Cora B. (Dolven) R.; m. L. Lynne Jordan, Apr. 16, 1966; 1 dau., Lynda Sue. Student, No. Mont. Coll., Havre, 1946-48; B.S., Purdue U., 1951; M.S., Northwestern U., 1955; Ph.D., U. Pitts., 1962. Asst. prof. elec. engring. U. Pitts., 1955-57, 60-62, lectr., 1957-60, assoc. prof., 1962-68; engr. Westinghouse Electric Corp., Pitts., 1957-60; cons. Westinghouse Electric Corp., 1960-61, Nat. Acad. Sci., 1962-68; prof., chmn. dept. elec. engring. U. Idaho, Moscow, 1968-73; dean engring. Kans. State U., Manhattan, 1973—. Mem. City of Manhattan Community Devel. Com., 1975—; chmn. bd. Kans. Entrepreneurial Ctr., 1988—. Recipient Disting. Alumnus award U. Pitts., 1976. Mem. Manhattan C. of C. (dir. 1975-78, 84-87), Kans. Engring. Soc. (chmn. legislature 1981-85), Nat. Assn. State Univ. and Land Grant Colls. (vice chmn. engring. 1981-84), IEEE, Am. Soc. Engring. Edn. (dir. engring. deans council 1980-83), Mid.-Am. State Univs. Assn. (exec. com. 1973-76), NSPE (nat. edn. adv. group 1985—, nat. chmn. profl. engrs. in edn. 1988—, North Cen. v.p. 1984-86, v.p., nat. v.p. 1988—), Golden Key (hon.), Sigma Xi, Tau Beta Pi, Eta Kappa Nu, Alpha Nu Sigma (hon.), Phi Kappa Phi. Presbyterian (elder). Lodge: Rotary (pres. 1981-82). Home: 2813 Brad Ln Manhattan KS 66502

RATHBONE, JOHN RANKIN (TIM), member of Parliament; b. London, Mar. 17, 1933; s. John Rankin Rathbone and Lady Beatrice (Clough) Wright; m. Margarita Sanchez y Sanchez, Sept. 3, 1960 (div. 1981); children: John Paul, Tina, Michael; m. Susan Jenkin coles, Apr. 15, 1982; stepchildren: Charles, Lucinda, Thomas. Degree in politics, philosophy and econs. with honors, U. Oxford, 1956; PMD, Harvard U., 1966. Researcher Robert Benson Lonsdale, London, 1956-58; from trainee to v.p. Ogilvy & Mather, N.Y.C., 1958-66; chief publicity and pub. relations officer Conservative Cen. Office, London, 1966-68; dir. Charles Barker, London, 1968-87; mem. of Parliament of Eng. Lewes, 1974—; parliamentary pvt. sec. Minister for Health, 1979-81, Minister for Consumer Affairs, 1982-83, Minister for Arts and Civil Service, 1985; chmn. adv. com. Inst. Mgmt. Resources, Calif. and London, 1987—; mem. Brit. del. to Council of Europe and We. European Union, 1987—. vice chmn. Anglo-Japanese Parliamentary Group, Ho. of Commons, London, 1986—; chmn. All-Party Franchise Group, Drug Misuse Group, 1987—, Ho. of Commons, 1987—, ; mem. Nat. Com. for Electoral Reform, 1978—, Conservative Group for Europe, 1974—; mem. Brit.-So. African Group, Brit.-Chinese Group, Brit.-Latin Am. Group, All Party Human Rights Group. Served with King's Royal Rifle Corps, 1951-53. Fellow Royal Soc. Arts Mfrs. and Commmerce (council 1983-88). Mem. Ch. of Eng. Clubs: Brook's, Pratts (London); Sussex (Brighton). Office: House of Commons, London SW1A 0AA, England

RATHBUN, JOHN WILBERT, American studies educator; b. Sioux City, Iowa, Oct. 24, 1924; s. Wilbert W. and Paulina Amanda (Baldes) R.; m. Mary Regina Walsh, Aug. 2, 1947 (div. Sept. 19, 1985); children: Mary Walsh, John Philip. Ph.B., Marquette U., Milw., 1951, M.A., 1952; Ph.D., U. Wis., 1956. Mem. faculty Calif. State U., Los Angeles, 1956—; prof. English/Am. studies Calif. State U., 1959—, chmn. dept. am. studies, 1969-75. Author: American Literary Criticism, 1800-1860, vol. 1, 1979, (with Harry Hayden Clark) American Literary Criticism, 1860-1905, vol. 2, 1979, Literature and Literary Analysis, 1983; (with Monica Grecu) American Literary Critics and Scholars, 1800-1850, 1987; contbr. articles to profl. jours. Served with AUS, 1943-46. Recipient Service citation Calif. State U., Los Angeles, 1977, Univ. Meritorious Achievement award, 1986; Fulbright fellow Romania, 1979-81. Mem. Am. Studies Assn. (council 1974), So. Calif. Am. Studies Assn. (pres. 1973), Coll. English Assn. So. Calif. (pres. 1966-67), MLA. Democrat. Office: 5151 State University Dr Los Angeles CA 90032

RATHKOLB, OLIVER ROBERT, historian; b. Vienna, Austria, Nov. 3, 1955; s. Otto Aurelius and Margarete (Novy) R.; m. Lydia Ruecklinger, Dec. 30, 1987. LDD, U. Vienna, 1978, PhD, 1982. Sci. researcher Inst. Contemporary History, Vienna, 1981-84; sci. asst. Ludwig Boltzmann Inst. Geschichte Gesellschaftswissenschaften, Vienna, 1984—; sci. dir. Bruno Kreisky Archives, Vienna, 1985—. Editor and author: Gesellschaft und Politik in der Zweiten Republik, 1985; co-editor:Der Junge Kreisky 1931-1945, Verdraengte Schuld-Verfehle Suehne Entnazifizierung in Osterreich 1945-1955, 1986, Die veruntreute Wohrheit Hitler's Propagandisten in Osterreich, 1938, 1988. Mem. Social Dem. Party. Roman Catholic. Office: Inst Zeitgeschichte, Rotenhausgasse 6, 1090 Vienna Austria

RATHLE, SELIM I., architect; b. Cairo, Egypt, Jan. 5, 1936; came to France, 1954; s. Ibrahim Selim Bey and Maria Camilla (Angelides) R.; m. Irene Gorodecki, July 8, 1959 (div. 1966); 1 child, Thomas; m. Catherine dePonton D'Amecourt, Sept. 8, 1966; children: Lionel, Julien. Baccalaureat, Coll. Des Peres Jesuites, Le Caire, Egypte, 1959; Diploma, Ecole Speciale d'Architecture, Paris, 1959; postgrad. Institut d'urbanisme, Université de Paris, 1959-60. Ptnr. Claude Balick Architecte, Paris, 1960-78; chmn. Rathle and Assocs., Paris, 1978—; dir. A2i Architecture et Infomatique Internationale, Paris, Design Systems Ltd., Lagos, Nigeria. Mem. Ordre des Architectes, Conseil Regional de Paris. Grec. Catholique. Clubs: The Travellers (Paris); Guezireh Sporting (Cairo). Home: 8 Rue D'Anjou, 75008 Paris France Office: Rathle and Assocs, 28 Ave Matignon, 75008 Paris France

RATHOD, MULCHAND SHAMJIBHAI, mechanical engineering educator; b. Pathri, India, Mar. 3, 1945, came to U.S., 1970, naturalized, 1981; s. Shamjibhai Laljibhai and Ramaben Rathod; m. Damayanti Thakor, Aug. 15, 1970; children—Prerana, Falgun, Sejal. B.S. in Mech. Engring., Sardar Patel U., India, 1970; M.S., Miss. State U., 1972; Ph.D., 1975. Research grad. asst. Miss. State U., 1970-75; cons. engr. Bowron & Butler, Jackson, Miss., 1975-76; asst. prof. Tuskegee Inst., Ala., 1976-78; tech. staff Jet Propulsion Lab., Pasadena, Calif., summers 1980, 81; summer faculty IBM Corp., Endicott, N.Y., 1982-85; assoc. prof., coordinator M.E.T. program SUNY, Binghamton, 1979-87; dir. engring. tech. div. Wayne State U., Detroit, 1987—; cons. Interpine, Hattiesburg, Miss., 1977-79, Jet Propulsion Lab., 1980-83, IBM Corp., 1982-85; pres. Shiv-Parvati, Inc. 1982— . Patentee in field. Contbr. article to profl. jour. Den leader Susquehanna council Boy Scouts Am., Vestal, N.Y., 1983-84. Grantee SUNY Found., 1984, IBM, 1984-85, Dept. Energy, 1978. Mem. Am. Soc. Engring. Edn. (reviewer), ASME (Cert. Appreciation 1982, 83, 84, 85, 86, 87, NASA award for Tech. Innovation, 1981), ASHRAE, N.Y. State Engring. Tech. Assn., India Assn. Miss. State U. (pres. 1972-73), Pi Tau Sigma. Home: 1042 Woods Ln Grosse Pointe Woods MI 48236 Office: Wayne State U Div Engring Tech Detroit MI 48202

RATI, ROBERT DEAN, data processing executive; b. Pittsburg, Kans., Jan. 8, 1939; s. Steve Julius Rati and Dorothy Bill (Rodebush) McWilliams; m. Margaret Fort Henry, June 7, 1969; children: Susan Margaret, Robert Henry. BA, U. Kans., 1961; MA, Northeastern U., Boston, 1970; MBA, Columbia U., 1973. Systems engr. IBM Corp., Boston, 1965-72; mgr. mgmt. services Arthur Young and Co., N.Y.C., 1973-75; mgr. client systems Touche Ross and Co., N.Y.C., 1975-76; mgr. systems and programs Walker Mfg. div. Tenneco, Racine, Wis., 1976-78; mgr. data processing Schwitzer div. Household Internat., Indpls., 1979—. Contbr. articles to fraternal orgs. newsletters. Mem. Rep. Com., Ramsey, N.J., 1972-74; treas. Rep. Club Ramsey, 1972-75; vice chmn. Swimming Pool Commn., Ramsey, 1972-74; bd. dirs., exec. com. Near Eastside Multi-Service Ctr., Indpls., 1984-87; fin. com. Carmel (Ind.) United Meth. Ch., 1984-87, adminstrv. bd., 1987—. Served to lt. (j.g.) USN, 1961-64. Recipient Regional Mgrs. award, IBM Corp., 1967. Mem. Soc. Ind. Pioneers (bd. govs. 1985—), Huguenot Soc. Ind. (pres. 1985—), S.R. (Ill. pres. 1980-82, chmn. awards com. 1983—), Pi Mu Epsilon. Republican. Home: 12923 Andover Dr Carmel IN 46032 Office: Schwitzer Household Internat 1125 Brookside Ave Indianapolis IN 46202

RATIU, ION, author; b. Turda, Romania, June 6, 1917; s. Augustin Stefan and Eugenia (Turcu) R.; LLB, U. Cluj, 1938; MA, St. John's Coll., Cambridge U., 1943; PhD in Polit. Sci. Internat. Free U., Birmingham, Miss., 1987; m. Elisabeth Pilkington, Sept. 22, 1945; children—Indrei, Nicolae. Chancellor Romanian Legation, London, 1940; program asst. BBC, London, 1949-56; dir. Free Romanian Press, London, 1956-86; dir. The Free Romanian monthly; freelance journalist, broadcaster, lectr. fgn. affairs. Mem. exec. com. Free Romanian Movement, 1940-45, East Central European Commn. of European Movement, 1960—. Served to 2d lt. Romanian Army, 1938-39. Mem. Internat. Fedn. Free Journalists (chmn. 1957-84; hon. pres. 1984—), Brit.-Romanian Assn. (pres. 1965-85, hon. pres. 1985—), World Union Free Romanians (pres. 1984—), PEN Internat., PEN in Exile, Fgn. Press Assn. Mem. Romanian Peasant Party. Mem. Greek Catholic Ch. Author: General Theory of Tort, 1936; Succession Ab Intestat, 1937; Policy for the West, 1957; Contemporary Romania, 1975; Cartea Memorandului, 1979; Moscow Challenges the World, 1986; co-author: (play) Templeton, 1958; contbr. articles to mags., newspapers. Home: Chalet Lani, Steinmatte, 3290 Zermatt Switzerland also: 308 E Liberty St Savannah GA 31401 Office: 54-62 Regent St, London W1R 5PJ, England

RATJEN, KARL GUSTAF, manufacturing company executive; b. Berlin, June 18, 1919; s. G.A. and Martha (Schnitzler) R.; student U. Munich, U. Bonn.; m. Annette Grafin Lambsdorff; children: Bjorn, Felix. Practice law, Munich, 1950-51; asst. to comml. mng. dir. Sachtleben AG, Cologne, 1951, mem. mgmt. bd., from 1954; mem. bd. Metallgesellschaft, Frankfurt, 1964, chmn. bd., 1974-84, mem. supervisory bd., 1984—; chmn. L'Union des Industries de la Communauté Européenne, 1986—; mem. adv. com. Dresdner Bank AG; mem. supervisory bd. Gutehoffnungshuette AG, Harpen AG, Industriekreditbank AG, Maizena GmbH; chmn. supervisory bd. Volkswagenwerk AG, Kuhnle Kopp & Kausch AG, Kolbenschmidt AG, Norddeutsche Affinerie; mem. adminstrn. Stadelsches Kunstinstitut, Frankfurt. Club: Rotary. Office: Metallgesellschaft AG, Reuterweg 14, 6000 Frankfurt Federal Republic of Germany *

RATLIFF, CECIL WAYNE, computer scientist; b. Ironton, Ohio, Dec. 10, 1946; s. Cecil and Bonnie Jean (Hensley) R.; m. Carolyn Jean Schmidt; 1 step-child, Kimberlee Sue Morse. Student, U. Colo., Boulder, 1964-68; BS, Met. State Coll., Denver, 1973. Sr. group engr. Martin Marietta Corp., Denver, 1969-82; pres. Ratliff Software Prodn., La Crescenta, Calif., 1977-88, Los Osos, Calif., 1988—; chief scientist Ashton-Tate, Culver City, Calif., 1983-86; hon. chief scientist Migent Inc., Incline Village, Nev., 1986—. Author: Computer Program, d Base II, 1981 (PC World Class winner 1984); prin. author: d Base III, 1984, Emerald Bay Database Management System, 1988. Served with U.S. Army, 1969-71. John Kenney Meml. scholar Internat. Chem. Works, 1964. Mem. ACM, IEEE. Republican. Office: Ratliff Software Prodn Inc Los Osos CA 93402

RATNASAMY, FREDDY, engineering and construction executive; b. Pondicherry, India, May 29, 1948; arrived in France, 1972; s. Arokiasamy and Honorine (Maguimey) R.; m. Fatima Christine Tambou, July 16, 1977; children: Frank Joshi, Fritz Minou. B Tech. in Chem. Engring., Madras U., India, 1970; GIO in Indsl. Engring., U. Paris Orsay, 1973. Supr. Anglo-French Textiles, Ltd., Pondicherry, 1971-72; project engr. Speichim, Bondy, France, 1974-75; thermal engr. Ce-Lummus, France and U.S., 1975-80; project mgr. Proser, Creteil, France, 1981-83; area mgr. C.G. Doris, Paris, 1984; mgr. Pecquet Tesson, Viroflay, France, 1985—; cons. Risk Engring., Paris, 1984-85. Contbr. articles to profl. jours. Roman Catholic. Home: 8 Rue Des Loriots, 77360 Vaires Sur Marne France Office: Pecquet Tesson, 183 Ave Du Gen Leclerc, 78220 Viroflay France

RATNER, HAROLD, pediatrician, educator; b. Bklyn., June 19, 1927; s. George and Bertha (Silverman) R.; BS, Coll. City N.Y., 1948; MD, Chgo. Med. Sch., 1952; m. Lillian Gross, Feb. 4, 1961; children—Sanford Miles, Marcia Ellen. Intern, Jewish Hosp., Med. Center Bklyn., 1952-53, resident in pediatrics, 1953-55; practice medicine specializing in pediatrics, Bklyn.; clin. instr. pediatrics SUNY Downstate Med. Center, N.Y.C., 1955-67, clin. asst. prof., 1967-69, clin. asso. prof., 1969-87; lectr. pediatrics, 1987—; chief of pediatrics Greenpoint Hosp., Bklyn., 1967-80, pres. med. staff, 1970-71, 74-80; dir. ambulatory services Woodhull Med. and Mental Health Center, Bklyn., 1980-83; clin. assoc. prof. pediatrics SUNY-Bklyn., 1983-87, lectr., 1987—; clin. assoc. prof. pediatrics, N.Y.U., 1987—; med. specialist Nathan Kline Inst. for Psychiat. Research, Orangeburg, N.Y., Rockland Psychiat. Ctr., Orangeburg, N.Y., 1986-88, unit chief, med. services , 1988—; mem. adv. council to pres. N.Y.C. Health and Hosp. Corp., 1970-71, 74-80, 81-83, sec., 1975, v.p., 1976-80; mem. med. bd., dir. Camp Sussex, camp for underprivileged children; bd. dirs. Kings County Health Care Rev. Orgn., Bklyn., 1976-84, past co-chmn. hosp. rev. com., continuing med. edn., med. care evaluation com. Trustee Village of Saddle Rock (N.Y.), 1980—. Served with AUS, 1945-47. Diplomate Nat. Bd. Med. Examiners, Am. Bd. Pediatrics. Fellow Am. Pediatric Soc., Bklyn. Pediatric Soc., Kings County Med. Soc., Royal Soc. Health; mem. AMA, Soc. Clin. and Exptl. Hypnosis, Am. Pub. Health Assn., Am. Soc. Clin. Hypnosis, N.Y. State, Kings County, Pan-Am. med. socs. Democrat. Jewish. Contbr. articles on pediatrics to med. jours. Home: 55 Bluebird Dr Great Neck NY 11023

RATNER, LILLIAN GROSS, psychiatrist; b. N.Y.C., Aug. 18, 1932; d. Herman and Sarah (Widelitz) Gross; B.A., Barnard Coll., 1953; postgrad. U. Lausanne (Switzerland), 1954-56; M.D., Duke U., 1959; m. Harold Ratner, Feb. 4, 1961; children—Sanford Miles, Marcia Ellen. Intern, Kings County Hosp., Bklyn., 1959-60, resident, 1967-70, fellow in child psychiatry, 1969-70, psychiatrist devel. evaluation clinic, 1970-72; resident Jewish Hosp. Bklyn., 1960-62, fellow in pediatric psychiatry, 1962-63; physician in charge pediatric psychiat. clinic Greenpoint (N.Y.) Hosp., 1964-67; pvt. practice psychiatry, Great Neck, N.Y., 1970—; clin. instr. psychiatry Downstate Med. Center, Bklyn., 1970-74, clin. asst. prof., 1974—; lectr. in psychiatry Columbia U., 1974—; psychiat. cons. N.Y.C. Bd. Edn., 1972-75, Queens Children's Hosp., 1975—; mem. med. bd. Camp Sussex (N.J.), 1963—, Saras Center, Great Neck, N.Y., 1977—. Diplomate Am. Bd. Pediatrics, Am. Bd. Psychiatry and Neurology, Am. Bd. Child Psychiatry. Fellow Am. Acad. Pediatrics, Am. Acad. Psychiatry, Am. Acad. Child Psychiatry; mem. Am., Nassau, Bklyn. psychiat. assns., Bklyn. (sr. mem.), Nassau pediatric socs., Soc. Adolescent Psychiatry, N.Y. Council Child Psychiatry, Soc. Clin. and Exptl. Hypnosis, Am. Med. Women's Assn. (pres. Nassau), AMA, N.Y., Kings County med. socs., Am. Soc. Clin. Hypnosis, N.Y. Soc. Clin. Hypnosis (pres.). Home and Office: 55 Bluebird Dr Great Neck NY 11023

RATSIRAKA, DIDIER, president of Democratic Madagascar; b. Vatomandry, Madagascar, Nov. 4, 1936; student Coll. St. Michel, Tananarive, Lycee Henri IV, Paris, Ecole Navale, Lanveoc-Poulimic (France), Ecole des Officiers Transmissions, Les Bormettes, Ecole Superieure de Guerre Navale, Paris. Holder several naval positions, 1963-70; mil. attache Madasgascar embassy, Paris, 1970-72; minister fgn. affairs, 1972-75; pres. Supreme Council Revolution, 1975—, prime minister and minister of def., 1975, pres. Democratic Republic Madagascar, 1976—. Sec.-gen. Arema; pres. Front Nat. pour la Def. de la Revolution, 1977—. Serves as adm. Navy. Address: Cabinet du President, Antananarivo Madagascar *

RATTLE, SIMON, symphony conductor; b. Liverpool, Eng., 1955; studied conducting and piano Royal Acad. Music. PhD (hon.) Birmingham U., 1985. At age 15 occasional percussion player Royal Liverpool Philharmonic Orch.; prin. condr., artistic adv. City of Birmingham Symphony Orch., 1980—; prin. guest condr. Los Angeles Philharm. Orch., 1981—, Rotterdam Philharm. Orch., 1981-84; prin. condr. London Choral Soc., 1979-84; assoc. condr. Royal Liverpool Philharmonic Orch., 1977-80, BBC Scottish Symphony Orch., 1977-80; artistic dir. South Bank Summer Music, 1981-83; asst. condr. Bournemouth Symphony Orch. and Bournemouth Sinfonietta, 1974-76; debut at Glyndebourne Festival Opera, 1977, appeared regularly since then. Recipient 1st prize John Player Internat. Condrs. Competition, 1974, Comdr. of the British Empire, 1987. Office: care Harold Holt Ltd, 31 Sinclair Rd, London W14 ONS, England also: care Pub Relations Office Capitol Records Inc 1370 Avenue of the Americas New York NY 10019

RATZ, ALEKSANDER, automobile company executive; b. Krakow, Poland, June 11, 1946; s. Martin and Emilia (Endler) R.; m. Teofila Trokki, June 6, 1970; children: Martin, Jacob, Benjamin. MSc, Chalmers U., 1971; MBA, U. Göteborg, Sweden, 1986. Home: Utlandagatan 25, 41261 Göteborg Sweden Office: Volvo Data AB, S-405 08 Göteborg Sweden

RATZINGER, JOSEPH ALOIS CARDINAL, archbishop, cardinal; b. Marktl, Germany, Apr. 16, 1927; s. Joseph and Maria (Peintner) R.; ed. U. Munich. Ordained priest Roman Catholic Ch.; chaplain, 1951; archbishop, 1977; cardinal, 1977; prof. theology U. Freising, 1951, U. Bonn, 1958, U. Munster, 1963, U. Tubingen, 1966, U. Regensburg, 1969; now archbishop of Munich-Freising, chmn. Bavarian Bishops Conf. Author books and articles. Office: Postfach 360, D-8000 Munchen 33 Federal Republic of Germany *

RAU, LEE ARTHUR, lawyer; b. Mpls., July 22, 1940; s. Arthur W. and Selma A. (Lund) R.; m. Janice R. Childress, June 27, 1964; children—Brendan D., Patrick C., Brian T. B.S.B., U. Minn., 1962; J.D., UCLA, 1965. Bar: Calif. 1966, U.S. Ct. Mil. Appeals 1966, U.S. Supreme Ct. 1971, D.C., 1972, U.S. Ct. Appeals (D.C. cir.) 1972, U.S. Dist. Ct. (D.C.) 1973, U.S. Ct. Appeals (3d cir.) 1975, U.S. Ct. Appeals (6th cir.) 1980, Va. 1986; U.S. Dist. Ct. (ea. dist.) Va. 1988, U.S. Ct. Appeals (4th cir.) 1988. Trial atty. evaluation sect. antitrust div. U.S. Dept. Justice, Washington, 1965-66, appellate sect., 1970-72; assoc. Reed Smith Shaw & McClay, Washington, 1972-74, ptnr., 1975—; mem. constl. and adminstrv. law adv. com. Nat. Chamber Litigation Ctr. Inc. Contbr. articles to profl. jours. Sec. bd. dirs. Reston Found., 1982—; bd. dirs. Reston Interfaith Inc., 1973, pres., 1984—, Greater Reston Arts Ctr.; mem. Washington Dulles Task Force, 1982—, United Way Social Needs com., 1986—, regional council; chmn. Reston Transp. Com. Served to capt. JAGC, U.S. Army, 1966-70. Decorated Commendation medal with oak leaf cluster. Mem. ABA (antitrust, adminstrv. law, corp. banking and bus. sic. and tech. sects.), D.C. Bar Assn. (past chmn. energy study group), Calif. Bar Assn., Fairfax Bar Assn., U.S. C. of C. (antitrust policy com.), Fairfax County C. of C., Phi Alpha Delta. Democrat. Lutheran. Home: 1930 Upper Lake Dr Reston VA 22091 Office: Reed Smith Shaw & McClay 8201 Greensboro Dr Suite 820 McLean VA 22102

RAUCH, ARTHUR IRVING, consultant; b. N.Y.C., Sept. 18, 1933; s. David and Miriam (Frankel) R.; BA magna cum laude (Rufus Choate scholar), Dartmouth Coll., 1954, MS, Amos Tuck Sch. Bus. Adminstrn., 1955; m. Roxane M. Spiller, Aug. 19, 1962 (div. 1977); children—David S., Janine B. Security analyst Lionel D. Edie & Co., N.Y.C., 1959-64; group dir. research Eastman Dillon, Union Securities & Co., N.Y.C., 1964-68; v.p., sr. analyst Laird, Inc., N.Y.C., 1968-69, dir. research, 1969-71, sr. v.p., 1970-73; ptnr. Oppenheimer & Co., N.Y.C., 1973-77; v.p. corp. devel. Rorer Group Inc., Ft. Washington, Pa., 1977-84; v.p. corp. fin. Arnhold & S. Bleichroeder, Inc., 1984-88; cons. corp. devel. ICN Pharms. Inc., N.Y.C., 1988—; mem. investment com. Becker Fund, 1969-73; bd. dirs. Sonomed Tech., Inc. Exec. com. Dartmouth Class of 1954, 1968-79. Served to lt. (j.g.) USNR, 1956-59. Chartered fin. analyst. Mem. N.Y. Soc. Security Analysts, Assn. Corp. Growth, Fin. Analysts Fedn. (corp. info. com.), Phi Beta Kappa. Home: 1185 Park Ave New York NY 10128 Office: 375 Park Ave New York NY 10152

RAUCH, HELMUT, physicist, educator; b. Krems, Austria, Jan. 22, 1939; s. Hans and Hermine (Weidenauer) R.; m. Annemarie Krutzler; children: Peter, Astrid, Christoph. Diploma in physics, Tech. U., Vienna, 1962, D of Tech., 1965, dozent, 1970. Asst. prof. Atominstitut, Vienna, 1962-72, dir., 1972—; prof. physics Tech. U., Vienna, 1972—; v.p. Austrian Nat. Sci. Found., 1985—. Editor Atomkernenergie, 1977—; contbr. 150 articles on neutron physics to profl. jours. Recipient Erwin Schrödinger award Austrian Acad. Scis., 1977, Kardinal Innitzer award Innitzer Found., 1986. Mem. Austrian Physical Soc., German Physical Soc. Roman Catholic. Office: Atominstitut, Schuettelstr 115, A-1020 Vienna Austria

RAUH, RICHARD PAUL, architect; b. Covington, Ky., Mar. 27, 1948; s. Robert Paul and Pauline (Farmer) R.; m. Mary Darlene Bailey, Oct. 6, 1975. A.B., Columbia U., 1970; B.Arch., M.Arch., Harvard U., 1974; D.M.D., U. Ky., 1980. Registered architect, 28 states; lic. dentist, Ky., Va. Asst. prof. U. Ky. Coll. Arch., Lexington, 1976-80, adj. asst. prof., 1980-81; prin. Carpenter/Rauh, Lexington, 1978-80; prin. Rabun Hatch Portman McWhorter Hatch & Rauh Architects, Atlanta, 1981-85; prin. Richard Rauh & Assocs., Architects, Atlanta, 1984—. Works include: Norfolk Hilton Hotel, Va., 1985, Netherland Plaza Hotel restoration, Cin., 1982-83, Bridgeport Plaza Hotel, Conn., 1985, Carew Tower Block restoration, Cin., 1983, master plan Ctr. for Humanities U. Ky. Lexington, 1984, La Concha Hotel, Key West, Fla., 1986, Carolina Head Injury Ctr., Durham, N.C., 1987, Albany (Ga.) Holiday Inn Hotel, 1988, Bay Valley Hotel, Bay City, Mich., 1988; author (with David G. Wright) Design Courses at Schools of Architecture in Western Europe: A Documentary Study, 1975. Pres., Hist. South Hill Assn., Lexington, 1978-80; bd. dirs. Margaret Mitchell House, Inc., 1987—. Sheldon fellow, Harvard U., 1974-75, Appleton fellow, 1974-75; recipient LUMEN excellence award Illuminating Engring. Soc. N.Am., 1985; Harvard Book award Harvard Club Cin., 1965; U.S. Dept. Interior grantee Ky. Heritage Commn., 1978, U.S. Dept. of HUD Urban Devel. Action grantee, 1988; recipient honor awards Nat. Trust Historic Preservation U.S., 1985, AIA South Atlantic Regional council, 1984, Ga. Assn. AIA, 1984, Ky. Soc. Architects AIA, 1986, Nat. award Soc. Am. Reg. Architects, 1986; Greater Cin. Beautiful award City of Cin., 1984, Ohio Hist. Soc., 1987, Fla. Keys Preservation Bd, 1987. Democrat. Presbyterian. Home: 3605 Stratford Rd NE Atlanta GA 30342 Office: Richard Rauh & Assocs 3300 Piedmont Rd NE Atlanta GA 30305

RAUSCHENBERG, ROBERT, artist; b. Port Arthur, Tex., Oct. 22, 1925; m. Sue Weil, 1950 (div. 1952); 1 son, Christopher. Student, U. Tex., Austin, Kansas City Art Inst. and Sch. Design, Academie Julian, Paris, France, Black Mountain Coll., N.C., Art Students League, N.Y.C. One man shows, Parsons Gallery, N.Y.C., 1951, Stable Gallery, N.Y.C., 1953, White Chapel Art Gallery, London, 1964, Leo Castelli Gallery, 1972, 73, Galerie Ileana Sonnabend, Paris, 1971, 72, 73, Ace Gallery, Los Angeles, 1973, Vancouver Art Gallery, 1978, Tate Gallery, London, 1981, Phoenix Art Mus., 1982, G.H. Dalsheimer Gallery, Balt., 1983, Castell Graphics, 1984, others; exhbt. art constrns., Rome and Florence Italy, 1953, Leo Castelli Gallery, N.Y.C., 1957—; rep. internat. art festivals, Carnegie Inst. Internat. exhbns., Sao Paulo Biennial, 1959, Exposition Internat. du Surrealisme, Paris, 1959-60, Amsterdam, others; group shows Sixteen Americans at, Mus. Modern Art, 1959, Art of Assemblage at, Guggengeim Mus., 1961, N.Y. Collection in, Stockholm, 1972, Whitney Ann., N.Y.C., 1972, 73, Garage Show, Rome, 1973, Automme Festival d'Artes, Paris, 1973, Mus. South Tex., Corpus Christi, 1974, N.Y. Cultural Center, 1973, retrospective exhbn., Nat. Collection Fine Arts, Smithsonian Inst., Washington, 1976, Mus. Modern Art, N.Y.C., 1977, Albright Knox Gallery, 1977, San Francisco Mus. Modern Art, 1977, Art Inst. Chgo., 1977, Staatliche Kunsthalle, Berlin, 1980, Kunsthalle, Düsseldorf, 1980, Louisiana Mus., Copenhagen, 1980, Stadelsches Kunstinstitut, Frankfurt, 1981, Städtische Galerie im Lembachhaus, Munich, 1981, Tate Gallery, London, 1981, The Real Big Picture, Queen's Mus., N.Y., 1986, reprodn. photographs by silk screen stenciling technique to allow change in scale, on tour as set and costume designer, lighting expert, stage mgr., Merce Cunningham Dance Co., 1964; choreographer: dance Pelican; others; works include electronic sculpture Soundings; paintings Tut-Scape. Served with USNR, World War II; neuropsychiat. tech. Calif. Naval Hosps. Recipient 1st prize Internat. Exbn. Prints Gallery Modern Art, Ljubljana, Yugoslavia, 1963, 1st prize Venice Biennelle, 1964, 1st prize Corcoran Biennial Contemporary Am. Painters, 1965, Showhegan Sch. Painting and Sculpture medal, 1982, NAD assoc., 1983, Grammy award, 1984. Mem. Am. Acad. and, Inst. Arts and Letters. Office: care Leo Castelli Gallery 420 W Broadway New York NY 10012 *

RAVEN, JAMES RUSSELL, history educator; b. Colchester, Essex, Eng., Apr. 13, 1959; s. Leonard Ernest and Eileen Leonora (Wightman) R. MA, Cambridge U., 1984, PhD, 1985. Fellow Pembroke Coll. Cambridge U., Eng., 1985—. Author: British Fiction 1750-1770, 1987, Popular Writing and the Image of Business in Eighteenth Century Britain, 1988. Newberry Library fellow, Chgo., 1986; Peterson fellow Am. Antiquarian Soc., Worcester, Mass., 1986; recipient Thirlwall prize and Seeley medal U. Cambridge, 1986. Mem. Inst. Hist. Research, English-Speaking Union (chmn. Cambridge U. chpt. 1981-83, com. mem. 1982-87, com. mem. East region 1982—), Bibliog. Soc. Club: Dartmouth House (London).

RAVEN, RONALD JACOB, education educator, researcher, consultant; b. San Francisco, Jan. 7, 1935; s. Jacob and Ella (O'Connor) R.; m. Cynthia Opacinch; children—Michael, Julie. B.S., U. San Francisco, 1952-56; M.A., Calif. State U. at San Francisco, 1960; Ed.D., U. Calif.-Berkeley, 1965. Tchr. Campbell High Sch., Calif., 1959-62; lectr. in biology Fullerton Coll., Calif., 1962-63; prof. SUNY-Amherst, 1965—; vis. prof. U. Calif.-Berkeley, summer 1968, Ontario Inst. for Edn. Studies, summer 1970, U. Iowa, Iowa City, summer 1973, U. Minas Gerais, Belo Horizonte, Brazil, summer 1976; cons. NSF, Nat. Assessment of Ednl. Progress. Author tests: Raven Test of Logical Ops., 1980; Raven Test of Sci. Reasoning, 1982. Mem. editorial bd. Sci. Edn., 1970—, Jour. Research in Sci. Teaching, 1970-83. Served to 1st lt. U.S. Army-Armor, 1964. Fellow AAAS; mem. Assn. for Edn. Tchrs. Sci. (bd. dirs. 1973-76), Assn. for Research in Sci. Teaching (exec. bd., bd. dirs. 1976-80), Nat. Sci. Tchrs. Assn., Am. Ednl. Research Assn. Roman Catholic. Avocations: piano, tennis. Home: 53 Wellingwood Dr East Amherst NY 14051 Office: SUNY Amherst NY 14051

RAVILY, GILBERT, physician, consultant; b. Lannion, France, Nov. 22, 1951; s. Jean Ravily and Marie Cojean; m. Colette Poisson, 1972 (div. 1981); children: Laurence, Christelle; m. Martine Descottes, Aug. 29, 1981. MD, U. Nantes, France, 1976. Gen. practice medicine Meaux, France, 1976—; educator medicine pvt. schs. and univs., Paris, 1982—; cons. mesotherapy Necker Hosp., Paris, 1979—. Author: Clinical Atlas of Mesotherapy, 1988, Yearbook of Mesotherapy, 1987; mgr. Med. Congress, Versailles, France, 1983—. Fellow Internat. Mesotherapy Soc. (founder), French Mesotherapy Soc.; mem. Hosp. Mesotherapy Soc. (founder, pres.-elect 1983—). Lodge: Rotary (fellow Meaux chpt. 1985). Home and Office: Le Connetable, de Richemont 1 BP 162, 77100 Meaux France

RAVITZ, LEONARD J., JR., physician, scientist, consultant; b. Cuyahoga County, Ohio, Apr. 17, 1925; s. Leonard Robert and Esther Evelyn (Skerball) R. BS, Case Western Res. U., 1944; MD, Wayne State U., 1946; MS, Yale U., 1950. Diplomate Am. Bd. Psychiatry and Neurology. Research asst. EEG, Harper Hosp., Detroit, 1943-46; spl. trainee in hypnosis to Milton H. Erickson Wayne County Gen. Hosp., Eloise, Mich., 1945-46; rotating intern St. Elizabeths Hosp., Washington, 1946-47; jr., sr. asst. resident in psychiatry, Yale-New Haven Hosp.; asst. in psychiatry and mental hygiene, Yale Med. Sch., 1947-49, research fellow sect. neuro-anatomy, 1949-50; sr. resident in neuropsychiatry Duke Hosp., instr. Duke U. Hosp., Durham, N.C., 1950-51, assoc. in neuropsychiatry, Duke U. Med. Sch., 1951-53; asst. dir. profl. edn. in charge tng. U. Wyo. Nursing Sch. affiliates; chief research rehab. bldg. Downey VA Hosp. (now called VA Hosp.), North Chicago, Ill., 1953-54; assoc. in psychiatry Sch. Medicine and Hosp. U. Pa., Phila., 1955-58; dir. tng. and research Ea. State Hosp., Williamsburg, Va., 1958-60; practice medicine specializing in psychiatry, Norfolk, Va., 1961—; psychiatrist, cons. Div. Alcohol Studies and Rehab., Va. Dept. Health (later Va. Dept. Mental Health and Mental Retardation), 1961-81; clin. asst. prof. psychiatry, psychiatrist Health Sci. Ctr. SUNY, Bkyln., 1983—staff Med. Ctr. Hosps., Norfolk Gen. Div., 1961—; psychiatrist Greenpoint Clinic, Bklyn., 1983-87, 17th St. Clinic, N.Y.C., 1987—; clin. asst. prof. psychiatry SUNY Health Sci. Ctr. (Downstate Med. Ctr.), 1983—; vis. asst. prof. Meharry Med. Coll., Nashville, 1953; sec.-treas. Euclid-97th St. Clinic, Inc., Cleve., 1956-63, pres., 1963-69; pvt. cons., Cleve., 1960-69, Upper Montclair, N.J., 1982—; lectr. sociology and criminology Old Dominion U., Norfolk, 1961-62, cons. nutrition research project, research found., 1978—; spl. med. cons. Frederick Mil. Acad., Portsmouth, Va., 1963-71; cons. Tidewater Epilepsy Found., Chesapeake, Va., 1962-68, electrodynamic field research project, Yale U., 1972-74, USPH Hosp. Alcohol Unit, Norfolk, 1980-81, Nat. Inst. Rehab. Therapy, Butler, N.J., 1982—; invited lectr., U.S., Fed. Republic Germany; participant 5th Internat. Congress for Hypnosis and Psychosomatic Medicine, Gutenburg U., Mainz, Fed. Republic Germany, 1970; organizer symposia in field. Discoverer electromagnetic field measurement of hypnotic states, 1948-50; asst. editor Jour. Am. Soc. Psychosomatic Dentistry and Medicine, 1980-83; mem. editorial bd. Internat. Jour. Psychosomatics, 1984—; contbr. sects. to books, articles, book revs., abstracts to profl. publs. Sr. v.p. Willoughby Civic League, 1971-75. Served to 1st lt. AUS, 1943-46. Lyman Research Fund grantee, 1950-53. Fellow Am. Psychiat. Assn., AAAS, N.Y. Acad. Scis., Am. Soc. Clin. Hypnosis (charter), Royal Soc. Health (London), Am. Psychiat. Assn., ; mem. Va. Soc. Clin. Hypnosis (founding pres. 1956-60), Norfolk Acad. Medicine, Sigma Xi, Nu Sigma Nu.

RAVNIHAR, BOZENA, oncology educator; b. Ljubljana, Yugoslavia, Mar. 18, 1914; d. Vladimir and Antonija (Sterle) R.; MD, U. Belgrade, 1940. Head labs. Inst. Oncology, Ljubljana, Yugoslavia, 1946-48, head radiotherapy, 1949-66, head cancer registry, 1950-75, dir., 1964-82, sci. cons., 1982-84, prof. oncology and radiotherapy Med. Faculty, U. Ljubljana, 1955-84, prof. emeritus, 1984—, chair dept. oncology and radiotherapy, 1967-84. Mem. Council of the Socialist Republic of Slovenia, 1983—. Served with M.C., Nat. Liberation Army, 1942-45. Mem. Internat. Assn. Cancer Registries, Yugoslav Assn. Radiology and Nuclear Medicine, Slovenian Med. Soc., Assn. Yugoslav Cancerologists. Home: Ulica 29 hercegovske, divizije 2, 61000 Ljubljana Yugoslavia Office: Inst Oncology, Vrazov trg 4, 61105 Ljubljana Yugoslavia

RAVOIRA, JAMES, artist; b. Weirton, W.Va., Sept. 4, 1933; s. James and Josephine; B.A., W. Liberty State Coll., 1962; M.A., Kent State U., 1966, M.F.A., 1977; m. LaWanda Faye Pugh, Nov. 19, 1977. Asst. prof. Indian River Community Coll., Ft. Pierce, Fla., 1967-69; faculty Thornton Community Coll., Harvey, Ill., 1969-70; asst. prof. The Citadel, Charleston, S.C.,

1971-74; prof. art U. S.C., Myrtle Beach, 1974-77; art dir. State Fla. grant U. North Fla., Jacksonville, 1983; one-man show Myrtle Beach Conv. Ctr., 1977, Lynn Kottler Galleries, N.Y.C., 1977, 78; group shows include Fed. Bldg., Ft. Lauderdale, Fla., 1986, Centro Studi E Richerche Delle Nazioni (World Culture Prize) 1985; pub. in Artist/USA, 1977, The Experiment, 1978; actor Guys and Dolls, 1984. Recipient Eleanor D. Caldwell award Bethany (W.Va.) Coll., 1961, Carnegie Library award, 1961, Krasner Pollock Found. award, N.Y.C., 1987. Mem. Coll. Art Assn., Accademia Italia delle Arti e del Lavoro (Gold medal). Included in Internat. Dictionary of Contemporary Artists. Home: 3521 NW 34th Ave Fort Lauderdale FL 33309 Address: 110 Powers Rd Weirton WV 26062

RAWL, ARTHUR JULIAN, accountant, consultant; b. Boston, July 6, 1942; s. Philip and Evelyn (Rosoff) R.; m. Karen Lee Werby, June 4, 1967; 1 child, Kristen Alexandra. BBA, Boston U., 1967. CPA, Mass., N.Y., La. Audit mgr. Touche Ross & Co., Boston, 1967-77; audit mgr. Touche Ross & Co., N.Y.C., 1977-79, ptnr., 1979; ptnr. Touche Ross & Co., Newark, 1980-88, N.Y.C., 1988—; mem. adj. faculty Boston U., 1971-75. Contbr. articles to profl. journals. Mem. Newton Upper Falls Hist. Commn., 1977; dir. Sherburne Scholarship Fund Boston U., 1977-80; mem. Englewood (N.J.) Planning Bd., 1981-83; trustee, Englewood Bd. Edn., 1983-85; trustee, treas., Englewood Econ. Devel. Corp. 1986—; fin. and compensation com. Dwight Englewood Sch., 1985—. Served to 2d class petty officer USN, 1960-63. Fellow Am. Inst. CPA's, Mass. Soc. CPA's, N.Y. Soc. CPA's; mem. Am. Legion, Navy League U.S., N.J. Hist. Soc. (bd. govs., exec. com., nominating com., treas. 1987—). Clubs: Essex (Newark); Englewood Field, Englewood. Lodge: Order St. John (knight). Home: 72 Booth Ave Englewood NJ 07631 Office: Touche Ross & Co Gateway 1 Newark NJ 07102

RAWL, LAWRENCE G., petroleum company executive; b. 1928. Grad. Okla. U., 1952. With Exxon Corp, 1952—, asst. mgr. East Tex. prodn. div., 1965-66, mgr. ops. 1966-67, exec. asst. to chmn., 1967-69, gen. mgr. supply Exxon Co. USA div. then v.p. mktg., 1969-72, v.p. then sr. v.p., 1972-76, exec. v.p. Exxon Co. USA div., 1976-80, sr. v.p. Exxon Corp., N.Y.C., 1980-86, pres., 1986, chmn., chief exec. officer, 1986—, also dir. Office: Exxon Corp 1251 Ave of the Americas New York NY 10020 *

RAWLES, EDWARD HUGH, lawyer; b. Chgo., May 7, 1945; s. Fred Wilson and Nancy (Hughes) R.; m. Margaret Mary O'Donoghue, Oct. 20, 1979; children—Lee Kathryn, Jacklyn Ann. B.A., U. Ill., 1967; J.D. summa cum laude, Ill. Inst. Tech., 1970. Bar: Ill., 1970, U.S. Dist. Ct. (cen. dist.) Ill. 1970, U.S. Supreme Ct. 1973, U.S. Ct. Appeals (7th cir.) 1983, Colo. 1984. Assoc. Reno, O'Byrne & Kepley, Champaign, Ill., 1970-73, ptnr., 1973-84; v.p. Reno O'Byrne & Kepley P.C., Champaign, 1984—; mem. student legal service adv. bd. U. Ill., Urbana, 1982—; hearing officer Ill. Fair Employment Practice Commn., Springfield, 1972-74. Diplomate Nat. Bd. Trial Advocacy, 1983. Fellow Ill. State Bar Found., 1984. Mem. Assn. Trial Lawyers Am., Ill. Trial Lawyers Assn., Ill. Bar Assn., Colo. Trial Lawyers Assn., Bar Assn. 7th Fed. Cir., Kent Soc. Honor Men, Phi Delta Theta. Roman Catholic. Home: Rural Rt 1 Box 137 White Heath IL 61884 Office: Reno O'Byrne & Kepley 501 W Church PO Box 693 Champaign IL 61820

RAWLINGS, BOYNTON MOTT, lawyer; b. El Paso, Tex., Dec. 6, 1935; s. Junius Mott and Laura Bassett (Boynton) R.; m. Nancy Mary Peay, Aug. 24, 1962 (div. 1973); children—Laura Bassett, James Mott; m. Judith Reed, Dec. 10, 1977; 1 child, William Reed. A.B., Princeton U., 1958; LL.B., Stanford U., 1961; Diploma, U. Strasbourg (France), 1963. Bar: Calif., 1962, D.C., 1980, Conseil Juridique Paris, 1973. Assoc. Broad, Busterud & Khorie, San Francisco, 1963-65, Homer G. Angelo, Brussels, 1966; assoc., ptnr. S.G. Archibald, Paris, 1967-74; ptnr. Boynton M. Rawlings, Paris, Los Angeles, 1974-84, Kevorkian & Rawlings, Paris, 1984—; dir. Central Soya France, S.A., Trappes, France. Contbr. articles to profl. jours. Mem. Los Angeles Bar Assn. (bd. dirs. sect. internat. law 1975-82), French Am. C. of C. (bd. dirs., v.p. 1985—). Republican. Episcopalian. Avocations: music; tennis; skiing; hiking. Home: 53 Ave Montaigne, 75008 Paris France Office: Kevorkian and Rawlings, 46 Ave D'Iena, 75116 Paris France

RAWLINGS, JAMES W., diplomat; b. Provo, Utah, Oct. 12, 1929; m. Joan E. Berkhimer; 5 children. BA, Brigham Young U., 1955; KD, U. Utah, 1958. Assoc. Chadbourne, Parke, Whiteside and Wolff, N.Y.C., 1958-60; counsel metals div. Union Carbide Corp., 1960-66; counsel Union Carbide Eastern, Inc., 1966, v.p. fin., metals div., 1969-72, v.p., gen. mgr. mining ops. for metals div., 1972-78; vice-chmn. Union Carbide Africa and Middle East, Inc., 1978-79; chmn. and pres. Union Carbide So. Africa, Inc., 1979-86; U.S. ambassador to Zimbabwe 1986—. Served with USAF, 1950-54. *

RAWLINGS, JERRY JOHN, head of state of Ghana; b. Accra, Ghana, June 22, 1947; s. Victoria Abbotoi; m. Nana Konadu Agyeman; 4 children. Ed. Achimota Sch. and Ghana Mil. Acad., Teshie. Commd. Pilot officer Ghanaian Air Force, 1969, advanced through grades to flight-lt., 1978; arrested for leading mutiny of jr. officers, 1979; leader mil. coup which overthrew Govt. of Supreme Mil. Council, 1979; chmn. Armed Forces Revolutionary Council (head of state), 1979; ret. from armed forces, 1979; handed over to elected govt., 1979; leader mil. coup which overthrew Govt. of Dr. Hilla Limann, 1981; chmn. Provisional Nat. Def. Council, 1981—; head of state Ghana, Accra, 1982—, chief of def. staff., 1982—. Office: Office Head of State, Provisional Nat Def Council, Accra Ghana

RAWLINGS, PATRICIA ELIZABETH, association executive, researcher; b. London, Jan. 27, 1939; d. Louis and Mary (Boas de Winter) R.; m. David Wolfson, Dec. 18, 1962 (div. 1967). B.A. in English Lit., U. Coll. London, 1979; postgrad. London Sch. Econs., 1983-86. Dir. French Art Auction Co., Rheims and Laurin, 1968-71, Contemporary Fine Arts Gallery Nigel Greenwood Inc., 1969—, Textile Co., 1971-82; chmn. appeals British Red Cross Soc., London br., 1970—; researcher Ctr. for Policy Studies Arms Control, 1984—; mem. Peace Through NATO Council, 1985-86. Mem. Conservative Women's Nat. Com., 1983—; mem. govt. com. Video Censors, 1985—; bd. dirs. English Chamber Orch. and Music Soc., 1980-85; Conservative candidate Gen. Election for Sheffield Central, 1983, for Council Election for Westminster City Council, Bayswater, 1986, for Doncaster Central, 1987; polit. advisor on inner cities to minister Dept. The Environment, 1987. Recipient Nat. Badge of Honor, Brit. Red Cross Soc., London, 1981; selected conservative candidate Essex S.W. seat, 1988. Mem. European Union of Women (commr.), Royal Inst. Internat. Affairs, Internat. Inst. Strategic Studies, Chatham House. Club: Queen's Tennis (London). Avocations: music; art; golf. Home: 86 Eaton Sq, London SW1 England

RAWLINS, HARRY ERLE, JR., realtor; b. Lancaster, Tex., Oct. 13, 1907; s. H. Erle and Maude Trigg (White) R.; m. Virginia Louise Marvin, Dec. 5, 1944 (dec. 1967); children—H. Erle, Susan Rawlins Weaver. B.A., Rice U., 1931, postgrad. Lic. realtor, Tex. With Remington Rand, Houston, 1931-35; officer mgr. Diamond Alkali, Dallas, 1936-39; co-owner Erle Rawlins Jr. Realtors, Dallas, 1945—; restorer town square, Lancaster, Tex. Bd. dirs. Dallas Ballet, Hist. Preservation League, Oak Lawn Preservation Soc., Dallas Mus. Fine Art. Served to lt. comdr. USNR, 1941-45. Mem. Dallas Bd. Realtors. Episcopalian. Clubs: Dallas Country, Lancers. Office: 6801 Snider Plaza Dallas TX 75205

RAWLS, CATHERINE POTEMPA, commodity futures executive, financial futures analyst; b. Chgo., Mar. 19, 1953; d. Stanley Louis and Mary Ann (Kuczmarski) Potempa; m. Stephen Franklin Rawls, July 30, 1983. B.A., Marquette U., 1975. Mem. Chgo. Bd. Trade, 1977-79, 83—; fin. futures analyst Geldermann Inc., Chgo., 1979-82, dir. research, 1982-86 ; pres. Tiare Trading Co. 1987—; mem. Chgo. Merc. Exchange, 1982. Editor Fax & Figures newsletter, 1983, Geldermann-Peavey newsletter, 1983-86 . Recipient award Marquette U. chpt. Women in Communications, 1975. Mem. Futures Industry Assn. Roman Catholic. Home: 421-C Sandhurst Circle Glen Ellyn IL 60137 Office: O'Connor & Co 141 W Jackson 28th Floor Chicago IL 60604

RAWLS, FRANK MACKLIN, lawyer; b. Suffolk, Va., Aug. 24, 1952; s. John Lewis and Mary Helen (Macklin) R.; m. Sally Hallum Blanchard, June 26, 1976; children—Matthew Christopher, John Stephen, Michael Andrew. B.A. cum laude in History, Hampden Sydney Coll., 1974; J.D., U. Va., 1977. Bar: Va. 1977, U.S. Dist. Ct. (ea. dist.) Va. 1977, U.S. Ct. Appeals (4th cir.) 1977. Assoc. Rawls, Habel & Rawls, Suffolk, 1977-78, ptnr., 1978—; bd. dirs. Suffolk Title Ltd., 1986—. Elder, clk. of session Westminster Presbyn. Ch., Suffolk, 1984—; chmn. bd. dirs. Suffolk Crime Line, 1982—, Suffolk Cheer Fund, 1982—, Covenant Christian Schs., Suffolk, 1982-84; treas., Suffolk Fellowship, city wide prayer breakfast com.; mem. adv. bd. dirs. Salvation Army, Suffolk, 1977-84; treas., bd. dirs. L.T. and Margaret W. Reid Scholarship Fund, 1984—, Suffolk YMCA, 1988—. Mem. Suffolk Bar Assn., Va. Bar Assn., Christian Legal Soc., Va. Trial Lawyers Assn., ABA, Assn. Trial Lawyers Am., Suffolk Bar Assn. Lodge: Rotary. Home: 613 N Broad St Suffolk VA 23434

RAWSON, KENNETT LONGLEY, publishing company executive; b. Chgo., 1911; s. Frederick Holbrook and Edith (Kennett) R.; m. Eleanor MacMannis, 1954; children: Linda Kennett, Kennett Longley. Student, Phillips Acad., Andover, Mass., 1926-29; A.B., Yale, 1933. Mem. Arctic expdns. led by Comdr. Donald MacMillan, 1925, 26, 27, 29; navigator 2d Byrd Antarctic Expdn., 1933-35; editorial dept. G.P. Putman's Sons, 1936, editor firm, 1938-41, editor, 1945, v.p., editor in chief, dir., 1947-50; pres. David McKay Co., Inc., N.Y.C., 1950-74, Rawson, Wade Pubs., Inc., N.Y.C., 1974-81; chair publs. com. Rawson Assocs. a div. of Macmillan Publ. Co., N.Y.C., 1981—; sr. v.p. Scribner Book Cos., Inc., N.Y.C., 1981-86. Author: A Boy's Eye View of the Arctic, 1926. Emeritus, bd. dirs. Mather Hosp., Port Jefferson, N.Y. Served as lt. comdr. USNR, 1941-45; communications, navigating officer, comdg. officer. Decorated Navy Cross. Mem. Century Assn. Clubs: Yale (N.Y.C.); Oldfield, Setauket Yacht. Home: Blueberry Bay Farm 23 Brewster Ln E Setauket NY 11733 Office: 866 3d Ave New York NY 10022

RAY, CHARLES DEAN, neurosurgeon; b. Americus, Ga., Aug. 1, 1927; s. Oliver Tinsley and Katherine (Broadfield) R.; A.B., Emory U., 1950; M.S., U. Miami (Fla.), 1952; M.D., Med. Coll. Ga., 1956; m. Roberta L. Mann, Dec. 17, 1978; children—Bruce, Kathy, C. Marlene, Thomas, John, Blythe. Intern, Baptist Meml. Hosp., Memphis, 1956-57; resident, research assoc. neurosurgery U. Tenn. Hosp., Memphis, 1957-62; fellow, research asst. Mayo Clinic and Found., Rochester, Minn., 1962-64; asst. prof. neurosurgery, lectr. bioengring. Johns Hopkins U. Med. Sch., Balt., 1964-68; chief dept. med. engring. F. Hoffmann-LaRoche, Basel, Switzerland, also lectr. U. Basel, 1968-73; practice medicine, specializing in neurosurgery, Mpls., 1973—; staff Sister Kenny Inst., Children's, Abbott-Northwestern hosps., Mpls., clin. assoc. prof. medicine U. Minn., Mpls., 1973—; v.p. med research Medtronic Inc., Mpls., 1972-79; chmn. bd., pres. Cedar Devel. Corp., Cedar Surg. Inc., 1985—; cons. in field. Chmn. com. materials and devices World Fedn. Neurosurg. Socs., 1977—; vestry St. Martin's Episcopal Ch., Wayzata, Minn., 1976-79. Served with USN, 1945-49. Diplomate Am. Bd. Neurol. Surgery. Fellow ACS, Royal Soc. Health; mem. Pan-Am. Med. Assns., AMA, Am. Assn. Neurol. Surgeons, Congress Neurol. Surgeons, W. Ger. Armed Forces Med. Soc., IEEE, Internat. Fedn. Med. Biol. Engring., Internat. Soc. Stereotaxic and Functional Neurosurgery, ASTM, Internat. Orgn. Standardization, Sigma Xi, others. Clubs: Cosmos, Lafayette, Minneapolis. Author: Principles of Engineering Applied to Medicine, 1964; Medical Engineering, 1974; Lumbar Spine Surgery, 1988; contbr. articles to profl. publs. Home: 19550 Cedarhurst Wayzata MN 55391 Office: Inst for Low Back Care Sister Kenny Inst 2737 Chicago Ave Minneapolis MN 55407

RAY, DARRELL MORRIS, financial planning company executive, religious school administrator , educator; b. Findlay, Ohio, Mar. 22, 1959; s. Sherman Hodge and Delores (Lowe) R.; m. Julia Ann Corbin, Oct. 6, 1978; children: Jeremy James, Stephen Michael. BA, Bapt. Bible Coll., Springfield, Mo., 1981; student, Southwest Mo. State U., 1981, Pensacola (Fla.) Christian Coll., summer 1986, U. Mich., 1987; cert. in real estate fin., U. Toledo. Cert. Life Underwriting Tng. Council. Sales rep. Life Ins. Co. Va., Toledo, 1982-84; owner, pres. Darrell Ray and Assocs., Financial Planning Agy., Inc., Westland, Mich. and Toledo, 1982—; pres. Bus. Opportunity Search Partnership, Toledo, 1986—; bus. dir. United Bapt. Ch., Springfield, 1977; dir. bus., sr. citizens and children's ministries Trinity Bapt. Ch., 1978-80; adminstr. G.B. Vick Meml. Christian Schs., Garden City, Mich., 1986—. Vol. various Rep. polit. campaigns; past pres. Springfield area Coll. Reps.; past chmn. 7th Congrl. Dist. Coll. Reps.; past 2d v.p. Greene County Young Reps.; mgr., advisor campaigns Green County Reps. 1977-78, 80-81; candidate Findlay City Council 1979; dir. Ch. Polit. Awareness Program (forerunner Ohio Moral Majority) 1978-80; active Mo. Moral Majority 1980-81; mem. Lucas County Rep. Cen. Com. 1982-84. Mem. Nat. Assn. Life Underwriters, Ohio Assn. Life Underwriters, ToledoAssn. Life Underwriters, Nat. Bd. Realtors, Ohio Bd. Realtors, Toledo Bd. Realtors, Internat. Assn. Fin. Planning, Nat. Arbor Day Found., Inst. Cert. Fin. Planners, Ohio Bapt. Bible Fellowship. Office: Darrell Ray & Assocs Fin Planning Agy Inc 400 Renaissance Ctr Suite 500 Detroit MI 48243 also: GB Vick Meml Christian Schs 33443 Fernwood Westland MI 48185 Office: Bus Opportunity Search 5917 Rounding River Ln Toledo OH 43611

RAY, FRANK ALLEN, lawyer; b. Lafayette, Ind., Jan. 30, 1949; s. Dale Allen and Merry Ann (Fleming) R.; m. Carol Ann Olmutz, Oct. 1, 1982; children—Erica Fleming, Robert Allen. B.A., Ohio State U., 1970, J.D., 1973. Bar: Ohio 1973, U.S. Dist. Ct. (so. dist.) Ohio 1975, U.S. Supreme Ct. 1976, U.S. Tax Ct. 1977, U.S. Ct. Appeals (6th cir.) 1977, U.S. Dist Ct. (no. dist.) Ohio 1980, Pa. 1983, U.S. Dist. Ct. (ea. dist.) Mich. 1983, U.S. Ct. Appeals (1st cir.) cert. civil trial adv. Nat. Bd. Trial Advocacy. Asst. pros. atty. Franklin County, Ohio, 1973-75, chief civil counsel, 1976-78; dir. econ. crime project Nat. Dist. Attys. Assn., Washington, 1975-76; assoc. Brownfield, Kosydar, Bowen, Bally & Sturtz, Columbus, Ohio, 1978, Michael F. Colley Co., L.P.A., Columbus, 1979-83; pres. Frank A. Ray Co., L.P.A., Columbus, 1983—; mem. seminar faculty Nat. Coll. Dist. Attys., Houston, 1975-77; mem. nat. conf. faculty Fed. Jud. Ctr., Washington, 1976-77. Editor: Economic Crime Digest, 1975-76. Mem. fin. com. Franklin County Republican Orgn., Columbus, 1979-84. Served to 1st lt. inf. U.S. Army, 1973. Named to Ten Outstanding Young Citizens of Columbus, Columbus Jaycees, 1976; recipient Nat. award of Distinctive Service, Nat. Dist. Attys. Assn., 1977. Fellow Columbus Bar Found., Roscoe Pound Found.; mem. Columbus Bar Assn., Ohio State Bar Assn., ABA, Assn. Trial Lawyers Am., Ohio Acad. Trial Lawyers (trustee 1984-87, sec. 1987-88, pres.-elect 1988—, legis. coordinator 1986—, Pres.' award 1986), Franklin County Trial Lawyers Assn. (trustee 1982-83, treas. 1984-85, chmn. com. negligence law 1983-87, sec. 1985-86, v.p. 1986-87, pres. 1987-88). Presbyterian. Home: 5800 Olentangy Blvd Worthington OH 43085 Office: 330 S High St Columbus OH 43215

RAY, FRANK DAVID, government agency official; b. Mt. Vernon, Ohio, Dec. 1, 1940; s. John Paul and Lola Mae (Miller) R.; BS in Edn., Ohio State U., 1964, JD, 1967; m. Julia Anne Sachs, June 11, 1976. Bar: Ohio 1967, U.S. Dist. Ct. 1969, U.S. Cir. Ct. Appeals (6th cir.) 1970, U.S. Supreme Ct. 1971. Legal aide to atty. gen. Ohio, 1965-66; bailiff probate ct., Franklin County, Ohio, 1966-67, gen. referee, 1967-68; with firm Stouffer, Wait and Ashbrook, Columbus, Ohio, 1967-71; jour. clk. Ohio Ho. of Reps., 1969-71; dist. dir. SBA, 1971—; mem. Ohio Pub. Defender Commn., 1983—; mem. U.S. Dept. Commerce So. Ohio Dist. Export Council, 1988—; mem. Columbus Mayor's Econ. Devel. Council, 1983-84; mem. Small Bus. and High Tech. adv. com. Ohio Div. Securities, 1983-84; mem. tech. alliance Central Ohio Adv. Bd., 1983—. Mem. Upper Arlington (Ohio) Bd. Health, 1970-75; pres. Buckeye Republican Club, 1970, Franklin County Forum, 1970; chmn. Central Ohio chpt. Nat. Found.-March of Dimes, 1974-77; trustee Columbus Acad. Contemporary Art, 1976. Recipient Service award Nat. Found.-March of Dimes, 1974, 75, 76, 77; Am. Jurisprudence award for Excellence, 1967, In Search of Excellence award SBA, 1985; named Ohio Commodore, 1973. Mem. Delta Upsilon, Alpha Epsilon Delta. Clubs: Ohio Press, Ohio State U. Pres. Home: 4200 Dublin Rd Hilliard OH 43026

RAY, JOHN JOSEPH, writer; b. Innisfail, Queensland, Australia, July 15, 1943; s. Frank Edward and Margaret (Copelin) R.; m. Joyce Anne Burns Petrie (div. 1984); m. Jennifer Ann Lucas; Nov. 30, 1985; 1 child, Joseph Henry. BA with honors, U. Queensland, Brisbane, 1967; MA with honors, U. Sydney, Australia, 1968; PhD, Macquarie U., Sydney, 1970. Tutor psychology Macquarie U., 1969-70; lectr. sociology U. New South Wales, Sydney, 1971-83; freelance writer Mt. Gravatt, Australia, 1983—. Author: Conservatism as Heresy, 1974; contbr. over 200 papers to sci. jours. Home: 23 Camlet St, Mount Gravatt, Queensland 4122, Australia

RAY, JOHN WALKER, physician, educator; b. Columbus, Ohio, Jan. 12, 1936; s. Kenneth Clark and Hope (Walker) Ray; m. Susanne Gettings, July 15, 1961; children: Nancy Ann, Susan Christy. AB magna cum laude, Marietta Coll., 1956; MD cum laude, Ohio State U., 1960; postgrad. Temple U., 1964, Mt. Sinai Hosp. and Columbia U., 1964, 66, Northwestern U., 1967, 71, U. Ill., 1968, U. Ind., 1969, Tulane U., 1969. Intern, Ohio State U. Hosps., Columbus, 1960-61, clin. research trainee NIH, 1963-65, resident dept. otolaryngology, 1963-65, 1966-67, resident dept. surgery 1965-66, instr. dept. otolaryngology, 1966-67, 70-75, clin. asst. prof., 1975-82, clin. assoc. prof., 1982—; active staff, past chief of staff Bethesda Hosp.; staff, chief of staff Good Samaritan Hosp., Zanesville, Ohio, 1967-86; courtesy staff Ohio State U. Hosps., Columbus, 1970—; radio-TV health commentator, 1982—. Past pres. Muskingum chpt. Am. Cancer Soc.; trustee Care One Health Systems, Ohio Med. Polit. Action Com. Served to capt. USAF, 1961-63. Recipient Barraquer Meml. award, 1965; named to Order of Ky. Col., 1966. Diplomate Am. Bd. Otolaryngology. Fellow ACS, Am. Soc. Otolaryn. Allergy, Am. Acad. Otolaryngology (gov.), Am. Acad. Facial Plastic and Reconstructive Surgery; mem. Nat. Assn. Physician Broadcasters, Muskingum County Acad. Medicine, AMA (del. hosp. med. Staff sect.), Ohio Med. Assn. (del.), Columbus Ophthalmol. and Otolaryngol. Soc. (past pres.), Ohio Soc. Otolaryngology (past pres.), Pan-Am. Assn. Otolaryngology and Bronchoesophagology, Pan-Am. Allergy Soc., Am. Council Otolaryngology, Am. Auditory Soc., Am. Soc. Contemporary Medicine and Surgery, Phi Beta Kappa, Alpha Tau Omega, Alpha Kappa Kappa, Alpha Omega Alpha, Beta Beta Beta. Republican. Presbyterian. Contbr. articles to sci., med. jours. Collaborator, surg. motion picture Laryngectomy and Neck Dissection, 1964. Office: 2825 Maple Ave Zanesville OH 43701

RAY, JUDITH DIANA, physical education educator; b. St. Louis, Sept. 14, 1946; d. Arthur Charles and Pauline (Malloyd) R.; A.B. in Edn., Harris Tchrs. Coll., 1968; M.A. in Edn., Washington U., St. Louis, 1972; M.S., Wash. State U., 1979. Tchr., St. Louis Bd. Edn., 1968-72; teaching asst. Washington U., 1970-72; lectr. phys. edn. York Coll., CUNY, 1972-75; teaching and research asst Sch. Vet. Medicine, Wash. State U., 1975-78; asst. prof. phys. edn. West Chester (Pa.) U. 1978—; reflexologist; dance tchr.; equine researcher Wash. State U., 1975-80; mem. Earthwatch team, archaeol. dig, eura de Vetralla, Italy, 1982. Vol. participant 1984 Olympics. Mem. AAHPER, ASTM, Internat. Soc. Biomechanics, Am. Soc. Biomechanics, AAUP, U.S. Fencing Assn., U.S. Fencing Coaches Assn., Internat. Soc. Biomechanics in Sport, U.S. Tennis Assn., U.S. Profl. Tennis Assn., Alpha Kappa Alpha, Phi Delta Kappa. Office: 307SC West Chester Univ West Chester PA 19380

RAY, RICHARD SCHELL, veterinarian, emeritus educator; b. Antwerp, Ohio, May 21, 1928; s. Alton D. and Dorothy Fransis (Schell) R.; m. Diane Maxine Foster, June 12, 1954; children—Kathleen F., David A., Elizabeth A. B.A., Ohio State U., 1950, D.V.M., 1955, M.S., 1958, Ph.D., 1963. Accredited Ohio Bd. Vet. Examiners, U.S. Dept. Agr. Practice vet. medicine, Toledo, 1955. Instr. vet. physiology and pharmacology and Grad. Sch. Ohio State U., Columbus, 1955-63, asst. prof., vet. clin. scis., 1963-67, assoc. prof., 1967-73, prof., 1973-84, prof. emeritus, 1984—; teaching team leader, 1969-74, 77-83; cons. forensic pharmacology and metabolic disease; dir. Pre-and Post-Race Drug Detection Lab., Ohio State U., 1969-82. Contbr. articles to profl. jours. Grantee Harness Racing Inst., 1965-68, N.Y. Racing Assn., 1965-68, Jockey Club, 1965-68, U.S. Trotting Assn., 1969, 71, Horseman's Benevolent Protective Assn., 1971, Nat. Assn. State Racing Commrs., 1976, Snyder Mfg. Co., 1970, USPHS, 1967-71, HEW, NIH, 1973, Ohio Thoroughbred Fund, 1967-83. Fellow Am. Coll. Vet. Pharmacology and Therapeutics; mem. Am. Soc. Vet. Physiologists and Pharmacologists, World Assn. Vet. Physiologists, Pharmacologists and Biochemists, Assn. Ofcl. Racing Chemists, Assn. Drug Detection Labs., Am. Chem. Soc., Am. Assn. Vet. Clinicians, Am. Assn. Equine Practitioners, Phi Zeta, Omega Tau Sigma, Alpha Sigma Phi. Republican. Methodist. Lodge: Masons. Home: 2752 Folkstone Rd Columbus OH 43220 Office: 1935 Coffey Rd Columbus OH 43210

RAY, ROBERT D., physician, educator; b. Cleve., Sept. 21, 1914; s. Clifford A. and Edna (Durant) R.; m. Genevieve Triau, Dec. 19, 1953; children—Frances Carol, Robert Triau, Esten Bernard, Gisele Antoinette, Charles Alexander. B.A. cum laude, U. Calif., 1936, M.A., 1938, Ph.D., 1948; M.D., Harvard U., 1943; Hon. H.D. (Docent), Umeö, Sweden. Diplomate Am. Bd. Surgery. Teaching asst. in anatomy U. Calif. Med. Sch., 1937-38, Carnegie research fellow, 1938-40, instr. anatomy, 1947-48; postgrad. tng. U. Calif. Hosp., San Francisco, 1949; intern Peter Bent Brigham Hosp., Boston, 1943; resident orthopaedic surgery Children's Hosp., Boston, 1944-45; asst. orthopaedic surgery Harvard U. Med. Sch., 1944-45; asst. prof. surgery, head orthopaedic surgery U. Wash. Sch. Medicine, 1948-51, asso. prof. surgery, 1954-56; prof., chmn. dept. orthopaedic surgery Presbyn.-St. Luke's Hosp., 1956-70; also U. Ill. Med. Sch., Chgo., 1956-85; ret. 1985; chief surgery 61st Sta. Hosp.; theatre cons. orthopaedic surgery MTOUSA, 1945-47. Contbr. articles to profl. publs. Recipient ann. award for outstanding orthopaedic research Kappa Delta, Chgo., 1954. Mem. Am. Orthopaedic Assn., Orthopaedic Research Soc., Soc. Nuclear Medicine, Internat. Assn. Orthopaedics and Traumatology, AAAS, Am. Assn. Anatomists, Am. Acad. Orthopaedic Surgery, A.C.S., Sigma Xi, Phi Sigma. Home: 2200 Laguna Vista Dr Novato CA 94945

RAY, SAMARJIT, mechanical engineering educator; b. Brahminbarya, Bengal, India, Dec. 13, 1945; s. Kulendra Kishor and Taru (Rani); m. Kabita Chatterjee, Aug. 11, 1979; 1 child, Debashish. B in Engring., Bengal Engring Coll., India, 1970, M in Engring., 1973, PhD in Mech. Engring., 1983. Engr. Indian Mechanisation & Allied Products Ltd., Calcutta, India, 1972-75; demonstrator mech. engring. Bengal Engring. Coll., 1975-79, lectr. mech. engring., 1979—. Contbr. articles to profl. jours. Mem. Assn. Engrs. Club: Profs. Common Room (cultural sec. 1975-76). Home: B-14/340, Kalyani, Nadia, West Bengal 741 235, India Office: Bengal Engring Coll, Mech Engring Dept Howrah, West Bengal 711103, India

RAY, SATYAJIT, film producer, director; b. Calcutta, India, May 2, 1921; s. Sukumar and Suprabha (Das) Ray; studied Ballygunge Govt. Sch., also Presidency Coll., Calcutta; B.A., U. Calcutta, 1974; D.Litt. (hon.), Royal Coll. Art, London, 1974, Oxford U., 1978; m. Bijoya Das, 1949; 1 son. Visualizer, D.J. Keymer & Co., advt. firm, 1943, art dir., 1949-56; film producer dir., 1953—; produced first feature film Pather Panchali, 1955 (Cannes Spl. award 1956, San Francisco Best film, 1957); other films include Aparajito (Venice Grand Prix 1957, San Francisco best direction); Jalsaghar, 1958; Devi, 1959; Apur Sansar, 1959 (Selznick award, Sutherland trophy 1960); Teen Kanya, 1961, Kanchanjangha, 1962; Two Daughters, 1963; Mahanagar, 1964; Charulata, 1964; The Coward and the Holy Man, 1965; The Hero, 1965; The Adventures of Goopy and Bagha, 1968; Days and Nights in the Forest, 1969; The Adversary, 1970; Company Limited, 1971; Distant Thunder, 1973 (Berlin Film Festival Prize 1973); Golden Fortress, 1974; The Middle Man, 1975; The Chessplayers, 1977; The Kingdom of Diamonds, 1980; Pikoo, 1982. Founder Film Soc., Calcutta, 1947. Decorated Order Yugoslav Flag, 1971. Composer background music for own films, from 1960. Editor Sandesh, children's mag., from 1961. Author: (essays) Our Films, Their Films, 1976; (with Sukumar Ray) Nonsense Rhymes, 1975, also novels, short stories, film articles. Address: Flat 8, 1-1 Bishop Lefroy Rd, Calcutta 20 Bengal, India

RAY, WILLIAM F., banker; b. Cin., Sept. 17, 1915; s. William F. and Adele (Daller) R.; m. Helen Payne, 1939; children: Katharine Ray Sturgis, Barbara Ray Stevens, Mary Ray Struthers, Margaret Ray Gilbert, Whitney Ray Dawson, William F. III, Susan. A.B., U. Cin., 1935; M.B.A., Harvard, 1937. With Brown Bros. Harriman & Co., 1937—, asst. mgr., 1944-49; mgr. Brown Bros. Harriman & Co., Boston, 1950-67; partner Brown Bros. Harriman & Co., N.Y.C., 1968—; trustee emeritus Atlantic Mut. Ins. Co., N.Y.C.; mem. internat. bd. advice Australia and New Zealand Banking Group, Ltd. Bd. dirs., v.p. Robert Brunner Found.; bd. dirs. Downtown-Lower Manhattan Assn., Inc., Am. Australian Bicentennial Found. Mem. Bankers Assn. for Fgn. Trade (pres. 1966-67), Harvard Bus. Sch. Assn. (pres. 1963-64, exec. council), Robert Morris Assocs. (pres. N.E. 1962-63), Pilgrims U.S., Am. Australian Assn. (pres.), Phi Beta Kappa Assocs. (v.p., dir.), Order of Australia (officer, hon.), Sons of the Revolution (life), Am. Assn. Sovereign Mil. Order of Malta, Phi Beta Kappa. Republican. Clubs: Skating (Boston) (pres. 1956-58); Country (Brookline, Mass.); Union, India

House (N.Y.C.); Apawamis (Rye, N.Y.); Fishers Island (N.Y.) Country, Ardsley (N.Y.) Curling; Mountain Lake (Lake Wales, Fla.). Home: 1 East End Ave New York NY 10021 Office: 59 Wall St New York NY 10005

RAYBAUD, CHARLES ANTOINE, radiologist, educator; b. Marseille, France, Sept. 4, 1943; s. Antoine Marc and Marie Louise (Saillet) R.; m. Francoise Suzanne Causse, Dec. 11, 1970; children: Phillipe, Olivier, Sebastien, Catherine. MD, Med. Sch. Marseille, 1970. Resident U. Hosp. Marseille, 1967-71; radiology resident Washington U., St. Louis, 1972-73; asst. prof. Timone U. Hosp., Marseille, 1973-80; assoc. prof. U. Aix-Marseille II, 1980; vis. prof. radiology U. Wis., Madison, 1984-85; head radiology Nord U. Hosp., Marseille, 1985—; cons. pediatric neuroradiology Timone Children's Hosp., Marseille, 1985—. Mem. editorial bd. Jour. Neuroradiology, Paris, 1978—, Pediatric Neurosci., Basel, Switzerland, 1985—; contbr. articles on pediatric neuroradiology. Mem. Council Radiology Prof. France, Paris, 1980—, Sci. Council Regional Obs. Health, Marseille, 1985. Served with Civil Service, 1968-69. Mem. European Soc. Neuroradiology, French Soc. Neuroradiology, European Soc. Pediatric Radiology, Am. Soc. Neuroradiology, Radiol. Soc. of N. Am., French Coll. Interventional Radiology. Home: Traverse de L'Aumone, 13400 Aubagne France Office: Radiology Hosp Nord Ch Des Bourrelly, 13015 Marseille France

RAYL, GRANVILLE MONROE, religious association executive, founder; b. Sedalia, Mo., Aug. 21, 1917; s. Burley and Cordelia (Swope) R.; m. Hazel Arlene Gruver, June 8, 1952; children: Janet Arlene, Granville Alan. BTh, Faith Bible Coll. and Theol. Sem., 1964; DD, The Evang. Evangelism Crusades, 1962; ThD, Faith Bible Coll. and Theol. Sem., 1965. Ordained to ministry Fundamental Ministers and Chs., 1957. Regional dir. Fundamental Ministers & Chs., Inc., Kansas City, 1957-62; pres. Internat. Bible Coll. & Sem., DeSoto, Mo., 1963—, Assn. Internat. Gospel Assemblies, Inc., DeSoto, 1962—. Republican. Office: Assn Internat Gospel Assemblies Inc 411 S Third St DeSoto MO 63020

RAYMOND, CHARLES MICHAEL, lawyer; b. Chester, Pa., May 22, 1953; s. Charles Anthony and Theresa (Curney) R.; m. Sandra H. Brabham, May 22, 1984. B.A., La. State U., 1975; J.D., Loyola U., New Orleans, 1978. Bar: La. 1979, U.S. Supreme Ct. 1984, U.S. Ct. Appeals (5th cir.) 1979, U.S. Dist. Ct. (mid. dist.) La. 1981, (so. dist.) Tex. 1984, (we. dist.) Mo. 1984, (ea. dist.) La. 1983, D.C. 1987, U.S. Ct. Appeals (11th cir.) 1985, U.S. Ct. Appeals (D.C. cir.) 1987. Asst. city-parish atty. City of Baton Rouge and Parish East Baton Rouge, 1979-84; atty. Gill & Bankston, Baton Rouge, 1982-84, Camp, Carmouche, Barsh, Hunter, Gray Hoffman & Gill, Baton Rouge, 1984-86, E & P litigations Shell Oil Co., 1986—. Exec. v.p. La. Young Democrats, 1977-78; mem.-at-large East Baton Rouge Parish Dem. Exec. Com., 1979-83; coordinator City-Parish Atty.'s Office United Way Campaign, Baton Rouge, 1983. Moot Ct. judge, So. U. Sch. Law, 1983. Mem. Assn. Trial Lawyers Am., ABA, La. Trial Lawyers Assn., La. Bar Assn., Fed. Bar Assn., Pi Sigma Alpha. Democrat. Roman Catholic. Home: 241 10th St New Orleans LA 70124 Office: One Shell Sq Shell Legal Div Suite 4961 701 Poydras St New Orleans LA 70139

RAYMOND, GENE, actor, producer; b. N.Y.C., Aug. 13, 1908; s. LeRoy D. and Mary (Smith) Guion; m. Jeanette MacDonald, June 16, 1937 (dec. Jan. 14, 1965); m. former Mrs. Nel Bentley Hees, Sept. 8, 1974. Student, Profl. Children's Sch., N.Y.C. Broadway debut in: The Piper, 1920; other Broadway appearances include Eyvind of the Hills, 1921, Why Not?, 1922, The Potters, 1923, Cradle Snatchers, 1925, Take My Advice, 1927, Mirrors, 1928, Sherlock Holmes, 1928, Say When, 1928, The War Song, 1928, Jonesy, 1929, Young Sinners, 1929, A Shadow of My Enemy, 1957; other theater appearances include The Man in Possession, Dennis, Mass., 1946; other theater appearances include The Guardsman, 1951, The Voice of the Turtle, 1952, Angel Street, Richmond, Va., 1952, Petrified Forest, 1952, Call Me Madam, 1952, Private Lives, 1953, The Moon is Blue, 1953, Be Quiet, 1953, My Love, 1953, Detective Story, 1954, The Devil's Disciple, 1954, The Fifth Season, 1955, Will Success Spoil Rock Hunter, Los Angeles, San Francisco, 1956, Los Angeles, San Francisco, 1956, Romeo and Juliet, 1956, The Seven Year Itch, 1958, Holiday for Lovers, Chgo., 1959; appeared as Joseph Cantwell in nat. touring co.: The Best Man, 1960; other theater appearances include Majority of One, 1962, Write Me A Murder, 1962, Mr. Roberts, 1962, Kiss Me Kate, 1962; other roles include Candida, 1961, The Moon is Blue, 1963, Madly in Love, 1963; film appearances include Personal Maid, 1931, Stolen Heaven, 1931, Ladies of the Big House, 1932, The Night of June 13th, 1932, Forgotten Commandments, 1932, If I Had a Million, 1932, Red Dust, 1932, Ex-Lady, 1933, The House on 56th Street, 1933, Zoo in Budapest, 1933, Brief Moment, 1933, Ann Carver's Profession, 1933, Flying Down to Rio, 1933, Sadie McKee, 1934, I Am Suzanne, 1934, Coming Out Party, 1934, Transatlantic Merry-Go-Round, 1934, Behold My Wife, 1935, The Woman in Red, 1935, Seven Keys to Baldpate, 1935, Hooray for Love, 1935, Love on a Bet, 1936, Walking on Air, 1936, The Bride Walks Out, 1936, The Smartest Girl in Town, Transient Lady, 1936, There Goes My Girl, 1937, Life of the Party, 1937, That Girl From Paris, 1939, Mr. and Mrs. Smith, 1939; film appearances include: Cross-Country Romance, 1940, Smilin' Thru', 1941; film appearances include The Locket, 1946, Assigned to Danger, 1948, Million-Dollar Weekend, 1948, Sofia, 1948, Hit the Deck, 1955, Plunder Road, 1957, The Best Man, 1964, I'd Rather Be Rich, 1964; TV appearances include: U.S. Steel Hour, The Defenders, Playhouse 90, Ironside, Name of the Game, Judd for the Defense, Bold Ones, Mannix, others; author: teleplay Prima Donna; composer: songs Release, Will You?, Let Me Always Sing. Past v.p. Arthritis Found. So. Calif.; pres. Motion Picture and TV Fund, 1980; trustee Falcon Found., USAF Acad. Served with USAAF, 1942-45, ETO; served to col. USAFR, 1945-68. Decorated Legion of Merit and others.; Recipient Disting. Service award Arthritis Found.; Humanitarian award Air Force Assn.; Better World award VFW; Bronze Halo award So. Calif. Motion Picture Council. Mem. Screen Actors Guild (dir.), Acad. TV Arts and Scis. (bd. dirs.), Air Force Assn. (pres. Los Angeles chpt.). Clubs: Players (N.Y.C.); N.Y. Athletic; Bel Air Country (Los Angeles); Army and Navy (Washington); Order of Daedalians. Address: 9570 Wilshire Blvd Beverly Hills CA 90212

RAYMOND, JACK, journalist, public relations executive, foundation executive; b. Lodz, Poland, Oct. 6, 1918; s. Harry and Anna (Lange) R.; m. Gertrude Silverman, Oct. 6, 1946; children: David Alan, Judith. Student, CCNY, 1939. Sports writer N.Y. World-Telegram, 1934-38; ct. reporter, city editor, columnist N.Y. Daily North Side News, 1938-40; Corr. N.Y. Times, 1940-66, Berlin, 1946-47, Frankfurt, 1947-49, Bonn, 1949-52, Balkans, Belgrade, 1952-56, Moscow, 1956; Pentagon corr. N.Y. Times, Washington, 1956-66; pub. relations exec., pres. Thomas J. Deegan Co., Washington and N.Y.C., 1966-70; v.p. Bryan Publs., N.Y.C., 1970-74; founding pres. Internat. Inst. Environ. Affairs, 1970; pres. Dialog div. J. Walter Thompson Co., 1973-75; pres. Jack Raymond & Co., Inc., N.Y.C., 1975-87, chmn., 1987—; acting communications dir. Commonwealth Fund, 1987; Book reviewer The Villager, N.Y.C., 1970-74; cons. UN Conf. on Human Environment, 1972, also; Aspen Inst. Humanistic Studies, HABITAT, UN Conf. Human Settlements; adv. com. Center for Environ. Info. UN Assn./U.S., 1975-78; mem. Rumanian-U.S. econ. council U.S. C. of C., 1973-75; project dir. 1987 Workshop Internat. Environ. Bur. Internat. C. of C. Author: Power at Pentagon, 1964, Your Military Obligations and Opportunities, 1963; co-author: This is Germany, 1950; editor Upton Nooz, 1942-43; combat correspondant Stars and Stripes, news editor Naples and Rome edits., mng. editor Marseilles edit.; combat correspondant, war editor, editor Stars and Stripes mag. Paris edit., combat correspondant, news editor Frankfurt edit., 1943-45; also author articles. Trustee N.Y. Urban League, 1969-72; bd. dirs. Internat. Inst. Environ. Affairs, N.Y.C., 1970-74, pres., 1970-73; bd. dirs. Internat. Inst. Environment and Devel., London, 1974—, mem. adv. council, 1978-82, mem. exec. com., 1982—; bd. dirs. Epoch B Found., La Jolla, Calif., acting pres., 1977-85; trustee Moroccan-Am. Found., 1982—; bd. overseers Heller Grad. Sch., Brandeis U. Served with AUS, 1942-45. Decorated 5 Battle Stars, Bronze Star, Purple Heart. Mem. Council on Fgn. Relations. Clubs: Overseas Press Am. (N.Y.C.) (pres. 1972-76), Century Assn. (N.Y.C.), Friars (N.Y.C.); Nat. Press (Washington), Internat. (Washington). Home: Flintlock Ridge Rd RFD 3 Katonah NY 10536 Office: Look Bldg 488 Madison Ave New York NY 10022

RAYMOND, WILLIAM FRANCIS, agricultural research consultant; b. Weston, Somerset, Eng., Feb. 25, 1922; s. Leonard William and May (Bennett) R.; m. Amy Elizabeth Kelk; children: Christopher, Karen, Robin, Charles. BA in Natural Sci., Queen's Coll., Oxford, Eng., 1940-43, MA, 1950. Research sci. Med. Research Council Inst., London, 1943-45; head, biochemistry, animal nutrition, asst. dir. Grassland Research Inst., Berkshire, Eng., 1945-72; dep. chief scientist Ministry Agriculture, Fisheries and Food, London, 1972-80, chief scientist, 1981-82; ind. cons. Watlington, Eng., 1982—; vis. prof. Wye Coll. U. London, 1979-84; cons. Food Appointment Orgn., Rome, 1984, Commn., European Communities, Brussels, 1982—, World Bank, Washington, 1985-86. Author: Forage Conservation and Feeding, 4th edit., 1987; contbr. Alternative Uses in Agriculture and on the Land, 1987. Hon. treas. Rural (U.K.) Soc. for Responsible Use of Resources in Agriculture and on the Land. Recipient Research medal Royal Agriculture Soc. Eng., 1969; named Commdr. of Brit. Empire by Queen of Eng., 1978. Fellow Royal Soc. Chemistry, Brit. Grassland Soc. (pres. 1975), Brit. Soc. Animal Prodn. (pres. 1981). Anglican. Club: Farmers. Home: Periwinkle Cottage, Christmas Common, Watlington OX9 5HR, England

RAYNAUD, BERNARD MARCEL, physician; b. Paris, June 3, 1943; s. Andre and Barbara (Spiegel) R.; m. Daniele Chabot, Aug. 3, 1968; children: Helene, Stephane. MD, U. Lyon, France, 1970. Physician French Air Force, Metz, France, 1970-74; pvt. practice medicine Marly, France, 1974—; administering physician Moselle, France, 1975—; physician French Football League, Lorraine, France, 1976—, French Rys., Metz, 1976—. Author: The Story of the French Postal Service, 4 Volumes. town councillor Marly Town, 1974-77; served to capt. French Med. Air Force, 1963-74. Mem. Rassemblement pour la République Party. Roman Catholic. Clubs: GUVF, ACEMA. Office: Cabinet Med, 33 rue de la Croix St Joseph, 57157 Marly, Moselle France

RAYNAUD, JEAN-PIERRE, pharmaceutical company executive, researcher; b. Mazamet, Tarn, France, Sept. 24, 1938; s. Paul Jules and Simone Pauline (Cormary) R.; m. Claude Suzanne Jeanne Jammet, June 26, 1963; children—Isabelle, Anne-Charlotte, Luc. Degree in Electronics Engring., U. Toulouse, 1962; MSc, Laval U., 1964; D es Sci., Paris U., 1971; postgrad. Harvard U. Bus. Sch., 1980. Head biophysics lab., dir. biol. research Roussel-Uclaf Research Ctr., Romainville, France, 1966-80; dir. innovation Roussel-Uclaf Group, Paris, 1980—; mem. WHO task forces, Geneva, 1971-75; mem. DGRST Grants Commn., Paris, 1975-79; mem. biotech. com. Ministry Industry and Research, Paris, 1981-82; head biotech. relations Que. and France Ministry Affairs, Paris, 1981—; pres., ARIBIO, Paris, 1982—; v.p., Organibio, Paris, 1983—. Editor: Progesterone Receptors in Normal and Neoplastic Tissues, 1977; Hormones and Cancer, 1984; Medical Management of Endometriosis, 1984; mem. editorial bd. Jour. Steroid Biochemistry, 1981, Biofutur, 1982, Hormones: reproduction-metabolisme, 1984; contbr. over 200 sci. articles to profl. jours.; patentee in field. Sworn expert Ct. Appeals of Paris. Mem. Endocrine Soc., Harvard Bus. Club. Home: 51 Blvd Suchet, Paris France Office: Roussel Uclaf, 35 Bd des Invalides, 75007 Paris France

RAYNAULD, ANDRE, economist, educator; b. Quebec, Que., Can., Oct. 20, 1927; s. Léopold and Blanche (Gauthier) R.; m. Michelle Nolin, Oct. 15, 1951; children: Francoy, Olivier, Dominique, Isabelle. B.A. cum laude, U. Montreal, 1948, M.A. in Indsl. Relations magna cum laude, 1951; D.Econs., U. Paris, 1954; D.Econs. (hon.), U. Ottawa, 1976, U. Sherbrooke, 1976. Mem. faculty U. Montreal, 1954-71, founder, dir. Ctr. Econ. Research and Devel., 1970-72; vis. prof. U. Toronto, 1962-63; chmn. Economic Council Can., Ottawa, 1971-76; mem. Parliament for Que. Province, 1976-80; prof. U. Montreal, 1980—; exec. com. Canadian Social Sci. Research Council, 1961-63, 64-65; pres. Inst. Canadien Affaires Publiques, 1961-62; bd. govs. Canadian Labour Coll., 1962-66; dir., exec. com. CBC, 1964-67; trustee CBC Pension Fund, 1967-70; pres. Soc. Canadienne de Sci. Economique, 1967-69; mem. Royal Commn. Bilingualism and Biculturalism, 1969-70, Canadian Council Urban and Regional Research, 1971, Quebec Council Planning and Devel., 1971; chmn. com. inquiry French-lang. tchr.-tng. Western provinces Dept. Sec. State, 1971; mem. interfutures study group OECD, Paris, 1976-78; mem. bd. Inst. Research Pub. Policy, 1980—; research fellow Devel. Ctr. OECD, Paris, 1986-87. Author: Economic Growth in Quebec, 1961; The Canadian Economic System, 1967; La propriete des entreprises au Quebec, 1974, Institutions Economiques Canadiennes, 2nd edition, 1977, Le financement des exportations, 1979, Government Assistance to Export Financing, 1984; co-editor: Canadian Journal of Economics, 1965-70. Recipient ann. award des Diplomes de l'U. de Montreal, 1974; apptd. Officer of Order of Can., 1986; fellow Walter Levy Council on Fgn. Relations, Boston, 1977. Fellow Royal Soc. Can.; mem. Canadian Econs. Assn. (pres. 1983-84), Am. Econs. Assn. Liberal. Roman Catholic. Home: 4820 Roslyn St, Montreal, PQ Canada H3W 2L2 Office: Dept Econs, U Montreal, Montreal, PQ Canada H3C 3J7

RAYNER, LORD DEREK GEORGE, business executive; b. Norwich, Norfolk, Eng., Mar. 30, 1926; s. George William and Hilda Jane (Rant) R. Student City Coll., Norwich, Selwyn Coll., Cambridge U. (hon. fellow 1983). Joint mng. dir. Marks and Spencer, London, 1973—, joint vice-chmn., from 1982, chief exec., 1983-88, chmn., 1986— . Spl. adviser to Her Majesty's Govt., 1970; chief exec., procurement exec. MOD, 1971-72; mem. U.K. Permanent Security Commn., 1977-80; dep. chmn. Civil Service Pay Bd., 1978-80; mem. Design Council, 1973-75, Council RCA, 1973-76; adviser to Prime Minister on improving efficiency and eliminating waste in govt., 1979-83. Served with RAF, 1946-48. Fellow Inst. Purchasing and Supply, 1970. Office: Mark and Spencer, Michael House, Baker St, London W1A 1DN England

RAYNER, STEVE, cultural anthropologist, technology policy researcher; b. Bristol, Eng., May 22, 1953; came to U.S., 1980; s. Harold Frank and Esmé(Britton) R.; m. Patricia Lund, Oct. 25, 1987. BA in Philosophy, Theology, U. Kent, Canterbury, Eng., 1974; Ph.D. in Social Anthropology, U. Coll. London, 1979. Lectr. U. London, 1977-78; research assoc. Ctr. Occupational Community Research, London, 1978-80, Russell Sage Found., N.Y.C., 1980-81; sr. research assoc. Ctr. Occupational Community Research, 1981-86; research staff. Oak Ridge Nat. Lab., Tenn., 1983—. Author: (with J.L. Gross) Measuring Culture, 1985, (with J.G. Flanagan) Rules, Decisions and Inequality, 1987; contbr. articles to profl. jours. Vis. scholar Boston U. Sch. Pub. Health, 1982, Columbia U. dept computer sci., 1981, 82. Fellow Royal Anthropol. Inst.; mem. Am. Anthropol. Assn., Am. Sociol. Assn., Assn. Social Anthropologists of Commonwealth, Soc. for Risk Analysis, Internat. Research Group on Risk Communication, So. Sociol. Soc., East Tenn. Wine Soc., Sigma Xi. Avocations: cooking; wine tasting; canoeing; folk music. Home: 111 Grandcove Ln Oak Ridge TN 37830 Office: Oak Ridge Nat Lab PO Box 2008 Oak Ridge TN 37831-6206

RAZ, AVI, pharmacist, retail pharmacy executive; b. Insterburg, Germany, Feb. 18, 1926; came to Israel, 1936; s. Willy and Gertrud (De Vries) R.; m. Rina Ben-Avi, Oct. 20, 1946; children: Ittamar, Jaqueline, Ron. B in Pharmacy, London U., 1950; B in Econs., Hebrew U., 1955. Cert. pharmacist. Pharmacist St. Thomas Hosp., London, 1950-51; chief pharmacist Alba Ltd., Jerusalem, 1951-81, chmn. bd. dirs., 1980—; dir. Sci. Based Industries Camps Ltd., Jerusalem. Chmn. bd. dirs. Jerusalem Econ. Corp., 1981; bd. govs. Hebrew U., 1983. Served to lt. col. M.C. Israeli Army, 1950-83. Mem. Israel Pharm. Soc. (chmn. 1988—). Mem. Liberal party. Jewish. Home: 14 Gichon St, Jerusalem Israel Office: Jerusalem Econ Corp, 12 Sarei Israel St, Jerusalem Israel

RAZ, IGAL, chemical engineer; b. Haifa, Israel, July 25, 1937; s. Sheraga and Yaffa (Stienwoorztell) R.; m. Nicole Ninnette Castro/Raz, June 21, 1981; children—Hila, Gilad; children by previous marriage—Sigal, Abigail, Michal. B.Sc., Technion, 1959, Diplom Engr., 1961. Project engr. Israel Atomic Energy, Beer-Sheva, 1959-65; prodn. engr. Berk Ltd., London, 1965-66; process engr. Nuclear Chem. Plant, London, 1966-67, sr. processing and cost engr. IMI, Haifa, 1967-70, comml. mgr., 1970-76, dep. mng. dir., 1976-86, sr. v.p., 1986—; dir. Solida Bonding Ltd., Potassium Nitrates. Served with Israeli Army, 1959-62. Mem. Licensing Execs. Soc., am. Inst. Cost Engrs. Home: 27 Yael St, Kiriat Motzkin 26323, Isreal Office: IMI, PO Box 313, Haifa 31002, Israel

RAZAFIMAHATRATRA, VICTOR CARDINAL, archbishop of Tananarive; b. Ambanitsilena-Ranomansina, Madagascar, Sept. 8, 1921; Joined S.J., 1945, ordained priest Roman Cath. Ch., 1956; rector of Fianarantsoa Minor Sem., 1960-63; superior Jesuit residence at Ambositra, 1963-69; rector of Tananarive Maj. Sem., 1969-71; bishop of Farafangana, 1971; archbishop of Tananarive, 1976—; elevated to Sacred Coll. Cardinals, 1976; titular ch. Holy Cross in Jerudalem; pres. Madagascar Episcopal Conf.; mem. Congregation Evangelization of Peoples, Commn. Revision Code Canon Law. Address: Archeveche Andohalo, Antananarive Democratic Republic of Madagascar *

RAZALI, SYAHRUM, architect; b. Tanjung Balai, North Sumatera, Indonesia, May 10, 1941; s. Razali Sulaiman and Mahani (Ani) Wahab; m. Tieke Merdikanti, May 22, 1971; children: Arkinova, Arry Saladdin, Mohamad Rizki. Grad., Bandung Inst. Tech., Indonesia, 1972. Cert. engr. in architecture. Head bldg. permit dept. City of Medan, Indonesia, 1972-76; lectr. architecture planning and design Faculty Engring., U. Indonesia, Jakarta, 1976-77; housing estate project mgr. Nat. Housing Corp., Cirebow, Indonesia, 1977-79; head estate mgmt. dept. Nat. Housing Corp., Jakarta, 1979-81; dist. mgr. Nat. Housing Corp., Medan, 1981-84; dir. P. T. Cail Indonesia Cons., Medan, 1987—; architect Medan Architect Services P.T., 1972-76; sr. architect P. T. Cipta Pura Inc., Jakarta, 1976-77; lectr. Pub. Work's Acad. Engring., Cirebon, 1977-79, Medan Inst. Tech., 1981—. Fellow Inst. Architects Indonesia (chmn. 1982), Real Estate Indonesia; mem. Indonesia Inst. Engring. Golongan Karya. Moslem. Club: Tsi. Lodge: Rotary. Home: 45 S Jalan Brigjen Katamso, 20151 Medan Nort Sumatera, Indonesia Office: Medan Inst Tech, Jalan Gedung Arca 52, 20151 Medan Nort Sumatera, Indonesia

RAZI, NAZIM HASAN, airline executive; b. Karachi, Sind, Pakistan, Apr. 15, 1951; s. Mohammed Razi Uddin Hasan and Ishrat Razi; m. Shehla Razi. BS, Islamia Coll., Lahore, Panjab, Pakistan, 1970; M in Bus. Edn., U. Panjab, Lahore, 1975. Sr. ops. and mgmt. analyst Pakistan Internat. Airlines, Karachi, 1975-78; indsl. engring. officer Pakistan Airlines, Karachi, 1978-81, remuneration planning officer, 1983-86, mgr. coordination to dir. adminstrn., 1986-87, asst. mgr. policies and procedures, 1987—; cons., advisor Booz Allen & Hamilton (N.Y.C.), Karachi, 1981-83. Club: YMCA (Karachi). Home: B-195 Block D, North Nazimabad, Karachi-33 Pakistan Office: Pakistan Internat Airlines, Head Office Bldg, Karachi Pakistan

RAZZANO, PASQUALE ANGELO, lawyer; b. Bklyn., Apr. 3, 1943; s. Pasquale Anthony and Agnes Mary (Borgia) R.; m. Maryann Walker, Jan. 29, 1966; children—Elizabeth, Pasquale, Susan, ChristyAnn. B.S.C.E., Poly. Inst. Bklyn., 1964; student law, NYU, 1964-66; J.D., Georgetown U., 1969. Bar: Va. 1969, N.Y. 1970, U.S. Ct. Appeals (2d, 3d, 9th and fed. cirs.), U.S. Supreme Ct., U.S. Dist. Ct. (so., ea. and western dists.) N.Y., U.S. Dist. Ct. (we. dist.) Tex. Examiner U.S. Patent Office, 1966-69; assoc. Curtis, Morris & Safford, P.C., 1969-71, ptnr., 1971—; guest lectr. U.S. Trademark Assn., Practicing Law Inst., N.Y.U. Law Ctr. Bd. editors: Merchandising Reporter, 1986—, Trademark Reporter, 1987—. Republican committeeman Rockland County. Recipient Robert Ridgeway award, 1964. Mem. Fed. Bar Assn., N.Y. Patent Law Assn. (bd. dirs. 1985—, sec. 1988—), Am. Patent Law Assn., N.Y. Bar Assn., Va. Bar Assn., Fed. Bar Assn., ABA. Republican. Roman Catholic. Club: N.Y. Athletic, Minute Man Yacht. Address: 15 White Woods Ln Westport CT 06880 also: 14 Deerwood Trail Lake Placid NY 12946

READ, CHARLES ARTHUR, lawyer; b. Washington, Dec. 14, 1919; s. Ernest James and Florence Albertine (Gude) R.; m. Marian Berky, May 23, 1953; children: Susan, Charles, Andrew. B.S. in Commerce, U. Va., 1941, J.D., 1947. Bar: Va. 1947, N.Y. 1948, U.S. Supreme Ct. 1962, D.C. 1965. Biology instr. U. Va., 1938-40; instr. naval scis. Notre Dame U., 1942-43; asst. prof. naval scis. Ga. Inst. Tech., 1946; assoc. Reid & Priest, N.Y.C., 1947-55, ptnr., 1956-86, mng. ptnr., 1981-86, sr. counsel, 1987—; gen. counsel Pub. Power Corp., Athens, Greece, 1950-52. Chmn. Republican Party, Upper Montclair, N.J., 1960-72; chmn. bd. Perkiomen Sch., 1971-79. Served to lt. USNR, 1942-46. Recipient Raven award U. Va., 1941. Mem. ABA, N.Y. State Bar Assn., Va. Bar Assn., D.C. Bar Assn., U. Va. Alumni Assn. (trustee 1976-82, pres. 1980-81), U. Va. Law Sch. Alumni Assn. (trustee 1982-87, pres. 1987—), Beta Gamma Sigma, Omicron Delta Kappa. Episcopalian. Clubs: Union League, Down Town Assn., Club at World Trade Center, Wall St., Montclair Golf, Farmington Country. Home: 162 Inwood Ave Upper Montclair NJ 07043 Office: 40 W 57th St New York NY 10019

READ, ELEANOR MAY, financial analyst; b. Arcadia, N.Y., July 4, 1942; d. Henry and Lena May (Fagner) Van Koevering; 1 child, Robin Jo. Typist, clk., sec., credit corr. Sarah Coventry, Inc., Newark, N.Y., 1957-61; exec. sec. Mobil Chem. Co., Macedon, N.Y., 1961-68; bus. mgr. Henry's Hardware, Newark, 1968-72; with Xerox Corp., Fremont, Calif., 1973—, internat. clk. analyst, personnel adminstrv. asst., employment coordinator, exec. sec., cycle count analyst., tax preparer H&R Block, 1985—. Mem. Xerox/Diablo Mgmt. Assn., Am. Mgmt. Assn., Profl. Businesswomen's Assn. Office: 910 Page Ave FM-239 Fremont CA 94538

READER, AUGUST LAFAYETTE, III, neurophthalmologist; b. Ft. Worth, Feb. 24, 1949; s. August Lafayette and Charlotte Ann (Perkins) R.; children; Adrienne Marie, Elizabeth Ann, Jessica Caryn; m. Nanette Marie Starke, May 11, 1984. B.S. in Biology, U. Tex., 1970, M.D., 1974. Diplomate Nat. Bd. Med. Examiners, Am. Bd. Ophthalmology. Intern in neurology Nat. Naval Med. Ctr., Bethesda, Md., 1974-75, resident in ophthalmology, 1975-76; fellow in neuroophthal E.S. Harkness Eye Inst., N.Y.C., 1978-79; neuroophthalmologist dept. ophthalmology Naval Hosp., San Diego, 1979-83, asst. chmn., 1983; neuroophthalmologist, ptnr. Beverly Hills Eye Med. Group, Los Angeles, 1983—; staff ophthalmologist Children's Hosp., Los Angeles, 1983—, Midway Hosp., Los Angeles, 1983—, Cedars-Sinai Med. Ctr., Los Angeles, 1984—; asst. clin. prof. U. So. Calif., Los Angeles, 1983—. Contbr. articles to med. jours. Served to lt. comdr. USN, 1973-83. Recipient cert. of appreciation from Alfred Atherton, U.S. Ambassador to Egypt, 1982. Fellow Am. Acad. Ophthalmology; mem. AMA, Calif. Med. Assn., Los Angeles County Med. Assn., Frank Walsh Soc. Democrat.

REAGAN, NANCY DAVIS (ANNE FRANCIS ROBBINS), wife of President U.S.; b. N.Y.C., July 6, 1923; d. Kenneth and Edith (Luckett) Robbins; step dau. Loyal Davis; m. Ronald Reagan, Mar. 4, 1952; children: Patricia Ann, Ronald Prescott; stepchildren: Maureen, Michael. BA, Smith Col.; LLD (hon.), Pepperdine U., 1983; LHD (hon.), Georgetown U., 1987. Contract actress, MGM, 1949-56; films include The Next Voice You Hear, 1950, Donovan's Brain, 1953, Hellcats of the Navy, 1957; Author: Nancy, 1980; formerly author syndicated column on prisoner-of-war and missing-in-action soldiers and their families; author: (with Jane Wilkie) To Love a Child. Civic worker, visited wounded Viet Nam vets., sr. citizens, hosps. and schs. for physically and emotionally handicapped children, active in furthering foster grandparents for handicapped children program; hon. nat. chmn. Aid to Adoption of Spl. Kids, 1977; spl. interest in fighting alcohol and drug abuse among youth: hosted first ladies from around the world for 2d Internat. Drug Conf., 1985; hon. chmn. Just Say No Found., Nat. Fedn. of Parents for Drug-Free Youth, Nat. Child Watch Campaign, President's Com. on the Arts and Humanities, Wolf Trap Found. bd. of trustees, Nat. Trust for Historic Preservation, Cystic Fibrosis Found., Nat. Repbulican Women's Club; hon. pres. Girl Scouts of Am. Named one of Ten Most Admired Am. Women, Good Housekeeping mag., ranking #1 in poll, 1984, 85, 86; Woman of Yr. Los Angeles Times, 1977; permanent mem. Hall of Fame of Ten Best Dressed Women in U.S.; recipient humanitarian awards from Am. Camping Assn., Nat. Council on Alcoholism, United Cerebral Palsy Assn., Internat. Ctr. for Disabled; Boys Town Father Flanagan award; 1986 Kiwanis World Service medal; Variety Clubs Internat. Lifeline award; numerous awards for her role in fight against drug abuse. Home and Office: The White House 1600 Pennsylvania Ave Washington DC 20500

REAGAN, REGINALD LEE, biologist, clinical pathologist; b. Broadford, Pa., July 19, 1910; s. James Blaine and Helen (McLaughlin) R.; Ph.D., U. Md., 1956; m. Marie Ann Johnson, Mar. 5, 1932 (dec. 1980); children—Nelda (Mrs. Dan Cullivan), Helen (Mrs. Bill Savage), Bill Olsen, Elsa (Mrs. Leo Sullivan); m. 2d, Ruth R. Rafferty, July 9, 1982. Joined U.S. Army, 1928, advanced through grades to maj., 1946; Rockefeller Found. Research asso. Rockefeller Inst., N.Y.C., 1936-40; faculty U. Md., College Park, 1946-61, asso. prof., 1948-52, prof. med. virology, 1952-61; chief virologist Jen-Son Lab., Kansas City, Mo., 1961-62; biologist Nat. Cancer Inst., Bethesda, Md., 1962-80. Mem. N.Y. Acad. Sci., Soc. Exptl. Biology and Medicine, Electronmicroscopic Soc., Ret. Officers Assn., Soc. Clin. Pathologists, AAUP. Author: One Man's Research, 1980; contbr. over 300 articles to profl. jours. Home: PO Box 6 Ohiopyle PA 15470

REAGAN, RONALD WILSON, President of U.S.; b. Tampico, Ill., Feb. 6, 1911; s. John Edward and Nelle (Wilson) R.; m. Jane Wyman, Jan. 25, 1940 (div. 1948); children: Maureen E., Michael E.; m. Nancy Davis, Mar. 4, 1952; children: Patricia, Ronald. AB, Eureka Coll., 1932. Gov. State of Calif., 1967-74; businessman, rancher, and commentator on public policy 1975-80, Pres. of U.S., 1981-89. Sports announcer, motion picture and TV actor, 1932-66. Served as capt. USAAF, 1942-45. Mem. Screen Actors Guild (pres. 1947-52, 59), Tau Kappa Epsilon. Republican. Home and Office: The White House 1600 Pennsylvania Ave Washington DC 20500 *

REAM, CAROLYN, job placement specialist, consultant; b. Tulsa, Feb. 17, 1920; d. John Clarence and Zelma Constance (Garner) Ghormley; m. Errol Jefferson, Sept. 15, 1951; 1 son, Eric Jeffrey. Student Okla. Sch. Bus., Accountancy, Law and Fin., 1937-38, U. Nev.-Las Vegas, 1968-69, Sacramento State U., 1974, San Diego State U., 1975. Cert. rehab. specialist. Personnel asst. U. Nev., Las Vegas, 1966-70; job devel. specialist Employment Security Dept., Las Vegas, 1970-74, State Bur. Vocat. Rehab., Las Vegas, 1974-76; counselor Nev. Indsl. Commn., Las Vegas, 1976-77, job placement specialist and pub. relations coordinator Jean Hanna Clark Rehab. Center (State Indsl. Ins. System, formerly Nev. Indsl. Commn.), 1977-84; pvt. practice cons. labor market access determinations, career devel., discriminatory employment practices against disabled, Las Vegas, 1983—; oral exam. bd. mem. State of Nev. Personnel Div., Las Vegas, 1967-84; cons., lectr. career orientation Clark County Sch. Dist., Las Vegas, 1971-73; cons., lectr. So. Nev. Meml. Hosp., Las Vegas, 1974-84; cons., advisor vocat. rehab., Tex. Inst. Rehab. and Research, Houston, 1975; cons., trainer Nev. Commn. on Equal Rights of Citizens, Las Vegas, 1975-76; cons., workshop coordinator Ohio Rehab. Services Commn., Columbus, 1978; cons., advisor Valley Hosp., Las Vegas, 1982; cons. accreditation William A. Callahan Rehab. Center, Wilsonville, Oreg., 1982; cons. accessibility for handicapped sta. KVBC-TV, Las Vegas, 1982; mem. Sr. Citizens Adv. Bd. City of Las Vegas, 1988—. Writer, producer shows: Jobortunity, sta. KLAS-TV, 1973; contbr. articles to mag.; author booklets in field. Chmn., Econ. Opportunity Bd. Clark County Adv. Bd. on Transp. for Handicapped and Srs., Las Vegas, 1975—; bd. dirs., sec. United Way Services, Inc., 1975—, chmn. budget com.; vice chmn. So. Nev. Com. on Employment of Handicapped, 1977—, chmn., 1984-85; mem. Winchester Town Adv. Bd., 1978—; mem. adv. bd. Nev. Assn. Handicapped/Ctr. for Ind. Living, 1985—. Recipient cert. of merit, Employment Security Dept., Las Vegas, 1973, cert. of apppreciation Nev. Spl. Olympics, 1973-74, Am. Lung Assn. Nev., 1982-83, Multiple Sclerosis Soc., 1982. Mem. Nat. Rehab. Assn. (Margaret Fairbairn award job placement div. 1975, Pacific region rep. 1984—), So. Nev. Personnel Assn. (dir. 1980), Phi Mu Alumnae (coll. advisor Las Vegas 1971, treas. 1972). Democrat. Congregationalist. Home: 400 Greenbriar Townhouse Way Las Vegas NV 89121

REAM, NORMAN JACOB, management consultant; b. Aurora, Ill., June 20, 1912; s. Edward Franklin and Margaret E. (Colbert) R.; m. Eileen Margaret Bouvia, May 24, 1952; children—Judith Ellen (Mrs. William B. Miles), Patricia Margaret (Mrs. Paul W. Michel), Norma Jane (Mrs. Robert Yamaguchi), John Patrick. B.S. in Accountancy, U. Ill., 1934; postgrad., Northwestern U., 1940-41. C.P.A., Calif., Ill., N.Y. Mem. controllers staff Pure Oil Co., 1934-41; accountant Touche, Niven & Co. (C.P.A.'s), Chgo., 1941-42; sr. cons. George Fry & Assos., Chgo., 1942-47; dir. accounting research IBM Corp., 1947-50; asst. treas. Lever Bros., 1950-53; corp. dir. systems planning Lockheed Aircraft Corp., 1953-65; dir. Inst. Computer Scis. and Tech., Nat. Bur. Standards, 1965-66; spl. asst. to sec. navy, also mem. navy secretariat 1966-69; prin. S.D. Leidesdorf & Co., 1969-71; chmn. Jamerica Cons. Group, 1971—; guest lectr. Japan Mgmt. Assn., Japan Productivity Center, 1963-67, Japan Acad. Sci., Hiroshima, 1965; Mem. U.S del. UN Conf. Application Sci. and Tech. for Benefit Less Devel. Areas, Geneva, Switzerland, 1963; speaker Internat. Mgmt. Congress CIOS XV, Tokyo, Japan, 1969, Constl. Assembly of Inter-Am. Center Tax Adminstrn., 1967, 1st Internat. Conf. on Communications, Tokyo, 1972. Contbr. articles to profl. jours. Gen. chmn. Incorporation City of Downey, Calif., 1954-56. Decorated Distinguished Civilian Service medal USN. Mem. Am. Inst. C.P.A.'s (hon.), Calif. Soc. C.P.A.'s, N.Y. Soc. C.P.A.'s, Am. Accounting Assn., IEEE (life), Inst. Mgmt. Scis., Am. Mgmt. Assn. (sr. planning council 1962—). Home: 511 Avenida San Juan San Clemente CA 92672

REAMS, BERNARD DINSMORE, JR., lawyer, educator; b. Lynchburg, Va., Aug. 17, 1943; s. Bernard Dinsmore and Martha Eloise (Hickman) R.; m. Rosemarie Bridget Boyle, Oct. 26, 1968; children: Andrew Dennet, Adriane Bevin. B.A., Lynchburg Coll., 1965; M.S., Drexel U., Phila., 1966; J.D., U. Kans., 1972; Ph.D., St. Louis U., 1983. Bar: Kans. 1973, Mo. 1986. Instr., asst. librarian Rutgers U., 1966-69; asst. prof. law, librarian U. Kans., Lawrence, 1969-74; mem. faculty law sch. Washington U., St. Louis, 1974—, prof. law, 1976—, librarian, 1974-76, acting dean univ. libraries, 1987—. Author: Law For The Businessman, 1974, Reader in Law Librarianship, 1976, Federal Price and Wage Control Programs 1917-1979: Legis. Histories and Laws, 1980, Education of the Handicapped: Laws, Legislative Histories, and Administrative Documents, 1982, Housing and Transportation of the Handicapped: Laws and Legislative Histories, 1983, Internal Revenue Acts of the United States: The Revenue Act of 1954 with Legislative Histories and Congressional Documents, 1983 Congress and the Courts: A Legislative History 1978-1984, 1984, University-Industry Research Partnerships: The Major Issues in Research and Development Agreements, 1986, Deficit Control and the Gramm-Rudman-Hollings Act, 1986, The Semiconductor Chip and the Law: A Legislative History of the Semiconductor Chip Protection Act of 1984, 1986, American International Law Cases, 2d series, 1986, Technology Transfer Law: The Export Administration Acts of the U.S., 1987; co-author: Segregation and the Fourteenth Amendment in the States, 1975, Historic Preservation Law: An Annotated Bibliography, 1976, Congress and the Courts: A Legislative History 1787-1977, 1978, Federal Consumer Protection Laws, Rules and Regulations, 1979, A Guide and Analytical Index to the Internal Revenue Acts of the U.S., 1909-1950, 1979, The Numerical Lists and Schedule of Volumes of the U.S. Congressional Serial Set: 73d Congress through the 96th Congress, 1984, Human Experimentation: Federal Laws, Legislative Histories, Regulations and Related Documents, 1985, American Legal Literature: A Guide to Selected Legal Resources, 1985, The Constitution of the United States: A Guide and Bibliography, 1987, The Congressional Impeachment Process and the Judiciary, 1987. Thornton award for Excellence Lynchburg Coll., 1986. Mem. ABA, Am. Assn. Higher Edn., ALA, Spl. Libraries Assn., Internat. Assn. Law Libraries, Am. Assn. Law Librarians, Southwestern Assn. Law Librarians (pres. 1977-78), ABA, Nat. Assn. of Coll. and Univ. Attys., Order of Coif, Phi Beta Kappa, Beta Phi Mu, Phi Delta Phi, Phi Delta Epsilon, Kappa Delta Pi., Pi Lambda Theta. Home: 3051 Thornbury Town and Country MO 63131 Office: Washington U Law Sch Box 1120 Saint Louis MO 63130

REASONER, GREGORY ALAN, electronics company executive; personnel mgr.; b. Marion, Ohio, July, 18, 1953; s. Irl and Nancy Jane Reasoner; BA, Miami U., Oxford, Ohio, 1976, MS, 1977; Dir. counseling services Chatfield Coll., 1977-78; dir. personnel Smith Clinic, Marion, 1978-80; corp. mgr. manpower and staffing Borden, Inc., Columbus, Ohio, 1980-81; mgr. personnel Advanced Robotics Corp., Hebron, Ohio, 1981-82; dir. human resources Gould, Inc., 1982-86; mgr. personnel NCR Corp., Cambridge, Ohio, 1986—; instr. Marion Tech. Coll., 1979-80; chmn. personnel council Marion Area C. of C., 1980-81. Bd. dirs. Cambridge Performing Arts Ctr. Mem. Am. Soc. Personnel Adminstrn., Marion Econ. Council, Med. Group Mgmt. Assn., Marion Assn. Tng. and Devel. Home: 424 N 10th St Cambridge OH 43725 Office: NCR Corp PO Box 728 Cambridge OH 43725

RÉAU, JEAN-PAUL, diplomat; b. Bordeaux, France, Aug. 26, 1941; s. Louis Henri and Jeanne (Sarthou) R.; children: Anne-Francois, Armel, Agnès, Delphine. Diplôme de Malais-Indonesien, Orientales, Paris, 1966; Diplome de Chinois, Ecole des LanguesOrientales, Paris, 1966; Licencées Lettres, U. Sorbonne, Paris, 1967. Licence en Droit. Asst. prof. Faculté de Droit, Lille, 1968-70; 2d sec. French Embassy, Beijing, 1970-74; head China desk Ministry of Fgn. Affairs, Paris, 1974-75; 1st sec., counsellor French Embassy, London, 1975-79; counsellor French Embassy, Washington, 1979-84; minister counsellor French Embassy, Beijing, 1984-87; insp. of fgn. affairs Ministry of Fgn. Affairs, Paris, 1987—. Office: Ministère des Affaires, Étrangères, 37 Quai d'orsay, 75007 Paris France

REBBECK, LESTER JAMES, JR., artist; b. Chgo., June 25, 1929; s. Lester J. and Marie L. (Runkle) R.; B.A.E., Art Inst. Chgo., 1953, M.A.E., Art Inst. Chgo. and U. Chgo., 1959; m. Paula B. Phillips, July 7, 1951; 1 son, Lester J. Asst. prof. art William Rainey Harper Coll., Pallatine, Ill., 1967-72; dir. Countryside Art Gallery (Ill.), 1967-73; gallery dir. Chgo. Soc. Artists, 1967-68; now artist, tchr.; one man exhbns. include Harper Jr. Coll.; group exhbns. include Univ. Club, Chgo., 1980, Art Inst., Chgo., 1953. Served with U.S. Army, 1951-52. Mem. NEA, Ill. Edn. Assn., Ill. Art Educators Assn., Chgo. Soc. Artists, Coll. Art Assn., Art Inst. Chgo. Alumni Assn. Republican. Presbyterian. Home: 2041 Vermont St Rolling Meadows IL 60008

REBEIZ, CONSTANTIN ANIS, plant physiology educator; b. Beirut, July 11, 1936; came to U.S., 1969, naturalized, 1975; s. Anis C. and Valentine A. (Choueyri) R.; m. Carole Louise Conness, Aug. 18, 1962; children: Paul A., Natalie, Mark J. B.S., Am. U., Beirut, 1959; M.S., U. Calif. - Davis, 1960, Ph.D., 1965. Dir. dept. biol. scis. Agrl. Research Inst., Beirut, 1965-69; research assoc. biology U. Calif. - Davis, 1969-71; assoc. prof. plant physiology U. Ill., Urbana-Champaign, 1972-76; prof. U. Ill., 1976—. Contbr. articles to sci. publs. plant physiology and biochemistry. Recipient Beckman research awards, 1982, 85, Funk award, 1985, John P. Trebellas Research Endowment, 1986; named One of 100 Outstanding Innovators, Sci. Digest, 1984-85. Mem. Am. Soc. Plant Physiologists, Comite Internat. de Photobiologie, Am. Soc. Photobiology, AAAS, Lebanese Assn. Advancement Scis. (exec. com. 1967-69), Sigma Xi. Greek Orthodox. Home: 301 W Pennsylvania Ave Urbana IL 61801 Office: Vegetable Crops Bldg U Ill Urbana IL 61801

REBELLO DA SILVA, LUIS A., glass company executive; b. Albergaria-A-Velha, Portugal, Sept. 20, 1931; s. Luis A. and Maria Jose (Roque) Rebello DaS.; m. Maria Teresa Bonneville Nesbitt, Dec. 22, 1958; children—Maria Margarida, Maria Teresa, Ana Filipa, Luis Augusto. Lic. mech. engrng. U. Lisbon, 1955. With Sorefame, Vigola, Productora (all Lisbon), 1957-64; factory mgr. Produtora Garrafas, Marinha Grande, 1964-66; sr. exec. CIVE, Lisbon, Portugal, 1967-70; mng. dir. Barbosa & Almeida, Oporto, 1971-77; gen. mgr. J.M. Fonseca Internat. Vinhos, Azeitao-Setubal, 1978-80; chmn. bd. Covina Co., Sta Iria de Azoia, Lisbon, 1980-88, ACTA Co., Lisbon, 1988—; lectr. Instituto Superior Tecnico, Lisbon, 1954-55, 1956-57, 61-62; dir. Fundicai de Oeiras, Lisbon, 1987—. Chmn., Juventude Escola Catolica Portugal, 1952-56, Juventude Universitaria Catolica, 1954-58. Mem. Soc. Glass Tech., Ordem Dos Engenheiros. Roman Catholic. Clubs: Sporting, Gremio Literario, American (Lisbon). Home: Av de Sintra 19-R/C Esq, Cascais 2750, Lisbon Portugal Office: Acta Actividedes Elēctricas Associadas SA, Av. Casal Ribeiro 18 80, Lisbon 1096 Portugal

RECANATI, RAPHAEL, shipping and banking executive; b. Salonique, Greece, Feb. 12, 1924; s. Leon and Mathilde (Saporta) R.; m. Diane Hettena, Oct. 8, 1946; children: Yehuda, Michael. Student Israel and Eng. Chmn. El-Yam Ships Ltd., 1953—; chmn. Discount Bank & Trust Co., Geneva, Switzerland, 1970; chmn., mng. dir. IDB Bankholding Ltd., 1970—. Home: 944 Fifth Ave New York NY 10021 Office: 511 Fifth Ave New York NY 10017

RECHCIGL, MILOSLAV, JR., government official; b. Mlada Boleslav, Czechoslovakia, July 30, 1930; s. Miloslav and Marie (Rajtrova) R.; came to U.S., 1950, naturalized, 1955; m. Eva Marie Edwards, Aug. 29, 1953; children: John Edward, Karen Marie. BS, Cornell U., 1954, M of Nutrition Sci., 1955, PhD, 1958. Teaching asst. Cornell U., Ithaca, N.Y., 1953-57, grad. research asst., 1957-58, research assoc., 1958; USPHS research fellow Nat. Cancer Inst., 1958-60, chemist enzymes and metabolism sect., 1960-61, research biochemist, tumor host relations sect., 1962-64, sr. investigator, 1964-68; grants assoc. program NIH, 1968-69; spl. asst. for nutrition and health to dir. Regional Med. Programs Service, Health Services and Mental Health Adminstrn., HEW, 1969-70, exec. sec. nutrition program adv. com. Health Services and Mental Health Adminstrn., 1969-70; nutrition adviser AID, Dept. State, Washington, 1970—, chief Research and Instl. Grants div., 1970-73, exec. sec. research and instl. grants council, 1970-74, exec. sec. AID research adv. com., 1971-83, AID rep. USC/FAR com., 1972-82, asst dir. Office Research and Instl. Grants, 1973-74, acting dir., 1974-75, dir. interregional research staff, 1975-78, devel. studies program, 1978, chief research and methodology div., 1979-82, research mgmt. and rev. dir. Office of the Sci. Advisor, 1982—; del. White House Conf. on Food, Nutrition and Health, 1969, Agrl. Research Policy Adv. Com. Conf. on Research to Meet U.S. and World Food Needs, 1975; cons. Office Sec. Agr., 1969-70, Dept. Treasury, 1973, Office Technol. Assessment, 1977, FDA, 1979, Nat Acad. Sci. NRC, 1985—. Author: The Czechoslovak Contribution to World Culture, 1964, Czechoslovakia Past and Present, 1968, (with Z. Hruban) Microbodies and Related Particles: Morphology, Biochemistry and Physiology, 1969, Russian edit., 1972, Enzyme Synthesis and Degradation in Mammalian Systems, 1971, (with Eva Rechcigl) Biographical Directory of the Members of the Czechoslovak Society of Arts and Sciences in America, 1972, 3d edit., 1978, 4th edit., 1983, 6th edit., 1988, Food, Nutritio983n and Health: A Multidisciplinary Treatise Addressed to the Major Nutrition Problems from a World Wide Perspective, 1973, Man, Food and Nutrition: Strategies and Technological Measures for Alleviating the World Food Problem, 1973, World Food Problem: A Selective Bibliography of Reviews, 1975, Carbohydrates, Lipids and Accessory Growth Factors, 1976, Nutrient Elements and Toxicants, 1977, Nitrogen, Electrolytes, Water and Energy Metabolism, 1979, Nutrition and the World Food Problem, 1979, Educators with Czechoslovak Roots: A U.S. and Canadian Faculty Roster, 1980, Physiology of Growth and Nutrition, 1981, Handbook of Nutritional Requirements in a Functional Context, 2 vols., 1981, Handbook of Agricultural Productivity, 2 vols., 1981, Handbook of Nutritive Value of Processed Food, 2 vols., 1982, Handbook of Foodborne Diseases of Biological Origin, 1983, Handbook of Naturally Occurring Food Toxicants, 1983, Handbook of Nutitional Supplements, 2 vols, 1983, U.S. Legislators with Czechoslovak Roots from Colonial Times to Present, 1987, others; co-editor: Internat. Jour. of Cycle Research, 1969-74, Jour. Applied Nutrition, 1970-82; series editor: Comparative Animal Nutrition, 1976-81; editor-in-chief: (series) Nutrition and Food, 1977—; mem. editorial bd.: Nutrition Reports Internat., 1977-80; translator: Chemical Abstracts, 1959—; contbr. articles to sci. jours. Organizer, mem. council Montrose Civic Assn., Rockville, Md. Nat. Acad. Scis. grantee, 1962. Fellow AAAS, Am. Inst. Chemists (councilor 1972-74, program chmn. 1974 ann. meeting, mem. program com. 1980 meeting), Internat. Coll. Applied Nutrition, Intercontinental Biog. Assn.. Washington Acad. Scis. (del. 1972—); mem. Am. Inst. Nutrition (com. Western Hemisphere Nutrition Congress 1971, 74, program com. 1979-82), Am. Soc. Biol. Chemists, Am. Chem. Soc. (joint bd.-council com. on internat. activities 1975-76), D.C. Inst. Che(pres. 1972-74, councilor 1974-80), Am. Inst. Biol. Scis., Soc. for Exptl. Biology and Medicine, Am. Soc. Animal Sci., Internat., Am. socs. cell biology, Soc. for Developmental Biology, Am. Assn. for Cancer Research, Soc. for Biol. Rhythm, Am. Pub. Health Assn., N.Y. Acad. Scis., Chem. Soc. Washington (symposium com. 1970, 71), Internat. Coll. Applied Nutrition, Internat. Soc. for Research on Civilization Diseases and Vital Substances, Soc. for Geochemistry and Health, Soc. for Internat. Devel., Internat. Platform Assn., Am. Assn. for Advancement Slavic Studies, Czechoslovak Soc. Arts and Scis. in Am. (hon., dir.-at-large 1962—, dir. publs. 1962-68, 70-74, v.p. 1968-74, pres. 1974-78, pres. collegium 1978—), History of Sci. Soc., Soc. Research Adminstrs., Sigma Xi, Phi Kappa Phi, Delta Tau Kappa (hon.). Clubs: Cosmos, Cornell (Washington). Home: 1703 Mark Ln Rockville MD 20852 Office: Office of Sci Advisor AID Washington DC 20523

RECINOS ARGUELLO, ORLANDO MAURICIO, electronic company executive; b. San Salvador, El Salvador, Mar. 9, 1939; s. Jose Alberto and Elvira (Arguello) R.; B.E.E., U. N.Mex., 1963; m. Paquita Casanovas, Nov. 6, 1965; children: Orlando Maruicio, Fernando Jose, Maria Elena. Constrn. elec. supr. Guajoyo Hidroelectric Project, El Salvador, 1962-64; asst. to gen. supt. Comision Ejecutiva Hidroelectrica del Rio Lempa, El Salvador, 1964-66, substas. supt., 1966-71; owner, pres. Autoconsa, El Salvador, 1971—; founder, pres. Meditron S.A., El Salvador, 1974—; founder, dir. Compucom S.A. de C.V.; dir. J.A. Recinos hijos Cia. UN for Indsl. Devel. fellow, Sweden, 1969. Mem. IEEE. Roman Catholic. Clubs: Circulo Deportivo Internacional, Centro Español. Home: la y 3a CP y Pasaje, Campos Colonia Escalon, San Salvador El Salvador Office: 37 Ave sur 543, Col Flor Blanca, San Salvador El Salvador

RECK, MICHAEL PIERCE, writer, American literature educator; b. Washington, July 27, 1928; s. Alfred and Daisy (Darling) R.; m. Hanne-Gabriele Baumann; divorced; children: Michael Hunter, Claudio, Christoph.; m. Margaret Elizabeth Mortimer, 1987. BA, Harvard U., 1950, MA, 1957; DrPhil, Ludwig-Maximilian U., Munich, 1968. Prof. U. P.R., Rio Piedras, 1962-83, U. Erlangen, Fed. Republic Germany, 1983, U. Bamberg, 1984—; columnist San Juan Star, P.R., 1981-83. Author: Ezra Pound, A Close-Up, 1967, 68, 73, 76 (in Spanish), 87 (in Japanese). Recipient Madeline Sadin award N.Y. Quarterly, 1978. Anglican. Home: Krimpling 331, A-5071 Wals bei Salzburg Austria

RECK, W(ALDO) EMERSON, retired university administrator, public relations consultant, writer; b. Gettysburg, Ohio, Dec. 28, 1903; s. Samuel Harvey and Effie D. (Arnett) R.; m. Hazel Winifred January, Sept. 7, 1926; children: Phyllis (Mrs. Louis E. Welch, Jr.), Elizabeth Ann (Mrs. Gabriel J. Lada). A.B., Wittenberg U., 1926; A.M., U. Iowa, 1946; LL.D., Midland Coll., 1949. Reporter Springfield (Ohio) News, 1922-26; publicity dir. Midland Coll., Fremont, Nebr., 1926-28; dir. pub. relations, prof. journalism Midland Coll., 1928-40; dir. pub. relations Colgate U., 1940-48; v.p. Wittenberg U., Springfield, Ohio, 1948-70; v.p. emeritus Wittenberg U., 1970—; pub. relations specialist Cumerford Corp., 1970-78; hist. columnist Springfield Sun, 1973-81; spl. corr. Asso. Press, 1928-38; mng. editor Fremont Morning Guide, 1939; vis. lectr. pub. relations State U. Iowa, summers 1941, 42, U. Wyo., summer 1948; lectr. pub. relations and hist. subjects. Co-dir. Seminar on Pub. Relations for High Edn., Syracuse U., summers 1944, 45, 46; Mem. commn. on ch. papers United Luth. Ch., 1951-62, cons. com. dept. of press, radio and TV, 1955-60; mem. commn. on ch. papers Luth Ch. in Am., 1962-64, 70-72, mem. exec. com., also chmn. com. periodicals of bd. publs., 1962-72; mem. mgmt. com. Office of Communications, 1972-76; chmn. pub. relations com. Council Protestant Colls. and Univs., 1961-65. Author: Public Relations: a Program for Colleges and Universities, 1946, The American College (with others), 1949, Public Relations Handbook (contbr.) , 1950, 62, 67, The Changing World of College Relations, 1976, Father Can't Forget, 1982, A. Lincoln: His Last 24 Hours, 1987; editor: Publicity Problems, 1939, College Publicity Manual, 1948; contbr. hist. and pub. relations articles to gen., ednl., profl. mags. Recipient award Am. Coll. Pub. Relations Assn. for distinguished service, 1942, for outstanding achievement in interpretation of higher edn., 1944, 47; award Council for Advancement and Support of Edn., 1977; medal of honor Wittenberg U., 1982. Mem. Am. Coll. Pub. Relations Assn. (v.p. in charge research 1936-38, editor assn. mag. 1938-40, pres. 1940-41, chmn. plans and policies com. 1944-50, dir. 1956, historian 1966-76), Luth. Coll. Pub. Relations Assn. (pres. 1951-53), Pub. Relations Soc. Am. (nat. jud. council 1952), Assn. Am. Colls. (mem. com. on pub. relations 1945-48), AAUP, Nat. Luth. Ednl. Conf. (chmn. com. pub. relations 1949-50), Ohio Coll. Pub. Relations Officers (pres. 1954-55), Clark County Hist. Soc. (pres. 1985-86), Nat. Trust for Hist. Preservation, Smithsonian Assos., Archives Assos., Nat. Hist. Soc. (founding asso.), Abraham Lincoln Assn., Blue Key, Sigma Delta Chi, Pi Delta Epsilon, Delta Sigma Phi, Omicron Delta Kappa. Home: 3148 Argonne Ln N Springfield OH 45503

RECTO, RAFAEL SUNICO, JR, orthopedic surgeon; b. Manila, Oct. 20, 1934; s. Rafael San Jose and Nicanora Paras (Sunico) R.; m. Aurora Santiago Cifra, Feb. 1, 1962; children: Rafael III, Isabelita, Ronaldo, Ruel. BA, U. Philippines, Quezon City, 1954; MD, U. Philippines, Manila, 1959. Resident, then chief resident Philippines Gen. Hosp., Manila, 1959-64; registrar Nuffield Orthopedic Ctr., Oxford, Eng., 1966-67; fellow Queen Mary's Hosp. Limb Fitting Ctr., Roehampton, Eng., 1967-68; research fellow Blodgett Meml. Hosp., Grand Rapids, Mich., 1968; chmn.dept. orthopedics Philippines Gen. Hosp., Manila, 1968-86; dir. Nat. Orthopedic Hosp. Rehab. Med. Ctr., Quezon City, 1987—; cons. Philippine Gen. Hosp.; mem. staff Med. Ctr. Manila, Makati Med. Ctr. Contbr. articles to profl. jours. Fellow Philippine Coll. Surgeons, Philippine Orthopedic Assn. Inc., Philippine Assn. Spine Surgeons, Western Pacific Orthopedic Assn., ACS, La Soc. Internat. Chirurgie Orthopedic et Traumatologie,; mem. Philippine Med. Assn., Internat. Soc. Prosthetics Orthopedics. Home: 34 Abueva St, Corinthian Gardens, Quezon City Philippines Office: Medical Center Manila, 1122 Gen Luna Ermita, Suite 304, Manila Philippines

REDD, JANET FAITH, librarian; b. Albany, Calif., May 24, 1945; d. Joseph Patrick and Faith Pauline (Schoen) R. B.A., U. Calif.-Berkeley, 1967, M.L.S., 1968; M.A., San Jose State U., 1974; Ph.D., Stanford U., 1980, postdoctoral scholar, 1984-86. Standard services credential, supervision-library services, Calif. Reference evening librarian asst. cataloger De Anza Coll., Cupertino, Calif., 1968-70, circulation librarian, 1970-77, acquisitions and periodicals librarian, 1978 , pres. faculty senate, 1984-85. Contbr. articles to various publs. Calif. State Scholarships fellow, 1963-68; U. Calif.-Berkeley scholar, 1963-67. Mem. ALA, Calif. Library Assn., Calif. Assn. Research Libraries, Am. Assn. Higher Edn., Assn. Coll. and Research Libraries, Am. Ednl. Research Assn., Wildlife Rescue Assn., Campanile Club, Tower and Flame, Phi Beta Kappa, Beta Phi Mu. Home: 21995 Via Regina Saratoga CA 95070 Office: De Anza Coll Learning Ctr 21250 Stevens Creek Blvd Cupertino CA 95070

REDDAN, E. DOUGLAS, financial consultant, investor; b. East Orange, N.J., Aug. 7, 1916; s. William J. and Catherine E. (Tansey) R.; student Stevens Inst. Tech., 1934-37, Newark Coll. Engring., 1938-40; m. Marian Williams, May 29, 1948; children—Susan (Mrs. Robert Maquire III), Jeffrey, Polly, Lisa Paige. Mech. engr. Aerospace div. Walter Kidde & Co., Inc., Belleville, N.J., 1937-42, sales mgr., 1946-52; v.p. Mil. div. Electronics Corp. Am., Cambridge, Mass., 1952-57; founder, chief exec. officer, dir. Infrared Industries, Inc., Santa Barbara, Calif., 1957-65, chmn. bd., 1965-66; dir. Nash Controls, Inc., Caldwell, N.J., 1961-64, Exotech, Inc., Falls Church, Va., 1961-65; dir. Electro-Nuclear Labs, Inc., Mountain View, Calif., 1961-65, pres., 1961-63; chmn. bd., chief exec. officer Rolair Systems Inc., Santa Barbara, 1970-76; vice chmn., dir. Century Mortgage Co., Fin. Corp. Santa Barbara, Santa Barbara Savs. & Loan. Bd. dirs. Santa Barbara Symphony Orch. Assn., Santa Barbara Mus. Art, Santa Barbara Med. Found., Music Acad. West, Santa Barbara, LaGuna Blanca Sch., Santa Barbara, Am. Nat. Red Cross, Cottage Hosp., Santa Barbara, vice chmn. Arthritis Inst., Arlington, Va. Served to lt. AC, USNR, 1942-46. Mem. Am. Ordnance Assn., Optical Soc. Am., ASME, Am. Mgmt. Assn., I.E.E.E. Clubs: Valley of Montecito (pres., gov.); Santa Barbara (gov.), Birnham Wood Golf. Contbr. articles on flight safety devices, electro-optical techniques to indsl. and aerospace to profl. publs. Patentee in field. Home: 475 Crocker Sperry Dr Santa Barbara CA 93108 Office: 1129 State St Suite 28 Santa Barbara CA 93101

REDDICK, W(ALKER) HOMER, social worker; b. River Junction, Fla., Mar. 26, 1922; s. Walker H. and Lillian (Anderson) R.; B.S., Fla. State U., 1951, M.S.W., 1957; m. Anne Elizabeth Hardwick, Sept. 7, 1947; children—Walker Homer, Andy Hardwick (dec.). Chief juvenile probation officer Muscogee County Juvenile Ct., Columbus, Ga., 1952-53; sr. child welfare worker Floyd County Dept. Pub. Welfare, Rome, Ga., 1955-56; chief social worker Montgomery County Dept. Pub. Health, Montgomery, Ala., 1957-59; dir. social services Ala. Bapt. Children's Home, Troy, 1959-64; casework supr. Youth Devel. Center, Milledgeville, Ga., 1964-71; dir. Family Counseling Center, Macon, Ga., 1972-81; cons. Appleton Ch. Home for Girls Group Homes, Macon, 1974-81; community columnist Macon (Ga.) Telegraph, 1980-81. Pres. Council Service Agys., Macon, 1975. Mem. Ala. State Adv. Com. on Children and Youth, 1961-64. Bd. dirs. Middle Ga. Drug Council. Served with AUS, 1940-43. Licensed marriage and family counselor, Ga. Fellow Royal Soc. Health; mem. Nat. Am. Legion, Assn. Social Workers (charter; bd. mem.-at-large Ga. chpt.), Acad. Cert. Social Workers, Am. Assn. Marriage and Family Therapists, Transactional Analysis Study Group of Macon (dir. 1974), DAV, 121st Inf. Assn. (historian 1981—). Episcopalian. Club: Masons. Contbr. articles to profl. jours. Address: 2485 Kingsley Dr Macon GA 31204

REDDIEN, CHARLES HENRY, JR., lawyer, business executive, securities financial consultant; b. San Diego, Aug. 27, 1944; s. Charles Henry and

Betty Jane (McCormick) R.; m. Paula Gayle, June 16, 1974; 1 son, Tyler Charles. BSEE, U. Colo.-Boulder, 1966; MSEE, U. So. Calif., 1968; JD, Loyola U., Los Angeles, 1972. Bar: Calif. 1972, Colo. 1981, U.S. Dist. Ct. 1981. Mgr., Hughes Aircraft Co., 1966-81; sole practice law, 1972—; owner, broker, real estate brokerage firm, 1978—; mem. spl. staff, co-dir. tax advantage group OTC Net Inc., 1981-82; pres., chmn. Heritage Group Inc., investment banking holding co., 1982-84, Plans and Assistance Inc., mgmt. cons., 1982-83, Orchard Group Ltd., investment banking holding co., 1982-84, J.W. Gant & Assocs., Inc., investment bankers, 1983-84; mng. ptnr., chief exec. officer J.W. Gant & Assocs., Ltd., 1984-85; chmn. bd. Kalamath Group Ltd., 1985-87, Heritage group Ltd. Investment Bankers, 1985-87; dir. Virtusonics Corp., 1985—; v.p., dir. Heritage Fin. Planners Inc., 1982-83; pres., chmn. PDN Inc., 1987—; exec. v.p., dir. World News Digest Inc., 1987—. Recipient Teaching Internship award, 1964. Mem. Calif. Bar Assn., Nat. Assn. Securities Dealers, IEEE (chmn. U. Colo. chpt. 1965), Am. Inst. Aero. and Astronautical Engrs., Phi Alpha Delta, Tau Beta Pi, Eta Kappa Nu. Contbr. articles to profl. jours. Office: Denver Pl Suite 2730 999 Eighteenth Denver CO 80202

REDDIX, JOSEPH WILLIAM, computer company consultant; b. Gary, Ind., June 26, 1949; s. James David and Ophelia (Valentine) R.; m. Cynthia Ann Ramseur, June 11, 1977; 1 child, Bryan Joseph. Student, Purdue U., 1973-76. Coil feeder Gary Sheet & Tin Co., Ind., 1972-73; programmer/analyst Gary Nat. Bank, 1973-77, United Airlines, Elk Grove Village, Ill., 1978-79; systems analyst Allied Van Lines, Broadview, Ill., 1977-78; project mgr. Am. Express Co., Phoenix, 1979-83; dist. systems cons./telecommunications Wang Labs., Phoenix, 1983-87; sr. telecommunications cons., Computer Task Group, Phoenix, 1987; sr. systems engr. Ariz. Pub. Service Co., 1987—; prin. systems cons. Mem. NAACP (Maricopa County Br.), Phoenix Urban League. Served with USN, 1968-72. Democrat. Baptist. Home: 17434 N 36th Dr Glendale AZ 85308

REDDY, MARAMREDDY PEDDA MADDULETI, oceanographer, educator; b. Suddamalla, A.P., India, July 2, 1935; s. Maramreddy Chinna Madduleti and Maramreddy Maddamma R.; M.Sc., Andhra (India) U., 1959, Ph.D., 1963; m. M. Kamala Reddy, Oct. 12, 1964; children—M. Manohar, M. Malathi. Council of Sci. and Indsl. Research sr. research fellow Andra U., Waltair, India, 1963-64; Nat. Research Council of Can. postdoctoral research fellow Bedford Inst. Oceanography, Dartmouth, Can., 1964-68; sci. pool officer Nat. Inst. Oceanography, Panjim, Goa, India, 1969-71; asso. prof. fishery oceanography, head dept. fishery hydrography Coll. of Fisheries, U. Agrl. Scis., Mangalore, India, 1971-84, prof., head dept. fishery oceanography, 1984—; mem. bd. of studies, mem. acad. council, 1972—; examiner in oceanography for various univs. India, 1972—; mem. selection coms. in oceanography and fishery sci. in India, 1981—; sr. v.p. (hon.) Siveast Cons., Inc., Dover, Del., 1982—. Contbr. articles on oceanography and fishery oceanography to sci. jours.; research in coastal oceanography, fishery oceanography. Home: 8 Hat-Hill Officers Quarters, Mangalore 575 006, India Office: Coll of Fisheries, U Agrl Scis, Mangalore, Karntaka 575 002, India

REDDY, PALAKURU CHENGAL, anthropology educator; b. Paleru, Andhra Pradesh, India, July 1, 1947; s. Palakuru Doraswamy and Palakuru Kristhnamma Reddy; m. Palakuru Gayatridevi, June 26, 1980; children: Palakuru Surya Swetha, Palakuru Surya Sreeram. BS, Govt. Coll., Andhra Pradesh, 1970; MS, Sri Venkateswara (Tirupati, India) U., 1973, PhD, 1980. Lectr. Sri Venkateswara U., 1979-85, reader, 1985—. Contbr. articles to profl. jours. Recipient career award U. Grants Commn., New Delhi, 1985-88. Mem. Indian Anthrop. Soc. (life), Indian Soc. Human Genetics (life), Current Anthrop. Assn. (assoc.). Home: 9-71 Padmavathi Nagar, Tirupati 517 502, India Office: Sri Venkateswara U, Tirupati 517 502, India

REDDY, YENAMALA RAMACHANDRA, metal processing executive; b. Polavaram, Andhra, India, Feb. 12, 1939; came to U.S., 1974; s. Y. Venkata and Y. Lakshamamma Reddy; m. Y. Uma Reddy, May 30, 1965; children: Y. Sharath, Y. Jay. BME, S.V. U., Andhra, 1961; M in Tech., IIT, Bombay, 1966, PhD, 1970. Lic. profl. engr., Wis. Asst. prof. IIT, Bombay, 1966-69; research and devel. mgr. Jyoti Pumps, Baroda, 1973-74; chief engr. Patterson Pumps, Toccoa, Ga., 1974-80; pres. R.B. Pump Co., Baxley, 1980—, U.B. Cons., Ga., 1980—. Contbr. articles to tech. jours. Postdoctoral fellow U. of Tech., Loughborough, Eng., 1970-73. Mem. Am. Soc. of Mech. Engrs. Office: R B Pump Co #1 Dixie Dr PO Box 557 Baxley GA 31513

REDEBAUGH-LEVI, CAROLINE LOUISE, senior action center coordinator, registered nurse; b. Dixon, Ill., May 23, 1910; d. Charles R. and May Caroline (Barnes) Kreger; m. Richard E. Belcher, Nov. 24, 1934 (dec. 1964); children—Richard Charles, Mary; m. Charles H. Redebaugh, Dec. 3, 1966 (dec. 1979); m. Paul Levi, July 20, 1985. R.N., Katherine Shaw Bethea Sch. Nursing, 1930. Nurse, various hosps., 1930-49; adminstr. Orchard Glen Nursing Home, Dixon, Ill., 1949-77; coordinator Sr. Action Ctr., Springfield, Ill., 1977—; mem. various adv. coms. advocating for srs. Contbr. articles to profl. jours. Mem. nat. adv. com., del. White House Conf. on Aging, 1981; v.p. Ill. Joint Council to Improve Health Care for Aged, 1953, pres., 1954. Mem. Capitol City Republican Women (v.p. 1983-84), State Council on Aging, Am. Coll. Nursing Home Adminstrs. (charter, edn. com., pres.), Am. Nursing Home Assn. (v.p. 1953), Ill. Nurses Assn. (bd. dirs.). Home: 1420 Eustace Dr Dixon IL 61021

REDELBACH, ANDRZEJ, legal educator, barrister; b. Wielkopolska, Poland, Mar. 12, 1946; s. Thadeusz Antoni and Izabela Irena (Jankowska) R.; m. Lucyna Teodora Kryńska, July 16, 1967; children: Michael Jakub, Marta Barbara Malgorzata Maria. LLM, Adam Mickiewicz U., 1969, Doctorate, 1972, habilitation, 1980. Asst. Adam Mickiewicz U., Poznán, Poland, 1969-71, sr. asst., 1971-72, lectr., 1972-81, assoc. prof. Faculty of Law, 1981—; legal advisor local govt. of Poznáń, 1982-83; barrister Barrister Chamber, Poznáń, 1983—, mem. disciplinary ct., 1986—. Author: National Unity Front--Its Constitutional Function, 1974 (Minister of Higher Edn's award 1975), National Unity Front--Model and Functioning of the National Front in Poland, 1978; co-author: The Growth of the Importance and The New Tasks of the Cooperative Movement, 1977, The Origin and the Substance of the Political Parties in the Western Countries, 1980, The Transformations in the Electoral Law in Poland, 1981, Protection of the Right to Life by Law and by Other Means, 1985. Recipient Medal of Merit local govts. of Szczecin, Poland, 1976, Kalisz, Poland, 1977, Poznáń, Poland, 1980. Fellow Soc. of Friends of Sci. Roman Catholic. Home: Slowakiego 47, 3 60-521 Poznán Poland Office: Adam Mickiewicz U, Faculty of Law, ul Wieniawskiego 1, Poznán Poland

REDELL, HOLLY M., communications consultant, writer; b. Bklyn., May 23, 1945; m. Donald W. Redell, Mar. 13, 1973 (dec. Nov. 1980); 1 child, Charles Walter. B.A., Adelphi U., 1966, M.A., 1968. Mgr. audio visual distbn. Nat. Edn. TV, N.Y.C., 1972-75, mgr. affiliate relations Eastern div. Group W Satellite Communications, Stamford, Conn., 1981-82; exec. dir. Am. Soc. Journalists and Authors, N.Y.C., 1976-80; pres. Spl. Program Sales, N.Y.C., 1980-84; dir. adminstrn. and devel. Inst. for Relationship Therapy, 1984-85; exec. dir. Council of Writers Orgns., N.Y.C., 1987—; cons. Reuters, Ltd., N.Y.C., 1983, Port of Seattle, 1984. Mng-editor Jour. Am. Soc. Journalists and Authors. Barbara Berry scholar, teaching fellow Adelphi U., 1964, 1966; broadcaster "Daywatch" Sta.-WMCA, as N.Y. expert, 1988; columnist N.Y. Parents and Kids Directory. Mem. Pi Delta Epsilon. Democrat.

REDFERN, WALTER DAVID, academic educator; b. Liverpool, Eng., Feb. 22, 1936; s. Walter Barton and Charlotte (Jones) R.; m. Angela Kirkup, Mar. 30, 1963; children: Kate, Sam. BA, Cambridge U., Eng., 1957, MA, PhD, 1960. Asst. lectr. U. Reading, Eng., 1960-63, lectr., 1963-72, reader, 1972-80, prof., 1980—; vis. prof. U. Ill., Urbana, 1981-82. Author: Paul Nizan, 1972, Puns, 1984, Georges Darien, 1984, A Calm Estate, 1987. Fulbright travel scholar, 1981-82. Home: 8 Northcourt Ave, Reading RG2 7HA, England Office: Univ of Reading, Whiteknights, Reading RG6 2AA, England

REDFORD, GARY WILLIAM, management consultant; b. Ogden, Utah, Jan. 13, 1951; s. James William and Lillian (Schmidt) R.; m. Marsha Adams, Sept. 9, 1978; 1 child, Joshua Weir. AAS, Utah Tech. Coll., 1974; BS, Weber State Coll., 1977; MBA, U. Utah, 1979. Programmer, analyst Surety Life Ins. Co., Salt Lake City, 1974-77, Skaggs Cos., Inc., Salt Lake City, 1977-78; sr. programmer, analyst dept. data processing U. Utah, Salt Lake City, 1978-80; prin., cons. G&M Cons., Salt Lake City, 1980-85, Lexus Group, Inc., Salt Lake City, 1984-85; v.p. Carter, Whitlock, Redford & Byrd, Inc., Salt Lake City, 1985-87; pres. G.W. Redford and Assocs., Salt Lake City, 1987—; prin. Tarrance Software, 1986—; instr. U. Utah, Salt Lake City, Weber State Coll., Ogden, 1980-86. Mem. Ch. Jesus Christ and Latter-Day-Saints mission to Mex., 1970-72. Republican. Mormon. Home: 1211 E 300 N Layton UT 84041 Office: GW Redford and Assocs 50 W Broadway Suite 1000 Salt Lake City UT 84101

REDFORD, MARCIA EMMALINE, library administrator; b. Moose Jaw, Sask., Can., Nov. 20, 1938; d. Charles William and Ruth Esther (Monkhouse) Wellington; m. David Arthur Redford, May 18, 1960; children—Karen, Keith, Holly. B.A., U. Sask., 1959; cert. Tchr. Coll., Moose Jaw, 1957; B.L.S., U. Alta., 1974. Library asst. Regina Pub. Library, Sask., 1959-60; tchr. Huron County Sch. Bd., near Exeter, Ont., Can., 1960-61, Our Lady of the Angels Sch., Fort Saskatchewan, Alta., Can., 1969-70; asst. librarian No. Sask. Inst. Tech. (now Kelsey Inst.), Saskatoon, 1965-66; dir. Fort Saskatchewan Mcpl. Library, 1975—. Contbr. weekly library column to The Record, Fort Saskatchewan, 1975—. Mem. council First United Ch., Fort Saskatchewan, 1983—. Mem. Can. Library Assn., Alta. Library Assn. Home: Box 3004, Fort Saskatchewan, AB Canada T8L 2T1 Office: Fort Saskatchewan Mcpl Library, 10011 102d St, Fort Saskatchewan, AB Canada T8L 2C5

REDGRAVE, VANESSA, actress; b. London, Jan. 30, 1937; d. Michael and Rachel (Kempson) R.; m. Tony Richardson, Apr. 28, 1962 (div.); children: Natasha Jane, Joely Kim. Student, Central Sch. Speech and Drama, London, 1955-57. Prin. theatrical roles include Helena in Midsummer Night's Dream, 1959, Stella in Tiger and the Horse, 1960, Katerina in The Taming of the Shrew, 1961, Rosaline in As You Like It, 1961, Imogene in Cymbeline, 1962, Nina in The Seagull, 1964, Miss Brodie in The Prime of Miss Jean Brodie, 1966; other plays include Cato Street, 1971, Threepenny Opera, 1972, Twelfth Night, 1972, Anthony and Cleopatra, 1973, Design for Living, 1973, Macbeth, 1975, Lady from the Sea, 1976, 78, 79; film roles include Leonie in Morgan-A Suitable Case for Treatment, 1965 (Best Actress award Cannes Film Festival 1966), Sheila in Sailor from Gibraltar, 1965, Anne-Marie in La Musica, 1965, Jane in Blow Up, 1967, Guinevere in Camelot, 1967, Isadora in Isadora Duncan, 1968 (Best Actress award Cannes Film Festival); other films include The Charge of The Light Brigade, 1968, The Seagull, 1968, A Quiet Place in the Country, 1968, Daniel Deronda, 1969, Dropout, 1969, The Trojan Women, 1970, The Devils, 1970, The Holiday, 1971, Mary Queen of Scots, 1971, Murder on the Orient Express, 1974, Winter Rates, 1974, 7 per cent solution, 1975, Julia, 1977, Agatha, 1978, Yanks, 1978, Bear Island, 1979, Playing for Time, 1980, My Body My Child, 1981, Wagner, 1982, The Bostonians, 1984, Wetherby, 1985, Prick Up Your Ears, 1987, Comrades, 1987; TV film and miniseries appearances include Snow White and the Seven Dwarfs, 1985, Three Sovereigns for Sarah, 1985, Peter the Great, 1986, Second Serve, 1986; Author: Pussies and Tigers, 1964. Bd. govs. Central Sch. Speech and Drama, 1963—. Decorated comdr. Order Brit. Empire; recipient Drama award Evening Standard, 1961, Best Actress award Variety Club Gt. Brit., 1961, 66, Best Actress award Brit. Guild TV Producers and Dirs., 1966, Golden Globe award, 1978, Acad. award for best supporting actress, 1977, Emmy award for best actress in limited series or special, 1980. *

REDHE, SVEN OLLE, dental surgeon, photographer; b. Falun, Sweden, Aug. 3, 1932; s. Olov Sigfrid and Martha Elizabeth (Johansson) R.; m. Solveig Ingalill Kronander, June 19, 1958; children: Ulf Olov Magnus, Eva Margareta. DDS, Tandlakarhogskolan, Malmo, Sweden, 1958. Pvt. practice dental surgery Falun, 1958—; cons. R-Dental AB, Falun, 1964—, The Central Inst. Dental Ergonomics, 1974—, Fedn. Dentaire Internat., 1977—. Author, editor: Are Your Teeth Your Headache?, 1985; photographer The Colorphoto Book, 1967, A Picturecavalcade With Photos by Olle Redhe, 1988; contbr. articles to profl. jours. and mags. Recipient Award of Excellence, Creativity 86, Communications Arts Mag., 1984. Fellow Internat. Coll. Dentists; mem. Brit. Dental Migraine Study Group, Acad. Gentium Pro Pace, Am. Equilibration Soc. Office: Falugtan 1, S79171 Falun Sweden

REDHEAD, MICHAEL LOGAN GONNE, history and philosophy of science educator; b. London, Dec. 30, 1929; s. Robert Arthur and C. (Browning) R.; m. Jennifer Anne Hill, Oct. 3, 1964; children: Alexander, Julian, Roland. BS, Univ. Coll., U. London, 1950, PhD, 1970. Dir. Redhead Properties Ltd., London, 1962—; ptnr. Galveston Estates, London, 1970—; lectr. Chelsea Coll., London, 1981-83, sr. lectr., 1983-84, prof., 1984-85; prof. King's Coll., London, 1985-87, U. Cambridge, Eng., 1987—; fellow Wolfson Coll., Cambridge, 1988—. Author: Incompleteness, Nonlocality and Realism, 1987; contbr. articles to profl. jours. Fellow Inst. Physic; mem. Brit Soc. Philosophy of Sci. Club: Hurlingham, commd. Queen's. Home: 34 Coniger Rd, London SW6 3TA, England Office: Cambridge U Dept Hist Phil Sci, Free Sch Ln, Cambridge CB2 3RH, England

REDLICH, MARC, lawyer; b. N.Y.C., Nov. 25, 1946; s. Louis and Mollie Redlich; m. Janis Redlich, Jan. 16, 1982; 1 child, Alison. B.A., Queens Coll., 1967; J.D., Harvard U., 1971. Bar: Mass. 1971, U.S. Dist. Ct. 1971, U.S. Ct. Appeals (1st cir.) 1974, U.S. Ct. Appeals (5th cir.) 1984. Assoc. Guterman, Horvitz, Rubin & Rudman, Boston, 1971-75; mem., sr. dir. Widett, Slater & Goldman, Boston, 1975-84; prin. Law Offices of Marc Redlich, Cambridge, Mass., 1984—. Mem. ABA, Mass. Bar Assn., Boston Bar Assn., Assn. Trial Lawyers Am., Nat. Assn. Coll. Univ. Attys., Cambridge C. of C., Phi Beta Kappa. Club: Harvard (Boston). Office: 1000 Massachusetts Ave Cambridge MA 02138

REDMAN, CLARENCE OWEN, lawyer; b. Joliet, Ill., Nov. 23, 1942; s. Harold F. and Edith L. (Read) R.; m. Barbara Ann Pawlan, Jan. 26, 1964 (div.); children—Scott, Steven; m. 2d, Carla J. Rozycki, Sept. 24, 1983. B.S., U. Ill., 1964, J.D., 1966, M.A., 1967. Bar: Ill. 1966, U.S. Dist. Ct. (ea. dist.) Ill. 1966, U.S. Dist. Ct. (no. dist.) Ill. 1970, U.S. Ct. Appeals (7th cir.), 1973, U.S. Ct. Appeals (4th cir.) 1982, U.S. Supreme Ct. 1975. Assoc., Keck, Mahin & Cate, Chgo., 1969-73, ptnr., 1973—, chief exec. officer, 1986—; spl. asst. atty. gen. Ill., 1975-81. Served to capt. U.S. Army, 1967-69. Decorated Bronze Star. Mem. Ill. State Bar Assn. (chmn. young lawyers sect. 1977-78, del. assembly 1978-81, 84-87), Chgo. Bar Assn., ABA, Seventh Cir. Bar Assn. Republican. Clubs: Union League, Met. (Chgo.). Am. Legion (Roselle, Ill.). Office: 8300 Sears Tower 233 S Wacker Dr Chicago IL 60606

REDMOND, DAVID DUDLEY, lawyer; b. Hartford, Conn., May 12, 1944; s. Robert LaVere and Dorothy Iva (Mylchreest) R.; m. Eugenia Blount Scott, Aug. 24, 1968; children—R. Scott, Sarah D. B.A., Washington and Lee U., 1966, LL.B., 1969. Bar: Va. 1970, U.S. Dist. Ct. (ea. dist.) Va. 1972, U.S. Ct. Appeals (4th cir.) 1972. Ptnr. Christian Barton Epps Brent & Chappell, Richmond, Va., 1972—. Served to capt. U.S. Army, 1970-71. Decorated Bronze Star. Mem. ABA, Va. State Bar, Va. Bar Assn., Richmond Bar Assn. (exec. com. 1980), Washington and Lee U. Alumni Assn. (pres. Richmond chpt. 1980-82), Omicron Delta Kappa. Editorial bd. Washington and Lee U. Law Rev., 1968-69. Office: Suite 1200 Mutual Bldg Richmond VA 23219

REDO, S(AVERIO) FRANK, surgeon; b. Bklyn., Dec. 28, 1920; s. Frank and Maria (Guida) R.; m. Maria Lappano, June 27, 1948; children—Philip, Martha. B.S., Queens Coll., 1942; M.D., Cornell U., 1950. Diplomate: Am. Bd. Thoracic Surgery, Am. Bd. Surgery (pediatric surgery). Intern in surgery N.Y. Hosp., N.Y.C., 1950-51; asst. resident surgeon N.Y. Hosp., 1951-56, resident surgeon, 1956-57, asst. attending surgeon, 1958-60, asso. attending surgeon, 1960-66, surgeon in charge pediatric surgery, 1960, attending surgeon, 1966—; practice medicine specializing in surgery; clin. asso. prof. surgery Cornell U. Med. Coll., 1963-72, prof., 1972—. Author: Surgery in the Ambulatory Child, 1961, Principles of Surgery in the First Six Months of Life, 1976, Atlas of Surgery in the First Six Months of Life, 1977; contbr. articles to profl. jours. Served to capt. USAAF, 1942-46. Fellow A.C.S., Am. Coll. Chest Physicians; mem. Harvey Soc., Pan Am. Med. Assn., Soc. Univ. Surgeons, Am. Acad. Pediatrics, Am. Fedn. for Clin. Research, Internat. Cardiovascular Soc., Am. Surg. Assn., Am. Assn. Thoracic Surgery, Soc. for Surgery Alimentary Tract, Am. Soc. Artificial Internat. Organs, Am. Acad. Pediatrics, Assn. Advancement Med. Instrumentation, Soc. Thoracic Surgeons, Internat. Soc. Surgery, N.Y. Gastroent. Soc., N.Y. Acad. Sci., N.Y. Cardiovascular Soc., N.Y. Acad. Medicine, N.Y. Soc. Thoracic Surgery, N.Y. Pediatric Soc., Med. Soc. County N.Y., Queens Coll. Alumni Assn. (gov. 1962—), Sigma Xi. Home: 435 E 70th St New York NY 10021 Office: 525 E 68th St New York NY 10021

REDSTONE, SUMNER MURRAY, theatre executive, lawyer; b. Boston, May 27, 1923; s. Michael and Belle (Ostrovsky) R.; m. Phyllis Gloria Raphael, July 6, 1947; children—Brent Dale, Shari Ellin. B.A., Harvard U., 1944, LL.B., 1947. Bar: Mass. 1947, U.S. Ct. Appeals (1st cir.) 1948, U.S. Ct. Appeals (8th cir.) 1950, U.S. Ct. Appeals (9th cir.) 1948, D.C. 1951, U.S. Supreme Ct. 1952. Law sec. U.S. Ct. Appeals for 9th Circuit, San Francisco, 1947-48; instr. law and labor mgmt. U. San Francisco, 1947; spl. asst. to U.S. atty. gen., Washington, 1948-51; partner firm Ford, Bergson, Adams, Borkland & Redstone, Washington, 1951-54; pres., chief exec. officer Natl. Amusements, Inc., Dedham, Mass., 1967—, also chmn. bd. dirs., 1986—; chmn. bd. Viacom Internat., Inc.; prof. Boston U. Law Sch., 1982, 85-86. Chmn. met. div. NE Combined Jewish Philanthropies, Boston, 1963; mem. corp. New Eng. Med. Center, 1967—; trustee Children's Cancer Research Found.; chmn. Am. Cancer Crusade, State of Mass., 1984-86; Art Lending Library; sponsor Boston Mus. Sci.; chmn. Jimmy Fund Found., 1960; v.p., mem. exec. com. Will Rogers Meml. Fund; bd. dirs. Boston Arts Festival; bd. overseers Dana Farber Cancer Center, Boston Mus. Fine Arts; mem. presdl. adv. com. on arts John F. Kennedy Center for Performing Arts; bd. dirs. John F. Kennedy Library Found. Served to 1st lt. AUS, 1943-45. Decorated Army Commendation medal; recipient William J. German Human Relations award Am. Jewish Com. Entertainment and Communication Div., 1977, Silver Shingle award Boston U. Law Sch., 1985; named one of ten outstanding young men Greater Boston C. of C., 1958, Communicator of Yr. B'nai B'rith Communications/Cinema Lodge, 1980. Mem. Am. Congress Exhibitors (exec. com. 1961—), Theatre Owners Am. (asst. pres. 1960-63, pres. 1964-65), Nat. Assn. Theatre Owners (chmn. bd. dirs. 1965-66), Motion Picture Pioneers (bd. dirs.), Am., Boston, Mass. bar assns., Harvard Law Sch. Assn., Am. Judicature Soc. Clubs: Mason, University, Variety New Eng., Harvard (Boston). Home: 98 Baldpate Hill Rd Newton Centre MA 02159 Office: Nat Amusements Inc 200 Elm St Dedham MA 02026

REED, ADAM VICTOR, psychologist, engineer; b. Torun, Poland, Jan. 11, 1946; came to U.S., 1959, naturalized, 1965; s. Henry Kenneth and Eva (Tenenbaum) R.; B.S. in E.E., M.I.T., 1967, M.S. in Biology and M.S. in E.E., 1970; Ph.D., U. Oreg., 1974; m. Barbara Irene Birnbaum, Dec. 26, 1982; 1 child, Halina Brooke. Research programmer Artificial Intelligence Lab., M.I.T., Cambridge, 1965; research engr. Hewlett Packard Co., Palo Alto, Calif., 1966-67; mem. research staff Riverside Research Inst., N.Y.C., 1970-71; postdoctoral fellow, adj. asst. prof. Rockefeller U., N.Y.C., 1974-78; asst. prof., vis. lectr. psychology Grad. Faculty Social and Polit. Sci., New Sch. Social Research, N.Y.C., 1977-82; mem. tech. staff AT&T Bell Labs., AT&T Info. Systems, 1981—; peer rev. referee NSF, others. Sci. and tech. adv. Libertarian Party v.p. candidate Tonie Nathan, 1972. NDEA Title IV fellow, 1967-70; NSF fellow, 1970-73; NIMH Research Service fellow, 1974-77. Mem. N.Y. Acad. Sci., IEEE, Am. Psychol. Assn., Soc. Engring. Psychologists, Assn. Computing Machinery, Am. Soc. Cybernetics, AAAS, Sigma Xi, Tau Beta Pi, Eta Kappa Nu. Libertarian. Patentee in field; contbr. articles to profl. jours.

REED, A(LFRED) BYRON, retired apparel manufacturing company executive; b. Indpls., June 30, 1916; s. Alfred Lumpkin and Myrtle (Wood) R.; m. Mary Ellen Myers, Sept. 1, 1950; 1 child, Charles W. BS., Butler U., 1939; postgrad., U. Chgo., 1946-47. Asst. brokerage mgr. Conn. Gen. Life Ins. Co., Chgo., 1939-41; sales mgr., mktg. mgr., asst. gen. mgr. Vassar Co., Chgo., 1946-57; gen. mgr. women's div. Munsingwear, Inc., Mpls., 1958-66; pres., chief exec. officer Munsingwear, Inc., 1966-79, chmn., 1979-81, also dir.; dir., trust com., exec. com. 1st Nat. Bank Mpls., Hoerner Waldorf Co., St. Paul, 1973-77, Murphy Motor Freight; mem. mgmt.-labor textile adv. com. U.S. Dept. Commerce. Chmn. Nat. Alliance Businessmen, Mpls., 1971-72; mem. Adv. Council U.S.-Japan Econ. Relations, Washington, also exec. com.; adviser Council Fin. Aid to Edn.; chmn. U.S. Savs. Bond Drive, 1975-76; Bd. dirs. Better Bus. Bur. Mpls., 1973-74, Minn. Pvt. Coll. Fund, Mpls. YMCA; trustee Butler U. Served to lt. USNR, 1942-46. Mem. Am. Apparel Mfrs. Assn. (chmn. bd. dirs., exec. com.), U.S. C. of C. (internat. policy com., internat. trade subcom.), Mpls. C. of C. (dir.), Phi Delta Theta. Republican. Episcopalian. Clubs: Minneapolis, Minikahda (Mpls.); Mission Viejo (Calif.) Country. Home: 23521 Via Murillo Mission Viejo CA 92692 also: 16750 Iroquois Dr Indian Wells CA 92210

REED, CHRISTOPHER ROBERT, civil engineer; b. Charleston, W.Va., Feb. 12, 1948; s. Clarence Milton and Anne (Schaffner) R.; m. Mary Dandridge Kennedy, Mar. 4, 1983. Student W.Va. Inst. Tech., 1966-70, 76-77, Ga. State U., 1973-74. Designer, Sverdrup & Parcel, Charleston, 1970-72; asso. project engr. Mayes, Sudderth & Etheredge, Atlanta, 1973-76; project mgr. Sverdrup & Parcel, Washington, 1976-79; estimator Deleuw, Cather/Parsons, Washington, 1979-80; project mgr. Parsons Brinckerhoff, McLean, Va., 1980-85; assoc. Loledeaman Assocs., Inc.; Rockville, Md., 1985-86; assoc. Post Buckley Schuh and Jernigan Inc., Arlington, Va., 1986—. Mem. Constrn. Specifications Inst., Am. Assn. Cost Engrs., Am. Ry. Engring. Assn., Soc. Am. Mil. Engrs., Am. Pub. Transit Assn., ASTM. Home: 2334 Generation Dr Reston VA 22091 Office: 2000 15th St N Suite 506 Arlington VA 22201

REED, JANE GARSON, controller, accounting educator; b. Cleve., Jan. 11, 1948; d. Joseph John Guzowski and Irene Sophie (Dominic) Garson; m. Wayne Ellis Reed, May 17, 1969; children: Craig Michael, Kevin Matthew. BBA magna cum laude, Baldwin Wallace Coll., 1977; MBA, Case Western Res. U., 1983. CPA, Ohio. Letter carrier U.S. Postal Service, Brecksville, Ohio, 1966-76; sr. asst. acct. Deloitte, Haskins & Sells, Cleve., 1977-78; sr. corp. auditor White Motor Corp., Beachwood, Ohio, 1979-81; instr. acctg. Cuyahoga Community Coll., Parma, 1981-82; ind. contractor State of Wash., Olympia, 1982-84; dir. fin. The Montefiore Home, Cleveland Heights, Ohio, 1985-86; controller, bus. mgr. Western Res. Human Services, Inc., Akron, Ohio, 1986-87; lectr. mgmt. acctg. U. Akron, 1987-88; controller Multi-Care Mgmt. Co., Beachwood, 1988—; instr. acctg. Cuyahoga Community Coll., Parma, Ohio, 1981, 82. Fin. sec. to bd. dirs. Prince of Peace Luth. Ch., Medina, Ohio, 1978-79; mem. budget and fin. com. Wooster (Ohio) dist. office United Meth. Ch., 1983-84; mem. Brunswick High Sch. Band and Choir Boosters, 1984—; cub scout leader Boy Scouts Am., Brunswick, 1978-79; agt. Trinity High Sch. Alumni; mem. fin. com. Brunswick United Meth. Ch., 1988—, also budget com., 1988—. Mem. Am. Inst. CPA's, Am. Women's Soc. CPA's, Ohio Soc. CPA's (mem.-in-industry com. 1980-82), Nat. Assn. Accts., Soc. for Advancement Mgmt. (reactivated chpt. pres 1976-77). Methodist. Home: 1254 Hadcock Rd Brunswick OH 44212 Office: Multi-Care Mgmt 3659 S Green Rd Suite 320 Beachwood OH 44122

REED, JESSE FRANCIS, entrepreneur, artist, inventor, theologian, business consultant; b. Federalsburg, Md., June 6, 1925; s. Homer F. and Lola Irene (Stevens) R.; BFA, Montclair Coll., 1950; D.D., Gnostic Sem., 1968; m. Mary Grace Mayo, July 9, 1944; 1 son, Gary. Owner, Reed's Frozen Foods, Paterson, N.J., 1950-59; pres. A.E. Inc., N.Y.C., 1959-72, Intercontinental Bus. Research & Devel. Inc., San Francisco, 1959-72, chmn. bd., pres. Dallas and Washington, 1972—, Intercontinental Oil & Ore Inc., Carson City, Nev. and Dallas, 1972—; chmn. bd., pres. COSMO U.S.A., Inc., Dallas and Washington, 1974—, Internat. Art Exchange Ltd., Dallas and Los Angeles, 1980—; chmn. bd. Gnosis, 1980—. Chmn. bd. Internat. Arts Soc., Inc., Dallas, 1981—; dir. XTR Corp. Bd. dirs. Am. Art Alliance, Inc., Internat. Fine Art, Inc., Worldwide Art Exchange, Inc. Gnostic Ch. Served with USN, 1942-46. Recipient various Art Show awards in Tex., Calif., N.J., N.Y., Ga., Fla., Wash., Ill., Hawaii, Minn., Nev., N.Mex., Oreg., Mo., Can., Eng., France, Belgium, Norway, Sweden, Denmark, Switzerland, Australia, N.Z. Mem. Screen Writers Guild, Cattlemen's Assn. Inventor protein converter (controlled environ. food prodn. chain), visual edn. system to translate all edml. disciplines into their pictorial presentations, modular prefabricate bldg. systems, solar energy systems, hydroponics systems, plasma energy systems, elect. vehicle systems, subliminal learning systems. Home and Office: Box 12488 Dallas TX 75225

REED, JOHN SHEPARD, banker; b. Chgo., Feb. 7, 1939; married; 4 children. BA, Washington and Jefferson Coll., 1959; BS, MIT, 1961; MS, Sloan Sch., 1965. Former systems analyst Goodyear Tire & Rubber Co.; with Citibank N.A., 1965—, former vice chmn., now chmn., chief exec. officer, dir.; with Citicorp (parent), N.Y.C., sr. exec. v.p. individual banking, then vice-chmn., 1982-84, chmn., chief exec. officer, 1984—, dir.; dir. Philip Morris, Inc., United Techs. Corp., Rand Corp., Monsanto Co. Mem. Meml. Sloan-Kettering Cancer Ctr, MIT, Ctr. for Advanced Study in Behavioral Scis., Woodrow Wilson Internat. Ctr. for Scholars in Smithsonian Inst.; bd. dirs. Russell Sage Found., Sloan Kettering Inst. for Cancer; bd. dirs., chmn. N.Y. Blood Ctr.; chmn. Russell Sage Found. Served with C.E., U.S. Army, Korea. Democrat. Office: Citicorp 399 Park Ave New York NY 10043 *

REED, JOSEPH HOWARD, banker, investor, oil operator, rancher; b. Medford, Okla., June 15, 1930; s. Harold Dehorty and Verna Lee (Elder) R.; m. Paula Sue Nyswonger, Dec. 20, 1952; children—Jason Howard, Renee Suzanne. B.S., Okla. State U., Stillwater, 1952; postgrad., Mexico City Coll., 1953; J.D., Georgetown U., 1957; M.A., Calif. Western U., Santa Ana, 1976; postgrad., Oxford U., 1986. Bar: D.C. 1957, Okla. 1957. Vice pres. Grant County Bank, Medford, Okla., 1957-68, pres., 1968—; pres. Reed Enterprise Inc., Medford, 1977—, Reed Properties Inc., Medford, 1977—; farmer, rancher Medford, 1954—; dir. Adams Hard-Facing Co. Inc., Guymon, Okla., 1975—. Contbr. articles to profl jours. Mem. Gov.'s Commn. on Reform of State Govt., Okla., 1984—; state chmn. Com. of Employer Support for Guard and Res., Okla., 1984—; mem. Gov.'s Jobs for Vets., 1984—, Democratic Nat. Fin. Council, Washington, 1984—; centennial adv. commn. Okla. State U., 1985; adv. com. Sen. Nickles, 1985; mem. Sooner Sports Games Council, 1986; dir. Okla. Found. for Excellence in Edn.; gov's. com. Okla. Vets. Meml. Task Force, 1986; bd. govs. Okla. State U. Found., 1986—. Served to 1st lt. U.S. Army, 1953-55; brig. gen. Okla. NG, 1983—. Decorated Legion of Merit, Meritorious Service medal, others; mem. Okla. State U. Coll. of Bus. Adminstrn. Hall of Fame, 1986. Mem. Internat. Platform Assn., Okla. Bankers Assn., Res. Officers Assn., Nat. Mil. Intelligence Assn., Former Intelligence Officers Assn., Nat. Guard Assn., U.S. C. of C. (pres. Medford chpt. 1975), VFW, Am. Legion, Phi Kappa Phi. Office: Grant County Bank 1122 S Main St Medford OK 73759

REED, KATHLYN LOUISE, occupational therapist, educator; b. Detroit, June 2, 1940; d. Herbert C. and Jessie R. (Krehbiel) R. B.S. in Occupational Therapy, U. Kans., 1964; M.A., Western Mich. U., 1966; Ph.D., U. Wash., 1973; MLS, U. Okla., 1987. Occupational therapist in psychiatry Kans. U. Med. Center, Kansas City, 1964-65; instr. occupational therapy U. Wash., Seattle, 1967-70; assoc. prof. dept. occupational therapy U. Okla. Health Scis. Center, Oklahoma City, 1973-77; prof. U. Okla. Health Scis. Center, 1978-85, chmn. dept. occupational therapy, 1973-85; librarian edn. info. servicesHouston Acad. of Medicine Tex. Med. Ctr. Library, 1988—; cons. to Okla. State Dept. Health, 1976-77, Children's Convalescent Center (Oklahoma City), 1977-80, Oklahoma City public schs., 1980-81. Author: (with Sharon Sanderson) Concepts of Occupational Therapy, 1980, 2d edit., 1983, Models of Practice in Occupational Therapy, 1983, author, 1983. Vol. crisis counselor Open Door Clinic, Seattle, 1968-72; mem. exec. bd. Seattle Mental Health Inst., 1971-72; Mem. Citizen Participation Liaison Council, Seattle, 1970-72. Recipient Award of Merit, Can. Assn. Occupational Therapists, 1988. Fellow Am. Occupational Therapy Assn. (Merit award 1983, Slagle lecture award 1985, Service award 1985); mem. World Fedn. of Occupational Therapists, Council Exceptional Children, Occupational Therapy Assn. (pres. 1974-76), ALA, Med. Library Assn. (Rittenhouse award 1987), Spl. Library Assn., Nat. Rehab. Assn., Am. Occupational Therapy Found. (cert. appreciation 1987), Alpha Eta. Democrat. Home: 7600 Kirby Dr Apt 207 Houston TX 77030

REED, MARSHA LEE, personnel agency executive, consultant; b. Pitts., Sept. 8, 1953; d. Milton and Ruth (Farber) Denmark; m. David P. Reed, Sept. 4, 1977; children—Diane, Robert. B.Gen. Studies, Ohio U., 1975. Cons. Devonshire Personnel, Garden Grove, Calif., 1977-79, Mgmt. Recruiters, Miami, Fla., 1979-80; unit mgr. Dunhill Personnel, Miami, 1980-82; owner, pres. Markett Personnel, Miami, 1982—. Mem. Nat. Assn. Personnel Cons., Nat. Assn. Female Execs., Nat. Assn. Female Bus. Owners, Fla. Assn. Personnel Cons., Bus. and Profl. Women, Greater Miami Jewish Fedn., Kappa Delta (social chmn. 1973-75), Kappa Delta Alumni Assn. Democrat. Club: Hadassah (Miami). Avocations: reading; piano playing. Home: 11124 SW 132d Ct Miami FL 33186 Office: Markett Personnel PO Box 162-211 Miami FL 33116

REED, (ROBERT) OLIVER, actor; b. London, Feb. 13, 1938; s. Peter and Marcia (Andrews) R.; children—Mark Thurloe, Sarah. Student, Homewood House, Ewell Castle Sch. Prin. films include: Lion in the Desert, Women in Love, The Devils, Oliver, Three Musketeers, Tommy, Royal Flash, Prince and the Pauper, The Big Sleep, 1978, Condorman, 1981, The Sting II, 1983, Dragonard, 1987; numerous TV films include The Seekers, 1979, Scruples, 1980, Heroine, 1985, Castaway, 1986, Wheels of Terror, 1986, Dragonard, 1987, Rage to Kill, 1987, Coast of Skeletons, 1987, Master of Dragonard Hill, 1987, Adventures of Baron Munchaosen, 1987. Vice pres. Rosslyn Park Rugby Club, 1973—. Served with Brit. Army. Named Master Arts and Sci., Musketeer (France). Club: White Elephant (London). Office: Maddens, 500 Reigate Rd, Tadworth, Surrey KT20 5PF, England

REED, RONALD LOUIS, chemical engineer; b. Long Beach, Calif., July 26, 1926; s. Louis Archibald and Ruth Sellers (Ferguson) R.; B.S.-Ch.E., Northwestern U., 1946; M.S. in Chem. Engring., U. Kans., 1948, Ph.D. in Math. Physics, 1954; m. Margaret Jane Chastain, Mar. 27, 1948 (dec. Jan. 1986); children—Ronald Christopher, Marianna, Michael Allen. Systems analyst Sandia Corp., Albuquerque, 1954-56; supr. new recovery processes Gulf Research & Devel. Co., Pitts., 1956-62; asso. prof. petroleum engring. U. Tex., Austin, 1962-64; prof. mech. engring. Drexel Inst. Tech., Phila., 1964-66; prof. chem. engring. U. Houston, 1966-70; supr. chem. recovery processes Exxon Prodn. Research Co., Houston, 1970-76; vice chmn. Gordon Conf. on Fluids in Permeable Media, Meridan, N.H., 1979, co-chmn., Tilton, N.H., 1981; referee nat. and internat. engring. and sci. jours. Youth baseball coach, 1972, 74. Served with USNR, 1943-46. Mem. Soc. Petroleum Engrs. (chmn. nat. com. on fluid mechanics and oil recovery processes 1980, named Enhanced Oil Recovery Pioneer 1988), Am. Petroleum Inst., Sigma Xi, Tau Beta Pi, Pi Mu Epsilon, Phi Eta Sigma, Pi Epsilon Tau. Republican. Presbyterian. Author tech. publs. Patentee oil recovery processes. Home: 12502 Winding Brook Houston TX 77024 Office: PO Box 2189 Houston TX 77001

REED, STANLEY FOSTER, lecturer, editor, publisher; b. Bogota, N.J., Sept. 28, 1917; s. Morton H. and Beryl (Turner) R.; m. Stella Swingle, Sept. 28, 1940 (div. 1978); children: Nancie, Beryl Ann, Alexandra; m. Shirley Weihman, Sept. 28, 1985 (dec. Feb. 1988). Student, George Washington U., 1939-40, Johns Hopkins, 1940-41; M.B.A., Loyola U. Md., 1981. Registered profl. engr., D.C. With Bethlehem Steel Corp., Balt., 1940-41; cons. engr. 1942-44; founder, pres. Reed Research, Inc., Washington, 1945-62; pres. Reed Research Inst. Creative Studies, Washington, from 1951; founder, chmn. LogEtronics, Inc., 1955; founder, pres., chmn. Tech. Audit Corp., 1962; assoc. Mgmt. Analysis Corp., 1978-81; sr. cons. Hay Assocs., Phila., 1980-83; prin. Reed Assocs., McLean, Va.; co-chmn. semi-ann. Merger Week Northwestern U.; lectr. numerous U.S. and fgn. groups and instns. including Union Theol. Sem., U. Pa., Pa. State U., U. Colo., Georgetown U., Rensselaer Poly. Inst., Am. U., Claremont Coll., So. Meth. U., Pace U., Wayne State U., U. Oreg., U. Conn., St. John's U., Pepperdine U., Loyola Coll. of Md., San Francisco State U., U. Pitts., U. R.I., Marquette U., Vanderbilt U., Boston U., U. Cin., Gustavus Adolphus Coll., U. Mo., Mich. State U., Lehigh U., Calif. Inst. Tech., Denver U., George Washington U., Elmhurst Coll.; vis. fellow Wilton Pk. Conf., Eng., 1968. Author: Merger/Acquisition/Buyout Guide, 1988; founder, editor, pub.: Mergers & Acquisitions Mag., 1965—, Dirs. and Bds. Mag., 1976—; founder, editor pub.: Campaigns & Elections mag., 1979—; founder, pub. Export Today mag., Export Data Line, Export Update Newsletter, 1984; contbr. articles to leading jours.; chpts. in books. Bd. dirs. Nat. Patent Council, 1970—; founder, chmn. annual Merger Week, Washington, 1973-76. Mem. Soc. Naval Architects and Marine Engrs. (life), Am. Econ. Assn. Clubs: N.Y. Yacht; International (Washington); Racquet (Phila.); Pelham Country (N.Y.). Home and Office: 1621 Brookside Rd McLean VA 22101

REED, WILLIAM EDWARD, government official, educator; b. Columbia, La., July 15, 1914; s. William Reed and Virginia (Barnes) R.; m. Mattye Marie Scott, Aug. 27, 1942; children: Edwarda Marie (Mrs. Lucien L. Johnson), Carol Ann, Beverlyn Bernetiae. B.S., So. U., 1937; M.S., Iowa State U., 1941; Ph.D., Cornell U., 1946. County agrl. agt. Agr. and Home Econs. Extension Service, La. State U., 1937-41; lectr. soil sci. and chemistry So. U., 1942-47; agrl. research specialist U.S. Econ. Mission to Liberia, 1947-49; dean agr. Agrl. and Tech. Coll. N.C., 1949-61; mem. U.S. del. Russia; rep. ICA in Togo, 1961; asst. dir. AID Mission to Nigeria, 1961-68; mem. U.S. del. to UN Conf. on Application Sci. and Tech., 1963; dep. dir. AID Mission to Ethiopia, 1968-72; fgn. service officer in residence N.C. A. & T. State U., Greensboro, 1972-74; spl. asst. to chancellor for internat. programs N.C. A. & T. State U., 1974-76, asso. dean research and spl. projects, 1976-78, dir. internat. programs, 1978-84; cons. in field 1984—. State rep. Sisters Cities Internat. Mem. Nat. Planning Assn., Am. Fgn. Service Assn., Am. Freedom Assn. (dir.), Am. Security Council (adv. bd.), Atlantic Council U.S.A. (adv. bd.), Assn. U.S. Dirs. Internat. Agrl. Programs (dir.), Sigma Xi, Phi Kappa Phi, Beta Kappa Chi, Sigma Pi Phi, Gamma Sigma Delta. Episcopalian. Home: 2711 McConnell Rd Greensboro NC 27401

REEDER, F. ROBERT, lawyer; b. Brigham City, Utah, Jan. 23, 1943; s. Frank O. and Helen H. (Heninger) R.; m. Joannie Anderson, May 4, 1974; children—David, Kristina, Adam. J.D., U. Utah, 1967. Bar: Utah 1967, U.S. Ct. Appeals (10th cir.) 1967, U.S. Ct. Mil. Appeals 1968, U.S. Supreme Ct. 1972, U.S. Ct. Appeals (D.C. and 5th cirs.) 1979. Shareholder, dir., officer Parsons, Behle & Latimer, Salt Lake City, (1968—). Bd. dirs., chmn. Holy Cross Hosp. Found. (1979—). Served with U.S. Army, 1967-68. Mem. ABA, Utah State Bar, Salt Lake County Bar. Clubs: University (Salt Lake City), Cottonwood (pres. 1981, 82, bd. dirs. 1979-82). Office: Parsons Behle & Latimer PO Box 11898 Salt Lake City UT 84147

REEDER, FRANK FITZGERALD, marketing research co. exec.; b. Big Stone Gap, Va., Apr. 9, 1932; s. Andrew Horatio and Suzanne Fitzgerald (Bourdon) R.; B.S. in Econs., U. Va., 1954; postgrad. Columbia, 1955; m. Judith Ann Sands, Feb. 16, 1957; children—Diane Frances, Gail Sands. Asst. to pres. Advt. and Mktg. Cons., Inc., Princeton, N.J., 1954-57; gen. service exec. Gallup & Robinson, Inc., Princeton, 1957-60; research group head Colgate Palmolive Co., N.Y.C., 1960-63; account research mgr. J. Walter Thompson Co., N.Y.C., 1964-72; v.p. Research 100, Inc., Princeton, 1972-73; pres. Frank Reeder Mktg. Research Co., Princeton, 1973—. Lt. gov. Princeton Co. Recipient Wall St. Jour. award, 1954. Mem. Am. Mktg. Assn., Mktg. Research Assn., Jamestowne Soc., U. Va. Alumni Assn. Republican. Episcopalian. Author: Big Is Bad-A Treatise on Individualism, 1977. Patentee disposable fire extinguisher. Home: 62 Herrontown Circle Princeton NJ 08540 Office: PO Box 532 Palmer Sq Princeton NJ 08540

REEDER, ROBERT HARRY, lawyer; b. Topeka, Dec. 3, 1930; s. William Harry and Florence Mae (Cochran) R. A.B. Washburn U., 1952, J.D., 1960. Bar: U.S. Dist. Ct. Kans. 1960, Kans. 1960, U.S. Supreme Ct. 1968. Research asst. Kans. Legis. Council Research Dept., Topeka, 1955-60; asst. counsel Traffic Inst., Northwestern U., Evanston, Ill., 1960-67, gen. counsel, 1967—; exec. dir. Nat. Com. on Uniform Traffic Laws and Ordinances, Evanston, 1982—. Co-author: Vehicle Traffic Law, 1974; The Evidence Handbook, 1980. Author: Interpretation of Implied Consent by the Courts, 1972. Served with U.S. Army, 1952-54. Mem. Com. Alcohol and Other Drugs (chmn. 1973-75). Republican. Methodist. Office: Nat Com on Uniform Traffic Laws PO Box 1409 405 Church St Evanston IL 60204

REEDER, VIRGINIA LEE (FOSTER), educator; b. Tuskahoma, Okla., Jan. 25, 1929; d. Clarence William and Alice (King) Foster; m. Walter Lee Reeder, July 24, 1950; children: Ralph Wesley, Alice Jean. BA, U. Redlands, 1974; MS, Pepperdine U., 1976. Elem. tchr. Harbor City Pub. Schs., 1960-61, First Bapt. Sch., Compton, Calif., 1961-64, Compton Unified Sch., 1980—; head start tchr. Compton Community Youth Ctr., Compton, 1964-76, Charles R. Drew Sch., Compton, 1976-80; tchr. early childhood edn. Compton Coll., 1974—. Democrat. Baptist. Home: 11919 E 161st St Norwalk CA 90650

REES, CHARLES H. G., financial consultant, investor; b. Trenton, Mar. 6, 1922; s. Albert H. and Helen (Gallagher) R.; m. Nancy Thomas, Oct. 30, 1954; children: Liberty, Camilla, Nancy, Hilleary. B.A., Princeton U., 1948. Salesman John A. Roebling's Sons Co., Trenton, N.J., 1948-50; staff officer CIA, Washington, 1951-54; assoc. J.H. Whitney & Co., N.Y.C., 1954 59; gen. ptnr. Whitcom Investment Co., N.Y.C., 1967-85; with Whitney Communications Corp., N.Y.C., 1960-85, pres., 1982-85, dir., 1960-85; bd. dirs. Mich. Energy Resources, Inc., Monroe, Mich. Trustee Riverside Research Inst., N.Y.C. Served to capt. U.S. Army, 1942-46, 50-51. Decorated Bronze Star. Republican. Clubs: Ivy, Nassau (Princeton, N.J.); Misquamicut (Watch Hill, R.I.); Watch Hill Yacht (R.I.); Brook, Pilgrims, Princeton, Union (N.Y.C.). Home: Ocean View Hwy Watch Hill RI 02891 also: 1130 Park Ave New York NY 10128

REES, DAVID ROY, aerospace company executive; b. Penclawdd, Wales, U.K., Oct. 13, 1933; arrived in Australia, 1967; s. John Norcliffe and Margaret Elveira (Jones) R.; m. Sandra Muriel Hansen, Feb. 10, 1968; children: Catharine Lynden, Samuel David Rothwell. BS, U. London, 1955. Tech. officer B.O.A.C. Airline, Eng., 1958-59; design engr. Hawker Aircraft Ltd., Eng., 1959-62; project design leader Hawker Siddeley Aviation Ltd., Eng., 1962-67; sr. aerodynamicist Commonwealth Aircraft Corp. Ltd., Australia, 1967-72, project mgr., 1972-75, mgr. planning and prodn. control, 1975-78, mktg. exec., 1978-88; planning exec. Ansett Airlines of Australia, Melbourne, 1988—. Co-author: The Future of Tactical Airspace in the Defense of Australia, 1976. Royal MIT bus. adminstrn. fellow, Melbourne, 1976; MIT sr. fellow, Boston, 1983. Mem. Royal Aero. Soc. (pres. Australian div. 1985-87), Instn. Engrs. Australia, Metal Trades Industry Assn. (pres. export group 1981-86). Anglican. Clubs: Naval and Mil. (Melbourne); Sorrento Sailing. Home: 80 Cole St, Gardenvale, Victoria 3185, Australia Office: Ansett Airlines of Australia, Operations Rd, Melbourne Airport, Victoria 3185, Australia

REES, GARETH, environmental science educator, administrator; b. Pencoed, Wales, Sept. 7, 1951; s. Ronald Thomas and Josephine Gwendoline (Hughes) R.; m. Peta Anne Hyett, July 26, 1978; children: Luke Owen, Samuel Huw, Benjamin Ewan. BS in Marine Zoology, U. Coll. Wales, Aberstwyth, 1973; MS in Biodeterioration, Portsmouth Poly., 1976, PhD in Marine Mycology, 1982. Schoolmaster Dwr-Y-Felin Comprehensive Sch., Neath, West Glamorgan, Wales, 1973-75; research asst. Portsmouth Poly., 1976-80; from lectr. to head dept. Sci. and Environ. Tech. Farnborough (Hampshire, Eng.) Coll. Tech., 1980—; edn. commr. Internat. Union for Conservation of Nature and Natural Resources, Gland, Switzerland, 1985—; bd. dirs. Internat. Ctr. Environ. Ops., Farnborough, 1986—; bd. dirs. Microbiological Services Ltd., Farnborough, 1985—. Contbr. articles to profl. jours. Mem. British Mycology Soc., Soc. Applied Bacteriology, Inst. Environ. Scis. Home: 36 Churchfields, Kingsley, Bordon GU35 9PJ, England

REES, WILLIAM LINFORD LLEWELYN, psychiatrist, educator; b. Burry Port, Wales, Oct. 24, 1914; s. Edward Parry and Mary (John) R.; B.Sc., U. Wales, 1935, M.B., B.Ch., 1938, M.D., 1943, LL.D. (hon.), 1981; D.Sc., U. London, 1978; m. Catherine Magdalen Thomas, June 15, 1940; children—David, Angharad, Vaughan, Catrin. Regional adv. in psychiatry, Wales and Monmouthshire, 1948-54; cons. physician Maudsley and Bethlem Royal Hosps., 1954-66; physician in charge dept. psychol. medicine St. Bartholomew's Hosp., 1959—; prof. psychiatry U. London, 1966-80, prof. emeritus, 1980—. Decorated comdr. Order Brit. Empire; freeman City of London. Fellow Brit. Med. Assn., Royal Coll. Psychiatrists (hon.), Am. Psychiat. Assn. (disting.); hon. mem. Swedish Psychiat. Assn., Venezuelan Soc. Psychiatry and Neurology, Inst. Group Analysis, Am. Coll. Psychiatrists, Pakistan Psychiat. Assn., others. Club: Athenaeum. Author: A Short Textbook of Psychiatry, 3d edit., 1982; editor: Anxiety in Comprehensive Medical Care, 1973; contbr. 250 articles to profl. jours. Home: 62 Oakwood Ave, Purley Surrey England Office: Charter Clinic, Radnor Walk, London SW3 4BP, England

REESE, TED M., dentist; b. Dayton, Ohio, Jan. 21, 1959; s. Virgil Marion and Elizabeth June (Holmes) R. Student, Anderson (Ind.) Coll., 1977-80; DDS with distinction, Ind. U., Indpls., 1984. Gen. practice dentistry Clinton, Ind., 1984-87; practice specializing in implant dentistry Indpls., 1987—; co-founder, pres. Med./Den. Missions, Inc., 1988—. Vol. Project Ptnr. in Christ, Middletown, Ohio, 1984, Good Shepherd Ministries, Rockledge, Fla., 1985, Orphans, Inc., 1984; profl. edn. chmn. Am. Cancer Soc., Vermillion County, Ind., 1986. Mem. ADA, Ind. Dental Assn., Acad. Gen. Dentistry, Am. Acad. Implant Dentistry (supporting), Internat. Congress of Oral Implantology. Republican. Office: 8202 Madison Ave Indianapolis IN 46227

REESE, WILLIAM WILLIS, banker; b. N.Y.C., July 8, 1940; s. Willis Livingston Meiser and Frances Galletin (Stevens) R.; B.A., Trinity Coll., 1963; M.B.A., J.D., Columbia U., 1970. Admitted to N.Y. bar, 1972; research analyst Morgan Guaranty Trust Co., N.Y.C., 1971-73, investment research officer, 1973-77, asst. v.p., 1977-86, v.p., 1986— . Bd. dirs. N.Y.C. Ballet, 1975-87, Counseling and Human Devel. Center, 1977—, 3d St. Music Sch. Settlement, 1976—; trustee Millbrook Sch., 1972—. Served with USAF, 1963-67. Mem. Am., Inter-Am., N.Y. State (sec. com. on internat. law 1973-76), Dutchess County bar assns., N.Y. Soc. Security Analysts, Certified Fin. Analysts, Assn. Bar City N.Y. Republican. Episcopalian. Clubs: Union, Racquet and Tennis, Rockaway Hunt, Mt. Holyoke Lodge. Home: 910 Park Ave New York NY 10021

REESE, WILLIS LIVINGSTON MESIER, legal educator; b. Bernardsville, N.J., June 16, 1913; s. William Willis and Augusta (Bliss) R.; m. Frances Gallatin Stevens, June 26, 1937; children: William Willis, Frances Gallatin, John Rathbone, George Bliss, Alexander Stevens. Grad., St. Paul's Sch., N.H., 1931; AB, Yale U., 1935, LLB, 1938; LLB, U. Leuven, Belgium, 1972, Trinity Coll., 1979. Bar: N.Y. 1938, U.S. Supreme Ct. 1945. Law clk. Judge Thomas Swan, 1938-39; asso. Winthrop, Stimson, Putnam & Roberts, N.Y.C., 1939-41; from asst. prof. to Charles Evans Hughes prof. law Columbia, 1946—; dir. Parker Sch. Fgn. and Comparative Law, 1955-80; Lectr. Hague Acad. Internat. Law, 1964, 76, mem. curatorium, 1975—; mem. Inst. Internat. Law, 1971—, adv. com. on pvt. internat. law Sec. of State, 1964—; U.S. del. Hague Conf. Pvt. Internat. Law, 1956, 60, 64, 68, 72, 76, 80, 84, 85, ; reporter restatement (2d) conflict laws Am. Law Inst. Author: (with Rosenberg) Cases and Materials on Conflict of Laws, 1984. Bd. dirs. Episc. Ch. Found., 1979—, N.Y. Legal Aid Soc., 1951-71; chmn. Community Action for Legal Services, 1967-70; mem. N.Y. Law Revision Commn., 1973-83; Pres. bd. trustees Millbrook Sch., 1968-77; pres. Five Towns United Fund, 1959, chmn. bd., 1958, 60. Served as capt. AUS, 1941-46. Mem. Am. Assn. Comparative Study Law (sec., dir. 1955-80), Joint Conf. Legal Edn. (1st v.p.), Assn. Bar City of N.Y., Internat. Law Assn. (Am. br.), Am. Bar Assn., Am. Soc. Internat. Law, Am. Fgn. Law Assn. (pres. 1964-67), Am. Assn. UN (pres. Five Towns chpt. 1962-63, 77-81), Acad. Polit. Sci. (life), Inst. Internat. Law, Phi Beta Kappa, Order of Coif. Episcopalian (sr. warden, sec. standing com. Diocese N.Y. 1963-65). Clubs: Century, Rockaway Hunting, Union. Home: 345 Meadowview Ave Hewlett NY 11557 Office: 435 W 116th St New York NY 10027

REES-MOGG, SIR WILLIAM, business executive, journalist; b. Temple Cloud, Somerset, Eng., July 14, 1928; s. Edmund Fletcher and Beatrice (Warren) R-M; m. Gillian Shakespeare Morris, 1962; 3 children. Student, Oxford (Eng.) U.; LLD (hon.), Bath U., 1977. Pres. Oxford Union, Eng., 1951; with Fin. Times, Eng., 1952-60, asst. editor, 1957-60; city editor Sunday Times, Eng., 1960-61; polit. and econ. editor Sunday Times, 1961-63, dep. editor, 1964-67; mem. exec. bd. Times Newspapers Ltd., 1968-81, dir., 1978-81; dir. The Times Ltd., 1968-81; vice-chmn. bd. of govs. BBC, 1981-86; chmn., owner Pickering and Chatto Ltd., 1981—; chmn. Broadcasting Std. Council, 1988—; dir. Gen. Electric Co., 1981—, Sidgwick and Jackson, 1985—, Arts Council of Great Britain, 1982; mem. internat. com. Pontifical Council for Culture, 1983—; treas. Inst. of Journalists, 1960-63, 66-68, pres., 1963-64; vis. fellow Nuffield Coll., Oxford U., 1968-72. The Reigning Error: the crisis of world inflation, 1974, An Humbler Heaven, 1977, How to Buy Rare Books, 1985. Vice-chmn. Conservative Party's nat. adv. com. on polit. edn., 1961-63; contested Chester-le-St. Co. Durham By-election, 1956, Gen. Election, 1959; High Sheriff, Somerset, 1978. Mem. English Assn. (pres. 1983-84). Club: Garrick. Home: 3 Smith Sq, London SW2, England Office: The Old Rectory, Hinton Blewitt near Bristol, Avon England *

REEVE, JAMES KEY, art consultant, writer; b. Lewistown, Mont.; s. John Rumsey and Isabelle (Key) R. B.A., U. Tulsa, 1950; M.A., N.Y. U., 1954; postgrad., U. London, 1961-63; tuition scholar, Nat. Trust Summer Sch. Study of Hist. Arch. of Eng., summer 1962. Lectr. on architecture Mus. Modern Art, N.Y.C., 1950, Toledo Mus. Art, 1954-58, Am. Art USIS, London, 1961-63; asst. prof. art, curator Univ. Art Gallery, U. Notre Dame, 1958-61; asst. prof., curator Anglo-Am. Art Mus., La. State U., 1963-66; curator Am. art Toledo Mus. Art, 1966-71; gen. curator Philbrook Art Center, Tulsa, 1972-74; ind. mus. cons. 1974-75; adj. lectr. art history U. Tulsa, 1972-74; adj. prof. art history Oklahoma City U., 1976-78; dir. Okla. Mus. Art, Oklahoma City, 1975-81; adj. assoc. prof. dept. art history Sch. Art, U. Okla., 1981-82; art and mus. cons., 1981—; Active archtl. preservation groups. Author: The Art of Showing Art, 1986. Designer author exhbn. catalogues. Mem. Old West End Dist. Council, Toledo, 1970-71; 2d v.p. Internat. Inst. Greater Toledo, 1969-71. Served with USCG, 1943-46. Mem. Am. Assn. Museums, Internat. Council Museums, Nat. Trust Historic Preservation. Home: 4913 E 27th St Tulsa OK 74114

REEVE, JANET WHEELER, landscape company executive; b. Balt., Feb. 20, 1941; d. James Donald Wheeler and Dorothy Meehan (Chandler) Wheeler Kirby; m. John Landon Reeve IV, Feb. 3, 1962; children—Deonne Justine, James Donald. B.S., U. Md., 1965; postgrad. Hood Coll., 1973-75, Goucher Coll., 1975-76. Tchr. Baltimore County Bd. Edn., Towson, Md., 1961-62, Howard County Bd. Edn., Columbia, Md., 1962-63; with Chapel Valley Landscape Co., Woodbine, Md., 1968—, pub. relations mgr., 1976-82, sec./treas., 1968-84, v.p., 1984—. Mem. Landscape Contractors Assn. Met. Washington (awardee), assoc. Landscape Contractors Am. (sec., bd. dirs., v.p., pres. Womens Group, awardee), Am. Soc. Landscape Architects (awardee), Nat. Landscape Assn. (awardee). Am. Assn. Nurserymen (awardee), Md. Nurserymens Assn. Republican. Avocations: Swimming; tennis; skiing; writing. Home: 3275 Jennings Chapel Rd PO Box 159 Woodbine MD 21797 Office: Chapel Valley Landscape Co PO Box 159 Woodbine MD 21797

REEVES, MICHAELYN MARIE, communications technician; b. S.I., N.Y., Nov. 3, 1956; d. Clyde James and Dorothy Grace (Brown) Tuggle; m. Robert Owen Reeves, Sept. 24, 1976 (div. Apr. 1978). Cashier I. Magnin, Pasadena, Calif., 1979-80; communication technician AT&T Communications, Los Angeles, 1980—. Served with USAF, 1974-79. Roman Catholic. Home: 14634 Vose St Van Nuys CA 91405

REEVES, PATRICIA, engineering and commercial writer; b. Seattle, Jan. 15, 1926; d. Thurlow Johnson and Dorothy (Todd) R.; m. Daniel Pershing Yates, 1944 (div. 1967). Student Los Angeles State U., 1965-67, Johns Hopkins U., 1967-68, UCLA, 1980-83, Institut de France Allience Francaise, Paris, 1971-72. Free-lance cons./writer tech. publs., 1950—; co-owner, dir. Falcon Press, La Jolla, Calif. and Beverly Hills, Calif., 1978-84; prin. Reeves Assocs., Ltd. , London, 1984—. Mem. MENSA, Nat. Acad. TV Arts and Scis., Am. Mgmt. Assn., Soc. Tech. Communication (sr.), ACLU. Republican. Author numerous tech. publs.; clients include: Bechtel Corp., Westinghouse, Lockheed, Philco-Ford, Martin-Marietta, Northrop Aircraft, Litton Data Systems, Lear-Siegler, N.V. Philips Telecommunicatie Industrie, Philips Centre Technique et Industriel, Messerschmitt-Bolkow-Blohm, Societa Italiana Avionica. Home: Le Floriana, 406 Chemin de St Claude, 06600 Antibes France Office: Reeves & Assocs Ltd, Standbrock House, 2-5 Old Bond St, London W1X 3TD, England

REEVES, PAUL ALFRED, governor general of New Zealand; b. Dec. 6, 1932; s. D'Arcy Lionel and Hilda Mary Reeves; m. Beverley Gwendolen Watkins; 3 children. Student Wellington Coll., New Zealand, 1946-51; M.A., Victoria U. of Wellington, 1956; L.Th., St. John's Theol. Coll., Auckland, 1959; M.A., St. Peter's Coll., U. Oxford, 1964. Ordained deacon Anglican Ch., 1958, priest, 1960. Curate, Tokoroa, N.Z., 1958-59, St. Mary the Virgin, Oxford, 1959-61, Kirkley St. Peter, Lowestoft, 1961-63; vicar St. Paul, Okato, N.Z., 1964-66; lectr. in ch. history St. John's Coll., Auckland, N.Z., 1966-69; dir. Christian Edn. Dio, Auckland, 1969-71; bishop of Waiapu,

1971-79; bishop of Auckland, 1979-85; archbishop and primate of New Zealand, 1980-85; gov. gen. of New Zealand, 1985—; chmn. Environ. Council, 1974-76. Address: Office of Gov Gen, Wellington New Zealand *

REEVES, ROY RUSSELL, osteopathic physician; b. Waco, Tex., Apr. 27, 1952; s. George A. and Doris (McKiddy) R.; m. Vicki Sharon Cain, Mar. 2, 1974 (div. May 1983); 1 child, David Nathan. BA, Union Coll., Barbourville, Ky., 1971; MS, Morehead (Ky.) State U., 1972; PhD, U. So. Miss., 1975; DO, Kirksville (Mo.) Coll. Osteo. Med., 1979. Emergency dept. physician Kirksville Osteo. Health Ctr., 1980-82, Cameron (Mo.) Community Hosp., 1982-87; resident in neurology Sch. Medicine U. N.Mex., Albuquerque, 1987—. Contbr. articles to profl. jours. mem. Am. Osteo. Assn., Am. Coll. Emergency Physicians, Am. Coll. Osteo. Emergency Physicians, Am. Coll. Neuropsychiatrists, Drs. for Life. Republican. Home: 614 Palomas SE Albuquerque NM 87108 Office: U NMex Sch Medicine Dept Neurology Albuquerque NM 87131

REEVES, WILLIAM HATTON, electronics and chemical company executive; b. Phila., Jan. 18, 1937; s. Jonathan Hatton and Eugene Sue (Headley) R.; m. Carole Lynne Cargal, Aug. 4, 1962; children: Mark Stephen, Jonathan Wyatt, Marion Alicia. Student, U. W.Va., 1955-56; BS in Chemistry and Zoology, Marshall U., 1959; postgrad., Universite Louis Pasteur, Strasbourg, France, 1976-81. Dir. product devel. Internat. Paper Co., N.Y.C., 1967-69; nat. sales mgr. Sherwood Med. Industries, St. Louis, 1969-73; v.p. mktg. Logos Internat., Plainfield, N.J., 1973-76; chmn., founder Vectra Corp., Columbia, Md., 1976-81, Magnum Electronics, Englewood, Ohio, 1981-86; pres., founder Chronodynamics, Ltd., Dayton, Ohio, 1986—; cons. Rhom Pharma NA, Durmstadt, Fed. Republic Germany, 1981—, QMax Tech., Dayton, 1981—; bd. dirs. MedTech Inc., Dayton, Thermology Labs., Centerville, Ohio. Holder 4 patents. Served with U.S. Army, 1959-62. Fellow Am. Acad. Thermology, Internat. Soc. Christian Counselors. Republican. Presbyterian. Home: 1308 Norwich Ln Centerville OH 45459 Office: Chronodynamics Ltd 6012 N Dixie Dr Dayton OH 45404

REEVES, WILLIAM RAY, franchising company executive; b. Corbin, Ky., Feb. 8, 1937; s. Leslie Joseph and Phoebe Mae (Hale) R.; B.Chem. Engring., U. Cin., 1959; postgrad. Harvard U., 1960-61; M.B.A., U. Va., 1964; m. Mary Agnes O'Rourke, Dec. 30, 1972; children—Katherine Margaret, David William Joseph, Robert Sean Hale. Cons., Fantus div. Dun & Bradstreet, N.Y.C., 1969-70; pres. Barnett Chem. Products, Inc., Phila., 1970-72; cons. Nat. Center for Resource Recovery, Washington, 1972-73; v.p. Interstate Gen. Corp., St. Charles, Md., San Juan, P.R., 1973-81; pres. New Energy Investment Services, Inc., Washington, 1981-83; pres. CFM of Md., Inc., St. Charles, 1983—. Served as capt. U.S. Army, 1960-61. Registered profl. engr., Ohio, Md. Mem. Port Tobacco Restoration Soc. (pres., dir. 1976—), Charles County (Md.) Heart Assn. (chmn. 1976-77), Met. Washington Bd. Trade, Harvard Bus. Sch. Club Washington. Club: Hawthorne Country. Patentee radio controlled fishing boat, 1968. Home: Sunnytop Farm Port Tobacco MD 20677 Office: 109 Post Office Rd PO Box 966 Saint Charles MD 20601

RÉFEGA, ANTÓNIO AUGUSTO GUERRA, educator; b. Milhão-Bragança, Feb. 14, 1935; s. António Cândido and Alice Augusta (Guerra) R.; Eng. Agrónomo, Tech. U. Lisbon, 1960; postgrad. Inst. Superior de Agronomia; D. Agronomy, 1973; m. Maria Isabel Lopes, Apr. 17, 1960; children: Paulo Antonio Lopes Guerra. Research asst. Portuguese Overseas Research Bd., 1959-65; lectr., asst. prof. U. Luanda, 1965-74; head bd. dirs. Inst. Politécnico de Vila Real, 1974-77; asst. prof. Inst. Universitário de Évora (Portugal), 1976-79; asst. prof. Univ. Nova de Lisboa, Lisbon, Portugal, 1979—, cathedratic prof., 1981—; v.p. Inst. de Investigação Lientifica Tropical, 1985; adviser Minister Edn., 1976— ; collaborator Ctr. de Estudos Florestais and Ctr. de Pedologia da Univ. Técnica de Lisboa; nat. del. Research and Devel. of EEC. Recipient Melo Geraldes prize Inst. Superior de Agronomia, 1959; citation Ministry Edn., 1976; citation Sec. of State for Higher Edn., 1982, 83, 85; Gulbenkian Found. fellow, 1969-70, U. Luanda grantee, 1970-71. Mem. Internat. Soil Sci. Soc., Portuguese Soil Sci. Soc., Portuguese Agrarian Sci. Soc., Portuguese Soc. Electronic Microscopy, Geol. Soc. Portugal, Environ. Protection League. Roman Catholic. Home: Lt 11-c 4o Av do Ultramar, Oeiras Codex 2780, Portugal Office: 86 Rua da Jurqueira, 1300 Lisbon Portugal

REFSLAND, GARY ARLAN, gerontology center administrator, sociology educator; b. Big Timber, Mont., May 5, 1944; s. William Anton and Agnes Eline (Freeberg) R.; m. Judith Estelle Hall, Aug. 20, 1969 (div. Aug. 1974). BS in Sociology, Mont. State U., 1970, MS in Sociology, 1971; postgrad., Internat. Grad. Sch., Stockholm, 1970; AA in funeral directing, Calif. Coll. Mortuary Sci., 1973. Cert. funeral dir., mortician. Instr. sociology Mont. State U., Bozeman, 1971-72, lectr., 1976—, coordinator of aging services Coll. Letters and Sci., 1976-77, acting dir. Ctr. Gerontology, 1977-79, dir. Mont. Ctr. Gerontology, 1979—; mortician Dokken Nelson Funeral Service, Bozeman, 1974-76; cons. State Agy. Aging, 1979—, Legacy Legis., 1987—; program coordinator Mont. Area Health Edn. Ctr./Office Rural Health, 1987—; mem. adv. bd. Sr. Community Services Employment program, Mont., 1983—, Regional Edn. and Tng. program Fed. Region VIII, 1980-82, Mont. State U., 1986—, Mont. Area Health Edn. Ctr., 1987; mem. planning com. Gov.'s Adv. Council, Mont. Aging Policy Perspectives: 1990, 1987—; mem. Gov.'s Third Priorities for People, 1988; state coordinator White Ho. Conf. on Aging, 1981-82. Writer, producer (TV show) Mont.'s Priorities for Aging, 1981; writer, exec. producer (videotape) Senior Centers.: Opportunities for Older Montanans; contbr. articles to profl. jours. Pres. Gallatin County Housing Authority Bd., Bozeman, 1981-82, sec. 1978-81; pres. Sourdough Ridge Property Owners Assn., Bozeman, 1982-84, Gallatin County Council on Aging, 1978-80. Served with USN, 1962-66. Recipient Armed Forces Community award San Diego C. of C., 1966; Cert. Appreciation U.S. Dept. Health and Human Services, Denver, 1982; named one of Outstanding Young Men Am., U.S. Jaycees, 1981. Mem. Am. Soc. Aging, Mont. Gerontology Soc. (charter officer 1982-83), Nat. Council on Aging (del. council 1982-83), Am. Legion, Alpha Kappa Delta. Home: 212 Ridge Trail Rd Bozeman MT 59715 Office: Mont State U Ctr Gerontology Bozeman MT 59717

REGAN, DONALD THOMAS, financier, writer, lecturer; b. Cambridge, Mass., Dec. 21, 1918; m. Ann G. Buchanan, July 11, 1942. BA, Harvard U., 1940; LLD (hon.), Hahnemann Med. Coll. Hosp., 1968, U. Pa., 1972, Pace U., 1973; DHL (hon.), Colgate U. With Merrill Lynch, Pierce, Fenner & Smith Inc. (and predecessor), 1946-81, sec., dir. adminstrv. div., 1960-64, exec. v.p., 1964-68, pres., 1968-70, chmn., chief exec. officer, 1971-80; chmn. bd., chief exec. officer Merrill Lynch & Co. Inc., 1973-81; sec. Dept. of Treasury, Washington, 1981-85; White House chief of staff Washington, 1985-87; vice chmn., dir. N.Y. Stock Exchange, 1972-75. Author: A View from the Street, 1972, For the Record, 1988. Trustee Charles E. Merrill Trust, 1961-80; chmn. bd. trustees U. Pa., 1974-78, life trustee, 1978-80; mem. policy com. Bus. Roundtable, 1978-80; trustee Com. for Econ. Devel., 1978-80. Served to lt. col. USMCR, World War II. Clubs: Army-Navy, Metropolitan (Washington); Burning Tree. Office: 11 Canal Ctr Plaza Suite 301 Alexandria VA 22314

REGAN, FREDERIC DENNIS, cardiologist, internist; b. Newburyport, Mass., Aug. 21, 1921; s. Dennis and Catherine R. (Haley) R.; m. Margaret amary Regan. Student Syracuse U., 1940-42; M.D., U. Buffalo, 1945; children—Denise, Frederic, Michael. Intern, USPHS Hosp., S.I., N.Y., 1945-46, research fellow in cardiology, 1947, resident in medicine, dep. chief medicine, chief cardiac clinic, 1950-52; practice medicine specializing in cardiology and internal medicine; chief of medicine Richmond Meml. Hosp. and Health Ctr.; instr. medicine N.Y. Hosp. Diplomate Am. Bd. Internal Medicine. Fellow ACP, Am. Coll. Cardiology, N.Y. Cardiology Soc.; mem. Richmond County Med. Soc. (pres. 1961-62). Office: 347 Edison St Staten Island NY 10306

REGAN, JOHN DENNISS, insurance company executive; b. Bklyn., Oct. 29, 1943; s. Cornelius and Margarite Regan; m. Lynda Louise Heider, May 5, 1968; children: Alysia, Melissa. CLU, Chartered Fin. Cons. Agt. Washington Nat. Ins. Co., San Francisco, 1968-73; pres. Regan Co., Sausalito, Calif., 1973-84, Regan Group Ins. Mktg., Sausalito, 1979-86; pres. & chief exec. officer Gen. Services Life Holding Co. and Gen. Services Life Ins. Co., Novato, Calif., 1986—; chmn. bd. Melal Printing & Pub. Co., Sausalito; bd. dirs. Comprehensive Benefit Services, Calif. Retirement Services, Sausalito; frequent speaker various groups. Author: Complete Book of Retired Lives Reserves, 1979; contbr. numerous articles to profl. jours. Founder, bd. dirs. Nat. Ins. Polit. Action Com., Washington, 1984—. Mem. Ins. Coalition Am. (founding), Assn. for Advanced Life Underwriting, Nat. Assn. Life Underwriters, Internat. Assn. Fin. Planners, Million Dollar Round Table, Internat. Forum, Top of Table. Republican. Roman Catholic. Office: 201 Alameda del Prado Novato CA 94949

REGAN, MICHAEL PATRICK, lawyer; b. Bklyn., Feb. 22, 1941; s. Cornelius Francis and Marguerite (Cann) R.; m. Susan Ann Light, July 13, 1974; children—Michael Patrick, Brian Christopher, Mark Dennis. B.A. in English, U. Notre Dame, 1963; LL.B., Albany Law Sch., Union U., 1967, J.D., 1968. Bar: N.Y. 1967, Va. 1975. Assoc. Medwin & McMahon, Albany, N.Y., 1967-69; asst. dist. atty. Albany County, N.Y., 1969; corp. atty. Mohasco Corp., Amsterdam, N.Y., 1969-74; asst. gen. csl. Dan River Inc., Danville, Va., 1975-81, assoc. gen. csl., 1981—, asst. sec., 1984—; assoc. gen. counsel, asst. sec. Dan River Holding Co., 1984—; asst. sec. Dan River Service Corp. of Va., 1984—. Sec. Dan Pac, polit. action com., Danville; clarinetist, saxophonist Tightsqueeze Philharm. Band; leader: The Dance-Notes. Mem. ABA, N.Y. State Bar Assn., Va. Bar Assn., Danville Bar Assn., Union Internationale des Avocats, Internat. Platform Assn. Republican. Roman Catholic. Club: Rotary (Danville). Home: 236 Cambridge Circle Danville VA 24541 Office: 2291 Memorial Dr Danville VA 24541

REGAN, PATRICK JOSEPH, investment company executive, author, consultant; b. San Francisco, July 2, 1947; s. John Joseph and Marion Gertrude (Sayers) R.; m. Kathleen Mary Bisazza, July 11, 1970; 1 child, Michael. BS in Fin., U. San Francisco, 1969; MBA, U. Calif., Berkeley, 1971. Chartered fin. analyst. Sr. security analyst Merrill Lynch, N.Y.C., 1972-76; v.p. BEA Assocs., Inc., N.Y.C., 1976—; panel advisor Pension Benefit Guaranty Corp., Washington, 1977-78, 85-86; mem. pension task force Fin. Acctg. Standards Bd., Stamford, Conn., 1982-85; mem. investment adv. council N.Y.C. Pension Fund, 1982. Author: (with Jack L Treynor and William W. Priest, Jr.) The Financial Reality of Pension Funding Under ERISA, 1976. Columnist, Fin. Analysts Jour., 1978—. Contbr. to various books and mags. Mem. N.Y. Soc. Security Analysts, Analysts Club N.Y. (pres. 1983). Home: PO Box 442 Greens Farms Ct 06436 Office: BEA Assocs Inc 153 E 53d St 58th Floor New York NY 10022

REGAN, SUZANNE MARIE, food company executive; b. Camden, N.J., May 11, 1950; d. Cornelius Joseph and Jeannette (Way) R.; B.S., U. Conn., 1972; M.B.A., Drexel U., 1978; m. Ronald L. Feldberg, Apr. 10, 1976; 1 son, Matthew Regan. Acctg. procedures analyst Campbell Soup Co., Camden, N.J., 1972-74, mktg. research analyst, 1974-77, asst. mktg. mgr. Swanson div., 1977-78, mktg. mgr. Swanson div., 1978-81, mktg. dir. Pet Food unit, 1981-85, pres., gen. mgr. Pet Food unit (Champion Valley Farms) 1985-87, gen. mgr. refrigerated deli unit, 1987-88, gen. mgr. Marie's Salad Dressing, 1988—. Mem. Am. Mgmt. Assn., Nat. Assn. Female Execs. Home: 59 Woodhurst Dr West Berlin NJ 08091 Office: Campbell Pl Camden NJ 08101

REGAZZI, JOHN HENRY, corporate executive; b. N.Y.C., Jan. 4, 1921; s. Caesar B. and Jennie (Moruzzi) R.; m. Doris Mary Litzau, Feb. 16, 1946; children—Mark, Dale. B.B.A., Pace Coll., 1951. C.P.A., N.Y. Mgr. Price Waterhouse, N.Y.C., 1946-62; comptroller ABC, N.Y.C., 1962-70; sr. v.p., chief fin. officer Avnet, Inc., N.Y.C., 1970—. Contbr. articles to profl. jours. Pres. bd. River Dell Regional High Sch., Oradell, N.J., 1962-65; trustee, treas. Oradell Pub. Library, 1970-79; councilman Borough of Oradell, 1979—. Served as staff sgt. USAF, 1942-45. Mem. Fin. Execs. Inst., Am. Inst. C.P.A.s, Nat. Assn. Accts. Republican. Roman Catholic. Lodge: Lions. Home: 637 Park Ave Oradell NJ 07649 Office: Avnet Inc 767 Fifth Ave New York NY 10153

REGENSTREIF, HERBERT, lawyer; b. N.Y.C., May 13, 1935; s. Max and Jeannette (Hacker) R.; m. Patricia Friedman, Dec. 20, 1967 (div. July 1968); m. Charlotte Lois Levy, Dec. 10, 1980; 1 child, Cara Rachael. BA, Hobart Coll., 1957; JD, N.Y. Law Sch., 1960; MS, Pratt Inst., 1985. Bar: N.Y. 1961, Ky. 1985, U.S. Dist. Ct. (ea. and so. dists.) N.Y. 1962, U.S. Tax Ct. 1967, U.S. Ct. Appeals (2d cir.) 1962, U.S. Supreme Ct. 1967. Ptnr., Fried & Regenstreif, P.C., Mineola, N.Y., 1963—; cons. in field. Contbr. articles to profl. jours. County committeeman Dem. Com., Queens County, N.Y., 1978-79; arbitrator N.Y. City Civil Ct., 1984-86. Mem. Bar Assn. Nassau County, Phi Delta Phi, Beta Phi Mu. Jewish. Club: Hobart of N.Y. (gov. 1968-69).

REGER, GARY L., ancient history educator; b. Elmhurst, Ill., Mar. 19, 1954; s. Joseph L. and Loveta M. (Richardson) R.; m. Edith A. Folta. BA in History, U. Ill., 1975; MA in Greek, U. Wis., 1983, MA in History, 1984, PhD, 1987. Asst. prof. Trinity Coll., Hartford, 1987—. Fulbright fellow, Munich, Fed. Republic Germany, 1986-87; Heinrich Schliemann fellow Am. Sch. in Athens, 1984-85; fellow Am. Numismatic Soc., 1986. Mem. Am. Philol. Assn., Archael. Inst. Am., Assn. Ancient Historians. Office: Trinity Coll Box 1343 Hartford CT 06106

REGES, MARIANNA ALICE, consumer products company executive; b. Budapest, Hungary, Mar. 23, 1947; came to U.S., 1956, naturalized, 1963; d. Otto H. and Alice M. R.; m. Charles P. Green, Feb. 15, 1975; children: Rebecca, Charles III. AAS with honors, Fashion Inst. Tech., N.Y.C., 1967; BBA magna cum laude, Baruch Coll., 1971, MBA in Stats., 1978. Media research analyst Doyle, Dane, Bernbach Advt., N.Y.C., 1967-70; research supr. Sta. WCBS-TV, N.Y.C., 1970-71; research mgr. Woman's Day mag., N.Y.C., 1971-72; asst. media dir. Benton & Bowles Advt., N.Y.C., 1972-75; mgr. research and sales devel. NBC Radio, N.Y.C., 1975-77; sr. research mgr. Ziff-Davis Pub. Co., N.Y.C., 1977-84; mgr. media research Bristol-Myers Co., 1984—. Mem. Vt. Natural Resources Council, 1977—; advisor Baruch Coll. Advt. Soc., 1975—. Mem. Am. Mktg. Assn., Am. Advt. Fedn., Media Research Dirs. Assn., Radio and TV Research Council, Beta Gamma Sigma, Sigma Alpha Delta. Home: 140 E 83d St New York NY 10028 Office: Bristol-Myers Co 345 Park Ave New York NY 10154

REGIRER, WALTER WLODZIMIERZ, lawyer; b. Warsaw, Poland, Dec. 22, 1913. Student Law Sch., Lille, France, 1932; LL.M., U. Warsaw, 1937; J.D., U. Richmond (Va.), 1949. Bar: Va. 1949, U.S. Supreme Ct. 1954. Adminstrv. asst. U.S. Econ. Mission to Monrovia, Liberia, 1945; with export dept. Montgomery Ward, Chgo., 1947; mem. Purcell, Regirer, House & Hall, Richmond, Va., 1949-60; sole practice, Richmond, 1960—; consul. for Mex. in U.S., 1975—; pres., gen. counsel Health of Va., also Plyler's, The Windsor, University Park, 1949—; lectr. internat. law Coll. William and Mary, Richmond, 1955-59; U.S. exhbn. mgr. U.S. Dept. Commerce with embassies Rio de Janeiro, Guatemala, San Salvador, Montevideo and U.S. consulates gen., Zurich and Barcelona, 1963-68; instr. internat. law JAGC Sch., Charlottesville, Va., 1966-70; dir.-gen. Internat. Consular Acad. Served to lt. col. JAGC, USAR, 1949-74. Aide-de-camp to gov. Va., 1958—; col. JAGC Va. Defense Force. Decorated Brit. Star, 1939-45, Order of Consular Merit, gran official Instituto Consular Interamericano, 1977; recipient Disting. Service award P.R. Consular Corps, 1977. Mem. Nat. Lawyers Club (Washington), ABA (chmn. diplomatic and consular law com.), Fed. Bar Assn. (v.p. 1960-61), Va. State Bar (bar council 1960-64, chmn. internat. health, sr. lawyers sects.), 4th U.S. Circuit Jud. Conf. Editor Consular Rev. (Hardy Cross Dillard Meml. award 1985). Home: 9 Roslyn Hills Dr Richmond VA 23229 Office: 2420 Pemberton Rd Richmond VA 23233-2099

REGNART, CLAUDIA SWANNACK, educator; b. Spokane, Wash., Aug. 11, 1937; d. John William and Leone Estelle (Roth) Swannack; B.A., U. Puget Sound, 1959; postgrad. E. Wash. Coll. Edn., summers 1958, 60, U. Wash., summer 1966, Alaska Pacific U., 1968-69, 84, U. Alaska, summers 1972, 74, 82; m. Ronald I. Regnart, Nov. 21, 1962; children—Jeffrey, Patrick. Tchr., Anchorage Sch. Dist., 1959-63, 64-65, 67, Nome (Alaska) Sch. Dist., 1963-64; tchr., owner Rabbit Creek Pre-Sch., Anchorage, 1972—. Chmn. PTA, Anchorage, 1970—; den mother Boy Scouts Am., 1973-79; vol. worker Cancer Fund, Heart Fund, FISH, Little League. Mem. Alaska Edn. Assn., NEA, Am. Assn. for Edn. of Young Children. Methodist. Club: Order Eastern Star. Home and Office: 4900 Rabbit Creek Rd SRA Book 476A Anchorage AK 99516

REGNIER, CLAIRE NEOMIE, marketing and business consultant; b. Fort Riley, Kans., May 2, 1939; d. Eugene Arthur and Claire Janet (Macfarlane) Regnier; B.S. cum laude in Journalism, Trinity U., San Antonio, 1961. Advt. cons., San Antonio, 1961-68; editor Paseo del Rio Showboat newspaper, San Antonio, 1968-81; exec. dir. San Antonio River Assn., San Antonio, 1968-81; pres. Regnier, Valdez & Assoc., San Antonio, 1981—. Chmn. Centro 21 Downtown Revitalization Task Force, San Antonio; rep. San Antonio River Corridor Com.; mem. Fiesta San Antonio Commn., San Antonio Parks and Recreation Adv. Bd.; bd. dirs., chmn. public relations com. San Antonio Area council Girl Scouts U.S.A. Recipient awards of excellence for Showboat, Alamo Bus. Communicators, 1970, 71, 73, 74; Headliner award San Antonio chpt. Women in Communications, 1980. Mem. Internat. Assn. Bus. Communicators (Bronze Quill award 1986), Women in Communications (Southwest region banner award 1981, Proliner awards 1984-87), Tex. Public Relations Assn., Alamo Bus. Communicators (Communicator of Yr. 1977), San Antonio Mus. Assn., San Antonio Conservation Soc. Home: 7772 Woodridge St San Antonio TX 78209 Office: Regnier Valdez & Assoc 5152 Fredricksburg #205 San Antonio TX 78229

RÉGNIER, FRANÇOIS JEAN, pharmaceutical company executive; b. Dudweiler, Fed. Republic Germany, Sept. 12, 1933; s. Paul Gustave and Jeanne (Soenen) R.; m. Edith Marie Haushalter, Nov. 13, 1959; children: Caroline Régnier Guillon Verne, Raphaëlle Régnier Aellig. MD, Nancy U., France, 1960. Registered in pharm. medicine. Area mgr. Dausse Labs., Nancy, 1962-78; med. advisor Synthélabo, 1979-80; project mgr. LERS-Synthélabo, Paris, 1981-82, dir. French unit, 1982—; cons. in field; sci. coordinator editorial bd. Prospective et Santé, 1983—. Author: L'information Médicale et le Médicament, 1973, La Médecine: pour ou contre les Hommes?, 1976; contbr. articles to profl. jours.; inventor l'Abaque de Régnier. Recipient Prix Baron Larrey, Nat. Acad. Medicine, 1980. Mem. Found. L'industrie Pharm. pour la Recherche (pres. sci. com. 1988—). Home: 6 rue de la Source, 54000 Nancy France Office: LERS-Synthelab, 58 rue de la Glaciere, 75013 Paris France

REH, THOMAS EDWARD, radiologist, educator; b. St. Louis, Sept. 12, 1943; s. Edward Paul and Ceil Anne (Golden) R.; m. Benedette Texada Gieselman, June 22, 1968; children: Matthew J., Benedette T., Elizabeth W. BA, St. Louis U., 1965, MD, 1969. Diplomate Am. Bd. Radiology, Nat. Bd. Med. Examiners. Intern St. John's Mercy Med. Ctr., St. Louis, 1969-70; resident St. Louis VA Hosp., 1970-73; fellow in vascular radiology Beth Israel Hosp., Boston, 1973-74; radiologist St. Mary's Health Ctr., St. Louis, 1974—, chmn. dept. radiology, 1986—; clin. asst. prof. radiology St. Louis U. Sch. Medicine, 1978—. Mem. Am. Coll. Radiology, AMA, Radiol. Soc. N.Am., St. Louis Met. Med. Soc., Alpha Omega Alpha, Alpha Sigma Nu, Delta Sigma Phi. Republican. Roman Catholic. Clubs: St. Louis, Confrerie des Chevaliers du Tastevin. Home: 9850 Waterbury Dr Saint Louis MO 63124 Office: Bellevue Radiology Inc 1699 S Hanley Rd Saint Louis MO 63144

REHA, ROSE KRIVISKY, business educator emeritus; b. N.Y.C., Dec. 17, 1920; d. Boris and Freda (Gerstein) Krivisky; m. Rudolph John Reha, Apr. 11, 1941; children: Irene Gale, Phyllis. BS, Ind. State U., 1965; MA, U. Minn., 1967, PhD, 1971. With U.S. and State Civil Service, 1941-63; tchr. pub. schs., Minn., 1965-66; teaching assoc., part-time instr. U. Minn., Mpls., 1966-68; prof. Coll. Bus., St. Cloud (Minn.) State U., 1968-85, prof. emeritus, 1985—, chmn. bus. edn. and office adminstrn. dept., 1982-83; cons., lectr. in field. Reviewer of bus. communications and consumer edn. textbooks; contbr. articles to profl. jours. Camp dir. Girl Scouts U.S.A., 1960-62; active various community fund drives; sec., mem. relicensure rev. Com. Minn. Bd. Teaching Continuing Edn., 1984—. Recipient Achievement award St. Cloud State U., 1985, St. Cloud State U. Research and Faculty Improvement grantee, 1973, 78, 83. Mem. Am. Vocat. Assn., Minn. Econ. Assn., Minn. Women of Higher Edn., NEA, Minn. Edn. Assn. (pres. women's caucus 1981-83, award 1983), St. Cloud U. Faculty Assembly (pres. 1975-76), St. Cloud State U. Grad. Council (chmn. 1983-85), Pi Omega Pi (sponsor St. Cloud State U. chpt. 1982—), Phi Chi Theta, Delta Pi Epsilon, Delta Kappa Gamma. Jewish. Home: 1725 13 Ave SE Saint Cloud MN 56304 Office: St Cloud State Univ Coll Bus Saint Cloud MN 56301

REHAK, JAMES RICHARD, orthodontist; b. Chgo., Jan. 2, 1938; s. James Joseph and Lydia Ann (Thomas) R.; BS, U. Ill., 1960, DDS cum laude, 1962, M.S., 1967, cert. in orthodontics, 1965; m. Joann Marie Tabbert, Oct. 15, 1969; 1 dau., Suzanne Therese. Practice dentistry, Chgo., 1962-63, practice orthodontics, Chgo., Arlington Heights, Ill., Cape Coral and Naples, Fla; asst. prof. U. Ill. Coll. Dentistry, 1966-68. Kellogg Found. fellow, 1958. Fellow Royal Soc. Health; mem. ADA, Ill. Dental Assn., Chgo. Dental Soc., Fla. Dental Assn., West Coast Dental Soc., Collier County Dental Assn., Am. Assn. Orthodontists, Am. Assn. Lingual Orthodontists, So. Soc. Orthodontists, Fedn. Dentaire Internationale, Internat. Platform Assn., Psi Omega, Omicron Kappa Upsilon. Home: 859 Nelson's Walk Naples FL 33940 Office: 785 Central Ave Naples FL 33940

REHBEIN, EDWARD ANDREW, exploration geologist; b. Portland, Oreg., Aug. 13, 1947; s. Edward Louis and Marjorie Ann (Simshaw) R.; m. Phyllis Jean Boyer, June 23, 1973; children: Matthew Louis, Angela Mae. BS in Geology, Calif. Inst. Tech., 1969. Geologist U.S. Forest Service, Elkins, W.Va., 1972-74, U.S. Geol. Survey, Billings, Mont., 1974-76; coal geologist W.Va. Geologic Survey, Morgantown, 1977; cons. Morgantown, 1978; geologist Allied Corp., Beckley, W.Va., 1979; sr. exploration geologist Kerr-McGee Corp., Beckley, 1980-82, regional mgr. exploration, Reno, Nev., 1983-85; exploration geologist, Oklahoma City, 1985—. Contbr. articles to profl. jours. Mem. Am. Assn. Petroleum Geologists, Am. Inst. Profl. Geologists. Club: Shotokan Karate Am. Office: Kerr McGee Corp 123 Robert S Kerr Ave MT 2706 Oklahoma City OK 73162

REHBERGER, GUSTAV, artist; b. Riedlingsdorf, Austria, Oct. 20, 1910; s. Joseph and Elizabeth (Piff) R.; brought to U.S., 1923, naturalized, 1928; student Art Inst. Chgo., 1924-27, Art Instrn. Schs., Mpls., 1926-28. Staff art dir. Esquire mag., N.Y.C., 1949-60, Coronet mag., 1949-62; prof. art Old Mill Art Ctr. Adirondacks, 1964-66, Am. Art Sch., N.Y.C., 1969-72, Art Students League N.Y., 1972—. Fine arts painter, also former illustrator for nat. mags., motion picture promotion, books; designer, illustrator nat. advt. campaigns; one-man shows: Library, North Canton, Ohio, 1940, Stevens-Gross Gallery, Chgo., 1950, Soc. Illustrators, N.Y.C., 1957, 65, Old Mill Art Ctr. of Adirondacks, Elizabethtown, N.Y., 1964, 65, 66, Nat. Arts Club, Montreal, 1967, Wyoming Valley Art League, Wilkes-Barre, Pa., 1967, Wickersham Gallery, N.Y.C., 1971, Jacques Seligmann Gallery, N.Y.C., 1977; exhibited in group shows: NAD, N.Y.C., Audubon Artists, N.Y.C. (Most Creative Painting award 1949, award 1966), Allied Artists Am., N.Y.C., Painters in Casein, N.Y.C., Internat. Water Color Show at The Art Inst. Chgo., 1938, Chgo. and Vicinity Exhbn. The Art Inst. Chgo., 1935-40, Pastel Society Am., Wichita, Kans., The Oldfield Gallery, Pitts., 1983, Abelle Gallery, Princeton, N.J., 1985, Nat. Galleries, London, Nat. Gallery, Washington, Oldfield Gallery, Pitts., Abelle Gallery, Princeton, N.J., Am. Water Color Soc., N.Y.C., Nat. Drawing Exhbn., Oklahoma City; represented in permanent collections: Lyman Allyn Mus., New London, Conn., St. Johns U., N.Y.C., Sports Hall, Peking, China, also pvt. collections in U.S., Can., Europe, China, Saudi Arabia; commissioned works include: World War II Murals at Union Sta., Chgo., 1942, portrait of "Mama" Kutsher Kutsher's Resort, Monticello, N.Y., 1965, painting of Beethoven for the Beethoven Soc., Fed. Republic Germany, 1979; invited by city of Bonn, Fed. Republic Germany, to present art/music performance tributing Beethoven, 1986 (resulting painting presented to the Beethoven Archives); subject of articles in several mags. including Newsweek, Am. Artist; lectr., painting and drawing demonstrator The Spirit of Form, Movement and Expression; condr. nationwide workshops anatomy and figure drawing. Served with USAAF, 1943-45, ETO. Recipient award for creative painting 7th Ann. Audubon Artists Exhbn.; Art Dirs. Show award, N.Y.C., 1954, 55; Soc. Typographic Arts award, Chgo., 1936; Minnie R. Stern award 24th Ann. Audubon Artists Exhbn., 1966; Paul Puzinas Meml. award Allied Artists Am., 1974; Tiro A. Segno Found. award Pastel Soc. Am., 1976, Dirs. award, 1979, Exceptional Merit award, 1981, Dr. Leonard Cammer award, Lever House award, 1982, elected master pastelist, 1984, assn. award, 1984, Popular Vote award, 1985; Knickerbocker Artists award, 1984; named to Pastel Soc. Am. Hall of Fame, 1988. Mem. Allied Artists Am., (award in oil painting 1974, 81), Pastel Soc. Am. (founding mem., former 1st v.p., mem. adv. bd.), Audubon

Artists, Allied Artists, Am. Acad. Taos. Pioneer in use expressionism in Am. illustration and design. Address: Carnegie Hall Studio 1206 New York NY 10019

REHKOPF, CHARLES FREDERICK, church executive; b. Topeka, Dec. 24, 1908; s. Frederick A. and Mary G. (Jennings) R.; m. Dorothy A. Getchell, July 30, 1936; children—Frederick, Jeanne, Susan. B.S., Washburn Coll., 1932; certificate Episcopal Theol. Sch., 1935. Civil engr. Kans. Engrng. Co., Topeka, 1927-30; rector Trinity Episc. Ch., El Dorado, Kans., 1935-44, St. John's Episc. Ch., St. Louis, 1944-52; archdeacon and exec. sec. Diocese Mo., Protestant Episc. Ch., St. Louis, 1953-76; chmn. dept. research and planning Met. Ch. Fedn. Greater St. Louis, 1954-64; chmn. div. adminstrn. Mo. Council Chs., 1965-68, chmn. div. communications, 1970-72, chmn. div. Christian unity, 1972-73; registrar Diocese of Mo., 1949—; staff Episc. Ch., Webster Groves, Mo., 1976—. Editor The Historiographer's News Letter. Author articles pub. profl. jours. Trustee Episcopal Presbyn. Found. for Aging, Inc., mem. Religious Pub. Relations Council. Mem. Soc. Am. Archivists, Hist. Soc. Protestant Episc. Ch. (dir.). Home: 642 Clark Ave Webster Groves MO 63119 Office: 1210 Locust St Saint Louis MO 63103

REHM, JOHN EDWIN, manufacturing company executive; b. Bucyrus, Ohio, Oct. 20, 1924; s. Lester Carl and Mary O'Dale (Myers) R.; student Heidelberg U., 1942; U. Ala., 1943-44; Ohio State U., 1946-49. Asst. plant engr. Shunk Mfg. Co., Inc., Bucyrus, 1949-53, prodn. mgr., 1951-61, plant mgr., 1961-65, mgr. prodn. services, 1965-68, mgr. customer service dept., 1968-69, ops. mgr., 1969-70, v.p. ops., 1970-71; materials mgr. Oury Engrng. Co., Marion, Ohio, 1971-73, W.W. Sly Mfg. Co., Cleve., 1973-79, 84—; v.p., gen. mgr. Moody Mfg. Co., Inc., Maben, Miss., 1979-84. Bd. dirs. Bucyrus United Community Fund, 1969-70. Served with AUS, 1943-46, PTO. Decorated Bronze Star with oak leaf cluster. Mem. Am. Soc. Personnel Adminstrn., Bucyrus Area C. of C. (v.p. 1966, pres. 1967). Republican. Lodges: Elks, Rotary. Home: 5246 Manchester Circle North Ridgeville OH 44039

REHMATULLAH, ABED MAHMOOD, taxation administrator; b. Massawa, Ethiopia, Feb. 17, 1948; s. Mahmood Rehmatullah MAngroo and Khatuon Suleiman Yousef. Student, Aden Comml. Inst., Aden, Dem. Yeman, 1976, 78; diploma in fin. ecomomy, Fachshüle Für Finanzwritzchaft, Dem. Republic Germany, 1984. Taxation officer Dept. Taxes, Aden, 1967-73, sr. taxation officer, 1974-87, head traders, profls. and self employeed div., 1987—. Mem. Aden Trade Union. Home: House #76/27 Sect E St #2, PO Box 4523, Aden Yemen

REHNQUIST, WILLIAM HUBBS, Supreme Court justice; b. Milw., Oct. 1, 1924; s. William Benjamin and Margery (Peck) R.; m. Natalie Cornell, Aug. 29, 1953; children: James, Janet, Nancy. BA, MA, Stanford, 1948; MA, Harvard, 1949; LLB, Stanford, 1952. Bar: Ariz. Law clk. to former justice Robert H. Jackson, U.S. Supreme Ct., 1952-53; with Evans, Kitchel & Jenckes, Phoenix, 1953-55; mem. Ragan & Rehnquist, Phoenix, 1956-57; ptnr. Cunningham, Carson & Messenger, Phoenix, 1957-60, Powers & Rehnquist, Phoenix, 1960-69; asst. atty.-gen. office of legal counsel Dept. of Justice, Washington, 1969-71; assoc. justice U.S. Supreme Ct., 1971-1986, chief justice, 1986—; mem. Nat. Conf. Commrs. Uniform State Laws, 1963-69. Contbr. articles to law jours., nat. mags. Served with USAAF, 1943-46, NATOUSA. Mem. Fed., Am. Maricopa (Ariz.) County bar assns., State Bar Ariz., Nat. Conf. Lawyers and Realtors, Phi Beta Kappa, Order of Coif, Phi Delta Phi. Lutheran. Office: Supreme Ct US 1 First St NE Washington DC 20543 *

REHPENNING, WOLFGANG, statistician; b. Heringsdorf, Ger., Oct. 20, 1938; s. Hans-Harald and Margarete (Eggert) R.; m. Lotte Detenhoff, Feb. 10, 1987. Diploma in math. Westfälische Wilhelms-Universität Münster, 1967, Ph.D. in Astronomy, 1976, habilitation, 1982. Statistician, U. Hamburg, 1972—, U. Eppendorf, 1972—, U. Krankenhaus, 1972—. Mem. Gesellschaft Deutscher Naturfreunde und Ärtze, Astronomische Gesellschaft, Biometrical Soc. (German region). Home: Willi-Hill-Weg 7, 2000 Hamburg 53 Federal Republic of Germany Office: Martinistrasse 52, 2000 Hamburg Federal Republic of Germany

REIBSTEIN, RICHARD JAY, lawyer; b. Phila., Mar. 12, 1951; s. Albert Simon and Alma (Wilf) R.; m. Susan Barbara Fisch, May 18, 1975. BA with distinction, U. Rochester, 1973; JD with honors, George Washington U., 1976. Bar: Pa. 1976, N.Y. 1979, N.J. 1979, U.S. Dist. Ct. (so. dist.) N.Y. 1979, U.S. Dist. Ct. (ea. dist.) N.Y. 1979, N.J. 1979, U.S. Ct. Appeals (3d cir.) 1980, U.S. Ct. Appeals (2d cir.) 1982, U.S. Supreme Ct. 1983. Staff atty. Dept. Labor, Washington, 1976; counsel NLRB, Washington, 1976-78; assoc. Seham, Klein & Zelman (formerly Surrey, Karasik, Morse & Seham), N.Y.C., 1978-81; assoc. Epstein Becker & Green, P.C., N.Y.C., 1981-86, ptnr., 1986—; arbitrator Better Bus. Bur. Met. N.Y. Co-author: Negligent Hiring, Fraud, Defamation, and Other Emerging Areas of Employer Liability, 1988; contbr. articles to legal jours. Mem. ABA (devel. of law under NLRA com., sect. labor and employment law 1976—), N.Y. State Bar Assn. (labor arbitration and collective bargaining com., sect. labor and employment law 1980—). Democrat. Office: Epstein Becker & Green PC 250 Park Ave New York NY 10177

REICH, JACK EGAN, insurance company executive; b. Chgo., June 17, 1910; s. Henry Carl and Rose (Egan) B.; m. Jean Grady, Apr. 30, 1935; children: Rosemary (Mrs. Jerry Semler), Judith (Mrs. Dan Hoyt). Student, Purdue U., 1928-31; LLD (hon.), Butler U., 1973; PhD (hon.), Marian Coll., 1983; LLD (hon.), Ind. U., 1986. With Inland Steel Co., East Chicago, Ind., 1925-31; field dir. gross income tax and employment security divs. State of Ind., 1933-40; field dir. Ind. C. of C., 1940-52, exec. v.p., 1952-62; chmn. bd., pres. Indpls. Water Co., 1962-67, now mem. exec. com., dir.; chmn. bd., chief exec. officer Am. United Life Ins. Co.; bd. dirs., past pres. Assn. Ind. Life Ins. Cos.; bd. dirs. 1st Nat. Bank East Chicago, Ind., Indpls. Water Resources, Indpls. Health Inst., Inc.; bd. dirs., exec. com. Banc One Ind. Corp., Bank One Indpls., N.A. Bd. dirs., past pres. Greater Indpls. Progress Com.; bd. dirs., pres. Ind. Legal Found.; past chmn. Assoc. Colls. Ind.; bd. govs., past campaign chmn., chmn. bd., pres. United Way Greater Indpls.; bd. dirs. Corp. Community Council, Commn. for Downtown; past mem. bd. lay trustees St. Mary-of-the-Woods Coll.; mem. adv. bd. St. Vincent Hosp.; pres. Ind. Acad.; past local and state pres., nat. v.p. Jr. C. of C. Mem. Ind. C. of C. (dir., past chmn.), Indpls. C. of C. (dir.), Health Ins. Assn. Am. (nominating com., pub. relations policy com.), Pi Kappa Alpha. Clubs: Economic (past pres.), Columbia, Indpls. Athletic, Indpls. Press, Meridian Hills Country, Skyline 100 (chmn.), (Indpls.); Ind. Soc. (Chgo.). Home: 7404 N Pennsylvania St Indianapolis IN 46240 Office: Am United Life Ins Co 1 American Sq PO Box 368 Indianapolis IN 46206

REICH, KATHLEEN JOHANNA, librarian, educator; b. Mannheim, Germany, May 1, 1927; came to U.S., 1955, naturalized, 1958; d. Robert and Luise Charlotte Helene (Kurowsky) Weichel; 1 child, Robert Weichel. MAT in English, Rollins Coll., 1976, EdS, 1981, postgrad. U. Leipzig, U. Mainz. With Orlando (Fla.) Pub. Library, 1955-57; cataloguer, instr. U. Detroit, 1957-60, Trinity U., San Antonio, 1960-61; adminstr. Fla. Book Processing Ctr., Orlando, 1961-68; bur. chief, div. library services Fla. State Dept., Winter Park, 1968-71; assoc. prof. library sci. Rollins Coll., Winter Park, 1971—, asst. dean faculty, 1981-83, dir. overseas studies, 1983-84; head archives and spl. collections Rollins Coll., 1983—; acad. dean Prew Prep. Sch., Sarasota, Fla., 1983-85. Mem. AAUP, African Lit. Assn., Am. Water Ski Assn., Soc. Am. Archivists, Soc. Fla. Archivists, Fla. Historical Assn., Winter Park Historical Soc. (bd. dirs.), Kappa Delta Pi. Home: 211 Fawsett Rd Winter Park FL 32789 Office: Rollins Coll Winter Park FL 32789

REICH, NATHANIEL EDWIN, physician, artist, educator; b. N.Y.C., May 19, 1907; s. Alexander and Betty (Feigenbaum) R.; m. Joan Finkel, May 22, 1943; children: Andrew, Matthew. B.S., NYU, 1927; student, Marquette U. Coll. Medicine, 1927-29; M.D., U. Chgo., 1932. Diplomate Am. Bd. Internal Medicine. Intern, resident pathologist City Hosp., N.Y.C., 1931-33; emeritus attending physician Kingsbrook Jewish Med. Center Hosp.; mem. exec. bd., vis. physician Kings County Hosp., Bklyn.; mem. exec. bd.; attending physician State U. Hosp.; faculty SUNY Downstate Med. Center, 1938—, asso. clin. prof. medicine, 1952-74, clin. prof., 1974-77, emeritus prof., 1977—; vis. prof. San Marcos U. Coll. Medicine, Lima, Peru, 1968, U. Afghanistan, 1970, U. Indonesia, 1972, U. Sri Lanka, 1975; asst. attending physician N.Y. Postgrad. Hosp., Columbia U., 1940; cons. Long Beach Meml. Hosp.; cardiac cons. U.S. R.R. Retirement Bd., 1965—; program cons. Acad. Family Physicians, 1973, N.Y. State Disability Determinations; lectr. univs., Rome, Moscow, Rijeka, Haiti, Jerusalem, Cairo, Athens, Bangkok, Bucharest, Manila, Lisbon, Beijing, Shanghai, Witwatersrand, Capetown, Natal, Lima, Buenos Aires, Rio de Janeiro, Quito; lectr. univs. U. Madras (India), 1969, Spain, 1971, Auckland, N.Z., Sydney, Australia, also; lectr. univs. Japan Med. Assn., Philippine Heart Assn., Royal Thai Air Force Med. Service, China Med. Assn., Shanghai, 1978, Nat. Taiwan U., Taipei, 1978, Beijing Cardiac Inst., 1986; chmn. internat. cardiology sect. Congress Chest Diseases, Cologne, Germany, 1956; impartial specialist N.Y. State Dept. Labor, U.S. Fed. Employees; cons. N.Y. State Bur. Disability Determinations, N.Y.C.; Office Vocat. Rehab., U.S. R.R. Retirement Bd., Dept. Health and Human Services, 1965—; chief med. examiner SSS, 1942-44 (Presdl. commendation). Exhibited one-man show, L.I. U., 1961, N.Y.U. Loeb Center, 1962, 72, 74, Greer Gallery, 1962, 64, St. Charles, La., 1964, Nyack, N.Y., 1986, Prospect Park Central Art Show, 1966, Art Inst. Boston, 1970, 76, George Wiener Gallery, 1972; group shows Little Studio, 1952, Mus. Modern Art, Paris, 1970, Bodley Gallery, 1965, 69, Nyack, N.Y., 1987, others; represented permanent collections, Huntington Hartford collection N.Y. Cultural Center, 1969, Washington County Mus. of Fine Arts, Hagerstown, Md., Evansville (Ind.) Mus. Arts, Joe and Emily Lowe Mus. U. Miami, Coral Gables, Fla., also several univs., many pvt. collections; Author: Diseases of the Aorta, 1949, The Uncommon Heart Diseases, 1954, (with Dr. R.E. Fremont) Chest Pain: Systematic Differentiation and Treatment, 1959; numerous articles cardiology and internal medicine; contbr. to 3 encys. Served from 1st lt. to maj. M.C., AUS, 1944-47. Recipient St. Gaudens award, 1923; 1st prize Art Assn. AMA, 1948; 1st prize Art Assn. Literary Soc., 1949. Fellow ACP, Royal Soc. Medicine, Am. Coll. Cardiology, Am. Coll. Angiology (med. honor awards 1956, 59), Am. Coll. Legal Medicine (founder), Am. Coll. Chest Physicians (chmn. exhibits com. 1961, cardiovascular rehab. com. 1965, coronary disease com. 1968, pres. N.Y. state chpt. 1970); mem. Am. Arbitration Assn., N.Y. State Med. Soc. (vice chmn. space med. sect. 1967, 75, chmn. chest sect. 1972), Internat. Soc. Internal Medicine, World Med. Assn., Am. Heart Assn. (council on thrombosis), N.Y. Heart Assn., N.Y. Cardiol. Soc. (pres., chmn. exec. bd.), Am. Geriatrics Soc., Am. Soc. Law and Sci., Am. Med. Authors Soc., AMA (physicians Recognition award 1970, 74, 77, 80, 83, 86), Kings County Med. Soc. (chmn. radio com., cultural, program and social coms.), Am. Soc. Internal Medicine, Royal Soc. Health, N.Y.C. Hosp. Alumni Soc., Explorers Club, Phi Delta Epsilon, Kappa Alpha (hon.), Sigma Psi (hon.). Clubs: Temple (v.p.), Doctors (vice chmn. bd. govs. Bklyn.), Circumnavigators, Explorers. Home: 1620 Ave I Brooklyn NY 11230 Office: 135 Eastern Pkwy Brooklyn NY 11238

REICH, OTTO JUAN, diplomat, political analyst; b. Havana, Cuba, Oct. 16, 1945; came to U.S., 1960; s. Walter and Graciela Maria (Fleites) R.; m. Connie Lynn Dillinger, Apr. 19, 1975; children: Adrienne Michelle, Natalie Lauren. BA, U. N.C.-Chapel Hill, 1966; MA, Georgetown U., 1973; grad., Officers Candidate Sch., U.S. Army, 1967. Civil affairs officer U.S. Army, Panama, 1967-69; staff asst. U.S. Ho. Reps., Washington, 1970-71; v.p. Cormorant Enterprises, Miami, Fla., 1972-73; internat. rep. Fla. Dept. Commerce, Coral Gables, 1973-75; community devel. coordinator City of Miami, Fla., 1975-76; dir. Washington ops. Council of the Americas, 1976-81; asst. adminstr. U.S. AID, Washington, 1981-83; spl. adv. for pub. diplomacy to sec. state with rank of ambassador U.S. Dept. State, Washington, 1983-86; U.S. ambassador to Venezuela Caracas, 1986—. Bd. dirs. Human Rights, Washington, 1979-81; co-dir. com. hemispheric priorities Am. Enterprise Inst., Washington, 1979-81. Served to 1st lt. U.S. Army, 1966-69; C.Z. Recipient commendation medal for meritorious service Panama Canal Zone U.S. Army, 1969; Georgetown Ctr. Strategic and Internat. Studies fellow, 1971. Mem. Am. Council Young Polit. Leaders, Council of Am. Ambassadors. Home and Office: US Embassy Caracas APO Miami FL 34037 Office: US Ambassador to Venezuela care Dept of State Washington DC 20520

REICH, ROBERT CLAUDE, metallurgist, physicist; b. Paris, France, Nov. 2, 1929; s. Felix and Nelly (Belestin) R.; Engr., Ecole Nationale Supérieure de Chimie Paris, 1953; Licence ès Sciences Physiques, U. Paris, 1954, Docteur ès Sciences Physiques, 1965; m. Francoise Thiébault, June 10, 1972; m. Michele Helene Brand'Huy, Dec. 29, 1981. Attaché de recherche Centre Nat. de La Recherche Scientifique, Centre d'Etudes de Chimie Métallurgique, Vitry sur Seine, France, 1953-54, 58-65; chargé de recherche Laboratoire de Physique des Solides, Orsay, France, 1965-71, maître de recherche, 1971-83, dir. research, 1984—. Mem. Société Française de Physique, Société Française de Métallurgie, European Phys. Soc., Electrochem. Soc. (U.S.), Internat. Soc. Electrochemistry (sec. French sect.), Am. Soc. Metal. Research and publs. on purification of metals by zone-melting, elec. resistivity of metals versus purity (observed temperature squared term of ideal resistivity in non-magnetic metals), deviations from Matthiessen's rule, supra conducting transition in tin, determination of characteristic Debye temperatures, ferminology studies in mercury, size-effect, ionic interactions in solutions, electrolyte glass transitions, anodic dissolution of metals, corrosion and superconducting oxides. Home: 3 Allée des Mouille-Boeufs, 92290 Châtenay-Malabry France Office: Lab de Physique des Solides, Bâtiment 510/ U Paris-Sud, 91405 Orsay-Cedex France

REICHARD, JOHN FRANCIS, association executive; b. Abington, Pa., June 2, 1924; s. Francis Radcliffe and Katherine (Butler) R.; m. Ruth Naomi Nachod, Aug. 5, 1950; children—Scot, John Nicholas. B.A., Wesleyan U., 1949, postgrad. (Winchester fellow), 1949-50; postgrad. (Fulbright scholar) Glasgow U., 1950-51. Instr. English/humanities Wesleyan U., Middletown, Conn., 1951-52, Ohio Wesleyan U., Delaware, 1952-54; internat. campus adminstr. U.S. Nat. Student Assn., Cambridge, Mass., 1954; exec. dir. Internat. Student Assn. Greater Boston, 1955-60; pres. Phila. Council for Internat. Visitors, 1960-73; internat. coordinator Phila. 76, 1973-75; exec. dir. Global Interdependence Ctr., 1975-79; exec. v.p. Nat. Assn. for Fgn. Student Affairs, Washington, 1980—. Counselor Meridian Houe Internat.; travel adv. com. U.S. Travel Service, 1963-64; pres. Nat. Council Internat. Visitors, 1963-65; organizer, co-chmn. Internat. Yr. of Child, UNICEF, Phila., 1977-78; internat. adv. bd. Bryn Mawr Coll., 1975-79; chmn. schools com. Phila. steering com. on alumni affairs Wesleyan U., 1968-76; adv. bd. Hariri Found.; mem. Nat. Liaison Com. on Fgn. Student Admissions. Contbr. articles to profl. jours. Served with USAAF, 1943-46. Recipient Tribute of Appreciation, U.S. Dept. State, 1973. Mem. Am. Council on Edn. (secretariat, commn. on internat. edn.), Internat. Ednl. Exchange Liaison Group, Test of English as a Fgn. Lang. (policy council), Fulbright Alumni Assn. (v.p. 1978-80), Phi Beta Kappa. Democrat. Club: Cosmos. Home: 4974 Sentinel Dr 301 Bethesda MD 20816 Office: Nat Assn for Foreign Student Affairs 1860 19th St Washington DC 20009

REICHARD, SHERWOOD MARSHALL, radiobiologist, scientist, educator; b. Easton, Pa., June 24, 1928; B.A., Lafayette Coll., 1948; M.A. in Physiology, N.Y. U., 1950, Ph.D. in Endocrine Physiology (AEC fellow), 1955; postgrad. (Am. Heart Assn. and Muscular Dystrophy Assn. fellow) McCollum Pratt Inst., Johns Hopkins U., 1957-60, Army Chem. Sch., summer 1964, Inst. Biophysics, U. Freiburg (Ger.), summer 1970; m. Janet Williamson, June 24, 1954; children—Jon Lanier, Deborah L., Stuart B. Vis. investigator Armed Forces Inst. Pathology, Washington, 1958-60; asst. prof. physiology dept. biol. scis. Fla. State U., Tallahassee, 1960-63, dir. Radiation Biology Inst., 1961-63; asso. prof. radiology and physiology Med. Coll. Ga., Augusta, 1964-69, prof. radiology and physiology, 1969—, Regents' prof. radiology, 1979—, prof. physiology Sch. Grad. Studies, 1969—, dir. div. radiobiology, 1969—; radiobiologist Med. Coll. of Ga. Hosp. and Clinics, Augusta, 1966—; disting. lectr. Bryn Mawr Coll., 1965; sci. adv. EPA, 1979; research advisor E.I. Du Pont de Nemours & Co., 1973, Warner-Lambert/Parke-Davis, 1978; vis. lectr. various univs. in U.S., Japan, Europe and Israel, 1958-80; participant various internat. symposia on radiology and shock, 1958-82; cons. NASA, 1963-67, Graniteville Co., 1978-82; pres. Chem. Cons., Augusta, 1978—. Bd. dirs. Health Center Credit Union, 1976-81, chmn., 1976-81, pres., 1976-81, hon. chmn., 1981—. Served with M.S.C., U.S. Army, 1955-57. Recipient Founder's Day award NYU, 1956; Zoology medal Internat. Congress Zoology, 1963; Outstanding Tchr. award U.S. Army Chem. Sch., 1964; Outstanding Faculty award Med. Coll. Ga., 1978, Chair's Disting. Service award, 1982; NIH grantee, 1966-80; Upjohn grantee, 1981. Fellow AAAS, N.Y. Acad. Sci.; mem. Am. Physiol. Soc., Soc. for Leukoeyte Biology (hon. life), Georgia Acad. of Sci. (pres. 1988), Internat. Trade Council, Internat. Devel. Inst., Am. Soc. Zoologists, Radiation Research Soc., Radiol. Soc. N.Am., Reticuloendothelial Soc. (pres. 1973-74, council 1965-82, Silver Medallion award 1976, parliamentarian 1977-82, exec. dir. 1982—), Endocrine Soc. (Fred Conrad Koch travel award 1970), Soc. Nuclear Medicine, Shock Soc. (sec. 1978-80, pres. 1981-82, exec. dir. 1983—), Internat. Union Reticuloendothelial Socs. (pres. 1978-84, sec. gen. 1985—), Internat. Inflammation Club, Am. Assn. Anatomists, Soc. Exptl. Biology and Medicine, Mgmt. Assn. for Profl. Socs. (pres., fin. advisor), AAUP (pres. 1970-72), Sigma Xi (pres. 1982), Beta Beta Beta, Sigma Pi Sigma. Author: RES Functions, 1974; Tax Sheltered Annuities: A Comparative Analysis, 1980; contbr. numerous articles on radiobiology, the reticuloendothelial system, shock and cancer to sci. publs.; editor Jour. Reticuloendothelial Soc., 1970-73; editor Advances in Biology and Medicine, 1976; The Reticuloendothelial System: A Comprehensive Treatise, 1980-87; Advances in Shock Research, 1982-84; Progress in Leukocyte Biology; reviewer books in biology; contbr. numerous articles on physiology and radiation research to sci. jours. Home: 1122 Johns Rd Augusta GA 30904 Office: Med Coll Ga Div Radiobiology Augusta GA 30912

REICHELT, FERDINAND HERBERT, insurance and real estate corporation executive; b. Chgo., Jan. 26, 1941; s. Ferdinand W. and Justine E. (Schuetpelz) R.; m. Diane Bethel Peters, Nov. 14, 1964; children—Christine, Brian. B.S., U. Ill., 1963; postgrad. Loyola U., Chgo., 1964. C.P.A., Ill. Supr., mgr. Peat Marwick & Mitchell, Chgo., 1963-70; actuary, 1966-68, mgr., Omaha, 1970-72; chief fin. officer CMI Investment Corp. and subs., Madison, Wis., 1972-78; exec. v.p. Verex Corp. and subs., Madison, 1978-85, chief operating officer, 1983-86, pres., chief exec. officer, 1986-88, Gemini Corp., 1988—, also bd. dirs. Treas. Madison Civic Ctr. Found., 1981—; bd. dirs. Festival of Lakes; chmn. Friends of WHA-TV, Inc., 1983; trustee Edgewood Coll.; mem. bd. advisors Clin. Cancer Ctr., U. Wis., Elvehjem Art Ctr., Madison, 1986—. Served with USAF, 1963-69. Mem. Nat. Assn. Accts., Nat. Investor Relations Inst., Wis. Inst. C.P.A.s, Ill. Inst. C.P.A.s, Nebr. Inst. C.P.A.s, Nat. Assn. Ind. Insurers, Fin. Execs. Inst, Madison C. of C. (bd. dirs.). Lutheran. Clubs: PGA Nat. Golf (Palm Beach Gardens, Fla.); Nakoma Golf, Madison (Madison). Editor: Secondary Mortgage Market Handbook; guest columnist Barrons; contbr. to profl. publs. Office: Gemini Corp 301 N Broom St Madison WI 53703

REICHLE, FREDERICK ADOLPH, surgeon, educator; b. Neshaminy, Pa., Apr. 20, 1935; s. Albert and Ernestine R. BA summa cum laude, Temple U., 1957, MD, 1961, MS in Biochemistry, 1961, MS in Surgery, 1966. Diplomate Am. Bd. Surgery. Intern Abington Meml. Hosp., 1962; resident Temple U. Hosp., Phila., 1966, surgeon, 1966—; practice medicine specializing in surgery Phila., 1966—; assoc. attending surgeon Epis. Hosp., St. Mary's Hosp., St. Christopher's Hosp. for Children, Phoenixville Hosp.; cons. VA Hosp., Wilkes Barre, Pa., Germantown Dispensary and Hosp.; site visitor Can. Dept. Health and Welfare Program Br., 1977; chmn. dept. vascular surgery Presbyn.-U. Pa. Med. Ctr., 1980—; prof. surgery U. Pa., 1980—. Contbr. articles to profl. jours. Recipient Surg. Residents Research Paper award Phila. Acad. Surgery, 1964, 66, Gross Essay prize, 1976; Am. Heart Assn. grantee, 1973. Fellow ACS, Coll. Physicians Phila.; mem. Am. Surg. Assn., Soc. Univ. Surgeons, AMA, Pa. Med. Soc., Assn. Acad. Surgery, Chilean Surg. Soc., Royal Soc. Medicine, N.Y. Acad. Sci., AAAS, Am. Fedn. Clin. Research, Nat. Assn. Professions, Am. Gastroent. Assn., Am. Assn. Cancer Research, Am. Heart Assn., Phila. Acad. Surgery, Heart Assn. Southeastern Pa., Internat. Soc. Thombosis and Haemostasis, Nat. Kidney Found., Soc. for Surgery Alimentary Tract, Soc. Vascular Surgery, Colleguim Internationale Chirurgie Digestivae, Am. Soc. Pharmacology and Exptl. Therapeutics, Am. Inst. Ultrasound in Medicine, Am. Physiol. Soc., Soc. Internationale de Chirurgie, Am. Soc. Abdominal Surgeons, Surg. Hist. Soc., Am. Aging Assn., Am. Geriatrics Soc., Gerontol. Soc., Am. Diabetes Assn., Surg. Biology Club, Omega Alpha, Sigma Xi, Phi Rho Sigma. Office: 51 N 39th St Philadelphia PA 19104

REICHSTEIN, ANDREAS V., television producer; b. Freiburg, Fed. Republic Germany, Feb. 22, 1953; s. Barbara (Lepke) R.; m. Renate Böker, Dec. 11, 1980; children: Georg Alexander, Angelika Rebecca. B in Law, U. Freiburg, 1977, MA in History, 1979, PhD in History, 1983. TV producer and program mgr. N. German Radio and TV, Hamburg, Fed. Republic Germany, 1985—. Author: (book) Der Texanische Unabhängigkeitskrieg 1935/36, 1984; (TV series) Movies and Justice, 1986; (radio feature) Das Attentat auf John F. Kennedy, 1985; contbr. articles in field. Recipient Research stipend John F. Kennedy Inst., Berlin, 1979, Internat. Exchange grantee, U. Tex., 1980, research grantee German Acad. Exchange Service, 1982, John F. Kennedy Found., Boston, 1987. Mem. Am. Film Inst., Orgn. Am. Historians, Tex. State Hist. Assn., German Soc. Am. Studies, Nat. Geog. Soc. Roman Catholic. Home: Ebeersreye 120, 2000 Hamburg 72 Federal Republic of Germany Office: NDR-Redaktion Film Theatre, Jenfelder Allee 80, 2000 Hamburg 70 Federal Republic of Germany

REICHSTEIN, TADEUS, scientist, educator; b. Wloclawek, Poland, July 20, 1897; s. Isidor and Gustava (Brokman) R.; student Industrieschule, Zurich, 1914-16; Diploma in chem. Engring., Eidg. Tech. Hochschule, Zurich, 1920, Dr. Ing.-Chem., 1922, D.Sc. (hon.), Sorbonne, Paris, 1947, U. Basel, 1951, U. Geneva, 1967, U. Abidjan, 1967, U. London, 1968, U. Leeds, 1970; m. Luise Henriette Quarles v. Ufford, July 21, 1927; children—Margrit, Ruth. Prof. Eidg. Techn. Hochschule, 1934-38; prof. U. Basel (Switzerland), 1938-67, prof. emeritus, 1967—, dir. Pharmacol. Inst., 1938-48, dir. Inst. Organic Chemistry, 1946-67; research botanist on ferns, 1967—. Recipient Marcel-Benoist prize, 1948; co-recipient Nobel prize in physiology or medicine, 1950, various other prizes. Fellow Royal Soc. London, Nat. Acad. Sci. (Washington), Royal Irish Acad., Chem. Soc. London (hon.), Swiss Med. Acad. (hon.), Indian Acad. Sci. (hon.); mem. Mus. Hist. Nat. Paris (corr.), Med. Faculty U. Basel (hon.). Contbr. articles to profl. pubs. Home: 22 Weissensteinstrasse, CH-4059 Basel Switzerland Office: Inst fur Organische Chemie, St Johanns-Ring 19, CH-4056 Basel Switzerland

REICIN, RONALD IAN, lawyer; b. Chgo., Dec. 11, 1942; s. Frank Edward and Abranita (Rome) R.; m. Alyta Friedland, May 23, 1965; children—Eric, Kael. B.B.A., U. Mich., 1964, M.B.A., 1967, J.D. cum laude, 1967. Bar: Ill. 1967, U.S. Tax Ct. 1967. Mem. staff Price Waterhouse & Co., Chgo., 1966; ptnr. Jenner & Block, Chgo., 1967—. Bd. dirs. Nat. Kidney Found. Ill., 1978—, Scoliosis Assn. Chgo., 1981—, Ruth Page Found. Mem. Chgo. Bar Assn., Internat. Conf. Shopping Ctrs., ABA, Ill. Bar Assn., Chgo. Mortgage Attys. Assn., Phi Kappa Phi, Beta Gamma Sigma, Beta Alpha Psi. Clubs: Executive, Legal (Chgo.). Home: 1916 Berkeley Rd Highland Park IL 60035 Office: Jenner & Block 1 IBM Plaza 43d Floor Chicago IL 60611

REICKERT, ERICK ARTHUR, automotive executive; b. Newport, Tenn., Aug. 30, 1935; s. Frederick Arthur and Reva M. (Irish) R.; m. Diane Lois Comens, June 10, 1961 (div. Jan. 1979); children: Craig A., Laura L.; m. Heather Kathleen Ross, Sept. 1, 1982. BSEE, Northwestern U., 1958; MBA, Harvard U., 1965. Various positions Ford Motor Co., Dearborn, Mich., 1965-74, exec. dir. small car planning, 1979-84; v.p. export ops. Ford Motor Co., Brentwood, Eng., 1974-79; v.p. advance product devel. Chrysler Motors, Detroit, 1984-86, v.p. program mgmt., 1986-87; v.p., mng. dir. Chrysler Mexico, 1987—. Mem. Soc. Automotive Engrs., Engring. Soc. Detroit, Harvard Bus. Sch. Club of Detroit. Club: Univ. of Mexico City. Office: Chrysler Motors 12000 Chrysler Dr Highland Park MI 48288 also: Chrysler de Mex SA, Lago Alberto 320, 11320 Mexico City Mexico

REID, BELMONT MERVYN, brokerage house executive; b. San Jose, Calif., May 17, 1927; s. C. Belmont and Mary Irene (Kilfoyl) R.; B.S. in Engring., San Jose State U., 1950, postgrad.; m. Evangeline Joan Rogers, June 1, 1952. Pres., Lifetime Realty Corp., San Jose, 1969-77, Lifetime Fin. Planning Corp., San Jose, 1967-77; founder, chmn. bd. Belmont Reid & Co., Inc., San Jose, 1960-77; gen. ptnr., registered investment adv. JOBEL Fin. Inc., Carson City, Nev., 1980—; pres., chmn. bd. Data-West Systems, Inc., 1984-86 . County chmn. 1982-85, Carson City Rep. Cen. Com., treas., 1979-81; mem. Brewery Arts Ctr., chmn. Carson City Gen. Obligation Bond Commn., 1986—; rural county chmn., 1984-88. Nev. Rep. Cen. Com., 1984—; vice chmn. Carson City Charter Rev. Com., 1986—. Served with USN, 1945-46, 51-55. Decorated Air medals. Mem. Nat. Assn. Securities Dealers, Mcpl. Securities Rulemaking Bd., Nat. Futures Assn., Carson City C. of C. (pres., dir. 1986-87). Clubs: Capital of Carson City. Lodge: Rotary (chpt. sec. 1983-84, 86-87, pres.1988—). Home: 610 Bonanza Dr Carson City NV 89701 Office: 711 E Washington St Carson City NV 89701

REID, BONNIE LEE, junior high school principal; b. St. Louis, Jan. 30, 1937; d. William Charles Lovrenic and Fern Lee (Swingler) Reiman; m. Thomas James Fitzsimmons, Aug. 16, 1958 (div. Aug. 1966); children: Susan Lee, Scott James; m. Donald Francis Reid, Nov. 18, 1966; stepchildren: Christopher Kearns, Donald Francis Jr., Connie Ann, Britton Anthony, Douglas Nye. BE, U. Mo., 1958; MA in Adminstrn., Washington U., St. Louis, 1977, postgrad., 1978-80. Cert. tchr., Mo.; cert. secondary adminstr., Mo. Tchr. Webster Groves (Mo.) High Sch., 1958-60; tchr., dept. chmn. Parkway Sch. Dist., Chesterfield, Mo., 1971-81, asst. prin., 1982-83, assoc. prin., 1984, interim prin., 1985; prin. Parkway E. Jr. High Sch., Chesterfield, 1986—; mem. governance com. Gov.'s Conf. Edn., 1978; prin. Nat. Secondary Sch. Recognition Sch., 1986-87. Fellow Prin.'s Acad.; mem. Nat. Assn. Secondary Sch. Prins., Assn. Supervision and Curriculum Devel. (consortium sch. team leader 1986—) , Nat. Middle Sch. Assn. (conf. edn.), Mortar Bd., Mo. State Future Tchrs. Am., Parkway Ind. Community Tchrs. Assn., Greater St. Louis Tchrs. Assn., Delta Kappa Gamma, Kappa Alpha Theta, Pi Lambda Theta, Phi Sigma Iota, Kappa Epsilon Alpha, Sigma Rho Sigma. Republican. Presbyterian. Office: Parkway E Jr High Sch 181 Coeur De Ville Creve Coeur MO 63141

REID, BRIAN HOLDEN, historian, educator; b. Dec. 4, 1952; s. Robert Holden and Doreen Joan (Kempton) R. BA in History, U. Hull, Eng., 1974; MA in Am. Studies, U. Sussex, Eng., 1975; PhD in War Studies, King's Coll., London, 1983. Lectr. in modern history Polytech. North London, London, 1978-80; lectr. in modern history dept. extra-mural studies U. London, 1981-87, research assoc. dept. war studies, 1983-84, lectr. in war studies, 1987—; resident historian Brit. Army Staff Coll., Camberley, Surrey, Eng., 1987—; cons. Ministry of Def., London, 1987—; co-chmn. mil. history research seminar Inst. Hist. Research, London, 1987—. Author: J.F.C. Fuller: Military Thinker, 1987; editor Royal U.S. Inst. Jour., London, 1984-87; contbr. articles to profl. jours. Isodarco scholar, Verona, Italy, 1982. Fellow Royal Hist. Soc. Club: Reform (London). Home: 22 Danesfield, Benfleet, Essex SS7 5EF, England Office: King's Coll, Dept War Studies, Strand, London WC2R 2LS, England

REID, EVANS BURTON, chemist, artist, educator; b. Brock Twp., Ont., Can., Mar. 29, 1913; came to U.S., 1941, naturalized, 1944; s. William Thomas and Ethel Elizabeth (Burton) R.; m. Isabel Sue Lewin, Apr. 2, 1942 (dec. Nov. 3, 1962); 1 child, Nicholas Evans David; m. Dorothy Pearson, Aug. 12, 1963. B.Sc. with first class honors, McGill U., 1937, Ph.D. cum laude, 1940. Grad. asst. chem. engring. McGill U., 1937-38, demonstrator organic chemistry, 1938-40; research chemist Dominion Tar & Chem. Co., Montreal, 1940-41; instr. chemistry Middlebury Coll., 1941-43, asst. prof., 1943-46; asst. prof. chemistry Johns Hopkins, 1946-54; cons. Tainton Products, Balt., 1951-54; Merrill prof. chemistry, chmn. dept. Colby Coll., 1954-78, prof. emeritus, 1978—, acting dean faculty, 1967-68; dir. Coll. NSF Summer Sci. Inst., 1958-73; cons. to NSF, 1963-65; corporator Maine Med. Care Devel., Inc., 1968-76; Smith-Mundt vis. prof. chemistry U. Baghdad, 1960-61; Mem. screening panel for Nat. award in pure chemistry, 1953. Adv. council World Who's Who in Sci, 1968; contbr. to profl. jours. and encys.; painting student with Allan Lehtis, 1979-81; art exhbns. include Tony Vaj's Meml. Arts Festival, Waterville, 1980, 81, St. Mark's Ch., Waterville, 1981, Last Unicorn, 1981, 86, Learning Resources Ctr., U. Maine-Augusta, 1982, Thomas Coll. Waterville, 1983, Art Ctr., Ogunquit, Maine, 1983, 84, Thayer Gallery, 1984, Harlow Gallery, Hollowell, 1984, 86, Maine Biennial (juried), Portland Mus. Art, 1985. Recipient J. Shelton Horsley award Va. Acad. Scis. (with Albert W. Lutz), 1955. Home and Studio: 11 Highland Ave Waterville ME 04901

REID, HARRY, U.S. senator; b. Searchlight, Nev., Dec. 2, 1939; s. Harry and Inez Reid; m. Landra Joy Gould; children—Lana, Rory, Leif, Josh, Key. AA in Sci., U. So. Utah, 1959; LLD (hon.), South Utah State Coll., 1984; BS, Utah State U., 1961; JD, George Washington U., 1964. Bar: Nev. 1963, U.S. Supreme Ct. City atty. Henderson, Nev., 1964-66; trustee So. Nev. Meml. Hosp. Bd., 1967-69, chmn. bd. trustees, 1968-69; mem. Nev. Assembly, 1969-70; lt. gov. Nev., 1970-74; chmn. Nev. Gaming Commn., 1977-81; mem. 98th-99th Congresses, 1983-87; U.S. senator from Nev. 1987—, mem. appropriations, environ. and pub. works, aging coms., 1987—; sec., treas. Calif. Dem. Congl. Del. Mem. Helsinki Commn. Named Nev. Jaycees Outstanding Young Man of Yr., 1970, Man of Yr., City of Hope, 1970; recipient Nat. Jewish Hosp.-Asthma Ctr. Humanitarian award, 1984, Honor award Am. Lung Assn., 1987. Mem. Nev. Bar Assn., Am. Bd. Trial Advocates, Phi Kappa Phi. Office: US Senate Washington DC 20510

REID, INEZ SMITH, lawyer, educator; b. New Orleans, Apr. 7, 1937; d. Sidney Randall Dickerson and Beatrice Virginia (Bundy) Smith. BA, Tufts U., 1959; LLB, Yale U., 1962; MA, UCLA, 1963; PhD, Columbia U., 1968. Bar: Calif. 1963, N.Y. 1972, D.C. 1980. Assoc. prof. Barnard Coll. Columbia U., N.Y.C., 1972-76; gen. counsel youth div. State of N.Y., 1976-77; dep. gen. counsel HEW, Washington, 1977-79; inspector gen. EPA, Washington, 1979-81; chief legis. and opinions, dep. corp. counsel Office of Corp. Counsel, Washington, 1981-83; corp. counsel D.C., 1983-85; counsel Finley, Kumble, Wagner (now Laxalt, Washington, Perito & Dubuc), Washington, 1986—; William J. Maier, Jr. vis. prof. law W.Va. U. Coll. Law, Morgantown, 1985-86. Author: Together Black Women, 1972; contbr. articles to profl. jours. and publs. Bd. dirs. Homes and Ministries Bd. United Ch. of Christ, N.Y.C., 1978-83, vice chmn., 1981-83; chmn. bd. govs. Antioch Law Sch., Washington, 1979-81; chmn. bd. trustees Antioch U., Yellow Springs, Ohio, 1981-82. Recipient Emily Gregory award Barnard Coll., 1976, Arthur Morgan award Antioch U., 1982, Service award United Ch. of Christ, 1983, Disting. Service (Profl. Life) award Tufts U. Alumni Assn., 1988. Office: Laxalt Washington Perito et al 1120 Connecticut Ave NW Suite 1100 Washington DC 20036

REID, LOREN DUDLEY, speech educator; b. Gilman City, Mo., Aug. 26, 1905; s. Dudley Alver and Josephine (Tarwater) R.; m. Mary Augusta Towner, Aug. 28, 1930; children: Jane Ellen, John Christopher, Stephen Dudley Towner, Don Anthony. A.B., Grinnell Coll., 1927; A.M., State U. Iowa, 1930, Ph.D., 1932. Tchr. Vermillion (S.D.) High Sch., 1927-29; instr. State U. Iowa, 1931-33; tchr. Westport High Sch., Kansas City, Mo., 1933-35; English instr. U. Mo., 1935-37, asst. prof., 1937-39; asst. prof. and later asso. prof. of speech Syracuse U., 1939-44; prof. of speech U. Mo., 1944—, chmn. dept. speech, 1947-52; vis. prof. speech U. So. Calif., summer, 1947; summer lectr. La. State U., 1949, Mich., 1950, 56; summer lectr. State U. Iowa, 1952, Denver, 1960, Oklahoma, 1962; vis. prof. U. Utah, summer 1952, San Diego State Coll., summer 1954, U. So. Calif., summer 1954; European staff U. Md., 1952-53, summer, 1955, 1961-62, London; European staff U. Mich., summer 1957, State U. Iowa, summer 1958; Carnegie vis. prof. U. Hawaii, 1957, La. State U., 1985; vis. lectr. Kyoto (Japan) Sangyo U., 1987. Author: Charles James Fox: An Eighteenth Century Parliamentary Speaker, 1932, Course Book in Public Speaking, (With Gilman and Aly) Speech Preparation, (with Gilman and Aly), 1946, Fundamentals of Speaking, (with Gilman and Aly), 1951, Teaching Speech in High School, 1952, Teaching Speech, rev. edit, 1960, 4th edit., 1971, First Principles of Public Speaking, 1960, rev. edit., published in 1962, Studies in American Public Address, 1961, Speaking Well, 4th edit, 1982, Hurry Home Wednesday (Mo. Writers Guild award 1979), 1978 (Mo. Library Assn. Lit. award 1979), Finally It's Friday, 1981, Japanese edit., 1986, Charles James Fox (James A. Winans award 1969), 1969 (Golden Anniversary award 1970); also mem. editorial bd.: Speech Monographs, 1960-62, Speech Tch, 1964-66, Quar. Jour. Speech, 1966-68; Contbr. profl. jours. Recipient Alumni Achievement award Grinnell Coll., 1962; Disting. prof. awards U. Mo., 1970, 71; Andersch award Ohio U., 1981. Fellow Royal Hist. Soc.; mem. Eastern Pub. Speaking Conf., Speech Assn. Am. (exec. sec. 1945-51, pres. 1957, Disting. Service award 1981), N.Y. State Speech Assn. (pres. 1942-44, recipient special award for outstanding service 1967), Central States Speech Assn. (exec. sec. 1937-39, Disting. Service award 1979), Speech and Theatre Assn. Mo. (Disting. Service award 1982), AAUP, Mo. Tchrs. Assn., Hansard Soc. London, Internat. Soc. Study Rhetoric, Assn. Phoné tique Internationale, Conf. on Brit. Studies, Sigma Delta Chi, Kappa Tau Alpha. Democrat. Episcopalian. Club: University of Missouri (pres. 1947). Home: 200 E Brandon Rd Columbia MO 65203

REID, RALPH WALDO EMERSON, management consultant; b. Phila., July 5, 1915; s. Ralph Waldo Emerson and Alice Myrtle (Stuart) R.; m. Ruth Bull, Dec. 7, 1946; 1 child, Robert. Student, Temple U., 1932-34; B.S., Northwestern U., 1936; M.A., U. Hawaii, 1938; Ph.D., Harvard U., 1948. Cert. mgmt. cons. Asst. to v.p. Northwestern U., Evanston, Ill., 1938-40; chief mcpl. govt. br., spl. asst. govt. sect. Supreme Comdr. Allied Powers, 1946-47; spl. asst. Under Sec. of Army, 1948-49; chief Far Eastern affairs div. Office Occupied Areas, chief econs. div. Office Civil Affairs and Mil. Govt., Dept. of Army, 1950-53; asst. to dir. U.S. Bur. of Budget, Washington, 1953-55, asst. dir., 1955-61; resident mgr. A.T. Kearney Inc., Washington, 1961-72, mng. dir., Tokyo, 1972-81, cons., Alexandria, Va., 1981—; former dir. Nihon Regulator Co., Tokyo, Yuasa-Ionics Ltd., Tokyo, Japan DME, Tokyo. Served to comdr. USNR, 1941-46, PTO. Decorated Commendation Ribbon, Order of Rising Sun (3d class) (Japan); recipient Exceptional Civilian Service award U.S. Army, 1954. Mem. Inst. Mgmt. Consultants, Am. Polit. Sci. Assn., Am. Soc. Pub. Adminstrn. Republican. Am. Baptist. Clubs: Cosmos, Capitol Hill (Washington); Union League (Chgo.). Home: 412 Monticello Blvd Alexandria VA 22305 Office: A T Kearney Inc PO Box 1405 Alexandria VA 22313

REID, ROSS, lawyer, retired business executive; b. Spokane, Wash., Mar. 9, 1917; s. William George and Margaret (Gamble) R.; m. Sara Falknor, Dec. 31, 1940 (div.); 1 dau., Heather (Mrs. Edmund A. Schaffzin); m. Marney Sick Meeker, Jan. 19, 1966. A.B., Whitman Coll., 1938; student, U. Wash. Sch. Law, 1938-40; J.D., Northwestern U., 1942. Bar: Ill. 1941, N.Y. 1943, D.C. 1960. Assoc. firm Root, Clark, Buckner & Ballantine, N.Y.C., 1942-53; mem. firm Dewey, Ballantine, Bushby, Palmer & Wood (and predecessors), N.Y.C., 1954-62; v.p., dir., gen. counsel Beechnut Life Savers, Inc., 1962-68; sr. v.p., dir., gen. counsel, exec. com. Squibb Corp., 1968-83, dir. exec. com., 1983-84; dir. Allegheny Power System, Inc.; trustee Emigrant Savs. Bank; mem. N.Y State Lawyers Com. to Support Ct. Reorgn., 1958-60. Chmn. bd. Am. Heart Assn., 1972-74; chmn. N.Y. Heart Assn., 1964-72, exec. com.; bd. dirs. Internat. Cardiology Found.; bd. mem. 1st v.p. Internat. Soc. and Fedn. Cardiology; trustee Whitman Coll., Robert A. Taft Inst. Govt., Food and Drug Law Inst. Served with USAAF, 1945. Recipient Gold Heart award Am. Heart Assn., 1970. Fellow Am. Bar Found.; mem. Am., N.Y., Assn. Bar City N.Y. (chmn. membership com. 1961-64, exec. com. 1962-66), Jud. Conf. Second Circuit (exec. sec. plans com. 1960-64), Am. Judicature Soc., Order of Coif, Beta Theta Pi, Delta Sigma Rho, Delta Theta Phi. Clubs: University (N.Y.C.), West Side Tennis (N.Y.C.); Coral Beach and Tennis (Bermuda); Seattle Tennis. Home: 142 E 71st St New York NY 10021 Office: 40 W 57th St New York NY 10019

REID, SHERRI JO, tax preparation company executive; b. Maquoketa, Iowa, June 22, 1941; d. William Earle and Luella Augusta (Teters) Wells; m. Gary Harrison Hicks, July 2, 1958 (dec. Apr. 1973); children: Bryon Keith, Scott Allen; m. Ronald Dwight Reid, July 21, 1977; stepchildren: Mark Douglas, Dwight David, Curtis Duane. Grad. pub. schs., Maquoketa. Enrolled to practice before IRS. Proof operator Jackson (Iowa) State Bank, 1958-61; co-owner, mgr. Hicks TV & Appliances, Maquoketa, 1961-72; tax practitioner Schoenthaler & Schoenthaler, Roberg, Maq Iowa, 1972-75; owner, tax cons. Sherri's Tax Service, Onslow, Iowa, 1975—; enrolled agt., owner, computer programmer Reid Enterprises, Onslow, 1975—. Mem. Nat. Assn. Tax Practitioners, Nat. Fedn. Ind. Bus., Nat. Assn. Enrolled Agts., Nat. Assn. Pub. Accts. Republican. Methodist. Clubs: Garden (Maquoketa); Claytonian (Onslow). Avocations: geology, science, fishing, crafts, flower arranging. Home and Office: Sherri's Tax Service Box 790 1000 E Platt Maquoketa IA 52060

REID, WILLIAM HOWARD, psychiatrist; b. Dallas, Apr. 10, 1945; s. Howard Clinton and Lucile (Lattanner) R. B.A., U. Minn., 1966, M.D., 1970; M.P.H., U. Calif.-Berkeley, 1975. Diplomate Am. Bd. Psychiatry and Neurology. Intern, U. Calif.-Davis, 1970-71, resident in psychiatry, 1973-75; clin., research and forensic psychiatrist, asso. prof., vice chief of staff Nebr. Psychiat. Inst., Omaha, 1977-86; med. dir. Colonial Hills/Hosp., San Antonio, 1986—; clin. prof. psychiatry U. Tex. Health Sci. Ctr.; lectr. in psychiatry Northwestern U., vis. asso. prof. and forensic cons. Rush Med. Coll., 1978-81; chair research sect. Cross Keys Internat. Conf. Psychiat. Aspects of Terrorism; v.p. Nat. Assn. State Mental Health Research Insts; pres. Am. Acad. Psychiatry & Law. Served with M.C., AUS, 1971-73. Mem. Am. Psychiat. Assn., AMA, Am. Acad. Psychiatry and the Law (pres. 1988-89). Author: The Psychopath: A Comprehensive Study of Antisocial Disorders and Behaviors, 1978; Psychiatry for the House Officer, 1979; Basic Intensive Psychotherapy, 1980; The Treatment of Antisocial Syndromes, 1981; Treatment of the DSM-III Psychiatric Disorders, 1983. Co-editor: Terrorism: Interdisciplinary Perspectives, 1983; Assaults Within Psychiatric Facilities, 1983; Unmasking the Psychopath, 1986; The Treatment of Psychiatric Disorders, 1988, Training Guide to DSM-III-R, 1988. Contbr. articles to sci. jours. Composer 15 mus. compositions.

REID CABRAL, DONALD, Dominican Republic government official; b. June 9, 1923; s. William C. Reid and Auristela Cabral de Reid; m. Clara A. Tejera, 1949; 2 daughters. Student, U. Santo Domingo, Dominican Republic. Pres. Reid & Pellerano C.A., 1949—; v.p. Council of State, 1962-63; minister fgn. affairs Dominican Republic, 1963-64, ambassador to UN, 1963, ambassador to Israel, 1963, minister armed forces, 1964-65, now sec. state of fgn. relations; pres. Triumvirate which ruled the Dominican Republic, 1963-65. Home: Cervantes 8, Santo Domingo DN Dominican Republic Office: Sec State Fgn Relations, Santo Domingo Dominican Republic *

REIDER, HARRY ROBERT, management consultant; b. Phila., Nov. 28, 1940; s. Benjamin and Esther (Weiss) R. BSBA, Drexel U., 1963, MBA, 1966; PhD in Organizational and Mgmt. Psychology, Southwest U., Phoenix, 1982. CPA, Pa. Corp. systems analyst Campbell Soup Co., Camden, N.J., 1963-66; mgr. corp. systems devel. Leeds & Northrup, North Wales, Pa., 1966-69; mgr., mgmt. cons. Peat, Marwick, Mitchell & Co., Phila., 1969-76; pres. Reider Assocs., mgmt. cons., Huntingdon Valley, Pa. and Santa Fe, 1976—; lectr., cons. in field. Author: Operational Auditing, 1983; EDP Auditing, 1983; Developing a Consulting Practice, 1985; General Practice Management, 1985; Microcomputer Fundamentals, 1985; Microcomputer Hardware and Software Selection Process, 1985; Developing an MAS Practice, Self Study Course, 1987; other books; contbr. articles to profl. jours. Mem. Pa. Inst. C.P.A.s (chmn. social responsibility com. 1980-81), Am. Inst. C.P.A.s (Discussion Leader of Yr. 1986-87). Office: Reider Assocs 348 Meadowbrook Dr Huntingdon Valley PA 19006

REIDINGER, RICHARD BARBER, economist; b. Chattanooga, Jan. 6, 1943; s. Cleon A. and Faith (Barber) R.; B.A., Coll. Wooster, 1965; Ph.D., Duke U., 1971; postdoctoral fellow U. Calif., Davis, 1971; m. Judith G. Barry, June 5, 1965; children—Shaunti C., Richard C. Peace Corps vol., Haryana, India, 1965-67; research contract economist U.S. AID, New Delhi, India, 1970; postdoctoral research agrl. economist U. Calif., Davis, 1971; cons. World Bank, 1972; agrl. economist Econ. Research Service, U.S. Dept. Agr., Washington, 1972-77; agrl. economist World Bank, Washington, 1977-81, sr. agrl. economist, 1981—. Pres., Nat. Drug Abuse Found., 1979-86. Recipient U.S. Dept. Agr. honor award for group achievement, 1975, also cert. of merit, 1975. Fulbright Research fellow, 1969; NDEA Title VI fellow, 1967-69. Mem. Am. Econs. Assn., Am. Agrl. Economic Assn., Internat. Commn. on Irrigation and Drainage. Presbyn. Home: 6500 Randall Pl Falls Church VA 22044 Office: 1818 H St NW Washington DC 20433

REIFF, JEFFREY MARC, lawyer; b. Phila., Jan. 24, 1955; s. Morton William and Phyliss (Rubin) R.; m. Dominiqus F. Edrei, June 3, 1979; children—Justin Alexander, Collin Michael. B.S., B.A. magna cum laude in Mktg. Fin., Am. U., 1976; J.D., Temple U., 1976. Bar: Pa. 1979, U.S. Dist. Ct. Pa. 1975, N.Y. 1985. Ptnr. Sablosky, Wertheimer & Reiff, Phila., 1979-82, Mozenter, Durst & Reiff, Phila., 1982-85; prin., founder Reiff, Haaz and Assocs. and predecessor firms, Phila., 1985—. Mem. young leadership bd. Fedn. Jewish Agys., Phila., 1982—; bd. dirs. Golden Slipper Charities, Phila., 1979—, Solomon Schecker Schs., Phila., 1984. Mem. Phila. Bar Assn. (com. chmn. 1984—), Pa. Bar Assn. (com. chmn., mem. lawyers reference com. young lawyers div. 1980—), Am. Trial Lawyers Assn., Pa. Trial Lawyers Assn., Phila. Trial Lawyers Assn. Clubs: Locust, Golden Slipper (bd. dirs. 1980—), Abington Country (Phila.). Home: 229 Holmecrest Rd Jenkintown PA 19046 Office: Jeffrey M Reiff & Assocs 1324 Walnut St Philadelphia PA 19107

REIFSNYDER, CHARLES FRANK, lawyer; b. Ottumwa, Iowa, Sept. 6, 1920; s. Charles L. and Lena (Emery) R.; A.B., George Washington U., 1944, LL.B., 1946; m. Sally Ann Evans, Dec. 27, 1948; children—Daniel Alan, Jeremy Evans; m. 2d, Nancy Lee Laws, Mar. 4, 1960; 1 son, Frank Laws. Admitted to D.C. bar, 1945; sec. Judge T. Alan Goldsborough, U.S. Dist. Ct., Washington, 1945; law clk. Chief Judge Bolitha J. Laws, U.S. Dist. Ct., 1946-47; asst. U.S. atty., Washington, 1947-51; spl. asst. to Atty. Gen. U.S., 1950-51; asso. Hogan & Hartson, Washington, 1951-58, partner, 1959-85; chmn. personnel security rev. bd. Energy Research and Devel. Adminstrn. (formerly AEC). Trustee, Legal Aid Agy. (now Public Defender Service), Washington, 1960-67; bd. dirs. Nat. Jud. Coll., Reno, 1968-70. Fellow Inst. Jud. Adminstrn., N.Y.C., 1967-68. Fellow Internat. Soc. Barristers, Am. Bar Found.; mem. Am. (chmn. spl. com. coordination jud. improvements 1971-74, mem. spl. com. atomic energy law 1969-73, chmn. div. jud. adminstrn. 1967-68, del. 1968-69), Fed., Fed. Energy (pres. 1981-82, chmn. com. natural gas 1967-68), D.C. (dir. 1955-56) bar assns., Am. Arbitration Assn., (nat. panel arbitrators), Am. Judicature Soc. (dir. 1972-76), Am. Law Inst., Phi Delta Phi, Sigma Nu. Episcopalian. Clubs: Met., Nat. Lawyers, Barristers, Lawyers (Washington); Gibson Island (Md.) Yacht Squadron; Annapolis (Md.) Yacht, Farmington Country (Charlottesville, Va.). Home: Gibson Island MD 21056

REIG, JOSÉ ALBERTO, nuclear engineer; b. Havana, Cuba, Sept. 20, 1945; came to U.S., 1962; s. José María and Dulce María (Ynastrilla) R.; m. Sonia Magarita León, May 7, 1977. AA, Montgomery Coll., 1970; BSE, U. Md., 1973. Registered profl. engr., Va., Md., Washington, Del.; cert. energy mgr. Draftsman Syska & Hennessy, Washington, 1965-69, mech. engr., 1975-76; plumbing designer Perkins & Will, Washington, 1969-70; nuclear engr. Babcock & Wilcox, Lynchburg, Va., 1973-75; pres. Energy Systems Engring., Inc., Kensington, Md., 1977—; cons. engr. Pan Am. Health Orgn., Washington, 1978, 87-88. Mem. Montgomery County Energy Adv. Com., Rockville, Md., 1980-83. Mem. ASHRAE (Regionnaire award 1984, pres. nat. capital chpt. 1983-84, regional vice chmn. energy mgmt. 1985-88, soc. dir. 1988—), NSPE (bd. dirs. Potomac chpt. 1980-84, pres. 1986-87), ASME (assoc.). Home: 10816 Horde St Wheaton MD 20902 Office: Energy Systems Engring Inc 10400 Connecticut Ave Suite 500 Kensington MD 20895

REIJNST, BERNARD ANTONY, metals, mining and processing executive; b. Jakarta, Indonesia, Aug. 18, 1924; s. Antonie Jacobus Willem and Cornelia (De Zwart) Reynst; m. Kerstin Margaretha Brännman, Aug. 28, 1954 (div. 1973); children: Ingrid, Märith, Angelica, Patrick, Sisismund; m. Birgitta Margaretha Brännman; 1 child, Bernarda. Degree in mining engring., Technische Hogeschool, 1955. Mine surveyor LKAB, Kiruna, Sweden, 1955-56; chief engr. San Antonio de Esquilache, Puno, Peru, 1957; chief engr. Emp. Monera de Mantos Blancos S/A, Antofagasta, Chile, 1957-61, mine supt., 1961-67, gen. supt., 1968-69, asst. gen. mgr. ops., 1970-75, gen. mgr. ops., 1976-86, resident dir., 1987—. Mem. Mijnbouwkundig Genootschap, Soc. Mining Engrs., Inst. Ingenieros de Mina de Chile. Home: Colo Colo 112, Pucon Chile

REILEY, THOMAS PHILLIP, food company executive; b. Ft. Lewis, Wash., May 5, 1950; s. Thomas Phillip and Anne Marie (Russick) R.; B.Sc. in Biophysics, Pa. State U., 1973; postgrad. in Bus. Adminstrn., Rutgers U. Inventory supr. Leland Tube Co., S. Plainfield, N.J., 1973-76; prodn. inventory control supr. Bomar Crystal Co., Middlesex, N.J., 1976-79; prodn. control mgr. Codi Semicondr. Inc., Linden, N.J., 1979-81; mfg. systems analyst Western Union Info. Systems, Mahwah, N.J., 1981-85; sr. systems analyst Nabisco Brands Biscuit Div., Parsippany, N.J., 1985—. Mem. Am. Prodn. and Inventory Control Soc. (chmn. ednl. com. Raritan Valley chpt.), N.Y. Acad. Scis., Assn. M.B.A. Execs., Mensa. Republican. Home: 56 Carlton Club Dr Piscataway NJ 08854 Office: Nabisco Brands Plaza Parsippany NJ 07054

REILLY, EDWARD ARTHUR, lawyer; b. N.Y.C., Dec. 17, 1943; s. Edward Arthur and Anna Marguerite (Sautter) R.; m. Patricia Brien, Feb. 8, 1969; children—M. Teresa, Edward A. A.B., Princeton U., 1965; J.D., Duke U., 1968. Bar: N.Y. 1969, N.C. 1971, Fla. 1979, Conn. 1983. Asst. dean Duke U. Law Sch., 1970-72; assoc. Shearman & Sterling, N.Y.C., 1972-80, ptnr., 1980-87; ptnr. Harlow, Reilly, Derr & Stark, Research Triangle Park, N.C., 1988—. Served to lt. USNR, 1968-70. Fellow Am. Coll. Probate Counsel; mem. ABA, N.Y. State Bar Assn., N.Y. County Lawyers Assn., Assn. Bar City N.Y., N.C. Bar Assn., Fla. Bar Assn., Conn. Bar Assn. Roman Catholic. Office: Harlow Reilly Derr & Stark Park Forty Plaza PO Drawer 13448 Research Triangle Park NC 27709

REILLY, FRANK KELLY, business educator; b. Chgo., Dec. 30, 1935; s. Clarence Raymond and Mary Josephine (Ruckrigel) R.; m. Therese Adele Bourke, Aug. 2, 1958; children: Frank Kelly III, Clarence Raymond II, Therese B., Edgar B. B.B.A., U. Notre Dame, 1957; M.B.A., Northwestern U., 1961, U. Chgo., 1964; Ph.D., U. Chgo., 1968. Chartered fin. analyst. Trader Goldman Sachs & Co., Chgo., 1958-59; security analyst Tech. Fund, Chgo., 1959-62; asst. prof. U. Kans., Lawrence, 1965-68, assoc. prof., 1968-72; prof. bus., assoc. dir. div. bus. and econ. research U. Wyo., Laramie, 1972-75; prof. fin. U. Ill., Champaign-Urbana, 1975-81; Bernard J. Hank prof. U. Notre Dame, Ind., 1981—, dean Coll. Bus. Adminstrn., 1981-87; bd. dirs. First Interstate Bank of No. Ind. Author: Investment Analysis and Portfolio Management, 1979, 2d edit., 1985, 3d edit., 1989, Investments, 1982, 2d edit., 1986; Editor: Readings and Issues in Investments, 1975; Assoc. editor: Fin. Mgmt, 1977-82, Quar. Rev. Econs. and Bus, 1979—, Fin. Rev, 1979—, Jour. Fin. Edn., 1981—. Arthur J. Schmidt Found. fellow, 1962-65; U. Chgo. fellow, 1963-65. Mem. Midwest Bus. Adminstrn. Assn. (pres. 1974-75), Am. Fin. Assn., Southwestern, Western Fin. Assn. (exec. com. 1973-75), Eastern Fin. Assn. (exec. com. 1979-84, pres. 1982-83), Midwest Fin. Assn., Fin. Analysts Fedn., Fin. Mgmt. Assn. (pres. 1983-84, chmn. 1985—; bd. dirs. Acad. Fin. Services), Nat. Bur. Econ. Research, Beta Gamma Sigma. Roman Catholic. Office: Coll Bus Adminstrn U Notre Dame Notre Dame IN 46556

REILLY, JEANETTE P., clinical psychologist; b. Denver, Oct. 19, 1908; d. George L. and Marie (Bloedorn) Parker; A.B., U. Colo., 1929; M.A., Columbia U., 1951, Ed.D., 1959; m. Peter C. Reilly, Sept. 15, 1932; children—Marie Reilly Heed, Sara Jean Reilly Wilhelm, Patricia Reilly Davis. Lectr. psychology Butler U., Indpls., 1957-58, 60-65; cons. child psychologist Mental Hygiene Clinic, Episcopal Community Services, Indpls., 1959-65; cons. clin. psychologist VA Hosp., Indpls., 1965-66; Christian Theol. Sem., 1968-70; pvt. practice clin. psychology, Indpls., 1967—; cons. clin. psychologist St. Vincent's Hosp., 1973—; adv. cons. middle mgmt. group Indpls. City Council, 1980-81. Mem. women's aux. council U. Notre Dame, 1953—; trustee Hanover (Ind.) Coll., 1975—; bd. dirs. Community Hosp. Found., Indpls., 1978—, Indpls. Mus. Art, 1987—; mem. Ind. Bd. Examiners in Psychology, 1969-73; mem. Com. for Future of Butler U., 1985-86. Mem. Am. Psychol. Assn., Am. Personnel and Guidance Assn., Am. Vocat. Assn., Ind. Psychol. Assn., Central Ind. Psychol. Assn., Ind. Personnel and Guidance Assn., Nat. Registry Psychologists in U.S.A. Office: 3777 Bay Rd N Dr Indianapolis IN 46240

REILLY, PATRICK JOHN, engineering-construction company executive; b. Nutley, N.J., Oct. 10, 1925; s. Philip and Anna (Cox) O'Reilly; m. Marcia Garcia Vazquez, July 27, 1957; children: Anne Maria, Patrick John, Thomas J., Frank P. BSCE, NYU, 1950; cert. practical constrn. law, U. Santa Clara, 1977. Lin. gen. engring. contractor, Calif. Shaft engr. Lincoln Tunnel third tube Walsh Constrn. Co., N.Y.C., 1950-54; asst. equipment mgr. Brown-Raymond-Walsh, Madrid, 1954-55, project engr., 1955-57; v.p., project mgr. wastewater treatment plants Shanley Constrn. Co., San Francisco, 1957-65; constrn. mgr. W.W. Kimmins and Sons, Buffalo, 1965-70, gen. supt. hwy., utilities and underground constrn., 1970; dir. mcpl. waste projects, constrn. mgr. Monsanto Environ. Chem. Co., Chgo., 1970-74; v.p., project mgr., dir. constrn. and regional constrn. mgr. solid waste facilities BSP div. Envirotech Corp., Menlo Park, Calif., 1974-84, v.p. project mgmt., 1984—. Served with USAAF, 1943-45. Decorated D.F.C., Air medal with 5 oak leaf clusters. Mem. ASCE, Am. Arbitration Assn. (panel arbitrators). Roman Catholic. Home: 20719 Woodward Ct Saratoga CA 95070 Office: 3000 Sand Hill Rd Menlo Park CA 94025

REILLY, PETER C., chemical company executive; b. Indpls., Jan. 19, 1907; s. Peter C. and Ineva (Gash) R.; A.B., U. Colo., 1929; M.B.A., Harvard U.,

1931; m. Jeanette Parker, Sept. 15, 1932; children—Marie (Mrs. Jack H. Heed), Sara Jean (Mrs. Clarke Wilhelm), Patricia Ann (Mrs. Michael Davis). With accounting dept. Republic Creosoting Co., Indpls., 1931-32; sales dept. Reilly Tar & Chem. Corp., N.Y.C., 1932-36, v.p., Eastern mgr., 1936-52; v.p. sales, treas. both cos., Indpls., 1952-59, pres., 1959-73, chmn. bd., 1973-75, vice chmn., 1975-82, chmn., 1982—; dir. Environ. Quality Control Inc.; past dir. Ind. Nat. Corp., Ind. Union Ry., Ind. Nat. Bank. Dir. Goodwill Industries Found.; past bd. dirs. United Fund Greater Indpls., Indpls. Symphony Orch.; bd. govs. Jr. Achievement Indpls. Mem. adv. council U. Notre Dame Sch. Commerce, 1947—; mem. adv. council Winona Meml. Hosp. Recipient Sagamore of Wabash award. Mem. Chem. Spltys. Mfg. Assn. (life; treas. 1950-60, past dir.), Chem. Mfrs. Assn. (past dir.), Am. Chem. Soc., Soc. Chem. Industry (past dir. Am. sect. 1979—). Clubs: Union League, Harvard, Chemist (N.Y.C.); Larchmont (N.Y.) Yacht; Indianapolis Athletic, Pine Valley Golf (N.J.), Meridian Hills Country, Columbia (Indpls.); Rotary, One Hundred (past dir.); Crooked Stick Golf. Home: 3777 Bay Rd North Dr Indianapolis IN 46240 Office: Reilly Tar & Chem Corp Market Sq Ctr 151 N Delaware St #1510 Indianapolis IN 46204

REILLY, ROBERT FREDERICK, valuation consultant; b. N.Y.C., Oct. 3, 1952; s. James J. and Marie (Griebel) K.; m. Janet H. Steiner, Apr. 16, 1975; children: Ashley Lauren, Brandon Christopher. BA in Econs., Columbia U., 1974, MBA in Fin., 1975. CPA. Sr. cons. Booz, Allen & Hamilton, Cin., 1975-76; dir. corp. planning Huffy Corp., Dayton, Ohio, 1976-81; v.p. Arthur D. Little Valuation, Inc., Chgo., 1981-85; ptnr., mng. dir. Valuation Engring. Assocs. and ptnr. of Touche Ross & Co., Chgo., 1985—; adj. prof. accounting U. Dayton Grad. Sch. Bus., 1977-81; adj. prof. fin. econs., Elmhurst (Ill.) Coll., 1982-87; adj. prof. fin. Ill. Inst. Tech. Grad. Sch. Bus., Chgo., 1985-87; adj. prof. taxation U. Chgo. Grad. Sch. Bus., 1985-87. Contbr. articles to profl. jours. Mem. Am. Soc. Appraisers (bd. examiners 1985—), Nat. Assn. Accts.(chpt. dir. 1976—), Inst. Property Taxation, Soc. Mfg. Engrs., Am. Inst. CPAs, Ill. Soc. CPAs, Ohio Soc. CPAs (chpt. dir. 1978-81). Home: 310 Algonquin Rd Barrington Hills IL 60010 Office: Touche Ross & Co 111 E Wacker Dr Chicago IL 60601

REILLY, WILLIAM FRANCIS, publishing company executive; b. N.Y.C., June 8, 1938; s. William F. and Genevieve Reilly; m. Ellen Chapman, Nov. 19, 1966; children: Anthony Chapman and Jane Wasey (twins). AB cum laude, U. Notre Dame, 1959; MBA, Harvard U., 1964. Mgr. fin. analysis W.R. Grace & Co., N.Y.C., 1964-67, asst. to pres., 1969-71, chief exec. officer Bekaert Textile div., 1971-74, group exec. mdse. products group, 1974-75, dep. chief exec. consumer products group, 1974-75; asst. fin. adminstr. City of N.Y., 1967-69; pres. Herman's World of Sporting Goods, Carteret, N.J., 1976-77; v.p. W.R. Grace & Co., N.Y.C., 1977-80, pres. Home Center Div., 1979-80; exec. v.p. Macmillan, Inc., N.Y.C., 1980, pres., chief operating officer, 1981—; pres. Macmillan Pub. Co. div. Macmillan, Inc., N.Y.C., 1987—. Served to 1st lt. U.S. Army, 1959-61. Home: 8 E 96th St New York NY 10128 Office: Macmillan Inc 866 Third Ave New York NY 10022

REIMAN, DONALD HENRY, English educator; b. Erie, Pa., May 17, 1934; s. Henry Ward and Mildred Abbie (Pearce) R.; m. Mary Warner, 1958 (div. 1974); 1 child, Laurel Elizabeth; m. Hélène Liberman Dworzan, Oct. 3, 1975. A.B., Coll. of Wooster, 1956, Litt.D., 1981; M.A., U. Ill., 1957, Ph.D., 1960. Instr. English Duke U., 1960-62, asst. prof., 1962-64; assoc. prof. U. Wis., Milw., 1964-65; adj. assoc. prof. grad. program in English CUNY, 1967-68; adj. prof. English Columbia U., 1969-70, sr. research assoc. in English, 1970-73; vis. prof. St. John's U., Jamaica, N.Y., 1974-75; editor Shelley and His Circle, Carl H. Pforzheimer Library, N.Y.C., 1965-86, N.Y. Pub. Library, 1986—; vis. lectr. U. Ill., 1963; vis. prof. U. Wash, Seattle, summer 1981; Lyell Reader in Bibliography Oxford U., 1988-89; cons. Harvard U. Press, Yale U. Press., Princeton U. Press, John Hopkins U. Press, Garland Pub. Inc., Macmillan & Co., Oxford U. Press. Author: Shelley's The Triumph of Life, A Critical Study, 1965, 2d edit., 1979, Percy Bysshe Shelley, 1969, 2d edit., 1974; (with D.D. Fischer) Byron on the Continent, 1974; English Romantic Poetry, 1800-1835, 1979, Romantic Texts and Contexts, 1987, Intervals of Inspiration: The Skeptical Tradition and the Psychology of Romanticism, 1988; editor: Shelley and His Circle, Vols. V-VI, 1973, Vols. VII-VIII, 1986, The Romantics Reviewed: Contemporary Reviews of English Romantic Writers, 9 vols., 1972; (with S.B. Powers) Shelley's Poetry and Prose: A Norton Critical Edition, 1977; The Romantic Context: Poetry, 128 vols., 1976-79; (with M.C. Jaye and B.T. Bennett) The Evidence of the Imagination, 1978; gen. editor Manuscripts of the Younger Romantics, 1984—; editor-in-chief The Bodleian Shelley Manuscripts, 1984—; mem. editorial com. adv. bd. Publs. of MLA, 1969-70; mem. editorial bd. Keats-Shelley Jour., 1968-73; mem. adv. bd. Milton and the Romantics, 1975-80, Studies in Romanticism, 1977—, Romanticism Past and Present, 1980-86, Text, 1981—, Nineteenth-Century Literature, 1986—, Nineteenth-Century Contexts, 1987—; contbr. articles to books and profl. jours. Active Common Cause, Better World Soc. Fellow Am. Council Learned Socs., 1963-64, Wesleyan Ctr. Advanced Studies, 1963-64, NEH, 1978; grantee Am. Council Learned Socs., 1961, NEH, 1983-86, 86—. Mem. AAUP, MLA (life), Modern Humanities Research Assn. (life), Wordsworth-Coleridge Assn. Am. (founder), Byron Soc. (Am. com. 1973—), Keats-Shelley Assn. Am. (dir. treas. 1973—, Disting. Scholar award 1987), Bibliog. Soc. Am., Soc. Textual Scholarship (exec. com. 1981—), Charles Lamb Soc., Assn. for Documentary Editing. Democrat. Presbyterian. Home: 6495 Broadway 6M Bronx NY 10471 Office: care Pforzheimer Collection New York Pub Library 5th Ave at 42d St New York NY 10018

REINER, PAULA, consulting company executive; b. N.Y.C., Apr. 3, 1950; d. Samuel Reiner and Elaine (Klein) Blau. B.A. cum laude, Bklyn. Coll., 1971; M.B.A., N.Y. U., 1977. Systems engr. ICL Inc., N.Y.C., 1977-78; sr. systems engr. NCR Corp., N.Y.C., 1978-79; sr. mgmt. adv. services cons. Price Waterhouse & Co., N.Y.C., 1979-80; data processing mgr. Recs. for the Blind, Inc., N.Y.C., 1980-81; pvt. practice systems cons., N.Y.C., 1981—; pres. SIGCONSULT of Greater N.Y., 1987—; vice chmn. Interex SIGCONSULT, 1986—. Mem. NOW (dir. N.Y.C. chpt. 1981), Women in Info. Processing, Hewlett Packard Computer Systems Users Group (vice chair spl. cons. interest group 1986—). Office: 319 E 24th St New York NY 10010

REINHARD, WOLFGANG, history educator; b. Pforzheim Baden, Germany, Apr. 10, 1937; s. Rudolf and Maria (Maurer) R.; m. Gudrun Graner, June 8, 1965; children: Johannes, Judith, Jakob. Staatsexamen, U. Freiburg, Fed. Republic Germany, 1962, PhD, 1963, habilitation in History, 1973. Tchr. Freiburg, 1962-65; adminstr. Land Baden-Wuerttemberg, Freiburg, 1965-66; research fellow Goerres-Gesellschaft, Rome, 1966-69, Deutsche Forschungsgemeinschaft, Rome, Freiburg, 1970-71, Fazit Stiftung, Freiburg, 1971-73; dozent Freiburg U., 1973-77; prof. Augsburg U., Fed. Republic Germany, 1977—; vis. prof. Emory U., Atlanta, Ga., 1985-86. Author: eight books including Geschichte der europaeischen Expansion I-IV, 1983; editor six books; contbr. numerous articles to profl. jours. Office: U Augsburg, Universitaetsstrasse 10, D8900 Augsburg Federal Republic of Germany

REINHARDT, ALFRED, retired educator, consultant; b. Berthelsdorf, Saxony, Germany, Aug. 12, 1921; arrived in Fed. Republic Germany, 1945; s. Edwin and Alma (Fiedler) R.; m. Gisela Maria Cecilia Göddertz, Sept. 23, 1960; children: Ulrike, Birgit. Diplom in Engring., Tech. U., 1953, Doctor in Engring., 1960. Registered profl. engr. Asst. Tech. U., Hannover, Fed. Republic Germany, 1955-60; planungsingenieur, AEG, Frankfurt, Fed. Republic Germany, 1960-62, mgr., 1962-71, oberingenieur, 1970; tchr. Tech. High Sch., Hannover, 1971-75, prof., 1975-86; cons. Kraftwerk Union, Erlangen, Germany, 1971-82. Author VDE-Forschungsheft 482, 1960; ATKE-Contribution, 1970, also numerous papers in field. Served as sgt. German Army, 1940-45. Mem. Verband, Deutscher Elektrotechniker, Kerntechnische Gesellschaft, Nachrichtentechnische Gesellschaft, VDI/VDE-Ausschuss Reaktor-Leittechnik. Evangelic Lutheran. Home: Herderstrasse 17, D3003 Ronnenberg, Niedersachsen Federal Republic of Germany

REINHARDT, KURT, retired physician, educator; b. Limbach, Saar, Feb. 18, 1920; s. Friedrich and Elisabeth (Hock) R.; student U. Berlin, 1939-40, U. Heidelberg, 1940-45; Cand.-Med., U. Innsbruck, 1945; m. Maria Lefeber, Dec. 29, 1951. Resident dept. radiology U. Homburg, 1951-58; head physician, dept. radiol. nuclear medicine Kreiskrankenhaus Volklingen, from 1958, habilitation, 1958, prof., from 1964, now ret. Decorated Cross of Merit 1st class Fed. Republic of Germany. Mem. Deutsche Roentgengesellschaft, Internat. Skeletal Soc. Author 10 monographs and books including Krankhafte Haltungs-änderungen Skoliosen und Kyphosen; contbr. 200 articles to med. jours. Home: 32 am Kirschenwaldchen, Volklingen Federal Republic of Germany

REINHARDT, MAX, publisher; b. Istanbul, Nov. 30, 1915; s. Ernest and Frieda (Darr) R.; student English High Sch. for Boys, Istanbul, Ecole des Hautes Etudes Commerciales, Paris, London Sch. Econs., m. Joan MacDonald, 1957; 2 daus. Chmn., HFL (Publishers) Ltd. (now Reinhardt Books Ltd.), London, 1948-87; chmn. Max Reinhardt Ltd., London, 1948—, Nonesuch Press, Ltd., 1985—; bd. dirs. The Badley Head, chmn. 1982-87. Mem. council Royal Acad. Dramatic Art, 1965—. Mem. Publishers Assn. (mem council 1963-69). Address: 16 Pelham Crescent, London SW7 2NR, England

REINING, BETH LAVERNE (BETTY), public relations consultant, journalist; b. Fargo, N.D.; d. George and Grace (Twiford) Reimche; student N.D. State Coll., U. Minn., Glendale Community Coll., Calif. State Coll., Carson; 1 dau., Carolyn Ray Toohey Hiett; m. Jack Warren Reining, Oct. 3, 1976 (div. 1984). Originated self-worth seminars in Phoenix, 1970-76; owner Janzik Pub. Relations, 1971-76; talk show reporter-hostess What's Happening in Ariz., Sta. KPAZ-TV, 1970-73; writer syndicated column People Want to Know, Today newspaper, Phoenix, 1973; owner JB Communications, Phoenix, 1976-84; owner, pres. Media Communications, 1984—; freelance writer; tchr. How to Weigh Your Self-Worth courses Phoenix Coll., Rio Solado Community Coll., Phoenix, 1976-84; muralist, works include 25 figures in med. office. Founder Ariz. Call-A-Teen Youth Resources, Inc., pres., 1975-76, v.p., 1976-77, now bd. dirs. Recipient awards including 1st pl. in TV writing Nat. Fedn. Press Women, 1971-88, numerous state awards in journalism Ariz. Press Women, 1971-76, Good Citizen award Builders of Greater Ariz., 1961. Mem. Ariz. Press Women, No. Ariz. Press Women (pres. 1983), Nat. Fedn. Am. Press Women, Pub. Relations Soc. Am., Phoenix Pub. Relations Soc., Nat. Acad. TV Arts and Scis., Phoenix Valley of Sun Convention Bur., Verde Valley C. of C. (bd. dirs., tourism chmn. 1986-87, Best Chair of Yr. award 1986), Phoenix Metro C. of C. Cottonwood C. of C. (chmn. of Yr. award, 1986). Inventor stocking-tension twist footlet, 1962. Club: Phoenix Press. Office: PO Box 10509 Phoenix AZ 85064 Address: PO Box 10509 Phoenix AZ 85016

REINSCH, JAMES LEONARD, cable company executive; b. Streator, Ill., June 28, 1908; s. Henry Emil and Lillian (Funk) R.; m. Phyllis McGeough, Feb. 1, 1936; children: Penelope Luise (Mrs. Bohn), James Leonard. B.S., Northwestern U., 1934. With radio sta. WLS, Chgo., 1924; former chmn. bd. Cox Broadcasting Corp.; chmn. bd. Sunbelt Cable Co., 1983-86; pres. Nat. Cable Communications Inc., 1986—; former dir. 1st Nat. Bank Atlanta; also cable cons. Former chmn. U.S. Adv. Commn. Information; radio adviser to White House, 1945-52; TV and radio cons. Democratic Nat. Com.; exec. dir. Democratic Nat. Conv., 1956, 60-64, also arrangements dir., 1968, TV-radio dir. Dem. presdl. campaign, 1960; mem. Carnegie Commn. on Future Public Broadcasting. Author: Radio Station Management, 1948, rev. edit., 1960, Getting Elected, 1987. Bd. dirs., exec. com. Am. Cancer Soc. Recipient D.F. Keller award Northwestern U., Distinguished Bus. Mgmt. award Emory U., 1968, award Am. Women in Radio and TV, 1975, Disting. Service award Nat. Assn. Broadcasters, 1978. Mem. Atlanta Art Assn., Internat. Radio and TV Soc. (Gold medal 1973), Cable Pioneers, Sigma Delta Chi, Di Gamma Kappa. Clubs: Capital City (Atlanta), Peachtree Golf (Atlanta); Burning Tree (Washington); Broadcast Pioneers (N.Y.C.); Nat. Capital Democratic (Washington); Palm Beach Polo and Country, Palm Beach Yacht, Wellington. Lodge: Rotary. Home: 4553 Upper Roswell Rd Marietta GA 30062 also: 11730 Maidstone West Palm Beach FL 33414

REINSDORF, JERRY MICHAEL, lawyer, professional athletic franchise executive, real estate executive; b. Bklyn., Feb. 25, 1936; s. Max and Marion (Smith) R.; m. Martyl F. Rifkin, Dec. 29, 1956; children: David Jason, Susan Janeen, Michael Andrew, Jonathon Milton. B.A., George Washington U., 1957; J.D., Northwestern U., 1960. Bar: D.C., Ill. 1960; CPA, Ill.; cert. specialist real estate securities, rev. appraiser; registered mortgage underwriter. Atty. staff regional counsel IRS, Chgo., 1960-64; assoc. law firm Chapman & Cutler, 1964-68; ptnr. Altman, Kurlander & Weiss, 1968-74; of counsel firm Katten, Muchin, Gitles, Zavis, Pearl & Galler, 1974-79; gen. ptnr. Carlyle Real Estate Ltd. Partnerships, 1971, 72; former pres. Balcor Co., Skokie, Ill.; chmn. bd. Balcor Co., 1974—; chmn. Chicago White Sox, 1981—, Chgo. Bulls Basketball Team, 1985—; mng. partner TBC Films, 1975—; lectr. John Marshall Law Sch., 1966-68; bd. dirs. Shearson Lehman Bros, Inc., John Howard Assn., Tax Mgmt. Adv. Bd. on Real Estate, Ednl. Tape Recording for Blind, Project Academus of DePaul U., Chgo., 1987—, Sports Immortals Mus., 1987—, Com. Commemorate U.S. Constitution, 1987; lectr. in real estate and taxation. Author: (with L. Herbert Schneider) Uses of Life Insurance in Qualified Employee Benefit Plans, 1970. Co-chmn. Ill. Profls. for Sen. Ralph Smith, 1970; bd. dirs. Gastro-Intestinal Research Found., 1981-86, Chgo. Promotional Council, 1981-85, Ednl. Tape Recording for the Blind, 1979—, Sports Immortals Mus. Bd., 1987—; mem. Chgo. Region Bd. Anti-Defamation League, 1986—; adv. bd. Project Academus, 1987—. Mem. ABA, Ill. Bar Assn., Chgo. Bar Assn., Fed. Bar Assn., Nat. Assn. Rev. Appraisers and Mortgage Underwriters, Northwestern Law Sch. Alumni Assn. (bd. dirs.), Order of Coif, Omega Tau Rho. Office: Bojer Fin Ltd 980 N Michigan Ave Suite 1011 Chicago IL 60611

REINSTEDT, ROBERT NELSON, educational administrator; researcher, lecturer; b. Detroit, May 21, 1926; s. Albert Peterson and Mayme May (Bowlin) R.; m. Jean Kirkup; children by previous marriage: Lee N., Bruce R., Jane Barry. A.B., DePauw U., 1950, M.A., 1955; postgrad. Ind. U. 1955, Whittier Coll., 1957, UCLA, 1960. Dean of students Whittier Coll., Calif., 1955-58; with Rand Corp., 1958-86, assoc. dept. head, 1972-77, sr. researcher behavioral scis. dept., 1977-86; pres. computer personnel research group 1970-72; lectr. in field; dir. Rand Employees Fed. Credit Union, trustee Pension Trust Fund; lectr. in field. Contbr. chapters various books. Mem. AAAS, Am. Psychol. Assn., Calif. Psychol. Assn., Western Psychol. Assn., DePauw U. Alumni Assn. (past pres. Los Angeles chpt.) Office: Rand Corp 1700 Main St Santa Monica CA 90406

REINVANG, IVAR REINHOLT, psychologist; b. Halden, Norway, Apr. 20, 1944; s. Egil and Elsa (Karlsen) R.; m. Jette Larsen, Dec. 28, 1968 (div. Sept. 1975); children: Rasmus, Line; m. Toril Bjorg, Mar. 4, 1984. Degree in psychology, U. Oslo, Norway, 1969, PhD, 1983. Research fellow Norwegian Council for Research, Oslo, 1970-73; postdoctoral fellow MIT, Cambridge, 1970-72; dir. inst. Nat. Assn. Health, Oslo, 1973-77; psychologist Sunnaas Rehab. Hosp., Nesoddtangen, Norway, 1978-85; prof. psychology U. Oslo, 1981—; psychologist Nat. Hosp., Oslo, 1986—; sec. Com. on Strokes, Oslo, 1983-86; mem. grant rev. bd. Norwegian Council for Research, 1987—. Author: Afasi: Språkfortyrrelse, 1978, Aphasia and Brain Organization, 1985; contbr. articles to profl. jours. Mem. Norsk Psykologforening (chair subcom. 1986-87), Am. Psychol. Assn., Internat. Neuropsychol. Assn., Acad. Aphasia, Council for Coronary and Vascular Diesease. Office: Nat Hosp, Pilestredet 32, 0027 Oslo Norway

REIS, CARLOS MANUEL VIEIRA, surgeon, writer; b. Chaves, Vila Real, Portugal, Jan. 19, 1935; s. Manuel Rodrigues Reis and Julieta Vieira Reis; children: Helena, Manuel, Carlos, João. M.D., Faculdade de Medicina, Lisboa, 1960; postgrad. Inst. Med. Tropical, Lisboa, 1961, Inst. Nacional Educaç ão Fisica, Lisboa, 1966, Faculdade de Letras, Lisboa, 1968, 83, Instituto de Altos Estudos Militares, Lisboa, 1973. All degrees of surg. career Civic Hospitals, Lisboa, 1960-67; surgery and emergency services dir. Hosp. Militar Principal, Lisboa, 1972-81; clin. dir. Casa de Saude de Familia Militar, Lisboa, 1981; main hosp. subdir. Hosp. Militar Principal, Lisboa, 1981-82; health service cons. Estado Maior Gen. des Forças Armadas, Lisboa, 1982-86; sub dir. Mil. Health Service Sch., 1986; surgery cons. Centro Policlinico, Almada, 1978—; surgeon examiner Correios, Telefones, CTT, TLP, Marconi, police, banks, Lisboa, 1979; pres. Comissão de Farmácia e Terapêutica do Hosp. Militar Principal, Lisboa, 1980-84; rep. for Portugal, Euromed, Holland, The Hague, 1983—; surgery asst. prof. Faculdade de Ciências Médicas, Lisboa, 1976-84. Author: Prazer em conhecê-lo, 1984; author, editor weekly radio program Poesia, Música e Teatro-Trilogia necessá ria, 1977; corr. Med. Corps Internat., Portugal. Redactor chief Revista Portuguesa de Medicina Militar, 1984—. Contbr. articles on surgery and history of medicine to profl. jours. Co-founder Espaco A-Clube Cinquenta, Lisboa, 1983, NOEI-Cons. for Devel., Lisboa, 1983. Served to col. Portuguese Health Service, 1961. Mem. Sociedade Portuguesa de Medicina Desportiva, Sociedade Internactional de Psicologia Desportiva, Sociedade das Ciê ncias Mé dicas de Lisboa, Sociedade Portuguesa de Cirurgia, Associacion de Cirujanos de los Cursos del Hosp. San Pablo, Barcelona, Associaç ã o Portuguesa de Pacing, Sociedade Portuguesa de Histó ria da Medicina, Sociedade Portuguesa de Escritores Médicos, União Mundial Escritores Médicos, Soc. Española Médicos Escritores. Club: Lisbon Sports (Lisboa). Avocations: art collector; medals collector. Home: Rua Coelho da Rocha, 11-5 Dto, 1300 Lisbon Portugal Office: ESSM Escola do Servico de Saude, Militar, Rua Infantaria 16 No 30, 1300 Lisbon Portugal

REIS, DONALD JEFFERY, neurologist, neurobiologist, educator; b. N.Y.C., Sept. 9, 1931; s. Samuel H. and Alice (Kiesler) R.; m. Cornelia Langer Noland, Apr. 13, 1985. A.B., Cornell U., 1953, M.D., 1956. Intern N.Y. Hosp., N.Y.C., 1956; resident in neurology Boston City Hosp.-Harvard Med. Sch., 1957-59; Fulbright fellow, United Cerebral Palsy Found. fellow London and Stockholm, 1959-60; research asso. NIMH, Bethesda, Md., 1960-62; spl. fellow NIH, Nobel Neurophysiology Inst., Stockholm, 1962-63; asst. prof. neurology Cornell U. Med. Sch., N.Y.C., 1963-67; asso. prof. neurology and psychiatry Cornell U. Med. Sch., 1967-71, prof., 1971—, First George C. Cotzias Disting. prof. neurology, 1982—; Mem. U.S.-Soviet Exchange Program; adv. councils NIH; bd. sci. advisers Merck, Sharpe and Dohm; cons. biomed. cos. Contbr. articles to profl. jours.; mem. editorial bd. various profl. jours. Recipient CIBA Prize award Am. Heart Assn. Mem. Am. Physiol. Soc., Am. Neurol. Assn., Am. Pharmacol. Soc., Am. Assn. Physicians, Telluride Assn., Am. Soc. Clin. Investigation, Phi Beta Kappa, Sigma Xi, Alpha Omega Alpha. Club: Century Assn. Home: 190 E 72d St New York NY 10021 Office: 1300 York Ave New York NY 10021

REISLER, HELEN BARBARA, publishing and advertising executive; b. N.Y.C., June 21; d. George and Elizabeth Lois (Schultz) Gottesman; B.S., in Edn., N.Y. U., 1954; M.S. in Edn. and Reading, L.I. U., 1978; m. Melvin Reisler, June 5, 1955; children—Susan O'Brien, Karen Reisler, Keith James. Elem. tchr., N.Y.C., 1954-78; instr. grad. sch., adj. lectr. L.I. U., Bklyn., 1978; account exec. N.Y. Yellow Pages, Inc., N.Y.C., 1979, personnel mgr., 1979, adminstrv. dir., 1980-83, v.p. personnel, 1983-84, v.p. adminstrn./personnel, 1984-85, also dir.; staff specialist sales and market support Southwestern Bell Publs., 1985-88, NY. mgr. pub. relations and recruitment N.Y. Yellow Pages/Mast Advt. and Publs., Inc. of Southwestern Bell, 1988—; recruiter Northeast Region, N.Y. area community relations rep.; moderator weekly cable TV show New York Business Forum, N.Y.C., 1983-85. Named Ptnr. in Edn., N.Y.C. Bd. Edn., 1984. Mem. Sales Execs. Club N.Y. (bd. dirs., reception, membership and mem. relations coms., chmn. youth edn., v.p. 1987—), Execs. Assn. Greater N.Y. (chmn. com. Sec. Day). Clubs: NYU, Heritage Hills Country (Westchester), Sales Execs. (v.p.). Profiled in various bus. publs. Lodge: Rotary. Home: 47 Plaza St Park Slope Brooklyn NY 11217 Office: Southwestern Bell Publs 91 Fifth Ave New York NY 10003

REISS, FRED, educator; b. Phila., Dec. 22, 1946; s. Manny M. and Yetta Reiss; B.S. in Physics, Rutgers-The State U., 1968; M.A. in Curriculum Devel. and Supervision, Glassboro Coll., 1979; m. Diane Skobeloff, June 9, 1968; children—Joel, Susan. Tchr. physics Camden (N.J.) High Sch., 1968-76, chmn. sci. dept., 1976-84, supr. computer edn., 1984-87, dir. research, planning and tech., 1987—, coordinator Orbit '81, 1977-84; prin. Temple Sinai Religious Sch., Cinnaminson, N.J., 1975-88; NASA cons. to Get-Away Spl. space shuttle high sch. projects. Winner Nat. Contest on Aerospace Papers, Smithsonian Inst., 1979; recipient cert. of recognition N.J. State Sch. Bd., 1982; Excellence in Sci. Edn. award Nat. Sci. Tchrs. Assn., 1982; prize for disting. secondary sch. teaching Princeton U., 1983; Phila. Bd. Edn. scholar, 1964-68; NASA grantee, 1979-80. Mem. Am. Phys. Soc., Am. Assn. Physics Tchrs., Assn. Supervision and Curriculum Devel., IEEE Computer Soc., Internat. Council for Computing Educators. Author books, most recent being: Creation and Mysticism, 1982; Ants in Space: A High School Prepares for the Space Shuttle, 1982; Standard Guide to the Jewish and Civil Calendar, 1986; Space Science and the Space Shuttle, 1986. Office: Adminstrv Annex 1656 Kaighn Ave Camden NJ 08103

REISS, JEROME, lawyer; b. Bklyn., Dec. 7, 1924; s. William and Eva (Marenstein) R.; m. Naomi Betty Plutzik, June 15, 1947; children—Robert Scott, Harlan Morgan, Andrea Ellen, Samantha Glynis. B.A., Bklyn. Coll., 1948; J.D., Harvard U., 1951. Bar: N.Y. 1951, D.C. 1967. Staff atty. civil br. Legal Aid Soc., 1951-54; asst. corp. counsel City of N.Y., 1954-58; assoc. Max E. Greenberg, 1958-67; sr. ptnr. Max E. Greenberg, Trayman, Cantor, Reiss & Blasky, 1967-80, Max E. Greenberg, Cantor & Reiss, N.Y.C., 1980-87, Blodnick, Pomeranz, Reiss, Schultz & Abromowitz, N.Y.C., 1988—; lectr.on constitutional law; Small Claims Ct. arbitrator, 1960—. Served to cpl. USAAF, 1943-46. Mem. Am. Judges Assn., ABA. Contbr. articles to profl. jours., chpts. in books.

REISSMULLER, JOHANN GEORGE, editor-in-chief; b. Leitmeritz, Bohemia, Czhechoslovak Socialist Republic, Feb. 2, 1932; s. Karl Georg and Margarethe (Trummer) R. LLM, U. Tübingen, Fed. Republic of Germany, 1952, LLD, 1955. Editor Juristenzeitung, Tübingen, 1956-61, Frankfurter Allgemeine Zeitung, Franfurt am Main, Fed. Republic of Germany, 1961-67; correspondent Frankfurter Allgemeine Zeitung, Belgrad, Yugoslavia, 1967-71; sr. editor Frankfurter Allgemeine Zeitung, Frankfurt am Main, 1971-74, editor in chief, 1974—. Author: Jugoslawien, 1971, Die vergessene Hälfte, 1986. Office: Frankfurter Allgemeine Zeitung, Hellerhofstr 2-4 Postfah 2901, 6000 Frankfurt am Main Federal Republic of Germany

REISTAD, ALF, engineering association executive; b. Bergen, Norway, Apr. 7, 1933; s. Manfelt and Liv Margrethe (Hagen) R.; m. Wenche Strandmoe, Oct. 19, 1957 (div. 1975); children: Anne, Ole, Maria, Ingrid, Alf Magnus, Berthe, Peder; m. Mai Nagell, Aug. 28, 1976. Grad., Oslo U., Norway, 1959. Cert. nuclear physics. Fellow in research NAVF, Norway, 1957-60; asst. prof. Oslo U., 1960-61; cons. Norway Civil Defense, 1961-63; chief edn. dept. Noway Soc. Chartered Engrs., 1963-78, research and devel. exec., 1978—. Mem. Noway Soc. Chartered Engrs., Norway Physicist Soc., Norway Soc. Sanitary Engrs., Norway Polytech. Soc., Norway Inst. Personnel Adminstrs., Clean Air Soc. (sec.), Maintenance Soc. (sec.), Value Analysis Soc. (sec.), Norway Inst. Mgmt. (bd. dirs.), Student Soc. Math-Nat (chmn.). Home: Hallagerbk 96A, 1256 Oslo 12 Norway

REISTLE, CARL ERNEST, JR., petroleum engineer; b. Denver, June 26, 1901; s. Carl E. and Leonora I. (McMaster) R.; m. Mattie A Muldrow, June 23, 1922; children: Bette Jean (Mrs. George F. Pierce), Mattie Ann (Mrs. James Tracy Clark), Nancy L. (Mrs. Travis Parker), Carl Ernest III. B.S., U. Okla., 1922; postgrad., Harvard Sch. Bus. Adminstrn., 1948. Petroleum chemist U.S. Bur. Mines, 1922-29, petroleum engr., 1929-33; chmn. East Tex. Engring. Assn., 1933-36; engr. in charge Humble Oil & Refining Co., 1936-40, chief petroleum engr., 1940-45, gen. supt. prodn., 1945-46, mgr. prodn. dept., 1946-51, dir., 1948-51, dir. in charge prodn. dept., 1951-55, v.p., 1955-57, exec. v.p., 1957-61, pres., 1961-63, chmn. bd., chief exec. officer, 1963-66, ret., 1966, cons., 1966-69; dir. Eltra Corp.; dir., chmn. exec. com. Olinkraft, Inc., 1967-78. Contbr. numerous articles to profl. jours. Bd. dirs. Tex. Tech Coll., Lubbock, 1966-69, U. Okla. Research Inst., Norman. Recipient Anthony F. Lucas Gold medal Am. Inst. Mining, Metall. and Petroleum Engrs., 1958. Mem. Am. Petroleum Inst., Am. Inst. Mining, Metall. and Petroleum Engrs. (pres. 1956), Sigma Xi, Tau Beta Pi, Sigma Tau, Alpha Chi Sigma. Clubs: Ramada, Petroleum, River Oaks Country. Home: 3196 Chevy Chase Houston TX 77019 Office: 1100 Milam Bldg Suite 4601 Houston TX 77002

REITAN, DANIEL KINSETH, electrical and computer engineering educator; b. Duluth, Minn., Aug. 13, 1921; s. Conrad Ulfred and Joy Elizabeth R.; m. Marian Anne Stemme, July 18, 1946; children: Debra Leah, Danielle Karen. B.S.E.E., N.D. State U., 1946; M.S.E.E., U. Wis., 1949, Ph.D., 1952. Registered profl. engr., Wis. Control engr. Gen. Electric Co., Schenectady, N.Y., 1946-48; transmission line engr. Gen. Telephone Co., Madison, Wis., 1949-50; mem. faculty Coll. Engring. U. Wis., Madison, 1952—; prof. elec. and computer engring. Coll. Engring. U. Wis., 1962-85, dir. power systems simulation lab., 1968-84, also dir. wind power research Energy Ctr.; cons. in field, U.S. Nat. Bur. Standards. Contbr. articles to profl. jours. Served with U.S. Army, World War II. Recipient Outstanding Tchr. award Polygon Engring. Council., Gov.'s citation for service to State of Wis. Fellow IEEE (Centennial medal and cert. for outstanding achievement 1984, IEEE Power Engring., Computer, Control, Indsl. Applications, and Edn. Socs.), Conf. Internat. des Grands Reseaux Electriques a Haute Tension, Am. Soc. Engring. Edn., Wis. Acad. Scis., Am. Wind Energy Assn., Sigma Xi, Tau Delta Pi, Tau Beta Pi, Eta Kappa Nu, Kappa Eta Kappa. Lutheran. Office: Elec and Computer Engring Dept 1425 Johnson Dr Madison WI 53706

REITEN, IDUN, mathematics professor; b. Trondheim, Norway, Jan. 1, 1942; parents: Ivar and Alma (Braa) R. BA, U. Trondheim, 1964; MA, U. Oslo, 1968; PhD, U. Ill., 1971. Research asst. U. Oslo, 1966-69; lectr. MIT, Boston, 1973; lectr. U. Trondheim, 1974-79, assoc. prof., 1979-81, prof., 1982—. contbr. articles to profl. jours. Fellow Norwegian Research Council, U. Ill. and Brandeis, 1971-73. Office: U Trondheim AVH, 7055 Dragroll, Trondheim Norway

REITER, JOSEPH HENRY, lawyer; b. Phila., Mar. 21, 1929; s. Nicholas and Barbara (Hellmann) R. A.B., Temple U., 1950, LL.B., 1953. Bar: D.C. 1953, Pa. 1954. Atty. advisor U.S. Army, 1955-61; asst. U.S. atty. Ea. Dist. Pa., 1961-63, asst. U.S. atty. in charge of civil div., 1963-69; chief organized crime and racketeering strike force Western N.Y. State, U.S. Dept. Justice, 1969-70, sr. trial atty. tax div. 1970-72, regional dir. office of drug abuse law enforcement, 1972-73; dep. atty. gen., dir. Drug Law Enforcement Office of Pa., 1973-77; ptnr. Stassen, Kostos and Mason, Phila. 1978-85, Kostos Reiter & Lamer, 1985—; mem. adv. com. Joint State Commn. on Procurement; lectr. in field. Contbr. articles to profl. jours. Mem. Citizens Crime Commn. Pa. Served with U.S. Army, 1953-55. Recipient Meritorious Service award U.S. Atty. Gen. Clark, 1967, Spl. Commendation Asst. U.S. Atty. Gen. Tax Div., 1969, Outstanding Performance award U.S. Atty. Gen. Richardson, 1973. Mem. ABA, Fed. Bar Assn., D.C. Bar Assn., Pa. Bar Assn., Phila. Bar Assn. Democrat. Club: Vesper (Phila.). Office: 1608 Walnut St Suite 1300 Philadelphia PA 19103

REITER, JOZSEF, research chemist, research administrator; b. Kassa, Hungary, Nov. 1, 1939; s. Jozsef and Erzsebet (Hanka) R.; m. Klara Esses, Apr. 10, 1965; children—Klara-Marta, Jozsef-Ferenc. Degree in Chemistry and Physics, Charles U., Prague, Czechoslovakia, 1961, Degree in Edn., 1961; Spl. Engr. for Pharm. Chemistry degree, Tech. U., Budapest, Hungary, 1971; Ph.D., Eotvos Lorand U., Budapest, 1973; C.Sc., Hungarian Acad. Scis., Budapest, 1973, D.Sc., 1988. Asst. lectr. P.J. Safarik U., Kosice, Czechoslovakia, 1961-63; researcher Chinoin Pharm. Factory, Budapest, 1963-65; researcher Inst. for Drug Research, Budapest, 1965-71, sr. research worker, 1971-74, head research group, 1974-77, head research dept., 1977-81; head synthetical research dept. EGIS Pharmaceuticals (formerly Egyt Pharmacochem. Works), Budapest, 1981—; vis. Fulbright scholar, U.S., 1985. Contbr. numerous papers on synthetical organic chemistry, spectroscopy, medicinal chemistry to internat. profl. jours. Mem. Hungarian Heterocyclic Soc., Hungarian Alkaloid Soc., Internat. Soc. Heterocyclic Chemistry; fellow Royal Soc. Chemistry (chartered chemist). Roman Catholic. Home: 32/b Mihalyfi E u, 1022 Budapest Hungary Office: EGIS Pharmaceuticals, 30-38 Kereszturi u, 1106 Budapest Hungary

REITER-SCOTT, GAYLA DENISE, labor union official; b. Beloit, Kans., Sept. 12, 1945; d. Gail Francis and Vivian Maxine (Lagle) R.; m. Stephen C. Chappell, Apr. 10, 1976 (div. 1980); m. Wilfred Joseph Scott, July 4, 1982; 1 child, Layla Diana Scott (dec.), BS magna cum laude, Portland State U., 1967; cert. Chemeketa Community Coll., 1973; labor studies credential San Francisco City Coll., 1982; grad. trade union program Harvard U., 1987. Pub. affairs specialist Social Security Adminstrn., San Francisco, 1974-75, mgr., 1975-80, claims specialist, 1980-87; sr. personnel specialist, U. Calif., Davis, 1987-88; pres. local 3172, Am. Fedn. Govt. Employees, San Francisco, 1979-86, exec. v.p. Nat. Council 220, 1982—, pres. regional council 147, San Francisco, 1982-87; chief litigator, 1982—; pres. No. Calif. Sudden Infant Death Syndrome adv. bd., 1988—; statewide legislative dir. Sudden Infant Death adv. councils; del. San Mateo County Labor Council, Calif., 1982—. Co-editor Union Line from Region Nine, 1980-87 (outstanding Regional Paper 1983). Co-dir., fundraiser SIRS Hunger Project, San Francisco, 1982; legis. chmn. Calif. adv. council SIDS Found., 1984—, pres. 1988—; co-chmn. combined fed. campaign United Good Neighbors, San Francisco, 1984-86; chmn. Nat. Legis. Polit. Action Comm., 1984—, regional chmn. 1980-84. Recipient Gov.'s award State of Oreg., 1971, Superior Achievement award Social Security Adminstrn., Seattle, 1973, Nat. SIDS Found. Congrl. Leadership award 1986; named to San Mateo Womens Hall of Fame. Mem. Am. Fedn. Govt. Employees (nat. polit. action coordinator for Calif., Nev., Ariz. 1984-87, legis. rep. Congl. testimony 1982—; del., com. chmn. nat. conv. Cleve., 1984; del., 1st v.p. officer no. council of locals 1982-86; nat. leadership award 1982), ACLU, NOW, Women Execs. San Francisco (v.p., publicist 1975—), Coalition Labor Union Women, LWV (moderator various ednl. TV programs, redevel. com., 1988—), Phi Beta Kappa (v.p. Outstanding Speaker award 1967), Alpha Sigma Omega (Outstanding Woman award 1966). Democrat. Clubs: Masters Swim Program, Soroptimist (pres., v.p. 1976-80), Women's Spiritual Network.

REITER-SOFFER, DOMY, choreographer, dancer, director, artist; b. Tel-Aviv, Oct. 24, 1948; s. Meir and Rosa (Obadiah) S. Student, Habimah Sch. Dramatic Art, Tel-Aviv, 1960-64, Music Acad. Art, Jerusalem and copenhagen, 1961-65; studies with Mia Arbatova, Tel Aviv; studies with Vera Volkova, Copenhagen; studies with Dame Peggy van Praagh, Martha Graham, Audrey de Vos. Prin. dancer London Dance Theatre, 1966-68, Western Theatre Ballet, London, 1968-70, Scottish Ballet, Glasgow, 1970-72; artistic advisor Irish Nat. Ballet, 1973—; resident choreographer Bat Dor Dance Co., Israel, 1970—. Choreographer of over 30 ballets in the past 20 yrs. for ensembles that include Dance Theatre of Harlem, Australian Ballet, La Scala Ballet-Milan, Am. Ballet Theatre 2, Ruth Page's Chgo. Ballet, Louisville Ballet, Pitts. Ballet Theatre; creator over 14 ballets for Bat Dor Dance Co., Israel including Journey, Visitors of Time, Prophetic Visions, Notturni Ed Alba; choreographer-dir. for ballets including Cul-De-Sac, Irish Theatre Ballet, 1969, Quarto de Sonata, Scottish Ballet, 1970, "I Shall Sing to Thee", Bat Dor Dance Co., 1971, Children of the Sun, Am. Ballet Theatre II, 1973, Women, Irish Nat. Ballet, 1974, Romances, Israel Ballet, 1976, Romeo and Juliet, Irish Nat. Ballet, 1977, Elusive Garden, Am. Ballet Theatre II, 1978, House of Bernarda Alba, Ballet Met. Columbus, Ohio, 1980, Equus (Best Ballet Yr. award N.Y. Dailey News, 1982), Md. Ballet, 1980, Night Spells, Extemporary Co., 1980, In The Mood, Irish Nat. Ballet, 1985, Dear Mr. Gershwin, Divertimento, Bat Dor Dance Co., 1987, Sinfonia Antartica, Irish Nat. Ballet, 1987, Paradise Gained, Irish Nat. Ballet, 1980 and Louiville Ballet, 1987, Lady of the Camellias, Irish Nat. Ballet and Finnish Nat. Ballet, both 1984; choreographer operas including Don Quixote, Wexford Festival, Carmen, Irish Grand Opera; dir. plays including The Fantastic, Dublin Theatre, 1976, Eve, Irish Theatre, 1978, Mary Make Believe, Abbey Theatre, 1982 (nominated 1 of best plays Dublin Theatre Festival); one-man shows include Yaffa Gallery, Israel, 1974, Hansen Gallery, Copenhagen, 1974, Leopold Gallery, London, 1978, 80, Wayne Gallery, London, 1981, Alpine Gallery, London, 1988. Office: Irish Nat Ballet, Ib Emmet Place, Cork County Cork, Ireland

REITZ, RICHARD ELMER, physician, laboratory administrator; b. Buffalo, Sept. 18, 1938; s. Elmer Valentine and Edna Anna (Guenther) R.; m. Gail Ida Pounds, Aug. 20, 1960; children—Richard Allen, Mark David. B.S., Heidelberg Coll., 1960; M.D., SUNY-Buffalo, 1964. Intern Hartford (Conn.) Hosp., 1964-65, resident in medicine, 1966-67; asst. resident in medicine Yale U., 1965-66; vis. research assoc. NIH, Bethesda, Md., 1967-68; research fellow in medicine Harvard Med. Sch., Mass. Gen. Hosp., Boston, 1967-69; asst. dir. clin. investigation ctr. Naval Regional Med. Ctr., 1969-71; dir. Endocrine Metabolic Center, Oakland, Calif., 1973—; asst. prof. medicine U. Calif.-San Francisco, 1971-76; assoc. clin. prof. medicine U. Calif.-Davis, 1976-86 ; clin. prof. med. 1986—; chief endocrinology Providence Hosp., Oakland, Calif., 1972—. Contbr. articles to profl. jours., chpt. to book. Mem. scholarship com., Bank of Am., San Francisco, 1983. Served to lt. comdr. USNR, 1969-71. Mem. Endocrine Soc., Am. Soc. Bone and Mineral Research, Am. Fedn. Clin. Research, Am. Fertility Soc., Am. Soc. Internal Medicine, AAAS. Democrat. Lodge: Rotary. Home: 867 Stonehaven Dr Walnut Creek CA 94598 Office: Endocrine Metabolic Ctr 3100 Summit St Oakland CA 94623

REJNA, FILIPPO GIUSEPPE MARIA, chemical company executive; b. Milan, Apr. 22, 1948; s. Alberto and Luciana (Bramardi) R.; m. Gabriella Bianchi; children: Chiara, Alberto Maria. Grad., U. Milan, 1972. Production leader Savid SPA, Como, Italy, 1973-74, mgr. production, 1974-76, product mgr., 1976-86, mgr. profit ctr., 1986-87, gen. mgr., 1987—. Patentee in field; contbr. articles to profl. jours. Adminstr. Mezzegra (Como) Civic Community, 1975-80, sr. adminstr., 1980—; pres. Mezzegra Pub. Water Supply, 1978—. Mem. Federchimica (chmn. powder paint nat. group 1986-87, nat. del. mem.), European Powder Paint Assn. Home: Via 4 Novembre 2, 22010 Mezzegra Italy Office: DSM Italia, Via Silvio Pellico 12, 22100 Como Italy

RELIER, JEAN PIERRE, pediatrician; b. Paris, May 16, 1935; s. Jean Albert and Renée Faust (Allart) R.; m. Ruth Margrit Sauberli; children: Jean Noel, Delphine, Guillaume, Damien. MD, U. Paris, 1962. Resident pediatrics Hosp. of Paris, 1963-68, chief resident, 1968-70, 72-75; resident pediatrics Hosp. Cantonnal, Lausanne, Switzerland, 1965-66; prof. pediatrics U. René Descartes, Paris, 1975—; research fellow Vanderbilt U., Nashville, 1070-72; chief neonatal unit Hosp. Port Royal, Paris, 1987—; bd. dirs. Ctr. Recherche Biologie Devel. Foetal Neonatal Assn. Claude Bernard, Paris, 1983—. Author: Pediatrie d'urgence, 1977, Flammarion, 1981, Physiologie de la grossesse, 1982, Masson Biologie du Developpement, 1981, Medecine Neonatale, 1985, Perinatologie, 1985; editor: Biology of the Neonate, 1983—, Karger. Mem. Soc. France Neonatologie (chief sec. 1983—), Brit. Neonatal Soc., European Soc. Perinatal Medicine, Soc. France Med. Perinatale, Italian Soc. Pediatrics (hon.). Office: Hosp Port Royal, 123 bd de Port Royal, 75674 Paris Cedex 14, France

RELLY, GAVIN WALTER HAMILTON, mining company executive; b. Cape Town, Republic of South Africa, Feb. 6, 1926; s. Cullis Hamilton and Helen Rose (Stanford) R.; m. Jane Margaret Relly, Aug. 4, 1951; 3 children. MA in Politics, Philosophy and Econs., Trinity Coll., Oxford, 1948. With Anglo Am. Corp. South Africa Ltd., 1949—, mgr. coal div., 1955-58, mgr. chmn.'s office, 1958-65; in charge Zambia ops. Anglo Am. Corp. South Africa Ltd., Lusaka, 1965-66; exec. dir. Anglo Am. Corp. South Africa Ltd., 1966-70; head N.Am. interests Anglo Am. Corp. South Africa Ltd., Toronto, Ont., Can., 1970-73; dep. chmn. corp. Anglo Am. Corp. South Africa Ltd., 1977, chmn. exec. com., 1977-83, chmn., 1983—, also bd. dirs.; chmn. AECI Ltd.; bd. dirs. De Beers Consol. Mines Ltd., Minorco, Anglo Am. Indsl. Corp. Ltd., Anglo Am. Coal Corp. Ltd., Anglo Am. Farms Ltd., Anglo Am. Gold Investment Co. Ltd., Anglo Am. Investment Trust Ltd., Boart Internat. Ltd., Charter Consol. PLC, Highveld Steel and Vanadium Corp. Ltd., Minerals and Resources Corp. Ltd., Mondi Paper Co. Ltd., South African Eagle Ins. Co. Ltd., South African Motor Corp. (Pty.) Ltd., Standard Bank Investment Corp. Ltd., Vaal Reefs Exploration and Mining Co. Ltd., Zambia Copper Investments Ltd. Pres. South Africa Found., Johannesburg, 1981-83; chmn. St. George's Home for Boys, 1956-65; bd. govs. U. Witwatersrand Found.; trustee U. South Africa Found., Johannesburg, 1975—, Urban Found., Johannesburg, 1985—, U. Zululand Found., Natal, 1986—. Clubs: River, Country (Johannesburg). Office: Anglo Am Corp South Africa Ltd, 44 Main St, Johannesburg 2001, Republic of South Africa

REM, MARTINUS, computer science educator, consultant; b. Koog Aan De Zaan, The Netherlands, Sept. 22, 1946; s. Martinus and Gerritje (Schoute) R.; m. Eleonora H. C. Bervoets, July 7, 1972; children: Coen, Bart. MS in Math., U. Amsterdam, The Netherlands, 1971; PhD in Computer Sci., U. Eindhoven, The Netherlands, 1976. Asst prof. Calif. Inst. Tech., Pasadena, 1976-78; prof. U. Eindhoven, 1978—; vis. prof. Calif. Inst. Tech., 1978—; cons. Philips Research, Eindhoven, 1985—. Editor Science of Computer Programming, 1983—. Lodge: Rotary. Home: Sagittalaan 15, 5632 AK Eindhoven The Netherlands Office: U Eindhoven, Den Dolech 2, 5600 Eindhoven The Netherlands

REMBSKI, STANISLAV, artist, portrait painter; b. Sochaczew, Poland; s. Ludwik and Magdalena (Liechtenstein) R.; came to U.S., 1922, naturalized, 1929; student Technol. Inst. Warsaw, Ecole des Beaux Arts, Royal Acad. Fine Arts (Berlin); m. Isabelle Walton Everett, Dec. 24, 1927; m. Dorothy Mann Klein, Aug. 21, 1981. Prin. works include Nude, Newark Mus.; portraits of notable public figures, educators, and clergyman in ednl., public and pvt. collections, among more recent being: Adm. William S. Pye, Naval War Coll., Newport; Adm. of the Fleet, William D. Leahy, Washington; Pres. Woodrow Wilson, Woodrow Wilson Nat. Shrine, Washington; Pres. Franklin D. Roosevelt, F.D.R. Meml. Library, Hyde Park, N.Y.; Comdr. Joshua Barney, Naval Mus., Washington; Dr. Maurice J. Pincoffs, Dr. Eduard Uhlenhuth (U. Md. Med. Sch.); Dr. Hubert McNeill Poteat (Wake Forest Coll.); Dr. John B. Zinn (Gettysburg Coll.); Col. William Baxter, Dr. Thomas G. Pullen, Senator George L. Radcliffe, J. Harold Grady (mayor Balt.), Gov. J. Millard Tawes of Md., Maj. Gen. William Purnell, Howard MacCarthy, Jr., Lawrence Cardinal Shehan, Commodore Thomas Truxton, USN, Frigate Constellation, Balt., Thomas Jefferson and the 4 Md. Signers of Declaration of Independence McDonogh Sch., Md., Count Casimir Pulaski War Meml., Balt., Commodore Joshua Barney, Meml. Naval Mus., Brigham Young U., others; murals: Triptych, 19x22 feet, St. Bernard of Clairvaux at St. Bernard's Sch. for Boys, Gladstone, N.J.; I Am the Life, Meml. Episcopal Ch., Episcopal, Balt.; wives 5 Md. govs. for Govt. House, Annapolis; Babe Ruth, Babe Ruth Mus., Balt. Lectr., vis. critic Md. Inst. Art, 1952-55. Mem. Allied Artists Am., Nat. Soc. Mural Painters, Am. Artists Profl. League. Clubs: Univ. (Balt.), Churchman's; Paint and Powder; Salmagundi (N.Y.C.). Home and Office: 1404 Park Ave Baltimore MD 21217

RÉMÉDIANI, FRANCIS MARIUS ROSÉ, pediatrician; b. Nice, France, Nov. 9, 1938; s. Antoine and Felicie (Bailet) R.; m. Anne Marie Fürbacher, Jan. 16, 1965; children: Carine, Nathalie. D. U. Montpellier, France, 1965, diploma in Pediatrics, 1970. Extern pediatrics Ctr. Hosp. U. Montpellier, 1964-67; pediatric staff Service Professeur Chaptal, Montpellier, 1968-71; pediatrician Beausoleil (France) Consulting Room, 1971—; pediatric staff Hosp. Princess Grace, Monaco, 1986—. Author: Children's Nyctherae Ral Biologic Variations, 1965. Served to lt. French mil., 1965-67. Club: Round Table (Monaco).

REMENCHIK, ALEXANDER PAVLOVICH, physician; b. Chgo., Sept. 13, 1922; s. Paul Samuelovich and Irina Alexandra (Babich) R.; m. Mary Margaret Mays, Apr. 19, 1947; children: Alex Kevin, Ellen Jean, Karen Ann, Margaret Lynn. BS in Physics, U. Chgo., 1943, MD, 1951. Diplomate Am. Bd. Internal Medicine. Intern Cook County Hosp., Chgo., 1951-52; resident U. Ill. Research and Ednl. Hosps., 1952-53, fellow, 1953-54; clin. investigator VA Hosp., Hines, Ill., 1960-62; practice medicine specializing in internal medicine, Chgo., 1953-72, Montclair, N.J., 1972-74, Houston, 1974—; asst. med. supt. Mcpl. Contagious Disease Hosp., Chgo., 1953-59; instr. medicine U. Ill., Chgo., 1954-59; asst. prof. medicine Stritch Sch. Medicine, Loyola U., Maywood, Ill., 1960-63, assoc. prof., 1964-67, prof., 1967-72, pres. Faculty Collegium, 1970-71, asst. chmn. dept. medicine, 1964-70; dir. dept. nuclear medicine Loyola U. Hosp., 1969-71; attending physician Cook County Hosp., 1959-72; Mountainside Hosp., Montclair, 1972-74, dir. med. edn., 1972-74; attending mem. active staff Parkway Hosp., 1974-79, Citizens Gen. Hosp., 1974-86, chief med. service, 1977, chief of staff, 1979, 82-83, mem. governing bd., 1977-86; mem. staff Eastway Gen. Hosp., 1974—, chmn. dept. medicine, 1976-80; pres. East Loop Emergency Med. Clinic, Houston, 1979-82, East Loop Cardio Pulmonary Ctr., Inc., 1979-85; mem. med. adv. bd. Seminars and Symposia Inc., chmn. continuing med. edn. com. Editor: (with P.J. Talso) Mechanisms of Disease, 1968; contbr. over 50 articles on internal medicine to profl. jours. Mem. Zoning Commn. Oak Park (Ill.), 1969-72; trustee Unitarian-Universalist Ch. of Oak Park, 1969-70. Served to lt. (j.g.) USN, 1943-46. Fellow ACP; mem. Houston Soc. Internal Medicine, Soc. Exptl. Biology and Medicine, Am. Fedn. Clin. Research, Harris County Med. Soc., AMA, Tex. Med. Assn., Am. Heart Assn., Am. Diabetes Assn., Soc. Critical Care Medicine, Houston Cardiology Soc., Sigma Xi. Home: 9330 Oakford Ct Houston TX 77024 Office: 8799 N Loop East Houston TX 77029

REMICK, ROBERT JEROME, electrochemist; b. Williamsport, Pa., Dec. 16, 1945; s. Robert Jervine and Katherine Jane (Reiff) R.; B.S., Lock Haven (Pa.) State Coll., 1968; M.Ed., Millersville (Pa.) State U., 1972; Ph.D., Pa. State U., 1978; m. Joyce Marie Villello, Aug. 24, 1968. Tchr. chemistry Middletown (Pa.) public schs., 1968-75; research asst. Pa. State U., 1975-78; mgr. electrochem. research Inst. Gas Tech., Chgo., 1978—. Pres. Royalton (Pa.) Borough Council, 1972-75. Mem. Am. Chem. Soc., AAAS, Electrochem. Soc., Sigma Xi (chpt. research award 1977). Republican. Lutheran. Author, patentee in field. Office: 3424 S State St Chicago IL 60616

REMINE, WILLIAM HERVEY, JR., surgeon; b. Richmond, Va., Oct. 11, 1918; s. William Hervey and Mabel Inez (Walthall) ReM.; m. Doris Irene Grumbacher, June 9, 1943; children—William H., Stephen Gordon, Walter James, Gary Craig. B.S. in Biology, U. Richmond, 1940, D.Sc. (hon.), 1965; M.D., Med. Coll. Va., Richmond, 1943; M.S. in Surgery, U. Minn., Mpls., 1952. Diplomate Am. Bd. Surgery. Intern Doctor's Hosp., Washington, 1944; fellow in surgery Mayo Clinic, Rochester, Minn., 1944-45, 47-52; instr. surgery Mayo Grad. Sch. Medicine, Rochester, Minn., 1954-59, asst. prof. surgery, 1959-65, assoc. prof. surgery, 1965-70, prof. surgery, 1970-83, prof. surgery emeritus, 1983—; surg. cons. to surgeon gen. U.S. Army, 1965-75. Sr. author: Cancer of the Stomach, 1964, Manual of Upper Gastro-intestinal Surgery, 1985; editor: Problems in General Surgery, Surgery of the Biliary Tract, 1986; mem. editorial bd. Rev. Surgery, 1965-75, Jour. Lancet, 1968-77; contbr. 200 articles to profl. jours. Served to capt. U.S. Army, 1945-47. Recipient St. Francis surg. award St. Francis Hosp., Pitts., 1976, disting. service award Alumni Council, U. Richmond, 1976. Mem. ACS, AAAS, Am. Assn. History of Medicine, AMA, Am. Med. Writers Assn., Am. Soc. Colon and Rectal Surgeons, Soc. Surgery Alimentary Tract (v.p. 1983-84), Am. Surg. Assn., Assn. Mil. Surgeons U.S., Internat. Soc. Surgery, Digestive Disease Found., Priestley Soc. (pres. 1968-69), Central Assn. Physicians and Dentists (pres. 1972-73), Central Surg. Assn., Soc. Med. Cons. Armed Forces, Mayo Clinic Surg. Soc. (chmn. 1964-66), Soc. Head and Neck Surgeons, Soc. Surg. Oncology, So. Surg. Assn., Western Surg. Assn. (pres. 1979-80), Minn. State Med. Assn., Minn. Surg. Soc. (pres. 1966-67), Zumbro Valley Med. Soc., Sigma Xi; hon. mem. Colombian Coll. Surgeons, St. Paul Surg. Soc., Flint Surg. Soc., Venezuelan Surg. Soc., Colombian Soc. Gastroenterology, Dallas So. Clin. Soc., Ga. Surg. Soc., Soc. Postgrad. Surgeons Los Angeles County, Japanese Surg. Soc., Argentine Surg. Digestive Soc., Bassanese Surg. Assn. (Italy), Tex. Surg. Soc., Omicron Delta Kappa, Alpha Omega Alpha, Beta Beta Beta. Methodist. Home: 600 4th St SW Rochester MN 55902 Office: Mayo Clinic 200 1st St SW Rochester MN 55905

REMINGER, RICHARD THOMAS, lawyer; b. Cleve., Apr. 3, 1931; s. Edwin Carl and Theresa Henrietta (Bookmyer) R.; m. Billie Carmen Greer, June 26, 1954; children—Susan Greer, Patricia Allison, Richard Thomas. A.B., Case-Western Res. U., 1953; J.D., Cleve.-Marshall Law Sch., 1957. Bar: Ohio 1957, Pa. 1978, U.S. Supreme Ct. 1961. Personnel and safety dir. Motor Express, Inc., Cleve., 1954-58; mng. ptnr. Reminger & Reminger Co., L.P.A., Cleve., 1958—; dir. U.S. Truck Lines, Inc., Del. Cardinal Casualty Co.; mem. nat. claims council adv. bd. Comml. Union Assurance Co., 1980—; lectr. transp. law Fenn Coll., 1960-62, bus. law, Case Western Res. U., 1962-64. Mem. joint com. Cleve. Acad. Medicine-Greater Cleve. Bar Assn.; trustee Cleve. Zool. Soc., exec. com., 1984—, v.p., 1987—; trustee Andrew Sch., Huron Rd. Hosp., Cleve., Cleve. Soc. for Blind, 1987—. Served with AC, USNR, 1950-58. Mem. Fedn. Ins. and Corp. Counsel, Trial Attys. Am. (mem. sect. litigation, also tort and ins. practice), Fed. Bar Assn., ABA (com. on law and medicine, profl. responsibility com. 1977—), Internat. Bar Assn., Ohio Bar Assn. (council dels. 1987—), Pa. Bar Assn., Cleve. Bar Assn. (chmn. med. legal com. 1978-79, profl. liability com. 1977—), Transp. Lawyers Assn., Cleve. Assn. Civil Trial Attys., Am. Soc. Hosp. Attys., Soc. Ohio Hosp. Attys., Ohio Assn. Civil Trial Attys., Am. Judicature Soc., Def. Research Inst., Maritime Law Assn. U.S., Am. Coll. Law and Medicine, 8th Jud. Bar Assn. (life Ohio dist.). Clubs: Mayfield Country (pres. 1980-82), Union, Cleve. Playhouse, Hermit (pres. 1973-75) (Cleve.); Lost Tree, Everglades (Fla.); Kirtland Country (Cleve.); Rolling Rock (Pa.). Home: 34000 Hackney Rd Hunting Valley OH 44022 Office: The 113 St Clair Bldg Cleveland OH 44114

REMMERS, JOHANN JACOB, banker; b. Wittmund, Fed. Republic of Germany, Mar. 28, 1934. PhD in Econs., U. Hamburg, Fed. Republic of Germany, 1968. Various positions Raiffeisenbank Wittmund, 1951-59, Nordd. Genossenschaftsbank, Hannover, Fed. Republic of Germany, 1959-65; various positions DG Bank, Frankfurt on the Main, Fed. Republic of Germany, 1965-81, mng. dir., 1981—; chmn. supervisory bd. DEFO Deutsche Fonds fuer Immobilienvermoegen GmbH, Franfourt on the Main; vice-chmn. supervisory bd. Deutsche Immobilien Fonds AG, Hamburg, Suedwestbank AG, Stuttgart, Fed. Republic of Germany; bd. dirs. Centralgenossenschaft Vieh und Fleisch eG, Hannover, Fed. Republic of Germany, Fidinam Cons. and Holding S.A., Zug, Switzerland, London & Continental Bankers Ltd., London, Spar Handels AG, Hamburg, Duesseldorf, Munich. Office: Deutsche Genossenschaftsbank, Am Platz der Republik, D6000 Frankfurt am 1 Federal Republic of Germany

REMPFER, ROBERT WEIR, mathematics educator; b. Parkston, S.D., Apr. 14, 1914; s. William Christian and Helen Irene (Weir) R.; B.S. summa cum laude, U. S.D., 1933; M.S., Northwestern U., 1934; Ph.D. in Math., U. Ill., 1937; m. Gertrude Marjorie Fleming, Sept. 25, 1942; children—Richard Fleming, Jean Trudi, Anne Louise (dec.), William Curry, Rhoda Anne. Mem. faculty Rensselaer Poly. Inst., 1937-44; with Manhattan Project, Columbia U., 1944-45; math. physicist Farrand Optical Co., N.Y., 1945-50; prof. math. Antioch Coll., 1950-53, Fisk U., 1953-57; prof. math. Portland (Oreg.) State U., 1957—, chmn. dept., 1957-61; adj. prof. biostats. Oreg. Health Scis. U., 1969-81. Translator, Cons.' Bur., Plenum Pub. Corp., 1969-79; v.p. Applied Math. Assocs., Inc., Portland, 1962-71; dir. NSF Summer Insts., Portland State U., 1958, 63, 64; lectr. Oreg. Acad. Sci., 1963-64. Mem. AAUP (pres. Oreg. State Fedn. 1962-63), NAACP (life), Soc. Indsl. and Applied Math., Math. Assn. Am. (lectr. 1960-63), Am. Math. Soc. Home: Box 268B Rt 1 Forest Grove OR 97116 Office: Portland State U Math Dept Portland OR 97207

RENARDY, YURIKO YAMAMURO, mathematician, educator; b. Sapporo, Japan, Jan. 15, 1955; came to U.S., 1980; d. Sadayuki and Akiko (Maeda) Yamamuro; m. Michael Renardy, Apr. 9, 1981; 1 child, Sylvia. BS with honors, Australian Nat. U., 1977; PhD, U. Western Australia, 1981. Research assoc. Math. Research Ctr., U. Wis., Madison, 1980-83, program coordinator, 1983-86; instr. U. Minn., Mpls., 1981-82; asst. prof. math. Va. Polytech. Inst. and State U., 1986—. Contbr. articles to profl. jours. NSF research grantee, 1986—. Mem. Am. Phys. Soc. (div. fluid dynamics), Soc. for Indsl. and Applied Math. Office: Va Polytech and State U Math Dept 460 McBryde Hall Blacksburg VA 24061

RENDELL, RUTH BARBARA, novelist; b. Feb. 17, 1930; d. Arthur Grasemann and Ebba Kruse; m. Donald Rendell, 1950; 1 son. Student, Loughton County High Sch., Eng. Author: From Doon with Death, 1964, To Fear a Painted Devil, 1965, Vanity Dies Hard, 1966, A New Lease of Death, 1967, Wolf to the Slaughter, 1967, The Secret House of Death, 1968, The Best Man to Die, 1969, A Guilty Thing Surprised, 1970, One Across Two Down, 1971, No More Dying Then, 1971, Murder Being Once Done, 1972, Some Lie and Some Die, 1973, The Face of Trespass, 1974, Shake Hands for Ever, 1975, A Demon in my View, 1976, The Fallen Curtain, 1976, A Judgement in Stone, 1977, A Sleeping Life, 1978, Make Death Love Me, 1979, Means of Evil, 1979, The Lake of Darkness, 1980, Put on by Cunning, 1981, Master of the Moor, 1982, The Fever Tree, 1982, The Speaker of Mandarin, 1983, The Killing Doll, 1984, The Tree of Hands, 1984, An Unkindness of Ravens, 1985, The New Girl Friend, 1985, Live Flesh, 1986, Heartstones, 1987, Talking to Strange Men, 1987; (as Barbara Vine) A Dark-Adapted Eye, 1986, A Fatal Inversion, 1987. Recipient Arts Council Nat. Book award, 1981. Address: Nussteads, Polstead, Suffolk England *

RENDL-MARCUS, MILDRED, artist, economist; b. N.Y.C., May 30, 1928; d. Julius and Agnes (Hokr) Rendl; BS, NYU, 1948, MBA, 1950; PhD (Dean Bernice Brown Cronkhite fellow 1950-51), Radcliffe Coll., 1954; m. Edward Marcus, Aug. 10, 1956. Economist, Gen. Electric Co., 1953-56, Bigelow-Sanford Carpet Co., Inc., 1956-58; lectr. econs. evening sessions CCNY, 1953-58; research investment problems in tropical Africa, 1958-59; instr. econs. Hunter Coll. CUNY, 1959-60; lectr. econs. Columbia U., 1960-61; research econ. devel. Nigeria, W. Africa, 1961-63; sr. economist Internat. div. Nat. Indsl. Conf. Bd., 1963-66; asst. prof. Grad. Sch. Bus. Adminstrn., Pace Coll., 1964-66; asso. prof. Borough of Manhattan Community Coll., City U. N.Y., 1966-71, prof., 1972-85; vis. prof. Fla. Internat. U., 1986; prin.

MRM Assos., Rendl Fine Art; corp. art econ. cons.; fine arts appraiser; participant Internat. Economical Meeting, Amsterdam, 1968, Econs. of Fine Arts in Age of Tech., 1984, Internat. Economic Assn. North Am., Laredo, Tex., 1987-88, Soc. Southwestern Economists, San Antonio, 1988. Exhibited New Canaan Art Show, 1982, 83, 84, 85, New Canaan Soc. for Arts Ann., 1983, 85, New Canaan Arts, 1985, Silvermine Galleries, 1986, Stamford Art Assn., 1987, Women in the Arts at Phoenix Gallery, Group Show, N.Y.C., 1988; symposium participant Sienna, Italy, 1988; contbr. articles to Women in the Arts newsletter, 1986-87, Coalition Womens Art Orgns., 1986-87. Bd. dirs. N.Y.C. Council on Econ. Edn., 1970— ; mem. program planning com. Women's Econ. Roundtable; participant Eastern Econ. Assn., Boston, 1988; Participant Art and Personal Property Appraisal, N.Y.U., 1986-88. Recipient Disting. Service award CUNY, 1985. Fellow Gerontol. Assn.; mem. Internat. Schumpeter Econs. Soc. (founding), Am. (vice chmn. ann. meeting 1973), Met. (sec. 1954-56) econ. assns., Indsl. Relations Research Assn., Audubon Artists and Nat. Soc. Painters in Casein (assoc. 1987-88) Allied Social Sci. Assn. (vice chmn. conv. 1973), AAUW, N.Y.C. Women in Arts, Women's Econ. Roundtable, N.Y. U. Grad. Sch. Bus. Adminstrn. Alumni (sec. 1956-58). Clubs: Radcliffe; Women's City (art and landmarks com.). Author: (with husband) Investment and Development of Tropical Africa, 1959, International Trade and Finance, 1965, Monetary and Banking Theory, 1965; Economics, 1969; (with husband) Principles of Economics, 1969; Economic Progress and the Developing World, 1970; Economics, 1978; also monographs and articles in field. Econ. and internat. research on industrialization less developed areas, internat. debtor nations and workability of buffer stock schemes; columnist economics of art Women in Art. Home: 928 West Rd New Canaan CT 06840 Office: PO Box 814 New Canaan CT 06840 also: 7441 Wayne Ave Miami Beach FL 33141

RENE, FRANCE ALBERT, president of Seychelles; b. Seychelles, Nov. 16, 1935; s. Price and Louisa (Morgan) R.; ed. St. Louis Coll., Seychelles, St. Moritz, Switzerland, St. Mary's Coll., Southampton, Eng., King's Coll., U. London, London Sch. Econs. and Polit. Sci.; m. Karen Handley, 1956; 1 child; m. Geva Adam, 1975; 1 child. Called to bar, 1957; practiced Law, 1958-75; founder, leader Seychelles People's United Party, 1964—; mem. Legis. Council, 1965—, Governing Council, 1967, Legis. Assembly, 1970, 74; minister of works and land devel., 1975-77; prime minister, 1976-77; pres. of Seychelles, 1977—, also minister for def., 1986, now minister for adminstr., minister for agrl., minister for external relations, minister for health, minister for industry, minister for tourism, minister for trans.; pres.Seychelles People's Progressive Front, 1978-84, sec.-gen., 1984—. Address: Office of Pres, State House, Victoria, Mahé Seychelles

RENE-WORMS, GEORGES, management consultant; b. Paris, Aug. 23, 1945; s. Rene and Marthe (Heymann) W.; m. Chantal May, Nov. 28, 1958; children: Pierre, Sophie Carole, Marc. Grad., Ecole Supérieure des Sci. Econ. et Commerciales, Paris, 1947. Clk. Barclays Bank, Paris, 1948-52; adminstrv. dir. Galeries Lafayette, Casablanca, Morocco, 1952-55; buyer Galeries Lafayette, Paris, 1956-59; mgr. Scapa, Paris, 1960-63, Primagel, Paris, 1963-68, Dorothee Bis, Paris, 1969-72; pres. Cons. Assocs., Paris, 1972—, 4T, Paris, 1983, Gerclaus, Paris, 1984. Editor: Poivre & Sel mag., 1980; contbr. articles on devel. of frozen food market to various publs. Served with French Army, 1944-45. Home: 1 Avenue Bugeaud, 75116 Paris France Office: Compagnie des Cons Assocs, 3 rue de l'Arrivee, 75015 Paris France

RENFREW, ANDREW COLIN, archaeologist and academic administrator; b. Stockton-on-Tees, Eng., July 25, 1937; s. Archibald and Helena Douglas (Savage) R.; B.A., St. John's Coll., Cambridge U., 1962, M.A., 1964, Ph.D., 1965, Sc.D., 1976; m. Jane Margaret Ewbank, Apr. 21, 1965; children—Helena Margaret, Alban Robert, Magnus Archibald. Lectr. archaeology U. Sheffield, 1965-72; vis. lectr. UCLA, 1967; prof. U. Southampton, 1972-81; Disney prof. archaeology Cambridge U., 1981—, fellow St. John's Coll., 1981-86; master, Jesus Coll., Cambridge, 1986—. George Grant McCurdy lectr. Harvard U., 1977; Patten lectr. Ind. U., 1982; field excavations in Saliagos, 1962-64, Sitagroi, 1968-70, Quanterness, Orkney, 1972-74, Phylakopi, Melos, 1974-76. Served with RAF, 1956-58. Recipient Rivers Meml. medal Royal Anthrop. Inst., 1979. Fellow Brit. Acad., Soc. Antiquaries London; mem. Ancient Monuments Bd. (ad.v com.). Clubs: Athenaeum, United Oxford and Cambridge. Author: The Emergence of Civilisation, 1972; Before Civilisation, 1973; Investigations in Orkney, 1979; Problems in European Prehistory, 1979; editor: The Explanation of Culture Change, 1973; (with K.L. Cooke) Mathematical Approaches to Culture Change, 1979; (with M. Wagstaff) An Island Polity, 1982; Approaches to Social Archaeology, 1984; The Archaeology of Cult, 1984, Archaeology and Language, 1987; editor: The Prehistory of Orkney, 1988; presenter TV films: The Tree That Put the Clock Back, 1970; Islands Out of Time, 1973; Orkney Underground, 1974; Aphrodite's Other Island, 1977; Bronze Age Blast Off, 1978; Lost Kings of the Desert, 1980; The Emperor's Immortal Army, 1981; City of the Dead, 1982; Who Built Stonehenge, 1986. Office: Dept Archaeology, Downing St, Cambridge SB2 3DZ, England

RENFREW, GLEN MCGARVIE, world news service executive; b. Aberdare, New South Wales, Australia, Sept. 15, 1928; s. Robert and Jane Grey (Watson) R.; m. Daphne Ann Hailey, Feb. 20, 1954; children: Barry Glen, Ann Gladys (dec.), Susan Jane, Judith Hailey. B.A., Sydney (Australia) U., 1949. With Reuters News Service, 1952—; began in Reuters News Service, London, Eng., 1952; then served in reporting and mgmt. posts in Africa, Europe and Far East, mgr. computer div. Reuters News Service, London, 1964-70; mgr. N.Am. Reuters News Service, 1971-81; now mng. dir., chief exec. officer Reuters Holdings PHC, London and N.Y.C.; chmn. IDR Inc. (mfr. info. retrieval systems and equipment, subs. Reuters News Service), 1973—, also dir.; chmn. Rich Inc., 1985—. Clubs: Manhassett Bay Yacht, Nat. Press. Office: 1700 Broadway New York NY 10019

REN JIANXIN, judge, government official. Dir. dept. legal affairs China Council for Promotion of Internat. Trade, from 1980, sec.-gen. Fgn. and Econ. Trade Arbitration Commn., 1981-86, vice-chmn., from 1981; vice chmn. jud. com. Nat. People's Congress Standing Com., from 1983; v.p. Supreme People's Ct., 1984-88, Pres., 1988—. Office: Supreme Peoples Ct, Dongjiaomin Xiang, Beijing Peoples Republic of China *

RENKIS, ALAN ILMARS, plastics formulating company executive; b. Preili, Latvia, Apr. 16, 1938; came to U.S., 1950; naturalized, 1958.; s. Joseph and Malvine (Sturitis) R.; m. Inara Balodis, July 15, 1961; children: Martin Alan, Laura Alise. BSChemE, Pa. State U., 1960. With product devel. and tech. service div. Diamond Alkali Co., Painesville, Ohio, 1960-63; tech. dir. G.S. Plastics Co., Cleve., 1963; founder, pres. Thermoclad Co., Erie, Pa., 1963—, Riverside, Calif., 1972—, Ocala, Fla., 1985—. Developer comml. PVC resins for formulating fluidized bed coating powders; formulations and compounding techniques. Mem. Young Pres. Orgn., Soc. Plastics Engrs., Sigma Pi, Fraternitas Metropolitana (Latvian student frat.). Clubs: University, Erie, Aviation, Kankwa (Erie). Home: 5109 Watson Rd Erie PA 16505 Office: 361 W 11th St Erie PA 16501

RENNE, ARNOLD MARINUS J., retail executive; b. Haarlem, Netherlands, Feb. 15, 1929; s. Marinus and Maria (Hulsebosch) R.; m. Ursel I. Koster; 3 children. Grad., Tech. Coll., Haarlem, 1952. Sales mgr. Benelux, Guldner-Motorenerke AG, Aschaffenburg, Fed. Republic Germany, 1955-64; sales dir. IHC Shipyards, Rotterdam, The Netherlands, 1964-70; mng. dir. Pioneer Laura BV, Kerkrade, The Netherlands, 1970-75, V Berkel, Leidsohendam, The Netherlands, 1975-82; gen. mgr. Boschhaven Group of Cos., Nieuwegein, The Netherlands, 1982—. Conservative. Roman Catholic. Home: Populierenlaan 6, 3735 LH Bosch en Duin The Netherlands Office: Boschhaven Group of Cos, Overysselhaven 30, 3433 PH Nieuwegein The Netherlands

RENNIE, HEUGHAN BASSETT, lawyer; b. Wanganui, New Zealand, Apr. 7, 1945; s. William Stanley Norman and Reta (Bassett) R.; m. Caroline Jane Harding, Dec. 2, 1967; children: Jonathan, Thomas, Barnaby. BA, Victoria U. of Wellington, New Zealand, 1966, LLB, 1969. Bar: New Zealand 1970. Ptnr. Macalister Mazengarb, Wellington, 1972—; chmn. Broadcasting Corp. of New Zealand, Wellington, Fourth Estate PUb. Group, Wellington. Mem. New Zealand Council Law Reporting, Soc. for Computers and Law, Commonwealth Lawyers Assn. Presbyterian. Club: Wellington. Home: 31 Pitt St, Wellington 6001, New Zealand Office: Broadcasting Corp of New Zealand, Bowen St Bldg POB 98, Wellington New Zealand

RENOFF, PAUL VERNON, ret. elec. mfrs. rep.; b. Balt., July 17, 1911; s. Henry John and Mary E. (Snyder) R.; B.E.E., Johns Hopkins U., 1932; m. Margaret Hamilton Houghton, June 18, 1937; children—Ronald Hamilton, Lois Ellen (Mrs. Henry Ward Brockett), Cynthia Houghton (Mrs. George A. Taler). Engr., H.R. Houghton, 1933-36; partner Houghton & Renoff, 1936-45, Paul V. Renoff Co., 1945-66; pres. Renoff Assos., Inc. 1966-73; former dir. Edwin L. Wiegand Co., Skan-A-Matic Corp., United Co. Past pres., Roland Ct. Maintenance Corp.; past pres. Arundel Beach Improvement Assn.; mem. Magothy River Assn.; former dir. Roland Park Civic League. Registered profl. engr., Md. Mem. Md. Acad. Sci., IEEE, U.S. Power Squadron, Md. Hist. Soc. Democrat. Episcopalian. Clubs: Engineers; Johns Hopkins, Chartwell Golf & Country (Severna Park, Md.). Died Sept. 19, 1987. Home: 4326 Roland Ave Baltimore MD 21210 Home: 454 Arundel Beach Rd Severna Park MD 21146 Home: PO Box 1 Sugar Loaf Shores FL 33044

RENS, MAX JOANNES LEOPOLD MARIA, automotive company executive; b. Maastricht, The Netherlands, Feb. 2, 1947; s. Max J.R.M. and May L. (Olieslagers) R.; divorced; children: Paul, Sander; m. Chella A. Sluis, June 21, 1985; 1 child, Rachel. Degree in law, U. Leiden, The Netherlands, 1974. Asst. controller Fokker-VFW Internat. BV, Schiphol, The Netherlands, 1974-76, corp. sec. and gen. counsel, 1976-80; dir. industry relations Fokker BV, Amsterdam, The Netherlands, 1980-83; v.p. mktg. Volvo Car BV, Helmond, The Netherlands, 1983—. Home: Egelantier 35, 5708 DZ Helmond The Netherlands Office: Volvo Car BV, PO Box 1015, 5700 MC Helmond The Netherlands

RENSCH, JOSEPH ROMAINE, public utility holding company executive; b. San Bernardino, Calif., Jan. 1, 1923; s. Joseph R. and Lucille (Ham) R.; m. June Elizabeth Burley, Mar. 25, 1946; children: Steven R., Jeffrey P. BS, Stanford U., 1947; JD, Golden Gate U., 1955. Bar: Calif.; registered profl. engr., Calif. Successively sales engr., regional gas engr., asst. regional gas supt., asst. mgr. gas supply and control Coast Counties Gas & Electric Co., San Francisco, 1947-54; sr. pipeline operations engr. Pacific Gas & Electric Co., 1954-56; prodn. control supt. Western div. Dow Chem. Co., Pittsburg, Calif., 1956; asst. counsel So. Counties Gas Co. of Calif., Los Angeles, 1957-58; asst. v.p., spl. counsel Pacific Lighting Gas Supply Co., Los Angeles, 1958- 61, v.p., bd. dirs., 1962-65; sr. v.p. Pacific Lighting Service Co., 1965-67, exec. v.p., 1967-69, pres., 1969-71, chmn. bd., 1971-73; exec. v.p., dir. Pacific Lighting Corp., Los Angeles, 1968-72, pres., 1972-86, vice chmn., 1986-88; bd. dirs. McKesson Corp. Served with USNR, 1942-46. Mem. Pacific Coast Gas Assn. (pres. 1966-67), Am. Gas Assn., Tau Beta Pi, Alpha Tau Omega. Office: Pacific Enterprises 810 S Flower St Los Angeles CA 90017

RENSHAW, CHARLES CLARK, JR., retired publishing executive; b. Chgo., Aug. 22, 1920; s. Charles Clark and Nanna Lou (Nysewander) R.; m. Elizabeth Campbell Fly, Apr. 11, 1953 (div. Jan. 1960); 1 dau., Nina Renshaw Griscom. Student, Hill Sch., Pottstown, Pa., 1934-39, Trinity Coll., Hartford, Conn., 1939-41. Reporter, feature writer, book critic Chgo. Herald-Am., 1943-46; asso. editor Finance mag., Chgo., 1947; writer, articles editor American Weekly, N.Y.C., 1948-61; sr. editor, asst. mng. editor, mng. editor World Book Ency. Year Book, Chgo., 1962-67; free-lance writer N.Y.C., 1968-70; sr. editor Nat. Wildlife mag., Milw., 1970-72; editor Prism (the Socio-econ. Mag. of AMA), 1972-75; editor-in-chief Socioecon. Publs. AMA, Chgo., 1975-78; v.p., editorial dir. non-sci. publs. AMA, 1978-81, v.p., editorial dir. Consumer Book Div., 1981-85, cons., Office of Internat. Med., 1988—. Home: 1360 N Lake Shore Dr Chicago IL 60610

RENSHAW, PATRICK RICHARD GEORGE, history educator, writer; b. West Ham, London, Eng., Feb. 26, 1936; s. George Albert and Winifred Norah (Thorpe) R.; m. Mary Davies, Aug. 29, 1959; children: Donovan, Caradoc, Nan, Richard. BA, Oxford (Eng.) U., 1959, MA, 1963; postgrad. Northwestern U., 1961-62. Journalist, Westminster Press, Bedford and Oxford, Eng., 1961-68; lectr. Sheffield (Eng.) U., 1968-76, sr. lectr. in history, 1976—; examiner A-level Cambridge (Eng.) U. Bd., 1974—; Ph.D., examiner Oxford, Kent, London, Glasgow and Sheffield univs., 1977—. Author: The Wobblies, 1967, Italian transl., 1970, Japanese transl., 1973; The General Strike, 1975; Nine Days In May, 1976; contbr. numerous articles to various publs. Bd. dirs. Nat. Union Journalists, Oxford, 1965-67. Served to sr. aircraftsman RAF, 1954-56. Rockefeller fellow, 1960-61; Nuffield Coll. grantee U.S. libraries, 1966; Fulbright fellow, Syracuse, N.Y., 1971-72; Am. Council Learned Soc. fellow, Binghamton, N.Y., 1981-82. Fellow Royal Hist. Soc.; mem. Brit. Assn. Am. Studies, Orgn. Am. Historians. Mem. Labour Party. Club: Oxford (Eng.) Union. Avocations: swimming, tennis, walking, politics. Office: Sheffield Univ, Dept History, Sheffield S10 2TN, England

RENSIN, HOWARD M., lawyer; b. Syracuse, N.Y., July 31, 1943; s. Kenneth Coleman and Ethel (Bloom) R.; m. Katherine Kallet, June 13, 1964; children—Joseph, Samuel, David, Deborah. B.A., Syracuse U., 1964; LL.B., George Washington U., 1967, J.D., 1978. Bar: D.C. 1967, Md. 1968, U.S. Supreme Ct. 1971. Law clk. Taylor & Waldron, Washington, 1965-67, assoc., 1967-68; assoc. Schwartzbach & Wortman, Washington, 1968-70; assoc. Lesser & Lesser, Washington, 1970-72; sole practice, Hyattsville, Md., 1972—. Trustee Silver Spring Civic Assn., Md., 1972-79; synagogue trustee, Silver Spring, Md., 1978-80, v.p., 1980-82, chmn. bd., 1982-84. Recipient Amateur Radio Disaster Traffic award, 1982. Mem. Md. Bar Assn., D.C. Bar Assn., Prince George's County Bar Assn., Assn. Trial Lawyers Am., Am. Arbitration Assn. (arbitrator), Am. Radio Relay League, Md. Emergency Traffic Network. Home: 15221 Centergate Dr Silver Spring MD 20904

RENSON, MARCEL GILLES, psychosociologist, international consultant; b. Liege, Belgium, June 17, 1926; s. Gilles and Marie (Berry) R.; m. Christine Pauletter Hansen-Soulie, Feb. 2, 1986. Student, State U., Liege, 1947; grad. psychosociology, State U., 1949; grad. Gestalt Therapy, Cleve.; diploma in musicology, State Conservatory, Liege, 1979. First asst. UNESCO, Paris, 1949; promotion mgr. P.C.B., Brussels, 1949; gen. mgr. Internat. Union Advertisers, Brussels, 1958, Renson Internat. Mktg. Co., Brussels, 1968; seminar exec. State U., Liege, 1976—; pres. exec. programs EPI Ctr., Brussels, 1976; chmn. III European Congress Distbn., Brussels, 1958; internat. reporter VI European Congress for Humanistic Psychology, Paris, 1986. Author: European Youth, Future Leadership; contbr. articles on social work and mktg. mgmt. to profl. jours. Bd. dirs. Assn. for Cultural Devel. Wallonie, Liege, 1975, North Atkantic Inst., 1975; gen. sec. Liege Inst. Musicology, 1975. Served to 2d lt. 14th Inf. Regt. Belgium Army, 1946. Decorated knight Equestrian Order Holy Sepulchre Jerusalem. Mem. French Soc. Gestalt (bd. dirs. 1981), NATO Belgian Assn. (bd. dirs 1975), Internat. C. of C. (internat. reporter 1958). Mem. Secular Order of St. Benedict. Home: Domaine d'Aprebois, 2 Allee de Muguet, 60305 Apremont France Office: EPI, 58 eu Vandenbussche, Brussels B 1030, Belgium

RENTSCHLER, ALVIN EUGENE, mechanical engineer; b. Havre, Mont., Oct. 24, 1940; s. Alvin Joseph and Pauline Elizabeth (Browning) R.; m. Marilyn Joan Bostrom, Dec. 7, 1974; children—Elizabeth Louise, Richard Eugene, Alison Lynn. BS, Mont. State U., 1964. Sci. and math. instr. Helena (Mont.) Pub. Schs., 1964-66; dist. mgr. Woodmen Accident and Life Co., Helena, 1966-69; profl. med. rep. Abbott Labs., Great Falls, Mont., 1969-72; sales engr. Agribest, Inc., Great Falls, 1973; design engr. Anaconda Co., Mont., 1974-77; ops. and maintenance engr. Rochester Meth. Hosp., Minn., 1977-85; maintenance supervisor, 1985—; mem. engring. coordinating com. Franklin Heating Sta., 1977-85. Bd. dirs. Mont. affiliate Am. Diabetes Assn., 1975-78, pres. Butte-Anaconda chpt., 1974-77; mem. citizens adv. com. Rochester Tech. Inst., 1977— (chmn. 1987—). Recipient Greatest Achievement award Combined Tng., Inc., 1977, Pres.' Club award Woodmen Accident & Life Co., 1968. Mem. ASME, Am. Soc. Hosp. Engring., Internat. Congress Hosp. Engring. Mem. Covenant Ch.

RENTSCHLER, WILLIAM HENRY, newspaper publisher, business executive; b. Hamilton, Ohio, May 11, 1925; s. Peter Earl and Barbara (Schlosser) R.; A.B., Princeton U., 1949; m. Sylvia Gale Angevin, Dec. 20, 1948; children—Sarah Yorke, Peter Ferris, Mary Angevin, Phoebe Mason; m. Martha Guthrie Snowdon, Jan. 20, 1967; 1 dau., Hope Snowdon. Reporter, Cin. Times-Star, 1946; reporter, asst. to exec. editor Mpls. Star & Tribune, 1949-53; 2d v.p. No. Trust Co., Chgo., 1953-56, pres. Martha Washington Kitchens, Inc., 1957-68, Stevens Candy Kitchens, Inc., 1957-66; investor closely-held cos.; bus. and mktg. cons., 1970-81; chmn., chief exec. officer Medart, Inc., Greenwood, Miss., 1981, Jakes Mfg. Corp., Greenwood, 1983, Roper Whitney Corp., Rockford, Ill., 1986, Berkley Small Corp, Medina, Ohio, 1986. Editor, pub. News Voice Newspapers, Inc., Highland Park, Ill., 1983, San Francisco Progress, Inc., 1986; pres. sta. WNVR, Lake Forest, Ill., 1988. Spl. adviser Pres.'s Nat. Program for Vol. Action, 1969; chmn. Ill. Low Tech./High Return Adv. Bd.; exec. com. Nat. Council Crime and Delinquency, also mem. Council of Judges; bd. dirs. Better Boys Found.; pres. John Howard Assn., 1985-87; Republican candidate U.S. Senate, 1960, 70; chmn. Ill. Citizens for Nixon, 1968; pres. Young Reps. Ill., 1957-59; exec. com. United Rep. Fund Ill., 1963-69; former trustee Rockford Coll., Goodwill Industries, Chgo. Council Fgn. Relations; mem. mayor's fiscal adv. com., blue ribbon com. on bus., 1987. Recipient 1st Ann. Buddy Hackett award for service to young men, 1968, Voice for Children award Coleman Advocates,San francisco; Pulitzer prize nominee, 1985, 87. Mem. Am. Newspaper Pubs. Assn. Clubs: Onwentsia (Lake Forest, Ill.); Execs., Economic, City, Chicago Presidents, Tavern (Chgo.); Princeton (N.Y.C.); Press (San Francisco). Home: 450 W Deerpath Rd Lake Forest IL 60045 Office: The Medart Cos 950 N Western Ave Lake Forest IL 60045

REPHAN, JACK, lawyer; b. Little Rock, Mar. 16, 1932; s. Henry and Mildred (Frank) R.; m. Arlene Clark, June 23, 1957; children: Amy Carol, James Clark. B.S. in Commerce, 1954; LL.B., U. Va., 1959. Bar: Va. 1959, D.C. 1961. Asso. Kanter & Kanter, Norfolk, Va., 1959-60; law clk. to Judge Sam E. Whitaker, U.S. Ct. Claims, Washington, 1960-62; asso. Pierson, Ball & Dowd, Washington, 1962-64; ptnr. Danzansky, Dickey, Tydings, Quint & Gordon, Washington, 1964-77; mem. Braude, Margulies, Sacks & Rephan, Washington, 1977-87; ptnr. Porter, Wright, Morris & Arthur, Washington, 1987-88; with Sadur and Pelland, Washington, 1988—; mem. nat. panel arbitrators Am. Arbitration Assn.; lectr. joint com. continuing legal edn. State Bar Va. Contbr. articles to legal jours. Pres. Patrick Henry PTA, Alexandria, Va., 1968-69; treas. John Adams Middle Sch. PTA, Alexandria, 1970-71; pres. Seminary Ridge Citizens Assn., 1976-77; Democratic candidate for Alexandria City Com., 1969. Served to 1st lt. AUS, 1955-57. Mem. ABA (chmn. subcom. procurement jud. remedies, pub. contract sect. 1973-74), Va. Bar Assn. (gov. sect. constrn. law 1979—, vice chmn. 1980-81, chmn. 1981-82), D.C. Bar Assn., Phi Epsilon Pi, Phi Alpha Delta. Jewish. Clubs: Kiwanis (pres. Landmark club, Alexandria 1969), Westwood Country (v.p. 1977-78), Belle Haven Country. Home: 7203 Park Terrace Dr Alexandria VA 22307 Office: 2000 L St NW Suite 612 Washington DC 20036

REPPERT, NANCY LUE, county official; b. Kansas City, Mo., June 17, 1933; d. James Everett and Iris R. (Moomey) Moore; student Central Mo. State U., 1951-52, U. Mo., Kansas City, 1971-75; cert. legal asst., Rockhurst Coll., Kansas City, Mo., 1980; cert. risk mgr., 1979; m. James E. Cassidy, 1952 (div.); children: James E., II, Tracy C. With Kansas City (Mo.) chpt. ARC, 1952-54, N. Central region Boy Scouts Am., 1963-66, Clay County Health Dept., Liberty, Mo., 1966-71, City of Liberty, 1971-80; risk mgr. City of Ames (Iowa), 1980-82; risk mgr. City of Dallas, 1982-83; dir. Dept. Risk Mgmt., Pinellas County, Fla., 1984—; mem. faculty William Jewell Coll., Liberty, 1975-80; vis. prof. U. Kans., 1981; seminar leader, cons in field. Lay minister United Meth. Ch., 1965—; dir. youth devel. Hillside United Meth. Ch., Liberty; co-chmn. youth dir. Collegiate United Meth. Ch. scouting coordinator Palm Lake Christian Ch., Exec. Fellow U. South Fla., mem. Council of Ministries; advancement chmn. Mid-Iowa Council Boy Scouts Am., membership chmn. White Rock Dist. council, health and safety chmn. West Central Fla. council, 1985—; scouting coordinator Palm Lake Christian Ch., 1987—; skipper Sea Explorer ship, 1986—. Recipient Order of Merit, Boy Scouts Am., 1979, Living Sculpture award, 1978,79; Service award Rotary Internat., 1979; Exec. fellow U. South Fla., 1988. Mem. Am. Mgmt. Assns., Internat Platform Assn., Risk and Ins. Mgrs. Soc., Public Risk and Ins. Mgmt. Assn., Am. Soc. Profl. and Exec. Women, Am. Film Inst., U.S. Naval Inst., Nat. Assn. Female Execs., Nat. Inst. Mcpl. Law Officers. Author: Kids Are People, Too, 1975. Pearls of Potentiality, 1980; also articles. Home: Blind Pass Marina 9555 Blind Pass Rd St Petersburg Beach FL 33706 Office: 315 Court St Clearwater FL 33516

REPSTAD, PAAL STEINAR, political science educator; b. Kristiansand, Agder, Norway, Feb. 21, 1947; s. Laurits and Signe (Ditlefsen) R.; m. Kari Grete Haakonsen, Aug. 1, 1970; children: Haakon, Mari. Cand. Polit., U. Oslo (Norway), 1973. Assoc. prof. Rogaland Coll., Stavanger, Norway, 1973-78; prof. Agder Coll., Kristiansand, 1978-79, 79—. Editor: Det Religiose Norge, 1977; author: Raud Preikestol?, 1973, Mellom Himmel Og Jord, 1981, Institusjonssosiologi, 1983, Fra Ilden Til Asken, 1984, Mellom Naerhet Og Distanse, 1987. Vice chmn. Sosialistisk Folkeparti, Stavanger, 1974-75; mem. Kristiansand Bystyret, 1984-87. Mem. Norsk Statsvitenskapelig Forening, Norwegian Union of Polit. Scientists (bd. dirs. 1982-84). Left Socialists. Lutheran Ch. of Norway. Home: Knarrevikveien 6, N-4638 Kristiansand Norway Office: Agder Coll, Gyldenloevesgate 14, N-4601 Kristiansand Norway

RESETTA, LUIGI GERMANICO, marketing manager; b. Saarbrucken, Fed. Republic Germany, Jan. 2, 1939; s. Carlo and Enrica (Zuzzi) R.; m. Sonia Dubost, Jan. 25, 1964; children: Pascal, Caroline. BA, U. Paris, 1965. Market researcher De La Rue, London, 1965-68; sales mgr. Elf-Aquitaine, Paris, 1968-73; mktg. mgr. Thomson-Brandt, Mainz, Fed. Republic Germany, 1973-75; gen. mgr. Huit Deutschland, Offenbach, Fed. Republic Germany, 1976-77; export mgr. Europe Blaupunkt, Hildesheim, Fed. Republic Germany, 1978-80; export dir. Karlsberg, Honburg-Saarbrucken, 1981-84; mktg. mgr. Clarion Co., Frankfurt, Fed. Republic Germany, 1984—. Mem. Mktg. Club Frankfurt. Club: Main Taunus Golf (pub. relations officer 1983-87). Home: Drei Linden Strasse 19, 6232 Hessen, Bad Soden Am Taunus Federal Republic of Germany

RESHTIA, SAYED QASSEM, writer, diplomat; b. Kabul, Afghanistan, Mar. 21, 1913; s. Sayed Habib and Zainab (Azimi) R.; m. Noorjahan Ziaee, May 17, 1930 (dec. Sept. 1946); children: Sayed Ehsanullah, Leila Enayat-Seraj; m. Golalai Seraj, Dec. 19, 1971. Student, Kabul U., 1935-39, 54-56. Editor Kabul Almanch and Kabul Mag., 1936-38; v.p. publs. div. Afghan Acad., 1938, dir.-gen. publs., press dept., 1940-44, pres., 1948; planning bd. liaison officer UN Tech. Coop. Mission, Afghanistan, 1950; pres. econ. planning bd. 1950-51, head govt. co-op. orgn., 1951-54, Minister of Info., 1956-60, 1963-64, Minister of Fin., 1964-65, vice-chmn. Com. to Draft Constitution, 1964; ambassador to Czechoslovakia, Poland, and Hungary, 1960-62, to United Arab Republic, Lebanon, Sudan, and Greece, 1962-63, to Japan, 1970-73. Author: Afghanistan in the 19th Century, 1947, Jawani Afghan, 1949, Jamaluddin Afghani, 1977, The Second Anglo-Afghan War, 1978, The Price of Liberty, the Tragedy of Afghanistan, 1984; also several novels. Address: 13 rue des Boudines, Apt 51, 1217 Meyrin Switzerland

RESINK, DICK EVERHARDUS, marketing professional; b. Almelo, Overijssel, The Netherlands, July 31, 1954; s. Johannes Henricus Franciscus and Riek (Nijenhuis) R.; m. Judy Van der Haar, Dec. 20, 1980; children: Jan Pieter, Annemarijn. Degree in econs. and mktg., U. Econs. and Bus. Adminstrn., Enschede, The Netherlands, 1979; degree in advanced advt., S.R.M. Utrecht, The Netherlands, 1983; degree in internat. product mgmt., Mgmt. Coll. Europe, Brussels, 1983; degree in advanced mktg., Mgmt. Coll., Ashridge, Eng., 1987. Jr. product mgr. Kimberly-Clark Benelux, Veenendaal, The Netherlands, 1980-82, product mgr., 1983-84; group product mgr. Theodorus-Niemeyer, Groningen, The Netherlands, 1985-86, mgr./cons. mktg., 1987—. Recipient Advt. award Internat. Advt. Festival, 1986. Roman Catholic. Home: Rembrandtweg 46, 9761 HT Eelde, Drente The Netherlands Office: Theodorus-Niemeyer, Paterswoldseweg 43, 9726 BB Groningen The Netherlands

RESNAIS, ALAIN, motion picture director; b. Vannes, France, June 3, 1922; s. Pierre and Jeanne (Gachet) R. m. Florence Malraux, Oct. 7, 1969. Ed. Coll. St. Francois Xavier, Vannes. Co-dir. Guernica, 1950. Les Statues Meurent Aussi, 1951; dir. Nuit et Brouillard, 1955. Hiroshima Mon Amour (Cannes award), 1959, L'Annee Derniere A Marienbad (Gold Lion award Venice Film Festival 1961), 1961; Muriel, 1963; La Guerre Est Finie, 1966; Je t'aime, 1968; Stavisky, 1974; Providence, 1977; Mon Oncle d'Amerique,

1980; La Vie Est un Roman, 1984; L'Amour a Mort, 1984, co-dir. Loin de Vietnam, 1967; also numerous short films, 1948—. Author: (photog. album) Reperages. Recipient Grand Nat. prize cinema, 1976, Louis Lumiere award, 1983. Office: Artmedia, 10 ave George V, 75008 Paris France *

RESNICK, MARK JEFFREY, psychologist; b. Balt., Mar. 3, 1955; s. Martin Ronald and Thalia Ann (Dragon) R. BA, Oglethorpe U., 1977; MA, Loyola Coll., Balt., 1980; PhD, U. Kans., 1987. Staff psychologist Glover-Tillman Learning Ctr. and Glover-Tillman Child Mental Health Service, Balt., 1979-80; psychologist Shawnee Mission (Kans.) Pub. Schs., 1980-84, Gardner-Edgerton-Antioch Unified Sch. Dist. 231, 1984-85; instr. psychology Penn Valley Community Coll., Kansas City, 1982-85; behavioral cons. Responsive Mgmt. Clinic, Overland Park, Kans., 1982-84; sch. psychologist Carroll County Pub. Schs., Westminster, Md., 1985—; pvt. practice psychology Towson, Md., 1986—; instr. psychology Essex Community Coll., Balt., 1986—. Mem. Am. Psychol. Assn. (assoc.), Nat. Assn. Sch. Psychologists, Md. Sch. Psychologists' Assn., Soc. for Research in Child Devel., Md. State Tchr. Assn., Nat. Edn. Assn. Republican. Jewish. Home: 267 Cedarmere Circle Owings Mills MD 21117 Office: Carroll County Bd Edn Dept Spl Edn 55 N Court St Westminster MD 21157 Office: Hampton House PH 14 204 E Joppa Rd Towson MD 21204

RESNIK, HARVEY LEWIS PAUL, psychiatrist; b. Buffalo, Apr. 6, 1930; s. Samuel and Celia (Greenberg) R.; m. Audrey Ruth Frey, Aug. 30, 1964; children—Rebecca Gabrielle, Henry Seth Maccabee, Jessica Ruth. B.A. magna cum laude, U. Buffalo, 1951; M.D., Columbia, 1955; grad., Phila. Psychoanalytic Inst., 1967. Diplomate: Am. Bd. Psychiatry and Neurology. Intern Phila. Gen. Hosp., 1955-56, resident, 1956-57; resident Jackson Meml. Hosp., Miami, Fla., 1959-61; fellow U. Pa. Hosp., 1961-62, mem. staff, 1962-67; instr. Sch. Medicine, U. Pa., 1962-66; instr. med. hypnosis Sch. Medicine, U. Pa. (Grad. Sch. Medicine), 1963-65; clin. dir. psychiatry E. J. Meyer Meml. Hosp., Buffalo, 1967; dir. E. J. Meyer Meml. Hosp., 1968; assoc. prof. psychiatry Sch. Medicine, SUNY at Buffalo, 1967, prof., 1968-70, dep. chmn. dept. psychiatry, 1968-69; chief Nat. Center for Studies of Suicide Prevention, NIMH, 1969-74, chief mental health emergencies sect., 1974-76; with Reproductive Biology Research Found., St. Louis, 1971; clin. prof. psychiatry Sch. Medicine, George Washington U., 1969—; lectr. Sch. Medicine, Johns Hopkins, 1969-71; adj. prof. Johns Hopkins U. Sch. Pub. Health, 1981-82; prof. community health Fed. City Coll., 1971-75; med. dir. Human Behavior Found., 1975—, Johns Hopkins U. Compulsive Gambling Ctr. (now Wash. Ctr. for Pathologic Gambling); instr. Del. Valley Group Therapy Inst.; vis. prof. Katholike Universiet, Leuven, Belgium, 1986—; cons. to Sec.-Gen. Ministry of Health, Belgium, 1986—, NATO, 1986-87, Ten Kerselaere Psycho-Geriatric Hosp., Belgium; cons. Marriage Council Phila., Phila. Gen. Hosp., Pa. Hosp., Danville State Hosp., WHO, Nat. Naval Med. Center, ARC, Nat. Cancer Inst., Mental Health Assn. Southeastern Pa., Dept. Def. Author: Suicidal Behaviors: Diagnosis and Management, 1968, (with M. E. Wolfgang) Treatment of the Sexual Offender, 1971, Sexual Behaviors: Social, Clinical and Legal Aspects, 1972, (with B. Hathorne) Suicide Prevention in the Seventies, 1973, (with H.L. Ruben) Emergency Psychiatric Care, 1974, (with others) The Prediction of Suicide, 1974, Emergency and Disaster Management, 1976; (with J.T. Mitchell) Emergency Response to Crisis, 1981; Editor: Bull. Suicidology, 1969-74; Contbr. (with others) articles on hypnosis, sexual offenders, marriage and sexual dysfunction treatment, suicide, death and dying, emergency psychiatric care. Mem. Addictions Adv. Bd. Prince George's County . Served to capt. USAF, 1957-59, ETO-Middle East; capt. USNR. Fellow Am. Psychiat. Assn., Am. Coll. Psychiatrists, Am. Coll. Mental Health Adminstrn.; mem. Med-Chi of Md., Prince Georges County Med. Assn., Phila. Psychoanalytic Soc., Phi Beta Kappa, Beta Sigma Rho (grand Vice-warden 1963). Jewish. Club: Cosmos (Washington). Office: Univ Med Center 4700 Berwyn House Rd #201 College Park MD 20740 also: 18572 Office Park Dr Gaithersburg MD 20879

RESNIK, SOL LEON, manufacturing executive; b. Providence, May 16, 1930; s. Nathan and Fanny (Priest) R.; m. Esther Petersohn, June 20, 1954; children: David, Marcia, Linda. Pres. Emblem & Badge Inc., Providence, 1954-87, also chmn. bd. dirs.; ptnr. Village Park Realty, 1970—, Eleven-Eleven Assocs., Providence, 1974-76; chmn., bd. dirs. Polar Cap Inc., Providence, Plasticity Inc., Providence, Promotion Corp. Am., Providence, 1970-76; pres. Resnik Realty, 1978—. Bd. dirs. Providence Hebrew Day Sch., 1960-73, R.I. Broadway Theatre League, 1965-73, R.I. Jewish Community Ctr., 1974-76, Jewish Fedn. R.I., 1973-76, 77-88, Temple Emanu-El, Narragansett Bay Devel. Soc., 1974-87; v.p. Soc. Friends of Touro Synagogue. Mem. Mfg. Jewelers and Silversmiths Am. Clubs: Masons (32 deg.), Shriners. Office: 859 N Main St Providence RI 02940

RESTER, GEORGE G., architect; b. Ponchatoula, La., Oct. 5, 1923; s. Kelly Caldwell Rester and Myra Vira (Adams) Smith; m. Virginia Wilhelmena, June 25, 1955; children: Gina Louise, Taira Elizabeth, Licia Therese. Student, U.S. Army Engring. Sch., Ft. Belvor, Va., 1943, Soulé Coll., 1945-48, Delgado Tech. Inst., 1949-50, Art Ctr. Coll. Design, 1961-62. Registered architect, La., Calif., Fla., Colo., N.Y., Ariz., Tex., N.J., Mich., Minn., Wash., N.Mex. Architect, designer, draftsman various firms, New Orleans, 1953-60; pvt. practice architecture Culver City, Calif., 1960-61; project architect Welton Beckett Architect, Beverly Hills, Calif., 1961-64; chief architect, dir. archtl. design and prodn. Walt Disney Imagineers, Glendale, Calif., 1965-87; prin. George G. Rester Architect & Assocs., Rolling Hills Estates, Calif., 1987—; founder, pres., chief exec. officer New Visions Resorts Inc., Rolling Hills Estates, 1987—. Served as pfc. C.E., U.S. Army Engrs., 1943-45, ETO, Africa, Mid. East. Mem. AIA, Internat. Platform Assn., Smithsonian Instn. Republican. Roman Catholic. Club: New Orleans Amateur Artists Soc. (founding pres. 1940-42). Home and Office: 26337 Dunwood Rd Rolling Hills Estates CA 90274

RESTON, JAMES BARRETT, author, newspaperman; b. Clydebank, Scotland, Nov. 3, 1909; s. James and Johanna (Irving) R.; brought to U.S., 1910; student Vale of Leven Acad., Alexandria, Scotland, 1914-20; B.S., U. Ill., 1932, LL.D. (hon.), 1962; Litt.D., Colgate U., 1951, Oberlin Coll., 1955, Rutgers U., 1957; LL.D. (hon.), Dartmouth, 1959, N.Y. U., 1961, Boston Coll., 1963, Brandeis U., 1964; D.H.L., Kenyon Coll., 1962, Columbia, 1963, U. Mich., 1965, Harvard, 1970, Stanford, 1972, U. Utah, 1973, Kent State U., 1974, Colby Coll., 1975, Yale U., 1977, Miami U., Oxford, Ohio; hon. degrees U. Md., Northeastern U., 1976, U. Glasgow, 1983; m. Sarah Jane Fulton, Dec. 24, 1935; children: Richard Fulton, James Barrett, Thomas Busey. With Springfield (Ohio) Daily News, 1932-33; with publicity dept. Ohio State U., 1933; publicity dir. Cin. Baseball Club, 1934; reporter A.P., N.Y.C., 1934-37, London, 1937-39; reporter London bur. N.Y. Times, 1939-41, Washington bur., 1941—, chief Washington corr., bur. chief, 1953-64, asso. editor, 1964-68, exec. editor, 1968-69, v.p., 1969-74, columnist, cons., 1974—, also dir. N.Y. Times Co.; co-pub. The Vineyard Gazette, 1968—. Recipient Pulitzer prize for nat. corr., 1945, nat. reporting, 1957; Overseas Press Club award for interpretation internat. news, 1949, 51, 53; George Polk Meml. award for nat. reporting, 1954; U. Mo. medal, 1961; J.P. Zenger award, 1964; Elijah Parrish Lovejoy award, 1974; Helen B. Bernstein Excellence in Journalism award, 1988; decorated Legion d'Honneur (France); ordre National du Mérite (France); Order St. Olav (Norway), Order of Merit (Chile); comdr. Order Brit. Empire. Clubs: Century (N.Y.C.); Metropolitan (Washington); Chevy Chase (Md.). Author: The Artillery of the Press, 1967; Sketches in the Sand, 1967. Office: New York Times 1000 Connecticut Ave Washington DC 20036 *

RESTREPO, URIBE-RESTROD, magistrate; b. Bogotá, Columbia, Apr. 11, 1929; s. Félix and Ana (Restrepo) Uribe; m. Cecilia Restrepo; children: Luis Fernando, Ana Cecilia, Miguel Ignacio, Daniel Alberto, Félix Alfredo, Juan Pablo, Tomás Esteban. BA, U. Pontifica Bolivariana, Madellín, Columbia, 1948, D en Dercho, 1952; MA in Social Scis., Cath. U. Am., Washington, 1955. Jefe departmento Suramericana de Seguros, Medellín, 1955-60; v.p. Nat. Assn. Industries, Medellín, 1960-78; magistrate Supreme Ct. Justice, Bogotá, 1978-85, pres. supreme ct., 1985-87; magistrate Tribunal Andino de Justicia, Quito, Ecuador, 1987—; consejo de administración Internat. Labor Orgn., Ginebra, Suiza, 1975-78, comité de expertos, 1979—; pres. Consejo Directivo COMFANA, Madellin, 1970-78; prof. U. Pontificia Bolivariana, U. Nat. , Bogotá, U. Javeriana, Bogotá, U. Externado, Bogotá. Mem. Assn. Abogados Laboralistas (hon.), Assn. Iberoamericana D. del Trabajo. Conservative. Roman Catholic. Clubs: Campestre (Medellán), Chiris (Quito). Office: Palacio de Justicia, Plaza de Bolivar, Bogotá Colombia

RETHORE, JOELLE, linguistics educator; b. Safi, Morocco, Sept. 4, 1945; came to France, 1960; d. Jacques and Anne-Marie (Gribelin) Daillier; m. Andre Rethore, Sept. 30, 1969 (div. Nov. 1985). Lic., U. Paris, 1968, Maitrise, 1969; Dr. 3d Cycle, Maitrise, 1973, LittD in Linguistics, 1988. Lectr. linguistics U. Paris VIII, 1969-74; sr. lectr. U. Perpignan, France, 1974—, conf. organizer, 1883, 86, 87; tchr. secondary pvt. sch., Paris Vincennes, 1970-72, refresher course Montpellier Edn. Offices, Perpignan, 1976—. Coeditor spl. issue on Peirce for sci. jour., 1988; contbr. articles to profl. jours. Mem. Assn. Francaise Semiotique (treas. 1986—), Assn. Internat. Semiotique. Clubs: Aero Roussillon (Perpignan); Portail a Roulettes (Salses, France). Home: 2 Impasse de L'Eglise, 66540 Baho France Office: U Perpignan, Ave de Villeneuve, 66025 Perpignan France

RETI, TAMAS, economist; b. Budapest, Hungary, July 9, 1951; arrived in Hungary, 1987; s. Pal and Gizella (Farago) R.; m. Maria Kemeny, 1978 (div. 1984); children: Anna, Peter. Grad., U. Econs., Budapest, 1973, PhD, 1979. Research fellow Inst. World Economy, Budapest, 1974-88, Inst. Econ. and Market Research and Informatics, Budapest, 1988—. Contbr. articles to profl. jours. Fellow Hungarian Govt., 1982, Hungarian Acad. Scis., 1983, Woodrow Wilson Ctr. Washington, 1987. Home: Pusztaszer ut 53, 1025 Budapest Hungary Office: Inst Econ Market Res and Informatics, Dorottya u 6, 1051 Budapest Hungary

RETORE, GUY, theatre director; b. Apr. 7, 1924. Student U. Paris. With pub. relations dept. SNCF, until 1955; actor, producer Theatre de Boulevard until 1955; formed La Guilde, theatrical co., Menilmontant, East Paris, 1954; opened Theatre de Menilmontant, 1958; dir. Maison de la Culture, Menilmontant, 1962—; dir. Theatre de l'Est Parisien. Producer plays include La fille du roi (Cosmos), 1955, Life and Death of King John, 1956, Grenadiers de la reine (Farquhar, adapted by Cosmos), 1957, L'avare (Moliere), Les caprices de Marianne (Musset), la fleur a la bouche (Pirandello), Le medecin malgre lui (Moliere), Le manteau (Gogol, adapted by Cosmos), 1963, La Locandiera (Goldoni), Arden of Faversham, 1964, Monsieur Alexandre (Cosmos), 1964, MacBeth (Shakespeare), 1964, Turcaret (Lesage) 1965, Measure for Measure (Shakespeare), 1965, Le voyage de Monsieur Perrichon (Labiche), 1965, Live Like Pigs (Arden), The Silver Tassie (O'Casey), 1966-67, Les 13 soleils de la rue St. Blaise (A. Gatti), La machine (Jean Cosmos), 1968-69, Lorenzaccio (Musset), L'opera de quat'sous (Brecht), Major Barbara (Shaw), 1969-70, Les ennemis (Gorki), L'ane de l'hospice (Arden), 1970-71, Sainte Jeanne des abattoirs (Brecht), 1971-72, Macbeth (Shakespeare), 1972-73, Androcles et le lion (Shaw), 1974-75, Coquin de coq (O'Casey), 1975-76, L'otage (Claudel), 1976-77, Le camp du drap d'or, (Rezvani), 1980; Fin. de Partie (S. Beckett), 1980-81, Tueur sans Gages (E. Inonesco), 1981-82, Promethee (Eschylel Heiner Müller), 1982-83, Le Chantier (C. Tordsman), 1983-84, Clair D'usine (D. Besnehard), 1983-84, 325.000 Francs (R. Vailland), George Dandin (Holiere), 1985-86. Decorated officier des Arts et des Lettres, Chevalier Legion of Honor. Office: 159 Ave Gambetta, 75020 Paris France *

RETTENMAIER, MARVIN JOSEPH, manufacturing company official, mosaicist; b. Carroll, Iowa, Mar. 23, 1924; s. Edward E. and Bernadine (Bernholtz) R. Student Mpls. Inst. Art, 1945-46, U. Minn., 1947-48, Milw. Sch. Engring., 1966. Aircraft mechanic Northwest Orient Airlines, St. Paul, 1942-45; master stencil artist Photoplating Co., Mpls., 1945-49; 3d officer, purser North Central Airlines, Mpls., 1953; chief insp. W.H. Brady Co., Milw., 1953—; exhbn. micro mosaics include: Putnam Mus., Davenport, Iowa, Milwaukee County Pub. Mus., Morristown (N.J.) Coll., Cath. U. Library, Washington, First Wis. Ctr., Milw. represented in permanent collections: Alcoa Co., Pitts., Oberlin Coll., Wildwood Mus., Cape May, N.J., Ripley Internat., Toronto. Served with AUS, 1949-53. Mem. Am. Soc. Quality Control, (charter mem. insp. div.). Roman Catholic. Lodge: Eagles. Office: 2221 W Camden Rd PO Box 2131 Milwaukee WI 53201

RETTER, CATHARINE JOSEPHINE, marketing director; b. Amsterdam, Holland, Nov. 3, 1946; came to Australia, 1952; d. Elias Liko and Elisabeth Antonia (Boissevain) Krejcik; m. Peter Owen Retter, Feb. 9, 1974. Diploma Sydney Tech. Coll., New South Wales, Australia, 1964; Student Macquarie U., New South Wales, 1982-83. Sec., asst. Leo Burnett, Sydney, Australia, 1968-70; account mgr. Grey Advt., Sydney, 1972-79; account dir. Fountain Huie Fish, Sydney, 1979-82; dir. and ptnr. Retter Advt., Sydney, 1982-85; dir. mktg. Australian Bicentennial Authority, Sydney, 1985—; dir. Retter Advt. Mem. Australian Mktg. Inst. (assoc.). Avocations: dressage; reading; walking. Office: Australian Bicentennial Authority, 88 George St, Sydney, New South Wales 2000, Australia

RETTERSTOL, NILS, psychiatrist; b. Oslo, Norway, Oct. 3, 1924; s. Kittel and Kathrine (Steen) R.; M.D., U. Oslo, 1950, Dr.med., 1966; m. Kirsten Christensen, Aug. 16, 1958; children: Trine Lise, Kjetil, Lars Jorgen. Med. officer Dikemark Hosp., Ulleval Hosp., Oslo, 1952-56, Runwell Hosp., Eng., 1956-57; resident in psychiatry Ulleval Hosp., Oslo, 1957-58; asso. prof., dep. dir. Univ. Psychiat. Clinic, Oslo, 1959-68; prof. psychiatry U. Bergen, head dir. Neevengarden Hosp., Bergen, 1969-73; prof. psychiatry U. Oslo, 1973—; head dir. Gaustad Hosp., Oslo, 1973—; head Norwegian Info. Bank for Narcotic problems; chmn. Norwegian Commn. for Forensic Pschiatry, 1983; cons. in field. Served to capt. Norwegian Army. Recipient gold medal for psychiat. research, H.M. The King of Norway; prize for research Norwegian Council Humanities and Sci., 1978; comdr. The Royal St. Olav Order, 1984. Mem. Norwegian Acad. Sci. (hon.), Swedish Psychiat. Assn., German. Assn. Neurology and Psychiatry, Finnish Assn. Psychiatry, Norwegian Med. Soc., Norwegian Psychiat. Soc., Internat. Assn. Suicide Prevention and Crisis Intervention (dir.). Author: 25 books including Paranoid and Paranoiac Psychoses, 1966; Prognosis in Paranoid Psychoses, 1970 (with L. Eitinger) Crisis and Neuroses, 4th edit., 1984, Forensic Psychiatry, 3d edit., 1984, Psychoses, 3d edit., 1984; editor Scand. Med. Yearbook, 1972, Eur. Archives of Phychiatry and Neurological Scis., 1975—; European editor Jour. Drug Issues, 1980; co-editor Psychopathology, 1983. Home: Nordseterveien 20 A, Oslo 11 Norway Office: Gaustad sykehus, Boks 24 Gaustad, H0320 Oslo 3 Norway

RETTIG, TERRY, veterinarian, wildlife consultant; b. Houston, Jan. 30, 1947; s. William E. and Rose (Munves) R.; m. Anne Calhoun Martin, Aug. 29, 1970; children—Michael Thomas, Jennifer Suzanne. B.S. in Zoology, Duke U., 1969, M.A.T. in Sci., 1970; D.V.M., U. Ga., 1975. Resident veterinarian, mgr. animal health The Wildlife Preserve, Largo, Md., 1975-76; wildlife veterinarian Dept. Environ. Conservation, State of N.Y., Delmar, 1976-77; owner Atlanta Animal Hosp., 1976—; pres., chmn. Atlanta Animal Services, P.A., 1983—; sec., dir. Atlanta Pet Supply, Inc., 1983—; cons. Six Flags Over Ga., Yellow River Game Ranch, Stone Mountain Park Animal Forest, Atlanta Zoo; Author: (with Murray Fowler) Zoo and Wild Animal Medicine (Aardvark award 1978), 1978, 2d edit., 1986 (Order of Kukukifuku award 1986); contbr. articles to profl. jours. Del., Dekalb County Republican Conv., 1983. Spl. scholar Cambridge U. Coll. Vet. Medicine, 1973-74. Mem. AVMA, Ga. Vet. Med. Assn., Greater Atlanta Vet. Med. Assn., Dekalb Vet. Soc., Acad. Vet. Medicine, Am. Assn. Zoo Veterinarians, Am. Assn. Zool. Parks and Aquaria, Nat. Wildlife Health Found., Nat. Wildlife Assn., Atlanta Zool. Soc., Am. Fedn. Aviculturists, Cousteau Soc., Am. Assn. Avian Veterinarians, Am. Animal Hosp. Assn., Internat. Wildlife Assn., Soc. Aquatic Veterinary Medicine, Am. Buffalo Assn. Presbyterian. Home: 5082 Wickford Way Dunwoody GA 30338 Office: Atlanta Animal Hosp 2482 C Mt Vernon Rd Dunwoody GA 30338 also: Atlanta Animal Hosp 5005 Kimball Bridge Rd Alpharetta GA 30201

REUBEN, ALVIN BERNARD, entertainment executive; b. Harrisburg, Pa., Aug. 11, 1940; s. Maurice and Lillian (Katzef) R.; m. Barbara Ann Harrison, Mar. 18, 1967; 1 dau., Mindee Jill. B.S. in Commerce, Rider Coll., 1962. Buyer Pomeroy's div. Allied Stores Corp., Harrisburg, 1962-67; sales rep. Random House, Inc., N.Y.C., 1967-74; dir. mktg. Ballantine Books, Inc. (div. Random House), N.Y.C., 1974-76; v.p. sales Simon & Schuster, N.Y.C., 1976-79, sr. v.p. sales Pocket Books div., 1979-81, sr. v.p. mktg., 1981-82, pres. promotional pub. group, 1982-83, exec. v.p. electronic pub. div., 1983-85; exec. v.p. Prentice Hall div. Simon & Schuster, 1985-86; sr. v.p. mktg., sales and distbn. Vestron, Inc., 1986—; instr. edn. in pub. program, grad. program SUNY; active problem solving seminar Pubs. Weekly, N.Y.C., 1980. Trustee Marlboro (N.J.) Jewish Center. Served with USAFR, 1963-69. Mem. Assn. Am. Pubs. (mktg. com.), Jewish Book Council, Tau Kappa Epsilon. Home: 54 High Point Rd Westport CT 06880 Office: 1010 Washington Blvd Stamford CT 06901

REUBI, FRANCOIS CHARLES, medical educator; b. Neuchatel, Switzerland, July 10, 1917; s. Charles H. and Marie (Grisel) R.; m. Claudine Petitpierre, Apr. 12, 1944; children—Jean Claude, Monique F. M.D., U. Geneva, Switzerland, 1941. Resident in pathology U. Geneva, 1942-43; resident in medicine U. Berne (Switzerland), 1944-46, 49-53, assoc. prof. dept. medicine, 1951-53, prof. medicine, 1954—, dir. outpatient dept., 1954—; research fellow Barnes Hosp., St. Louis, 1947-48; mem. Fed. Drug Com. Switzerland, 1973—. Author: Renal Diseases, 3d edit., 1960; L'Hypertension Arterielle, 1976; Clearance Tests in Medicine, 1963; editor: Essential Hypertension, 1960; The Nephrotic Syndrome, 1963. Hon. mem. Societe Hopitaux de Paris, Austrian Soc. Nephrology; mem. League Against Hypertension (pres. 1976-80), Swiss Found. (pres. 1971—), Internat. Soc. Nephrology (v.p. 1963-66), French Renal Assn. (past pres.), German Renal Assn. (past pres.), Swiss Renal Assn. (past pres.). Home: Chemin Du Village 44, CH 1012 Lausanne Switzerland Office: Medizinische Poliklinik, Freiburgstrasse 3, CH 3000 Berne CH Switzerland

REUNANEN, MIKKO SAKARI, surgeon; b. Poytya, Finland, Nov. 18, 1944; s. Kaarlo Kalervo and Saima Salli (Hirvijoki) R.; m. Hellevi Tuulikki Helenius, Aug. 20, 1977; children—Juho Kalle Mikael, Karoliina Veera Maria. Med. Lic., Turku U. Hosp., Finland, 1971, Surgeon, 1979, Pediatric Surgeon, 1979. Chief surgeon Naantali Health Spa, Finland, 1985-87; gen. surgeon Turunmaan Sairaala, 1987; sr. pediatric surgeon TUCH, Turku, 1979-85, 87—; surgeon Turku Rys., 1972—; cons. surgeon Orgn. of Invalids of War, Turku area, 1975—; pediatric surgeon cons. Pvt. Health Central Vagus, Turku, 1979—, Pvt. Health Central Paaskyvuori, Turku, 1983—, Pvt. Health Central Pulssi, Turku, 1984—. Served with Finnish Army, 1971-72. Mem. Finnish Surgeons, Finnish Union Pediatricians, Finnish Union Radiologists, Finnish Union Pediatric Surgeons, Finnish Union Doctors of Rys. Mem. Center Party. Lutheran. Clubs: Tennis (Turku). Avocations: collecting money; reading. Home: Tammikko, SF-20660 Littoinen Finland Office: TUCH Pediatric Surgery Clinics, SF-20520 Turku Finland

REUSCHE, FRANK LOUIS, ceramic decorating supply company executive; b. Bklyn., Feb. 17, 1925; s. Frank Louis and Marjorie Theresa (Ryan) R.; grad. Fordham Prep. Sch., 1941; B.S., Bethany Coll., 1944; postgrad. Ohio State U., 1945, Rutgers U., 1947-48; m. Amelia V. Ozimek, Sept. 18, 1949 (dec. Oct. 1972); children—Frank Louis III, Thomas R., Marjorie A., Mary T., Madeline C.; m. 2d, Jane Fabian Verney, Dec. 28, 1975; stepchildren—Bruce, Kim, Kerry and Alison Verney. Grad. chemist So. Acid & Sulfur Co., Columbus O., 1945; chemist research and devel. L. Reusche & Co., Newark, 1947-51, v.p., 1951-66. pres., 1966—. Served with USAAF, 1945-47. Mem. Soc. Glass and Ceramic Decorators, Stained Glass Assn. Am., Am., N.J. ceramic socs., Sigma Nu. Patentee in field. Home: 164 Canoe Brook Pkwy Summit NJ 07901 Office: 2-6 Lister Ave Newark NJ 07105

REUTER, THOMAS, electrical engineer; b. Koblenz, Fed. Rep. Germany, Oct. 7, 1957; s. Robert and Anita (Neubauer) R.; m. Margot-Christel Einsfeld. Diploma, Rheinisch West-fälische Technische Hochschule, Aachen, 1982. Registered profl. engr. Researcher, project leader Heinrich-Hertz Inst., Berlin, Fed. Rep. Germany, 1982. Contbr. articles to profl. jours. Recipient Literature award, Info. technische Gesellschaft, 1987. Office: Heinrich-Hertz Inst, Einstein Ufer 37, 1000 Berlin 10 Federal Republic of Germany

REVAH, YVES, obstetrician; b. St. Pierre de Fursac, Creuse, France, July 22, 1944; s. Israel Salvator and Claire Mathilde (Lievre) R.; married; children: Bertrand, Emilie, Julien. MD, Faculté de Médecine, Paris, 1964. Diplomate in Ob-Gyn. Obstetrician Clinique du Val de Marne, Champigny-sur-Marne, France, 1973—; cons. staff Pitiè Salpetriere Hosp., Paris, 1970—. Office: Clinique du Val de Marne, 12 Rue de la Plage, 94507 Champigny CEDEX France

REVEL, GARY NEAL, music publishing executive; b. Florala, Ala., June 29, 1949; s. Leamon Curtise and Martha Marie (Mitchell) R.; m. Linda Marie Willis, Jan. 23, 1973; children: Gary Neal Jr., Curtise Leamon II, Mary Noel, Rebecca Ann, Elisabeth Marie, Sonny Americas. BA in Advanced Theology, Am. Bible Coll., Pineland, Fla., 1983. Pres., chief exec. officer Star City Records, Inc., Nashville, 1979-80; songwriter Milene-Opryland Music, Nashville, 1975—; owner, pub., songwriter Gary Revel Music, Hollywood, Calif., 1980—, Jongleur Music, Hollywood, 1983—; owner, chief exec. officer, recording artist Top's Records, Hollywood, 1983—; cons. Friends Indeed, Hollywood, 1980-84. Author: (novel) Midnight's Calling; (poems) The Poet's Fare, 1986, Wanderings, 1987; (play) And Then I Went Away, 1971; composer (songs) Treat America Like a Lady, 1985, I Know (We're Gonna Make It Love), 1988, I've Got Tears, 1988, songwriter soundtrack (film) Last of the American Hoboes, 1971. Founder Ams. for Worldwide Prison Reform; bd. dirs. Citizens Com. for Civic Betterment; past scoutmaster Boy Scouts Am. Served with USN, 1967-69. Recipient Humanitarian award So. Calif. Motion Picture Council, Los Angeles Freedoms Day award Citizens Com. for Civic Betterment, Angel Victory cert. award and Angel Victory Patriotic award, Mus and Performing Arts Angels. Named one of Outstanding Ams. under the age of 40 Esquire, 1984, 85. Mem. ASCAP, So. Calif. Motion Picture Council, Internat. Platform Assn., Am. Legion. Home and Office: 9015 Owensmouth Ave #106 Canoga Park CA 91304

REVEL, JACQUES MICHEL, history, social sciences educator; b. Avignon, France, July 25, 1942; s. Paul I. and Jeanne (Dreyfus) R.; m. Michèle Mac Aleese, Sept. 30, 1965; children: Judith, Jeanne, Ariane. Student, Ecole Normale Superieure, Paris, 1963-68; Licence, Sorbonne U., 1965, Agrégation Histoire, 1968. Asst. prof. Sorbonne U., Paris, 1969-70; researcher Ecole Francaise de Rome, 1970-73; researcher attache Nat. Ctr. for Sci. Research, Paris, 1973-77, mem. nat. com., 1975-81; assoc. prof. social scis. Ecole Hautes in Sciences Sociales, Paris, 1977-83, prof., 1983—; vis. prof. NYU, Cornell U., U. Mich., U. Calif., Berkeley, U. Tel Aviv, Acad. Social Scis., Beijing; sec. then dir. Annales, economies, societes civilisations, 1975—. Author: Une Politique de la Langue, 1975, La Nouvelle Histoire, 1978, Les Lyceen et Leurs Etudes, 1983, Logiques de la Foule, 1988; author/editor: Les Universites Europeenes a L'Epoque Moderne, 1986, 1988. Office: Maison des Sciences de l'Homme, 54 Blvd Raspail, 75006 Paris France

REVELEY, LOUIS RAMON, pathologist; b. San Antonio, Nov. 13, 1951; s. Marciano Contreras Gonzalez and Marietta Augusta Reveley; m. Suzanne Morrissey, Jan. 14, 1978; 1 child, Todd Raymond. B.A. with honors, U. Tex., Austin, 1973; M.D., U. Tex.-Dallas, 1978. Diplomate Am. Bd. pathology, Nat. Bd. Med. Examiners. Resident in pathology Parkland Meml. Hosp., Dallas, 1978-82; assoc. pathologist Brown & Assocs. Med. Labs., Houston, 1982—, tech. dir. clin. pathology reference lab., 1982-85; ptnr. Brown and Assocs. Med. Labs., Houston, 1985—; staff pathologist Park Plaza Hosp., Houston, 1982-83; dir. labs. Polly Ryon Hosp., Richmond, Tex., 1983—, sec. med. staff, 1985, 86; med. dir. med. lab. technologist tng. program San Jacinto Coll. Central, Pasadena, Tex., 1984—. Am. Cancer Soc. clin. fellow in radiation oncology St. Paul Hosp., Dallas, 1974; Southwestern Med. Found. scholar, 1974. Active Tex. Longhorn Ednl. Found. Fellow Am. Soc. Clin. Pathologists, Coll. Am. Pathologists (insp. lab. accreditation program, dep. sate commr. lab accredation program, 1986—); mem. N.Y. Acad. Scis., Internat. Acad. Pathology, AMA, Am. Assn. Blood Banks, Am. Soc. Cytology, So. Med. Assn., Tex. Med. Assn., Tex. Soc. Pathologists, Calif. Soc. Pathologists, Ind. Soc. Pathologists, Am. Chem. Soc., Am. Heart Assn., Nat. Com. for Clinical Lab. Standards, Harris County Med. Soc., Houston Soc. Clin Pathologists, Am. Soc. Microbiology, Tex. Hist. Assn., San Jacinto Mus. History Assn., Republican. Methodist. Club: The Briar, The 200 Horns, Houston Longhorn (bd. dirs.). Home: 2130 Swift St Houston TX 77030 Office: Brown & Assocs Med Labs 1213 Hermann Dr Suite 220 Houston TX 77004

REVELEY, MICHAEL AUGUST, psychiatrist; b. San Antonio, June 14, 1944; arrived in Eng., 1977; s. Hugh Price and Evelyn Elsa (Woeltz) R.; m. Adrianne Moore, May 12, 1975; children: Colin, Thomas. BA, U. Tex., Austin, 1966; MD, SW Med. Sch., 1970; PhD, U. London, 1988. Intern

Barnes Hosp.-Washington U. Sch. Med., St. Louis, 1970-71, resident in psychiatry, then chief resident, 1973-77; NIMH fellow in psychopharmacology Queen Charlotte's Hosp.-U. London, 1977-80; lectr. psychiatry U. London Inst. Psychiatry, 1980-81, sr. lectr., 1982-85; lectr. psychiatry Charing Cross Hosp. Med. Sch., London, 1981-82; sr. lectr. psychiatry London Hosp. Med. Coll.-U. London, 1985—. Asst. editor Brit. Jour. Psychiatry, 1985—; contbr. articles to profl. publs. Served with USPHS, 1970-71. Fellow Royal Soc. Medicine; mem. Brit. Soc. Biol. Psychiatry (sec.-treas. 1985), Royal Coll. Psychiatrists (research prize and bronze medal 1983), Brit. Assn. Psychopharmacology, Am. Psychiat. Assn., European Coll. Neuropsychpharmacology. Office: London Hosp Med Coll, Univ Dept Psychiatry, Alexandra Wing Turner St, London E1 2AD, England

REVELL, JOHN HAROLD, dentist; b. Lead, S.D., Dec. 12, 1906; s. Aris LeRoy and Margaret (O'Donnell) R.; A.B. in Engring., Stanford, 1930; postgrad. McGill Med. Sch., 1930; D.D.S. summa cum laude, U. So. Calif., 1941; postgrad. in Maxillo Facial and Plastic Surgery, Mayo Found., U. Minn., 1944; m. Catherine Cecelia Gerrard, Sept. 14, 1936; children—Mary Margaret (Mrs. Irwin Goodwin), Kathleen Dianne Revell, Timothy John, Maureen Frances Brown, Dennis Cormac. Engaged as instr. U. So. Calif. Dental Coll., Los Angeles, 1941-42; practice oral surgery, maxillo facial-plastic surgery, Shafter, Calif., 1946—; mem. staff Mercy Hosp., Bakersfield, Calif., 1948—, chmn. dental sect., 1955-60, 70-71; mem. surg. staff San Joaquoin Hosp., Bakersfield; lectr. on applied nutrition; internat. pioneer lectr. surg. orthodontics. Served with AUS, 1932-37, 42-46; now maj. ret. Recipient of Special Clinic award Am. Soc. Dentistry for Children, 1964; Rotary Internat. Presdl. citation, 1982. Diplomate Internat. Bd. Applied Nutrition. Fellow Internat. Coll. Applied Nutrition; mem. ADA (life), Calif. Dental Assn. (life), Ventura Dental Soc. (life), So. Calif., Kern County (dir.), Los Angeles County (award 1941), Santa Barbara-Ventura County dental assns., Am. Acad. Dental Medicine, Am. Acad. Applied Nutrition, Am. Soc. Dentistry for Children (life), Pierre Fauchard Acad., Shafter C. of C. (dir. 1948-50), Alpha Tau Epsilon, Omicron Kappa Upsilon, Phi Kappa Phi, Theta Xi. Democrat. Roman Catholic. Rotarian (pres. Shafter 1950-51, dir. 1951-52). Patentee precisioner. Research on maxillary dental papilloma, rotation unerupted impacted teeth, channeling for extensive movement of teeth; also clin. research in cleft palate surgery; inventor rapid fabrication device for infant feeding; pioneer in pre-fab. bldgs. and homes while constrn. officer U.S. Army, 1932; developer prototype WW-2 Jeep machine gun mount. Author publs. in field; all research data presented to and housed at La. State U. Dental Coll., New Orleans. Home: 81 620 Ave 49 Indio CA 92201

REVESZ, PAL, mathematics educator; b. Budapest, Hungary, June 6, 1934; s. Mark and Olga (Deutschlander) R.; m. Klara Földesi, May 25, 1963; children: Agnes, Zsuzsanna. PhD, U. Budapest, 1958. Asst. prof. of math. U. Budapest, 1956-63; research fellow Math. Inst., Budapest, 1963-85; prof. Technische U., Wien, Austria, 1985—, Tech. U. Budapest. Author: Strong Approximation in Probability and Statistics, 1981. Fellow Inst. Math. Statistics; mem. Bernoulli Soc. (pres. 1981-83), Hungarian Acad. Sci. Home: Herbert Rauchgasse 1-I, 2361 Laxenburg Austria Office: Technische U Wien, Wiedner Hauptstr 8-10, 1040 Vienna Austria

REVIRON, JEAN, immunohematologist; b. Chateauroux, France, May 29, 1924; s. Marcel Henry and Solange (Villeneuve) R.; m. Roselyne Robinet, Sept. 12, 1951; 1 child, Denis. Diploma in aero. medicine, Faculty of Medicine, Paris, 1951, MD, 1952, cert. in hematological spl. studies, 1964; competence in ob-gyn, Nat. Physicians Order, Paris, 1954. Specialist in blood tranfusion Departmental Blood Transfusion Ctr., Paris, 1949-54; dir. La Salpetriere Hosp. Blood Bank, Paris, 1954-64, Saint-Louis Hosp. Blood Transfusion Ctr., Paris, 1964—; fundamental scis. asst. Saint-Antoine Hosp. Univ. Ctr., Paris, 1966-69; clin. teaching attaché Lariboisiere-St. Louis Faculty of Medicine, Paris, 1971-77, dir., 1978—; expert nat. Pharmacopeia Commn., Paris, 1986—; founder Assn. Research and Transfusion, 1968, Immunobiol. Reagents Research Inst., 1985. Contbr. articles to profl. jours., 1954—. Mem. Universal Movement for Sci. Responsibility, Paris, 1988. Named prof. Medicine Coll. Paris Hosps., 1984. Mem. Internat. Soc. Blood Transfusion, Nat. Soc. Blood Transfusion, French Soc. Immunology. Club: Hemobios. Home: 17 Bis Rue de Champigny, 94430 Chennevieres France Office: Saint-Louis Hosp, 1 Ave Claude Vellefaux, 75010 Paris France

REX, ROBERT RICHMOND, prime minister of Niue Island b. Alofi, Niue Island, Jan. 25, 1909; s. Leslie Lucas Richmond and Monomono (Paea) R.; m. Tuagatagaloa Patricia Vatolo, Oct. 5, 1941; children: Mathinna Fitiamonomono, Robert Richmond, John Hector Richmond, Ethel Maile Waiwera. Ed. Tufukia Tech. Sch., Niue. Ofcl. interpreter Niue Govt., Alofi, 1934-52, politician, 1952-74, prime minister, 1974—, also minister for govt. adminstrn., housing, immigration, inland revenue, police, transport, and minister for fin.; mng. dir. RR Rex & Sons Ltd., Alofi, 1952—; mem. Niue Island Council, 1952-60, exec. com. Assembly, 1960-66, leader of govt. bus., 1966-74. Decorated Order Brit. Empire, companion St. Michael and St. George; created Knight. Mem. Niue Sports Club (Alofi patron 1952—). Office: Office of the Premier, Alofi Niue Island *

REY, ANTHONY MAURICE, hotel executive; b. N.Y.C., Mar. 31, 1916; s. Anthony A. and Madeleine (Lauper) R.; student NYU, 1933-34, L'Ecole Hoteliere, Lausanne, Switzerland, 1934-35; m. Dorothea M. Carley, June 2, 1934; children—Anthony Maurice, Donna Christine, Jamie Elisabeth R. Di Giovanni, Andrea Michele (dec.), Cynthia Anne Higbee. With Waldorf-Astoria Hotel, N.Y.C., 1934-58; gen. mgr., v.p. Astor Hotel, N.Y.C., 1958-65; pres., dir. Chalfonte Haddon Hall, 1965-76; pres. dir. Resorts Internat. Hotel Casino Co., 1976-80, also dir.; v.p. Resorts Internat. Inc., 1979-82, sr. v.p., 1982-86; dir. Bancorp. Atlantic City (N.J.), Guarantee Bank, Atlantic City; sec. E.J.H. Co. Commr., bd. dirs. Atlantic Area council Boy Scouts Am., 1965-87; commr., vice chmn. Atlantic County Improvement Authority, 1965-74; bd. dirs. Miss Am. Pageant, 1966-80; chmn. exec. com. Atlantic City Conv. Bur., 1967-81, chmn. bd., 1975-81; v.p., trustee So. N.J. Devel. Council, 1971-86; chmn. Conv. Liaison Council, 1967-74; bd. dirs. Atlantic County United Fund, 1967-69; trustee Internat. Restaurant and Hotel Union Pension Trust, 1975-76, Am. Hotel Ednl. Inst.; adv. council Culinary Inst. Am., 1980—, Weidner U. Restaurant and Hotel Sch., 1980—, Johnson & Wales Coll. Hotel and Restaurant Sch. Served with USNR, 1942-45. Decorated Bronze Star, Presdl. citation; named N.J. Innkeeper of Year, 1971, Am. Hotel Resort Exec. of 1979, Hotel Man of Yr., State of N.J., 1980; named to Hospitality Hall of Fame, 1969; recipient Arthur Goldman Innkeeper award, 1986, Disting. Citizen award Boy Scouts Am., 1981; Community Services award Anti-Defamation League of B'nai B'rith 1986; hon. dept. fire chief N.Y.C., 1963—. Mem. Greater Atlantic City C. of C. (pres. 1969-71, chmn. bd. 1971-73), N.J. C. of C. (dir. 1973-86), Internat. Hotel Sales Mgmt. Assn., Am. Hotel Motel Assn. (industry adv. council 1974—, trustee Ednl. Inst. 1978-87, Lamplighter award 1986, writer food and beverage manual; chmn. resort com. 1978, chmn. bd. 1979), N.J. Hotel Motel Assn. (pres. 1971-72, chmn. bd. 1972-75, trustee, life mem., Arthur Goldman award 1976), Atlantic City Hotel Assn. (trustee 1976—, pres. 1980-82, chmn. 1982-84, chmn. emeritus 1984), mem. Confrerie dela Chaines des Rotisseurs Bailli, Atlantc City, 1980-87, chmn. emeritus, 1987—. Mem. NYU Hotel and Restaurant Soc. (hon. life), Hotel and Restaurant Mgmt. Soc. Fairleigh Dickenson U. (life), Ednl. Inst. Am. Hotel/Motel (Ambassador at large 1986, cert. hotel adminstr., cert. food and beverage exec.), Waldorf Astoria Disting. Alumni Assn. (chmn. 1973—), Am. Legion. Episcopalian. Clubs: Skal, Lambs (N.Y.C.); Circus Saints and Sinners (life); Seaview Country (Absecon, N.J.). Home: 1 S Somerset Ave Ventnor NJ 08406

REYES, CANDACE MULCAHY, business administrator; b. Chgo., Feb. 16, 1946; d. Robert Emmet and Rita Helen (Schultz) Mulcahy; m. Phillip John Manzella, Aug. 18, 1964 (div. May 1967); 1 child, Janet Manzella; m. James Theodore Shell, Aug. 13, 1971 (div. May 1976); 1 child, Julia; m. Jaime Magbual Reyes, Aug. 12, 1978 (July 1987). Commodity broker Earl K. Riley, Chgo., 1968-72; acct. R.J. O'Brien, Chgo., 1974-75; commodity broker E.F. Hutton, Chgo., 1975-77; make-up artist Elizabeth Arden, Chgo., 1977-78; acct. Crocker Nat. Bank, San Francisco, 1978-80; bus. adminstr. Jaime Reyes, Casa Grande, Ariz., 1980—. Fund raiser Pinal County Med. Soc. Aux., Casa Grande, Ariz., 1983—. Fellow AMA Aux. (del. 1984), Nat. Assn. Female Execs., Pinal County Med. Soc. Aux. (pres. 1984-85), Assn. Phillippine Practicing Physicians Ariz. Aux. (sec. 1983, treas. 1982), Internat. Platform Assn. Roman Catholic. Home: 5265 W Devon Ave Chicago IL 60646 Office: 1131 Avenida Fresca Casa Grande AZ 85222

REYES, PEDRO M., JR., pediatric surgeon; b. Manila, Nov. 11, 1919; s. Pedro Ysidro and Mariquita (Ochinngco) R.; m. Virginia Evanugzelista Reyes; children: Pedro III, Dennis, Ariel. MD, U. Philippines, Manila, 1944. Assoc. prof. surgery U. Philippines Philippine Gen. Hosp., 1958-84, Far Eastern U. Inst. Medicine, 1970-88; head dept. pediatric surgery Philippine Children's Hosp., Quezon City, 1970-86; med. dir., chief surgeon Childrens Med. Ctr., Quezon City, 1976—; med. dir., chief surgeon Childrens Med. Ctr., Quezen City, 1976—. Contbr. profl. jours. and textbooks. Fellow Am. Coll. Surgeons, Am. Acad. Pediatrics; mem. Brit. Assn. Pediatric Surgeons, Internat. Coll. Pediatrics, Asian Assn. Pediatric Surgeons (treas. 1976-88). Home: 109 Apo St Sta Mesa Hts, Quezon City Philippines Home: Childrens Med Ctr, 11 Banawe St, Quezon City Philippines

REYNDERS, MICHEL ALBERT JOSEPH P., pathologist; b. Brussels, Belgium, June 29, 1931; s. Joseph Henri J. and Ludwine Ida (Viscountess de Preud'homme d'Hailly de Nieuport) R.; came to U.S., 1961, naturalized, 1966; M.D., U. of Louvain, (Belgium), 1959; m. Colette De Peet; children—Jean-Noel, Dominique. Freelance journalist, Belgium, 1952-59; intern and surg. resident U. Louvain Med. Center, Belgium, 1958-61; resident U. Colo. Med. Center, Denver, 1961-66; practice medicine specializing in pathology; asso. pathologist Bergen Pines Hosp., Paramus, N.J., 1967; pathologist Porter Meml. Hosp., Denver, 1967—; assoc. clin. prof. pathology Sch. Medicine, U. Colo., 1967—. Diplomate Am. Bd. Pathology. Named hon. vice-consul Belgium. Fellow Coll. Am. Pathologists, Internat. Soc. Hematology, Internat. Soc. Thrombosis Haemostasis, Am. Soc. Coagulationist (founding); mem. AMA, Colo., Denver med. socs., Am. Soc. Abdominal Surgeons, Am. Soc. Cytology, Internat. Soc. Hematology, Mediterranean League Thrombo-Embolic Diseases, Alliance Francaise de Denver (dir., editor newsletter), Chevaliers du Tastevin. Roman Catholic Home: 131 S Birch St Denver CO 80222 Office: 2525 S Downing St Denver CO 80210

REYNOLDS, ARTHUR SIMPSON, investment banker; b. Hartford, Conn., Mar. 25, 1944; s. Arthur Simpson and Virginia (Richardson) R.; m. Catharine Prendergast, June 9, 1967; 1 child, Christopher. AB, Columbia U., 1965; MA, Cambridge U., 1967; MBA, NYU, 1977. Asst. treas. Morgan Guaranty Trust Co., N.Y.C., 1973-75; mgr. J.P. Morgan Interfunding Corp., N.Y.C., 1975-77; v.p. Banque de la Société Financiere Européene, N.Y.C., 1977-78; dir. Merrill Lynch Internat. Bank, Ltd., London, 1979-82; mng. dir. Ferghana Ltd., London, 1982—; mng. dir. London and Overseas Ltd., 1986—. Treas. Barnsley Parish Ch. Council, Gloucestershire, 1982—; chmn. Bells Appeal, Barnsley, Gloucestershire, 1986—. Mem. Oriental Ceramic Soc. (treas. 1979—). Clubs: Union, Racquet and Tennis (N.Y.C.). Home: 6 Swan Walk, London SW3 4JJ, England Office: Ferghana Ltd, 25 Queen Anne St, London W1M 9FB, England

REYNOLDS, DANA DRUMMOND, development executive; b. Flemington, W.Va., Nov. 22, 1908; s. Wayland Fuller and Inez (Brohard) R.; m. Lorna Woollacott Murphy, Sept. 12, 1933; children: Winifred W. (Mrs. R. Garcia), Deirdre A. Madden, Lorna Jean, John Dana. AB, W.Va. U., 1930; postgrad., George Washington U., 1943, 46, Am. U., 1948. Editorial asst. Agr. Extension Service, W.Va. U., 1927, asst. editor, 1928, acting editor, 1929; staff office of info. Dept. Agr., 1930-33, 36-43, 46-48; staff President's Inter-Agy. Com. for Upper Monongahela Valley, acting sec. for preparation of report, 1934-35; liaison agrl. information Dept. Agr.-ECA, 1949-50; food and agrl. specialist ECA-Mut. Security Agy., 1951-52; chief agr. instns. br. FOA-ICA, 1953-58; adv. com. sci. communications service Inter-Am. Inst. Agrl. Scis., Turrialba, 1955-58; dep. food and agr. officer U.S. Ops. Mission to, Libya, 1958-60; extension tng. adviser to U.S. Ops. Mission to, Afghanistan, 1960-63; cons. AID, other orgns., 1963- 68; pvt. cons. internat. devel. strategy 1968-70; pres. Internat. Center for Dynamics of Devel., 1971—; organized world conf. Country Strategies to Involve People in Devel., 1975; Center co-sponsor with UN Inst. for Tng. and Research 2 internat. Symposia on Nat. Strategies To Build Support for Devel. in Context of New Internat. Econ. Order, 1979; organizer, coordinator Gross Nat. Waste Product Forum, 1987. Editor: symposium papers Unity and Development in the Middle East; Center report Creating Political Will for Orderly Change-10 Year Sampling of Strategies Toward Global Unity and Development. Served as lt. USNR, 1944-45. Mem. Soc. for Internat. Devel., The Networking Inst., Planetary Citizens, AAAS, Found. for Peace, Am. Acad. Polit. and Social Sci., World Future Soc., Common Cause, Acad. Polit. Sci., Center Study of Presidency, Global Tomorrow Coalition, Better World Soc., Ctr. for Study Democracy, Nat. Dem. Inst., Nat. Mus. Women in the Arts, Kappa Tau Alpha. Address: 4201 S 31st St #616 Arlington VA 22206

REYNOLDS, DAVID, educator; b. Gosport, Hants., Eng., May 3, 1949; s. Colin and Joyce (Jones) R. B.Sc. in Sociology, U. Essex, Eng., 1971. Sci. staff Med. Research Council, Cardiff, Wales, 1971-75; lectr. Univ. Coll. Cardiff, 1975—; hon. clin. tchr. Wales Nat. Sch. Medicine, 1972-82; vis. fellow Cornell U., Ithaca, N.Y., summer 1981; polit. adv. Welsh Nationalist Party, House of Commons, London, 1982—; cons. in field. Edn. editor Arcade Mag., 1981-83; author: Studying School Effectiveness, 1985; Bringing Schools Back In, 1986; The Comprehensive Experiment, 1987; Education Policy, 1987; also articles in profl. jours. Cornell U. scholar, 1977; Welsh Office grantee, 1978-82, 86; Spencer Found. grantee, 1977-81; Manpower Services Commn. grantee, 1981-82. Mem. Internat. Sociol. Assn., Welsh Union of Writers. Welsh Nationalist. Club: BBC. Office: Univ Coll Cardiff, PO Box 78, Cardiff Wales

REYNOLDS, DAVID PARHAM, metals company executive; b. Bristol, Tenn., June 16, 1915; s. Richard S. and Julia L. (Parham) R.; m. Margaret Harrison, Mar. 25, 1944; children: Margaret A., Julia P., Dorothy H. Student, Princeton U. With Reynolds Metals Co., Louisville, 1937—, salesman, 1937-41, asst. mgr. aircraft parts div., 1941-44, asst. v.p., 1944-46, v.p., 1946-58, exec. v.p., 1958-69, exec. v.p., gen. mgr., 1969-75, vice chmn., chmn. exec. com., 1975-76, chief exec. officer, 1976-86, chmn. bd., 1986—; also dir., chmn. Eskimo Pie Corp. Trustee Lawrenceville Sch. (N.J.), U. Richmond; bd. dirs. United Negro Coll. Fund.; mem. Bus. Com. for the Arts. Mem. Internat. Primary Aluminum Assn. (past chmn.), AIA (hon.). Office: Reynolds Metals Co 6601 Broad Street Rd Richmond VA 23261

REYNOLDS, JO (SCHOLZE), educational administrator; b. Sarasota, Fla., Aug. 15, 1941; d. Joseph Wendling and Frances (Amsden) Scholze; m. James Hooks Reynolds, Dec. 27, 1959 (div. May 1985); children: Jamie Jo, James Burton. AA, Palm Beach Jr. Coll., 1967; BS, Fla. Atlantic U., 1968, MEd, 1973; EdD, Nova U., 1987. Tchr. J.I. Leonard High Sch., Lake Worth, Fla., 1968-73; dean Conniston Jr. High Sch., West Palm Beach, Fla., 1973-76, Congress Middle Sch., Boynton Beach, Fla., 1976-79; asst. prin. Forest Hill High Sch., West Palm Beach, 1979-83; prin. Palm Beach pub. sch., Fla., 1983-87, Wellington Landings Community Middle Sch., Fla., 1987—; chmn. county secondary curriculum com., 1985-86. Contbr. poetry to various publs. Former Tchrs. Sarasota scholar, 1959; Selby Found. scholar and grantee, 1967. Mem. Nat. Assn. Secondary Sch. Prins., fla. Assn. Secondary Sch. Prins., Am. Assn. Sch. Adminstrs., Palm Beach C. of C. Democrat. Baptist. Office: Wellington Landings Mid Sch 1100 Aero Club Dr West Palm Beach FL 33414

REYNOLDS, JOSEPH MELVIN, university official, physicist, educator; b. Woodlawn, Tenn., June 16, 1924; s. James Jennings and Frances (Shelby) R.; m. Ruth Anna Heise, Sept. 2, 1950; children: Molly Elizabeth Reynolds Kuribayashi, John Shelby, Wendy Lee. B.A., Vanderbilt U., 1946; M.S., Yale U., 1947, Ph.D., 1950. Asst. prof. physics La. State U., Baton Rouge, 1950-54, assoc. prof., 1954-58, prof. physics, 1958-62, Boyd prof., 1962—, v.p. instrn. and research, 1965-81, v.p. acad. affairs, 1981-85; v.p. emeritus La. State U., 1985—; vis. prof. Kamerlingh Onnes Lab., U. Leiden, Netherlands, 1959, Stanford U., 1969-70; mem. nat. sci. bd. NSF, 1966-78; mem. naval studies bd. Nat. Acad. Scis., 1974-79, chmn. panel on advanced nav. tech., 1978—, mem. space sci. bd., 1988—; chmn. PACE sci. rev. bd. NASA, 1983—; mem. task force on sci. uses of space sta. NASA/Space and Earth Scis. Adv. Com., 1984-87; mem. space sta. lab. module adv. group George C. Marshall Space Flight Ctr., 1985-87; NASA rep. on Internat. Forum on Sci. Uses of Space Sta., 1985-87. Contbr. articles to profl. jours. Bd. visitors Bernice P. Bishop Mus., Honolulu, 1978-84. Sheffield-Loomis fellow, 1948; Guggenheim fellow, 1958. Fellow Am. Phys. Soc., AAAS; mem. Am. Inst. Astronautics and Aeros., Am. Inst. Physics (bd. govs. 1987—), Sigma Xi. Clubs: Cosmos, So. Yacht. Home: 998 W Lakeview Dr Baton Rouge LA 70810 Office: La State U Dept Physics and Astronomy Baton Rouge LA 70803

REYNOLDS, LINDA CAROLINE, writer, educator; b. Ft. Worth, Jan. 20; d. James Daniel and Martha Caroline (Valigura) Little; BBA, Tex. Christian U., 1965, MBA, 1970. Tchr., Ft. Worth Pub. Schs., 1965-73; instr. Tarrant County Jr. Coll., 1974-75, Tex. Christian U., Ft. Worth, 1976-85; self-employed writer, lectr. and cons., Ft. Worth, 1976—. Bd. dirs. Mus. Western Transp.; active Van Cliburn INternat. Friends, Opera Guild. Mem. Am. Vocat. Assn., Am. Bus. Communication Assn., Tex. Bus. Edn. Assn., Nat. Bus. Edn. Assn. Author: Snow Country Typewriting Practice Set, 1974; Air Country Typewriting Practice Set, 1980; Gymnastics Unlimited Typewriting Practice Set, 1987; Letters PLUS, 1987; Dimensions in Personal Development, 1976; Dimensions in Professional Development, 1982, 3d edit., 1988. Office: PO Box 100534 Fort Worth TX 76185

REYNOLDS, NANCY BRADFORD DUPONT (MRS. WILLIAM GLASGOW REYNOLDS), sculptor; b. Greenville, Del., Dec. 28, 1919; d. Eugene Eleuthere and Catherine Dulcinea (Moxham) duPont; student Goldey-Beacom Coll., Wilmington, Del., 1938; m. William Glasgow Reynolds, May 18, 1940; children—Kathrine Glasgow Reynolds, William Bradford, Mary Parminter Reynolds Savage, Cynthia duPont Reynolds Farris. Exhibited one-woman shows: Rehoboth (Del.) Art League, 1963, Del. Art Mus., Wilmington, Caldwell, Inc., 1975, Wilmington Art Mus., 1976; exhibited group shows: Corcoran Gallery, Washington, 1943, Soc. Fine Arts, Wilmington, 1937, 38, 40, 41, 48, 50, 62, 65, NAD, N.Y.C., 1964, Pa. Mil. Coll., Chester, 1966, Del. Art Center, 1967, Met. Mus. Art, N.Y.C., 1977, Lever House, N.Y.C., 1979; represented in permanent collections: Wilmington Trust Co., E.I. duPont de Nemours & Co., Children's Home, Inc., Claymont, Del., Children's Bur., Wilmington, Stephenson Sci. Center, Nashville, Lutheran Towers Bldg., Travelers Aid and Family Soc. Bldg., Wilmington, Bronze Fountain Head, Longwood Gardens, Kennett Square, Pa. Guide, mem. research staff Henry Francis DuPont Winterthur Mus., 1955-63. Organizer vol. service Del. chpt. ARC, 1938-39; chmn. Com. for Revision Del. Child Adoption Law, 1950-52; pres. bd. dirs. Children Bur. Del.; pres., trustee Children's Home, Inc. Recipient Confrerie des Chevaliers du Tastevin Clos de Vougeot-Bourgogne France, 1960; Hort. award Garden Club Am., 1964, medal of Merit, 1976; Dorothy Platt award Garden Club of Phila., 1980; Alumni medal of merit Westover Sch., Middlebury, Conn. Mem. Pa. Hort. Soc., Wilmington Soc. Fine Arts, Mayflower Descs., Del. Hist. Soc., Colonial Dames, League Am. Pen Women, Nat. Trust Hist. Preservation. Episcopalian. Clubs: Garden of Wilmington (past pres.), Garden of Am. (past asst. zone 4 chmn.), Vicmead Hunt, Greenville Country, Chevy Chase (Washington); Colony (N.Y.C.). Contbr. articles to profl. jours. Address: PO Box 3919 Greenville DE 19807

REYNOLDS, PETER JAMES, physicist; b. N.Y.C., Nov. 19, 1949; s. Rudolph and Lydia Mary (Schanzer) R.; m. Louise Perini, Aug. 7, 1982. AB in Physics, U. Calif., Berkeley, 1971; Ph.D., MIT, 1979. Research assoc. and lectr. Boston U., 1979, asst. research prof., 1979-83; mem. sci. staff Nat. Resource for Computation in Chemistry, Lawrence Berkeley Lab., U. Calif., 1980-81, mem. research staff materials and chem. scis. div., 1982—; vis. scientist NEC Fundamental Research Lab., Kawasaki, Japan, 1986; adj. assoc. prof. dept. chemistry San Francisco State U., 1988—; vis. research chemist, U. Calif., Berkeley, 1988—; lectr. and researcher in field of chem., statis. and computational physics and Monte Carlo Methods. Contbr. chpts. to books, articles in field to profl. jours. NSF fellow, 1971-74, IBM fellow, 1975; Lawrence Berkeley Lab. grantee, 1982-83. Mem. AAAS, Am. Phys. Soc., N.Y. Acad. Scis., Phi Beta Kappa, Sigma Xi. Lutheran. Office: Office Naval Research Physics Div 800 N Quincy St Arlington VA 22217

REYNOLDS, R. WALLACE, technical writer, emeritus educator; b. Pitts., Apr. 30, 1914; s. Raymond O. and Anna May (Kime) R.; BS, California U. Pa. (name formerly State Tchrs. Coll.), 1940; MS, Purdue U., 1946; postgrad. U. Pitts., 1946, U. So. Calif., 1948; m. Marjorie Frances Johnson, June 25, 1943; children—Marjorie Wallace, Timothy Lincoln. Engr., Douglas Aircraft Co., 1942, Naval Ordnance Lab., 1942-46; prof., chmn. engring. drawing Washington & Jefferson Coll., 1946-47, U. Santa Clara, 1947-48, West Coast U., 1949-52, Calif. Poly. State U., 1953-79, prof. emeritus, 1979—; mgr. R. Wallace Reynolds Drafting Service, San Luis Obispo, 1968-78; cons. U.S. Bur. Ships, 1955-58; sr. engr. design sect. Jet Propulsion Lab., Pasadena, 1975. Dem committeeman, San Luis Obispo County, 1956-63. Recipient certificate of commendation, U.S. Naval Ordnance Lab., 1945; Excellence award Visual Communications Industry, 1968. Fellow Am. Soc. Cert. Engring. Technicians; mem. Am. Soc. Engring. Edn. (sec. Pacific Southwest sect. 1969-75, chmn. 1976-77, 78-80, nat. dir. 1978-80, life mem.), Am. Inst. Drafting and Design (v.p. edn. Calif. chpt. 1967-69, dir. Central Coast 1972-75), Nat. Assn. Civilian Conservation Corps Alumni, (exec. dir. 1981-82, gen. chmn. 5th biennial nat. conv. 1987), Phi Sigma Pi, Tau Alpha Pi. Author: Problems for Modern Engineering Drawing, 1956-67. Home: 577 Princeton Pl San Luis Obispo CA 93401

REYNOLDS, ROBERT GREGORY, toxicologist, management consultant; b. Chgo., July 29, 1952; s. Robert G. and Loys Delle (Kever) R.; m. Phyllis Thurrell, May 1983. B.S. in Nutrition and Food Sci., MIT, 1973, postgrad. in toxicology, 1973-78; postgrad. in mgmt. Sloan Sch. Mgmt., 1977-78. Mng. editor The Graduate Mag., MIT, 1975-78; v.p. Internat. Contact Bur., Ft. Lauderdale, Fla., 1977—; staff toxicologist, asst. to v.p. mktg. Enviro Control, Inc., Rockville, Md., 1978-79; dir. tech. resources Borriston Research Labs., Inc., Temple Hills, Md., 1979-80; dir. mktg. Northrop Services Inc., Research Triangle Park, N.C., 1980-88, mgr. bus. devel., NSI Tech. Services Corp., 1988—; mgmt. cons., 1981—; toxicol. cons. Energy Resources Co., Inc., Cambridge, 1976-77. NSF fellow, 1973. Mem. Am. Acad. Clin. Toxicology, Air Pollution Control Assn., AAAS. Episcopalian. Contbr. chpts. to textbook, lab. manual, sci. jours. and govt. publs. Office: NSI Technology Services Corp PO Box 12313 Research Triangle Park NC 27709

REYNOLDS, THOMAS ELLIOTT, public relations executive; b. New Orleans, Jan. 11, 1953; s. Jack Maurice and Mary Jean (Keith) R.; m. Deborah Kay Hart, May 1, 1976; children: Heather Elizabeth, Elisabeth Anne. Student Mich. State U., 1971-72; AB cum laude, U. Detroit, 1975. Staff writer, feature writer New Orleans Daily Record, 1974-75; freelance writer, public relations cons., Detroit and New Orleans, 1975-76; assoc. dir. instl. advancement Detroit Coll. Law, 1977-86; account supr. P.R. Assocs., Inc., Detroit, 1986—. Mem. Pub. Relations Soc. Am., Detroit Sports Broadcasters Assn., Sigma Delta Chi. Author: Renaissance Center-The Symbol of a Great City's Rebirth, 1980; The Detroit College of Law Student Guide, 1980. Clubs: Adcraft.

REYNOLDS, THOMAS MORGAN, chemical company executive; b. Jackson, Tenn., Nov. 28, 1943; s. Albert Morgan and Tommie Orleigh (Melton) R.; student So. Ill. U., 1962-63; B.S.B.A., Roosevelt U., 1982; 1 son, Brent Morgan. With Wyandotte Chems., St. Louis, 1965-68, Allied-Kelite Div., Witco, Chgo., 1969-82; electronic industry mgr. M & T Chems., Chgo., 1982-84; v.p. NCA Systems, Chgo., 1984-85, pres. Reynolds & Co., 1985—, v.p. Lamina, Inc., 1985—. Mem. Electronic Connector Study Group (founder Midwest chpt.), Am. Electroplaters Soc., Am. Soc. Metals, Interconnection Packaging Circuitry, Midwest Circuit Assn. (founder). Home: 1605 E Central Rd Arlington Heights IL 60005 Office: 30 N 8th Ave Maywood IL 60153

REYNOLDS, WILLIAM GLASGOW, lawyer; b. Dover, Tenn., July 15, 1911; s. John Lacey and Harriett Edwina (Glasgow) R.; m. Nancy Bradford du Pont, May 18, 1940; children: Katherine Glasgow (Mrs. John M. Sturges, Jr.), William Bradford, Mary Parminter (Mrs. John Schofield Savage), Cynthia du Pont (Mrs. Kermit Nelson Farris). A.B., Vanderbilt U., 1932, J.D. summa cum laude, 1935. Bar: Tenn. 1935, D.C. bar 1964, also U.S. Supreme Ct 1945. Gen. practice Nashville, 1934-35; with E. I. du Pont de Nemours & Co., 1935-71, chief counsel advt., pub. relations and central research depts., 1954-71; with firm Morris, Nichols, Arsht & Tunnell, Wilmington, Del., 1972—; resident counsel Remington Arms Co., Bridgeport,

Conn., 1940-41; with Office Gen. Counsel, U.S. Navy, 1942-43, Exec. Office Sec. Navy, 1944, Office Asst. Sec. Navy, 1945; Permanent mem. jud. conf. 3d Jud. Circuit U.S., 1955—; rep. chem. industry Water Resources Policy Com., 1950; mem. adv. com. Patent Office, Dept. Commerce, 1954; mem. Internat. Conf. Indsl. and Municipal Air Pollution, 1949; chmn. Nat. Com. Assay U.S. Mints, 1958; Am. indsl. rep. Com. Experts on Internat. Trademark Treaties, 1969-71, U.S. Govt. rep., 1972-73; del. numerous internat. confs.; dir. Del. Trust Co., Wilmington, 1974-85, mem. exec. com., 1976-85, trust com., 1976-85; mem. vis. com. Law Sch., Vanderbilt U., 1968, mem. chancellor's council, 1968—, chmn. Law Sch. devel. council, 1968. Author: The Law of Water and Water Rights in the Tenn. River Valley, 1934, Local Restrictions on the Pollution of Inland Waters, 1948, Trademark Management—A Guide for Businessmen, 1955, Trademark Selection, 1960, The Chemical Engineer and Public Liability Law, 1962, A Brief for Corporate Counsel, 1964, Legal Servicing of Industrial Publicity, 1967, Planning a Bonsai Collection, 1968, Reynolds History Annotated, 1978, also numerous articles, treatises. Alternate del. Republican Nat. Conv., 1956; mem. Rep. Nat. Com. Assos., 1956-65; Bd. dirs., sec. Rencourt Found. Del., 1955—; bd. dirs. United Community Fund No. Del., 1948-53, exec. com., 1949-51; trustee, chmn. bldg. com. Children's Home, Claymont and Wilmington, 1946-47, pres., 1947-51; bd. dir., mem. bldg. com. Del. Art Center, 1948-64. Recipient Founders medal Vanderbilt U. Law Sch., 1935, U.S. Navy commendations, 1943, 45. Mem. Mfg. Chemists Assn. (chmn. lawyers adv. com. 1954), U.S. Trademark Assn. (chmn. bd., pres. 1964-65), Assn. Internationale pour la Protection de la Propertie Industrielle, Am., Fed., D.C., Del. bar assns., Del., Tenn. trial lawyers assns., Nashville Bar Assn., Navy League U.S., Vanderbilt Alumni Assn. (bd. dirs. 1961-64), Vanderbilt Law Alumni (pres. 1970-71), Am., Pa. Bonsai societies, Sons Colonial Wars in Am., SAR, Order of Coif, Phi Kappa Psi. Episcopalian (past warden, vestryman, chmn. bldg. com.). Clubs: Confrerie des Chevaliers du Tastevin (grand officier Wilmington chpt. 1972, mem. nat. council 1973, grant intendant Eastern U.S. 1975, delé ge general 1976, grand pelier gen. U.S. 1977, of N. Am. 1978, bd. dirs., pres. found. 1979-81), Chevy Chase (Md.) Country; Griffith Island (Ont., Can.); Aurora Gun (Greenville, Del.), Greenville Country (Greenville, Del.) (bd. dirs. 1962-65), Vicmead Hunt (Greenville, Del.); Wilmington. Home: PO Box 3919 Greenville DE 19807 Office: 1702 Am International Bldg Wilmington DE 19801 *Died Jan. 29, 1987.*

REYNOLDS, WILLIAM JENSEN, church musician, hymnologist, composer; b. Atlantic, Iowa, Apr. 2, 1920; s. George Washington and Ethel (Horn) R.; student Okla. Baptist U., 1937-39; A.B., Southwest Mo. State Coll., 1942; M.S.M., Southwestern Bapt. Theol. Sem., 1945; M.M., N. Tex. State U., 1946; Ed.D., George Peabody Coll. Tchrs. 1961; m. Mary Lou Robertson, July 6, 1947; children—Timothy Jensen, Kirk Mallory. Minister of music First Bapt. Ch., Ardmore, Okla., 1946-47, First Bapt. Ch., Oklahoma City, 1947-55; music editor Ch. Music dept. Bapt. Sunday Sch. Bd., Nashville, 1955-62, dir. editorial services, 1962-67, supr. music publs., 1967-71, head ch. music dept., 1971-80; guest prof. Southwestern Bapt. Theol. Sem., Ft. Worth, 1980—, prof. ch. music Sch. Ch. Music, 1981—; music dir. So. Bapt. Conv., Houston, 1958, Phila., 1972, Portland, Oreg., 1973, Dallas, 1974, Miami Beach, 1975, Norfolk, 1976, Kansas City, 1977, 83, 84, Atlanta, 1978, 86, Houston, 1979, St. Louis, 1980, Los Angeles, 1981, New Orleans, 1982, Pitts., 1983, Dallas, 1985; music dir. Bapt. World Alliance, Rio de Janeiro, 1960, Stockholm, 1975, Toronto, 1980, Los Angeles, 1985; music dir. Bapt. World Youth Conf., Toronto, 1958, Beirut, 1963, Berne, 1968; nat. cons. Ctr. for Study of So. Culture, U. Miss.; mem. hymnal com. Baptist Hymnal, 1956; chmn. hymnal com., gen. editor Baptist Hymnal, 1975; gen. editor New Broadman Hymnal, 1977; composer: Ichthus, 1971; Reaching People, 1973; Share His Word, 1973; Bold Mission, 1977; numerous choral anthems, hymn tunes, songs, etc.; dir. Sacred Harp Pub. Co.; lectr., clinician, condr. seminars and workshops in ch. music; adjudicator music festivals. Author: A Survey of Christian Hymnody, 1963; Hymns of our Faith, 1964; Christ and the Carols, 1967; Congregational Singing, 1975; Companion to the Baptist Hymnal, 1976; Christian Hymnody, 1983; co-author: A Joyful Song: Christian Hymnody, 1977, A Survey of Christian Hymnody, 1987; compiler: Building an Effective Music Ministry, 1980; weekly newspaper columnist History of Hymns. Bd. dirs. John W. Work Meml. Found. Recipient B.B. McKinney Found. award, 1960; W. Hines Sims Achievement award, 1971; N. Tex. State U. Sch. Music Alumni citation, 1972. Mem. Hymn Soc. Am. (pres. 1978-80), Ch. Music Pubs. Assn. (v.p. 1973-75), ASCAP, Nat. Acad. Rec. Arts and Scis., Gospel Music Assn., So. Bapt. Ch. Music Conf., Harpeth Valley Sacred Harp Singing Assn. (pres. 1966-80). Home: 6750 Cartagena Ct Fort Worth TX 76133

REYNOSO, REMEDIOS LOPEZ, dermatologist; b. Indang, Cavite, Philippines, Nov. 22, 1940; d. Buenaventura Mojica and Juana Cruzena (Umali) L.; m. Luis Dinginbayan Reynoso; children: Cynthia, Allan, Zoraida, Newson, Frances Ian. MD, Manila Cen. U., 1969. Practicing medicine specializing in gen. practice 1969-73; resident Dermatology Research and Tng. Ctr., 1975-76; lectr. 1976-80, practicing medicine specializing in dermatology, 1976—; sr. cons.dermatology Office of Pres. Malacanang Clinic, 1980—; therapist in chelation treatment, 1981—; founder, dir. Logevity Health Ctr., Phila., 1981; lectr. and cons. in field. Recipient Plaque Appreciation Ministry Health, Internat. Recognition award Schering Berlin Inc., 1f977, cert. Appreciation Office Prime Minister of Thailand, 1978, Kaunlaran award Oriental and Civic Fellowship of Phila. Inc., 1981 and numerous other awards. Mem. Am. Coll. Advancement Medicine, Phila. Med. Assn., Internat. Coll. Tropical Dermatology, Phila. Soc. Dermatology and Aesthetic Medicine. Home: 112 Tipas, Taguig, Metro Manila Philippines 3136 Office: PDC Bldg, 1440 Taft Ave, Manila Philippines 500-2528

REY PALENZUELA, JAVIER, service company executive; b. Bilbao, Vizcaya, Spain, Jan. 6, 1938; s. Teofilo and Rosario (Palenzuela) Rey J.; m. Teresa Tobalina, July 24, 1964; children: Javier, Asuncion, Agueda, Monica. Diploma in Tech. Engring., Tech. Engring. Sch., Bilbao, 1958; M in Engring., Engring. High Sch., Bilbao, 1965. Dir. orgn. Babcock & Wilcox Spain, Bilbao, 1966-70, foundry and forging dir., 1970-76, dir. indsl. relations, 1976-78; group tech. dir. Eulen Group, Bilbao, 1978-84; dir., v.p. Eulen Group, Madrid, 1984—. Author: Process of Fabricating for Steel Castings, 1975; contbr. articles to profl. jours. Served with Spanish Navy, 1958-59. C. of C. grantee Bilbao, 1952. Mem. Coll. Master Indsl. Engrs. Roman Catholic. Office: Eulen SA Carretera de La Coruña, Km 17900, 28230 Las Rozas Madrid Spain

REZEK, EDWARD ANTHONY, electrical engineer; b. Omaha, July 19, 1954; s. Edward George and Elizabeth Helen (Kuckta) R.; m. Gloria Elia Lopez-Sauer, Nov. 14, 1981. B.S. in Elec. Engring., Washington U., St. Louis, 1976; A.B. in Physics, 1976; M.S. in Elec. Engring., U. Ill., Urbana, 1977, Ph.D., 1980. Mem. tech. staff TRW Tech. Research Ctr., El Segundo, Calif., 1980-84; sect. head TRW Electro-Optics Research Ctr., Redondo Beach, Calif., 1984-85, dept. mgr., 1985-86, program mgr., 1986—. Contbr. articles to profl. jours. Patentee crystal growth technique, optoelectronic devices Mem. IEEE, Electrochem. Soc., Am. Phys. Soc., AAAS, Tau Beta Pi, Eta Kappa Nu, Omicron Delta Kappa, Phi Kappa Phi. Republican. Roman Catholic. Home: 4720 Paseo de las Tortugas Torrance CA 90505

REZZONICO, RENZO, lawyer; b. Lugano, Switzerland, Nov. 18, 1929; s. Nino and Blanche (Schlaeppi) R. Doctorate summa cum laude, U. Basle, 1955; postgrad. in econs., U. Lausanne, 1956. Sec. Swiss Fed. Tribunal, Lausanne, 1956-58; sole practice, Lugano, Switzerland, 1958—. Author, editor: Helbing and Lichtenhahn, 1955. Mem. Internat. Bar. Assn., Internat. Tax Planning Assn. Home: Via Orbisana 37, 6932 Biogno di Breganzona Switzerland Studio: Studio Legale-Notarile Avv, Renzo Rezzonico, Piazza Dante, 6901 Lugano Switzerland

RHEE, JIN HONG, orthopaedic surgeon; b. Choong Ju, Korea, Feb. 6, 1939; came to U.S., 1969, naturalized, 1978; s. Chol Kyu and Hae Ok (Park) R.; M.D., Seoul Nat. U., 1965; m. Chong Ja Kim, Oct. 30, 1968; children—David, Patricia, Paul. Resident in gen. surgery Jewish Meml. Hosp., N.Y.C., 1970-71; resident in orthopaedic surgery Thomas Jefferson U. Hosp., Phila., 1971-74; fellow in hand surgery Columbia Presbyn. Hosp., N.Y.C., 1974; practice medicine specializing in orthopaedic surgery, Havre de Grace, Md., 1975—; attending orthopaedic surgeon Harford Meml. Hosp., Havre de Grace, 1975—, Fallston (Md.) Gen. Hosp., 1975-78. Diplomate Am. Bd. Orthopaedic Surgery. Fellow Am. Acad. Orthopaedic Surgeons; mem. AMA, Am. Acad. Orthopaedic Surgery, Med. and Chirurg. Faculty of State of Md. Home: 3653 Harmony Church Rd Havre de Grace MD 21078 Office: 601 S Union Ave Havre de Grace MD 21078

RHEE, YANG HO, radiologist; b. Kunsan, Republic of Korea, Mar. 22, 1943; came to U.S., 1973; s. Young Whan and Ae Wol (Rah) R.; m. Shin Ae Kang; children: Hoyeon, Thomas, Karen. MD, Chonnam Med. Sch., Kwangj, Republic of Korea, 1968. Diplomate Am. Bd. Radiology. Intern Seoul Adventist Hosp., Republic of Korea, 1972-73, Cook County Hosp., Chgo., 1973-74; resident Hines (Ill.) VA Hosp., 1974-77; staff physician Illini Hosp., Silvis, Ill., 1977—. Chmn. bd. trustees Quad City Korean Assn., Ill. and Iowa, 1986—, v.p., 1980-81; mem. adv. council on peaceful unification policy Republic of Korea, 1984—; chmn. dept. radiology Illini Hosp., Silvis, Ill., 1988—. Served to capt. Korean Army, 1968-72, Korea and Vietnam. Mem. AMA, Am. Coll. Radiology, Radiol. Soc. N.Am., Soc. Nuclear Medicine, Am. Inst. Ultrasound in Medicine. Office: 801 Hospital Rd Silvis IL 61282

RHEINSTEIN, PETER HOWARD, government official, physician, lawyer; b. Cleve., Sept. 7, 1943; s. Franz Joseph Rheinstein and Hede Henrietta (Neheimer) Rheinstein Lerner; m. Miriam Ruth Weissman, Feb. 22, 1969; 1 child, Jason Edward. B.A. with high honors, Mich. State U., 1963, M.S., 1964; M.D., Johns Hopkins U., 1967; J.D., U. Md., 1973. Bar: Md., D.C.; diplomate Am. Bd. Family Practice. Intern USPHS Hosp., San Francisco, 1967-68; resident in internal medicine USPHS Hosp., Balt., 1968-70; practice medicine specializing in internal medicine Balt., 1970—; instr. medicine U. Md., Balt., 1970-73; med. dir. extended care facilities CHC Corp., Balt., 1972-74; dir. drug advt. and labeling div. FDA, Rockville, Md., 1974-82, acting dep. dir. Office Drugs, 1982-83, acting dir. Office Drugs, 1983-84, dir. Office Drug Standards, 1984—; adj. prof. forensic medicine George Washington U., 1974-76; WHO cons. on drug regulation Nat. Inst. for Control Pharm. and Biol. Products, People's Republic of China, 1981—; advisor on essential drugs WHO, 1985—; FDA del. to U.S. Pharmacopeial Conv., 1985—. Co-author: (with others) Human Organ Transplantation, 1987; spl. editorial advisor Good Housekeeping Guide to Medicine and Drugs, 1977—; mem. editorial bd. Legal Aspects Med. Practice, 1981—, Drug Info. Jour., 1982-86; contbr. articles to profl. jours. Recipient Commendable Service award FDA, 1981, group award of merit, 1983, 1988. Fellow Am. Coll. Legal Medicine (bd. govs. 1982—, treas., chmn. fin. com. 1985-88 , Pres.'s award 1985, 86), Am. Acad. Family Physicians; mem. Drug Info. Assn. (bd. dirs. 1981—, pres. 1984-85, immediate past pres. 1985-86, v.p. 1986-87, pres. elect 1987-88, pres. 1988—), Fed. Bar Assn. (chmn. food and drug com. 1976-79, Disting. Service award 1977), AMA, ABA, Med. and Chirurgical Faculty Md., Balt. City Med. Soc., Johns Hopkins Med. and Surg. Assn., Am. Pub. Health Assn., Md. Bar Assn., Math. Assn. Am., Soc. for Indsl. and Applied Math., Mensa (life), U.S. Power Squadrons, Mich. State U. Alumni Assn. (life), U. Md. Alumni Assn. (life), Johns Hopkins U. Alumni Assn., Delta Theta Phi. Clubs: Chartwell Golf and Country (Severna Park, Md.), Annapolis (Md.) Yacht, Johns Hopkins, Univ. (Balt.). Home: 621 Holly Ridge Rd Severna Park MD 21146-3520 Office: Dir Office Drug Standards FDA 5600 Fishers Ln Rockville MD 20857

RHIEW, FRANCIS CHANGNAM, physician; b. Korea, Dec. 3, 1938; s. Byung Kyun and In Sil (Lee) R.; came to U.S., 1967, naturalized, 1977; B.S., Seoul Nat. U., 1960, M.D., 1964; m. Kay Kyungja Chang, June 11, 1967; children—Richard C., Elizabeth. Intern, St. Mary's Hosp., Waterbury, Conn., 1967-68; resident in radiology and nuclear medicine L.I.U.-Queens Hosp. Center, N.Y., 1968-71; instr. radiology W. Va. U. Sch. Medicine, Morgantown, 1971-73; mem. staff Mercy Hosp. and Moses Taylor Hosp., Scranton, Pa., 1973—, also dir. nuclear medicine; clin. instr., Temple U., 1987—; pres. Radiol. Consultants, Inc., 1984—. Served with M.C., Korean Army, 1964-67. Recipient Minister of Health and Welfare award, 1963; certified Am. Bd. Nuclear Medicine. Mem. Soc. Nuclear Medicine, Radiol. Soc. N.Am., Am. Coll. Nuclear Medicine, Am. Coll. Radiology, Am. Inst. Ultra Sound, AMA. Clubs: Country of Scranton, Pres.'s U. Scranton. Lodge: Elks. Home: 101 Belmont Ave Clarks Summit PA 18411 Office: 746 Jefferson Ave Scranton PA 18501

RHIJNSBURGER, LOUISE MARINA, marketing professional; b. The Hague, The Netherlands, Aug. 13, 1950; d. Simon and Hendrika Maria (De Meyer) R.; m. Arnold Nicholaas Tuytel, Aug. 23, 1984; 1 child, Jean-Marc Roger Michel. 1st diplomaStichting Reklame en Mktg., SRM, Rotterdam, The Netherlands, 1981, 2d diploma, 1982. With export dept. Sierra, The Hague, 1974-76; sales mgr. Benelux Hellma, The Hague, 1976-78; mktg. analyst Moore Internat. B.V., The Hague, 1978-88; tchr. personal computer software Compu'Train, Utrecht, The Netherlands, 1985—; Dutch-English interpretor various cos. Clubs: Personal Computer (Zeist, The Netherlands); Hobby Computer (Amsterdam). Home: Trompweg 10, 2253 XP Voorschoten The Netherlands

RHIND, DAVID WILLIAM, geographer, educator; b. Berwick, Northumberland, Eng., Nov. 29, 1943; s. William and Christina (Abercrombie) R.; m. Christine Young, Aug. 22, 1966; children: Jonathan Dalgety, Samantha Letitia, Zoe Danielle. BSc, Bristol (Eng.) U., 1965; PhD, Edinburgh (Scotland) U., 1968. Research asst. U. Edinburgh, 1968-69; research fellow Royal Coll. Art, London, 1969-73; lectr. U. Durham, Eng., 1973-78, reader, 1978-81; prof. geography Birkbeck Coll., U. London, 1982—; mem. United Kingdom Govt. Com. Enquiry on Handling Geographic Infos., 1985-87. Co-author: Land Use, 1980, People in Britain, 1980, Census Users Handbook, 1983; contbr. articles to profl. jours. Fellow Royal Geog. Soc.; mem. Inst. Brit. Geographers. Club: Athenaeum (London). Office: U London Birkbeck Coll, 7-15 Gresse St, London W1P 1PA, England

RHIND, JAMES THOMAS, lawyer; b. Chgo., July 21, 1922; s. John Gray and Eleanor (Bradley) R.; m. Laura Haney Campbell, Apr. 19, 1958; children: Anne Constance, James Campbell, David Scott. Student, Hamilton Coll., 1940-42; A.B. cum laude, Ohio State U., 1944; LL.B. cum laude, Harvard U., 1950. Bar: Ill. bar 1950. Japanese translator U.S. War Dept., Tokyo, Japan, 1946-47; congl. liaison Fgn. Operations Adminstrn., Washington, 1954; since practiced in Chgo.; atty. Bell, Boyd & Lloyd, 1950-53, 55—, partner, 1958—; Dir. Kewaunee Scientific Corp., Wilmette, Ill., Lindberg Corp., Chgo., Microseal Corp., Zion, Ill. Commr. Gen. Assembly United Presbyn. Ch., 1963; vice chmn., trustee Hamilton Coll., Clinton, N.Y.; vice chmn., trustee U. Chgo., Northwestern Univ. Assocs.; chmn. Cook County Young Republican Orgn., 1957; Ill. Young Rep. nat. committeeman, 1957-58; v.p., mem. bd. govs. United Rep. Fund Ill., 1965-84; Pres. Ill. Childrens Home and Aid Soc., 1971-73, now life trustee; vice chmn. Ravinia Festival Assn., 1980-84, now life trustee; bd. dirs. E.J. Dalton Youth Center, 1966- 69; governing mem. Orchestral Assn., Chgo.; mem. Ill. Arts Council, 1971-75; mem. exec. com. div. Met. Mission and Ch. Extension Bd., Chgo. Presbytery, 1966-68; trustee Presbyn. Home, W. Clement and Jessie V. Stone Found., U. Chgo. Hosps. Served with M.I. AUS, 1943-46. Mem. ABA, Ill. Bar Assn., Chgo. Bar Assn. (bd. mgrs. 1967-69), Fed. Bar Assns., Chgo. Council on Fgn. Relations, Japan Am. Soc. Chgo., Legal Club Chgo., Law Club Chgo., Phi Beta Kappa, Sigma Phi. Presbyterian (elder). Clubs: Chicago (Chgo.), Glen View (Chgo.), Commercial (Chgo.), Attic (Chgo.), Economic (Chgo.). Home: 830 Normandy Ln Glenview IL 60025 Office: Three First Nat Plaza Chicago IL 60602

RHOADS, JONATHAN EVANS, surgeon; b. Phila., May 9, 1907; s. Edward G. and Margaret (Ely Paxson) R.; m. Teresa Folin, July 4, 1936 (dec. 1987); children: Margaret Rhoads Kendon, Jonathan Evans, George Grant, Edward Otto Folin, Philip Garrett, Charles James. B.A., Haverford Coll., 1928, D.Sc. (hon.), 1962; M.D., Johns Hopkins U., 1932; D. Med. Sci., U. Pa., 1940, LL.D. (hon.), 1960; D.Sc. (hon.), Swarthmore Coll., 1969, Hahnemann Med. Coll., 1978, Duke U., 1979, Med. Coll. Ohio, 1985; D.Sci. (Med.) (hon.), Med. Coll. Pa., 1974, Georgetown U., 1981; Litt.D. (hon.), Thomas Jefferson U., 1979. Intern Hosp. of U. Pa., 1932-34, fellow, instr. surgery, 1934-39; asso. surgery, surg. research U. Pa. Med. Sch., Grad. Sch. Medicine, 1939-47, asst. prof. surg. research, 1944-47, asst. prof. surgery, 1946-47, assoc. prof., 1947-49; J. William White prof. surg. research U. Pa., 1949-51; prof. surgery U. Pa. (Grad. Sch. Medicine), 1950—; prof. surgery and surg. research U. Pa. Sch. Med., 1951-57, prof. surgery, 1957-59; provost U. Pa., 1956-59, provost emeritus, 1977—, John Rhea Barton prof. surgery, chmn. dept. surgery, 1959-72, prof. surgery, 1972—, asst. dir. Harrison dept. surg. research, 1946-59, dir., 1959-72; dir. surgery Pa. Hosp., 1972-74; surg. cons. Pa. Hosp., Germantown (Pa.), Phila. VA hosps.; mem. staff Hosp. of U. Pa.; Dir. J. E. Rhoads & Sons, Inc.; Mem. bd. pub. edn., City of Phila., 1965-71; co-chmn. Phila. Mayor's Commn. on Health Aspects of Trash to Steam Plant, 1986; former mem. bd. mgrs. Haverford Coll., chmn., 1963-72, pres. corp., 1963-78; bd. mgrs. Friends Hosp. of Phila.; trustee Inst. Med. Research, 1957—, v.p. sci. affairs, 1964-76; trustee Gen. Motors Cancer Research Found.; chmn. bd. trustees Measey Found.; trustee emeritus Bryn Mawr Coll.; mem. com. in charge Westtown Sch.; treas. Germantown Friends Sch.; cons. Bur. State Services, VA, 1963; nat. adv. gen. medical scis. council USPHS, 1963; cons. to div. of medical scis. NIH, 1962-63; adv. council Life Ins. Med. Research Fund., 1961-66; Pres. Phila. div., 1955-56; chmn. adv. commn. on research on pathogenesis of cancer Am. Cancer Soc., 1956-57, del., 1956-61, dir. at large, 1965—, pres., 1969-70, past officer dir., 1970-77, hon. life mem., 1977—; chmn. surgery adv. com. Food and Drug Adminstrn., 1972-74; chmn. Nat. Cancer Adv. Bd., 1972-79; Mem. Am. Bd. Surgery, 1963-69, sr. mem., 1969—. Author, co-editor: Surgery: Principles and Practice, 1957, 61, 65, 70; author: (with J.M. Howard) The Chemistry of Trauma. mem. editorial bd.: Jour. Surg. Research, 1960-71, Oncology Times, 1979—; editor: Jour. Cancer, 1972—; mem. editorial bd. Annals of Surgery, 1947-77, emeritus, 1977—, chmn., 1971-73; mem. editorial adv. bd. Guthrie Bull., 1986—; contbr. articles to med. jours. and chpts. to books. Trustee John Rhea Barton Surg. Found. Recipient Roswell Park medal, 1973, Papanicolaou award, 1977, Phila. award, 1976, Swanberg award, 1987, Benjamin Franklin medal Am. Philos. Soc., Medal of the Surgeon Gen. of U.S.; hon. Benjamin Franklin fellow Royal Soc. Arts. Fellow Am. Med. Writers Assn., Am. Philos. Soc. (sec. 1963-66, pres. 1977-84), ACS (regent, chmn. bd. regents 1967-69, pres. 1971-72), Royal Coll. Surgeons (Eng.) (hon.), Royal Coll. Surgeons Edinburgh (hon.), Deutsches Gesellschaft für Chirurgie (corr.), Assn. Surgeons India (hon.), Royal Coll. Physicians and Surgeons Can. (hon.), Coll. Medicine South Africa (hon.), Polish Assn. Surgeons (hon.), AAAS (sec. med. sci. sect. 1980-86); mem. Hollandsche Maatschappij der Wetenschappen (fgn.), Am. Public Health Assn., Assn. Am. Med. Colls. (chmn. council acad. socs. 1968-69, disting. service mem. 1974—), Fedn. Am. Socs. Exptl. Biology, Am. Assn. Surgery Trauma, Am. Trauma Soc. (founding mem., v.p., chmn. bd. dirs. 1986), AMA (co-recipient Goldberger award 1970, Dr. Rodman and Thomas G. Sheen award 1980), Pa. Med. Soc. (Disting. service award 1975), Phila. County Med. Soc. (pres. 1970, Strittmatler award 1968), Coll. Physicians Phila. (v.p. 1954-57, pres. 1958-60, Disting. Service award 1987), Phila. Acad. Surgery (pres. 1964), Phila. Physiol. Soc. (v.p. 1945-46), Am. Surg. Assn. (pres. 1972-73, Disting. Service medal, trustee found.), Pan Pacific Surg. Assn. (v.p. 1975-77), So. Surg. Assn., The Internat. Surg. Group (pres. 1958), Internat. Fedn. Surg. Colls. (v.p. 1972-78, pres. 1978-81, hon. pres. 1987—), Fellows of Am. Studies, Soc. of U. Surgeons, Soc. Clin. Surgery (pres. 1966-68), Am. Assn. for Cancer Research, Am. Chem. Soc., Am. Physiol. Soc., Internat. Soc. Surgery (hon.) N.Y. Acad. Scis., Surg. Infection Soc. (pres. 1984-85), Surgeons Travel Club (pres. 1976, hon. mem.), Am. Inst. Nutrition, World Med. Assn., Am. Acad. Arts and Scis., Inst. of Medicine (sr.), Soc. for Surgery Alimentary Tract (pres. 1967-68), Southeastern Surg. Congress, Soc. Surg. Chmn. (pres. 1966-68), Buckingham Mountain Found. (sec., treas.), Phi Beta Kappa, Alpha Omega Alpha, Sigma Xi. Clubs: Phila. Art Alliance, Rittenhous, Union League, Philadelphia; Cosmos (D.C.). Office: 3400 Spruce St Philadelphia PA 19104

RHODES, CECIL GLENN, metallurgist; b. Leesville, Ohio, Oct. 17, 1933; s. Lloyd Howard and Sibyl Imogene (Price) R.; B.S. in Math., Calif. State U., Northridge, 1968; m. Lois Irene Spellman, Jan. 1, 1953; children—Pamela Kay, Diane Christine. Metallographer, Battelle Meml. Inst., Columbus, Ohio, 1953-56, Gen. Electric Co., Cin., 1956-59; mem. tech. staff Rockwell Internat. Co., Thousand Oaks, Calif., 1959—. Mem. AIME (publns. com. Metall. Soc.), Electron Microscopy Soc. Am., So. Calif. Electron Microscopy Soc. Author papers in field. Office: PO Box 1085 Rockwell Internat Co Thousand Oaks CA 91360

RHODES, DONALD FREDERICK, research physicist, educator; b. Johnstown, Pa., July 1, 1932; s. Frederick D. and Irene M. (Ankney) R.; m. Patricia J. Beaumariage, Dec. 22, 1956. B.S., U. Pitts., 1954, M.Litt., 1956; Ph.D., Pacific Western U., 1982. Instr. physics U. Pitts., 1954-55; engr. Westinghouse Electric Pitts., 1956-57; research physicist Gulf Research & Devel., Pitts., 1958-86; educator aviation tech., Pitts., 1975—; ind. cons. 1986—. Recipient IR 100 award Indsl. Research, 1968. Mem. Am. Nuclear Soc., Health Physics Soc. Club: Aero of Pitts. Patentee nuclear instrumentation. Home: 439 Trestle Rd Pittsburgh PA 15239 Office: Gulf Research & Devel Co PO Drawer 2038 Pittsburgh PA 15230

RHODES, ERIC FOSTER, editor, publisher; b. Luray, Va., Feb. 5, 1927; s. Wallace Keith and Bertha (Foster) R.; A.A., George Washington U., 1949, A.B., 1950, M.A., 1952, Ed.D., 1967; m. Barbara Ellen Henson, Oct. 19, 1946; children—Roxanne Jane, Laurel Lee; m. 2d, Lorraine Endresen, July 29, 1972; m. 3d, Daisy Chun, May 31, 1980. Tchr. high sch., Arlington, Va., 1950-52; counselor Washington Lee High Sch., Arlington, 1952-53, dir. publs., 1953-54, chmn. dept. English, 1954-55; exec. sec. Arlington Edn. Assn., 1952-53, Montgomery County (Md.) Edn. Assn., 1955-57; lectr. edn. George Washington U., 1955-60, 65-70; salary cons. NEA, Washington, 1957-58, asst. dir. membership div., 1958-60, dir. N.Y. regional office, N.Y.C., 1960-64, ednl. cons. Ednl. Research Services, White Plains, N.Y., 1964-65; pres. Ednl. Service Bur., Inc., Arlington, 1965-72, chmn. bd., 1972-80; pres. Negotiations Consultation Services, Inc., 1969-80, Eastern States Advt. Inc., 1970-79, EFR Corp., 1972—; exec. dir. Assn. Negotiators and Contract Adminstrs., 1981—; dir. Employee Futures Research, 1980-87, pres. 1988—; asst. supt. for adminstrn. Brighton (N.Y.) Schs., 1983-88; owner Frederick Foster Galleries, 1974—; cons. Va. Dept. Community Colls., 1965-77; employee relations ofcl. City of Orlando, 1980-83; vice chancellor Va. Community Coll. System, 1970-71; lectr. edn. Frostburg (Md.) State Coll., 1967. Mem. Civil Rights Commn., Franklin Twp., N.J., 1962-64; mem. Franklin Twp. Bd. Edn., 1964-65; mem. adv. bd. Keep Am. Beautiful, 1964-75, nat. chmn., 1968. Served with AUS, 1945-47. Mem. Am. Assn. Sch. Adminstrs., Internat. Assn. Sch. Bus. Officials, NEA, Edn. Press Assn., Nat. Assn. Ednl. Negotiators (exec. dir. 1971-81), Phi Delta Kappa (chpt. pres. 1959-60), Fed. Schoolmen's Club, N.Y. Schoolmasters Club. Club: Lions. Author: Negotiating Salaries; 41 Ways to Cut Budget Costs. Editor: Inside Negotiations, Wages and Benefits; Employers' Negotiating Service. Home: 114 N Court St Luray VA 22835

RHODES, FRANK HAROLD TREVOR, university president, geologist; b. Warwickshire, Eng., Oct. 29, 1926; came to U.S., 1968, naturalized, 1976; s. Harold Cecil and Gladys (Ford) R.; m. Rosa Carlson, Aug. 16, 1952; children: Jennifer, Catherine, Penelope, Deborah. BSc., U. Birmingham, 1948, Ph.D., 1950, D.Sc. (hon.), 1963; LL.D. (hon.), Coll. Wooster, 1976, Nazareth Coll. Rochester, 1979; L.H.D. (hon.), Colgate U., 1980, John Hopkins U., 1982, Wagner Coll., 1982, Hope Coll., 1982, Rensselaer Poly Inst., 1982, LeMoyne Coll., 1984, Pace U., 1986, Alaska Pacific U., 1987, Hamilton Coll., 1987; D.Sc. (hon.), U. Wales, 1981; D.Sci. (hon.), U. Ill., 1986; DLitt, U. Nev., Las Vegas, 1982. Post-doctoral fellow, Fulbright scholar U. Ill., 1950-51, vis. lectr. geology, summers 1951-52; lectr. geology U. Durham, 1951-54; asst. prof. U. Ill., 1954-55, assoc. prof., 1955-56; dir. U. Ill. Field Sta., Wyo., 1956; prof. geology, head geology dept. U. Wales, Swansea, 1956-68, dean faculty of sci., 1967-68; prof. geology and mineralogy Coll. Lit., Sci. and Arts, U. Mich., 1968-77, dean, 1971-74, v.p. for acad. affairs, 1974-77; pres., prof. geology Cornell U., Ithaca, N.Y., 1977—; Gurley lectr. Cornell U., 1960; Bownocker lectr. Ohio State U., 1966; Case lectr. U. Mich., 1976; dir. NSF, Am. Geol. Inst., summer field inst., 1963; Australian vice-chancellors' visitor to Australian univs., 1964; vis. fellow Clare Hall, Cambridge, Summer 1982; Bye fellow Robinson Coll., Cambridge, Summers, 1986, 87; Am. Fulbright Disting. fellow, Kuwait, 1987. Author: The Evolution of Life, 1962, 2d edit., 1976, Fossils, 1963, Geology, 1972, Evolution, 1974, Language of the Earth, 1981; author numerous articles and monographs on sci. and edn. Trustee Carnegie Found. for Advancement Teaching, 1978-86, vice chmn., 1983-85, chmn. 1985-86; trustee Gannett Found., 1983—; trustee Com. for Econ. Devel., 1984—; bd. trustees Andrew W. Mellon Found., 1984; bd. dirs. KMI Continental, Inc., 1979-86, Tompkins County Trust Co., 1984—, Gen. Electric Co., 1984—, Nat. Broadcasting Corp., 1986—, Am. Council on Edn., 1983—, vice chair, 1985-86, chair, 1986-88; bd. overseers Meml. Sloan-Kettering Cancer Ctr., 1979—; chmn. adv. bd. Gannett Ctr. for Media Studies, 1984—; mem. Nat. Sci. Bd., 1987—, Internat. Exec. Service Corps Council, 1984—. NSF sr. vis. research fellow, 1965-66; mem. Nat. Sci. Bd., 1987—. Fellow Geol. Soc. London (council 1963-66, Bigsby medal

1967); mem. Palaeontol. Assn. (v.p. 1963-68), Brit. Assn. Advancement Sci., Geol. Soc. Am., Am. Assn. Petroleum Geologists, Soc. Econ. Paleontologists and Mineralogists, Phi Beta Kappa (hon.). Office: Cornell Univ Office of Pres Ithaca NY 14853

RHODES, HARLAN NEWELL, petroleum executive; b. Wayne, Nebr., Apr. 26, 1926; s. Harley N. and Emma Jane (Schroeder) R.; m. Betty Lou Etz, June 1, 1951; children—William Frederick, Kristen Elizabeth, Patricia Lou. B.S. in Petroleum Engring., N. Mex. Sch. Mines., 1953. Registered profl. petroleum engr. N.Mex. 1957. Vice pres., dir. Petro Search, Inc., Denver, 1971-77; v.p. Patrick Petroleum Corp., Denver, 1977-79; sr. v.p., vice chmn. EMCOR Petroleum Corp., 1979-83; prin. H.N. Rhodes, P.E., Denver, 1984—;owner Circle "R" Aviation Co. Inc., Denver. Served to sgt. USMC, 1943-46 PTO. Mem. Ind. Petroleum Assn. Am. (past v.p., exec. com. 1986—), Soc. Petroleum Engrs. AIME, Ind. Petroleum Assn. Mountain States (pres.). Republican. Presbyterian. Clubs: Denver Petroleum; Abilene Petroleum (Tex.), Valley Country (Denver). Home: 4714 S Jasper St Aurora CO 80015 Office: 3325 Anaconda Tower 555 17th St Denver CO 80202

RHODES, JEROME DOMINIC, management consultant; b. London, June 7, 1930; s. Cecil William and Gwen Mona (Shortridge) R.; m. Patricia Anne Rhodes, July 4, 1953 (div. 1980); children: Peter, Joanna, Philippa, Michael; m. Susan Alice Thame, Dec. 29, 1982. MA, U. Oxford, Eng., 1953, Diploma in Edn., 1954. Tchr. Whittlebury Sch., Northampton, Eng., 1954-58; salesman, staff instr., area mgr. Hoover Ltd., Cambridge, Eng., 1958-63; mgr. London branch Guest, Keen & Nettlefolds, 1963-65; mgr. edn. and tng. Rank Xerox U.K., London, 1965-68; mgmt. devel. advisor Rank Orgn., London, 1968-70; mng. dir. Kepner Tregoe Ltd., Slough, Eng., 1970-75; dir. Joint Devel. Resources, London, 1975—. Author: The Colours of Your Mind, 1988; co-author: (with others) Management Development and Training Handbook, 1975; inventor in field. Served with Royal Navy, 1948-50. Fellow Brit. Inst. Mgmt.; mem. Inst. Personnel Mgmt. Conservative. Roman Catholic.

RHODES, KENT, publishing company executive; b. Bklyn., Feb. 5, 1912; s. Clarence and Louise (Rhodes) Klinck; m. Christina Riordan, July 19, 1952; children: David Christian, Jean Louise, Brian Mark. B.S., Amos Tuck Sch., Dartmouth, 1933; L.H.D. (hon.), Mercy Coll., 1978. Editor, pub. Dartmouth Pictorial, 1931-33; with Time Inc., 1933-44, Reader's Digest Assn., Inc., Pleasantville, N.Y., 1944-78; dir. Reader's Digest Assn., Inc., 1965-78, exec. v.p., 1970-75, pres., 1975-76, chmn. bd., 1976-78; bd. dirs. Mag. Pubs. Assn., N.Y.C., 1956-78, chmn., 1958-60, pres., 1979-82. Bd. dirs. Reader's Digest Found., 1970-86, pres., 1974-86; chmn. Reader's Digest Fund for Blind, 1973-86; trustee Outward Bound, 1966—, pres., 1971-72, chmn. bd., 1973; trustee Hurricane Island Outward Bound Sch., Maine, 1971-77, Harvey Sch., Katonah, N.Y., 1966-77, Internat. Exec. Service Corps., 1973-78, Internat. House, 1977—, Inst. Internat. Edn., 1978—, Taft Inst. for Two-Party Govt., 1986—; bd. dirs. Advt. Council, 1979-82, Nat. Accreditation Council, 1986—; mem. Presdl. Commn. on Postal Service, 1976-77. Recipient William Caxton Human Relations award Am. Jewish Com., 1965. Mem. Assn. Publ. Prodn. Mgrs. (founder, 1st pres. 1939—), Nat. Inst. Social Sci., Westchester County Assn. (bd. dirs. 1972-83, vice chmn. 1975-77, chmn. 1978—), Direct Mail Mktg. Assn. (dir. 1964-72, vice chmn. 1971), Pilgrims of U.S., Zeta Psi. Clubs: Knickerbocker, Dartmouth, University, N.Y. Athletic (N.Y.C.); Fishers Island (N.Y.). Home: 17 W 54th St New York NY 10019

RHODES, PATRICK L., counselor; b. Santa Barbara, Calif., Mar. 17, 1946; s. George and Edwina (Burruss) R. BA, Guilford Coll., 1972; MS, James Madison U., 1974; EdD, U. N.C., Greensboro, 1981. Dir. behavior modification Youth Rehab. Ctr., Roanoke, Va., 1972-73; asst. prof. Tidewater Community Coll., Portsmouth, Va., 1974-77; mgr. Youth Care Inc., Greensboro, N.C., 1982-83; dir. Office of Youth Services, Waynesboro, Va., 1983—; project adminstr., Va. Dept. Corrections, 1983—; youth counselor City of Waynesboro, 1983-88; mem. social services bd. dirs. City of Staunton, Va., 1984—; VISTA site supr., 1985-86; mem. Interagy. Com. Concerned With Truancy, 1983-87, chmn., 1985-87; mem. adv. council 70001, Ltd. Youth Employment Program, 1984-85; mem. research rev. com. DeJarnette Ctr. for Human Devel., 1985-86; mem. adv. bd. WMRA Pub. Radio for Shenandoah Valley, 1984-85; vol. adv. com. Emergency Foster Care, 1986-88. Mem. Waynesboro Explorer Scout Exec. Com., 1983-87, chmn., 1984-86. Served with AUS, 1968-70. Mem. Am. Soc. Pub. Adminstrn., Va. Delinquency Prevention and Youth Devel. Assn. (mem. exec. com. 1984-86, sec. 1985-86), Phi Delta Kappa, Psi Chi. Lodge: Rotary (mem. service com. Waynesboro chpt. 1985-88). Office: Box 1554 Waynesboro VA 22980

RHODES, WILLIAM REGINALD, banker; b. N.Y.C., Aug. 15, 1935; s. Edward R. and Elsie R.; divorced; 1 child, Elizabeth. B.A. in History, Brown U., 1957. Sr. officer internat. banking group-Latin Am. and Caribbean Citibank, N.A., N.Y.C., 1977-80; sr. corp. officer Latin Am. and Caribbean Citibank, N.A., 1980-84, chmn. restructuring com., 1984—, group exec., 1986—, also chmn. bank adv. coms. for Brazil, Argentina, Peru, and Uruguay, 1982—, co-chmn. bank adv. com. for Mexico, 1982—. Decorated Orden Mérito en el Trabajo, 1st class, Orden Francisco Miranda, 1st and 3d classes (Venezuela). Mem. Americas Soc. (bd. dirs.), Council of Ams. (trustee), Bankers Assn. for Fgn. Trade (bd. dirs., past pres.), Council Fgn. Relations, Venezuelan-Am. C. of C. (past pres.). Office: Citicorp 399 Park Ave New York NY 10043

RHYNE, CHARLES SYLVANUS, lawyer; b. Charlotte, N.C., June 23, 1912; s. Sydneyham S. and Mary (Wilson) R.; m. Sue Cotton, Sept. 16, 1932 (dec. Mar. 1974); children: Mary Margaret, William Sylvanus; m. Sarah P. Hendon, Oct. 2, 1976; children: Sarah Wilson, Elizabeth Parkhill. B.A., Duke U., 1934, LL.D., 1958; J.D., George Washington U., 1937, D.C.L., 1958; LL.D., Loyola U. of Calif., 1958, Dickinson Law Sch., 1959, Ohio No. U., 1966, De Paul U., 1968, Centre, 1969, U. Richmond, 1970, Howard U., 1975, Belmont Abbey, 1982. Bar: D.C. 1937. Since practiced in Washington; sr. partner Rhyne & Rhyne; gen. counsel Nat. Inst. Municipal Law Officers; professorial lectr. on aviation law George Washington U., 1948-53; gen. counsel Fed. Commn. Jud. and Congl. Salaries, 1953-54; spl. cons. Pres. Eisenhower, 1957-60; Dir. Nat. Savs. & Trust Co.; Mem. Internat Commn. Rules Judicial Procedures, 1959-61, Pres.'s Commn. on UN, 1969-71; spl. ambassador, personal rep. of Pres. U.S. to UN High Commr. for Refugees, 1971. Author: Civil Aeronautics Act, Annotated, 1939, Airports and the Courts, 1944, Aviation Accident Law, 1947, Airport Lease and Concession Agreements, 1948, Cases on Aviation Law, 1950, The Law of Municipal Contracts, 1952, Municipal Law, 1957, International Law, 1971, Renowned Law Givers and Great Law Documents of Humankind, 1975, International Refugee Law, 1976, Law and Judicial Systems of Nations, 1978, Law of Local Government Operations, 1980; editor: Municipal Attorney; Contbr. articles in field. Trustee Geo. Washington U., 1957-67, Duke U., 1961—. Recipient Grotius Peace award, 1958; Freedoms Found. award for creation Law Day-U.S.A., 1959; Alumni Achievement award George Washington U., 1960; Nat. Bar Assn. Stradford award, 1962; gold medal Am. Bar Assn., 1966; 1st Whitney M. Young award, 1972; Harris award Rotary, 1974; U.S. Dept. State appreciation award, 1976; D.C. Bar Assn. Distinguished Service award, 1976; Nansen Ring for refugee work, 1976, 1st Placemaker award Rotary, 1988. Mem. World Peace Through Law Center (pres. 1963—), ABA (pres. 1957-58, chmn. ho. dels. 1956-58, chmn. commn. world peace through law 1958-66, chmn. com. aero. law 1946-48, 51-54, chmn. internat. and comparative law sect. 1948-49, chmn. UN com., chmn. commn. on nat. inst. justice 1972-76, nat. chmn. Jr. Bar Conf. 1944-45), D.C. Bar Assn. (pres. 1955-56), Inter-Am. Bar Assn. (v.p. 1957-59), Am. Bar Found. (pres. 1957-58, chmn. fellows 1958-59), Internat. Bar (v.p. 1957-58), Am. Judicature Soc. (dir.), Am. Law Inst., Am. Soc. Internat. Law (life), Nat. Aero. Assn. (dir. 1945-47), Washington Bd. Trade, Duke U. Alumni Assn. (chmn. nat. council 1955-56, pres. 1959-60), Delta Theta Phi, Order of Coif, Omicron Delta Kappa, Scribes. Clubs: Metropolitan, Nat. Press, Barristers, Congressional, Nat. Lawyers, Easton (Md.) Broadcasters. Home: 1404 Langley Pl McLean VA 22101 Office: 1000 Connecticut Ave NW Suite 800 Washington DC 20036

RIACHI, ANTOINE AYOUB, socio-economist; b. Zahlé, Lebanon, Nov. 27, 1933; immigrated to France, 1961; s. Ayoub and Laurice (Kassis) R.; m. Sabah Adib Mawad, Nov. 27, 1969; children: Daoud Ghanem, Nada Ghanem, Rania. B.Philosophy, Coll. des Apôtres, Lebanon, 1955; D.E.A., Ecolé Pratique des Hautes Etudes, Paris; Doctorat Economie Sociale, U. Paris (Sorbonne), 1968. Analyst/statisician Ministry Social Affairs, Lebanon, 1957-58; journalist Arabic programs O.R.T.F., Paris, 1962-64; researcher/expert for Middle East and Africa, Arnold Bergstraesser Inst., Freiburg, Fed. Republic of Germany, 1966-69; mem. com. del. to EEC, del. to Africa (Congo), 1968; dir. internat. affairs Econs. Research Center, Beirut, Lebanon, 1971-75; dir-gen. ECOGROUP-France, Paris, 1981—; lectr. Lebanese Civic Council. Editor/analyst various Arabic publs., 1974; editor in chief ECO Press Revs.; author: Disparity of Social Classes in Lebanon, Social Structure of Confessions in Lebanon, The New Trend of Socialism in the World, Security in the Gulf, 1985. Home: 25 rue de Bellevue, 94190 Villeneuve Saint Georges France Office: ECOGROUP, 23 rue Washington, 75008 Paris France

RIALS, STÉPHANE CLAUDE GERMAIN ROBERT, law educator; b. Paris, Apr. 3, 1951; s. André and Jeannine-Marie (Coni-Fabre) R.; m. Sophie-Anastasie Mintz, Oct. 31, 1978; children: Constance-Louise, Louis-Cyprien. Diploma, Inst. d'Etudes Politiques, Paris, 1975; Laureate, U. Paris, 1978; Agrégé, Facultés de Droit, 1979. Monitor history of law, U. Paris X, 1971-73; asst. in pub. law U. Paris II, 1975-79; prof. pub. law U. Metz, France, 1979-81, U. Caen, France, 1981-87, U. Paris 2, 1987; gen. sec. Société pour l'histoire des facultés de droit et de la Science Juridique, 1983—; pres. Institut de recherches politiques, administratives et juridiques, 1982—; dir. Droits-Revue française de theorie juridique, Droit Fondamental, Léviathan. Author: le Juge administratif francais et la technique du standard, 1980; la Presidence de la Republique, 1981; le Premier ministre, 1981; Votre commune et la mort, 1981; Exercices pratiques de droit constitutionnel, 3d edit., 1981; Textes constitutionnels étrangers, 1982; Textes constitutionnels français, 1982; le Légitimisme, 1983; Textes politiques français, 1983; Paris de Trochu Thiers, 1985; Destin du Fédéralisme, 1986; Le miracle carpétien, 1987; Révolution en contre-révolution au XIX's Siéche, 1987;Droit Constitutionnel, 1989; Les Défenseurs du droit, 1989; others. Contbr. articles to profl. jours. Decorated Chevalier de L'Ordre èquestre du Saint-Sé pulcre de Jerusalem, 1982; Chevalier pontifical, 1983; Chevalier de l'Ordre des Arts et Lettres, 1986; Chevalier de l'Ordre du Mérit, 1988. Roman Catholic. Clubs: Automobile of France, Saint-Germain-des-Prés. Home: 11 cité Charles Godon, 75009 Paris France Office: U Paris Sch Econ, Soc Sci, 12 place de Pantheon, 75005 Paris France

RIBADENEIRA, MARIO, Ecuadorian diplomat; b. Guayaquil, Ecuador, Mar. 1, 1933; d. Modesto and Beatriz (Traversari) R.; m. Concha Quevedo, Aug. 2, 1958; children—Felipe, Manuela, Joaquin. D. Engring., Princeton U., 1954. Dir., pres., chmn. bd. numerous Ecuadorian corps., 1958—; Ecuadorian ambassador to U.S., Washington, 1984—. Mem. Trade Mission to Japan, 1976, to China, 1984; bd. dirs. Roman Catholic. Home: 2515 Massachussetts Ave NW Washington DC 20008 Office: Embassy of Ecuador 2535 15th St NW PO Box 625 Washington DC 20009

RIBARIC, MARJAN, physicist, mathematician; b. Ljubljana, Yugoslavia, Mar. 12, 1932; s. Miho and Joza (Kramer) R.; m. Pavla Peternelj, Dec. 12, 1959; children: Samo, Peter. Diploma in Physics, U. Ljubljana, 1954; PhD, 1959. Research fellow Inst. J. Stefan, Ljubljana, 1954-62; sr. sci. Inst. J. Stefan, 1964-71, heda applied math., 1969—, sci. counselor, 1971—, habilitation for asst. prof. math analysis, 1971, assoc. prof., 1979-86, prof., 1986—; resident research assoc. Argonne (Ill.) Nat. Lab., 1962-64. Author: Functional-Analytic Concepts and Structures of Neutron Transport Theory, 1973, Thermodynamics of Linear Transport Processes, 1975, Computational Methods for Parsimonious Data Fitting, 1984; contbr. articles to profl. jours. Decorated Order of Republic with Bronze Wreath; recipient Kidrič Found. Praise for sci. achievement, 1966, 85. Mem. Yugoslav Soc. Math. and Physicists, Gesellschaft fuer Angewandte Math. und Mechanik, European Phys. Soc. Home: 51 Trzaska, 61000 Ljubljana Yugoslavia Office: Inst J Stefan, 39 Jamova, 61000 Ljubljana Yugoslavia

RIBE, MARTIN GUSTAF, statistician, mathematician; b. Stockholm, Dec. 25, 1945; s. Sten Emil and Maja (Hok) R. B.A., U. Stockholm, 1967; Ph.D., Linkoping U., 1972. Fellow Institut MittagLeffler, Djursholm, 1972-74; sr. statistician Statistics Sweden, Stockholm, 1977—. Contbr. articles to profl. jours. Mem. Swedish Math. Soc., Swedish Statis. Assn., Am. Math. Soc., Am. Statis. Assn., Bernoulli Soc. Avocation: mathematical research work. Home: Lostigen 1, 17171 Solna Sweden Office: Statistics Sweden, 11581 Stockholm Sweden

RIBEIRO, ANTONIO CARDINAL, Cardinal, Patriarch of Lisbon (Portugal); b. Gandarela, Archdiocese of Braga, May 21, 1928. Appointed Patriarch of Lisbon, 1971, proclaimed cardinal, 1973—. Address: Campo de Santana 45, Lisbon Portugal *

RIBEIRO, LAIR G(ERALDO) T(HEODORO), clinical research director, educator; b. Juiz De Fora, Minas, Brazil, July 6, 1945; came to U.S., 1976; s. Francisco and Ruth (Reis) R.; m. Edna May Ottoni Porto, Jan. 1, 1968 (div. 1978); children: Frederico, Claudia; m. Mary Miller, May 22, 1979; 1 dau., Christine. B.S., Fundação Machado Sobrinho, 1967; M.D., Juiz De Fora Med. Sch., 1972. Teaching asst. in anatomy Med. Sch. of Fed. U., Juiz de Fora, 1969-71, teaching asst. in cardiology, 1971-72; resident in cardiology Pontificia Universidade Catolica do Rio de Jeneiro, Brazil, 1973, instr. cardiology, 1974; cardiologist Cantral Army Hosp., Rio de Jeneiro, 1974; asst. prof. cardiology Med. Sch., Barbacena, Brazil, 1975-76; research fellow in medicine Peter Bent Prigham Hosp. and Harvard Med. Sch., Boston, 1976-78; fellow in cardiology Meth. Hosp.-Baylor Coll. Medicine, Houston, 1978-80; asst. dir. Deborah Cardiovascular Research Inst., Browns Mills, N.J., 1980-82; dir. clin. research-domestic Merck Sharp & Dohme Research Labs., West Point, Pa., 1982-85; exec. dir. cardiovascular clin. research Pharms. div. Ciba-Geigy Corp., Summit, N.J., 1985—; adj. assoc. prof. physiology Thomas Jefferson Coll. Medicine, Phila., 1981—. Author: Coronary Spasm, 1983; co-author: Myocardial Ischemia, 1978, Platelets and Prostaglandins, 1981; contbr. articles to profl. jours. Served with Brazilian Army, 1964. Recipient 1st place in cardiology postgrad. tng. Cath. U., 1973. Fellow Am. Coll. Cardiology; mem. Brazilian Cardiology Soc., Am. Fedn. Clin. Research, N.Y. Acad. Scis. Home: 117 High Oaks Dr Watchung NJ 07901 Office: Ciba-Geigy Corp Pharms Div Summit NJ 07901

RICCI, FRANCO MARIA MARCHESE, publisher, designer; b. Parma, Italy, Dec. 12, 1936; s. A. and Carolina (Vitali) R. Grad. in Geology, U. Parma, 1958. Publs. include: facsimile edit. of Ency. by Diderot et d'Alambert, 1979, various series of art books, FMR (art mags.), 1965—. Recipient Les insignes de Chevalier dans l'ordre des Arts et des Lettres, France, 1980. Club: Grolier (N.Y.C.). Office: Via Durini 19, 20122 Milan Italy

RICCI, GIOVANNI MARIO, finance company executive, government consultant; b. Barga, Lucca, Italy, Aug. 7, 1929; s. Ettore and Jolanda (Bardoni) R.; m. Lia Cheli, Feb. 14, 1949 (div. 1970); children: Ettore, Franco, Cristiana; m. Angela Carbognin, Oct. 21, 1973; children: Mariangela, Rebecca. Ed. Italian schs.; D.h.c. in Theology, 1983. fin. advisor Seychelles Republic, 1974—; owner, GMR Group, Lugano, Switzerland, 1975—; fin. adv. Seychelles Republic, 1974—, ambassador, plenipotentiary minister Order Copts Cath. Knights of Malta, 1984—; rep. for Africa Holy Copt Cath. Ch., 1986—. Journalist, corr. ANSA (Italian News Agy.), 1980—. Office: GMR Group, PO Box 267, Victoria, Mahe Seychelles

RICCIARELLI, KATIA, soprano; b. Rovigo, Italy, Jan. 18, 1946. Grad. summa cum laude, Benedetto Marcello Conservatory, Venice, Italy. Debuts include: Mimi in La Boheme, Mantua, Italy, 1969, I Due Foscari, Lyric Opera, Chgo., 1972; Mimi in La Boheme, Covent Garden, London, 1974, Suor Angelica, La Scala, Milan, 1976, La Boheme, Met. Opera Co., N.Y.C., 1975; appeared throughout U.S. and Europe including San Francisco Opera, Paris Opera, Verona Festival; leading roles in Anna Bolena; operatic recordings include: I Due Foscari, Turandot, Carmen, Aida, Un Ballo in Maschera, Falstaff, Il Travatore, La Boheme, Tosca. Office: care Columbia Artists Mgmt 165 W 57th St New York NY 10019 also: Via Magellana 2, I-20097 Corsica Milano, Italy *

RICE, DENIS TIMLIN, lawyer; b. Milw., July 11, 1932; s. Cyrus Francis and Kathleen (Timlin) R.; children: James Connelly, Tracy Ellen. A.B., Princeton U., 1954; J.D., U. Mich., 1959. Bar: Calif. 1960. Practiced in San Francisco, 1959—; assoc. firm Pillsbury, Madison & Sutro, 1959-61, Howard & Prim, 1961-63; prin. firm Howard, Rice, Nemerovski, Canady, Robertson & Falk, 1964—; dir. Gensler & Assocs., Inc., San Francisco; chmn., mng. com. San Francisco Inst. Fin. Services. Councilman, City of Tiburon, Calif., 1968-72, mayor, 1970-72, dir., Marin County Transit Dist., 1970-72, 77-81, chmn., 1979-80; supr. Marin County, 1977-81, chmn., 1979-80; commr. Marin Housing Authority, 1977-81; mem. San Francisco Bay Conservation and Devel. Commn., 1977-83; bd. dirs. Planning and Conservation League, 1981—, Marin Symphony, 1984—, Marin Theatre Co., 1987—; mem. Met. Transp. Commn., 1980-83; mem. bd. visitors U. Mich. Law Sch. Served to 1st lt. AUS, 1955-57. Recipient Freedom Found. medal, 1956. Mem. State Bar Calif. (vice chmn. exec. com. bus. law sect.), ABA (Fed. Regulation of Securities com.), San Francisco Bar Assn., Am. Judicature Soc., Order of Coif, Phi Beta Kappa, Phi Delta Phi. Clubs: Univ., Bankers, Tiburon Peninsula, Corinthian Yacht (Tiburon); Nassau (Princeton, N.J.). Home: 1850 Mountain View Dr Tiburon CA 94920 Office: Suite 700 3 Embarcadero Ctr San Francisco CA 94111

RICE, GEORGE LAWRENCE, III, lawyer; b. Jackson, Tenn., Sept. 24, 1951; s. George Lawrence Jr. and Judith W. (Pierce) R.; m. Joy Gaia, Sept. 14, 1974; children: George Lawrence IV, Amy Colleen. BA with honors, Southwestern Coll., 1974; JD, Memphis State U., 1976; student, Nat. Coll. Advocacy. Bar: Tenn. 1977, U.S. Supreme Ct. 1980. Assoc. Pierce & Rice, Memphis, 1976-81, ptnr., 1981—; lectr. Memphis Cablevision, Sta. WHBQ, Memphis, U. Chgo. Law Sch. Author: Divorce Practice in Tennessee, 1987, 2d. edit., 1988, Professionalism and Competency, 1987, Divorce Practice for Legal Secretaries and Paralegals, 1987, Domestic Relation, 1988. Mem. ABA, Tenn. Bar Assn. (chmn. family law sect., litigation sect. council), Memphis Bar Assn. (founding chmn. div. and family law sect.), Assn. Trial Lawyers Am., Tenn. Trial Lawyers Assn. Memphis Trial Lawyers Assn. Unitarian. Office: Pierce Rice 147 Jefferson St #600 Memphis TN 38104

RICE, IVAN GLENN, gas turbine consulting engineer; b. Phoenix, July 24, 1924; s. Harvey Clifford and Charlotte Abegail (Burre) R.; student Phoenix Coll., 1946-47; B.S.M.E. with high distinction, U. Ariz., 1950; Carolyn Ruth Keyes, June 16, 1950; children—Thomas Glenn, Kathleen Elizabeth, James Nelson. With Gen. Electric Co., 1950-69, gas turbine application engr., for S.W. U.S.A., Houston, 1957-64, regional turbine engr. for U.S., Can. and Mexico, Houston, 1964-69; mgr. nat. and worldwide mktg. DeLaval Turbine Inc., Houston, 1969-74; cons. engr., Spring, Tex., 1974—. Mem. adv. com. Turbo-Machinery Symposium, Tex. A&M U., 1972—; mem. planning com. First Offshore Tech. Conf., Houston, 1969. Pres. Spring High Sch. PTA, 1972-73; mem.-at-large Sam Houston Area council Boy Scouts Am.; chmn. Harris County Republican Precinct 110, 1976-78. Served with Transp. Corps, AUS, 1943-46; ETO. Recipient Mgmt. awards Gen. Electric Co., 1955, 61, 66, Breakthrough 60 award Gen. Electric Co., 1960, Scouters award Boy Scouts Am., 1966. Fellow ASME (Meritorious Service award 1968, gas turbine div. commendation 1971, chmn. South Tex. sect. 1975-76, chmn. div. gas turbine 1976-77, Council award 1977, 80, Centennial medallion 1980, Region X award 1984); mem. Nat., Tex. socs. profl. engrs., Soc. Petroleum Engrs., AAAS, Houston Engring. and Sci. Soc., Pi Mu Epsilon, Phi Kappa Phi, Tau Beta Pi, Pi Tau Sigma. Republican. Lutheran (adminstrv. bd. 1975-76). Contbr. articles on gas turbines to profl. jours. Patentee gas turbine heat rate control; internat. patentee reheat-gas turbine combined cycle control; steam-blade cooling of reheat-gas turbine. Home: 1007 Lynwood St Spring TX 77373 Office: PO Box 233 Spring TX 77383

RICE, JERRY DARREL, architectural designer; b. Longview, Wash., Mar. 14, 1939; s. Harry Franklin and Alma Ida (Skalitzky) R.; Frank Lloyd Wright Found. fellow, apprentice archtl. designer Frank Lloyd Wright Sch. Architecture, 1963-68; A.A. in Horticulture, Central Ariz. Coll., 1977. Mem. staff Frank Lloyd Wright Sch. Architecture-Taliesin Asso. Architects, Spring Green, Wis., Scottsdale, Ariz., 1968-70; owner, pres., chief exec. officer, developer, cons. Habitats of Optimum Mobility and Environ. Systems, Inc., (subs.) Criterion Consortium Network, Joint Ventures, Cockeyed Cowgirl Silver and Saddle Shop, Critter's Corner, Western Trader; div. mgr. Joint Ventures; instr. landscape design, archtl. drafting and design. Served with U.S. Army, 1961-63. Mem. Am. Inst. Bldg. Design (designer registration), Nat. Ski Patrol (Nat. Honor award 1957). Prin. archtl. work includes Wintergreen Ski Area; research and devel. in solar energy systems, earth covered and berm structures. Office: 2027 N 39th St Phoenix AZ 85008

RICE, JOHN RAY, social worker; b. Covington, Tenn., Jan. 3, 1949; s. Luttrell and Mary Alma (Walker) R. ABS, George Williams Coll., 1971, MSW, 1977. Lic. therapist, Ill. Psychiat. social worker Kane/Kendall County Mental Health Ctr., Ill., 1971-74; young adult coordinator Thresholds, Chgo., 1974-77; pvt. practice therapy, Chgo., 1977—; camp dir. Unions for Youth, Nat. Football League Players Assn., Elmhurst, Ill., 1979, Winchendon, Mass.; social worker, instr. Behavior Sci.-Family Practice Residency Tng. Program, Ill. Masonic Ctr., Chgo., 1980; child-family therapist Habilitative Systems, Inc., Chgo., 1985-86, coordinator clin. services, 1986-86; unit coordinator Valley Inst. Psychiatry, Owensboro, Ky., 1987—; field instr. George Williams Coll. Sch. Social Work Edn. Author: Thank You for Loving Me. Mem. YMCA World Service, Bogota, Columbia, 1967; mem. coms. Ill. Comm. on Children. Mem. Nat. Assn. Social Workers (cert.), Nat. Assn. Black Social Workers. Baptist. Home: 1200 E Byers Ave B224 Owensboro KY 42301 Office: Valley Inst Psychiatry 1000 Industrial Dr Owensboro KY 42301

RICE, JOSEPH ALBERT, banker; b. Cranford, N.J., Oct. 11, 1924; s. Louis A. and Elizabeth J. (Michael) R.; m. Katharine Wolfe, Sept. 11, 1948; children—Walter, Carol, Philip, Alan. B.Aero. Engring., Rensselear Poly. Inst., 1948; M.Indsl. Engring., NYU, 1952, MA, 1968. With Grumman Aircraft Engring. Corp., 1948-53; with IBM, N.Y.C., 1953-65, mgr. ops., real estate, constrn. divs., 1963-65; dep. group exec. N.Am. comml. telecommunications group, pres. telecommunications div. ITT, N.Y.C., 1965-67; sr. v.p. Irving Trust Co., N.Y.C., 1967-69, exec. v.p., 1969-72, sr. exec. v.p., 1972-73, vice chmn., 1973-74, pres., from 1974, chmn., 1984—, bd. dirs.; exec. v.p. Irving Bank Corp., 1971-74, vice chmn., 1974-75, pres., 1975-84, chmn. bd., chief exec. officer, 1984—, also bd. dirs.; dir., Internat. Comml. Bank PL.C., N. Am. Phillips Corp., Avon Products, Inc., Wing Hang Bank, U.S. Philips Corp., Downtown-Lower Manhattan Assn.; trustee Banking Research Fund. Trustee John Simon Guggenheim Meml. Found., Hist. Hudson Valley Restorations. Served to 1st lt. C.E. AUS, 1943-46. Mem. Assn. Bank Holding Cos., Council Fgn. Relations, Banking Roundtable. Clubs: University (N.Y.C.), Links (N.Y.C.), Sky (N.Y.C.) (bd. govs.); Sleepy Hollow Country (Scarborough, N.Y.). Office: Irving Bank Corp One Wall St New York NY 10005

RICE, KENNETH LLOYD, finance company executive; b. St. Paul, June 17, 1937; s. Irving James and Anne Louise (Rogers) R.; m. Elizabeth Lyman Vankat, May , 1963 (div. June 1980); children: Anne Louise, Kenneth L. Jr., Elizabeth Ellen, Stephen James. BBA, U. Wis., 1959; postgrad., N.Y. Inst. Finance, 1960-64; completed Advanced Mgmt. Program, Harvard U., 1975. Trainee corp. finance Irving J. Rice & Co., St. Paul, 1959-64; asst. branch mgr. DB Marron & Co. Inc., St. Paul, 1964-65; mgr. corp. finance JW Sparks & Co. Inc., St. Paul, 1965-69, The Milw. Co., St. Paul, 1969-70; dir. finance Cedar Riverside Assocs. Inc., Mpls., 1970-71; prin. Kenneth L. Rice & Assocs., St. Paul, 1971—; MN Hon. Consul Rep. Togo; MN del. World Trade Cens. Assn., 1987, Budapest, Hungary. Founder Chimera Theatre, St. Paul, 1969; vice moderator Presbytery of the Twin Cities, Mpls., 1976; pres. Liberty Plaza Non-Profit Housing Project, St. Paul, 1975-77; judge Leadership Fellows Bush Found., St. Paul, 1985—; co-chmn. Parents Fund, Macalester Coll., St. Paul, 1985-87. Mem. Real Estate Securities Syndication Inst. (chpt. pres. 1977, disting. service award 1978). Presbyterian. Club: Harvard Bus. (local bd. dirs. 1978-83). Lodges: Optimists (local v.p. 1986-88), Masons, KT, Shriners. Office: 220 S Robert St Suite 208 Saint Paul MN 55107

RICE, MABEL MCCULLOUGH (MRS. CLINTON D. RICE), motor co. exec.; b. Lamoni, Iowa, Jan. 8, 1904; d. Issac and Bertha (Naylor) Bedell; B.Bus. Law, Blackstone Coll., Chgo., 1954-60; m. Guy Leroy McCullough, Aug. 1, 1921; 1 son, Gary; m. 2d, Clinton D. Rice, Aug. 13, 1948 (dec. Nov. 1980); 1 son, Clinton Thane. With McCullough Motor Co., Groundbirch, B.C., Can., 1936—, pres., 1948—, dir., 1936-72; officer Ringduck Corp., Mt.

Ayr, Iowa; dir. Mt. Ayr Developing Co. Bd. dirs. Ringgold County Hosp. Mem. Bus. and Profl. Women's Club. Republican. Methodist. Lodge: Order of Eastern Star (worthy matron 1928). Developer of land in Can. Address: 117 E Madison St Mount Ayr IA 50854 Office: 1201 116th Ave, Dawson Creek, BC Canada V1G 4P5

RICE, MICHAEL CHARLES, educator; b. St. Ann's, Eng., Aug. 4, 1939; arrived in Republic of South Africa, 1946; s. Thomas Inglis and Flora McDonald (Bland) R.; m. Ruth Lucille Collett, Apr. 2, 1966 (dec. 1975); children: Brendan, Dammon; m. Ruth Emelie Fischer, Apr. 12, 1986; 1 child, Gretel. BA, U. South Africa, Pretoria, 1967; BA with honors, U. South Africa, 1969, MA, 1975; DLitt, PhD, Rand Afrikaans U., Johannesburg, 1984. Tchr. Cape Edn. Dept., Cape Town, Republic South Africa, 1965-71; lectr. U. North, Pietersburg, Republic South Africa, 1972-75; sr. lectr. Coll. Edn., Pretoria, Republic South Africa, 1976; assoc. head dept. Johannesburg Coll., Republic South Africa, 1977—; visiting lectr. U. Witwatersrand, Johannesburg, 1984, U. Cape Town, 1985. Translator: Christine (play), 1984; contbr. articles on apartheid. Active Detainees Parents Support Com.; organized Free the Children Alliance; testified Lawyers for Human Rights Under Law Conf. Children in Detention South Africa., Washington, 1987. Home: 37 Fawley Ave, Auckland Park, Johannesburg 2092, Republic of South Africa Office: Johannesburg Coll Edn, 27 St Andrews Rd, Parktown, Johannesburg Transvaal 2193, Republic of South Africa

RICE, OTIS LAVERNE, nursing home builder and developer; b. Emerson, Iowa, June 24, 1922; s. William Reuben and Bonnie Elizabeth (Edie) R.; m. Ferill Jeane Dalton, Mar. 7, 1946; children: LeVeria June McMichael, Larry Lee. Student Fox Valley Tech. Sch., 1971-72. Lic. electrician and contractor. With Tumpane Electric, Omaha, 1949-53; ptnr., pres. Rice & Rice, Inc., Kaukauna, Wis., 1953—. Ptnr. Rice Enterprises. Served with U.S. Army, 1942-46. Decorated Bronze Stars. Mem. Associated Builders and Contractors, Fenton Art Glass Collectors of Am. Inc. (founder), Internat. Carnival Glass Collectors, Am. Carnival Glass Collectors, Heisey Collectors of Am. Republican. Clubs: Masons, Shriners, Eastern Star.

RICE, RAMONA GAIL, physiologist, phycologist, educator, consultant; b. Texarkana, Tex., Feb. 15, 1950; d. Raymond Lester and Jessie Gail (Hubbard) R.; m. Carl H. Rosen. BS, Ouachita U., 1972; MS, U. Ark., 1975, PhD, 1978; postgrad. Utah State U., 1978-80. Undergrad. asst. Ouachita U., Arkadelphia, Ark., 1970-72; grad. teaching asst. U. Ark., Fayetteville, 1972, 77-78, grad. research asst., 1973-77; asst. research scholar, scientist Fla. Internat. U., Miami, 1980-85; research coordinator, faculty Pratt Community Coll., Kans., 1985—; adj. instr. Miami Dade Community Coll., 1984-85, Wichita (Kans.) State U., 1986—. Contbr. articles to profl. jours. Judge Pratt County Sci. Fairs, Dade County Sci. Fair, Fla., 1981-85, Barber County Sci. Fairs; tchr. Sunday Sch. First Baptist Ch., South Miami, Fla., 1982-85, leader girls in action, 1982-83, youth chaperone, 1982-85; patron Pratt Community Concert Series. Grantee NSF, 1981-83, Am. Biog. Inst. Disting. Leadership award, 1987. Fla. Dept. Environ., 1981-83, EPA, 1983-85, So. Fla. Research Ctr., Everglades Nat. Park, 1983-86. Mem. AMA, Ninescah Valley Med. Soc. Aux., Pratt Higher Edn. Assn. (sec. 1987-88), Fla. Acad. Scis., AAAS, Phycological Soc. Am., Soc. Limnology and Oceanography, Sigma Xi. Democrat. Avocations: pianist, crochet, needlework, photography, reading. Office: Pratt Community Coll Dept Biol Scis Pratt KS 67124

RICE, RICHARD CAMPBELL, state official, retired army officer; b. Atchison, Kans., Dec. 11, 1933; s. Olive Campbell and Ruby Thelma (Rose) R.; m. Donna Marie Lincoln, Aug. 4, 1956; children—Robert Alden, Holly Elizabeth. B.A. in History, Kans. State U., 1955; M.A. in Social Studies, Eastern Mich. U., 1965; grad. U.S. Army Command and Gen. Staff Coll., 1968, U.S. Army War Coll., 1977, grad. program for sr. execs. in state and local govt., Harvard U., 1985. Commd. 2d lt. U.S. Army, 1955; advanced through grades to col., 1976; with Joint Chiefs of Staff, Washington, 1975-76; faculty U.S. Army War Coll., Carlisle Barracks, Pa., 1977-79; chief of staff Hdqrs. 3d ROTC Region, Ft. Riley, Kans., 1982-83; ret. 1983; dir. Mo. State Emergency Mgmt. Agy., Jefferson City, 1983-85, dir. Mo. Dept. Pub. Safety, Jefferson City, 1985—. Mem. Coordinating Council Health Edn., Mo.'s Children and Adolescents., Mo. Jail and Prison Overcrowding Task Force, Gov.'s Domestic Violence Task Force, Gov.'s Conf. Health Needs Children, Gov's Commn. on Crime, Gov's Adv. Council on Driving While Intoxicated, Mo. Children's Services Commn., Blue Ribbon Commn. on Services to Youth, Campaign to Protect Our Children; chmn. Gov.'s Cabinet Council for Justice Administrn., Mo. Statistical Analysis Ctr. adv. bd., adv. bd. Mo. Criminal Hist. Records; bd. dirs. Mo. Law Enforcement Meml. Found. Decorated Legion of Merit, Bronze Star (3), Meritorious Service medal (4), Air medal (2), Joint Service Commendation medal, Army Commendation medal (2); Republic of Vietnam Cross of Gallantry with Silver Star. Mem. Nat. Eagle Scout Assn., Assn. U.S. Army, Soc. First Div., Am. Legion, VFW, Disabled Am. Vets., Nat. Soc., Sons Am. Revolution, Internat. Assn. Chiefs of Police, Mo. Police Chiefs Assn., Mo. Peace Officers Assn., The Retired Officers Assn., Nat. Fedn. of Grand Order Of Pachyderms, Nat. Criminal Justice Assn. (bd. dirs. 1987—), Am. Soc. Pub. Administrn., Mo. Inst. Pub. Adminstrn. Theta Xi. Republican. Lodges: Rotary. Avocation: sailing. Office: Public Safety Dept 301 W High St Jefferson City MO 65102

RICE, SUSAN JOETTE, nurse; b. Topeka, Nov. 15, 1946; d. Claude Harvey and Martha May (McClellan) R.; student Pasadena Nazarene Coll., 1964-66; B.S. in Nursing, Calif. State U., Los Angeles, 1969, M.S.N., 1982; postgrad Cambridge Grad. Sch. Psychology, Los Angeles, 1985—. Staff nurse Children's Hosp. Los Angeles, 1969-75, asst. head nurse, 1972-74, nurse mgr., 1974-75; nursing unit coordinator newborn and neonatal intensive care nurseries, perinatal clinician Glendale (Calif.) Adventist Med. Center, 1976-78; neonatal clin. specialist Huntington Meml. Hosp., Pasadena, 1981-85; staff nurse mental health unit Glendale Adventist Med. Ctr., 1985-88; practicum field worker Treatment Ctrs. Am. Panorama City, Calif., 1988—. Vol. counselor Pasadena Mental Health Ctr., 1985—. Mem. Am. Assn. Critical Care Nurses, Calif. Perinatal Assn., Nat. Assn. Neonatal Nurses, Pasadena Area Psychol. Assn. Republican. Mem. Nazarene Ch. Home: 133 E Pamela Rd Monrovia CA 91016

RICE, TIMOTHY MILES BINDON, writer, broadcaster; b. Amersham, Eng., Nov. 10, 1944; s. Hugh Gordon and Joan Odette (Bawden) R.; m. Jane McIntosh, Aug. 19, 1974; children: Eva Jane Florence, Donald Alexander Hugh. Student, Lancing Coll., Sussex, 1958-62. Solicitor's articled clk. Pettit & Westlake, London, 1963-66; mgmt. trainee E.M.I. Records Manchester Sq., London, 1966-68; record producer Norrie Paramor Orgn., London, 1968-69; ind. writer, record producer London, 1969—; broadcaster BBC Radio and TV, Ind. TV, U.K., 1973—. Author: libretto Joseph and The Amazing Technicolor Dreamcoat, 1968, expanded for stage, 1973, Jesus Christ Superstar, 1970, extra material for film, 1973, Evita, 1976, for stage, 1978, Blondel, 1983, Chess, 1984; (with others) Guinness Book of British Hit Singles; co-founder, dir. Pavilion Books, 1981; editor: Lord Taverner's Sticky Wicket Book, 1979. Clubs: Marylebone Cricket, Heartaches Cricket. Address: 196 Shaftesbury Ave, London WC2, England

RICE, WILLIAM DAVID, advertising agency executive; b. Salt Lake City, Jan. 30, 1920; s. William and Elsie (Cohn) R.; m. Adrienne G. Schwartz, Mar. 3, 1957 (dec. May 1964); children—William E., Taylor D.; m. Jo Anne Twelves, Nov. 9, 1966; children—Robert G., James A. B.S. in Chemistry, U. Utah, 1942. Vice pres. Cooper & Crowe Advt., Salt Lake City, 1947-53; pres. Demiris, Rice & Assocs. Advt., Salt Lake City, 1953—. Pres., Salt Lake Mental Health Assn., 1961-62, Utah Assn. Mental Health, 1964-66, Utah Traveler's Aid Soc., 1972-73; v.p. communications Nat. Assn. Mental Health, 1973-75; chmn. Utah Mental Health Adv. Council, 1978-80; bd. dirs. Hospice of Salt Lake City, 1978—, chmn., 1979-86; chmn. Com. for Severely Mentally Impaired, 1979-81, Mental Health Media Devel. Com., 1983—; chmn. Community Nursing Service, 1986—; trustee Utah Mil. Vet. Affairs Com., 1986—. Served to comdr. USN, 1942-46. Recipient Disting. Service award Utah Med. Assn., 1975, Nat. Assn. Mental Health, 1975. Fellow Am. Inst. Mgmt. (pres.'s council 1971-72); mem. Utah Assn. Advt. Agys., Internat. Platform Assn., Salt Lake Advt. Club. Clubs: University (Salt Lake City) (pres. 1982-83); Mensa (proctor 1970—). Office: Demiris Rice & Assocs Inc 50 S Main Suite 420 Salt Lake City UT 84144

RICE, WILLIAM HENRY, aviation marketing and communications consultant, writer, editor; b. Halifax, N.S., Can., Apr. 3, 1931; s. William Henry and Edith Mary (Dawes) R.; m. Evelyn Marie Svrcek, Feb. 1, 1958; children—William Henry, Douglas Walter. B.A., Sir George Williams U., 1956. Writer, producer CBC, Montreal, Que., 1961-66; producer Westinghouse Broadcasting Co., Phila., 1966-68, Triangle Broadcasting div. Triangle Publs., Phila., 1968-71; contbg. editor Pvt. Pilot mag. and Aero mag., Phila., 1971-76, Eastern editor, 1976—; contbg. editor Can. Aviation, 1977—; aviation cons. to advt. industry, 1976—; pres. Bill Rice Assos.; communications cons. to aviation industry, 1976—. Producer films: Art Scholl Story (Oberhausen award, Kranj award, Golden Eagle award), 1970; Portrait of a Rodeo (Award of Excellence, Cowboy Hall of Fame), 1971. Served with U.S. Army, 1956-59. Mem. Aircraft Owners and Pilots Assn., Seaplane Pilots Assn. Episcopalian. Office: 275 S Byrn Mawr Ave Sutie B-32 Bryn Mawr PA 19010

RICE, WINSTON EDWARD, lawyer; b. Shreveport, La., Feb. 22, 1946; s. Winston Churchill and Margaret (Coughlin) R.; student Centenary Coll. La., 1967; m. Barbara Reily Gay, Apr. 16, 1977; 1 child, Andrew Hynes; children by previous marriage: Winston Hobson, Christian MacTaggart. JD, La. State U., 1971. Bar: La. Cons. geologist Crosby Mineral Co., Gulfport, Miss., 1968-70; partner firm Phelps, Dunbar, Marks, Claverie & Sims, New Orleans, 1971-88; sr. ptnr. Rice, Fowler, Kingsmill, Vance & Flint, New Orleans, 1988—; instr. law La. State U., Baton Rouge, 1970-71. Assoc. editor La. Law Rev., 1970-71. Mem. ABA (vice-chmn. com. on admiralty and maritime law 1979-84), La. Bar Assn., New Orleans Bar Assn., New Orleans Assn. Def. Counsel, Maritime Law Assn. U.S. (chmn. subcom. on offshore exploration and devel. 1985—), Assn. Average Adjusters U.S., Assn. Average Adjusters (U.K.), Order of Coif, Phi Delta Phi, Phi Kappa Phi, Kappa Alpha. Republican. Episcopalian. Clubs: Mariners (treas. 1974-75, 78-79, sec. 1975-76, v.p. 1976-77, pres. 1977-78), Boston, Stratford, Bayou Racquet, Petroleum (New Orleans); Coral Beach and Tennis (Bermuda). Office: 650 Poydras St Suite 1920 New Orleans LA 70130

RICH, CHRISTOPHER CHARLES, state official, lawyer; b. Brookline, Mass., June 8, 1952; s. Francis Patrick and Catherine Louise (Lochiatto) R. B.S., Boston Coll., 1974; J.D., Suffolk U., 1978. Bar: Mass. 1978, U.S. dist. ct. Mass. 1979, U.S. Ct. Appeals (1st cir.) 1979, U.S. Supreme Ct. 1984. Br. mgr. Logan Equipment Corp., Boston, 1972; spl. police officer Dennis (Mass.) Police Dept., 1973-75, Harwich (Mass.) Police Dept., 1974-75, Suffolk County (Mass.) Dist. Atty.'s Office, 1974-78, asst. dist. atty. maj. violations div. Suffolk Ct., Suffolk County Dist. Atty., 1979; asst. chief legal counsel Mass. Dept. Pub. Works, 1979; dep. sec. Mass. Dept. Pub. Utilities, Boston, 1979—; spl. police officer Saugus (Mass.) Police Dept., 1982—; sole practice, Boston, 1982-83; sr. assoc. atty. Mass. office Hayt, Hayt & Landau, 1983-84; ptnr., 1984-87; mng. ptnr. Law Offices Christopher C. Rich, P.C., 1987—; bus. cons. Mem. Saugus Town Meeting, 1975-78; keyperson United Way Fund Drive, 1982-83. Recipient John B. Atkinson award Boston Coll., 1974. Mem. Mass. Bar Assn., ABA, Justinial Law Soc., New Eng. Narcotic Enforcement Officers Assn. (dir., gen. counsel), Internat. Narcotic Enforcement Officers Assn., Phi Delta Phi. Roman Catholic. Club: Saugus Italian Am. (gen. counsel 1983—). Home: 94 Saugus Ave Saugus MA 01906 Office: 187 Condor St East Boston MA 02128 also: 99 Walnut St Suite G1 Saugus MA 01906

RICH, ERIC, plastics company executive; b. Znojmo, Czechoslovakia, Oct. 1, 1921; came to U.S., 1955, naturalized, 1962; s. Sandor and Alice (Shifferes) Reich; m. Ilse L.B. Renard, Nov. 14, 1959; children—Susan Frances, Sally Dora, Charles Anthony. Ed., U. Coll., Wales, Bangor, U.K. Export sales mgr. Pilot Radio, Ltd., London, Eng., 1945-49; dir. Derwent Exports, Ltd., London, 1949-55; export sales mgr. Am. Molding Powder & Chem. Corp., N.Y.C., 1956-58; with Gering Plastics Co. div. Monsanto Chem. Co., Kenilworth, N.J., 1958-67; v.p., gen. mgr. Goldmark Plastics Internat., Inc., New Hyde Park, N.Y., 1967—. Served with RAF, 1941-45. Decorated Gallantry medal, 1939-43, Star Atlantic Star. Home: 111 7th St Garden City NY 11530 Office: Nassau Terminal Rd New Hyde Park NY 11040

RICH, MICHAEL JOSEPH, lawyer; b. N.Y.C., June 19, 1945; s. Jesse and Phyllis (Sternfeld) R.; m. Linda Christine Kubis, July 19, 1969; children—David Lawrence, Lisa Diane. B.A., Gettysburg Coll., 1967; J.D., Am. U., 1972. Bar: Del. 1973, U.S. Dist. Ct. Del. 1973, U.S. Supreme Ct. 1976, Pa. 1981. Law clk. Del. Supreme Ct., Georgetown, 1972-73; assoc. Tunnell & Raysor, Georgetown, 1973-76; ptnr. Morris, Nichols, Arsht & Tunnell, Georgetown, 1983—; ptnr. Dunlap, Holland & Rich, Georgetown, 1976-80; gen. counsel Pearlette Fashions Inc., Lebanon, Pa., 1981-83; minority counsel Del. Ho. of Reps., Dover, 1977-79; mem. Del. Gov's Magistrate Commn., 1980, 1983-86; sec. Del. Gov's. Jud. Nominating Commn., 1986—. Bd. dirs. People's Place II, Inc., Milford, Del., 1973-77; pres. Bi-County United Way, Inc., Milford, 1977-78; mem. Partnership Greater Milford Commn., 1987—. Served to 1st lt. U.S. Army, 1967-69, Vietnam. Dean's fellow Am. U., 1971-72. Mem. ABA, Del. Bd. of Bar Examiners, Del. Bar Assn. (v.p. at large 1987—), Sussex County Bar Assn. (pres. 1987—). Office: Morris Nichols Arsht & Tunnell PO Box 231 Georgetown DE 19927

RICH, PAUL BENJAMIN, education educator; b. Colchester, Essex, Eng., Mar. 25, 1950; s. Charles Austin and Clare (Young) R. BA, U. Sussex, Brighton, Eng., 1972; PhB, U. York, Eng., 1973; PhD, U. Warwick, Coventry, Eng., 1980. Research fellow Ctr. Research in Ethnic Relations U. Warwick and U. Aston, Coventry, Eng., 1980-85; fellow in politics U. Warwick, Coventry, Eng., 1985-86; lectr. politics U. Bristol, Eng., 1986-87, U. Warwick, Coventry, 1987—. Author: White Power and the Liberal Conscience, 1984, Race and Empire in British Politics, 1986, Race, Government and Politics in Britain, 1986, Prospero's Return: Essays on Race, Class and Culture in Britain, 1988. Recipient writing grant British Acad., 1985; research fellow The Leverhulme Trust U. Bristol, 1986. Mem. Polit. Studies Assn., Internat. Soc. for Study European Ideas, Am. Hist. Assn., Royal Inst. Internat. Affairs. Mem. Ch. of Eng. Home: 4 Gleeson Dr, Warwick CV34 5VA, England Office: Univ of Warwick, Conventry England

RICH, ROBERT GRAHAM, JR., diplomat; b. Gainesville, Fla., Nov. 15, 1930; s. Robert Graham and Lula A. (Hawkins) R.; m. Mary Ann M. Coté, June 27, 1987; children: Susan, Nan, Catherine, Caroline. BS, U. Fla., 1952; postgrad., Cornell U., 1955-57; student, Nat. Def. U., Washington, 1971-72. Research asst. U. Fla., Gainesville, 1954-55; jr. research engr. Sperry Rand Corp., Little Neck, N.Y., 1955; grad. teaching asst. Cornell U., Ithaca, N.Y., 1955-57; dep. chief missions State Dept., Manila, 1982-85; ambassador to Belize 1987—. Served to lt. USNR, 1952-54. Office: US Ambassador to Belize care Department of State Washington DC 20520

RICH, ROBERT STEPHEN, lawyer; b. N.Y.C., Apr. 30, 1938; s. Maurice H. and Natalie (Priess) R.; m. Myra N. Lakoff, May 31, 1964; children: David, Rebecca, Sarah. AB, Cornell U., 1959; JD, Yale U., 1963. Bar: N.Y. 1964, Colo. 1973, U.S. Tax Ct. 1966, U.S. Sup. Ct. 1967, U.S. Ct. Clms. 1968, U.S. Dist. Ct. (so. dist.) N.Y. 1965, U.S. Dist. Ct. (ea. dist.) N.Y. 1965, U.S. Dist. Ct. Colo. 1980, U.S. Ct. Apls. (2d cir.) 1964, U.S. Ct. Appeals (10th cir.) 1978; conseil juridique, Paris, 1968. Assoc. Shearman & Sterling, N.Y.C., Paris, London, 1963-72; ptnr. Davis, Graham & Stubbs, Denver, 1973—; Am. Coll of Tax counsel, 1987—; adj. faculty U. Denver Law Sch., 1977—; bd. dirs. Clos du Val Wine Co. Ltd., Danskin Cattle Co., Areti Wine Imports, Ltd., Taltarni Vineyards, Rocky Mountain Internat. Bus. Service Ctr., 1987—, several other corps.; mem. Colo. Internat. Trade Adv. Council, 1985—. Author treatises on internat. taxation; contbr. articles to profl. jours. Bd. dirs. Denver Internat. Film Festival, 1978-79, Alliance Française, 1977—; actor, musician N.Y. Shakespeare Festival, 1960; trustee, sec. Denver Art Mus., 1982—. Served to capt., AUS, 1959-60. Fellow Am. Coll. of Tax Counsel; mem. ABA, Union Internationale des Avocats, Internat. Fiscal Assn., Internat. Bar Assn., Colo. Bar Assn., N.Y. State Bar Assn., Assn. of Bar of City of N.Y. Clubs: Denver, Yale (N.Y.C.). Office: Davis Graham & Stubbs PO Box 185 Denver CO 80201

RICH, WAYNE ADRIAN, retired lawyer; b. Piner, Ky., Aug. 8, 1912; s. Shirley S. and Edna Jane (Mann) R.; m. Ellen Peters, Sept. 4, 1937 (dec. Dec., 1966); children—Wayne A., Ellen Randolph Williams; m. Frances Runyan, Oct. 4, 1968; 1 stepchild, Charles Hamilton West. A.B., U. Cin., 1935; J.D., Harvard U., 1938. Bar: W.Va., U.S. Supreme Ct., U.S. Tax Ct. Sole practice law, Charleston, W.Va., 1938-77, ret., 1977—; dir. City Nat. Bank, Charleston, 1956-77, pres., 1967-68, chmn. bd., trust officer, 1968-77. Mem. Kanawha Juvenile Council, Charleston, 1955-62; bd. dirs. Kanawha Welfare Council, 1957-63; trustee Greater Kanawha Valley Found., 1968-77; mem. City Council, Charleston, 1955-59, Mcpl. Planning Commn., Charleston, 1962-77; mem. W.Va. adv. council SBA, 1962-63. Served to comdr. USN, 1943-46. Mem. W.Va. State Bar Assn., Kanawha County Bar Assn. (v.p. 1953, 59), Tau Kappa Alpha, Omicron Delta Kappa, Sigma Chi. Republican. Presbyterian. Club: Kingsmill Golf (Williamsburg). Avocation: golf. Home: 12 Ensigne Spence Williamsburg VA 23185

RICHARD, BETTY BYRD, geriatric fitness educator, consultant, writer; b. Charleston, W.Va., Aug. 30, 1922; d. Ernest O'Farrell and Blanche Elizabeth (Davenport) Byrd; m. Samuel Jackson Richard, Jr., June 12, 1943 (dec. Nov. 1987); children—Caroline Byrd Richard Rossman, Samuel Jackson III. B.A. in Sociology, U. Charleston (W.Va.), 1977. Research assoc. exercise planning and design Frankel Found., Charleston, 1966-70; assoc. adminstr., 1970-79; cons. geriatric fitness W.Va. Commn. on Aging, 1979-83; dir. Gerokinetics, Charleston, 1984—; W.Va. co-originator co-dir. Preventicare program, 1970-79; coordinator 1st Appalachian Conf. on Phys. Activity and Aging, 1973; coordinator Gerokinesiatrics Conf. on Aging, 1977; author books including: Be Alive as Long As You Live, rev. edit. 1977; Age and Mobility, 1979; contbr. to Guide to Fitness After Fifty, 1977; producer gerokinetics program on audio cassette, 1980, gerokinetics slide/tape program, 1985; featured on weekly pub. TV series on exercise programs for sr. citizens, 1974-75. Recipient Gov.'s Sr. Service award, 1982. Republican. Presbyterian. Lodge: Eastern Star. Home: 321 Mountain View Dr Charleston WV 25314 Office: Gerokinetics 401 4th Ave S Charleston WV 25303

RICHARDS, ADRIAN FRANK, marine consulting company executive; b. Worcester, Mass., Apr. 1, 1929; s. Oscar White and Cecilia (Rosser) R.; m. Joan Adgie, 1952 (div. 1972); children—Ronald, Bronwyn, Eric; m. Berry Gargal, 1975 (div. 1985); m. Efrosine A. Yeannakopoulos, 1986. B.S., U. N.Mex., 1951; Ph.D., UCLA, 1957. Geol. oceanographer U.S. N. Hydrographic Office, Suitland, Md., 1957-60; resident research assoc. U.S. Navy Electronics Lab., San Diego, 1960-61; head earth scis. br. U.S. Office Naval Research, London, 1961-63; postdoctoral fellow Norwegian Geotech. Inst., Oslo, 1963-64; assoc. prof. U. Ill., Urbana, 1964-68, prof., 1969; dir. Marine Geotech. Lab., prof. oceanography and ocean engring. Lehigh U., Bethlehem, Pa., 1969-82; sr. cons., v.p. research and devel. Fugro B.V., Leidschendam, Netherlands, 1982-87; pres. A. F. Richards & Assocs., Inc., Bethlehem, Pa., 1975-83, dir., 1983-87; pres. Adrian Richards Co., Aalsmeer, 1987—; prof. Tech. U. of Delft, 1988—; cons. ocean engring. UNESCO, Paris, 1974, 1979—; cons. ocean energy UN, N.Y.C., 1979; advisor Nat. Oceanic, Rockville, Md., 1977-81. Editor: Marine Geotechnique, 1967; European Sci. Notes (jour.), 1963; assoc. editor Jour. Ocean Engring., 1975—; editor-in-chief Jour. Marine Geotechnology, 1975-83, assoc. editor for Europe, 1983—; mem. editorial bd. Indsl. Council Oceanology Jour., 1987—. Recipient C. A. Hogentoger award ASTM, 1973. Fellow Geol. Soc. Am., Geol. Soc. London, ASCE, Marine Tech. Soc. (v.p. 1969-71), AAAS; mem. Am. Geophys. Soc., Brit. Geotech. Soc., Internat. Soc. Soil Mechanics and Found. Engring., Royal Geol. and Mining Soc. Netherlands, Royal Inst. Engrs. Netherlands, Soc. Underwater Tech., Strategic Planning Soc. Home: Uiterweg 309, 1431 AJ Aalsmeer The Netherlands Office: Adrian Richards Co, Uiterweg 309, 1431 AJ Aalsmeer The Netherlands

RICHARDS, ARTHUR GUYON, physician, medical sociologist; b. Burgess Hill, Sussex, Eng., Dec. 13, 1918; arrived in Can., 1948; s. Walter Guyon and Ellen Ruth (Chaffers Welsh) R.; m. Elizabeth Mary Mitchell, May 27, 1943; children: John Guyon, Simon Gerald, Guy Alfred. BA in Natural Sci. with Honors, Cambridge U., 1939; MB BChir, 1942; MA in Sociology, U. Sask., 1972. Trainee in pathology Cambridge (Eng.) U., 1946-48; bacteriologist U. Sask., Saskatoon, Can., 1948-50; med. sociologist U. Sask., Saskatoon, 1972-87; gen. practice medicine Saskatoon, 1952-87. Contbr. articles to profl. jours. Pres. Amnesty Internat., Saskatoon, 1977-79. Mem. Coll Physicians and Surgeons Sask., Physicians for Social Responsibility, Western Assn. Sociologists and Anthropologists (sec. 1973-74), Am. Humanist Assn. (bd. dirs. 1966-69). Mem. New Democratic Party. Home: 327 666 Leg in Boot Square, Vancouver, BC Canada V5Z 4B3

RICHARDS, DARRIE HEWITT, investment company executive; b. Washington, May 31, 1921; s. George Jacob and Esmee (MacMahon) R.; m. Patricia Louise Moses, Jan. 1, 1947; children: Hilary Wade, Craig Hewitt, Lynn Cotter. Student, Brown U., 1937-39; B.S., U.S. Mil. Acad., 1943; M.S., Princeton U., 1949. Commd. 2d lt. U.S. Army, 1943, advanced through grades to maj. gen., 1970; mem. Army Gen. Staff Logistics, 1962-66; brigade comdr., logistics staff officer Europe, 1966-68; comdr. Qui Nhon (Vietnam) Support Command, 1968-69, Western Area Mil. Traffic Mgmt. and Terminal Service, 1969-70; asst. dep. chief staff for logistics Dept. Army, 1970-73; dep. dir. Def. Logistics Agy., 1973-74, ret., 1974; v.p. Capital Resources Inc., Washington, 1974-75; asso. Devel. Resources, Inc., Alexandria, Va., 1975-79; pres. the Montgomery Corp., Alexandria, 1976-84; gen. partner Craighill Co., Alexandria, 1980—. Author publs. on devel allied strategy in World War II, also nat. transp. policy. Decorated D.S.M. with oak leaf cluster, Legion of Merit with 3 oak leaf clusters, Bronze Star, Air medal with 3 oak leaf clusters; Order Chung Mu Republic Korea; Disting. Service Order; Honor medal 1st class Vietnam. Mem. Def. Mgmt. Assn. (v.p. 1973-74), Am. Def. Preparedness Assn. (nat. council 1974-76), Assn. U.S. Army (pres. Heidelburg chpt. 1967-68), alumni assns. U.S. Mil Acad., Princeton U., Brown U. Episcopalian. Home: 1250 S Washington St Apt 709 Alexandria VA 22314 Office: 300 Montgomery St Alexandria VA 22314

RICHARDS, DAVID ALAN, lawyer; b. Dayton, Ohio, Sept. 21, 1945; s. Charles Vernon and Betty Ann (Macher) R.; m. Marianne Catherine Del Monaco, June 26, 1971; children: Christopher, Courtney. BA summa cum laude, Yale U., 1967, JD, 1972; MA, Cambridge U., 1969. Bar: N.Y., 1973. Assoc. Paul, Weiss, Rifkind, Wharton & Garrison, N.Y.C., 1972-77, Coudert Bros., N.Y.C., 1977-80, ptnr., 1981-82; ptnr., head real estate group Sidley & Austin, N.Y.C., 1983—; gov. Anglo-Am. Real Property Inst. U.S./U.K., 1983—, sec., 1988—. Contbr. articles to profl. jours. Trustee Scarsdale Pub. Library, 1984—, pres., 1988—. Mem. ABA (real property, probate and trust sect., council 1982—, bd. dirs. real property div., 1988—, Am. Coll. Real Estate Lawyers (chmn. amicus curiae brief com. 1985—, gov. 1987—), Internat. Bar Assn., Assn. Bar City N.Y. (real property com. 1978-80, 84-87). Democrat. United Ch. of Christ. Club: Shenorock Shore (Rye, N.Y.). Home: 18 Forest Ln Scarsdale NY 10583 Office: Sidley & Austin 875 3d Ave New York NY 10022

RICHARDS, FREDERICK FRANCIS, JR., manufacturing company executive; b. Payette, Idaho, Jan. 28, 1936; s. Frederick Francis and Dorothy Lucille (Taylor) R.; B.S. in Indsl. Engring., So. Meth. U., 1959; M.B.A., Harvard U., 1961; m. DeAnne Aden, Aug. 10, 1959; children—Frederick Francis III, Craig, Jeffrey. Indsl. engr. Collins Radio Inc., 1955-59; research asst. Harvard U., 1961-62; fin. analyst H.F. Linder & William T. Golden, N.Y.C., 1962-65; pres. Adrich Corp. and subs., Dallas, 1965—; v.p. and prin. Capital Alliance Corp., Dallas, 1985—; v.p. GTex., Inc., Dallas, 1986-87; pres. AR Assocs., internat. mgmt. cons., Dallas, 1972—; dir. Dallas Pub. Inc., DPIM, Inc., Alt. Energy Resources, Global Link, Aden-Richards, Inc. Mem. Am. Inst. Indsl. Engrs. (sr.), ASTM, Airplane Owners and Pilot Assn., Am. Soc. Indsl. Security, Internat. Assn. Chiefs Police, Nat. Pilots Assn., Exptl. Aircraft Assn. Club: Harvard (N.Y.C.). Author papers in field; bus. columnist. Home: 3 Cumberland Pl Richardson TX 75080 Office: 1111 W Mockingbird Ln Suite 737 Dallas TX 75247

RICHARDS, GERALD THOMAS, lawyer, consultant; b. Monrovia, Calif., Mar. 17, 1933; s. Louis Jacquelyn Richards and Inez Vivian (Richardson) Hall; children: Patricia M. Richards Grauf, Laura J., Dag Hammarskjold; m. Mary Lou Richards, Dec. 27, 1986. BS magna cum laude, Lafayette Coll., 1957; MS, Purdue U., 1963; JD, Golden Gate U., 1976. Bar: Calif. 1976, U.S. Dist. Ct. (no. dist.) Calif. 1977, U.S. Patent Office 1981, U.S. Ct. Appeals (9th cir.) 1984, U.S. Supreme Ct. 1984. Computational physicist Lawrence Livermore (Calif.) Nat. Lab., 1967-73., planning staff lawyer, 1979, mgr. tech. transfer office, 1980-83, asst. lab. counsel, 1984—; sole practice, Livermore, 1976-78; mem. exec. com., policy advisor Fed. Lab. Consortium for Tech. Transfer, 1980—; panelist, del. White House Conf. on Productivity, Washington, 1983; del. Nat. Conf. on Tech. and Aging, Wingspread, Wis.,

1981. Commr. Housing Authority, City of Livermore, 1977, vice chairperson, 1978, chairperson, 1979; pres. Housing Choices, Inc., Livermore, 1980-84; bd. dirs. Valley Vol. Ctr., Pleasanton, Calif., 1983, pres., 1984-86. Recipient Engring. award Gen. Electric Co., 1956. Served to maj. U.S. Army, 1959-67, Korea. Korea. Mem. ABA, San Francisco Bar Assn., Alameda County Bar Assn., Livermore-Amador Valley Bar Assn. (sec. 1978), Phi Beta Kappa, Tau Beta Pi, Sigma Pi Sigma. Club: Commonwealth Calif. Home: 1070 Shady Creek Pl Danville CA 94526 Office: Lawrence Livermore Nat Lab PO Box 808 L-701 Livermore CA 94550

RICHARDS, LACLAIRE LISSETTA JONES (MRS. GEORGE A. RICHARDS), social worker; b. Pine Bluff, Ark.; d. Artie William and Geraldine (Adams) Jones; B.A., Nat. Coll. Christian Workers, 1953; M.S.W., U. Kans., 1956; postgrad. Columbia U., 1960; m. George Alvarez Richards, July 26, 1958; children—Leslie Rosario, Lia Mercedes, Jorge Ferguson. Diplomate Clin. Social Work; cert. gerontologist. Psychiat. supervisory, teaching, community orgn., adminstrv. and consultative duties Hastings Regional Center, Ingleside, Nebr., 1956-60; supervisory, consultative and adminstrv. responsibilities for psychiat. and geriatric patients VA Hosp., Knoxville, Iowa, 1960-74, field instr. for grad. students from U. Mo., EEO counselor, 1969-74, 78—, com. chmn., 1969-70, Fed. women's program coordinator, 1972-74; sr. social worker Mental Health Inst., Cherokee, Iowa, 1974-77; adj. asst. prof. dept. social behavior U. S.D.; instr. Augustana Coll., 1981-86; outpatient social worker VA Med. and Regional Office Center, Sioux Falls, S.D., 1978—; EEO counselor. Mem. Knoxville Juvenile Adv. Com., 1963-65, 68-70, sec., 1965-66, chmn., 1966-68; sec. Urban Renewal Citizens' Adv. Com., Knoxville, 1966-68; mem. United Methodist Ch. Task Force Exptl. Styles Ministry and Leadership, 1973-74, mem. adult choir, mem. ch. and society com.; counselor Knoxville Youth Line program; sec. exec. com. Vis. Nurse Assn., 1979-80; canvasser community fund drs., Knoxville; mem. Cherokee Civil Rights Commn.; bd. dirs., pub. relations, membership devel. and program devel. cons. YWCA, 1983-85. Named S.D. Social Worker of Yr., 1983. Mem. Nat. Assn. Social Workers (co-chmn. Nebr. chpt. profl. standards com. 1958-59), Acad. Cert. Social Workers, S.D. Assn. Social Workers (chmn. minority affairs com., v.p. S.E. region 1980, pres. 1980-82 exec. com. 1982-84, mem. social policy and action com.), Nebr. Assn. Social Workers (chmn. 1958-59), AAUW (sec. Hastings chpt. 1958-60), AMA Aux., Seventh Dist. S.D. Med. Soc. Aux., Coalition on Aging, NAACP (chmn. edn. com. 1983—). Methodist (Sunday sch. tchr. adult div.; mem. commn. on edn.; mem. Core com. for adult edn.; mem. Adult Choir; mem. Social Concerns Work Area). Home: 1701 Ponderosa Dr Sioux Falls SD 57103

RICHARDS, MARTIN GERARD, entomologist; b. Oxford, Eng., June 10, 1956; s. Bruce William and Grace Maud (Mitchell) R.; m. Margaret Jane Steward, June 9, 1984. BSc in Agrl. Zoology, U. Newcastle, Eng., 1977; MSc in Applied Entomology, U. London, 1980, PhD in Entomology, 1984. Postgrad. researcher Glasshouse Crops Research Inst., Eng., 1980-84; program mgr. entomology Microgenesys, Inc., West Haven, Conn., 1984-86; mgr. product devel. Agrl. Genetics Co., Cambridge, Eng., 1986—. Contbr. sci. papers to profl. jours. Fellow Royal Entomol. Soc. Mem. Ch. of Eng. Office: Agrl Genetics Co Ltd, Unit 154/155, Cambridge, Sci Park, Milton Rd, Cambridge CB4 4GG, England

RICHARDS, ROGER THOMAS, acoustical scientist; b. Akron, Ohio, June 19, 1942; s. Clyde Irvin and Thelma Josephine (Whitaker) R.; BS in Physics, Westminster Coll., New Wilmington, Pa., 1964; MS in Physics, Ohio U., 1968; PhD in Acoustics, Pa. State U., 1980. Grad. asst. in physics Ohio U., 1965-67, research asst. in acoustics, 1967-68; asso. engr. transducer lab. Gen. Dynamics/Electronics Co., Rochester, N.Y., 1968-69, engr. acoustics dept., 1969-71; NASA trainee Pa. State U., 1971-74, grad. asst. in acoustics, 1974-80; staff asso. Applied Research Lab., State College, Pa., 1976-80; tech. staff marine systems div. Rockwell Internat., Groton, Conn., 1980-84; sr. scientist Bolt Beranch & Newman, New London, Conn., 1984-87; physicist Nav. Underwater System Ctr., New London, 1987—. Fellow NASA. Mem. Acoustical Soc. Am., AIAA, Nat. Speleological Soc. (life, vice chmn. Nittany Grotto 1975-76), Am. Cryptographic Assn., AAAS, U.S. Chess Fedn. (capt. Pa. State U. team 1973, cert. tournament dir., life), Am. Go Assn., Am. Contract Bridge League (pres. local club 1970-71), U.S. Othello Assn. (corp. dir. 1979-84, Midwestern Othello champion 1979-84), Pa. State U. Alumni Assn. (alumni council and exec. bd. 1973-74), Sigma Xi, Kappa Mu Epsilon, Sigma Pi Sigma (nat. del. 1967). Contbg. editor Othello Quar., 1979—, editorial staff The Cryptogram, 1984—; contbr. articles to profl. jours.; research in acoustic propagation and scattering, sonar transducer and array design. Home: 34 Coveside Ln Stonington CT 06378 Office: Nav Underwater System Ctr New London CT 06320

RICHARDS, THOMAS JEFFREY, physicist; b. Berwyn, Ill., Feb. 28, 1944; s. James Henry and Caroline Emily (Patha) R. B.A., Lake Forest Coll., 1966; M.A., Wake Forest U., 1968; Ph.D., St. Louis U., 1972. Sr. research engr. Caterpillar, Inc., Peoria, Ill., 1973-76, project engr., 1976-81, staff engr., 1981—. Patentee in field. Mem. Am. Phys. Soc., AAAS. Office: Caterpillar Inc Research Dept TC-A Peoria IL 61629

RICHARDS, WILLIAM GEORGE, retired savings and loan executive; b. Lockhart, Tex., Feb. 20, 1920; s. Cyrus F. and Gussie (Baldridge) R.; LL.B., U. Tex., 1948; m. Winnifred Adams, Nov. 23, 1940 (dec. May 1969); children—Bettye Ann (Mrs. Rogers), Mark Andrew; m. 2d, Corrie Marsh, Mar. 29, 1972. Admitted to Tex. bar, 1948; practiced law with father, Lockhart, 1948-55; v.p., atty., dir. Lockhart Savs. & Loan Assn., 1948-55; exec. v.p. Benjamin Franklin Savs. & Loan Assn., 1955-64, pres., 1964-74, vice-chmn. bd., 1974-75; chmn. bd., chief exec. officer Surety Savs. Assn., Houston, 1975-78; trustee Savs. & Loan Found., Inc., 1957-59. Mem. Tex. Ho. of Reps., 1947-50; mayor of Lockhart, 1954-55. Mem. adv. com. Coll. Bus. Adminstrn. U. Houston, 1966-70. Served with USNR, 1942-45. Mem. Nat. League Insured Savs. Assns. (exec. com. 1962-66), Houston C. of C. (dir. 1966, 68-73), Tex. Savs. and Loan League (dir. 1953-63, 63-66; pres. 1967-68), Phi Delta Phi. Democrat. Episcopalian. Clubs: Onion Creek, The Citadel, Austin (Austin). Home: 11007 Pinehurst Dr Austin TX 78747

RICHARDSON, DAVID WALTHALL, cardiologic educator, consultant; b. Nanking, China, Mar. 22, 1925; s. Donald William and Virginia (McIlwaine) R.; m. Frances Lee Wingfield, June 12, 1948; children—Donald, Sarah, David. B.S., Davidson Coll., 1947; M.D., Harvard U., 1951. Diplomate Am. Bd. Internal Medicine, Am. Bd. Cardiology. Intern, resident Yale New Haven Hosp., Conn., 1951-53; resident, fellow Med. Coll. Va., Richmond, 1953-56, assoc. prof. to prof. medicine, 1962—, chmn. div. cardiology, 1972-87; chief cardiology, assoc. chief staff for research VA Hosp., Richmond, 1956-61; vis. scientist Oxford U., Eng., 1961-62; vis. prof. U. Milan, Italy, 1972-73. Contbr. articles to profl. jours. Moderator Hanover Presbytery, Presbyterian Ch. U.S., Richmond, 1970. Served with USN, 1944-46. Fellow. Am. Coll. Cardiology (gov. VA. 1970-72), Am. Heart Assn. (council clin. cardiology); mem. Am. Soc. Clin. Investigation, Am. Clin. and Climatol. Assn. Current work: Cardiac arrhythmias, hypertension, clinical trials. Subspecialties: Cardiology; Internal medicine. Home: 5501 Queensbury Rd Richmond VA 23226

RICHARDSON, DONALD CHARLES, engineer, consultant; b. Glendale, Calif., June 6, 1937; s. George Robert and Margaret Josephine (Buchholz) R.; m. Helen Mary Boyd, Aug. 9, 1984. B.A. in Sci., Calif. State U., 1965; M.S. in Engring., Queens U., 1981, M.Ed., 1983; Ph.D., Clarkson U., 1988. Sr. engr. Control Data Corp., Toronto, Ont., Can., 1972-75; tchr. Algonquin Coll., Kingston, Ont., Can., 1975-79; assoc. prof. Royal Mil. Coll. of Can., Kingston, 1982-84; instr. Clarkson U., Potsdam, N.Y., 1988; superconductor cons., MIT. Author of engring. papers. Served to lt. comdr. USN, 1964-69, Vietnam. Electrochem. Soc. fellow, 1984. Mem. Am. Soc. Engring. Edn., Mensa, Sigma Xi. Lodge: Fraternal Order of Seals.

RICHARDSON, EMILIE WHITE, manufacturing company executive, investment company executive, lecturer; b. Chattanooga, July 8; d. Emmett and Mildred Evelyn (Harbin) White; B.A., Wheaton Coll., 1951; 1 dau., Julie Richardson Morphis. With Christy Mfg. Co., Inc., Fayetteville, N.C., 1952—, sec. 1956-66, v.p., 1967-74, exec. v.p., 1975-79, pres., chief exec. officer, 1980—; v.p. E. White Investment Co., 1968-83, pres., 1983—; cons. Aerostatic Industries, 1979—; v.p. Gannon Corp., 1981—; cons. govt. contacts and offshore mfg., 1981—; lectr., speaker in field. Vice pres. public relations Ft. Lauderdale Symphony Soc., 1974-76, v.p. membership, 1976-77, adv. bd., 1978—; active Atlantic Found., Ft. Lauderdale Mus. Art, Beaux Arts, Freedoms Found.; mem. East Broward Women's Republican Club, 1968—, Americanism chmn., 1971-72. Mem. Internat. Platform Assn., Nat. Speakers Assn., Fla. Speakers Assn. Presbyterian. Clubs: Toastmasters, Green Valley Country. Home: 1531 NE 51st St Fort Lauderdale FL 33334 Office: 3311 Ft Bragg Rd Fayetteville NC 28303

RICHARDSON, GRAHAM FREDERICK, senator; b. Kogarah, New South Wales, Australia, Sept. 27, 1949; s. Frederick James and Catherine Maud (Graham) R.; m. Cheryl Ruth Gardner, Apr. 18, 1973; children: Matthew, Kate. Student law sch., Sydney U., 1969-71. State organizer New South Wales br. Australian Labor Party, 1971-76, del. to nat. conf., 1977—, convenor nat. industry platform com. including portfolios resources and energy, primary industry, sport and tourism, sci., industry, tech. & commerce, gen. sec., 1976-83, nat. exec., from 1979, v.p., 1986; senator from New South Wales Australian Parliament, 1983, mem. numerous coms. including fin. and govt. ops., mem. electoral reform com., chmn. Estimates"A", 1986—, mem. sen. select TV equalization com., 1987—, minister for arts, sport, the environment, tourism and the territories, 1987—. Roman Catholic. Clubs: Tattersalls, Killara Golf (Sydney); St. George Leagues. Office: Morgan Grenfell Bldg 10th Floor, 56 Phillip St, Sydney, New South Wales 2000, Australia

RICHARDSON, (ROBERT) IAN, management consulting company executive; b. Cavan, Ireland, Jan. 20, 1951; s. Robert Mason and Elizabeth Margaret (Hamilton) R.; m. Linda Margaret Bell, Apr. 3, 1976; children—Gemma Jane, Amy Louise. B.Social Scis., Queen's U., Belfast, No. Ireland, 1973. Sr. mgr. Civil Service, No. Ireland, 1973-78; research mgr. Pvt. Bus. Forum, Eng., 1979-80; recruitment cons. Hoggett Bowers P.L.C., Manchester, Eng., 1980-81; recruitment mgr. K.B.S. Ltd., Liverpool, Eng., 1981-84; mng. dir. Meridian (U.K.) Ltd., Crewe, Eng., 1984-86; mng. dir. Link Resources div. Link Orgn. Ltd., 1986—. Editor, contbr. Referendum mag., 1979—. Seale Found. scholar, 1965. Fellow Inst. Employment Cons., Nat. Chamber of Trade Gt. Britain. Social Democrat. Anglican. Avocations: theatre; board games; travel. Office: Link Recruitment Group, 3 Macon Ct, Crewe, Cheshire CW1 1EA, England

RICHARDSON, IAN WILLIAM, actor; b. Edinburgh, Scotland, Apr. 7, 1934; s. John and Margaret R.; m. Maroussia Frank, Feb. 2, 1961; children—Jeremy, Miles. Diploma in Acting and Teaching, Royal Scottish Acad. Music and Drama. Actor Royal Shakespeare Co., Stratford on Avon and London, 1960-75, Shaw Festival Theatre, Niagara, Ont., Can., 1977. Appeared in numerous plays, including: My Fair Lady, Broadway, 1976-77; films and TV plays include: Tinker, Tailor, Soldier, Spy, Private Shulz, The Sign of Four, The Hound of the Baskervilles; films: Brazil, Whoops!, Apocalypse, The Fourth Protocol, Cry Freedom; tv includes: Star Quality, Porterhouse Blue; author prefaces to Shakespearean works. Fellow Royal Scottish Acad. Music and Drama; mem. Brit. Actors Equity, Actors Equity, Screen Actors Guild. Clubs: Garrick (London); players (N.Y.C.). Office: care London Mgmt, 231-245 Regent St, London W1, England

RICHARDSON, JACQUES GABRIEL, editor, author; b. Balt., Jan. 20, 1924; s. John Benjamin and Adrienne Marguerite (Bit) R.; student Concordia U., 1940-42, Trinity Coll., 1942; B.A., U. Mich., 1947; m. Erika Buggert; children: Pamela A., Michelle D. With Guide Pubs., Inc., Balt., 1948-49, USIA, Washington, 1950-54, Office of Q.M. Gen., Dept. Army, Washington, 1955-60, Office Chief of Staff, Washington, 1960-61, Conover-Mast Pub., Inc., N.Y.C. and Paris, 1962-68; European dir. Tech. Communication, Inc., Paris, 1968-70; assoc. pub. La Recherche, Paris, 1971-72; editor-in-chief Impact of Sci. and Soc., head Sci. and Soc. sect. UNESCO, Paris, 1972-85; lectr. Seikei Gakuin U., Tokyo, 1955-60; cons. in tech. communication, 1968—. Mem. corp. Am. Hosp. in France, 1970—; mem. Democrats in France, 1978—. Served with U.S. Army, 1943-48. Decorated Bronze Star (U.S.); Ordre du Merite Social de Belgique. Mem. Union Internat. Tech. Assns. (bd. dirs.), AAAS, Pugwash Confs. on Sci. and World Affairs (French sect.), Association des Journalistes Scientifiques de la Presse d'Information. Clubs: Am. of Paris, Vienna. Contbr. articles to profl. jours.; editor: Integrated Technology Transfer, 1979; (with Buzatti-Traverso) La Sfida della Scienza, 1976; (with Baker and Green) Julian Huxley, Scientist and World Citizen, 1978; (with Kinnon and Kholodilin) The Impact of Modern Scientific Ideas on Society, 1981; editor: Models of Reality: Shaping Thought and Action, 1984; Managing The Ocean—Resources, Research, Law, 1985; Windows on Creativity and Invention, 1988. Home: 78 ave de Suffren, 75015 Paris France Office: Cidex 400, Authon la Plaine, 91410 Dourdan France

RICHARDSON, JOHN, international relations executive; b. Boston, Feb. 4, 1921; s. John and Hope (Hemenway) R.; m. Thelma Ingram, Jan. 19, 1945; children: Eva Selek Teleki, Teren de Cossy, Hope H., Catherine Barrett), Hetty L. A.B., Harvard U., 1943, J.D., 1949. Bar: N.Y. 1949. Assoc. Sullivan & Cromwell, N.Y.C., 1949-55; with Paine, Webber, Jackson & Curtis, N.Y.C., 1955-69, gen. ptnr., 1958-61, ltd. ptnr., 1961-69; pres., chief exec. officer Free Europe, Inc. (Radio Free Europe), 1961-68; asst. sec. for ednl. and cultural affairs Dept. State, 1969-77, also acting asst. sec. state for pub. affairs, 1971-73; exec. dir. for social policy Ctr. for Strategic and Internat. Studies; research prof. internat. communication Sch. Fgn. Service, Georgetown U., Washington, 1977-78; pres., chief exec. officer Youth for Understanding, Inc., 1978-86; counsellor U.S. Peace Inst., Washington, 1987—; spl. advisor Aspen Inst. Humanistic Studies, 1977-80. Mem. Council Fgn. Relations, 1957—, Citizens Commn. on S.E. Asian Refugees, 1978—; founder Polish Med. Aid Project, 1957-61; pres. Internat. Rescue Com., 1960-61, bd. dirs., 1958-61, 78—; chmn. N.Y.C. Met. Mission, United Ch. of Christ, 1966-69, Am. Council for United Nations U., 1977-87, Consortium for Internat. Citizens Exchange, 1980-84—; bd. dirs. Freedom House, 1963-69, pres., 1977-84; chmn. Nat. Endowment for Democracy, 1984-88, bd. dirs., 1984—; bd. dirs. Kennedy Ctr. for Performing Arts, 1970-77, Inter-Am. Found., 1970-77, East-West Ctr., 1975-77, Fgn. Policy Assn., 1958-68, 77-86, Japan-U.S. Friendship Commn., 1976-77, Global Perspectives in Edn., 1977—, Inst. Psychiatry and Fgn. Affairs, 1977—, Meridian House Internat., 1978-83, Atlantic Council of U.S., 1982-84, Fgn. Student Service Council, 1978-82. Served with paratroops, World War II. Home: 7401 Bradley Blvd Bethesda MD 20817 Office: US Inst Peace 1550 M St NW Suite 700 Washington DC 20005-1708

RICHARDSON, MILDRED LOVINA TOURTILLOTT, psychologist; b. North Hampton, N.H., May 8, 1907; d. Herbert Shaw and Sarach Louise (Fife) Tourtillott; m. Harold Wellington Richardson, June 25, 1932; children: Elizabeth Fern Ruben, Constance Joy Van Valer, Carol Louise Dennis, Sarah Louise. AB, Bates Coll., 1930; MA, U. Mich., 1948; EdS, Butler U., 1961; PhD, Ind. U., 1965. Diplomate Am. Bd. Profl. Psychology, Nat. Register Health Service Providers in Psychology; cert. clin. and sch. psychology, Pa., Ind. Tchr. math. and sci. Norwich (Conn.) Free Acad., 1930-32, Port Huron (Mich.) High Sch., 1943-45; dir. intermediate girls Interlochen Nat. Music Camp, Mich., 1953, asst. dean univ. women, 1954; tchr., guidance counselor Community Sch. Corp., Franklin, Ind., 1956-64; supr. tng. Devereux Found., Devon, Pa., 1965-78, cons. clin. tng. in sch. and clin. psychology, 1975-78; tchr. psychology of spl. edn. Pa. State U.ext., King of Prussia, 1966-68; sch. psychologist Johnson County (Ind.) Spl. Services, 1979-82; head clin. psychology Community Psychiat. Ctrs. Valle Vista Hosp., Greenwood, Ind., 1983—; pvt. practice health service provider in psychology Greenwood, 1985—; clin. assoc. prof. Hahnemann Med. Coll., Phila., 1973-78, dir. seminar on psychodiagnostics; assoc. prof. sch. psychology, grad. seminar and practicum Ind. U., Bloomington, 1982; pvt. practice psychology, 1970—; bd. examiners Midwest Regional Bd. Am. Bd. Profl. Psychology; bd. dirs. Johnson County (Ind.) Assn. Mentally Retarded Citizens, 1982-84; participant Internat. Sch. Psychology Colloquium, 1975, Ind. State Tchrs. Assn., Ind. Psychol. Assn. Contbr. articles to profl. jours. Recipient Headliner award Theta Sigma Phi, 1964. Fellow Am. Psychol. Assn.; mem. Inst. Clin. Tng. (hon.), Internat. Council Psychologists, Internat. Sch. Psychology Com., Soc. Ret. Execs., Devereux Found. (hon.), Phi Kappa Phi. Republican. Baptist. Home: 477 Oakwood Dr S Greenwood IN 46142 Office: Community Psychiat Ctrs Valle Vista Hosp 898 E Main St Greenwood IN 46142

RICHARDSON, ROBERT OWEN, lawyer; b. Gallatin, Mo., Sept. 7, 1922; s. Denver Oscar and Opal (Wellman) R.; m. Carroll Sparks, July 7, 1951 (div.); children—Robert Steven, Linda Colleen; m. 2d, Viola Kapantais Wempe, Dec. 22, 1977. B.S. in Physics, Drury Coll., 1946; LL.B., George Washington U., 1954, J.D., 1968; M.S., Fla. Inst. Tech., 1977. Bar: U.S. Dist. Ct. (D.C.) 1954, U.S. Patent Office 1954, U.S. Ct. Customs and Patent Appeals 1958, Calif. 1958, N.H. 1961, Iowa 1976, U.S. Supreme Ct. 1961, Can. Patent Office, 1962, U.S. Ct. Appeals (fed. cir.) 1982. Patent examiner U.S. Patent Office, Washington, 1949-54; patent atty. Navy Electronics Lab., San Diego, 1954-56, Gen. Dynamics, San Diego, 1956-60; chief patent counsel Sanders Assoc., Nashua, N.H., 1960-62; patent atty. TRW, Canoga Park, Calif., 1963-64, McDonnell Douglas, Santa Monica, Calif., 1964-75; patent counsel U.S. Army Armament Munitions Chem. Command, Rock Island, Ill., 1975-85; patent arbitrator Am. Arbitration Assn., 1984—; judge pro tem Los Angeles Mcpl. Ct., 1967-68. Author: How To Get Your Own Patent, 1981. Democratic nominee for Congress from Mo. 6th Dist., 1951. Served to lt. comdr. USNR, 1942-73. Mem. MENSA, Govt. Patent Lawyer's Assn., Am. Patent Law Assn., Patent Law Assn. San Diego, Patent Law Assn. Los Angeles, Patent Law Assn. Boston, Patent Law Assn. Iowa. Lodges: Masons, Shriners.

RICHARDSON, TIMOTHY SCOTT, barrister; b. Auckland, N.Z., Nov. 24, 1946; s. Murray and Beatrice Ruth (Waite) R.; m. Susan Elaine Low, July 24, 1976 (div. 1984); 1 child, Emily Clare. LLB, U. Auckland, 1972. Solicitor, barrister N.Z., 1969. Barrister, solicitor, prin. Osborne Handley Gray and Richardson, Whakatane, N.Z., 1973-85; sole practice Tauranga, N.Z., 1985—; bd. dirs. Bell-Air Exec. Air Travel, Whakatane; tutor Bay of Plenty Poly., Tauranga, 1987—. Contbr. articles to profl. jours. Mem. Auckland Dist. Law Soc. (costs reviser 1986—), Auckland Med.-Legal Soc., Energy and Nat. Resources Law Assn. of N.Z. Inc., Auckland U. Rowing Club (life), Whakatane Rowing Club (pres. 1980-83), Tauranga Rowing Club (coach 1985—). Presbyterian. Home: 3/136 Fraser St, Tauranga, Bay of Plenty New Zealand Office: Trustbank Bldg Devonport Rd., Tauranga,, Bay of Plenty New Zealand

RICHARDSON, TONY, stage and film producer; b. Shipley, Yorkshire, Eng., June 5, 1928; came to U.S., 1974; s. Clarence Albert and Elsie Evans (Campion) R.; m. Vanessa Redgrave, 1962 (div. 1967); children—Natasha, Joely, Katharine Grimond. B.A., Wadham Coll. Oxford U. (Eng.), 1950. Assoc. artistic dir. Royal Ct. Theatre, 1956-64; dir. Woodfall Film Prodns. Ltd., London, Eng., 1958—; plays: (produced or directed) Look Back in Anger, The Chairs, Pericles and Othello (Stratford), The Entertainer, Luther, The Seagull, St. Joan of the Stockyards, Hamlet, Threepenny Opera, I Claudius, Arturo Ui, A Taste of Honey, Lady From the Sea, As You Like It (Los Angeles); films: (produced or directed): Look Back in Anger, 1958, The Entertainer, 1959, Saturday Night and Sunday Morning, 1960, A Taste of Honey, 1961, The Loneliness of the Long Distance Runner, 1962, Tom Jones (recipient Acad. award), 1963, The Loved One, 1964, Mademoiselle, 1965, The Sailor from Gibraltar, 1965, Red and Blue, 1966, The Charge of the Light Brigade, 1967, Laughter in the Dark, 1968, Hamlet, 1969, Ned Kelly, 1969, A Delicate Balance, 1973, Dead Cert 1973, Joseph Andrews 1977, Death in Canaan, 1978, The Border, 1981; The Hotel New Hampshire, 1984, Penalty Phase, 1986, Antony and Cleopatra, 1987. Office: care Dirs Guild Am 17950 Sunset Blvd Los Angeles CA 90046

RICHER, STEPHEN BRUCE, state official; b. Newark, N.J., Aug. 18, 1946; s. Seymour Albert Richer and Rosalind (Greenberg) Anderson; m. Kathleen Shagner Richer, Jan. 10, 1981; children—Sean Edmund and Jack Albert. A.B. in Politics, Princeton U., 1968. Dep. dir. N.J. Bicentennial Commn., Trenton, N.J., 1975-77; spl. asst. to gov. N.J., Trenton, 1977-80; dir. N.J. Div. of Tourism, Trenton, 1980-82; pres. Travel & Recreation Info. Products, Randolph, N.J., 1982-83; exec. dir. Nev. Commn. on Tourism, Carson City, 1983—; vice chmn. Visit US West; mem. fed. agy. Nev. dist. Export Council, Reno, 1984—. Mayor, councilman Randolph Twp., Randolph, N.J., 1974-80; mem. N.J. County and Mcpl. Govt. Study Commn., Trenton, 1979-82; chmn. Pine Nut (Nev.) dist. merit badge com. Eagle Scout, 1986—. Recipient Tourism award N.J. Hotel and Motel Assn., 1980. Mem. Nat. Govs. Assn. (staff adv. com. on internat. trade and Fgn. relations 1984—), Nat. Council State Travel Dirs. (bd. dirs. 1980-82, 86—), Nev. Hotel-Motel Assn. (ex. officio bd. dirs. 1984—), Am. Bus. Assn., Nat. Tour Assn., Am. Soc. Travel Agts. Travel Industry Assn. Am. (Outstanding Mkgt. award 1980). Democrat. Jewish. Club: Princeton (chmn. schs. com. Northwestern, N.J. 1972-81, Nev. 1985—). Club: Skal of No. Nev. Lodge: Kiwanis (pres. Dover, N.J. 1974). Office: Nev Tourism Commn State Capitol Complex Carson City NV 89710

RICHESON, HUGH ANTHONY, JR., lawyer; b. Aberdeen, Md., Apr. 22, 1947; s. Hugh Anthony Sr. and Mary Evelyn (Burford) R.; m. Melissa Anne Baum, Apr. 4, 1970; children: Hugh Anthony III, Heidi E., Holly K., Hagin G., Herald Joshua. BBA, U. Richmond, 1969; JD, U. Fla., 1973. Bar: Fla. 1974, U.S. Dist. Ct. (mid. dist.) Fla. 1975. Assoc. Bryant, Dickens, Rumph, Franson & Miller, Jacksonville, Fla., 1974-76, ptnr., 1977; sole practice Orange Park, Fla., 1977-82; ptnr. Smith, Hallowes & Richeson, Orange Park, 1982-83; sole practice Palm Harbor, Fla., 1984—. Pres. Full Gospel Bus. Men's Fellowship Internat., Orange Park, 1983-84, Palm Harbor, 1985—, field rep., 1987—; chmn. North Pinellas (Fla.) Pregnancy Ctr., Palm Harbor, 1986—. Mem. Clay County Bar Assn. (pres. 1981-82), Clearwater Bar Assn., Assn. Trial Lawyers Am., Acad. Fla. Trial Lawyers, Fla. Council Bar Assn. Pres.'s (life), Christian Legal Soc., Phi Delta Phi. Republican. Mem. Christian Ch. Home: 2463 Indian Trail E Palm Harbor FL 34683 Office: 1209 US Hwy 19 N Suite 251 PO Box 99 Palm Harbor FL 34682

RICHEY, PHIL HORACE, former manufacturing executive, consultant; b. Detroit, July 30, 1923; s. Lawrence Kennedy and Hazel Annsonia (Stuckey) R.; children: Karen L. Richey Forrester, Ann C. Richey Zepke; stepchildren: Gregory F. Lloyd, Charles E. Lloyd III.; m. Mary Elizabeth McCulloch, June 30, 1984; stepchildren—Julie Ann McCulloch Beal, Mary Elizabeth McCulloch, Claire May McCullough. B.A. with distinction, U. Mich., 1948. With Detrex Chem. Industries Inc., Detroit, 1948-56; group v.p. Detrex Chem. Industries Inc., 1962-71; with Allied Research Products Co., 1956-59, v.p. fin., 1958-59; with U.S. Chem. Milling Co., Manhattan Beach, Calif., 1959-61; v.p. U.S. Chem. Milling Co., 1960-61; with Olin Corp., Stamford, Conn., 1971-81; corp. v.p., pres. Winchester group, 1977-81; mgmt. cons., 1981—; dir. LCI Ltd., Trinity Am. Corp., Gen. Am. Corp., Assoc. Chems. & Services Inc.; adj. prof. U.S. Internat. U., San Diego. Served as 1st. lt. AUS, 1942-46. Mem. Phi Kappa Phi, Beta Gamma Sigma. Home and Office: 342 Winamar Ave La Jolla CA 92037

RICHIR, MARC, philosopher; b. Charleroi, Belgium, Feb. 2, 1943; s. Jean and Jeanine (de Valeriola) R.; m. France Crenier, Aug. 18, 1964; 1 child, Vincent. Lic. in Phys. Scis., State U. of Liège, Belgium, 1964; Lic. in Philosophy, Free U., Brussels, 1968, PhD, 1973. Research worker Inst. Astrophysics, Liège, Belgium, 1964-65; stagiaire de recherches Fonds Nat. Research Sch., Brussels, 1968-69; aspirant Fonds Nat. Research Sch., Brussels, 1969-73, chargé de recherches, 1973-77, chercheur qualifié, 1977—; prof. Free U. of Brussels, 1978—; dir. seminar Collège Internat. de Philosophie, Paris, 1986-88. Author: Au-delà du renversement copernicien, 1976, Recherches phénoménologiques, 1981, vol. II, 1983, Phénomènes temps et êtres, 1987, vol. II, 1988. Recipient Prix Picard award Free Acad. Belgium, 1971. Mem. Belgian Soc. Philosophy (chmn. 1981-84), Ctr. Advanced Research in Phenomenology (internat. bd. advisors 1984—), Royal Acad. Belgium (corr.). Home: Les Bonsjeans, 84 410 Les Baux, Bedoin France Office: Institut de Philosophie, 143 Ave Ad Buyl, 1050 Brussels Belgium

RICHLER, MORDECAI, writer; b. Montreal, Que., Can., Jan. 27, 1931; s. Moses Isaac and Lily (Rosenberg) R.; m. Florence Wood, July 27, 1959; children: Daniel, Noah, Emma, Martha, Jacob. Student, Sir George Williams U., 1948-50. Vis. prof. Carleton U., Ottawa, Ont., 1972-74; assoc. judge for Can., Book-of-the-Month Club, 1974, also mem. editorial bd., N.Y. Author: novels The Acrobats, 1954, Son of a Smaller Hero, 1955, A Choice of Enemies, 1957, The Apprenticeship of Duddy Kravitz, 1959, Stick Your Neck Out, 1963, Cocksure, 1967, St. Urbain's Horseman, 1971, Joshua Then and Now, 1980; essays Notes on an Endangered Species, 1974, Home Sweet Home, 1984; stories The Street, 1975; childrens books Jacob Two-Two Meets The Hooded Fang, 1975, Jacob Two-Two and the Dinosaur, 1987; film The Apprenticeship of Duddy Kravitz (Acad. award nomination 1974), 1974 (Writers Guild of Am. award 1974), Joshua, Then and Now, 1985; also articles.; editor: The Best of Modern Humor, 1983. Recipient Gov.-Gen.'s award for lit., 1968, 71, Paris Rev. Humour prize, 1968; Guggenheim fellow, 1961; various Can. Council fellows. Club: Montreal Press. Address: 1321 Sherbrooke St W, Apt 80C, Montreal, PQ Canada H3Y 1J4

RICHMAN, ANTHONY E., textile rental company executive; b. Los Angeles, Dec. 13, 1941; s. Irving M. and Helen V. (Muchnic) R.; m. Judy Harriet Richman, Dec. 19, 1964; children: Lisa Michele, Jennifer Beth. BS, U. So. Calif., 1964. With Reliable Textile Rental Services, Los Angeles, 1964—, service mgr., 1969, sales and service mgr., 1970-73, plant mgr., 1973-75, gen. mgr., bd. dirs., 1975-78, chief exec. officer, 1978-82, v.p., sec.-treas., 1975-82, exec. v.p., chief exec. officer, 1982-84, pres., chief exec. officer, 1984—. Bd. dirs. Guild for Children, 1979—, Valley Guild for Cystic Fibrosis, 1974—; Cystic Fibrosis Found., 1985—; founding mem. Patrons for Cystic Fibrosis, 1983—. Recipient cert. of Achievement Linen Supply Assn. Am., 1979. Mem. Textile Rental Services Assn. Am. (past bd. dirs.). Office: Reliable Textile Rental Services 3200 N Figueroa St Los Angeles CA 90065

RICHMAN, JOHN MARSHALL, business executive, lawyer; b. N.Y.C., Nov. 9, 1927; s. Arthur and Madeleine (Marshall) R.; m. Priscilla Frary, Sept. 3, 1951; children: Catherine, Diana H. B.A., Yale U., 1949; LL.B., Harvard U., 1952. Bar: N.Y. 1953, Ill. 1973. Assoc. Leve, Hecht, Hadfield & McAlpin, N.Y.C., 1952-54; mem. law dept. Kraft, Inc., Glenview, Ill., 1954-63, gen. counsel Sealtest Foods div., 1963-67, asst. gen. counsel, 1967-70, v.p., gen. counsel, 1970-73, sr. v.p., gen. counsel, 1973-75, sr. v.p. adminstrn., gen. counsel, 1975-79, chmn. bd., chief exec. officer, 1979—; chmn. bd., chief exec. officer Dart & Kraft, Inc. (became Kraft, Inc. 1986), Glenview, Ill., 1980. Congregationalist. Clubs: Commercial (Chgo.), Economic (Chgo.), Mid-Am. (Chgo.); Union League (N.Y.C.); Westmoreland Country (Wilmette, Ill.). Office: Kraft Inc Kraft Ct Glenview IL 60025

RICHMAN, MARVIN JORDAN, real estate developer; b. N.Y.C., July 13, 1939; s. Morris and Minnie (Graubart) R.; m. Amy Paula Rubin, July 31, 1966; children—Mark Jason, Keith Hayden, Susanne Elizabeth, Jessica Paige. B.Arch., MIT, 1962; M.Urban Planning, N.Y. U., 1966, postgrad., 1967-69; M.B.A., U. Chgo., 1977; U.S. Dept. State fellow U. Chile, 1960. Architect, planner Skidmore, Owings & Merrill, N.Y.C., 1964, Conklin & Rossant, N.Y.C., 1965-67; ptnr. Vizbaras & Assos., N.Y.C., 1968-69; v.p. Urban Investment & Devel. Co., Chgo., 1969-79, sr. v.p., 1979; pres. First City Devels. Corp., Beverly Hills, Calif., 1979-80, Olympia & York Calif. Equities Corp., Los Angeles, 1981— Olympia & York Calif. Devel. Corp., 1981—, O&Y Hope St. Mgmt. Corp., 1982—, O&Y Homes Corp., 1983—; lectr. N.Y. U., 1967-69, Nat. Humanities Inst., other univs. Adv. Nat. Endowment for Arts. Mem. UCLA Ctr. Fin. and Real Estate Bd. Advisors. Served with USAF, 1963-64. Registered architect; lic. real estate broker. Mem. AIA, Am Planning Assn., Am. Arbitration Assn., Internat. Council Shopping Centers, Los Angeles World Affairs Council, Urban Land Inst., Nat. Assn. Office and Indsl. Parks, Chief Exec.'s Round Table, Air Force Assn., Lambda Alpha. Home: 3238 Fond Dr Encino CA 91436 Office: Olympia & York Cos 11601 Wilshire Blvd Los Angeles CA 90025

RICHMAN, PETER, electronics executive; b. N.Y.C., Nov. 7, 1927; s. Emil H. and Janet (Seidler) R.; B.S., M.I.T., 1946; M.S., N.Y. U., 1953; m. Vivian Hoffman, July 29, 1951; children—Meredith, Jeremy. Asst. chief engr. Reeves Instrument Corp., Garden City, N.Y., 1948-58; chief engr. Epsco, Inc., Cambridge, Mass., 1959-60; v.p., co-founder Rotek Instrument Corp., Watertown, Mass., 1960-64; v.p. Weston-Rotek, Lexington, Mass., 1964-67; cons. electronics engr., Lexington, 1967—; founder, pres. KeyTek Instrument Corp., 1976—; mem. NRC/Nat. Acad. Scis./Nat. Acad. Engring. Evaluation Panel for electricity div. Nat. Bur. Standards; mem. sci. adv. groups for several indsl. and sci. orgns. Fellow IEEE; mem. Instrument Soc. Am. (sr.), Sigma Xi, Tau Beta Pi. Patentee in precision electronic instrumentation; pioneer in precision dc and audio-frequency measurements, surge electrostatic discharge generation and electrostatic discharge measurements. Contbr. articles to profl. jours.

RICHMAN, SHELDON BARNETT, lawyer, author; b. N.Y.C., Mar. 1, 1944; s. Harry L. and Jean B. (Weinstein) R.; m. Arleen B. Friedel, May 26, 1970. BA, CUNY, 1965, JD, Bklyn. Law Sch., 1968. Bar: N.Y. 1968. Ptnr. Zik & Richman, N.Y.C., 1969-70; adminstrv. asst. Empresa Falconi, Quito, Ecuador, S.Am., 1970-71; legal editor Securities Regulation & Law Report, Bur. Nat. Affairs, Inc., Washington, 1972-75, mng. editor Antitrust & Trade Regulation Report, 1975—; lectr. on continuing legal edn.; pres. dir. River Farms Conservancy, 1982—; book rev. editor Anti-Trust Mag., 1987—; Mem. ABA (antitrust law, litigation and bus. law sects.), Internat. Bar Assn. (sect. bus. law), Repporteur, Anti-Trust and Trade Law Com., Nat. Health Lawyers Assn., D.C. Bar Assn., Anti-Trust Inst. (bd. dirs. 1976—). Lodges: Masons (master 1987-88), Masters & Wardens Assn. (pres. 1988), Tall Cedars of Lebanon. Home: 2741 Carter Farm Ct Alexandria VA 22306 Office: 1231 25th St NW Washington DC 20037

RICHMAN, STEPHEN I., lawyer; b. Washington, Pa., Mar. 26, 1933; m. Audrey May Gefsky. BS, Northwestern U., 1954; JD, U. Pa., 1957. Bar: Pa. 1958. ptnr. Ceisler, Richman, Sweet Law Firm, P.A., Washington. Lectr. W.Va. U. Med. Ctr., Grand Rounds. Mem. Am. Coll. Chest Physicians, Pa. Thoracic Soc., Am. Thoracic Soc., The Energy Bur., Coll. of Pathologists, Allegheny County Health Dept., Am. Pub. Health Assn., Indsl. Health Assn., Self-Insurers Assn., Am. Iron and Steel Inst., Can. Thoracic Soc., ABA, Pa. Chamber of Bus. and Industry, Internat. Conf. Pneumoconiosis. Author: Meaning of Impairment and Disability, Chest, 1980, Legal Aspects for the Pathologist, in Pathology of Occupational and Environmental Lung Disease, 1988, Current Medical Methods in Diagnosing Coal Workers Pneumoconiosis, A Review of the Medical and Legal Definitions of Related Impairment and Disability, Labor and the Congress, 1986, Medicolegal Aspects of Asbestos for Pathologists, Arch. Pathology and Laboratory Medicine, 1983, The Franklin Report to The Congress, 1983, Struggle for Reason and Accountability, 1986, Compensation for Occupational Lung Disease, Legal Insight, 1988, other publs. Mem. legal com. Indsl. Health Found., Pitts. Mem. ABA (vice chair workers compensation and employers liability law com.), Pa. Bar Assn. (governing council worker's compensation sect.), Assn. Trial Lawyers Am., Pa. Chamber Bus. and Industry (workers' compensation com., chmn. subcom. on legis. drafting). Home: 820 E Beau St Washington PA 15301 Office: Suite 200 Washington Trust Bldg Washington PA 15301

RICHMOND, JOHN, lawyer; b. Oakland, Calif., Dec. 10, 1907; s. Samuel and Sarah (Stein) R. B.S., U. Calif.-Berkeley, 1928, M.S., 1934; LL.B., Oakland Coll. Law, 1942; Ph.D. (hon.), Hamilton State U., 1973. Bar: Calif. Pres., Richmond Enterprises, Berkeley, 1928—, atty., 1946—; sole practice Berkeley, 1946—. Co-chmn. Lincoln and Washington patriotic program, City Berkeley, 1962, gen. chmn. Marin Point Aquatic Park Meml. Services, 1963. Served with USAF, 1942-45. Mem. Calif. Bar Assn., Nat. Lawyers Club, U. Calif. Alumni Assn., Alameda County Bar Assn., Berkeley-Albany Bar Assn., ABA, Fed. Bar Assn., Supreme Ct. Hist. Soc., VFW (comdr. 1962, nat. membership com. 1980-81). Republican. Clubs: Masons.

RICHOZ, ANDRE HILAIRE, engineering and manufacturing executive; b. Billens, Fribourg, Switzerland, May 26, 1947; Arrived in Japan, 1985; s. Henri and Leonie (Raboud) R.; m. Marguerite Pittet, Oct. 30, 1976; children: Alexander, Isabelle, Stephanie. MS, Swiss Inst. Tech., Zurich, 1972; PhD, U. Zurich, Switzerland, 1975; MBA, European Inst. Bus. Adminstrn., Foutainebleau, France, 1977. Project leader Research Lab., Zurich, 1975-78, Swiss Credit Bank, 1978-79; corp. planner Sulzer Bros. Ltd., Winterthur, Switzerland, 1979-80; plant mgr. Sulzer Bros. Ltd., Johannesburg, Republic South Africa, 1981-85; pres. Sulzer Bros. Japan Ltd., Tokyo, 1985—. Served to bn. comdr., Swiss army. Fellow Swiss Inst. Tech., others. Roman Catholic. Home: 2-25-15 Higashi-Tamagawa, Tokyo 158, Japan Office: Sulzer Bros Japan Ltd, Asahi-Tokai Bldg, 6-1 2-Chome Otemachi, Tokyo 100, Japan

RICHSTEIN, ABRAHAM RICHARD, lawyer; b. N.Y.C., Apr. 18, 1919; s. Morris and Ida (Stupp) R.; m. Rosalind Bauman; children: Eric, Jonathan. B.S., CCNY, 1939; J.D., Fordham U., 1942; LL.M. in Internat. Law, NYU, 1956; M.S. in Internat. Affairs, George Washington U., 1966; diploma, Command and Gen. Staff Coll., 1958, Nat. War Coll., 1966. Bar: N.Y. 1942, U.S. Supreme Ct 1956, D.C. 1977. Enlisted as pvt. U.S. Army, 1942, advanced through grades to col., 1966; served with Mil. Intelligence, U.S. 9th Army U.S. Army, Europe, 1944; legal staff U.S. War Crimes Commn. U.S. Army, Ger., 1946; staff officer UN Command (U.S. Army), Far East, 1951-53; mil. law judge (Hdqrs. First Army), 1954-57; chief internat. affairs Office Judge Adv., Hdqrs. US Army Europe U.S. Army, 1960-63; chief plans office Office Judge Adv. Gen., Washington, 1963-64; judge adv. Hdqtrs. U.S. Army Combat Devels. Command, 1964-66; ret. 1969; asst. gen. counsel AID, State Dept., 1969-81; gen. counsel ACDA, Washington, 1981-83; mem. faculty Nat. War Coll., 1966-68; joint staff planner, policy and planning directorate Joint Chiefs Staff, Washington, 1968-69. Editorial bd.: Mil. Law and Law of War Rev, 1960-63; Book rev. editor: Fordham Law Rev, 1941-42. Decorated Bronze Star.; recipient AID Superior Honor award, 1980, ACDA Meritorious Honor award, 1983. Mem. Am. Soc. Internat. Law. Home: 8713 Mary Lee Ln Annandale VA 22003

RICHTER, BURTON, physicist, educator; b. N.Y.C., Mar. 22, 1931; s. Abraham and Fanny (Pollack) R.; m. Laurose Becker, July 1, 1960; children: Elizabeth, Matthew. B.S., MIT, 1952, Ph.D., 1956. Research assoc. Stanford U., 1956-60, asst. prof. physics, 1960-63, assoc. prof., 1963-67, prof., 1967—, Paul Pigott prof. phys. sci., 1980—, tech. dir. Linear Accelerator Ctr., 1982-84, dir. Linear Accelerator Ctr., 1984—; cons. NSF, Dept. Energy; dir. Teknowledge Inc., Middlefield Capital Corp. Contbr. over 200 articles to profl. publs. Recipient E.O. Lawrence medal Dept. Energy, 1975; Nobel prize in physics, 1976. Fellow Am. Phys. Soc., AAAS; mem. Nat. Acad. Sci. Research elementary particle physics. Office: Stanford U SLAC PO Box 4349 Stanford CA 94305

RICHTER, JOHN GROVES, management consultant; b. Westville, N.J., Feb. 26, 1929; s. Horace Freytag and Sophie Louise (Moe) R.; m. Florence M. Clarke, Sept. 14, 1957; 1 child, John Groves. BSBA, Temple U., 1962; postgrad., U. Houston, 1977, Temple U., 1963-64, 76-77, U. Pa., 1962-63, Rutgers U., 1967-68, State Coll. Pa., 1949-50. With Reliance Ins. Cos., Phila., 1961-77; cons. engring. support/document control dept. Stone & Webster Engring. Corp., Cherry Hill, N.J., 1977-78; cons., acting supr. engring support/document control dept. N.J. Bur. Archives and History, 1978-79; mgr. adminstrv. systems/records mgmt. Reliance Group Inc., Phila., 1979-82; cons., actg. mgr. records mgmt. dept. Power Authority State of N.Y., White Plains, 1982-83; mgr. records, forms and reprographics Phila. Life Ins. Co., 1983-86; mgmt. cons., 1986—; lectr. in field. Author: Vital Records Manual, 1976, The Records Retention Manual, 1964, rev., 1975. Served with USN, 1948-53. Decorated Navy Commendation medal. Mem. Assn. Records Mgrs. and Adminstrs. (chpt. pres. 1975-76, bd. dirs. 1969-77, Mem. of Yr. 1976), Nat. Micrographic Assn. (bd. dirs. 1977-79), Am. Mgmt. Assn., Temple U. Alumni Assn. Republican. Episcopalian. Lodge: Masons, Artisan Order Mutual Protection (master 1973-75). Home: 132 Merion Ave Haddonfield NJ 08033 Office: 132 Merion Ave Haddonfield NJ 08033

RICHTER, MARTIN EDWARD, lawyer, law educator; b. Baker, Oreg., June 3, 1947; s. Forrest Edward and Pauline (Hudgens) R.; m. Pamela Ann Mollenhauer, Oct. 28, 1967; children: Sean Martin, Shannon Michelle. BBA in Mktg., North Tex. State U., 1973; JD, St. Mary's Sch. Law, San Antonio, 1975. Bar: Tex. 1976, U.S. Ct. Appeals (5th and 11th cirs.) 1977, U.S. Dist. Ct. (no. and ea. dists.) Tex. 1985. Assoc. Rivera & Ritter, San Antonio, 1976-77, Rivera, Ritter & Richter, San Antonio, 1977-78; prin. Law Office Martin E. Richter P.C. San Antonio, 1978-84; asst. gen. counsel State Bar Tex., Dallas, 1984—; mcpl. judge City of Balch Springs, Tex., 1988—. Served with USMC, 1966-70. Mem. ABA, Assn. Trial Lawyers Am., Tex. Bar Assn. (state bar coll. 1988), Dallas Bar Assn., Tex. Trial Lawyers Assn. Office: Office Gen Counsel State Bar Tex 714 Jackson St Suite 850 Dallas TX 75202

RICHTER, ROBERTA BRANDENBURG (MRS. J. PAUL RICHTER), educator; b. Osborn, Ohio, Dec. 29; d. Warren F. and Mary M. (Davis) Brandenburg; student Miami-Jacobs Coll., 1930, Wittenberg U., 1930-31, Coll. Music, U. Cin., 1931-32, U. Dayton, 1954, 64; B.S., Miami U., Oxford, Ohio, 1958, M.Ed., 1959; postgrad. Wright State U., 1966-70; doctoral candidate Ohio State U., 1969; m. Jean Paul Richter, Oct. 6, 1934; 1 son, James Paul. Bus. mgr. T.D. Peffley, Inc., 1929-32; sec., prodn. mgr. Delco Products div. Gen. Motors, 1932-34; exec. sec. Meth. Union, 1932-38, LWV, 1935-38, Elder & Johnston Dept. Store, 1938-40; ct. reporter Common Pleas Ct. Montgomery County, 1940-46; adminstrv. asst. Ch. Fedn. Greater Dayton, Ohio, 1946-50; audio-visual cons. schs., chs. Twyman Films, 1950-53; legal asst. Nadlin Law Offices, 1953-58; instr. stenotype, office practice Miami-Jacobs Coll., Dayton, 1941-48; tchr. stenotype, guidance counselor Stebbins High Sch., Dayton, 1958-82; vocat. guidance coordinator Mad River Planning Dist., Montgomery County, Ohio, 1968-73. Instr. workshops in stenotype for ct. reporting Wright State U., Dayton, 1970—; 1st cellist youth div. Symphony Orch.; dir. Lang. Unlimited, Inc., Lake Forest, Ill. Supt., tchr., adviser youth div. Grace United Meth. Ch., Dayton, 1942-72, sec. adminstrv. bd., 1940—, council on ministries, 1972-74, past pres. Excel Club, circle leader, hospitality chmn., pres. homebuilders class, program chmn., laywoman chmn. Christian higher edn.; instr., counselor Camp Miniwanca, Am. Youth Found., 1949-68. Mem. Am., Ohio, Miami Valley personnel and guidance assns., Nat., Ohio bus. tchrs. assns., Am., Ohio sch. counselor assns., Nat., Ohio edn. assns., Nat. Vocat. Guidance Assn., Dayton Area Bus. Soc. (v.p. 1969-82), Nat. Shorthand Reporters Assn., Delphian Soc. (past pres.), Pub. Speaker Bur., Council World Affairs, AAUW, LWV (past pres. and treas.), Internat. Platform Assn., World Trade Club (1st woman), Greater Dayton C. of C., Bus. and Profl. Women (past pres.), Pi Omega Pi. Clubs: Order Eastern Star, Progressive Mothers (chmn. program Dayton 1969-70). Author ednl. handbooks, pamphlets. Contbr. articles to profl. jours.; lectr. in field. Home: 3865 Seiber Ave Dayton OH 45405

RICHTER, SVIATOSLAV THEOFILOVICH, pianist; b. Zhitomir, Russia, Mar. 20, 1915; grad. piano class Moscow Conservatory, 1947; m. Nina Dorliak. Rehearsals condr. Odessa Theater Opera and Ballet, 1934-37; debut concert pianist, Odessa, 1935; won 1st prize Third USSR Competition of Executant Musicans, 1945, since has made extensive concert tours of Europe, U.S. Recipient Stalin prize, 1950; Lenin prize, 1961; decorated Order of Lenin; named People's Artist of USSR, 1961. Address: care Moscow State Philharm Soc, 31 Ulitsa Gorkogo, Moscow USSR other: care Victor Hochhauser Ltd, 4 Holland Park Ave, London W11 England *

RICKIN, SHEILA ANNE, personnel executive; b. N.Y.C., Oct. 13, 1945; d. Louis and Ethel (Schmukler) Bernstein; BA, CCNY, 1966; postgrad. N.Y.U.; MBA, Pace U., 1988. Research asst. pre-baccalureate program CCNY, 1966-68; placement counselor Elaine Revell, Inc., N.Y.C., 1968; adminstr. asso. to chief exec. officer Planned Parenthood Fedn. of Am., N.Y.C., 1969-74; personnel mgr. Family Circle Mag./N.Y. Times Mag. Group, 1974-87; sr. human resources rep., Drexel Burnham Lambert, 1987—. Mem. Am. Soc. Personnel Adminstrs., Am. Mgmt. Assn., N.Y. Human Resources Planners, N.Y. Personnel Mgrs. Assn. (program com.), Mag. Pubs. Assn. (personnel com. 1978-87). Office: Drexel Burnham Lambert 2 Broadway New York NY 10004

RICKLIN, BEDA ROMAN, sales manager; b. Wattwil, Switzerland, Sept. 16, 1955; s. Beda Karl and Rita (Isenschmid) R. Student, Middle Mgmt. Sch., Lucerne, Switzerland, 1985-87. Apprentice Heberlein & Co. AG, Wattwil, 1971-74; sales clk. Hetex Garn AG, Wattwil, 1974-76; from asst. area sales mgr. to area sales mgr. Viscosuisse AG, Emmenbruecke, Switzerland, 1977-87, dist. mgr., 1987—; English educator Viscosuisse Fibres, Ltd., Manchester, Eng., 1978-80. Served as soldier Switzerland Telecom, 1974—. Mem. Switzerland Fedn. Textile. Roman Catholic. Club: Sports. Office: Viscosuisse AG Dept VE2, CH-6020 Emmenbruecke Switzerland

RICKMAN, HANS PETER, philosopher, educator, writer; b. Prague, Czechoslavakia, Nov. 11, 1918; came to Eng., 1938; s. Ernst and Grete (Wollin) Weisskopf. BA, U. London, 1941; D Philosophy, Oxford U., 1943, MA, 1948. Freelance lectr. adult edn., London, 1947-49; staff tutor U. Hull, Eng., 1949-61; sr. lectr. City U. London, reader, 1962-82, vis. prof. philosophy, 1982—. Author: The Adventure of Reason, 1983, Understanding and the Human Studies; Dilthey Today, 1988; contbr. articles to profl. jours. Served with Brit. mil., 1943. Mem. Soc. Authors, PEN, CRUSE, Assn. U. Tchrs. Conservative. Home: 12 Fitzroy Ct, 57 Shepherds Hill, London N6 5RD, England Office: The City U Northampton Sq, London EC1V 0HB, England

RICKS, DAVID ARTEL, business educator, editor; b. Washington, July 21, 1942; s. Artel and Focha (Black) R.; m. Lesley A. Williams, July 3, 1976. B.S., Brigham Young U., 1966; M.B.A., Ind. U., 1968, Ph.D., 1970. Asst. prof. Ohio State U., 1970-75, assoc. prof., 1975-81; prof. internat. bus. U. S.C., Columbia, 1981—; editor Kent Pub. Co., Boston, 1978—. Author books, articles in field, including Directory of Foreign Manufactures in the U.S. (Best Reference Book 1974 ALA, 1975). Editor-in-chief Jour. of Internat. Business Studies, 1984—. Mem. Acad. Internat. Bus. (treas. 1981-82), Acad. Mgmt. (chmn. internat. div. 1988-89). Home: 828 Kilbourne Rd Columbia SC 29205 Office: U SC Coll of Bus Columbia SC 29208

RICO, FRANCISCO, Medieval and Renaissance literature educator; b. Barcelona, Spain, Apr. 28, 1942; s. Cipriano Rico and Maria Manrique; m. Victoria Camps, Sept. 19, 1966; children: Daniel, Guillermo, Felix. DPhil. and Letters, U. Barcelona, 1966. Asst. prof. U. Barcelona, 1964-70; prof. Medieval and Renaissance lit. Autonomous U., Barcelona, 1971—; vis. prof. Johns Hopkins U., Balt., 1966-67, Warburg Inst., London, 1972, Princeton (N.J.) U., 1981; dir. book series Letras e ideas, 1970, Filologia, T Letras Hispanicas, 1983. Author: El pequeno mundo del hombre, 1970, 2d edit., 1986 (transl. into Italian), The Spanish Picaresque Novel and the Point of View, 1970, 3d edit., 1982 (transl. into English, Italian and Japanese), Vida u obra de Petrarca, Vol. I, 1974 (transl. into Italian and English); editor: Historia y critica de la literature espanola, 8 vols., 1980-84. Gen. dir. Ctr. Spanish Letters, Spanish Ministry Culture, 1985-86. Mem. Royal Spanish Acad., Praemium Erasmianum (internat. com. 1982—), Hispanic Assn. Medieval Lit. (pres. 1984—), Ente Nazionale Francesco Petrarca (cons. 1985—). Roman Catholic. Home: 38 Santa Teresa, 08190 Sant Cugat del Valles Spain Office: Autonomous Univ, Barcelona Apartado 1, 08290 Bellaterra Spain

RIDDELL, ALICE MARY, educator; b. N.Y.C., Aug. 12, 1928; d. Arthur Edward and Alice Mary (McAuliffe) Robertson; B.A., Queens Coll., 1963, M.S., 1966; profl. diploma, St. John's U., 1973; m. Robert Lawrence Riddell, Jan. 17, 1948; 1 son, Jeffrey Lawrence. Tchr. and narcotics coordinator N.Y.C. Bd. Edn., Queens, 1963-70; dist. narcotics coordinator Community Sch. Dist. 25, Flushing, N.Y., 1970-71, dir. Project 25, 1971—; asst. adj. prof. Queens Coll., Flushing, 1970-78. Mem. N.Y. State Adv. Council on Substance Abuse, 1978-83; mem. Borough Pres.' Adv. Council on Substance Abuse, 1970—; co-chmn. Greater Flushing Substance Abuse Conf., 1980, Women in Crisis Conf., Drug Abuse Task Force, 1981; bd. trustees and bd. govs. Daytop Village, Inc., 1972—; bd. dirs. College Point Sports Assn., 1981—; mem. N.Y. State Bd. Regents Com. for Profl. Assistance, 1986—; vestryman Ch. St. Uriel the Archangel, Sea Girt, N.J., 1988—. Recipient Merit cert. Flushing Drug Alert Com., 1972, Frank DeSilva Meml. award N.Y. State, 1982, N.Y. State award for Excellence in Prevention, 1986; named Educator of Yr., N.Y.C. Bd. Edn., 1985, Cath. Tchrs. Assn. Bklyn. and Queens, 1985. Mem. N.Y. State Assn. Substance Abuse Programs (dir.), N.Y.C. Coalition Dirs. Sch.-Based Drug Prevention Programs, N.Y. State Assn. Sch.-Based Prevention Profls. (pres., award for Excellence in Prevention Programming 1986), Assn. Curriculum and Supervision, N.Y.C. Adminstrv. Women in Edn., Chancellor's Task Force for Sch.-Based Drug Programs, Internat. Platform Assn., Ladies of Charity, Phi Delta Kappa. Democrat. Roman Catholic. Clubs: N.Y. Univ., Ft. Hamilton Officers. Author: (with others) NCCJ Handbook for School Staffs Re: Alcohol & Drugs, 1981; contbr. articles to profl. jours.; editor Quar., 1981—. Home: 46 Linden Dr Box 528 Spring Lake NJ 07760 Office: Project 25 144-80 Barcly Ave Flushing NY 11355

RIDDEZ, PAUL MICHEL, airline sales executive; b. Stockholm, Aug. 1, 1956; s. Jose Harald and Solveig Riddez; m. Eva-Marie, Mar. 8, 1956; children: Victor, Isabelle. Student in French Studies, Inst. Francais, Perpignan, France, 1976; Student in Sales, Mktg., R M I, Stockholm, 1983-85. Traffic agt. Scandinavian Airlines, Stockholm, 1976-80; sales rep Sabena Belgian World Airlines, Stockholm, 1980-85, sales mgr., 1985—. Office: Sabena Birger, Jarlsgatan 13, 111 45 Stockholm Sweden

RIDDICK, FRANK ADAMS, JR., physician; b. Memphis, June 14, 1929; s. Frank Adams and Falba (Crawford) R.; m. Mary Belle Alston, June 15, 1952; children: Laura Elizabeth Dufresne, Frank Adams III, John Alston. BA cum laude, Vanderbilt U., 1951, MD, 1954. Diplomate: Am. Bd. Internal Medicine (bd. govs. 1973-80). Intern Barnes Hosp., St. Louis, 1954-55, resident in medicine, 1957-60; fellow in metabolic diseases Washington U., St. Louis, 1960-61; staff Ochsner Clinic (Ochsner Found. Hosp.), New Orleans, 1961—; head sect. endocrinology and metabolic disease Ochsner Clinic (Ochsner Found. Hosp.), 1976—, asst. med. dir., 1968-72, assoc. med. dir., 1972-75, med. dir., 1975—; clin. prof. medicine Tulane U., New Orleans, 1977—; trustee Alton Ochsner Med. Found., 1973—; chmn. bd. Ochsner Health Plan, 1983—; pres. Orleans Service Corp., 1976-80, South La. Med. Assocs., New Orleans, 1978—; dir. Brent House Corp., New Orleans, 1980—. Trustee St. Martin's Protestant Epis. Sch., Metairie, La., 1970-84; bd. govs. Isidore Newman Sch., New Orleans, 1987—. Served to maj. U.S. Army, 1955-57. Recipient Disting. Alumnus award Castle Heights Mil. Acad., 1979; recipient teaching award Alton Ochsner Med. Found., 1969, Physician Exec. award Am. Coll. Med. Group Adminstrs., 1984, Disting. Alumnus award Vanderbilt U., 1988. Fellow ACP, Am. Coll. Physician Execs. (pres. 1987—); mem. Am. Soc. Internal Medicine (trustee 1970-76 disting. internist award), AMA (ho. of dels. 1971, chmn. council on med. edn. 1983-85), Endocrine Soc., Am. Diabetes Assn., Nat. Acad. Scis. Inst. Medicine, Soc. Med. Adminstrs., Accreditation Council on Grad. Med. Edn. (chmn. 1986-87), Nat. Resident Matching Program (v.p. 1986—). Clubs: Boston, New Orleans Country, Internat. House; Plimsoll (New Orleans). Home: 1923 Octavia St New Orleans LA 70115 Office: Ochsner Clinic 1514 Jefferson Hwy New Orleans LA 70121

RIDDLE, DAVID ANDREW, lawyer, educator; b. Ft. Belvoir Va., Aug. 5, 1952; s. Howard Dean and Joan Helena (Carroll) R.; m. Linda Wilkinson, June 2, 1979. BA with high honors, U. Hawaii, 1974; JD, Calif. Western Law Sch., 1977; LLM cum laude in internat. and comparative law U. Brussels, 1985. Bar: Hawaii 1978, U.S. Dist. Ct. Hawaii 1978, U.S. Ct. Appeals (9th cir.). Commd. officer U.S. Army JAG, advanced through grades to capt., 1978; prosecutor, Fed. Magistrate Ct., Honolulu, 1977-78; chief prosecutor Ft. Shafter, Hawaii, 1978-79, def. counsel chief, legal assistance, 1979, chief legal asst., Seoul, Korea, 1979-80, chief fgn. claims div., Seoul, 1980-82; chief fgn. claims commns., Mannheim, W.Ger., 1982-84, officer-in-charge U.S. Claims Office, Brussels, 1984-86, civilian govt. atty., advisor Nuremberg (Fed. Republic Germany) Law Ctr., 1986—; instr. bus. law U. Md., Seoul, 1980-81; lectr. internat. law Boston U. Grad. Internat. Relations Program, Brussels, 1985-86. Mem. Korean Am. Friendship Assn., 1981-82. Recipient Arthur Lyman Dean prize U. Hawaii, 1973-74, Meritorious Service medal U.S. Dept. Def., 1982, Superior Civilian Service award, 1988. Mem. ABA (fgn. claims com. sect. internat. law), Fed. Bar Assn., Internat. Bar Assn., Am. Soc. Internat. Law. Club: Mid Pacific Road Runners. Office: US Army HQS 1st Armored Div Nuremberg Law Ctr APO New York NY 09696

RIDDLE, MAXWELL, newspaper columnist; b. Ravenna, Ohio, July 29, 1907; s. Henry Warner and Mary E. (Fitz-Gerald) R.; BA, U. Ariz., 1929; m. Martha A. Hurd, Mar. 31, 1933 (dec. 1982); children—Betsy Riddle Whitmore, Henry W. III; m. Lenora Romain, 1985. Turf editor, columnist NEA Service, 1930, 39; kennel editor, columnist, pets columnist Cleve. Press, 1938-69; columnist Columbia Features, Inc., 1959-66; columnist Ledger Syndicate, 1966-73, Scott Editor Service, 1973—, Allied Feature Syndicate, 1975—; all breed dog judge, fgn. countries, 1955. U.S., 1960—. Recipient Cruikshank medal, 1941; named Dog Writer of Yr., 1949, 61, 83, Dogdom's Man of the Yr., 1968, Dog Journalist of Yr., 1970, 72; inducted into Kennel Ration Hall of Fame, 1987. Mem. Ohio Dog Owners Assn., Dog Writers Assn. (past pres.), Sigma Delta Chi, Delta Upsilon. Clubs: Western Reserve Kennel, Ravenna Kennel. Author: The Springer Spaniel, 1939; The Lovable Mongrel, 1954; This Is the Chihuahua, 1959; The Complete Book of Puppy Training and Care, 1962; Dog People are Crazy, 1966; Your Show Dog, 1968; A Quick Guide to the Standards of Show Dogs, 1972; (with Mrs. M.B. Seeley) The Complete Alaskan Malamute, 1976. The Complete Brittany Spaniel, 1974, The New Complete Brittany, 1987; The New Shetland

Sheepdog, 1974; The Wild Dogs in Life and Legend, 1979; Your Family Dog, 1981, Dogs Through History, 1987 (best of yr. award Dog Writers Assn. Am., 1987); also articles; contbr. Hunters Ency., 1948, New Dog Ency., 1967, Internat. Dog Ency., 1972, World Book Ency.; assoc. editor Dog World mag., 1961—. Home: 5374 Riddle Rd PO Drawer 110 Ravenna OH 44266

RIDENOUR, JAMES FRANKLIN, coll. adminstr.; b. Peoria, Ill., Aug. 2, 1932; s. Arthur S. and Ruth O. (Ohlzen) R.; B.S., Ill. Wesleyan U., 1954; M.S., Ill. State U., 1970; m. Doris K. Maxeiner, June 21, 1958; children—James, David Arthur, Eric Carl, Anne Catherine. Mktg. rep. Armstrong Cork Co., 1955-67; assoc. dir. devel. Ill. Wesleyan U., 1967-73; v.p. devel. Western Md. Coll., Westminster, 1973-84; v.p. devel. Berry Coll., Rome, Ga., 1984—. Chmn., Carroll County Tourism Council, 1976-79; active Boy Scouts Am.; bd. dirs. YMCA, 1976-79; chmn. Families of Evenglow, 1979—. Mem. Council Advancement and Support of Edn. (com. gift standards 1977—), Pi Gamma Mu, Gamma Upsilon. Republican. Episcopalian. Club: Center (Balt.). Lodge: Rotary. Office: Berry Coll Mount Berry Sta Rome GA 30149

RIDER, JAMES LINCOLN, lawyer; b. Newburgh, N.Y., Feb. 11, 1942; s. Meyer J. Rider and Marion (Weinberg) Levin; m. Eleanor Yazbeck, Nov. 5, 1977; children—Jordan E., Michael J. B.A., Lafayette Coll., Easton, Pa., 1963; J.D., Fordham U., 1966. Bar: N.Y. 1966, D.C. 1971, Va. 1972, U.S. Dist. Ct. D.C. 1971, U.S. Dist. Ct. (ea. dist.) Va. 1972, U.S. Dist. Ct. Md. 1973, U.S. Ct. Appeals (D.C. cir.) 1971, U.S. Ct. Appeals (4th cir.) 1972, U.S. Ct. Appeals (8th cir.) 1976, U.S. Supreme Ct. 1975. Ptnr., Margolius, Davis & Rider, Washington, 1971—. Advisor Parents Without Ptnrs., No. Va., 1979—; trustee Somerset Sch., Washington, 1983—. Served to capt. U.S. Army, 1967-71. Decorated Disting. Service medal. Mem. D.C. Bar, Va. Bar Assn., Assn. Trial Lawyers Am. Office: Margolius Davis & Rider 1503 21st St NW Washington DC 20036

RIDER, MORRETTE LEROY, music educator, university dean; b. New Cumberland, Pa., May 3, 1921; s. Ira M. and Rhoda Anna (Morrette) R.; student U. Pa., 1938-39; B.Mus., U. Mich., 1942, M.Mus., 1947; D.Ed., Columbia U., 1955; postgrad. L'Ecole Monteux, Hancock, Maine, 1950-52, Berkshire Music Center, 1949, 65, U. Vienna (Austria), 1958, U. Rochester, 1964; m. Wanda Nigh, Jan. 6, 1946; 1 dau., Rhonda. Asst. prof. music Hope Coll., 1947-50, assoc. prof., 1950-55, prof., 1955-67, dean for acad. affairs, 1968-75, assoc. dir. Inst. European Studies, Vienna, Austria, summer 1958; adminstrv. asst. to pres. U. Wash., 1967-68; dean Sch. Music, U. Oreg., Eugene, 1975-86; pres. Ship's Carpenter Mfg. Co., Holland, Mich., 1957-65; bd. dirs. Gt. Lakes Colls. Assn.-U. Novi Sad, Urban Studies Center, Yugoslavia, 1970; dean theatre and art summer session, Dubrovnik, Yugoslavia, 1972; dean English Center for Internat. Music Edn., Reading, Eng., 1977-79; curriculum cons. Music Hochschulen, W. Ger., 1979; cons. to state arts councils; mem. exec. bd. Mich. Council for Arts, 1957-66; mem. exec. bd. Eugene Jr. Symphony Assn. Served with U.S. Army, 1942-45, CBI. Time-Life grantee, 1964, 66; Den Uyl Found. grantee, 1965; Ford Found.-Am. Council Edn. grantee, 1967-68. Mem. Am. Symphony Orch. League, Nat. Sch. Orch. Assn. (exec. bd., chmn. N.W. region 1979-81), Nat. Assn. Schs. Music (vice-chmn. N.W. div. 1976-78, chmn. div. 1978-82, exec. bd. 1978-82), Music Educators Nat. Conf., Am. String Tchrs. Assn. (pres. Mich. chpt. 1963-65), Music Tchrs. Nat. Assn., CBI Vets.' Assn., Coll. Music Assn., Mich. Sch. Band and Orch. Assn. (hon. life mem.), Internat. Soc. Music Edn. (bd. dirs.; organizer 16th world conf. 1984), Eugene Symphony Orch. Assn. (exec. bd.), Eugene-Univ. Music Assn. (exec. bd.), U.S. Power Squadrons, Phi Mu Alpha Sinfonia, Pi Kappa Lambda (founder 2 chpts.), Delta Omicron. Republican. Methodist. Contbr. articles to profl. jours., U.S., Europe; writer, producer: History of the Symphony Orchestra, Music of the 20th century, Time-Life TV programs, 1966-67; Jazz in America, Music Since 1900, radio programs, 1975-76; condr. numerous orch. concerts throughout U.S., 1950—. Home: 1847 Fircrest Dr Eugene OR 97403 Office: Sch Music U Oreg Eugene OR 97403

RIDGWAY, DAVID WENZEL, educational film producer, director; b. Los Angeles, Dec. 12, 1904; s. David Nelson and Marie (Wenzel) R.; A.B., UCLA, 1926; M.B.A., Harvard U., 1928; m. Rochelle Devine, June 22, 1955. With RKO Studios, Hollywood, Calif., 1930-42; motion picture specialist WPB, Washington, 1942-43; prodn. mgr., producer Ency. Brit. Films, Wilmette, Ill., 1946-60; dir. film activities, exec. dir. Chem. Edn. Material Study, U. Calif. at Berkeley, 1960—; producer, on-screen interviewer Am. Chem. Soc. TV series Eminent Chemists, 1981; cons. TV project Mech. Universe, Calif. Inst. Tech., 1983 also Am. Inst. Biol. Scis.; introduced CHEM study films to People's Republic of China, 1983. Served to lt. comdr. USNR, 1943-46. Recipient Chris award for prodn. CHEM Study Ednl. Films in Chemistry, Film Council Greater Columbus, 1962-63; Bronze medal, Padua, Italy, 1963; CINE Golden Eagle awards, 1962-64, 73; Gold Camera award for film Wondering About Things, U.S. Indsl. Film Festival, 1971; diploma of honour Internat. Sci. Film Assn. Festival, Cairo, 1st prize Am. Biol. Photog. Assn. for film MARS: Chemistry Looks for Life, 1978. Mem. Soc. Motion Pictures and Television Engrs. (chmn. San Francisco sect. 1970-72), Am. Sci. Film Assn. (trustee 1974-81), Delta Upsilon, Alpha Kappa Psi. Clubs: Faculty (U. Calif.), Bohemian (San Francisco). Author: (with Richard J. Merrill) The CHEM Study Story, 1969; also articles in ednl. jours. Home: 1735 Highland Pl Berkeley CA 94709 Office: U Calif Lawrence Hall of Sci Berkeley CA 94720

RIDGWAY, ROZANNE LEJEANNE, foreign service officer; b. St. Paul, Aug. 22, 1935; d. H. Clay and Ethel Rozanne (Cote) R.; m. Theodore E. Deming. B.A., Hamline U., 1957, LL.D. (hon.), 1978. Entered Fgn. Service, 1957; assigned Dept. State, Washington, 1957-59, 64-67, 70-73, Am. embassy, Manila, 1959-61, U.S. Consulate Gen., Palermo, Italy, 1962-64, Am. embassy, Oslo, 1967-70; dep. chief mission Am. embassy, Nassau, 1973-75; dep. asst. sec. state, ambassador for oceans and fisheries affairs 1975-77, ambassador to Finland, 1977-80; counselor of the Dept., Washington, 1980-81; spl. asst. to sec. state 1981; ambassador to German Dem. Republic, 1982-85; asst. sec. state Europe and Can. 1985—. Recipient Profl. awards Dept. State, 1967, 70, 75, 81, Joseph C. Wilson internat. relations achievement award, 1982; named Person of Year Nat. Fisheries Inst., 1977. Office: Dept State Bur European & Can Affairs Room 6226 Washington DC 20520

RIDLEY, BETTY ANN, educator, church worker; b. St. Louis, Oct. 19, 1926; d. Rupert Alexis and Virginia Regina (Weikel) Steber; B.A., Scripps Coll., Claremont, Calif., 1948; m. Fred A. Ridley, Jr., Sept. 8, 1948; children—Linda Drue Ridley Archer, Clay Kent. Christian Sci. practitioner, Oklahoma City, 1973—; Christian Sci. tchr., 1983—; nat. bd. trustees Adventure/Unlimited; mem. Christian Sci. Bd. Lectureship, 1980-85. Found. Bibl. Research and Preservation Primitive Christianity. Mem. Jr. League Am. Home: 7908 Lakehurst Dr Oklahoma City OK 73120 Office: 3000 United Founders Blvd Suite 100-G Oklahoma City OK 73112

RIDLON, MARGARET AGNES, retired social worker; b. Pittsburg, Kans., Feb. 27, 1923; d. Evan Anthony and Agnes Jessie (Staib) Naylor; B.A., B.S., Pittsburg State U., 1943; M.S. in Social Work (fellowship 1969-71, univ. grantee 1971), U. Tenn., 1971; lic. cert. social worker; children—Evan Anthony, William Frank, II. Med. supr. Ark. Social Services, 1967-71, utilization rev. supr., 1971-73; social work supr. Ark. State Hosp., Little Rock, 1973-76; counselor supr. Ark. Mental Retardation Dept., 1976-81; client and family support dir. S.E. Ark. Human Devel. Ctr., Warren, 1981-87, dir., Arkadelphia Human Devel. Ctr., 1987—; diplomate Clinical Social Work, 1987; mem. Ark. Comprehensive Health Planning Commn., 1972-76, Environ. Barriers Council, 1977-87; field instr. U. Ark. Sch. Social Work; bd. dirs. N. Central Ark. Mental Health, 1974-76. Mem. Am. Assn. Mental Deficiency (chmn. social work Ark. 1979-85), Nat. Assn. Social Workers, Acad. Cert. Social Workers, Sigma Delta Chi, Alpha Sigma Alpha. Democrat. Methodist. Home: 212 Indianhead Dr Sherwood AR 72116

RIDOUT, JOHN EDWARD, holding company executive; b. Deal, Dent, Eng., May 24, 1936; s. Edward Albert and Margaret Mary (Sloan) R.; m. Barbera Mary Hodgeson, Mar. 25, 1967; 1 child, Matthew John. Higher nat. cert. in Engring., Dover Tech. Coll., 1957. Apprentice engring. draftsman Petbow, Ltd., Sandwich, Kent, Eng., 1951-56, mech./elec. draftsman, 1957-58, control system designer, 1959-60, estimator power plant, 1961-62, asst. sales mgr., 1963-69, sales and publicity mgr., 1970-80, sales mgr. European div.,, 1981-82; mktg. mgr. Petbow Holdings Plc., Sandwich, 1983-84, group mktg. mgr., 1985—. Editor: 50 Years in Power, 1983; contbr. articles on elec. power, world markets and power plants to tech. jours. Mem. Inst. Mktg. (com. mem. Kent br. 1982-85). Mem. Ch. of Eng. Home: Sea Lodge, Kingsdown Rd Walmer, Kent CT14 8AR, England Office: Petbow Ltd, Sandwich, Kent CT13 9NE, England

RIEBESEHL, E. ALLAN, lawyer; b. N.Y.C., July 7, 1938; s. Harold J. and Phyllis R.; m. Suzanne C. Moore, July 28, 1963; children: Gregory, Christopher. BA, CCNY, 1961; JD, Fordham Law Sch., 1966; LLM, NYU, 1972. Bar: N.Y. 1966, U.S. Tax Ct. 1968, U.S. Supreme Ct. 1970, U.S. Ct. Appeals (2d cir.) 1971, U.S. Dist. Ct. (ea. dist.) N.Y. 1973, U.S. Dist. Ct. (so. dist.) N.Y., 1974. Tax atty. Kennecott Copper Corp., N.Y.C., 1966-69, Celanese Corp., 1969-70, Pan Am. World Airways, N.Y.C., 1970-71; sole practice, Mineola, N.Y., 1971—. adj. prof. Touro Law Sch. Past pres. Woodbury-Syosset Republican Club; past v.p. Syosset Hosp. Community Adv. Bd. Served with USMC, 1961-66. Fellow Am. Acad. Matrimonial Lawyers; mem. ABA, Am. Judicature Soc., C.W. Post Tax Inst., Am. Arbitration Assn., Cath. Lawyers Guild (exec. v.p.), N.Y. State Bar Assn., Nassau County Bar Assn. (bd. dirs.), Suffolk County Bar Assn., Nassau Lawyers Assn., Lawyers in Mensa. Club: Kiwanis (past pres.) (Mineola, N.Y.). Co-author: New York Practice Guide: Domestic Relations; contbr. articles to profl. jours. Office: 999 Brush Hollow Rd Westbury NY 11590

RIEBOLD, GILBERT ADRIEN, management consultant; b. Nancy, France, Jan. 13, 1921; came to U.S., 1957; naturalized,; s. Adrien Joseph and Fernande Riebold. JD, U. Nancy, 1945; Diploma in Bus., Grad. Sch. Bus. Adminstrn., Paris, 1948; postgrad., La Salle Coll., 1957-60. Tax cons. Soc. Juridique et Fiscale de France, 1945-50; mgr. auditing and mgmt. services Fiduciaire de France et Morocco, Casablanca, 1950-56; controller S.G.T.M., Paris, 1956-57; sr. acct., auditor Eby, Blake & Cullen, Pasadena, Calif., 1960-63, ZTB&G, Las Vegas, Nev., 1964; adminstrv. asst. to pres. Westgate Builders Inc., Las Vegas, 1965; controller Frederic Apcar Enterprises, Las Vegas, 1965-66; mgmt. cons. and statutory auditor Commissaire aux Comptes, Paris, 1967—. Author: The Cash Flow, 1968, U.S. Methods of Business Evaluation, 1973, External Audit-A Service to Managers, 1975, Accounting for Non-Account Managers, 1975, Finance for Non-Financial Managers, 1984, Cash Flow and the Integral Cash Flow Statement, 1984; contbr. numerous articles to profl. jours. Mem. Calif. Soc. CPA's. Office: 108 Ave Felix Faure, 75015 Paris France

RIECKER, JOHN E(RNEST), lawyer, banker; b. Ann Arbor, Mich., Nov. 25, 1930; s. Herman H. and Elizabeth (Wertz) R.; m. Margaret Ann Towsley, July 30, 1955; children: John Towsley, Margaret Elizabeth. AB with distinction, U. Mich., 1952, JD with distinction, 1954. Bar: Mich. 1954, Calif. 1955, U.S. Tax Ct., U.S. Supreme Ct., U.S. Treasury. Assoc. Bonisteel & Bonisteel, Ann Arbor, 1954-55; ptnr. Francis, Wetmore & Riecker, Midland, Mich., 1958-65; ptnr. Gillespie Riecker & George, Midland, 1966-85; sr. ptnr. Riecker, George, Hartley & Van Dam and Camp, P.C., 1985—; chmn. bd. First Midland Bank & Trust Co., 1970-78; bd. dirs. Comerica Bank-Midland; sec., bd. dirs. numerous Mich. corps.; mem. NAM trade mission to EEC, 1964. Mem. bd. editors Mich. Law Rev., 1953-54; contbr. articles to profl. jours. Trustee, treas. Delta Coll., 1965-68; mem. bd. mgrs. United Fund Midland 1960-64, chmn., 1980—; sec. Midland City Charter Rev. Com., 1964, mem. Spl. Charter Commn., 1972; bd. dirs. Midland Found., 1974; mem. Bd. Ethics State of Mich., 1976—; sec. Dow Found., Towsley Found. Ann Arbor; mem. exec. com. Mich. United Fund, 1970-72; bd. govs. Northwood Inst., 1969-71; benefactor U. Mich.; vice chmn. bd. dirs. U. Mich. Devel. Council, 1982—; chmn. bd. dirs. Cen. Mich. U. Devel. Council, 1983-86; bd. govs. Cranbrook Acad. Art, 1980-84; chmn. Matrix, Midland, 1981-83; bd. dirs. steering com. U. Mich. Grad. Sch. Bus., 1982—; mem. com. visitors U. Mich. Law Sch., 1981—; vice chmn. Campaign for Mich., 1984; bd. dirs., chmn. fin. com. Hillsdale Coll., 1985—; exec. com., trustee Mich. Hist. Soc., 1985—. Served as 1st lt., Judge Adv. Gens. Corps, AUS, 1955-58, now capt. Res. Recipient U. Mich. Outstanding Alumni award, 1984. Mem. Midland County (pres. 1962-63), ABA, Calif. Bar Assn., Mich. Bar Assn. (mem. tax council), Midland C. of C. (pres. 1971), Phi Beta Kappa, Phi Kappa Phi, Phi Eta Sigma, Sigma Iota Epsilon, Alpha Delta Phi, Phi Delta Phi. Republican. Episcopalian. Clubs: Benmark, Midland Country, Saginaw, Saginaw Valley Torch; Detroit Athletic, Renaissance; Pres.'s, Benefactors (Ann Arbor). Home: 3211 Valley Dr Midland MI 48640 Office: 414 Townsend St Midland MI 48640

RIEFENSTAHL, LENI, author, photographer, film director b. Berlin, Aug. 22, 1902; d. Alfred and Berta (Scherlach) R.; m. Peter Jacob, Mar. 21, 1944 (div. 1946). Student Russian Ballet, Mary Wigmann Sch. for Dance Dresden, Jutta Klamt Sch. for Dance, Berlin. Modern dance, Germany and abroad, 1923-24; actress various prodns. including Der Heilige Berg, 1926, Der Grosse Sprung, 1927, Das Schicksaal derer von Habsburg, 1928, Die Weisse Holle von Piz Palu, 1929, Sturm uber dem Montblanc, 1930, Der Weisse Rausch, 1931, SOS Eisberg, 1932; founder L.R. Film Prodn., Berlin, 1931; producer, dir. actress Das Blaue Licht, 1931, Tiefland, 1954; dir. Sieg des Glaubens, 1933; producer, dir. Triumpf des Willens, 1934, Tag der Freiheit, 1935, Olympia, part 1, part 2, 1936-38; author: Kampf in Schnee und Eis, 1933, Schonheit in Olympische Kampf, 1938, The Last of the Nuba, 1974, The People of Kau, 1976, Coral Gardens, 1978, Mein Afrika, 1982; one person photography show, Tokyo, Japan, 1980. Recipient Silver medal (Das Blaue Licht) Biennale Venice, 1932, Gold medal (Triumpf des Willens), 1935, Gold medal (Olympia films), 1938, Gold medals World Exposition (Triumpf des Willens, Das Blaue Licht), 1937, 1st prize and Olympic Gold medals (Olympia films), 1948, Best Photography of Yr., Art Dirs. Club, 1977. Address: 20 Tengstrasse, 8000 Munich 40 Federal Republic of Germany

RIEGEL, BYRON WILLIAM, ophthalmologist, educator; b. Evanston, Ill., Jan. 19, 1938; s. Byron and Belle Mae (Huot) R.; B.S., Stanford U., 1960; M.D., Cornell U., 1964; m. Marilyn Hills, May 18, 1968; children—Marc William, Ryan Marie, Andrea Elizabeth. Intern, King County Hosp., Seattle, 1964-65; asst. resident in surgery U. Wash., Seattle, 1965; resident in ophthalmology U. Fla., 1968-71; pvt. practice medicine specializing in ophthalmology, Sierra Eye Med. Group, Inc., Visalia, Calif., 1972—; mem. staff Kaweah Delta Dist. Hosp., chief of staff, 1978-79; mem. staff Visalia Community Hosp.; med. staff ophthalmology Valley Med. Center-Univ. Calif. Fresno Med. Edn. Program, 1972—; asst. clin. prof. ophthalmology U. Calif., San Francisco, 1981—. Bd. dirs., asst. sec. Kaweah Delta Dist. Hosp., 1983—. Ka. Served as flight surgeon USN, 1966-68. Co-recipient Fight-for-Sight citation for research in retinal dystrophy, 1970. Diplomate Am. Bd. Ophthalmology, Nat. Bd. Med. Examiners. Fellow A.C.S., Am. Acad. Ophthalmology; mem. AMA, Calif. (del. 1978-79), Tulare County med. assns., Calif., Am. assns. ophthalmology, Am. Soc. Cataract and Refractive Surgery, Internat. Phacoemulsification and Cataract Methodology Soc. Roman Catholic. Club: Rotary (Visalia). Home: 1101 W Whitendale St Visalia CA 93277 Office: 2830 W Main St Visalia CA 93291

RIEGER, ELLEN LUNDE, commodity exchange executive; b. N.Y.C., June 30, 1952; d. Steen and Barbara A. (Baylis) Lunde; m. Peter C. Brathauer, Aug. 17, 1974 (div. Sept. 1977); m. Thomas Muller Rieger, June 22, 1983. BA cum laude, St. John's U., N.Y.C., 1974. Banquet mgr. Princeton Club N.Y., 1975-80; asst. to ptnr. East View Co., N.Y.C., 1980-84; v.p. Windsor-Birch, Ltd., N.Y.C., 1983-86; exec. asst. to pres., Commodity Exchange, Inc., N.Y.C., 1986-87, exec. asst. to chmn., 1987—. Mem. DAR (regent Peter Minuit chpt. 1984-887, chmn. Greater N.Y. Regent's Round Table 1986-87, sec. 1987-88). Home: 1192 Park Ave New York NY 10128 Office: Commodity Exchange Inc 4 World Trade Ctr New York NY 10048

RIEGER, MITCHELL SHERIDAN, lawyer; b. Chgo., Sept. 5, 1922; s. Louis and Evelyn (Sampson) R.; m. Rena White Abelmann, May 17, 1949 (div. 1957); 1 child, Karen Gross Cooper; m. Nancy Horner, May 30, 1961 (div. 1972); step-children—Jill Levi, Linda Hanan, Susan Felsenthal, James Geoffrey Felsenthal; m. Pearl Handelsman, June 10, 1973; step-children—Steven Newman, Mary Ann Malarkey, Nancy Newman. A.B., Northwestern U., 1944; J.D., Harvard U., 1949. Bar: Ill. 1950, U.S. Dist. Ct. (no. dist.) Ill. 1950, U.S. Supreme Ct. 1953, U.S. Ct. Mil. Appeals 1953, U.S. Ct. Appeals (7th cir.) 1954. Legal asst. Rieger & Rieger, Chgo., 1949-50, assoc., 1950-54; asst. U.S. atty. No. Dist Ill., Chgo., 1954-60; 1st asst. No. Dist Ill., 1958-60; assoc. gen. counsel SEC, Washington, 1960-61; ptnr. Schiff Hardin and Waite, Chgo., 1961—; instr. John Marshall Law Sch. Chgo., 1952-54. Contbr. articles to profl. jours. Mem. Chgo. Crime Commn., 1965—; pres. Park View Home for Aged, 1969-71; Rep. precinct committeeman, Highland Park, Ill., 1964-68; bd. dirs. Spertus Mus. Judaica. Served to lt. (j.g.) USNR, 1943-46, PTO. Fellow Am. Coll. Trial Lawyers; ABA, Chgo. Bar Assn., Ill. State Bar Assn., Am. Judicature Soc., 7th Circuit Bar Assn., Fed. Bar Assn. (pres. Chgo. chpt. 1959-60, nat. v.p. 1960-61), Phi Beta Kappa. Jewish. Clubs: Standard, Metropolitan, Law of Chgo., Cliff Dwellers, Vail Racquet. Home: 4950 Chicago Beach Dr Chicago IL 60615 Office: Schiff Hardin & Waite 7200 Sears Tower 233 S Wacker Dr Chicago IL 60606

RIEGGER, VOLKER, research institute executive, strategist, consultant; b. Aalen, Baden-Wuerttemberg, Fed. Republic Germany, Dec. 5, 1942; s. Franz and Julie (Burry) V.; m. Brigitte Keul, Apr. 20, 1966; 1 child Jacob. Diploma in econs., U. Munich, 1969. Bus. editor Wiesbadener Kurier, Wiesbaden, Fed. Rep. Germany, 1962-64; research asst. econs. U. Munich, 1969-72; campaign mgr. Headquarter Social Dem. Party: Willy Brandt, Helmut Schmidt, Bonn, Fed. Republic Germany, 1972-86; bd. dirs. Infratest Forschung, Munich, 1986—; bd. dirs. TV network Zweites Deutsches Fernsehen, Mainz, Fed. Republic Germany, 1981-86; lectr. Hochschule der Kuenste, Berlin, 1986—. Mem. Am. Econ. Assn., List Soc., Internat. Assn. Pol. Cons., European Soc. for Opinion and Mktg. Research. Office: Infratest Forschung, Landsberger-Str 330, 8000 Munich Federal Republic of Germany

RIEGLE, DONALD WAYNE, JR., U.S. senator; b. Flint, Mich., Feb. 4, 1938; s. Donald Wayne and Dorothy (Fitchett) R.; m. Lori L. Hansen, May 20, 1978; 4 children. Student, Flint Jr. Coll., 1956-57, Western Mich. U., 1957-58; B.A., U. Mich., 1960; M.B.A., Mich. State U., 1961; postgrad., Harvard U., 1964-66; LL.D., St. Benedict's Coll., 1970, Defiance Coll. Sr. pricing analyst with IBM Corp., 1961-64; faculty Mich. State U., 1962, Boston U., 1965, Harvard U., 1965-66; cons. Harvard U. MIT Joint Center Urban Studies, 1965-66; mem. 90th-94th congresses from 7th Dist. Mich.; mem. U.S. Senate from Mich. 1977—. Author: O Congress, 1972. Named one of America's 10 Outstanding Young Men U.S. Jr. C. of C., 1967, one of Two Best Congressmen of Yr., The Nation mag., 1967. Democrat. Office: 105 Dirksen Senate Bldg Washington DC 20510

RIEGLE, ROBERT ROY, agricultural products executive; b. Greenville, Ohio, July 30, 1927; s. Alvin N. and Nola M. (Dickey) R.; student Internat. Coll., 1952-53; children—Kirk, Karen. Acct., Coopers & Lybrand, Fort Wayne, 1953-67; mgr. corp. acctg. Peter Eckrich & Sons, Inc., Fort Wayne, 1967-69; v.p., sec., controller E.W. Kneip, Inc., Forest Park, Ill., 1969-85, Beatrice Meats, Inc., Oakbrook, Ill., 1985-87, also bd. dirs., Bodee Wholesale Flower Inc., Burr Ridge, Ill., 1987—. Mem. Am. Inst. CPA's, Ind. Assn. CPA's, Nat. Inst. Controllers, Nat. Assn. Accts., Adminstrv. Mgmt. Soc., Am. Mgmt. Assn. Lodge: Lions (local pres. 1975). Home: 507 Windgate Ct Arlington Heights IL 60005 Office: 161 Tower Dr Suite J Burr Ridge IL 60521

RIELLI, ROBERTO RADICI, electromechanic engineer; b. Bergamo, Lombardia, Italy, Apr. 25, 1947; arrived in Mex., 1976; s. Mario and Maria (Radici) R.; m. Luisa Sandoval, May 5, 1977. Grad., Inst. Pesenti, Bergamo, 1968; perito industriale, Colegio Graduados Alta Direccion, Mex., 1985-87. Proyector elec. substation Magrini Galileo, Bergamo, 1970-76; coordinator installation elec. distbn. Sicartsa, Lazaro Cardenas, Mex., 1976-80; with Magrini Galileo, Mexico City, 1980-81; tech. and comml. dir. Ansaldo De Mex. S.A. de C.V., Mexico City, 1981-83; mng. dir. Ansaldo Electromecanica S.A.C.V., Mexico City, 1983-84, Ansaldo De México, S.A. de C.V., Mexico City, 1984—; advisor Camara Comercio Italiana, Mex. Served with the Italian Navy, 1969-71. Mem. Caname, Canacintra. Club: Mundet. Office: Ansaldo De Mexico SA de CV, Rousseau No 14 - 3er piso, 11590 Mexico City Mexico

RIEPE, DALE MAURICE, philosopher, educator, Asian art dealer; b. Tacoma, June 22, 1918; s. Rol and Martha (Johnson) R.; m. Charleine Williams, 1948; children: Kathrine Leigh, Dorothy Lorraine. B.A., U. Wash., 1944; M.A., U. Mich., 1946, Ph.D., 1954; postgrad. (Rockefeller-Watamull-McInerny fellow), U. Hawaii, Banaras and Madras, India, Tokyo and Waseda, Japan, 1949. Instr. philosophy Carleton Coll., 1948-51; asst. prof. U. S.D., 1952-54; asso. prof. U. N.D., 1954-59, prof., 1959-62, chmn. dept., 1954-62; prof., chmn. C.W. Post Coll., 1962-63; prof. philosophy State U. N.Y., Buffalo, 1963—; chmn. dept. social scis., asso. dean State U. N.Y. (Grad. Sch.), 1964—; exchange lectr. U. Man., 1955; vis. lectr. Western Wash. Coll., 1961; Marine instr. electricity Naval Tng. Program, Seattle, 1943-45; mem. nat. screening bd. South Asia, Fulbright Selection, 1968-70, Asia, 1970-72; chmn. Fulbright Selection Com. for Asia, 1972, 82; vis. Fullbright lectr. Tokyo U., 1957-58, vis. lectr. Delhi U., 1967; exchange lectr. Moscow State U., 1979, Beijing Higher Edn. Inst., 1984; docent Albright-Knox Art Gallery; cons. Ctr. for Sci., Tech. and Devel., Council of Sci. and Indsl. Research, Govt. India, 1978—, Inst. Fang Studies, 1987—; del. Cuban-N.Am. Philosophy Conf., Cuban Inst. Social Sci., 1982, Fang Centennial, Taiwan Nat. U., Taipeh, 1987, Hungarian-Am. Philos. Conf., Budapest, 1988. Author: The Naturalistic Tradition in Indian Thought, 1961, The Philosophy of India and its Impact on American Thought, 1970, East-West Dialogue, 1973, Indian Philosophy Since Independence, 1979, The Owl Flies by Day, 1979, Asian Philosophy Today, 1981, Objectivity and Subjectivism in the Philosophy of Science, 1985, Philosophy and Revolutionary Theory, 1986, also articles in field.; editor: Phenomenology and Natural Existence, 1973, Philosophy and Political Economy; Co-editor: The Structure of Philosophy, 1966, Contributions of American Sankritists in the Spread of Indian Philosophy in the United States, 1967, Radical Currents in Contemporary Philosophy, 1970, Reflections on Revolution, 1971, Philosophy at the Barricade, 1971, Contemporary East European Philosophy, 1971, Essays in East-West Dialogue, 1973, Explorations in Philosophy and Society, 1978; editorial com.: Chinese Studies in History, 1970—, Chinese Studies in Philosophy, 1970—; publs. bd.: Conf. for Asian Affairs; Editor various series.; Editorial bd.: Philos. Currents and Revolutionary World, 1972, Soviet Studies in Philosophy, 1979-87, Marxist Dimensions, 1987—,. Mem. com. overseers Chung-an U., Korea. Fulbright scholar India, 1951-52; Fulbright lectr. U. Tokyo, 1957-58; Carnegie Corp. fellow Asian Studies, 1960-61; grantee 4th East-West Philosophers Conf., 1964; Penrose fund Am. Philos. Soc., 1963; State U. N.Y. Research Found., 1965, 66, 67, 69, 72, 73; State U. N.Y. Research Found. Bulgarian Acad. Sci., 1975; Am. Inst. Indian Studies research fellow, 1966-67; London Sch. Oriental and African Studies grantee, 1971. Fellow Royal Asiatic Soc.; mem. Conf. Asian Affairs (sec. 1955), Am. Oriental Soc., Am. Philos. Soc., Indian Inst. Psychology, Philosophy and Psychical Research (hon. adviser), Soc. for Am. Philosophy (chmn. 1960), Am. Inst. Indian Studies (trustee 1965-66), Soc. for Creative Ethics (sec.), Am. Archaeol. Soc., ACLU, Eastern Inst., AAAS, Am. Archeol. Soc., Am. Assn. Asian Studies, Am. Math. Soc., Am. Aesthetics Soc., Am. Soc. Comparative and Asian Philosophy, Asiatic Soc. (Calcutta), Soc. for Philos. Study Dialectical Materialism (founding sec.-treas. 1962—), Soc. for Philos. Study Marxism (publs. sec. 1973—), Union Am. and Japanese Profls. against Nuclear Omnicide (treas. U.S. sect. 1978—), Internat. Philosophers for Prevention Nuclear Omnicide, United Univ. Profs of SUNY-Buffalo (v.p.), Wash. State Hist. Assn., Alpha Pi Zeta. Clubs: Tumwater Valley. Home: 3138 SE Lorne Olympia WA 98501 Office: 605 Baldy Hall State U NY Buffalo NY 14261

RIES, EDWARD RICHARD, petroleum geologist, consultant; b. Freeman, S.D., Sept. 18, 1918; s. August and Mary F. (Graber) R.; student Freeman Jr. Coll., 1937-39; A.B. magna cum laude, U. S.D., 1941; M.S., U. Okla., 1943, Ph.D. (Warden-Humble fellow), 1951; postgrad. Harvard, 1946-47; m. Amelia D. Capshaw, Jan. 24, 1948 (div. Oct. 1956); children—Rosemary Melinda, Victoria Elise; m. 2d, Maria Wipfler, June 12, 1964. Asst. geologist Geol. Survey S.D., Vermillion, 1941; geophys. interpreter Robert Ray Inc., Oklahoma City, 1942; jr. geologist Carter Oil Co., Mont., Wyo., 1943-44, geologist Cutbank, Mont., 1944-49; sr. geologist Standard Vacuum Oil Co., India, 1951-53, sr. regional geologist, Indonesia, 1953-59, geol. adviser for Far East and Africa, White Plains, N.Y., 1959-62; geol. adviser Far East, Africa, Oceania, Mobil Petroleum Co., N.Y.C., N.Y., 1962-65; geol. adviser for Europe, Far East, Mobil Oil Corp., N.Y.C., 1965-71, sr. regional explorationist Far East, Dallas, 1971-73, Asia-Pacific, Dallas, 1973-76, 1976-79, assoc. geol. advisor Regional Geology-Geophysics, Dallas, 1979-82, geol.

cons., 1982-83; ind. geol. cons., Dallas, 1983—. Grad. asst., teaching fellow U. Okla., 1941-43, Harvard, 1946-47. Served with AUS, 1944-46. Mem. N.Y. Acad. Scis., Am. Assn. Petroleum Geologists (asso. editor 1976-83). Geol. Soc. Am., Am. Hort. Soc., Internat. Platform Assn., Am. Geol. Inst., A.A.A.S., Nat. Audubon Soc., Nat. Wildlife Fedn., Soc. Exploration Geophysicists, Wilderness Soc., Am. Legion, Phi Beta Kappa, Sigma Xi, Phi Sigma, Sigma Gamma Epsilon. Republican. Mennonite. Club: Harvard (Dallas). Contbr. articles to profl. jours. Home: 6009 Royal Crest Dr Dallas TX 75230 Office: 7200 N Stemmons Dallas TX 75247

RIESCO, ARMANDO, II, management consultant, educator; b. Cuba, May 21, 1943; s. Armando Riesco Puyol and Bertha Cartaya Gutierrez; m. Blanca Rosa Farinas Torres, Dec. 16, 1972; children: Natascha Beatrice, Armando, Alejandro Jose. Student U. Bridgeport, 1960-61; BS in Indsl. Engring. magna cum laude, U. Fla., 1965, MS in Indsl. Engring., 1967, PhD in Indsl. and Systems Engring. and Ops. Research, 1970. Prof. indsl. engring. U. P.R., Mayaguez, 1970-79; pres. Sistema Inc., Guaynabo, P.R., 1979—; vis. prof. indsl. and systems engring. U. Fla., Gainesville, 1976-77; sr. cons., cofounder Mgmt. Systems Design and Analysis, 1974-79; pvt. practice cons., 1967-74, corps. including Citibank, Electronic Data Systems, IBM, Pfizer Corp., Fed. Savs. Bank P.R., First Fed. Savs. Bank, govt. agys. including NASA, govts. P.R., Costa Rica, Dominican Republic, Jamaica; chmn., dir. organizational meetings profl. orgns.; lectr. in field. OAS fellow, 1968-70. Mem. Inst. Indsl. Engrs., Ops. Research Soc. Am., Inst. Mgmt. Scis., Phi Kappa Phi, Alpha Pi Mu (past regional v.p.), Sigma Xi, Tau Beta Pi. Roman Catholic. Contbr. sci. papers to profl. confs. and publs. Office: SISTEMA Inc Call Box 7886 Suite 515 Banco de San Juan Ctr Guaynabo PR 00657

RIESENHUBER, HEINZ FRIEDRICH RUPPERT, West German minister of research and technology; b. Frankfurt, Ger., Dec. 1, 1935; s. Karl Eugen and Elisabeth (Birkner) R.; m. Beatrix Walter, 1968; children—Maximilian, Eva, Katharina, Felix. Dr.rer.nat., U. Frankfurt, 1965. Ofcl. expert Erzgesellschaft mbH, Frankfurt, 1966; head clk. Metallgesellschaft AG, Frankfurt, 1967, mng. dir., 1968-71; tech. mng. dir. Synthomer-Chemie Gmbh, Frankfurt, 1971-82; fed. minister research and tech. W.Ger., 1982—. Contbr. numerous articles to profl. jours. Mem. regional party exec. bd. Christian Democratic Union, 1965—. Roman Catholic. Office: Bundesminist fur Forschung/Tech, Heinemannstr 2 PF 200706, 5300 Bonn 2 Federal Republic of Germany

RIETZ, KENNETH CHARLES, advertising executive, political consultant; b. Appleton, Wis., May 3, 1941; s. Howard K. and Catherine (Abbey) R.; 1 child, Kenneth Charles. Grad. George Washington U., 1973. Dep. chmn. Republican Nat. Com., 1973; v.p. MGM Records, Los Angeles, 1974, Mike Curb Prodns., 1974-76; pres. Ken Rietz & Co., Los Angeles, 1976—. Chmn. 70001 Tng. and Employment Inst., bd. trustees Fund for Am. Studies; bd. dirs. VOR Found. Mem. Am. Assn. Polit. Cons., Am. Council Young Polit. Leaders, Rep. Eagles. Presbyterian. Office: PO Box 691821 Los Angeles CA 90069

RIFA'I, ZEID SAMEER, prime minister and minister of defense Hashemite Kingdom of Jordan; b. Amman, Jordan, 1936; s. Sameer Rifai; married; 2 children. B.A. in Polit Sci., Harvard U., 1957; M.A. in Law and Internat. Affairs, Columbia U., 1958. Attache, Ministry Fgn. Affairs, 1957; sec. Jordanian embassy, Cairo, 1957, sec., Beirut, 1957, 1st sec., London, 1962-64, ambassador, London, 1970-71; sec. Jordanian del. UN, 1957-59; head internat. orgns. dept. Ministry of Fgn. Affairs, 1959-62; asst. chief Royal Ct., 1964, 66, dep. chief, 1969, chief, 1969; head Royal Protocol, 1964, 66-67; head polit. dept. Ministry Fgn. Affairs, 1964-65; del. to Gen. Assembly, 1958-65; head Royal Protocol, pvt. sec. to King Hussein, 1967; sec. gen. Royal Ct.; polit. advisor to King Hussein, 1973; prime minister, 1973—; minister def., 1973—; minister fgn. affairs, 1973, 74-76; mem. Upper House Parliament, 1979—. Decorated Independence medal, Jordanian Star medal, several fgn. medals. Office: Office of Prime Minister, PO Box 80, Amman Jordan *

RIFAI, ZEIN SAMIR, Jordanian diplomat; b. Amman, Jordan, June 28, 1944; d. Samir and Alia (Shukri) R. B.A., Oxford U., 1964, M.A., 1967. Second sec. Ministry of Fgn. Affairs, Govt. Jordan, 1967-71; 1st sec. Ministry of Info., Govt. Jordan, 1971-75; counsellor Jordan Embassy in London, 1975—, now minister Plenipotentiary. Moslem. Avocations: reading; gardening; theatre. Office: Jordan Embassy, 6 Upper Phillimore Gardens, London W8 7HB England

RIFBJERG, KLAUS THORVALD, writer; b. Copenhagen, Dec. 15, 1931; s. Thorvald Frants and Lilly (Nielsen) R.; ed. U. Copenhagen, Princeton U.; m. Inge M.G. Andersen, May 28, 1955; children—Lise Beate, Synne Marie, Frands Carl. Freelance writer, poet and dramatist; lit. critic Info., 1955-57, Politiken, from 1959; lit. dir. Gyldendal Pubs., 1984—. Author (novels) Den Kroniske Uskyld, 1958, Til Spanien, 1971, Brevet til Gerda, 1972, Det sort hul, 1980, numerous others, (short stories) Og Andre Historier, 1964, Sommer, 1974, (plays) Gris Pa Gaflen, 1962, Udviklinger, 1965, numerous other books of short stories, plays, also criticism. Recipient award Danish Acad., 1967; Nordic Council prize, 1970; Holberg medal, 1979; others. Mem. Danish Acad. Arts and Letters, Danish Gastronomic Acad. Clubs: Princeton Colonial (hon.); Princeton (N.Y.C.). Office: care Gyldendal Pubs, 3 Klarenboderne, 1001 Copenhagen Denmark *

RIFKIND, MALCOLM (LESLIE), secretary of state for Scotland; b. Scotland, June 21, 1946; s. E. Rifkind; m. Edith Amalia Steinberg, 1970; 1 son, 1 dau. LLB, George Watson's Coll., Edinburgh; MSc, Edinburgh U. Bar: Scotland, 1970. Lectr. U. Rhodesia, Republic of South Africa, 1967-68; opposition front bench spokesman on Scottish affairs Parliament, London, 1975-76, under sec. of state, Scottish Office, 1979-82, under sec. of state Fgn. & Commonwealth Office, 1982-83, minister of state Fgn. & Commonwealth Office, 1983-86, sec. of state for Scotland Fgn. & Commonwealth Office, 1986—; hon. pres. Scottish Young Conservatives, Fed. Conservative Students; mem. Edinburgh Town Council, 1970-74; chmn. Scotish Conservative Devolution Com., 1976; joint sec. Conservative Fgn. and Commonwealth Affairs Com., 1978; mem. Select Com. on European Secondary Legis., 1975-76; Select Ccom. on Overseas Devel., 1978-79. Address: House of Commons, SW1A 0AA London England *

RIFKIND, RICHARD ALLEN, physician; b. N.Y.C., Oct. 26, 1930; s. Simon H. and Adele (Singer) R.; B.S., Yale U., 1951; M.D., Columbia U., 1955; m. Carole Lewis, June 24, 1956; children—Barbara, Nancy. Intern. Presbyn. Hosp. N.Y.C., 1955-56, resident, 1957-61, dir. hematology, 1972-81; asst. prof. dept. medicine Columbia U., 1963-67, asso. prof., 1967-70, prof., 1970-81, dir. comprehensive Cancer Center, 1980-81, chmn. dept. genetics, 1980-81; dir. Grad. Sch. Meml. Sloan-Kettering Cancer Center, N.Y.C., 1981—, research chmn. Sloan-Kettering Inst., 1983—. Served to capt. M.C., USAF, 1957-59. Diplomate Am. Bd. Internal Medicine. Mem. Am. Soc. Clin. Investigation, Am. Assn. Physicians, Am. Soc. Hematology. Democrat. Jewish. Contbr. articles in field. *

RIFMAN, AVRUM KATZ, lawyer; b. Balt., Oct. 19, 1905; s. Hyman Shemon and Zeesla Baile (Katz) R.; m. Ruth Pell, May 4, 1935; children—Samuel Sholom, Melvin Sadler. LL.B., U. Md., 1926. Bar: Md. 1926, U.S. Dist. Ct. Md. 1927, U.S. Ct. Appeals (4th cir.) 1946, U.S. Supreme Ct. 1950. 1st asst., chief, trial div. City of Balt., 1943-45; trial magistrate So. Dist. Balt., 1951-53; Md. mem. Nat. Conf. Commrs. of Uniform State Laws, 1957-61; judge Mcpl. Ct. of Balt., 1968-70; master-in-chancery Supreme Bench of Balt., 1971-75; judge Archdiocesan Ct. Balt., 1977—; panel chmn. malpractice claims Md. Health Claims Arbitration Act, 1977—. Mem. ABA, Md. Bar Assn., Baltimore City Bar Assn., Jewish Hist. Soc. Md. Jewish. Clubs: Mason, Allied, B'nai B'rith. Contbr. articles of legal jours.

RIGBY, KENNETH, lawyer; b. Shreveport, La., Oct. 20, 1925; s. Samuel and Mary Elizabeth (Fearnhead) R.; m. Jacqueline Carol Brandon, June 10, 1951; children—Brenda, Wayne, Glen. B.S. magna cum laude, La. State U., 1950, J.D., 1951. Bar: La. 1951, U.S. Ct. Appeals (5th cir.) 1966, U.S. Supreme Ct. 1971, U.S. Tax Ct. 1981, U.S. Ct. Appeals (11th cir.) 1982. Ptnr. Love, Rigby, Dehan, Love & McDaniel, 1951—; mem. Marriage-Persons Com. La. Law Inst., 1981—, mem. council, 1988—. Sec. madatory continuing legal edn. com. La. Supreme Ct., 1987—. Served with USAAF, 1943-46. Fellow Am. Acad. Matrimonial Lawyers; mem. ABA, Assn. Trial Lawyers Am., La. Trial Lawyers Assn., Shreveport Bar Assn. (pres. 1973-74), La. State Bar Assn. (chmn. com. on continuing legal edn. 1974-75, chmn. family law sect. 1981-82, bd. of govs. 1986-88). Methodist. Contbr. articles to profl. jours. Office: Johnson Bldg 6th Floor 412 Milam St Shreveport LA 71101

RIGDON, RONALD MILTON, management consultant; b. Balt., Jan. 15, 1937; s. Leland Sanford and Betty Berniece (Roe) R.; student Kansas City (Mo.) Art Inst., 1958-60, William Jewell Coll., Liberty, Mo., 1955-58, 62-63; m. Arlene June Eddington, May 26, 1962; children—Ryan Todd, Rebecca Erin. Field adjuster CNA Ins. Corp., Kansas City, Mo., 1962-63; asst. mgr. Anchor Fin. Corp. Ins. Agy., Overland Park, Kans., 1963-64; mgr. First Mortgage Investment Co. Ins. Agy., Kansas City, Mo., 1964-67; pres. Programming Inst., Mission, Kans., 1967-70, RMR & Assos., Inc., Overland Park, 1970—; dir. Assn. Cons., Inc., Scheduling Systems, Inc. First v.p. Johnson County Mental Health Assn., 1968-70, Kans. Mental Health Assn., 1969-70. Mem. Mgmt. Cons. Inst., Profl. Ins. Mass-Mktg. Assn., Am. Mgmt. Assn., Assn. Chief Exec. Officers, Am. Profl. Assn. Group Ins. Adminstrs., U.S. Dressage Fedn., Kansas City Dressage Soc. Republican. Baptist. Author: Work Flow-Cost Reduction a Management Control System, 1978. Home: 12200 Big Bone Trail Olathe KS 66061 Office: 10875 Benson Dr Suite 103 Overland Park KS 66210

RIGG, DIANA, actress; b. Doncaster, Yorkshire, Eng., July 20, 1938; d. Louis and Beryl (Helliwell) R.; m. Manahem Gueffen, July 6, 1973 (div. Sept. 1976); m. Archibald Hugh Stirling, Mar. 25, 1981; 1 child, Rachael Atlanta. Grad., Fulneck Girls' Sch., Pudsey, Yorkshire; student, Royal Acad. Dramatic Art, London. Stage debut as Natella Abashwilli in The Caucasian Chalk Circle, Theatre Royal, York, Eng., 1957; joined Royal Shakespeare Co., Stratford-on-Avon, 1959, debut as Andromache in Troilus and Cressida, 1960; London debut as Philippe Trincant in The Devils, London, 1961; numerous repertory appearances; joined Nat. Theatre, 1972, appeared in Jumpers, Macbeth, The Misanthrope, Pygmalion; film appearances include A Midsummer Night's Dream, The Assassination Bureau, On Her Majesty's Secret Service, Julius Caesar, The Hospital, The Great Muppet Caper, Evil Under the Sun; co-starred as Emma Peel in Brit. TV series The Avengers, 1965-67; star TV series Diana, 1973-74; numerous TV movies including Bleak House, 1984, Wildlife, 1986, Follies, 1987, A Hazard of Hearts, 1987; author: No Turn Unstoned, 1982, U.S. edit., 1983. Recipient Tony award nomination as best actress in Abelard and Heloise and The Misanthrope; Plays and Players award for Phaedra Britannica and Night and Day; Variety Club Great Britain award for best actress for Evil Under the Sun; decorated Comdr. British Empire, 1988. Mem. United Brit. Artists (co-founder, dir. 1982—). Office: care London Mgmt, 235 Regent St, London W1A 2JT, England *

RIGGS, DONALD EUGENE, university librarian; b. Middlebourne, W.Va., May 11, 1942; m. Jane Vasbinder, Sept. 25, 1964; children: Janna Jennifer, Krista Dyonis. BA, Glenville State Coll., 1964; MA, W.Va. U., 1966; MLS, U. Pitts., 1968; EdD, Va. Poly. Inst. and State U., 1975. Head librarian, tchr. sci. Warwood (W.Va.) High Sch., 1964-65; head librarian, audiovisual dir. Wheeling (W.Va.) High Sch., 1965-67; sci. and econs. librarian California State Coll. of Pa., 1968-70; dir. library and learning center Bluefield State Coll., 1970-72; dir. libraries and media services Bluefield State Coll., Concord Coll., Greenbrier Community Coll., and So. campus W.Va. Coll. of Grad. Studies, 1972-76; dir. libraries U. Colo., Denver, Met. State Coll., and Community Col. of Denver—Auraria Campus, 1976-79; univ. librarian Ariz. State U., 1979—; adj. prof. Calif. State Coll., 1968-70, W.Va. U., 1970-72, U. Colo., 1977-79, U. Ariz., 1985; fed. relations coordinator Am. and W.Va. library assns., 1970-75; chmn. bd. dirs. Cen. Colo. Library System, 1976-79; chmn. Colo. Council Acad. Libraries, 1977-78; exec. bd. Colo. Alliance Research Libraries, 1978-79; cons. to libraries. Contbr. articles to profl. publs.; editor W.Va. Libraries, 1973-75; assoc. editor: Southeastern Librarian, 1973-75; contbg. author: Libraries in the Political Process, 1980; contbg. author, editor: Library Leadership: Visualizing the Future, 1982; contbg. author: Options for the 80s, 1982, Library and Information Technology: At the Crossroads, 1984; author: Strategic Planning for Library Managers, 1984, History of the Arizona State University Libraries, 1986, (with Rao Aluri) Expert Systems in Libraries, 1988, (with Gordon Sabine) Libraries in the '90s: What Leaders Expect, 1988; editorial bd. Jour. Library Adminstrn., 1987—; editorial bd. Am. Libraries, 1987—, editor Library Adminstrn. and Mgmt., 1987—. Trustee Mesa (Ariz.) Pub. Library, 1980-86, chmn., 1985-86; mem. Ariz. State Library Adv. Council, 1981-84; bd. dirs. Documentation Abstracts, Inc., 1986—. Named Outstanding Young Educator Ohio County Schs., 1966; Council on Library Resources grantee, 1985. Mem. ALA (councilor-at-large 1982-86, chmn. council's resolutions com. 1985-86), Ariz. Library Assn. (pres. coll. and univ. div. 1981-82, pres. 1983-84, Spl. Service award 1986), Colo. Library Assn. (pres. 1978-79), W.Va. Library Assn. (pres. 1975-76), Assn. Coll. and Research Libraries (pres. Tri-State chpt. 1972-74, pres. Ariz. chpt. 1981-82), So. Library Assn. (chmn. coll. and univ. sect. 1982-83), Assn. Research Libraries (mem. 100th meeting planning com. 1982), AMIGOS Bibliograph. Council, Inc. (trustee 1986—, del. users council online computer library ctr., 1987—, chair artificial intelligence and expert systems nat. group, 1987), Library Adminstrn. and Mgmt. Assn. (bd. dirs. 1987—), Library Info. and Tech. Assn., Mountain Plains Library Assn. (bd. dirs. 1987—), Beta Phi Mu, Chi Beta Phi, Phi Delta Kappa, Phi Kappa Phi. Home: 2120 E Knoll Circle Mesa AZ 85213 Office: Ariz State U Tempe AZ 85287

RIGGS, JEANETTE TEMPLETON, civic worker; b. Little Rock, Mar. 13, 1933; d. Donald M. and Fay (Templeton) Brewer; student Little Rock U., 1950-51, Tex. Coll. for Women, 1951-52; B.S., U. Ark., 1955; m. Byron Lawrence Riggs, June 1955; children—Byron Kent, Ann Templeton. Founder, Rochester (Minn.) Ballet Guild, 1970, pres., 1974; mem. establishing bd., exec. bd. Rochester Arts Council, 1972, producer, dir. T.S. Elliot's The Rock, 1970; founder, performer So. Minn. Ballet Co., 1974; sponsor Nat. Ballet Cos., Rochester, 1970-75; exec. bd. for restoration 1875 Pattern Book House, Rochester Heritage Assn., 1975-77; exec. bd. Savino Ballet Nat., 1975-78; founder, exec. bd. Citizens Action Com., 1977-79; asso., commentator Women, Cable TV Program for Women, Rochester, 1979; mem. Mayor's Com. on Drug Abuse, 1979-80; mem. Olmsted County Steering Com. for George Bush, 1979-80, a founder, mem. exec. bd. Olmsted County Republican Women's Orgn., 1979—, mem. Olmsted County Rep. Central Com., 1979—, exec. bd. issues com., 1979-80. Home: 432 SW 10th Ave Rochester MN 55901

RIGGS, ROBERT MELDRUM, French educator; b. Washington, Aug. 1, 1932; s. Theodore Scott and Phillis Wey (Symmonds) R.; B.A. with distinction, George Washington U., 1955; Fulbright scholar, U. Toulouse (France), 1955-56; M.A. (Miller fellow), U. Ill., 1957, postgrad., 1957-62. Grad. asst. U. Ill., 1957-62; instr. French, then asst. prof. George Washington U., 1964-70, asst. to chmn. dept. Romance langs., 1963-70; assoc. prof. French, Frostburg (Md.) State Coll., 1970—, chmn. dept. fgn. langs., 1984—. Bd. dirs. Allegany County Mental Health Assn., 1975-81; layreader, chmn. Christian edn. com. Emmanuel Episcopal Ch., Cumberland, 1979—, vestryman, 1981-85. Mem. Am. Assn. Tchrs. of French, Soc. War 1812, Nat. Trust Hist. Preservation, Denison Soc., Gallup Family Assn., Allegany County Hist. Soc. (curator 1976-78, 1st v.p. 1978-80, trustee 1980-82), Phi Beta Kappa, Phi Kappa Phi, Omicron Delta Kappa, Pi Delta Epsilon, Pi Delta Phi, Sigma Delta Pi, Acacia. Democrat. Home: 101 Washington St Cumberland MD 21502 Office: Frostburg State Coll Frostburg MD 21532

RIGHI-LAMBERTINI, EGANO CARDINAL, clergyman; b. Cassalecchio di Reno, Bologna, Italy, Feb. 22, 1906. Ordained priest, 1929. Titular archibishop of Docles, 1960-79; elevated to Sacred Coll. of Cardinals, 1979; mem. Council for Pub. Affairs of the Church, Sacred Congregation for the Bishops, Secretariat for Non-Christians; hon. pres. Commn. for Sacred Art in Italy; deacon of S. Giovanni Bosco in Via Tuscolana. Address: Piazza della Citta Leonina 9, 00193 Rome Italy *

RIHMER, ZOLTÁN, psychiatrist, neurologist; b. Pécs, Baranya, Hungary, Mar. 25, 1947; s. Zoltán Rihmer and Erzsébet Csizmadia; m. Lídia Harmati, Aug. 23, 1969; children: Zoltán, Annamária. MD, Med. U. of Pécs, 1971; cert. in psychiatry, Postgrad. Med. Sch., Budapest, Hungary, 1975, cert. in neurology, 1979. Psychiat. intern Psychiat. Inst. Pomáz, Hungary, 1971-73; psychiat. intern Nat. Inst. for Nervous and Mental Diseases, Budapest, 1973-75, neurology intern, 1976-79, chief psychiat. dept., sec. sci. com., 1982—; assoc. prof. psychiatry Semmelweis Med. Sch., Budapest, 1984; lectr. in psychiatry Postgrad. Med. Sch., 1980—. Editor: (with I. Bitter) Practical Psychopharmacology, 1986; contbr. more than 70 articles to sci. publs. Mem. med. sect. Hungarian Trade Union, Budapest, 1969—. Mem. Assn. Hungarian Neurologists and Psychiatrists (sec. 1977-80), Hungarian Psychiat. Assn. (sec. sect. psychopathology). Mem. Communist Party. Home: Magyar Jakobinusok Tere 6, 1122 Budapest Hungary Office: Nat Inst Nervous/Mental Diseases, 116 Voroshadsereg, 1281 Budapest Hungary

RIIHENTAUS, LEO JUHANI, mathematics educator, docent; b. Helsinki, Finland, Mar. 4, 1942; s. Leo and Leeni Lemmikki (Saarnilahti) R.; m. Leena Anneli Laurio, Nov. 6, 1965; children: Jyrki Juhani, Aila Marjaana. PhD, U. Helsinki, 1976. Asst. U. Jyväskyla, Finland, 1966-68; asst., dep. assoc. prof. Helsinki Inst. Tech., 1969-70, Lappeenranta Inst. Tech., Finland, 1970-71; lectr. U. Joensuu, Finland, 1972-76; math. educator Oulu Coll. Tech., Finland, 1977—; docent U. Joensuu, 1980—, U. Oulu, 1983—. Contbr. articles profl. jours. Mem. Finnish Math. Soc., Am. Math. Soc. (reviewer 1983—), Math. Assn. Am. Evangelical Lutheran. Home: Kosteperankatu 2 B 84, SF-90100 Oulu Finland

RIJKEBOER, GIJSBERT JAAP, marketing professional; b. Groningen, The Netherlands, Jan. 26, 1942; s. Cornelis J. and Rie (De Vries) R.; m. Lieve P. Perilleux, Dec. 27, 1969. Degree, U. Antwerp, Belgium, 1969. Attache Bank of Brussels, 1969-73; acct. mgr. Publicis Conseil, Brussels, 1973-74; internat. advt. coordinator Franklin Advt. Services, London, 1974; mktg. mgr., mktg. dir., gen. mgr. The Franklin Mint, various locations, 1975-82; pvt. practice mktg. cons. Brussels, 1983-84; gen. mgr. The Bradford Exchange, Ltd., London, 1984-88; mng. dir. Nightingale-Conant Corp., London, 1988—. Served to 1st lt. The Netherlands' Army, 1963-65. Mem. Inst. Dirs., Inst. Mgmt., Brit. Direct Mktg. Assn. (mem. trade practices com.). Office: The Citybridge House, 235-245 Goswell Rd, London EC1V 7JD, England

RILEY, ANN PEOPLES, marketing professional; b. Mooreland, Okla., Dec. 31, 1947; d. Estel Paul and Mary Jane (Munkres) Peoples; m. Michael Edward Riley, June 6, 1970 (div. Nov. 1985); children: Timothy, Andrea. BA, U. Okla., 1970, MA, 1973; JD, Temple U., 1979. Mgmt. cons. Software Inc., Norman, Okla., 1971-72; adj. prof. law Burlington Community Coll., Cinnaminson, N.J., 1979-81, Camden County Coll., Blackwood, N.J., 1981-82; with mktg. support IBM Office Products Div., Phila., 1981-82; program adminstr. nat. mktg. div. IBM, Phila., 1981-83; product mktg. mgr. nat. distbn. div. IBM, Princeton, N.J., 1983-86; program mgr. IBM-Asia Pacific Group, Tokyo, 1986—; prof. law Newport U., Tokyo, 1988—. Mem. Timbercrest Civic Assn., Mt. Laurel, N.J., 1979-86, Tokyo Am. Club, 1986—. Mem. Fgn. Exec. Women Tokyo. Democrat. Roman Catholic. Home: 7-18 MotoAzabu, 3-chome Minato-Ku, Tokyo 106, Japan Office: IBM Asia Pacific Group, IBM Kamiyacho Bldg, 3-9 Toranomon 4-chome, Minato-Ku, Tokyo 105, Japan

RILEY, BRIDGET LOUISE, painter; b. London, 1931; student Goldsmith's Sch. Art, London, 1949-52, Royal Coll. Art, London, 1952-55. With J. Walter Thompson, London, 1958-59, part-time, 1960-61; lectr. Loughborough Art Sch., 1959-60; part-time tchr. Hrnsey Coll. Art, London, 1960-61, Croydon Coll. Art, Surrey, Eng., 1961; exhibitor internat. shows; works represented public and pvt. collections world wide. Decorated comdr. Order Brit. Empire; recipient Peter Stuyvesant Found. travel bursary, 1964, AICA critics prize John Moores Exhbn., Liverpool, 1963, internat. prize for painting XXXIV Venice Biennale, 1968, Ohara Mus. Prize, Tokyo Print Biennale, 1972, gold medal Grafikk-bienniale, Fredrikstad, 1980. Office: Juda Rowan Gallery, 11 Tottenham Mews, London W1P 9PJ, England *

RILEY, DONALD CROSBY, marketing consultant, real estate broker; b. Oklahoma City, Sept. 27, 1926; s. Robert and Leila (Crosby) R.; m. Dorothy Donahue, Jan. 10, 1950 (div.). BBA, Ohio State U., 1945; MBA, Met. Collegiate Inst. London, 1947; PhD, Pacific Northwestern U., 1949; cultural doctorate, World U., 1986. Dir. profl. relations Pfizer Labs. div. Chas. Pfizer & Co., Inc., N.Y.C., 1950-61; N.Y. regional sales mgr. Victoreen Nuclear Electronics, Inc., 1960-66; owner Riley Mktg. Assocs., N.Y.C., 1966-72; v.p. internat. ops. Manhattan Pub. Co., Inc., N.Y.C., 1972-75; v.p. sales and mktg. A.M.S., Inc., N.Y.C., 1975-78; v.p. Cross & Brown Co., N.Y.C., 1978-82; mktg. cons., real estate broker, 1982—; prin. Jara Constrn. Corp.; mem. U.S. Congl. Adv. Bd. Commr. of Deeds City of N.Y., 1980—; mem. Nat. Trust for Hist. Preservation, Nat. Rep. Senatorial Club; trustee, charter mem. Rep. Presdl. Task Force; charter mem. U.S. Def. Com., Nat. Security Council, Carnegie Council on Ethics and Fgn. Affairs, Aviation Hall of Fame, 1978-81; mem. adv. bd. Fla. Crime Prevention Commn., Am. Security Council. Mem. Data Processing Mgmt. Assn. Internat. (chpt. exec. com. 1980-81), Asia Soc., Nat. Com. Am. Fgn. Policy, Sales Execs. Club N.Y., Sales and Mktg. Execs. Internat., Nat. Realty Club, Real Estate Bd. N.Y. Home: 40 Central Park S New York NY 10019 Office: 40 W 59th St New York NY 10019

RILEY, JAMES JOSEPH, union executive; b. Cleve., Nov. 12, 1919; s. Frank James and Mary Jane (Connor) R.; m. Ruth Marie Pearce, Apr. 10, 1939; children—Janet M., Nancy C., Catherine A., James F., Thomas M., Dennis J., Ruth E., Mary H., John R. B.S., Western Res. U., 1940. Mem. Cleve. Motion Picture Operators Union, Local 160, 1941—; partner Electric Speed Indicator Co. (weather instrument maker), Cleve., 1965-67; bus. agt. Internat. Alliance of Theatrical Stage Employees and Moving Picture Operators of U.S. and Can., Cleve., 1967-78; internat. gen.-sec. treas. Internat. Alliance of Theatrical Stage Employees and Moving Picture Operators of U.S. and Can., N.Y.C., 1978—, internat. trustee, 1969-78; v.p. Union Label and Service Trades dept. AFL-CIO, 1979—. Editor: Bull., Internat. Alliance Quar, 1978—. Served to lt. USNR, 1943-46, PTO. Roman Catholic. Home: 15801 Edgecliff Rd Cleveland OH 44111 Office: Suite 601 1515 Broadway New York NY 10036

RILEY, JOHN WINCHELL, JR., consulting sociologist; b. Brunswick, Maine, June 10, 1908; s. John Winchell and Marjorie Webster (Prince) R.; m. Matilda White, June 19, 1931; children—John Winchell, Lucy Ellen. A.B., Bowdoin Coll., 1930, LL.D., 1972; M.A., Harvard U., 1933, Ph.D., 1936. Mem. faculty Marietta Coll., 1933-35; mem. faculty Wellesley Coll., 1935-37, Douglass Coll., 1937-45; mem. faculty Rutgers U., 1945-60, prof. sociology, chmn. dept., 1945-60; v.p., dir. social research Equitable Life Assurance Soc. of U.S., N.Y.C., 1960-68, v.p. corp. relations, 1968—, sr. v.p. corp. relations, 1968-72, sr. v.p. social research, 1972-73, cons., 1973—; mem. faculty Harvard U., 1955; cons. Am. Council Life Ins., 1973—, WHO, 1984—, Internat. Fedn. Aging, 1983—, Scripps Found., 1987—, numerous others; vis. scholar Ctr. for Advanced Study in Behavioral Sci., 1978-79; mem. adv. bd. Carnegie Instn.'s Aging Soc. project, 1982—, U. Mich. Inst. Gerontology, 1987—; lectr. in field. Author: (with Bryce Ryan, Marcia Lifshitz) The Student Looks at His Teacher, 1950; (with Wilbur Schramm) The Reds Take A City, 1951; (with Matilda W. Riley, Jackson Toby) Sociological Studies in Seale Analysis, 1954; (with Matilda W. Riley, Marilyn Johnson) Aging and Society, Vol. II, 1969; editor: The Corporation and Its Public, 1963; contbr. Ency. of Aging, 1987, Nationalization of the Social Sciences, 1987; sr. cons. Internat. Glossary of Social Gerontology, 1983; sr. cons. editorial bds. numerous profl. jours.; adv. com. Sociol. Practice Rev., 1987; frequent program contbr. Internat. Soc. Assn., Internat. Soc. for the Study of Behavioral Devel., World Assn. for Pub. Opinion Research, Internat. Gerontol. Assn., others. Trustee Am. Found. Blind, Inst. Ednl. Devel., Nat. Urban League; trustee Industrywide Network Social Rural and Rural Efforts, sec., 1980—; mem. capital campaign com. Bowdoin Coll., 1984. Served with OWI, Psychol. Warfare Div., AUS, 1944, Far Eastern Research Group, USAF, 1950-51. Recipient numerous awards for profl. excellence. Fellow AAAS; mem. Sociol. Research Assn. (pres. 1964-65), Oliver Wendall Holmes Assn. (trustee), Am. Sociol. Assn. (sec. 1950-55, dist. career award 1987, award for practice 1983), Eastern Social Soc., Osborne Assn. (trustee), Am. Assn. Pub. Opinion Research (pres. 1961-62, award 1983), Market Research Council, Am. Assn. Internat. Aging (trustee), Am. Sociol. Found., D.C. Sociol. Soc. (co-pres. 1984-85). Home: 4701 Willard Ave Apt 1607 Chevy Chase MD 20815

RILEY, MATILDA WHITE (MRS. JOHN W. RILEY, JR), science adminstrator, emeritus sociology educator; b. Boston, Apr. 19, 1911; d. Percival and Mary (Iiff) White; m. John Winchell Riley, Jr., June 19, 1931; children: John Winchell III, Lucy Ellen Riley Sallick. A.B., Radcliffe Coll., 1931, M.A., 1937; D.Sc., Bowdoin Coll., 1972; L.H.D. (hon.), Rutgers U., 1983. Research asst. Harvard U., 1932; v.p. Market Research Co. Am., 1938-49; chief cons. economist WPB, 1941; research specialist Rutgers U., 1950, prof., 1951-73, emeritus prof., 1973—, dir. sociology lab., 1959-73, chmn. dept. sociology and anthropology, 1959-73; Daniel B. Fayerweather prof. polit. econ. and sociology Bowdoin Coll., 1974-81, prof. emeritus, 1981—; assoc. dir. Nat. Inst. on Aging, 1979—; mem. faculty Harvard, summer 1955; staff asso., dir. aging and society Russell Sage Found., 1964-73, staff sociologist, 1974-77; chmn. com. on life course Social Sci. Research Council, 1977-80; sr. research assoc. Center for Social Scis., Columbia U., 1978-80; adv. bd. Carnegie "Aging Soc." Project, 1985-87; mem. Commn. on Coll. Retirement, 1982-86; vis. prof. NYU, 1954-61; cons. Nat. Council on Aging, Acad. Ednl. Devel.; mem. study group NIH, 1971-79, Social Sci. Research Council Com. on Middle Years, 1973-77. Author: (with P. White) Gliding and Soaring, (with Riley and Toby) Sociological Studies in Scale Analysis, 1954, Sociological Research, vols. I, II, 1964, (with others) Aging and Society, vol. I, 1968, vol. II, 1969, vol. III, 1972, (with Nelson) Sociological Observation, 1974, Aging from Birth to Death: Interdisciplinary Perspectives, 1979, (with Merton) Sociological Traditions from Generation to Generation, 1980, (with Abeles and Teitelbaum) Aging from Birth to Death: Sociotemporal Perspectives, 1982, (with Hess and Bond) Aging in Society, 1983; co-editor: Perspectives in Behavioral Medicine: The Aging Dimension, 1987; Social Change and the Life Course, Vol. I. Social Structures and Human Lives (with B. Huber and B. Hess); Vol. II. Sociological Lives, 1988; editorial com.: Ann. Rev. Sociology, 1978-81, Social Change and the Life Course, Vol. 1, Social Structures and Human Lives, (with B. Huber and B. Hess) Sociological Lives, 1988; contbr. articles to profl. jours. Trustee The Big Sisters Assn. Recipient Lindback Research award Rutgers U., 1970; Social Sci. award Andrus Gerontology Center, U. So. Calif., 1972; fellow Advanced Study in Behavioral Scis., 1978-79; Matilda White Riley Award in Research Methodology established Rutgers U., 1977; Radcliffe Alumnae award, 1982, Commonwealth award 1984; Kesten Lecture award U. So. Calif., 1987; Winkleman Lectr., U. Mich., 1984; Selo Lectr., U. No. Calif., 1987; membership lectr. Am. Philos. Soc., 1987. Fellow AAAS (chmn. sect. on social and econ. scis. 1977-78); mem. Inst. Medicine of Nat. Acad. Scis. (sr.), Acad. Behavioral Medicine Research, Am. Sociol. Assn. (exec. officer 1949-60, v.p. 1973-74, pres. 1986, chmn.-elect sect. on Sociology of Aging 1988), Am. Assn. Public Opinion Research (sec.-treas. 1949-51, Disting. Service award 1983), Eastern Sociol. Soc. (v.p. 1968-69, pres. 1977-78, Disting. Career award 1986), Soc. for Study Social Biology (bd. dirs. 1986—), Am. Acad. Arts and Scis., D.C. Sociol. Soc. (co-pres. 1983-84), Sociol. Research Assn., Internat. Orgn. Study Human Devel., Am. Philos. Soc., Phi Beta Kappa, Phi Beta Kappa Assos. Home: 4701 Willard Ave Apt 1607 Chevy Chase MD 20815 Office: NIH Nat Inst on Aging 9000 Rockville Pike Bethesda MD 20205

RILEY, PATRICK ANTHONY, pathologist; b. Paris, Mar. 22, 1935; s. Bertram Hurrell and Olive (Stephenson) R.; m. Christine Elizabeth Morris, July 5, 1958; children—Sian Isobel, Caroline Anthea, Benjamin Patrick Hurrell. M.B., B.S., U. Coll., London, 1960, Ph.D., 1965. Research fellow Med. Research Council, London, 1969-71, Beit Meml. Univ. Coll., London, 1971-74; lectr. chem. pathology dept. Univ. Coll. London, 1974-76, reader biochem. pathology dept., 1976-84, prof. cell pathology, 1984—. Editor: Hydroxyanisole, 1984. Contbr. articles to sci. publs. Fellow Royal Coll. Pathologists, Linnean Soc., (mem. council 1980-84), Inst. Biology; mem. Biol. Council of Gt. Britain (mgmt. com. 1982—), Royal Instn. Avocations: reading; walking; skiing; 3-D photography. Office: University Coll, University St, London WC1E 6JJ, England

RILEY, ROBERT ANNAN, III, social services administrator, financial consultant; b. Balt., Jan. 2, 1955; s. Robert Jr. and Elfrieda Bertha (Mueller) R.; m. Adama Ly, July 31, 1987. BA in English, Yale U., 1979. Vol. Peace Corps, Gabon, Africa, 1979-83, adminstr. tng., 1983-84, assoc. dir. adminstrn., 1984—. Author of several computer fin. software programs, 1985—. Recipient Peace Corps Outstanding Achievement award, 1985, 87, Peace Corps award for Spl. Act of Service, 1986. Democrat. Episcopalian. Home: Boite Postale 85, Bamako Mali Office: Dept of State Bamako Mali Washington DC 20520-2050

RILEY-DAVIS, SHIRLEY MERLE, advertising agency executive, marketing consultant, writer; b. Pitts., Feb. 4, 1935; d. William Riley and Beatrice Estelle (Whittaker) Byrd; m. Louis Davis; 1 child, Terri Judith. Student U. Pitts., 1952. Copywriter, Pitts. Mercantile Co., 1954-60; exec. sec. U. Mich., Ann Arbor, 1962-67; copy supr. N.W. Ayer, N.Y.C., 1968-76, assoc. creative dir., Chgo., 1977-81; copy supr. Leo Burnett, Chgo., 1981-86; freelance advt. and mktg. cons., 1986—. Writer of print, radio, and TV commercials. Former bd. dirs. Epilepsy Services Chgo. Recipient Grand and First prize N.Y. Film Festival, 1974, Gold and Silver medal Atlanta Film Festival, 1973, Gold medal V.I. Film Festival, 1974, 50 Best Creatives award Am. Inst. Graphic Arts, 1972, Clio award, 1973, 74, 75, Andy Award of Merit, 1981, Silver medal Internat. Film Festival, 1982; Senatorial scholar. Mem. Women in Film, Facets Multimedia Film Theatre Orgn. (bd. dirs.), Nat. Assn. Female Execs., Greater Chgo. Council for Prevention of Child Abuse (bd. dirs.). Democrat. Roman Catholic. Avocations: dance, poetry, design.

RILEY-SMITH, JONATHAN SIMON CHRISTOPHER, history educator; b. Harrogate, North Yorkshire, Eng., June 27, 1938; s. William Henry D. and Elspeth Agnes M. (Craik Henderson) Riley-Smith; m. Marie-Louise Jeannetta Field, July 27, 1968; children: Tobias Augustine William, Tamsin Elspeth Hermione, Hippolyta Clemency Magdalen. Student, Eton Coll., Windsor, Eng., 1951-56; BA, Cambridge U., 1960, MA, PhD, 1964. Asst. lectr. Dept. Medieval History U. St. Andrews, Scotland, 1964-65, lectr., 1966-72; asst. lectr. Cambridge U., 1972-75, lectr., 1975-78; prof. U. London, 1978—; fellow, dir. studies in history Queens Coll., Cambridge U., 1972-78. Author: The Knights of St. John in Jerusalem and Cyprus, 1967, The Feudal Nobility and the Kingdom of Jerusalem, 1973, What Were the Crusades, 1977, The First Crusade and the Idea of Crusading, 1986, The Crusades: A Short History, 1987; co-author: Ayyubids, Mamlukes, and Crusaders (2 vols.), 1971, The Crusades: Idea and Reality, 1981. Named Librarian Priory, Most Venerable Order of St. John, 1966-78, Knight of Justice, 1969, Grand Priory 1982—. Fellow Royal Hist. Soc.; mem. Soc. for Study of Crusades and Latin East (founding, sec. 1980-82), Internat. Com. on False Orders St. John (hist. advisor 1974—), Sovereign Mil. Order of Malta (Knights of Magistral Grace 1971, Officer Merit, Order Pro Merito Melitensi 1984). Roman Catholic. Office: Royal Holloway and, Bedford New Coll, Egham Hill, Surrey TW20 0EX, England

RILL, JAMES FRANKLIN, lawyer; b. Evanston, Ill., Mar. 4, 1933; s. John Columbus and Frances Eleanor (Hill) R.; m. Mary Elizabeth Laws, June 14, 1957; children: James Franklin, Roderick M. AB cum laude, Dartmouth Coll., 1954; LLB, Harvard, 1959. Bar: D.C. bar 1959. Legis. asst. Congressman James P. S. Devereux, Washington, 1952; sole practice Washington, 1953—; assoc. Steadman, Collier & Shannon, 1959-63; ptnr. Collier, Shannon & Rill, 1963-69, Collier, Shannon, Rill & Scott, 1969—; bd. dirs. The Winston Group, Inc., Washington, Marshall Durbin Food Corp., Birmingham, Ala. Contbr. articles to profl. jours. Trustee Bullis Sch., Potomac, Md. Served to 1st lt. arty. AUS, 1954-56. Mem. ABA (past chmn. legis. com., mem. council, chmn. sect. of antitrust law, vice chmn. com. agy. adjudication sect. adminstrv. law), D.C. Bar Assn., Phi Delta Theta. Clubs: Met., Loudon Valley. Home: 7305 Masters Dr Potomac MD 20854 Office: Suite 308 1055 Thomas Jefferson St NW Washington DC 20007

RILLING, HELMUTH, conductor, educator; b. Stuttgart, Germany, May 29, 1933; s. Eugen and Hildegard (Plieninger) R.; m. Martina Greiner, 1967; 2 children. Student in organ, composition, conducting, Staatliche Hochschu Musik Stuttgart; student organ, Conservatorio de S. Cecilia Roma; student conducting with Leonard Bernstein, N.Y.C.; Dr. Phil. (hon.), Baldwin Wallace Coll Cleve. U., 1976; ThD (hon.), U. Tubingen, 1985. Founder, dir. Gächinger Kantorei Stuttgart, 1954—, Figuralchor of Gedächtniskirche, Stuttgart, 1957-80; tchr. organ and conducting Berliner Kirchenmusikschule Spandau; dir. Spandauer Kantorei, 1963-66; founder, dir. Bach-Collegium Stuttgart, 1965—, Summer Acad. Johann Sebastian Bach Stuttgart, 1979—, Internat. Bach Acad., Stuttgart, 1981—; prof. conducting, Staatliche Hochschule Musik, Frankfurt/Main, 1966-85; dir. Frankfurter Kantorei, 1969-81; founder, dir. Oreg. Bach Festival, Eugene, 1970—; cooperator Israel Philharmonic Orch., 1976—; mem. faculty Ind. U., Bloomington, 1976, 77; ensemble performer, guest conductor, guest prof. Bach Acads. in Tokyo, Buenos Aires, Poland, Czechoslovakia, U.S.S.R. Performer numerous records including all sacred cantatas and oratorioes of Bach, numerous TV and film Appearances. Recipient disting. service award U. Oreg., 1985. Office: Internat Bachakademie, Johan Sebastian Bach, Platz D 7000, Stuttgart 1, Federal Republic of Germany

RIM, JEONG DAE, mathematics educator; b. Seoul, Korea, May 30, 1930; s. Ilann and Soonam (moon) R.; m. Bunshik Rim; children: Yongjae, Songjae, Yumee Rim. BS, Yonsei U., Seoul, 1954, MS, 1957; PhD, Kyongbook U., Taegu, Korea, 1975. Lectr. Yonsei U., 1957-62, asst. prof., 1962-67, assoc. prof., 1967-70, chmn. dept., 1969-71, prof., 1970—; researcher U. Wash., Seattle, 1963-64; vis. scholar King's Coll. London Cu., 1979-80. Author: Introduction to Mathematical Logic, 1980, Mathematical Entities and Knowledge, 1985. Mem. Korean Math. Soc. (pres. 1986—). Office: Yonsei Univ, Seoul Republic of Korea

RIMBERG, KJELD, consulting and planning executive; b. Bergen, Norway, Nov. 25, 1943; s. Sverre Johan and Eli (Lien) R.; m. Reidun Tvedt, Oct. 15, 1965; children: Ina, Janne, Linn. Vordiplom, Eidenossische Technische Hochshule, Zurich, 1966; MSc, NTH, Trondheim, Norway, 1969. Cons. Søfteland & Jacobsen, Bergen, 1970-71; sci. asst. NTH, Trondheim, 1971-74; scientist Sintef, Trondheim, 1974-76; sec. NTNF, Oslo, 1976-81; mng. dir. Asplan, Berum, Norway, 1982—; mng. dir. Norwegian Bldg. Research Inst., Oslo, 1985-86; chmn. bd. Nat. Wine and Spirits Monopoly Ltd., Oslo; bd. dirs. Kongsberg Vapen Ltd., Byggholt Berum Ltd. Office: Asplan, Box 25, 1301 Sandvica Norway

RIMOIN, DAVID LAWRENCE, physician, geneticist; b. Montreal, Que., Can., Nov. 9, 1936; s. Michael and Fay (Lecker) R.; m. Mary Ann Singleton, Sept. 9, 1962 (div. 1979); 1 dau., Anne; m. Ann Piilani Garber, July 27, 1980; children: Michael, Lauren. BSc, McGill U., Montreal, 1957, MSc, MD, CM, 1961; PhD, Johns Hopkins U., 1967. Asst. prof. medicine, pediatrics Washington U., St. Louis, 1967-70; assoc. prof. medicine, pediatrics UCLA, 1970-73, prof., 1973—, chief med. genetics, Harbor-UCLA Med. Ctr., 1970-86; dir. dept. pediatrics, dir. Med. Genetics and Birth Defects Ctr., Cedars Sinai Med. Ctr., 1986—. Co-author: Principles and Practice of Medical Genetics, 1983; contbr. articles to profl. jours., chpts. to books. Recipient Ross Outstanding Young Investigator award Western Soc. Pediatric Research, 1976, E. Mead Johnson award Am. Acad. Pediatrics, 1976. Fellow ACP; mem. Am. Fedn. Clin. Research (sec./treas. 1972-75), Western Soc. Clin. Research (pres. 1978), Am. Bd. Med. Genetics (pres. 1979-83), Am. Soc. Human Genetics (pres. 1984), Am. Pediatric Soc., Soc. Pediatric Research, Am. Soc. Clin. Investigator, Assn. Am. Physicians. Home: 512 N Palm Dr Beverly Hills CA 90210 Office: Cedars Sinai Med Ctr 8700 Beverly Blvd Los Angeles CA 90048

RIMÓN, RANAN HILEL, psychiatry educator; b. Turku, Finland, Apr. 3, 1938; s. Salomon and Polja (Kagan) Portnoj; m. Anni Helena Laakso, June 16, 1967; children: Iris Bracha, Markus Mikael, Arje Salomon, Sonja Ilana. Lic. Medicine, U. Turku, 1963, MD, 1969. Commd. lt. Finnish Med. Corps, 1960, advanced through grades to maj., 1973, resigned, 1974; asst. clin. chief physician U. Turku, 1967-70, asst. prof. psychiatry, 1969-72; asst. clin. prof. U. Calif., San Diego, 1971; prof., chmn. psychiatry U. Kuopio, Finland, 1974-75; vis. prof., sr. scientist Hebrew U., Israel, 1975-79; asst. prof. U. Helsinki, Finland, 1971-74, prof., 1980—. Contbr. articles to profl. jours. Mem. Finnish Med. Assn., Finnish Psychiat. Assn., Israel Med. Assn. Assn. Mil. Surgeons Finland, Assn. Scandinavian Mil. Surgeons, Scandinavian Assn. Psychopharmacologists. Home: Italahdenkatu 1 B, SF-00210 Helsinki Finland Office: U Helsinki Dept Psychiatry, Lapinlahdentie, SF-00180 Helsinki Finland

RIMPELÄ, MATTI KEIJO, physician; b. Pori, Finland, Aug. 7, 1942; parents: Frans Keijo and Ihanelma (Levänen) R.; m. Ulla Mattelmäki, 1967 (dec. 1979); m. Arja Hannele Eskola, 1982; children: Jami, Riku, Anssi, Manu. MD, U. Turku, Finland, 1972; PhD, U. Tampere, Finland, 1980; MS in Sociology, U. London, 1985. Researcher Finnish Acad. Scis., Tampere, 1974-78; med. officer Nat. Bd. Health, Helsinki, Finland, 1978-82; assoc. prof. med. sociology U. Helsinki, 1982-86; sr. research fellow Finnish Acad. Scis., Helsinki, 1984; head physician Health Dept., City of Hyvinkää, Finland, 1986—; European adviser WHO. Author approximately 300 scientific papers on prevention, health promotion, perceived health and health policy. Sec. Working Party on Health Policy, Social Dem. Party, 1976-82. Recipient Health Edn. award Internat. Union for Health Edn., 1984. Mem. Finnish Acad. Scis. (med. research council 1978-80). Office: Health Dept, PO Box 90, 05801 Hyvinkää Finland

RIMPILA, JULIAN JOHN, gastroenterologist; b. Chgo., Apr. 19, 1940; s. Charles Einar and Verna Catherine (Swanson) R.; B.A., Knox Coll., 1962; M.S., U. Chgo., 1966, M.D., 1966; m. Beverly Rose Dahlen, Apr. 30, 1966; children—John-Eric, Carl, Kari, Siiri, Heidi. Intern in medicine Northwestern U.-Evanston Hosp., 1966-67, resident in internal medicine, 1967-70; fellow in gastroenterology U. Chgo., 1973-76; practice medicine specializing in gastroenterology, Chgo., 1976—; chmn. dept. med. Henrotin Hosp., Chgo., 1984-86; mem. med. staff Grant Hosp., Lutheran Gen. Hosp., Lincoln Park, Gottlieb Hosp.; mem. cons. staff Christ Hosp. Asst. scoutmaster Boy Scouts Am., Westchester, Ill., 1980—; councillor U. Chgo. Alumni Council, 1976-80. Served with M.C., U.S. Army, 1970-73; also lt. col., USAR. Recipient Leadership and Service award Boy Scouts Am., 1978, 79, 80. Mem. ACP, AMA, Am. Soc. Gastrointestinal Endoscopy, Chgo. Med. Soc., Assn. U.S. Army, Res. Officers Assn. U.S., Am. Scandinavian Found., Phi Beta Kappa, Tau Kappa Epsilon (Delta award Delta chpt. 1985). Sigma Xi. Republican. Lutheran. Mem. editorial bd. Medicine on the Midway, 1980—. Home: 11049 Windsor Dr Westchester IL 60153 Office: 505 N Lake Shore Dr Suite 406 Chicago IL 60611

RINALDO, HELEN, interior designer; b. Manville, N.J., July 5, 1922; d. Zigmond and Kate (Szymanski) Ossowski; student summer and evening classes N.Y. Sch. Interior Design, 1964; student N.Y. U., 1964, Somerset County (N.J.) Coll., 1975-76; m. Nicholas Rinaldo, Feb. 7, 1948; children—Linda Ann, Lorraine Ann. Interior designer W. & J. Sloane, Red Bank and Short Hills, N.J., 1981, Lord & Taylor, Paramus, N.J., 1974; owner Rinaldo Interiors, Scotch Plains, N.J., 1959-65; designer local firms; speaker career day local sch. Mem. Hist. Commn. Twp. of Branchburg (N.J.), until 1982. Mem. Allied Bd. Trade (N.Y.C.), Internat. Platform Assn. Home and Office: 69 Partridge Ln Cherry Hill NJ 08003

RINDERKNECHT, HANS ULRICH, lawyer; b. Zurich, Switzerland, May 13, 1920; s. Hans Jakob and Lina (Moos) R. Student Zurich Jr. Coll., 1933-36; B.A., Zurich Tchrs. Coll., 1940; B.L., Zurich and Berne U. Law Schs., 1944. Prin. Rinderknecht & Co. AG, attys., Zurich, 1944—; chmn. bd. DHJ Industries AG, Zug, Switzerland, 1973—, Taurean Investments N.V., Curacao, N.A., 1972—, Taurean Films S.A., Zug, 1972—, MEMCO S.A., Zurich, Emma Kunz Heilprodukte AG, Wuerenlos, Switzerland, 1985—, Steinwerke A. Meier AG, Wuerenlos, 1985—; vice chmn. Allied Chem. S.A., Zug, 1963—; dir. Figgie Internat., Inc., Richmond, Va., Paradise Island Bridge Co. Ltd., Nassau, Bahamas, Ticketmaster Ltd., Georgetown, Cayman Islands; chmn. Ticketmaster AG, Zurich, 1979—, Trammo Hydrocarbons & Chems. AG, Zurich, 1983—, Transammonia AG, Zurich, 1984—, Grover Trading Corp., Zurich, 1984—, Spanset Inter AG, Zurick, 1984—, Ansi Valve Trading AG, Zug, 1984—, Ramot SA, Zurich 1984—, Trammochem AG, Pfaeffikon, 1987—. Trustee Am. Coll. in Switzerland, Leysin, 1984. Mem. Am. C. of C. Switzerland (dir., treas. 1967-71). Clubs: Baur au Lac, Zurich. Home: 77 Zuercherstrasse, Rapperswil Switzerland Office: 7 Beethovenstrasse, 8022 Zurich Switzerland

RINEHART, GEORGINA HOPE, prospecting company executive; b. Perth, Western Australia, Australia, Feb. 9, 1954; d. Langley George and Hope Margaret (Nicholas) Hancock; m. Frank Rinehart; children: John Langley, Bianca Hope, Hope, Ginia Hope. Grad. U. Sydney, 1973. Dir., Hancock Prospecting Pty. Ltd. and subs. cos., Perth and Sydney, Australia, 1973—. Contbr. articles to mags. Organizer election compaign Westralian Secession Movement, Perth, 1974. Mem. Minerals and Energy Club Australia, Taxpayers United. Anglican. Clubs: Royal Kings Park Tennis (Perth); Harvard, Metropolitan (N.Y.C.). Office: Hancock Prospecting Pty Ltd, 49 Stirling Hwy, Nedlands, Western Australia 6009, Australia

RING, ALVIN MANUEL, pathologist; b. Detroit, Mar. 17, 1933; s. Julius and Helen (Krolik) R.; m. Cynthia Joan Jacobson, Sept. 29, 1963; children—Jeffrey, Melinda, Heather. B.S., Wayne State U., 1954; M.D., U. Mich., 1958. Intern Mt. Carmel Hosp., Detroit, 1958-59; resident in pathology Michael Reese Hosp., Chgo., 1960-62; asst. pathologist Kings County Hosp., Bklyn., 1962-63; assoc. pathologist El Camino Hosp., Mountain View, Calif., 1963-65; chief pathologist, dir. labs. St. Elizabeth's Hosp., Chgo., 1965-72, Holy Cross Hosp., Chgo., 1972-87; instr. SUNY, 1962-63, Stanford U., 1963-65; asst. prof. pathology U. Ill., Chgo., 1966-69, assoc. prof., 1969-78, prof., 1978—; adj. clin. prof. No. Ill. U., 1981—; chmn. histotech. Nat. Accrediting Agy. for Clin. Lab. Scis., 1977-81; mem. spl. adv. com. Health Manpower, 1966-71; pres. Spear Computer Users Group, 1981-82; mem. adv. com. Mid-Am. chpt. ARC, 1979-85; pres. Pathology and Lab. Cons., Inc., 1985—; originator, coordinator pathology courses Cook County Grad. Sch. Medicine, 1981—; bd. trustees Analytical Lab. for Environ. Excellence, 1987—; exec. con. Exec. Service Corp., 1987—. Author: Laboratory Correlation Manual, 1968, 82, 86, Laboratory Assistant Examination Review Book, 1971, Review Book in Pathology, Anatomic, 1986, Review Book in Pathology, Clinical, 1986; mem. editorial bd. Laboratory Medicine, 1975-87; contbr. articles to med. jours. Fellow Coll. Am. Pathology (insp. 1973—), Am. Soc. Clin. Pathology; mem. AMA, Ill. Med. Soc., Chgo. Med. Soc. (alt. councilor 1980-85, mem. adv. com. on health care delivery), Ill. Pathol. Soc., Chgo. Pathol. Soc. (censor 1980—, exec. com. 1985—), Am. Assn. Blood Banks, Phi Lambda Kappa. Home: 6843 N Lamon St Lincolnwood IL 60646 Office: 485 Frontage Rd Burr Ridge IL 60521

RING, BARBARA ANN, management consultant; b. St. Louis, Mar. 7, 1945; d. Oliver C. and Ann (McCarron) Garleb; 1 son, Michael Francis Ring. AA in Nursing, El Camino Coll., 1964; BA, UCLA, 1967, JD, 1971; BS in Mgmt., Pacific Christian Coll., 1976; BS in Nursing, Am. Nat. U., 1980, MBA, 1982; postgrad. U. So. Calif.; 1 son, Michael Francis. With Harbor Gen. Hosp., Torrance, Calif., 1964-66, Gardena Meml. Hosp., 1967-68, UCLA Med. Ctr., 1969-70, Brotman Meml. Hosp., Culver City, 1971-73; cardiac specialist Calif. Hosp. Med. Ctr., Los Angeles, 1974-77; asst. dir. nurses Fountain Valley Community Hosp. (Calif.), 1978-79; cons. Upjohn Health Care Services, 1980-84; mgmt. cons. Ind. Contractor. Dir. Charter Counseling Ctr., De Anza, Riverside; youth camp dir. YMCA, also caravan dir.; bd. dirs. U. Calif. riverside Athletic Assn., Urban League; mem. Jurupa 2001 steering com. Bank Am. scholar, 1962; Westmont Coll. scholar, 1962; recipient Woman of Achievement award Riverside YWCA. Mem. Am. Mgmt. Assn., Nat. Assn. Female Execs., Critical Care Nurses Assn. NOW, ACLU, Christian Bus. Women's Fellowship, Riverside C. of C. (ambassador, bd. dirs., steering com.), Jurupa C. of C. (bd. dirs.). Lodge: Soroptimist.

RING, LEONARD M., lawyer; b. Taurage, Lithuania, May 11, 1923; came to U.S., 1930, naturalized, 1930; s. Abe and Rose (Kahn) R.; m. Donna R. Cecrle, June 29, 1959; children—Robert Steven, Susan Ruth. Student, N.Mex. Sch. Mines, 1943-44; LL.D., DePaul U., 1949, J.D. Bar Ill. 1949. Spl. asst. atty. gen. State Ill., Chgo., 1967-72; spl. atty. Ill. Dept. Ins., Chgo., 1967-73; spl. trial atty. Met. San. Dist. Greater Chgo., Chgo., 1967-77; lectr. civil trial, appellate practice, tort law Nat. Coll. Advocacy, San Francisco, 1971, 72; mem. com. jury instrns. Ill. Supreme Ct., 1967—; nat. chmn. Attys. Congl. Campaign Trust, Washington, 1975-79. Author: (with Harold A. Baker) Jury Instructions and Forms of Verdict, 1972. Editorial bd. Belli Law Jour., 1983—; adv. bd. So. Ill. U. Law Jour., 1983—. Contbr. chpts. to books including Callaghan's Illinios Practice Guide, Personal Injury, 1988 and chpt. 6 (Jury Selection and Persuasion) for Masters of Trial Practice, also numerous articles to profl. jours. Trustee, Roscoe Pound-Am. Trial Lawyers Found., Washington, 1978-80; chmn. bd. trustees Avery Coonley Sch., Downers Grove, Ill., 1974-75. Served with U.S. Army, 1943-46. Decorated Purple Heart. Fellow Am. Coll. Trial Lawyers, Internat. Acad. Trial Lawyers, Internat. Soc. Barristers; mem. Soc. Trial Lawyers, Am. Judicature Soc., Appellate Lawyers Assn. (pres. 1974-75), Assn. Trial Lawyers Am. (nat. pres. 1973-74), Ill. Trial Lawyers Assn. (pres. 1966-68), Trial Lawyers for Pub. Justice (founder), Chgo. Bar Assn. (bd. mgrs. 1971-73), ABA (council 1983—, sect. tort and ins. practice, vice chair 1987—), Ill. Bar Assn., Kans. Bar Assn. (hon. life), Lex Legio Bar Assn. (pres. 1976-78), Inner Circle Advocates. Clubs: Metropolitan, Plaza, Meadow, River; Monroe (Chgo.). Home: 6 Royal Vale Dr Ginger Creek Oak Brook IL 60521 Office: 111 W Washington St Chicago IL 60602

RINGADOO, VEERASAMY, governor general of Mauritius; b. 1920; married; 2 children. LL.B. with honors, London Sch. Econs., 1948; D.C.L. (hon.), U. Mauritius, 1976; D.Litt. (hon.), Andhra U., 1978. Bar: Mauritius 1949. Mem. legis. council for Moka-Flacq, Mauritius, 1951-67, for Quartier Militaire/Moka, 1967-82, minister of labour & social security, 1959-63, minister of edn., 1964-67, minister of agr. & natural resources, 1967-68, minister of fin., 1968-82, gov.-gen., comdr.-in-chief of Mauritius and dependencies, 1986—; mcpl. councillor, Port Louis, 1956; participant London Constl. Conf., 1965; chmn. ADB/ADF Bd. Govs., 1977-78, gov. IMF/ADB, 1970-82. Decorated Officier de l'Ordre Nat. Malgache, 1969; Medaille de l'Assemblee Nat. Francaise, 1971; knighted, Mauritius, 1975; fellow London Sch. Econs., 1976; decorated Queens Counsel, 1983; knight grand cross of the Order of St. Michael and Saint George, 1986. Address: Office of the Gov-Gen, LeReduit, Port Louis Mauritius *

RINGE, MARION KAY, non-profit organization development executive; b. Detroit, Apr. 23, 1946; d. Norman Fred and Gladys Leona (Gohlke) R. B.A., Wayne State U., 1970, M.A., 1977. Asst. to v.p. advancement Merrill-Palmer Inst., Detroit, 1971-78; asst. dir. devel. Detroit Inst. Arts, 1978-80; asst. dir. devel. Harper-Grace Hosps., Detroit, 1980-85, dir. ann. support, 1985-88; dir. current giving The Detroit Med. Ctr., 1988—. Mem. Nat. Assn. Hosp. Devel., Mich. Assn. Hosp. Devel., Nat. Soc. Fund Raising Execs (cert.). Republican. Lutheran. Home: 23416 Wilmarth Farmington MI 48024 Office: The Detroit Med Ctr Devel Office 4160 John R St Ste 616 Detroit MI 48201

RINGELMANN, WALTER JOHANNES, city official; b. Pietermaritzburg, Natal, Republic of South Africa, Oct. 28, 1925; s. Andreas Walter and Minna (Stielau) R.; m. Waltraut Böhmer, May 16, 1953; children—Margret, Walter, Sigrid. B.Sc. in Engring., Natal U., 1947; Diploma in Pub. Adminstrn. U. Pretoria, 1985. Engr. Rand Water Bd., Johannesburg, Transvaal, Republic South Africa, 1948-52; tech. officer South African Bur. Standards, Pretoria, Transvaal, 1952-56; mech. engr. Natal Roads Dept., Durban, 1956-68; prin. engr. Dept. Forestry, Pretoria, 1968-70; chief engr., 1970—. Sec. Glenmore Ratepayers Assn., Durban, 1966-68; mem. Menlo Park Ratepayers Assn., 1968—. Fellow Engrs. Assn. South Africa; mem. South African Council Profl. Engrs. Lutheran. Avocations: photography; gardening. Home: 23 14th St Menlo Pk, Pretoria, Transvaal 0081, Republic South Africa Office: Dept Forestry, corner Pretorius/Vander Walt St, 0001 Pretoria Republic of South Africa

RINGLE, BRETT ADELBERT, lawyer; b. Berkeley, Calif., Mar. 17, 1951; s. Forrest A. and Elizabeth V. (Darnall) R.; m. Sue Kinslow, May 26, 1973. B.A., U. Tex., 1973, J.D., 1976. Bar: Tex. 1976, U.S. Dist. Ct. (no. dist.) Tex. 1976, U.S. Supreme Ct. 1980, U.S. Ct. Appeals (5th cir.) 1984. Ptnr., Shank, Irwin & Conant, Dallas, 1976-86, Jones, Day, Reavis & Pogue, Dallas, 1986—; adj. prof. law So. Meth. U., Dallas, 1983. Author: (with J. W. Moore and H. I. Bendix) Moore's Federal Practice, Vol. 12, 1980, Vol. 13, 1981, (with J. W. Moore) Vol. 1A, 1982. Mem. Dallas Bar Assn. Home: 6423 Malcolm Dr Dallas TX 75214 Office: Jones Day Reavis & Pogue 2001 Ross Ave PO Box 660623 Dallas TX 75266

RINGOIR, SEVERIN MARIA GHISLENUS, medical educator, physician; b. Aalst, Belgium, June 17, 1931; s. Benoni and Mariette (Vlasschaert) R.; children: Marc, Yves. MD, U. Gent, Belgium, 1956, PhD, 1967. Resident Med. Clinic U. Gent, 1958-61, instr., 1961-71, assoc. prof., 1971-75, prof. nephrology, 1975—, chief renal div., 1971—, chmn. medicine, 1981-84;

chmn. 1st Internat. Symposium Single Needle Hemodialysis, Tampa, Fla., 1984. Inventor pressure-pressure single needle hemodialysis; contbr. sci. articles to profl. jours. Served to maj. Mil. Health Service, 1956-58, Res., 1958—. Decorated comdr. Order of Leopold, officer Order of Crown (Belgium); recipient J. Lemaire prize, 1970. Fellow Royal Soc. Medicine; mem. Royal Acad. Medicine Belgium, Am. Soc. Artificial Internal Organs, N.Y. Acad. Scis., Swiss, German, French, Dutch Soc. Nephrology, European Dialysis and Transplant Assn. (council 1981-84, pres. 1985 Congress), European Soc. for Artifical Organs, (gov. 1988—, pres.-elect congress), Internat. Soc. Artificial Organs (v.p. 1981-85, gen. sec. 1984—). Christian Democrat. Roman Catholic. Home: Vaderlandstraat 44, B9000 Gent Belgium Office: Univ Gent, De Pintelaan 185, B9000 Gent Belgium

RINKENBERGER, RICHARD KRUG, physical scientist; b. Gridley, Ill., May 15, 1933; s. Burl E. and Olive J. (Krug) R.; divorced; children: Janice L., Ginger R., Rebekah P.; m. Ida Lee Vaughn, Mar. 22, 1985; children: Douglas W., Angela D. BA in Geology, U. Colo., 1959. Dir. prospecting Grubstake Assn., Sask., Can., 1958-59; engr. Martin-Marietta Aerospace Co., Denver, 1960-75; geologist U.S. Geol. Survey, Denver, 1975; geologist remote sensing U.S. Mine Safety and Health Adminstrn., Denver, 1975-79; pres., exploration geologist Banner Set, Ltd., Denver, 1980-84; pres., cons. geologist R.K. Rinkenberger & Assocs., Aurora, Colo., 1979-87; phys. scientist Dept. Energy, Germantown, Md., 1987—; educator prospecting Denver Sch. Prospecting, 1968-71, U. Colo, Denver, Boulder, 1970-75; research geochemist Heritage Chem. Co., Englewood, 1984-85; prospecting researcher R.K. Rinkenberger & Assocs., Aurora, 1965—. Contbr. articles to profl. jours. Mem. parent adv. bd, supt. of schs. Westminster, Colo., 1982-83. Recipient High Quality Performance award U.S. Mine Safety and Health Dept., 1977; grantee U.S. Geol. Survey, 1978. Mem. Am. Soc. Photogrammetry and Remote Sensing, Assn. Exploration Geochemists, Sigma Gamma Epsilon. Mem. Ch. Nazarene. Home: 16709 Frontenac Terr Rockville MD 20855 Office: PO Box 5523 Rockville MD 20855

RINMAN, THORSTEN JAN, newspaper editor; b. Gothenburg, Sweden, Apr. 4, 1934; s. Ture and Mary (Porter) R.; children—Johannes, Christoffer. Master Mariner, Gothenburg U., 1958. News editor Scandinavian Shipping Gazette, Gothenburg, 1959-69, chief editor, 1970—. Author: Shipping--How it Works, 1978; The Commerical History of Shipping, 1983. Home: Skolgatan 13, 440 60 Skarhamn Sweden Office: Scandinavian Shipping Gazette, Avenyen 1, PO Box 53088, 400 14 Gothenburg Sweden

RINNOOY KAN, ALEXANDER HENDRIK GEORGE, university professor; b. The Hague, The Netherlands, Oct. 5, 1949; s. Alfred and Eleanor Frances (Goodrich) R.; m. Eva M. van der Dussen, May 27, 1981; children: Robert Frederik, Willemijn Francesca. Doctoral in math., U. Leiden, The Netherlands, 1972; cand. econometrics, U. Amsterdam, The Netherlands, 1972; PhD in Math., U. Amsterdam, 1976. Asst. prof. Grad. Sch. Bus., Delft, The Netherlands, 1972-77; prof. Erasmus U., Rotterdam, The Netherlands, 1977—, rector, 1986—. Office: Erasmus U, PO Box 1738, 3000 DR Rotterdam The Netherlands

RINSER, LUISE, author; b. Pitzling/Oberbayern, Germany, Apr. 30, 1911; d. Joseph and Luise Rinser; m. Horst-Guenther Schnell, 1939 (dec.); 2 children; m. Carl Orff (dec. 1982). Sch. tchr. 1935-39; works banned, 1941; imprisoned, 1944-45; after World War II became literary critic of Neue Zeitung, Munich; now free-lance writer. Author: Die glasernen Ringe, 1940; Mitte des Lebens, 1950; Daniela, 1953; Abenteuer der Tugend, 1957; Tobias, 1968; Der schwarze Esel, 1974; Mirjam, 1983; (short stories) Ein Bundel weisser Narzissen, 1956; (essays) Schwerpunkt, Uber die Hoffnung, Vom Sinn der Traurigkeit, Unterentwickeltes Land Frau, Wie, wenn wir armer wurden 1974, Dem Tode geweiht, 1974; letters, diaries. Mem. Akad. der Kunste, PEN Ctr. of Fed. Republic Germany. Avocations: politics; theology. Address: Rocca di Papa, I-00040 Rome Italy *

RINSKY, JOEL CHARLES, lawyer; b. Bklyn., Jan. 29, 1938; s. Irving C. and Elsie (Millman) R.; m. Judith L. Lynn, Jan. 26, 1963; children: Heidi M., Heather S., Jason W. BS, Rutgers U., 1961, LLB, 1962, JD, 1968. Bar: N.J. 1963, U.S. Dist. Ct. N.J. 1963, U.S. Supreme Ct. 1967, U.S. Ct. Appeals (3d cir.) 1986. Sole practice Livingston, N.J., 1964—. Mem. exec. com. Essex County (N.J.) Dems., 1983—; Dem. com. person Millburn-Short Hills, N.J., 1982—, vice chmn. 1983—; bd. govs. Lake Naomi Assn. Pocono Pines, Pa., 1983—; trustee Student Loan Fund, Millburn, 1983—. Fellow Am. Acad. Matrimonial Lawyers; mem. N.J. Bar Assn., Essex County Bar Assn., N.J. Automobile Arbitration Program (arbitrator). Jewish. Home: 23 Winthrop Rd Short Hills NJ 07078 Office: 600 South Livingston Ave Livingston NJ 07039

RINSLAND, ROLAND DELANO, university official; b. Low Moor, Va., Apr. 11, 1933; s. Charles Henry and Lottie (Parks) R.; A.B. with distinction, Va. State U., 1954; A.M., Tchrs. Coll., Columbia U., 1959, profl. diploma, 1960, Ed.D., 1966. Asst. to dean of men Va. State Coll., Petersburg, 1952-54; asst. purchasing agt. Glyco Products Co., Inc., N.Y.C., 1956-57; asst. office of registrar Tchrs. Coll., Columbia U., N.Y.C., 1957-66, registrar, 1966-72, asst. dean for student affairs, also registrar, dir. office doctoral studies, 1972—; mem. Tchrs. Coll. Devel. Council, 1974-76. Served to 1st lt. AUS, 1954-56. Designated Important and Valuable Human Resource of USA Am. Heritage Research Assn. First Am. Bicentenium. Mem. N.Y. State Personnel and Guidance Assn., Am. Coll. Personnel Assn., Nat. Soc. Study Edn., Am. Ednl. Research Assn., Middle States, Am. (inter-assn. rep. to state edn. depts. on tchr. cert. 1973-74, mem. com. on orgn. and adminstrn. registrars activities 1973, 74-76) assns. collegiate registrars and admission officers, Assn. Records Execs. and Adminstrs. (charter mem., by-laws and program chmn. 1969), Am. Acad. Polit. and Social Sci., Am. Assn. Higher Edn., Assn. Instl. Research, Internat. Assn. Applied Psychology, Soc. Applied Anthropology, Am. Assn. Counseling and Devel., Assn. Study of Higher Edn., Am. Acad. Polit. and Social Sci., AAAS, N.Y. Acad. Scis., Met. Opera Guild, NEA (Leah B. Sykes award for life mem.), Scabbard and Blade, Kappa Phi Kappa, Phi Delta Kappa, Kappa Delta Pi. Home: 25 W 68th St New York NY 10023 Office: 525 W 120th St New York NY 10027

RINSLEY, DONALD BRENDAN, psychiatrist; b. N.Y.C., Jan. 31, 1928; s. Louis and Annamay (Hindle) R.; m. Charlotte Anne Trowbridge; 1 child, Eve Anne. A.B. with honors, Harvard U., 1949, postgrad., 1949-50; M.D., Washington U., St. Louis, 1954; diploma in child psychiatry (hon.), Menninger Found., 1975. Diplomate Am. Bd. Psychiatry and Neurology, Am. Bd. Med. Psychotherapists (fellow). Intern in pediatrics St. Louis Children's Hosp., 1954-55; fellow in psychiatry Menninger Found., Topeka, 1955-56, 58-60; staff psychiatrist Dept. Justice, U.S. Med. Center for Fed. Prisoners, Springfield, Mo., 1956-58; resident psychiatrist Topeka State Hosp., 1955-56, 58-60, asst. chief adolescent unit, childrens sect., 1960-68, chief, 1968-70, dir. sect., 1970-75; asso. chief psychiatry edn. Colmery-O'Neil VA Med. Center, Topeka, 1975—; cons. psychiatrist C.F. Menninger Meml. Hosp., 1976—; cons. psychiatrist children's div. Menninger Found., 1981—, Skillman prof. child psychiatry, 1983-84; asst. in pediatrics Washington U. Sch. Medicine, St. Louis, 1954-55; faculty gen. psychiatry Karl Menninger Sch. Psychiatry and Mental Health Scis., Topeka, 1960—, faculty child psychiatry, 1968—, exec. com. faculty in child psychiatry, 1969-75, 77-79; asso. clin. prof. psychiatry U. Kans. Sch. Medicine, 1970-77, clin. prof., 1977—; sr. asst. surgeon to surgeon USPHS, 1956-80; affiliate prof. psychiatry Oral Roberts U. Sch. Medicine, 1987—. Author: Treatment of the Severely Disturbed Adolescent, 1980; Borderline and Other Self Disorders, 1982; mem. editorial bd. Internat. Jour. Med. Psychotherapy, Adolescent Psychiatry; cons. editor Bull. Menninger Clinic; hon. cons. editor: Argentine Jour. Child and Adolescent Psychiatry and Psychology; contbr. articles to profl. jours. Recipient Edward A. Strecker Meml. award Inst. Pa. Hosp., 1968; William C. Menninger award Menninger Found., 1982; Spencer Found. fellow in advanced studies Menninger Found., 1976-79; fellow in interdisciplinary studies, 1979—. Fellow Am. Psychiat. Assn. (br. chmn. com. research 1964-65), Am. Coll. Psychoanalysts, Royal Soc. Health, AAAS, N.Y. Acad. Scis., Am. Soc. Adolescent Psychiatry, Am. Assn. Childrens Residential Centers; mem. Assn. for Research Nervous and Mental Disease, Soc. for Acad. Psychiatry, Am. Acad. Psychoanalysis, Am. Acad. Child and Adolescent Psychiatry, Canadian Psychiat. Assn. (corr.), Am. Assn. Psychiat. Services for Children, Sigmund Freud Soc. (Vienna), Argentine Assn. Child and Adolescent Psychiatry and Psychology (hon.), Sigma Xi (zone cons. to chpt. at large 1969-71, mem. com. on membership at large 1972-75). Club: Harvard-Radcliffe of Kansas City. Home: 4521 W 33d St Terr Topeka KS 66614 Office: Colmery-O'Neil VA Med Ctr 2200 SW Gage Blvd Topeka KS 66622

RIO, ELISEO DIANALA, electronics manufacturing executive; b. Escalante, Negros Occidental, Philippines, Oct. 14, 1919; s. Domingo Estandarte and Paz (Dianala) R.; m. Estela Tansingco Mijares, Dec. 20, 1943; children: Eliseo Jr., Elisela, Ephraim, Evaristo, Encarnacion, Ernesto, Estela. BS with honors, Philippine Mil. Acad., 1942; MS, U. Md., 1951. Comd. 3d lt. Philippine Army, 1942, advanced through grades to col., 1960; with 1st Regular Div., Bataan, Philippines, 1942; Panay guerilla 6th Mil. Dist., Philippines, 1942-45; student officer U.S. Army Engring. Sch., Ft. Belvoir, Va., 1945; camp engr. 5th Camp Compliment, Iloilo, Philippines, 1946; plans and tng. officer ROTC Silliman U., Dumaguete, Philippines, 1946-47; instr. math, physics Philippine Mil. Acad., 1947-49, 51-60; ret. Philippine Army, 1960; mgr. Radiowealth Inc., Metro Manila, 1960-61, v.p. for mfg., consumer electronics group, 1973-80; asst. to pres. REHCO, Metro Manila, 1961-63, v.p. research and devel., 1965-67; dir. 6th MD Vet. Devel. Corp., Metro Manila, 1973-83; gen. mgr. Veterans Electronics Communication Inc., Metro Manila, Philippines, 1980—; instr. Silliman U., 1946-47, Baguio Colls., 1948-49, 51-60. Pantentees in field. Decorated Bronze Star, Mil. Merit medal. Recipient Acad. award Bagui Colls. Found., 1961, Cavalier award Philippine Mil. Acad., 1962, Outstanding Alumni award Cen. Philipines U., 1963, Award Distinction 6th Mil. Dist. Veterans, 1979, Golden Imprints award Print Media Assn. Philippines, 1986. Home: #5 Greenhill St, White Plains, Quezon City Philippines Office: Veterans Electronics Comm Inc, Fort Bonifacio, Metro Manila Philippines

RÍOS, JUAN, poet, dramatist, journalist, critic; b. Barranco, Perú, Sept. 28, 1914; s. Rogelio and Victoria (Rey) R., m. Rosa Saco, Sept. 16, 1946; 1 child, Dulcinea. Author: Canción de Siempre, 1941; La Pintura Contemporánea en el Perú, 1946; Teatro 1, 1961; Ayar Manko, 1963; Primera Antología Poética, 1982. Recipient Nat. prize for playwriting, 1946, 50, 52, 54, 60; Nat. prize for poetry, 1948, 53. Mem. Acad. Peruana de la Lengua Correspondiente a la Real Acad. de la Lengua Española.

RIOUX, JEAN-PIERRE, historian; b. Clichy, France, Feb. 15, 1939; s. Rioux Fernand and Barriere Augustine Rioux; m. Hélene Cassagne, Mar. 25, 1963; children: Emmanuelle, Rémy. Agregation in history, U. Sorbonne, 1964. Asst. U. Paris, 1972-78, prof. history, 1979-80; researcher CNRS, Paris, 1980-86; dir. research Inst. Hist. to Present Time, 1986—; prof. Inst. Polit. Studies, Paris, 1977-85; pres. research council Culture Office, Paris, 1984—. Columnist L'Histoire, Paris, 1978—, Le Monde, Paris, 1985—; editor Vingtieme Siecle-Revue D'Histoire, Paris, 1984—; producer France Culture Radio, Paris, 1985—; author 5 books, 40 articles; editor: Mendes France Government, 1985, French Communism (1938-1941), 1987. Mem. Soc. Study Jauresiennes (gen. sec. 1973-79). Roman Catholic. Home: Damremont St 25, 75018 Paris France Office: Inst d'Histoire du Temps, Present De L'Amiral, Mouchez St 44, 75014 Paris France

RIP, ARIE, sociologist, educator; b. Kethel & Spaland, The Netherlands, June 13, 1941; s. Arie and Catharina (Vandenberg) R.; m. Marjan Buys; children: Ceciel Henriette, Carolien. BS in Chemistry, U. Leiden, 1962; BA in Philosophy, U. Leider, 1963, MS in Chemistry, 1965, PhD in Sci. and Soc., 1981. Instr. in chemistry U. Leiden, The Netherlands, 1961-65; lectr. in chemistry U. Leiden, 1965-68, asst. prof. chemistry, 1968-74, assoc. prof. chemistry, soc., 1974-84, sr. researcher social policy research, 1982-84; prof. sci. dynamics U. Amsterdam, The Netherlands, 1984-87; prof. philosophy of sci. and tech. U. Twente, The Netherlands, 1987—; bd. dirs. Netherlands Orgn. Tech. Assessment, U. Twente Ctr. for Studies Sci., Tech., and Soc.; cons. in field. Author: Wetenschap als Mensenwerk, 1978, Macht over Kennis, 1980, Mapping the Dynamics of Science and Technology, 1986. Ministry Educ. and Scis. grantee, U. Leiden, 1981. Mem. Royal Netherlands Chem. Soc. (editorial advisor 1976-83), Soc. for Social Studies Sci. (pres. 1987-89), European Assn. for Study Sci. and Tech. (sec.-treas. 1981-86, newsletter editor 1982—), Internat. Council Sci. Policy Studies. Office: De Boerderij, U Twente, P O Box 217, 7500 AE Enschede The Netherlands

RIPA DI MEANA, CARLO, parliamentarian, editor; b. Marina di Pietrasanta, Italy, Aug. 15, 1929; m. Marina Punturieri. Editor Il Lavaro, Unita, Rome, 1950-53; rep. Internat. Student Union, 1953-56; editor, cofounder Passato E Presente, Rome, 1957-58; pub. Feltrineli and Rizzoli, Rome, 1958-66; councillor from Lombardy dist. Italy, 1970-82; mem. European Parliament, Brussels, 1979-84, Commn. European Communities, Brussels, 1985—. Author: A Voyage to Vietnam, 1956, A Tribute to Raymond Rouseel and His Impressions of Africa, 1965, Audovisual Government, 1973; editor, co-founder Nuova Generazione. Pres. Santi Inst., Unitary Fedn. Italian Press Abroad.; rep. leadership Union of Socialist Parties. Mem. Italian Socialist Party. Clubs: Turati (Milan) (sec.-gen. 1967-76), Crocodile (founder). Office: care/Commn European Communities, 200 rue de la Loi, 1049 Brussels Belgium

RIPINSKY-NAXON, MICHAEL, archaeologist, art historian; b. Kutaisi, USSR, Mar. 23, 1944; s. Pinkus and Maria (Kokielov) R.; div.; 1 son, Tariel. A.B. in Anthropology with honors, U. Calif.-Berkeley, 1966, Ph.D. in Archeology and Art History, 1979. Research asst. Am. Mus. Natural History, N.Y.C., 1964, U. Calif.-Berkeley, 1964-66; mem. faculty dept. anthropology and geography of Near East, Calif. State U.-Hayward, 1966-67; asst. prof. Calif. State U.-Northridge, 1974-75; researcher, assoc. UCLA, 1974-75, sr. research anthropologist Hebrew U., Hadassah Med. Sch., Jerusalem, 1970-71; curator Anthropos Gallery of Ancient Art, Beverly Hills, Calif., 1976-78; chief research scientist Archaeometric Data Labs., Beverly Hills, 1976-78; dir. Ancient Artworld Corp., Beverly Hills, 1979-82; conducted excavations Israel, Egypt, Jordan, Mesopotamia, Mexico, Cen. Am; specialist in phenomenon of origins of domestication and camel ancestry; expert on art works from French Impressionists to ancient Egypt and classical world. Contbr. articles to sci. and scholarly jours. Recipient Cert. of Merit for Sci. Endeavour, Dictionary of Internat. Biography, 1974. Mem. Archaeol. Inst. Am. (life), Soc. for Am. Archaeology, Israel Exploration Soc., Am. Anthropol. Assn., Royal Anthropol. Inst., Am. Oriental Soc., Am. Geog. soc., Am. Ethnol. Soc., History of Sci. Soc., Ancient Art Council of Los Angeles County Museum of Art, Am. Chem. Soc., Soc. Archeol. Scis. (life), New England Appraisers Assns. Home: 472 Burton Way Palm Springs CA 92262

RIPLEY, STUART MCKINNON, real estate cons.; b. St. Louis, July 28, 1930; s. Rob Roy and Nina Pearl (Young) R.; B.A., U. Redlands, 1952; M.B.A., U. Calif., Berkeley, 1959; m. Marilyn Haerr MacDiarmid, Dec. 28, 1964; children—Jill, Bruce, Kent. Vice pres., dir. J.H. Hedrick & Co., Santa Barbara and San Diego, 1958-63; v.p. mktg. Cavanaugh Devel. Co., San Gabriel, Calif., 1963-65; v.p. mktg. dir. Calabasas Park, Bechtel Corp., Calabasas, Calif., 1967-69; v.p. mktg. Avco Community Developers, Inc., La Jolla, Calif., 1969-74; mktg. dir. U.S. Home Corp., Fla. Div., Clearwater, 1974-75; pres., dir. Howard's Camper Country, Inc., National City, Calif., 1975-77; v.p., mktg. dir. Valcas Internat. Corp., San Diego, 1976-77, pres., 1977-79; pres. Stuart M. Ripley, Inc., 1977—, Sunview Realty, Inc., a Watt Industries Co., Santa Monica, Calif., 1979-80; owner Everett Stunz Co., Ltd., La Jolla, 1981—; exec. v.p. Harriman-Ripley Co., Fallbrook, Calif.; avocado rancher, Fallbrook, 1978—; lectr. UCLA, 1961. Served with USN, 1952-55. U. Redlands fellow, 1960—. Mem. Nat. Assn. Homebuilders, Sales and Mktg. Council, Sales and Mktg. Execs., Pi Chi. Republican. Episcopalian. Club: Elks. Home: 13180 Portofino Dr Del Mar CA 92014 Office: 7644 Girard Ave La Jolla CA 92037

RIPPEL, JULIUS ALEXANDER, business and foundation executive; b. Newark, July 22, 1901; s. Albert A. and Caroline (Greig) R.; B.S., Dartmouth Coll., 1923; L.H.D. (hon.), Med. Coll. Pa., 1972, Upsala Coll., 1977; Sc.D. (hon.), Georgetown U. Sch. Medicine, 1977; m. Carol W. Richards, 1924; children—Susan J., Eric R. With J.S. Rippel & Co., Newark, 1923-38, v.p., 1933-38; pres. Julius A. Rippel, Inc., Newark, 1938-55, Rippel & Co., Newark, 1955-82; dir. emeritus NUI Corp. Pres., dir., chmn. Fannie E. Rippel Found., 1953-83, trustee, 1953—. Recipient Outstanding Citizen award Advt. Club Newark, 1943; Hosp. Achievement award N.J. Hosp. Assn., 1969; Heart award N.Y. Cardiology Soc., 1969; spl. citation United Hosps. of Newark, 1969; Disting. Service award Am. Heart Assn., 1970; Dignity-of-Man award Kessler Inst. Rehab., 1971; Merit citation Upper N.J. chpt. Nat. Multiple Sclerosis Assn., 1971; Man of Yr. award Mt. Carmel Guild N.J., 1972; spl. award Columbus Hosp., Newark, 1973; cert. of Achievement, Assn. Advancement Med. Instrumentation, 1974; Thanks award St. Michael's Med. Center, Newark, 1974; Citizens award Acad. Medicine N.J., 1976; achievement award Ariz. State U., 1977; Dartmouth Coll. Alumni award, 1980; Albert Gallatin fellow NYU, 1977. Mem. Am. Hosp. Assn. (hon.), Phi Beta Kappa Assos., Kappa Sigma. Clubs: Baltusrol Golf (Springfield, N.J.); Morris County Golf (Convent, N.J.); Essex (Newark). Home and Office: Madison NJ 07940

RIPPIN, DAVID WILLIAM THACKER, chemical engineer, educator; b. Retford, Eng., Jan. 14, 1935; arrived in Switzerland, 1970; s. Horace and Norah Eileen (Thacker) R.; m. Anne Crossland, Apr. 13, 1963; children: Sarah Jane, Jonathan David, Thomas Mark. BA, MA in Natural Scis. and Chem. Engring., Cambridge (Eng.) U., 1956, PhD, 1959. Chartered engr. Nato postdoctoral fellow U. Del., 1959-60; lectr. chem. engring. Imperial Coll., U. London, 1961-66; sr. lectr. systems engring. U. Lancaster, Eng., 1966-70; prof. chem. engring. Swiss Fed. Inst. Tech., Zurich, 1970—. Co-editor: Computers and Chem. Engring. jour., 1983—. Recipient Chemviron prize, 1977, medal City of Paris, 1986. Office: Swiss Fed Inst Tech, Technisch-Chemisches Lab, 8092 Zurich Switzerland

RIPPY, FRANCES MARGUERITE MAYHEW, educator; b. Ft. Worth, Sept. 16, 1929; d. Henry Grady and Marguerite Christine (O'Neill) Mayhew; m. Noble Merrill Rippy, Aug. 29, 1955 (dec. Sept. 1980); children: Felix O'Neill, Conrad Mayhew, Marguerite Hailey. BA, Tex. Christian U., 1949; MA, Vanderbilt U., 1951, PhD, 1957; postgrad., U. London, 1952-53. Instr. Tex. Christian U., 1953-55; instr. to asst. prof. Lamar State U., 1955-59; asst. prof. English, Ball State U., Muncie, Ind., 1959-64; assoc. prof. English, Ball State U., 1964-68, prof., 1968—, dir. grad. studies in English, 1966—; editor Ball State U. Forum, 1960—; vis. asst. prof. Sam Houston State U., 1957; vis. lectr., prof. U. P.R., summers 1959, 60, 61; exchange prof. Westminster Coll., U. Oxford, Eng., 1988; cons.-evaluator North Central Assn. Colls. and Schs., 1973—, commn.-at-large, 1987—; cons.-evaluator New Eng. Assn. Schs. and Colls., 1983—. Author: Matthew Prior, 1986. Contbr. articles to profl. jours., chpt. to anthology. Recipient McClintock award, 1966; Danforth grantee, summer 1964, Ball State U. Research grantee, 1960, 62, 70, 73, 76, 87, Lilly Library Research grantee, 1978; Fulbright scholar, U. London. Mem. MLA, Coll. English Assn., Ind. Coll. English Assn. (pres. 1984-85), Johnson Soc. Midwest (sec. 1961-62), AAUP, Nat. Council Tchrs. English, Am. Soc. 18th Century Studies. Home: 4709 W Jackson St Muncie IN 47304

RIRIE, CRAIG MARTIN, periodontist; b. Lewiston, Utah, Apr. 17, 1943; s. Martin Clarence and VaLera (Dixon) R.; m. Becky Ann Ririe, Sept. 17, 1982; children: Paige, Seth, Theron, Kendall, Nathan, Derek, Brian, Amber, Kristen. AA, San Bernadino Valley Coll., 1966; DDS, Creighton U., 1972; MSD, Loma Linda U., 1978. Staff mem. Flagstaff (Ariz.) Med. Ctr., 1974—; pvt. practice dentistry specializing in periodontics Flagstaff, 1974—; assoc. prof. periodontics No. Ariz. U., Flagstaff, 1979—, chmn. dept. dental hygiene, 1980-81; med. research cons. W.L. Gore, Flagstaff, 1983—. Contbr. articles to profl. jours. Health professions scholarship Creighton U., Omaha, 1969-71; recipient Mosby award Mosby Pub. Co., 1972; research fellowship U. Bergen, Norway, 1978-79. Mem. ADA, Am. Acad. Periodontology (cert.), Western Soc. Periodontology (chmn. com. on research 1982—, bd. dirs. 1983—), No. Ariz. Dental Soc., Am. Acad. Oral Implantologists, Internat. Congress Oral Implantologists, Ariz. Dental Assn. Republican. Mormon. Lodge: Rotary. Home: 1320 N Aztec Flagstaff AZ 86001 Office: 1421 N Beaver Flagstaff AZ 86001

RISCH, HUBERT, physician; b. Mulhouse, Alsace, France, Oct. 4, 1924; s. Paul and Paule (Meyer) R.; 1 child, Francoise. MD, U. Paris, 1950, Cert. Gastro Enterology, 1958, Cert. in Psychology, 1980. Prof. Inst. France d'Acupuncture, Paris, 1972. Author: Acupuncture Raisonneée, 1974, Auto-Evaluation en Acupuncture, 1987. Mem. Syndicat Nat. Médecins Acupunct France (pres. 1984), Assn. Francaise d'Acupuncture (v.p. 1978), Soc. Internat. d'Acupuncture (v.p. 1980), Soc. Francaise d'Acupuncture (treas. 1985), Assn. Mondiale Phyothérapie (GI sec. 1983), Mensa. Lodge: Lions.

RISELEY, MARTHA SUZANNAH HEATER (MRS. CHARLES RISELEY), psychologist, educator; b. Middletown, Ohio, Apr. 25, 1916; d. Elsor and Mary (Henderson) Heater; B.Ed., U. Toledo, 1943, M.A., 1958; Ph.D., Toledo Bible Coll., 1977; student Columbia U., summers 1943, 57; m. Lester Seiple, Aug. 27, 1944 (div. Feb. 1953); 1 son, L. Rolland, III; m. 2d, Charles Riseley, July 30, 1960. Tchr. kindergarten Maumee Valley Country Day Sch., Maumee, Ohio, 1942-44; dir. recreation Toledo Soc. for Crippled Children, 1950-51; tchr. trainable children Lott Day Sch., Toledo, 1951-57; psychologist, asst. dir. Sheltered Workshop Found., Lucas County, Ohio, 1957-62; psychologist Lucas County Child Welfare Bd., Toledo, 1956-62; tchr. educable retarded, head dept. spl. edn. Maumee City Schs., 1962-69; pvt. practice clin. psychology, 1956—; instr. spl. edn. Bowling Green State U., 1962-65; instr. Owens Tech. Coll., 1973-78; interim dir. rehab. services Toledo Goodwill Industries, summer 1967, clin. psychologist Rehab. Center, 1967—; staff psychologist Toledo Mental Health Center, 1979-84. Dir. camping activities for retarded girls and women Camp Libbey, Defiance, Ohio, summers 1951-62; group worker for retarded women Toledo YWCA, 1957-62; guest lectr. Ohio State U., 1957. Health care profl. mem. Nat. Osteoporosis Found., 1988—. Mem. Ohio Assn. Tchrs. Trainable Youth (pres. 1956-57), NW Ohio Rehab. Assn. (pres. 1961-62), Toledo Council for Exceptional Children (pres. 1965), Greater Toledo Assn. Mental Health, Nat. Assn. for Retarded Children, Ohio Assn. Tchrs. Slow Learners, Am. Assn. Mental Deficiency, Am. Soc. Psychologists in Marital and Family Counseling, Psychology and Law Soc., Am. (asso.), Ohio, NW Ohio (sec.-treas. 1974-77, pres. 1978-79) psychol. assns., Ohio Psychol. Assn. (continuing edn. com. 1978—), NEA, AAUW, Am. Soc. Psychologists in Pvt. Practice (nat. dir. 1976—), State Assn. Psychologists and Psychol. Assts., Bus. and Profl. Women's Club, (pres. 1970-72), Ohio Fedn. Bus. and Profl. Women's Clubs (dist. sec. 1970-71, dist. legis. chmn. 1972-74), Toledo Art Mus., Women's Aux. Toledo Bar Assn., League Women Voters, Zonta Internat. (local pres. 1973-74, 78-79, area dir. 1976-78), Maumee Valley Hist. Soc., MBLS PEO (chpt. pres. 1950-51), Toledo Council on World Affairs, Internat. Platform Assn. Baptist. Home: 2840 Broadway Toledo OH 43614 Office: 940 S Detroit Ave Toledo OH 43614

RISI, LOUIS J., JR., business executive; b. Highland Park, Ill., July 2, 1937; s. Louis J. and Ann E. R.; m. Mary Jean Anson, Jan. 15, 1955; children—Steven, Janet, Andrew. B.S., Bradley U., 1959. On mgmt. staff Arthur Young & Co., Chgo., 1959-69; pres., dir. Norin Corp., Miami, Fla., 1970-80; chmn. bd., chief exec. officer Nat. Investors Fire & Casualty Co., 1975-77; exec. comm., dir. Upper Lakes Shipping, Ltd., 1970-76, Port Weller and St. Lawerance Dry Dock, Ltd., 1971-76; pres., dir. Norris Grain Co., 1980-82; chmn. bd., chief exec. officer CTC Corp., 1981-83; chmn. bd., chief exec. officer Assured Group; exec. v.p., dir. Detroit Red Wings Hockey Club, Inc., 1980-82; bd. govs. Nat. Hockey League, 1980-82; dir. Chgo. Rock Island R.R., Bankmgrs. Corp. Mem. Am. Inst. C.P.A.'s, Ill. Soc. C.P.A.'s, Fin. Execs. Inst. Clubs: Ocean Reef Yacht, Bath, Jockey, Bankers. Home: 10915 SW 53d Ave Miami FL 33156 Office: 51 W Mowry St Homestead FL 33030

RISIK, PHILIP MAURICE, lawyer; b. N.Y.C., Jan. 18, 1914; s. Isidor Morton and Celia (Merken) R.; m. Natalie Wynn, Nov. 5, 1948; children: David, Stephen, Elizabeth. BS, NYU, 1932, JD, 1936. Bar: N.Y. 1937, Md. 1975, U.S. Dist. Ct. (so. dist.) N.Y. 1940, U.S. Dist. Ct. (D.C. dist.) 1970, U.S. Dist. Ct. Md. 1982, U.S. Ct. Claims 1975, U.S. Ct. Appeals (D.C. cir.) 1975, U.S. Ct. Appeals (8th cir.) 1979, U.S. Ct. Appeals (fed. cir.) 1987, U.S. Supreme Ct. 1975, U.S. Ct. Appeals (4th and 5th cirs.) 1986. Practice, N.Y.C., 1937-41, 46-49; counsel N.Y. QM Procurement Agy., N.Y.C., 1949-51; procurement specialist Office Sec. Def., Washington, 1953-62; adminstrv. judge Armed Services Bd. Contract Appeals, Washington, 1962-74; of counsel Wachtel Ross & Matzkin, Chevy Chase, Md., 1974—; lectr. So. Meth. U. Law Sch., other law schs. and univs.; mem. adv. bd. Fed. Contract Reports., Bur. Nat. Affairs; umpire emeritus U.S. Tennis Assn. Contbr. articles to George Washington U. Law Rev., Fed. Bar Jour. Area v.p. Montgomery County PTAs, Rockville, Md., 1969; trustee sch. dist., Kemp Mill, Md., 1967. Served to col. U.S. Army, 1941-46, 51-53; ETO. Decorated Bronze Star; recipient Conspicuous Service Cross, State of N.Y., 1947, Meritorious Civilian Service medal Sec. Def., 1974. Mem. ABA (council) pub.

contract law sect. 1969), Am. Arbitration Assn. (nat. panel arbitrators). Jewish. Lodges: Masons (sr. steward 1949). Home: 10224 Windsor View Dr Potomac MD 20854 Office: Wachtel Ross & Matzkin 5530 Wisconsin Ave Chevy Chase MD 20815

RISS, ERIC, psychologist; b. Vienna, Austria, Oct. 10, 1929; s. David S. and Rebecca (Schneider) R.; came to U.S., 1940, naturalized, 1945; B.A., Bklyn. Coll., 1950; Ph.D., NYU, 1958; diplomate Am. Bd. Psychotherapy; m. Miriam Barbara Schoen, July 22, 1956; children—Arthur, Suzanne, Wendy. Pvt. practice psychotherapy, family therapy, marriage counseling, N.Y.C., 1952—; sr. psychologist N.Y.C. Diagnostic Center, 1954-57; with Marriage and Family Life Inst., N.Y.C., 1956—; cons., 1956-58, dir. pub. edn., 1960-73, chmn. bd. dirs., 1961-73, dir., 1973—; mem. attending staff, supr. psychotherapy and family therapy Payne Whitney Psychiat. Clinic, N.Y. Hosp., N.Y.C., 1971-78; clin. instr. psychology and psychiatry Cornell U. Med. Coll., 1971-72, clin. asst. prof., 1973-78; dir. Inst. for Exploration of Marriage, 1976-84; chief psychologist Artists, Writers and Performers Psychotherapy Center, 1978—; lectr. Bklyn. Coll., 1955-62; cons. Fordham Hosp., 1956-68; psychotherapist N.Y. Neuropsychiat. Center, 1958-60; psychotherapist Community Guidance Service, N.Y.C., 1958-61. Mem. Am. Acad. Psychotherapy, N.Y. State Marriage, Family and Child Counseling Assn. (pres. 1971-72), Acad. Family Psychology, Am., N.Y. State psychol. assns. Contbr. numerous articles to profl. jours. Office: 174 E 73d St New York NY 10021

RISS, ROBERT BAILEY, corporate executive; b. Salida, Colo., May 27, 1927; s. Richard Rol and Louise (Roberts) R.; children: Edward Stayton, G. Leslie, Laura Bailey, Juliana Warren. B.S. in Bus. Adminstrn, U. Kans., 1949. Pres. Riss Internat. Corp., Kansas City, 1950-80; chmn. bd. Riss Internat. Corp., 1964-86; pres. Grandview Bank and Trust Co., Mo., 1964-86; Founder, chmn. bd., pres. Republic Industries, Inc., Kansas City, Mo., 1969-86; chmn. bd. Grandview Bank and Trust Co., 1969-86, Commonwealth Gen. Ins. Co., 1986—; Bd. dirs., chmn. exec. com. Heart of Am. Fire and Casualty Co.; chmn. bd. dirs. Comml. Equipment Co., Commonwealth Gen. Ins. Co. Mem. exec. com., bd. dirs. Kansas City Area Council Boy Scouts Am., 1971—; vice chmn. bd. trustees Kansas U. Endowment Assn., 1980—; mem. exec. com., advisory bd. Sch. of Bus., U. Kans., 1971—, mem. athletic bd., 1977-80; also mem. Chancellor's Assos. Recipient Silver Beaver award Kansas City Area council Boy Scouts Am., 1972; Disting. Service citation U. Kans., 1976; Fred Ellsworth medal U. Kans., 1979; named Most Outstanding Young Man in Mo. U.S. Jr. C. of C., 1956. Mem. Am. Royal Assn. (gov. 1972—, dir. 1979—, v.p. 1980—), Kans. U. Alumni Assn. (nat. pres. 1969-70, bd. dirs., exec. com. 1968-74), Sigma Nu. Episcopalian.

RIST, HAROLD ERNEST, consulting engineer; b. Newcomb, N.Y., Aug. 6, 1919; s. Ernest DeVerne and Iva Cardine (Braley) R.; m. Vera Leona Basuk, July 30, 1942 (div. June 1980); children: Cherry Diana Rist Chapman, Harold Ernest II, Byron Basuk; m. Ruth Ann Mahony, Aug. 16, 1980. BCE, Rensselaer Poly. Inst., 1950, MCE, 1952. Registered profl. engr., N.Y., N.J., N.H., Vt., Mass., Pa., Md., Ky. Project mgr. Seelye, Stevenson, Value & Knecht, N.Y.C., 1952-58; found., prin. Harold E. Rist, Assocs., Glens Falls, N.Y., 1958-60; ptnr., chief exec. officer Rist, Bright & Frost, Glens Falls, 1960-63, Rist, Frost & Assocs., Glens Falls, 1963-79; pres., chief exec. officer Rist, Frost Assocs., P.C., Glens Falls, 1979-84, chmn. bd., 1984—; pres. chief exec. officer 21 Bay Corp., Glens Falls, 1970—, Hudson Heights Moreau, Inc., Glens Falls, 1972—, Mech. Elec. Systems, Inc., Glens Falls, 1983—, Glens Falls Communications Corp., 1985—. Contbr. articles to profl. jours. Bd. dirs. Adirondack (N.Y.) North County Assn., 1960—, v.p., 1986—; commr. Hudson River Valley Commn.. Tarrytown, N.Y., 1970-78. Served to staff sgt. U.S. Army, 1942-44. Mem. NSPE, Cons. Engrs. Council N.Y. (pres. 1966-68), Am. Cons. Engrs. Council (v.p. 1970-72), Profl. Services Council (bd. dirs. 1972-85), N.Y. State Assn. of The Professions (charter), Adirondack Regional C. of C. (vice chmn. 1984—). Republican. Mem. Methodist Episcopal Ch. Clubs: The Gooley (Glen Falls) (pres. 1964-66); Lake George (Diamond Point, N.Y.); Safari Club Internat.; Surfside Vacation, Kehei, Maui Hawaii (pres.); Lodge: Masons. Home: Lake Shore Dr Box A 1 Diamond Point NY 12824 Office: Rist Frost Assocs P C 21 Bay St Glen Falls NY 12801

RISTOW, BRUNO VON BUETTNER, plastic surgeon; b. Brusque, Brazil, Oct. 18, 1940; came to U.S., 1967, naturalized, 1981; s. Arno and Ally Odette (von Buettner) R.; student Coll. Sinodal, Brazil, 1956-57, Coll. Julio de Castilhos, Brazil, 1957-58; M.D. magna cum laude, U. Brazil, 1966; m. Urania Carrasquilla Gutierrez, Nov. 10, 1979; children by previous marriage: Christian Kilian, Trevor Roland. Intern in surgery Hosp. dos Estrangeiros, Rio de Janeiro, Brazil, 1965, Hospital Estadual Miguel Couto, Brazil, 1965-66, Instituto Aposentadoria Pensão Comerciarios Hosp. for Gen. Surgery, 1966; resident in plastic and reconstructive surgery, Dr. Ivo Pitanguy Hosp. Santa Casa de Misericordia, Rio de Janeiro, 1967; fellow Inst. of Reconstructive Plastic Surgery, N.Y. U. Med. Center, N.Y.C., 1967-68, jr. resident, 1971-72, sr. and chief resident, 1972-73; practice medicine specializing in plastic surgery, Rio de Janeiro, 1967, N.Y.C., 1968-73, San Francisco, 1973—; asst. surgeon N.Y. Hosp., Cornell Med. Center, N.Y.C., 1968-71; clin. instr. surgery N.Y. U. Sch. of Medicine, 1972-73; chmn. plastic and reconstructive surgery div. Presbyn. Hosp., Pacific Med. Center, San Francisco, 1974—. Served with M.C., Brazilian Army Res., 1959-60. Decorated knight Venerable Order of St. Hubertus; Knight Order St. John of Jerusalem; fellow in surgery Cornell Med. Sch., 1968-71; diplomate Am. Bd. Plastic and Reconstructive Surgery. Fellow A.C.S., Internat. Coll. Surgeons; mem. Am. Soc. Aesthetic Plastic Surgery, Am. Soc. Plastic and Reconstructive Surgeons, Internat. Soc. Aesthetic Plastic Surgeons, Calif. Soc. Plastic Surgeons, AMA (Physician's Recognition award 1971-83), Calif. Med. Assn., San Francisco Med. Assn. Republican. Mem. Evang. Lutheran Ch. Club: San Francisco Olympic. Contbg. author: Cancer of the Hand, 1975; contbr. articles on plastic surgery to profl. publs. Office: Pacific Presbyn Med Bldg 2100 Webster St Suite 502 San Francisco CA 94115

RITCH, KATHLEEN, diversified company executive; Harbor Beach, Mich., Jan. 23, 1943; d. Eunice (Spry) R.; B.A., Mich. State U., 1965: student Katharine Gibbs Sch., 1965-66. Exec. sec., adminstrv. asst. to pres. Katy Industries, Inc., N.Y.C., 1969-70; exec. sec., adminstrv. asst. to chmn. Kobrand Corp., N.Y.C., 1970-72; adminstrv. asst. to chmn. and pres. Ogden Corp., N.Y.C., 1972-74; asst. sec., adminstr. office services, asst. to chmn. Ogden Corp., N.Y.C., 1974-81, corporate sec., adminstr. office services, 1981-84, v.p., corporate sec., adminstr. office services, 1984—; part-owner Unell Mfg. Co., Port Hope, Mich., 1966-87. Mem. Am. Soc. Corporate Secs. Home: 500 E 77th St New York NY 10162 Office: Ogden Corp Two Pennsylvania Plaza New York NY 10121

RITCH, ROBERT HARRY, ophthalmologist, educator; b. New Haven, May 14, 1942; s. Edward Lewis and Minerva (Grosberg) R.; B.A. cum laude (hon. scholar), Harvard, 1965, M.A. (NSF fellow), 1967; postgrad. (Harvard traveling fellow), Rice U., 1967-68; M.D., Albert Einstein Coll. Medicine, 1972. Diplomate Am. Bd. Ophthalmology, Am. Bd. Laser Surgery. Intern, St. Vincent's Med. Center, N.Y.C., 1972-73; resident in ophthalmology Mt. Sinai Sch. Medicine, N.Y.C., 1973-75, chief resident, 1975-76, Heed Ophthalmic Found. fellow, 1976-77, NIH-Nat. Research Service fellow, 1976-78, asst. clin. ophthalmologist, 1976-77, instr., 1977-78, asst. prof., 1978-80, assoc. prof., 1980-82; attending ophthalmologist Beth Israel Med. Center, N.Y.C., 1978-82; cons. ophthalmologist VA Hosp., Bronx, 1978-82; dir. glaucoma service Elmhurst Hosp., 1978-82, acting dir. dept. ophthalmology, 1979-82; chief glaucoma service N.Y. Eye and Ear Infirmary, N.Y.C., 1983—; prof. clin. ophthalmology N.Y. Med. Coll., Valhalla, 1983—; sec., treas., chmn. sci. adv. bd. Glaucoma Found., 1984—; mem. glaucoma adv. com. Nat. Soc. to Prevent Blindness, 1986—; organizing chmn. Bankok Opthal. Cong., 1985—; external assessor U. Malaya, 1988—. Acad. Investigator award NIH, 1978-81; Disting. Service award Internat. Ctr. N.Y., 1981, Exec. Dirs. award, 1985; Founders award Nat. Exhibits by Blind Artists, 1985. Fellow Am. Acad. Ophthalmology (Honor award 1985), N.Y. Acad. Medicine; mem. AMA, N.Y. State Med. Soc., N.Y. County Med. Soc., Assn. Research in Vision and Ophthalmology, Am. Assn. Ophthalmology, Ophthal. Soc. U.K., Internat. Assn. Ocular Surgeons, N.Y. Intra-Ocular Lens Implant Soc., Manhattan Ophthol. Soc., Internat. Soc. Eye Research, Soc. for Clin. Trials, Pan-Pacific Anterior Segment Soc. (v.p.), AAAS, N.Y. Acad. Sci., Ophthalmic Laser Surg. Soc. (sec.-treas. 1982—), N.Y. Soc. Clin. Ophthalmology (rec. sec. 1988—), Am. Soc. Cell Biology, Internat. Fedn. Cell Biologists, Pan-Am. Assn. Ophthalmology, N.Y. Soc. Electron Microscopy, Philippine Soc. Ophthalmology (hon.), Thailand Ophthal. Soc. (hon.), La.-Miss. Ophthal. and Otolarygol. Soc. (hon.), Can. Implant Soc. (hon.), English Speaking Union, Restaurant Soc. N.Y. (treas.). Clubs: Harvard (N.Y.C.); Harvard (So. Conn.). Author: (with M.B. Shields) The Secondary Glaucomas, 1982, (with M.B. Shields and T. Krupin) The Glaucomas, 1988. Home: 17 E 96th St New York NY 10028 Office: NY Eye and Ear Infirmary 310 E 14th St New York NY 10003

RITCHEY, KENNETH WILLIAM, special education administrator; b. Washington, June 7, 1947; s. Conrad Monroe and Katherine Costance (Sheris) R.; m. Nancy Jayne Kirk, Aug. 22, 1970; children: Kirk Damon, Erin Kathryn (dec. Apr. 1988). BS in Edn., Shippensburg U., 1969; MEd, in Spl. Edn., U. Va., 1972; MS in Ednl. Adminstrn., U. Dayton, 1980. Spl. edn. tchr. Shippensburg (Pa.) Area Sch. Dist., 1969-71; head cross country coach Shippensburg U., 1970-74; master tchr., coordinator work experience program Lincoln Intermediate Unit, New Oxford, Pa., 1971-76; adult edn. tchr. Franklin County Prison, Chambersburg, Pa., 1972-76; asst. supt. mgmt. services Montgomery County Bd. Mental Retardation and Devel. Disabilities, Dayton, Ohio, 1977-83, supt. bd., 1983—; mem. part-time faculty edn. dept. U. Dayton, 1983—; mem. community and mil. adv. com. ARC, 1986—, needs and priorities com. Human Services Levy Council, 1982-84, 87—. Former editor statewide newsletter for tchrs. and profls. in Work Experience. Vol., mem. C.A.R. council United Way; bd. dirs., pres.-elect Ohio Pub. Images, Inc. Mem. Am. Assn. Mental Retardation, Assn. Supervision and Curriculum Devel., Am. Assn. Sch. Adminstrs., Profl. Assn. Retardation, Ohio Assn. Supts. County Bds. Mental Retardation, Supts. Assn. (exec. com.), Phi Delta Kappa. Democrat. Methodist. Home: 454 W Hudson Ave Dayton OH 45406 Office: 8114 N Main St Dayton OH 45415

RITCHIE, CEDRIC ELMER, banker; b. Upper Kent, N.B., Can., Aug. 22, 1927; s. E. Thomas and Marion (Henderson) R.; m. Barbara Binnington, Apr. 20, 1956. Student pub. schs., Bath, N.B. With The Bank of N.S., Bath, 1945—; chief gen. mgr. The Bank of N.S., Toronto, Ont., Can., 1970-72, pres., 1972-79, chief exec. officer, 1972—, chmn. bd., 1974, also dir.; chmn. bd., dir. The Bank N.S. Channel Islands Ltd., The Bank N.S. Asia Ltd., The Bank N.S. Trust Co. Channel Islands Ltd., Scotiabank (U.K.) Ltd., Scotia Realty Ltd., The Bank N.S. Trust Co. (Bahamas) Ltd., The Bank N.S. Trust Co. (Caribbean) Ltd., BNS Internat. (U.K.) Ltd., The Bank N.S. Jamaica Ltd., The Bank N.S. Trust Co. Trinidad and Tobago Ltd., 1st So. Bank Ltd., Scotia Leasing Ltd., The West India Co. Mcht. Bankers Ltd., The Bank of N.S. Internat. Ltd., The Bank N.S. Trinidad & Tobago Ltd., Ingersoll-Rand Co., The Bank N.S. Trust Co. (Cayman) Ltd.;chmn, chief exec. officer, dir. The Bank of Nova Scotia Properties Inc.; dir. numerous companies; mem. adv. council for Can. Exec. Service. Mem. sch. of bus. adminstrn. adv. com. U. Western Ont., Internat. adv. council Ctr. for Inter-Am. Relations; mem. chmn.'s council Ams. Soc.; bd. govs. Dalhousie U., gov. Jr. Achievement Can., Olympic Trust Can. Decorated Officer Order of Can., 1981. Clubs: Canadian, Donalda, Mt. Royal, Mid Ocean, National, Toronto, York, Lyford Cay. Office: The Bank of NS, 44 King St W, Toronto, ON Canada M5H 1H1

RITCHIE, JOHN BENNETT, commercial and industrial realtor; b. West Point, N.Y., Sept. 23, 1924; s. Isaac and Charlotte (Bennett) R.; B.A., Yale, 1946; postgrad. student George Washington U., 1946, U. Wash. Law Sch., 1948-50; m. Suzanne Raisin, Dec. 27, 1952; children—Randolph, Charlotte, Mark, Victoria. Pres. Ritchie & Ritchie Corp., indsl. and comml. realtors, San Francisco, Oakland, San Jose, Calif., Ritchie & Ritchie Ins. Brokers, Inc.; v.p. Cotton-Ritchie Corp., San Diego, Ritchie MacFarland Corp., Portland, Oreg.; owner, trustee Ritchie-Chancery Bldg., Barrett-Ritchie Block, Ritchie & Ritchie Devel. Co., Ritchie Western Mortgage Corp., Ritchie Western Equities Co.; past mem. San Francisco Planning Commn.; past mem. San Francisco Landmarks Bd.; hon. counsul Uruguay. Served with AUS. Mem. Soc. Indsl. Realtors, Calif. Assn. of Realtors (v.p. 1967), San Francisco (pres. 1966), Oakland, San Jose real estate bds., San Francisco C. of C., Calif. Hist. Soc. (pres. 1973, trustee), Japan Soc. San Francisco (pres. 1976). Republican. Mem. Ch. of Jesus Christ of Latter-day Saints (elder). Clubs: Concordia Argonaut, Presidio Golf (San Francisco); Athenian-Nile (Oakland, Calif.); Alta (Salt Lake City); Brook (N.Y.); Caledonian (London); Outrigger Canoe (Honolulu). Home: 2 Presidio Terr San Francisco CA 94118 Home: 209 S Meadow Rd Glenbrook NV 89413 Home: 989 Rutherford Cross Rd Rutherford CA 94573 Office: 41 Sutter St San Francisco CA 94104 also: 200 Ritchie Chancery Bldg San Francisco CA 94612 also: 363 15th St Oakland CA 94612 also: 34 W Santa Clara St San Jose CA 95112 also: 233 A St Suite 1400 San Diego CA 92101 also: 133 SW 2d Ave Portland OR 97205 also: 989 Rutherford Cross Rd Rutherford CA 94573 also: 247 Beach Walk Waikiki Honolulu HI 96815

RITCHIE, ROYAL DANIEL, economic development executive; b. Takoma Park, Md., Dec. 28, 1945; s. Thomas Joseph and Dorothy Queen (Royal) R.; student Glassboro State U., 1965-66, Columbia Union Coll., 1966-67; V.p., dir. Asso. Developers Internat., Inc., Washington, 1968-75, Internat. Fin. and Mgmt. Corp., Washington, 1975-77; project mgr. Sheraton Corp., Washington, 1977-78; v.p. East Balt. Developers, Inc., 1979-82, East Balt. Contractors, Inc., 1979-82; dir. econ. devel. East Balt. Community Corp., 1979-82; pres. IFM Credit Corp., Balt., 1976—; with Stouffer Hotel Co., Balt., project mgr., Solon, Ohio, 1988—; mng. gen. ptnr. HFA Homes for Ams.; ltd. ptnr. C & R Contracting Assocs.; pres. RDR Contracting Assn., Inc.; pres. Hanlon Park Condominimum Assn., Inc. , 1st v.p. Prince George's Rep. Club, 1982-85; chmn. Com. for Better Govt., Riverdale, Md., 1984—; mem. 22d legis. dist. cen. com. Md. Reps., 1982-86; 2d v.p. Prince George's Civic Fedn., Inc., 1984, pres. 1985-86, 88—. Adventist. Home: 4715 Oliver St Riverdale MD 20737 Office: Stouffer Hotel Co 202 E Pratt St Baltimore MD 21202

RITTER, ANN L., lawyer; b. N.Y.C., May 20, 1933; d. Joseph and Grace (Goodman) R. B.A., Hunter Coll., 1954; J.D., N.Y. Law Sch., 1970; postgrad. Law Sch., NYU, 1971-72. Bar: N.Y. 1971, U.S. Ct. Appeals (2d cir.) 1975, U.S. Supreme Ct. 1975. Writer, 1954-70; editor, 1955-66; tchr., 1966-70; atty. Am. Soc. Composers, Authors and Pubs., N.Y.C., 1971-72, Greater N.Y. Ins. Co., N.Y.C., 1973-74; sr. ptnr. Brenhouse & Ritter, N.Y.C., 1974-78; sole practice, N.Y.C., 1978—. Editor N.Y. Immigration News, 1975-76. Mem. ABA, Am. Immigration Lawyers Assn. (treas. 1983-84, sec. 1984-85, vice chair 1985-86, chair 1986-87), N.Y. State Bar Assn., N.Y. County Lawyers Assn., Assn. Trial Lawyers Am., N.Y. State Trial Lawyers Assn., N.Y.C. Bar Assn. Democrat. Jewish. Home: 47 E 87th St New York NY 10128 Office: 420 Madison Ave New York NY 10017

RITTER, DEBORAH BRADFORD, lawyer; b. Boston, Nov. 4, 1953; d. Edmund Underwood and Priscilla (Rich) R. BA, Yale U., 1974; JD, Boston Coll., 1980. Bar: N.H. 1980, Mass. 1981. Assoc. McLane, Graf, Raulerson & Middleton, P.A., Manchester, N.H., 1980-82, Singer, Stoneman, Kunian & Kurland, P.C., Boston, 1983—; dir. N.H. Legal Assistance Corp., Concord, 1982-84. Sec. N.H. Performing Arts Ctr., 1980-85; bd. dirs. Yale Alumni Schs. Com., Boston, 1982—. Mem. ABA, Mass. Bar Assn., N.H. Bar Assn. Home: 413 Hammond St Chesnut Hill MA 02167 Office: Singer Stoneman Kunian & Kurland PC 100 Charles River Plaza Boston MA 02114

RITTER, GERHARD A., historian, educator; b. Berlin, Mar. 29, 1929; s. Wilhelm Erich Albert and Martha Ida (Wietasch) R.; m. Gisela Ritter, June 18, 1955; children: Michael, Clemens. PhD, Free U., Berlin, 1952; B litt., U. Oxford (Eng.), 1959; Habilitation, U. Berlin, 1961. Researcher, St. Antony's Coll., Oxford, Eng., 1952-54; asst. Free U., Berlin, 1954-61, prof. polit. sci., 1962-65; prof. modern history U. Munster (Germany), 1965-74, U. Munich, 1974—; vis. prof. St. Antony's Coll., Oxford, 1965-66, 72, Washington U., St. Louis, 1965, U. Calif.-Berkeley, 1971-72, U. Tel Aviv, 1973. Author: Die Arbeiterbewegung im Wilhelminischen Reich, 2d edit., 1963, Parlament und Demokratie in Grobritannien, 1972, Arbeiterbewegung, Parteien und Parlamentarismus, 1976, Das Deutsche Kaiserreich 1871-1914, 4th edit., 1981, Die II Internationale 1918-1919, 1980, Arbeiterschaft und Arbeiterbewegung in Deutschland, 1980, Sozialversicherung in Deutschland und England, 1983, Die deutschen Parteien 1830-1914, 1985, Social Welfare in Germany and Britain: Origins and Development, 1986; co-author: (with J. Kocka) Deutsche Sozialgeschichte 1870-1914, 3d edit., 1982; editor: Handbuch der Geschichte des deutschen Parlamentarismus, 6 vols., Geschichte der Arbeiter und der Arbeiterbewegung in Deutschland seit seit dem Ende des 18th Jahrhunderts, 3 vols; author: (with Merith Niehuss) Wahlen in der Bundesrepublik Deutschland, 1987. Mem. Senate, main com. German Research Assn., 1973-76; chmn. Assn. Historians of Germany, 1976-80; mem. Bavarian Acad. Sci. Internat. Commn. for the History of Parliamentary and Representative Instns. Hon. fellow St. Antony's Coll. Oxford; mem. Historische Kommission zu Berlin, Historische Kommission der Bayer, Akademie der Wissenschaften, Kommission für Geschichte des Parlamentarismus ünd der politischen Parteien, Beirat Institut fur Zeitgeschichte Munich, Beirat Deutsches Historisches Institut London. Home: Bismarckweg 3, D8137 Berg Starnberger See 3 Federal Republic of Germany Office: Univ Munich, Trautenwolfstr 3/I, D8000 Munich 40 Federal Republic of Germany

RITTER, ROBERT FORCIER, lawyer; b. St. Louis, Apr. 7, 1943; s. Tom Marshall and Jane Elizabeth (Forcier) R.; m. Karen Gray, Dec. 28, 1966; children: Allison Gray, Laura Thompson, Elisabeth Forcier. BA, U. Kans., 1965; JD, St. Louis U., 1968. Bar: Mo. 1968, U.S. Dist. Ct. (ea. and we. dists.) Mo. 1968, U.S. Ct. Mil. Appeals 1972, U.S. Supreme Ct. 1972, U.S. Ct. Appeals (8th cir.) 1980, U.S. Dist. Ct. (so. dist.) Ill. 1982. Assoc. Gray & Sommers, St. Louis, 1968-71; ptnr. Gray & Ritter, 1974—; bd. dirs. United Mo. Bank of St. Louis; adv. com. 22d cir. Supreme Ct., 1985—; lectr., author in field. Bd. dirs. Cystic Fibrosis Found. (Gateway chpt.). Served to capt. USAR, 1968-74. Recipient Law Week award Bur. Nat. Affairs, 1968. Fellow Internat. Soc. Barristers, Am. Coll. Trial Lawyers, Internat. Acad. Trial Lawyers; mem. Bar Assn. Met. St. Louis (chmn. trial sect., 1978-79, exec. com. 1980-82, award of merit 1976, award of achievement 1982, chmn. bench bar conf. 1983), Mo. Bar Assn. (council practice and procedure com. 1972—, council tort law com. 1982—, bd. govs. 1984—, fin. com. 1984—), Mo. Bar Found. (outstanding trial lawyer award, 1978), ABA, Lawyers Assn. St. Louis (exec. com. 1976-81, pres. 1977-78), Mo. Assn. Trial Attys. (bd. govs. 1984—), Assn. Trial Lawyers Am. Presbyterian. Clubs: Media, Racquet, Mo. Athletic, Bellerive Country, John's Island; Racquet of Ladue. Contbr. articles to law jours. Office: 1015 Locust St Suite 900 Saint Louis MO 63101

RITTER, ROBERT JOSEPH, lawyer; b. N.Y.C., Aug. 11, 1925; s. Robert Reinhart and Mary (Mandracchia) R.; m. Barbara Willis Foust, Oct. 1, 1955 (div. May 1977); children—Robert Thornton, Jan Willis, Nancy Carol. Student Bklyn. Poly. Inst., 1943; B.A. cum laude, Queens Coll., 1949; J.D., NYU, 1953, LL.M. in Internat. Law, 1955. Bar: N.Y. 1953. Acct. UN Secretariat, N.Y.C., 1949-54; asst. counsel RCA Corp., N.Y.C., 1955-58; atty. CIBA-GEIGY Corp., Ardsley, N.Y., 1958-60; atty. AT&T Bell Telephone Labs., Inc., Murray Hill, N.J., 1960-70; tax atty. AT&T Technologies, Inc., N.Y.C., 1970-85; mgr. fin. AT&T Corp. Hdqrs., Parsippany, N.J., 1985-87; asst. sec. 14 AT&T subs. telephone cos.; v.p. CPPS Income Tax Cons., N.Y.C., 1987—. Contbr. articles to legal jours. Pres. Harry B. Thayer chpt., Telephone Pioneers of Am., N.Y.C., 1983-84; corp. program dir. Vol. Action Ctr. of Middlesex County, N.J., 1988—; adv. council Project Resources, State N.J., 1987—; bd. dirs. Somerset Hills YMCA, Bernardsville, N.J., 1971-73; candidate (Democratic) N.Y. State Assembly, Westchester County, N.Y., 1965; chmn. Am. Cancer Soc. Fund Drive, Bronxville, N.Y., 1964. Served with USAAF, 1943-46; ATO. Recipient Crusade award Am. Cancer Soc., 1965, Masonic Service award, 1947, Am. Legion Citizenship award, 1943, Eagle Scout award Boy Scouts Am., 1941. Mem. Nat. Tax Assn.-Tax Inst. Am. (chmn., advisor state sales and use taxation com. 1984—, chmn. prodn. exemption subcom. 1978-84), Assn. Bar N.Y., Legal Aid Soc., NYU Law Alumni Assn., Sigma Alpha. Democrat. Episcopalian. Clubs: Rossmoor Tennis (pres. 1987—), Church of N.Y. Lodge: Kiwanis (1st v.p. 1970-71). Home: 3-N Village Mall Jamesburg NJ 08831 Office: CPPS Income Tax Cons PO Box 7022 Yorkville Station New York NY 10128

RITTERMAN, STUART I., speech pathologist, educator; b. Bklyn., May 21, 1937; s. Nathan and Ettie (Fried) R.; m. Sharen Bruneau, 1977; children: Moriah, Joshua. B.A., NYU, 1959; postgrad., CUNY, 1962-64; Ph.D., Case Western Res. U., 1968. Speech clinician Bklyn. Coll. Clinic, CUNY, Bklyn., g963, Bergen Pines County Hosp., Paramus, N.J., 1963-64; Vocat. Rehab. adminstrn. trainee Cleve. Hearing and Speech Center, 1964-66; speech clinician Benjamin Rose Hosp., Cleve., 1965-66; NIH career investigator trainee Case Western Res. U., Cleve., 1966-68; research asso. in dental edn. Case Western Res. U., 1967-68; asst. prof. dept. communication disorders U. Okla. Med. Center, Oklahoma City, 1968-69; dir. diagnostic services in speech pathology U. Okla. Med. Center, 1968-69; asst. prof. dept. communicology U. South Fla., Tampa, 1969-71; assoc. prof. U. South Fla., 1972-76, prof., 1976—, dir. diagnostic services, 1969-71, dir. research in communicology, 1976—, acting dir. program in speech pathology and audiology Coll. Social and Behavioral Sci., 1971, dir., 1971; vis. prof. phonetics U.E.R. Angellier U. Lille (France), 1984; pres. Cypher Research Consortium. Contbr. articles to profl. jours. HEW grantee, 1971; Office of Edn. grantee, 1971; Fla. Dept. Edn. grantee, 1971. Fellow Royal Soc. Health, Acad. for Forensic Application of Communication Process; mem. Am. Speech and Hearing Assn., Fla. Speech and Hearing Assn., Internat. Soc. Phonetic Sci., Inst. for Advanced Study of Communication Process, Computer Users Speech & Hearing. Home: 181 Ellerbee Rd Wesley Chapel FL 34249 Office: U South Fla CBA 241 Tampa FL 33620

RITTHALER, GERALD IRVIN, diversified company executive; b. Fremont, Nebr., May 27, 1930; s. Irvin Peter and Jessie (Vaughan) R.; m. Barbara Jane Brown, Aug. 17, 1952; children: Daniel Vaughan, Elizabeth Ann, John Charles. B.A., Wayne State Coll., 1953; postgrad., Drake U., 1958. Staff acct. Dennis West (C.P.A.), Shenandoah, Iowa, 1953-55; office mgr. Imperial Chem. Co., Shenandoah, 1955-57; asst. comptroller Boss Hotels Co., Des Moines, 1957-62; tax supr. Ernst & Whinney, Houston, 1963-65; tax mgr. Gulf & Western Industries, Inc., N.Y.C., 1965-67; v.p. Gulf & Western Industries, Inc., 1967-79, sr. v.p., 1979-83; pres. Simmons Ams. Corp., 1984—; ptnr. Argus Internat., 1984—; pres. Industrias Tecnolégicas Induteca C.A., Caracas, Venezuela, 1986—. Mem. Am. Inst. C.P.A.s. Presbyterian. Mailing Address: INDUTECA M 369 Jet Cargo Internat PO Box 020010 Miami FL 33102 Office: Apdo Postal 70090-1071-A, Caracas Venezuela

RIVAS, ERNESTO, newspaper columnist; b. N.Y.C., Dec. 19, 1924; s. Gabry and Sara (Solís) R.; m. Cocó, Dec. 8, 1969; children: Martín Javier, Gabriela. B of Arts and Sci., Colegio Centroamérica, Granada, Nicaragua. Press div. clk. UN, N.Y.C., 1947-48; reporter La Nueva Prensa, Managua, Nicaragua, 1949-52; dir. Radio Panamericana, Managua, 1952-60; with pub. relations dept. Nicaragua Mission to UN, N.Y.C., 1960-62; dir. news Radio 590, Managua, 1963-66; columnist La Noticia, Managua, 1967-77; with pub. relations dept. Emp. Nacional de Lyz y Fuerza, Managua, 1978-79; UPI corr., Managua, 1979-80; columnist Diario Las Américas, Miami, Fla., 1981—. Mem. UDN 1981-86, Acción Democrética, Miami, 1986—. Republican. Roman Catholic. Club: Nejapa Country and Terrzaz (Managua).

RIVAS, HUMBERTO ENRIQUE, polyethylene company executive; b. Maracaibo, Zulia, Venezuela, Sept. 18, 1944; s. Maria Rivas; m. Rosa Ana Sandrea, Dec. 22, 1967; children: Gabriela, Maria Eugenia, Hernando, Patricia, Pedro. Pub. acct., U. Del Zulia, 1970; stock broker, Comision Nacional de Valores, 1985. Sr. Price Waterhouse, Maracaibo, 1966-72; adminstrn. mgr. Polimeros Del Lago, C.A., Maracaibo, 1972-86, gen. mgr., 1987—; v.p. Bolsa de Valores de Maracaibo, 1986. Mem. Colegio Contadores Estado Zulia. Club: Centro Gallego. Home: Ave 14F No 56A 80, Maracaibo Zulia Venezuela Office: Polimeros del Lago CA, Ave 9B Entre Calle 77 y 78, Maracaibo Zulia 4002, Venezuela

RIVERA, ALBERTO, consulting engineering company executive; b. Mex. City, Aug. 14, 1935; s. Alberto and Maria Cruz (Gonzalez) R.; m. Gertrud Enander; 1 child, Maria Patricia. Diploma in Civil Engring., Universidad Puebla, 1958; M in Sanitary Engring., U. Nat. Autonoma Mex., 1959. Structural engr. Matthews & Mumby Ltd., Manchester, Eng., 1960-61, Ove Arup & Ptnrs., London, 1961-62 64-66; cons. engr. Fencing Stadium Olympic Games, Mex. City, 1968, on long span suspended structures, Mex. City, 1968-69; stagiere Assn. Stages Techniques, Paris, 1970; dir., ptnr. Habimex SA Constrn., Puebla, 1971—; dir., ptnr. Habimex Ingenieria SCP, Puebla, 1983—. Pres. Alliance Francaise, Puebla, 1979-82. Roman

Catholic. Club: Golf Campestre (Puebla). Office: Habimex, 5 A Sur 4508-A, 72530 Puebla, Pue Mexico

RIVERA-EMMANUELLI, RAFAEL LUIS, banker; b. Guayanilla, P.R., Apr. 11, 1933; s. Rafael and Luisa Maria (Emmanuelli) Rivera-Rivera; B.B.A., Cath. U. P.R., 1960; grad. Bank Adminstrn. Inst., 1965, Am. Inst. Banking, P.R., 1966; m. Maria Maiz de Rivera, Dec. 22, 1955; children—Rafael, Naida, Mayra, Roberto. Asst. auditor Arthur Andersen & Co., San Juan, P.R., 1960; officer trainee Banco Credito Ahorro Ponceno, Ponce, P.R., 1960-61, acct., 1961-64, asst. comptroller, 1964-67; dir. computer ctr., San Juan, 1967-68; asst. v.p. trust ops., 1968-69; bank cons. Peat Marwich, Mitchell & Co., San Juan, 1969-70; v.p., controller Banco Economias, San Juan, 1970-72, sr. v.p., 1972-74; bank cons. Rivera Emmanuelli Assocs., San Juan, 1974-75; pres. Banco Financiero Ahorro Ponce, 1975-78; exec. v.p. Girod Trust Co., San Juan, 1978-84; pres. Fidelity Data Corp., 1984—; instr. Am. Inst. Banking (P.R.), Instituto Cultural Comunidad, Cath. U. P.R., 1966. Served with U.S. Army, 1953-55. Mem. Fin. Execs. Inst., Nat. Assn. Accts., Bank Adminstrn. Inst. P.R. (pres. 1971-72), Club Ponce Mus. Art, Exchange Club Perla del Sur, Phi Sigma Alpha. Roman Catholic. Clubs: El Vigia Rotary; P.R. Bankers; Ponce Yacht and Fishing, Deportivo de Ponce; Atrium (N.Y.C.). Author: Principios de Operaciones Bancarias, 1979. Home: PO Box 2924 San Juan PR 00936-0092 Office: Fidelity Data Corp Calle Marginal Alameda 3-C Rio Piedras PR 00926

RIVERO, ANGEL, construction company executive, structural engineer; b. Carolina, P.R., Sept. 20, 1930; s. Jose L. Rivero and Carmen Cervera; B.S. in Civil Engring., U. P.R., 1956; postgrad. Los Angeles City Coll., 1958, 61, U. P.R., 1964; m. Sandra M. Serra, Dec. 24, 1958; children: Myrna, Dennis, Angel L., Diana. Asst. instr. Material Testing Lab., U. P.R., Mayaguez campus, 1956; engr. stress analysis airplane structures N. Am. Aviation Co., Los Angeles, 1957, dept. public utilities and transp. City of Los Angeles, 1957, dept. public works, 1958-59, supr., engr., 1959-61; engr. estimating and cost control Blythe Industries, Inc., San Juan, P.R., 1962-63, supr. and chief estimator engring. dept., 1963-72, v.p. adminstrv. procedures, cost control, 1972-78; partner, v.p. Calzadilla Constrn. Corp., San Juan, 1978-82; pres. Rivero Constrn. Corp., Trujillo Alto, P.R., 1978—, BB&S Constrn. Corp., Charlotte, N.C., 1981-83; ptnr., v.p. H.E. Constrn. and Leasing, Inc., San Juan, 1984-86. Pres., Comité Cívico Round Hill, 1969-70. Served with U.S. Army, 1953-55; Korea. Mem. Inst. Civil Engrs., ASCE, Am. Water Works Assn., Sociedad de Ingenieros de P.R., Water Pollution Control Fedn., P.R. Volleyball Fedn. (1st v.p. 1975-77, 2nd v.p. 1986—), Phi Delta Gamma (pres. 1956). Roman Catholic. Home: 121 Romerillo Santa María Rio Piedras PR 00927 Office: PO Box 1918 Trujillo Alto PR 00760

RIVERS, MARIE BIE, broadcasting executive; b. Tampa, Fla., July 12, 1928; d. Norman Albion and Rita Marie (Monrose) Bie; m. Eurith Dickinson Rivers, May 3, 1952; children—Eurith Dickinson, III, Rex B., M. Kells, Lucy L., Georgia. Student, George Washington U., 1946. Engaged in real estate bus. 1944-51, radio broadcasting, 1951—; chmn., part owner, Sta. WGUN, Atlanta, 1951-87, Sta. KWAM, KRNB, Memphis, Sta. WEAS-AM-FM, Savannah, Ga., Sta. WGOV, WAAC, Valdosta, Ga., Sta. WSWN-AM-FM, Belle Glade, Fla.; owner, chmn. Sta. WXOS, Islamorada, Fla.; chmn. The Gram Corp., Dee Rivers Group, Ocala; pres. real estate cos., Creative Christian Concepts Corp., 1985, United States K-9 Acad., Ocala, broadcast receivables cons., 1986, Deesown, Inc., Suncoast Broadcasting Inc.; owner Laser Acceptance Corp., 1988. Author: A Woman Alone, 1986; contbr. articles to profl. jours. Youth dir. Fla. Appaloosa Horse Club, 1972—. Mem. Fla. Assn. Broadcasters (bd. dirs.), Kappa Delta. Republican. Roman Catholic. Clubs: La Gorce Country (Miami Beach, Fla.); Coral Reef Yacht (Coconut Grove, Fla.); Sweetwater Country (Orlando, Fla.). Home: 7055 SW 70th Ave Ocala FL 32676 Office: GRAM Corp 2801 SW Coll Rd Suite 22 Ocala FL 32674

RIVIERE, JAMES CHARLES, computer systems company executive; b. Monticello, Ark., June 21, 1941; s. James Horace and Elsie Nora (Douglass) R.; student Southwestern at Memphis, 1959-62; B.A., U. Wash., 1966; M.B.A., Am. Grad. U., 1976; m. Adrienne Delensyl Gehman; children—Jean-Marie, William Douglas, Robert Wayne, John Patrick, Joseph Andrew, Louis Richard, James Paul. With The Boeing Co., Seattle, 1962-63, New Orleans, 1963-67; mcpl. real estate and property mgr. City of Seattle 1970-72; asst. treas. System Devel. Corp., Santa Monica, 1972-73, corp. dir. adminstrn., 1974-75, v.p., gen. mgr. electronic pub. systems div., 1975-76, corp. v.p. ops., 1977-82; v.p. planning and logistics Burroughs Corp., 1982-84; chief exec. officer Riviere Cos., Inc., 1984-86; pres., chief exec. officer United States Storage Co., 1986—; bd. dirs. Am. Bldg. Services, Hanna Transfer and Storage; affiliated profl. Pa. State U. Mem. Nat. Better Bus. Bur., Washington. Recipient award Math. Assn. Am. Mem. Nat. Contract Mgmt. Assn., Am. Soc. Mfg. Engrs., Am. Mgmt. Assn., Am. Inst. Indsl. Engrs., Nat. Council on Phys. Distbn. Mgmt., Pi Kappa Alpha. Republican. Presbyterian. Home: 4541 45th St NW Washington DC 20016 Office: 2033 M St NW Washington DC 20036

RIXEY, CHARLES WOODFORD, engineering company executive; b. Ferrelview, Mo., Apr. 15, 1926; s. Joseph Woodford and Genevieve (Hoskins) R.; m. Mary Joe Douglas, June 6, 1948; children: Susan, Sallie, Joseph. AB, William Jewell Coll., 1948; MBA, U. Pa., 1950; MS, Navy Engring. Sch., 1961. Enlisted USN, 1943, advanced through grades to rear admiral, 1975, ret., 1978; v.p. Am. Mgmt. Systems Inc., Arlington, Va., 1978—; pres. Tech. Systems subs. Am. Mgmt. Systems Inc., Arlington, 1982—. Mem. Navy League, Sigma Xi. Presbyterian. Club: Army-Navy Country (Arlington). Office: Am Mgmt Systems Inc 1777 N Kent St Arlington VA 22209

RIZOPOULOS, ANDREAS C(HRISTOS), daily newspaper publisher, public relations consultant; b. Patras, Greece, July 3, 1941; s. Christos A. and Anna S. (Economopoulos) R.; m. Charíclia Th. (Nana) Tsekouras, June 23, 1966; children—Anna Christina, Paul Christos. M.A. in Polit. Sci., Panteios U., Athens, 1973. Owner, C&A Pub. Relations, Athens, 1967—, Imera Pub. Co. S.A., Patras, Greece, 1974—. Translator 3 books; contbr. numerous articles to profl. jours. Active Boy Scouts Greece, Athens, 1953—. Served with Greek Army, 1962-64. Mem. Inst. Pub. Relations U.K., Brit. Inst. Mgmt., Fgn. Press Assn. Greece, Daily Newspaper Pubs. Assn. Lodge: Etairia Filikon, Quatuor Coronati. Home: 5Miltiadou St, 155 62 Holargos Athens Greece

RIZOS, JASON D., architect; b. Athens, Attiki, Greece, Nov. 1, 1923; s. Dimitri Rizos and Fani Athanasopoyloy; m. Dimitra Bourbouhaki, Dec. 28, 1953; children: Dimitri, Marilena. Diploma in Arch. Engring., Metsovion Nat. Poly., Athens, 1950. Architect Office of Mr. Kapsanbelis, Athens, 1953-58; advisor Nat. Bd. Electricity, Athens, 1957-64, Ktimatiki Bank of Greece, Athens, 1976-78, Nat. Enterprise of Programming and Design, Athens, 1978-79, Borough of Athens, 1987. Contbr. articles to profl. jours. Recipient Silver medal of bravery Greek Army Headquarters, 1949. Clubs: Marine (Pireus), Golf (Glyfada). Office: 10 Merlin St, 10671 Athens Greece

RIZZA, PETER JOSEPH, JR., educational consultant; b. Brookline, Mass., Jan. 21, 1947; s. Peter J. and Madge M. (Horton) R.; B.S. in Edn., Boston U., 1968, Ed.M., 1972; Ph.D., Pa. State U., 1974; m. Elizabeth Virginia Solis-Cohen, July 5, 1970; children—Daniel Hays, Emily Katherine. Tchr. Wayland, Mass., 1968-72; grad. asst. Pa. State U., 1972-74; ednl. cons. mgr. Control Data Corp., Bloomington, Minn., 1974-82, computer-based edn. specialist, 1974-76, mgr. acad. products, 1976-78, mgr. product specification and design, 1978-80; cons. Edn. Tech. Center, 1981-82, Eastern Regional Mgr. Edn. Systems, Control Data, Edison, N.J., 1982-85; dir. edn. product mktg. Software Mgmt. Service Inc., 1985—; pres. Princeton Ctr. Edn. Services, 1985-88; tech. cons. U.S. AID, Brasilia, Brazil, 1975-76. Recipient Tarpon award for Outstanding Service to Edn., Control Data Corp., 1977, also Outstanding Achievement award for Profl. Service, 1981, Outstanding Young Men of Am. Award, 1975. Contbr. articles on computer based edn. to profl. publs.; also papers presented to nat. and internat. confs. Home: 104 Jamieson Dr Pennington NJ 08534 Office: PO Box 397 Princeton NJ 08540

RIZZATO, GIANFRANCO, pulmonary internist, educator; b. Milan, Italy, July 27, 1939; s. Mario and Carolina (Battaglia) R.; MD, U. Milan, 1963; specialist in cardiology U. Turin, 1966; specialist in internal medicine, U. Parma, 1970, specialist in pneumology, 1974; m. Nanni Silvia Ida, Oct. 15, 1966. Intern, Ospedale Maggiore di Milano, 1960-63, med. asst., 1963-71; med. asst. Ospedale Regionale Niguarda, 1972-82, vice chmn., 1982—, chmn., 1988—; prof. med. semeiotics U. Milan, 1972—; med. writer Corriere della Sera newspaper, 1979—, Corriere Medico, 1980—. Founder Sarcoidosis, 1984; founder, sec. World Assn. on Sarcoidosis and other Granulomatous Disorders. Fellow Am. Coll. Chest Physicians; mem. Lombard Assn. Pneumology (mng. bd.), Italian Soc. Pneumology, European Soc. Pneumology (founder), Brit. Thoracic Soc., N.Y. Acad. Scis., Internat. Com. Sarcoidosis, Italian Com. on Sarcoidosis (founder, sec.). Contbr. articles in field to profl. jours. Home: 9 Juvara, 20129 Milan Italy

RIZZI, ARTHUR WILLIAM, mathematician; b. Jersey City, June 7, 1946; arrived in Sweden, 1977; s. John and Anna (Gasber) R.; m. Kerstin Elna-Maria Assarsson, Sept. 25, 1971; children: David, Ellen. BS, Pa. State U., 1967; MS, Stanford U., 1968, PhD, 1971. Research scientist NASA, Mountain View, Calif., 1970-77; chief scientist Flygtekniska Forsoksanstalten, Stockholm, 1977—; prof. Royal Inst. Tech., Stockholm, 1984—; Fellow Inst. Math. and Applications, London, 1981—; indsl. cons. Messerschmitt-Boelkow-Blohm Munich Control Data, Munich and Mpls., 1983—. Recipient Busk prize in Aerodyns. Royal Aero. Soc., London, 1985. Mem. Am. Inst. Aero. & Astronautics, Soc. Indsl. & Applied Math., German Assn. Applied Math. and Mechanics. Roman Catholic. Home: Faeltvaegen 30 A, 16358 Sponga Sweden Office: Aero Res Inst, 12 Ranhammarsv, 16111 Bromma Sweden

RIZZO, TERRIE LORRAINE HEINRICH, aerobic fitness executive; b. Oneonta, N.Y., Dec. 15, 1946; d. Steven Joseph Heinrich and Grace Beatrice (Davis) Chamberlin; m. Michael Louis Rizzo, Dec. 28, 1968; 1 child, Matthew Michael. BA, Pa. State U., 1968; MA, Johns Hopkins U., 1971. Tchr. Balt. County Sch. System, 1968-79; asst. dir. univ. relations U. Md., Catonsville, 1980-81; exec. dir. Aerobic Danse de Belgique, Brussels, 1981—; pres. Eurobics Inc., Sunnyvale, Calif., 1984—; aerobics dir. Green Valley Health Clubs, San Jose, Calif., 1985; pres. Personally Fit, 1986; cons. Belgian Ministry Sport, Sabena Airlines, others; lectr., syndicated columnist, 1986—. Author: Sittercise, 1985, How To Keep Fit While You Sit, 1988, Stress Relief Through Exercise, 1988; contbr. articles to profl. jours. Pres. Internat. Study Group, Brussels, 1983-84. Named Marketeer of Yr. Am. C. of C. in Belgium, 1987. Mem. Internat. Dance Exercise Assn., Assn. for Fitness in Bus., Aerobics and Fitness Assn. Am., Pa. State Alumni Assn. (bd. dirs. 1979-88), Brussels and Sunnyvale C. of C., San Francisco VCB, Mensa, Pi Gamma Mu, Phi Alpha Theta. Democrat. Roman Catholic. Clubs: Am. Women's (Brussels) (dir. 1983-84); San Jose Quota (bd. dirs. 1986-87). Avocations: traveling, oenology, gourmet cooking. Home: 19755 Lanark Ln Saratoga CA 95070 Office: 108 E Fremont Ave Sunnyvale CA 94087

RIZZUTO, CARMELA RITA, nursing educator, continuing professional education consultant; b. Waterbury, Conn., Aug. 26, 1942; d. Joseph Anthony and Carmella Rose R.; m. Thomas Lee Chernesky, Aug. 28, 1982. B.S., St. Joseph Coll., 1965; M.S., Boston Coll., 1971; Ed.D., Sch. Edn., UCLA, 1983. R.N., Calif. Nursing instr. Samaritan Hosp. Sch. Nursing, Troy, N.Y., 1969; med. nursing coordinator, clin. specialist Harvard Community Health Plan, Boston, 1971-72; instr. inservice edn. Tufts-New Eng. Med. Center, Boston, 1972-73; instr. inservice edn. St. John's Hosp. and Health Center, Santa Monica, Calif., 1974-76; asst. clin. prof. Sch. Nursing, UCLA, 1976-79; educator, continuing edn. for nurses, Calif. State U., Los Angeles, 1979-80, U. Calif., Santa Barbara, 1981-83; assoc. dir. nursing edn. St. Francis Hosp. of Santa Barbara, 1981-83; asst. dir. nursing edn. and research Stanford U. Hosp., 1983—; USPHS coronary care nurse trainee, 1968; USPHS nurse trainee, 1969-71; recipient Chancellor's Patent Fund, UCLA, 1972-73. Mem. Am. Assn. Critical Care Nurses. Contbr. articles to profl. publs. Office: Dept Nursing Research Stanford U Hosp Stanford CA 94305

ROACH, ARVID EDWARD, II, lawyer; b. Detroit, Sept. 6, 1951; s. Arvid Edward and Alda Elizabeth (Buckley) R. B.A. summa cum laude, Yale U., 1972; J.D. cum laude, Harvard U., 1977. Bar: D.C. 1978, N.Y. 1978, U.S. dist. ct. D.C. 1978, U.S. dist. ct. (so. dist.) N.Y. 1978, U.S. Ct. Appeals (10th cir.) 1980, U.S. Ct. Appeals (2d cir.) 1981, U.S. Ct. Appeals (D.C. cir.) 1981, U.S. Ct. Appeals (7th and 9th cirs.) 1982, U.S. Supreme Ct. 1983, U.S. Dist. Ct. Md., 1985. Law clk. to judge U.S. Dist. Ct., 1977-78; assoc. Covington & Burling, Washington, 1978-85, ptnr., 1985—. Mem. ABA, ACLU. Contbr. articles to legal jours.

ROACH, GARY FRANCIS, mathematics educator; b. Penpedairheol, Wales, Oct. 8, 1933; s. John Francis and Bertha Mary (Walters) R.; married, Sept. 3, 1960. BS, University Coll., Cardiff, Wales, 1955; MS, Birkbeck Coll., London, 1961; PhD, U. Manchester, Eng., 1964. Research mathematician British Petroleum, London, 1958-61; lectr. U. Manchester, 1961-66; vis. prof. U. B.C., Vancouver, Can., 1966-67; lectr. U. Strathclyde, Glasgow, 1967-70, sr. lectr., 1970-71, reader, 1971-1979, prof., 1979—, dean Sch. of Sci., 1982—. Author: Green's Functions. Served as flying officer RAF, 1955-58. Fellow Inst. Math. Applications, Royal Astronomical Soc., Royal Soc. Edinburgh; mem. Edinburgh Math. Soc. (pres. 1982-83). Home: 11 Menzies Ave, Fintry, Glasgow G63 0YE, Scotland Office: U Strathclyde, Richmond St, Glasgow G1 1XH, Scotland

ROACH, JOHN VINSON, II, retail company executive; b. Stamford, Tex., Nov. 22, 1938; s. John V. and Agnes M. (Hanson) R.; m. Barbara Jean Wiggin, Mar. 31, 1960; children: Amy, Lori. B.A. in Physics and Math, Tex. Christian U., 1961, M.B.A., 1965. V.p. Radio Shack, 1972-75, Radio Shack Mfg., 1975-78; exec. v.p. Radio Shack, 1978-80; Gen. mgr. data processing Tandy Corp., Ft. Worth, 1967-73, pres., 1980—, chief exec. officer, 1981—, chmn., 1982—, also dir.; dir. Tex. Am. Bancshares, Inc., Justin Industries. Bd. dirs. Ft. Worth Country Day Sch., N.Tex. Commn., Van Cliburn Found. Arts Council, Univ. Christian Ch., Tex. Christian U. Club: Rotary. Office: Tandy Corp 1800 One Tandy Center Fort Worth TX 76102

ROACH, WILLIAM RUSSELL, business executive; b. Bedford, Ind., Jan. 1940; s. George H. and Beatrice M. (Schoenlaub) R.; B.S., UCLA, 1961; m. Margaret R. Balogh, 1961; children—Kathleen L., Keith W. Internal auditor Hughes Aircraft Co., Los Angeles, 1961-62, Lockheed Aircraft Corp., Los Angeles, 1962; sr. acct. Haskins & Sells, Los Angeles, 1962-66; asst. to group v.p. Lear Siegler, Inc., Santa Monica, Calif., 1966-71; v.p. fin., sec. Paul Hardeman Engrs. & Constructors, Inc., Los Angeles, 1971-72; exec. v.p., corp. sec., dir. Optimum Systems Inc., Santa Clara, Calif., 1972-79; pres., dir. Banking Systems Inc., subs. Optimum Systems Inc., Dallas, 1976-79; pres., dir. BancSystems, Inc., Santa Clara, 1976-79, DMA/Optimum, Honolulu, 1978-79; pres. W.R. Assos., Menlo Park, Calif., 1979—; v.p. URS Corp., San Mateo, Calif., 1979-81; pres. URS Internat., Inc., 1980-81; pres., chief exec. officer, dir. Applied Learning Internat., Inc. (formed from merger of Advanced Systems, Inc. and Deltak Training Corp.), Arlington Heights, Ill., 1981—. Mem. Am. Inst. C.P.A.s, Calif. Soc. C.P.A.s, Theta Delta Chi. Clubs: Commonwealth (San Francisco); The Meadow (Chgo.). Home: 45 Hawthorne Ln Barrington Hills IL 60010 Office: Applied Learning Internat Inc 155 E Algonquin Rd Arlington Heights IL 60005

ROAN, FORREST CALVIN, JR., lawyer, title company executive; b. Waco, Tex., Dec. 18, 1944; s. Forrest Calvin and Lucille Elizabeth (McKinney) R.; m. Vickie Joan Howard, Feb. 15, 1969 (div. Dec. 1983); children: Amy Katherine, Jennifer Louise. BBA, U.Tex., Austin, 1973, JD, 1976. Bar: Tex. 1976, U.S. Dist. Ct. (we. dist.) Tex. 1977, U.S. Ct. Appeals (5th cir.) 1977, U.S. Ct. Appeals (11th cir.) 1981, U.S. Supreme Ct. 1979. Prin. Roan & Assos., Austin, 1969-71; counsel/com. dir. Tex. Ho. of Reps., 1972-75; assoc. Heath, Davis & McCalla, Austin, 1975-78; prin. Roan & Gullahorn, P.C., Austin, 1978-85, Roan, Simpson and Autrey (formerly Roan & Simpson), P.C., 1986—; bd. dirs. Pioneer Title Co., 1980—; bd. dirs. Waterloo Fin. Services, Inc., Capital Nat. Corp., Capital Nat. Life Ins. Co., Natesco Underwriters, Tex. Lawyers Credit Union, chmn., 1982, 83; dir. pub. law sect. State Bar Tex., 1980-84. Served with US Army NG, 1966-74. Mem. Travis County Bar Assn., ABA, Heritage Soc. Austin, Knights of the Symphony, Tex. Lyceum Assn. (v.p., bd. dirs. 1983-87), Austin C. of C. Methodist. Clubs: Citadel, Austin, Headliners, Capital. Lodges: Masons, Shriners (Parsons Masonic Master 1976-77). Office: Roan Simpson and Autrey 710 First Bank Tower 400 W 15th St Austin TX 78701

ROARK, ROBERT CAMERON, insurance agency executive; b. San Diego, Jan. 11, 1931; s. Alfred T. and Virginia J. Roark; A.B. in Journalism, San Diego State U., 1954; m. Lois Joan Maynard, July 19, 1952; children—Cynthia, Susan, Kellie, Robert. Agt., Mass. Mut. Life Ins. Co., San Diego, 1955-57; agy. supr. John Hancock Mut. Co., San Diego, 1957-59; gen. agt. Am. Mut. Life Ins. Co., San Diego, 1959-64; Southwestern regional v.p. Northwestern Life Ins. of Seattle, 1965-68; owner Roark Ins. Co., San Juan Capistrano, Calif., 1968—. Pres., bd. dirs. Mission Hills Homeowners Assn., San Juan Capistrano, Calif., 1972-73, Marinita Homeowners Assn., Dana Point, Calif., 1981-82; regional treas., bd. dirs. Orange County chpt. Am. Youth Soccer, 1977-80. Flotilla commdr. U.S. Coast Guard Aux. of Newport Beach, 1987. Republican. Club: Lions (pres., dir. Capitstrano 1970-71, zone chmn. South Orange County 1971-72).

ROBATI, PUPUKE, prime minister of Cook Islands. Prime minister, minister of info., marine resources, outer island affairs, minister responsible for pub. service, minister trade, labor and transport Cook Islands. Office: Office of Prime Minister, Avarva Cook Islands *

ROBB, CHARLES SPITTAL, lawyer, former governor of Virginia; b. Phoenix, June 26, 1939; s. James Spittal and Francis Howard (Woolley) R.; m. Lynda Bird Johnson, Dec. 9, 1967; children: Lucinda Desha, Catherine Lewis, Jennifer Wickliffe. Student, Cornell U., 1957-58; B.B.A., U. Wis., 1961; J.D., U. Va., 1973. Bar: Va. 1973, U.S. Supreme Ct. 1976. Law clk. to John D. Butzner, Jr., U.S. Ct. Appeals, 1973-74; atty. Williams Connolly & Califano, 1974-77; lt. gov. Va., 1978-82, gov., 1982-86; ptnr. Hunton & Williams, Richmond, Norfolk, and Fairfax, Va., Washington; bd. dirs. Crestar Fin. Corp.; chmn. Nat. Conf. Lt. Govs., 1979-80; chmn. Am. Council Young Polit. Leaders del. to Peoples Republic of China, 1979; chmn. Edn. Comm. of the States, 1985; vis. prof. pub. affairs George Mason U., spring 1987. Mem. bd. assocs. U. Richmond, 1974—; active Carnegie Found., Enterprise Found.; chmn. Jobs for Am.'s Grads., Inc., 1985—; gov. Atlantic Inst. for Internat. Affairs, 1987; chmn. Dem. Leadership Council, 1986—; active Dulles Area Rail Transp., Inc., Washington-Dulles Task Force, Nat. Leadership Commn. on Health Care, The Ctr. for the Study of the Vietnam Generation, The MacArthur Found.; chmn. 20th Century Fund's Task Force and Study Group on Sr. Exec. Service, Nat. Commn. on Pub. Service. Decorated Bronze Star, Vietnam Service medal with 4 Stars; Vietnamese Cross of Gallantry with Silver Star; recipient Raven award, 1973, Seven Soc. award U. Va. Mem. ABA, Va. Bar Assn., D.C. Bar Assn., Va. Trial Lawyers Assn., So. Govs. Assn. (chmn.), Dem. Govs. Assn. (chmn.), Coalition for Dem. Majority, Res. Officers Assn., USMC Res. Officers Assn., U. Va. Law Alumni Assn. (bd. dirs. 1974-85), Am. Legion, Raven Soc., Navy League U.S., Council on Fgn. Relations, Omicron Delta Kappa. Episcopalian. Office: Hunton & Williams 3050 Chain Bridge Rd Fairfax VA 22030

ROBB, FELIX COMPTON, association executive, consultant; b. Birmingham, Ala., Dec. 26, 1914; s. Felix Compton and Ruth (Nicholson) R.; m. Virginia Lytle Threlkeld. A.B. summa cum laude, Birmingham-So. Coll., 1936; M.A., Vanderbilt U., 1939; student, George Peabody Coll., 1939-40; Ed.D., Harvard U., 1952; D.Ped., W.Va. Wesleyan Coll., 1968; LL.D., Mercer U., 1968, U. S.C., 1978; D.H.L., U. Ala. System, 1975, Jacksonville U., 1981; H.H.D., Birmingham So. Coll., 1979. Tchr. jr. high sch. Irondale, Ala., 1936-37; tchr. Ensley High Sch., Birmingham, Ala., 1937-38; instr. English Birmingham-So. Coll., 1940-42, successively alumni sec., registrar, 1946; asst. to pres. Peabody Coll., 1947-51; acting dir. Peabody Coll. (Library Sch.), 1947-48, acting dean of coll., 1948-49, asso. prof. higher edn., 1950-53, prof., 1953-66, acting dir. surveys and field services, summer 1951, dean instrn., 1951-61, coll. pres., 1961-66; dir. So. Assn. Colls. and Schs., Atlanta, 1966-79; exec. dir. So. Assn. Colls. and Schs., 1979-82, exec. dir. emeritus, 1982—; pres. Ginge, Inc., 1982—; sec., treas. So. Edn. Exec. Search Assocs.; coordinator edn. project in, Korea, 1956-58, Dir. Carnegie fellowships in teaching, 1950-60; dir. Peabody Bldg. Fund Campaign, 1958; chief of staff The Study of Coll. and Univ. Presidency, 1958-60; mem. Tenn. Adv. Council on Tchr. Edn. and Certification, 1954-58; case writer Inst. for Coll. and Univ. Adminstrs., Harvard, 1955; nat. selection com. Fulbright awards, 1955-57; dir. workshops in TV, ednl. TV program series, Nashville, chmn. gov.'s conf. edn. beyond high sch., 1958; mem. com. specialized personnel Dept. Labor, Tenn. Commn. Human Relations, 1964-66; exec. com. Met. Action Commn., 1965-66; chmn. S.E. Manpower Adv. Com., 1965-68; mem. bd. So. Edn. Reporting Service, 1961-69; mem. nat. adv. com. Acad. of Sr. Profls. at Eckerd Coll. Trustee, chmn. scholarship com. Presser Found.; trustee, chmn. fin. com. United Meth. Children's Home; trustee Longview Found., Reinhardt Coll.; trustee, chmn. acad. affairs com. Eckerd Coll.; mem. Cleveland Conf.; mem. devel. council Birmingham-So. Coll., adv. bd. Southall Trust; bd. dirs. Atlanta Partnership of Bus. and Edn. Served to lt. USNR, 1943-46. Mem. So. Council Tchr. Edn. (pres. 1956-57), Am. Soc. Assn. Execs., Loulie Compton Sem. Alumni Assn. (pres.), Phi Beta Kappa, Omicron Delta Kappa, Phi Delta Kappa, Kappa Phi Kappa, Pi Gamma Mu, Kappa Alpha Order, Kappa Delta Pi (Laureate mem., vice chmn. ednl. found.). Methodist (trustee, chmn. adminstrv. bd. 1974). Club: Rotarian. Home: 377 Camden Rd NE Atlanta GA 30309 Office: So Assn Colls and Schs 1866 Southern Ln Decatur GA 30033-4097

ROBBE-GRILLET, ALAIN, author, film-maker; b. Brest, Aug. 18, 1922; s. Gaston and Yvonne (Canu) R.; m. Catherine Rstakian, 1957. Ed. Lycee Buffon, Lycee St. Louis and Inst. Nat. Agronomique, Paris. Charge de Mission, Inst. Nat. de la Statistique, 1945-48; engr. Inst. des Fruits Tropicaux (French Guina, Morocco, Martinique and Guadeloupe), 1949-51; lit. adviser Editions de Minuit, 1955-84; dir. Ctr. Sociology of Lit. U. Brussels, 1985-87; author: (novels) Les gommes, 1953, Le voyeur, 1955, La jalousie, 1957, Dans le labyrinthe, 1959, La maison de rendez-vous, 1965, Projet pour une revolution a New York, 1970, Topologie d'une cite fantome 1976, La belle captive, 1977, Un regicide 1978, Souvenirs du triangle d'or 1978, Djinn 1981, Le Miroir Qui revient, 1985, Angélique ou l'Enchantement, 1988; short stories: Instantanes, 1962; essay: Pour un nouveau roman, 1964; films: L'annee derniere a Marienbad, 1961; dir. films: L'immortelle, 1963, Trans-Europ-Epress, 1967, L'homme qui ment, 1968, L'Eden et apres, 1970, Glissements progressifs du plaisir, 1974, Le jeu avec le feu 1976, La belle captive, 1983. Decorated chevalier Legion d'Honneur; officier Ordre nat. du merit; recipient Prix Louis Delluc, 1963. Office: 7 rue Bernard Palissy, 75006 Paris France

ROBBINS, FREDERICK CHAPMAN, physician, emeritus medical school dean; b. Auburn, Ala., Aug. 25, 1916; s. William J. and Christine (Chapman) R.; m. Alice Havemeyer Northrop, June 19, 1948; children: Alice, Louise. A.B., U. Mo., 1936, B.S., 1938; M.D., Harvard U., 1940; D.Sc. (hon.), John Carroll U., 1955, U. Mo., 1958; D.Sci. (hon.), U. N.C., 1979, Tufts U., 1983, Med. Coll. Ohio, 1983; LL.D., U. N.Mex., 1968. Diplomate Am. Bd. Pediatrics. Sr. fellow virus disease NRC, 1948-50; staff research div. infectious diseases Children's Hosp., Boston, 1948-50, assoc. physician, assoc. dir. isolation service, asso. research div. infectious diseases, 1950-52; instr., assoc. in pediatrics Harvard Med. Sch., 1950-52; dir. dept. pediatrics and contagious diseases Cleve. Met. Gen. Hosp., 1952-66; prof. pediatrics Case-Western Res. U., 1952-80, dean Sch. Medicine, 1966-80, Univ prof., dean emeritus, 1980—, Univ. prof. emeritus, 1987—; pres. Inst. Medicine, Nat. Acad. Scis., 1980-85; vis. scientist Donner Lab., U. Calif., 1963-64. Served as maj. AUS, 1942-46; chief virus and rickettsial disease sect. 15th Med. Gen. Lab. investigations infectious hepatitis, typhus fever and Q fever. Decorated Bronze Star, 1945; recipient 1st Mead Johnson prize application tissue culture methods to study of viral infections, 1953; co-recipient Nobel prize in physiology and medicine, 1954; Med. Mut. Honor Award for, 1969; Ohio Gov.'s award, 1971. Mem. Nat. Acad. Scis., Am. Acad. Arts and Scis., Am. Soc. Clin. Investigation (emeritus mem.), Am. Acad. Pediatrics, Soc. Pediatric Research (pres. 1961-62, emeritus mem.), Am. Pediatric Soc., Am. Philos. Soc., Phi Beta Kappa, Sigma Xi, Phi Gamma Delta. Office: Case Western Res U Sch Medicine 2119 Abington Rd Cleveland OH 44106 *

ROBBINS, HAROLD, author; b. N.Y.C., May 21, 1916; m. Lillian Machnivitz (div.); m. Grace Palermo; children: Caryn, Adreana. Student pub. schs., N.Y.C. In food factoring bus. until 1940; shipping clk. Universal Pictures, N.Y.C., 1940-46. Author: Never Love a Stranger, 1948, The Dream Merchants, 1949, A Stone for Danny Fisher, 1951, Never Leave Me, 1953, 79 Park Avenue, 1955, Stiletto, 1953, The Carpetbaggers, 1961, Where

Love Has Gone, 1962, The Adventurers, 1966, The Inheritors, 1969, The Betsy, 1971, The Pirate, 1974, Lonely Lady, 1976, Dreams Die First, 1977, Memories of Another Day, 1979, Goodbye, Janette, 1981, Spellbinder, 1982, Descent from Xanadu, 1984, The Storyteller, 1985. Office: care Ernst Cane Berner & Gitlin 7 W 51st St New York NY 10019 also: care Simon & Schuster 1230 6th Ave New York NY 10009

ROBBINS, JEROME, choreographer, director; b. N.Y.C., Oct. 11, 1918; s. Harry and Lena (Rips) R. Student, NYU, 1935-36, hon. degree, 1985; D.F.A. (hon.), Ohio U., 1975; studied ballet, modern, Spanish and Oriental dance.; hon. degree, CUNY, 1980. Mem. panel N.Y. Council on Arts, 1973-77, Nat. Council on Arts, Nat. Endowment for Arts, 1974-80. Debut as dancer Sandor-Sorel Dance Center, 1937; dancer Broadway musicals Straw Hat Review, 1938-40, Ballet Theatre, N.Y.C., 1940-44, soloist, 1941-44; choreographer Ballet Theatre, 1944-48; choreographer N.Y.C. Ballet, 1949—, assoc. artistic dir., 1949-59, ballet master, 1969-83, co-ballet master in chief, 1983—, dir., Ballets: U.S.A., 1958-61, Jerome Robbins Chamber Dance Co. tour Peoples' Republic China (sponsored by U.S. Internat. Communications Agy.), 1981; ballets also in repertories of Am. Ballet Theatre, Joffrey Ballet, Royal Swedish Ballet, Batsheva Ballet, Royal Danish Ballet, Boston Ballet, Nat. Ballet Can., Harkness Ballet, Royal Ballet, London, Australian Ballet, San Francisco Ballet, Pa. Ballet, Dance Theatre of Harlem, Paris Opera Ballet, Bayerischen Staatsoper Munich, La Scala, Opernhaus, Zurich; ballets choreographed include Fancy Free, 1944, Interplay, 1945, The Cage, 1951, Fanfare, 1953, Afternoon of a Faun, 1953, N.Y. Export: Opus Jazz, 1958, Moves, 1959, Les Noces, 1965, Dances at a Gathering, 1969, In the Night, 1970, The Goldberg Variations, 1971, Requiem Canticles, 1972, (with Balanchine) Dumbarton Oaks, 1972, Watermill, 1972, Scherzo Fantastique, 1972, Circus Polka, 1972, Dybbuk Variations, 1974, Concerto in G (later in G Major), 1975, Ma Mere l'oye, 1975, Chansons Madecasses, 1975, Other Dances, 1976, The Four Seasons, 1979, Opus 19: The Dreamer, 1979, Rondo, 1981, Andantino, 1981, Piano Pieces, 1981, (with Pulchinella 1972 and Firebird 1970) Allegro con Grazia, 1981, The Gershwin Concerto, 1982, Four Chamber Works, 1982, Glass Pieces, 1983, I'm Old Fashioned, 1983, Antique Epigraphs, 1984, Brahms/Handel (with Twyla Tharp), 1984, Eight Lines, 1985, In Memory Of . . . , 1985; choreographer Broadway musicals On the Town (based on ballet Fancy Free), 1945, Billion Dollar Baby, 1946, High Button Shoes, 1947, Miss Liberty, 1949, Call Me Madam, 1950, The King and I, 1951, Two's Company, 1952; dir. and choreographer stage musicals Peter Pan, 1954, Bells Are Ringing, 1956, West Side Story, 1957 (Donaldson and Antoinette Perry awards); Gypsy, 1959, Fiddler on the Roof, 1964 (Antoinette Perry awards for choreography and direction), 1980; TV versions Peter Pan, 1955-60 (Emmy award); nat. tour, 1981; co-dir. (with George Abbott) Pajama Game (stage version), 1952; prodn. supr. Funny Girl (stage version), 1964; choreographer motion pictures The King and I, 1956, West Side Story, 1960 (Academy Awards for choreography and direction, Screen Dirs. Guild award, Laurel award); dir. plays Oh Dad, Poor Dad, Mama's Hung You in the Closet and I'm Feeling So Sad, 1962, Mother Courage and Her Children, 1963; TV credits include Two Duets, 1980, Live from Studio 8H (An Evening of Jerome Robbins Ballets), 1980. Decorated chevalier Order Arts and Letters (France); recipient numerous awards for prodns. including 5 Donaldson awards, 4 Antoinette Perry awards, 2 Academy Awards, and Sylvania, Emmy, Dance Magazine, Box Office Blue Ribbon, Evening Standard Drama (London), Screen Dirs. Guild, Laurel, Drama Critics, and City of Paris awards, Capezio Dance award (1976); recipient Handel medallion N.Y.C., 1976, Kennedy Ctr. honors, 1981; named best choreographer Theatre des Nations, 1959; recipient Brandeis U. Creative Arts award, 1984; Lifetime Achievement award (Astaire awards), 1985. Mem. Am. Acad. and Inst. Arts and Letters (hon.). Office: NYC Ballet NY State Theater Lincoln Ctr New York NY 10023 *

ROBBINS, KENNETH CHARLES, health care executive, lawyer; b. Boston, Oct. 26, 1942; s. Charles F. and Dorothy Rae (Gillis) R.; m. Marjorie Helen Dumas, June 25, 1965; children—Kimberly, Kerri, Susan. A.B., U. Mass., 1965; J.D., Suffolk U., 1973. Bar: Mass. 1973, Ill. 1976. Research dir. Com. Govt. Regulations Mass. Legislature, 1972-73, legal counsel, staff dir., 1973-76; ptnr. Pearlman & Robbins, 1974-76; dir. med.-legal affairs Ill. Hosp. Assn., Naperville, 1976-79, v.p., asst. gen. counsel, 1979-82, pres., 1983—; exec. dir. Ill. State Cost Containment Com., 1978, lectr. health care law Northwestern U. Served to capt. USAF, 1965-70; lt. col. Ill. Air N.G., 1976—. Mem. ABA, Ill. State Bar Assn., Am. Acad. Hosp. Attys., Ill. Assn. Hosp. Attys., Ill. Hosp. Assn. Execs. Forum, N.G. Assn. U.S., N.G. Assn. Ill. Roman Catholic. Clubs: University, Econ. (Chgo.). Office: Ill Hosp Assn 1151 E Warrenville Rd Naperville IL 60566

ROBBINS, VERNON EARL, lawyer, accountant; b. Balt., Aug. 16, 1921; s. Alexander Goldborough and Anne Jeanette (Bubb) R.; m. Ruth Adele Holland, Oct. 21, 1941; m. 2d, Alice Sherman Meredith, Feb. 17, 1961; 1 dau., Sharon Holland; 1 stepdau., Susan Victoria Causey. A.B.A., Md. Sch. Acctg., 1941; J.D., U. Balt., 1952. Bar: Md. 1952. Internal revenue agt. IRS, Balt., 1943-52, ptnr. Robbins, Adam & Co., C.P.A. firm, Cambridge, Md., 1952—; sole practice law, Cambridge, 1952—; mem. adv. bd. Cambridge Balt. Fed. Savs. & Loan Assn.; bd. dirs. Bank of Eastern Shore. Served with U.S. Maritime Service, 1941-45. Named Boss of Yr., Tidewater chpt. Nat. Secs. Assn., 1978. Mem. ABA, Md. bar Assn., Am. Inst. C.P.A.s, Md. Assn. C.P.A.s, Am. Assn. Atty.-C.P.A.s, Am. Judicature Soc., Navy League, Dorchester County Hist. Soc., Dorchester Art Center. Democrat. Methodist. Club: Cambridge Yacht. Lodges: Elks, Masons, Shriners. Office: PO Box 236 118 Cedar St Cambridge MD 21613

ROBEIN, JEAN-ANTOINE, urologist, surgeon; b. Strasbourg, France, May 4, 1946; s. Antoine and Jeanne R.; m. Pierquin Pascale, Sept. 20, 1969; children: Helene, Agnes, Gabrielle, Pierre. MD, U. Nancy, France, 1972. Resident Metz, France, 1968-72; resident Univ. Hosp., Besancon, France, 1973-76, resident chief, 1977-79; resident U. Montreal, Que., Can., 1976-77; ambulance surgeon Natitingou, Benin, 1972-73; practice medicine specializing in urology and surgery Centre Medico-Chirurgical, Chaumont, France, 1979—; pres. surveillance council Centre Medico-Chirurgical, Chaumont, 1983-84, pres. dir., 1984-86. Mem. French Assn. Urology. Office: Centre Medico Chirurgical, 17 Ave des Etats-Unis, 52000 Chaumont France

ROBERT, PHILIPPE, sociologist; b. Pau, France, July 23, 1939; s. Jean and Suzanne (Sarrat) R.; m. Maryse de Maqueville; children: Olivier, Frédéric, Isabelle, Emmanuel. PhD, U. Bordeaux, France, 1967. Head service d'Etudes pénales criminologiques Nat. Ctr. for Sci. Research and Ministry of Justice, Paris, 1969-83, dir. ctr. recherches sociologiques sur le droit les instns. pénales, 1983—. Author: Les Bandes d'Adolescents, 1966, Traité de Droit des Mineurs, 1969, 1981, La Question Pénale, 1984, Les Comptes du Crime, 1985; co-author: Les Bandes d'Adolescents, Une Théorie de la Ségrégation, 1984, Images du Viol Collectif, 1976, Le Coût de Crime, 1977, La Justice et Son Public, 1978, Les Forces Cachées de la Justice, 1981. Recipient Gold medal Univ. Liege, 1971, Chevalier Ordre National du merite. Mem. Soc. Francaise Sociologie, Soc. Francaise Criminologie, Assn. Internat. Sociologues Langue Francaise, Am. Soc. Sociology, Internat. Soc. Sociology. Office: CESDIP, 4 rue de Mondovi, F-75001 Paris France

ROBERTS, ALLEN EARL, film producer, author; b. Pawtucket, R.I., Oct. 11, 1917; s. John and Lillian Phillips (Wilson) R.; student public schs., also Internat. Corr. Schs., Armed Forces Inst., T. C. Williams Law Sch.; m. Dorothy Grimes, June 12, 1946; children—Allen E., R. Wayne, Kenneth D., Marcia L., Brian K. With U.S. Govt., 1946-50, Bank of Va., 1950-52, Henrico County (Va.), 1952-54, Capitol City Iron Works, 1954-56, Va. Bur. Correctional Field Units, 1956-72; owner Imagination Unltd. and Anchor Communications, Highland Springs, Va., 1969—; producer, author, dir. numerous films including: Saga of the Holy Royal Arch of Freemasonry, 1974; series Leadership Training Films, 1969-75; The Brotherhood of Man, 1975; Challenge!, 1977; Precious Heritage, 1977; Lonely World, 1980; Virtue Will Triumph, 1982; Living Stones, 1984; author: House Undivided, 1961; Freemasonry's Servant, 1969; Key to Freemasonry's Growth, 1969; The Craft and Its Symbols, 1974; G. Washington: Master Mason, 1976; Frontier Cornerstone, 1980; Shedding Light on Leadership, 1982; Freemasonry in American History, 1984, Brother Truman, 1986, The Diamond Years, 1987, The Search for Leadership, 1987, Seekers of Truth, 1988; others. Served with USNR, 1942-45. Recipient Masonic awards; Silver award Internat. Film and TV Festival N.Y., 1974, 75, 77, Gold award, 1977; Freedoms Found. award, 1981. Fellow Philalethes Soc.; mem. Acad. Cert. Adminstrv. Mgrs., Info. Film Producers Am., Soc. Motion Picture and TV Producers. Methodist. Club: Masons. Home: 110 Quince Ave Highland Springs VA 23075 Office: PO Box 70 Highland Springs VA 23075

ROBERTS, ARCHIBALD EDWARD, retired army officer, author; b. Cheboygan, Mich., Mar. 21, 1915; s. Archibald Lancaster and Madeline Ruth (Smith) R.; grad. Command and Gen. Staff Coll., 1952; student U.S. Armed Forces Inst., 1953, U. Md., 1958; m. Florence Snure, Sept. 25, 1940 (div. Feb. 1950); children—Michael James, John Douglas; m. 2d, Doris Elfriede White, June 23, 1951; children—Guy Archer, Charles Lancaster, Christopher Corwin. Enlisted U.S. Army, 1939, advanced through grades to lt. col., 1960; served in Far East Command, 1942, 1953-55, ETO, 1943-45, 57-60; tech. info. officer Office Surgeon Gen., Dept. Army, Washington, 1950, Ft. Campbell, Ky., 1952-53, info. officer, Camp Chicamauga, Japan, Ft. Bragg, N.C., Ft. Campbell, Ky., 1953-56, Ft. Campbell, 1956-57, Ft. Benning, Ga., Wurzburg, Germany, 1957-58, spl. projects officer Augsburg, Germany, 1959-60, U.S. Army Info. Office, N.Y.C., 1960-61; writer program precipitating Senate Armed Services Hearings, 1962; ret., 1965; mgr., salesman Nu-Enamel Stores, Ashville, N.C., 1937-38; co-owner, dir. Roberts & Roberts Advt. Agy., Denver, 1946-49; pres. Found. for Edn., Scholarship, Patriotism and Americanism, Inc.; founder, nat. bd. dirs. Com. to Restore Constn., Inc., 1965—; Recipient award of merit Am. Acad. Pub. Affairs, 1967; Good Citizenship medal SAR, 1968; Liberty award Congress of Freedom, 1969; Man of Yr. awards Women for Constl. Govt., 1970, Wis. Legislative and Research Com., 1971; medal of merit Am. Legion, 1972; Speaker of Year award We, The People, 1973; Col. Arch Roberts Week named for him City of Danville, Ill., 1974; recipient Spl. Tribute State of Mich., 1979. Mem. Res. Officers Assn., Airborne Assn., SAR, Sons Am. Colonists. Author: Rakkasan, 1955; Screaming Eagles, 1956; The Marne Division, 1957; Victory Denied, 1966; The Anatomy of a Revolution, 1968; Peace: By the Wonderful People Who Brought You Korea and Viet Nam, 1972; The Republic: Decline and Future Promise, 1975; The Crisis of Federal Regionalism: A Solution, 1976; Emerging Struggle for State Sovereignty, 1979; How to Organize for Survival, 1982; The Most Secret Science, 1984; also numerous pamphlets and articles. Home: 2218 W Prospect PO Box 986 Fort Collins CO 80522

ROBERTS, ARTHUR STANLEY, JR., systems company executive, dentist; b. Indpls., Jan. 21, 1946; s. Arthur Stanley and Rosemary Jane (Morris) R.; m. Karen Sue Strawn, Aug. 17, 1968; children—Meredith Holly, Arthur Stanley. Student Earlham Coll., 1964-65, Ind. U., 1965-67, postgrad., 1978-80; D.D.S., Ind. U.-Indpls., 1971. Intern William Beaumont Gen. Hosp., Ft. Bliss, Tex., 1971-72; staff dental officer USARSUPTHAI, Bangkok, Thailand, 1972-73; gen. practice dentistry, Rushville, Ind., 1973-81; pres. Geneva Cons., Shelbyville, Ind., 1981-83; chmn., founder, chief exec. officer Alpha Systems Resource Co., Shelbyville, 1983-86; pres. Mgmt. Research Corp., 1986—; research assoc. oral facial genetics Ind. U. Med. Ctr., Indpls., 1981-83; faculty extramural Ind. U. Med. Ctr., Indpls., 1979-85. Nat. bd. advisors Rose Hulman Inst. Tech. Co-inventor pill mill. Acad. Gen. Dentistry fellow, 1980. Fellow Royal Soc. Health, Info. Industry Assn., Acad. Gen. Dentistry Clubs: Ind. Rugby, Columbia (Indpls.) Avocations: skiing; anthropology; sailing. Home: 203 W Washington St Shelbyville IN 46176

ROBERTS, B. K., lawyer, former judge; b. Sopchoppy, Fla., Feb. 5, 1907; s. Thomas and Florida (Morrison) R.; m. Mary Newman, Aug. 20, 1937; children: Mary Jane, Thomas Frederick. J.D., U. Fla., 1928; LL.D., U. Miami, 1954; D.H.L., Fla. State U., 1980. Bar: Fla. 1928. Practiced in Tallahassee, 1928-49; justice Supreme Ct. of Fla., 1949-77, chief justice, 1953-54, 61-63, 71-72, ret., 1977; sr. partner firm Roberts, Baggett, LaFace & Richard, and predecessor, 1977—; v.p., dir. Tallahassee Bank & Trust Co. (now Barnett Bank), 1948-49; Mem. awards jury Freedoms Found. at Valley Forge, 1962; mem. Fla. Constl. Revision Commn., 1966, 77; chmn. subcom. on human rights; chmn. Jud. Council Fla., 1962-77; mem. exec. com. Nat. Conf. Chief Justices, 1966, dep. chmn., 1972-73. Chmn. trustees Fla. State U. Found.; bd. counselors Fla. Presbyn. Coll. Served as lt. comdr. USCG; Served as lt. comdr. 1942-45; shipping commr. 1943-45, Port Jacksonville, Fla. Recipient Distinguished Citizen award Stetson U. Coll. Law (2). Mem. Internat. Bar Assn. (patron), Inter-Am., ABA (UN com., world order under law com.; ofcl. ct. rep. London meeting 1957), Fla. Bar Assn. (past v.p.), Tallahassee Bar Assn. (past pres.), Am. Judicature Soc., Am. Law Inst., Newcomen Soc. Eng., Am. Legion (mem. nat. distinguished guests com.), Alpha Kappa Psi, Fla. Blue Key, Fla State U. Gold Key, Soc. of Wig and Robe, Phi Alpha Delta, Delta Chi. Democrat. Presbyterian. Clubs: Governor's, Killearn Golf and Country, Hendersonville (N.C.) Country. Lodges: Masons; Shriners; Elks; Odd Fellows; Kiwanis. Home: MSS Box 3005 Tallahassee FL 32303 Office: PO Drawer 1838 Tallahassee FL 32302 also: 101 E College Ave Tallahassee FL 32302

ROBERTS, BRYNLEY FRANCIS, librarian; b. Aberdare, Wales, Feb. 3, 1931; s. Robert Francis and Laura Jane (Williams) R.; m. Rhiannon Campbell; children: Rolant Lloyd, Owen Maredudd. BA with hons., U. Coll. Wales, Aberystwyth, 1951, MA, 1954, PhD, 1969. Lectr., sr. lectr., reader U. Coll. Wales, 1957-78; prof., dept. head U. Coll. Swansea (Wales), 1978-85; librarian Nat. Library Wales, Aberystwyth, 1985—. Author: Edward Lhuyd, 1980; editor Gwassanaeth Meir, 1961, Brut y Brenhinedd, 1971, Cyfranc Lludd a Llefelys, 1975. vis. fellow Jesus Coll., Oxford, 1973-74. Fellow Soc. Antiquaries. Office: Nat Library Wales, Aberystwyth Dyfed SY23 3BU, Wales

ROBERTS, CORNELIUS SHELDON, materials scientist, consultant; b. Rupert, Vt., Oct. 27, 1926; s. Cornelius Vivian and Lola Jones (Sheldon) R.; m. Patricia Rose Wiseman, Oct. 21, 1950; children—David M., Steven H., Wayne E. B.Met.E., Rensselaer Poly. Inst., 1948; S.M., MIT, 1949, Sc.D., 1951; D. Eng. (hon.) Rensselaer Poly. Inst., 1988. Lic. profl. engr., Calif. Research metallurgist Dow chem. Co., Midland, Mich., 1951-56; sr. staff mem. Shockley Labs., Palo Alto, Calif., 1956-57; co-founder, head materials Fairchild Semicondr. Corp., Palo Alto, 1957-61; co-founder, head spl. devices Amelco Semicondr. div. Teledyne Inc., Mountain View, Calif., 1961-63; cons. materials and processes, Los Altos, Calif., 1963-78, San Jose, Calif., 1978-84, Sunriver, Oreg., 1984—. Author: Magnesium and Its Alloys, 1958; also numerous articles. Trustee Rensselaer Poly. Inst., 1972—, San Francisco Conservatory Music, 1983—. Served with USNR, 1944-46. Recipient Alfred Noble award Combined Engring. Socs., 1954. Mem. Am. Soc. Metals (trustee 1984-87), IEEE, AIME, Soc. Air Safety Investigators, Sigma Xi, Tau Beta Pi. Republican. Methodist. Club: University (N.Y.C.). Lodge: Elks. Current work: Electronic microchip technology; failure analysis, materials and aircraft. Subspecialties: Electronic materials; Materials processing. Home: 4 Grouse Ln Sunriver OR 97707 Office: PO Box 4576 Sunriver OR 97707

ROBERTS, DOUGLAS STUART, architect; b. Harare, Zimbabwe, Republic of South Africa, Mar. 24, 1938; s. Claude Leonard and Theresa (Winifred) R.; m. Mary Ann Nicholls, 1973; children: Caroline, Jonathan. BArch, U. Cape Town, Republic of South Africa, 1961; postgrad., Sch. de Arte, Venezia, 1962; MArch, Yale, 1963. Archtl. asst. Pallet & Pryce Architects., Harare, 1957-61, Cowper Poole & Ptnrs., London, 1962, Paul Rudolf, New Haven, 1963; prin. Douglas Roberts Architects, Cape Town, 1964-81; ptnr. Douglas Roberts Peter Loebenberg Architects, Cape Town, 1981—; studio master U. Cape Town, 1966-69; mem. various coms. Cape Provincial Inst. Architecture , 1970—; lectr. U. Cape Town, 1983. Various bldgs. illustrated in numerous nat. and internat. books, jours. and newspapers. Rotary Found. fellow, 1962; recipient Mayor's Greening of City award, 1986-87, South African Property Owner's Assn. award, 1987. Club: Netherlands. Lodge: Rotary (pres. 1983). Home: 2 Higgo Rd, Higgovale, Cape Town 8001, Republic of South Africa Office: Loenberg Architects CC, 5th Floor 35 Wale St, Cape Town 8001, Republic of South Africa

ROBERTS, FRANCIS STONE, advertising executive; b. Scranton, Pa., Aug. 15, 1944; s. Gordon Link and Eleanor Swartz (Stone) R.; m. Anne Carter Housh, Dec. 21, 1974; children: Francis Stone, Link McGregor. B.A., Grove City (Pa.) Coll., 1966; A.M.P., U. Chgo., 1984. With media dept., then account exec. Compton Advt. Inc., N.Y.C., 1966-69; account exec. Tatham-Laird & Kudner Advt., N.Y.C., 1969-70; account supr., v.p. SSC&B Advt. Inc., N.Y.C., 1970-78, sr. v.p., mgmt. supr., 1978-81; exec. v.p. Lintas Advt. Inc., 1981-86, group exec. v.p., 1987—, mem. policy and ops. coms., chmn. strategy rev. bd., also dir. Mem. William Penn Charter Alumni Assn. (pres. N.Y. chpt. 1984—). Republican. Presbyterian. Club: New Canaan Field, New Canaan Winter. Home: 208 Canoe Hill Rd New Canaan CT 06840 Office: Lintas Worldwide Advt Inc 1 Dag Hammarskjold Plaza New York NY 10017

ROBERTS, GEORGE CHRISTOPHER, manufacturing executive; b. Ridley Park, Pa., May 27, 1936; s. George H. and Marion C. (Smullen) R.; m. Adriana Toribio, July 19, 1966; children—Tupac A., Capac Y. Sr. engr. ITT, Paramus, N.J., 1960-65; program mgr. Arde Research, Mawah, N.J., 1965-67; Space-Life Sci. program mgr., research div. GATX, 1967-69; dir. research and devel. Monogram Industries, Los Angeles, 1969-71; chmn. Inca Mfg. Corp, 1970-72, pres. 1971—; pres. Environ. Protection Center, Inc., Los Angeles, 1970-76. Bd. dirs., trustee Fairborn Obs.; founder Culver Nat. Bank, 1983; trustee Calif. Mus. Sci. and Industry, 1988—; trustee Internat. Am. Profl. Photoelectric Photometrists, 1983—, Buckley Sch., 1984—; chmn. solar and stellar physics Mt. Wilson Research Corp., 1984-87; mem., dir., v.p. Peruvian Found. Mem. Am. Astron. Soc., Astron. Soc. Pacific. Patentee advanced waste treatment systems, automotive safety systems.

ROBERTS, HYMAN JACOB, physician, researcher, author; b. Boston, May 29, 1924; s. Benjamin and Eva (Sherman) R.; m. Carol Antonia Klein, Aug. 9, 1953; children: David, Jonathan, Mark, Stephen, Scott, Pamela. M.D. cum laude, Tufts U., 1947. Diplomate Am. Bd. Internal Medicine. Intern, resident Boston City Hosp., 1947-49; resident Mcpl. Hosp., Washington, 1949-50; research fellow, instr. med. Tufts Med. Sch., Boston, 1948-49, Georgetown Med. Sch., Washington, 1949-50; fellow in medicine Lahey Clinic, Boston, 1950-51; mem. sr. active staff Good Samaritan and St. Mary's Hosps., West Palm Beach, Fla., 1955—; dir. Palm Beach Inst. Med. Research, West Palm Beach, 1964—; lectr. two day seminar on "The New Frontiers in Leagal Medicine". U.S. rep. Council of Europe for Driving Standards, 1972 . Author: Difficult Diagnosis, Spanish and Italian edits, 1958; The Causes, Ecology and Prevention of Traffic Accidents, 1971; Is Vasectomy Safe?, 1979, Reactions to Aspartame, 1988; (play) My Wife, The Politician; assoc. editor: Tufts Med. Alumni Bull, Boston, 1978—; contbr. sci. and med. articles to profl. and theol. jours. Pres. Jewish Community Day Sch., West Palm Beach, Fla., 1975-76; disting. mem. pres. council U. Fla., Gainesville, 1974—; founder, dir. Jewish Fedn. Palm Beach County, West Palm Beach, 1960-72. Served to lt. USNR, 1951-54. Named Fla. Outstanding Young Man Jr. C. of C. Fla., 1958; hon. Ky. col.; recipient Gold Share cert. and silver certs. Inst. Agr. and Food Scis., U. Fla., 1974-78; Paul Harris fellow Rotary Found., 1980; hon. Ky. col. Fellow Am. Coll. Chest Physicians, Am. Coll. Nutrition, Stroke Council; mem. AMA, ACP, Am. Soc. Internal Medicine, Endocrine Soc., Am. Diabetes Assn., Am. Heart Assn., Am. Fedn. Clin. Research, Am. Coll. Angiology (gov. 1981), Pan Am. Med. Assn. (chmn. endocrinology 1982), So. Med. Assn., N.Y. Acad. Scis., Am. Physicians Fellowship of Israel Med. Assn., Confrerie de la Chaine des Rotisseurs, Alpha Omega Alpha, Sigma Xi. Club: Governors of West Palm Beach (a founder), Executive (founder). Lodges: Rotary; B'nai B'rith. Research in med diagnosis, diabetes, hypoglycemia, postvasectomy state, Vitamin E metabolism, pentachlorophenol and heavy metal toxicity, narcolepsy, traffic accidents, thrombophlebitis, aspartame, nutrition and bioethics. Home: 6708 Pamela Ln West Palm Beach FL 33405 Office: Palm Beach Inst Med Research 300 27th St West Palm Beach FL 33407

ROBERTS, JOHN ARTHUR, architect; b. Lincoln, Lincolnshire, Eng., Sept. 1, 1930; s. Arthur Clarence and Gladys (Reynolds) R.; m. Carole Maureen Martin, Feb. 25, 1965 (div. 1979); children: Simon Marcus, Lucy, Jonathan Martin. Diploma, Leicester (Eng.) Sch. Architecture, 1954. Chartered architect. Ptnr. Parker and Roberts, Lincoln, 1953-63; prin. John Roberts Assocs., Lincoln, 1963—, Ian Fraser, John Roberts & Ptnr., Lincoln, 1971—, John Roberts Architects, Ltd., Lincoln, 1986—. Prin. works include Civic Trust bldg. (16 awards), Cen. Council for Disabled bldg., Lincoln Civic Award bldg. Life mem. Lincoln Civic Trust; mem. Lloyds of London. Fellow Royal Inst. Brit. Architects, Chartered Soc. Designers; mem. London Archtl. Assn., London Cement and Concrete Assn., London Concrete Soc., Lincolnshire Soc. Architects (founding pres. 1967-70), Nottinghamshire and Derby Soc. Architects (v.p. 1965-69), Am. C. of C., Brit.-Arab C. of C. (mem. panel 1985—), Guild of Air Pilots and Air Navigators. Mem. Conservative Party. Mem. Ch. of Eng. Home: Burton Hall, Lincoln, Lincolnshire LN2 1RD, England Office: 1 James St, Lincoln, Lincolnshire LN2 1QD, England

ROBERTS, JOHN BENJAMIN, II, public policy consultant, writer; b. Albrook AFB, C.Z., Oct. 10, 1955; s. Robert Benjamin and Mary Pauline (Porath) R.; m. Karen Jeanne Jones, July 25, 1981; 1 child, John Benjamin III. BA, U. Calif., Irvine, 1973; MA with honors, Oxford U., Eng., 1978. Assoc. editor Handgunner, Ltd., London, 1979-80; press aide Reagan-Bush Campaign, Arlington, Va., 1980, sr. policy analyst, Washington, 1984; dep. dir. communications Rep. Nat. Com., Washington, 1981; dir. editorial policy U.S. Dept. Edn., Washington, 1981-83; assoc. dir. office planning and evaluation White House, Washington, 1983-84, assoc. dir. office polit. and govtl. affairs, 1985-86; sr. v.p. Russo, Watts & Rollins Inc., Washington, 1986-88, pres. Roberts & Watts Communications, Washington, 1988—; cons. Citizens for Republic, Santa Monica, Calif., 1982—, One on One, 1987, McLaughlin Group, 1987—; mem. steering com. Fund for America's Future, Washington, 1985—. Author: Entitlement Spending, 1984. Contbr. articles to newspapers, mags. Named one of Outstanding Young Men of Am., 1987. Bd. dirs U.S. Tall Ship Found., 1988. Mem. Am. Council Young Polit. Leaders, Oxford U. Pistol Club (Half-Blue Varsity award 1978), U.K. Practical Shooting Assn. (founder, life mem.), Oxford Soc., N.Am. Alliance for Keble Coll. (bd. dirs. 1986). Avocations: competitive marksmanship, backpacking, photography. Home: 2009 Mason Hill Dr Alexandria VA 22307 Office: Robert & Watts Communications 655 50th St NW Suite 300 Washington DC 20005

ROBERTS, JOHN KENYON, librarian; b. Leeds, Yorkshire, Eng., Jan. 10, 1940; s. Stanley and Jenny (Reeds) R.; m. Norma Elaine Critchley, Feb. 22, 1975; 1 child, Sarah Ann. BS, U. Manchester, Eng., 1962, MS, 1972. Asst. librarian Bradford Inst. Tech., Eng., 1963-66; sub librarian U. Manchester Inst. Sci. & Tech., 1966-70; sub librarian U. Wales Inst. Sci. & Tech., Cardiff, 1970-73, acting librarian, 1973-75, librarian, 1975-88; librarian U. Wales Coll. of Cardiff, 1988—; bd. dirs. Swalcap Library Services Ltd. Mem. Library Assn., Brit. Computer Soc. Anglican. Office: U Wales Coll of Cardiff, Library, PO Box 430, Cardiff CF1 3XT, Wales

ROBERTS, JOSEPH BOXLEY, JR., educator, writer; b. Yazoo City, Miss., Feb. 13, 1918; s. Joseph Boxley and Sheila (Hill) R.; B.A., U. Ala., 1950; M.A. (Rockefeller Found. scholar), U. N.C., 1954; Ph.D., U. Denver, 1959; m. Enyd Turner, Nov. 19, 1945; children—Joseph Boxley III, Sheila Anne Roberts Tweed. Served as enlisted man U.S. Army Air Corps, 1942-43, officer U.S. Army Air Force, 1943-46, recalled to active duty U.S. Air Force, 1951, advanced through grades to lt. col., 1966; asst. prof. English, U.S. Mil. Acad., West Point, N.Y., 1953-56; asso. prof. English, dep. head dept. U.S. Air Force Acad. (Colo.), 1956-63; dir. info. Office Aerospace Research, Washington, 1963-66; chief ops. Psychol. Ops. Directorate, Vietnam, 1966-67; head psychol. ops. civic action dept. Spl. Air Warfare Sch., Hurlburt Field, Fla., 1967-68; ret., 1968; instr. English, U. Ala., Huntsville, 1950; prof. English, Troy (Ala.) State U., 1968-81, prof. emeritus, 1981—, chmn. dept., 1968-71, dean Coll. Arts and Scis., 1971-72. Weekly newspaper columnist It Seems to Me, 1973-79, syndicated by Contemporary Features Syndicate, Inc., 1976-79. Decorated Bronze Star medal, Commendation medal. Mem. Modern Lang. Assn. Am., Nat. Council Tchrs. English, Conf. on Coll. Composition and Communication, South Atlantic Modern Lang. Assn., Troy C. of C. (chmn. edn. com. 1969-70), Air Force Assn., Ret. Officers Assn., Phi Beta Kappa. (pres. Troy Assn. 1969-70), Phi Eta Sigma, Phi Kappa Phi (pres. Troy State U. chpt. 1972-73), Sigma Tau Delta (adviser 1974-76). Episcopalian (vestryman 1974-77). Rotarian (dir. 1970-71). Author: Airway to India, 1945; Faint Voice Calling, 1945; Beginner's Handbook of Gold and Tropical Fish, 1947, rev. edit., 1952; Pet Shop Manual, 1953; Web of Our Life, 1957; The Sound of Wings, 1957; On Poetry and the Poetic Process, 1971; Of Time and Love, 1980. Home: 107 Richmond Ave Troy AL 36081 Office: Troy State U Dept English Troy AL 36081

ROBERTS, JUDITH MARIE, librarian, educator; b. Bluefield, W.Va., Aug. 5, 1939; d. Charles Bowen Lowder and Frances Marie (Bourne)

Lowder Alberts; m. Craig Currence Jackson, July 1, 1957 (div. 1962); 1 son, Craig, Jr.; m. 2d, Milton Rinehart Roberts, Aug. 13, 1966 (div. 1987). B.S., Concord State Tchrs. Coll., 1965. Librarian, Cape Henlopen Sch. Dist., Lewes, Del., 1965—. Pres. Friends of Lewes Pub. Library, 1986—; chmn. exhibits Govs. Conf. Libraries and Info. Services, Dover, Del., 1978; mem. Gov.'s State Library Adv. Council, 1987—. Mem. ALA, NEA, Del. State Edn. Assn., Sussex Help Orgn. for Resources Exchange (pres. 1984-85), Del. Library Assn. (pres. 1982-83), Del. Learning Resources Assn. (pres. 1976-77). Methodist. Home: 42 DeVries Circle Lewes DE 19958 Office: Cape Henlopen High Sch Kings Hwy Lewes DE 19958

ROBERTS, KEITH EDWARD, SR., lawyer; b. White Hall, Ill., Apr. 27, 1928; s. Victor Harold and Ruby Harriet (Kelsey) R.; m. Marthan Dusch, Sept. 4, 1954; 1 son, Keith Edward. Student, Western Ill. U., 1946-47, George Washington U., 1947-48; B.S., U. Ill., 1951, J.D., 1953. Bar: Ill. 1953, U.S. Dist. Ct. (no. dist.) Ill. 1957, U.S. Dist. Ct. (so. dist.) Ill. 1961, U.S. Dist. Ct. (no. dist.) Ohio 1960, U.S. Ct. Mil. Appeals 1954, U.S. Ct. Appeals (7th cir.) 1968. Assoc. J.D. Quarant, Elizabethtown, Ill., 1953-56; staff atty. Pa. R.R. Co., Chgo., 1957-60; assoc. Henslee, Monek & Henslee, Chgo., 1960-67; sole practice, Naperville, Ill., 1967-68; ptnr. Donovan, Atten, Mountcastle, Roberts & DaRosa, Wheaton, Ill., 1968-77; pres. Donovan & Roberts, P.C., Wheaton, 1977—. Served to capt. U.S. Army, 1954-57. Mem. ABA, Assn. Trial Lawyers Am., Ill. Bar Assn., DuPage County Bar Assn. (gen. counsel 1976-86). Democrat. Presbyterian. Office: PO Box 417 Wheaton IL 60187

ROBERTS, MARIE DYER, computer systems specialist; b. Statesboro, Ga., Feb. 19, 1943; d. Byron and Martha (Evans) Dyer; B.S., U. Ga., 1966; student Am. U., 1972; cert. systems profl., cert. in data processing; m. Hugh V. Roberts, Jr., Oct. 6, 1973. Mathematician, computer specialist U.S. Naval Oceanographic Office, Washington, 1966-73; systems analyst, programmer Sperry Microwave Electronics, Clearwater, Fla., 1973-75; data processing mgr., asst. bus. mgr. Trenam, Simmons, Kemker et al, Tampa, Fla., 1975-77; mathematician, computer specialist U.S. Army C.E., Savannah, Ga., 1977-81, 83-85, Frankfurt, W. Ger., 1981-83; ops. research analyst U.S. Army Contrn. Research Lab., Champaign, Ill., 1985-87; data base adminstr., computer systems programmer U.S. Army Corps of Engrs., South Pacific div., San Francisco, 1987—; instr. computer scis. City Coll. of Chgo. in Franfurt, 1982-83. Recipient Sustained Superior Performance award Dept. Army, 1983. Mem. Am. Soc. Hist. Preservation, Data Processing Mgmt. Assn., Assn. of Inst. for Cert. Computer Profls., Assn. Women in Computing, Assn. Women in Sci., Nat. Assn. Female Execs., Am. Film Inst., U. Ga. Alumni Assn., Sigma Kappa. Author: Harris Computer Users Manual, 1983.

ROBERTS, MARY BELLE, clinical social worker; b. Akron, Ohio, Sept. 27, 1923; d. Joseph Gill and Inez Wilson (Garvey) Roberts; BS, U. Mich., 1948, MSW, 1950. Cert. social worker, Md., lic. clin. social worker, Fla. Instr. dept. psychiatry U. Ala. Med. Coll., 1950-53; psychiat. social worker div. mental hygiene Ala. Dept. Pub. Health, 1950-52, acting dir., dir., 1952-53; sr. psychiat. social worker bur. mental health div. community service Pa. Dept. Welfare, 1954-55; cons. psychiat. social work community service br. NIMH, USPHS, HEW, 1955-64; pvt. practice psychiat. social work, 1964-68; caseworker Family Service, Miami, Fla., 1968-70, Family and Childrens Service, Miami, 1971-75; casework cons. United Family and Childrens Services, Miami, 1975-85, Family Counseling Services, Miami, 1985—. Home: 501 Valencia Ave #2 Coral Gables FL 33134 Office: 2190 NW 7th St Miami FL 33125

ROBERTS, MELVILLE PARKER, JR., neurosurgeon, educator; b. Phila., Oct. 15, 1931; s. Melville Parker and Marguerite Louise (Reimann) R.; m. Sigrid Marianne Magnusson, Mar. 27, 1954; children: Melville Parker III, Julia Pell, Erik Emerson. B.S., Washington and Lee U., 1953; M.D. (James Hudson Brown research fellow), Yale U., 1957. Diplomate: Am. Bd. Neurol. Surgery. Intern Yale Med. Center, 1957, neurosurg. resident, 1958-60, 62-64, Am. Cancer Soc. fellow in neurosurgery, 1962-64, instr., 1964; asst. prof. surgery U. Va. Sch. Medicine, Charlottesville, 1965-69; practice medicine specializing in neurol. surgery Hartford, Conn., 1970—; mem. sr. staff Hartford Hosp., John Dempsey Hosp.; asst. prof. surgery U. Conn. Sch. Medicine, Farmington, 1970-71; asso. prof. U. Conn. Sch. Medicine, 1972-75, asso. prof. neurology, 1974-77, chmn. div. neurosurgery, 1971-84, prof. surgery, 1975—, acting chmn. dept. neurology, 1973-77, acting chmn. dept. surgery, 1974-77, William Beecher Scoville prof. neurosurgery, 1976—; cons. Milford Hosp.; cons. neurosurgeon Cedarcrest Regional Hosp., Newington, Conn., Johnson Meml. Hosp., Stafford Springs, Conn. Author: Atlas of the Human Brain in Section, 1970, 2d edition, 1987; mem. editorial bd.: Conn. Medicine, 1973—; contbr. articles to profl. jours. Served as capt. M.C. U.S. Army, 1960-61. Fellow ACS; mem. Am. Assn. Neurol. Surgeons, Soc. Neurol. Surgeons, Congress. Neurol. Surgeons (bd. dirs. joint spinal sect. with Am. Assn. Neurol. Surgeons, chmn. annual meeting 1987, sci. program chmn. ann. meeting 1988), Assn. for Research in Nervous and Mental Diseases, Am. Assn. Anatomists, New Eng. Neurosurg. Soc. (bd. dirs. 1976-79, 86—), Soc. Brit. Neurol. Surgeons, Royal Soc. Medicine (London), Research Soc. Neurol. Surgeons, Soc. Research into Hydrocephalus and Spina Bifida, Vereingung Schweizer Neurochirurgen, Sigma Xi. Episcopalian. Clubs: Mory's Assn., Graduates (New Haven); Yale (N.Y.C.); Sloane (London); Farmington Country. Home: 10 Mountain Spring Rd Farmington CT 06032 Office: 85 Seymour St Hartford CT 06106

ROBERTS, MICHAEL ANDERSON, lawyer; b. Albemarle, N.C., Dec. 9, 1917; s. Ray Crouse and Bessie Lee (Cloniger) R.; m. Ruth Carolyn Covington, Jan. 17, 1942; children—Carolyn C. Roberts Schuft, Michael Anderson, Laura L. Roberts Kawecki. A.B. in Econs., U. N.C., 1940, M.S. in Indsl. Relations, 1950, J.D., 1952; LL.M., N.Y.U., 1955. Bar N.C. 1952, N.Y., 1955, U.S. Supreme Ct. 1968, Fla. 1973. With sales dept. A. H. Thomas Lab. Equipment, Phila., 1941-42; indsl. engr. Armstrong Cork Co., Lancaster, Pa., 1942-47; asst. personnel mgr. Armstrong Cork Co., Fulton, N.Y., 1948-49; asst. div. personnel mgr. Kraft Foods Co., N.Y.C., 1952-55; labor relations mgr. Curtiss Wright Corp., Woodridge, N.J., 1955-57; labor relations rep. St. Regis Corp., (now Champion Internat. Corp.), N.Y.C., 1957-60, indsl. relations mgr., Tacoma, 1960-64, mgr. labor law services, N.Y.C., 1964-68, mgr. manpower planning, N.Y.C., 1968-72, mgr. EEO, 1972-78, dir. EEO affairs, 1978-81, asst. to v.p. human resources, 1982-83; cons. in field, 1983—Charter mem. Republican Presdl. Task Force, 1982. Served to lt. USNR, 1942-46; PTO. Mem. ABA. Contbr. articles to legal jours. Office: 57 Canterbury Dr Ramsey NJ 07446

ROBERTS, PAUL CRAIG, III, economics educator, author, consultant; b. Atlanta, Apr. 3, 1939; s. Paul Craig and Ellen Lamar (Dryman) R.; m. Linda Jane Fisher, July 3, 1969; children—Pendaran Struan Sherman, Becky Ellen, Stephanie Bradford. B.S., Ga. Inst. Tech., 1961; postgrad., U. Calif., Berkeley, 1962-63, Merton Coll., Oxford (Eng.) U., 1964-65; Ph.D. Earhart fellow, U. Va., 1967. Asst. prof. econs. Va. Poly. Inst., 1965-69; assoc. prof. U. N.Mex., 1969-71; research fellow Hoover Instn., Stanford U., 1971-77, sr. research fellow, 1978—; mem. U.S. Congl. Staff, 1975-78; asst. sec. of treasury for econ. policy Dept. Treasury, Washington, 1981-82; William E. Simon prof. polit. economy Georgetown U. Center for Strategic and Internat. Studies, Washington, 1982—; chmn. Inst. Polit. Economy, 1985—; adj. scholar Cato Inst., 1987—; assoc. editor, columnist Wall St. Jour., N.Y.C., 1978-80; columnist Bus. Week, 1983—, Fin. Post, Can., 1988, Liberation, Paris, 1988, Erfolg, Fed. Rep. of Germany, 1988, Washington Times, 1988, San Diego Union, 1988; mem. Pres.-elect Reagan's Task Force on Tax Policy, 1980; dir. Value Line Investment Funds, N.Y.C.; cons. Morgan Guaranty Trust Co., Lazard Freres Asset Mgmt.; pres. Econ. & Communication Services Inc.; cons. Dept. Commerce, 1983, Dept. Def., 1983-84; mem. adv. bd. Marvin and Palmer; mem. Wright Investors' Service Internat. Bd. Econ. and Investment Advisors; bd. dirs. Com. on Present Danger; trustee Intercollegiate Studies Inst., Com. on Developing Am. Capitalism; mem. selection com. Frank E. Seidman Disting. Award in Polit. Economy. Author: Alienation and the Soviet Economy, 1971, Marx's Theory of Exchange, 1973, new edit., 1983, The Supply-Side Revolution: An Insider's Account of Policymaking in Washington, 1984, The Cost of Corporate Capital in the U.S. and Japan, 1985; mem. editorial bd. Modern Age, Intercollegiate Rev.; contbg. editor Harper's Mag. Recipient Meritorious Service award Dept. Treasury, 1982; Am. Philos. Soc. grantee, 1968; named to Chevalier de la Légion d'Honneur, 1987; Nat. Chamber Found. fellow, 1984-85. Mem. Acad. Polit. Sci., Am. Econ. Assn., Mont Pelerin Soc., N.Y. Acad. Scis., World Affairs Council, Beethoven Soc., U.S. C. of C. (taxation com.), Lehrman Inst. Republican. Clubs: International, (Washington). Office: Center for Strategic Internat Studies 1800 K St NW Washington DC 20006

ROBERTS, RICHARD, artist; b. Phila., June 26, 1925; s. Harold Roberts and Lily Herbst; m. Roslyn Cutler, Mar. 1, 1951. Exhbns. include: Mus. Fine Art, Srpingfield, Mass., 1953, Pa. Acad., Phila., 1953, Whitney Mus., N.Y.C., 1954, Balt. Mus., 1955. Recipient Emily Lowe Purchase prize, 1953; Louis Comfort Tiffany Found. fellow, 1954; Butler Inst. Am. Art Purchase prize, 1954; Delgado Mus. Purchase prize, 1955; Ward Ranger Purchase award Nat. Acad. Art, 1978; Ralph Fabri medal Nat. Soc. Painters Casein and Acrylic, 1988. Home: 175 W 12th St New York NY 10011

ROBERTS, SANDRA BROWN, realty company executive; b. Boston, May 26, 1939; d. Frederick Thomas and Christine (Peyton) Brown; m. Joseph Peter Roberts, Aug. 26, 1962 (div. May 1984); children—Christine, Joseph, Paul. B.A., Boston Coll., 1981. Lic. real estate broker, Mass. Owner, mgr. real estate, Wellesley, Mass., 1963—; pres. Riverview Realty, Wellesley, 1970—; comml. realtor, Boston, 1974—; cons. Berkshire Hathaway, New Bedford, Mass., 1983—. Founder, pres., bd. dirs. Friends of Ft. Washington, Inc.; active Friends of Boston Ballet, 1983—. Mem. New Eng. Women in Real Estate, DAR (Boston Tea Party chpt. regent 1983-84, 84-85). Navy League of U.S., New Eng. Hist. Geneal. Soc. Republican. Roman Catholic. Club: College (Boston). Lodge: Order of Crown of Charlemagne (life mem.), Order of Lafayette (bd. dirs.). Home: 52 Kenilworth Rd Wellesley MA 02181 Office: DAR Boston Tea Party Chpt 51 River St Wellesley MA 02181

ROBERTS, THOMAS GEORGE, retired physicist; b. Ft. Smith, Ark., Apr. 27, 1929; s. Thomas Lawrence and Emma Lee (Stanley) R.; m. Alice Anne Harbin, Nov. 14, 1958; children: Lawrence Dewey, Regina Anne; foster child, Marcia Roberts Dale. AA, Armstrong Coll., 1953; BS, U. Ga., 1956, MS, 1957; PhD, N.C. State U., 1967. Research physicist U.S. Army Missile Command, Huntsville, Ala., 1958-85; cons. industry and govt. agys., 1970—. Contbr. articles to profl. jours. Patentee in field. Served to sgt. USAF, 1948-52. Fellow Am. Optical Soc.; mem. Am. Phys. Soc., IEEE, Huntsville Optical Soc. Am. (pres. 1980). Episcopalian. Club: Toastmaster Internat. (pres. 1963). Current work: Laser physics, optics, particle beams and instrumentation; diagnostic devices and techniques development. Subspecialties: Laser physics; Plasma physics. Office: Technoco PO Box 4723 Huntsville AL 35815

ROBERTSHAW, JAMES, lawyer, pilot; b. Greenville, Miss., May 19, 1916; s. Frank Newell and Hannah Mary (Aldridge) R.; m. Sylvia Schively, Apr. 26, 1956; children: Mary Nicholson, Sylvia Yale, Frank Paxton. SB, Miss. State U., 1937; JD, Harvard U., 1940, Vet.'s Cert., Harvard Bus. Sch., 1946; postgrad. Command and Gen. Staff Sch., 1943. Bar: Miss. 1940, U.S. Dist. Ct. (no. dist.) Miss. 1951, U.S. Ct. Appeals (5th cir.) 1954, U.S. Supreme Ct. 1967, U.S. Dist. Ct. (so. dist.) Miss. 1984. Sole practice, Greenville, Miss., 1940, 46-62; ptnr. Robertshaw & Merideth, 1962-84; ptnr. Robertshaw, Terney & Noble, Greenville, 1984—. Chmn. Community and County Devel. Com., Miss. Econ. Council, 1968-70; mem. Miss. Ho. of Reps., 1953-56; chmn. Greenville Airport Commn., 1967-73, Indsl. Found., 1974; mem. com. tech. in the cts., mem. complaint tribunal Miss. Supreme Ct., 1987—. Served to col. U.S. Army, 1941-46. Decorated Legion of Merit, Croix de Guerre (France). Mem. Am. Judicature Soc., Miss. Bar Found. Episcopalian. Clubs: University (Washington), Greenville Golf and Country. Home: PO Box 99 Greenville MS 38702 Office: Robertshaw Terney Noble & Smith 128 S Poplar St Greenville MS 38702

ROBERTSON, ARMAND JAMES, II, lawyer; b. San Diego, Sept. 23, 1937; s. Armand James and Muriel H. R.; m. Marion Sperry, Aug. 11, 1962; children: Armand James, Laura Marie. A.M. in Econs, Stanford U., 1960; LL.B., Harvard U., 1965. Bar: Calif. 1966. Law clk. to Charles M. Merrill, U.S. Ct. Appeals 9th Circuit, 1965-66; asso. firm Howard, Prim, Rice, Nemerovski, Canady & Pollak, San Francisco, 1966-71; partner Howard, Prim, Rice, Nemerovski, Canady & Pollak, 1971-77; dir. Howard, Rice, Nemerovski, Canady, Robertson & Falk (P.C.), San Francisco, 1977—; lectr. antitrust law U. New South Wales, Sydney, Australia, and Monash U., Melbourne. Served to lt. (j.g.) USN, 1960-62. Mem. Am. Law Inst., ABA (antitrust sect.), Phi Beta Kappa. Clubs: Bohemian, Olympic, Commonwealth (San Francisco). Home: 178 Edgewood Ave San Francisco CA 94117 Office: 3 Embarcadero Ctr Suite 700 San Francisco CA 94111

ROBERTSON, CELESTE BERNARDINE, educator; b. Portsmouth, Va., Feb. 27, 1947; d. Eddie and Mildred Virginia (Harris) R.; m. John Kofi Abu, June 12, 1983; 1 child, Nichole Rochelle Robertson. B.A., Norfolk State U., 1971; M.Ed., Tex. So. U., 1973. Personnel mgmt. specialist Dept. Navy, Harrisburg, Pa., 1969-70; vol. Peace Corps, Ivory Coast, W. Africa, 1971-74; coordinator English Lang. Inst., Ivory Coast, 1974-77; internat. devel. specialist AID/Dept. State, Washington, 1979-82, asst. program officer, Niger, W. Africa, 1982-85, dep. program officer, Mali, W. Africa, 1985-87; program analyst Africa Bur. U.S. AID, Washington, 1987-88; publicity officer Internat. Women's Assn. Mali, 1986-87; prof. Tidewater Community Coll. Portsmouth, Va. 1987—. Recipient 10 Yr. Service award AID/Dept. State, 1985. Mem. Nat. Assn. Female Execs., Smithsonian Inst., Nat. Trust for Historic Preservation, Nat. Wildlife Preservation and Trust, Profl. Women of Mali Assn., NAACP. Democrat. Baptist. Avocations: gourmet cooking, reading. Home and Office: 1505 1/2 Lockport St Portsmouth VA 23704

ROBERTSON, DAVID WINFIELD, transportation engineer; b. Winston-Salem, N.C., Sept. 27, 1952; s. Henry Winfield and Ruby (Leftwich) R. B.S. with honors in Civil Enginrg., N.C. State U., 1974, M.S. in Civil Enginrg., 1975. Registered profl. engr. Transp. engr. intern City of Greensboro (N.C.), summers 1972-74; traffic signals engr. City of Raleigh (N.C.), 1974, assoc. traffic engr., 1974-80, traffic engr., 1980-84; hwy. engr. N.C. Dept. Transp., 1984—. traffic engring. cons. Research Engrs., Inc., Research Triangle Park, N.C. Mem. exec. bd. March of Dimes, 1981; West Raleigh coordinator Heart Fund, 1981; bus. coordinator United Fund Raleigh, 1981. Recipient Friendship Force Ambassador to Eng., 1980; Fed. Hwy. Adminstrn. grad. fellow, 1974; Vocat. Rehab. grantee, 1970. Mem. Nat. Soc. Profl. Engrs., ASCE, Inst. Transp. Engrs., Soil Conservation Soc. Am., N.C. Land Use Congress, Inc., Jaycees (dir. 1980-81, 83). Republican. Methodist. Author reports in field. Home: 3309 Mesa Ct Raleigh NC 27607 Office: NC Dept Traffic Engring PO Box 25201 Raleigh NC 27602

ROBERTSON, GORDON ARTHUR, geologist; b. Saskatoon, Sask., Can., July 29, 1934; s. Arthur William and Anne Jean (James) R.; m. Valerie Castle; children: Ross G., Craig J., Leslie A., David S. BS in Geology, U. Okla., 1956. Trainee geophysics Gulf Corp., Calgary, Can., 1956-57, geologist, 1957-59, exploration geologist, 1959-60, 62-63, exploitation geologist, 1960-63; sr. geologist Supertest Petroleum Co., Calgary, 1963-67; chief geologist Santos Ltd., Adelaide, Australia, 1967-70; div. geologist Burmah Oil Co. of Australia, Sydney and Perth, 1970-71; mgr. exploration Perth, 1973-77; mgr. exploration Woodside Petroleum N.L., Melbourne, Australia, 1971-72, asst. gen. mgr., 1972-73; mgr. exploration Melbourne & Vamgas Ltd., 1971-72, gen. mgr., 1972-73; mgr. exploration Burmah Oil Australia, Perth West, 1973-76; cons. petroleum Calgary, 1977; mgr. exploration Gt. No. Oil Co., Calgary, 1977-79; v.p., gen. mgr. Natomas Exploration of Can., Ltd., Calgary, 1979-83, Diamond Shamrock Exploration of Can., Ltd., Calgary, 1979-87; v.p., gen. mgr. Maxus Energy Can., Ltd., Calgary, 1987—, also bd. dirs.; v.p. Maxus Energy Corp., Dallas, 1987; dir. Independent Petroleum Assn. Canada, 1985—. Fundraiser Glenbow Mus., Calgary, 1984-87. Mem. Assn. Profl. Geologists and Geophysicists Alta., Can. Soc. Petroleum Geologists, Am. Assn. Petroleum Geologists, Ind. Petroleum Assn. Can. (bd. dirs.). Clubs: Calgary Petroleum, Bow Valley. Office: Maxus Energy Can Ltd, 1600 250-6th Ave SW, Calgary, AB Canada T2P 3H7

ROBERTSON, IAN CHARLES MACLAY, industrial multinational executive; b. Kirkcaldy, Scotland, Jan. 19, 1938; s. William Kirk Maclay and Catherine Mary (Guthrie) R.; m. Edith Margaret Hendry, Dec. 18, 1965; children—Dugald, Catriona, Seonaid. Ed. Edinburgh U. (Scotland), 1956-59. Chartered acct., Scottish Inst. Mem. staff to mgr. Deloitte Haskins & Sells, London, 1961-70, ptnr., 1970-79; v.p., counsel for internat. corp. practices TBG Holdings nv, Monaco. 1979-83, v.p., controller, 1983-87 ; advisor Brit. Govt., 1973-77; lectr. in field. Author: Companies Act 1976, 1976; Counter-Inflation Controls-Pay and Prices, 1976; Price Controls: 1977 and Beyond, 1977; contbr. articles to profl. jours. Chmn. Young Conservative Assn., Kirkcaldy, 1959-61. Mem. Inst. Chartered Accts. Scotland, Parl. and Law, Research, Audit Pract. Commns. Club: Gresham (London). Office: TBG Management sam, 3 Rue Louis Aureglia, BP 89, Monte Carlo 98007, Monaco

ROBERTSON, IAN HAMILTON, clinical psychologist; b. Glasgow, Scotland, Apr. 26, 1951; s. John McLean and Anne Dempster (Hamilton) R.; m. Fiona O'Doherty, July 13, 1984. BSc in Psychology with honors, U. Glasgow, 1973; M Philosophy in Clin. Psychology, U. London, 1978. Tchr. Govt. Fiji, Lautoka, 1974-75; clin. research psychologist Tayside Health Bd., Dundee, Scotland, 1978-80, sr. clin. psychologist, 1980-82; sr. clin. psychologist Lothian Health Bd., Edinburgh, Scotland, 1982-84, prin. clin. psychologist, 1984—; hon. fellow U. Edinburgh, 1982—; mem. council Alcohol Edn. and Research Council Gt. Britain, 1987—; vis. cons. South Australia Drug and Alcohol Authority, 1985. Co-author: Controlled Drinking, 1981, 2d edit., 1983, Problem Drinking, 1986, Let's Drink to Your Health, 1987; editor: The Misuse of Alcohol, 1985; contbr. articles to profl. jours. Scottish Home and Health Dept. grantee, 1985—. Mem. Brit. Psychol. Soc., Brit. Assn. Behavioral Psychotherapy, Soc. for Research in Rehab. Office: Dept Clin Psychology, Astley Ainslie Hosp, Grange Loan, Edinburgh EH9 2HL, Scotland

ROBERTSON, JAQUELIN TAYLOR, architect, educator; b. Richmond, Va., Mar. 20, 1933; s. Walter Spencer and Mary Dade (Taylor) R.; B.A. cum laude, Yale U., 1955, M.Arch., 1961; postgrad. (Rhodes scholar) Oxford U., 1957; m. Marianna Neese, Sept. 15, 1962. Archtl. designer Sir Leslie Martin, Cambridge, Eng., 1961-62, Edward L. Barnes Assos., N.Y.C., 1963-66; lectr. architecture Yale U., 1964-65, Columbia U., 1965-67; prin. urban designer N.Y.C. Planning Commn., 1967-69; dir. Office Midtown Planning & Devel., N.Y.C., 1969-72; lectr. The New Sch., N.Y.C., 1973; city planning commr., N.Y.C., 1973; vis. faculty Salzburg (Austria) Seminar, 1974; v.p. Arlen Realty Devel., N.Y.C., 1974-75; mng. dir. Llewelyn-Davies Va Shoraka, Tehran, Iran, 1975-77; chmn. Llewelyn-Davies Assos., N.Y.C., 1977-78; prin. Jaquelin Taylor Robertson FAIA, N.Y.C., 1978-80; prin. Design Devel. Resources, N.Y.C., 1980-88, Eisenman-Robertson Architects, N.Y.C., 1980-88; ptnr. Cooper-Robertson, N.Y.C., Charlottesville, Va., 1988— ; dean Sch. Architecture, U. Va., Charlottesville, 1980-88, Commonwealth prof. architecture, 1985—; vis. prof. archtl. design R.I. Sch. Design, Providence, 1979; William Henry Bishop prof. Yale U., 1980. Chmn. policy panel Design Arts Program, Nat. Endowment for Arts, 1979-83; vis. com. Harvard Grad. Sch. Design, 1983—; trustee Inst. Architecture and Urban Studies, N.Y.C., 1984-85; bd. dirs. Parks Council, N.Y.C., 1971-75, Mcpl. Arts Soc., N.Y.C., 1971-75, Archtl. League N.Y., 1972-75, 79-81, Ctr. for Study of Am. Architecture, Columbia U., 1984—; adviser Aga Khan Program for Study of Islamic Art & Architecture, Harvard and MIT, 1983—; trustee Va. Mus. of Fine Arts, 1985—; mem. art and architecture rev. council State of Va., 1982-88. Recipient numerous awards for design. Fellow AIA; mem. Am. Inst. Cert. Planners, Am. Planning Assn. Episcopalian. Clubs: Bullingdon (Oxford); Century, Knickerbocker (N.Y.C.); Pundits, St. Anthony Hall (New Haven); Country of Va. (Richmond); Maidstone (Easthampton, N.Y.). Exhbns. include Inst. Architecture and Urban Studies, N.Y.C., 1975, Archtl. League and Mcpl. Arts Soc., 1969, Mus. Modern Art, N.Y.C., 1967, others. Contbr. articles to profl. jours., mags. Home: Hotel D East Range U Va Charlottesville VA 22903 Office: U Va Sch Architecture Campbell Hall Charlottesville VA 22903 also: 211 E 70th St New York NY 10021

ROBERTSON, JOSEPH EDMOND, grain processing company executive; b. Brownstown, Ind., Feb. 16, 1918; s. Roscoe Melvin and Edith Penina (Shields) R.; m. Virginia Faye Baxter, Nov. 23, 1941; 1 son, Joseph Edmond. BS, Kans. State U., 1940, postgrad., 1940. Cereal chemist Ewing Mill Co., 1940-43, flour milling engr., 1946-50, feed nutritionist, 1951-59; v.p., sec. Robertson Corp., Brownstown, Ind., 1960-80, pres., 1980—. Pres. Jackson County (Ind.) Welfare Bd., 1948-52. mem. Ind. Port Commn., 1986—. Served with USAAF, 1943-45. Mem. Hardwood Plywood Mfrs. Assn. (v.p. affiliate div. 1971-73, 87-88), Am. Assn. Cereal Chemists, Assn. Operative Millers, Am. Legion, Brownstown C. of C. (dir. All Am. city program 1955), Kans. State U. Alumni Assn. (life), Blue Key, Phi Delta Theta, Phi Kappa Phi, Alpha Mu. Presbyterian. Clubs: Country (Seymour, Ind.); Hickory Hills Country (Brownstown, Ind.); Internat. Travelers Century (Los Angeles). Lodge: Elks. Home: Rt 1 Lake and Forest Club Box A Brownstown IN 47220 Office: 200 Front St Brownstown IN 47220

ROBERTSON, LENARD BELL, management consultant; b. Chgo., Apr. 11, 1937; s. Harold Paul and Lee Anna (Bell) Henson; ASE cum laude and ASBA cum laude, Tidewater Community Coll., 1975; BABA cum laude, Upper Iowa U., 1976; MBA, So. Ill. U., 1978; PhD in Mgmt. Am. Western U., 1981; m. Emma Butler; children: Jacqueline Delores, Pamela Renee, Lenard Bell II, Chandra. Commd. pvt. U.S. Marine Corps, 1955, advanced through grades to sgt., 1956; conterintelligence asst., Japan and Jacksonville, N.C., 1955-64; ret., 1964; enlisted in U.S. Air Force, 1964; intelligence analyst, Riverside, Calif., 1964-65, Omaha, 1965-66; bomb damage assessment statistician Def. Intelligence Agy., Pentagon, 1966, programmer, 1966-68; ret., 1968; taskleader Computer Scis. Corp., Arlington, Va., 1968-70, site mgr., Norfolk, Va., 1970-71, sect. mgr., Hampton, Va., 1971-77; head sect. system design and programming ITT, Nutley, N.J., 1977-81, dir., mgmt. info. system Systems-East div. Conrac Corp., West Caldwell, N.J., 1981-86; sr. instr. project mgmt. workshop AT&T Bell Labs., Whippany, N.J., later mgr. project mgmt. data measurements ; pres. Robertson's Mgmt. Assistance Corp., Inc., motivation and fin. cons., 1981—. Pres. Holland Elementary Sch. PTA, Va. Beach, 1971; legal rep. Virginia Beach City (Va.) PTA, 1971-72; assoc. pastor Emmanuel Bapt. Ch., Chgo. Mem. Tidewater Area Bus. League, IEEE, Nat. Urban League. Republican. Author articles on computer industry personnel selection and tng., on computer communication systems design and architecture on structured programming techniques. Home: PO Box 1303 South Holland IL 60473

ROBERTSON, LESLIE EARL, structural engineer; b. Los Angeles, Feb. 12, 1928; s. Garnett Roy and Tina (Grantham) R.; m. Saw-Teen See, Aug. 11, 1982; children: Jeanne, Christopher Alan, Sharon Miyuki, Karla Mei. BS, U. Calif., Berkeley, 1952; DSc (hon.), Rensselaer Polytech. Inst., 1986, U. Western Ontario, 1988. Structural engr. Kaiser Engrs., Oakland, Calif., 1952-54, John A. Blume, San Francisco, 1954-57, Raymond Internat. Co., N.Y.C., 1957-58; mng. ptnr. Skilling, Helle, Christiansen, Robertson, N.Y.C., Seattle and Anchorage, 1958-82; chmn. Robertson, Fowler & Assocs., P.C., N.Y.C., 1982-85, Leslie E. Robertson Assocs., structural engrs., 1986—; chmn. Council on Tall Bldgs. and Urban Habitat; , mem. Com. on Natural Disasters; commr. NRC; dir. Wind Engring. Research Council, lectr. Rensselaer Poly. Inst., 1984, Johns Hopkins U., 1985, Nat. Bur. Standards, 1986, Cornell U., Hong Kong U., 1986. Author papers in field. Mem. Engring. Coll. Council Cornell U. Served with USNR, 1944-46. Fellow ASCE (Raymond C. Reese Research prize 1974); mem. Nat. Acad. Engring. Home: 45 E 89th St New York NY 10128 Office: 211 E 46th St New York NY 10017

ROBERTSON, RUTHERFORD NESS, chemical biologist; b. Melbourne, Australia, Sept. 29, 1913; s. Joshua and Josephine (Hogan) R.; B.Sc., U. Sydney, 1934, D.Sc., 1961; Ph.D., U. Cambridge, 1939, Sc.D. (hon.), 1970; D.Sc. (hon.), U. Tasmania, 1965, Monash U., 1971, Australian Nat. U., 1979; m. Mary Helen Bruce Rogerson, Sept. 9, 1937; 1 son, Robert James. Linnean Macleay fellow Sydney (Australia) U., 1935-36, lectr., sr. lectr., 1939-46, hon. visitor Sch. Biol. Scis., 1978-87; scholar Royal Exhbn. of 1851, Cambridge (Eng.) U., 1936-39; research officer, later chief research officer Div. Food Preservation and Transport, Commonwealth Sci. and Indsl. Research Orgn., 1946-59, mem. exec., 1959-62; prof. botany Adelaide (Australia) U., 1962-69; master Univ. House, Australian Nat. U., Canberra, 1969-72, dir. Research Sch. Biol. Scis., 1973-78, pro-chancellor, 1984-86; vis. prof. UCLA, 1958-59; Kearney lectr. U. Calif., Berkeley, 1959; found. chmn. Australian Research Grants Com., 1965-69; dep. chmn. Australian Sci. and Tech. Council, 1977-81; mem. Australia-China Council, 1979-81; pres. 13th Internat. Bot. Congress, 1981. Decorated companion Order of St. Michael and St. George; knight bachelor; companion Order of Australia; recipient Clarke Meml. medal Royal Soc. New South Wales, 1954, Farrar Meml. medal, 1963, Australian and New Zealand Assn. Advancement of Sci. medal,

1968, Mueller medal, 1970, Burnet medal, 1975. Fellow Australian Acad. Sci. (pres. 1970-74), Royal Soc. London, St. John's Coll. Cambridge (hon.), Royal Soc. Edinburgh (hon.); fgn. assoc. mem. U.S. Nat. Acad. Scis.; mem. Am. Philos. Soc. (fgn.), Am. Soc. Plant Physiologists (corr.), Royal Soc. N.Z. (hon.), Am. Acad. Arts and Scis. (hon. fgn.). Club: Union (Sydney). Author: (with G.E. Briggs, A.B. Hope) Electrolytes in Plant Cells, 1961; Protons, Electrons, Phosphorylation and Active Transport, 1968; The Lively Membranes 1983. Contbr. many articles to sci. jours. Home: Muirhead PO Box 9, Binalong, New South Wales 2584, Australia other: care Royal Soc, 6 Carlton House Terr, London SW1Y 5AG, England

ROBERTSON, SAMUEL HARRY, III, transportation safety research engineer, educator; b. Phoenix, Oct. 2, 1934; s. Samuel Harry and Doris Byrle (Duffield) R.; m. Nancy Jean Bradford, Aug. 20, 1954; children: David Lyle, Pamela Louise. BS, Ariz. State U., 1956; D in Aviation Tech. (hon.), Embry-Riddle Aero. U., 1972. Registered profl. engr. Chief hazards div. Aviation Safety Engring. and Research, Phoenix, 1960-70; pres. Robertson Research Engrs., 1960-70; research prof., dir. Safety Ctr. Coll. Engring. and Applied Scis., Ariz State U., Tempe, 1970-79; pres. Robertson Research Inc., 1970—, Robertson Aviation Inc., 1977—, Internat. Ctr. for Safety Edn., 1982—; pres., chief exec. officer Robertson Research Group, Inc., Tempe, 1987—; cons. design and accident investigation of airplanes, 1961—; instr. Inst. Aerospace Safety, U. So. Calif., 1962-70, Armed Forces Inst. Pathology, 1970—, Dept. Transp. Safety Inst., 1970—; pres. Flying R Land & Cattle Co., 1976—. Contbr. 60 articles to profl. jours. and pubs.; patentee applying plastic to paper, fuel system safety check valves, crash resitant fuel system, safety aircraft seats; holder FAA STC's various fuel systems, fuel system components; designer, developer, mfr. crash resistant fuel systems for airplanes, helicopters, championship racing cars. Served as pilot USAF, 1956-60, Ariz. Army NG 1960-61, 70-74, Ariz. Air NG, 1961-69. Recipient Contbns. Automotive Racing Safety award CNA, 1957, Adm. Luis DeFlorez Internat. Flying Safety award, 1969, Cert. Commendation Nat. Safety Council, 1969, Gen. W. Spruance award for safety edn., SAFE Soc., 1982. Mem. Internat. Soc. Air Safety Investigators (Jerome Lederer internat. award 1981), Aerospace Med. Assn., AIAA, AMA, Soc. Automotive Engrs., Am. Helicopter Soc., Nat. Fire Protection Assn., Aircraft Owners and Pilots Assn., U.S. Automobile Club (mem. tech. com.). Office: 1024 E Vista del Cerro Tempe AZ 85281

ROBERTSON, WILLIAM HOWARD, physician, educator; b. Nashville, July 1, 1921; s. William Perry and Mary (Henderson) R.; m. Jennie May Webb, Oct. 29, 1940; children: Melissa Turpin, Jennifer Webb, William Webb. Student, Birmingham So. Coll., 1939-41; BS, U. Ala., 1947; MD, Med. Coll. Ala., 1951. Diplomate Am. Bd. Ob-Gyn. Intern U. Hosp., Birmingham, Ala., 1951-52, resident in ob-gyn, 1953-56; practice medicine specializing in ob-gyn, Birmingham, 1956—; assoc. clin. prof. Med. Coll. Ala., 1975—; lectr., Broadbeach, Australia. Author: The History of Contraception, 1987; med. writer Miles Pharms., West Haven, Conn.; contbr. articles to profl. jours. Chmn. United Way, Birmingham, 1977—, Arts Hall of Fame, Birmingham; chmn. bd. dirs. Birmingham Civic Ballet. Served with U.S. Army, 1942-46. Recipient medal Bayer AG Grer. Fellow ACS, Internat. Soc. Study of Vaginal Diseases; mem. AMA, So. Med. Assn., Royal Soc. Medicine, Pan Am. Med. Assn., Am. Fertility Soc., Birmingham Ob-Gyn Soc., Ala. Ob-Gyn Soc., Birmingham Surg. Soc., Internat. Soc. for Vulva Disease (chmn. vaginitis com.), AAAS, Internat. Soc. Reproductive Medicine (mem. internat. research bd.), N.Y. Acad. Sci., Nat. Arts Club, Alpha Omega Alpha. Office: 2660 10th Ave S Birmingham AL 35205

ROBEY, KATHLEEN MORAN (MRS. RALPH WEST ROBEY), club woman; b. Boston, Aug. 9, 1909; d. John Joseph and Katherine (Berrigan) Moran; B.A., Trinity Coll., Washington, 1933; m. Ralph West Robey, Jan. 28, 1941. Actress appearing in Pride and Prejudice, Broadway, 1935, Tomorrow is a Holiday, road co., 1935, Death Takes a Holiday, road co., 1936, Left Turn, Broadway, 1936, Come Home to Roost, Boston, 1936; pub. relations N.Y. Fashion Industry, N.Y.C., 1938-43. Mem. Florence Crittenton Home and Hosp., Women's Aux. Salvation Army, Gray Lady, ARC; mem. Seton Guild St. Ann's Infant Home. Mem. Christ Child Soc., Fedn. Republican Women of D.C. English-Speaking Union. Republican. Roman Catholic. Clubs: City Tavern, Cosmos (Washington), Nat. Woman's Republican. Home: 4000 Cathedral Ave NW Washington DC 20016

ROBICHAUD, PHYLLIS IVY ISABEL, artist, educator; b. Jamaica, West Indies, May 16, 1915; came to U.S., 1969, naturalized, 1977; d. Peter C. and Rose Matilda (Rickman) Burnett; grad. Tutorial Coll., 1933, Kingston, Jamaica, Munro Coll., St. Elizabeth, Jamaica, 1946; student Central Tech. Sch., Toronto, Ont., Can., 1960-63, Anderson Coll., Can., 1968-69; m. Roger Robichaud, July 22, 1961; children by previous marriage—George Wilmot Graham, William Henry Heron Graham, Mary Elizabeth Graham Watson, Peter Robert Burnett Graham. Sec. to supr. of Agr., St. Elizabeth, 1940-50; loans officer and cashier Confederation Life Assn., Kingston, 1950-53; tchr. art Jamaica Welfare Ltd., 1963; tchr. art recreation dept. New Port Richey, Fla., 1969-77; tchr. art Pasco Hernando Community Coll., New Port Richey, 1977—; demonstrator various organizations including West Pasco Art Guild, New Port Richey, Ace Artists, New Port Richey; propr., mgr. Band Box Dress Shop, Kingston, Jamaica, 1954-57; numerous one-woman shows of paintings including various banks, libraries, Kingston, 1963-64, 67, Toronto, 1968, New Port Richey, 1969, 70, 73, 76, Tampa, Fla., 1974, 75, 76, Omaha Cattle Company restaurant, Clearwater Fla., 1982; numerous group shows, latest being: Sweden House, Tampa, 1977-78, Chasco Fiesta, New Port Richey, 1977, Magnolia Valley Golf and Country Club, New Port Richey, 1978, W. Pasco Art Guild, New Port Richey, 1978, 79, Indian Rocks Beach, 1985, other cities in Fla.; executed murals, New Port Richey and Kingston; represented in permanent collections: New Port Richey C. of C., Magnolia Valley Golf and Country Club, also pvt. collections. Patron, St. Alban's 4H Club, 1942; sec. Sunday sch. Ch. of Eng., Kingston, 1937-39. Recipient award T. Eaton Co. of Can., 1961, cert. of merit, Mayor of New Port Richey, 1976, appreciation award New Port Richey Recreation Dept., 1977; award Fla. Heart Fund. Mem. Nat. League Am. Pen Women (v.p. Tampa br. 1978-80, dir. 1969—), West Pasco Art Guild (Blue ribbons 1978, 79), Fla. Fine Arts Guild. Republican. Roman Catholic. Address: 7032 Lenox Dr New Port Richey FL 34653

ROBINS, GERALD BURNS, educator; b. Salem, Ark., Jan. 24, 1924; s. Gerald Alfred and Lucille (Burns) R.; m. Fay Ann Kennan, Sept. 1, 1946; children: Gerald Kennan, James Dow. B.S. in Edn. cum laude, U. Ark., 1948, M.S., 1950; Ed.D., U. Ga., 1954. Asst. prof., chmn. dept. distbv. edn., chmn. dept. bus. edn. U. Ga., 1950-57, prof. higher edn., 1970-73; pres. Augusta (Ga.) Coll., 1957-70, Tex. A&I U., Kingsville, 1973-77; sr. prof. Tex. A&I U., 1977—; owner RobArt Sculpture; cons. Air Force ROTC, 1954; chmn. edn. com. Ga.-S.C. Nuclear Council, 1969; acad. dean CAP Cadet Officers Sch., 1970-71. Author: Understanding the College Budget, 1973, Campus, 1980, 1975. Trustee Lawton B. Evans Ednl. Fund, Barrett Sch. Nursing, Augusta Prep. Sch.; bd. dirs., v.p. Tex. A & I Fed. Credit Union; mem. Friends of John E. Conner Mus. Served with USAAF, 1943-46; lt. col. USAF Res. (ret.). Decorated Air medal; Recipient Disting. Alumnus award U. Ark., 1974; Donaghey fellow, 1943; Kellogg fellow, 1953-54; Paul Harris fellow. Mem. Am. Assn. State Colls. and Univs. (com. on studies), Assn. Tex. Colls. and Univs. (commn. on acad. affairs), Internat. Assn. U. Pres.'s, Internat. Council Edn. for Teaching, Nat. Collegiate Athletic Assn. (pres. Lone Star Conf.), Kleberg (Tex.) Hist. Commn. (chmn.), So. Tex. Hist. Soc. (dir.), Ret. Officers Assn. (life, pres.), Navy League, Res. Officers Assn. (life), Ga. Ret. Tchrs. Assn. (life), Kappa Sigma (alumni advisor), Kappa Delta Pi, Phi Kappa Phi, Omicron Delta Kappa, Psi Chi, Phi Delta Kappa (emeritus mem., charter chpt. pres.). Methodist. Clubs: Masons (32 deg.), Rotary (club pres., dist. gov., scholarship trustee, instr. assembly 1985), Pinnacle, Kingsville Country. Home: 515 University Blvd Kingsville TX 78363

ROBINSON, ADELBERT CARL, lawyer, justice; b. Shawnee, Okla., Dec. 13, 1926; s. William H. and Mayme (Forston) R.; m. Marilyn Ruth Stubbs, Dec. 28, 1963 (div.); children: William, James, Schuyler, Donald, David, Nancy, Lauri. Student Okla. Baptist U., 1944-47; JD, Okla. U., 1950. Bar: Okla. 1950. Practice, Muskogee, Okla., 1956—; with legal dept. Phillips Petroleum Co., 1950-51; adjuster U.S. Fidelity & Guaranty Co., 1951-54, atty., adjuster-in-charge, 1954-56; ptnr. Fite & Robinson, 1956-62, Fite, Robinson & Summers, 1963-70, Robinson & Summers, 1970-72, Robinson, Summers & Locke, 1972-76, Robinson, Locke & Gage, 1976-80, Robinson, Locke, Gage & Fite, 1980-83, Robinson, Locke, Gage, Fite & Williams, Muskogee, 1983—; police judge, 1963-64; mcpl. judge, 1964-70; prin. justice Temp. Div. 36 Okla. Ct. Appeals, 1981—; pres., dir. Wall St. Bldg Corp., 1969-78, Three Forks Devel. Corp., 1968-77, Rolo Leasing, Inc., 1971—, Suroya II, Inc., 1977—; sec., dir. Weddles Food Stores, Muskogee Tom's Inc., Blue Ridge Corp., Harborcliff Corp.; bd. dirs. First Bancshares of Muskogee, Inc., First of Muskogee Corp., First City Bank, Tulsa; adv. dir. First Nat. Bank & Trust Co. of Muskogee; mng. ptnr. RLG Ritz, 1980—; ptnr. First City Real Estate Partnership, 1985—. Chmn. Muskogee County (Okla.) Law Day, 1963; chmn. Muskogee Area Redevel. Authority, 1963; chmn. Muskogee County chpt. Am. Cancer Soc., 1956; pres. bd. dirs. Muskogee Community Council; bd. dirs. United Way of Muskogee, Inc., 1980—, v.p., 1982, pres. 1983; bd. dirs. Muskogee Community Concert Assn., Muskogee Tourist Info. Bur., 1964-68; bd. dirs., gen. counsel United Cerebral Palsy Eastern Okla., 1964-68; trustee Connors Devel. Found., Connors Coll., 1981—, chmn., 1987—. Served with if. AUS, 1945-46. Mem. ABA, Okla. Bar Assn. (chmn. uniform laws com. 1970-72, chmn. profl. coop. com. 1965-69, past regional chmn. grievance com.), Muskogee County Bar Assn. (pres. 1971, mem. exec. council 1971-74), Okla. Assn. Def. Counsel (dir.), Okla. Assn. Mcpl. Judges (dir.), Muskogee C. of C., Delta Theta Phi. Methodist. Club: Rotary (pres. 1971-72). Home: 2800 Robin Ln Muskogee OK 74403 Office: 530 Court St PO Box 87 Muskogee OK 74401

ROBINSON, ALEXANDER JACOB, clinical psychologist; b. St. John, Kans., Nov. 7, 1920; s. Oscar Frank and Lydia May (Beitler) R.; m. Elsie Louise Riggs, July 29, 1942; children: Madelyn K., Alicia A., David J., Charles A., Paul S., Marietta J., Stephen N. BA in Psychology, Ft. Hays (Kans.) State U., 1942, MS in Clin. Psychology, 1942; postgrad., U. Ill., 1942-44. Cert. psychologist, sch. psychologist. Chief psychologist Larned (Kans.) State Hosp., 1948-53, with employee selection, outpatient services, 1953-55; sch. psychologist County Schs., Modesto, Calif., 1955-61, Pratt (Kans.) Jr. Coll., 1961-66; fed. program developer Better Edn. Services Today, Pratt, 1966-70; dir. spl. edn., researcher Stafford County Schs., St. John, 1970-81, ret., 1981; writer, asst. dir. Best Exemplary Federally Funded Program on Spl. Edn., Pratt, 1966-70; fed. grantee, researcher, writer, study dir. Edn. for the High-Performance Child, St. John, 1970—; supr. research Ft. Hays State U., Kans., 1946. Minister, Ch. of Jesus Christ. Served to 2d lt. U.S. Army, 1944-46, PTO. Lodge: Lions (program chmn. St. John 1974-76). Home: Rt 1 Box 121A Saint John KS 67576

ROBINSON, ALLYN PRESTON, JR., emeritus college president, lecturer; b. Center Moriches, N.Y., Mar. 24, 1909; s. Allyn Preston and Madeline Joy (Penny) R.; m. Elizabeth Schenck, Sept. 15, 1934; children: Sarah Elizabeth Robinson Munson, Allyn Preston. BA, Columbia U., 1931; M in Divinity, Union Theol. Sem., 1933; HHD, Wilberforce U., 1956; DHL, Dowling Coll., 1977; LittD, Adelphi U., 1977. Ordained to ministry, Congregational Ch., 1933. Minister Puritan Congl. Ch., Wilkes-Barre, Pa., 1933-38, United Ch., Raleigh, N.C., 1938-46; instr. English N.C. State Coll., 1944-46; dir. N.C. region NCCJ, 1946-49, dir. Greater N.Y. area, 1956-65, dir. com. on religious orgn., 1949-56; dean Adelphi Suffolk Coll., Oakdale, N.Y., 1965-68; pres. Dowling Coll., Oakdale, N.Y., 1968-77, pres. emeritus, 1977—; cons. police tng. programs, labor mgmt. Author: Our Moral and Religious Resources, 1954, And Crown Thy Good, 1955, American Catholics: A Protestant Jewish View, 1959, Roots of Anti-Semitism in American Life, 1960, When Christmas Brings Conflict, 1962. Chmn. Islip Housing Authority, 1971-77; exec. council Boy Scouts Am., 1965-77; sec. L.I. Regional Adv. Council on Higher Edn.; trustee nat. bd. NCCJ; bd. dirs. WAKE, ACLU, Lisle Fellowship. Recipient Edn. award NCCJ, Gov. of L.I. award L.I. Pub. Relations Assn., L.I. Disting. Leadership award, cert. spl. achievement HUD, citation Town of Islip, citation Suffolk County, award Suffolk Human Rights Commn., Sr. Citizens Day award, 1984. Clubs: Lions (hon. pres.); Princeton (N.Y.C.), N.C. State U. Home: 328 Springmoor Dr Raleigh NC 27615

ROBINSON, ARTHUR NAPOLEON RAYMOND, prime minister, minister of finance and the economy; b. Trinidad and Tobago, Dec. 16, 1926; s. James and Isabella R.; married; 2 children. Student, Castara Meth. Sch., 1931-38, Bishop's High Sch., 1938-45; LLB, London U., 1949; honors, St. John's Coll., Oxford, U.K. Acting 2d class clk. Magistracy, Tobago, Trinidad, 1946, St. George West, Trinidad, 1946; 2d class clk. Social Services Dept., 1947; registrar Gen. Dept., 1951; with Sir Courtenay Hannays, barrister, Port of Spain, Scarborough, Trinidad and Tobago, 1955; treas. Peoples Nat. Movement, Trinidad, 1956-1959; mem. Fed. Parliament Trinidad, 1956; 1st minister of fin. Trinidad and Tobago, 1961-67; dep. polit. leader People's Nat. Movement, Trinidad and Tobago, 1966, minister of external affairs, 1967-70; leader Action Group of Dedicated Citizens (later Action Com. of Dedicated Citizens and Dem. Action Congress), Trinidad and Tobago, 1970-1976; mem. of opposition Tobago parliament, Trinidad and Tobago, 1976-1981; chmn. Tobago House of Assembly, Trinidad and Tobago, 1981-85; pollt. leader Nat. Alliance for Reconstruction, Trinidad and Tobago, 1985; prime minister, minister of fin. Port of Spain, Trinidad and Tobago, 1988—; cons. to UN on Internat. criminal law and human rights. Author: The Mechanics of Independence, 1971; contbr. articles to profl. jours. and article on Trinidad and Tobago to Encyclopedia Brittanica, 1971 edit. Office: Office of Prime Minister, Port of Spain Trinidad and Tobago *

ROBINSON, CHARLES BROOK, JR., management consultant; b. Meridian, Miss., Jan. 20, 1927; s. Charles Brook Sr. and Rubye (Ford) R.; m. Janet Cutter, Mar. 21, 1959; children: Christopher Brook, Lisa Barr. BS in Indsl. Engring., Ga. Inst. Tech., 1948; student, Sorbonne U., Paris, 1949-50. Mgr. Steel Heddle Mfg. Co., Greenville, S.C., 1950-56; assoc. McKinsey & Co., Inc., Washington, 1956-62; prin. McKinsey & Co., Inc., Amsterdam, The Netherlands, 1962-66; dir. McKinsey & Co., Inc., London, 1966-74, Cons. Ptnrs., Inc., London, 1974-77; mng. v.p. Booz, Allen & Hamilton, Inc., London, 1978-82; mng. dir. Robinson & Assocs., Inc., London, 1982—. Served with USAF, 1944-46. Presbyterian. Clubs: Reform, St. George's Tennis (London). Office: Robinson & Assocs Inc, 87 Jermyn St, London SW1 Y6JD, England

ROBINSON, DAVID HOWARD, lawyer; b. Hampton, Va., Nov. 24, 1948; s. Bernard Harris and Phyllis (Canter) R.; m. Nina Jane Briscoe, Aug. 20, 1979. B.A., Calif. State U., Northridge, 1970; J.D., Cabrillo Pacific U., 1975. Bar admittee: Calif., 1977, U.S. Dist Ct. (so. dist.) Calif., 1977, U.S. Ct. Claims, 1979, U.S. Supreme Ct., 1980. adminstr. Cabrillo Pacific U. Coll. Law, 1977; assoc. Gerald D. Egan, San Bernardino, Calif., 1977-78, Duke & Gerstel, San Diego, 1978-80, Rand, Day & Ziman, San Diego, 1980-81; sole practice, San Diego, 1981-88; ptnr. Robinson and Rubin, San Diego, 1988—. Mem. San Diego County Bar Assn., San Diego Trial Lawyers Assn.

ROBINSON, FRANCIS EDWIN, state legislator; b. Markesan, Wis., Dec. 24, 1909; s. Earl Paul and Sibyl (Fritz) R.; m. Elizabeth Walton, June 18, 1961; 1 child by previous marriage, James Francis. B.A., U. N.H., 1931, M.A., 1933. Exec. sec. N.H. Farm Bur., Concord, 1934-40; regional rep. U.S. Dept. Agr., Upper Darby, Pa., 1940-41; regional dir. market reports U.S. War Food Adminstrn., N.Y.C., 1942-44; asst. to pres., dir. publ info. U. N.H., Durham, 1944-52; staff mem. New Eng. Council, Boston, 1952-61; exec. sec. N.H. Assn. Savs. Banks, Concord, N.H., 1961-73; pres. Durham Trust Co., 1973-76; ret. 1977; dir. Mathes Assocs., Manchester, N.H., 1973-75, Fin. Life Ins. Co., 1970-76; pres. Putnam Agrl. Found., Concord, 1960-88; mem. N.H. Ho. of Reps., 1979-80, 83—, floor leader, 1985. Moderator, Town of Durham, 1962-72; trustee Berwick Acad., Maine, 1973-79, pres., 1978-79, trustee U. N.H., Durham, 1974-78, pres. U. N.H. Pres. Council, 1987—, Wentworth Douglass Hosp., Dover, 1982-88, vice chmn., 1984-86, chmn. 1986—; mem. N.H. Constl. Conv., 1974—; chmn. Health Circle Inc., 1985-88. Recipient Alumni Meritorious award U. N.H., 1982, Trustee Recognition award Berwick Acad., 1979, others. Republican. Congregationalist. Lodge: Rotary. Avocations: sailing; photography; travel. Home: Durham Point Rd RFD 2 Durham NH 03824

ROBINSON, GILBERT DE BEAUREGARD, mathematics educator, researcher; b. Toronto, Ont., Can., June 3, 1906; s. Percy James and Esther Toutant (de Beauregard) R.; m. Joan Loudon Howard, Sept. 1, 1936 (dec. Nov. 1982); children—Gilbert John, Nancy Alice Robinson Hill. B.A., U. Toronto, 1927; Ph.D., Cambridge U., Eng., 1931. With Nat. Research Council Can., Ottawa, 1941-45; prof. math U. Toronto, v.p. research, 1965-71, adminstr. Inst. Environment, 1971-72, researcher Coll. Edn., 1972-74; vis. prof. Mich. State U., 1953, Osaka, Japan and Melbourne, Australia, 1958, Vancouver, B.C., 1963, Christchurch, N.Z., 1968. Author: Representation Theory of the Symmetric Group, 1961, History of Mathematics Department of University of Toronto, 1979; (biography) P. J. Robinson, 1981; Sermons at Go Home Bay, 1983, Recollections of Gilbert de Beauregard Robinson; also 5 biographies, numerous articles. Pres. Univ. Settlement, Toronto, 1948-68. Decorated mem. Order Brit. Empire; recipient Centennial medal Govt. of Can., 1967, 25th Anniversary medal, 1977; award City of Toronto, 1985. Fellow Royal Soc. Can. (pres. sect. III 1960-62, prodn. mgr. Math. Reports 1979—); mem. Can. Math. Soc. (mng. editor jour. 1949-77, hon. mng. editor 1977—, pres. 1953-57), Am. Math. Soc. (council 1959-61), Can. Soc. History of Math. (pres. 1979-81), Univ. Research Assn. (regional trustee 1970-73), Math. Assn. Am. Liberal. Mem United Ch. Can. Clubs: Madawaska (pres. 1947-53); Arts and Letters, Faculty (pres. 1960-62) (Toronto). Home: 877 Yonge St, Apt 305, Toronto, ON Canada M4W3M2 Office: U Toronto, Room 185, Univ Coll, Toronto, ON Canada M5S 1A1

ROBINSON, IRWIN JAY, lawyer; b. Bay City, Mich., Oct. 8, 1928; s. Robert R. and Anne (Kaplan) R.; m. Janet Binder, July 7, 1957; children: Elizabeth Binder Robinson Schubiner, Jonathan Meyer, Eve Kimberly. AB, U. Mich., 1950; JD, Columbia U., 1953. Bar: N.Y. 1956. Assoc. Breed Abbott & Morgan, N.Y.C., 1955-58; asst. to ptnrs. Dreyfus & Co., N.Y.C., 1958-59; assoc. Greenbaum Wolff & Ernst, N.Y.C., 1959-65; ptnr. Greenbaum Wolff & Ernst, 1966-76; sr. ptnr. Rosenman & Colin, N.Y.C., 1976—; bd. dirs. Bernard Chaus, Inc., N.Y.C.; treas. Saarsteel, Inc., Whitestone, N.Y., 1970—; sec. Takara Toy Corp., N.Y.C., 1983—. Bd. dirs. Henry St. Settlement, N.Y.C., 1960-85, Nat. Jewish Welfare Bd., N.Y.C., 1967—, Philippine-Am. C. of C., 1970—, Am.-Asean Trade Council, Inc., N.Y.C., 1978—, Heart Research Found., 1988—. Served as sgt. U.S. Army, 1953-55. Mem. ABA, N.Y. State Bar Assn., Assn. Bar City N.Y., Internat. Bar Assn. Republican. Jewish. Clubs: Sunningdale Country (Scarsdale, N.Y.); Rockefeller Ctr. (N.Y.C.). Home: 4622 Grosvenor Ave Riverdale NY 10471 Office: Rosenman & Colin 575 Madison Ave New York NY 10022

ROBINSON, JACK F(AY), clergyman; b. Wilmington, Mass., Mar. 7, 1914; s. Thomas P. and Ethel Lincoln (Fay) R.; A.B., Mont. State U., 1936; D.B., Crozer Theol. Sem., 1939; A.M., U. Chgo., 1949, postgrad., 1950-52; m. Eleanor Jean Smith, Sept. 1, 1937 (dec. 1966); 1 dau., Alice Virginia Dungey; m. Lois Henze, July 16, 1968. Ordained to ministry Baptist Church, 1939; minister Bethany Ch., American Falls, Idaho, 1939-41, 1st Ch., Council Grove, Kans., 1944-49; ordained (transfer) to ministry Congregational Ch., 1945; minister United Ch., Chebanse, Ill., 1949-52, 1st Ch., Argo, Ill., 1954-58, Congl. Ch., St. Charles, Ill., 1958-64; assoc. minister Plymouth Congregational Ch., Lansing, Mich., 1964-66; tchr. Chgo. Pub. Schs., 1966-68; minister Waveland Ave. Congl. Ch., Chgo., 1967-79, interim pastor Chgo. Met. Assn., 1979—, First Congl. Ch., Des Plaines, Ill., 1979, Bethany Congl. Ch., Chgo., 1980, Eden United Ch. of Christ, Chgo., 1983-84, St. Nicolai Ch., Chgo., 1984, Grace United Ch. of Christ, Chgo., 1985-86, Christ Ch. of Chgo., 1987—, First Congl., Evanston, Ill., 1987-88; hist. cons. Bell & Howell Co., Chgo., 1981-82. Assoc. Hyde Park dept. Chgo. YMCA, 1942-44. U. Chgo. Library 1952-54; chmn. com. evangelism Kans. Congl. Christian Conf., 1947-48; city chmn. Layman's Missionary Movement, 1946-51; trustee Congl. and Christian Conf. Ill., v.p., 1963-64; mem. exec. council Chgo. Met. Assn. United Ch. of Christ, 1968-70, sec. ch. and ministry com., 1982—; mem. gen. bd. Ch. Fedn. Greater Chgo., 1969-71; mem. Library Bd. Council Grove, 1945-49; city chmn. NCCJ, 1945-49; dean Northside Mission Council United Ch. of Christ, 1975-77, sec. personnel com. Ill. Conf. United Ch. of Christ, 1986—. Mem. Am. Soc. Ch. History, Am. Acad. Polit. Sci., Am. Hist. Assn., C. of C. (past dir.), Internat. Platform Assn. Author: The Growth of the Bible, 1969; From A Mission to a Church, 1976; Bell & Howell Company: A 75 Year History, 1982, (co-author) Harza: 65 Years, 1986. Home: 2614 Lincolnwood Dr Evanston IL 60201 Office: PO Box 4578 Chicago IL 60680

ROBINSON, J(AMES) BRADFORD, freelance writer, musicologist; b. Sacramento, Sept. 16, 1947; arrived in Fed. Republic Germany, 1975; s. James William Robinson and June (Viner) Goman; m. Judith Dale McBeath, Apr. 15, 1977; children: Melanie, Angela, Tilman. AB cum laude, Harvard U., 1969; MA, U. Calif., Berkeley, 1972. Area editor Grove's Dictionary Music, London, 1972-76; freelance writer various publishers and broadcasting systems, Munich and Berlin, 1976—; prin. adviser Grove Dictionary of Am. Music, N.Y.C., 1983-85. Translator: C. Dahlhaus: Foundations of Music History, 1988; contbr. articles to profl. jours. Home: Ferd Kobell Str 64, Munich-Haar Federal Republic of Germany

ROBINSON, JAMES DIXON, III, corporate executive; b. Atlanta, Nov. 19, 1935; s. James Dixon Jr. and Josephine (Crawford) R.; m. Bettye Bradley (div.); children: Emily E. Robinson-Cook, James Dixon IV; m. Linda Gosden, July 27, 1984. BS, Ga. Inst. Tech., 1957; MBA, Harvard U., 1961; LHD (hon.), Spelman Coll., 1982; LLD (hon.), Adelphi U., 1982. Officer various depts. Morgan Guaranty Trust Co. of N.Y., N.Y.C., 1961-66, asst. v.p., staff asst. to chmn. bd. and pres., 1967-68; gen. partner corp. fin. dept. White, Weld & Co., 1968-70; exec. v.p. Am. Express Co., N.Y.C., 1970-75, pres., 1975-77, bd. dirs., 1975—, chmn. bd. dirs., chief exec. officer, 1977—; pres., chief exec. officer Am. Express Internat. Banking Corp., 1971-73; dir. Bristol-Myers Co., Coca Cola Co., Fireman's Fund Ins. Cos.; mem. adv. council on Japan-U.S. Econ. Relations; mem. U.S. sect. European Community-U.S. Businessmen's Council; bd. dirs. Econ. Devel. Council N.Y.C., Inc., Shearson Lehman Hutton Holdings, Inc. Chmn. Meml. Hosp. for Cancer and Allied Diseases; vice chmn. bd. overseers, bd. mgrs. Meml. Sloan Kettering Cancer Ctr.; mem. council Rockefeller U.; chmn. bd. govs. United Way Am.; chmn. N.Y. State Savs. Bond Co., 1980-81. Served to lt. USNR, 1957-59. Mem. Bus. Roundtable, N.Y. C. of C. and Industry (dir.), Bus. Council (vice chmn.), Council Fgn. Relations. Clubs: Economic (N.Y.C.); Pilgrims of U.S. Office: Am Express Co 200 Vesey St New York NY 10285-5100

ROBINSON, JOHN CHARLES, horticulturist; b. Widnes, Lancashire, Eng., Apr. 20, 1943; s. Basil Charles Hardy Robinson and Elsie (Millar) Wingrove; m. Jennifer Elizabeth Stacey, Nov. 14, 1981; children: Paul, Mark, Kate. BS in Agr. with honors, U. London, Harare, Zimbabwe, 1964; PhD in Horticulture, U. London, 1974. Research horticulturist Dept. Agr., Chiredzi, Zimbabwe, 1966-70; officer in charge Horticultural Research Ctr. Dept. Agr., Marondera, Zimbabwe, 1975-76, head Horticultural Research Inst., 1976-79; sr. agrl. researcher Dept. Agr., Nelspruit, Republic of South Africa, 1980-86, specialist scientist Citrus and Subtropical Fruit Research Inst., 1986—; external examiner dept. horticulture U. Natal, Pietermaritzburg, Republic of South Africa, 1981—. Mem. editorial adv. bd. Elsevier Sci. Pubs., Amsterdam, Holland, 1985—; contbr. articles to profl. publs. Served to corp. Zimbabwe Air Force Res., 1966-79. Mem. South African Soc. for Crop Prodn. (Nico Viljoen trophy for applied horticulture 1985), Internat. Soc. for Horticultural Sci., Internat. Group on Horticultural Physiology Bananas. Methodist. Home: 6 Bluegrass St, Nelspruit 1200, Republic of South Africa Office: Citrus Subtropical Fruit Research Inst, Pvt Bag X11208, Nelspruit 1200, Republic of South Africa

ROBINSON, JOHN MINOR, lawyer, business executive, retired; b. Uniontown, Pa., Mar. 18, 1910; s. John M. and Martha (Downs) R. A.B., Harvard U., 1932, LL.B, 1935. Bar: Calif. 1936. Assoc. firm Macdonald & Pettit, 1935-41; partner firm Musick, Peeler & Garrett, 1947-77; v.p., sec. Consol. Western Steel div. U.S. Steel Corp. (and predecessors), 1941-57. Clubs: Calif. (past pres.), Los Angeles Country (Los Angeles); Pacific Union (San Francisco); Cypress Point (Pebble Beach, Calif.); The Old Capital (Monterey, Calif.); Royal and Ancient Golf of St. Andrews (Fife, Scotland). Home: 1472 Oleada Rd Pebble Beach CA 93953 Office: 9500 Center St Carmel CA 90017

ROBINSON, MARK LEIGHTON, oil company executive, petroleum geologist, horse farm owner; b. San Bernardino, Calif., Aug. 4, 1927; s. Ernest Guy and Florence Iola (Lemmon) R.; m. Jean Marie Ries, Feb. 8, 1954; children: Francis Willis, Mark Ries, Paul Leighton. AB cum laude in Geology, Princeton U., 1950; postgrad. Stanford U., 1950-51. Geologist Shell Oil Co., Billings, Mont., Rapid City, S.D., Denver, Midland, Tex., 1951-56, dist. geologist, Roswell, N.Mex., 1957-60, div. mgr., Roswell, N.Mex., 1961-

63, Jackson, Miss., 1964-65, Bakersfield, Calif., 1967-68, mgr. exploration econs., N.Y.C., 1969; mgmt. advisor BIPM (Royal Dutch Shell Oil Co.), The Hague, The Netherlands, 1966; pres., chmn. bd. dirs. Robinson Resource Devel. Co., Inc., Roswell, 1970—. Campaign chmn. Chaves County Republican Com., Roswell, 1962; mem. alumni schs. com. Princeton U., 1980—. Served with USNR, 1945-46. Mem. Roswell Geol. Soc. (trustee 1972), Am. Assn. Petroleum Geologists, Stanford U. Earth Scientists Assn., Yellowstone Bighorn Research Assn., Am. Horse Shows Assn., SAR, Sigma Xi. Episcopalian. Discovered Lake Como oil field, Miss., 1971, McNeal oil field, Miss., 1973, North Deer Creek Gas Field, Mont., 1983, Bloomfield East Oil Field, Mont., 1986. Home: Rt 1 Box 31D Roswell NM 88201 Office: Robinson Resource Devel Co Inc PO Box 1227 Roswell NM 88201

ROBINSON, ORMSBEE W., educational consultant; b. Bklyn., June 17, 1910; s. Harry Alexander and Claire (Wright) R.; A.B. cum laude, Princeton U., 1932, M.S.S., New Sch. Social Research, 1937; M.A., Columbia U. Tchrs. Coll., 1942, Ed.D., 1949; m. Janet MacNaughton Miller, June 22, 1935; children—Heather (Mrs. Phillips Thorp), John Alexander. Exec. sec. Plainfield Inst., N.J., 1934-35; high sch. instr., 1935; dir. adult edn. Soc. Ethical Culture, N.Y.C., 1935-41; tchr. ethics Fieldston Sch., N.Y.C., 1935-42; exec. dir. Assoc. Jr. Work Camps, Inc., 1940-42; assoc. OPA, Region II, 1942-46; dir. admissions and public relations Bard Coll., 1946-50, v.p., 1950-54; ednl. cons. for higher edn. Conn. State Dept. Edn., 1954-55, chief Bur. Higher and Adult Edn., 1955-57; exec. sec. Conn. Council Higher Edn., 1954-57; cons. in exec. devel., IBM, 1957-61; program dir. IBM Exec. Sch., 1962; dir. ednl. affairs IBM, 1962-70, dir. univ. relations planning, 1970-75; adv. Assn. for Internat. Practical Tng.; dir. internat. program Nat. Council on Philanthropy, 1975-79, acting pres., 1977-78; cons. Eugenio Mendoza Found. and Venezuelan Fedn. Pvt. Founds., Caracas, Venezuela, 1979-83, Technoserve, Inc., 1980-83; assoc. Columbia U. seminar on technology and social change, 1962-75; chmn. bus. edn. adv. bd. Com. Econ. Devel., 1963-68, mem. Council Devel., Edn., Tng. Nat. Indsl. Conf. Bd., 1960-68; faculty Salzburg Seminar in Am. Studies, 1968; mem. U.S. Nat. Commn. UNESCO, 1971-74, exec. com., 1972-74, chmn. adv. com. on bus. and internat. edn., 1971-72, chmn. membership com., 1974; mem. standards com. Am. Assembly Coll. Schs. of Bus., 1971-72, chmn. internat. affairs com., 1973-75, bd. dirs., 1974-75; mem. task force bus. and internat. edn. Am. Council on Edn., 1975-76. Bd. dirs. World Affairs Ctr., Hartford, 1982-83; adv. council Am. Ditchley Found., 1969-86; mem. Granby Bd. Edn., Conn., 1979-83; bd. founders U. Hartford; bd. dirs. United Way of Chatham County; chmn. adv. council Orinoco Found., Palo Alto, Calif., 1980-83; chmn. devel. com. N.C. Bot. Garden; adv. Chatham County Agrl. Extension Service. Mem. Soc. Internat. Devel., S.R., Soc. Colonial Wars. Clubs: Princeton (N.Y.); Fearrington Garden; Men's Garden of Chapel Hill. Co-author: Education in Business and Industry, 1966. Editorial adv. bd. Indian Adminstrv. and M gmt. Rev., New Delhi, 1968-75. Contbr. to profl. jours. Home: Fearrington Post Box 241 Pittsboro NC 27312

ROBINSON, PEGGY MADSEN, administrative librarian, archivist; d. Carl Westergard and Margaret (Kennedy) Madsen. A.A., Stephens Coll.; B.A., Loretto Heights Coll., 1973; M.L.S., U. Denver, 1973, archival cert., 1975. Asst. librarian Loretto Heights Coll., Denver, 1973-77, art curator, 1974-77; adminstrv. librarian U.S. Dept. Army, Germany, 1977-79; tech. process intern Jefferson County Sch. Dist., Denver, 1980, archivist, 1981-82; dir. N.E. Colo. Regional Library, Wray, 1983-84; head librarian Periodicals dept. U. So. Colo., 1984—; adminstrv. librarian Friends of Children-Viet Nam Internat. Adoption Orgn., Denver, 1984—; instr. English U. Without Walls, Denver, 1973-77. Mem. ALA, Colo. Library Assn. Mountain Plains Library Assn., Soc. Scholarly Pub., SLA, AAUW (rep. commn. women, publicity chair), Wyoming Hist. Soc. (v.p. Washakie chpt.), U. Denver Alumni Assn. (sec.), Stephens Coll. Alumni Assn. (pres.), Citizen Ambassador China, 1985.

ROBINSON, RICHARD ALAN HODGSON, historian; b. Penrith, England, Oct. 9, 1940; s. Alan and Annie Elizabeth (Hodgson) R. MA, St. John's Coll., Oxford, Eng., 1963, PhD, 1968. Asst. lectr. U. Birmingham, Eng., 1965-68, lectr., 1968-74, sr. lectr., 1974-85, reader in Iberian history, 1985—. Author: The Origins of Franco's Spain, 1970, Contemporary Portugal, 1979; contbr. articles to profl. jours. Recipient Bolseiro award Fundação C. Gulbenkian, Lisbon, Portugal, 1973-74. Fellow Royal Hist. Soc. Anglican. Office: U Birmingham, Sch of History, Birmingham B15 2TT, England

ROBINSON, RICHARD ALLEN, JR., consultant, human resources development trainer; b. Ellensburg, Wash., Aug. 21, 1936; s. Richard Allen and Rosa Adele (Oswalt) R.; m. R. Elaine Whitham, Sept. 8, 1956; children—Sharon E. Robinson Losey, Richard Allen, René L. B.A., U. Wash., 1958; postgrad. U.S. Army Command and Gen. Staff Coll., 1969-70; M.A., U. Mo., 1971. Commd. 2d lt. U.S. Army, 1958, advanced through grades to lt. col., 1972, various infantry assignments including command, 1958-72, research and devel. assignments including dep. dir. test of behavioral sci., dep. commandant U.S.A. Organizational Effectiveness, 1975-77, ret., 1979; chief mgmt. devel. Wash. Dept. Social and Health Services, Olympia, 1979—; pvt. practice orgn. and mgmt. devel. cons./trainer, 1979—. Decorated Legion of Merit with oak leaf cluster, Bronze Star. Mem. Am. Soc. Tng. and Devel., Organizational Devel. Network, Internat. Platform Assn., Mass. Hort. Soc. Contbg. author: Games Trainers Play, vol. II, 1983. Office: DSHS Mail 8315 W 27th St Tacoma WA 98466

ROBINSON, RICHARD GARY, management consultant; b. Oakland, Calif., Aug. 17, 1931; s. William Albert and Inez Wilhelmina (Zetterblad) R.; B.B.A., U. Minn., 1955; grad. Indsl. Coll. Armed Forces, 1972; M. Internat. Mgmt., Am. Grad. Sch. Internat. Mgmt., 1980; m. Lorraine Mary Deshaies, Nov. 13, 1965 (dec.); children—Elisabeth Claudine (dec.), Christopher Paul. CPA, Colo.; cert. mgmt. cons. Commd. 2d lt. U.S. Air Force, 1956, advanced through grades to maj.; dir. radar ops. tactical air warfare, comdr. strategic missile operation and maintenance functions, project mgr., dir. mgmt. info. systems Dept. Def. activities, S.E. Asia; ret., 1976; mgmt. cons., Colorado Springs, Colo., 1976—; pres. Bus. Devel. Specialists; dir., chief fin. officer Unique Equipment Co.; bd. dirs. United Air Frieght Ltd.; mem. adj. faculty Embry Riddle Aero. U., Luke AFB, Ariz.; asst. prof. econs. and bus. Colorado Springs br. Regis Coll.; U. So. Colo. Mem. bus. adv. council Colo. Internat. Trade Office. Decorated Meritorious Service medal with oak leaf cluster, AF Commendation medal with 2 oak leaf clusters. Mem. Internat. Trade Assn. Colo. (pres.), Am. Mktg. Assn., Armed Forces Communications and Electronics Assn., Am. Mgmt. Assn., Nat. Assn. Accts., Inst. Mgmt. Cons., Assn. Polit. Risk Analysts, N.Am. Soc. Corp. Planning. Lutheran. Home: 1610 McKay Way Colorado Springs CO 80915 Office: 2340 Robinson St Suite 113 PO Box 2714 Colorado Springs CO 80901

ROBINSON, ROBERT ARMSTRONG, pension fund executive; b. Waterbury, Conn., Sept. 11, 1925; s. Robert and Ethel (Armstrong) R.; m. D. Ann Harding, June 7, 1947; 1 dau., Gayllis Robinson Ward. A.B. magna cum laude, Brown U., 1950, M.A., 1952; postgrad., U. Ill., 1954-55; Litt. D., Episcopal Theol. Sem. Ky., 1971; D.C.L., U. South, 1972; LL.D., Nashotah House, Oconomowoc, Wis. Instr. English Brown U., 1950-53; instr. English, asst. prof. rhetoric U. Ill., 1953-56; trust officer Colonial Bank & Trust Co., Waterbury, 1956-63; v.p., trust officer Colonial Bank & Trust Co., 1963-65, sr. trust officer, 1965-66; v.p., sec. Ch. Pension Fund and Affiliates, Ch. Life Ins. Corp., Ch. Ins. Co., Ch. Agy. Corp., Ch. Hymnal Corp., 1966-67, exec. v.p., 1967-68, pres., dir., 1968—; dir. Seabury Press, Inc., Mariners Instl. Funds, Inc., Mariner Tax Free Instl. Fund, UST Master Funds, Morehouse-Barlow Co., Inc., Mariner Funds Trust, Mariner Equity Trust, Pigmy Corp., U.S.T. Master Money Funds, Rosiclare Lead and Flourspar Mining Co., others; cons. to exec. dir. Pension Benefit Guaranty Corp. Trustee Hillspeak, Eureka Springs, Ark., Canterbury Cathedral Trust in Am., Washington Nat. Cathedral, Nashotah Theol. Sem., Wis., H.B. and F.K. Bugher Found., Living Church Found.; mem. exec. com. N.Y. councils Boy Scouts Am., Ch. Pensions Conf.; mem. econ. adv. bd. Columbia U. Grad. Sch. Bus. Adminstrn. Served with inf. AUS, 1943-46. Decorated Bronze Star, Purple Heart with oak leaf cluster, Knights of Malta, Order St. John. Mem. Conn. Bankers Assn. (v.p., head trust div.), Am. Numis. Assn., Newcomen Soc., Phi Beta Kappa. Republican. Episcopalian (vestryman). Clubs: St. Andrew's Soc. (N.Y.C.), Brown (N.Y.C.), Union League (N.Y.C.), Church (N.Y.C.); Country of New Canaan; Athenaeum (London); Pilgrims, Union; Met. (Washington); Yeaman's Hall (Charleston, S.C.). Home: 251 Laurel Rd New Canaan CT 06840 Office: 800 2d Ave New York NY 10017

ROBINSON, SHIRLIE LORENE, educator, political worker; b. Port Townsend, Wash., Mar. 27, 1933; d. Joel Craft and Berniece Ardelle (Ricker) Waddell; B.S. in Edn., Gorham (Maine) State Tchrs. Coll., 1949-53; M.S. in Edn., Calif. State U., Hayward, 1976; postgrad. U. Maine, Orono, 1957-63, Coll. Notre Dame, Belmont, Calif., 1971, U. Calif., Santa Cruz, 1976; m. Frederick Leroy Robinson, Sept. 19, 1953; children—Dana Lee, Dion Jay. Tchr., Emerson Elem. Sch., Portland, Maine, 1954-56; spl. edn. tchr. North Sch., Portland, 1961-62, Brown Elem. Sch., South Portland, Maine, 1962-64; spl. edn. tchr. John F. Kennedy High Sch., Fremont, Calif., 1965-69, 70-71, dep. head spl. edn. dept., 1970-71, work experience coordinator spl. edn. dept., 1970-71; sect. chmn. Fremont United Sch. Dist. Secondary Level Educable Mentally Retarded Com., 1968-69, mem. com. to develop grading philosophy for secondary level educable mentally retarded pupils, 1968, mem. secondary level educable mentally retarded curriculum guide com., 1968; tutor spl. edn. South Portland Sch. Dist., 1981-83. Publicity chmn. Tri-City, Am. Cancer Soc., 1973; mem. Fremont Democratic Women's Forum, Fremont, Calif., 1975—, sec., 1976-77, chmn., 1977-79, legis. reporter; mem. steering com. South Alameda County Dem. Hdqrs., Hayward, Calif., 1977-79; mem. Calif. State Dem. Central Com., 1978-80, del. Calif. state conv., 1979, secretarial co-asst. Calif. 25th Assembly Dist. Steering Com., Santa Clara County, Calif., 1980; del. Maine state dem. conv., 1988. Mem. Nat. Tchrs. Assn., Vols. in Politics. Address: 772 Gray Rd South Windham ME 04082

ROBINSON, WALTER STITT, JR., historian; b. Matthews, N.C., Aug. 28, 1917; s. Walter Stitt and Mary Irene (Jamison) S.; m. Constance Lee Mock, Mar. 18, 1944; children—Ethel Barry, Walter Lee. B.A. summa cum laude, Davidson (N.C.) Coll., 1939; M.A., U. Va., 1941, Ph.D., 1950. Asst. prof., then assoc. prof. history Florence (Ala.) State Coll., 1946-48; mem. faculty U. Kans., Lawrence, 1950—; prof. history U. Kans., 1959—, chmn. dept., 1968-73; mem. Nat. Civil War Centennial Commn., 1961-65, Kans. Com. Humanities, 1971-78, chmn., 1976-77. Author: Land Grants in Virginia, 1607-1699, 1957, The Southern Colonial Frontier, 1607-1763, 1979; editor: Indian Treaties of Colonial Virginia, 2 vols. 1983, Indian Treaties of Colonial Maryland, 1987; editorial bd.: 18th century bibliography in Philos. Quar, 1975-78; contbr. articles to profl. jours. Mem. adminstrv. bd. First United Methodist Ch., Lawrence, 1952—; exec. com., bd. dirs. Kans. Sch. Religion, pres., 1983-86. Served to capt. AUS, 1941-45. Decorated Bronze Star; recipient Disting. Scholarship award U. Kans., 1976; grantee Social Sci. Research Council, 1959-60; Am. Philos. Soc. grantee, 1967, 83. Mem. Am. Hist. Assn., Orgn. Am. Historians (chmn. program com. 1959), So. Hist. Assn., Kans. Hist. Soc. (dir.), Douglas County Hist. Soc. (pres. 1979-81), Raven Soc., Phi Beta Kappa, Phi Alpha Theta (internat. council 1978-80, adv. bd. 1980-81, 86-87, pres. 1984-85). Home: 801 Broadview Dr Lawrence KS 66044 Office: Dept History U Kans Lawrence KS 66045

ROBINSON, W(ILLIAM) CARY, electronic engineer, educator; b. Norwalk, Ohio, Dec. 24, 1910; s. Junius Cary and Marion Lois (Lucas) R.; m. Thelma Marguerite Pheanis, Aug. 1, 1940; children—Penn Robinson Ansorg, Quinn Cary. B.A., Miami U., Oxford, Ohio, 1932, postgrad., 1937-41; B.S.Ed., Bowling Green State U., 1937; postgrad. U. Chgo., 1941. Cert. tchr., Ohio. Tchr. pub. schs., Ohio, 1937-42; radar instr. USAF Tech. Sch., Boca Raton, Fla., 1942-44, chief instr., chief tng. research and devel., 1944-47; tng. supr. Air Force Radar Tech. Sch., Keesler AFB, Biloxi, Miss., 1947-49; staff supervisory aircraft electronics research and devel. engr. USAF Hdqrs, Washington, 1949-57, U.S. Army Signal Corps Hdqrs., 1957-62, U.S. Army Material Command Hdqrs., 1962-71; tech. rep. Dept. Def., various mil. and civilian orgns., Washington, 1949-71; mem. nat. aircraft collision prevention adv. group Charter Dept. Army, 1959-70; chair Joint Army/Navy Aircraft Instrumentation Research Program, 1960-61. Past mem. U.S. Civil Service Bd. of Examiners for Electronic Engr. and related fields, 1956-58; elected mem. state governing bd. Common Cause of Va., 1986—; founder, pres. Buckingham County Friends of the Library, 1976—; founder, pres. Buckingham County Pub. Library Bd. Dirs., 1983—; exec. dir. Buckingham County Library and Community Ctr., 1985—; del. Americans for Democratic Action, Washington, 1972—; founder Friends World Coll., L.I., N.Y., 1964; candidate Bd. Suprs., Buckingham County, Va., 1979; pres. Community Health Ctr., Buckingham County, 1979-80, Buckingham County Indsl. Devel. Corp., 1979-81, v.p., 1981—; bd. dirs. Va. Action, Richmond, 1982-85. Recipient Meritorious Civilian Service award, Dept. Army, 1962. Mem. AAAS, Fedn. Am. Scientists, Am. Mensa Ltd., Sigma Tau Delta. Club: Ruritan (v.p. 1974, pres. 1975, dir. 1976-80, Buckingham County Citizenship award 1978). Address: RD 3 Box 79 Dillwyn VA 23936

ROBINSON, WILLIE EDWARD, law educator, consultant; b. Harrisburg, Pa., Feb. 22, 1952; s. Hazel and Mamie (Mingo) R.; m. Brenda Twyner, Sept. 20, 1980; children—Bryant Francis, Alexandra Rosemary. B.A., Yale U., 1974; J.D., U. Va., 1977. Bar: Ga. 1977, U.S. Dist. Ct. (no. dist.) Ga. 1978, U.S. Ct. Appeals (5th cir.) 1978, U.S. Ct. Appeals (11th cir.) 1982, U.S. Supreme Ct. 1983. Assoc. Powell, Goldsteinet al, Atlanta, 1977-80, Parks, Jackson, et al, Atlanta, 1980-81; adj. prof. law Woodrow Wilson U., Atlanta, 1980-81; asst. prof. law Emory U., Atlanta, 1981-84; sole practice Atlanta, 1983—; vis. asst. prof. U. Va. Law Sch., Charlottesville, 1984—; of counsel Sumner & Hewes, Atlanta, 1983-87, Rogers & Hardin, Atlanta, 1987-88; v.p. Charlee Homes Inc., Atlanta, 1980—; pres. Select Sports Profls., Inc., 1987—; spl. advisor Nat. Bar Assn., Washington, 1984—. Contbr. articles to profl. jours. Chmn. Joint Com. to Study Standard of Need AFDC Payments, Atlanta, 1984; v.p. Residential Care Facilities for Elderly of Fulton County, Atlanta, 1983. Mem. Gate City Bar Assn. (sec. 1979, pres.-elect 1988), Atlanta Bar Assn., Nat. Bar Assn., Order of Coif. Methodist. Clubs: Handlers Ltd. (Atlanta), Atlanta City. Home: 900-5 Durant Pl NE Atlanta GA 30309 Office: 138 Peachtree St NW Atlanta GA 30303

ROBISON, JAMES EVERETT, business consultant; b. Alfred, N.D., Nov. 22, 1915; s. John J. and Myrtle (Klundt) R.; m. Jeanette Hoffman, June 6, 1942 (dec.); 1 child, Martha Ann Davies. A.B., U. Minn., 1938; M.B.A., Harvard U., 1940; Sc. D. (hon.), Suffolk U., 1968. Sales dept. Nashua Mfg. Co., N.Y.C., 1940-46, Textron, Inc., N.Y.C., 1947-53; chief textile br. OPS, Washington, 1951; pres., chief exec. officer, dir. Indian Head, Inc., N.Y.C., 1953-67; chmn. bd., chief exec. officer Indian Head, Inc., 1967-72, chmn. fin. com., 1971-76; pres. Lonsdale Enterprises, Inc., 1976—; bd. dirs. Houbigant, Inc. Mem. com. univ. resources Harvard U., 1966-69; vis. com. Grad. Sch. Bus. Adminstrn., 1966-72, 73-79; chmn. bd. Assos. Harvard Bus. Sch., 1968-70, bd. dirs. 1988—; trustee Air Force Aid Soc., 1968—, fin. com., 1969—; bd. dirs. Bus. Com. for Arts, 1973-80; trustee Com. Econ. Devel., 1965-74, Calif. Inst. Tech., 1970—; vice chmn. Pres.'s Council Sch. of Bus. U. Vt. Served to maj. USAAF, 1942-46. Decorated D.F.C., Air Medal with three oak leaf clusters; recipient Distinguished Service award Harvard Bus. Sch. Assn., 1969; Outstanding Alumni award U. Minn., 1974. Mem. Conf. Bd., Harvard Bus. Sch. Assn. (exec. council 1968-71), Am. Textile Mfrs. Inst. (dir. 1961-64), Soaring Soc. Am., U.S. C.of C., Air Force Res. Assn., Phi Delta Theta. Clubs: Harvard, Racquet and Tennis, Harvard Bus. Sch. Greater N.Y. (past dir., pres. 1967-68) (N.Y.C.); Stanwich (Greenwich, Conn.); Stowe (Vt.) Country; Bedford (N.Y.) Golf and Tennis; Lyford Cay (Bahamas). Home: Windmill Farm 12 Spruce Hill Rd Armonk NY 10504 Office: 20 Haarlem Ave White Plains NY 10603

ROBISON, KENNETH GERALD, naval officer; b. Great Falls, Mont., Sept. 30, 1938; s. Perry Russell and Ruth Elsie Helen (Johnson) R.; m. Mary Margaret Michele Crovitz, Mar. 6, 1964; children—Karin Michele, Mark Charles. Student U. Wash., 1958; B.A., U. Mont., 1960, postgrad., 1965. Commd. ensign U.S. Navy, 1960, advanced through grades to capt., 1980; intelligence officer; asst. naval attache U.S. Embassy, Stockholm, Sweden, 1975-78; asst. chief of staff intelligence U.S. Naval Forces Europe, London, 1980-84; dir. plans, policy and requirements Office Naval Intelligence, Washington, 1984—; mem. inter-agy. com. prisoners of war, missing in action, com. on imagery requirements and exploitation . Author: Prisoner of War Debrief—Capt. James Bond Stockdale, 1973. Decorated comdr. Order No. Star (Sweden). Mem. Mont. Hist. Soc., Nat. Geneal. Soc., U.S. Naval Inst., Phi Alpha Theta, Delta Sigma Phi. Republican. Presbyterian. Club: Army and Navy. Avocations: western Americana; genealogical research; squash; tennis. Home: 8241 Taunton Pl Springfield VA 22152 Office: Office of Chief Naval Ops Dept Navy OP-009P Washington DC 20350

ROBLEK, BRANKO, science educator; b. Yugoslavia, Jan. 9, 1934; s. Viktor and Marija (Kern) R. Diploma in Physics, Univ. FNT, Ljubljana, Yugoslavia, 1959, 1962 diploma in math., 1962, prof. math., 1964. Tchr. primary sch., Zg. Gorje, Yugoslavia, 1960-62, secondary sch., Skofja Loka, 1962-69, 73-81; insp., cons. Inst. Edn., Ljubljana, 1969-73; tchr. math., physics and computer sci., Edn. Ctr., Skofja Loka, 1981—; cons. Soc. Computer Sci., Ljubljana, 1973-81; mem. physics edn. faculty Inst. Edn., Ljubljana, 1981—. Author: (with others) AAAIII Zbirka vaj, 1969; Racunalnistvo ZN, 1980. Chmn. Syndicate of Civilizing Workers, Skofja Loka, 1966. Fellow Soc. Mathematicians; mem. Physicists and Astronomers of SR Slovenia. Home: Partizanska 46, 64220 Skofja Loka PO15 Yugoslavia

ROBY, DANIEL ARTHUR, lawyer; b. Anderson, Ind., Aug. 16, 1941; s. Virgil A. and Frances E. R.; m. Carolyn Sue Eaton, June 14, 1964; 1 dau., Kerilynn. A.B. with honors, Ind. U., 1963, J.D., 1966. Bar: Ind. 1966, U.S. Dist. Ct. (no. dist.) Ind. 1967, U.S. Dist. Ct. (so. dist.) Ind. 1966, U.S. Ct. Appeals (7th cir.) 1968. Practice law, Anderson, and Ft. Wayne, Ind.; faculty lectr. Ind. U.; mem. Allen County Jud. Nominating Commn., 1983—. Past pres. Allen County (Ind.) Heart Assn., Northeastern Ind. Heart Assn.; chmn. bd. Ind. affiliate Am. Heart Assn.; past pres. bd. mgrs. Faith Baptist Ch.; past pres. Interagy. Drug and Alcohol Council. Mem. Ind. State Bar Assn., Allen County Bar Assn. (bd. dirs. 1983), Assn. Trial Lawyers Am., Ind. Trial Lawyers Assn. (exec. com., bd. dirs. 1980—, named Lawyer of Yr. 1986), Am. Arbitration Assn. (bd. arbitrators). Club: Shriners. Contbr. articles to legal jours. Home: 6224 Cordava Ct Fort Wayne IN 46815 Office: 127 W Berry St Fort Wayne IN 46802 also: 420 E 8th St Anderson IN 46015

ROCA, JEAN CLAUDE EDOUARD, allergist; b. Tarbes, France, July 27, 1945; s. Joseph and Yvette Lucienne (Labarraque) R.; m. Annie Jeannine Desclaux, July 24, 1968; children: Philippe, Ghislaine, Eric, Herve. MD, U. Bordeaux, 1971, Cert. in Allergology, 1971. Extern Ctr. Hosp. U., Bordeaux, France, 1968; intern Ctr. Hosp. U., Bordeaux, 1969-71; practice medicine specializing in allergies Tarbes, France, 1971—; expert in allergy Ct. of Appeals, Pau, France, 1978, Ministry of Health, Paris, 1982. Author: Publication Fisons, Tome I, 1972; contbr. sci. revs. to numerous publs. Pres. Mutuelle Pyrenees-Bigorre, Tarbes, 1981—, Univ. TLB, Tarbes, 1983. Fellow Am. Coll. Allergists; mem. European Acad. Allergology and Clin. Immunology, French Soc. Allergology, Bordeaux Pharmacy Soc., French Soc. Chimie Biologique, Soc. Americanistes, Soc. Academique, Internat. Gesellschaft Aerosole in Medizin, Internat. Assn. of Asthmology, Pharmacy History Soc. Roman Catholic. Home: 10 rue Georges Ledormeur, 65000 Tarbes France Office: 8 Blvd Claude Debussy, 65000 Tarbes France

ROCALVE, PIERRE, diplomat; b. Montrejeau, Haute Garonne, France, Oct. 7, 1925; s. Paul and Gilberte (Manieval) R. BL, U. Paris; diploma, Inst. d'Etudes Politiques, Paris, Ctr. d'Etudes d'Arabe Moderne, Lebanon. Attaché Residence-Gen. of France to Tunis, Tunisia, 1953-55; sec. to French Ambassador to Tunisia, 1957, French Ambassador to Libya, 1957-59, French Ambassador to Lebanon, 1960-63; 1st sec. French Embassy, Cairo, 1963-66; dir. econ. and fin. affairs Ministry of Fgn. Affairs, Paris, 1967-70; councillor French Embassy, Washington, 1971-74; chargé de mission Del.-Gen. of Energy, Paris, 1974-75; minister-councellor French Embassy, Madrid, 1975-80; French ambassador to Iraq 1980-81, French ambassador to Saudi Arabia, 1981-85, Inspector-Gen. of fgn. affairs Paris, 1986—. Decorated Chevalier de la Legion d'Honneur, Chevalier de l'Ordre du Merite. Office: Ministry of Fgn Affairs, 37 Quai d'Orsay, 75007 Paris France

ROCARD, MICHEL LOUIS LÉON, prime minister of France; b. Courbevoie, France, Aug. 23, 1930; s. Yves Rocard and Renée Favre; m. Michèle Legendre, 1972; children: Sylvie, Francis, Olivier, Loic. Ed., U. Paris, Ecole Nat. Adminstrn. Nat. sec. Parti Socialiste Unifié, 1967-73; dep. to Nat. Assembly, Paris, 1969-73, 78-81; mem. Parti Socialiste, 1974, mem. exec. bur., 1975—, nat. sec. in charge of pub. sector, 1975-79; mayor Conflans-Sainte-Honorine, 1977—; minister state, minister planning and regional devel. France, Paris, 1981-83, minister agr., 1983-85, prime minister, 1988—. Address: Office Prime Minister, Paris France *

ROCES, FELIX CADAG, JR., petrochemical company executive; b. Pilar, Sorsogon, Philippines, Nov. 27, 1936; s. Alfeo A. and Caridad M. (Cadag) R.; m. Adelaida Caoangan Castro, Aug. 18, 1962; children: Felix Cadag III, Edmund, Rowena. BSEE, Mapua Inst. Tech., Manila, 1960; BA in Mfg. Mgmt., Kensington U., 1984. Diplomate Philippines Mktg. Inst. Process operator Bataan Refining Corp., Limay, Bataan, Philippines, 1960-63; start-up advisor ESSO, Port Dickson, Malaysia, 1963-64; from start-up assoc. to prodn. supt. Planters Products Inc., Limay, 1964-76; from ops. mgr. to dir. LMG Chems. Inc., Pascual, Batangas, Philippines, 1976—. Author: Utilities Operating Manual, 1970. Trainer Boy Scouts of Philippines, Bataan, 1973-76; pres. Philiplpine Rosicrucian Found., Manila, 1987. Mem. Safety Orgn. Philippines, Soc. Mfg. Engrs., Internat. Airline Passenger Assn. Roman Catholic. Club: Banaba Golf (San Pascual, Batangas). Lodge: Pliippine Amorc (master 1987-88), Lions. Office: LMG Chems Inc, San Pascual Batangas Philippines

ROCHA, ARMANDINO CORDEIRO DOS SANTOS, accountant, educator; b. Porto, Portugal, Oct. 19, 1934; s. Marios Dos Santos and Maria Da Conceicão (Cordeiro) R.; m. Maria Laura Oliveira Silva, Sept. 1, 1957 (div. 1977); children: Isabel Maria, Mario Rui; m. Ana Rosalina Sa Ribeiro, July 2, 1977; 1 child, Ana Sofia. B in Acctg., Inst. Comercial, Porto, 1962; B in Social Polit., Inst. Estudos Sociais, Lisbon, Portugal, 1969; B in Sociology, Inst. Superior Ciencias, 1982; BBA, Inst. superior C. Trab. Empresas, 1975. Fin. dir. Fabrica Fiacão E Tecidos Da Portela, Delães, Portugal, 1960-72, Tinturaria Vaz Ferreira, S. Mamede De Infesta, Portugal, 1962-73; regional dir. Companhia Seguros Bonanca, Porto, 1973-87; auditor Emaco, Sa, Lisboa, Porto, 1979-85, Imobur S.A. and Riguadiana S.A., Porto, 1979-85, Estaleiros Navais De Viana, Porto, 1979-82; auditor Efi-Ed Ferreirinha and Irmão S.A., Porto, 1984—, Feruni-Sociedade de Fundicão S.A., Trofa, Portugal, 1984—, Portocork, Internat., Lds, Feira, Portugal, 1987—, Copo Atlantico, Industria De Poliuretano S.A., Santo Tirso, Portugal, 1987—; instr. acctg. U. Do Minho, Braga, Portugal, 1980—. Author: Principios Do Seguro, 1982; contbr. articles to profl. jours. Mem. Assn. Para O Desenvowimento Economico E Social, Portugal Economists Assn., Portugal Mgmt. Assn., Inst. Dos Actuários Portugueses. Clubs: Vigorosa Sport, Fenianos. Home: 357-2 Raria Guimaraes, P-4000 Porto Portugal Office: Universidade Do Minho, Castelo, P-4119 Braga Portugal

ROCHA, FERNANDO AUGUSTO, recording communications specialist; b. Pacos Brandao, Feira, Portugal, Feb. 23, 1958; s. Fernando Figueiredo Rocha and Rosa Oliveira Pais. Freelance musician Oporto, Portugal, 1977-83; audio engr. Aura Studio LDA, Pacos de Brandao, 1985-86; studio mgr. Aura Studio LDA, Portugal, 1987—. Composer: (album) Procurem Na Sara, 1982; (score) Ballet De Espinho, 1982; (soundtrack) Cinanima '86, 1986. Dir. art. dept. Circulo Recreio Atre E Cultura, Pacos De Brandao. Mem. Audio Engrng. Soc. (assoc.). Office: Aura Studio LDA, Barroso, 4535 Pacos De Brandao Portugal

ROCHA, GUY LOUIS, archivist, historian; b. Long Beach, Calif., Sept. 23, 1951; s. Ernest Louis and Charlotte (Sobus) R.; m. Pamela Marie Parsons, Jan. 4, 1980. B.A. in Social Studies and Edn., Syracuse U., 1973; M.A. in Am. Studies, San Diego State U., 1975; postgrad., U. Nev., 1975—. Tchr., Washoe County Sch. Dist., Reno, Nev., 1975-76; history instr. Western Nev. Community Coll., Carson City, 1976; curator manuscripts Nev. Hist. Soc., Reno, 1976-81, interim asst. dir., 1980, interim dir., 1980-81; state archivist Nev. Div. Archives and Records, Carson City, 1981—; hist. cons. Janus Assocs., Tempe, Ariz., 1980, Rainshadow Assocs., Carson City, 1983—. Co-author The Ignoble Conspiracy: Radicalism on Trial in Nevada, 1986; contbr. to book and govt. study. Mem. Washoe Heritage Council, Reno, 1983-85; editorial bd. Nev. Hist. Soc., Reno, 1983—; mem. Washoe County Democratic Central Com., Reno, 1984—. Mem. Conf. Intermountain Archivists (Council mem 1979-87, v.p. 1984-85, pres. 1985-86), State Hist. Records Adv. Bd. (dep. coordinator 1984-86, coordinator 1986—), Westerners Internat. Nev. Corral (dep. sheriff 1980-81, sheriff 1984-85, mem. state coordinators steering com. 1985-87, vice chmn. 1986-87), Soc. Am. Archivists, Western History Assn., Nat. Assn. Govt. Archives and Records Adminstrs. Democrat. Home: 14485 Huron Trail Reno NV 89511-9012 Office: Nev State Library and Archives Div Archives and Records 101 S Fall St Carson City NV 89710

ROCHA, TOMAZ ANDRADE, lawyer; b. Lisbon, Portugal, June 3, 1931; s. Tomaz Parreira Rocha and Beatriz (Andrade) R.; LL.B. with 1st class honours, U. Lisbon, 1953; m. Isabel Pereira David, Mar. 3, 1956; children—Tomaz, Rita, Pedro, Tiago, Mateus. Admitted to Portuguese bar, 1955; pvt. practice, Lisbon, 1955—; atty. Portuguese and fgn. cos. in Portugal; dir. Moagem e Panificacao Nova Moapão, Auto-Ind., Tecnicar-Automoveis, Paraglas-Soc. de Acrilicos, Bayer Portugal, Esab-Comercio e Industria de Soldadura, Moagens Associadas, Progresso-Administradora TOMROCHA-Imob., TOMROCHA-Agri., NALCO PORTUGUESA Soc. Ind. Alianca, Soc. Al. Moagem, Sonel-Soc. Nac. de Electrodos, Daimon Duracell (Pilhas) Lda;chmn. fiscal bd. Esso Protugesa, SOFINLOC. Served with Portuguese Army, 1953-55. Mem. Ordem dos Advogados; internat. asso. Am. Bar Assn. Roman Catholic. Home: Lote 1 10th Floor, Rua das Murtas, 1700 Lisbon Portugal

ROCHAT, JEAN-PAUL, translator; b. Oran, Algeria, North Africa, Feb. 22, 1943; s. Lucien Henri and Manuela (Luis) R.; m. Alice Staeheli, Apr. 26, 1965; children: Janine Alice, Marcel Jean-Paul. Swiss and French nat. Lycée français, Sch. Interpreters, Zurich, 1966; Ph.D., Sussex Coll. Tech., Eng., 1972; D honoris causa, Thomas Jefferson U., 1984, D honoris causa en Ciencias Linguisticas, U. El Salvador, 1985, D honoris causa en Ciencias Sociales U. Politécnica de El Salvador, 1986. Interpreter, translator Wild Heerbrugg AG, 1961-63; translator Pro Jurentute, Zurich, 1964; translator F. Hoffman-La Roche & Co. S.A., Basle, Switzerland, 1965; translator, asst. mgr. Doetsch, Grether & Co. AG, Basle, 1966; translator, sales mgr. Agence Economique et Financiere, Zurich, 1967; owner Translation Agy., 1969—. Author: La Traduction en Suisse, 1972. Named a hon. col. a.d.c. Ala. State Militia, 1985. Mem. Swiss Assn. Translator and Interpreter (founder), Swiss Assn. Translation Agys. (pres. 1983). Home: Seestrasse 231, 8700 Kusnacht, Zurich Switzerland Office: Forchstrasse 108, 8032 Zurich Switzerland

ROCHE, JEAN FRANÇOISPAUL ANTOINE, physician; b. Neuilly, France, Nov. 20, 1938; s. Tony Andre and Marcelle (Eyraud) R.; m. Annie Claude Celine Degremont; children: Emmanuel, Jean Daniel, Anne Cecile. BSc in Math. and Physics, Paris, MD, 1969, spl. studies in anesthesiology, 1970. Resident Paris, 1969-70; anesthetist Clinique de L'Archette, Olivet, France, 1970—. Vice mayor St. Pryvé City Council, 1977-83; pres. Reformed Ch. Parish, Orleans, France, 1978-88. Mem. French Anesthetists Assn., French Speaking Anesthetists, European Soc. Regional Anesthesia, Palliative Care Assn., European Soc. Parenteral Nutrition. Home: 360 Rt de Saint Mesmin, 45750 Loiret, Saint Pryve France

ROCHE, MARCEL, research scientist, editor; b. Caracas, Venezuela, Aug. 15, 1920; s. Luis Roche and Beatrice Dugand; m. Maria Teresa Rolando, May 25, 1947 (dec.); children—Antoinette, Noelle, Christian, Diana; m. 2d, Flor Blanco-Fombona, Apr. 29, 1972. Bachilier, Sainte Croix de Neuilly, Paris, 1938; B.S., St. Joseph's Coll., 1942; M.D., Johns Hopkins U., 1946; Dr. Med., Universidad Central de Venezuela, 1954; Dr. Sc. (hon.), Case Inst. Tech., 1965, Universidad de Los Andes-Merida-Venezuela, 1973. Dir. Inst. de Investigaciones Medicas, Caracas, Venezuela, 1952-58, Inst. Venezolano de Investigaciones Cientificas, Caracas, 1958-69; pres. Nat. Research Council, 1969-72; investigator titular, Caracas, 1959—; editor Interciencia, Caracas, 1976—; cons. WHO, Geneva, Switzerland, 1964-69, Pan Am. Health Orgn., Washington, 1960-69, IBRD, Washington, 1965; rep. from Venezuela UNESCO, 1984. Contbr. articles to profl. jours. Recipient Nat. Sci. prize Venezuela, 1956; Premio G.E.N., Venezuela, 1957; Premio Jose Gregorio Hernandez, Venezuela, 1969; Premio Jose Moradell, Venezuela, 1982. Fellow AAAS; mem. Pontifical Acad. Scis. Club: Harvard (N.Y.C.). Home: Nunez Ponte No 88, Lomas del Mirador, Caracas 1060, Venezuela Office: Dept Estudio de la Cienci-IVIC, Apartado 1827, 1010-A Caracas Venezuela *

ROCHE, MARK CLIFFORD, architect; b. London, Oct. 24, 1953; s. Albert Noel and Valerie (Olwen) R. BS, U. Calif., San Luis Obispo, 1977, MArch, 1979. Registered architect, Eng. Architect Chapman Taylor Ptnrs., London, 1980-82; prin. architect Richard Rogers Partnership, London, 1982—; bd. dirs. Arete Designs, London. Prin. works include: a Cambridge U. lab., 1984, Citicorp Hdqrs., 1986, Reuters News Hdqrs., 1988; exhibited at Royal Acad. Summer Exhibition, London, 1983. Mem. Royal Inst. Brit. Architects.

ROCHEROLLE, EUGENIE KATHERINE, composer, lyricist, pianist, educator; b. New Orleans, Aug. 24, 1936; d. Gustave Joseph and Katherine Lucille (Schlegel) Ricau; m. Didier Andre Rocherolle, May 14, 1960; children—Valerie, Laurent, Damien, Justin. B.A. in Music, Sophie Newcomb Coll. Tulane U., 1958. Composer, lyricist 44 anthems for chorus, 3 band works, 1 work for band and chorus; composer 22 books for piano; composer musicals, chamber works, string orch. work, radio commls.; performance of Vignette for flute and piano, Kennedy Ctr., Washington, 1988; commd. piano solo Clavier Mag., 1983; commd. anthem Wilton Congregational Ch. (Conn.), 1976; featured Am. composer and judge Audrey Thayer Meml. Piano Competition, Avon, Conn., 1986; guest composer Anne Arundel State Music Teachers Assn., Annapolis, Md., 1987, Del. State Music Tchrs. Assn., Dover, Del., 1987, Piano Festival, Anderson (S.C.) Coll., 1988, Hartford chpt. Conn. State Music Tchrs. Assn., 1986; featured composer Profl. Devel. for Piano Tchrs, Montgomery (Md.) Coll., 1988, featured composer Profl. Devel. for Piano Tchrs., Montgomery Coll, Rockville, Md., 1988, Piano Festival Concerto Competition and Concert Series, Anderson Coll., S.C., 1988; Mem. Women's Republican Club, Wilton, 1980—, exec. bd., 1982-86; mem. exec. bd., sec. Wilton Orch., 1983-86. Mem. Nat. League Am. Penwoman (co-state chmn. music 1983-85, v.p. Pioneer br. 1986-88 , 1st prize-choral competition 1986, competition for piano composition for the left hand prizewinner 1988), Nat. Fedn. Music Clubs (judge jr. festivals 1982—), ASCAP, Conn. Composers Inc., sec. Wilton Orch. 1983-86). Roman Catholic. Clubs: DAR (chaplain Drum Hill chpt. 1982-86, Drum Hill chpt. vice regent 1987—); Shubert of Fairfield County (bd. dirs. 1986-88).

ROCHETTE, JACQUES HENRI JEAN, physician; b. Robiac, Gard, France, Dec. 19, 1944; s. Henri Jean Baptiste and Marie-Louise Celine (Folcher) R.; m. Claude Marie Catanzano; children: Anne, Celine, Claude. MS in Cardiology, U. Montpellier, France, 1974, MD, 1976. Intern then resident in cardiology Hosp. of U. Montpellier, 1966-72; asst. to faculty U. Montpellier, 1969-73; cons. La Seyne sur Mer (France) Hosp., 1977—, Toulon (France) Polyclinic, 1982—; cons. physician Préfecture du Var, Toulon, 1980—. Lodge: Rotary. Office: Cardiology Consulting Room, 2 Ave Marcel Dassault, Le Quadrige, 83500 La Seyne sur Mer, Var France

ROCHETTO, EVELYN MARIE, educator; b. Chgo.; d. Lucius J. and Clara M. (Jung) Young; Ph.B., Northwestern U., 1952; m. Paul A. Rochetto, June 9, 1937. Profl. musician, 1930-50; membership sec. Internat. Soc. for Gen. Semantics, 1950-55, exec. sec., 1955-68, dir., 1952-68; tchr. Aurora Coll., 1968—; counselor State of Ill., 1970—. Pres., Chgo. Story League. Dir. Pan Am. Bd. Edn. Mem. AAUW (pres. Chgo. br. 1956—, mem. bd. 1953—), Am. Legion Auxiliary (mem. bd.), Alpha Sigma Lambda (dir.). Club: Woman's University (pres. 1966—). Home: 5240 N Sheridan Rd Chicago IL 60640

ROCHWARGER, LEONARD, financial services company executive; b. Buffalo, Aug. 3, 1925; s. Max and Sarah (Wallace) R.; m. Arlene Bassuk, June 19, 1949; children: Jeffrey Alan, Michelle. BS, U. Buffalo, 1949; LHD (hon.), Canisius Coll. Chief auditor Western N.Y. State, Buffalo, 1949-61; sr. ptnr. S. L. Horowitz & Co., Buffalo, 1961-65; chmn., chief exec. officer Firstmark Corp., Buffalo, 1965-87; U.S. ambassador to Fiji, Republic of Kiribati, Kingdom of Tonga and Tuvalu, 1988—; chmn. bd. Indpls. Morris Plan Corp., Firstmark Fin. Corp., 1972-87; chmn. bd. Israel Am. Leasing Ltd., 1971-87; dir. Marine Midland Bank-Western, Nat. Fuel Gas Co.; chmn. Rockmont Corp., Buffalo, 1988. Past gen. chmn. United Way Buffalo and Erie Co., 1973; trustee, past chmn. bd. regents Canisius Coll.; past chmn. United Jewish Appeal, Buffalo, 1969; past. pres., life dir. Buffalo Jewish Center; nat. bd. dirs. NCCJ; past bd. dirs., past pres. Nat. Jewish Welfare Bd.; past pres. Jewish Fedn. Greater Buffalo; bd. dirs. Council Jewish Fedns.; mem. adv. council Johns Hopkins U. Sch. Adv. Internat. Studies, Washington; past pres. Found. Jewish Philanthropies, Buffalo. Served with AUS, 1943-46. Decorated Bronze Star, Conspicious Service Cross. Mem. Am. Assn. Equipment Lessors (past pres., dir.), Beta Gamma Sigma., B'nai B'rith (dir. 1960-63). Jewish. Home: 81 Nottingham Terr Buffalo NY 14216 Office: Rockmont Corp 135 Delaware Ave Buffalo NY 14202

ROCKAWAY, ROBERT ALLEN, history educator, researcher; b. Detroit, Jan. 27, 1939; came to Israel, 1971; s. Jack and Betty (Kaluzny) R.; m. Batya Mirzoeff, Jan. 27, 1976; children—Eytan Nahum, Shiran Devorah. A.B., Wayne State U., 1961; M.A., U. Mich., 1962, Ph.D., 1970. Teaching fellow U. Mich., Ann Arbor, 1964-67; asst. prof. U. Tex., El Paso, 1970-71; lectr. Tel-Aviv U. (Israel), 1971-74, sr. lectr., 1974—; vis. scholar Brandeis U., Waltham, Mass., 1975-76; adj. assoc. prof. Boston U., 1975-76; cons. Beth Hatefutsoth Mus. of Diaspora, Tel-Aviv, 1974—; dist. vis. prof. Lipinsky Inst. Judaic Studies, San Diego State U., 1986-87. Author: The Jews of Detroit: From the Beginning, 1762-1914, 1986. Co-editor: Michael X: On the History of the Jews in the Diaspora, 1986. Contbr. articles to profl. jours. Chmn. com. on overseas student problems Israel Council for Higher Edn., Jerusalem, 1978. Recipient Rabbi Franklin Meml. award Hebrew Union Coll., 1979; named Hon. Citizen, El Paso, 1986; Meml. Found. Jewish Culture research grantee, 1979. Mem. Israel Assn. Am. Studies (pres. 1982—), Am. Hist. Assn., Orgn. Am. Historians, Assn. Jewish Studies, Internat. Assn. Study Peace and Prejudice, Immigration History Soc., World Union Jewish Studies, Phi Kappa Phi, Alpha Epsilon Pi. Jewish. Home: 67 Kdoshei Hashoa, Herzlia Pituah 46767, Israel Office: Tel Aviv U, Jewish History Dept, Ramat-Aviv 69978, Israel

ROCKEFELLER, DAVID, banker; b. N.Y.C., June 12, 1915; s. John Davison Jr. and Abby Greene (Aldrich) R.; m. Margaret McGrath, Sept. 7, 1940; children: David, Abby A., Neva, Margaret D., Richard G., Eileen M. B.S., Harvard U., 1936, LL.D., 1969; Ph.D., U. Chgo., 1940; LL.D., Columbia U., 1954, Bowdoin Coll., 1958, Jewish Theol. Sem., 1958, Williams Coll., 1966, Wagner Coll., 1967, Harvard U., 1969, Pace Coll., 1970, St. John's U., 1971, U. Liberia, 1979. Sec. to Mayor Fiorello H. La Guardia, 1940-41; asst. regional dir. Office Def., Health and Welfare Services, 1941-42; 2d v.p. Chase Nat. Bank, 1948-49, v.p., 1949-51, sr. v.p., 1951-55; sr. v.p. Chase Nat. Bank (merged with); Bank of Manhattan; exec. v.p. Chase Manhattan Bank, 1955-57, vice chmn. bd., 1957-61, chmn. bd., 1961-81, pres., chmn. exec. com., 1961-69, chief exec. officer, 1969-80, chmn. internat. adv. com., 1981—, also dir.; chmn. bd. Rockefeller Center, Inc. Author: Unused Resources and Economic Waste, 1940, Creative Management in Banking, 1964. Mem. exec. com. Downtown Lower Manhattan Assn., 1958—, chmn., 1958-75; trustee, chmn. bd. Rockefeller U., 1950-75, chmn. exec. com., 1975—; chmn., trustee Rockefeller Bros. Fund; hon. trustee Rockefeller Family Fund; life trustee U. Chgo.; trustee, vice chmn. exec. com. Mus. Modern Art; bd. overseers Harvard Coll., 1954-60, 62-68, 73-74; chmn. Americas Council. Served to capt. AUS, 1942-46. Decorated Legion of Honor France; Order of Merit, Italy; recipient award of merit N.Y. chpt. AIA, 1965; medal of Honor for City Planning N.Y.C., 1968; Charles Evans Hughes award NCCJ, 1974. Mem. Internat. Exec. Service Corps (dir., chmn. 1964-68), Center Inter-Am. Relations (dir., hon. chmn.), Council Fgn. Relations (dir. 1949—, v.p. 1951-70, chmn.). Clubs: Harvard, Univ., Century, Links, Knickerbocker. Address: 30 Rockefeller Plaza New York NY 10112 *

ROCKEFELLER, JOHN DAVISON, IV, senator, former governor West Virginia; b. N.Y.C., June 18, 1937; s. John Davison III and Blanchette Ferry (Hooker) R.; m. Sharon Percy, Apr. 1, 1967; children—Jamie, Valerie, Charles, Justin. B.A., Harvard U., 1961; student, Japanese lang. Internat. Christian U., Tokyo, 1957-60; postgrad. in Chinese, Yale U. Inst. Far Eastern Langs., 1961-62. Apptd. mem. nat. adv. council Peace Corps, 1961, spl. asst. to dir. corps, 1962, ops. officer in charge work in Philippines, until 1963; desk officer for Indonesian affairs Bur. Far Eastern Affairs, U.S. State Dept., 1963; later asst. to asst. sec. state for Far Eastern affairs; cons. Pres.'s Commn. on Juvenile Delinquency and Youth Crime, 1964; field worker Action for Appalachian Youth program, from 1964; mem. W.Va. Ho. of Dels., 1966-68; sec. of state W.Va., 1968-72; pres. W.Va. Wesleyan Coll., Buckhannon, 1973-75; gov. State of W.Va., 1976-84; U.S. senator from W.Va. 1985—, mem. fin. com., mem. transp. com., mem. vets. affairs com.; chmn. natural resources and environ. com. Nat. Govs. Assn., 1981-84; mem. fin. com., commerce, sci. and transp. com., vets. affairs com. Contbr. articles to mags. including N.Y. Times Sunday mag. Trustee U. Chgo., 1967—; chmn. White House Conf. Balanced Nat. Growth and Econ. Devel., 1978, Pres.'s Commn. on Coal, 1978-80, White House Adv. Com. on Coal., 1980; active Commerce, Sci., and Transp. Com., Fin. Com., Vet. Affairs Com. Office: Office of the Senate 724 Hart Senate Bldg Washington DC 20510

ROCKEFELLER, LAURANCE S., business executive, conservationist; b. N.Y.C., May 26, 1910; s. John Davison, Jr. and Abby Greene (Aldrich) R.; m. Mary French, Aug. 15, 1934; children: Laura Rockefeller Chasin, Marion French Rockefeller Weber, Lucy Rockefeller Waletzky, Laurance. B.A., Princeton U., 1932; LL.D. (hon.), SUNY Sch. Forestry at Syracuse U., 1961; D.Pub. Service (hon.), George Washington U., 1964, U. Vt., 1968; L.H.D. (hon.), Tex. Tech. Coll., 1966, Duke U., 1981, Marymount Coll., 1983, Princeton U., 1987. Chmn. Rockefeller Center, Inc., 1953-56, 58-66, dir., 1936-78; pres., chmn. Rockefeller Bros. Fund, 1958-80, vice chmn., 1980-82, adv. trustee, 1980—; dir. emeritus Rockresorts Inc.; chmn. Woodstock Resort Corp.; dir. Reader's Digest Assn., 1973—. Chmn. Citizens Adv. Com. on Environ. Quality, 1969-73; pres. Jackson Hole Preserve, Inc., Palisades Interstate Park Commn., 1970-77; commr. emeritus, 1978—; hon. chmn. N.Y. Zool. Soc.; chmn. Outdoor Recreation Resources Rev. Commn., 1958-65, White House Conf. on Natural Beauty, 1965; life mem. corp. MIT; charter trustee Princeton U.; trustee Alfred P. Sloan Found., 1950-82, Greenacre Found., Nat. Geog. Soc., Nat. Park Found., 1968-76; trustee Sleepy Hollow Restorations, 1975, chmn., 1981-85; hon. chmn. Meml. Sloan-Kettering Cancer Center, 1982—; bd. dirs. Community Blood Council Greater N.Y., Nat. Park Found. Served from lt. (j.g.) to lt. comdr. USNR, 1942-45. Decorated commandeur de Ordre Royal du Lion, Belgium, 1950; comdr. most excellent Order Brit. Empire; recipient Conservation Service award U.S. Dept. Interior, 1956, 62, Horace Marden Albright Scenic Preservation medal, 1957; Disting. Service medal Theodore Roosevelt Assn., 1963; Audubon medal, 1964; Nat. Inst. Social Scis. award, 1959, 67; Alfred P. Sloan, Jr. Meml. award Am. Cancer Soc., 1969; Medal of Freedom, 1969; Cert. of Award Am. Assn. for Cancer Research, 1980; James Ewing Layman's award Soc. Surg. Oncology, 1980. Clubs: River, Princeton, University, Brook, Links, Boone and Crockett, Knickerbocker, Lotos (N.Y.C.); Cosmos, Metropolitan (Washington). Office: care Rockefeller Bros Fund 1290 Ave of the Americas New York NY 10104 *

ROCKEFELLER, WILLIAM, lawyer; b. N.Y.C., Dec. 4, 1918; s. William Avery and Florence (Lincoln) R.; m. Mary D. Gillett, July 3, 1947; children: Mary Gillett Fogarty, Edith McKee Laird, Sarah Stillman Bogdanovitch. Grad., St. Paul's Sch., 1936; A.B., Yale U., 1940; student, U. Wis., 1940-41; LL.B., Columbia U., 1947. Bar: N.Y. 1948. Asso. firm Dorr, Hammond, Hand & Dawson, 1947-55, Shearman & Sterling, N.Y.C., 1955-57; partner Shearman & Sterling, 1957—; Dir. Cranston Print Works Co., R.I., Indian Spring Land Co., Conn., Oneida Ltd. Trustee, sec. Meml. Sloan-Kettering Cancer Center; bd. dirs. Am. Soc. Prevention Cruelty to Animals, pres., 1956-64; hon. chmn. Met. Opera Assn.; chmn. Geraldine R. Dodge Found.; trustee Paul Smith's Coll. Served to lt. comdr. USNR, 1941-46. Decorated Bronze Star; recipient gold medal Nat. Inst. Social Sci., 1977, Yale Medal, 1987. Mem. Am., N.Y. bar assns., Assn. Bar City N.Y., Zeta Psi, Phi Delta Phi. Episcopalian. Clubs: N.Y. Yacht, Links, Anglers, Metropolitan Opera, Westminster Kennel (N.Y.C.); American Yacht (Rye), Apawamis (Rye), Racquet and Tennis. Home: 84 Grandview Ave Rye NY 10580 Office: 153 E 53 St New York NY 10022

ROCKEL, JOHN EDWARD, lawyer; b. Cin., Sept. 30, 1944; s. Edwin Louis and Cecilia (Lasita) R.; m. Rita Martinelli, Oct. 10, 1970; children: Brian Louis, Jason Edward, Jennifer Lillian. BS, U. Cin., 1970; JD, No. Ky. State U., 1975. Bar: Ohio 1975, U.S. Dist. Ct. (so. dist.) Ohio 1975, U.S. Ct. Appeals (6th cir.) 1975, U.S. Supreme Ct. 1980. Sole practice Cin., 1980—. Served with USN, 1962-64. Home: 5851 Rapid Run Cincinnati OH 45233 Office: 5 W 4th Suite 2300 Cincinnati OH 45202

ROCKELÉ, RONALD FRANÇOIS, medical devices company executive; b. Reet, Antwerp, Belgium, Sept. 24, 1947; s. Gustaaf J. and Lydie T. (Van Frausum) R.; divorced; 1 child, Sofie. Grad. in applied internat. econs., U. St. ignatius, Antwerp, 1969. Market analyst Sewab SA Lugano, Switzerland, Lagos, Nigeria, 1970-71; sales mgr. Europe GTE-Sylvania-Brussels, Belgium, 1971-74; mgr. mktg. and sales 3M Belgium, Diegem, 1975-82; mgr. Davis and Geck Benelux div. Am. Cyanamid, Belgium, 1982-85; European mgr. Storz Instrument div. Fed. Republic Germany, 1987—; mgr. internat. acquisitions Idem, Belgium, 1985-87; cons. wood industry, Belgium, 1974-75. Home: 12 Im Eichwald, D6900 Heidelberg-Boxberg Federal Republic of Germany Office: Storz Instrument GMBH, Im Schumachergewann 4, D6900 Heidelberg 1 Federal Republic of Germany

ROCKEMANN, DAVID DOUGLAS, marketing director of health services; b. Jefferson City, Mo., Mar. 9, 1954; s. Raymond William and Irene Pauline (Strobel) R.; m. Margaret Ann Perkinson, June 20, 1986. BA in Sociology, U. Mo., 1976, MS in Community Devel., 1978. State health planner State Health Planning Devel. Agy., Jefferson City, 1978; health cons., research assoc. Syncaredian Health Assn., Walnut Creek, Calif., 1978-79; asst. dir. day care Jewish Home for the Aged, San Francisco, 1979; adminstr. St. Regis Retirement Ctr., Hayward, Calif., 1979-82; dir. aging services Community and Econ. Devel. Assn., Chgo., 1982-86; exec. dir. Community Nutrition Network, Chgo., 1986-87; v.p. Biotech. Cons., Kansas City, Mo., 1987—; dir. of bus. devel. Health Services div. John Knox Village, Lee's Summit, Mo., 1988—; cons. Wade West Inc., San Francisco, 1979; researcher Calif. Dept. Health Services, San Francisco, 1978-79; research asst. Ctr. for Research in Social Behavior, Columbia, Mo., 1977-79; gerontology research cons. Ctr. for Aging, U. Mo., Kansas City, 1987—. Author: Outreach to the Elderly, 1983; (with others) Health Care Trends, 1978, Consumer's Guide to Nursing Homes, 1978. Mem. adv. council Suburban Cook County Area Agy. on Aging, Chgo., 1983-84; legis. adv. State of Ill. Spl. Com. on Aging, Chgo., 1985; coordinator, moderator Mid-Am. Congress on Aging, Kansas City, Mo., 1985; mem. planning com. Mid-Am. Congress on Aging, Chgo., 1986. Adminstrn. on Aging scholar U. Mo., 1977-78; Older Americans Act grantee, 1982-87. Mem. Gerontol. Soc. Am., Am. Soc. on Aging, Nat. Council on Aging, Community Devel. Soc. Am., Nat. Assn. of Nutrition and Aging Services Programs. Lutheran. Office: John Knox Village 400 N Murray Rd Lee's Summit MO 64081

ROCKWELL, ELIZABETH DENNIS, financial planner; b. Houston; d. Robert Richard and Nezzell Alderton (Christie) Dennis. Student Rice U., 1939-40, U. Houston, 1938-39, 40-42. Purchasing agt. Standard Oil Co., Houston, 1942-66; asst. sec. Heights Savs. Assn., Houston, 1967-70, asst. v.p., 1970-75, v.p. mktg., 1975-82; sr. v.p., fin. planner Oppenheimer & Co., Inc., Houston, 1982—; 2d v.p. Desk and Derrick Club Am., 1960-61; instr. Coll. of Mainland, Texas City, Tex.; instr. Downtown Coll. and Continuing Edn. Ctr., U. Houston; mem. Dean's adv. bd. U. Houston, alumni bd. 1987—, treas., 1988. Bd. dirs. ARC, 1985—, Houston Heights Assn., 1973-77, 85—; active Houston Jr. League, 1986-87. Named Outstanding Woman of Yr., YWCA. Mem. Am. Savs. and Loan League (state dir. 1973-76, chpt. pres. 1971-72; pres. S.W. regional conf. 1972-73; Leaders award 1972), Savs. Inst. Mktg. Soc. Am. (Key Person award 1974), Inst. Fin. Edn., Fin. Mgrs., Soc. Savs. Instns., U.S. Savs. and Loan League (com. on deposit acquisitions and adminstrn.), Spring Branch Meml. C. of C., Internat. Platform Assn., Houston Heights Assn. (charter, dir. 1973-77), Houston North Assn., Harris County Heritage Soc., Rice U. Bus. and Profl. Women, River Oaks Bus. Womens Exchange Club, U. Houston Bus. Womens Assn. (pres. 1986). Club: Forum. Author articles on retirement planning and tax options. Home: 3617 Yoakum Blvd Houston TX 77006 Office: Oppenheimer & Co Inc 333 Clay St Suite 4700 Houston TX 77002

ROCKWELL, WILLIAM HEARNE, lawyer; b. Taunton, Mass., Oct. 28, 1919; s. Julius and Alice (Hearne) R.; grad. Philips Acad.; A.B., U. Mich., 1941, M.A., 1947; LL.B., Columbia, 1950; m. Elizabeth Virginia Goode, Feb. 3, 1948; children—Enid Rockwell, Karen Rockwell, William Goode Rockwell (dec.). Bar: N.Y. 1950. Assoc. Donovan, Leisure, Newton & Irvine, 1950-51; asst. sec. The Valve Mfrs. Assn., 1951-55; sec. Am. Carpet Inst., Inc., 1956-66, sec., treas., 1966-68; sec., gen. counsel Am. Nat. Standards Inst., N.Y.C., 1969—, v.p., 1984—; gen. counsel Contemporary Dance, Inc., 1962—, Rondo Dance Theatre, Inc., 1970—, Montserrat Found., 1972—, Turns and Caicos Found., 1985—, Product Liability Prevention Conf., 1974—. Mem. bd. ethics Town of Pound Ridge, N.Y. Served from pvt. to maj. Transp. Corps, AUS, 1941-46. Mem. Assn. Bar City N.Y., ABA. (mem. anti-trust com.), Am. Soc. Assn. Execs. (legal com.), N.Y. Soc. Assn. Execs., Nat. Safety Council, Nat. Panel Arbitrators, Am. Arbitration Assn., Columbia Law Sch. Alumni Assn. (dir.), Pound Ridge Land Conservancy, Heritage Hills Soc., Ltd. (bd. dirs.). Clubs: Belham River Valley Country; Montserrat Yacht; Pound Ridge Tennis; New York Athletic; University (Washington), Heritage Hills Golf. Home: 957 D Heritage Hills Somers NY 10589 Office: 1430 Broadway New York NY 10018

RODAN, MENDI, conductor, music educator; b. Jassy, Romania, Apr. 17, 1929; s. Solomon and Miriam R.; m. Judith Rodan, Oct. 10, 1953; children: Aviad, Orly. MA, Acad. of Music, Bucharest, Romania, 1948. Conductor Radio Broadcasting Authority, Bucharest, 1953-58; prof. conducting Acad. Music, Jerusalem, 1962—, dep. dir., 1965-70, dean and dep. head, 1972-80, head, 1983—; dir. music and conductor Kol-Yisrael Broadcasting co., Jerusalem, 1963-72, Yerusalem Chamber Orch., Jerusalem, 1966-70; permanent guest conductor Israel, Europe, U.S., Far East, Australia, 1972-77; dir. music and chief conductor Israel Sinfonietta, B. Sheva, 1977—, Belgium Nat. Orch., Brussels, 1983—. Mem. bd. editors Ariel Pubs., Israel, Music in Time, Jerusalem. Bd. dirs. Council of Music, Israel, 1983—, music com. Am. Israel Cultural Found., N.Y.C, 1980—, various coms. of music and the arts. Named Officer of Merit, Italy, 1986, hon. citizen Tucson, 1974. Home: 6 Shiler St, Jerusalem 96227, Israel Office: Orch Nat de Belgique, 18 Flagey Plein, 1150 Brussels Belgium 1150

RODDER, WILHELM, mathematics educator; b. Remscheid, Fed. Republic Germany, Mar. 12, 1942; s. Walter and Herta (Pott) R.; m. Irmgard Rodder, Sept. 27, 1966 (div. Aug. 1986); children: Norbert, Melanie, Patrick. MS in Math., U. Cologne, Fed. Republic Germany, 1968; PhD, Rheinisch-Westfälische Tech. U., Aachen, Fed. Republic Germany, 1972; Dr.habil., Rheinisch-Westfälische Tech. U., 1986. Prof. Rheimisch-Westfälische Tech. Coll., 1968-78, 83—; head dept. U. Fed. Santa Cabarine, Florianpolis, Fed. Republic Germany, 1979-83; vis. prof. U. Panama, Panama City, 1987; cons. Inform, Aachen, 1976-79, Ministry Def., Bonn, Fed. Republic of Germany, 1978-79, Ministry Edn., Brazil, 1981-83, Volkswagen/Volvo, Wolfsburg, Holland, 1985-87. Contbr. numerous articles to profl. jours. Mem. Deutsche Gesellschaft fur U. Forschung. Home: Bogenstr 30, 5100 Aachen Federal Republic of Germany Office: RWTH, 5100 Aachen Templergraben Federal Republic of Germany

RODENGEN, JEFFREY LEE, nationally syndicated columnist, motion picture producer and director; b. Mpls., June 5, 1949; s. Marvin Albany and Geraldine Maude (Wooley) R.; m. Susan H. Olsonoski, June 23, 1973 (div. 1985); m. Karine N. Chapus, Nov. 3, 1985; student Moorhead (Minn.) State U., 1967-68, Universidad de las Americas, 1968-69, Riverside City Coll., 1969-70; B.A., U. Calif., Riverside, 1972; M.S., Ph.D. in Systems and Design Engring., U. Beverly Hills, 1982. Pres., Pythagoras Instruments, 1972, D.C. Recording Studios, Riverside, Calif., 1972, AVIII, Inc., 1973-78, AV Am., 1979-80; exec. producer, dir. mktg. Lights & Sounds Images, Tustin, Calif., 1979-81; pres. Grand Illusions Unltd., Las Vegas, 1981-83; Write Stuff Syndicate, 1986—; maj. prodns. include: Libra Colony, 1977, Latin Lasers, 1978, Galactic Laser Experience, 1978, Beyond Magic, 1981; Knowledge, 1978; Achieving Excellence, 1979; Celebrate, 1978; Fiesta Fantastico, 1979. Mem. Riverside Adminstrv. Bd. Appeals, 1973-77. Named Best Actor, Riverside Community Players, 1974; recipient Silver Cindy award, 1977; Honor award Soc. Tech. Communicators, 1984; holder Black Belt in Karate; lic. single and multi-engine pilot, instrument rating. Mem. Internat. Film Producers Am., Assn. Multi-Image, Aircraft Owners and Pilots Assn., Soc. Tech. Writers, Boating Writers Assn. Democrat. Presbyterian. Author: The Legend of Chris-Craft, 1987, Iron Fist: The Authorized Biography of Carl Kiekhaefer, 1988; inventor photo-optical laser and holographic devices, electronic ruler, space-docking game for Am.-Soviet space flight; patentee in field. Home and Office: 1108 Citrus Isle Fort Lauderdale FL 33315

RODERICK, JOHN PRESCOTT, journalist, lecturer, freelance writer; b. Waterville, Maine, Sept. 15, 1914; s. John Baptist and Emma (Toulouse) R. BA, Colby Coll., 1936, LHD, 1966; postgrad. in Japanese studies, Yale U., 1943. Reporter The Sentinel, Waterville, 1930-37; corr. A.P., Portland, Maine, 1937-42, Washington, 1942; fgn. corr. A.P., China, Middle East, London, Paris, North Africa, Indochina, Hong Kong,, Japan, 1945-84; bur. chief A.P., Hong Kong, 1956-58; bur. chief A.P., Beijing, 1979-80, spl. corr., 1977-84; lectr., free-lance writer, editor, 1984—; editor-in-residence East-West Ctr., Honolulu, 1985; disting. lectr. China, Colby Coll., 1986; lectr. U. Copenhagen, Arhus U., 1987. Author: What You Should Know about China, 1972; contbr. numerous articles on China and Japan to mags., Ency. Brit., chpts. to books. Served with U.S. Army, 1942-45, CBI. Decorated Order of Sacred Treasure (Japan); recipient Headliner's award for best article on China, AP Mng. Editors, 1971, Peace award Sokagakkai, 1986. Democrat. Clubs: Fgn. Corrs. of Japan (life; pres. 1965-66), Oriental (London). Home: 5-15-3 Kajiwara, Kamakura 247, Japan

RODGERS, FREDERIC BARKER, judge, lawyer; b. Albany, N.Y., Sept. 29, 1940; s. Prentice Johnson and Jane (Weed) R.; m. Judy Reed, Feb. 24, 1973. AB, Amherst Coll., 1963; JD, Union U., 1966. Bar: N.Y. 1966, U.S. Ct. Mil. Appeals 1968, Colo. 1972, U.S. Supreme Ct. 1974, U.S. Ct. Appeals (10th cir.) 1981. Chief dep. dist. atty., Denver, 1972-73; commr. Denver Juvenile Ct., 1973-79; mem. Mulligan Reeves Teasley & Joyce, P.C., Denver, 1979-80; pres. Frederic B. Rodgers, P.C., Breckenridge, Colo., 1980—; county judge County of Gilpin, 1987—; presiding mcpl. judge cities of Breckenridge, Blue River, Black Hawk, Central City, Edgewater, Empire, Idaho Springs and Westminster, Colo., 1979—; chmn. com. on mcpl. ct. rules of procedure Colo. Supreme Ct., 1984—. Mem. Colo. Commn. on Children, 1982-85. Served with JAGC, U.S. Army, 1967-72; to maj. USAR, 1972—. Decorated Bronze Star with oak leaf cluster, Air medal. Recipient Spl. Community Service award Colo. Am. Legion, 1979. Mem. ABA, Colo. Bar Assn. (bd. govs. 1986-88), Denver Bar Assn. (bd. trustees 1979-82), Continental Divide Bar Assn., First Judicial Dist. Bar Assn., Colo. Mcpl. Judges Assn. (pres. 1986-87), Nat. Conf. Spl. Ct. Judges (chmn.-elect), Denver Law Club (pres. 1981-82), Am. Judicature Soc., Marines Meml. Club. Episcopalian. Club: University (Denver). Contbr. articles to profl. jours.. Home: 210 E 4th High St Central City CO 80427-0398 Office: 11072 N State Hwy 9 PO Box 567 Breckenridge CO 80424

RODGERS, GARY ROLAND, investment banker; b. San Angelo, Tex., Oct. 21, 1946; s. Virgil D. and Hazel Alyne (Nutt) R.; m. Patricia Ann Lowe, Aug. 17, 1968; children: Gary Douglas, Trish Christine. BBA, U. Tex-Austin, 1969. CPA, Tex. Dep. commr. State Securities Bd., Austin, 1969-81; prin., sec.-treas. Tex. Capital Markets Group, Austin, 1981-83; pres., chmn. bd. Texvest Securities Corp., Austin, 1983—, Texvest Fin. Corp., 1987—; pres., chmn. bd. Texvest Realty Corp., Austin, 1983—; pres., chmn. bd. Texvest Mgmt. Corp., Austin, 1984—, Texvest Properties Corp., Austin, 1984—, pres., chmn. bd. Texvest Ins. Agy. Corp.; v.p., treas., dir. Devel. & Investment Group, Inc., Austin, 1983—, chmn. state employee incentive commn., Austin. Chmn. Employees Retirement System of Tex., 1983—; mem. Gov.'s Task Force on Health Ins., Austin, 1984; mem. Tex. Ho. of Reps. Select com. on state employee productivity, Austin, 1980. Mem. Austin Investment Assn., Tex. Pub. Employees Assn. (pres. 1979-80), Am. Inst. CPA's, Tex. Soc. CPA's. Democrat. Baptist. Clubs: Onion Creek, Capital, Austin. Home: 10922 Preston Trails Dr Austin TX 78747 Office: Texvest Securities Corp 900 Congress Ave Suite #405 Austin TX 78701

RODGERS, JOE M., diplomat; b. Bay Minette, Ala., Nov. 12, 1933; m. Helen Martin; two children. B.C.E., U. Ala., 1956. Chief engr. Burgess, Inc., 1959-63; mgr. sales and prodn. Dixie Concrete Pipe Co., 1963-66; pres., chmn. bd. Rodgers Constrn. Internat., 1966-76; proprietor JMR Investments, Nashville, 1976—; chmn., pres. Am. Constructors, Inc., 1979-85; fin. chmn. Republican Nat. Com., 1979-81; chmn. bd. CRC Equities, Inc., 1980-85; U.S. commr. gen. U.S. sect. 1982 World's Fair, 1982; mem. Pres.'s Fgn. Intelligence Adv. Bd., 1981-85; fin. chmn. Reagan-Bush '84 Campaign Com., 1984, 50th Am. Presdl. Inauguration Com.; U.S. ambassador to France Dept. State, Washington, 1985—. Bd. dirs. James S. Brady Presdl. Found., Fellowship of Christian Athletes, Randolph-Macon Women's Coll. Served to lt. USCG and Geod. Survey, 1956-58. Mem. Ams. for Responsible Govt. *

RODGERS, LOUIS DEAN, surgeon; b. Centerville, Iowa, Nov. 24, 1930; s. John James and Anna Alice (Spraguer) R.; m. Gretchen Lynn Hendershot, Feb. 19, 1954; children—Cynthia Ann, Elizabeth Dee. M.D., U. Iowa, 1960. Diplomate Am. Bd. Surgery. Intern, Broadlawns Hosp., Iowa, 1960-61; resident Meth-Hosp., Des Moines, 1961-65; practice medicine specializing in gen. surgery, Des Moines, 1965—; chmn. dept. surgery Iowa Methodist Ctr., Des Moines, 1980-84, chief gen surgery, 1982—; clin. assoc. prof. surgery U. Iowa, Iowa City, 1983—. Mem. steering com. Gov.'s Campaign, Republican Party, Iowa, 1982; bd. dirs. Iowa Meth. Med. Found., Des Moines, 1983, Des Moines Symphony, 1984—, Des Moines Children's Home, 1987. Served to staff sgt. U.S. Army, 1951-54. Named Surg. Tchr. of Yr., Iowa Meth. Med. Ctr. Dept. Surgery, 1978, 84. Fellow ACS (liaison to cancer com. 1973); mem. Western Surg. Assn. (mem. Iowa trauma com. 1983), Iowa Acad. Surgery (pres. 1982-83), Throckmorton Surg. Soc. (pres. 1986). Republican. Club: Des Moines Golf and Country. Home: 715 53d St Des Moines IA 50312 Office: Surgery PC 1212 Pleasant St #211 Des Moines IA 50309

RODGERS, MARY COLUMBRO, university chancellor, English language educator; b. Autora, Ohio, Apr. 17, 1925; d. Nicola and Nancy (DeNicola) Columbro; m. Daniel Richard Rodgers, July 24, 1965; children: Robert, Patricia, Kristine. A.B., Notre Dame Coll., 1957; M.A., Western Res. U., 1962; Ph.D., Ohio State U., 1964; postgrad. Fulbright scholar, U. Rome, 1964-65; Ed.D., Calif. Nat. Open U., 1975, D.Litt., 1978. Tchr. English Cleve. elem. schs., 1945-52, Cleve. secondary schs., 1952-62; supr. English student tchrs. Ohio State U., 1962-64; asst. prof. English U. Md., 1965-66; assoc. prof. Trinity Coll., 1967-68; prof. English D.C. Tchrs. Coll., 1968—; pres. Md. Nat. U., 1972—; chancellor Am. Open U., 1965—. Author numerous books and monographs; (latest works include) A Short Course in English Composition, 1976, Chapbook of Children's Literature, 1977, Comprehensive Catalogue: The Open University of America System, 1978-80, Open University of America System Source Book, V, VI, VII, 1978, Essays and Poems on Life and Literature, 1979, Modes and Models: Four Lessons for Young Writers, 1981, Open University Structures and Adult Learning, 1982, Papers in Applied English Linguistics, 1982, Twelve Lectures on the American Open University, 1982, English Pedagogy in the American Open University, 1983, Design for Personalized English Graduate Degrees in the Urban University, 1984, Open University English Teaching, 1945-85: Conceptual History and Rationale, 1985, Claims and Counterclaims Regarding Instruction Given in Personalized Degree Residency Programs Completed by Graduates of California National Open University, 1986, The American Open University, 1965 t0 1985: History and Sourcebook, 1986, New Design II: English Pedagogy in the American Open University, 1987, The American Open University, 1965 to 1985: A Research Report, 1987, The American Open University and Other Open Universities: A Comparative Study Report, 1988, others. Fellow Ship of Catholic Scholars; mem. Am. Open U. Acad., Poetry Soc. Am., Nat. Council Tchrs. English, Am. Ednl. Research Assn., Pi Lambda Theta. Roman Catholic. Home and Office: Coll Heights Estate 3916 Commander Dr Hyattsville MD 20782

RODGERS, RICHARD RANDOLPH, association executive; b. Madison, Ind., July 28, 1948; s. Richard Payne and Marjorie Jean (Bishop) R.; BS in Acctg., U. Ky., 1970, postgrad., 1972-73; postgrad. U. Md., 1984-85; m. Sharron Kaye Manley, Aug. 15, 1970; 1 child, Leigh Walker. Acct., Sullivan and Clancy, C.P.A.'s, Lexington, Ky., 1969-72; pvt. practice acctg., Lexington, 1972-73; comptroller Council of State Govts., Lexington, 1973-75; dir. adminstrn. and fin. Nat. Gov.'s Assn., Washington, 1975-86 , sec.-treas., 1977-86 , treas. Center for Policy Research, 1977-86 ; chmn. bd. State Services Orgn.; v.p. Adminstrn. Mortgage Bankers Assn. Am., 1986—. Pres., Lansdowne Neighborhood Assn., 1972-73; vice chmn. bd. deacons McLean Baptist Ch., 1979-80. Served with Army. N.G., 1970-76. C.P.A., Va. Mem. Am. Soc. Assn. Execs., Washington Soc. Assn. Execs., Ky. Soc. of Washington, U. Ky. Alumni Assn., Phi Gamma Delta. Baptist. Home: 1119 Brentfield Dr McLean VA 22101 Office: Suite 700 1125 15th St NW Washington DC 20005

RODIN, ERNST ANTON, neurologist; b. Vienna, Austria, Aug. 30, 1925; came to U.S., 1950, naturalized, 1955; s. Mathias and Erna (Diner) R.; m. Martha Joanne Kinscher, Dec. 23, 1951; children: Krista, Peter, Eric. M.D., U. Vienna, 1949; M.S., U. Minn., 1955. Diplomate Am. Bd. Neurology and Psychiatry. Intern S.I. Hosp., N.Y., 1950-51; fellow dept. neurology Mayo Found., 1951-55; instr., then asst. prof. psychiatry U. Mich. Med. Sch., 1955-58; mem. faculty Wayne State U. Med. Sch., Detroit, 1958—, prof. neurology, 1970-81; clin. prof. dept. neurology Wayne State U. Med. Sch., 1983-84, prof. dept. neurology, 1984—; clin. prof. dept. neurology U. Mich., Ann Arbor, 1981-82; chief neurology and EEG Lafayette Clinic, Detroit, 1958-80; med. dir. Epilepsy Ctr. Mich., 1971—; dir. EEG lab. Children's Hosp. Mich., Detroit, 1962-80; dir. epilepsy program and electroencephalography lab. Henry Ford Hosp., Detroit, 1981-82; med. dir. Holden Lab. for Clin. Neurophysiology, Harper-Grace Hosp., Detroit, 1984—. Author: The Prognosis of Patients with Epilepsy, 1969; also articles. Mem. Am. EEG Soc. (pres. 1975-76), AMA, Am. Acad. Neurology (S. Weir Mitchell award 1957), Am. Epilepsy Soc., Central EEG Soc. (past pres.), Eastern EEG Soc. (past pres.), Mich. Neurol. Assn. Club: Grosse Pointe Sail. Home: 773 Balfour St Grosse Pointe Park MI 48230 Office: 3800 Woodward Ave 7th Floor Detroit MI 48201

RODINO, ELAINE ANN, psychologist; b. N.Y.C., Apr. 16, 1940; d. Americo Joseph and Rachel (Cafiero) Lamberti; B.S. cum laude, C.W. Post Coll., L.I. U., 1961; M.A., Hofstra U., 1963; Ph.D., Calif. Sch. Profl. Psychology, 1978; m. Robert J. Rodino, July 3, 1965; 1 dau., Michelle Lyn. Sch. pyschologist Long Beach (N.Y.) City Sch. Dist., 1964-67, 70-71, Roslyn (N.Y.) Sch. Dist., 1971-76, Gt. Neck (N.Y.) Sch. Dist., 1973-75; mem. supervisory staff Center for Legal Psychiatry, Santa Monica, Calif., 1978-83; pvt. practice clin. psychology, Santa Monica, 1978—; psychologist Los Angeles Suicide Prevention Center, 1978-84; psychologist, clin. dir., 1982-84; cons. ABC After-Sch. spl. on Teen Suicide Prevention, 1986; mem. Calif. Task Force on Positive Parenting, 1978-79. Mem. Los Angeles County Psychol. Assn. (pres. 1983, bd. dirs. 1982-83, 85—), Am. Psychol. Assn. (mem. div. psychotherapy, com. chair div. ind. practitioners, mem. div. media psychology), Calif. State Psychol. Assn. (div. media psychology, div.clin. psyhology, Western Psychol. Assn., Los Angeles Soc. Clin. Psychology, Am. Assn. Suicidology, Pi Gamma Mu, Psi Chi. Office: 233 Wilshire Blvd Suite 910 Santa Monica CA 90401

RODKEY, FREDERICK STANLEY, JR., lawyer; b. Urbana, Ill., Oct. 25, 1930; s. Frederick Stanley and Temple (Ryan) R.; m. Suzanne Ooms, June 15, 1963; children—Gretchen, Geoffrey. B.A., Stanford U., 1953; postgrad. Boalt Hall Sch. Law, U. Calif., 1954; J.D., Chgo.-Kent Coll. Law, 1956. Bar: Ill. 1957. Atty., Chgo. Title & Trust, 1956-57; assoc. Newton, Wilhelm & Kennedy, Chgo., 1957-59; atty. Household Fin. Corp., Chgo., 1959-64; counsel Res. Ins. Co., Chgo., 1964-66; ptnr. Crandall & Rodkey, Evanston, Ill., 1966-67; sole practice, Freeport and Lena, Ill., 1967—; atty. Village of German Valley, Ill., 1973—, Village of Ridott, Ill., 1974—, Village of Lena, 1977—, Village of Cedarville, Ill., 1979—; spl. asst. atty. gen. State of Ill., 1973-76; asst. pub. defender Stephenson County, Ill., 1971—; atty. Lena Park Dist., 1977—. Chmn. Central com. Stephenson County Republican Party, 1972-74. Mem. Ill. Bar Assn., Chgo. Bar Assn., Stephenson County Bar Assn., Chgo.-Kent Alumni Assn., (past treas.), Stephenson County Hist. Soc., Stanford Alumni Assn., Alpha Sigma Phi, Pi Sigma Alpha, Nu Beta Epsilon. Mem. United Ch. of Christ. Clubs: Lions (past pres.), Men's Garden Club of Freeport (past pres.), Elks. Home: 1126 S Benson Blvd Freeport IL 61043 Office: 200 Post Office Bldg Freeport IL 61032

RODMAN, ALPINE CLARENCE, arts and crafts wholesaler, entrepreneur; b. Roswell, N.Mex., June 23, 1952; s. Robert Elsworth and Verna Mae (Means) R.; m. Sue Arlene Lawson, Dec. 13, 1970; 1 child, Connie Lynn. Student Colo. State U., 1970-71, U. No. Colo., 1983—. Ptnr. Pinel Silver Shop, Loveland, Colo., 1965-68, salesman, 1968-71; real estate salesman, Loveland, 1971-73; mgr. Traveling Traders, Phoenix, 1974-75; owner Deer Track Traders, Loveland, 1975-85, pres. Deer Track Traders, Ltd., 1985—. Author: The Vanishing Indian: Fact or Fiction?, 1985. Mem. Civil Air Patrol, 1965-72, 87—, CAP, Ft. Collins, Colo., 1968, 70, Colo. rep. to youth tng. program, 1969, U.S. youth rep. to Japan, 1970. Mem. Bur. Wholesale Sales Reps., Mountain States Men's, Boy's and Western Apparel Club, Eastern States Western Salesman's Assn., Internat. Platform Assn., Indian Arts and Crafts Assn. (bd. dirs. 1988). Republican. Baptist. Clubs: Crazy Horse Grass Roots. Office: Deer Track Traders Ltd PO Box 448 Loveland CO 80539

RODOLITZ, GARY MICHAEL, civil engineer, consultant; b. N.Y.C., July 25, 1950; s. Abraham Jonas and Anna (Cohen) R.; m. Barbara Gale Friedman, Jan. 13, 1974; children—Lauren Sara, David Evan. B.A., NYU, 1973, B.S.C.E., 1973. Registered profl. engr., N.Y. Mng. ptnr. Profl. Engring. Assocs., Woodmere, N.Y., 1979-82; pres., chief exec. officer Corp. Ctr. Communications, Westbury, N.Y., 1985—, David Lauren Assocs., Ltd., Westbury, 1983—; mng. ptnr. Rodolitz Orgn., Westbury, 1984—; chief exec. officer Mitchel Field Bldg. and Contracting Corp., Westbury, 1982—; cons. Inc. Village of Freeport, N.Y., 1982—, City of Long Beach, N.Y., 1983-84. Designer, builder Mitchel Field Corp. Ctr., Garden City Corp. Ctr., Nassau County, N.Y. Mem. L.I. Bus. Devel. Council; bd. dirs. Assn. for a Better L.I.; trustee, bd. dirs. Bi-County Polit. Action Com. Mem. ASCE, N.Y. Acad. Scis., Nat. Soc. Profl. Engrs., N.Y. State Soc. Profl. Engrs., Nat. Com. Furtherance Jewish Edn. (bd. dirs., Edn. award 1986), Am. Mus. Natural History. Jewish. Avocations: photography, reading, guitar. Office: Rodolitz Orgn 1600 Stewart Ave Westbury NY 11590

RODRIGUEZ, CARLOS RAFAEL, economist, Cuban government official; b. Cienfuegos, Cuba, May 23, 1913; s. Pedro Rodriguez Villametide and Antonia Rodriguez R.; m. Mirta Rodriguez, Feb. 12, 1976; children—Anabelle, Dania, Enrique. D. Law, Dr. Social, Polit. and Econ. Scis. magna cum laude, Havana U., 1939. Bar: Cuba 1939. Mayor of Cienfuegos, 1933-34; minister without portfolio Cuban Govt., 1944; rep. Socialist Popular Party in Sierra Maestra, 1958-59; editor Party newspaper News of Hoy, 1959-62; pres. Nat. Inst. Agrarian Reform, Ministry Agr. and Animal Prodn., 1962-65; pres. Nat. Commn. Econ., Sci. and Tech. Collaboration, 1965-75; permanent rep. Cuba to Council of Mut. Econ. Aid; v.p. Council of State, v.p. council ministers charge fgn. affairs, fgn. trade, Nat. Bank Cuba, Com. Econ. Collaboration, 1976—; v.p. Councils of State and Ministers, 1976—; prof. econs. Havana U., 1960-62, dean Sch. Econs., 1961-62; mem. South Commn., Geneva, 1987. Author: Marxism in Cuban History, 1943; Jose de la Luz y Caballero, 1947; Welles Mission, 1957; Four Years of Agrarian Reform, 1962; Lenin and the Colonial Question, 1970; Marti, Contemporary and Companion, 1973; The Cuban Transition Toward Socialism 1959-63, 1978; Letra con Filo 3 vol., 1984, 88; Palabras en los 70, 1985. Contbr. articles to profl. jours. Mem., Revolutionairies Integrated Orgns., United Party Socialist Revolution Cuba; mem. central com., mem. secretariat Community Party Cuba, 1975-78, mem. polit. bur., 1975—. Recipient Cuban Nat. González Lanusa award, 1939, Nat. Essay award, 1938, Nat. Journalism award, 1939, XX Ann. Revolution medal, 1973; Orden Frank Pais, 1983; Orden Juan Marinello, 1983; named Prof. emeritus Havana U., 1983; also numerous decorations, Poland, Rumania, Bulgaria, U.S.S.R., Czechislovakia. Mem. Nat. Assn. Econs., Nat. Lawyers Guild. Address: Palace of Revolution, Havana Cuba

RODRIGUEZ, FILEMON CATARROJA, civil engineer; b. Quezon, Philippines, Dec. 25, 1903; d. Felix Romero and Brigada (Lorezca) Catarroja R.; m. Pilar Alonzo Tolentino, Jan. 6, 1932; children: Pilar, Filemon, Fernando, Manuel, Alberto, Cecilia, Eduardo, Jose, Cristina. BSCE cum laude, U. Philippines, 1926; PhD in Econs. with Honors, Philippines Women's U., 1974. Cert. engr. Philippines. Mem. irragation investigation com. Dept. Pub. Works and Communications, Philippines, 1929-30; tech. adviser Dept. Pub. Works and Communications, 1932-35; govt. scholar U. Calif., U.S. Bur. Reclamation, 1930-31; hydraulic engr. Nat. Devel. Co. on Investigation of Power Sites of Philippines, 1935-36, Nat. Power Corp., Philippines, 1937-39; chief engr. Nat. Power Corp., 1940-47, gen. mgr., 1948-54; chmn. Nat. Econ. Econ. Council & Coordinator of U.S. Aid, Philippines, 1954-55; dir. Philippine Bank Commerce, 1954-57; spl. tech adviser to pres. Philippines 1955-57; pres. Engring and Devel. Corp. of Philippines, 1955-57; chmn. Filoil Refinery Corp., Philippines, 1960-75; chmn. Nat. Econ. Devel. Council, Philippines, 1966; mem. Manpower Devel. Council of Philippines, 1966-67; mem. gooverning council Asian Inst. Econ. Devel. and Planning, 1966-68; v.p., bd. dirs. Elizalde Steel Rolling Mills, Philippines, 1968-75; chmn. Trans-Asia Oil & Mineral Devel. Corp., Philippines, 1969-77; pres. Philippine Internat. Trading Corp., 1974-76; chmn.; pres. Engring. and Devwl. Corp. Philippines, 1981—; vice chmn., cons. Bacnotan Conslidated Industries Inc., Cen. Cement Corp.; chmn. emeritus Philippine Investment Mgmt. Cons., Inc.; chmn. Phinma-EDCOPúDIAZ Internat. Corp., PHINMA-Atchison Cons. Inc., PHINMAúag Sugar Co., Inc.; mem. bd. trustees Philippine Women's U.; vice chmn. Kabankalan Sugar Co. Inc., Filagro Devel. Corp.; bd. dirs. FCI Devel. Corp., United Paper & Pulp Co. Inc.; cons. and lectr. in field. Author: Our Struggle for Power, 1967; Our Strategy of Survival, 1971; I Believe: A Testament of Faith, 1979; contbr. articles to profl. jours. Active numerous civic orgns. Recipient awards for excellence from numerous engring. and govt. service orgns. Fellow Acad. Internat. de l'Orgn., Phi Kappa Phi; mem. Nat. Research Council Philippines, Philippine Soc. Civic Engrs., Am. Judicature Soc., Philippine Soc. Agrl. Engrs. (Hon.), Philippine Inst. Chem. Engrs. (hon.), Philippine C. of C. Roman Catholic. Office: Engring Devel Corp of Philippines, EDCOP Bldg, Bengcal Makati, Metro Manila 3116, Philippines

RODRÍGUEZ, GILBERTO, marine biologist, researcher; b. Caracas, Venezuela, May 12, 1929; s. Tomás Rodríguez-Vázquez and Blanca Rami rez de Rodri guez; B.Sc., U. Central Venezuela, 1955; M.Sc., U. Miami, 1957; Ph.D., U. Wales, 1970; m. Selva Díaz, May 1, 1959; children: Sonsoles, Iliana, Gloria, Carolina, Elías, Isabel. Asst. dir. Oceanographic Inst., U. de Oriente, Venezuela, 1959; researcher, head Center of Ecology, Venezuelan Inst. for Sci. Research, Caracas, 1960—, investigator, 1979—; prof. marine biology U. Central de Venezuela. Mem. Nat. Agrl. Council, 1966-68; Venezuelan del. to UN Law of Sea Conf., 1971-76; del. Nat. Council Research and Tech., 1981-83. Mem. Soc. Exptl. Biology (London), Groupe Europeen de Recherrche sur l'evolution des Malacostraces, Sociedad Venezolana de Ciencias Naturales, The Crustacean Soc. (bd. govs. S.Am. 1986—). Author 4 books; contbr. articles to profl. jours. Office: Inst Venezolano de Investigaciones, Apartado 1827, Caracas Venezuela

RODRIGUEZ, JUAN ALFONSO, technology corporation executive; b. Santiago, Cuba, Feb. 10, 1941; came to U.S., 1953; s. Alfonso and Marie Madeleine (Hourcadette) R.; m. Alicia Sama, July 23, 1964; children: Juan V., Diego A., Silvia M., Carlos D. B.E.E., CCNY, 1962; M.E.E., NYU, 1963. Engr. IBM, Poughkeepsie, N.Y. and Boulder, Colo., 1963-68; engring. mgr. IBM, 1968-69; dir. tech. Storage Tech. Corp., Louisville, Colo., 1969-74, v.p. engring., 1974-77, v.p., gen. mgr. disk, 1977-79; v.p., gen. mgr. optical disk Storage Tech. Corp., Longmont, Colo., 1979-85; pres., chief exec. officer Exabyte Corp., Boulder, 1985-87, chmn., chief exec. officer, 1987—; dir. Iomega, Odgen, Utah, 1980-87. Patentee in field. Bd. dirs. Boulder YMCA, 1982-87. Recipient Outstanding Contbn. award IBM, 1967. Mem. Soc. Photo-Optical Instrumentation Engrs., IEEE (sr.; steering com. mass storage Computer Soc. 1981—). Republican. Roman Catholic. Office: Exabyte Corp 1745 38th St Boulder CO 80301

RODRIGUEZ, JUAN GUADALUPE, entomologist; b. Espanola, N.Mex., Dec. 23, 1920; s. Manuel D. and Lugardita (Salazar) R.; m. Lorraine Ditzler, Apr. 17, 1948; children: Carmen, Teresa, Carla, Rosa. BS, N.Mex. State U., 1943; MS, Ohio State U., 1946, PhD, 1949. Asst. entomologist U. Ky., Lexington, 1949-55, assoc. entomologist, 1955-61, prof. entomology, 1961—; adv. entomology U. de San Carlos, Guatemala, 1961; vis. scientist Warsaw U., 1961; sec. V Internat. Congress Acarology, 1978; del. internat. confs. Vienna, Moscow, San Jose, Costa Rica, Nottingham, Eng., Prague, Saalfelden, Austria, Kyoto, Japan, Edinburgh, Scotland, Hamburg, Fed. Republic Germany. Bd. dirs. Lexington chpt. NCCJ. Served with inf., AUS, World War II. Recipient Disting. Research award U. Ky. Alumni Assn., 1963; Thomas Poe Cooper award U. Ky. Coll. Agr., 1972, Outstanding Acarologist award Am. Registry Profl. Entomologists, 1984. Mem. Am. Inst. Biol. Scis., Acarol. Soc. Am. (governing bd.), Ky. Acad. Sci. (pres. 1982-83; pres. Found. 1982—, Disting. Scientist award 1985, exec. sec. 1988—), AAAS, Can. Entomol. Soc., Ont. Entomol. Soc., Entomol. Soc. Am. (br. sec.-treas. 1963-65, br. com. man at large 1968-71, br. pres. 1982-83, North Cen. States br. rep. to governing bd. 1984-87, chmn. centennial com. 1987—), Order Ky. Cols., Sigma Xi (pres. U. Ky. chpt. 1977, Gamma Alpha, Gamma Sigma Delta. Roman Catholic. Editor: Insect and Mite Nutrition, 1972, Recent Advances in Acarology, vols. I and II, 1979; co-editor: Current Trends in Insect Endocrinology and Nutrition, 1981, Leafhoppers and Planthoppers, 1985, Nutritional Ecology of Insects, Mites and Spiders, 1987; mem. editorial bd. Internat. Jour. Acarology; contbr. articles to profl. jours. Home: 1550 Beacon Hill Rd Lexington KY 40504

RODRIGUEZ, LEONARD, public relations executive; b. Phoenix, Jan. 27, 1944; s. Jesus H. and Manuela (Razo) R.; m. Jo Ann Gama, Jan. 16, 1965; 1 child, Lena Teresa. BS in Mktg., Ariz. State U., 1981. Cert. tchr., Ariz. Adminstrv. services officer Title XX Adminstrn., Phoenix, 1979-81, Block Grants Adminstrn., Phoenix, 1981-84; property mgmt. mgr. State of Ariz., Phoenix, 1984-86; pres. LTR Mgmt. Services, Phoenix, 1986—; adj. clin. instr., faculty assoc. Ariz. State U., 1979—; cons. Applied Econs. Curriculum, Jr. Achievement of Cen. Ariz., Inc., 1987. Chmn. community relations Ariz. State U. Minority Recruitment Program, Tempe, 1985-86; bd. dirs. Friendly House Inc., Phoenix, 1985—, vice chmn., 1986, pres., 1987; mem. community problem solving coordinating com. Valley of the Sun United Way, 1988—. Mem. Ariz. Adminstrs. Assn., Counterparts (founder 1986), Hispanic C. of C. Club: Vesta (Phoenix) (chmn. scholarship com. 1983). Lodge: Rotary (sgt. at arms 1985-86, sec. 1986—87, voting del. internat. conv., Munich, 1987, pres. 1987-88). Home: 7650 S 14th St Phoenix AZ 85040 Office: LTR Mgmt Services 3225 N Central Ave Suite 1618 Phoenix AZ 85012

RODRIGUEZ, MAURICIO, chemical company executive; b. Bogota, Colombia, Mar. 5, 1958; s. Jorge Enrique and Cecilia (Munera) R.; m. Carla Tarditi, Aug. 14, 1981; children: Santiago, Federico. BBA, C.E.S.A., Bogota, 1980; postgrad., U. S.C., 1981, Harvard U., 1983. Credit officer Citibank, Bogota, 1979-80; mgr. planning Dow Chem. Co., Miami, Fla., 1981-82; mgr. planning Dow Chem. Co., Bogota, 1982-83, v.p. fin., 1983—; rep. Nat. Bus. Adminstrn. Council, Bogota, also bd. dirs.; prof. fin. theory fin. grad. program Universidid de Los Andes . Contbr. articles to profl. jours. Bd. dirs. Colegio de Estudias Superiores de Adminstracion, Bogata, PUNCH, Leasing Srancol. Mem. Conservative Party. Roman Catholic. Home: CRA 8#83-50 Apt 202, Bogota Colombia Office: Dow Chem Co, Transversal 18 78-80, Bogota Colombia

RODRIGUEZ, MIGUEL, bishop; b. Mayaguez, P.R., Apr. 18, 1931. Student, St. Mary's Minor Sem., Pa. Ordained priest Roman Cath. Ch., 1958. Bishop Arecibo, P.R., 1974—. Office: Bishop's House Bx 616 Arecibo PR 00613

RODRIGUEZ, OSCAR, bank executive, industrial engineer; b. San Jose, Costa Rica, Aug. 25, 1951; s. Edwin and Matilde (Ulloa) R.; m. Marisol Fernandez de Rodriguez; children: Diana, Anabelle. BS in Indsl. Engring., Ga. Inst. Tech., 1974; MBA, INCAE, Nicaragua, 1976. Fin. mgr. Metalco, San Jose, Costa Rica, 1976-78; div. mgr. Matra div. Caterpillar Mfg. Co., San Jose, Costa Rica, 1978-81; gen. mgr. Banco Banex, San Jose, Costa Rica, 1981—; bd. dirs. Asociacion Bancaria Costarricense, Comite Nal. de Incae. Mem. Nat. Assn. Indsl. Engrs., Alpha Pi Mu. Home: PO Box 5806, San Jose Costa Rica

RODRÍGUEZ-CAMPOAMOR, HERNÁN, international civil servant; b. Buenos Aires, Nov. 26, 1921; arrived in Switzerland, 1963; s. Julián and Castora (Campoamor) Rodríguez; m. Blanca Ethel Giovo, Feb. 22, 1952; children: Alejandro Hernán, Géraldine Nina, Kaarina Blanca. BS, Col. Nat. Justo José Urquiza, Buenos Aires, 1938; MA, CUNY, 1965. Editor Revista Internal de Trabajo, Geneva, 1965-66; research sociologist Internat. Labor Office, Geneva, 1966-72; dep. dir. area office Internat. Labor Office, Buenos Aires, 1972-78; acting dir. area office Internat. Labor Office, Mexico City, 1978-80; chief editor Spanish Internat. Labor Office, Geneva, 1980-83; chief Spanish linguistic unit Intergovtl. Com. for Migration, Geneva, 1983—; cons. in field. Author: Psicologia y Cibernética, 1958, La Automatización en Perspectiva, 1959; editor: Hachette, Ariel, Siglo XX, 1945-78. Bd. dirs. student ctr. Faculty of Philosophy and Letters, Buenos Aires U., 1940-43; mem. Friends of the Museum of Fine Arts of Geneva. Recipient linguistic achievement award Argentine-Brazilian Cultural Inst., Buenos Aires, 1974, Platero prize

Spanish Book Club of the UN, Geneva, 1986. Mem. Soc. Suisse des Américanistes, Pro Novioduno. Roman Catholic. Club: Tennis of Nyon. Home: 15 Ave des Eules, CH 1260 Nyon Vaud Switzerland

RODRIGUEZ-DIAZ, JUAN E., lawyer; b. Ponce, P.R., Dec. 27, 1941; s. Juan and Auristela (Diaz-Alvarado) Rodriguez de Jesus; m. Sonia de Hostos-Anca, Aug. 10, 1966; children: Juan Eugenio, Jorge Eduardo, Ingrid Marie Rodriguez. BA, Yale U., 1963; LLB, Harvard U., 1966; LLM in Taxation, N.Y.U., 1969. Bar: N.Y. 1968, P.R. 1970. Assoc. Baker & McKenzie, N.Y.C., 1966-68; assoc. McConnell, Valdes, Kelley, Griggs, Sifre & Ruiz-Suria, San Juan, P.R.; undersec. Dept. Treasury P.R., 1971-73; mem. Sweeting, Pons, Gonzalez & Rodriguez, 1973-81; sole practice, Hato Rey, P.R., 1981—; dir. Ochoa Indsl. Sales Corp., Camaleglo Corp., Ochoa Telecom, Inc., Las Americas Trust Co., Ital/Americas Foods Corp., Paramount Foods Corp., Farmacias José Guillermo, Inc., Drug Cosmos, Inc. Bd. govs. Acqueduct and Sewer Authority P.R., 1979-84; mem. adv. com. collective bargaining negotiation of P.R. Elec. Power Authority to Gov. P.R., 1977-78; bd. govs. P.R. council Boy Scouts Am., mem. transition com., 1984-85. Mem. ABA, N.Y. State Bar Assn., P.R. Bar Assn. Roman Catholic. Clubs: AFDA, San Juan Yacht. Home: Calle Fresno #1 Urb San Patricio Caparra Heights PR 00921 Office: Suite 920 Chase Bldg 416 Ponce de Leon Ave Hato Rey PR 00918

RODRIGUEZ-IBANEZ, JOSE E., sociologist, educator; b. Zaragoza, Spain, Feb. 25, 1948; s. Hermenegildo and Encarnacion (Ibanez) R.; m. Maria Jesus Gil, June 27, 1973. Licenciado en Derecho, U. Madrid, 1971, Doctor en Derecho, 1980; MA in Sociology, U. Calif., Santa Barbara, 1976, PhD, 1985. Research asst. U. Madrid, Spain, 1976-80, asst. prof., 1980-82; prof. sociology U. Malaga, Spain, 1983-87; vocal-asesor Centro de Estudios Constitucionales, Madrid, 1987—. Author: Teoria Critica y Sociologia, 1978, El Sueno de la Razon, 1982, Despues de una Dictadura, 1987. Mem. Spanish Sociol. Assn., Spanish Soc. Sociology Profs. (dir. 1986—), Revista Espanola de Investigaciones Sociologias (editorial bd. 1982—), Revista de Occidente (editorial bd. 1986—), Sistema (editorial bd. 1979—). Home: Paseo de la Habana 70, 28036 Madrid Spain

RODRIGUEZ PADRON, JORGE, literature teacher; b. Las Palmas, Spain, June 11, 1943; s. Jorge Rodríguez Benítez and Iris Padrón Hernández; m. McDolores Vázquez-Dodero, June 24, 1967; children: Jorge, Gonzalo. MD in Romanic Lang., U. Madrid, 1966; PhD, U. La Laguna, Spain, 1977. Author: Domingo Rivero, Poeta del Cuerpo, 1967, Octavio Paz, 1976; editor: Antologia Poesia Hispanoamericana, 1984; contbr. articles to profl. jours. Mem. Litterary Critics Spanish Assn. Home: Descubridores 23 4B, Tres Cantos, 28760 Madrid Spain

RODRIQUEZ, RODRIGO, furniture company executive; b. Rome, July 29, 1937; s. Michele and Margherita (Costantini) R.; m. Adele Cassina, Jan. 9, 1963; children: Emanuele, Giovanni, Chiara, Francesco. Degree in law, U. Rome, 1960; degree Istituto Post Università per l'Organizzazione Aziendale, Torino, Italy, 1961; postgrad., Glacier Inst. Mgmt., London, 1965. Vice-chmn., co-pres. Cassina S.p.A., Milan, Italy, 1982—; chmn. Marcatre S.p.A., Milan, 1978—; dir. Flos S.p.A., Brescia, Cassina Japan K.K., Tokyo, Marcatre Ltd., London, CIPIEMME Costruzioni Parti Metalliche S.p.A, Carugo; pres. Europeenne de l'Ameublement, Brussels, 1986—. Home: Il Ronco 45, Carimate, 22060 Como Italy Office: Cassina SpA, Meda, Milan Italy

RODRIQUEZ COSTANTINO, EDUARDO JOSÉ, plastic company executive; b. Buenos Aires, June 15, 1941; s. José and Catalina (Costantino) R.; m. Josefina María Rauqel Aponte, July 7, 1976; children: María Victoria, María Catalina, María Florencia. Diploma, Facultad de Ciencias Médicas, Buenos Aires, 1960, Facultad de Ciencias Económicas, Buenos Aires, 1962. Mgr. adscript Salvat S.A., Capital Federal, Argentina, 1961-70; mgr. comml. El Monaguillo S.A., Capital Federal, 1970-75; mgr. ops. Flor de Lis S.A., Capital Federal, 1975-80; mgr. comml. Ferrum S.A., Capital Federal, 1980-82; gen. mgr. Hunter Douglas, San Martin, Buenos Aires, 1982-86; dir. comml. Cinplast S.A., Capital Federal, 1985—; cons. Plumari S.A., Lanös, Argentina, 1983. Mem. Assn. Argentina de Mktg. Roman Catholic. Lodge: Dr. Rosenfeldt. Home: Olaguer 3006 7 C, 1426 Capital Federal Argentina Office: Viamonte 748 4 Piso, 1053 Capital Federal Argentina

RODY, WALTER WILLIAM, shipbuilding company executive; b. St. Petersburg, Fla., Aug. 16, 1926; s. Walter and Mary (Fleitas) R.; BE in Civil Engring., Tulane U., 1948; MBA, La. State U., 1969; m. Joyce Dolores Van Sandt, July 27, 1949; children: Walter Wayne, Wendelyn Wren, Wendell Wesley. Office engr. Mene Grande Oil Co., San Tome, Venezuela, 1948-50; constrn. engr. A.N. Goldberg, New Orleans, 1950-52; prodn. engr. Avondale Shipyards, New Orleans, 1952-53, chief cost engr., 1953-54, chief engr., 1954-58, asst. to pres., 1958-59, prodn. mgr., 1959-65, v.p., 1966-69; dir. prodn. planning and control Ingalls/Litton Shipbldg., Inc., Pascagoula, Miss., 1969-71, dir. shipbldg., 1971-72; marine and indsl. cons., 1972-78; pres. Port Allen Marine Services, Inc., Baton Rouge, 1978-86; marine, environ. cons., Baton Rouge, 1987—. Chmn. adv. bd. Salvation Army, New Orleans, 1965, Baton Rouge, 1983; v.p. United Way, Baton Rouge, 1984-86; exec. v.p. Boy Scouts Am., Baton Rouge, 1986—; pres. Met. Crime Commn. New Orleans, 1965-66; chmn. Nat. Brotherhood of Christians and Jews Week, 1966; sustaining membership chmn. Boy Scouts Am., 1984-85. Recipient Disting. Service award New Orleans Jaycees, 1962; Citizen of Yr. award Jefferson Parish Sheriffs Assn., 1966. Mem. Am. Waterway Operators (chmn. Am. Waterway Shipyard Conf. 1985, exec. com. and bd. dirs. 1985-86), ASTM (chmn. Gulf Region 1969), Traffic Club Baton Rouge, ASCE, Tulane Engrs. Club. Methodist. Clubs: Skyline Country, World Trade Ctr., Plimsoll, Internat. House, City. Lodges: Rotary (Baton Rouge); Masons (past master), Shriners, Grand Consistory of La. (knights comdr. ct. of honor), Royal Order of Jesters (New Orleans). Contbr. articles to profl. jours. Home: 10 Oak Alley Baton Rouge LA 70806 Office: P O Box 14861 Baton Rouge LA 70898

ROE, KEITH, researcher; b. Plymouth, Great Britain, Aug. 9, 1949; s. Bernard Arnold and Eileen Julia Gertrude (Easton) R. BS, Loughborough U., 1971; MEd, Nottingham U., 1978, postgrad.; PhD, Lunds U., Sweden, 1983. Tchr. Kursversammeen Vidlunds U., Lund, Sweden, 1977-82; research asst. U. Lund, 1980-86; research fellow U. Gothenburg, Sweden, 1986—. Author: Mass Media and Adolescent Schooling: Conflict of Co-Existence, 1983; contbr. articles to profl. jours. Grantee Bank of Sweden, 1983-86, Swedish Social Sci. Research Council, 1988—. Mem. Internat. Communications Assn., Internat. Assn. Mass Communications Researchers, Internat. Assn. Study of Popular Music (sec., treas. 1986—), Assn. Swedish Mass Communicators (exec. com. 1983-85), Internat. Assn. Popular Music (treas. Nordic sec., treas. 1986—). Office: U Gothenberg, Box 5048, 40221 Gothenburg Sweden

ROE, KENNETH KEITH, utility service company executive; b. Phila., Oct. 17, 1945; s. Kenneth Andrew and Hazel (Thropp) R.; m. Elizabeth Eaton, June 28, 1975; children: Kenneth Andrew, Whitney Elizabeth, Edward Scott, Graham Bradford. B.S. in Mech. Engring., Princeton U., 1968; degree in Nuclear Engring., MIT, 1974, M.S. in Nuclear Engring., 1974; postgrad. in mgmt. devel., Harvard Bus. Sch., 1980. Registered profl. engr., Calif., N.Y., Wash., P.R., N.H. Engr., asst. project mgr. Burns and Roe, Inc., Hempstead, N.Y., 1971-75, Oradell, N.J., 1975-77; project engr., resident project mgr. Burns and Roe, Inc., P.R., Woodbury, N.Y., Richland, Wash., 1977-78; project engr. mgr., asst. project mgr. Burns and Roe, Inc., Oradell, 1978-79, asst. to pres., 1979-80, v.p., 1980-82, exec. v.p., 1982-85, dir., 1971—; pres. Burns and Roe Enterprises, Inc., 1985—. Chmn. pastor-parish relations com. First Ch. of Round Hill, Greenwich, Conn., from 1981; mem. adv. council dept. mech. engr. Columbia U., N.Y.C., 1982—. Served as lt. (j.g.) USN, 1969-71. Sloan Found. fellow, 1971. Mem. Am. Nuclear Soc. (corp. rep.), ASME (sec. exec. com. Met. Sect. 1981-82, 82-83, region II 1987—, chmn. 1983-84, Outstanding Leadership award 1986-87, chmn. nat. agenda bd.), AAAS, Water Pollution Control Assn. (P.R.), Colegio de Ingenieros (P.R.), Young Pres.'s. Assn., Sigma Xi. Republican. Clubs: Princeton (N.Y.C.); Stanwich (Greenwich); Sankaty Head Golf (Nantucket, Mass.); Coral Beach and Tennis (Paget, Bermuda). Office: Burns and Roe Enterprises Inc 800 Kinderkamack Rd Oradell NJ 07649

ROEBLING, MARY GINDHART, banker; b. West Collingswood, N.J.; d. I.D., Jr. and Mary W. (Simon) Gindhart; m. Siegfried Roebling (dec.); children: Elizabeth (Mrs. D.J. Hobin), Paul. Student bus adminstrn., econs. and fin., U. Pa., econs. and fin., NYU; LLD (hon.), Ithaca Coll., 1954; DS in Bus. Adminstrn. (hon.), Bryant Coll.; DSc (hon.), Muhlenberg Coll.; HHD (hon.), Wilberforce U.; DFA (hon.), Rider Coll.; DCS (hon.), St. John's U.; LHD (hon.), Marymount Coll., Rutgers U., 1987. Former chmn. bd. Nat. State Bank N.J., Women's Bank, Denver, now chmn. emeritus; chmn. N.Y. World's Fair Corp., 1964-65; dir. Companion Life Ins. Co., N.Y. Mem. adv. com. U.S. commr. gen. for Expo '67; nat. bd. dirs. U.S.O.; pub. gov. Am. Stock Exchange, 1958-62; mem. Regional Adv. Com. on Banking Policies and Practices; econ. ambassador State N.J. Chmn., N.J. Citizens for Clean Water, 1969-70; mem. Ann. Assay Commn., 1971, Nat. Bus. Council on Consumer Affairs; mem. adv. com. N.J. Museum. Life trustee George C. Marshall Research Found., N.J. Dental Service Plan; mem. nat. adv. council Nat. Multiple Sclerosis Soc.; trustee Invest-in-America; adv. bd. Assn. U.S. Army, civilian aide emeritus to Sec. Army, First Army; bd. govs. Del. Valley Council; chmn. N.J. Savs. Bond Com.; mem. 4th dist. Adv. Council Naval Affairs; bd. govs. Swedish Hist. Found.; nat. bd. Jr. Achievement Inc.; emeritus mem. def. adv. com. on women in services Dept. Def.; citizens adv. council Com. on Status of Women; bd. dirs. Am. Mus. Immigration; chmn. N.J. Hospitalized Vets.'s Service; comptroller Trenton Parking Authority; founder Donnelly Meml. Hosp. Women's Com. Decorated Royal Order Vasa (Sweden); commendatore Order Star Solidarity (Italy); recipient Brotherhood award NCCJ; Nat. Assn. Ins. Women award; Distinguished Service award Marine Corps League; Golden Key award N.J. Fedn. Jewish Philanthropies; Spirit of Achievement award women's div. Albert Einstein Coll. Medicine; Holland award N.J. Fedn. Women's Clubs; Outstanding Civilian Service medal Dept. Army, 1969; Humanitarian award N.J. chpt. Nat. Arthritis Found., 1970; Four Chaplains award, 1969; Trenton chpt. Nat. Secs. Boss of Year award, 1969, Internat. Boss of Year award, 1972; Golden Plate award Am. Acad. Achievement; Jerusalem Holy City of Peace award State of Israel; Dept. of Def. medal for Disting. Pub. Service, 1984; others. Mem. Nat. Def. Transp. Assn. (life mem.), U.S. Council of I.C.C. (trustee), N.J. Conf. Christians and Jews, Swedish Colonial Soc., League Women Voters, Am. Inst. Banking, N.J. Investment Council, Am. Bankers Assn., Soc. Mayflower Descs., Colonial Daus. 17th Century, Trenton C. of C., N.J. Firemen's Mut. Benevolent Assn. (hon. life), DAR, Geneal. Soc. Pa., Bus. and Profl. Women's Club, Daus. Colonial Wars, Pilgrim John Howland Soc. Clubs: Zonta, Trenton Country; Colony (N.Y.C.), Sea View Country, Contemporary (Trenton), Greenacres Country (Lawrenceville); Overseas Press (assoc.); Am. Newspaper Women's (asso.), 1925 F Street (Washington); Union League (Phila.). Address: 120 Sanhican Dr Apt 3C Trenton NJ 08618

ROEG, NICOLAS JACK, film director; b. London, Aug. 15, 1928; s. Jack Nicolas and Mabel Getrude (Silk) R.; m. Susan Rennie Stephen, May 12, 1957; children—Joscelin Nicolas, Nicolas Jack, Lucien John, Sholto Jules; m. 2d Theresa Russell, 1985; children: Maximilian Nicolas Sextus, Statten Jack. Student Brit. schs. Cinematographer: films The Caretaker, 1963, Masque of Red Death, 1964, Fahrenheit 451, 1966, A Funny Thing Happened on The Way to the Forum, 1966, Far From the Madding Crowd, 1967, Petulia, 1968; co-dir.: films Performance, 1970; dir.: films Walkabout, 1970, Don't Look Now, 1973, The Man Who Fell to Earth, 1976, Bad Timing, 1980, Eureka, 1982, Insignificance, 1985, Castaway, 1986, Track 29, 1987, Aria, 1988, The Witches, 1988. Mem. Dirs. Guild Am., Assn. Cinematograph, Television and Allied Technicians. Address: 14 Courtnell St, London W2, England

ROEGIEST, EUGEEN HERMAN JOSEPH, linguist, educator; b. Deurne, Antwerp, Belgium, Oct. 31, 1946; s. Lode and Maria (Baten) R.; m. Agnes G. Detollenaere, June 28, 1974; children: Isabel, Olivier. MA, U. Ghent, Belgium, 1968, PhD, 1976. Asst. prof. State U. of Ghent, 1969-83, lectr., 1983—, prof., 1985—, dir. Dept. Romance Linguistics, 1985—, dir. Post-grad. Bus. Lang. and Communications, 1987—; prof. Sch. Interpreters, Ghent, 1978-85, cons. mem. commn. of adminstrn., 1985—. Author: Prepositions in Modern Spanish, 1980; editor (book) Verb and Verb Phrases in Romance Languages, 1983; contbr. articles to profl. jours. Mem. Soc. de Linguistique Roman, Belgian Linguistics Soc. Office: State U Ghent, Blandijnberg 2, B-9000 Ghent Belgium

ROEGNER, GEORGE PETER, industrial designer; b. Flushing, N.Y., Sept. 3, 1932; s. George Elmer and Margaret (Hanna) R.; B.F.A., Pratt Inst., 1954; m. Jane R. Kramer, Aug. 29, 1959; children—George Curtis, John Hanson, Nicholas Meade. Staff designer Gen. Motors Corp., 1954-55, Raymond Loewy Assocs., N.Y.C., Westinghouse Corp., Metuchen, N.J., 1960-66; product design mgr. RCA, Indpls., 1966-70; dir. design Lenox Inc., Trenton, 1972-74; pres. Curtis Hanson Meade Inc., Far Hills, N.J., 1974—; partner Furniture Concepts Internat. Ltd.; dir. Cove House Corp. Bd. dirs. Clarence Dillon Library; vice chmn. Far Hills Bd. Adjustment; councilman Borough of Far Hills, 1982—, police chmn., 1984—. Served with U.S. Army, 1956-58. Recipient design awards ID Mag., Nat. Paper Box, Consumer Electronics Show, Printing Industries, Print Mag., Wescon. Mem. Indsl. Designers Soc. Am. (past nat. com. chmn.), Somerset Hills Assn., Raritan Valley Watershed Assn. Republican. Clubs: Eastward Ho Country, Stage Harbor Yacht. Designs shown at Mus. Modern Art, Smithsonian Instn., N.Y. World's Fair, Brussels, Zagreb Fairs, Indpls. Art Mus. also: 120 Woodland Way Chathamport MA 02650

ROEHL, JERRALD J(OSEPH), lawyer; b. Austin, Tex., Dec. 6, 1945; s. Joseph E. and Jeanne Foster (Scott) R.; m. Nancy J. Meyers, Jan. 15, 1977; children: Daniel J., Katherine C., J. Ryan, J. Taylor. BA, U. N.Mex., 1968; JD, Washington and Lee U., 1971. Bar: N.Mex. 1972, U.S. Ct. Appeals (10th cir.) 1972, U.S. Supreme Ct. 1977. Practice of Law, Albuquerque, 1972—; pres. Jerrald J. Roehl & Assocs., 1976-84, Roehl & Henkel, P.C., 1984—. lectr. to profl. groups; real estate developer, Albuquerque. Bd. dirs. Rehab. Ctr. of Albuquerque, 1974-78; mem. assocs. Presbyn. Hosp. Ctr., Albuquerque, 1974-82. Recipient award of recognition State Bar N.Mex., 1975, 76, 77. Mem. ABA (award of achievement Young Lawyers div. 1975, council econs. of law practice sect. 1978-80, exec. council Young Lawyers div. 1979-81, fellow div. 1984—, council tort and ins. practice sect. 1981-83), N.Mex. Bar Assn. (pres. young lawyers sect. 1975-76), Albuquerque Bar Assn. (bd. dirs. 1976-79), N.Mex. Def. Lawyers Assn. (pres. 1983-84), Sigma Alpha Epsilon, Sigma Delta Chi, Phi Delta Phi. Roman Catholic. Clubs: Albuquerque Country, Albuquerque Petroleum. Bd. advs. ABA Jour., 1981-83; bd. editors Washington and Lee Law Rev., 1970-71. Home: 4000 Aspen Ave NE Albuquerque NM 87110 Office: Roehl & Henkel 300 Central Ave SW 3d Central Plaza Suite 2500 E Albuquerque NM 87102

ROEHL, JOSEPH E., lawyer; b. Albuquerque, Feb. 17, 1913; s. H.C. and Elizabeth J. (Walsh) R.; m. Jeanne F. Scott, Nov. 1, 1938; children: James F., Jerrald J., Virginia J. B.A., U. N.Mex., 1936, postgrad., 1936-37; LL.B., U. Tex., 1946. Bar: Tex. 1946, N.Mex. 1946. News columnist, bus. mgr. N.Mex. Lobo, Albuquerque, 1934-36; spl. events, sports announcer sta. KOB, Albuquerque, 1935-37; advt. mgr. N.Mex. Sentinel, Santa Fe, 1938-40; owner operator Gas Palace, Albuquerque, 1940-42; asst. adminstr. OPA, 1942-44; promotion, merchandising mgr. sta. KNOW, Austin, Tex., 1945-46; librarian Supreme Ct. Tex., Austin, 1945-46; practice in Albuquerque, 1946—; law clk. U.S. Circuit Judge Sam G. Bratton, Albuquerque, 1946-47; assoc. Simms & Modrall, 1947-53; mng. partner Modrall, Seymour, Sperling, Roehl & Harris, 1954-74; sr. ptnr. Modrall, Sperling, Roehl, Harris & Sisk, 1953—, also dir.; chmn. com. uniform jury instrns. Supreme Ct. N.M., 1962-83; dir. Mountain States Mut. Casualty Ins. Co., 1977—; Pres., gen. mgr. Rio Grande Lumber Co., 1959-68; pres. Rico, Inc. Co-author, editor: New Mexico Civil Jury Instruction, 1966, 2d edit., 1981; Contbr. articles on law office econs. and mgmt. profl. jours.; speaker before profl. groups. Recipient First Nat. award for state bar activities, 1962. Mem. Fellows Am. Bar Assn., Am., Tex., N.Mex. bar assns., Sigma Chi. Roman Catholic. Clubs: Elk, Albuquerque Country, Albuquerque Petroleum. Home: 4010 Avenida La Resolana NE Albuquerque NM 87110 Office: 1000 SunWest Bldg Albuquerque NM 87102

ROELKE, ADA E(LLEN), social services adminstrator; b. Cumberland, Md., Aug. 24, 1928; d. George William Knock and Mary Emma (Roelke) Eichelberger; children: Karen Bahnsen, Steven Leveen. BA, Syracuse U., 1950; MSW, San Diego State U., 1967; PhD, Profl. Sch. of Psychol. Studies, 1986. Lic. clin. social worker, Calif. Tchr. pub. schs., Syracuse, N.Y., 1960-61; social worker Dept. Pub. Welfare, San Diego, 1964-66; psychiat. social worker State of Calif., Bakersfield, 1967-68; child protection worker Dept. Social Service, San Diego, 1968-77; coordinator, psychotherapist, Chronic Program Grantville Day Treatment Ctr., San Diego, 1977-81; chief social services Edgemoor Geriatric Hosp., Santee, Calif., 1981—; pvt. practice psychotherapy, La Mesa, Calif., 1969—; clin. cons. Fellow Nat. Assn. Social Workers; mem. Marriage Family and Child Counselors Assn., Lic. Clin. Social Workers Assn., Mineral and Gem Soc., Lapidary Soc. Unitarian. Home: 4015 King St La Mesa CA 92041 Office: Edgemoor Geriatric Hosp 9065 Edgemoor Dr Santee CA 92071

ROEMER, CHARLES ELSON, III, governor; b. Shreveport, La., Oct. 4, 1943; s. Charles E. and Adeline (McDade) R.; m. Patti Crocker; children: Caroline Elizabeth, Charles Elson, Dakota Frost. B.A., Harvard U., 1964, M.B.A., 1967. V.p. sales Innovative Data Systems Inc.; ptnr. Scopena Plantation; mem. 97th-100th Congresses from 4th Dist. La., 1981-87; gov. La., 1988—. Chmn. Bossier Heart Fund Drive, 1973; past v.p. La. Alliance for Good Govt.; mem. Bossier and La. Farm burs.; trustee Physicians and Surgeons Hosp., Shreveport Bossier Urban League, Alliance for a Better Community; chmn. Minuteman Orgn.; bd. dirs. Diabetic Bd. N. La.; del. La. Constl. Conv., 1972. Named Outstanding Young Man Bossier Parish, 1970. Democrat. Methodist. Office: Office of Gov PO Box 94004 Baton Rouge LA 70804-9004 *

ROES, NICHOLAS A., communications executive; b. Jersey City, Dec. 26, 1952; s. Nicholas R. and Mimi (Maresca) R.; m. Nancy Bennett. BS in Edn., U. Bridgeport, 1974, MA in Bus. and Pub. Mgmt., 1983. Registered investment advisor (SEC). Chmn. bd. Tchr. Update, Inc., Saddle River, N.J., 1976—; pres., cons., author Nicholas A. Roes & Assocs., Saddle River, 1979—; ptnr. Barryville (N.Y.) Investors, 1985—; dir. investor relations Gambling Times, Inc., Los Angeles, 1984—, NAR Prodns., 1987. Author: Helping Children Watch TV, 1982, America's Lowest Cost Colleges, 1985, Gambling for Fun, 1988; editor newsletter Tchr. Update, 1977—; (column) The Investment Column, 1980—. Mem. Internat. Assn. Fin. Planners, Direct Mail Club of N.Y., EDPRESS, C. of C., Mensa, Internat. Platform Assn. Office: PO Box 205 Saddle River NJ 07458

ROESCH, MAURICE ALBERT, III, marine corps officer, systems engineer; b. Phila., Aug. 22, 1940; s. Maurice Albert and Anne Catherine (Whitsky) R.; children—Timothy Patrick, Thomas Jonathan. B.S.M.E., Va. Poly. Inst. and State U., 1962; M.S. in Ops. Research, U.S. Naval Postgrad. Sch., 1970; Ph.D. in Systems Engring., U. Va., 1979. Commd. 2d lt. USMC, 1962, advanced through grades to col., 1983, ret., 1987; platoon comdr. 1st Marine Div., Camp Pendleton, Calif., 1963-64, co. comdr., 1965; co. comdr. 3d Marine Div., Vietnam, 1965-66; base maintenance officer Marine Corps Logistics Support Base, Albany, Ga., 1966-68; div. engr. 3d Marine Div., Okinawa, 1970-71; project mgr. Marine Air Ground Intelligence System, Marine Corps Devel. Ctr., Quantico, Va., 1971-75; marine office instr. NROTC unit U. Va., Charlottesville, 1976-79; comdg. officer wing engr. squadron 2d Marine Air Craft Wing, Cherry Point, N.C., 1979-80, asst. chief of staff G-4 (logistics), 1981; student Indsl. Coll. Armed Forces, Ft. McNair, Washington, 1981-82; acquisition sponsor project officer engr. equipment Hdqrs. Marine Corps, Washington, 1982-83; asst. dir. def. tech. and systems White House Sci. Office, Washington, 1983-87; dir. advanced systems initiatives TRW Space & Def., Redondo Beach, Calif., 1987—; assoc. prof. naval sci. U. Va., 1976-79; adj. prof. U. So. Calif., Los Angeles, 1980-82; instr. econs. Golden Gate U., 1981. Decorated Def. Superior Service medal and Navy Commendation medal. Mem. ASME, AIAA, AAAS, Tau Beta Pi, Sigma Xi. Roman Catholic. Home: 7300 Via Marie Celeste Rancho Palos Verdes CA 90274 Office: TRW Inc Space-Defense Sector One Space Park Bldg E-2 Room 10063 Redondo Beach CA 90278

ROESELER, ALBRECHT JOHANNES, newspaper editor; b. Berlin, Jan. 29, 1930; m. Brigitte Noack, Aug. 28, 1957; children: Caroline, Daniel, Emanuel. Teaching cert., Detmold (Fed. Republic Germany) Music Acad., 1950; PhD in Musicology, Berlin U., 1957; postgrad., Indiana U., 1953-54. Music editor Sikorski Publishers, Hamburg, Fed. Republic Germany, 1957-60; editor-in-chief Ullstein Book Pub., Frankfurt, Fed. Republic Germany, 1960-64, Piper Book Pub., Munich, Fed. Republic Germany, 1965-73; sr. editor Arts sect. Süddeutsche Zeitung, Munich, 1973—. Author: Heinrich Schütz, 1958, Grosse Geiger unseres Jahrhunderts, 1987. Office: Südeutsche Zeitung, Sendlingerstrasse, 8000 Munich 2, Federal Republic of Germany

ROESELER, WOLFGANG GUENTHER JOACHIM, city planner; b. Berlin, Mar. 30, 1925; s. Karl Ludwig and Therese (Guenther) Ph.D., Philipps State U. of Hesse, Marburg, W.Ger., 1946-49; LL.B., Blackstone Sch. Law, Chgo., 1958; m. Eva Maria Jante, Mar. 12, 1947; children—Marion, Joanie, Karl. Asso. planner Kansas City (Mo.) Planning Commn., 1950-52; city planning dir. City of Palm Springs, Calif., 1952-54; sr. city planner Kansas City, 1954-56; prin. asso. Ladislas Segoe & Assocs., Cin., 1956-64; dir. urban and regional planning Howard, Needles, Tammen & Bergendoff, cons. Kansas City, N.Y.C., 1964-68; owner W.G. Roeseler, Cons. City Planner and Transp. Specialist, Bryan, Tex., 1969—; head dept. urban and regional planning Tex. A&M U., 1975-81, 85-88, prof., 1975—, dir. Tex. A&M Ctr. Urban Affairs, 1984-88, exec. officer for edn. College of Architecture, 1988—. Fellow Inst. Transport Engrs.; mem. Am. Inst. Cert. Planners, Am. Planning Assn. Author: Successful American Urban Plans, 1982. Contbr. articles to profl. jours. Home: 2508 Broadmoor PO Box 4007 Bryan TX 77801 Office: Tex A&M U College Station TX 77843

ROESS, MARTIN JOHN, lawyer, banker; b. Ocala, Fla., Dec. 18, 1907; s. Martin John and Mary (Anderson) R.; m. Alice Guion, Nov. 21, 1981; children—Diane Celeste, Robert Thornton, Martin John, Mary Susan, Morgan Leslie, Sherry Allison, Lori. A.B., Cornell U., 1930, LL.D., 1931. Bar: Fla. 1932, D.C. 1938, U.S. Supreme Ct. 1935. Assoc. Rogers & Towers, Jacksonville, Fla., 1931-34; chief counsel Large Scale Housing div. FHA, Washington, 1934-37, dist. dir., Jacksonville, 1947-48; assoc. gen. counsel Internat. Paper & Power Co., N.Y.C., 1937-38; practice, St. Petersburg, Fla., 1938—; gen. counsel A. Lloyd Goode Contracting Co., Washington, 1938-43; pres., gen. counsel Builders Mortgage Corp., St. Petersburg, 1948-51; assoc. atty. Holland & Runyon, St. Petersburg, 1948-51; acting dir. Shelter div. Fed. CD Authority, Washington, 1951-52; owner, operator Martin Roess Co., Jacksonville, 1952-55; judge Fla. 6th Jud. Cir., 1967-68; owner, chmn. Am. Nat. Bank, South Pasadena, St. Petersburg, 1963-74; organizer, chmn. Am. Nat. Bank, Tyrone, St. Petersburg, 1972-74; chmn. Am. Nat. Bank, Clearwater, Fla., 1955-74; organizer, chmn. N.Am. Mortgage Corp., St. Petersburg, 1955-74; chmn., pres. N. Am. Ins. Agy., Inc., St. Petersburg, 1955-84; owner, dir. Lawyers Land Title Corp., St. Petersburg, 1958-85; founder, chmn., pres. Guaranty Savs. and Loan Assn., St. Petersburg, 1960-82; founder, pres. Internat. Travel Assoc., Inc., St. Peterburg, 1976—, Tour Hosts of Fla., Inc., 1977—; of counsel Jacobs, Robbins-Gaynor, P.A. Past bd. dirs. Fla. Council of 100; past chmn. Oceanography Com. Fla., Mem. ABA, St. Petersburg Bar Assn., Fla. Bar Assn., Fla. Bankers Assn., Am. Bankers Assn., Mortgage Bankers Assn., St. Petersburg Bd. Realtors, Fla. Savs. and Loan League, U.S. League Savs. Assns., U.S. C. of C., St. Petersburg C. of C., Ind. Bankers Fla. (past dir.), Cornell Law Assn., Phi Beta Kappa, Phi Delta Phi. Clubs: University (Washington); Cornell (N.Y.C.); River (Jacksonville); Yacht (St. Petersburg); Centre (Tampa). Office: PO Box 40070 Saint Petersburg FL 33743

ROETHLE, JOHN DONALD, corporate executive; b. Milw., Mar. 2, 1933; s. Rueben Henry and Helen Irene R.; m. Janet Y. Zemlicka, Sept. 19, 1960; children: Elizabeth Ann, John Henry, Christopher Charles. BA in Econs., Loras Coll., 1958; MBA, Northwestern U., 1959. Sales and adminstrv. asst. Rexnord, Milw., 1959-61; gen. mgr., treas. Wis. Capital Corp., Milw., 1961-62; v.p. fin. Romar Filter Corp., Milw., 1962-63; exec. v.p. Anderson/Roethle & Assocs., Inc., Milw., 1963-70; pres. Anderson/Roethle, Inc., Milw., 1970—; instr. fin. Marquette U., Milw., 1959-72; lectr. U. Wis., Madison, Milw., Milw. Sch. Engring, 1964-70; bd. dirs. Capital Investments, Inc. Contbr. articles to profl. publs. Bd. dirs. Milw. Tennis Classic Found., 1976—, Friends of the Mus., 1979-83. Mem. Inst. Mgmt. Cons. (dir. 1980—, pres. elect 1985, pres. 1985-87), Ind. Bus. Assn. Wis. (pres. 1988), Internat. Council Mgmt. Cons. Inst. (chmn. 1987). Republican. Episcopalian. Club: University. Lodge: Rotary (dir. 1976-79, treas. 1978-79). Home: 6311 N Berkeley Blvd Whitefish Bay WI 53217 Office: 811 E Wisconsin Ave Milwaukee WI 53202

ROEVER, FREDERICK HENRY, physician; b. Phila., June 9, 1940; s. Henry Frederick and Irma Suzanna (Lux) R.; B.S., Haverford Coll., 1962; M.D., Hahnemann Med. Coll., 1966; m. Patricia Anne Ayars, Sept. 4, 1965; children—Christopher Paul, Cynthia Patricia. Chief med. resident Mercy Catholic Med. Center, Phila., 1972; dir. med. edn. Tarpon Springs (Fla.) Hosp., 1973—, chief dept. medicine, 1976—, also mem. staff; practice medicine, specializing in internal medicine, Tarpon Springs; lectr. U. S.Fla. Served to capt., inf., U.S. Army, 1968-69; Vietnam. Decorated Bronze Star, Air medal, Vietnamese Honor medal 1st class. Diplomate Am. Bd. Internal Medicine. Fellow ACP; mem. AMA (student teaching award 1976), Undersea Med. Soc., Christian Med. Soc., Am. Soc. Internal Medicine, Assn. U.S. Army, VFW, Am. Legion. Democrat. Lutheran. Office: 1 E Valencia Dr New Port Richey FL 33552

ROFF, ALAN LEE, lawyer; b. Winfield, Kans., July 2, 1936; s. Roy Darlus and Mildred Marie (Goodale) R.; m. Molly Gek Neo Tan, July 21, 1980: 1 child: Cynthia Lee Edwards. BA with honors and distinction, U. Kans., 1964, JD with distinction, 1966. Bar: Okla. 1967. Staff atty. Phillips Petroleum Co., Bartlesville, Okla., 1966-75, sr. atty., 1976-85, sr. counsel, 1986—; statutory auditor Phillips Petroleum Toray Inc., Japan; bd. dirs. Singapore Chems. Phillips Petroleum, Singapore. Editorial bd. Kans. Law Rev., 1965-66. Precinct com. man Rep. Party, Lawrence, Kans., 1963-64; assoc. justice Kans. U. Chancery Club; mem. Kans. U. Young Reps. Elizabeth Reeder scholar U. Kans., 1965-66, Eldon Wallingford award, 1964-66. Mem. ABA, Okla. Bar Assn., Washington County Bar Assn., Order of Coif, Phi Alpha Delta, Pi Sigma Alpha. Mem. First Christian Ch. Club: Phoenix (Bartlesville) (bd. dirs. 1985-86, gen. counsel 1986—). Lodge: Masons. Office: 1209 Adams Bldg 4th and Keeler Bartlesville OK 74004

ROFF, J(OHN) HUGH, JR., energy company executive; b. Wewoka, Okla., Oct. 27, 1931; s. Hugh and Louise Roff; m. Ann Green, Dec. 23, 1956; children—John, Charles, Andrew, Elizabeth, Jennifer. A.B., U. Okla., 1954, LL.B., 1955. Bar: Okla., Mo., N.Y. Law clk. to presiding justice U.S. Ct. Appeals (10th cir.), 1958; atty. Southwestern Bell Telephone Co., St. Louis, 1959-63, AT&T, N.Y.C., 1964-68; v.p., gen. atty. Long Lines, N.Y.C., 1969-73, gen. atty., 1973-74; chmn., pres., chief exec. officer United Energy Resources, Houston, 1974-86; chmn. PetroUnited Terminals Inc. and Ala. Methane Prodn. Co., Houston, 1986—. Past chmn. Central Houston, Inc.; mem. adv. bd. Ctr. for Strategic and Internat. Studies, Washington; mem. council of overseers Rice U. Jones Sch. Bus. Adminstrn.; trustee Baylor Coll. Medicine; pres. Houston Symphony. Served to 1st lt. JAGC, U.S. Army, 1955-58. Mem. Order of Coif, Phi Beta Kappa. Clubs: Houston Country, Houston, Coronado, Houstonian. Office: United Energy Resources Inc United Energy Plaza Box 1478 Houston TX 77001

ROFFEY, LEANE ELIZABETH, insurance company systems analyst programmer; b. Chgo., Mar. 17, 1949; d. Joseph Andrew and Ethel Antoinette (DeSalvo) Accomando; m. Arthur Roffey, 1972 (div. 1973). B.A., Wayne State U., 1972. Indsl. cons. Computype Corp., Ann Arbor, Mich., 1976-77; project leader Manufacturing Data Systems, Ann Arbor, 1978-80; info. mgmt. supr. First Variable Life Ins. Co., Little Rock, 1980-82; programmer/analyst First Pyramid Life, Little Rock, 1982-83, Ark. Blue Cross and Blue Shield, Inc., Little Rock, 1983-85, Am. Security Life Ins. Co., San Antonio, 1985—. Fellow Life Mgmt. Inst.; mem. Mensa, Phi Theta Kappa. Republican. Episcopalian. Avocations: vocal coach, classic car restoration, auto racing.

ROGALSKI, LOIS ANN, speech and language pathologist; b. Bklyn., Dec. 17, 1947; d. Louis J. and Filomena Evelyn (Maro) Giordano; B.A., Bklyn. Coll., 1968; M.A., U. Mass., 1969; Ph.D., N.Y. U., 1975; m. Stephen James Rogalski, June 27, 1970; children—Keri Anne, Stefan Louis, Christopher James, Rebecca Blair. Speech, lang. and voice pathologist Rehab. Center of So. Fairfield County, Stamford, Conn., 1969, Sch. Health Program-P.A. 481, Stamford, 1969-72; pvt. practice speech, lang. and voice pathology, Scarsdale, N.Y., 1972—; cons. Bd. Coop. Ednl. Services, 1976-79, Handicapped Program for Preschoolers for Alcott Montessori Sch., Ardsley, N.Y., 1978—; research methodologist Burke Rehab. Center, 1977. Mem. profl. adv. bd. Found. for Children with Learning Disabilities, 1978—. Lic. speech and lang. pathologist, N.Y. State; Rehab. Services Adminstrn. fellow, 1968-69; N.Y. Med. Coll. fellow, 1972-75. Bd. dirs. United Way of Scarsdale-Edgemont, 1988—. Mem. N.Y. Speech and Hearing Assn., Westchester Speech and Hearing Assn., Am. Speech, Hearing and Lang. Assn. (cert. clin. competence), Council for Exceptional Children, Assn. on Mental Deficiency, Am. Acad. Pvt. Practice in Speech Pathology and Audiology (bd. dirs., treas. 1983-87, pres. 1987—), Internat. Assn. Logopedics and Phoniatrics, Sigma Alpha Eta. Contbr. articles to profl. jours. Office: PO Box 1242 Scarsdale NY 10583

ROGAN, ROBERT WILLIAM, management educator, osteopath; b. Buffalo; s. Rudolph Roland and Alice May (Saville) R. BA, SUNY, Buffalo, 1965, MBA, 1967; DO, W.Va. Sch. Osteo. Medicine, 1983; postgrad., Virginia Beach, 1986-88. Cert. data processor, data educator; diplomate Nat. Bd. Examiners for Osteo. Medicine and Surgery. Assoc. prof. bus. West Liberty (W.Va.) State Coll., 1976-79; intern Metro Health Ctr., Erie, Pa., 1983-84; asst. prof. computer sci. Gannon U., Erie, Pa., 1984-85; asst. prof. mgmt. Slippery Rock (Pa.) U., 1985-86; practice medicine specializing in osteopathy Harborcreek Family Practice, Erie, Pa., 1985. Couns. Contact Crisis Care, Lewisburg, W.Va., 1980-81; med. vol. in Jamaica, West Indies, 1988. Named one of Outstanding Young Men Am., 1978; recipient Hon. Sci. award Bausch and Lomb, 1960, scholarship U. Buffalo, 1960, two scholarships N.Y. State Regents, 1960-64; grantee NSF, Cornell U., 1959. Mem. Am. Osteo. Assn., Am. Coll. Gen. Practitioners, Mensa. Home: 3853 N Buffalo Rd Orchard Park NY 14127

ROGENSKI, THEODORE JOSEPH, financial services executive; b. Moline, Ill., Mar. 20, 1941; s. Felix Joseph and Stella Agnes (Borowski) R.; m. Nancy Elizabeth Moore, July 2, 1966; children: Jeffrey, Mark, Kerry. BBA, U. Wis., 1964; MBA, U. Chgo., 1970. Asst. cashier Am. Nat. Bank, Chgo., 1964-70; dist. mktg. mgr. Greyhound Leasing and Fin, Chgo., 1970-71; v.p. mktg. Am. Fletcher Leasing Corp., Chgo., 1971-74; regional v.p. Wells Fargo Leasing Corp., Phoenix, 1974-75; sr. v.p. Wells Fargo Leasing Corp., San Francisco, 1976-80, pres., chief exec. officer, 1981—, also bd. dirs.; bd. dirs. Wells Fargo Capital Markets, San Francisco, 1983—. Bd. dirs. Oberlin Dance Co., San Francisco, 1987—. Mem. Am. Assn. Equipment Lessors (bd. dirs. 1988—). Republican. Roman Catholic. Office: Wells Fargo Leasing Corp 101 California St San Francisco CA 94111

ROGER, JEAN GÉRARD, physician; b. Strasbourg, France, Oct. 28, 1933; s. Jean and Marie Helene (Berthelen) R.; m. Monique Werner, Nov. 5, 1955; children: Cathie, Alain, Philippe. MD, U. Strasbourg, 1964. Pvt. practice medicine specializing in arteriology, phlebology, lymphology Strasbourg, 1965; attache in cardiovascular diseases CHU, Strasbourg. Mem. French Coll. Vascular Pathology, French Soc. Phlebology, Assn. Regionale Angiologues Alsace-Lorraine (pres. 1982). Home: 17 Rue de Bourgogne, 67540 Ostawald France Office: 16 Rue du Vieux-Marché-, aux Grains, 67000 Strasbourg France

ROGERS, ALICE BRADSHAW, public relations and advertising executive; b. Dayton, Tex., Sept. 18, 1911; d. William Benjamin and Mannie Willis (Davis) Bradshaw; m. Evert A. Rogers, Aug. 17, 1934 (div. May 1950); children—Jane Rogers Matthews, Elizabeth Rogers Bannister, Nancy Lynn Rogers Stephanow. Student U. Tex., 1927-29, U. Houston, 1953, 59. Sec., Henry L. Doherty, stocks and bonds, 1930-33, L.E. Norton Real Estate, 1933-34, Fisk Electric Co., 1934-37; sec.-treas. Art Engraving Co., 1937-49, pres., 1949-50; pres. Advt. Arts Bldg. Corp., 1952-54, Houston Tradetypers, 1955-57, Goodwin-Dannenbaum Advt. Agy., 1957; dir., sec.-treas., pres. Art Engraving Co., Inc.; dir., pres. Advt. Arts Bldg. Corp.; pub. relations dir. Houston Youth Symphony, 1962-64; bus. relations dir. Better Bus. Bur., Houston; community club awards dir. Houston Chronicle, 1963-64; activities coordinator Houston Club, editor, bus. mgr. The Houston Clubber, 1964-83. Mem. adv. bd. Achievement Rewards Coll. Scientists Found.; dist. chmn. publicity bd. Girl Scouts U.S.A., 1946-50; mem. publicity com. United Fund, 1952-54; mem. advt. program com. Pin Oak Horse Show, Houston Fat Stock Show. Mem. Advt. Fedn. Am. (dir. 10th dist. 1955-81, Sterling Silver award 1978), Houston Advt. Fedn. (Outstanding Woman of Yr. award 1981, Alice B. Rogers Ednl. Fund established 1982), Houston Soc. Assn. Execs., Houston Advt. Club (hon. life, v.p., dir., sec.-treas., Disting. Service mem., Silver medal award 1979), Harris County Heritage Soc., Houston C. of C., Gamma Alpha Chi. Clubs: Press (life) (Houston); Mothers (Zeta Tau Alpha). Home: 2501 Lazy Hollow Apt 110B Houston TX 77063

ROGERS, BERNARD WILLIAM, military officer; b. Fairview, Kans., July 16, 1921; s. William Henry and Lora (Haynes) R.; m. Ann Ellen Jones, Dec. 28, 1944; children—Michael W., Diane E., Susan A. Student, Kans. State Coll., 1939-40; B.S., U.S. Mil. Acad., 1943; B.A. (Rhodes scholar), Oxford (Eng.) U., 1950, M.A., 1954, D.C.L. (hon.), 1983; grad., Command and Gen. Staff Coll., 1954-55, Army War Coll., 1959-60; LL.D. (hon.), Akron U., 1978, Boston U., 1981. Commd. lt. U.S. Army, 1943, advanced through grades to gen., 1974; aide to supt. U.S. Mil. Acad., 1945-46, comdt. cadets, 1967-69; aide to high commr. Austria Gen. Mark W. Clark, 1946-47; bn. comdr. Korea, 1952; exec. to comdr.-in-chief Far East Command, 1953-54; mil. asst. to Chief Staff U.S. Army, 1956-59; exec. to chmn. (Joint Chiefs of Staff), 1962-66; asst. div. comdr. (1st Inf. Div.), Vietnam, 1966-67; comdg. gen. (5th Inf. Div.), Ft. Carson, Colo., 1969-70; chief legis. liaison Dept. Army, 1971-72, dep. chief of staff for personnel, 1972-74; comdg. gen. U.S. Army Forces Command, 1974-76; chief of staff U.S. Army, 1976-79; supreme allied comdr. Europe; comdr. in chief (U.S. European Command), 1979-87; sr. cons. Coca Cola Co.; bd. dirs. Gen. Dynamics Corp., The Kemper Ins. Group, Inst. Def. Analyses, Atlantic Council U.S., Am. Council on Germany. Decorated D.S.C., Def. D.S.M., Silver Star, Legion of Merit with 3 oak leaf clusters, D.F.C. with 2 oak leaf clusters, Bronze Star medal with V device, hon. fellow Univ. Coll., Oxford U.; recipient Dist. Service Citation U. Kans., 1984. Mem. Council on Fgn. Relations, Assn. U.S. Army, Legion of Valor, Assn. Am. Rhodes Scholars, Soc. 1st Inf. Div., Am. Soc. French Legion of Honor, Phi Delta Theta. Club: Army-Navy Country. Office: c/o SHAPE Liaison Office Room 1A711 Pentagon Washington DC 20310

ROGERS, CHARLES CLAYTON, news anchor and reporter; b. Shreveport, La., Dec. 4, 1957; s. John Irwin and Ila (Milton) R.; m. Jane Elizabeth Safly, May 12, 1984. BA, U. Ark., 1979; M in Pub. Adminstrn., So. Meth. U., 1981; postgrad. in Journalism, Iowa State U., 1982-83. Pub. affairs rep. Exxon Co., USA, Houston, 1981-82; news anchor, reporter Sta. WOI-TV, Ames, Iowa, 1983-84, Sta. WMBD-TV, Peoria, Ill., 1984-87, Sta. WBNS-TV, Columbus, Ohio, 1987—; vol. TV cons. Ill. Dept. Children, Family Services, Peoria, 1984—. Co-producer, host TV spl., Somebody's Child, 1984-87 (named Best Feature AP 1986), Drunk Driving, 1986. Telethon host Muscular Dystrophy Assn., Peoria, 1986; adminstrv. bd. mem. 1st United Meth. Ch., Peoria, 1985-87; adminstrv. asst. WIlliamson for Mayor Campaign, Shreveport, 1982; state campaign staff coordinator Williamson for Ins. Commr. Campaign, Baton Rouge, 1979. Recipient Humanitarian Service award Ill. Dept. Children Family Services, 1986, Humanitarian Service award Luth. Social Services, 1986, Humanitarian Service award Counseling and Family Services, 1986, Humanitarian Service award One Ch. One Child of Ill., 1986, Spl. Citation for Outstanding work with children in need of adoption Gov. of Ill., 1987; Best Pub. Affairs Program Ill. Broadcasters Assn. for spl. report on drunk driving, 1986; named one of Outstanding Young Men of Am. U.S. Jaycees, 1981, 83. Mem. Ill. News Broadcasters Assn., Delta Upsilon (bd. dirs. 1978-79). Office: WBNS-TV Columbus OH

ROGERS, GARDNER SPENCER, railroad company executive, retired, consultant; b. Bryn Mawr, Pa., Sept. 16, 1926; s. Gardner Spencer and Frances (Lloyd) R.; m. Margaret Elizabeth Windsor, July 18, 1954; children: Ann Windsor, Barbara Lloyd. Student Episcopal Acad., 1940-44, MIT, 1944-45; BS, U. Colo., 1951. Registered profl. engr., Calif. With Western Pacific R.R. Co., San Francisco, 1947-70, engr. costs, valuation and stats., 1964-69, asst. to gen. mgr. planning and control, 1969, asst. gen. mgr., 1970; gen. mgr. Civil & Mech. Maintenance Pty. Ltd., 1970-77; mgr. Western Australian ops. Fluor Australia Pty. Ltd., 1971-73, gen. mgr. ry. div., 1973-77; gen. mgr. Pilbara Industries, 1971-73; dir. budgets and control Consol. Rail Corp., 1978-79, sr. dir. budgets, planning and control, 1980, dir. corp. planning, 1981-87; cons., 1987—; mem. spl. adv. team R.R. ofcls. to U.S. Govt., 1962; adv. com. on R.R. property ICC, 1966-70. Mng. trustee Daniel B. Gardner Trust, Chgo.; alt. trustee Cathedral Sq. Found., Perth; vestryman Ch. of Eng., 1971-77, mem. synod and provincial synod, 1973-77, mem. diocesan council, 1974-77, bd. dirs. sch.'s trust, 1975-77. Mem. Instn. Engrs. Australia, Am. C. of C. in Australia (bd. dirs., v.p., chmn. Western Australian exec. com. 1976-77), Swanleigh (chmn. exec. com. 1974-77, council), Am. Mgmt. Assn., Am. Ry. Engr. Assn. (sec. com. 11), Ry. and Locomotive Hist. Soc., Soc. of Cin., Mil. Order Loyal Legion (vice comdr.), Colo. Alumni Assn. No. Calif. (pres. 1951-52), Alpha Tau Omega (high council 1964-68, 82—). Republican. Clubs: Berkeley Tennis, Pacific Railway (San Francisco); Commonwealth (Calif.); Australian-Am. (Perth). Home and Office: Rt 1 9 Mal Paso Rd Carmel CA 93923

ROGERS, JAMES BEELAND, JR., investment company executive; b. Balt., Oct. 19, 1942; s. James Beeland and Ernestine Barbara (Brewer) R.; B.A. cum laude, Yale U., 1964; B.A. with honors, M.A. in Politics, Philosophy and Econs., Balliol Coll., Oxford (Eng.) U., 1966. Investment analyst Bache & Co., N.Y.C., 1966-69, R. Gilder & Co., N.Y.C., 1969-70; asst. to chmn. Neuberger & Berman, N.Y.C., 1970-71; with Arnhold and S. Bleichroeder Inc., 1971-73; exec. v.p. Soros Fund Mgmt. N.Y.C., 1973-80; chmn. bd. Rogers Holdings, 1980—; adj. prof. Columbia U. Sch. Bus., 1983-85, prof. fin., 1986—. Served to lt. U.S. Army, 1966-68. Home: 352 Riverside Dr New York NY 10025

ROGERS, JAMES THOMAS, lawyer; b. Denver, Oct. 3, 1941; s. John Thomas and Elizabeth (Milligan) R. J.D., U. Wis., 1966. Bar: Wis. 1966, U.S. Tax Ct. 1976, U.S. Ct. Claims, 1975, U.S. Ct. Customs and Patent Appeals, 1975, U.S. Supreme Ct. 1973. Chmn., Madison (Wis.) Legal Aid Soc., 1965-66; dist. atty. Lincoln County (Wis.), 1967, 69-73; spl. dist. atty. pro tem Oneida County (Wis.), 1972, Price County (Wis.), 1972-76, Lincoln County (Wis.), 1976-84; spl. city atty. City of Wausau (Wis.), 1973, 74, 77; ptnr. Rogers & Bremer, Merrill, Wis., 1973—. Chmn. Judiciary Com., N.E. Crime Control Commn., 1971-72. Chmn., Lincoln County Republican Com., 1971-73; bd. dirs. Pub. Defender State of Wis., 1988—. Mem. State Bar Wis. (spl. com. on prosecutorial improvements 1983—, spl. com. to rev. criminal sanctions 1987—), Lincoln County Bar Assn. (pres. 1969-70), Wis. Dist. Attys. Assn. (life), ABA (drunk driving com. of criminal justice sect., vice chmn. asset and investment mgmt. com. sec. econs. of law practice, marriage and cohabitation com. family law sect., def. services commn. criminal law sect.), Nat. Assn. Criminal Def. Lawyers, Assn. Trial Lawyers Am. (constl. challenge com. 1988—), Wis. Acad. Trial Lawyers (bd. dirs. 1985—), Tex. Trial Lawyers Assn., N.Y. State Trial Lawyers Assn., Personal Injury Lawyers Assn., Wis. Assn. Criminal Def. Lawyers (sec. 1986-87, pres.-elect 1987-88, pres. 1988—, bd. dirs. 1986—). Club: Wausau. Home: 1408 E 8th St Merrill WI 54452 Office: Rogers & Bremer 120 S Mill St Merrill WI 54452-0438

ROGERS, JANSIE, art and decorating company executive; b. Lenoir, N.C., Feb. 22, 1939; d. Raymond L. and Ruth (Henley) Setzer; m. G.R. Walter Rogers, June 23, 1963; (div. July 1984); children: Rob, Sharon. BA, James Madison U., 1961. Cert. custom decorator. Pub. sch. tchr., Baltimore County, Md., 1960-63, Perryville, Md., 1975-77; custom decorator Transart Industries, Woodstock, Ga., 1977-78, design dir., 1978-82, nat. dir. Trans Designs, Woodstock, 1982—. Bd. dirs. YMCA, Nat. Multiple Sclerosis Soc., Arthritis Found. Recipient awards including trips abroad, mink coats, diamonds TransDesigns, 1977-86. Mem. The Female Exec., Am. Bus. Women's Assn., LWV, Howard County C. of C. Democrat. Avocations: tennis, racquetball. Home and Office: 7554 Weatherworn Way Columbia MD 21046

ROGERS, KELLY WALTER, internat. transp. co. exec.; b. Chgo., July 26, 1930; s. Kelly Howard and Sophie Dolores (Bednarczyk) R.; student Chgo. and Calvert City (Ky.) pub. schs., 1936-48; m. Celeste Fern Mykol, Oct. 4, 1962; children—Derrick, Karla, Blake. Truck driver various firms, 1957-61; regional mgr. northwestern states Republic Van Lines, Seattle, 1961-63; regional mgr., western area Greyhound Van Lines div. Greyhound, Corp., Los Angeles, 1964-71; exec. v.p., gen. mgr. Hawaiian Hauling Service, Honolulu, 1971-74; asst. gen. mgr. Atlas Van Lines Internat., Evansville, Ind., 1974, v.p. and gen. mgr., 1974-76, exec. v.p., 1976, pres., chief operating officer, 1976-84, pres., chief exec. officer, dir., 1984-87; pres., owner Ambassador Travel, Inc., Evansville, 1987—; Ambassador Inst. Travel, Evansville, 1987—. Served with U.S. Army, 1948-53. Named Boss of Year, Internat. Secs. Assn., 1976; commd. Ky. Col., 1976; recipient Apollo d'Oro trophy European C. of C., 1983. Mem. Nat. Def. Transp. Assn., Household Goods Forwarders Assn. Am., Bus. Council for UN, Nat. Com. on Am. Fgn. Policy. Republican. Baptist. Club: Oak Meadow Golf & Country. Home: 410 Kings Valley Rd Evansville IN 47711 Office: 1310 N Green River Rd Evansville IN 47715

ROGERS, LEE JASPER, lawyer; b. Fort Monmouth, N.J., May 6, 1955; s. Peter and Ethel Mae (Williams) R.; m. Vanessa Walisha Yarbrough, Apr. 18, 1981; 1 child, Stephanie Alexandria. Student Drew U., 1975, Monmouth Coll., 1975; BA in History, Hampton Inst., 1977; JD, Howard U., 1980. Sole practice law, Red Bank, N.J., 1981—; vol. counsel Pro Bono Legal Services, Red Bank, 1982—; pres., chmn. bd. Jay-Mar Entertainment Enterprises Inc., 1986—. Author numerous poems. Mem. exec. com. NAACP, Red Bank, 1983-86. Mem. Assn. Trial lawyers Am., ABA. Baptist. Lodge: Elks (past acting recording sec.). Home: 112 Catherine St Red Bank NJ 07701-1244 Office: 298 Shrewsbury Ave Red Bank NJ 07701-1319

ROGERS, LLEWELLYN L., financial consultant, accountant; b. Greene, N.Y., May 30, 1909; s. Fred Leroy and Leora French (Burrows) R.; m. Mildred Ethel Hodge, Feb. 28, 1935; 1 child, Evelyn M. B.S., Pace Coll., 1929; grad. Nat. Exec. Tng. Sch., Mendham, N.J., 1934. C.P.A., N.Y. Staff acct. Touche, Ross & Co., N.Y.C., 1932-41; asst. treas. Clark Assocs., Inc., Binghamton, N.Y., 1946-53; sr. ptnr. Rogers & Patterson, Oneonta, N.Y., 1957-83; cons. to various pvt. founds., 1976—; lectr. acctg. and estate planning. Chmn. Milford Planning Bd., N.Y., 1968-70. Served to lt. USNR, 1942-45. Mem. Am. Inst. C.P.A.s, N.Y. State Soc. C.P.A.s (dir. 1959-61, pres. Binghamton chpt. 1956-58). Lodges: Rotary (dir. Oneonta 1960-63), Masons, Elks. Home: 5 Journey's End RD 1 Box 1216 Maryland NY 12116

ROGERS, MICHAEL BRUCE, orthodontist; b. Augusta, Ga., Oct. 25, 1945; s. Bruce Latimer and Dorothy (Baird) R.; m. Elizabeth Bennett, Dec. 21, 1968; children—Bruce, Kay, Alison, Lisa. Student Emory U., 1963-65, D.D.S., 1969; cert. in Orthodontics, Med. Coll. Ga., 1973. Diplomate Am. Bd. Orthodontists. Pvt. practice orthodontia, Augusta, Ga., 1973—; part time asst. clin. prof. Sch. Dentistry, Med. Coll. Ga., Augusta, 1973—. Served to capt. Dental Corps U.S. Army, 1971-73. Fellow Internat. Acad. Dental Studies; mem. ADA, Ga. Dental Assn. (del.), Am. Assn. Orthodontists (Ga. del.), Eastern Dist. Dental Soc. (pres. 1982-83), Ga. Soc. Orthodontists (v.p. 1983-84, pres. 1984-85), Med. Coll. Ga. Orthodontic Alumni Assn. (pres. 1981-83), Augusta Dental Soc. (pres. 1986-87), Psi Omega (pres. 1967-68), Omicron Kappa Upsilon. Roman Catholic. Avocations: golf; boating. Home: 3214 Candace Dr Augusta GA 30909 Office: 3545 Wheeler Rd Augusta GA 30909

ROGERS, ROBERT LEE, physician; b. Sabetha, Kans., Jan. 29, 1930; s. William Henry and Lora B. (Haynes) R.; B.A., Kans. U., 1952, M.D., 1955; m. Marjory Elaine Bauerle, Aug. 10, 1952; children—Clark William, Hugh Alan, Emily Sue. Intern, Mpls. Gen. Hosp., 1955-56; staff Gelvin-Haughey Clinic, Concordia, Kans., 1958-60; resident in ENT, Kans. U. Med. Center, Kansas City, 1960-63; practice medicine, specializing in otolaryngology Otolaryngic Med. Group, Kansas City, Mo., 1963-83, v.p., 1968-83; pvt. practice, Kansas City, Mo., 1983—; asso. clin. prof. ENT, Kans. U. Med. Center, 1964—; staff and chief ENT, Research Med. Center, Menorah, Bapt., St. Joseph hosps. Served with U.S. Army, 1956-58. Mem. Jackson County Med. Soc., Mo. Med. Soc., AMA, Kansas City Soc. Ophthalmology and Otolaryngology, Am. Soc. for Head and Neck Surgery, ACS, Am. Soc. Otology, Rhinology and Laryngology, Phi Beta Kappa, Alpha Omega Alpha. Republican. Lutheran. Club: Indian Hills Country. Contbr. articles to profl. jours. Office: Research Med Office Tower Suite T-401 6320 Prosepct St Kansas City MO 64132

ROGERS, ROBERT REED, manufacturing company executive; b. Oak Park, Ill., Feb. 22, 1929; s. Glen Charles and Lucile (Reed) R.; m. Barbara June Fain, Feb. 22, 1951 (div.); children—Robin, Janeen, Kevin. B.S. in Chemistry, Berea Coll., 1951; M.B.A., Ill. Inst. Tech., 1958, postgrad., 1959-62. Asst. mgr. metallurgy research dept. Armour Research Found., Ill. Inst. Tech., 1955-56, mem. faculty, econs. dept., 1956-62; cons. McKinsey & Co., Inc., 1962-64; mgr. devel. planning, profl. group Litton Industries, Inc., 1964-67; pres. N.Am. subs. Muirhead & Co., Ltd., 1967-68; group v.p. Am. Electric Inc. subs. City Investing Co., 1968-70; pres. Cleartight Corp., 1971-73; pres. Newport Internat. Metals Corp., 1973-76; pres. Kensington Assocs., Inc., Newport Beach, Calif., 1976-83; pres., chmn. bd. Proteus Group, Inc., Newport Beach, 1981-85, pres., chmn. bd. Comparator Systems Corp., Costa Mesa, Calif., 1983—. Served as officer USN, 1951-55. Decorated Knight of Grace Sovereign Order St. John; Machinery and Allied Products Inst. fellow, 1956-62; Berea Coll. grantee, 1947-51. Mem. Navy League, Ferrari Owners Club. Republican. Mem. Ch. of Religious Sci. Club: Lido Isle Yacht. Home: 2800 Broad St Newport Beach CA 92663 Office: Comparator Systems Corp 18552 MacArthur Blvd Suite 400 Irvine CA 92715

ROGERS, RUTH LOTTE, fashion consultant; b. Vienna, Austria, Dec. 31; came to U.S., 1938; d. Arnold and Elsie (Zemanek) Karplus; m. Martin C. Rogers, 1938 (div. 1950); m. Hans C. Altmann, Oct. 8, 1965; children: Susan Friedman, Victoria Thorson. Diploma, Kunst Gewerbe Akadamie, Vienna. Design cons. Herzmansky, Vienna, White Stag, N.Y.C., Koret of Calif., N.Y.C.; exec. v.p. R.R.J. Industry, N.Y.C.; now pres. Ruth Rogers Enterprises Internat., N.Y.C.; cons. Oxford Industries, Inc., The Forgotten Woman Stores; cons. Met. Mus. Costume Inst., N.Y.C.; panelist Am. Woman's Econ. Devel. Corp., N.Y.C.; lectr. Shenkar Coll., Tel-Aviv, Israel, Fashion Inst. Tech., N.Y.C. Author fashion and color forecast Burlington Industry; columnist: Knit Notes. Mem. Fashion Group Inc. (chairperson knits com. forecasting trendbook), Fashion News Workshop, Designers Group Nat. Knitwear and Sportswear Assn. (exec. com.), Woman's Fashion Network (charter). Avocations: painting, skiing, art. Home: 71 Park Ave New York NY 10016 Office: 71 Park Ave New York NY 10016

ROGERS, THEODORE COURTNEY, investment company executive, consultant; b. Lorain, Ohio, Aug. 25, 1934; s. William Theodore and Leona Ruth (Gerhart) R.; B.S. in Social Sci., Miami U., Oxford, Ohio, 1956; postgrad. Johns Hopkins U., 1957; M.B.A. summa cum laude, Marquette U., 1968; m. Elizabeth B. Barlow, June 28, 1984; children by previous marriage—Pamela Anne Rogers Harmon, Theodore Courtney Jr. With Armco Inc., 1958-80; pres. Olympic Fastening Systems, 1970-74, with Bathey Mfg. Co. subs., 1970, group v.p. indsl. products, 1971-74, exec. v.p. Nat. Supply Co. subs., Houston, 1974-76, pres., 1976-80, v.p. parent co., 1976-79, group v.p. parent co., 1979-80; pres., chief operating officer NL Industries, Inc., N.Y.C., 1980-82, pres., chief exec. officer, 1982-83, chmn., pres., chief exec. officer, 1983-87; ptnr. Am. Indsl. Ptnrs., N.Y., 1987—; cons. Valhi Corp., Dallas, 1987—. dir. Allied Signal Inc., Allied Stores Corp., MCorp. Bd. dirs. Nat. Corp. Fund for Dance, United Cerebral Palsy Research and Ednl. Found., Inc.; chmn. N.Y.C. Cerebral Palsy Fund Drive; chmn. nat. com. Houston Ballet; mem. devel. bd. U. Tex. Health Sci Ctr.; mem. campaign com. United Way Tri State; mem. fund leadership com. Lincoln Ctr.; chmn. bd. N.Y.C. Ballet. Served as lt. USN, 1956-58. Mem. Petroleum Equipment Suppliers Assn. (bd. dirs.), Young Pres. Orgn., Bus. Roundtable, Dir.'s Table, Beta Gamma Sigma (dirs.' table), Kappa Phi Kappa. Clubs: Ramada, Houston Country; Links, Sky, Economic (N.Y.C.); Metropolitan (Washington). Office: Am Indsl Ptnr 200 Park Ave Suite 3122 New York NY 10166-0114

ROGERS, VAN RENSSELAER, adminstrative and sales consultant; b. nr. Lexington, Ky., Jan. 9, 1914; s. Edgar Alfred and Nellie Estella (Burton) R.; grad. Cleve. Inst. Art, 1937; m. Ruth Charlotte Reichelt, Aug. 3, 1941; 1 son, Peter Van. Commd. sculptor Walt Disney Enterprises, Hollywood, Calif., 1937-38; co-founder Rogers Bennett Studios, Cleve., 1938; pres., owner Rogers Display Studios div. NESCO, Inc. (now Rogers Displays Inc.), Cleve., 1959—; founder Van R. Rogers Prodns., Inc., 1983—; profl. sculptor, artist, designer, painter. Asst. registrar John Huntington Poly. Inst., Cleve., 1938-41, producer sculptural artwork and household decorative artifacts, 1986. Chmn. Zoning Commn., Russell Twp., Geauga County, Ohio, 1974. Served to lt. comdr. USNR, 1942-46. Named to Hon. Order Ky. Cols. Mem. Exhibit Designers and Producers Assn. (pres. Ohio chpt. 1964-65), Nat. Trade Show Exhibitor Assn. (founder, citation as Godfather of orgn. 1977), Archaeol. Soc. Ohio, Dunham Tavern Soc. Collectors, Ohio

Hist. Soc., Geauga County Hist. Soc., Russell Twp. Hist. Soc., Nat. Trust Hist. Preservation, Found. Ill. Archeology, North and South Skirmish Assn., Nat. Muzzle Loading Rifle Assn., Greater Cleve. Growth Assn., Nat. Hist. Soc., Western Reserve Hist. Soc., Northwestern Archaeol. Soc., Genuine Indian Relic Soc., Nat. Hist. Soc., Ohio Acad. History, Archaeology Inst. Am., Imperial German Mil. Collectors Assn., Great Lakes Hist. Soc., Exhibit Designers and Producers Assn. (pres. Ohio Chpt. 1964-65), Am. Heritage Soc., Early Am. Soc., Nat. Hist. Soc. Club: Advertising. Lodges: Masons (32 deg.), K.T. Office: Rogers Displays Inc 26470 Lakeland Blvd Cleveland OH 44132

ROGERS, WILLIAM FENNA, JR., supermarket executive, management consultant; b. Higginsville, Mo., Dec. 25, 1912; s. William Fenna and Emily S. (Moose) R.; m. Thelma Ann Hooper, June 15, 1940 (dec. Mar. 1982); m. Ethel Allene Burgess, Aug. 6, 1983; stepchildren—Dorothy H. Nance, Linda H. Connors. B.A., Ark. Coll., 1933; postgrad. U. Ark., 1933, Tulane U., 1935, U. Fla., 1938-39. Vocat. adv. Nat. Youth Adminstrn., Little Rock, 1936-38; chief field ops. U.S. Employment Service, Little Rock, 1938-43, chief supr. tng., Washington, 1946-47; asst. dir. Civilian Personnel Div., U.S. Dept. Navy, Washington, 1947-55; member productivity team Nat. Mgmt. Council, Paris, 1952;lectr. U.S. Internat. Fair, Amsterdam, 1963; v.p. indsl. relations Giant Food, Inc., Washington, 1955-75; mgmt. cons., Falls Church, Va., 1975—; trustee Teamster Warehouse Fund, 1956—, Carpet Layers Funds, 1968—; lectr. Am. U., 1949-69; pres. Chateau Devel. Corp., Fairfax, Va., 1978-83. Mem. selection bd. U.S. Postal Service, 1969-77; elder New York Ave. Presbyterian Ch., Washington, 1948-72, Falls Church Presbyn. Ch., 1980-83; mem. Falls Church Village Preservation and Improvement Soc., 1967—; cons. Lincoln commn. New York Ave. Presbyn. Ch., 1984—; chmn. bur. edn. and employment Greater Washington Bd. Trade, 1974-76. Served to lt. comdr. USNR, 1943-64. Mem. Am. Soc. Tng. and Devel. (life), Am. Legion Res. Officers Assn., Naval Res. Assn., Alpha Psi Omega, Kappa Gamma, Pi Kappa Delta, Iota Lambda Sigma. Club: International Town and Country (dir. 1959-61) (Fairfax, Va.). Avocations: golf; fishing. Home: 214 Van Buren St Falls Church VA 22046

ROGGE, DWAINE WILLIAM, investment banker, counselor; b. Auburn, Nebr., Apr. 5, 1938; s. Elmer John and Gertrude Luella (Gerdes) R.; m. Wanda Lucille Teten, Aug. 17, 1958; children—Dwaine Scott, Shari Louise, Paul Alan. B.Sc. in Civil Engring., U. Nebr., 1960; M.B.A., Harvard U., 1962. Mgmt. trainee Archer Daniels Midland Bank, Mpls., 1962-64; corp. fin. dir. research First Mid.-Am., LIncoln, Nebr., 1964-74, exec. v.p., 1974-75; pres. Commerce Capital Inc., Lincoln, 1975—, Commerce Properties, Lincoln, 1979—, Commerce Commodities, Lincoln, 1975—, chmn., pres. Commerce Fin. Group, Inc. 1987—, Commerce Total Return Fund, Inc., 1987—; founder, stockholder Commerce Energy of Nebr., Lincoln, 1974—; founder, chmn. bd. Cartender Internat., Lincoln, 1984—. Pres. Family Service Assn. Lincoln, 1975, bd. dirs., 1969-75; mem. adv. bd. State Fin. com. Nebr. Republican Com., 1983-84. Served as lt. U.S. Army, 1962. Mem. Omaha-Lincoln Soc. Security Analysts (treas., bd. dirs. 1983-84), U. Nebr. Engring. and Tech. Alumni Assn. (pres. 1983-84). Lutheran. Home: 1835 Monterey Dr Lincoln NE 68506 Office: Commerce Capital Inc 846 NBC Ctr Lincoln NE 68508

ROGGE, JAN-UWE, researcher; b. Stade, W.Ger., Dec. 4, 1947; s. Ernst-Gunther and Anni (Bastein) R.; m. Brigitte Kreuscher, Mar. 23, 1973 (div. 1982); m. Regine Venzlaff, Dec. 2, 1983. Abitur, Atheneum, Stade, 1967; Dr. rer. soc., U. Tubingen, 1981. Research fellow U. Tubingen (Germany), 1977-86. Author: Medienmarkt für Kinder, 1980; Kinderfernsehsendungen, 1981; Kinderkultur in der DDR, 1984; Heidi, PacMan und die Video-Zombies, 1985; contbr. articles on media culture to profl. jours. Served to lt. German Navy, 1967-71. Mem. Union Children, Books, Media, Union Mass Media and Edn., Deutsche Gesellschaft fur Volkskunde. Home: Bachstrasse 140, D-2072 Bargteheide Federal Republic of Germany Office: Jan Uwe Rogge Gmbh, Bachstr 140, 2072 Bargteheide Federal Republic of Germany

ROGNAN, LLOYD NORMAN, artist, illustrator; b. Chgo., June 14, 1923; s. John and Gertrude Sophia (Hagen) R.; student Am. Acad. Art, 1941, 50, 51; diploma Acad. de la grande Chamiere, 1949; m. Sylvia Marcella Erickson, July 18, 1953; children—Bruce Byron, Cindy Lou. Cover artist French edit. Ellery Queen, Paris, 1947-49; religious film strip artist Concordia Pubs., St. Louis, 1950-53; art dir. Jahn & Ollier Engraving Co., 1954—; sci. fiction cover artist Greenleaf Publs., Evanston, Ill., 1956-58; with Meyer and Booth Studio, Chgo., 1958-61; biol. artist Golden Books Press, N.Y.C., 1961-63; cartoonist United Card Co., Rolling Meadows, Ill., 1966-71; art dir. Gallant Greetings, Chgo., 1972; artist, advt. posters (silk screen), Chgo., 1973-75; calendar artist Brown & Bigelow, St. Paul, 1976-79, Baumgarth, Brown & Bigelow, 1976-84, with Saga, Inc., ltd. edits. Western prints Albuquerque, 1977—; ltd. edit. plates Picard, Inc., Antioch, Ill., 1983-84; art dir., creative editor United Card Co., Arlington Hts., Ill., 1978—; represented in permanent collection Vesterheim Mus., Decorah, Iowa. Art counsellor Boy Scouts Am. Served with U.S. Army, 1943-46; ETO. Decorated Purple Heart. Home and Studio: 3620 Linneman St Glenview IL 60025

ROGNONI, PAULINA AMELIA, cardiologist; b. Panama City, Panama, Mar. 21, 1947; d. Mario Carlos-Enrique and Isabel Maria (Rodriguez) R.; B.S. in Chemistry (Tulane scholar), Tulane U., New Orleans, 1969, M.D., 1973. Rotating intern Gorgas Hosp., C.Z., Panama, 1973-74; intern internal medicine Touro Infirmary, New Orleans, 1974-75; resident in internal medicine Charity Hosp., New Orleans, 1975-77; fellow in cardiology Charity Hosp., 1977-79, VA Hosp., New Orleans, 1979-80; compulsory rural intern Panamanian Govt., Hosp. Amador Guerrero, Panam, 1980-81; dir. intensive care unit Gorgas Army Hosp., Meddac, Panama; cardiology cons. Clinica San Fernando. Mem. ACP, Med. Assn. Panama Canal Area, Am. Coll. Cardiology (asso.), Am. Med. Women's Assn., Am. Heart Assn., Mussor-Burch Soc., AMA. Assn. Mil. Surgeons U.S., Sociedad Panamena de Cardiologia, Sociedad Panamena de Mecidina Interna, Chi Beta, Beta Beta Beta, Alpha Epsilon Delta. Roman Catholic. Club: Panama Soroptimists. Home: U South Am Meddac, Panama Gorgas Army Hosp, Dept of Medicine, 34004-5000 Panama City Panama

ROHDE, JAMES VINCENT, software systems company executive; b. O'Neill, Nebr., Jan. 25, 1939; s. Ambrose Vincent and Loretta Cecilia R.; children: Maria, Sonja, Daniele. BCS, Seattle U., 1962. Chmn. bd. dirs., pres., Applied Telephone Tech., Oakland, 1974; v.p. sales and mktg. Automation Electornics Corp., Oakland, 1975-82; pres., chmn. bd. dirs. Am. Telecorp, Inc., 1982—. Pres. Council Regents Heritage Coll., Toppenish, Wash., 1985—; chmn. exec. com. Council Regents Heritage Coll. Republican. Roman Catholic. Office: Am Telecorp Inc 10 Twin Dolphin Dr Redwood City CA 94065

ROHLICEK, RUDOLF, government official Czechoslovakia; b. Malacky, July 14, 1929. Ed. Sch. Econs., Bratislava; postgrad. studies, 1960-63. Head dept. Investment Bank, Bratislava, 1948-58; chief sec. dist. com. Communist Party of Slovakia, 1958-60, in various offices central com., 1964-67; ofcl. central com. Communist Party of Czechoslovakia, 1963-64, head dept., central com., 1967-69, mem. central com., 1971—; minister of fin. Fed. Govt. Czechoslovakia, 1969-73, dep. prime minister, 1973-86, 1st dep. prime minister, 1986—; head Czechoslovak del. to CMEA Permanent Commn. for Fin. Questions, 1970-73, permanent rep. to CMEA, 1973; dep. House of People, Fed. Assembly CSSR, 1971—; chmn. CSSR Govt. Commn. for Questions of Rationalization of State Adminstrn., 1970-74; chmn. Council for Internat. Econ. and Sci. Tech. Cooperation, 1974—; chmn. Govt. Com. for Fgn. Tourism, 1976-82; chmn. Govt. Com. for Questions of Planned Mgmt. of Nat. Economy, 1985—. Author: Finance and Technical Progress, 1966; Finance and Efficiency, 1974. Decorated Order of Labour, Order of Victorious February. Office: Govt Presdium Czechoslovakia, nabr kpt Jarose 4, Prague Czechoslovakia

RÖHLING, HORST RUDOLF, librarian; b. Zwickau, Germany, Oct. 28, 1929; s. Rudolf Paul and Elisabeth Helene (SüB) R. Dr.phil. in Slavistics, Eastern Chs., 1956. Librarian, Univ. Library, Bochum, Fed. Republic Germany, 1964-69, Oberbibliotheksrat, 1969—; sec. Verband der Bibliotheken des Landes Nordrhein-Westfalen, Fed. Republic Germany, 1964-75. Author: Studien zur Geschichte der Balkanslavischen Volkspoesie, 1975; Slavica-Bibliotheca-Ecclesia Orientalis, 1981; Drei Bulgaro-Germanica, 1983. Editor: Arbeiten und Bibliographien zum Buch-und Bibliothekswesen; contbr. articles to profl. publs. Active Four Cs Club, Study Group on 18th Century Russia. Mem. Verein Deutscher Bibliothekare, Deutsche Gesellschaft für die Erforschung des 18 Jahrhunderts, Südosteuropa-Gesellschaft, Wolfenbütteler Arbeitskreis fur Geschichte des Buchwesens, Wolfenbütteler Arbeitskreis für Bibliotheksgeschichte, Study Group on 18th Century Russia, Internat. Adv. Panel of Solanus. Lutheran. Avocations: music, theatre, walking, drinking tea. Home: Unterkrone 37, 5810 Witten, Westfalia Federal Republic of Germany Office: Univ Library, Box 10 21 48, 4630 Bochum Federal Republic of Germany

ROHMER, ERIC (JEAN-MARIE MAURICE SCHERER), film director; b. Tulle, France, Mar. 21, 1920. Journalist until 1951; film critic for Revue du cinema, Arts, Temps modernes, La Parisienne; formerly co-editor and founder La Gazette du cinema; formerly co-editor Cahiers du cinema; co-dir. Soc. des Films du Losange. Dir. films: Le Signe du Lion, 1959; La Boulangère de Monceau, 1962, La Carrière de Suzanne, 1963, La Collectionneuse, 1967, My Night at Maud's, 1970 (Prix Max Ophuls 1970), Claire's Knee, 1970, Cloe in the Afternoon, 1972, Die Marquise von O, 1975, Perceval le Gallois, 1978, Comédies et Proverbes (La Femme de l'Aviateur), 1981, Le Beau Mariage, 1982, Pauline àla Plage, 1983; Full Moon in Paris, 1984, Le Rayon Vert, 1986, Quatre aventures de Reinette et Mirabelle, 1987, L'Ami de mon amie, 1987; made ednl. films for French TV, 1964-70; Author: (with Claude Chabrol) L'Organisation de l'espace le Faust de Murnau, 1977, Six Moral Tales, 1980. Recipient Prix Louis-Delluc, Prix du Meilleur Film dur Festival de Saint-Sebastien, Prix Melies (all for Claire's Knee), 1971. *

ROHNER, LOUIS, lawyer; b. Heerbrugg, Switzerland, Sept. 11, 1949; s. Otto Niklaus R. Dr.Jur., U. Zurich, 1976; LL.M., Harvard U., 1978. Dir. numerous Swiss and internat. cos. Mem. ABA, Swiss Bar Assn., Zurich Bar Assn. Home: Widmerstrasse 27, 8038 Zurich Switzerland Office: Rohner & Knecht, Ramistrasse 8, 8024 Zurich Switzerland

ROHRER, HEINRICH, physicist; b. Buchs, Switzerland, June 6, 1933. Diploma in Physics, Swiss Inst. Tech., Zurich, 1955, PhD in Physics, 1960; D. Sci. (hon.), Rutgers U., 1987. Research asst. Swiss Inst. Tech., Zurich, 1960-61; post-doc. Rutgers U., New Brunswick, N.J., 1961-63; with IBM Research Lab., Zurich, 1963—, now mgr. Physics dept.; vis. scholar U. Calif., Santa Barbara, 1974-75. Co-recipient King Faisal Internat. prize for sci., 1984, Hewlett Packard Europhysics prize, 1984, Nobel prize for Physics, 1986, Cresson medal Franklin Inst., Phila., 1987; IBM fellow, 1986. Office: IBM Zurich Reseach Lab, Saumerstrasse 4, CH-8803 Ruschlikon Schweig Switzerland *

ROHRMAN, DOUGLASS FREDERICK, lawyer; b. Chgo., Aug. 10, 1941; s. Frederick Alvin and Velma Elizabeth (Birdwell) R.; m. Susan Vitullo; children: Kathryn Anne, Elizabeth Clelia, Alessandra Claire. AB, Duke U., 1963; JD, Northwestern U., 1966. Bar: Ill. 1966. Legal coordinator Nat. Communicable Disease Center, Altanta, 1966-68; assoc. Keck, Mahin & Cate, Chgo., 1968-73, ptnr., 1973—; exec. v.p., dir. Kerogen Oil Co., 1967—. Vice chmn., commr. Ill. Food and Drug Commn., 1970-72. Served as lt. USPHS, 1966-68. Mem. Am., Chgo. (chmn. com. on food and drug law 1972-73), 7th Circuit bar assns., Am. Soc. Law and Medicine, Selden Soc. Democrat. Episcopalian. Clubs: Legal, Kenilworth, Metropolitan, River, Wigmore, Washington Duke. Co-author: Commercial Liability Risk Management and Insurance, 2 vols., 1978, 1986. Contbr. articles on law to profl. jours. Home: 520 Brier St Kenilworth IL 60043 Office: 8300 Sears Tower Chicago IL 60606

ROH TAE WOO, president of Republic of Korea; b. 1932; m. Kim Ok Sook, May 31, 1959. Grad., Korean Mil. Acad., 1955. With Korean Mil.; head Mil. Intelligence, 1980, ret. as Gen., 1981; fgn. relations minister, then home minister Govt. of Republic of Korea; mem. Nat. Assembly, 1985; chmn. Dem. Justice Party, 1985; pres. Republic of Korea, 1987—. Office: Office of the Pres, Seoul Republic of Korea *

ROISINBLIT, JORGE MARIO, cardiologist; b. Buenos Aires, Nov. 19, 1947; s. Adolfo and Meri Paulina (Martoy) R.; m. Sonia Haydee Brasch, Nov. 20, 1970; children: Ariela Vanina, Gustavo Walter, Diego Axel. B, San Martin Mil. Lyceum, 1963. Diplomate med. dr. Intern internal medicine U. Buenos Aires, 1970-71, resident internal medicine, 1971-74, docent internal medicine, 1974-75, asst. physician in cardiology, 1975-84; 2d chief lab. echocardiography Hosp. De Clinicas U. Buenos Aires, 1984—; v.p. Argentine Coll. of Cardiac Doppler, 1988—. Co-author: Restrictive Cardiomyopathy, 1987. Mem. Argentine Soc. Cardiology, Argentine Council Echocardiology (counselor 1986—). Club: Swiss Lawn Tennis (Buenos Aires). Home: Virrey Arrendondo 2529 1P, 1426 Buenos Aires Argentina Office: Hosp De Clinicas, Cordoba 2351, 1120 Buenos Aires Argentina

ROITSCH, PAUL ALBERT, pilot; b. Hermosa Beach, Calif., Oct. 15, 1926; s. George Arthur and Margaret (Pattillo) R.; m. Phyllis T.A. McCoy, Aug. 26, 1955; children—Sharon Elise, Alison Carol, Paul Eric. BA, U. So. Calif., 1952; postgrad. U.S. Navy Test Pilot Sch., 1965. Copilot, navigator Pan Am. Airways, San Francisco, 1952-53, pilot, 1955-64, asst. chief pilot tech., Jamaica, N.Y., 1965-69, chief pilot tech., 1969-73, line pilot, 1973-86, pres. Paul Roitsch Assocs., Internat. Aviation Cons., Greenwich, Conn., 1986—, pilot Civil Air Transport, 1954-55. Served with USN, 1944-49, 53-54. Mem. AIAA, Soc. Automotive Engrs. (safety standardization adv. com., airplane handling qualities and flight deck design com., recipient cert. of appreciation 1981), Internat. Soc. Air Safety Investigators. Home: John St Greenwich CT 06831 Office: PO Box 786 Greenwich CT 06836-0786

ROIZ, MYRIAM, foreign trade firm executive; b. Managua, Nicaragua, Jan. 21, 1938; came to U.S., 1949; d. Francisco Octavio and Maria Herminia (Briones) R.; m. Nicholas M. Orphanopoulos, Jan. 21, 1957 (div.); children—Jacqueline Orphanopoulos-Doggwiler, Gene E. Orphanopoulos, George A. Orphanopoulos. BA cum laude in Interdisciplinary Social Sci., San Francisco State U., 1980. Lic. ins. agt. Sales rep. Met. Life Ins. Co., San Francisco, 1977-79; mktg. dir. Europe/Latin Am., Allied Canners & Pachers, San Francisco, 1979-83; mktg. dir. Europe/Latin Am., M-C Internat., San Francisco, 1983—. Mem. Common Cause; coordinator Robert F. Kennedy Presdl. campaign, Millbrae, San Mateo County, local mayoral campaign, Millbrae, 1975; dir., organizer fund-raising campaign for earthquake-devastated Nicaragua; active Brown U. World Hunger Program. Named Outstanding Employee of Yr. Hillsborough City Sch. Dist., 1973; recipient Sales award Met. Life Ins. Co., 1977. Mem. Am. Soc. Profl. and Exec. Women, AAUW. Democrat. Roman Catholic. Club: Latino de Foster City. Office: M-C Internat 742 Market St 4th Floor San Francisco CA 94102

ROIZMAN, BERNARD, educator, virologist; b. Chisinau, Rumania, Apr. 17, 1929; came to U.S., 1947, naturalized, 1954; s. Abram and Liudmilla (Seinberg) R.; m. Betty Cohen, Aug. 26, 1950; children: Arthur, Niels. B.A., Temple U., 1952, M.S., 1954; Sc.D. in Microbiology, Johns Hopkins, 1956; D.H.L. (hon.), Gov.'s State U., 1984. From instr. microbiology to asst. prof. Johns Hopkins Med. Sch., 1956-65; mem. faculty div. biol. scis. U. Chgo., 1965—, prof. microbiology, 1969—, prof. biophysics, 1970—, chmn. com. virology, 1969-85, Joseph Regenstein prof., 1981—, Joseph Regenstein disting. service prof., 1984—, chmn. dept. molecular genetics and cell biology, 1985—; convener herpesvirus workshop, Cold Spring Harbor, N.Y., 1972; lectr. Am. Found. for Microbiology, 1974-75; mem. spl. virus cancer program, devel. research working group Nat. Cancer Inst., 1967-71, cons. inst., 1967-73; mem. steering com. human cell biology program NSF, 1971-74, cons. found., 1972-74; mem. adv. com. cell biology and virology Am. Cancer Soc., 1970-74; chmn. herpesvirus study group for Internat. Commn. Taxonomy of Viruses, 1971—; mem. Internat. Microbiol. Genetics Commn., Internat. Assn. Microbiol. Scis., 1974-86; sci. adv. council N.Y. Cancer Inst., 1971—; med. adv. bd. Leukemia Research Found., 1972-77; mem. herpesvirus working team WHO/FOA, 1972-81; mem. bd. sci. consultants Sloan Kettering Inst., N.Y.C., 1975-81; mem. study sect. on exptl. virology NIH, 1976-80; mem. task force on virology Nat. Inst. Allergy and Infectious Disease, 1976-77; mem. external adv. com. Emory U. Cancer Ctr., 1973-81, Northwestern U. Cancer Center, 1979—; cons. Institut Merieux, Lyon, France.; mem. sci. adv. com. Internat. Assn. for Study and Prevention Virus Assoc. Cancers, 1983—; mem. com. to establish vaccine priorities Nat. Inst. Medicine, 1983-85; chmn. sci. adv. bd. Showa U. Inst. Biol. Scis., 1983—. Author sci. papers, chpts. in books; mem. editorial bd.: Jour. Hygiene, 1958-61; editor: Herpes viruses, Vol. 1, 1982, Vol. 2, 1983, Vols. 3 and 4, 1985; mem. editorial bd.: Infectious Diseases, 1965-69, Jour. Virology, 1970—, Jour. Intervirology, 1972-85, Archives of Virology, 1975—, Virology, 1976-78, 83—, Microbiologica, 1978—, Cell, 1979-80; adv. editor: Progress in Surface Membrance Sci, 1972. Trustee Goodwin Inst. for Cancer Research, 1977—. Recipient Lederle Med. Faculty award, 1960-61, Career Devel. award USPHS, 1963-65, Pasteur award Ill. Soc. Microbiology, 1972, Esther Langer award for achievement in cancer research, 1974, Outstanding Alumnus in Pub. Health award Johns Hopkins U., 1984; named hon. prof. Shand oug Acad. Med. Scis., People's Republic of China, 1985; Am. Cancer Soc. scholar cancer research at Pasteur Inst. Paris, 1961-62; ICN Internat. prize in virology, 1988; faculty research assoc., 1966-71; traveling fellow Internat. Agy. Research Against Cancer, Karolinska Inst., Stockholm, Sweden, 1970; grantee USPHS/NIH, 1958—; grantee Am. Cancer Soc., 1962—; grantee NSF, 1962-79; grantee Whitehall Found., 1966-74. Hon. fellow Pan Am. Cancer Soc.; mem. Nat. Acad. Scis., Am. Assn. Immunologists, Am. Soc. Microbiology, Am. Soc. Virology, Am. Soc. Biol. Chemists, Brit. Soc. Gen. Microbiology. Club: Quadrangle (Chgo.). Home: 5555 S Everett Ave Chicago IL 60637

ROKKANEN, PENTTI UOLEVI, orthopedic surgeon; b. Helsinki, July 14, 1927; s. William and Ada (Kontio) R.; Lic. med., Helsinki U., 1953; M.D.Sci., Helsinki, 1962; asst. surgeon Lahti Hosp., Helsinki, 1955-64; cons. orthopedic surgeon Helsinki U. Hosp., 1964-71; surgeon in chief Central Hosp. Middle Finland, Jyvaskyla, 1972-75; prof. surgery Tampere (Finland) U., 1975-80; prof. orthopedics and traumatology Helsinki U., 1981—, dean med. faculty, 1984-87. Served to lt. Finnish Army, 1954. Recipient Silver medal Disabled Ex-Service Mens Assn. Finland, 1969, Finnish Med. Assn., 1973. Mem. Finnish Med. Assn. (pres. 1970-72), Finnish Orthopedic Assn. (pres. 1976-79, hon. mem. 1988), Duodecim, Finnish Surg. Assn., Nordic Surg. Assn., Scandinavian Orthopedic Assn. (pres. 1988—), Internat. Coll. Surgeons, European Soc. Surg. Research, Soc. Internationale de Chirurgie Orthopedique et de Traumatologie (nat. del.), Royal Soc. Medicine. Contbr. articles to profl. jours. Home: Marjaniemenranta 29, SF-00930 Helsinki 93 Finland Office: Toolo Hospital, Topeliuksenk 5, SF00260 Helsinki Finland

ROKKANEN, SEPPO OLAVI, administration research and consultancy company executive; b. Helsinki, Aug. 21, 1945; s. Väinö and Martta Maria (Pajunen) R.; 1 child, Laura Maria. BSC in Econs., Helsinki Sch. Econs., 1973, MSc in Econs., MBA, 1976. Product mgr. Oy Hedengren Ab, Helsinki, 1971-73; head dept. Oy Lohja Ab, Lohja, Finland, 1973-74; freelance researcher, cons. Cent. Africa, 1975-78; pres. Viemartek Oy, Helsinki, 1978—, Seppo Rokkanen Ltd., 1981—. Contbr. articles and columns in field of mgmt. Served to sr. 1st lt. Finnish Army, 1968-70. Lutheran. Office: Viemartek Oy, Box 179, SF-00131 Helsinki Finland

ROLAND, BILLY RAY, electronics company executive; b. Grandview, Tex., June 12, 1926; s. Marvin Wesley and Minnie Mae (Martin) R.; m. Ruth Ranell Sheets, Mar. 9, 1950 (div. 1982); children—Carl Ray and Darla Kay (twins); m. Linda Sue Leslie, Feb. 21, 1986. B.S., Tex. Christian U., 1954. C.P.A., Tex. Ticket and baggage agt. Southwestern Greyhound Co., Ft. Worth, 1943-44, 46-51; supr. acctg. dept. Tandy Leather Co., 1954-60; controller, asst. sec., treas. Tandy Corp., 1960-75, Tandy crafts, Inc., 1975-78; v.p. Tandy Corp., 1978-85. Vice pres., treas. David L. Tandy Found., 1966—; mng. trustee James L. and Eunice West Charitable Trust, 1980—; treas. Benjamin F. Johnston Found., 1984—; retired 1985. Served with inf. U.S. Army, 1944-46. Mem. Am. Inst. C.P.A.s, Tex. Soc. C.P.A.s, Ft. Worth Soc. C.P.A.s, Ft. Worth C. of C. Democrat. Methodist. Clubs: Colonial Country, Petroleum, Lake Country Golf and Country. Home: 8937 Random Rd Fort Worth TX 76179

ROLET, BERNARD JEAN-MARIE, international business consultant; b. Metz, France, June 23, 1927; s. Francis Eugene and Edith Marie (Hennequin) R.; m. Huguette Marcelle Richard, Aug. 13, 1951; children—Francois, Sylvie Dubourg, Anne Vallin. Mathematiques Speciales, Lycee Henri IV, Paris, 1947; Hon. engr., Ecole Centrale des Arts et Manufactures, Paris, 1950. Engr. to chief engr. Houilleres du Bassin de Lorraine, St. Avold, France, 1950-68; tech. mgr. CdF Chimie S.A., Paris, 1968-79; mng. dir. CdF Chimie Internat., Paris, 1980-87; vice-chmn. C.L.E.C., 1982-87; official adviser french fgn. trade, 1981— . Decorated chevalier Ordre du Merite (France). Roman Catholic. Lodge: Rotary (permanent mem. of honor) (St. Avold, France, A.C.F., Paris). Home and Office: 8 Residence du Parc, 78150 Rocquencourt Yvelines France

ROLFE, MICHAEL N., accounting firm executive; b. Chgo., Sept. 9, 1937; s. Mark Alexander and Antoinette (Wittgenstein) R.; m. Judith Mary Lewis, June 16, 1959; children—Andrew, Lisa, James. A.B. in Econs., U. Mich., 1959; postgrad., Grad. Sch. Bus., U. Chgo., 1963-65. Sales staff Lewis Co., Northbrook, Ill., 1961-62; systems mgmt. staff Brunswick Corp., Chgo., 1962-68; v.p. Kearney Mgmt. Cons., Chgo., 1968-81; ptnr. Peat, Marwick, Main & Co., Chgo., 1981—. Author: AMA Management Handbook, 1969. Bd. dirs. Common, Chgo., 1972-75, U. Chgo. Cancer Research, 1985-88, Am. Cancer Soc., Chgo., 1985—; trustee Michael Reese Med. Ctr., 1986—; pres. Sch. Bd. Dist. 113, Highland Park, Ill., 1977-83. Served to lt. (j.g.) USNR, 1959-61. Clubs: Northmoor Country (Highland Park); Standard, Mid Am. (Chgo.). Home: 1730 Overland Trail Deerfield IL 60015 Office: Peat Marwick Main & Co 303 E Wacker Dr Chicago IL 60601

ROLLE, GUSTAVOUS BERKLEY, public utilities executive; b. Nassau, Bahamas, Sept. 11, 1938; s. George Raleigh and Maria (Tucker) R.; m. Marina Major; children: Patricia, Bridget, Gustavous Jr., Gregory, Tanya, Tiffany. Diploma in bookkeeping, Gordon Arlen Coll., London, 1969; diploma, Inst. Purchasing and Supply, Stamford, Eng., 1981. Sr. asst. Bahamas Electricity Corp., Nassau, 1958-65, asst. acct., 1966-69, expenditure acct., 1970-76, purchasing mgr., 1976—. Active Bahamas Nat. Trust, Bahamas Kidney Found., Bahamas Red Cross. Mem. Purchasing Mgr.'s Assn., Nat. Assn. Purchasing Mgmt., Inst. Materials Handling, Inst. Purchasing and Supply, Alexander Hamilton Inst. Baptist. Lodges: Kiwanis, Masons. Home: PO Box GT-2395, Nassau The Bahamas Office: Bahamas Electricity Corp, PO Box N-7509, Nassau The Bahamas

RÖLLER, WOLFGANG, banker; b. Uelsen, Fed. Republic Germany, Oct. 20, 1929. Grad., U. Berlin, 1951, PhD in Econs., 1957. With Dresdner Bank AG, Frankfurt, Fed. Republic Germany, 1951-55, dep. mem. bd. mng. dirs., 1971-73, full mem. bd. mng. dirs., 1973-85, chmn. bd. dirs., 1985—; chmn. supervisory bd. Bank für Handel und Industrie, Deutscher Investment-Trust Gesellschaft für Wertpapieranlagen, Dresdnerbank Investment Mgmt. Kapitalanlagegesellschaft, ABD Securities Corp., N.Y.C., Dresdner-ABD Securities, Hong Kong, Tokyo. Mem. Assn. German Banks (pres. 1987—). Office: Dresdner Bank AG, Jurgen-Ponto-Platz 1, 6000 Frankfurt 1 Federal Republic of Germany

ROLLHAUS, PHILIP EDWARD, JR., diversified manufacturing corporation executive; b. Phila., Sept. 29, 1934; s. Philip Edward and Elizabeth Snow (Bedford) R.; m. Jacqueline Merrill, Feb. 13, 1965 (div. 1975); children: Natalie, Philip Edward III; m. Barbara Lynn Walker, Oct. 8, 1983. B.A. in English Lit., Wesleyan U., 1956. Dir. gen. Société Rollhaus, Paris, 1960-64; regional mgr. Bus. Internat., Chgo., 1964-67; mgr. pvt. placements Woolard & Co., Chgo., 1967-69; founder, chmn., pres., chief exec. officer Quixote Corp., Chgo., 1969—; bd. dirs. Chgo. Capital Fund. Bd. dirs. DeVry, Inc., 1987—, Keller Grad. Sch. Mgmt., Chgo., 1974-87; chmn. Starlight Found., Chgo., 1986-88, Gastro-Intestinal Research Found., Chgo., 1984—; trustee Inst. Psychoanalysis, Chgo., 1983—; mem. Am. Bus. Conf., Washington, 1987—. Served to lt. (j.g.) USN, 1956-60. Mem. Newcomen Soc. U.S., Econ. Club of Chgo., Soc. Mayflower Descs. Republican. Presbyterian. Clubs: Chicago, Racquet, Tavern (Chgo.); Bath and Tennis (Palm Beach, Fla.); Michigan City Yacht (Ind.). Home: 1500 N Lake Shore Dr Chicago IL 60610 Office: Quixote Corp One E Wacker Dr Chicago IL 60601

ROLLIER, PHILIPPE REMY, manufacturing company executive; b. St. Etienne, France, Feb. 19, 1943; s. Francois and Louise (Germain de Montauzan) R.; m. Anne Le Conte de Poly; children: Guillaume, Violaine, Stephanie, Ariane. Degree in Agronomy Engring., Ensag, Paris, 1967; postgrad. degree in Polit. Sci., IEP, Paris, 1969. Attached to fin. dir. Lafarge, Paris, 1969-73; sales mgr. Can. Cement Lafarge, Calgary, Alta.,

1973-77; fin. mgr. Can. Cement Lafarge, Montreal, 1977-79; dep. mng. dir. Doulton San. Ware, Stoke-on-Trent, Eng., 1979-82; mng. dir. Allia Group, Paris, 1982—. Mem. Union Mfrs. Ceramic Sanitaryware (v.p.). Club: Cercle du Bois de Boulogne (Paris). Home: 6 Sq du Trocadero, 75116 Paris France Office: Allia Group, 61 Rue des Belles Feuilles, 75116 Paris France

ROLLINGS, JOANN, nurse, army officer; b. St. Louis, Feb. 13, 1947; d. Edward Charles and Dorothy Jane (Horak) R. BS in Nursing, Baylor U., 1969; MS in Nursing, U. Tex.-El Paso, 1982; postgrad. U. Calif.-San Francisco, 1984—. Registered nurse, Tex. Commd. Nurse Corps, U.S. Army, 1969, advanced through grades to lt. col., 1986; clin. staff nurse Irwin Army Hosp., 1969-70, 95th Evacuation Hosp., DaNang, Vietnam, 1970-71; chief nursing inservice edn. and tng. Letterman Gen. Hosp., 1971-72; asst. prof. Walter Reed Army Inst. of Nursing, U. Md. Sch. Nursing, Washington, 1974-78; critical care clin. nurse specialist William Beaumont Army Med. Ctr., 1979-82; chief clin. nursing service U.S. Army Community Hosp., Seoul, Korea, 1982-83; quality assurance cons. Letterman Army Med. Ctr., 1985—; adj. clin. faculty Sch. Nursing, U. Tex.-El Paso, 1980-82, Sch. Nursing, San Francisco State U., 1983-84; cons. to Surgeon Gen. for Critical Care Nursing, 1976—; co-chmn. Maryland Ctr. Vietnamese Relocation Project, 1977-78. Contbr. articles to profl. jours. Health cons. Girl Scouts U.S.A., Rockville, Md., 1975-77. Decorated Bronze Star medal, Army Commendation medal with oak leaf cluster, Meritorious Service medal with 2 oak leaf clusters; Commendation medal (Vietnam); U.S. Army Nurse Corps scholar, 1985. Mem. Am. Nurses Assn., Am. Assn. Critical Care Nurses, Calif. Nurses Assn., Nurses Christian Fellowship, Sigma Theta Tau.

ROLLINSON, MARK, lawyer; b. Chattanooga, Dec. 8, 1935; s. Turner Earl and Josephine (Orput) R.; m. Barbara Crain, Sept. 7, 1957; children—Barbara Louis, Alice Orput, Marjorie Ann, Amy Claire; m. 2d, Carole Seliger, Oct. 30, 1971. A.B. in Econs., Duke U., 1958; LL.B., George Washington U., 1962. Bar: D.C. 1964, Md. 1975, Va. 1982, U.S. Dist. Ct. Md. 1976, U.S. Dist. Ct. (ea. dist.) Va. 1982, U.S. Ct. Appeals (D.C. cir.) 1963, U.S. Ct. Appeals (4th cir.) 1984, U.S. Ct. Appeals (5th cir.) 1987. Asst. trust officer Nation Savs. and Trust Co., 1958; staff economist Foster Assoc., 1959; treas., exec. com. Human Scis. Research, Inc., 1960-62; v.p. Greater Washington Investors, Inc., 1963-71; ptnr. Rollinson & Schaumberg, Washington, 1972-77; resident ptnr. Dykema, Gossett, Spencer, Goodnow & Trigg, Washington, 1978-81; ptnr. Smith Rollinson, Alexandria, Va., 1982—; mem. task force on inflation White House Conf. on Small Bus., 1979-80, exptl. research and devel. incentives program NSF, 1974-75; bd. dirs. Panel Arbitrators, NASD, N.Y. Stock Exchange, AAA. Mem. ABA (taxation sect., corp., banking and bus. law sect., internat. law sect., standing com. on law and tech., 1980-81, governing com. of forum com. on franchising, 1976-81, planning coms. confs.), D.C. Bar Assn. (chmn. com. on computer-assisted legal research), Internat. Bar Assn. (sect. bus. law). Republican. Episcopalian. Clubs: Belle Haven Country, Lawyers, Alexandria Business-men's. Contbr. writings to legal publs.; speaker in field seminars and schs. Office: 603 King St Alexandria VA 22314

ROLLS, JOHN MARLAND, JR., lawyer, law educator; b. San Francisco, Nov. 18, 1937; s. Jack M. and Margaret Rita (Tracy) R.; m. Dorothy K. Higa, Oct. 2, 1976; children: Dana Kimiko, Jennifer Mariko. BA, Stanford U., 1959, LLB, 1962. Bar: Hawaii 1965, U.S. Dist. Ct. Hawaii 1965, U.S. Ct. Appeals (9th cir.) 1967, U.S. Supreme Ct. 1970. Asst. prof. dept. social scis. U.S. Mil. Acad., West Point, N.Y., 1962-65; assoc. Ashford & Wriston, Honolulu, 1965-68, ptnr. 1970—; instr. Grad. Realtors Inst., Hawaii Assn. Realtors, Honolulu, 1976-84; adj. prof. U. Hawaii Sch. Law, Honolulu, 1980-84; mem. adv. com. to commr. fin. instns., State of Hawaii, 1985—. Co-editor: Hawaii Conveyance Manual, 1979, 3d edit. 1987. Served to maj. U.S. Army, 1962-65, 68-69, Vietnam, col. Res. Decorated Bronze Star. Mem. ABA, Hawaii Bar Assn. (bd. dirs. real property and fin. services sect. 1983—, vice-chmn. 1986, chmn. 1987). Republican. Episcopalian. Office: Ashford & Wriston 235 Queen St Honolulu HI 96813

ROLSTON, HOLMES, III, philosopher, educator; b. Staunton, Va., Nov. 19, 1932; s. Holmes and Mary Winifred (Long) R.; m. Jane Irving Wilson, June 1, 1956; children: Shonny Hunter, Giles Campbell. BS, Davidson Coll., 1953; BD, Union Theol. Sem., 1956; MA in Philosophy of Sci., U. Pitts., 1968; PhD in Theology, U. Edinburgh, Scotland, 1958. Ordained to ministry Presbyn. Ch., 1956. Pastor Walnut Grove Presbyn. Ch., Bristol, Va., 1959-67; prof. philosophy Colo. State U., Ft. Collins, 1968—; vis. scholar Ctr. Study of World Religions, Harvard U., 1974-75. Author: The Cosmic Christ, 1966, John Calvin versus the Westminster Confession, 1972, Religious Inquiry--Participation and Detachment, 1985, Philosophy Gone Wild, 1986, Science and Religion: A Critical Survey, 1987, Environmental Ethics, 1988; assoc. editor Environ. Ethics, 1979—; mem. editorial bd. Reidel Series in Applied Philosophy and Pub. Policy; contbr. chpts. to books, articles to profl. jours. Recipient Pennock award Disting. Scholarship Colo. State U., 1984; NSF and NEH grantee. Mem. Am. Acad. Religion, AAAS, Am. Philos. Assn. Home: 1712 Concord Dr Fort Collins CO 80526 Office: Colo State U Dept Philosophy Fort Collins CO 80523

ROMAHI, SEIF AHMED WADY, government official; b. Muzeira, Palestine, Dec. 28, 1938. BA in Polit. Sci. and Econs., Lebanese State U., Beirut, 1960; cert. with distinction in Internat. Law, City of London Coll., 1960; MA in Govt. Studies, So. Ill. U., 1966, PhD, 1970; PhD, U. Birmingham (Eng.), 1981. Educationalist Ministry of Edn. in Qatar, Mid. East, 1960-63; dep. dir. to Emiri Ct., Palace Office of Ruler of Abu Dhabi, 1968-70; dir. League of Arab States Office, Dallas, 1970-72; minister plenipotentiary Ministry of Fgn. Affairs, Embassy of United Arab Emirates, Tripoli, Libya, 1973-75, Tokyo, Japan, 1976-80, supr. diplomatic tng., Abu Dhabi, 1980-83, 86—; minister plenipotentiary fin. affairs, chief rep. Nat. Bank of Abu Dhabi, Tokyo, 1983-86; vis. prof. Sophia U., Tokyo, 1977-80; prof. Internat. U. of Japan, 1983-86; mem. fgn. dels. Co-author: Abu Dhabi Public Civil Service Code of 1969, 1972; author: Economics and Political Evolution in the Gulf States, 1980; U.A.E. Challenges the Desert to Bloom, 1976; The Palestine Question and International Law, 1979; Studies in International Law and Diplomatic Practice, 1980; contbr. articles to profl. jours.; author speeches and lectures. Recipient Student of Yr. from Mid. East award So. Ill. U., 1965-66; Inst. Internat. Edn. award, N.Y., 1965-66; Am. Friends of Mid. East scholar, 1965-66; So. Ill. U. Grad. fellow, 1966-70; Brit. Council Scholar award, 1966-67; decorated 2d Class Order of Ind.award King Hussein of Jordan, 1969. Mem. Am. Soc. Internat. Law, Arab Am. Univ. Grads., Acad. Islamic Research, Japanese Acad. Oriental Studies, Mid. East Studies Assn. N.Am., Brit. Soc. Mid. Ea. Studies. Home: PO Box 8222, Abu Dhabi United Arab Emirates Other: PO Box 651, Tela Ali, Amman Jordan

ROMANI, FRANCO ALESSANDRO, economics educator; b. Verolanuova, Brescia, Italy, Apr. 13, 1935; s. Antonio and Elsa (Scaietti) R.; m. Josik Borvo, July 25, 1964 (dec. June 1976); 1 child, Heloïse; m. Maria Teresa Guerra de Jamblinne, Feb. 17, 1979. JD, Law Sch. Pavia, Italy, 1958; Libera Docenza in Pub. Econs., U. Rome, 1967. Prof. pub. econs. Dept. Econs. and Banking, U. Sienna, Italy, 1968-74, dean, 1973-74; prof. pub. econs. Law Sch., U. Rome, 1974-76, prof. polit. economy, 1976—; bd. dirs. Italcalble, Italy. Author: Incrementi Patrimoniali and Imposta sul Reddito, 1964 (Vanoni prize 1967); editor: Analisi Economiche Interpretazione Giuridica, 1982; contbr. articles to scientific jours. Mem. Comitato Per L'Attuzione Riforma Tributaria, Ministry Fin., Rome, 1978-82, Commissione Centrale Tributaria, Rome, 1974-86; chmn. Commissione Per La Concorrenza, Ministry Trade, 1986-87. Served to lt. Italian Air Force, 1961-63. Home: Via Ruffini 2A, 00195 Rome Italy Office: U Lasapienza Fac Giurisprudenza, Ple Aldo Moro, 00100 Rome Italy

ROMANI, PAUL NICHOLAS, government official; b. L.I., N.Y., May 14, 1943; s. Nicholas Oliver and Rita (Gripp) R.; m. Patricia Elsie Riley, July 26, 1968; children—Michele P., Christopher P. B.B.A., George Washington U., 1967, M.B.A., 1968, D.P.A. with distinction, 1975. Lic. in real estate, Va.; cert. EEO counselor. McGraw-Edison fellow George Washington U., 1971-73, assoc. professorial lectr., 1970-72; sci. adminstr. NSF, Washington, 1972-82; sci. and tech. fellow The White House, 1982-83, dir. fin. and adminstrn. Automated Systems Div., 1983-85, dir. adminstrv. ops. The White House, 1985—; cons. to Pres. Nixon's Adv. Council on Mgmt. Improvement, 1970. Contbr. articles to profl. jours. Humble Oil fellow, 1968. Mem. Am. Soc. Pub. Adminstrn., Soc. Gen. Systems Research, Alpha Kappa Psi. Roman Catholic. Office: Office of Adminstrn The White House Washington DC 20500

ROMANO, JOHN, psychiatrist; b. Milw., Nov. 20, 1908; s. Nicholas Vincent and Frances Louise (Notari) R.; m. Miriam Modesitt, May 13, 1933; 1 child, David Gilman. BS, Marquette U., 1932, MD, 1934; DSc (hon.), Med. Coll. Wis., 1971, Hahnemann Med. Coll., 1974, U. Cin., 1979. Diplomate Am. Bd. Psychiatry and Neurology. Asst. biochemistry Marquette U. Sch. Medicine, 1929-30; extern psychiatry Milw. County Asylum for Mental Diseases, 1932-33; intern medicine Milw. County Hosp., 1933-34; asst. psychiatry Yale Sch. Medicine, 1934-35; intern, asst. resident psychiatry New Haven Hosp., 1934-35; Commonwealth Fund fellow psychiatry U. Colo., 1935-38; asst. psychiatrist Colo. Psychopathic Hosp., Denver, 1935-38; fellow neurology Boston City Hosp., 1938-39; Rockefeller fellow neurology Harvard Med. Sch., 1938-39, asst. medicine, 1939-40, instr. medicine, 1940-42; asso. medicine Peter Bent Brigham Hosp., 1939-42; Sigmund Freud fellow psychoanalysis Boston Psychoanalytic Soc., 1939-42; dir. dept. psychiatry Cin. Gen. Hosp., 1942-46; prof. psychiatry U. Cin. Coll. Medicine, 1942-46; psychiatrist in chief Strong Meml. Hosp., Rochester, 1946-71; prof. psychiatry, chmn. dept. U. Rochester Sch. Medicine, 1946-71, distinguished univ. prof. psychiatry, 1968-79, disting. univ. prof. emeritus, 1979—; lectr. in field; vis. prof. U. Toronto, Ont., Can., 1972; physician-in-residence U.S. VA, 1975—; qualified psychiatrist N.Y. State Dept. Mental Hygiene, 1954—; Salmon lectr. N.Y. Acad. Medicine, 1976; nat. adv. mental health council USPHS, chmn. mental health career investigator selection com., 1956-61; chmn. adv. com. human growth and emotion devel. Social Sci. Research Found., 1953; cons. health div. Ford Found., adv. com. behavioral scis. div., rep., Europe, 1956; cons. surgeon gen. U.S. Army Europe, 1955; exam. com. Examination Medicine, Part II, Nat. Bd. Med. Examiners, 1953-56; bd. psychiat. exams. N.Y. Dept. Mental Hygiene, 1963-65; mem. med. adv. com. Phillips Exeter Acad., 1964—; mem. bd. health sci. policy Inst. Medicine, Nat. Acad. Sci., 1985; mem. sci. council Nat. Alliance Research on Schizophrenia and Depression, 1985—. Mem. editorial bd. Jour. Psychiatric Research, 1961—, Schizophrenia Bull, 1971—; mem. panel of editors: Year Book of Psychiatry and Applied Mental Health, 1972—; sr. editor The Merck Manual, 15th edit., 1987; contbr. articles to profl. jours. Served as vis. neuropsychiat. cons. 8th Service Command AUS, 1943-44; cons. psychiatry AUS, 1945, ETO. Commonwealth Fund advanced fellow European study, 1959-60; recipient William J. Kerr Lecture award U. Calif., San Francisco, 1972, William C. Menninger Meml. award A.C.P., 1973, Disting. Profl. Achievement award Genesee Valley Psychol. Assn., 1975, Disting. Service award Am. Coll. of Psychiatrists, 1987, Sigmund Freud award Am. Assn. Psychoanalytic Physicians, Erik Stromgren medal Aarhus, Denmark, 1981. Fellow Acad. Arts and Scis., Royal Coll. Psychiatrists (hon.); mem. Assn. Research in Nervous and Mental Disease (1st v.p. 1955), Am. Psychiat. Assn. (Psychiatrist of Year Area II 1976, Disting. Service award 1979), Physicians for Social Responsibility (adv. bd. Rochester chpt. 1985—), Am. League Against Epilepsy, Am. Soc. Research Psychosomatic Problems, Nat. Com. Mental Hygiene, Am. Neurol. Assn., AAAS, Inst. Medicine, Nat. Acad. Scis. (sr.), Am. Soc. Clin. Investigation, Monroe County Soc. Mental Hygiene (dir.), N.Y. Acad. Medicine (Salmon com. on psychiatry and medicine 1970—, Salmon medal 1984), Phi Beta Kappa (v.p. Iota chpt. 1983-85), Sigma Xi, Alpha Omega Alpha. Unitarian. Clubs: Cosmos (Washington); Fortnightly. Home: 240 Chelmsford Rd Rochester NY 14618

ROMANO, PAUL EDWARD, pediatric ophthalmologist, educator; b. N.Y.C., Oct. 30, 1934; s. Paul Salvatore and Mary Elizabeth (Simms) R.; m. Judith Ann Robinson, Oct. 18, 1969. A.B., Cornell U., 1955, M.D., 1959; M.S. with distinction in Ophthalmology, Georgetown U., 1967. Diplomate Am. Bd. Ophthalmology. Intern in surgery Albany Med. Ctr. Hosp., N.Y., 1959-60, residency in gen. surgery, 1960-61; residency in ophthalmology Georgetown U. Hosp., Washington, 1964-67; fellow in ophthalmology Armed Forces Inst. Pathology, Washington, 1967, Wilmer Ophthal. Inst., Johns Hopkins Hosp., Balt., 1967-69; dir. ophthalmology Children's Meml. Hosp., Chgo., 1970-80; asst. prof. Northwestern U. Med. Sch., Chgo., 1969-73, assoc. prof., 1973-80; prof. ophthalmology U. Fla. Coll. Medicine, Gainesville, 1980—; cons. VA Med. Ctr., Gainesville, 1980—, Naval Regional Med. Ctr., Jacksonville, Fla., 1981—. Founding editor Binocular Vision Jour., 1985—. Contbr. over 150 articles to sci. jours. Served to capt. U.S. Army, 1961-64. Fellow Heed Found., 1968, NIH, 1968-69. Fellow Am. Acad. Ophthalmology, Am. Acad. Pediatrics; mem. Internat. Assn. Ocular Surgeons (charter), Internat. Strabismus Assn., Am. Assn. for Pediatric Ophthalmology (charter), Assn. for Research in Vision and Ophthalmology, AAUP, Fla Med. Assn., Fla. Soc. Ophthalmology, Alachua County Med. Soc., Soc. Heed Fellows, Wilmer Residents' Assn. Avocation: auto racing (owner and driver). Home: 2500 NW 23d Terr Gainesville FL 32605 Office: U Fla Coll Medicine Dept Ophthalmology Box J-284 Gainesville FL 32610

ROMANOFF, MILFORD MARTIN, building contractor, architectural designer; b. Cleve., Aug. 21, 1921; s. Barney Sanford and Edythe Stolpher (Bort) R.; student Coll. Arch., U. Mich., 1939-42; B.B.A., U. Toledo, 1943; m. Marjorie Reinwald, Nov. 6, 1945; children—Bennett S., Lawrence M., Janet Beth (dec.). Pres., Glass City Constrn. Co., Toledo, 1951-55, Milford Romanoff Inc., Toledo, 1956—. Co-founder, Neighborhood Improvement Found. Toledo, 1960; mem. Lucas County Econ. Devel. Com., 1979—; mem. citizens adv. bd. Recreation Commn. Toledo, 1973-86; mem. campus adv. com. Med. Coll. Ohio, 1980—; trustee Cummings Treatment Center for Adolescents, 1981—; mem. Children's Services Bd. Lucas County, 1981—; pres. Ohio B'nai B'rith, 1959-60, Toledo Lodge, 1958-59; bd. dirs. Anti-Defamation League, 1955-60, Ohio Hillel Orgns.; chmn. Toledo Amateur Baseball and Softball Com., 1979-81; mem. Democratic Precinct Com., 1975-78; trustee Temple Brotherhood, 1956-58, bd. dirs., 1981—; pres. Cherry Hill Nursing Home, 1964-85; cons. U.S. Care Corp., 1985—; mem. Crosby Gardens Bd. Adv., 1983—; bd. govs. Toledo Housing for Elderly, 1982—; bd. advisors Ret. Sr. Vol. Program, 1987—; mem. adv. bd. Salvation Army (vice chmn. 1986—), chmn. Mental Health Adv. Bd., 1983—; bd. dirs. Kidney Found. Northwestern Ohio, 1986—. Mem. U. Toledo Alumni Assn., Toledo Mus. Art (asso.), U. Mich. Alumni Assn., Toledo Zool. Soc., Zeta Beta Tau. Clubs: Masons; B'nai B'rith (pres. Toledo lodge 1958-59, statewide pres. 1959-60), Hadassah (assoc. Toledo chpt.). Home and Office: Milford Romanoff Inc 2514 Bexford Pl Toledo OH 43606

ROMANSKY, MONROE JAMES, physician, educator; b. Hartford, Conn., Mar. 16, 1911; s. Benjamin and Henrietta (Levine) R.; m. Evelyn Muriel Lackman, Jan. 10, 1943; children: Stephen, Gerald, Michael, Richard. A.B., U. Maine, 1933; M.D., U. Rochester, 1937. Diplomate: Am. Bd. Internal Medicine. Intern Strong Meml. Hosp.-U. Rochester, N.Y., 1937-38; asst. resident Strong Meml. Hosp.-U. Rochester, 1938-39, James Gleason Research fellow studies on relationship of kidneys to hypertension, 1939-40, chief resident, 1940-41, instr. in medicine, 1941-42; investigator Office Sci. Research and Devel., Surgeon Gen. U.S., 1941-42; chief biochemistry and antibiotic research Walter Reed Army Hosp., 1942-46; asso. prof. Sch. Medicine, George Washington U., Washington, 1946—; prof. medicine Sch. Medicine, George Washington U., 1957—; dir. George Washington U. med. div. D.C. Gen. Hosp., 1950-69; dir. infectious diseases research lab. and infectious diseases div. D.C. Gen. Hosp., 1950-69; cons. internal medicine antibiotics Walter Reed Army Hosp., Washington, 1946—; Cons. internal medicine antibiotics VA Hosp., Washington, 1952—, NIH, Bethesda, Md., 1953—, Surgeon Gen. USAF, 1966—; mem. Asian influenza adv. com. D.C., 1956-61; mem. ad hoc adv. com. Bur. Medicine FDA, 1966-67; examiner Am. Bd. Internal Medicine, 1965, 67, 69. Editorial bd.: Antimicrobial Agts. and Chemotherapy, 1961-72; Contbr. to profl. jours. Trustees council U. Rochester, 1965—. Served with M.C., AUS, 1942-46. Decorated Legion of Merit; recipient Founders award Tau Epsilon Phi, Disting. Career award U. Maine. Fellow ACP (adv. bd. to gov. D.C. 1969—); mem. Am. Soc. Internal Medicine, Am. Fedn. Clin. Research, Soc. Exptl. Biology and Medicine, Am. Soc. Microbiology, Infectious Diseases Soc. (founding council 1963-66), Soc. Med. Cons. to Armed Forces, Sigma Xi, Alpha Omega Alpha. Club: Woodmont Country. Home: 6609 32d Pl NW Washington DC 20015 Office: 5480 Wisconsin Ave Chevy Chase MD 20815

ROMBERG, LESLIE HOLMES, international marketing management company executive; b. Bklyn., Aug. 11, 1941; d. Alton Butler and Margaret Nichol (Arnett) H.; m. Jon Word Blaschke, Aug. 20, 1966 (div. June 1968); m. Conrad Louis Romberg, Jan. 6, 1985; 1 stepdaughter, Allison Romberg. Student, Baylor Coll. Dentistry, 1959-60, U. Tulsa, 1962-64; BS in Chemistry and Biology, Cen. State U., Edmond, Okla., 1966; PhD in Biochemistry, U. Okla., 1968. Head internat. ops. New Eng. Nuclear Corp., Boston, 1969-77 (name now DuPont-NEN); sales engr. Tracor Analytic, Des Plaines, Ill., 1977-79; internat. mktg. and product mgr. Zoecon Industries, Dallas, 1979-80; owner, operator Tex-Am. Internat., Dallas, 1980—; ptnr. Twin Assocs. Engring. Cons., Olten, Switzerland. V.p. Richardson Unitarian Ch., 1985-86, pres., 1986-87, bd. dirs. 87—, sec. 1988-89; bd. dirs. Greenhill Parents Assn., 1987-88; founder Greenhill Former Parents' Assn., 1988. Mem. Dallas C. of C., Rowlett C. of C. (exec. com.), North Dallas Network Career Women. Republican. Home and Office: PO Box 549 Rowlett TX 75088

ROMBS, VINCENT JOSEPH, accountant, lawyer; b. Newport, Ky., Mar. 8, 1918; s. John Thomas and Mathilda (Fromhold) R.; m. Ruth Burns, Aug. 15, 1942; 1 child, Ellen (Mrs. James P. Herman). Student Xavier U., 1936-37; BS with honors, Southeastern U., 1941; JD, Loyola U., Chgo., 1952. Bar: Ill. 1952; CPA, Ill. Tax ptnr. with local and nat. pub. acctg. firms, Chgo., 1952—; assoc. Laventhol & Horwath, Chgo., 1970-75; of counsel Edelman Chartered, 1975—; Ostrow Reisin Berk & Abrams, Ltd., 1977—; pres. Vincent J. Rombs, Ltd., 1982-88. Bd. dirs. Miller Found. Served to lt. comdr., USNR, 1941-46. Recipient Scholarship Key award Delta Theta Phi, 1953. Mem. Am. Inst. CPA's, Ill. Soc. CPA's, Ill. Bar Assn. Home: 915 E Golf Rd Apt 3 Arlington Heights IL 60005 Office: 1 N LaSalle St Suite 1714 Chicago IL 60602 also: 676 Saint Clair St Suite 2100 Chicago IL 60611

ROME, DONALD LEE, lawyer; b. West Hartford, Conn., May 17, 1929; s. Herman Isaac and Juliette (Stern) R.; m. Sheila Ward, Apr. 20, 1958; children: Adam Ward, Lisa, Ethan Stern. SB, Trinity Coll., 1951; LLB, Harvard U., 1954. Bar: Conn. 1954, U.S. Dist. Ct. 1955, U.S. Cir. Ct. Appeals 1965, U.S. Supreme Ct. 1965. Assoc. Ribicoff and Kotkin, Hartford, Conn., 1954-58, ptnr., 1958-67; ptnr. Rosenberg, Rome, Barnett, Sattin & Santos and predecessor, Hartford, 1967-83; now ptnr. Robinson & Cole, Hartford, 1983—; mem. Conn. Gov.'s Study Commn. on Uniform Consumer Credit Code, 1969-70; chmn. Conn. bar advisory com. of attys. to make recommendations to U.S. dist. ct. for proposed changes of bankruptcy rules in dist. Conn., 1975-77; mem. Bankruptcy Merit Screening Com. for Dist. Ct., 1980-81; lectr. in law U. Conn., 1965-74, 81-83; mem. faculty Sch. Banking of the South, La. State U., 1982-84; lectr. continuing legal edn. on secured creditors' rights, comml. fin., bankruptcy and uniform comml. code, 1958—; corp. adv. bd. dirs. Conn. Nat. Bank. Co-author: A Comparative Analysis and Study of the Uniform Consumer Credit Code in Relation to the Existing Consumer Credit Law in Connecticut, 1970; author: Business Workouts Manual, 1985; contbg. author: Connecticut Practice Book, 1978, Collier Bankruptcy Practice Guide, 1981, Asset-Based Financing: A Transactional Guide, 1984; contbr. articles to profl. jours. Past mem. bd. dirs. New Eng. region Am. Jewish Com., also Hartford chpt., Hebrew Home for Aged, Hartford; past mem. bd. trustees Temple Beth Israel, West Hartford. Mem. ABA (bus. bankruptcy com. and comml. fin. services com., sect. on corp., banking and bus. law), Fed. Bar Assn. (bankruptcy law com.), Conn. Bar Assn. (chmn. sect. comml. law and bankruptcy 1977-80, chmn. spl. com. scope and correlation 1983-84), Hartford County Bar Assn. (continuing legal edn. com.), Conn. Bar Found., Assn. Comml. Fin. Attys. (pres. 1978-80), Am. Arbitration Assn. (mem. panel comml. arbitrators), Am. Bankruptcy Inst., Comml. Law League Am., Harvard Law Sch. Assn. Conn. (pres. 1970-71). Clubs: Hartford, Harvard of N.Y.C, Trinity. Lodge: Masons (32 deg., trial commn. Conn. grand lodge 1970-82). Home: 46 Belknap Rd West Hartford CT 06117 Office: Robinson & Cole 1 Commercial Plaza Hartford CT 06103-3597

ROMER, RENE ANTONIO, government official; s. Ciro Jose and Johanna Maria (Gorsira) R.; m. Jacqueline Carola Ignatia de Vreese, May 26, 1958; children: René Philippe, Alexandra Mercedes, Ligia Maria. BA in Polit. and Social Scis., U. Nymegen, Holland, MA in Social Sci., PhD in Sociology, U. Leiden, Holland. Head Bur. for Culture and Edn., Govt. of Netherlands Antilles, 1959-74, sr. lectr. Sociology Caribbean, U. Netherlands Antilles, 1974-81, prof. 1981-83, pres. 1981-83; gov. Netherlands Antilles, 1983—. Author: Samenleving op eew Caribisch Eiland, Curacao, 1981, Cultureel Mozaiek van de Nederlandse Antillen Zutphen (Holland), 1979, Un pueblo na Kaminda, Zutphen 1977; contbr. articles to profl. jours. Lodge: Rotary. Address: Office of the Gov, Fort Amsterdam, Willemstad, Antilles The Netherlands

ROMER, ROY R., governor of Colorado; b. Garden City, Kans., Oct. 31, 1928; s. Irving Rudolph and Margaret Elizabeth (Snyder) R.; B.S. in Agrl. Econs., Colo. State U., 1950; LL.B., U. Colo., 1952; postgrad. Yale U.; m. Beatrice Miller, June 10, 1952; children—Paul, Mark, Mary, Christopher, Timothy, Thomas, Elizabeth. Engaged in farming in Colo., 1942-52; admitted to Colo. bar, 1952; ind. practice, Denver, 1955-66; mem. Colo. Ho. of Reps., Dist., 1958-62, Colo. Senate, 1962-66; owner, operator Arapahoe Aviation Co., Colo. Flying Acad., Geneva Basin Ski Area; engaged in home site devel.; owner chain farm implement and indsl. equipment stores in Colo.; commr. agr. State of Colo., 1975, state treas., 1977-86; gov. State of Colo., 1987—; chief staff, exec. asst. to gov. Colo., 1975-77, 83-84; chmn. Gov. Colo. Blue Ribbon Panel, Gov. Colo. Small Bus. Council; mem. agrl. adv. com. Colo. Bd. Agr. Past trustee Iliff Sch. Theology, Denver. Served with USAF, 1952-54. Mem. Colo. Bar Assn. (gov.), Order of Coif. Democrat. Presbyterian. Bd. editors Colo. U. Law Rev., 1960-62. Office: Office of the Gov State Capitol Bldg Room 136 Denver CO 80203 •

ROMERO, ANDRES FERNANDEZ, consulting company executive; b. Puenteareas, Pontevedra, Spain, Apr. 15, 1930; s. Andres Fernandez and Isabel Romero (Garcia) Pereira; m. Antonia Lozano de las Heras, Aug. 15, 1955; children: Maria Isabel, Andres Antonio, Ignacio, Carlos. Lic. in Econs., Cen. U., Madrid, 1955; prof. in mercantilism, Sch. of Commerce, Vigo, Spain, 1954. Fin. exec. Metalúrgica de Santa Ana, Madrid, 1957-62; chief dept. TEA-CEGOS, Madrid, 1962-69; pres. Consultores Españoles, Madrid, 1969-79; planning dir. Nat. Inst. Industry, Madrid, 1974-85; pres. Orgn. of Cons., Madrid, 1985—; chmn. Grupo de Empresas Alvarez, Vigo, 1979-83. Author: Método de Cálculo, 1966, Control e Información, 1968, Plan a Largo Plazo, 1972. Mem. Assn. Española Planificación (chmn. 1986). Roman Catholic. Home: Felix Boix 8-5 B, 28036 Madrid Spain Office: Orgn de Consultores SA, D Ramón de la Cruz 39-1, 28001 Madrid Spain

ROMERO-BARCELÓ, CARLOS ANTONIO, former governor of Puerto Rico; b. San Juan, P.R., Sept. 4, 1932; s. Antonio and Josefina (Barcelo-Bird) Romero-Moreno; BA, Yale U., 1953; LLB, U. P.R., 1956; LLD (hon.), U. Bridgeport, 1977; m. Kathleen Donnelly, Jan. 2, 1966; children: Juan Carlos, Melinda Kathleen; children by previous marriage: Carlos, Andrés. Admitted to P.R. bar, 1956; mem. firm Herrero-Frank & Romero-Barceló, 1956-58; partner firm Rivera-Zayas, Rivera-Cestero & Rúa, San Juan, 1958-63, Segurola, Romero & Toledo, 1963-68; pres. Citizens for State 51, 1965-67; mayor, San Juan, 1969-77; gov. P.R., 1977-85. Pres. New Progressive Party, 1974-86. Recipient Hoey award for Interracial Justice, Cath. Interracial Council of N.Y., 1977, Spl. Gold Medal award Spanish Inst., N.Y., 1979, U.S. Atty.-Gen.'s medal, 1981. Mem. Nat. Govs. Assn., So. Govs. Conf. (chmn. 1980-81), Conf., Nat. League Cities (pres. 1975), U.S. Conf. Mayors (dir.). Roman Catholic. Author: Statehood is for the Poor; contbr. articles to profl. jours. Office: GPO Box 4109 San Juan PR 00936

ROMERO-FIGUEROA, ANDRES ANTONIO, linguist; b. Cumaná, Sucre, Venezuela, Oct. 31, 1947; s. Jesus María and María (Figueroa) R.; m. Sonia Elena Rojas, Nov. 29, 1971; children: Andrés, Esmeralda. Edn. licenciate, U. Oriente, Cumaná, 1973; MS in Linguistics, Georgetown U., 1979; PhD in Anthropology, U. Man., Winnipeg, Can., 1986. Asst. prof. U. Oriente, 1975-77, assoc. prof., 1982—; exec. sec. staff classification com. Univ. Oriente, 1980-82; dir. extra-mural studies Univ. Oriente, 1986-87. Contbr. articles to profl. jours. Recipient Ipspudo Research award Ipspudo Fin. Trust, 1980-82. Mem. Linguistic Soc. Am., Assn. Venezolana de Linguistica, Can. Linguistic Soc., Finno-Ugric Lang. Soc. Mem. Social Democrat Party. Roman Catholic. Office: U Oriente, Cerro-Colorado-, Núcleo de Sucre, Cumaná, Sucre 6101, Venezuela

ROMERO SANCHO, SANTIAGO, business executive; b. Zaragoza, Spain, Sept. 27, 1947; s. Santiago Romero Sancho and MaTose Sancho Faure; m. Isabel Lacasa Suarez, Apr. 8, 1972; children: Eduardo Romero Lacasa,

Virginia Romero Lacasa. BS, Inst. Goya, Zaragoza, 1965; MBA, Oxford U. Cert. mech. engr. Mgr. Industrias Luzmetal S.A., Zaragoza, 1972-76; sr. cons. Centro Superior de Estudios Aplicados, Barcelona, Spain, 1977-86; owner, cons. Santiago Romero & Assocs., Zaragoza, 1987—; developer seminars on new techs. and strategies. Mem. Engrs. Assn. Zaragoza. Roman Catholic. Club: Tennis (Zaragoza). Home: Fernando el Catolico 14-4, 50 009 Zaragoza Spain Office: Santiago Romero & Assocs, Fernando el Catolico 11, 50 006 Zaragoza Spain

ROMINE, THOMAS BEESON, JR., consulting engineering firm executive; b. Billings, Mont., Nov. 16, 1925; s. Thomas Beeson and Elizabeth Marjorie (Tschudy) R.; m. Rosemary Pearl Melancon, Aug. 14, 1948; children—Thomas Beeson III, Richard Alexander, Robert Harold. Student, Rice Inst., 1943-44; B.S. in Mech. Engring, U. Tex., Austin, 1948. Registered profl. engr., Tex., Okla., La., Ga. Jr. engr. Gen. Engring. Co., Ft. Worth, 1948-50; design engr. Wyatt C. Hedrick (architect/engr.), Ft. Worth, 1950-54; chief mech. engr. Wyatt C. Hedrick (architect/engr.), 1954-56; pres., chief mech. engr. Thomas B. Romine, Jr. (cons. engr. (now Romine Romine & Burgess, Inc. cons. engrs.)), Ft. Worth, 1956—; mem. heating, ventilating, and air conditioning controls com. NRC, 1986-88. Author numerous computer programs in energy analysis and heating and air conditioning field; contbr. articles to profl. jours. Mem. Plan Commn., City of Ft. Worth, 1958-62; mem. Supervisory Bd. Plumbers, City Ft. Worth, 1963-71, chmn., 1970-71; chmn. Plumbing Code Rev. Com., 1968-69; mem. Mech. Bd., City Ft. Worth, 1974—, chmn., 1976—; chmn. plumbing code bd. North Central Tex. Council Govts., Ft. Worth, 1971-75; Bd. mgrs. Tex. Christian U.-South Side YMCA, 1969-74; trustee Ft. Worth Symphony Orch., 1968—, Orch. Hall, 1975—. Served with USNR, 1943-45. Fellow ASHRAE (pres. Ft. Worth chpt. 1958, nat. committeeman 1974—), Am. Cons. Engrs. Council, Automated Procedures Engring. Cons. (trustee 1970-71, 75, 1st v.p. 1972-73, internat. pres. 1974); mem. Nat. Soc. Profl. Engrs., Tex. Soc. Profl. Engrs. (dir. 1956, treas. 1967), Cons. Engrs. Council Tex. (pres. North Tex. chpt., also v.p. state orgn. 1965, dir. state orgn. 1967), Starfish Class Assn. (nat. pres. 1970-73, nat. champion 1976), Delta Tau Delta (v.p. West div. 1980—), Pi Tau Sigma. Episcopalian (vestryman). Clubs: Colonial Country, Rotary. Home: 3232 Preston Hollow St Fort Worth TX 76109 Office: Romine Romine & Burgess 300 Greenleaf St Fort Worth TX 76107

ROMITI, CESARE, industrial executive; b. Rome, June 24, 1923; m. Luigina Gastaldi; children: Piergiorgio, Maurizio. Degree in econs. and commerce, 1945. Joined Bombrini, Parodi, Delfino, Italy, 1947, gen. mgr. for fin. and coordination SNIA-BPD, 1968-70; mng. dir., gen. mgr. Alitalia Airlines, 1970-73; mng. dir., gen. mgr. Italstat, 1973-74; head corporate fin. planning and control dept. Fiat S.p.A., 1974-76; mng. dir., 1976—. Chmn. FIDIS, 1976—, Gilardini, 1976—, SNIA-BDP, 1984—, Gemina, 1985—; vice-chmn. I.H.F., 1976—; adv. bd. Deutsche Bank. Mem. Italian Stock Cos. Assn. (mem. exec. com., gen. advisor), Turin Indsl. Assn. (bd. dirs.), Aspen Inst. Italia, Trilateral Commn. Office: Fiat SpA, Corso Marconi 10, 10125 Torino Italy

ROMLEY, DEREK VANDERBILT, architect; b. Boston, June 16, 1935; s. Frederick Joseph and Cora-Marie (Sherman-Kenealy) R.; m. Elizabeth Colloredo-Mansfeld, Aug. 28, 1960 (div. June 1972). With various architects, N.Y., Paris, Lima, Milan, and Calif., until 1976; B.A., Harvard U., 1957; B.Arch., Yale U., 1964, M.Arch., 1965. Registered architect, Mass., Fla., Calif.; cert. Nat. Council Archtl. Registration Bds.; lic. contractor and real estate broker, Mass. instr. design Pratt Inst., 1969-70; vis. critic Sorbonne, Paris, U. Houston, UCLA, U. Calif.-Santa Barbara; prin. Derek Romley, Architects, Palm Beach Fla., 1976—. Author: play The Men, 1987; work pub. in archtl. mags., Vogue, Life, Look, House Beautiful; features in Los Angeles Times, Paris Herald, N.Y. Times, Houston Chronicle, Cape Cod newspapers and periodicals. Chmn. Dennis Planning Bd., 1977-78, Dennis Archtl. Rev. Bd., 1977-81. Winner passive solar award cycle 5, HUD; design award; constrn. grantee. Mem. AIA, Boston Soc. Architects. Christian Scientist. Clubs: Harvard (Cape Cod, Mass.); Yale, Hyannis Yacht. Home and Office: 100 Centre St RR 1 South Dennis MA 02660-3626

ROMPIS, OSCAR, contractor, corporate executive; b. Balikpapan, East Kalimantan, Indonesia, Oct. 31, 1944; s. Dipan and Helena Maria (Kambey) R.; m. Hemina Pinontoan, Oct. 27, 1970; children: Jerry H., Marleyn M., Marlon M. MA, U. Jakarta, Indonesia, 1983. Dir. P.T. Malakuru Ltd., Jakarta, 1977-80; chmn. Y P K, Jakarta, 1979—, Kukmi Jakarta Utara, 1985—; pres., dir. P.T. Jemar Baru Ltd., Jakarta, 1980—; advisor Kadin Jakarta Utara, 1986—. Seminar speaker Indonesian Protection Found., 1986-87. Mem. World Fedn. Bldg. Service Contractors (bd. dirs. 1986-88), Bldg. Service Contractors Assn. Internat. (zone chmn. 1985—), Indonesian Bldg. Maintenance Assn. (sec. gen. 1986—), Jakarta Utara C. of C. (advisor 1985—). Mem. Golkar Party. Roman Catholic. Club: Orari (Jakarta). Lodge: K K K. Home: Jalan Agung Jaya 5/10-A, Podomoro, Jakarta Utara 14350, Indonesia Office: PT Jemar Baru Ltd, Jalan Kenari 18-20, Cilincing, Jakarta Utara 14130, Indonesia

RONAN, WILLIAM JOHN, business executive; b. Buffalo, Nov. 8, 1912; s. William and Charlotte (Ramp) R.; m. Elena Vinadé, May 29, 1939; children: Monica (Mrs. Bruce Nourie), Diana (Mrs. Alan Quasha). A.B., Syracuse U., 1934; Ph. D., N.Y. U., 1940, LL.D., 1969; certificate, Geneva Sch. Internat. Studies, 1933. Mus. asst. Buffalo Mus. Sci., 1928-30; with Niagara-Hudson Power Co., 1931; transfer dept. N.Y.C.R.R., 1932; Penfield fellow internat. law, diplomacy and belles lettres 1935, Univ. fellow, 1936; editor Fed. Bank Service, Prentice-Hall, Inc., 1937; instr. govt. N.Y. U., 1938, exec. sec. grad. div. for tng. in pub. services, 1938, asst. dir., 1940, asst. prof. govt., dir. grad. div. for tng. pub. service, 1940, assoc. prof. govt., 1946-47, prof., 1947, dean, grad. sch. pub. adminstrn. and social service, 1953-58; Cons. N.Y.C. Civil Service Commn., 1938; prin. rev. officer, negotiations officer U.S. Civil Service Commn., 1942; prin. div. asst. U.S. Dept. State, 1943; cons. Dept. State, 1948, Dept. Def., 1954; dir. studies N.Y. State Coordination Commn., 1951-58; project mgr. N.Y. U.-U. Ankara project, 1954-59; cons. ICA, 1955, N.Y. State Welfare Conf.; adminstrv. co-dir. Albany Grad. Program in Pub. Adminstrn.; 1st dep. city adminstr. N.Y.C., 1956-57; exec. dir. N.Y. State Temporary Commn. Constl. Conv., 1956-58; sec. to Gov. N.Y., 1959-66; chmn. interdept. com. traffic safety; commr. Port Authority N.Y. and N.J., 1967—, vice chmn., 1972-74, chmn., 1974-77; trustee Crosslands Savs. Bank; chmn. bd. L.I. R.R., 1966-74; Chmn. Tri-State Transp. Com., N.Y., N.J., Conn., 1961-67; chmn. interstate com. New Haven R.R., 1960-63; chmn. N.Y. com. on L.I. R.R., 1964-65; mem. N.Y. State Commn. Interstate Coop., 1961, N.Y. State Com. Fgn. Ofcl. Visitors, 1961, N.Y. State Coordination Commn., 1960; mem. N.Y. Civil Service Commn., Temporary State Commn. on Constl. Conv., 1966-67; chmn. N.Y. State Met. Commuter Transp. Authority, 1965-68, Met. Transp. Authority, 1968-74, Tri-Borough Bridge and Tunnel Authority, 1968-74, N.Y.C. Transit Authority, 1968-74, Manhattan and Bronx Surface Transit Operating Authority, 1968-74; chmn. bd., pres. 3d Century Corp., 1974—; mem. Commn. Critical Choices for Am., 1973—, acting chmn., 1975—; mem. urban transp. adv. com. U.S. Dept. Transp.; sr. adviser Rockefeller family, 1974-80; pres. Nelson Rockefeller Collection, Inc., 1977-80; trustee Power Authority of State of N.Y., 1974-77; cons. to trustees Penn Central Transp. Co.; vice chmn. bd. CCX, Inc.; sec.-treas. Sarabam Corp. N.V.; chmn., dir. UTDC (U.S.A.) Inc., 1987—; bd. dirs. Crosslands Savs. Bank L.I., Metal Powder Products Inc., Prometech, Inc.; chmn. N.Y. and N.J. Inland Rail Rate Com.; Dir. Nat. Mgmt. Council, 1951. Author: Money Power of States in International Law, 1940, The Board of Regents and the Commissioner, 1948, Our War Economy, 1943, (with others), articles in profl. jours.; adviser: Jour. Inst. Socio-Econ. Studies. Mem. U.S. FOA, Am. Public Health Assn.; staff relations officer N.Y.C. Bd. Edn.; Mem. Nat. Conf. Social Work, Nat. Conf. on Met. Areas, Citizens Com. on Corrections, Council on Social Work Edn.; bd. dirs. World Trade Club; adv. bd. World Trade Inst.; mem. 42d St. Redevel. Corp., chmn., 1980—; mem. Assn. for a Better N.Y.; bd. advisers Inst. for Socioecon. Studies, 1977—; dir. Nat. Health Council, 1980-86; dep. dir. policy Nelson Rockefeller campaign for Republican presdl. nomination, 1964; mem. N.Y. State Gov.'s Com. on Shoreham Nuclear Plant, 1983—, Nassau County Indsl. Devel. Authority, 1982—, U.S. Dept. Transp. Com. on Washington and Capital Dist. Airports, 1985-86; bd. dirs. Ctr. Study Presidency, 1986—, Alcoholism Council of N.Y., 1986—; trustee N.Y. Coll. Osteopathic Medicine, 1986—. Served as lt. USNR, 1943-46. Mem. Am. Polit. Sci. Assn., Am. Acad. Public Adminstrn., Am. Soc. Public Adminstrn., Civil Service Assembly of U.S. and Canada, Internat. Assn. Met. Research and Devel., Nat. Municipal League, Municipal Personnel Soc., Citizens Union of N.Y., Nat. Civil Service League, Am. Acad. of Polit. and Social Sci., L.I. Assn. Commerce and Industry (dir.), Internat. Inst. Adminstrv. Scis., N.E.A., Am. Fgn. Law Assn., Internat. Union Pub. Transport (mgmt. com.; v.p.), Am. Pub. Transit Assn. (chmn. 1974-76), Nat. Def. Transportation Assn. (v.p. for Mass. transit). Clubs: Metropolitan Opera, Maidstone, Devon Yacht, Knickerbocker, Hemisphere, Harvard, Creek, Wings, Traffic, University, Railroad, (N.Y.C.); American (Riviera). Home: 655 Park Ave New York NY 10021 also: Villa La Pointe Du Cap, Ave de La Corniche, 06230 Saint Jean Cap Ferrat France also: 9500 S Ocean Blvd Hutchinson Island FL 33457 Office: 689 Fifth Ave New York NY 10022 also: Port Authority of NY and NJ 1 World Trade Center New York NY 10048

RONAYNE, MICHAEL RICHARD, JR., university administrator; b. Boston, Apr. 29, 1937; s. Michael Richard and Margaret (Fahey) R.; m. Joanne Marie, Aug. 7, 1971; 1 child, Michelle Eileen. B.S., Boston Coll., 1958; Ph.D., U. Notre Dame, 1962. Instr. chemistry Providence Coll., 1962-63, asst. prof. chemistry, 1963-64; research chemist Panametrics, Inc., Waltham, Mass., 1964-66; asst. prof. chemistry Suffolk U., Boston, 1966-67, assoc. prof., 1967-70, prof., chmn. dept. chemistry, 1970-72, dean Coll. Liberal Arts and Sci., 1972—; reaccreditation vis. team mem. New Eng. Assn. Schs. and Colls., Winchester, Mass., 1974-80, Mass. Dept. Edn., Boston, 1975; mem. acad. adv. com. Mass. Bd. Higher Edn., Boston, 1977. Mem. Winchester Sch. Com., 1983—, chmn., 1984-85, 86-87; mem. Winchester Town Meeting, 1983—, mem. town capital planning com., 1983-84, town council on youth, 1987-88; mem. exec. com., bd. dirs. Mass. Bay Marine Studies Consortium, 1985-87; project dir. U.S. Dept. of Edn. Title III Grants. Shell Oil Corp. fellow, 1958-59; AEC fellow 1959-62. Mem. Am. Chem. Soc., Am. Conf. Acad. Deans, Sigma Xi, Phi Alpha Theta, Phi Gamma Mu, Sigma Tau Delta. Contbr. articles to sci. jours., profl. publs. Office: Suffolk U Beacon Hill Boston MA 02114

RONDEAU, CLEMENT ROBERT, petroleum geologist; b. Ironwood, Mich., July 6, 1928. BS, Tulane U., 1955. Geol. supr. Texaco, Inc., New Orleans, 1955-63; area mgr. Pubco Petroleum Corp., New Orleans, 1963-69; cons. petroleum geologist Harahan, La., 1969—; owner Natural Gas Exploration Co., Harahan, 1977—. Mem. Am. Assn. Petroleum Geologists, Soc. Exploration Geophysicists, New Orleans Geol. Soc., AAAS, Explorers Club, Ind. Petroleum Assn., N.Y. Acad. Sci., Internat. Platform Assn., Internat. Oil Scouts Assn., Phi Beta Kappa, Sigma Gamma Epsilon. Democrat. Roman Catholic. Clubs: New Orleans Athletic; Bay/Waveland Yacht (Miss.). Home: 632 Stratford Dr Harahan LA 70123 Office: Natural Gas Exploration Co 958 Hickory Suite A Harahan LA 70123

RONDEAU, DORIS JEAN, entrepreneur, consultant; b. Winston-Salem, N.C., Nov. 25, 1941; d. John Delbert and Eldora Virginia (Klutz) Robinson; m. Robert Breen Corrente, Sept. 4, 1965 (div. 1970); m. Wilfrid Dolor Rondeau, June 3, 1972. Student Syracuse U., 1959-62, Fullerton Jr. Coll., 1974-75; BA in Philosophy, Calif. State U.-Fullerton, 1976, postgrad., 1976-80. Ordained to ministry The Spirit of Divine Love, 1974. Trust real estate clk. Security First Nat. Bank, Riverside, Calif., 1965-68; entertainer Talent, Inc., Hollywood, Calif., 1969-72; co-founder, dir. Spirit of Divine Love, Capistrano Beach, Calif., 1974—; pub., co-founder Passing Through, Inc., Capistrano Beach, 1983—; instr. Learning Activity, Anaheim, Calif., 1984—; chmn. bd., prin. D.J. Rondeau, Entrepreneur, Inc., Capistrano Beach, 1984—; co-founder, dir. Spiritual Positive Attitude, Inc., Moon In Pisces, Inc., Vibrations By Rondeau, Inc., Divine Consciousness, Expressed, Inc., Capistrano Beach. Author, editor: A Short Introduction To The Spirit of Divine Love, 1984; writer, producer, dir. performer spiritual vignettes for NBS Radio Network, KWVE-FM, 1982-84; author: Spiritual Meditations to Uplift the Soul, 1988. Served with USAF, 1963-65. Recipient Pop Vocalist First Place award USAF Talent Show, 1964, Sigma chpt. Epsilon Delta Chi, 1985, others. Mem. Hamel Bus. Grads., Smithsonian Assocs., Am. Mgmt. Assn., Nat. Assn. Female Execs. Avocations: long-distance running, body fitness, arts and crafts, snorkeling, musical composition.

RONDON, FERNANDO E., U.S. ambassador to Ecuador; b. Los Angeles, May 6, 1936; s. Fernando and Martha (Seldner) R.; m. Marian Hand, Mar. 3, 1962; children—Mark, Lawrence, Susan. B.S., U. Calif., Berkeley. Dep. dir. East Coast, South Am. U.S. Dept. of State, Washington, 1976-78; dep. chief mission Am. Embassy, Tegucigalpa, Honduras, 1978-80; ambassador to Madagascar U.S. Dept. State, Antananarivo, 1980-83, ambassador to Comoros, 1982-83; Andean dir. U.S. Dept. State, Washington, 1983-85; ambassador to Ecuador U.S. Dept. State, Quito, 1985—. Served with U.S. Army, 1961. Mem. Phi Beta Kappa. Office: Am Embassy Ecuador APO Miami FL 34039

RONEY, ALICE LORRAINE MANN, poet; b. Hartford, Mich., Dec. 6, 1926; d. Paul Douglass and Margaret Alice (Widener) Mann; A.A., Santa Monica Coll., 1946; B.A., U. Calif. at Los Angeles, 1950; m. Robert Kenneth Roney, Oct. 6, 1951; children—Stephen Paul, Karen Margaret. Tech. writer Hughes Aircraft Co., Culver City, Calif., 1949-52; chmn. Ebell Jr. Blind Recording, Los Angeles, 1959-63; librarian St. Augustine-by-the-Sea Episcopal Day Sch., Santa Monica, Calif., 1961-68; author: Those Treasured Moments, 1972; The Seeds of Love, 1975; Psalms for My Lord, 1975; contbr. to anthologies, 1971—; contbr. poetry to mags., 1972—. Recipient Ebell Jr. Service award, 1959; hon. mentions Major Poets Poetry Contest, 1972; 2d place for poetry creative writing div. marina dist. Calif. Fedn. Women's Clubs Fine Arts Festival, 1979, 3d place for inspirational poetry, 1979, 2d and 3d place, 1981, 1st and 2d place, 1982, 1st place, 1985, 2d place, 1986, 3d place for light verse, 1980, 1st place for children's stories, 1983, 85. Fellow World Lit. Acad.; mem. Centro Studi e Scambi Internazionali, Academia Internazionale Leonardo da Vinci, World (life), Internat., Calif. State, Ky. State poetry socs., Nat. Fedn. State Poetry Socs., P.E.O. (pres. chpt. QB, 1969-71, 76-78, 86—). Episcopalian (mem. sch. bd. 1964-67, asst. directress altar guild 1967-69, directress altar guild 1969-71, treas. Diocese of Los Angeles Churchwomen 1970-73). Clubs: Santa Monica Bay Woman's (1st v.p. 1980-82, pres. 1982-84, 86—, 2d v.p. 1984-86). Home and Office: 1105 Georgina Av Santa Monica CA 90402

RONHOVDE, VIRGINIA SEDMAN, political and civic worker; b. Missoula, Mont., Dec. 17, 1909; d. Oscar Alfred and Harriet Laura (Rankin) Sedman; student U. Mont., 1925-27; B.A., Wellesley Coll., 1929; M.A., Columbia U., 1930; postgrad., 1930-33; postgrad. (Columbia U. fellow) U. Berlin, 1933-35; m. Andreas G. Ronhovde, Apr. 7, 1936; children—Erik Sedman, Andrea Rankin, Nora Montana Ronhovde Hohenlohe, Kent McGregor. Instr. sociology and labor problems Rutgers U., 1935-36; salesman Boss and Phelps, Inc., Simmons Properties, Washington, 1954-76. Sec., League Rep. Women, Washington, 1969-71, bd. dirs., 1971-73, 75-77, 1st v.p., 1973-75; del. Nat. Fedn. Rep. Women Conv., Dallas, 1975; del., mem. permanent orgn. com. Rep. Nat. Conv., 1976; mem. cen. com. D.C. Rep. Com., 1976-80, 80-84, alt. nat. committeewoman, 1980-84; mem. Missoula Design Rev. Bd. Mem. Missoula Rep. Women's Club, Kappa Kappa Gamma. Episcopalian. Home: 600 Beverly Ave Missoula MT 59801

RONTY, BRUNO GEORGE, phonograph record mfg. co. exec., tenor; b. Lwow, Poland, June 10, 1922; came to U.S., 1946, naturalized, 1955; s. Leon and Hermine (Elsner) R.; student Lwow Lyceum of Humanities, 1938-40; B.A., Conservatory, 1939, M.A., M.F.A., 1941, Ph.D. in History and Polit. Sci., 1945; m. Wanda von Rudolph, Nov. 3, 1943 (div. 1959); 1 dau., Maria; m. 2nd, Michele van Beveren, June 12, 1962 (div. 1972). Tenor, USSR, Poland, Sweden, U.S., 1940-50; pres. Colosseum Records, Inc., N.Y.C., 1950—, Musicart Internat., Ltd., N.Y.C., Wilton, Conn., 1958—; pres. Acropole Corp. Am., N.Y.C., 1972—; producer Bruno Hi-Fi Records; voice instr. N.Y.C.; tenor, gen. dir. cultural exchange program Musica Nostra et Vostra, Nat. Corp. Am., 1973—. Contrbr. articles to profl. jours. Bd. dirs. Ministry Culture, Art, Poland, 1945; pres. Narcolepsy and Cataplexy Found. Am., 1975—, Cultural Exchange Soc. Am., 1976—. Served with Polish Army, 1942-45. Decorated Grunwald Cross; Polonia Restituta; recipient 1st prize USSR Internat. Competition, 1940. Roman Catholic. Club: YMCA Greater N.Y. (life mem.). Office: Suite 2D Box 22 1410 York Ave New York NY 10021

ROOMANN, HUGO, architect; b. Tallinn, Estonia, Mar. 25, 1923; came to U.S., 1951, naturalized, 1957; s. Eduard August and Annette (Kask) R.; m. Raja R. Suursoho, Sept. 15, 1945; children—Katrin-Kaja, Linda-Anu. B.S., Inst. Tech. Carolo Wilhelmina, Braunschweig, W. Ger., 1950; M.F.A. in Arch. (scholar 1956-57), Princeton U., 1957. Archtl. engr. Austin Co., Roselle, N.J., 1951-54; archtl. designer Epple & Seaman, Newark, 1954-55, 57-61; propr. Hugo Roomann, Cranford and Elizabeth, N.J., 1961-66; partner A.M. Kinney Assocs. (Architects and Engrs.), Cin., N.Y.C. and Chgo., 1966—; dir. architecture, v.p. corp. ops. A.M. Kinney, Inc., Cin., 1967, 77; dir. Walter Kidde Constructors, Inc., 1973, A.M. Kinney, Inc., A.M. Kinney Assocs. Inc., Chgo.; pres. Design Art Corp., 1986. Prin. works include Grad. Research Center for Biol. Scis, Ohio State U., 1970, Lloyd Library, Cin., 1968, offices, labs. and mfg. facilities, Miles Labs., West Haven, Conn., 1969, Am. Mus. Atomic Energy, Oak Ridge, 1975, Renton K. Brodie Sci. Center, U. Cin., 1970. Pres. Citizens League, Elizabeth, N.J., 1966. Recipient Top Ten Plant award Factory mag., 1967, Top Ten Plant award Modern Mfg. mag., 1970. Mem. AIA (Ohio chpt. award for Renton K. Brodie Sci. Center, U. Cin. 1971), Soc. Archtl. Historians. Lutheran. Club: Princeton. Office: 2900 Vernon Pl Cincinnati OH 45219

ROONEY, FRANCIS CHARLES, JR., corporate executive; b. North Brookfield, Mass., Nov. 24, 1921; s. Francis Charles and Evelyn Fullerbrown (Murray) R.; m. Frances Elizabeth Heffernan, June 10, 1950; children—Peter, Michael, Stephen, Jean, William, Carol, Frances, Clare. B.S. in Econs., U. Pa., 1943; D.Comml. Sci. (hon.), Suffolk U., 1968, St. John's U., 1973; PhD (hon.), Boston Coll., 1986. Mem. sales staff John Foote Shoe Co., Brockton, Mass., 1946-48; mem. sales staff Florsheim Shoe Co., Chgo., 1948-53; various positions Melville Shoe Co., N.Y.C., 1953—; pres. Thom McAn div. Melville Shoe Corp., N.Y.C., 1961-64; pres., chief exec. officer Melville Corp., Harrison, N.Y. and N.Y.C., 1964-77; chmn., pres., chief exec. officer Melville Corp., Harrison, 1977-80, chmn., chief exec. officer, 1980-86, chmn. exec. com., 1987—; dir. Bankers Trust Co., N.Y.C., Crystal Brands Inc., Southport, Conn., N.Y.C., The Neiman Marcus Group, Chestnut Hill, Mass. Bd. dirs. United Cerebral Palsy, N.Y.C., 1960, Smithsonian Assocs., 1975; overseers Wharton Sch. U. Pa.; trustee March of Dimes, N.Y. Med. Coll.; bd. dirs. Wilfred Am. Ednl. Corp. Served to lt. (j.g.) USN, 1943-46. Republican. Roman Catholic. Clubs: Round Hill (Greenwich); Links (N.Y.C.); Winged Foot (Mamaroneck, N.Y.). Office: 60 Arch St Greenwich CT 06830

ROONEY, GEORGE WILLARD, lawyer; b. Appleton, Wis., Nov. 16, 1915; s. Francis John and Margaret Ellen (O'Connell) R.; m. Doris I. Maxon, Sept. 20, 1941; children—Catherine Ann, Thomas Dudley, George Willard. B.S., U. Wis., 1938; J.D., Ohio State U., 1948. Bar: Ohio 1949. Assoc. Wise, Roetzel, Maxon, Kelly & Andress, Akron, Ohio, 1949-54; ptnr. Roetzel & Andress, and predecessor, Akron, 1954—; dir. Bank One of Akron, Duracote Corp. Nat. bd. govs. ARC, 1972-78; v.p. Akron council Boy Scouts Am., 1975-88; pres. Akron Automobile Assn., 1980, trustee, 1986—; chmn. bd. Akron Gen. Med. Center, 1981-86, trustee, mem. exec. com., 1986—; trustee Mobile Meals Found., Bluecoats, Inc.. Served to maj. USAAF, 1942-46. Decorated D.F.C. with 2 oak leaf clusters, Air medal with 3 oak leaf clusters; recipient Disting. Community Service award Akron Labor Council, 1973; Disting. Service award Summit County chpt. ARC, 1978. Mem. ABA, Ohio Bar Assn. Akron Bar Assn. Am. Judicature Soc. Republican. Roman Catholic. Clubs: Rotary (past pres.), Portage Country (past pres.), Cascade (bd. govs.) (Akron), KC. Home: 2863 Walnut Ridge Rd Akron OH 44313 Office: 75 E Market St Akron OH 44308

ROONEY, JAMES PATRICK, international business consultant; b. Lewiston, Idaho, Apr. 25, 1938; arrived in Thailand, 1971; s. Harry Needham and Ruth (Hartley) R.; m. Dawn W. Fairley, Jan. 28, 1967; 1 child, Sarah W. B.A., Pomona Coll., 1960; postgrad. Inst. Far Eastern Studies, Yale U., 1966; M.A. in Fgn. Trade, Am. Grad. Sch. Internat. Mgmt., 1967. Officer Citibank, Hong Kong, 1967-69; mgr. Citicorp. Devel. and Fin. Corp., Bangkok, Thailand, 1969-73; mng. dir. Bangkok 1st Investment & Trust, 1973-75; mng. dir. J.P. Rooney & Assocs., Ltd., Bangkok, 1976—; dir. Taxplan Ltd., Bangkok, Taxplan Inc., Manila, Taxplan Ltd., Singapore. Bd. dirs. ASEAN-Am. Trade Council, N.Y.C., 1982-83, Thailand Bd. Trade, 1976, Bangkok YMCA, 1982—; mem. exec. council Ctr. for Internat. Pvt. Enterprise, Washington, 1983-85; mem. ASEAN-U.S. Bus. Council, Washington, 1984-85; mem. fgn. investment adv. com. Prime Minister of Thailand, 1976; mem. Securities Exchange Formation com. Bank of Thailand, 1973-75. Served to 1st lt. AUS, 1961-65. Mem. Asia Pacific Council of Am. C. of C. (chmn. 1981-82, vice chmn. 1980-85), Am. C. of C. in Thailand (pres. 1976, dir. 1973-74, 77-80, 82—), Investment Adv. Com. of the Thai Fund, adv. com. to Royal Thai Army for the Devel. of N.E. Thailand, C. of C. of U.S. (mem. Council Small Bus. 1981-84, mem. internat. trade and investment com. 1981-82, mem. task force on export policy, 1981-82), Thai Fin. & Sec. Assn. (founding dir. 1973-74), Thailand Mgmt. Assn. (bd. dirs. 1972-75). Episcopalian. Clubs: Royal Bangkok Sports (dir. 1976—, vice chmn. 1987), British, Chaine de Rotissuers, Fgn. Corrs. of Thailand, Siam Soc., Thailand Sub-Aqua; Asia Soc. (N.Y.C.); Oriental Ceramic Soc. (various chpts.), orgns. in London, Hong Kong, Singapore and Japan. Office: J P Rooney & Assocs Ltd, 4th Floor Panunee Bldg, 518/3 Ploenchit Rd, Bangkok Thailand

ROONEY, JOHN LOSSIN, telecommunication educator; b. Oak Park, Ill., Oct. 10, 1940; s. James J. and Dorothy W. (Lossin) R.; children: James, Jenny, Jeffrey. BS, U. So. Calif., 1965, MBA, 1966, MS, 1974. Mgr. Ralphs, Los Angeles, 1961-78; dir. FedMart, San Diego, 1978-83; asst. prof. tech. Nat. U., San Diego, 1983-85, chmn., prof. telecommunications, 1985. Home: 1844 Chickasaw Los Angeles CA 90041 Office: Nat U 6672 University Ave San Diego CA 92115

ROOS, JEF RENE, metallurgical engineering educator; b. Aalst Belgium, Mar. 15, 1943; s. Jules B. and Irene M. (Goeman) R.; m. Martine A. Boel, Oct. 6, 1965; children—Evie, Jan, Hilde. Metall. Engr., Katholieke Universiteit Leuven (Belgium), 1966; M.Sc. in Metall. Engring., Colo. Sch. Mines., 1967, Ph.D. in Metall. Engring., 1969. Research fellow Colo. Sch. Mines, Golden, 1966-69; asst. prof. metall. engring. Katholieke Universiteit Leuven, 1969-74, assoc. prof., from 1974, prof., 1976—, head dept. metall. engring., 1983—; v.p. Benelux Metallurgie, 1982—; con.to industry and govt.; bd. dirs. Belgian Nuclear Research. Author: Extractive Metallurgy, 1982; contbr. numerous articles to profl. jours., 1969—; patentee alloys, 1977—. Recipient Vincotte award, 1980; Fulbright awardee, 1966; grantee Belgian Nat. Sci. Found., 1972-84, European Econ. Community, 1983. Fellow Inst. Metal Finishing; mem. AIME. Office: Katholeike U, Dept Metal and Materials Engring, 2 De Croylaan, B3030 Leuven Belgium

ROOS, LARS ERIK, corporate executive; b. Luleå, Sweden, Sept. 6, 1944; s. Karl Simeon and Ellen C. (Eriksson) R.; m. Gunilla Petersson, Apr. 11, 1946; children: Martin, Fredrik. Degree in econs., U. Stockholm, 1970; M in Civil Engring., Royal U. Tech., Stockholm, 1970; degree in mgmt., Inst. för Företags Ledning, Stockholm, 1984. Planning engr. Rationell Planering AB, Stockholm, 1970-71; prodn. engr. Loussauvara Kirunauaara AB, Malmberget, Sweden, 1972-76; plant mgr. Rockwool AB, Gimo, Sweden, 1977-79; mining cons. Hierro Patagónico de Sierra Grande S.A., Sierra Grande, Argentina, 1980; mng. dir. Upplandsinvest AB, Uppsala, Sweden, 1981; div. mgr. Holmens Bruk AB, Vrena, Sweden, 1982; mng. dir. Swedeboard Vrena AB, Vrena, 1983—; pres. Swedeboard Inc., Atlanta, 1985—; dir. Lamiflex Gmbh, Düsseldorf, Fed. Republic Germany, 1986—; chmn. Swedish Wallboard Fedn., Stockholm, 1984-85, Nordic Fiberboard Fedn., Stockholm, 1984-85; v.p. Feropa, Fed. Republic Germany, 1984-85; bd. dirs. Scanpac, Tunbridge Wells, Eng., 1982. Inventor fiberpellets, 1979. Mem. Swedish Cicil Engrs., C. of C. (rep. 1982—). Club: Exec. Home: Snackvagen 35, 61300 Oxelösund Sweden Office: Swedeboard Vrena AB, 61056 Vrena Sweden

ROOS, LARS HAKAN, jewelry firm executive; b. Malmö, Sweden, Feb. 28, 1955; s. Axel Bernard and Lena Lillemor (Bertenius) R.; m. Karin Helene Sterne. MBA, Stockholm Sch. Econs., 1979. Mng. dir. C.G. Hallbergs Goldsmiths Inc., Malmö and Stockholm, 1981—, Trift Computers Ltd., Malmö, 1986-88; owner, pres. Wheel Products-Kleber Sweden, Helsingborg, 1985—; bd. dirs. Transferator Fondkommission Ltd. Mem. Malmö Mktg. Assn. (bd. dirs. 1986-88), Stockholm Sch. Econs. Alumni Assn. (chmn. 1977-78). Home: Radjursstigen 16, 23600 Hollviken Sweden Office: Hallbergs Goldsmiths Ltd, PO Box 105, 20121 Malmö Sweden

ROOS, PIERRE GERHARD, optometrist; b. Standerton, Republic South Africa, Dec. 20, 1923. Diploma in Optometry, Witwatersrand Tech. Sch., Johannesburg, Republic South Africa, 1945. Registered optometrist, Republic South Africa. Pvt. practice optometry Bloemfontein, Republic South Africa, 1945—; mem. profl. bd. optometry. Fellow Assn. Contact Lens Practitioners; mem. South African Optometric Soc. (various offices), SAMDC (profession bd.). Office: Floreat Mall 1st Floor Suite, Box 1110, Bloemfontein 9301, Republic of South Africa

ROOSE, DIRK ALBERT FLORIMOND, computer science educator; b. Brussels, Dec. 25, 1954; s. Juliaan and Simone (Waerebeke) R.; m. Mieke Ransschaert, July 27, 1977; children: Liesbet, Ine, Annelore. M in Computer Sci., Katholieke U., Leuven, Belgium, 1978, PhD in Applied Scis., 1985. Registered profl. engr. Research asst. Katholieke U., 1978-85, sr. asst., 1985-86, lectr., 1986—; cons., 1986—. Contbr. articles to profl. jours. Katholieke U.-Ministry Sci. grantee, 1987, IBM-Nat. Sci. Found. Belgium grantee, 1987; Von Humboldt research fellow, 1988. Home: Rerum Novarumlaan 44, B-3200 Leuven Belgium Office: Katholieke U Dept Computer Scis, Celestijnenlaan 200A, B-3030 Leuven Belgium

ROOSJEN, SIERD KEIMPE, pharmaceutical company executive; b. Hardenberg, The Netherlands, Mar. 9, 1942; arrived in France, 1985; s. Douwe and Sytske (Plat) R.; m. Maria Louise Hendriks, Jan. 27, 1966; children: Barbara, Bob. BBA, Nyenrode Bus. Sch., The Netherlands, 1963. Mgmt. trainee Curacao Trading Co., Amsterdam, The Netherlands, 1965-66; asst. gen. mgr. Curacao Trading Co., Tegucigalpa, Honduras, 1966-69; mgmt. trainee AK20 Pharm., Oss, The Netherlands, 1970-71; gen. mgr. AK20 Pharm., Caracas, Venezuela, 1976-81, Regional Ctr. Africa, Casablanca, Morocco, 1971-76; regional dir. Duphar, Amsterdam, 1981-83, exec. v.p., 1983-85; pres. Duphar, Villeur Banne, France, 1985—; cons. in field. Served as sgt. The Netherlands Service, 1963-65. Club: Country. Home: 252 Rt Mont Verdun, Villa Arena, F-69760 Limonest France Office: Duphar, 60 Rue de Verdun, F-69604 Villeur Banne France

ROOT, ALLEN WILLIAM, pediatrician, educator; b. Phila., Sept. 24, 1933; s. Morris Jacob and Priscilla R.; m. Janet Greenberg, June 15, 1958; children: Jonathan, Jennifer, Michael. A.B., Dartmouth Coll., 1955; postgrad., Dartmouth Med. Sch., 1954-56; M.D., Harvard U., 1958. Intern Strong Meml. Hosp., Rochester, N.Y., 1958-60; resident in pediatrics Hosp. U. Pa., Phila., 1960-62; fellow in pediatric endocrinology Children's Hosp. of Phila., 1962-65; assoc. physician in pediatrics U. Pa. Sch. Medicine, 1964-66, asst. prof. pediatrics, 1966-69; assoc. prof. pediatrics Temple U. Sch. Medicine, Phila., 1969-73; prof. Temple U. Sch. Medicine, 1973; asst. physician in endocrinology Children's Hosp. Phila., 1965-69; chmn. div. pediatrics Albert Einstein Med. Center., Phila., 1969-73; prof. pediatrics U. South Fla. Coll. Medicine, St. Petersburg, 1973—; assoc. chmn. dept. pediatrics U. South Fla. Coll. Medicine, 1974—, dir. sect. pediatric endocrinology, 1973—; dir. univ. teaching services All Children's Hosp., St. Petersburg, 1973—; mem. Fla. Infant Screening Adv. Council, 1979—, Hillsborough County Thyroid Adv. Com., 1980; mem. med. adv. com. Nat. Pituitary Agy., 1974-78, mem. growth hormone subcom., 1972-79, 81-85; mem. sub-bd. pediatric endocrinology Am. Bd. Pediatrics, 1985—. Author: Human Pituitary Growth Hormone, 1972; Editor: (with C. La Cauza) Problems in Pediatric Endocrinology, 1980. Mem. editorial bd.: Jour. Pediatrics, 1973-81, Jour. Adolescent Health Care, 1979—, Jour. Pediatric Endocrinology, 1985—. Contbr. articles to med. jours. USPHS grantee; Birth Defects Found. grantee. Mem. Am. Pediatric Soc., Soc. Pediatric Research, Lawson Wilkins Pediatric Endocrine Soc. (treas. 1979-88, pres. elect 1987-88, pres. 1988—), Endocrine Soc., Am. Acad. Pediatrics, Am. Fedn. Clin. Research, AAAS, Soc. Exptl. Biology and Medicine, Soc. Nuclear Medicine, N.Y. Acad. Sci., Phila. Coll. Physicians, Phila. Endocrine Soc. (pres. 1972-73), Phila. Pediatric Soc. (dir. 1971-72, treas. 1973), Dartmouth Coll. Alumni Council. Club: Dartmouth (Tampa) (pres. 1987—). Office: 801 6th St S Saint Petersburg FL 33731

ROOT, NILE, photographer, educator; b. Denver, Dec. 11, 1926; s. Victor Nile and Ella May (Holaway) R.; student U. Denver, 1968; M.S. in Instructional Tech., Rochester Inst. Tech., 1978; m. Abigail Barton Brown, Feb. 5, 1960; 1 son, James Michael. Microphotographer, U.S. Dept. Commerce, Fed. Republic Germany, 1946-48; free-lance photographer, 1949-51; pres. Photography Workshop, Inc., Denver, 1952-60; dir. dept. biophotography and med. illustration Gen. Rose Meml. Hosp., Denver, 1960-70; dir. med. illustration dept. Children's Hosp., Denver, 1970-71; dir. Photography for Sci., Denver, 1971-72; prof. biomed. photog. communications Rochester Inst. Tech. (N.Y.), 197213 , chmn. dept., 1974-86, prof. emeritus, 1986—. dir. HEW project for devel. of field, 1974-77. Served with USN, 1945-46. Recipient numerous awards for sci. photographs; Eisenhart Outstanding Tchr. award Rochester Inst. Tech., 1986; 1st Ann. Faculty fellow Sch. Photog. Arts and Scis., Rochester Inst. Tech., 1979. Fellow Biol. Photog. Assn. (registered, bd. govs. 1977-79, Louis Schmidt award 1986); mem. Astron. Soc. Pacific, Soc. Photog. Edn., Friends of Photography, Internat. Mus. Photography. Democrat. Contbr. illustrations to med. textbooks; represented in numerous mus. photog. exhibits. Home and Office: 2-3 Higashi Yamate Machi, 301, Nagasaki 850, Japan

ROOTS, JOHN MCCOOK, author, lecturer, foreign correspondent; b. Hankow, China (parents Am. citizens) Oct. 27, 1903; s. Logan Herbert and Eliza Lydia (McCook) R. B.A. cum laude, Harvard Coll., 1925. Contbr. New York Times, Herald Tribune, Atlantic Monthly, Asia, Pace, Look, Reader's Digest, Time, Saturday Rev., others, 1927—; traveling rep., dir. Moral Re-Armament teams, S. Africa, 1929-31, U.S., 1932, Great Britain, France, Switzerland, The Netherlands, Germany, Italy, Can. Belgium, East Africa, Greece, Middle East 1932-68; lectr. U.S. and Can., 1964-81; fgn. corr. various publs., numerous countries including China, Egypt, Israel, Jordan, Lebanon, Syria, Saudi Arabia, Indonesia, Iran, 1927-80; assoc. Up With People orgn., 1968—; author: Chou: a Biography of China's Legendary Chou En-lai, 1978. Recipient Washburn Prize for History, Harvard Coll., 1925. Clubs: Harvard (N.Y.C.), Army and Navy (Washington) Home and Office: 158 Graham Ave Saint Ignace MI 49781

ROOTS, PETER CHARLES, data processing company executive; b. Munich, W. Ger., Mar. 19, 1921; came to U.S., 1939, naturalized, 1943; s. Josef and Ruth R.; B.S., Sch. Fgn. Service, Georgetown U., 1948, LL.B., J.D., 1952; m. Sachiko Tamura; children—Stephanie E. Roots-Karsten, Judith A. Roots-Carver, David H., Catherine E. Admitted to Md. bar, U.S. Tax Ct. bar, 1952; atty. Sperry-Rand Corp., N.Y.C., 1952-65; exec. Sperry-Rand Corp. fgn. subs., Germany, Japan, 1965-70; pres. Inverdata GMBH, W. Ger., 1970—. Served with AUS, 1943-46. Mem. ABA. Club: Kronberg Golf & Land (W. Ger.). Author: (with Greene & Thompson) Developing Munitions for War, 1952. Home: Habicht Strasse 1, D6078 Neu Isenburg Federal Republic of Germany Office: Inverdata Electronics, Paul-Ehrlich Strasse 17, D-6074 Roedermark Federal Republic of Germany also: 1666 Newport Blvd Suite E Costa Mesa CA 92627

ROPCKE, GUNTHER BENDORFF, surgeon, educator; b. Vamdrup, Denmark, Sept. 15, 1941; s. Werner Ernest and Mathilde (Bendorff) R.; m. Vibeke Pedersen, May 31, 1980; children—Karsten, Diana, Philip, Stephanie. M.D., U. Arhus, 1969. Educator U. Arhus, Denmark, 1965-78; resident Arhus County Hosp., 1970-73; sub-chief Grenia Hosp., 1975-78, Randers Central Hosp., 1978-82; surgeon Surg. Clinic, Arhus, 1977—. Served to sgt. Infantry, 1960-62. Mem. Soc. Danish Drs., Soc. Med. Specialists. Home: Gammel Stillingvej 10, Mesing, 8660 Skanderborg Denmark Office: Surgical Clinic, Aboulevarden 3, 8000 Aarhus Denmark

ROPKEY, ANN SAMONIAL, educator, lecturer; b. Vincennes, Ind., Jan. 31, 1917; d. Charles Edward and Martha Ann (Love) Samonial; A.A., Vincennes U., 1936; B.S., Peabody Coll., 1938, M.A., 1941; postgrad. Vanderbilt U.; Litt.D. (hon.), Steed Coll., 1957; m. Stewart Winning McClelland, Aug. 2, 1947 (dec. Feb. 1977); m. 2d, F. Noble Ropkey, Aug. 16, 1980. Tchr., Bogalusa (La.) High Sch., 1938, Holmes High Sch., Covington, Ky., 1939-45; instr. Okla. Coll. Women, 1938-39; dean women Lincoln Meml. U., 1945-47; sponsor Dale Carnegie courses, Fla., Ind., 1947—; assoc. with Mrs. Dale Carnegie in Dorothy Carnegie Courses Women, 1956—. Pres. Decorative Arts Soc. (two-time program chmn.), Indpls. Mus. Art; state chmn. DAR Mus., Washington; mem. adv. bd. Pompeiiana, Inc. Recipient faculty citation Vincennes U., 1983. Fellow Royal Soc. Arts (London) (life); mem. Indpls. Propylaeum (past pres.), Internat. Platform Assn., AAUW, Wedgwood Internat. Seminar, Wedgwood Soc. (London), English Speaking Union, DAR (past chmn. Wheel and Distaff, chmn. nat. def. com. 1984-85, past hon. regent Caroline Scott Harrison chpt. 1975-77, lifemem. and past pres. Ind. Officers Club), Children's Mus. of Ind., Hon. Order Ky. Cols., Blair Mus. Lithophanes, Indpls. Mus. Art, Am Ceramic Circle, Kappa Kappa Kappa, Pi Gamma Chi. Republican. Roman Catholic. Clubs: Fortnightly, Contemporary, Alpha Beta Latreian (Indpls.). Authority on Coin glass, Lithophanes and Wedgwood, Fore-edge books. Home: 6360 W 79th St Indianapolis IN 46278

ROPOHL, GUENTER, engineering educator; b. Cologne, Germany, June 14, 1939; s. Franz and Lilly (Muller) R.; m. Ursula Pattberg, Jan. 29, 1965; 1 son, Ralph Manuel. Dipl. Ing., U. Stuttgart, 1964, Dr. Ing., 1970. Prof. gen. tech. U. Karlsruhe (W.Ger.), 1979-81, U. Frankfurt (W.Ger.), 1981—. Author: Flexible Fertigungssysteme, 1971; Eine Systemtheorie der Technik, 1979; Die unvollkommene Technik, 1985; editor: Systemtechnik, 1975; Interdisziplinaere Technikforschung, 1981; Arbeit im Wandel, 1985; Technik und Ethik, 1987 . Home: Kelterstrasse 34, 7500 Karlsruhe Durlach Federal Republic of Germany Office: U Frankfurt, Dantestrasse 5, 6000 Frankfurt Federal Republic of Germany

RORER, LEONARD GEORGE, psychology educator; b. Dixon, Ill., Dec. 24, 1932; s. Leonard Gleason and Marion Emma (Geyer) R.; B.A., Swarthmore (Pa.) Coll., 1954; Ph.D., U. Minn., 1963; m. Gail Evans, Apr. 30, 1958; children—Liat, Eric Evans; m. 2d, Nancy McKimens, Jan. 9, 1969; 1 dau., Mya Noelani. Research asso., then asso. dir. Oreg. Research Inst., Eugene, 1963-75; prof. psychology Miami U., Oxford, Ohio, 1975—, dir. clin. psychology tng. program, 1976-86 ; pres. Oreg. Psychol. Assn., 1973-75. NIMH spl. research fellow, 1967-68; fellow Netherlands Inst. Advanced Study, 1971-72; postdoctoral fellow Inst. for Rational-Emotive Therapy, 1982-83. Fellow Am. Psychol. Assn. (council reps. 1968-72); mem. Ohio Psychol. Assn., Midwestern Psychol. Assn., Assn. Advancement Behavior Therapy, Soc. Multivariate Exptl. Psychology. Author articles in field, mem. editorial bds. profl. jours. Home: 327 W Sycamore St Oxford OH 45056 Office: Psychology Dept Miami U Oxford OH 45056

RORISON, MARGARET LIPPITT, reading consultant; b. Wilmington, N.C., Feb. 6, 1925; d. Harmon Chadbourn and Margaret Devereux (Lippitt) R.; A.B., Hollins Coll., 1946; M.A., Columbia U., 1956; Diplôme de langue, L'Alliance Française, Paris, 1966; postgrad. U. S.C., 1967-70, 81—. Market and editorial researcher Time, Inc., N.Y.C., 1949-55; classroom and corrective reading tchr. N.Y.C. public schs., 1956-65; TV instr. ETV-WNDT, Channel 13, N.Y.C., 1962-63; grad. asst., TV instr. U. S.C., Columbia, 1967-70; instrnl. specialist in reading S.C. Office Instrnl. TV and Radio, S.C. Dept. Edn., Columbia, 1971-81; reading cons. S.C. Office Instructional Tech., 1982—. Active Common Cause. Mem. Internat. Reading Assn., Am. Ednl. Research Assn., Assn. Supervision and Curriculum Devel., Nat. Soc. Study of Edn., AAUW. Phi Delta Kappa, Delta Kappa Gamma. Episcopalian. Author instrnl. TV series: Getting the Word (So. Ednl. Communications Assn. award 1972, Ohio State award 1973, S.C. Scholastic Broadcasters award 1973), Getting the Message, 1981. Home: 1724 Enoree Ave Columbia SC 29205

ROSAR, VIRGINIA WILEY, librarian; b. Cleve., Nov. 22, 1926; d. John Egbert and Kathryn Coe (Snyder) Wiley; m. Michael Thorpe Rosar, April 8, 1950 (div. Feb. 1968); children: Bruce Wiley, Keith Michael, James Wilfred. Attended, Oberlin Coll., 1944-46; BA, U. Puget Sound, 1948; MS, C.W. Post Coll., L.I.U., Greenvale, N.Y., 1971. Cert. elem. music teacher, N.Y.; cert. sch. library media specialist. Music programmer Station WFAS, White Plains, N.Y., 1948; prodn. asst. NBC-TV, N.Y.C., 1948-50; tchr. Portledge Sch., Locust Valley, N.Y., 1967-70; librarian Syosset (N.Y.) Schs., 1970-71, Smithtown (N.Y.) Schs., 1971—; pres. World of Realia, Woodbury, N.Y., 1969-86; founder Cygnus Pub., Woodbury, 1985-87. Active local chpt. ARC, 1960-63, Community Concert Assn., 1960-66, Leukemia Soc. Am., 1978—. Mem. Suffolk Sch. Library Media Assn., AAAS, N.Y. Acad. Scis., Am. Mus. Natural History (assoc.), Am. Library Assn., L.I. Alumnae Club of Pi Beta Phi (pres. 1964-66). Republican. Presbyterian. Home: 10 Warrenton Ct Huntington NY 11743

ROSBERG, CARL GUSTAF, political science educator; b. Oakland, Calif., Feb. 28, 1923; s. Carl Gustaf and Ethel (Moore) R.; m. Elizabeth Joanna Wilson, Oct. 23, 1954; children—James Howard, David Nils. B.S., Georgetown U., 1948, M.S., 1950; D.Phil., Oxford (Eng.) U., 1954. Asst. prof., research asso. African studies program Boston U., 1955-58; vis. asst. prof. U. Calif., Berkeley, 1958-59; asst. prof. dept. polit. sci. U. Calif., 1959-63, asso. prof., 1963-67, prof., 1967—, chmn. dept. polit. sci., 1969-74, dir. Inst. Internat. Studies, 1973—. Author: (with John Nottingham) The Myth of Mau Mau: Nationalism in Kenya, 1966, (with George Bennett) The Kenyatta Election: Kenya, 1960-61, 1961, (with Robert Jackson) Personal Rule in Black Africa: Prince, Autocrat, Prophet, Tyrant, 1982; editor: (with James S. Coleman) Political Parties and National Integration in Tropical Africa, 1964, (with William H. Friedland) African Socialism, 1964, (with Thomas Callaghy) Socialism in Sub-Saharan Africa, (with Robert M. Price) The Apartheid Regime: Political Power and Racial Domination, 1980. Served with USAAF, 1943-45. Decorated Purple Heart, Air medal.; Ford Found. fellow, 1954-55. Mem. Royal African Soc., African Studies Assn. (past pres.). Home: 1015 Cragmont Ave Berkeley CA 94708 Office: Dept Polit Sci U Calif Berkeley CA 94720

ROSBOROUGH, JOSEPH ROBERT, lawyer; b. Moline, Ill., Jan. 13, 1911; s. Caldwell Robert and Nellie (Ball) R.; m. Jean Bowman, Oct. 7, 1939; children: Nancy, Barbara Jo, Margaret Ann. BS, U. Ill., 1933, JD, 1935; postgrad., Harvard U., 1942. Bar: Ill. 1936, U.S. Supreme Ct. 1939. Sole practice Moline, 1936—; asst. atty. gen. State of Ill., Moline, 1968-82. Served to lt. comdr. USN, 1942-45. Mem. ABA, Ill. Bar Assn. Republican. Clubs: Rock Island (Ill.) Arsenal Golf; Davenport (Iowa) Outing; Union League (Chgo.), South Park Tennis. Lodges: Rotary, Elks. Home: 1825 29th St Moline IL 61265 Office: 501-15th St Suite 609 Moline IL 61265

ROSE, ARTHUR MORRIS, wholesale hardware executive; b. Bklyn., Mar. 7, 1943; s. Lawrence and Lillian (Rosen) R.; B.S., N.Y. U., 1964; M.B.A. with distinction, Adelphi U., 1978; m. Nadine Posner; children—Sharon Elisabeth, Kevin Benjamin, Amy Meredith, Erica June, Jonathan Calman. Exec. trainee, mgr. boy's dept. Gertz Dept. Stores, Hicksville, N.Y., 1966; registered rep. Loeb Rhoades & Co., N.Y.C., 1967; pres. L. Rose Hardware Inc., Bklyn., 1968—. Mem. Am. Mgmt. Assn., U.S. Power Squadron, Am. Radio Relay League, Delta Mu Delta. Jewish. Club: Steppingstone Sailing. Home: 33 Georgian Ln Great Neck NY 11024 Office: L Rose Hardware Inc 201 Snediker Ave Brooklyn NY 11207

ROSE, CAROLYN BRUCE, interior designer, educator; b. Gunnison, Miss., Oct. 10, 1930; d. John Douglas and Emmye Elizabeth (Bowe) Simmons; m. James Frederic Rose, Sept. 7, 1953; children: James Frederic, Phillip Douglas, Elizabeth Bowe. BS, Miss. Women's U., 1952; MS, Delta State U., 1952. Tchr. Inverness (Miss.) High Sch., 1952; elem. sch. tchr. John D. Overstreet Elem. Sch., Starkeville, Miss., 1952-53, Misawa (Japan) AFB Dependent Sch., 1954-55; nursery sch. tchr., Long Island, N.Y., 1954-55; owner Rose Designs, Dallas, 1975—; exec. v.p., Handel's Specialty Shops, Dallas, 1988. Sec. women's com. Dallas Theatre Ctr., 1965-74; bd. dirs. women's com. Dallas Civic Opera, 1978-83; bd. dirs. Family Restoration Network, 1985; mem. Opera Action, 1965-70; research com. head Noted Cookery Cookbook, Dallas Symphony Orch., 1968; chmn. charity events Investment Bankers Wives' Com., 1978; local chmn., judge Dallas County 4-H; bd. dirs. Chorus of Santa Fe, 1985-86, Family Restoration Network, Dallas, 1986, Scarborough Prodns., Dallas Communications Ctr., 1986; nat. adv. bd. Santa Fe Opera, 1986-87. Home chosen for Dallas Designer's Homes Tour, 1981. Mem. Miss. Edn. Assn. Republican. Episcopalian.

ROSE, DANIEL, real estate company executive, consultant; b. N.Y.C., Oct. 31, 1929; s. Samuel B. and Belle (Bernstein) R.; m. Joanna Semel, Sept. 16, 1956; children: David Semel, Joseph Benedict, Emily, Gideon Gregory. Student, Yale U., 1947-50; cert. of proficiency in Russian lang., U.S. Air Force Program, 1951; B.A., Syracuse U., 1952; postgrad., U. Paris. With Dwelling Mgrs., Inc., N.Y.C., 1954—; exec. v.p. charge mgmt. Dwelling Mgrs., Inc., 1957-60, pres., 1960—; dir. Dreyfus Tax Exempt Bond Fund Inc., 1976-82; pres. Rose Assocs., Inc., N.Y.C., 1980—; dir. U.S. Trust Corp., Boston Brit. Properties, Town and City Properties Ltd.; trustee Corporate Property Investors, U.S. Trust Co. of N.Y.; advisor to sec. HUD, 1972; cons. U.S. commr. edn., 1974; mem. N.Y. Gov.'s Task Force on Housing, 1975; mem. task force on taxation Municipal Assistance Corp., 1976—. Chmn. bd. trustees Horace Mann Sch., 1971-74; trustee, asst. treas. Police Athletic League N.Y.; former trustee Fedn. Jewish Philanthropies N.Y.; asso. fellow Pierson Coll. of Yale; mem. council fellows New Sch. Social Research; also bd. overseers Center N.Y.C. Affairs; pres. Nat. Jewish Welfare Bd., 1974-78; past pres. YM and YWHA, Bronx; trustee Citizens Union, N.Y.C., Rand Inst., Mus. City of N.Y., 1984—; trustee, treas. Citizens Housing and Planning Council N.Y.; mem. adv. bd. NYC Municipal Broadcasting System, 1977-78, CUNY-TV Channel, 1986—, vice chmn. Trilling Seminars Columbia U., 1977—; bd. dirs. N.Y. Inst. Humanistic Studies NYU, 1977—, N.Y. Council for Humanities, 1980—, N.Y. Convention Center Devel. Corp., 1980—; v.p. N.Y. Landmarks Conservancy, 1979—; mem. adv. com. Harvard U. Grad. Sch. Design, 1986—; advisor MIT Ctr. for Real Estate Devel., 1983—; mem. bd. trustees Mus. City of N.Y.; chmn. Democratic Platform Adv. Com., 1984. Served with USAF, 1951-54. Mem. Am. Arbitration Assn. (nat. panel), N.Y. Bldg. Supts. Assn. (hon., Real Estate Man of Year 1961), Fgn. Policy Assn. (dir., mem. exec. com., chmn. assos), Am. Technion Soc. (dir.), Council Fgn. Relations, Real Estate Bd. N.Y. (gov., chmn. housing programs com.), Assn. Yale Alumni (assembly del.-at-large 1978—). Clubs: Century Assn., Coffee House, Yale (N.Y.C.); Cosmos (Washington); Racquet and Tennis, Union (Boston). Home: 895 Park Ave New York NY 10021 Office: 380 Madison Ave New York NY 10017

ROSE, HORACE CHAPMAN, lawyer; b. Columbus, Ohio, Feb. 11, 1907; s. Henry Nelson and Grace (Chapman) R.; m. Katherine Cast, Oct. 1, 1938; 1 son, Jonathan Chapman. A.B., Princeton U., 1928; LL.B., Harvard U., 1931. Bar: Ohio 1933, D.C. 1946. Sec. to Oliver Wendell Holmes (assoc. justice Supreme Ct. U.S.), 1931-32; assoc. Jones, Day, Cockley & Reavis (formerly Tolles, Hogsett & Ginn), Cleve., 1933-38; partner Jones, Day Reavis & Pogue, Cleve., Washington, 1939-42, 46-52, 56-76; of counsel Jones, Day Reavis & Pogue, 1977-82; dir. Office of Contract Settlement, Washington, 1946; asst. sec. treasury, 1953-55, undersec. treasury, 1955-56. Trustee Cleve. Orch., Cleve. Council World Affairs; bd. dirs. Atlantic Council, Washington; trustee emeritus Princeton U., Brookings Instn. Served to col. AUS, 1942-45. Decorated Legion of Merit. Mem. Am., Ohio, Cleve. bar assns., Am. Law Inst. (council), Phi Beta Kappa. Republican. Episcopalian. Clubs: Union (Cleve.), Tavern (Cleve.), Kirtland Country (Cleve.); Princeton (N.Y.C.); Metropolitan (Washington), Burning Tree (Washington), Chevy Chase (Washington). Home: 2701 31st St NW Washington DC 20008 Office: Met Sq 655 15th St NW Washington DC 20005

ROSE, JAMES TURNER, aerospace executive; b. Louisburg, N.C., Sept. 21, 1935; s. Frank Rogers and Mary Burt (Turner) R.; m. Daniele Raymond, Sept. 15, 1984; children by previous marriage—James Turner, Katharine S. B.S. with high honors, N.C. State U., 1957. Aero. research engr. NASA, Langley Field, Va., 1957-59; project engr. NASA (Mercury and Gemini), Langley Field, Va. and Houston, 1959-64; program systems mgr. McDonnell Douglas Astronatuics Co (MDAC), St. Louis, 1964-69, mgr. shuttle ops. and implementation, 1969-72, mgr. shuttle support, 1972-74, mgr. space processing programs, 1976-83, dir. electrophoresis ops. in space, 1983-86; dir. space shuttle engrng. NASA, Washington, 1974-76, asst. adminstr. comml. programs, 1987—. Mem. Phi Kappa Phi. Episcopalian. Office: NASA Hdqrs 600 Independence Ave SW Washington DC 20546

ROSE, JONATHAN CHAPMAN, lawyer; b. Cleve., June 8, 1941; s. Horace Chapman and Katherine Virginia (Cast) R.; m. Susan Anne Porter, Jan. 26, 1980; 1 son, Benjamin Chapman. A.B., Yale U., 1963; LL.B. cum laude, Harvard U., 1967. Bar: Mass. 1968, D.C. 1972, U.S. Supreme Ct. 1976, Circuit Ct. Appeals 1977, Ohio 1978. Law clk. Justice R. Ammi Cutter, Mass. Supreme Jud. Ct., 1967-68; spl. asst. to U.S. pres., 1971-73; gen. counsel Council on Internat. Econ. Policy, 1973-74; assoc. dept. atty. gen. U.S. Dept. Justice, 1974-75; dept. asst. atty. gen. U.S. Dept. Justice (Antitrust Div.), 1975-77; asst. atty. gen. Office of Legal Policy, 1981-84; ptnr. firm Jones, Day, Reavis & Pogue, Washington, 1977-81, 84—. Served to 1st lt. U.S. Army, 1969-71. Mem. Adminstrv. Conf. of U.S., Am. Bar Assn., D.C. Bar Assn., Mass. Bar Assn., Ohio Bar Assn., Fed. Bar Assn., Am. Law Inst. Republican. Episcopalian. Clubs: Met, Chevy Chase, Union, Yale, Harvard. Office: Jones Day Reavis & Pogue Metropolitan Sq 1450 G St NW Suite 600 Washington DC 20005

ROSE, ROSEMARY S. CATHERINE, business executive, financial consultant; b. Antigo, Wis., Jan. 2, 1931; d. Ernest J. and Rose F. Slizewski; 1 child, Ted R. Secretarial cert. Bryant-Stratton Sch., Milw., 1953; real estate course Spencerian Sch., Milw., 1964-65; Am. Inst. Paralegal Studies, 1985-86. Lic. real estate broker, Wis. Adminstrv. asst. H. R. Salen, Waukesha, Wis., 1964—; owner, operator Country Motel, Brookfield, Wis., 1951-55; co-owner Al's Super Service, Lannon, Wis., 1955-65; exec. sec. E.P. Hoyer, New Berlin, Wis., 1960-65; owner, operator Sanitation Service Inc., Menomonee Falls, Wis., 1967-70, North Twin Supper Club, Phelps, Wis., 1970-74; exec. sec., v.p. O.L. Schilffarth Co. div. Crown Industries, Milw., 1975-79; gen. mgr. Hotel Rogers, Beaver Dam, Wis., 1979-82; prin. Alrose Realty Co., 1980—, owner R-Service Co., Germantown, Wis., 1980—; exec. housekeeper Park East Hotel, Milw., 1983-84; office mgr. Cedar Disposal, Inc., Menomonee Falls, 1984-85; adminstr. A-1 Service Co., Inc., Germantown, 1985-87; mem. Research Bd. of Advisors Nat. Div. Am. Biographical Inst., Inc. Mem. Internat. Platform Assn., Nat. Assn. Female Execs., Nat. Rifle Assn. Home: N105 W15750 Hamilton Ct Germantown WI 53022 Office: A-1 Services Co N 104 W 13075 Donges Bay Rd Germantown WI 53022

ROSE, SHIRLEY, publisher; b. Kansas City, Mo., Mar. 12, 1921; d. Harry G. and Esther (Mendelson) Mallin; B.A., U. Mo., 1941; m. Stanley Jay Rose, Oct. 7, 1942; children—Roberta Susan, Stephen Frederick. Co-founder, co-pub. Sun Newspapers, Overland Park, Kans., 1950—; sec., dir. Sun Publs. Inc., 1973—. Treas. Kans. div. Am. Cancer Soc.; pres. Johnson County Cancer unit; mem. adv. bd. U. Kans. Med. Ctr., CASA. Recipient Bea Johnson Meml. cancer award, 1975, 76, honoree for outstanding achievement in journalism Women in Communication, 1979. lectr. on Soviet Union, China, Vietnam, Cambodia, Middle East. Mem. Overland Park C. of C. (dir.), Theta Sigma Phi. Republican. Club: Soroptimist. Avocation: photographer. Home: 8600 Mission Rd Shawnee Mission KS 66207 Office: Sun Publs Bldg 7373 W 107th St Overland Park KS 66212

ROSE, STANLEY JAY, newspaper executive; b. Kansas City, Mo., June 3, 1918; s. Joseph and Mae (Lund) R.; m. Shirley Mallin, Oct. 7, 1942; children: Roberta Susan Rose Small, Stephen F. AA, Los Angeles City Coll., 1939; BJ, U. Mo., 1941. Chmn. bd., pub. Sun Publs., Inc., Overland Park, Kans., 1950—; pub. Kansas City (Mo.) Jewish Chronicle, Inc., 1964—, College Blvd. News, 1984—, Atlanta Jewish Times, 1986—, Olathe (Kans.) Life, 1980. Author: Memo from Russia, 1986. Bd. dirs. Kaw Valley Heart Assn., Heart of Am. council Boy Scouts Am.; past chmn. bd. trustees Humana Med Ctr.; trustee William Allen White Found.; mem. adv. council U. Kans. Med. Center, K.U. Chancellor's Cabinet, 1986—. Served to lt. (j.g.) USNR, World War II; PTO. Recipient Sweepstakes, 1st place awards Kans. Better Newspaper Contest, 1968-70, 72, 73, William Allen White News Enterprise award, 1975, Bea Johnson award Am. Cancer Soc., 1st place winner for gen. excellence Suburban Newspapers Am., 1983-84; honoree Matrix Table, 1980; hon. col. Kans. Cav. Mem. Overland Park C. of C. (dir.), Kans. Assn. Commerce and Industry (dir.), Sigma Delta Chi. Club: Kansas City (Mo.) Press. Lodges: Masons, Shriners, Rotary (Paul Harris fellow 1985). Home: 8600 Mission Rd Prairie Village KS 66207 Office: Sun Publs Bldg Overland Park KS 66212

ROSE, WILLIAM ALLEN, JR., architect; b. Flushing, N.Y., Nov. 26, 1938; s. William Allen and Josephine (Grohe) R.; m. Sandra L. Latham, June 24, 1961; children: Lindsay E., Lesley A. B.A. cum laude, Harvard U., 1960; M.Arch., Columbia U., 1964. Architect Rose Beaton Corsbie Dearden & Crowe, N.Y.C. and White Plains, N.Y., 1964-69; ptnr. Rose Beaton & Rose, White Plains, 1969—. Chmn. White Plains Citizens Adv. Com., 1970-73; pres. Hillair Circle Civic Assn., White Plains, 1972-76; mem. White Plains City Council, 1974-78, pres., 1976-78; bd. dirs. White Plains YMCA, 1970-73, chmn. bd. trustees, 1981-83; bd. govs. YMCA Central and No. Westchester, 1983—, vice-chmn., 1983-85, chmn., 1985-87; chmn. bd. mgrs.

McBurney Sch., N.Y.C., 1973-76, trustee, 1981-86; trustee Rye Country Day Sch., N.Y., 1981-87; trustee Baldwin League of Ind. Schs., 1986-88; trustee Mercy Coll., 1980—, vice-chmn., 1982-88, chmn. 1988—; bd. dirs. Burke Rehab. Inst., 1979-84, v.p., 1981-84; chmn. Commn. Fed. Procurement of Archtl. and Engring. Services, 1983-84. Recipient Robert Ross McBurney medal McBurney Sch., 1956; recipient Design award Bell System, 1971, 76, Honor award for Archtl. Excellence L.I. Assn., 1971, 76, Del Gaudio award N.Y. State Assn. Architects-AIA, 1982, Gold medal Westchester chpt. AIA, 1983, award Westchester Easter Seals, 1976, Outstanding Citizenship award United Way White Plains, 1980, World Fellowship award, 1988. Fellow AIA (pres. chpt. 1975-76, regional dir. 1978-81, nat. v.p. 1982, trustee Polit. Action Com. 1981-82, bursar Coll. of Fellows 1986-88, vice chancellor 1988—); mem. N.Y. State Assn. Architects (pres. 1977-78, trustee Polit. Action Com. 1981-84, Columbia Archtl. Alumni Assn. v.p. 1969), St. Andrew's Soc. N.Y. Republican. Congregationalist. Clubs: New York Athletic (N.Y.C.); Harvard of Westchester (pres.) (1974-76); Sunningdale Golf (Berkshire, Eng.); Winged Foot Golf (sec. 1980-82), John's Island. Lodge: Rotary. Office: Rose Beaton & Rose 81 Main St White Plains NY 10601

ROSEBERG, CARL ANDERSSON, sculptor, educator; b. Vinton, Iowa, Sept. 26, 1916; s. Swan Bernard and Selma (Olson) R.; m. Virginia M. Gorman, Aug. 23, 1942. B.F.A., U. Iowa, 1939, postgrad., 1939-41, M.F.A., 1947; postgrad., Cranbrook Acad. Art, summers 1947-48, U. Hawaii, 1950-51, U. Va., summer 1964, Mysore (India) U., summer 1965, Tyler Sch. Art, Temple U., summer 1967. Faculty Coll. William and Mary, Williamsburg, Va., 1947—; prof. fine arts Coll. William and Mary, 1966-82, prof. emeritus, 1982—, William and Mary Heritage fellow, 1968-82; founding bd. mem. 20th Century Gallery, Williamsburg.; active judge various art groups. Exhibited one man shows at Radford Coll., 1962, Roanoke Fine Art Gallery, 1962-63, Norfolk Mus., 1963, Asheville (N.C.) Gallery Art, 1963, Longwood Coll., 1966, Phi Beta Kappa Hall, William and Mary Coll., 1970; 35 yr. retrospective William and Mary Coll., 1982; retrospective Twentieth Century Gallery, 1983; exhibited in numerous group shows; represented in permanent collections at U. Iowa, Springfield (Mo.) Mus., Va. Mus. Fine Arts, Colonial Williamsburg, Chrysler Mus. Norfolk, Rockingham County Citizens Com., Longwood Coll., Farmville, Va., Thalhimer Bros., Inc., others; designer, creator bronze meml. plaque honoring Donald W. Davis for, Millington Hall, Coll. William and Mary, 1970, bronze plaque honoring William G. Guy, Rogers Hall, 1975; I.L. Jones, Jr., Bruton Parish Ch., 1985. designer: James City County Bicentennial Medallion, 1976. Served to comdr. USNR, 1941-45, 50-52; ret. Res. Recipient Thomas Jefferson award, 1971, numerous art awards. Fellow Internat. Inst. Arts and Letters; mem. Audubon Artists Am., Tidewater Artists Assn., Asian Soc., Res. Officers Assn. Am., Va. Watercolor Soc., Navy League U.S., Lambda Chi Alpha. Presbyn. Clubs: Mason, Williamsburg German. Home: 4998 Hickory Signpost Rd Williamsburg VA 23185

ROSELLE, WILLIAM CHARLES, librarian; b. Vandergrift, Pa., June 30, 1936; s. William John and Suzanne Esther (Clever) R.; m. Marsha Louise Lucas, Aug. 2, 1959; 1 child, Paul Lucas. BA, Thiel Coll., 1958; MLS, U. Pitts., 1963. Lic. profl. guide State of Mont., 1978. Mem. faculty Milton Hershey (Pa.) Sch., 1960-62; trainee Pa. State Library, 1962-63; asst. catalog librarian Pa. State U., 1963-65; engring., math. librarian U. Iowa, 1965-66, library adminstrv. asst., 1966-69, asst. dir. libraries, 1969-71; prof., dir. library U. Wis.-Milw., 1971—; chmn. Morris Fromkin Meml. Lectr. Com., 1972—; chmn. planning task force on computing U. Wis. System, 1973-74, mem. library planning study com., 1978-79, co-chmn. library automation task force, 1983-85; chmn. computing mgmt. rev. team U. Wis.-Stout, 1976; chmn. Council for U. Wis. Libraries, 1981-82; library cons. Grambling (La.) State U., Viterbo Coll., LaCrosse, Wis., N.C. A&T U., Greensboro, Mt. Mary Coll., Milw., U. Ill. at Chgo., Milw. Sch. Engring., Bklyn. Coll., U. South Ala., Concordia Coll., Milw., Metrics Research Corp., Cardinal Stritch Coll., Milw., N.Y. Inst. Tech., Indiana U. of Pa., Med. Coll. Wis., Wis. Luth. Coll., Milw.; participant Library Adminstrs. Devel. Program, U. Md., 1973, micrographics seminar Nat. Microfilm Assn., 1973, Mgmt. Skills Inst., Assn. Research Libraries, Kansas City, Mo., 1977, Meadowbrook Symposium Midwest Library Network, 1976; mem. sect. geography and map libraries Internat. Fedn. Library Assns. and Instns., 1978-83; mem. bldg. com. Ctr. for Research Libraries, 1980-82. Editorial cons. The Quest for Social Justice, 1983, Current Geographical Publications, 1978—; contbr. articles to profl. jours. Bd. dirs. Charles Allis Art Mus., 1979-84. Served with AUS, 1958-60. Named Disting. Alumnus, Thiel Coll., 1985. Hon. fellow Am. Geog. Soc.; mem. Spl. Libraries Assn. (spl. citation 1979), ALA (life), Iowa Library Assn. (chmn. audit com. 1968-70, chmn. intellectual freedom com. 1969-70), Wis. Library Assn., Midwest Acad. Librarians Conf. (chmn. 1969-71), AAUP (treas. U. Iowa chpt. 1969-70), Council Wis. Libraries (chmn. 1973-74), Soc. Tympanuchus Cupido Pinnatus, Milw. Civil War Round Table, Beta Beta Beta, Beta Phi Mu, Phi Alpha Theta, Phi Kappa Phi, Phi Delta Kappa. Lutheran. Home: 324 Sunny Ln Thiensville WI 53092 Office: U Wis Milw Golda Meir Library PO Box 604 Milwaukee WI 53201

ROSEMOND, KENNETH B., electronics company executive; b. Greenville, S.C., Dec. 24, 1956; s. Oscar Rosemond and Frances R. Gordon. BA in Polit. Sci., Benedict Coll., Columbia, S.C., 1978. With Digital Equipment Corp.; mgr. Rosemond Campaign, Greenville, 1984—. Pres. Youth Conf. Club, 1986-87; vol. Leadership Devel. Program, Greenville. Club: Groove Phi Groove (Columbia) (pres.). Home: 214 Bluff Dr Greenville SC 29605

ROSEN, EMANUEL SAUL, consulting ophthalmic surgeon; b. Hull, Yorkshire, Eng., Sept. 23, 1936; s. Lionel and Leah R.; m. June Avis Lever, Sept. 9, 1962; children—Caroline Alexandra, William David, Edward Leon. B.Sc., Manchester U., 1957, M.B.Ch., 1961, M.D., 1967. Intern, Manchester Royal Infirmary (Eng.), 1962; resident, Manchester Royal Eye Hosp., 1964, now mem. staff; practice medicine specializing in ophthalmic surgery, cons., Manchester; mem. staff dept. ophthalmology U. Manchester. Author: Fluorescence Photography of the Eye, 1969; Basic Ophthalmoscopy, 1972; co-editor: Intraocular Lens Implantation, 1983; Implant, European Jour. Implant and Refractive Surgery; Seminars in Opthalmolgy. Fellow Royal Photog. Soc., Am. Acad. Ophthalmology, Royal Coll. Surgeons, Royal Coll. Surgeons (Edinburgh); mem. U.K. Intraocular Implant Soc. (sec. 1983), European Intraocular Implant Club, Internat. Intraocular Implant Club, European Intraocular Lens Implant Council (pres. 1987—). Home: 10 St John St,, Manchester M3 4DY England

ROSEN, FREDERICK, political science educator; b. N.Y.C., Sept. 13, 1938; s. David and Rae (Reich) R.; m. Maria Rosaline Barron, May 25, 1968; children: Gregory, Alexander. BA, Colgate U., 1960; MA, Syracuse U., 1963; PhD, U. London, 1965. Asst. prof. Franklin and Marshall Coll., 1966-68; lectr. City Univ. London, 1968-70; lectr., then sr. lectr. London Sch. Econs., 1970-86; research asst. Univ. Coll. London, 1965-66; reader in history of polit. thought Univ Coll. London, 1986—; dir. Bentham Project, Univ. Coll., 1986—. Author: Jeremy Bentham and Representative Democracy, 1983, Progress and Democracy: William Goodwin's Contribution to Political Philosophy, 1987; gen. editor: The Collected Works of Jeremy Bentham, 1983—; editor: The Jeremy Bentham Newsletter, 1984—; co-editor: Bentham's Constitutional Code., Vol. 1, 1983, Lives, Liberties, and the Public Good, 1987. Office: Univ Coll London, Gower St, London WC1, England

ROSEN, GERALD HARRIS, physicist, educator; b. Mount Vernon, N.Y., Aug. 10, 1933; s. David A. and Shirley (Schapiro) R.; m. Sarah Louise Sweet, June 8, 1963; children: Lawrence Alexander, Karlyn Penelope. B.S.E. (Guggenheim Jet Propulsion scholar, Whiton Engring.-Physics scholar), Princeton U., 1955, M.A. (NSF predoctoral fellow), 1956, Ph.D., 1958. NSF predoctoral fellow Inst. Theoretical Physics, Utrecht, Netherlands, 1957-58; research asso. dept. aero. engring. Princeton, 1958-59; NSF postdoctoral fellow Inst. Theoretical Physics, Stockholm, 1959-60; tech. cons. weapon systems evaluation div. The Pentagon, 1960; prin. scientist Martin-Marietta Aerospace div., Balt., 1960-63; cons. to a tech. v.p. Southwest Research Inst., 1963-66; prof. physics Drexel U., Phila., 1966-73; M.R. Wehr prof. physics Drexel U., 1973—; Cons. indsl. and govt. agys., 1966—. Reviewer: Math. Revs, 1964—; jours. Am. Phys. Soc, 1960—; assoc. editor: Bull. Math. Biol., 1982—; Author: Formulations of Classical and Quantum Dynamical Theory, 1969; contbr. articles to profl. jours. Sponsor San Antonio Chamber Music Soc., 1963-66; mem. Franklin Inst., 1967—; mem. publ. bd. Soc. Math. Biol., 1983—. Fellow Am. Phys. Soc., AAAS; mem. Am. Math. Soc. Home: 415 Charles Ln Wynnewood PA 19096 Office: Drexel U Dept Physics Philadelphia PA 19104

ROSEN, MARTIN HOWARD, biochemist, educator; b. Bklyn., July 29, 1942; s. Edward M. and Gussie (Klar) R.; BS in Biology, Bklyn. Coll., 1964, MA, 1967; PhD in Biochemistry, NYU, 1974; m. Beth D. Werfel, June 9, 1968. Lectr. dept. biology N.Y.C. Community Coll., 1966-67; teaching fellow Bklyn. Coll., 1966-67; lectr. Queensborough Community Coll., Queens, N.Y., 1968, Kingsborough Community Coll., 1968; instr. dept. biology Manhattan Community Coll., 1969, summer, 1970; assoc. prof. dept. biology Coll. of S.I. (N.Y.), 1968—, evening session supr., 1973-76, 77-86, dep. chmn. dept. biology, 1978-86; assoc. research pathologist dept. pathology S.I. Hosp., 1986—; research assoc. biochem. dept. biology N.Y.U. Grad. Sch., 1974-78, research assoc. dept. dermatology N.Y.U. Med. Center, 1978-82; research asst. Beth Israel Hosp., N.Y.C., 1965-67. Bd. dirs. Found. for Research Against Disease, 1979-84, S.I. Zool. Soc., 1981— (bd. trustees). NSF grantee M.I.T., 1977; IBA fellow, Cambridge, Eng., 1985, World Lit. Acad. life fellow, Cambridge, 1987. ; mem. N.Y. Acad. Scis., AAAS, Royal Dublin Soc., Met. Assn. Coll. and Univ. Biologists (dir. 1977-79), Sigma Xi. Original photomicrographs: Handbook of Microscopic Anatomy for the Health Sciences, 1975; contbr. articles on enzymology to profl. pubs.

ROSEN, MATTHEW STEPHEN, botanist, consultant; b. N.Y.C., Oct. 7, 1943; s. Norman and Lucille (Cass) R.; m. Deborah Louise Mackay, June 16, 1974 (div. Feb. 1983); children—Gabriel Mackay, Rebecca Mackay; m. Kay Eloise Williams, July 11, 1987. M.F.Sc., Yale U., 1972; B.S., Cornell U., 1967. Instr. ornamental horticulture SUNY-Farmingdale, 1968-69; landscape designer Manhattan Gardener, N.Y.C., 1969-70; instr. ornamental horticulture McHenry County Coll., Crystal Lake, Ill., 1972-74; coordinator agrl. studies, asst. prof. biology, chemistry Mercer County Community Coll., West Windsor, N.J., 1974-79; adminstr. Des Moines Botanical Ctr., 1979—; cons. in field. Contbr. articles to profl. jours. Com. chmn. United Way Cen. Iowa, 1982, div. chmn. 1983-86, 88, group chmn. 1987, chmn. arts adv. com. 1985-86, pres. 1986, bd. dirs. Arts and Recreation Council, 1985-86; mem. career vocat. com. Des Moines Indsl. Sch. Dist., 1986, co-chmn., 1987; chmn. Two Rivers Festival, 1987-88. Mem. Am. Assn. Botanical Gardens and Arboreta (edn. com.), Greater Des Moines C. of C. (team leader), Phi Kappa Phi, Pi Alpha Xi. Democrat. Jewish. Avocations: photography, reading, model trains, collecting old books, writing. Home: 1042 22d St W Des Moines IA 50265 Office: Des Moines Botanical Ctr 909 E River Dr Des Moines IA 50316

ROSEN, RICHARD LEWIS, lawyer, real estate developer; b. N.Y.C., Mar. 6, 1943; s. Morris and Lorraine (Levy) R.; m. Doris Ellen Bloom, Aug. 28, 1983. BA, Cornell U., 1965; JD, N.Y. Law Sch., 1968; cert. N.Y.U. Real Estate Inst., 1980; bar: N.Y. 1968, Fed. Cts. 1972. Sole practice, N.Y.C., 1971-73; ptnr. Rosen, Wise, Felzen & Salomon, N.Y.C., 1973-79; ptnr. Rosen & Felzen, N.Y.C., 1979-84, Rosen, Rudd, Kera, Graubard & Hollender, 1985—. Mem. ABA (mem. franchising com. anti-trust div.), Red Key Hon. Soc., Cornell U., Sphinx Head Hon. Soc., Cornell U., Ea. Intercollegiate Athletic Assn. Lightweight Football All Ea. Selection, 1963, 64; Ea. States Lightweight Weightlifting Champion, 1968. Home: 181 E 73d St New York NY 10021

ROSEN, RONALD STANLEY, lawyer; b. Los Angeles, July 22, 1932; s. Daniel and Florence Edyth (Hirsch) R.; A.B. cum laude, Stanford, 1954, LL.B., 1957; postgrad. (scholar) London Sch. Econs., 1953; m. Judith Berenice Friedman, June 26, 1955; children—Philip James, Matthew Howard. Admitted to Calif. bar, 1958; asst. U.S. atty., So. Dist. Calif., Los Angeles, 1958-59; asso. firm Pacht, Ross, Warne & Bernhard, Los Angeles, 1959-62; partner Silverberg, Rosen & Leon (now Silverberg, Rosen, Leon & Behr), 1962—; officer, dir. numerous corps.; guest lectr. U. So. Calif. Law Ctr., 1984, Georgetown Law Ctr., 1984, 85, Stanford Law Sch., 1986. Chmn., Fed. Indigent Def. Com., Los Angeles, 1966-68, Lawyer's Reference Com., Los Angeles, 1969-70. Bd. dirs. Elsie DeWolfe Found.; trustee Young Musicians Found., 1973—; pres., bd. dirs. Los Angeles Chamber Orch., 1982—, pres., 1985-88, chmn., 1988— . Mem. ABA, Los Angeles County, Beverly Hills bar assns., State Bar Calif. (adminstrv. com. 1969—, chmn. 1972—, mem. state bar disciplinary com. 1975—, exec. com. 1975-76, disciplinary referee 1975—), Phi Beta Kappa, Phi Delta Phi. Clubs: Los Angeles, Los Angeles Tennis. Home: 16613 Oldham Pl Encino CA 91436 Office: 2029 Century Park E #1900 Century City Los Angeles CA 90067

ROSEN, SIDNEY MARVIN, lawyer; b. Detroit, June 27, 1939; s. Fred A. and Gertrude (Cole) R.; m. Babette Van Praag, July 3, 1971; children: Jordan, Aviva. BS, U. Ariz., 1961, JD, 1964. Bar: Ariz. 1964, U.S. Dist. Ct. Ariz. 1964, Calif. 1965, U.S. Dist. Ct. Calif. 1965, U.S. Supreme Ct. 1971. Asst. atty. gen. State of Ariz., Phoenix, 1964-66, spl. asst. atty. gen., 1968-69; assoc. Kirkwood, Kaplan, Russin & Vechi, Bangcock, Thailand and Saigon, Vietnam, 1967-68; ptnr. Rosen, Waters & Enriquez and predecessor firm, Phoenix, 1970—; co-founder, law instr. Ariz. Bar Rev. Course, 1965-73; prof. internat. law Grad. Sch. Phoenix, 1975-76; former gen. counsel Nat. Speakers Assn., 1973-85. Candidate Dem. nomination for atty. gen. State of Ariz., 1974, U.S. Congress, 1976; mem. Ariz.-Mex. Gov.'s Commn., 1974—, counsel commerce and industry sect., 1974—; chmn. campaign Bonds for Israel, Ariz., 1980-85. Mem. Ariz. Bar Assn. (latin Am. relations com.), Calif. Bar Assn., Maricopa County Bar Assn., World Assn. Lawyers, Nat. Speakers Assn. (founder, former gen. counsel 1973-85), World Affairs Council, Hospitality Internat. (host), FIABCI (Internat. Real Estate Fedn., gen. counsel Ariz. chpt. 1985—), Ariz. World Trade Assn. (former bd. dirs.), Jaycees (treas. Ariz. chpt. 1969-70, ambassador to Philippine Islands 1969-70), Phi Alpha Delta. Democrat. Jewish. Lodge: Kiwanis. Home: 119 E Alvarado Rd Phoenix AZ 85004 Office: Rosen Waters & Enriquez 4323 N 12th St Suite 104 Phoenix AZ 85014

ROSENBAUM, RALPH ERNEST, accountant; b. Bklyn., June 20, 1952; s. Ben and Gertrude (Podhaicier) R.; m. Beatrice Friedfertig, Nov. 20, 1976. BA, Bklyn. Coll., 1974; MBA, L.I. U., 1979. CPA, N.Y. Staff assoc. Manes Orgn., N.Y.C., 1977-78; semi-sr. acct. Wolf & Wolf CPAs, N.Y.C., 1978-79; sr. acct. Weissbarth, Altman & Miller, CPAs, N.Y.C., 1979-81; dir. fin. ops. Belding Heminway Co. Inc., N.Y.C., 1981-84; asst. dir. fin. acctg. Nat. Cleaning Contractors, N.Y.C., 1984-86; pvt. practice acctg., 1986—; staff mem. N.Y. State Soc. C.P.A.s Com. on Interim Fin. Statements, N.Y.C., 1983-85; instr. Hudson County Community Coll. cons. Physicians Tax Service, East Hanover, N.J., 1981—. Treas. Temple Beth Ahm. Mem. Am. Inst. CPAs, N.Y. State Soc. CPAs, N.J. State Soc. CPAs. Office: 26 Fair Ln Aberdeen NJ 07747

ROSENBERG, ALAN DAVID, accountant; b. Mt. Vernon, N.Y. Apr. 11, 1946; s. Benjamin B. and Miriam (Nierenberg) R.; m. Wendy Patricia Cutler, May 25, 1975; children—Kerri Leigh, Joshua Zade, Brian Scott. B.S., N.Y.U., 1967; M.B.A., Baruch Coll., 1970. C.P.A. N.Y. Sr. acct. Ernst & Ernst, N.Y.C., 1967-70; asst. to pres. Wall St. Resources, N.Y.C., 1970-71; dir. acctg., New Am. Industries, N.Y.C., 1971-73; dir. fin. and adminstrn. Eve of Roma, N.Y.C., 1973-75; adjunct lectr., Baruch Coll., N.Y.C., 1972-75, Hunter Coll., 1975-76; instr. Fairleigh Dickinson U., Tenneck, N.J., 1970-72; pres. Alan D. Rosenberg C.P.A., P.C., N.Y.C., 1975—. Recipient NY U. Founders Day award, 1967; award Accountant Most Likely to Succeed, 1967; mem. Am. Inst. C.P.A.'s, N.Y. State C.P.A.'s, Natl. assn. Accts., Am. Accts. Assn., Beta Alpha Psi (pres. 1966-67), N.Y.U. Alumni Fund (committeeman 1975—). Jewish.

ROSENBERG, ALAN SPENCER, organization development consulting firm executive; b. Staten Island, N.Y., Aug. 24, 1940; s. Milton and Dorothy (Meltzer) R.; B.S. in Bus. Psychology, Pa. State U., 1962; M.Ed. in Adult Edn., Temple U., 1973; M.A. in Indsl. Relations, St. Francis Coll., 1975; m. Marsha Leinhardt, Dec. 3, 1960; children—Louis Robert, Milton David. Nat. employment and recruiting mgr. McCrory Stores div. McCrory Corp., York, Pa., 1969-71; employment and tng. mgr. E.I. DuPont de Nemours & Co., New Cumberland, Pa., 1971-73; dir. human resources Giant Food Stores, Inc., Carlisle, Pa., 1973-76; pres. Alan S. Rosenberg Assos., Inc., York, 1976—; mng. partner Mid Hill Profl. Center, York, 1977—; pres. Spencer Cons., York, 1969-76; mem. adj. faculty York Coll. Pa., 1974—, Pa. State U., 1975—; jobs dir. NAB, 1968. Adult leader Boy Scouts Am., 1973—; bd. dirs. Ohev Sholom Synagogue, York, 1971-72, Community Progress Council, 1974, Susquehanna Manpower Devel. Corp., 1974-76. Contbr. articles on human resource utilization to profl. jours. Mem. Am. Soc. Tng. and Devel., Am. Soc. Personnel Adminstrn. (accredited personnel diplomate), Asso. Builders and Contractors, Soc. Advancement of Mgmt., Indsl. Relations Research Assn., York Soc. Personnel Adminstrn. (pres. 1986—), Pa. Retailers Assn., Pa. Petroleum Assn., Republican. Jewish. Contbr. numerous articles to nat. profl. jours.; developer tax recovery system and govt. subsidized tng. programs for employers. Home and Office: 441 Hunting Park Ln York PA 17402

ROSENBERG, DENNIS MELVILLE LEO, surgeon; b. Johannesburg, South Africa, Jan. 27, 1921; came to U.S., 1946, naturalized, 1953; s. Nathan and Dorothy (Lee) R.; m. Jeanna Van der Kar, Jan., 1947. B.Sc. with honors, U. Witwatersrand, South Africa, 1941, M.B., B.Ch., 1945. Intern Johannesburg Gen. Hosp., 1946; resident in surgery Tulane U. Ochsner Found. Hosp., 1947-51, Children's Hosp., Johannesburg, 1952; asst. thoracic surgeon Biggs Hosp., Ithaca, N.Y., 1953-54; practice medicine specializing in cardiovascular and thoracic surgery New Orleans, 1955—; sr. surgeon Touro Infirmary, New Orleans, 1955—; chief dept. cardiovascular and thoracic surgery Touro Infirmary, 1972-85; mem. staffs St. Charles Gen. Hosp., New Orleans, Mercy Hosp., New Orleans; cons. surgeon Charity Hosp., New Orleans, 1962—; sr. investigator Touro Research Inst., 1964—; prof. surgery Tulane U. Served with M.C. South African Army, 1940-45. Fellow A.C.S.; mem. Am. Coll. Chest Physicians, Am. Coll. Cardiology, AMA, Am. Heart Assn., Am. Assn. Thoracic Surgery, So. Thoracic Surg. Assn., Internat. Cardiovascular Soc., Am. Thoracic Soc., Soc. Thoracic Surgeons, Soc. Vascular Surgery, Soc. Internationale de Cirugie, Royal Soc. Medicine, So. Assn. Vascular Surgery, Soc. Clin. Vascular Surgery. Home: 3115 Prytania St New Orleans LA 70115 Office: 3525 Prytania St New Orleans LA 70115

ROSENBERG, HENRI, advocate, Rabbinic barrister; b. Antwerp, Belgium, May 1, 1950; s. Salomon and Gerda (Tobias) R.; m. Anita Kaszirer, May 23, 1974; children: Natasha Bella, Amanda Ethel, David, Salomon, Gershon. Licenciate in polit. ans social scis., Cath. U., Louvain, 1974; grad. Jewish legal studies, Cen. Talmudic Acad., Jerusalem and Boston, 1977; LLD, U. Antwerp, 1985; M of Rabbinic Law, United Israel Insts., Jerusalem, 1985; postgrad. in Am. law, Columbia U., 1986, Leyden U., 1986; postgrad. in port and maritime law, U. Ghent, 1986; grad. parapsychology, Acad. Paranormal Scis., 1986; postgrad. internat. banking and fin., City U., London, 1987; student, U. Ghent, 1987—. Asst. mgr. Scientific Translation Internat., Jerusalem, 1974-76; mgr. chem. dept. McGison PVBA, Antwerp, 1976-78; mng. dir. Intra Diamond Co. NV, Antwerp, 1978-85; advocate, Rabbinic barrister, researcher Inter-Univ. Ctr. for State Law, Brussels, 1987—. Author: Israel and the USSR: 20 Years of Diplomatic Negotiations, 1947-67, 1974, Aspects of Jewish Law: A Compilation, 1984. Founder, adminstrv. pres. Belgian Jewish Students' Front, 1970; co-founder, mem. com., spokesman coordinating com. Belgian Jewish Youth Orgns., 1971; mem. Israelite Community of Antwerp; pres. Keren Tobias Found. Home: Belgielei 195, 2018 Antwerp Belgium Office: Belgielei 195B, 2018 Antwerp Belgium

ROSENBERG, JOEL BARRY, government economist; b. Bronx, N.Y., Aug. 14, 1942; s. Benjamin and Miriam Dorothy (Yellin) R.; B.A., Queens Coll., 1964, M.A., 1966; Ph.D., Brown U., 1972; m. Judith Lynne Jackler, Aug. 26, 1965; children—Jeffrey Alan, Marc David. Cons., Commonwealth Services, Washington, 1970-71; asst. prof. econs. SUNY, Geneseo, 1971-75, Case Western Res. U., Cleve., 1975-76; industry economist IRS, Washington, 1976—. NDEA fellow, Brown U., 1966-69. Mem. Am. Econ. Assn., Nat. Assn. Bus. Economists, Am. Statis. Assn. Contbr. articles to profl. jours. Home: 13 Glazebrook Ct Gaithersburg MD 20878 Office: 1201 E St NW Washington DC 20226

ROSENBERG, PETER DAVID, lawyer, patent examiner, educator; b. N.Y.C., Aug. 2, 1942; s. Frederick and Martha (Grossman) R. BA, NYU, 1962, B in Chem. Engring., 1963; JD, N.Y. Law Sch., 1968; LL.M., George Washington U., 1971. Bar: N.Y. 1970, U.S. Ct. Appeals (2d cir.) 1970, U.S. Dist. Ct. (so. and ea. dists.) N.Y. 1971, U.S. Supreme Ct. 1973, U.S. Dist Ct. (no. and we. dists.) N.Y. 1979, U.S. Ct. Appeals D.C. 1982, U.S. Ct. Internat. Trade 1982, U.S. Ct. Mil. Appeals 1982. Examiner U.S. Patent and Trademark Office, Washington, 1968—; assoc. professorial lectr. George Washington U.; Recipient Silver Medal award U.S. Dept. Commerce, 1981. Mem. ABA (antitrust sect.). Author: Patent Law Fundamentals, 1975, 2d edit. 1980, revised 1988; assoc. editor Jour. Patent and Trademark Office Soc.; contbr. articles to profl. jours. Home: 1400 S Joyce St Arlington VA 22202

ROSENBERG, PIERRE MAX, museum curator; b. Paris, Apr. 13, 1936; s. Charles and Gertrude (Nassauer) R.; m. Béatrice de Rothschild, July 29, 1981. Baccalauréat, Lycée Charlemagne, Paris; Licence, Law Faculty, Paris; Diplome, Louvre Sch., Paris. Chief curator dept. paintings Musée du Louvre, Paris; curator in charge Musée Nat. de l'Amitié et des Relations franco-américaines de Blérancourt Author: Chardin, 1963; Peyron, 1983; (catalogue) La peinture française du XVIIe siècle dans les coll. américaines, 1981; (catalogue) Watteau, 1984, Fragonard, 1987. Decorated chevalier des Arts et des Lettres, 1971, Chevalier de l'Ordre National du Mérite, 1984. Mem. Société de l'Histoire de l'Art Français (pres. 1982-84), Comité Français d'Histoire de l'Art (pres. 1984). Home: 35 rue de Vaugirard, 75006 Paris France Office: Musée du Louvre, 34 quai du Louvre, 75041 Paris France Other: Musée Nat de la, Coop Franco-Am, Château de Blérancourt, 02300 Chauny France

ROSENBERG, RUDY, chemical company executive; b. Charleroi, Belgium, Feb. 26, 1930; came to U.S., 1949, naturalized, 1954; s. Hilaire and Frieda (Friedemann) R.; student in classical studies Atheneum Leon Lepage, Brussels, 1946; m. Rose H. Wauters, Nov. 7, 1953; 1 child, Rudy. Buyer, Lever Bros., Brussels, 1946-49; head Biochem. div. Mann Research Labs., N.Y.C., 1954-61, Gallard-Schlesinger, Carle Place, N.Y., 1961-75; pres. Accurate Chem. & Sci. Corp., Westbury, N.Y., 1975—; prin., v.p., Leeches U.S.A. Ltd. Served with U.S. Army, 1951-53. Mem. Reticuloendothelial Soc. Internat. Democrat. Clubs: Antique Automobile, Rolls Royce, Puppetry Guild Greater N.Y. Home: 68 Custer Ave Williston Park NY 11596 Office: 300 Shames Dr Westbury NY 11590

ROSENBERG, VICTOR I., plastic surgeon; b. N.Y.C., Nov. 15, 1936; s. Leonard C. and Sarah G. (Berger) R.; A.B., N.Y.U., 1957; M.D., Chgo. Med. Sch., 1961; m. Deborah Iskoe, Jan. 2, 1966; children—Spencer, Ria. Intern, Beth Israel Hosp., N.Y.C., 1961-62, resident, 1962-63, 64-66; resident Beckman Downtown Hosp., 1963-64, Bronx Mcpl. Hosp., 1966-67, Mt. Sinai Hosp., N.Y.C., 1967-68; practice medicine specializing in plastic surgery, N.Y.C., 1968—; assoc. attending surgeon Beth Isreal Hosp., 1968—; asso. attending surgeon Beekman Downtown Hosp., 1968—, chief plastic surgery, 1976-80; attending surgeon N.Y. Infirmary-Beekman Downtown Hosp., 1980—, dir. cosmetic surgery, 1984—; sr. clin. asst. Mt. Sinai Hosp., N.Y.C., 1968—; asso. dept. plastic surgery City U. N.Y., N.Y.C. Served to comdr. USN, 1968-70. Diplomate Am. Bd. Plastic Surgery. Fellow ACS, Internat. Coll. Surgeons; mem. Am., N.Y. Regional socs. plastic and reconstructive surgeons, Am. Soc. Aesthetic Plastic Surgery, AMA, Am. Cleft Palate Assn., N.Y. Acad. Medicine, N.Y. State, N.Y. County Med. Socs., Pan Am. Med. Assn. (diplomate sect. plastic surgery). Club: Friars, Atrium. Office: 4 Sutton Pl New York NY 10022

ROSENBERGER, GERHARD, mathematics educator; b. Wentorf, Germany, Dec. 8, 1944; s. Horst and Jutta (Bless) R.; m. Katariina Kangas, July 24, 1976. Grad. U. Hamburg, Fed. Republic Germany, 1973, Inauguration, 1974. Asst., U. Hamburg, 1972-76; professorial chair rep. U. Bielefeld, Fed. Republic Germany, 1976-77; prof. math. U. Dortmund, Fed. Republic Germany, 1977—. Contbr. research articles to math. jours. Mem. Hamburger Math. Gesellschaft, Deutsche Mathematikervereinigung, Am. Math. Soc., Suomen Matemaattinen Yhdistys, Hochschulverband, Deutsch-Finnische Gesellschaft, London Math. Soc. Lutheran. Office: U Dortmund, Abt Mathematik, Postfach 50 05 00, 4600 Dortmund 50 Federal Republic of Germany

ROSENBERGER, JUDITH BRAILEY, psychotherapist, psychoanalyst; b. Columbus, Ohio, Mar. 24, 1943; d. Lester George and Helen Cornelia (Castle) Brailey; B.S., Purdue U., 1965; M.A., U. Mich., 1967, Ph.D., 1973; M.S.W., Hunter Coll., 1976; cert. psychoanalysis, Postgrad. Ctr. for Mental

Health, 1982; m. Ernst H. Rosenberger, June 10, 1978; children: John Brailey, Anne Elizabeth. Intern in counseling, student services counseling center, U. Mich., Ann Arbor, 1967-70; counselor Wayne State U., Detroit, 1970-71; lectr. Herbert N. Lehman Coll., City U. N.Y., 1971-82; pvt. practice psychotherapy and psychoanalysis, N.Y.C., 1978—; faculty Postgrad. Center for Mental Health, N.Y.C., 1985—; summer faculty Smith Coll. Sch. Social Work, 1984, 85; asst. prof. Hunter Coll. Sch. Social Work, 1985—; invited presenter, Mary Gottesfeld lectr. Hunter Coll., 1987; presenter at confs. Assn. Children and Adults with Hearing Disabilities, 1988, Am. Orthopsychiat. Conf., 1988. Profl. project dir. Profl. Staff Congress, Bd. Higher Edn. research project, 1977-79; invited presenter, trustee, bd. dirs. Gateway Sch. of N.Y., 1987—; bd. dirs. Postmasters Program in Clin. Social Work, 1986—. Cert. psychologist, Mass.; cert. social worker, N.Y. Mem. Am. Psychol. Assn. (div. psychoanalysis), AAUP, Acad. Cert. Social Workers, N.Y. Soc. Clin. Social Work Psychotherapists, Nat. Assn. Social Workers, Postgrad. Psychoanalytic Soc., Nat. Assn. Advancement Psychoanalysis, Am. Orthopsychiat. Assn. (bd. dirs. 1988—), Assn. Children and Adults with Learning Disabilities (bd. dirs. 1988—). Author: The Identity Experience of College Women: Some Contributing Factors, 1973; Women Who Aspire to be Police Officers, 1979. Office: 315 E 68th New York NY 10021

ROSENBLATT, JULIA CARLSON, journalist, psychology educator; b. Orange, N.J., Dec. 26, 1940; d. Harold S. and Anabel (Alberts) Carlson; m. Albert M. Rosenblatt, Aug. 23, 1970; 1 child, Betsy L. BA, Upsala Coll., East Orange, N.J., 1962; MA, U. Iowa, 1964, PhD, 1965. Postdoctoral fellow Ednl. Testing Service, Princeton, N.J., 1965-67; asst. prof. psychology Vassar Coll., Poughkeepsie, N.Y., 1967-73; freelance journalist Pleasant Valley, N.Y., 1973—; instr. Mohawk Mountain Ski Sch., Cornwall, Conn., 1983—; bd. dirs. Poughkeepsie Savs. Bank, 1979-88. Co-author: Dining with Sherlock Holmes, 1976; also articles. Bd. dirs. Dutchess County Assn. Sr. Citizens, Poughkeepsie, 1980-86, Mid-Hudson Civic Ctr., Poughkeepsie, 1982—, Dorothy Albertson Fund for Little People, Pleasant Valley, 1984—; treas. Ret. Sr. Vol. Program, Poughkeepsie, 1980-81. USPHS fellow, 1962-65. Mem. Am. Psychol. Assn., Eastern Ski Writers Assn., U.S. Ski Writers Assn. Profl. Ski Instrs. Am. Avocations: photography, skiing. Home and Office: Freedom Rd Pleasant Valley NY 12569

ROSENBLATT, LESTER, naval architect; b. N.Y.C., Apr. 13, 1920; s. Mandell and Rosa (Wolff) R. BS, CCNY; BS in Naval Architecture and Marine Engring., U. Mich., 1942. Registered profl. engr., N.Y., Mass. Naval architect John H. Wells, Inc., 1942-47; co-founder, chmn., chief exec. officer, naval architect M. Rosenblatt & Son Inc., Naval Architects and Marine Engrs., N.Y.C. and throughout U.S., 1947—; designer maj. ships, U.S. and fgn.; trustee Webb Inst. Naval Architecture. Contbr. numerous tech. papers. Mem. United Jewish Appeal of N.Y., Maritime Friends of Seamen's Church Inst. Recipient U. Mich. Sesquicentennial award in ship design, 1967, Harold Saunders award ASNE, 1987. Mem. Soc. Naval Architects and Marine Engrs. (pres. 1978-80, nat. chmn. membership com. 1964-78, mem. council and exec. com.; Land medalist, fellow, hon. mem., chmn. N.Y. met. sect. 1961-62), Am. Bur. Shipping, Bur. Veritas, Am. Soc. Naval Engrs. (Harold Saunders award 1987); hon. mem. Marine Soc. N.Y. Club: N.Y. Yacht. Home: 8 E 83d St Apt 12B New York NY 10028-0418 Office: M Rosenblatt & Son Inc 350 Broadway New York NY 10013

ROSENBLITH, WALTER ALTER, scientist, educator; b. Vienna, Austria, Sept. 21, 1913; came to U.S., 1939, naturalized, 1946; s. David A. and Gabriele (Roth) R.; m. Judy Olcott Francis, Sept. 27, 1941; children: Sandra Yvonne, Ronald Francis. Ingenieur Radiotelegraphiste, U. Bordeaux, 1936; Ing. Radioelectricien, Ecole Supérieure d'Electricité, Paris, 1937. Research engr. France, 1937-39; research asst. N.Y. U., 1939-40; grad. fellow, teaching fellow physics U. Calif. at Los Angeles, 1940-43; asst. prof., asso. prof., acting head dept. physics S.D. Sch. Mines and Tech., 1943-47; research fellow Psycho-Acoustic Lab., Harvard U., 1947-51; lectr. otolaryngology Mass. Eye and Ear Imfirmary, 1957-76, Harvard Med. Sch., 1969—; asso. prof. communications biophysics Mass. Inst. Tech., 1951-57, prof., 1957-84, Inst. prof., 1975—; staff Research Lab. Electronics, 1951-69, chmn. faculty, 1967-69, asso. provost, 1969-71, provost, 1971-80; dir. Kaiser Industries, 1968-76; chmn. com. electronic computers in life scis. Nat. Acad. Scis.-NRC, 1960-64, mem. brain scis. com., 1965-68, chmn., 1966-67; mem. central council Internat. Brain Research Orgn., 1960-68, mem. exec. com., 1960-68, hon. treas., 1962-67; cons. life scis. panel Pres.'s Sci. Adv. Com., 1961-66; mem. council Internat. Union Pure and Applied Biophysics, 1961-69; inaugural lectr. Tata Inst. Fundamental Research, Bombay, 1962; Weizmann lectr. Weizmann Inst. Sci., Rehovoth, Israel, 1962; U.S. Nat. Pure and Applied Biophysics of Communication and Control Processes, 1964-69; mem. Pres.'s Com. Urban Housing, 1967-68; cons. communications scis. WHO, 1964-65; mem. bd. medicine Nat. Acad. Sci., 1967-70; charter mem. Inst. Medicine, 1970—, mem. council, 1970-76; mem. adv. com. to dir. NIH, 1970-74; mem. governing bd. NRC, 1974-76; mem. adv. com. med. sci. AMA, 1972-74; mem. exec. com. Tyler Prize for Environ. Achievement, 1973—; chmn. sci. adv. council Callier Center for Communication Disorders, 1968—; chmn. research com of the Health Effects Inst., 1981—; chmn. internat. adv. panel of Chinese U. Devel. Project, 1986— ; mem. Com. on Scholarly Communication with People's Republic of China, 1977-86; counsel Fgn. Relations, 1983—. Bd. Fgn. Scholarships, 1978-81, chmn., 1980-81; co-chmn. NRC-IOM com. for study of saccharin and food safety policy, 1978-79; cons. Carnegie Corp. N.Y., 1986—. Contbr. articles and chpts. to profl. publs. Bd. govs. Weizmann Inst. Sci., 1973-86; chmn. nat. com. on rehab. of physically handicapped NRC, 1975-77; trustee Brandeis U., 1979—. Fellow Acoustical Soc. Am., World Acad. Art and Sci., Am. Acad. Arts and Scis. (exec. bd. 1970-77), AAAS, IEEE; mem. Internat. Council Sci. Unions (v.p. 1984—), Biophys. Soc. (council 1957-61, 69-72, exec. bd. 1957-61), Nat. Acad. Engring., Nat. Acad. Scis. (fgn. sec. 1982-86), Soc. Exptl. Psychologists. Office: MIT Cambridge MA 02139

ROSENBLOOM, MORRIS VICTOR, publisher, public relations executive, government official; b. Pitts., Oct. 25, 1915; s. Alfred A. and Corinne (Lorch) R.; m. Ronda Rose Robins, May 16, 1953 (div. 1975). B.A., U. Pitts., 1936. Dir. research stats. for Edward L. Bernays, N.Y.C., 1937; asst. to pres. Ruffsdale Distilling Co., Braddock, Pa., 1937-39; founder, dir. Am. Industries Surveys, N.Y.C., 1939-41; reactivated as Am. Surveys, 1947, dir., 1947-54, pres., 1955—; pres. Am. Surveys Internat., 1965—; sabbatical yr. as bus. liaison officer U.S. Customs Service, Washington, 1983-84; sr. economist OPM, 1941-42; prin. indsl. specialist, chief consumers durable goods and service equipment W.P.B., later asst. to vice chmn. civilian requirements, 1942-43; v.p. charge sales Diamond Prodns. Inc., 1946-47; mktg. and sales cons. to pres. Publicker Industries, Inc., Phila.; sales mgr. subs. Publicker Industries, Inc., 1947-50; program coordinator, asst. to chmn. NSRB, 1950; spl. asst. dept. adminstr. DPA, 1951-52; founder, exec. dir. Inst. on Econs. Def. Moblzn., sponsored by Am. U., ODM, 1951-52; exec. dir. def. materials operating and policy coms. ODM, 1953; asso. Coates & McCormick, Inc., Washington and N.Y.C., 1954. Author: The Liquor Industry, 1935, rev. edit., 1937; Bottling for Profit (with A.B. Greenleaf), 1940; Peace Through Strength: Bernard Baruch and a Blueprint for Security, 1953; contbr. articles to profl. jours.; lectr. Dir. ops. Nat. Citizens Com. for Hoover Report; sponsor Atlantic Council; mem. pub. relations adv. com. Fair Campaign Practices Com.; mem. Nat Council, nat. communications com. Boy Scouts Am.; also mem. adv. bd. and chmn. pub. relations com. Nat. Capital Area Council; chmn. alumni regional council U. Pitts., 1960-61. Served with USNR, 1943-46; comdg. officer submarine chaser. Recipient Silver Beaver award Boy Scouts Am., 1963. Mem. Nat. Eagle Scout Assn., Def. Orientation Conf. Assn. (charter, v.p. 1955-56), Pub. Relations Soc. Am. (accredited, dir. Washington chpt., chmn. govt. affairs adv. com., mem. exec. com. counselors sect.), Internat. Pub. Relations Assn., Res. Officers Assn. U.S., Ret. Officers Assn., U.S. Naval Inst., Friends of Kennedy Ctr. (founder), Internat. Platform Assn., Am. Arbitration Assn., Pi Lambda Phi (Big PII award 1973). Clubs: Army and Navy (Washington), Pitt. (Washington). Home: Embassy Sq Washington DC 20036-2311 Office: Am Surveys Internat 2000 N St NW Washington DC 20036-2311

ROSENBLUM, MARTIN JEROME, ophthalmologist; b. N.Y.C., Apr. 7, 1948; s. Philip and Rita (Steppel) R.; m. Zina Zarin, May 31, 1975; children—Steven David, Richard James. B.S., Bklyn. Coll., 1968; M.D., U. Ariz., 1973. Diplomate Am. Bd. Ophthalmology, Nat. Bd. Med. Examiners. Intern Cornell U., N.Y.C., 1974-75; resident N.Y. Med. Coll., 1975-78, instr., 1978-79; resident Columbia U., 1977; practice medicine specializing in eye surgery, St. Petersburg, Fla., 1979—; asst. clin. prof. ophthalmology, U. So. Fla. Fellow Am. Acad. Ophthalmology, ACS, Am. Intraocular Implant Soc.; mem. AMA, Fla. Med. Assn., Fla. Soc. Ophthalmology. Republican. Jewish. Club: Seminole Lake Country. Avocation: tennis. Home: 9035 Baywood Park Dr Seminole FL 33543 Office: 2200 16th St N Saint Petersburg FL 33704

ROSENBLUTH, MORTON, periodontist, educator; b. N.Y.C., Sept. 28, 1924; s. Jacob and Eva (Bigeleissen) R.; B.A., N.Y.U., 1943, grad. program in periodontia, oral medicine, D.D.S., 1946; m. Sylvia Fradin, July 2, 1946; children—Cheryl Bonnie, Hal Glen. Intern, Bellevue Hosp. N.Y.C., 1946-47, resident, 1947; individual practice dentistry, N.Y.C., 1947-59; individual practice periodontia, North Miami Beach, Fla., 1960—; periodontist Mt. Sinai Hosp., N.Y., Polyclinic Hosp. and Med. Sch. N.Y., Mt. Sinai Hosp., Miami Beach, Fla., Parkway Gen. Hosp.; chief dental dept. North Miami Gen. Hosp.; chmn. periodontia sect. Dade County Research Ctr.; clin. assoc. prof. div. oral and maxillofacial surgery U. Miami Sch. Medicine; assoc. clin. prof. Southeastern Osteo. Coll. Medicine; lectr. throughout U.S.A., Israel, Mexico, Rome, Teheran, Bangkok, Hong Kong, Tokyo, Honolulu, Jamaica, Paris, London, Sicily, Budapest, Berlin, Luxembourg, South Africa, and others; vis. lectr. U. Tenn. Dental Coll., N.Y.U. Dental Coll.; cons. VA Hosp., Miami. Mem. adv. bd. U. Fla. Coll. Dentistry; mem. profl. adv. bd. North Dade Children's Center, Hope Sch. Mentally Retarded Children; mem. sci. adv. com. United Health Found. Chmn. Dental div. United Fund of Dade County, Combined Jewish Appeal; nat. chmn. Hebrew U. Sch. Dental Medicine; bd. dirs. Health Planning Council S. Fla.; pres. Condominium Assn. Jockey Club III. Served with AUS, 1943-44, as capt. USAF, 1951-52. Recipient Maimonides award State of Israel, 1979; diplomate Am. Bd. Periodontology. Fellow Am. Coll. Dentists, Internat. Coll. Dentists; mem. Am. Acad. Periodontology, Am., Fla. socs. periodontists, Am. Assn. Hosp. Dental Chiefs, Am. Acad. Dental Medicine, Am. Soc. Advancement Gen. Anesthesia in Dentistry, ADA, Northeastern Soc. Periodontists, Fla. (chmn. council on legislation), Miami, Miami Beach, East Coast (sec.-treas. 1968, pres. 1971-72), North Dade (pres. 1963-64) dental socs., Fedn. Dentaire Internationale, Fla. Acad. Dental Practice Adminstrn., Alpha Omega (pres. 1967-68, internat. regent 1973-75, internat. editor 1975-77, internat. pres.-elect 1977-78, internat. pres. 1979, chmn. bd. Alpha Omega Found.) Am. Dental Interfrat. Council (pres. 1981-82). Jewish (trustee congregation 1961-64). Clubs: Nocoma (pres. 1958-60), N.Y.U. Century (local chmn.), Jockey Club (bd. of govs.). Lodges: KP, Masons, Kiwanis (dir. 1965). Contbr. articles to profl. jours. Home: 11111 Biscayne Blvd Apt 857 North Miami FL 33161 Office: Profl Center 1100 NE 163d St North Miami Beach FL 33162

ROSENDAHL, PATRICIA MCGARVEY, lawyer; b. Galveston, Tex., Sept. 1, 1952; d. James Ligon and Elvera (McCoy) McGarvey; m. Torben Erik Rosendahl, July 3, 1976; children—James, Erik, Alicia, Jennifer. AA, Palomar Coll., 1974; BA, U. Tex., 1975; postgrad. U. Houston Law Sch., 1984-87 ; assoc. McLeod, Alexander, Powel and Apffel. Cert. social worker. Med. social worker Tex. Dept. Health, Galveston, 1977-84; head articles editor Houston Jour. Internat. Law, 1986-87 . Mem. ABA, Fed. Bar Assn., State Bar Tex., Order of Barons, Admiralty Law Soc. (sec. 1985-86), Health Law Orgn., Phi Delta Phi, Phi Kappa Phi. Episcopalian. Avocations: travel, writing, reading. Home: 1807 Austin Dr LaMarque TX 77568

ROSENDIN, RAYMOND JOSEPH, electrical contracting company executive; b. San Jose, Calif., Feb. 14, 1929; s. Moses Louis and Bertha C. (Pinedo) R.; m. Jeanette Marie Bucher, June 30, 1951 (dec. Feb. 1967); children: Mark R., Patricia A., Debra M., Cynthia C., David R.; m. Nancy Ann Burke, July 6, 1984; children: Raymond M., Callie R., Blake W. Student engring., San Jose State U., 1947-48; B.S.E.E., Heald's Engring. Coll., San Francisco, 1950. Vice pres. Rosendin Electric, Inc., San Jose, Calif., 1953-59, exec. v.p., 1959-75, pres., 1975—; former dir. Community Bank, San Jose. Bd. fellows U. Santa Clara, Calif., 1966—, pres. bd., 1969-72, bd. regents, 1972-82; bd. dirs. United Way, Santa Clara, 1970-74, O'Connor's Hosp., San Jose, 1979—, Community Hosp., Los Gatos, Calif., 1968-74. Recipient Man of Yr. award Santa Clara Valley Youth Village, 1963, Optimist of Yr. award Optimist Club, San Jose, 1970. Mem. C. of C. Greater San Jose (past dir.), Nat. Elec. Contractors Assn. (past pres., gov., dir.). Republican. Roman Catholic. Club: St. Claire (San Jose). Office: Rosendin Electric Inc 880 N Mabury Rd San Jose CA 95133

ROSENFELD, ISADORE, medical educator, cardiologist, lecturer; b. Montreal, Que., Can., Sept. 7, 1926; came to U.S., 1958; s. Morris and Vera (Friedman) R.; m. Camilla Master, Aug. 19, 1956; children—Arthur, Stephen, Hildi, Herbert. B.S., McGill U., 1947, M.D.C.M., 1951, diploma internal medicine, 1956. Intern Royal Victoria Hosp., Montreal; also resident Balt. City Hosp.; clin. asst. prof. medicine Cornell Med. Coll., N.Y.C., 1964-71, clin. assoc. prof., 1971-79, clin. prof., 1979—, now hon. fellow; attending N.Y. Hosp., N.Y.C., 1964—; pres. Rosenfeld Heart Found., N.Y.C., 1974—; juror Lasker Sci. Awards, 1972—; chmn. Found. Bio-Med. Research, N.Y.C., 1982—; lectr., TV commentator.; vis. prof. Baylor U. Coll. Medicine, 1982. Author: ECG and X-Ray in Diseases of the Heart, 1963, The Complete Medical Exam, 1978, Second Opinion, 1981; Modern Prevention, 1986, Symptoms, 1988. Bd. dirs. N.Y. Heart Assn., 1979-82; mem. nat. adv. com. Harriman Inst. Advanced Study of Soviet Union, 1982—; bd. overseers Cornell U. Med. Coll., 1980—; bd. visitors U. Calif. Sch. Medicine, Davis, 1983—. Recipient Vera award The Voice Found., 1981. Fellow ACP, Am. Coll. Chest Physicians, Am. Coll. Cardiology, Royal Coll. Physicians Can., N.Y. County Med. Soc. (bd. censors 1979-83, v.p. 1983-84, pres. 1984-85, trustee 1985—), Am. Physician's Fellowship for Israel (hon. nat. pres. 1975—), Cornell Alumni Assn. (hon.). Jewish. Research on hypertension, angina pectoris, sudden cardiac death, arteriosclerosis. Office: 125 E 72d St New York NY 10021

ROSENFELD, JOSEPH, development corporation executive; b. Medway, Mass., Dec. 3, 1907; s. Abraham and Annie (Candleman) R.; student pub. schs., Milford, Mass. Mgr., Abraham Rosenfeld Sand & Gravel Co., Milford, 1925-32; owner, operator Rosenfeld Washed Sand & Stone Co., Hopedale, Mass., 1932-85, also concrete plants, Dedham, Plainville, Ashland, Walpole, and Weymouth, Mass., pres. Rosenfeld Devel. Corp., Milford, 1986—; vice chmn., clk., dir. Home Nat. Bank and Home Nat. Corp., Milford; dir. Milford Water Co., Milford Indsl. Com., 1966; chmn. Milford Indsl. Devel. Commn., 1966-76. Pres., Milford Combined Charities, 1958-59; mem. gifts com. Milford Hosp., 1961, mem. bd. mgrs., trustee; v.p., bd. dirs. Milford Whitinsville Hosp.; hon. chmn. Milford Heart Fund; mem. Milford Town Meeting, 1935-73; mem. men's assocs. Jewish Meml. Hosp., 1969; chmn. Milford area Mass. Assn. for Mental Health, 1967—; sponsor Nat. Jewish Hosp., 1969, Greater Boston Assn. Retarded Children, Milford and Hopedale Little League, Hopedale Women's Softball League, Babe Ruth League; mem. adv. bd. Algonquin council Boy Scouts Am., recipient Disting. Citizen award, 1974; mem. com. Speakers Ann. Charity Ball, 1965-67; mem. Milford Sch. Bldg. Com.; donor bldg. for Rosenfeld Hebrew Sch., Milford; hon. chmn. Milford Area March of Dimes campaign, 1970; Bd. dirs. Worcester chpt. Prevention Cruelty to Children, 1971, Central chpt. Mass. Heart Assn., 1967, Mass. 4-H Found. Recipient citation United Jewish Appeal, 1953, Milford Hebrew Assn., 1958, Milford Kiwanis Club, 1960, Community Service award V.F.W. Post 9373, 1961, citation Trustees Kiwanis-Rotary Pub. Service Trust, Greater Boston Assn. Retarded Children, Inc., Worcester chpt. Milford Heart Fund, 1966; Certificate of appreciation Nat. Found.-March of Dimes, 1968; Community leader of Am. award, 1969; State of Israel award, 1973; other awards. Mem. Asso. Gen. Contractors Am., Mass. Bldg. Congress, Utility Contractors New Eng., Home Builders Assn. Greater Boston, Nat. Assn. Home Builders U.S., Mass. Motor Truck Assn. Inc., Mass. Concrete Inst. (dir.), Milford (dir., mem. exec. bd., Distinguished Service award 1976), Greater Boston chambers commerce, A.I.M. (pres.'s council 1966), Milford Hebrew Assn. (trustee), Art Inst. Boston. Republican. Jewish religion. Lion (charter Milford, pres. 1956-57), Elk; mem. B'nai B'rith (25 year silver honor certificate for humanitarian programs 1961). Clubs: Century; Hopedale Country; Portuguese de Instrucao E Recreio Inc. (Milford) (hon. life mem.; citation 1965); Milford Sons of Italy Dramatic and Sportsman's (hon.); Bungay Brook Sporting (hon.) (Bellingham). Home and Office: 34 Cedar St Milford MA 01757

ROSENFIELD, JOHN MAX, art educator; b. Dallas, Oct. 9, 1924; s. John M. and Claire (Burger) R.; student U. Tex., 1941-43; B.A., U. Calif. at Berkeley, 1945; B.F.A., So. Meth. U., 1947; M.F.A., U. Iowa, 1949; Ph.D., Harvard U. 1959; m. Ella Hopper, Jan. 2, 1948; children—Sarah, Paul Thomas. Instr. art U. Iowa, 1949, 52-54, asst. prof. UCLA, 1957-60; research fellow Harvard U., 1960-65, faculty, 1965—, prof. art, 1968—, Abby Aldrich Rockefeller prof. Oriental art, 1974—, chmn. dept. fine arts, 1971-76, acting dir. Art Mus., 1982-85. Trustee Mus. Fine Arts, Boston, 1975-77. Served with AUS, 1943-46, 50-51. Mem. Assn. Asian Studies, Coll. Art Assn., Am. Acad. Benares, Am. Acad. Arts and Scis. Author: Dynastic Arts of the Kushans, 1967; Japanese Art of the Heian Period, 1967; co-author: Traditions of Japanese Art, 1970; Courtly Tradition of Japanese Art and Literature, 1972; Journey of Three Jewels, 1979; Song of the Brush, 1979, Masters of Japanese Calligraphy, 1984; editor Archives of Asian Art, 1973-84, Japanese Arts Library, 1977—. Research history Buddhist art and Japanese art. Home: 75 Coolidge Rd Arlington MA 02174 Office: Fogg Art Mus Harvard Univ 32 Quincy St Cambridge MA 02138 *

ROSENGARTEN, FREDERIC, JR., author, spice company executive; b. Phila., Oct. 4, 1916; s. Frederic and E. Marion (Sims) R.; A.B., Princeton U., 1938; m. Miriam B. Osterhoust, June 18, 1941; children: Miriam Suydam Rosengarten Lansing, Clara Rosengarten Urbahn, Lynn Rosengarten Horowitz, Joan Rosengarten Van Der Grift. Mgr. v.p. Exptl. Plantations, Inc. subs. Merck & Co., C.A., 1940-43, in charge quinine plantations in Guatemala and Costa Rica, 1940-43; self-employed producer coffee, spices, essential oils in Guatemala, 1947-58; pres. Monte de Oro, S.A., Guatemala Corp., Guatemala City, Guatemala, 1958-72; dir. U. of Valley of Guatemala Found. Trustee, Escuela Agrícola Panamericana, El Zamorano, Honduras, Pacific Tropical Bot. Garden. Served from pvt. to 1st lt., AUS, 1944-46. Decorated Order of the Quetzal (Guatemala); hon. research fellow econ. botany Harvard U. Fellow Linnean Soc. (London). Episcopalian. Clubs: Guatemala Country (pres. 1957); Seminole Golf (Palm Beach, Fla.); Phila. Developer of Guatemalan cardomon. Author: The Book of Spices, 1969; Freebooters Must Die!, 1976; The Book of Edible Nuts, 1984. Home: 247 Jungle Rd Palm Beach FL 33480

ROSENGREN, BJÖRN ERIC, solicitor; b. Stockholm, Jan. 8, 1944; s. Eric August Magnus and Eva Margareta Knutsdotter (Holmberg) R.; divorced; children: Josephine, David. Officer cert., Coast Arty., 1964; LLB, U. Stockholm, 1968. Bar: Sweden, 1974. Asst. solicitor Advokatfirman Henning Sjöström, Stockholm, 1968-78; owner Advokatfirman Björn Rosengren, Stockholm, 1978—. Served to lt. Swedish Coast Arty., 1962-64. Mem. Swedish Boxing Assn. (chmn. bd. 1978-83, hon. chmn. 1983—), Swedish Olympic Com. (bd. dirs. 1984—), Swedish Cen. Assn. Promotion Sports (bd. dirs. 1985—), Ct. Arbitration for Sport, European Boxing Assn. (tech. and rules commn.). Office: Advokatfirman Björn Rosengren, Birger Jarlsgatan 73-75, 113 56 Stockholm Sweden

ROSENGREN, GUNNAR ARVID, investment company executive; b. Bredestad, Sweden, Jan. 16, 1943; s. Arvid and Ingeborg (Rosengren) Karlsson; m. Anita Gunilla Edstrom, Aug., 1966; children: Joakim, Gabriella. M.Law, Stockholm U., 1967. Legal adviser Lagerlof's Law Firm, Stockholm, 1970-73; legal advisor Saleninvest AB, Stockholm, 1973, asst. to former pres., 1974-77; pres. Salen Dry Cargo AB, Stockholm, 1977-82; pres., chief exec. officer, Saleninvest Group, Stockholm, 1982-84; pres. Rosengren & Åström Ptnrs. AB, 1985—; pres., chief exec. officer Uddevalla Shipping AB, 1986—. Office: Rosengren & Astrom Ptnrs AB, Skinnarviksringen 4, 117 26 Stockholm Sweden

ROSENGREN, INGER TILLY, linguist, educator; b. Aarhus, Denmark, July 14, 1934; arrived in Sweden, 1946; d. Theo and Gertrud (Morlock) Hofmann; m. Karl Erik Rosengren, Dec. 29, 1956; children: Anders, Jörgen, Staffan. Fil Dr in German lang., U. Lund, Sweden, 1966. Assoc. prof. German U. Lund, 1966-71, prof., 1971—. Author, co-author, editor numerous books on German linguistics; editor Lunder Germanistische Forschungen, 1971—; contbr. articles to profl. jours. Recipient numerous grants Swedish Council Res Humaniker and Social Scis., Bank of Sweden Tercentenary Found., Bd. of Info. Support. Mem. Internat. Assn. Tchrs. German (sec. gen. 1974-77). Home: Vittnesgrand 39, S222 47 Lund Sweden Office: U Lund Dept German, Helgonabacken 14, S223 62 Lund Sweden

ROSENGREN, KARL ERIK, sociology educator; b. Malmoe, Scania, Sweden, Mar. 3, 1932; s. Bengt Erik and Nanna Karolina (Larsson) R.; m. Inger Tilly, Dec. 29, 1956; children: Anders, Jörgen, Staffan. DLitt, U. Lund, Sweden, 1966, D Sociology, 1968. Lectr. sociology U. Lund, Sweden, 1966-69, assoc. prof., 1969-74, prof. sociology, 1986—; research fellow Swedish Social Sci. Council, Stockholm, 1975-82; prof. mass. communications U. Gothenburg, Sweden, 1982-86; cons. Swedish Com. on Press, 1972-75, Bank of Sweden Tercentenar Found., 1975-86, Swedish Bd. Medicine and Social Conditions, 1987—. Founding editor European Jour. Communications, London, 1986—, also numerous books on the sociology of culture and communication; contbr. articles to profl. jours. Recipient numerous grants Swedish Social Sci. Council, Bank of Sweden Tercentenary Found., and Swedish Bd. Psychol. Def., Stockholm. Mem. Internat. Sociolog. Assn., Am. Sociolog. Assn., Internat. Inst. Communication, Internat. Communication Assn. Home: Vittnesgrand 39, S222 47 Lund Sweden Office: U Lund Dept Sociology, Box 114, S222 47 Lund Sweden

ROSENKILDE, CARL EDWARD, physicist; b. Yakima, Wash., Mar. 16, 1937; s. Elmer Edward and Doris Edith (Fitzgerald) R.; m. Bernadine Doris Blumenstine, June 22, 1963; children: Karen Louise, Paul Eric. B.S. in Physics, Wash. State Coll., 1959; M.S. in Physics, U. Chgo., 1960, Ph.D. in Physics, 1966. Postdoctoral fellow Argonne (Ill.) Nat. Lab., 1966-68; asst. prof. math. NYU, 1968-70; asst. prof. physics Kans. State U., Manhattan, 1970-76, assoc. prof., 1976-79; physicist Lawrence Livermore (Calif.) Nat. Lab., 1979—, cons., 1974-79. Contbr. articles on physics to profl. jours. Woodrow Wilson fellow, 1959, 60. Mem. Am. Phys. Soc., Am. Astron. Soc., Soc. for Indsl. and Applied Math., Am. Geophys. Union, Acoustical Soc. Am., Phi Beta Kappa, Phi Kappa Phi, Phi Eta Sigma, Sigma Xi. Republican. Presbyterian. Club: Tubists Universal Brotherhood Assn. (TUBA). Current Work: Nonlinear wave propagation in complex media. Subspecialties: Theoretical physics; Fluid dynamics.

ROSENKRANZ, GEORGE, chemical executive; b. Budapest, Hungary, Aug. 20, 1916; naturalized Mexican citizen, 1949; s. Bertalan and Stella (Weiner) R.; degree as chem. engr., dr. tech. scis. E.T.H. Zurich, Switzerland, 1939, postgrad., 1940-41; D (hon.) U. of las Ams. m. Edith Stein, Sept. 20, 1945; children—Robert Peter, Gerald Michael, Richard Thomas. Tech. dir. Labs. Vieta-Plasencia, Havana, Cuba, 1941-45; with Syntex, S.A. (name later changed to Syntex Corp.), Mexico City, 1945—, tech. dir., 1945-47, research dir., 1947-49, v.p. research, 1949-51, v.p. research and prodn., 1951-53, exec. v.p. 1953-56, pres., chmn. bd., 1956-76, chmn. bd., 1976-81, founding chmn. bd., 1981—, chief exec. officer, 1976-80. Bd. govs. U. Tel Aviv, Israel; bd. govs. mem. sci. commn. Weizmann Inst., Israel; mem. council Rockefeller U., N.Y.C. Created comdr. Order Vasco Nunez de Balboa, Panama. Fellow Internat. Coll. Dentists; mem. Am. Chem. Soc., AAAS, Royal Chem. Soc. Gt. Britain, Nat. Acad. Medicine in Mex. (hon.), Chem. Soc. Switzerland. Author: The Romex System, A Dynamic Approach to Bidding; Win with Romex, Key to Accurate Bidding; Bid Your Way to the Top; Modern Ideas in Bidding, Bridge: The Bidders Game, Everything You Always Wanted to Know About Trump Leads; contbr. articles to profl. publs.; patentee in field. Home: Parque Via Reforma 1730, Delegación Miguel, 11000 Chapultepec, Mexico City Mexico Office: Syntex Corp, Apartado Postal 2679, Mexico City Mexico

ROSENKRANZ, ROBERTO PEDRO, pharmacologist; b. Mexico City, Mar. 30, 1950; s. George and Edith R.; m. Heather Blum, Aug. 21, 1983; 1 child, Tamara Ann. A.B. in Psychology, Stanford U., 1971; Ph.D. in Comparative Pharmacology/Toxicology, U. Calif.-Davis, 1980. Neurobiologic researcher Instituto Nacional de Neruologia, Mex., 1971-72; Mexican del. Internat. Group on Drug Legis. and Programs, Geneva, 1971-73; dir. research Centro Mexicano de Estudios en Farmacodependencia, 1972-73; research fellow dept. medicine Stanford U., Calif., 1980-82; research sect. leader Syntex Research, Palo Alto, Calif., 1982—; cons.; pres. Lic. Luis Echeverria Alvarez. Contbr. articles on pharmacology to profl. jours. Mex. del. Joint U.S.-Mex. Exec. Conf. on Drug Abuse Planning, 1972; Mexican del. UN Social Def. Research Inst., Rome, 1971-72. Mem. AAAS, N.Y. Acad. Scis., Soc. Neurosci., Am. Soc. Pharmacology and Exptl. Therapeutics, Western Pharmacology Soc. (sec. 1988—), Internat. Soc. Study of Xenobiotics, Internat. Soc. Cardiovascular Pharmacology. Office: Syntex Research 3401 Hillview Palo Alto CA 94304

ROSENN, HAROLD, lawyer; b. Plains, Pa., Nov. 4, 1917; s. Joseph and Jennie (Wohl) R.; m. Sallyanne Frank, Sept. 19, 1948; 1 child, Frank Scott. BA, U. Mich., 1939, JD, 1941. Bar: Pa. 1942, U.S. Supreme Ct. 1957. Ptnr. Rosenn & Rosenn, Wilkes Barre, Pa., 1948-54; ptnr. Rosenn, Jenkins & Greenwald, Wilkes Barre, 1954-87, of counsel, 1988—; asst. dist. atty Luzerne County, Pa., 1952-54; mem. Gov's. Justice Commn., Pa., 1968-73, Crime Commn., Pa., 1968-73, Fed. Judicial Nominating Com., Pa., 1977-79, Appellate Ct. Nominating Com., Pa., 1979-81; bd. dirs. Franklin 1st Fed. Savs. and Loan Assn., Wilkes-Barre. Chmn. ARC, Wilkes Barre, 1958-60; pres. Pa. Council on Crime and Delinquency, Harrisburg, 1969-71; bd. dirs. Coll. Misericordia, Dallas, Pa., 1976-86, Hoyt Library, Kingston, Pa., 1971-78, Nat. Council on Crime and Delinquency, N.Y.C., 1969-71; chmn. United Way Campaign of Wyoming Valley, 1975; pres. United Way, Wyoming Valley, 1978-80. Served to capt. USAAF, 1942-45, ETO. Named Honoree, Wyo. Vally Interfaith Council, 1986; recipient Erasmus medal Dutch Govt., 1985. Mem. ABA, Pa. Bar Assn., Am. Judicature Soc., Pa. State Bd. Law Examiners. Republican. Jewish. Clubs: U. Mich. (N.E. Pa.) (pres. 1946-76), Westmoreland (Wilkes Barre). Lodge: B'nai Brith (pres. Wilkes Barre 1952-53, Community Service award 1976). Home: 29 Hedge Pl Kingston PA 18704 Office: Rosenn Jenkins & Greenwald 15 S Franklin St Wilkes-Barre PA 18711

ROSENSAFT, LESTER JAY, management consultant, reorganization lawyer, business executive; b. Leominster, Mass., Jan. 11, 1958; s. Melvin and Beatrice (Golombek) R. BS in Econs., Wharton Sch., U. Pa., 1978; JD, Case Western Res. U., 1981, MBA, 1981; LLM in Corporate Law, NYU, 1983. Bar: Ohio 1981, U.S. dist. ct. (no. dist.) Ohio 1982, U.S. dist cts. (ea., we., no., so. dists.) N.Y. 1982. Practice corp. and comml. law, Ohio, 1981—, reorgn. law fed. cts. Ohio, N.Y., 1982—; mem. firm Hall, Rosensaft & Yen, Cleve. and Singapore, 1981—; with Cons. to Mgmt., Inc., Cleve., N.Y.C., Boston, Hong Kong, 1977—, v.p., 1977-80, pres. and chief exec. officer, 1980-83, chmn., 1983—; pres. and chief exec. officer Eljay Devel. Corp., 1985-86; chmn., chief exec. officer Logistix Ltd., 1987—; ptnr. Sanctuary Assocs., Boston, 1988—; vice chmn. bd. Paramount Systems Design Group, Inc., N.Y.C., 1982—; v.p. corp. devel., mem. bd. dirs. Ameritec Corp., N.Y.C., 1983—; v.p., chief fin. officer, mem. bd. dirs. Chipurnoi Inc., L.I. City, N.Y., 1983—; v.p., chief fin. officer Kinnerton Industries, N.Y.C. and London, 1983—; vice chmn., gen. counsel, mem. bd. dirs. GIOIA Couture, Inc., Akron, Ohio, 1984-86; dir. Honeybee Robotics Ltd., Taiwan and N.Y.C., dir. Pelletier Brothers, Inc., 1986— , Advanced Radiator Techs., Inc., Fitchburg, Mass., 1987—; ednl. cons.; advisor indsl. devel. and strategic urbanism; cons. federally funded biomed. research projects; active Combined Jewish Philanthropies; participant 40th Anniversary II Pres.'s Mission, 1987; chmn. Region V Outreach Mission, 1988; mem. Russian Resettlement Com., 1988; active U. Pa. Secondary Com. of Cen. Mass. Co-author (with Melvin Rosensaft): Industrial Development Survey for City of Leominster, 1978. Contbr. articles to profl. jours. Mem. exec. adv. council Keene State Coll., 1984—. Mem. ABA, Greater Cleve. Bar Assn., Ohio State Bar Assn., Assn. Bar City N.Y., Assn. Trial Lawyers Am., Am. Mgmt. Assn., Am. Mktg. Assn. Wharton Club Cleve. (exec. com.), Wharton Club N.Y., U. Pa. Clubs Cleve., U. Pa. Club N.Y., Bankruptcy Lawyers Bar Assn., N.Y.C. Reorgn. Roundtable, Internat. Soc. Strategic Planning Cons., Soc. Profl. Mgmt. Cons., Inst. of Mgmt. Cons. (cert. mgmt. cons.), North Cen. Mass. C. of C. (indsl. devel. com. 1984—), Phi Alpha Delta (vice justice). Clubs: Boca Beach, Boca Pointe Golf and Racquet, Boca West, Boca Raton Hotel and Club (Boca Raton, Fla.). Home: 59 Crescent Rd Leominster MA 01453

ROSENSAFT, MENACHEM ZWI, lawyer, author, community leader; b. Bergen-Belsen, Germany, May 1, 1948; came to U.S., 1958, naturalized, 1962; s. Josef and Hadassah (Bimko) R.; m. Jean Bloch, Jan. 13, 1974; 1 child, Joana Deborah. BA, MA, Johns Hopkins U., 1971; MA, Columbia U., 1975, JD, 1979. Bar: N.Y. 1980. Adj. lectr. dept. Jewish studies CCNY, 1972-74, professorial fellow, 1974-75; research fellow Am. Law Inst., 1977-78; law clk. to U.S. Dist. Ct. judge (so. dist.), N.Y.C., 1979-81; assoc. Proskauer, Rose, Goetz & Mendelsohn, N.Y.C., 1981-82, Kaye, Scholer, Fierman, Hays & Handler, N.Y.C., 1982—. Author: Moshe Sharett, Statesman of Israel, 1966, Fragments, Past and Future (poetry), 1968, Not Backward to Belligerency, 1969; editor Bergen Belsen Youth mag., 1965; book rev. editor Columbia Jour. Transnat. Law, 1978-79; co-editor (with Yehuda Bauer) Antisemitism: Threat to Western Civilization, 1988; contbr. to various publs. including The New York Times, The New York Post, Columbia Human Rights Law Rev., Jewish Social Studies, Leo Baeck Inst. Year Book XXI, Columbia Jour. Environ. Law, Reform Judaism, Letzte Nayes, Tel Aviv, Asahi Evening News, Tokyo, Midstream. Chmn. Internat. Network of Children of Jewish Holocaust Survivors, 1981-84, founding chmn., 1984— chmn. 2d Generation Com. Am. Gathering of Jewish Holocaust Survivors, 1982-85, chmn. action com., 1985—; chmn. commn. on human rights World Jewish Congress, 1986—, chmn. exec. com. Am. sect., 1986—; mem. Gen. Council World Zionist Orgn, 1987—; chmn. 2d Generation Adv. Com. to U.S. Holocaust Meml. Council, 1983-87; mem. N.Y.C. Holocaust Meml. Commn., 1982— (chmn. collections com., 1987—); mem. Tribunal Am. Zionist Fedn., 1988—; organizer, leader demonstration against President Reagan's visit to Bitburg cemetery, Bergen-Belsen, 1985; pres. Labor Zionist Alliance, 1988—. Recipient Parker Sch. recognition of achievement with honors in internat. and fgn. law, 1979; Harlan Fiske Stone scholar, 1977-79. Mem. ABA, Assn. Bar City N.Y., Phi Beta Kappa. Home: 179 E 70th St New York NY 10021 Office: Kaye Scholer Fierman Hays & Handler 425 Park Ave New York NY 10022

ROSENSCHEIN, GUY RAOUL, surgeon; b. Paris, July 28, 1953; s. Maurice and Caroline (Meller) R. M.D., Lariboisiere-St. Louis, Paris, 1977. Intern, Hôpital Saint-Louis, 1973-74, Hôpital Lariboisière, 1975-76; resident Hôpitaux de Paris, 1977-80, Hôpital Bretonneau, 1977-78, Hôpital Lariboisière, 1979-80; resident Hôpital de Monaco, Monte Carlo, 1980-81; resident Hôpital St. Vincent de Paul, Paris, 1981-82, attache, 1982-84, asst., 1984-86; chef de clinique U. Paris, 1984-86; attache Hôpital de Villeneuve St Georges, 1987—; maitre de stage hospitalier Faculté de Médecine de Creteil, 1987—. Author: Pancreatite non traumatique et non infectieuse de l'enfant, 1982. Served to capt., M.C., French Armed Forces, 1977. Mem. Conseil Nat. de L'ordre des Medecins. Jewish. Club: A.C. Renault (Chavenay, France). Avocation: flying. Home: 61 rue de Picpus, 75012 Paris France Office: Centre Hospitalier Intercommunal, de Villeneuve, Saint Georges, 94190 Villeneuve Saint Georges France also: Clinique Chirurgicale, 20 Ave Maurice Berteaux, 78500 Sartrouville France

ROSENSTEIN, ALLEN BERTRAM, electrical engineering educator; b. Balt., Aug. 25, 1920; s. Morton and Mary (Epstein) R.; m. Betty Lebell; children: Jerry Tyler, Lisa Nan, Adam Mark. B.S. with high distinction, U. Ariz., 1940; M.S., UCLA, 1950, Ph.D., 1958. Elec. engr. Consol. Vultee Aircraft, San Diego, 1940-41; sr. elec. engr. Lockheed Aircraft Corp., Burbank, Calif., 1941-42; chief plant engr. Utility Fan Corp., Los Angeles, 1942-44; prof. engring. UCLA, 1946—; founder, chmn. bd. Inet, Inc., 1947-53, cons. engr., 1954—; founder, chmn. bd. dirs. Pioneer Magnetics, Inc., Pioneer Research Inc., Anadex Instruments Inc.; dir. Internat. Transformer Co., Inc., Fgn. Resource Services; cons. ednl. planning UNESCO, Venezuela, 1974-76. Author: (with others) Engineering Communications, 1965, A Study of a Profession and Professional Education, 1968; contbr. articles to profl. jours.; patentee in field. Bd. dirs. Vista Hill Psychiat. Found. Served with USNR, 1944-46. Fellow IEEE; mem., Am. Soc. Engring. Edn., N.Y. Acad. Scis., AAAS, Sigma Xi, Phi Kappa Phi, Delta Phi Sigma, Tau Beta Pi. Home: 314 S Rockingham St Los Angeles CA 90049

ROSENSTEIN, ROBERT BRYCE, lawyer, financial advisor; b. Santa Monica, Calif., Feb. 26, 1954; s. Franklin Lee and Queen Esther (Shall) R.; m. Resa Shanee Brookler, Nov. 30, 1980; children: Shaun Franklin, Jessica Laney. BA, Calif. State U., Northridge, 1976; JD, Southwestern U., 1979. Bar: Calif. 1979, U.S. Dist. Ct. (cen. dist. Calif.) 1980, U.S. Tax Ct. 1981. Service rep. Social Security Adminstrn., Los Angeles, 1974-77; tax cons. Am. Tax Assocs., Los Angeles, 1970-78, ptnr., 1978; prin., pres. Robert B. Rosenstein, PC, Los Angeles, 1979-84; ptnr. Rosenstein and Werlin, Los Angeles, 1984-87; sr. ptnr. Robert Bryce Rosenstein Ltd., Los Angeles, 1987—; chief fin. officer and corp. counsel BSE Mgmt. Inc., Los Angeles, 1987—; corp. counsel Sirius Computer Corp., Spartan Computer, Unicomp, Inc., Palmadale Investment Inc., Bldg. Systems Evaluation Inc., Diagnostic Engring. Inc., 1986—; pres. Will Find Inc., 1986—. Recipient Am. Jurisprudence award Bancroft Whitney. Mem. ABA (taxation com.), Assn. Trial Lawyers Am., Los Angeles Bar Assn. Republican. Jewish. Lodges: Masons, Ionic, Composite. Office: La Cienega Blvd Suite 815 PO Box 92971 Los Angeles CA 90009-2971

ROSENTHAL, ABRAHAM MICHAEL, editor; b. Sault St. Marie, Ont., Can., May 2, 1922; came to U.S., 1926, naturalized, 1951; s. Harry and Sarah (Dickstein) R.; m. Ann Marie Burke, Mar. 12, 1949; children: Jonathan Harry, Daniel Michael, Andrew Mark; m. Shirley Lord, June 10, 1987. B.S. in Social Sci., CCNY, 1944, LL.D. (hon.), 1974; hon. degree, SUNY, 1984. Staff N.Y. Times, 1944—, UN corr., 1946-54; assigned N.Y. Times, India, 1954-58, Warsaw, Poland, 1958-59, Geneva, Switzerland, 1960-61, Tokyo, 1961-63; met. editor N.Y. Times, 1963-66, asst. mng. editor, 1967-68, asso. mng. editor, 1968-69, mng. editor, 1969-77, exec. editor, 1977-86, assoc. editor and columnist, 1986-87, columnist, 1987—; editor at large, editorial cons. G.P. Putnam, 1988—; Pres. Fgn. Corr. Assn. India, 1957. Author: 38 Witnesses; co-author: One More Victim; co-editor: The Night the Lights Went Out, The Pope's Journey to the United States; contbr.: articles Foreign Affairs. Recipient citation for work in India Overseas Press Club, 1956, for work in India and Poland, 1959, for two fgn. affairs mag. articles, 1965; Pulitzer prize for internat. reporting, 1960; Number One award Overseas Press Club, 1960; George Polk Meml. award, 1960, 65; Page One award Newspaper Guild N.Y., 1960; Hon. award Assn. Indians in Am., 1974; New York County Bar Assn. award, 1978. Office: care NY Times 229 W 43d St New York NY 10036

ROSENTHAL, ALBERT LESTER, dermatologist; b. New Bedford, Mass., July 25, 1926; s. Myer and Ruth Naomi (Gourse) R.; m. Carol Ash, July 30, 1969; children—Robert, Jill, Bruce. BA magna cum laude, Tufts U., 1946, MD, 1951. Intern, R.I. Hosp., Providence, 1951-52, asst. resident surgery, 1952-53; asst. resident dermatology Mass. Gen. Hosp., Boston, 1955-56; asst. in dermatology N.Y. U., 1958-60; practice medicine specializing in dermatology, Trenton, N.J., 1958—; attending and chief dermatologist Mercer Hosp., 1958—; chief dermatology Helene Fuld Hosp., 1973-85; asso. in dermatology U. Pa., Phila., 1969-73; asso. prof. dermatology Hahnemann Med. Coll., Phila., 1973-87, clin. prof., dermatologist, 1987— ; mem. staff Grad. Hosp. of Pa., 1969-73; mem. staff Hamilton Hosp., chief dermatologist, 1972-76. Contbr. numerous articles on dermatology to med. jours. Trustee, Friends of the N.J. State Mus., 1972—, chmn. bd. trustees, 1980-82, v.p. fine arts, 1978-80; mem. Mercer County Cultural and Heritage Commn., 1982—, chmn., 1984—. Served to capt., M.C., USAF, 1953-55. Diplomate Am. Bd. Dermatology. Mem. Am. Acad. Dermatology, Pa. Acad. Dermatology, Noah Worcester Dermatology Soc., Phila. Dermatology Soc. (pres. 1984-85), N.J. Dermatology Soc., N.J. Med. Soc., Mercer Med. Soc., AMA. Jewish. Office: 74 Franklin Corner Rd Lawrenceville NJ 08648

ROSENTHAL, LUCY GABRIELLE, writer, editor; b. N.Y.C.; d. Henry Moses and Rachel (Tchernowitz) R. AB, U. Mich., 1954; MS, Columbia U., 1955; MFA, Yale Sch. Drama, 1961. Asst. editor Radiology mag., Detroit, 1955-57; freelance editorial cons. various pub. houses, lit. agts. N.Y.C., 1957-73; mem. admissions staff U. Iowa Writers Workshop, Iowa City, 1965-68; editor Book-of-the-Month Club, N.Y.C., 1973-74; mem. editorial bd. judges Book-of-the-Month Club, 1974-79, sr. editorial adv., 1979-87; mem. biography jury Pulitzer Prize, 1980; mem. bd. Am. Book Awards, 1981-82; adj. prof. English, NYU, spring, fall 1986, spring, fall 1988; mem. faculty dept. humanities 92d St. YM-YWHA, fall 1987; adj. prof. NYU Sch. Continuing Edn., spring, 1988. Produced plays at Eugene O'Neill Meml. Theatre Ctr., 66, 67; author: The Ticket Out, 1983; editor: Great American Love Stories, 1988; contbr. articles and revs. to various mags. and periodicals including Book World, Saturday Rev., Ms. mag., Mich. Quar. Rev., N.Y. Times Book Rev. Pulitzer fellow critical writing, 1968. Mem. Authors Guild, Nat. Book Critics Circle, Women's Media Group (dir. 1979-81), PEN, Eugene O'Neill Meml. Theater Center, Phi Beta Kappa, Phi Kappa Phi. Office: care Wendy Weil Agy Inc 747 3d Ave New York NY 10017

ROSENTHAL, MARA ELENA, archaeologist; b. Washington, Dec. 8, 1959; d. Irving and Suzanne (Geist) R. BA cum laude, Cornell U., 1980; MA in Prehistory, U. London, 1981; postgrad., U. chgo. Asst. curator, researcher Brit. Mus. N.Am. Indian Collections, 1980-81; anthropologist Govt. of Niger, Oullam Arrondissement, 1982; research specialist Argonne (Ill.) Nat. Labs., 1985; dir. archaeol. study Southeastern Viti Levu, Fiji, 1985-88; dir. Nasilai Archaeology Project for Fiji Mus., Suva, 1987; speaker profl. meetings. Contbr. articles to profl. jours.; surveyor, draftsman archtl illustrations and maps. Fellow U. Chgo., 1983-84, Smithsonian Inst., 1988-89; grantee Margary, 1980, Wenner-Gren, 1988; Hirsch scholar, 1979, Fulbright scholar, 1985-87. Jewish. Office: Fiji Mus, PO Box 2023 Government Bldgs, Suva Fiji

ROSENTHAL, MYRON MARTIN, electrical engineer, educator, author; b. Bklyn., Nov. 5, 1930; s. Murray Morris and Selma Locke (Belsky) R.; (divorced); children: Lynn, Debbie, Richard. BEE, CCNY, 1953; MS, Adelphi U., 1957. Registered profl. engr., N.J.; lic. public acct., N.J. Sr. engr. Republic Aviation Corp., Farmingdale, L.I., 1955-61; pres. Myron M. Rosenthal & Staff, Farmingdale, L.I., 1957-61; program mgr. Loral Electronics, Bronx, N.Y., 1962-64; engring. mgr. Singer-Kearfott div. The Singer Co., Wayne, N.J., 1964-87; prof. Poly. U., Bklyn., N.J., 1954-87; bd. dirs. Electronics and Aerospace Conv., 1971-82, treas., 1972-82, chmn. bd., 1974; bd. dirs. Nat. Aerospace and Electronics Conf., 1972-75; notary pub., N.J., N.Y. Founder Randal Carter PTA cultural workshop, Wayne, 1965; lighting commr. Wayne, 1956. Recipient Picatinny Arsenal U.S. Army Engring. and Leadership commendations, 1969, 71, 73; Poly. U. N.Y. faculty award, 1975 Disting. Faculty award, 1982; Nat. Aerospace and Electronics Conf. award, 1968, 75, 76; Electronics and Aerospace Conv. award, 1974, 80, 82; Poly Service award, 1984. Mem. IEEE (sr. mem., award 1972, 74, Centennial medal 1984), Nat. Soc. Profl. Engrs., AIAA, ASME, ASCE, Illuminating Engring. Soc., Am. Assn. Clin. Chemistry, Am. Inst. Indsl. Engrs., Audio Engring. Soc., Cincinatus Soc., Forest Products Research Soc., Am. Inst. Chemists, Nat. Fire Protection Assn., Nat. Rehab. Assn., Assn. U.S. Army, Navy League, U.S. Naval Inst., Marine Corps Assn., Am. Def. Preparedness Assn., Air Force Assn., ASTM, Aerospace Electronics and Systems Soc. (bd. govs. 1968-82, v.p. 1972, chmn. N.Y.-N.J. Met. chpt. 1972-82, Disting. Service award 1972, 74, 79, 82), Armed Forces Communications and Electronics Assn., AAUP, N.Y. Acad. Sci., Am. Soc. Indsl. Security, Am. Chem. Soc., Am. Assn. Physics Tchrs., Am. Physics Soc., Am. Soc. Safety Engrs. (profl. mem.), Am. Vocat. Assn. (life), Constrn. Specifications Inst., Am. Soc. Public Adminstrn., Am. Public Works Assn., Am. Assn. Cost Engrs., Am. Ceramic Soc., Nat. Mgmt. Assn. (certified), Nat. Council Tchrs. of Math., Nat. Council Tchrs. of English, Adult Edn. Assn., Inst. Cert. Profl. Mgrs. (cert.), Am. Radio Relay League, Nat. Assn. Accts., Nat. Soc. Public Accts., ALA, Soc. Automotive Engrs., Am. Craft Council, Nat. Soc. Architects, Am. Soc. Interior Design, Nat. Sci. Tchrs. Assn., Soc. Plastics Engrs., Audio Engring. Soc., Internat. Assn. Assessing Officers, Am. Hist. Assn., Am. Philos. Assn., MLA, Inst. of Nav. (program com. 1978), Am. Judicature Soc., Aircraft Owners and Pilots Assn., Refrigeration Service Engrs. Soc., AAAS, Boat Owners Assn., Am. Assn. Higher Edn., Nat. Aeros. Assn., Nat. Assn. Social Workers, Nat. Council Young Israel, Am. Rose Soc., Nat. Audubon Soc., Nat. Assn. of Deaf, Nat. Eye Research Found., Am. Council for Blind, Am. Diabetes Assn., Nat. Rehab. Assn., Am. Jewish Congress, Workmen's Circle, Am. Council Museums, Triple Nine Soc., Mensa, Intertel, Am. Nuclear Soc., United Otomy Assn., Sigma Xi, Eta Kappa Nu. Republican. Jewish. Clubs: B'nai B'rith (trustee 1976-77), Toastmasters (pres. 1969, area gov. 1970, best speaker of the year 1967, 68, 69, 75, 77). Home: 6858 Giralda Circle Boca Raton FL 33433 Office: 333 Jay St Brooklyn NY 11201

ROSENWALD, PETER JOSEPH, marketing consultant; b. N.Y.C., Nov. 9, 1935; s. Joseph Sanger and Elsa (Jacob) R.; m. Fenella Roberts, Dec. 27, 1968; children—Patricia Jeanne, David Joseph, Celia Janet. B.A., Princeton U., 1957. Mgr. advt. Book Find Club and Seven Arts Book Soc., N.Y.C., 1957-59; pub. book div. Am. Heritage Pub. Co., N.Y.C., 1959-62; dir. internat. cons. Pubaid, S.A. (Swiss), London, 1962-68; pres. Wunderman Internat. Group, London, 1968-78, N.Y.C., 1978-81; sr. v.p. Reeves Communications Corp., N.Y.C., 1981-82; pres. Peter J. Rosenwald & Internat. Assocs., Inc., N.Y.C., 1983-85; internat. chmn. Saatchi & Saatchi Direct Worldwide, London; dir. Internat. Assocs., Zurich, Fin. Agy. Mgmt. Ltd., London, Haircuts, Inc., NDL Internat., U.K. Mem. exec. com. U.S. Democrats Abroad Assn., 1964-74; adv. 92d St. YMHA, 1979—, Big Apple Circus, 1982-87; bd. dirs. Ballet Rev., 1982—; mem. dance panel N.Y. State Council Arts, 1983-84. Decorated cavaleiro Order Cruzeiro do Sul (Brazil), 1979. Mem. U.S. Direct Mail Mktg. Assn., Brit. Direct Mktg. Advt. Assn. (dir.), Dance Critics Assn., European Direct Mktg. Assn. Clubs: Century, Overseas Press (N.Y.C.). Dance critic Wall St. Jour., 1971—; articles in Horizon, N.Y. Mag., New West, Dance News, European Travel & Life. Home: 39 Drayton Gardens, London SW10 9RY, England Office: Saatchi & Saatchi Direct, 80 Charlotte St, London W1, England Office: Internat Assocs, Hagenholtzstrasse 81, CH8050 Zurich Switzerland

ROSENZWEIG, NORMAN, psychiatry educator; b. N.Y.C., Feb. 28, 1924; s. Jacob Arthur and Edna (Braman) R.; m. Carol Treleaven, Sept. 20, 1945; 1 child, Elizabeth Ann. MB, Chgo. Med. Sch., 1947, MD, 1948; MS, U. Mich., 1954. Diplomate Am. Bd. Psychiatry and Neurology. Asst. prof. psychiatry U. Mich., Ann Arbor, 1963-67, assoc. prof., 1967-73; prof. Wayne State U., Detroit, 1973—; chmn. dept. psychiat. Sch. Med. Wayne State U., Detroit, 1987—, Sinai Hosp., Detroit, 1961—; spl. cons., profl. advisor Oakland County Community Mental Health Services Bd., 1964-65; mem. protem med. adv. panel Herman Kiefer Hosp., Detroit, 1970, psychiat. task force N.W. Quadrangle Hosps., Detroit, 1971-78, planning com. mental health adv. council Dept. Mental Health State of Mich., Lansing, 1978-81, tech. adv. research com., 1978-82; psychiat. bed need task force Office Health and Med. Affairs State of Mich., 1980-84, facility bed needs task force, 1984—; bd. dirs. Alliance for Mental Health, Farmington Hills, Mich.; speaker in field. Author: Community Mental Health Programs in England: An American View, 1975; co-editor: Psychopharmacology and Psychotherapy-Synthesis of Antithesis?, 1978, Sex Education for the Health Professional: A Curriculum Guide, 1978; contbr. articles to profl. jours. and chpts. to books. Mem. profl. adv. bd. The Orchards, Livonia, Mich., 1963. Served as capt. USAF, 1955-57. Recipient Appreciation and Merit cert. Mich. Soc. Psychiatry and Neurology, 1970-71. Fellow Am. Coll. Mental Health Adminstrn., Am. Coll. Psychiatrists (hon. membership com., com. on regional ednl. programs, liaison officer to The Royal Australian and New Zealand Coll. Psychiatrists 1984-88), Am. Psychiat. Assn. (life fellow, council on internat. affairs 1970-79, chmn. 1973-76, assembly liaison to council on internat. affairs 1979-80, 82-84, reference com. 1973-76, nominating com. 1978-79, internat. affairs survey team 1973-74, assoc. representing Am. Psychiat. Assn. to Inter-Am. Council Psychiat. Assns. 1973-75, others, Rush Gold Medal award 1974, cert. Commendation, 1973-76, 78-80, Warren Williams award 1986); mem. AAAS, AAUP, AMA (Physician's Recognition award 1971, 74, 77, 80-81, 84), Am. Assn. Dirs. Psychiat. Residency Tng. (nominating com. 1972-74, task force on core curriculum 1972-74), Am. Assn. Gen. Hosp. Psychiatry, Puerto Rico Med. Assn. (hon. sect. psychiatry, neurology and neurosurgery, Presdl. award 1981), Am. Hosp. Assn. (governing council psychiat. services sect. 1977-79, ad hoc com. on uniform mental health definitions, chmn. task force on psychiat. coverage under Nat. Health Ins. 1977-79, others), Brit. Soc. Clin. Psychiatrists (task force on gen. hosp. psychiatry 1969-74), Can. Psychiat. Assn., Mich. Assn. Professions, Mich. Hosp. Assn. (psychiat. and mental health services com. 1979-81), Mich. Psychiat. Soc. (com. on ins. 1965-69, chmn. com. on community mental health services 1967-68, chmn. com. on nominations of fellows 1972-73, mem. com. on budget 1973-74, task force on pornography 1973-74, chmn. commn. on health professions and groups 1978-81, chmn. com. on liaison with hosp. assns. 1979-81, chmn. subcom. on liaison with Am. Hosp. Assn. 1979-81, numerous others, Past Pres. plaque, 1978, cert. Recognition, 1980, Disting. Service award 1986), Mich. State Med. Soc. (vice chmn. sect. psychiatry 1972-73, chmn. sect. psychiatry 1974-75, mem. com. to improve membership 1977-78, alt. del for Mich. Psychiat. Soc. to House of Dels. 1978-79, del. from Wayne County Med. Soc. to Mich. Med. Soc. House of Dels. 1982-88), N.Y. Acad. Scis., Pan Am. Med. Assn., Wayne County Med. Soc. (com. on hosp. and prof. relations 1983-84, com. on child health advocacy 1983-87, med. edn. com. 1983-87, mental health com. 1983-87), Royal Australian and New Zealand Coll. Psychiatrists (hon.), Indian Psychiat. Soc. (hon. corr.), World Psychiat. Assn., Sect. Gen. Hosp. Psychiat. Home: 1234 Cedarholm Ln Bloomfield Hills MI 48013 Office: Sinai Hosp Detroit 6767 W Outer Dr Detroit 8235

ROSETT, RICHARD NATHANIEL, educator, economist; b. Balt., Feb. 29, 1928; s. Walter and Essie (Stofberg) R.; m. Madelon Louise George, June 24, 1951; children: Claudia Anne, Martha Victoria, Joshua George, Sarah Elizabeth, Charles Richard. B.A., Columbia U., 1953; M.A., Yale U., 1954, Ph.D., 1957. Instr. Yale U., 1956-58; mem. faculty U. Rochester, 1958-74, chmn. dept. econs., 1966-74, prof. econs., 1967-74, prof. preventive medicine and community health, 1969-74; prof. bus. econs. Grad. Sch. Bus., U. Chgo., 1974-84, dean, 1974-83; dean Faculty Arts and Scis. Washington U., 1984-87, prof. econs., 1984—; bd. dirs. Hutchinson Techs., Inc., Kemper Corp., Gen. Instrument Corp. Editor: The Role of Health Insurance in the Health Services Sector, 1976; Contbr. articles to profl. jours. Bd. dirs., chmn. Nat. Bur. Econ. Research, 1986—. Served with USNR, 1944-45. Mem. Am. Econ. Assn., Mont Pelerin Soc., Phi Beta Kappa, Beta Gamma Sigma. Clubs: Cosmos; Chgo., Quadrangle (Chgo.). Home: 7057 Westmoreland Dr Saint Louis MO 63130

ROSHON, GEORGE KENNETH, manufacturing company executive, b. Pottstown, Pa., July 30, 1942; s. George Washington 3d and Ellen Eleanor (Knopf) R.; B.S. in Elec. Engring., Pa. State U., 1964; M.S., Drexel U., Phila., 1974, postgrad., 1974-75; m. Ella Maye Barndt, Nov. 21, 1964; 1 dau., Kirsten Renee. Sr. engr. Am. Electronics Labs., Inc., Colmar, Pa., 1966-69; v.p. engring. Acrodyne Industries, Inc., Montgomeryville, Pa., 1969-74; mgr. electric design W-J div. Hayes-Albion Corp., Norristown, Pa., 1974-78; mgr. quality assurance PSMBD, Gen. Electric Co., Phila., after 1978, mem. exec. com. electronics test council after 1980, mgr. advanced systems engring., 1983-84, mgr. communications engring., Malvern, Pa., 1984-86; v.p. quality assurance Hercules Aerospace Display Systems, Inc., Hatfield, Pa., 1986—. Patentee in field. Served to lt. USNR, 1964-66. Registered profl. engr., Pa. Mem. Nat. Soc. Profl. Engrs., Am. Soc. Quality Control (cert. quality engr.), Pa. Soc. Profl. Engrs., Gen. Electric Mgmt. Assn., Elfun Soc., Drexel U. Alumni Assn., Pa. State U. Alumni Assn., Tri-County Arabian Horse Assn. Home: 454 Eagle Ln Lansdale PA 19446 Office: 2321 Topaz Dr Hatfield PA 19440

ROSHONG, DEE ANN DANIELS, educator; b. Kansas City, Mo., Nov. 22, 1936; d. Vernon Edmund and Doradell (Kellogg) Daniels; B.Mus.Ed., U. Kans., 1958; M.A. in Counseling and Guidance, Stanford U., 1960; postgrad. Fresno State U., U. Calif.; Ed.D., U. San Francisco, 1980; m. Richard Lee Roshong, Aug. 27, 1960 (div.). Counselor, psychometrist Fresno City Coll., 1961-65; counselor, instr. psychology Chabot Coll., Hayward, Calif., 1965-75; coordinator counseling services Chabot Coll., Valley Campus, Livermore, Calif., 1975-81, asst. dir. student personnel services, 1981—; writer, coordinator I, a Woman Symposium, 1974, Feeling Free to be You and Me Symposium, 1975, All for the Family Symposium, 1976, I Celebrate Myself Symposium, 1977, Person to Person in Love and Work Symposium, 1978; The Healthy Person in Body, Mind and Spirit Symposium, 1979; Feelin' Good Symposium, 1980, Change Symposium, 1981; Sources of Strength Symposium, 1982; Love and Friendship Symposium, 1983, Self Esteem Symposium, 1984, Trust Symposium, 1985, Prime Time: Making the Most of this Time in Your Life Symposium, 1986, Symposium on Healing, 1987, How to Live in the World and Still Be Happy Symposium, 1988, Student Success is a Team Effort, others; mem. cast TV prodns. Eve and Co., Best of Our Times, Cowboy; chmn. Calif. Community Coll. Chancellor's Task Force on Counseling; Statewide Conf. on Emotionally Disturbed Student in Calif. Community Colls., 1982—, Conf. on the Under represented Student in California Community Colleges, 1986. Mem. Assn. Humanistic Psychologists, Western Psychol. Assn., Nat. Assn. Women. Deans and Counselors, Assn. for Counseling and Devel., Calif. Assn. Community Colls. (chmn. commn. on student services 1979-84), Calif. Community Colls. Counselors Assn. (Service award 1986, 87, award for Outstanding and Disting. Service, 1986, 87), Alpha Phi. Author: Counseling Needs of Community Coll. Students, 1980. Home: 808 Comet Dr Foster City CA 94404 Office: 3033 Collier Canyon Rd Livermore CA 94550

ROSICKY, BOHUMIR, parasitologist, educator; b. Brno, Apr. 18, 1922; Dr.rer.nat., Dr.Sc., Charles U., Prague, Czechoslovakia. Mem. staff Rovnost (Brno daily paper), 1945-46; chem. research worker, lab. head, chem. industry, 1947-50; specialist Central Biol. Inst., Prague, 1950-53; head dept. parasitology Biol. Inst., Czechoslovak Acad. Scis., Prague, 1954-61; dir. Inst. Parasitology, Prague, 1962-80, Inst. Hygiene and Epidemiology, 1980—; prof. natural scis. Comenius U., Bratislava, 1965—; dep. Czech Nat. Council, 1969—, mem. presidium, from 1969; WHO cons., India, 1964-65; mem. Joint WHO/FAO UN Panel of Zoonoses. Author: Czechoslovak Fauna-Aphaniptera, 1957; co-author: Modern Insecticides, 1951, Parasitologische Arbeitsmethoden, 1965; author numerous papers on ecology, taxonomy, entomology, med. zoology and parasitology. Decorated Order Cyril and Method (Bulgaria), Krzyz Oficerski (Poland), Order Labor; recipient State prize, 1954, G. Mendel Gold medal, 1970; co-recipient Klement Gottwald State prize, 1956, 72. Mem. Czechoslovak Acad. Scis. (academician 1970—, v.p. 1970-77, Silver plaque 1972), Bulgarian Acad. Scis. (corr.). Office: Inst of Hygiene and Epidemiology, Sroberove 48, 110-42 Prague Czechoslovakia

ROSKAM, HENRI, banker; b. Amsterdam, The Netherlands, Apr. 8, 1929; m. Gertrude T. Houting; children: Alexandra, Andrea, Saskia, Hugo. Grad., Netherlands Coll. for Fgn. Service, 1980. With The Netherlands Fgn. Service, 1950-55; mgr. internat. dept. Union Trust Co., Washington, 1955-58; rep. to Middle East Bank of Am., Beirut, 1958-62; European rep. Intra Bank, Geneva, 1962-63; sr. v.p. Crocker Nat. Bank, San Francisco, 1964-85; mng. dir. Dawn Investments BV, Amsterdam, The Netherlands, 1985—; European rep. Al Baraka Group, London, Amsterdam, Jeddah, 1985—; bd. dirs. Multitrade, The Netherlands, Saks, N.Y.C., Lease Line, The Netherlands; gen. consul Mauritius, Amsterdam, 1982—. Fulbright scholar U. Cin. Mem. Overseas Bankers Club, Industrieele Grote Club. Club: Hilversum Golf. Home: Heidelaantje 2, 1272 PE Huizen The Netherlands Office: Al Baraka Group, Keizersgracht 534, 1017 EK Amsterdam The Netherlands

ROSKOVENSKY, VINCENT JOSEPH, II, lawyer; b. Uniontown, Pa., Mar. 15, 1950; s. Vincent S. and Gertrude F. Roskovensky; m. Christine D. Bruni, July 16, 1977; 1 child, Vincent M. BA, U. Pitts., 1971; JD, Duquesne U., 1974. Bar: Pa. 1974, U.S. Dist. Ct. (we. dist.) Pa. 1975. Sole practice, Uniontown, 1974—; asst. dist. atty. Fayette County (Pa.), 1975-77; solicitor Smithfield Borough, Smithfield, Pa., 1980-88, Albert Gallatin Mcpl. Authority, Lake Lynn, Pa., 1980—; pres. Poca Coal Land Co., Uniontown. Treas., past pres. Fayette County Children and Youth Adv. Com., Uniontown. Mem. Pa. Bar Assn., Fayette County Bar Assn., Assn. Trial Lawyers Am., ABA. Democrat. Roman Catholic. Club: Exchange. Home: Heritage Hills Rd Uniontown PA 15401 Office: 9 Court St Uniontown PA 15401

ROSKY, BURTON SEYMOUR, lawyer; b. Chgo., May 28, 1927; s. David T. and Mary W. (Zelkin) R.; m. Leatrice J. Darrow, June 16, 1951; children: David Scott, Bruce Alan. Student, Ill. Inst. Tech., 1944-45; B.S., UCLA, 1948; J.D., Loyola U., Los Angeles, 1953. Bar: Calif. 1954, U.S. Supreme Ct 1964, U.S. Tax Ct 1964; C.P.A., Calif. Auditor City Los Angeles, 1948- 51; with Beidner, Temkin & Ziskin (C.P.A.s), Los Angeles, 1951-52; supervising auditor Army Audit Agy., 1952-53; practiced law Los Angeles, Beverly Hills, 1954—; partner Duskin & Rosky, 1972-82, Rosky, Landau & Fox, 1982—; lectr. on tax and bus. problems. Judge pro tem Beverly Hills Mcpl. Ct.; mem. Los Angeles Mayor's Community Adv. Council. Contbr. profl. publs. Charter supporting mem. Los Angeles County Mus. Arts; contbg. mem. Assocs. of Smithsonian Instn.; charter mem. Air and Space Mus; mem. Am. Mus. Natural History, Los Angeles Zoo; sustaining mem. Los Angeles Mus. Natural History; mem. exec. bd. So. Calif. council Nat. Fedn. Temple Brotherhoods, mem. nat. exec. bd. Served with USNR, 1945-46. Walter Henry Cook fellow Loyola Law Sch. Fellow Jewish Chautauqua Soc. (life mem.); mem. Am. Arbitration Assn. (nat. panel arbitrators), Am. Assn. Attys.-C.P.A.s (charter mem. pres. 1968), Calif. Assn. Attys.-C.P.A.s (charter mem., pres. 1963), Calif. Soc. C.P.A.s, Calif., Beverly Hills, Century City, Los Angeles County bar assns., Am. Judicature Soc., Chancellors Assocs. UCLA, Tau Delta Phi, Phi Alpha Delta.; mem. B'nai B'rith. Jewish (mem. exec. bd., pres. temple, pres. brotherhood). Club: Mason. Office: 8383 Wilshire Blvd Beverly Hills CA 90211

ROSLOW, SYDNEY, marketing educator; b. N.Y.C., July 29, 1910; s. Joseph and Anna (Lipman) R.; B.S., N.Y. U., 1931, M.A., 1932, Ph.D., 1935; m. Irma Sternberg, Oct. 21, 1932; children—Richard Jay, Susan Jane, Peter Dirk. Research asst. in market, indsl., personnel research Psychol. Corp., 1931-41; sch. psychologist, mem. bd. edn., Hastings on Hudson, N.Y., 1937-48; pub. opinion research program surveys div. Dept. Agr., 1939-43; founder Pulse, Inc., market and audience research in radio, television, advt. industries, N.Y.C., 1941-78; adj. assoc. prof. Baruch Coll. CUNY, 1967-75; assoc. prof. dept. mktg. Fla. Internat. U., 1976-83, prof. mktg., assoc. dean Coll. Bus. Adminstrn., 1983—. Fellow Am. Psychol. Assn.; mem. Am. Mktg. Assn. (pres. Miami chpt. 1980-82), Market Research Council, Radio-Television Research Council (past pres.) Radio and Television Execs. Soc., Phi Beta Kappa. Contbr. articles to profl. jours. Home: 1035 NE 202d Terr N Miami Beach FL 33179

ROSLUND, ULLA-BRITT, business consultant, accountant; b. Vena, Sweden, July 5, 1941; d. Elmer Johan and Ruth H. (Nilsson) Danielsson; m. Bengt Erik Roslund, Jan. 25, 1965; children: Helena, Hubert. B.Bus.Econs., U. Lund (Sweden), 1964. Authorized pub. acct. Auditor of taxes State Govt. Linkoping, 1964-66, State Govt. Västerås, 1966-67; head audit devel. Savs. Banks Auditing Co., Stockholm, 1967-80; mem. audit devel. staff PK Banken Ltd., Stockholm, 1980-82; pub. acct., 1982-84; bus. cons. B. Olssons Cons.s Co. Ltd., 1985—; authorised pub. acct. B. Olssons Ltd., 1985—; mem. working com. vulnerability analysis method Data Insp. Bd., Stockholm, 1982-83. Contbr. articles on EDP security to profl. jours. Mem. Inst. Internal Auditors (chmn. edn. com. 1976-78), Inst. Chartered Accts., Data Mgmt. Assn. (EDP security com. 1979—), Inst. Authorized Pub. Accts., Data Mgmt. Assn. Home: Flygarvagen 48, 17563 Järfälla Sweden Office: Bertil Olssons Ltd, Kungsgal 37, Stockholm Sweden

ROSMINI, GARY DAVID, financial marketing executive, consultant; b. Sewickley, Pa., Dec. 20, 1952; s. Silvio and Evelyn (Casciola) R.; m. Vivian Hooks, Jan. 7, 1978 (div. July 1984). BA, Pa. State U., 1975. Acct. mgr. Atwood-Vandell Assocs., Inc., N.Y.C., 1976-80, Clayton Brokerage, N.Y.C., 1980-81; assoc. v.p. Whitehall Investors Internat., Inc., N.Y.C., 1981-82; v.p. Monetary Futures Inc., N.Y.C., 1982-84; regional mktg. dir. Barrick Group, New Haven, Conn., 1984-86; pres. Rosmini Assocs., San Raphael, Calif., 1986—; regional mgr. Dunhill Investments, Emeryville, Calif., 1987-88, Donato, Calif., 1988—; mem. bd. advisors Pacific Investment Banking Group, Portland, Oreg., 1986—; bd. dirs. Superior Robotics Am., Petaluma, Calif., 1983-84; cons. in field. Creative dir. corp. brochure, 1986; copy writer bus. publ., 1983-84. Foster parent Save the Children, Ind., 1983-86; counselor Found. for Inner Peace, N.Y.C., 1976-78; choir dir. Saint Frances Cabrini Ch., Monaca, Pa., 1970-72; mem. Sewickley (Pa.) Civic Symphony, 1970-72, N.Y.C. Choral Soc., 1979-81. Recipient Billy Mitchell award CAP, 1970. Mem. Internat. Assn. Fin. Planning. (bd. dirs. 1981-84), Pa. State Alumni Assn. Home: 125 Wild Horse Valley Dr Novato CA 94947

ROSNESS, BETTY JUNE, advertising and public relations agency executive; b. Oklahoma City, Mar. 4, 1924; d. Thomas Harrison and Clara Marguerite (Stubblefield) Pyeatt; student Oklahoma City U., 1940-41; m. Joseph H. Rosness, Aug. 5, 1960; children—Melody L. Johnson (dec.), Michael C., Randall L., Melinda Rosness Mason, John C. Continuity dir. Sta. KFBI, Wichita, Kans., 1957-58; sales exec. Sta. KFH, Wichita, 1958-60; U.S. senatorial press sec., 1961-66; dir. advt. and public relations Alaska State Bank, Anchorage, 1966-68; prin. Rosness Advt. Assocs., Goleta, Calif., 1968—; bd. dirs. Fin. Corp. Santa Barbara (Calif.), Santa Barbara Savs. & Loan. Pres., Goleta Valley Girls Club, 1972-75, Ret. Officers Womens Assn., 1970; v.p. Santa Barbara Symphony Assn., 1977-80; bd. dirs. Channel City Womens Forum, 1976—, Goleta Valley Community Hosp.; Chmn. U. Calif. at Santa Barbara Affiliates, Pvt. Industry Council Santa Barbara County, 1985-86; bd. dirs. Cancer Found., Santa Barbara, 1978-82, founding mem. Goleta Beautiful, Club West Track and Field; mem. allocations com., bd. dirs. United Way, Santa Barbara; founding mem., bd. dirs. Children's World of Hospice; mem. evangelism com. Good Shepherd Lutheran Ch. Named Woman of Year, Santa Barbara County, 1978, Affiliate of Yr., U. Calif.-Santa Barbara, 1983-84. Mem. Greater Santa Barbara Advt. Club. (past v.p.), Goleta Valley C. of C. (past dir.), Santa Barbara C. of C. (bd. dirs. 1982-86), Goleta Valley C. of C. Address: 669 Larchmont Pl Goleta CA 93117

ROSOFF, WILLIAM A., lawyer; b. Phila., June 21, 1943; s. Herbert and Estelle (Finkel) R.; m. Beverly Rae Rifkin, Feb. 7, 1970; children: Catherine D., Andrew M. BS with honors, Temple U., 1964; LLB magna cum laude, U. Pa., 1967. Bar: Pa. 1968, U.S. Dist. Ct. (ea. dist.) Pa. 1968. Law clk. U.S. Ct. Appeals (3d cir.), 1967-68; instr. U. Pa. Law Sch., Phila., 1968-69; assoc. Wolf, Block, Schorr & Solis-Cohen, Phila., 1969-75, ptnr., 1975—, chmn. exec. com., 1987-88; bd. dirs. Korman Co.; guest lectr. confs. and seminars on tax law; mem. Commerce Clearing House Tax. Trans. Adv. Bd., 1983—; mem. legal activities policy bd. Tax Analysts, 1978—. Editor U. Pa. Law Rev., 1965-67; mem. bd. contbg. editors and advisors Jour. Partnership Taxation, 1983—; author reports and papers on tax law. Bd. dirs. Phila. chpt. Am. Soc. for Technion; dir., mem. com. on law and social action, Phila. Council Am. Jewish Congress. Fellow Am. Coll. Tax Counsel; mem. Am. Law Inst. (cons. taxation of partnerships 1976-78, assoc. reporter taxation of partnerships, 1978-82, mem. adv. group, adv. group on fed. income tax project 1982—), Order of Coif, Beta Gamma Sigma, Beta Alpha Psi. Club: Locust. Office: 15th and Chestnut Sts Packard Bldg 12th Floor Philadelphia PA 19102

ROSS, ADRIAN E., diamond drilling company executive; b. Clintonville, N.Y., Mar. 6, 1912; s. James A. and Bertha (Beardsley) R.; B.S. in Elec. Engring., M.I.T., 1934, M.S. in Elec. Engring., 1935; m. Ruth T. Hill, Mar. 2, 1934; children—James A., Daniel R. Materials engr. USN, 1935-37; devel. engr. Electrolux Corp., 1937-41; chief engr. and asst. to pres. Sprague & Henwood, Inc., Scranton, Pa., 1946-53, dir., 1951—, pres., 1953-74, chmn. bd., 1963—; pres., dir. Sprague & Henwood de Venezuela; dir. Hands Eng. Ltd., Scranton Lackawanna Indsl. Bldg. Co. (emeritus), N.E. Bank of Pa. (emeritus), profl. engrs. Past chmn. bd., dir. emeritus Keystone Jr. Coll.; pres., dir. James A. Ross Found., Sprague & Henwood Found.; former chmn. bd., dir. emeritus Johnson Sch. Tech. Served from lt. to lt. col. Air Communication. USAAF, 1941-46. Registered profl. engr., Pa. Mem. Diamond Core Drill Mfrs. Assn. (past pres.), AIME, ASCE, Soc. Profl Engrs., U.S. Nat. Council Soil Mechanics, Indsl. Diamond Assn. Am. (past pres.), C. of C. Presbyn. Clubs: Mining (N.Y.C.); Scranton, M.I.T. (Scranton, Pa.). Contbr. articles to Mining Congress Jour., Mining Engring., Engring. and Mining Jour., Diamond Drill Handbook. Home: 5 Overlook Rd Clarks Green PA 18411 Office: 221 West Olive St Scranton PA 18501

ROSS, ANDREW, publisher; b. Oct. 23, 1930. MA, Oxford (Eng.) U. Mng. dir. NTP Bus. Jours., 1968-70, FT Bus. Pubs., 1970-72; mng. dir. Morgan-Grampian Profl. Press, 1973-78, dir., 1973-83; mng. dir. Fin. Weekly, 1979-82; chmn. The Countryman, Ltd., 1984—, Geog. Press, Ltd., 1984—; dir. Punch Pubs., Ltd., 1987—. contbr. numerous articles to various newspapers. Mem. Inst. of Dirs., Peridocial Pubs. Assn. Office: United Newspapers plc, 23-27 Tudor St, London EC4Y OHR, England

ROSS, CARLOS EDGAR, technology consultant; b. Monterrey, Mexico, Nov. 29, 1947; s. Gaston and Lilly (Scheede) R.; m. Maria Elena Eager, Sept. 10, 1971. BS in Mech. Engring., U. Tex., 1970, MS in Ops. Research, 1971; MBA, Inst. Tech. de Estudios Superiores de Monterrey, 1976. Systems analyst Grupo Vitro, Monterrey, 1971-74; mgr. informatics planning Grupo Cydsa, S.A., Monterrey, 1975-80; ptnr. Proa Consultores, S.C., Monterrey, 1981—; cons. curriculum devel. U. Regiomontana, Monterrey, 1982-83, tech. devel. Consejo Nat. de Ciencia y Tech., Mexico City, 1984-86. Developer TEAM group integration model, 1980. Mem. Assn. Mexican Info. Profls. (founder, sec. 1983-85), U. Tex. Ex-Alumni Assn. (founder, v.p. 1979-86), World Future Soc. Club: Sierra Madre Tennis (Garza Garcia, Mex.) (pres. 1987—). Home: Plaza de San Marcos 208, Valle de San Angel Garza Garcia, 66290 Nuevo Leon Mexico Office: Proa Cons SC, Calzada del Valle 400 Local 77, Garza Garcia, 66220 Nuevo Leon Mexico

ROSS, CHESTER WHEELER, clergyman; b. Evansville, Ind., Nov. 3, 1922; s. Mylo Wheeler and Irma (Berning) R.; A.B. cum laude, Kans. Wesleyan U., 1952; M.Div., Garrett Theol. Sem., 1954; D. Ministry, St. Paul Sch. Theology, 1979; m. Ruth Eulaine Briney, Aug. 30, 1949; children—James W., Deborah R., Judith R., Martha S., John W. Ordained to ministry United Meth. Ch., 1953; enlisted pvt. USAAF, 1942, advanced through grades to lt. col., 1968; chaplain, Africa, Europe, Alaska, Greenland, Taiwan; installation chaplain, Columbus AFB, Miss., 1972-75; ret., 1975; pastor Unity Parish, Iuka, Kans., 1975-80, Ness City (Kans.) United Meth. Ch., 1980. Instr. Parent Effectiveness Tng., 1st aid ARC; cubmaster, scoutmaster, dist. chmn. Boy Scouts Am., recipient Silver Beaver award, 1975; vol. parolee counselor; mem. USD 303 Sch. Bd. Paul Harris fellow Rotary Internat.; Decorated Air medal (2), Meritorious Service medal (2). Mem. Ness City Ministers Assn., Conf. Council on Fin. and Adminstrn., Mil. Chaplains Assn., Acad. Parish Clergy, Ret. Officers Assn., Res. O ficers Assn., Air Force Aid, Air Force Assn., Nat. Hist. Soc., Am. Assn. Christian Counselors, Appalachian Trail Conf., Menninger Found., Kans. Sheriffs Assn. Assn. Ret. Persons, Order Ky. Col., Am. Legion, VFW. Lodge: Rotary. Address: 1102 Arcade Goodland KS 67735

ROSS, CLIVE RONALD, accountant; b. Calcutta, Bengal, India, Dec. 29, 1939; arrived in Australia, 1966; s. Dennis Eric Arnold and Catherina Myrtle (Farnworth) R.; m. Jean Margaret Mercer, Feb. 4, 1961; children: Richard, Alison, Jacqueline, Felicity. B in Bus., West Australian Inst. Tech., Perth, 1980. With News Ltd., Perth, 1967—, acct., 1973-75, fin. acct., 1975-84, chief acct., 1985—. Mem. Inst. Chartered Secs. and Adminstrs., Australian Inst. Mgmt., Nat. Inst. Accts., Inst. Personnel Mgmt. Australian, Alexander Hamilton Inst. U.S.A. Mem. Liberal Party. Roman Catholic. Clubs: Sundowners (treas. 1973-82), St. Thomas' Old Pupils Assn. (treas. 1987—). Home: 7 Stedman Pkwy, Leeming, Western Australia 6155, Australia Office: News Ltd, 34 Stirling St, Perth, Western Australia 6000, Australia

ROSS, COLEMAN DEVANE, accountant; b. Greensboro, N.C., Mar. 18, 1943; s. Guy Matthews and Nancy McConnell (Coleman) R.; B.S. in Bus. Adminstrn., U. N.C., 1965; postgrad. Sch. of Banking of South, 1982-84; m. Carol Louise Morde, Aug. 26, 1965; children—Coleman, Jonathan, Andrew. With Price Waterhouse, Tampa, 1965-76, Toronto, 1970, Hartford, Conn., 1976—, ptnr., 1977—, mng. ptnr. Nat. Ins. INdustry Services Group, 1988—. Exec. bd., Long Rivers Council, Boy Scouts Am., 1978—, pres. 1985-88, exec. bd. Northeast Region, Boy Scouts Am., 1988—, pres. New Eng. area, 1988—; div. campaign chmn. United Way of Capital Area, 1984; bd. dirs., treas. Family Service Soc. Greater Hartford, 1977-80. C.P.A., C.L.U.; chartered bank auditor. Fellow Life Mgmt. Inst.; mem. Am. Inst. C.P.A.s (ins. cos. com. 1985—, reins. auditing and acctg. task force 1979-85, relations with actuaries com. 1982-85), N.C. Assn. C.P.A.s, Conn. Soc. C.P.A.s, Soc. Ins. Accts., Am. Soc. CLUs, Nat. Soc. chartered bank auditors. Clubs: Hartford (bd. govs. 1977-84), Hop Meadow Country. Home: 11 Neal Dr Simsbury CT 06070 Office: 1 Financial Plaza Hartford CT 06103

ROSS, DALE GARAND, therapist, programming consultant, speaker, writer; b. Detroit, May 31, 1948; s. Stanley Anthony and Kathleen Mary (Moore) Jamros. B.S. in Psychology, Mich. State U., 1970; M.S.W., Wayne State U., 1980. Cert. Nat. Acad. Cert. Social Workers, Nat. Cert. Counselor, Cert. Social Worker, State Mich. Ptnr. Unicorns, Detroit, 1970-76; pres. Realities, Ltd., Birmingham, Mich., 1976-78; counselor I univ. counseling Wayne State U., Detroit, 1980-82, counselor II ednl. resources/disabilities, 1982-84, counselor II, univ. counseling, 1984-85; therapist Substance Abuse Ctr., Warren, Mich., 1985 ; pvt. practice, Southfield, Mich., 1985—; mem. Wellness Networks, Inc., Detroit, 1983-84; cons. in field; presenter programs. Contbr. articles to profl. jours. Pres., chmn. protem, founding mem. Wellness House Mich., 1985-87; mem. steering com. Venereal Disease Action Coalition United Community Services, 1986—, steering com. Macomb County AIDS Community Council, chmn. 1988, Hospice AIDS Task Force, 1986—, AIDS Related Communication Coalition, 1986—; mem. AIDS speakers bur. and AIDA phone network Mich. State Med. Soc., 1987. Program chmn. Motor City Bus. Forum, 1983-84, chmn. community ctr. com., 1982-83. Recipient Am. Legion award, 1966, Library Key award Hazel Park Pub. Schs., 1966; Mich. Bd. Govs. grantee, 1978-79, 79-80. Mem. Nat. Assn. Social Workers, Am Coll. Personnel Assn., (men's task force), Nat. Orgn. for Changing Men (co-chmn. job-work satisfaction task group 1986), Internat. Platform Assn., Mich. Orgn. for Human Rights, World Future Soc., Mich. Alcohol and Addiction Assn., Am. Assn. Counseling Devel. Avocations: antiques; ceramics. Home: 2366 Earlmont Berkley MI 48072 Office: 206 Americana Plaza 28475 Greenfield Southfield MI 48076

ROSS, DIANA, singer, actress, entertainer, fashion designer; b. Detroit, Mar. 26, 1944; d. Fred and Ernestine R.; m. Robert Ellis Silberstein, Jan. 1971 (div. 1976); children: Rhonda, Tracee, Chudney; m. Arne Naess, Oct. 23, 1985; 1 son: Ross Arne. Grad. high sch. Pres. Diana Ross Enterprises, Inc., fashion and merchandising, Anaid Film Prodns., Inc., RTC Mgmt. Corp., artists mgmt., Chondee Inc., Rosstown, Rossville, music pub. Lead singer until 1969, Diana Ross and the Supremes; solo artist, 1969—; albums include Diana Ross, 1970, 76, Everything Is Everything, 1971, I'm Still Waiting, 1971, Lady Sings The Blues, 1972, Touch Me In The Morning, 1973, Original Soundtrack of Mahogany, 1975, Baby It's Me, 1977, The Wiz, 1978, Ross, 1978, 83, The Boss, 1979, Diana, 1981, To Love Again, 1981, Why Do Fools Fall In Love?, 1981, Silk Electric, 1982, Swept Away, 1984, Eaten Alive, 1985, Chain Reaction, 1986; films include Lady Sings the Blues, 1972, Mahogany, 1975, The Wiz, 1978; NBC-TV spl., An Evening With Diana Ross, 1977, Diana, 1981, numerous others. Recipient citation Vice Pres. Humphrey for efforts on behalf Pres. Johnson's Youth Opportunity Program, citation Mrs. Martin Luther King and Rev. Abernathy for contbn. to SCLC cause, awards Billboard, Cash Box and Record World as worlds outstanding singer, Grammy award, 1970, Female Entertainer of Year NAACP, 1970, Cue award as Entertainer of year, 1972, Golden Apple award, 1972, Gold medal award Photoplay, 1972, Antoinette Perry award, 1977, nominee as best actress of year for Lady Sings the Blues Motion Picture Acad. Arts and Scis., 1972, Golden Globe award, 1972; named to Rock and Roll Hall of Fame, 1988. Office: RTC Mgmt PO Box 1683 New York NY 10185 also: care Shelly Berger 6255 Sunset Blvd Los Angeles CA 90028 *

ROSS, DONALD EDWARD, engineer; b. N.Y.C., May 2, 1930; m. Jeanne Ellen McKessy, Apr. 4, 1954; children—Susan, Christopher, Carolyn. B.A., Columbia U., 1952, B.S. in Mech. Engring., 1953; M.B.A., NYU, 1960. Registered profl. engr., N.Y., N.J., Calif. Engr. Carrier Corp., N.Y.C., 1955-70; v.p. Dynadata, 1970-71; with. Jaros, Baum & Bolles, 1971—, ptnr. 1977— . Chmn. profl. liability com. Am. Cons. Engrs. Council, Washington, 1984—; mem. engring. council Columbia U. Sch. Engring and Applied Sci. Mem. faculty and alumni adv. council Columbia U. Served to lt. (j.g.) USN, 1953-55. Fellow ASHRAE; mem. ASME, Nat. Soc. Profl. Engrs., N.Y. Assn. Cons. Engrs. (pres. 1984-86, council on tall bldgs. and urban habitat), Nat. Bur. Engrs. Clubs: Univ. (N.Y.C.), Nassau Country (Glen Cove, N.Y.). Office: Jaros Baum & Bolles 345 Park Ave New York NY 10154

ROSS, DONALD KEITH, insurance company executive; b. Rochester, N.Y., July 1, 1925; s. Alexander L. and Althea G. (Granger) R.; m. Mary F. Fyffe, June 4, 1949; children: Catherine (Mrs. Charles P. Lesher), Susan (Mrs. William Gardner Morris, Jr.), Donald Keith, Deborah Anne (Mrs. Michael Holt). B.E., Yale U., 1946; M.B.A., Harvard U., 1948. With N.Y. Life Ins. Co., N.Y.C., 1948—, exec. v.p., 1974-79, vice chmn., 1979-80, pres., 1980-81, chmn. bd., chief exec. officer, 1981—, also dir.; trustee Consol. Edison of N.Y. Trustee Colonial Williamsburg (Va.) Found.; chmn. N.Y. Life Found.; chmn. bd. dirs. YMCA. Club: Links. Office: NY Life Ins Co 51 Madison Ave New York NY 10010

ROSS, DORIS G., civic worker; b. Thompsonville, Conn.; d. Philip A. and Eva (Saffir) Sisitzky; student Barnard Coll., Max Reinhardt Drama Workshop, N.Y. U. Radio Workshop, Lee Strasberg Theatre Inst., Royal Acad. Dramatic Arts; m. Lewis H. Ross, Jan. 4, 1942; children—Phyllis, Allyne. Dir. New Eng. Zionist Youth Com., 1943-45; dir. theatre arts Manchester Inst. Arts and Scis., 1947-48; pres. Manchester Girls Clubs, 1950-51, dir., 1949-53, 54-58, 59-69, chmn. nat. adv. bd. Girls Clubs Am., 1955-57, v.p., 1956-57, pres., 1957-59, chmn. 15th Ann. Conf., 1960, first acting chmn. past pres. com., 1974, 1st pres. past pres. club, 1975-77, chmn. 15th ann. conf., 1960, chmn. silver jubilee com., 1969-70, chmn. directions and social concerns com., 1978-79, founder Children's Creative Theatre, 1978, chmn., 1979-81; hon. mem., 1981—; exec. com. Girls Clubs N.Y., 1970-73, bd. dirs., 1970-73, sustaining dir., 1973—, co-chmn. long range planning com., 1970-71; 1st pres. Theatre Art Players, Temple Emanuel, N.Y.C., 1970-71; trustee Actors Studio, 1978-82, 84, conceived Actors Studio Achievement awards celebration, 1981; dir. Manchester Settlement Assn., 1951-54, Manchester Vis. Nurses Assn., 1955-61; del. Nat. Soc. Welfare Assembly, 1957-59, White House Conf. on Children and Youth, 1960, voting del. nat. council state coms., 1960, mem. N.H. state exec. com., 1960, N.H. state sub-com. on Leisure Times Activities chmn., 1960; charter colleague Nat. Assembly Nat. Voluntary Health and Welfare Orgns., Inc., 1976—, mem. Nat. Juvenile Justice Program Collaboration, Mem. Pres.'s Citizens Adv. Com. on Fitness of Am. Youth, 1958-60; mem. exec. com. Gov.'s Com. on Children and Youth, 1961-63; Gov.'s rep. to Pres.'s Conf. on Youth Fitness, 1962; pres. Manchester Garden Club, 1963-64; dir. Opera League New Hampshire, Inc., 1964-69; trustee Actors Studio, 1978-82. Mem. Hadassah (pres. Manchester chpt. 1943-44, dir. Manchester chpt. 1942-49, New Eng. regional v.p. 1944-46). Address: 985 Fifth Ave New York NY 10021

ROSS, EDWARD, physician; b. Fairfield, Ala., Oct. 10, 1937; s. Horace and Carrie Lee (Griggs) R.; B.S., Clark Coll., 1959; M.D., Ind. U., 1963; m. Catherine I. Webster, Jan. 19, 1974; children—Edward, Ronald, Cheryl, Anthony. Intern, Marion County Gen. Hosp., Indpls., 1963; resident in internal medicine Ind. U., 1964-66, 68, cardiology research fellowship, 1968-70, clin. asst. prof. medicine, 1970; cardiologist Capitol Med. Assn., Indpls., 1970-74; pvt. practice medicine, specializing in cardiology, Indpls., 1974—; staff cardiologist Winona Meml. Hosp., Indpls.; Methodist Hosp., Indpls. Mem. Central Ind. Health Planning Council, 1972-73; dir. Ind. chpt. Am. Heart Assn., 1973-74; dir. multiphasic screening East Side Clinic, Flanner Ho. of Indpls., 1968-71; med. dir. Nat. Center for Health Service Research and Devel., HEW, 1970; consumer rep. radiologic device panel Health, Food and Drug Adminstrn., 1988—; dir. hyptertensive screening State of Ind., 1974. Served to capt., MC, USAF, 1966-68. Woodrow Wilson fellow, 1959; Nat. Found. Health scholar, 1955; Gorgas Found. scholar, 1955. Diplomate Am. Bd. Internal Medicine. Fellow Royal Soc. Promotion of Health (Eng.), Am. Coll. Angiology (v.p. fgn. affairs), Internat. Coll. of Angiology, Am. Coll. Cardiology; mem. AMA, Am. Soc. Contemporary Medicine and Surgery, Nat. Med. Assn. (council sci. assembly 1985-89), Ind. Med. Soc., Marion County Med. Soc., Am. Soc. Internal Medicine, Am. Heart Assn., Ind. Soc. Internal Medicine (pres. 1987-89), Ind. State Med. Assn. (chmn. internat. medicine sect. 1987-89), Aesculapean Med. Soc., Hoosier State Med. Assn. (pres. 1980-85), NAACP, Urban League, Alpha Omega Alpha, Alpha Kappa Mu, Beta Kappa Chi, Omega Psi Phi. Baptist. Sr. editor Jour. Vascular Medicine, 1983—. Office: 3171 N Meridian St Suite 201 Indianapolis IN 46208

ROSS, IAN MUNRO, electrical engineer; b. Southport, Eng., Aug. 15, 1927; came to U.S., 1952, naturalized, 1960; m. Christina Leinberg Ross, Aug. 24, 1955; children: Timothy Ian, Nancy Lynn, Stina Marguerite. BA, Gonville and Caius Coll., Cambridge (Eng.) U., 1948; MA in Elec. Engring, Cambridge U., 1952, PhD, 1952; DSc (hon.), N.J. Inst. Tech., 1983; D of Engring. (hon.), Stevens Inst. Tech., 1983. With AT&T Bell Labs. (and affiliates), 1952—, exec. dir. network planning div., 1971-73, v.p. network planning and customer services, 1973-76; exec. v.p. systems engring. and devel. AT&T Bell Labs. (and affiliates), Holmdel, N.J., 1976-79; pres. AT&T Bell Labs. (and affiliates), 1979—; dir. Thomas & Betts Corp., B.F. Goodrich Co. Recipient Liebmann Meml. prize IEEE, 1963, Pub. Service award NASA, 1969, Founders medal IEEE, 1988. Fellow IEEE (Liebmann Meml. prize 1963, Founders medal 1988), Am. Acad. Arts and Scis.; mem. Nat. Acad. Engring. Home: 5 Blackpoint Horseshoe Rumson NJ 07760 Office: AT&T Bell Labs Crawfords Corner Rd Holmdel NJ 07733

ROSS, J. ANDREW, mathematics and physics advisor, researcher, writer; b. Luton, U.K., Nov. 13, 1949; s. Robert and Elizabeth (Appleyard) Pigdon. MA, U. Oxford, 1972, MS, 1974, M Philosophy, 1976, M Litt, 1980. Philosophy tutor N.E. London Poly., 1973-74, St. Annes Coll., Oxford, Eng., 1976-77; adminstrv. trainee Ministry of Def., London, 1977-78; ad. rep. Internat. Pub. Corp., London, 1979; English tutor Oxford Sch. English, 1980; physics tutor Davies Laing, Dick, London, 1980-81; English tutor Green English Sch., Shizuoka, Japan, 1981-82; physics and math. lectr. Lansdowne Coll., London, 1982-87; editor in physics and math. Springer-Verlag, Heidelberg, Fed. Republic of Germany, 1987—; freelance journalist Internat. Pub. Corp., London, 1979-80. Author: Dialectical Logic I, 1975, Dialectical Logic II, 1977, Dialectical Logic III, 1979, Life: The Past and Future Evolution of Human Civilization, 1985. Action coordinator UN Assn., Oxford, 1970; com. mem. 1st Div. Assn., London, 1978. Leverhulme studentship London Sch. Econs., 1972-74, Amelia Jackson studentship Exeter Coll., Oxford, 1974-77. Mem. Am. Physical Soc., Am. Math. Soc., Planetary Soc. Home: St Peter St 17, 6900 Heidelberg Federal Republic of Germany

ROSS, JOHN MUNDER, psychologist, educator; b. N.Y.C., June 20, 1945; s. Nathaniel and Barbara Evangela (Munder) R.; BA magna cum laude, Harvard Coll., 1967; PhD, NYU, 1974; Cert., N.Y.U. Med. Ctr. Psychoanalytic Inst., 1984. m. Katherine Ball, Aug. 17, 1974; 1 son, Matthew Ross. Asst. prof. Ferkauf Grad. Sch., 1976-78; vis. asst. prof. Albert Einstein Coll. Medicine, 1977-78; clin. asst. prof. Downstate Med. Center, Bklyn., 1978-80, clin. assoc. prof., 1980-84; clin. instr. Cornell Med. Coll., N.Y.C., 1978-80, adj. asst. prof., 1980-84, adj. assoc. prof., 1984—, clin. assoc. prof., 1985—; faculty mem. The Psychoanalytic Inst. NYU Med. Ctr. Bd. dirs. Bank St. Fatherhood Project. Recipient Detur Prize Harvard Coll.; Disting. Teaching award Downstate Med. Center, 1979; award for outstanding book in behavioral scis. Am. Assn. Pubs., 1982; Leverhulme fellow, 1968-69; NIMH fellow, 1967-68, 69-71. Mem. Am. Psychol. Assn., Am. Psychoanalytic Assn., Internat. Psychoanalytical Assn., N.Y. State Psychol. Assn., Phi Beta Kappa. Democrat. Club: Harvard (N.Y.C.) Editor: (with S. H. Cath, A. R. Gurwitt) Father and Child, 1982, (with G. Pollock) The Oedipus Papers, 1988, (with W.A. Myers) New Concepts in Psychoanalytic Psychotherapy, 1988; author (with Sudhir Kakar) Tales of Love, Sex and Danger; editor-in-chief Internat. Jour. Psychoanalytic Psychotherapy, 1984—; research editor Psychoanalytic Edn., 1984—; contbr. articles to profl. jours. Home: 277 West End Ave New York NY 10023 Office: 243 West End Ave New York NY 10023

ROSS, JUDITH PARIS, life insurance executive; b. Boston, Dec. 23, 1939; d. Max and Ruth Paris; ed. Boston U., 1961, UCLA, 1978; grad. Life Underwriting Tng. Council, 1978; 1 son, Adam Stuart. Producer, co-host Checkpoint TV show, Washington, 1967-71; hostess Judi Says TV show, Washington, 1969; brokerage supr., specialist impaired risk underwriting Beneficial Nat. Life Ins. Co. (now Nat. Benefit Life), Beverly Hills, Calif., 1973-82, dir. Salary Savs. program for West Coast, 1982-87; ins. and benefits specialist, cons. Alliance Assocs., 1987—; mktg. dir. Brougher Ins. Group, 1982-87; ins. and benefits specialist Alliance Assocs., Beverly Hills, 1987—; featured speaker ins. industry seminars. Active local PTA, Boy Scouts Am., Beverly Hills local politics; mem. early childhood edn. adv. com. Beverly Hills Unified Sch. Dist., 1977. Mem. Nat. Assn. Life Underwriters, Calif. Assn. Life Underwriters (dir. W. Los Angeles 1980—, v.p. chpt. 1982—, chmn. pub. relations), West Los Angeles Life Underwriters Assn. (v.p. fin. 1983-84). Office: Alliance Assocs 449 S Beverly Dr #206 Beverly Hills CA 90212

ROSS, MALCOLM MACKENZIE, English literature educator, consultant; b. Fredericton, N.B., Can., Jan. 2, 1911; s. Charles Duff and Cora Elizabeth (Hewitson) R.; m. Lois Natalie Hall; 1 child, Julie Martha. B.A., U. N.B., 1933, D.Litt. (hon.), 1962; M.A., U. Toronto, 1934; Ph.D., Cornell U., 1941; LL.D. (hon.), St. Thomas U., Fredericton, N.B., 1976, Dalhousie U., Halifax, N.S., 1983; D. Litt. (hon.), Trent U., Peterborough, Ont., 1982, U. Edinburgh, 1986. Asst. prof., assoc. prof., then prof. English lit. U. Man., Winnipeg, 1945-50; prof. Queen's U., Kingston, 1950-57, chmn. dept., 1957-62, James Cappon prof., 1960-62; prof. Trinity Coll., U. Toronto, 1962-68, dean of arts, 1965-68, acting provost, 1967-68; prof. Dalhousie U., Halifax, N.S., 1968—, Thomas McCulloch prof., 1973-82, prof. emeritus, 1982—; vis. prof. U. Edinburgh, Scotland, 1982-83; mem. acad. panel Can. Council, Ottawa, Ont., 1966-68, vice-chmn. arts panel, 1980-84, mem. awards juries, 1974-76; mem. grants com. Nuffield Found., 1961-62; bd. dirs. Nat. Library Can., Ottawa, 1977-80, Can. Inst. Hist. Microreprodns., Ottawa, 1979—; mem. council. Can. Inst. Advanced Research, Toronto, 1982—. Author: Milton's Royalism, 1943; Poetry and Dogma, 1954; The Impossible Sum of our Traditions, 1986. Editor: Our Sense of Identity, 1954; New Canadian Library, 196 vols., 1958—; Man and His World, 1961; Queen's Quarterly, 1953-56; The Arts in Canada, 1958; mem. editorial bd. Lit. History of Can., Can. Poetry, English Studies in Can. Contbr. articles and original poetry to publs. Mem. Halifax com. Atlantic Symphony, 1970-73; bd. dirs. Neptune Theatre, Halifax, 1973-76; mem. ministries com. Diocese of N.S., 1977-81. Guggenheim fellow, 1949-50; grantee Nuffield Found., 1957, Can. Council, 1959; officer Order Can.; recipient award in Can. Studies No. Telecom Internat., 1985. Fellow Royal Soc. Can. (pres. acad. II 1970-71; Lorne Pierce medal 1982); mem. Humanities Assn. Can., Assn. Can. Univ. Tchrs. English. Anglican. Avocation: music. Home: 1750 Connaught Ave, Halifax, NS Canada B3H 4C8 Office: Dalhousie U Dept English, 1434 Henry St, Halifax, NS Canada B3H 3J5

ROSS, MICHAEL AARON, lawyer; b. Newark, Sept. 15, 1941; s. Alexander Ash and Matilda (Blumenthal) R.; m. Leslie Gordon, June 26, 1976; children—Christopher Gordon, Alan Gordon. B.A., Franklin and Marshall Coll., 1963; J.D., Columbia U., 1966; M.S. in Econs., U. London, 1967. Bar: N.Y. 1968. Assoc., then ptnr. Shearman & Sterling, N.Y.C., 1967—; dir. MFY Legal Services Inc. Mem. ABA, New York County Lawyers Assn., Bar City N.Y. Club: University. Office: Shearman & Sterling 599 Lexington Ave at 53rd St New York NY 10022

ROSS, OTHO BESCENT, III, lawyer; b. Charlotte, N.C., July 23, 1951; s. Otho B. Jr. and Dorothy (Lowe) R. BS in Engring. magna cum laude with distinction, Duke U., 1974; JD, U. N.C., 1977. Bar: N.Y. 1978, U.S. Dist. Ct. (so. and ea. dists.) N.Y. 1978, U.S. Ct. Claims, 1987, U.S. Patent and Trademark Office, 1987. Assoc. Gaston, Snow, Beekman and Bogue, N.Y.C., 1980-83; sr. atty. Sony Corp. Am., Park Ridge, N.J., 1983-87; assoc. Stiefel, Gross and Kurland, N.Y.C., 1987-88, atty. IBM Corp., East Fishkill, N.Y., 1988—; mem. Vol. Lawyers for the Arts, N.Y.C., 1987. Research editor N.C. Law Rev., 1976; contbr. articles to Jour. Patent Office Soc. Mem. Assn. Bar City N.Y., ABA, N.Y. Patent, Trademark and Copyright Law Assn., Eta Kappa Nu. Avocations: music, tennis. Home: 30 Waterside Plaza #30-G New York NY 10010

ROSS, RANDOLPH ERNEST, portfolio manager; b. N.Y.C., Mar. 17, 1955; s. David Harvey and Pearl (Frandsen) R.; m. Joan Frances Healey, Apr. 2, 1982. A.B. in History, Brown U., 1977; M.B.A. in Fin., Columbia U., 1981. Chartered fin. analyst. Nat. editor WEAN Radio (CBS affiliate), Providence, 1977-79; research analyst, asst. v.p. Kidder, Peabody & Co., Inc., N.Y.C., 1981-85; research analyst First Manhattan Co., N.Y.C., 1985-86; portfolio mgr. Brundage, Story and Rose, N.Y.C., 1986—. Fundraiser Brown U., Providence, 1981-87, Grad. Sch. of Bus., Columbia U., 1985. Fellow Fin. Analysts Fedn.; mem. Inst. Chartered Fin. Analysts, N.Y. Soc. Security Analysts, N.Y. Hist. Soc., L.I. Hist. Soc. Republican. Clubs: Columbia (N.Y.C.), Brown. Avocations: sailing; archtl. and urban history; fiction; music. Office: Brundage Story and Rose One Broadway New York NY 10004

ROSS, ROBERT DONALD, librarian; b. N.Y.C., Mar. 28, 1931; s. William and Ceceile (Cross) Rosenfeld; B.A., CCNY, 1954; postgrad. NYU, 1960-64, Columbia U., 1968; M.L.S., Rutgers U., 1966; m. Madeleine Ladner, May 28, 1961; children—Jeffrey Laurence, Jodie Dianne. Reference librarian Bklyn. Pub. c Library, 1965; reader services librarian, asst. prof. Suffolk County (N.Y.) Community Coll., 1966-69; dir. South Brunswick (N.J.) Pub. Library, 1969-73, Ridgewood (N.J.) Pub. Library, 1973—; adj. prof. Middlesex County (N.J.) Community Coll., 1973-76. Mem. exec. bd. South Brunswick Community Council, 1970-73; adv. com. Nat. Project Center for Film and Humanities, N.Y.C., 1971-75; treas. Bergen-Passaic Regional Library Coop., 1987—, mem. exec. bd., 1986—; mem. Ridgewood Bicentennial Commn., 1975-76. Mem. ALA (chmn. discussion group com. fund raising and fin. devel. sect. library adminstrn. and mgmt. div. 1984-85), N.J. Library Assn. (library devel. com. 1977—, chmn. edn. for librarianship com. 1982-83, govt. relations com. 1982-86, 100th anniversary com. 1988—), Libraries of South Middlesex (chmn. 1970-73), North Bergen Fedn. Libraries (chmn. dirs. council 1975), Bergen County Coop. Library System (pres., treas. 1982-83, 86-87, exec. bd. computer consortium 1987—), Ridgewood C. of C. (bd. dirs. 1983-88, treas. 1988—), Soc. Valley Hosp. Club: Ridgewood Kiwanis (pres., treas. 1987-88, Disting. Club Pres. award 1983). Home: 351 Walthery Ave Ridgewood NJ 07450 Office: Ridgewood Pub Library 125 N Maple Ave Ridgewood NJ 07450

ROSS, ROBERT LIVINGSTONE, development banker; b. Washington, Nov. 18, 1933 s. Emerson Adams and Florence Laverne (Atkins) Dunham R.; m. Myriam Briones, May 15, 1965; children: Christopher, Charlotte, Andrea. Student Université de Neuchâtel, Switzerland, 1950-51; cert. Ecole Nat. des Langues Orientales Vivantes, Paris, 1952; B.A. in Econs., Harvard U., 1956; M.A. in Econs., Georgetown U., 1964. News writer Voice of Am., Washington, 1959-60; adminstrv. asst. UN Econ. Commn. for Latin Am., Washington, 1960-61, economist, Port-au-Prince, Haiti, 1961-62; economist UN Inst. for Econ. and Social Planning, Santiago, Chile, 1962-65; v.p. Adela Investment Co., Washington, Lima, Peru, 1965-72; pres. Latin Am. Agribus. Devel. Corp., Coral Gables, Fla, 1972—; dir. Trade Wind Industries, Turks and Caicos, Hortifrut S.A., Chile. Mem. Presidential Task Force on Agrl. Devel. in Central Am. and the Caribbean, 1979-80; mem. Presidential Task Force on Agrl. Devel. in Peru, 1982; adj. prof. Grad. Sch. Internat. Studies, U. Miami, Coral Gables, Fla., 1983—; trustee Miami Project to Cure Paralysis. Served with U.S. Army, 1956-58. Mem. Coral Gables C. of C. Club: Country (Coral Gables). Office: Latin Am Agribus Devel Corp 306 Alcazar Suite 3A Coral Gables FL 33134

ROSS, RUSSELL, pathologist; St. Augustine, Fla., May 25, 1929; s. Samuel and Minnie (DuBoff) R.; A.B., Cornell U., 1951; D.D.S., Columbia U., 1955; Ph.D., U. Wash., 1962; DSc (hon.), Med. Coll. Pa., 1987; m. Jean Long Teller, Feb. 22, 1956; children—Valerie Regina, Douglas Teller. Intern, Columbia-Presbyn. Med. Center, 1955-56, USPHS Hosp., Seattle, 1956-58; spl. research fellow pathology U. Wash. Sch. Medicine, 1958-62, asst. prof. pathology and oral biology U. Wash. Sch. Medicine and Dentistry, 1962-65, asso. prof. pathology, 1965-69, prof., 1969—, chmn. dept., 1982—, adj. prof. biochemistry, 1978—, assoc. dean for sci. affairs Sch. of Medicine, 1971-78; vis. scientist Strangeways Research Lab., Cambridge, Eng.; mem. research com. Am. Heart Assn.; mem. adv. bd. Found. Cardiologique Princess Liliane, Brussels, Belgium; mem. nat. research adv. bd. Cleve. Clinic Found.; vis. fellow Clare Hall, Cambridge U. Recipient Gordon Wilson med. Am. Clin. and Climatol. Assn., 1981. John Simon Guggenheim fellow, 1966-67; mem. nat. heart, lung and blood adv. council Nat. Heart, Lung and Blood Inst., NIH, 1978-81. Fellow Japan Soc. for Promotion of Sci.; mem. Am. Soc. Cell Biology, Tissue Culture Assn., Gerontol. Soc., Am. Assn. Pathologists, Internat. Soc. Cell Biology, Electron Microscope Soc. Am., Am. Heart Assn. (fellow Council on Arteriosclerosis), Royal Microscopical Soc., AAAS, Belgian Acad. Medicine (fgn. corr. mem.), Nat. Acad. Scis., Inst. Medicine, Harvey Soc. (hon.). Sigma Xi. Mem. editorial bds. Proceedings Exptl. Biology and Medicine, 1971—, Jour. Cell Biology, 1972-74, Exptl. Cell Research, Am. Jour. Pathology; asso. editor Jour. Cell Physiology, Jour. Cellular Biochemistry, Arteriosclerosis, and other jours. Contbr. articles in field of arteriosclerosis research and wound healing to profl. jours. Home: 4811 NE 42d St Seattle WA 98105 Office: U of Wash Sch Medicine SM-30 Seattle WA 98195

ROSS, STANLEY, editor, publisher; b. N.Y.C., Jan. 18, 1914; s. Harry Paul and Bella R.; m. Eleanore Lyle, July 1, 1948 (dec. Feb. 1960); 1 child, Michael Stanley; m. Countess Margarita Theresa Parravicini. Student, CCNY, 1932-36, U. Caracas, Venezuela, 1941-43. Editor The Argus, 1932-34; owner of 9 weeklies under corporate name Stanley Ross Assos., 1936; N.Y. Times corr. Venezuela and other S.Am. countries, 1940-43; pub. relations adviser to Pres. of Venezuela, 1941-43; traveled widely through Latin and S.Am. for U.S. mags. 1940-47; AP and NBC corr. Argentina, 1943-45; organized Latin Am. Press Syndicate (serving 700 Latin Am. papers), 1946; founder, pub., editor El Caribe and El Urgente (daily papers), Dominican Republic, 1947-49; pub., editor The Star, Wilmington, Del., 1948-50; editor N.Y. Amsterdam News, 1951; editor in chief, assoc. pub. El Diario de Nueva York (daily newspaper), 1955-62; editor-in-chief Bklyn. Eagle, 1962-63, La Prensa (daily), 1961-62; editor, pub. El Tiempo, N.Y.C., 1963-69, 73-75, El Mundo, N.Y.C., 1969-71; also editor in chief L.I. (N.Y.) Post; internat. editor ABC of the Americas and, Madrid; cons. on Latin Am. Affairs Dept. Justice; lectr. Latin Am. affairs, throughout U.S., 1948. Author semi-weekly articles appearing in 245 Latin Am. papers.; Author: Communism in Latin America, 1947, The War for Trade in Latin America, 1947, Axel Wenner-Gren, The Sphinx of Sweden, 1948. Decorated comdr. Order Ruben Dario (Nicaragua). Mem. Assn. de Escritores Americanos (1st U.S. citizen elected pres. 1946, 47), Nat. Soc. Prevention Juvenile Delinquency (hon. pres.), N.Y. Advt. Club. Republican. Clubs: Masons, Overseas Press. Home: 230 E 48th St New York NY 10017

ROSS, STEVEN J., communications company executive; b. N.Y.C., 1927. Student, Paul Smith's Coll., 1948. Pres., dir. Kinney Services Inc., 1966-72; chmn. bd., chief exec. officer Warner Communications Inc., N.Y.C., 1972—, pres., from 1972; Bd. dirs. N.Y. Conv. and Visitors Bur., N.Y. State Alliance to Save Energy; mem. bd. sports medicine Lenox Hill Hosp. Office: Warner Communications Inc 75 Rockefeller Plaza New York NY 10019 *

ROSS, SUZANNE IRIS, fund raising executive; b. Chgo., Feb. 2, 1948; d. Irving and Rose (Stein) R. BA in Secondary Edn., Western Mich. U., 1971. Dir. youth employment Ill. Youth Services Bur., Maywood, Ill., 1978-79; exec. dir. Edn. Resource Ctr., Chgo., 1979-82; asst. dir. devel. Art Inst. Chgo., 1982-83, mgr. govt. affairs, 1983-84, dir. govt. affairs, 1984-85; v.p. devel. Spertus Coll. Judaica, Chgo., 1985—; lectr. Sch. Art Inst., Chgo., 1982-85, Ill. Fire Inspectors Assn., Mt. Prospect, Ill., 1982-84, Episcopalian Archdiocese, Chgo., 1984, Nat. Soc. Fund Raising Execs. and Donor's Forum, Chgo., 1987; instr. DePaul U. Sch. for New Learning, 1987, Columbia Coll., Chgo., 1980—. Mem. adv. council Citizens Com. on Media, Chgo., 1978-80; adv. panelist Chgo. Office Fine Arts, 1981-82; mem. adv. council Greater Chgo. Food Depository, 1984-85; exec. com. Chgo. Coalition Arts in Edn., 1981-82; mem. info. services com. Donors' Forum Chgo., 1986—, mem. adv. bd. Chgo. Moving Co., 1987—. Mem. Nat. Soc. Fund Raising Execs., Am. Assn. Mus., Am. Council Arts, Ill. Arts Alliance. Democrat. Jewish. Avocation: attending cultural events. Home: 3709 N Janssen #2RB Chicago IL 60613 Office: Spertus Coll Judaica 618 S Michigan Ave Chicago IL 60605

ROSS, WILLIAM DEE, JR., economist; b. Jackson, Miss., May 16, 1921; s. William Dee and Betty (Biggs) R.; m. Nell Triplett, July 25, 1944; 1 child, William Dee III. BA, Millsaps Coll., 1942; MA, Duke U., 1947, PhD, 1951. Economist U.S. Mil. Govt. for Germany, Berlin, 1945-46; instr. econs. Duke U., Durham, N.C., 1946-49; assoc. prof. La. State U., Baton Rouge, 1949-54, prof. econs., 1954-56, dean Coll. Bus. Adminstrn., 1956-76; pres. Fin. Cons. Services, Inc., Baton Rouge, 1976—; bd. dirs. Am. Bank, Baton Rouge, Piccadilly Cafeterias Inc., others; dir. La. Hwy. Fin. Study, La. Legis. Council, 1953-54; cons. Joint House-Senate Hwy. Com., La. Legislature, La. Dept. Hwys., 1955-56; lectr. exec. devel. programs Mich. State U., Ga. Inst. Tech., La. State U.; mem. dept. econs., fin. and adminstrn. Hwy. Research Bd., Nat. Acad. Scis., Washington, 1957-64; mem. adv. council Tax Inst. Am., 1961-63. Author (with B.U. Ratchford) Berlin Reparations Assignment, 1947, Financing Highway Imporvements in Louisiana, 1955, Business in a Free Society, 1966; contbr. articles to profl. jours. Bd. dirs. area council Boy Scouts Am. Served to 1st lt. USAAF, 1943-45. Mem. Am. Assn. Collegiate Schs. Bus., Am. Econ. Assn., So. Econ. Assn. (exec. com. 1960-62), Nat. Tax Assn. (exec. com. 1960-63, editorial com. Nat. Tax Jour. 1959-62), Am. Fin. Assn., So. Fin. Assn. (pres. 1962-63), Southwestern Social Sci. Assn., Omicron Delta Kappa, Beta Gamma Sigma. Methodist. Lodge: Rotary. Home: 2763 Bocage Ct E Baton Rouge LA 70809 Office: Fin Cons Services 8555 United Plaza Blvd Suite 407 Baton Rouge LA 70809

ROSS, WILLIAM JARBOE, lawyer; b. Oklahoma City, May 9, 1930; s. Walter John and Bertha (Jarboe) R.; m. Mary Lillian Ryan, May 19, 1962; children: Rebecca Anne, Robert Joseph, Molly Kathleen. B.B.A., U. Okla., 1952, LL.B., 1954. Bar: Okla. 1954. Since practiced in Oklahoma City; asst. municipal counselor Oklahoma City, 1955-60; mem. firm Rainey, Ross, Rice & Binns, 1960—, partner, 1965—; bd. dirs. PetroUnited Terminals, Inc., PetroUnited Holdings, Inc. Bd. dirs. St. Anthony's Hosp. Found., First Interstate Bank of Okla. Mem. Okla. Bar Assn., Okla. Heritage Assn. (chmn. edn. com.), The Newcomen Soc., Phi Alpha Delta, Beta Theta Pi. Clubs: Oklahoma City Golf and Country, Econ. (Okla.). Lodges: Rotary, K.C. Home: 6923 Avondale Ct Oklahoma City OK 73116 Office: Rainey Ross Rice & Binns 735 First National Ctr W Oklahoma City OK 73102

ROSS, YAN MICHAEL, lawyer; b. N.Y.C., Dec. 2, 1942; s. Herman J. and Pauline (Chodeck) R.; m. Deedee Corradini, Mar. 21, 1981; children—Matthew Kennett, Elizabeth Feiga. A.B., Princeton U., 1964; J.D., Yale U., 1967. Bar: D.C. 1969, U.S. Supreme Ct. 1973, U.S. Ct. Appeals (10th cir.) 1980, Utah 1982. Counsel to Republican mems. banking com. U.S. Ho. of Reps., Washington, 1970-75; alt. U.S. exec. dir. Inter-Am. Devel. Bank, Washington, 1975-77; ptnr. Metzger, Shadyac & Schwarz, Washington, 1977-82; ptnr. Parsons, Behle & Latimer, Salt Lake City/Washington, 1982-87; counsel LeBoeuf, Lamb, Leiby & MacRae, Salt Lake City, 1988—; adj. prof. grad. sch. bus. U. Utah, 1986—. Trustee, Utah Heritage Found., 1982—, Utah Air Travel Commn., 1983—, chmn., 1986—. trustee Internat. Vis. Utah Council, 1986—, Salt Lake Vis. & Conv. Bur., 1988—; chmn. nat. adv. council Ballet West, 1984— Served to 1st lt. USAF, 1968-70. Mem. ABA, Fed. Bar Assn., Inter-Am. Bar Assn., Salt Lake Area C. of C. (chmn. fed. issues com. 1983-86). Episcopalian. Clubs: Ft. Douglas (Salt Lake City), Capitol Hill (Washington). Office: LeBoeuf Lamb Leiby & MacRae 136 S Main St Salt Lake City UT 84101

ROSSEL, SVEN HAKON, literature educator; b. Bangkok, Thailand, Oct. 25, 1943; came to U.S., 1974; s. Leo Hancke and Maria Katharina (Muller) R.; m. Dominika Jagiella; 1 child, Eva Maria Katharina. Ph.D., U. Copenhagen, 1968. Asst. prof. U. Hamburg, Fed. Republic of Germany, 1968-69; asst. prof. U. Kiel, Fed. Republic of Germany, 1969-71; research fellow U. Copenhagen, Denmark, 1971-74; assoc. prof. U. Wash., Seattle, 1974-80, prof., 1980—, chmn. Scandinavian dept., 1981—. Author: Den litteraere vise, 1971; A History of Scandinavian Literature, 1982; Scandinavian Ballads, 1982; Johannes V. Jensen, 1984. Co-editor: Danmarks gamle Folkeviser, 1976, H. C. Andersen's Tales, 1980, Scandinavian Literature in a Transcultural Context, 1986. Contbr. articles, revs. and translations to profl. jours. Recipient Honor award Denmark-Am. Found., Copenhagen, 1980; State of Wash. Spl. award, 1981; Am. Scandinavian Found. award, 1985. Grundtvig-Olrik grantee, 1976, 80, 83, 85, 88. Mem. Soc. for Advancement of Scandinavian Studies, Internat. Assn. Scandinavian Studies, Arbeitsgemeinschaft Norden-Deutschland, Danish Folklore Soc., Medieval Assn. of Pacific. Roman Catholic. Club: Danish (Seattle) (v.p. 1975-76). Home: 6368 NE 193rd Pl Seattle WA 98155

ROSSELOT, MAX B., university administrator; b. West Elkton, Ohio, June 30, 1913; s. Harvey L. and Gertrude (Vance) R.; A.B., Denison U., 1935; A.M., Miami U., Oxford, Ohio, 1950; postgrad. Ind. U., 1953-54, summer 1960; M.A., Columbia U., 1982; Ed.M., Columbia U., 1984; m. Lillian Anna Draut, Oct. 5, 1940; children—Deborah Rosselot Bramlage, Michael T., Keith V. (dec.), Bruce E., Rome H. Sales corr. Armco Internat. Corp., Middletown, Ohio, 1936-43; asst. to pres. E.B. Thirkield & Sons, Franklin, Ohio, 1943-46; pres. M.B. Rosselot Sales Co., Middletown, 1946-47; asst. prin., tchr. Monroe (Ohio) High Sch., 1947-49; mem. faculty Miami U., Oxford, 1949-68, assoc. registrar, asst. prof. office skills and mgmt., 1956-60, registrar and asso. prof., 1960-68; dir. univ. records and studies SUNY, Stony Brook, from 1968, dean for student adminstrv. services, from 1971, dean emeritus student adminstrv. services, psychol. counselor in gerontology; case mgr., social worker dept. for aging, City of N.Y. and Queens div. N.Y. Urban League, 1988—; cons. U. Ibadan (Nigeria), 1966-67, vis. registrar, cons. in the registry, 1972-74; cons. N.Y. State Edn. Dept. Bd. dirs. Hamilton County council Boy Scouts Am. Grantee SUNY, Rockefeller Found.; Brookdale Inst. fellow, 1982-83; recipient citation U. Ibadan. Mem. Am. Assn. Higher Edn., NEA, Am. Council on Edn., Nat. Office Mgmt. Assn. (dir., Butler County chpt. sec. 1958-60), Am. (chmn. research in admissions ann. meeting 1970, chmn. nat. standing com. 1970-72), Ohio (past sec., treas., pres. elect) assns. collegiate registrars and admissions officers, SUNY Registrars Assn. (v.p. 1974-75), AAUP (sec. Miami U. chpt. 1954-55), Common Cause, Am. Acad. Polit. and Social Scis., Nat. Assn. Student Personnel Adminstrs., Am. Acad. Arts and Scis., Assn. Community and Univ. Cooperation (v.p. 1975-76), Am. Mgmt. Assn., L.I. Coll. Student Personnel Assn. (pres. 1978-79), N.Y. Zool. Soc., Am. Mus. Natural History, ACLU, Theta Chi, Delta Pi Epsilon, Phi Delta Kappa, Kappa Delta Pi. Episcopalian. Clubs: Masons, Rotary, Old Field (gov.). Home: 96 Christian Ave Stony Brook NY 11790 also: 43-15 45th St Apt 6J Long Island City NY 11104

ROSSEY, PAUL WILLIAM, superintendent schools; b. Richmond, Ind., July 7, 1926; s. Chris C. and Lela (Longman) R.; m. Adelaide Elizabeth Finnegan; 1 dau., Joanne Rossey Sczubelek. B.S., Jersey City State Coll., 1952, Litt. D., 1971; M.A., NYU, 1953, Ed.D. (Kellogg Found. fellow 1955), 1958. Head jr. sch. Peddie Sch., Hightstown, N.J., 1952-53; cons., elem. sch. instr. West Hempstead, N.Y., 1953-55; prin. elem. sch. Dobbs Ferry, N.Y., 1955-58; supt. schs. Litchfield, Conn., 1958-60, Scotch Plains-Fanwood, N.J., 1960-67; dist. supt. schs. Nassau County, N.Y., 1967-69; pres. West Chester (Pa.) State U., 1969-74; supt. schs. Millburn-Short Hills, N.J., 1974—; lectr. NYU, 1954-67. Contbr. articles to profl. jours. County dir. Boy Scouts Am.; v.p. YMCA.; bd. dirs. Garbe Found., Community Fund; trustee NYU, 1970-74, The Peddie Sch., 1974—; mem. exec. com. N.J. Council Edn., 1977-83. Served with USNR, 1944-46; served with USMCR, 1972-86 ret. Named Outstanding Alumnus, Jersey City State Coll., 1962; recipient NYU medallion, 1966, Ernest O. Melby award human relations, 1970. Mem. Am. Assn. Sch. Adminstrs. (chmn. N.J. 1965-67), Am. Council Edn., Aircraft Owners and Pilots Assn., N.J. Assn. Sch. Adminstrs. (exec. com. 1964-67, 81-85), Horace Mann League U.S. (nat. pres. 1977-78), Kappa Delta Pi, Phi Delta Kappa. Republican. Presbyn. Clubs: Exchange (dir.), N.J. Schoolmasters. Home: 219 Summit Ave Summit NJ 07901 Office: 434 Millburn Ave Millburn NJ 07041

ROSSI, AGNELO CARDINAL, former archbishop of Sao Paulo; b. Joaquim Egidio, Brazil, May 4, 1913. Ordained priest Roman Cath. Ch., 1937; bishop of Barra do Pirai, 1956; archbishop of Riberoa Preto, 1962-64, of Sao Paulo, 1964-70; cardinal, 1965; titular ch. Mother of God; prefect Congregation for Evangelism of Peoples 1970-84; bishop Subrubicarian Title of Sabina and Poggio Mirteto, 1984; pres. Adminstrn. Patrimony of Holy See, 1984; grand chancellor Pontifical Urban U.; mem. Council Public Affairs of Ch., Congregation of Clergy, Congregation Doctrine of Faith, Congregation of Bishops, Congregation Oriental Chs., Congregation Causes of Saints, Congregation Religious and Secular Insts., Congregation Cath. Edn., Commn. Revision Oriental Code Canon Law, Commn. Works Religion. Address: 00121 Vatican City Vatican *

ROSSI, BRUNO, physicist; b. Venice, Italy, Apr. 13, 1905; s. Rino and Lina (Minerbi) R.; m. Nora Lombroso, Apr. 10, 1938; children—Florence S., Frank R., Linda L. Student, U. Padua, 1923-25, U. Bologna, 1925-27; hon. doctorate, U. Palermo, 1964, U. Durham, Eng., 1974, U. Chgo., 1977. Asst. physics dept. U. Florence, 1928-32; prof. physics U. Padua, 1932-38; research assoc. U. Manchester, Eng., 1939; research assoc. in cosmic rays U. Chgo., 1939-40; asso. prof. physics Cornell U., 1940-43; prof. physics Mass. Inst. Tech., 1946—, Inst. prof., 1966-70, Inst. prof. emeritus, 1970—; Mem. staff Los Alamos Lab.; 1943-46, hon. fellow Tata Inst. Fundamental Research, Bombay, India, 1971; mem. physics com. NASA; hon. prof. U. Mayor, San Andres, La Paz, Bolivia. Author: Rayons Cosmiques, 1935, (with L. Pincherle) Lezioni di Fisca Sperimentale Elettrologia, 1936, Lezioni di Fisica Sperimentale Ottica, 1937, Ionization Chambers and Counters, 1949, (with Staub), High Energy Particles, 1952, Optics, 1957, Cosmic Rays, 1964, (with S. Olbert) Introduction to the Physics of Space, 1970, Momenti nella vite di uno Scientiato, 1987. Recipient Cresson medal Franklin Inst., 1974, Nat. Medal of Sci., 1983, Wolf award, 1987; decorated Order of Merit (Republic of Italy). Mem. Am. Acad. Arts and Scis. (Rumford prize 1976), Nat. Acad. Sci. (space sci. bd., astronomy survey com.), Deutsche Akademieder Naturforscher Leopoldina, Am. Phys. Soc., Am. Inst. Physics, Accademia dei Lincel (Internat. Feltrinelli award 1971), Internat. Astron. Union, Am., Royal astron. socs., Accademia Patavina di Scienze, Letteree Arti, Accademia Ligure di Scienze e Lettere, Bolivian Acad. Scis. (corr.), AAAS, Am. Philos. Soc., Italian Phys. Soc. (Gold medal 1970), Inststuto Veneto di Science, Lettere e Arti, Sigma Xi. Address: 221 Mt Auburn St Cambridge MA 02138 also: Wolf Found care Mr Yaron Gruder, PO Box 398, Herzlia Bet 46103, Israel

ROSSI, GUIDO ANTONIO, mathematics educator, researcher; b. Moretta, Cuneo, Italy, Jan. 17, 1944; s. Giulio Cesare and Anna Maria (Ferraris di Celle) R.; m. Maria Emilia Zucchi, Mar. 27, 1978. Dr. in Math., Universita di Torino, Italy, 1967. Asst. Universita di Torino, 1969-82, asst. prof. Facolta di Economia e Commercio, 1971-82, assoc. prof. math. Istituto di Matematica Finanziaria, 1982-86, prof. math., 1986—, dir., 1974-81, 83-85. Contbr. articles to profl. jours. Served to lt. Italian Army, 1967-68. Mem. Unione Matematica Italiana, Associazione per lu Matematica Applicata alle Scienze Economiche Sociali, Associazione Museo Ferroviario Piemontese (pres. 1986—), Am. Mathematical Soc. Roman Catholic. Lodge: I Neoteri. Avocations: railways and models; sailing; skiing. Office: Istituto di Matematics Finanziaria, Via Assarotti 3, I-10122 Torino Italy

ROSSI, NICK, opera administrator, author, educator; b. San Luis Obispo, Calif., Nov. 14, 1924; s. Nicholas Louis and Lillian Alice (McCurry) R.; Mus.B., U. So. Calif., 1948, Mus.M., 1952; Ph.D., Sussex Coll. Tech., 1971. Music cons. secondary schs., Los Angeles City Sch. Dist., 1948-68; dir. various mus. comedies and operettas North Hollywood High Sch., Calif., 1949-68; producer, stage dir. opera Hollywood Theater Arts Workshop, 1963-64; condr., stage dir. Infancy of Christ (oratorio), Congl. Ch. of Glendale (Calif.), 1959; prodn. supr. TV high sch. talent series Sta. KHJ-TV, Los Angeles, 1961-62, dir., condr. Oklahoma, 1957; program dir. choral ensembles Sta. KFI, Los Angeles, 1959-60, 61-62, 62-63; dir. Romeo and Juliet, ABC-TV, Los Angeles, 1964; stage dir., producer operas including: Aucassin et Nicolette, 1965, Four Saints in Three Acts, 1962, 71, Song of Songs, 1973, Importance of Being Earnest, 1974, Crazy to Do My Act, 1979, Trial of St. Joan, 1973, L'importanza di esser Franco, 1984, Muzio Scevola, 1985, Il principe Barbablu, 1986, Il filosofo di campagna, 1986, Il geloso shernito, 1986, Amor soldato, 1987, La Pentola, 1987, Cosi fan tutte, 1988, Dialoghi d'amore, 1988, others; chmn. music edn. U. Bridgeport, Conn., 1970-74, organizer, dir. Virgil Thomson festival, 1971, Norman Dello Joio Festival, 1972, Don Juan in the Performing Arts Festival, 1973, Castelnuovo-Tedesco Festival, 1974, Carman Moore Festival, 1976, Women in Music Festival, 1978; adminstrv. dir. Studio Lirico Italy, 1983—; coordinator music and dance LaGuardia Community Coll., L.I., N.Y., 1974-86; adminstrv. dir. Internat. Festa Musicale Stiana, 1985—; assoc. prof., 1974-86; assoc. editor Keyboard Publs., div. Am. Book Co., N.Y.C., 1962-80; dir. chorus Los Angeles Ann. Bach Festival, 1962-65; guest lectr. various internat. music edn. orgns., 1962—; music critic The Christian Sci. Monitor, 1985—, Italy for Opera Can., 1988—, CD Classica, Italy, 1988—; foreign correspondent Italy for Musical Am., 1983—, Gramophone, 1986—. Author: (with Sadie Rafferty) Music Through the Centuries, 1963, 3d edit., 1981; (with Robert A. Choate) Music of Our Time, 1969; From Jazz to Rock, 1970; Pathways to Music, 1970; A Musical Pilgrimage, 1971; Electronic Music, 1971; Twentieth-Century Music and Art, 1972; Hearing Music, 1981; J.S. Bach: A Biography in Pictures, 1981; European Opera for the Record, 1983—; Notes from Abroad, 1983. Contbr. articles to profl. jours. Served with U.S. Army, 1942-46. Recipient ASCAP/Deems Taylor award, 1984, Research award New York City U., 1984; Named Andrew Mellon fellow, 1985. Mem. Am. Choral Condrs. Assn., Am. Musicological Soc., Choral Condrs. Guild of Am. (hon.), Internat. Folk Music Council, ASCAP, Soc. for Ethnomusicology, Internat. Castelnuovo-Tedesco Soc. (founder, pres. 1975—), Nat. Assn. for Am. Condrs. and Composers, Oceanic Soc. Am. Mus. Natural History, Pi Kappa Lambda. Christian Scientist. Home: Via Pian delle Macchie 100,, I-50063 Figline Valdarno FI Italy

ROSSI, OPILIO CARDINAL, clergyman; b. N.Y.C., May 14, 1910; Italian citizen. Ordained priest Roman Cath. Ch., 1933; served in nunciatures in Belgium, Netherlands and Ger., 1938-53; titular archbishop of Ancyra, 1953; nuncio in Ecuador, 1953-59, in Chile, 1959-61, in Austria, 1961-76; cardinal, 1976; deacon S. Maria Liberatrice (on the Monte Testaccio); mem. Council Public Affairs of Ch., Congregation of Bishops, Congregation Oriental Chs., Congregation Sacraments and Divine Worship, Congregation Religious and Secular Insts., Congregation Evangelization of Peoples; pres. Commn. Council for Laity, Cardinalatial Com. Sanctuaries of Pompei and Loretto; mem. Apostolic Signatura Tribunal, Authentic Interpretation of Code of Canon Law Commn. Address: Via della Scrofa 70, 00186 Rome Italy

ROSSI, ROBERT JOHN, newspaper executive; b. Pitts., Jan. 5, 1928; s. John Baptist and Carmella Marie (Pastore) R.; B.A., Denison U., 1950; postgrad. 1963; m. Mary Kathryn Rust, June 30, 1951; children—Shannon Elizabeth, Claudia Irene. Advt. dir., bus. mgr. Willoughby (Ohio) News-Herald, 1953-60; advt. dir. Elgin (Ill.) Courier-News, 1960-64; editor and pub. New Albany (Ind.) Tribune and Sunday Ledger, 1964-71; mgmt. cons. Thomson Newspapers, Inc., Chgo., 1971, gen. mgr. So. div., Tampa, Fla., 1972-73; v.p., chief newspaper ops. officer Park Communications Inc., Inc., Ithaca, N.Y., 1974-79, 85—, also dir.; editor, gen. mgr. Courier News, Blytheville, Ark., 1983-85, also Osceola Times, Ark.; Bd. dirs. Ky. Opera Assn., Ky.-Ind. Comprehensive Health Planning Council. Served with U.S. Army, 1946. Mem. Am., So. newspaper pubs. assns., Internat. Execs. Service Corps. Club: Filson. Republican. Presbyterian. Home: 323 Winthrop Dr Ithaca NY 14850 Office: PO Box 550 Ithaca NY 14851

ROSSI DI MONTELERA, LUIGI, member of Italian Parliament; b. Turin, Italy, May 14, 1946; s. Napoleone and Niccoletta (Niccolini di Camugliano) Rossi di Montelera; m. Maria Giulia Malvezzi Campeggi, Sept. 15, 1975; children: Niccoletta, Anna Maria, Leone. D. Law, U. Turin, 1969. Dir. Martini & Rossi, Turin, 1972—; counselor for tech. problems Gen. Beverage Mgmt., Geneva, 1980—; mem. Italian Parliament, Rome, 1976—; v.p. Federvini, Rome; bd. dirs. Unione Industrale, Torino; Under-Sec. of State for Tourism and Entertainment, 1987-88. Author: Racconto di un sequestro, 1977. Mem. Fédération Internationale Vins et Spiritueux (hon. pres.), Unione Cristiana Imprenditori Dirigenti, Rotary. Roman Catholic. Clubs: Circolo Subalpino, Circolo Whist, Circolo Della Caccia. Office: Via Pomba 4, I-10123 Torino Italy

ROSSIENSKY, JEAN-PAUL, software company executive; b. St. Raphael, Var, France, May 12, 1941; s. Georges and Luce Etienne Rossiensky; m. Monique Veber, July 20, 1963; children: Francois, Nathalie. Diploma in Engring., Ecole Poly., Paris, 1963; MS in Computer Scis., Stanford U., 1967. Engr. French Atomic Energy Commn., Saclay, 1964-70; mng. dir. Cegos & Sligos, Paris, 1970-75, Alvan, Paris, 1975-77; chmn., chief exec. officer Transtec, Paris, 1977—, also bd. dirs.; chmn. R.I.S.L., London, 1980—, also bd. dirs.; chmn., chief exec. officer Cassie, Paris, 1982—, also bd. dirs.; chmn. Cisi-Systemes, Paris, 1985—. Contbr. articles to profl. jours. Served to lt. French Air Force, 1963-64. Home: 2 Delieuses, Louveciennes, 78430 Yvelines France Office: Transtec, 32 Rue de Ponthieu, 75008 Paris France

ROSSITER, MARTIN EDWARD, food company executive; b. Llandrindod, Wells, Wales, U.K., Dec. 25, 1940; s. Edward Charles and Phyllis Marion (Weston) R.; m. Jennifer Margaret Paul, Oct. 9, 1965; children—Peter, Sophie. Mgr. J. Lyons & Co., London, 1964-68; regional mgr. Banquets of Oxford, Oxon, 1968-71; chmn. Leisure & Pleasure Catering Services Ltd., Whaley Bridge, Cheshire, 1971-74; chmn. Sports & Leisure Foods Group, Macclesfield, Cheshire, 1974—; chmn. Custombetter Foodservice, Ltd., London, 1987—; bd. dirs. Country Moment Hotels, Ltd., Beaumaris, Anglesey, Scandinavian Health Systems, Macclesfield, Cheshire. Contbr. articles to profl. jours. Chmn. social com. Parish Council of Whaley Bridge, 1985-87, council mem., 1982—; sponsor Community of the King of Love, Whaley Bridge, 1985—. Office: Sports & Leisure Foods Group, George Street House, Macclesfield SK11 6HS, England

ROSSLYN, FELICITY MARGARET, English educator; b. Epsom, Eng., Sept. 28, 1950; d. Raymond and Audrey Joyce Mary (Minney) R.; m. Piotr Kuhivchak, Mar. 27, 1987. BA, Cambridge (Eng.) U., 1972, PhD, 1978. Lectr. English U. Lancaster, Eng., 1978—; vis. lectr. U. Sarajevo, Yugoslavia, 1983-84, U. Warsaw, Poland, 1985. Editor: The Cambridge quarterly, 1986—, Pope's Iliad, 1985; contbr. articles to profl. jours. Recipient Ivo Andric prize Andric Found., 1982; Harvard U. fellow, 1972-74. Office: U Lancaster English Dept, Lancaster LA1 4YT, England

ROSSMANN, PAVEL, pathologist; b. Bratislava, Czechoslovakia, Jan. 4, 1933; s. Zdenek and Marie (Dolezelova) R.; m. Svetluse Valentova, July 18, 1968; children: Michael, Zdenek. MD, Charles U., Prague, Czechoslovakia, 1957, CSc, 1965; DrSc, Czechoslovakia Acad. Sci., Prague, 1986. Mem. staff med. faculty Inst. Pathology, Charles U., Hradec Kralove, Czechoslovakia, 1957-60, Prague, 1960-62; researcher Inst. Clin. and Exptl. Medicine, Prague, 1962-79, cons. pathologist clin. transplantation program, 1979—; stagiaire etranger Clin. Nephrologique Hopital Necker, Paris, 1965-66; leading researcher dept. immunology Inst. Microbiology, Czechoslovak Acad. Sci., 1979—. Author: Rejection Nephropathy (Sci. prize Czechoslovakia Ministry Health 1980), 1979; contbr. articles to profl. jours. Recipient Sci. award Lit. Fund, Prague, 1980. Mem. Czechoslovak Med. Assn. (Sci. prizes 1970, 73, 76, 88), Czechoslovak Immunol. Assn. Club: Czechoslovak Alpine (Prague) (tng. officer 1963—). Office: Czechoslovak Acad Scis, Inst Microbiology Dept 113, 142 20 Prague 4 Czechoslovakia

ROSSMILLER, RICHARD ALLEN, educational administration educator, consultant; b. Burlington, Wis., May 25, 1928; s. Harold Curtis and Lydia Sophia (Keller) R.; m. Lois Catherine Koch, July 5, 1952; children—Daniel, Stuart, David. B.S., U. Wis.-Madison, 1950, M.S., 1958, Ph.D., 1960. Supt. Racine County Agrl. Sch., Rochester, Wis., 1954-57; prin. Evanston Twp. High Sch., Ill., 1960-61; supt. Muskego-Norway Schs., Wis., 1961-62; prof. ednl. adminstrn. U. Wis.-Madison, 1962—; vis. prof. U. Fla., Gainesville, 1967-68, Pontificial Cath. U., Rio de Janeiro, Brazil, 1977; cons. RAND Corp., Santa Monica, Calif., 1977-81, CAPES Ministry of Edn. and Culture, Brasilia, Brazil, 1975, OECD; mem. Nat. Commn. on Excellence in Ednl. Adminstrn., 1985-87; mem. planning com. Internat. Intervisitation Program, 1987—. Author: Opportunities Unlimited, 1959, 1983. Co-author: The Law and Public School Operation, 1969, 1978; Individual Guided Education, 1977; Dimensions of Educational Need, 1969. Dir. State Supts. Task Force on Teaching, Madison, 1983; pub. mem. Wis. Legis. Council, Madison, 1975, 1978. Recipient Benjamin Constant medal Inst. of Edn. of Rio de Janeiro, 1980. Mem. Am. Edn. and Fin. Assn. (pres. 1981), Univ. Council Ednl. Adminstrn. (pres. 1984-85), Am. Ednl. Research Assn., Council for Ednl. Devel. and Research (pres. 1975-76), Nat. Orgn. Legal Problems of Edn. Democrat. Lodge: Rotary (dir. 1982-83). Avocation: photography. Home: 5806 Cable Ave Madison WI 53705 Office: Dept Ednl Adminstrn 1025 W Johnson St Madison WI 53706

ROSTENBACH, KEVIN VICTOR, infosystems specialist, consultant; b. Davenport, Iowa, Sept. 23, 1959; s. Marvin Henry and Loisfaye (Bahr) R.; m. Jean Lee Sasser, Aug. 16, 1978 (div. June, 1980); m. Karla Lynn Bowden, Nov. 22, 1986 (div. July, 1988). Postgrad., Am. Inst. Commerce, 1982. Data processing coordinator Am. Inst. Commerce, Bettendorf, Iowa, 1982-87; personal computer analyst, programmer First Fed. Savs. and Loan, Davenport, Iowa, 1987—; ptnr. Profl. Assment Cons., Computer Aided Tools for Psychologists; chief exec. officer KVR Systems; cons. Vera French Mental Health Ctr., Davenport. Mem. Soc. Data Educators, Data Processing Mgmt. Assn. (exec. v.p. Ill. chpt., 1985, local pres. 1986), Internat. Platform Assn. Home: PO Box 2358 Davenport IA 52809 Office: First Fed Savs and Loan 131 W 3d St Davenport IA 52801

ROSTINSKY, JOSEPH NORMON, East European studies educator, consultant; b. Brno, Moravia, Czechoslovakia, Oct. 14, 1945; came to U.S., 1969; s. Frantisek and Anna (Kolaya) R. Ph.C., Masaryk U., Brno, Czechoslovakia, 1969; M.A., SUNY-Albany, 1972; M.A., Harvard U., 1975; Ph.D., Brown U., 1980. Preceptor Harvard U., Cambridge, Mass., 1973-75; instr. U.S. Def. Lang. Inst., Calif., 1977; lectr. U. Tex., Austin, 1975-77; instr. Brown U., Providence, 1978-80; prof. East European studies Tokai U., Tokyo, 1980—; cons. Info. Communication Systems, Tokyo, 1984; curriculum analyst Brown U., Providence, 1978-79; research analyst Nat. Acad. Scis., Washington, 1974. Co-chmn., Koji Chikugo Fund. Author: Credo, 1984. Contbr. articles to profl. jours. Chmn. drama Semiotic Soc. U.S. Symposium, Providence, 1978. Harvard U. fellow, Cambridge, Mass., 1973-75, Humanities research grantee Tokai U., Tokyo, 1983. Recipient Nat. Def. F.L. award Brown U., 1976-77. Mem. Japanese Soc. Slavic and Ea. European Studies, Czech Acad. Arts and Scis., Czechoslovac History Conf., Harvard Slavic Conf. Assn. (pres. 1974-75), Brown U. Slavic Conf. (pres. 1978), Am. Assn. Advancement Slavic Studies, Modern Lang. Assn. Am., Toronto Semiotic Circle. Roman Catholic. Clubs: Internat. House of Japan, Brown U. of Japan, Harvard of Japan. Office: Tokyo U, East European Dept, 1117 Kita Kaname, Hiratsuka 259 12, Japan

ROSTROPOVICH, MSTISLAV LEOPOLDOVICH, musician; b. Baku, USSR, Mar. 27, 1927; s. Leopold and Sofia (Fedotova) R.; m. Galina Vishnevskaya; children: Olga, Elena. Grad., Moscow Conservatory 1948; numerous hon. doctorate degrees. Faculty mem. Moscow Conservatory, 1953, prof., 1960; head cello and double-bass dept., formerly prof. Leningrad Conservatory; music dir. Nat. Symphony Orch., Washington, 1977—; hon. prof. Cuban Nat. Conservatory, 1960-78; co. dir. Aldeburg Festival, U.K., 1977—; pres. Evian Internat. Music Festival. Debut as violoncellist, 1935; performer world concert tours, Moscow Philharm. Orch. Decorated Hon. Knight of the Brit. Empire, 1987, Commdr. French Legion of Honor, 1987; recipient Stalin prize, 1951, 53, Lenin prize, 1963, Life in Music prize, 1984, Albert Schweitzer Music award, 1985, Grammy awards, 1970, 77, 80, 84, Presdl. Medal Freedom, 1987; named Musician of Yr., Mus. Am., 1987. Mem. Am. Acad. Arts and Scis., Union Soviet Composers, Brit. Royal Acad. Music (hon.). Address: care Nat Symphony Orch John F Kennedy Ctr Performing Arts Washington DC 20566 *

ROSZEL, STEPHEN SAMUEL, JR., oil company executive; b. Middleburg, Va., Sept. 22, 1921; s. Stephen Samuel and Rosa Dulany (Hall) R.; student architecture Va. Poly. Inst., 1939-41, U. Va., 1941-42; m. Susan Katherine Hull, Mar. 5, 1949; children—Susan, Stephen, Thomas. Vice pres. Pan Air Corp., New Orleans, 1947-48, Superior Oil Co., Lafayette, La., 1949-55; gen. sales mgr. Eastman Oil Well Survey Co., Denver, 1955-58; mgr. indsl. and public relations J. Ray McDermott & Co., Inc., New Orleans, 1959-64; officer, dir. Petroleum Exploration, Inc., 1964-67; sales mgr. Ingram Contractors Australia, 1967-68; sr. v.p. Ingram Internat., S.A., 1969-72; v.p. ops. Ingram Far East Pte. Ltd., 1969-72; mgr. Ingram Contractors Indonesia, 1969-72; mgr. sales-Far East, Oceanic Contractors, Inc., McDermott S.E. Asia, 1972-73; pres. Jardine Offshore, Ltd., Singapore, 1973-77, ETPM-USA, Inc., Houston, 1977-79, Essarco, Inc., Houston and Warrenton, Va., 1979—, Anacoco Corp., DeRidder, La.; chmn. Eurasia Trading Corp., Houston; dir. Malaco Chem. Co., Singapore, Petroleum Cons., Ltd., Hong Kong, Educoin Co., Inc., New Orleans, Plastiflex Corp., Houston, Houtex Oil & Gas Corp., MME Internat., Houston, Essarco, Inc. writer, photographer, producer indsl. films, 1948—. Served in RAF, also to maj. USAAF, World War II. Decorated Allied Service medal. Mem. Houston Engring. and Sci. Soc., Quiet Birdmen, Ox-5 Soc. Episcopalian. Clubs: Masons; Corpus Christi Yacht; Univ. (Houston); Holiday of New Orleans (past pres.); Sugar Creek Country; RACV (Melbourne); Singapore Petroleum, Tanglin, American, Singapore Yacht (Singapore); Fauquier (bd. govs.), Fauquier Springs Country (Warrenton, Va.). Office: PO Box 627 Warrenton VA 22186

ROT, SANDOR, linguist, philologist, educator; b. Turjaremete, Hungary, Nov. 1, 1921; s. Mavrikey and Fani (Gruenberger) R.; M.A., Charles U., Prague, 1946; Ph.D., Moscow U., 1955, Inst. Fgn. Langs., Moscow, 1957, Budapest U., 1978; D.Sc., Inst. Linguistics, Moscow, 1969, Hungarian Acad. Scis., 1975; m. Ita Belenkaya, July 19, 1952; 1 son, Antal. Successively lectr., sr. lectr., asst. prof., prof., head depts. linguistics and philology Uzhgorod State U., Transcarpathia, 1949-74; prof. English and linguistics Eotvos U., Budapest, Hungary, 1974—; lectr., Fulbright scholar Brown U. and Harvard U., 1981-82; vis. prof. numerous European, Am. and Asian univs. Decorated golden degree Order of Labor. Mem. Union Hungarian Writers, Internat. PEN Club, Societas Linguistica Europaea, Internat. Assn. Univ. Profs. English, Hungarian Acad. Scis., Hungarian Linguistic Soc., Soc. for Popularization of Sci. Knowledge, Assn. Modern Philology. Author 26 monographs, textbooks, dictionaries, and over 580 papers on linguistics, philology, lit., translations into 11 langs.; editor: New Trends in British and American Studies, 1978; mem. editorial bd. Philol. Studies (in Hungarian), Acta Linguistica Hungarian Acad. Scis. Home: 13 Zsindely, 1025 Budapest Hungary Office: 1 Pesti Barnabas, 1052 Budapest Hungary

ROTCHFORD, PATRICIA KATHLEEN, general counsel, lawyer; b. Chgo., Nov. 17, 1945; d. Charles E. Sr. and Mary (Rodde) R.; 1 child, John. BA with honors, Rosary Coll., River Forest, Ill., 1966; JD, No. Ill. U., 1979. Bar: Ill. 1979. Tchr. pub. schs. Schiller Park, Ill., 1966-76; sole practice Elmhurst, Ill., 1977-79; assoc. Shand, Morahan, Evanston, Ill., 1979-83; corp. counsel CNA Fin., Chgo., 1983-86; gen. counsel, v.p. and corp. sec. MMI Cos., Bannockburn, Ill., 1986-87; gen. counsel, v.p., corp. sec. Inland Group, Northbrook, Ill., 1987—; legal counsel/fin. and ins. advisor Nat. Med. Assoc., Washington, 1988—; mem. nat. bd. dirs. NAFWIC. Author: (pamphlet) Handle Your Own Claims, 1983, (book) Women's Resource Guide, 1988, Women's Insurance and Financial Resource Guide, 1988. Counselor for battered women. Mem. Womens Bar Assn. Ill. (active coms. and activities), Corp. Councils Am., Womens Exec. Network, Nat. Assn. Women in Careers. Office: Inland Group 5 Revere Dr Suite 200 Northbrook IL 60062

ROTH, EDITH ELIZABETH, account executive, securities trader, political campaign consultant; b. Budapest, Hungary, June 2, 1935; came to U.S., 1949; d. Edmond and Mary (Bertalan) Rockenstein; m. Mickey Moshe Roth, Apr. 9, 1964; children: Leonora Rose, Adrienne Haddassah. BA, Cleve. State U., 1981; MA, Kent State U., 1982. Coordinator re-entry women's program Cleve. State U., 1981; pvt. practice campaign cons., Ohio, 1982—; div. mgr. First Investors Corp., 1985—; co-owner Imagination in Plastic, Cleve., 1982—. Trustee Heights Community Congress, Cleveland Heights, Ohio, 1977-80; chairperson Severance Devel. Commn., Cleveland Heights, 1978; pres. Millikin Neighbors, Inc., Cleveland Heights, 1978-82; mem. fin. com. City Council, Cleveland Heights, 1979-81. Mem. Pi Sigma Alpha. Clubs: Cleveland Heights Democratic. Home: 3691 Blanche Rd Cleveland Heights OH 44118 Office: Dean Witter Reynolds Inc 24400 Chagrin Blvd Beachwood OH 44122

ROTH, ETIENNE GEORGES ALFRED, chemistry educator; b. Strasbourg, France, June 6, 1922; s. Georges Jules and Marguerite (Neymarck) R.; m. Francoise Alice Hirsch, June 3, 1949; children—Catherine, Elisabeth, Marianne, Brigitte. D. in Engring., Ecole Polytech. Paris, 1946; D.Sc., Sorbonne, 1960. Research scientist Atomic Energy Commn., France, 1946-54, head stable isotope sect., 1954-59, head stable isotope service, 1959-71, head dept. research and analysis, 1971—, dep. dir. chemistry, 1978—, dir. research, 1980-87; prof. applied nuclear chemistry Conservatoire Nat. Des Arts et Metiers, Paris, 1963—; chmn. Atomic Weights Commn., 1971-77. Recipient Chemistry award French Acad. Scis., 1969; Decorated Chevalier De La Legion D'Honneur. Contbr. articles to profl. jours. Mem. Soc. Chem. Physics, Am. Nuclear Soc., European Phys. Soc. Home: 103 Brancas, 92310 Sevres France Office: Desicp CEN Saclay Gif, 91191 Sur Yvette France

ROTH, HADDEN WING, lawyer; b. Oakland, Calif., Feb. 10, 1930; s. Mark and Jane (Haley) R.; married 1959 (div. 1972); 1 child, Elizabeth Wing; m. Alice Becker, Aug. 7, 1987. AA, Coll. Marin, 1949; BA, U. Calif., Berkeley, 1951; JD, U. Calif., San Francisco, 1957. Bar: Calif. 1958, U.S. Dist. Ct. (no. dist.) Calif. 1958, U.S. Ct. Appeals (9th cir.) 1958, U.S. Supreme Ct. 1966. Ptnr. Roth, Thorner and Curtin, San Rafael, Calif., 1957-63; sole practice San Rafael, 1963—; dep. atty. City of San Rafael, 1958-60, City of Sausalito and Mill Valley, Calif., 1964-66; dep. dist. atty. County of Marin, 1960-63; judge Marin County Mcpl. Ct., 1966-70; cons. Marin Muni Water Dist., Corte Madera, Calif.; atty. Town of Ross and San Anselmo, Calif.; lectr. law Golden Gate Coll. Law, San Francisco, 1971-73. Chmn. Marin Coll. Bond Campaign, 1971, Prison Task Force, 1973; bd. dirs. Marin Gen. Hosp., 1964-66. Served to corp. U.S. Army, 1952-54. Named Outstanding Citizen of Yr., Coll. Marin, 1972. Mem. Marin County Bar Assn. Home: 343 Fairhills Dr San Rafael CA 94901 Office: Roth & Thorner 1050 Northgate Dr San Rafael CA 94903

ROTH, OLIVER RALPH, radiologist; b. Cumberland, Md., Nov. 30, 1921; s. DeCoursey Andrew and Mabel (Lathrum) R.; B.S., Frostburg (Md.) State Coll., 1942, D.Sc. (hon.), 1980; M.D., U. Md., 1950; m. Virginia McBride, June 2, 1943; 1 dau., Tiija. Diplomate Am. Bd. Radiology. Resident, Johns Hopkins Hosp., Balt., 1954-57; cancer research fellow Middlesex Hosp., London, 1957-58; founder dept. radiation oncology Presbyn. Hosp., Charlotte, N.C., 1958-62; attending radiologist King's Daus. Hosp., Ashland, Ky., 1962-80; radiologist Our Lady of Bellefonte Hosp., 1981—; mem. adv. com. Ky. Cancer Commn., 1978; bd. dirs. Boyd County chpt. Am. Cancer Soc., 1978. Served with USN, 1942-45. Commanded to Buckingham Palace, June 17, 1958; recipient Disting. Alumni award Frostburg State Coll., 1979. Mem. AMA, Am. Coll. Radiology, Radiol. Soc. N.Am., Am. Radium Soc., Royal Faculty Radiology, Brit. Inst. Radiology. Democrat. Lutheran. Club: Shriners (Cumberland, Md.). Book reviewer Radiology, 1954-55. Home: 2912 Cogan St Ashland KY 41101

ROTH, PHILIP, author; b. Newark, Mar. 19, 1933; s. Herman and Bess (Finkel) R.; student Newark Coll. of Rutgers U., 1950-51; A.B., Bucknell U., 1954; M.A., U. Chgo., 1955; m. Margaret Martinson, Feb. 22, 1959 (dec. 1968). Tchr. English, U. Chgo., 1956-58; short story writer, novelist, works pub. in Harper's, New Yorker, Epoch, Commentary, others, also reprints in Best Am. Short Stories of 1956, 59, 60, O'Henry Prize Stories of 1960; faculty Iowa Writers Workshop, 1960-62; writer in residence Princeton U., 1962-63; adj. prof. U. Pa., 1967-77. Recipient Aga Khan prize for fiction, 1958; Guggenheim fellow, 1959-60; Rockefeller fellow, 1966; award Nat. Inst. Arts and Letters, 1960; Daroff award Jewish Book Council, 1960. Mem. Nat. Inst. Arts and Letters. Author: Goodbye, Columbus (Nat. Book award), 1959, Letting Go, 1962, When She Was Good, 1967, Portnoy's Complaint, 1969, Our Gang, 1971, The Breast, 1972, The Great American Novel, 1973, My Life as a Man, 1974, Reading Myself and Others, 1975, The Professor of Desire, 1977, The Ghost Writer, 1979, A Philip Roth Reader, 1980, Zuckerman Unbound, 1981, The Anatomy Lesson, 1983, Zuckerman Bound, 1985, The Prague Orgy, 1985, The Counterlife (Nat. Book Critics Circle award for fiction, 1988), The Facts, 1988. Address: care Farrar Straus & Giroux 19 Union Sq New York NY 10003 *

ROTH, ROBERT EARL, radiologist, educator; b. Springfield, Ill., Mar. 3, 1925; s. Earl Andrew and Aldine (Schockley) R.; m. Joanne Seneff, June 26, 1948; children—Michael Gordon, Nicholas Brian, Andrew John, Emily Dean, Laura Seneff. Student, Columbia U., 1943-45, U. Ill., Chgo., 1947; M.D., U. Ill., 1949. Diplomate Am. Bd. Radiology. Intern St. Louis County Hosp., Clayton, Mo., 1949-50; resident U.S. Naval Hosp., San Diego, VA Hosp., Vanderbilt U., Nashville, 1950-54; practice medicine specializing in radiology Birmingham, Ala., 1955; asst. chief radiology VA Hosp., Nashville, 1954-55; asst. prof. radiology, chief radiation therapy U. Ala. Med. Coll., Birmingham, 1957-58, assoc. prof., chief radiation therapy, 1958-59, prof., chmn. dept., 1959-69; acting chief radiology V.A. Hosp., Birmingham, 1959-69, chmn. dept. radiation oncology, 1950-85; radiation oncologist Norwood Clinic, Birmingham, 1985—; cons. radiology; radiologist-in-chief U. Ala. Hosps. and Clinics, 1959-69, radiation oncologist-in-chief, 1969-85. Served to lt. M.C. USNR, 1949-52. Fellow Am. Coll. Radiology; mem. AAAS, Am. Soc. Therapeutic Radiologists (emeritus), Am. Coll. Radiology, Radiol. Soc. N.Am., N.Y. Acad. Scis., So. Radiol. Conf., Soc. Nuclear Medicine (emeritus), Ala. Med. Soc., Jefferson County Med. Soc., Pan Am. Can Cytology Soc., Ala. Roentgen Ray Soc. (past pres.), Ala. Soc. Radiation Oncologists (sec., treas.), Birmingham Surgeons Soc.

ROTH, WILLIAM STANLEY, hospital foundation executive; b. N.Y.C., Jan. 12, 1929; s. Sam Irving and Louise Caroline (Martin) R.; A.A., Asheville-Biltmore Jr. Coll., 1948; B.S., U. N.C., 1950; m. Hazel Adcock, May 6, 1963; children—R. Charles, W. Stanley. Dep. regional exec. Nat. council Boy Scouts Am., 1953-65; exec. v.p. Am. Humanics Found., 1965-67; dir. devel. Bethany Med. Center, Kansas City, Kans., 1967-74; exec. v.p. Geisinger Med. Center Found., Danville, Pa., 1974-78; pres. Found., Baptist Med. Centers, Birmingham, Ala., 1978—. Mem.-at-large Nat. council Boy Scouts Am., 1972-86; chmn. NAHD Ednl. Fund, 1980-82; ruling elder John Knox Kirk, Kansas City, Mo., Grove Presbyn. Ch., Danville, Pa. Recipient Silver award United Methodist Ch., 1970, Mid-West Health Congress, 1971; Seymour award for outstanding hosp. devel. officer 1983. Fellow Nat. Assn. Hosp. Devel. (nat. pres. 1975-76); mem. Nat. Soc. Fund Raising Execs. (pres. Ala. chpt. 1980-82, nat. dir. 1980-84, cert. fund raising exec., Outstanding Fund Raising Exec., Ala. chpt. 1983). Mid-Am.Hosp. Devel. Assn. (pres. 1973-74), Mid-West Health Congress (devel. chmn. 1972-74), Am. Soc. for Hosp. Mktg. and Pub. Relations, Ala. Soc. for Sleep Disorders, Ala. Heart Inst., Alpha Phi Omega (nat. pres. 1958-62, dir. 1950—, Nat. Disting. Service award 1962), Delta Upsilon (pres. N.C. Alumni 1963-65). Clubs: Rotary (pres. club 1976-77), Relay House, Green Valley (bd. govs.), Elks, Order Holy Grail, Order Golden Fleece, Order of The Arrow (Nat. Disting. Service award 1958). Editor Torch and Trefoil, 1960-61. Home: 341 Laredo Dr Birmingham AL 35226 Office: 2700 Hwy 280 S Birmingham AL 35223

ROTH, WILLIAM V., JR., senator; b. Great Falls, Mont., July 22, 1921; m. Jane K. Richards; children: William V. III, Katharine Kellond. B.A., U. Oreg.; M.B.A., LL.B., Harvard. Bar: Del. bar, U.S. Supreme Ct. Mem. 90th-91st congresses at large from, Del., 1967-71; senator from Del., 1971—; mem. fin., govt. affairs coms, joint econ. com.; Chmn. Del. Republican State Com., 1961-64; mem. Rep. Nat. Com., 1961-64. Served to capt. AUS, 1943-46. Decorated Bronze Star medal. Mem. Am., Del. bar assns. Episcopalian. Office: 104 Hart Senate Bldg Washington DC 20510

ROTHBERG, GERALD, editor, publisher; b. Bklyn., Oct. 29, 1937; s. Abraham and Pauline Rothberg; m. Glenda Fay Morris, June 18, 1970; children: Laura, Abigail. B.A., Bklyn. Coll., 1960; postgrad., Dickinson Law Sch., 1962. Spl. projects editor Esquire (mag.), 1963-66; owner, editor, pub., founder Circus (mag.), N.Y.C., 1966—; owner, founder, editor Sci. and Living Tomorrow, 1980—, Who's In, 1981; founder, editor Sports Mirror mag., 1983—, MGF mag., 1985—. Mem. Periodical and Book Assn. Am. (pres.). Office: 3 W 18th St New York NY 10011

ROTHENBERG, ELLIOT CALVIN, lawyer, writer; b. Mpls., Nov. 12, 1939; s. Sam S. and Claire Sylvia (Feller) R.; m. Sally Smayling; 1 child, Margaret. B.A. summa cum laude, U. Minn., 1961; J.D., Harvard U. (Fulbright fellow), 1964 Assoc. project dir. Brookings Inst., Washington, 1966-67; fgn. service officer, legal advisor U.S. Dept. State, Washington, 1968-73; nat. law dir. Anti-Defamation League, N.Y.C., 1973-74; legal dir. Minn. Public Interest Research Group, Mpls., 1974-77; admitted to Minn. bar, 1966, D.C. 1968, N.Y., 1974; pvt. practice law, Mpls., 1977—; adj. prof. William Mitchell Coll. Law, St. Paul, 1983—. State bd. dirs. YMCA Youth in Govt. Program, 1981-84 ; v.p. Twin Cities chpt. Am. Jewish Com., 1980-84 ; mem. Minn. House of Reps., 1978-82, asst. floor leader (whip), 1981-82; pres., dir. North Star Legal Found., 1983—; Legal affairs editor Public Research Syndicated, 1986—; Mem. citizens adv. com. Voyageurs Nat. Park, 1979-81. Recipient Legis. Evaluation Assembly Legis. Excellence award, 1980, Vietnam Civilian Service medal U.S Dept. State, 1970, North Star award, U. Minn., 1961. Mem. Am. Bar Assn., Harvard Law Sch. Assn., Minn. Bar Assn., Am. Legion, Mensa, Phi Beta Kappa. Republican. Jewish. Contbr. articles to profl. and scholarly jours., newspapers, popular magazines; author: (with Zelman Cowen) Sir John Latham and Other Papers, 1965. Home: 3901 W 25th St Saint Louis Park MN 55416 Office: 500 Plymouth Bldg Minneapolis MN 55402

ROTHENBERG, IRWIN Z., laboratory administrator; b. Bklyn., Feb. 17, 1944; s. Alex and Tillie (Rothstein) R.; B.S., Bklyn. Coll., City U. N.Y., 1965; MS, Colo. State U., 1969; MT, Good Samaritan Sch. Med. Tech., 1973. Staff technologist in microbiology Carl Hayden Community Hosp., Tucson, 1974; adminstrv. technologist McKee Med. Center, Loveland, Colo., 1974-79; lab. mgr. Crittenden Meml. Hosp., West Memphis, Ark., 1979—, AIDS edn. coordinator/counselor, 1987—. Active Tenn. AIDS council, 1987—. NSF exchange scientist, Antarctica, 1967-68. Mem. ACLU (state bd. dirs. 1984—), Am. Soc. Clin. Pathology, Am. Soc. Med. Tech., Clin. Lab. Mgmt. Assn., Black and White Men Together (nat. bd. dirs., 1985-87, co-founder Memphis chpt.), Sigma Xi, Phi Kappa Phi. Jewish. Home: 1471 North Pkwy Memphis TN 38112 Office: 200 Tyler Ave West Memphis AR 72301

ROTHENBERG, ROBERT EDWARD, physician, author; b. Bklyn., Sept. 27, 1908; s. Simon and Caroline A. (Baer) R.; m. Lillian Babette Lustig, June 8, 1933 (dec. Jan. 1977); m. Eileen Fein, Nov. 3, 1977 (dec. Aug. 1987); children: Robert Philip, Lynn Barbara (Mrs. Richard L. Kay). A.B., Cornell U., 1929, M.D., 1932. Diplomate: Am. Bd. Surgery. Intern Jewish Hosp., Bklyn., 1932-34; attending surgeon Jewish Hosp., 1955-75; postgrad. study Royal Infirmary, Edinburgh, 1934-35; civilian cons. U.S. Army Hosp., Ft. Jay, N.Y., 1960-66; attending surgeon French Polyclinic Med. Sch. and Health Center, N.Y.C., 1966-76; pres. 1973—, trustee, 1972-76; attending surgeon Cabrini Health Care Center, 1976-86; cons. surgeon Cabrini Med. Ctr., 1986—, dir. surg. research, 1981—; clin. asst. prof. environ. medicine and community health State U. Coll. Medicine, N.Y.C., 1950-60; clin. prof. surgery N.Y. Med. Coll., 1981-86, prof. emeritus, 1986—; pvt. practice 1935-86; pres. Medbook Publs., Inc.; chmn. Med. Group Council, 1947-64; cons. Office and Profl. Employees Internat. Union (local 153) Health Plan, 1960-82, United Automobile Workers (local 259) Health Plan, 1960-86, Sanitationmen's Security Benefit Fund, 1964-83; dir. Surgery Internat. Ladies Garment Workers Union, 1970-85; med. adv. bd. Hotel Assn. and Hotel Workers Health Plan, 1950-60, Hosp. Workers Health Plan, 1970-76. Author and/or editor: Group Medicine and Health Insurance in Action, 1949, Understanding Surgery, 1955, New Illustrated Med. Ency., 4 vols., 1959, New Am. Med. Dictionary and Health Manual, 1962, Reoperative Surgery, 1964, Health in Later Years, 1964, Child Care Ency., 12 vols., 1966, Doctor's Premarital Medical Adviser, 1969, The Fast Diet Book, 1970, The Unabridged Medical Encyclopedia, 20 vols., 1973, Our Family Medical Record Book, 1973, The Complete Surgical Guide, 1973, What Every Patient Wants to Know, 1975, The Complete Book of Breast Care, 1975, Disney's Growing Up Healthy, 4 vols., 1975, First Aid—What to Do in an Emergency, 1976, The Plain Language Law Dictionary, 1980; contbr. articles to med. jours. Served to lt. col. M.C., AUS, 1942-45. Mem. ACS, AMA, Bklyn. Surg. Assn., N.Y. County Med. Soc., Alpha Omega Alpha. Home: 35 Sutton Pl New York NY 10022 also: Monterosso, Camaiore Italy

ROTHERMEL, RICHARD LLOYD, publishing sales company executive; b. Reading, Pa., May 10, 1926; s. Lloyd Rahn and Naomi (Brensinger) R.; m. Josephine Cecelia Stahler, Sept. 2, 1950; children—Cynthia M. Rothermel Edington, Kathy Jo Rothermel Hatch, David Lloyd. BS in Econs., Albright Coll., Pa., 1950. With Curtis Pub. Co., Phila., 1950-64; subscription mgr. McCall Pub. Co., N.Y.C., 1964-67; circulation dir. Dell Pub. Co., Inc., N.Y.C., 1967-71; v.p. mktg. Perfect Subscription Co., Phila., 1971-72; pres., chief exec. officer Keystone Readers' Service, Inc., Phila., 1972-80, Mag. Service Bur., Inc., Wayne, Pa., 1980—. Served with USNR, 1944-46, ETO. Am. Legion scholar, 1940. Mem. Soc. Preservation and Encouragement of Barbershop Quartet Singing in Am. (past chpt. pres.), XYZ Club (dir. 1969, 83), 100 Million Club. Republican. Presbyterian. Lodges: Masons, Shriners. Avocations: barbershop singing; tennis; bridge; golf; reading. Home: 713 Larchwood Ln Villanova PA 19085 Office: 151 S Warner Rd Wayne PA 19087

ROTHHAMMER, FRANCISCO, human geneticist, researcher, educator; b. Santiago, Chile, Nov. 9, 1940; s. Francisco and Tona (Engel) R.; m. Maria Olga Achondo, May 2, 1970 (div.); children: Francisco, Paula; m. Elena Llop, Nov. 6, 1980; children: Sebastian, Matias. DDS, U. Chile, Santiago, 1964, PhD, 1977. Assoc. prof. genetics U. Chile Med. Sch., 1970-75, prof., 1975—; prof. Austral U. Chile, Valdivia, 1973-77; dir. dept. cellular biology and genetics, faculty medicine U. Chile, 1974-76, 79-83; head unit human genetics, councilman U. Chile Faculty of Medicine, 1986—. Author: Curso Basico De Genetica Humana, 1977, 2d rev. edit., 1983, Genetica De Poblaciones Humanas, 1977, Desarrollo De Las Teorias Evolutivas Despues De Darwin, 1981; contbr. articles to profl. jours.; assoc. editor Revista Chilena Historia Natural, Santiago, 1983—; mem. editorial Archivos De Biologia Experimentales, Santiago, 1977—, Medio Ambiente, Valdivia, 1982—; mem. editorial com., chumgara, Arica, 1986—. NIH fellow U. Mich., 1970-73; Guggenheim fellow, 1986-87. Mem. Genetics Soc. Chile (pres. 1975-77), Biol. Soc. Chile, Archaelogical Soc. Chile, Physiol. Soc. Chile, Human Biology Council, Am. Assn. Phys. Anthropologists, Am. Soc. Human Genetics, Internat. Congresses Human Genetics (permanent com.). Home: Los Refugios 17241, Santiago Chile Office: U Chile Faculty Medicine, Dept Cellular Biology Genetics, Independencia 1027, Santiago Chile

ROTHMAN, BERNARD, lawyer; b. N.Y.C., Aug. 11, 1932; s. Harry and Rebecca (Fritz) R.; m. Barbara Joan Schaeffer, Aug. 1953; children—Brian, Adam, Helene. B.A. cum laude, CCNY, 1953; LL.B., NYU, 1959. Bar: N.Y. 1959, U.S Dist. Ct. (ea. and so. dists.) N.Y. 1962, U.S. Ct. Apls. (2d cir.) 1965, U.S. Supreme Ct. 1966, U.S. Tax Ct. 1971. Assoc. Held, Telchin & Held, 1961-62; asst. U.S. atty. U.S. Dept. Justice, 1962-66; assoc. Edward Gettinger & Peter Gettinger, 1966-68; ptnr. Schwartz, Rothman & Abrams, P.C., 1968-78; ptnr. Finkelstein, Bruckman, Wohl, Most & Rothman, N.Y.C., 1978—; acting judge Village of Larchmont, 1981-87, dep. Village atty., 1974-81, former arbitrator Civil Ct. N.Y.C., family disputes panel Am. Arbitration Assn., guest lectr. domestic relations and family law Cardozo Law Sch., Albert Einstein Coll. Med.; mem. exec. bd., past v.p. Westchester Putnam council Boy Scouts Am., past mem. nat. council, 1977-81, recipient Silver Beaver award, Wood Badge award; past pres. Congregation B'Nai Israel, 1961-63; pres. B'Nai B'rith, Larchmont chpt., 1981-83. Fellow Am. Acad. Matrimonial Lawyers (co-chmn. interdisciplinary com. on mental health and family law 1986—, bd. govs. N.Y. chpt. 1986—); mem. ABA (family law sect.), N.Y. State Bar Assn. (exec. com. family law sect. 1982, co-chmn. com. on mediation and arbitration 1982, com. on legis. 1978-86, com. on child custody 1985, contbr. articles Family Law Review, co-author Leaving Home, 1987), Assn. of Bar of City of N.Y., N.Y. State Magistrates Assn., Westchester Magistrates Assn. Democrat. Clubs: N.Y. Road Runners, Limousine 6 Track. Office: Finkelstein Bruckman Wohl Most & Rothman 801 2d Ave New York NY 10017

ROTHMAN, STEWART NEIL, photographer; b. Rochester, N.Y., Dec. 27, 1930; s. Morris Zeus and Rose Mary (Cotler) R.; student Wayne State U., 1952-54; m. Shirley Mae Derry, Sept. 12, 1957; children—Leslie Paula, Karen Pat. Free-lance photographer, Detroit, 1952-57; photographer NASA, Gilmore Creek, Alaska, 1965-68; writer, photographer Jessen's Daily, Fairbanks, Alaska, 1968-69; propr. The Lens Unlimited, Fairbanks, 1959—; staff photographer Gen. Mac Arthur's Hdqrs., Tokyo, 1948-50; pres., chmn. bd. Arctic Publs., 1968-72; pres. Public Relations Specialists Co., 1973—; editor Arctic Oil Jour., 1968-72, This Month in Fairbanks, 1974--85; pub. The Fairbanks Mag., 1985—. Publicity adviser to mayor of Fairbanks; pres. Tanana-Yukon Hist. Soc. Served with U.S. Army, 1948-52, Korea, then USAF, 1957-65. Decorated Purple Heart with oak leaf cluster. Fellow Master Photographers Assn. Gt. Britain; mem. European Council Photographers, Fairbanks C. of C. Club: Farthest North Press. Lodges: Lions (pres.), Elks. Author: Nudes of Sixteen Lands, 1971; Hobo and Dangerous Dan McGrew, 1975; The Lens is My Brush, 1977; China, The Opening Door, 1980; Pope John Paul II's First Visit to Alaska, 1981; Window on Life, 1982; The Pope and the President, 1984. Home and Office: 921 Woodway St Fairbanks AK 99709

ROTHSCHEIN, KAREL, chemist; b. Lomnice u Tisnova, Czechoslovakia, Dec. 18, 1935; s. Karel and Kamila (Havelka) R.; grad. U. Brno, 1958; C.Sc., Tech. U., Pardubice, 1974; m. Anna Cuprova, Mar. 31, 1959; children—Karel, Marie, Tom, Monika, Marketa, David. Tech. info. Vertex, Litomysl, Czechoslovakia, 1958-61, chemist devel., 1961-70, sci. group leader, 1970-74, research scientist, 1974—, tech. cons., 1994—. Mem. Soc. Sci. and Technology. Roman Catholic. Patentee in field; contbr. in field. Home: 121 Koncinska, 57001 Litomysl Czechoslovakia

ROTHSCHILD, DONALD PHILLIP, legal educator, arbitrator; b. Dayton, Ohio, Mar. 31, 1927; s. Leo and Anne (Office) R.; m. Ruth Eckstein, July 7, 1950; children—Nancy Lee, Judy Lynn Hoffman, James Alex. A.B., U. Mich., 1950; J.D. summa cum laude, U. Toledo, 1965; LL.M., Harvard U., 1966. Bar: Ohio 1966, D.C. 1970, U.S. Supreme Ct. 1975. Teaching fellow Harvard U. Law Sch., Cambridge, Mass., 1965-66; instr. solicitor's office U.S. Dept. Labor, Washington, 1966-67; vis. prof. U. Mich. Law Sch., Ann Arbor, 1976; prof. law George Washington U. Nat. Law Ctr., Washington, 1966—, dir. Consumer Protection Ctr., 1971—; dir. Inst. Law and Aging, Washington, 1973—, Ctr. for Community Justice, Washington, 1974—, Nat. Consumers League, Washington, 1981—; v.p. Regulatory Alternatives Devel. Corp., Washington, 1982—; cons. Washington Met. Council Govt., 1979-82; mayoral appointee Adv. Com. on Consumer Protection, Washington, 1979-80; chmn. bd. dirs. D.C. Citizens Complaint Ctr., Washington, 1980. Co-author: Consumer Protection Text and Materials, 1973; Collective Bargaining and Labor Arbitration, 1979; Fundamentals of Administrative Practice and Procedure, 1981. Contbr. numerous articles to profl. publs. Mem. FTC Adv. Council, Washington, 1970. Recipient Community Service award Television Acad., Washington, 1981. Mem. Nat. Acad. Arbitrators, Fed. Mediation and Conciliation Service, Am. Arbitration Assn., ABA, D.C. Bar Assn., Phi Kappa Phi. Jewish. Home: 2450 Virginia Ave NW Washington DC 20037 also: Shadow Farm Unit #4 Wakefield RI 02879 Office: George Washington U Nat Law Ctr Washington DC 20052

ROTHSCHILD, JOHN DAVID, art dealer; b. Chgo., June 22, 1940; s. Seymour Hampton Rothschild and Louise (Guthman) Fink; m. Carolyn Anita Kohl, Nov. 26, 1966. BS, MIT, 1962; MBA, Columbia U., 1964. Mktg. exec. Young & Rubicam, Inc., N.Y.C., 1964-77; owner, treas. Rothschild Fine Arts, Inc., N.Y.C., 1977—; dir. 205 West End Ave. Owners Corp., 1987—.

ROTHSCHILD, KURT WILHELM, professor emeritus, consultant; b. Vienna, Austria, Oct. 21, 1914; s. Ernst and Phillippine (Hollub) R.; m. Valerie Kunke, Aug. 10, 1938; children: Thomas, Elisabeth. JD, Vienna U., 1938; MA in Econs., Glasgow U., 1940; Dr h.c., U. Aachen, 1987. Asst. lectr. econs. U. Glasgow, Eng., 1940-47; sr. researcher Austria Inst. Econ. Research, Vienna, 1947-66; prof. econs. U. Linz, Austria, 1966-85; prof. emeritus U. Linz, Linz, Austria, 1985—. Author; Theory of Wages, 1954, Economic Forecasting, 1969, Economics of Power, 1971, Unemployment, 1988. Recipient Sci. reward City of Vienna, 1980, Sci. medal City of Linz, 1982; Order of Merit, Austrian Rep., 1986. Mem. Austria Econ. Assn., Royal Econs. Soc. Club: Rome. Home: Doeblinger Haupstrasse 77a, A1190 Vienna Austria

ROTHSCHILD, V. HENRY, II, lawyer; b. N.Y.C., Apr. 4, 1908; s. Victor Sidney and Lily (Sulzberger) R.; m. Ann Eleanor Hatfield, May 29, 1939 (div.); children: Thomas Adams, V. Henry III; m. Jacqueline Dury Roy; stepchildren: Michel, Serge, Christian Roy. A.B. with honors, Cornell U., 1929; LL.B. with honors, Yale U., 1932. Bar: N.Y. 1934. Since practiced in N.Y.C; asso. Root, Clark, Buckner & Ballantine (now Dewey, Ballantine, Bushby, Palmer & Wood), N.Y.C., 1932-40; mem. Rothschild & Salwen, N.Y.C., 1955-81; counsel Lord Day & Lord, Barrett Smith, N.Y.C., 1981—; mem. Salary Stblzn. Bd., 1951-52, chief counsel, 1951, vice chmn., 1952; lectr. Practising Law Inst., NYU Inst. Fed. Taxation. Author: (with William J. Casey) Pay Contracts with Key Men, 1952; (with J.K. Lasser) Deferred Compensation for Executives, 1955, Compensating the Corporate Executive, 1962; (with George Thomas Washington), 3d edit., 1962; (with Myer Feldman) Executive Compensation and Federal Securities Legislation, 1957, Financing Stock Purchases, 1957, Expense Accounts for Executives, 1958, Business Gifts as Income, 1961, The New Stock Option, 1965, Top Management Compensation Outlook, 1966, The Restricted Stock Arrangement, 1968; (with Peter Miller) Employee Stock Options and the New Maximum Tax Rate on Earned Income, 1971, Stock Option Plans in France, 1972; (with Jack B. Salwen) Stock Option Plans in Transition, 1973, Regulation of Deferred Compensation for Executives by the Pension Reform Act, 1975, Funding Deferred Compensation Arrangements, 1976; (with Robert J. Salwen) Protecting the Executive against Inflation, 1980; (with Arthur D. Sporn) Executive Compensation, 1984, 2d edit.; contbg. author: Executive Compensation, a Road Map for the Corporate Advisor, 1984; contbr. articles to legal and non-legal publs.; editor: Yale Law Sch. Jour., 1930-32. Hon. trustee Asso. YM-YMCA Greater N.Y. Mem. ABA (mem. sect. corp., banking and bus., com. on employee benefits, tax), N.Y. State Bar Assn. (chmn. com. on employee benefits 1968-70, chmn. com. retirement plan 1971-76), N.Y.C. Bar Assn., Am. Arbitration Assn. (nat. panel), Am. Pension Conf. (steering com. 1966-70), Phi Beta Kappa, Phi Kappa Phi, Pi Lambda Phi. Clubs: Sky (N.Y.C.), Yale (N.Y.C.). Home: 25 E 92d St New York NY 10128 also: PO Box 935 Truro MA 02666 Office: Lord Day & Lord 25 Broadway New York NY 10004

ROTHSTEIN, SAMUEL, librarian, educator; b. Moscow, Russia, Jan. 12, 1921; emigrated to Can., 1922, naturalized, 1929; s. Louis Israel and Rose (Checov) R.; m. Miriam Ruth Teitelbaum, Aug. 26, 1951; children: Linda Rose, Sharon Lee. B.A., U. B.C., 1939, M.A., 1940; student, U. Calif. at Berkeley, 1941-42, B.L.S., 1947; student, U. Wash., 1942-43; Ph.D. (Carnegie Corp. fellow 1951-54), U. Ill., 1954; D.Litt., York U., 1971. Teaching fellow U. Wash., 1942-43; prin. library asst. U. Calif. at Berkeley Library, 1947—; mem. staff U. B.C. Library, 1946-51, 54-62; acting univ. librarian U. B.C., 1961-62, prof. library sci., 1961—, dir. Sch. Librarianship,, 1961-70; vis. prof. U. Hawaii, 1969, U. Toronto, 1970, 79, Hebrew U., Jerusalem, 1973; Mem. Commn. Nat. Plan Library Edn., 1963—; mem. assoc. com. sci. information Nat. Research Council Can., 1962—; councillor B.C. Med. Library Service, 1961, Pacific div. Canadian Jewish Congress, 1962—, Internat. House Assn. B.C., 1959-60; mem. Canadian Adv. Bd. Sci. and Tech. Info.; pres. Vancouver Pub. Library Trust, 1987-88. Author: The Development of Reference Services, 1955, (with others) Training Professional Librarians for Western Canada, 1957, The University-The Library, 1972; also articles.; Co-editor: As We Remember It, 1970. Bd. dirs. Jewish Community Centre of Vancouver, pres., 1972-74. Served with Canadian Army, 1943-46. Recipient Helen Gordon Stewart award, 1970, ALISE award Assn. Library Info. Sci. Edn., 1987. Mem. Assn. Am. Library Schs. (pres. 1968-69), Can. Assn. Library Schs. (pres. 1982-84), ALA (council 1963-69, Beta Phi Mu award 1988), B.C. Library Assn. (pres. 1959-60, hon. life mem.), Pacific N.W. Library Assn. (pres. 1963-64, hon. life mem.), Canadian Library Assn. (council 1958-60, Outstanding Service to Librarianship award 1986), Bibliog. Soc. Can. (council 1959-63), Canadian Assn. U. Tchrs. Home: 1416 W 40th Ave, Vancouver, BC Canada

ROTHWELL, VICTOR HOWARD, historian, educator; b. Hyde, Cheshire, Eng., Apr. 11, 1945; s. Harry and Hilda (Holland) R.; m. Margaret Cowin, Mar. 27, 1971; children: Sonya Jane, Nyree Margaret. BA, Nottingham U., 1966; PhD, Leeds U., 1969. Asst. prof. U. Edinburgh, Scotland, 1970—. Author: British War Aims 1914-18, 1971, Britain and the Cold War 1941-47, 1982; contbr. articles to profl. publs. Office: Dept History U Edinburgh, Robertson Bldg, George Sq, Edinburgh EH8 9JY, Scotland

ROTOLO, ELIO RICHARD, management consultant; b. N.Y.C., Jan. 2, 1924; s. Rosario and Antoinette Carbonaro; student Bklyn. Coll., 1942; B.S., Lehigh U., 1949; postgrad. Rutgers U., 1953-55, Stevens Inst., 1963-66; children—Claudia Ann, Debra Carla. Mgr. indsl. engring. Dollin Corp., Irvington, N.J., 1952-60; prin. Arthur Young & Co., N.Y.C., 1960-70; dir. mfg. engring. ITT, N.Y.C., 1970-75; v.p. Security Pacific Nat. Bank, Los Angeles, 1975-82; pres. Rotolo & Whitney, Inc., Pasadena, Calif., 1982—; sr. v.p. Fin. Corp. Am., 1984—; mem. faculty Sch. Bank Adminstrn., Madison, Wis. Chmn., Los Angeles County Productivity Adv. Com.; Republican county committeeman, Union, N.J., 1955-60; chmn. bd. dirs. Productivity Ctr. S.W.; bd. dirs. Opera Guild So. Calif. Served to 1st lt. AUS, 1942-45. Registered prof. engr., Calif. Fellow Am. Inst. Indsl. Engrs. (nat. pres. 1967-68); mem. Engrs. Joint Council (dir.), Office Automation Council (dir.), Nat. Soc. Profl. Engrs., Newcomen Soc. Lodge: Lions. Contbr. articles to profl. jours.; editorial adv. bd. Office Adminstrn. and Automation mag.; editor-in-chief: Handbook of Office and Information Automation. Home: 4369 LaBarca Dr Tarzana CA 91356 Office: 15260 Ventura Blvd Suite 1500 Sherman Oaks CA 91403

ROTTER, PAUL TALBOTT, retired insurance executive; b. Parsons, Kans., Feb. 21, 1918; s. J. and LaNora (Talbott) R.; m. Virginia Sutherlin Barksdale, July 17, 1943; children—Carolyn Sutherlin, Diane Talbott. B.S. summa cum laude, Harvard U., 1937. Asst. mathematician Prudential Ins. Co. of Am., Newark, 1938-46; with Mut. Benefit Life Ins. Co., Newark, 1946—; successively asst. mathematician, asso. mathematician, mathematician Mut. Benefit Life Ins. Co., 1946-59, v.p., 1959-69, exec. v.p., 1969-80, ret., 1980. Mem. Madison Bd. Edn., 1958-64, pres., 1959-64; Trustee, mem. budget com. United Campaign of Madison, 1951-55; mem. bd., chmn. advancement com. Robert Treat council Boy Scouts Am., 1959-64. Fellow Soc. Actuaries (bd. govs. 1965-68, gen. chmn. edn. and exam. com. 1963-66, chmn. adv. com. edn. and exam. 1969-72); mem. Brit. Inst. Actuaries (asso.), Am. Acad. Actuaries (v.p. 1968-70, bd. dirs., chmn. edn. and exam. com. 1965-66, chmn. rev. and evaluation com. 1968-74), Asso. Harvard Alumni (regional dir. 1965-69), Actuaries Club N.Y. (pres. 1967-68), Harvard Alumni Assn. (v.p. 1964-66),Am. Lawn Bowls Assn. (pres. SW div.), Phi Beta Kappa Assos., Phi Beta Kappa. Clubs: Harvard N.J. (pres. 1956-57); Harvard (N.Y.C.); Morris County Golf (Convent, N.J.). Home: 18278 Canfield Pl San Diego CA 92128

ROTTGERS, KURT, philosopher, educator; b. Marienwerder, Germany, July 21, 1944; s. Heinz and Ursula (Engel) R.; children: Tanja, Silja, Janko. Dr Phil, U. Bochum, 1972; habilitation, U. Giessen, 1981. Asst. U. Bielefeld, Fed. Republic Germany, 1970-83; privat dozent U. Giessen, Fed. Republic Germany, 1981-84; prof. U. Hagen, Fed. Republic Germany, 1984—. Author: Kritik und Praxis, 1975, Gewalt, 1978, Der Kommunikative Text, 1982, Texte und Menschen, 1983. Office: Fernuniversitat Gesamthochschule, Postfach 940, 5800 Hagen 1, Federal Republic of Germany

ROTUNDA, DONALD THEODORE, corp. communications ofcl.; b. Blue Island, Ill., Feb. 14, 1945; s. Nicholas and Frances (Manna) R.; B.A., Georgetown U., 1967; M.A., London Sch. Econs., 1968, Ph.D., 1972. Analyst, NASA, Washington, 1972; lectr. in econs. U. D.C., 1973; legis. asst. Ho. of Reps., Washington, 1974-76, economist budget com., 1977; mgmt. analyst Office Mgmt. and Budget, Washington, 1977-81; cons., 1981-82; mgr. editorial services United Technologies Corp., Hartford, Conn., 1982-87, mgr. editorial services, Pepsico, Purchase, N.Y., 1987—. Roman Catholic. Contbr. numerous articles to Washington Post, New Republic, Saturday Rev. Home: 20 Church St Apt A-64 Greenwich CT 06830 Office: Pepsico Purchase NY 10577

RÖTZSCH, HELMUT KARL WERNER, library director; b. Leipzig, Germany, Dec. 17, 1923; s. Karl and Helene (Hennig) R.; m. Ursula Heinz, Sept. 1, 1951; 1 son, Michael. Bookseller, Booksellers' Tng. Coll., Leipzig, 1941; M.A., Karl Marx U., 1950, Ph.D., 1969. Head adminstrn. and personnel dept. Deutsche Bücherei, Leipzig, German Democratic Republic, 1950-53, head acquisitions dept., 1953-59, dep. dir.-gen., 1959-61, dir. gen., 1961—; titular prof. Karl Marx U., 1970; Oberbibliotheksrat, 1983; mem. UNESCO-Kommission der DDR, 1973—. Author booklets: Der Börsenverein der Deutschen Buchhändler zu Leipzig und die Deutsche Bücherei, 1962; Die Deutsche Bücherei— die deutsche Nationalbibliothek, 1962; Anton Graff und seine Buchhändlerporträts, 1965; co-author: Die Deutsche Bücherei in Leipzig, 1987; editor: Deutsche Bücherei— 1912-1962, 1962; co-editor yearbook: Jahrbuch der Deutschen Bücherei, 1965; co-editor series: Beiträge zur Geschichte des Buchwesens, 1965. Town councillor City of Leipzig, 1961—. Decorated Order Banner of Labor, 1976; recipient Disting. Service medal of German Democratic Republic, 1959, Nat. Disting. Service Bronze medal of German Dem. Republic, 1964, Nat. Disting. Service Silver medal of German Dem. Republic, 1980. Mem. Bibliotheksverband of D.D.R. (pres.1968-74), Nationaler Rat der D.D.R. zur Pflege und Verbreitung des Deutschen Kulturerbes. Office: Deutsche Bücherei, Deutscher Platz 1, 7010 Leipzig German Democratic Republic

ROU, HENRY JENNINGS, II, citrus company executive; b. Leesburg, Fla., Feb. 13, 1935; s. Henry Jennings and Martha (Albright) R.; m. Ann Huffstetler, Nov. 13, 1960; children: Jennifer E. Woodburry, Henry Jennings III, Alison W. BS, Fla. So. Coll., 1960. Pres., chmn. bd. H. Jennings Rou Inc., Citrus, Eustis, Fla., 1966—; dir. Foremost Fertilizer Co., Leesburg, First Union Nat. Bank, Eustis; trustee Fla. Citrus Showcase, Winter Haven, 1980—; pres., bd. dirs. Fla. Orange Marketers, Leesburg, 1988—; chmn. Lake-Orange Extension Citrus Adv. Com., 1985-87; bd. dirs. Fla. Citrus Packers, Lakeland. Served with USAF, 1953-57. Recipient Outstanding Service award Citrus Inst., Fla. So. Coll., 1977, cert. of appreciation, Fla. Citrus Mut., Lakeland, 1976. Mem. Fla. Fruit and Vegetable Assn. (dir. Orlando 1982—). Republican. Presbyterian. Clubs: Pine Meadow Country (Eustis) (pres. 1977-78); Florida (Winter Haven); Citrus (Orlando). Lodges: Kiwanis (v.p. Eustis 1974), Elks. Home: 2000 Country Club Dr Eustis FL 32726 Office: PO Box 1130 400 S Bay St Eustis FL 32727-1130

ROUAULT DE LA VIGNE, HENRI, physician; b. Dinan, Brittany, France, May 5, 1953; s. Alain and Elisabeth (Rousselin) Rouault de la V.; m. Sabine de Gouzillon de Belizal, Sept. 19, 1981; children: Nicolas, Gabrielle, Cecile. MD, Faculte de Med., Rennes, France, 1982. Gen. practice medicine St. Georges de Reintembault, France, 1982—. Home: Chateau du Logis, 35420 Poilley France Office: 25 rue Leclerc, 35420 Saint Georges de Reintembault France

ROUCHITSAS, SPIROS, marketing executive, consultant; b. Pireas, Attica, Greece, Sept. 2, 1955; s. Panagiotis and Katerina Rouchitsas; m. Isabelle Houdement, Aug. 24, 1985. BBA, Athens Bus. Sch., 1978; MBA, Dalhousie U., 1980. Analyst Athens Stock Exchange, Greece, 1981; trainee Soc. Gen., Paris, France, 1982, Bank de la Henin, Paris, 1982-83; group product mgr. Unilever, Greece, 1983—; co-owner cons. firm Athens, 1985. Mem. Internat. students Assn. (exchange controller 1975, v.p. 1976, cons. 1981), Greek

Mktg. Assn., Greek Adv. Assn. Home and Office: 3 Laodikias St, 18453 Nikea, Pireas Greece

ROUDYBUSH, ALEXANDRA, novelist; b. Hyres, Cote d'Azur, France, Mar. 14, 1911; d. Constantine and Ethel (Wheeler) Brown; student St. Paul's Sch. for Girls, London; m. Franklin Roudybush, 1942. Journalist, London Eve. Standard, 1931, Time mag., 1933, French News Agy., 1935, CBS, 1936, MBS, 1940; White House corr. MBC Radio, 1940-48; author: Before the Ball Was Over, 1965; Death of a Moral Person, 1967; Capital Crime, 1969; House of the Cat, 1970; A Sybaritic Death, 1972; Suddenly in Paris, 1975; The Female of the Species, 1977; Blood Ties, 1981. Mem. Crime Writers Am. and Brit. Democrat. Episcopalian. Clubs: Am. Woman's (Paris); Miramar Golf (Porto, Portugal).

ROUDYBUSH, FRANKLIN, diplomat, educator; b. Washington, Sept. 17, 1906; s. Rumsey Franklin and Frances (Mahon) R.; student U. Vienna, 1925, Ecole National des Langues Orintales Vivantes, Paris, 1926, U. Paris, 1926-28, U. Madrid, 1928, Academie Julian, Paris, 1967; B.Fgn. Service, Georgetown U., 1930; postgrad. Harvard U., 1931; M.A., George Washington U., 1944; Ph.D., U. Strasbourg (France), 1953; m. Alexandra Brown, May 22, 1941. Dean Roudybush Fgn. Service Schs., Washington, Los Angeles, Phila., N.Y.C., 1932—. Prof. internat. econ. relations Southeastern U., Washington, 1938-42; dir. Pan Am. Inst., Washington, 1934; editor Affairs, 1934-45; commodity economist, statistician Dept. State, 1945; with Fgn. Service Inst., Dept. State, 1945-48, Council of Europe, Strasbourg, 1948-54, Am. Embassy, Paris, 1954, Pakistan, 1955, Dublin, 1956. Mem. Am. Soc. Internat. Law, Brit. Inst. Internat. and Comparative Law (London), Delta Phi Epsilon. Clubs: Assns des Amis du Salon d'Automne (Paris); France Amerique; English Speaking Union (London); Nat. Press (Washington); Harvard (Paris), Royal Aberdeen Golf; Miramar Golf (Oporto, Portugal), Yacht (Angiers, France); Pormarnock Golf (Dublin); Les Societe des Artistes Independants Grand Palais (Paris). Author: The Twentieth Century; The Battle of Cultures; Diplomatic Language; Twentieth Century Diplomacy; The Present State of Western Capitalism, 1959; Diplomacy and Art, French Educational System, 1971; The Techniques of International Negotiation, 1979; The Diplomacy of the Cardinal, Duke de Richilieu, 1980. Home: Villa St Honoré, Moledo do Minho, Minho Portugal Office: 15 Ave du President Wilson, Paris 16, France also: Sauveterre de Rouerque, 12800 Aveyron France

ROUGÉ, BERNARD, image processing engineer; b. Montpellier, France, Dec. 31, 1943; s. Pierre and Marcelle Rougé. D of Math., U. Paris, 1970. Researcher Ctr. Nat. Recherche Scientifique, Paris, 1970; engr. Electricité de France, Paris, 1971-72; image processing engr. Ctr. Nat. d'Etudes Spatiales, Toulouse, France, 1973—. Inventor image mosaic, image clustering. Home: 19 Bonnat St, 31400 Toulouse France Office: Ctr Nat d'Etudes Spatiales, 18 Ave Edouard Belin, 31055 Toulouse France

ROUGEMONT, MICHEL, physician; b. Bourg en Bresse, France, Sept. 19, 1946; s. Jean and Rene (Ladre) R.; m. Josette Chichoux, Sept. 4, 1971; children: Real, Alexis. MD, U. Lyon, 1975. Resident in surgery Hosp. Vienne, France, 1972-73; asst. for surgery research Hosp. Sherbrooke, Que., Can., 1973-75; resident medicine Hosp. Valence, France, 1975; gen. practice medicine Bourg en Bresse, 1976—; mem. com. for County of Ain in charg of career placement of handicapped citizens, France, 1977—; med. expert ins. cos., France 1976—, Ct. of Appeals of Lyon and Mcpl. Cts. Bourg en Bresse, 1978—, social security, France, 1981—; forensic expert county of Ain, France, 1983—. Assoc. Judge Mcpl. Ct. (concerning children), Bourg en Bresse, 1978—; chmn. Club-Avenir et Liberte, County of Ain, 1982—; nat. sec. Assn. Health Profls. for Prevention of Nuclear-Biol.-Chem. Warfare, France 1985—; mem. exec. intelligence review Biol. Holocaust Task Force USA, 1985—; chmn. Club-Sante Liberte, County of Ain, 1987—. Office: Ave des Belges No 6, 01000 Bourg en Bresse France

ROUGEMONT, MICHEL, physician, medical expert; b. Bourg en Bresse, France, Sept. 19, 1946; s. Jean and Renee (Ladre) R.; m. Josette Chichoux, Sept. 4, 1971; children: Real, Alexis. MD, U. Lyon, France, 1975. Cert. medical accident expert, forensic medicine practitioner. Resident in surgery Hospital Vienne, France, 1972-73; asst. surgery research U. Sherbrooke Hosp., Quebec, Can., 1973-75; resident in medicine Hosp. Valence, France, 1975; gen. practice medicine Bourg en Bresse, 1976—; med. expert various ins. French cos., 1976—, Lyon Appeals Ct. and Municipal Ct. Bourg en Bresse, 1978—, Social Security France, 1981—; assoc. judge Municipal Ct. Bourg en Bresse, 1978—; forensic expert Ain County, 1983—. Mem. Com. Career Placement for Handicapped Citizens, Ain County, 1977—, exec. intelligence rev. Biol. Holocaust Task Force USA, 1985—; chmn. Club Avenir et Liberte, Ain County, 1982—. Mem. Assn. of Health Profls. for the Prevention of Nuclear-Biol.-Chem. Warfare (nat. sec. 1985—), Club Avenir et Liberte (chmn. Ain County, 1982—). Office: Avenue des Belges No 6, 01000 Bourg en Bresse France

ROUHANI, MEHRDAD ZIA, transportation executive, consultant; b. Dubai, United Arab Emirates, Oct. 11, 1959; s. Zia Khalil and Shidrokh Misaghi R. BS, U. Calif., Davis, 1981; MS, Cranfield (Eng.) Inst. Tech., 1984. Data processing mgr. Rouhani Showrooms, Dubai, 1981-82, br. mgr., 1984—. Mem. Am. Inst. Aeronautics & Astronautics, Royal Aeronautical Soc., Chartered Inst. Transport. Baha'i Faith. Home: PO Box 616, Dubai United Arab Emirates

ROUHBAN, BADAOUI MICHEL, civil engineer; b. Zgharta, Lebanon, June 29, 1951; came to France, 1974; s. Michel Youssef and Maria (Zaloua) R. Diplôme of Civil Engring., Ecole Supérieure d'Ingénieurs-Lebanon, 1974; Cert., CHEBAP, Paris, 1974-75; Dr.Engring. U. Pierre et Marie Curie, 1978. Civil engr. SODETEG, Paris, 1980-81; cons. UNESCO, Paris, 1981-83, program specialist, 1983—. Co-editor: Assessment and Mitigation of Earthquake Risk in the Arab Region, 1984. Contbr. articles to profl. jours. Mem. Seismological Soc. Am., Am. Geophys. Union, Assn. Française de Génie Parasismique, Earthquake Engring. Research Inst. Home: 4 Villa Poirier, 75015 Paris France Office: UNESCO div Earth Scis, 7 Place Fontenoy, 75007 Paris France

ROUILLON, FERNAND MARIE JOSEPH, former French ambassador to Turkey; b. Condrieu, France, Dec. 11, 1920; s. Albert and Marguerite (Bassieux) R.; m. Annick Chavoix, July 13, 1946; children: Anne, Giselle, Françoise, Perrine, Nathalie, Alice, Juliette, Vincent, Stephanie. Licencie es lettres, Bordeaux U. (France), 1942; diplôme d'etudes supèrieures de droit, 1942; diplôme de l'Ecole libre des sciences politique, Paris Sch. Polit. Sci., 1943. With French Fgn. Service, 1944—, 2d, then 1st counselor to UN, 1963, ambassador to Syria, 1975-81, Turkey, Ankara, 1982-86. Decorated French Legion d'Honneur, French Merite Nat. Order, numerous fgn. decorations. Home: 78 Rue du Chateau, 75014 Paris France Office: Foreign Ministry, 37 Quai d'Orsay, Paris France

ROUND, NICHOLAS GRENVILLE, language educator; b. Looe, Cornwall, Eng., June 6, 1938; s. Isaac Eric and Laura Christabel (Poole) R.; m. Ann Le Vin, Mar. 29, 1966; 1 child, Gráine Ann. BA in Spanish and French with honors, Oxford U., 1959, MA, 1964, PhD, 1967. Lectr. in Spanish Queen's U., Belfast, 1962-71, reader in Spanish, 1971-72; Stevenson prof. Hispanic studies U. Glasgow, Scotland, 1972—. Author: Abel Sanchez: A Critical Guide, 1974, The Greatest Man Uncrowned, 1986; editor, translator: Tirso de Molina: Damned for Despair, 1986; editor: Studies for Geoffrey Connell, 1985; mem. editorial bd. BHS Hispanic Texts and Monographs series, 1986, Westfield Coll. Medieval Studies Newsletter, 1987—, Bull. Hispanic Studies, 1987—; contbr. to numerous jours. Mem. regional exec. council Labour party, Strathclyde, 1986—. Grantee Brit. Acad., 1978, 83. Mem. Assn. Hispanists Gt. Britain and Ireland (nat. com. 1970-73), Modern Humanities Research Assn., MLA, Soc. Study Medieval Langs. and Lit., Internat. Assn. Hispanists. Home: 11 Dougalston Ave, Milngavie Glasgow G62 6AS, Scotland Office: U Glasgow, Dept Hispanic Studies, Glasgow G12 8QL, Scotland

ROUNICK, JACK A., lawyer; b. Phila., June 5, 1935; s. Philip and Nettie (Brownstein) R.; B.B.A., U. Mich., 1956; J.D., U. Pa., 1959; m. Noreen A. Garrigan, Sept. 4, 1970; children—Ellen, Eric, Amy, Michelle. Admitted to Pa. bar, 1960, U.S. Dist. Ct. (ea. dist.) Pa., 1960; spl. asst. atty. gen., 1963-71; ptnr. Israelit & Rounick, 1960-67, Moss & Rounick, 1968-69, Moss, Rounick & Hurowitz, Norristown, Pa., 1969-72, Moss & Rounick, Norristown, 1972-73; ptnr. Pechner, Dorfman, Wolffe, Rounick and Cabot, Norristown, 1973-87; v.p., gen. counsel Martin Lawrence Ltd. Editions, Inc., 1987—; dir. Martin Lawrence Ltd. Editions, Inc., 1984—, Deb Shops, Inc., 1974—. Fin. chmn. Pa. Young Rep., 1964-66, treas., 1966-68, chmn., 1968-70. Recipient Boss of Yr. award Montgomery County Legal Secs. Assn., 1970, cert. of appreciation Pa. Bar Inst., 1980. Fellow Am. Acad. Matrimonial Lawyers (pres. Pa. chpt. 1982-84, gov. 1983-85, v.p. 1985-87); mem. ABA, (council family law sect. 1982-87, chmn. scope and correlation com. family law sect. 1984-86), Pa. Bar Assn. (past chmn. family law sect.; Spl. Achievement award 1979-80), Montgomery Bar Assn., Am. Friends of the Hebrew U. (Phila. chpt. pres. 1988—). Republican. Jewish. Author: Pennsylvania Matrimonial Practice, 3 vols., 1982. Editor, Pa. Family Lawyer, 1980-87. Contbr. articles to profl. jours. Office: Martin Lawrence Galleries 151 E 10th Ave Conshohocken PA 19428

ROUQUIER, FREDERIC PAUL, physician; b. Kankan, Guinea, Nov. 11, 1956; s. Maurice Jean and Alice Celine Daniele (Rigal) R.; m. Rosetti Augusta; children: Celine, Emile, Sandrine. MD, diploma in Tropical Medicine, Hosp. of Pitie-Salpetriere, 1982. Physician Mimongo, Gabon, 1983; gen. practice medicine St.-Cezaire-sur-Siagne, France, 1984—. Home and Office: Rue Issaurat, 06780 Saint-Cezaire-sur-Siagne France

ROUS, STEPHEN NORMAN, physician, educator, editor; b. N.Y.C., Nov. 1, 1931; s. David H. and Luba (Margulies) R.; m. Margot Woolfolk, Nov. 12, 1966; children: Benjamin, David. A.B., Amherst Coll., 1952; M.D., N.Y. Med. Coll., 1956; M.S., U. Minn., 1963. Diplomate: Am. Bd. Urology. Intern Phila. Gen. Hosp., 1956-57, resident, 1959-60; resident Flower-Fifth Ave. and Met. Hosp., N.Y.C., 1957-59, Mayo Clinic, Rochester, Minn., 1960-63; practice medicine specializing in urology San Francisco, 1963-68; asso. prof. urology N.Y. Med. Coll., N.Y.C., 1968-72; asso. dean N.Y. Med. Coll., 1970-72; prof. surgery, chief div. urology Mich. State U., East Lansing, 1972-75; prof., chmn. dept. urology Med. U. S.C., Charleston, 1975-88; urologist-in-chief Med. U. S.C. and County hosps., Charleston, 1975-88; editorial dir. Norton Med. Books div. W.W. Norton and Co., 1988—; adj. prof. urology U. S.C., 1988—, adj. prof. surgery Dartmouth Med. Sch., 1988—; cons. urologist Saginaw VA Hosp., 1972-75, Charleston VA Hosp., 1975-88; hon. cons. St. Peter's Hosp., London, 1981-82; sr. vis. fellow Inst. Urology, London, 1981-82; mil. cons. in urology USAF Surgeon Gen., 1982-85; chmn. alumni devel. com. Mayo Clinic, 1979-82; hon. staff The Exeter Hosp., N.H., 1988—. Author: Understanding Urology, 1973, Urology in Primary Care, 1976, Spanish edit., 1978, Russian edit., 1979, Urology: A Core Textbook, 1985, The Prostate Book, 1988; editor: Urology Annual, 1987, 88, Stone Disease: Diagnosis and Management, 1987; contbr. articles to profl. jours. Mem. East Lansing Planning Commn., 1974-75; vestryman, jr. warden All Saints Episcopal Ch., 1974-75, lay reader, mem. diocesan com. on continuing edn., 1975-86 ; vestryman St. Michael's Episcopal Ch., 1979-82, chmn. every mem. canvas, 1979, 80, chmn. lay readers, 1983-86. Apptd. col. USAFR, 1980-85, USAR, 1985—. Fellow ACS, Am. Acad. Pediatrics; mem. Soc. Univ. Urologists, Internat. Soc. Urology, Am. Urol. Assn., AMA, Nat. Urologic Forum, Soc. Pediatric Urology, Brit. Assn. Urological Surgeons, German Urological Assn. (hon. 1986), Mayo Alumni Assn. (v.p. 1979-81, pres. 1983-85), Alpha Omega Alpha (hon. 1987). Republican. Clubs: Army and Navy (Washington), Lotos (N.Y.C.). Home: 32 Sanborn Rd Hampton Falls NH 03844 Office: The Long Block 4 Franklin St Exeter NH 03833

ROUSE, ELOISE MEADOWS, foundation executive; b. Shreveport, La., July 22, 1931; d. Curtis Washington and Lucille Eloise (Loyd) Meadows; m. Dudley Lee Rouse, Aug. 26, 1952; children: Deborah L., Lee, Elizabeth M. B of Music Edn., Baylor U., 1952. Tchr. 1st grade Brentwood Elem. Sch., Austin, Tex., 1953-55; v.p., dir., mem. grants rev. com., The Meadows Found., Dallas, 1979—. Mem. honor bd. New Horizons Ranch and Ctr. Home for Troubled Youth, Goldthwaite, Tex.; mem. exec. bd. Meadows Sch. of the Arts, So. Meth. U., Dallas; mem. exec. com., bd. dirs. Dallas Summer Musicals; bd. dirs., mem. exec. com. Nat. Wildflower Research Ctr.; mem. adv. com. Baylor U. Sch. Music; chair, mem., 2d v.p. program com. Conf. S.W. Founds.; mem. landscape devel. com. Dallas Garden Ctr.; active Dallas Mus. Art, Wadley Guild, Dallas Summer Musicals Guild; mem. exec.'s Bible class 1st Bapt. Ch. Dallas, past Sunday sch. tchr., past mem. music com. Mem. Nat. Trust Hist. Preservation, Park Cities Hist. Soc., Internat. Platform Assn., DAR, Council on Founds., Independent Sector. Clubs: Village Gardeners' Garden (former 1st v.p.), Marianne Scruggs Garden, Crystal Charity Ball Com., Dallas Country, Dallas Women's, Lancers (Dallas); Ponte Vedra (Fla.) Inn and Club, Tournament Players; Pelican (Galveston, Tex.). Office: The Meadows Found 2922 Swiss Ave Dallas TX 75204

ROUSE, STANLEY HARRY, retired securities and insurance executive; b. Cin., Sept. 4, 1927; s. Clifford S. and Ada Z. (Rolf) R.; m. Virginia P. Richardson, Apr. 29, 1950; children: Deborah Rouse Aliberti, Gregory Stanley. Student U. Cin., 1945-48. Mgr. Westheimer & Co., Cin., 1948-61; v.p., sec. Robinson-Humphrey Co., Inc., Atlanta, 1961-68, 75-77; prin. Stanley H. Rouse & Co., from 1978, now ret. v.p. Courts & Co., Atlanta, 1968-69; sr. v.p., treas. Roberts, Scott & Co., Inc., San Diego, 1969-71; sr. v.p. First Albany Corp., Albany, N.Y., 1971-74; supr. Paul Revere Life Ins. Co., Albany, 1974-75; allied mem. N.Y. Stock Exchange. Mem. exec. com., dad's com. Stephens Coll., Columbia, Mo., 1971-72. Served with USNR, 1945. Mem. Nat. Machine Accts. Assn. (pres. 1957), Nat. Assn. Securities Dealers (regulation T com. N.Y. 1973-74).

ROUSSEAU, DANICK JEAN, manufacturing executive; b. Boulogne, France, Dec. 13, 1937; s. Jean Armand and Gisele (Levaillant) R.; m. Therese de Cherisey, July 8, 1967 (div. Oct. 1978); children: Axel, Robin, Fabrice; m. Francoise Gouffault, Oct. 30, 1982; 1 stepchild, Julien Goupil. Student, Ecole Poly., Paris, 1956-58, Ecole des Ponts et Chaussees, Paris, 1959-61; MBA, Harvard U., 1964. Cert. engr. Cons., gen. mgr. SEMA, Paris, 1968-72; v.p. plastics div. Hutchinson, Paris, 1979-80, dir. corp. strategy, 1981-84, v.p. spl. products, 1984, exec. v.p., 1984—. Served to lt. French Army, 1959, 61-62. Club: Harvard Bus. Sch. France. Home: 65 Rue La Fontaine, 75016 Paris France Office: Hutchinson, 2 Rue Balzac, 75008 Paris France

ROUSSEAU, FRANÇOIS-OLIVIER, writer; b. Paris, Sept. 20, 1947; m. Joanna Ekaterina Kouklakis, Feb. 28, 1975. Licence de lettres, U. Paris X, U. Paris-Sorbonne, 1969. Author: Le Regard du Voyageur, 1978, L'Enfant D'Edouard, 1981 (Prix Médicis 1981), Sebastien Dore, 1985 (Prix Marcel Proust 1986). Home: 18 Alexander Dr, Douglas Isle of Man

ROUSSEAU, WILLIAM CAUBU, chemical engineer, educator; b. San Francisco, Sept. 16, 1913; s. Oliver M. and Irene (Caubu) R.; AB in Chemistry, Stanford U., 1934; MS in Chem. Engring., MIT, 1936; m. Margaret Hutchinson, May 1, 1939; 1 son, William. Process design engr., then contracts engr. E.B. Badger & Sons, Boston and Phila., 1936-51; with Badger Co., Inc., Cambridge, Mass., 1951-79, exec. v.p., 1965-68, vice chmn. bd., 1968-74, advisor, 1974-79; vis. lectr. dept. chem. engring. MIT, Cambridge, 1974—. Registered profl. engr., Mass. Mem. Am. Inst. Chem. Engrs., Am. Chem. Soc., AAAS, Soc. Chem. Industry, Nat. Soc. Profl. Engrs. Clubs: MIT Faculty (Cambridge); Chemists (N.Y.C.); St. Botolph (Boston); Boat (Cambridge); Royal Bermuda Yacht; Royal Hamilton Amateur Dinghy, Coral Beach, Mid Ocean (Bermuda); Lost Tree (North Palm Beach, Fla.), Beach (Palm Beach). Home: 12166 West End North Palm Beach FL 33408 Office: MIT Room 66-513 Cambridge MA 02139

ROUSSELOT, EDOUARD, automotive parts company executive; b. Montpellier, France; s. Jean Marie and Jeanne (Andre) R.; m. Laurence deTricornot de Rose, Oct. 30, 1969; children—Jean, Laetitia, Vanessa. Ingenieur Civil, Ponts et Chaussees, Paris, 1964; M.B.A., Harvard U., 1966. Mktg. mgr. Rousselot S.A., Paris, 1969-70, asst. to pres., 1971-72; dir. Tyre div. Dunlop S.A., Paris, 1980-84; pres.-dir. gen. Signal-Vision S.A., Bondoufle, France, 1984-86; dir. eclairage signalisation div. Neiman S.A., 1987-88; dep. gen. mgr. SPIE-TRINDEL, Parc St. Christophe cagy Pontoise, France. Served to 2d lt. French Air Force, 1966-68. Mem. Rubber Profl. Assn. (bd. dirs. 1982-84), Automotive Part Profl. Assn. (bd. dirs. 1986-88), Automobile Club de France. Club: Tennis Club de Paris. Home: 1 rue Dauphine, 75006 Paris France Office: Signal Vision SA, 2 rue Gustave Eiffel, 91032 Bondoufle France

ROUSSIN, ANDRE JEAN PAUL, playwright; b. Marseille, France, Jan. 22, 1911; s. Honore and Suzanne (Gardair) R.; student Inst. Melizan, Marseille; m. Lucienne Deluy, 1947; 1 dau., Jean-Marie. Founder, Le Rideau Gris; plays; Am-stramgam, Une grande fille toute simple, Jean-Baptiste le mal-aime, Le tombeau d'Achille, La sainte famille, La petite hutte, Les oeufs de l'Autruche, Nina, Bobosse, Lorsque l'enfant parait, La main de Cesar, Le mari, la femme et la mort, L'amour fou, La mamma, Une femme qui dit la verité, Les Glorieuses, L'Ecole des autres, Un amour qui ne finit pas, La voyante, la locomotive, on ne sait jamais, Le claque, La Vie est trop courte, La coquine; author adaptations for films. Recipient Officer Legion d'honneur, Commdr. Ordre des arts et des lettres, commdr. Order national du Merite. Mem. Academie Française, Soc. des Auteurs et Compositeurs Dramatiques (pres. 1984, 86). Author essays: Patience et impatiences, 1953, Un contentement raiso-nable, 1965, La boite a couleurs, 1974, Le Rideau rouge, 1982, Rideau Gris et habit vert, 1983. Office: 12 Place des Victoires, 75002 Paris France *

ROUTSON, RONALD CHESTER, soil scientist; b. Chewelah, Wash., Dec. 12, 1933; s. Chester A. and Lucille F. R.; Ph.D. in Soil Sci., Wash. State U., 1970; m. Mary Joan Boning, Dec. 26, 1958; 1 dau., Kelly L. Prin. soil chemist Battelle Pacific N.W. Lab., 1967-78, Rockwell Hanford Ops., Richland, Wash., 1978-87, Westinghouse, Hanford, Conn., 1987—. Served with U.S. Army, 1958-62; mem. Res. NDEA fellow, 1964-68. Mem. Am. Soc. Agronomy, Soil Sci. Soc. Am., Am. Nuclear Soc., N.W. Sci. Assn., Western Soil Sci. Soc., Sigma Xi, Alpha Zeta. Republican. Roman Catholic. Home: Rt 1 Box 1351 Benton City WA 99320 Office: PO Box 1972 Richland WA 99352

ROUX, AMBROISE MARIE CASIMIR, utility executive; b. Piscop, France, June 26, 1921; s. Andre and Cecile (Marchilhacy) R.; m. Françoise Marion, June 17, 1946; children: Christian, Véronique. Student, Coll. Stanislas, Paris, 1932-40, Ecole Polytechnique, 1940-41, Ecole des Ponts & Chausées, 1942-44, Ecole Supérieure d'Electricité, 1945-46. Engr. Dept. Civil Engring., France, 1944-51; exec. dir. Office Sec. States for Industry and Commerce, 1952-55; sr. v.p. Compagnie Générale d'Electricité, Paris, 1955-63, pres., 1963—, chmn. bd., 1970-82, hon. chmn., 1982—, dir., 1986—; also hon. chmn. Pétrofigaz, Afnor; chmn. AGREF, 1976-82, Association Française des entreprises Privées, 1983—; chmn. Compagnie Industrielle des Télécommunications (CIT-Alcatel), 1966-82, hon. chmn., 1982—; chmn. Compagnie Electro-Financière, 1969-82, hon. chmn., 1982—; vice chmn. Sté. des Plantations des Terres Rouges; dir. Barclays Bank, 1983—, vice chmn., 1985—; chmn. Générale Occidentale, 1987—, also dir.; dir. Société La Radiotechnique, Compagnie Generale des Eaux, Mines de Kali Sainte-Thérèse, Sté. du Louvre, Cie Financière Paribas, Presses de la Cité. Author: La Science et les Pouvoirs Psychiques de l'Homme. Decorated grand officer Légion d'Honneur, comdr. Mérite Comml., comdr. Instrn. Publique. Mem. Fedn. French Industries (vice chmn. 1966-75, 1st vice chmn. 1975—, hon. 1st vice chmn. 1982—). Home: 17 place des Etats-Unis, 75116 Paris France Office: 8 bis rue Margueritte, 75017 Paris France

ROUX, HUBERT, rheumatologist, educator; b. Marseille, France, Mar. 16, 1934; s. Jean Baptiste and Jeanine (Bonnafoux) R.; m. Anne Santini, Mar. 16, 1963; children: Denis, Jean-Jaques, Christian. B in math., U. Marseille, 1953, MD, 1965. Intern Hosp. Marseille, 1961-66, asst. chief of clinic, 1966-69, chief rheumatology ward, 1977—; prof. rheumatology U. Marseille, 1969—. Author: Scapuloperoneal Syndrom, 1979, Magnetic Resonance Imaging, 1986. Mem. Nat. Counsil Univs.; founder Mediterranean Rheumatology, 1982—. Served to lt. French armed forces health service, 1961-63. Recipient Titre de reconnaissance de la nation War Ministry of France, 1963. Mem. French Soc. Rheumatology, Royal Soc. Medicine, European Assn. Study Diabetes, other profl. orgns. Roman Catholic. Home: Residence Marie Christine Villa 28, 58 Ave des Caillols, 13012 Marseille France Office: Hosp La Conception, 147 Blvd Baille, 13385 Marseille France

ROUX, LOUIS-JOANNY, British literature and civilization educator; b. S'Etienne, France, Aug. 26, 1939; s. Roux Marius Antoine and Roux Jeanne (Bauquis) R.; m. Claudette Reymondon, Jan. 2, 1968; children—Anne, Xavier. Agrege del' Universite, France, 1964; Docteur es Lettres, France, 1979. Prof. Universite de Saint-Etienne, 1980—. Editor of books and contbr. articles to profl. jours., 1971—. Author: Thomas Hobbes, 1973, 77, 82. Recipient Officier Ordre des Palmes Academiques. Home: 31 rue R Goblet, 42100 Saint-Etienne France Office: CIEREC, 35 rue du Onze-Novembre, 42023 Cedex 2, Saint Etienne France

ROVATTI, PIER ALDO, philosopher, educator; b. Modena, Italy, Apr. 19, 1942; s. Ugo and Anita (Casari) R.; 1 child, Toni. BA in Philosophy, U. Milan, 1967. Asst. faculty of letters and philosophy U. Milan, 1967-75; contract prof. faculty of letter and philosophy U. Trieste, Italy, 1976-82, assoc. prof. faculty of letters and philosophy, 1983—. Author: Sartre, 1969, La Filosofia del Processo, 1969, Critica e Scientificita in Marx, 1973, Bisogni e Teoria Marxista, 1976, Il Pensiero Debole, 1983, Intorno a Levinas, 1987, La Posta in Gioco, 1987, Il Declino della Luce, 1988; editor Bergson, Opere, 1986; mem. editorial bd. Jour. Aut Aut, Milan, 1973. Home: 61 Via Catalani, 20131 Milan Italy

ROVELLI, FAUSTO, cardiologist, consultant; b. Milan, Nov. 10, 1918; s. Riccardo and Emma (Fusi) R.; m. Adele Helg, June 23, 1951; children: Riccardo, Sistina, Francesca. MD, State U., Milan, 1943, accreditation for univ. teaching in medicine, 1960. Clin. asst. Hosp. Ca' Granda, Milan, 1955-62, chief cardiological div., 1962-86, dir. cardiological dept., 1986—. Promoter, dir. Giornale Italiano Di Cardiologica, 1970-72; editor various annual courses in cardiology, 1967-87; contbr. over 300 articles to profl. jours. Chmn. Regional Cardiological Com., Milano, 1972; v.p. Bd. European Soc. Cardiology, 1976-80; mem. nat. cardiological com. Health Ministry, Rome, 1980-87. Recipient Gold medal Health Ministry, 1974. Fellow Am. Coll. Cardiology; mem. European Pediatric Cardiology (hon.), Italian Soc. Cardiology (v.p. 1977-79), Italian Assn. Hosp. Cardiologists (v.p. 1974-76). Roman Catholic. Lodge: Rotary. Home: Via Quadronno 24, 20122 Milan Italy Office: Ospedale Ca Granda, Piazza Ospedale Maggiore 3, 20162 Milan Italy

ROVERE, GIOVANNI OSVALDO, language educator; b. Basle, Switzerland, July 31, 1950; s. Osvaldo and Anna (Zuccolin) R.; m. Beatrice Pia Fenati. D, U. Basle, 1976. Habilitation, U. Basle, 1981. Asst. U. Basle, 1974-82, instr., 1981-83; prof. U. Heidelberg, Federal Republic Germany, 1983—. Author: Testi di Italiano Popolare, 1977, Il Discorso Omiletico, 1982, Il Plurilinguismo in Suizzera, 1982. Roman Catholic. Home: Mühltalstr 137, 6900 Heidelberg Federal Republic of Germany Office: Inst fur Überstzen, und Dolmetschen, Plock 57a, 6900 Heidelberg Federal Republic of Germany

ROVIARO, SUSAN ELIZABETH, clinical psychologist; b. Pittsfield, Mass., Sept. 10, 1949; d. Louis Peter and Elizabeth (Angelini) R.; m. Robert Paul Wisdom, June 18, 1983. B.A., U. Mass., 1971; M.A., U. Kans., 1977, Ph.D., 1981. Lic. psychologist. Grad. research and teaching asst. dept. psychology U. Kans., Lawrence, 1974-77; psychologist in tng. VA Med. Center, Topeka, 1975-77, research asst. depts. neuropsychology and medicine, 1977-79; predoctoral fellow dept. psychiatry Mount Zion Hosp. and Med. Center, San Francisco, 1979-80; clin. dir. Pawnee Mental Health Services, Manhattan, Kans., 1980—; health profl. affiliate Meml. and St. Mary's hosps., Manhattan. Mem. Am. Psychol. Assn., Kans. Psychol. Assn. (bd. govs. 1984-86), Phi Beta Kappa. Home: 812 Colorado St Manhattan KS 66502 Office: 2001 Claflin Rd Manhattan KS 66502

ROVINE, ARTHUR WILLIAM, lawyer; b. Phila., Apr. 29, 1937; s. George Isaac and Rosanna (Lipsitz) R.; m. Phyllis Ellen Hamburger, Apr. 7, 1963; children: Joshua, Deborah. AB, U. Pa., 1958; LLB, Harvard U., 1961; PhD, Columbia U., 1966. Bar: D.C. 1964, N.Y. 1984. Assoc. Curtis, Mallet-Prevost, Colt & Mosle, N.Y.C., 1964-66; asst. prof. Cornell U., Ithaca, N.Y., 1966-72; editor Digest of U.S. Practice in International Law U.S. Dept. State, Washington, 1972-75, asst. legal adviser, 1975-81; agt. U.S. Govt. to Iran-U.S. Claims Tribunal U.S. Dept. State, The Hague, Netherlands, 1981-

83; of counsel Baker & McKenzie, N.Y.C., 1983-85, ptnr., 1985—; adj. prof. law Georgetown U., Washington, 1977-81. Author: The First Fifty Years: The Secretary-General in World Politics, 1920-1970, 1970; editor: Digest of U.S. Practice in International Law, 1973, 74; co-editor: The Case Law of the International Court of Justice, 1968, 1972, 1974, 1976; bd. editors Am. Jour. Internat. Law, 1977-87; also articles on internat. law. Mem. ABA (chmn. internat. law sect. 1985-86), Am. Soc. Internat. Law (cert. of merit 1974, exec. council 1975-77), U.S. Council for Internat. Bus. (arbitration com.), Ctr. for Pub. Resources (panel on settlement of transnat. bus. disputes), Am. Arbitration Assn. (panel of arbitrators), Council on Fgn. Relations. Home: 150 E 61st St New York NY 10021 Office: Baker & McKenzie 805 3rd Ave New York NY 10022

ROWAN, ALEXANDRA MCINTOSH, speech pathology lecturer; b. Glasgow, Scotland, Oct. 14, 1935; d. Peter and Robina (McIntosh) McCartney; m. John David Barr Rowan, July 23, 1960 (dec. Aug. 1984); children: Fiona, David Peter. Licentiate of the Coll. of Speech Therapists, Glasgow Sch. Speech Therapy, 1956; MA in Psychology of Mental Handicap, U. Keele, 1986. Speech therapist Schs. Health Service, County of Aberdeen, 1956-57, City of Glasgow, 1957-59; from speech therapist to chief therapist Ayrshire & Arran Health Bd., Ayr, 1959-72; sr. therapist Spastics Soc., Watford, Eng., 1973-75, Midland Spastics Assn., Birmingham, Eng., 1975-76; sr. lectr. speech pathology City Birmingham Poly., 1976—; external examiner Coll. Speech Therapists, 1976-82, Leicester Poly., 1983-87, Manchester Poly., 1987—. Mem. Coll. Speech Therapists. Home: 123 Court Oak Rd, Birmingham B17 9AA, England Office: Dept Health Scis, Birmingham Poly, Franchise St, Birmingham B42 2SU, England

ROWAN, RONALD THOMAS, lawyer; b. Bozeman, Mont., Nov. 6, 1941; s. Lawrence Eugene and Florence M.; m. Katherine Terrell Sponenberg, Sept. 4, 1964; children—Heather, Nicholaus, Matthew. B.A., Wichita U., 1964; J.D., U. Denver, 1969. Bar: Colo. 1969, U.S. Dist. Ct. Colo. 1969. Asst. city atty. City of Colorado Springs, Colo., 1969-71; asst. dist. atty. 4th Jud. Dist., Colorado Springs, 1971-79; gen. counsel U.S. Olympic Com., Colorado Springs, 1979—. Chmn. CSC, Colorado Springs, 1975—; chmn. Criminal Justice Adv. Bd., 1983—; chmn. El Paso Crimnal Justice Adv. Com.; bd. dirs. Crimestoppers, 1982-87, past pres. 1985-87, Internat. Anti-counterfeiting Coalition; chmn. Community Corrections Bd., 1981, 86, 87. Mem. ABA, Colo. Bar Assn., El Paso County Trial Lawyers (pres. 1972), El Paso County Bar Assn., U. Denver Law Alumni (chmn.), Colo. Trial Lawyers Assn. Republican. Roman Catholic. Home: 2915 Nevermind Ln Colorado Springs CO 80917 Office: US Olympic Com 1750 E Boulder St Colorado Springs CO 80909-5760

ROWE, BRUCE MACHIN, executive search company executive; b. Nottingham, England, Mar. 18, 1936; came to France, 1974; s. Herbert Stanley and Frances Mary (Machin) R.; m. Angela Pritchard, Aug. 20, 1958; children: Julian, Amanda, Philippa, Alexander. BA in Lit. and Humanities honors, Oxford U., Eng., 1961. Mgr. brand Procter & Gamble Ltd., Gosforth, Eng., 1961-65; mgr. group product Nabisco Foods Ltd., Welwyn Garden City, Eng., 1965-66; mgr. group mktg. Smiths Food Group Ltd., Brentford, Eng., 1966-70; joint mng. dir. Snakpak Food Products Ltd., Cardiff, Wales, 1967-69; dir. cons. for Europe Glendinning Assocs. Internat., London, 1970-74; coordinator Internat. Playtex Inc., Slough, Eng., 1974; pres., dir. gen. Playtex France, Paris, 1974-77; sr. ptnr. Baritault SA, Paris, 1977-85; mng. ptnr. Rowe Internat., Paris, 1985—. Served to 2nd lt. Royal Arty., 1955-57. Fellow Inst. Dirs. Club: United Oxford, Cambridge U. (London). Office: Rowe Internat, 9 ave de Friedland, 75008 Paris France

ROWE, CHRISTOPHER JAMES, classicist; b. March, Cambridgeshire, Eng., Mar. 17, 1944; s. Daniel Francis and Edith Mary (Ashford) R.; m. Heather Jean Knight, July 31, 1965; children: Daniel Geoffrey, Sarah Anne Mary. BA, Trinity Coll., Cambridge, Eng., 1965, PhD, 1968. Lectr. Classics U. Bristol, Eng., 1968-82; jr. fellow Ctr. Hellenic Studies, Edinburgh, Scotland, 1974-78; sr. lectr. Classics U. Bristol, Eng., 1982-85, reader in Classics, 1985—; vis. fellow U. Edinburgh, Scotland, 1972; vis. prof. U. Tex., Austin, 1979. Author: The Eudemian and Nicomachean Ethics, 1971, Plato, 1984, Plato: Phaedrus, 1986; contbr. articles to profl. jours. Chmn. govs. Backwell Sch., Bristol, 1985—. Fulbright scholar, 1974-75. Mem. Hellenic Soc., History of Polit. Thought (editorial bd. 1980—), Classical Assn., Council of Univ. Classical Depts. (mem. standing. com. 1985—). Office: Univ of Bristol, Bristol BS8 1TH, England

ROWE, GENEVA LASSITER, psychotherapist, counseling center administrator; b. Atlanta, Aug. 11, 1927; d. Hoyt Cleveland and Tinie (Gresham) Lassiter; m. Fred Earnest Rowe, May 3, 1958; children: Carol, Vickie, Randall. BA, Oglethorpe U., 1968; MSW, U. Ga., 1970; PhD, Fla. State U., 1978. Accredited Acad. Cert. Social Workers; lic. marriage and family therapist, Ga.; approved AAMFT supr., 1986. Alcohol and drug counselor Georgian Clinic, Atlanta, 1968; outpatient counselor DeKalb Guidance Clinic, Atlanta, 1969; protective services supr. DeKalb Family and Children Services, Decatur, Ga., 1970-72; outpatient therapist Cen. DeKalb Mental Health Ctr., 1972-75; marriage and family therapist Fla. State U., 1977; lectr. sociology Oglethorpe U., 1978-81; psychotherapist, clin. supr., dir., owner N.E. Counseling Ctr., P.C., Atlanta and Lawrenceville, Ga., 1978—; clin. supr. master's students in practicum Ga. State U., 1980—; approved AAMFT supr., 1986—; allied health prof. CPC Parkwood Hosp., 1987—. Fellow Am. Orthopsychiat. Assn., Internat. Council Sex Edn. and Parenthood; mem. Am. Assn. Marriage and Family Therapy (clin. mem., approved supr.), AAUW, Ga. Assn. Marriage and Family Therapy (pub. relations chmn. 1984-86), Gwinnett County C. of C., Young Women of Arts. Methodist. Home: 2005 Woodsdale Rd NE Atlanta GA 30324 Office: NE Counseling Ctr PC 2995 Lawrenceville Hwy Lawrenceville GA 30245

ROWELL, EDWARD MORGAN, foreign service officer; b. Oakland, Calif., Oct. 13, 1931; s. Edward Joseph and Mary Helen (Mohler) R.; m. Lenora Mary Wood, Aug. 23, 1957; children: Edward Oliver, Karen Elizabeth Schuler, Christopher Douglas. B.A. in Internat. Relations, Yale U., 1953; postgrad., Stanford U., 1964-65, Stanford Bus. Sch., 1970-71. Fgn. service insp. U.S. Govt., Washington, 1971-74; dep. dir., econ. officer Office Iberian Affairs, Washington, 1974-75; dep. dir. Office West European Affairs, Washington, 1975-76, dir., 1977-78; minister-counselor U.S. Embassy, Lisbon, Portugal, 1978-83; mem. Bur. Consular Affairs, Washington, 1983-85, dep. asst. sec., 1983-85; U.S. ambassador to Bolivia La Paz, 1985-88; U.S. ambassador to Portugal Lisbon, 1988—. Treas. Cleveland Park Congl. Ch., Washington, 1984-85. Served to cpl. U.S. Army, 1953-55. Scholar Yale U., 1949, 50, 51, 52; U. Calif. fellow, 1953; Una Chapman Cox Found. grantee, 1984. Mem. Am. Fgn. Service Assn., Stanford U. Alumni Assn., Yale U. Alumni Assn., Arena Stage Assocs. Home: 1409 Oxford St Apt 6 Berkeley CA 94709 Office: Dept of State US Embassy Portugal Washington DC 20521

ROWE-MAAS, BETTY LOU, real estate investor; b. San Jose, Calif., Apr. 2, 1925; d. Horace DeWitt and Lucy Belle (Spiker) Rowe; children: Terry Lee, Clifford Lindsay, Craig Harrison, Joan Louise. Real estate investor, Saratoga, Calif., 1968—. Mem. Nat. Trust Hist. Preservation, Smithsonian Instn., San Jose Mus., Saratoga Mus., San Francisco Mus., Los Gatos Mus., San Jose Symphony, Moltalvo; bd. dirs. Valley Inst. Theatre Arts; San Francisco Ballet, City Ctr. Ballet of San Jose and Cleve., Music and Arts Found.; mem. Route 85 Task Force, 1978—, treas., 1984-89; mem. Saratoga Good Govt., 1970—; treas. Traffic Relief for Saratoga. Mem. LWV. Republican. Clubs: Commonwealth of Calif. (life), Saratoga Country. Home: 20360 Saratoga Los Gatos Rd Saratoga CA 95070

ROWEN, RUTH HALLE, musicologist, educator; b. N.Y.C., Apr. 5, 1918; d. Louis and Ethel (Fried) Halle; m. Seymour M. Rowen, Oct. 13, 1940; children: Mary Helen Rowen, Louis Halle Rowen. B.A., Barnard Coll., 1939; M.A., Columbia U., 1941, Ph.D., 1948. Mgmt. ednl. dept. Carl Fischer, Inc., N.Y.C., 1954-63; assoc. prof. musicology CUNY, 1967-72, prof., 1972—, mem. doctoral faculty in musicology, 1967—. Author: Early Chamber Music, 1948, reprinted, 1974; (with Adele T. Katz) Hearing-Gateway to Music, 1959, (with William Simon) Jolly Come Sing and Play, 1956, Music Through Sources and Documents, 1979, (with Mary Rowen) Instant Piano, 1979, 80, 83; contbr. articles to profl. jours. Mem. ASCAP, Am. Musicol. Soc., Music Library Assn., Coll. Music Soc., Nat. Fedn. Music Clubs (nat. musicianship chmn. 1962-74, nat. young artist auditions com. 1964-74, N.Y. state chmn. Young Artist Auditions 1981, dist. coordinator 1983), N.Y. Fedn. Music Clubs (pres.), Phi Beta Kappa. Home: 115 Central Park W New York NY 10023

ROWLAND, CAROLE ANN, air force officer; b. Oskaloosa, Iowa, Mar. 30, 1952; d. Willis Marion and Majorie Ann (Lamb) R. B.S. in Edn., Northeast Mo. State U., 1975, M.A. in Phys. Scis., 1976; grad. Squadron Officer Sch., Montgomery, Ala., 1985. Prof. sci. Northeast Mo. State U., Kirksville, 1975-76; asst. maintenance supr. Davis-Monthan AFB, Ariz., 1978-81; chief equipment allowance sect. Hdqrs. TAC, Langley AFB, Va., 1981-84; equipment maintenance squadron officer-in-charge maintenance br. 363 Tactical Fighter Wing, Shaw AFB, 1984-85, maintenacne supr., 1985-86, comdr., 1986; dep. comdr. for maintenance Det 4 81 Tactical Fighter Wing, Norvenich Air Base, Germany, 1986—; officer's club rep., 1985-86; resident cons. for mil. women Davis-Monthan AFB, Ariz., 1980-81. Editor film Grand Canyon Adventure, 1975; also articles; mural artist. 4-H leader, Sumter, S.C., 1985-86; base donation organizer ARC, Tucson, 1978-81. Served to capt. USAF, 1976—. Mem. Nat. Assn. Female Execs., Fed. Women's Program (program and publicity com.), Nat. Wildlife Fedn. (life), Nat. Parks and Conservation Assn. (life), Alpha Sigma Tau, Sigma Zeta. Avocations: photography, basketball, racquetball, art, softball.

ROWLAND, JAMES A., supermarket chain executive. With Safeway Stores, Inc., mgr. ops. Amarillo and So. Calif., 1956-66, mgr. Little Rock div., 1966-70, v.p., 1970-72, v.p., mgr. midwest region, 1972-76, v.p. adminstrn. from 1976, now pres., chief operating officer, dir. Office: Safeway Stores Inc 201 4th St Oakland CA 94660 *

ROWLAND, ROBERT JOSEPH, JR., classicist, educator; b. Shenandoah, Pa., Mar. 27, 1938; s. Robert Joseph and Catherine (Brennan) R.; m. Carole S. Ricords, Aug. 16, 1960; children: Robert Joseph III, Francine Marie, Patrick Brennan, Maria Danielle. B.A., LaSalle Coll., 1959; M.A., U. Pa., 1961, Ph.D., 1964. Instr. LaSalle Coll., Phila., 1959-65; instr., asst. prof. Vallanova U., Pa., 1961-67; vis. asst. prof. U. Pa., Phila., 1965; assoc. prof. classics U. Mo., Columbia, 1967-72, assoc. prof. history, 1972-74, prof., 1974-84; prof., chmn. classics dept. U. Md., 1984—. Author: Ritrovamenti Romani in Sardegna, 1981; editor: Vergil and the American Experience, 1988; (with M.S. Balmuth) Studies in Sardinian Archaeology, 1983, The Augustan Age, 1981—; (with R.M. and M.P. Wilhelm) The Aeneid Institute Papers, 1987; (with J.F. O'Connor) Teaching Classical Mythology, 1987; contbr. articles on ancient and medieval history, lit. and archaeology to profl. jours. Am. Council Learned Socs. grantee in aid, 1974, 76, 81, 86; Am. Philos. Soc. grantee, 1972; Am. Council Learned Socs. travel grantee, 1983; NEH grantee, 1984, 86, 87. Mem. Vergilian Soc. Am. (exec. sec. 1980—), Classical Assn. Midwest and South (pres. so. sect. 1982-84), Am. Philol. Assn., Friends of Ancient History (pres. 1984), Am. Assn. Ancient Historians, Soc. for Promotion Roman Studies, Archeol. Assn. Am. (bd. govs. D.C. Chpt., 1986—), Classical Assn. Atlantic States (2d v.p., 1987, 1st v.p., 1988). Democrat. Roman Catholic. Club: Cosmos. Office: Univ Md Dept Classics College Park MD 20742

ROWLEY, CHARLES KERSHAW, economics educator; b. Southampton, Eng., June 21, 1939; came to U.S., 1984; s. Frank and Ellen (Beal) R.; m. Betty Silverwood, June 19, 1961 (div. 1971); m. Marjorie Isobel Spillets, July 17, 1972; children: Amanda, Sarah. Lectr. U. Nottingham, Eng., 1962-65; lectr., then sr. lectr. U. Kent, Canterbury, Eng., 1965-70; reader U. York, Eng., 1970-72; prof. econs. U. Newcastle, Eng., 1972-83, George Mason U., Fairfax, Va., 1984—, dean Grad. Sch., 1987—; sr. research assoc., Ctr. for Study of Pub. Choice, 1987—; cons. Office Fair Trading, London, 1980-83; research assoc. Wolfson Coll., Oxford, 1984—. Author numerous books in econ., pub. choice and law. Contbr. articles to profl. jours. Grantee Bank of Eng., 1965, Social Sci. Research Council, London, 1970-72, Dept. Environ., London, 1974-80. Mem. Mont Pelerin Soc., Am. Econ. Assn., Royal Econ. Soc., Pub. Choice Soc., European Pub. Choice Soc. (pres. 1980-82) Home: 5188 Dungannon Rd Fairfax VA 22030 Office: George Mason U The Grad Sch 4400 University Dr Fairfax VA 22030

ROWSE, ALFRED LESLIE, British historian, poet, writer; b. St. Austell, Cornwall, Dec. 4, 1903. Emeritus fellow All Souls Coll., Oxford. Author: Sir Richard Grenville of the Revenge, 1937; Tudor Cornwall, 1941; Poems of a Decade 1931-41, A Cornish Childhood, 1942; The Spirit of English History, 1943, Poems Chiefly Cornish, 1944, The English Spirit, 1944; West Country Stories, 1945; The Use of History, 1946; The End of an Epoch, 1947; The England of Elizabeth, 1950; The English Past (revised edit. entitled Times, Persons, Places 1965), 1951; The Expansion of Elizabethan England, 1955; The Early Churchills, 1956; The Later Churchills, 1958; Poems Partly American, 1959; The Elizabethans and America, 1959; Appeasement: A Study in Political Decline, 1961; Raleigh and the Throckmortons, 1962; William Shakespeare: A Biography, 1963; Christopher Marlowe: A Biography, 1964; A Cornishman at Oxford, 1965; Shakespeare's Southampton, 1965; Bosworth Field and the Wars of the Roses, 1966; Poems of Cornwall and America, 1967; Cornish Stories, 1967; A Cornish Anthology, 1968; The Cornish in America, 1969; The Elizabethan Renaissance: Vol. I The Life of the Society, 1971, Vol. II The Cultural Achievement, 1972; The Tower of London in the History of the Nation, 1972, Shakespeare the Man, 1973 (rev. 1988); Simon Forman: Sex and Society in Shakespeare's Age, 1974; Windsor Castle in the History of the Nation, 1974; (with Sir John Betjeman) Victorian and Edwardian Cornwall, 1974, Oxford in the History of the Nation, 1975; Discoveries and Reviews from Renaissance to Restoration, 1975; Jonathan Swift, Major Prophet, 1975; A Cornishman Abroad, 1976; Brown Buck: A Californian Fantasy, 1976; Matthew Arnold: Poet and Prophet, 1976; Shakespeare the Elizabethan, 1976; Homosexuals in History: Ambivalence in Society, Literature and the Arts, 1977; Milton the Puritan, 1977; Heritage of Britain, 1977; The Road to Oxford: Poems, 1978; The Byrons and Trevanions, 1978; Night at the Carn: Stories; A Man of the Thirties, 1979, Portraits and Views, 1979, Story of Britain, 1979, Memories of Men and Women, 1980, A Life: Collected Poems 1981, Eminent Elizabethans, 1983, Shakespeare's Sonnets, with prose versions (rev. edit.), 1983; Stories from Trenarren, 1986; Reflections on the Puritan Revolution, 1986; The Little Land of Cornwall, 1986; Glimpses of the Great, 1986; Hakluyt's Voyages of North America, 1986; The Poet Auden: A Personal Memoir, 1988; Quiller Couch: Portrait of Q, 1988; Froude the Historian, 1988; A.L. Rowse's Cornwall, 1988; Friends and Contemporaries, 1989. Editor: The Poems of Shakespeare's Dark Lady 1978; The Contemporary Shakespeare. Address: Trenarren St Austell, Cornwall England

ROY, ASIM, business educator; b. Calcutta, India, May 5, 1948; came to U.S., 1975; s. Samarendra Nath and Chhaya (Mukherjee) R.; m. Suchandra Mukherjee, Feb. 10, 1974; 1 child, Sion Roy. B.E., Calcutta U., 1971; M.S. (scholar), Case Western Res. U., 1977; Ph.D., U. Tex.-Austin, 1979. Foreman, Guest, Keen, Williams, Calcutta, 1972-74; mgr. optimization group Execucom Systems Corp., Austin, 1980-82; asst. prof. U. Nebr.-Omaha, 1983, Ariz. State U., Tempe, 1983—; cons. Mid-Am. Steel Corp., 1976-77, Fabri-Centre, Inc., Cleve., 1976; pres., chief exec. officer Decision Support Software, Inc. Author software: IFPS/Optimum. Contbr. articles to profl. jours. Calcutta U. Merit scholar, 1967; U. Tex. research scholar, 1978-80. Mem. Inst. Mgmt. Sci., Ops. Research Soc. Am. Hindu. Home: 1401 E Brentrup Dr Tempe AZ 85283 Office: Ariz State U Tempe AZ 85287

ROY, CATHERINE ELIZABETH, physical therapist; b. Tucson, Jan. 16, 1948; d. Francis Albert and Dorothy Orme (Thomas) R.; m. Richard M. Johnson, Aug. 31, 1968 (div. 1978); children: Kimberly Anne, Troy Michael. BA in Social Sci. magna cum laude, San Diego State U., 1980; MS in Phys. Therapy, U. So. Calif., 1984. Staff therapist Sharp Meml. Hosp., San Diego, 1984—, chairperson patient and family edn. com., 1986-87, chairperson sex edn. and counselling com., 1987—, chairperson adv. bd. for phys. therapy, asst. for edn. program, 1987—; ptnr. C&J Assocs., San Diego, 1987—; lectr. patient edn., family edn., peer edn.; mem. curriculum rev. com. U. So. Calif. Phys. Therapy Dept., 1982; bd. dirs. Ctr. for Edn. in Health; writer, reviewer licensure examination items for phys. therapy Profl. Examination Services.. Researcher: Consumer Education: Physical Therapy, 1984-85. Tennis coach at clinics Rancho Penasquitos Swim and Tennis Club, San Diego, 1980-81; active Polit. Activities Network, 1985. Mem. Am. Phys. Therapy Assn. (research presenter nat. conf. 1985, del. nat. conf. 1986-88, rep. state conf. 1987, 88, Mary McMillan student award 1984, mem. exec. bd. San Diego dist. 1985—), AAUW, Nat. Assn. Female Execs., Am. Coll. Sports Medicine, Am. Congress Rehab. Medicine, Phi Beta Kappa, Phi Kappa Phi, Chi Omega. Home: 13133 Via del Valedor San Diego CA 92129 Office: Sharp Meml Rehab Ctr 7901 Frost St San Diego CA 92123

ROY, DAVID TOD, Chinese literature educator; b. Nanking, Peoples Republic China, Apr. 5, 1933; s. Andrew Tod and Margaret (Crutchfield) R.; m. Barbara Jean Chew, Feb. 4, 1967. AB, Harvard U., 1958, AM, 1960, PhD, 1965. Asst. prof. Princeton (N.J.) U., 1963-67; assoc. prof. U. Chgo., 1967-73, prof., 1973—, chmn. com. on Far Eastern Studies, 1968-70, chmn. dept. Far Eastern Langs. and Civilizations, 1972-75. Author: Kuo Mo-jo: The Early Years, 1971; co-editor: Ancient China: Studies in Early Civilization, 1978. Served with U.S. Army, 1954-56. Ford Found. fellow, 1958-60, Jr. fellow Harvard Soc. Fellows, 1960-63, fellow Fulbright-Hays Commn., 1967; grantee Am. Council Learned Socs., 1976-77, NEH, 1983-86. Mem. Am. Oriental Soc., Assn. for Asian Studies, Chinese Lang. Tchrs. Assn. Democrat. Club: Quadrangle (Chgo.). Home: 5443 S Cornell Ave Chicago IL 60615 Office: Univ Chgo 5736 S Woodlawn Ave Chicago IL 60637

ROY, HAROLD EDWARD, research chemist; b. Stratford, Conn., June 2, 1921; s. Ludger Homer and Meta (Jepsen) R.; B.A., Duke U., 1950; m. Joyce E. Enslin, Oct. 9, 1946 (div. 1975); children—Glenn E., Barbara Anne, Suzanne Elizabeth. Chemist research div. Lockheed Propulsion Co., Redlands, Calif., 1957-61; sec., treas. The Halgene Corp., Riverside, Calif., 1961-63; self-employed chemist, Glendora, Calif., 1963-64; chief engr. propellant devel. Rocket Power, Inc., Mesa, Ariz., 1964-65; cons., Glendora, 1965-66; engrng. specialist Northrop Corp., Anaheim, Calif., 1966-69; pres. Argus Tech., Beverly Hills, 1969-70, dir. Harold E. Roy & Assos., Glendora, 1969—. Served to lt. (j.g.) USNR, 1943-46. Mem. Exptl. Aircraft Assn., Am. Ordnance Assn., Am. Inst. Aeros. and Astronautics, Internat. Platform Assn., Acad. Parapsychology and Medicine, Calif. Profl. Hypnotists Assn., World Future Soc. Republican. Home: 7344 N Barranca Glendora CA 91740

ROY, KENNETH RUSSELL, educator; b. Hartford, Conn., Mar. 29, 1946; s. Russell George and Irene Mary (Birkowski) R.; B.S., Central Conn. State Coll., New Britain, 1968, M.S., 1974; 6th yr. degree in profl. edn. U. Conn., 1981, Ph.D., 1985; m. Marisa Anne Russo, Jan. 27, 1968; children—Lisa Marie, Louise Irene. Tchr. sci. Rocky Hill (Conn.) High Sch., 1968-73, N.W. Cath. High Sch., West Hartford, Conn., 1973-74; sci. and math. coordinator Bolton (Conn.) High Sch., 1974-78; chmn. scis. Bacon Acad., Colchester, Conn., 1978-81; K-12 dir. sci. Glastonbury (Conn.) Pub. Schs., 1981—; mem. adj. faculty Manchester Community Coll., 1976—, Tunxis Community Coll., 1975—; instr. U. Conn. Coop. Program, 1974-78; cons./adv. Project Rise, 1978-81; lectr., sci. curriculum cons. various Conn. sch. dists.; nat. dir. Nat. Sci. Suprs. Assn., 1988—. Co-editor Conn. Jour. Sci. Edn., 1984-88. Contbr. articles to profl. jours. Mem. St. Christopher Sch. Bd., 1982-83. Named Tchr. of Yr., Colchester, 1980; NSF grantee, 1968, staff devel. grantee, 1979, 80, Nat. Sci. Supr. Leadership Conf. grantee, 1980. Mem. Nat. Sci. Tchrs. Assn., Nat. Sci. Suprs. Assn. (pres.-elect 1986-87, pres. 1987-88), Nat. Assn. Secondary Sci. Suprs., Nat. Assn. Supervision and Curriculum Devel., Conn. Sci. Tchrs. Assn., Conn. Sci. Suprs. Assn. (pres. 1985-86), Conn. Assn. Profl. Devel., Conn. Assn. Supervision and Curriculum Devel., Glastonbury Adminstrs. and Suprs. Assn., Nat. Ctr. Improvement Sci. Teaching and Learning (mem. adv. bd. 1988—), Internat. Council Assns. Sci. Edn. (nat. rep. 1987-88), Phi Delta Kappa. Roman Catholic. Office: Glastonbury Pub Schs Glastonbury CT 06033

ROY, KULDIP KUMAR, editor; b. Lahore, Pakistan, Feb. 28, 1935; s. Ram Nath and Shanti (Devi) R.; B.A. with honours, Punjab U., 1954, J.D., 1954; D.Litt., U. Canberra (Australia), 1971; m. Vimala Goyal, July 19, 1959; 5 children. Editor, School World, 1956-58, Hosp. Digest, 1958-66, Asian and African Books Newsletter, 1966-69, Africa Letter, 1969-72, Bibliographia Asiatica, 1972-73, History of Agr., 1973-75, Library History Rev., 1975-76, Legal History, 1976-78, Asian Jour. European Studies, Multicultural Children's Lit. and Research in Tourism, 1978—; cons. editor univ. presses; dir. K.K. Roy Ltd., Intertrade Publs. (India) Ltd., Royson (Fire Engrs.) Pvt. Ltd. Recipient Valor award, N.Y.C., 1966; Bruce Hartmann trophy, Sydney, Australia, 1970; Edward Hartton award, London, 1971; hon. fellow Magdalen Coll., Oxford U., 1972. Fellow Royal Asiatic Soc., Theosophical Soc., Royal Soc. Medicine; mem. Internat. Assn. History Agr., Internat. Agy. Research Library History, Indian Inst. Legal History, Assn. Sci. Exports in Tourism, Indo-Latin Am. C. of C. (exec. dir.), Indo-Australian C. of C. (exec. dir.). Club: Calcutta Tennis. Author: Stray Thoughts and Other Poems; Mirza Ghalib; Waris Shah; Subramanya Bharati; The Swami and the Comrade; Living My Own Death; Old Paths, New Ruts. Home: 55 Gariahat Rd, PO Box 10210, Calcutta 700 019 India Office: Suite 1-2 Presidency Ct, Gariahat Rd, Calcutta 700 019, India

ROY, PIERRE-GEORGES, financier; b. Normandin, Quebec, Can., Aug. 22, 1937; s. Louis Nazaire and Rita (Morin) R.; divorced; children: Anne Chantal, Pierre-Georges. BA, Church Point (N.S.) Coll., 1954; CE, Tri-State Coll., Angola, Ind., 1962; MBA, Harvard U., 1964. Pres. OMCO S.A., Aalter, Belgium, 1973-78, Transact Internat. S.A., Paris, 1978-83, Transact Internat., Ltd., London, 1983—.

ROY, SABITENDRANATH, publishing company executive, journalist; b. Calcutta, India, Nov. 1, 1934; s. Surendranath and Nivedita Roy; m. Archana Roy, Dec. 12, 1970; children: Indrani, Sarbani. BS, Calcutta U., 1953. Editor Katha-Sahitya jour., Calcutta, 1967-84; joint mng. dir. Mitra & Ghosh Pubs. Pvt. Ltd., Calcutta, 1984—; reviewer All India Radio, 1982. Editor: Syed Mujtaba' Ali, 1978, Anthology of Bibhuti Bhusan Banerjee, 1979. Mem. Pubs. and Booksellers Guild, Paschimbana Sahitya Prakashak Sanstha (pres. 1983). Avocation: reading. Office: Mitra & Ghosh Pubs, 10 Shyamacharande St, Calcutta 700 073, India

ROY, TUHIN KUMAR, engineering company executive; b. Monghyr, India, Aug. 1, 1923; s. Rakhal Raj and Bijoyini (Gupta) R.; B.Sc., Calcutta U., 1943, M.Sc., 1945; M.S., M.I.T., 1949, Sc.D., 1951; m. Silva Mardiste, Jan. 1, 1951; children—Dipak, Rupak, Indrek. Head metals research Chem. Constrn. Corp., N.Y.C., 1951-54; prof., head chem. engrng. dept. Jadavpur U., 1954-56, 58-60; cons. Freeport Minerals Co., New Orleans, 1956-58; mng. dir. Indsl. Cons. Bur., New Delhi, 1960-63; sr. exec. Sci. Design Co., N.Y.C., 1963-65; mng. dir. Chem. and Metall. Design Co. Pvt. Ltd., New Delhi, 1966—; v.p. SLBR Internat. Ltd., Hamilton, Ont., Can.; dir. Nat. Research Devel. Corp., Consultancy Consortium P. Ltd., Okhla Chems. Ltd. Mng. trustee B. Jagtiani Charitable Trust. Fellow Indian Acad. Scis., Indian Nat. Acad. Engrng.; mem. Am. Inst. Chem. Engrs., Indian Inst. Chem. Engrs. (Chem. Engr. of Yr. award 1983), Nat. Assn. Cons. Engrs. New Delhi (past pres.). Hindu. Contbr. articles to profl. jours. Patentee in field. Home: C 6/3 Safdarjung Dev Area, New Delhi 110016, India Office: 511 Mansarovar Nehru Pl, New Delhi PIN 110019, India

ROYCE, RAYMOND WATSON, lawyer, rancher, citrus grower; b. West Palm Beach, Fla., Mar. 5, 1936; s. Wilbur E. and Veda (Watson) R.; m. Catherine L. Setzer, Apr. 21, 1979; children: Raymond, Steven, Nancy, Kathryn. BCE, U. Fla., 1958, JD, 1961. Bar: Fla. 1961, U.S. Dist. Ct. (so. dist.) Fla. 1961, U.S. Ct. Appeals (5th cir.) 1961, U.S. Ct. Appeals (11th cir.) 1981. Assoc. William W. Blakeslee, Palm Beach, Fla., 1961-62; with Scott, Royce, Harris & Bryan P.A., Palm Beach, Fla., 1962—, pres., 1982—; bd. dirs. Econ. Council. Mem. Fla. Bar (bd. govs. 1974-78), Palm Beach County Bar Assn. (pres. 1973-74), Am. Judicature Soc., Fla. Trial Lawyers Assn., Fla. Citrus Mut., Fla. Cattleman's Assn., Internat. Brangus Breeders Assn., Fla. Blue Key, Phi Delta Phi. Democrat. Presbyterian. Home: 5550 Whirlaway Rd Palm Beach Gardens FL 33418 Office: Scott Royce Harris & Bryan 450 Royal Palm Way Palm Beach FL 33480

ROZANSKI, EDWARD C(ASIMIR), retired editor, manager newspapers, deacon; b. Chgo., Mar. 7, 1915; s. Casimir Joseph and Bess (Kilinski) R.; m. Leocadia Procanin, Aug. 24, 1940. O.D., Ill. Coll. Optometry, 1948; Ordained deacon Roman Cath. Ch. Photographer, Washington Photo Studio, Chgo., 1931-39; photographer-reporter Zgoda, Polish daily, Chgo., 1939-42, 45-50, gen. mgr., editor, 1975-85; deacon St. Hyacinth Ch., Chgo., 1979—; field advocate, notary Met. Tribunal, Archdiocese Chgo., 1985—; shift supr. wet plate process chart and map reprodn. for U.S. Navy, U.S. Army, and U.S. Army Air Force with U.S. Coast and Geodetic Survey, USN, Washington, 1942-45; color specialist, gravure Cuneo Press, Chgo., 1950-75; gen. mgr. Dziennik Zwiazkowy, Polish daily, Chgo., 1975-85; mem.

adv. bd. Chgo. Cath., 1983. Bd. dirs. Chgo. Access Corp.; v.p. sch. bd. St. Hyacinth Ch., Chgo., 1982—; mem. Ill. Hist. Records Adv. Bd.; active Polish Nat. Alliance, 1932—; v.p. PNA Youth Home Corp., 1975-86; sec. Dist. XIII Polish Nat. Alliance, 1979—; monuments chmn. for Paul Sobolewski, 1963, St. Kociemski, 1969, Mieczislaus Haiman, 1985, Rev. Jerzy Popieluszko, 1985, Teofila Samolinska Monument, 1988; active Ill. Civil War Centennial Commn., Am. Heritage Commn., Cook County Sesquicentennial Commn., Ill. Bicentennial Commn., also treas. Decorated chevalier Ordre Souverain Et Militaire du Temple de Jerusalem (France); cavalier and officers cross Order Polonia Restituta, Gold Cross Legion of Honor, Gold Cross of Merit, Gen. Haller's Swords, Krzyz Zaslugi Cross of Merit (Poland); comdr. Order St. Lazarus of Jerusalem (Malta); Order Lafayette (U.S.); recipient citation Polish Legion Am. Vets, 1962, 63; citation Polish Combatans World War II, (4), Silver Emblem, 1968, Gold emblem, 1983; citation Polish Welfare Council Schenectady, 1964, Polonus Philatelic Soc., 1964; Lincoln plaquette Sta. WGN-Radio-TV, 1965, medal Pope Paul VI, 1971, Silver medal Nat. Library Poland, 1980, Bronze medal Gen. Pulaski Museum, Warka, Poland, 1981, Legion of Honor medal Polish Falcons Am., 1982, Haiman's Silver medal award Polish Am. Hist. Assn., 1986. Mem. Profl. Photographers Am., Photog. Soc. Am. (cornerstone mem.), Winona Sch. Profl. Photography (cornerstone mem.), Orchard Lake Schs. Alumni Assn. (hon.), Ill. Hist. Soc. (life), Societe Historique et Litteraire Polonaise (Paris life), Polish Mus. Am. (life), Polish Am. Congress (pres. Ill. div. 1966-70, 78-79, archivist, Heritage award 1983). Democrat. Lodges: KC (Sir Knight Lafourths 1966), Giller Zann Soc., Polish Roman Cath. Union, others. Publisher: 100 Years of Polish Press in America, 1963; The Battle That Changed The Destiny of Europe, 1982; King John Sobieski, 1983; Life of Teofila Samolinska, 1980; Memoirs of General Kriz—Krzyzanowski Civil War General, 1963; editor PNA Almanac, 1977-84, Zgoda, 1982-86. Home: 5319 N Delphia Unit 219 Chicago IL 60656 Office: St Hyacinth Ch 3636 W Wolfram Chicago IL 60618

ROZANSKI, MORDECHAI, historian, university dean; b. Lodz, Poland, July 4, 1946; came to U.S., 1968; s. Louis and Bertha R.; B.A., McGill U., 1968; postgrad. Columbia U., 1970, New Asia Coll., 1971-72; Ph.D., U. Pa., 1974; m. Bonnie Gail Asher, May 30, 1970; 1 son, Daniel K. Instr. history U. Pa., Phila., 1969-71; assoc. prof. Asian history Berry Coll., Rome, Ga., 1974-76; asst. prof. Asian history, dir. Office of Internat. Edn. and fgn. area studies program Pacific Luth. U., Tacoma, 1976-82; assoc. dean for internat. studies Adelphi U., Garden City, N.Y., 1982-84, assoc. provost, 1984-86; dean Coll. Liberal Arts, Fairleigh Dickinson U., Teaneck, N.J., 1986—; dir. programs Nat. Council on Fgn. Langs. and Internat. Studies, 1983-86. Trustee, World Affairs Council, Seattle, 1978-81; vice chmn. Nat. Com. on Internat. Studies and Program Adminstrs., 1979-80; chmn. Pacific N.W. Internat./Intercultural Edn. Consortium, 1979-82. Que. Province fellow, 1967; Wilson Meml. scholar, 1968; U. Pa. fellow, 1968-71; Am. Hist. Assn. Am.-East Asian Relations fellow, Columbia U., 1970; Can. Council doctoral fellow, 1971-73; U.S. Office of Edn. research grantee, 1977; Lilly Found. fellow Stanford U., summer 1978. Author: Manual of World History, 1975; Guide to U.S. State Papers on China, 1979. Office: Fairleigh Dickinson U Liberal Arts Office Dean Teaneck NJ 07070

ROZELL, JOSEPH GERARD, accountant; b. Kansas City, Kans., Mar. 20, 1959; s. Joseph Frank and Frances Elizabeth (Gojmeric) R. BSBA, Rockhurst Coll., 1981. Staff acct. Donnelly, Meiners & Jordan, Kansas City, Mo., 1981-82, Francis A. Wright & Co., Kansas City, Mo., 1982—. Mem. Am. Inst. CPA's, Mo. Soc. CPA's (legis. com., liaison com.), Greater Kansas City Jaycees (treas.). Republican. Roman Catholic. Home: 8741 Chestnut Cir #306 Kansas City MO 64131-2850

ROZENTAL, ANDRÉS, bank executive, former ambassador; b. Mexico City, Apr. 27, 1945; arrived in Sweden, 1983; s. Leonid Rozental and Neoma (Gutman) Castañeda; m. Vivian Holzer; children: Tamara, Sandra. BA, U. Americas, Mexico City, 1966; MA, U. Pa., 1968. Vice consul Mexican Consulate, Phila., 1967-68; sec. Ministry for Fgn. Affairs, Mexico City, 1968-71; counselor, dep. rep. to OAS Washington, 1971-74; counselor Mexican Embassy, London, 1974-76; sr. advisor to Fgn. Minister Mexico City, 1977-79, dir. gen. for N.Am. Affairs, 1979-82; Mexican ambassador to UN Geneva, Switzerland, 1982-83; Mexican ambassador to Sweden Stockholm, 1983-88; sr. v.p. Banco Nacional de Mexico SNC, 1988—. Recipient Order of Polar Star King of Sweden, 1981. Office: Banco Nacional de Mexico, Andrés Bello 45, 11560 Mexico City Mexico

ROZES, SIMONE, lawyer; b. Paris, Mar. 29, 1920; d. Leon Ludwig and Marcelle Cetre; m. Gabriel Rozes, 1942; 2 children. Licence en droit, Ecole Libre des Sciences Politiques, U. Paris. Traine lawyer, Paris, 1947-49; surrogate judge, Bourges, France, 1949-50; attache Justice Dept. France, 1951-58, adminstrn. chief cabine of minister of justice, 1958-62, judge, 1962-69; v.p. Tribunal Grande Instance Paris, 1969-73, pres., 1976-81; dir. reformatory edn., 1973-76; mem. crime prevention and control com. UN, 1977—; adv. gen. European Ct. of Justice, 1981-82, 1st adv. gen., 1982-84; pres. Cour de Cassation, Paris, 1984—. Decorated officier Legion d'Honneur, officier Ordre National du Merite, medaille de l'Education Surveillee, medaille de l'Administration Penitentiaire; comdr. cross Order Merit (Fed. Republic Germany). Avocations: skiing; mountaineering.

ROZHDESTVENSKY, GENNADI NIKOLAEVICH, conductor; b. Moscow, May 4, 1931; m. Victoria Postnikova. Ed. Moscow State Conservatory. Condr., Bolshoi Theatre, 1951-60, prin. condr., 1965-70; prin. condr., mus. dir. USSR Radio and TV Symphony Orch., 1960-65, 70-74, also Moscow Chamber Orch., 1974-83; prin. condr. Stockholm Philharmonic, 1974-77; prin. condr. BBC Symphony Orch., 1978-81; condr. Vienna Symphony Orch., from 1981; founder, artistic dir., chief condr. State Symphony Orch. of Ministry of Culture, 1983—; guest condr. Europe, Am., Asia. Decorated Order of Red Banner of Labour; named Merited and People's Artist R.S.F.S.R., 1966; recipient Lenin prize, 1970. Mem. Royal Swedish Acad. (hon.). Address: care Victor Hochhausen Ltd, 4 Holland Park Ave, London W11 England *

ROZHDESTVENSKY, ROBERT IVANOVICH, poet; b. Kosiha, Altai, Russia, June 20, 1932; s. Ivan Ivanovich and Vera Paulovna (Fedorova) R.; m. Alla Borisovna Kireeva, Nov. 14, 1953; children—Ekaterina Robertovna, Ksenya Robertovna. Ed. U. Petrozavodsk (USSR), 1950-51, Inst. Lit., Moscow, 1951-56. Writer, 1950—; spl. corr. Izvestya newspaper, Moscow, 1969—; mem. editorial bd. Smena, Moscow, 1977—; mem. jury Cannes Film Festival, France, 1968, 74, 79. Author of more than 90 books on the langs. of the nations of USSR; author numerous working papers and articles to profl. jours.; host TV program, Moscow, 1973—. Dep., Moscow Soviet, 1975; v.p. European Cultural Soc., Venice, Italy, 1981; v.p. Soviet Peace Com. Peace Fund, Moscow, 1981; mem. Union Trade Council, Moscow, 1981, Nat. Olympic Com., 1981. Recipient Golden Laurel Wreath, Struga Poetry Festival, Yugoslavia, 1969; State award for Lit., Moscow, 1979; recipient numerous other state awards for excellence in lit. Mem. Union Soviet Writers (sec. 1970—), Central Lit. Club (pres. 1980—). Mem. CPSU. Office: Union Soviet Writers, Ulitsa Vorovskogo 52, Moscow USSR *

ROZRAN, JACK LOUIS, courier service executive; b. Chgo., Mar. 4, 1939; s. Philip Reuben and Rose (Rosenberg) R.; m. Dawn Faulkner, May 25, 1986; children: Claire Ashley, Ryan Bjur. BA, Northwestern U., 1960; JD, Harvard U., 1963. Bar: Ill. 1963. Law clk. to judge U.S. Dist. Ct. Ill., 1963-64; v.p. Cannonball, Inc., Chgo., 1964-66, pres., 1966—. Trustee Hull House Assn., 1972—, v.p. 1987; sec. Erikson Inst., 1982, trustee, 1971—. Mem. Messenger Service Assn. Ill. (pres. 1987—), Air Courier Conf. Am. (treas. 1980-82, pres. 1982-84, bd. dirs. 1976—), ABA, Chgo. Bar Assn., Beta Alpha Psi. Club: Economic (Chgo.). Home: 2650 N Lakeview Ave Chicago IL 60614 Office: Cannonball Inc 875 W Huron St Chicago IL 60622

RUANO, MIGUEL, aeronautical engineer; b. Tangier, Morocco, Spain, July 29, 1928; s. Miguel and M. Dolores (Quero) R.; children: Miguel, Jose C., Fernando, Beatriz, Gonzalo. Degree in Aero. Engring., A.M. Ingenieros Aeronauticos, Madrid, Spain, 1953; D in Aero. Engring., E.S. Ingenieros Aeronauticos, Madrid Spain, 1967. Registered profl. engr. Commd. Spanish Air Force, 1947, advanced through grades to capt.; shop supr. Son Bonet Air Force Depot, Majorca, Spain, 1953-56; maintenance comdr. Spanish Air Force, Son San Juan AFB, Majorca, 1956-59; inspection supr. Spanish Air Force, Barcelona, Spain, 1959-60; head dept. E.N. Motores De Aviacion, Barcelona, Spain, 1960-62; tech. mgr. Fundiciones Industriales, Barcelona, 1962-73; gen. mgr. Sirma, Barcelona, 1973-74, Metron, Barcelona, 1974-82; mng. dir. Corp. Indsl. Catalana, Barcelona, 1982—. Recipient Aero. Merit Cross Ministerio Del Aire, Madrid, 1953. Mem. Assn. Ingenieros España, Assn. Ingenieros Aeronauticos, Colegio Ingenieros Aeronauticos. Office: Corp Industrial Catalana, Pau Claris 165, 08037 Barcelona Spain

RUBAN, GERHARD, crystallographer; b. Motzen, Fed. Republic Germany, July 3, 1926; s. Herman and Gertrud (Schulze) R.; m. Sigrid Franke; 1 child, Wolfram R. Diploma in Chemistry, Free U. Berlin, 1957; Dr. rer. nat., Free U., 1961. Research asst. Fritz Haber Inst., Berlin, 1960-66; research assoc. U. Del., Dover, 1966-67; research asst. Free U. Berlin, 1967-71, prof. crystallography, 1971—. Author research papers. Home: 15 Reichensteiner Weg, D1000 Berlin 33 Federal Republic of Germany Office: 6 Takustrasse, D1000 Berlin 33 Federal Republic of Germany

RUBB, PEGGY-GRACE PLOURD, artistic director, dancer; b. Hartford, Conn., Sept. 27, 1931; d. Launcelot J. and Margaret (Feeney) Plourd; m. Milton Robert Rubb, June 6, 1953; children—Bonnie Leigh, Eric John, Michael Robert. Student Hartt Conservatory of Music, Hartford, 1938-49, Shenandoah Conservatory, Winchester, Va., 1949-51, Froman Profl. Ballet Sch., New London, Conn., 1959-62, Hampton Acad. Ballet, Va., 1962-63, Nat. Ballet, Washington, 1963-66. Tchr., R.H. Lee Elem. Sch., Glen Burnie, Md., 1951-52; dancer Common Glory Jamestown Corp., Williamsburg, Va., 1963; accompanist Annapolis Modern Dance Assn., Md., 1973; ballet mistress dance studio, Crofton, Md., 1974-78; dance instr. gymnastics camp Washington Coll., Chestertown, Md., 1977; dance coach Glen Burnie Artistic Skate Club, 1980-81; artistic dir. Crofton-Bowie Sch. of Ballet and affiliated cos., 1978—; choreographer Tom Thumb Players, Annapolis, 1972; dancer Hampton Roads Civic Ballet, Va., 1962-63. Choreographer; composer; lyricist. Bd. dirs. Annapolis Children's Theatre, 1977-78, choreographer Nat. Assn. for Regional Ballet, Inc. Choreography Conf., 1987. Mem. Md. Council for Dance, Nat. Assn. Female Execs., Profl. Dance Tchrs. Assn., Inc., Internat. Platform Assn., Phi Beta Sigma. Club: U.S. Naval Acad. Class '53 Wives (pres. San Diego 1957-58, pres. New London 1959-60). Avocations: sketching; painting. Home: 1 Pennsylvania Ave Edgewater MD 21037 Office: 2411 Crofton Ln Chelsea House Suite 2 Crofton MD 21114

RUBBIA, CARLO, physicist; b. Georizia, Italy, Mar. 31, 1934; s. Silvio and Bice (Liceni) R.; m. Marisa Rome, June 27, 1960; children—Laura, Andrea. Diploma, Scuola Normale, Pisa, 1958; A.M. (hon.), Harvard U., 1970. Research fellow Columbia U., N.Y.C., 1960-61; asst. prof. physics U. Rome, 1961-62; prof. physics Harvard U., Cambridge, Mass., 1960—; sr. research physicist European Orgn. for Nuclear Research, Geneva, 1962—. Recipient Nobel prize in physics, 1984. Mem. European Physics Soc., Am. Physics Soc.; fgn. assoc., Nat. Acad. Scis. Office: CERN, Lab for Particle Physics, 1211 Geneva 23, Switzerland *

RUBEN, LAWRENCE, real estate developer, building company executive, lawyer; b. Bklyn., Sept. 28, 1926; s. Irving and Minnie (Sruelif) R.; m. Selma Belfer, Dec. 20, 1952; children: Richard Gordon, Lenore Denise Spiegel, Rochelle Gail. BA, NYU, 1949; LLB, Bklyn. Law Sch., 1951. Bar: N.Y. 1952. Gen. practice law N.Y.C., 1952-53; pres. Ru-Min Constrn. Co., N.Y.C., 1953-54; exec. v.p. Belco Petroleum Corp., N.Y.C., 1954-64, dir., 1954-85; v.p. Fundamental Bldg. Corp., 1952—; pres. Randall Devel. Co., Aragon Devel. Corp., Lawrence Ruben Co., Inc.; ptnr. Lexington Madison Co., Tower Plaza Assocs., Devonshire Assocs., Boylston Ptnrs., Devonshire Constrn. Co. Inc., Lawrence Assocs.; pres. Washington Mgmt. Corp. Chmn. N.Y. Builders and Realtors Fellowship Fund; trustee Nat. Jewish Ctr. for Immunology and Respiratory Medicine, Denver; patron Albert Einstein Coll. Medicine; sponsor Grad. Sch. Sci.; and mem. bd. Cardoza Sch. Law at Yeshiva U.; chmn. United Jewish Appeal, Scarsdale, N.Y., 1974-75. Served with AUS, 1945-46. Mem. ABA. Clubs: Fenway Golf, Boca Rio Golf. Office: 600 Madison Ave New York NY 10022

RUBIN, ARTHUR HERMAN, university administrator; b. N.Y.C., Aug. 14, 1927; s. Samuel and Bessie (Moritt) R.; BS, N.Y. U., 1950, MA, 1951; m. Janice Levy, Apr. 9, 1950 (div. 1965); children: Renee Ellen, Linda Joy; m. 2d, Audrey M. Schmidt, July 1, 1973. Adminstrv. asst. to asst. dean Sch. Edn., N.Y. U., 1947-54, lab. asst. bus. edn. dept., 1950-54, instr., 1954-56, program dir. grad. students orgn., 1954-63, dir. tours, 1955-58, co-ordinator summer sessions activities, 1959-64, dir. Bur. Pub. Occasions, 1963-74, dir. Bur. Conf. Facilities, 1968-69, asst. v.p. pub. occasions, 1974-75, dir. extramural affairs Coll. Dentistry, 1976, assoc. dean adminstrn., 1976-80, adj. asst. prof. behavioral scis. and community health, 1976-80, dir. alumni relations Sch. of Med., 1980—, dir. alumni relations and spl. events med. ctr., 1988—; tchr. Patrick Henry Jr. High Sch., N.Y.C., 1949-58; acting asst. prin. Robert F. Wagner Jr. High Sch., N.Y.C., 1958-63; cons. in field. Trustee Agnew Found., 1967—. Recipient N.Y. U. Presdl. citation, 1971; GSO award, 1980; Ernest O. Melby award Sch. Edn. Alumni Assn., 1976; citation Bus. Edn. Assn. Met. N.Y., 1976; Sesquicentennial award N.Y.U. Alumni Fedn., 1982, Meritorious Service award, 1985. Mem. Eastern Bus. Tchrs. Assn. (chmn. exhibits 1953-74, exec. bd. 1969-71, pres. 1972-73, award 1974), Bus. Edn. Assn. of Met. N.Y. (mem. exec. bd. 1962-83), Bus. Edn. Securities Club, Inc. (pres. 1963-66, v.p. ops. 1967-68), Arch Securities Club, Inc. (pres. 1963-66, v.p. ops. 1967-68), Nat. Bus. Edn. Assn. (mem. exec. bd. 1972-74, conv. mgr. 1974—), N.Y. Acad. Pub. Edn. (bd. dirs. 1979—), Educators Securities Club, Inc. (v.p. ops. 1966-68), N.Y. U. Edn. Alumni Assn. (v.p. 1961-62, 64-67), Delta Pi Epsilon (Service awards Alpha chpt. 1971, 81), Kappa Phi Kappa, Alpha Delta Pi Securities Club, Inc. (pres. 1963-66, v.p. ops. 1967-68). Club: N.Y. U. (bd. govs. 1972-78, 79—, v.p. 1983-86, chmn. bd. 1986-87). Home: 110 Bleecker St Apt 29E New York NY 10012 Office: NYU Med Ctr 550 1st Ave New York NY 10016

RUBIN, BURTON JAY, lawyer, editor; b. Bklyn., Jan. 23, 1946; s. Samuel and Sidell (Greenfield) R.; m. Janice Ann Edelstein, Feb. 17, 1974; 1 dau., Jennifer Sidell. A.B. in Biology, Guilford Coll., Greensboro, N.C., 1966; J.D., U. N.C., 1969. Bar: Va. 1971; U.S. Ct. Customs and Patent Appeals 1975. Legal editor Labor Relations Reporter, Bur. Nat. Affairs, Inc., Washington, 1970; asst. editor U.S. Law Week, 1970-74, asst. mng. editor Patent, Trademark and Copyright Jour., 1974-75, mng. editor U.S. Patents Quar., 1975-85; gen. counsel Am. Soc. Travel Agts., 1985—; cons. Roundhouse Sq. Psychiat. Ctr., Alexandria, Va. Mem. Fairfax County Water Authority, Va.; mem. Fairfax County Police-Citizens Adv. Council, 1982-83, alt. mem., 1984-85; mem. West Springfield Police-Citizens Adv. Com., 1979-85, chmn., 1981; bd. dirs. Bur. Nat. Affairs, 1984-85; mem. Fairfax County Rep. Com., 1982-85. Mem. ABA. Contbr. articles to profl. jours. Office: 1101 King St Alexandria VA 22314

RUBIN, IRVIN I., plastics company executive; b. Bklyn., Feb. 27, 1919; B.S. in Chemistry, CCNY, 1938; postgrad. Bklyn. Coll., 1939-40; children—Jesse, Julie. Pres., Robinson Plastics Corp., Hoboken, N.J., 1940-42, 44—; engr. Montrose Chem., Newark, 1942-45; prin. Robinson, Lewis & Rubin, Inc., N.Y.C., 1957-70; adj. prof. plastics N.Y. Inst. Tech., 1960-63; mem. Plastics Ednl. Commn., Adv. Bd. Vocat. and Extension Edn., Bd. Edn. N.Y.C., 1960-71; cons. Dupont, Am. Optical, Kodex, Mem. Soc. Plastic Engrs. (pres. N.Y. sect.). Author: Injection Molding Theory and Practice, 1973. Office: 527 Clinton St Hoboken NJ 07030

RUBIN, LAWRENCE GILBERT, laboratory manager, physicist; b. Bklyn., Sept. 17, 1925; s. Harry E. and Ruth (Feirberg) R.; m. Florence Ruth Kagan, Feb. 11, 1951; children: Michael G., Richard D., Jeffrey N. Student, Cooper Union, N.Y.C., 1943, 46-47; B.S. in Physics, U. Chgo., 1949; M.A. in Physics, Columbia U., 1950. Staff mem., physicist research div. Raytheon Co., Waltham, Mass., 1950-64; group leader Nat. Magnet Lab., MIT, Cambridge, Mass., 1964-78, div. head high magnetic field facility, 1978—; Nat. Acad. Scis. adv. panel Nat. Bur. Standards, 1976-82, 85—; dir. Lake Shore Cryotronics, Inc., Columbus, Ohio, 1982—; gen. chmn. 6th Internat. Temperature Symposium, Washington, 1982. Editor sect. of book; mem. editorial bd.: Rev. Sci. Instruments, 1968-70, 79-81, Two Instrumentation Encys., 1985—; chmn. adv. com. Physics Today Buyers' Guide; contr. articles to physics jours. Concord Band, Big Band Inc. Served with U.S. Army, 1943-46, ETO. Fellow Am. Phys. Soc. (organizer and 1st chmn. new instrument and measurement sci. group 1985), IEEE; mem. Instrument Soc. Am. (sr.), Am. Vacuum Soc. Jewish. Home: 1504 Centre St Newton Centre MA 02159 Office: Nat Magnet Lab MIT Bldg NW14 170 Albany St Cambridge MA 02139

RUBIN, MARTIN N., meeting planner, consultant; b. N.Y.C., Aug. 9, 1928; s. Max and Esther (Chernow) R.; m. Shirley Anne Rubin, Aug. 22, 1954 (div. Aug. 1964); m. Karen Anne O'Brien, Sept. 21, 1981. AB, U. Mich.; AM, Miami U., Oxford, Ohio; PhD., Sussex U., Eng. Lic. psychologist. With Dayton (Ohio) Sch. System, 1951-60, West Alexandria (Ohio) Sch. System, 1961-63; instr. Wright State U., Dayton, 1961-63; with Devereux Found., Pa., N.Y. Dept. Corrections, Bklyn., 1971-73, Council for Retarded Children, Albany, N.Y., 1973-75; prin. M. Rubin & Co., Inc., Mount Vernon, N.Y., 1975—. Author: Developmentally Disabled, 1965. Candidate Dem. State Legis., 1982; adv. bd. Mt. Vernon Mental Health Bd., 1985. Master's degree scholar Miami U., 1958; Guidance Inst. grantee Miami U., 1959. Fellow Am. Assn. Mental Deficiency (pres. 1967); mem. Soc. Assn. Execs. (bd. dirs. 1985—). Lodge: Masons (sr. warden 1983).

RUBIN, SEYMOUR JEFFREY, lawyer, educator; b. Chgo., Apr. 6, 1914; s. Sol and Sadie (Bloom) R.; m. Janet Beck, Mar. 26, 1943. B.A., U. Mich., 1935; LL.B. magna cum laude, Harvard U., 1938, LL.M., 1939. Bar: Ill. 1939, D.C. 1941. Mem. U.S. Reparations Del., 1945, Inter-Am. Conf. on Problems of War and Peace, 1945; chief U.S. Delegation on Post-War Problems, Portugal, Spain, Sweden, 1946; asst. legal adviser econ. affairs Dept. State, 1946-48; legal adviser U.S. dels. to organizing confs. GATT, 1947-48; practiced law Washington, 1948-61; mem. Spl. Presdl. Mission to Bolivia, 1961; personal rep. Pres. to Bolivia wih rank of spl. ambassador 1962; gen. counsel ICA and AID, 1961-62; U.S. rep. Devel. Assistance Com., 1962-64; U.S. rep. to spl. com. UN Security Council, 1964-65; counsel Surrey, Karasik & Morse, 1964-75; U.S. rep. UN Commn. on Internat. Trade Law, 1967-69; prof. Am. U. Law Sch., 1973-85, prof. emeritus, 1985—; exec. v.p. Am. Soc. Internat. Law, 1975-85, sr. adviser, 1985—; mem. Inter Am. Juridical Commn., 1974—; U.S. rep. UN Commn. on Transnat. Corps., 1975-87; mem. U.S. del. UNCTAD Tech. Transfer Conf., 1978; mem. panel of conciliators Internat. Centre for Settlement of Investment Disputes, 1981—; cons. U.S. Dept. State, Brookings Instn., 1948-49; chief U.S. del negotiating Marshall Plan Agreements, 1951-52; dep. adminstr. Mut. Def. Assistance Control Act, 1952-53; pub. mem. Commn. on Internat. Rules Jud. Procedure, 1961-62; adj. prof. Georgetown U. Law Ctr., Washington, 1964-72; lectr. Sloan Sch. Bus. Adminstrn., MIT, Cambridge, 1969; pres. InterAm. Legal Services Assn., 1980-82; sr. cons. Am. Soc. Internat. Law; lectr. in field at various univs. worldwide, 1949—; chmn. Bellagio Trade Conf., 1985, Symposium on U.S.-European Community trade issues, Boston, 1987; chmn. U.S. Govt. Constitution Com. on Dem. Instns., 1987—; cons. legal issues of trade and investment. Author: Private Foreign Investment, 1956, The Conscience of the Rich Nations - The Common Aid Effort and the Development Assistance Committee, 1966, (with others) The International Corporation, 1970, Global Companies, 1975, Emerging Standards for Internat. Trade and Investment, 1983, Managing Trade Relations in the 1980s, 1984; editor, contbr.: Foreign Development Lending—Legal Aspects, 1971, Environment and Trade, 1981; editor: Avoidance and Settlement of International Trade Disputes, 1986; contbr. (with others) articles in field to profl. jours. Mem. bd. Inst. Internat. Law, Consumers for World Trade. Recipient Sesquicentennial award U. Mich., 1967; Grand Silver medal Austria, 1967. Mem. Am. Soc. Internat. Law, Internat. Law Assn., Council on Fgn. Affairs, Am. Law Inst., Am. Bar Assn., Interam. Bar Assn., Soc. for Internat. Devel. Democrat. Home: 1675 35th St NW Washington DC 20007 Office: 2223 Massachusetts Ave NW Washington DC 20008

RUBIN, STANLEY CREAMER, producer; b. N.Y.C., Oct. 8, 1917; s. Michael Isaac and Anne (Creamer) R.; m. Elizabeth Margaret von Gerkan (actress Kathleen Hughes), July 25, 1954; children: John, Chris, Angela, Michael. Student, UCLA, 1933-37. Writer Universal Studios, Universal City, Calif., 1940-42, Columbia Pictures, Los Angeles, 1946-47; writer, producer NBC-TV, Burbank, Calif., 1948-49; theatrical film producer various studios, 1949-55; TV producer CBS-TV, Los Angeles, 1956-59, Universal Studios, Universal City, 1960-63, 20th Century-Fox, Los Angeles, 1967-71, MGM Studios, Culver City, Calif., 1972-77; pres. TBA Prodns., Los Angeles, 1978—. Producer theatrical films including The Narrow Margin, 1950, My Pal Gus, 1950, Destination Gobi, 1951, River of No Return, 1952, Promise Her Anything, 1966, The President's Analyst, 1967; TV prodns. include G.E. Theatre, 1959-63, Ghost and Mrs. Muir, 1968-69, Bracken's World, 1969-71; writer, producer TV film The Diamond Necklace, 1948 (Emmy award 1949); producer TV films including Babe, 1975 (Hollywood Fgn. Press Golden Globe award, Christopher medal), And Your Name is Jonah, 1978 (Christopher medal 1979), The Story of Satchel Paige, 1980 (Image award 1981); exec. producer TV prodn. Escape from Iran: The Canadian Caper, 1981. Producer spl. programming Dem. Nat. Conv., San Francisco, 1984, Columbia Pictures and Rastar Prdns., 1988—. Served to 1st lt. USAAF, 1942-46. Mem. Writers Guild Am. (dir. 1941-42), Producers Guild Am. (bd. dirs. 1968-74, pres. 1974-79, v.p. 1987—), Acad. Motion Picture Arts and Scis., Acad. TV Arts and Scis. (bd. govs. 1971, 73), Phi Beta Kappa. Home and Office: TBA Prodns Inc 8818 Rising Glen Pl Los Angeles CA 90069

RUBIN, WLADYSLAW CARDINAL, Polish ecclesiastic; b. Toki, Lwow, Poland, Sept. 20, 1917. Student St. Joseph U., Beirut. Ordained priest Roman Catholic Ch., 1946. Served as chaplain for Polish community and Polish refugees in Italy, 1953-58, rector Polish Coll., Rome, 1964; titular bishop of Serta and aux. bishop for Gniezno, 1964-79; sec. gen. Synod of Bishop, 1967-79; elevated to Sacred Coll. Cardinals, 1970; prefect Sacred Congregation for Eastern Chs., 1980-85; mem. Sacred Congregations for Doctrine of Faith and for Causes of Saints; mem. Supreme Tribunal for Apostolic Signature; sec. for Promoting Christian Unity, Pontifical Com. for Rev. of Oriental Canon Law, Sacred Congregation for Doctrine of Faith, for Religious and Secular Insts., for Evangelization of People, for Causes of Saints, for Cath. Edn., Supreme of Apostolic Signature; sec. for Christian Unity, Pontifical Com. for Revision of Codex of Eastern Canonical Law; deacon of St. Maria in Via Lata. Address: Palazzo dei Convertendi, Via della Conciliazione 34, 00193 Rome Italy *

RUBINO, PETER JAMES, civil engineer; b. Torrington, Conn., Aug. 24, 1952; s. Bernard Paul and Katherine Emile (Bzullak) R.; m. Mahvash Sedigheh Tahtolkassaie, Aug. 20, 1978; children—Jasper Antoni, Jason Cyrus. B.S. in Civil Engring., U. Conn., 1974; M.B.A., U. Okla., 1985. Registered profl. engr., Conn., Tex. Acting mng. dir. I.H.L., Baghdad, Iraq, 1976, asst. project mgr., Bandar Abbas, Iran, 1976-77, office/field engr., Tehran, Iran, 1977-78; office engr. IRATEX, Houston, 1978-80; project engr. ARAMCO, Dhahran, Saudi Arabia, 1980-86; sr. facility engr., team leader leased facilities projects Intel Corp., Chandler, Ariz., 1987— . Designer Jordan Army Dining Hall, 1977. Mem. ASCE, Nat. Soc. Profl. Engrs. Republican. Avocations: photography; home computers; investment; swimming; biking; woodworking. Home and Office: 5000 W Chandler Blvd Chandler AZ 85224

RUBINSTEIN, HYMAN SOLOMON, neurologist, psychiatrist, psychoanalyst; b. Leeds, Eng., Mar. 16, 1904; s. Myer David and Rose (Schneederman) R.; m. Ellen Steinhorn, July 21, 1929; children: Madelyn Shapiro, Roberta Rubinstein. Ph.G., U. Md., 1924, M.D., 1928, B.S., 1932, Ph.D., 1934; student, Henry Phipps Psychiat. Clinic, Johns Hopkins, 1932-35, George Washington U., 1935-36, Washington-Balt. Psychoanalytic Inst., 1946-51; diploma, Washington Sch. Psychiatry, 1952; certificate in psychoanalysis, William Alanson White Inst., 1958. Diplomate: Am. Bd. Psychiatry and Neurology. Intern Sinai Hosp., Balt., 1927-29; asst. medicine Sinai Hosp., 1929-30; instr. neuroanatomy and neurology U. Md., 1930-33; asso. neuroanatomy, chief neurol. clinic 1933-35; dir. lab. neuroendocrine research Sinai Hosp., 1935-45, chief div. psychiatry, 1945-47, psychiat. research, 1945-51; cons. psychiatry USPHS, 1937-42; cons. psychiatrist U.S. Fed. Ct., 1942-50, Jewish Big Brother League; attending physician neurology and psychiatry U.S. Army Hosp., Aberdeen Proving Ground, 1951-54; faculty Washington Sch. Psychiatry, 1952-56; pvt. practice psychiatry and psychoanalysis; mem. staff Sinai Hosp.; supervising psychiatrist Seton Psychiat. Inst., Balt., 1965-73; chmn. vis. staff Seton Psychiat. Inst., 1972-73. Author: (with C. L. Davis) Laboratory Manual of Neuroanatomy, 1937, Stereoscopic Atlas of Neuroanatomy, 1947, The Study of the Brain, 1953, Interpersonal Conflict, 1960; Contbg. author: The Pituitary Gland, 1938; Contbr.: World Book Ency.; Editor-in-chief: Quar. Phi Lambda Kappa and

Med. Students Aid Soc, 1964-66; Cons. psychiatry: Current Med. Digest, 1960-75. Chmn. commn. on law and social action, 1958-61; chmn. commn. on internat. affairs Md. chpt. Am. Jewish Congress, 1961, pres. Md., 1964-69, mem. nat. governing council of congress, 1958-62, 64—; pres. Med. Students Aid Soc., 1959-63; bd. dirs. Hebrew Immigrant Aid Soc., pres., 1969-71; bd. dirs. Asso. Jewish Charities and Welfare Fund, 1969-71; bd. dirs. Histadrut Council of Greater Balt., pres., 1975-80. Named Big Brother of Year for Md. by Jewish Big. Bro. League Balt. and Big Bros. Affiliates of Big Bros. Am., U.S. and Can., 1964; recipient Sidney Hollander award Md. chpt. Am. Jewish Congress, 1973, cert. distinction Alumni Assn. Sch. Pharmacy U. Md., 1974, cert. service to mankind Alumni Assn. Sch. Medicine U. Md., 1978. Fellow Am. Acad. Psychoanalysis (life), Am. Psychiat. Assn., AAAS; mem. AMA, William A. White Psychoanalytic Soc., Soc. Med. Psychoanalysts, Am. Physicians Fellowship for Israel Med. Assn. (pres. Md. chpt. 1957-67, mem. nat. exec. com., nat. v.p.), Israel Med. Assn. (hon. corr. mem.), Alumni Assn. Peabody Conservatory Johns Hopkins U., Sigma Xi, Phi Sigma Delta, Phi Lambda Kappa (nat. bd. govs., nat. pres. 1966-67, Grand Sci. award particularly for research in neuroendocrinology and neuropsychiatry 1986). Jewish (bd. electors Balt. Hebrew congregation 1966-69). Club: Music (Balt.). Address: 3900 N Charles St Baltimore MD 21218

RUBINSTEIN, LOUIS BARUCH, lawyer, consultant; b. Providence, Dec. 5, 1908; s. Israel Sessel and Fannie Rebecca (Rubin) R.; m. Lillian Berger, Dec. 20, 1950; children—Louis H., Michael L.; m. 2d, Dorothy L. Gottlieb, June 6, 1982. B.A., Yale U., 1931, J.D., 1934. Bar: D.C. 1936, R.I. 1938, U.S. Supreme Ct. 1974. Counsel, advisor on internat. law U.S. Dept. State, 1934-38; chief legal officer Dept. Employment Security State of R.I., 1965-76; counsel Zietz, Mittleman & Webster, 1950-82; mem. Gates, Mellion & Rubinstein, Providence, 1982—; master in chancery Superior Ct. R.I.; lectr. in field. Hon. dir. Temple Emanuel Jewish Community Ctr.; hon. pres. R.I. Region Jewish Nat. Fund; hon. sec. Jewish Fedn. of R.I., 1982—. Served with USAF, 1942-45. Mem. R.I. Bar Assn. (award of merit 1977, 82, 85, mem. exec. com. 1977-81, editor in chief Jour. 1977-81), Am. Arbitration Assn. (arbitrator labor-mgmt. panel). Democrat. Clubs: Kirkbrae Country (Lincoln, R.I.); Boca Teeca Country (Boca Raton, Fla.), Yale of R.I., Masons (past master), Shriners. Contbr. articles to profl. jours. Address: 299 NW 52d Terrace #417 Boca Raton FL 33431

RUBINSTEIN, SHIRLEY JOY, nursing service executive; b. Toronto, Ont., Can., Nov. 19, 1927; came to U.S., 1928, naturalized, 1948; d. Harry Hyman and Ida Ruth (Albert) Adel; m. Philip F. Rubinstein, Aug. 17, 1947; children—David Brian, Wendy Sue, Hope Terri. With Jewish Agy. for Palestine, Washington, 1947-49; coordinator Nursing Staff, Inc., 1975-78; co-founder, pres. Nursing Services, Inc., Silver Spring, Md., 1978—; founder, pres. Fantasy Factory Inc., Pegasus Limosine Services. Democrat. Jewish. Club: B'nai Birth. Office: PO Box 4133 Silver Spring MD 20904

RUBINSTEIN, WILLIAM DAVID, professor, author; b. N.Y.C., Aug. 12, 1946; s. Jack and Enid Victoria (Rubenstein) R.; m. Hilary Louise Manns, Jan. 2, 1968; 1 child, Paul Benjamin. BA, Swarthmore Coll., 1968; PhD, Johns Hopkins U., 1975. Research assoc. Dept. History U. Lancaster, Eng., 1974-75; research fellow Dept. Sociology Australian Nat. U., Canberra, 1976-78; lectr. Sch. Social Scis., Geelong, Victoria, Australia, 1978-81; sr. lectr. Deakin U., Australia, 1982-84, assoc. prof., 1985-88, prof., 1988—; research cons. Australian Inst. Jewish Affairs, Melbourne, Australia, 1984—. Editor: Wealth and the Wealthy in the Modern World, 1980, Men of Property: The Very Wealthy in Britain since the Industrial Revolution, 1981, The Left, The Right, and the Jews, 1982 (translated into Italian 1986), The Jews in Australia, 1986, Wealth and Inequality in Britain, 1986, Elites and the Wealthy, in Modern British History, 1987, Jews in the Sixth Continent, 1987; contbr. articles to prfl. jours. Fellow Australian Acad. of Humanities, Royal Hist. Soc.; mem. Econ. History Soc., Social History Soc., Australian Assn. Jewish Studies (v.p. 1987), Australian Jewish Hist. Soc. (v.p. 1985). Office: Deakin U, Sch Social Scis, Victoria 3217, Australia

RUBINYI, PAUL, management consultant; b. Budapest, Hungary, Oct. 28, 1921; arrived in Can., 1957; s. Andor and Regina Rubinyi; m. Lea Hirsch; 1 child, Katherine. PhD in Econs., Bolyai U., Romania, 1946; PhD in Managerial Cybernetics, Brunel U., London, 1980. Exec. officer Cen. Planning Authority, Hungary, 1946-56; cons. various firms, Can., 1957-69; dir. cen. planning and programming Govt. of Can., Ottawa, Ont., 1969-86; ptnr. Ernst & Whinney, Montreal, Que, Can., 1987—; head Paul Rubinyi and Assocs., Montreal, 1987— ; pvt. cons. various firms, 1987—. Mem. Am. Econs. Assn., Inst. Chartered Accts. Can., Soc. for Gen. Systems Research, Am. Cybernetics Assn. Home: 1405 Dumfries Rd, Montreal, PQ Canada H3P 2R2

RUBIO, LUIS F., political scientist; b. Mexico City, Aug. 19, 1955; s. Boris and Paulina (Freidberg) R.; m. Martha Kaufer; 1 child, Erika. Licenciatura, U. Iberoam., Mexico City, 1976; MA, Brandeis U., 1978, PhD, 1982—. Planning dir. Citibank NA, Mexico City, 1978-81; advisor Secretaria de Hacienda y Crèdito Pub., Mexico City, 1980-81; dir. gen. IBAFIN Centro de Investigación para el Desarrollo, Mexico City, 1981—; advisor Ctr. for Strategic and Internat. Studies, Washington, 1984-87; bd. dirs. Banco Obrero; assoc. prof. U. Iberoam., Mexico City, 1978—. Author: (with others) Mexico's Dilemma, 1984 (Assn. Polit. Risk Analysts award 1985), A Mexican Response, 1987, (author/editor with others) El Reto del Sistema Financiero Mexicano, 1986; editorial bd. Global Risk Assessment, Los Angeles, 1984—; contbr. articles to profl. jours. v.p. Mexico City Preparatory and Secondary Sch., 1981—. Mem. Assn. Polit. Risk Analysts (bd. dirs.), Council on Fgn. Relations, Internat. Polit. Sci. Assn. Office: IBAFIN, Jaime Balmes 11-D-2, 10 Mexico City Mexico

RUBIO, PEDRO ANTONIO, cardiovascular surgeon; b. Mexico City, Dec. 17, 1944; came to U.S., 1970; s. Isaac and Esther; children: Sandra, Edward, MD, U. Nacional Autónoma de Méx., 1968; MS in Surg. Tech., Pacific Western U., 1981, PhD in Biomed. Tech., 1982. Diplomate Am. Bd. Surgery; profl. cert. law enforcement sci., Nat. Com. Profl. Law Enforcement Standards, 1972. Prof. neurology Escuela Normal de Especialización, Secretaria De Educación Publica, Mexico City, 1968-69; asst. instr. dept. surgery Baylor Coll. Medicine, Houston, 1971-76; clin. instr. dept. surgery U. Tex. Med. Sch., Houston, 1978—; clin. supr. psychiatry residency tng. program Tex. Research Inst. Mental Scis., Houston, 1979-85; surgeon, dir. Cardiovascular Surg. Ctr., Houston, 1976-85, Houston Cardiovascular Inst., 1985— ; chmn. surgery dept. HCA Med. Ctr. Hosp., Houston, 1978—; research projects with FDA, NCI, HEW, VA ; pres. exec. com. Houston Chamber Singers, 1982-83. Decorated Palms Honor Cross (hon.), Mex. Army; recipient Recognition diploma bachelor's class Universidad Nacional Autonoma de Mex., 1961, Facultad de Medicina, 1966; named Outstanding Surg. Intern, Baylor Coll. Medicine, 1970-71. Fellow Academia Mexicana de Cirugia, ACS (Best Paper award South Tex. chpt. 1976), Am. Coll. Angiology, Am. Coll. Chest Physicians, Houston Acad. Medicine. Internat. Coll. Angiology, Internat. Coll. Surgeons (pres. U.S. sect. 1987-88, 89—, pres. Tex. div. 1983-85, historian 1985—, chmn. membership com. U.S. sect. 1984-86, 3d pl. sci. motion picture 1980), Israel Med. Assn. USA, Royal Soc. Medicine, Am. Heart Assn. (stroke council), Am. Geriatrics Soc., AMA (Recognition award 1971, 73—), Am. Trauma Soc., Denton A. Cooley Cardiovascular Soc., Harris County (Tex.) Med. Soc., Houston Surg. Soc. (1st pl. essay 1973, 75), Internat. Assn. Study Lung Cancer, Internat. Cardiovascular Soc., Sociedad Mexicana de Angiologia (1st pl. nat. essay contest 1974), Soc. Internat. Chirurgie, Tex. Med. Assn., World Med. Assn. Lodge: Rosicrucian. Author: (with E.M. Farrell) Atlas of Angioaccess Surgery, 1983; Atlas of Stapling Techniques, 1986; contbr. 165 sci. articles to publs.; patentee med. instrumentation. Office: Houston Cardiovascular Inst 7400 Fannin Suite 1240 Houston TX 77054

RUBLOFF, BURTON, real estate broker, appraiser; b. Chisholm, Minn., June 1, 1912; s. Solomon W. and Mary R.; m. Patricia F. Williams, July 17, 1943; 1 dau., Jenifer. Grad, Northwestern U., 1940. With Arthur Rubloff & Co. (now Rubloff Inc.), Chgo., 1930—; v.p. Arthur Rubloff & Co. (now Rubloff Inc.), 1947-76, sr. v.p., 1976—. Bd. dirs. Mcpl. Art League Chgo.; mem. Urbanland Inst. Served with U.S. Army, 1943-46, ETO. Mem. Am. Inst. Real Estate Appraisers (life mem. chpt. 6), Nat. Ill., Chgo. (hon. life mem.) assns. real estate bds., Chgo. Real Estate Bd. (ethics com.), Bldg. Mgrs. Assn. Chgo., Urban Land Inst., Greater State St. Council (real estate com.), Lambda Alpha Internat. (Ely chpt.). Clubs: John Evans (Northwestern U.); City (Chgo.). Office: Rubloff Inc 111 W Washington St Chicago IL 60602

RUBY, CHARLES LEROY, educator, lawyer, civic leader; b. Carthage, Ind., Dec. 28, 1900; s. Edgar Valentine and Mary Emma (Butler) R.; certificate Ball State U., 1921-22; AB, Cen. Normal Coll., 1924, LLB, 1926, BS, 1931, BPE, 1932; MA, Stanford, 1929; JD, Pacific Coll. of Law, 1931; PhD, Olympic U., 1933; m. Rachael Elizabeth Martindale, Aug. 30, 1925; children: Phyllis Arline (Mrs. Norman Braskat), Charles L., Martin Dale. Prin., Pine Village (Ind.) High Sch., 1923-25; Glenwood (Ind.) Pub. Schs., 1925-26; tchr. El Centro (Calif.) Pub. Sch., 1926-27, Central (Calif.) Union High Sch., 1927-29; prof. law Fullerton Coll., 1929-66; prof. edn. Armstrong Coll., summer 1935, Cen. Normal Coll., summers 1929-33; admitted to Ind. bar, 1926, U.S. Supreme Ct. bar, 1970; pres. Ret. Service Vol. Program, North Orange County, Calif., 1973-76, 83-84; dir. North Orange County Vol. Bur., Fullerton Sr. Citizens Task Force. Life trustee, Continuing Learning Experiences program Calif. State U., Fullerton, hon. chmn. fund com. Gerontology Bldg; founder, dir. Fullerton Pub. Forum, 1929-39; founder Elks Nat. Found.; co-founder, benefactor Gerontology Ctr. Calif. State U., Fullerton; pres. Fullerton Rotary, 1939-40, hon. mem., 1983—; mem. U.S. Assay Commn., 1968—; mem. Orange County Dem. Cen. Com., 1962-78; bd. dirs. Fullerton Sr. Multi-purpose Ctr., 1981—; bd. dirs. Orange County Sr. Citizens Adv. Council; mem. pres.'s com. Calif. State U., Fullerton. Recipient Medal of Merit, Am. Numis. Assn., 1954, Spl. Commendation, Calif. State Assembly, 1966, Calif. State Senate, 1978, 86, Commendation, Ind. Sec. of State, 1984, Commendation, Bd. Suprs. Orange County, 1985, Commendation, Fullerton City Council, 1986, Commendation, Orange County Bd. Supervisors, 1986, Commendation, Calif. State Senate, 1986, Commendation, Exec. Com. Pres. Calif. State U., Fullerton, 1986; Charles L. and Rachael E. Ruby Gerontology Ctr. named in his and late wife's honor, Calif. State U., Fullerton. Fellow Ind. Bar Found.; mem. Pres. Assocs. Calif. State U. Fullerton, Fullerton Coll. Assocs. (named Spl. Retiree of Yr. 1986, Commendation, 1986), Calif. (life, pres. So. sect. 1962-63, treas. 1964-65, pres. 1960-61, dir. 1956-65), Orange County Tchrs. Assn. (pres. 1953-55), Fullerton Coll. (pres. 1958-60) Tchrs. Assn., NEA (life), Ind. Bar Assn., Stanford U. Law Soc., Calif. State Council Edn., Am. Numismatic Assn. (gov. 1951-53, life adv. bd.), Ind. Bar Assn. (hon. life), Calif. Bus. Educators Assn. (hon. life), Calif. Assn. Univ. Profs., Pacific S.W. Bus. Law Assn. (pres. 1969-70, life), Numismatic Assn. So. Calif. (life, pres. 1961), Calif. Numis. Assn., Indpls. Coin Club (hon. life), Los Angeles Coin Club (hon. life), U.S. Supreme Ct. Hist. Soc., Calif. Town Hall, North Orange County Mus. Assn. (life, benefactor dir.), Stanford U. Alumni Assn., Old Timers Assay Commn. Methodist. Clubs: Elks, Fullerton Jr. Coll. Vets. (hon. life). Contbr. articles in field to profl. jours. Home: 308 N Marwood Ave Fullerton CA 92632

RUBY, SALLY ANNE, city official; b. Hershey, Pa., Sept. 25, 1944; d. Edward Mark and Sarah Ellen (Tobias) Keeney; B.S., Labanon Valley Coll., Annville, Pa., 1973; M.Ed., Millersville (Pa.) State Coll., 1974. Counselor, Fla. Div. Corrections, 1974-76; compliance coordinator City of Clearwater (Fla.), 1976—. Mem. loan com. Neighborhood Housing Service, Clearwater; mem. bi-racial com. Pinellas County Sch. Bd.; mem. task force Project Self-Sufficency; program chair 3d Ann. State Civil Rights Conf., chairperson fundraising project Family Service Ctr., 1987, mem. devel. com.; sec. adv. bd. Clearwater Adult Eve. Sch.; bd. dirs. Pinellas Opportunity Council. Mem. NAACP (life), Nat. Assn. Human Rights Workers, Internat. Assn. Ofcl. Human Rights Agys., NOW, Fla. Assn. Community Relations Profls., Millersville U. Alumni Assn., Nat. Orgn. on Disability. Home: 416 N Lincoln Ave Clearwater FL 34615 Office: PO Box 4748 Clearwater FL 33618

RUCH, WILLIAM VAUGHN, educator, consultant; b. Allentown, Pa., Sept. 29, 1937; s. Weston H. and Dorothy D. (Daubert) R.;. BA, Moravian Coll., 1959; MA in Communications, Syracuse U., 1969; MBA, Fairleigh Dickinson U., 1972; PhD, Rensselaer Poly. Inst., 1980; JD, Western State U. Coll. Law, 1983. Reporter Call-Chronicle Newspapers, Allentown, Pa., 1959-60; tchr. English conversation Jonan Sr. High Sch., Matsuyama, Japan, 1960-62; asst. editor Dixie News, Am. Can Co., Easton, Pa., 1964-65; fin. editor Pa. Power & Light Co., Allentown, 1967-69, sales promotion writer, 1965-66, advt. asst., 1966-67; tech. writer, editor Space Tech. Ctr., Allentown, 1966-67, Gen. Electric Co., King of Prussia, Pa., 1969; prof. mgmt. Monmouth Coll., West Long Branch, N.J., 1985-88; corp. communications cons. Madison, N.J., 1988—; asst. editor Bell System Tech. Jour., Bell Telephone Labs., Murray Hill, N.J., 1969-71; field rep. N.W. Ayer & Son, Inc., N.Y.C., 1972-73; asst. prof. bus. communications Fairleigh Dickinson U., Madison, N.J., 1974-75, Bloomsburg (Pa.) State Coll., 1975-76; lectr. Sch. Bus. and Pub. Adminstrn., Calif. State U., Sacramento, 1977-79; asst. prof. bus. writing Coll. Bus. Adminstrn., San Diego (Calif.) State U., 1979-84; lectr. European div. U. Md., 1984-85; cons. Corporate Communications, 1988—. Author: Corporate Communications: A Comparison of Japanese and American Practices, 1984, Business Reports: Written and Oral, 1988. Mem. Acad. Mgmt., Assn. for Bus. Communication Assn., Internat. Assn. Bus. Communicators, Internat. Platform Assn. Republican. Mem. United Ch. of Christ. Home: 288F Main St Madison NJ 07940

RÜCKER, GÜNTHER, artist; b. Liberec, Czechoslovakia, Feb. 2, 1924; arrived in Germany, 1945; s. Thomas and Johanna (Schmidt) R.; m. Anke Wagemann, May 20, 1940; children: Nina, Jenny. Grad., Mendelssohn Acad., Leipzig, German Democratic Republic, 1949. freelance artist. Author, dir. various radio plays (Prix Italia 1977); dir. various films (Nat. award 1956, Grand Prix 1980); author various stories (Nat. award 1980). Mem. Akademie der Künste der DDR (head. dept. literary sect. 1972-82).

RUDA, JOSE MARIA, judge International Court of Justice; b. Buenos Aires, Aug. 9, 1924; s. Jose Maria and Margarita (Comas) R.; Dr. Law and Social Scis., U. Buenos Aires, 1949; LL.M., N.Y. U., 1955; LL.D. (hon.), Punjab (India) U.; m. Mariá Haydée Arnold (dec. 1981); 5 children; m. Ruth Guevara Achaval, 1983. With Office Legal Affairs, UN, 1950-55; sec. state Salta Province, Argentina, 1956-57; counsellor Argentine embassy, La Paz, Bolivia, 1957-59; chief cabinet Minister Fgn. Affairs and Worship, 1959-61; mem. Argentine del. to UN, from 1959, chmn., 1965; permanent rep. to UN, 1965-70; asso. prof. internat. law U. Buenos Aires Law Sch., 1959-71, prof., 1971—; undersec. state for fgn. affairs and worship, 1970-72; mem. Internat. Ct. Justice, The Hague, 1973—; vis. prof. Colegio de Mex., 1963; mem. UN Internat. Law Commn., 1964-73, chmn., 1968; mem. Permanent Ct. of Arbitration, 1977; mem. com. experts ILO, 1978—; del. numerous internat. confs. Mem. Inst. Internat. Law, Internat. Law Assn., Inter.-Am. Inst. Internat. Juridical Studies, Hispano-Luso-Am. Inst. Internat. Law, Internat. Inst. Space Law, Argentine Internat. Law Assn. Author: The Powers of the General Assembly of the UN in Political and Security Matters, 1956; Jurisdiction of the International Court, 1959; Relations Between the United Nations and the Organization of American States in Connection with International Peace and Security, 1959; A Study in Politics and Law: The United Nations, 1962; The Evolution of International Law; International Instruments, 1976; International Law, Vol. I, 1980; The Purposes and Principles of the United Nations Charter (a legis. history of the Preamble, articles 1 and 2), 1983. Address: Internat Ct Justice, Peace Palace, 2517 The Hague The Netherlands

RUDACILLE, SHARON VICTORIA, medical technologist; b. Ranson, W. Va., Sept. 11, 1950; d. Albert William and Roberta Mae (Anderson) R.; B.S. cum laude, Shepherd Coll., 1972. Med. technologist VA Center, Martinsburg, W. Va., 1972—, instr. Sch. Med. Tech., 1972-76, asso. coordinator edn., 1976-77, edn. coordinator, 1977-78, quality assurance officer clin. chemistry, 1978-80, lab. service quality assurance and edn. officer, 1980-84, clin. chemistry sect. leader, 1984—; adj. faculty mem. Shippensburg (Pa.) State Coll., 1977-78. Mem. Am. Soc. Med. Tech., Am. Soc. Clin. Pathologists, W.Va. Soc. Med. Technologists, Shepherd Coll. Alumni Assn., Sigma Pi Epsilon. Baptist. Home: PO Box 14 Ranson WV 25438

RUDDICK, STEPHEN RICHARD, state representative, lawyer, political consultant; b. Denver, Nov. 6, 1954; s. Paul Richard and Myra Jane (Brooks) R.; m. Ana Maria Peters, June 16, 1984. B.A., Met. State U., Denver, 1977; J.D., U. Denver, 1980. Bar: Colo. 1980, U.S. Dist. Ct. Colo. 1980, U.S. Ct. Appeals (10th cir.) 1980. Steward, I.B. of Teamsters, Denver, 1979; law clk., later assoc. law firm Anderson, Calder & Lembke, P.C., Aurora, Colo., 1979-80; sole practice law, Aurora, Colo., 1980-81; asst. city atty. City Atty.'s Office, Aurora, Colo., 1981—; state rep. Colo. Gen. Assembly, 1987-89. Chmn., 18th Jud. Dist. Dem. Cen. Com., 1983—; vice-chmn. Arapahoe County Dem. Com., 1983-85; mem. Colo. ACLU, Colo. Common Cause, Arapahoe-Denver NOW. Mem. Aurora Bar Assn. (sec.-treas. 1983-84, v.p. 1984-85, pres. 1985-86), Colo. Bar Assn. Democrat. Roman Catholic. Club: Aurora East Lions. Lodge: Masons (master mason 1983—). Home: 1031 Sable Blvd Aurora CO 80011 Office: Office of City Atty 1470 S Havana St Aurora CO 80012

RUDDY, FRANK S., ambassador, lawyer; b. N.Y.C., Sept. 15, 1937; s. Francis Stephen and Teresa (O'Neil) R.; m. Kateri Mary O'Neill, Aug. 29, 1964; children—Neil, David, Stephen. A.B., Holy Cross Coll., 1959; M.A., NYU, 1962, LL.M., 1967; LL.B., Loyola U., New Orleans, 1965; Ph.D., Cambridge U., Eng., 1969. Bar: D.C., N.Y., Tex., U.S. Supreme Ct. Faculty Cambridge U., 1967-69; asst. gen. counsel U.S. Info. Agy., Washington, 1969-72, 73-74; sr. atty. Office of Telecommunication Policy, White House, Washington, 1972-73; counsel Exxon Corp., Houston, 1974-81; asst. adminstr. AID (with rank asst. sec. state) Dept. State, Washington, 1981-84; U.S. ambassador to Equatorial Guinea 1984-88 . Author: International Law in the Enlightenment, 1975; editor: American International Law Cases (series), 1972—; editor-in-chief Internat. Lawyer, 1978-83; contbr. articles to legal jours. Bd. dirs. African Devel. Found., Washington, 1983-84. Served with USMCR, 1956-61. Mem. ABA (council internat. law sect. 1978-83), Am. Soc. Internat. Law, Internat. Law Assn., Hague Acad. Internat. Law Alumni Assn. Republican. Roman Catholic. Clubs: Oxford and Cambridge (London); Conservative, Internat. (Washington). Home: 10839 Britoak Houston TX 77079 Office: US Embassy Equatorial Guinea Dept of State Washington DC 20520

RUDENIUS, ARNE ROLF, manager, engineer, consultant; b. Växö, Småland, Sweden, May 9, 1938; s. Einar Fritz Harry and Sally Åhild (Lund) R.; m. Monica Holgersson, Sept. 16, 1961 (div. Dec. 1987); children: Susanne, Stefan. BS, Karlskrona Tech. Sr. Sch., Sweden, 1961. Sect. engr. Nat. Housing Bd., Sweden, 1961-64; head Dept. for Bldg. Project A-Betong AB, Sweden, 1964-76; head Patent Dept. A-Betong Sabema, Sweden, 1976-82, head Devel. Dept., 1982-87; European patent atty. Awapatent AB, Sweden, 1987-88, head local office, 1988—. Chmn. local br. Swedish Union Clerical and Tech. Employees in Industry, 1978-81. Mem. Swedish Cement and Concrete Research Inst. (mem. project bd. new concrete materials 1986—), Swedish Nat. Bldg. Standardization Inst. (mem. tech. com. bldg. tolerance 1982—), Swedish Inst. Bldg. Documentation (mem. project bd. future orgn. of info. to Swedis bldg. sect.), Inst. Profl. Reps. Before the European Patent Office. Home: Engelbrektsgatan 57, S-412 52 Gothenburg Sweden Office: Awapatent AB, Kungsportsavenyn 18, Box 53252, S-200 71 Malmö Sweden

RUDING, HERMAN ONNO, Dutch minister of finance; b. Aug. 15, 1939; m. Renee V.M. Hekking; 2 children. M.A. in Econs., Netherlands Sch. Econs. (Erasmus U.), 1964, Ph.D. in Econs. cum laude, 1969. Head div. internat. monetary affairs Treas. Gen. of Ministry of Fin., The Hague, Netherlands, 1965-70; joint gen. mgr. Amsterdam-Rotterdam Bank N.V., Amsterdam, 1971-76; exec. dir. IMF, Washington, 1977-80; bd. mng. dirs. Amsterdam-Rotterdam Bank N.V., 1981-82; minister of fin. Netherlands, The Hague, 1982—. Contbr. articles to profl. jours. Bd. dirs. Foster Parents Plan Internat., 1981-82. Mem. Christian Democratic Alliance. Office: Ministry of Fin, Korte Voorhout 7, 2511 The Hague The Netherlands *

RUDISILL, ROBERT MACK, JR., lawyer; b. Charlotte, N.C., Apr. 15, 1945; s. Robert Mack and Lucretia Rose (Hall) R.; m. Frances Barbara McMillan, Aug. 17, 1968 (div. 1983); children: David Stuart, Michael Joseph. Cert., U. Geneva, Switzerland, 1965; B.A., U. Fla., Gainesville, 1967, Hague Acad., Netherlands, 1969; J.D., Duke U., 1970. Bar: Mich. 1970, U.S. Ct. Claims 1971, U.S. Supreme Ct. 1977, Fla. 1978. Assoc. Warner, Norcross & Judd, Grand Rapids, Mich., 1970-74; asst. counsel Mellon Bank, N.A., Pitts., 1975-76; dir. affiliate legal affairs Southeast Banking Corp., Miami, Fla., 1976-80; v.p., gen. counsel Sun Banks, Inc., Orlando, Fla., 1980-86; ptnr. Smith, Mackinnon, Mathews, Harris and Christiansen, Orlando, Fla., 1986—; course coordinator Sch. Banking of South, Baton Rouge, 1985-86; moderator Robert Morris Assocs. nat. workshops on comml. loan documentation, Phila, 1978—. Chmn. mass transit com. Grand Rapids C. of C., Mich., 1973. Served with USAFR, 1963-69. Mem. ABA, Fla. Bar Assn. (chmn. corp. counsel com. 1980-82, co-chmn. fin. instns. com. 1988—), The Banking Law Inst. (adv. council), Mensa. Republican. Episcopalian. Office: Smith Mackinnon Mathews Harris & Christiansen 255 S Orange Orlando FL 32801

RUDLOFF, ENRIQUE, financial adviser, software company executive, agricultural entrepreneur; b. Santiago, Chile, Apr. 29, 1943; s. Luis and Erika (Wachtel) R.; m. Christine Bossonney, Sept. 12, 1969; children: Candice, Natalie, Dominique. Comml. Engr., U. Chile, 1967, Auditor, 1967. Adminstrv. and fin. advisor Federación Nacional de Cooperativas de Ahorroy Prestamo, Santiago, 1964; asst. auditor Co. Acero del Pacif, Santiago, 1965-66; adminstr., fin. Sindelen S.A.I.C., Santiago, 1965-67; fin. mgr. Maestranza Cerrillos, Santiago, 1968; fin. and adminstrn. mgr. Sindelen S.A.I.C., Santiago, 1968-72; fin. and adminstrv. area mgr. Gildemeister S.A.C., Santiago, 1974-87; gen. mgr. Sociedad Inversiones Proandes S.A., Santiago, 1988—; pres. Soc. Agricola Rudloff, Santiago; exec. dir. Soc. Inversiones Gildemeister, Santiago. Mem. Colegio de Ingenieros de Chile. Author: Working Capital, 1968; Administration of Credit According to Cash Flow, 1973. Club: Deportivo Manquehue (Santiago). Home: Camino El Algarrobo, 9540 Los Dominicos, Santiago Chile

RUDMAN, WARREN BRUCE, U.S. senator; b. Boston, May 18, 1930; s. Edward G. and Theresa (Levenson) R.; m. Shirley Wahl, July 9, 1952; children: Laura, Alan, Debra. B.S., Syracuse (N.Y.) U., 1952; LL.B., Boston Coll., 1960. Bar: N.H. 1960. Mem. firm Rudman & Gormley, Nashua, N.H., 1960-69; counsel to Gov. Walter Peterson, Concord, N.H., 1970; atty. gen. State of N.H., Concord, 1970-76; mem. firm. Sheehan, Phinney, Bass & Green, 1976-80; mem. U.S. Senate from N.H., 1980—. Founder, 1965; since chmn. bd. trustees Daniel Webster Jr. Coll., also, New Eng. Aero. Inst.; chmn. consumer protection com. Nat. Assn. Attys. Gen., 1974, pres., 1975; chmn. Citizens Alliance Against Casinos, 1977. Served to capt. AUS, 1952-54, Korea. Decorated Bronze Star, Combat Inf. Badge. Mem. Am. Legion. Republican. Office: 530 Hart Senate Bldg Washington DC 20510 *

RUDNIKOFF, ISADORE, physician; b. Montreal, Can., Feb. 19, 1909; s. Max and Sophie (Izenson) R.; B.S., Coll. City N.Y., 1929, M.D., N.Y. U., 1933; m. Sarah Robowsky, Aug. 19, 1933; children—Carol Joan, Barbara, Robert William. Intern, Lebanon Hosp., N.Y.C., 1933-36; practice medicine, Yonkers, N.Y., 1936—; dir. medicine, pres. med. bd. chief internal medicine, attending cardiologist Yonkers Gen. Hosp.; attending physician Yonkers Profl. Hosp.; active staff Boswell Meml. Hosp., Sun City, Ariz.; dir. medicine Valley View Community Hosp., Youngstown, Ariz. Med. adv. com. to Mayor; med. adviser Selective Service System; bd. dirs. Ariz. State U. Sch. Music, Phoenix Chamber Music Soc.; bd. dirs.Ariz. State U. Friends of Music; awarded Presdl. medal for services. Diplomate Am. Bd. Internal Medicine. Fellow A.C.P., N.Y. Acad. Medicine, N.Y. Diabetes Assn., Am. Geriatrics Soc., Westchester Acad. Medicine; mem. Am. Soc. Internal Medicine, Internat. Soc. Internal Medicine, World Med. Assn. (founder), Yonkers Acad. Medicine (past pres.), Am. Heart Assn., Royal Soc. Medicine (affiliate), AAAS, Smithsonian Assocs. (charter), Phi Beta Kappa. Mem. B'nai B'rith. Home: 6126 E Charter Oak Rd Scottsdale AZ 85254 Office: Maricopa County Gen Hosp Phoenix AZ 85008

RUDOLF, BERNHARD, sound engineer; b. Konstanz, W. Germany, Sept. 13, 1956; s. Kurt and Erna R. Degree, U. Heidelberg, W. Germany, 1987. Dir. Ingenieurbüro Sch., Konstanz, W. Germany, 1983-87; owner Klang and Hammer Recording Studio, Konstanz, 1983—; dir. Lake People, Konstanz, 1986-87; owner Ingenieurbüro, Konstanz, 1987—. Mem. Audio Engring. Soc. Office: Klang and Hammer Recording Studio, Bückle str 33, D7750 Konstanz Federal Republic of Germany

RUDOLF, MAX, symphony and opera conductor; b. Frankfurt-Am-Main, Germany, June 15, 1902; came to U.S., 1940, naturalized, 1946; student Goethe-Gymnasium, Frankfurt, Hoch Conservatory Music, Frankfurt U.; pvt. mus. instrn.; D.Mus. (hon.), Cin. Conservatory Music; L.H.D. (hon.), U.

Cin., 1960, Miami U., 1963, Curtis Inst. Music, 1972; D.Mus., Baldwin-Wallace Coll., 1973, Temple U., 1975; m. Liese Ederheimer, Aug. 4, 1927; children—William, Marianne. Asst. condr. Freiburg (Germany) Municipal Opera, 1922-23; condr. State Opera of Hesse, Darmstadt, Germany, 1923-29, German Opera, Prague, 1929-35; guest condr. Gothenburg (Sweden) Orch. Soc., also choral dir. radio concerts Swedish Broadcasting Corp., 1935-40; mem. faculty Central YMCA Coll., Chgo., 1941-43; condr. New Opera Co., N.Y.C., 1944; mem. mus. staff Met. Opera Assn., N.Y.C., 1945-58, artistic adminstr., 1950-58; adminstr. Kathryn Long opera courses Met. Opera, N.Y.C., 1949-58; mus. dir. Cin. May Festival, 1963-70; music dir., condr. Cin. Symphony Orch., 1958-70, world-wide concert tour, 1966; condr. Met. Opera Assn., N.Y.C., 1973-75; mem. faculty Curtis Inst. Music, Phila., 1970-73, 83—; tchr. conducting Ford Found. project, Balt., 1962-64, Tanglewood, 1964; Distinguished Service prof. U. Cin., 1966-68; condr. Columbia Records, Book of Month Club Music Appreciation Series, Cetra (Italy), Decca; guest condr. symphony orchs. throughout U.S., Italy; panel mem. Nat. Endowment for Arts, Washington, 1970-73; artistic adviser Dallas Symphony Orch., 1973, N.J. Symphony Orch., 1976-77, Detroit Symphony Orch., 1983, Exxon/Art Endowment Condrs. Program, 1977—. Recipient Alice M. Diston award, 1964; 1st recipient of Theodore Thomas award Conductors' Guild, 1988. Mem. Pi Kappa Lambda. Author: The Grammar of Conducting, 1950, 2d edit., 1980. Home: 220 W Rittenhouse Sq Philadelphia PA 19103

RUDOLPH, ANDREW HENRY, dermatologist, educator; b. Detroit, Jan. 30, 1943; s. John J. and Mary M. (Mizesko) R.; M.D. cum laude (Regent's scholar), U. Mich., 1966; m. Mary Martha Fox, Aug. 17, 1963; children—Kristen Ann, Kevin Andrew. Intern, Univ. Hosp., U. Mich. Med. Center, Ann Arbor, 1966-67, resident dept. dermatology, 1967-70; practice medicine specializing in dermatology, 1972—; asst. prof. dermatology Baylor Coll. Medicine, Houston, 1972-75, assoc. prof., 1975-83, clin. prof., 1983—; chief dermatology service VA Hosp., Houston, 1977-82; mem. staff Meth. Hosp., Women's Hosp., Ben Taub Gen. Hosp., Jefferson Davis Hosp., Houston VA Hosp., Tex. Children's Hosp., St. Luke's Episcopal Hosp., Hermann Hosp., Tex. Inst. for Rehab. and Research. Served as surgeon USPHS, 1970-72. Diplomate Am. Bd. Dermatology. Fellow Am. Acad. Dermatology; mem. Am. Dermatol. Assn., AMA, So. Med. Assn., Tex. Med. Assn., Harris County Med. Soc., Houston Dermatol. Soc. (past pres.), Tex. Dermatol. Soc., Am. Geriatric Soc., Assn. Mil. Dermatologists, Internat. Soc. Tropical Dermatology, Royal Soc. Health, N.Y. Acad. Scis., Royal Soc. Medicine, Dermatology Found., Pan Am. Med. Assn., Skin Cancer Found., Internat. Soc. Dermatopathology, Am. Venereal Disease Assn. (past pres.), Am. Public Health Assn., Assn. Mil. Surgeons U.S., Am. Soc. for Dermatol. Surgery, Soc. for Investigative Dermatology, S. Central Dermatologic Congress, Mich. Alumni Assn. (life), Alpha Omega Alpha, Phi Kappa Phi, Phi Rho Sigma, Theta Xi. Mem. editorial bd. Jour. of Sexually Transmitted Diseases, 1977-85. Contbr. to med. jours., periodicals and textbooks. Office: Surlock Tower Suite 724 6560 Fannin Houston TX 77030

RUDOLPH, CHARLES HERMAN, computer software development executive; b. Balt., Mar. 14, 1953; s. Charles Henry and Margaret Theresa (McCarron) R.; m. Terri Gay; 1 child, Kristin Margaret. B.S. summa cum laude, King's Coll., 1975. Asst. mgr. product mktg. Datapoint Corp., San Antonio, 1977-78, mgr. systems planning, 1978-79, mgr. software devel., 1979-82, dir. software devel., 1982-84; sr. dir. Custom Systems, San Antonio, 1984-85; dir. engring. Digital Communications Assocs., Atlanta, 1985-88; v.p. mktg. Crosstalk Communications, Roswell, Ga., 1988—. Republican. Lutheran. Home: 2480 Roxburgh Dr Roswell GA 30076 Office: Crosstalk Communications Suite 440 1000 Holcomb Woods Pkwy Roswell GA 30076

RUDOLPH, MALCOLM ROME, investment banker; b. Balt., Sept. 22, 1924; s. Louis and Sara E. (Rome) R.; m. Zita Herzmark, July 1, 1956 (div. 1979); children—Madelon R. II, Margot R.; m. Barbara J. Girson, 1979. A.B., Harvard U., 1947; postgrad., Grenoble U., France, 1948, Hayden Stone Mgmt. Sch., 1965. With div. internat. confs. U.S. Dept. State, Paris, France, 1949; registered rep. trainee Orvis Bros. & Co., N.Y.C., 1949, rep., asst. mgr., acting mgr., 1950-64; mgr. Hayden Stone Inc., Washington, 1964-68, ptnr., 1968-69; chmn. bd. Donatelli, Rudolph & Schoen Inc., Washington, 1970-74; chmn. bd. Multi-Nat. Fin. Group, Inc., Washington, 1974-79, pres., 1979-86; chmn. Multi-Nat. Precious Metals Corp., 1974-75; chmn. bd. Multi-Nat. Money Mgmt. Co. Inc., 1974-79, pres., 1979—; pres. Rudolph & Schoen Inc., 1975-85; sr. v.p., dir. Laidlaw Adams & Peck Inc., 1975-79; pres. Laidlaw Resources Inc., 1976—, Sutton Energy, Inc., 1976—, DeRand Resources Corp., 1979—; sr. v.p., dir. DeRand Corp. Am., 1979—; chmn. bd. Arlington Energy Corp., 1980—; mem. Phila.-Balt.-Washington Stock Exchange, 1972-75; pres. Rome Resources Corp., 1982—, Investment Bankers and Cons.; assoc. mem. Pitts., Boston, Montreal stock exchanges, 1972-75; allied mem. N.Y. Stock Exchange, 1975-79. Mem. Presdl. Inaugural Com., 1960, 64. Served with USNR, 1943-46. Mem. Assn. Investment Brokers Met. Washington (v.p. 1965-66, pres. 1967), Bond Club Washington, Ohio Oil and Gas Assn., Ind. Oil and Gas Assn. of W. Va., Ind. Petroleum Assn. Am., Southeastern Ohio Oil and Gas Assn., Washington Met. Bd. Trade, Internat. Assn. Fin. Planners. Clubs: Internat., Harvard (asst. treas. 1957-60, treas. 1960-64, exec. com. 1957-67), Nat. Aviation (Washington). Home: Willow Oak Farm Bozman MD 21612 Office: 2201 Wilson Blvd Arlington VA 22201

RUDOWSKI, WITOLD JANUSZ, surgeon, educator; b. Piotrkow Trybunalski, July 17, 1918; s. Maksymilian and Stefania R.; M.D., Clandestine U., Warsaw; Dr. (hon.), Poznan Med. Acad., 1975, Warsaw Med. Sch., 1979; Lodz Med. Sch., 1980, Wroclaw Med. Sch., 1982, Edinburgh U., 1983; m. Irena, 1940; 3 children. Assoc. prof. surgery Warsaw U., 1954-61, prof. extraordinary, 1961-70, prof., 1971—; cons. surgeon, sr. research worker Madame M. Curie Cancer Inst. in Warsaw, 1948-64; dir., head dept. surgery Inst. Haematology and Blood Transfusion, Warsaw, 1964—; chmn. Sci. Council to Minister of Health and Social Welfare, 1970-75; expert WHO, 1975—, mem., vice-chmn. exec. bd., 1985—. Recipient Silver Cross of Virtuti Militari, 1944, Gold Cross of Merit, 1956, Commdr. Cross Order of Polonia Restituta, 1979, Medal for Warsaw, 1970, State prize 2d Class, 1972, State prize 2d Class collective, 1978. Fellow ACS (hon.), Royal Coll. Surgeons Edinburgh, Royal Coll. Surgeons Eng., Royal Coll. Physicians and Surgeons Can., Coll. Dutch Surgeons, Swedish Surg. Soc., Royal Coll. Surgeons Ireland, Royal Australasian Coll. Surgeons; mem. Internat. Fedn. Surg. Colls. (v.p., pres. Internat. Fedn. Surg. Coll., Polish Haematological Soc., Polish Surgeons Soc, Polish Acad. Scis., N. Pacific Surg. Assn., Italian Soc. Surg. Research, West African Coll. Surgeons, Czechoslovakian Soc. Physicians. Author: Burn—Therapy and Research, 1976, Disorders of Hemostasis in Surgery, 1977, Surgery of the Spleen, 1987; contbr. numerous articles in field to profl. jours. Office: Research Inst Hematology and Blood Transfusion, Chocimska 5, 00 957 Warsaw Poland

RUDY, WILLIS, historian; b. N.Y.C., Jan. 25, 1920; s. Philip and Rose (Handman) R; B.S.S., CCNY, 1939; M.A., Columbia U., 1940, Ph.D., 1948; m. Dorothy L. Richardson, Jan. 31, 1948; children—Dee Dee, Willis Philip, Willa. Instr. Coll. City N.Y., 1939-49; instr., lectr. Harvard U., 1949-52, 53, 57, 58; prof. Mass. State Coll., Worcester, 1953-63; prof. history Fairleigh Dickinson U., Teaneck, N.J., 1963-82, prof. emeritus, 1982—; editorial bd. Fairleigh Dickinson U. Press, 1966-77. Mem. Am. Hist. Assn., Orgn. Am. Historians, Phi Beta Kappa. Author: The College of the City of New York, A History, 1847-1947, 1949; 1976; The American Liberal Arts College Curriculum, 1960; Higher Education in Transition, 1958, 68, 76; Schools in an Age of Mass Culture, 1965; The Universities of Europe: a History, 1984. Home: 161 W Clinton Ave Tenafly NJ 07670 Office: Fairleigh Dickinson U Dept of Hist Teaneck NJ 07666

RUEDEN, HENRY ANTHONY, accountant; b. Green Bay, Wis., Dec. 25, 1949; s. Bernard M. and Audrey Virgin R. BS, U. Wis., Green Bay, 1971; MBA, U. Wis., Oshkosh, 1973; postgrad., Internat. Grad. Sch., St. Louis, 1984—. CPA, Ill., Wis.; cert. mgmt. acct.; cert. internal auditor; cert. info. systems auditor; cert. cost analyst. Auditor U.S. Customs Service, Chgo., 1974-86; systems acct. U.S. R.R. Retirement Bd., Chgo., 1986—. Leader 4-H. Mem. CPAs For The Pub. Interest, Nat. Wildlife Fedn., Inst. Cost Analysis, Nat. Audubon Soc., Wis. Farm Bur., Wis. State Hist. Soc., Wis. Farm Bur. Fedn., Future Farmers Am., Am. Inst. CPA's, Wis. Inst. CPA's, Nat. Assn. Accts., Assn. Govt. Accts. Roman Catholic. Home: 2661 S Pine Tree Rd De Pere WI 54115

RUEGG, WALTER HENRI, sociology educator; b. Zurich, Switzerland, Apr. 4, 1918; s. Walter Henri and Margrit (Braun) R.; children—Elisabeth Andreas, Helena. B.A., State Coll., Schaffhausen, Switzerland, 1936; postgrad. Sorbonne, U. Paris, 1938-39; Ph.D., U. Zurich, 1944, Diploma coll. tchr., 1946. Lectr. U. Zurich, 1950-59, asst. prof., 1959-62; sec. gen. European Wrought Aluminum Assn., Zurich, 1956-62; full prof. sociology U. Frankfurt (W.Ger.), 1962-73, dean Faculty Econs., 1963-64, rector univ., 1965-70; full prof. U. Berne (Switzerland), 1973-86, prof. emeritus, 1986—, dean Faculty Law and Econs., 1975-76; guest lectr. U. Cologne (W.Ger.), 1948, 51, U. Frankfurt, 1952, U. Chgo., 1953; vis. prof. U. St. Gallen (Switzerland), 1956-58, 79-80; v.p. West German Rectors Conf., Bonn., 1966-71, pres., 1968-69. Author: Cicero und der Humanismus, 1946; Soziologie, 1969; Anstoesse (Collected Essays) 1945-1967, 1973; Bedrohte Lebensordnung (Collected Essays) 1968-1977, 1978; Konkurrenz der Kopfarbeiter, 1985; Zementierung oder Innovation, 1987. Decorated commandeur des palmes academiques (France); recipient medalha do Merito en ouro Universitade Federal Santa Maria (Brazil), 1967. Mem. Wissenschaftliche Gesellschaft Frankfurt, Gesellschaft Schweizer Akademiker (pres. 1956-62, 73—), Internat. Fedn. Social Sci. Assns. (pres. 1976-78), Schweizer Arbeitskreis Militaer und Sozialwissenschaften (pres. 1976-87). Club: PEN of Switzerland. Lodge: Rotary (Frankfurt and Berne). Home: Eisselweg 26, Belp, CH3123 Berne Switzerland

RUEGSEGGER, DONALD RAY, JR., radiological physicist, educator; b. Detroit, May 29, 1942; s. Donald Ray and Margaret Arlene (Elliot) R.; B.S., Wheaton Coll., 1964; M.S., Ariz. State U., 1966, Ph.D. (NDEA fellow), 1969. Diplomate Am. Bd. Radiology; m. Judith Ann Merrill, Aug. 20, 1965; children—Steven, Susan, Mark, Ann. Radiol. physicist Miami Valley Hosp., Dayton, Ohio, 1969—, chief med. physics sect., 1983—; physics cons. X-ray dept. VA Hosp., Dayton, 1970—; adj. asst. prof. physics Wright State U., Fairborn, Ohio, 1973—, clin. asst. prof. radiology, 1976-81, clin. assoc. prof. radiology, 1981—, group leader in med. physics, dept. radiol. scis. Med. Sch., 1978—. Mem. Am. Assn. Physicists in Medicine (pres. Ohio River Valley chpt. 1982-83, co-chmn. local summer sch. arrangements com. 1986), Am. Coll. Radiology, Am. Coll. Med. Physics (founding chancellor), Am. Phys. Soc., AAAS, Ohio Radiol. Soc., Health Physics Soc. Baptist. Home: 2018 Washington Creek Ln Centerville OH 45458 Office: Radiation Therapy Miami Valley Hosp 1 Wyoming St Dayton OH 45409

RUEGSEGGER, PAUL MELCHIOR, physician, researcher; b. Berne, Switzerland, June 27, 1921; came to U.S., 1948, naturalized, 1954; s. Paul and Frieda Beatrice (Schmocker) R.; m. Freya Bundi Wipf, Sept. 6, 1948; children—Theodore Bernard, Christine Monica, Carole Suzanne. M.D., Ph.D., U. Zurich, Switzerland, 1946. Diplomate: Am. Bd. Internal Medicine. Intern Bellevue Hosp., N.Y.C., 1948-51, resident, 1951-52; resident in cardiology Meml. Sloan Kettering Cancer Center, N.Y.C., 1952-53, 55-56; asst. prof. clin. medicine Cornell U. Med. Sch., N.Y.C., 1959; research assoc. Sloan Kettering Inst., N.Y.C., 1959-67; attending physician Meml. Center for Cancer, N.Y.C., 1959-69, N.Y. Hosp., 1956-69; research dir. Med. Imaging Lab. (name now Biotronics Inst.), N.Y.C., 1970—; aero-med. cons. Swissair Lines, N.Y.C., 1956—; thermography cons. Trial Lawyers Assn., N.Y.C., 1982—; cons. med. imaging Hoffmann-LaRoche Corp., Nutley, N.J., 1969—. Author: Transaminase Tests, 1956, Coronary Thrombolysis, 1959, Walking EKG Stress Test, 1963, Thermography of Pain, 1969, 81. Served to capt. USAF, 1953-55; Japan. Recipient Young Investigators award Nat Heart Inst., 1958. Mem. N.Y. Acad. Scis., Am. Fedn. Clin. Research, Harvey Soc. N.Y., N.Y. County Med. Soc., Am. Acad. Thermology, European Thermology Soc., Am. Soc. Internal Medicine, Zool. Soc. N.Y., N.Y. Bot. Garden, Swiss Soc. N.Y. Office: Biotronics Inst 115 E 61st St New York NY 10021

RUFF, DARRYL EVERETT JOHN, real estate consultant, executive; b. Camrose, Alta., Can., Mar. 27, 1938; s. Everett Emil and Rehilda (Klatt) R.; m. Sharyn Elizabeth Muir, Aug. 1, 1964; children: Darin, Jason. Grad. high sch., Camrose. Supr. Polychemical Industries Ltd., Edmonton, Alta., 1956-59; underwriter Can. Merit Ins. Co., Montreal, 1959-65; sr. adjustor McLaren & Lockie Adjustors, Kelowna, B.C., Can., 1965-67; mng. dir. H.A. Roberts Gallery/Homes Ltd., Kelowna, 1967-76; pres., mgr. Magnum Group Cos., Kelowna, 1976—; cons. City of Kelowna, 1983—, West Kootenay Power & Light, Trail, B.C., 1983—. Author monthly newsletter of entrepreneur club, 1985; inventor Magic-Ads, 1984. Bd. dirs. Kelowna Regatta Assn., 1967, Provincial Ministry Tourism Recreation Culture, Kelowna, 1986. Recipient Mcpl. award, Kelowna, 1983. Mem. Internat. Festival Arts. Mem. Provincial-Social Credit Nat. Conservative Party. Baptist. Club: Camera. Office: Magnum Group of Cos, PO Box 692, Station A, Kelowna, BC Canada V1Y 7P4

RUFF, ROBERT LOUIS, neurologist, physiology researcher; b. Bklyn., Dec. 16, 1950; s. John Joseph and Rhoda (Alpert) R.; m. Louise Seymour Acheson, Apr. 26, 1980. BS with highest honors, Cooper Union, 1971; MD with highest honors in Medicine, U. Wash., 1976, PhD in Physiology. Diplomate Am. Bd. Neurology and Psychiatry. Asst. neurologist N.Y. Hosp., Cornell Med. Sch., N.Y.C., 1977-80; asst. prof. physiology and medicine U. Wash., Seattle, 1980-84; assoc. prof. neurology Case Western Res. Med. Sch., Cleve., 1984; chief dept. neurology Cleve. VA Med. Ctr., 1984—; adv. Child Devel. and Mental Retardation Ctr., Seattle, 1980-84, Burien Devel. Disability Ctr., Wash., 1982-84; mem. med. adv. bd. Muscular Dystrophy Assn., Seattle, 1984, NE Ohio chpt. Multiple Sclerosis Soc., 1986—; chmn. med. adv. bd. NE Ohio chpt. Myasthemia Gravis Found., 1987—. Contbr. articles to profl. jours. and chpts. to books. Recipient Tchr. Investigator award NIH; NSF fellow, 1971; NIH grantee, Muscular Dystrophy Assn. grantee; N.Y. State Regents med. scholar, 1971. Fellow Am. Heart Assn. (stroke council); mem. Am. Physics Soc., Am. Acad. Neurology, AMA, Neurosci. Soc., Biophys. Soc., Am. Neurol. Assn., N.Y. Acad. Sci., Am. Geriatrics Soc., Sigma Pi Sigma (v.p. 1970-71), Alpha Omega Alpha (v.p. 1975-76). Democrat. Home: 2572 Stratford Rd Cleveland Heights OH 44110 Office: VA Med Ctr 10701 East Blvd127-W Cleveland OH 44106

RUFFIN, CRAIGE, lumber-millwork executive; b. Richmond, Va., May 11, 1902; s. Thomas Champion and Grace Helen (Spear) R.; m. Marjorie Belvin, Oct. 20, 1934; 1 dau., Marjorie Belvin. B.S., U. Va., 1923. Gen. clk. Ruffin & Payne, Inc., Richmond, 1923-25, shipping clk., 1925-28, buyer, 1928-30, v.p., 1930-73, exec. v.p., 1972-79, pres., 1979-83, chmn., pres., 1983-84, chmn. 1984—; dir. Dominion Nat. Bank, Richmond, 1967-78 (ret.). Past pres. Salvation Army Hosp.; past dir. United Givers Fund, Richmond Community Council; former vestryman St. Stephens Episc. Ch. Mem. Archtl. Woodwork Internat. (past dir.), Richmond C. of C. (past dir.), Richmond Retail Mchts. Assn. (past dir.), Va. Forests (past dir.), Va. Bldg. Materials Dealers Assn. (past pres., dir.), Nat. Lumber Dealers Assn. (past dir.), Lumber Dealers Research Council (past dir.). Republican. Clubs: Commonwealth, Country of Va. (past dir.). Lodges: Masons (past master), Rotary (past pres.).

RUFFINELLI, JORGE, Spanish and Portuguese language educator; b. Montevideo, Uruguay, Dec. 16, 1943; s. Agustin Francisco and Iris Selika (Altesor) R.; m. Cristina Hernández, 1968 (div. 1982); children: Alvaro, Andrea; m. Cecilia Gonzalez, 1978; 1 son, Gerardo; m. Cristina Meneghetti, 1983; 1 dau., Paula. Degree in Lit., U. Uruguay, 1963-68. Prof. U. Buenos Aires, 1973-74, U. Veracruzana, México, 1974-86; dir. Centro de Investigaciones Linguistico-Literarias, 1974-86; prof. dept. Spanish and Portuguese Stanford (Calif.) U., 1986—; vis. prof. U. Calif., San Diego, 1980, U. Calif. Santa Cruz, 1981, U. Wis., Madison, 1982, U. So. Calif., 1985. Author: Palabras en orden, 1974, 2d revised edit., 1985, José Revueltas, 1977, El otro México, 1978, Crítica en Marcha, 1979, Las Infamias de la inteligencia burguesa, 1979, El lugar de Rulfo, 1980, El primer Mariano Azuela, 1982 (Nat. award México), John Reed, Villa y la Revolución Mexicana, 1983, Poesía y descolonización, 1985, La escritura invisible, 1986; editor: Texto crítico, Nuevo texto Crítico. Mem. Marcha (dir. lit. sect. 1968-74). Office: Stanford U Dept Spanish Portuguese Stanford CA 94305

RUFIN, PATRICK, allergist; b. Bayeux, Normandie, France, June 19, 1947; s. Jacques and Marie-Therese (Reveillon) R.; m. Marie-Claude Veronique Bourdon; children: Christophe, Stéphanie, Thomas. MD, UER Necker U. René Descartes, Paris, 1974. Cert. in allergology. Tchr. allergology Paris V U., 1977—; pres. Commn. Nat. de Recherch sur les Aérosols Tests, 1981—; editorial bd. for abstracts in Revue Française d'Allergologie et d'Immunologie Clinique. Editor: (book) Les Tests de Provocation Bronchique et Nasale, 1986. Mem. Soc. Franç d'Allergologie, Internat. Assn. Allergology and Clin. Immunology, Internat. Assn. Asthmology, European Acad. Allergology and Clin. Immunology, British Soc. for Allergy and Clin. Immunology. Office: 61 rue de Passy, 75016 Paris France

RUGAMBWA, LAUREAN CARDINAL, archbishop of Dar es Salaam; b. Bukongo, Tanzania; July 12, 1912; s. Domitian Rushubirwa and Asteria Mukaboshezi; student Rutabo, Rubya Sem., 1926-33, Katigondo Sem., 1933-43; D.Canon Law, U. Propaganda, Rome, 1951; LL.D. (hon.), Notre Dame U., 1961, Georgetown U., 1961, Rosary Coll., Buffalo, 1965; LH.D. (hon.) Coll. of New Rochelle, 1961, also others. Ordained priest Roman Cath. Ch., 1943; bishop of Rutabo, 1952-60; elevated to Sacred Coll. Cardinals and bishop of Bukoba, 1960; archbishop of Dar es Salaam, 1969—; mem. congregation of Causes of Saints. Mem. Knights of St. Peter Claver, KC. Office: Bishop's House, Bukoba Tanzania *

RUGER, WILLIAM BATTERMAN, firearms manufacturing company executive; b. Bklyn., June 21, 1916; s. Adolph and May R.; m. Mary Thompson, Aug. 26, 1938; children: William Batterman, Carolyn Amalie Ruger Vogel, James Thompson. Student, U. N.C. Firearms design engr. U.S. Armory, Springfield, Mass., 1939-40; machine gun designer Auto Ordnance Corp., Hartford, Conn., World War II; founder, pres. Ruger Corp. (hand tool mfrs.), Southport, Conn., 1946-48; co-founder 1948; since pres., chmn. bd., treas. Sturm, Ruger & Co., Inc., Southport; v.p. Sporting Arms and Ammunition Inst., 1978—; past bd. dirs. Nat. Shooting Sports Found. Author, editor. Trustee Salisbury (Conn.) Sch., 1970-75, Naval War Coll. Found., Buffalo Bill Hist. Ctr. Recipient Nat. Leadership award Hunting Hall of Fame, 1979; named Handgunner of Year Am. Handgunner Found., 1975. Mem. Nat. Rifle Assn. (past dir.), Blue Mountain Forest Assn., Vintage Sports Car Club Am., Auburn-Cord Duesenberg, Rolls Royce Owners Club, Rolls Royce Silver Ghost Assn., Am. Bugatti Club, Bugatti Owners' Club, Bentley Drivers Club, Delta Kappa Epsilon. Lutheran. Clubs: Campfire, Pequot Yacht, N.Y. Yacht, Boone and Crockett, Cat Cay, Clambake (Newport). Office: Sturm Ruger & Co Lacey Pl Southport CT 06490

RUGGIERI, DAVID THOMAS, marketing executive, consultant; b. Providence, Sept. 3, 1947; s. Rizieri and Dorothy (DiMeo) R., m. Marie Milosovic, Dec. 7, 1975; children: Christopher, Vanessa. BBA, Nat. U., 1975. Dir. Cabrillo Pacific U., San Diego, 1976-78; v.p. sales Nat. Edn. Corp., Newport Beach, Calif., 1978-80; v.p. Mid-Western Edn. Systems, Phoenix, 1983-85; owner, pres. Career Mktg. System, Los Angeles, 1980—; pres. Chgo. Model Mgmt., 1985-87; chmn. Western Edn. and Tng. Systems, Inc., 1987—; bd. dirs., v.p. Chgo. Career Ctrs., 1985—; cons. Drake Coll, Mid-West Ednl. Author: Sales Management, 1978, Telephone Marketing, 1979, Admissions Management, 1980, Sales Strategy for Colleges, 1980-81. Served to lt. USAF, 1968-71. Mem. Am. Mktg. Assn., Sales Execs. Internat. Office: 250 4th St San Francisco CA 94103

RUGGIU, DENIS FRANCOIS, physician; b. Bone, Algeria, May 29, 1939; s. Francois and Marie Jeanne (Giardino) R.; m. Marie Jose Hillairet de Boisferon, July 31, 1965; children: Francois Joseph, Jean Sylvain, Louis Emmanuel. Dr. medicine, Bordeaux U., France, 1965. Diplomate French Bd. Family Practice. Extern Holitaux, Bordeaux, 1964; resident Hosp. Bordeaux, 1964-67; gen. practice medicine Gradignan, France, 1968—; gen. mgr. Pub. Co. Home Saint Gabriel, Gradignan, 1987—. Dep. mayor City of Gradignan, 1977; pres. Music Sch. Violin, 1987. Mem. Ordre des Medecins. Lodge: Lions. Home and Office: 166 Cours General de Gaulle, 33170 Gradignan France

RUGH, WILLIAM ARTHUR, diplomat; b. N.Y.C., May 10, 1936; s. Roberts and Harriette (Sheldon) R.; m. Andrea Scott Bear, July 12, 1958; children—David William, Douglas Edward, Nicholas Alexander. Student, Hamburg U., Germany, 1958-59; B.A., Oberlin Coll., 1958; M.A., Johns Hopkins U., 1961; Ph.D., Columbia U., 1967. Near East policy dir. USIA, Washington, 1971-72, dep. asst. dir., 1973-76; pub. affairs counsellor U.S. Embassy, Cairo, 1976-81; dep. chief of mission U.S. Embassy, Damascus, Syria, 1981-84; ambassador U.S. Embassy, Sanaa, Yemen, 1984-87; diplomat in residence Fletcher Sch. Tufts U., Medford, Mass., 1987—. Author: Riyadh, a History, 1969; The Arab Press, 1979, 87; also contbr. articles and chpts. to books. Council on Fgn. Relations fellow, 1972-73; recipient Presdl. award U.S. Pres., 1983. Mem. Middle East Inst., Middle East Studies Assn. Home: 114 South St Medford MA 02155 Office: Tufts U Fletcher Sch Medford MA 02155

RUGMAN, ALAN MICHAEL, international business educator; b. Bristol, Eng., June 9, 1945; came to Canada, 1968, naturalized, 1973; s. Kenneth M. and Dorothy Irene Rugman; m. Helen Scruton, 1970; 1 child, Andrew. B.A. in Econs. with Honors, U. Leeds (Eng.), 1966; M.Sc. in Econs., U. London, 1967; Ph.D. in Econs., Simon Fraser U., Can., 1974. Lectr. econs. U. Winnipeg (Can.) 1970-73, asst. prof., 1973-78, assoc. prof., 1978-79; assoc. prof. fin. Concordia U., Montreal, 1979-80; assoc. prof. bus. adminstrn. Dalhousie U., Halifax, N.S., Can., 1980-82, prof., 1982-87, dir. research Ont. Ctr. Internat. Bus., 1989—; prof. mgmt. U. Toronto, 1987—, research dir. internat. bus. ctr., Ont., Can., 1988—; vis. assoc. prof. internat. bus. Columbia U., 1978-79, vis. prof., 1982; vis. scholar Ctr. for Internat. Affairs, Harvard U., 1984; vis. prof. London Bus. Sch., 1985, U. Hawaii, 1985, U Alberta, 1988; mem. internat. trade adv. com. Govt. of Can., 1986-88. Author: International Diversification and the Multinational Enterprise, 1979; Multinationals in Canada: Theory, Performance and Economic Impact, 1980; Inside the Multinationals: The Economics of Internal Markets, 1981, Outward Bound: Canadian Direct Investment in the United States, 1987; co-author: International Business: Firm and Environment, 1985; Megafirms: Strategies for Canada's Multinationals, 1985, Administered Protection in America, 1987; editor: New Theories of the Multinational Enterprise, 1982; Multinationals and Technology Transfer: The Canadian Experience, 1983; co-editor: Multinationals and Transfer Pricing, 1985, business Strategies and Free Trade, 1988; referee manuscripts for numerous profl. jours.; reviewer manuscripts for numerous publishers; contbr. articles, book revs. to profl. jours.; lectr. to profl. confs.; contbr. chpts. to books. Soc. Scis. and Humanities Research Council Can. grantee, 1983, 84. Mem. Acad. Internat. Bus., North Am. Econ. and Fin. Assn. (bd. dirs. 1979—, pres. 1984), Acad. Mgmt., Can. Econs. Assn., Am. Econ. Assn. Office: U Toronto Faculty Mgmt, 246 Bloor St W, Toronto, ON Canada M5S 1V4

RUHE, DAVID SIEGER, medical educator, religious organization administrator; b. Allentown, Pa., Jan. 3, 1914; arrived in Israel, 1968; s. Percy Bot and Amy Catherine (Sieger) R.; m. Margaret Rosa Kunz, Sept. 7, 1940; children: Christopher Kunz, Douglas Frederic. BS, Mich. State Coll., 1936, MS, 1937; MD, Temple U., 1941, ScD (hon.), 1956. Commd. intern USPHS, 1941, advanced through grades to sr. surgeon, 1954; prof. med. communication, assoc. prof. preventive medicine U. Kans. Coll. Medicine, 1954-63; sec. Nat. Spiritual Assembly Baha'i of USA, Wilmette, Ill., 1963-68; mem. Universal House of Justice Baha'i Internat. Community, Haifa, Israel, 1968—; past med. acad. appointments Emory U. Coll. Medicine, N.Y. Coll. Medicine, U. Ill. Coll. Medicine; cons. in field. Author: Door of Hope, 1983; (with others) Films in Psychiatry and Mental Health, 1953, Films in the Cardiovascular Diseases, 1953; writer, dir. and producer 29 films in medicine and health (Golden Reel award 1956, TV Raster award 1967). Mem. Com. Am. VA's, 1946-48; mem. Human Rights Council Wilmette, 1964-68. Fellow Am. Pub. Health Assn.; mem. United World Federalists, AMA, Phi Kappa Phi, Alpha Omicron Alpha. Office: Baha'i World Ctr, PO Box 155, Haifa Israel

RUHFUS, JÜRGEN, ambassador; b. Bochum, Fed. Republic of Germany, Aug. 4, 1930; s. Heinz and Grete (Rose) R.; m. Karin Engel, 1958; children: Andrea, Maren, Antje. Student, U. Munich, U. Denver; PhD in Law, U. Münster, Fed. Republic of Germany, 1965. Entered Fgn. Service, Bonn, Fed. Republic of Germany, 1955-57; assigned to consulates Geneva, Dakar, Senegal, Athens, Greece, 1957-63; from dep. spokesman to spokesman Fgn. Service, Bonn, 1964-70; ambassador to Kenya Nairobi, 1970-73; head UN directorate Fgn. Service, Bonn, 1973-74, head polit. directorate for We. Hemisphere, 1974-75; advisor on fgn. affairs and security matters Fed. Chancellery, Bonn, 1976-79; ambassador to U.K. and No. Ireland London, 1980-83; head of polit. directorate-gen. for third world countries Fgn. Service, Bonn, 1983-84, state sec., 1984-87; ambassador to U.S. Washington,

1987—. Fulbright scholar U. Denver, 1952-53. Home: 1900 Foxhall Rd NW Washington DC 20007 Office: Embassy of Fed Republic of Germany 4645 Reservoir Rd NW Washington DC 20007

RUHLI, EDWIN, educator; b. Schaffhausen, Switzerland, Feb. 15, 1933; s. Eugen and Anna (Winzeler) R.; Ph.D. in Bus. Adminstrn., U. Zurich, 1961; m. Margrit Bachtold, July 18, 1959; children—Markus, Margret, Frank. Asst. to dir. Nestle, Vevey, Switzerland, 1960-64; planning cons. Swiss Dept. Def., 1964-67; prof. U. Zurich, 1967—; dir. Buhrle Co.; cons. to Swiss Fed. Govt. Served as gen. staff officer Swiss Army, 1968—. Mem. Verband der Hochschullehrer fur Betriebswirtschaft e.V., Vorstandmitglied. Clubs: Lions, Harvard of Switzerland. Author: Unternehmungsfuhrung und Unternehmungspolitik, 2 vols., 1976; contbr. articles on mgmt., orgn. theory and theory of investment to profl. jours. Home: Oberbalm, 8330 Auslikon Switzerland Office: 62 Ramistrasse, 8001 Zurich Switzerland

RUHLMAN, HERMAN C(LOYD), JR., manufacturing company executive; b. Warren, Pa., Jan. 17, 1949; s. Herman Cloyd and Virginia Lee (Wimer) R.; B.S. in Indsl. Tech., California (Pa.) State Coll., 1974; divorced; children—Brian, Jason, Chad; m. Lorraine; stepchildren: Bethany, Michelle, Randy. Gen. mgr. Rand Machine Products, Inc., Falconer, N.Y., 1974-80, pres., chmn. bd. dirs., 1980—; pres. Spartan Tool Co., Gerry, N.Y., 1986—. Active local Boy Scouts Am. Served with USAF, 1968-72. Mem. Epsilon Pi Tau. Republican. Home: PO Box 284 15 Annis St Frewsburg NY 14738 Office: PO Box 72 Allen St Extension Falconer NY 14733

RUIZ CASTAÑEDA, MARIA DEL CARMEN, academic administrator; b. Tampico, Mex., Aug. 24, 1926; d. Arturo and Luz Maria Ruiz. Master's, Univ. Autónoma de Mexico, Mexico City, 1944-46, Doctorate. Dir. Hemeroteca Nacional, Mexico City, 1973-78, Inst. de Investigaciones Bibliográficas, Mexico City, 1978-84, 1984—; adv. Consejo Univ. UNAM, Mexico City, 1978—; mem. Fideicomiso del Premio Rafael Heliodoro Valle, Mexico City, 1978—. Author: La Prensa Periodica en Torno a la Constitución de 1857, 1959, El Periodismo en Mexico: 450 Años de Historia, 1980, Catálogo de Seudónimos, Anagramas y Otros Alias, 1985, Diccionario de Seudónimos, 1988. Recipient Condecoración Chevalier de L'Ordre Nat. du Mérite, France, 1988. Mem. Asociacion de Bibliotecarios Edn. Superior e Investigación. Home: Mar de la Tranquilidad 34, 04890 Mexico City Mexico Office: Biblioteca Nacional Insurgentes, Sur Cen Cultural Ciudad U, 04510 Mexico City Mexico

RUIZ-SURIA, FERNANDO, lawyer; b. San Juan, P.R., May 18, 1916; s. Abelardo and Teresa (Suria) R.; m. Irma Bosch, Aug. 18, 1946; children—Fernando, Vanessa, Ivan, Mimi. B.A., U. P.R., 1938, LL.B., 1940. Bar: P.R. 1941, U.S. Dist. Ct. P.R. 1941, U.S. Ct. Appeals (1st cir.) 1959, U.S. Supreme Ct. 1963, U.S. Ct. Appeals D.C. 1977, Temporary Emergency Ct. Appeals 1980. House counsel Shell Co. Ltd., San Juan, 1942-53; sr. ptnr. Sifre & Ruiz-Suria, San Juan, 1953-67, McConnell Valdes Kelley Sifre Griggs & Ruiz-Suria, San Juan, 1967-81; of counsel McConnell Valdes et al; dir. corps.; mem. jud. confs.; former mem. P.R. Bar Examiners; former mem. Evidence Rules Com. Fellow Am. Coll. Trial Lawyers; mem. ABA, Colegio de Abogados de P.R., Sara Bay C. of C., Meadows C. of C. Roman Catholic. Clubs: Bird Key Yacht (Sarasota, Fla.); Bankers (San Juan, P.R.). Office: McConnell Valdes et al Royal Bank Ctr San Juan PR 00918

RUIZ-VALERA, PHOEBE LUCILE, librarian; b. Barranquilla, Colombia, Jan. 27, 1950; d. Ramon and Marion (Mehlman) Ruiz-Valera; m. Thomas Patrick Winkler, Mar. 27, 1981. BA cum laude, Westminster Coll., 1971; MLS, Rutgers U., 1974; MA, NYU, 1978. Library trainee Passaic (N.J.) Pub. Library, 1973-74, reference librarian, 1974; library assoc., cataloger NYU Law Library, N.Y.C., 1974-79, asst. curator, cataloger, 1979-81; librarian III, cataloger Rutgers U. Library, New Brunswick, N.J., 1981-82; chief cataloger Assn. Bar City N.Y., 1982-85, head tech. services, 1985—. Mem. ALA, Am. Assn. Law Libraries, Law Library Assn. Greater N.Y., Reforma, Salalm. Democrat. Presbyterian. Office: Assn Bar City NY 42 W 44th St New York NY 10036

RULAU, RUSSELL, numismatic consultant; b. Chgo., Sept. 21, 1926; s. Alphonse and Ruth (Thorsen) R.; student U. Wis., 1946-48; m. Hazel Darlene Grizzell, Feb. 1, 1968; children by previous marriage—Lance Eric, Russell A.W., Marcia June, Scott Quentin, Roberta Ann, Kyle Christopher; 1 step-dau., Sharon Maria Kenowski. Entered U.S. Army, 1944-1950, served to master sgt. USAF, 1950-62; resigned active duty, 1962; asst. editor Coin World newspaper, Sidney, Ohio, 1962-74, editor World Coins mag., 1964-74, Numis. Scrapbook mag., 1968-74; editorial coordinator How to Order Fgn. Coins guidebook, 1966-74; editor in chief World Coin News newspaper, 1974-84, Bank Note Reporter, 1983-84; fgn. editor Numis. News newspaper, 1974-77; cons. editor Standard Catalog of World Paper Money, 1975-83; contbg. editor Standard Catalog of World Coins, 1974-81; pres. House of Rulau, 1984—; v.p. Keogh-Rulau Galleries, Dallas, 1984-85, Pobjoy Mint Ltd., Iola, Wis., 1985—. Mem. U.S. Assay Commn., 1973. Sec., Numismatic Terms Standardization Com., 1966 71; vice chmn. Waupaca County Republican party, 1977-79, chmn., 1979-82; chmn. county chairmen, 3d vice chmn. Wis. Rep. Party, 1981-83; del. Rep. Nat. Conv., 1980; exec. com. 6th Wis. Dist. Rep. Com., 1984—. Fellow Royal Numis. Soc., Am. Numis. Soc. (asso.); mem. Token and Medal Soc. (editor 1962-63), Am. Numis. Assn., Canadian, S. African numis. assns., Mont. Hist. Soc., Am. Vecturist Assn., Numis. Lit. Guild (dir. 1974-78, editor 1984—), VFW (post commdr. 1985—). Lutheran. Author: (with George Fuld) Spiel Marken, 1962-65, American Game Counters, 1972; World Mint Marks, 1966; Modern World Mint Marks, 1970; (with J. U. Rixen and Frovin Sieg) Seddelkatalog Slesvig Plebiscit Zone I og II, 1970; Numismatics of Old Alabama, 1971-73; Hard Times Tokens, 1980; Early American Tokens, 1981; U.S. Merchant Tokens 1845-1860, 1982; U.S. Trade Tokens 1866-1889, 1983, Tokens of the Gay Nineties, 1987; (with George Fuld) Medallic Portraits of Washington, 1985. Contbr. numis. articles to profl. jours. Home: N7747 County J Iola WI 54945 Office: Pobjoy Mint USA Ltd PO Box 153 Iola WI 54945

RULLIERE, ROGER PIERRE, internist, educator; b. Paris, Dec. 16, 1926; s. Francisque and Suzanne (Mancel) R. Degree, Interne des Hôpitaux Paris, 1952; MD, U. Paris, 1957. Intern, Paris, 1952-57; asst. Hosp. de Paris, 1957-59, physician, 1962-72; chief cardiology and internal medicine service Hosp. Broussais, Paris, 1972—; prof. history of medicine U. Paris VI, 1979—. Author: Abrege de Cardiologie, 1971, 4th rev. edit. 1987, ABCs d'Electrocadiographie, 1975, 3d rev. edit. 1984, ABCs de Soins Intensif Cardiologiques, 1977, 3d rev. edit. 1984, Histoire de la Medicine, 1981, Electrocardiographie Clinique, 1969, 2d rev. edit. 1978; contbr. articles to scis. jours. Mem. 12 French and fgn. sci. Home: 6 rue de Bassano, 75116 Paris France Office: Hosp Broussais, 96 rue Didot, 75614 Paris Cedex 14 France

RUMBAUGH, MAX ELDEN, JR., professional society administrator; b. Ada, Okla., Dec. 11, 1937; s. Max E. and Gertrude (Gulker) R.; m. Joan E. Brockway; children: Maria, Max E. III. BS in Engring., U.S. Mil. Acad., 1960; MS in Engring. Scis., Purdue U., 1965, MBA, 1972. Instr. Purdue U., West Lafayette, Ind., 1964-65; corp. officer Midwest Applied Sci. Corp., West Lafayette, 1965-72; chief engr. advanced tech. Schwitzer div. Wallace-Murray Corp., Indpls., 1972-77, dir. research, 1977-81; mgr. engring. activities div. Soc. Automotive Engrs., Warrendale, Pa., 1981-84, v.p., asst. gen. mgr., 1984-86, exec. v.p., 1986—; pres. Soc. Research Adminstrs. Internat., 1973-74; chmn. Ind. sect. Soc. Automotive Engrs., 1978-79; bd. dirs. Am. Nat. Standards Inst., N.Y.C., 1986-88. Author mag. column Focus, 1986-87. Bd. dirs. Jr. Achievement of Western Pa., Pitts., 1986—, YMCA, North Hills, Pitts., 1985—. Served to 1st lt. U.S. Army, 1960-63. Mem. ASME. Lodge: Rotary (bd. dirs. 1982-84). Home: 2274 Wood Acres Ct Pittsburgh PA 15237 Office: Soc of Automotive Engrs Inc 400 Commonwealth Dr Warrendale PA 15096-0001

RUMMEL, CHRISTOPH HANS, managment consultant; b. Heidelberg, W. Ger., Nov. 3, 1949; s. Christoph Joseph and Elisabeth (von Kleinsorgen) R.; m. Heidi Renate Grau, Mar. 10, 1980. M.B.A., U. Mannheim, Ph.D. in Bus. Adminstrn., 1977. Personnel officer Perkin-Elmer, Überlingen, W.Ger., 1978-79; personnel dept. mgr. Avon Cosmetics GmbH, Munich, W.Ger., 1980-81, div. sales mgr., 1981-83; European dir. human resources Mallinckrodt, Inc., Neunkirchen-Seelscheid W.Ger. and St. Louis, 1984-87; br. mgr. Baumgartner and Partner, Duesseldorf, 1987—. Co-author: Manpower Planning, 1974; author: Worker's Participation in Management in West Germany, 1977; contbr. article to profl. jour. W.Ger. govt. scholar, 1972-75; research fellow McMaster U., Can., 1975-76. Home: Opladener Strasse 221, 4019 Monheim Federal Republic of Germany

RUMMERFIELD, BENJAMIN FRANKLIN, geophysicist; b. Denver, May 25, 1917; s. Lawrence L. and Helen A. (Roper) R.; Engr. Geology, Colo. Sch. Mines, 1940; grad. Harvard U. Advanced Mgmt. Program, 1947, Aspen Inst. Humanistic Studies, 1958, Indsl. Coll. Armed Forces, 1963; m. Mary Merchant, Feb. 16, 1979; children: Ann S., Michael J., Benjamin F., Mary Susan, Lila, Sonya, Karim. Asst. mgr. Seismograph Service Corp., Mexico City, 1947-50, Venezuela and Colombia, 1945-47; exec. v.p. Century Geophys. Corp., Tulsa, 1950-60, also dir.; pres. GeoData Corp., Tulsa, 1960—, Gulf Coast GeoData, Houston, 1962—; dir. GeoData Index Internat. Ltd., East Grinstead, West Sussex, U.K., Permian Exploration, Custom Data Services; cons. Petróleos Mexicanos. Bd. dirs. YMCA, Tulsa, 1955—, pres., 1956-59. Recipient Outstanding Service award YMCA, Tulsa, 1958, 63, Disting. Achievement medal Colo. Sch. Mines, 1978, hon. mention for painting Philbrook Art Mus., 1961. Mem. Tulsa Geol. Soc., Colo. Sch. Mines Alumni Assn. (pres. 1953), Asociación Mexicana de Geólogos Petróleos, Am. Assn. Petroleum Geologists, Soc. Exploration Geophysicists (life, nat. v.p. 1958), Sigma Gamma Epsilon. Clubs: Tulsa, Harvard (Tulsa). Contbr. numerous articles to profl. jours. Home: 6787 Timberlane Dr Tulsa OK 74105 Office: care GeoData Corp 211 South Cheyenne Tulsa OK 74101

RUMP, SIEGFRIED MICHAEL, mathematics educator; b. Wuppertal, Federal Republic of Germany, Mar. 3, 1955; s. Hubert A. and Elisabeth (Ghiselli) R.; m. Angelika D. Vierl, July 6, 1979; children: Dorothea A., Mathias S. M in Math., U. Kaiserslautern, Federal Republic of Germany, 1977; PhD in Math., U. Karlsruhe, Federal Republic of Germany, 1980; Habilitation degree, U. Karlsruhe, 1983. Project leader German br. IBM Corp., Boeblingen, 1983-87; prof. Tech. U. Hamburg, Federal Republic of Germany, 1987—; project mgr. univ. research activities IBM Corp., Boeblingen, 1983—. Co-author 3 sci. books in math. and related fields; coauthor and patentee on highly accurate and fast arithmetic; contbr. over 50 articles on math. and related subjects to internat. jours. Mem. Soc. Indsl. and Applied Math., Gesellschaft für Informatik, Gesellschaft für Angewandte Mathematik and Mechanik, Deutsche Mathematiker Vereinigung. Office: Tech U Informatik III, Eissendorfer Str 38, 2100 Hamburg 90 Federal Republic of Germany

RUMPF, FRANCOIS MAX EDOUARD, banker, economist; b. Lausanne, Switzerland, Dec. 6, 1941; s. Jean J. A. and Antoinette M. (Reymond) R.; m. Juliette J. W. Roussy, Nov. 19, 1965; children—Sophie, Joelle, Laetitia. Licencie es sciences economiques, U. Lausanne, 1965, Docteur es sciences economiques, 1981. Travel agt. Wagons Lits Cook, Montreux, Switzerland, and Geneva, 1959-62; economist Swiss Bank Corp., Lausanne, 1965-74, first v.p., Monaco, 1974-82, first v.p. gen. mgmt., Basle, Switzerland, 1982-85, 1st v.p. SBC Geneva, 1986—. Author: Wall Street et les agents de change americains en suisse, 1981. Pres. Colonie Suisse, Monaco, 1979-82. Served to maj. Swiss Army, 1984—. Mem. Alumni Insead, Association Suisse des Banquiers. Clubs: Automobile Suisse, Bentley Drivers, Abbaye de l'Arc (Lausanne). Office: Swiss Bank Corp, 2 Rue de Confederation, 1211 Geneva Switzerland

RUMPF, MICHAEL, architectural company executive; b. Giessen, Fed. Republic Germany, Mar. 29, 1946; s. Walter and Irene (Gail) R.; m. Iraci Prado de Calasans, 1981; children: Christian Philip, Nathalie Isabelle. Dr. oec., Hochschule State Gallen, Switzerland, 1972. Pres. Gail do Brasil, Sao Paulo, 1972-81; chief exec. officer Gail AG, Giessen, 1982—; pres. Fachverband Baukermik und Spaltplatten e.V., Frankfurt, 1982-86. Mem. C. of C. Home: Suedhang 7, Giessen Federal Republic of Germany Office: Gail AG, Postfach 5510, D6300 Giessen Federal Republic of Germany

RUNCIE, ROBERT ALEXANDER KENNEDY, archbishop of Canterbury; b. England, Oct. 2, 1921; s. Robert Dalziel and Anne R.; m. Angela Rosalind Turner, 1957; children: James, Rebecca. B.A. in Classics, Brasenose Coll., Oxford (Eng.) U.; M.A., Westcott House, Cambridge (Eng.) U., 1948, D.D., 1980. Ordained deacon Anglican Ch., 1950, priest, 1951; curate All Saints Ch., Gosforth, 1950-52; chaplain Westcott House, 1953-54, vice prin., 1954-56; fellow, dean, asst. tutor Trinity Hall, Cambridge U., 1956-60, hon. fellow, from 1975—; prin. Cuddesdon Coll., also vicar of Cuddesdon 1960-69, bishop of St. Albans, 1970-80, canon and prebendary of Lincoln, 1969-70, archbishop of Canterbury, 1980—. Editor: Cathedral and City: St. Albans and Modern, 1978. Served with Brit. Army, 1939-45. Decorated Mil. Cross; Squire Minor scholar; hon. fellow Brasenose Coll., Oxford U., 1979. Club: Athenaeum (London). Address: Lambeth Palace, London SE1 7JU, England also: Old Palace, Canterbury Kent England

RUNCIMAN, SIR STEVEN (JAMES COCHRAN STEVENSON), historian; b. Northumberland, Eng., July 7, 1903; s. 1st Viscount Runciman and Hilda Stevenson; ed. Eton Coll., Trinity Coll., Cambridge; hon. degrees: Litt.D., Cambridge (Eng.) U., U. Chgo., U. Durham, U. London, Oxford U., St. Andrews U.; Birmingham U., NYU; LL.D., U. Glasgow; D.Phil., U. Salonika; D.D., Wabash Coll.; D.Litt. Hum., Ball State U. Fellow Trinity Coll., Cambridge, 1927-38, lectr., 1931-38; press attache Brit. Legation, Sofia, 1940-41; prof. Byzantine studies Istanbul U., 1942-45; rep. of Brit. Council, Greece, 1945-47; chmn. Anglo-Hellenic League, 1951-67; trustee Brit. Mus., 1960-67. Knighted; decorated Companion of Honour, Knight Comdr. Order of Phoenix (Greece; recipient Silver PEN award, 1969; appted by Ecumenical Patriarch, Grand Orator of the Gt. Ch., 1970. Fellow Brit. Soc., Brit. Acad.; mem. Acad. Athens (hon.), Royal Irish Acad. (hon.), Am. Philos. Soc. (fgn. mem.). Author: The Emperor Romanus Lecapenus, 1929; The First Bulgarian Empire, 1930; Byzantine Civilisation, 1933; The Medieval Manichee, 1947; History of the Crusades (3 vols.), 1951-54; The Eastern Schism, 1955; The Sicilian Vespers, 1958; The White Rajahs, 1960; The Fall of Constantinople 1453, 1965; The Great Church in Captivity, 1968; The Last Byzantine Renaissance, 1970; The Orthodox Churches and the Secular State, 1972; Byzantine Style and Civilisation, 1975; The Byzantine Theocracy, 1977; Mistra, 1979. Address: Elshieshields, Lockerbie, Dumfriesshire DG11 1LY, Scotland Office: British Acad, 20-21 Cornwall Terrace, London NW1 4QP, England

RUNDELL, ORVIS HERMAN, JR., psychologist; b. Oklahoma City, June 16, 1940; s. Orvis Herman and Virginia Reid (George) R.; B.S., U. Okla., 1962, M.S., 1972, Ph.D., 1976; m. Jane Shannon Brians, June 25, 1966; children—Leslie Jane, Anne Reid. Lab. mgr. Okla. Center Alcohol and Drug-Related Studies, Oklahoma City, 1969-76, staff scientist, 1974—; asst. prof. psychiatry and behavioral scis. U. Okla. Health Sci. Center, 1976—; dir. clin. physiology and sleep disorders ctr. Presbyterian Hosp., Oklahoma City, 1982—; cons. in field. Bd. dirs. Hist. Preservation, Inc., Oklahoma City, 1978—. Served with USAR, 1963-69. Grantee Nat. Inst. Drug Abuse, Nat. Inst. Alcohol Abuse and Alcoholism, Kerr Found. Fellow Clin. Sleep Soc.; mem. Am. Psychol. Assn., Soc. Psychophysiol. Research, Internat. Soc. Chronobiology, N.Y. Acad. Scis., Research Soc. Alcoholism, Southwestern Psychol. Assn., Okla. Psychol. Assn., Evaluation Research Soc., Psi Chi, Phi Gamma Delta. Author articles, papers in field, chpts. in books; asst. editor Alcohol Tech. Reports, 1976—; cons. editor Psychophysiology, 1974—. Home: 431 NW 20th St Oklahoma City OK 73103 Office: Northeast 13th St at Lincoln Blvd Oklahoma City OK 73104

RUNDLETT, DONALD HODGMAN, banker; b. New Rochelle, N.Y., July 5, 1935; s. Raymond Crawford and Eunice Wade (Hodgman) R.; m. Mary Jane Keller, Oct. 11, 1958; children—Deborah, Raymond, Elizabeth, Donald Hodgman. B.A., Bowdoin Coll., 1957. Account exec. Mobil Oil Co., Inc., N.Y.C., 1958-62; sr. account exec. Merrill Lynch Pierce, Fenner & Smith, Inc., N.Y.C., 1962-71; sr. v.p. White, Weld & Co., Inc., N.Y.C., 1971-77, also dir.; sr. v.p., head div. pvt. banking Citibank, N.A., N.Y.C., 1977-80; pres. Merrill Lynch Pvt. Capital Inc., N.Y.C., 1981-85; chmn., chief exec. officer Pvt. Capital Ptnrs., Inc., N.Y.C., 1985—. Pres. United Fund, Bronxville, Eastchester, Tuckahoe, N.Y., 1974; pres. bd. govs. Lawrence Hosp., Bronxville; elder, v.p. Consistory Reformed Ch. Bronxville. Served to capt. armored div. USAR, 1958-64. Recipient Citizenship award Am. Legion, Eastchester, N.Y., 1978. Republican. Clubs: River (N.Y.C.); Siwanoy Country, Bronxville Field (Bronxville); Farmington Country (Charlottesville, Va.); Nat. Golf Links Am.; Seminole Golf (North Palm Beach, Fla.); Castle Pines (Colo.) Golf; Honors Course (Chattanooga). Office: 535 Madison Ave New York NY 10022

RUNDLETT, ELLSWORTH TURNER, III, lawyer; b. Portland, Maine, Jan. 12, 1946; s. Ellsworth Turner II and Esther (Stevens) R.; m. Lisa Warren, Oct. 25, 1964 (div. June 1967); 1 child, Ellsworth Turner IV; m. Jamie Donnelly, June 7, 1982. AB cum laude, Bowdoin Coll., 1968; JD, U. Maine, 1973. Bar: Maine 1973, U.S. Dist. Ct. Maine 1973, U.S. Ct. Appeals (1st cir.) 1973. Bowdoin Coll. intern U.S. Senate, Washington, 1967; law clk. Superior Ct. Maine, Portland, 1972-73; asst. corp. counsel City of Portland, 1973-76; ptnr. Childs, Emerson, Rundlett, Fifield & Childs, Portland, 1980—. Contbr. legal articles to Maine Bus. Digest, 1978-84. Pres. Pine Tree Alcohol Treatment Ctr., Windham, Maine, 1978-80; trustee Portland Players, Inc., South Portland, Maine, 1977-84, pres., 1985-87. Mem. Cumberland County Bar (trustee 1983-84, 86-87, v.p. 1988—), Maine Bar Assn., Am. Trial Lawyers Assn., Maine Trial Lawyers Assn., U. Maine Law Alumni (bd. dirs. 1984-87, v.p. 1988). Clubs: Cumberland, Portland (gov. 1983-86), Bowdoin of Portland (pres. 1978) (Portland). Office: Emerson Rundlett & Fifield 257 Deering Ave Portland ME 04103

RUNG, RICHARD ALLEN, air force officer; b. Rome, N.Y., Dec. 16, 1929; s. George Stuart and Ruth Marie (Henderberg) R.; m. Yolande Moalli, June 15, 1957; children: Michael, Bruce, Colette. B.A. summa cum laude, St. Michael's Coll., 1957; J.D., Syracuse U., 1960. Bar: N.Y. 1961. Law partner Lawler & Rung, DeWitt, N.Y., 1960-61; law assoc. J. F. Ferlo Law Office, Rome, N.Y., 1961-63; commd. 2d lt. USAF, 1952, advanced through grades to col., 1979; USAF fighter pilot 1952-55; USAF fighter pilot and flight comdr. La., Spain, Vietnam, N.Y., 1963-74; USAF flight safety evaluator and cons. Norton AFB, Calif., 1974-79; prof. aerospace studies, Air Force ROTC detachment comdr. U. Ill., Champaign-Urbana, 1979-82; commandant AFJROTC Pompano Beach High Sch., (Fla.), 1982-85, Northeast High Sch., (Fla.), 1985—. Decorated Legion of Merit, D.F.C., Air medal with 7 oak leaf clusters; recipient award Aerospace Safety Hall Fame, 1979; Disting. Service award Am. Vets, 1980. Mem. Delta Epsilon Sigma, Sigma Nu, Phi Delta Phi. Roman Catholic. Home: 2672 Emerald Way N Deerfield Beach FL 33441 Office: AFJROTC Northeast High Sch Oakland Park FL 33304

RUNNETTE, ALAN CHARLES, aeronautical engineer; b. Islington, Eng., June 27, 1937; s. Charles Washington and Jessie Mary (Funnell) R.; m.; children: Darren Charles, Emma Louise. BS in Aeronautical Engring., Bristol U., Eng., 1962. Engr. project Rolls Royce, Hertfordshire, Eng., 1952-62, Hunting Engring. Ltd., Bedfordshire, Eng., 1962-72; liason engr. Associated Engring., Warwickshire, Eng., 1972-74; mgr. project Pitney Bowes Ltd., Essex, Eng., 1974-76; mgr. regional Electrovert Ltd., Royal Berkshire, Eng., 1976-81; cons. production John Minister Automation Ltd., Kent, Eng., 1981-86; mgr. sales Thorn EMI Datatech Ltd., London, 1986—. Served with Coldstream Guards, 1955-57. Mem. Inst. Metal Finishing Prodn. Engrs. Anglican. Home: 28 The Chase, Watford Hertfordshire WD1 7SQ, England

RUNQUIST, MERRELL PHILIP, clinical psychologist; b. Sturgeon Bay, Wis., Nov. 18, 1945; s. Philip Frederick and Helen Elvira (Merrell) R.; student U. Ill., 1963-65; BS, U. Wis.-Oshkosh, 1968; PhD, U. Nebr., 1975; m. Bonnie Catherine Cady, Oct. 18, 1980; 1 dau., Sonya; step children—Christian Esch, Peter Esch. Clin. psychology intern U. N.C. Sch. Medicine, 1970-71; teaching asst. U. Nebr., 1971-72, asst. dir. Project Early Aid, 1972-73, co-dir. project, 1973-76, clin. asst. prof., 1975-76; asst. prof. psychology and psychiatry U. Va. Sch. Medicine, 1976-82, dir. psychology tng., 1979-82; faculty Inst. Clin. Psychology U. Va., 1981—; clin. asst. prof. behavioral medicine, psychiatry and psychology, 1982—; clin. staff U. Va. Hosps., 1976-86; clin. staff Charter Hosp. Charlottesville, Va., 1986—; pvt. practice clin. psychology; v.p., sec. clin. Psychology Assocs., P.C.; cons. Little Keswick (Va.) Sch., Charlottesville Ctr. Dyslexia; cons. in field. Mem. Va. Mental Health Adv. Council; bd. dirs. clin. centers. VA traineeship. Treas., v.p. Va. Psychol. Found. NIH grantee; recipient numerous awards for work in field. Lic. psychologist, clin. psychologist, Va. Mem. Va. Psychol. Assn. (dir., treas.), Am. Assn. Psychiat. Services for Children, Am. Psychol. Assn. (cons.), Va. Acad. Clin. Psychologists, Psi Chi. Democrat. Contbr. articles to profl. jours. Home: Buck Falls Farm Star Route 1 Box 63 Earlysville VA 22936 Office: 408 E Market St Suite 103 Charlottesville VA 22901

RUNYON, JOHN HAROLD, management consultant; b. Reading, Pa., June 30, 1945; s. James Hilliard and Ruth Emma (Kantner) R.; B.A. (Rose Meml. honor scholar), Drew U., 1967; student London City Coll., 1965; postgrad. Union Theol. Sem., 1967-68; M.A., Rutgers U., 1969; m. Sally Sutphen, July 8, 1967; 1 dau., Erica Lyn. Rockefeller Found. fellow Union Theol. Sem., 1967-68; asst. dir. Center for State Legislative Research and Service, Eagleton Inst. Politics, Rutgers U., 1969-71, asst. to pres., 1971-73; adminstr. Twp. of East Brunswick, N.J., 1973-84; pres. Community Mgmt. Assocs., 1984—; cons. ABC Election News Coverage N.J., 1970-80, N.J. Pub. Broadcasting System, 1971; tabulation coordinator News Election Service, 1970. Trustee Drew U., Madison, N.J., 1971-76; chmn. Middlesex County 208 Water Quality Mgmt. Planning Program, 1975-79; mem. East Brunswick Planning Bd., 1974-84; mem. East Brunswick Council Econ. Health, 1977—, Middlesex County Fair, 1978—, South River basic council Middlesex County WRA, 1978-84; mem. N.J. Clean Water Council, 1979-84, chmn., 1980-82; founding trustee, pres. East Brunswick Mus. Corp., 1978—; commr. Township of East Brunswick Septic System Mgmt. Area, 1979-82; chmn. Middlesex County Water Resources Assn., 1979-81; mem. mcpl. mgmt. clearinghouse steering com. Council NE Econ. Action, 1979—, Middlesex County Overall Econ. Devel. Planning Com., 1979—; mem. water research adv. bd. Water Research Inst., Rutgers U., also mem. adv. bd. Eagleton Inst. Politics. Mem. Nat. Council Urban Econ. Devel., N.J.-East Brunswick Hist. Soc. Author: (with others) Source Book of American Presidential Campaign and Election Statistics, 1972. Home and Office: 162 Main St East Brunswick NJ 08816

RUONA, ARTHUR ERNEST, marine engineer, astronomer; b. Fairfax, Minn., Oct. 4, 1920; s. Ernest and Emma Elma (Pudas) R.; m. Darlene Debbie Nelson, Sept. 21, 1967; 1 child, Laura Tola. Student, U. Minn., 1946-47; B Laws, LaSalle U., 1963. Marine engr. MEBA, San Francisco, 1957-84; instr. engring. Lake Carriers, Cleve., 1953-56. Patentee in field. Served to sgt. U.S. Army, 1942-46, ETO. Mem. Marine Engrs., Naval Inst., Air Force Assn., Am. Legion (life). Republican. Lutheran. Home and Office: RFD #1 Box 62 Fairfax MN 55332

RUPP, GEORGE ERIK, university president; b. Summit, N.J., Sept. 22, 1942; s. Gustav Wilhelm and Erika (Braunoehler) R.; m. Nancy Katherine Farrar, Aug. 22, 1964; children: Katherine Heather, Stephanie Karin. Student, Ludwig Maximilians U., Munich, Germany, 1962-63; A.B., Princeton U., 1964; B.D., Yale U., 1967; postgrad., U. Sri Lanka, Peradeniya, 1969-70; Ph.D., Harvard U., 1972. Ordained to ministry Presbyn. Ch. U.S.A., 1971; faculty fellow in religion, vice chancellor Johnston Coll., U. Redlands, Calif., 1971-74; asst. prof. Harvard Div. Sch., Harvard U., Cambridge, Mass., 1974-76; asso. prof. Harvard Div. Sch., Harvard U., 1976-77, prof., dean, 1979-85; prof., dean acad. affairs U. Wis., Green Bay, 1977-79; pres. prof. Rice U., Houston, 1985—; bd. dirs. Inst. Internat. Edn., Inst. European Studies, Tex. Commerce Bank, CORETECH, Cameron Iron Works. Author: Christologies and Cultures: Toward a Typology of Religious Worldviews, 1974, Culture Protestantism: German Liberal Theology at the Turn of the Twentieth Century, 1977, Beyond Existentialism and Zen: Religion in a Pluralistic World, 1979; contbr. articles to profl. jours. Bd. dirs. Amigos de las Americas, Meth. Hosp., St. John's Sch., Forum Club Houston, Houston Symphony Orch. Danforth Grad. fellow, 1964-71. Mem. Soc. for Values in Higher Edn., Am. Acad. Religion, AAAS, Houston Philos. Soc., Houston Com. on Fgn. Relations, Yale U. Com. on Religious Life. Office: Rice Univ Office of Pres PO Box 1892 Houston TX 77251

RUPPE, RICHARD JAMES, computer supply company executive; b. Cleve., July 18, 1938; s. Rudolf and Antonia (Petsche) R.; m. Joanne Marie Marinko, Sept. 7, 1968; children: Mark James, Christine Marie, Michael David. Student, Cleve. State U., 1958-61, 68-69, Case-Western Res. U., 1964-68. Account rep. A.B. Dick Co., Cleve., 1961-69; account mgr. Graphic Sci., Cleve., 1969-74; owner Imaging Products, Chesterland, Ohio, 1974—. Vol. project drive United Way Services, Chardon, Ohio, 1984.

Mem. Nat. Assn. for Self-Employed, Nat. Office Machine Dealers Assn., U.S. Table Tennis Assn., Am. Mutual LIfe Assn. Republican. Roman Catholic. Clubs: Orchard Hills, Country, Berkshire Hills Country (Chesterland, Ohio).

RUPPEL, HOWARD JAMES, JR., sociologist, sexologist, educator; b. Orange, N.J., July 22, 1941; s. Howard J. and Lillian M. (Wordley) R.; B.A., St. Joseph's Coll., Ind., 1963; M.A., No. Ill. U., 1968; postgrad. U. Iowa, 1968—; m. Barbara Margaret Wiedemann, June 3, 1967. Instr. social sci. St. Francis High Sch., Wheaton, Ill., 1963-65, debate coach, 1963-65; instr. sociology St. Dominic Coll., St. Charles, Ill., 1966-67; instr. sociology Cornell Coll., Mt. Vernon, Iowa, 1969-70, asst. prof., 1970-72, lectr., 1972-73; research dir. Social Sci. Research Assos., Cedar Rapids, Iowa, 1973-80; founder, co-dir. Center for Sexual Growth and Devel., Mt. Vernon, 1980—; instr. Sch. Social Work, U. Iowa, 1976-78, adj. asst. prof., 1979-81, adj. assoc. prof., 1981—; exec. dir. Soc. for Sci. Study of Sex, 1988—; cons. Iowa Dept. Social Services, Abbe Mental Health Ctr., Cedar Rapids, Families Inc., West Branch; bd. dirs. The Human Outreach and Achievement Inst., Boston, 1988—. NSF fellow, 1968. Cert. sexologist Am. Coll. Sexologists. Mem. Am. Sociol. Assn., Harry Benjamin Internat. Gender Dysphoria Assn., Midwest Sociol. Soc., Nat., Iowa (sec. 1983-84, treas. 1985) councils family relations, Changing Family Conf. (bd. dirs. 1983-87), Soc. Sci. Study of Religion, Soc. Study of Social Problems, Soc. Sci. Study of Sex Inc. (bd. dirs. 1983-88, pres. Midcontinent Region, 1984-85, treas. 1986-88, chmn. membership com. 1983-85, chmn. exhibits com. 1983-88, ann. meeting chmn. 1986), Assn. Sexologists, Am. Assn. Sex Educators, Counselors and Therapists (cert. sex educator), Sex Info. and Edn. Council U.S. (assoc.), Soc. Sex Therapy and Research (research mem.), Harry Benjamin Internat. Gender Dysphoria Assn., Nat. Forensic League, No. Ill. U. Alumni Assn., Alpha Kappa Delta. Democrat. Co-editor: Sexuality and the Family Life Span, 1983; contbr. articles on complex orgns., marriage and the family, sexual attitudes and behavior, childhood and preadolescent sexuality, methodology and child care theory to profl. publs. Home: 608 5th Ave N Mount Vernon IA 52314 Office: SSSS PO Box 208 Mount Vernon IA 52314

RUPRECHT, DIETRICH, publisher. PhD, U. Freiburg, Fed. Republic of Germany, 1956. Pub. Verlag Vandenhoeck & Ruprecht, Göttingen, Fed. Republic of Germany, 1958—. Office: Vandenhoeck Und Ruprecht, Theaterstr 13 Postfach 3753, D3400 Göttingen Federal Republic of Germany

RUS, JAN, III, anthropologist; b. Ithaca, N.Y., Jan. 9, 1948; arrived in Mex., 1985; s. Jan and Mary Jean (Hayes) R.; m. Diane Louise Crow, June 15, 1968; children: Jan IV, Jacob R. AB summa cum laude, Harvard U., 1969, MA, 1976. Tutor in anthropology and Latin Am. studies Harvard U., Cambridge, Mass., 1972-74; field dir. Harvard-Chiapas Project, San Cristobal, Mex., 1975-76; prof. Autonomous U. Chiapas an Cristobal, 1976-78; investigator U.S.-Mex. Border Task Force, Pasadena, Calif., 1978-81; dir. native lang. project Maya Region Applied Anthropology Inst., San Cristobal, 1985—; lectr. Latin Am. studies Stanford U., 1988; editor, 1985—. Author: Guerra de Castas de Quien, 1988. Vol. Peace Corps, 1969-71; mem. Cath. Com. Against Hunger, 1985—. Doherty Found. fellow, 1975; Wenner-Glen Found. grantee, 1981-82. Mem. Latin Am. Studies Assn., Soc. Mexican Anthropologists, Phi Beta Kappa. Home: Ejercito Nacional 64, San Cristobal de Las Casas, 29200 Chiapas Mexico Office: INAREMAC, Apt #6, 29200 San Cristobal Chiapas Mexico

RUSH, JULIA ANN HALLORAN (MRS. RICHARD HENRY RUSH), artist, writer; b. St. Louis, Oct. 25, 1927; d. Edward Roosevelt and Flavia Hadley (Griffin) Halloran; m. Richard Henry Rush, Aug. 15, 1956; 1 child, Sallie Haywood. Student Washington U., St. Louis, 1945-47; B.A., George Washington U., 1949. One-woman shows: Fort Amador Officers Club, Panama Canal Zone, El Panama Hotel, Panama, George Washington U., Statler Hotel, Roosevelt Hotel, Washington, Newspaper Women's Club, Washington, Waukegan Library, Ill., Epworth Heights Hotel, Ludington, Mich.; exhibited in group shows: Panama Art League, Corcoran Gallery; represented in permanent collections: U. Panama; also pvt. collections; model John Robert Powers Agy., 1950; sec.-treas., dir. N.Am. Acceptance Corp., 1956-58; v.p. Rush and Halloran, Inc., 1957-58, ptnr., 1954-57; research asst. to husband's bi-weekly newsletter Art/Antiques Investment Report, 1973—. Illustrator: Antiques As An Investment (author Richard H. Rush), 1968; research asst.: Investments You Can Live With and Enjoy (author: Richard H. Rush), 1974, 2d, edit., 1975, 3d edit., 1976; Photographer: Automobiles as an Investment, 1982; Investing in Classic Cars, 1984. Recipient 1st prize (Panama) Newspaper Women's Club, 1953; First Prize Panama Art League, 1953. Mem. DAR, Nat. League Am. Penwomen, Florence Crittenton Circle (rec. sec. 1968-69), Kappa Kappa Gamma. Club: Washington.

RUSH, KENNETH, lawyer, industrialist, government official; b. Jan. 17, 1910; s. David Campbell and Emma Kate (Kidwell) R.; m. Jane Gilbert Smith, June 12, 1937; children: George Gilbert (dec.), David (dec.), Malcolm, Cynthia Shepherd (Mrs. Thomas J. Monahan), John Randall, Kenneth. AB, U. Tenn., 1930; JD, Yale U., 1932; LLD (hon.), Tusculum Coll., 1961; HHD (hon.), The Citadel, 1982. Asso. Chadbourne, Parke, Whiteside & Wolff, N.Y.C., 1932-36; asst. prof. Duke U. Law Sch., 1936-37; with Union Carbide Corp., N.Y.C., 1937-69; v.p. Union Carbide Corp., 1949-61, exec. v.p., 1961-66, pres., 1966-69, dir., 1958-69, mem. exec. com., 1966-69, chmn. gen. operating com., 1965-69; dir. Bankers Trust Co., 1966-69, Amstar Corp., 1962-69, Bankers Trust N.Y. Corp., 1966-69; U.S. ambassador to Germany 1969-72; also Am. negotiator and signer Quadripartite Agreement on Berlin, 1971; dep. sec. def. U.S., 1972-73; dep. sec. of state 1973-74, sec. ad interim, 1973, mem. cabinets Presidents Nixon and Ford as counsellor for econ. policy, 1974, ambassador to France, 1974-77. Editor: Yale Law Jour, 1930-32. Mem. Pres. Johnson's Pub. Adv. Com. U.S. Trade Policy, 1968-69; chmn. Bd. Fgn. Service, 1973-74; mem. Nat. Security Council, 1973-74; chmn. Council Internat. Econ. Policy, Pres.'s Com. East-West Trade Policy, Pres.'s Food Com., Council Wage and Price Stability, Joint Presdl.-Congl. Steering Com. for Conf. on Inflation, all 1974, Atlantic Council, 1978-85, Exec. Council on Fgn. Diplomats, 1977-78; mem. Commn. on Jud. Fellows, U.S. Supreme Ct.; bd. dirs. Alliance To Save Energy, 1977—; trustee Taft Sch., 1957-62, Richard Nixon Predl. Archives Found., 1982—, Inst. Study Diplomacy Georgetown U., 1980—, Am. Inst. Contemporary German Studies Johns Hopkins, 1983—; Found. for Commemoration of the Constitution, vice chmn. 1986; chmn. Presdl. Com. For German-Am. Tricentennial, 1983-84; bd. govs. Am. Nat. Red Cross, 1972-74; chmn. personnel com., mem. audit and planning com. Smithsonian Instn.; chmn. Council Am. Ambassadors, Youth for Understanding. Recipient Distinguished Pub. Service medal Dept. Def., 1972; gold medal French Senate, 1977; decorated Grand Cross Order Merit Germany, 1972. Mem. Internat. C. of C. (trustee U.S. council 1955-69), Yale Law Sch. Assn. (exec. com. 1952-62), Fgn. Policy Assn. (dir. 1964-69), Council Fgn. Relations, Am. Acad. Diplomacy, Supreme Ct. Hist. Soc. (chmn.), Phi Beta Kappa. Episcopalian. Address: 200 N Ocean Blvd Apt 8N Delray Beach FL 33483

RUSH, RICHARD WILLIAM, geologist, consultant; b. Austin, Minn., July 14, 1921; s. James Francis and Irene Evelyn (Peterson) R.; m. Florence Allison Rayman, Sept. 6, 1945 (div. 1972); children: Richard William, Lucy E., Frederick J., Cynthia I. B.A., U. Iowa, 1945; M.A., Columbia U., 1948; Ph.D., 1954; tchrs. cert. U. Iowa, 1961; diploma Nat. Tech. Schs., Los Angeles, 1976. Registered geologist, Calif., Ariz., Alaska. Instr. Colby Coll., Waterville, Maine, 1949-51; chief geologist Plateau Exploration & Devel. Corp., Cortez, Colo., 1951-52; asst. prof. U. Tex., Austin, 1952-57; sr. scientist Creole Petroleum Corp., Caracas, Venezuela, 1957-59; vis. prof. U. Iowa, Iowa City, 1960; cons. River Products Co., Iowa City, 1961-64; assoc. prof. No. Ariz. U., Flagstaff, 1963-69; cons. geologist, Phoenix, 1969—; cons. U.S. Steel, Que., Can., 1960; chief geologist Plateau Exploration and Devel. Corp., Cortez, Colo., 1951-52; cons. Exxon Corp., Midland, Tex., 1971, Mobil Oil Corp., Houston, 1972-73, Seneca Upshur Petroleum Co., Buckhannon, W.Va., 1981, 84; pres. JLC Corp., Los Angeles, 1974-75, WESGOE, Denver, 1982. Editor, geologist: Conceptual Design and Engineering, Economic and Environmental Analysis of Surface Pit Slope Caving Mining System, 1977. Supt. Episcopal Ch. Schs., Flagstaff, Ariz., 1965-67. Mem. enforcement adv. com. Ariz. Bd. Tech. Registration Geologists, 1984—. Recipient medal of merit Presdl. Task Force, 1984; Fulbright scholar, Brazil, Boliva, 1967, 68. Fellow AAAS, Geol. Soc. Am.; mem. Am. Inst. Profl. Geologists (charter, mem. exec. com. Ariz. sect.), Am. Assn. Petroleum Geologists (cert. of recognition 1982, 84), Am. Geophys. Union. Republican. Episcopalian. Office: 337 W Pasadena Suite 16 Phoenix AZ 85013

RUSHDIE, (BUTT) SALMAN, author; b. Bombay, India, June 19, 1947; s. Anis Ahmed and Negin Rushdie; m. Clarissa Luard, 1976; 1 child, Zafar. Ed. Cathedral Sch., Bombay; M.A. in History with honors, King's Coll., Cambridge U. (Eng.), 1968. Author: Grimus, 1975; Midnight's Children (Booker McConnell prize for fiction, James Tait Black Meml. Book prize, E.SU Lit. award), 1981; Shame, 1983, The Jaguar Smile: A Nicaraguan Journey, 1987; contbr. to Firebird 1: Writing Today, 1982, London Rev. of Books, Anthology One, 1982, Shakespeare Stories, 1982, Authors Take Sides on the Falklands, 1982. Fellow Royal Soc. Lit.; mem. Internat. PEN, Soc. Authors, Nat. Book League (exec. com.). Office: care Deborah Rogers Ltd, 49 Blenheim Crescent, London W11, England also: 19 Raveley St, London NW5 2HX England *

RUSHLOW, PHILIP LEO, marketing systems company executive; b. Covington, Ky., Feb. 2, 1929; s. Leo Bernard and Elinor Victoria (Slater) R.; m. Bonnie Miller, June 25, 1945; children—Philip Lee, David Robert. B.A., Wayne U., 1949; M.A., Mich. State U., 1956. Regional mgr. B.F. Goodrich Co., Detroit, 1945-56; pres. Lansing Gen. Co., East Lansing, Mich., 1956-59, Azura Internat. Corp., Lansing Mich., 1959-61, Fashion Industries, Inc., Miami, Fla., 1961-71; pres., chmn. Group Three Corp., Ft. Lauderdale, Fla., 1971—; mktg. cons., dir. The First Bankers Corp., Pompano Beach, Fla., 1973-86; ptnr. Leo Bernard & Co., Pompano Beach, Fla., 1978—; dir. Richelieu Assocs., Inc., Ft. Lauderdale, Rushlow, Philips & David Corp., Ft. Lauderdale. Contbr. to mktg., advt. and research publs. Fellow Aspen Inst. Humanities. Clubs: Lighthouse Point (Fla.); Beech Mountain Country (N.C.). Home: Hillsboro Shores FL Office: Group Three Corp 3200 NE 14th Causeway Pompano Beach FL 33062

RUSHNELL, SQUIRE DERRICK, television executive; b. Adams Center, N.Y., Oct. 31, 1938; s. Reginald Grant and Erica Mifanwy Redwood Sedgemore (Squire) R.; m. Jinny Schreckinger, Feb. 29, 1980; 1 child, Squire Grant Sedgemore; children by previous marriage—Robin Tracy, Hilary Adair. Ed., Syracuse U., 1956-60. Disc jockey WOLF, WHEN, WFBL, Syracuse, N.Y., 1958-61, WTRL, Bradenton, Fla., 1961-62; exec. producer Contact, WBZ Radio-TV, Boston, 1962-67; program dir. KYW News-Radio, Phila., 1968; exec. producer Kennedy & Co., WLS-TV, Chgo., 1969-71; program dir. WLS, 1971-73; v.p. programs ABC owned TV stas., N.Y.C., 1973-74; v.p. childrens TV ABC-TV Network, N.Y.C., 1974-78, v.p. Good Morning Am. and childrens programs, 1978-81, v.p. long range planning and Children's TV, 1981-87; v.p. late night and children's TV ABC Entertainment, N.Y.C., 1987—. Author: The Kingdom Chums Greatest Stories, 1986, Sing-Me-A-Story Books, 1987; co-author: Broadcast Programming, 1981, Broadcast/Cable Programming, 1984, rev. edit., 1987. Recipient Emmy awards, 1975, 76, 77, 78, 79, 80, 81, 82, 83, 84, 58, 86, TV Critics Circle award, 1976, all for outstanding childrens television programming, Am. Children's TV Festival award, 1985, 87. Mem. Acad. Television Arts and Scis., Nat. Acad. Arts and Scis., Internat. Radio and Television Soc., Action for Childrens Television (award for outstanding childrens television programming). Office: ABC Entertainment 1330 Avenue of the Americas New York NY 10019

RUSKIN, ROBERT EDWARD, science consultant; b. Sioux Falls, S.D., Oct. 30, 1916; s. Edward Vance and Leona Opal (Knapp) R.; A.B., Kans. State Tchrs. Coll., 1940; postgrad. U. Mo., 1940-42; m. Thelma B. Gipe, Aug. 23, 1942 (dec. Sept. 1982); children—Robert Sterling, Nancy Jean; m. Louise Deane, Aug. 18, 1984. Physicist uranium isotope project Naval Research Lab., Navy Dept., 1942-47, head instrument sect. atmospheric physics br., Washington, 1947-73, head exptl. cloud physics sect., 1973-76, asst. head atmospheric physics br., 1976-80; vis. prof. atmospheric scis. Colo. State U., 1970; sci. cons. AMAF Industries, Columbia, Md., 1980-83; freelance sci. cons., 1984—. Pres., Hillcrest Heights Citizens Assn., 1952-60; del. Prince Georges County Civic Fedn., 1952-72; treas. Alice Ferguson Found., 1967-70, pres., 1970-76, dir., 1976-78. Recipient Meritorious Civilian Ser. award Naval Research Lab., 1945, 78; Superior Civilian Accomplishment award, 1965. Mem. Am. Meterol. Soc., Am. Phys. Soc., Research Soc. Am., Sigma Pi Sigma. Editor: Humidity and Moisture, Vol. 1, 1965. Contbr. articles to tech. jours. Patentee in field. Home: 1406 Ruffner Rd Alexandria VA 22302

RUSS, HUMPHREY, marketing executive; b. Newbury, Berkshire, Eng., Sept. 30, 1944; s. Albert Stewart and Norah Jean (Humphries) R.; m. Josephine Lynn Staples, Aug. 15, 1971; children: Carolyn Sheila, Gillian Emma. Higher nat. cert., Reading Tech. Coll., 1966. Chartered electronics engr. Apprentice Isotope Devels. Ltd., Beenham, Eng., 1960-65; design engr. Nuclear Enterprises, Beenham, 1965-70; sales, sr. sales engr. Ampex (GB) Ltd., Reading, Eng., 1970-80, mktg. mgr., 1980—. Mem. Inst. Sales and Mktg. Mgmt. Mem. Ch. of Eng. Home: Folly Cottage, Greenlands Rd, Newbury Berkshire RG14 7JU, England Office: Ampex (GB) Ltd, Acre Rd, Reading Berkshire RG2 OQR, England

RUSSELL, ALEXANDER, pediatrics educator, clinical researcher; b. Newcastle upon Tyne, Eng., Jan. 13, 1914; s. Solomom Hyett and Sylvia R.; m. Haya Hirshberg, Jan. 1946; children: Lorna, Sharon. MB BS, U. Durham (Eng.), 1935, B of Hygiene DPH, 1936, DCH, 1947, MD with distinction, 1952. Asst. prof. pediatrics Hosp. for Sick Children U. London and Queen Elizabeth Hosp., London, 1950-54; cons. pediatrician Queen Elizabeth Hosp. for Children and Chelsea & Kensington Group of Hosps., 1954-66; prof. pediatrics and child care, head Hadassah Med. Ctr. Hebrew U., Jerusalem, 1966-82, emeritus prof., 1982—; dir. gen. Jerusalem Variety Ctr. for Child and Family Devel. Habilitation, Harley St. cons. practice, 1954-66. Co-editor: World Pediatrics and Child Care, Pediatric Reviews and Communications; contbr. over 200 articles to med. jours. Served to wing comdr. RAF, 1940-46. Recipient Bela Schick award Mt. Sinai Hosp., N.Y.C., 1972; mentioned twice in Despatches. Fellow Royal Coll. Physicians; mem. Internat. Coll. Pediatrics (pres.), Internat. Acad. Pediatric Transdisciplinary Edn. (pres.), European Soc. Pediatric Research (hon. elder), Royal Soc. Medicine (hon., London chpt., endocrine sect.), Rodin Inst. for Research in Learning Disability. Address: 32 27 King David Gardens, King David St, Jerusalem Israel also: 6 7 Upper Harley St, London NW1 PS4, England

RUSSELL, CHARLES ROBERTS, chemical engineer; b. Spokane, Wash., July 13, 1914; s. Marvin Alvin and Dessie Corselia (Price) R.; m. Dolores Kopriva, May 17, 1943; children—Ann E., John C., David F., Thomas R. B.S. in Chem. Engring, Wash. State U., 1936; Ph.D. in Chem. Engring. (Procter and Gamble Co. fellow 1940-41), U. Wis., 1941. Egr. div. reactor devel. AEC, Washington, 1950-56; engr. Gen. Motors Tech. Center, Warren, Mich. and Santa Barbara, Calif., 1956-68; assoc. dean engring. Calif. Poly. State U., San Luis Obispo, 1968-73; prof. mech. engring. Calif. Poly. State U., 1973-80; sec. adv. com. reactor safeguards AEC, 1950-55. Author: Reactor Safeguards, 1962, Elements of Energy Conversion, 1967. Served with USNR, 1944-46. Mem. Am. Chem. Soc. Republican. Roman Catholic. Club: Channel City (Santa Barbara). Home and Office: 3071 Marilyn Way Santa Barbara CA 93105

RUSSELL, DAVID GRAHAM, barrister; b. Dalby, Queensland, Australia, Dec. 2, 1950; s. Charles Wilfred and Hilary Maude (Newton) R.; m. Deborah Ann Campbell, Sept. 19, 1975; children: Andrew Robin Campbell. BA, U. Queensland, Brisbane, 1970, LLB, 1973, LLM, 1980. Solicitor Cannan & Peterson, Brisbane, 1974; personal asst. to dir.-gen. Conservative Cen. Office, London, 1974; sec. Logan Downs Proprietary Ltd., Brisbane, 1975-77; sole practice barrister at law Brisbane, 1977—; bd. dirs. Logan Downs Proprietary Ltd. Contbr. articles to profl. jours. Mem. state mgmt. com. Nat. Party Australia, Queensland, 1984—, chmn. conf. agenda com., 1986—, chmn. policy standing com., 1987—. Recipient Queen's Counsel award Gov.-in-Council on recommendation of Chief Justice, 1986. Anglican. Clubs: Queensland, Australasian Pioneers. Office: 1201-1202 MLC Ctr, 239 George St, Brisbane, Queensland 4000, Australia

RUSSELL, DAVID L(AWSON), psychology educator; b. Apr. 1, 1921; m. Jean Williams; children: David W., Nancy K. B.A. in Psychology with honors, Wesleyan U., 1942; postgrad., Columbia U., summers 1942, 46; Ph.D. in Psychology, U. Minn., 1953. Lic. psychologist, Ohio. Adminstrv. fellow Office Dean of Students, U. Minn., Mpls., 1947; teaching asst. dept. psychology U. Minn., 1947-48; clin. fellow Student Counseling Bur., 1948-50; dir. student counseling Bowdoin Coll., Brunswick, Maine, 1950-59; instr. Bowdoin Coll., 1950-54, asst. prof. psychology, 1954-59; asso. prof. Ohio U., 1959-67, prof., 1967—, asst. chmn. dept. psychology, 1968, chmn., 1969-72; vis. prof. U. N.H., summer 1958; mem. faculty NDEA Counseling and Guidance Inst. at Ohio U., 1961, 63, 65, 1966-67; pres. Maine Psychol. Assn., 1956-57; chmn. Maine Bd. Examiners Psychologists, 1959; cons. Div. Undergrad. Edn. in Sci., NSF, 1965, 70, 71; sec. Nat. Council Chairmen Grad. Depts. Psychology, 1971-72. Author: (with others) Applied Psychology, 1966; contbr. articles to profl. publs. Mem. Superintending Sch. Com., Town of Topsham (Maine), 1953-59, chmn., 1953-54, 56-57, mem. sch. bldg. com., 1953-55, com. chmn., 1953-55; sec. Joint-Com. Maine Sch. Union 46, 1953-59; mem. Topsham Zoning Com., 1956-57; bd. dirs. United Srs. of Athens County, 1986—; mem. adv. bd. Athens County Dept. Human Services, 1987—; mem. regional adv. council on aging, 1988—; mem. Athens County council on aging, 1988—. Served to lt. USCGR, 1943-52. Mem. Am. Psychol. Assn., Midwestern Psychol. Assn., Am. Assn. Counseling and Devel., Nat. Council on Aging, Am. Ednl. Research Assn., Gerontol. Soc. Am., Mass. Audubon Soc., Buckeye Trail Assn., Vergilian Soc., Ohio U. Soc. Alumni and Friends of Coll. Arts and Scis. (exec. sec. 1985—), Sierra Club, Sigma Xi (pres. Ohio U. chpt. 1972-73), Psi Chi., Sigma Phi Omega. Club: Appalachian Mountain. Home: 41 Elmwood Pl Athens OH 45701 Office: Dept Psychology Ohio U Athens OH 45701

RUSSELL, DAVID WILLIAMS, lawyer; b. Lockport, N.Y., Apr. 5, 1945; s. David Lawson and Jean Graves (Williams) R.; A.B. (Army ROTC scholar, Daniel Webster scholar), Dartmouth Coll., 1967, M.B.A., 1969; J.D. cum laude, Northwestern U., 1976; m. Frances Yung Chung Chen, May 23, 1970; children—Bayard Chen, Ming Rennick. English tchr. Talledega (Ala.) Coll., summer 1967; math. tchr. Lyndon Inst., Lyndonville, Vt., 1967-68; instr. econs. Royalton Coll., South Royalton, Vt., part-time 1968-69; asst. to pres. for planning Tougaloo (Miss.) Coll., 1969-71, bus. mgr., 1971-73; mgr. will and trust rev. project Continental Ill. Nat. Bank & Trust Co. Chgo., summer 1974; law clk. Montgomery, McCracken, Walker & Rhoads, Phila., summer 1975; admitted to Ill. bar, 1976, Ind. bar, 1983; Winston & Strawn, Chgo., 1976-83; ptnr. Klineman, Rose, Wolf & Wallack, Indpls., 1983-87, Johnson, Smith, Densborn, Wright & Heath, 1987—; cons. Alfred P. Sloan Found., 1972-73; dir., sec. Forum for Internat. Profl. Services, 1985—; U.S. Dept. Justice del. to U.S. China Joint Session on Trade, Investment & Econ. Law, Beijing, 1987—; lectr. Ind. Law, Gov's Ind. Trade Mission to Japan, 1986, internat. law Ind. Continuing Legal Edn. Forum, 1986, chmn., 1987. Mem. Ind. ASEAN Task Force, 1988—, nat. selection com. Woodrow Wilson Found. Adminstrv. Fellowship Program, 1973-76; vol. Lawyers for Creative Arts, Chgo., 1977-83; dir. World Trade Club of Ind., 1987—; v.p., dir., Sister Cities of Ind., 1988—; dir. Internat. Ctr. Indpls., 1988—. Woodrow Wilson Found. Adminstrv. fellow, 1969-72. Mem. Am., Ill., Ind., Indpls., bar assns., Dartmouth Lawyers Assn., Indpls. Assn. Chinese Ams., ACLU, Chinese Music Soc., Zeta Psi. Presbyterian. Club: Dartmouth of Ind. (sec. 1986-87, pres. 1987-88). Home: 10926 Lakeview Dr Carmel IN 46032 Office: 1800 One Indiana Square Indiana Nat Bank Tower Indianapolis IN 46204

RUSSELL, EUGENE, III, chemist, laboratory administrator; b. Juniper, Ga., Feb. 23, 1944; s. Eugene Jr. and Viola S. R.; m. Betty Jean Ousley, Mar. 25, 1967; children: Chandra Patriece, Tania Cherie, Eugene IV. BS, Albany State Coll., 1966; MS in Med. Tech., Ga. State U., 1980. Tchr. sci. Fulton County Sch. Systems, College Park, Ga., 1969-72; technologist S.W. Community Hosp., Atlanta, 1972-74; asst. supr. Ga. Bapt. Hosp., Atlanta, 1974—; pres., adminstrv. dir. Acculabs Inc., Atlanta, 1981—; chief technologist dept. medicine Emory U., Atlanta, 1975-80. Vol. faculty Med. Lab. for Primary Health Care Ctrs., 1978-80. Served with U.S. Army, 1966-69, Korea. Recipient cert. Appreciation Ga. Dept. Human Resources, 1979. Mem. Am. Soc. Clin. Pathologists (cert. technologist/chemist), Nat. Certification Agy. (cert. clin. lab. dir.), Am. Pub. Health Assn., Clin. Lab. Mgmt. Assn., Alpha Phi Alpha. Democrat. Baptist. Lodge: Masons. Home: 3470 Old Fairburn Rd SW Atlanta GA 30331 Office: 730 Peachtree St NE Suite 1020 Atlanta GA 30308

RUSSELL, JAMES DOUGLAS, power industry executive; b. Vancouver, B.C., Can., Dec. 14, 1952; s. Douglas Keith and Barbara Jane (Gray) R.; m. Vicki Suzanne Gray, Oct. 14, 1977. BASc, U. Toronto, Ont., Can., 1976. Registered profl. engr., Can. With U. Toronto Inst. for Aerospace Studies, 1974-75; prodn. engr. Triple-A Mfg. Co., Toronto, 1975-76; mgr. mfg. engring. Babcock & Wilcox Internat., Cambridge, Ont., 1976—. Author: History and Design of Tunnel Hulls, 1981, Nuclear Steam Generator Tube Materials; contbr. articles to profl. jours. Mem. Assn. Profl. Engrs. Ont., Can. Nuclear Soc., Can. Boating Fedn., Can.-Am. Prodn. and Inventory Control Soc. Home: 67 Highland Crescent, Cambridge, ON Canada N1S 1M1 Office: Babcock & Wilcox Internat, Coronation Blvd, Cambridge, ON Canada N1R 5V3

RUSSELL, JAMES SARGENT, retired naval officer; b. Tacoma, Mar. 22, 1903; s. Ambrose J. and Loella Janet (Sargent) R.; B.S., U.S. Naval Acad., 1926; M.S., Calif. Inst. Tech., 1935; m. Dorothy Irene Johnson, Apr. 13, 1929 (dec. Apr. 1965); children—Donald Johnson, Kenneth McDonald; m. 2d, Geraldine Haus Rahn, July 12, 1966. Served with Mcht. Marine, 1918-22; commd. ensign U.S. Navy, 1926, advanced through grades to adm., 1958; naval aviator, 1929-65; comdg. officer aircraft sqdn. VP 42, Aleutians and Alaska, 1941-42; chief of staff to comdr. Carrier Div. Two, Pacific campaigns of Palau, P.I., Iwo Jima, Okinawa, 1944-45; bombing survey, Japan, 1945; comdg. officer U.S.S., Bairoko, 1946-47, U.S.S. Coral Sea, 1951-52; with aircraft carrier desk Bur. Aero., 1939-41, dir. mil. requirements, 1943-44; dept. dir. mil. application AEC, 1947-51; dir. air warfare div. Office Chief Naval Ops., 1952-54; comdr. carrier div. 17 & 5, Pacific Fleet, 1954-55, chief Bur. of Aero., 1955-57; dep. comdr. Atlantic Fleet, 1957-58, vice chief Naval Ops., 1958-61; comdr. NATO forces in So. Europe, 1962-65, ret., 1965; recalled to active duty, 1967, 68; mem. various Navy adv. bds.; cons. Boeing Co. Decorated D.S.M. (2), Legion of Merit (3), D.F.C., Air medal (U.S.); grand cross Royal Order King George I (Greece); Grand Ofcl. Order Republic of Italy; comdr. Legion of Honor (France); Gt. Cross Peruvian Cross of Naval Merit; Grand Officer Order of Naval Merit (Brazil); recipient Collier-Trophy, 1956. Fellow AIAA. Home: 7734 Walnut Ave SW Tacoma WA 98498

RUSSELL, JOHN DRINKER, legal educator and administrator, consultant; b. Portland, Oreg., Sept. 19, 1911; s. Charles Bert and Alice Eleanor (Drinker) R.; m. Lucille Erica Umbreit, July 11, 1953. B.A., Stanford U., 1931, M.A., 1941; LL.B., Northwestern Sch. Law, Lewis and Clark Coll., 1935. Bar: Oreg. 1935, U.S. Dist. Ct. Oreg. 1936. Ptnr. Berg, Jones & Russell, Portland, 1935-38; counselor, instr. Menlo Coll., Menlo Park, Calif., 1938-42, dir. admissions, registrar, 1946-55, prof. domestic and internat. comml. law, 1946-77, dir. top acad. adminstr., 1955-77, part time prof. law and internat. bus., 1977-81, prof. emeritus, 1981—. Active Menlo Park Master Plan Com., 1955-56. Served to comdr. USNR, 1942-63. Mem. ABA, Inter-Am. Bar Assn., Internat. Bar Assn., Am. Bus. Law Assn., Am. Soc. Internat. Law, Law Assn. for Asia and Western Pacific, Oreg. State Bar, Union Internationale des Avocats, Internat. Law Assn., Am. Legion, Am. Assn. Ret. Persons, Res. Officers Assn., Ret. Officers Assn., Delta Sigma Pi, Delta Theta Phi, Phi Delta Kappa. Republican. Presbyterian. Club: Rotary (pres. Menlo Park 1952-53, chmn. Rotary Found. scholarships com. Dist. 513 1981—). Home: Channing House 850 Webster St #714 Palo Alto CA 94301 Office: Menlo Coll Menlo Park CA 94025

RUSSELL, JOHN ST. CLAIR, JR., lawyer; b. Albany, N.Y., Mar. 21, 1917; s. John St. Clair and Hazel (Barbiers) R.; m. Betty Kixmiller, Sept. 12, 1941; children—Patricia Russell, John St. Clair, III (dec.), David K. A.B. cum laude, Dartmouth Coll., 1938; LL.B., Yale U., 1941. Bar: N.Y. 1942, D.C. 1965. Mem. Hale Russell & Gray (and predecessors), N.Y.C., 1948-85, Winthrop, Stimson, Putnam & Roberts, N.Y.C., 1985—; dir. Brit. Aerospace Holdings, Inc., A. Johnson & Co. Inc., Acoustiguide, Inc. Mem., Irvington (N.Y.) Zoning Bd. Appeals, 1955—; chmn. Raoul Wallenberg Com. of U.S., 1985—. Served to maj. USMCR, 1942-46. Decorated Order of Vasa Sweden; recipient medal of merit Swedish Red Cross. Mem. Assn. Bar City N.Y., Am. Bar Assn., Phi Beta Kappa, Phi Sigma Kappa. Clubs:

Dartmouth, Downtown Assn. (N.Y.C.). Office: 40 Wall St New York NY 10005

RUSSELL, JOSIAH COX, historian, educator; b. Richmond, Ind., Sept. 3, 1900; s. Elbert and Lieuetta (Cox) R.; m. Ruth Winslow, Sept. 15, 1924; children: Elbert Winslow, Walter Howard, Joan. A.B., Earlham Coll., 1922; M.A., Harvard U., 1923, Ph.D., 1926. Asst. in history Radcliffe Coll., 1923-24, Harvard U., 1924-26; asst. prof. Colo. Coll., 1927-29; prof. history and head social sci. dept. N.Mex. Highlands U., 1929-31; instr. to assoc. prof. U. N.C., 1931-46; chmn. history dept. U. N.Mex., 1946-53, prof., 1946-65, prof. emeritus, 1965—; prof. Tex. A & I U., 1965-71, Piper prof. (hon.), 1971. Author: Dictionary of Writers of Thirteenth Century England, 1936, British Medieval Population, 1948, Late Ancient and Medieval Population, 1958, Medieval Regions and Their Cities, 1972, Twelfth Century Studies, 1978, Control of Late Ancient and Medieval Population, 1985, Medieval Demography, 1987; contbr. chpt. to Fontana Economic History of Europe, Historia Universal, Salvat, vol. IV; contbr. numerous articles to profl. jours. Chmn. Orange Dist. com. Boy Scouts Am., 1945-46. Fulbright lectr. Univ. Coll., Wales, 1952-53; research grantee Guggenheim Found., 1930-31, Am. Council Learned Socs., summers 1933, 34, Social Sci. Research Council, summers 1938, 49, 51, Am. Philos. Soc., 1938-39, 61; fellow Islamic Seminar Princeton, summer 1935; cons. Fulbright Brit. Empire Prof. Selection, 1955. Fellow Mediaeval Acad. Am.; mem. Am. Hist. Assn. (mem. Pacific Coast council 1964-65), Population Assn. Am., Soc. of Friends, AAUP (state chmn. 1951-52, nat. council 1953-56), Phi Alpha Theta. Address: 16 South Wind Circle Saint Augustine FL 32084

RUSSELL, MARTIN, publications consultant; b. Setauket, N.Y., June 5, 1923; s. John Winter and Emma Sargent R.; B.S., CCNY, 1947; A.M., Harvard U., 1949; m. Esther Kart, Sept. 2, 1947; children—Lanning Philip, Amelie, Jeffrey Winter. Tutor, CCNY, 1946; geologist, asst. sect. chief U.S. Geol. Survey, 1949-59; mng. editor tech. publs. Am. Geol. Inst., Washington, 1959-65; mng. editor Geol. Soc. Am., N.Y.C., 1965-67; tech. editor, chief standards and procedures sect. policies and resources planning div. Dept. Tech. Coop. for Devel., UN, N.Y.C., 1968-83; publs. cons., 1983—. Pres., U.N. Philatelic Soc., 1974-78. Served with U.S. Army, 1943-46. Mem. Soc. Tech. Communication, Assn. Earth Sci. Editors, Soc. Scholarly Publs., Geosci. Info. Soc. Author: United Nations and Related World-Wide Stamps, 1973; (with E.S. Russell) The Ever-widening Circle, 1983. Home and Office: 61 Kincaid Dr Yonkers NY 10710

RUSSELL, MICHAEL ANDRÉ, automobile sales professional; b. Tyler, Tex., Aug. 19, 1956; s. Jeraldine (Lane) R. A.S., Tyler Jr. Coll., 1977, A.A., 1977; B.A., Fisk U., 1979; M.B.A., Atlanta U., 1981. Mktg. rep IBM, Atlanta, 1980-82; asst. brand mgr. USA Nat. Coca-Cola Hdqrs., Atlanta, 1983-86; candidate Gen. Motors Dealer Devel. Acad., Detroit, 1986—. Vice-chmn. bd. trustees Simpson St. Ch. of Christ, Atlanta, 1982; bd. dirs. Butler St. YMCA, Atlanta, 1983; active High Mus. Art/Young Careers, Atlanta, 1984, NAACP, Atlanta, 1983; mem. Atlanta Sesquicentennial Mayor's Commn. on the Future of Atlanta, 1987. Mem. Nat. Black M.B.A. Assn. (mktg. chmn. 1979), Am. Mktg. Assn. (pres. chpt. 1979-80), Fisk U. Alumni Assn. (exec. com. 1980, chpt. pres. 1984), Kappa Alpha Psi. Democrat. Mem. Ch. of Christ. Club: Atlanta City.

RUSSELL, ROBERT BONNELL, petroleum geologist; b. Wylie, Tex., Oct. 5, 1919; s. Vaughn Heywood and Maude Louise (Adams) R.; m. Lettye Louise Smith, Oct. 16, 1948; children: Susan Jo McDaniel, Robert Van, Robin Everett. BA in Geology, Tex. Christian U., 1953. Cert. petroleum geologist. Geologist, Conoco Inc., 1953-55, petroleum geologist, Midland, Tex., 1955-65, staff geologist, Casper, Wyo., 1966-67, sr. geologist, Denver, 1967-81; ind. petroleum geologist, Lakewood, Colo., 1981—; exploration ptnr. cons. petroleum exploration cos. Compiler data: RMAG Guide Book, 1954. Served with U.S. Army, 1940-42; to 1st lt. USAAF, 1942-48, ETO. Mem. Am. Assn. Petroleum Geologists, Fifteenth Air Force Assn. Baptist. Club: Caterpillar. Home: 2696 S Ammons Way Lakewood CO 80227

RUSSELL, ROBERT EMERSON, JR., marketing and fund raising executive, consultant; b. Indpls., Aug. 1, 1937; s. Robert E. and Nancy Schwenk (Kalleen) R.; B.A., Wabash Coll., 1959; postgrad. Nat. Indsl. Conf. Bd., 1965; m. Ruth Ellen Drake, May 26, 1967; children—Kristen Kalleen, Robert Emerson III. Advt. and pub. relations Armstrong Cork Co., Lancaster, Pa., 1963-67; devel. officer Wabash Coll., Crawfordsville, Ind., 1967-68, dir. devel. and alumni affairs, 1968-71; dir. devel. Rosary Coll., River Forest, Ill., 1971-72; dir. devel. and pub. affairs Rehab. Inst. of Chgo., 1972-76, assoc., 1976—; pres. Robert Russell & Assocs., Inc., Chgo. and Geneva, Ill., 1976—; v.p. mktg. Hillsdale Coll., 1983-86; devel. counsel The Heritage Found., 1987—; mem. adv. bd. Inst. Ednl. Affairs, 1987—; John T. McCarty Meml. Found., 1986—. Mem. task force Chgo. Community Trust Edn. Network, 1977; chmn. conf. Nat. Assn. Hosp. Devel., 1975; pres., bd. dirs. operation ABLE Chgo., 1977-80;pres. Wabash Club of Chgo., 1974-78. Served with U.S. Army, 1960-63. Recipient Capital Funds award Nat. Assn. Hosp. Devel., 1975; Golden Trumpet award Chgo. Pub. Assn., 1974. named Outstanding Young Man of Mem. Nat. Soc. Fund Raising Execs., Nat. Assn. Hosp. Devel., Council Advancement and Support of Edn., Am. Mktg. Assn., SAR, Nat. Assn. Wabash Men (dir.), Blue Key, Sigma Chi, Alpha Psi Omega. Republican. Episcopalian. Club: University (Chgo). Office: PO Box 206 Naperville IL 60540 Office: Hillsdale Coll Hillsdale MI 49242

RUSSELL, ROBERT GILMORE, lawyer; b. Detroit, May 22, 1928; s. William Gilmore and Esther Marion (Redmond) R.; m. Martha Jones, July 9, 1955; children: Robin Russell Millstein, Julie Russell Smith. AB, U. Mich., 1951, JD, 1953. Bar: Mich. 1954. Atty. Kerr, Russell & Weber (and predecessors), Detroit, 1953—; ptnr. Kerr, Russell & Weber (and predecessors), 1959—; instr. Wayne State U. Law Sch., 1954-60. Assoc. editor Mich. Law Rev., 1952-53. Fellow Am. Coll. Trial Lawyers, Am. Bar Found. (sustaining life), Mich. Bar Found.; mem. ABA, Mich. Bar Assn. (chair negligence council 1988-89), Detroit Bar Assn. (dir. 1977—, pres. 1981-82), Am. Judicature Soc., Internat. Assn. Def. Counsel, Assn. Def. Trial Counsel Detroit (pres. 1973-74), Mich. Assn. Def. Counsel, Barristers, Order of Coif, Mimes, Theta Xi, Phi Delta Phi, Phi Eta Sigma. Clubs: Detroit, Thomas Cooley. Home: 879 Sunningdale Dr Grosse Pointe Woods MI 48236 Office: Comerica Bldg Detroit MI 48226

RUSSELL, ROBERT LEONARD, association executive; b. Mt. Vernon, Ill., July 18, 1916; s. Charles Arthur and Edna Mabel (Yearwood) R.; m. Jeanne Lucille Tackenberg, May 21, 1942. Student, St. Petersburg Jr. Coll., 1971-72; BS, U. Mid. Fla., 1973, MS, 1974. Reporter Peoria (Ill.) Jour., 1939-42, 46-47, Chgo. Daily News, 1947-57; asst. exec. dir. Profl. Golfers Assn., Dunedin, Fla., 1957-65; exec. dir. United Vol. Services, San Mateo, Calif., 1965-66; reporter St. Petersburg (Fla.) Evening Ind., 1967-70; pres. Aldrich & Assocs., 1967-70; exec. v.p. Fla. Health Care Assn. (formerly Fla. Nursing Home Assn.), Orlando, 1970-77; exec. v.p. Mortgage Bankers Assn. Fla., Orlando, 1977—, Mortgage Bankers Assn. Cen. Fla., Orlando, 1978—; exec. v.p. Mortgage Bankers Ednl. Found. Fla., Orlando, 1986—; adminstr. Fla. Health Care Self Insurers Fund, 1972-78; sec.-treas. Mortgage Bankers Fla. Polit. Action Com., 1977-85, treas., 1987—; pres. Profl. Assn. Services, Inc., 1977-81, chmn. bd., 1981—. Editor: Profl. Golfer mag., 1957-65, Nat. Golfer mag., 1965-66, Communicator, 1977-80, Bull., 1980-81, The Messenger, 1986—; exec. editor Rx Sports and Travel mag., 1966-67. Elder Park Lake Presbyn. Ch., Orlando, 1979-83, St. Paul's Presbyn. Ch., Orlando, 1983-87, Presbyn. Ch. of Lakes, 1987—. Served with USAAF, 1942-46. Mem. Am. Soc. Assn. Execs. (cert.), Fla. Soc. Assn. Execs., Cen. Fla. Soc. Assn. Exec., Am. Coll. Health Care Adminstrs. (hon.), Fla. Sheriffs Assn. (hon.), U.S. Basketball Writers Assn. (pres. 1956-57), Football Writers Assn. Am. (bd. dirs. 1955-57), Nat. Rifle Assn. (life), Am. Legion. Republican. Home: 6586 Kreidt Dr Orlando FL 32818 Office: 4401 Vineland Rd Suite A-11 Orlando FL 32811

RUSSELL, VIRGINIA WILLIS, foundation administrator, researcher; b. Buffalo, Feb. 13, 1913; d. Jay Burroughs and Faith Lillian (Wright) Willis; m. James Washington Russell; children—James Willis, Brian Jay, Robert Alan, Gary Lloyd. B.A., SUNY-Buffalo, 1934, postgrad., 1934-47. Mem. staff Erie County Emergency Walfare Services, 1941-45; research assoc. physics SUNY-Buffalo, 1959-65; tree farmer, Buffalo, 1952—; founder, dir. Universal Field Found., Buffalo, 1958—. Contbr. articles to profl. jours.; editor Audubon Outlook. Mem. Erie County Bd. Suprs.; N.Y. State chmn. conservation Fedn. Women's Clubs' chmn. Women's Day 125th Anniversary Buffalo; dirs. Erie County LWV. Recipient Civil Def. award, Republican woman of Yr. award. Mem. N.Y. Acad. Sci., AAAS, Am. Chem. Soc., Planetary Soc., History of Sci. U. Buffalo Alumni Assn. (treas, v.p.), Tesla Soc. (dir.), AAUW, Buffalo Soc. Natural Sci. Republican. Presbyterian. Club: Sierra. Current work: Writing patents on control of Radiation emissions; researching Universal Field equations. Home and Office: Unbiversal Field Found 435 Crescent Ave Buffalo NY 12414

RUSSELL, WALTER JAMES, radiologist; b. Seattle, Apr. 25, 1923; s. Walter James and Viola Maurine (Cooke) R.; m. Mitsuko Chijiiwa, June 2, 1974; children—Mai Theresa, James Frederick, Mia Elizabeth, Walter James, Mary Katherine. A.B., Whitman Coll., 1945; B.S., Seattle Coll., 1947; B.Ph. cum laude, Seattle U., 1949; M.D., St. Louis U., 1952; D.M.Sc., Kyushu U., 1971. Intern Providence Hosp., Seattle, 1952-53; radiology resident Sacred Heart Hosp., Spokane, 1953-54, Providence Hosp., Children's Orthopedic Hosp., King County Hosp., Seattle, 1954-55, Meml. Ctr. for Cancer and Allied Diseases, N.Y.C., 1958-59; Nat. Cancer Inst. fellow, 1958-59, Nat. Acad. Scis., 1959—; chief radiology Atomic Bomb Casualty Commn., Hiroshima, 1959-75; chief radiology dept. Radiation Effects Research Found., Hiroshima, 1975-85, editor-in-chief, chmn. editorial bd., 1976-85; research cons., 1985—; cons. radiologist Sta. Hosp., USMC Air Sta., Iwakuni, Japan, 1959-75, Sta. Hosp., U.S. Fleet Activities, Sasebo, Japan, 1959-71; mem. Fulbright Reviewing Com. for U.S. Ednl. Commn. in Japan, 1962; lectr. Hiroshima U. Sch. Medicine, 1967-76. Editor supplement Jour. Radiation Research, Vol. 16, 1975. Contbr. articles to profl. jours. Served to lt. USNR, 1943-46, 55-58. Recipient Irie award Kyushu U., 1973, medal for extraordinary service Nat. Acad. Scis., 1975, Cert. of Commendation, Kyushu U., 1979, award for promoting postgrad. med. edn., 1984; medal Atomic Bomb Casualty Commn./Radiation Effects Research Found., 1980. Fellow Am. Coll. Radiology; mem. AMA, Am. Inst. Ultra sound in Medicine, Am. Roentgen Ray Soc., Health Physics Soc., Internat. Radiation Protection Assn., Radiol. Soc. N.Am., Meml. Sloan-Kettering Inst. Alumni Assn., Soc. Nuclear Medicine, St. Louis U. Alumni Assn., Cornell U. Alumni Assn., Japanese Assn. Radiol. Physicists, Japan Radiol. Soc., Domon-Kai Soc. of Kyushu U., Pan Am. Med. Assn., Tau Kappa Epsilon, Phi Chi. Roman Catholic. Club: Washington Athletic. Office: Radiation Effects Research Found, 5-2 Hijiyama Park, Minami Ward, Hiroshima-shi 732, Japan also: Atomic Bomb Casualty Commn USMC Air Sta FPO Seattle WA 98764

RUSSELL, WILLIAM ARTHUR, JR., international trade and telecommunications consultant; b. Erie, Pa., Mar. 10, 1947; s. William Arthur and Hulda Carolyn (Gregory) R.; m. Barbara Jane Walker, Aug. 26, 1978 (div. Mar. 1981). B.S. in Polit. Sci., U. Tenn., 1969; postgrad. U. N.C. Sch. Law, 1969-71, Georgetown U., 1968. Adminstrv. aide Gov. James Holshouser, Raleigh, N.C., 1973-76; field rep. Republican Nat. Com., Washington, 1976-77; dir. field ops. John Warner for Senate campaign, Alexandria, Va., 1977-78; pres. William Russell & Assocs., Washington, 1977-81; adminstrv. asst. Office of Pres.-Elect, Washington, 1980-81; dir. Office of Pub. Affairs, FCC, Washington, 1981-86; pres. William Russell and Assocs., Inc., Washington, 1986—; exploratory com. Dole for Pres., 1987. Author: Legislative Campaign Manual, 1974. Recipient Good Citizen award N.C. Rep. Party, 1972. Mem. Am. Conservative Union, U.S. Yacht Racing Union, Archeol. Inst. Am. Methodist. Home: 5340 Holmes Run Pkwy #712 Alexandria VA 22304 Office: William Russell and Assocs Inc 1701 Pennsylvania Ave NW Suite 1000 Washington DC 20006

RUSSELL-HUNTER, W(ILLIAM) D(EVIGNE), zoology educator, research biologist, writer; b. Rutherglen, Scotland, May 3, 1926; came to U.S., 1963, naturalized, 1968; s. Robert R. and Gwladys (Dew) R-H.; m. Myra Porter Chapman, Mar. 22, 1951; 1 child, Peregrine D. B.Sc. with honors, U. Glasgow, 1946, Ph.D., 1953, D.Sc., 1961. Sci. officer Bisra, Brit. Admiralty, Millport, Scotland, 1946-48; asst. lectr U. Glasgow, Scotland, 1948-51, univ. lectr. in zoology, 1951-63; examiner in biology Pharm. Soc. Gt. Britain, Edinburgh, 1957-63; chmn. dept. invertebrate zoology Marine Biol. Lab., Woods Hole, Mass., 1964-68, trustee, 1967-75, 77—; prof. zoology Syracuse U., N.Y., 1963—; cons. editor McGraw-Hill Encys., 1977—; bd. dirs. Upstate Freshwater Inst., Syracuse, 1981—. Author: Biology of Lower Invertebrates, 1967, Biology of Higher Invertebrates, 1968, Aquatic Productivity, 1970, A Life of Invertebrates, 1979, The Mollusca: Ecology, 1983; mng. editor: Biol. Bull. Woods Hole, Mass., 1968-80; contbr. over 120 articles to sci. jours. Carnegie and Browne fellow, 1954; research grantee NIH, 1964-70, NSF, 1971-81, U.S. Army C.E., 1985-87; confirmed Scottish armiger, 1967. Fellow Linnean Soc. London, Royal Soc. Edinburgh, Inst. Biology U.K., AAAS; mem. Ecol. Soc. Am., AAUP. Office: Syracuse U 029L Lyman Hall Syracuse NY 13244

RUSSO, IRMA HAYDEE ALVAREZ DE, pathologist; b. San Rafael, Mendoza, Argentina, Feb. 28, 1942; came to U. S., 1972; d. Jose Maria and Maria Carmen (Martinez) de Alvarez; BA, Escuela Normal M.T.S.M. de Balcarce, 1959; MD, U. Nat. of Cuyo, Mendoza, 1970; m. Jose Russo, Feb. 8, 1969; 1 child, Patricia Alexandra. Intern, Sch. of Medicine Hosps., Argentina, 1969-70; resident in pathology Wayne State U. Sch. Medicine, Detroit, 1976-80; research asst. and instr. Inst. of Histology and Embryology Sch. Medicine U. Nat. of Cuyo, 1963-71, asso. prof. histology Faculty of Phys., Chem. and Math. Scis., 1970-72; research asso. Inst. for Molecular and Cellular Evolution, U. Miami, Fla., 1972-73; research asso. exptl. pathology lab. div. biol. scis., Mich. Cancer Found., Detroit, 1973-75, research scientist, 1975-76, vis. research scientist, 1976-82, asst. mem., pathologist, 1982—, co-dir. pathology reference lab., 1982-86; co-dir. Mich. Cancer Found. Lab. Services, 1986—; chief resident physician dept. pathology Wayne State U. Sch. Medicine, 1978-80, asst. prof., 1980-82; mem. staff Harper-Grace Hosps., Detroit, 1980-82; Rockefeller grantee, 1972-73; Nat. Cancer Inst. grantee, 1978-81, 84-87; Am. Cancer Soc. grantee 1988-89; guest lectr. dept. obstetrics Sch. Medicine U. Nat. of Cuyo, 1965-71. Diplomate Am. Bd. Pathology. Mem. AAAS, Coll. Am. Pathologists, Am. Soc. Clin. Pathologists, Am. Assn. for Cancer Research, Mich. Soc. Pathologists, Am. Assn. Clin. Chemistry, Electron Microscopy Soc. Am., Mich. Electron Microscopy Forum, Sigma Xi. Roman Catholic. Contbr. numerous articles on pathology to profl. jours. Office: 110 E Warren Ave Detroit MI 48201

RUSSO, PAUL A., ambassador; b. Cleve., July 21, 1943; s. Michael J. and Marie R.; m. Kathie A. Regan, Dec. 25, 1985. B.S., Ohio State U., 1968; postgrad., Case Western Res. U., 1968. With Robert Taft Senate Campaign, 1969; mem. Republican Nat. Com., Washington, 1970; asst. to Gov. Reagan, State of Calif., 1972-74; dir. polit. action com. Senator Bob Dole, 1977-78; mem. Reagan for Pres. Com., 1976, 80; spl. asst. to Pres. for polit. affairs Washington, 1981-83; dep. under sec. labor Dept. Labor, Washington, 1983-84; pres. Capitol Cons., Washington, 1984-86; ambassador to eastern Caribbean Dept. State, 1986—. Republican. Office: Am Embassy Bridgetown US Dept State Washington DC 20520 *

RUST, DOUGLAS CRAIG, electronics engineer; b. Lexington, Ky., Sept. 29, 1955; s. Charles Manning and Louise Iola (Bryant) R. B.S., Devry Inst. Tech., 1976. Engring. and sci. asst. Sandia Nat. Labs., Albuquerque, 1976-84; project supr., sr. field engr. Secure Engring. Services Inc., Columbia, Md., and Lobbach-Lobenfeld, W.Ger., 1984—. Mem. Am. Soc. Indsl. Security, Internat. Platform Assn. Democrat. Lutheran. Avocations: snow skiing; hiking; golf; travel, skydiving. Home: Ostring 16, 6719 Kerzenheim Federal Republic of Germany Office: Secure Engineering Services Inc, Rosenweg 16, Lobenfeld Federal Republic of Germany also: Columbia Profl Ctr 10840 Little Patuxent Pkwy Suite 405 Columbia MD 21044

RUST, EDWARD BARRY, JR., insurance company executive, lawyer; b. Chgo., Aug. 3, 1950; s. Edward Barry Sr. and Harriett B. (Fuller) R.; m. Sally Buckler, Feb. 28, 1976; 1 child, Edward Barry III. Student, Lawrence U., Appleton, Wis., 1968-69; BS, Ill. Wesleyan U., Bloomington, 1972; JD and MBA, So. Meth. U., Dallas, 1975. Bar: Tex. 1975, Ill. 1976. Mgmt. trainee State Farm Ins. Cos., Dallas, 1975-76; atty. State Farm Ins. Cos., Bloomington, 1976, sr. atty., 1976-78, asst. v.p., 1978-81, v.p., 1981-83, exec. v.p., 1983-85, pres. and chief exec. officer, 1985—; pres. and bd. dirs. State Farm Investment Mgmt. Corp., State Farm Internat. Services, Inc., State Farm Cos. Found.; chmn. State Farm Mut. Automobile Ins. Co., 1987; bd. dirs. exec. and investment coms. State Farm Annuity and Life Ins. Co., State Farm Mut. Automobile Ins. Co., State Farm Life Ins. Co., State Farm Fire and Casualty, State Farm Gen. Trustee Ill. Wesleyan U., 1985—. Mem. ABA, Tex. State Bar Assn., Ill. Bar Assn., Am. Inst. Property and Liability Underwriters (trustee 1986—), Ins. Inst. Am. (trustee 1986—), Inst. for Civil Justice (bd. overseers). Office: State Farm Fire & Casualty Co 1 State Farm Plaza Bloomington IL 61704

RUST, JOHN NEVILLE, psychologist; b. Scunthorpe, Lincolnshire, Eng., Nov. 25, 1943; s. John Cyprian Walcot and Francis Mary (Walshaw) R.; m. Susan Esther Golombok, Feb. 22, 1978; 1 child, Jamie Carlos; 1 child by previous marriage: Naseem Azure. BSc with 1st class honors, U. London, 1970, MA in Philosophy, 1976; PhD in Psychology, Inst. Psychiatry, London, 1974. Med. technician Churchill Hosp., Oxford, Eng., 1963, Pub. Health Lab., Lincoln, Eng., 1964, Udaipur Gen. Hosp., India, 1965; psychiatric nurse Maudsley Hosp., London, 1966-67; research psychologist U. London, Inst. Psychiatry, 1972-74, lectr. psychology, 1974-76; lectr. psychometrics U. London, Inst. Edn., 1976-86, sr. lectr. psychometrics, 1986, head dept. psychology, 1984—; senator U. London, 1983-87; cons. Brit. Library, London, 1987—, Nat. Westminster Bank, 1987—. Contbr. articles to profl. jours.; author psychol. tests; editor (jour. series) Philos. Psychology, 1987. Inter-U. Council scholar, 1977, 78, Brit. Council scholar, 1986. Fellow Royal Statis. Soc., Brit. Psychol. Soc.; mem. Soc. for Philosophy and Psychology, Brit. Computer Soc., Am. Psychol. Soc. Home: 173 Shakespeare Tower, The Barbican, London EC2Y 8DR, England Office: Inst Edn U London, 25 Woburn Sq, London WC1H 0AA, England

RUST, LIBBY KAREN, fund raising counsel; b. York, Maine, Feb. 8, 1951; d. Myron Davis and Meta Mildred (Libby) R.; B.A., Wheaton Coll., 1973; M.S., Columbia U., 1977. Day care field asst. Childhood Ednl. Enrichment Program, Waterville, Maine, 1974-75; cons. Center for Community Planning and Cons., N.Y.C., 1975-76; intern Morgan Guaranty Trust Co., N.Y.C., 1976; staff asst. subcom. on mental health Task Force on N.Y.C. Fiscal Crisis, 1976-77; auditor AT&T, N.Y.C., 1977; budget examiner Legis. Office of Budget Rev., N.Y.C., 1977-78; exec. dir. Strafford County Human Services, Dover, N.H., 1978-79; dir. allocations and agy. relations United Way, Inc., Portland, Maine, 1979-82, planning and allocations div. dir., 1982-84; exec. dir. Seacoast United Way, Portsmouth, N.H., 1984-87; dir. Devel. Am. Cancer Soc., Los Angeles, 1987—. Mem. budget com. Town of York, 1979-80. Mem. Jr. League Portland, Jr. League Los Angeles, Kents Hill Sch. Alumni Assn. (bd. dirs.). Republican. Clubs: Portland Wheaton; Rolling Hills Racquet. Home: Neuyorkholme Mitchell Rd York ME 03909

RUSTEN, ELMER MATHEW, dermatologist; b. Pigeon Falls, Wis., Oct. 5, 1902; s. Ener E. and Clara L. (Benrud) R.; B.A., St. Olaf Coll., 1925; B.S., U. Minn., 1928, B.M., 1928, M.D., 1929, postgrad., 1929-31, U. Vienna, 1932; m. Helen Marthine Steidl, July 19, 1930; 1 son, Elmer Michael. Intern, Mpls. Gen. Hosp., 1929, resident, 1929-31; practice medicine specializing in dermatology, Mpls., 1933-82; instr. dermatology U. Minn., Mpls., 1934-38, clin. instr., 1938-42, clin. asst. prof., 1942-71; mem. cons. staff Mpls. Gen. Hosp., 1933-40, 51-60, Glen Lake Sanatorium, Oak Terrace, Minn., 1936-60; mem. attending staff Methodist Hosp., St. Louis Park, Minn., 1959-77, Abbott Hosp., Mpls., Minn., 1935—, Asbury Hosp., Mpls., 1934-50. Del. to 14th Internat. Tb Conf., New Delhi, India, 1957. Mem. Minn. Citizens Council, 1963-66; bd. dirs. Correctional Service of Minn., pres., 1963-67; bd. dirs. Minn. Dermatol. Found., 1950-54, Central Luth. Found., 1952-84. Diplomate Am. Bd. Dermatology. Mem. Am., Minn. med. assns., Mpls. Acad. Medicine (past pres.), Am. Acad. Dermatology, Soc. for Investigative Dermatology, Minn. Dermatol. Soc. (past pres.), Chgo. Dermatol. Socs., Internat. Soc. Tropical Dermatology, Am. Acad. Allergy, Internat. Corrs. Soc. of Allergists, Hennepin County Med. Soc., Alaska Territorial Assn. (hon.), Phi Beta Kappa, Phi Beta Pi (past pres. North Central chpt.). Republican. Lutheran. Clubs: Rotary (pres. 1961, Paul Harris fellow 1983), Boone and Crockett (hon. life mem., chmn. Big Game Competition 1961, 64, v.p. 1965-74), Big Game (pres. 1940, dir. Spl. Projects Found. 1970—). Author: Wheat, Egg and Milk-Free Diets, 1932; contbr. to Ofcl. Scoring System for N. Am. Big Game, 1971. Home: 18420 D 8th Ave N Plymouth MN 55447

RUSTIA, SERGIO ORTIZ, physician, educator; b. Manila, Feb. 17, 1931; s. Roman Javier Rustia and Caridad Concepcion Ortiz; m. Carmencita Valero, Feb. 17, 1962; children: Maria Beatriz, Maria Caridad. AA, U. St. Tomas, Manila, 1950, MD, 1955. Diplomate Philippine Bd. Internal Medicine. Asst. instr. U. Mo., 1958-59; resident New England Deaconess Hosp., Boston, 1959-60; fellow medicine Joslin Clinic, Boston, 1960-61; instr. U. St. Tomas, 1967-70, asst. prof., 1970-80, assoc. prof., 1980—; chief subsect. endocrine U. St. Tomas Hosp., 1987-88; prof., dept. chmn. Fatima Coll. Medicine, Valenzuela, Philippines, 1980—; cons., head of internal medicine Meralco Hosp., Cotton Hosp., Pasig, Philippines. Author: Review of Medical Endocrinology, 1962; contbr. articles to profl. jours. Pres. Philippine Diabetic Assn., 1973-74. Recipient over 25 certs. and plaques from various med. orgns. Fellow Philippine Soc. Endocrinology and Metabolism, Philippine Coll. Physicians. Club: Harvard. Home: 21 Arguilla, San Lorenzo, Makati Metro Manila Philippines Office: John F Cotton Hosp, Ortigas Ave, Pasig Metro Manila Philippines

RUSTIGIAN, STELLA SACHAKLIAN, interior designer; b. Boston, May 10, 1912; d. Aaron Harutune and Eliza (Der Melkonian) Sachaklian; m. Jacob Rustigian, May 30, 1937 (dec. June 1968); children—George, Arsine Rustigian Oshagan, Jackie. B.F.A. in Interior Design, Syracuse U., 1933; student in History, Edn., Trinity Coll., 1956-60; M.A. in Edn., U. Conn., 1979, postgrad. in Edn., 1983—. Free-lance interior designer, Syracuse, N.Y., 1933-37; interior designer S. H. Sachaklian's, Hartford, Conn., 1937-39, G. Fox & Co., Hartford, 1961-75; personnel asst. Trinity Coll., Hartford, 1955-61; specialist Armenian World Externs Program, U. Conn., 1979—, mem. steering com. Armenian studies, 1984—, mem. adv. bd.,1987—; asst. dir., lectr. Armenian Relief Soc. Summer Studies, U. Pa., U. Conn., 1979, 82. Author: Armenian Day School Movement in the U.S., 1979; editorial staff Armenian Weekly, 1934—. Contbr. articles to The Armenian Rev., 1948-82. Mem. Hartford Mayor's All-Ams. Council, 1971-78; vol. translator ARC, Hartford, 1977—, spl. cons., 1987; co-chairperson Conn. State Ethnic Adv. Council, Hartford, 1983—, chmn. cultural research com., 1983; mem. World Edn. Fellowship, Conn., 1975—, treas. 1985. Recipient cert. Hartford All-Ams. Festival, 1972, citation Hartford chpt. ARC, 1977; citation Conn. State Dept. Edn., 1977; resolution of commendation Hartford City Council, 1978. Mem. Am. Soc. Interior Designers (profl. mem.), Armenian Studies Assn., Armenian Relief Soc. N.Am. (exec. bd., regional bd. 1986-88), Armenian Relief Soc. (internat. body, various exec. positions Hartford chpt. 1942—), Armenian Nat. Edn. Com., Pi Lambda Theta, Tau Sigma Delta, Tau Epsilon. Republican. Armenian Apostolic. Lodge: Order Eastern Star (worthy matron 1958-59).

RUSTON, WALTER RALPH, chemical engineer; b. Vienna, Austria, Jan. 25, 1916; came to Belgium, 1945; s. Victor Charles and Elisabeth Marie (Maltzan) R.; m. Edda Adeline Keinert, Apr. 12, 1945; 1 dau., Beatrix. Dipl.Ing., Tech. U. Vienna, 1943. Asst., Inst. Inorganic Chemistry, Tech. U. Vienna, 1943-45; researcher Coal Stratigraphy and Paleontology Assn., Brussels, 1945-46; Assn. pour les Etudes Texturales, Brussels, 1946-55; mgr. Soc. Applied Indsl. Research, Brussels, 1955-58; gen. mgr., mng. dir. SERAI, Brussels, 1958-69; pres., mng. dir. Ruston Tech. Services Internat., Brussels, 1969—; dir. Profl. Nuclear Industry Group, 1961-69; advisor metallurgy Nuclear Research Ctr., Belgium, 1963-69; dir. Profl. Assn. Space Activities, 1965-69; advisor to UNIDO, 1974-80. Author numerous articles profl. jours. Mem. Am. Chem. Soc., AAAS, Assn. Aeronautique et Astronautique de France, Deutsche Gesellschaft fur Chemisches Apparatewesen DECHEMA, Gesellschaft für Chemiewirtschaft, Societe Royale Belge des Ingenieurs des Industriels, Brit. Nuclear Energy Soc., Chem. Inst. Can., Iron and Steel Inst. Japan, N.Y. Acad. Scis. Home: Ave Jeanne 10 Bte 8, B1050 Brussels Belgium

RUTENBER, RALPH DUDLEY, JR., teacher; b. Bardonia, N.Y., Aug. 3, 1905; s. Ralph Dudley and Margaret (Gerow) R.; grad. Blackburn Acad., Carlinville, Ill., 1922; A.B., Princeton U., 1926; postgrad. Cornell U., 1930; A.M., Columbia U., 1940; Litt.D., Am. Internat. Coll., 1959; m. Cleminette Downing, Dec. 29, 1932; children—Anne Downing (Mrs. Roger L. Clifton), John Downing. Master in Latin, Choate Sch., 1926-28; head English dept. Wooster Sch., Danbury, Conn., 1928-33, sr. master, 1933-41; headmaster MacDuffie Sch. for Girls, Springfield, Mass., 1941-72, pres., 1975-78; ednl.

cons., 1972-75; lectr. edn., lit. and religion; past dir. Community Sch. Religious Edn., Springfield. Past dir. Ind. Schs. Found. of Mass.; former bd. dirs. Ind. Sch. Assn. Mass.; former trustee Springfield Library and Mus., Mental Health and Retardation Area Bd., trustee MacDuffie Sch. Mem. Nat. Assn. Prins. of Schs. for Girls (sec. 1964-66, mem. council, pres. 1971-73), Headmasters Assn., Authors Guild, Phi Beta Kappa. Episcopalian. Author: How to Bring Up 2000 Teenagers, 1979; also articles, essays and reviews. Home and Office: 334 Maple St Springfield MA 01105

RUTERBUSCH, PAUL HUGO, electro-optical systems engineer; b. Bay City, Mich., Oct. 25, 1953; s. Eldon Lorey and Rosemary Helen (Gollin) R. A.S., Delta Coll., 1975; B.S., Saginaw Valley State Coll., 1979; M.S., Pa. State U., 1981. Lab. asst. Saginaw Valley State Coll., University Center, Mich., 1978-79; research asst. Wayne State U., Detroit, 1979-80; research asst. Pa. State U., University Park, 1980-82; ptnr. Applied Optical Tech., Bay City, Mich., 1982-83; optical engr. Gen. Electric Co., Syracuse, N.Y., 1983-85, project engr., 1985-86; electro-optical systems engr. Gen. Electric Co., 1986—. Contbr. articles to profl. jours; patentee in field. Mem. Optical Soc. Am. Lutheran. Current work: Holography, holographic interferometry, optical image processing, solar energy collection systems, photography, optomechanical design. Subspecialties: Holography; Optical engineering.

RUTH, FRANKLIN WILLIAM, JR., manufacturing company executive metal cutting tools; b. Dayton, Ohio, Oct. 14, 1917; s. Frank William and Florence U. (Iobst) R.; m. Pearl Showers, Mar. 23, 1940; children: Betsy Ann (Mrs. Derle M. Snyder), Pamela Jane, Franklin William III. BA, Pa. State Coll., 1939. Supr. bookkeeper Pa. Treasury dept., 1942; sr. accountant Main & Co. C.P.A.s, Harrisburg, Pa., 1942-44; chief accounting officer Reiff & Nestor, Co., Lykens, Pa., 1944-46; sec., dir. Reiff & Nestor, Co., 1946-83, gen. mgr., 1951-83, treas., 1965-83; sec. dir., gen. mgr. Medco Developing Co. Inc., Lykens, 1955-83; treas. Medco Developing Co. Inc., 1965-83; sec., gen. mgr. Medco Process Inc., Lykens, 1957-83, treas., 1965-83, dir., 1957—; bd. dirs. Miners Bank Lykens, 1987, sec. 1962-87, pres. 1987—; treas. New Eng. Tap Co. Inc., 1967-83; also dir.; dir., mem. exec. com. Capital Blue Cross, Harrisburg, vice chmn. bd., 1980-82, chmn. bd., 1982—; dir. Camp Hill Ins. Co. Trustee Pa. State U., 1956-63; sec., dir. Nestor Charitable Found., 1953-83, treas., 1965-83; sec., dir. Mary Margaret Nestor Found., 1953-83, treas., 1965-83; chmn. Upper Dauphin Area Sch. Authority, 1972-80. Mem. N.A.M., Nat. Soc. Pub. Accountants, Am. Soc. Tool and Mfg. Engrs. Methodist. Club: Mason (Shriner). Home: 422 S 2d St Lykens PA 17048

RUTH, JAN-ERIK UNO, gerontologist, educator; b. Borgå, Nyland, Finland, Apr. 5, 1944; s. Erik Uno Ruth and Vivi Sofia (Stohlstedt) Laine; m. Vineta Julia, Apr. 1, 1971 (div. Jan. 1986); children: Emelie Caroline, Julia Charlotta, Inge-Maj Eriksson. M of Polit. Sci., Åbo (Finland) Acad., 1970, degree in polit. sci., 1978; MA, U. So. Calif., 1976, PhD, 1981. Asst. tchr. edn. ÅBo Acad., 1971, mem. faculty humanities, 1972-74, asst. tchr. psychology, 1972-79; researcher Åbo Acad. Found., 1980-82; researcher Ctr. for Gerontol. Tng. and Research, Kuntokallio Found., stersundom, Finland, 1983-84, dir. research, 1985—; docent Helsinki (Finland) U., 1984; cons. Med. Bd. Finland, Helsinki, 1985—, Social Bd. Finland, Helsinki, 1986—; head Social-Gerontol. Network Researchers, 1986—. Author, editor: Aging in Finland, 1983, Dimensions of Creativity, 1984, Death and Life, 1985, Care of the Demented Patient, 1987, The Human Life Span, 1988; editor: (jours.) Comprehensive Gerontology, 1987—, Gerontologia, 1987—. Fulbright scholar, 1975. Mem. Soc. for Growth and Aging Research (founder, mem. steering bd. 1981—). Greek Orthodox. Home: Brunnsgatan 12V, 06100 Borga Finland Office: Kuntokallio Found, Ctr for Gerontol Tng/Research, 01100 Ostersundom Finland

RUTHVEN, ADRIENNE NICHOLA NUNAN, geophysicist, geologist; b. Cork, Ireland, Nov. 9, 1956; came to U.S., 1958, naturalized, 1963; d. Timothy Raymond and Bridget Carmel (Cotter) N.; m. Les D. Ruthven, Jan. 3, 1987. BS in Geology with honors, U. Ala., 1979; MS in Geology, U. N.C., 1983. Research and teaching asst. geology dept. U. Ala., Birmingham, 1976-79, U. N.C., Chapel Hill, 1980-83; geologist Law Engring. and Testing Co., Atlanta, 1979-80, Miami, Fla., 1980; sr. petroleum geophysicist Exxon Co., U.S.A., Houston, 1983—. Contbr. abstracts to profl. jours. Participant Exxon Vol. Involvement Program, Woodland Heights Civic Assn. Martin fellow U. N.C., 1981. Mem. Geol. Soc. Am. (Exxon Co. USA co. rep. 1985—), Am. Assn. Petroleum Geologists, Am. Geophys. Union, Phi Kappa Phi. Club: Houston Bicycle, Houston Proud. Current work: Geophysical and geological exploration for petroleum resources in Exxon's Offshore/Alaska division, currently focused on offshore Gulf of Mexico. Subspecialties: Geology, Geophysics. Home: 708 Euclid Houston TX 77009

RUTINS, KARLIS VISVALDIS, corporate executive; b. Riga, Latvia, May 17, 1937; s. Alfreds Karlis and Anna Lepik R.; student Brown U., 1955-58; B.S.M.E., Newark Coll. Engring., 1963; M.S.I.E., Columbia U., 1965; m. Margita Anderson, July 9, 1966; 1 son, Erik Karlis. Indsl. engr. Eastman Kodak, Rochester, N.Y., 1963-64; systems engr. IBM, N.Y.C., 1965-66; systems mgr. Am. Hoechst Corp., Somerville, N.J., 1966—, v.p. info. systems, 1980—, v.p. organizational planning, 1983-86, pres., Chief operating officer Strategic Procurement Group, Inc., Martinsville, N.J., 1986—. Mem. Am. Inst. Indsl. Engrs., Nat. Council Phys. Distbn. Mgmt., N.Am. Soc. Corp. Planning, Am. Productivity Mgmt. Assn., World Future Soc.

RUTKOWSKI, BOGDAN, archeologist; b. Torun, Poland, June 26, 1930; s. Czeslaw and Maria (Michalak) R.; m. Barbara Szubinska, June 25, 1963. PhD, Acad Scis., Warsaw, 1963; Habilitation, 1971. Head dept. classical archaeology inst. history material culture Polish Acad. Scis., Swierczewskiego, 1973—, prof., 1977—. Author: Fruhgriechische Kultuarstellungen, 1981, The Cult Places of the Aegean, 1986, and many others. Mem. German Archaeol. Inst. Home: PL 00979 PO Box 82, 34 Warsaw Poland Office: Polish Acad Scis, Ul Swierczewskiego 105, 00141 Warsaw Poland

RUTLEDGE, JOHN WILLIAM, watch company executive; b. Eureka, Calif., Mar. 12, 1923; s. William Eugene and Ellen Agnes (Jordan) R.; m. Mary Jo McKinley, Nov. 23, 1951; children: Ellen, John William, Amy. B.S., Northwestern U., 1943; M.B.A., Harvard U., 1947; MA. in Archaeology, Yale U., 1985. Tchr. Charlestown State Penitentiary, Boston, 1946-47; salesman Lahey Fargo & Co., 1947-48; asst. controller Lehigh Coal & Navigation Co., 1948-54; sr. v.p., dir. Xerox Corp., Stamford, Conn., 1954-71; sr. v.p. home furnishings group, dir. Magnavox Co., N.Y.C., 1971-73; pres., dir. Bulova Watch Co., N.Y.C., 1973-79; dir. Nat. Telecommunications and Tech., Network Controls, Nat. Aviation & Tech. Corp., Orion Capital Corp. Served to lt. USNR. Mem. Sigma Alpha Epsilon. Clubs: Harvard (N.Y.C.), N.Y. Athletic (N.Y.C.). Home: 127 Dunning Rd New Canaan CT 06840 also: 893 S County Rd Palm Beach FL 33480

RUTTER, JOHN WESTHEAD, mathematics educator; b. Bolton, Eng., Oct. 2, 1935; s. Wilfred George and Ethel (Westhead) R.; m. Eileen Hall Hartley, Apr. 11, 1959(div. June 1976); children: Catherine Ethel, Sasha Clare, Frances Georgina, Tanya Christine Hall. BA in Math. with 1st class honors, U. Oxford, Eng., 1958, PhD, 1963. Tchr. math. Queens Coll. U. Oxford, 1958-59, jr. lectr. Magdalen Coll., 1959-61; lectr. U. Liverpool, Eng., 1961—; vis. lectr. Stanford (Calif.) U., 1964-65. Contbr. over 20 research articles in field. Mem. London Math. Soc., Am. Math. Soc. Home: 14 The Priory, Sandown Rd, Liverpool L15 4JD, England Office: U Liverpool, Dept Math, Liverpool L69 3BX, England

RUUSUVUORI, AARNO EMIL, architect; b. Kuopio, Jan. 14, 1925; s. Armas Ruusuvuori and Aune Hamalainen; m. Anna Marie E. Jaameri, 1970; 2 children. Ed. Helsinki Tech. U. Asst. in architecture Helsinki Tech. U. (Finland), 1952-59, acting prof. architecture, 1959-63, prof., 1963-66; prin. own drawing office, 1952—; dir. Mus. Finnish Architecture, 1975-78, 83-88; state prof. art, 1978-83. Prin. works include: Parish Cens: Hyvinkaa Church, 1961, Huutoniemi Ch., 1963, Tapiola Ch., 1964; Printing Works of Weilin and Goos, 1964-66; Police Hdqrs., Mikkeli, 1968; Helsinki City Hall renovation, 1970-88; Rauhanummi Chapel, Hyvinkaa, 1972; Paragon Office Bldg., 1973; REDC Bldg., Addis Ababa, Ethiopia, 1976; Parate Printing Works, 1979; Hotel Al Rashid, Riyadh, Saudi Arabia, 1980; editor Architect-Arkitekten mag., 1952-55, chief editor, 1956-57. Decorated Order of Lion of Finland. Recipient Vaino Vahakallio award, 1955; 1st prize award Nat. Mus., 1987. Fellow AIA (hon.); mem. Finnish Assn. Architects (pres. 1982). Office: Annankatu 15 B 10, 00120 Helsinki 12 Finland

RUWE, LESTER NICHOLAS, ambassador to Republic of Iceland; b. Grosse Pointe Farms, Mich., Sept. 22, 1933; s. Lester Frederick and Ruth M. (Devoy) R.; m. Nancy Lammerding, Feb. 13, 1975. B.A., Brown U., 1955. Mem. staff Nixon for Pres., Washington, 1960; mem. staff John Tower for Senate, Houston, 1961, Nixon for Gov., Los Angeles, 1962, Charles Percy for Gov., Chgo., 1964; mem. sr. staff Nixon for Pres., N.Y.C., 1968; asst. chief of protocol Dept. State, Washington, 1969-76; U.S. ambassador to Iceland Dept. State, Reykjavik, 1985—; mem. sr. staff Reagan for Pres., Los Angeles and Washington, 1979-80; chief of staff Office of Richard Nixon, N.Y.C., 1980-84; sr. cons. Reagan-Bush '84, Washington, 1984. Clubs: Everglades (Palm Beach, Fla.); Chevy Chase (Md.). Office: Am Embassy-Reykjavik FPO New York NY 09571

RUYS, MANU EDOUARD, editor; b. Antwerp, Belgium, Feb. 25, 1924; s. Emmanuel Peter and Eveline Cornelia (Thomas); m. Greta Paule de Keuster; children: Iris, Francis, Robert. MA, U. Louvain, Belgium, 1948. Parliamentary journalist De Standaard, Brussels, 1949-60, chief polit. sect., 1960-75, editor in chief, 1975—. Author: The Flemings, 1972, Vijfentwintig jaar Kongo Zaire, 1985. Dir. Ho. Reps., Belgium, 1982—. Recipient prize Flemish Press Club, 1968, Press award Union European Federalists, Antwerp, 1975. Mem. Internat. Press Inst. Home: Roostat 2A, 1860 Meise, Brussels Belgium Office: Krantengroep De Standaard, Ave Gosset 30, Dilbeek, Brussels Belgium

RWAKISETA-TINAAKO, F., chemical company executive; b. Uganda, Oct. 21, 1941; s. Shem and Janet Rwakiseta; married; children: Isaac, Brenda, Sharon, Moses, Andrew. BSE, Makerere U., 1968. Factory chemist Uganda, 1969-70, mgr., 1971-72, gen. mgr., 1973-77; gen. mgr. Tororo Indsl. Chems. & Fertilizers, Kampala, Uganda, 1977—. Club: Golf. Lodge: Lions. Home and Office: PO Box 7042, Kampala Uganda

RYAN, CLARENCE AUGUSTINE, JR., biochemistry educator; b. Butte, Mont., Sept. 29, 1931; s. Clarence A. Sr. and Agnes L. (Duckham) R.; m. Patricia Louise Meunier, Feb. 8, 1936; children: Jamie Arlette, Steven Michael, Janice Marie, Joseph Patrick. BA in Chemistry, Carroll Coll., 1953; MS in Chemistry, Mont. State U., 1956, PhD in Chemistry, 1959. Postdoctoral fellow in biochemistry Oreg. State U., Corvallis, 1959-61; postdoctoral fellow in biochemistry U.S. Western Regional Lab., Berkeley, Calif., 1961-63, chemist, 1963-64; asst. prof. biochemistry Wash. State U., Pullman, 1964-68, assoc. prof., 1968-72, prof., 1972—, chmn. dept. agrl. chemistry, 1977-80, fellow Inst. Biol. Chemistry, 1980—; visiting scientist dept. biochemistry U. Wash., 1981—, Harvard U. Med. Sch., 1982; cons. Kemin Industries, Des Moines, 1981—, Plant Genetics, Davis, Calif., 1987—; research adv. bd. Frito-Lay, Inc., Dallas, 1982, Plant Genetic Engring. Lab., N.M. State U., Las Cruces, 1986—; mgr. biol. stress program USDA Competitve Grants Program, Washington, 1983-84; former mem. adv. panels for Internat. Potato Ctr., Lima, Peru, Internat. Ctr. Genetic Engring. and Biotech., New Delhi, Internat. Ctr. Tropical Agr., Cali, Columbia; mem. grant rev. panels NSF, NIH. Mem. edit. bd. several biochem. and plant physiology jours.; contbr. articles to profl. publs., chpts. to books; co-editor 2 books. Grantee USDA, NSF, NIH, Rockefeller Found.; recipient Merch award for grad. research Mont. State U., 1959, career devel. awards NIH, 1964-74, Alumni Achievement award Carroll Coll., 1986, Pres.'s Faculty Excellence award in research Wash. State U., 1986; named to Carroll Coll. Alumni Hall Fame, 1981; Carroll Coll. Basketball Hall Fame, 1982. Mem. AAAS, Nat. Acad. Scis. (elected), Am. Chem. Soc., Am. Soc. Plant Physiology, Am. Soc. Exptl. Biology, Biochemical Soc., Internat. Soc. Chem. Ecology, Internat. Soc. Plant Molecular Biology (bd. dirs.), Phytochem. Soc. N.Am., Phi Kappa Phi (Recognition award 1976). Democrat. Roman Catholic. Office: Wash State Univ Inst Biol Chemistry Pullman WA 99164

RYAN, FRANK JAMES, financial analyst.; b. Boston, May 22, 1934; s. James Francis and Edna Anna (Schnaufer) R.; B.Sc., Cornell U., 1955, M.B.A., 1959, M.A., 1959; postgrad. N.Y.U. Sch. Law, 1961-62; m. Catherine Joyce Fujiwara, July 15, 1966; children—Nicole Melia, Todd Thomas, Scott James. With fgn. investment dept. Goodbody & Co., N.Y.C., 1959-61; asst. v.p. fgn. investment Am. Fgn. Ins. Assn., N.Y.C., 1962-66; asst. treas. fgn. investment Am. Life Ins. Co., Bermuda, 1966-69; v.p. fgn. investment C.V. Starr & Co., N.Y.C., 1969-78; v.p. InterSec Research Corp., N.Y.C., 1978-79; investment mgr. Abu Dhabi Investment Authority, Abu Dhabi, United Arab Emirates, 1979—. Trustee Am. Community Sch., Abu Dhabi. Served with AUS, 1955, 58-59. Mem. Acad. Polit. Schi., Am. Acad. Polit. and Social Sci., Am. soc. Internat. Law, Cornell Soc. Engrs., Cornell Soc. Hotelmen, Internat. Studies Assn., N.Y. Soc. Security Analysts, Fin. Analysts Fedn., Internat. Soc. Fin. Analysts, Fgn. Analysts Fedn., La Chaine des Rotisseurs. Club: N.Y. Athletic. Office: PO Box 3600, Abu Dhabi United Arab Emirates

RYAN, JAMES WALTER, physician, medical researcher; b. Amarillo, Tex., June 8, 1935; s. Lee W. and Emma E. (Haddox) R.; children: James P.A., Alexandra L.E., Amy J.S. A.B. in Polit. Sci., Dartmouth Coll., 1957; M.D., Cornell U., 1961; D.Phil., Oxford U. (Eng.), 1967. Diplomate: Nat. Bd. Med. Examiners. Intern, Montreal (Que.) Gen. Hosp., McGill U., Can., 1961-62; asst. resident in medicine Montreal (Que.) Gen. Hosp., McGill U., 1962-63; USPHS research asso. NIMH, NIH, 1963-65; guest investigator Rockefeller U., N.Y.C., 1967-68; asst. prof. biochemistry Rockefeller U., 1968; asso. prof. medicine U. Miami (Fla.) Sch. Medicine, 1968-79, prof. medicine, 1979—; sr. scientist Papanicolaou Cancer Research Inst., Miami, 1972-77; hon. med. officer to Regius prof. medicine Oxford U., 1965-67; vis. prof. Clin. Research Inst. Montreal, 1974; mem. vis. faculty thoracic disease div., dept. internal medicine Mayo Clinic, 1974; cons. Ventrex Labs., Inc., Chugai Pharm. Co., Ltd., Tokyo. Contbr. numerous articles on biochem. research and pathology to sci. jours. Rockefeller Found. travel awardee, 1962; William Waldorf Astor travelling fellow, 1966; USPHS spl. fellow, 1967-68; Pfizer travelling fellow, 1972; recipient Louis and Artur Luciano award for research of circulatory diseases McGill U., 1984-85. Fellow Am. Inst. Chemists; mem. Am. Chem. Soc., Biochem. Soc., Am. Soc. Biol. Chemists, Am. Heart Assn. (mem. council cardiopulmonary diseases 1972—, Council for High Blood Pressure Research 1976—), Microcirculatory Soc., So. Soc. Clin. Investigation, AAAS, N.Y. Acad. Scis., Sigma Xi. Baptist. Club: United Oxford and Cambridge U. (London); The Fisher Island (Miami). Home: 3420 Poinciana Ave Miami FL 33133 Office: 1399 NW 17th Ave Miami FL 33125

RYAN, JOHN THOMAS, JR., business executive; b. Pitts., Mar. 1, 1912; s. John Thomas and Julia (Brown) R.; m. Irene O'Brien, Aug. 1, 1939; children: John, III, Irene (Mrs. L. Edward Shaw, Jr.), Michael, Daniel, Julia (Mrs. Robert F. Parker), William. B.S., Pa. State Coll., 1934; M.B.A., Harvard U., 1936; D.Sc. (hon.), Duquesne U.; LL.D., U. Notre Dame, 1973. Engr. with Mine Safety Appliances Co., 1936-38, asst. gen. mgr., 1938-40, gen. mgr., 1940-48, exec. v.p. and dir., 1948-53, pres., dir., 1953-63, chmn., 1963—. Mem. exec. com. Allegheny Conf. Community Devel.; trustee emeritus U. Notre Dame; bd. dirs. Children's Hosp. Pitts.; trustee Thomas A. Edison Found. Mem. Am. Mining Congress (dir. mfg. div.), Council on Fgn. Relations, Am. Inst. Mining and Metall. Engrs., ASME, Phi Delta Theta, Tau Beta Pi, Pitts. Athletic Assn. Roman Catholic. Clubs: Pitts. Golf, University, Duquesne; N.Y. Yacht, Union League (N.Y.C.); Chicago; Metropolitan (Washington); Fox Chapel (Pa.); Rolling Rock (Ligonier, Pa.), Allegheny (Laurel Valley). Lodge: Knights of Malta. Home: W Woodland Rd Pittsburgh PA 15232 Office: Mine Safety Appliances Co PO Box 426 Pittsburgh PA 15230

RYAN, JOHN WILLIAM, association executive; b. Manchester, N.H., Sept. 16, 1937; s. William Charles and Mary Ann (Marcoux) R.; m. Carol Jean Battaglia, Sept. 17, 1960; children: James, Kathleen, John, Michael. A.B., St. Anselm Coll., 1959; M.A., Niagara U., 1960; Ph.D., St. John's U., 1965. Asst. prof. history Gannon U., Erie, Pa., 1965-66; edn. specialist, div. grad. programs U.S. Office Edn., Washington, 1966-68; regional coordinator, grad. acad. programs U.S. Office Edn., 1968-70; dir. univ. programs Univ. Assos., Inc., Washington, 1970-72; asst. to pres., sec. Council of Grad. Schs. in U.S., Washington, 1972-80; exec. v.p. Renewables Research Inst., Annandale, Va., 1980-81; exec. dir. Worcester (Mass.) Consortium Higher Edn., 1981—. Contbr. articles to profl. jours. Mem. Am. Assn. Higher Edn. Club: Worcester. Office: 37 Fruit St Worcester MA 01609

RYAN, JOHN WILLIAM, emeritus university president; b. Chgo., Aug. 12, 1929; s. Leonard John and Maxine (Mitchell) R.; m. D. Patricia Goodday, Mar. 20, 1949; children: Kathleen Elynne Ryan Acker, Kevin Dennis Mitchell, Kerrick Charles Casey. B.A., U. Utah, 1951; M.A., Ind. U., 1958, Ph.D., 1959; LL.D. (hon.), U. Notre Dame, 1978, Oakland City Coll., 1981, St. Joseph Coll., 1981, Hanover Coll., 1982, DePauw U., 1983, Manchester Coll., 1983, U. Evansville, 1985, Wabash Coll., 1986; D.Litt., Coll. St. Thomas, 1977. Research analyst Ky. Dept. Revenue, Frankfort, 1954-55; vis. research prof. Ind. U. project at U. Thammasat, Bangkok, Thailand, 1955-57; asst. dir. Inst. Tng. for Public Service, Ind. U., 1957-58; successively asst. prof., asso. prof. polit. sci., asso. dir. Bur. Govt., U. Wis., 1958-62; exec. asst. to pres., sec. of univ. U. Mass., Amherst, 1962-63; chancellor U. Mass., Boston, 1965-68; v.p. acad. affairs Ariz. State U., 1963-65; v.p., chancellor regional campuses Ind. U., Bloomington, 1968-71, pres., 1971-87, also prof. pub. and environ. affairs and prof. polit. sci.; bd. dirs. Ind. Bell Telephone Co., Bank One Ind. Corp., Forum Group, State Life; chmn. Nat. Adv. Bd. on Internat. Edn. Programs, 1985—. Author papers and reports in field. Bd. govs. Pub. Broadcasting Service, 1973-82; chmn. bd. dirs. Ind. U. Found., from 1972; trustee Coll. St. Thomas, from 1975; bd. visitors Air U., 1974-81; chmn. Air Force Inst. Tech Subcom., 1976-81; mem. univ. adv. com. Am. Council Life Ins.;bd. dirs. Corp. Community Council, 1976; mem. nat. adv. council Pan Am. Games, 1985; mem. adv. bd. Assocs. for Religious and Intellectual Life, from 1984; mem. United Way of Ind. Centennial Commn. Mem. Am. Soc. Public Adminstrn. (pres. Ind. chpt. 1969-70, nat. chpt. 1972-73, nat. council from 1970, Ind. Soc. Chgo. (non-resident v.p. from 1976, Am. Polit. Sci. Assn., Assn. Asian Studies, Am. Council Edn., Am. Judicature Soc., Assn. Am. Univs. (exec. com. from 1978, chmn. com. on coms. 1984, health edn. com. from 1978, chmn. 1981-82), Ind. Soc. N.Y.C., Ind. Soc. Washington, Nat. Acad. Public Adminstrn., Ind. Acad., Explorers Club, Adelphia (hon.), Phi Kappa Phi, Phi Alpha Theta, Pi Sigma Alpha, Beta Gamma Sigma, Kappa Sigma (worthy grand master 1985-87). Club: Circumnavigators, N.Y. Lodges: K.C., Rotary, Elks. Office: SPEA 316 Ind Univ Bloomington IN 47405

RYAN, LEO VINCENT, university professor; b. Waukon, Iowa, Apr. 6, 1927; s. John Joseph and Mary Irene (O'Brien) R. B.S., Marquette U., 1949; M.B.A., DePaul U., 1954; Ph.D., St. Louis U., 1958; postgrad., Catholic U. Am., 1951-52, Bradley U., 1952-54, Northwestern U., 1950; LLD, Seton Hall U., 1988. Joined Order Clerics of St. Viator, 1950; mem. faculty Marquette U., Milw., 1957-65; dir. continuing edn. summer sessions, coordinator evening divs. Marquette U., 1959-65, prof. indsl. mgmt., 1964; prof. and chmn. dept. mgmt. Loyola U., Chgo., 1965-66; adj. prof. mgmt. Loyola U., 1967-69; dep. dir. Peace Corps, Lagos, Nigeria, 1966-67; dir. Western Nigeria Peace Corps, Ibadan, 1967-68; asst. superior gen. and treas. gen. Clerics of St. Viator, Rome, 1968-69; dir. edn. Am. province Clerics of St. Viator, Arlington Heights, Ill., 1969-74; pres. St. Viator High Sch., 1972-74; dean Coll. Bus. Adminstrn. U. Notre Dame, Ind., 1975-80, Coll. Commerce, DePaul U., 1980-88; dir. Peace Corps. tng. programs Marquette U., 1962-65; adj. prof. human devel. St. Mary's Coll., Winona, Minn., 1972-74; mem. sch. bd. Archdiocese Chgo., 1972-75, vice chmn., 1973-75; mem. nat. edn. com. U.S. Cath. Conf., 1971-75, mem. exec. com., 1973-75; mem. nat. adv. bd. Benedictine Sisters of Nauvoo, 1973— ; mem. nat. adv. council SBA, 1982-85, vice chmn. minority bus., 1982-85, exec. com. Chgo. chpt., 1982-84; vis. prof. U. Ife, Ibadan, 1967-68; bd. dirs. 1st Bank-Milw., chmn. trust audit com., 1980-85, chmn. audit and trust com., 1985—; bd. dirs. 1st Bank-LaCrosse, Vilter Mfg. Co., McHugh-Freeman Assos., Filbert Corp., Vilter Sales & Service, Vilter Internat., Henricksen & Co., Inc., Gebhardt Refrigeration Co.; mem. fin. commn. Clerics of St. Viator, 1978—, mem. provincial chpt., 1985—; cons. Pontifical Commn. on Justice and Peace, 1968-70; vis. scholar Grad. Sch. of Bus. U. Calf. Berkeley. Mem. Pres.'s Com. on Employment Handicapped, 1959-65, Wis. Gov.'s Com. on Employment Handicapped, 1959-65, Wis. Gov.'s Com. on UN, 1961-64, Burnham Park Planning Commn., 1982—; bd. dirs. Ctr. Pastoral Liturgy U. Notre Dame, 1976-79; trustee St. Mary of Woods Coll., 1978-81; regent Seton Hall U., 1981-87, mem. acad. affairs com., 1981-87, chmn., 1983-87. Recipient Freedom award Berlin Commn., 1961; chieftaincy title Asoju Atoaja of Oshogbo Oba Adenle I, Yorubaland, Nigeria, 1967; Brother Leo V. Ryan award created in his honor Cath. Bus. Edn. Assn., 1962; named Man of Year Jr. C. of C. Milw., 1959, Marquette U. Bus. Adminstrn. Alumni Man of Year, 1974, Tchr. of Yr. U. Notre Dame, 1980; recipient B'nai B'rith Interfaith award Milw., 1963; Distinguished Alumnus award DePaul U., 1976; Tchr. of Yr. award Beta Alpha Psi, Notre Dame U., 1980, Scholar-in-Residience award The Mgmt. Sch., Imperial Coll. of Sci. and Tech., U. of London, 1988; Centennial Alumni Achievement award Marquette U., 1981; Milw. Bd. Realtors travelling fellow, 1964; Nat. Assn. Purchasing Agts. faculty fellow, 1958; German Am. Acad. Exchange Council fellow, summer 1983; Presidl. fellow Am. Grad. Sch. of Internat. Mgmt. Mem. Cath. Bus. Edn. Assn. (nat. pres. 1960-62, nat. exec. bd. 1960-64), Assn. Sch. Bus. Ofcls. (nat. com. chmn. 1965-67), Am. Assembly Collegiate Schs. Bus. (com. internat. affairs 1977-84, chmn. 1981-84, bd. dirs. 1981-87, program chmn. 1979-80, exec. com., chmn. projects/service mgmt. com. 1984-86), Am. Fgn. Service Assn., Acad. Internat. Bus., Acad. Mgmt., August Derleth Soc., Econ. Club Chgo., Chgo. Counvil Fgn. Relations, Council Fgn. Relations (Chgo. com.), Alpha Sigma Nu, Alpha Kappa Psi (Bronze Disting. Service award 1949, silver Disting. Service award 1958), Beta Alpha Psi, Beta Gamma Sigma (co-chair 75th Anniversary committee), Delta Mu Delta, Pi Gamma Mu, Tau Kappa Epsilon. Club: Milw. Press (hon.). Office: De Paul U Coll Commerce Mgmt Dept 25 E Jackson Blvd Chicago IL 60604-2287

RYAN, LEONARD EAMES, lawyer, public affairs consultant; b. Albion, N.Y., July 8, 1930; s. Bernard and Harriet Earle (Fitts) R.; m. Ann Allen, June 18, 1973; 1 child, Thomas Eames Allen-Ryan. Grad., Kent Sch., 1948; A.B., U. Pa., 1954; J.D., N.Y. U., 1962. Bar: D.C., N.Y. bars 1963, U.S. Ct. of Appeals, D.C 1963, U.S. Dist. Ct. for So. and Eastern Dists. of N.Y 1965, U.S. Ct. of Appeals for the Second Circuit 1966, U.S. Supreme Ct. bar 1967. Reporter Upper Darby (Pa.) News, 1954; newsman AP, Pitts., Phila., Harrisburg, N.Y.C., 1955-62; reporter, spl. writer on law N.Y. Times, 1962-63; info. adviser corp. hdqrs. IBM, N.Y.C., 1963; atty. firm Perrell, Nielsen & Stephens, N.Y.C., 1964-66; trial atty. Civil Rights Div. Dept. Justice, Washington, 1966-68; asst. to dir. bus. affairs CBS News, N.Y.C., 1968; program officer Office Govt. and Law, Ford Found., N.Y.C., 1968-74; sole practice, cons. pub. affairs N.Y.C., 1974—; v.p., sec. W.P. Carey & Co., Inc., N.Y.C., 1976-81; adminstrv. law judge N.Y. State Div. Human Rights, 1976—, N.Y. State Dept. Health, 1982—, N.Y. State Dept. Agr. and Mkts., 1987—; impartial hearing officer Office for Handicapped, N.Y.C. Bd. Edn., 1976—; hearing examiner Family Ct. of State of N.Y., N.Y. County, 1981-82; arbitrator Small Claims Ct., N.Y.C., 1974-84; bd. dirs. Community Action for Legal Services Inc., N.Y.C., 1971-77, vice-chmn., 1975-77; co-chmn. Citizens Com. to Save Legal Services, N.Y.C., 1975-76; bd. dirs. Lower East Side Service Center, N.Y.C., 1977—. Author: (with Bernard Ryan Jr.) So You Want to Go Into Journalism, 1963; contbr. articles to profl. jours. Served with USAR, 1950-57. Mem. Am. Judicature Soc., Assn. of Bar of City of N.Y., N.Y. State Bar Assn. Democrat. Clubs: St. Elmo, Phila. Office: 32 Orange St Brooklyn NY 11201

RYAN, MARLEIGH GRAYER, college dean, Japanese language educator; b. N.Y.C., May 1, 1930; d. Harry and Betty (Hurwick) Grayer; m. Edward Ryan, June 4, 1950; 1 child, David Patrick. B.A., NYU, 1951; M.A., Columbia U., 1956, Ph.D., 1965; Cert., East Asian Inst., 1956; postgrad., Kyoto U., 1958-59. Research assoc. Columbia U., N.Y.C., 1960-61, lectr. Japanese, 1961-65, asst. prof., 1965-70, assoc. prof., 1970-72; vis. asst. prof. Yale U., New Haven, 1966-67; assoc. prof. U. Iowa, Iowa City, 1972-75, prof., 1975-81, chmn. dept., 1972-81; dean liberal arts and scis., prof. Japanese SUNY-New Paltz, 1981—; vice chair seminar on modern Japan, Columbia U., 1984-85, chair, 1985-86; co-chmn. N.Y. State Conf. on Asian Studies, 1986. Co-author: (with Herschel Webb) Research in Japanese Sources, 1965; author: Japan's First Modern Novel, 1967, The Development of Realism in the Fiction of Tsubouchi Shoyo, 1975; assoc. editor: Jour. Assn. Tchrs. Japanese, 1962-71, editor, 1971-75. East Asian Inst. fellow Columbia U., 1955; Ford Found. fellow, 1958-60; Japan Found. fellow, 1973, Woodrow Wilson Ctr. Internat. Scholars fellow, 1988-89; recipient Van. Am. Disting. Book award Columbia, 1968. Mem. MLA (sec. com. on teaching

Japanese Lang. 1962-68, mem. del. assembly 1979-87, mem. exec. com. div. Asian lit. 1981-86), Assn. Tchrs. Japanese (exec. com. 1969-72, 74-77), Assn. Asian Studies (bd. dirs. 1975-78), Midwest Conf. Asian Studies (pres. 1980-81). Office: SUNY FT 614 New Paltz NY 12561

RYAN, MARY ELLEN, advertising materials distributing business official; b. Chgo., Oct. 24, 1951; d. Albert John and Helen Mary (Heinlein) Gubricky; m. Patrick M. Ryan. Cert. Arts, Richard J. Daley Jr. Coll., Chgo., 1972; B.S.Ed., No. Ill. U., 1974; M.A. in Curriculum Devel., U. Conn., 1977, postgrad., 1980-84. With Ill. Bell Telephone Co., Chgo., 1969-71; internat. acct. Mex. br. Ency. Brit. Ednl. Corp., Chgo., 1974-76; advt. cons. Buzz Barton & Assos., Inc., Chgo., 1977-78; varied advt. positions Dimensional Mktg. Inc., Chgo., 1978; tchr. Nativity of Our Lord Sch., Chgo., 1979; tchr. Mother McAuley High Sch., Chgo., 1979-82; substitute tchr. Oak Lawn and Evergreen Park, Ill., 1983-84; tchr. Montessori Elem. Sch., Blue Island, Ill., 1984; customer service rep. Martin Brower (M-B Sales), Chgo., 1985—.

RYAN, PAUL RYDER, JR., editor, writer; b. Mineola, N.Y., Jan. 5, 1932; s. Paul Ryder Ryan and Lillian (Roos) Doyle; m. Ruthann Tobin, Aug. 12, 1958; children—Liane, Bethann, Paul III, Michael. Student Boston U., 1954-55, Mex. City Coll., 1955-58; B.A., Harvard U., 1981. Editor, reporter Reuters, Eng., 1960-63, N.Y. Times, Paris and N.Y.C., 1964-68; asst. to news dir. Radio Free Europe, Munich, W.Ger., 1968-70; exec. editor Drama Rev., NYU, N.Y.C., 1970-75; editor Oceanus mag. Woods Hole Oceanographic Instn., (Mass.), 1975—. Editor: Seabirds, Sharks and Marine Animals, 1984; contbr. articles to profl. jours. and mags. Bd. dirs. Woods Hole Theater Co., 1979-83, also dir., actor, playwright; trustee Falmouth Theater Guild (Mass.), 1984. Served with USAF, 1950-54. Recipient Acad. award for Best Fgn. Film, Acad. Motion Picture Arts and Scis., 1967, 88—; Fulbright research scholar Japan, 1988. Mem. Am. Soc. Mag. Editors, Council Biology Editors, Soc. Scholarly Pub. Democrat. Roman Catholic. Clubs: Harvard; Harvard Faculty (Cambridge). Home: Box 637 10 Hinckley Rd Woods Hole MA 02543 Office: Oceanus Mag Woods Hole Oceanographic Instn Woods Hole MA 02543

RYAN, READE HAINES, JR., lawyer; b. Plainfield, N.J., Jan. 4, 1937; s. Reade Haines and Anne Mary (Moment) R.; m. Joan Louise Larson, June 16, 1966; children—Reade Haines III, Rebecca Marie. A.B., Princeton U., 1959; LL.B., Harvard U., 1965. Bar: N.Y. 1966, Calif. 1985. Assoc. firm Shearman & Sterling, N.Y.C., 1965-73; ptnr. Shearman & Sterling, 1973—; lectr. Practicing Law Inst., 1977-88, Am. Law Inst.-ABA, 1979-88. Trustee Brentwood Sch., Calif. Assn. Ind. Schs. Served to lt. USN, 1959-62. Mem. Internat. Bar Assn., ABA, Calif. State Bar, N.Y. State Bar Assn., Assn. Bar City N.Y., Los Angeles County Bar Assn., Beverly Hills Bar Assn. Republican. Club: Los Angeles Athletic. Home: 201 Homewood Rd Los Angeles CA 90049 Office: Shearman and Sterling 725 S Figueroa St Suite 2190 Los Angeles CA 90017-5430 also: Shearman & Sterling 599 Lexington Ave at 53rd St New York NY 10022

RYAN, ROBERT J., JR., diplomat; b. Washington, Aug. 11, 1939; s. Robert J. and Mary Francis (O'Leary) R.; m. Clare Pope, June 10, 1960; children—Susan Marie, Sean Patric. B.A., Johns Hopkins U., 1960; M.A., MIT, 1967. Vice-consul Am. Consulate, Ponta Delgada, Azores, Portugal, 1961-63; asst. comml. attache Am. Embassy, Rio de Janeiro, Brazil, 1964-66; econ. officer Am. Embassy, Pretoria, South Africa, 1967-69; program analyst staff Nat. Security Council, Washington, 1969-71; econ. officer Am. Embassy, Paris, France, 1971-73; counselor for econ. affairs Am. Embassy, Rabat, Morrocco, 1973-74; dir. office of monetary affairs Dept. of State, Washington, 1974-77, ambassador, coordinator Caribbean Basin Initiative, 1981-82, dep. asst. sec. for inter-Am. affairs, 1983; mem. Exec. Seminar on Nat. and Internat. Affairs, Washington, 1977-78; dep. permanent rep. U.S. Mission to OECD, Paris, 1978-81; ambassador to Mali Bamako, from 1984; now with Africa Desk, Dept. of State Washington, D.C. Recipient Meritorious Honor award Dept. of State, Washington, 1983, Presdl. Meritorious award White House, Washington, 1984, Superior Honor award Dept. State. Mem. Am. Fgn. Service Assn., Phi Beta Kappa. Club: Internat. (Washington). Office: Dept of State US Embassy to Mali Washington DC 20520 *

RYAN, SHEENA ROSS, financial planner; b. Perth, Scotland, Aug. 1, 1944; came to U.S., 1972; d. Douglas George Haig and Johanna Adams (Brown) Ross; m. Raymond John Ryan, Dec. 17, 1978 (div. Feb. 1985); 1 child, Ross McCarthy. Assoc., Inst. Bankers, Glasgow, Scotland, 1964; B. Profl. Studies, Pace U., 1985. Banker, Clydesdale Bank, Glasgow, 1962-65; acct. Newmont Pty. Ltd., Melbourne, Australia, 1965-72; acctg. mgr. Hertz Internat., N.Y.C., 1972-73; asst. controller M&M Internat., N.Y.C., 1974-76; v.p. human resource planning Marsh & McLennan, N.Y.C., 1976-80; dir. data processing, Town of Ridgefield, Conn., 1986-87, Rotondo Real Estate, Katonah, N.Y., 1981-87; dir. corp. info. systems, asst. to v.p. fin. Children's TV Workshop, N.Y.C., 1988—; v.p., trustee Hammond Mus., N. Salem, N.Y., 1988—, founder, dir. New Eng. Sch. of Needle Art, Wilton, Conn., 1985-86; dir. Rotondo Real Estate, Katonah, N.Y. Editor: Human Resource Planning newsletter, 1979. Mem. Embroiderers Guild Am., Mensa. Avocation: reading.

RYAN, WILLIAM FRANK, management consultant, insurance and risk consultant; b. Inkster, Mich., May 6, 1924; s. William Henry and Gertrude Mary (Kling) R.; m. Loke Waiau Akoni, Oct. 5, 1963; children—Ilima, Lokelani, Eugene. Student Georgetown U., 1948-49, Columbia U., 1951-52, U. Padua (Italy), 1950-51; B.A., U. Mich., 1948. Diplomatic assignments in Russia, Italy and Japan, 1949-53; investment broker N.Y.C., Detroit and Honolulu, 1953-63; mgmt. cons. Bus. Mgmt. Internat., Honolulu, 1963-68; officer, dir. numerous corps.; ins. and risk mgr. U. Mich., Ann Arbor, 1969—; mem. Nat. Univ. Property Pool Ins. Study Group, 1969-70; chmn. ins. com. Mich. Council State Coll. Pres., 1971-73; mem. Nat. Task Force on Instl. Liability, 1974-76; exec. cons. William Ryan Risk Mgmt. Assocs., 1984—; chmn. adv. com. Assoc. Degree program in health care risk mgmt. Oakland Community Coll., 1984—; pres. Veritas Ins. Corp, 1986—; pres. Risk Mgmt. Internat. Ltd., 1986—. Trustee Assn. Ind. Colls. and Univs. Mich. Workers Compensation Self-Ins. Fund. Served to lt. (j.g.) USN, 1943-46. Recipient Instl. Risk Mgr. of Yr. award Bus. Ins. mag., 1981, Disting. Service award Assn. Ind. Colls. and Univs. of Mich., 1986. Mem. Am. Soc. Hosp. Risk Mgmt. (bd. dirs. 1981-84, pres. 1983), Univ. Risk Mgmt. and Ins. Assn. (dir.), Mich. Coll. and Univ. Risk Mgmt. Officers Assn. (chmn. 1973-75), Midwest Univ. Risk and Ins. Mgmt. Assn. (chmn. 1977-78), Hist. Soc. Mich., Nat. Trust for Hist. Preservation, Irish Georgian Soc., Am. Com. for Irish Studies, Royal O'Connor Clan Assn. Democrat. Roman Catholic. Home: 801 Center Dr Ann Arbor MI 48103 Office: 400 N Ingalls Bldg Ann Arbor MI 48109

RYBERG, LENNART, manufacturing executive; b. Malmö, Sweden, Nov. 7, 1947; s. Hans and Inga (Reynold) R.; m. Carin Pihlsgard, July 8, 1982; children: Sarah, Fredrik. BA in Econs., U. Lund, 1972. Area sales mgr. Perstorp AB, Sweden, 1976-80; product mgr. Sondex AB, Malmö, 1980—; deputy mng. dir. Sundex Co., Malmö, 1986—. Home: Astrakanvaegen 2, 22356 Lund Sweden Office: Sondex AB, Limmamnsvaegen 108-110, Malmö Sweden

RYBURN, SAMUEL MCCHESNEY, business executive; b. Morristown, Tenn., Oct. 25, 1914; s. Samuel McChesney and Mary Belle (Whittaker) R.; m. Margaret Beverly Huse, June 5, 1943; children: John Huse, Marie DuPlessis. B.S., U. Ala., 1936; postgrad., U. Vienna, Austria, 1937-38; M.B.A., Boston Coll., 1962. Vice pres. Boston Capital Corp., 1960-72; v.p. Urban Nat. Corp., Boston, 1972-73, Am. Research and Devel. Co., Boston, 1973-77; pres. Textron Adv. Group Inc., Providence, 1977-80; adv. Egypt-Sudan Integration Fund, Cairo, 1985; advisor Mohammad Ali Habib Group, Karachi, Pakistan, 1986, Capital Markets Authority Govt. of Egypt, 1987, agy. for investment and free zones Govt. of Egypt, 1988. Pres. bd. trustees Charles River Sch., Dover, Mass., 1961-64; trustee Hale Reservation, Boston, 1963-69; v.p. Dover Found., 1965-67, Nat. Inst. Campus Ministries, Boston, 1980-81. Served as lt. comdr. USN, 1941-45, PTO. Recipient Gamma Sigma Epsilon award, Internat. Scholarship award. Mem. Am. Chem. Soc., Nat. Venture Capital Assn., Am. Rock Garden Soc. (chmn. New Eng. chpt.), Phi Gamma Delta. Roman Catholic. Clubs: Dedham Country and Polo, Marshall St. Hist. Home: 33 Wilsondale St Dover MA 02030

RYDBERG, ULF S., psychiatrist, educator; b. Stockholm, Sept. 9, 1940; s. Sixten G. and R. Vera (Andersson) R.; m. Inga E. Fahlstrom, Aug. 21, 1976; 1 son, U Marcus. B.Medicine, Karolinska Inst., Stockholm, 1961, M.D., 1968, Ph.D., 1972. Med. Diplomate, Sweden. Research asst. dept. alcohol research Karolinska Inst., 1960-69, vice chmn., 1969-78; fellow alcohol research Swedish Med. Research Council, 1969-72; resident Clinic Alcohol Diseases, Karolinska Hosp., Stockholm, 1972-78; head drug and alcohol dependence unit Psychiat. Clinic Huddinge U. Hosp. (Sweden), 1978-87; prof., head dept. clin. alcohol and drug addiction research Karolinska Inst., Stockholm, 1987—; med. expert Com. on Alcohol Policy, Swedish State. Dept. Treasury, 1970-74, Council of Europe, Strasbourg, 1980-81, State Commn. on Narcotics, State Dept. Social Affairs, 1982-84; mem. sci. bd. Nat. Bd. Health and Social Welfare, Stockholm, 1983—; mem. adv. panel alcohol and dependence- producing drugs WHO, 1985—. Co-editor: Alcohol and the Developing Brain, 1985. Contbr. numerous articles to profl. jours. Mem. Swedish Med. Assn., Swedish Soc. Med. Scis., Collegium Internationale Neuropsychopharmacologicum, Internat. Soc. for Biomed. Research on Alcoholism, World Psychiat. Assn. (mem. alcohol and drug sect. 1983), Nordic Council on Alcohol and Drug Research. Office: Karolinska Hosp, Dept Clin Alcohol and Drug Addiction, Box 60500, S104 01 Stockholm Sweden

RYDÉN, MATS LENNART EDVARD, researcher, educator; b. Motala, Sweden, Aug. 27, 1929; s. Sam and Elin (Mogren) R.; m. Karin Monica Elisabet Liljefelt, 1963; children: Johan, Elisabet. Fil. mag., U. Uppsala, 1954, Fil. Lic., 1962, Fil. Dr., 1966. Asst. lectr. Stockholm U., 1966-74, assoc. prof., 1974—; lectr. Linköping U., 1977; prof. Umeå U., 1986—. Humanistisk-samhällsvetenskapliga forskningsrådet grantee, 1977, 79, 83. Author: Relative Constructions in Early 16th Century English, 1966; Shakespearean Plant Names, 1978; An Introduction to the Historical Study of English Syntax, 1979; The English Plant Names in The Grete Herball (1526), 1984; (with Sverker Brorstrom): The Be/Have Variation with Intransitives Vin English, 1987; contbr. articles on English linguistics and philology to profl. jours. Office: Umeå Univ, English Dept, S901 87 Umeå Sweden

RYDER, DEAN MATTHEW, film producer, distributor, consultant; b. Amityville, N.Y., Aug. 10, 1956; s. Donald and Ellen (Wyman) R. BA with honors, U. Vt., 1977, MA, 1979. Dealer ancient, medieval and modern coins, Burlington, Vt. and Madison, Wis., 1975-84, Hollywood, Calif., 1984—; cataloger John H. Kent collection Greek, Roman, and Byzantine coins U. Vt., 1975; mgr. ancient and medieval dept. Internat. Coins and Currency, Montpelier, Vt., 1976, 77; founder Dean M. Ryder Co., 1978, pres. Dean M. Ryder Corp., Madison, 1979-84, Hollywood, 1984—; film prodn. and distbn., cons. Author: Index to the Canadian Numismatic Journal, 1967-76, 1977; The John H. Kent Collection of Greek, Roman, and Byzantine Coins, 1977; The Development of Greek Coinage, 1977; also articles. John H. Kent scholar, 1977. Royal Numis. Soc. fellow; mem. Am. Numis. Soc., Can. Numis. Assn., Soc. Ancient Numismatics, Am. Film Inst. Office: 1930 N Vermont Ave Suite 310 Hollywood CA 90027

RYDER, IAN KENNETH, computer company executive; b. Manchester, Eng., May 11, 1951; s. Kenneth and Olive (Thorley) R.; m. Christine Elizabeth Bucke, Apr. 28, 1973. Mgmt. Studies, S. Cheshire Coll., 1975. Dep. computer mgr. ICI, Alderley Edge, Cheshire, 1974-79; computer mgr. Alcan Aluminium, Banbury, Oxon, 1979-80; mktg. mgr. Nat. Computing Centre, Manchester, Eng., 1980-84; Hewlett-Packard Ltd., Berks, Eng., 1984-87; mgr. European mktg. Wyse Tech., Berks, 1987—; cons. Young Enterprise, Macclesfield, Cheshire, 1975-76. Fellow Inst. Dirs.; mem. Inst. Mktg., Inst. Data Processing Mgrs., Inst. Supervisory Mgmt. Methodist. Avocations: squash; golf; tennis. Home: 14 Manor Park Dr, Deerhurst Manor Park, Wokingham Berks England Office: Wyse Tech Ltd, 1 The Pavilions, Twyford, Berks England

RYDER, MICHAEL LAWSON, biologist, consultant; b. Leeds, Eng., July 24, 1927; s. Cecil and Alice (Lawson) R.; m. Mary Nicholson, Sept. 1952; children: Stephen, Jonathan. BSc, U. Leeds, 1951, MSc, 1954, PhD, 1956. With biology dept. Wool Industries Research Assn., Leeds, 1951-59; sr. lectr. U. New Eng., Australia, 1960-62; prin. sci. offr. Animal Breeding Research Orgn., Edinburgh, Scotland, 1962-84; prin. sci. officer Hill Farming Research Orgn., Edinburgh, 1964-87; hon. lectr. Univ. Edinburgh, 1966—; cons. in field. Co-author: Wool Growth, 1968; author: Animal Bones in Archaeology, 1969, Hair, 1973, Sheep and Man, 1983. Served as lt. Brit. Army, 1945-48. NSF grantee, 1974-75. Fellow Inst. Biology (cert., mem. Scottish com. 1980-83); mem. Soc. Authors. Home and Office: 4 Osprey Close, Southampton S01 8EX, England

RYDIN, BO GORAN, agricultural executive; b. Frinnaryd, Sweden, May 7, 1932; m. Monika Aureus; children—Goran, Johan, Helena, Kristina. BBA, 1956. With Stockholms Enskilda Bank, 1956-57; asst. to pres. Marma Långrör AB, 1957-60; pres., chief exec. officer Gullhogens Bruk, Skovde, Sweden, 1960-71, Svenska Cellulosa, Aktiebolaget, 1972-88, chmn., chief exec. officer, 1988—. Bd. dirs. Svenska Handelsbanken, Skandia Ins. co., Nobelindustrier, PWA Papierwerke Waldhof Aschaffenburg, IBM World Trade Corp., Skandia Ins. Co., Svensk Intercontinental Lufttrafik AB, AB Aerotransport,; vice chmn. Volvo, Euroc, Svenska Handelsbanken; chmn. Transatlantic, Swedish Employer's Confedn. Industrivarden. Recipient King's Medal, 12th Dimension, of Order of Seraphim. Mem. Royal Swedish Acad. Engring. Scis., Royal Swedish Acad. Agriculture and Forestry, Internat. C. of C., Royal Swedish Opera (chmn.). Lodge: Rotary. Avocation: golf, hunting. Home: Allegatan 2, Sundsvall Sweden Office: Svenska Cellulosa AB, S-85188 Sundsvall Sweden

RYDNING, ANTIN FOUGNER, translator, educator; b. Oslo, Aug. 29, 1949; s. Nicolay A. and Colette (Mary) Fougner; m. Pal Rydning; children: Céline, Palnic, Christian. Masters degree, U. Paris Sorbonne, 1972, diploma in translating, 1973, translatology degree, 1982, interpretation degree, 1984. Tchr. Malselv High Sch., Norway, 1974; pub. relations cons. Nissen-Lie Cons., Oslo, 1975-76; lectr. Agder Regional Coll., Kristiansand, Norway, 1977-82, 1987—; lectr. Ecole Superieure d'Interprètes et de Traducteurs, Paris, 1983; researcher Norwegian Council Sci. Research, U. Oslo, 1984-87; free-lance translator, interpreter, Norway and France, 1974-87. Mem. Norwegian Translator's Guild (pres. 1983-85). Home: Setravei 4b, 0390 Oslo 3 Norway Office: U Oslo, Blindern, 1067 Oslo 3 Norway

RYERSON, W. NEWTON, association executive; b. N.Y.C., Sept. 29, 1902; s. William Newton and Martha (Taft) R.; m. Jean Hamilton, May 15, 1936 (dec. Sept. 1973); children: Timothy (dec.), Amy Ryerson Borer, Marjorie, William N.; m. Henriette Keil, July 13, 1974. BS in Engring., Yale U., 1925. Cadet engr. to personnel supr. Phila. Gas Works Co., 1927-44; various positions with Sun Oil Co., Phila., 1944-67; dir. placement Vt. Tech. Coll., Randolph Center, Vt., 1967-82; exec. dir. Randolph C. of C., 1983—; bd. mem. Green Mountain Econ. Devel. Corp., Am. Heart Assn. White River Valley unit; vis. instr. Pa. State U., University Park, 1962-68. Vice pres. Swarthmore Sch. Bd. (Pa.), 1956-62; chmn. troop Boy Scouts Am., Swarthmore, 1952-55; mem. Republican Com., Swarthmore, 1951-55; jr. warden Trinity Ch. Vestry, Swarthmore, 1953-56. Recipient Disting. Service award Vt. Tech. Coll., 1982. Mem. Vt. Assn. Chamber Execs., Vt. Soc. Career Counselors, Vt. Soc. Assn. Execs., Tau Alpha Pi. Episcopalian. Club: Phila. Foremen's, Appalachian Mountain. Home: Randolph Center VT 05061 Office: Randolph C of C PO Box 9 Randolph VT 05060

RYMER, S. BRADFORD, JR., retired appliance manufacturing company executive; b. Cleveland, Tenn., May 30, 1915; s. S. Bradford and Clara Ladosky (Gee) R.; m. Anne Roddye Caudle, Nov. 7, 1942; children: Anita Elise, S. Bradford III. Grad., Fishburne Mil. Sch., 1933; BS in Indsl. Mgmt, Ga. Inst. Tech., 1937; D of Bus. Adminstration (hon.), Wesleyan Coll. Indsl. engr. Dixie Foundry Co., Inc., Cleveland, Tenn., 1937-40, sec.-treas., dir. prodn., 1940-50, pres., 1950-87; pres., chmn. Dixie Foundry Co., Inc., Cleveland, 1972-87; chmn. Magic Chef, Inc. div. Maytag Corp., Cleveland, 1986-87, ret., 1987; past chmn. Dixie-Narco, Inc., Ranson, W. Va.; dir. Munford Co.; former dir. Provident Life and Accident Ins. Co., Citizens & So. Nat. Bank, Atlanta. Past pres. Cleveland Asso. Industries; past trustee Tenn. Wesleyan Coll.; past bd. dirs. Bradley County Meml. Hosp.; trustee Fishburne Mil. Sch., Hiwassee Coll. Civilian flight instr. World War II; former trustee Ga. Tech. Found.; former nat. dir. Jr. Achievement; former dir. Allied Arts of Chattanooga. Mem. Am. Gas Assn. (past exec. com., dir.), NAM (past dir.); Chief Execs. Orgn. (pres. 1971, dir.), Gas Appliance Mfrs. Assn. (pres. 1965), Young Pres. Orgn. (past dir., area v.p., chmn. Rebel chpt.), Ga. Tech. Nat. Alumni Assn. (past trustee), Phi Gamma Delta. Methodist (chmn. bd. trustees). Home: 1790 Ocoee St NE Cleveland TN 37311 also: 1326 Lake Worth Ln Lost Tree Village North Palm Beach FL 33408

RYNDERS, LEO JULIAN, real estate appraiser; b. Ft. Smith, Ark., Mar. 18, 1912; s. Wesley N. and Ella (Brownfield) R.; B.A., B.J., U. Mo., 1934; m. Kathryn Elizabeth Schwartz, Aug. 19, 1939; children—Ray David, Ronald Edward, Carol Ann. With Rynders & Rynders, Ft. Smith, 1934-37; partner Ark. Democrat, Little Rock, 1937; dist. mgr. subscription sales Curtis Pub. Co., Phila., 1937-38; with Am. News Co., Dallas, St. Louis and Abilene, Tex., 1938-41, div. mgr. W. Tex. and Eastern N.Mex., 1941-55; salesman Henley Realty Co., 1955-59; sales mgr., appraiser Dick Lawrence Assos., Realtors and Appraisers, 1959-77; owner Leo J. Rynders, Sr. Residential Appraiser, Abilene, Tex., 1977—; chmn. multiple listing service Abilene Bd. Realtors, 1969, 75. Active Boy Scouts Am. Mem. Soc. Real Estate Appraisers (contbr. article to assn. jour.), Abilene Bd. Realtors, Tex. Assn. Realtors (lt. gov. 1961-62, vice chmn. bd. govs. 1962), Nat. Assn. Realtors (Grad. Realtors Inst. designation), Tex. Profl. Photographers Assn., Photog. Soc. Am. (contbr. articles to jour.), Kappa Tau Alpha, Sigma Delta Chi, Delta Tau Delta. Republican. Methodist. Club: Kiwanis (pres. Key City 1975-76). Exhibited photographs at Abilene Fine Arts Mus., La. Fine Arts Mus., Amy Graves Ryan Fine Arts Mus., Abilene. Home and Office: 2042 Sayles Blvd Abilene TX 79605

RYNN, MIDORI YAMANOUCHI, sociology and anthropology educator, management consultant; b. Osaka, City, Japan, Jan. 8, 1928; came to U.S., 1956, naturalized, 1961; d. Shin'ichi and Fumiko (Urai) Yamanouchi; B.A., Sophia U., Tokyo, 1956; M.A.L.S., U. Mich., 1959; M.A., Mich. State U., 1958, Ph.D., 1973; m. Edward J. Rynn, Sept. 10, 1975. Librarian, bibliographer Mich. State U. Libraries, East Lansing, 1959-67; asst. prof. sociology Marshall U., Huntington, W.Va., 1967-70; asst. prof. sociology and anthropology Fisk U., Nashville, 1970-72; asso. prof. Livingstone Coll. and Katawba Coll., Salisbury, N.C., 1972-74; vis. prof. sociology and anthropology Frostburg State Coll., 1974-75; assoc. prof. sociology and anthropology U. Scranton (Pa.), 1975—. Nat. Endowment for Humanities grantee, summer 1980. Mem. Assn. for Gen. and Liberal Studies (exec. council 1975-78), Am. Mktg. Assn., Assn. Japanese Bus. Studies, Am. Sociol. Assn., North Cen. Sociol. Assn., Pa. Sociol. Soc. (Disting. Sociologist award 1987), Am. Anthropol. Assn., Soc. Psychol. Study of Social Issues, Soc. Study of Social Problems, Assn. for Asian Studies, Am. Future Soc., AAUW, Internat. Soc. Comparative Study of Civilizations, Alpha Tau Kappa, Pi Gamma Mu. Republican. Zen Buddhist. Contbr. articles to profl. jours. Home: RD 1 Box 531 Lake Ariel PA 18436 Office: Univ of Scranton St Thomas Hall Scranton PA 18510

RYPKA, EUGENE WESTON, microbiologist; b. Owatonna, Minn., May 6, 1925; s. Charles Frederick and Ethel Marie (Ellerman) R.; m. Rosemary Speeker, June 1, 1967; 1 child, Barbara. Student, Carleton Coll., 1946-47; BA, Stanford U., 1950, PhD, 1958. Prof. microbiology, systems, cybernetics U. N.Mex., Albuquerque, 1957-62; bacteriologist Leonard Wood Meml. Lab. Johns Hopkins U., Balt., 1962-63; sr. scientist Lovelace Med. Ctr., Albuquerque, 1963-71, chief microbiologist, 1971—; adj. prof. U. N.Mex., 1973—; cons. Hoffmann-LaRoche Inc., Nutley, N.J., 1974—, Airline Pilots Assn., Washington, 1976, Pasco Lab., Denver, 1983—; advisor Nat. Com. Clinic Lab. Standards, Pa., 1980-84. Contbr. articles to profl. jours. Served with USNR, USMC 1943-46. Fellow AAAS; mem. IEEE, Internat. Soc. Gen. Systems Research. Republican. Presbyterian. Home: PO Box 8345 Albuquerque NM 87198

RYSANEK, LEONIE, soprano; b. Vienna, Austria, Nov. 14, 1926; d. Peter and Josefine (Hoeberth) R.; m. Ernst-Ludwig Gausmann, Dec. 23, 1968. Student, Vienna Conservatory, 1947-49. First singing engagements include, Bayreuth, (Sieglinde-Die Walkure), 1951, San Francisco Opera, (Senta-Der Fliegende Hollaender), 1956, Metropolitan Opera, (Lady Macbeth), 1959; now appears in world's foremost opera houses, N.Y.C., Vienna, Milano, San Francisco, London, Paris, (Chrysothemis-Elektra, 1973, Berlin, (Gioconda, 1974, Munich, Hamburg, Budapest, Moscow, (Parsifal, 1975; and festivals of, Salzburg, (Kaiserin-Die Frau Ohne Schatten, 1974, Bayreuth, Orange, (Salome, 1974, Sieglinde-Die Walkuere, 1975, Aix en Provence, Athens, (Medea, 1973, Edinburgh, recordings, RCA Victor, Deutsche Grammophon, London Records, EMI and Philips, Kundry, Parsifal (Stuttgart 1978), Kammersangerin of Austria and Bavaria, Kostelkidca, Australian Opera, 1985, Vienna, 1986, San Francisco, 1986, N.Y. Carnegie Hall, 1988. Recipient Chappel Gold medal of singing London; Silver Rose Vienna Philharmonic; Austrian Gold Cross 1st class for arts and scis.; San Francisco medal. Hon. mem. Vienna Staatsoper. Office: care Herbert H Breslin Inc 119 W 57th St New York NY 10019

RYSKAMP, CARROLL JOSEPH, chemical engineer; b. Grand Rapids, Mich., Dec. 25, 1930; s. Henry C. and Edna E. (Robinson) R.; m. Joanne Ruth Winter, Nov. 17, 1951; children: Jan C., John M., Julie K., Jay A. BS in Chem. Engring., Wayne State U., 1953. Registered profl. control systems engr. Chem. engr. Reichhold Chem. Co., Ferndale, Mich., 1953-55; process supv. and specialist Marathon Oil Co., Detroit, 1955-65; process control coordinator Marathon Oil Co., Findlay, Ohio, 1965-70; control cons. Foxboro (Mass.) Co., 1970-85; owner Process Performance Co., Foxboro, 1986. Contbr. articles to profl. jours.; patentee in field. Bristol fellow, The Foxboro Co., 1985. Sr. mem. Instrument Soc. Am. (Philip T. Sprague award, 1981). Republican. Home and Office: Process Performance Co 48 Prospect St Foxboro MA 02035

RYSZKA, FRANCISZEK, history and political science educator; b. Kniaziowka, Sokolka, Poland, Aug. 4, 1924; s. Jozef and Anna (Wankowicz) R.; m. Romana Mroczkowska, Aug. 1, 1949 (div. 1964); children: Anna Cybulski, Lydia Scannell; m. Elzbieta Grabczak, June 16, 1964; 1 child, Dominika Ryszka-Pasek. MA, U. Wroclaw, Poland, 1950, PhD in Law, 1951. Asst. prof. dept. law U. Wroclaw, 1950-53; asst. prof. Inst. History, Polish Acad. Scis., Warsaw, 1953-63, prof., 1963-85; prof. Inst. Polit. Sci., U. Warsaw, 1986—; vis. prof. U. Hamburg, Fed. Republic Germany, 1973, Ecole des Hautes Etudes en Sci. Sociales, Paris, 1980-81, U. Saarbrücken, Fed. Republic Germany, 1984; chmn. longterm research U. Warsaw, 1983—; part-time prof. Warsaw Theatre and Drama Acad., 1982—. Author: Night and Fog: Germany in the Hitler's Time, 1962, Literature under the Pressure of History, 1967, Politics and War, 1975, Reflection on Literature, 1978, Nuremberg, 1982, Political Science, 1984, The Martial Law State: on the State and Legal System of the Third Reich, 1985, 3rd rev. ed.; co-author Between Utopia and Despair: on Marshall McLuhan and Herbert Marcuse, 1970, History of Political and Legal Doctrines, 1983 ; editor (book) Polska Ludowa, 1974. Sci./academic adviser Glowna Komisja Badania Zbrodni Hitlerowskich, Warsaw, 1965—. Served as sgt. inf. Polish Army, 1944-46. Decorated Mil. Cross, Polonia Resituta Cross. Mem. Polskie Towarzystwo Nauk Politycznych (v.p. 1965-66), Komitet Polskiej Akademii Nauk (v.p. 1983-85). Roman Catholic. Home: Zwciezcow 4m 84, 03-941 Warsaw Poland Office: U Warsaw Inst Nauk Politycznych, Krakowskie Przedmiescie 3, 00-047 Warsaw Poland

RYTTERBORG, ULF, editor, publishing executive; b. Karlskrona, Sweden, Mar. 29, 1942; s. Sven and Siri (Hultberg) R.; m. Suzanne Beskow; 1 son, Jacob. Student schs., Sweden. Polit. columnist Kvällsposten, Malmö, Sweden, 1965-68, dep. polit. editor, 1968-78, editor-in-chief, 1978-85, pub., 1983-85; v.p., mem. bd. Sydsvenska Dagbladets Inc. and Kvällspostens Inc., 1978-85; pres., chmn. bd. Tricordia Inc., 1985—; v.p., chmn. bd. Marknad-sByrå Inc., 1986—. Counsellor City of Malmö, 1967-71, Wasa Ins., 1984. Clubs: Press of South Sweden (pres. 1977-83), Royal Swedish Automobile. Lodge: Rotary. Home: Rudbecksgatan 47, S216 22 Malmö Sweden Office: Box 22103, S200 63 Malmö Sweden

RYU, JAI HYUN, scientist, educator; b. Ham-nam, Korea, Oct. 27, 1940; s. Chang Yul and Byung Sun (Park) R.; came to U.S., 1960, naturalized, 1973; B.S.E. in Aerospace Engring., U. Mich., 1966, M.S.E. in Bio-Mech. Engring., 1972; Ph.D. in Bio-Systems Engring., U. Iowa, 1979; m. Jacqueline Ellen Brisbin, June 16, 1973; children—Juliette Jaie, Jessica Jaie, Jennifer Jaie.

Research asst. dept. otorhinolaryngology U. Mich., 1961-66; asso. research scientist dept. otolaryngology U. Iowa, 1966-74, research scientist, 1974-80, dir. vestibular research labs., 1974-80, assoc. prof., dir. research, 1980-84, prof. surgery (otolaryngology); dir. research Bowman Gray Sch. Medicine, Wake Forest U., 1984—. Mem. Barany Soc., AIAA, Aerospace Med. Assn., Soc. Neurosci., Bioengring. Soc., Am. Acad. Otolaryngology, N.Y. Acad. Sci., Centurion Deafness Research Found., Korean Otolaryngology Soc., Am. Neurotology Soc., Assn. for Research in Otolaryngology, Sigma Xi. Author: The Vestibular System, 1975; Vestibular Physiology in Understanding the Dizzy Patient, 1980; contbr. articles to profl. jours. Home: 1007 Kendale Dr Winston-Salem NC 27104 Office: Bowman Sch Med, Wake Forest U Dept Surgery, Sect Otolaryngology 300 S Hawthorne Rd Winston-Salem NC 27103

RYUYTEL, ARNOLD FEDOROVICH, Soviet state official; b. 1928, Island of Saaremaa. Grad. Esthonian Acad. Agrarian Scis., agronomist, cand. Agrarian Scis. Agronomist agrl. sect. Kuressaarsk, served in navy, tchr. Sch. for Mechanization of Agr. in Tartu, 1949-57; chief tech. zoologist RTjachtvere research sta.; dep. dir. Esthonian Sci. Research Inst. of Animal Husbandry and Vet. Sci., 1957-63; rector Esthonian Acad. Agrarian Scis., 1969-77; cand. mem. 1966-71, mem. Central Com. Esthonian Communist Party, 1971—; mem. Bur. Central Com., 1977—; 1st dep. chmn. Council of Ministers Esthonian SSR, 1979-83; dep. chmn. USSR Supreme Soviet Presidium, 1983—. Address: Office of Deputy Chmn, USSR Supreme Soviet, Moscow USSR *

RYZHKOV, NIKOLAI IVANOVICH, chairman Council of Ministers of Soviet Union; b. Sept. 28, 1929. Grad. Uralsk Polytechnik Inst., Sverdlovsk, 1959. Mem. Communist Party of Soviet Union, 1956—; chief engr. Uralmash Plant, 1951-70, dir. 1970-71, gen. dir. Uralmash Prodn. Assn., 1971-75; dep. to USSR Supreme Soviet, 1974—; 1st dep. Ministry of Heavy and Transport Machine Building, 1975-79, 1st dep. chmn. GOSMOPLAN, 1979-82, mem. Cen. Com., 1981—, sec. Cen. Com., 1982-85, full mem. Politburo, 1985—, chmn. Council of Ministers, 1985—. Address: Chmn Council of Ministers, The Kremlin, Moscow USSR *

RZEPA, TERESA KURYLCZYK, psychology educator; b. Kalisz Pomorski, Poland, Feb. 3, 1952; d. Hieronim Kurylczyk and Helena (Bielska) K. Pulwin; m. Krzysztof Rzepa, Mar. 3, 1974; children: Tymoteusz, Lukasz. Grad. with distinction, U. Poznań, Poland, 1974; D Humanities Scis., U. Poznań, 1979. Asst. U. Poznań, 1974-79; asst. prof. Inst. Psychology, U. Poznań, 1979—; cons. Acad. Cath. Theology, Warsaw, Poland, 1984-85. Author: Orientation in Measure of Objects, Features and Events, 1986, The Relations Between Linguistic and Individual Experience, 1988; co-author: Psychology of Work, 1979 (Rector award 1980); contbr. articles to profl. jours. Exec. NSZZ "Solidarność", Inst. Psychology, U. Poznań, 1980, editor info. service, 1981. Recipient sci. research awards Rector U. Poznań, 1984, 86, 87. Mem. Polish Psychol. Assn., Polish Semiotics Assn. Roman Catholic. Home: Szamotulska 38a, 60366 Poznan Poland Office: U Poznan Inst Psychology, Szamarzewskiego 89, 60586 Poznan Poland

SAAD, EDSON ABDALLA, cardiologist, educator; b. Igarapava, São Paulo, Brazil, July 12, 1935; s. Calim Abdalla and Evelina (Fayad) S.; m. Monica Benchimol, July 21, 1962; children: Marcelo, Sergio, Eduardo. MD, Fed. U. Rio de Janeiro, 1959. Intern Nat. Med. Faculty Hosp. Moncorvo Filho, Rio de Janeiro, 1959; resident, chair for tropical and infectious diseases Hosp. São Francisco de Assis, Rio de Janeiro, 1960-62; instr. in medicine nat. med. faculty Fed. U. Rio de Janeiro, 1960-62, asst. prof. nat. med. faculty, 1963-69, assoc. prof. nat. med. faculty, 1969-78, prof. cardiologynat. med. faculty, 1978—, 1979—, chief medicine, 1979-85; prof. cardiology Fed. Fluminense U., Rio de Janeiro, 1972-87; adviser Fundaç'28o Zerbini U. São Paulo Heart Inst., 1986—; cgmn. bd. dirs. SAB Trading, Rio de Janeiro. Recipient Gerhardt Dogmak medal Bayer, 1964. Fellow Am. Coll. Cardiology, N.Y. Acad. Scis.; mem. Brazilian Soc. Cardiology (treas. 1970-78), Soc. Cardiology Rio de Janeiro (dir. edn. 1984-87). Club: Iate (Rio de Janeiro). Home: Rua Bernardino dos Santos 2, Rio de Janeiro 20241, Brazil Office: U Hosp Fed U, Ave Brigadeiro, Trompowski s/nq, Rio de Janeiro 20241, Brazil

SAADE, NICOLAS ANTONIO, JR., finance company executive, consultant; b. Barranquilla, Colombia, Jan. 11, 1950; s. Nicolas Toufic and Alexandra (Haraoui) S.; m. Roula Marie Saade, June 5, 1976; children: Nicholas III, Sandra. Honours BA in Econs. with distinction, McMaster U., Hamilton, Ont., Can., 1973; MBA, U. Pa., 1975. Trainee Toronto-Dominion Bank, Ont., 1975-76, chief credit analyst, 1977; rep. Toronto (Ont.) Dominion Bank, 1978-79, mgr., 1979, mktg. rep., 1980; dep. gen. mgr. Banque Banafrique, Abidjan, Ivory Coast, 1980-85; regional mgr. Banque du Liban et d'Outre-Mer, Dubai, Sharjah, United Arab Emirates and Oman, 1985-87; chief exec., fin. cons. Legal Services, Dubai, 1987—; educator econs. Wharton Community Ednl. Program, U. Pa., Phila., 1974-75; fin. cons. Tescon, Sharjah, 1987—, Al-Sultan, Abu Dhabi, United Arab Emirates, 1987—. Contbr. articles to Euromoney mag. and other Middle Ea. periodicals. Chmn. Wharton Alumni Interviewing, Toronto, 1976-80. Mem. Investment Internat. Club. Club: Wharton Alumni of Mid. East (pres. 1975) (Beirut, Lebanon). Office: Legal Services, PO Box 3376, Dubai United Arab Emirates

SAARI, BRUCE BERNARD, industrial psychologist; b. Mpls., Aug. 25, 1950; s. Bernard Waldemar and Patricia Ann (Tweed) S.; m. Cynthia Jo Petersen, Aug. 16, 1969; 1 child, Trevor Jon. BA, U. Minn., 1972; MA, Mich. State U., 1975, PhD, 1976. Staff psychologist LWFW Inc., Houston and Dallas, 1976-80; dir. human resources Computer Lang. Research Co., Dallas, 1980-81, Pepsi-Cola Co., Purchase, N.Y., 1981-86; v.p. personnel resources Pepsi-Cola Co., Somers, N.Y., 1987; v.p. employee relations Pepsi-Cola Co., Dallas, 1988—; adj. prof North Tex. State U., 1981. Contbr. articles to profl. jours. Mem. Am. Psychol. Assn., Phi Beta Kappa. Home: 4625 Conner Circle Plano TX 75093 Office: Pepsi Cola Co South 12750 Merit Dr Dallas TX 76000

SAASK, AAPO, research company executive; b. Tartu Estonia, Mar. 22, 1943; came to Sweden, 1944; s. Alexander and Asta (Kallas) S.; m. Helny Cecilia Sundin, July 15, 1966; children: Fredrik, Markus. BA, Brown U., 1964; postgrad. Rutgers U., 1964-65; M in Polit. Sci. and Philosophy, U. Stockholm, 1968; MSc.in Edn., U. Linkoping (Sweden), 1970; MBA, U. Stockholm, 1973. Ptnr., Scarab Devel. Group, Stockholm, 1973-77; mng. dir. AB Scarab Devel., Stockholm, 1977-83, 83—; chmn. Scarab Energy AB, Taby, Sweden, 1983—; pres. Internat. Coconut Devel. Assn., Stockholm, 1979-86. Author: Integrated Processing of Coconuts, 1981; pub. Coconut Industries Quarterly, 1978-82; contbr. articles on coconuts, desalination to profl. jours. Mem. Internat. Desalination Assn. (Topsfield, Mass.), Coconut Industries Consultancy Service (London), Mem. European Desalination Assn. (Glasgow). Office: Scarab, Gardesvagen 11, 18330 Taby Sweden

SAATCHI, CHARLES, communications and marketing company executive; b. June 9, 1943; m. Doris Lockart, 1973. Student, Christ's Coll., Finchley. Assoc. dir. Collett Dickenson Pearce, 1966-68; dir. Cramer Saatchi, 1968-70, Saatchi & Saatchi, 1970—. Office: Saatchi & Saatchi Co, 15 Lower Regent St, London SW1Y 4LR, England

SAATCHI, MAURICE, communications and marketing company executive; b. June 21, 1946; s. Nathan and Daisy Saatchi; m. Josephine Hart, 1984; 1 son, 1 stepson. BS in Econs., London Sch. Econs. and Polit. Sci. Co-founder Saatchi & Saatchi Co., 1970, chmn., 1984—. Office: 80 Charlotte St, London W1A 1AQ, England also: Saatchi & Saatchi Co, 15 Lower Regent St, London SW1Y 4LR, England

SABA, SHOICHI, manufacturing company executive; b. Tokyo, Feb. 28, 1919; s. Wataru and Sumie (Uemura) S.; m. Fujiko Saito, 1945; children: Hiroko, Kazuhisa, Shunji. Grad. Imperial U., Tokyo, 1941. With Toshiba Corp., Tokyo, 1942-87, mng. dir., 1972-74, exec. v.p., 1974-76, sr. exec. v.p., 1976-80, pres., chief exec. officer, 1980-86, chmn., exec. officer, 1986-87, adviser to bd., 1987—; dir. numerous cos.; vice chmn. Keidanren (Japan Fedn. Econ. Orgns.); non exec. dir. Imperial Chem. Industries PLC, England. Recipient Progress prize Japan Inst. Electric and Electronics Engrs., 1958; Blue Ribbon medal Govt. of Japan, 1980; Commander's Cross of Order of Merit F.R. Germany, 1988. Mem. Electronic Industries Assn. of Japan (chmn. 1986—, adviser 1987—), Japan Electronics Industry Promotion Assn. (dir., vice chmn. 1980—), Japan Inst. Indsl. Engring. (chmn. 1982—). Office: Toshiba Corp, 1-1 Shibaura 1-chome, Minato-ku, Tokyo 105, Japan

SABATH, KENNETH MICHAEL, lawyer; b. Newark, Sept. 12, 1956; s. Vincent Frank and Nellie (Barauskis) S.; m. Lanko Shoji, Mar. 21, 1985. BA, Bates Coll., 1977; JD, Suffolk U., 1980. Bar: Hawaii 1980, U.S. Dist Ct. Hawaii 1980, U.S. Ct. Appeals (9th cir.) 1980, U.S. Ct. Mil. Appeals 1984. Sole practice Honolulu, 1984—; cons. Honolulu Legal Secretaries Assn., 1986—; ct. observer Ambassador Mike Mansfield, Am. embassy, Tokyo, 1982-84. Mem. U.S. Armed Services Com., Honolulu, 1986—. Served to lt. (judge adv.) USN, 1980-84. Recipient certs. appreciation ARC, U.S. Navy Family Advocacy, 1982-84. Mem. Internat. Legal Soc., ABA (certs. of appreciation 1986, 87), Assn. Trial Lawyers Am., Judge Advs. Assn., Hawaii State Bar Assn., Hawaii C. of C., Soc. Chinese Profls., Pacific and Asian Affairs Council, Japan-Am. Soc. of Honolulu, Honolulu Acad. Arts, Japanese Culture Study, Semantics. Republican. Roman Catholic. Home: 2452 Tusitala St #806 Honolulu HI 96815 Office: 1188 Bishop St #3210 Honolulu HI 96813

SABATIER, ROBERT, writer; b. Paris, Aug. 17, 1923; s. Pierre and Marie (Exbrayat) S.; m. Christiane Lesparre, 1957. Books include: Alain et le negre, 1953, Le marchand de sable, 1954, Le gout de la cendre, 1955, Les fêtes solaires, 1955, Boulevard, 1956, Canard au sang, 1958, Saint Vincent de Paul, 1959, Dédicace d'un naviere, 1959, La Sainte-Farce, 1960, La mort du figuier, 1962, Dessin sur un trottoir, 1964, Les poisons delectables (poems), 1965, Le Chinois d'Afrique, 1966, Dictionnaire de la mort, 1967, Les chateaux de millions d'annees (poems), 1969, Les allumettes suedoises, 1969, Trois sucettes a la menthe, 1972, Noisettes sauvages, 1974, Histoire de la poésie francaise des origines a nos jours, 1975, Icare et autres poemes, 1976, Les enfants de l'été, 1978, Les fillettes chantantes, 1980, L'oiseau de demain, 1981; Les années secrètes de la vie d'un homme, 1984; David et Olivier, 1986; lecture, producer jour, 1987. La Cassette; press positions French U., 1951-64; lit. dir. editions Albin Michel, 1965-72. Recipient Grand Prix de Poesie de l'Academie francaise, 1969; Antonin-Artaud prize; Prix Apollinaire for poems Les fetes solaires; decorated officier de la Legion d'honneur, commandeur de l'ordre national du Merite. Address: 64 blvd Exelmans, 75016 Paris France

SABATO, ERNESTO, author; b. Rojas, Argentina, June 24, 1911; s. Francisco and Juana (Ferrari) S.; Ph.D. in Physics, U. La Plata, 1937; postgrad, (scholar) Curie Labs., Paris, 1938, M.I.T., 1939; m. Matilde Kusminsky-Richter, May 24, 1936; children—Jorge, Mario. Lectr. univs. in France, U.S., Spain, Italy, W. Ger., Can. and Poland; author: Uno y el Universo, 1945; (novel) El Tunel, 1948; Hombres y Engranajes, 1951; Heterodoxia, 1953; (novel) Sobre Heroes y Tumbas, 1961; El Escritor y sus Fantasmas, 1963; Tres Aproximaciones a la Literature da Nuestro Tiempoa, 1969; (novel) Abaddon el Exterminador, 1974; El Angel de las Tinieblas, 1976. Decorated chevalier Ordre des Arts et des Lettres (France); recipient Ribbon of Honour, Argentine Soc. Letters; prize Inst. Fgn. Relations, Stuttgart, W. Ger.; grand prize Argentine Writers Soc.; Prix au meilleur Livre Etranger, Paris, 1976, commendation of civil merit Italy, 1982, commendation of arts and letters, France, 1983, Gabriela Mistral prize, 1984, Miguel de Cervantes prize Spain, 1984; decorated chevalier Legion of Honor (France); Grand Cross (Spain); ofcl. Grand Order of Merit (Italy). Mem. Com. pour l'Univ. de l'Unesco, Jerusalem Com., Club Rome. Address: Severino Langeri 3135, Santos Lugares, 1676 Buenos Aires Argentina *

SABATTANI, AURELIO CARDINAL, church administrator; b. Casal Fiumanese, Italy, Oct. 18, 1912. Ordained priest Roman Catholic Ch., 1935. Various assignments, Imola, Italy; judge ofcl. ecclesiastical tribunal, Bologna, Italy; prelate auditor Roman Rota, 1955; ordained titular archbishop of Justinian Prima, 1965; prelate of Loreto, 1965-71; sec. Supreme Tribunal of Apostolic Signatura, 1971, pro-prefect, 1982-83, prefect, 1983; consultor Secretariat of State, 1971; elevated to Sacred Coll. of Cardinals, 1983; archpriest St. Peter's Basilica, Vatican, 1983; deacon St. Apollinaris. Mem. Council for Pub. Affairs of Ch., Congregation Bishops. Address: Vatican City Vatican

SABAU, CARMEN SYBILE, chemist; b. Cluj, Romania, Apr. 24, 1933; naturalized U.S. citizen; d. George and Antoinette Marie (Chiriac) Grigorescu; m. Mircea Nicolae Sabau, July 11, 1956; 1 dau., Isabelle Carmen. M.S. in Inorganic and Analytical Chemistry, U. C.I. Parhon, Bucharest, Romania, 1955; Ph.D. in Radiochemistry, U. Fridericiana, Karlsruhe, W.Ger., 1972. Chemist, Argonne (Ill.) Nat. Lab., 1976—. Internat. Atomic Energy Agy. fellow, 1967-68; Humboldt fellow, 1970-72. Mem. Am. Chem. Soc., Am. Nuclear Soc., Am. Romanian Acad. Arts and Sci., Assn. for Women in Sci., N.Y. Acad. Sci., Sigma Xi. Author: Ion-exchange Theory and Applications in Analytical Chemistry, 1967; contbr. articles to profl. jours. Home: 6902 Martin Dr Woodridge IL 60517 Office: Argonne Nat Lab 9700 S Cass Ave Bldg 205 Argonne IL 60439

SABBAGHA, RUDY E., obstetrician, gynecologist, educator; b. Tel Aviv, Oct. 29, 1931; s. Elias C. and Sonia B. S.; m. Asma E. Sahyouny, Oct. 5, 1957; children: Elias, Randa. BA, MD, Am. U., Beirut. Sr. physician Tapline, Saudi Arabia, 1958-64, ob-gyn specialist, 1969-70; teaching fellow U. Pitts., 1965-68; asst. prof. ob-gyn, 1970-75; prof. Northwestern U., Chgo., 1975—; obstetrician, gynecologist Prentice Women's Hosp., Chgo. Author: Ultrasound-High Risk Obstetrics, 1979; editor: Ultrasound Applied to Obstetrics and Gynecology, 1980, 2d edit., 1987; contbr. articles to profl. jours. Fellow Am. Coll. Obstetricians and Gynecologists; mem. Soc. Gynecologic Investigation, Central Assn. Obstetricians and Gynecologists, Assn. Profs. Ob-Gyn, Am. Inst. Ultrasound in Medicine. Research on diagnostic ultrasound, obstetrics and gynecology. Home: 2415 Meadow Dr Wilmette IL 60091 Office: Prentice Women's Hosp Chicago IL 60611

SABBAR, ABDALLA MOHAMMED, engineering company executive, architect, planner; b. Wadi Halfa, Sudan, May 6, 1939; s. Mohammed Abdel Halim Sabbar and Nazla Abdel Ghafour Abdu. B.Sc. in Architecture, U. Khartoum, Sudan, 1964, MArch; A.A.Dip., Archtl. Assn., London, 1966, A.A.Dip. in Planning, 1971; diploma (fellow) MIT, 1973. Head dept. architecture Khartoum Poly., 1964-65; urban planner Greater London Council, 1967-68; sr. planner Colin Buchanan & Ptnrs., London and Kuwait, 1969-71; sr. planning adviser Planning Bd. Kuwait Govt., 1971-72; dri., sr. planner, ptnr. Tech. Studies Bur., Kuwait, 1974—, cons. Saudi Arabia, Iraq and Oman, 1974—. Editor: Hawally Dist. Master Plan, Kuwait, 1982; Khaitan/Farwaniya Study, 3 vols., 1985. Editor: Salmiya Dist., Kuwait, 1977. Ford Found. fellow, 1972; recipient Archtl. Design award Arab Authority Agrl. Investment and Devel., 1982, Sheikh Mustafa Amin, 1985, Design award Faisal Islamic Bank New Comml Ctr., Khartoum. Fellow Sudanese Inst. Architects; mem. Sudan Engrs. Union, Engring. Council Sudan, Soc. Engrs. Kuwait, Iraq Engrs. Union. Avocation: photography. Office: Tech Studies Bur, (TEST) Kuwait, PO Box 2399, Safat 13024, Kuwait Other: Tech Studies Bur (TEST), Sudan PO Box 2849, Khartoum Sudan

SABEL, ROBERT WALTER, security company executive; b. Chgo., Oct. 22, 1920; s. Walter Reuben and Ella Elizabeth (Andersson) S.; student Coe Coll., 1939-40, U. Md., 1948-49, El Camino Coll., 1980; m. Faith Carol Hammarlund, Dec. 9, 1950; children—Karen L., Ingrid M., James R., John G., Paul F., Kristin E. Mgr. nuclear research and devel. Cook Electric Co., Chgo., 1952-55; mem. tech. staff Ramo-Wooldridge Corp., Los Angeles, 1955-57; western regional mgr. Control Data Corp., Los Angeles, 1957-62; v.p. Electro Vision Industries, Los Angeles, 1962-65; owner Sabel Assos., Los Angeles, 1965-79; pres., dir. Zenith Internat. Protection, Inc., Redondo Beach, Calif., 1979—; lectr. Internat. Police Acad., 1969-72, U. So. Calif. Pres., chmn. Liaison League Rehab. Group, Inc. Served to lt. col. USAF, 1941-50. Decorated D.F.C. with 1 oak leaf cluster, Air medal with 3 oak leaf clusters; Croix de Guerre with Palm (France). Mem. Internat. Assn. Identification, Calif. Peace Officers Assn., Internat. Acad. Criminology, Calif. Assn. Lic. Investigators, Res. Officers Assn. U.S., Am. Law Enforcement Officers & Assn., VFW. Republican. Baptist. Clubs: Army-Navy (Washington); Elks, Masons. Home: 341 Paseo de Gracia Redondo Beach CA 90277

SABHARWAL, RANJIT SINGH, mathematician; b. Dhudial, India, Dec. 11, 1925; came to U.S., 1958, naturalized, 1981; s. Krishan Ch and Devti (An) S.; m. Pritam Kaur Chadha, Mar. 5, 1948; children—Rajinderpal, Amarjit, Jasbir. B.A. with honors, Punjab U., 1944, M.A., 1948; M.A. U. Calif, Berkeley, 1962; Ph.D., Wash. State U., 1966. Lectr. math. Khalsa Coll., Bombay, India, 1951-58; teaching asst. U. Calif., Berkeley, 1958-62; instr. math. Portland (Oreg.) State U., 1962-62, Wash. State U., 1963-66; asst. prof. Kans. State U., 1966-68; mem. faculty Calif. State Hayward, 1968—, prof. math., 1974—. Author papers on non-Desarguesian planes. Mem. Am. Math. Soc., Math. Assn. Am., Sigma Xi. Address: 27892 Adobe Ct Hayward CA 94542

SABIN, ALBERT BRUCE, physician, scientist, emeritus educator; b. Bialystok, Poland, Aug. 26, 1906; s. Jacob and Tillie (Krugman) S.; m. Heloisa Dunshee de Abranches, July 28, 1972; children: Deborah, Amy. B.Sc., M.D., NYU, 1931; recipient 31 hon. degress from U.S. and fgn. univs. Research assoc. NYU Coll. Medicine, 1926-31; house physician Bellevue Hosp., N.Y.C., 1932-33; NRC fellow Lister Inst., London, 1934; mem. sci. staff Rockefeller Inst. for Med. Research, N.Y.C., 1935-39; asso. prof. pediatrics U. Cin. Coll. Medicine and Children's Hosp. Research Found., 1939-43, prof. research pediatrics, 1946-60, Disting. Service prof., 1960-71, Emeritus Disting. Service prof., 1971—; pres. Weizmann Inst. of Sci., Rehovot, Israel, 1970-72; bd. govs. Weizmann Inst. of Sci., 1965—; cons. U.S. Army, 1941-62; mem. Armed Forces Epidemiological Bd., 1963-69; cons. NIH, USPHS, 1947-73; mem. Nat. Adv. Council Nat. Inst. Allergy and Infectious Diseases, 1965-70; Fogarty scholar Fogarty Internat. Center for Advanced Study in Health Scis., NIH, 1973; mem. adv. com. on med. research Pan Am. Health Orgn., 1973-76; expert cons. Nat. Cancer Inst., 1974; mem. U.S. Army Med. Research and Devel. Adv. Panel, 1974-79; cons. Surgeon Gen., U.S. Army, 1974—; Disting. Research prof. of biomedicine Med. U. S.C., Charleston, 1974-82, emeritus, 1982—; sr. expert cons. Fogarty Internat. Ctr., NIH, 1984-86; cons. to asst. sec. for health HEW, 1975-77. Author over 300 papers in field. Bd. govs. Hebrew U. Jerusalem, 1965—; trustee N.Y. U., 1966-70. Served to lt. col. U.S. Army, 1943-46. Decorated Legion of Merit.; Recipient Antonio Feltrinelli prize in med. and surg. sci. Accademia Nazionale dei Lincei, Rome, 1964; Albert Lasker clin. medicine research award, 1965; gold medal Royal Soc. Health, London, 1969; U.S. Nat. Medal of Sci., 1971; Disting. Civilian Service medal U.S. Army, 1973; Presdl. Medal of Freedom, 1986, Medal of Liberty, 1986, Order of Friendhsip Among Peoples, USSR, 1986; many other awards. Mem. Nat. Acad. Scis., Am. Acad. Arts and Scis., Assn. Am. Physicians, Am. Pediatric Soc., Infectious Diseases Soc. Am. (pres. 1969), numerous other U.S. and hon. fgn. memberships. Home: Sutton Towers Apt 1001 3101 New Mexico Ave NW Washington DC 20016 Office: NIH Bldg 38A Room B2N13 Bethesda MD 20892 *

SABIN, GARY BYRON, financial company executive, investment advisor; b. Provo, Utah, Apr. 7, 1954; s. Marvin Elmer and Sylvia (Wall) S.; m. Valerie Purdy, Aug. 18, 1976; children: Kimberly, Justin, Spencer, Jennifer. AA in Lang., Brigham Young U., 1976, BS in Fin., 1977; CFP, Coll. Fin. Planning, 1981; postgrad. (Sloan fellow) Stanford U. Grad. Sch. Bus., 1984-85. Regional gen. mgr. Investors/N.Am. Mgmt., Orem, Utah, 1975-77; pres., chief exec. officer Excel Interfin. Corp., San Diego, 1977—; chmn. Warner Beck, Inc., San Diego, 1983—; gen. ptnr. various cos., San Diego, 1979—. Recipient Outstanding Young Man of Am. award U.S. Jaycees, 1983. Mem. Inst. Cert. Fin. Planners, Nat. Assn. Securities Dealers (registered prin. 1982—), Young Pres.'s Orgn. Republican. Mormon. Home: 16289 Oak Creek Trail Poway CA 92064 Office: Excel Interfin Corp 15010 Ave of Science Suite 100 San Diego CA 92128

SABIN, JACK CHARLES, engineering and construction firm executive; b. Phoenix, June 29, 1921; s. Jack Byron and Rena (Lewis) S.; B.S., U. Ariz., 1943; B.Chem.Engring., U. Minn., 1947; m. Frances Jane McIntyre, Mar. 27, 1950; children—Karen Lee, Robert William, Dorothy Ann, Tracy Ellen. With Standard Oil Co. of Calif., 1947-66, sr. engr., 1966—; pres., dir. Indsl. Control & Engring., Inc., Redondo Beach, Calif., 1966—; owner/mgr. Jack C. Sabin, Engr.-Contractor, Redondo Beach, 1968—; staff engr. Pacific Molasses Co., San Francisco, 1975-77; project mgr. E & L Assos., Long Beach, Calif., 1977-79; dir. Alaska Pacific Petroleum, Inc., 1968—, Marlex Petroleum, Inc., 1970, 71—. Served with U.S. Army, 1942-46; capt. Chem. Corps, Res., 1949-56. Registered profl. engr., Calif., Alaska; lic. gen. engring. contractor, Ariz., Calif. Mem. Nat. Soc. Profl. Engrs., Ind. Liquid Terminals Assn., Conservative Caucus, Calif. Tax Reduction Com., Tau Beta Pi, Phi Lambda Upsilon, Phi Sigma Kappa. Republican. Clubs: Elks; Town Hall of Calif. Address: 151 Camino de las Colinas Redondo Beach CA 90277

SABISTON, DAVID COSTON, JR., educator, surgeon; b. Onslow County, N.C., Oct. 4, 1924; s. David Coston and Marie (Jackson) S.; m. Agnes Foy Barden, Sept. 24, 1955; children: Anne Sabiston Leggett, Agnes Sabiston Butler, Sarah Coston. BS, U. N.C., 1943; MD, Johns Hopkins U., 1947. Diplomate: Am. Bd. Surgery (chmn. 1971-72). Successively intern, asst. resident, chief resident surgery Johns Hopkins Hosp., 1947-53; successively asst. prof., assoc. prof., prof. surgery Johns Hopkins Med. Sch., 1955-64, Howard Hughes investigator, 1955-61; Fulbright research scholar U. Oxford, Eng., 1960; research assoc. Hosp. Sick Children, U. London, Eng., 1961; James B. Duke prof. surgery, chmn. dept. Duke Med. Sch., 1964—; Hunterian lectr.; chmn. Accreditation Council for Grad. Med. Edn., 1985-86. Editor: Textbook of Surgery, Essentials of Surgery; co-editor: Gibbon's Surgery of the Chest; chmn. editorial bd.: Annals of Surgery; mem. editorial bd.: Jour. Thoracic and Cardiovascular Surgery, Circulation, Annals Clin. Research, ISI Atlas of Surgery: The Classics of Surgery Library, Surgery, Gynecology and Obstetrics, Jour. Applied Cardiology, Jour. Cardiac Surgery, World Jour. Surgery. Mem. State of N.C. Awards com. Served to capt., M.C. AUS, 1953-55. Recipient Career Research award NIH, 1962-64; N.C. award in Sci., 1978; Disting. Achievement award Am. Heart Assn. Sci. Council, 1983; named Significant Sigma Chi awardee, 1987; College medalist Am. Coll. Chest Physicians, 1987. Mem. ACS (chmn. bd. govs. 1974-75, regent 1975-86, chmn. bd. regents 1982-84, pres. 1985-86), Am. Surg. Assn. (pres. 1977-78), So. Surg. Assn. (sec. 1969-73, pres. 1973-74), Am. Assn. Thoracic Surgery (pres. 1984-85), Soc. Clin. Surgery, Internat. Soc. Cardiovascular Surgery, Soc. Vascular Surgery (v.p. 1967-68), Soc. Univ. Surgeons (pres. 1968-69), Halsted Soc., Surg. Biology Club II, Soc. Thoracic Surgery, Soc. Surgery Alimentary Tract, Johns Hopkins U. Soc. Scholars, Soc. Surg. Chairmen (pres. 1974-76), Soc. Thoracic Surgeons Great Britain and Ireland, Royal Coll. Surgeons Edinburgh (hon.), Royal Coll. Surgeons Eng. (hon.), Asociació n de Cirugí a del Litoral (Argentina) (hon.), Royal Coll. Physicians and Surgeons Can. (hon.), Royal Coll. Surgeons Ireland (hon.), Royal Australasian Coll. Surgeons (hon.), German Surgical Soc. (hon.), Colombian Surg. Soc. (hon.), Brazilian Coll. Surgeons (hon.), Japanese Coll. Surgeons (hon.), Phi Beta Kappa, Alpha Omega Alpha. Clubs: Cosmos (Washington). Home: 1528 Pinecrest Rd Durham NC 27705

SACASAS, RENE, lawyer; b. N.Y.C., July 10, 1947; s. Anselmo and Orlanda (Soto) S.; m. Cathy Lee Van Natta, Jan. 24, 1970. BA, Am. U., 1969; JD, Emory U., 1975. Bar: Fla. 1976, U.S. Dist. Ct. (so. dist.) Fla. 1976, U.S. Ct. Appeals (5th cir.) 1976, U.S. Supreme Ct. 1980, U.S. Ct. Appeals (11th cir.) 1983. Law clk. McLarty and Aiken, Atlanta, 1974-76; assoc. Welbaum, Zook, Jones, Williams, Miami, Fla., 1976-79; ptnr. Darrach, Merkin and Sacasas, Miami, 1979-83, Merkin & Sacasas, Miami, 1984-86; of counsel Welbaum, Zook & Jones, Miami, 1986—; asst. prof. bus. law U. Miami, 1985—. Mem. ABA, Fla. Bar Assn. (vice chmn. grievance com. 1981-84), Dade County Bar Assn., Latin Am. C. of C., U.S. Jaycees, Cuban Am. Bar Assn., Phi Sigma Kappa (ET chpt. pres. 1968). Contbr. articles profl. jours. Home: 3790 Kent Ct Miami FL 33133 Office: Welbaum Zook & Jones 2701 S Bayshore Dr Penthouse Suite Miami FL 33133

SACCI MORSIANI, GIANGUIDO, lawyer, professor, financial executive; b. Scandiano, Reggio Emilia, Italy, Oct. 8, 1934; m. Maria Ghetti; two children. JD. Pres. Cassa di Risparmio, Bologna, Italy, 1980—; bd. dirs. Immobiliare Nettuno, Produttori Sementi S.p.A., Magazzini Centrali Italiani, Assn. of EEC Savings Banks, ABI (Italian Banking Assn.), GERIT S.p.A., Finemiro S.p.A., Eptaconsors S.p.A., Società Eptafund p.A., Meliorconsorzio (exec. com.), SIL-Società Italiana Leasing S.p.A., ISEA (Inst. Econ. Devel.

North and Cen. Appennines); pres. Siomatica S.p.A., Fed. of Savings Banks and Banche del Monte della Emilia Romagna, Prolingest, ICCRI (Cen. Inst. of Italian Savings Banks), 1986—; v.p. ANERT (Nat. Assn. Collectors of Direct Taxes and Treas. of Local Bodies); mem. commn. for internal relations, ACRI (Assn. Italian Savings Bansks). Recipient Umberto Borsi award for best mongraph on adminstrv. law, 1969-70. Mem. Guglielmo Marconi Found. and Univ. Interprovincial Consortium of Bologna (bd. dirs.), UCID (v.p.), Nat. Acad. Agr. (corr.), Historic and Artistic Bologna (hon.). Home: Via Loderingo degli Andalo 9, 40124 Bologna Italy Office: Cassa di Risparmio in Bologna, Via Farini 22, 40124 Bologna Italy

SACDALAN, FELIPE JORDAN, film director, equipment rental company executive; b. Bulacan, Phillipines, Apr. 30, 1916; s. Jacinto Aguilar and Antonina (Jordan) S.; m. Felicitation Nicolas Mendoza, 1935; children: Flordeliza, Benjamin. Grad. high sch., Bulacan, 1934. Still-man then asst. cameraman Fillipine Films Inc., Manila, 1939-42; cameraman Royal Prodns., Inc., Quezon City, Phillipines, 1943-50; dir. photography Premier Prodns., Inc., Caloocan City, Phillipines, 1951-54, Lynn-Romero Prodns., Inc., N.Y.C., 1955, Harry Smith Prodns., Hollywood, Calif., 1956, New World Prodns., Inc., Los Angeles, 1956; propr. F.J. Sacdalan Movie Camera Rental and Service, Quezon City, 1970—; movie cons. Nat. Media Prodns., Manila, 1980, Film Acad. Phillipines, Manila, 1980-85; lectr. Dirs. Guild, Quezon City, 1980—. Recipient 5 cinematography awards Filipino Acad. Movie Arts & Sci., 1954-80, named to Hall of Fame, 1983; recipient Best Cinematography award Manila Film Festival, 1960. Mem. Filipino Soc. Cinematographers (pres. 1969-80, 82-83, lectr. 1980—, Pioneer Achievement award 1987, Lifetime Achievement award for Cinematography, 1988), Am. Film Inst. Liberal. Adventist. Home and Office: 57 Tolentino St SFDM, 1104 Quezon City Philippines

SACERDOTI, GIORGIO G., lawyer, educator; b. Nice, France, Mar. 2, 1943; s. Piero and Ilse (Klein) S.; m. Liliana D. Konigsman, June 26, 1982; 1 child, Margherita. JD, U. Milan, 1965; M in Civil Law, Columbia U., N.Y.C., 1967. Bar: Milan, 1969. Asst. prof. internat. trade law Bari U., Italy, 1971-76; prof. internat. orgn. Urbino U., Italy, 1976-77; prof. internat. law Bergamo U., Italy, 1977—, Bocconi U., Milan, 1985—; ptnr. F. Formiggini Pasotelli, Milan, 1969-81; sole practice Milan, 1982—. Author: State Contracts in International Law, 1972, (with others) International Economic Law, 1982. Pres. Jewish Community, Milan, 1982—; bd. dirs. Union of Italian Jewish Communities, Rome, 1976—; vis. assoc. Cleary, Gottlieb, Steen & Hamilton, N.Y.C., 1967-68. Served to lt. Alpine Troops, 1965-66. Mem. Milan Bar Assn., Am. Soc. Internat. Law, Internat. Law Assn., Columbia Law Sch. Alumni Assn. Lodge: Rotary. Office: Via Visconti Di Modrone 32, 20122 Milan Italy

SACERDOTTI COEN, GIANNI, advertising executive; b. Florence, Italy, Jan. 7, 1943. Student, Bocconi, Milan, 1971. Area mgr. Italian State Steel Co., Milan, 1971-74; cons. J.R. Cegos Consulting Co., Milan, 1974-78; advt. mgr. Edisport Pub. House, Milan, 1978-83; gen. mgr. GSE S.P.A. Advt. Co., Milan, 1984—. Author: Sailing, 1981; contbr. articles to profl. jours. Office: GSE SPA, 7 Via Trentacoste, 20123 Milan Italy

SACHAU, WILLIAM HENRY, diversified energy co. ofcl.; b. Ridgewood, N.Y., Feb. 6, 1924; s. Hans Richard Koenig and Christiana H. (Betke) S.; B.S. in Bus. Adminstrn., Duquesne U., 1950; M.B.A., U. Denver, 1953; m. Dorothy Jean Fjone, Nov. 1, 1952; children—Christy Jean. Susan Melinda, William Eric. X-ray technician Presbyn. Hosps. Med. Center. N.Y.C. and Pitts., 1946-50; staff mem. Ralph B. Mayo & Co., C.P.A.s, Denver. 1951-54; auditor Ford Motor Co., Dearborn, Mich., 1954-59; auditor Collins Radio Co., Dallas, 1959-60, supr. ops. control, 1960-62, mgr. auditing and procedures. 1962-71, mgr. acctg. and consolidations, 1971-74; mgr. auditing Cities Service Co., Tulsa, 1974-82 ; audit chmn. Syncrude Ltd., 1980—; corp. mgr. internal audit Occidental Petroleum, 1983-85, mgr. audit coordination, ops. and systems analyst 1985—; instr. So. Methodist U.; lectr., mem. adv. bd. North Tex. U. Mem. Dallas United Fund, 1968-72; active Boy Scouts Am.; judge, timer Pard Swim Team, Richardson, Tex., 1966-73. Bd. dirs. Richardson Credit Union, 1971-76, Karios Counseling Ctr., Tulsa. Served with Armored Div., AUS, 1943-45, ETO; 1951-52, Korea; capt. Res. ret. Decorated Bronze Star, Commendation medal, Purple Heart; named Outstanding Mem., Inst. Internal Auditors of Dallas, 1964-65; cert. internal auditor. Mem. Inst. Internal Auditors (internat. dir. 1966-67, regional dir. 1967-70, research com. mem. 1970-80, 82-87, internat. sec. 1980-81), Am. Acctg. Assn., Nat. Assn. Accts., Am. Assn. Cost Engrs., Am. Inst. C.P.A.s (com. on internal acctg. control). Republican. Lutheran (council 1955-68, 75-79). Contbr. articles to profl. jours. Home: 4123 E 85th St Tulsa OK 74137 Office: PO Box 300 Tulsa OK 74101

SACHS, EKKEHARD WOLFGANG, mathematics educator; b. Frankfurt, Fed Republic Germany, June 19, 1950; s. Hermann and Helene (Stallgies) S.; m. Maria Luise Gorgasser, Apr. 30, 1977; children: Sandra, Stephen. Diploma in Math., Techn. Hochschule, Aachen, Fed. Republic Germany, 1973; PhD, Techn. Hochschule, Darmstadt, Fed. Republic Germany, 1975, Habilitation, 1980. Asst. Techn. Hochschule, Darmstadt, Fed. Republic Germany, 1976-78; asst. prof. math. Techn. Hochschule, Berlin, 1978-81; asst. prof. N.C. State U., Raleigh, 1982-85, assoc. prof., 1985-86; prof. U. Trier, Fed. Republic Germany, 1986—. co-author: Algorithmic Methods in Optimal Control, 1981. Mem. Soc. for Indsl. and Applied Math. (edit. bd. Soc. Indsl. Applied Math. Rev.1985—), Gesellschaft für Angewandte Mathematik und Mechanik. Home: Januarius-Zick-Str 77, 5500 Trier Federal Republic of Germany Office: Universität Trier, FBIV-Mathematik Postfach 3825, 5500 Trier Federal Republic of Germany

SACHS, IRVING JOSEPH, lawyer, accountant, pension consultant; b. Chgo., Sept. 12, 1922; s. Philip and Ida (Camras) S.; m. Bettie Taub, June 8, 1947 (dec. Jan. 1964); children—Richard, Melissa, Ilene, Philip; m. 2d Francine Lee Rodbard, Aug. 15, 1965; children—Marc, Jan, Wayne, Jason. B.S. in Acctg., DePaul U., 1948, J.D., 1951. Bar: Ill. 1951; C.P.A., Ill. Sr. ptnr. Sachs, Shapiro & Silver, Chgo. and Skokie, Ill., 1954-65, Sachs, Rosenberg & Kosin, Chgo., 1954-62; sole practice, Chgo. and Highland Park, Ill., 1962-76; pres. Nat. Pension Consultants, Inc., Chgo., 1978-79, Alliance Pension Consultants, Inc., Skokie, 1979—. Served with Signal Corps, U.S. Army, 1943-46, ETO, PTO. Jewish. Office: Alliance Pension Cons Inc 9933 Lawler Ave Suite 505 Skokie IL 60077

SACHSSE, ULRICH, psychoanalyst, psychiatrist; b. Beuel, Fed. Republic Germany, Apr. 15, 1949; s. Heinz and Anna (Hooge) S.; m. Margit Ilona Gatke, Dec. 21, 1973; children—Tilmann, Miriam. Med. Examination, U. Goettingen, 1974, med. approbation, 1976, Dr. Med., 1980; postgrad. Inst. Psychoanalysis (Goettingen), 1984. Physician, head physician Clinic for Psychogenic and Psychosomatic Disorders, Tiefenbrunn, Lower Saxony, 1976-82; physician Psychiat. State Hosp., Goettingen, 1982-85, Neurol. Clinic Schildautal, Seesen, 1985, head physician Psychiat. State Hosp., Goettingen, 1986—; lectr. Inst. Psychoanalysis, Goettingen, 1985—. Author: Group Psychotherapy with Guided Affective Imagery; contbr. articles to profl. jours. Mem. German Psychoanalytic Assn., Internat. Soc. Guided Affective and Mental Imagery Techniques (sec. 1980—), Mensa Internat. Lutheran. Avocations: classical music; mystery stories. Home: An den Teichen 2A, D3405 Rosdorf Federal Republic of Germany Office: Psychiatric State Hosp, Rosdorfer Weg 70, D3400 Goettingen, Lower Saxony Federal Republic of Germany

SACINO, SHERRY WHEATLEY, public relations executive; b. Wilmington, Del., July 14, 1959; d. Lawrence McClusky and Carolyn Aria (Alexander) W.; m. Ronald Anthony Sacino, Dec. 29, 1984. BA, Ariz. State U., 1980. Pub. relations exec. Phoenix Pro Soccer, 1980-81; owner, pres. Wheatley Advt. and Pub. Relations, Phoenix, 1981-83; owner, pres. Sherry Wheatley Sacino, Inc., 1983—; dir. news Kzzz/KAAA radio, Kingman, Ariz., 1976-77; promotional dir. KUPD/KUKQ radio, Phoenix, 1979-80; acct. supr. Wood, Cohen, Leonard & Bush Advt. and Pub. Relations, Tampa, Fla., 1983-84; mem. exec. com. Super Task Force, Tampa; founder, exec. dir. Tampa Bay Council for Internat. Visitors, Inc., 1984-87; exec. dir. Internat. Culinary Festival, Tampa, 1984; owner Ariz. Coaching Acad., Phoenix, 1981-83; pub. relations dir. Richard Simmons Concert, Phoenix, 1982, Phoenix Clean Community System, 1982-83, Larry's Ice Cream Exchange, USSR, 1987; nat. spokesperson McDonald's Restaurant, 1977. Creator Ruby Slippers Kit, 1983. Vol. pub. relations coordinator Muscular Dystrophy Assn., Ariz. and Fla., 1974-84, Arthritis Assn., Ariz. and Fla., 1980-84; dir. pub. relations Dan Fogelbert Concert for Ariz. Gov. Babbitt, Phoenix, 1982; mem. Ariz. Gov.'s Council on Health and Fitness, 1983; mem. Global Family Citizens Moscow Summit, 1988, Handshake Exchange Moscow Summit, 1988; bd. dirs. Pinellas County March of Dimes; mem. Tampa Bay Internat. Trade Council. Recipient award Phoenix Clean Community System, 1982. Mem. Phoenix AD2 Club (v.p. 1983), Sigma Delta Chi (sec. 1978-80). Republican. Roman Catholic. Avocations: developing cultural awareness, aviation. Home: 2507 Pass-A-Grille Way Pass-A-Grille Beach FL 33706 Office: 214 First Ave N Saint Petersburg FL 33701

SACK, MERLIN FRANK, polygraphist; b. Lincoln, Nebr., Oct. 7, 1934; s. Merlin M. and H. Leone (Mooberry) S.; student Doane Coll., Crete, Nebr., 1953-57; A.S., Mohawk Valley Community Coll., Utica, N.Y., 1974; grad. with high honors Nat. Tng. Ctr. of Polygraph Sci., N.Y.C., 1975; B. Profl. Studies, Loyola U., 1978, M.S. in Psychology, 1979, Ph.D. in Behavioral Sci., 1980; M in Polygraph Nat. Tng. Ctr., 1987; m. Mary Ann Salvatore, Dec. 31, 1970; children—Lynne Anne, John Martin, Rebecca Anne. Established Am. Polygraph Centers, 1976, exec. dir., 1978-84; guest lectr. Mohawk Valley Community Coll., 1975—, SUNY, Utica, 1979, Mohawk Valley Police Acad., 1987—; instr. N.Y. State Dept. Mental Health. Marshal, City of Utica, 1970—; bd. dirs. Jewish Community Council, Utica, 1977-78. Cert. polygraphist. Mem. Acad. Cert. Polygraphists (exec. sec. 1978, dir. media relations 1983-88, legis. com. 1988—), Am. Assn. Police Polygraphists (charter), Am. Polygraph Assn., Internat. Assn. Identification, N.Y. State Polygraphists, Inc. (bd. dirs. 1977—, treas. 1987—). Jewish. Lodges: KP, B'nai B'rith. Pub. Am. Personnel Profiles Am. Personnel Rev.; editor Tracings, 1981-83. Office: 240 Genessee St Utica NY 13502

SACKLOW, HARRIETTE LYNN, advertising agency executive; b. Bklyn., Apr. 12, 1944; d. Sidney and Mildred (Myers) Cooperman; m. Stewart Irwin, July 2, 1967; 1 son, Ian Marc. BA, SUNY-Albany, 1965, postgrad., 1967-69; postgrad. Union Coll., 1969-70, Telmar Media Sch., N.Y.C., 1981. Tchr. math. Guilderland Cen. Schs. (N.Y.), 1967-76; v.p. Wolkcas Advt., Inc., Albany, N.Y., 1975—; supr. internship programs Coll. St. Rose, Albany, N.Y., 1981; lectr. to area colls., Albany, 1981-83. Vice pres. Sisterhood Congregation Ohav Sholom, Albany, 1983-84; mem. bd. Congregation Ohav Sholom, Albany, 1983—, bd. dirs. northeastern N.Y. chpt. Arthritis Found.; advisor Ronald McDonald House. Mem. Nat. Assn. Female Execs., Am. Women in Radio and TV (pres. 1982-84, chmn. task force for new mem. acquisition, v.p. Northeast area 1987—, chmn. area conf. 1987, pres. 1982-84, speaker, dist. dir.). Club: Advt. of the Capital Dist., Albany (N.Y.) Yacht. Office: Wolkcas Advt Inc 435 New Karner Rd Albany NY 12205

SACKTON, FRANK JOSEPH, university official, lecturer, retired army officer; b. Chgo., Aug. 11, 1912; m. June Dorothy Raymond, Sept. 21, 1940. Student, Northwestern U., 1936, Yale, 1946, U. Md., 1951-52; B.S., U. Md., 1970; grad., Army Inf. Sch., 1941, Command and Gen. Staff Coll., 1942, Armed Forces Staff Coll., 1949, Nat. War Coll., 1954; M.Pub. Adminstrn., Ariz. State U., 1976. Mem. 131st Inf. Regt., Ill. N.G., 1929-40; commd. 2d lt. U.S. Army, 1934, advanced through grades to lt. gen., 1967; brigade plans and ops. officer (33d Inf. Div.), 1941, PTO, 1943-45; div. signal officer 1942-43, div. intelligence officer, 1944, div. plans and ops. officer, 1945; sec. to gen. staff for Gen. MacArthur Tokyo, 1947-48; bn. comdr. 30th Inf. Regt., 1949-50; mem. spl. staff Dept. Army, 1951; plans and ops. officer Joint Task Force 132, PTO, 1952; comdr. Joint Task Force 7, Marshall Islands, 1953; mem. gen. staff Dept. Army, 1954-55; with Office Sec. Def., 1956; comdr. 18th Inf. Regt., 1957-58; chief staff 1st Inf. Div., 1959; chief army Mil. Mission to Turkey, 1960-62; comdr. XIV Army Corps, 1963; dep. dir. plans Joint Chiefs Staff, 1964-66; army general staff mil. ops. 1966-67, comptroller of the army, 1967-70, ret., 1970; spl. asst. for fed./state relations Gov. Ariz., 1971-75; chmn. Ariz. Programming and Coordinating Com. for Fed. Programs, 1971-75; lectr. Am. Grad. Sch. Internat. Mgmt., 1973-77; vis. asst. prof., lectr. public affairs Ariz. State U., Tempe, 1976-78; dean Ariz. State U. Coll. Public Programs, 1979-80; prof. public affairs Ariz. State U., 1980—, v.p. bus. affairs, 1981-83, dep. dir. intercollegiate athletics, 1984-85. Contbr. articles to public affairs and mil. jours. Mem. Ariz. Steering Com. for Restoration of the State Capitol, 1974-75, Ariz. State Personnel Bd., 1978-83, Ariz. Regulatory Council, 1981—. Decorated D.S.M., Silver Star, also Legion of Merit with 4 oak leaf clusters, Bronze Star with 2 oak leaf clusters, Air medal, Army Commendation medal with 1 oak leaf cluster, Combat Inf. badge. Mem. Ariz. Acad. Public Adminstrn., Pi Alpha Alpha (pres. chpt. 1976-82). Clubs: Army-Navy (Washington); Arizona (Phoenix). Home: 7814 E Northland Dr Scottsdale AZ 85251 Office: College Public Programs Ariz State U Tempe AZ 85287

SACRE, ROBERT ANTOINE, surgeon, oncologist; b. Antwerp, Belgium, Apr. 4, 1944; s. Arthur and Maria (Stuyts) S.; m. Liliane Smits, Sept. 12, 1970; children—Ariane, Corinne. M.D., Vrije Universiteit Brussel, 1970. Tng. surgeon Bordet Inst., Brussels, 1970-73, St. Pieters Hosp., Brussels, 1973-79; head clinic Acad. Hosp. V.U.B., Brussels, 1979—; oncologic and head and neck surgery Oncologic Ctr. AC. Hosp. V.U.B., Brussels, 1979—. Author: (with others) Leerboek Chirurgie, 1983; Gynecologie-Obstetrie, 1984. Contbr. articles to profl. jours. Mem. European Orgn. Research on Treatment Cancer, European Soc. Surgical Oncology, Belgium Med. Soc. Avocations: skiing; travel. Home: Ch Plisnierlaan 23, B1070 Brussels Belgium Office: Acad Hosp VUB, Laarbeeklaan 101, B1090 Brussels Belgium

SADDAM HUSSEIN See HUSSEIN, SADDAM

SADDLER, GEORGE FLOYD, economic adviser; b. Memphis, Sept. 27, 1925; s. Henry Rutherford and Ludorn Myrtle (Woods) S.; m. Pauline Evelyn McKissack, Jan. 3, 1944; children—Paula Frederica, Paulette Yvonne. B.S., NYU, 1950; postgrad. Northwestern U., Chgo., 1954, U. Chgo., 1961-62. Supr. acctg. dept. Aldens, Inc., Chgo., 1950-57; sr. acct. City of Chgo., 1957-65; internat. adminstrn. officer U.S. Dept. State, Washington, 1965-68; chief budget sect. UN, N.Y.C., 1968-74; dir. fin. UN Devel. Program, N.Y.C., 1974-78; minister-counselor U.S. Mission to UN, N.Y.C., 1978-81; asst. dir. gen. UNESCO, Paris, 1981-86; sr. econ. adviser U.S. Mission to UN, N.Y.C., 1986—. Served as cpl. U.S. Army, 1944-46. Club: NYU (N.Y.C.). Office: US Mission to UN 799 UN Plaza New York NY 10017

SADÉE, CONSTANT FRANÇOIS, engineering company executive, consultant; b. Rotterdam, Netherlands, Apr. 9, 1920; s. Karel Louis Marie Hubert and Johanna Alexandrina Lambert; m. Jeanne Ferdinande Ghislaine deMassart, Aug. 8, 1953; children—Dominique, Marie-Madeleine. Student Aviation-Automobile Engring. Coll., Eng., 1937-39. Dep. mgr. Schelling's Oliehandel N.V., Schiedam and Gulf Oil, Rotterdam, Netherlands, 1945-53; dep. mgr. Ingenieurs-bureau Fulgor NV, Bilthoven, Netherlands, 1953-54, mgr. Son and Eindhoven, Netherlands, 1954-56, gen. mgr., v.p., 1956-61, pres., owner, 1962—; cons. Officer Resistance Movement, Holland, World War II. Served with Dutch Army, 1939-40. Decorated Resistance Cross, Queen of Netherlands, 1981. Mem. Liberal Party. Roman Catholic. Clubs: OSL Stichting (Berkel), KNAC (The Hague). Home: PO Box 1, NL-5690 Aasen The Netherlands Office: PO Box 1, Oranjestraat 1, NL 5690 Assen The Netherlands

SADIE, STANLEY JOHN, writer, editor; b. London, Oct. 30, 1930; s. David and Deborah (Simons) S.; m. Adèle Simmons, Dec. 10, 1953 (dec. May 1978); children: Graham Robert, Ursula Joan, Stephen Peter; m. 2d Julie Anne McCornack, July 18, 1978; children: Celia Kathryn, Matthew David. M.A., Ph.D., Mus.B., Cambridge U. (Eng.), 1950-56; Litt.D. (hon.), Leicester U. (Eng.), 1982. Music critic The Times, London, 1964-81; editor Musical Times, London, 1967-87. Author: Mozart, 1966; Handel, 1962; joint author: Opera Guide, 3d edit., 1984; Stanley Sadie's Music Guide, 1986; editor: New Grove Dictionary Music and Musicians, 20 vols., 1980, Master Musicians, 1976—, New Grove Dictionary of Musical Instruments, 3 vols., 1984; joint editor New Grove Dictionary of American Music, 4 vols., 1986; editor: Norton/Grove Concise Encyclopedia of Music, 1988. Decorated comdr. Order Brit. Empire. Fellow Royal Soc. for Arts; hon. mem. Royal Acad. Music; mem. Royal Mus. Assn. (v.p.), Am. Musicol. Soc., Internat. Musicol. Soc. (mem. directorium), Critics' Circle. Office: New Grove Dictionary, 4 Little Essex St, London WC2R 3LF England

SADILEK, VLADIMIR, architect; b. Czechoslovakia, June 27, 1933; came to U.S., 1967, naturalized, 1973; s. Oldrich and Antoine (Zlamal) S.; Ph.D. summa cum laude in City Planning and Architecture, Tech. U. Prague, 1957; m. Jana Kadlec, Mar. 25, 1960; 1 son, Vladimir, Jr. Chief architect State Office for City Planning, Prague, 1958-67; architect, designer Bank Bldg. Corp., St. Louis, 1967-70, asso. architect, San Francisco, 1970-74; owner, chief exec. officer Bank Design Cons., San Mateo, Calif., 1974-81, West Coast Development Co., San Mateo, 1975—; pres., chief exec. officer Orbis Devel. Corp., San Mateo, 1981—. Served with Inf. of Czechoslovakia, 1958. Recipient awards of excellence from Bank Building Corp. and AIA for planning and design of fin. instns. in Hawaii, Calif. (1971), Ariz., N.Mex., Tex. (1972), Colo., Wyo. (1973), Idaho, Oreg., Washington (1974); lic. architect, 28 states. Republican. Roman Catholic. Home: 80 Orange Ct Hillsborough CA 94010 Office: 1777 Borel Pl San Mateo CA 94402

SADJADI, FIROOZ AHMADI, electrical engineer, consultant, researcher; b. Tehran, Iran, Mar. 18, 1949; came to U.S., 1968; s. Akbar Ahmadi and Fakhri (Mohsen) S.; m. Carolyn JoAnne Elkins; 1 child, Farzad. BEE, Purdue U., 1972, MEE, 1974; E.E.E., U. So. Calif., 1976; postgrad. U. Tenn., Knoxville, 1983. Research asst. Image Processing Inst., U. So. Calif., Los Angeles, 1974-76; cons. Oak Ridge Lab., Knoxville, 1980; researcher dept. elec. engring. U. Tenn., 1977-83; sr. research scientist Honeywell Systems and Research Ctr., 1983—. Mem. IEEE (sr.), Soc. Photo-Optical Instrumentation Engrs., Am. Assn. for Artificial Intelligence, Sigma Xi. Contbg. author numerous profl. publs. Office: Honeywell Systems and Research 3660 Technology Dr MN65-2300 Minneapolis MN 55418

SADLER, ERNEST ELMORE, electronics company executive; b. Bklyn., May 15, 1932; s. Ernest Elmore and Faith Myrtle (Jeffers) S.; B.A., U. Mass., 1959, M.S., 1961; m. Maureen Sheila Downey, Feb. 19, 1955; children—Kathleen, Faith, Amy, Sean. Research asst. U. Mass., 1958-61; research engr. N. Am. Rockwell, Anaheim, Calif., 1961-64; mem. tech. staff Rockwell Internat., Anaheim, 1964-70; v.p., gen. mgr. Good Taste Ltd., Reseda, Calif., 1970-74; v.p. ops. Unisen, Inc., Irvine, Calif., 1974-85, pres., 1985—, also dir. Served with USN, 1949-54; ETO. Mem. Human Factors Soc., Am. Psychol. Assn., Soc. Engring. Psychologists, AMVETS, Vets. Fgn. Wars, DAV, Sigma Xi. Lodge: Elks. Contbr. articles to profl. jours. Home: 405 S West St Anaheim CA 92805 Office: Unisen Corp 14352 Chambers Rd Tustin CA 92680

SADLER, PHILIP JOHN, management educator; b. London, Jan. 27, 1930; s. Edward John and Adelaide Violet (Parish) S.; m. Teresa Jacqueline Colley, July 11, 1964; children: Matthew John, Jonathan. BA, U. London, 1953. Prin. sci. officer U.K. Ministry of Def., London, 1954-63; sr. research officer Nat. Econ. Devel. Office, London, 1964; dir. research Ashridge Mgmt. Coll., Berkhamstead, Eng., 1964-68, prin., 1969-87; chief exec. officer Ashridge Mgmt. Coll., Berkhamstead, 1988—; regional dir. Lloyds Bank PLC, London, 1985—; bd. dirs. Williams Lea Group Ltd., London, Broadway Lodge, Weston-super-Mare, Eng. Named Companion to Brit. Empire, 1986. Fellow Internat. Acad. Mgmt., Inst. of Dirs., Inst. Personnel Mgmt.; mem. Brit. Inst. Mgmt. (pres. Luton br., Gold medal 1972), Strategic Planning Soc. (v.p. 1985—). Home: 115 Cross Oak Rd, Berkhamstead HP4 3HZ, England Office: Ashridge Mgmt Coll, Berkhamstead HP4 1NS, England

SADOUL, PAUL LOUIS CHARLES, physician, educator; b. Tours, France, 1918; s. Charles and Anna (Claude) S.; M.D., U. Nancy (France), 1949; postgrad. U. Rochester (N.Y.), 1951-52; m. Colette Noviant, Feb. 8, 1945; children: Pascale Sadoul Rollin, Jean-Charles, Helene Sadoul Delva, Marie Sadoul Lanternier, Nicolas, Remy. Mem. faculty U. Nancy I, 1955—, prof. medicine, 1960-86; sci. dir. research unit 14, INSERM, 1961-84; mem. med. research com. European Community, 1960-82. Mem. Musée Lorrain. Decorated Chevalier Legion of Honor. Mem. European Soc. Clin. Respiratory Physiology (pres. 1966-73, hon. pres. 1974—), Soc. d'Archéologie Lorraine (pres. 1987). Roman Catholic. Home: 28 rue Pasteur, 54500 Vandoeuvre les Nancy France Office: Faculte de Medicine, BP 184, 54505 Vandoeuvre les Nancy France

SADOWSKI, JOHN STANLEY, utility executive; b. Maspeth, N.Y., Oct. 29, 1948; s. John Thomas and Mary Ann (Roman) S.; m. Jessica, May 21, 1977; children: Daniel John, Christopher Brendan. BBA, Hofstra U., 1976; MBA with distinction, N.Y. Inst. Tech., 1979. Acctg. asst. Consol. Edison Co. N.Y., N.Y.C., 1973-76, staff acct., 1976, analyst forecasting and econ. analysis, 1976-77, supr. acctg. and stats., 1977-78; mgr. gas supply N.J. Natural Gas Co., Asbury Park, 1978-82; mgr. gas supply planning and regulatory affairs UGI Corp., 1982-85; dir. mktg. HNG/North Gas Mktg., Inc., Malvern, Pa., 1985; account exec. HNG/Internorth Gas Mktg., Inc., Malvern, 1985-86; dir. Eastern region Enron Gas Mktg., Malvern, 1986-87, dir. planning and analysis, Houston, 1987-88, gen. mgr. ea. div. sales, 1988—; rep. operating com. Assoc. Gas Distbrs., 1978-85; prof. bus. mgmt. Kutztown State U. Served with U.S. Army, 1969-73. Mem. Am. Gas Assn., Assn. MBA Execs. Roman Catholic. Lodge: K.C.

SADR-AMELI, MOHAMMAD ALI, cardiologist, educator; b. Tehran, Iran, Dec. 23, 1951; s. Mehdi Sadr-Ameli and Tahereh Sadr; m. Minoo Amirjamshidi; 1 child, Davoud. MD, Tehran U., 1979; grad. in cardiology, Tehran Heart Hosp., 1983. Research fellow in electrophysiology Sacre Coeur Hosp., Montreal, Que., Can., 1984-86; asst. prof. cardiology Tehran Heart Hosp., 1986—, dir. electrophysiologic lab., 1987—. Contbr. articles to med. jours.; editor-in-chief Cardiovascular Jour., Tehran, 1987. Home: PO Box 19395, 4313 Tehran Iran Office: Heart Hosp, Valiasr St, Tehran Iran

SADRUDDIN, MOE, oil company consultant; b. Hyderabad, India, Mar. 3, 1943; came to U.S., 1964; m. Azmath Oureshi, 1964; 3 children. BSME, Osmania U., Hyderabad, 1964; MS in Indsl. Engring., NYU, 1966; IE in Indsl. Engring., Columbia U., 1970, MBA, 1978. Cons. project engr. Ford, Bacon & Davis, N.Y.C., 1966; staff indsl. engr. J.C. Penney, N.Y.C., 1966-68; sr. cons. Drake, Sheahan, Stewart & Dougall, N.Y.C., 1968-70, Beech-Nut Inc. subs. Squibb Corp., N.Y.C., 1970-72; founder, pres. Azmath Constrn. Co., Englewood, N.J., 1972-77; crude oil cons., fgn. govt. rep. 1977—; pres. A-One Petroleum Co., Fullerton, Calif., 1985—; govt. advisor Puerto Rico, 1980-82, Dominica Kenya, 1983-84, St. Vincent, 1981-82, Kenya, 1983-84, Belize 1984-85, Costa Rica 1983-86, Paraguay 1984-87; mem. Los Angeles World Affairs Council. Mem. Los Angeles World Affairs Council. Mem. Internat. Platform Assn. Address: A-One Petroleum Co 2656 Camino Del Sol Fullerton CA 92633

SADUN, ALFREDO ARRIGO, neuro-ophthalmologist; b. New Orleans, Oct. 23, 1950; s. Elvio H. and Lina (Ottoleghi) S.; m. Debra Leigh Rice, Mar. 18, 1978; children: Rebecca Eli, Elvio Aaron, Benjamin Maxwell. BS, MIT, 1972; PhD, Albert Einstein Med. Sch., Bronx, N.Y., 1976, MD, 1978. Intern Huntington Meml. Hosp. U. So. Calif., Pasadena, 1978-79; resident Harvard U. Med. Sch., Boston, 1979-82, HEED Found. fellow in neuro-ophthalmology Mass. Eye and Ear Inst., 1982-83, instr. ophthalmology, 1983, asst. prof. ophthalmology, 1984; dir. residential tng. U. So. Calif. Dept. Ophthalmology, Los Angeles, 1984-85; asst. prof. ophthalmology and neurosurgery U. So. Calif., Los Angeles, 1984-87, assoc. prof., 1987—; prin. investigator Howe Lab. Harvard U., Boston, 1981-84, E. Doheny Eye Found., Los Angeles, 1984—. Author: Optics for Opthalmologists, 1988; contbr. articles to profl. jours. Fellow Am. Acad. Ophthalmology; mem. NIH (Med. Scientist Tng. award, 1972-78), Soc. to Prevent Blindness, Nat. Eye Inst. (New Investigator Research award 1983-86), Soc. Neuroscis., Assn. Research in Vision and Ophthalmology, Am. Assn. Anatomists, N.Am. Neuro-Ophthal. Soc. Home: 2478 Adair St San Marino CA 91108 Office: U So Calif E Doheny Eye Inst 1355 San Pablo Los Angeles CA 90033

SADURSKI, WOJCIECH, legal philosophy educator; b. Warsaw, Poland, June 5, 1950; s. Franciszek and Anna (Lenkiewicz) S.; m. Romana Gurgul, Apr. 20, 1974. LLM, U. Warsaw, 1972, PhD, 1976; diploma in etudes internats., U. Nice, 1977. Lectr. U. Warsaw, 1972-80; lectr. U. Sydney, 1981-82, sr. lectr., 1986—; research fellow Australian Nat. U., Canberra, 1983; lectr. U. Melbourne, Australia, 1983-85. Author: Giving Desert Its Due, 1985; contbr. articles to profl. jours. Mem. Internat. Assn. Philosophy of Law and Social Philosophy (sec. gen. 1987—), Australian Soc. Legal Philosophy (sec. 1986—). Office: U Sydney, Sch Law, 173 Phillip St, Sydney, New South Wales 2000, Australia

SAEBOE, MAGNE, theology educator; b. Fjelberg, Norway, Jan. 23, 1929; s. Samson and Malla (Oelfaernes) S.; m. Mona Uni Bjoernstad, June 27, 1953; children: Snorre, Lars Arnljot, Jan Eystein. Cand. theol., Free Faculty of Theology, Oslo, 1956; D. Theol., U. Oslo, 1969. Tchr. Hebrew U. Oslo, 1961-70; lectr. O.T. Free Faculty of Theology, Oslo, 1969-70, prof. O.T., 1970—, dean, 1975-77, 1988—. Author: Sacharja 9-14. Untersuchungen von Text und Form, 1969, Gjennom alle tider, 1978, Ordene og Ordet. Studier, 1979, Kommentar til Ordspråkene, Forkynnren, Høysangen, Klagesangene, 1986; contbr. articles to profl. jours. Chmn. Lut. European Consultation on the Ch. and Jewish People, Hannover, Fed. Republic Germany, 1979-82. Mem. Wiss. Gesellschaft fur Theologie, The Royal Norwegian Soc. of Scis. and Letters, Norwegian Acad. Scis. and Letters, Nathan Soderblom-Sallskapet, Norwegian Bible Soc. (chmn. Old Testament translation com. 1968-78). Home: Lars Muhles vei 34, N-1300 Sandvika Norway Office: The Free Faculty of Theology, Gydas vei 4, Oslo 3 Norway

SAEED, KHAWAJA AMJAD, marketing professional, educator; b. Amritsar, India, Mar. 21, 1936; s. Khawaja Abdul and Zubadia Rashid; m. Fauzia Naheed, Nov. 21, 1965; children: Javaria, Asjad, Rabia, Asad. M of Commerce, Hailey Coll., Lahore, Pakistan, 1959; MBA, Am. U. Beirut, 1970; LLB, U. Punjab, 1976; PhD, Century U., 1981. Jr. exec. Colony Group Industries, Lahore, 1958-59; sr. audit in charge A.F. Ferguson and Co., Lahore, 1959-64; managerial exec. P. Leiner & Sons Group, Lahore, 1964-65; prof., chmn. dept. bus. adminstrn. U. Punjab, Lahore, 1965—; econ. cons. Lahore Stock Exchange, 1980—. Author: Economic Structure of Pakistan, 1977 (Writers Guild award 1979), 20 books on fin., commerce, and bus. adminstrn.; contbr. over 250 articles to scholarly jours. Pres. mosque, Lahore, 1982—; mem. Zakat Com., Lahore, 1983—. Mem. Inst. Chartered Accts. Pakistan, Inst. Cost and Mgmt. Accts. Pakistan, Inst. Mktg. Mgmt. (pres. 1986—). Club: Acctg. (Lahore) (pres. 1958-59). Home: U Punjab, Lahore 20, Pakistan

SAEED, MOHAMMAD, electrical engineer; b. Shahjhanpur, India, May 14, 1950; arrived in Pakistan, 1950.; s. Mazhar Ahmed and Zakia Begum; married Nov. 22, 1974; children: Ijlal, Oraiba, Bilal. Higher secondary sch. cert., Islamia Coll., Sukkur, Sind, 1965; BEE, Sind U. Engring. Coll., Jamshoro, Sind, 1969. Apprentice engr. Mehran Sugar Mills, Hyderabad, Sind, 1970-71; asst. elec. engr. Mehran Sugar Mills, Hyderabad, 1972-73, Sui Gas Transmission Co., Karachi, Sind, 1973-77; sales engr. Greaves Cotton and Co. Ltd., Karachi, 1977-80; sales mgr. Allied Engring. and Services Ltd., Karachi, 1980—. Mem. Inst. Engring., Inst. Elec. Engrs., Pakistan Engring Council. Home: B-515 Block 13 F B Area, Karachi, Sind Pakistan

SAEKI, AKIRA, electronics company executive; b. Mar. 8, 1917; m. Sachiko Saeki. Mng. dir. Hayakawa Kinzoku Kogyo Lab., from 1958; currently pres. Sharp Corp., Osaka, Japan. Mem. Japan Electric Mfrs. Assn. (trustee). Home: 8-36 Kitabatake, 1-chome Abeno-ku, Osaka 545, Japan Office: Sharp Corp, 22-22 Nagaike-Cho, Abeno-ku, Osaka 545, Japan *

SAELS, GUY JEAN, paper company executive; b. Schaerbeek, Belgium, Feb. 3, 1935; s. Antoine Lambert and Marie Françoise Saels; m. Marie Louise Behets Wydemans, Dec. 28, 1958; children: Jean, Anne. Ptnr., dir. Asco, Lubumbashi, Republic of Zaire, 1962—, Pagerbel, Brussels, 1970—, Drenko, Brussels, 1970—. Mem. Aneza. Lodge: Rotary (pres. 1986—). Home: Ave Fr Roosevelt 89, 1050 Brussels Belgium Office: Asco, PO Box 73, Lubumbashi Shaba Zaire

SAENGER, BRUCE WALTER, consulting firm executive; b. Hanover, N.H., July 16, 1943; s. Werner Hugo and Natalie Bertha (Brown) S.; m. Cheryl Jeanne Bouchard, Nov. 6, 1976. B.A., Pa. State U., 1969; postgrad. Am. Coll., Bryn Mawr, Pa., 1979, Coll. Fin. Planning, Denver, 1980; C.P.C.U., Am. Inst., Malvern, Pa., 1981. Chartered fin. cons; C.L.U. Agt., Nationwide Ins., Lansdale, Pa., 1969-73, dist. sales mgr., Springfield, Ma., 1973-75; dist. sales mgr. Am. Mut., Braintree, Ma., 1975-77; dir. mktg. Bankers Life & Casualty, Chgo., 1977-78; pres., founder Sales Tng. Techs., Southboro, Mass., 1979-81, The Saenger Orgn., Medway, Mass., 1981—; faculty Notre Dame U., South Bend, Ind., 1977-78, Northeastern U., Boston, 1984—; commr. RHU Commn., Washington, 1979-81; dir. Northeastern U. Ins. Inst., Boston, 1985—; cons. in field. Author: Series 6 Study Book, 1983, Series 22 Study Book, 1984, Tax Shelter Market Guide, 1985, Marketing Mutual Funds, 1985; also articles. Bd. dirs. Lansdale Gen. Hosp., Pa., 1971-73. Served with U.S. Army, 1960-66. Recipient Ednl. Achievement award Profl. Ins. Agts. Assn., 1983. Fellow Soc. C.L.U.s (ednl. adv., bd. dirs. 1987—), Soc. C.P.C.U.s (ednl. adv.), Life Mgmt. Inst. (Outstanding Lectr. award 1984); mem. Internat. Assn. Fin. Planners (ednl. adv., bd. dirs. 1986—), Soc. Cert. Ins. Counselors (ednl. adv.), Life Underwriters Assn. (ednl. adv.). Republican. Roman Catholic. Avocations: golf, fishing. Home: 1 Stephanie Dr Medway MA 02053 Office: The Saenger Orgn 89 Main St Suite 213 Medway MA 02053

SAENT-JOHNS, GERALDINE MCCORMICK, painter, miniaturist, sculptor; b. Montreal, Que., Can., Sept. 12, 1930; d. Alexander Gerald and Anne (Lubkowski) McCormick; came to U.S., 1952, naturalized, 1965; student McGill U. Freelance artist, 1969—; owner, operator Eden Mood Studios 1973—; lectr. animals in art; miniature painting on gemstone rep. in collection of 8th Duke of Wellington, Pres. and Mrs. Gerald Ford. Mem. East African Wild Life Soc., N.Am. Falconers Assn., Nat. Wildlife Fedn., Aircraft Owners and Pilots Assn., Canadian Nature Fedn. Republican. Home: 4800 Lander Rd Chagrin Falls OH 44022

SAENZ, MARIA T., manufacturing company executive; b. LaPaz, Bolivia, Sept. 18, 1930; d. Carlos and Lily (Estenssoro) Viaña; m. Jorge Saenz, Apr. 9, 1951; children: Rossie, Georgette, Tabbie. Cert., Michael Ham Meml. Coll., Buenos Aires, 1947; BS in Bus. and Mktg., U. LaPaz, 1951. Mgr. internat. import dept. Mfrs. Rep. Co., LaPaz, 1952-57, gen. mgr., 1957-66, dir., 1967-72, pres., 1972; exec. chmn. Industrias Unidas "El Progreso" S.A., LaPaz, 1971—. Hon. consul Costa Rica in LaPaz, 1981-87. Mem. Bolivian Fgn. Consular Assn. (v.p. 1984-85). Roman Catholic. Clubs: La Paz Tennis, Bridge, Brit. Women's (pres. 1985). Home: PO Box 543, La Paz Bolivia

SAFAR, MAHMOOD MOHAMMAD, civil engineering educator; b. Makkah, Saudi Arabia, Oct. 27, 1940; s. Mohammad Mahmoud Safar and Noor Bakre Abu Laban; m. Lamyazal Abdul Rahman Qutob; children: Medhat, Mazin, Maie, Maha, Mozon. B in Engring., Cairo U., 1964; M in Civil Engring., Stanford U., 1968; PhD in Soil Mechanics and Found. Engring., N.C. State U., 1972. Demonstrator faculty engring. King Saoud U., Riyadh, Saudi Arabia, 1964-65, assoc. prof. faculty engring., 1972-76, dean of students, 1973-75; sec. gen. Supreme Council Univs. of Saudi Arabia, Riyadh, 1975-84; vice minister higher edn. Riyadh, 1976-84; prof. civil engring. King Fahad U. Petroleum and Minerals, Dhahran, Saudi Arabia, 1984—; pres. Arabian Gulf U., Bahrain, Saudi Arabia, 1984—; chmn. supervising com. Internat. Conf. Islamic Solidarity in Sci. and Tech., 1974-76; initiator, organizer Project on Devel. Higher Edn. in Saudi Arabia, 1975-84; rapporteur gen. 1st Conf. Ministers Higher Edn. and Sci. Research of Arab States, Algiers, Algeria, 1982. Author: Development as an Issue, Civilization as a Challenge, Information as an Attitude, Productivity of a Society; contbr. articles to profl. jours. Pres. Saudi Arabia Nat. Com. Equivalence of University Degrees, 1976-84; v.p. Supreme Bd. King Faisal Scholarships, 1976-84; mem. Saudi Arabia Higher Com. on Info., 1979-82, UN Univ. Consultation Com., Tokyo, 1980-83; trustee U. of East and West, Chgo., 1979. Decorated Order Bright Star, People's Republic of China, 1978. Mem. Civil Engring. Soc. U.S., Council on Higher Edn. for Arab Gulf States. Moslem. Home and Office: PO Box 18370, Riyadh 11415, Saudi Arabia

SAFAR, MICHEL EMILE, internist, educator; b. Algiers, Algeria, Mar. 17, 1937; s. Henri Zacharie and Josette (Chiche) S.; married, 1967; children: Marie-Claude, Helene, Pierre. MD, Broussais-Hôtel Dieu, Paris, 1966. Intern Hosp. Broussais, Paris, 1966, chief diagnosis ctr.; assoc. prof. Paris VI U., 1972-81, prof., 1981—; mem. Cleve. Council for High Blood Pressure. Author: Mechanisms of Hypertension, Clinical Pharmacology of Hypertension, Arterial and Nervous System in Hypertension, 1987. Mem. Internat. Soc. Arterial Hypertension (bd. dirs.), Internat. Soc. nephrology, Am. Soc. Arterial Hypertension (bd. dirs.), N.Y. Acad. Scis. Home: 10 blvd Emile Augier, 75016 Paris France Office: Hôpital Broussais, Diagnostic Ctr, 96 rue Didot, 75016 Paris France

SAFAR, SERGE ELIE, psychiatrist; b. Paris, Jan. 15, 1926; Andre and Blanche S.; m. Micheline Sonigo. MD. Chef Clinique Neuropsychiatrique U. Alger; chef de Lab. Hospital de la litié, Paris. Mem. Soc. D'Encouragement au Progrès. Office: 17 Neuro-psychiatre, 9 T Blvd du Montparnasse, 75006 Paris France

SAFARS, BERTA See FISZER-SZAFARZ, BERTA

SAFDIE, MOSHE, architect; b. Haifa, Israel, July 14, 1938; s. Leon S.; m. Nina Nusynowicz, Sept. 6, 1959 (div. 1981); children: Taal, Oren; m. Michal Ronnen, June 7, 1981; children: Carmelle, Yasmin. B.Arch, McGill U., 1961; LL.D. (hon.), 1982. With H.P.D. Van Ginkel (architect), Montreal, Can., then Louis I. Kahn, Phila.; assoc. David, Barrott and Boulva, Montreal; in pvt. practice Boston; with brs. in Montreal, Jerusalem; prof. architecture and urban design, dir. urban design program Harvard U. Grad. Sch. Design, 1978-84, Ian Woodner Studio prof. architecture and urban design, 1984—. Participated on master plan for Expo 67; executed: Habitat 67; other works include: Coldspring New Town, Balt., Tampines New Community, Singapore, Yeshivat Porat Joseph, Jerusalem, Cambridge Ctr. Complex, Mass., Robina New Town, Gold Coast, Australia, master plan for renewal of North Sta. area, Boston, Nat. Gallery, Can., Hebrew Union Coll., Jerusalem, Musée de la civilisation, Que., Columbus Ctr., N.Y.C., Montreal Mus. Fine Arts, Que., Hebrew Union Coll. Cultural Ctr. for Am. Jewish Life, Los Angeles, Yad Vashem Children's Meml., Jerusalem, Toronto Ballet Opera House, Ont.; author: Beyond Habitat, 1970, 2d edit., 1987, For Everyone A Garden, 1974, Form and Purpose, 1980, Harvard Jerusalem Studio: Urban Design for the Holy City, 1986, Rebuilding Jerusalem: The Future of the Past, 1988. Recipient Massey medal in architecture; Lt. Gov. Can. Gold medal; Urban Design Concept award HUD, 1980; Internat. Design award in urban design Am. Soc. Interior Designers, 1980, Le Priz d'excellence in Architecture Que. Order Architects, 1988. Fellow Royal Inst. Architects Can.; mem. Order Architects Province Que., Ont. Assn. Architects, AIA. Home: 4 Buckingham St Cambridge MA 02138 Office: 100 Properzi Way Somerville MA 02143

SAFER, JOHN, sculptor, banker; b. Washington, Sept. 6, 1922; s. John M. and Rebecca (Herzmark) S.; m. Joy Scott; children: Janine Whitney, Thomas. A.B., George Washington U., 1947; LL.B., Harvard, 1949. chmn. bd. Sovran Bank/D.C. Nat.; chmn. exec. com. Fin. Gen. Bankshares, 1977-80. Represented in permanent collections at Balt. Mus. Art, Corcoran Gallery Art, Nat. Air and Space Mus., Washington, High Mus. Art, Atlanta, Milw. Mus. Art, Harvard Law Sch., Harvard Bus. Sch., Phila. Mus. Art, San Francisco Mus. Art, Georgetown U., Williams Coll., Mus. Fine Arts, Caracas, Venezuela, Royal Collection Madrid; pub. sculpture includes World Series of Golf Trophy, Timepiece, Internat. Sq. Bldg., Washington, Christa McAuliffe Meml., Bowie, Md. Served as 1st lt. USAAF, 1942-46. Clubs: Cosmos, Burning Tree, Harvard, Woodmont (Washington); Harvard (N.Y.); Lyford Cay (Nassau); Mid-Ocean (Bermuda); Linville Ridge (N.C.). Office: Sovran Bank 1801 K St NW Washington DC 20006

SAFFIR, HERBERT SEYMOUR, structural engineer, consultant; b. N.Y.C., Mar. 29, 1917; s. A.L. and Gertrude (Samuels) S.; m. Sarah Young, May 9, 1941; children: Richard Young, Barbara Joan. BS in Civil Engring. cum laude, Ga. Inst. Tech., 1940. Registered profl. engr., Fla., N.Y., Tex., P.R., Miss. Civil engr. TVA, Chattanooga, 1940, NACA, Langley Field, Va., 1940-41; structural engr. Ebasco Services, N.Y.C., 1941-43, York & Sawyer & Fred Severud, N.Y.C., 1945; engr. Waddell & Hardesty, Cons. Engrs., N.Y.C., 1945-47; asst. county engr. Dade County, Miami, Fla., 1947-59; cons. engr. Herbert S. Saffir, Coral Gables, Fla., 1959—; Adj. lectr. civil engring. Coll. Engring., U. Miami, 1964—; adviser civil engring. Fla. Internat. U., 1975-80; cons. on bldg. codes Govt. Bahamas; cons. on engring. in housing to UN; past chmn. Met. Dade County Unsafe Structures Bd., vice chmn.; mem. Am. Nat. Standards Inst. Commn. Bldg. Design Loads, Nat. Adv. Group on Glass Design; cons. to govt. and industry, condr. seminars, Australia; reviewer for NSF. Author: Housing Construction in Hurricane Prone Areas, 1971, Nature and Extent of Damage by Hurricane Camille, 1972; contbg. author: Wind Effects on Structures, 1976; editor Wind Engr.; contbr. articles to profl. jours. Served with AUS, 1943-44. Recipient Outstanding Service award Fla. Profl. Engrs., 1954, Pub. Service award Nat. Weather Service, 1975, Disting. Service award Nat. Hurricane Conf., 1987; named Miami Engr. of Year, 1978, Gov.'s Design award, 1986, Gov. Gilchrist award for Profl. Excellence, 1988. Fellow ASCE (past pres., sec., aerodynamics com. 1983—, mem. mitigation of wind damage com. 1985—), Fla. Engring. Soc. (award for outstanding tech. achievement 1973, Community Service award 1980); mem. Soc. Am. Mil. Engrs., Am. Concrete Inst., ASTM (mem. com. performance bldg. constrn.), Prestressed Concrete Inst., Internat. Assn. for Bridge and Structural Engring., Colegio de Ingenieros P.R., Am. Meteorol. Soc., Am. Arbitration Assn., Wind Engring. Research Council (past bd. dirs.), Coral Gables C. of C. (bd. dirs., past pres.), Tau Beta Pi, Chi Epsilon (hon.). Club: Country of Coral Gables. Home: 4818 Alhambra Circle Coral Gables FL 33146 Office: 255 University Dr Coral Gables FL 33134

SAGAN, CARL EDWARD, astronomer, educator, author; b. N.Y.C., Nov. 9, 1934; s. Samuel and Rachel (Gruber) S.; m. Ann Druyan; children by previous marriages: Dorion Solomon, Jeremy Ethan, Nicholas; 1 dau., Alexandra. A.B. with gen. and spl. honors, U. Chgo., 1954, B.S., 1955, M.S., 1956, Ph.D., 1960; Sc.D. (hon.), Rensselaer Poly. Inst., 1975, Denison U., 1976, Clarkson Coll. Tech., 1977, Whittier Coll., 1978, Clark U., 1978, Am. U., 1980; D.H.L. (hon.), Skidmore Coll., 1976, Lewis and Clark Coll., 1980, Bklyn. Coll., CUNY, 1982; LL.D. (hon.), U. Wyo., 1978. Miller research fellow U. Calif.-Berkeley, 1960-62; vis. asst. prof. genetics Stanford Med. Sch., 1962-63; astrophysicist Smithsonian Astrophys. Obs., Cambridge, Mass., 1962-68; asst. prof. Harvard U., 1962-67; mem. faculty Cornell U., 1968—, prof. astronomy and space scis., 1970—, David Duncan prof., 1976—, dir. Lab. Planetary Studies, 1968—, assoc. dir. Center for Radiophysics and Space Research, 1972-81; pres. Carl Sagan Prodns. (Cosmos TV series), 1977—; nonresident fellow Robotics Inst., Carnegie-Mellon U., 1982—; NSF-Am. Astron. Soc. vis. prof. various colls., 1963-67, Condon lectr., Oreg., 1967-68; Holiday lectr. AAAS, 1970; Vanuxem lectr. Princeton U., 1973; Smith lectr. Dartmouth Coll., 1974, 77; Wagner lectr. U. Pa., 1975; Bronowski lectr. U. Toronto, 1975; Philips lectr. Haverford Coll., 1975; Disting. scholar Am. U., 1976; Danz lectr. U. Wash., 1976; Clark Meml. lectr. U. Tex., 1976; Stahl lectr. Bowdoin Coll., 1977; Christmas lectr. Royal Instn., London, 1977; Menninger Meml. lectr. Am. Psychiat. Assn., 1978; Carver Meml. lectr. Tuskegee Inst., 1981; Feinstone lectr. U.S. Mil. Acad., 1981; Pal lectr. Motion Picture Acad. Arts and Scis., 1982; Dodge lectr. U. Ariz., 1982; other hon. lectureships; mem. various adv. groups NASA and Nat. Acad. Scis., 1959—; mem. council Smithsonian Instn., 1975—; vice chmn. working group moon and planets, space orgn. Internat. Council Sci. Unions, 1968-74; lectr. Apollo flight crews NASA, 1969-72; chmn. U.S. del. joint conf. U.S. Nat. and Soviet Acads. Sci. on Communication with Extraterrestrial Intelligence, 1971; responsible for Pioneer 10 and 11 and Voyager 1 and 2 interstellar messages; mem. Voyager Imaging Sci. Team; judge Nat. Book Awards, 1975; mem. fellowship panel Guggenheim Found., 1976—. Author: Atmospheres of Mars and Venus, 1961, Planets, 1966, Intelligent Life in the Universe, 1966, Planetary Exploration, 1970, Mars and the Mind of Man, 1973, The Cosmic Connection, 1973, Other Worlds, 1975, The Dragons of Eden, 1977, Murmurs of Earth: The Voyager Interstellar Record, 1978, Broca's Brain, 1979, Cosmos, 1980, Contact, 1985, (novel) Comet, 1985; also numerous articles; editor: Icarus: Internat. Jour. Solar System Studies, 1968-79, Planetary Atmospheres, 1971, Space Research, 1971, UFO's: A Scientific Debate, 1972, Communication with Extraterrestrial Intelligence, 1973; editorial bd.: Origins of Life, 1974—, Icarus, 1962—, Climatic Change, 1976—, Science 80, 1979-82. Recipient Smith prize Harvard U., 1964; NASA medal for exceptional sci. achievement, 1972; Prix Galabert, 1973; John W. Campbell Meml. award, 1974; Klumpke-Roberts prize, 1974; Priestley award, 1975; NASA medal for disting. pub. service, 1977, 81; Pulitzer prize for lit., 1978; Washburn medal, 1978; Rittenhouse medal, 1980; Peabody award, 1981; Hugo award, 1981; Seaborg prize, 1981; Roe medal, 1981; NSF fellow, 1955-60; Sloan research fellow, 1963-67. Fellow AAAS (chmn. astronomy sect. 1975), Am. Acad. Arts and Scis., AIAA, Am. Geophys. Union (pres. planetology sect. 1980-82), Am. Astronautical Soc. (council 1976-81, Kennedy award 1984), Brit. Interplanetary Soc., Explorers Club (75th Anniversary award 1980); mem. Am. Phys. Soc., Am. Astron. Soc. (councillor, chmn. div. for planetary scis. 1975-76), Fedn. Am. Scientists (council 1977-81), Am. Com. on East-West Accord, Soc. Study of Evolution, Genetics Soc. Am., Internat. Astron. Union, Internat. Acad. Astronautics, Internat. Soc. Study Origin of Life (council 1980—), Planetary Soc. (pres. 1979—), Authors Guild, Phi Beta Kappa, Sigma Xi. Address: Cornell Univ Space Sci Bldg Ithaca NY 14853 *

SAGAN, FRANÇOISE (FRANÇOISE QUOIREZ), writer; b. Cajarc, France, June 21, 1935; d. Pierre and Marie (Laubaed) Quoirez; ed. Convent des Oiseaux and Convent du Sacre Coeur, Paris; m. Guy Schoeller, 1958; m. Robert Westhoff, 1962 (div.); 1 son, Denis. Books include: Bonjour tristesse (Prix des Critiques), 1954; Un certan sourirer, 1956; Dans un Mois, dans un an, 1957; Aimez-vous Brahms, 1959; La chamade, 1965; Le garde du coeur, 1968; Un peu de soleil dans l'eau froide, 1969; Des bleus a l'ame, 1972; Il est des Parfums (with Guillaume Hanoteau), 1978; Les merveilleux nuages, 1973; Un profil perdu, 1974; Reponses, 1975; Des yeux de soie, 1976; The Painted Lady, 1983; Incidental Music, 1984; Pretenders, 1984; scenario for ballet Le rendez-vous manque (with Michel Magne); own film adaptation of Dans un mois, dans un an; dir. Les fougeres bleues (film), 1976; plays include: Chateau en Suede, 1959; Les violons parfois, 1961; La robe mauve de valentine, 1963; Bonheur, impair et passe, 1964; Le cheval evanoui, 1966; l'echarde, 1966; Un piano dans l'herbe, 1970; Zaphorie, 1973; Le lit defait, 1977; other books include: Pol Vandromme, 1978; Il fait beau jour et nuit, 1978; Le Chien Couchant, 1980; Salad Days, 1984. Office: Ramsay, 9 rue du Cherche-Midi, 75006 Paris France also: Editions Flammarion, 26 rue Racine, 75006 Paris France *

SAGAR, PREM THIRUVEETHI, civil engineer; b. Salem, India, Jan. 18, 1924; s. Radakrishnan and Mangalambal; m. Minoo Michael, Aug. 29, 1959; children—Sujata, Sanjay. B.C.E. with honors, U. Madras, India, 1945; M.S. in Hwy. Engring., Stanford U. and U. Utah, 1947; M.Phil in Civil and Hwy. Engring., U. Utah, 1969. Asst. engr. Dept. Hwys. and Rural Works, Govt. Madras, 1950-51; ops. engr. ESSO, India, 1951-60; engr. Earthmoving and Constrn. Equipment div. William Jacks & Co., Ltd., Bombay, India, 1960-61, roads div. Ministry of Works, Govt. Eastern Nigeria, 1961-67; transport and communications adviser, civil engr. UN in Tanzania, 1967-71; transport engr., transport economist Commonwealth Secretariat, Commonwealth Fund for Tech. Cooperation in Nigeria, London, 1972-76; prin. resident engr. Ove Arup & Ptnrs., Cons. Engrs., Nigeria, 1976-80; project coordinator, chief tech. adviser UN ILO, Addis Ababa, 1980-81; sr. engr. road and bridge div. Dorsch Cons. in Iraq, Munich, Fed. Republic Germany, 1982-86; mng. dir. North-West Lines, Ltd., Nigeria, 1974-76, Rima Transport Co., Ltd., Nigeria, 1975-76. U. Utah fellow, 47-49. Indian Govt. scholar, 1945. Fellow Instn. Civil Engrs. (chartered engr.), Instn. Hwy. Engrs. U.K., ASCE, Instn. Engrs. India, Brit. Inst. Mgmt. U.K., Internat. Assn. Project Mgmt. Switzerland.

SAGAR, VIRENDRA, publishing company executive; b. Pakistan, Feb. 10, 1946; came to India, 1947; s. Bansilal and Shanti Rani Sagar; m. Madhu Sagar, Feb. 24, 1973; children—Shikha, Nikhar. Grad. high sch., Allahabad, Uttar Pradesh, India, 1963. Mgmt. trainee Law Pubs. (India) Pvt. Ltd., Allahabad, 1963-66, mgr., 1967-76, gen. mgr., 1976-83, ptnr., 1983-84, chief exec., 1985—, dir., 1986—; dir. Character Types Pvt. Ltd., Allahabad, 1976—; ptnr. Eastern Printers, Allahabad, 1966—. Avocations: religious reading; reading management books. Home: 8-C Strachy Rd, Allahabad Uttar, Pradesh 211 001, India Office: Law Pubs (India) Pvt Ltd, 15 Sardar Patel Marg, Allahabad Uttar Pradesh 211 001, India

SAGER, CLIFFORD JULIUS, psychiatrist, educator; b. N.Y.C.; s. Max and Lena (Lipman) S.; m. Anne; children from previous marriage: Barbara L., Philip T., Rebecca J., Anthony F. B.S., Pa. State U., 1937; M.D., N.Y. U., 1941; cert. in psychoanalysis, N.Y. Med. Coll., 1949. Diplomate: Am. Bd. Psychiatry and Neurology. Rotating intern Montefiore Hosp., N.Y.C., 1941-42; resident Bellevue Hosp., N.Y.C., 1942, 46-48; practice medicine specializing in psychiatry N.Y.C., 1946—; dir. therapeutic services, asso. dean Postgrad. Ctr. Mental Health, 1948-60; vis. psychiatrist, med. bd. Flower and Fifth Ave Hosp., 1960-71, Met. Hosp., 1960-71; dir. psychiat. tng. and edn. N.Y. Med. Coll., 1960-61; attending psychiatrist Bird S. Coler Hosp., 1960-71; clin. dir. N.Y. Med. Coll., 1960-63, assoc. prof. psychiatry, 1960-65, prof., 1966-71, dir. partial hosp. programs and family treatment and study unit, 1964-71; clin. prof. psychiatry Mt. Sinai Sch. Medicine, 1971-80, N.Y. Hosp.-Cornell Univ. Med. Ctr., 1980—; attending psychiatrist N.Y. Hosp.-Payne Whitney Clinic, 1980—; attending psychiatrist Mt. Sinai Hosp., 1971-80; chief behavioral scis. Gouverneur Hosp.; chief family treatment unit Beth Israel Med. Ctr., 1970-71, assoc. dir. family and group therapy, 1971-74; psychiat. dir. Jewish Family Service, 1974-77; dir. family psychiatry Jewish Bd. Family and Children's Services., 1978—. Mem. editorial bd.: Am. Jour. Orthopsychiatry, 1960-69, Internat. Jour. Group Psychotherapy, 1968—, Family Process, 1969—, Divorce, 1977—, Comprehensive Rev. Jour. Family and Marriage, 1978—; cons.: Sexual Medicine, 1974—; co-editor: Jour. Sex and Marital Therapy, 1976—, Jour. Marriage and Family Counseling, 1977—, Internat. Jour. Family Counseling, 1977—; author: Marriage Contracts and Couple Therapy, 1976, Intimate Partners, 1979, Treating the Remarried Family, 1983; co-author: Black Ghetto Family in Therapy, 1970; editor: Progress in Group and Family Therapy, 1972; contbr. over 90 articles to profl. jours., chpts. to books. Served as capt. M.C. AUS, 1942-46. Recipient Am. Family Therapy Assn. award for Outstanding Contribution to Family Therapy 1983, Assn. Marriage and Family Therapists award for Outstanding Contributions to the field of Marital and Family Therapy, 1984. Fellow Am. Psychiat. Assn. (life), Am. Orthopsychiat. Assn. (life), Acad. Psychoanalysis, Am. Group Psychotherapy Assn. (pres. 1968-70, dir. 1962-74), Soc. Med. Psychoanalysts (pres. 1960-61, dir. 1958-62); mem. AMA, Am. Soc. Advancement of Psychotherapy (dir. 1954-60), N.Y. Soc. Clin. Psychiatry, Soc. for Sex Therapy and Research (pres. 1976-77), Am. Assn. Marital and Family Therapists. Office: 65 E 76th St New York NY 10021

SAGESSER, RENE WALTER, bank executive; b. Zurich, Switzerland, June 18, 1949; arrived in Eng., 1987; s. Friedrich Ernst and Ella (Heimberg) S. Diploma in banking, Comml. Coll., Zurich, 1970; student in bus. adminstrn. and econs., McGill U., Montreal, Can., 1976; diploma in securities, Can. Bankers Assn., 1977. Orgn. specialist Credit Suisse, Zurich, 1970-74; asst. to mgr. ops. Montreal, 1975-79; project mgr. Hong Kong, 1980, Cairo, 1981; project mgr., cons. N.Y.C., 1982; asst. v.p. orgns. abroad Zurich, 1983-85, dep. v.p. orgns. abroad, 1986; v.p. orgn. and automation London, 1987—. Contbr. articles to local newspapers. V.p., then pres. Youth Orgn. Comml. Coll., Zurich, 1968-72. Serving with logistics br. Switzerland Army. Recipient Hon. award Town of Opfikon, Switzerland, 1969. Mem. Swiss Nat. Soc. (treas. 1976-79). Home: The Coachhouse, 4 Putney Park Ave, London SW15 5QN, England Office: Credit Suisse, 24 Bishopsgate, London EC2N 4BQ, England

SAGIV, EITAN, export cargo service executive, consultant; b. Isfahan, Iran, Sept. 7, 1941; arrived in Israel, 1968; s. Jacob and Rachel (Motahedeh) Sohayegh; m. Iafa Sagiv, July 6, 1967; children: Irit, Alon, Ron, Nurit. Export mgr. Skyways Travel Ltd., Teheran, Iran, 1960-67, U.S. Embassy customs rep., Army attache, 1962-67; export cargo services mgr. Israel Airlines Ltd., Lod Airport, Israel, 1969-87; mgr. dangerous goods safe handling, sales and spl. projects Flying Cargo Ltd., Tel Aviv, 1987—. Home: Kriat Shmoneh 3/3, Holon 58483, Israel

SAGSTETTER, WILLIAM EDWARD, freelance film producer; b. Denver, Jan. 10, 1945; s. William Edward and Pauline Elizabeth (Strouse) S.; m. Elizabeth Miller, Apr. 16, 1976. Freelance filmmaker, photographer Denver, 1970—; instr. filmmaking U. Colo., Denver, 1977-82; freelance photographer Denver Post, 1981-82; instr. history Denver Auraria Community Coll., 1984; cons. Adrienne Hynes & Assocs., Denver, 1984—; freelance photographer for mags. and newspapers, 1978—. Producer: (TV films) Mystery of Huajatolla, 1978, Caverna del Oro, 1970, The Bartered Tribe, 1973, Tarahumara: The People Who Run, 1976, Perspectives on Aging, 1982; patentee in field. Recipient Spl. Film award Aspen Arts Film Festival, 1978. Home and Office: 2217 Grove Denver CO 80211

SAHA, INDRAJIT KUMAR, paper company executive; b. Comilla, Bangladesh, Mar. 1, 1935; s. Jnanendra Chandra and Kula Bala (Saha) S.; m.

Gouri Poddar, Mar. 7, 1964; children: Indrani, Indraneel. BA with honors, Scottish Ch. Coll., Calcutta, India, 1955; postgrad. diploma in personnel mgmt. and indsl. relations, Tata Inst. Social Scis., Bombay, 1957. Personnel officer Lipton India Ltd., Calcutta, 1957-64; head personnel dept. Union Carbide India Ltd, Calcutta, 1964-73; dir. personnel Tribeni Tissues Ltd., Calcutta, 1974-87, v.p., 1987—; examiner, paper setter Calcutta U.; mem. guest faculty Indian Inst. Mgmt., Indian Inst. Social Welfare and Bus. Mgmt., Calcutta. Fellow Nat. Inst. Personnel Mgmt., Brit. Inst. Mgmt.; mem. Nat. Inst. Personnel Mgmt. India (life, past chmn.), Calcutta Mgmt. Assn. (pres. 1987), India Mgmt. Assn. (exec. council). Clubs: Calcutta, Calcutta Rowing. Home: 58/1 Ballygunge Circular Rd, Calcutta 700 019, India

SAHA, NILMANI, human geneticist and physiologist; b. Jhikira, India, Mar. 1, 1935; s. Gajendra Nath and Krishna Mati; B.Sc., Calcutta U., 1957, M.B.B.S., 1960, Ph.D. in Medicine, 1972; M.D., Panjab U., 1966; married; children—Swaroopa, Sabari. Tutor, lectr., asst. prof. med. colls., India, 1960-66; lectr. physiology med. faculty U. Singapore, 1966-72; research fellow dept. human biology John Curtin Sch. Med. Research, Australia Nat. U. Canberra, 1972-73; prof. physiology U. Khartoum (Sudan), 1973-80; hon. research fellow Galton Lab., Univ. Coll., London, 1974-75, 76-78; vis. prof. dept. med. genetics U. Umea, Sweden, 1980-81; asso. prof. physiology med. faculty Nat. U. Singapore, 1981-84, research scientist, 1987—; vis. scientist insts. human genetics, Hannover, Hamburg, Marburg, W.Ger. Internat. Child Health Found. fellow, 1966. Fellow Inst. Biology (cert.), Genetical Soc. United Kingdom; mem. Am. Soc. Human Genetics, Soc. Study Human Biology, Internat. Assn. Human Biologists, Human Biology Council, Internat. Fedn. Body Builders (med. com.), Indian Soc. Human Genetics, Indian Sci. Congress, Nutrition Soc., Inst. Biology, European Assn. Human Biologists, Calcutta Med. Club. Contbr. 100 articles on human genetics and human nutrition to internat. jours. Home: 30 Lornie Rd, Singapore 1129, Singapore Office: Faculty Medicine, Nat Univ Singapore, Singapore 0511, Singapore

SAHA, SUBRATA, bioengineering educator; b. Kushtia, India, Nov. 2, 1942; came to U.S., 1968, naturalized, 1976; s. Jaladhar K. and Sushama S.; m. Pamela Sunday, Oct. 30, 1972; children—Sunil, Supriya. B.S., Calcutta U., 1963; M.S., Tenn. Tech. U., 1969; Ph.D., Stanford U., 1973. Engr. cons. firms, 1963-67; research and teaching asst. Tenn. Tech. U., Cookeville, 1968-69, Stanford U., 1969-73; research assoc. Yale U. Sch. Medicine, 1974; asst. prof. Yale U., 1974-79; assoc. prof., coordinator bioengring. La. State U. Med. Center, Shreveport, 1979-84, prof., coordinator bioengring., 1984—. Editorial bd. Jour. Bioelectricity, Jour. Biomed. Material Research, Biotelemetry and Patient Monitoring, Biomaterials, Medical Devices and Artificial Organs. Contbr. numerous articles to nat. and internat. jours., books; also abstracts. Recipient Research Career Devel. award NIH, 1978-83, U.S.-India Exchange Scientist award, 1978; Fulbright award, 1982; C. William Hall Research award, 1987. Fellow ASME (Engring. Achievement award 1984); mem. Soc. Exptl. Stress Analysis, Soc. Biomaterials, Orthopaedic Research Soc., Biomed. Engring. Soc., Am. Soc. Biomechanics, IEEE (sr.), So. Bioengring. Conf. (founder), ASCE, Am. Acad. Mechanics, Sigma Xi. Home: 7601 Old Spanish Trail Shreveport LA 71105 Office: Dept Orthopaedic Surgery La State U Med Ctr PO Box 33932 Shreveport LA 71130

SAHAY, ANANT, infosystems specialist; b. Patna, Bihar, India, May 26, 1952; s. Hemant Kumar and Urmilla (Varma) S.; m. Naintara Motwani, Dec. 21, 1980; children: Nishant, Harshvardhan. BSc, Bihar Inst. of Tech., 1974; postgrad. diploma in bus. mgmt., Xavier Labour Relations Inst., Jamshedpur, 1980. Grad. apprentice Tata Engring. Co., Jamshedpur, 1974-76; asst. indsl. engr. 1976-77, programmer analyst, 1977-80, systems analyst, 1980-81; systems analyst Tata Engring. Services Ltd., Singapore, 1981-83; analyst programmer Gulf Air Co., Bahrain, 1983; sr. analyst programmer 1983—. Home: Villa 1702 Rd 1555, Saar 515 Bahrain Office: Gulf Air Co, Muharque Bahrain

SAHB, ABDALLAH LEON DE (MARQUIS), economics consultant; b. Aleppo, Syria, June 20, 1921; s. Leon and Guitta (Shelhot) de S.; LL.M., U. Beirut (Lebanon), 1945, Pharmacist, 1967; M.S., U. Sorbonne (Paris), 1950; Chem. Engr., E.N.S.C., Paris, 1950; Ph.D., U. Paris, 1969; Electronics Engr., ESIEE, Paris, 1981; m. Odile Samman, June 18, 1955; children—Dalal-Guitta, Mathilda, Leon, Rima-Ghislaine, Nahla-Helen, Namir-Nicolas. Dir. gen. No. Syria, Wheat Collection Scheme Govt. Syria, 1946-47; founder, chief exec. Marquis Leon de Sahb & Sons, Aleppo, 1951-61, Nat. Foundries & Mech. Workshops, Aleppo, 1952-66, Syrian Swedish Trading Co., Aleppo, Damascus, Syria, 1953-62, Transcontinental Econ. & Devel. Corp., Beirut, 1961-66, United Pharm. & Chem. Corp., Beirut, 1967-76, Al-Omrane Cons., Beirut, 1968—, Establissements A. de Sahb, internat. econ. cons., Beirut, 1970—; vis. prof. Dauphine U., Paris, 1978—; cons., expert Chamber Commerce and Industry, Paris, 1979—; lectr., cons. in field. Mem. Ministerial Com. Syrian 5-Yr. Plan, Damascus, 1960-61. Decorated Knight Holy Sepulchre, Cross Sci. Merit Paris, Grand Officer Order Constantine the Gt., Order Cedar Pres. Lebanon. Mem. Assn. Anciens Eleves de l'Ecole Nat. Superieure de Chimie, Paris, Nat. Order Pharmacists Lebanon, N.Y. Acad. Scis. Club: Vision (Paris). Author: Developpement et Questions d'Orient, 1972; Iran: A Front Page Candidate for Industrialization, 1974; Saudi Arabia: Pressing for Oil to Change into Lifeblood, 1974; From Petrodollars to Arab Steel, 1976; Egypt's Industrial Vocation, 1976; Saudi Arabia in the 1980's, 1978; Development of Expert Systems and the Resources of the Mind, 1988. Home: 97 Blvd Murat, 75016 Paris France Office: Starco Center, PO Box 11-5564, Beirut Lebanon

SAHGAL, NAYANTARA, writer; b. Allahabad, India, May 10, 1927; d. Ranjit Sitaram and Vijaya Lakshmi (Nehru) Pandit; m. Gautam Sahgal, Jan. 2, 1949 (div. Mar. 1967); children: Nonika, Ranjit, Gita; m. Edward Nirmal Mangat-Rai, Sept. 17, 1979. BA in History, Wellesley Coll., 1947. Freelance writer Dehra Dun, India, 1947—; writer-in-residence So. Meth. U., Dallas, 1973, 77; vis. scholar Radcliffe Inst., Cambridge, Mass., 1976. Author: Prison and Chocolate Cake, 1954, A Time to be Happy, 1958, From Fear Set Free, 1962, This Time of Morning, 1965, Storm in Chandigark, 1969, The Day in Shadow, 1972, A Situation in New Delhi, 1977, Indira Gandhi: Her Road to Power, 1982, Rich Like Us, 1985 (Sinclair prize 1985), Plans for Departure, 1986 (Sahitya Akoderm award 1987, Commonwealth Writer's prize 1987). Hindu. Home and Office: 181-B Rajpur Rd, Dehra Dun 248 009, India

SAHIB, MOHAMMED ALI, statistician; b. Lautoka, Fiji Islands, Aug. 6, 1929; s. Nanhu and Hussain B. S.; B.A. with honors, Govt. Coll., Lahore, Pakistan, 1955; M.A. in Stats. (Gold medal), U. Panjab, Lahore, 1957; M.A. in Econs., U. Ottawa (Ont., Can.), 1962; m. Hussain Sahib, May 3, 1958; children—Mazhar Ali, Azhar Ali. Trade stats. officer, customs dept. Govt. Fiji, 1957-60, statistician commerce and industries dept., 1962-67, dep. govt. statistician Bur. Stats., 1967-69, govt. statistician, 1969-74; econ. affairs officer stats. div. UN Econ. and Social Commn. Asia and Pacific (ESCAP), Bangkok, Thailand, 1974-79, chief stats. div., 1979—, mem. several policy and functional coms.; nat. dir. Fiji Fertility Survey, 1973-74. Commonwealth fellow, 1960-62, Internat. Monetary Fund fellow, 1969; recipient Fiji Independence medal, 1970. Fellow Inst. of Statisticians of London; mem. Internat. Statis. Inst., Am. Statis. Assn., Am. Sociol. Assn., Internat. Assn. Ofct. Stats. (v.p.), Internat. Union Sci. Study Population. Islam. Clubs: UN Golf. Author: Economic Development of Fiji, 1961; Life Tables of Fiji, 1967; Fiji Fertility Survey Report, 1976; numerous papers on statis. orgns. in developing countries and promotion of nat. statis. capability bldg. 1974—. Office: ESCAP Secretariat, UN Bldg, Rajdamnern Ave, Bangkok 10200 Thailand

SAHLIN, MAURITZ, manufacturing executive; b. Karlskoga, Sweden, June 14, 1935; s. Mauritz and Inga (Hessle) S.; m. Barbro Rönnholm; children: Annika, Katarina, Mauritz; m. Ulla Hilding; 1 child, Charlotte Hilding. Degree in Marine Engring., Royal Swedish Naval Staff Coll., Stockholm, 1960; MS, Royal Inst. Tech., Stockholm, 1960. Head cold forming sect. Bulten-Kanthal AB, Hallstahammer, Sweden, 1960-62, mgr. indsl. engring., 1962-69, gen. mgr. Bulten div., 1969-72; dep. gen. mgr. SKF Göteborg, Sweden, 1972-73; mng. dir. SKF Schweinfurt, Fed. Republic Germany, 1973-78; dep. mng. dir. SKF Group, Göteborg, 1975-85; dir. European Bearing Div. AB SKF, Göteborg, 1978-85; pres., group chief exec. SKF Group, 1985—. Mem. Swedish Assn. Mech. Engring. (chmn. 1984-87), Ovako Steel AB (chmn. 1986—), AB Export Invest, AB Saab-Scania, Fedn. Swedish Industries. Home: Gotabergsgatan 34, 411 34 Goteberg Sweden Office: AB SKF, 415 50 Goteborg Sweden

SAHNI-KHANPURI, CHATTAR SINGH, insurance executive; b. Khanpur, Pakistan, Sept. 20, 1926; s. Budh Singh and Ram Lubhai S.; m. Ranjiit Kaur Sahni, May 11, 1949; children: Jaghans, Maniderjeet, Parvinder, Harvinder, Inderbir. BA, Forman Christian Coll., 1947; FCII, Chartered Ins. Inst., 1968; student, U. London, 1970. Mng. ptnr. R.S. & C.S. Shipping and Clearing Co., Khorramshahr, Iran, 1947-50, Khanpuri TRading Co., Ltd., Tehran, Iran, 1950-57; mgr. overseas br. Bimeh Bazarganan, Tehran, 1957-59; mgr. A.R. Albisher & Z. Alkazemi, Kuwait City, Kuwait, 1959-65, gen. mgr. Guardian Royal Exchange Assurance, 1965—. Editor Folio, 1946-47; contbr. articles to various pubs. Fellow Chartered Ins. Inst., Brit. Inst. Mgmt.; mem. Kuwait Ins. Assn. (chmn. 1975-76, 78-79, 83—). Clubs: Gazelle, Govt. Sea, Indian Arts Circle (Kuwait). Home: PO Box 2334, Safat, Kuwait City 13024, Kuwait

SAHNOUN, MOHAMED, diplomat; b. Chlef, Algeria, Apr. 8, 1931; m. Hadjira Bachtarzi, Oct. 1967; children—Kamel, Hania. Higher edn. cert., Sorbonne U., Paris; BA, MA in Sociology, NYU. Dir. polit. affairs Algerian Ministry of Fgn. Affairs, Algiers, 1962-64; dep. sec. gen. polit. affairs and decolonization Orgn. African Unity, Addis-Ababa, Ethiopia, 1964-73; dep. sec. gen. African affairs League of Arab States, Cairo, 1973-74; Algerian ambassador to Fed. Republic Germany Bonn, 1975-79; ambassador to France Paris, 1979-82; ambassador, chief of permanent mission of Algeria UN, N.Y.C., 1982-84; Algerian ambassador to U.S. Washington, 1984—; mem. UN World Commn. on Environment and Devel., various internat. panels on UN reforms and conflict resolutions. Mem. FLN Party (mem. cen. com.). Office: Embassy of Algeria 2118 Kalorama Rd NW Washington DC 20008

SAHU, SAHEB, pediatrician; b. Mulbar, India, May 3, 1944; came to U.S., 1970, naturalized, 1972; s. Bidyadhar and Sakuntala Sahu; M.D., All-India Inst. Med. Scis., 1969; m. Krishna, June 8, 1970; children—Raj, Neil. Resident in pediatrics Raymond Blank Meml. Hosp. for Children, Des Moines, 1970-72; fellow in neonatology Med. Coll. Wis., Milw., 1972-73; asst. prof. U. Osteopathic Medicine and Surgery, Des Moines, 1973-76, asso. prof., 1976-77, prof., 1978—; dir. neonatal ICU, Mercy Hosp. Med. Center, Des Moines, 1974—; cons. to sec. Dept. Health and Human Services, 1980. Sec.-treas. Children Health Care Fund Assn., Des Moines. Fellow Am. Acad. Pediatrics, Internat. Coll. Pediatrics; mem. AMA, Iowa Med. Soc., Polk County Med. Soc., Indo-Am. Assn. Des Moines (founding pres. 1975), World Med. Assn. Lodge: West Des Moines Rotary. Author 2 med. texts. Contbr. articles to med. jours. Home: 8117 52d St West Des Moines IA 50265 Office: 412 Laurel St Mercy Med Plaza Suite 304 Des Moines IA 50314

SAI, ZAIJU, architectural firm executive; b. Republic of Korea, Feb. 1, 1927; m. Nin-nen Kim; children: Kazuko, Kazuei, Kazuhide. BS, Kanto Gakuin U., Yokohama, Japan, 1952. Registered archtl. engr., Japan. Staff Ishii Archtl. Research Inst., Tokyo, 1952-55, v.p., 1956-61; lectr. Kanto Gakuin U., Yokohama, 1959-63; dir. Homat Homes, Ltd., Tokyo, 1954—; pres. Sai Archtl. Research Inst. Co., Ltd., Tokyo, 1961—; advisor Homat Homes Ltd., Tokyo, 1954—. Mem. Japan Inst. Architects. Avocation: gardener. Home: Tsurugamine 2-29-2, Asahiku, Yokohama 241, Japan Office: Sai Archtl Research Co Ltd, 31-17 Shiba 2-chome, Minato-ku, Tokyo 105, Japan

SAICH, ANTHONY JAMES, Sinologist; b. London, Apr. 1, 1953; arrived in The Netherlands, 1982; s. James William and Queenie Elsie (Holden) S.; m. Mieke Kerkhoven. BA with Honors, U. Newcastle-upon-Tyne, England, 1975; Diploma in Chinese History, Nanjing (People's Republic China) U., 1977; MS in Econs., Sch. Oriental and African Studies, London, 1978; PhD, State U. Leiden, The Netherlands, 1986. Lectr. U. Newcastle-upon-Tyne, 1978-82; prof. State U. Leiden, 1982—; bd. dirs. Sawadee Travel, Amsterdam. Author: China: Politics and Government, 1981, China's Science Policy in the Eighties, 1987; author, editor: The Henk Sneevliet Archives, 1987; editorial bd. Jour. Communist Studies, 1985—; editor China Information, Leiden, 1986—; contbr. numerous articles to profl. jours. Assn. Commonwealth Univs. research fellow, 1978. Mem. Royal Dutch Acad. Scis. (China com. 1985—), Brit. Assn. Chinese Studies (exec. com. 1980-82), European Assn. Chinese Studies, European Consortium for Polit. Research (Standing Group for Eastern Asia). Office: Sinologisch Inst, Posthus 9515, Leiden 2300 RA, The Netherlands

SAID, GILLES EMILE, pediatrician; b. Blida, France, May 18, 1926; s. Avellan and Cécile (Attia) S.; m. Françoise Lion, Aug. 26, 1957; children: Isabelle, Catherine. MD, Fac Medicine of Paris, 1957. Extern Hosp. of Paris, 1959; Lauréat Acad. Medicine, France, Price of comité National de l'Enfance. Contr. articles to profl. jours. Mem. adminstrv. com. Nat. League Against Cancer. Jewish. Home: 70 Avenue De Bourg La Reine, 92220 Bagneux France

SAID, MOHSIN M., insurance company executive, consultant; b. Cairo, Egypt, Nov. 7, 1954; came to U.S., 1978, naturalized 1981; s. M. Said and Hanem (Hagag) Mohamoud; m. Therese Hanson, Nov. 7, 1977; children: Sharif, Summe, Jihan. BA in Phys. Edn., Cairo U., 1976. Fin. planner Aetna Ins., Milw., 1978-79; ins. exec. Lincoln Fin. Resources, Milw., 1979—; dir. Lincoln Fin. Resources Fin. & Investment Corp., Milw., 1979—. Active Republican Party, Washington, 1983—. Mem. Internt. Assn. Fin. Planners (accredited), Nat. Assn. Life Underwriters (life, Nat. Sales Achievement award, 1981-87), Nat. Assn. Health Underwriters (life, leading producer roundtable, Nat. Quality award 1981-87). Club: Athletic. Avocations: soccer, bicycling, traveling, tennis, stamp collecting. Home: 14505 Watertown Plank Rd Elm Grove WI 53122 Office: Lincoln Fin Resources Bishops Woods West I 150 S Sunnyslope Rd Suite 101 Brookfield WI 53005

SAIDI, AHMAD, export company executive; b. Khoy, Iran, Jan. 28, 1904; came to U.S., 1931, naturalized, 1950; s. Abol Hassan and Khanombozorg (Abolghassemi) S.; B.A., U. Okla., 1935; M.A., George Washington U., 1937; m. Elizabeth Gettner, Feb. 12, 1954; 1 child, Ali Emerson. Asst. to pres. M. Dilmaghani & Co., Scarsdale, N.Y., 1938-41; instr. Persian Inst., 1942; chief Persian Desk, OWI, N.Y.C., 1942-43; chief Persian sect. Dept. Def., N.Y.C., 1943-45; exec. sec. Iran Am. C. of C., N.Y.C., 1945-75; pres. Gen. Fgn. Sales Corp., Scarsdale, N.Y., 1946-68, chmn. bd. 1968-75; pres. Iran Trading Corp., Scarsdale, 1949-68; chmn. bd. Export Promotion Center, Tehran, Iran, 1967-68. Inaugurated, dir. Voice of Am. broadcasts to Iran, 1943. Mem. high coordinating econ. com., Tehran, Iran, 1967-68. Mem. nat. gift com. NCCJ, 1964. Decorated Order of Homayoon, Shah of Iran, 1962. Mem. Nat. Geog. Soc., Pi Sigma Alpha. Contbg. author: Sufi Studies: East and West. Editor: Iran Am. Monthly Newsletter, 1950-75, Iran Am. Rev., 1945-75. Numerous articles in Persian and English. Home: 1416 Gray Bluff Trail Chapel Hill NC 27514

SAIEH, ALVARO BENDECK, bank executive, educator; b. Villanueva, Colombia, Sept. 14, 1949; arrived in Chile, 1953; s. José and Elena (Bendeck) S.; m. Ana Victoria Guzmán; children: Jorge Andrès, María Soledad, María Francisca, María Catalina, María Consuelo. Degree in Engring., U. Chile, Santiago, 1976-77; MA, U. Chgo., 1976, PhD in Econs., 1980. Cons. Cen. Bank Chile, Santiago, 1976-77, Econ. Commn. Latin Am., Santiago, 1977-78; chief economist Cen. Bank Chile, 1979-80; dean faculty econs. and bus. U. Chile, 1980-81, chmn. dept. econs. and bus. univ., 1985-86, exec. dir. Found. Monetary Fin. Studies, 1985-86; gen. mgr. Banco Osorno Unión, Santiago, 1986—. Office: Banco Osorno y La Unión, Bandera 66, PO Box 57-D, Santiago Chile

SAIGER, GEORGE LEWIS, physician, epidemiologist, statistician, educator, medical research consultant; b. Burlington, Vt., Dec. 5, 1922; s. Simeon Hillel and Sophie (Snider) S.; m. Faye Toby Diamond, Nov. 4, 1948 (dec. Sept. 1976). Cert., Stanford U., 1944; B.S., U. Vt., 1945, M.D., 1948; M.P.H., Columbia U., 1951, Dr.P.H., 1955. Intern U.S. Marine Hosp., Cleve., 1948-49; asst. county health officer chronic disease div. USPHS, Prince Georges County, Md., 1949-50; instr. biostats. Columbia U., 1951-52; med. research cons., part-time pvt. practice Ft. Lee, N.J., 1952-53; prof. biostats. Columbia U., 1956-59, prof. epidemiology, 1959-64; also cons. med. research and biometric; med. cons. Bur. Medicine, FDA, Washington, 1963; dir. div. research and reference and FDA info. center on adverse reactions and hazards Bur. Medicine, FDA, 1963-64; cons. med. research Palisade and Ft. Lee, N.J., 1964-67; owner-dir. George L. Saiger & Assos., Cons. in Med. Research, Palisade and Ft. Lee, 1967-72, Englewood Cliffs, N.J., 1972—; land acquisition and devel., 1969—; vis. lectr. SUNY, Bklyn., 1952; asst. prof. preventive medicine La. State U., 1955; cons. med. jours., 1952—; med. research cons. Rand Corp., 1955-57; med. research cons., chief biometrician, asst. to dir. Army Med. Research Lab., Ft. Knox, Ky., 1953-55; Rockefeller Found. fellow U. Aberdeen, Scotland, 1959; mem. thesis exam. com. and mental, cardiovascular, radiation research coms. Columbia U. and Argonne Nat. Lab., 1956-63; mem. adv. com. model prescription rec. system study Sch. Pharmacy, U. Pitts., 1963-64; guest speaker spl. conf. on drug info. services Am. Soc. Hosp. Pharmacists, 1964; med. sect. Pharm. Mfrs. Assn., 1964. Author: Tables of the Normal, t, F and Chi-Square Distributions, 1953, A Laboratory Manual of Biometry, 1953, 54, Techniques in Multivariate Analysis as Applied to Medical Data, 1955, Medical Biometry, A Course Outline for Medical Students, 1958, Fundamentals of Epidemiology, 1961, Chemical and Biological Effects of Chemosol, a Tobacco Additive, 1976, Reductol V in Perspective, 1980; contbr. articles to profl. jours. Expert witness Com. on Commerce, U.S. Senate, 1965; expert witness Com. on Interstate and Fgn. Commerce, Ho. of Reps., 1965, 69. Served with AUS, 1943-46; capt. M.C. 1953-55; asst. surgeon (R) USPHS, 1948-53. Recipient Nat. Found. Infantile Paralysis fellowship award, 1951; Social Sci. Research Council Internat. Conf. Travel grantee, 1961. Fellow Am. Public Health Assn., Am. Geriatrics Soc., AAAS, N.J. Acad. Sci.; mem. World Med. Assn. (U.S. com.), Internat. Platform Assn., Am. Statis. Assn. (N.Y.C. Met. Area and No. N.J. chpts.), Biometric Soc. (Eastern N.Am. region), Assn. Alumni Columbia Sch. Public Health and Adminstrv. Medicine, Assn. Tchrs. Preventive Medicine, U. Vt. Med. Alumni Assn., Alumni Fedn. Columbia U. Address: 28 John St Englewood Cliffs NJ 07632-2908

SAIKKONEN, PEKKA JUHANI, physicochemist, process metallurgist; b. Helsinki, Finland, July 3, 1946; s. Eino Sulo and Salli Matilda (Laakso) S.; m. Raili Anneli Leino, Dec. 28, 1968; 1 child, Riku Juhani. M.Sci., Helsinki U. Tech., 1970. Research asst. Helsinki U. Tech., Espoo, Finland, 1969-70, asst., 1971-82, researcher phys. chemistry, 1982—. Contbr. articles to profl. jours.; patentee in field of extractive process metallurgy. Served to 1st lt. Finnish Army, 1970-71. Mem. Finnish Tech. Soc., Finnish Chem. Soc., AIME. Home: Alakartanontie 4B 63, 02360 Espoo Finland Office: Helsinki Univ Technology, Otakaari 1, 02150 Espoo Finland

SAILLARD, MICHEL RENE, engineer; b. Paris, Mar. 21, 1928; s. Rene Frederic and Helene Marguerite (Dupont) S.; m. Claude Marguerite Mougrnot, Aug. 6, 1956; children: Dominique, Frederic. Ingenieur, Ecole Polytechnique, Paris, 1951, Ecole des Ponts et Chaussées, Paris, 1953. Ingenieur prin. Travaux Publics, Sfax, Tunisia, 1953-57; ingenieur en chef Navigation Seine, Paris, 1957-58; dir. Société Centrale pour L'equipment du Territore, Paris, 1958-64; sec. gen. Scoiété Centrale Immobiliere, Paris, 1966-67; dir. gen. de la SCIC, Paris, 1967-82; pres., dir. gen. Société Française d'Etudes et de Réalisations d'Equipements Gaziers, Paris-Clichy, 1983-84, pres. dir. gen., 1984—; prof. Ecole des Ponts et Chaussées, 1980—. Contbr. articles to profl. jours. Served to capt. Arty., French Army, 1948-51. Decorated chevalier Legion D'Honneur, 1972; officer Merite National, 1977. Roman Catholic. Club: Cercle DuBois de Boulogne (Paris). Office: Sofregaz, 92 Blvd Victor Hugo, 92-115 Clichy sur Seine France

SAILLON, ALFRED, psychiatrist; b. Haïfa, Israel, Apr. 13, 1944; arrived in France, 1963; s. Joseph and Andree (Gemayel) Sahyoun; m. Anne Crouzat, Mar. 19, 1965; children: Helene, Marc, Antoine. Student, Am. U., Beirut, 1963; MD, Paris Med. Sch., 1971, psychiatry, 1974. Intern various hosps., Paris, 1971-74; pvt. practice specializing in psychiatry Fontainebleau, France, 1974—; asst. Hosp. de Coulommiers, 1976; pres. Les Jardins D'Eleusis, France, 1986. Contbr. articles to profl. jours. Mem. Assn. Pour la Prevention des Comportements Toxico Maniaques (pres. 1985-87). Home and Office: 3 Bld Thiers, 77300 Fountainbleau France

SAINER, LEONARD, lawyer, business executive; b. London, Oct. 12, 1909; s. Archer and Sarah (Lewis) S. Ed., Univ. Coll., London, London Sch. Econs. Formerly sr. ptnr., now cons. Titmuss Sainer & Webb, London; life pres. Sears plc, London. Office: Sears PLC, 40 Duke St, London W1M 6AN, England

SAINI, GULSHAN RAI, soil physicist; b. Hoshiarpur, India, Oct. 1, 1924; s. Ram Saran and Parmeshri Devi (Bhondi) S.; B.Sc., U. Panjab, 1945, M.Sc., 1956; Ph.D., Ohio State U., 1960; m. Veena Chaudhri, Jan. 14, 1950; 1 son, Vikas. Research asst. Govt. Agrl. Coll., Ludhiana, India, 1945-57; research assoc. Ohio State U., Columbus, 1957-60; asst. prof. Punjab Agrl. U., Ludhiana, India, 1960-61; research scientist Can. Dept. Agr., Fredericton, N.B., 1962-84; adj. prof. Faculty of Forestry, U. N.B., Fredericton, 1968-76; vis. prof. Rutgers U., 1984-85. Mem. Indian Sci. Congress Assn. (life), Multicultural Assn. Fredericton (life, pres. 1980-81), Profl. Inst. Pub. Service Can. (nat. v.p. 1980, 81, chmn. Atlantic regional council 1978, 79), Sigma Xi, Phi Lambda Upsilon. Contbr. articles to profl. jours. Home: 24 Brook St Brookline MA 02146

SAINI, RAJENDAR MOHAN, orthodontist; b. Hoshiarpur, India, Sept. 17, 1940; came to U.S., 1963; s. Dev Raj and Durga (Devi) S.; B.D.S., Dental Coll. Asr. India, 1962; M.S.D., N.Y.U., 1966; D.D.S., U. Toronto (Ont., Can.), 1970; m. Indira Chaudhary, Aug. 23, 1967; children—Renu, Tarun, Bela. Asst. prof. Howard U. Coll. Dentistry, Washington, 1966-69, U. Md., Balt., 1970-76; practice dentistry specializing in orthodontics, Columbia, Md., 1970—; orthodontic cons. Montgomery County Health Dept., Rockville, Md., 1970—. Chmn., GNFA Inc. (Punjab/Indian Community/Religious Assn.), 1978-79. Named Outstanding Lectr., Howard U. Coll. Dentistry, 1969; diplomate Am. Bd. Orthodontics. Mem. ADA, Am. Assn. Orthodontists, Internat. Assn. for Dental Research, Howard County Dental Assocs. (charter pres. 1984-85). Club: Rotary (club pres. 1979-80, gov. 85-86, nat. coordinator internat. polio plus project 1986-88). Home: 11413 High Hay Dr Columbia MD 21044 Office: 10776 Hickory Ridge Columbia MD 21044

ST. CLAIR-GEORGE, MICHAEL ANTHONY, plantation company executive, consultant; b. Bengal, India, Sept. 17, 1942; s. Lionel Aram and Pearl Leonora (Pedroza) George; m. Elizabeth Ann St. Clair-Pedroza, June 1, 1973; children: Jeremy James, Jane Elizabeth. Student, St. Michaels Coll., Hitchin, Hertfordshire, Eng., 1956-60. Auditor Carter, Son & White, London, 1961-69; chief acct. Davu Wire and Cables Ltd., London, 1969-73; fin. controller, dir. Harrison & Crosfield, Kuala Lumpur, Malaysia, 1973-82; dir. fin. Harrisons Malaysian Plantations, Kuala Lumpur, 1982—; cons. Harrisons Flemming Adv. Services, London, 1973—; cons., bd. dirs. HMPB Consultancy Services, Kuala Lumpur, 1982—. Fellow Inst. Chartered Accts. Eng. and Wales. Conservative. Roman Catholic. Clubs: Lake (Kuala Lumpur), Commonwealth (London). Office: Harrisons Malaysian Plantations, Menara PNB, 201-A Jalan Tun Razak, 50734 Kuala Lumpur Malaysia

ST. CLEMENT, COURTNEY TOLSON, advertising executive; b. Fort Worth, Nov. 8, 1951; d. J.B. and Dorothy Allison (Marshall) Tolson; m. Reginald St. Clement, Sept. 13, 1981. Art dir. Bloom Advt., Dallas, 1973-77, Cunningham & Walsh, N.Y.C., 1977-82; pres., creative dir. St. Clement Group, N.Y.C., 1982—. Bd. dirs. East Meets West. Recipient Mead award Mead Paper, 1976; Silver Microphone award All Star Radio, 1985. Mem. Dutch Reform Ch. Clubs: Snarks (N.Y.C.); Bklyn. Equestrian. Office: St Clement Group 106 E 19th St New York NY 10003

ST. GERMAIN, JEAN MARY, medical physicist; b. N.Y.C.; d. Herbert and Mary J. (Newman) S.; B.S., Marymount Manhattan Coll., 1966; M.S., Rutgers U., 1967. Fellow radiol. health USPHS, Rutgers U., New Brunswick, N.J., 1967; fellow dept. med. physics Meml. Hosp., N.Y.C., Cornell U. Med. Coll., 1967-68, asst. physicist, 1968-71, instr. radiology (physics), 1971-78, clin. asst. prof., 1979—; asst. attending physicist Meml. Sloan-Kettering Cancer Center; cons. in field. Diplomate Am. Bd. Health Physics. Mem. Am. Inst. Physics (gov. bd.), Health Physics Soc. Am. Assn. Physicists in Medicine (sec., dir.), Soc. Nuclear Medicine, Radiol. Soc.

N.Am., N.Y. Acad. Scis., Radiol. and Med. Physics Soc. N.Y. (past pres.), Nat. Soc. Arts and Letters (regional dir., pres. N.Y. chpt.). Iota Sigma Pi (treas., pres. V chpt.). Author: The Nurse and Radiotherapy, 1978; contbr. articles, chpts. to med. jours., texts. Office: 1275 York Ave New York NY 10021

ST. JOHN, ADAM, artist, designer, consultant, instructor; b. Tampa, Fla., Feb. 24, 1952; 1 child, Aprile Danyse. Prin., ASJ Assoc., Houston and Dallas, 1980—; creator, lectr. seminar The Simplified Art of Faux Finishing, 1985—; . Contbr. articles to numerous popular mags. including Los Angeles Times mag, Texas Homes, Houston Home & Garden, Dallas-Fort Worth Home & Garden, Austin Homes & Gardens, San Antonio Homes and Gardens, So. Accents, Playboy; also European mags.; exhibited in group shows at Chair Fair, N.Y.C., 1986-87, Sq. One LA, Los Angeles, 1986-87, The Homestead, San Antonio, 1986, Arresta, Dallas, 1986, EQU, Dallas, 1986-87, Domo, inc., Houston, 1986-87, World Trade Ctr., Dallas, 1987, Parkerson Gallery, Houston, 1987, AES Gallery, Chgo., 1987, San Francisco Mus. Modern Art, 1987; represented in permanent collections in Mus. Fine Arts, Houston, San Antonio Museum Assn. Coll., San Francisco Mus. Modern Art. Recipient Best Show award Greater Denton Arts Council, Honor award Tex. Homes Furniture Design Competition, 1986. Mem. Am. Soc. Furniture Designers, Art League Houston (bd. dirs.), Am. Craft Council, Mensa. Office: ASJ Assoc 2615 Waugh Dr Suite 216 Houston TX 77006

ST. JULIAN, GRANT, JR., microbiologist; b. Beaumont, Tex., Feb. 13, 1931; s. Grant and Leah (Hebert) St. J.; m. Cora Jeanne Wood, Dec. 26, 1955; children: Grant, Andrea Renee, Tanya Suzanne. BS, Samuel Huston Coll., 1951; BA, Huston-Tillotson Coll., 1954; MS, U. Tex., 1957; postgrad. Bradley U., 1964-65, MIT, 1967. Research microbiologist agrl. microbiology unit, fermentation lab. No. Regional Research Ctr., U.S. Dept. Agr., Peoria, Ill., 1961—. Cons. dept. biochemistry U. Oxford (Eng.), Internat. Ctr. Insect Physiology and Ecology, Nairobi, Kenya, 1982. Chmn. Human Relations Commn. Peoria, 1960-64, mem. Fire and Police Commn., 1964-70; chmn. bd. dirs. Peoria Tri-County Urban League, 1969-71; mem. Mayor's Drug Abuse Task Force, 1970-71; bd. dirs. Ill. Arthritis Found, 1970-71, Tri-County Comprehensive Health Planning Commn., 1977; mem. priorities com. Heart of Ill. United Way, 1972-73, adv. bd. Salvation Army. Served with U.S. Army, 1952-54. Recipient Cert. of Merit, Human Relations Commn. Peoria, 1963; Humanitarian award State of Ill., 1965; Ralph Bunche Humanitarian award Peoria Bus. Assn., 1966; Paul Schlink Good Govt. award Peoria C. of C., 1968; Disting. Citizen award Urban League, 1976; Cert. of Merit, No. Regional Research Ctr., Peoria, 1979; Disting. Speaker award Am. Chem. Soc., 1980. Mem. N.Y. Acad. Scis., Ill. Acad. Sci., Internat. Invertebrate Pathology, Am. Soc. Microbiology, Ill. Soc. Microbiology, Entomol. Soc. Am., Sigma Xi. Democrat. Roman Catholic. Contbr. 60 articles to profl. jours. Home: 5609 Stephen Dr Peoria IL 61615 Office: 1815 University Peoria IL 61604

ST. LANDAU, NORMAN, lawyer; b. Vienna, Austria, Apr. 14, 1920; s. Henry M. and Anka (Nemirovska) St. L.; m. Maisie Dennis, July 18, 1942; children—Lorraine, Jon L., Norman D. B.S., A.B. with honors, U. Ill., 1941; LL.B., Rutgers U., 1948; LL.M., NYU, 1951. Bar: D.C. 1948, U.S. Supreme Ct. 1952, N.J. 1958. With Pitts. Plate Glass Co., Ohio, 1941-42; with Johnson & Johnson, New Brunswick, N.J., 1942-84, internat. counsel, 1957-84, chief trademark counsel, 1961-84; dir., officer numerous affiliates Johnson & Johnson Internat.; of counsel Lalos, Leeds, Keegan, Lett & Marsh, Washington, 1983-85, Durand, Gorman, Heher, Imbriaco & Morrice, Princeton, N.J., 1984-86, Brylawski, Cleary & Leeds, 1985—; ptnr. Heher, Clarke & St. Landau, Princeton, 1987—; chmn. bd. Action Law Systems, Inc., 1987—; mem. adv. com. U.S. Sec. State and Commr. Patents, 1975—. Co-author: Trademark Management, 1987, (with others) Guide to Patent Arbitration, 1987; fgn. editor Les Nouvelles, 1965—. Mem. N.J. State Bar Assn. (div. chmn., vice-chmn. immigration and nationality sect. 1988—), Nat. Fgn. Trade Council (chmn. indsl. property com.), N.J. Patent Law Assn. (past pres.), Nat. Council Patent Law Assns. (sec.-gen.), Nat. Panel Arbitrators, Am. Arbitration Assn., ABA, Am. Chem. Soc. (nat. councillor), Am. Patent Law Assn. (bd. mgrs.), Am. Immigration Lawyers Assn., Inter-Am. Assn. Indsl. Property (exec. com.), Internat. Patent and Trademark Assn., Lic. Execs. Lawyers. Club: Nassau. Lodge: Rotary. Home: 822 E Meadow Dr Bound Brook NJ 08805 Office: Heher Clarke & St Landau 105 College Rd E Forrestal Ctr Princeton NJ 08540

SAINT LAURENT, YVES (HENRI DONAT MATHIEU), couturier; b. Oran, Algeria, Aug. 1, 1936; s. Charles Mathieu and Lucinne-Andree (Wilbaux) Saint L.; diploma secondary studies. Collaborator, 1954, then successor of Christian Dior, 1957-60; adminstr. Société Yves Saint Laurent, 1962—; costume design for Cyrano de Bergerac Ballet, 1959; stage sets and costumes Les Chants de Meldoror, 1962, Zizi Jeanmaire Spectacles, 1962, 63; costume designs for Mariage de Figaro, 1964, ballets Adage et Variations, also Notre-Dame de Paris, 1965, Delicate Balance, 1967; costume designs for films Belle-de-Jour, 1967, Chamade, 1968; illus. La Vilaine Lulu, 1967. Recipient Neiman-Marcus award for fashions, 1958; Oscar from Harper's Bazaar, 1966. Office: 5 ave Marceau, 75016 Paris 16e France *

SAINT-MARTIN, JACQUES EDOUARD, pediatrician; b. Compiegne, France, Nov. 17, 1934; s. Lucien Joseph and Genevieve Alexandrine (Fournival) S.; m. Lily Charlotte Afifi, fJan. 28, 1958; children: Guy, Caroline, Valerie, Arnaud, Jerome. MD, Faculty of Medicine, Paris, 1967. Intern Hosp des enfants malades, Paris, 1963-67; asst. prof. pediatrics Hosp St. Vincent de Paul, Paris, 1967-72; head dept. pediatrics Gen. Hosp., Pau, 1972—; tchr. pediatrics Faculty Medicine, Phonm Penh, Kampuchea, 1988; mem. working party on pediatrics French Ministry of Health, 1985—. Contbr. articles to profl. jours. Tchr. care of newborn babies UNICEF, Vietnam, 1984-85. Recipient award Birth in Finland, Council of Europe, 1981, Birth in Sweden WHO, 1984. Fellow French Soc. Intensive Care Medicine, French Soc. Pediatrics. Roman Catholic. Office: Gen Hosp, 4 Boulevard Hauterive, 64015 Pau France

SAINT-MLEUX, ANDRE LEÒN, former minister of state Monaco, assn. adminstr.; b. St.-Malo, France, Sept. 25, 1920; s. Andre and Mary. Faculte de droit de Paris; m. Danielle Ramfos, Feb. 8, 1961; children: Andre, Arnaud, Armelle. Minister of state Govt. of Monaco, 1972-81. Served as officer French Army, 1943-45. Decorated Croix de Guerre, Legion of Honor (France). Pres., del. Société Des Bains de Mer et du Cercle Des Etrangers, Monte Carlo. Office: Société des Bains der Mer, Monte Carlo Monaco

SAINT-PIERRE, MICHAEL ROBERT, funeral director, consultant; b. Indpls., July 12, 1947; s. Robert Ross and Gaile Russell (Cousins) S.; m. Betty Carolyn Wilhoit, Jan. 14, 1967; children: Michelle René, Paul Christopher. Student Milligan Coll., 1965-67, Butler U., 1966; B.S., East Tenn. State U., 1969; diploma Ind. Coll. Mortuary Sci., 1970; postgrad. Nat. Found. Funeral Service, 1970, 71, 73, 74, 76, Ind. U., Indpls., 1977. Intern, Hamlett-Dobson, Kingsport, Tenn., 1967-69; pres. J.C. Wilson & Co., Inc., Indpls., 1969—, St. Pierre Funeral Mgmt. Corp., 1984—; evaluator/practitioner rep. Am. Bd. Funeral Service Edn., 1980—; prof., trustee Ind. Coll. Mortuary Sci., 1971-76; prof. Nat. Found. Funeral Service, 1987—; bd. advisors Nat. Bank Greenwood (Ind.), 1978-80; bd. dirs. Premier Mgmt. Corp., Metro Media Inc. Contbr. articles to profl. jours. Bd. dirs. Central Ind. Better Bus. Bur., Indpls., 1982-86, Adult/Child Mental Health Ctr., Indpls., 1982-85, Allied Meml. Council, Indpls., 1979—; elder Greenwood (Ind.) United Presbyn. Ch., 1976; past mem., treas. bd. dirs. Consumer Info. Bur., Inc.; past mem. bd. dirs. Center for Life/Death Edn., Indpls. Recipient Nat. Bd. Cert., Conf. Funeral Service Exam. Bd., 1970; Disting. Service awards Ind. Coll. Mortuary Sci., Indpls., 1978, Mid Am. Coll. Funeral Service, Jeffersonville, Ind., 1982. Fellow Nat. Found. Funeral Service (pres. alumni assn. 1978); mem. Associated Funeral Dirs. Service Internat. (pres. 1981), Nat. Selected Morticians, Nat. Funeral Dirs. Assn. (practitioner, resource and ourtreach, edn., supplementary speakers bur. and arbitration coms., chmn. employee/employer task force, chmn. mgmt. practice com.), Acad. Profl. Funeral Service Practice, Ind. Funeral Dirs. Assn. (bd. dirs., pres. 1982-83), Funeral Dirs. Forum, Prearrangement Assn. Am., Marion County Funeral Dirs. Assn. (pres. 1974), Nat. Eagle Scout Assn. Republican. Presbyterian. Clubs: Valle Vista Country, Skyline. Lodges: Rotary (past pres., Paul Harris fellow), Masons (past master), Scottish Rite, Shriners; Order Eastern Star. Office: Wilson St Pierre Funeral Service PO 147 481 W Main St Greenwood IN 46142

ST. PIERRE, ROGER, communications specialist; b. Weymouth, Dorset, England, Nov. 8, 1941; s. Alexander Richard and Caroline Amelia (Borrett) St.P.; m. Lesley Constantine, Oct. 10, 1975 (div. 1982); children: Richard Alexander, Danielle Jane, Nicole Marie. Grad. high sch., Essex, Eng. Editor Ford Motor Co., Dagenham, Eng., 1962-64, Internat. Pub. Co., London, Eng., 1964-66; publicity dir. Beacon Records, Eng., 1967-68; proprietor, U.K. publicist for Marvin Gaye, James Brown, Glen Campbell and others St. Pierre Publicity, Dulwich, London, Eng., 1968—. Author 17 pub. titles including Book of The Bicycle, Rock Handbook, 1966—; editor: Brit. Midland Airways Mag.; contbr. articles to profl. jours. Mem. Nat. Union Journalist, Rhythm and Blues Assn. (bd.dirs. 1966-70). Club: Zeus Racing (London) (sec. 1959-62), Havering Cycling (London) (sec. 1962-69). Home and Office: 24 Beauval Rd, Dulwich, London SE22 8UQ, England

SAINT-REMY, PIERRE LEON, import-export executive; b. Gonaïves, Artibonite, Haiti, Mar. 8, 1934; s. Leon and Yvonne (Forbin) Saint-R.; m. Michaelle Marie Delaquis, July 29, 1961; children: Pierre Leon Jr., Nathalie. BA, Coll. St. Martial, Port-au-Prince, Haiti, 1954; BS in acctg. and fin., NYU, 1958. With Madame Leon Saint-Remy Import-Export, Gonaïves, 1958-60, dir. export dept., 1961-69, under-dir. gen., 1969-73, dir. gen., 1973-76, pres., dir. gen., 1976—; pres., dir. gen. Les Allumettes Haïtiennes, S.A., Gonaïves, 1976—. Mem. Constitutional Assembly, Haiti, 1987; bd. dirs. Assn. for the Def. of the Constitution, 1987. Mem. Assn. des Industries d'Haiti (exec. bd. 1984), Soc. Financiere Haitienne de Devel. (exec. bd. 1986). Roman Catholic. Club: Cercle Bellevue (Port-au-Prince). Home: Ave des Dattes, Gonaives Haiti also: Rue Ludovie, Chante Brise, Delmas 83, Port-Au-Prince Haiti Office: Les Allumettes Haitiennes SA, Detour Laborde, Gonaives Haiti

SAITO, EISHIRO, steel company executive; b. Niigata-ken, Japan, Nov. 22, 1911; s. Tooru and Tome S.; B.Econs., Imperial U. Tokyo, 1935; m. Toshiko Kato, May 28, 1939; children: Satoko Saito Takasu, Hideki. With Japan Iron & Steel Co. Ltd., 1941-62; with Yawata Iron & Steel Co. Ltd., 1951, mng. dir., 1962-68, sr. mng. dir. 1968-70; sr. mng. dir. Nippon Steel Corp., Tokyo, 1970-73, exec. v.p., 1973-77, pres., 1977-81, rep. dir., 1977—, chmn. bd., 1981—; vice chmn. Keizai Doyu Kai, 1975; exec. dir. Keidanren, 1977, vice chmn., 1980, chmn., 1986—; chmn. Internat. Iron and Steel Inst., 1977-79, Keizai Koho Ctr. Recipient medal honor with blue ribbon Govt. of Japan, 1967, 1st Class Order Sacred Treasure (Japan); Ordem de Rio Branco (Brazil), 1978; Order of Bernard O'Higgins (Chile). Mem. Japan Iron and Steel Fedn. (chmn. 1979—). Office: Nippon Steel Corp, 6-3 Otemachi 2-chome, Chiyoda-ku, Tokyo 100, Japan *

SAITO, NOBUO, trading company executive; b. Tokyo, Fukuoka, Japan, Nov. 10, 1932; s. Eiichi and Masa S.; m. Sachiko Muramatsu, Aug. 10, 1965 (div. Apr. 1971); m. Kayoko Shimura, Feb. 3, 1972; 1 child, Yasuko. M.Ph., Tokyo U. With overseas procurement Nichimen Co., Tokyo, 1956-65; export mgr. Osawa Machine Co., Kawasaki, Japan, 1965-68; customer service mgr. Motorola Semiconductors, Tokyo, 1968-70; exec. dir. Peer Internat. Ltd., Tokyo, 1970—. Mem. Japan Seiki Gakkai. Liberal Democrat. Buddist. Clubs: Club VIVI, Internat. House of Japan (Tokyo). Avocation: speed racing. Home: 3-8-11-301 Nishiazabu, Minatoku, Tokyo 106, Japan Office: Peer Internat Ltd 2-4-2, 2-4-2 Nagata-cho, Chiyoda-Ku, Tokyo 100, Japan

SAITOH, MAMORU, textile company executive; b. Okazaki, Aichi, Japan, Jan. 1, 1935; s. Tamotsu and Kiyoko Saitoh; m. Minako Hayakawa, May 20, 1962; children: Kayoko, Yumiko. B in Engring., Nagoya U., Japan, 1958. Design engr. textile machinery div. Toyoda Automatic Loom Works Co., Kariya, Japan, 1958-71; chief design engr. Toyoda-Sulzer Mfg., Ohbu, Japan, 1971-82; chief design engr. Toyoda Automatic Loom Works Co., Kariya, 1982-84, asst. dir., 1984—. Mem. Japan Textile Machinery Assn. Buddhist. Club: Fuji Kani Country. Home: 4-23 Tosakishinmachi, Okazaki 444, Japan Office: Textile Machinery Engring, 2-4 Toyota-cho, Kariya 466, Japan

SAJJADI, SHAHRDAD GHOTB, theoretical physicist, mathematician, educator; b. Tehran, Iran, Feb. 1, 1961; s. Shamsedin and Parry (Badie) S.; m. Megan Louise Davies, Aug. 18, 1984; (div. Oct. 1986). BSc, Coventry (Eng.) Poly., 1982, PhD, 1984. Research officer Rutherford Appleton Lab., Didcot, Eng., 1982-84; lectr. math. Coventry Poly., 1984-85, sr. research fellow, 1985-88; sr. research fellow Cranfield Inst. Tech., 1988—; research cons. Rutherford Appleton Lab., Didcot, 1984—. Editor: Air-Sea Interfaces, 1987; conbtbr. articles to profl. jours. Mem. Inst. Math. and its Applications, Soc. Indsl. Applied Math., Am. Math. Soc.

SAKAI, KATSUO, electrophotographic engineer; b. Matsumoto, Nagano, Japan, Apr. 9, 1942; s. Mototeru and Fumi (Iida) S.; m. Toshiko Hagiwara, Feb. 7, 1976; children: Asako, Akiharu, Hirohiko. B in Applied Physics, Waseda U., Tokyo, 1967. Engr. Ricoh Co. Ltd., Tokyo, 1967—; lectr. in field. Contbr. articles to profl. jours.; inventor, patentee two-color electrophotography, 1980. Mem. Soc. Electrophotography of Japan, Soc. for Imaging Sci. and Tech. Club: Minami Fuji Country. Home: 25-64 Moegino Midori-ku, Yokohama 227, Japan Office: Ricoh Co Ltd, 1-3-6-Nakamagome, Ohta-ku, Tokyo 143, Japan

SAKAI, MAMORU, banker; b. Mar. 30, 1924; married. Grad., Kyushu U., 1947. With Kangyo Bank, from 1948; with Long-Term Credit Bank of Japan Ltd., 1952—, now pres., rep. dir. Home: 3-14 Midori-cho, 2-chome Tanashi-ku, Tokyo Japan Office: Long Term Credit Bank Japan, 2-4 Otemachi, 1-chome Chiyoda-ku, Tokyo Japan *

SAKAI, SHOICHIRO, mathematics educator; b. Kanuma, Tochigi, Japan, Jan. 2, 1928; s. Hajime and Moto (Kojima) S.; m. Yoshiko Sasaki, July 5, 1958; children—Masato, Kiyoshi. Ph.D., Tohoku U., Sendai, Japan, 1961. Research asst. Tohoku U., Sendai, 1953-60; asst. prof. math. Waseda U., Tokyo, 1960-62; vis. lectr. Yale U., New Haven, 1962-64; assoc. prof. U. Pa., Phila., 1964-67, prof., 1967-81; prof. Nihon U., Tokyo, 1981—. Author: C* Algebras and W* Algebras, 1971. Contbr. articles to profl. jours. Guggenheim fellow, 1970-71; invited speaker Internat. Congress for Mathematicians, Helsinki, Finland, 1978. Mem. Am. Math. Soc., Japan Math. Soc. (editor jours. 1984—), N.Y. Acad. Scis. Home: 205 Green Heights 5-1-6 Odawara, Sendai 983 Japan Office: Dept Math Nihon U, Sakura-Josui, Setagaya-ku, Tokyo Japan

SAKAI, SUMIKO, bank executive; b. Osaka City, Osaka, Japan, Nov. 25, 1932; d. Chozaburo and Shigeru S. Grad. high sch., Toyokawa City. With Gamagori br. The Nagoya Sogo Bank Ltd., Japan, 1952-57, with Toyohashi br., 1957-63, with gen. affairs div., 1963-69, with personnel div., 1969-71, asst. mgr. personnel div., 1971-75, mgr. personnel div., 1975-83, gen. mgr. Toyotahomi br., 1983-86, gen. mgr. Umemori br., 1986—; com. mem. Woman's Labour Problem, Nagoya, Japan, 1977, A Meeting Of Woman's Ednl. Test Research, Aichi Prefecture, Japan, 1977—, Audience Conf. NHK, 1983—, Indsl. and Ednl. council, Aichi Prefecture, 1984—. Mem. Internat. Fedn. Bus. Profl. Women. Home: 42-4 Ikeda, Yatsurugicho, Iwakura-city 482, Japan Office: The Nagoya Sogo Bank Ltd, Umemori Br, 2-519, Umemorizaka-nishi Meito-ku, Nagoya Japan

SAKAI, YOSHIRO, chemistry educator; b. Nagasaki, Japan, Dec. 28, 1935; s. Tsuyoshi and Rei (Ikeno) S.; m. Mutsuko Abe, Oct. 18, 1964; children: Hideaki, Masako. BS, Kyushu U., Fukuoka, Japan, 1958, ScD, 1970. Research fellow Govt. Indsl. Research Inst., Nagoya, Japan, 1958-68; assoc. prof. Ehime U., Matsuyama, Japan, 1968-74, prof. chemistry, 1974—. Mem. Chem. Soc. Japan, Soc. Polymer Sci., Electrochem. Soc. Japan. Home: 225-4 Shin-ishite, Matsuyama 790, Ehime Japan Office: Ehime Univ, Bunkyo-cho Matsuyama, Ehime Japan

SAKAKIBARA, SHUMPEI, chemical company executive; b. Kobe, Japan, Oct. 26, 1926; s. Yasukichi and Sofu (Shigeno) S.; m. Keiko Kado, Apr. 24, 1955; children—Toshiro, Tomoko. Ph.D., Osaka U., 1960. Assoc. prof. Osaka U., Japan, 1963-71; dir. Protein Research Found., Minoh, Japan, 1971—; pres. Peptide Inst. Inc., Minoh, 1977—. Editor: Peptide Chemistry, 1982, 87. Mem. Japan Chem. Soc., Am. Chem. Soc., Gesellschaft Deutscher Chemiker. Home: 23-3, Fujishirodai 2, Suita-shi, Osaka 565, Japan Office: Protein Research Found, 1-2 Ina-4 Minoh-shi, Osaka 562, Japan

SAKALAUSKAS, VITAUTAS VLADOVICH, Soviet government official; b. Lithuania, USSR, 1933. Grad., Poly. Inst. Kaunas, USSR. Mem. Communist Party Soviet Union, 1960—; sr. master, head sect., chief engr., dir. Priekalas enterprise, Kaunas, 1957-65; dep. head, dept. head Cen. Com. Lithuanian Communist Party, 1968-69; chair exec. com. Vilnius City Soviet People's Deps., USSR, 1969-74; mem. Cen. Com. Lithuanian Communist Party, Vilnius, 1971—, 1st city sec., 1974—, mem. bur., 1974-76; dep. USSR Supreme Soviet, 1974—; now chmn. Council of Ministers, Vilnius, Lithuanian Soviet Socialist Republic. Office: Council Ministers, Office of Chmn, Vilnius Lithuanian SSR, USSR *

SAKAMOTO, MASAE, data processing executive; b. Minami, Saku-gun, Japan, Dec. 7, 1931; s. Enjuro and Komachi S.; m. Chieko Sato, June 25, 1961; children: Asami, Tetsuya, Kozo. BBA, Meiji U., Tokyo, 1956. With statistics bur. Supply Hdqrs. U.S. Air Force Far East, Tokyo, 1956-61; with Okamura Mfg. Co., Kanagawa, Japan, 1961-62, Nippon Bus. Automation Co., Tokyo, 1962-64, Data Service Co., Tokyo, 1964—. Office: Data Service Co, 31F Shinjuku Center Bldg, 1-25-1 Nishi-Shinjuku, Shinjuku-ku Tokyo Japan 163

SAKHAROV, ANDREY DIMITRIYEVICH, physicist; b. Moscow, May 21, 1921; grad. Moscow State U., 1942; PhD 1953; m. Yelena Bonner, 1971; 2 children. Physicist, P.N. Lebedev Physics Inst., Acad. of Scis., Moscow, 1945-80; achieved important breakthrough in controlled nuclear fusion leading to devel. of Soviet hydrogen bomb; founder Human Rights Comm., 1970; active Soviet human rights campaign; in internal exile, 1980—. Decorated Order of Lenin; recipient Eleanor Roosevelt Peace award, 1973; Cino del Duca prize, 1974; Stalin prize; Reinhold Niebohr prize U. Chgo., 1974; Nobel Peace prize, 1975. Mem. Am. Acad. Arts and Scis., Nat. Acad. Scis., French Acad. Sci. (fgn. assoc.), Soviet Acad. Scis. Author: Progress, Peaceful Co-existence and Intellectual Freedom, 1968; Sakharov Speaks, 1974; My Country and the World, 1975; Alarm and Hope, 1979, also, others. Address: 214 Gagarin Prospect,, Sherpinki 2, Flat 3,, Gorky USSR *

SAKITA, MASAAKI, architect; b. Maizuru, Japan, Feb. 13, 1939; s. Manzo and Aiko (Inaba) S.; m. Aiko Sonoda, Oct. 17, 1970; children: Hajime, Atsushi. B in Engring., Fukui U., 1961. Registered architect, Japan. Mem. staff Yamada Mamoru Archtl. Firm and Assocs., Tokyo, 1961-66; job capt. Yamada Mamoru Architects and Engrs., Osaka City, Japan, 1966-80; assoc. Osaka Yamada Mamoru Architects and Engrs., Osaka City, 1980—. Prin. works include Naruto and Maizuru Hosp.; co-author: Knowledge of Comfortable House Making, 1979, Let's Live in an Amenity, 1985. Mem. Japan Inst. Architects, Sakai Designers Assn., Osaka Registered Architects Assn., Archtl. Inst. Japan. Home: 4-323-6 Hamadera, Suwanomori Nishi, Sakai City, Osaka 592, Japan Office: Osaka Yamada Mamoru Archs & Engrs, 6-2-26 Ue Hon Machi, Tennoji ku, Osaka City, Osaka 543, Japan

SAKONG, IL, minister of finance; b. Kunwi, Kyung-buk, Korea, Jan. 10, 1940; s. Don and Jum Bun (Park) Sa K.; m. Young Hee Lee, May 10, 1974, children: Jin, In. BA in Commerce, Seoul Nat. U., Republic of Korea, 1964; MBA, UCLA, 1966, PhD, 1969. Asst. prof. NYU, 1969-73; dir. research Korea Devel. Inst., Seoul, 1973-82; sr. economist Presdl. Council Econ. and Sci. Affairs, Seoul, 1980; sr. counsellor to Dep. Prime Minister Republic of Korea, Seoul, 1982; v.p. Korea Devel. Inst., Seoul, 1982-83; pres. Korea Inst. Econ. and Tech., Seoul, 1983; sr. sec. to pres. for econ. affairs Office of the Pres., Seoul, 1983-87; minister Ministry of Finance, Seoul, 1987—. Author: Government and Business, 1980, Macroeconomic Aspect of Public Enterprise, 1979; contbr. articles to profl. jours. Named to Order of Civil "Moran medal" Govt. of Korea, 1983, Order of Crown Kingdom of Belgium, 1986, Order of Brilliant Star with Grand Cordon Republic of China, 1987. Home: 85-702 Hyndai, Apt Abgujung Dong, 135 Seoul Republic of Korea Office: Ministry of Finance, 2nd Govt Bldg, 1 Jungang-Dong, 171 11 Kwachon Kyungai-Do Republic of Korea

SAKOVER, RAYMOND PAUL, radiologist; b. Chgo., Oct. 8, 1944; s. Max and Lena (Berardi) S.; B.S. (James scholar), U. Ill., 1965, M.D., 1969; m. Patricia Ellyn Taylor, June 7, 1969; children—Shelley Lynn, Michael Paul, David Evan, Raymond Taylor. Intern, St. Francis Hosp., Evanston, Ill., 1969-70, resident, 1970-73; practice medicine specializing in radiology, Riverside, Calif., 1975—; staff radiologist Riverside Community Hosp., 1975-86, pres. Computerized Diagnostic Imaging, 1986—; clin. instr. Loma Linda (Calif.) U. Med. Center, 1976—. Bd. dirs. Lung Assn. Riverside, 1978-83, Riverside Humane Soc., 1980—. Served with USNR, 1973-75. Diplomate Am. Bd. Radiology. Mem. Am. Coll. Radiology, Soc. Nuclear Medicine, AMA, Calif. Med. Soc., N.Am., Calif. radiol. socs. Roman Catholic. Lodge: Rotary. Contbr. articles in field to profl. jours. Office: Riverside Radiology 6941 Brockton Ave Riverside CA 92506

SAKS, JUDITH-ANN, artist; b. Anniston, Ala., Dec. 20, 1943; d. Julien David and Lucy-Jane (Watson) S.; student Tex. Acad. Art, 1957-58, Mus. Fine Arts, Houston, 1962, Rice U., 1962; BFA, Tulane U., 1966; postgrad. U. Houston, 1967; m. Haskell Irvin Rosenthal, Dec. 22, 1974; 1 son, Brian Julien. One-man shows include: Alley Gallery, Houston, 1969, 2131 Gallery, Houston, 1969; group shows include: Birmingham (Ala.) Mus., 1967, Meinhard Galleries, Houston, 1977; Galerie Barbizon, Houston, 1980, Park Crest Gallery, Austin, 1981; represented in permanent collections including: L.B. Johnson Manned Space Mus., Clear Lake City, Tex., Harris County Heritage Mus., Windsor Castle, London, Smithsonian Instn., Washington: commns. include: Pin Oak Charity Horse Show Assn., Roberts S.S. Agy., New Orleans; curator student art collection U. Houston, 1968-72; artist Am. Revolution Bicentennial project Port of Houston Authority, 1975-76. Recipient art awards including: 1st prize for water color Art League Houston, 1969, 1st prize for graphics, 1969, 1st prize for sculpture, 1968, 1st place award for original print, DAR, Am. Heritage Com., 1987. Mem. Art League Houston, Houston Mus. Fine Arts, DAR (curator 1983-85, contbr. Tex. sesquicentennial drawing for DAR mag.), Daus. Republic Tex. Home: PO Box 1793 Bellaire TX 77401

SAKSENA, JAGDISH PRASAD, operations researcher; b. Etawah, India, June 29, 1932; s. Guizari Lal and Krishna Devi Saksena; children: Pravin, Atul, Dipti. MS in Math., Allahabad (India) U., 1952; PhD in Ops. Research, Poona (India) U., 1966. Sr. sci. officer Arament Research and Devel. Establishment, Poona, 1961-66; mem. staff Indian Statis. Inst., Calcutta, India, 1967-70; ops. research analyst Bharat Heavy Electronics Ltd., Hardwar, India, 1970-73; dir. ops. research Nat. Product Council, New Delhi, 1973—. Author, reviewer research papers, books. Mem. Ops. Research Soc. Am., Ops. Research Soc. India. Office: Nat Product Council, Lodi Rd, New Delhi 110 003, India

SAKURAI, ISAMU, pathologist, educator; b. Tono, Iwate, Japan, June 9, 1933; s. Tadashi and Etsu (Yamanaka) S.; m. Shizuko Taniide, Mar. 27, 1964; children: Ayah, Yuki, Ken. MD, Nihon U., Tokyo, 1959, Sci. D. in Medicine, 1964. Cert. pathologist and clin. pathologist. Intern Tokyo Police Hosp., 1959-60; grad. student 1960-64; asst. prof. pathology Nihon U. Sch. Medicine, Tokyo, 1964-67, 70-73; research fellow pathology U. Chgo. and U. Hawaii, 1967-70; asst. dean in research Nihon U. Sch. Medicine, Tokyo, 1979-83, assoc. prof. pathology, 1973-79, prof. pathology, 1979—, asst. dean in edn., 1983—. Co-author: Arteriosclerosis, 1979, Surg. Pathology, 1984, Circulatory Diseases, 1985. Recipient Med. Research award Japan Med. Assn., Tokyo, 1979; Scientific research grantee Ministry Edn. and Culture, 1978-70, 83-85, 86— Circulatory Disease Research grantee, Scientific Research grantee, 1979-80. Fellow Internat. Coll. Angiology; mem. Japan Med. Assn., Internat. Acad. Pathology, Internat. Soc. Leprosy, Japanese Pathological Soc. (councilor), Japanese Assn. Clin. Pathology (councilor), Japan Atherosclerosis Soc. (councilor), Panama Soc. Surgery (hon.). Democrat. Roman Catholic. Home: 2-6-35 Hayamiya Nerima-ku, Tokyo 176, Japan Office: Nihon U Sch Medicine, Ohyaguchi-kami-machi Itabashi-ku, Tokyo 173, Japan

SAKUTA, MANABU, neurologist, educator; b. Ichikawa, Japan, Oct. 31, 1947; s. Jun and Shizuko (Tsuji) S.; m. Yuko Fukushi, June 17, 1973; children—Akiko, Junko, Ken-Ichi. M.D., U. Tokyo, 1973, Ph.D., 1978; M.S.

in Neurology, U. Minn., 1981. Med. diplomate. Diplomat Japanese Bd. Neurology. Asst. Dept. Neurology U. Tokyo, Japan, 1980; research fellow Dept. Neurology U. Minn., Mpls., 1980-81, asst. prof., 1981-82; head Dept. Neurology Japanese Red Cross Med. Ctr., Tokyo, 1982—; prof. Japanese Red Cross Women's Coll. Sch. Nursing, Tokyo, 1983-85, instr. 1986—; lectr. Dept. Neurology, U. Tokyo, 1984—; cons. Nakayama Hosp., Ichikawa, Japan, 1980—. Mem. Japanese Soc. Internal Medicine, Japanese Soc. Neurology (mem. council, 1985—, mem. council Kanto Br., 1984—, pres. Kanto Br. 1984), Japanese Soc. Diabetology, Japanese Soc. Electroencephalography and Electromyography, Japanese Soc. Autonomic Nervous System (mem. council). Liberal. Buddhist. Clubs: U. Minn. Alumni (Mpls.). Tetsumon (Tokyo). Conbr. articles to profl. jours. Office: Japanese Red Cross Med Ctr, 4-2-22 Hiroo, Shibuya-ku, 150 Tokyo Japan

SALA, LUIS FRANCISCO, surgeon; b. N.Y.C., Dec. 13, 1919; s. Luis and Josefina (Goenaga) S.; m. Judith Colon, June 5, 1943; children: Luis E., Francisco A., Jorge P., Jose M. B.S. cum laude, Georgetown U., 1939, M.D., 1943; M.Sc. in Surgery, U. Pa., 1951. Diplomate: Am. Bd. Surgery. Intern, resident Presbyn. Hosp., San Juan, P.R., 1943-45; resident Presbyn. Hosp., 1944-45; chief resident Grad. Hosp. U. Pa., 1947-51, instr. surgery, 1950-51; clin. asst. surgery Med. Coll. Pa.; practice medicine, specializing in surgery Ponce, P.R., 1951—; chmn. dept. surgery Damas Hosp., Ponce, 1955—; prof. surgery U. P.R. Sch. Medicine, 1968—; pres., dean Ponce Sch. of Medicine, 1988—; del. P.R. Med. Assn., 1960-80, pres., 1965-66. Author: Consideraciones Basicas para la Acreditacion de Hospitales, 1978; contbr. chpts. to books, articles to profl. jours. Active Boy Scouts Am., 1955-74; pres. adv. com. to pres. Cath. U. P.R., 1963-72; bd. dirs. Boys Home of Ponce, 1966-76; bd. regents Amigos Museo de Arte de Ponce, 1968-73, Cath. U., 1972—; pres. bd. regents Ponce Med. Sch. Found., 1980—. Served with M.C. U.S. Army, 1945-47. Recipient Silver Beaver award, 1965; named lt. P.R. Equestrian Order of Holy Sepulchre of Jerusalem, 1982. Fellow A.C.S. (gov. for P.R. 1965-74), Internat. Soc. Surgery, AMA. Republican. Roman Catholic. Home: 6 Almena Alhambra Ponce PR 00731 Office: 43 Concordia Ponce PR 00731

SALA, MARIUS SABIN, linguist, researcher; b. Vascău, Bihor, Romania, Sept. 8, 1932; s. Sabin Sala and Eleonora (Bogdan) Tocoianu; m. Florica Indreica, July 29, 1958; 1 child, Iulia Elena. BA in Philosophy, Fac. Philology, Bucharest, Romania, 1955, PhD, 1967. Researcher Inst. Linguistics, Bucharest, 1955-67, sr. researcher, head Romance linguistics sect., 1967—. Author: Contributions to the Historical Phonetics of the Romanian Language, 1970 (Prize of Romanian Acad.), Estudios Sobre el Judeo-Español de Bucarest, 1970, Phonétique et Phonologie du Judéo-Español de Bucarest, 1971, Le Judéo-Español, 1976, Contributions a la Phonétique Historique du Roumain, 1976, El Problema de las Lenguas en Contacto, 1988 (with others) El Léxico Indígena del Español Americano, Apreciaciones Sobre su Vitalidad, 1977 (Prize of Mex. Acad. Centennial), El Español de Am. Léxico, 1981, The Languages of the World. A Concise Encyclopaedia, 1981, Les Langues du Monde, 1984, Limba Romana si Etimologia, 1987, Vocabularul Reprezentativ al Limbilor Romanice, 1988; contbr. articles to profl. jours. Mem. Internat. Com. Onomastic Studies, Internat. Com. of Mediterranean Linguistic Atlas, Junta of Assn. of Hispanists, Com. Soc. Romance Linguistics, Com. Internat. of Linguists. Communist. Orthodox. Home: Aleea Bistra 1, E 1, Ap 39, 77314 Bucharest Romania Office: Institutul de Lingvistica, Str Spiru Haret, 12, 79368 Bucharest Romania

SALABOUNIS, MANUEL, computer information scientist, mathematician, scientist; b. Salonica, Greece, Apr. 15, 1935; came to U.S., 1954; s. Anastasios and Marietta (Mytonidis) Tsalabounis; m. Mary Louise Turk, Apr. 26, 1966 (div. Sept. 1978); children: Stacy, Mary E., John; m. Baerbel Thekla Rushford, July 2, 1988. Cert., Anatolia Coll., Salonica, Greece, 1954; student, Morris Harvey Coll., 1954-56; BS in Engring. Sci., Cleve. State U., 1960; MS in Math., Akron U., 1964. Master Univ. Sch., Shaker Heights, Ohio, 1960-62; mathematician Babcock and Wilcox, Alliance, Ohio, 1962-66; dir. computer ctr. John Carroll U., University Heights, Ohio, 1966-68; pres. Electronic Service Assocs. Corp., Euclid, Ohio, 1968-73; v.p. North Am. Co., Chgo., 1974-79; sr. project leader Hibernia Bank, New Orleans, 1979-83; project mgr. Compuware Corp., Birmingham, Mich., 1984—. accomplishments include work in internat. banking applications, 3 dim. thermostress analysis, generic tool definitions and design, and others. Vol. Saint Constantine Ch., Saint Helen Ch., Cleve., 1956-58, Saint Nicholas, Detroit, 1986. Home: 28238 Westerleigh Farmington Hills MI 48018 Office: Compuware Corp 32100 Telegraph Rd Birmingham MI 48010

SALAH, ABDULLAH A., diplomat; b. Tulkarm, Jordan, Dec. 31, 1932; m. Fadwa Salah; 1 child, Hanya Salah. BA in Polit. Sci., Am. U., Beirut, 1944; JD, Jerusalem Law Classes, 1948. Officer field edn. UN Relief and Work Agy. for Palestine Refugees, 1950-62; Jordan ambassador to Kuwait, 1962-63, India, 1963-64; fgn. minister Jordan, 1966-67, 70-72; Jordan ambassador to France, 1967-70, U.S. and Mex., 1973-80, Switzerland and Austria, 1980-83, permanent rep. Jordan Mission to UN, N.Y.C., 1983—. Several Jordanian and fgn. decorations. Home: 126 E 72d St New York NY 10021 Office: Jordan Mission to UN 866 United Nations Plaza New York NY 10017

SALAHUDDIN ABDUL AZIZ SHAH, sultan of Selangor; b. Istana Bandar, Kuala Langat, Malaysia, Mar. 8, 1926; s. Sultan Hisamuddin 'Alam Shah; student Malay Coll., Kuala Langsar, 1936-41, Sch. Oriental and African Studies, U. London, 1947; m. Raja Saidatul Hisham, 1943; 7 children; m. 2d, Tengku Rahimah, 1956; 2 children. Pres. Council of Regency, Selangor, 1952, regent, 1953, 59; sultan of Selangor, 1959—; col. Royal Malaysian Air Force, 1966; chancellor U. Agr. Malaysia, 1977. Address: care Press Attache Malaysian Embassy 2401 Massachusetts Ave Washington DC 20008 *

SALAM, ABDUS, physicist, educator; b. Jhang, Pakistan, Jan. 29, 1926; s. student Govt. Coll., Lahore, Pakistan, 1938-46, St. John's Coll., Cambridge (Eng.) U., 1946-49; B.A., Cambridge, 1949, Ph.D., 1952; 20 D.Sc. hon. degrees including, Panjab U., 1957, U. Edinburgh, 1971, Hindu U., 1981, U. Chittagong, 1981, U. Bristol, 1981, U. Maiduguri, 1981, U. Khartoum, 1983, U. Complutense de Madrid, 1983. Prof., Govt. Coll., Lahore, 1951-54, U. Panjab, 1951-54; fellow St. John's Coll. Cambridge, 1951-56; prof. theoretical physics Imperial Coll., London, 1957—; dir. Internat. Centre for Theoretical Physics, Trieste, Italy, 1964—; mem. AEC Pakistan, 1958-74, Pakistan Nat. Sci. Council, 1963-75, South Commn., 1987; hon. sci. adviser Pres. Pakistan, 1961-74; mem. sci. and tech. adv. com UN, 1964-75; gov. Internat. Atomic Energy Agy., Vienna, 1962-63. Recipient Hopkins prize Cambridge U., 1957, Adams prize, 1958; Maxwell medal and prize London Phys. Soc., 1961; Hughes medal Royal Soc. London, 1964; Atoms for Peace prize, 1968; Oppenheimer prize and medal, 1971; Guthrie medal and prize IPPS, 1976; Matteucci medal Accademia Nazionale dei XL, Rome, 1978; John Torrence Tate medal Am. Inst. Physics, 1978; Nobel Prize in Physics, 1979; Einstein medal, 1979, Josef Stefan medal, 1980; Peace medal, 1981; Lomonosov gold medal USSR Acad. Scis., 1983; also numerous decorations. Fellow Royal Soc. London (medal 1978), Royal Swedish Acad. Scis.; fgn. assoc. U.S. Nat. Acad. Scis., Accademia dei Lincei (Rome); fgn. mem. Acad. Scis. USSR, Internat. Union Pure and Applied Physics (v.p.); mem. Third World Acad. Sci. (founding, pres.). Author: Symmetry Concepts in Modern Physics, 1965; Aspects of Quantum Mechanics, 1972. Office: Imperial Coll, Prince Consort Rd, London SW7, England also: Internat Ctr for Theoretical Physics, PO Box 586, I-34100 Trieste Italy

SALAMA, HUSSEIN SAMIR ABDEL RAHMAN, entomologist, educator; b. Kafr El-Zayat, Egypt, Jan. 26, 1936; s. Abdel Rahman Ahmed and Aisha (Mohamed) S.; m. Zeba Mohamed Zaki, June 21, 1973; children: Hussam, Sameh. BS with honors, Ain Shams U., Cairo, 1955, MS in Entomology, 1959; PhD in Entomology, Cairo U., 1962, DS in Entomology, 1987. Researcher Nat. Research Ctr., Cairo, 1962-67, assoc. research prof., 1967-73, research prof., 1973—, head labs. of pests and plant protection, 1976—, head agrl. research div., 1978-80, chief fgn. research contracts dept., 1979-85, v.p., 1985-87, pres., 1988—. contbr. numerous research papers to profl. jours., also chpts. to books. Recipient state prize of Biol. Sci. Acad. Sci. Research and Tech., 1973, State prize Agrl. Sci., 1983, medal Scis. and Arts First Rank Pres. Republic, 1975, 85. National Democrat. Club: Shooting (Cairo). Home: 76 Mohyee Aboul-Ezz St, Dokki, Cairo Arab Republic of Egypt Office: Nat Research Ctr, El Tahrir St, Dokki, Cairo Arab Republic of Egypt

SALAMON, DIETMAR ARNO, mathematics educator; b. Bremen, Fed. Republic Germany, Mar. 7, 1953; came to Eng., 1986.; s. Artur and Helga (Straube) S. Diploma in math., U. Bremen, 1977, PhD, 1982. Research asst. Forschungsschwerpunkt Dynamische Systeme, Fed. Republic Germany, 1978-83; research assoc. math. research ctr. U. Wis., Madison, 1983-85; vis. acad. Forschungsinstitut Für Mathematik, Zürich, Switzerland, 1985-86; lectr. math. U. Warwick, Coventry, Eng., 1986—. Author: Control and Observation of Neutral Systems, 1984. Mem. Am. Math. Soc., Soc. Indsl. and Applied Math. Home: 9 Victoria St, Leamington Spa CV31 3PU, England Office: Math Inst, U Warwick, Coventry CV4 7AL, England

SALAMON, FRANK RICHARD, educator, author; b. Norwich, Conn., June 7, 1927; s. Francis Henry and Valeria Mary (Czarn) S.; B.S., Central Conn. State Coll., 1950; M.Ed., U. Hartford, 1956; postgrad. Columbia U., 1959-60; m. Dorothy Marie Kleinhenn, Apr. 6, 1951; children—Frank William, Joan Marie Salamon Israelson. Social worker State of Conn., 1950-52; secondary sch. tchr., Canton, Conn., 1952-54; elem. sch. tchr., West Hartford, Conn., 1954-56, sci. cons., 1956-61; assoc. exec. sec., elem. sch. sci. cons. Nat. Sci. Tchrs. Assn., Washington, 1961-65; sci. editor Addison-Wesley Pub. Co., Menlo Park, Calif., 1965-66; free-lance writer, edn. cons., 1966-70; prof. child study St. Joseph Coll., West Hartford, 1970—; vis. prof. edn. Conn. Wesleyan U., Middletown, 1981—; vis. prof. sci. edn. U. Victoria (B.C., Can.), summer 1981, U. No. Colo., Greeley, summer 1975; cons. Man. (Can.) Dept. Edn., 1978—, Ohaus Scale Corp., Florham Park, N.J., 1973-75, also state agys. Mem. Montgomery County (Md.) Democratic Com., 1962-64, Ridgefield (Conn.) Bd. Edn., 1969-70; trustee North Canton (Conn.) Community United Methodist Ch., 1980—. Served with U.S. Army, 1945-47. Recipient Outstanding Teaching award West Hartford, 1956; ESSO grantee, summer 1957; NSF fellow, summer 1959; U.S. Office Edn. grantee, summer 1976; U.S. Dept. Energy grantee, summer 1980; HEW grantee, 1980. Mem. AAAS, AAUP, Nat. Sci. Tchrs. Assn. (life), Conn. Sci. Tchrs. Assn., Assn. Supervision and Curriculum Devel., Council Elem. Sci. Internat. (past pres.), Conn. Assn. Colls. and Univs. for Tchr. Edn. (past pres.), Sierra Club, Phi Delta Kappa. Club: Hartford Bridge. Co-author: Addison-Wesley Science, 1984; Science series, 1980; Les Chemins de la Science, 1978; Ciencias, 1976; Space, Time, Energy and Matter, 1972; author: An Introduction to Mathematical Concepts, 1972. Home: 37 Wright Rd Collinsville CT 06022 Office: 1687 Asylum Ave W Hartford CT 06117 also: Wesleyan U Room 128 Science Tower Middletown CT 06457

SALAMON, MICHAEL JACOB, psychologist, health care and psychology educator, researcher; b. Bklyn., Oct. 18, 1951; s. Milton and Bessie (Kessler) S.; B.A., Queens Coll., 1974, M.A., 1977; M.A., Hofstra U., 1981, Ph.D., 1983. Project dir. Nat. Council Sr. League, Far Rockaway, N.Y., 1974-78; dir., founder Adult Devel. Ctr., Hewlett, N.Y., 1978—; dir. research Gustave Hartman YM-YWHA, Far Rockaway, 1978-82; asst. prof. psychology L.I. U., 1981-83; gerontology cons. St. Johns Hosp., Far Rockaway, 1980-83; adult devel. cons. CSE, 1980-83, N.Y. State Dept. of Labor, 1978-80; dir. research div. Hebrew Home for Aged at Riverdale, 1983-85; dir. psychology St. John's Home and Hosp., 1986—; vis. scholar Brookdale Found., Jerusalem, 1985. Assoc. bd. dirs. Democratic Club of Rockaways, 1981; bd. dirs. Young Israel of Woodmere, 1982. Bruner Found. grantee, 1979; N.Y. State Dept. Social Services grantee, 1982. Mem. Am. Psychol. Assn., Gerontol. Soc. Am. (research fellow 1983), Northeastern Gerontol. Soc., Assn. Jewish Scientists, Am. Psychiat. Assn. Democrat. Jewish. Author: Adult Assessment Scale, 1982; textbook on gerontology; editor: Jour. Clin. Gerontology; contbr. articles to profl. jours. Office: Adult Devel Ctr 920 Broadway #1A Woodmere NY 11598

SALARIYA, ELLENA MADGE, nurse, midwife; b. Ardallie, Aberdeenshire, Scotland, Aug. 17, 1931; d. James Morrison and Gladys Murray (Moir) Stewart; m. Basil Piara Salariya, Sept. 5, 1953; children: David, Leonard. RN, Maryfield Hosp., Dundee, Scotland, 1952; cert. in midwifery, So. Gen. Hosp., Glasgow, Scotland, 1953. Staff midwife Maryfield Hosp., Dundee, 1953-54, 61-64; staff midwife Royal Infirmary, Dundee, 1955-58, sister, 1973-74; sister Community Midwifery, Dundee Corp., 1964-73; sister Ninewells Hosp., Dundee, 1974-85, postgrad. research midwife, 1985—. Contbr. articles to profl. jours. Mem. Children's Panel, Tayside, 1978-87. Grantee Florence Nightingale Trust, 1980. Mem. Royal Coll. Midwives (infant feeding working group, 1986-87, policy working group 1987, chmn. Dundee br. 1970, 80, 87). Office: Ninewells Hosp, Level 8 Midwifery Dept, Dundee DD1 9SY, Scotland

SALAS, MARILYN SUE, academic director; b. Sabetha, Kans., June 4, 1943; d. Lee R. and Agnes M. (McPeak) Cashman; m. Henry C. Salas, Aug. 1, 1970. Student, Kans. State U., 1961-62, Kans. U., 1962-64; BA in Bus. Adminstrn., Emporia State U., 1965. Cert. secondary bus. edn. and psychology tchr., Kans., Calif. High sch. tchr. Pacifica High Sch., Garden Grove, Calif., 1966-68; word processor Orange County, Calif., 1968-72; ednl. service rep. IBM, Anaheim, Calif., 1969-70; coll. instr. Cerritos Coll., Norwalk, Calif., 1970-74; adult edn. instr. Lincoln Edn. Tng., Garden Grove, 1972-78; coll. instr. Golden West Coll., Huntington Beach, Calif., 1973-80, Orange Coast Coll., Costa Mesa, Calif., 1976-79, Cypress (Calif.) Coll., 1977-79; freelance word processor Burlington Northern, Newport Beach, Calif., 1978-79; cons. in field, Orange County, 1979; coll. instr. Saddleback Coll., Mission Viejo, Calif., 1979; dir. The Word Processing and Computer Sch., Anaheim, 1980-87. Mem. Assn. Info. Systems Profls. (mem. ednl. task force), Am. Soc. Tng. and Devel., Calif. Bus. Educators Assn., Anaheim C. of C., Nat. Assn. Trade and Tech. Schs. Accrediting Agy. (accredited). Democrat. Methodist. Home: 41105 Valle Vista Murrieta CA 92362

SALAS, OMAR, natural resources company executive; b. Montevideo, Uruguay, Jan. 15, 1944; s. Octavio and Sofia (Costabel) S.; m. Petrona Sarti, July 24, 1968; children: Sofia, Mariana. B of Commerce, Concordia U., Montreal, Can., 1981; MBA, McGill U., Montreal, 1987. Cert. mgmt. acct. Mgr. adminstrn. Domtar, Inc., Montreal, 1981-88; mgr. adminstrv. services McGill U., Montreal, 1988—; speaker Quebec U., Montreal, 1985-87. Mem. Project Mgmt. Inst. Home: 22 Nelson, Outremont, PQ Canada H2V 3Z6 Office: McGill U Dept Physical Plant, 840 Docteur Penfield, Montreal, PQ Canada H3A 1A4

SALAS, RANDALL, automotive company executive; b. Willemstad, Curazao, Venezuela, Oct. 20, 1945; s. Herbert and Claire (Nouel) S.; m. Silvia M. Mago, Feb. 16, 1974; children: Maria Silvia, Claudia Isabel-la. Student, Santiago de León, Caracas, Venezuela, 1965; BS in Indsl. Engring., Cath. U., Caracas, 1971, BA in Journalism, 1976. Pilots coordinating engr. Gen. Motors de Venezuela, Caracas, 1971-73, methods engr., 1973-76, gen. supply products facilitator, 1976-78, products facility mgr., 1978-80, prodn. mgr., 1980-81, dir. personnel, 1981-86, dir. personnel and pub. govtl. relations, v.p., 1987—; bd. dirs. Camara Automotriz de Venezuela, Caracas. Named to Labor Merit Order 1st Degree, Ministry of Labor, 1987. Mem. Coll. Engrs. Venezuela, Assn. Venezolana de Ejecutivos, Nat. Assn. Indsl. Relations Execs. Roman Catholic. Club: Lagunita Country (Caracas). Office: Av Principal La Castella, Edif Banco Lara 4 Piso, 1010 Caracas Venezuela

SALASIN, PONG, government official; b. Bangkok, July 16, 1927; s. Pote and Siri Sarasin; m. Khunying Malinee; 3 children. BS in Bus. Adminstrn., Boston U., 1951. Dep. prime minister Govt. Thailand, Bangkok, 1986—; bd. dirs. Thai Pure Drinks Ltd., Bangkok, Siam Comml. Bank, Bangkok. Sec. gen. Social Action Party, Bangkok, 1985-87, also vice chmn., m.p. Mem. Boston U. Alumni Assn. Club: RBSC (chmn.). Office: Thai Pure Drinks Co, 24800 Hua Mark Rd, Bangkok Thailand

SALAZAR-CARRILLO, JORGE, economics educator; b. Havana, Cuba, Jan. 17, 1938; came to U.S., 1960; s. Jose Salazar and Ana Maria Carrillo; m. Maria Eugenia Winthrop, Aug. 30, 1959; children—Jorge, Manning, Mario, Maria Eugenia. B.B.A., U. Miami, 1958; M.A. in Econs., U. Calif.-Berkeley, 1964, cert. in econ. planning, 1964, Ph.D. in Econs., 1967. Sr. fellow, non-resident staff mem. Brookings Instn., Washington, 1965—; dir., mission chief UN, Rio de Janeiro, Brazil, 1974-80; prof. econs. Fla. Internat. U., Miami, 1980—, chmn. dept. econs., 1980—; advisor U.S. Info. Agy., advisor, contbg. editor Library of Congress, Washington, 1972—; editorial bd. Jour. of Banking and Fin.; chmn. program com. Hispanic Profs. of Econs. and Bus.; cons. econs. Agy. for Internat. Devel., Washington, 1979—; council mem. Internat. Assn. Housing, Vienna, 1981—; exec. bd. Cuban Nat. Planning Council, Miami, 1982—; bd. dirs. Insts. of Econ. and Social Research of Caribbean Basin, Dominican Republic, 1983—, U.S.-Chile Council, Miami, 1984—. Co-author: Trade, Debt and Growth in Latin America, 1984; Prices for Estimation in Cuba, 1985; The Foreign Debt and Latin America, 1983; External Debt and Strategy of Development in Latin America, 1985; The Brazilian Economy in the Eighties, 1987, Foreign Investment, Debt and Growth in Latin America, 1988; author: Wage Structure in Latin America, 1982. Fellow Brit. Council, London, 1960, Georgetown U., Washington, 1961-62, OAS, Washington, 1962-64, Brookings Instn., Washington, 1964-65. Mem. Am. Econ. Assn., Internat. Assn. Research in Income and Wealth, Econometric Soc. Latin Am., N.Am. Econs. and Fin. Assn., Internat. Assn. Energy Economists (pres. Fla. chpt.), Nat. Assn. Forensic Economists, Latin Am. Studies Assn. Roman Catholic. Lodge: Knights of Malta. Home: 1105 Almeria Ave Coral Gables FL 33134 Office: Fla Internat U Tamiami Campus DM 347 Miami FL 33199

SALAZAR LOPEZ, JOSE CARDINAL, archbishop; b. Ameca, Mexico, Jan. 12, 1910. Ordained priest Roman Cath. Ch., 1934; named titular bishop of Prusiade 1961, named bishop of Zamora, 1967-70, named archbishop of Guadalajara, 1970—. Office: Arzobispado Apartado, Postal 1-331, Guadalajara, Jalisco 44100, Mexico *

SALCEDO FERNANDEZ DEL CASTILLO, TOMÁS DE LA CUADRA, Spanish government official; b. 1946; married; 2 children. Lectr. adminstrv. law U. Madrid; legal adviser Cuadernos para el dialogo mag., 1968; lawyer specializing in adminstrv. law Gregorio Peces-Barbo, until 1982; minister territorial adminstrn. Spain, 1982-86; pres. Council of State, Madrid, 1986—. Address: El Consejo del Estado, Madrid Spain *

SALE, TOM S., economist, educator; b. Haynesville, La., July 27, 1942; s. Thomas and Mary Belle (Fagg) S.; BA, Tulane U., 1964; MA, Duke U., 1965; PhD, La. State U., 1972; m. Liza Spivey, July 13, 1966 (div. June 1988); children: Thomas Sanderson IV, Jennifer Elizabeth, Sarah Elaine. Mem. faculty La. Tech. U., Ruston, 1965—, prof. econs., 1975—, head dept. econs. and fin., 1974-86, dir. grad. studies Coll. Adminstrn and Bus., 1988—. Bd. dirs. La. Council for Econ. Edn., 1974—. Chartered fin. analyst. Mem. Am. Econs. Assn., So. Econs. Assns., Southwestern Fin. Assn. (pres. 1985-86), Am. Fin. Assn., Inst. Chartered Fin. Analysts (exam. com.), SW Fedn. Adminstrv. Disciplines (v.p. 1988-89), Dallas Assn. Fin. Analysts, Omicron Delta Kappa, Omicron Delta Epsilon. Episcopalian. Contbr. articles to profl. jours. Home: PO Box 1365 Ruston LA 71273 Office: La Tech U Ruston LA 71272

SALEH, ABDUL AZIZ, marketing professional; b. Rengat, Riau, Indonesia, Sept. 10, 1937; s. Saleh and Hadijah S.; m. Auda Syamsuddin, Dec. 12, 1969; children: Fadil, Farid. MSc in Pharmacy, Padjadjaran U., Banduc, Indonesia, 1966. Lic. pharmacist. Sales supr. Pfizer Indonesia, Jakarta, 1968-73, prodn. mgr., 1973-74, mktg. mgr., 1976-78; mktg. mgr. Pfizer Malaysia/Singapore, Jakarta, 1978-79; mktg. mgr. Pfizer Indonesia, Jakarta, 1980-87, mgr. bus. devel., 1988—; asst. lectr. Padjadjaran U., Banduc, 1962-66, lectr., 1966-70. Home: JL Raya Cipayung Kav I/1, 13480 Jakarta Timur Indonesia

SALEH, MOHAMAD, medical educator, chairman cardiac center; b. Jakarta, Indonesia, Aug. 2, 1930; s. Mohamad Arpan Soemodikoro and Moeamanah Soemodikoro; m. Annie Soebianti Soedewo, Feb. 19, 1956; children—Mohamad Syahrial, Maya Syahrina, Meralda Syahwina, Moira Syahfauzia, Harris Syahrazad, Myrna Syahraya. M.D., U. Airlangga, 1960. Specialist in internal medicine and cardiology. Resident intern U. Airlangga, Surabaya, Indonesia, 1963, sr. lectr. in internal medicine, 1967-76, head div. cardiology dept. medicine, 1976—, chmn. and head dept. of medicine, 1977—, prof. medicine, 1980—; postgad. fellow in cardiology U. Indonesia, Jakarta, 1968; first chmn. Indonesian Heart Found. East Java Br., 1983. Author: Basic Principles of Electrocardiography, 1979; chief editor Indonesian Heart Jour., 1979—; contbr. articles to med. jours. Recipient Setyalencana Karya Setya, Govt. Republic of Indonesia, 1983. Mem. N.Y. Acad. Scis., Indonesian Med. Assn., Indonesian Heart Assn., Indonesian Assn. Internal Medicine, Internat. Fedn. and Soc. Cardiology. Club: Lions. Home: Jalan Dr Soetomo 101, Surabaya East Java, Indonesia Office: Dept Medicine, Airlangga Univ, Jalan Dharmahusada 47, Surabaya Indonesia

SALEM, CARLITO ARIEL CAPILI, pediatrician; b. Luisiana, Laguna, Philippines, June 2, 1946; s. Gregorio Lupaz and Esther Suello (Capili) Salem; m. Melva Auto Navaja, Oct. 25, 1980; children: Dylan, Daryl, Dawn, Diana. MD, Southwestern U., Cebu City, Philippines, 1974. Intern Davao Gen. Hosp., Davao City, Philippines, 1974-75; resident in pediatrics, medicine Davao Doctor's Hosp., Davao City, 1976-77; Arakan Outreach program dir. Brokenshire Meml. Hosp., Arakan Valley, Philippines, 1977-79; head Dept. of Community Health Brokenshire Meml. Hosp., 1978-79; vis. pediatrician Cotabato City (Philippines) Med. Soc., 1979-84; practice medicine Salem Child Health Clinic, Midsayap, Cotabato, 1979—; med. examiner Insular LIfe Ins. Corp., Midsayap, 1983—, Philippine Crop Ins. Corp., Midsayap, 1987—, Creative Lng. Ctr., Midsayap, 1987—; prof. dept. midwifery So. Christian Coll., Midsayap, 1983—, dept. head 1984—. Health cons. Midsayap-Goshen Malnutrition Charity Clinic, 1986—; trustee So. Christian Coll., Midsayap, 1979-85. Mem. Cotabato City Med. Soc. (v.p. 1980-81), Philippine Acad. Family Physician, Philippine Med. Soc., Med. Allied Services Assn. (pres. 1980), Alumni Assn. So. Christian Coll. (pres. 1979-86), Philippine Jaycees (Award of Distinction 1981). Mem. United Ch. of Christ. Clubs: Karate (Cotabato City), Tennis (Midsayap). Lodge: Masons (jr. warden 1986-87, worshipful master 1988). Home: Facultyville Poblacion 8, Midsayap 9330, Philippines Office: Salem Child Health Clinic, 277 Quezon Ave, Midsayap, Cotabato 9410, Philippines

SALES, JAMES BOHUS, lawyer; b. Weimar, Tex., Aug. 24, 1934; s. Henry B. and Agnes Mary (Pesek) S.; m. Beuna M. Vornsand, June 3, 1956; children: Mark Keith, Debra Lynn, Travis James. B.S., U. Tex., 1956, LL.B. with honors, 1960. Bar: Tex. 1960. Practiced in Houston, 1960—; sr. ptnr. firm Fulbright & Jaworski, 1960—; advocate, Am. Bd. Trial Advocates; pres.-elect State Bar of Tex., 1987-88. Contbr. articles legal publns. Trustee South Tex. Coll. Law, 1982—. Served with USMCR, 1956-58. Fellow Internat. Acad. Trial Lawyers, Am. Coll. Trial Lawyers, Am. Bar Found., Tex. Bar Found., Houston Bar Found. (chmn. bd.); mem. Internat. Assn. Ins. Counsel, ABA (ho. of dels. 1984-88), Def. Research Inst., So. Tex. Coll. Trial Advocacy (dir. 1983—), Fed. Bar Assn., State Bar Tex. (pres.-elect 1987-88, pres. 1988-89, bd. dirs. 1983-86, chmn. bd. 1985-86), Tex. Assn. Def. Counsel (v.p. 1977-79, 83-84), Houston Bar Assn. (pres. 1980-81, Outstanding Service award 1977, 78, Pres.'s and Bd. Dirs. award 1983), Gulf Coast Legal Found. (dir. 1982-85), Houston C. of C., The Forum. Roman Catholic. Clubs: Westlake (bd. govs.), Houston Athletic, Inns of Ct. Home: 10803 Oak Creek Houston TX 77024 Office: Fulbright & Jaworski 1301 McKinney St Houston TX 77010

SALET, EUGENE ALBERT, retired army officer, college administrator; b. Standish, Calif., May 25, 1911; s. August and Marie (Irigary) S.; B.A., U. Nev., 1934, LL.D. (hon.), 1968; student Nat. War Coll., 1955; Advanced Mgmt. Program, Harvard U., 1958; LL.D. (hon.), Dickinson Law Sch., 1966; D.D. (hon.), Am. Theol. Sem., 1985; m. Irene Taylor, June 13, 1936; children—Suzette Taylor Salet Cook, Eugene Michael. Commd. 2d lt. U.S. Army, 1934, advanced through grades to maj. gen., 1962, ret., 1970; trust devel. officer 1st Nat. Bank & Trust Co., Augusta, Ga., 1970-73; pres. Ga. Mil. Coll., Milledgeville, 1973-85; pres. U.S. Army War Coll., 1964-67; sec. NATO mil. comm., 1955-58. Decorated D.S.M., Silver Star, Legion of Merit with 2 oak leaf clusters, Bronze Star with 2 oak leaf clusters; Mil. Valor Cross (Italy), Croix de Guerre (France), Fourragere (France), others; named Disting. Nevadan, 1967. Mem. Assn. Pvt. Colls. and Schs. (pres. 1984-85), Assn. Mil. Colls. and Schs. U.S. (pres. 1983-84), 3d Inf. Div. Assn., VFW, Ret. Officers Assn. Republican. Roman Catholic. Clubs: Kiwanis; Harvard (Atlanta). Home: Conifer Place 77 Bristlecone Ln Augusta GA 30909

SALGADO, FELIX YAP, obstetrician, gynecologist; b. Laguna, Philippines, July 29, 1951; s. Godofredo and Arsenia (Yap) S.; m. Ma Rebecca C. Castañeda, Apr., 1978; children: Paolo Mikel, Nikolai Felix, Julian Santino. BS, U. Philippines, Quezon City, 1971; MD, U. Philippines, Manila, 1975; postgrad., Harvard U., 1981. Intern Philippine Gen. Hosp. Med. Ctr., Manila, 1975-76, resident, 1977-80, chief resident, 1980; fellow Mass. Gen. Hosp., Boston, 1981; postgrad. fellow Balt. City Infectious Disease Ctr., Johns Hopkins Hosp., 1981; clin. asst. prof. U. Philippines, Manila, 1983—; med. cons. dept. ob-byn Philippine Gen. Hosp. Med. Ctr., Manila, 1983—; fellow Kobe U. Sch. Medicine, Japan, 1984; cons. Fatima Sch. Medicine and Hosp., Valenzuela, Philippines, 1981—, Mary Johnston Hosp. Fertility Care Ctr., Manila, 1981-84, Cardinal Santos Meml. Hosp., Quezon City, 1981-84, Manila Doctors Hosp., 1983—; coordinator Total Maternal Care Program, Manila, 1980—, Rural Surgical Sterilization Program, Philippines, 1981—; founder, coordinator Women Health Car Ctr., Philippines, 1985—. Contbr. articles on ob-gyn to jours. Fellow Am. Assn. Gynecol. Laparoscopists; mem. Am. Venereal Disease Assn., Philippine Assn. for Study of Sterilization, Family Planning Orgn. of Philippines, Philippine Med. Assn., Philippine Assn. Gynecol. Endoscopy and Microsurgery. Home: 46 MH Del Pilar St, Calamba, Laguna Philippines Office: Manila Doctors Hosp, United Nations Ave, Manila Philippines

SALGO, NICOLAS M., U.S. government official; b. Budapest, Hungary, Aug. 17, 1914; naturalized citizen, 1953.; LL.D., U. Budapest, Hungary, 1937, Ph.D., 1937. Trainee, export mgr. Manfred Weiss Co., Budapest, Hungary, 1933-36; trainee, export mgr. Manfred Weiss Co., Geneva, Switzerland, 1936-39; ptnr., dir. Salvaj and Cie, Geneva, Switzerland, 1939-48; owner, pres. Indeco Corp., Coal Credit Corp., Salvaj and Co., N.Y.C., 1948-58; exec. v.p. Webb and Knapp, N.Y.C., 1950-57; pres., chief exec. officer Norbute Corp., Butte, Mont., 1954-60; founder, owner Nicolas Salgo and Co., N.Y.C., 1959-83; vice chmn., then chmn. Bangor Punta Corp. and subs., Greenwich, Conn., 1960-74; co-owner, pres. ZX Ranch, Paisley, Oreg., 1966-80; founder, ltd. ptnr. Watergate Improvement Assocs., 1960-77; chmn. Watergate Cos., 1977—; cons. USIA, 1972—; mem. Internat. Pvt. Enterprise Task Force, 1983—; U.S. ambassador Dept. State, Budapest, Hungary, 1983-86; with Dept. State, Washington, 1986—. Office: Dept of State Office Fgn Missions Washington DC 20520 *

SALGO, PETER LLOYD, anesthesiologist, consultant; b. N.Y.C., Nov. 9, 1949; s. Michael Nicholas and Ruth F. Salgo; B.A., Columbia U., 1971, M.D., 1975. Intern in internal medicine Columbia Presbyn. Med. Center, N.Y.C., 1975-76; resident in internal medicine, 1976-78; vis. faculty fellow specializing in intensive care medicine and anesthesiology, dept. anesthesiology Columbia U., 1979-81; lectr. Harvard Med. Sch., Boston; asst. prof. anesthesia Columbia U.; staff anesthesia and medicine Mass. Gen. Hosp., Boston; attending in anesthesia Presbyn. Hosp., N.Y.C.; host nat. radio med. program PRN-Radio, 1979-81; writer, producer, host med. info. broadcast Sta. WCBS-TV, N.Y.C., 1980; med. corr. WCBS News, 1981—; syndicated CBS Network Newsfeed, 1981—, corr. CBS Network Radio News, 1982—, host Healthtalk, 1982—; cons. to networks on med. content of TV programs. Recipient Leonard Pullman award Columbia U., 1971, Blakesley award, Am. Heart Assn., Journalism award, Medic-alert Found., Honorable Mention Journalism, UPI; Alumni Assn. medal Columbia U. Coll. Physicians and Surgeons, 1975; diplomate Am. Bd. Internal Medicine, Am. Bd. Anesthesiology; lic. physician, N.Y., Calif., Mass. Fellow ACP; mem. AMA, N.Y. State Med Soc., N.Y. County Med. Soc., Am. Soc. Anesthesiologists, AAAS, AFTRA. Home: 115 Bedford St New York NY 10014 Office: Mass General Hospitol Dept Anesthesiology Boston MA 02114

SALGUERO, CARLOS EDUARDO, tobacco company executive; b. Viota, Colombia, Oct. 10, 1929; s. Luis A. and Maria K. (Munar) S.; m. Ann Holden Lesure, Aug. 10, 1949; children: Linda Kathleen, Suzanne, Ricardo A., Jeffrey, Stephen. B.A., Facultad de Ciencias Economics, Bogota, Colombia, 1948; postgrad., Albany (N.Y.) Bus. Coll., 1948-49. Asst. export mgr. Bristol Labs. Inc., Syracuse, N.Y., 1950-57; with Philip Morris Internat., N.Y.C., 1957—; exec. v.p. Philip Morris Internat., 1980—. Clubs: Metropolitan (N.Y.C); Real De Puerta de Hierro (Madrid, Spain), Real Madrid (Madrid, Spain), Financiero (Madrid, Spain). Home: Guecho 22, Madrid Spain Office: Philip Morris Internat 120 Park Ave New York NY 10017

SALIB, ADEL ANDRÉ, physico-chemist; b. Alexandria, Egypt, June 27, 1940; arrived in Switzerland, 1970; s. André and Sophie (Sidhom) S.; m. Ingrid Hagedorn, June 20, 1968; children: André, Alexandra. BSc in chem. and physics, Alexandra (Egypt) U., 1963. Analytical chemist for Dr. Zoernig, Koeln, Fed. Republic Germany, 1964-66; info. specialist Dynamit Nobel AG, Troisdorf, Fed. Republic Germany, 1966-69, CIBA-GEIGY AG, Basle, Switzerland, 1970-79; info. mgr. CIBA-GEIGY AG, Basle, 1979—; lectr. Swiss Assn. for Documentation, 1977-82, sci. publ. info retrieval. Office: CIBA-GEIGY AG, R 1066 5 46, CH-4002 Basel Switzerland

SALIH, ALI ABDULLAH, president Yemen Arab Republic, army officer; b. 1942. Security chief Taiz Province, until 1978; mem. Provisional Presdl. Council, dep. comdr.-in-chief Armed Forces, 1978; pres., comdr.-in-chief armed forces Yemen Arab Republic, 1978—. Address: Office of Pres, Sana'a Yemen Arab Republic *

SALIM, ABDULLAH, JR. (REGINALD ARMISTICE HAWKINS), lawyer, consultant; b. Charlotte, N.C., May 18, 1948; s. Reginald Armistice and Catherine Elizabeth (Richardson) H.; m. Umme Salma, June 2, 1972; children: Salah, Abdullah, Salma. BA, U. N.C., 1970; postgrad. Howard U., 1970-71, U. Md., 1976; JD, Goerge Mason U., 1981. Bar: Md. 1983, U.S. Ct. Appeals Md. 1983. Library asst. Smithsonian Inst. Mus. Natural History, Washington, 1966; writer, researcher Pride Inc., Washington, 1970; temp. tchr. D.C. Pub. Schs., 1970-71; sr. appraiser, claim rep. Aetna Life & Casualty Co., McLean, Va., 1971-78; mgr. Assocs. IV Theaters, Oxon Hill, Md., 1974-75; pub. transport mgr. D.C. Barwood Cabs, Washington, 1977-78; mgr. E & S Cons., Washington, 1981-82; material damage cons. Crawford & Co., Fairfax, Va., 1982-84; sole practice law, Silver Spring, Md., 1983—; hist. cons. Abdullah Salim & Assocs., Silver Spring, 1983—. Mem. Md. Black Reps. council, 1984; coach Little League Baseball, Rockville, Md. and Silver Spring, 1984; nat. assoc. Smithsonian Inst., Washington, 1984; trustee A.L. Richardson scholarship fund, 1984—. Hurbert Lehman scholor, 1966; recipient Immigration Law award Ayuda Neighborhood Services, 1981. Mem. Am. Soc. Internat. Law, Nat. Bar Assn., ABA, Am. Trial Lawyers Assn., Md. Trial Lawyers Assn., George Mason U. Internat. Law Soc. (v.p. 1980-81), George Mason U. Black Law Students Assn. (chmn. 1980-81), Internat. Platform Assn., U. N.C. Alumni Assn., George Mason U. Alumni Assn., Phi Delta Phi. Republican. Muslim. Home: 1016 Merrimac Dr Silver Spring MD 20903 Office: 4500 College Ave Suite 201 College Park MD 20740

SALIM, SALIM AHMED, deputy prime minister of Tanzania; b. Zanzibar, Jan. 23, 1942; s. Ahmed Salim Ali and Maryam Ali Ahmed; certificate Lumumba Coll., Zanzibar, 1960; corr. study U. Delhi (India), 1965-67; M.Internat. Affairs, Columbia U., 1975; m. Amne Ali Rifai, Apr. 17, 1964. Founder, 1st v.p. All Zanzibar Students Union, also sec.-gen. of youth movement, 1960; dep. chief rep. Zanzibar office, Havana, Cuba, 1961-62; chief editor Zanzibar daily paper, also sec.-gen. All Zanzibar Journalists Orgn., 1963, ambassador to United Arab Republic, Cairo, 1964-65; high commr. to India, 1965-68; dir. African and Middle East affairs div. Tanzania Ministry Fgn. Affairs, 1968-69; ambassador to People's Republic China, Democratic People's Republic Korea, 1969; permanent rep. to UN, N.Y.C., 1970-80, pres. UN Security Council, 1976; also ambassador to Cuba, high commr. to Guyana, 1970-80, Barbados, 1971-80, Jamaica, 1971-80, Trinidad-Tobago, 1971-80; minister of fgn. affairs Tanzania, 1980-84, prime minister, 1984-85; now dep. prime minister and minister of Def. and Nat. Service, 1985—; chmn. UN Com. on Decolonisation, 1972-75, UN Security Council Com. on Sanctions against So. Rhodesia, from 1975; now minister for fgn. affairs. Mem. Tanganyika African Nat. Union and Afro-Shirazi party. Office: Dep Prime Minister, Box 9544, Dar es Salaam Tanzania *

SALIM, SURYA CHANDRA, corporate executive; b. Tebing, Tinggi, Indonesia, Oct. 28, 1949; s. Mustafa Kemal Salim and Nurhana Siregar; m. Siti Fatimah Salim, July 3, 1978; children: Pasoka Permana, Yuki Marina, Zulia Kartika Sandra. BS, U. S.U., 1977. Mem. staff P.T. Industira, Jakarta, Indonesia, 1978-79, mgr., 1980-84, asst. mktg. dir., 1984-86, jr. mktg. dir., 1986—. Mem. Soc. Indonesian Engrs. Home: J1K H Mas Mansyur #25A, 10240 Jakarta Indonesia Office: PT Industira, Hayam Wuruk Plaza Tower, Floor 9 Hayam Wuruk 108, 11160 Jakarta Indonesia

SALINAS, WILLIAM EDWARD, computer company executive; b. Mexico City, Apr. 25, 1960; s. Hugo and Esther (Salinas) S.; m. Lilia Trevino, May 12, 1984; children: Guillermo Andres, Federico Eugenio. Degree in acctg., I.T.E.S.M., Monterrey, Mex., 1978-82. Data processing asst. Elektra, Mexico City, 1978-80; chief exec. officer, co-founder Dataflux, Monterrey, 1982—; bd. dirs. Elektra, Mexico City, Agimex, Monterrey. Club: Campestre. Office: Dataflux, Calz del Valle # 109 Ote, 66220 Garza Garcia Mexico

SALISBURY, HELEN HOLLAND, educator; b. Bedford, Ind., Dec. 15, 1923; d. Deward Julius and Zella (Kinser) Holland; B.S. in Home Econs., Ind. U., 1957; M.Ed., U. Va., 1967; Ed.D., Temple U., 1979; m. Charles Jackson Salisbury, Jan. 10, 1942; children—Creggie Helen Salisbury Henderson, Andrew Jackson II. Plating chemist Curtiss-Wright, Indpls., 1943; supr. sch. lunch program Charlottesville (Va.) Pub. Schs., 1963-65; dir. Harcum Jr. Coll. Lab. Sch., Bryn Mawr, Pa., 1966-68; prof. edn. Harcum Jr. Coll., Bryn Mawr, 1965-73; teaching assoc. Temple U., Phila., 1974; early childhood cons., 1979—; prof. edn. Harcum Jr. Coll., Bryn Mawr, 1982—, dir. infant devel. practice, 1982—; early childhood cons. Head Start, 1965. Mem. Nat. Assn. Edn. Young Children, Delaware Valley Assn. Edn. Young Children, Orgn. Mondiale pour L'Education Prescolaire, Assn. Supervision and Curriculum Devel., DAR, Kappa Alpha Theta, Episcopalian. Co-author: Diagnosing Individual Needs for Early Childhood Education, 1975. Home: 315 Strathmore Dr Rosemont PA 19010 Office: Harcum Jr Coll Montgomery Ave Bryn Mawr PA 19010

SALITERMAN, LAURA SHRAGER, pediatrician; b. N.Y.C., June 26, 1946; d. Arthur M. and Ida (Wildman) Shrager; m. Richard Arlen Saliterman, June 15, 1975; 1 child, Robert Warren. AB magna cum laude, Brandeis U., 1967; MD, NYU, 1971. Intern Montefiore Hosp. and Med. Ctr., Bronx, N.Y., 1971-72, resident in pediatrics, 1972-74; pediatrician Morrisania Family Care Ctr., N.Y.C., 1974-75; pediatrician Share Health Plan, St. Paul, 1975-85, dir. pediatrics, 1976-82; pediatrician Aspen Med. Group, St. Paul, 1985—; clin. asst. prof. U. Minn. Med. Sch. Mem. Am. Acad. Pediatrics (chair accident prevention com. Minn. chpt. 1985—), Phi Beta Kappa. Club: Oak Ridge. Home: 11911 Live Oak Dr Minnetonka MN 55343 Office: 1020 Bandana Blvd W Saint Paul MN 55108

SALITERMAN, RICHARD ARLEN, lawyer, educator; b. Mpls., Aug. 3, 1946; s. Leonard Slitz and Dorothy (Sloan) S.; m. Laura Shrager, June 15, 1975; 1 child, Robert Warren. BA summa cum laude, U. Minn., 1968; JD, Columbia U., 1971; LLM, N.Y.U., 1974. Bar: Minn. 1972, D.C. 1974. Mem. legal staff U.S. Senate Subcom. on Antitrust and Monopoly, 1971-72; acting dir., dep. dir. Compliance and Enforcement div. Fed. Energy Office, N.Y.C., 1974; mil. atty. Presdl. Clemency Bd., White House, Washington, 1975; sr. ptnr. Saliterman Law Firm, Mpls., 1975—; adj. prof. law Hamline U., 1976-81. Chmn. Hennepin County Bar Jour., 1985-87. Bd. dirs. Mpls. Urban League, 1987—, pres. Am. Jewish Com., Mpls. St. Paul chpt., 1988—. Served with USN, 1972-75. Mem. ABA, Minn. State Bar Assn., Hennepin County Bar Assn. (governing council 1985-87). Clubs: Oakridge Country (Hopkins, Minn.), Mpls. Club, Wyazata Yacht (Minn.).

SALIWANCHIK, ROMAN, lawyer, consultant; b. Michigan City, Ind., Nov. 12, 1926; s. John Reuben and Mary Alice (Kuta) S.; m. Doris Mae Colligan, May 30, 1954; children—Doris, Michael, David. B.S., Purdue U., 1952; J.D., Ind. U., 1961. Bar: U.S. Dist. Ct. (so. dist.) Ind. 1961, U.S. Dist. Ct. (we. dist.) Mich. 1963, U.S. Patent and Trademark Office 1963, U.S. Ct. Customs and Patent Appeals 1968, U.S. Supreme Ct. 1978, U.S. Ct. Appeals (Fed. cir.) 1982. Chemist, microbiologist Eli Lilly & Co., Indpls., 1952-61; patent Lawyer Upjohn Co., Kalamazoo, Mich., 1961-84; sole practice, Richland, Mich., 1984—, Gainesville, Fla., 1984—. Author: Legal Protection for Microbiological and Genetic Engineering Inventions, 1982, Protecting Biotechnology Inventions: A Guide for Scientists, 1988. Editor Ind. U. Law Jour., 1959-61. Contbr. articles to profl. jours. Served with USCG, 1944-46, PTO. Mem. Mich. Bar Assn. (mem. council 1974-77, com. chmn. 1977-78), Am. Intellectual Property Law Assn., Soc. Indsl. Microbiology (chmn. com. 1977—), Am. Soc. Microbiology, Am. Chem. Soc., U.S. Fedn. for Culture Collections (mem. exec. bd. 1984—), Phi Alpha Delta. Office: 529 NW 60th St Suite B Gainesville FL 32607

SALK, JONAS EDWARD, physician, scientist; b. N.Y.C., Oct. 28, 1914; s. Daniel B. and Dora (Press) S.; m. Donna Lindsay, June 8, 1939; children: Peter Lindsay, Darrell John, Jonathan Daniel; m. Francoise Gilot, June 29, 1970. B.S., CCNY, 1934, LL.D. (hon.), 1955; M.D., NYU, 1939, Sc.D. (hon.), 1955; LL.D. (hon.), U. Pitts., 1955; Ph.D. (hon.), Hebrew U., 1959; LL.D. (hon.), Roosevelt U., 1955; Sc.D. (hon.), Turin U., 1957, U. Leeds, 1959, Hahnemann Med. Coll., 1959, Franklin and Marshall U., 1960; D.H.L. (hon.), Yeshiva U., 1959; LL.D. (hon.), Tuskegee Inst., 1964. Fellow in chemistry NYU, 1935-37, fellow in exptl. surgery, 1937-38, fellow in bacteriology, 1939-40; Intern Mt. Sinai Hosp., N.Y.C., 1940-42; NRC fellow Sch. Pub. Health, U. Mich., 1942-43, research fellow epidemiology, 1943-44, research asso., 1944-46, asst. prof. epidemiology, 1946-47; asso. research prof. bacteriology Sch. Medicine, U. Pitts., 1947-49, dir. virus research lab., 1947-63, research prof. bacteriology, 1949-55, Commonwealth prof. preventive medicine, 1955-57, Commonwealth prof. exptl. medicine, 1957-63; dir. Salk Inst. Biol. Studies, 1963-75, resident fellow, 1963-84, founding dir., 1976—, 1976—, disting. prof. internat. health scis., 1984—; developed vaccine, preventive of poliomyelitis, 1955, cons. epidemic diseases sec. war, 1944-47, sec. army, 1947-54; mem. commn. on influenza Army Epidemiol. Bd., 1944-54, acting dir. commn. on influenza, 1944; mem. expert adv. panel on virus diseases WHO; adj. prof. health scis., depts. psychiatry, community medicine and medicine U. Calif., San Diego, 1970—. Author: Man Unfolding, 1972, The Survival of the Wisest, 1973, (with Jonathan Salk) World Population and Human Values: A New Reality, 1981, Anatomy of Reality, 1983; Contbr. sci. articles to jours. Decorated chevalier Legion of Honor France, 1955, officer, 1976; recipient Criss award, 1955, Lasker award, 1956, Gold medal of Congress and presdl. citation, 1955, Howard Ricketts award, 1957, Robert Koch medal, 1963, Mellon Inst. award, 1969; Presdl. medal of Freedom, 1977; Jawaharlal Nehru award for internat. understanding, 1976. Fellow AAAS, Am. Pub. Health Assn., Am. Acad. Pediatrics (hon., assoc.); mem. Am. Coll. Preventive Medicine, Am. Acad. Neurology, Assn. Am. Physicians., Soc. Exptl. Biology and Medicine, Inst. Medicine (sr.), Phi Beta Kappa, Alpha Omega Alpha, Delta Omega. Office: Salk Inst for Biol Studies PO Box 85800 San Diego CA 92138

SALKIN, GERALDINE (JERI) FAUBION, dancer, dance therapist, educator; b. Denver, Mar. 18, 1916; d. George Everett and Hanna Viola (Harvey) Faubion; student Lester Horton Dance Theater, Carmelita Maracci, Trudi Schoop, Los Angeles, 1937-47, Doris Humphrey, N.Y.C., 1952-53, Rudolf Von Laban, London, 1956-57, Hanna Fenichel, Ph.D.,Westwood, Calif., 1965-70, UCLA, 1959-60; Ph.D., 1978; m. Leo Salkin, June 29, 1936; 1 dau., Lynn Salkin Sbiroli. Concert dancer Lester Horton Dance Group, Los Angeles, 1937-47, tchr. creative modern dance, 1939-47; tchr. creative modern dance Dance Assos., Hollywood, Calif., 1949-53, Am. Sch. of London (Eng.), 1956-57, Jeri Salkin Studio and Ctr. for Child Study, Hollywood, 1968-73; developer body ego technique Camarillo (Calif.) State Hosp., 1957-64; movement specialist Nat. Endowment Arts grantee, 1973—; dir., body ego technique dept. Cedars-Sinai Thalians Community Mental Health Ctr., Los Angeles, 1965—; dance cons., tchr. Nat. Head Start Program, Calif., 1964; conductor yearly workshops for tchrs., dancers, psychologists, psychiatrists, therapists, Rome, 1979—, mem. aux. faculty Goddard Coll., Antioch Coll., various hosps. and univs. Calif. Dept. Mental Hygiene grantee, 1960-63. Mem. Am. Dance Therapy Assn., AAHPER, Calif. Dance Educators Assn., Calif. Assn. Health, Phys. Edn. Dance and Recreation, Nat. Assn. Edn. Young Children, Assn. Child Devel. Specialists, Com. Research in Dance. Democrat. Author: Body Ego Technique, an Educational and Therapeutic Approach to Body Image and Self-Identity, 1973; author, choreographer film (with Leo Salkin and Trudi Schoop) Body Ego Technique, 1962 (U.S. Golden Eagle Council on Internat. Nontheatrical Events award 1963). Home: 3584 Multiview Dr Hollywood CA 90068 Office: 3584 Multiview Dr Hollywood CA 90068

SALKO, HENRY S., textile company executive; b. N.Y.C., Feb. 24, 1925; s. Max and Louise M. (Ginsberg) S.; BS in Econs., Wharton Sch. Fin., U. Pa., 1949; children: Richard Michael, Karen Leslie, Amy Lynn. With Max Salko Corp., N.Y.C., 1949—, v.p., 1958—; bd. dirs. Ritz Tower Hotel. Chmn. Citizens for Eisenhower; pres. Young Reps. Larchmont Mamaroneck, 1953; mem. Rep. Town Com., Mamaroneck, 1953-56; trustee Harrison (N.Y.) Jewish Community Ctr., 1970-73; mem. Pub. Employees Relations Bd. Harrison, 1970-73. Served with 75th Inf. Div., U.S. Army, 1943-45. Decorated Bronze Star, Purple Heart. Mem. N.Y. Acad. Sci., Retail Assocs. Group, Delta Sigma Rho, Alpha Epsilon Pi. Clubs: Textile Sq., Wharton, City Athletic. Lodge: B'nai B'rith (N.Y. state regional bd. Anti-Defamation League 1979-83, chmn. various coms., pres. Westchester Putnam council 1984-85, v.p. Dist. 1: Northeastern U.S., internat. bd. govs.). Home: Palmer Landing 123 Harbor Dr #209 Stamford CT 06902 Office: Max Salko Corp 17 W 31st St New York NY 10001

SALKOLA, ASKO LAURI, export-import executive; b. Helsinki, Finland, Aug. 6, 1937; s. Yrjö and Ingrid Alexandra (Piirainen) S.; m. Anita Bergman, Sept. 8, 1962; 1 child, Lars. BA in Econs., Helsinki State Coll., 1958. Clerk Mercantile, Helsinki, 1959-61; purser Swedish Am. Line, Gothenburg, 1961-62; clerk real estate Santa Rosa, Calif., 1963-65; transport mgr. Bilspedition Group, Gothenburg, 1965-76, Confracta, Gothenburg, 1976-83; pres. Intergarment, Gothenburg, 1983—. Served to sgt. Finnish Army, 1958-59. Home: Utlandagatan 8-C, 41261 Gothenburg Sweden Office: Intergarment, Ekonomivägen 4, 43681 Askim Sweden

SALLAH, MAJEED JIM, real estate developer; b. Boston, Aug. 5, 1920; s. Herbert K. and Rose (Karem) S.; student Gloucester (Mass.) Pub. Schs.; m. Aline C. Powers, Apr. 10, 1970; children—Christopher M., Melissa Rose. Pres., dir. Glo-Bit Fish Co., Gloucester, 1947-48, Live-Pak of Ohio, Inc., 1947-51, Cape Ann Glass Co., Inc., Gloucester, 1950-72, Cape Ann Realty Corp., Gloucester, 1961—, Marias Restaurant, Gloucester, 1960—; pres., treas., dir. Gloucester Hot-Top Constrn. Co., Gloucester, 1967-75; pres., treas. Points East, Inc.; trustee Christopher Investment Trust; dir. Lutsal, Inc. Pres. Lebanese-Am. Bus. Men's Club; treas. Lebanese-Maronite Soc. Served with U.S. Army, 1942-45. Decorated Bronze Star. Mem. Gloucester Assocs., Cape Ann Investment Corp., Am. Legion, Amvets, Hon. Order Ky. Cols. Roman Catholic. Lodges: Lions, Elks, Moose. Home: 56 Hilltop Rd Gloucester MA 01930 Office: 56 Hilltop Rd Gloucester MA 01930

SALLAMAA, KARI MATTI EINAR, literature educator; b. Helsinki, Finland, Mar. 19, 1942; s. Eilif Karl Einar and Aino Ida Elise (Ervasti) S.; m. Kaisu Emilia Karna, July 20, 1966; children: Outi Maretta, Silva Piritta Karintytar. Candidate in Philosophy, U. Helsinki, 1969; Licenciate in Philosophy, U. Oulu, Finland, 1987. Journalist various newspapers and mags., Oulu and Helsinki, 1968-79; lectr. Inst. Lit. U. Oulu, 1980—. Author: The World of P. Haanpaa, 1985, The Short Stories of the Group Kiila, 1987; short stories; editor lit. anthologies; contbr. numerous articles to profl. pubis. Served to 2d lt. Finnish Antiaircraft Forces, 1962-63. Mem. Assn. Lit. Researchers, Internat. Comparative Lit. Assn., Writers and Artists Group Kiila (pres. Helsinki chpt. 1975-77). Home: 90470 Varjakka Finland Office: U Oulu Inst Lit, Kasarmintie 8, 90100 Oulu Finland

SALLEN, DAVID URBAN, lawyer; b. Ft. Madison, Iowa, June 23, 1952; s. Urban Frank and Lillian Virginia (Ashby) S.; m. Sheila Marie Strang, Jan. 5, 1985. BA in Sociology and Philosophy, St. Ambrose Coll., 1974; JD, U. Iowa, 1977. Bar: Iowa 1977, U.S. Dist. Ct. (no. and so. dists.) Iowa 1977, U.S. Ct. Appeals (8th cir.) 1978, U.S. Supreme Ct. 1980. Assoc., Morr & Shelton, Chariton, Iowa, 1977-79; asst. county atty. Lucas County (Iowa), 1977-79; pub. defender Lee County, Ft. Madison, 1979—; sole practice, Ft. Madison, 1982—. Chairperson Ft. Madison Human Rights Commn., 1980—, Lee County Community Action Agy., 1982—; mem. jud. coordinating com. Iowa Supreme Ct., Des. Moines, 1981—, mem. commn. indigent def. transition com., 1985-87; council mem. St. Marys Parish, Ft. Madison, 1982-84; elected councilman 1st ward Ft. Madison City Council, 1988—; pres. Iowa Pub. Defenders Assn., 1982-83; sec. Community Services Council, 1983—; mem. com. drinking drivers Iowa State Legislature, Des Moines, 1984-85. Recipient Cert. of Appreciation, Southeast Iowa Community Action Agy., 1983, Friends Reach Out, Inc., 1982. Mem. Nat. Assn. Crim. Def. Lawyers, Nat. Legal Aid and Defender Assn., Iowa State Bar Assn., ABA, Lucas County Bar Assn. (pres. 1978-79), Am. Judicature Soc., Lee County Bar Assn. Club: Dominic. Lodge: K.C. Home: 309 6th St Fort Madison IA 52627 Office: 707 1/2 Ave G Fort Madison IA 52627

SALLET, DIRSE WILKIS, mechanical engineering educator; b. Washington, Aug. 10, 1936; s. Richard and Margarete Louise (Stolzenbach) S.; m. Martha Jane Obert, June 9, 1963 (div.); children: Stefan and Michael (twins), Bonnie, Johnny. B.S.M.E., George Washington U., 1961; M.S.M.E., U. Kans., 1963; Dr.Ing., U. Stuttgart, Germany, 1966. Registered profl. engr., Md. Research asso. Inst. Aero and Gas Dynamics, U. Stuttgart, 1963-66; research mech. engr. Naval Ordnance Lab., Silver Spring, Md., 1966-67; asst. prof. mech. engrng. U. Md., College Park, 1967-70; assoc. prof. U. Md., 1970-76, prof., 1976—; vis. scientist Max-Planck-Inst. for Fluid Mechanic Research, Göttingen, Germany, also Aerodynamische Versuchsanstalt Göttingen, 1973-74; vis. research scientist Center for Nuclear Research, Karlsruhe (Germany) Inst. for Nuclear Reactor Components, 1980-81; cons. in field; vis. prof. Tech. U. of Munich, Fed. Republic of Germany, 1987; mem. Bd. of Boiler Rules State of Md. Contbr. articles to profl. jours. Recipient numerous research contracts Dept. Transp., numerous research contracts Dept. Def.; recipient Alexander von Humboldt Prize, 1985. Mem. ASME, Am. Phys. Soc., Washington Acad. Scis., Philos. Soc. Washington (pres. 1984-85), Gauss Gesellschaft Göttingen, Sigma Xi, Pi Tau Sigma. Home: 4205 Tuckerman St University Park MD 20782 Office: Dept Mech Engrng U Md College Park MD 20742

SALLOUM, ANTOINE ABDULLAH, pharmacist; b. Amyoun, Lebanon, Feb. 20, 1913; came to U.S., 1937, naturalized, 1943; s. Albert and Fontaine (Easa) S.; m. Violet Khouri, Dec. 31, 1943; children—Lulie (dec.), Leah. B.A., Am. U. Beirut, 1936; B.S., U. Pitts., 1940; Ph.D. in Pharmacy (hon.), Mass. Coll. Pharmacy and Allied Health Services, 1982. Owner, mgr. Sullivan's Pharmacy, Roslindale, Mass., 1945-76. Trustee Mass. Coll. Pharmacy and Allied Health Scis.; life mem. Shriners Hosp. for Crippled Children and Burn Ctr. Served with USN, 1942-45. Recipient citations Am. Legion, 1956, White House, 1965, Pres. Nixon, 1971, Mass. Ho. of Reps., 1974, Pa. Ho. of Reps., 1982. Mem. DAV (life). Clubs: Home and Sch. Assn. (Roslindale pres. 1965-80); Kiwanis, Am. Legion (comdr.). Lodges: Masons, Shriners, Lebanese Internat., Cultural Union Greater Boston. Home: 2772 NE 3rd St Pompano Beach FL 33062

SALMAWY, MOHAMMED, playwright, editor, literary writer; b. Cairo, May 26, 1945; B.A. in Lit., Cairo U., 1966; postgrad. in lit. (Univ. scholar) Birmingham (Eng.) U., summer 1969; M.A. in Mass Communications, Am. U., Cairo, 1974; m. Nazli Madkour, Mar. 23, 1970; children—Seif, Sara. Tchr. lang. and lit. Cairo U., 1966-70; announcer, editor cultural and polit. programs Radio Cairo, 1966-77; editor fgn. news Al-Ahram newspaper, Cairo, 1970—; dir. Egyptian Press Syndicate, 1983—; mem. faculty Am. U., Cairo, 1978-79; apptd. Undersec. of State for Culture, 1988—; Imprisoned for polit. activity following Food Riots, 1977, released without bail. Mem. Egyptian Press Syndicate, Union Arab Journalists, Old Victorian Assn., Amnesty Internat. Clubs: Maadi and Yacht, Guezira Sporting; Rotary (Cairo). Author: The Foreign Editor, 1976; Origins of British Socialism, 1978; The Public Image of Gamal Abdel-Nasser, 1983; The Man Who Regained His Memory and other short stories, 1983, The Nay Concerto (short stories), 1988; Come Back Tomorrow: two one-act plays, 1984; On Nasserism 1984; Salome (play) 1985; Come Back Tomorrow & other plays, 1985; Murderer at Large (play), 1986 (play) Two Down the Drain, 1987; contbr. articles to The Guardian, Le Monde, Politique Internationale; subject of BBC interviews and articles in The Times, London, Canberra Times and Le Monde as polit. writer, playwright. Home: 9 Rd 216 Maadi, Cairo Arab Republic of Egypt

SALMEN, WALTER, musicologist, educator; b. Paderborn, Fed. Republic Germany, Sept. 20, 1926; s. Josef and Elisabeth (Hollman) S.; m. Gabriele Busch. Dr. Philosophy Habil., U. Heidelberg, Fed. Republic Germany, 1949. Dir. inst. musicology U. Kiel, Fed. Republic Germany, U. Innsbruck, Austria, 1979—; 6-74. Home: Purnhofweg 37, A6020 Innsbruck Austria Office: Innsbruck U, Karl-Schönherr-Strasse 3, A6020 Innsbruck Austria

SALMERON, FERNANDO, philosopher, researcher; b. Córdoba, Veracruz, Mex., Oct. 30, 1925; s. Fernando Salmerón-Díz and Ana María Salmerón Roiz; m. Alicia Castro; children: Fernando, Leonardo, Jorge, Alicia, Gabriel, Ana María. Lic. in law, U. Veracruzana, Veracruz, 1948, DHC (hon.), 1980; M of Philosophy, UNAM, Mex., 1955, PhD, 1965. Dir. faculty philosophy U. Veracurzana, 1956-58, rector, 1961-63; dir. Inst. Philos. Research, UNAM, 1966-78, researcher complete time, 1981—; rector iztapalapa sect. Met. Autonomus U., Mex., 1978-79, gen. rector, 1979-81. Author: Las mocedades de Ortega, 1959, 3d edit., 1983, Cuestiones educativas y Págs sobre Mexico, 1962, 2d edit., 1980, La filosofía y las actitudes morales, 1971, 3d edit., 1986, Ortega y Gasset, 1984, Etica y análisis, 1985, Ensayos filosóficos, 1988. Rockefeller Found. scholar, 1959-60; Sistema Nacional Investigadores fellow, Mex., 1984—. Mem. Colegion Nacional, Inst. Internat. Philosophie, Acad. Investigación Científica, Acad. Mex. Lengua, Assn. Filosófica Mex. (pres. 1988—). Home: Congreso 70, 14000 Tlalpan Mexico Office: El Colegio Nacional, Luis Gonzalez Obregon 23, Mexico City 1, Mexico

SALMOIRAGHI, GIAN CARLO, physiologist, educator; b. Gorla Minore, Italy, Sept. 19, 1924; came to U.S., 1952, naturalized, 1958; s. Giuseppe Carlo and Dina (Rinetti) S.; m. Eva Tchoukourlieva, Dec. 5, 1970; 1 child, George Charles. M.D., U. Rome, 1948; Ph.D., McGill U., 1959. Sr. med. officer Internat. Refugee Orgn., Naples, Italy, 1949-52; research fellow Cleve. Clinic Found., 1952-55; lectr. dept. physiology McGill U., Montreal, Que., Can., 1956-58; from neurophysiologist to dir., div. spl. mental health research NIMH, Washington, 1959-73; assoc. commr. research N.Y. State Dept. Mental Hygiene, Albany, 1973-77; assoc. dir. for research Nat. Inst. Alcohol Abuse, HHS, Bethesda, Md., 1977-84; prof. neurology and physiology Hahnemann U., Phila., 1984-85, vice provost for research affairs, 1984-85, chmn. dept. physiology, asst. v.p research, 1985—; clin. prof. psychiatry George Washington U., 1966-73. Contbr. articles to profl. jours. Recipient Superior Service award HEW, 1970. Fellow Am. Coll. Neuropsychopharmacology; mem. AAAS, Am. Physiol. Soc., Am. Soc. Pharmacology and Exptl. Therapeutics, Internat. Brain Research Orgn., Internat. Soc. Psychoneuroendocrinology, Am. Psychiat. Assn., Soc. Neurosci., Royal Soc. Medicine, Soc. Biol. Psychiat., Assn. Research Neurol. and Mental Disease, Research Soc. Alcoholism, Assn. Chmn. Dept. Physiology, Sci. Research Soc., Sigma Xi. Club: Cosmos (Washington). Home: 212 W Gravers Ln Philadelphia PA 19118 Office: Hahnemann U Broad and Vine Sts Philadelphia PA 19102

SALMON, LOUIS, lawyer; b. Mobile, Ala., Aug. 30, 1923; s. Maurice Louis and Wertie (Williams) S.; m. Elisabeth Echols Watts, June 11, 1948; children—John Houston, Margaret Elisabeth. BS, U. Ala., 1943, LLB, 1948; LLD (hon.), U. Ala., Huntsville. Bar: Ala. bar 1949. Instr. acctg. U. Ala., 1946-48; pub. accountant Smith, Dukes & Buckalew, Mobile, 1949-50; practice in Huntsville, 1950—; mem. firm Watts, Salmon, Roberts, Manning & Noojin and predecessor firms, 1950—; gen. counsel 1st Ala. Bank of Huntsville (N.A.); dir. Dunlop Tire Corp., First Ala. Bancshares; past v.p., sec., trustee Huntsville Indsl. Assos. Mem. exec. com. Ala. Rep. Com., 1969-70; mem. Madison County Rep. Exec. Com., Ala.; pres. Huntsville Indsl. Expansion Com., 1968-70; past bd. dirs. Ala. Christian Coll.; mem. pres.'s cabinet U. Ala.; trustee Randolph Sch.; chmn. bd. trustees U. Ala. Huntsville Found.; bd. dirs. Ala. Sports of Fame. Served to capt. AUS, 1943-46, ETO. Decorated Purple Heart; recipient Disting. Service award Huntsville C. of C., 1987. Mem. ABA, Ala. Bar Assn., Huntsville Bar Assn., Ala. C. of C. (pres., dir.), Order of Coif., Kappa Alpha, Phi Alpha Delta. Mem. Ch. of Christ. Club: Huntsville Country (past pres.). Lodge: Rotary (past pres.). Home: 2201 Briarcliff Rd SE Huntsville AL 35801 Office: Terry-Hutchens Bldg Suite 1000 Jefferson St Huntsville AL 35801

SALMON, WATT THOMAS, psychiatrist; b. Erath County, Tex., Jan. 30, 1927; s. Thomas Harvey and Katie (Knick) S.; BS, So. Meth. U., 1950; MD, U. Tenn., Memphis, 1954; m. Barbara Jean Smith, 1962; children—Amelia Gail, Thomas Harald. Fellow, Menninger Sch. Psychiatry, Topeka, 1957-60, mem. faculty, 1960-69, 76-77; chief outpatient services Topeka VA Hosp., 1965-69; staff Menninger Meml. Hosp. and Menninger Found., 1969-77; pvt. practice medicine specializing in psychiatry, Amarillo, Tex., 1977-81; med. dir. outpatient services Amarillo Psychiat. Pavilion, 1978-81; asso. prof. Tex. Tech. Med. Sch., 1978—, dir. residency tng., 1982—, chief psychiatry Amarillo VA Center, 1981—; mem. staff NW Tex. Hosp., High Plains Bapt. Hosp. St. Anthonys Hosp., Amarillo; dir. Psychiat. Ambulatory Clinic, 1978-82. Served with USNR, 1944-46. Recipient service award Menninger Found., 1977. Diplomate Am. Bd. Psychiatry. Mem. Am. Psychiat. Assn., Alumni Assn. Menninger Sch. Psychiatry. Office: 1400 Wallace Blvd Amarillo TX 79106

SALOMA-OROZCO, ABRAHAM EDUARDO, biochemist, food technologist; b. Mexico City, July 19, 1941; s. Abraham and Hortensia (Orozco) Saloma-Cordova; B.Sc., Tex. A&M U., 1963, M.Sc., 1966, Ph.D., 1970; children: Abraham Eduardo, Rafael Ricardo, David Antonio, Begona Elizabeth, Mikel Imanol. Tech. dir. Kraft Foods, Mexico City, 1969-74; asso. prof. U. Iberoamericana, Mexico City, 1971-74; prof. Instituto Politécnico Nacional, Mexico City, 1971-74; dir. research Industrias Cárnicas Navarras, S.A., Pamplona, Spain, 1974-80; dir. for Latin Am., Protein div. Ralston Purina Co., St. Louis, 1980—; cons. Industrias Ilsa-Frigo, Mexico City, 1971—, Alimentos Porta, S.A., Huesca, Spain, 1980—. Named Hon. Fellow, Elintarvikeylioppilaiden Yhdistys LIPIDI, R.Y., U. Helsinki, Finland, 1979. Fellow Am. Inst. Chemists; mem. Am. Mktg. Assn., Am. Chem. Soc., Am. Oil Chemists Soc., Inst. Food Technologists, Am. Dairy Sci. Assn., AAAS, Poultry Sci. Assn., N.Y. Acad. Sci., Am. Meat Sci. Assn., Sociedad Chilena de Tecnología de Alimentos, Sigma Xi. Roman Catholic. Club: The Madrid Tex. Aggie. Contbr. articles to profl. jours. Home: 735 Louwen Saint Louis MO 63124 Office: Checkerboard Sq 14-T Saint Louis MO 63164

SALOMON, CAMHI AVAYÚ, architect; b. Temuco, Chile, June 14, 1936; s. Darío and Raquel (Avayú) C.; m. Estrella Cohen Icahaj, Nov. 17, 1962; children: Dari René, Marcelo. Grad., U. Chile, Santiago, 1961; postgrad. Inter-Am. Ctr., Loyola U., New Orleans, 1971. Design provectist Braden Cooper Co., Santiago, 1962-63; architect Municipalidad de La Reina, Santiago, 1969-74, dir. Direccion Obras Municipales, 1969-74; pvt. practice architecture Santiago, 1975—. Named Hon. Citizen New Orleans, 1971; recipient Cert. Achievement U.S. Dept. State Agy. Internat. Devel., 1971. Mem. Colegio de Arquitectos. Jewish. Clubs: Israelita Stadium, La Dehesa Golf (Santiago). Home: Los Trigeles 7800, Santiago Chile Office: Coyancura 2270, Santiago Chile

SALOMONE, A. WILLIAM, historian, educator, writer; b. Guardiagrele, Italy, Aug. 18, 1915; came to U.S., 1927, naturalized, 1942; s. Michael and Italia (Scioli) S.; m. Lina Palmerio, Sept. 13, 1941; 1 child, Ilia Susan. B.A., LaSalle Coll., 1938; M.A., U. Pa., 1940, Ph.D. (Social Sci. Research Council fellow), 1943. Instr. history, Italian civilization Haverford Coll., 1942-43; instr. modern European history U. Pa., 1944-45; successively instr., asst. prof., asso. prof., prof. N.Y. U., 1945-62; Wilson prof. modern European and Italian history U. Rochester, 1962—; vis. prof. Columbia U., 1961-62, 64; Pres. Am. div. Instituto per la Storia del Risorgimento, 1959-60; cons. in Italian history Collier's Ency.; Mem. selection com. Italian govt. scholarships, Fulbright Italian history fellowships. Author: Italian Democracy in the Making, 1945, L'Età Giolittiana, 1949, (with A. Baltzly) Readings in Twentieth-Century European History, 1950, Italy in the Giolittian Era, 1960, Italy from the Risorgimento to Fascism, 1970; mem. editorial bd. Jour. Modern History, 1965-68, Italian Quar., 1974—, Jour. Ital. History, 1977-82; editorial coordinator Italian sect. International Dictionary of Great Historians, forthcoming auspice Comité Internationale des Science, Historiques, Commission de l'Historiographie, 1984—, preface to S. Di Scala's Renewing Italian Socialism, 1988; contbr. articles to profl. jours. Recipient Herbert Baxter Adams prize Am. Hist. Assn., 1946; Social Sci. Research Council fellow, 1942-43, 55-56; Guggenheim fellow, 1951- 52; Nat. Found. for Humanities Sr. fellow, 1967-68; decorated knight-officer Order Merit Italian Republic, 1960; recipient citation Soc. Italian Hist. Studies, 1967; synposium held in his honor U. Rochester, 1981; conf. in his honor Columbia U., 1982. Mem. Am. Hist. Assn. (session held in his honor 1983), Assn. European Historians N.Y. (pres. 1970-72), Renaissance Soc. Am., Am. Assn. Tchrs. Italian, Am. Acad. Polit. Sci., Soc. for Italian Hist. Studies (pres.), Am.-Italy Soc., Matteotti Internat. Symposium (pres. 1975). Home: 124 Whitemarsh Rd Ardmore PA 19003

SALOMONSSON, ANDERS, archivist, educator; b. Vaxjo, Sweden, May 23, 1946; s. Allan and Margit (Holgersson) S.; m. Violet Johansson, May 25, 1968; children: Linda, Jonna. PhD, U. Lund., 1982. Mus. curator Gotlands Fornsal, Visby, Sweden, 1972-79; head mus. Ystads Museer, Sweden, 1979-81; research asst. dept. ethnology U. Lund, Sweden, 1981-83, archivist, 1983—; docent, asst. prof. U. Lund, 1986. Author: Vader-och vattenkvarnar pa Gotland, 1977, Gotlandsdricka, 1979, Mera än mat, 1987. Home: Sunnanvag 10-0, 222 26 Lund Sweden Office: U Lund Dept Ethnology, Finngatan 8, 223 62 Lund Sweden

SALONEN, ESA-PEKKA, conductor; b. Helsinki, Finland, June 30, 1958. Student, Sibelius Acad., Helsinki; studies with Rautavarra and Panula. Condr. Finnish Radio Symphony, 1979, Philharmonia Orch., London, 1983; guest condr. orchs. London, Berlin, Paris, Los Angeles, Toronto, Phila., St. Louis, Minn.; prin. guest condr. London Philharmonia Orch., 1984, Swedish Radio Symphony Orch., 1985, Oslo Philharm. Orch., 1985—; artistic advisor New Stockholm Chamber Orch., 1986. Office: Oslo Philharm Orch, PO Box 1607 Vika, Munkedamsueien 14, N-0119 Oslo 2 Norway *

SALOOM, KALISTE JOSEPH, JR., judge, lawyer; b. Lafayette, La., May 15, 1918; s. Kaliste and Asma Ann (Boustany) S.; m. Yvonne Adelle Nassar, Oct. 19, 1958; children: Kaliste, Douglas James, Leanne Isabelle, Gregory John. BA with high distinction, U. Southwestern La., 1939; JD, Tulane U., 1942. Bar: La. 1942. Atty. City of Lafayette (La.), 1948-52; judge City and Juvenile Ct., Lafayette, 1952—; tech. adviser Jud. Adminstrn. of Traffic Cts.; mem. jud. council La. Supreme Ct., 1960-64; bd. dirs. Nat. Ctr. for State Cts., Williamsburg, Va., 1978-84, adv. council, 1984—, mem. assocs. com., 1986— (Disting. Service award Trial Judge on State Level 1988); mem. Nat. Hwy. Traffic Safety Adminstrn. Adv. Com., U.S. Dept. Transp., 1977-80, Nat. Com. on Uniform Traffic Laws, 1986. Served with U.S. Army, 1942-45. mem. editorial bd. Tulane Law Rev., 1941; contbr. articles to profl. jours. Recipient Civic Cup, City of Lafayette, 1965, Pub. Service award U.S. Dept. Transp., 1980, Disting. Jurist award Miss. State U. Pre-Law Soc., 1987, Disting. Service award Nat. Ctr. for State Cts., 1988. Mem. ABA (Benjamin Flaschner award 1981), Am. Judges Assn. (William H. Burnett award 1982), Nat. Council Juvenile Ct. Judges, La. City Judges Assn. (past pres.), La. Juvenile Ct. Judges Assn. (past pres.), Am. Judicature Soc., Order of Coif. Democrat. Roman Catholic. Clubs: Oakbourne Country (Lafayette). Lodge: KC. Home: 502 Marguerite Blvd Lafayette LA 70503 Office: 211 W Main St Lafayette LA 70501

SALTER, CHARLES AUGUST, psychologist, army officer; b. Ft. Worth, Oct. 12, 1947; s. Simon August and Doris Rebecca (Robinson) S.; student U. Leeds (Eng.), 1967-68; BS magna cum laude, Tulane U., 1969; MA, U. Pa., 1970, PhD, 1973; MS, Harvard U., 1987; m. Carlota Luisa Delerma, May 13, 1972; children—Brian, Valerie, Carolyn. Assoc. prof. psychology Spring Hill Coll., Mobile, Ala., 1973-80; pres. Intellect Corp., Mobile, 1977-80; research cons. Berkley-Small, Inc., Mobile, 1977-80; commd. capt. Med. Service Corps, U.S. Army, 1980, advanced through grades to maj., 1986; research psychologist U.S. Army Natick Research and Devel. Labs. (Mass.), 1981-84. Pres., Mobile Cinema Workshop, 1974. Mem. Am. Psychol. Assn., Phi Beta Kappa, Kappa Delta Pi. Editor: Knight's Food Service Dictionary, 1987; author: Psychology for Living, 1977, Guide to Kitchen Management, 1985, Foodservice Standards in Resorts, 1987, On The Frontlines, 1988, Getting It Off; Keeping It Off, 1988; also articles in profl. jours., mags.; syndicated columnist Suburban Features; editor: Readings in Introductory Psychology, 1975; Alternative Careers for Academics Bull., 1978. Office: US Army Natick Research Devel and Engring Ctr Behavioral Scis Div Natick MA 01760

SALTINI, IVAN RICCARDO, electronics executive; b. Modena, Italy, Sept. 17, 1948; s. Noé Guido and Argia (Gasparini) S.; m. Rossella Pierozzi, Sept. 23, 1973 (dec. 1982); 1 child, Veronica. BSEE, Univ. Bologna, Italy, 1974. Digital designer S.M.A. Corp., Firenze, Italy, 1975-78, radar systems designer, 1978-82, supr. electronic design, 1983-86; exec. dir. Perseo, Bologna, 1986, Informatica 1, Bologna, 1986-87; chief exec. officer Caesar Co., Bologna, 1987—; cons. Data-B, Milan, 1978-84. Contbr. articles to profl. jours. Mem. Internat. Material Mgmt. Soc. Roman Catholic. Home: Via de Tommasi 6, 50142 Florence Italy Office: Caesar Spa, Via Corassori 54, 40100 Modena, Emilia Italy

SALTMAN, DAVID, graphic arts and publishing consultant; b. Glasgow, Scotland, Oct. 25, 1912; came to U.S., 1921, naturalized, 1933; s. Gilbert and Sophia (Ziontz) S.; student CCNY, 1930-33; m. Henrietta Roskin, Dec. 5, 1942 (dec. 1976); children—Gilbert Martin, Elliot Barry; m. Elaine Dworkin, 1977. Gen. mgr., prodn. mgr. Cowan Pub. Corp., N.Y.C., 1940-41, 45-58, 60; mgr. printing dept. United Tech. Pub., Garden City, N.Y., 1958-59; pres. Elgin Press Inc., 1960-83; pub. and printing cons., N.Y.C., 1950—; mem. faculty NYU, 1952-77, adj. asst. prof. graphic design, 1969-77; instr. edn. dept. Printing Industries Met. N.Y., 1977-79; chmn. in-plant printing seminar Am. Mgmt. Assn., 1971; condr. graphic arts seminars, Atlanta, May, 1977, Nat. Assn. Printers and Lithographers, St. Louis, Dec., 1978, Web Offset sect. Printing Industries Am., Denver, May, 1980, Printfest, Printing Industries Am., Arlington, Va., Sept., 1980, Mgmt. Services, Assn. Graphic Arts Cons., New Orleans, 1986. Explorer commr., troop com. chmn. Boy Scouts Am., 1960-76. Served with FA, AUS, World War II. Recipient Golden Keys award Club Printing House Craftsmen, citation Nat. Assn. Recycling Industries, 1974. Mem. Res. Officers Assn. (chpt. pres. 1952-54, 70-74, 85-86, conv. chmn. N.Y. State dept. 1974, mem. nat. publs. com. 1976—), Internat. Graphic Arts Edn. Assn., TAPPI, Assn. Graphic Arts Cons. Printing Industries Am. (v.p. 1983-84, pres. 1984-86), Mil. Order of World Wars (vice comdr. N.Y. chpt. 1978-88), Am. Legion. Clubs: Wantagh (N.Y.) Camera (pres. 1971-72), Wantagh Chess (pres. 1973-75), Navigators (pres. 1976-77). Author: Production Planning and Impositions Simplified, 1976, Paper Basics, 1978, Lithography Primer, 1986, Pulp and Paper Primer, 1981; editor-in-chief: Top Management Guide for Printers and Publishers, 1984. Home: 1252 Campbell Rd Wantagh NY 11793 Office: PO Box A127 Wantagh NY 11793

SALTZMAN, BENJAMIN NATHAN, physician, health department administrator; b. Ansonia, Conn., Apr. 24, 1914; s. Joseph N. and Frances (Levine) S.; m. Ruth Elizabeth Bohan, Dec. 19, 1941; children—Sue Ann, John Joseph, Mark Stephen. B.A., U. Oreg., 1935, M.A., 1936, M.D., 1940. Diplomate Am. Bd. Family Practice. Intern, then resident Gorgas Hosp., Ancon, Panama, 1940-42; gen. practice medicine Saltzman Clinic, Mountain Home, Ark., 1946-74; prof. family and community medicine U. Ark. Coll. Medicine, Little Rock, 1974-81; prof. emeritus U. Ark. Coll. Medicine; dir. Ark. Dept. Health, Little Rock, 1981-87; dir. Pulaski county unit Ark. Dept. Health, 1987—. Contbr. articles to profl. jours. Alderman Mountain Home City Council, 1947-55; pres. Ark. Brotherhood NCCJ, 1986—; sr. bd. pres. Florence Crittendon Home Services, Ark., 1986—. Served to capt. AUS, 1942-46, lt. col. Res. ret. Recipient Ark. Man of Yr. award Ark. Democrat, 1975, Will Ross award Am. Lung Assn., 1979; Tom T. Ross award Ark. Pub. Health Assn., 1975, Outstanding Achievement award, 1975, Ark. Human Relations award, 1980; Disting. Leadership award Am. Rural Health Assn., 1985; named Arkansan of Yr., Ark. Gerontological Soc., 1987. Fellow Am. Acad. Family Physicians (chmn. rural health and mental health com. 1956-71), Am. Coll. Preventive Medicine; mem. AMA (chmn. council on rural health 1966-69), Ark. Acad. Family Physicians (pres. 1955-56), Ark. Med. Soc. (pres. 1974-75), Gerontologic Soc. (Arkansas of the yr. 1987), Mountain Home C. of C. (pres. 1955-68). Lodges: Rotary (bd. dirs. 1961-63, trustee Rotary Found. 1965-67, bd. dirs. internat. chpt.), Masons, Elks (state pres. 1956-59). Home: 224 N Palm St Little Rock AR 72205 Office: Ark Dept Health Pulaski County Unit 1700 W 13th St Little Rock AR 72202

SALTZMAN, FLORY, small business owner; b. Colon, Republic of Panama, Jan. 31, 1927; d. Abraham Abadi Balid and Zakie Mizrachi; m. Jacob Saltzman, Aug. 30, 1953; children: Jon Michael, Lynne Harriet, Daniel Alan. Grad. high sch., Israel. Sec. Brit. Mil. Service, Palestine, Israel, 1946-48; mgr. Casa Fachlich Jewelry Store, Republic of Panama, 1956-61; acting ptnr. Flory Saltzman-Molas (formerly La Innovacion Gift Shop), Republic of Panama, 1961-71, owner, 1971—. Served with Israeli Army, 1948-50. Office: La Innovacion Gift Shop, Box 1719, Balboa Republic of Panama

SALTZMAN, JACK DAVID, elec. co. exec.; b. N.Y.C., Aug. 4, 1920; s. Morris and Regina (Bauch) S.; B.S. in Elec. Engring., N.Y. U., 1940; m. Margaret Decker, Nov. 4, 1960; children—Mark David, Lisa Rachel, Ira Robert. Engr., Fischbach & Moore, Inc., 1940-48, chief engr., project mgr., 1948; chmn., bd. dirs. Consol. Electric Supply Inc. div. Wilcox & Gibbs, N.Y.C., 1987—, Wilcox & Gibbs, N.Y.C., Consol. Internat. div., Art Craft Electric Supply div., Calcon Electric Supply Co. div., SEB Assocs. div.; treas. Mid Eastern Funding, Union, Seigler Assos., East Orange, N.J., Mansion Assos., N.Y.C.; v.p. Hwy. Leasing Corp., Jersey City, Hwy. Terminal Corp., Jersey City; mem. N.Y. Stock Exchange; pres. M.R. Saltzman, Deal. Chmn., Israel Bond Dr., Deal. Chmn. bd. Hillel Sch., N.J., Monmouth County YW-YMHA; former chmn. bd., v.p. Jewish Hosp. and Rehab. Center N.J.; bd. dirs. Kingsbrook Jewish Med. Center, Bklyn., Salvation Army, Jersey City, Fight for Sight; a founder Technion Inst. Israel; trustee, prin. Saltzman Found.; bd. dirs., v.p. Hillel Sch., Miami; trustee Jewish Fedn. S. Broward (Fla.); v.p. Am. Friends of Hebrew U. Home: 19624 Oakbrook Circle Boca Raton FL 33434 Office: 7000 NW 52d St Miami FL 33166

SALVADORI, ANNA, mathematician, educator; b. Perugia, Italy, Oct. 16, 1952; d. Sante and Jole (Pompei) S. Laurea in math., U. Perugia, 1975. Assoc. prof. math. U. Perugia, Italy, 1978—. Office: U Perugia, Dept Math, Via Pascoli, 06100 Perugia Italy

SALVATORELLI, JOSEPH J., engineer, consultant; b. Phila., Oct. 22, 1924; s. Luigi and Agnes (D'Amario) S.; m. Dolores A. Biello, Aug. 11, 1946; 1 son, Joel Girard. Diploma in Civil Engring., Drexel U., 1954, B.S.C.E., 1956. Registered profl. engr. N.J., Pa., Md., Va., Del., N.Y., Nebr.; lic. sewage/water treatment plant operator; registered land surveyor; diplomate Am. Acad. Environ. Engrs.; With Albright & Friel, Inc., Phila., 1946-71, ptnr., 1959-71, v.p., 1962-71, also dir.; sr. assoc. Taylor Wiseman Taylor, Mt. Laurel, N.J., 1971-75, v.p., ptnr., 1975-85; ret.; cons. in field, 1986—; mem. research adv. council P.S.E.G. Research Corp., 1986—. Contbr. to profl. publs. Pres. Assn. Island House Unit Owners, 1974-76, 79-84; pres. Island House Condominium Assn., Margate, N.J., 1976-77. Served as sgt. U.S. Army, 1943-46, PTO. Recipient Alumni Achievement award Drexel U., 1959, named Alumnus of Yr., 1976. Mem. Nat. Soc. Profl. Engrs., Franklin Inst., Water Pollution Control Assn. Pa. (life, pres. 1971-72; High Hat award 1975, Hazeltine award 1980), Water Pollution Control Fedn. (dir. 1973-76; Arthur Sidney Bedell award 1973, Service award 76), Eastern Pa. Water Pollution Control Operators Assn. (life, Service award 1973, Bolenius-Wiest Clean Streams award 1983), ASCE (dir. Phila. sect., chmn. san. engring. div. 1968-69), Am. Water Works Assn., N.J. Water Pollution Control Assn., Pa. Mcpl. Authorities Assn., Authorities Assn. of N.J. (dir. 1972-74), Alpha Sigma Lambda (ETA chpt.). Roman Catholic. Lodge: Yeadon Kiwanis (sec. 1968-70, pres. 1972, dir.) (Pa.). Current work: Consultant in environmental engineering, engineering management, forensic engineering. Subspecialties: Civil engineering; Environmental engineering.

SALVERSON, CAROL ANN, library administrator, clergywoman; b. Buffalo, June 30, 1944; d. Howard F. and Estella G. (Zelie) Heavener; B.A. in Philosophy, SUNY, Buffalo, 1966; M.S. in Library Sci., Syracuse U., 1968; grad. Sacred Coll. Jamilian Theology and Div. Sch., 1976. Library trainee and research asst. SUNY, Med. Center, Syracuse, 1966-67; asst. editor SUNY Union List of Serials, Syracuse, 1967-68; readers services librarian, asst. prof. Jefferson Community Coll., Watertown, N.Y., 1968-75; ordained to ministry Internat. Community of Christ Ch., 1974; adminstr. public services dept. Internat. Community of Christ, Chancellery, Reno, 1975-84, dir. Jamilian Theol. Research Library, 1975—; mem. faculty Sacred Coll. Jamilian U. of the Ordained, Reno, 1979—, Jamilian Parochial Sch., Internat. Community of Christ, 1978—. Chmn. religious edn. com. All Souls Unitarian-Universalist Ch., Watertown, N.Y., 1970-71, treas., 1974-75; trustee North Country Reference and Research Resources Council, Canton, N.Y., 1974-75; dir. Gene Savoy Heritage Museum and Library, 1984—; violist Symphonietta, Reno, 1983—. Mem. ALA, Nev. Library Assn., Friends of Library Washoe County, Friends of Library U. Nev. Club: Coll. Women's. Contbr. articles on library sci. to profl. jours. Home: 2025 La Fond Dr Reno NV 89509 Office: Internat Community of Christ Chancellory 643 Ralston St Reno NV 89503

SALVESON, MELVIN ERWIN, business executive, educator; b. Brea, Calif., Jan. 16, 1919; s. John T. and Elizabeth (Green) S.; m. Joan Y. Stipek, Aug. 22, 1944; children: Eric C., Kent Erwin. B.S., U. Calif. at Berkeley, 1941; M.S., Mass. Inst. Tech., 1947; Ph.D., U. Chgo., 1952. Cons. McKinsey & Co., N.Y.C., 1948-49; asst. prof., dir. mgmt. sci. research U. Calif. at Los Angeles, 1949-54; mgr. advanced data systems Gen. Electric Co., Louisville and N.Y.C., 1954-57; pres. Mgmt. Scis. Corp., Los Angeles, 1957-67; group v.p. Control Data/CEIR, Inc., 1967-68; pres. Electronic Currency Corp., 1968—; chmn. OneCard Internat., Inc., 1983—; bd. dirs. OneCard Internat. Inc., Diversified Earth Scis., Inc., Algeran, Inc., Electronic Currency Corp.; founder Master Card System, Los Angeles, 1966; chmn. Corporate Strategies Internat.; prof. bus. Pepperdine U. 1972-85; adj. prof. U. So. Calif.; adviser data processing City of Los Angeles, 1962-64; futures forecasting IBM, 1957-61; adviser strategic systems planning USAF, 1961-67; info. systems Calif. Dept. Human Resources, 1972-73, City Los Angeles Automated Urban Data Base, 1962-67; tech. transfer NASA, 1965-70, others; mem. bd. trustees, Long Beach City Coll. Contbr. articles to profl. jours. Served to lt. comdr. USNR, 1941-46. Named to Long Beach City Coll. Hall of Fame. Fellow AAAS; mem. Inst. Mgmt. Sci. (founder, past pres.). Republican. Club: Founders (Los Angeles Philharmonic Orch.), Calif. Yacht. Home: 1577 N Bundy Dr Los Angeles CA 90049

SALVO, ANDRÉ BERNARD, urologist; b. Marseilles, Bouches du Rhone, France, July 4, 1931; s. Antoine and Dorothy Vivienne (Bryett) S.; m. Nadia Nowak, Dec. 19, 1963; children: Nicole, Noell, Alexis. Degree, Ext. Hôpitaux, Assistance Publique, Marseilles, 1955; MD, U. Aix-Marseilles, 1963. Diplomate Nat. Med. Bd. Resident intern St. Joseph's Hosp., Marseilles, 1964—, asst. urologist, 1965-77, chief of staff, 1978—; educator attaché U. Aiz-Marseilles, 1969—; mem. med. counsel, 1969; expert Social Security France, 1969—; med. examiner St. Joseph's internship, 1985, 1988. Contbr. articles to profl. jours. Mem. polit. bur. Rassemblement pour la Republique, Ileme circonscription Marseille, 1984-86. Served to sub lt. M.C., French mil., 1958-60. Mem. French Urol. Assn., S.E. Urol. Soc., Internat. French Speaking Urodynamic Soc., Med. St. Joseph's Hosp. (pres. 1982—). Roman Catholic. Club: Lacydon Nautical (Marseilles). Office: Saint Joseph's Hosp, 26 bd de Louvain, 13008 Marseilles France

SAM, PIERRE DESFORGES, ambassador; b. St. Louis North, Haiti, May 23, 1925; s. Felix D. and Exantucia (Poux) S.; m. Conceptia Geffrar; children: Jean-Renaud, Pierre Richard, Marlene, Donald. BS in Agrl. Engring., U. Haiti, 1945; BSA, U. Mayaguez, P.R., 1946; certification, U. New Mex., 1951; student, IICA, Costa Rica, 1957. Bar: Haiti, 1953. Project mgr. U.S. Ops. Mission, Gonave, St. Raphael, Haiti, 1945-53; nat. supr. U.S. Ops. Mission Extension, Port-Au-Prince, Haiti, 1953-55; project. mgr. SCIPA, Haiti, 1955-62; regional officer U.N., Rome, 1962-63; extension officer Gov. of Haiti, Africa, S. Am., Africa, 1963-80; Minister of Planning Gov. of Haiti, Port-Au-Prince, 1981-82, Minister of Agriculture, 1982; Hatian Ambassador Washington, 1986-88; sr. cons., pvt. cons., mgr. U.S. AID/Soc. d'Etudes et de Mise en Valeur, Haiti. Minister of State, Haiti, 1981-82. Recipient rank of Rising Star from Pres. of Taiwan, 1981, Chevalier of the Order of Nat. Merit Haiti; Hon. Citizen of Los Angeles, 1987, Oakland, Calif., 1987. Mem. U.S. Nat. Assn. of Agrl. Engrs., U.S. Acad. of Scis., FAO/UN Internat. Group on Agrl. Extension, Smithsonian. Roman Catholic. Clubs: Nat. Press, Washington Internat. Lodge: Rotary. Office: Embassy of Haiti 2311 Massachusetts Ave NW Washington DC 20008

SAM, SEONG KIN, comsumer products executive; b. Macao, Apr. 17, 1953; s. Chak Lam Sam and Fun Hoo (Tsang) S. B in Adminstrn., Concordia U., Montreal, 1979. Managerial exec. Victor Corp., Macao, 1972-76; head advtg. and sales promotion Macao Indsl. Ltd., 1979-82; exec. Govt. Macoa, 1982-84; regional mgr. Man Weng Corp., Macao, 1984—. Mem. Am. Statistical Assn., Adminstrv. Mgmt. Assn. Home: 21 Beco Da Boa Vista, 10 Andar Macao (via Hong Kong) Macao

SAMAAN, NAGUIB ABDELMALIK, endocrinologist; b. Girga, Egypt, Apr. 2, 1925; s. Abdelmalik and Amasil Hanna S.; m. Jean Moffatt, Nov. 18, 1961; children—Sarah Ann, Mary Elizabeth, Jane Susan, Catherine Thia,

Michael James. M.B., Ch.B., Alexandria (Egypt) U., 1951; D.M. in Internal Medicine, 1953; Ph.D. in Medicine, U. London, 1964. Rotating intern Alexandria U. Hosp., 1951-52, resident, 1952-54, sr. med. resident, instr., 1954-55; sr. research fellow Chest Inst., Brompton Hosp., London, 1955-56, Neurology Inst., Queen Sq., London, 1956; clin. fellow Postgrad. Med. Sch., London, 1957; clin. asst. prof. dept. endocrinology and therapeutics, asst. physician Royal Infirmary, Edinburgh, Scotland, 1957; sr. med. resident North Cambridge (Eng.) Hosps., 1958-60; staff physician, asst. prof., sr. research fellow Royal Postgrad. Med. Sch., London, 1960-64; research asso., asst. physician and endocrinologist Case Western Res. U., Cleve., 1964-66; staff physician, asst. prof. dept. internal medicine U. Iowa Hosps., Iowa City, 1966-69; med. staff physician and endocrinologist VA Hosp., Iowa City, 1966-69; chief sect. endocrinology U. Tex. M.D. Anderson Hosp. and Tumor Inst., Houston, 1969—; asso. internist, asso. prof. medicine U. Tex. M.D. Anderson Hosp. and Tumor Inst., 1969-72, internist, prof. medicine, 1972—; prof. medicine and physiology U. Tex. Grad. Sch. Biomed. Scis., Houston, 1969-72, prof., 1972—; prof. internal medicine U. Tex. M.D. Anderson Hosp. and Tumor Inst. and U. Tex. Med. Sch., Houston, 1973—, dep. chmn. dept. of medicine, 1983—; cons., attending physician dept. internal medicine Hermann Hosp., Houston, 1970—. Contbr. numerous articles to med. jours. Brit. Med. Research Council grantee, 1962-64; NIH grantee, 1969—; Am. Cancer Soc. grantee, 1971—. Fellow Royal Coll. Physicians (Scotland) Royal Coll. Physicians (Eng.), A.C.P.; mem. Brit. Med. Assn., AMA, Am. Endocrine Soc., Am. Fedn. Clin. Research, Am. Physiol. Soc., Fedn. Am. Socs. Exptl. Biology, Central Soc. Clin. Research, Soc. Gynecologic Investigation, N.Y. Acad. Sci., Harris County Med. Soc., Houston Soc. Internal Medicine, Am. Thyroid Assn., Am. Diabetes Assn. Club: Nottingham Forest (Houston). Home: 14315 Heatherfield St Houston TX 77024 Office: MD Anderson Hosp and Tumor Inst 6723 Bertner Ave Houston TX 77030

SAMAAN, SELIM TAWFICK, surgeon; b. Alexandria, Egypt, Jan. 23, 1932; s. Tawfick Elias and Eva Nichola (Hamoui) S.; came to U.S., 1960, naturalized, 1971; M.B.B.Ch., Alexandria U., 1951, M.D., 1958; m. Judith Lane Watson, Dec. 29, 1962; children—Eva, Peter, Andrew, Catherine. Intern, Harlem Hosp., N.Y.C., 1960-61, resident surgery Union Meml. Hosp., Balt., 1961-63, chief resident in surgery, 1964-65; resident in colon and rectal surgery Lahey Clinic, Boston, 1965-66, asst. staff, 1966-67; practice medicine specializing in colon and rectal surgery, Garden City, N.Y., 1967—; chief colon and rectal surgery Mercy Hosp., 1975—; asst. clin. prof. SUNY. Diplomate Am. Bd. Surgery, Am. Bd Colon and Rectal Surgery. Fellow ACS, AMA, Am. Soc. Colon and Rectal Surgery; mem. N.Y., Nassau County med. socs., N.Y. Soc. Surgeons, N.Y., Pa. socs. colon and rectal surgery. Republican. Greek Orthodox. Club: Cherry Valley. Office: 520 Franklin Ave Garden City NY 11530

SAMAHA, FRANCIS JOSEPH, periodontist; b. Washington, Apr. 16, 1928; s. Toufig Nickolas and Edna (George) S.; D.D.S., Georgetown U., 1951; m. Lili Ann Sheahin, July 4, 1951; children—Jeffrey F., Gary M., Lisa M., Richard G.; m. 2d, Gina A. Rota, Sept. 15, 1973; 1 dau., Nina M. Commd. 2d lt. USAF, 1950, advanced through grades to col., 1968; intern Fitzsimmons Army Hosp., Denver, 1951-52; assigned Bergstrom AFB, Tex., 1952-56; resident Tufts U., Boston, 1956-58; assigned Ramey AFB, P.R., 1958-61, Andrews AFB, Md., 1961-69, Clark Air Base, Philippines, 1969-70; ret., 1970; practice dentistry, 1970—; asso. prof., dir. grad. periodontics Georgetown U., Washington, 1970-72, U. Md., 1972-73. Cons. to surgeon gen. USAF, 1961-69; nat., internat. lectr. in field. Pres., Holy Name Soc., Bergstrom AFB, 1955-56; coach, mgr. Little League Baseball, Andrews AFB, 1961-64. Bd. dirs. Prince Georges County Boys Club, 1965-67. Decorated Legion of Merit, Commendation medal; diplomate Am. Bd. Periodontology. Fellow Am. Coll. Dentists, Va. Dental Assn., Am. Acad. Occlusodontia; mem. ADA, Am. Acad. Oral Medicine, Am. Acad. Periodontology, Am. Acad. Oral Pathology, No. Va. Dental Soc. (pres. 1984-85), Greater Washington Soc. Periodontology (pres. 1967-68), Omicron Kappa Upsilon. Melkite Catholic. Home: 4741 Rock Spring Rd Arlington VA 22207 Office: 6845 Elm St Suite 607 McLean VA 22101

SAMALIN, EDWIN, lawyer, educator; b. N.Y.C., Sept. 19, 1935; s. Harry Louis and Sydell (Fisher) S.; m. Sheila Karen Samalin, Oct. 12, 1961; children—David Seth, Andrew Evan, Jonathan Daniel. B.S., U. R.I., 1957; J.D., N.Y. Law Sch., 1962. Bar: N.Y. 1963, U.S. Supreme Ct. 1976. Tax atty. Electric Bond & Share Co., N.Y.C., 1963; ptnr. Samalin & Sklaver, Yorktown Heights, N.Y., 1969-78; sole practice, Yorktown Heights, 1963-69, 78-84; ptnr. Samalin & Bock, Yorktown Heights, 1984—; adj. faculty Mercy Coll., Dobbs Ferry, N.Y., 1974—; commodity cons. Murlas Commodities, Yorktown Heights, 1982—; ptnr. Patterson (N.Y.) Realty Assn., 1983—; pres. Sammark Realty Corp., Westchester, N.Y., 1984—; commodity cons. Dem. candidate for County Legislature, 1973. Served to capt. U.S. Army, 1957-59. Mem. N.Y. State Bar Assn., Westchester County Bar Assn., Yorktown Bar Assn. (pres. 1982, Man of Yr. 1983), Am. Arbitration Assn. (arbitrator 1974—), Phi Delta Phi. Home: 951A Heritage Hills Somers NY 10589 Office: Samalin & Bock PC 2000 Maple Hill St Yorktown Heights NY 10598

SAMANTAR, MOHAMMED ALI, prime minister Somalia; b. Chisimaio, Somalia, 1931. Ed., Mil. Acad. Rome, Mil. Acad. Moscow. Comdt. Somali Police, 1956; maj.-adj. Somalian Armed Forces, 1958-65; brig.-gen. Nat. Army Somalia, 1967, maj.-gen., 1973; v.p. Supreme Revolutionary Council, 1971-76; sec. state for def. Somalia, 1971-76; comdr.-in-chief Somalian Armed Forces, 1971-78; former v.p. polit. bur. Somali Socialist Revolutionary Party; minister def. 1976-81, from 82; chair def. and security com. Supreme Council of the Revolution, 1980-82, v.p., 1981-82; now prime minister Somalia. Address: Office Prime Minister, Mogadishu Somalia *

SAMARANCH, JUAN ANTONIO, International Olympic Committee president; b. Barcelona, Spain, July 17, 1920; s. Francisco and Juana (Torello) S.; m. Maria Teresa Salisachs, Dec. 1955; children: Maria Teresa, Juan Antonio. Student Higher Inst. Bus. Studies, Barcelona; Doctor Honoris Causa, U. Alberta, Can., U. Trois Riviéres, Can., U. Sofia, Bulgaria. With Spanish Olympic Com., from 1954, pres., 1967-71; mem. Internat. Olympic Com., Lausanne, Switzerland, 1966—, v.p., 1974-78, pres., 1980—; bd. dirs. Banco Exterior, Zurich; pres. Caja de Pensiones para la Vejez y de ahorros de Cataluna y Baleares, Spain, 1987; Spanish Ambassador to USSR, 1977-80; mcpl. councillor, Barcelona; nat. del. for phys. edn. and sports, 1967-71; pres. Diputacion, Barcelona, 1973-77. Decorated Grand Croix. Roman Catholic. Home: Ave Pau Casals 24, Barcelona 21 Spain Office: Internat Olympic Com, Chateau de Vidy, 1007 Lausanne Switzerland

SAMARAWICKRAMA, GERVIN PANDUKA, academic administrator, medical educator; b. Colombo, Sri Lanka, July 5, 1938; s. Stephen and Darlina (Wijeratne) S.; m. Sunethra Manthri Kehelpannala, July 11, 1966; 1 child, Rajeeva. MBBS, U. Ceylon, Sri Lanka, 1967; MS, U. London, 1975; PhD, Med. Research Council Toxicology Unit, Surrey, Eng., 1979. Med. officer-in-charge Veneral Diseases Clinic, Galle, Sri Lanka, 1968-69, Govt. Hosp., Hurikaduwa, Sri Lanka, 1969-71; lectr., then sr. lectr. U. Peradeniya, Sri Lanka, 1971-80; prof. community medicine U. Ruhuna, Matara, Sri Lanka, 1980—, vice chancellor, 1982—; vis. prof. Postgrad. Inst. Medicine, Colombo, 1980—, mem. bd. study community medicine; chmn. com. vice-chancellors and dirs., Sri Lanka, 1985, Univ. Grants Commn.; mem. task force WHO, Stockholm, 1981; bd. dirs. State Mortgage and Investment Bank of Sri Lanka. Contbr. articles to profl. jours. and chpts. to books. WHO fellow, London, 1974-79. Mem. Sri Lanka Med. Assn., Sri Lanka AAAS. Buddhist. Home: 35/2 Hosp Quarters, Karapitiya, Galle Sri Lanka Office: U Ruhuna, Office Vice Chancellor, Matara Sri Lanka

SAMAY, Z. LANCE, lawyer; b. Janoshaza, Hungary, Dec. 2, 1944; B.A., Rutgers U., 1967; J.D., Seton Hall U., 1970. Bar: N.J. 1970, U.S. Ct. Appeals (3d cir.) 1974, U.S. Supreme Ct. 1976, N.Y. 1988. Law sec. Appellate div. Superior Ct. N.J., 1970-71; asst. U.S. Atty. Dist. N.J., 1971-76; chief Environ. Protection Div., Office of U.S. Atty. Fed. Dist. N.J., 1972-74, chief Civil Div., 1974-76; now pres. Z. Lance Samay, P.C., Morristown, N.J.; adj. prof. environ. law Seton Hall U. Sch. Law, 1973, 74, 76; trial instr. Atty. Gen.'s Advocacy Inst., 1975, 76; vice chmn. consumer affairs com. Fed. Exec. Bd., 1973-74, chmn. human resources com., 1974-75, chmn. relations with academia com., 1975-76. Recipient U.S. Atty. Gen's spl. commendation for outstanding service, 1973; U.S. Dept. Justice spl. achievement award for sustained superior performance, 1972, 76. Mem. US Atty.'s Alumni Assn., Morris County Bar Assn., Seton Hall Law Alumni Assn. (adv. com. to dean 1971-72, trustee 1975-80, treas. 1975-76, pres. 1976-79, mem. deans search com. for Seton Hall Law Ctr. 1977-78). Co-founder, notes and rewrite editor Seton Hall Law Rev., 1969-70, case notes editor Seton Hall Law Jour., 1969. Club: Mountain Lakes (bd. govs.). Home: Mountain Lakes and Bernardsville NJ 07046 Office: One Washington St Morristown NJ 07960

SAMBAR, DAVID H., investment banker; b. Haifa, Palestine, Aug. 19, 1930; in Eng., 1976, naturalized; s. Habib David and Georgette (El Khoury) S.; m. Salma Renee Zacca, Oct. 15, 1966; children—Habib David, Syma Karine. B.A., London U., 1951; M.A. in Econs., Am. U., Beirut, 1962; Doctorate magna cum laude Faculty Econs. and Bus. Adminstrn., Lyon, France, 1975; hon. doctorate Mex. Acad. Internat. Law, 1980. Asst. auditor, auditor Chase Bank, Beirut, 1955-62, from asst. mgr. to mgr. to v.p., 1962-73, v.p., N.Y.C., 1973-77; chmn. Sharjah Investment, London, 1977-81, Strategic Investment Planning, London, 1982-86, Sambar Internat. Investments Ltd., 1986—; chmn. D.H. Sambar Investments, Geneva, 1981—; mem. Lloyds of London, 1984—; adviser various cos. Editor articles and speeches various U.S. and European pub. and profl. orgns. Mem. Stanford Research Inst., 1979—; counsellor internat. fin. affairs Peoples for UN, N.Y.C., 1979—; trustee Princeton in Asia, 1965—, Ctr. for Internat. Bus., Dallas, 1978—. Roman Catholic. Clubs: Hurlingham (London); Metropolitan (N.Y.C.). Avocations: tennis, skiing. Office: Sambar Internat Investments Ltd, 96 Park Ln, London W1, England

SAMBROOK, ARTHUR JAMES, English literature, language educator; b. Nuneaton, Warwicks, Eng., Sept. 5, 1931; s. Arthur and Constance Elizabeth (Gapper) S.; m. Patience Ann Crawford, Mar. 25, 1961; children: John Arthur, William James, Robert Joseph, Thomas Daniel. BA in English Language, Lit., U. Oxford, 1955; PhD, U. Nottingham, 1957; MA in English Language, Lit., U. Oxford, 1959. Lectr. English lang., lit. U. Wales, Lampeter, 1957-64; lectr. U. Southampton, Eng., 1964-71; sr. lectr. U. Southampton, 1971-75, reader, 1975-81, prof., 1981—. Author: A Poet Hidden, The Life of Richard Watson Dixon 1833-1900, 1962, William Cobbet, an Author Guide, 1973, Pre-Raphaelitism, 1976, English Pastoral Poetry, 1983, The Eighteenth Century: The Intellectual and Cultural Context of English Literature, 1700-1789, 1986; editor: The Scribleriad, 1742, 1967, The Seasons (James Thomson), 1981, Liberty, The Castle of Indolence and Other Poems (James Thomson), 1986; contbr. articles to profl., academic jours. Killham Sr. research fellow Dalhousie U., Halifax, Nova Scotia, 1968-69, vis. fellow Newberry Library, Chgo., 1969, Leverhulme research fellow, 1974-75, Brit. Acad., Folger Shakespeare Library, Washington, 1974, 82, Magdalen Coll. U. Oxford, 1984, St. John's Coll. U. Oxford, 1985, Humanities Research Ctr. Australian Nat. U. Canberra, 1988. Office: U Southampton, Southhampton SO9 5NH, England

SAMEK, EDWARD LASKER, service company executive; b. N.Y.C., Oct. 26, 1936; s. Richard E. and Jane L. Samek; B.S. in Commerce and Fin., Bucknell U., 1958; M.B.A., Columbia U., 1960; m. Marthann Lauver, June 26, 1960; children—Anne, Margaret, Elizabeth. Brand mgr. Procter & Gamble Co., Cin., 1960-62; dir. New products Johnson & Johnson, New Brunswick, N.J., 1962-67; v.p., gen. mgr. Avon Products Inc., N.Y.C., 1967-75; pres., chief exec. officer Childcraft Edn. Corp., Edison, N.J., 1975-78, also dir.; pres. Hudson Pharm. Corp., W. Caldwell, N.J., 1978-82; chmn. bd., pres. Secrephone Ltd., Jenkintown, Pa., various locations, 1982—. Pres. bd. trustees Hartridge Sch., Plainfield, N.J., 1969-76; v.p. bd. trustees Wardlaw-Hartridge Sch., Plainfield and Edison, 1975—; trustee, v.p. bd. Plainfield Symphony, 1976—. Served with Ordnance Corps, U.S. Army, 1958-59. Mem. Young Pres.'s Orgn. Clubs: Williams, Metuchen (N.J.) Golf and Country, World Bus. Council. Home: 1717 Woodland Ave Edison NJ 08820

SAMELSON, LINCOLN RUSSELL, publisher; b. N.Y.C., Mar. 30, 1926; s. John Sommer and Marjorie (Don) S.; m. Marie Janet Schupmann, Nov. 16, 1957; children: Scott Lincoln, Kevin Russell, Quentin Barth, Susan Marie, Timothy Charles, Jeffrey Lincoln. Student, Columbia U., 1944-45; B.S. with honors in Journalism, U. Ill., 1947. Advt. mgr. Commonwealth Life Ins. Co., Louisville, 1947-48; advt. and promotion mgr. Insulation Mfrs. Corp., Chgo., 1948-54; editor, co-pub. Lake Pub. Co., Lake Forest, Ill., 1954-58; pres., pub. Lake Pub. Corp., Libertyville, Ill., 1958—; pub. dir. Electronic Mfg., Elec. Mfg., 1958—; pub. Microelectronic Mfg. and Testing, 1978—, Hybrid Circuit Tech., 1985—, Connection Tech., 1985—, Child Care Ctr., 1986—, Surface Mount Tech., 1987—; mem. conf. on elec. insulation NRC, 1956—; mem. exec. com. Elec.-Electronics Insulation Conf., 1958—, gen. chmn., 1973. Served with USNR, 1943-46. Mem. IEEE, Internat. Electronic Packaging Soc., Surface Mount Tech. Assn., Soc. Plastic Engrs., Small Motor Mfrs. Assn., Internat. Soc. Hybrid Microelectronics, ASTM, AAAS, Electrochem. Soc., Bus.-Profl. Advt. Assn., Internat. Coll. Winding Assn., Power Conversion Products Council Internat. Republican. Lutheran. Clubs: TF (Chgo.). Home: 920 Hawthorne Ln Libertyville IL 60048 Office: Lake Pub Corp 17730 W Peterson Rd Libertyville IL 60048

SAMET, CHARLES MERLE, physician; b. Mpls., May 27, 1928; s. Joseph and Rela (Greenberg) S.; B.A. magna cum laude, U. Minn., 1948, B.S., 1950, M.B., 1952, M.D., 1953; m. Rochelle Renee Rosenberg, June 19, 1955 (dec. June 1983); children—Rhonda Claire, Jeffrey Allen. Intern, Boston City Hosp., 1952-53, resident in internal medicine, 1953-54; resident in internal medicine Boston VA Hosp., 1956-57; fellow in infectious disease Tufts U.-New Eng. Center Hosp., Boston, 1957-59; practice medicine specializing in internal medicine and infectious diseases, Manhasset, N.Y., 1959—; former assoc. prof. clin. medicine SUNY-Stony Brook; clin. asst. prof. medicine Cornell U. Med. Sch., Ithaca, N.Y.; cons. medico-legal aspects of infectious disease; mem. med. advisory com. Vis. Nurse Assn. L.I. Served with M.C., USAF, 1954-56. Fellow ACP, Infectious Diseases Soc. Am.; mem. Am. Fedn. Clin. Research, N.Y. Acad. Sci., Alpha Omega Alpha. Jewish. Contbr. articles on infectious diseases to med. jours. Home: 22 Olive St Lake Success NY 11020 Office: 1201 Northern Blvd Manhasset NY 11030

SAMII, MASSOOD VAJED, economist, civil servant; b. Tehran, Iran, Aug. 17, 1945; came to Austria, 1979; s. Nasser and Gritty (Sheybani) Vajed-Samii; m. Farideh NemaziúShiraz, Nov. 17, 1978; children: Babak, Leila. BS, U. Hartford, 1968; MBA, Western New Eng. Coll., Springfield, Mass., 1970; PhD, SUNY, Albany, 1975. Sr. economist plan and budget orgn. Got. Iran, Tehran, 1975-76; acting head Internat. Econ. Bur., 1976-77; sr. economist OPEC, Vienna, 1979-83, head internat. money and fin. unit, 1983-84, head fin. sect., 1984—; adj. prof. planning Coll. Computer and Planning, Tehran, 1975-76; adj. prof. econs. Iran-Zamin Coll., Tehran, 1977-79; adj. prof. energy/econs. Webster U., Vienna, 1982-84. Contbr. articles to profl. jours. Mem. Assn. Energy Economists, Assn. Am. Econs. Home: 32/4 Gallmayergasse 18, 1190 Vienna Austria

SAMIIAN, BARAZANDEH, corporate executive; b. Tehran, May 13, 1939; came to U.S., 1958. B.A., Woodbury U., Los Angeles, 1961; B.A., Immaculate Heart Coll., Los Angeles, 1979; M.A., Webster U., Geneva, 1981. 1 child, Mina P. Cullimore. Cons., Design & Architecture, Tehran, 1965-72; bus. cons. multinat. corps., Calif., 1970-77; co-owner Samiian and Solomon Assocs., Geneva, 1978-86; owner, B. Samiian Assocs., Jacksonville, Fla., 1987—; dir., Internat. Cons. Found. Bd., 1987—; adj. prof. Webster U., Geneva, 1981—; cons. and lectr. human resources devel.; bd. dirs. Internat. Cons. Found., 1987. Named Woman of Yr., 1983; recipient Gov's. citation State of Md., 1983. Office: B Samiian Assocs PO Box 23825 Jacksonville FL 32241-3825

SAMMARCO, PAUL WILLIAM, marine ecologist; b. Hackensack, N.J., Oct. 18, 1948; s. Giacomo and Esther (Galanti) S.; m. Jean Sogioka, Aug. 8, 1971; children: Mimi Cecile, Dustin Paul, Jack Isao. BA, Syracuse U., 1970, postgrad., 1970-71; cert. Marine Biology Lab., Woods Hole, Mass., 1971, Fairleigh Dickinson U. W.I. Lab., U.S. V.I., 1972; Ph.D., SUNY-Stony Brook, 1977. Teaching asst. Syracuse U. (N.Y.), 1970-71, Discovery Bay Marine Lab., SUNY-Stony Brook Overseas Acad. Program, Jamaica, 1974, SUNY-Stony Brook, 1971-77; asst. prof., Clarkson Coll., Potsdam, N.Y., 1977-79; vis. asst. prof. tropical ecology, in St. Croix, V.I., SUNY-Potsdam, 1979; sr. research scientist Australian Inst. Marine Sci., Townsville, Queensland, 1979—, coordinator Shelf Seas Research Program 1985-86, dir. research seminar program, 1979-83; dir. inter-univ. seminar program Assn. Colls. St. Lawrence Valley, Potsdam, 1977-79. Composer ballads; contbr. numerous articles to profl. jours.; editorial advisor Marine Ecology Progress Series, 1985—; co-editor, mem. editorial bd. Proceedings Inaugural Great Barrier Conf., 1983; editorial bd. Proceedings 6th Internat. Coral Reef Symposium, 1988. NSF grantee, 1973-75, Internat. Sci. Exchange award, 1988-89; Mem. Australian Marine Scis. Assn. (keynote speaker 1981, counselor 1984—, chmn., organizer nat. conf. 1987), Ecol. Soc. Am., Internat. Soc. Reef Studies, Australian Coral Reef Soc., Am. Soc. Limnology and Oceanography, Assn. Island Marine Labs. Carribbean, Australian Soc. Phychological Botany, Internat. Soc. Tropical Ecology, Malacology Soc. London, Nat. Geographic Soc., Smithsonian Assn., Western Soc. Nat., Australasian Performing Rights Assn., Nashville Songwriters Assn., Sigma Xi. Democrat. Mem. Uniting Ch. of Australia. Home: 25 Deschamp St, Gulliver, Townsville 4812, Australia Office: Australian Inst Marine Sci, PMB 3, Townsville 4810, Australia

SAMMARTINO, SYLVIA, university co-founder; b. Boston, Dec. 5, 1903; d. Louis J. and Anna E. (Bianchi) Scaramelli; m. Peter Sammartino, Dec. 5, 1933. A.B., Smith Coll., 1925; M.A., Columbia U., 1926; LL.D. (hon.), Kyung Hee U., Korea, 1964; D.H.L. (hon.), Fairleigh Dickinson U., 1966. Tchr. public high sch. N.Y.C., 1927-28, 33-35; treas. Scaramelli & Co., Inc., N.Y.C., 1928-33; ednl. editor Atlantica, 1933-35; circulation mgr. La Voix de France, N.Y.C., 1935-37; registrar Fairleigh Dickinson U., Rutherford, N.J., 1942-50; dir. admissions Fairleigh Dickinson U., 1950-59, dean of admissions, 1959-67. Chmn. N.J. Commn. on Women, 1971; mem. bd. govs. N.Y. Cultural Center, 1968-73; mem. exec. com. Restore Ellis Island Commn., 1974-79; pres. Garden State Ballet Found., 1975-80; trustee Newark Symphony Hall, 1976-79, William Carlos Williams Center for Performing Arts, Rutherford, N.J., 1980—; trustee, chmn. Integrity, Inc., 1980—; trustee, sec.-treas. Williams Inst., 1981—. Decorated knight Order of Merit Italy; comdr. Order Star of Africa Liberia; officer Order Nat. Ivory Coast; recipient Amita award, 1960; Smith Coll. medal, 1967; President's medal Mercy Coll., 1980, Humanitarian award William Carlos Williams Ctr. for the Arts, 1988; named Woman of Yr., Rutherford C. of C. Home and Office: 140 Ridge Rd Rutherford NJ 07070

SAMMS-MOULTRY, EVA DOLORES, educator; b. Quitman, Ga., Mar. 25, 1937; d. Benjamin Franklin and Ruby Lee (Mitchell) Watts; m. Royce Moultry; children—Rory C. Thomas, Enrique S. Samms. B.A., Shaw U., Raleigh, N.C., 1976; M.S., Nova U., Ft. Lauderdale, 1978, Ed.S., 1982, postgrad., 1982—. Cert. vocat. and adult edn. tchr. Fla. Legal sec. Legal Services of Greater Miami, Fla., 1967-70, Storer Broadcasting Co., Balharbour, Fla., 1970-72; sec., bookkeeper Dade County Pub. Schs., Miami, 1973-76, bus. tchr., 1976-84, vocat. and adult edn. tchr., 1984—; curriculum writer Dade County Schs., 1982—, software evaluator, 1986; pres., cons. Triangle Mgmt., Miami, 1985—. Author: (curriculum) Professional Secretary, 1978. Precinct capt. Democratic Party, Miami, 1977-83, com. woman, 1984—; dep. registrar Voter Registration, Miami, 1980—; pres. Minority Women, Miami, 1982, 84. Recipient Outstanding Service Plaque, Miami Lakes Jr. High Sch., 1981, Service award United Tchrs. of Dade County, 1984, 85; Letter of Commendation, Area Supt., North Miami, 1984. Mem. Vocat. Bus. Edn. Assn., Assn. Supervision and Curriculum Devel., Booker T. Washington Alumni (Miami, pres. 1984-85), Phi Delta Kappa, Beta Tau Zeta. Democrat. Am. Baptist. Club: Scruples (Miami). Avocations: gardening; sports; dancing; people. Office: Lindsey Hopkins Vocat & Tech Ctr 750 NW 20th St Miami FL 33127

SAMOZVANTSEV, ANDREI MICHAILOVICH, Sanskritologist; b. Moscow, Nov. 20, 1949; s. Michail Pavlovich and Tamara Sergeevna (Surova) S.; m. Natalia Vladimirovna Alexandrova, 1982; 1 child, Gleb Andreevich. PhD, Moscow State U., 1975. Jr. research scholar Inst. Oriental Studies of USSR Acad. Scis., Moscow, 1975-84, sr. research scholar, sanskritologist, 1984—. Author: Theory of Property in Ancient India, 1978, Society State and Law in Ancient India, 1985; contbr. articles to profl. jours. Mem. Assn. of Oriental Studies of USSR, Internat. Assn. Sanskrit Studies. Home: Nemansky Proezd, 12381 Moscow USSR Office: Acad Sci USSR, Inst Oriental Studies, Zhdanova St 12, 103777 Moscow USSR

SAMPEDRO, JOSÉ LUIS, novelist, economist; b. Barcelona, Spain, Feb. 1, 1917; s. Luis and Matilde (Saez) S.; m. Isabel Pellicer, July 10, 1944; 1 child, Isabel. D.Econ.Scis., Universidad Complutense, Madrid. Asst. lectr. faculty econs. U. Madrid, 1949-55, prof. econs., 1955-72; adviser Spanish Ministry Commerce, 1951-57, Ministry Fin., 1957-62; econ. adviser Banco Exterior de España, 1948-68, 77-82; v.p. Fundacion Banco Exterior, Madrid, 1982-84; rep. to OECD, Paris, 1958-62; mem. Spanish mission to UN, 1956; mem. III UNCTAD, Santiago de Chile, 1972, FMI/Banco Mundial de Tokyo, 1964. Author: (novels) Congreso en Estocolmo, 1952; El Rio que nos Lleva, 1961; Octubre, Octubre, 1981; La Sonrisa Etrusca, 1985; (play) La Paloma de Carton (Nat. prize Calderon de la Barca 1950), 1950; also other plays and fiction, several works on econs. Mem. Spanish Senate, 1977-78. Mem. Colegio de Economistas, Asociacion Española de Ciencia Regional, Sociedad de Autores de España. *

SAMPLE, STEVEN BROWNING, university administrator; b. St. Louis, Nov. 29, 1940; s. Howard and Dorothy (Cunningham) S.; m. Kathryn Brunkow, Jan. 28, 1961; children: Michelle Louise, Melissa. B.S.E.E., U. Ill., 1962, M.S., 1963, Ph.D., 1965. Sr. scientist Melpar, Inc., Falls Church, Va., 1965-66; assoc. prof. elec. engring. Purdue U., 1966-71; dep. dir. Ill. Bd. Higher Edn., Chgo., 1971-74; exec. v.p. acad. affairs U. Nebr., 1974-82; pres. SUNY-Buffalo, 1982—; bd. dirs. D&M Corp., Connersville, Ind., Moog Inc., Buffalo, Dunlop Tire Corp.; chmn. We. N.Y. Regional Econ. Devel. Council, 1984—; NASULGC, 1986-87; cons. in field. Contbr. articles to profl. jours.; patentee in field. Mem. Nebr. Ednl. TV Commn., 1974-82; bd. mgrs. Buffalo and Erie County Hist. Soc., 1982—; bd. dirs. Buffalo Philharm. Orch., 1982—, U. at Buffalo Found., 1982—, United Way of Buffalo and Erie County, 1985—, research found. SUNY, 1987—; chmn. bd. dirs. Calspan-UB Research Ctr., Inc., Buffalo, 1983—; chmn. council of pres.'s Nat. Assn. of State Univs. and Land-Grant Colls., 1985-86, mem. ednl. and tech. com., 1986-87, mem. exec. com., 1987—. Recipient Disting. Alumnus award Dept. Elec. Engring. U. Ill., 1980; Engr. of Yr., Citation award Buffalo Council on World Affairs, 1984—, N.Y. State Soc. Profl. Engrs., 1985; Alumni Honor award Coll. Engring., U. Ill., 1985; Sloan Found. fellow, 1962-63; NSF fellow, 1963-65; NSF grantee, 1968-73. Mem. Nat. Assn. State Univs. and Land-Grant Colls. (ednl. telecommunications com., chmn. council of pres. 1985-86, edn. and tech. com. 1986—, exec. com. 1987—), Council on Fgn. Relations, IEEE, Greater Buffalo C. of C. (bd. dirs. 1985—), Sigma Xi. Episcopalian. Clubs: Buffalo; University (N.Y.C.). Home: 889 LeBrun Rd Amherst NY 14226 Office: SUNY Capen Hall Buffalo NY 14260 *

SAMPSON, ANTHONY TERRELL SEWARD, author; b. Billingham, Durham, Eng., Aug. 3, 1926; s. Michael Treviskey and Phyllis Marion (Seward) S.; m. Sally Virginia Sampson, May 31, 1965; children—Katharine, Paul. Degree in English, Oxford U., 1947-50. Editor Drum Mag., Johannesburg, South Africa, 1951-55; mem. editorial staff Observer newspaper, London, 1955-74; editorial adviser Brandt Commn., 1979-83; assoc. prof. U. Vincennes, Paris, 1969-81. Author: Drum: A Venture into the New Africa, 1955; The Treason Cage, 1958; Commonsense About Africa, 1960; Anatomy of Britain, 1962; Anatomy of Britain Today, 1965; Macmillan: A Study in Ambiguity, 1967; The New Europeans, 1968; The New Anatomy of Britain, 1971; The Sovereign State of ITT, 1973; The Seven Sisters, 1975; The Arms Bazaar, 1977; The Money Lenders, 1981; The Changing Anatomy of Britain, 1982; Empires of the Sky, 1984; (with Sally Sampson) The Oxford Book of Ages, 1985; editor The Sampson Letter, 1984-86, Black and Gold, 1987. Clubs: Beefsteak (London), Groucho.

SAMPSON, STEVEN LEWIS, social anthropologist; b. Phila., Sept. 7, 1948; s. Horace N. and Dorothy (Madway) S.; m. Vibeke Petersen; children: Anna, Andreas. BA, Antioch Coll., Yellow Springs, Ohio, 1971; MA, U. Mass., 1974, PhD, 1980. Fulbright scholar U.S. Dept. Edn., Romania, 1975-76; research fellow Ford Found. U. Mass., 1976-77; instr. U. Copenhagen, 1978-80; research fellow Social Sci. Research Council, Denmark, 1980-82; instr. U. Copenhagen, 1982-83; research fellow Inst. Ethnology and Anthropology U. Copenhagen, 1983-86, Social Sci. Research Council, Copenhagen, 1987—; translator Danish-English, Copenhagen. Author: The Planners and the Peasants: An Anthropological Study of Urban Development in Romania, 1982, National Integration through Socialist Planning: An Anthropological study of a Romanian New Town, 1984; author, editor: (with others) Uden Regning (Danish Underground Economy), 1986; contbr.

articles to profl. jours. Mem. Am. Anthrop. Assn., Am. Assn. Slavic and East European Studies, Romanian Studies Assn., British Nat. Assn. Soviet and East European Studies, Danish Ethnographica 1 Soc., Anthrop. Assn. of Denmark. Home: 2720 Vanlose, Hasselvej 26 Denmark

SAMPSON, WILLIAM ROBERT, JR., communication and theater arts educator, administrator; b. Detroit, Apr. 23, 1942; s. William Robert and Alice Juanita (Jones) S.; m. Sharon Kay Miner, Feb. 27, 1970 (div. Jan. 1982); children: William Robert, Michael Stanton; m. Karin Lee Menzel, Jan. 31, 1983; 1 child, Andrew Peter. BA, Western Mich. U., 1964; MA, Wayne State U., 1967, PhD, 1973. Tchr. Utica (Mich.) Community Schs., 1964-66; instr. Macomb County Community Coll., Mich., 1966-68; asst. prof. Ferris State Coll., Big Rapids, Mich., 1968-72, assoc. prof., 1972-76; assoc. prof. Ea. Mich. U., Ypsilanti, 1976-80; dir. grad. bus. programs, 1978-80, assoc. dean Coll. Bus., 1979-80; chmn., prof. dept. communication and theater arts U. Wis., Eau Claire, 1980—; organizational communication tng. and devel. cons. Editor Wis. Communication Assn. Jour. Bd. dirs. Chippewa Valley Theatre Guild. Recipient Ferris State Coll. Bd. Control, 1972. Mem. Acad. Mgmt., Am. Soc. Tng. and Devel., Internat. Communication Assn., Speech Communication Assn. Congregationalist. Home: 6650 S Shore Dr Altoona WI 54720 Office: U Wis Dept Communication and Theatre Arts Eau Claire WI 54701

SAMS, ERIC SYDNEY, musicologist; b. London, May 3, 1926; s. Henry Sydney and Violet Lois (Hill) S.; m. Enid Mary Tidmarsh, June 30, 1952; children: Richard, Jeremy. BA, Cambridge U., 1950, PhD, 1973. Prin. officer Dept. Employment, 1950-78. Author: The Songs of Hugo Wolf, 1961, 2nd edit., 1983, The Songs of Robert Schumann, 1969, 2nd edit., 1975, Brahms Songs, 1971, Shakespeare's Lost Play: Edmund Ironside, 1985, 2d edit., 1986; contbr. articles to profl. jours. Served with Intelligence Corps, Brit. Army, 1944-47. Home and Office: 32 Arundel Ave, Sanderstead Surrey CR2 8BB, England

SAMTER, MAX, physician, educator; b. Berlin, Germany, Mar. 3, 1908; came to U.S., 1937; s. Paul and Claire (Rawicz) S.; m. Virginia Svarz Ackerman, Oct. 17, 1947; 1 dau., Virginia Claire. Student, U. Freiburg, Germany, 1926, U. Innsbruck, Austria, 1928; M.D., U. Berlin, 1933. Diplomate: Am. Bd. Internal Medicine (past chmn. bd. allergy), Am. Bd. Allergy and Immunology. Intern, resident Medizinische Universitätsklinik der Charité, Berlin, 1931-33; practice medicine Berlin-Karow, Germany, 1933-37; asst. dispensary physician hematology Johns Hopkins Hosp., 1937-38; guest fellow anatomy U. Pa. Sch. Medicine, 1938-43; research asso. dept. biochemistry U. Ill., Chgo., 1946-47; instr. asst. prof., asso. prof., prof. dept. medicine, 1948-69; prof. medicine Abraham Lincoln Sch. Medicine, 1969—, asso. dean for clin. affairs, 1974-75; chief staff U. Ill. Hosp., 1974-75; sr. cons. Max Samter Inst. Allergy and Clin. Immunology, Chgo., 1975—; cons. in allergy U.S. VA, 1962—. Editor: American Lectures in Allergy, 1950, (with Oren C. Durham) Regional Allergy, 1954, (with Harry L. Alexander) Immunological Diseases, 1965, 71, 78, 88, Excerpts from Classics in Allergy, 1969, (with Charles W. Parker) Hypersensitivity to Drugs, 1972; also articles in field. Served to capt. M.C. AUS, 1943-46, ETO. Recipient Disting. Faculty award U. Ill. Coll. Med. 1987. Fellow ACP; mem. AMA, Am. Acad. Allergy (past pres.), Internat. Assn. Allergology (past pres.), Phila. Coll. Physicians (hon.), Interasma (hon.), Sigma Xi, Alpha Omega Alpha. Home: 645 Sheridan Rd Evanston IL 60202 Office: 550 W Webster Ave Chicago IL 60614

SAMUDIO MOLINA, RAFAEL, military officer; b. Bucaramanga, Santander, Colombia, Jan. 3, 1932; s. Arturo and Jacinta (Molina) S.; m. Margarita Lizcano, Apr. 18, 1959; children: Sandra, Adriana, Mauricio, Monica, Paola Andrea. Abogado, U. Gran Colombia, 1963. Advanced through ranks to gen. Infanteróa, Columbia; comandante Quinta Brigada del Ejército, Bucaramanga, Columbia, 1978-80; dir. Escuela Militar de Cadetes, Bogotá, Columbia, 1980-81; sugjefe estado mayor conjunto Comando Gen. Fuerzas Militares, Bogotá, 1981-82; procurador delagado Fuerzas Militares, Bogotá, 1982-83, inspector gen., 1983-84; jefe estado mayor Comando del Ejército, Bogotá, 1984-85; comandante Ejército Nacional, Bogotá, 1985-86; ministro de defensa Gobierno Nacional, Bogotá, 1986; prof. militar invitado Fort Gulich Panamá, 1970-71; adjunto militar Emgajada de Colombia, Washington, 1975-76. Recipient Orden de Boyacá, José María Córdova from Gran Cruz, Antonio Narino Comendador y Gran Cruz, Legion of Merit U.S.A., 1985, 87. Home: Calle 89 No 9-61, Bogotá DE Colombia Office: Ministerio de Defensa Nacional, Avenida Eldorado - CAN, Bogotá Colombia

SAMUEL, ARYEH HERMANN ALBERT, research scientist; b. Hildesheim, Germany, Feb. 19, 1924; came to U.S., 1941, naturalized, 1957; s. Rudolf and Erna (Ballheimer) S.; m. Betty Roth, Mar. 28, 1954 (dec. 1983); 1 son, Joshua Reuven. BS, U. Ill., 1943; MS, Northwestern U., 1946; PhD, U. Notre Dame, 1953. Research scientist Broadview Research, Burlingame, Calif., 1956-60, Stanford Research Inst., Menlo Park, Calif., 1960-65, 67-72; research mgr. Gen Precision Research Lab., Little Falls, N.J., 1965-67; ops. analyst Vector Research, Inc., Ann Arbor, Mich., 1974-77; prin. research scientist Battelle Meml. Inst., Washington, 1977-87, ret., 1987. Served with Israeli Army, 1948-49. Mem. Ops. Research Soc. Am. (Lanchester prize 1962). Research on analysis of pub. sector systems (especially mil., postal); radiation chemistry, mass spectrometry. Home: 10861 Bucknell Dr Wheaton MD 20902

SAMUEL, LAWRENCE, hotel executive; b. Castries, St. Lucia, West Indies, Nov. 19, 1955; s. James and Josephine (Isidore) S.; children: Elizabeth, Afka, Diane, Samuel. Student, parochial schs., Ft. St. Lucia, 1972-75. Office clk. Halcyon Days Hotel, St. Lucia, 1972-75, asst. acct., 1975-77, office mgr., 1977-79, chief acct., 1979-80; fin. controller/asst. mgr. Halcyon Beach Club, Castries, 1980-82; group controller Carribean Hotel Mgmt. Services, Castries, 1982-83; resident mgr. St. Lucian Hotel, Castries, 1983-87, gen. mgr., 1987—, also bd. dirs.; spl. adviser Aqua Action Com., Castries, 1982—. Mem. St. Lucia Hotel Assn. (1st v.p. 1985-87). Home and Office: PO Box 512, Castries, Saint Lucia West Indies

SAMUEL, PAUL, physician; b. Janoshaza, Hungary, Feb. 17, 1927; came to U.S., 1954, naturalized, 1960; s. Adolf and Magda (Zollner) S.; m. Gabriella R. Zeichner, Mar. 27, 1954; children—Robert Mark, Adrianne Jill. Baccalaureat, Kemeny Zsigmond Gymnasium, Budapest, 1945; M.D., U. Paris, 1953. Intern Queens Hosp. Ctr., N.Y.C., 1954-55; resident L.I. Jewish Med. Ctr., New Hyde Park, N.Y., 1959-61; adj. prof. Rockefeller U., N.Y.C., 1971-81; adj. prof. medicine Cornell U., N.Y.C., 1979—; clin. prof. medicine Albert Einstein Coll. Medicine, Bronx, 1981—; dir. Arteriosclerosis Research Lab., L.I. Jewish-Hillside Med. Ctr., New Hyde Park, 1962—; chmn. N.Y. Lipid Research Club, Rockefeller U., 1977-78. Contbr. articles to profl. jours. Pres. Am. Heart Assn., Nassau County, 1980. Fellow Am. Coll. Cardiology; mem. Am. Heart Assn. (fellow council on arteriosclerosis, Disting. Achievement award 1975), Am. Fedn. Clin. Research, Harvey Soc., ACP. Home: 25 Nassau Dr Great Neck NY 11021 Office: Albert Einstein Coll Medicine 1300 Morris Park Ave Bronx NY 10461

SAMUEL, PIERRE, mathematics educator; b. Paris, Sept. 12, 1921; s. Raymond and Jacqueline (Dalmeyda) S.; m. Nicole Herrmann, July 23, 1948; children: Laurent, Fabien. Lic. in Scis., U. Grenoble, France, 1942; MA, PhD, Princeton U., 1947; D in Scis., U. Paris, 1949. Agrégation Ecole Normale Supérieure. Prof. U. Clermont-Ferrand, France, 1949-61, U. Paris, 1961-69, U. Paris-Sud, Orsay, 1969—; vis. prof. numerous internat. univs. Author 11 math. books; contbr. over 90 article on math. to profl. jours. Chmn. Les Amis de la Terre, Paris, 1979—. Mem. Soc. Math. France, Am. Math. Soc., Ligue des Droits de l'Homme, Found. Cousteau, Assn. pour le Droit de Mourir dans la Dignité. Home: 3 av du Lycee Lakanal, F-92340 Bourg-la-Reine France

SAMUEL, ROBERT THOMPSON, optometrist; b. Kansas City, Mo., June 27, 1944; s. Manlius Thompson and Helen Evelyn (Syverson) S. B.A., William Jewell Coll., 1966; postgrad. U. Mo.-Kansas City, 1967, M.S. U. Mo., 1968; D. Optometry, U. Tenn.-Memphis, 1971. Cert. optometrist, Mo. Buyer Recco, Inc., Kansas City, Mo., 1963-67; histology lab. instr. William Jewell Coll., Liberty, Mo., 1965-66; pvt. practice optometry Gladstone, Mo., 1972—; panel doctor Ford Motor Co., Claycomo, Mo., 1985—, Union Pacific R.R., Kansas City, 1985—. Publicity coordinator Republican Party, Kansas City, Mo., 1975-76; chmn. Save Your Vision Week, Kansas City, 1977; mem. Theatre League of Kansas City, 1976—, Friends of Art, 1985. Recipient Outstanding Young Men of Am. award Jaycees, 1978. Mem. Am. Optometric Assn., Mo. Optometric Assn., Heart of Am. Contact Lens Congress, Am. Acad. Sports Vision, Smithsonian Assocs. Republican. Lutheran. Lodge: Lions (exec. bd. dirs. Lions Eye Clinic 1974-84, bd. dirs. Lions Eye Clinic 1982—, Outstanding Service award 1973, 74, editor Lions Optometric Ctr. Quar., 1974-84). Avocations: photography, music, piano, swimming. Home: 6325 N Monroe St Gladstone MO 64119 Office: 2700 Kendallwood Pkwy Suite 109 Gladstone MO 64119

SAMUELS, IVOR, advertising executive; b. London, May 11, 1936. MA, U. Cambridge, Eng., 1959; BA, Open U., Milton Keynes, Eng., 1982. Asst. mng. dir. Benton & Bowles Ltd., London, 1959-74; mng. dir. Samuels Jones Isaacson Page Ltd., London, 1974-80; chmn., chief exec. officer BBDO Ltd., London, 1981-85; chmn. Watson Ward Albert Varndell Ltd., London, 1981-88. Served Brit. Army, 1954-56. Fellow Inst. Practioners in Advt. (council mem. 1971—). Mem. Social Democratic Party. Jewish. Office: WWAV Ltd, 31 Saint Petersburgh Pl, London W2 4LA, England

SAMUELS, JANET LEE, lawyer; b. Pitts., July 18, 1953; d. Emerson and Jeanne (Kalish) S.; m. David Arthur Kalow, June 18, 1978; children—Margaret Emily Samuels-Kalow, Jacob Richard Samuels-Kalow. B.A. with honors, Beloit Coll., 1974; J.D., NYU, 1977. Bar: N.Y. 1978, D.C. 1980. Staff atty. SCM Corp., N.Y.C., 1977-80, corp. atty., 1980-83, sr. corp. atty., 1983-85, assoc. gen. counsel Allied Paper div., 1983-86, Holtzmann, Wise & Shepard, 1986—. Adviser student adviser program NYU Law Sch., 1982—. Mem. ABA, Assn. Bar City N.Y., Assn. Trial Lawyers Am., N.Y. State Bar Assn., Mortar Board, Phi Beta Kappa. Office: Holtzmann Wise & Shepard 745 Fifth Ave New York NY 10151

SAMUELS, RICHARD MEL, clinical psychologist, communications executive; b. Bklyn., Mar. 22, 1943; s. Murray and Rose S.; Assoc. Applied Sci., SUNY, 1961; B.A., Hofstra U., 1965, M.A., 1967; Ph.D., City U. N.Y., 1973; post-doctoral diploma Human Sexuality dept. Ob/Gyn N.J. Med. Sch. m. Linda Nersesian, Dec. 2, 1984; children: Lisa, David; stepchildren: Michelle, Michael. Adj. assoc. prof. City U. N.Y., 1970-73; sr. clin. psychologist N.J. Med. Sch., Newark, 1973-74, sr. clin. prof. human sexuality program, dept. ob-gyn also adj. asst. prof. dept. psychiatry, 1974-76, dir. gender dysphoria clinic, 1974-76; clin. psychologist, creator 2d self discovery program ; dir. Human Insights Assocs.; pres., chief exec. officer Ambivision Oradell, producer video programming; chmn., exec. v.p. Travelvues, Oradell and Cin.; mem. clin. faculty Sch., Applied and Profl. Psychology, Rutgers U. Grad. Sch.; cons. Teaneck Group Home for Girls. Recipient Albert J. Harris award City U. N.Y., 1967; N.J. Med. Sch. fellow, 1973-74; diplomate Am. Bd. Clin. Psychology. Fellow Behavior Therapy and Research Soc., Eastern Assn. Sex Therapists (charter), Am. Psychol. Assn. (past pres. div. ind. practice of psychology, chmn. com. on expanded psychol. practice); mem. AAAS, Assn. Advancement of Behavior Therapy, N.J. Psychol. Assn., N.J. Assn. for Advancement Psychology (pres.), N.J. Acad. Psychology. Author: Sex During Pregnancy and the Postpartum Period, 1976, A Gender Dysphoria Clinic in New Jersey, 1977, Computers, An Extension of the Psychologists Mind; cons. editor Behavior Therapy, 1973-80 ; editor Pvt. Practitioner, 1976-82; software rev. editor Jour. Psychotherapy and Pvt. Practice. Office: Ambivision 1 Kinderkamack Rd Oradell NJ 07649

SAMUELSON, KENNETH LEE, lawyer; b. Natrona Heights, Pa., Aug. 22, 1946; s. Sam Abraham and Frances Bernice (Robbins) S.; m. Marlene Ina Rabinowitz, Jan. 1, 1980; children: Heather, Cheryl. BA magna cum laude, U. Pitts., 1968; JD, U. Mich., 1971. Bar: Md. 1972, D.C. 1980, U.S. Dist. Ct. Md. Trial Bar 1984. Assoc. Weinberg & Green, Balt., 1971-73; assoc. Dickerson, Nice, Sokol & Horn, Balt., 1973; asst. atty. gen. State of Md., 1973-77; sole practice, Balt., 1978; ptnr. Linowes and Blocher, Potomac, Md. and Washington, 1979—. Author in field. Bd. dirs. D.C. Assn. for Retarded Citizens, Inc., 1981—. Served to capt. U.S. Army, to 1976. Mem. ABA (chmn. subcom. of the comml. leasing com., sect. real property, probate and trust law 1985—, moderator program 1987), D.C. Bar (comml. real estate com.), Md. State Bar Assn. (real property, planning and zoning sect., chmn. environ. subcom., 1987—, litigation sect. 1982-84, chmn. comml. trans. com., speaker Md. Inst. Continuing Profl. Edn. Lawyers, 1988; moderator of program before ABA on comml. leases, 1987, Internat. Council Shopping Ctrs. U., 1988; speaker before D.C. Bar program on lawyer's opinion letters in real estate transactions, 1987), Montgomery County Bar Assn. (judicial selections com. 1988—), Phi Beta Kappa. Address: 12613 Exchange Ct N Potomac MD 20854

SAMUELSON, PAUL ANTHONY, economics educator; b. Gary, Ind., May 15, 1915; s. Frank and Ella (Lipton) S.; m. Marion Crawford, July 2, 1938 (dec.); children: Jane Kendall, Margaret Wray, William Frank, Robert James, John Crawford, Paul Reid.; m. Risha Eckaus, 1981. B.S., U. Chgo., 1935; M.A., Harvard U., 1936, Ph.D. (David A. Wells prize 1941), 1941; hon. degrees:; LL.D., U. Chgo., Oberlin Coll., 1961, Boston Coll., 1964, Ind. U., 1966, U. Mich., 1967, Claremont Grad. Sch., 1970, U. N.H., 1971, Keio U., 1971, Widener Coll., 1982, Cath. U. at Riva Aguero U., Lima, Peru, 1980; D.Sc., East Anglia U., Norwich, Eng., 1966; D.Litt. (hon.), Ripon Coll., 1962, No. Mich. U., 1973; L.H.D., Seton Hall Coll., 1971, Williams Coll., 1971; D.Sc., U. Mass., 1972, U. R.I., 1972; LL.D., Harvard, 1972, Gustavus Adolphus Coll., 1974, U. So. Calif., 1975, U. Pa., 1976, U. Rochester, 1976, Emmanuel Coll., 1977, Stonehill Coll., 1978, Widener Coll., 1982; Doctorate Honoris Causa, U. Catholique de Louvain, Belgium, 1976, City U., London, 1980, New U. Lisbon, 1985; DLitt., Valparaiso U., 1987; DLitt, Columbia U, 1988; DSc, Tufts U., 1988. Prof. econs. Mass. Inst. Tech., 1940—, inst. prof., 1966; mem. staff Radiation Lab., 1944-45; prof. internat. econ. relations Fletcher Sch. Law and Diplomacy, part-time, 1945; cons. Nat. Resources Planning Bd., 1941-43, WPB, 1945, U.S. Treasury, 1945-52, 61—, Bur. Budget, 1952, RAND Corp., 1948-75, Fed. Res. Bd., 1965—; council Econ. Advisers, 1960—; econ. adviser to Pres. Kennedy; sr. adviser Brookings Panel on Econ. Activity; mem. spl. commn. on social scis. NSF, 1967—; cons. int Econ. Council, Congl. Budget Office; Inst. prof., Inst. prof. emeritus, Gordon Y Billard Fellow MIT, Boston, 1986—; vis. prof of polit. econ. Ctr. Japan-U.S. Bus. and Econ. Studies, NYU, 1987—; Stamp Meml. lectr., London, 1961, Wicksell lectr., Stockholm, 1962, Franklin lectr., Detroit, 1962; Hoyt vis. fellow Calhoun Coll., Yale, 1962; Carnegie Found. reflective year, 1965-66; John von Neumann lectr. U. Wis., 1971; Gerhard Colm Meml. lectr. New Sch. for Social Research, N.Y.C., 1971; Davidson lectr. U. N.H., 1971; Sulzbacher Meml. lectr. Columbia Law Sch., N.Y.C., 1974; J. Willard Gibbs lectr. Am. Math. Soc., San Francisco, 1974; John Diebold lectr. Harvard, 1976; Horowitz lectr. Jerusalem and Tel Aviv, 1984; lectr. Harvard 350 Symposium, Harvard U., 1986, many other lectureships; acad. cons. Fed. Reserve Bd. Author: Foundations of Economic Analysis, 1947, enlarged edit., 1983, Economics, 1948-85, Readings in Economics, 1955, (with R. Dorfman and R.M. Solow) Linear Programming and Economic Analysis, 1958, Collected Scientific Papers, 5 vols., 1966, 72, 78, 86; co-author numerous other books.; Contbr. numerous articles to profl. jours.; Columnist for, Newsweek, 1966-81; assoc. editor: J. Pub. Econs., J. Internat. Econs., J. Fin. Econs., J. Nonlinear Analysis; adv. bd. Challenge Mag.; editorial bd. Proceedings Nat. Acad. Scis. Chmn. Pres.'s Task Force Maintaining Am. Prosperity, 1964; mem. Nat. Task Force on Econ. Edn., 1960-61; econ. adviser to Pres. John F. Kennedy, 1959-63; mem. adv. bd. Nat. Commn. Money and Credit, 1958-60. Hon. fellow London Sch. Econs. and Polit. Sci. Guggenheim fellow, 1948-49; Ford Found. research fellow, 1958-59; Recipient John Bates Clark medal Am. Econ. Assn., 1947; Alfred Nobel Meml. prize in econ. sci., 1970; Medal of Honor U. Evansville, Ill., 1970; Albert Einstein Commemorative award, 1971; Distinguished Service award Investment Edn. Inst., Nat. Assn. Investment Clubs, 1974; Alumni medal U. Chgo., 1983. Fellow Brit. Acad. (corr.), Am. Philos. Soc., Econometric Soc. (v.p. 1950, pres. 1951), Am. Econ. Assn. (hon.; pres. 1961); mem. Com. Econ. Devel. (commn. on nat. goals, research adv. bd. 1959-60), Am. Acad. Arts and Scis., Internat. Econ. Assn. (pres. 1966-68, hon. pres.), Nat. Acad. Scis., Leibniz-Akademie der Wissenschaften und der Literatur (corr. mem. 1987—), Phi Beta Kappa, Omicron Delta Kappa (trustee). Home: 75 Clairemont Rd Belmont MA 02178 Office: MIT Dept of Economics Cambridge MA 02139

SAMUELSSON, BENGT INGEMAR, medical chemist; b. Halmstad, Sweden, May 21, 1934; s. Anders and Stina (Nilsson) S.; m. Inga Karin Bergstein, Aug. 19, 1958; children: Bo, Elisabet, Astrid. DMS, Karolinska Inst., Stockholm, 1960, MD, 1961; DSc (hon.), U. Chgo, 1978., U. Ill., 1983. Asst. prof. Karolinska Inst., 1961-66, prof. med. and physiol. chemistry, 1972—, chmn. physiol. chemistry dept., 1973-83, dean Med. Faculty, 1978-83, pres., 1983—; research fellow Harvard U., 1961-62; prof. med. chemistry Royal Vet. Coll., Stockholm, 1967-72; Harvey lectr., N.Y.C., 1979; mem. Nobel Com. Physiology and Medicine, 1984-86, chmn. com., 1987—; mem. research adv. bd. Swedish Govt., 1985—; mem. Nat. Commn. Health Policy, 1987—. Contbr articles to profl. jours. Recipient A. Jahres award Oslo U., 1970, Louisa Gross Horwitz award Columbia U., 1975, Albert Lasker basic med. research award, 1977, Ciba-Geigy Drew award in biomed. research, 1980, Lewis S. Rosentiel award in basic med. research Brandeis U., 1981, Gairdner Found. award, 1981, Heinrich Wieland prize, 1981, Nobel prize in physiology of medicine, 1982, award medicinal chemistry div. Am. Chem. Soc., 1982, Waterford Bio-Med. Sci. award, 1982, Internat. Assn. Allergology and Clin. Immunology award, 1982, Abraham White sci. achievement award, 1984. Mem. Royal Swedish Acad. Scis., Mediterranean Acad.; hon. mem. Assn. Am. Physicians, AAAS, Swedish Med. Assn., Am. Soc. Biol. Chemists, Italian Pharm. Soc., Acad. Nat. Medicina de Buenos Aires, Internat. Soc. Hematology, Fgn. Assn. U.S. Nat. Acad. Scis. Office: Karolinska Inst, Solnavagen 1, S-10401 Stockholm Sweden

SAMUELSSON, GUSTAV BENNY ROGER, chemical executive; b. Uddevalla, Sweden, May 18, 1942; s. G.P. Wenzel and Greta J. (Johansson) S.; m. Anne-Marie Kruckenberg, Jan. 2, 1965; 1 child, Johanna. BS, U. Göteborg, Sweden, 1965, lic., 1970, PhD, 1970. Group leader Hässle AB div. Astra Cardiovascular, Mölndal, Sweden, 1971-77, asst. dept. mgr., 1977-79; dir. research Gambro AB, Lund, Sweden, 1979-81, v.p. research and devel., 1981-86; pres., chief exec. officer Excorim KB, Lund, 1985—. Contbr. articles to profl. jours.; patentee in field. Served as sgt. with Swedish Army, 1961-62. Mem. Swedish Assn. Chemists, Internat. Soc. Artificial Organs, European Dialysis and Transplant Assn., Swedish-German Research Assn., Swedish Assn. Pharmacists. Home: Getgatan 58, 21616 Malmo Sweden Office: Excorim KB, Box 10101, 22010 Lund Sweden

SAMYN, PHILIPPE EUGÉNE, architect, civil engineer; b. Gent, Vlaanderen, Belgium, Sept. 1, 1948; s. Edouard and Isaline (Delmotte) S.; m. Beatrice Ralet, July 27, 1972; children: Virginie, Amandine, Fabrice. Degree in civil engring., U. Libre Bruxelles, Brussels, 1971, degree, 1973; MS in Civil Engring., MIT, 1973; degree in architecture, Inst. Supérieur Architecture L'Etat La Cambre, Brussels, 1985. Registered architect, Belgium, France; profl. engr. Assoc. architect A.J. De Doncker Assoc., Brussels, 1972-74; structural engr. Verdeyen Moenaert, Brussels, 1972-74; ptnr. A.J. De Doncker and Samyn, Brussels, 1975-77; prin. ptnr. Samyn and Ptnrs. Architects and Engrs., Brussels, 1977—; ptnr. Setesco S.A., Civil Engrs., Brussels, 1986—. Home: Ave Victor Emmanuel III, 54, 1180 Uccle, Brussels Belgium Office: Ave H Boulenger 25, 1180 Uccle, Brussels Belgium

SAMZ, JANE DEDE, editor, writer; b. Closter, N.J., Jan. 2; d. Benjamin and Ruth (Burstein) S. A.B. in Math., Smith Coll., 1969; postgrad., U. Ky., 1969-70; M.A. in History of Sci., U. Wis.-Madison, 1971. Teaching asst. physics dept. U. Ky., Lexington, 1969-70; editorial asst. Sci. World mag., Scholastic Mags., Inc., N.Y.C., 1972-73, asst. editor, 1973-76, assoc. editor, 1976-79, editor, 1979-87, sr. editor, sci. cons., 1987-88; lectr. communications dept. Stanford U., Calif., 1979; freelance writer Grolier Ency. Yearbook, 1977-79, Funk & Wagnalls Ency. Yearbook, 1981-83, Prentice-Hall, Inc.; also freelance cons. Author: Drugs & Diet, 1988; creator, author: Matter - Science World Visuals 9, 1975; co-author: Voyage to Jupiter, 1980; freelance writer, editor: Curriculum Concepts, Inc., N.Y.C., 1987; contbr. articles to Sci. World, World Book Science Year, 1988, World Book Health and Medical Annual, 1988, Futures, Creative Classroom, World Book Science Year Annual, 1988. Camille and Henry Dreyfus Found. sci. writer's fellow Stanford U., 1978-79. Mem. AAAS, Am. Mus. Natural History, N.Y. Acad. Scis., N.Y. Newspaper Guild. Clubs: Smith-Princeton Chamber Singers; The Planetary Soc. Home: 55-612 River Dr S Jersey City NJ 07310

SAN, NGUYEN DUY, psychiatrist; b. Langson, Vietnam, Sept. 25, 1932; s. Nguyen Duy and Tran Tuyet (Trang) Quyen; came to Can., 1971, naturalized, 1977; M.D., U. Saigon, 1960; postgrad. U. Mich., 1970; m. Eddie Jean Ciesielski, Aug. 24, 1971; children—Megan Thuloan, Muriel Mylinh, Claire Kimlan, Robin Xuanlan, Baodan Edward. Intern, Cho Ray Hosp., Saigon, 1957-58; resident Univ. Hosp., Ann Arbor, Mich., 1968-70, Lafayette Clinic, Detroit, 1970-71, Clarke Inst. Psychiatry, Toronto, Ont., Can., 1971-72; chief of psychiatry South Vietnamese Army, 1964-68; sr. psychiatrist Queen St. Mental Health Center, Toronto, 1972-74; unit dir. Homewood San., Guelph, Ont., 1974-80; cons. psychiatrist Guelph Gen. Hosp., St. Joseph's Hosp., Guelph; practice medicine specializing in psychiatry, Guelph, 1974-80; unit dir. inpatient service Royal Ottawa (Ont., Can.) Hosp., 1980-84, dir. psychiat. rehab. program, 1985 87; asst. prof. psychiatry U. Ottawa Med. Sch., 1980-85, assoc. prof. psychiatry, 1985-87; bd. dirs. Hong Fook Mental Health Service, Toronto, 1987—, dir. East-West Mental Health Ctr., Toronto, 1987—; chmn., bd. dirs. Access Alliance Multicultural Health Ctr., Toronto, 1988—; cons. UN High Commr. for Refugees, 1987—. Served with Army Republic of Vietnam, 1953-68. Mem. Can. Med. Assn., Can., Am. psychiat. assns., Am. Soc. Clin. Hypnosis, Internat. Soc. Hypnosis, N.Y. Acad. Scis. Buddhist. Author: Etude du Tetanos au Vietnam, 1960; (with others) The Psychology and Physiology of Stress, 1969, Psychosomatic Medicine, theoretical, clinical, and transcultural aspects, 1983, Uprooting, Loss and Adaptation, 1984, 87, Southeast Asian Mental Health, 1985. Office: 2238 Dundas St W, Suite 306, Toronto, ON Canada M6R 3A9

SAN AGUSTIN, JOE TAITANO, Guam senator, financial institution executive, management researcher; b. Agana, Guam, Oct. 15, 1930; s. Candido S. and Maria P. (Taitano) San A.; m. Carmen Santos Shimizu, June 18, 1955; children—Mary, Ann, Joe, John. B.A., George Washington U., 1954, M.A., 1965. Chief budget and mgmt. Office of Govt. Guam, Agana, 1966-68; dir. dept. adminstrn. Govt. Guam, Agana, 1968-74; senator Guam Legislature, Agana, 1976—, minority leader 16th Guam Legislature, 1981-82, vice-speaker 17th Guam Legislature, 1983—, chmn. com. on ways and means 17th and 18th Guam Legislatures, 1983-86; chmn. Com. on Ways and Means 17th and 18th, 1983-86; chmn. bd. dirs. Guam Greyhound, Inc., Agana, 1975-86; dir. Bank of Guam, Agana. Democrat. Roman Catholic. Office: 163 Chalan Santo Papa Agana GU 96910

SANANMAN, MICHAEL LAWRENCE, neurologist; b. Bklyn., Oct. 11, 1939; s. Jack and Sarey (Bykofsky) S.; A.B., Swarthmore Coll., 1960; M.D., Columbia U., 1964; m. Elisa Joan Freeman, Apr. 12, 1964; children—Amy, Peter. Intern, Univ. Hosp., San Francisco, 1964-65; resident in neurology N.Y. Neurol. Inst., N.Y.C., 1966-69; practice medicine specializing in neurology, Elizabeth, N.J., 1972—; cons. neurologist St. Elizabeth's Hosp., Elizabeth Gen. Hosp., Alexian Bros. Hosp., Rahway (N.J.) Hosp.; instr. neurology Columbia U., N.Y.C., 1971-75; asso. clin. prof. neurology U. Medicine and Dentistry N.J., Newark, 1975—; mem. advisory council N.J. chpt. Multiple Sclerosis Soc. Served to lt. comdr. M.C., USNR, 1969-71. Diplomate Am. Bd. Psychiatry and Neurology. Mem. Am. Acad. Neurology, AMA, Am. Epilepsy Soc. (advisory council N.J. chpt.), N.J. Acad. Medicine (chmn. neurology sect.), Am., Eastern EEG socs., Am. Assn. EMG and Electrodiagnosis. Office: 700 N Broad St Elizabeth NJ 07208

SANCHEZ SANCHEZ, LUIS ALBERTO, first vice president of Peru, lawyer, writer, educator; b. Lima, Peru, Oct. 12, 1940; s. Alberto and Maria Sanchez; m. Rosa Dergan; children—Aurora, Luisa, Cesar, Jose, Luis, Salma. Ph.D., U. Lima, 1922, law degree, 1926; hon. degree U. Nacional Federico Villareal, 1983. Editor Mercurio Peruano, 1919, Revista Hogar, 1920, Revista Mundial, 1921; founder Diario la Tribuna, 1931; dep. for Lima, 1931-36, 45; asst. dir. pub. house Ercilla, 1934-49, dir. after 1939; prof. U. San Marcos, after 1927; asst. dir. Nat. Library of Lima, 1928-31; rector U. Nacional Mayor de San Marcos, 1946-61, 66; elected mem. Peruvian Senate, 1963, 80, 85, pres. of Senate, from 1985; mem. Constituent Assembly, 1979; 1st v.p. of Peru, Lima, 1985—. Author: Haya de la Torre o El Politico, 1934; Historia Contemporanea; Historia de la Literature Americana; La Literature en el Peru; Historia General de America; Peru: Retrato de un pais adolescente; Testimonio Personal: Memoria de un peruano del Siglo XX; Bolivar; numerous other publs. Mem. nat. exec. com. Partido Aprista

Peruano, 1931-32, 33-34, pres. polit. commn., 1984. Decorated gran oficial de la Orden del Sol del Peru, gran cruz de la Orden del Sol, gran cruz del Aguila Azteca de Merito, gran cruz de la Orden de Blasco Nunez de Balboa, gran cruz de la Orden del Congreso del Peru, Palmas Magisteriales, gran cruz de la Orden Alfonso El Sabio, Palmas Magisteriales-Grado Amauta, Condecoracion del la Guardia Civil en el Grado de Gran Cruz, Condecoracion de Sanidad de las Fuerzas Policiales, Condecoracion de la Guardia Republicana; caballero de la Orden de Merito de Chile, comendador de la Orden del Merito de Chile; gran cruz de la Orden Sor Juana Ines de la Cruz (Mex.). Mem. Lima Coll. Law, Peruvian Coll. Journalism, Peruvian Coll. Lang., Instituto Iberoamericano de Literatura (Spain), PEN Club. Office: Palacio de Gobierno, Lima 1 Peru *

SANDAGE, ALLAN REX, astronomer; b. Iowa City, June 18, 1926; s. Charles Harold and Dorothy (Briggs) S.; m. Mary Lois Connelley, June 8, 1959; children—David Allan, John Howard. A.B., U. Ill., 1948, D.Sc. (hon.), 1967; Ph.D., Calif. Inst. Tech., 1953; D.Sc. (hon.), Yale U., 1966, U. Chgo., 1967, Miami U., Oxford, Ohio, 1974; LL.D. (hon.), U. So. Calif., 1971; Sc.D. (hon.), Graceland Coll., Iowa, 1985. Astronomer Mt. Wilson Obs., Palomar Obs., Carnegie Instn., Washington, 1952—; Peyton postdoctoral fellow Princeton U., 1952; asst. astronomer Hale Obs., Pasadena, Calif., 1952-56, astronomer, 1956—; sr. research astronomer Space Telescope Sci. Inst. NASA, Balt., 1986—; Homewood Prof. of Physics Johns Hopkins U., Balt., 1987-88; Hitchcock prof. U. Calif., Berkeley, 1988—; mem. permanent organizing com. Solvay Conf. in Physics; vis. lectr. Harvard U., 1957; mem. astron. expdn. to South Africa, 1958; cons. NSF, 1961-64; Sigma Xi nat. lectr., 1966; vis. prof. Mt. Stromlo Obs., Australian Nat. U., 1968-69, ; vis. research astronomer U. Basel, 1985; research astronomer U. Calif., San Diego, 1985-86; vis. astronomer U. Hawaii, 1986. Served with USNR, 1944-45. Recipient gold medal Royal Astron. Soc., 1967, Pope Pius XI gold medal Pontifical Acad. Sci., 1966, Rittenhouse medal, 1968, Nat. Medal Sci., 1971; Fulbright-Hayes scholar, 1972. Mem. Am. Astron. Soc. (Helen Warner prize 1960, Russell prize 1973), Royal Astron. Soc. (Eddington medal 1963, Gold medal 1967), Astron. Soc. Pacific (Gold medal 1975), Franklin Inst. (Elliott Cresson medal 1973), Phi Beta Kappa, Sigma Xi. Home: 8319 Josard Rd San Gabriel CA 91775 Office: 813 Santa Barbara St Pasadena CA 91101

SANDAGE, ELIZABETH ANTHEA, advertising educator; b. Larned, Kans., Oct. 13, 1930; d. Curtis Carl and Beulah Pauline (Knupp) Smith; student Okla. State U., 1963-65; B.S., U. Colo., 1967; M.A., 1970; Ph.D. in Communications U. Ill., 1983; m. Charles Harold Sandage, July 18, 1971; children by previous marriage—Diana Louise Danner White, David Alan Danner. Pub. relations rep., editor Martin News, Martin Marietta Corp., Denver, 1960-63, 65-67; retail advt. salesperson Denver Post, 1967-70; instr. advt. U. Ill., 1970-71, vis. lectr. advt., 1977-84; v.p., corp. sec., dir. Farm Research Inst., Urbana, 1984—. Exec. dir. Sandage Charitible Trust, 1986—. Mem. Kappa Tau Alpha. Republican. Presbyterian. Editor: Occasional Papers in Advertising, 1971; The Sandage Family Cookbook, 1976, 2d edit., 1986; The Inkling, Carle Hosp. Aux. Newsletter, 1975-76. Home: 106 The Meadows Urbana IL 61801

SANDAGE, SHIRLEY MARIE, social scientist; b. Mason City, Iowa, May 5, 1927; d. Jack D. and Flossie M. (Reynolds) Farrer; m. Richard Sandage, Feb. 10, 1946; children: Richard, John, Scott. Student Cornell Coll., Mt. Vernon, Iowa, 1949. Exec. dir. Migrant Action Program, Iowa and Minn., 1965-69; dep. dir. Migrant Research Project, Washington, 1969-72; cons. welfare reform office Sec. Labor, 1972-73; leader spl. task force U.S. Employment Service, Washington, 1972-74; dir. hazaradous waste project study in Iowa, Garrity-Sandage Assos., 1974-76; exec. dir., The Door Opener, center for women, Mason City, 1976-83; exec. dir. Older Women's League, Washington, 1983-85; U.S. field rep. Christian Children's Fund, Washington, 1985-88; mgmt. cons., Arlington, 1988—; pres. bd. Displaced Homemaker Network, 1981-82; mem. Iowa Health Care Commn. Recipient Achievement award Mason City YWCA, 1978; Spl. Recognition award for significant contbn. to welfare of Iowa, Gov. of Iowa, 1982. Mem. Rural Am. Women, Bus. and Profl. Women, Older Women's League (nat. bd. dirs.), Am. Assn. Ret. Persons, Am. Soc. for Tng. and Dvel., Women in Devel. Democrat. Mem. Christian Ch. (Disciples of Christ). Author: Child of Hope, 1964, Suffer Little Children, 1988, Children at Risk: America's Legacy for the Future, 1988; also articles. Home: 500 S Taylor St Arlington VA 22204-1447 Office: 5 G St NW Washington DC 20005

SANDBERG, ARNE JOHN, data processing company executive; b. Oslo, July 18, 1940; s. Josef and Anna (Andersen) S.; m. Kari Langer, Aug. 6, 1947; 1 child, Geir. Degree in Bus. Econs., Bedriftsokonomisk Inst., Oslo, 1977. Systems cons. IBM, Oslo, 1962-64; systems cons. Singer Co., Oslo, 1964-67, mgr. sales, 1973-75; systems mgr. Data Processing Bur., Oslo, 1967-72; mgr. sales ICL, Oslo, 1977-83; mgr. div. data processing Nixdorf Computer A/S, Oslo, 1983—. Contbr. articles to data processing mags. Served with Norwegian Army, 1962-62. Conservative. Mem. Norwegian State Ch. Lodge: Rotary. Home: Stasjonsveien 19, 1482 Nittedal Norway Office: Nixdorf Computer A/S, Drammensvn 134, Oslo 2, Norway

SANDBERG, ARTHUR GUNNAR, airline executive, civil aviation consultant; b. Nora, Sweden, Oct. 3, 1916; s. Arthur Anton and Berta Helena (Gustafson) S.; m. Karin Magnusson, June 24, 1942; 1 child, Britt Karin Helén. Degree in Bus. Econs., Stockholm, 1948; postgrad. in Advanced Mgmt., Grad. Engring. Assn., Stockholm, 1955; postgrad., Internat. Conf. of Sr. Execs., Centre d'Etude Ind.-elles, Geneva, 1974. Mem. staff to head State Power Bd., Stockholm, 1939-58; v.p. adminstrn. State Power Bd., 1962-68; v.p. procurement Scandinavian Airlines, Stockholm, 1959-61; sr. v.p. adminstrn. Scandinavian Airlines, 1969-81; sr. ptnr., pres. Scanavia, cons. in field of aviation 1981—. Decorated Knight of the Order of Royal North Star, The King of Sweden, Stockholm, 1958, Comdr. of the Order of Royal North Star, 1968; UN fellow in mgmt.; Elec. Power Bus., various areas in U.S.A., 1952. Mem. Royal Swedish Aero Club, Assn. Bus. Econonmoists (chmn. 1978-80), Assn. Swedish Purchasers (chmn. 1982-83), Airline Mgmt. Devel. Assn. (chmn. 1975-82). Moderate Party. Lutheran. Club: Swedish Cruizing (Stockholm). Home: Lappstigen 5A, S162 40 Vallingby, Stockholm Sweden Office: Scanavia AB, Drottningholmsvagen 31-33, S112 42 Stockholm Sweden

SANDBERG, SIR MICHAEL (GRAHAM RUDDOCK), bank executive; b. May 31, 1927; s. Gerald Arthur Clifford and Ethel Marion Sandberg; m. Carmel Mary Roseleen, 1954; 4 children. Student, St. Edward's Sch., Oxford, Eng.; LLD (hon.), U. Hong Kong, 1984, Pepperdine U., 1986. Joined The Hong Kong and Shanghai Banking Corp., 1949, chmn., 1977-86; mem. exec. council Hong Kong, 1978-86; chmn. The Brit. Bank of the Middle East, 1980-86; treas. U. Hongkong, 1977-86. Served with Brit. Army, 1945. Decorated Knight, 1986, CBE, 1982. Clubs: Royal Hong Kong Jockey (steward 1972-76, chmn. 1981-86), Cavalry and Guards, Carlton, Portland, MCC, Surrey CCC. Office: Hong Kong and Shanghai Bank Corp, 1 Queen's Rd Central, Hong Kong Hong Kong *

SANDER, LOUIS WILSON, psychiatry educator, researcher; b. San Francisco, July 31, 1918; s. Louis Francis and Emily (Wilson) S.; m. Betty Estelle Thorpe, Apr. 25, 1953; children—Mark, Rebecca, David. A.B., U. Calif.-Berkeley, 1939; M.D., U. Calif.-San Francisco, 1942. Diplomate Am. Bd. Psychiatry and Neurology. Intern U. Calif. Hosp., San Francisco, 1942-43; resident psychiatry Worcester State Hosp., Mass., 1947, Judge Baker Guidance Ctr., Boston, 1949-50; resident psychiatry Mass. Meml. Hosps., Boston U. Sch. Medicine, 1947-49, resident in neurology, 1950; from instr. to assoc. prof. psychiatry Boston U. Sch. Medicine, 1949-68, prof., 1968-78; prof. psychiatry U. Colo. Sch. Medicine, Denver, 1978-87; prof. emeritus, 1987—; prin. investigator 25 yr. longitudinal study Boston U. Sch. Medicine-U. Colo. Sch. Medicine, 1981—; prin. investigator research Boston U. Sch. Medicine, 1954-78; vis. prof. U. Calif., Davis, 1979; Simpson vis. prof. U. Calif., San Francisco, 1984. Editor: (with others) Infant Psychiatry: A New Synthesis, 1976. Inventor/developer non-invasive infant bassinet monitor, 1958, infant state and infant caregiver systems regulation monitor, 1987. Contbr. articles, book chpts., and revs. to profl. publs., 1962-83. Served to maj. USAAF, 1943-46. Recipient Research Career Devel. awards USPHS, 1963-78; research grantee USPHS, March of Dimes, W. Grant Found., MacArthur Found., Spencer Found., Developmental Psychobiology Research Group-Colo. U., Nat. Council on Alcoholism, Univ. Hosp., Boston. Fellow Am. Coll. Psychoanalysts, Denver Psychoanalytic Soc.; mem. Am. Psychiat. Assn., Am. Acad. Child Psychiatry (sec. 1960-61), Boston Psychoanalytic Soc., AAAS, Soc. for Research in Child Devel. (governing council 1975-77), Phi Beta Kappa, Alpha Omega Alpha. Home: 2525 Madrona Ave Saint Helena CA 94574 Office: Univ Colo Med Sch 4200 E 9th St Denver CO 80262

SANDERS, CURTIS REMMELL, management and investment consultant; b. Jonesboro, Ark., Mar. 12, 1929; s. Macon Remmell and Dorothea Auttie Irene (McAuliffe) M.; m. Dorothy Elizabeth Dalton, Sept. 6, 1950; children: Elizabeth, Linda, Eric. BS in Chemistry, San Diego State U., 1958; student, U. So. Calif. and UCLA, 1962-66. Dir. product forecasting IBM Product Group div. IBM Corp., U.S.A., 1972-74; group dir. bus. vols. IBM Europe div. IBM Corp., 1974-79; dir. bus. plans IBM Office Products div. IBM Corp., U.S.A., 1979-82; dir. market research IBM Corp., White Plains, N.Y., 1982-87; pres., chief exec. officer Haigh Assoc., Inc., Stamford, Conn., 1983—. Served with USN, 1946-49, PTO. Mem. Mktg. Sci. Inst., Conf. Bd. Council on Mktg. Research.

SANDERS, DIANE KATHLEEN, dietitian; b. Kansas City, Mo., Oct. 26, 1950; d. C.R. and E.E. (Ernst) Sanders. BS, Kans. State U., 1973, MS, 1974. Registered dietitian; cert. culinary educator. Clin. dietician St. Mary Hosp., Manhattan, Kans., 1973-75; instr. U.S.D. #383, Manhattan, 1975—; cons. Manhattan area nursing homes, 1974—; vol. nutritionist Head Start, Manhattan, 1973-74; coordinator Food Service Supr. Program, Manhattan, 1977—, continuing edn. course food service workers, Manhattan, 1982—. Bd. dirs. Wharton Manor Nursing Home, 1973-81, chmn., 1979. Avocations: water skiing, sailing. Home: 5012 Vista Acres Dr Manhattan KS 66502 Office: Manhattan Vocat Sch 3136 Dickens Ave Manhattan KS 66502

SANDERS, GARY GLENN, electronics engineer, consultant; b. Gettysburg, Pa., Dec. 21, 1944; s. James Glenn Sanders and Martha Maybelle (Fleming) Ehlert; m. Elizabeth Marie Rega, Sept. 9, 1977 (div. Sept. 1981). Cert. med. technologist, Chgo. Inst. Tech., 1970; AA, Mayfair Coll., 1972; BS in Electronic Engring., Cooks Inst., Jackson, Miss., 1982. Cons. engr. Electronics Design Services, Chgo., 1977-79; applications engr. Nationwide Electronics Systems, Streamwood, Ill., 1979-80; mng. engr. Electronics Design Ctr. Case Western Res. U., Cleve., 1980-82; sr. project mgr. Scott Fetzer Co., Cleve., 1982—. Contbr. articles on medicine and biology to profl. confs. and publs.; patentee in biomed. electronics and indsl. instrumentation fields. Alumni mem. Boy Scouts Am. Served with U.S. Army, 1962-68, Vietnam. Decorated DFC, Bronze Star, Air medal. Fellow Internat. Coll. Med. Technologists; mem. IEEE, AAAS, Instrument Soc. of Am., Internat. Soc. Hybrid Microelectronics, N.Y. Acad. Scis., DAV, Am. Legion, Ohio Acad. Sci., Nat. Eagle Scout Assn. Republican. Home: 1360 Brockley Ave Lakewood OH 44107-2415 Office: Scott Fetzer Co Meriam Div 10920 Madison Ave Cleveland OH 44102

SANDERS, GILBERT OTIS, research psychologist, consultant, educator; b. Oklahoma City, Aug. 7, 1945; s. Richard Allen and Evelyn Wilmoth (Barker) S.; m. Marline Marie Lairmore, Nov. 1, 1969 (dec.); 1 dau., Lisa Dawn; m. Lidia Julie Grados-Ventura, Aug. 31, 1984. A.S., Murray State Coll, 1965; B.A., Okla. State U., 1967; M.S., Troy State U., 1970; Ed.D., U. Tulsa, 1974; postdoctoral St. Louis U., Am. Tech. U. Research psychologist U.S. Army Research Inst., Ft. Hood, Tex., 1978-79; engring. psychologist U.S. Army Tng. and Doctrine Command Systems Analysis Activity, White Sands Missile Range, N. Mex., 1979-80; project dir./research psychologist Applied Sci. Assocs., Ft. Sill, Okla., 1980-81; research psychologist Res. Components Personnel and Adminstrn. Ctr., St. Louis, 1981-83; pres. Southwestern Behavioral Research and Mktg. Co., Oklahoma City, 1984—; pvt. counseling practice, Oklahoma City, 1984—; cons. behavioral sci., St. Louis, 1981-84; adj. prof. bus. and psychology Columbia Coll.-Buder Campus, St. Louis, 1982-84; assoc. prof. Pittsburgh State U., Kans., 1983-85; adj. prof. Columbia Pacific U., 1984—, U.S. Army Command Staff and Gen. Coll., Ft. Leavenworth, Kans., 1983—; chmn. dept. computer sci., dir. computer services Calumet Coll., Whiting, Ind., 1975-78; dir. edn. Am. Humane Edn. Soc., Boston, 1975. Prin. editor: TRADOC Training Effectiveness Analysis Handbook, 1980; author research reports. Hon. col. Okla. Gov.'s Staff, Oklahoma City, 1972; hon. ambassador Gov. Okla., 1974. Recipient Kavanough Found. Community Builder award, 1967. Mem. Am. Psychol. Assn., Okla. Psychol. Assn., Tex. Psychol. Assn., Mo. Psychol. Assn., Am. Assn. Counseling and Devel., Tex. Assn. Counseling and Devel., Am. Mental Health Counselors Assn., Human Factors Soc., Okla. Hist. Soc., Reserve Officers Assn. Lodge: Masons. Office: 5404 NW 65th St Oklahoma City OK 73132 also: 3805 W Gore Lawton OK 73505

SANDERS, HOWARD, investment company executive; b. Phila., June 30, 1941; s. Louis and Freda (Liss) S.; m. Dale Rosenberg, Dec. 15, 1963; children: Lee Michael, Kimberly Joy. B.S. in Acctg., Temple U., 1962; M.Acctg., Ohio State U., 1963. C.P.A. Acct., Price, Waterhouse & Co., Phila., 1962-65; asst. prof. acctg. Temple U., 1965-72; v.p. Revere Fund, Inc., Phila., 1966-76; pres. Revere Mgmt. Co., Inc., Phila., 1966-72; chmn. bd. Ladies Center of Nebr., Inc., 1976—, Volk Footwear and Findings Co., 1977-78, Mister Plywood Enterprises, Inc., 1970-82; pres. Sanders Fin. Mgmt., Inc., Fort Lauderdale, 1972—; chmn. bd. Am. Carpet Backing Distbg. Inc., 1978-80, Polis-Sanders Real Estate Corp., 1981—. Contbg. author: How to Start a Mutual Fund, 1970. Mem. adv. bd. Phila. Assn. for Retarded Children, 1970-72; chmn. bd. Women's Med. Center of Providence, Inc., 1977—, Women's Med. Center of North Jersey, Inc., 1977-82, Women's Med. Center of Atlanta, Inc., 1977—, Cherry Hill Women's Center, Inc., 1978—, Metairie Women's Center of New Orleans, Inc., 1980-84, Hartford Gynecol. Center, 1980—. Kaiser Aluminum and Chem. Co. fellow, 1962-63. Mem. Am. Inst. C.P.A.s, Pa. Inst. C.P.A.s (award for paper 1961), Phila. Jaycees (dir. 1966), Nat. Assn. Accts., B'rith Shalom Assn., Beta Gamma Sigma, Beta Alpha Psi, Tau Epsilon Phi. Home and Office: 410 Sea Turtle Terr Plantation FL 33324

SANDERS, MARVIS CLAIRE, travel journalist; b. Fairland, Okla., Dec. 10, 1930; d. Jacob Monroe and Jessie Augusta (James) England; m. Delmer Marion Sanders, Apr. 10, 1950; children—George Gregory, Marcia Lynn. Student Contra Costa Jr. Coll., 1968; B.A., Calif. State U.-Fresno, 1981; A.A., Coll. Sequoias, 1976. Library clk. City of Richmond, Calif., 1966-71; with Contra Costa County, Richmond, 1971; reporter Mineral King Publs., Exeter, Calif., 1971-80, editor, 1980-85. Leader, Campfire Girls, Richmond, 1964-66; chmn. Alvarado Sch. PTA Library, Richmond, 1962-68. Mem. Calif. Congress of Parents and Tchrs. (hon. life). Democrat.

SANDERS, MICHAEL LEWIS, historian, educator; b. Fulmer, Eng., Oct. 27, 1943; s. Cyril Lewis and Alice (Brown) S.; m. Kay Christine Porter, Aug. 13, 1966 (div. 1975); children: Neil, Julie; m. N. Lynn Darmstadt, Dec. 14, 1985. BA, Queens' Coll., Cambridge, Eng., 1965, MA, 1969; M. Phil., London Sch. Econs. and Polit. Sci., 1972. Cert. edn. King's Coll., 1966. Asst. master St. Clement Dane's Sch., London, 1966-68, Royal Liberty Sch., Romford, Eng., 1968-71; head history Highams Park Sr. High Sch., London, 1971-73; lectr. in edn. Trent Park Coll., Enfield, Eng., 1973-75; sr. lectr. in history Middlesex Polytech., Barnet, Herts, Eng., 1975-87; vis. prof. Calif. State U., Hayward, 1980-81, SUNY, New Paltz, 1984-85, 87—; external examiner Inst. Edn., London, 1972-73, Council Nat. Acad. Awards, London, 1985-86; tutor, Open U., London, 1979-80. Author: British Propaganda, 1982; contbr. articles to profl. jours. Recipient scholarship Eng. Dept. Edn., 1962, Queens' Coll., 1962. Home: 35 Wurts St Kingston NY 12401

SANDERS, SHIRLEY, clinical psychologist; b. Phila., Nov. 8, 1935; d. Samuel and Nellie (Shor) S. A.B., U. Miami, 1963; M.A., U. Ky., 1965, Ph.D., 1967. Lic. psychologist, N.C. Asst. prof. U. N.C., Chapel Hill, 1968-77, assoc., 1977-81, clin. assoc. prof., 1981-84, clin. prof., 1984—; practice psychology, Chapel Hill, 1981—; cons. Randolph County Mental Health, Asheboro, N.C., 1968-70; dir. Project Redirect, Siler City, N.C., 1975-78. Contbr. articles to profl. jours. Recipient N.C. State Dept. Catthel award 1976. Fellow Am. Psychol. Assn., Am. Soc. Clin. Hypnosis (pres. 1982; recognition award 1982), Soc. Clin. and Exptl. Hypnosis (recipient Morton Prince award 1981). Avocations: photography; dance; music. Home: 209 Ferguson Rd Chapel Hill NC 27516 Office: 1829 E Franklin St Suite 101 Chapel Hill NC 27514

SANDERSON, MICHAEL DAVID, marketing company executive; b. Bristol, Eng., June 7, 1943; s. Arthur Joseph and Betty (Potter) S.; m. Mariana Welly, July 21, 1967; children—Charles Sebastian, Victoria Elizabeth. B.Sc. in Chemistry with honors, U. Reading, Eng., 1964; Ph.D., U. Leeds, Eng., 1968. Tech. dir. Wilkinson Sword Ltd., London, 1971-78, mktg. dir., 1978-82; engring. dir. AMF Legg, Andover, Eng., 1982-83, acting mng. dir., 1983-84; assoc. dir. Oakland Mgmt. Holdings Ltd., Eng., 1984-85; export dir. Lansing Bagnall Ltd., Basingstoke, Eng., 1985-87, group dir., 1987—. Contbr. articles to profl. jours. Patentee surface coating. Fellow Inst. Materials Mgmt.; mem. Inst. Metals, Inst. Corrosion Sci. and Tech. Conservative. Mem. Ch. Eng. Home: 145 Hill Ln, Southampton SO1 5AF, England Office: Lansing Bagnall Ltd, Kings Clere Rd, Basingstoke RG21 2XJ, England

SANDIFORD, LLOYD ERSKINE, prime minister; b. Porters, St. James, Barbados, Mar. 24, 1937; s. Cyril Gordon and Eunice (Bend) S.; m. Angelita Petrona Ricketts; children: Garth, Sheree-Ann, Inga. BA (hons.) in English, U. Coll. of West Indies, 1957-60; MA in Econs., U. Manchester (Eng.), 1961-63. Asst. master Modern High Sch., Barbados, 1956-57, Kingston Coll., Jamaica, 1960-61; asst. master Harrison Coll., Barbados, 1963-64, sr. grad. master, 1964-66; part-time tutor and lectr. U. West Indies, Barbados, 1963-65; mem. senate Dem. Labour Party Govt. of Barbados, Bridgetown, 1967-71, mem. of house of assembly, 1971—, personal asst. to prime minister, 1966-67, minister of edn., 1967-71, minister of edn., youth affairs, community devel. and sports, 1971-75, minister of health and welfare, 1975-76, dep. prime minister and minister of edn. and culture, 1986-87, prime minister and minister of econ. affairs and minister of fin., 1987—; asst. tutor Barbados Community Coll., 1976-86. Mem. Dem. Labour Party, 1964—, v.p., 1972-74, 75-76, pres., 1974-75, 87—; founder Acad. of Politics. Office: Prime Minister's Office, Govt Headquarters, Bridgetown Barbados West Indies

SANDIN, BONIFACIO, psychotherapist, educator, researcher; b. San Pedro de Zamudia, Zamora, Spain, Dec. 25, 1948; s. Bonifacio Sandin and Benilde Ferrero. PhD in Psychology, U. Complutense de Madrid, 1981. Prof. psychophysiology Centro Estudios Universitarios, Madrid, 1975-84, chief div. psychobiol., 1981-84; prof. psychodiagnostic U. Nacional de Educacion a Distancia, Madrid, 1976-82, prof. psychopathology, 1983—; becario programa formacion de personal investigador U. Complutense, Madrid, 1976-78. Author: Aportaciones Recientes en Psicopatologia, 1986, Procesos Emocionales y Salud, 1988, Investigations on Relationships Between Skin and Salivary pH and Anxiety, 1988; cons. editor Psiquis. Rev. Psychiat. Psychol. Psychosom., 1981—, Internat. Jour. Psychosomatics, Phila., 1984—; exptl. works on neurosis conditioning; contbr. scientific articles to profl. jours. Recipient Disting. Premio Extraordinario de Licenciatura U. Complutense, 1976. Mem. Internat. Psychosomatics Inst., Sociedad Española de Psicologia, Sociedad Española de Evaluacion Psicologica, Asociacion Española de Terapia del Comportamiento. Home: Paseo Juan XXIII No 3, 28040 Madrid Spain Office: Universidad Nacional, de Educacion a Distancia, PO Box 60148, 28040 Madrid Spain

SANDLER, ALBERT N(ATHAN), radiologist; b. St. Louis, Dec. 1, 1930; s. Lewis N. and Dorothy (Zimmerman) S.; m. Lillian Jean Muchnick, Aug. 1965; children: Scott Louis, Bradley Jay. BS, MA in Edn., Northeast Mo. State U., 1962; DO, Kirskville Coll. Osteopathic Medicine, 1970. Diplomate Am. Bd. Radiology. Tchr., coach Webster Groves Sch., Mo., 1961-62, Parkway Sch. Dist., Chesterfield, Mo., 1962-66; emergency physician Normandy (Mo.) Osteopathic Hosp., 1970-73, resident in radiology, 1973-76; radiologist Radiol. Cons., Des Peres, Mo., 1977—; head resident program Radiol. Cons., 1982-83, 85—, chief radiology dept. Active Am. Cancer Soc., St. Louis; mem. Friends of St. Louis Art Mus., 1984, Mo. Hist. Soc., 1984, Wildlife Soc, St. Louise, 1984. Served to cpl. U.S. Army, 1952-54. Mem. Am. Coll. Osteopatic Radiology (cert.), Am. Coll. Radiology, Mo. Osteopathic Assn., St. Louis Osteopathic Assn., Mo Osteopathic Radiologists. Republican. Home: #7 Clayton Hills Ln Town and Country MO 63131 Office: Normandy Osteopathic Hosp S 530 Des Peres Rd Des Peres MO 63131

SANDLIN, GEORGE WILSON, real estate broker, mortgage banker; b. Glen Rose, Tex., May 13, 1912; s. Walter Algie and Margaret (Parks) S.; student pub. schs., also Schreiner Inst.; m. Ruth Ina Zollinger, Sept. 21, 1941 (dec. 1975); children—George Walter Raoul, Carole Ruth, Sarah Louise, Margaret Ina; m. Ann Marie Anderson, Nov. 11, 1984. Field rep. HOLC, San Antonio, 1934-36; pres. Sandlin Mortgage Corp., Austin, Tex.; owner Sandlin & Co., 1936—; pres., dir. Trans-Pacific Resorts, Inc.; pres. Profl. Arts, Inc.; ind. fee appraiser. Chmn., Tex. Real Estate Commn., 1949-55. Mem. Austin City Planning Commn., 1947-52, chmn., 1951-52. Chmn., Tex. Dem. Exec. Com., 1954-56. Pres. chmn. bd. Tex. Found., 1955—. Served as lt. comdr. USNR, World War II; PTO. Recipient Silver Citizenship medal VFW, 1957. Mem. Tex. Assn. Realtors (dir., pres. 1979, Realtor of Yr. 1981), Austin Real Estate Bd. (past pres.), Inst. Real Estate Mgmt., Inst. Real Estate Brokers, Mortgage Bankers Assn., Nat. Assn. Realtors (dir., chmn. polit. action com. 1982), Am. Legion, V.F.W. Episcopalian. Clubs: Austin Country, Headliners. Home: 11301 Spicewood Pkwy Austin TX 78750 Office: 6010 Balcones Dr Austin TX 78731

SANDOR, JEAN-MARIE, physician; b. Morthomiers, Cher, France, July 25, 1943; s. Ladislas Sandor and Marie-Madeleine Lenkey; m. Marlene Glaçon; children: Rodolphe, Dorothee, Valery. MD, Univ. Lille, 1970. Practice medicine Henin-Beaumont, France, 1972—; researcher in informatic smart cards in patients' file field and telematic. Author: Spasmophily, 1985, Enuresie, 1986. Mcpl. officer City of Henin-Beaumont, 1977—; officer Am. Field Service, Paris, 1981-85, S.O.S. Internat., Paris, 1983-84, Centre Nat. Info. Sur La Drogue Catholique, 1982. Served with French Air Force, 1970-71. Mem. No. Formation Med. Doctors (officer), Assn. Departementale de Devel. Sanitaire (pres.). Mem. Parti Democrate. Roman Catholic. Lodge: Order St. Jean de Jerusalem. Home: 196 Ave Victor Hugo, 62110 Henin-Beaumont Pas de Calais France Office: 284 Ave Victor Hugo, 62110 Henin-Beaumont Pas de Calais France

SANDOVAL, MARCIAL CERRATO, advertising executive; b. Tegucigalpa, Honduras, June 29, 1937; s. Encarnación Cerrato and Mercedes Sandoval; m. Norma Sabillon Greenwood, June 20, 1964; children: Norma Allegra, Pedro Marcial, Angel Humberto. Grad. in Law, U. Nacional Autonoma Honduras, Tegucigalpa, 1967. Post master Dirección Gral. de Correos, Comayagüela, Honduras, 1957-63; chief of bills Servicio Autónomo Nat. de Acueductos y Alcantarillados, Tegucigalpa, 1964-67; account exec. McCann-Erickson, Tegucigalpa, 1967-71; v.p. Banco Atlántida, Tegucigalpa, 1971-80; pres. Mercadeo Integral, Tegucigalpa, 1980—; cons. Calderón Publicidad, Tegucigalpa, 1984—, Banco Capitalizadora Hondureña, S.A., Tegucigalpa, 1984—; cons., instr. Financiera Centroamericana Tegucigalpa, 1986—. Author: Advertising and Public Relations, 1980, Bank's Operation, 1981, Banking Laws, 1982, Bank's Marketing, 1984. Pres. Inst. de Cultura Interamericano, Tegucigalpa, 1984-85, Fundación Hondureña de Rehab. del Limitado, Tegucigalpa, 1986, Patronato de Rehab. del Ciego, Tegucigalpa. Recipient Diploma, Dirección de Folklore, 1971, Nat. Library, 1976, Assn. de Prensa Hondureña, 1981, Gold Laurel, Ministerio de Cultura, 1976. Mem. Ctr. Asesor Para El Desarrollo de los Recursos Humanos de Honduras, Jr. C. of C. Internat. Mem. Liberal Party. Roman Catholic. Home: la Avenida F8, Col 15 de Setiembre, Comayagüela Honduras

SANDRED, KARL INGE, English language educator; b. Uppsala, Sweden, May 7, 1925; m. Gunvor Elisabeth Klinga, 1952; children: Jan, Gunnel Elisabeth, Orjan. MA, Uppsala U., 1952, fil. lic., 1959, PhD, 1963. Tchr. 1952-63; docent Uppsala U., 1963, sr. reader, 1969, acting prof. English, 1984; sr. reader English Umeå U., 1968, acting prof. English, 1973, 79-80; No. Scholars lectr. Edinburgh U., 1970. Author: English Place-Names in stead, 1963, (with G. Holm) En diskussion om sta-namnen, 1967, A Middle English Version of the Gesta Romanorum, 1971, (with T. Andersson) The Vikings, 1978, Good or Bad Scots?, 1983. Served with Swedish Army, 1945-46. British Council scholar Univ. Coll. London, 1959; Leverhulme European vis. fellow, 1971-72, Vis. Research fellow Edinburgh U., 1975, Nottingham U. vis. fellow. Mem. Royal Swedish Gustav Adolf Acad., Philol. Soc. London, Linguistic Soc. Am., Societas Linguistica Europaea, English Place Name Soc., Uppsala Place Name Soc. (sec., editorial bd.). Office: Box 10034, 750 10 Uppsala Sweden

SANDS, RICHARD, banker, accountant; b. Nassau, The Bahamas, May 20, 1956; s. Harry Zedekiah and Dorothy (Perpall) S. B in Commerce, U. Windsor, Can., 1981. Cert. gen. acct. Acct. Ministry of Fin., Nassau, 1982-84, fin. officer, 1984-86; banker Bank of Nova Scotia, Nassau, 1986—; asst. fin. officer Commonwealth Heads Govt. Meeting, 1985; alt. mem. ad-hoc com. Acctg. Legis. Coach Becks Cougars Basketball Club, Bahamas, 1982-84. Mem. Cert. Gen. Accts. Assn. Can. (v.p. 1988—), Cert. Gen. Accts. Assn. Bahamas (treas. 1986). Baptist.

SANDY, WILLIAM HASKELL, training and communications systems company president; b. N.Y.C., Apr. 28, 1929; s. Fred and Rose S.; A.B., U. Md., 1950, J.D., 1953; postgrad. Advanced Mgmt. Program, Harvard Bus. Sch., 1970-71; m. Marjorie Mazor, June 15, 1952; children—Alan, Lewis, Barbara. Admitted to Md. bar, 1953; planner-writer, account exec., account supr. Jam Handy Orgn., Detroit, 1953-64, v.p., 1964-69, sr. v.p., 1969-71; pres. Sandy Corp., Troy, Mich., 1971—. Bd. govs. Northwood Inst., 1976-80; bd. dirs. Cranbrook Sci. Inst.; mem. nat. exec. council Harvard Bus. Sch., 1985—. Mem. Am. Mktg. Assn. (pres. Detroit chpt. 1975), Am. Soc. Tng. and Devel., Southeastern Mich. Better Bus. Bur. (bd. dirs.), Adcraft Club, Nat. Assn. Ednl. Broadcasters. Clubs: Harvard Bus. Sch. (pres. Detroit club 1983-85), The Hundred. Home: 596 Rudgate Bloomfield Hills MI 48013 Office: Sandy Corp 1500 W Big Beaver Rd Troy MI 48084

SANEFUJI, TAKASHI, petrochemical company executive; b. Sao Bento Sapucaí, São Paulo, Brazil, Oct. 10, 1937; s. Kamenosuke and Kiyono (Nagano) S.; m. Mieko Sanefuji; children: Roberto Takashi, Claudia. BSME, U. São Paulo, 1962; postgrad., Washington U., St. Louis, 1974-76. Controller energy yield São Paulo Light Co., 1963-66; project mgr. Squibb, São Paulo, 1967-69; mgr. investment devel. Monsanto, São Paulo and Rio de Janeiro, 1970-73; mgr. planning devel. Monsanto, St. Louis, 1974-76; dir. adminstrn. Monsanto, São Paulo, 1976; dir., pres. CIA Brasileira de Estireno, São Paulo, 1976—; bd. dirs. Siresp Synthetic Resins Prodn. Syndicate, Sinproquim Chem. Producers Syndicate, São Paulo, v.p., 1984—. Mem. Abiquim Chem. Industry Assn. (bd. dirs.), AMA Pres. Assn., Engring. Inst. Office: CIA Brasileira de Estireno, Rua Paes Leme #524 9 Andar, Sao Paulo 05424, Brazil

SANETO, RUSSELL PATRICK, neurobiologist; b. Burbank, Calif., Oct. 10, 1950; s. Arthur and Mitzi (Seddon) S. B.S. with honors, San Diego State U., 1972, M.S., 1975; Ph.D., U. Tex. Med. Br., 1981. Teaching asst. San Diego State U. 1969-75; substitute tchr. Salt Lake City Sch. Dist., 1975; teaching and research asst. U. Tex. Med. Br., 1976-77, NIH predoctoral fellow, 1977-81, postdoctoral fellow, 1981; Jeanne B. Kempner postdoctoral fellow UCLA, 1981-82, NIH postdoctoral fellow, 1982-87; asst. prof. Oreg. Regional Primate Research Ctr. div. Neurosci., Beaverton, 1987; asst. prof. dept. cell biology and anatomy Oreg. Health Scis. U.; asst. prof. dept. cell biology and anatomy Oreg. Health Scis. U., Portland; lectr. research methods Grad. Sch., 1982; vis. scholar in ethics So. Baptist Theol. Sem., Louisville, 1981. Contbr. articles to profl. jours. Recipient Merit award Nat. March of Dimes, 1978; named one of Outstanding Young Men in Am., 1979, 81, Man of Significance, 1985. Mem. Bread for World, Save the Whales, Sierra Club, Am. Soc. Human Genetics, AAAS, Winter Confs. Brain Research, Neuroscis. Study Program, N.Y. Acad. Scis., Am. Soc. Neurochem., Soc. Neurosci., Am. Soc. Neurochemistry, Soc. Neurosci. Democrat. Mem. Evangelical Free Ch. Club: World Runners. Office: Oreg Regional Primate Research Ctr Div Neurosci 505 NW 185th Ave Beaverton OR 97006

SANFORD, CHARLES STEADMAN, JR., banker; b. Savannah, Ga., Oct. 8, 1936; s. Charles Steadman and Ann (Lawrence) S.; m. Mary McRitchie, June 19, 1959; children: Ann Whitney, Charles Steadman III. AB, U. Ga., 1958; MBA, U. Pa., 1960. Vice pres. nat. div., account officer Bankers Trust Co., N.Y.C., 1961-68, 1st v.p., asst. to head resources mgmt., 1969-71, sr. v.p., 1973, exec. v.p., head resources mgmt., from 1972, pres., 1983-86, dep. chmn., from 1986, chmn., chief exec. officer, 1987—, mem. mgmt. com., 1979—; chmn. N.Y. Clearing House Com.; dir. Gen Re Corp., Council for Aid to Edn., Inc., Internat. Monetary Conf., Wharton Bus. Sch. Club N.Y. Mem. bd. overseers Wharton Sch. of the U. Pa.; trustee U. Ga. Found., Com. for Econ. Devel. Served with arty. U.S. Army, 1958-59. Mem. Public Securities Assn. (dir. 1977-78), Securities Industry Assn. (exec. com. gov., dir., mem., 1976), Assn. Res. City Bankers (dir.), Council Fgn. Relations Inc., The Conf. Bd., Econ. Club of N.Y., Bond Club of N.Y., Inc. Office: Bankers Trust Co 280 Park Ave New York NY 10017

SANFORD, TERRY, U.S. senator, former governor, former university president; b. Laurinburg, N.C., Aug. 20, 1917; s. Cecil and Elizabeth (Martin) S.; m. Margaret Rose Knight, July 4, 1942; children: Elizabeth Knight, Terry. AB, U. N.C., 1939, JD, 1946; 24 hon. degrees from colls. and univs. Bar: N.C. 1946. Asst. dir. Inst. Govt., U. N.C., 1940-41, 46-48; spl. agt. FBI, 1941-42; practiced in Fayetteville, 1948-60; ptnr. Sanford, Adams, McCullough & Beard, Raleigh, N.C. and Washington, 1965-86; gov. State of N.C. 1961-65; pres. Duke U., Durham, N.C., 1969-85; U.S. Senator from N.C. 99th-100th Congresses, Washington, 1986—; public gov. Am. Stock Exchange, 1977-83; Dir. Study of Am. States, Duke U., 1965-68; mem. Carnegie Commn. Ednl. TV, 1964-67; pres. Urban Am., Inc., 1968-69; chmn. ITT Internat. Fellowship Com., Am. Council Young Polit. Leaders. Author: But What About the People?, 1966, Storm Over the States, 1967, A Danger of Democracy, 1981. Sec.-treas. N. C. Port Authority, 1950-53; mem. N.C. Senate, 1953-54; pres. N.C. Young Dem. Clubs, 1949-50; del. Nat. Dem. Conv., 1956, 60, 64, 68, 72, 84; chmn. Nat. Dem. Charter Commn., 1972-74; mem. governing bd. Nat. Com. for Citizens in Edn., Am. Art Alliance; trustee Cordell Hull Found. Internat. Edn., Am. Council Learned Socs., 1970-73, Nat. Humanities Center, Meth. Coll., Howard U.; bd. dirs. Children's TV Workshop, 1967-71, Council on Founds., 1971-76, N.C. Outward Bound, 1981—, Nat. Acad. Public Adminstrs.; chmn. So. Regional Edn. Bd., 1961-63, Sta. ACSN (The Learning Channel), 1980-86, Assn. Am. Univs., 1980-81, Nat. Civic League. Served to 1st lt. AUS, 1942-46. Mem. ABA, Am. Acad. Polit. and Social Sci., Council Fgn. Relations, Am. Judicature Soc., Nat. Civ. League (chmn. 1985-86), AAAS. Methodist. Office: US Senate 716 Hart Senate Bldg Washington DC 20510 also: 9050 W Main St Suite 24-B Durham NC 27701

SANGER, FREDERICK, retired molecular biologist; b. Rendcomb, Gloucestershire, Eng., Aug. 13, 1918; s. Frederick and Cicely S.; B.A., St. John's Coll., Cambridge U., 1940, Ph.D., 1943; D.Sc. (hon.) Leicester U., 1968, Oxford U., 1970, Strasbourg U., 1970; m. Joan Howe, 1940; children—Robin, Peter Frederick, Sally Joan. Beit Meml. Med. Research fellow U. Cambridge, 1944-51, research scientist dept. biochemistry, 1944-61; research scientist, div. head Med. Research Council Lab. of Molecular Biology, Cambridge, 1962-83. Recipient Nobel prize for chemistry, 1958, 80; Gairdner Found. ann. award, 1971, 79, William Bate Hardy prize Cambridge Philos. Soc., 1976, Copley medal Royal Soc., 1977; fellow King's Coll., Cambridge U., 1954. Mem. Am. Acad. Arts and Scis. (hon. fgn. mem.), Am. Soc. Biol. Chemists (hon.), Fgn. Assn., Nat. Acad. Scis. Contbr. articles in field to sci. jours. Home: Far Leys, Fen Ln, Swaffham Bulbeck, Cambridge CB5 ONJ, England Office: MRC Lab of Molecular Biology, Hills Rd, Cambridge CB2 2QH, England

SANGHVI, MANOJ KUMAR DALICHAND, oil company executive; b. Morvi, India, Sept. 13, 1928; came to U.S., 1952; s. Dalichand Hakubhai and Navalben Jagannath (Sanghani) S.; m. Shobhana Hiralal Shah, Apr. 1, 1958; children: Sunil, Parag, Pulin. BS with honors, U. Bombay, 1949, BS in Tech., 1951; MS, Ohio State U., 1953, PhD, 1956. Research fellow Govt. India Council Sci. and Indsl. Research, Bombay, 1951-52; research fellow Ohio State U., Columbus, 1953-55, research assoc., 1955-56; vis. fellow Ohio State U., 1956-57; project chem. engr. Standard Oil Co., Whiting, Ind., 1956-60; economiste conseil Société Civile Amoco, Paris, 1960-62; chief economist Amoco Ltd., London, 1962-63; econ. adviser Far East div. Amoco Internat. Oil Co., N.Y.C., 1963-65; sr. tech. coordinator Amoco India, Inc., New Delhi, 1965-68; coordinator corp. planning Standard Oil Co., Chgo., 1968-74, sr. coordinator planning and econs., 1974-83, now dir. internat. industry analysis; mem. Chgo. adv. bd. Coll. Engring., Ohio State U., 1988—. Trustee ILA Found., 1981—, pres., 1984-87. Contbr. articles to profl. jours. Fulbright fellow Ohio State U.; Ford Found. scholar Ohio State U. Mem. Am. Inst. Chem. Engrs. (chmn. nat. program com., mgmt. sci. 1972-78, chmn. mgmt. group 1980-82), India League Am. (v.p., bd. dirs. 1974-81, pres. 1978), Ill. Asian Am. Adv. Council to Gov., Sigma Xi, Phi Lambda Upsilon. Lodge: Rotary. Home: 1024 Heatherfield Lane Glenview IL 60025 Office: 200 E Randolph Dr Chicago IL 60601

SANGIORGI, MARIO, internal medicine educator; b. Catania, Italy, July 20, 1922; s. Giuseppe and Enrica (D'Alessandro) S.; m. Michela De Petra, Feb. 2, 1961; child, Giuseppe. MD, U. Bari, Italy, 1945. Resident in internal medicine Inst. Med. Clinic, Catania, 1946-51, asst., 1952-71; assoc. prof. cardiology 1st Univ., Rome, 1969-72, prof. med. semeiology, 1973-77; prof. internal medicine 2d Univ., Rome, 1983—. Contbr. articles to profl. jours. Recipient Internat. prize Gastroenteology, Rio de Janeiro, 1956, prize Cardiology Recordati, Milan, 1954. Fellow Acad. Medica di Roma (hon.), Acad. Lancisiana di Roma (hon.), Royal Coll. Physicians Ireland (hon.), Soc. Médicale des Hopitaux de Paris (hon.), Am. Coll. Chest Physicians; mem. Acad. Nacional de Medicina de Buenos Aires, Deutsche Akademie der Naturforscher Leopoldina (hon.), Soc. Portuguesa de Cardiol., Assn. Européenne Médecine Interne (pres. 1977-81), Internat. Soc. of Internal Medicine (pres. 1986-88).. Lodge: Lions. Home: Via C Maes 50, 00162 Rome Italy Office: Clinica Medica, Ospedale S Eugenio ple delé, 'Umanesimo, 00144 Rome Italy

SANGSTER, ROBERT EDMUND, international horse racing syndicate; b. Liverpool, Eng., May 23, 1936; s. Vernon S. Student Repton Coll. Race horse owner, including The Minstrel (won Epsom Derby, 1977); Alleged (won Prix de l'Arc de Triomphe, 1977, 1978); Detroit (won Prix de l'Arc de Triomphe 1980); Beldale Ball (won Melbourne Cup 1980); Our Paddy Boy (won Australian Jockey Club Cup 1981); Golden Fleece (won Epsom Derby 1982); Assert (won French Derby 1982); Lomond (won 2,000 Guineas 1983); Caerleon (won French Derby 1983); Gildoran (won Ascot Gold Cup 1984, 85); Marooned (won Sydney Cup 1986); Marauding (won Golden Slipper 1987); Midnight Fever (won Blue Diamond 1987); Bluebird (won King Stand 1987); Prince of Birds (won Irish 2000 Guineas 1988); Lady Liberty (won South Australian Oaks 1988); Handsome Sailor (won William Hill Sprint championship 1988); chmn. Vernons Pools, Liverpool. Leading winning racehorse owner, 1977, 78, 82-84 seasons; Leading owner Royal Ascot, 1977, 79, 84, 87, Australia, 86, 87. Office: The Nunnery, Douglas Isle of Man

SANGUINETI, EDOARDO, writer, educator; b. Genoa, Italy, Dec. 9, 1930; s. Giovanni and Giuseppina (Cocchi) Sanguineti; m. Luciana Garabello, Sept. 30, 1954; children—Federico, Alessandro, Michele, Giulia. B.A., U. Turin, 1956. Asst. prof. U. Turin, 1957-68, tchr., 1963-64; tchr. U. Salerno, 1968-70, prof., 1970-74; prof. Italian Lit., U. Genoa, 1974—. Author: Capriccio Italiano, 1963; Il Giuoco dell'Oca, 1967; author poetry: Laborintus, 1956; Opus metricum, 1960; Triperuno, 1964; Wirrwarr, 1972; Postkarten, 1978; Stracciafoglio, 1980; Segnalibro, 1982; Alfabeto Apocalittico, 1984; Novissimum Testamentum, 1986; Bisbidis, 1987; contbr. articles, essays to jours. Town councillor Commune Genoa, 1976-81; mem. chamber of deps. Italian Parliament, Rome, 1979-83. Office: Istituto di Letteratura Italiana, via Balbi 6, 16126 Genoa Italy

SANGUINETTI, JULIO MARIA, president of Uruguay, lawyer; b. Montevideo, Jan. 6, 1936. Grad. Faculty of Law and Social Scis., U. Montevideo, 1961; m. Marta Canessa; children: Julio Luis, Emma. Mem. Gen. Assembly, 1962-73; minister of labour and industry, 1969-72, minister of edn. and culture, 1972-73; pres. Comision Nacional de Artes Plasticas, 1967; then pres. of UNESCO commn. for promotion of books in Latin Am.; pres. of Uruguay, 1985—; leader Colorado Party, 1981—. Pres. Nat. Fine Arts Council. Contbr. articles to profl. jours. Address: Oficiena del Presidente, Montevideo Uruguay *

SANJURJO, F. JAVIER, textile company executive; b. Valencia, Spain, July 7, 1952; s. Francisco and Asuncion Sanjurjo; m. Carmen Banuls, July 19, 1980; children: Patricia, Javier. Licenciado, 1975. Lab. chief Textiles y Confecciones Europas, SA, Jativa, Spain, 1977-78, factory subdir., 1978-80, tech. mgr., 1980-87, gen. product mgr., 1987—. Mem. Am. Assn. Textile Chemists and Colorists, Assn. Espanola Quimicos y Coloristas. Liberal. Roman Catholic. Home: Gregorio Molina 6, Jativa, Valencia Spain Office: Textiles y Confecciones, Europeas SA, c/de Barcheta, Jativa Spain

SANKHYAN, ANEK RAM, anthropologist, researcher; b. Bilaspur, India, Aug. 20, 1951; s. Govind Ram and Bholand Sankhyan. BSc, Punjab U., 1972, MSc in Anthropology, 1974. Research assoc. Anthrop. Survey India, Dehra Dun, 1975—. Contbr. articles to profl. jours. Mem. Indian Sci. Congress Assn. Home: V Chunjhani PO Lehri Sarail, Bilaspur 174 027, India Office: Anthrop Survey India, 192/1 Kaulagarh Rd, Dehra Dun 248 195, India

SANKS, CHARLES RANDOLPH, JR., psychotherapist, clergyman; b. Yonkers, N.Y., Feb. 14, 1928; s. Charles Randolph and Myrtle Elizabeth (Bunn) S.; m. Jacquelyn Gibson, Nov. 11, 1949; children: Charlene Cynthia Saunders, Valeri Ann. B.A. cum laude, Stetson U., 1956; B.Div., Southeastern Sem., 1960; M.Th., Union Sem., 1961; postgrad., U. Salamanca, Spain, 1975; D.Ministry, Wesley Theol. Sem., 1977. Ordained to ministry Baptist Ch., 1957. Minister Judson Meml. Bapt. Ch., Fayetteville, N.C., 1957-60; interim minister First Bapt. Ch. of South Miami, Fla., 1961-62, Sunset Heights Bapt. Ch., Hialeah, Fla., 1962; sr. minister Starling Ave. Bapt. Ch., Martinsville, Va., 1963-69; assoc. pastor 1st Bapt. Ch., Washington, 1969-82, minister to Pres. U.S., 1976-80; developer ministry to community foster-care patients, 1975; dir. Pastoral Counseling Ctr. Greater Marlboro, Md., 1982-87; sr. counselor Washington Pastoral Counseling Service, 1982—; dir. clin. mgmt. Washington Pastoral Counseling Service, 1988—; ptnr. Pastoral Psychotherapy Assocs., Washington, 1984—; fellow Am. Assn. Pastoral Counselors, 1984—; trainer Journeyman Program, Fgn. Mission Bd., So. Bapt. Convention, 1968; mem. exec. com. D.C. Bapt. Conv., 1971-77; leader, speaker in liturgics and worship N.C. Bapt. Conv. Conf., 1972, 75; cons. Pastoral Psychotherapy Assocs., Washington, 1981-84; lectr. on worship and liturgics So. Bapt. Theol. Sem., Louisville, 1978; lectr. Stetson U., Deland, Fla., 1978, So. Ecumenical Conf., Atlanta, 1978. Bd. dirs. Uplift House, Washington, 1970-73, Day Care Ctr., Martinsville, Va., 1963-69, Big Brother Orgn. and Sheltered Workshop, Martinsville, Va., 1963-69. Served to cpl. USMC, 1946-49. Fellow Interpreters' House, Lake Junaluska, N.C., 1968-79; guest Oxford U., Eng., 1981. Mem. Am. Digestive Disease Soc. (bd. dirs. 1979-87). Democrat. Baptist. Avocations; travel; horseback riding; music; art. Home: 1090 Larkspur Terr Rockville MD 20850

SAN MIGUEL, MANUEL, painter, historian; b. Guayama, P.R., Sept. 29, 1930; s. Manuel and Luisa (Griffo) San M.; ed. U. P.R., 1947-51, U. Pa., 1966-68, Arts Students League, N.Y.C., 1968-69; m. Sandra Bonilla, July 12, 1969; children—Manuel, Ana. Historian, San Juan Nat. Historic Site, Nat. Park Service, 1953-63; exec. sec. Acad. Arts and Scis., San Juan, 1963-64; painter, writer, musician, 1964—; bd. advisors Am. Biog. Inst.cons. in field. Contbr. poetry to anthologies including Anthology of Latin American Poets, vol. III, 1987; rec. artist popular music of P.R. Served to capt. U.S. Army, 1951-53, Korea. Decorated Bronze Star with oakleaf cluster, Purple Heart, Combat Infantryman Badge, others; recipient citation Nat. Park Service, 1964, Am. Biog. Inst. Medal of Honor, 1987. Mem. Acad. Arts and Scis., Ateneo de Puerto Rico, Inst. Puerto Rican Culture (cons.), Internat. Platform Assn. Club: Lions (Lion of Yr. 1962-63). Home: 1214 Howell Creek Dr Winter Springs FL 32708

SANNA, RICHARD JEFFREY, lawyer; b. N.Y.C., July 20, 1949; s. Francis and Ann (Bryant) S.; m. Rosemarie A. Lagnena, Nov. 21, 1971; children: John, Kristin, Michele, Elisabeth, Kelly. BA, St. Johns U., Jamaica, N.Y., 1971; JD, Del. Law Sch., 1975. Bar: N.Y. 1977, U.S. Dist. Ct. (so. dist.) N.Y. 1978, U.S. Dist. Ct. (ea. dist.) N.Y. 1979, U.S. Ct. Appeals (2d cir.) 1979, U.S. Supreme Ct. 1980. Assoc. McKay, King, Castricone & Piazza, Queens, N.Y., 1978-80; sr. ptnr. Sarisohn, Sarisohn, Thierman, Carner & LeBow, Commack, N.Y., 1980-82; ptnr. Migliore, Sanna & Infranco P.C., Commack, 1982-85; sole practice Hauppauge, N.Y., 1985-86, Commack, 1986—. Cubmaster Cub Scouts Am., Bethpage, 1982-84; mem. adv. council St. Martins of Tours Ch., Bethpage, N.Y., 1983—; atty. Bethpage Civic Assn., 1985—. Mem. N.Y. State Bar Assn., Suffolk County Bar Assn. (chmn. fee dispute com. 1984-86), Assn. Trial Lawyers Am., N.Y. Trial Lawyers Assn., Columbian Lawyers Assn. Republican. Roman Catholic. Lodge: K.C. Home: 91 Sycamore Ave Bethpage NY 11714 Office: 320 Veterans Memorial Hwy Commack NY 11725

SANNIG, JESPER UFFE, pharmaceutical company executive; b. Copenhagen, Jan. 27, 1943; s. Arne Harry and Gunhild (Jensen) S. M.D., U. Copenhagen, 1963. Hosp. salesman Upjohn Pharms., Copenhagen, 1974-78; product mgr. OEC Scandinavia, Copenhagen, 1978-82, Radiometer, med. product advisor, Copenhagen, 1982-87; coordinator Clin. Trails, Dunnex, Ltd., 1987—; cons. educator Union of Danish Med. Students, Copenhagen, 1966-68. Author: Dialysis and Ventilation, 1967. Treas., Union of Old Pupils at Akademisk Studenterkursus, Copenhagen, 1970, chmn., 1971. Served with Danish Air Force, 1973-74. Recipient Mgmt. by Objective award Mercuri Inst., 1975; Shock Symposion award Freie Universitat Berlin, 1977; Psykofarmakology, Medicin Importor Foreningen, 1978; Product Tng. Course award Seton Group of Cos., 1978. Mem. Clin. Chemistry Data Communication Group. Home: Bryggervej 1B, 3200 Helsinge Denmark Office: Dumex Ltd, Prags Blvd 32, DK-2300 Copenhagen S Denmark

SANNITA, WALTER GEROLAMO, medical educator; b. Stazzano, Piedmont, Italy, May 29, 1945; s. Giuseppe Carlo and Elodia (Marchiori) S.; m. Titty Uglioni. MD, Med. Sch.-Univ., Genova, Italy, 1970; cert. in neurology, Med. Sch.-Univ., Parma, Italy, 1977; cert. in clin. neurophysiology, Med. Sch.-Univ., Genova, Italy, 1981. Cert. Ednl. commn. for fgn. med. grads., N.Y., 1976. Instr. Med. Sch.-Univ., Genova, 1970-76, asst. prof., 1977—; asst. prof. SUNY, Stony Brook, 1975-76, assoc. prof., 1976—; cons. Nat. Council of Research, Genova, 1977—; head Centre Neuroactive Drugs, Genova, 1980—. Adv. editor Research Communications Psychiatry Psychology Behavior, Rivista Italiana EEG Neurofisiol.; contbr. articles to profl. and scientific jours. Research fellow Nat. Council of Research, 1970-76, J.W. Goethe U., 1971-72. Fellow Internat. Pharmaco-EEG; mem. Internat. Soc. Clin. Electrophysiology Vision, Am. Acad. Clin. Neurophysiology, Italian EEG Soc., Italian League against Epilepsy. Lodge: Lions. Office: Inst of Neurophysiopathology, Ospedale San Martino, 16132 Genoa Italy

SANO, HIDEO, intelligence circulation agency administrator; b. Tokushima, Shikoku, Japan, Apr. 28, 1926; s. Jukichi and Fumi Sano. Grad. high sch., Okayama, Japan. From clk. to vice chief Tokushima Prefectural Port Authority, 1950-84; chief gen. affairs sect. Prefectural Civil Engring. Assn., Tokushima, 1984-86; promoter, chief Intelligence Circulation Agy., Tokushima, 1986—. Insp. Tokushima Civic Theatre, 1967—. Mem. Internat. Concord Conversation Seminar (proxy), Tokushima Worker's Music Assn. (vice chief, chief, advisor 1954—). Home: 3-34 Sarugaku Otanicho, 770 Tokushima, Shikoku Japan Office: Intelligence Circulation Agy, 1 Kachidokibashdori, 770 Tokushima, Shikoku Japan

SANO, KEIJI, neurosurgeon; b. Shizuoka Prefecture, Japan, June 30, 1920; s. Takeo and Haru (Sase) S.; m. Yaeko Sano. M.D., U. Tokyo, 1945, D.M.Sc., 1951. Asst., U. Tokyo, 1945-56, lectr., chief out patient clinic, 1956-57, asso. prof. neurosurgery, 1957-62, prof., 1962-81, emeritus prof., 1981—; prof., dir. dept. neurosurgery Teikyo U., 1981—; pres. 5th Internat. Congress Neurol. Surgery, 1973; chmn., dir Nat. Com. for Brain Research, Sci. Council of Japan, 1987—; bd. dirs. Fuji Brain Trust. Mem. Japan Neurosurg. Soc. (pres. 1965), Japanese Assn. Research in Stereoancephalotomy (pres. 1966), Asian and Australasian Soc. Neurol. Surgeons (pres. 1967-71, hon. life pres. 1971—), World Fedn. Neurosurg. Socs. (pres. 1969-73, hon. life pres. 1973—), Japanese Soc. CNS CT (pres. 1978—), Am. Assn. Neurol. Surgeons (hon.), Deutsche Gesellschaft für Neurochirurgie (hon.), Academia Eurasiana Neurochirurgica (pres. 1986); Soc. Neurol. Surgeons (hon.), Am. Acad. Neurol. Surgery (hon.), Congress Neurol. Surgeons (hon.), Scandinavian Neurosurg. Soc. (corr.), Am. Surg. Assn. (sr.), Am. Neurol. Assn. (corr.), ACS (hon.). Research on treatment of brain tumors, aneurisms, stereo-encephalotomy, vascular lesions. Home: 4-22-6 Den-en-chofu, Ota-ku, Tokyo Japan

SANO, RICHARD MITSUTO, medical manufacturing comany executive; b. Chgo., Apr. 9, 1940; s. Clifford Minoru and Lillian Yuri (Matsukawa) S.; student U. Chgo., 1956-59, U. Miami (Fla.), 1959-61; m. Marjorie Hersh Rosenblum, Oct. 9, 1966; children: Leslie Marer, Laura Davey, Lanie Veith. Research asso. neurology and med. instrumentation U. Miami Med. Sch., 1962-68; corp. sec. Phys. Instruments, Inc., Coral Gables, Fla., 1961-64; cons. Nuclear Data Co., 1963, N. Am. Aviation Co., 1963-64, Hewlett Packard Co., 1965-67; asst. product mgr. Picker Corp., Northford, Conn., 1967-69, product mgr., 1970-74, product line mgr., 1975-76, mgr. tech. resources, clin. diagnostic systems, 1977-80, mng. editor quar. Picker Nuclear Instrumental Jour., 1980; mgr. dept. med. applications Philips Med. Systems, Inc., Shelton, Conn., 1980-83, mgr. NMR sci. and med. applications dept., 1983-87; title med. research mgr. Philips Med. Systems N.Am., Inc., 1988—; U.S. indsl. rep. Internat. Electrotech. Commn., Internat. Congress Radiation Protection, 1983-86; cons. Soc. Nuclear Medicine, 1977-80. Concert pianist, soloist Chgo. Symphony Orchestra, 1955-56. Mem. Nat. Elec. Mfrs. Assn., (chmn. magnetic resonance sect. 1983-88, bd. dirs. diagnostic imaging and therapy div. 1983-88), Sci. Apparatus Makers Assn., Soc. Magnetic Resonance in Medicine. Author papers in field. Home: 153 Sanford Ln Stamford CT 06905 Office: Philips Med Systems N Am 710 Bridgeport Ave Shelton CT 06484

SANO, YOSHIAKI, manufacturing executive; b. Ichinomiya, Aichi, Japan, Nov. 16, 1930; s. Kumasaburo and Chitose Sano; m. Sakiko Oda, Oct. 7, 1958; children: Reiko, Yoshiko Honguu. BA in Engring., Gifu Univ., Japan, 1954. Various positions Matsushita Electric Indsl. Co., Ltd., Osaka, Japan, 1954-60; engring. supr. Rice Cooker div. Matsushita Electric Indsl. Co., Ltd., Osaka, 1960-66; engring. mgr. Rice Cooker div. Matsushita Electric Indsl. Co., Ltd., Osaka, Japan, 1966-72, gen. mgr. Rice Cooker div., 1972-82, exec. dir. Rice Cooker div., 1982-84, exec. dir. Kitchen Appliances Div., 1984—. Holder numerous patents. Recipient OHM Tech. award OHM Assn. Tech., 1962, Progress award Japan Elec. Mfrs. Assn., 1963, Gov.'s award Prefecture of Osaka, 1963, Nat. Commendations for Inventiveness, Japan Invention Assn., 1969. Mem. Acad. Light Metals (councilor Tokyo 1981—). Buddhist. Home: 3-8-98 Kouyoudai, Kawanishi City, Hyoogo 666-01, Japan Office: Matsushita Kitchen Appliance Div, 3-8-3 Himesato, Nichiyodogawa-ku, Osaka 555, Japan

SANSEVERINO, RAYMOND ANTHONY, lawyer; b. Bklyn., Feb. 16, 1947; s. Raphael and Alice Ann (Camerano) S.; m. Karen Marie Mooney, Aug. 24, 1968 (dec. 1980); children—Deirdre Ann, Stacy Lee; m. Victoria Vent, June 6, 1982. A.B. in English Lit., Franklin & Marshall Coll., 1968; J.D. cum laude, Fordham U., 1972. Bar: N.Y. 1973, U.S. Dist. Ct. (so. dist. and ea. dist.) N.Y. 1973, U.S. Ct. Appeals (2d cir.) 1974, U.S. Supreme Ct. 1986. Assoc. Rogers & Wells, N.Y.C., 1972-75, Corbin & Gordon, N.Y.C., 1975-77; ptnr. Corbin Silverman & Sanseverino, N.Y.C., 1978—. Contbr. articles to profl. jours. Articles editor Fordham Law Review, 1971-72. Recipient West Pub. Co. prize, 1972. Mem. ABA, Assn. of Bar of City of N.Y., N.Y. State Bar Assn. Republican. Roman Catholic. Clubs: Twin Oaks Swim and Tennis (Chappaqua, N.Y.) (bd. dirs. 1981—). Office: Corbin Silverman & Sanseverino 805 3d Ave New York NY 10022

SANSONE, FREDRICK RAWLS, television producer, gallery executive; b. Miami, May 11, 1952; s. Alfred G. and Rose Anne (Malyk) S. B.G.S., U. Miami, 1974. Producer, The Larry King Show, Sta. WIOD, Miami, 1975-78; ops. mgr. Sta. WNWS, Miami, 1978-79, exec. producer, 1985-86; producer To the Point, Sta. WCIX, Miami, 1979-81; exec. producer Frankly Speaking with Dr. Kathy Peres, Sta. WCIX, Miami, 1981-84, exec. producer Frankly Speaking with Chuck Zink, 1984-85, sta. editorial coordinator, 1983-85; v.p. Sadler Galleries, North Lauderdale, Fla., 1984—; producer, dir. Miami-Dade Community Coll., 1984-85. Recipient Outstanding Media award Dade County Psychol. Assn., 1982. Mem. Assn. Media Psychology, Nat. Acad. TV Arts and Scis. (Emmy award 1979, 82), Mensa.

SANTAELLA, IRMA VIDAL, N.Y. State supreme court justice; b. N.Y.C., Oct. 4, 1924; d. Rafael and Sixta (Thillet) Vidal; children: Anthony, Ivette. Acctg. degree, Modern Bus. Coll., 1942; BA, Hunter Coll., 1959; LLB, Bklyn. Law Sch., 1961, JD, 1967. Bar: N.Y. 1961. Sole practice N.Y.C., 1961-63, with ptnr., 1966-68; dep. commr. N.Y.C. Dept Correction, 1963-66; mem. N.Y. State Human Rights Appeal Bd., N.Y.C., 1968-83, chmn., 1975-83; justice N.Y. State Supreme Court, N.Y.C., 1983—; mem. N.Y.C. Adv. Council on Minority Affairs, 1982—, N.Y.C. Commn. on Status of Women, 1975-77. Founder, chmn. Legion of Voters, 1962-68; nat. del. Presdl. Democratic Convs., 1968, 72, 76, 80; vice chmn. N.Y. State del. 1976 Conv.;

founder Nat. Assn. for Puerto Rican Civil Rights, 1962, Hispanic Community Chest Am., 1972; chmn. bd. dirs. Puerto Rican Parade, 1962-67; bd. dirs. Catholic Interracial Council, 1968-81; nat. co-chmn. Coalition Hispanic People, 1970; fund raiser Boy Scouts Am., 1962-63; chmn. Children's Camp, South Bronx (N.Y.) 41st Police Precinct, 1967; active City-Wide Steering Com. for Quality Edn., 1962-64, Community Service Soc., 1972-74, Talbott Perkins Children's Services, 1973-75, Planned Parenthood Assn., 1968-69, Puerto Rican Crippled Children's Fund, 1965-69; founder N.Y. chpt. Clinica Grillasca, P.R. Cancer Assn., 1974—. Recipient citations for civic work Gov. Rockefeller, 1972, Gov. Carey, 1982; citations for work on voting and human rights N.Y. State Assembly, 1982, P.R. Senate, 1982, others. Mem. Am. Judicature Soc. Roman Catholic. Home: 853 Seventh Ave New York City NY 10019 Office: Supreme Ct State NY 60 Centre St New York NY 10003

SANTANGELO, MARIO VINCENT, dentist, association executive, educator; b. Youngstown, Ohio, Oct. 5, 1931; s. Anthony and Maria (Zarlenga) S.; student U. Pitts., 1949-51; D.D.S., Loyola U. (Chgo.), 1955, M.S., 1960. Instr. Loyola U., Chgo., 1957-60, asst. prof., 1960-66, chmn. dpt. radiology, 1962-70, dir. dental aux. utilization program, 1963-70, assoc. prof., 1966-70, chmn. dept. oral diagnosis, 1967-70, asst. dean, 1969-70; practice dentistry, Chgo., 1960-70; cons. Cert. Bd. Am. Dental Assts. Assn., 1967-76, VA Research Hosp., 1969-75, Chgo. Civil Service Commn., 1967-75; counselor Chgo. Dental Assts. Assn., 1966-69; mem. dental student tng. adv. com. Div. Dental Health USPHS, Dept. Health, Edn. and Welfare, 1969-71; cons. dental edn. rev. com. NIH, 1971-72; cons. USPHS, HEW, Region IV, Atlanta, 1973-76, Region V, Chgo., 1973-77; mem. Commn. on Dental Edn. and Practice, Fedn. Dentaire Internationale, 1984—. Bd. visitors Sch. Dental Medicine, Washington U., St. Louis, 1974-76. Served to capt. USAF, 1955-57. Recipient Dr. Harry Strusser Meml. award NYU Coll. Dentistry, 1985. Fellow Am. Coll. Dentists; mem. AMA (mem. edn. work group 1982-86), Assembly Specialized Accrediting Bodies (council on postsecondary accreditation 1981—), Am. Assn. Dental Schs., Odontographic Soc. Chgo., Am. (asst. sec. council dental edn. 1971-81, acting sec. 1981-82, sec. 1982—, asst. sec. commn. on dental accreditation 1975-81, acting sec. 1981-82, sec. 1982—, acting sec. commn. on continuing dental edn. 1981-82, sec. 1982-85), Ill., Chgo. dental assns., Am. Acad. Oral Pathology, Am. Acad. Dental Radiology, Am. Acad. Oral Medicine, Omicron Kappa Upsilon (pres. 1967-68), Blue Key, Xi Psi Phi. Contbr. articles to profl. jours. Home: 1440 N Lake Shore Dr Chicago IL 60610 Office: 211 E Chicago Ave Chicago IL 60611

SANTARELLO, PIERO ENRICO, computer company executive; b. Asmara, Ethiopia, Nov. 10, 1942; arrived in Italy, 1981; s. Angelo and Carla (Seroni) S.; m. Mariangela Albertin; children: Aurelio, Daniela. Grad., Comboni Coll., Khartoum, Sudan, 1962. Machine operator Olivetti Corp., Milan, 1962; salesman Addis Ababa, Ethiopia, 1963-64; salesman NCR, Addis Ababa, 1965, sales mgr., 1966-68; salesman Accra, Ghana, 1968, sales mgr., 1969-70; salesman Bologna, Italy, 1971-76, area mgr., 1976-80; pres., chief exec. officer SMC Computers, Carpi, Italy, 1981—. Office: SMC Computers, Via Nuova Ponente, 41012 Carpi Italy

SANTASALO, LAURI NIILO JOHANNES, engineering company executive; b. Helsinki, Finland, Nov. 21, 1924; s. Niilo Viljo and Maria Rakel (Saksa) S.; m. Hilkka Inkeri Engblom, June 16, 1951 (dec. Jan. 1973); children: Niilo Timo, Tuomas Rurik, Laura Inkeri; m. May-Inga Falck, Mar. 30, 1974. MSc in Engring., Tech. U., Helsinki, 1951. Sales engr. Santasalo-Sohlberg Corp., Helsinki, 1951-58, asst. mgr., 1958-64, pres., 1964-79, chmn., 1979-86, sr. cons. research and devel., 1979—; chmn. —, Hyryla, Finland, 1986—, research dir., 1987—. Contbr. articles on distilling and sterilization to profl. publs.; patentee in fields of water stills and sterilizing methods. Served with arty. Finnish Army, 1943-45. Decorated knight Order of Finnish White Rose. Mem Finnish Tech. Soc., ASME, Parenteral Drug Assn. Mem. Conservative Party. Lutheran. Home: Kuusisaarenpolku 7, SF 00340 Helsinki Finland Office: Santasalo Sohlberg Corp, Teollisuustie 2, SF 04300 Hyryla Finland

SANTEMMA, JON NOEL, lawyer; b. Oceanside, N.Y., Dec. 24, 1937; s. Esterino E. and Emilie E. (Davis) S.; m. Lynne Maurer, Dec. 27, 1960 (div. 1987); children: Suzanne, Deborah, Jon E., Christopher Jon; m. Carol Marie Hoffman, July 16, 1988. BA, Cornell U., 1960; JD, Fordham U., 1963. Bar: N.Y. 1963, U.S. Ct. Mil. Appeals 1969, U.S. Ct. Claims 1969, U.S. Supreme Ct. 1969, U.S. Dist. Ct. (ea. dist.) N.Y. 1977. Assoc. Parnell Callahan, N.Y.C., 1963-64; assoc. Warburton, Hyman, Deeley & Connolly, Mineola, N.Y., 1964-66; law sec. to adminstrv. judge of Nassau County, Mineola, 1966-71; sole practice, Mineola, 1971-74; ptnr. Santemma & Murphy, P.C., Mineola, and East Norwich, N.Y., 1974—; lectr. in field. Trustee Inc. Village of Laurel Hollow (N.Y.), 1979—; mem. Nassau County Republican Law Com., 1979—. Recipient Outstanding Man of Yr. in Law award L.I. U., 1976. Mem. Am. Bar Found., N.Y. Bar Found., N.Y. State Bar Assn. (ho. of dels. 1980—, mem. exec. com. 1984-85, v.p. 1986—), Nassau County Bar Assn. (pres. 1979-80, pres.'s award for outstanding service 1981), N.Y. State Trial Lawyers Assn., Suffolk County Bar Assn., Assn. Bar City N.Y. Clubs: Huntington Country, Winter, Elks (Huntington); Cold Spring Harbor (N.Y.) Beach; Garden City Golf. Contbr. articles to profl. jours. Address: 170 Old Country Rd Mineola NY 11501

SANTER, JEAN JACQUES, Luxembourg prime minister; b. Waaserbillig, Luxembourg, May 18, 1937; s. Joseph and Marguerite (Hengen) S.; B.S., Athenee, Luxembourg, 1956; Ph.D., Inst. Polit. Scis., Paris, 1960; m. Daniele Binot, Mar. 31, 1967; children—Patrick, Jerome. Lawyer, 1961-66, 74-79; Parliamentary Sec., Luxembourg, 1966-72; state sec. for social and cultural affairs, Luxembourg, 1972-74; minister fin., labor and social security, Luxembourg, 1979-84; prime minister, minister of fin., 1984—, minister of planning, post, telephone and telegraph . Mem. Luxembourg Parliament, 1974-79; mem. European Parliament, 1975-79, v.p., 1975-77; chmn. Christian Social Party, 1974-82. Served with Luxembourg Army, 1961-62. Christian Democrat. Roman Catholic. Office: Hotel de Bourgogne, 4 rue de la Congregation, Luxembourg-Ville Luxembourg *

SANTESSON, MANS OLOF MANSSON, journalist; b. Lund, Sweden, Oct. 15, 1932; s. Mans F.R. and Marta (Anderson) S.; m. My Stromberg, July 27, 1965; children: Helena, Rebecka, Gabriella. BA, U. Stockholm, 1956. Reporter Dagens Nyheter, Stockholm, 1956-59, polit. corr., 1959-62, leader writer, 1962-72, fgn. editor, 1973—. Home: Skeppargatan 48, S-114 58 Stockholm Sweden Office: Dagens Nyheter, S-105 15 Stockholm Sweden

SANTHANARAJ, STEPHEN, electronics manufacturing company executive, trainer; b. Kuala Lumpur, Selangor, Malaysia, Jan. 22, 1947; s. Joseph Baratharaj and Mary Thangam (Fernando) B. B.A., U. Malaya, Malaysia, 1971; Diploma in Personnel Mgmt., Singapore Inst. of Mgmt., 1979; MBA, Asian Inst. Mgmt., Philippines, 1981; Diploma in Tng. and Devel., Slough Coll., U.K., 1985. Asst. supt. customs Customs and Excise Dept., Singapore, 1971-76, supt. customs, 1976-81; tng. officer Philips Singapore Pte. Ltd., Singapore, 1981-82, sr. tng. officer, 1982, tng. mgr., 1983—; lectr. Singapore Inst. Mgmt., 1985, 86. Govt. Australia fellow, 1977, UN fellow, 1980. Mem. Asian Inst. Mgmt. Alumni of Singapore, Singapore Tng. and Devel. Assn., Am. Mgmt. Assn., Nat. Productivity Bd., Malaysia and Singapore Vintage Car Register. Roman Catholic. Clubs: Guild House, Singapore Cricket. Avocations: squash; tennis; reading; travel. Home: 7 Jalan Gapis, Singapore 2775, Singapore Office: Philips Singapore Pte Ltd, Lorong 1 TOA Payoh Lorong 1, Singapore 1231, Singapore

SANTIAGO, ROSA EMILIA, sales and marketing executive, entrepreneur; b. Havana, Cuba, Nov. 17, 1935; came to U.S., 1960; d. Emilio and Rosa (Fernandez) S.; m. Pedro P. Llaguno, July 19, 1963 (div. 1976); children—Rosa E., Peter E., Paul E. BA with honors, Fla. Internat. U., 1977. With sales and mktg. dept. Holiday Inn, Coral Gables, Fla., 1975-78, mktg. dir., 1983-86; sales mgr. Holiday Rent-a-Car, St. Petersburg, Fla., 1978-79, v.p., 1981; mktg. dir. Ramada Inn/Airport, Miami, 1981; S.E. dist. mktg. dir. Holiday Rent-a-Car System, Miami, 1981-82; pres. Amcrest Internat. Corp. sponsor U.S. Aviation Showcase and Exhbn.: Women in Arts, 1986—; instr. div. tourism St. Thomas U., Miami, 1980—, assoc. editor tourism mag., 1976-83; membership chmn. Tequesta dist. Boy Scouts Am.; bd. mem. at large Miami Forum; mentor Dade Found. Recipient Wood badge Boy Scouts Am., 1978, Dist. award of merit, 1984, Silver Beaver award, 1985. Mem. Women's C. of C. South Fla. (charter mem.), Brazilian Am. C. of C., Coral Gables C. of C. (bd. dirs., chmn. tourism com.), Internat. Council Air Shows, Council for Internat. Visitors (v.p.), League of Women Voters (bd. dirs.) Women in Arts (exec. dir. 1987—), Internat. Platform Assn., Coalition Hispanic-Am. Women, Alexander von Humboldt Soc. Ams. (pres.), Nat. Aeronautics Assn., New Theatre (bd. dirs.), Greater Miami Aviation Assn., Phi Lambda Pi. Democrat. Roman Catholic. Club: Miami Press. Home: 1510 Bird Rd Coral Gables FL 33146-1059 Office: Amcrest Internat 799 Brickell Plaza Suite 600 Miami FL 33131

SANTILLAN, ANTONIO, banker, motion picture finance executive; b. Buenos Aires, May 8, 1936; naturalized, 1966; s. Guillermo Spika and Raphaella C. (Abaladejo) S.; children: Andrea, Miguel, Marcos. Grad., Morgan Park Mil. Acad., Chgo., 1954; student, Coll. of William and Mary, 1958. Cert. real estate broker. Asst. in charge of prodn. Wilding Studios, Chgo., 1964; pres. Adams Fin. Services, Los Angeles, 1965-88. Writer, producer, dir. (motion pictures) The Glass Cage, co-writer Dirty Mary/Crazy Harry, Viva Knievel; contbg. writer Once Upon a Time in America; TV panelist Window on Wall Street; contbr. articles to profl. fin. and real estate jours. Served with USNR, 1959. Recipient Am. Rep. award San Francisco Film Festival, Cork Ireland Film Fest, 1961. Mem. Writer's Guild Am., Los Angeles Bd. Realtors, Beverly Hills Bd. Realtors (income/investment div. steering com.), Westside Realty Bd. (bd. dirs.), Los Angeles Venture Assn. (bd. dirs.). Lodge: Rotary. Office: Winning Visions Inc 425 N Alfred St Los Angeles CA 90048

SANTONOCITO, PAULA JOAN, bank executive, purchasing director; b. Riverhead, N.Y., Apr. 1, 1957; d. Anthony Philip and Clara Joan (Doman) S.; m. Francis Thaddeus Kennedy, Feb. 4, 1983. Student, L.I. U., 1975-78. Asst. mgr. legal advt. dept. San Diego Daily Transcript, 1979; methods analyst Saks Fifth Ave., N.Y., 1979-80, forms analyst, 1980-81, corp. purchasing exec., 1981-84; asst. cashier, mgr. materials mgmt. Midlantic Nat. Bank, Edison, N.J., 1984-85; asst. v.p., dir. materials mgmt. Midlantic Nat. Bank, Edison, 1985-87, v.p. materials mgmt., 1987—. Author poetry (3 poems) pub. in Street Mag., 1980. Vol. tutor Literacy Vols. Am., Woodbridge, N.J., 1983-84. Mem. Nat. Assn. Purchasing Mgmt, Purchasing Mgmt. Assn. N.J., Internat. Platform Assn. Club: Barefoot Bay Golf and Country (Sebastian, Fla.). Office: Midlantic Nat Bank 10 Jersey Ave Metuchen NJ 08840

SANTOPIETRO, ALBERT ROBERT, lawyer; b. Providence, R.I., Oct. 18, 1948; s. Alfred and Marie (Epifanio) S.; m. Linda Williams Standridge, Nov. 22, 1974; children: Hope, Spencer, Anna. BA, Brown U., 1969; JD, U. Va., 1972. Bar: R.I. 1973, U.S. Dist. Ct. R.I. 1973, Ill. 1974, Conn. 1983. Atty. Met. Life Ins. Co., Oak Brook, Ill., 1974-75, Seligman Group, N.Y.C., 1975-76; atty. Mut. Benefit Life Ins. Co., Newark, 1976-78, asst. counsel, 1978-81; atty. Aetna Life and Casualty, Hartford, Conn., 1981-82, counsel, 1982—. Mem. ABA, Am. Corp. Counsel Assn. Office: Aetna Life and Casualty City Pl Hartford CT 06156

SANTOS, EUGENIO MIGUEL, molecular biologist, researcher; b. Salamanca, Spain, May 5, 1953; came to U.S., 1979; s. Julian Santos and Angela De Dios; m. Isabel Santos, Jan. 3, 1982; children: Miguel, Javier. B.Sc., U. Salamanca, Spain, 1975, M.Sc., 1975, Ph.D., 1978. Postdoctoral fellow Roche Inst. Molecular Biology, Nutley, N.J., 1979-81; vis. fellow Nat. Cancer Inst., Bethesda, Md., 1981-84; prof. microbiology Salamanca U., Spain, 1984; staff scientist Nat. Cancer Inst., Frederick, Md., 1984-85; vis. scientist lab molecular microbiology NIH, Nat. Cancer Inst., Bethesda, 1985—. Contbr. articles to profl. jours. and books. Spanish-N. Am. Com. Sci. Coop. fellow, 1981; Fundacion Juan March, fellow, 1982; recipient medal U. Salamanca, 1983; Annual Monographic award Spanich Assn. against Cancer, 1984; 1st Severo Ochoa award for biomed. research, 1985. Mem. Am. Soc. Microbiology, Spanish Biochem. Soc., Spanish Soc. Microbiology, AAAS, Royal Acad. Medicine (Salamanca, Spain). Roman Catholic.

SANTOS, JOSE DA CONCEICAO, sales executive; b. Tomar, Portugal, Sept. 25, 1943; s. Francisco and Vitalina (Conceicao) S.; m. Guilhermina Lopes Machado, July 12, 1964; 3 children. Degree in Proficiency, Brit. Inst. of Lisbon, 1970-78; PhD in Mgmt., Instituto de Novas Profissões U., Lisbon, 1985. Med. rep. Beecham Portuguesa, Lison, 1970-73, supr., 1973-80, tng. mgr., 1980-85, sales mgr., 1985—. Served to lt. Portuguese Armed Forces, 1961-69. Roman Catholic. Home: Rua de Ceuta Lote, 158 17C, 2795 Lisbon Portugal Office: Beecham Portuguesa, Rua Sebastiao e Silva 56, 2745 Queluz Portugal

SANTOS, LEONARDO DIAZ, pathologist, educator; b. Talavera, Philippines, Aug. 5, 1951; s. Pablo C. and Demetria (Diaz) S.; m. Ofelia Ludovice, Dec. 21, 1975; children: Joseph Allan, Mary Desiree, Mary Carmel, Joseph Raymond. BS, U. of the East, 1972, MD, 1976. Diplomate Philippine Soc. Pathologists. Intern Dr. P.J. Garcia Meml. Research Ctr., Cabanatuan City, Philippines, 1976-77; residency in anatomic pathology U. of the East Ramon Magsaysay Meml. Med. Ctr., Quezon City, Philippines, 1978-81; head of lab. Good Samaritan Hosp., Cabanatuan City, 1981-85; med. specialist Quirino Meml. Gen. Hosp., Quezon City, 1982—; asst. prof. pathology Manila Cen. U.-Filemon D. Tanchoco Med. Found., Caloocan, Philippines, 1983-87, Angeles U. Found., Angeles City, Philippines, 1984—; cons. pathologist Quezon City Gen. Hosp., 1987—. Author: Manual in Pathology, 1984, (with others) Sylabus in Pathology, 1982. Research fellow U.S. Naval Med. Research Unit No. 2, Philippine Soc. for Microbiology and Infectious Diseases, 1987-88. Fellow Anatomic Pathology Soc. of the Philippines, Philippine Soc. of Pathologists. Roman Catholic. Home: 12 Quirino St, Valley Subdiv, Marikina Philippines Office: Angeles U Found, Dept Pathology, Angeles City Philippines

SANTOS SILVA, ARTUR EDUARDO, banker; b. Oporto, Portugal, May 22, 1941; s. Artur Morgado Ferreira and Alda (Brochado Oliveira) S.; m. Teresa Maria Rodrigues Vaz Osório, July 20, 1968; children: Artur Bernardo, Maria, Eduardo Nuno, Rodrigo. Degree in law, U. Coimbra, Portugal, 1963; grad. exec. program, Stanford U., 1985. Asst. prof. law U. Coimbra, 1963-67, prof., 1980-82; mgr. Banco Portuguès do Atlântico, Porto, Portugal, 1968-75; sec. treasury Ministry of Fin., Lisbon, Portugal, 1975-76; dep. gov. Cen. Bank, Lisbon, 1977-78; prof. Cath. U. Oporto, Porto, 1982-85; pres., chief exec. officer Portuguese Soc. Investment, Porto, 1981-85; pres. Portuguese Investment Bank, Porto, 1985—; mem. auditing bd. Sedes, Lisbon, 1979—; mem. adv. council Sch. Econs., New U. Lisbon, 1984—; mem. internat. council European Inst. Bus. Adminstrn., 1987—; chmn. auditing bd. Portuguese Indsl. Confedn., Porto, 1987—, Portuguese Indsl. Assn., Porto, 1987—. Mem. supervisory bd. Portuguese Assn. Integração Europe, Lisbon, 1978—; mem. supervisory bd. Nat. Inst. Adminstrn., Lisbon, 1982—, Oliveira Martins Found., Lisbon, 1983—. Served with Portuguese Navy, 1964-67. Named to Nat. Order of Merit as officer, French Govt., 1986. Mem. Comml. Assn. Porto, Brit.-Portuguese C. of C. (v.p. Lisbon chpt. 1987—). Clubs: Grémio Literário (Lisbon); Portuense, Lawn Tennis da Foz (Porto). Office: Portuguese Investment Bank, 284 Rua Tenente Valadim, 4100 Porto Portugal

SAN YU, president of Burma; b. Prome, Burma, 1919; student U. Rangoon, Commd. officer Burmese Army, 1942, advanced through grades to brig. gen.; mil. sec. to chief gen. staff, 1956-59, officer commanding North and Northwest mil. areas; mem. Revolutionary Council; dep. chief of gen. staff, commdr. land forces; minister fin. and revenue, 1963; gen. sec. Central Organizing com. Burmese Socialist Programme Party, from 1965, minister nat. planning, fin. and revenue, 1969-72; dep. prime minister, 1971-74; minister def., 1972-74; chief gen. staff, 1972-74; sec. Council State, 1974-81, chmn., 1981—; vice chmn. Socialist Econ. Planning Com. Address: Office of the President, Ady Rd, Rangoon Burma *

SAOULIS, ANTHONY CONSTANTINE, industrialist; b. Alexandria, Egypt, May 18, 1920; s. George and Jane (Dracopoulo) S. (parents Greek citizens); M.Sc. in Chem. Engring., Athens (Greece) Tech. U., 1943; student mgmt. sci. Delft (Netherlands) U., 1958-59; m. Angela Georgelou; 1 dau., Jane. Tech. mgr. Canellatos Ceramic Industry, Alexandria, 1946-60, gen. mgr., 1949-60; mng. dir. Hellenit Asbestos-Cement Industry, Athens, 1960—, pres. 1970—; chmn. bd. Kerem Ceramic Industry, Athens, 1960-83; v.p. Belplast Industry for Plastic Pipes, Athens, 1971-82, pres., 1983—; v.p., later pres. Evelit Industry for Bldg. Materials, Athens, 1978-82; chmn. bd. Neolit Gypsum and Gypsum Products Industry, Athens, also pres., 1983—. Served with Greek Air Force, 1944-45. Decorated Spl. award for action against forces of occupation. Mem. Hellenic Exporters Assn. (v.p. Athens chpt. 1975—), Fedn. Greek Industries-Athens (dir. 1976—, v.p., 1978—), Hellenic Standardization Orgn.-Athens (dir. 1976-82), Hellenic Asbestos and Asbestos-Cement Assn. (pres. 1978—), Indsl. Products Exporters Assn. Athens (v.p. 1980-82, pres. 1983—). Clubs: Athenian, Yacht of Greece, Glyfada Golf. Research on Greek industry, exports. Home: 15 Pindarou, 106-73 Athens Greece Office: 8 Omirou, 105-64 Athens Greece

SAPARDAN, WALUYO SUDIBIO, physician, consultant; b. Medan, North Sumatera, Indonesia, July 8, 1940; s. Herman and Siti Wulandari (Tjiptodharsono) S.; m. Siti Hermandari Kartowisastro, July 31, 1968; children: Wantya Nayadi, Widya Handarani. MD, U. Indonesia, 1965; degree in ob-gyn., U. Indonesia, Jakarta, 1969; degree in maternal-fetal medicine, Free U., Amsterdam, 1975. Intern Jakarta, 1963-65, resident, 1966-69; research fellow U. Indonesia, 1969-70; cons. Province Hosp., Jambi, Indonesia, 1971-73; dept. head Pertamina Hosp., Jakarta, 1973-76; sr. lectr. Cath. U. Med. Sch., Jakarta, 1976-85; bd. dirs., cons. Pondok Indah Hosp., Jakarta, 1986—; cons. in field; dir. hosp. Asih Maternity Hosp., Jakarta, 1984-86. Founder Pondok Indah Hosp., Jakarta, 1985. Mem. Internat. Assn. Ob-Gyn. (co-chmn. 1980—), Nat. Assn. Ob-Gyn. (treas. 1985-87), Jakarta Assn. Ob.-Gyn. Office: Private Clinic, Jl Panglima Polim 9/5, 12160 Jakarta Indonesia

SAPORTA, JACK, clinical psychologist, educator; b. N.Y.C., Oct. 21, 1927; s. David and Victoria (Fils) S.; m. Judith Hammond, May 28, 1967 (div. 1979); children: David, Victoria. AB cum laude, Adelphi U., 1951; PhD, U. Chgo., 1962. Diplomate Am. Bd. Profl. Psychology; registered psychologist. Supt. Tinley Park (Ill.) Mental Health Ctr., 1975-78; chief manpower tng. and devel. Ill. Dept. Mental Health, Chgo., 1978-82; dean, prof. Forest Inst. Profl. Psychology, Des Plaines, Ill., 1982-85; core faculty Fielding Inst., Santa Barbara, Calif., 1984—, Ill. Sch. Profl. Psychology, Chgo., 1985—; adj. instr. psychology Lake Forest Grad. Sch. Mgmt., 1988—; Mem. Ill. State Psychology Exam Com., Springfield, Ill., 1984—, profl. staff Forest Hosp., Des Plaines, 1977—, Luth. Gen. Hosp., Park Ridge, Ill., 1986—. Served with U.S. Army, 1946-47, Germany. Named Educator of Yr., Forest Inst., 1982. Mem. Am. Acad. Psychotherapists, Am. Psychol. Assn. (accreditation site vis. team), Ill. Psychol. Assn.; fellow Nat. Tng. Labs. Inst. (adj. staff). Home: 3201 California Ave Rolling Meadows IL 60008 Office: 2604 Dempster St Des Plaines IL 60016

SAPORTA, MARC, author, editor; b. Constantinople, Turkey, Mar. 20, 1923; came to France, 1929; s. Jaime and Simone (Nahmias) S. D. Law, U. Madrid, 1948; M.A. in Philosophy, U. Sorbonne, Paris, 1954. Research asst. UNESCO, Paris, 1948-53; literary critic L'Express, Paris, 1954-71; dep. editor-in-chief USIS, Paris, 1954-71, editor-in-chief, 1971-84. Author: Le Furet, 1959; La Distribution, 1961; La Quete, 1961; Composition No One, 1962; Les Invites, 1964; Le Grand Defi USA-URSS, vol. I, 1967, vol. II, 1968; Le Tour des Etats-Unis en 80 Jours, 1958; La Vie Quotidienne aux U.S.A., 1972; Go West, 1976; Vivre Aux Etats-Unis, 1986; Histoire du Roman Americain, 1970; editor, joint author essays: William Faulkner, 1983; Henry James, 1983; Isaac Bashevis Singer, 1984; Nathalie Sarraute, 1984; Henry Miller, 1985; Marguerite Duras, 1985; Mem. Pen Club. Home: 9 Rue Saint Didier, 75116 Paris France

SAPP, BARBARA DIANE, data process executive, realtor; b. Wenatchee, Wash., Nov. 27, 1940; d. John Franklin and Dorothy Doris (Kelsay) Cool; m. Leroy Sapp, Dec. 12, 1959 (div. 1975); children: Michael, Patrick, Stephen. BSBA, U. Redlands, 1979. Tape clk. GTE Data Services, Marina del Rey, Calif., 1975-76, IM-programmer, 1976-77, IM-programmer analyst, 1977-79, IM-systems analyst, 1979-80, IM-sr. tech. analyst, 1980-81; IM-supr. data resource mgmt. Gen. Telephone, Marina Del Rey, 1981-87; IM supr. tech. support systems, 1987—; GTE Calif., Thousand Oaks, Calif. Mem., organizer Conejo Valley Community Ctrs., Newbury Park, Calif., 1976 (council rep. 1988-89). Mem. Gen. Telephone Good Govt. Club, C.S.V.C. (pres. 1988—), Beta Sigma Phi (pres. 1974-75, 87-88, council pres. 1988—), Lambda Omega (preceptor, pres. 1987-88, ways and means 1988-89). Republican. Methodist. Avocations: flying, backpacking. Home: 3441 Frankie Dr Newbury Park CA 91320 Office: GTE of Calif 112 Lakeview Canyon Rd Thousand Oaks CA 91362

SAPP, DONALD GENE, minister; b. Phoenix, Feb. 27, 1927; s. Guerry Byron and Lydia Elmeda (Snyder) S.; m. Anna Maydean Nevitt, July 10, 1952 (dec.); m. Joann Herrin Mountz, May 1, 1976; children: Gregory, Paula, Jeffrey. AB in Edn., Ariz. State U., 1949; M Sacred Theology, Boston U., 1952, M of Div., 1960; D in Ministry, Calif. Grad. Sch. Theology, 1975. Ordained deacon, 1950, ordained elder, 1952. Dir. youth activities Hyde Park (Mass.) Meth. Ch., 1950-52; minister 1st Meth. Ch., Peabody, Mass., 1952-54, Balboa Island (Calif.) Community Meth. Ch., 1954-57, Ch. of the Foothills Meth., Duarte, Calif., 1957-63; sr. minister Aldersgate United Meth. Ch., Tustin, Calif., 1963-70, Paradise Valley (Ariz.) United Meth. Ch., 1970-83; dist. supt. Cen. West Dist. of Desert S.W. Conf. United Meth. Ctr., Phoenix, 1983—. Editor Wide Horizons, 1983—; contbr. articles to profl. jours. Chaplain City of Hope Med. Ctr., Duarte, 1957-63; trustee Plaza Community Ctr., Los Angeles, 1967-70; corp. mem. Sch. Theology at Claremont, Calif., 1972-80; pres. Met. Phoenix Commn., 1983-85; del. western jurisdictional conf. United Meth. Ch., 1982, 88, World Meth. Conf., Nairobi, Kenya, 1986, 88; bd. dirs. So. Calif. Council Chs., Los Angeles, 1963-67, Wesley Community Ctr., Phoenix, 1983—, Orange County (Calif.) Human Relations Council, 1967-70, Interfaith Counseling Service Found., 1982—. Served with USN, 1945-46. Mem. Ariz. Ecumenical Council, Kappa Delta Pi, Tau Kappa Epsilon, Blue Key. Democrat. Lodge: Rotary (pres.). Home: 5225 E Road Runner Rd Paradise Valley AZ 85253 Office: United Meth Ctr 1807 N Central Ave Suite 100 Phoenix AZ 84004-1508

SAPPAN, RAPHAEL, linguist; b. Tel Aviv, Israel, Apr. 10, 1928; s. Jacob and Hannah (Glant) Sapotinsky; M.A., Hebrew U. Jerusalem, 1967, Ph.D., 1975; research fellow Oxford Center Postgrad. Hebrew Studies, 1976. Lectr., U. Haifa, 1968-70; vis. asst. prof. U. Toronto, 1970-72; sr. lectr. U. Beer-Sheva, 1973-78; sr. vis. lectr. Bar-Ilan U., U. Haifa, 1979-80; vis. asso. prof. U. Man. (Can.), Winnipeg, 1981-82, Hebrew U. Jerusalem, 1982-83, U. Franch Comtè, Besançon, 1983-85, U. Lyon III, 1985-86; vis. fellow Oxford Ctr. Postgrad. Hebrew Studies, 1986-87; vis. prof. U. Toronto, 1987—. Served with Brit. Army, 1945-46, Israeli Army, 1948-49. Recipient Ansky prize City of Ramat-Gan, 1967. Mem. Israeli Assn. Applied Linguistics (secretariat 1976-78), Internat. Linguistic Assn., Assn. Jewish Studies, World Union Jewish Studies. Author: Syntax of the Poetical Dialect of the Old Testament, 1975; The Logical-Rhetorical Classification of Semantic Changes, 1983, 87. Home: Gibton, Rehovot 76910, Israel

SARAF, DILIP GOVIND, electronics executive; b. Belgaum, India, Nov. 10, 1942; s. Govind Vithal and Indira Laxman (Divekar) S.; m. Mary Lou Arnold, July 25, 1970; 1 son, Rajesh Dilip. B. Tech with honors, Indian Inst. Tech., Bombay, 1965; M.S.E.E., Stanford U., 1969. Sr. mgmt. trainee Delhi Cloth and Gen. Mills Co. (India), 1965-68; sr. research engr. SRI Internat., Menlo Park, Calif., 1969-78; project dir. Kaiser Electronics, San Jose, Calif., 1978-87; sr. engring. mgr. Varian Assocs., Santa Clara, Calif., 1987— ; cons. teaching U. Santa Clara, 1972, 73. Vice-chmn. bd. Peninsula Childrens' Ctr., Palo Alto, Calif. Mem. IEEE, Soc. Am. Inventors, Speakers' Bur. Contbr. articles to profl jours. Patentee in field. Club: Toastmasters. Home: 28050 Horse Shoe Ct Los Altos Hills CA 94022 Office: 3200 Patrick Henry Dr Santa Clara CA 95054

SARAFIAN, SYLVIA ANNETTE, computer systems specialist; b. Newton, Mass., June 16, 1931; d. Antranig Arakel and Elizabeth (Zorian) S.; B.A., Mt. Holyoke Coll., 1953. Chemist, Mass. Meml. Hosps., Boston, 1953-56; programmer, Honeywell Inc., Newton, Mass., 1956-58, System Devel. Corp., Santa Monica, Calif., 1958-61, Bedford, Mass., 1961-64, computer systems specialist, Santa Monica, 1966-71; programmer Bolt, Benarek & Newman, Cambridge, Mass., 1964-66; owner COMPUFARM and The Aurora, Marina Del Rey, Calif., 1971—, Advanced Bus. Microsystems, Marina Del Rey, 1981—; speaker symposium on computers in agr.; participant programs in field. Asso. mem. Calif. Republican State Central Com., 1975-76, 78; bd.

dirs. Marina Rep. Club, 1982; mem. Dornan for Congress campaign, 1976, 78, 80; active Calif. Women for Agr., 1977-79. Mem. Armenian Apostolic Church. Club: Appalachian Mountain. Author CompuFARM, computer system for agr., written for time-sharing, 1971, for microcomputers, 1981; author: The Aurora, written for time-sharing, 1977, for microcomputers, 1982; prodn. asst. for TV show Face to Face, 1976. Home: 519 Lantana St #138 Camarillo CA 93010 Office: PO Box 1909 Camarillo CA 93011

SARAGAT, GIUSEPPE, Italian government official; b. Sept. 19, 1898. Ed., U. degli Studi, Turin, Italy. Ambassador to France 1945-47; sec. Italian Socialist Labour Party, 1947-64; dep. prime minister Italy, Rome, 1947-49, 54-57, minister merchant marine, 1947-49, minister fgn. affairs, 1963-64, former mem. Senate; pres. Italian Republic, Rome, 1964-71, Social Dem. Party, Rome, 1975—; life senator. Address: Partito Socialista Democratico, Via Santa Maria in Via 12, 1-00187 Rome Italy *

SARAN, SANJAYA CHANDRA, mechanical engineer; b. Bombay, India, Feb. 6, 1951; s. Chandra Bhushan and Minal (Mehta) S.; m. Arati Pandit, Mar. 16, 1983; 1 child, Devaki. B.S. in Mech. Engring., Carnegie-Mellon U., 1973; M.B.A., Columbia U., 1975. Mng. dir. Saran Cons. Pvt. Ltd., Bombay, 1975-79; joint mng. dir. XLO India Ltd., Bombay, 1979-80, mng. dir., 1980—; chmn. XLO-GWB Cardan Shafts, Bombay, XLO United Clutch Products Ltd, Alwar, Rajasthan, India, BCL Forgings, Ltd., Bombay. Mem. Indian Machine Tool Mfrs. Assn., Soc. Automotive Engrs., Soc. Mech. Engrs. Club: Willingdon Sports (Bombay). Avocations: reading, squash. Home: 3 Westfield Estate B, Desai Rd, Bombay 400 026, India Office: XLO India Ltd, 78B Dr Annie Besant Rd, Bombay 400 018, India

SARANTOPOULOS, IOANNIS CONSTANTINOS, mathematics educator; b. Dorion, Messinia, Greece, Aug. 25, 1950; s. Constantinos G. and Emily I. (Katsambanis) S.; m. Dina D. Volga, 1987. Diploma, U. Patras, Greece, 1974; MS, U. Man., Winnipeg, Can., 1978; PhD, Brunel U., West London, 1987. Research fellow Nat. Tech. U. Athens, 1981-83; researcher Brunel U., London, 1983-85; research assoc. Kent (Ohio) State U., 1985-86; lectr. dept. math. Nat. Tech. U. Athens, 1987—. Contbr. articles to profl. jours. Mem. Greek Math. Soc., Am. Math. Soc. Home: Ionion Nison 28, 172 37 Athens Greece Office: Nat Tech U Athens, Zografou Campus, 157 73 Athens Greece

SARAPO, DONATO FRANK, physician; b. N.Y.C., July 2, 1925; s. Donato Frank and Theresa (Miglionico) S.; m. Joyce Sarapo; children—Terry, Nora, Guy, David. Student, Columbia U., 1949; M.D., N.Y. Med. Coll., 1952. Intern Detroit Gen. and VA hosps., Dearborn, Mich., 1952-53; resident Detroit Gen. and VA hosps., 1953-56; pvt. practice specializing in internal medicine Adrian, Mich., 1956—; chief of medicine, chief of staff Emma L. Bixby Hosp.; mem. Mich. State Bd. Med. Licensure 1969-78; pres., dir. Adrian Profl. Bldgs.; pres. Indsl. Medicine Assocs., Inc., 1985—; dir. Comml. Savs. Bank of Adrian. Alt. del. Rep. Nat. Conv., 1968; mem. Lenawee County Rep. Exec. Com.; treas. Lenawee County Reps., 1969-70; bd. dirs., pres. Cath. Social Services; bd. dirs. Detroit Cath. Charities, Goodwill Industries; mem. lay adv. bd., vice chmn. Siena Heights Coll., 1966-68, chmn., 1968-69, bd. dirs., 1970—; v.p., bd. dirs. Lenawee County Social Services Found.; bd. dirs. Guest House, 1970—; trustee Mercy Coll., Detroit, 1976-82. Served with U.S. Army, 1943-46. Mem. Mich. Med. Soc. (council mem. 1970—, del. 1960-70), Lenawee County Med. Soc., AMA, Mich. Soc. Internal Medicine, ACP, Mich. Assn. of Professions (dir. 1974-76), Adrian Area C. of C. Republican. Roman Catholic. Club: Rotary. Home: 1265 Cherry Dr Adrian MI 49221 Office: Mill St Profl Bldg Adrian MI 49221

SARASIN, KEN, trading company executive; b. London, Mar. 14, 1941; s. Kit and Bridie (Butler) S.; m. Sirichan Sarasin, Apr. 1, 1986. Engring. cert., Twickenham Coll., London; grad. Program for Mgmt. Devel., Harvard U., 1974. Asst. regional mgr. Worthington Corp., N.J., 1966-69; gen. sales mgr. Jardine Waugh, Bangkok, 1969-71; gen. mgr. Jardine Matheson (Thailand) Ltd., Bangkok, 1971-78, mng. dir., 1978—; bd. dirs. Oriental Hotel, Bangkok, Siam Flight Services, Bangkok, Jardine Schindler Co., Bangkok, Airside Co., Bangkok. Home: 26 Soi Nantha Sathorn, Bangkok Thailand Office: Jardine Matheson (Thailand) Ltd, 1032/1-5 Rama IV Rd, PO Box 40, Bangkok Thailand

SARAVAL, ENRICO, corporate executive; b. Venice, Italy, Nov. 25, 1940; s. Umberto and Ada (Vismara) S.; m. Maria Paleari-Henssler, Nov. 17, 1962 (div. Feb. 1981); children: Alessandra, Umberto, Elisabetta; m. Rosella Milesi, Sept. 26, 1981. BEE, Poly. U., Milan, 1972; AMP, Harvard U. Bus. Sch., 1986. Tech. employee C.E.I. S.p.A., Milan, 1964-66, comml. mgr., 1966-68, gen. mgr., 1968-72, mng. dir., 1972-79; co-mng. dir. Dravotec S.p.A., Milan, 1979-81, mng. dir., 1982—; chmn. La Finanziaria S.p.A., Compagnia Elettrotecnica Italiana S.p.A., Controlcei S.p.A., Dravo Costruttori S.p.A., Italservice S.p.A., Power Transmission Lines Ltd.; bd. dirs. Cementi Adriatico S.p.A. Office: Cei Holding SpA, Palazzo L1-Strada, 6-Milanofiori, 20089 Rozzano Italy

SARAZEN, RICHARD ALLEN, media company executive; b. Bklyn., June 27, 1933; s. Nicholas and Anna M. (Isacco) S.; m. Christine M. Horwith, July 27, 1974; children—Richard, Theresa, Mary, Barbara, David, Russell, Christina, Andrea. B.B.A., Hofstra U., 1955. C.P.A., N.Y., Pa., Calif. Acct. Arthur Young & Co., N.Y.C., 1955-58; ptnr. Alexander Grant & Co., N.Y.C., 1958-67; v.p. fin. Seeburg Corp., Chgo., 1967-69; mng. ptnr. Alexander Grant & Co., Pitts., Los Angeles, 1969-74; exec. v.p. News Am. Pub., Inc., N.Y.C., 1974-80; chmn. bd. XCor Internat., Inc., N.Y.C., 1980-82; chief fin. officer, dir. The News Corp. Ltd., Sydney, Australia, 1982—. Bd. dirs. N.Y.C. Center Found. Mem. Am. Inst. C.P.A.s, N.Y. State Soc. C.P.A.s. Republican. Roman Catholic. Club: Chgo. Athletic. Home: 1220 Park Ave New York NY 10028 Office: News America Pub Inc 10 E 53d St New York NY 10022

SARBANES, PAUL SPYROS, senator; b. Salisbury, Md., Feb. 3, 1933; s. Spyros P. and Matina (Tsigounis) S.; m. Christine Dunbar, June 11, 1960; children—John Peter, Michael Anthony, Janet Matina. A.B., Princeton, 1954; B.A. (Rhodes scholar), Oxford (Eng.) U., 1957; LL.B., Harvard, 1960. Bar: Md. bar 1960. Law clk. to Judge Morris Soper, 4th Circuit Ct. of Appeals, 1960-61; asso. Piper & Marbury, Balt., 1961-62; adminstrv. asst. Walter W. Heller; chmn. Council Econ. Advisers, 1962-63; exec. dir. Charter Revision Commn., Balt., 1963-64; asso. Venable, Baetjer & Howard, Balt., 1965-70; mem. 92d Congress from 4th Dist. Md., 93d-94th congresses from 3d Dist. Md., U.S. Senate from Md., 1977—. Mem. Md. Ho. of Dels., 1967-71. Democrat. Greek Orthodox. Office: 332 Dirksen Senate Bldg Washington DC 20510 also: Fed Office Bldg Baltimore MD 21201

SARDARI, AMIR MANSOUR, physician, consultant; b. Tehran, Iran, Sept. 23, 1923; s. Nasser Gholi and Nabir Almolouk (Ghajar Davalou) S.; children: Fereydoun Frederick, Catayoune Catherine. M.D., Faculté de Medecine, Paris. Specialist pneumologie Faculté de Medecine, Paris, 1954; resident, staff physician chest diseases Bellevue Hosp. Med. Ctr. Columbia U., N.Y.C., 1954-58; prof. U. Tehran, 1958-78; sec. for health population and social welfare Govt. of Iran, Tehran, 1965-77; dir. gen. Inst. Pasteur, Tehran, 1977-78; coordinator UN Fund for Population Activities, Haiti and Dominican Republic, 1979-80, Morocco, 1982-85, sr. adviser on population, UN coordinator, N.Y.C., 1980-82, Author: Population and Devel., 1969; Health and Population in Third World Countries, 1973, Primary Health CAre and Manpower Development in Developing Countries, 1974, Text Book on Chest Diseases, 1976. Mem. High Council Planning, Tehran, 1967-77, World Bank Panel for Future Policies on Health and Population, 1973; mem. expert com. on family health WHO, Geneva, 1974-80. Mem. Assn. Internat. for Promotion of Preventive Medicine. Avocations: photography; tennis; swimming; music. Home: 3 Rue Denis Poisson, 75017 Paris France

SARDI, EMILIO, pharmaceutical company executive, management consultant; b. Cali, Valle, Colombia, Oct. 29, 1943; s. Luis Emilio and Olga (Aparicio) S.; m. Liliana Blum, Dec. 19, 1970; children: Giovanna, Daniella. BS, MIT, 1964, MS, 1966. Asst. to pres. C.I.C.S.A., Cali, 1966-67; gen. mgr. Industrias TICO Ltd., Palmira, Colombia, 1967-68, Muebles Candle de Col. S.A., Palmira, 1968-74, IMPA Ltd., Palmira, 1974-78; gen. mgr. INFRA S.A., Cali, 1979-80, also bd. dirs.; v.p. Tecnoquimicas S.A., Cali, 1980—, also bd. dirs.; bd. dirs. Construcciones Populares S.A., Cali, Hotel Casablanca S.A., San Andrés, Colombia. Contbr. articles to profl. jours. Mem. Fedn. Colombiana de Golf (exec. com. 1982-83). Clubs: Colombia (bd. dirs. 1967-68), Campestre (bd. dirs. 1972-74). Office: Tecnoquimicas SA, Calle 23 No 7-39, Cali, Valle Colombia

SARGENT, DIANA RHEA, bookkeeper; b. Cheyenne, Wyo., Feb. 20, 1939; d. Clarence and Edith (de Castro) Hayes; grad. high sch.; m. Charles Sargent, Apr. 17, 1975; children: Rene A. Coburn, Rochelle A. Riddle, Weldy, Clayton R. Weldy, Christopher J.; stepchildren: Laurie Branch, Leslie E. Sargent. IBM proof operator Bank Am., Stockton, Calif., 1956-58, gen. ledger bookkeeper, Modesto, Calif., 1963-66; office mgr., head bookkeeper Cen. Drug Store, Modesto, 1966-76; pres. Sargent & Sargent Inc., Modesto, 1976—. Mem. Stanislaus Women's Center, Mem. NOW, San Francisco Mus. Soc., Nat. Soc. Public Accts. Office: 915 14th St Modesto CA 95353

SARGENT, WILLIAM EARL, educator, freelance writer; b. Balt., Aug. 2, 1919; s. Edward Brown and Lucy Edna (Simms) S.; grad. Balt. Poly. Inst.; B.A. in History, Am. U., 1953, M.Ed. in Adminstrn. and Supervision, 1963; postgrad. Va. Poly. Inst. and State U., 1976—. Dir., Burgundy Farm Country Day Sch., Alexandria, Va., 1960-63; elem. classroom tchr., Arlington County, Va., 1954-60, 67-70, 77-78, tchr. seminar for gifted elem. students, 1963-67, sch. social worker, 1970-72, child devel. cons., 1972-76, elem. sci. tchr., 1976-77, tchr. English as 2d lang., 1978-79; team leader, asst. to dir. Arlington-Trinity Tchr. Corps Project in Bilingual and Multicultural Edn., 1979, tchr. English as 2d Lang., 1980—, Dial-a-Tchr., 1984—; free lance writer 1981—; vol. Spanish Speaking Com. Va. Mem. Fairfax County Dem. Com., 1970; mem. Greenbelt Consumer Services Inc., 1979—. Served with USN, 1942-46; PTO. Fellow Am. Orthopsychiat. Assn.; mem. Am. Assn. Counseling and Devel., Am. Sch. Counselors Assn., United Teaching Profession, Assn. for Tchr. Edn., Irish Am. Cultural Inst., Clan Fraser Soc. N. Am., Clan Stewart Soc. in Am., Sim(ms)s Soc. (founder, chmn.), Scottish Heritage U.S.A., Wicomico County Hist. Soc., Furnace Town Found., Md. Hist. Soc., Friends of St. Andrews U., Scotland Internat. Platform Assn. Unitarian. Clubs: Conradh na Gaeilge (Washington); An Comunn Gaidhealach (Am. and Scotland). Home and Office: 902 Myers Circle SW Vienna VA 22180

SARIAN, JIRAIR NERSES, radiologist; b. Aintab, Turkey, Aug. 16, 1915; s. Nerses Sarkis and Nourita Hagop (Philipbossian) S.; B.A., Am. U. Beirut, 1937; M.D., U. Lausanne (Switzerland), 1940; B.D., Nazarene Theol. Sem., 1949; m. Jessie Helen Maghakian, Jan. 28, 1950; children—Norita, June, John. Rotating intern U. Lausanne Hosps., 1940-41, resident, 1941-44, chief asst., 1944-46; rotating intern Herrick Meml. Hosp., Berkeley, Calif., 1950-51; research and teaching fellow dept. oncology and radiology U. Kans. Med. Ctr., Kansas City, 1948-49, dept. radiology Huntington Meml. Hosp., Pasadena, Calif., 1951; practice medicine specializing in radiology, Los Angeles, 1951; asst. clin. prof. radiology U. Calif. Coll. Medicine, Irvine, 1965—; asst. clin. prof. U. of Calif., Los Angeles, Sch. of Nursing; med. dir. Union Rescue Mission; treas. bd. trustees Haigazian Coll. Author articles, books and booklets in English, Armenian and French. Recipient cert. of appreciation AMA, Am. Roentgen Ray Soc., 1963; Physicians Recognition award AMA, 1969, 72, 76. Diplomate Am. Bd. Radiology. Mem. Armed Forces Inst. Pathology (cert.), AMA, Calif., Los Angeles County med. assns., Am. Roentgen Ray Soc., Am. Coll. Radiology, Physicians Club. Home: 5305 Shenandoah Ave Los Angeles CA 90056 Office: 727 W 7th St Los Angeles CA 90017

SARIDJA, OZALP, economist; b. Nicosia, Cyprus, Dec. 25, 1932; s. Turgut and Hatice (Ismail) S.; divorced; children—Ruhsan, Emre. B.A. (hons.) DUnelm Politics & Econs., U. Durham, 1958; M.A., Columbia U., 1960. Econs. officer Ministry of Fin., Nicosia, Cyprus, 1960-62; dep. gov. Central Bank of Cyprus, Nicosia, 1962-64; dir. gen. Vakfs Orgn., Nicosia, 1964-68; sec.-gen. Econ. Planning Orgn., Nicosia, 1968-72; mng. dir. E.T.I. Ent., Ltd., Nicosia, 1972-81; mng. dir. Cypex Co. Ltd., Nicosia, 1981—; part-time lectr. econs. East Mediterranean U., Famagusta, North Cyprus. National Unity Party. Moslem. Home: Kervansaray No C110, Karaoglanoglu, Kyrenia North Cyprus Office: Cypex Co Ltd, Server Somuncuoglu St, Nicosia Cyprus

SARINO, EDGARDO FORMANTES, physician; b. Laoag City, Ilocos Norte, Philippines, Nov. 6, 1940; s. Epafrodito Cruz and Esperanza Raval Formantes S.; came to U.S., 1965, naturalized, 1983; M.D., Univ. of the East, 1964; m. Milagros Felix Ona, Dec. 6, 1965; children—Edith Melanie, Edgar Michael, Edenn Michele. Rotating intern St. Clare's Hosp., N.Y.C., 1965-66; resident in anatomical pathology Coney Island Hosp., N.Y.C., 1966; resident in gen. surgery Manhattan VA Hosp., N.Y.C., 1966-67, N.Y. U.-Bellevue Med. Center, N.Y.C., 1967-68; resident in radiology Manhattan VA Hosp., N.Y.C., 1968-71, fellow in diagnostic radiology, 1971-73; staff radiologist Mercer Med. Center, Trenton, N.J., 1973-83; chief nuclear medicine service, staff radiologist Louis Johnson VA Med. Ctr., Clarksburg, W.Va., 1983—; teaching asst. in gen. surgery N.Y. U.-Bellevue Med. Center, N.Y.C., 1967-68. Recipient Certificate of Merit, Mallinkrodt Pharm., 1969. Diplomate Am. Bd. Radiology. Mem. Soc. Nuclear Med., Am. Coll. Radiology, Radiol. Soc. N.Am., Harrison County Med. Soc., W.Va. Radiol. Soc., Assn. Philippine Practicing Physicans in Am., Philippine Radiol. Soc. Am. Contbr. articles to med. jours. Home: 96 Garden Circle Bridgeport WV 26330 Office: Louis Johnson VA Med Ctr Clarksburg WV 26301

SARKAR, SUBRATA KUMAR, engineer; b. Calcutta, India, Dec. 17, 1936; s. Dhirendra Nath and Puspila (Sinha) S.; B.Sc., Calcutta U., 1956; B.S. with honors, Glasgow U., 1965; M.S., Moore Sch. Pa. U., 1972; m. Eva Schaub, Dec. 22, 1961; children—Noemi, Andreas. Engr., Philips Labs., Zurich, Switzerland, 1962-63, Can. Marconi Co., Montreal, 1965-66; systems engr. RCA/Astro-Electronics div., Princeton, N.J., 1967-68; staff engr. Northrop-Page Communications Engrs., Washington, 1968-70; sci. tech. expert Gen. Directorate of Swiss Post, Telephone and Telegraph, Berne, 1970—. Mem. IEEE (Centennial medal 1984), Internat. Inst. Space Law, AIAA, Internat. Inst. Communication, Soc. Internat. Devel., World Future Soc. Club: Swiss Alpine. Home: Ackerweg, CH-3054 Schupfen Switzerland Office: Generaldirektion PTT, Viktoriastrasse 21, CH-3030 Berne Switzerland

SARKISYAN, FADEI TACHATOVICH, Soviet state official; b. 1923. Grad. Leningrad Mil. Acad. of Communications, 1946, Dr. of Tech. Sci., 1975; Academician of Acad. of Sci. Armenian SSR, 1977. Engring. posts in USSR Ministry of Def., 1946-63; dir. sci. research inst. in Armenian SSR, 1963-77; chmn. Council of Ministry, Armenian SSR, 1977—; mem. Politbur. Central Com., Armenian Communist Party, 1977—; dep. to USSR Supreme Soviet, from 1979; mem. Central Auditing Commn., Communist Party of Soviet Union, from 1981. Decorated USSR State Prize, 1971. Address: Armenian SSR Council of Ministry, Yerevan Armenian SSR USSR *

SARLEMIJN, ANDRIES, physics educator; b. Amsterdam, The Netherlands, Dec. 11, 1936; s. Willem Sarlemijn and Maria Baart; m. Lisette Fagnotti, July 7, 1984. Degree, U. Fribourg, Switzerland, 1969; postgrad., Den Haag (The Netherlands) Sch. of Econs. TSW, 1974. Asst. Inst. East European Studies, Fribourg, 1967-69; lectr. Social High Sch., Groningen, The Netherlands, 1969-70, Den Haag, 1970-71; lectr. Tech. U., Eindhoven, The Netherlands, 1971—; vis. prof. Univ. Bielefeld, Fed. Republic Germany, 1977-78. Author: Methodology of Technology, 1986, several other books; contbr. articles to profl. jours. Home: Dijkakkerweg 8, 5511 KX Knegsel The Netherlands Office: Eindhoven Tech U HG 9 02, PO Box 513, 5600 MB Eindhoven The Netherlands

SARMANTO, AUVO KALEVA, government executive, computer operations administrator; b. Helsinki, Finland, Mar. 3, 1923; s. Hillel and Laura (Pajumaki) S.; m. Kirsti M. Godenhjelm, Aug. 8, 1959; 1 child, Ari. MS, U. Helsinki, 1966. Temporary prof. computer sci. U. Jyvaskyla, Finland, 1967-70; project mgr. SITRA Fund of 50th Anniversary of Finland, Helsinki, 1970-71; computer chief Ministry of Edn., Helsinki, 1972—; mem. com. for. computer policy Govt. of Finland, 1972-74; chmn. Finnish-French Working Group New Tech. in Edn., 1982—; mem. Scandinavian Working Group New Tech. in Edn., 1983—; mem. Nordic Adv. Bd. for Computer Applications, 1987—. Decorated Officier dans l'Ordre des Palmes Academiques, France, 1985. Mem. Finnish Phys. Soc., Finnish Soc. for Future Research. Office: Ministry of Edn, Meritullinkatu 10, 00170 Helsinki Finland

SARMIENTO, RAMÓN COELLO, philologist, educator; b. Maceda, Orense, Spain, July 10, 1947; s. J. Ramón Sarmiento. m. Joaquina Guede, Aug. 7, 1976; children: Noemí, José Ramón. Grad., U. Autónoma, Madrid, 1973, PhD, 1977. Asst. prof. U. Autónoma, 1974-79, titular prof., 1980—. Editor: Historiografía de ling. Española, 1986, jour. Soc. Gen. de Librería Española, 1982—. Alexander von Humboldt fellow, 1987. Mem. Soc. Española de Lingüística, Soc. d'Histoire, Épistémologie, Langage, Internat. Conf. History Lang. Scis. Office: U Autónoma de Madrid, Cantoblanco, Madrid 28049, Spain

SARNEY COSTA, JOSÉ, president of Brazil, lawyer; b. Pinheiro, Brazil, Apr. 24, 1930; s. Sarney de Araujo Costa and Kiola Ferreira de Araujo Costa; m. Marly Macieira; children: Roseana, Fernando José, José Sarney Filho. LL.B., Maranhao Law Sch., 1953. Asst. to Maranhao State Gov., 1950-56, Maranhao State dep., 1956-65; gov. State of Maranhao, 1965-70; mem. Council Superintendency of the Devel. of the N.E., 1967; mem. Congress, 1956-66, majority asst. leader, 1961, senator, 1970-78, 79-86; vice-pres. of Brazil, 1985, pres., 1985—; asst. congl. leader Nat. Democratic Union, 1959-60, chair nat. bd., 1961-63; chair regional bd. for Maranhao, Nat. Renovator Alliance, 1970, chair nat. bd., 1979; chair nat. pro-tem bd. Social Dem. party, 1980, chair nat. bd., 1980; prof. law Social Service Sch., Maranhao Catholic U., 1957; prof. Brazilian issues Maranhao Bus. Adminstrn. Sch., 1957; hon. prof. Sch. Econs., Maranhao U.; lectr. War Coll., Rio de Janeiro, 1970-81, Mackenzie U., Sao Paulo, 1967, Navy War Coll., 1982, 83; del. numerous internat. confs. Author articles in field; poet. Mem. Maranhao Folklore Commn. Decorated Order of Cultural Merit (Maranhao); grand officer Brasilia Order of Merit, Order of Mil. Merit, Order of Naval Merit, Order of Air Force Merit, Rio Branco Order; recipient Machado de Assis medal Brazilian Acad. Letters; Found. of Sao Luis medal; Goncalves Dias medal; Pedro Alvares Cabral medal; Graca Aranha medal; Jose Bonifacio medal; grand officer Order of Ipiranga; others. Mem. Brazilian Acad. Letters, Brasilia Acad. Letters. Office: Office of President, Palacio do Planalto, 70150 Brasilia Brazil *

SARNI, VINCENT ANTHONY, manufacturing company executive; b. Bayonne, N.J., July 11, 1928; s. Alfred M. and Louise M. (Zoratti) S.; m. Dorothy Bellavance, Nov. 4, 1950; children: Louise Marie, Karen Lee, Vincent Anthony. B.S., U. R.I., 1949; postgrad., N.Y. U., 1950-52, Harvard U., 1973; LL.D. (hon.), Juniata Coll., 1979, U. R.I., 1985. Plant acct. Rheem Mfg. Co., Linden, N.J., 1950-53; dir. mfg. services Crown Can Co., Balt., 1953-57; dir. mktg. services Olin Corp., Stamford, Conn., 1957-68; with PPG Industries Inc., Pitts., 1968—, v.p. mktg. indsl. chem. dept., 1968-69, v.p., gen. mgr. indsl. chem. dept., 1969-75, v.p., gen. mgr. chem div., 1975-77, group v.p. chems. group, 1977-80; sr. v.p. PPG Industries Inc. (parent co.), Pitts., 1980-83, vice chmn., 1984, chmn., chief exec. officer, 1984—; bd. dirs. Brockway, Inc., Honeywell, Inc., Pitts. Baseball Assocs.; chmn. bus. adv. com. Inst. for Tng. of Handicapped in Advanced Tech. Exec. com. Allegheny Conf. on Community Devel.; trustee U. R.I. Found., Juniata Coll.; bd. dirs. Pitts. Guild for Blind, 1980; bd. dirs., vice chmn. Allegheny Gen. Hosp.; mem. bus. adv. council U. R.I., 1975—. Mem. Chem. Mfrs. Assn. (bd. dirs.), Soc. Chem. Industry, Bus. Higher Edn. Forum, Bus. Roundtable. Clubs: Duquesne, Rolling Rock, Laurel Valley Country, Chartiers Country, Allegheny, Point Judith Country. Office: PPG Industries Inc One PPG Place Pittsburgh PA 15272 *

SARNOFF, LILI-CHARLOTTE DREYFUS (LOLO SARNOFF), artist, business executive; b. Frankfurt, Germany (Swiss citizen), Jan. 9, 1916; d. Willy and Martha (Koch von Hirsch) Dreyfus; grad. Reimann Art Sch. (Germany), 1934, U. Berlin, 1935; student U. Florence (Italy), 1936-37; m. Stanley Jay Sarnoff, Sept. 11, 1948; children—Daniela Martha, Robert B.L. Came to U.S., 1941, naturalized, 1944. Research asst. Harvard Sch. Public Health, 1948-54; research asso. cardiac physiology Nat. Heart Inst., Bethesda, Md., 1954-59; pres. Rodana Research Corp., Bethesda, 1958-61; v.p. Catrix Corp., Bethesda, 1958-61; inventor FloLite light sculptures under name Lolo Sarnoff, 1968; one-woman shows: Agra Gallery, Washington, 1969, Corning Glass Center Mus., Corning, N.Y., 1970, Gallery Two, Woodstock, Vt., 1970, Gallery Marc, Washington, 1971, Hood Coll., Frederick, Md., 1972, Internat. Art Mart, Basel, Switzerland, 1972, Franz Bader Gallery, Washington, 1976, Art Barn, Washington, 1976, Art Fair, Washington, 1976, Gallery K, Washington, 1978, 81, Washington Project for Arts, 1980, Alwin Gallery, London, 1981, Galerie von Bartha, Basel, Switzerland, 1982, Gallery K, Washington, 1982, 83, 84, 85, La Galerie L'Hotel de Ville, Geneva, Switzerland, 1982, Washington Women's Art Ctr., 1985, Ctr. Internat. d'Art Contemporain, Paris, 1985, Pfalzgalerie, Kaiserlautern, Fed. Republic of Germany, 1985, Gallery K, Washington, 1987, Garden Show McCrillis Gardens, Bethesda, Md., 1987, Rockville (Md.) Recreational Ctr. Garden Show, 1988; represented in collections: Fed. Nat. Mortgage Assn., Washington, Corning Glass Center Mus., Nat. Air and Space Museum, Washington, David Lloyd Kreeger Collection, Washington, Kennedy Center, Washington, Nat. Acad. Sci., Chase Manhattan Bank, N.Y.C., Israel Mus., Jerusalem, Women in the Arts, Washington, others. Past trustee Nat. Ballet, Mt. Vernon Coll., Washington, Art Barn; past pres. "Arts for the Aging, Inc."; bd. dirs. Fgn. Student Service Council, Washington Performing Arts Soc. Mem. women's com., trustee Corcoran Gallery of Art. Recipient Gold medal Accademia Italia delle Arti e del Lavoro, 1980. Club: City Tavern (Washington). Democrat. Co-inventor electrophrenic respirator; inventor flowmeter. Home: 7507 Hampden Ln Bethesda MD 20814

SÁROSI, BÁLINT, ethnomusicologist; b. Rákos, Csik, Hungary, Jan. 1, 1925; s. István and Jozefa (Fülöp) S.; m. Jolán Benkö, Oct. 18, 1952; children: Sophie, Ursula. PhD, Pázmaány U., Budapest, Hungary, 1948; diploma in musicology, Acad. Music, Budapest, Hungary, 1956, diploma in composition, 1958. Research fellow Inst. Musicology, Budapest, 1958-74, head ethnomusicological dept., 1974. Author: Die Volksmusikinstrumente Ungarns, 1967, Gypsy Music, 1978, Folk Music, 1986. Mem. Internat. Council Traditional Music (bd. dirs. 1981). Home: Aldas u 11, H-1025 Budapest Hungary Office: Inst Musicology, Tancsics u 7, H-1014 Budapest Hungary

SARPANEVA, TIMO TAPANI, designer; b. Oct. 31, 1926; s. Akseli Johannes Sarpaneva and Martta Sofia Karimo; m. Ann-Mari Holmberg (div.); m. Marfatta Svennerig; 4 children. Ed. Indsl. Art Inst., Helsinki, Finland; Dr. Design (hon.), Royal Coll. Art, London, 1967. Designer, A. Ahlstrom Oy, Iittala Glassworks, 1950—; tchr. textile printing and design Indsl. Art Inst. Helsinki, 1953-57; artistic dir. Porin Puuvilla Cotton Mill, 1955-66; with AB Kinnasand Textile Mill, Sweden, 1964—; designer for Juhava Oy, Jughans AG, W.Ger., Opa Oy, Primo Oy, Rosenlew Oy, Roserthal AG, W.Ger., Villayhnyma; invited by Brazilian govt. to lectr. on and exhibit Finnish art glass, 1958; exhbn. architect for Finnish indsl. art exhbns., Europe, Japan, U.S.; architect Finnish sect. Expo 1967, Montreal, Que., Can.; bd. dirs. State Com. Design, Bd. Inst. Indsl. Design; exhibited in Finland, Sweden, Norway, Denmark, Iceland, Netherlands, Eng., Germany, France, Italy, U.S., Brazil, USSR. Decorated Order of Lion (Finland); recipient numerous awards, including 3 Grand prix Milan Triennali. Mem. Assn. Arts and Crafts (dir.). Address: Via Navegna 7, Minusio, Locarno Switzerland *

SARRAMON, JEAN-PIERRE FERNAND LOUIS, urologist, educator; b. Toulouse, France, Jan. 18, 1938; s. Henri and Jacqueline (Pellegrin) S.; m. Marie-France Lhez, Mar. 19, 1964; children: Christine, Benedicte. Baccalaureate in Lit. and Philosophy, St. Joseph Coll., Toulouse, 1956; M.D., Med. Faculty of Toulouse, 1970. Intern in medicine Univ. Hosp., Toulouse, 1964; prosector in anatomy Med. Sch., Toulouse, 1970, chief of clinic in surgery, 1970-71, chief of clinic in urology, 1971-77, asst. prof. urology, 1972-77, assoc. prof., 1978; chief of service urological transplantation dept. Univ. Hosp., 1982—; dir. exptl. surgery dept. C.H.U. Purpan, Toulouse, 1985—. mem. U. Nat. Counsel, 1987. Mem. editorial bd. Les Annales d'Urologie, Archivio Italiano di Urologia, Nephrologia Andrologia, 1988; contbr. chpts. to books. Served to commandant French Armed Forces, 1975—. Mem. French Transplantation Soc., French Soc. Urology, European Urol. Assn., Am. Urol. Assn. (corr.), Société Internat. d'Urologie, Belgium Urol. Assn., European Orgn. for Research in Treatment of Cancer, Internat. Microsurgery Soc., European Soc. for Organ Transplantation, Internat. Soc. Impotence Research, Rassemblement pour la République. Roman Catholic. Avocations: riding, mountaineering, sailing, golfing. Home: 6 Rue Darquie,

31000 Toulouse France Office: Urological Service CHU Purpan, Place du Docteur Baylac, 31000 Toulouse France

SARRAUTE, NATHALIE, author; b. Ivanowo, Russia, July 18, 1900; d. Ilya Tcherniak and Pauline Chatounowski; m. Raymond Sarraute, 1925; 3 children. Student Sorbonne, Ecole de Droit de Paris, Oxford U. Author: Tropismes, 1964; Portrait d'un inconnu, 1948, Portrait of a Man Unknown, 1959; Martereau, 1953, English transl., 1959, L'Ere du soupcon, 1956, English transl., The Age of Suspicion, 1964; Le Planetarium, 1959, English transl., The Planetarium, 1962; Les Fruits d'or, 1963, English transl., The Golden Fruits (Prix international de Litterature 1964), 1965; Entre la vie et la mort, 1968, English transl., Between Life and Death, 1969; Vous les entendez? (Do You Hear Them?) 1972; " disent les imbeciles" , 1976, English transl., " fools say" , 1977; L'usage de la parole, 1980, English transl., The Use of Speech, 1983; Enfance, 1983; plays: Le Silence, Le Mensonge, 1967, English transl., Silence and The Lie, 1969; Isma, 1970; C'est beau, 1973, English transl., It is Beautiful, 1978; Elle est la, 1978; Collected Plays, 1980; Pour un oui ou pour un non, 1982. Recipient Prix Internat. de Litterature, 1964; Grand Prix Nat., 1982; Prix Cavour, 1984. Office: 12 ave Pierre 1 de Serbie, 75116 Paris France

SARSFIELD, GEORGE P., lawyer; b. Vancouver, B.C., Can., Jan. 14, 1913 (parents Am. citizens); s. John M. and Margaret (LaValle) S.; B.A., J.D., U. Mont., 1950; m. Margeret Davis, May 23, 1942. Blk., laborer, miner, 1930-41; admitted to Mont. bar, 1950, since practiced in Butte. Past pres. Butte YMCA. Republican nominee Congress, 1st dist. Mont., 1960. Chmn. exec. bd. Mont. Coll. Mineral Sci. and Tech., 1968-71; chmn. bd. trustees U. Mont. Devel. Fund, 1967-70; adv. bd. Salvation Army, 1952—. Served from pvt. to capt. U.S. Army, 1941-46. Recipient Disting. Service award U. Mont., 1971, Pantzer award, 1975. Mem. Am., Mont. (past v.p.) bar assns., Am. Trial Lawyers Assn., U. Mont. Alumni Assn. (pres. 1964, chmn. bd. 1964-66), Mont. State Golf Assn. (past pres.), U.S. Golf Assn. (mem. sectional affairs com. 1968—), Phi Delta Phi, Alpha Kappa Psi, Phi Delta Theta. Clubs: Rotary (past local pres.; dist. gov. 1963-64, chmn. internat. constn. and by-laws com. 1969-70, internat. dir. 1973-75, internat. 1st v.p. 1974-75, chmn. exec. com. internat. bd. dirs. 1974-75). Club: Butte Country (past pres.). Former Mont. open golf champion; Mont. amateur golf champion, 4 years. Home: 2700 Floral Blvd Butte MT 59701 Office: Mayer Bldg Butte MT 59701

SARTRE, MAURICE, ancient history educator; b. Lyon, France, Oct. 3, 1944; s. Louis and Emma (Cusin) S.; m. Annie Fauriat, Dec. 23, 1971; children: Sophie, Thibaut. Agrégation d'Histoire, U. Lyon, 1968, DLitt, 1978. Asst. prof. U. Clermont-Ferrand, 1969-78; prof. U. Damascus, Syria, 1970-72; mem. Inst. Francais d'Archeologie du Proche Orient, Beirut, 1973-74; prof. ancient history U. Francois-Rabelais, Tours, France, 1978—, dean faculty human scis., 1980-83. Author: Trois Etudes Sur l'Arabie, 1982, Inscriptions Grecques et Latines de Syrie XIII, 1985, Bostra, 1985 (recipient prix Ambatielos, 1986). Decorated Chevalier des Palmes Academiques Ministry of Edn., 1985. Home: 30 rue des Perriers, 37170 Chambray-lés-Tours France Office: U Tours, 3 Rue des Tanneurs, 37000 Tours France

SARTZETAKIS, CHRISTOS, president of Greece; b. Thessaloniki, Greece, 1929; m. Efie Argyriou; 1 dau. Student U. Thessaloniki; grad. Salonika U.; postgrad. U. Paris, 1965-67. Bar: 1954. Judge Volos Ct. Misdemeanours, 1967-69; appeal judge, 1974-81; sr. appeal judge, Nafplion, 1981-85; pres. of Greece, 1985—. Office: Office of Pres, Athens Greece *

SARUNGU, SIMON TIRANDA, ophthalmologist, consultant; b. Rantepao, Indonesia, July 5, 1932; s. Jozef Sando Sarungu and Hana (Sea) Tarukbua; m. Esther Morra, Dec. 30, 1968; 1 child, Olivia Febrina. Diploma in medicine, U. Hasanuddin, Ujung Pandang, 1967. Dir. Makasar (Indonesia) Jr. High Sch., 1953-55, Surabaya (Indonesia) Sr. High Sch., 1957-60; lectr. Faculty of Medicine U. Hasanuddin, 1972-79, head tumor div. dept. ophthalmology, 1975-77, head dept. ophthalmology div. trauma, 1978—, sr. lectr. dept. ophthalmology, 1980—; cons. in field. Author: The Physiology of the Eye, 1980, Ocular Complications in Leprosy, 1985. Recipient cert. of merit The Netherlands of Tech. Help Orgn., 1972-73. Mem. Indonesian Med. Assn., Indonesian Ophthal. Assn. (cert. of merit). Club: Korpri (Ujung Pandang). Home: Jalan Gelora Massa 37, Ujung Pandang Indonesia Office: U Hasanuddin, Jalan Mesjid Raya 55, Ujung Pandang Indonesia

SARUYA, HIROMICHI, manufacturing executive; b. Japan, Sept. 21, 1941; s. Kakichi and Tokiko Saruya; m. Yukiko Saruya; 2 children. B in Econs., Kwansei-Gakuin U., Nishinomiya City, Japan, 1966. Mgr. procurement Sumitomo Heavy Industries Ltd., Osaka, Japan, 1980-87, Okayama, Japan, 1987—; mgr. V-E, market research Sumitomo Heavy Industries Ltd., Osaka, Japan, 1983-85. Inventor in field. Democrat. Buddhist. Home: 3-2-3 Nogami, Takarazuka City, Hyogo Prefecture 665, Japan Office: Sumitomo Heavy Industries Ltd, 8230 Shinminato Otoshima, Kurashiki, Okayama Japan

SASAKI, ITARU, architect; b. Hiroshima, Japan, Oct. 22, 1935; s. Shigeru and Yoshie (Kishima) S.; m. Fumiko Katamura, Jan. 8, 1987. B in Engring., Kanto Gakuin U., Yokohama, Japan, 1962. Registered architect. Mem. staff Tokoro Planning Office, 1963-65; architect Sasaki Itaru Archtl. Planning Room, Hiroshima, 1970—, also bd. dirs.; lectr. Kinki U., Kure, Japan, 1972—, Hiroshima Women's Coll., 1983—. Mem. Promotional Com. for Indsl. Design in Hiroshima, 1979-82; mem. Steering Council for Art Exhbn. in Hiroshima, 1986-87. Recipient 34th Shinseisaku-Kyokai Prize For New Artists, 1970, Prize for Fine Work Japan Sign Design Assn., 1988. Mem. Peace Studies Assn. Japan, Japan Design Network, Archtl. Inst. Japan, Japan Inst. Architects. Club: Nippon Harmonica (councilor). Office: Hiroshima Japan

SASAKI, TAKASHI, mechanical engineer; b. Miyako, Iwate, Japan, Apr. 28, 1952; s. Shozo and Reiko S.; m. Machiko Takeda, Apr. 27, 1980; children: Ayaka, Haruka. B in Engring., Yamagata U., Yonezawa, Japan, 1975; M in Engring., Hokkaido U., Sapporo, Japan, 1978. Supr. Mitsui Mining Co., Ltd., Sunagawa, Japan, 1979-87; engr. Dow Kakoh K.K., Kanuma, Japan, 1987—. Mem. Japan Soc. Mech. Engring., The Soc. Chem. Engring. Home: 8-23 Minami-Cho, Kanuma, Tochigi 322-05, Japan Office: Dow Kakoh KK Kanuma Plant, 11-1 Satsuki-Cho, Kanuma, Tochigi 322, Japan

SASAKI, Y. TITO, business services company executive; b. Tokyo, Feb. 6, 1938; came to U.S., 1967, naturalized, 1983; s. Yoshinaga and Chiyoko (Imada) S.; m. Janet Louise Cline, June 27, 1963; 1 child, Heather N. BS, Chiba U., 1959; postgrad. Royal Coll. Art, London, 1961, U. Oslo, 1962; MS, Athens Tech. Inst., Greece, 1964; postgrad. U. Calif., Berkeley, 1969. Chief designer Aires Camera Industries Co., Tokyo, 1958-59; tech. officer London County Council, 1961-62; researcher Athens Ctr. Ekistics, 1964-66; sr. researcher Battelle Inst., Geneva, 1966-68; project engr. Marin County Transit Dist., San Rafael, Calif., 1968-69; chief planning, research Golden Gate Bridge Dist., San Francisco, 1969-74; pres. Visio Internat. Inc., Somona, Calif., 1973—; chmn. steering com. Kawada Industries Inc., Tokyo, 1974-82; chief exec. officer Quantum Mechanics Corp., Somona, 1981—; bd. dirs., v.p. Sonoma Skypark, Inc., 1986—. Mem. Rep. Nat. Com. Mem. ASME, Am. Welding Soc., Helicopter Assn. Internat., AIAA, Am. Inst. Cert. Planners, World Soc. Ekistics, Brit. Soc. Long-Range Planning, Am. Vacuum Soc., Aircraft Owners and Pilots Assn. Roman Catholic. Office: Visio Internat Inc PO Box 1888 Sonoma CA 95476

SASLAW, LEONARD DAVID, chemist; b. Bklyn., Aug. 27, 1927; s. Issay and Sara (Singer) S.; B.S., CCNY, 1949; M.S., George Washington U., 1954; Ph.D. in Chemistry, Georgetown U., 1963. Chemist, Nat. Cancer Inst., NIH, Bethesda, Md., 1951-57, div. biophysics Sloan-Kettering Inst., N.Y.C., 1957-58, biochem. br. Armed Forces Inst. Pathology, Washington, 1958-65; dir. div. biochem. pharmacology, cancer chemotherapy dept. Microbiol. Assos., Bethesda, 1965-68; sr. biochemist Nat. Drug Co., Phila., 1968-69; chief lab. cellular biochemistry Albert Einstein Med. Center, Phila., 1969-70; clin. lab. dir. Med. Diagnostic Centers, Inc., Norristown, Pa., 1970-71; lab. dir. and research asso., renal lab., dept. medicine N.Y. Med. Coll., 1971-73; mgr. biochem. investigation Bio/Dynamics, Inc., East Millstone, N.J., 1973-74; profl. assoc. Smithsonian Sci. Info. Exchange, Washington, 1975-77; physiologist FDA, Washington, 1978-82, Rockville, Md., 1983—; lectr. residents' program in ophthalmology Washington Hosp. Center, 1967; cons. Burton, Parsons Co., Inc., Washington, 1978. Pres., Washington chpt. B'nai B'rith Young Men, 1954. Served in USN, 1945-46. Recipient Meritorious Achievement award Armed Forces Inst. Pathology, 1964. Mem. Am. Assn. Cancer Research, Am. Coll. Toxicology, Soc. of Toxicology (Mid-Atlantic chpt.), Am. Soc. Pharmacology and Exptl. Therapeutics, Sigma Xi. Democrat. Jewish. Contbr. articles to profl. jours. Home: 425 G St SW Washington DC 20024 Office: 5600 Fishers Ln Rockville MD 20857

SASMANNSHAUSEN, E.H. GUNTHER, geologist, metal corporation executive; b. Weidenau, Germany, June 3, 1930; diploma in geology, Aachen U. With Pressag AG, Hanover, W.Ger., 1955, tech dir., 1960, asst. dir., 1965, dir., 1968-72, pres., chief exec. dir., 1972—; chmn. Amalgamated Metal Corp. Ltd., London; pres. Neritschoftsvereinigung Metalle, Dusseldorf. Office: Pressag AG, Leibnizufer 9, 3000 Hanover Federal Republic of Germany also: Amalgamated Metal Corp PLC, Adelaide House, London Bridge, London EC4R 9DT England *

SASMOR, JAMES CECIL, publishing representative; b. N.Y.C., July 29, 1920; s. Louis and Cecilia (Mockler) S.; m. Jeannette L. Fuchs, May 30, 1965; 1 dau., Elizabeth Lynn. BS, Columbia U., 1942; MBA, Calif. Western U., 1977, PhD, 1979. Cert. Am. Bd. Med. Psychotherapists; cert. sex educator Am. Assn. Sex Educators, Counselors and Therapists. Advt. exec. N.Y. World Telegram, 1946-48, Chain Store Age, 1948-50, Am. Girl mag., 1950-59; registered rep. Nat. Assn. Security Dealers, 1956-57; founder, owner J.C. Sasmor Assocs. Publishing Reps., N.Y.C., 1959—; co-founder, pres., dir. adminstrn. Continuing Edn. Cons., Inc., Tampa, 1976—; pub. cons., 1959—; clin assoc., U. So. Fla. Coll. of Medicine, 1987-88; lectr. U. S. Fla. Coll. Nursing; dir. ednl. counseling U. So. Fla., Comprehensive Breast Cancer Ctr., Clin. Assoc. Coll. Medicine. Team tchr. childbirth edn. Am. Soc. Childbirth Educators; bd. dirs. Tampa chpt. ARC, also chmn. instructional com. on nursing and health; county nursing ednl. cons. ARC; dir. edn. counseling U. So. Fla. Comprehensive Breast Cancer Ctr. Served with USN, 1942-46. Recipient cert. appreciation ARC, 1979; Dept. Health and Rehab. Services award for Fla. Mental Health Inst. service, 1980. Internat. Council of Sex Edn. and Parenthood Am. U. fellow, 1981—. Mem. Assn. Pubs. Reps. (pres. 1965-66), Am. Soc. Psychoprophylaxis in Obstetrics (dir. 1970-71), Am. Assn. Childbirth Educators (co-founder, dir. 1972—), Nurses Assn. of Am. Coll. Obstetricians and Gynecologist (dir. Tampa chpt.), Health Edn. Media Assn., Nursing Educators Assn. Tampa. Contbr. chpts. to Childbirth Education: A Nursing Perspective, 1979; contbr. articles to profl. jours. Office: PO Box 16159 Tampa FL 33687

SASSER, JAMES RALPH, senator; b. Memphis, Sept. 30, 1936; s. Joseph Ralph and Mary Nell (Gray) S.; m. Mary Gorman, Aug. 18, 1962; children: Gray, Elizabeth. BA, Vanderbilt U., 1958, LLB, 1961. Bar: Tenn. 1961. Ptnr. Goodpasture, Carpenter, Woods & Sasser, Nashville, 1961-76; mem. U.S. Senate from Tenn., 1977—. Chmn. Tenn. State Dem. Exec. Com., 1973-76; so. vice chmn. Assn. Dem. State Chmn., 1975-76. Served with USMCR, 1958-65. Mem. ABA, NCCJ (dir. Nashville chpt.), UN Assn., Nashville Com. Fgn. Relations, Am. Judicature Soc. Office: Office of the Senate 363 Russell Senate Bldg Washington DC 20510 *

SASSOON, ADRIAN DAVID, art historian; b. London, Feb. 1, 1961; s. Hugh Meyer and Marion Julia (Schiff) S. Student, Wagner's, London, 1966-68, Sunningdale Sch., Berkshire, 1969-73, Eton Coll., Berkshire, 1974-78; diploma (hon.) in Fine Arts, Inchbald Sch. Design, London, 1979, Christie's Fine Arts Course, London, 1980. Curatorial asst. Dept. Decorative Arts, 1980-82; asst. curator The J. Paul Getty Mus., Malibu, Calif., 1982-84; asst. to mng. dir. Alexander & Berendt, Ltd., London, 1987—. Contbr. articles to profl. jours. Mem. French Porcelain Soc. (com. mem. 1985—). Club: Lyford Cay (Nassau).

SASSOU-NGUESSO, DENIS, president People's Republic of Congo; b. 1943. Mem. Council of State, 1976-77; 1st v.p. Mil. Com. Parti Congolais du Travail, 1977-79; minister of nat. def., 1977-79; pres. People's Republic of Congo, 1979—; also minister of def. and security. Address: Office of President, Parti Congolais du Travail, Brazzaville People's Republic of Congo *

SASTROWIDJOJO, HENDRO, physician; b. Surabaya, Indonesia, Mar. 23, 1941; s. Hiram Sastrowidjojo and Sharon Nugraha; m. Lana Wijaya; 1 child, Lily. Degree in medicine, U. Airlangga, Surabaya, 1965. Diplomate Indonesian Bd. Family Practice. Intern, then resident in general practice Dr. Soetomo Gen. Hosp., Surabaya, 1963-66; chief physician Pamekasan Dist. Hosp. Extension, Indonesia, 1966-67; dir. Pamekasan Dist. Health Service, 1967-70; med. officer Surabaya Municipality Health Ctr., 1970—. Contbr. articles to profl. jours. Project leader Surabaya Urban Leprosy Control Program, 1984—; sec. Indonesian Leprosy Found. Mem. Indonesian Med. Assn. Home: Iman Bondjol, Surabaya East Jawa, Indonesia Office: Surabaya Health Office, 5 Mergoyoso, Surabaya East Jawa, Indonesia

SASTRY, SHANKARANARAYANA, educator; b. Dodballapur, India, Nov. 4, 1938; s. Rama Jois and Lakshamma. BS honors in Math., Y. Mysore, India, 1959, MS in Math., 1960. Lectr. in math. Kle Soc.'s Coll., Belgaum, India, 1961-63, Haveri, India, 1963-67; tchr. math. Ethiopian Ministry Edn., Makele, 1967-73, Addis Ababa, 1973—. Contbr. articles, notes to profl. jours. Named Tchr. of Yr., Ethiopian Ministry Edn., 1971. Mem. Math. Assn. Am., Math. Assn. Gr. Britain. Hindu. Home and Office: Box 21862, Addis Ababa Ethiopia

SATARAWALA, KERSHASP TEHMURASP, ambassador; b. Satara, Maharashtra, India, Feb. 15, 1916; s. Tehmurasp Pirosha Satarawala and Meherbai Pirosha (Dinbai) Chhiber; m. Frainy Kaikhushru Bilimoria, Dec. 28, 1947; children: Phiroza, Anita, Ferida. BA with honors, Nowrosjee Wadia Coll., Poona, India, 1937; MA in Econs., Govt. Coll., Lahore, India, 1939; SC, Staff Coll., Quetta, India, 1944; cert., B.I.S.F. Mgmt. Coll., Ashorne Hill, Eng., 1963. Cert. E.R.T., Environ. Mgmt. Inst. 1979. Various governmental positions Indian Adminstrv. Service, 1947-75; sec. gen. Family Planning Assn. India, Bombay, 1976; mem. minorities commn., coordinator, vice chmn. IX Asian Games 1982 Govt. India, New Delhi, 1981; concurrently lt. gov. Goa, Daman and Diu, adminstr. Dadra, Nagar and Haveli Govt. India, Panaji, Goa, 1983; gov. Punjab Govt. India, Chandigarh, 1984; ambassador of India Govts. Mex., Guatemala, El Salvador, Mexico City, 1985—; bd. dirs. Tata Chems. Ltd., Bombay, Gujarat State Fertilizers Co. Ltd., Baroda, Gujarat, Indian Oil Corp., Bombay, Air India Internat., Bombay, Hindustan Aeronautics Ltd., Bangalore, Indian Electricity bd., Mineral Devel., Indian Devel., others; chmn. bd. Gujarat Aromatics Ltd., Baroda. Author: Gujarat Plan for Tourism and Civil Aviation, 1972, Gir Lion Sanctuary Project, 1972; editor Perspective Plan of Gujarat: 1974-84, 1972. Mem. exec. com. World Wildlife Fund, Bombay, 1976-81; founding mem. Nat. Trust for Art and Cultural Heritage; life mem. Soc. Clean Environ., Bombay, mem. Nat. Com. Environ. Planning, Indian Bd. Wildlife. Decorated Burma Star, India medal, War medal, Gen. Service medal with SE Asia clasp, Govt. India, 1940-45; recipient Padma Bushan Pres. India, 1983; fellow Nuffield Found., London, 1963, Modern Edn. Soc., Poona, 1967—. Zoroastrian. Club: Delhi Gymkhana, New Delhi. Home: K-423 Narangibag Rd, Pune Marashtra 411001, India Office: Embassy of India, Av Musset 325 Col Polanco, 11550 Mexico City Mexico

SATHIASEELAN, NAGAMONEY KANDIAH SINNADURAI, medical administrator; b. Kuala Lumpur, Malaysia, Sept. 2, 1948; s. Nagamoney Kandiah Sinnadurai and Sinnadurai Namakal; m. Cumarasamy Rathimalar; children: Mohana, Dharmenderi. MBBS, U. Mysore, India, 1975; M in Health Planning, U. New South Wales, Sydney, Australia, 1984. Intern Gen. Hosp., Seremban, Negri Sembilan, Malaysia, 1976-77; med. officer Gen. Hosp., Kuantan, Pahang, Malaysia, 1978-80; med. officer in charge Dist. Hosp., Tanjong Karang, Selangor, Malaysia, 1981-84, Mentakab, Pahang, Malaysia, 1985; asst. dir. planning Ministry Health, Kuala Lumpur, Malaysia, 1987—. Fellow Royal Australian Coll. Med. Adminstrs.; mem. Malaysian Med. Assn., Jaffnese Cooperative Soc., Jaffnese Cooperative Housing Soc., Selangor/Kuala Lumpur Ceylon Saivites Assn. Hindu. Home: 43 Jalan Raja Muda, 50300 Kuala Lumpur Malaysia Office: Ministry of Health, Jalan Duta, Kuala Lumpur Malaysia

SATHIRAKUL, KAMCHORN, bank executive; b. Nakorn Sri Thammarat, Thailand, Aug. 10, 1933; m. Khun Panee; 1 child. AB in Econs., U. Mich., 1955, AM in Econs.; postgrad., Nat. Def. Coll., Thailand, 1984. 2d grade customs officer div. stats. Govt. Thailand, 1960-64, insp., economist dept. customs, 1964-70, dir. div. customs tariffs, 1970-74, dir. assessment div., 1974-76, dep. dir.-gen. for policy and adminstrn., 1976-82; dir. tax policy div. Office Fiscal Policy, Ministry of Fin., 1972-74, dir.-gen., 1982-84; gov. Bank of Thailand, Bangkok, 1984—, also bd. dirs.; mem. Nat. Customs Tariffs Com., 1963-84; apptd. mem. Nat. Petroleum Com., 1977; spl. lectr. on econometrics and ops. analysis Faculty of Accountancy, Chulalongkorn U., Thailand, Faculty of Econs., Thammasat U., Bangkok; mem. exec. sub-com. Bd. Investment, 1981; chmn. bd. Securities Exchange Thailand; bd. dirs. Indsl. Estate Authority Thailand, Telephone Orgn. Thailand, Thai Airways Internat. Co. Senator Nat. Legis. Council, 1972-74, Nat. Assembly, 1974. Decorated Knight, Grand Cross. Office: Bank of Thailand, 273 Samsen Rd PO Box 154, Bangkok Thailand

SATKUNANANTHAM, KANDIAH, orthopedic surgeon; b. Malaysia, Dec. 22, 1949; arrived in Singapore, 1969; s. Vythilingam Kandiah and Poopathy Arulampalam; m. Bharathi R. Vaithinathan, Sept. 10, 1976; children: Neeta, Mala. MBBS, U. Singapore, 1974, M in Medicine, 1978. House officer Ministry of Health, Singapore, 1974-75, med. officer, 1975-78; lectr. Nat. U. Singapore, 1978-83, sr. lectr., cons. orthopedic surgery, 1983—; sr. lectr., cons. Singapore Gen. Hosp., 1978-85. Contbr. numerous articles to profl. jours.; author: (with others) Principles and Practices of Orthopaedic Surgery, Seminar in Orthopaedics, 1986. Recipient Howard Eddy Gold medal Royal Autralasian Coll. Surgeons, 1976. Fellow Royal Coll. Surgeons (Edinburgh); mem. Internat. Knee Soc., Western Pacific Orthopedic Assn. (asst. sec., sec. knee sect.), Singapore Med. Assn., Singapore Orthopedic Assn., Acad. Medicine Singapore. Home: 4 Sunset Crescent, Singapore 2159, Singapore Office: Nat U Hosp, Lower Kent Ridge Rd, Singapore 0511, Singapore

SATO, AISUKE, publishing company executive; b. Tokyo, Apr. 27, 1931; s. Ryutaro and Shizuko (Maruyama) S.; m. Yoko Kitazawa, Jan. 1, 1933; children: Mizuho, Chigusa, Asako, Kyoko. BA in Econs., Yokohama (Japan) Nat. U., 1955. Econ. reporter Toyo Keizai Shinpo Sha, Tokyo, 1956-70, chief editor kaishashikiho, 1970-72, chief editor weekly Toyokeizai, 1972-74; dir. Kansai bur. Toyo Keizai Shinpo Sha, Osaka, Japan, 1975-78; dir. editorial bd. Toyo Keizai Shinpo Sha, Tokyo, 1979-82, exec. dir. advt. bur., 1982—; lectr. econs. Shinshu U., Nagano, Japan, 1985-88; cons. policy Ministry Labour, tokyo, 1980—. Home: 1236 Takadacho Kohokuku, Yokohama 223, Japan Office: Toyo Keizai Shimposha, 1-2-1 Hongokucho Chuoku, Tokyo 103, Japan

SATO, HIDEO, political scientist, educator; b. Shimonita, Kanragun, Japan, Aug. 25, 1942; s. Kunio and Kikue (Morita) S.; m. Akiko Mano, Aug. 9, 1976; 1 child, Hideaki. BA in Social Sci., Internat. Christian U., Tokyo, 1967; MA in Internat. Relations, U. Chgo., 1970, PhD in Polit. Sci., 1976. Research assoc. The Brookings Instn., Washington, 1973-76; asst. prof. Yale U., New Haven, 1970-81, assoc. prof., 1981-82; prof. U. Tsukuba, Japan, 1982—, dean coll. internat. relations, 1988—; dir. Task force on Politics of Econ. Disputes, U.S.-Japan Econ. Relations Group, Washington and Tokyo, 1980-81; chmn. internat. polit. economy group Japan Internat. Relations Assn., Tokyo, 1987—. Co-author: Managing An Alliance, 1976, The Textile Wrangle, 1979, U.S. Policy Toward Japan and Korea, 1982, Coping with U.S.-Japanese Economic Conflicts, 1982, Canadian-Japanese Relations in Triangular Perspective, 1987. V.p. Am. Field Service Alumni Assn., Tsukuba br., 1987—. Fulbright All-Expense grantee, Washington, 1968; recipient Disting. Internat. Service award, Macalester Coll., Mpls.-St. Paul, 1969, Can.-Japan Research award Can. Govt., 1985; named to The Hon. Order of Ky. Cols., Commonwealth of Ky., 1987. Mem. Japan Internat. Relations Assn. (councilor), Japan Polit. Sci. Assn., Japan Am. Studies Assn., Am. Polit. Sci. Assn., Assn. for Asian Studies. Club: Internat. House of Japan. Office: U Tsukuba Shakai Kogakukei, 1-1-1 Tennodai, Tsukuba, Ibaraki 305, Japan

SATO, SHOZO, artist, educator; b. Kobe City, Japan, May 18, 1933; came to U.S., 1964; s. Takami and Midori Sato; m. Alice Y. Ogura, June 19, 1975. Degree in Fine Arts, Bunka Gakuin Coll., Japan, 1955; various diplomas in trad. arts. Dir. Kamakura Ryusei Sch. Fine Arts, Japan, 1959-64; faculty U. Ill., Urbana, 1964-66, 68—, artist-in-residence, prof. art, 1968—, dir. Japan House, 1976—, dir. opera, theatre prodns., 1965—; faculty U. Wis., Madison, 1966-67; vis. lectr. numerous colls. and univs. internationally, 1964—. Author: The Art of Arranging Flowers, 1966, The Appreciation of Oriental Art, 1967, The Art of Sumi-E, 1984: contbr. articles to profl. jours. Named Outstanding educator Am., 1975; recipient graphic design awards Prints Regional Design, 1979, 86, Joseph Jefferson award Chgo. Theatre Assn., 1982, 84, N.Y. Arts Dirs. award, 1984, 87, Bay Area Critics award, 1985, Faculty Achievement award Burlington No. Found., 1985, Hollywood Drama Logue award, 1985, Outstanding Achievement award Ryusei Sch. of Ikebana, Tokyo, 1987, Graphic design award Internat. Soc. Performing Arts Adminstrs., 1987, numerous other awards for Kabuki style adaptations. Mem. Am. Guild Mus. Artists, Gold Key (hon.). Office: U Ill 124 Fine Arts Bldg Champaign IL 61820

SATOH, ATSUKO, cooking instructor; b. Tokyo, June 1, 1953; parents: Yukinobu and Hiroko (Suzuki) S. BS in Analytical Chemistry, Tokyo U. Agr., 1977. Material analyst Hitachi Cen. Research Lab., Tokyo, 1977-84; pvt. practice cooking instr. Tokyo, 1984—; indexer Assist Systems, Tokyo, 1985—; cooking instr. Salon de Chie, Tokyo, 1986—; adv. specialist consumer affairs Ministry Internat. Trade and Industry, 1984—. Home: 3-17-3 Nukuikitamachi, Koganei-shi, Tokyo 184, Japan

SATOH, JIRO, machinery importing and office rental executive; b. Osaka, Japan, Jan. 12, 1935; s. Etsujiro and Tokino S.; m. Motoko Tomura, Nov. 14, 1959; children: Yuusuke, Shunsuke. M in Engring., Waseda U., Tokyo, 1958. Mgr. Chori Co., Ltd., Osaka, Tokyo, 1958-75, Sanjo Shoji Co., Ltd., Tokyo, 1976-86; pres. Mimimax Ltd., Tokyo, 1985—; pres. Tomura Satoh Ltd., Tokyo, 1983—. Mem. Tokyo Label Assn., Waseda Indsl. Mgmt. Assn. Home: 7-24-14 Kitakarasuyama, Setagaya-ku, 157 Tokyo Japan Office: Mimimax Ltd, 1-8-1 Tsukiji, Chuo-ku, 104 Tokyo Japan

SATOWAKI, JOSEPH ASAJIRO CARDINAL, archbishop of Nagasaki (Japan); b. Shittsu, Japan, Feb. 1, 1904. Ordained priest Roman Catholic Ch., 1932; served in various pastoral capacities in Nagasaki archdiocese after ordination; apostolic adminstr. Taiwan (Japanese possession), 1941-45; dir. Nagasaki temporary major sem., 1945-57; vicar gen. of Nagasaki, 1945; ordained 1st bishop of Kagoshima, Japan, 1955; archbishop of Nagasaki, 1968—; pres. Japanese Episcopal Conf., 1979—; elevated to cardinal, 1979; titular ch. St. Mary of Peace; mem. commn. Revision of Code of Canon Law. Mem. Congregation: Evangelization of Peoples; secretariat: Non-Christians. Office: Catholic Ctr, 10-14 Venomachi, Nagasaki Japan *

SAUCY, MIREILLE ELISABETH, public relations consultant; b. Les Genevez, Switzerland, Mar. 30, 1945; d. Gerald and Felicia (Kirchhof) S. Grad. Classical Sch., 1962, Comml. Sch., Zurich, 1965. Advt. asst. Wild Advt., Zurich, 1963-77; pub. relations cons. Swiss Fashion Assn., Zurich, 1966-71; advt. cons. BxW Advt., Zurich, 1971-73; pub. relations cons. Karl F. Schneiders, Zurich, 1973-81, M.E.S. Pub. Relations, Zurich, 1981—, also pres. bd., owner. Chief editor PR Rev., periodical, 1982—. Mem. Swiss Pub. Relations Soc. (dir.), Profl. Groups Swiss Public Relations Assn. Home: Hofwiesenstrasse 27, 8057 Zurich Switzerland Office: Häldeliweg 35, 8044 Zurich Switzerland

SAUD AL-FAISAL, PRINCE, Saudi Arabian minister foreign affairs; b. Riyadh, Saudi Arabia, 1940; s. King Faisal; B.A. in Econs., Princeton U. Former dep. minister petroleum and mineral resources Govt. of Saudi Arabia; minister of state for fgn. affairs, 1975, minister fgn. affairs, 1975—; leader Saudi del. to UN Gen. Assembly, 1976; spl. envoy diplomatic efforts to resolve Algerian-Moroccan conflict over Western Sahara, and civil war in Lebanon; mem. Saudi del. to Arab restricted summit, Riyadh, 1976, also to Summit Conf., Arab League, 1976. Founding mem. Charity Soc. Office: Ministry Fgn Affairs, Jeddah Saudi Arabia *

SAUER, DAVID ANDREW, librarian; b. Urbana, Ill., Feb. 25, 1948; s. Elmer Louis and Frances (Hill) S. B.A., Northwestern U., 1970; M.S., Simmons Coll., 1975. Reference librarian Boston U., 1976-78, bibliographer, 1978-84, sci. bibliographer, 1984-88, head Stone Sci. Library, 1988—. Mem. S.W. Corridor Project, Boston, 1977—, Forest Hills Neighborhood Improvement Assn., Boston, 1977—. Mem. ALA, Spl. Libraries Assn., Assn. Coll. and Research Libraries, New Eng. Online Users Group. Democrat. Home: 66 Weld Hill St Boston MA 02130 Office: Boston U Stone Sci Library 675 Commonwealth Ave Boston MA 02215

SAUL, BRADLEY SCOTT, communications, advertising and entertainment executive; b. Chgo., June 29, 1960; s. Richard Cushman and Yolanda (Merdinger) S. BS, Northwestern U., 1981, MA, 1982; postgrad., Loyola U., 1983-84. With info. services dept. Sta. CBS/WBBM Radio, Chgo., 1978-80; gen. mgr. Sta. WEEF Radio, Highland Park, Ill., 1979-81, Sta. WONX, Evanston, Ill., 1981-83; faculty advisor Sta. WNUR Radio, Evanston, 1981-83; pres., ptnr., co-founder Pub. Interest Affiliates, Chgo., N.Y., 1981—; pres. Chgo. Antique Radio Corp., 1986—; prof. Columbia Coll., Chgo., 1985-87; bd. dirs. Lake View Mental Health Ctr., Chgo. Contbr. articles to prof. jours. Named Outstanding Investigative Journalist, Warner Books, 1977. Mem. Nat. Assn. Broadcasters, Ill. Assn. Broadcasters. Jewish. Club: East Bank (Chgo.). Office: Pub Interest Affiliates 680 N Lake Shore Dr Suite 800 Chicago IL 60611 also: 12 W 31st St New York NY 10001

SAUL, IRVING ISAAC, lawyer; b. Washington, Pa., July 9, 1929; s. Israel Jacob and Jennie (Green) S.; m. Lita Brown, Dec. 29, 1950; children: Joanne Ilene, Sandra Lynn. BA, Washington and Jefferson Coll., 1949; LLB, U. Pitts., 1952; postgrad. Georgetown U., 1949, Ohio State U., 1951. Bar: Ohio 1952, U.S. Supreme Ct. 1961, U.S. Ct. Appeals (6th cir.) 1966, U.S. Ct. Appeals (7th cir.) 1978, U.S. Ct. Appeals (4th cir.) 1978, U.S. Dist. Ct. (so. dist.) Ohio 1954, U.S. Dist. Ct. (no. dist.) Ohio 1967, U.S. Dist. Ct. (ea. dist.) Wis. 1973. Sole practice, Dayton, Ohio, 1952—; spl. counsel Coolidge, Wall, Womsley & Lombard Co., L.P.A., Dayton, 1986—; cons. in antitrust litigation; bd. advs. Fed. Civil Practice Abstracts, 1986-87, Ohio Dist. Ct. Rev., 1988—; lectr. in field. James Gillespie Blaine scholar, 1948. Mem. ABA, Ohio Bar Assn. (chmn. fed. cts. and practice com. 1977-79, chmn. pvt. enforcement com. 1979—, bd. govs. antitrust sect. 1982—), Dayton Bar Assn. (chmn. fed. ct. practice com. 1976-77, 78-80, chmn. com. on judiciary 1987-88), Am. Judicature Soc., Phi Beta Kappa. Jewish. Lodge: Masons (Shriner). Contbr. articles to profl. jours. Office: 113 Bethpolamy Ct Dayton OH 45415

SAUL, MARK E., mathematics educator, consultant; b. N.Y.C., June 17, 1948; s. Sidney R. and Shura (Camenir) S.; m. Carol Portnoy, June 26, 1968; children—Susanna, Michael, Peter. BA, Columbia U., 1969; MA, Courant Inst. Math. Scis., NYU, 1974; PhD, NYU, 1987. Tchr. math. and computer sci. Bronx High Sch. Sci., N.Y., 1969-85; teaching fellow Adm. Hyman H. Rickover Found., 1985; computer cons./coordinator Bronxville Schs., N.Y., 1985—; dir. Research Sci. Inst. Ctr. Excellence in Edn., Mclean, Va., 1987; mem. N.Y. State Com. on Problem Solving, 1985—; cons. computer graphics 1984 Olympics ABC-TV, N.Y.C., 1983-84; pres. N.Y.C. Interscholastic Math. League, N.Y.C., 1979—; cons. Ednl. Testing Service, Princeton, N.J., 1980-82; panelist/cons. LaGuardia High Sch. Performing Arts, N.Y.C., 1977-86; tchr. trainer N.Y.C. Bd. Edn., 1981; tchr.-coordinator computer sci. Hollingworth Ctr. for Gifted, Tchrs. Coll., Columbia U., 1984; instr. Lehman Coll., 1984-86; Johns Hopkins U. Ctr. Talented Youth, 1986; Sarah Lawrence Coll., 1987. Author: Science/Mathematics Research Programs in the High School, 1982, The New York City Contest Problem Book, 1986; co-author: Advanced Placement Computer Science, 1985; author of enrichment problems in Leadership Manual for High School Supervisors in Mathematics, 1982; author, translator of articles, problems, and solutions, Crux Mathematicorum, 1980—; contbr. Jour. N.Y. State Assn. Computers and Tech. in Edn. Judge Internat. Math. Olympiad, Washington, 1981; author contest questions Mass. Math. League Ann. Contest, 1981. Recipient Presdl. award for Excellence in Teaching Math., NSF, 1984. Mem. Assn. Tchrs. Math. (exec. bd. mem. 1980-85), Am. Regions Math. League (exec. bd. mem., 1977—), Math. Assn. Am. (mem. com. on high sch. contests 1981—), Nat. Council Tchrs. Math., N.Y. Acad. Scis. Home: 711 Amsterdam Ave New York NY 10025 Office: Bronxville Sch 7710 Old Springhouse Rd Bronxville NY 10708

SAUL, SAMUEL BERRICK, academic administrator; b. West Bromwich, Eng., Oct. 20, 1924; s. Ernest and Maud (Eaton) S.; m. Sheila Stenton, Aug. 4, 1953; children: Christopher, Judith. B Com., Birmingham U., Eng., 1949; PhD, Birmingham U., 1953; LLD, York U., Can., 1981; Dr hc, Edinburgh U., Scotland, 1986. Lectr. Liverpool U., Eng., 1951-63; prof. Edinburgh U., 1963-78, dean faculty social scis., 1970-75, vice prin., acting prin., 1975-78; vice chancellor U. York, 1978—; vis. prof. U. Calif., Berkeley, 1959, Columbia U., N.Y.C., 1959, Stanford U., Palo Alto, Calif., 1969, Harvard U., Cambridge, Mass., 1973. Author: Studies in British Overseas Trade 1870-1914, 1960, The Myth of the Great Depression, 1969, Technological Change: The U.S. and Britain in the 19th Century, 1970; (with A.S. Milward) The Economic Development of Continental Europe 1780-1870, 1973, The Development of the Economies of Continental Europe 1850-1914, 1977. Chmn. Standing Conf. on Univ. Entrance, 1986—, Cen. Council Edn. and Tng. in Social Work, 1987—. Served to lt. British Army, 1943-47. Mem. Research Council European U. Inst. Social Dem. Home: Vice-Chancellor's House, Spring Lane, Heslington York Y01 5DZ, England Office: U York, Heslington, York Y01 5DD, England

SAULAT, QAMAR, physician; b. Bulundsher, Pakistan, June 28, 1945; parents Ibne Hasan and Jameela Khatoon; m. Saulat Majeed, Oct. 17, 1970; children: Bilal, Numairah, Naaima, Shamila. MD, Fatima Jinah Med. Coll., Lahore, Pakistan, 1966. Med. officer Pakistan Ordnance Factories Hosp., Wah Cantt, 1969-83, med. supr., 1983—. Moslem. Office: Pakistan Ordnance Factory Hosp, Wah Cantt Pakistan

SAULTER-HEMMER, JANET LYNN, computer programmer; b. Glen Ridge, N.J., Nov. 25, 1954; d. Lajoie Alvin and Nancy Harriet (Leatherberry) Saulter; m. Benjamin Joseph Singerline, Dec. 11, 1976 (div. 1981); 1 son, Scott Benjamin; m. Thomas Paul Hemmer, Oct. 7, 1984. AA, Thomas A. Edison Coll., Trenton, N.J., 1977, BA, 1983; grad. Chubb Inst. Computer Tech., Parsippany, N.J. Sec. to v.p. Rapidata Co., Fairfield, N.J., 1974-76; office mgr. Scottish Pedlar Co., South Orange, N.J., 1976-77; contract adminstr. McGraw-Edison Service, Fairfield, 1979-84; computer programmer Dun's Mktg. Services div. Dun & Bradstreet, 1984-87; tech. cons., Tiffany Computer Systems, 1987—; Recycling co-ordinator Presbyn. Ch., West Caldwell, N.J.; organizer, N.J. state pres. Orgn. Enforcement Child Support, past pres., West Caldwell; former mem. Essex County Adv. Commn. on Status of Women; chmn. Foster Grandparents Program, West Caldwell; former dir. Camp Fatima N.J., Livingston; youth adv. del. Presbytery of Newark; elder Presbyn. Ch. of West Caldwell; mem. Cub Scout Pack 177 and Boy Scout Troop 177 (com. chmn.); mem. Morris County Family Ct. Child Placement Rev. Bd., 1987-88. Mem. Jaycee-ettes (state dir. 1979-80, officer yr. 1980). Democrat. Club: Jr. Woman's (West Essex, N.J.). Lodge: Order Easter Star. Home: 8 Maple Ln Lake Hiawatha NJ 07034-1125 Office: Tiffany Computer Systems 170 Changeloride Rd Suite A2 Montville NJ 07054

SAUMIER, ANDRE, finance executive; b. Montreal, Que., Can., Aug. 26, 1933; s. Robert and Georgette (Sansoucy) S.; m. Suzel Brunel, Jan. 26, 1972; children—Sonia, Genevieve, Verushka. BA, U. Montreal, 1950; LTh, Angelicum U., Rome, 1955; MA, U. Chgo., 1958; MBA, Harvard U., 1962. Research assoc. Battelle Inst., Columbus, Ohio, 1962-63; dir. research Urban Affairs Council, Ottawa, Ont., Can., 1963-67; asst. dep. minister Can. Govt., Ottawa, Ont., Can., 1967-75; dep. minister Que. Govt., Quebec City, 1975-79; sr. v.p. Richardson Greenshields Co., Montreal, 1979-85; pres., chief exec. officer Montreal Exchange, 1985-87; chmn. Saumier Morrisson & Davidson Ptnrs. Inc., Investment Bankers, Montreal, 1987—; bd. dirs., chmn. Société Nationale de L'Amiante, Montreal, Seleine Mines Inc., Montreal, Unilever Can. Ltd., Davidson Ptnrs. Ltd., Toronto. Contbg. author books on environment. Bd. dirs. Nouveau-Monde Theater, Montreal, 1983—; v.p. Wilfrid Pelletier Found., Montreal, 1983—; chmn. Hotel-Dieu Found., Montreal, 1985—. Named officer Nat. Order of Niger, 1972; recipient Merit award Montreal C. of C., 1985. Club: University (Montreal). Home: 65 St Paul W Apt 403, Montreal, PQ Canada H2Y 3S5 Office: Saumier Morrisson & Davidson, Ptnrs Inc 800 Sq Victoria, PO Box 394, Montreal, PQ Canada H4Z 1J2

SAUNDERS, BASIL, public relations consultant; b. Rosyth, Fife, Scotland, Aug. 12, 1925; s. John Edward and Marjorie (Purdon) S.; m. Betty Smith, Jan. 7, 1957; children: Bill, Kate, Louisa, Etta, Eddie, Charlotte. MA, Oxford U., Eng., 1950. English asst. Coll. Tarascon, France, 1950-51; writer, editor Gen. Electric Corp., U.S., 1952-53; officer pub. relations Brit. Inst. Mgmt., 1954-57; assoc. dir. Pritchard, Wood & Ptnrs., U.K., 1957-63; head pub. relations Wellcome Found., U.K., 1963-78; dir.-gen. Assn. Spl. Libraries and Info. Bureaux, U.K., 1978-80; bd. dirs. Charles Barker Traverse-Healy Ltd., London, 1981—. Author: Crackle of Thorns, 1968; contbr. short stories to mags., articles to Manchester Guardian. Served to sub.-lt. Royal Naval Vol. Res., 1944-46. Fellow Inst. Pub. Relations. Office: Charles Barker, Traverse-Healy Ltd, 30 Farringdon St, London EC4A 4EA, England

SAUNDERS, BETTY HUEY (MRS. AULUS WARD SAUNDERS), journalist, playwright; b. St. Louis, July 11, 1909; d. Leslie and Kathryn Artimissia (Hyer) Huey; AA, Stephens Coll., 1929; BJ, U. Mo., 1931; m. Aulus Ward Saunders, June 12, 1931; children: Alan Ward, Susan Beth (Mrs. William Harry Cook). Staff writer, corr., columnist, advt. salesman News-Champion, St. Louis County, Mo., 1920-37; writer Oswego Palladium-Times, 1937-80; playwright one-act plays and radio plays, 1930—; contbg. author Oswego County (N.Y.) Messenger, 1981—; freelance writer with works pub. in newspapers and mags. including Reader's Digest, New Yorker, St. Louis Post-Dispatch, Wall St. Jour., People, Upstate, numerous others; author, dir. hist. musical SUNY centennial celebration, 1961. Pub. relations chmn., playwright, v.p. Oswego (N.Y.) Players, 1941-69; cons. pub. relations to N.Y. community theatres, 1949-69; lit. critic Nat. Writers Club, 1964—; pub., staged plays The Happy Medium, A Spinster's Telephone Call, Never Laugh At a Burglar, Meet My Deadline, Don't Argue with a Ghost, The Happy Medium; playwrighting cons. Oswego (N.Y.) Chancel Theatre Group, 1973-77. Formerly mem. exec. bd., chmn. pub. relations Oswego County chpt. ARC, also Community Chest. Recipient Jay L. Torrey scholarship U. Mo. Sch. Journalism, 1930; poetry and short story writing prizes Nat. Writers Club Contests, 1959, 64; prize N.Y. State Drummond One-Act Playwriting Contest, 1956; honored by Oswego Congregational Ch. of Christ for 50 yrs. in its choir, 1988. Mem. Bus. and Profl. Women's Club., Women in Communications, Alpha Gamma Delta (pres. 1930-31). Congregationalist. Editor The Grail, weekly religious mag., 1928-30. Editor-agt.-collaborator (with Dan Saunders) non-fiction books and articles on Alaska; model for Miss Am. on St. Louis gold medal for Charles Lindbergh, 1927. Address: 165 E 3d St Oswego NY 13126

SAUNDERS, DONALD LESLIE, hotel executive, real estate company executive; b. Brookline, Mass., Jan. 28, 1935; s. Irving Matthew Saunders and Shirley Brown; m. Liv Ullmann; children—Lisa M., Pamela R. AB in Econs., Brown U., 1957; grad., Inst. Real Estate Mgmt., 1963. Real estate broker, R.I., Mass. Pres., chief exec. officer Saunders & Assocs., Boston, 1957—; chmn., treas. The Boston Park Plaza Hotel Operating Co. Inc., 1976—, gen. ptnr.; co-owner Copley Square Hotel, Boston; trustee The Stoneholm Trust, Boston; bd. dirs. Hotel Lenox of Boston Inc. Bd. dirs. Park Sch. Corp., Brookline, Mass., The Jerusalem Found. Inc.; pres. Farview Inc.; vice chmn. Brown U. Corp. Facilities and Design Com.; advisor Coll. Mental Health Ctr. Inc., Boston; trustee emeritus Brown U., 1972—; bd. dirs., corp. mem. U.S. Com. for UNICEF; trustee The Boston Theatre Dist. Assn. Inc., The Boston Ballet Co.; trustee-at-large Combined Jewish Philanthropies of Greater Boston Inc.; bd. dirs. Jerusalem Inst. Mgmt. Inc. at Harvard Bus. Sch., Cambridge, Mass.; bd. dirs. Alzheimer's Disease and Related Disorders Assn. Mass. Recipient Nat. Jewish Hosp. and Research Ctr. Nat. Asthma Ctr. Humanitarian award, 1979, Back Bay Fedn. Community Devel. Ann. award, 1981, Historic Neighborhoods Found. award, 1986. Mem. Bldg. Owners & Mgrs. Assn., Greater Boston Real Estate Bd., Internat. Real Estate Fedn., Internat. Hotel Assn., Inst. Real Estate Mgmt., Mass. Assn. Corp. Real Estate Execs., Mass. Assn. Corp. Real Estate Execs., Nat. Assn. Realtors, Mass. Rental Housing Assn., New Eng. Innkeepers Assn. Inc., N.Y. Bd. Realtors, N.H. Bd. Realtors, R.I. Bd. Realtors, Urban Land Inst. Clubs: Lotos (N.Y.C.), Players (N.Y.C.), Union League (N.Y.C.); The Hope (Providence); 100 of Massachusetts (Boston), Tennis and Racquet (Boston); Eastern Point Yacht (Gloucester, Mass.); Belmont Country (Belmont, Mass.). Office: Saunders & Assocs 20 Park Plaza Boston MA 02116-4399

SAUNDERS, GEORGE LAWTON, JR., lawyer; b. Mulga, Ala., Nov. 8, 1931; s. George Lawton and Ethel Estell (York) S.; m. Joanne Rosa Helperin, Dec. 4, 1959 (div.); children: Kenneth, Ralph, Victoria; m. Terry M. Rose, Sept. 21, 1975. B.A., U. Ala., 1956; J.D., U. Chgo., 1959. Bar: Ill. 1960. Law clk. to chief judge U.S. Ct. Appeals (5th cir.), Montgomery, Ala., 1959-60; law clk Justice Hugo L. Black, U.S. Supreme Ct., Washington, 1960-62; assoc. Sidley & Austin, Chgo., 1962-67, ptnr., 1967—. Served with USAF, 1951-54. Mem. ABA, Ill. State Bar Assn., Chgo. Bar Assn., Am. Coll. Trial Lawyers, Order of Coif, Phi Beta Kappa. Democrat. Baptist. Clubs: Chicago, Saddle and Cycle, Mid-Am., Quadrangle, Law, Legal (Chgo.). Home: 179 E Lake Shore Dr Chicago IL 60611 Office: Sidley & Austin 1 First Nat Plaza Chicago IL 60603

SAUNDERS, JOSEPH ARTHUR, office products manufacturing company executive; b. Creston, Mont., July 9, 1926; s. Albert Henry and Edith Margaret (Rhodes) S.; m. Lois Evelyn White, June 19, 1948 (dec. Oct. 1986); children: Albert Henry II, Margaret Jean; m. Eva Homor, July 18, 1987; stepchildren: Rodney, Charmaine. Ed. pub. schs., Youngstown, Ohio and Winthrop, Maine. With Saunders Mfg. Co. Inc., Winthrop, 1947—, exec. v.p., 1967-77, pres., 1977-88 , chief exec. officer, 1967—, chmn. bd., 1988—; chmn. Saunders Internat. B.V., Netherlands; co-founder, sec., bd. dirs. Dirigo Bank and Trust Co., Augusta, Maine, 1969-86. Served with U.S. Army, 1945-47. Patentee in field. Mem. Maine C. of C. and Industry (bd. dirs. 1976-81, chmn. mfg. council 1978-82), Maine Metal Products Assn. (bd. dirs. 1983-84), Soc. Mfg. Engrs. (cert. new product engr.), Internat. Bus. Forms Industries (chmn. assocs. 1976-77, co-chmn. exhbts. com. 1978-82), Nat. Bus. Forms Assn., Nat. Office Products Assn., Am. Mgmt. Assn., Maine Metal Products Assn., Printing Industries New Eng. Am. Soc. Metals, Printing Industries Am., Am. Legion, others. Lodges: Masons, Shriners. Home: Touisett Point Readfield ME 04355 Office: Saunders Mfg Co Box 243 Winthrop ME 04364

SAUNDERS, LONNA JEANNE, lawyer, newscaster; b. Cleve., Nov. 26, 1952; d. Jack Glenn and Lillian Frances (Newman) Slaby. Student, Dartmouth Coll., 1972-73; AB, Vassar Coll., 1974; JD, Northwestern U., 1981. Bar: Ill. 1981. News dir., morning news anchor Sta. WKBK-AM, Keene, N.H., 1974-75; reporter Sta. KDKA-AM, Pitts., 1975; pub. affairs dir., news anchor Sta. WJW-AM, Cleve., 1975-77; morning news anchor Sta. WBBG-AM, Cleve., 1978; talk host, news anchor Sta. WIND-AM, Chgo., 1978-82; atty. Arvey, Hodes, Costello & Burman, Chgo., 1981-82; host, news anchor WCIU-TV, Chgo., 1982-85; staff atty. Better Govt. Assn., Chgo., 1983-84; news anchor, reporter Sta. WBMX-FM, Chgo., 1984-86; sole practice Chgo., 1985—; news anchor Sta. WKQX-FM, Chgo., 1987; talk host Sta. WMAQ-AM, Chgo., 1988—; instr. Columbia Coll., Chgo., 1987; guest talk host sta. WMCA, N.Y.C., 1983; host, producer "The Lively Arts" Cablevision Chgo., 1986; atty. Lawyers for Creative Arts, Chgo., 1985—. Contbg. editor Chgo. Life mag., 1986—; contbr. articles to profl. jours.; creator (pub. affairs program) "Ask The Schools" WBBM-AM. Recipient Akron Press Club award (best pub. affairs presentation); Scripps Howard found. grantee, 1978-79, 80-81; AFTRA George Heller Meml. scholar, 1980-81. Mem. Dartmouth Lawyers Assn., Women's Bar Assn. Ill., Investigative Reporters and Editors, Nat. Acad. TV Arts and Scis., ABA (exec. coms. Lawyers and the Arts, Law and Media), Sigma Delta Chi. Roman Catholic. Clubs: Chgo. Vassar, Vassar (N.Y.C.), Chgo. Dartmouth. Home: 1212 S Michigan Ave #2206 Chicago IL 60605

SAUNDERS, OWEN (ALFRED), mechanical engineer, educator; b. Sept. 24, 1904; s. Aldred George and Margaret Ellen (Jones) S.; ed. Birbeck Coll., London, Trinity Coll., Cambridge (Eng.) U.; m. Marion Isabel McKechney, 1935 (dec. 1980); 3 children; m. 2d Daphne Holmes, 1981. Sci. officer Dept. Sci. and Indsl. Research, 1926; lectr. applied math. physics Imperial Coll., 1932; Clothworkers' Reader in applied thermodynamics U. London, 1937, prof., from 1946, head dept., 1946-65, pro-rector, 1964-67, acting rector, 1966-67, vice chancellor, 1967-69, dean City and Guilds Coll., 1955-64, prof. emeritus; on loan Directorate Tubine Engines, MAP, 1942-45. Pres. Brit. Flame Research Com., British Assn., 1949; chmn. council Royal Holloway Coll., 1971-86; founder Fellowship of Engring., 1976. Author: The Calculation of Heat Transmission, 1932; An Introduction to Heat Transfer, 1950; contbr. articles to profl. jours. Created knight, 1965. Fellow Royal Soc.; hon. mem. Yugoslav Acad., Japan Soc. Mech. Engrs., ASME, Assn. Nat. Acad. Engring. Home: Oakbank, Sea Ln, Middleton Sussex, England *

SAUNDERS, PAUL CHRISTOPHER, lawyer; b. N.Y.C., May 21, 1941; s. John Richard and Agnes Grace (Kelly) S.; m. Patricia Newman, Sept. 14, 1968; children—Paul Christopher, Michael Eagan. A.B., Fordham Coll., 1963; J.D., Georgetown U., 1966; Certificat d'Études Politiques, Institut d'Études Politiques, Paris, 1962. Bar: N.Y. 1966, D.C. 1967, U.S. Supreme Ct. 1969, U.S. Ct. Appeals (2d cir.) 1971, U.S. Ct. Appeals (5th cir.) 1980, U.S. Ct. Appeals (11th cir.) 1981, U.S. Ct. Appeals (6th cir.) 1982, U.S. Ct. Appeals (9th cir.) 1985. Assoc. Cravath, Swaine & Moore, N.Y.C., 1971-77, ptnr., 1977—. bd. editors Georgetown Law Jour. Trustee Fordham prep. sch.; v.p., dir. Legal Aid Soc. Served to capt. JAGC, U.S. Army, 1967-71. Decorated Knight of Malta, 1982. Fellow Am. Bar Found.; mem. ABA, N.Y.C. Bar Assn., Cardinal's Com. of Laity. Democrat. Roman Catholic. Clubs: Apawamis, Westchester Country (Rye, N.Y.). Home: 1220 Park Ave New York NY 10128 also: Polly Park Rd Rye NY 10580 also: Cravath Swaine & Moore 1 Chase Manhattan Plaza New York NY 10005

SAUNDERS, ROBERT NORMAN, pharmacologist; b. Fairbury, Ill., Sept. 25, 1938. B.S., Purdue U., 1961, M.S., 1966, Ph.D., 1968. Research investigator Searle Labs., Skokie, Ill., 1968-74, group leader, 1974-79; sect. head Sandoz, Inc., E. Hanover, N.J., 1980-84, dept. head, 1984-85, dir. dept., 1985—. Current work: Platelets, thrombosis, platelet-activating factor, platelet-derived growth factor, atherosclerosis. Subspecialties: Cell biology (medicine); Pharmacology.

SAUNDERS, STUART JOHN, university administrator; b. Capetown, Republic South Africa, Aug. 28, 1931; s. Albert Frederick and Lillian Emily (Roe) S.; m. Noreen Merle Harrison, Oct. 6, 1956 (dec. 1983); children: John Stuart, Jane Noreen; m. Anita Louw, Feb. 5, 1984. MD, U. Capetown, U. Capetown, 1987. FRCP, FCPSA. Registrar in pathology and medicine Groote Shuur Hosp., U. Capetown, 1955-58, from lectr. to sr. lectr., 1961-71, prof., head med. dept., 1971-80; dep. prin. for planning U. Cape Town, 1978-80; research asst. Royal Postgrad. Med. Sch., London, 1959-60; vice-chancellor U. Capetown, 1981—; fellow in medicine Harvard Med. Sch. & Mass. Gen. Hosp., 1971-80; Contbr. numerous articles to profl. jours. Pres. South Africa Inst. Race Relations, 1986-87. Adams fellow, Eng., 1959; Internat. Research Fellow USPHS, 1964. Fellow Royal Coll. Physicians, Coll. Physicians of South Africa. Club: Owl (Captetown). Home: Glenara Burg Rd, Rondebosch 7700, Republic of South Africa Office: Univ of Cape Town, Pvt Bag, Rondebosch, Cape Town 7700, Republic of South Africa

SAUNDERS, TREVOR JOHN, classicist, educator; b. Corsham, Wiltshire, Eng., July 12, 1934; s. William John and Phyllis Margaret (Escott) S.; m. Teresa Mary Louisa Schmitz, Sept. 5, 1959; children: Clare Catherine Anne, Angela Mary Veronica. BA in Classics with honors, Univ. Coll., London, 1956; PhD, Cambridge U., 1962. Various lectureships U. London, U. Hull, U. Newcastle upon Tyne, Eng., 1959-72; sr. lectr. in Classics U. Newcastle upon Tyne, 1972-78, reader in Greek Philosophy, 1978, prof. Greek, 1978—; head dept. Classics U. Newcastle-upon-Tyne, 1976-82, 87—, dean faculty Arts, 1982-85; vis. mem. Inst. for Advanced Study, Princeton, 1971-72, 86; vis. fellow Humanities Research Ctr., Australian Nat. U., Canberra, 1986. Author: Notes on the Laws of Plato, 1972, Biliography on Plato's Laws, 1975; translator: Plato, The Laws, 1970, Aristotle, The Politics, 1981; contbg. editor Plato, Early Socratic Dialogues, 1987; contbr. articles to profl. jours. Active U. Newcastle upon Tyne Senate, Ct., Council, 1977—. Mem. Classical Assn. (mem. council 1973-79), Soc. for Promotion of Hellenic Studies (mem. council 1968-71, 1974-77), Cambridge Philol. Soc., Council Univ. Classics Depts. (chmn. 1981-84). Roman Catholic. Office: U Newcastle upon Tyne, Dept Classics, Newcastle upon Tyne NE1 7RU, England

SAUNDERS, WILLIAM LOCKWOOD, financial consultant; b. Seattle, Dec. 13, 1911; s. William Guy and Elizabeth (Ruggles) S.; m. Marjorie Allen, Nov. 30, 1945 (dec.); 1 dau., Mary Lee; m. Margaret Cella, Feb. 13, 1959. B.A., U. Wash., 1948; M.B.A., Northwestern U., 1950. Resident mgr. Drumheller Ehrlichman & White, Aberdeen, Wash., 1933-36; with W.L. Saunders (investments), 1936-42; sales mgr. H. Irving Lee & Co., San Jose, Calif., 1946; fin. cons. 1946-48; with A.G. Becker & Co., Inc., Chgo., 1949—; v.p. A.G. Becker & Co., Inc., 1951—, dir., 1960—; chmn. Oceanatic Steamship Co., 1958-61; pres. Gisholt Machine Co., Madison, Wis., 1963-66; also dir.; chmn. Long Island Tankers, 1958-60; dir. Oregon Am. Lumber Co., 1951-53, Pacific Far East Line, 1957-61, Gilman Engring. & Mfg., 1963, Enterprises Internat., Inc., 1973—, The George E. Taylor Fgn. Affairs INst., 1986—. Bd. dirs. John A. Johnson Found. Served to lt. comdr. USNR, 1943-46. Mem. Beta Gamma Sigma, Alpha Sigma Phi. Congregationalist. Clubs: Yacht (Seattle); Bohemian (San Francisco). Home: The Highlands Seattle WA 98177 Office: PO Box 33250 Seattle WA 98133

SAUNIER, BERNARD-MARIE, civil engineer; b. Cholet, France, July 6, 1948; s. Rene and Madeleine (Guerin) S.; m. Elisabeth Marie Raphaelle Levy, Sept. 8, 1973; children—Juliette, Xavier, Florence. Civil Engr., Enitrts (1), Strasbourg, France, 1971; San. engr. ENSP (2), Rennes-France, 1972; M.S. in Civil Engring., U. Calif.-Berkeley, 1973, Ph.D., 1976. Assoc. prof. ENSP (2), Rennes, France, 1971-72; research asst. Sanitary Engr. Research Lab., U. Calif., Berkeley, 1974-76; pres., gen. mgr. Saunier Eau et Environment, St. Gregoire, France, 1976—, SAFEGE, Nanterre, France, 1986—; lectr. in field. Contbr. articles to profl. jours. Patentee in field. Recipient 1st prize, Am. Water Works Assn. for Ph.D. thesis, 1976. Mem. Am. Water Works Assn., Am. Soc. Limnology and Oceanography, ASCE, Water Pollution Control Fedn., Internat. Water Supply Assn., Association generale des Hygienistes et Techniciens Muncipaux. Home: 25 rue Victor Hugo, 78420 Carriéres s/Seine France

SAUST, FRITJOF PALLE, manufacturing and trade company executive; b. Copenhagen, Jan. 2, 1933; s. Fritjof Leo and Elda Pauline (Hansen) S.; m. Anni Reuter, Oct. 8, 1956; 1 son, Kenneth Fritjof. Engr., Copenhagen Machine Sch., 1956; postgrad. Dif. Corr. Sch. Copenhagen, 1960-63. Supr., Danish Radio, Copenhagen, 1956-58; salesman Jens S. Christensen A/S, Copenhagen 1958-69, sales mgr., 1969-73, mng. dir., 1973—. Lodges: Den Danske Frimurer Orden, Grand Lodge of Denmark. Home: 27 Toftevangen, 4130-DK Sjaelland Denmark Office: Jens S Christensen A/S, 5 Brogrenen, 2635-SK Ishoej Denmark

SAUTAREL, FRANCOIS MICHEL, physician, medical manager; b. Monestier, Auvergne, France, Aug. 8, 1947; s. Albert Francois and Irène Marie-Antoinette (Bosdeveix) S. GCE, Rodin Secondary Sch., Paris, 1961-66; MD, Med. Faculty Pitie, 1974; cert. rheumatologic specialist, Med. Faculty Cochin, Paris, 1976. Intern and resident Hosp. Pitie-Salpetiere, Paris, 1967-73, Hosp. Cochin Paris, Paris, 1973-76, Hosp. Tenon, Paris, 1977-79; practice medicine specializing in thermal medicine Vichy, France, 1978—; practice medicine specializing in rheumatology France, 1976—; surgery attache Paris Hosp., 1976—; med. mgr. Compagnie Ferniere de Vichy div. Groupe Perrier, France, 1984; scientist advisor Merck-Sharp-Dome Lab., France, 1981-84. Contbr. med. articles to profl. jours. Office: 1 Ave Thermale, 03200 Vichy France

SAUTTER, EDOUARD ANDRE, international banking executive; b. Paris, Oct. 28, 1936; s. Sautter and Huguette (Duval) Yves; m. Christine Jeanne Dollfus, Sept. 3, 1962; children: Yves-Etienne, Fiona. M.S., Ecole Polytechnique, Paris, 1959; M.S., Stanford U., 1962, Ph.D., 1964. Economist, Electricité of France, Paris, 1964-66; mgmt. cons. Banque Nationale de Paris, 1967-69, dep. gen. mgr., London, 1970-75, sr. v.p., gen. mgr. Asia-Pacific div., 1980-84; dep. gen. mgr. Europe, Americas, Asia-Pacific div., 1985-86; chief operating officer Banque National de Paris World Corp. Banking Group; pres. French Bank of Calif., San Francisco, 1975-79; dir. French Am. Banking Corp., N.Y.C., Arjil SA, Banque National de Paris Luxembourg SA, Meunier Promotion SA, Paris. Trustee, Brighton Convalescent Home Found., London, 1972; dir. Ecole Alsacienne, Paris, 1981; pres. French Am.

C. of C., San Francisco, 1977. Served with French Navy, 1959-61. Ford Found. research asst., Stanford U., 1962. Club: Cercle Union Interalliée (Paris). Home: 71 Boulevard Raspail, 75006 Paris France Office: Banque Nationale de Paris, 20 Bld Italiens, 75009 Paris France

SAUVÉ, GEORGES, surgeon; b. Paris, Sept. 10, 1925; s. Louis de Gonzague and Marie (Bourdon) S.; m. Monique Lemaigre, June 11, 1955; children: Frédérique, Jacques-Philippe, Diane, Claire, Marie-Amelie, Béengère. MD, U. Paris, 1956. Intern Hosp. de Paris, 1955-57, chief of surgery, 1975-62; practice surgery, Laval, France, 1962—. Author: Les Fils de Saint Come, 1987. Mem. Internat. Coll. Surgeons. Roman Catholic. Home: 22 Place Du Gast, 53000 Laval France Office: Polyclinique du Maine, Ave Francais, Laval France

SAUVÉ, JEANNE, governor-general of Canada; b. Prud'homme, Sask., Can., Apr. 26, 1922; d. Charles Albert and Anna (Vaillant) Benoit; m. Maurice Sauvé, Sept. 24, 1948; 1 son, Jean-François. Grad., U. Ottawa, D (hon.); diploma in French Civilization, U. Paris, 1952; DSc (hon.), N.B. U., 1974; LHD (hon.), Mt. St. Vincent U., 1983, St. Lawrence U., 1987; LLD (hon.), U. Calgary, 1982, Queen's U., 1984, McGill U., 1984, Carleton U., 1986, U. Toronto, 1984, Laurentian U.; D (hon.), Laval U., 1984, U. Montreal, 1985; PhD in Polit. Sci. (hon.), Chulalongkorn U., Bangkok, 1987; LLD (hon.), Ottawa U., U. Moncton, 1988, U Man., 1988. Nat. pres. Jeuness Etudiante Catholique, Montreal, 1942-47; tchr. French London County Council, 1948-50; asst. to dir. youth sect. UNESCO, Paris, 1951; journalist, broadcaster 1952-72; bd. dirs. Union des Artistes, Montreal, 1961, v.p., 1968-70; v.p. Canadian Inst. on Pub. Affairs, 1962-64, pres., 1964; mem. Can. Centennial Commn., 1967; gen. sec. Fedn. des Auteurs et des Artistes du Can., 1966-72; mem. Parliament for Ahuntsic (Montreal), 1972-79, for Laval-des-Rapides, 1979-84; gov. gen. Canada, 1984—; minister of state in charge of sci. and tech., 1972-74, minister of environment, 1974-75, minister of communications, 1975-79; advisor for external affairs Sec. of State, 1978; speaker House of Commons, 1980-84. Decorated Commander of the Order Mil. Merit, Can. Forces Decoration; named Privy Councillor; recipient La Médaille de la Chancellerie des U. de Paris, Sorbonne U. Hon. fellow Royal Archtl. Inst. Can.; founding mem. Inst. Polit. Research. Mem. Liberal Party of Can. Roman Catholic. Office: Rideau Hall, 1 Sussex Dr, Ottawa, ON Canada K1A 0A1

SAVAGE, DANIEL ALEXANDER, librarian; b. Sherbrooke, Que., Can., Apr. 12, 1948; s. Thomas Alexander and Barbara Muriel (Lever) S.; m. Marilyn Sarah MacDonald, Aug. 1, 1981; children: Sarah Joanna, Heather Elizabeth, Peter Daniel. BA in Geography, Carleton U., Ottawa, Ont., Can., 1974; Diploma in Edn., Bishop's U., Lennoxville, Que., Can., 1975; Diploma in Spl. Edn., McGill U., Montreal, Que., Can., 1978; MLS, Dalhousie U., Halifax, N.S., Can., 1981. Tchr. La Tabatiere (Que.) Elem. Sch., Can., 1975-76, Drummondville (Que.) Elem. Sch., Can., 1976-78; librarian N.S. Dept. of Transp., Halifax, Can., 1979-81; chief librarian Redeemer Coll., Hamilton, Ont., Can., 1982—; cons., com. Ont. Theol. Sem., 1987; conducted workshops Ont. Christian Schs. Tchrs. Assn., 1984, 86. Mem. Am. Library Assn., Assn. of Christian Librarians, Assn. pour l'avancement des scis. et des techniques de la documentation, Can. Edn. Assn., Can. Library Assn., Can. Soc. for the Study of Edn., Can. Soc. for the Study of Higher Edn., Ont. Library Assn. Presbyterian. Home: 29 Belleau, Stoney Creek, ON Canada L8J 1N1

SAVAGE, EUGENE WILLIAM, finance director; b. Dublin, Ireland, May 18, 1936; s. Michael Patrick and Marie (Horne) S.; m. Elizabeth Ann Murphy, Feb. 25, 1963; children: Shirley, Janine, Yvonne, Adele. BA, Univ. Coll., Dublin, 1966. Adminstrn. officer Butler Bros. Ltd., Dublin, 1955-58; chief acct. A.F. Hastings & Co. Ltd., Dublin, 1958-60; fin. dir. Brunswick of Ireland Ltd., Dublin, 1960-69; dir. group fin. Irish Distillers Group PLC, Dublin, 1969—. Active local Rugby club (pres. 1970). Fellow Chartered Inst. Mgmt. Accts. (council mem., 1986—, mem. world body); Consultative Com. Accountancy Bodies of Ireland (chmn. comml. and indsl. mems. com. 1987—). Roman Catholic. Clubs: Fitzwilliam Lawn Tennis, Seapoint Rugby Football (Dublin) (pres. 1970). Office: Irish Distillers Group PLC, Bow St Distillery, Dublin Smithfield 7, Ireland

SAVAGE, JOHN WILLIAM, lawyer; b. Seattle, Oct. 11, 1951; s. Stanley and Jennie Sabina (Siggstedt) S.; m. Rebecca Lee Abraham, Oct. 1, 1983. Student Lewis and Clark Coll., 1969-71; B.A., U. Wash., 1973; J.D., Northwestern Sch. Law, Lewis and Clark Coll., 1977. Bar: Oreg. 1977, U.S. Dist. Ct. Oreg. 1977, U.S. Ct. Appeals (9th cir.) 1977, U.S. Supreme Ct. 1985. Sole practice, Portland, Oreg., 1977-79; ptnr. Bailey, Olstad, Rieke, Geil & Savage, P.C., Portland, 1979-80; ptnr., shareholder Rieke, Geil & Savage, P.C. Portland, 1980—; mem. Oreg. Literacy Inc., Portland, 1979-85. Mem. standing com. City Club, Portland, 1984—, chmn. law and pub. safety standing com. 1984-87. Mem. Multnomah Bar Assn. (v.p. young Lawyers sect. 1980, pres.-elect 1981, pres. 1982, Dist. Service award), ABA (chairperson Young Lawyers sect. Nat. Community Law Week 1983-84, Inmate Grievance Com. 1984—), Oreg. Bar Assn. (def. of indigent accused com. 1985—), Oreg. Criminal Def. Lawyers Assn. (bd. dirs. 1984-86). Home: 397 Furnace Lake Oswego OR 97034 Office: Rieke Geil & Savage PC 820 SW 2d Ave Suite 200 Portland OR 97204

SAVAGE, RICHARD NIGEL, travel firm executive, musician; b. Southport, Eng., May 15, 1948; s. Gilbert Richard and Eileen (Rowlandson) S.; m. Carol Hall, Mar. 2, 1974; children—Thomas, Katherine. B.A. in Natural Sci., Oxford U., 1969. Chmn., mng. dir. Specialised Travel Ltd., London, N.Y.C., 1980—; singing appearances, European cities, 1976—. Bd. dirs. St. Moritz Festival, Switzerland; trustee Schola Cantorum Oxford, 1985—, London Baroque Taverner Concerts Trust, David Reichenborg Arts Trust. Mem. Equity. Anglican. Club: Oxford and Cambridge (London). Avocations: squash; tennis. Home: 52 Avenue Rd, Highgate, London N6 5DR, England Office: Specialized Travel Ltd, 4 Hanger Green Park Royal, London W5 3EL, England

SAVAGE, WILLIAM WOODROW, educator; b. Onley, Va., Jan. 9, 1914; s. Frank Howard and Florence Elmira (Twyford) S.; m. Margaret Jane Clarke; children—Earl R., William W. A.B., Coll. William and Mary, 1937; M.A., U. Chgo., 1946, Ph.D., 1955; student, U. Va., summer 1951. Research editor, div. rural research Fed. Emergency Relief Adminstrn., Richmond, Va., 1935-36; div. mgr. Montgomery Ward & Co., Newport News, Va., 1937-38; statis. worker WPA, Richmond, 1938-39; counselor Va. Consultation Service, Richmond, 1939-42; acting dir. Va. Consultation Service, 1942-45; asst. state supr. guidance and consultation services Va. Dept. Edn., 1946-47; dean Longwood Coll., Farmville, Va., 1947-52; project coordinator, asso. dir. Midwest Adminstrn. Center, U. Chgo., 1952-56; dean Coll. Edn., U. S.C., 1956-65, prof. edn., 1956-79; curator U. S.C. Mus. Edn., 1973-85. Author: Interpersonal and Group Relations, 1968; Co-author: Readings in American Education, 1963; Editor: Work and Training, monthly Va. Bd. Edn, 1941-47, Administrator's Notebook, monthly Midwest Adminstrn. Center, 1954-56, U. S.C. Edn. Report, 1957-65, 67-85; adv. com.: Sch. Rev, 1954-56; Contbr. articles to jours. Mem. visitation and appraisal com. Nat. Council for Accreditation Tchr. Edn., 1964-67. Mem. S.C. Assn. Sch. Adminstrs., Univ. South Caroliniana Soc., Order White Jacket, Phi Delta Kappa. Methodist. Clubs: Wardlaw (pres. 1974-75), Torch. Home: 6316 Eastshore Rd Columbia SC 29206

SAVAGE, XYLA RUTH, government official; b. Norman, Okla., Dec. 17, 1937; d. Joel Frederick and Thelma Gladys (Burgess) Church; B.A., U. Okla., 1969; postgrad. U.S. Dept. Agr., 1971; m. John W. Savage, Jr., Jan. 18, 1955 (dec. Oct. 1982); children—Mark Wayne, John Christian. Interior designer Sears, Roebuck and Co., Petersburg, Va., 1966-67; head tech. illustration dept. ITT, Bladensburg, Md., 1967-69; supr. publs. dept. NASA, Greenbelt, Md., 1969-71; supr. illustration dept. VA, Washington, 1971-72; mgr. forms design and visual communications dept. Bur. Labor Stats., Washington, 1972—; instr. design U.S. Dept. Agr. Grad. Sch., evenings 1972—. Mem. Presidential sub-com. Questionnaire Design, 1987; chmn. publicity Band Parents; officer, parents orgn. Mem. Bus. Forms Mgmt. Assn., Printing Industries Am. Mem. Christian Ch. Author: Forms Design, 1975. Home: 12901 Chalfont Ave Fort Washington MD 20744 Office: 441 G St NW Room 2862 Washington DC 20212

SAVELL, EDWARD LUPO, lawyer; b. Atlanta, Apr. 29, 1921; s. Leon M. and Lillian (Lupo) S.; m. Bettie Patterson Hoyt, Oct. 11, 1944; 1 dau., Mary Lillian Savell Clarke. B.B.A., Emory U., 1947, LL.B., 1949. Bar: Ga. 1948. Practiced law Atlanta, 1948—; partner Savell & Williams, Atlanta, 1953—; instr. John Marshall Law Sch., 1952-56. Contbr. articles to legal jours. Served with USAF, 1942-45, CBI. Fellow Internat. Acad. Trial Lawyers (pres. 1978—, dean of acad. 1976); mem. Atlanta Bar Assn. (sec.-treas. 1953-54), ABA, State Bar Ga., Ga. Def. Lawyers Assn. (founder, v.p.), Internat. Assn. Ins. Counsel, Atlanta Claims Assn., Lawyers Club Atlanta, Chi Phi, Phi Delta Phi. Presbyterian. Clubs: Cherokee Town and Country, Commerce, Univ. Yacht (past commodore). Home: 4350 E Conway Dr Atlanta GA 30327 Office: Savell and Williams Healey Bldg 57 Forsyth St Atlanta GA 30303

SÄVE-SÖDERBERGH, BENGT, undersecretary of state for international development cooperation; b. Stockholm, Sweden, July 23, 1940. Student, Union Coll., Schenectady, N.Y., 1960-61; MBA, Stockholm Sch. Econs., 1965. With Swedish Internat. Devel. Authority, Stockholm, 1967-70; head of sect. Dept. Internat. Devel. Cooperation Ministry Fgn. Affairs, Stockholm, 1970-76; research sec. Swedish Trade Union Confedn., Stockholm, 1976-78; sec. gen. Internat. Ctr. Swedish Labour Movement, Stockholm, 1978-85; undersec. of state internat. devel. cooperation Ministry Fgn. Affairs, Stockholm, 1985—; gov. Asian Devel. Bank, African Devel. Bank, 1985—. Chmn. bd. The Ethnographical Mus. Sweden, Stockholm, 1983—. Office: Ministry for Fgn Affairs, 103 33 Stockholm Sweden

SAVIN, RONALD RICHARD, chemical company executive, inventor; b. Cleve., Oct. 16, 1926; s. Samuel and Ada (Silver) S.; m. Gloria Ann Hopkins, Apr. 21, 1962; children: Danielle Elizabeth, Andrea Lianne. Student, U. Cin., 1944-46; BA in Chem. and Literature, U. Mich., 1948; postgrad., Sorbonne, Paris, 1949-50; grad., Air War Coll., 1975, Indsl. Coll. Armed Forces, 1976. V.p. Premium Finishes, Inc., Cin., 1957-58, pres., owner, 1958—; dir., prin. stockholder LOBO S.A., Lyon, France. Contbr. articles on aerospace, marine industry and transp. to profl. jours.; mgmt. adv. council Chem Week mag; patentee corrosive prevention coatings for aerospace use. Served with USAF, 1950-55, Korea, col. Res. ret. Mem. Nat. Assn. Corrosion Engrs., Air Force Assn., Am. Internat. Club, Reserve Officers Assn. U.S. Club: Mission Hills Country (Rancho Mirage, Calif.). Office: Premium Finishes Inc 10448 Chester Rd Cincinnati OH 45215 also: LOBO, St Symphorien, Lyon France

SAVITT, SUSAN SCHENKEL, lawyer; b. Bklyn., Aug. 21, 1943; d. Edward Charles and Sylvia (Dlugatch) S.; m. Harvey Savitt, July 2, 1969 (div. 1978); children: Andrew Todd, Daniel Cory. BA magna cum laude, Pa. State U., 1964; JD, Columbia U., 1968. Bar: N.Y. 1968, U.S. Dist. Ct. (so. and ea. dists.) N.Y. 1973, U.S. Tax Ct. 1973, U.S. Ct. Appeals (2d cir.) 1981, U.S. Supreme Ct. 1980. Atty. Nassau County Legal Services, Freeport, N.Y., 1973-74; asst. corp. counsel City of Yonkers, 1977-78; adj. prof. Elizabeth Seton Coll., Yonkers, 1982-83; from assoc. to ptnr. Epstein, Becker, Borsody & Green, P.C., N.Y.C., 1978—; mem. exec. council Met. Ctr. for Ednl. Research, Devel. and Tng., 1987—. Mem. Hastings-on-Hudson (N.Y.) Sch. Bd., 1984—, v.p., 1986, 87—; trustee Westchester County Civil Liberties Union, White Plains, N.Y., 1976-77; v.p. PTSA, 1974-76. Mem. ABA, N.Y. State Bar Assn., N.Y. State Women's Assn., N.Y. State Sch. Bd. Attys. Assn., N.Y. State Pub. Employer Labor Relations Assn., Pa. State Alumni Club (v.p. Westchester County 1985-87), Westchester County C. of C., N.Y. C. of C. (mem. small bus. com.), Phi Beta Kappa, Alpha Kappa Delta, Phi Gamma Mu, Pi Kappa Phi. Office: Epstein Becker Borsody & Green PC 250 Park Ave New York NY 10177-0077

SAVITZ, SAMUEL J., actuarial consulting firm executive; b. Phila., Dec. 23, 1936; s. Paul and Ann (Gechman) S.; B.S. in Bus. Adminstrn., Temple U., 1958; postgrad. U. Pa., 1960-62, Temple U., 1965; m. Selma Goldberg, June 15, 1958; children—Jacqueline Beverly, Steven Leslie, Michelle Lynn. Pension analyst Provident Mut. Life Ins. Co., Phila., 1958-61; v.p. The Wirkman Co., Phila., 1961-64; pres. Samuel J. Savitz & Assoc., Inc., Phila., 1964-86; chmn. bd., cons. Exec. Compensation Plans, Inc., Phila., 1984—; sr. prin. Laventhol & Horwath, Phila., 1986—; mng. ptnr. Samuel J. Savitz & Assocs. div. Laventhol & Horwath, 1986—; vis. lectr. U. Pa., Phila., 1960, La. State U., 1972-74; faculty Villanova U., 1971-75; cons. in field. Mem. pension com. Fedn. Jewish Agencies, Phila., 1960; bd. dirs. Am. com. Weizmann Inst. Sci., 1984-85, Phila. All-Star Forum, 1987—. Served with USAR, 1954-62. Mem. Am. Soc. Pension Actuaries (dir. 1969-75), Am. Soc. C.L.U.'s, Assn. Advanced Life Underwriting. Jewish. Club: Locust. Contbr. articles in field to profl. jours. Home: 470 Conshohocken State Rd Bala Cynwyd PA 19004 Office: REBC Assocs 1845 Walnut St Philadelphia PA 19103

SAVOLA, KAI KARI AKSELI, theater executive; b. Helsinki, Finland, Sept. 30, 1931, S. Tauno Elias and Hilppa Marjatta (Korpinen) S.; m. Terttu Hellin Byckling, July 5, 1958; children—Tero Kristo, Maarit Pirjetta, Torsti Karel. Student Helsinki U., 1955-59. Adminstrv. mgr. Student Theatre, Helsinki, 1959-62; mng. dir. Theatre Orgn. TNL, Helsinki, 1962-65; dramaturg Helsinki City theatre, 1965-68; gen. mgr. Tampere Workers Theatre, 1968-73; asst. mgr. Finnish Nat. Theatre, Helsinki, 1973-74, gen. mgr., 1974—; mem. ITI Finland, 1963-69, adv. bd. Helsinki City Festivals, 1975—. Translator Drama from German, Swedish and English. Recipient Golden Badge of merit Tampere City, 1973. Home: Takametsantie 4 B, 00620 Helsinki Finland Office: Finnish Nat Theatre, Läntinen Teatterikuja 1B, 00100 Helsinki Finland

SAVOLAINEN, VELI-ANTTI, publishing company executive; b. Helsinki, Finland, June 30, 1948; s. Kalevi and Inkeri (Kiukkonen) S.; m. Pirjo Kyllikki Niemi, Sept. 25, 1982; children: Sonja-Maria, Samuel Eino Aleksanteri. Editor-in-chief Iltaset Evening Newspaper, Helsinki, 1973-75, Pääkaupunki Free Weekly Newspaper, Helsinki, 1976; mng. editor, editor-in-chief Uusi Suomi, Helsinki, 1977-80, 81-82; editor-in-chief Iltalehti Evening Newspaper, Helsinki, 1981-82, APU Nat. Weekly, Helsinki, 1983-85; dir. Uusi Suomi Group, Helsinki, 1986; editor-in-chief Iltalehti Newspaper, Helsinki, 1987—; sr. v.p., group pub. Uusi Suomi, Helsinki, 1987—; bd. dirs. Radio 1, Videoprodn. Provision Oy, Helsinki; chmn. bd. Intermer Oy, 1986—, Suoranava Oy, Helsinki, 1987—. Former mem. Nat. Council Liberal Party, Helsinki, 1968-72, 75-77, Nat. Exec. Bd., 1972-74, City Council of Espoo, 1973-80. Mem. Finnish-Australian Trade Assn. Home: Aurorankatu 17 A 8, 00100 Helsinki Finland Office: Uusi Suomi, Vetokuja 4, Vantaa Finland

SAVONA, MICHAEL RICHARD, physician; b. N.Y.C., Oct. 21, 1947; s. Salvatore Joseph and Diana Grace (Menditto) S.; B.S. summa cum laude, Siena Coll., 1969; M.D., SUNY, Buffalo, 1973; m. Dorothy O'Neill, Oct. 18, 1975. Intern in internal medicine, Presbyn. Hosp., Columbia U., N.Y.C., 1973-74, resident in internal medicine, 1974-76, vis. fellow internal medicine Delafield Hosp./Columbia U. Coll. Physicians and Surgeons, 1974-76; practice medicine specializing in internal medicine, Maui Med. Group, Wailuku, Hawaii, 1976-87; gen. practice medicine, 1987—; dir. ICU, Maui Meml. Hosp., also dir. respiratory therapy, CCU., chmn. dept. medicine, 1980—; clin. faculty John A. Burns Sch. Medicine, U. Hawaii. Bd. dirs. Maui Heart Assn.; dir. profl. edn. Maui chpt. Am. Cancer Soc.; mem. Maui County Hosp. Adv. Commn.; mem. council Community Cancer Program of Hawaii. Recipient James A. Gibson Wayne J. Atwell award, 1970, physiology award, 1970, Ernest Whitebsky award, 1971, Roche Lab. award, 1972, Pfiser Lab. award, 1973, Phillip Sang award, 1973, Hans Lowenstein M.D. Meml. award, 1973. Diplomate Am. Bd. Internal Medicine. Mem. AMA, Am. Thoracic Soc., Hawaii Thoracic Soc., Maui County Med. Assn. (past pres.), Hawaii Med. Assn., Hawaii Oncology Group, A.C.P., SW Oncology Coop. Group, Alpha Omega Alpha, Delta Epsilon Sigma. Office: 1830 Wells St Wailuku HI 96793

SAVOY, DOUGLAS EUGENE, explorer, writer, clergyman; b. Bellingham, Wash., May 11, 1927; s. Lewis Dell and Maymie (Janett) S.; m. Elvira Clarke, Dec. 5, 1957 (div.); 1 son, Jamil Sean (dec.); m. Sylvia Ontaneda, July 7, 1971; children: Douglas Eugene, Christopher Sean, Sylvia Jamila. Student, U. Portland; D.C.L. Engaged in newspaper publishing West Coast, 1949-56; began explorations in jungles east of Andes in Peru to prove his theory that high civilizations of Peru may have had their origin in jungles 1967; pres., founder Andean Explorers Club, Found., Reno; ordained minister; chancellor, founder Sacred Coll. of Jamilian Theology; founder, pres. Jamilian U. of Ordained; pastor Chapel of Holy Child, Reno, Nev. Author: Antisuyo, The Search for Lost Cities of the High Amazon, 1970, Vilcabamba, Last City of the Incas, 1970, The Cosolargy Papers, vol. 1, 1970, vol. 2-3, 1972, The Child Christ, 1973, Arabic edit., 1976, Japanese edit., 1981, The Decoded New Testament, 1974, Arabic edit., 1981, The Millenium Edition of the Decoded New Testament, 1983, On The Trail of The Feathered Serpent, 1974, Code Book and Community Manual for Overseers, 1975, Prophecies of Jamil, First Prophecy to the Americas, Vol. 1, 1976, Second Prophecy to the Americas, 1976, The Secret Sayings of Jamil, The Image and the Word, Vol. 1, 1976, Vol. 2, 1977, Project X—The Search For the Secrets of Immortality, 1977, Prophecy to the Races of Man, Vol. 2, 1977, Solar Cultures of The Americas, 1977, Dream Analysis, 1977, Vision Analysis, 1977, Christoanalysis, 1978, The Essaei Document: Secrets of an Eternal Race, 1978, Millennium edit., 1983, The Lost Gospel of Jesus: Hidden Teachings of Christ, Millennium edit., Secret Sayings of Jamil, Vol. 4, 1978, Prophecy to The Christian Churches, 1978, The Sayings, vol. 3, 1978, vol. 4, 1979, Solar Cultures of Oceania, 1979, Prophecy of The End Times, Vol. 4, 1980, Solar Cultures of Israel, The Holy Kabbalah and Secret Symbolism, Vols. 1 and 2, 1980, Solar Cultures of China, 1980, Christotheraphy, 1980, Christophysics, 1980, Christodynamics, 1980, Code Book of Prophecy, 1980, The Sayings, vol. 5, 1980, vol. 6, 1981, Solar Cultures of India, 1981, Prophecy on the Golden Age of Light and the Nation of Nations, Vol. 5, 1981, Solar Cultures of Israel, 1981, The Counsels, 1982, Prophecy of the Universal Theocracy, vol. 6, 1982, Prophecy of the New Covenant, vol. 7, 1982, The Book of God's Revelation, 1983, Miracle of the Second Advent, 1984; numerous others.; Contbr. articles on Peruvian cultures to mags., also articles on philosophy and religion. Trustee in Trust Episcopal Head Bishop Internat. Community of Christ. Served with AS USNR, 1944-46. Recipient numerous exploring awards. Mem. Geog. Soc. Lima, Authors Guild. Clubs: Explorers (N.Y.C.); Andean Explorers Found. and Ocean Sailing. Home: 2025 La Fond Reno NV 89509 Office: 643 Ralston St Reno NV 89503

SAWADA, HIDEO, chemical company executive, chemist; b. Kyoto, Japan, Jan. 29, 1934; s. Masao and Hiroko (Ohno) S.; m. Yoshiko Kasai, May 5, 1961; children—Yukari, Jun. B.S., Osaka U., 1956, D.S., 1965; student Cornell U., 1961-62. Cert. tchr. Research mgr. Daicel Ltd. Filter Lab., Osaka, Japan, 1973-80, gen. mgr., 1980—. Author: Thermodynamics of Polymerization, 1976; Encyclopedia of Polymer Science and Engineering, 1985. Mem. Am. Chem. Soc., Soc. Polymer Sci. Japan, Chem. Soc. Japan, Soc. Fiber Sci. and Tech., Internat. Union Pure and Applied Chemistry. Zen. Home: 2534 3-chome Sayama, 589 Sayama Osaka Japan Office: Daicel Chem Industries Ltd, 1 Teppo-cho, Sakai, Osaka 590, Japan

SAWALLISCH, WOLFGANG, conductor; b. Munich, Germany, Aug. 26, 1923; s. Wilhelm and Maria (Obermeier) S.; ed. Wittelsbacher Gymnasium of Munich, Musikalische Ausbildung, pvt. music studies; m. S. Mechthild, 1952. Condr., Augsburg, 1947-53; musical dir. Aachen, 1953-58, Wiesbaden, 1958-60, Cologne Opera, 1960-63; condr. Hamburg Philharm. Orch., 1960-73, hon. mem., 1973—; prin. condr. Vienna Symphony Orch., 1960-70, hon. mem.; also prof. Staatliche Hochschule für Musik, Cologne, 1960-63; musical dir. Bayerische Staatsoper Munich, 1971—, dir. Staatsoper Munich, 1982—; permanent condr. Teatro alla Scala, Milan; condr. many festivals; rec. artist U.S. and Britain; hon. condr. NHK Symphony Orch., Tokyo, 1967; artistic dir. Suisse Romande Orch., Geneva, 1973-80. Served with German Army, 1942-46; prisoner of war in Italy. Recipient Accademico Onorario Santa Cecilia, 1975; decorated Osterreichisches Ehrenkreuz für Kunst und Wissenschaft, Bundesverdienstkreuz, Bayerischer Verdienstorden, Verdienstkreuz (Fed. Republic Germany), Order of the Rising Sun Japan; recipient Bruckner-Ring, Vienna Symphony Orch., 1980; Bayerisches Maximiliansorder für Wissenschaft and Kunst, 1984. Mem. Richard Strauss Gesellschaft Munich (pres. 1976). Office: Bayerische Staatsoper Nat Theatre, Max-Joseph-Platz 2, D-8000 Munich 2 Federal Republic of Germany

SAWAN AL AWAMI, SAMIR, architecture company executive; b. Doha, Qatar, Sept. 23, 1953; s. Mahmood and Samiha (Abu Shamala) S.; m. Lina Nuseibeh, Sept. 8, 1960. Diploma in sports injury, physiotherapy, Army sports injury unit, Qatar, 1975; diploma in mgmt. and adminstrn., Transtutorial Coll., Eng., 1986-87. Cert. internat. coach, Volleyball Fedn. Egypt, 1974. Asst. coach Volleyball Fedn. Youth Nat. Team, Qatar, 1973-77; capt., mem. team Volleyball Fedn. Nat. Team, Qatar, 1972-80; exec. mgr. Design Studio Architects, Doha, 1978—. Recipient Honors award (Qatar), 1985; named to Guinness Book Records, 1985. Mem. Profl. Assn. Diving Instrs., U.S.A. Clubs: Doha, Al Sadd, Al Araabi. Office: Design Studio Architects, PO Box 5785, Doha Qatar

SAWAUMI, SHINICHI, electronics company executive; b. Kawasaki, Kanagawa, Japan, June 27, 1949; s. Tosuke and Kaoru (Miyoshi) S.; m. Yohko Goh, Nov. 23, 1972; children: Hokuto, Mao. MA in lit., Waseda U., Tokyo, 1972. Mgr. Mitsukoshi Transp. Co. Ltd., Tokyo, 1972-82, Signetics Japan Ltd., Tokyo, 1982-88; far east mktg. communications mgr., mgr. I.C. Products Philips Kabushiki Kaisha, Tokyo, 1988—. Club: Wakoh Marine (Ohshima). Office: Philips KK8-7 Sanbancho, Kowa Bldg 25 5th Floor, Tokyo 102, Japan

SAWH, LALL RAMNATH, urologist; b. Couva, Trinidad, June 1, 1951; s. Ramnath Rooplal and Ramkumaria (Sinanan) S.; m. Sylvia Sheila Ragobar, Dec. 22, 1973; children: Sean Lall, Shane Stefan. MBBS, U. W.I., Mona, Jamaica, 1975. Intern Gen. Hosp. San Fernando, Trinidad, 1975-76, sr. housr officer, 1976-77, sr. registrar in urology, 1980-86, acting cons. urologist, 1987—; clin. asst. Royal Infirmary Edinburgh, Scotland, 1978-79; clin. attachment Inst. Urology, London, 1979; examiner Nursing Council, Trinidad, 1984-86; cons. urologist Gen. Hosp., Port of Spain, Trinidad, Mar. 21, 1988. Author: Renal Hypothermic Surgery, 1982, Button-Hole Kidney Surgery, 1986. Commonwealth med. scholar, 1977. Fellow Royal Coll. Surgeons; mem. Med. Assn. Trinidad and Tobago (chmn. 1984-85), Endourol. Soc. U.S., Med. Bd. Trinidad and Tobago (specialist, med. officer), Surg. Edn. Com. (founder), Soc. Surgeons (treas. 1986-87). Club: Lawn Tennis (Point a Pierre, Trinidad). Office: Med Day Ctr, 15 Prince of Wales St, San Fernando Trinidad

SAWTELLE, CARL S., psychiatric social worker; b. Boston, July 14, 1927; s. Carl Salvador and Martha (Bellamacina) S.; B.A., Suffolk U., Boston, 1951; M.S.W., Simmons Sch. Social Work, 1953; m. Thelma Florence Ramsay, Aug. 20, 1950; children—Tracy Lynn, Lisa June. Social worker Tewksburry (Mass.) State Hosp., 1952; psychiat. social worker Taunton (Mass.) State Hosp., 1953-57, head psychiat. social worker, 1957-64, dir. clin. social work, 1964—; social worker Taunton Area Mental Health Clinic, 1958-61; co-chmn. Task Force Lic. and Registration Social Workers in Mass., 1970-71. Vice pres. Triumph, Inc., 1965-69. Served with USCG, 1944-46. 1st lic. social worker in Mass., 1980. Mem. Nat. Assn. Social Workers (co-founder, pres. Southeast Mass. 1957, dir. Mass. chpt., service award 1978), Acad. Cert. Social Workers, Am. Legion, Mass. Mental Health Social Workers Assn. (pres. 1972-74, co-founder). Initiator and primary motivator in achieving law requiring licensing and registration of Social Workers in Mass. Home: 9 Tracywood Rd Canton MA 02021 Office: Box 151 Taunton MA 02780

SAWYER, DONALD D., marketing executive, consultant, lecturer; b. Bklyn., June 3, 1933; s. Murry S. and Bobbe Rose (Black) Schneiderman; m. Dolores Inez Geller, Sept. 24, 1953; m. Janice Elaine Thorsten, Apr. 16, 1974; children—Charles S., Robert A., Brett R., Kirsten M. B.A., U. Miami, 1956; postgrad. Cambridge U., 1956-57. Vice-pres., Young & Rubicam, Inc., N.Y.C., 1962-67; pres. Donald Sawyer Assocs., Inc., Beverly Hills, Calif., 1967-75, pres. The Original Cookie Company, Inc., Los Angeles, 1974-75; chmn. Whimsy, Inc. div. Rapid Am., Inc., Los Angeles, 1976-79; v.p. Mattel, Inc., Hawthorne, Calif., 1979-82; pres. People Protections Products Inc., Hawthorne, 1981-82; chmn. bd. Cookhouse, Inc., Sherman Oaks, Calif., 1983—; pres., chief exec. officer The Famous Amos Chocolate Chip Cookie Corp., 1985-86; mng. dir. The Toppington Group Ltd., Beverly Hills, 1986-87; sr. v.p. HDM Advt., Los Angeles, 1987—; lectr. Sch. Bus., U. So. Calif.; dir. Atlanta Fin. Corp., Reese Finer Foods; cons. ARCORP mgmt. Bd. dirs. Los Angeles Better Bus. Bur., L.I. Heart Inst., Inc. Served to lt. USAR, 1957-59.

SAWYER, KATHERINE H. (MRS. CHARLES BALDWIN SAWYER), librarian; b. Cleve., July 11, 1908; d. Willard and Martha (Beaumont) Hirsh; AB, Smith Coll., 1930; MS in Library Sci., Western Res. U., 1956; m. Charles Baldwin Sawyer, Aug. 19, 1933; children: Samuel Prentiss, Charles Brush, William Beaumont. With Cleve. Pub. Library, profl. librarian hosps., instns. dept., 1956-61; med. librarian St. Luke's Hosp., Pittsfield, Mass., 1965-66; library cons. Ministry of Health, Guyana, S. Am., 1966-68; curator Sophia Smith Collection; counselor Friends of Smith Coll. Library, chmn. exec. com., 1959-65; chmn. Friends of Western Res. Hist. Library, 1973-78, hon. trustee, 1980—; dir., trustee Friends of Pima-Green Valley Library; trustee Episcopal Ch. Home, 1965— ; bd. govs. Western Res. U., 1957-66, bd. visitors Sch. Library Sci., 1958-68, 69-72; trustee Friends of Cleve. Pub. Library, 1962-67, Christian Residences Found., 1976-82, WRHS, 1979—; counselor Friends of Smith Coll. Library, 1962-68. Mem. Ariz. State Library Assn., Western Res. Hist. Soc., Archeol. Inst., Spl. Libraries Assn., Nat. League Am. Pen Women. Episcopalian (vestryman 1974-77). Clubs: Union, Allience Française; Green Valley Country; Intown. Co-author (talking books for blind) Gardening for Blind Persons, 1962; Beauty, Glamour and Style, 1963. Home: 525 Paseo del Mundo Green Valley AZ 85614

SAWYER, THOMAS EDGAR, management consultant; b. Homer, La., July 7, 1932; s. Sidney Edgar and Ruth (Bickham) S.; B.S., UCLA, 1959; M.A., Occidental Coll., 1969; m. Joyce Mezzanatto, Aug. 22, 1954; children—Jeffrey T., Scott A., Robert J., Julie Anne. Project engr. Garrett Corp., Los Angeles, 1954-60; mgr. devel. ops. TRW Systems, Redondo Beach, Calif., 1960-66; spl. asst. to gov. State of Calif., Sacramento, 1967-69; prin., gen. mgr. Planning Research Corp., McLean, Va., 1969-72; dep. dir. OEO, Washington, 1972-74; asso. prof. bus. mgmt. Brigham Young U., 1974-78; pres. Mesa Corp., Provo, 1978-82, chmn. bd., 1978-82; pres. and dir. Sage Inst. Internat., Inc., Provo, Utah, 1982—; dir. Insul Chem. Corp., Coal Reserves Inc., Intechna Corp., HighTech Corp., Nooraid Chem. Corp., Nat. Applied Computer Tech. Inc. (chmn.), Indian Affiliates, Inc. Chmn. Nat. Adv. Council Indian Affairs; chmn. Utah State Bd. Indian Affairs; mem. Utah Dist. Export Council; mem. Utah dist. SBA Council; chmn. So. Paiute Restoration Com.; mem. adv. council Nat. Bus. Assn.; mem. Utah Job Tng. Coordinating Council. Served with USMC, 1950-53. Mem. Am. Mgmt. Assn., Am. Soc. Public Adminstrn., Utah Council Small Bus. (dir.). Republican. Mormon. Club: Masons. Author: Assimilation Versus Self-Identity: A Modern Native American Perspective, 1976; Computer Assisted Instruction: An Inevitable Breakthrough. Home: 548 W 630 S Orem UT 84058 Office: Sage Inst Internat Inc 226 W 2230 N Provo UT 84604

SAWYERR, AKILAPA, academic administrator; b. Accra, Greater Accra, Ghana, Mar. 24, 1939; s. Akilagpa and Charlotte Amy (Mettle) S., m. Judith Sara Quitkin; children: Ayodele, Fashole. LLB, U. Durham, Eng., 1962; LLM, U. London, 1965, U. Calif., Berkeley, 1967; JSD, U. Calif., Berkeley, 1972. Lic. barrister-at-law, Lincoln's Inn, Eng., Supreme Ct., Ghana; barrister and solicitor, Supreme Ct. of Papua New Guinea. Sr. lectr. U. Dar Es Salaam, Tanzania, 1964-70; dir. research ctr. U. Dar Es Salaam, 1969-70; assoc. prof. law U. Ghana, Legon, 1970-81, vice-chancellor, 1985—; prof. U. Papua New Guinea, 1979-84; mem. panel arbitrators Internat. Ctr. Settlement of Investment Disputes, Washington, 1984—. Co-author: Doctrine of Precedent in Court of Appeal for East Africa, 1971; editor: East African Law and Social Change, 1967, Economic Development and Trade in Papua New Guinea, 1984; co-editor: Law and Social Change in Papua New Guinea, 1982; contbr. articles to profl. jours.; mem. adv. council Internat. Encyclopedia Comparative Law, Hamburg, Fed. Republic Germany, 1970—; editorial cons. Australian Jour. Law and Soc., 1981. Chmn. Nat. Minerals Commn., Ghana, 1984—; legal cons. Spl. Action Unit Govt. of Ghana, 1973; chief govt. negotiator Valco Agreement Renegotiation, Ghana, 1983-85; mem. Nat. Econ. Commn., Ghana, 1986—. Sailer fellow, 1967, fellow Max Planck Inst., 1969, Yale U., 1973. Mem. African Soc. Internat. and Comparative Law (bd. dirs. 1986—). Home and Office: Univ of Ghana, Vice-Chancellor's Office, Legon Ghana

SAWYERS, JOHN LAZELLE, physician; b. Centerville, Iowa, July 26, 1925; s. Francis Lazelle and Almira (Baker) S.; m. Julia Edwards, May 25, 1957; children: Charles Lazelle, Al Baker, Julia Edwards. A.B., U. Rochester, 1946; M.D., Johns Hopkins U., 1949. Diplomate: Am. Bd. Surgery (dir. 1981-87), Am. Bd. Thoracic Surgery. House officer surgery Johns Hopkins Hosp., Balt., 1949-50; asst. resident, resident in surgery Vanderbilt U. Hosp., Nashville, 1953-58; practice medicine specializing in surgery Nashville, 1958—; surgeon Edwards-Eve Clinic, 1958-60; chief surg. service Nashville Gen. Hosp., 1960-77; surgeon-in-chief St. Thomas Hosp., Nashville, 1977-82; prof. surgery Vanderbilt U., Nashville., chmn. dept. surgery, dir. sect. surg. scis., 1983—. Bd. dirs. Davidson County unit Am. Cancer Soc. Served from lt. (j.g.) to lt. M.C. USNR, 1950-52. Fellow A.C.S. (gov. 1974-80, pres. Tenn. chpt. 1974); mem. Am. Surg. Assn., Southeastern Surg. Congress (pres. 1980), So. Surg. Assn. (pres. 1987), Halsted Soc. (pres. 1981). Home: 403 Ellendale Dr Nashville TN 37205 Office: Dept Surgery T-2116 Vanderbilt U Nashville TN 37232

SAX, MARY RANDOLPH, speech pathologist; b. Pontiac, Mich., July 13, 1925; d. Bernard Angus and Ada Lucile (Thurman) TePoorten; B.A. magna cum laude, Mich. State U., 1947; M.A., U. Mich., 1949; m. William Martin Sax, Feb. 7, 1948. Supr. speech correction dept. Waterford Twp. Schs., Pontiac, 1949-69; lectr. Marygrove Coll., Detroit, 1971-72; pvt. practice speech and lang. rehab., Wayne, Oakland Counties, Mich., 1973—; adj. speech pathologist Southfield, Mich., Farmington, Mich.; mem. sci. council stroke Am. Heart Assn. Grantee Inst. Articulation and Learning, 1969, others. Mem. Am. Speech-Lang.-Hearing Assn., Mich. Speech Pathologists in Clin. Practice, Mich. Speech-Lang.-Hearing Assn. (com. community and hosp. services), Am. Heart Assn. of Mich., Stroke Com. of Am., AAUW, Internat. Assn. Logopedics and Phoniatrics (Switzerland), Founders Soc. of Detroit Inst. Arts, Mich. Humane Soc., Theta Alpha Phi, Phi Kappa Phi, Kappa Delta Pi. Contbr. articles to profl. jours. Home and Office: 31320 Woodside Franklin MI 48025

SAXBY, ROBIN KEITH, electronics executive; b. Chesterfield, Derby, Eng., Feb. 4, 1947; s. Keith William and Mary (Lowe) S.; m. Patricia Susan Saxby, Aug. 20, 1970; children: Katherine Helen, Neil Edward. BEE, Liverpool U., 1968. Registered profl. engr., UK. Engr. devel. Rank Bush Murphy Ltd., London, 1968-72; sr. design engr. Pye TMC Ltd., St. Mary Cray, Eng., 1972-73; mgr. strategy European systems Motorola Semiconductors, London, 1973-84; mng. dir. Henderson Security Systems Ltd., High Wycombe Bucks, Eng., 1984-86; dir., v.p. N. Europe European Silicon Structures, Bracknell, Bershire, Eng., 1986—; dir. N. Europe ES2 Ltd., Brachnell, 1986-87; mng. dir. Henderson Security Systems, Pitts Security Gates, Henderson Access Control, Visual Contact Ltd., Frontier Gate Systems. Contbr. chpts. to several engring. books; contbr. articles to profl. jours. Mem. IEE (assoc.), Royal TV Soc. Office: ES2 European Silicon Structures, Mount Lane, Bracknell RG12 3DY, England

SAXE, HARRY CHARLES, civil engineer, educator; b. Long Island City, N.Y., Mar. 18, 1920; s. Charles Lawrence and Alice (McGrath) S.; m. Margaret Veronica Bligh, Nov. 12, 1945 (dec. Aug., 1985); children: Janine Marie Saxe Sager, Coreen Marie Saxe Urbina; m. Mary Kay Stevens, Oct. 3, 1986. B.C.E., City Coll. N.Y., 1942; M.S.E., U. Fla., 1949; Sc.D., Mass. Inst. Tech., 1952. Registered profl. engr., N.Y., Ky., S.C. Grad. asst., instr. civil engring. U. Fla., 1948-50; grad. research asst. civil engring. Mass. Inst. Tech., 1950-52; asso. prof. civil engring. Ga. Inst. Tech., 1952-56; structural engr. Praeger-Kavanagh & Assos. (cons. engrs.), N.Y.C., 1956-57; asso. prof. Poly. Inst. Bklyn., 1957; U. Cin., 1957-59; prof. civil engring. U. Notre Dame, 1959-69, head dept., 1959-60, 61-65; acting dean U. Notre Dame (Coll. Engring.), 1960-61, 66-67, chmn. dept., 1967-69; pres. Inst. Indsl. Research U. Louisville, 1969-74, prof. civil engring., 1969-83, dean James Breckenridge Speed Sci. Sch., 1969-80, dean, prof. emeritus, 1983—, invited alumnus, 1982—; vis. prof. civil engring. Clemson U., 1980-81; Frederik Wachtmeister disting. prof. phys. scis. and vis. prof. civil engring. Va. Mil. Inst., spring 1983; Col. Louis S. LeTellier disting. vis. prof. The Citadel-Mil. Coll. S.C., Charleston, 1983—; spl. research structural engring. and mechanics; NSF sci. faculty fellow, vis. prof. civil engring. Imperial Coll. Sci. and Tech., U. London, Eng., 1965-66, U. Md., 1985; Cons. USAF Spl. Weapons Center, Albuquerque, 1961-66; mem. Ky. Bd. Registration for Profl. Engrs. and Land Surveyors, 1972-80, sec.-treas., 1979-80; mem. Ky. Sci. and Tech. Adv. Council, 1970-75; mem. energy research bd. Ky. Dept. Energy, 1976-80; mem. exec. bd. INCOME, Inc., 1978-80; cons. in forensic structural engring., 1980—. Served to capt., C.E. AUS and USAAF, 1942-48, ETO. Recipient Notre Dame U. Spl. Service award, 1967. Fellow ASCE; mem. Soc. Am. Mil. Engrs., Am. Soc. Engring. Edn., Am. Concrete Inst., NSPE, S.C. Soc. Profl. Engrs., Speed Alumni Found. (hon.), Sigma Xi, Tau Beta Pi, Phi Kappa Phi, Chi Epsilon, Sigma Tau, Pi Tau Sigma. Club: Charleston Civil Engrs.; Notre Dame of Charleston; The Citadel Brigadier. Home: 612 Harbor Creek Pl Charleston SC 29412 Office: Dept Civil Engring The Citadel-Mil Coll SC Charleston SC 29409

SAXENA, ARJUN NATH, physicist; b. Lucknow, India, Apr. 1, 1932; s. Sheo and Mohan (Piyari) Shanker; came to U.S., 1956, naturalized, 1976; B.Sc., Lucknow U., 1950, M.Sc., 1952, profl. cert. in German, 1954; Post M.S. diploma, Inst. Nuclear Physics, Calcutta, India, 1955; Ph.D., Stanford U., 1963; m. Veera Saxena, Feb. 9, 1956; children: Rashmi, Amol, Varsha, Ashvin. Research asst. Stanford U., 1956-60; mem. tech. staff Fairchild Semicondr. Co., Palo Alto, Calif., 1960-65; dept. head Sprague Electric Co., North Adams, Mass., 1965-69; mem. tech. staff RCA Labs., Princeton, N.J., 1969-71; pres., chmn. bd. Astro-Optics, Phila., 1972; pres. Internat. Sci. Co., Princeton Junction, N.J., 1973-74; vis. scientist Centre de Récherches Nucléaires, Strasbourg, France, 1973, 77; sr. staff scientist, mgr. engring. Data Gen. Corp., Sunnyvale, Calif., 1975-80; mgr. process tech. Signetics Corp., Sunnyvale, 1980-81; Gould AMI scientist, dir. advanced process devel. Gould AMI Semicondrs., Santa Clara, Calif., 1981-87; dir. Ctr. for Integrated Electronics, prof. dept. elec. and computer system engring. Rensselaer Poly. Inst., Troy, N.Y., 1987—. Treas. Pack 66, Boy Scouts Am., W. Windsor, N.J., 1970-74. Recipient Disting. Citizen award State of N.J., 1975. Mem. Am. Phys. Soc., IEEE, Electrochem. Soc., Stanford Alumni Assn. (life). Contbr. articles on semicondr. tech., optics, nuclear and high-energy physics to sci. jours., 1953—; patentee in field. Home: 2 Birch Hill Rd Ballston Lake NY 12019-9370 Office: Rensselaer Poly Inst Ctr Integrated Electronics Dept Elec/Computer Sci Engring Troy NY 12180-3590

SAXENA, SURENDRA KUMAR, geotechnical engineering educator, consultant, researcher; m. Sandra L. Pruitt; 1 child, Anil. B.S. Aligarh U., India, 1955; M.S., Duke U., 1965, Ph.D., 1971. Registered profl. engr., N.Y., N.J., Ill., Fla. Dist. engr. Pub. Works Dept., State Govt. Rajasthan, Jaipur, India, 1955-62; soils engr. Port Authority of N.Y., N.J., 1969-74; sr. engr. Dames & Moore, Cranford, N.J., 1974-76; assoc. prof. Ill. Inst. Tech., Chgo., 1976-81, prof., chmn. dept. civil engring., 1981—; apptd. to Gov.'s Commn. on Sci. and Tech., 1985—. Contbr. articles to profl. jours. and confs. Editor geotech. books. Fellow ASCE (past mem. publs. com. of Geotech. Jour., com. numerical methods of geotechnical div., current mem. com. on soil dynamics, chmn. geotech. div. Ill. sect. 1982); mem. ASTM (marine geotechnics com., past chmn. subcom. properties of soils), Transp. Res. Bd. (rigid pavement com. 1978—), Earthquake Engring. Research Inst. (pres. Great Lakes chpt. 1983-84), Internat. Soc. Soil Mechanics and Found. Engring., Assn. Asian Indians in Am. (pres. 1982-83, 84-85), Sigma Xi. Current work: Earthquake engineering, soil-structure interaction, static and dynamic soil properties, ballast-soil geotextile behavior, unsaturated soils, thermal properties of soils. Subspecialty: Civil engineering. Home: 1 South 130 Pine Ln Lombard IL 60148

SAXHAUG, GUNNAR, travel executive; b. Oslo, May 20, 1944; s. Juul and Harriet (Ostberg) S.; children: Torill Säthre, Geir; m. Jette Lokke, Dec. 11, 1982. BS, Oslo Mcpl. Coll., 1967, Norwegian Sch. Hotel Adminstrn., 1968. Hotel mgr. Norwegian Skiingn Assn., Norefjell, 1971-74; head conv. dept. Bennett Travel Bur. Ltd., Oslo, 1974-79; sales mgr. Finnair Region Norway, Oslo, 1979-85, adminstrv. mgr., 1985—; agts. investigating panel IAIA, Oslo, 1980-85. Mem. editorial com. Norwegian Hotel and Restaurant Assn., Oslo, 1976-79. Served to 2d lt. Norwegian reserve armed forces, 1984—. Mem. Internat. SkÅl Club. Officw: Finnair Region Norway, Rosenkrantzgt 17, 0160 Oslo Norway

SAXTON, LAWRENCE VICTOR, computer science educator, researcher; b. St. Catharines, Ont., Can., Mar. 26, 1946; s. Ronald Victor and Violet (Lawrence) S. B.Math., U. Waterloo, Ont., 1969, M.Math., 1970, Ph.D., 1973. Lectr. U. Waterloo, 1973; asst. prof. U. Regina, Sask., Can., 1973-78, assoc. prof., 1978-82, coop. coordinator, 1978-81, assoc. prof. computer sci., 1983—; vis. assoc. prof. Vanderbilt U., Nashville, 1982-83. Contbr. articles to profl. jours. Canvasser United Way of Regina, Sask., 1978-87. Ont. scholar Province of Ont., 1964, NRC grad. scholar, Can., 1969-73, Natural Scis. and Engring. Research Council operating grantee, 1974-78, 84-86. Mem. Assn. Computing Machinery (faculty advisor student chpt.), Soc. Indsl. and Applied Math., Canadian Info. Processing Soc. Anglican. Clubs: Lakeshore Tennis, Faculty (Regina) (dir. 1981-82). Avocations: tennis. Home: 53 Bobolink Bay, Regina, SK Canada S4S 4K2 Office: U Regina, Computer Sci Dept, Regina, SK Canada S4S 0A2

SAY, MARLYS MORTENSEN (MRS. JOHN THEODORE SAY), superintendent; b. Yankton, S.D., Mar. 11, 1924; d. Melvin A. and Edith L. (Fargo) Mortensen; B.A., U. Colo., 1949, M.Ed., 1953; adminstrv. specialist U. Nebr., 1973; m. John Theodore Say, June 21, 1951; children—Mary Louise, James Kenneth, John Melvin, Margaret Ann. Tchr. Huron (S.D.) Jr. High Sch., 1944-48, Lamar (Colo.) Jr. High Sch., 1950-52, Norfolk Pub. Sch., 1962-63; Madison County supt., Madison, Nebr., 1963—. Mem. N.E.A. (life), Am. Assn. Sch. Adminstrs., Dept. Rural Edn., Nebr. Assn. County Supts. (pres.), Nebr. Elementary Prins. Assn., AAUW (pres. Norfolk br.), N.E. Nebr. County Supts. Assn. (pres.), Assn. Sch. Bus. Ofcls., Nat. Orgn. Legal Problems in Edn., Assn. Supervision and Curriculum Devel., Nebr. Edn. Assn., Nebr. Sch. Adminstrs. Assn. Republican. Methodist. Home: 4805 S 13th St Norfolk NE 68701 Office: Courthouse Madison NE 68748

SAYAMPANATHAM, SATHIAMOORTHY RAMALINGAM, physician; b. Jaffna, Ceylon, Sept. 13, 1921; s. Victor Emmanuel and Margaret M. (Ramalingam) S.; m. Isabella T. Thuraiappah, Oct. 1955; children: Selan Reuben, Mark Sudhir. B in Medicine and Surgery, U. Singapore, 1953, diploma Pub. Health, 1958. Med. officer health Govt. of Singapore, 1954-62, sr. registrar, 1962-65, sr. health officer quaratine and epidemiology, 1965-78, sr. registrar, 1978-86; gen. practice medicine Singapore, 1986—; mem. expert panel on health of seafarers WHO, Geneva, 1964-87. Bd. dirs. People's Assn., Singapore, 1977-87; surgeon St. John Ambulance Brigade, Singapore, 1954-70, chief commr., 1970-80. Decorated Comdr. of Order St. John, 1983; recipient Pub. Service Star Singapore Govt., 1985. Fellow Royal Soc. for Promotion of Health of Eng.; mem. Acad. Medicine Singapore. Home: 9 Merryn Rd, Singapore 1129, Singapore

SAYASOV, YURI STEPANOVICH, scientific worker, educator; b. Moscow, Apr. 9, 1927; came to Switzerland, 1973; s. Stepan Nikolaevich and Irina (Raskina) S.; m. Vera Ivanovna Bikova, Jan. 5, 1968; 1 child, Andrej. Tchr. physics and math. Lenin's State Pedagogical Inst.-Moscow, 1948; Can. Phys. Math., Inst. Chem. Physics, USSR Acad. Scis., 1955, Dr. Phys. Math., 1966. Jr. sci. worker Inst. Chem. Physics, USSR Acad. Scis., Moscow, 1950-55, sr. sci. worker, 1955-67; vis. scientist, lectr. Kernforschungszentrum and U. Karlsruhe, Federal Republic Germany, 1982-83; sci. worker, lectr. Inst. Physics, U. Fribourg, Switzerland, 1973—; reviewer Inst. Sci. Info., Moscow, 1955-73; reviewer Math. Revs., U. Mich., 1974—. Contbr. articles to profl. jours. Mem. Am. Math. Soc., European Phys. Soc., Swiss Phys. Soc., Int. Gesellschaft für Menschenrechte. Russian Orthodox. Avocations: skiing, mountaineering. Home: CH 1607 Granges-Veveyse Switzerland Office: Univ Fribourg, Inst Physics, CH 1700 Perolles, Fribourg Switzerland

SAYEED, USMAN AHMED, general engineer; b. Nellore, India, Nov. 15, 1939; came to U.S., 1970, naturalized, 1979; s. Mohammad Saiduddin and Zainab Begum; m. Gurdev Kaur Singh, Oct. 1, 1969; children—Iqbal, Siraj, Yusef. B.Sc. with honors, Andhra U., Waltair, India, 1959, M.Sc., 1960; M.Sc., Meml. U. Nfld., St. Johns, Can., 1970; Ph.D., U. Nebr., 1973; M.B.A., CUNY, 1979. Research asst. India Inst. Tech., Kharagpur, 1960; geologist Geol. Survey, Calcutta, India, 1961-68; research asst. Meml. U. Nfld., 1968-70; grad. teaching asst. U. Nebr., Lincoln, 1970-73; adj. asst. prof. Hofstra U., Hempstead, N.Y., 1974, 75; asst. prof. Fla. Internat. U., Miami, 1975-78; mining engr. IRS, Pitts., 1979-87, IRS, Louisville, Ky., 1987— . Contbr. articles to profl. publs. Fellow Geol. Assn. Can., Geol. Soc. India; mem. Am. Geophys. Union, Assn. Geologists for Internat. Devel., Sigma Xi. Democrat. Muslim.

SAYERS, JANET VIRGINIA, psychologist, educator; b. London, Oct. 26, 1945; d. Norman Price and Shirley Kate (Dixon) Toulson; m. Sean Philip Sayers, Sept. 19, 1970; children: Nicholas, Daniel. BA, Cambridge (Eng.) U., 1968, Cambridge (Eng.) U., 1970; Diploma in Clin. Psychology, Tavisbock Clinic, 1970; PhD, U. Kent, Eng., 1986. Clin. psychologist Tavistock Clinic, London, 1968-70, St. Augustine's Hosp., Canterbury, Eng., 1970-71; ednl. psychologist Child Guidance Clinic, Canterbury, 1971-73; lectr. psychology U. Kent, Canterbury, 1974—; clin. psychologist Canterbury and Thanet Health Dist., 1986—. Author: Biological Politics, 1982, Sexual Contradictions, 1986; co-editor: Engels Revisted, 1987. Mem. Brit. Psychol. Soc. Office: U Kent, Keynes Coll, Canterbury CT2 7NP, England

SAY PHOUTHANG, government official. V.p. Council of State, Phnom Penh, People's Republic of Kampuchea. Office: Kampuchean People's, Revolutionary Party, Phnom-Penh People's Republic of Kampuchea *

SAYRE, JOHN MARSHALL, lawyer; b. Boulder, Colo., Nov. 9, 1921; s. Henry Marshall and Lulu M. (Cooper) S.; m. Jean Miller, Aug. 22, 1943; children—Henry M., Charles Franklin, John Marshall, Ann Elizabeth Sayre Taggart (dec.). B.A., U. Colo., 1943, J.D., 1948. Bar: Colo. 1948, U.S. Dist. Ct. Colo. 1952, U.S. Ct. Appeals (10th cir.) 1964. Law clk. trust dept. Denver Nat. Bank, 1948-49; asst. cashier, trust officer Nat. State Bank of Boulder, 1949-50; ptnr. Ryan, Sayre, Martin, Brotzman, Boulder, 1950-66, Davis, Graham & Stubbs, Denver, 1966—. Bd. dirs. Boulder Sch. Dist. 3, 1951-57; city atty. City of Boulder, 1952-55; gen. counsel Colo. Mcpl. League, 1956-63; counsel No. Colo. Water Conservancy Dist. and mcpl. subdist., 1964-87, spl. counsel, 1987, bd. dirs. dist., 1960-64; legal counsel Colo. Assn. Commerce and Industry. Served to lt. (j.g.) USNR, 1943-46. Decorated Purple Heart. Fellow Am. Bar. Found.; mem. ABA, Colo. Bar Assn., Boulder County Bar Assn., Denver Bar Assn., Nat. Water Resources Assn. (Colo. dir. 1980—, pres. 1984-86), Phi Beta Kappa. Republican. Episcopalian. Clubs: Denver Country, Denver, Petroleum. Office: PO Box 185 Denver CO 80201

SAYRE, ROBERT MARION, ambassador; b. Hillsboro, Oreg., Aug. 18, 1924; s. William Octavius and Mary (Brozka) S.; m. Elora Amanda Moyhihan, Dec. 29, 1951; children: Marian Amanda, Robert Marion, Daniel Humphrey. B.A. summa cum laude, Willamette U., 1949; J.D. cum laude (Alexander Welborn Weddell Peace prize 1956), George Washington U., 1956; M.A., Stanford U., 1960; LL.D., Willamette U., 1965. Bar: D.C. 1956, U.S. Ct. Appeals 1956, U.S. Supreme Ct. 1962, Fed. Bar 1986. Joined U.S. Fgn. Service, 1949; econ. adviser on Latin Am. 1950-52, mil. adviser, 1952-57, officer charge inter-Am. security affairs, 1955-57; chief polit. sect. embassy Lima, Peru, 1958-59; fin. attache embassy Havana, Cuba, 1960; exec. sec. Task Force Latin Am., State Dept., 1961, officer charge Mexican affairs, 1961-63; dep. dir. Office Caribbean and Mexican Affairs, 1963-64; dir. Office Mexican Affairs, 1964; sr. staff mem. White House, 1964-65; dep. asst. sec. Bur. Inter-Am. Affairs, Dept. State, 1965-67; acting asst. sec. Dept. State, 1968—; Am. ambassador to Uruguay 1968-69, to Panama, 1969-74; sr. insp. Dept. State, 1974-75, insp. gen., 1975-78; ambassador to Brazil 1978-81; chmn. U.S. Interdepartmental group on Terrorism, dir. Counter-terrorism and Emergency Planning Dept. State, 1981-85, sr. insp., 1985-86; ptnr. IRC Group, Inc., 1986-87; asst. sec. mgmt. OAS, 1987—; cons. Dept. State; sr. Councilor Atlantic Council U.S.; adviser to U.S. rep. OAS, 1986; asst. sec. Mgmt. Orgn. Am. States, 1987; mem. Washington Inst. Fgn. Affairs. Served to capt. AUS, World War II; col. Res. ret. Recipient Outstanding Employee award Dept. State, 1952, Superior Honor awards, 1964, 75, Disting. Honor award, 1978, Outstanding Performance award, 1982, 83, 84, 85; decorated So. Cross (Brazil), 1981, Cross of Balboa (Panama), 1974; Presdl. Meritorious award, 1986. Mem. Blue Key, Phi Delta Theta, Phi Eta Sigma, Tau Kappa Alpha. Episcopalian. Club: Cosmos. Home: 3714 Bent Branch Rd Falls Church VA 22041 Office: OAS 1889 F St NW Suite 600 Washington DC 20006

SBORDONE, CARLO, mathematics educator; b. Napoli, Italy, Nov. 23, 1948; s. Francesco and Maria (Colamonico) S.; m. Roberta D'Angelo, Feb. 2, 1954; children: Barbara, Francesco. Laurea, U. Napoli, 1971. Asst. U. Napoli, 1973-80, prof., 1980—; researcher Scuola Normale Superiore, Pisa, Italy, 1979-80; organizer Internat. Congress SAFA, Napoli, 1980. Contbr. articles to profl. jours.; mem. editorial bd. Ricerche di Matematica (internat. jour.) 1983-87. Recipient U. Nobile prize, U. Napoli, 1971, UMI-CNR prize, 1976, Bonavera prize Acad. Sci. Torino, 1978. Mem. Unione Mathematica Italiana, Am. Math. Soc., Accademia Pontaniana, Accademia Sci. Fis. Matematica. Home: Parco Griffeo 30, 80121 Napoli Italy Office: U Napoli Dept Math, Mezzocannone 8, 80136 Napoli Italy

SBORDONE, ROBERT JOSEPH, neuropsychologist, educator; b. Boston, May 6, 1940; s. Saverio and Phylliss (Dellaria) Vella; m. Melinda Welles, June 30, 1972 (div. 1977). A.B., U. So. Calif., 1967; M.A., Calif. State U.-Los Angeles, 1969; Ph.D., UCLA, 1976, postgrad., 1977. Cert. psychologist Calif.; diplomate Am. Bd. Profl. Neuropsychology, Am. Bd. Clin. Neuropsychology. Mem. staff psychology UCLA, 1977-78; sole practice psychology, Los Angeles, 1978-80; asst. prof. psychology U. Calif.-Irvine, 1980-82, asst. clin. prof., 1983—; pres. Robert Sbordone Inc., Calif., 1982—; bd. dirs. Neuropsychol. Assocs. Calif., 1984—; adv. bd. High Hopes Neurol. Recovery Group Orange County, Alzheimer's disease and Related Disorders Calif. Contbr. chpt. to book and articles to profl. jours.; editor: Clinical Neuropsychology jour, 1979—; editorial bd. Internat. Jour. Clin. Neuropsychology; edit. adv. bd. Jour. Head Trauma Rehabilitation. Goodwill ambassador to Middle East, 1963. Served with USAF, 1962-66. NIMH grantee, 1973-77. Fellow Nat. Acad. Neuropsychology; mem. Am. Psychol. Assn., Internat. Neuropsychol. Soc., Nat. Head Injury Found., Internat. Soc. Research in Aggression, N.Y. Acad. Scis. Subspecialties: Neuropsychology; Clinical Psychology. Current work: Neuropsychological assessment of brain injured; development of computer software for assessment and rehabilitation of brain injured patients. Developer of computer software, 1982. Home: 3591 Aquarius Dr Huntington Beach CA 92649 Office: Orange County Neuropsychology 8840 Warner Ave Suite 301 Fountain Valley CA 92708

SCAGLIA, MARIO, engineer; b. Milano, Italy, Aug. 12, 1934; s. Camillo and Luigia (Meroni) S.; m. Viky Radice, Oct. 29, 1960; children: Stefano, Riccardo, Federico. Dott. Ing., Politécnico, Milano, 1958. Registered profl. engr. Project engr. M. Scaglia Sp.A., Milano, 1960-68, mng. dir., 1968—; mng. dir. S.I.T., Brembilla, Italy, 1970—. Mayor, City Adminstrn., Brembilla, 1975-80; pres. Accademia Carrara, Bergamo, 1980—; peace judge Civic Adminstrn., Brembilla, 1981. Roman Catholic. Avocations: Italian baroque painting; hunting. Home: 10 Via Nirone, 20123 Milan Italy Office: SIT 15, Via Watt, 20143 Milan Italy

SCALE, IVAN EDWIN, electrical engineer; b. Melbourne, Victoria, Australia, Mar. 15, 1930; s. Herbert Hedley and Alice Ellen (Hill) S.; m. Elly Leonora Moerdijk, 1952 (div. 1970); children: Merilee Alice, Linlee Joy; m. Eleanor May Hawke, Sept. 7, 1970. Diplomas EE, ME, Swinburne Coll., Melbourne, 1950; BE with honors, U. New South Wales, Sydney, 1965; PhD in Engring., Newcastle U., 1973. Cadet engr. Rola Co., Melbourne, 1945-49, State Electricity Commn., Yallourn, Australia, 1950; design engr. Sanitarium Health Food Co., Cooranbong, 1952-65, chief engr., dir. plant devel. div., 1966-87, project mgr. Australasia, 1988—. Fellow Inst. Engrs. of Australia, Australian Inst. of Energy, Inst. of Instrumentation and Control; mem. Australian Soc. of Ops. Research. Adventist. Home: 10 Lindfield Ave, Cooranbong 2265, Australia Office: Sanitarium Health Food Co, 146 Fox Valley Rd, Wahroonga NSW 2076, Australia

SCALETTA, PHILLIP JASPER, lawyer, educator; b. Sioux City, Iowa, Aug. 20, 1925; s. Phillip and Louise (Pelmulder) S.; m. Helen M. Scaletta; children: Phillip R., Cheryl D. Kesler. BS, Morningside Coll., Sioux City, 1948; JD, U. Iowa, 1950. Bar: Iowa 1950, U.S. Dist. Ct. Iowa 1950, Ind. 1966, U.S. Supreme Ct. 1968. Ptnr. McKnight and Scaletta, Sioux City, 1950-51; field rep. Farmers Ins. Group, Sioux City, 1951-54, sr. liability examiner, Aurora, Ill., 1954-60; br. claims mgr., Ft. Wayne, Ind., 1960-66; prof. law Purdue U., West Lafayette, Ind., 1966—; dir. profl. masters programs of the Krannet Grad. Sch. of Mgmt. Purdue U., 1987—; of counsel with Mayfield & Brooks Attys. at Law, 1967—; arbitrator Panel of Arbitrators Am. Abritration Assn. Co-author: Business Law, Principles and Cases, 1982, 2d edit., 1985, Business Law Workbook, 1982, 2d edit., 1985, Foundations of Business Law, 1986, Student Workbook and Study Guide,

1986; contbr. numerous articles to profl. jours. Mem. Ind. Gov's Commn. Individual Privacy, 1975. Recipient Best Tchr. of Yr. award Standard Oil Ind. Found., 1972, Outstanding Tchr. award Purdue U. Alumni Assn., 1974. Mem. Am. Bus. Law Assn. (pres.), Tippecanoe County Bar Assn., Tri State Bus Law Assn., Midwest Bus. Adminstrn. Assn., Ind. Acad. Social Scis., Beta Gamma Sigma (bd. govs.). Office: Purdue U 511 Krannert Bldg West Lafayette IN 47906

SCALFI, CARLO GUISEPPE, business service company executive; b. Milan, Mar. 8, 1932; s. Franco Guiseppe and Rosa Maria (Beria) S.; m. Micheline Lacoste, Apr. 24, 1962; 1 child, Luigi. DChemE, Politecnico Milan, 1956. With S. Gobain-Chauny-Cirey, Rouen, France, 1958-60; with quality control dept., fiberglass Balzaretti Modigliani, Besana, Italy, 1960-61; plant mgr., glasswool Balzaretti Modigliani, Vidalengo, Italy, 1961-65; plant mgr., fiberglass Balzaretti Modigliani, Besana, Italy, 1965-71; sr. v.p. Balzaretti Modigliani, Milan, 1971-73; v.p. fiberglass div. Certain Teed Co., Valley Forge, Pa., 1973-75; licensing officer S. Gobain Industries, Paris, 1975-84; chief exec. officer ARXIN S.p.A, Milan, 1984—. Served as arty. officer. Named Hon. Citizen of Tex., 1973. Roman Catholic. Home: Piazzetta Bossi 1, 20121 Milan Italy

SCALIA, ANTONIN, justice; b. Trenton, N.J., Mar. 11, 1936; s. S. Eugene and Catherine Louise (Panaro) S.; m. Maureen McCarthy, Sept. 10, 1960; children—Ann Forrest, Eugene, John Francis, Catherine Elisabeth, Mary Clare, Paul David, Matthew, Christopher James, Margaret Jane. A.B., Georgetown U., 1957; student, U. Fribourg, Switzerland, 1955-56; LL.B., Harvard, 1960. Bar: Ohio 1962, Va. 1970. Assoc. Jones, Day, Cockley & Reavis, Cleve., 1961-67; assoc. prof. U. Va. Law Sch., 1967-70, prof., 1970-74; gen. counsel Office Telecommunications Policy, Exec. Office of Pres., 1971-72; chmn. Adminstrv. Conf. U.S., Washington, 1972-74; asst. atty. gen. U.S. Office Legal Counsel, Justice Dept., 1974-77; vis. prof. Georgetown Law Center, 1977, Stanford Law Sch., 1980-81; vis. scholar Am. Enterprise Inst., 1977; prof. Law Sch., U. Chgo., 1977-82; judge U.S. Ct. Appeals (D.C. Cir.), 1982-86; justice U.S. Supreme Ct., Washington, 1986—; cons. CSC, 1969, 77, FCC, 1977, FTC, 1978, 80; Bd. dirs. Nat. Inst. for Consumer Justice, 1972-73, Center for Adminstrv. Justice, 1972-74; adv. council for legal policy studies Am. Enterprise Inst., 1978—. Editor: Regulation mag, 1979-82. Sheldon fellow Harvard, 1960-61. Mem. ABA (council, sect. adminstrv. law 1974-77, chmn. sect. adminstrv. law 1981-82, chmn. conf. sect. chmn. 1982-83). Office: US Supreme Ct 1 1st St NE Washington DC 20543 *

SCALIA, AUGUSTO ANTONIO, physicist, educator; b. Catania, Sicily, Italy, Jan. 3, 1943; s. Salvatore and Maria (Consoli) S.; m. Carla Silvana Condorelli, Jan. 4, 1975; children: Emiliano, Fabio Arianna. BA in Physics, U. Catania, 1967. Assoc. researcher Nuclear Phys. Ctr., Catania, 1967—, Italian Nuclear Physics Inst., Catania, 1968—; asst. prof. physics U. Catania, 1971-85, prof., 1985—. Contbr. articles to profl. jours. Roman Catholic. Office: U Catania Dept Physics, Corso Italia 57, 95129 Catania Italy

SCAMMELL, GEOFFREY VAUGHAN, historian, educator; b. Wallasey, Cheshire, Eng., July 11, 1925; s. Edwin and Mabel Beatrice (Vaughan) S.; m. Jean Margaret Elders, Oct. 3, 1953; 1 child, Peter Geoffrey. BA, Emmanuel Coll., 1948, MA, 1953. Research asst. U. Durham, Eng., 1949-51; lectr. U. Durham, 1951-52; fellow Emmanuel Coll. U. Cambridge, Eng., 1952-53; lectr. U. Durham, 1953-65; lectr. U. Cambridge, 1965—, fellow, dir. studies in history Pembroke Coll., 1965-85, Leverhulme fellow Pembroke Coll., 1985-87; mem. council Soc. Nautical Research, 1963-66, Hakluyt Soc., 1981-86; chmn. Brit. com. Internat. Maritime History Com., 1978—. Author: Hugh Du Puiset, 1956, The World Encompassed, 1981, The Great Chartered Companies and the Sea, 1983; contbr. articles to profl. jours. Served to lt. Royal Navy, 1943-46. Recipient Prince Consort prize U. Cambridge, 1952, Notable Naval Book of 1982 award, U.S. Naval Inst., 1983. Fellow Royal Hist. Soc. Club: Little Ship. Home: 137 Huntingdon Rd, Cambridge CB3 0DQ, England Office: U Cambridge Pembroke Coll, Cambridge CB2 1RF, England

SCANAVINO, N. H. MARCO, real estate executive; b. Torino, Italy, Apr. 11, 1953; s. Cesare and Olga (Ghivarello) S. Ph.D. Acupuncture, Sch. Medicine U. Turin. Adminstr. M.A.S.T.E.R.S. Real Estate, Turin, 1980—; chmn. C.O.G.I.T.A., Turin, 1981—; ins. broker Augusta Assicurazioni (F.I.A.T. Group), 1986—. Clubs: Golf, Bridge. Office: C O G I T A, S S Quirico 115, 10020 Baldissero Torinese, Italy

SCANLAN, JOHN DOUGLAS, ambassador to Yugoslavia; b. Thief River Falls, Minn., Dec. 20, 1927; s. Paul Douglas and Ruby (Bennes) S.; m. Margaret Anne Calvi; children: Kathleen, Michael, Malia, John. B.A., U. Minn., 1952, M.A. in Russian Studies, 1955; postgrad. Fgn. Service Inst., 1960-61. Instr. U. Minn., 1955; Soviet research analyst U.S. Dept. State, Washington, 1956-58, third sec. Am. Embassy, Moscow, 1958-60, cultural attache Am. Embassy, Warsaw, 1961-65, second sec. Am. Embassy, Montevideo, 1966-67, prin. officer Am. Consulate, Poznan, Poland, 1967-69, sr. rep. to U.S. Dept. Defense, Washington, 1969-71, desk officer, U.S.-Soviet bilateral relations, 1971-73, Polit. counselor Am. Embassy, Warsaw, 1973-75, mem. st. exec. seminar, Washington, 1975-76, spl. asst. to Dir. Gen. of Fgn. Service, 1976-77, dep. dir. for Europe, USIA, 1977-79; dep. chief Mission in Belgrade, Yugoslavia, 1979-81; dep. asst. sec. of state for European affairs, 1981-82; fgn. affairs fellow Fletcher Sch. Law and Diplomacy, Tufts U., 1983-84; chmn. U.S. del. to Conf. on Security and Coop. in Europe, Cultural Forum Preparatory Conf., Budapest, 1984; mem. Bur. European Affairs, Dept. State, 1985; ambassador to Yugoslavia, 1985—. COntbr. articles on Soviet policy and U.S.-Soviet relations to profl. jours. Mem. Planning Commn., Falls Church, Va., 1972-73, City Council, 1975-79. Recipient Presdl. Meritorious Service award for Diplomacy, 1984. Address: care Dept of State US Ambassador to Yugoslavia Washington DC 20520

SCARBOROUGH, CHARLES BISHOP, III, broadcast journalist, writer; b. Pitts., Nov. 4, 1943; s. Charles Bishop and Esther Francis (Campbell) S.; m. Linda Anne Gross, Dec. 14, 1972; children: Charles Bishop, IV, Elizabeth Anne.; m. Anne Ford Uzielli, Oct. 2, 1982; stepchildren—Alessandro Uzielli, Allegra Uzielli. B.S., U. So. Miss., 1969. Prodn. mgr. Sta.-WLOX-TV, Biloxi, Miss., 1966-68; reporter, anchorman Sta.-WDAM-TV, Hattiesburg, Miss., 1968-69; reporter, anchorman, mng. editor Sta.-WAGA-TV, Atlanta, 1969-72; reporter, anchorman Sta.-WNAC-TV, Boston, 1972-74, NBC News, N.Y.C., 1974—. Author: novels Stryker, 1978, The Myrmidon Project, 1981. Served with USAF, 1961-65. Recipient awards for journalism AP (7), 1969-72, Emmy awards (15), 1974-79, award Aviation/Space Writers Assn., 1977, 78, 88, UPI award for journalism, N.Y. Press Club award, 1988, Sigma Delta Chi award, Deadline Club award. Mem. Phi Kappa Phi. Office: NBC News 30 Rockefeller Plaza New York NY 10020

SCARBOROUGH, CURTISS CLINTON, foundation executive; b. West Frankfort, Ill., Dec. 10, 1935; s. Curtis Clinton and Olive Jane (Keith) S.; B.A., So. Ill. U., 1956; B.C.M., Southwestern Bapt. Sem., 1959, M.R.E., 1959; M.A., Evangelical Coll., 1961; Ph.D., Columbia Pacific U., 1979; m. Ruth Ann Jent, Nov. 23, 1955; children—Karol Ruth, Keith Curtiss. Ordained to ministry Baptist Ch., 1964; minister First Bapt. Ch., Metropolis, Ill., 1959-61, Westview Bapt. Ch., Belleville, Ill., 1961-63, Water Tower Bapt. Ch., St. Louis, 1963-67, N. Side Bapt. Ch., Florissant, Mo., 1967-75; dir. communications Christian Civic Found., St. Louis, 1975-83; pres. Christian Civic Found., 1983—; pres., chmn. bd. Drug Alcohol Tobacco Edn., Inc., 1983—; exec. dir. Am. Council on Alcohol Problems, 1987—; pres. Temperance Edn. Inc., 1987—; trustee Christian Life Commn. So. Bapt. Conv., 1987—. Author: (with Cleveland R. Horne) Citizens, Under God, 1979; (with John D. King) An Ounce of Prevention, 1980; Basics on Abused Drugs, 1981; Take the Freeway, 1983; author, compiler (with Gerald Young) Choice Sermons from Missouri Pulpits, 1981; newspaper editor The Christian Citizen, 1975-83, Dateline, 1975-83; syndicated columnist Drug Quiz, 1979—. Home: 2476 Buttonwood Ct Florissant MO 63031 Office: 3426 Bridgeland Dr Bridgeton MO 63044

SCARLOT, ROBERT MARCEL BERNARD, nuclear medicine physician, anesthesiologist; b. Monaco, Mar. 24, 1936; d. Michel and Lucienne (Levantini) S.; m. Jeannine Gouy-Paillier, Dec. 23, 1961; 1 child, Florence. MD, U. Grenoble, France, 1965; cert. anesthesia, U. Lyon, France, 1966; cert. nuclear medicine, U. Marseille, France, 1980. Intern Grenoble Hosp., 1959-64; resident Lyon Hosp., 1964-67; adjoint chief Ctr. Hosp. Princess Grace, Monaco, 1967-86, chief dept., 1986—; med. dir. Formula One Orgn. Auto, Monaco, 1971. Named Order St. Charles, Monaco, 1984. Mem. Soc. Nuclear Medicine, Soc. Biophysics, Soc. Anesthesia, Automobile Club Monaco (chmn. med. commn. 1970—), Internat. Fedn. Automobile Paris (mem. med. commn. 1982—). Roman Catholic. Lodge: Rotary. Home: 1 Blvd De Suisse, MC98000 Monte Carlo Monaco Office: Ctr Hosp Princess Grace, Ave Pasteur, MC98000 Monaco Monaco

SCARZAFAVA, JOHN FRANCIS, lawyer; b. Oneonta, N.Y., Apr. 4, 1947; s. Francis R. and Nettie (Ho Talen) S.; m. Nettie Jean Chambers; 1 child, Robert Francis; stepchildren: Angela Atkinson, Amber Atkinson, Amy Atkinson. BA, St. Bonaventure U., 1973; JD, St. Mary's U., San Antonio, 1975. Bar: Tex. 1975, U.S. Ct. Appeals (5th cir.) 1976, U.S. Dist. Ct. (we. dist.) Tex. 1978, U.S. Supreme Ct. 1979, N.Y. 1981, U.S. Dist. Ct. (no. dist.) N.Y. 1982. Assoc. Gochman & Weir, San Antonio, 1975-77, ptnr., 1977-78; ptnr. Scarzafava & Davis, San Antonio, 1978-82; sole practice Oneonta, 1982—. Contbr. numerous articles to profl. law jours. Chmn. Dem. Com., Oneonta, 1982-85; Dem. committeeman, Otsego County, N.Y., 1982-85; bd. dirs. St. Bonaventure U. Nat. Alumni, v.p. 1986—; bd. dirs. St. Mary's U. Sch. Law Alumni, 1979; mem. Citizen's Bd., Hartwick Coll., 1984—. Served to sgt. USAF, 1967-70. Mem. Assn. Trial Lawyers Am. (nat. sec. Labor law Sect. 1980, lectr. nat. conv. 1982, 86, instr. various Nat. Coll. of Adv. 1979—), Tex. Trial Lawyers Assn., N.Y. State Trial Lawyers Assn., San Antonio Trial Lawyers Assn., Delta Theta Phi (Dean Bickett Senate 1977), St. Bonaventure U. Alumni Assn. (Pres. 1988—). Roman Catholic. Club: 6th Ward Athletic (bd. dirs. 1984-85), President's (St. Mary's U.). Home: RD 1 Box 70D Oneonta NY 13820 Office: 48 Dietz St Suite C Oneonta NY 13820

SCATTERGOOD, THOMAS W., planetologist, analytical chemist; b. Mt. Holly, N.J., Oct. 3, 1946; s. William E. and Grace (Paulin) S. B.S. in Chemistry, U. Del., Newark, 1968; M.S., SUNY-Stony Brook, 1972, Ph.D. in Chemistry, 1975. Teaching asst. SUNY-Stony Brook, 1970-72, research asst., 1972-75, research assoc., 1975-76, sr. research assoc., 1979—; research assoc. NRC, Nat. Acad. Scis., 1977-78, Mars Exobiology Research Consortium, NASA Ames Research Ctr., Titan Probe Sci. Study Group, NASA Ames Research Ctr., Moffett Field, Calif., 1979-81; adj. asst. prof. SUNY-Stony Brook ; adj. assoc. prof., 1987—. Contbr. articles to profl. publs. Treas. Central Coast Counties Camera Club Council. Mem. AAAS, Am. Geophys. Union, Am. Astron. Soc. (div. planetary scis.), Planetary Soc., Photog. Soc. Am., Internat. Soc. for Study of Origin of Life. Quaker. Club: Camaraderie Camera (Mountain View, Calif.). Office: NASA Ames Research Ctr MS 239-12 Moffett Field CA 94035

SCERBO, FRANCIS BARRY, university service administrator; b. Fulton, N.Y., Feb. 3, 1943; s. Francis Albert and Ahleen (Downing) S.; B.A. in Bus. Adminstrn., Hiram Scott Coll., 1971; children—Anthony J., Andrew A. Asst. dir. aux. services Hiram Scott Coll., Scottsbluff, Nebr., 1968-71; asst. dir. food service, Univ. Center, U. Mont., Missoula, 1971-72; dir. univ. food services De Paul U., Chgo., 1973-76; exec. dir., dir. dining services Aux. Campus Enterprises, SUNY, Binghamton, Inc., 1976-83; dir. univ. food service Duke U., Durham, N.C., 1983—. Tech. dir. Syracuse Symphony Opera, 1963, 64; dir. Wildcat Hills Pageant, Scottsbluff, 1970, 71; cub master Boy Scouts Am., 1979-83. Served with USAF, 1966-68. Mem. Nat. Restaurant Assn., Nat. Assn. Coll. Aux. Services, Nat. Assn. Coll. and Univ. Food Services, N.C. State Restaurant Assn., Internat. Platform Assn., Durham Univ. Club. Democrat. Roman Catholic. Lodges: Optimists, Toastmasters. Home: 3010 Harriman Rd Durham NC 27705 Office: Duke U PO Box 4853 Duke Station Durham NC 27706

SCHAAF, C(ARL) HART, former United Nations official, consultant, writer; b. Ft. Wayne, Ind., Jan. 14, 1912; s. Albert H. and Bertha May (Hart) S.; m. Barbara Joan Crook, Nov. 22, 1945; children: Albert H., Timothy H. Student, U. Montpellier, France, 1930-31, U. Stockholm, 1937-39; B.A., U. Mich., 1935, Ph.D. (Horace H. Rackham fellow), 1940. Instr. polit. sci. CCNY, summer 1940; asso. prof. public adminstrn. Richmond div. Coll. William and Mary, 1940-42; state rationing adminstr. for Va. U.S. OPA, 1942-43; asst. dep. dir. gen., also chief supply for Europe UNRRA, 1944-47; asso. prof. adminstrn. Sch. Bus. and Public Adminstrn., Cornell U., 1947-49; dep. exec. sec. UN Econ. Commn. for Asia and Far East, 1949-54; mem. UN Tech. Assistance Survey Mission to, Indonesia, 1950; spl. adviser to UN sec. gen. on relief and support civilian population Korea 1950-51; resident rep. in Israel UN Tech. Assistance Bd., 1954-57; resident rep. for UN Tech. Assistance Bd., Philippines, 1957-59; exec. agt. Com. Coordination Investigations Lower Mekong Basin, UN Econ. Commn. for, Asia and Far East, Com. Coordination Investigations Lower Mekong Basin, UN Econ. Commn. for Bangkok, 1959-69; resident rep. UN Devel. Program, Sri Lanka and Republic of Maldives, 1969-74; dep. exec. dir. ops. UN Fund for Population Activities, N.Y.C., 1974-77; team leader Basic Needs Assessment Missions to UN Fund for Population Activities, Nigeria, 1979, Tunisia, 1980, Maldives, 1981, Indonesia, 1984, Egypt, 1985; pres. C. Hart Schaaf Assos., Inc. (cons. econ. and social devel.), 1980—; Mem. Mekong Adv. Com. Bd., 1969-72. Author: play Partition, 1948; (with Russell H. Fifield) The Lower Mekong: Challenge to Cooperation in Southeast Asia, 1963; Contbr. articles to tech. and acad. jours. Recipient (with Mekong Com.) Ramon Magsaysay award for internat. understanding, 1966, Outstanding Achievement award U. Mich., 1966. Mem. Am. Polit. Sci. Assn., Soc. Internat. Devel. Home: 3525 Twin Branches Dr Silver Spring MD 20906

SCHAAF, LINDA ANN, nurse, educator; b. Balt., Feb. 15, 1944; d. Wilbert Frederick and Rosina Catherine (Lutz) S. Diploma, St. Agnes Hosp. Sch. Nursing, 1967; BSN, U. Md., 1971; MSN, Cath. U. Am., 1973. RN. Staff nurse, charge nurse St. Agnes Hosp., Balt., 1967-71; staff nurse Provident Hosp., Washington, 1972-73; pvt. duty nurse Med. Personnel Pool, Washington, 1973; practitioner, tchr. Rush-Presbyn. St. Luke's Med. Ctr., Chgo., 1973-80; staff nurse Critical Care Services, Inc., Chgo., 1980-82; assoc. prof. Ill. Benedictine Coll., Lisle, 1980—; clin. educator, cons. Glendale Heights (Ill.) Community Hosp., 1983—; cons. curriculum Trinity Coll., Washington Hosp. Ctr., Washington, 1976. Bd. dirs. Woodridge (Ill.) Unit Am Cancer Soc., 1984—; mem. Chgo. Heart Assn., 1973—. Mem. Am. Nurses Assn. (cert.), Ill. Nurses Assn., Am. Assn. Critical Care Nurses (cert. critical care RN), Nat. League for Nursing, Ill. League for Nursing (program developer 1976), Am. Heart Assn. (council on cardiovascular nursing 1970—), Sigma Theta Tau, Internat. Honor Soc. Nursing. Democrat. Roman Catholic. Office: Ill Benedictine Coll 5700 College Rd Lisle IL 60532

SCHAARSCHMIDT, HARRY FRED, manufacturing executive, product manager; b. Basel, Switzerland, Nov. 16, 1931; s. Fritz R. and Margrit E. (Mueller) S.; m. Claire M. Guldimann; children: Marc H., Karin D. Various studies in commerce and tech., 1949-56; degree in mgmt., Trey (Switzerland) Inst., 1952. In bldg. trade Nigeria, 1957-62; enlisted Swiss army, 1963, advanced through grades to sgt.-maj., 1970, served as instr., 1963-81, resigned, 1981; product mgr. U. Ammann Bldg. Equipment Ltd., Langenthal, Switzerland, 1981—. Served in Swiss army res., 1981-87. Home: Ruetistr 1, CH 4900 Langenthal Switzerland Office: U Ammann Building Equipment, Ltd, CH 4900 Langenthal Switzerland

SCHACHINGER, FRITZ JOHANN WOLFGANG, dental manufacturing company sales manager; b. Vienna, Austria, Sept. 16, 1956; s. Fritz and Edeltraud S.; m. Evamaria Schachinger, April 5, 1983; children: Michael, Katrin. MBA, Econ. U. of Vienna, 1982. Mktg. asst. Pepsico, Vienna, 1982-84; nat. mktg. mgr. Wilson Sporting Goods, Munich, 1984-85; export mgr. TRO Sports, Hohenems, Austria, 1985-86; sales mgr. Coltene, Altstaetten, Switzerland, 1986—. Served in Austrian army, 1974—, advanced through grades to capt., 1987. Mem. OEVP Conservative party. Roman Catholic. Club E.S.V. Tennis. Lodge: Rotary. Home: Austrasse 84, A-6805 Feldkirch Austria

SCHACHT, WILLIAM EUGENE, accountant; b. Kokomo, Ind., Nov. 6, 1941; s. Francis Albert and Estella Lillian (Brockman) S.; m. Lucia Fatima Camara, Nov. 21, 1985; children: Julie Ann, Susan Ruth, Randolph Lee. BS in Acctg., Ball State U., 1970. CPA, Calif. Acct. Davidson, Dreyer and Hopkins, CPA's, 1973-74, mgr., 1974-77; pvt. practice acctg. San Francisco, 1977-88; chief exec. officer BX-100 Corp., San Francisco, 1988—; chmn., treas. Unique Adventures, Inc.; bd. dirs. Rio-Cal, Inc., Tigs of San Francisco, Inc. Served with U.S. Army, 1959-62. Recipient Scholastic award Price-Waterhouse, 1968. Mem. Am. Inst. CPA's, San Francisco C. of C. Republican. Office: 140 2d St 6th Fl San Francisco CA 94105

SCHÄCHTER, LEON, nuclear engineer; b. Berlin, Germany, May 11, 1930; arrived in Romania, 1934.; B in Engring., Inst. Leningrad, USSR, 1955; postgrad. nuclear physics, engring., U. Bucharest, Romania, 1957; D in Nuclear Engring., Inst. Atomic Physics, Bucharest, 1975. Sr. scientist Inst. Atomic Phusics, Bucharest, 1970—. Contbr. articles to profl. jours. Recipient Constantin Miculescu prize Romanian Acad., 1974. Home: Bucharest Str Faurei 1, Bucharest Romania

SCHACK, ROBERT J., lawyer; b. N.Y.C., Jan. 8, 1944; s. Jerome Arthur and Elizabeth (Thompson) S. Cert. in Spanish U. Internacional Menendez-Pelayo, Santander, Spain, 1964; B.A. with honors, Haverford Coll., 1965; J.D., NYU, 1974. Bar: N.Y. 1975, U.S. Dist. Ct. (so. and ea. dists.) N.Y. 1978, U.S. Ct. Appeals (2d cir.) 1978, U.S. Supreme Ct. 1978. Staff counsel Citizens Com. for Children, N.Y.C., 1974-76; sr. atty. N.Y. State Mental Hygiene, N.Y.C., 1976-77; asst. atty. gen. State of N.Y., N.Y.C., 1977—; adj. prof. Baruch Coll., N.Y.C., 1984; vice-chmn. profl. conduct com. div. cen. screening for Family Ct. Panel, 1985—. Co-author: Undelivered Care: The Incapacitated and the Mentally Ill New York City Defendant, 1972. Contbr. articles to law and computer jours. Drafter social service legislation. Bd. editors, editor-in-chief law sch. and coll. newspapers. Trustee Inst. of Child Mental Health, N.Y.C., 1986—; co-founder, bd. dirs., past pres., co-counsel WNCN Listeners' Guild, N.Y.C., 1974-82; co-founder, bd. dirs. Saving Families for Children, 1976-81; Woodrow Wilson fellow 1965; recipient Kroner Meml. award NYU, 1974, Commendation award WNCN Listeners' Guild, 1976; cert. Liberty Through Law Program, 1984. Mem. N.Y. State Bar Assn. (chmn. subcoms. on juvenile justice and child welfare 1978—), N.Y. County Lawyers Assn. (chmn. subcom. family ct. com. 1986—, chmn. com. medicine and mental health 1983-85), Assn. Bar City of N.Y. (chmn. subcom. family ct. and family law com. 1982-83). Nat. Council Juvenile and Family Ct. Judges, ABA. Democrat. Jewish. Home: 330 E 71st St Apt 2F New York NY 10021 Office: New York State Dept Law 120 Broadway New York NY 10271

SCHAD, THEODORE GEORGE, JR., food company executive; b. N.Y.C., Mar. 4, 1927; s. Theodore George and Helen (Tennyson) S.; m. Karma Rose Cundell, Mar. 21, 1957 (dec. June 1978); children: Roberta Gay Hill, Theodore George III, Olive Schad Smith, Peter Tennyson.; m. Mary Nell Jennings, June 20, 1981. Student, Va. Mil. Inst., 1944-45; B.S. in Bus. and Econs, Ill. Inst. Tech., 1950, M.S. in Bus. and Econs, 1951. V.p. mktg. Great Western Savs. Co., Los Angeles, 1961-63; prin., nat. dir. mktg. and econs. cons. Peat, Marwick, Mitchell, N.Y.C., 1964-71; chmn. bd., pres., chief exec. officer Lou Ana Foods, Inc., Schad Industries, Inc. (formerly Lou Ana Industries, Inc.), 1971—, Lou Ana Industries Internat., 1971-84, Schad Industries Internat., Opelousas, La., 1985—, Lou Ana Foods of Tex., Inc., Kingwood, 1986—; instr. mktg. and econs. U. Calif., Riverside, U. So. Calif., Los Angeles State Coll., U. Calif., Los Angeles, 1956-63. Pres. Assn. Parents Retarded Children, Mamaroneck, N.Y., 1970-71; bd. dirs. Council for Better La., Baton Rouge, 1975-80, La. Assn. Bus. and Industry, 1980-85; chmn. U.S. Bus. and Indsl. Council, 1987—, bd. dirs., 1979-84, mem. exec. com., 1984-87, bd. dirs. U.S. Indsl. Council Ednl. Found., 1987—; trustee Va. Mil. Inst. Found., 1978—; v.p., mem. exec. bd. Evangeline Area council Boy Scouts Am., 1984-85. Recipient Disting. Eagle Scout award Boy Scouts Am., 1985; named Citizen of Yr. Opelousas, La., 1979, Man of Yr. Sertoma of Opelousas, 1978, Paul Harris fellow Rotary, 1987. Mem. Am. Mktg. Assn. (pres. So. Calif. chpt. 1961-62, dir. 1962-63). Republican. Methodist. Lodge: Sertoma (founding pres. local chpt. 1963). Office: Lou Ana Foods PO Box 591 Opelousas LA 70570

SCHAD, THEODORE MACNEEVE, science research administrator, consultant; b. Balt., Aug. 25, 1918; s. William Henry and Emma Margaret (Scheldt) S.; m. Kathleen White, Nov. 5, 1944; children: Mary Jane, Rebecca Christina. BSCE, Johns Hopkins U., 1939. Various positions water resources engring. U.S. Army C.E., U.S. Bur. Reclamation, Md., Colo., Oreg. Wash., 1939-54; prin. budget examiner water resources programs U.S. Bur. Budget, Exec. Office of Pres., 1954-58; sr. specialist engring. and pub. works, dep. dir. Congl. Research Service, Library of Congress, 1958-68; staff dir. U.S. Senate Com. Nat. Water Resources, 1959-61; exec. dir. Nat. Water Commn., 1968-73; exec. sec. Environ. Studies Bd., 1973-77; dep. dir. Commn. Natural Resources, Nat. Acad. Scis., Washington, 1977-83; exec. dir. Nat. Ground Water Policy Forum; exec. dir. The Conservation Found., Washington, 1984-86, sr. fellow, 1986—; U.S. commr. Permanent Internat. Assn. Nav. Congresses, Brussels, 1963-70, commr. emeritus, 1987—; cons. U.S. Senate Com. Interior and Insular Affairs, 1963, U.S. Ho. of Reps. Com. Sci. and Tech., 1964-65, Fed. Council Sci. and Tech., 1962-65, U.S. Office Saline Water, 1965-67, A.T. Kearney, Inc., Alexandria, Va., 1979-80, Chesapeake Research Consortium, 1984, Ronco Cons. Corp., 1986—, Gambia River Basin Devel. Commn., Dakar, 1986-87. Contbr. articles to Ency. Brit. and profl. jours. Treas. Nat. Speleol. Found., 1961-65, trustee, 1965—; bd. dirs. Vets. Coop. Housing Assn., Washington, 1958-81, v.p., 1960-72. Recipient Meritorious Service award U.S. Dept. Interior, 1950; recipient Icko Iben award Am. Water Resources Assn., 1978. Fellow ASCE (treas. Nat. Capital sect. 1952-55, v.p. 1967, pres. 1968), Nat. Speleol. Soc.; mem. Am. Water Works Assn. (hon.), Am. Geophys. Union, AAAS, Soc. Am. Acad. Environ. Engrs., Nat. Acad. Pub. Adminstrn., Permanent Internat. Assn. Nav. Congresses, Internat. Commn. Irrigation and Drainage. Clubs: Potomac Appalachian Trail; Cosmos (Washington); Colo. Mountain (Denver); Seattle Mountaineers. Home: 4138 26th Rd N Arlington VA 22207 Office: The Conservation Found 1255 23d St NW Washington DC 20037

SCHADE, ROBERT RICHARD, medical educator, researcher; b. Rockville Centre, N.Y., Jan. 5, 1948; s. Robert Richard and Loretta K. (McGovern) S.; m. Rosann Foster, Oct. 14, 1972; children—Danielle Nicole, Kimberly Anne, Allison Janine. A.B., Colgate U., 1969; M.D., George Washington U., 1973. Diplomate: Am. Bd. Internal Medicine Nat. Bd. Med. Examiners. Intern Rush-Presbyn. Med. Ctr., Chgo., 1973-74, resident in internal medicine, 1974-76; fellow liver disease unit Yale U., New Haven, 1976-78, fellow in gastroenterology, 1978-80; asst. prof. medicine U. Pitts. Med. Sch., 1980-86, assoc. prof., 1986—; dir. Clin. Gastrointestinal lab. Presbyn. U. Hosp., Pitts., 1982—; attending VA Hosp. of Oakland, Pitts., Children's Hosp. Pitts. Assoc. editor: Digestive Diseases and Sciences, 1988—; author book chpts. in med. texts; reviewer med. jours. Contbr. articles to profl. jours. Mem. sci. adv. bd. Pitts. chpt. Nat. Found. (sci. adv. bd. 1981-86). Ileitis and Colitis, 1981—. Fellow ACP, Am. Coll. Gastroenterology; mem. Am. Gastroent. Assn., N.Y. Acad. Sci., Midwest Gut Club, Pa. Soc. Gastroenterology, Am. Soc. Gastrointestinal Endoscopy, Am. Assn. Study Liver Disease, AAAS. Republican. Roman Catholic. Home: 338 Dewey Ave Pittsburgh PA 15218 Office: U Pitts 1000J Scaife Hall Pittsburgh PA 15261

SCHAEFER, CHARLES JAMES, III, advertising agency executive; b. Orange, N.J., Dec. 17, 1926; m. Eleanor Anne Montville, Apr. 8, 1961; 1 child, Charles James IV. A.B., Dartmouth Coll., 1948, M. Comml. Sci. Amos Tuck Sch., 1949. Vice pres. Dickie-Raymond, 1952-67; sr. v.p. Metromedia, 1968-69; exec. v.p., treas. The DR Group, Boston, 1969-76, pres., 1976—; exec. v.p., dir. Needham Harper Worldwide Inc., N.Y.C., 1984-87; chmn. bd. Marcoa Dr Group, Inc., N.Y.C., 1987—. Served with USN, 1945-46. Clubs: Dartmouth (pres. 1968-70), Lotos (treas. 1987— N.Y.C.); Canoe Brook Country (Summit, N.J.). Home: 307 Hobart Ave Short Hills NJ 07078 Office: Marcoa DR Group Inc 475 Park Ave S New York NY 10016

SCHAEFER, CHRISTOPHER BRIAN, county planning official, geographic information system company official; b. N.Y.C., June 27, 1949; s. Rudolf Franz and Florence (Rittenwagen) S.; m. Doris Bennett, Nov. 13, 1976; children—Justin, Kimberly, Nathaniel. B.S., U. Utah, 1972; M. Urban Planning, U. Pitts., 1979. Cert. planner. Sr. planner Davis County Planning Commn., Farmington, Utah, 1976—; prin. UNI-Graphic Systems Inc., Salt Lake City, 1984—; cons. planner various local communities, Utah, 1977—; speaker profl. conf., 1983. Planning asst. Squirrel Hill Urban Coalition, Pitts., 1975, People's Freeway Group, Salt Lake City, 1972. Co-author: Davis County Gig, The Hybrid Approach to Map Accuracy, 1986, The Challenge of Developing A Multi-purpose Cadagter-The Davis County Experience. Mem. Am. Inst. Cert. Planners, Am. Planning Assn., Urban and

Regional Info. Systems Assn. Mormon. Home: 445 S 925 E Kaysville UT 84037 Office: UNI-Graphic Systems Inc PO Box 520610 Salt Lake City UT 84152

SCHAEFER, GEORGE ANTHONY, manufacturing company executive; b. Covington, Ky., June 13, 1928; s. George Joseph and Marie Cecelia (Sandheger) S.; m. Barbara Ann Quick, Aug. 11, 1951; children: Mark Christopher, Sharon Marie. BS in Commerce, St. Louis U., 1951. With Caterpillar Inc., Peoria, Ill., 1951—, div. mgr., 1968-73; plant mgr. Caterpillar Inc., Decatur, Ill., 1973-76, v.p., 1976-81, dir., 1981-84; vice chmn., exec. v.p. Caterpillar Inc., Peoria, 1984-85, chmn., chief exec. officer, 1985—; fin. and acctg. mgr. Caterpillar France S.A., Grenoble, 1962-68; db. dirs. San Diego, 1st Chgo. Corp.; mem. bus. council Emergency Com. for Am. Trade Negotiations. Mem. adv. council Coll. Commerce and Bus. Adminstrn. U. Ill, Champaign, 1979; trustee Bradley U.; econ. devel. com. Proctor Community Hosp. Served with USMC, 1946-48. Mem. Bus. Council. Republican. Roman Catholic. Club: Peoria Country. Office: Caterpillar Inc 100 NE Adams St Peoria IL 61629

SCHAEFER, HELMUT HANS, mathematician; b. Grossenhain, Germany, Feb. 14, 1925; s. Hans Arwed and Marianne Ilse (Schmidt) S.; m. Käthe M. Heym, Aug. 15, 1951; children: Rhea, Christoph, Mark. Degree, U. Leipzig, 1951, Venia Legendi, 1954. Assoc. prof. Wash. State U., Pullman, 1958-60, U. Mich., 1960-63; prof. math. U. Tuebingen, Germany, 1963—; visiting prof. U. Ill., 1965-66, U. Md., 1969-70, 72-73, Calif. Inst. Tech., 1978-79, 84, Tex. A&M U., 1983. Author: Topological Vector Spaces, 1966, Banach Lattices and Positive Operators, 1974; contbr. articles to profl. jours; adv. bd. Mathematische Zeitschrift. Mem. Acad. Sci. Heidelberg, Deutscher Mathematiker Vereinigung, Am. Math. Soc.; Acad. Sci. Zaragoza (corr. mem.). Home: Raichbergstr 7, 7408 Wankheim Federal Republic of Germany Office: Math Inst of Tubingen, Auf der Morgenstelle 10, 7400 Tubingen Federal Republic of Germany

SCHAEFER, HENRY FREDERICK, III, chemistry educator; b. Grand Rapids, Mich., June 8, 1944; s. Henry Frederick Jr. and Janice Christine (Trost) S.; m. Karen Regine Rasmussen, Sept. 2, 1966; children: Charlotte, Pierre, Theodore, Rebecca, Caleb. BS in Chem. Physics, MIT, 1966; PhD in Chem. Physics, Stanford U., 1969. Asst. prof. chemistry U. Calif., Berkeley, 1969-74, assoc. prof., 1974-78, prof., 1978-87; Graham Perdue prof., dir. Ctr. for Computational Quantum Chemistry U. Ga., Athens, 1987—; Wilfred T. Doherty prof., dir. Inst. Theoretical Chemistry, U. Tex., Austin, 1979-80; endowed lectr. Nat. U. Mex., 1979, Johns Hopkins U., 1982, Brown U., 1985, U. Canterbury, Christchurch, New Zealand, 1986, U. Kans., 1986, Vanderbilt U., 1988, U. Va., 1988. Author: The Electronic Structure of Atoms and Molecules: A Survey of Rigorous Quantum Mechanical Results, 1972, Modern Theoretical Chemistry, 1977, Quantum Chemistry, 1984. Recipient Pure Chemistry award Am. Chem. Soc., 1979, Leo Hendrik Baekeland award, 1983; Sloan fellow, 1972, Guggenheim fellow, 1976-77; named One of the 100 Outstanding Young Scientists in Am., Sci. Digest, 1984. Fellow Am. Phys. Soc.; mem. Internat. Acad. Quantum Molecular Sci. Mem. Presbyterian Ch. in Am. Office: U Ga Dept Chemistry Athens GA 30602

SCHAEFER, KATHLEEN ANN, clinical instrument company executive; b. Racine, Wis., Aug. 12, 1948; d. Victor Louis and Mary Claire Weinfurter. B.S., U. Wis.-Whitewater, 1970; M.B.A., Lake Forest Grad. Sch. Mgmt., 1982. Staff technologist St. Luke's Meml. Hosp., Racine, Wis., 1970-72, Presbyn. Hosp. Center, Albuquerque, 1972-75; control analyst Hyland Diagnostics, div. Travenol Labs., Inc., Round Lake, Ill., 1976, sr. control analyst, 1976-78, supr. quality labs., 1978, supt. stability assurance, 1978-80, sect. mgr. quality assurance services, 1980-81, mgr. quality assurance labs., 1981-82; mgr. tng. and edn. Baker Instruments Inc. div. Richardson-Vicks, Allentown, Pa., 1982-83, mgr. tech. and ednl. services, 1983; dir. tech. services and edn. Kone Instruments, Inc., Bensenville, Ill., 1983-86, dir. mktg. services, 1986-87; asst. dir. instrument support group Rupp & Bowman Co., Irving, Tex., 1987—; adv. bd. Lake County Coll. Med. Technician Program. Mem. Am. Assn. for Clin. Chemistry, Am. Soc. Clin. Pathologists (asso. mem.), Nat. Assn. Female Execs. and Women in Healthcare, Assn. Field Service Mgrs. (mem. subcom. nat. com. clin. lab. standards), Regulatory Affairs Profl. Soc. Home: 6 Greentree Ln Bedford TX 76201 Office: Rupp & Bowman Co 9206 Royal Ln Irving TX 75063

SCHAEFER, PATRICIA, librarian; b. Ft. Wayne, Ind., Apr. 23, 1930; d. Edward John and Hildegarde Hartman (Hormel) S.; MusB, Northwestern U., 1951; MusM, U. Ill., 1958; MA in LS, U. Mich., 1963. With U.S. Rubber Co., Ft. Wayne, Ind., 1951-52; sec. to promotion mgr. Sta. WOWO, Ft. Wayne, Ind., 1952, sec. to program mgr., 1953-55; coordinator publicity and promotion Home Telephone Co., Ft. Wayne, 1955-56; sec. Fine Arts Found., Ft. Wayne, 1956-57; library asst. Columbus (Ohio) Pub. Library, 1958-59; audio-visual librarian Muncie (Ind.) Pub. Library, 1959-86, asst. library dir., 1981-86; library dir., 1986—; chmn. Ind. Library Film Circuit, 1962-63; treas. Ind. Library Film Service 1969-70, 83-85; mem. trustees adv. council Milton S. Eisenhower Library, Johns Hopkins U.; cons. in field. Weekly columnist Library Lines, Muncie Evening Press, 1981-83; Contbr. articles to profl. jours. Dir. Franklin Electric Co., Inc. Bd. dirs. Muncie Symphony Assn., 1964-74, 85—; bd. trustees Masterworks Chorale, Muncie Mcpl. Band; bd. dirs. Cen. City Bus. Assn. Mem. adv. com., bookshop dir. Midwest Writers Workshop, 1976-77; sec. Del. County Council for the Arts, 1978-79, pres., 1979-81, bd. dirs., 1985-86; mem. pres.'s council Berea Coll.; bd. dirs. Muncie YWCA, 1977-82, 85-86, treas., 1981-82, 88; gen. chmn. Ind. Renaissance Fair, 1978-79; pres. Muncie Matinee Musicale, 1965-67; past pres. Ind. Film and Video Council; mem. community adv. com. Minnetrista Cultural Ctr. Mem. Ind. Library Assn. (pres. 1987-88), ALA, Nat. League Am. Pen Women (pres. Muncie br. 1974-78), Am. Recorder Soc., Northeastern Ind. Recorder Soc., Delta Zeta, Mu Phi Epsilon. Republican. Roman Catholic. Clubs: Riley-Jones, Altrusa (Muncie) (pres. 1986-87). Home: 405 S Tara Ln Muncie IN 47304 Office: 301 E Jackson St Muncie IN 47305

SCHAEFER, WILLIAM DONALD, governor of Maryland, former mayor; b. Balt., Nov. 2, 1921; s. William Henry and Tululu (Skipper) S. LL.B., U. Balt., 1942, LL.M., 1951, LL.D. (hon.), 1976; J.D. (hon.), Loyola Coll., 1976; J.D., Goucher Coll., 1980; D.Public Service (hon.), U. Md., 1979, LL.D. (hon.), 1981; LL.D. (hon.), Morgan State U., 1983; D.H.L. (hon.), Towson State U., 1983. Bar: Md. 1943. Practiced in Balt., 1943—; mem. Balt. City Council, 1955-67, pres., 1967-71; mayor City of Balt., 1971-87; gov. State of Md., Annapolis, 1987—. Served with AUS, 1942-45; Col. Res. (ret.). Recipient numerous awards, including 1st ann. Civic Statesmanship award Citizens Planning and Housing Assn., Jefferson award for outstanding public service, 1979, Outstanding Leadership in Devel. and Support of Citizen Volunteerism U.S. Conf. Mayors, 1979, Michael A. DiNunzio award U.S. Conf. Mayors, 1981, award of excellence Urban Land Inst., 1980, Man of Decade award Advt. Club Balt., 1982, Disting. Mayor award Nat. Urban Coalition, 1982; named Alumni of Yr. U. Balt., 1971; Man of Yr. Jewish Nat. Fund, 1972. Mem. Nat. League Cities (dir.), Md. Assn. Counties, Md. Mcpl. League, Balt. Bar Assn., Citizens Planning and Housing Assn. Balt., Nat. Hist. Soc., Balt. Ecol. Soc., Md. Ret. Officers Assn., Balt. Assn. Retarded Citizens, Md. Acad. Scis., VFW, Navy League U.S., Am. Pub. Works Assn., Am. Inst. Banking (hon.), Am. Public Works Assn., AIA (hon. mem. Balt. chpt.), Md. Law Enforcement Officers, Md 4-H Club. Democrat. Club: Rotary (Balt.). Home: Govt House Annapolis MD 21401 Office: Office of Gov State House Annapolis MD 21401

SCHAEFFER, BARBARA HAMILTON, transportation company executive; travel consultant; b. Newton, Mass., Apr. 26, 1926; d. Peter Davidson Gunn and Harriet Bennett (Thompson) Hamilton; m. John Schaeffer, Sept. 7, 1946; children—Laurie, John, Peter. Student, Skidmore Coll., 1943-46; AB in English, Bucknell U., 1948; postgrad. Montclair State U., 1950-51, Bank St. Coll. Edn., 1959-61, Yeshiva U., 1961-62; student Daytona Beach Coll., 1984. Cert. primary, secondary tchr., N.J. Dir. Pompton Plains Sch., N.J., 1959-62; adviser Episcopal Sch., Towaco, N.J., 1968-70; v.p. Deltona-De-Land Trolley, Orange City, Fla., 1980-81; pres. Monroe Heavy Equipment Rentals, Inc., Orange City, 1981—, also Magic Carpet Travel subs., 1986—; cons. TLC Travel Club, Orange City, 1981—; lectr. on children's art, 1959-70. Contbr. articles to profl. publs. Mem. Internat. Platform Assn., Am. Soc. Travel Agts., Deltona C. of C., Orange City C. of C., Small Bus. Devel. Regional Ctr. (Stetson U. chpt.), DeLand Area C. of C. (transp. com. 1981-85). Episcopalian. Avocations: restoring old homes, oil painting, piano. Home: 400 Foothill Farms Rd Orange City FL 32763 Office: Magic Carpet Travel 2425 Enterprise Rd Orange City FL 32763

SCHAEFFER, KLAUS HEYMANN, urban planner, educator; b. Charlottenburg, Germany, Feb. 28, 1921; came to U.S. 1939, naturalized 1951; s. Ernst Johann Heymann and Olga Elisabet (Kurnik) S.; B.A., Oberlin Coll., 1943; postgrad. Yale U., 1943-44, U. Mich., 1949-51; B.D., Luth. Theol. Sem., Gettysburg, Pa., 1946; M.A., U. Nebr., 1947; m. Eunice Eileen Barth, Jan. 26, 1945; children—Mark H. (dec.), Frank H. Instr. German, Gettysburg Coll., 1945-46; instr. philosophy Coll. William and Mary, 1947-48; asst. prof. philosophy and psychology Alma Coll., 1948-50, prof., 1950-51; research staff and mgmt. positions U. Mich., 1951-58, Stanford Research Inst., Menlo Park, Calif., 1958-63, Mitre Corp., Bedford, Mass., 1963-69, Analytical Systems Corp., Burlington, Mass., 1969-70, Transp. Systems Center, U.S. Dept. Transp., Cambridge, Mass., 1970-83; pres. Assn. Public Transp., 1979-82; adj. prof. urban planning Columbia U., N.Y.C., 1983; lectr. Boston Archtl. Ctr., 1979—; cons., 1983—. Mem. Ops. Research Soc. Am., Transp. Research Forum. Author: (with Elliott Sclar) Access for All-Transportation and Urban Growth, 1975. Office: 3 Acacia St Cambridge MA 02138

SCHAEFFER, PIERRE HENRI MARIE, author, composer; b. Nancy, France, Aug. 14, 1910; s. Henri and Lucie (Labriet) S.; m. Elisabeth Schmitt, Feb. 1935 (dec. June 1941); 1 dau., Marie Claire; m. 2d, Jacqueline de Lisle, Oct. 31, 1962; 1 child, Justine. Student Ecole Polytechnique, Paris, 1929-31, Ecole superieure d'electricite, Paris, 1932-33, Ecole superieure des telecommunications, Paris, 1933-34. Founder Studio d'Essai, Radiodiffusion Francaise, 1942-45; founder Radio d'Outremer, France, 1950-55; founder, dir. Serviee de la Recherche, ORTF, France, 1960-75; founder Groupe de Rechrche Musique Electroacoustique, France; prof. Conservatoire National de Musique, Paris, 1968-76; mem. Haut Conseil de l'Audiovisuel, France, 1970-75; leader of movement to form musique concrete, France, from 1948. Composer: Etudes de Bruit, 1948; Symphonie pour un Homme Seul, 1950; Orphee, 1953; Etudes aux Objets, 1960; Triedre Fertile, 1975; author books, essays: Clotaire Nicole, 1935; Les enfants de coeur, 1948; Traite des Objets Musicaux, 1966; L'Avenir a reculons, 1967; Le gardien de volcan (prix Sainte-Beuve 1969), 1969; Machines a communiquer, vol. 1 Genese des simulacres, 1970, vol. 2 Pouvoir et Communciation, 1972; La Musique et les Ordinateures, 1970; de l'experience musicale a l'experience humaine, 1971; De la Musique concrete a la Musique meme, 1977; Les antennes de Jericho, 1978; Excusez moi je meurs, 1981; Psychanalyse et Musique, 1982; Prelude Choral et Fugue, 1983; Faber et Sapiens, enai, 1986. Decorated chevalier des Palmes academiques; officier Legion d'Honneur; grand officer Ordre National du Merite, comdr. des Arts et des Lettres.

SCHAEFFER, WENDELL GORDON, political science educator; b. Waverly, Ill., Nov. 5, 1917; s. Samuel Carlyle and Minnie Pearl (Morton) S.; B.S., U. So. Calif., 1939; M.A., U. Calif.-Berkeley, 1946, Ph.D., 1949; m. Luella Pauline Elmes, Nov. 24, 1939; children—Thomas Leslie, Wendy Elizabeth Brandeau. Asst. prof. history, polit. sci. U. Fla., 1948-50; publs. dir., hdqrs. supr., chief of party in El Salvador and Puerto Rico, resident rep. in Burma, Pub. Adminstrn. Service, Chgo., 1950-59; asso. prof. pub. affairs, prof. pub., internat. affairs, assoc. dean U. Pitts., 1959-66, dean faculties in Ecuador, 1963-66; pres. Govtl. Affairs Inst., Washington, 1966-69, chmn., 1968-70; Herman Brown disting. prof. polit. sci. Tex. Christian U., Ft. Worth, 1969-81, chmn. dept. polit. sci., 1969-76; sr. mgmt. specialist AID-Nat. Assn. Schs. Public Affairs and Adminstrn. Coop. Program, Washington, 1982-87; dir. Pre-Conv. Constl. Studies for Alaska Statehood Commn., 1955; cons. UN on local govt. in Latin Am., 1959, 68; cons. on program evaluation Brazil mission U.S. AID, 1969-70; mem. Three-Man Commn. to Rev. Program Tech. Cooperation of OAS, 1962; UN cons. adminstrv. regionalization for devel., Venezuela, 1971-72, Japan, 1972, Panama, 1974-75, 78; cons. AID, Colombia, 1974; project mgr. Mgmt. Tng. Needs Analysis for Southern African Devel. Coordination Conf., 1984-85. Mem. Am. Soc. Pub. Adminstrn. (mem. nat. council 1976-79, chmn. sect. internat. and comparative adminstrn. 1976-77, rep. on bd. Am. Consortium for Internat. Pub. Adminstrn. 1976-77), Am. Consortium Internat. Pub. Adminstrn. (sec. 1978-79, 82-84), Nat. Assn. Schs. Pub. Affairs and Adminstrn. (chmn. com. on internat. and comparative adminstrn. 1977-80, sect. on internat. activities 1980-82), Internat. Assn. Schs. and Insts. Adminstrn. (Am. vice chmn. 1977-81, v.p. programs 1981-86, pres. 1986—), Internat. Inst. Adminstrv. Scis. (exec. com. and council of adminstrn. 1986), Phi Beta Kappa. Presbyterian. Author: (with Donald Worcester) The Growth and Culture of Latin America, 2 vols., 1970; Modernizing Government Revenue Administration, 1961; Public Policy: An International Perspective, 1977; contbr. chpt. to Dynamics of Development: An International Perspective (Sudesh Kumar Sharma), 1977. Home: 2005 Lakewinds Dr Reston VA 22091 Office: 1120 G St NW, Suite 520 Washington DC 20005

SCHAFER, CARL WALTER, investment executive; b. Chgo., Jan. 16, 1936; s. MacHenry George and Gertrude (Herrick) S.; m. June Elizabeth Perry, Feb. 2, 1963; 1 child, MacHenry George II. BA with distinction, U. Rochester, 1958. Budget examiner Budget Bur., Exec. Office Pres., Washington, 1961-64, legis. analyst, 1964-66, dep. dir. budget preparation, 1966-68, dir. budget preparation, 1968-69; staff asst. U.S. Ho. of Reps. Appropriations Com., 1969; dir. budget Princeton (N.J.) U., 1969-72, treas., 1972-76, fin. v.p., treas., 1976-87, lectr. indsl. adminstrn., 1975; pres., chief exec. officer Palmer Square Inc., 1979-81; trustee, treas. McCarter Theatre Co. Inc., 1974-76; now a principal of Rockefeller & Co., Inc., 1987—, also a dir.; trustee Wainoco Oil Corp., Bio Techniques Labs. Inc., Ecova Corp., Electronic Clearing House Inc., the Kidder, Peabody Group of Mutual Funds, the Johnson Atelier and Sch. Sculpture; adv. dir. Princeton Bank, Horizon Trust Co., Hamilton and Co.; chmn. investment adv. com. Howard Hughes Med. Inst.; mem. adv. council Domain Ptnrs. Co-chmn. N.J. Gov.'s Task Force on Improving N.J. Econ. and Regulatory Climate, 1982-83; trustee Harbor Br. Oceanographic Inst. Inc., Am. Bible Soc., Jewish Guild for the Blind, Atlantic Found. Mem. Phi Beta Kappa. Republican. Episcopalian. Clubs: Princeton (N.Y.C.); Nassau (Princeton). Home: PO Box 1164 Princeton NJ 08542 Office: Rockefeller and Co Inc Room 5425 30 Rockefeller Plaza New York NY 10112

SCHÄFER, DIETER, biologist, researcher; b. Düren, Fed. Republic Germany, Feb. 15, 1935; s. Heinrich and Luise (Klein) S.; m. Silvia Danneel, Nov. 31, 1965; children: Jan Raimund, Jngo Christian, Carolin Christiane. Grad., Bonn (Fed. Republic Germany) U. Sci. asst. Kernforschungsanlage, Jülich, Fed. Republic Germany, 1965-70; scientist Max Planck Gesellschaft, Dortmund, Fed. Republic Germany, 1970—; senator Max Planck Gesellschaft, Munich, 1985—. Contbr. articles to sci. jours. Mem. Deutsche Zoologische Gesellschaft, Deutscher Gesellschaft für Electronenmikroskopie, Deutsche Gesellschaft fü Histochemie, Deutsche Gesellschaft für Zellbiologie, Gesellschaft Deutscher Naturforscher und Ärzte. Office: Max Planck Inst, Rheinlandamm 201, D-4600 Dortmund Federal Republic of Germany

SCHÄFER, PETER, educator; b. Hückeswagen, Fed. Republic Germany, June 29, 1943; s. Josef and Agnes (Fischer) S.; m. Barbara Siems; children: Ruth, Eva, Simon Peter. PhD, U. Freiburg, Fed. Republic Germany, 1968; Habilitation, U. Frankfurt, Fed. Republic Germany, 1973. Asst. U. Tübingen, Fed. Republic Germany, 1969-74; asst. U. Cologne, Fed. Republic Germany, 1974, prof., 1974-82, prof. Judaic Studies, 1982-83; prof. Judaic Studies U. Berlin, Fed. Republic Germany, 1983—. Author: Die Vorstellung vom Heiligen Geist in der Rabbinischen Literatur, 1972, Rivalität zwischen Engeln und Menschen, 1975, Studien zur Geschichte und Theologie des Rabbinischen Judentums, 1978, (with J. Maier) Kleines Lexikon des Judentums, 1981, Der Bar Kokhba-Aufstand, 1981, Synopse zur Hekhalot-Literatur, 1981, Geschichte der Juden in der Antike, 1983 (French: Histoire des Juifs, 1988), Geniza-Fragmente zur Hekhalot-Literatur, vol.1, 1984, Konkordanz zur Hekhalot-Literatur, vol. 1, 1986, vol. 2, 1988, Ubersetzung der Hekhalot-Literatur, vol. 2, 1987. Fellow Oxford Ctr. Postgrad. Hebrew Studies (sr. assoc.), Brit. Acad. (corr.). Office: Freie U Berlin Inst Judaistik, Schwendenerstrasse 27, 1000 Berlin 33 Federal Republic of Germany

SCHAFF, ADAM, philosopher, sociologist; b. Lwow, Ukraine, USSR, Mar. 10, 1913; s. Maks and Ernestyna (Feliks) S.; m. Anna Kibrik, 1935 (dec. Mar. 1975); 1 dau., Eva Schaff-Blass; m. Teresa Schaff, 1976. Degree, U. Lwow, 1935; cand. phil. Inst. Philosophy, Moscow Acad. Sci., 1941, Ph.D., 1945; Dr. h.c., U. Mich., 1967, Sorbonne, U. Paris, 1975, U. Nancy (France), 1982. Assoc. prof. U. Lodz (Poland), 1945-48; prof. U. Warsaw, 1948-70; hon. prof. U. Vienna, 1970-82; mem. Polish Acad. Scis., 1952—, European Ctr. for Social Scis., Vienna, Bulgarian Acad. Sci., Royal Spanish Acad. Sci. (pres. 1963-83). Author numerous books on philosophy and sociology; contbr. numerous articles to profl. publs. Mem. central com. Polish United Workers Party, Warsaw, 1955-68. Decorated Polonia Restituta. Mem. Internat. Inst. Philosophy. Club: Club of Rome (exec. com.).

SCHAFFER, GEORGE JOHN, lawyer; b. Pitts., July 1, 1907; s. George August and Philomena (Reese) S.; m. Winifred Mahen, 1933; children—Winifred, Marylyn F.; m. 2d, Mildred Annette Gerberding, Sept. 1, 1966. Ph.B., Northwestern U., 1959; J.D., Chgo.-Kent Coll. Law, 1954. Bar: Ill. 1955. With Bell Telephone of Pa., 1926-46, Ill. Bell Telephone Co., 1946-59; instr. Chgo.-Kent Coll. Law, 1959, prof., 1959-63; sole practice, Elmhurst, Ill., 1963-65, 82—; agt. estate and gift taxes, Chgo., 1965-72, regional analyst, 1972-74; tchr. comml. law Coll. of Du Page, Glen Allyn, Ill., 1969-70; tax. cons. Served with AUS, 1943-45. Mem. Ill. State Bar Assn., Fed. Bar Assn., Du Page County Bar Assn., Am. Legion. Republican. Presbyterian. Clubs: Medinah Temple, Mason, Shriners. Home and Office: 381 Ferndale Ave Elmhurst IL 60126

SCHAISON, GILBERT, medical educator; b. Paris, Oct. 15, 1934; s. Geoffroy and Germaine (Bloch) S. MD, Paris U., 1965. Resident Pub. Assistance Program, Paris, 1961-65, asst. prof., 1965-71, prof., 1971-81; chmn. dept. reproductive medicine Hosp. Bicetre, Paris, 1981; prof. U. Paris, 1981. Author: Reproductive Medicine; contbr. numerous articles on endocrinology to profl. jours. Served to capt. French Army, 1959-61. Inserm grantee, Paris, 1985. Mem. Endocrine Soc. (v.p. 1983-85). Home: 59 Blvd Arago, 75013 Paris France

SCHALLY, ANDREW VICTOR, medical research scientist; b. Poland, Nov. 30, 1926; came to U.S., 1957; s. Casimir Peter and Maria (Lacka) S.; married; children: Karen, Gordon; m. Ana Maria Comaru, Aug. 1976. B.Sc., McGill U., Can., 1955, Ph.D. in Biochemistry, 1957; 15 hon. doctorates. Research asst. biochemistry Nat. Inst. Med. Research, London, 1949-52; dept. psychiatry McGill U., Montreal, Que., 1952-57; research assoc., asst. prof. physiology and biochemistry Coll. Medicine, Baylor U., Houston, 1957-62; assoc. prof. Tulane U. Sch. Medicine, New Orleans, 1962-67, prof., 1967—; chief Endocrine Polypeptide and Cancer Inst. VA Med. Ctr., New Orleans; sr. med. investigator VA, 1973—. Author several books; contbr. articles to profl. jours. Recipient ; Van Meter prize Am. Thyroid Assn., 1969; Ayerst-Squibb award Endocrine Soc., 1970; William S. Middletown award VA, 1970; Ch. Mickle award U. Toronto, 1974; Gairdner Internat. award, 1974; Borden award Assn. Am. Med. Colls. and Borden Co. Found., 1975; Lasker Basic Research award, 1975; co-recipient Nobel prize for medicine, 1977; USPHS sr. research fellow, 1961-62. Mem. Endocrine Soc., Am. Physiol. Soc., Soc. Biol. Chemists, AAAS, Soc. Exptl. Biol. Medicine, Internat. Soc. Research Biology Reprodn., Soc. Study Reprodn., Soc. Internat. Brain Research Orgn., Mexican Acad. Medicine, Am. Soc. Animal Sci., Nat. Acad. Sci., Nat. Acad. Medicine Brazil, Acad. Medicine Venezuela, Acad. Sci. Hungary. Home: 5025 Kawanee Ave Metairie LA 70002 Office: VA Hospital 1601 Perdido St New Orleans LA 70146

SCHANKMAN, ALAN ROBERT, ophthalmologist; b. Bklyn., Jan. 1, 1947; s. Barnet and Sylvia (Barken) S.; m. Vicky Barbara Gellman, Dec. 10, 1973; children—Dana, Lauren, Alison, Michael. B.S., Bklyn. Coll., 1968; M.D., Downstate Med. Sch., SUNY-Bklyn., 1972. Diplomate Am. Bd. Ophthalmology. Intern Beth Israel Med. Ctr., N.Y.C., 1973; resident in ophthalmology E.J. Meyer Meml. Hosp., Buffalo, 1973-76; pvt. practice, N.Y.C., 1976-78, Los Angeles, 1978—; co-founder, v.p. and sec. S & S Med. Office Systems, Inc.; clin. instr. Jules Stein Eye Inst., UCLA Med. Sch., 1980—; co-founder, v.p. S&S Med. Office Systems, Inc.; cons. Braille Inst. Developer refractive eye surgery, myopia, 1980; investigator Yag laser surgery, 1982. Fellow Am. Acad. Ophthalmology; mem. Internat. Assn. Ocular Surgeons, Calif. Assn. Ophthalmology, Los Angeles County Ophthal. Soc., Calif. Med. Soc., Los Angeles County Med. Assn., Internat. Glaucoma Congress, Am. Soc. Contemporary Ophthalmology, Am. Assn. Ophthalmology, Keratorefractive Soc., N.Y. Acad. Scis. Office: 12840 Riverside Dr North Hollywood CA 91607

SCHAPIRA, HANS ERWIN, urologist; b. Vienna, Austria, Aug. 1, 1925; s. Paul and Felicitas (Mayer) S.; m. Ruth Jelinek, Aug. 31, 1957; children—Ralph Mark, Paul Victor. M.D. cum laude, U. Rome, 1955; came to U.S., 1956, naturalized, 1960. Intern, The Bronx Hosp., N.Y.C., 1957-58; resident in gen. surgery Beth Israel Hosp., N.Y.C., 1958-59; resident urology Mt. Sinai Med. Center, N.Y.C., 1959-62, clin. asst. urology, 1962-64, now attending in urology, asst. prof. urology, 1965 71, asso. prof., 1971—; clinical prof. urology, 1981; acting chief of service-urology, 1982-84; practice medicine specializing in urology, N.Y.C., 1962—; mem. staffs Mt. Sinai Med. Center. Diplomate Am. Bd. Urology. Fellow A.C.S.; mem. Am. Fertility Soc., N.Y. Acad. Medicine, Am. Urol. Assn. Jewish. Contbr. articles to profl. jours. Home: 335 W 246th St Bronx NY 10471 Office: 47 E 77th St New York NY 10021

SCHAPIRO, JEROME BENTLEY, chemical company executive; b. N.Y.C., Feb. 7, 1930; s. Sol and Claire (Rose) S.; B.Chem. Engring., Syracuse U., 1951; postgrad. Columbia U., 1951-52; m. Edith Irene Kravet, Dec. 27, 1953; children—Lois, Robert, Kenneth. Project engr. propellents br. U.S. Naval Air Rocket Test Sta., Lake Denmark, N.J., 1951-52; with Dixo Co., Inc., Rochelle Park, N.J., 1954—, pres., 1966—; lectr. detergent standards, drycleaning, care labeling, consumers standards, orgns., U.S., 1968—; U.S. del. spokesman on drycleaning Internat. Standards Orgn., Newton, Mass., 1971, Brussels, 1972, U.S. del. spokesman on dimensional stability of textiles, Paris, 1974, Ottawa, 1977, Copenhagen, 1981; chmn. U.S. del. com. on consumer affairs, Geneva, 1974, 75, 76, spokesman U.S. del. on textiles, Paris, 1974, mem. U.S. del. on care labeling of textiles, The Hague, Holland, 1974, U.S. del., chmn. del. council com. on consumer policy, Geneva, 1978, 79, 82, Israel, 1980, Paris, 1981; leader U.S. del. com. on dimensional stability of textiles, Manchester, Eng., 1984; fed. govtl. appointee to Industry Functional Adv. Com. on Standards, 1980-81. Mem. Montclair (N.J.) Sch. Study Com., 1968-69. Served as 2d lt. USAF, 1952-53. Mem. Am. Inst. Chem. Engrs., Am. Nat. Standards Inst. (vice chmn. bd. dirs., 1983-85 , exec. com. 1979-81, 83-85 , dir. 1979-85, fin. com. 1982-85 , chmn. consumer council 1976, 79, 80, 81, mem. steering com. to advise Dept. Commerce on implementation GATT agreements 1976-77, mem. exec. standards council, 1977-79), internat. standards council, chmn. internat. consumer policy adv. com. 1978-86), Am. Assn. Textile Chemists and Colorists (mem. exec. com. on research 1974-77, chmn. com. on dry cleaning 1976—, vice chmn. internat. test methods com.) Am. Chem. Soc., Standards Engring. Soc. (cert.), ASTM (award 1970, chmn. com. D-12, 1974-79, mem. standing com. on internat. standards 1980-84), Internat. Standards Orgn. (mem. internat. standards steering com. for consumer affairs 1978-81), Nat. Small Bus. Assn. (assoc. trustee 1983-85). Jewish (v.p., treas. temple). Mason. Home: 197 N Mountain Ave Montclair NJ 07042 Office: 158 Central Ave Rochelle Park NJ 07662

SCHARABI, MOHAMED, architect, educator; b. Cairo, Egypt, Jan. 28, 1938; arrived in Fed. Republic Germany, 1957; s. Mahmud and Naima (Ad-Digwi) S.; m. Regina Bartel, Aug. 27, 1966; children: Farid, Karim. Diploma in engring., Technische U., Berlin, Fed. Republic Germany, 1963, D of Engring. (hon.), 1968; D of Engring., Habilitation, Technische U., Darmstadt, Fed. Republic Germany, 1981. Architect Office of Fritz Bronemann, Berlin, 1961-64; lectr. Technische U., Berlin, 1964-66; asst. prof. Technische U., Darmstadt, 1968-81; town planner Municipality of Kuwait, Kuwait, 1966-68; prof. Technische U., Darmstadt, 1981—; cons. Govt. Saudi Arabia, Jeddah and Riyadh, 1972-84, Ministry Fgn. Affairs, Govt. Fed. Republic Germany, Bonn, 1985—. Author: École des Beaux-Arts und die Berliner Architektur, 1968, Der Bazar, 1985, Kairo der Kolonialzeit, 1988. Mem. Koldeway-Gesellschaft Für Bauforschung, Architektenkammer-Hessen. Home: Freiligrathstrasse 3, D-6100 Darmstadt, Hessen Federal Republic of Germany Office: Tech Univ THD FB15, Petersenstrasse 15, D-6100 Darmstadt, Hessen Federal Republic of Germany

SCHARDEIN, JAMES LOREN, toxicologist; b. Mt. Ayr, Iowa, Apr. 27, 1934; s. Glenn William and Margaret Louise (McCandless) S.; m. Mary Lorayne Miller, Nov. 26, 1954; children—Laura, Carolyn, Barbara. M.S., State U. Iowa, 1958, B.A., 1956. Sect. head Parke, Davis & Co., Ann Arbor, Mich., 1958-77; sect. dir. Warner-Lambert, 1977-81; dept. dir. Internat. Research & Devel. Corp., Mattawan, Mich., 1981-82, asst. div. dir., 1982-85, div. dir., 1985—. Author: Drugs as Teratogens, 1976; Chemically-Induced Birth Defects, 1985; contbr. articles to profl. jours. Bd. dirs. Chelsea Library Bd., 1972-74; mem. Chelsea Planning Commn., Mich., 1974-76; trustee Chelsea Village Council, 1976-80. Mem. Soc. Toxicology (sect. pres. 1984-85, exec. council 1985—, assoc. editor Fundamental and Applied Toxicology, 1986—), Teratology Soc., (council 1985-88), Midwest Teratology Assn. (pres. 1983-84), Am. Coll. Toxicology, European and Japanese Teratology Soc. Republican. Current work: Laboratory and clinical congenital malformations induced by drugs and chemicals. Subspecialties: Teratology; Toxicology (medicine). Home: 4179 N 6th St Kalamazoo MI 49009

SCHARF, DANIEL MASON, hospital administrator; b. Grand Junction, Colo., Aug. 18, 1947; s. Samuel R. and Shirley L. (Hickman) S.; m. Edna Margarite Kast, Sept. 14, 1974. A.A., Mesa Jr. Coll., 1971; B.A. in Psychology, Western Colo. U., 1973, M.A. in Rehab. Psychology, 1974; M.A. in Vocal. Rehab., U. No. Colo., 1975, Ed.D., in Counseling Psychology, 1977. Lic. Nursing Care Instn. Adminstr. Cert. vocat. guidance specialist, Colo. Instr. U. No. Colo., Greeley, 1976-77; adminstr. City of Greeley, Colo., 1977-78; counselor Aims Coll., Greeley, 1978-79; fellow George Washington U., Washington, 1979-80; market researcher Basic Telecommunications Corp., Ft. Collins, Colo., 1979-81; project coordinator Good Samaritan Med. Ctr., Phoenix, 1981-83, dir., 1983—; mem. adv. bd. Project with Industry, Ariz. Congress for Action; adminstrv. dir. Meridian Point Rehab. Hosp., 1988—; cons. in field. Contbr. articles to profl. jours. Narrator film See What I Can Do, 1980. Bd. dirs. United Way Campaign; vice chmn. Colo. Govs. Council, 1977-80; chmn. state adv. com., div. rehab. Dept. Social Services. Served with USCG, 1966-67. Recipient Presdl. citation, 1975. Mem. VA Tech. and Research Found., Rocky Mountain Spinal Cord Injury Found., Am. Vocat. Assn. (nat. chmn. consumer task force), Paralyzed Vets. (life men), DAV (life mem.; Vet. of Yr. award 1976), Kappa Delta Pi. Lodge: Lions Internat. Home: 2051 S Dobson #219 Mesa AZ 85202 Office: Good Samaritan Med Ctr 1111E McDowell Rd Phoenix AZ 85062

SCHARFF, MONROE BERNARD, investor relations consultant; b. Boston, Sept. 8, 1923; s. Bernard Wertheimer and Minette (Switzer) S.; m. Edwina Kuhn, June 30, 1949; children—Peter Bernard, Stuart Monroe. B.A., Columbia U., 1948. Vice pres. Cold Cathode Corp., N.Y.C., 1951-56; pres. Monroe B. Scharff & Co., N.Y.C., 1957—, Swofford & Scharff, N.Y.C., 1980-88, sr. cons. for investor relations, Doremus and Co. (merged with Swofford and Scharff), 1988—; dir. YMCA-Greater N.Y., 1970-85, Ingalls Assocs., Boston, 1983—, William H. Willis & Co., N.Y., 1975—. Trustee Forman Sch., Litchfield, Conn., 1968—, Portland Mus. Art, 1985; bd. dirs. Maine Capital Corp., 1982—, Found. for Blood Research, 1986—. Served to 1st lt. USAF, 1943-46, 1951-52. Clubs: Arundel Yacht, Camden Yacht, Kennebunk River, Army and Navy, Cumberland, City Midday. Republican. Jewish. Avocations: skiing, sailing. Office: Doremus and Co 120 Broadway New York NY 10022

SCHATZMAN, MICHELLE VERA, mathematician, educator; b. Paris, Dec. 8, 1949; d. Evry Leon and Ruth S.; m. Yves Pigier (div.); children: Claude, René. Docteur es sciences, U. Paris, 1979. Attaché de recherche Centre National Recherche Scientifique, Paris, 1972-79, chargé de recherche, 1979-84, mem. com. nat., 1976-81, 83-86; prof. U. Lyon, France, 1984—. Mem. Soc. Mathematique de France, Soc. Mathematiques Appliquées et Industrielles, Am. Math. Soc. Jewish. Office: U Lyon, 69622 Villeurbanne Cedex France

SCHAUB, SHERWOOD ANHDER, JR., management consultant; b. Rahway, N.J., Jan. 8, 1942; s. Sherwood Anhder Sr. and Doris (Beecher) S.; m. Diane Katherine Wells, July 29, 1967; children: Whitney, Kristen. BBA with honors, Nichols Coll., 1964; postgrad. in bus. adminstrn., Fairleigh Dickinson U., 1965-69. Dir. Gilbert Lane, N.Y.C., 1965-67; exec. v.p. Ward Clancy, N.Y.C., 1967-71; founder, chmn., chief exec. officer, sr. mng. ptnr. Goodrich & Sherwood Co., N.Y.C. 1971—; pres., chmn., chief exec. officer Reed, Cuff & Assocs., 1978—; pres., chief exec. officer Exec. Change, Inc. Author: Breakpoints, 1986, Doubleday; contbr. articles on mgmt. to mags. and profl. jours. Rep. Congl. advisor Pres. Ronald Reagan; head Bus. Task Force N.Y. for Reagan Adminstrn.; bd. dirs. Conn. Pub. Broadcasting. Mem. Nat. Human Resources Planners Assn., Young Pres. Orgn. (bd. dirs., vice chmn. met. chpt. sounding bd. com, hospitality com., edn. chmn.), Internat. Platform Assn., Pvt. Pilots Assn. (sr.), Nat. Ski Patrol, Safari Club Internat. (bd. dirs.), Madison Ave. Sports Car Driving and Chowder Soc., U.S. Equestrian Team. Congregationalist. Clubs: University, Ox Ridge Hunt, Westfield Tennis, New Canaan Racquet, New Cannan Field, Rolling Rock, Porcupine Rod and Gun, Mashomak Field and Game, Econ. of N.Y., Explorers (fellow), Madison Ave Sports Car Driving, Chowder Society, Safari Internat, Greenwich Polo. Avocations: scuba diving, equestrian riding, collecting and restoring vintage race cars, big and small game hunting. Office: Goodrich and Sherwood Co 521 5th Ave New York NY 10017 also: #4 Greenwich Office Park Greenwich CT 06830 also: The Office Ctr Plainsboro Rd Plainsboro NJ 08536 also: 177 Madison Ave Morristown NJ

SCHAUBEL, HOWARD JAMES, orthopedic surgeon; b. Grand Rapids, Mich., May 20, 1916; s. Charles Theodore and Jennie (Slager) S.; m. Marjorie Faye Moody, June 19, 1943; children: Candice, Janice, Wendy, Gayla. AS, Grand Rapids Jr. Coll., 1936; AB, Hope Coll., 1938; MD, U. Mich., 1942; cert. orthopaedic surgery, Duke U., 1946. Diplomate Am. Bd. Orthopaedic Surgeons. Intern Duke U. Hosp., Durham, N.C., 1942-43, chief orthopaedic resident, 1944-46; chief resident N.C. Orthopaedic Hosp., Gastonia, 1943-44; practice medicine specializing in orthopaedic surgery Grand Rapids, 1946—, Brownsville, Tex., 1982—; hosp. appointments Butterworth Hosp., Grand Rapids, 1946— (emeritus), Ferguson Hosp., Grand Rapids, 1946— (cons.); chief orthopaedic surgeon Saladin Temple Crippled Children's Clinic, 1947-73; orthopaedic cons. Shriner's Hosp., Chgo., 1950-73, U.S. Dept. Labor, Tex., 1985; dep. examiner Tex. div. Disability Determination, 1984—. Contbr. articles to profl. jours. Served to maj. M.C., U.S. Army, 1953-54. Recipient Disting. Service award Saladin Shrine Temple, Appreciation award Shriner's Hosp. of Chgo., Service award Ferguson Hosp., 1962-73, Service award Fishermen's Hosp., 1974, 75, 76, Disting. Service award Monroe County Med. Soc., 1977, Service award Key's Meml. Hosp., 1977, Disting. Alumni award Grand Rapids Jr. Coll., 1967, Disting. Service award Grand Rapids United Community Fund, 1973. Fellow Am. Acad. Orthopaedic Surgeons (emeritus), Internat. Coll. Surgeons; mem. AMA (Physician's Recognition award 1973-88), Mich. Orthopaedic Soc., Piedmont Orthopaedic Soc. (chmn. 1963), Eastern Orthopaedic Assn. (emeritus), So. Med. Assn. (life), Galens Hon. Med. Soc. U. Mich., So. Orthopaedic Assn. (charter), Tex. Orthopaedic Soc., The World Med. Assn., Mich. State Med. Soc., Ottawa County Med. Soc., Tex. Med. Assn., Cameron-Willacy County Med. Soc., Am. Occupational Med. Assn., Mich. Occupational Med. Assn., Monroe County Med. Soc. (pres. 1976), Internat. Soc. Aquatic Medicine, Phi Rho Sigma (officer1941-42). Republican. Congregationalist. Home: 10843 Lake Shore Dr West Olive MI 49460 Office: 456 Cherry St SE Grand Rapids MI 49503

SCHAUER, HANS, ambassador; b. Hannover, Federal Republic Germany, Aug. 12, 1926; s. Hans and Maria S.; m. Lisa Spornhauer, Dec. 21, 1956. Student, U. Göttingen, Fed. Republic Germany, Swarthmore (Pa.) Coll., U. Dijon, France. Foreign service Govt. Fed. Republic Germany, Stockholm, 1955-58, Zürich, 1958-59, Bern, Switzerland, 1959-62; with Pres.'s office Govt. Fed. Republic Germany, 1962-65, London, 1965-70; with chancellor's office Govt. Fed. Republic Germany, 1970-74, Washington, 1974-79; with chancellor's office Govt. Fed. Republic Germany, 1979-82, with foreign office, 1982-85; with foreign office Govt. Fed. Republic Germany, Canberra, 1985—. Recipient Officer's Cross of Order of Fed. Republic Germany. Office: Embassy Fed Republic of Germany, 119 Empire Circuit, Yarralumla ACT 2600, Australia

SCHAUER, THOMAS ALFRED, insurance company executive; b. Canton, Ohio, Dec. 24, 1927; s. Alfred T. and Marie A. (Luthi) S.; B.Sc., Ohio State U., 1950; m. Joanne Alice Fay, Oct. 30, 1954; children—Alan, David, Susan, William. Ins. agt., Canton, 1951—; with Schauer & Reed Agy., 1951—, Kitzmiller, Tudor & Schauer, 1957—, Webb-Broda & Co., 1971—, Foglesong Agy., 1972—; pres. Ind. Ins. Service Corp. Akron, Dover and Canton, Canton, 1964—, Laurenson Agy., 1978—, Wells-Williams, 1978—, J.D. Craig Agy., 1981—dir. Central Trust Co. NE Ohio (N.A.). Chmn., Joint Hosp. Blood Com., 1974; bd. dirs. Better Bus. Bur., Canton, 1970-81, chmn., 1979-80; bd. dirs. area YMCA, 1974, v.p., 1975-82, pres., 1982-84; trustee Canton Cemetery Assn., 1988—, Stark County Blue Coats, 1987—; bd. dirs. Hosp. Bur. Central Stark City, 1972-78; vice chmn. bd. Aultman Hosp., 1981-84, chmn., 1984-87; pres. Aultman Hosp. Found., 1987—; chmn. bd. JMS Found., 1968—; bd. dirs. United Way, 1974-84, pres., 1976-78; mem. distbn. com. Stark County Found., 1977-87, chmn. distbn. com.; 1984-87; adv. bd. Malone Coll., 1979—; trustee Kent State U., 1980-81, trustee emeritus, 1988—, N.E. Ohio Univs. Coll. Medicine, 1983-88; past trustee Canton Urban League, Boys Village (Smithville, Ohio), Canton Art Inst., Buckeye Council Boy Scouts Am. Served with USNR, 1946-48. C.L.U., C.P.C.U. Recipient Gold Key award United Way of Cen. Stark County, 1981, Award of Merit Canton C. of C., 1984, Red. Triangle award Canton Area YMCA, 1985. Mem. Chartered Ins. Inst. London, Nat. Assn. Mfg., Am. Soc. C.P.C.U.'s, Am. Soc. C.L.U.s, Am. Mgmt. Assn., Assn. Advanced Life Underwriters, Am. Risk and Ins. Assn., Am. Soc. Pension Actuaries, Stark County Accident and Health Underwriters (past pres.). Clubs: Canton, Brookside Country, Atwood Yacht. Home: 1756 Dunbarton Dr NW Canton OH 44708 Office: Carnegie Library Bldg 236 3d St SW Canton OH 44702

SCHAUFFLER, HARVEY ELLIOTT, JR., lawyer; b. Glassport, Pa., June 29, 1918; s. Harvey E. and Ada (Barlow) S. BA, U. Pitts., 1938, JD, 1942. Bar: Pa. 1943. sole practice, Pitts., 1946—; solicitor State Capital Savs. & Loan Assn., Harrisburg, Pa.; co-counsel Pitts. chpt. DAV. Chmn. Pa. Employ the Physically Handicapped Com., 1956, mem., 1979—; owner Sandybrook Egyptian Arabian Horse Industry, Beaver, Pa., 1986—; owner, developer Cascades Golf and Townhouse Complex, 1986—. Served to capt. USAF, 1942-46. Fellow Acad. Trial Lawyers Allegheny County; mem. Am. Arbitration Assn., Pa. Trial Lawyers Assn., Assn. Trial Lawyers Am., Allegheny County Bar Assn., Pa. Bar Assn. Internat. Platform Assn., Am. Legion, Pyramid Soc. Assn. Republican. Methodist. Clubs: Indian Creek Country, Surf, Palm Bay (Miami, Fla.); Youghiogheny Country. Home: 2829 NE 35th St Fort Lauderdale FL 33306 Office: 803 Frick Bldg Pittsburgh PA 15219

SCHAUFUSS, PETER, dancer, producer, choreographer, artistic director; b. Copenhagen, Denmark, Apr. 26, 1950; s. Frank Schaufuss and Mona Vangsaae S. Ed., Royal Danish Ballet Sch. Apprentice with Royal Danish Ballet, 1965; soloist Nat. Ballet Can., 1967-68, Royal Danish Ballet, 1969-70; prin. with LFB, 1970-74, N.Y.C. Ballet, 1974-77, Nat. Ballet Can., 1977-83; artistic dir. London Festival Ballet, 1984; guest appearances in Can., Denmark, France, Germany, Italy, Japan, U.K., U.S.A., USSR, Austria, S.Am.; presented BBC TV series Dancer, 1984; numerous other TV appearances; created roles include Rhapsodie Espagnole, The Steadfast Tin Soldier (Balanchine), Phantom of the Opera (Petit), Verdi Variations, Orpheus (MacMillan); ballets produced include La Sylphide (London Festival Ballet, Stuttgart Ballet, Roland Petit's Ballet de Marseille, Deutsche Oper Berlin, Teatro Comunale Firenze), Napoli (Nat. Ballet Can.), Folktale (Deutsche Oper Berlin), Dances From Napoli (London Festival Ballet), Bournonville (Aterballetto), The Nutcracker (London Festival Ballet). Recipient Solo award 2d Internat. Ballet Competition, Moscow, 1973, Star of the Yr. award Abendzeitung, Munich, 1978, Evening Standard award, 1979, Soc. of West End Theatres Ballet award (now Oliver), 1979. Address: care Papoutsis Rep Ltd, 18 Sundial Ave, South Norwood, London SE25 4BX, England also: London Festival Ballet, 39 Jay Mews, London SW7 2ES, England

SCHAUMBURGER, JOSEPH ZALMON, publishing executive; b. N.Y.C., June 28, 1930; s. Leo and Lillian Natalie (Fleck) S.; BA, CCNY, 1961; postgrad. NYU, 1971-72; m. Dorothy Constas, Sept. 11, 1959 (dec.); m. Nancy Engbretsen, Nov. 11, 1983. Head mail order dept. Haber & Fink, Inc., N.Y.C., 1953-55; sr. advt. billing exec. Gotham-Vladimir Advt., Inc., N.Y.C., 1955-56; asst. exec. sec. Synthetic Organic Chem. Mfrs. Assn., N.Y.C., 1956-61; asst. v.p., advt. mgr. Bus. & Profl. Books div. Prentice-Hall, Inc., Englewood Cliffs, N.J., 1961-81, asst. v.p., advt. mgr. Exec. Reports Corp., 1981-83, v.p., 1984-86; mng. editor DAW Books, Inc., 1986— . Committeeman 6th dist. Democratic Com., Closter, N.J., 1979-83. Served with U.S. Army, 1948-50. Mem. Direct Mail Mktg. Assn., Pascack Art Assn., Sci. Fiction Writers Am., N.J. Sci. Fiction Soc. (past pres.) Dickens Fellowship N.Y., Dickens Fellowship Westchester (pres., bd. dirs.), Nat. Fantasy Fan Fedn. Jewish. Author: Ultra-Psychonics, 1975. Home: 78 Westervelt Pl Cresskill NJ 07626 Office: DAW Books Inc 1633 Broadway New York NY 10019

SCHAWLOW, ARTHUR LEONARD, educator, physicist; b. Mt. Vernon, N.Y., May 5, 1921; s. Arthur and Helen (Mason) S.; m. Aurelia Keith Townes, May 19, 1951; children: Arthur Keith, Helen Aurelia, Edith Ellen. B.A., U. Toronto, 1941, M.A., 1942, Ph.D., 1949, LL.D. (hon.), 1970; D.Sc. (hon.), U. Ghent, Belgium, 1968, U. Bradford, Eng., 1970, U. Ala., 1984, Trinity Coll., Dublin, Ireland, 1986; D.Tech. (hon.), U. Lund, Sweden, 1987. Postdoctoral fellow, research asso. Columbia, 1949-51; vis. assoc. prof. Columbia U., 1960; research physicist Bell Telephone Labs., 1951-61, cons., 1961-62; prof. physics Stanford U., 1961—, now J.G. Jackson-C.J. Wood prof. physics, exec. head dept., 1966-70, acting chmn. dept., 1973-74. Author: (with C.H. Townes) Microwave Spectroscopy, 1955; Co-inventor (with C.H. Townes), optical maser or laser, 1958. Recipient Ballantine medal Franklin Inst., 1962, Thomas Young medal and prize Inst. Physics and Phys. Soc., London, 1963, Schawlow medal Laser Inst. Am., 1982; Nobel prize in physics, 1981; named Calif. Scientist of Year, 1973, Marconi Internat. fellow, 1977. Fellow Am. Acad. Arts and Scis., Am. Phys. Soc. (council 1966-70, chmn. div. electron and atomic physics 1974, pres. 1981), Optical Soc. Am. (hon. mem. 1983, dir.-at-large 1966-68, pres. 1975, Frederick Ives medal 1976); mem. Nat. Acad. Scis., IEEE (Liebmann prize 1964), AAAS (chmn. physics sect. 1979), Am. Philos. Soc. Office: Stanford U Dept of Physics Stanford CA 94305-4060

SCHECHTER, ARTHUR LOUIS, lawyer; b. Rosenberg, Tex., Dec. 6, 1939; s. Morris and Helen (Brilling) S.; m. Joyce Proler, Aug. 28, 1964; children—Leslie, Jennifer. B.A., U. Tex., 1962, J.D. 1964; postgrad. U. Houston, 1964-65. Bar: Tex. 1964, U.S. Dist. Ct. (ea. and so. dists.) Tex. 1966, U.S. Ct. Appeals (5th cir.), U.S. Supreme Ct. 1976, cert. Tex. Bd. Legal Specialization to Personal Injury Trial Law. Pres. firm Dowman, Jones & Schechter, Houston, 1964-76, Schechter and Eisenman, Houston, 1976—; dir. Bank of Harris County, Houston; speaker Marine Law Seminar, 1983. Contbr. to Law Rev., 1984. Bd. dirs. Theatre Under the Stars, Houston, 1972-78, Congregation Beth Israel, Houston, 1972-84, Am. Jewish Com., Houston, 1982-84; mem. fin. council Nat. Dem. Orgn., 1979; mem. Deans Council, U. Tex. Law Sch. Found., Austin, 1981-84; v.p. Beth Israel Congregation; chmn. fgn. relations commn. Am. Jewish Com. Recipient Service award Congregation Beth Israel, 1976. Mem. Tex. Trial Lawyers Assn. (chmn. admiralty sect.), Am. Jewish Com. (exec. com.), Houston Trial Lawyers Assn., Houston Bar Assn., Assn. Trial Lawyers Am. Democrat. Jewish. Clubs: Westwood Country (bd. dirs., sec.), Houston Racquet (Houston). Home: 519 Hunterwood Dr Houston TX 77024

SCHEDL, OTTO, former Bavarian minister; b. Sinzing, Germany, Dec. 10, 1912; s. Otto and Kreszenz (Kellner) S.; Dr. Phil., U. Wuerzburg, 1941; m. Maria Reuss, Apr. 11, 1942; m. 2d, Finny Wolf, Feb. 27, 1970; 2 children. Sec. gen. Christian Social Union, 1947-48; country mgr. Landrat, 1948-57; mem. Bundesrat, 1957-72; Bavarian minister economy and transport, 1957-70, of finance, 1970-72, dep. prime minister, 1967-72; mem. bd. suprs. Allianz Vers, 1972-84, Grundig AG, 1972-85, Suddeutsch Kalkstickstoffwerke, 1958-78, Dornier GmbH, 1972-85, Beirat Deutch Bank, 1969-85, Beirat Bay, Landesbank, 1973; mem. bd. suprs. Beirat Südaufbau Nürnberg, 1973-85; pres. suprs. Kapital und Wert, 1982-84; mem. Stiftungsrat Messerschmitt-stiftung, 1982. Roman Catholic. Clubs: Rotary, Super Sonic. Author: Die Lebenskreise Bei K.C.F. Krause, 1941; Wirtschaft in Grossraum, 1968; Neues Wirtschaftsprogramm der SPD-Weg in den Sozialistischen Staat, 1978; Kennkraft und kein Ende, 1980; Programmierte Energienotstand?, 1982; Energie für die Zukunft, 1982; Europu-Eine Illusion? Home: 6 Neuberghauserstrasse, D-8000 Munich Federal Republic of Germany

SCHEDLER, SPENCER JAIME, consultant; b. Manila, Philippines, Oct. 23, 1933; s. Edmund W. and Ruth (Spencer) S.; m. Judy Hamilton, Aug. 30, 1969; children: Ryan Edmund, Spencer Hamilton, Peter Joseph. BS, U. Tulsa, 1955; MBA, Harvard U., 1962. Petroleum engr., Humble Oil & Refining Co., 1957-60; fin. analyst Sinclair Oil Corp., Tulsa, 1963-65, asst. dir. budgets, N.Y.C., 1965-66, mgr. budgets and fin. analysis for mfg. and mktg., 1966-67, corp. mgr. budget and analysis, 1968-69; asst. Sec. of Air Force, 1969-73; exec. v.p. Hycel Inc., Houston, 1973-74; gen. mgr., asst. to vice chmn. fin. and adminstrn. Continental Can Co., Inc., N.Y.C., 1974-76; gen. mgr. corp. bus. devel. Continental Group, Inc., 1977-81, chief resources staff, 1981-82; v.p. Continental Resources Co., 1982-83; pres. Maxam Corp. (cons. in U.S. acquisitions to maj. fgn. cos.), 1984—; bd. dirs. Myers Group Inc., Nova Fund. Served as pilot USAF, 1955-58. Club: Innis Arden Golf. Office: PO Box 542 Old Greenwich CT 06870

SCHEEL, WALTER, former president Federal Republic Germany; b. Solingen, Germany, July 8, 1919 (dec. 1985); m. Mildred Wirtz, July 18, 1969; 4 children. Student Reform Gymnasium. Mgr. hardware factory, head market research orgn., ind. bus. cons., 1945-53; former mem. North Rhine-Westphalia Landtag; mem. Bundestag, 1953-74, v.p., 1967-69; fed. minister econ. coop. Fed. Republic Germany, 1961-66, fed. minister for fgn. affairs, dep. fed. chancellor, 1969-74, pres., 1974-79. Author: Outlines of a New World-Problems, Disillusionment and Opportunities of Industrial Nations, 1965; Formulas of German Policy, 1968; Co-determination-Why and How? A Discussion, 1970; Bundestagsreden, 1972; Reden und Interviews, Vols. 1 and 2, 1972-74, Vols. 1-5, 1974-79; The Other Person's Rights. Reflections on Freedom, 1977; The Future of Freedom, 1979; After Thirty Years. The Federal Republic of Germany-Past, Present and Future, 1979; The Other German Question. Cultural and Social Order of the Federal Republic of Germany after Thirty Years, 1981. Mem. Solingen City Council, 1948; mem. European Parliament, 1958-61; vice chmn. Friedrich Naumann Found., 1967-74, chmn. bd. trustees, 1979—; v.p. Liberal World Union, 1968-74; chmn. Free Democratic Party, 1968-74, hon. chmn., 1979—. Served with German Air Force, World War II. Decorated Order of Merit (Fed. Republic Germany); Order of Bath (Gt. Britain); Order of Isabel la Catolica (Spain); Legion of Honour (France); Order of Orange-Nassau (The Netherlands); numerous other fgn. decorations; recipient Wolfgang Doring medal, Theodor Heuss prize, Peace prize Kajima Inst. for World Peace, Internat. Charlemagne prize City of Aachen (W.Ger.), numerous other awards. Office: Lindenallee 23, 5000 Cologne-Marienburg Federal Republic of Germany *

SCHEFFLER, STUART JAY, lawyer; b. Phila., Oct. 9, 1950; s. Walter and Fritzy (Salkoff) S.; m. Barbara Jane Green, July 3, 1975. BA cum laude, Pa. State U., 1972, MPA, 1973; JD, Temple U., 1980. Bar: Pa. 1980, U.S. Dist. Ct. (ea. dist.) Pa. 1981, U.S. Ct. Appeals (3d cir.) 1983, U.S. Supreme Ct. 1986. Tchr. Sch. Dist. of Phila., 1974-75; claims authorizer Social Security Adminstrn., HEW, Phila., 1975-76, equal opportunity specialist Office of Civil Rights, 1976-77; paraprofessional Law Offices of Ronald A. Bell., Bala Cynwyd, Pa., 1978-80; assoc. Law Office of Robert B. Mozenter, Phila., 1980-81, Gekoski & Bogdanoff, Phila., 1981-82; ptnr. Rubin & Scheffler, Phila., 1982-84; sole practice, Phila., 1984—. Councilman Bakers Bay Condominium Assn., Phila., 1982. Fellow Acad. of Advocacy, mem. ABA (tort and ins. practice, sports and entertainment, civil litigation sects.), Pa. Bar Assn. (legis. liaison, medico-legal coms.), Phila. Bar Assn., Am. Trial Lawyers Assn., Phila. Trial Lawyers Assn., Pa. Trial Lawyers Assn., Drug Info. Assn., Phi Beta Kappa, Delta Sigma Rho, Tau Kappa Alpha, Zeta Beta Tau. Democrat. Club: Hartikvah Basketball Assn. (Phila.) (v.p. 1974—). Office: 1712 Locust St Philadelphia PA 19103

SCHEFTNER, GEROLD, marketing executive; b. Milw., June 1, 1937; s. Arthur Joseph and Alice Agnes (Gregory) S.; m. Chantal Scheftner; children: Mark A., Mary L., Scot P., Michael D. Student, Milw. Bus. Inst., 1953, Great Lakes Naval Acad. Sch. Dental-Med. Surgery, USAF, 1955-56, USAF Inst., 1959, Marquette U., 1959-60. Territorial rep. Mossey-Otto Co., Milw., 1960-63; with Den-Tal-Ez Mfg. Co., Des Moines, 1963—; dir. fgn. affairs Den-Tal-Ez Mfg. Co., 1969-71; dir. Far Eastern affairs, 1971-72, exec. dir. internat. sales/mktg., 1973, v.p., gen. mgr. internat. ops., 1974—, also corp. dir., 1969—; chmn. bd. Den-Tal-Ez Ltd., Gt. Britain, 1974—; pres., mktg. specialist Pennwalt/Jelenko; pres. S&S Scheftner Ltd, Biel/Bienne, Switzerland subs., Mainz, Germany; adviser Kuwait M.O.H.; pres., mktg. specialist Southern Dental Industries, Australia, Productivity Tng. Corp., Calif. Bd. dirs. Dist. Export Council of Iowa, 1976-77; mem. Lake Panorama (Iowa) Devel. Assn., 1972-73; chmn. World Trade Council Iowa, 1976-77; adv. bd. bldg. program St. Charles Boys Home, Milw., 1963. Served with USAF, 1955-59. Recipient Presdl. Mgr. of Year award Den-Tal-Ez Co., 1967, Lectr. award Faculdade de Odontologia, U. Ribeirao Preto, Brazil, 1974. Mem. Am. Dental Trade Assn., Am. Dental Mfrs. Assn., Hong Kong Dental Trade Assn. (hon.), Internat. Platform Assn., Greater Des Moines C. of C. (dir. 1976-77). Republican. Club: Lion. Office: Silbergasse 6, CH-2502 Biel/Bienne Switzerland

SCHEIBER, STEPHEN CARL, psychiatrist; b. N.Y.C., May 2, 1938; s. Irving Martin and Frieda Olga (Schor) S.; m. Mary Ann McDonnell, Sept. 14, 1965; children: Lisa Susan, Martin Irving, Laura Ann. BA, Columbia Coll., 1960; MD, SUNY, Buffalo, 1964. Diplomate Am. Bd. Psychiatry and Neurology. Intern Mary Fletcher Hosp., Burlington, Vt., 1964-65; resident in psychiatry Strong Meml. Hosp., Rochester, N.Y., 1967-70; asst. prof. U. Ariz., Tucson, 1970-76, assoc. prof., 1976-81, prof., 1981-86; exec. sec. Am. Bd. Psychiatry and Neurology, Inc., Deerfield, Ill., 1986—; prof. clin. psychiatry Northwestern U., Evanston, 1986—; adj. prof. psychiatry Med. Coll. Wis., Milw., 1986. Co-editor: The Impaired Physician, 1983; contbr. articles to profl. jours. Mem. med. adv. com. Casas de los Ninos, Tucson, 1974-86, mental health adv. com. Tucson Health Planning Council, 1974-75; mem. YMCA, Northbrook, Ill., 1986-87; med. student interviewer Office of Med. Edn., 1975. Served as surgeon USPHS, 1965-67. Grantee Group Therapy Outcome Studies on Inpatient Service, 1980, Dialysis and Schizophrenia Pilot Project NIH, 1978; recipient Outstanding Tchr. award U. Ariz., 1986. Fellow Am. Psychiat. Assn. (chmn. Impaired Physician com. 1985-88), Am. Coll. Psychiatrists; mem. Am. Assn. Dirs. of Psychiat. Residency Tng. (pres. 1981-82), Assn. Acad. Psychiatry (parliamentary sec. 1979-84, treas. 1984-88, pres.-elect 1988), Group for Advancement of Psychiatry (invited mem., chmn. med. edn. com. 1987—). Democrat. Jewish. Club: Oracle Heights (Tucson) (pres. 1983-84). Office: Am Bd Psychiatry and Neurology 500 Lake Cook Rd Suite 335 Deerfield IL 60015

SCHEIBNER, RUTH MARTIN (MRS. LAWRENCE F. SCHEIBNER, JR.), psychologist, emeritus educator; b. Phila., Aug. 24, 1921; d. James Frederick and Rebecca Bamford (Carmen) Martin; A.B., Temple U., 1960, M.A., 1962, Ph.D., 1969; m. Lawrence Frederick Scheibner, Jr., May 27, 1950; 1 dau., Judith (Mrs. John Joseph Massaro). Psychology intern VA Hosp., Coatesville, Pa., 1961-62, VA Hosp., Phila., 1962-63; instr., counseling psychologist, acad. adviser Temple U., 1963-69; sch. psychologist, Marlton, N.J., 1966-67; lectr. Thomas Jefferson U., 1968-69; asst. prof. Phila. Coll. Pharmacy and Sci., 1968-70, assoc. prof., 1971-75, prof., 1976-85, prof. emeritus, 1986—, chmn. dept. humanities and social scis., 1980-85; individual practice psychotherapy, 1968—; counsellor family relations com. Phila. Soc. Friends, 1969-75. Bd. dirs. Phila. br. human engring. lab. Johnson O'Connor Research Found., 1954-56. Recipient award for excellence in psychology Psi Chi, 1962. Mem. Am., Eastern, Pa. psychol. assns., AAUP, AAAS, Phila. Soc. Clin. Psychologists (past chmn. continuing edn. com., dir. Human Services Center 1977-80), Kappa Epsilon. Home: 1654 E Butler Pike Ambler PA 19002 Office: Phila Coll of Pharmacy and Sci 43d St and Woodland Ave Philadelphia PA 19104

SCHEINFELD, JAMES DAVID, travel agency executive; b. Milw., Nov. 11, 1926; s. Aaron and Sylvia (Rosenberg) S.; m. Mary Kathleen McGrew, Dec. 29, 1974; children by previous marriage: John Stephen, Nancy Ellen, Robert Alan. B.A. in Econs. magna cum laude, U. Wis., 1949. With Manpower, Inc., 1948-78; salesman Manpower, Inc., Chgo., 1949-51; br. mgr. Manpower, Inc., 1951-53; nat. sales mgr. Manpower, Inc., Milw., 1953-56; dir. sales, corp. sec. Manpower, Inc., 1956-59, v.p. sales, 1959-62, v.p. mktg., 1962-65, exec. v.p., 1965-70, sr. exec. v.p., chief ops. officer, 1970-76, v.p. spl. projects, 1976-78, cons., 1978-84, dir., 1959-76, mem. exec. com.;

exec. v.p., dir. Transpersonnel, Inc., Any Task, Inc., Manpower Argentina, Manpower Europe, Manpower Ltd. (U.K.), Manpower Australia, Manpower Japan, Manpower Germany GmbH, Manpower Norway, Manpower Denmark, Manpower Venezuela, 1966-76; pres. Aide Services, Inc., Tampa, Fla., 1976-81; pres., chief exec. officer Travel Power Inc., 1976-84; sr. v.p. Ask Mr. Foster Travel Service, 1984—. Contbr. articles to profl. jours. Chmn. Cancer Crusade Milw. County, 1970; bd. dirs. Mt. Sinai Med. Center, Better Bus. Bur. Milw.; trustee U. Wis.-Milw. Found., 1977—; mem. bus. adv. bd. U. Wis.-Milw., 1987—; mem. adv. bd. Sch. Fine Arts, U. Wis.-Milw., 1986—; chmn. bus. adv. bd. Santa Barbara City Coll., 1988—; mem. Greater Milw. Com., 1974—. Served with USNR, 1944-46. Mem. Nat. Assn. Temporary Services (pres. 1975-76, dir. 1969-77), Hickory Assn. (pres. 1980-82). Clubs: Univ. (Milw.); Coral Casino (Santa Barbara, Calif.). Lodge: Rotary. Home: #2301 Yankee Hill 626 E Kilbourn Milwaukee WI 53202 Office: 8911 N Port Washington Rd Milwaukee WI 53217

SCHEINMAN, STANLEY BRUCE, venture capital executive, lawyer; b. N.Y.C., Nov. 13, 1933; s. Samuel and Sadie (Seiffer) S.; m. Janet L. Donnelly, Dec. 30, 1975; children: Catherine Amy, Anthony Paul, Sarah Jean, Norah Jane. A.B., Cornell U., 1954; M.B.A., CCNY, 1957; J.D. (Harlan Fisk Stone scholar), Columbia U., 1960. Bar: N.Y. 1960. Assoc. firm Cravath, Swaine & Moore, N.Y.C., 1960-62; capital projects officer, legis. programs staff coordinator AID, Washington, 1962-64; sr. exec. officer Bur. Pvt. Enterprise AID, 1982-83; v.p. fin. and adminstrn. Services Industries div., also v.p., counsel Internat. div. PepsiCo. Inc., 1965-70; v.p. fin. and adminstrn. Pharm. div. Revlon, Inc., 1970-72; sr. v.p. MCI Communications, 1972-76; pres., chief operating officer FSC Corp., Pitts., 1976-81; pres. New Venture Capital Corp., Washington, 1984-85; prin. Re Venture Assocs., Salisbury, Conn., 1985-86; chmn., chief exec. officer Internat. 800 Telcom Corp., Geneva, 1987-88; pres., chief exec. officer Zurich Depository Corp, 1988—. Mem. Fin. Execs. Inst., Internat. Execs. Assn., Assn. Bar City N.Y. Clubs: Paris-Am, Foreign Service, Cornell. Home: Undermountain Rd Salisbury CT 06068

SCHEIRING, MICHAEL J., college administrator; b. Canton, Ohio, Oct. 11, 1949; s. Robert J. and Madonna L. (Geisigi) S.; m. Marcia L. Young, May 13, 1972; children—Kristy L., Lauren M. BA, Kent State U., 1971, MPA, 1972. Sect. supr. N.J. Dept. Treasury, Trenton, 1974-78; policy analyst to gov., Trenton, 1978-80; dir. adminstrn. N.J. Dept. Community Affairs, Trenton, 1980-82; dir. corp. budgeting N.J. Transit Corp., Newark, 1982-83; v.p. adminstrn. and fin. Thomas Edison Coll., Trenton, 1983—; trustee N.J. Ednl. Computer Corp., 1984—; trustee, comptroller Edison Found., Trenton, 1984—. Contbg. author: N.J. Zero-Based Budgeting, 1979. Mem. Am. Soc. Pub. Adminstrn. (council 1980-84, v.p. programs 1984, v.p. membership 1985, pres. 1987, 1988), Council Coll. Fiscal Officers N.J. (sec. 1984-87). Roman Cathlic. Home: 2 Lotus Ln Lawrenceville NJ 08648 Office: Thomas A Edison State Coll 101 W State St Trenton NJ 08625

SCHELER, WERNER, molecular pharmacologist; b. Coburg, Germany, Sept. 12, 1923; s. Karl and Elise (Vogel) S.; Dr.med., Friedrich Schiller U., 1951, Dr.sc.med., Humboldt U., Berlin, 1956; Dr. h.c., U. Vilnius, U.S.S.R., 1979, U. Greifswald (E. Ger.), 1981; m. Ingeborg Fischbach, Dec. 31, 1960; children: Karin, Ute, Heike. Sci. asst. Humboldt U., 1951-54; sr. asst. Acad. Scis., 1954-59; asst. prof. to prof. U. Greifswald, 1959-71, rector, 1966-70; dir. Research Center Molecular Biology and Medicine, German Dem. Republic Acad. Scis., Berlin, 1971-79, pres., 1979—. Mem. Volkskammer, 1963-66, 81—. Recipient Nat. prize for sci. and tech., German Dem. Republic, 1970. Mem. Deutsche Akademie der Naturforscher Leopoldina, 1978, Czechoslovak, Bulgarian, USSR Acad. Scis. (fgn. mem.), USSR Acad. Med. Scis., German Dem. Republic Research Council, Med. Research Council, Council Higher Edn., Internat. Soc. Biochem. Pharmacology, European Soc. Study of Drug Toxicity. Author: Grundlagen der Allgemeinen Pharmakologie, 1969, 80; chief editor Biomedica Biochimica Acta, 1958—; research on physico-chem. and functional properties of hemoproteins, ligand-protein interactions, pharmacodynamics. Home: 47 Lienhardweg, 1170 Berlin German Democratic Republic Office: Akademie der Wissenschaften, 22-23 Otto-Nuschke-Strasse, 1086 Berlin German Democratic Republic

SCHELL, MAXIMILIAN, actor, director; b. Vienna, Austria, Dec. 8, 1930; s. Hermann Ferdinand and Margarethe (Noé von Nordberg) S. Student, Humanistisches Gymnasium, Basel, Switzerland, Freies Gymnasium, Zürich, Switzerland, also univs., Zürich, Basel and Munich. Various appearances on stage in Switzerland and Germany, 1952-55; German film debut in Children, Mothers and a General, 1955; Am. film debut in Young Lions, 1958; on Broadway stage in Interlock, 1958; prin. roles in films Judgment at Nuremberg, 1961 (Acad. award Best Actor), Five Finger Exercise, 1961, Reluctant Saint, 1962, Condemned of Altona, 1962, Topkapi, 1963, Return from the Ashes, 1965, The Deadly Affair, 1966, Counterpoint, 1967, The Castle, 1968, Simon Bolivar, 1969, First Love, 1970, Pope Joan, 1971, Paulina 1880, 1972, The Man in the Glass Booth, 1974, The Odessa File, 1974, Assassination in Sarajewo, 1975, Cross of Iron, 1976, A Bridge Too Far, 1976, Julia, 1976, The Black Hole, 1979, Players, 1979, Avalanche Express, 1978, The Chosen, 1980, Les Iles, 1981, Man Under Suspicion, 1983, The Assisi Underground, 1984; various appearances on stage roles Hamlet, Prince of Homburg, Mannerhouse, Don Carlos, Durell's Sappho, A Patriot for Me, London, 1965, Broadway, 1969, Old Times Vienna, 1973, Everyman, Salzburg Festival, 1978-82, Poor Murderer, Berlin, 1982, Der Seidene Schuh, Salzburg Festival, 1985; producer, dir. films include The Pedestrian, 1973, End of the Game, 1975, Tales from the Vienna Woods, 1978; producer film Ansichten eines Clowns, 1975; dir., co-author screenplay, actor in film Marlene, 1983; stage dir. plays include All For the Best, Vienna, 1966, Hamlet, Munich, 1968, Pygmalion, Dusseldorf, 1970; (opera) La Traviata, 1975, Tales from the Vienna Woods, London, 1977, The Undiscovered Country, Salzburg Festival, 1979, 80, opera Cornet, Deutsche Opera, Berlin, 1985; prin. TV film appearances include Heidi, 1968, The Diary of Anne Frank, 1980, Phantom of the Opera, 1983, miniseries Peter the Great, 1986. Served as corporal in Swiss Army, 1948-49. Recipient N.Y. Critics Circle award, 1961, 78, 86, Acad. award, 1961, Golden Globe award, 1962, 74, Silver Shell award, 1970, 75, German Fed. award, 1971, 79, 80, 84, Chgo. Film Critics award, 1973, Golden Cup award, Germany, 1974, Gold Hugo award, 1979, Nat. Soc. Film Critics award, 1986; nominated Critics award (Broadway), 1961, Academy award, 1970, 74, 75, 78, 85. *

SCHELM, ROGER LEONARD, infosystems specialist; b. Kingston, N.Y., July 29, 1936; s. Frederick G. and Elizabeth M. (Wojciehowski) S.; m. Gloria Mae Dutterer, June 13, 1958; children—Sandra Lee, Theresa Jean, Ginger Lisa. B.A. in Polit. Sci., Western Md. Coll., 1958; M.A. in Pub. Adminstrn., Am. U., 1970; postgrad., U. Md. Law Sch., 1960-62. Analytic equipment programmer Nat. Security Agy., Ft. Meade, Md., 1958-60; computer cons. various cons. firms Balt. and Washington, 1960-68; mgr. army plans and programs Informatics Inc., Bethesda, Md., 1968; mgr. def. programs Automation Tech. Inc., Wheaton, Md., 1968-69; dir. advanced planning Genasys Corp., Washington, 1969-71; mgr. info. systems Ins. Co. North Am., Phila., 1971-72, sect. mgr. computing ops., 1972-74; mgr. tech. services INA Corp., Phila., 1974-75; mem. spl. tech. projects INA Corp. merger with Conn. Gen. Ins. Co. to form CIGNA Corp. 1982, Phila., 1975-76, asst. dir. tech. services, 1977, asst. dir. spl. tech. projects, 1977-78, asst. dir. adminstrn., 1978-79, asst. dir. resource mgmt., data ctr. design, contingency planning, 1979-80; dir. corp. info. tech. now CIGNA Corp., Phila., 1981-82, dir. planning and control ops. div., 1982-83, v.p. strategic planning, systems div., 1983-84, v.p. applied research/expert systems, systems div., 1984—; mem. adj. faculty Camden Coll., N.J., 1978-82; mem. Camden County EDP Adv. Com., 1980-82; mem. faculty Drexel U., Phila., 1984-85. Author Ednl. Computer Mag., 1982; editorial adv. bd., author Small Systems World Mag., 1982-84; editorial adv. bd. Spang-Robinson Report, 1986-87, Machine Intelligence News, 1987—, AI Expert Mag., 1987—; regional adv. bd. InfoSystems Mag., 1985—; cons. editor Expert Systems Jour., 1987—. Tech. advisor various sch. bds., colls., univs. and non-profit orgns. Served to capt. U.S. Army, 1959. Mem. Am. Assn. Artificial Intelligence, Assn. Computing Machinery (founder Delaware Valley chpt. vice. chmn., program chmn. 1983-84, chmn. 1984-85, founder Del. Valley Spl. Interest Group in Artificial Intelligence, 1985, vice chmn. 1985-87), World Future Soc. Home: 506 Balsam Rd Cherry Hill NJ 08003 Office: CIGNA Corp 1600 Arch St Philadelphia PA 19101

SCHEMAN, L. RONALD, lawyer; b. Bklyn., Aug. 9, 1931; s. Mac and Eleanor (Minkowitz) S.; B.A. with distinction cum laude (Rufus Choate scholar) Dartmouth Coll., 1953; J.D., Yale U., 1956; m. Ethel Goldman, June 5, 1955; children—Ann, Corinne, Jennifer, Daniel. Admitted to N.Y. bar, 1956, D.C. bar, 1979; practice law, Hartford, Conn., 1957, N.Y.C., 1958-59, Coudert Bros., Washington, 1984-85; Kaplan, Russin and Vecchi, 1987—; Inter-Am. Cultural Conv. fellow, Brazil, 1960-61; atty. dept. legal affairs OAS, Washington, 1961-64, planning officer, 1968-70, asst. sec. gen. for mgmt., 1975-83; exec. dir. Ctr. Advanced Studies of the Americas, 1985-87; secretariat Inter-Am. Commn. on Human Rights, 1961-64; exec. dir. Pan Am. Devel. Found., 1964-68; pres. Porter Internat. Co., Washington, 1970-75; v.p. fin. Robert R. Nathan Assocs., 1974-75; pub. Soviet Bus. and Trade, 1973-75; exec. v.p., dir. Intercomp, S.A., 1971-74; dir. Vision mag., 1973-74; asso. dir. Council of Ams., 1976—; professorial lectr. in internat. orgn. George Washington U., 1979-83. Asst. treas. Inter-Am. Bar Found., 1967-74, 87; trustee Pan Am. Devel. Found., pres., 1976-83, 87—; mem. exec. com. Am. Jewish Com. of Washington; bd. dirs. East-West Trade Council, 1974-75, Ctr. for Advanced Studies of the Ams., 1984—, Tools for Freedom Found., 1965, Inter-Am. Literacy Found., Inter-Am. Music Festival, 1979-82; mem. steering com. on governance in Western Hemisphere, Aspen Inst., 1981-82; mem. adv. panel on regionalism and devel. UNITAR, 1981-82. Decorated Order Bernardo O'Higgins (Chile), 1967. Mem. Washington Fgn. Law Soc. (bd. govs. 1965-67, pres. 1968), Am. Fgn. Law Assn. (v.p. 1971), Am. Soc. Internat. Law, Phi Beta Kappa. Clubs: Cosmos, Internat. (Washington). Author: Foundations of Freedom, 1966, The Inter-American Dilemma, 1988; bd. editors Mng. Internat. Devel. quar., 1984-86; contbr. articles on internat. orgn. and inter-Am. affairs to profl. jours. Home: 2500 Virginia Ave NW Washington DC 20037 Office: 1215 17th St NW Washington DC 20036

SCHEMBRI, CARMELO MARIA, judge; b. Mosta, Malta, Sept. 2, 1922; s. Joseph and Lucia (Tabone Adami) S.; m. Helen Holland, July 3, 1949; children—John, Robert, David, Rosanne, Lucia, Joseph, Connie, Mario, Michael, Christine, Angela. LL.D., U. Malta, 1947. Pvt. practice, Malta, 1947-54; asst. crown counsel, Malta Law Ctr., 1954-62, magistrate, 1962-78, judge, 1978-81, chief justice, 1981—; minister edn. Govt. of Malta, 1952-54. Recipient Coronation medal Queen Elizabeth of Eng., 1952. Roman Catholic. Club: Union (Sliema, Malta). Home: 2 Holland Ct, Bisazza St, Sliema Malta Office: Superior Cts, Valletta Malta

SCHENK, RICHARD CHARLES, priest, editor; b. Glendale, Calif., June 27, 1951; s. Robert C. and Betty K. (Groschong) S. BA, St. Albert's Coll., 1974; MA, Dominican Sch. Philosophy and Theology, 1977; ThD, Ludwig Max U., Munich, 1986. Ordained Dominican priest Roman Cath. Ch., 1978. Teaching asst. Dominican Sch. Philosophy and Theology, Berkeley, Calif., 1974, St. Mary's Coll., Moraga, Calif., 1975; sci. asst. U. Munich, 1982-85; editor medieval texts Bavarian Acad. Scis., Munich, 1986—. Author: Die Gnade Vollendeter Endlichkeit, 1988; contbr. articles to profl. jours. Home: Salvatorplatz 2/a, 8000 Munich 2 Federal Republic of Germany Office: Bavarian Acad Scis, Marstallplatz 8, 8000 Munich 22 Federal Republic of Germany

SCHENKEVELD, DIRK MARIE, professor of ancient Greek; b. Alkmaar, North Holland, The Netherlands, Jan. 6, 1934; d. Arie and Willemina Cornelia (Verburg) S.; m. Maria Adriana Van Der Dussen, Aug. 6, 1959; children: Arie Dirk, Willemina Margaretha. PhD, Vrye U., Amsterdam, The Netherlands, 1964. Tchr. of classics Eerste Chr. Lyceum, Haarlem, The Netherlands, 1959-62; univ. asst. Vrye U., Amsterdam, 1962-71, prof. ancient Greek, 1971—; vice chancellor Vrye U., Amsterdam, 1978-79. Author: Studies Demetrius, 1964; contbr. articles to profl. jours. Pres. Prins Bernhard Funds, Amsterdam, 1982-87; bd. dirs. European Cultural Found., Amsterdam, 1986-87. Mem. Plutarch Soc., Internat. Soc. History of Rhetoric, Hollandsche Maatschappy Der Weten-schappen (sec. 1986). Gereformeerd. Office: Vrye U, De Boelelaan 1105, 1081 HV Amsterdam The Netherlands

SCHENOWITZ, GERARD GASTON, gastroenterologist; b. Nice, France, Aug. 6, 1946; s. Guy and Paulette (Drau) S.; m. Carole Antonietti, July 3, 1970; children: Valerie, Yann. MD, U. Marseille, France, 1975. Intern Conception Hosp., Marseille, 1969-72; resident Digestive Diseases Hosp., Nice, 1972-75; cons. gastroenterology Nice. Hosp., 1975-78; practice medicine specializing in gastroenterology Nice, 1977—; pathology asst. U. Nice Med. Coll., 1975-76; dir. Dietetic Research Inst., 1984-86; cons. Pasteur Hosp., Nice, 1986—. Contbr. articles to profl. jours. Pres. Pupil Assn., Nice, 1982-86; mem. Club Reflexion Cabuneks Groupe Gasho Enterologie, 1980—. Mem. Endoscopy Tchg. Assn. (pres. 1979-86). Roman Catholic. Home: 10 Ave Therese, 06000 Nice France Office: 25 Blvd V Hugo, 06000 Nice France

SCHEPS, MARC, museum director; b. Basel, Switzerland, July 6, 1932; s. Samuel and Lily S.; student Ecole des Beaux-Arts, Geneva, 1949-53; m. Esther Jasinowsky, Jan. 2, 1955; children—Ohr, Yalon. Artist, Paris, 1960-70; asst. dir. to dir. Tel Aviv Mus., 1971-73, dir., chief curator, 1977-86, dir., 1986—; curator Israel Mus., Jerusalem; artistic advisor to Mayor of Jerusalem, 1973-76. Mem. Mus. Assn. Israel, Internat. Council Mus., Internat. Council Mus. and Collections of Modern Art (exec. com. of internat. com.). Home: 11 Beit Shamai St, Ramat Gan Israel Office: Tel-Aviv Mus, 27-29 Shderot Shaul Hamelech, Tel Aviv 64239, Israel

SCHEPS-DETTON, RUTH REGINE, radio producer; b. Geneva, Aug. 25, 1945; d. Samuel and Lily (Scheps) S.; children by previous marriage: Keren, Ioel, Emmanuel. M.Sc. in Biology, Geneva U., 1968; Ph.D. in Genetical Biochemistry, Weizmann Inst. Sci., Rehovot, Israel, 1973. Postdoctoral researcher European Molecular Biology Orgn., Paris, 1973-74; transdisciplinary researcher Sorbonne and Ecole Pratique des Hautes Etudes, Paris, 1974-76; radio producer Radio France (France-Culture), Paris, 1976—, radio-TV Suisse Romande, 1984. Mem. Société Civile des Auteurs multi-media. Jewish. Author sci. radio shows; contbr. articles to profl. jours. Home: 11-13 rue Gros, 75016 Paris France Office: Maison de Radio France, 116 av du Pres Kennedy, 75016 Paris France

SCHER, STANLEY JULES, lawyer; b. Bklyn., Dec. 19, 1929; s. Leo A. and Frances (Goldman) S.; m. Susan Goldman, June 16, 1957; children--William Goldman, Peter Lawrence, Alison Hope. LL.B., Bklyn. Law Sch., 1952. Bar: N.Y. 1954, U.S. Dist. Ct. (so. and ea. dists.) N.Y. 1960, U.S. Supreme Ct. 1970. Ptnr. Tullman, Fisher & Scher, N.Y.C., 1954-62; founder, sr. ptnr. Garbarini, Scher & DeCicco, P.C., N.Y.C., 1962—; med.-legal lectr. physicians, hosps., health-related facilities, 1970—; mem. faculty N.Y. State Trial Lawyers Assn., 1975—; lectr. Nassau Acad. Law, 1984, N.Y. State Bar Assn., 1983. Pres. Baker Hill Civic Assn., Great Neck, N.Y., past zone leader Great Neck Democratic Com., mem. Nat. CIC Orgn., Great Neck. Served with U.S. Army, 1952-54. Mem. ABA, Assn. Trial Lawyers Am., Soc. Med. Jurisprudence, N.Y. State Bar Assn., N.Y. County Lawyers Assn., Queens County Bar Assn., Nassau County Bar Assn. Jewish. Club: Temple Israel Couples (Great Neck, N.Y.) (past pres.). Lodge: B'nai B'rith. Home: 59 Essex Rd Great Neck NY 11023 Office: Garbarini & Scher PC 1114 Ave of the Americas New York NY 10036

SCHERECK, WILLIAM JOHN, retired historian, consultant; b. Chgo., Dec. 22, 1913; s. Frank and Adele (Schubert) S.; student Wofford Coll., 1950-51; B.S. in Sociology, U. Wis., 1952, postgrad., 1952-53; m. Flora Blanche George, May 19, 1943; children—Linda, William John, Ralph, George. With Crawford County (Wis.) Welfare Dept., 1938-42; with State Hist. Soc. Wis., Madison, 1953-79, research asst., 1954-55, field services supr., 1956-59, head Office Local History, 1960-79, Wis. Council Local History, from 1961, ret.; now researcher ancient histories and religions. Active Girls Scouts U.S.A., Spartanburg, S.C., 1947-48, Boy Scouts Am., Madison, 1956-58; established William J. Schereck Local History Promotional Fund, Inc., 1986; organizer, chmn. Lodi, Wis. Friends of the Library, 1988. Served to 2d lt. U.S. Army, 1942-45. Decorated Bronze star medal; recipient 1st place award S.C. State Coll. Press Assn., 1951, Crusade for Freedom awards, 1951, 1st place award for Sounds of Heritage, Am. Exhbn. Ednl. Radio and Television, 1955. Author, distbr. Simplified System of Cataloging local Hist. Soc. and Mus. Mem. Am. Legion, Ret. Officers Assn., Am. Fedn. State, County and Mcpl. Employees, Wis. Alumni Assn., Smithsonian Instn., Madison Civic Opera Guild, Costeau Soc., Field Mus. Natural History, Am. Assn. Ret. Persons. Episcopalian. Author numerous publs. State Hist. Soc. Am. Contbr. articles to mags. and newspapers. Home: W 11013 Harmony Dr Lodi WI 53555

SCHERER, ALFREDO VICENTE CARDINAL, former archbishop of Porto Alegre, Brazil; b. Bom Principio, Rio Grande do Sul, Brazil, Feb. 5, 1903; s. Pedro and Ana Oppermann Scherer; student Seminario Central de Sao Leopoldo and Pontifical Gregorian U., Rome. Ordained priest Roman Catholic Ch., Rome, 1926; pvt. sec. to archbishop of Porto Alegre, Brazil, 1927-33; organizer of Parishes of Tapes and Barra do Ribeiro, 1933-35; parish priest Sao Geraldo, Porto Alegre, 1935-46; aux. bishop of Porto Alegre, 1946; archbishop, 1946-81; elevated to Sacred Coll. of Cardinals, 1969. Address: Residencia Arquiepiscopal, Rua Espirito Santo 95, Porto Alegre RS, Brazil *

SCHERER, GORDON HARRY, lawyer, former congressman; b. Cin., Dec. 26, 1906; s. John E. and Minnie (Kuehnle) S.; m. Virginia E. Mottern, Feb. 18, 1933; children: Gordon Mottern, Suzanne Virginia (Mrs. Michael Kitei). Student, U. Cin.; LL.B., Salmon P. Chase Coll. Law, 1929; LL.D., Institutum Divi Thomae, 1961. Bar: Ohio 1929. Practiced in Cin. 1929—; asst. pros. atty. Hamilton County, Ohio, 1933-41; dir. safety City of Cin., 1943-44; mem. Planning Commn. Cin., 1946-47; mem. 83d-87th Congresses from 1st Dist. Ohio, mem. un-Am. activities com., pub. works com.; mem. U.S. nat. commn. UNESCO, 1970-73; U.S. mem. exec. bd. UNESCO, Paris, 1974-75; U.S. del. UNESCO Internat. Conf. on Programs for Devel. of Communications, Acapulco, Mex., 1982; U.S. rep. to UN, 1972-73; dir. Universal Guaranty Life Ins. Co. of Ohio, 1965-80; chmn. bd. Gentile Bros. Co., 1969-82; pres. bd. trustees Cin. So. Ry., 1968-81; Mem. Ohio Supreme Ct. Bd. Commrs. on Grievances and Discipline, 1970-76; Mem. bd. visitors USAF Acad., Colorado Springs, Colo., 1971-75; chmn. Republican Party of Hamilton County, 1962-68; mem. Ohio Rep. State Central and Exec. coms., 1964-70; mem. bd. elections, Hamilton County, 1968-78. Trustee Ams. for Constl. Action; mem. Cin. City Council, 1945-49. Recipient Patriotic Service awards Coalition Am. Patriotic Socs., Am. Legion, DAR; Disting. Service award Negro Citizens Cin. Mem. Am., Ohio, Cin. bar assns., Order of Curia, Phi Alpha Delta. Club: Mason (33 deg.). Home: 2101 Highland Towers 1071 Celestial St Cincinnati OH 45202 Office: 2103 Highland Towers 1071 Celestial St Cincinnati OH 45202

SCHERER, JEANNE CATHERINE, nurse, author; b. Buffalo, Apr. 8, 1928; d. Albert and Florence Rose (Steinman) Scherer. R.N., Buffalo Gen. Hosp. Sch. Nursing, 1954; B.S. in Nursing, D'Youville Coll., 1966; M.S., Canisius Coll., 1972. Staff nurse various hosps., 1954-66; clin. instr. Sisters Hosp. Sch. Nursing, Buffalo, 1966-68, 78-86 , asst. dir., med. surg. nursing coordinator, 1968-78, cons., 1986—. Author: Introductory Clinical Pharmacology, 1975, 3d edit., 1987; Introductory Medical-Surgical Nursing, 1977, 4th edit., 1986; Student Work Manual for Introductory Medical-Surgical Nursing, 1977, 4th edit., 1986; Student Work Manual for Introductory Clinical Pharmacology, 1982, 3d edit., 1987; Lippincott's Nurses' Drug Manual, 1985. Mem. Western N.Y. League for Nursing. Republican. Roman Catholic. Office: PO Box 763 West Seneca NY 14224

SCHERER, VICTOR RICHARD, physicist, computer specialist, musician; b. Poland, Feb. 7, 1940; came to U.S., 1941, naturalized, 1951; s. Emanuel and Florence B. Scherer; B.S. magna cum laude, CCNY, 1960; M.A., Columbia U., 1962; Ph.D., U. Wis., Madison, 1974; m. Gail R. Dobrofsky, Aug. 11, 1963; children—Helena Cecille, Markus David. Health physics asst. Columbia U., N.Y.C., 1961-63; research asst. dept. physics U. Wis., Madison, 1967-74, project asso., project mgr. Inst. for Environ. Studies, World Climate-Food Research Group, 1974-78, specialist computer systems Acad. Computing Center, 1978—. Concert pianist; tchr., promoter contemporary composers. AEC fellow, 1960-61. Mem. Am. Phys. Soc., Am. Meteorol. Soc., Am. Soc. Agronomy, Assn. Computing Machinery, Nat. Computer Graphics Assn., AAAS, Sigma Xi, Phi Beta Kappa. Researcher in particle physics, agroclimatology, soil-yield relationships and computer graphics; cons. on computer graphics and supercomputing applications. Office: U Wis Acad Computing Ctr 1210 W Dayton St Madison WI 53706

SCHERGER, MOZELLE SPAINHOUR (MRS. GEORGE RICHARD SCHERGER), librarian; b. Forsyth County, N.C., Dec. 17, 1916; d. Earnest Sidney and Mertie Blanche (Hauser) Spainhour; B.S., Appalachian State Tchrs. Coll., Boone, N.C., 1937; B.S. in L.S., U. N.C., 1943; m. George Richard Scherger, Feb. 23, 1946; children—Teresa Ann (Mrs. Richard Martin), George Richard, Joseph John, Daniel M. Tchr. English and French, sch. librarian Cramerton (N.C.) High Sch., 1937-42; librarian Laurinburg-Maxton AFB, 1943, Piedmont Jr. High Sch., 1944, Pope Field AFB, 1945-46, Charlotte (N.C.) Coll., 1957-64; documents and serials librarian U. N.C. at Charlotte, 1965-69, asst. reference librarian, 1969-78, reference librarian, 1979-80. Mem. AAUP. Home: 701 St Julien St Charlotte NC 28205

SCHERICH, ERWIN THOMAS, civil engineer, consultant; b. Inland, Nebr., Dec. 6, 1918; s. Harry Erwin and Ella (Peterson) S.; student Hastings Coll., 1937-39, N.C. State Coll., 1943-44; B.S., U. Nebr., 1946-48; M.S., U. Colo., 1948-51; m. Jessie Mae Funk, Jan. 1, 1947; children—Janna Rae Scherich Thornton, Jerilyn Mae Scherich Dobson, Mark Thomas. Civil and design engr. U.S. Bur. Reclamation, Denver, 1948-84, chief spillways and outlets sect., 1974-75, chief dams br., div. design, 1975-78, chief tech. rev. staff, 1978-79, chief div. tech. rev. Office of Asst. Commr. Engring. and Research Ctr., 1980-84; cons. civil engr., 1984—. Mem. U.S. Com. Internat. Commn. on Large Dams. Served with AUS, 1941-45. Registered profl. engr., Colo. Fellow ASCE; mem. Nat. Soc. Profl. Engrs. (nat. dir. 1981-87), Profl. Engrs. Colo. (pres. 1977-78), Wheat Ridge C. of C. Republican. Methodist. Home and office: 3915 Balsam St Wheat Ridge CO 80033

SCHEUER, PAUL JOSEF, emeritus chemistry educator; b. Heilbronn, Germany, May 25, 1915; came to U.S., 1938, naturalized, 1944; s. Albert and Emma (Neu) S.; m. Alice Elizabeth Dash, Sept. 5, 1950; children: Elizabeth E., Deborah A., David A.L., Jonathan L.L. B.S., Northeastern U., 1943; M.A., Harvard U., 1947, Ph.D., 1950. Asst. prof. U. Hawaii, Honolulu, 1950-55; assoc. prof. U. Hawaii, 1955-61, prof. chemistry, 1961-85, prof. emeritus, 1985—, chmn. dept., 1959-62; vis. prof. U. Copenhagen, 1977; Barton lectr. U. Okla., 1967; J.F. Toole lectr. U. N.B., 1977. Author: Chemistry of Marine Natural Products, 1973; Editor: Marine Natural Products: Chemical and Biological Perspectives, Vol. 1, 2, 1978, Vol. 3, 1980, Vol. 4, 1981, Vol. 5, 1983, Bioorganic Marine Chemistry, Vol. 1, 1987; mem. editorial council: Toxicon; mem. editorial bd.: Toxin Revs. Served with AUS, 1944-46. Recipient Outstanding Alumni award Northeastern U., 1984. Mem. Am., Swiss chem. socs., Royal Soc. Chemistry, AAAS, Sigma Xi, Phi Kappa Phi. Home: 3271 Melemele Pl Honolulu HI 96822

SCHIAVI, ROSEMARY FILOMENA, educator; b. Syracuse, N.Y., Feb. 20, 1947; d. Stefano and Rose (Falso) Schiavi; A.A., Maria Regina Coll., 1967; BA, Brescia Coll., 1969; MS, Syracuse U., 1973, cert. advanced studies tchr. edn. and curriculum devel., 1987. Tchr., Syracuse City Sch. Dist., 1969—, tchr. Meachem Sch., 1980-83, acting prin., 1979; asst. office of profl. devel. and field programs Syracuse U., 1984-85; adminstrv. intern West Genesee/Syracuse U. Teaching Ctr., Bus. Ednl. Exchange Com. Mem. exec. bd. Maria Regina Coll., pres. exec. alumni assn. Mem. S.C. Assn. for Supervision and Curriculum Devel., Am. Fedn. Tchrs., N.Y. United Tchrs. Assn., Syracuse Tchrs. Assn., N.Y. State Assn. Tchr. Educators, Brescia Coll. Alumni Assn., Syracuse U. Alumni Assn., Am. Edn. Research Assn., Assn. Tchr. Educators, Assoc. Photographers Internat., Nat. Assn. Female Execs., Audubon Soc., Phi Delta Kappa.

SCHICK, IRVIN HENRY, educator; b. Wilkes-Barre, Pa., Aug. 10, 1924; s. Irvin and Elizabeth (Valentine) S.; diploma Bliss Elec. Sch., 1947; B.E.E., George Washington U., 1958; M.S. in Elec. Engring. (NSF fellow), U. Md., 1961; m. Marilyn Freeman, July 17, 1954 (dec. Aug. 1961); m. 2d, Marjorie Bletch Beach, Dec. 23, 1967; 1 dau., Carolyn Patricia. Engring. asst. Jeddo-Highland Coal Co. (Pa.), 1942-43; instr. Bliss Elec. Sch., Washington, 1947-50; prof. math. and elec. engring., dept. head Montgomery Coll., Rockville, Md., 1950-65, dir. extension, 1965-67, dean adminstrn., 1967-75, adminstrv. v.p., 1975-78, prof. emeritus, adminstrv. v.p. emeritus, 1978—. Tchr., tutor, cons. indsl. cos. 1949—. Served with USAAF, 1943-46. Mem. AAUP, Montgomery County Edn. Assn., Md. State Tchrs. Assn., IEEE, Am. Assn. Sch. Adminstrs., Internat. Platform Assn., Bliss Elec. Soc. (bd. govs., past pres.), Theta Tau, Sigma Tau, Sigma Pi Sigma, Tau Beta Pi. Home: 105 Fleetwood Terr Silver Spring MD 20910

SCHIEMENZ, ROLF BERND, business educator; b. Frankfurt, West Germany, Nov. 11, 1939; s. Willi Max Paul and Anna Antonia (Noll) S.; m. Rita Maria Kollmann, Mar. 29, 1963; children: Kai Uwe, Kirsten Elena. Diploma in econs. and engring. Darmstadt Inst. Tech., 1964, Dr. rer.pol., 1969, Habilitation, 1978. Research and teaching asst. Darmstadt Inst. Tech., 1964-65, 67-68; cons. OECD, Paris, 1966; asst. prof. bus. adminstrn. Philipps-Univ., Marburg, W.Ger., 1969-72, prof., 1972—; dean dept. econs. U. Marburg, 1976-77. Author: Regelungstheorie und Entscheidungsprozesse, 1972; Automatisierung der Produktion, 1980; Betriebskybernetik, 1982; editor: Weltwirtschaftsordnung und Wirtschwiss, 1978; Angewandte Wirtschafts- und Sozialkybernetik, 1984. Mem. German Soc. Ops. Research, Soc. Econ. and Social Cybernetics (pres.), Verband der Hochschullehrer für Betriebswirtschaft. Home: Sonnenhang 5, D-3550 Marburg 1 Federal Republic of Germany Office: Philipps-Universitaet, Am Plan 2, D-3550 Marburg 1 Federal Republic of Germany

SCHIER, DONALD STEPHEN, educator; b. Ft. Madison, Iowa, Sept. 10, 1914; s. Francis and Marcella (Kenny) S. B.A., State U. Iowa, 1936; M.A., Columbia U., 1937, Ph.D., 1941. Mem. faculty State Tchrs. Coll., Bemidji, Minn., 1939-41, 41-42, Ill. Inst. Tech., 1946; mem. faculty Carleton Coll., Northfield, Minn., 1946-80; prof. French Carleton Coll., 1953-80; vis. prof. U. Wis., 1964-65; Brown tutor in French U. of South, Sewanee, Tenn., 1980-81. Author: Louis-Bertrand Castel, 1942; editor: (with Scott Elledge) The Continental Model, 1960, 2d edit., 1970; (Bertrand de Fontenelle), Nouveaux Dialogues des morts, 1965, rev. edit., 1974; translator: Letter on Italian Music (Charles de Brosses), 1978. Mem. selection com. Young Scholar Program, Nat. Found. Arts and Humanities, 1966-67. Served to capt. AUS, 1942-46. Mem. MLA, Am. Assn. Tchrs. French, Am. Soc. Eighteenth-Century Studies. Home: 1106 Carol Woods Chapel Hill NC 27514

SCHIER, RUDOLF, academic administrator, educator; b. Amsterdam, The Netherlands, Mar. 4, 1937; s. Rudolf and Emilie (Jarma) S.; m. Brigitte Angele; children: Michael, Stephanie, Christopher. BA, Amherst Coll., 1959; MA, Cornell U., 1960, PhD, 1965. From instr. to asst. prof. to assoc. prof. of comparative lit. U. Ill., Urbana, 1963-79; dir. Austria-Ill. Exchange Program, Baden, 1971-79, Inst. European Studies, Vienna, Austria, 1980—. Author: Die Sprache Georg Trakls, 1970; contbr. articles to profl. jours. Grantee Am. Philos. Soc., 1970; recipient award Austrian Ministry Edn., 1976, Nat. Assn. Fgn. Student Affairs, 1977; named hon. mem. edn. dept. John F. Kennedy Ctr. Performing Arts, 1984. Office: Inst European Studies, Johannesgasse 7, A-1010 Vienna Austria

SCHIESSWOHL, CYNTHIA RAE SCHLEGEL, lawyer; b. Colorado Springs, July 7, 1955; d. Leslie H. and Maime (Kascak) Schlegel; m. Scott Jay Schiesswohl, Aug. 6, 1977; children: Leslie Michelle, Kristen Elizabeth. BA cum laude, So. Meth. U., 1976; JD, U. Colo., 1978; postgrad. U. Denver, 1984. Bar: Colo. 1979, U.S. Dist. Ct. (Colo.) 1979, U.S. Ct. Appeals (10th cir.) 1984, Wyo. 1986, Ind. 1988. Research clk. City Atty.'s Office, Colorado Springs, 1976; investigator Pub. Defender's Office, Colorado Springs, 1976; dep. dist. atty., 4th Jud. Dist. Colo., 1979-81; sole practice law, Grand Junction, Colo., 1981-82, Denver, 1983-84; assoc. Law Offices of John G. Salmon P.C., 1984-85; sole practice, Laramie, Wyo., 1985-88, Indpls., 1988—; guest lectr. Pikes Peak Community Coll., 1980. Staff U. Colo. Law Rev., 1977. Advisor, Explorer Law Post, Boy Scouts Am., 1980-81; ex officio mem. ch. devel. com. Cen. Rocky Mt. region Christian Ch. (Disciples of Christ), 1986-88; hearing officer Wyo. Dept. Edn., 1987-88; vol. Project Motivation, Dallas, 1974; chairperson Wyo. Med. Rev. Panel, 1987. Mem. ABA, Wyo. State Bar, Colo. Bar Assn. (ethics com. 1984-85, long range planning com. 1985-88, chairperson 1986-87), Denver Bar Assn., Ind. State Bar Assn., Pi Sigma Alpha, Alpha Lambda Delta, Alpha Delta Pi. Republican. United Methodist (mem. evangelism commn. 1987-88, mem. fin. com. youth and music depts. 1979-81, lay del. to Rocky Mountain Ann. Conf. 1986-87).

SCHIFF, ANDRAS, musician; b. Budapest, Hungary, Dec. 21, 1953; s. Odon and Klara (Osengeri) S.; m. Yuuko Shiokawa, Oct. 1987. Student, Franz Liszt Acad. Music, Budapest; studies with George Malcolm. tchr. chamber music Internat. Musicians Seminar, Cornwall, Eng. Pianist various orchs. including N.Y. Philharm. Orch., Chgo. Symphony Orch., Vienna Philharm., Concertgebown, Orch. Paris, London Philharm. Orch., London Symphony Orch., Royal Philharm. Orch., Israel Philharm. Orch., Phila. Orch., Washington Nat. Symphony Orch.; performer numerous festivals including Salzburg (Austria) Festival, Edinburgh (Scotland) Festival, Aldeburgh (Eng.) Festival, Tanglewood Festival; rec. artist Decca Records; recs. include various Bach works, Mendelssohn 1, Mendelssohn 2, Schumann 2, Chopin 2, Mozart K453, Mozart K456, Tchaikovsky Concerto, (with Sandor Vegh) Beethoven Violin and Piano Sonatas. Recipient Tchaikovsky Competition prize, Moscow, 1974, Leeds (Eng.) Competition prize, 1974, Liszt prize, 1977. Address: Terry Harrison Artists Mgmt, 9a Penzance Pl, London W11 4PE, England

SCHIFF, MARTIN, physician, surgeon; b. Phila., July 16, 1922; s. Isidore and Cecelia (Miller) S.; m. Mildred Tepley, Jan. 5, 1946; children: Denise Schiff Simon, Michael, David. BS, Pa. State U., 1943; MD, U. Calif.-Irvine, 1951. Intern Los Angeles County Gen. Hosp., 1950-51; gen. practice medicine specializing in bariatrics Los Angeles, 1951—; mem. staff Brotman Meml. Hosp.; lectr. Los Angeles area community colls. Author: Eat & Stay Slim, 1972, Miracle Weight-Loss Guide, 1976, One-Day-At-A-Time Weight Loss Plan, 1980, (tape) Weight Loss Plan for Health, Happiness & A Longer Life Span, 1982, The Thin Connection, 1986. Served to lt. USN, 1943-45, PTO. Mem. AMA, Calif. Med. Assn., Los Angeles Med. Assn., Am. Soc. Weight Control Specialists. Home: 1220 Corsica Dr Pacific Palisades CA 90272 Office: 12900 Venice Blvd Los Angeles CA 90066

SCHIFFMAN, DANIEL, lawyer; b. N.Y.C., Nov. 7, 1932; s. Jacob and Eva (Katzin) S.; m. P.G. Galex, June 26, 1955 (div.). BBA, CCNY, 1959; JD, NYU, 1962. Bar: N.Y. 1962, U.S. Supreme Ct. 1975, U.S. Ct. Appeals (2d cir.) 1980 (3d cir.) 1966, U.S. Dist. Ct. (so. dist.) 1966 (ea. dist.) 1979. Musician, 1950-55, public acct. Meyerson and Levine, CPA, N.Y.C., 1959-61, legal sec. to Chief City Magistrate, N.Y.C., 1961-62, assoc. Maxwell and Diamond, N.Y.C., 1962-66, sole practice, N.Y.C., 1966-74, 78—, mem. Schiffman and Ellenbogen, N.Y.C., 1975-78; counsel to adminstr. Commonwealth of P.R. Econ. Devel. Adminstrn., 1971-73, counsel, migration div. Commonwealth of P.R. Labor Dept., 1970-72; dir. MAESTRO Found., London; cons., lectr. Practising Law Inst., N.Y.C., 1963-68, 82; moderator, panelist World Gaming Congress, 1987-88, ABA, 1988; advisor U.S. GSA, 1979; treas. Citizens for a Responsive Congress, 1978-80. Recipient Bancroft Whitney prize, 1959. Mem. ABA (gaming law com.), Assn. of Bar of City of N.Y., Internat. Bar Assn., Fed. Bar Council, Nat. Assn. Gaming Attys., N.Y.C. Jr. C. of C. (legal advisor), Am. Fedn. Musicians. Clubs: Nat. Arts (chmn. music com., bd. govs.), Bohemians, NYU (N.Y.C.). Mem. staff NYU Law Rev., 1961-62. Home: 903 Park Ave New York NY 10021 Office: 380 Lexington Ave Suite 4900 New York NY 10168

SCHIFFMAN, GERALD, microbiologist, educator; b. N.Y.C., May 22, 1926; s. Samuel and Mollie (Brookner) S.; m. Lillian Ebert, July 12, 1951; children: Stewart, Howard. B.A. cum laude, NYU, 1948, Ph.D., 1954. Asst. prof. microbiology Coll. Physicians and Surgeons, Columbia U., N.Y.C., 1960-63; asso. prof. dept. research medicine and microbiology U. Pa., Phila., 1963-70; prof. SUNY Health Sci. Ctr., Bklyn., 1970—; cons. Contbr. articles to profl. jours. Served in U.S. Army, 1943-45, ETO. Decorated Bronze Star; recipient Nichols award, 1947; Atomic Energy fellow, 1948-52; NIH grantee, 1974—. Mem. Am. Assn. Immunologists, Am. Chem. Soc., Am. Soc. Microbiology, AAAS, Harvey Soc., Soc. Complex Carbohydrates, Sigma Xi, Phi Beta Kappa, Mu Chi Sigma, Pi Mu Epsilon. Jewish. Office: 450 Clarkson Ave Brooklyn NY 11203

SCHIFFMAN, JOSEPH HARRIS, literary historian, educator; b. N.Y.C., June 13, 1914; s. Samuel and Norma Minnie (Berger) S.; B.A., L.I. U., 1937; M.A., Columbia U., 1947; Ph.D., NYU, 1951; m. Elizabeth Selsbee, Nov. 29, 1941; children—Jessica, Joshua. Instr. dept. English, L.I. U., 1945-49, asst. prof., 1949-51, assoc. prof., 1951-58, coordinator grad. program Am. studies, 1956-58; prof. English, Dickinson Coll., Carlisle, Pa., 1958-79, James Hope Caldwell prof. Am. studies, 1968-79, emeritus prof., 1979—, prof. continuing edn., 1979-86, chmn. dept. English, 1959-69; sr. Fulbright vis. prof., India, 1964, U. Bordeaux (France), 1965-66, U. Indonesia, 1981-82; vis. prof. U. Pa. Grad. Sch., summers 1960, 67, New Coll., U. South Fla., spring 1981; lectr. U. P.R., winter, 1984, Lifetime Learning, Sarasota, winters, 1984, 85, 86, 87, 88; fgn. expert vis. prof. East China Normal U., Shanghai, Spring 1985; founding dir. Am. Studies Research Centre, India, 1964; lectr. French Ednl. Radio System, 1966, acad. specialist program, Malaysia, Internat. Communication Agy., 1982; theses examiner various univs., India, 1970—. Served with U.S. Army, 1942-45; ETO. Recipient Lindback Found. Disting. Teaching award, 1962; Fulbright-Hays award U.S. State Dept., 1964, 65, 81. Mem. Am. Studies Assn. (pres. Met. N.Y. chpt. 1958-59), MLA (head Am. lit. internat. bibliography com. 1961-64), Nat. Council Tchrs. English. Author: (with Lewis Leary) American Literature: A Critical History from Its Beginning to the Present, Ency. World Lit., 1973; contbr. articles on Am. writers to lit. jours.; contbr. intros. to Looking Backward (Edward Bellamy), 1959, Brook Farm (Lindsay Swift), 1961, Three Shorter Novels of Herman Melville, 1962; contbr. numerous book revs. to scholarly jours.; editor: Edward Bellamy, Selected Writings on Religion and Society, 1955. Home: 551 S Hanover Carlisle PA 17013 Office: Dickinson College Carlisle PA 17013

SCHIFFMAN, LOUIS F., management consultant; b. Poland, July 15, 1927; s. Harry and Bertha (Fleder) S.;m. Mina R. Hankin, Dec. 28, 1963; children—Howard Laurence, Laura Lea. B.Chem. Engring., NYU, 1948, M.S., 1952, Ph.D., 1955. Research engr. Pa. Grade Crude Oil Assn., Bradford, 1948-50; teaching fellow in chemistry NYU, 1950-54; research chemist E.I. duPont de Nemours & Co., Wilmington, Del., 1954-56, Atlantic Refining Co., Phila., 1956-69; project leader, group leader, head corrosion sect. Amchem Products Inc., Ambler, Pa., 1959-70; pres. Techni Research Assocs. Inc., Willow Grove, Pa., 1970—; pub., editor Patent Licensing Gazette, 1968—, World Tech., 1975—; mem. adv. oversight com. NSF, 1975, moderator energy conf. ERDA, Washington, 1976, Las Vegas, 1977. Editor: (with others) Guide to Available Technologies, 1985; contbr. to Encyclopedia of Chemical Technology, 1967; contbr. articles to profl. jours. Patentee in field. Recipient Founders Day award NYU, 1956. Fellow Am. Inst. Chemists; mem. Am. Chem. Soc., N.Y. Acad. Scis., Lic. Execs. Soc., Am. Assn. Small Research Cos. (editorial contbr. newsletter), Sigma Xi, Phi Lambda Upsilon. Home: 1837 Merritt Rd Abington PA 19001 Office: Techni Research Assocs Inc Willow Grove Plaza Willow Grove PA 19090

SCHIFFRIN, MILTON JULIUS, physiologist; b. Rochester, N.Y., Mar. 23, 1914; s. William and Lillian (Harris) S.; m. Dorothy Euphemia Wharry, Oct. 10, 1942; children: David Wharry, Hilary Ann. AB, U. Rochester, 1937, MS, 1939; PhD cum laude, McGill U., 1941. Instr. physiology Northwestern U. Med. Sch., Evanston, Ill., 1941-45; lectr. pharmacology U. Ill. Med. Sch., 1947-57, clin. asst. prof. anesthesiology, 1957-61; with Hoffmann-La Roche, Inc., Nutley, N.J., 1946-79, dir. drug regulatory affairs, 1964-71, asst. v.p., 1971-79; pres. Wharry Research Assn., Port St. Lucie, Fla., 1979—; chmn. Everglades Health Edn. Ctr., 1986-87. Author: (with E.G. Gross) Clinical Analgetics, 1955; editor: Management of Pain in Cancer, 1957. Served to capt. USAAF, 1942-46. Mem. Am. Med. Writers Assn. (bd. dirs. 1967—, pres. N.Y. chpt. 1967-68, nat. pres. 72-73), Am. Physiol. Soc., Internat. Coll. Surgeons, Am. Therapeutic Soc., Coll. Clin. Pharmacology and Therapeutics, Am. Chem. Soc. Office: 1430 Sans Souci Ln Port Saint Lucie FL 34952-5726

SCHIFMAN, EDWARD JOSEPH, marketing executive; b. Kansas City, Mo., Mar. 10, 1949; s. Herman H. and Dorothy (Price) S.; m. Vicki F. Wellner, Aug. 8, 1971; children—Michael Aaron, Lori Ann. B.F.A., U. Kans., 1972; M.B.A., Internat. U., 1978. Product coordinator Aladdin Industries, Nashville, 1972-76; mgr. devel. Kenner Products, Cin., 1976-78; product mgr. Clopay Corp., Cin., 1978-80; v.p. mktg. I.D.I., Kansas City, Kans., 1981-84, pres., 1984—. Patentee mailbox, game board apparatus (2), cart, mounted planter box. Recipient awards Samsonite Corp., Indsl. Design Soc. Am. Mem. Sales and Mktg. Execs. Republican. Jewish. Club: Kansas City (Mo.). Lodge: B'nai B'rith. Home: 2512 W 118th St Leawood KS 66207 Office: 5101 Richland Ave Kansas City KS 66106

SCHILBRACK, KAREN GAIL, system analyst; b. Tomahawk, Wis., Sept. 28; d. Edward Richard and Irene Angeline (Ligman) S. Student U. Calif.-Santa Barbara, 1967-69; B.A. in Anthropology, U. Calif.-Davis, 1971; postgrad. in Edn. and Archeology, Calif. State Poly. U., San Luis Obispo, 1971-72. Cert. computer specialist; cert. data processing; lic. cosmetologist. Computer specialist Facilities Systems Office, Port Hueneme, Calif., 1975-78, sr. computer specialist, 1978-80, project mgr. U.S. Naval Constrn. Bn. Ctr., 1980—, tng. cons. FACSO, 1981, 82; curriculum cons. Ventura Community Coll., Calif., 1981—; instr. U.S. Navy, Port Hueneme, 1983, Civil Service Commn., Port Hueneme, 1978-80. Author: AMALGAMAN Run Procedures, 1976; Cobol Programming Efficiencies, 1978; co-author, editor: Training Manual for Direct Data Entry System, 1983. Vol. Vols. for Camarillo State Hosp., Camarillo, 1978-88, coordinator Ventura County, 1981; chmn. scholarship fund drive Ventura, Santa Barbara, Los Angeles, Counties, 1980. Named Young Career Woman of Yr., Calif. Bus. and Profl. Women, 1979. Mem. Young Ladies Inst. (pres. Santa Paula, dist. dep. Ventura/Santa Barbara Counties), Am. Biog. Inst. Research Assn. (lifetime dep. gov.). Lodge: Toastmistress. Home: 6993 Wheeler Canyon Santa Paula CA 93060 Office: FACSO Code 18211 USNCBC Port Nueneme CA 93042

SCHILDKNECHT, CALVIN E(VERETT), chemist, consultant, writer; b. Frederick, Md., Aug. 15, 1910; s. Calvin Ezra and Edith Julia (Fisher) S.; m. Althea Jean Schneider, Nov. 21, 1942; children—David, Eric. B.S., Gettysburg Coll., 1931; Ph.D., Johns Hopkins U., 1936. Research chemist DuPont Co., Arlington, N.J., 1936-43; with dept. research and devel. Gen. Aniline & Film, Easton, Pa. and N.Y.C., 1943-51, Celanese Corp. Am., Summit, N.J., 1951-53; assoc. prof. chemistry Stevens Inst. Tech., Hoboken, N.J., 1953-59; prof. Gettysburg Coll., 1959-79, cons., 1953—; lectr. in field. Author: Vinyl and Related Polymers, 1952; Polymer Processes, 1956; Allyl Compounds and Their Polymers, 1973; (with Irving Skeist) Polymerization Processes, 1977, Monocacy and Catoctin, 1985. Contbr. to encys. and profl. jours. Patentee in field. Mem. Am. Chem. Soc., Audubon Soc., Adams and Frederick County Hist. Soc., Sigma XI. Club: Appalachian Mt. Avocation: butterfly gardening. Home: 135 Doubleday Ave Gettysburg PA 17325 Office: Gettysburg Coll Dept Chemistry Gettysburg PA 17325

SCHILLING, GUIDO, physical education administrator; b. Basel, Switzerland, Mar. 17, 1939; s. Fritz and Maria (Weiss) S.; m. Anna Christina Thoeni, May 8, 1961; children: Saskia, Caroline, Tonia, Luzius. Ph.D., U. Zurich, 1967. Psychologist Swissair, Zurich, 1962-67; phys. edn. tchr. U. Zurich, 1967-68; psychologist Research Inst. Swiss Sch. for Sports Magglingen, 1969-73, phys. edn. tchr., 1973-82, vice-dir., 1983-85; dir. phys. edn. dept. Swiss Fed. Inst. Tech., Zurich, 1985—; cons. Hoffmann La Roche, Basel, 1972-73; mem. adv. bd. MRC, Zurich, 1971-82. Pres., European Fedn. Sports Psychology, 1973-83, mem. mng. council Internat. Soc. Sports Psychology, 1985—. Mem. Panathlon Club. Roman Catholic. Pub., Audiovisual Meansin Sports, 1980; Does Top Level Sport Still Have a Future?, 1985. Editor, Psychologie wofur?, 1974; co-editor, Praxis der Psychologie im Leistungssport, 1979; pub., Anxiety in Sport, 1983. Home: Alpenstrasse 4, CH-2532 Magglingen Switzerland

SCHILLING, JOHN ALBERT, surgeon; b. Kansas City, Mo., Nov. 5, 1917; s. Carl Fielding and Lottie Lee (Henderson) S.; m. Lucy West, June 8, 1957 (dec.); children: Christine Henderson, Katharine Ann, Jolyon David, John Jay; m. Helen R. Spelbrink, May 28, 1979. A.B. with honors, Dartmouth Coll., 1937; M.D., Harvard U., 1941. Diplomate Am. Bd. Surgery (chmn. 1969). Intern, then resident in surgery Roosevelt Hosp., N.Y.C., 1941-44; mem. faculty U. Rochester (N.Y.) Med. Sch., 1945-53, asst. prof. surgery, 1955-56; prof. surgery, head dept. U. Okla. Med. Sch., 1956-74; prof. surgery U. Wash. Med. Sch., Seattle, 1974—; chmn. dept. U. Wash. Med. Sch., 1975-83, prof. emeritus, 1988—; mem. bd. sci. counselors Nat. Cancer Inst., chmn., 1969; also mem. diagnosis subcom. breast cancer task force; chmn. adv. com. to surgeon gen. on metabolism of trauma Army Med. Research and Devel. Command; mem. surgery study sect., div. research grants NIH; chief surgery USAF Sch. Aviation Medicine, 1953-55; cons. Surgeon Gen. USAF, 1959-75. Author articles, chpts. in books, abstracts, reports.; editorial bd. Am. Jour. Surgery, Annals of Surgery. Served to maj. M.C. USAF, 1953-55. Grantee Army Office Surgeon Gen., 1956-80. Mem. ACS (bd. govs., chmn. com. surg. edn. in med. schs., 1st v.p. 1977-78), Am. S., Western, Pan-Pacific, N. Pacific, Pacific Coast surg. assns., Soc. Univ. Surgeons, Southwestern Surg. Soc., Central Surg. Soc., Southwestern Surg. Congress (hon. mem. 1978), Okla. Surg. Assn. (pres. 1970-71, hon. mem. 1974) Am. Assn. Surgery Trauma, Surg. Biology Club, Am. Physiol. Soc., Soc. Surg. Chmn., Am. Trauma Soc., Seattle Surg. Soc., Soc. Exptl. Pathology, Soc. Surgery Alimentary Tract, Explorers Club, Alpha Omega Alpha. Clubs: Yacht (Seattle), University (Seattle). Home: 9807 Lake Washington Blvd NE Bellevue WA 98004 Office: Dept Surgery (RF-25) Univ Wash Medical Sch Seattle WA 98195

SCHILLING, RICHARD SELWYN FRANCIS, physician; b. Kessingland, Suffolk, Eng., Jan. 9, 1911; s. George and Florence Louise (Loweth) S.; m. Heather Norman, Aug. 28, 1937; children—Christopher, Marguerite, Erica. M.B., B.S., London U., 1937, M.D., 1947, D.Sc., 1962. Diplomate English Bd. Occupational Medicine. Sec., Indsl. Health Research Bd., Med. Research Council, 1942-46; reader occupational health Manchester U., 1946-56; dir. U. London Inst. Occupational Health, 1956-76, cons., prof. emeritus, 1976—; vis. prof. Yale U., 1963, 75; dir. Possum Controls Ltd., Langley Slough, Eng. Editor: Modern Trends in Occupational Health, 1960; editor, author: Occupational Health Practice, 1972, 2d edit., 1981. Served to capt. Royal Army Med. Corps, 1939-40. Decorated comdr. Order Brit. Empire. Fellow Royal Soc. Medicine (hon.), London Sch. Hygiene and Tropical Medicine (hon.); mem. Am. Occupational Med. Assn. (hon.; award 1986). Mem. Ch. of Eng. Avocations: fishing; gardening. Home and Office: 11C Prior Bolton St, London N1 2NX England

SCHIMBERG, A. BRUCE, lawyer; b. Chgo., Aug. 26, 1927; s. Archie and Helen (Isay) S.; m. Barbara Zisook; children: Geoffrey, Kate. Ph.B., U. Chgo., 1949, J.D., 1952. Bar: Ohio 1952, Ill. 1955. Assoc. Paxton & Seasongood, Cin., 1952-55; ptnr. Schimberg, Greenberger, Kraus & Jacobs, Chgo., 1955-65, Leibman, Williams, Bennett, Baird & Minow, Chgo., 1965-72, Sidley & Austin, Chgo., 1972—; lectr. U. Chgo., 1961-62; gen. counsel Nat. Comml. Fin. Assn., 1978—. Mng. and assoc. editor U. Chgo. Law Rev., 1951-52; contbr. articles to legal jours. Bd. dirs. U. Chgo. Law Sch. Alumni Assn., 1969-72; dir. vis. com. U. Chgo. Law Sch., 1980-83. Served to 2d lt. U.S. Army, 1945-47. Mem. ABA, Ill. State Bar Assn., Chgo. Bar Assn., 7th Cir. Bar Assn. Clubs: Mid-Day; Lake Shore Country (Chgo.). Home: 209 E Lake Shore Dr Chicago IL 60611

SCHIMBERNI, MARIO, pharmaceutical company executive; b. Rome, Mar. 10, 1923. Degree in Econs. and Bus. Adminstrn., U. Rome, 1945. Asst. prof. econs. and bus. adminstrn. U. Rome, 1946-51; with Credito Italiano, Cementi Isonzo, Inam; then worked as fin. exec. and held managerial positions in various areas; gen. mgr. BPD, 1964; gen. mgr. Snia Viscosa, 1970, mng. dir., 1972-75; pres. Montefibre, 1975-77; dir., v.p. fin., auditing, personnel and legal affairs Montedison, 1977-80, pres., 1980—; v.p. Confindustria, 1983—; pres. Erbamont N.V., 1983—; v.p. Himont Inc., 1983, now pres. Decorated Knight of Labour merit, 1985. Home: Foro Buonaparte 31, I-20121 Milan Italy Office: Erbamont NV 1266 Main St Stamford CT 06902 also: Himont Inc 1313 N Market St Wilmington DE 19894 •

SCHIMMENTI, JOHN JOSEPH, lawyer; b. N.Y.C., Mar. 21, 1938; s. John Marcus and Mae M. (Miranti) S.; m. Mary Elizabeth Sleep, Apr. 18, 1964. B.A., Columbia Coll., 1959; J.D., Georgetown U., 1962, LL.M., 1964. Bar: D.C. 1962, N.Y. 1964, Calif. 1965, U.S. Dist. Ct. (cen. dist.) Calif. 1965, U.S. Ct. Appeals (9th cir.) 1966, U.S. Supreme Ct. 1971. Trial atty. Anti-Trust div. U.S. Dept. Justice, Washington, 1962-64, Lands div., Los Angeles, 1965-67; trial atty. Santa Fe R.R., Los Angeles, 1968-70; ptnr. Schimmenti, Mullins & Berberian, El Segundo, Calif., 1971—. Mem. S.W. Dist. Bar Assn. (pres. 1983), Los Angeles Bar Assn. (condemnation com. 1983), Columbia U. Alumni of So. Calif. (pres. 1978). Republican. Roman Catholic. Club: El Segundo Rotary (pres. 1977). Office: 426 Main St El Segundo CA 90245

SCHIMPF, KLAUS, physician; b. Osterode/Harz, Germany, Aug. 12, 1923; s. Robert and Ilse (Ungewitter) S.; state med. exam., U. Goettingen, 1953; M.D., 1954; habil., U. Heidelberg, 1965; m. Ursula Becker, Dec. 28, 1965; children—Rainer, Birgit, Axel. Sci. asst. Inst. Pharmacology, U. Goettingen, 1953-54; resident in internal medicine U. Heidelberg Faculty Medicine, 1954-64, head blood coagulation lab., dept. internal medicine, 1964-72, sr. lectr. internal medicine univ. hosps., 1965-72, assoc. prof., 1972—; med. dir. Rehab. Hosp., founder Hemophilia Center, Heidelberg, 1972—; del. Chamber Physicians No. Badonia. Served as officer German Army, 1942-44; prisoner-of-war, 1944-48. Mem. World Fedn. Hemophilia (med. adv. bd., med. sec. 1979-83, exec. mem. 1983—), German Hemophilia Soc. (exec. 1983-87, mem. med. adv. bd. 1987—), Internat. Soc. Thrombosis and Hemostasis, German Soc. Blood Coagulation Research (chmn. 1978-79), German Soc. Hematology, German. Soc. Internal Medicine, German Soc. Rehab. Author articles. Home: 15 Truebner Strasse, D-6900 Heidelberg Federal Republic of Germany Office: Rehab Hosp Heidelberg, Postfach 101409, D-6900 Heidelberg Federal Republic of Germany

SCHINAGLE, ALLAN CHARLES, consulting firm executive; b. Cleve., June 7, 1930; s. Elmer William and Mildred (Handlir) S.; B.S. in Bus. Adminstrn., Miami U., Oxford, Ohio, 1953, m. Cynthia Volz Robinson, Apr. 21, 1956; children—Cheryl Lynn, Allan Charles, Holly Anne, Penny Sue. Home office rep. group div. Aetna Life Ins. Co., Cleve. and Louisville, 1953-65, mgr. group div., Cleve., 1965-70; sr. account exec. Aetna Life & Casualty Co., Cleve., 1970-76; v.p. Rollins Burdick Hunter of Ohio, Inc., Cleve., 1976-82; pres. Consulting Services, Inc., 1982—; chmn. pres.'s adv. council Central Res. Life Ins. Co. N.Am. Mem. Republican state candidate screening com., 1974; chmn. Rep. exec. and central coms., Geauga County, Ohio, 1970-76; del. to Rep. Nat. Conv., 1976; mem. Geauga County Bd. Elections, 1974-78. Served with USN, 1948-49. Named Ky. col. Mem. Am. Mgmt. Assn., Internat. Platform Assn., Nat. Life Underwriters Assn., Ohio Life Underwriters Assn. Presbyterian. Clubs: Rotary (dir.), Hunting Creek Country (Louisville), Hillbrook, Chagrin Valley Athletic, Cotillion Soc., Cleve. BlueBook, Fork and Fiddle. Office: 45 Bell St Chagrin Falls OH 44022

SCHINDELIN, JUERGEN WOLFGANG, engineer, scientist; b. Bad Friedrichshall, Germany, Aug. 8, 1928; s. August Friedrich and Emma Maria (Mueller) S.; M.S. in Elec. Engring., U. Karlsruhe, 1953; M.S., UCLA, 1959; Dr.Ing., U. Brunswick, 1967; m. Karin Anna Schlieper, May 5, 1967; 1 child, Tanya. Research engr. Convair, San Diego, 1957-59; design specialist Martin Marietta Corp., Orlando, Fla., 1959-61; sr. staff scientist Friedrich Krupp, Essen, Fed. Republic Germany, 1961-67; tech. staff Bellcomm, Inc., and Bell Tel. Lab., Washington and Whippany, N.J., 1967-73; chief scientist Def. Systems Center, Computer Scis. Corp., Moorestown, N.J., 1973-74; tech. staff, sci. advisor Messerschmitt-Boelkow-Blohm, Munich, Fed. Republic Germany, 1974—. Served with German Army, 1944-45. Recipient NASA Apollo Achievement award, 1970; AT&T Manned Space Flight award, 1971; Convair grantee, 1958-59. Mem. IEEE, N.Y. Acad. Scis., Deutsche Gesellschaft für Luft-und Raumfahrt, Sigma Xi. Contbr. articles to sci. jours. Patentee in field. Home: 28 Winzerstrasse, D-7100 Heilbronn Federal Republic of Germany Office: PO Box 801160, D-8000 Munich Federal Republic of Germany

SCHINDLER, JIRI, microbiologist; b. Prague, Czechoslovakia, Jan. 6, 1931; s. Zdenek and Magdalena (Schindlerova) S.; M.D., Ph.D., Charles U., Prague, 1963; m. Emma Cerna, Aug. 2, 1958; children-Magdalena, Jiri. Univ. asst. Charles U., 1956—, asst. prof. dept. med. microbiology and immunology, 1969—; sr. lectr. Khartoum (Sudan) U. Med. Faculty, 1966-68; chief Nat. Reference Lab. for Automation in Microbiology, 1980—; mem. spl. com., cons. Ministry of Health, 1978, 80, sec. cons. bd.; mem. subcom. on numerical taxonomy Internat. Com. on Systematic Bacteriology, Internat. Union Microbiol. Socs., also mem. data coding com. World Fedn. Culture Collections. Diplomate in med. microbiology. Mem. Czechoslovak Microbiol. Soc., (chmn. commn. med. microbiology), Czechoslovak Med. Soc. Author: Automatic Diagnostics of Bacteria, 1984; contbr. articles to profl. jours. Patentee in field. Translator to Czech: The Andromeda Strain, The Terminal Man (both Michael Crichton). Home: 2356 K Mateji, CS-16000 Prague Czechoslovakia Office: 7 Studnickova, CS-12800 Prague Czechoslovakia

SCHINDLER, JOE PAUL, electronics company executive; b. Berlin, Apr. 8, 1927; came to U.S., 1942; s. Henry and Helen (Brenner) S.; m. Jane Clare Hoffberg, Oct. 30, 1955; children—Deborah, Rachel, Aaron. B.E.E., Bklyn. Poly. Inst., 1950, M.E.E., 1958. Project engr. Polarad Electronics Corp., L.I., N.Y., 1950-54, group leader, 1954-56, head equipment devel. sect., 1956-58, asst. to v.p. engring, 1958-65, pres., chmn., Lake Success, N.Y., 1979-87 ; v.p. mktg. Gen. Microwave Corp., 1987—; v.p. mktg. Narda Microwave Corp., Plainview, N.Y., 1965-79; pres., chief exec. officer Rohde & Schwarz Sales Co., Inc., Lake Success, 1982-87 ; dir. North Hills Electronics, Inc., Glen Cove, N.Y. Pres., PTA, Saddle Rock Sch., N.Y., 1965-68; bd. dirs. Safety First Corp., 1987—. Served with AUS, 1945-47. Mem. IEEE, Am. Electronics Assn., Sigma Xi, Tau Beta Pi, Eta Kappa Nu. Home: 118 Old Mill Rd Great Neck NY 11023 Office: Gen Microwave Corp 5500 New Horizons Blvd Amityville NY 11701

SCHINK, DAVID REGIER, oceanographer, educator; b. Los Angeles, Aug. 3, 1931; s. Clifford E. and Esther (Abrams) S.; B.A., Pomona Coll., 1952; M.S., Scripps Instn. Oceanography, 1953; M.S., Stanford U., 1958; Ph.D., U. Calif., San Diego, 1962; m. Lee Harrison Burnette, Sept. 16, 1951; children—Jonathan, Julian, Alison, Roger. Asst. prof. Grad. Sch. Oceanography U. R.I., 1962-66; mgr. air ocean studies Teledyne Isotopes, Palo Alto (Calif.) Labs., 1966-71; assoc. prof. dept. oceanography Tex. A&M U., 1972-76, prof., 1976—, asst. dean research Coll. Geoscis., 1972-73, assoc. dean, 1984-88 ; adminstrv. judge Atomic Safety and Licensing Bd. Panel, NRC, 1974—; mem. adv. com. for ocean scis. NSF, 1984—, adv. com. for earth scis. NSF, 1985-88 ; mem. group of experts for methods standards and intercalibration UN Intergovtl. Oceanographic Commn. Served with USNR, 1953-57. Mem. Am. Geophys. Union, AAAS, Am. Chem. Soc., Internat. Assn. Phys. Scis. of the Ocean, Sigma Xi. Democrat. Author: Radiochemistry of Silicon, 1968. Contbr. numerous articles to tech. jours. Editor: Symposium on Marine Geochemistry, 1965; assoc. editor: U.S. Quadrennial Report to Internat. Union Geodesy and Geophysics, 1979-82, 83-87, Progress in Oceanography, 1980—. Home: 1002 Arboles College Station TX 77840 Office: Tex A&M U Dept Oceanography College Station TX 77843

SCHINNAGEL, HENRY A(DOLPH), computer manufacturing and distribution company executive; b. N.Y.C., Feb. 4, 1927; s. Henry A. and Elizabeth (Knan) S.; m. June Conforti, Sept. 3, 1950; children—Judith, Elizabeth, Pamela. B.B.A., LaSalle U., 1972; postgrad. Drexel Inst., 1972-73, Temple U., 1973-74. With Sperry Corp., 1957-82, system maintainability dir., Blue Bell, Pa., 1969-80, dir., London, 1980-82; computer systems product line dir. Wang Labs., Inc., Lowell, Mass., 1982—. Asst. scout master Boy Scouts Am., Bklyn., 1953-56. Served as sgt. U.S. Army, 1945-54. Roman Catholic. Avocations: skiing; tennis; radio amateur; jogging. Home: 38 Turkey Hill Rd Merrimack NH 03054 Office: Wang Labs Inc 59 Electronics Ave Lowell MA 03054

SCHINNERER, ERICH, comparative law educator, consultant; b. Vienna, Austria, Mar. 14, 1908; s. Paul and Lydia (Hardy) S.; m. Eleonore von Kamler, Oct. 28, 1937; children: Helga, Klaus. JUD, U. Vienna, 1931; Dr. Jur. Habilitation, U. Berlin, 1935. With Dozent U., Berlin, 1935-39; prof. U. Prag, 1939-45; banksyndikus Credinnstalt, Vienna, 1951-74; prof. Wirtschaftsuniversitat, Vienna, 1962—; cons. banks, Austria, 1974—. Author: Bankvertrage, 3 vols., 3d edit., 1974-78; editor D. Osterr Kreditwesengesetze, 1980. Recipient I. Kl. Ez. Wissenschaft, 1974, Gr. Silb Ehrenz., Republic Osterr, 1984. Mem. Osterr Juristentag (hon.). Mem. Evangelical Reformed Ch. Lodge: Rotary (pres. 1977-78). Home and Office: Mosenthalweg 6, 1180 Vienna Austria

SCHIRRA, WALTER MARTY, JR., business consultant, former astronaut; b. Hackensack, N.J., Mar. 12, 1923; s. Walter Marty and Florence (Leach) S.; m. Josephine Cook Fraser, Feb. 23, 1946; children: Walter Marty III, Suzanne Karen. Student, Newark Coll. Engring., 1940-42; B.S., U.S. Naval Acad., 1945; D. Astronautics (hon.), Lafayette Coll., U. So. Calif., N.J. Inst. Tech. Commd. ensign U.S. Navy, 1945, advanced through grades to capt., 1965; designated naval aviator 1948; service aboard battle cruiser Alaska, 1945-46; service with 7th Fleet, 1946; assigned Fighter Squadron 71, 1948-51; exchange pilot 154th USAF Fighter Bomber Squadron, 1951; engaged in devel. Sidewinder missile China Lake, Calif., 1952-54; project pilot F7U-3 Cutlass; also instr. pilot F7U-3 Cutlass and FJ3 Fury, 1954-56; ops. officer Fighter Squadron 124, U.S.S. Lexington, 1956-57; assigned Naval Air Safety Officer Sch., 1957, Naval Air Test Ctr., 1958-59; engaged in suitability devel. work F4H, 1958-59; joined Project Mercury, man-in-space, NASA, 1959; pilot spacecraft Sigma 7 in 6 orbital flights, Oct. 1962; in charge operations and tng. Astronaut Office, 1964-69; command pilot Gemini 6 which made rendezvous with target, Gemini 7, Dec. 1965; comdr. 11 day flight Apollo 7, 1968; ret. 1969; pres. Regency Investors, Inc., Denver, 1969-70; chmn., chief exec. officer ECCO Corp., Englewood, Colo., 1970-73; chmn. Sernco, Inc., 1973-74; with Johns-Manville Corp., Denver, 1974-77; v.p. devel. Goodwin Cos., Inc., Littleton, Colo., 1978-79; ind. cons. 1979-80; dir. Kimberly Clark, Finalco, Net Air Internat. Decorated D.F.C.(3), Air medal (2), Navy D.S.M.; recipient Distinguished Service medal (2), also; Exceptional Service medal NASA. Fellow Am. Astronautical Soc., Soc. Exptl. Test Pilots. Home and Office: PO Box 73 Rancho Santa Fe CA 92067 *

SCHLAG, EDWARD WILLIAM, physical chemistry educator; b. Los Angeles, Jan. 12, 1932; s. Hermann and Hilda (Nolte) S.; m. Angela Gräfin zu Castell-Castell, 1955; children: Katherine, Karl, Elisabeth. BS in Chemistry, Occidental Coll., 1953; PhD, U. Wash., 1958; PhD (hon.), Hebrew U., Jerusalem, 1988. Postdoctoral researcher U. Bonn, Fed. Republic Germany, 1958; research scientist film dept. E. I. du Pont de Nemours, Buffalo, 1959; tech. adviser, Buffalo, 1960-62; asst. prof. chemistry Northwestern U., Evanston, Ill., 1960-64, assoc. prof., 1964-69, prof., 1969-71; prof. phys. chemistry Tech. U. Munich, Fed. Republic Germany, 1971—, dean Faculty Chemistry, 1982-84; mem. selection com. Alexander von Humboldt Found.; mem. governing com. Fritz Haber Ctr. at Hebrew U., Jerusalem; mem. selection com. U.S. Sr. Award Program; mem. selection com. German-Israeli Minerva Found., mem. sci. program com.; mem. Nat. Fulbright Com. for Germany, 1963; mem. internat. organizing com. Internat. Congress on Photochemistry. Minerva. Founder, editor Chem. Physics, 1973; mem. editorial bd. Chem. Physics Letters, 1973—, Internat. Jour. Mass Spectrometry and Iron Processes, Laser Chemistry, 1982—, Jour. Phys. Chemistry, 1982—. Alfred P. Sloane fellow, 1965. Fellow Am. Phys. Soc., Deutsche Bunsengesellschaft (steering com.); mem. Bayrische Akademie der Wissenschaften. Home: Osterwaldstrasse 91, 8000 Munchen 40 Federal Republic of Germany Office: Technische U, Inst Physikalishe Theoretische Chemie, Lichtenbergstrasse 4, 8046 Munchen Federal Republic of Germany

SCHLAM, MARK HOWARD, internat. mktg. exec.; b. Bklyn., Sept. 24, 1951; s. Murray J. and Sophia (Bonis) S.; B.S., Elec. Engring. (N.Y. State Regents scholar), Poly. Inst. Bklyn., 1972, M.S., 1973. Sales asso. F.W. Madigan Real Estate Co., Flushing, N.Y., 1973-74; sales engr. Dayton T. Brown, Inc., Bohemia, N.Y., 1975-77; sr. mktg. rep. advanced systems Sperry Marine Systems, Gt. Neck, N.Y., 1977-80; pres. Mark H. Schlam Co. Internat., Melville, N.Y., 1980—; asso. editor Poly. Press, Bklyn., 1969-76. Mem. Audio Engring. Soc., Acoustical Soc. Am., AIAA, Am. Soc. Naval Engrs., IEEE, Soc. Tech. Communication, Soc. Automotive Engrs., AAAS, Nat. Pilots Assn., Assn. Old Crows, Nat. Soc. Profl. Engrs., Realtors Nat. Mktg. Inst., Poly. Inst. N.Y. Alumni Assn. (asso. dir. 1973—), Tau Delta Phi. Club: Masons. Asst. editor: Computer Processing in Communications, 1970, Submillimeter Waves, 1971; asso. editor Computers and Automata, 1971, Computer-Communications Networks and Teletraffic, 1972, Optical and Acoustical Micro-Electronics, 1975, Computer Software Engineering, 1976. Office: PO Box 97 East Northport NY 11731-0097

SCHLANG, JOSEPH, business executive; b. N.Y.C., Feb. 24, 1911; s. Alexander and Blanche (Cohen) S.; m. Bernice S. Breitbart, June 8, 1944; 1 son, Stuart Alexander. B.C.S., N.Y. U., 1931. Organized firm of Schlang Bros. & Co. (real estate), N.Y.C., 1934; controlled bldgs. 80, 89, 67 and 41 Broad St., 100 Gold St., 132 Nassau St., 30 Pine St., 67 Wall St., 15 Moore St., 27 William St., and others; owner bldg. material co. of Candee, Smith & Howland Co., 1944-55; dir., part owner Fork Lift Truck Rental Corp., Bond Indsl. Maintenance Corp., 1956-57; owner 271 Central Park West, 1958-59; ltd. ptnr. 975 Park Ave., 1957-60, 1165 Park Av., 1957-60, Majidot Realty Corp., 1958-68, Maidgold Realty Corp., 1960-81, 67 Wall St. Co., 1957-81, 80 Broad St., 1945-61, 1036 Park Ave. Assocs., 1960-61, N.Y. Stock Exchange firm Kalb, Voorhis & Co., 1958-85; pres. Schlang Manuscript Co., Inc., 1965-85, Internat. Opera Co., 1969-85, Opera Gems, Inc., 1971-85, Opera Presentations, Inc., 1972—; founder, owner bank locations, N.Y., Fla., U.S.A.-Inc., Schlang Manuscript Co.; owner Plaza Hotel, Palm Beach, 1987—; pres. Brazilian Corp., Palm Beach, 1987—. Producer, sponsor, panelist: weekly radio programs Opera Stars of Tomorrow, 1973-79, 100 and More Ways to Improve New York City, WNYC, 1973-79; assoc. pub. Graphic History Jewish Heritage, 1963, The Bible and Modern Medicine, 1963; author: booklet Survey of the Financial District of New York City, 1940, Financial District of New York City, 1956, also numerous newspaper and mag. articles. Asst. treas. Downtown Hosp., 1945-47; nat. council N.Y. Met. Opera, 1960—, 1st patron, 1962—; bd. dirs. Bklyn. Lyric Opera Co., 1972—; life mem. Concert Artists Guild, 1972—; sponsor N.Y.C. Opera, 1962-63; patron Cultural Film Club, Palm Beach, Fla., 1974, Palm Beach Opera, Greater Miami Opera, Norton Gallery of Art, Hist. Assn. Palm Beaches; life mem., patron Round Table Palm Beach, Soc. Four Arts; founder, 1st chmn. bus. Com. for Arts of Palm Beach County, 1979-82; founder, creator Met. Opera Co., patron 1962, 1st patron 1962; adviser Library of Presdl. Papers, 1966-70; cons. Mayor's Cultural Com., Yonkers, 1972-74, Mamaroneck, 1972-73; sec., dir. Kehillah of N.Y.C. (Jewish community); sec., treas. Synagogue Council Am., 1953-57, mem. exec. com., dir., 1947-67; bd. dirs. Union Orthodox Jewish Congregations of Am., sec.-treas., 1944-74; pres. Schlang Found., Inc., Broad St. Found., Inc., Barclay Found., Inc., Joseph Schlang Found., Inc.; treas. Elias Cohen Found., Inc.; Found. For a Graphic History Jewish Lit., Inc.; trustee Cong. Kehilath Jeshurun N.Y., 1957-77; Founder Albert Einstein Coll. Medicine, 1961—; life mem. Technion Inst. Medicine, Technion Inst. in Israel; charter mem. Rep. Presdl. Task Force, 1982-88; life mem. Rep. Presdl. Cen. Task Force, 1988—; sponsor of GOP Victory Fund, 1987-88; sustaining mem. Rep. Nat. Com., 1987-88; patron Ronald Reagan Library Found., 1986, 87, 88. Recipient award Am. Jewish Lit. Found., 1960; Statesman award Synagogue Council Am., 1964; proclamations for presentation of free opera festivals from Gov. N.Y. and mayors of 9 cities; certificate of appreciation Mayor N.Y.C., 1974; proclamations County Exec. Nassau and mayors, N.Y.C.; proclamations County Exec. Nassau and mayors, Mamaroneck; proclamations Yonkers for Verdi Festival Periods, 1974. Mem. U.S. and N.Y. Power Squadron, N.Y. Real Estate Bd., Nat. Assn. Real Estate Boards, Numismatic Soc., Manuscript Soc. Am., Nat. Assn. Owners, Mgrs. and Builders, Am. Biographical Inst. (life dep. gov., bd. dirs., recipient medal of honor for lifelong achievement). Republican. Clubs: Town, 100 (co-founder 1938, v.p. 1970-72, pres. 1972-74), Lancers (v.p., pres. 1960-75), City, Colonial Yacht, Palm Beach Poinciana; Gov.'s (Palm Beach, Fla.) (founder, 1984—). Home: 35 E 84th St New York NY 10028 also: 190 Bradley Pl Palm Beach FL 33480 Office: 45 John St New York NY 10038 also: Plaza Hotel 215 Brazilian Ave Palm Beach FL 33480

SCHLEBUSCH, LOURENS, psychologist; b. Kokstad Natal, Republic of South Africa, Jan. 18, 1943; s. Louwrens Antonie and Nellie Johanna (Pelser) S. BA (hon.), U. South Africa, 1970; MA in Clin. Psychology, U. Natal, 1972, PhD, 1976. Tch./sr. tchr. Natal Edn. Dept., Durban, Republic of South Africa, 1963-70; counseling psychologist Natal Edn. Dept., Durban, 1970-72, clin. psychologist, 1974-75; intern clin. psychology Ft. Napier and Townhill Hosps., Pietermaritzburg, Republic of South Africa, 1973; pvt. practice clin. psychology Durban, 1974-76; sr. clin. psychologist, head Pinetown Sch. Psychol. Clinic, 1976, Clin. Psychol. Services, Dept. Psychiatry Addington Hosp., Durban, 1977-84; prin. clin. psychologist, head Clin. Psychol. Services Dept. Psychiatry Faculty Medicine U. Natal, Durban, 1984-87, assoc. prof. medically applied psychology, 1988, chief clin. psychologist, prof. and head sub-dept. of medically applied psychology, 1988—; cons. in forensic psychology Pre-sentence Assessment Panel, Law Cts., Durban, 1980—. Contbr. articles to profl. jours.; editorial bd. Psychiatric Insight, 1986—, Psychiatry and Clin. Psychology in Practice, 1986—; author books. Mem. nat. welfare com. Nat. Cancer Assn. South Africa, Johannesburg, 1985—; mem. Natal Coastal Psychiatric Coordinating Com., 1985—; mem. work com. Med. Research Council South Africa, Cape Town, 1986—; mem. Children's Assessment and Therapy Centre, Durban, 1976—; mem. welfare and related matters subcom. to deal with adjustment of nat. servicemen in civilian life Dept. Social Welfare and Pension, 1978-83; mem. selection com. for foster care prospective parents The Child and Family Welfare Assn., Durban, 1981-83; bd. dirs. Westridge Spl. Sch., 1980-86. Recipient Cert. of Appreciation, Carlswood Jaycees, 1981, Mensa, 1987; Med. Research Council South Africa grantee, 1986, 1988, Human Sci. Research Council South Africa grantee, 1988. Mem. South African Inst. Clin Psychology (Natal bd.1978-80), South African Soc. Brain Behavior Research, Psychol Inst. Republic of South Africa, Psychol. Assn. South Africa, South African Assn. Med. Edn. Club: Mensa (supervisory psychologist 1980—). Office: U Natal Dept Psychiatry, Faculty Medicine, PO Box 17039, Congella, Durban 4013, Republic of South Africa

SCHLEE, WALTER, mathematician, educator; b. Schwandorf, Bavaria, Germany, Sept. 12, 1942; s. Walter Konrad and Babette Maria (Birner) S.; Student Technische U. Munich (W. Ger.); Diplom-Mathematiker, 1967, Dr.rer.nat., 1970; m. Walburga Koessler, Mar. 15, 1974. Researcher, mem. faculty dept. math. Technische U. Munich, 1967—. Mem. Am. Statis. Assn., Deutsche Statistische Gesellschaft, Association des Statisticiens Universitaires, Bernoulli Soc. for Math. Stats. and Probability, Soc. de Statistique de Paris et de France. Author works on math. optimization, graph theory and nonparametric stats. in English, French German; contbr. articles and revs. to profl. jours. Office: Arcisstrasse 21, D-8000 Munich 2 Federal Republic of Germany

SCHLEGEL, JØRGEN ULRIK, surgeon, educator; b. Copenhagen, July 18, 1918; s. Carl Otto Emil and Ingeborg (Nielsen) S.; m. Birgitte Raffenberg; children: Nils Ulrik, Peter Ulrik. MD, U. Copenhagen, 1945, PhD, 1949; MD, Tulane U., 1959. Asst. prof. U. Copenhagen, 1945-49, U. Rochester, N.Y., 1949-59; prof., chmn. med. sch. Tulane U., New Orleans, 1959-82, prof. emeritus, 1982—; chief of staff Tulane Med. Ctr. Hosp., New Orleans, 1977-82. Contbr. over 200 articles to profl. jours and texts. Fellow ACS, Clin. Soc. G.U. Surgeons, Am. Assn. Genitourinary Surgeons, Am. Assn. Anatomists, Am. Physiol. Soc. Home: Apt 129, 45900 Chapala, Jalisco Mexico

SCHLEGELMILCH, REUBEN ORVILLE, electrical engineer, consultant; b. Green Bay, Wis., Mar. 8, 1916; s. Raymond Adolf and Emma J. (Schley) S.; m. Margaret Elizabeth Roberts, Aug. 22, 1943; children: Janet R., Raymond J., Joan C., Margaret Ann. BS in Elec. and Agrl. Engring., U. Wis., 1938; MS in Elec. and Agrl. Engring., Rutgers U., 1940; postgrad. in elec. engring., Cornell U., 1940-41, Poly. Inst. Bklyn., 1947-51, U. Ill., 1941-42; SM in Indsl. Mgmt., MIT, 1955; postgrad. in elec. engring., Syracuse U., 1956-59. Registered profl. engr., N.J. Dir. research and devel. Rome Air (Elec.) Devel. Ctr., N.Y., 1955-59; tech. dir. def./space, Westinghouse Elec., Corp. Hdqrs., Washington, 1959-63; mgr. adv. tech. and missiles Fed Systems IBM, Owego, N.Y., 1963-68; gen. mgr., pres. Schilling Industries, Galesville, Wis., 1968-71; mgr. systems design U.S. Army Adv. Systems Concepts Agy., Alexandria, Va., 1971-74; mgr. gun fire control systems, Naval Sea Systems Command, Washington, 1974-80; tech. dir. office research and devel. U.S. Coast Guard Hdqrs., Washington 1980-86; cons. in field, 1986—; govt. cons. electronics, Dept. Def. Research and Devel. Bd., 1949-54; indsl. cons. missile/space, Aerospace Industries Assn., 1959-63; chmn. profl. sci. com. Rome Air Devel. Ctr., 1956-59; mem. nat. com. Engring. Mgmt. Inst. Elec. Engring., N.Y.C., 1956-59. Patentee target position indicator; author tech. reports and articles. Vol. Annandale Christian Community for Action (Va.), 1973-84; mem. Winterset Civic Assn., Annandale, 1971-84. MIT Alfred P. Sloan fellow, 1954-55. Mem. IEEE (sr. life, sec., vice chmn., chmn. 1956-59, Recognition award 1959), Am. Def. Preparedness Assn. (chmn. So. Tier Empire Post 1967-68, recognition award 1968), NSPE, N.Y. Acad. Scis., Soc. Sloan Fellows MIT. Lodges: Masons, Rotary, Shriners. Home: 8415 Frost Way Annandale VA 22003

SCHLEGER, PETER RALPH, corporate communications specialist, writer; b. N.Y.C., Apr. 7, 1944; s. Hans Emil and Susan Erna (Jacoby) S.; m. Batya Kahane, Apr. 29, 1975; children—Shane, Jesse. B.S. in Bus. Adminstrn., Boston U., 1965; M.B.A., Pace U., 1969; M.A., U. So. Calif., 1977. Bus. mgr. N.Y.C. Bd. Edn., Bronx, 1968-70; owner, operator Sandwich City, Tel Aviv, 1971-73; writer Baer/Joelson Prodns., 1975-76; dir. communications Barkers, Bronx, 1977-80; prin. Peter Schleger Co., N.Y.C., 1980—; prodn. mgr. Fraternity Row, 1975; presenter various confs. Author screenplays The Assignment, 1975, Stanik & Catherine, 1976, Bridges, 1980; novel Tammuz Web, 1982. Contbr. articles to Tng. News and Tng. and Devel. Jour., Employee Benefits Jour., 1980-88, newspapers. Mem. Am. Soc. Tng. and Devel. (Communicator of Yr. 1981, exec. com. media div. 1981-83), Tau Kappa Epsilon. Democrat. Jewish. Lodge: Masons. Home and Office: 135 W 58th St New York NY 10019

SCHLEICHER, HEINZ ANTON, economics educator; b. Heilbronn, Germany, Jan. 11, 1938; came to France, 1971; s. Anton and Rosa (Waldenmaier) S.; m. Monique Jacquey, Aug. 17, 1967; children: Jerome, Agathe. Diploma, U. Munich, 1961; D. rer. pol., U. Vienna, 1964, Docent, 1969; Diploma, Inst. for Advanced Study, Vienna, 1966. Asst. U. Vienna, Austria, 1962-66; scholar Inst. for Advanced Study, Vienna, 1964-66; research assoc. Princeton U., N.J., 1966-68; asst. prof. Vienna U., Austria, 1968-70, docent, 1970-71; maitre de conference associe U. Paris XII, France, 1971-76, prof., 1976—; with ISMEA Coll. France, 1979-87; vis. prof. U. Bielefeld, W.Ger., 1982, prof. Inst. Math. Econs., 1980, U. Casablanca, Morocco 1977; vis. scholar C.V. Starr Ctr. Applied Econs. NYU, 1984; cons. Faculty Medicine U. Paris, 1975-77. Author: Kapitalbewegungen, Kapitalbildung, und wirtschaftliche Integration, 1969; Staatshaushalt und Strategie, 1971; Jeux, Information, et Groupes, 1979. Grantee German Acad. Exchange Service and Austrian Govt., Vienna, 1962-64, Inst. for Advanced Studies, Vienna, 1964-66, Fulbright Commn., Washington, 1966-68. Mem. Am. Econ. Assn., Econometric Soc., German Econ. and Social Scis. Assn., Assn. française de sciences económiques. Office: Univ Paris XII, 58 Ave Didier La Varenne, Saint Hilaire France

SCHLEICHER, KLAUS FRIEDRICH ALBERT, university administrator; b. Hamburg, Germany, June 11, 1935; s. Friedrich Hugo and Ida (Nessau) S.; m. Mechthildy Sophia Harmstorf, Mar. 25, 1960; children: Gabriele, Andreas, Roland, Reinhold, Dietrich. BA, U. Hamburg, Fed. Republic Germany, 1962; PhD, U. Hamburg, 1968. Asst. prof. U. Hamburg, 1968-69, lectr., 1969-72, prof., 1973—, dir. Inst. Comparative and Internat. Edn., 1976-88; prof. U. Bochum, Nordrheim, 1972; vis. prof. Kent (Ohio) State U., 1970, 73, Ind. U., Bloomington, 1982, Smith Coll., Northampton, Mass., 1985; advisor Council of Europe, Strasbourg, 1977-86, Swiss Broadcasting Corp., Zurich, 1978-88, Ministry of Social Affairs Nordrheim-Westfalia, 1979-81; mem. planning bd. JCUS, 1987—. Advisor Kubel Stiftung, 1978-84; cons. Waldorf-Schule Bergstedt, Hamburg, 1985-88. Fulbright scholar, 1973; grantee Brit. Council, 1972, Japanese Soc. Philosophy of East, 1976, U. Hamburg, 1979-80. Mem. World Assn. Ednl. Research, Brit. Comparative and Internat. Edn., Deutsche Hochschulverband. Home: Schaferkamp 31A, Ammersbek Federal Republic of Germany Office: U Hamburg Dept Edn, Sedanstrasse 18, Hamburg 13 Federal Republic of Germany

SCHLESINGER, ARTHUR (MEIER), JR., writer, history educator; b. Columbus, Ohio, Oct. 15, 1917; s. Arthur M. and Elizabeth (Bancroft) S.; m. Marian Cannon, 1940 (div. 1970); children: Stephen Cannon, Katharine Kinderman, Christina, Andrew Bancroft; m. Alexandra Emmet, July 9, 1971; 1 son, Robert Emmet Kennedy. A.B. summa cum laude, Harvard U., 1938, mem. Soc. of Fellows, 1939-42; postgrad. (Henry fellow), Cambridge (Eng.) U., 1938-39; hon. degrees, Muhlenberg Coll., 1950, Bethany Coll., 1956, U. N.B., 1966, Tusculum Coll., 1966, R.I. Coll., 1969, Aquinas Coll., 1971, Western New Eng. Coll., 1974, Ripon Coll., 1976, Iona Coll., 1977, Utah State U., 1978, U. Louisville, 1978, Northeastern U., 1981, SUNY-Albany, 1984, U.N.H., 1985, U. Oxford, 1987, Akron U., 1987. With OWI, 1942-43, OSS, 1943-45; assoc. prof. history Harvard U., 1946-54, prof., 1954-61; vis. fellow (Inst. Advanced Study), Princeton, N.J., 1966; Schweitzer prof. humanities City U. N.Y., 1966—; spl. asst. to Pres. of U.S., 1961-64; Mem. jury Cannes Film Festival, 1964; Mem. Adlai E. Stevenson campaign staff, 1952, 56; trustee Twentieth Century Fund, Robert F. Kennedy Meml. Author: Orestes A. Brownson, 1939, The Age of Jackson, 1945, The Vital Center, 1949, The General and the President, (with R. H. Rovere), 1951, The Crisis of the Old Order, 1957, The Coming of the New Deal, 1958, The Politics of Upheaval, 1960, Kennedy or Nixon, 1960, The Politics of Hope, 1963, A Thousand Days, 1965, The Bitter Heritage, 1967, The Crisis of Confidence, 1969, The Imperial Presidency, 1973, Robert Kennedy and His Times, 1978, The Cycles of American History, 1986. Contbr. articles to mags. and newspapers; film reviewer: Show mag, 1962-64, Vogue, 1967-72, Saturday Rev, 1977-80, Am. Heritage, 1981-82. Served with AUS, 1945. Recipient Pulitzer prize for History, 1946, Francis Parkman prize, 1957, Bancroft prize, 1958, Pulitzer prize for Biography, 1966, Nat. Book award, 1966, 79, Am. Inst. Arts and Letters Gold medal for History, 1967, Fregene prize for lit. (Italy), 1983. Mem. Mass. Hist. Soc., Colonial Soc. Mass., Am. Hist. Assn., Orgn. Am. Historians, Soc. Am. Historians, Am. Acad. and Inst. Arts and Letters (pres. 1981-84, chancellor 1984—), ACLU, Council Fgn. Relations, Ams. for Dem. Action (nat. chmn. 1953-54), Assn. Study Afro-Am. Life and History, Phi Beta Kappa. Democrat. Unitarian. Club: Century. Office: CUNY 33 W 42d St New York NY 10036 *

SCHLESINGER, JAMES RODNEY, economist; b. N.Y.C., Feb. 15, 1929; s. Julius and Rhea (Rogen) S.; m. Rachel Mellinger, June 19, 1954; children: Cora K., Charles L., Ann R., William F., Emily, Thomas S., Clara, James Rodney. A.B. summa cum laude, Harvard U., 1950, A.M., 1952, Ph.D., 1956. Asst. prof., then asso. prof. U. Va., 1955-63; sr. staff mem. RAND Corp., 1963-67; dir. strategic studies 1967-69; asst. dir. Bur. Budget, 1969, acting dep. dir., 1969-70; asst. dir. Office Mgmt. and Budget, 1970-71; chmn. AEC, 1971-73; dir. CIA, Feb.-July 1973; U.S. sec. def. 1973-75; vis. scholar Johns Hopkins Sch. Advanced Internat. Studies, 1976-77; asst. to Pres., 1977; sec. Dept. Energy, 1977-79; sr. advisor Center for Strategic and Internat. Studies, Georgetown U., 1979—; sr. adv. Shearson Lehman Bros., Inc., 1979—; cons. in field. Author: The Political Economy of National Security, 1960; co-author: Issues in Defense Economics, 1967. Frederick Sheldon prize fellow Harvard U., 1950-51. Mem. Phi Beta Kappa. Republican. Lutheran. Office: Georgetown U Ctr Strategic & Internat Studies 1800 K St NW Washington DC 20006 *

SCHLESINGER, JOHN RICHARD, film, opera and theatre director; b. London, Eng., Feb. 16, 1926; s. Bernard Edward and Winifred Henrietta (Regensburg) S. B.A., Balliol Coll., Oxford U., 1950. Dir. BBC TV, 1958-60. Dir. feature films including A Kind of Loving, 1962 (Golden Bear award Berlin Film Festival), Billy Liar, 1963, Darling, 1965 (N.Y. Critics award), Far From the Madding Crowd, 1966, Midnight Cowboy, 1968 (Acad. award, Brit. Acad. award), Sunday Bloody Sunday, 1970 (David di Donatello award, Brit. Acad. award), Day of the Locust, 1974, Marathon Man, 1976, Yanks, 1979 (Nat. Bd. Rev. award, New Standard award), Honky Tonk Freeway, 1980, Separate Tables, 1982, An Englishman Abroad, 1983 (Brit. Acad. award), The Falcon and the Snowman, 1983, The Believers, 1986; plays Days in the Trees, 1966, I and Albert, 1972, Heartbreak House, 1974, Julius Caesar, 1977, True West, 1981, Les Contes d'Hoffmann, 1980-81 (SWET award), Der Rosenkavalier, 1984-85; assoc. dir. Nat. Theatre, London, 1973—. Served with Royal Engrs., 1944-48. Recipient David di Donatello Spl. Dir. award, 1980, Shakespeare prize, 1981; decorated comdr. Order Brit. Empire. Address: care Duncan Heath Assocs, Paramount House, 162 Wardour St, London W1, England *

SCHLESINGER, RUDOLF BERTHOLD, lawyer, educator; b. Munich, Germany, Oct. 11, 1909; s. Morris and Emma (Aufhauser) S.; m. Ruth Hirschland, Sept. 4, 1942; children: Steven, June, Fay. Dr.Jur. summa cum laude, U. Munich, 1933; LL.B., Columbia, 1942. Law sec. to Chief Judge Irving Lehman, N.Y. Ct. Appeals, 1942-43; confidential law sec. Judges N.Y. Ct. Appeals, 1943- 44; asso. Milbank, Tweed, Hope & Hadley, N.Y.C., 1944-48; asso. prof. Cornell U., 1948-51, prof., 1951-75, William N. Cromwell prof. internat. and comparative law, 1956-75; prof. Hastings Coll. Law, U. Calif., 1975—, vis. prof., 1974; Cons. N.Y. State Law Rev. Commn., 1949—; mem. adv. com. internat. rules of jud. procedure, 1959-66; vis. prof. Columbia, 1952, Salzburg Seminar, 1964; Charles Inglis Thomson distinguished vis. prof. U. Colo., summer 1976. Author: Cases, Text and Materials on Comparative Law, 2d edit, 1959, 3d edit., 1970, 4th edit., 1980, 5th edit., 1987/88 (with Baade, Damaska & Herzog), Formation of Contracts: A Study of the Common Core of Legal Systems, 2 vols, 1968; others.; Editor-in-chief: Columbia Law Rev, 1941-42; bd. editors: Am. Jour. Comparative Law; Author articles legal topics. Trustee Cornell U., 1961-66. Carnegie Corp. Reflective year fellowship, 1962-63. Mem. Am. Law Inst. (life), Am. Bar Assn., Internat. Acad. Comparative Law, Phi Beta Kappa, Order of Coif. Home: 2601 Vallejo St San Francisco CA 94123

SCHLETTE, SHARON ELIZABETH, utility company executive; b. Bklyn., May 25, 1945; d. Albert Valentine and Dorothy Lee (Jacobs) Kunz; m. Arthur F. Schlette, Oct. 25, 1985. Student, St. Johns U., 1978-82. With Consol. Edison Co., 1963—, dist. office teller, 1967-69, acctg. clk., customer service rep., 1967-72, asst. supr. Manhattan customer service, 1972-78; unit mgr. Br. III-Westside, Manhattan customer service, 1978-81, Lincoln Center Br., 1981-82; unit mgr. Yorkville Br., 1982-87, with final accounts/collections dept., 1987—. Mem. Consol. Edison Engring. Soc., Nat. Rifle Assn., Nat. Assn. Female Execs., Aircraft Owners and Pilots Assn. (lic. pilot). Republican. Home: 446 Madison Ave Brentwood NY 11717 Office: 708 1st Ave New York NY 10017

SCHLIEKELMANN, ROBERT JACQUES, aeronautical engineer; b. Amsterdam, The Netherlands, Sept. 24, 1922; s. Leo Joseph and Johanna (van der Burg) S.; m. Maria Anna Hazes; children: Marguerite, Lilian, Rosemarie, Leo, Rob. M in Aero. Engring., Tech. U., Delft, The Netherlands, 1948; postgrad., MIT, 1951. With Royal Netherlands Aircraft Co., Fokker, Schiphol, 1948-84, v.p. research and devel., 1974-84, ret., 1984; cons. Ministry for Econ. Affairs, The Hague, 1984-87; mgr. Advanced Structures Materials and Process Engring. Cons., Amstelveen, The Netherlands, 1984—; pres. adhesion sect. B.V.M., Zwijndrecht, The Netherlands, 1965—. Author: Adhesive Bonded Structures, 1969, Metall Kleban, 1971, Durability Adhesive Bonded Structures, 1979, Progress in Advanced Materials, 1985; patentee in field. Decorated officer Order of Orange Nassau (The Netherlands), 1984; recipient U.S. Innovation award SPE/Tech. Conf., Los Angeles, 1980. Mem. AIAA, The Netherlands Soc. Material Scis. (pres. 1984—, Gold medal 1971), Soc. Materials and Processing Engrs. (internat. com. 1980—), Royal Inst. Engrs. (Research Gold medal 1975), Soc. Automotive Engrs. Roman Catholic. Lodge: Lions (pres. 1987-88). Home and Office: Advanced Structures Material, & Process Engring Cons, 451 Amsterdamseweg, NL 1181 BP Amstelveen The Netherlands

SCHLONDORFF, VOLKER, motion picture director; b. Wiesbaden, Germany, Mar. 31, 1939; s. Georg S. and Ilse (Loycke) S.; m. Margarethe von Trotta. Studied in France; degree in econs., polit. sci.; studied filmmaking, Institut des Hautes Etudes Cinematographiques. Asst. dir. for French dirs. Jean-Pierre Melville, Louis Malle, Alain Resnais, from 1959; dir. 1st feature film: Der Junge Torless, 1969; dir. films including: Baal, A Free Woman, Los Honour of Katharina Blum, The Tin Drum (Golden Palm, Cannes 1979, Acad. award for best fgn. film), Circle of Deceit, 1982, Swann in Love, 1983, Death of a Salesman, 1985; dir. operas: Katia Kabanova, 1974; Der Fluss, 1976. Mem. West German PEN Ctr. Office: Turkenstrasse 91, D-8000 Munich 40 Federal Republic of Germany Address: Turvenstr 91, Bioscop Ficor, D-8000 Munich 40 Federal Republic of Germany

SCHLOSS, BRIGITTE, applied linguistics educator, university administrator; b. Gnadau, Germany, Oct. 3, 1927; came to Can., 1950; d. Erwin J. and Emilie (Ruppert) S. Tchr. diploma in home econs. Fribourg, Switzerland, 1945; B.A. in Edn., Meml. U., St. John's Nfld., Can., 1965; M.A., Laval U., Quebec, Que., Can., 1969; diploma for teaching French by audiovisual methods U. St. Cloud, France, 1970; Ph.D., U. Toronto, Ont., Can., 1980. Tchr. Moravian finishing sch., Montmirail, Switzerland, 1947-49; tchr. Moravian Mission, Makkovik, Labrador, 1950-52; tchr. Moravian Mission, Nain, Labrador, 1952-55, prin., 1956-59; tchr., head French dept. Integrated Sch. Bd., Happy Valley, Labrador, 1960-63, 64-68, 69-71; grad. asst. Ont. Inst. for Studies in Edn., Toronto, 1971-77; from lectr. to asst. prof. U. Western Ont., London, 1978-81; coordinator native tchr. edn. program, asst. prof. applied linguistics Meml. U., 1981—; condr. workshops in field. Author: Jeux Linguistiques, 1977; The Uneasy Status of Literature in Second Language Teaching, 1981; author curriculum units, 1971-78; co-author (reading comprehension tests) Test de lecture, 1978. Active fundraising for new ch. Moravian Ch., Nain. Ont. Inst. for Studies in Edn. grad. fellow U. Toronto, 1971-74. Mem. Meml. U. Faculty Assn. Avocations: church; native language study; nature; needlework; reading. Home: 337 Maplewood Pl, Saint John's, NF Canada A1E 4L8 Office: Meml U, Faculty Edn Native and No Edn, Saint John's, NF Canada A1B 3X8

SCHLOSS, JO ANN BOCK, entrepreneur; b. Denver, Aug. 9, 1932; d. Samuel and Rose Bock; B.A. in Communications, U. Colo., 1972, M.A. in Orgnl. Behavior and Communications (grad. fellow 1975), 1975; m. Charles M. Schloss, Jr., Dec. 19, 1948; children—Charles M., III, Sindi Jo, Kristy Anne. Community relations cons. Denver Commn. Community Relations, 1972-73, project dir. commn. youth, 1973-75; with Central Bank of Denver, 1976-82, v.p. staff relations and devel., 1979-81, v.p. human resources planning and devel., 1981-82; chief operating officer Schloss & Shubart, Inc., 1983-84; pres., chief exec. officer Profitable Decisions, Inc., Englewood, Colo., 1985—. Chair Arap. County Pvt. Industry Council; Denver Lions Club, Rockies Venture Club; bd. dirs. Women's Resource Ctr., Arapahoe Community Coll. Named hon. faculty dept. communication U. Colo. Mem. Am. Soc. Tng. and Devel., Internat. Assn. Bus. Communicators, Human Resources Planning Soc., Internat. Assn. Quality Circles, Am. Soc. Personnel Adminstrs., Leadership Denver, Women's Forum Colo., World Future Soc., Women Bus. Owners Assn., Denver C. of C., (small bus. steering com., mgmt. assistance task force, chair course devel. task force), Phi Beta Kappa.

SCHLUTER, PETER MUELLER, electronics company executive; b. Greenwich, Conn., May 24, 1933; s. Fredric Edward and Charlotte (Mueller) S.; B.M.E., Cornell U., 1956; postgrad. Harvard U. Grad. Sch. Bus. Adminstrn., 1982; m. Jaquelin Ambler Lamond, Apr. 18, 1970; children—Jane Randolph, Charlotte Mueller, Anne Ambler. Sr. engr. Thiokol Chem. Corp., Brigham City, Utah, 1958-59; asso. Porter Internat. Co., Washington, 1960-65, v.p., 1965-66, pres., treas., dir., 1966-70; pres., treas. dir. Zito Co., Derry, N.H., 1970-72; internat. bus. cons., Washington, 1972-74; v.p., dir. Buck Engring. Co. Inc., Farmingdale, N.J., 1975, pres., chief exec. officer, dir., 1975—; dir. Keystone Forging Co., Northumberland, Pa. Mem. Republican Inaugural Book and Program Com., 1969; mem. community adv. bd. Monmouth council Girl Scouts U.S.; mem. adv. council Monmouth (N.J.) Coll. Sch. Bus. Admin.; bd. dirs. United Way of Monmouth County., trustee Monmouth Med. Ctr. Mem. Pi Tau Sigma. Clubs: Metropolitan (Washington); Rumson Country. Home: 1607 Channel Club Tower Monmouth Beach NJ 07750 Office: PO Box 686 Farmingdale NJ 07727

SCHLUTER, POUL HOLMSKOV, prime minister of Denmark; b. Tønder, Denmark, Apr. 3, 1929; s. Johannes S.; m. Lisbeth Schluter, 1979 (dec. Feb. 1988); 3 children. Student in law Aarhus U.; LL.B., Copenhagen U., 1957. Mem. Folketing, Copenhagen, 1964—, chmn. Joint Danish consultative council on UN, 1966-68, mem. Parliamentary fgn. affairs com., 1968, chmn. Parliamentary fgn. affairs com., 1982—, prime minister of Denmark, 1982—; former dep. mayor Gladsaxe, Denmark; mem. Council of Europe, 1971-74; chmn. Danish del. to Nordic Council and mem. presiding com., 1978-79. Nat. leader Conservative Youth Movement, 1951; del. Internat. Congress of World Assn. of Youth, 1951, 54; chmn. Young Conservatives and mem. exec. com. Conservative Party, 1952-55, 71; nat. chmn. Danish Jr. C. of C., 1961, v.p. Jr. C. of C. Internat., 1962; polit. spokesman Conservative Mems. Parliament Denmark, 1971-74, chmn., 1974-82—; chmn. Conservative Party Denmark, 1974—. Office: Office of Prime Minister, Christiansborg, Prins Jorgens Gaard 11, 1218 Copenhagen K, Denmark

SCHLYTER, ANDERS ERIK, retail executive, consultant; b. Stockholm, Apr. 3, 1936; s. Carl Erik and Disa Aurora (Spets) S.; m. Anna Jansson, Nov. 11, 1954; children: Camilla, Carl, Erik, Martin. Grad., Ecole de Commerce, Neuchatel, Switzerland, 1954, London Sch. Fgn. Trade, 1956; BIM, Newcastle (Eng.) Coll., 1959. Underwriter Phoenix of London, Vancouver, BC, Can., 1959-60; staff orgnl. devel. Nordiska Kompaniet, Stockholm, 1960-62; mgr. Office of Econs., Monte Carlo, Monaco, 1962-63; staff market devel. Sweda, Solna, Sweden, 1963-70; internat. market mgr. Litton Industries ARS, Morristown, N.J., 1970-73; mgr. mktg. Hugin, Stockholm, 1974-77; sr. cons. HAO, Stockholm, 1977-86; mng. dir. Gävleborgs KÖpmf, 1986—; bd. dirs. SEB Bank Gävle. Author publs. on retainling and computers. Lodge: Gefle Rotary (Gavle, Sweden). Office: Gavleborge Kopmannaf, N Kungsg 11, S-80352 Gavle Sweden

SCHMARAKKUL, KANES, government adminstrator; b. Bangkok, Thailand, July 24, 1944; s. Pao and Siamluang (Sae Tung) S.; m. Voraporn Punprasert, Nov. 13, 1971; children: Pitibom, Nithiphand. BA in Polit. Sci. with honors, Chulalongkorn U., Bangkok, 1967; Internat. Law Cert., The Haque Acad. Internat. Law, Netherlands, 1968; diploma ENS-PTT, Ecole Nationale Superieure des Postes et Telecoms, Paris, 1971; diploma in diplomacy, Inst. Internat. Adminstrn. Pub., Paris, 1969; PhD with highest honors, Paris U., 1974. Chief of telecom section Thailand Post and Telegraph Dept., Bangkok, 1974-76; chief of legal section Thailand Post and Telegraph Dept., 1977-78, chief of post section, 1979-80, dir. welfare div., 1981-84, asst. dir. of relations, 1984-85; dir., lectr., head of Internat. Officers Ctr. Asian-Pacfic Postal Trg. Ctr., 1986—; lectr. Borpitpimuk Coll., Bangkok, 1974-75, Ramhamhaeng U., 1975-76, Nat. Inst. Devel. Adminstrn., 1976-77. contbr. articles to profl. jours. Served with the Thai Army, 1970. Named Commander of the Most Exalted Order to the White Elephant His Majesty the King of Thailand, 1980, Officer of the Most Noble Order of the Crown of Thailand His Majesty the King of Thailand 1985. Buddhist. Home: Pongpet Villa, 200/53 Chaengwattana Rd 14, Laksi, Bangkok 10210, Thailand Office: The Asian-Pacific Postal Trg Ctr, Chaengwattana Laksi, Bangkok 10210, Thailand

SCHMAUS, SIEGFRIED H. A., consulting engineer; b. Muelheim/Ruhr, W. Ger., Dec. 23, 1915; s. Wilhelm Friedrich and Hedwig (Flader) S.; student Staatliche Ingineur Schule, Duisburg, W. Ger., 1940-41, Esslingen, W. Ger., 1945-46; m. A. Babette Schmid, Aug. 17, 1946. Apprentice-designer Demag A.G., Duisburg, 1930-36; designer/supr. Meissner, Cologne, W. Ger., 1936-38; designer aircraft engines Daimler-Benz A.G., Stuttgart, W. Ger., 1943-45; designer Fischer & Porter, Warminster, Pa., 1948-53, Ametek Inc., Sellersville, Pa., 1954-65; staff research engr. Fischer & Porter, Warminster, 1966-80; pres. Sensor Devel. Inc., Broomall, Pa., 1977—, Sensor Research Inc., Phila., 1980—. Sec. Humboldt Circle, 1955—. V.p. Friends Hist. Rittenhouse Town. Served with German Luftwaffe, 1938-42. Recipient Hess Ingenuity award, 1962. Mem. Franklin Inst. (sr., silver mem.), Instrument Soc. Am. (sr.), Am. Soc. Mfg. Engrs., German Soc. Pa. (v.p. 1984, Founders Medal 1987). Republican. Lutheran. Club: Masons. Patentee in field. Home and Office: 806 Powder Mill Ln Penfield Downs Philadelphia PA 19151

SCHMELKIN, BENJAMIN, accountant; b. N.Y.C.; s. Joseph and Lucy (White) S.; B.S., CCNY; postgrad. Baruch Sch. Bus.; m. Selma Landsman, June 18, 1944; children—Alan, Kenneth, Mark. Tchr. acctg. high sch., N.Y.C., 1932-36; partner Schmelkin & Schmelkin, C.P.A.s, 1932—; acct. Am. Acad. Dental Medicine. Mem. Muscular Dystrophy Com., 1956-58; leader fund drive Bronx div. Boy Scouts Am., 1951-52; mem. Israel Bond Drive Com., Bronx, 1955—; chmn. Lyric Cemetery, Bethel, N.J., 1956—; mem. Am. Israel Public Affairs Com.; past patron Mt. Vernon Y.M. Assn.; trustee, exec. bd. Zionist Orgn. Am.; bd. dirs. Menninger Found.; founding mem. West Point Jewish Chapel; founding mem., chmn. fin. com. Temple Beth Shalom. Served with AUS, 1942-43. Scholarship fund named in his honor Kfar Silver Sch., Israel. C.P.A. Mem. Am. Inst. C.P.A.s, C.P.A. Soc. N.Y., Alumni CCNY, ASC, Center Internat. Security Studies, Smithsonian Instn. Assos., Jewish War Vets., Internat. Platform Assn. Clubs: Odd Fellows (past dist. dep., past rep. convs.); Men's (past pres.), Emanuel (Mt. Vernon, N.Y.). Lodge: B'nai B'rith. Home: Guildford E 1073 Boca Raton FL 33434 Office: 54 W Broad St Mount Vernon NY 10552

SCHMERTZ, ERIC JOSEPH, lawyer, labor management arbitrator; b. N.Y.C., Dec. 24, 1925; married; 4 children. A.B., Union Coll., 1948, LL.D. (hon.), 1978; cert., Alliance Francaise, Paris, 1948; J.D., NYU, 1954. Bar: N.Y. 1955. Internat. rep. Am. Fedn. State, County and Mcpl. Employees, AFL-CIO, N.Y.C., 1950-52; asst. v.p., dir. labor tribunals Am. Arbitration Assn., N.Y.C., 1952-57, 59-60; indsl. relations dir. Metal Textile Corp. subs. Gen. Cable Corp., Roselle, N.J., 1957-59; exec. dir. N.Y. State Bd. Mediation, 1960-62, corp. dir., 1962-68; labor-mgmt. arbitrator N.Y.C., 1962—; mem. faculty Hofstra U. Sch. Bus., 1962-70; prof. Hofstra U. Sch. Law, 1970—, Edward F. Carlough disting. prof. labor law, 1981—, dean Sch. Law, 1982—; 1st Beckley lectr. in bus. U. Vt., 1981; dir. Wilshire Oil Co. cons. and lectr. in field. Co-author: (with R.L. Greenman) Personnel Administration and the Law, 1978; contbr. chpts. to books, articles to profl. jours., to profl. law confs., seminars and workshops. Mem. numerous civic orgns. Served to lt. USN, 1943-46. Recipient Testimonial award Southeast Republican Club, 1969; Alexander Hamilton award Rep. Law Students Assn. Mem. Nat. Acad. Arbitrators, Am. Arbitration Assn. (law com.; Whitney North Seymour Sr. medal 1984), Fed. Mediation and Conciliation Service, N.Y. Mediation Bd., N.J. Mediation Bd., N.Y. Pub. Employment Relations Bd., N.J. Pub. Employment Relations Bd. Clubs: NYU (bd. govs.); Hofstra U. Address: 685 W 247th St Riverdale New York NY 10471

SCHMETZER, ALAN DAVID, psychiatrist; b. Louisville, Sept. 3, 1946; s. Clarence Fredrick and Catherine Louise (Wootan) S.; m. Janet Lynn Royce, Aug. 25, 1968; children—Angela Beth, Jennifer Lorraine. B.A., Ind. U., 1968, M.D., 1972. Diplomate Am. Bd. Psychiatry and Neurology. Intern, Ind. U. Hosps., Indpls., 1972-73, resident, 1972-75; dir. clinics PCI, Inc., Anderson, Beech Grove and Kokomo, Ind., 1975-79; psychiat. cons. Community Addiction Services Agy., Indpls., 1975-80; instr. psychiatry in primary care Family Practice Residency Programs, St. Francis Hosp., St. Vincent's Hosp. and Ind. U. Hosps., Indpls., 1975—; med. dir. Child Guidance Clinic of Marion County, Indpls., 1980-81; chmn. psychiatry dept. St. Francis Hosp., Beech Grove, 1980-82; med. dir. Crisis Intervention Unit, Midtown Mental Health Center and coordinator emergency psychiat. services Ind. U. Med. Ctr., Indpls., 1980—, also asst. prof. psychiatry; primary psychiat. cons. Ind. Dept. of Mental Health. Served to maj. Ind. N.G., 1972-79. Decorated Army Commendation medal; recipient Physicians Recognition award AMA, 1978; Residents award for outstanding teaching 1985. Fellow Am. Psychiat. Assn., Am. Ortho-psychiat. Assn.; mem. AMA, Ind. Med. Assn., Marion County Med. Soc., Am. Psychiat. Assn., Ind. Psychiat. Soc., Am. Orthopsychiat. Assn., Am. Acad. Clin. Psychiatry, Alpha Phi Omega, Phi Beta Pi, Psi Chi, Alpha Epsilon Delta. Presbyterian. Club: Athenaeum Turnverein. Author: Crisis Intervention: The Psychotic Assaultive Patient, a videotape and workbook, 1981; Crisis Intervention: The Suicidal Patient, 1981. Office: 1001 W 10th St Indianapolis IN 46202

SCHMICKLER-HIRZEBRUCH, ULRIKE, mathematics editor; b. Princeton, N.J., Aug. 14, 1953; d. Friedrich Ernst Peter and Ingeborg Maria (Spitzley) Hirzebruch; m. Wolfgang Hermann Schmickler, Nov. 30, 1973. Degree in math., U. Bonn, Fed. Republic Germany, 1979. Author: Elliptische Flächen über PC; editor over 85 books in math. Mem. Deutsche Mathematiker Vereinigung, Am. Math. Soc. Club: Germania Wiesbaden Sports. Office: Vieweg Publ, Faulbrunnenstrasse 13, 6200 Wiesbaden Federal Republic of Germany

SCHMID, RUDI (RUDOLF), physician, educator, researcher; b. Switzerland, May 2, 1922; came to U.S., 1948, naturalized, 1954; s. Rudolf and Bertha (Schiesser) S.; m. Sonja D. Wild, Sept. 17, 1949; children: Isabelle S., Peter R. B.S., U. Zurich, 1941, M.D., 1947; Ph.D., U. Minn., 1954. Intern U. Calif. Med. Center, San Francisco, 1948-49; resident medicine U. Minn., 1949-52, instr., 1952-54; research fellow biochemistry Columbia U., 1954-55; investigator NIH, Bethesda, Md., 1955-57; assoc. medicine Harvard U., 1957-59, asst. prof., 1959-62; prof. medicine U. Chgo., 1962-66; prof. medicine U. Calif., San Francisco, 1966—, dean Sch. Medicine, 1983—; Cons. U.S. Army Surgeon Gen., USPHS, VA. Mem. editorial bd. Jour. Clin. Investigation, 1965-70, Jour. Lab. and Clin. Medicine, 1964-70, Blood, 1962-75, Gastroenterology, 1965-70, Jour. Investigative Dermatology, 1968-72, Annals Internal Medicine, 1975-79, Proc. Soc. Exptl. Biology and Medicine, 1976-84; cons. editor Gastroenterology, 1981-86. Served with Swiss Army, 1943-45. Fellow AAAS, N.Y. Acad. Scis.; mem. Nat. Acad. Scis., Am. Acad. Arts and Scis., Assn. Am. Physicians (pres. 1986), Am. Soc. Clin. Investigation, A.C.P. (master), Am. Soc. Biol. Chemists, Am. Soc. Exptl. Pathology, Am. Soc. Hematology, Am. Gastroenterol. Assn., Am. Assn. Study Liver Disease (pres. 1965), Internat. Soc. Study Liver (pres. 1980), Leopoldina. Home: 211 Woodland Rd Kentfield CA 94904 Office: U of Calif Med Ctr Office of Dean San Francisco CA 94143

SCHMID, WERNER, financial director; b. Lucerne, Do, Switzerland, Sept. 10, 1938; s. Karl and Lidwina (Forster) S.; married; children: Rolf, Christine, Jurg. D in Econs., Hochschule St. Gallen, St. Gall, 1970. Fin. dir. Viscosuisse S.A., Emmenbrücke, Switzerland, 1971—. Author: Rechnungswesen mit EDV, 1970. Mem. Swiss Ins. and Risk Mgrs., Assn. Swiss Fin. Execs. Lodge: Rotary (Emmenbrücke). Home: Riffighalde 14, CH-6020 Emmenbrücke Switzerland Office: Viscosuisse S A, Gerliswilstr, CH-6020 Emmenbrücke Switzerland

SCHMIDT, ALFRED OTTO, international engineering consultant; b. Mogilno, Germany, May 12, 1906; came to U.S., 1939, naturalized, 1945; s. Oskar and Emma (Schulz) S.; Mech.Engr., Ingenieurschule Ilmenau, Germany, 1928; M.S.E., U. Mich., 1940, D.Sc., 1943; m. Dorothy Lancaster, Dec. 19, 1941; children—Elsa, Margaret. Mech. engr. Carl Zeiss Jena, Germany, 1929-38; chief research engr. Kearney & Trecker Corp., Milw., 1943-61; prof. mech. engring. and indsl. engring. Colo. State U., Ft. Collins, Marquette U., Milw., Roorkee (India) U., U. Wis., Milw., U. R.I., Kingston, Pa. State U., University Park, 1963-71; adv. machine tools UN Indsl. Devel. Orgn., Israel, 1967, Argentina, 1968, 73, 78, 79, Brazil, 1972, Pakistan, 1970, Kenya, 1970, Sri Lanka, 1974; cons. Korea, 1979, China, 1980, India, 1981, Sri Lanka, 1981, Taiwan, 1982. Fellow ASME (life), Soc. Mfg. Engrs., Am. Soc. Engring. Edn., Sigma Xi. Unitarian-Universalist. Author: Effective Use of Machine Tools, 1972; patentee in field; contbr. research papers to engring. jours. Home: 634 W Prospect Ave State College PA 16801

SCHMIDT, BENNO CHARLES, JR., lawyer, educator; b. Washington, Mar. 20, 1942; s. Benno Charles and Martha (Chastain) S.; children by previous marriage—Elizabeth, Benno III; m. Helen Cutting Whitney, 1980; 1 child, Christina. BA, Yale U., 1963, JD, 1966; LLD (hon.), Princeton U., 1986; LittD (hon.), Johns Hopkins U., 1987; LLD (hon.), Harvard U., 1987. Bar: D.C. 1967. Law clk. Chief Justice Earl Warren, U.S. Supreme Ct, Washington, 1966-67; spl. asst., asst. atty. gen. Office Legal Counsel U.S. Dept. Justice, Washington, 1967-69; Harlan Fiske Stone prof. law Columbia U., N.Y.C., 1983-86, dean Law Sch., 1984-86; pres., prof. law Yale U., New Haven, 1986—; dir. Nat. Humanities Ctr., Chapel Hill, N.C., 1985—. Author: Freedom of the Press versus Public Access, 1974; (with A.M. Bickel) The Judiciary and Responsible Government 1910-1921, 1985. Office: Yale Univ Office of Pres New Haven CT 06520

SCHMIDT, CARL FREDERIC, retired educator, pharmacologist, physiologist; b. Lebanon, Pa., July 29, 1893; s. Jacob Charles and Mary Ellen (Greth) S.; A.B., Lebanon Valley Coll., 1914, D.Sc. (hon.), 1955; M.D., U. Pa., 1918, Sc.D. (hon.), 1965; D.S.M., Charles U., Prague, 1963; m. Elizabeth Viola Gruber, June 24, 1920; children—Carl F., Barbara Elizabeth. Intern, Hosp. U. Pa., 1918-19; instr. pharmacology U. Pa., 1919-22, asst. prof., 1924-29, assoc. prof., 1929-31, prof. pharmacology Med. Sch., 1931-59, emeritus prof. pharmacology, 1959—, Dental Sch., 1949-52; assoc. in pharmacology Peking (China) Union Med. Coll., 1922-24; guest lectr. Portland (Oreg.) Med. Soc., U. Oreg. Med. Sch., 1943; Mary Scott Newbold lectr. Coll. Physicians Phila., 1943; Commonwealth vis. prof. U. Louisville, 1946; Harvey lectr., N.Y., 1949, ann. lectr. in pharmacology U. London, 1949; Henry Lower lectr., Cleve., 1949; Hachmeister Meml. lectr. Georgetown U., 1951; Graves lectr. Ind. U., 1954; chmn. adv. com. Life Ins. Research Fund, 1954-55; cons. surgeon gen. U.S. Army and VA; vis. prof. U. Philippines, 1955; research dir. U.S. Naval Aerospace, med. research dept. Naval Air Devel. Center, Johnsville, 1962-69; clin. prof. pharmacology U. South Fla. Coll. Medicine, 1970—; mem. Unitarian Med. Mission to Germany, 1948; chmn. pharmacology study sect. USPHS, 1947-51, mem. phsyiology study sec., 1947-48; chmn. Internat. Fellowships Com., 1963-64; mem. drug research bd. Nat. Acad. Sci., 1963-69; mem. NRC, 1947-50, sec. subcom. oxygen and anoxia, 1941-45; chmn. panel on physiology Research and Devel. Bd., 1948-50; chmn. subpanel on med. aspects of chem. warfare, 1948-50; mem. adv. panel on physiology Office Naval Research, 1947-52. Served as 1st lt., Med. Res. Corps, U.S. Army, 1918-25. Mem. Internat. Union Physiol. Scis. (v.p., pres. sect. pharmacology 1959-65, pres. 1965-66, hon. pres. 1966—), Am. Heart Assn., Am. Soc. Pharmacology (v.p. 1940-42, pres. 1948-50), Am. Physiology Soc., Soc. Exptl. Biology and Medicine, Assn. Am. Physicians, AAAS, Physiology Soc. Phila., Penn Valley Assn. (pres. 1944-46), Nat. Acad. Scis., Am. Acad. Arts and Sci., Aerospace Med. Assn., Alpha Omega Alpha, Sigma Xi; hon. mem. Pharmacol. Soc., Argentine Med. Assn., others. Club: Merion Cricket (Haverford, Pa.). Mng. editor Jour. Pharmacology and Exptl. Therapeutics, 1940-42, Circulation Research, 1958-62; asso. editor Chem. Abstracts, 1942-48; author articles on respiration, cerebral and coronary circulation, action of Chinese drugs; kidney function, aerospace pharmacology to profl. jours. Home: 749 King of Prussia Rd Radnor PA 19087

SCHMIDT, EDWARD CRAIG, lawyer; b. Pitts., Nov. 26, 1947; s. Harold Robert and Bernice (Williams) S.; m. Elizabeth Lowry Rial, Aug. 18, 1973; children—Harold Robert II, Robert Rial. B.A., U. Mich., 1969; J.D., U. Pitts., 1972. Bar: Pa. 1972, N.Y. 1982, U.S. Dist. Ct. (we. dist.) Pa. 1972, U.S. Ct. Appeals (3d. cir.) 1972, U.S. Ct. Appeals (D.C. cir.) 1975, U.S. Ct. Appeals (9th cir.) 1982, U.S. Ct. Appeals (6th cir.) 1987, U.S. Supreme Ct. 1981. Assoc. Rose, Schmidt, Hasley & Di Salle, Pitts., 1972-77, ptnr., 1977—; mem. adv. com. Superior Ct. Pa., 1978—. Co-editor; Antitrust Discovery Handbook-Supplement, 1982. Asst. editor: Antitrust Discovery Handbook, 1980. Contbr. articles to profl. jours. Bd. dirs. Urban League, Pitts., 1974-77. Mem. ABA (mem. civil practice and procedures com. antitrust sect. 1974—), Supreme Ct. Hist. Soc., Pa. Bar Assn., D.C. Bar Assn., Allegheny County Bar Assn. (pub. relations com. council civil litigation sect. 1977-80), Acad. Trial Lawyers Allegheny County (bd. govs. 1985—), Am. Counsel Assn., Assn. Ins. Attys., U. Pitts. Law Alumni Assn. (bd. govs. 1980). Clubs: Rolling Rock (Ligonier, Pa.); Duquesne (Pitts.). Republican. Home: 5432 Northumberland St Pittsburgh PA 15217 Office: Rose Schmidt Hasley & DiSalle 900 Oliver Bldg Pittsburgh PA 15222

SCHMIDT, GARY EMIL, corporate exec. mgr.; b. Toledo, Oct. 30, 1940; s. Emil August and Edna (Mowery) S.; B.A., Northwestern U., 1962. Bus. editor Calif. Apparel news, weekly newspaper, Los Angeles, 1968-69; feature editor Men's Stylist mag., monthly, Los Angeles, 1970-71; mng. editor Style for Men, weekly, Los Angeles, 1971-72; pres. Am. Century Mktg., Inc., Los Angeles, 1973-79, also dir; investment adv., Studio City, Calif., 1979-88; pres. New Century Rhinoceros, Inc., Panorama City, Calif., 1988—, also dir. Served with U.S. Army, 1962-65. Mem. Authors League Am., Authors Guild. Republican. Unitarian. Home: 4000 Coldwater Canyon Ave Studio City CA 91604

SCHMIDT, HAROLD ROBERT, lawyer; b. Braddock, Pa., Sept. 4, 1913; s. Abraham I. and Gustella (Frankle) S.; m. Bernice V. Williams, June 24, 1941; children: Barbara N. Schmidt Wickwire, Edward C., Gordon W. AB, U. Mich., 1934; LLB, U. Pitts., 1937. Bar: Pa. 1937, D.C. 1976. Sr. ptnr. in charge litigation Rose, Schmidt, Hasley & DiSalle, Pitts., Washington, Harrisburg and Ann Arbor, Mich., Washington, Pa., 1946—; co-chmn. Lawyers Non-Partisan Com. to Secure Additional Judges for Ct. Common Pleas, Allegheny County, 1963; chmn. Com. to Modernize Jury Selection Procedures, Allegheny County, 1965; permanent mem. Jud. Conf. 3d Circuit; former govt. appeal agt. local bd. 19, SSS, Pitts.; panel participant 1st Internat. Med.-Legal Seminar Pitts. Inst. Legal Medicine, U. Rome, 1965; lectr. 3d seminar U. London Med. Coll., 1967; lectr. short course on antitrust law So. Meth. U., 1979, 80, 82-83. Author: Handbook and Guide to the Federal Coal Mine Health and Safety Act of 1969 and Related State Statutes, 1970; contbg. author: Antitrust Law and the Coal Industry, 1983; editor-in-chief: U. Pitts. Law Rev., 1936-37. Chmn. exec. com. Pitts. chpt. Am. Jewish Com.; emeritus bd. dirs. ann. giving fund U. Pitts.; bd. visitors Sch. Law, 1978—; mem. Ft. Pitt Mus. Assocs.; ann. fund leadership com. U. Mich.; mem. Gov.'s Trial Ct. Nominating Commn. of Allegheny County, Pa., 1979; chmn. 1985— Appellate Ct. Nominating Commn. Pa., 1985. Served to capt. AUS, World War II. Fellow Internat. Acad. Trial Lawyers (bd. dirs., dean acad. 1983, pres.-elect 1986, pres. 1987); mem. World Assn. Lawyers (founder, life mem.), ABA (mem. council sect. antitrust law 1984-85, vice chmn. civil practice and procedure com. sect. antitrust law 1980-82), Pa. Bar Assn., Allegheny County Bar Assn., Supreme Ct. Hist. Soc., Nat. Assn. R.R. Trial Counsel, JAG Assn., Acad. Trial Lawyers Allegheny County (past pres.), U. Pitts. Law Sch. Alumni Assn. (past pres.), Am. Law Inst., World Peace through Law Ctr., Am. Judicature Soc., Internat. Soc. Barristers (past gov.), Soc. Mining Law Antiquarians, Pa. Inst. Legal Medicine, Pa. Def. Inst., Def. Research Inst., Res. Officers Assn. U.S., Pa. Soc., Order of Coif, Phi Beta Kappa, Phi Kappa Psi, Phi Eta Sigma. Clubs: Duquesne, Concordia, U. Michigan (past pres.). Lodge: Masons. Home: 154 N Bellefield Ave The Bristol Apt #20 Pittsburgh PA 15213 Office: Oliver Bldg Pittsburgh PA 15222

SCHMIDT, JAKOB EDWARD, medical and medicolegal lexicographer, physician, author, inventor; b. Riga, Livonia, Latvia, June 16, 1906; came to U.S., 1924, naturalized, 1929; s. Michael E. and Rachel I. (Goldman) S. Grad., Balt. City Coll., 1929; Ph.G., U. Md., 1932, BS in Pharmacy, 1935, MD, 1937, postgrad., 1939. Intern Sinai Hosp., Balt.; gen. practice medicine Balt., 1940-53; resident Charlestown, Ind., 1953—; indsl. physician Ind. Ordnance Works, 1953-54; med. and medicolegal lexicographer 1950—; pres. Sculptural Med. Jewelers, 1973-76; mem. revision com. U.S. Pharmacopeia XI. Columnist What's the Good Word, Balt. Sun; Sharpen Your Tongue, Am. Mercury; The Medical Lexicographer, Modern Medicine; Medical Semantics, Medical Science; Underworld English, Police; Medical Vocabulary Builder, Trauma; English Word Power and Culture, Charlestown Courier, Understanding Med. Talk; assoc. med. editor, Trauma, 1959-88; editor: Medical Dictionary, 1959—; compiler: 50,000-word vocabulary test, 1956; contbr. numerous articles to med. jours., lay press, including Esquire, Playboy, also to press services, including UPI, NANA, others; cons. JAMA on med. terminology, also cons. med. terminology to legal profession and cts., to mfrs. on med. tradenames and trademarks; author: Terminology of Sensual Emotions, 1954, Medical Terms Defined for the Layman, 1957, REVERSICON, A Physician's Medical Word Finder, 1958, Medical Discoveries, Who and When, 1959, Dictionary of Medical Slang and Related Expressions, 1959, Narcotics, Lingo and Lore, 1959, The Libido, Its Scientific, Lay, and Slang Terminology, 1960, Baby Name Finder—The Source and Romance of Names, 1961, Schmidt's Illustrated Attorneys' Dictionary of Medicine and Word Finder, 1962, One Thousand Elegant Phrases, 1965, Medical Lexicographer, A Study of Medical Terminology, 1966, The Cyclopedic Lexicon of Sex Terminology, 1967, Police Medical Dictionary, 1968, Practical Nurses' Medical Dictionary, 1968, A Paramedical Dictionary, 1969, 2d edit., 1973, Structural Units of Medical and Biological Terms, 1969, English Word Power for Physicians and other Professionals, 1971, English Idioms and Americanisms, 1972, English Speech for Foreign Students, 1973, Textbook of Medical Terminology, 1973, Visual Aids for Paramedical Vocabulary, 1973, Analyzer of Medical-Paramedical Vocabulary, 1973, Index of Medical-Paramedical Vocabulary, 1974, Schmidt Diccionario para Auxiliares de la Medicina, 1976, Literary Foreplay, 1983, Romantic's Lexicon, 1987, Schmidt's Illustrated Attorneys' Dictionary of Medicine and Word Finder, 18th edit., 4 vols., 1981, 19th edit., 1985, 21th edit., 1987, 22d edit., 1988. Recipient Owl gold medal Balt. City Coll., 1929; Rho Chi gold medal U. Md. Sch. Pharmacy, 1932; gold medal for excellence in all subjects, 1932; cert. of honor U. Md. Sch. Medicine, 1937; award and citation N.Y. met. chpt. Am. Med. Writers' Assn., 1959. Mem. Am. Dialect Soc., Natural History Soc., Am. Name Soc., Am. Med. Writers' Assn., Internat. Soc. Gen. Semantics, AMA, Med. and Chirurgical Faculty of Md., Balt. City Med. Soc., Nat. Assn. Standard Med. Vocabulary, Nat. Soc. Lit. and Arts, Authors' Guild, Authors' League, Am. Mus. Natural History, Cousteau Soc., Smithsonian Instn., Planetary Soc., Nat. Writers' Club, Rho Chi, others. Home: 934 Monroe St Charlestown IN 47111 Office: 934 Monroe St Charlestown IN 47111

SCHMIDT, JOHN JOSEPH, consultant; b. Chgo., Jan. 13, 1928; s. William Fred and Mildred C. (Petrone) S.; m. Gail Bormann, Oct. 8, 1955; children: Cathleen M., Karen B., Linda G. B.S., DePaul U., 1951; J.D., Loyola U., Chgo., 1955. Bar: Ill. 1955. Trial atty. The Atchison, Topeka and Santa Fe Ry., Chgo., 1955-69; asst. v.p. exec. dept. The Atchison, Topeka and Santa Fe Ry., 1969-73; v.p. Santa Fe Industries, Inc., Chgo., 1969-73; exec. v.p. Santa Fe Industries, Inc., 1973-78, pres., 1978-83; chmn. bd., chief exec. officer Santa Fe So. Pacific Corp. (formerly Santa Fe Industries, Inc.), 1983-87; pvt. practice cons. Chgo., 1987—; bd. dirs. Bankment Fin. Corp., E-D Holdings Inc., Textron Inc., Harris Trust & Savs. Bank, Harris Bankcorp Inc. Mem. Zoning Bd. Appeals, Planning Commn. Village of Burr Ridge, Ill., 1973-84. Served with U.S. Army, 1945-47. Mem. Am., Ill., Chgo. bar assns., Am. Soc. Trial Lawyers (past dir.), Ill. Def. Council (past pres.), Nat. Assn. R.R. Trial Counsel (past pres.). Clubs: Chgo. Athletic, Chgo. Economic. Home: 6401 County Line Burr Ridge IL 60521 Office: So Pacific Co One Market Plaza Stewart St Tower San Francisco CA 94105

SCHMIDT, LOUIS BERNARD, JR., industrial distribution executive; b. Ames, Iowa, Sept. 19, 1922; s. Louis Bernard and Georgia Perle (Wilson) S.; m. Jeanette Hook, June 2, 1956. B.S., Iowa State U., 1944; post grad., 1948. Salesman, Agrl. Indsl., Pub. Works Distributive Co., Tucson, 1952-62, v.p. sales, Phoenix, 1962-72; mgr. engine, energy div. Ariz. Engine and Pump Co., div. I.S. Industries, Inc. Phoenix, 1972-85; stationary gas engine use advisor; speaker in field. Active Phoenix Rep. Forum; mem. Ariz.-Mexico Commn., Ariz. Nature Conservancy. Mem. Am. Water Works Assn., Ariz. Water and Pollution Control Assn., Soc. Mayflower Descs. Ariz. (state treas., nat. asst. gen.), SAR, Phoenix Press Club, Ariz. Acad. Pub. Affairs, Eddy Homestead Assn., Gamma Sigma Delta. Unitarian. Clubs: Sky Harbor, Bellota. Lodges: Kiwanis, Elks. Home: 313 W Lewis Ave Phoenix AZ 85003

SCHMIDT, REINER, law educator, banker; b. Hof, Germany, Nov. 13, 1936; s. Wilhelm and Gerda (Hagenmuller) S.; m. Maria Grafin zu Castell-Castell, July 30, 1965; children—Johannes, Caroline, Heinrich. 1 jur. Staatsexamen, Universitat Wurzburg (W.Ger.), 1958, Promotion Dr. iur., 1963, Habilitation, 1971; 2. jur. Staatsexamen, Munchen (W.Ger.), 1963. Ptnr., Schmidt Bank, Hof, 1959—; full prof. law Universitat Augsburg (W.Ger.), 1972—. Author: Wirtschaftspolitik und Verfassung, 1971, Einführung in das Ulmweltrecht, 1987; editor: Die Augsburger Juristenausbildung, 1979. Mem. Vereinigung der deutschen Staatsrechtslehrer. Lodge: Rotary (Ausburg). Home: Bachwiesenstrasse 4, 8901 Gessertshausen Federal Republic of Germany Office: U Augsburg, Eichleitnerstrasse 30, 8900 Augsburg Federal Republic of Germany

SCHMIDT, RICHARD MARTEN, JR., lawyer; b. Winfield, Kans., Aug. 2, 1924; s. Richard M. and Ida (Marten) S.; m. Ann Downing, Jan. 2, 1948; children—Eric, Gregory, Rolf (dec.), Heidi. A.B., U. Denver, 1945, J.D., 1948. Bar: Colo. bar 1948, D.C. bar 1968. Dep. dist. atty. City and County of Denver, 1949-50; mem. firm McComb, Zarlengo, Mott & Schmidt, Denver, 1950-54; partner firm Schmidt & Van Cise (and predecessor), Denver, 1954-65; 65; gen. counsel USIA, 1965-68; partner firm Cohn and Marks, Washington, 1969—; counsel spl. agrl. investing subcom. U.S. Senate, 1959-60; gen. counxel Am. Soc. Newspaper Editors, 1968; mem. Gov.'s Council Local Govt., Colo., 1963-64; chmn. Mayor's Jud. Adv. Com., Denver, 1963-64, Gov.'s Supreme Ct. Nominating Com., 1964-65; mem. Gov.'s Oil Shale Adv. Com., 1963-65, Colo. Commn. on Higher Edn., 1965; chmn. Washington Journalism Center, 1979-81. Trustee U. Denver. Mem. ABA (chmn. standing com. on assn. communications 1969-73, chmn. forum com. on communications 1979-81, co-chmn. nat. conf. lawyers and reps. of media 1984—), Colo. Bar Assn. (gov.), Denver Bar Assn. (pres. 1963-64), D.C. Bar Assn. Episcopalian. Clubs: Denver Law (pres. 1955-56), Denver Press; Federal City (Washington), Nat. Press (Washington). Home: 115 5th St SE Washington DC 20003 Office: Cohn and Marks 1333 New Hampshire Ave NW Washington DC 20036

SCHMIDT, ROBERT, mechanical and civil engineer educator, editor; b. Ukraine, May 18, 1927; came to U.S., 1949, naturalized, 1956; s. Alfred and Aquilina (Konotop) S.; m. Irene Hubertine Bongartz, June 10, 1978; 1 child, Ingbert Robert. B.S., U. Colo., 1951, M.S., 1953; Ph.D., U. Ill., 1956. Engr. C.E., U.S. Army, Omaha, 1951-52; asst. prof. mechanics U. Ill., 1956-59; assoc. prof. U. Ariz., Tucson, 1959-63; prof. mechanics and civil engring. U. Detroit, 1963—, chmn. dept., 1978-80. Editor: Indsl. Math., 1969—; contbr. 114 articles to profl. jours. NSF grantee, 1960-78. Mem. ASCE, ASME (cert. recognition 1977), Am. Acad. Mechanics (a founder), Indsl. Math Soc. (pres. 1966-67, 81-84, 1st Gold award 1986), AAUP, NEA, Sigma Xi. Office: U Detroit Coll Engring Detroit MI 48221-9987

SCHMIDT, TERRY LANE, health care executive; b. Chgo., Nov. 28, 1943; s. LeRoy C. and Eunice P. S.; m. Nancy Lee Anthony; children: Christie Anne, Terry Lane II. B.S., Bowling Green State U., 1965; M.B.A. in Health Care Adminstrn, George Washington U., 1971. Resident in hosp. adminstrn. U. Pitts. Med. Center, VA Hosp., Pitts., 1968-69; adminstrv. asst. Mt. Sinai Med. Center, N.Y.C., 1969-70; asst. dir. Health Facilities Planning Council of Met. Washington, 1970-71; asst. dir. dept. govtl. relations A.M.A., Washington, 1971-74; pres. Terry L. Schmidt Inc., health care cons., Washington, 1974—, Med. Cons. Inc., 1983-84; v.p. Crisis Communications Corp. Ltd., 1982—; pres. Washington Actions on Health, 1975-78; partner Washington counsel Medicine and Health, 1979-81; pres. Ambulance Corp. Am., La Jolla, Calif., 1984-87, Physicians Services Group, La Jolla, 1987—; lectr. dept. health care adminstrn. George Washington U., 1969-71, asst. prof., 1971—; asst. prof. Nat. Naval Sch. Health Care Adminstrn., 1971-80; mem. faculty CSC Legis. Insts., 1972-80, Am. Assn. State Colls. and Univs. Health Tng. Insts.; mem. adv. com. on ambulatory care standards Joint Commn. on Accreditation of Hosps., 1971-72; chmn. San Diego Venture Group, 1984-86. Author: Congress and Health: An Introduction to the Legislative Process and the Key Participants, 1976, A Directory of Federal Health Resources and Services for the Disadvantaged, 1976, Health Care Reimbursement: A Glossary, 1983; Mem. editorial adv. bd.: Nation's Health, 1971-73; Contbr. numerous articles to profl. jours. Bd. dirs. Nat. Eye Found., 1976-78. Fellow Am. Pub. Health Assn.; mem. Am. Hosp. Assn., Med. Group Mgmt. Assn., Assn. Am. Med. Colls., Group Health Assn. Am., Hosp. Fin. Mgmt. Assn., Emergency Medicine Mgmt. Assn., Assn. Venture Capital Groups (bd. dirs. 1984—), San Diego Venture Group (chair 1984-87), Alpha Phi Omega (pres. Bowling Green alumni chpt. 1967-70, sec.-treas. alumni assn. 1968-71). Clubs: George Washington University, Nat. Democratic (life), Nat. Republican (life), Capitol Hill. Office: 8950 Villa La Jolla Dr Suite 1200 La Jolla CA 92037 also: PO Box 90223 Washington DC 20900

SCHMIEDER, CARL, jeweler; b. Phoenix, Apr. 27, 1938; s. Otto and Ruby Mable (Harkey) S.; m. Carole Ann Roberts, June 13, 1959; children: Gail, Susan, Nancy, Amy. Student Bradley Horological Sch., Peoria, Ill., 1959-61; B.A., Pomona Coll., 1961; Owner timepiece repair service, Peoria, 1959-61; clock repairman Otto Schmieder & Son, Phoenix, 1961-65, v.p., 1965-70, pres., 1970—, chief exec. officer, 1970—. Mem. subcom. Leap Commn., 1966; area rep. Pomona Coll., 1972-76. Cert. jeweler; cert. gemologist, gemologist appraiser; recipient Design award Diamonds Internat., 1965, Cultured Pearl Design award, 1967, 68, Diamonds for Christmas award, 1970; winner Am. Diamond Jewelry Competition, 1973; bd. dirs. Lincoln Hosp., 1983—, Ariz. Mus., 1984—; delegate White House Conf. Small Bus., 1986; col. Confederate Air Force. Mem. Am. Gem. Soc. (dir. 1973-86, nat. chmn. nomenclature com. 1975-77, chmn. membership com. 1977-81, officer 1981-86), Ariz. Jewelers Assn. (Man of Yr. 1974), Jewelers Security Alliance (dir. 1974-78), Jewelers Vigilance Com. (dir. 1981-88), Jewelry Industry Council (dir. 1982—), 24 Karat Club So. Calif., Exptl. Aircraft Assn., Deer Valley (Ariz.) Airport Tenants Assn. (dir. 1980—, pres. 1983—), Ariz. C. of C. (bd. dirs. 1985—), Small Bus. Council (bd. dirs. 1985—, chmn. 1988, del. to White House Conf., 1986). Republican. Methodist. Lodges: Kiwanis (pres. Valley of the Sun chpt. 1975-76), Friends of Iberia. Home: 537 W Kaler St Phoenix AZ 85021 Office: Park Central Phoenix AZ 85013

SCHMIT, LAURENT, architect; b. Esch, Luxembourg, May 19, 1924; s. Nicolas Schmit and Marguerite Noesen. State Diploma in Architecture, Govt. of France, 1950. Pvt. practice architecture Grand Duchy, Luxembourg, 1952. Home and Office: 24 Arlon St, 1140 Grand Duchy Luxembourg

SCHMITT, CARVETH JOSEPH RODNEY, office supplies manufacturing official; b. Manitowoc, Wis., Sept. 10, 1934; s. Clarence C. and Thelma J. (White) S.; m. Carolyn Sue Jarrett, May 14, 1965. diploma in bus. adminstrn. and acctg. Skadron Coll. Bus., 1959; A.A. in Bus. Mgmt., San Bernardino Valley Coll., 1962; B.S. in Bus. Adminstrn., U. Riverside-Calif., 1970; M.A. in Edn.-Manpower Adminstrn., U. Redlands, 1975; B.S. in Liberal Studies, SUNY-Albany, 1977; B.A. in Social Sci., Edison State Coll., Trenton, 1978; cert. in Human Services, U. Calif. Extension, Riverside, 1977, postgrad., 1977-80. Registered rep. Ernest F. Boruski, Jr., N.Y.C., 1956-61; acct. Barnum & Flagg Co., San Bernardino, Calif., 1959-70; registered rep., ins. agt. (part-time) Inland Am. Securities, Inc., San Bernardino, 1966-70; registered rep. (part-time) Parker-Jackson & Co., San Bernardino, 1970-73, LeBarron Securities, Inc., 1973-74. credit mgr. Stationers Corp., San Bernardino, 1970-77, office mgr., credit mgr., 1977-83; internal auditor Stockwell & Binney Office Products Ctrs., San Bernardino, 1983-85, corp. credit mgr., 1985—. Served with USAF, 1954-58. cert. tchr., community coll. counselor and personnel worker, Calif. Mem. Nat. Geog. Soc., Nat. Rifle Assn. (life), Nevada Mining Assn., Colo. Mining Assn., N.W. Mining Assn., Am. Philatelic Soc., Nat. Travel Club, Edison State Coll. Alumni Assn., U. Redlands Fellows, Friends of Library Assn. U. Redlands, Valley Prospectors (life), SUNY Regents Alumni Assn., U. Redlands Alumni Assn., Am. Legion, Am. Assn. Ret. Persons, Gold Prospectors Assn. Am. (life mem.). Republican. Rosicrucian. Clubs: Fontana Tour, Hiking, Badminton, Bowling, Arrowhead Stamp, M & M Tour, Rosicrucian (San Jose). Lodge: Masons. Home: 538 N Pampas Ave Rialto CA 92376 Office: 420 South E St PO Box 5129 San Bernardino CA 92412

SCHMITT, ROBERT LEE, computer scientist; b. Astoria, N.Y., Oct. 1, 1948; s. Edward and Margaret Louise (Gleason) S.; A.A.S. in Data Processing, SUNY, Farmingdale, 1972; student Hofstra U., 1972-73; B.S. in Computer Sci., SUNY, Stony Brook, 1974, M.S. in Computer Sci., 1975; postgrad. in gen. adminstrn. U. Md., 1979-80. Computer programmer U.S. Army Environ. Hygiene Agy., Aberdeen Proving Ground, Md., 1976; data systems programmer Dept Def., Ft. George G. Meade, Md., 1976-78, data systems analyst, 1978-83, computer systems analyst, 1983-85, sr. computer system analyst, 1985-86, computer scientist, 1986—. Served with USNR, 1968-70. Cert. computer programmer, data processor, Inst. Cert. of Computer Profls. Mem. Assn. Computing Machinery, Human Factors Soc. Home: 1211 Scattered Pines Ct Severn MD 21144 Office: 9800 Savage Rd Fort George G Meade MD 20755

SCHMITT, ROLAND WALTER, university president; b. Seguin, Tex., July 24, 1923; s. Walter L. and Myrtle F. (Caldwell) S.; m. Claire Freeman Kunz, Sept. 19, 1957; children: Lorenz Allen, Brian Walter, Alice Elizabeth, Henry Caldwell. B.A. in Math, U. Tex., 1947, B.S. in Physics, 1947, M.A. in Physics, 1948; Ph.D., Rice U., 1951; D.Sc. (hon.), Worcester Poly. Inst., 1985, U. Pa., 1985; D.C.L. (hon.), Union Coll., 1985; DL (hon.), Lehigh U., 1986; D.Sc. (hon.), U. South Carolina, 1988. With Gen. Electric Co., 1951-88; research and devel. mgr. phys. sci. and engring. Gen. Electric Corp. Research and Devel. Gen. Electric Co., Schenectady, 1967-74; research and devel. mgr. energy sci. and engring. Gen. Electric Corp. Research and Devel. Gen. Electric Co., 1974-78, v.p. corp. research and devel. Gen. Electric Corp. Research and Devel., 1978-82, sr. v.p. corp. research and devel. Gen. Electric Corp. Research and Devel., 1982-86, sr. v.p. sci. and tech., 1986-88, ret., 1988; pres. Rensselaer Poly. Inst., Troy, N.Y., 1988—; past pres. Indsl. Research Inst.; mem. energy research adv. bd. Dept. Energy, 1977-83. Trustee Northeast Savs. Bank., 1978-84, bd. advisors Union Coll.; vice chmn. bd. dirs., chmn. investment rev. com. N.Y. State Sci. and Tech. Found., 1978-84; bd. govs. Albany Med. Center Hosp., 1979-82; trustee Union Coll., Schenectady, 1981-84, Argonne Univs. Assn., 1979-82, RPI, bd. trustees, 1982-88; bd. dirs. Sunnyview Hosp. and Rehab. Center, 1978-86; bd. govs. Albany Med. Ctr. Hosp., 1988—; dir. Gen. Signal Corp., 1987—; vice chmn., Council on Superconductivity for Am. Competitiveness, 1987—; mem. exec. com., NYS Ctr. for Hazardous Waste Mgmt., 1988—. Served with USAAF, 1943-46. Recipient award for disting. contbns. Stony Brook Found., 1985, Disting. Alumnus award Rice U., 1985. Fellow Am. Phys. Soc., Am. Acad. Arts and Scis., IEEE, AAAS; mem. Am. Inst. Physics (chmn. com. on corp. assocs., mem. governing bd. 1979-83), Nat. Acad. Engring. (council), Nat. Sci. Bd. (chmn. 1982-88), Dirs. Indsl. Research, Am. Nuclear Soc., Indsl. Research Inst., 1978-88. Club: Cosmos. Office: Rensselaer Poly Inst Office of Pres Troy NY 12180-3590

SCHMITZ, ANTHONY FRANCIS, retail books executive; b. The Hague, Netherlands, Apr. 23, 1944; arrived in Scotland, 1970; s. Hendrik Antonius and Caterina Adrianna (Heemelaar) S.; m. Judith Gail Tapson; children: Karl Anthony, Julian James, John Gerard Joseph. B of Philosophy, Heythrop Coll., Oxon, Eng., 1966. Editor Mambo Press, Harare, Zimbabwe, 1967-70; freelance journalist London, 1970; mgr. James G. Bisset's-A Blackwell Book Shop, Aberdeen, Scotland, 1970-73, dir., 1973-87, mng. dir., 1987—; ptnr. Palladio Press, Aberdeen, 1973-80, owner, pres., 1980—. Chmn. Soc. for Protection of Unborn Children, 1979; chmn. Lifeline Pregnancy Care Services, 1979-87; sec. Friends of Pitfodels Sch., Aberdeen, 1985; active Newman Assn. Mem. Catholic Bishops Bioethics Assn., Scottish Booksellers Assn. (exec. com.), Coll. and Univ. Booksellers Group (exec. com.). Roman Catholic. Club: Catenians. Home: 77 University Rd, Aberdeen AB2 3DR, Scotland Office: James G Bissets Ltd, 12 Upperkirkgate, Aberdeen AB9 1BG, Scotland

SCHMITZ, CHARLES EDISON, clergyman; b. Mendota, Ill., July 18, 1919; s. Charles Francis and Lucetta M. (Foulk) Schmitz Kaufmann; m. Eunice M. Ewy, June 1, 1942; children—Charles Elwood, Jon Lee. Student Wheaton Coll., 1936-37, summer 1937, 38, 39; A.B., Wartburg Coll., Waverly, Iowa, 1940; B.D., Wartburg Theol. Sem., Dubuque, Iowa, 1942, M.Div., 1977. Home mission developer and parish pastor Am. Luth. Ch., 1942-65, 73-86, Evang. Luth. Ch. Am., 1988—; served as founding pastor 14 parishes including Ascension (Los Angeles), Am. Evang. Luth. Phoenix, others in Prescott, Glendale, and Scottsdale, Ariz., Portales, N.Mex., Sebastian and Palm Bay; Fla.; founder and prin. parochial schs. in Los Angeles, Phoenix and Palm Bay, synodical Bible evangelist Am. Luth. Ch., 1965-73; dir. Intermountain Missions, 1948-60; sr. pastor Peace Luth. Ch., Palm Bay, Fla., 1973-—. Active Ariz. Christian Conf., Ariz. Alcohol and Narcotics Edn. Assn., Phoenix Council Chs., Evang. Ministers Assn.; pres. Intermountain Conf., 1954-65; vice chmn. Am. Luth. Ch. Worship and Ch. Music Commn., 1961-65; chmn. Billy Graham Ariz. Crusade, 1964, Nat. Luth. Social Welfare Conf., 1944-70; chmn. Space Coast Conf., Am. Luth. Ch., 1980-84, mem. southeastern dist. transition team council, Fla. synod Evang. Luth. Ch. Am., 1980-84; chief chaplain Maricopa County CD, 1961-65; chaplain Palm Bay C. of C., South Brevard Area C. of C., 1973—. Coeditor: The ABC's of LIfe. Editor: Body of Christ-Evangelism for the Seventies. Contbg. editor Good News mag., 1965-71. Referee Maricopa County Juvenile Ct., 1959-61; mem. Gov.'s Com. Marriage and Divorce Problems, 1962-64; mem. Palm Bay Planning Commn., 1975-82; mem. Palm Bay Mayor's Assistance Com., 1974—; chmn. Space Coast Luth. Retirement Ctr., 1984—. Recipient Disting. Alumni award Wartburg Coll., 1959; City of Palm Bay Citizen of Yr. award, 1979. Mem. South Brevard Ministerial Assn. (charter). Lion (charter sec. and bd. mem. North Phoenix 1952-65, founding officer Palm Bay 1975-—, transition com. Formation ELCA Fla. Synod 1987). Home and Office: 1801 Port Malabar Blvd NE Palm Bay FL 32905

SCHMITZ, EDWARD HENRY, electrical equipment manufacturing executive; b. Glenbeulah, Wis., June 21, 1929; s. John Charles and Angeline Ann (Gundrum) S.; m. Janyth Lanier, Dec. 26, 1959; stepchildren: Janyth Lynn, Leslee; children: Robert, Ellen. BS in Bus. Adminstrn., Bryant Coll., 1955. Cert. purchasing mgr. Mgr. purchasing and traffic Hooker Glass Co., Chgo., 1961-65; materials mgr. API Industries, Chgo., 1965-71; purchasing mgr. G&W Electric Co., Blue Island, Ill., 1971—; cons. engr. A. Proudfoot, Chgo., 1957-60. Served with U.S. Army, 1951-53. Mem. Purchasing Mgmt. Assn. (bd. dirs. Chgo. chpt. 1971-73, 83-85), Nat. Assn. Purchasing Mgmt. (dist. chmn. 1980—), Am. Prodn. and Inventory Control Soc. Home: 112 Elizabeth Ln Downers Grove IL 60516 Office: G&W Electric Co 3500 W 127th St Blue Island IL 60406

SCHMITZ, EUGENE GERARD, engineer; b. Brackenridge, Pa., Sept. 17, 1929; s. Wienand Gerard and Florence Marie (Grimm) S.; student Phoenix Coll., 1946-47, Ariz. State U., 1959-61; m. Anna May Lee, May 3, 1952; children—Joyce Marie, Michael Paul, Carol Ann, John David, Eugene Jr. Dist. mgr. Field Enterprise Ednl. Corp., Phoenix, 1955-59; designer, engr. Motorola Inc., Scottsdale, Ariz., 1961-67; project engr. space and reentry systems div. Philco-Ford Co., Palo Alto, Calif., 1967-70; engring. program adminstr. Memorex Equipment Co., Santa Clara, Calif., 1970-71; plant mgr. Tijuana (Mex.) ops. Philco-Ford, 1971-72; engring. cons. FMC Corp., San Jose, Calif., 1972-75; staff cons. engr. Stetter Assos., Inc., Palo Alto, 1975-80, Schmitz Engring. Assocs., 1980-82, 1986—; project engr. Ordnance div. FMC Corp., 1982-86; instr. electronic design Middlton Inst., Phoenix, 1965-66. Served with U.S. Army, 1948-55. Registered profl. engr., Calif. Mem. Soc. Mfg. Engrs. (cert.), Nat. Soc. Profl. Engrs., Profl. Engrs. in Pvt. Practice, Am. Inst. Indsl. Engrs. Republican. Home: 3061 Vesuvius Ln San Jose CA 95132 Office: 3061 Vesuvius Ln San Jose CA 95132

SCHMITZ, WOLFGANG KLEMENS, monetary consultant; b. Vienna, May 28, 1923; s. Hans and Maria (Habel) S.; children: Johanna, Dorothea Pfersmann, Theres Holzinger, Veronika, Stefan. Dr.jur., U. Vienna, 1949. Sole practice law, 1949-50; with Austrian Fed. Econ. Chamber, 1950-64; sec. econ. policy dept. Austrian nat. com. Internat. C. of C., 1950-64; chmn. Beirat fü r Wirtschafts-und Sozialfragen, 1963-64, head econ. policy dept., 1964;minister of fin. Govt. of Austria, 1964-68; pres. Austrian Nat. Bank, Vienna, 1968-73; gov. World Bank, Austria, 1964-68, IMF, 1968-73; Cons., lectr. in field. Author: International Investment, Growth and Crisis-A Plea for Freedom of Movement for International Private Investment Capital, 1975; Die antizyklische Konjunkturpolitik-eine Illusion, Grenzen der Machtbarkeit durch Globalsteuerung, 1976; Die Gesetzesflut-Folge und Ausdruck der Uberforderung des Staates, Gutachten fü r den Siebenten Osterreichischen Juristentag, 1979; Die Währung-eine offene Flanke staatlicher Verfassungsordnung, ihre Schliessung-ein Beitrag zur Festigung der freiheitlichen Demokratie, 1983. Contbr. articles to profl. jours. Mem. Verein fü r Socialpolitik, Ludwig Erhard-Stiftung, List Görres Gesellschaft. Roman Catholic. Home: Gustav Tschermak Gasse 3/2, 1180 Vienna Austria Office: Austrian Fed Econ Chamber, Wiedner Haupstrasse 63 PF-187, A-1045 Vienna Austria

SCHMOE, WILFRED PICKERING, chemical, oil and gas company executive; b. Seattle, June 18, 1927; s. Floyd Wilfred and Ruth (Pickering) S.; m. Lillian Agnes Standing, Aug. 26, 1947; children: Lee Alan, Lynne Marie Higerd, Lori Ann Schmoe Field. Student, Pasadena City Coll., 1947-48, U. Wash., 1948-50; BS in Mech. Engring., Okla. State U., 1953. With Conoco, Wyo., Colo., 1953-66; mgr. personnel Conoco, Houston, 1966-70, v.p. internat. prodn., 1980-81; mgr. internat. prodn. Stamford, Conn., 1970-75; vice-chmn. Conoco, Stamford, Conn., 1981-84; exec. v.p. Conoco North Sea, London, 1975-80, E.I. DuPont, Wilmington, Del., 1984—; chmn., mng. dir. Conoco U.K. Ltd., London, 1980-81; bd. dirs. E.I. DuPont de Nemours & Co., Bank of Del.; pres. U.K. Offshore Operators Assn., London, 1977-78. Trustee Med. Ctr. Del., 1986—. Mem. AIME, Am. Petroleum Inst. Republican. Clubs: Wilmington Country, Wilmington; Teton Pines (Jackson, Wyo.). Home: PO Box 906 Mendenhall PA 19357 Office: EI DuPont de Nemours & Co 1007 Market St Wilmington DE 19898

SCHMUHL, THOMAS ROEGER, lawyer; b. Phila., Oct. 4, 1946; s. Norman George and Ethel Sandt (Roeger) S.; m. Jean Giannone, Aug. 3, 1974; children—Andrew, Deborah. A.B., Johns Hopkins U., 1968, M.A., 1968; J.D., U. Pa., 1971. Bar: Pa. 1971, U.S. Dist. Ct. (ea. dist.) Pa. 1971, U.S. Supreme Ct. 1980. Assoc., Schnader, Harrison, Segal & Lewis, Phila., 1971-78, ptnr., 1979—, chmn. bus. dept., 1984—. Served to capt., USAR, 1968-75. Mem. Internat. Bar Assn., ABA, Phila. Bar Assn., Pa. Bar Assn., Nat. Assn. Bond Lawyers, Com. of Seventy. Club: Racquet of Phila. Office: 1600 Market St Philadelphia PA 19103

SCHMUTZ, JACQUES HENRI, physician; b. LaRochelle, Charente Mme, France, Sept. 25, 1938; s. Paul Camille and Suzanne Blanche (Bellot) S.; m. Francette Michelle Sorlut, Sept. 19, 1961; children: Richard Paul, Axel Luc. MD, U. Toulouse, 1961; diploma homoeopathy SMB, Paris, 1982. Intern Limoges Hosp., France, 1965, Rochefort Hosp., France, 1964-65, 66-67; gen. practice medicine Rochefort, 1967—. Author: Le Portugal et la mer, 1958. Served to lt., French mil., 1965-66. Home: 57 Rue Jean Jaures, 17300 Rochefort, Charente Mme France Office: 57 bis Rue Jean Jaurès, 17300 Rochefort Charente Mme France

SCHMUTZHART, BERTHOLD JOSEF, sculptor, educator, art and education consultant; b. Salzburg, Austria, Aug. 17, 1928; came to U.S., 1958, naturalized, 1963; s. Berthold Josef and Anna (Valaschek) S. Student, Acad. for Applied Art, Vienna, Austria, 1956. Cert. fed. tchr., Austria. Prof. Wekschulheim Felbertal, Salzburg, 1951-58; sculptor Washington, 1959-60; tchr. Longfellow Sch., Bethesda, Md., 1960-63; prof., chmn. dept. sculpture Corcoran Sch. Art, Washington, 1963—; designer art program for learning disabled Lab. Sch., Washington, 1966-70; lectr. Smithsonian Instn., Washington, 1968—. One-man shows include Fredericksburg Gallery Fine Art, Va., 1967-73, Franz Bader Gallery, Washington, 1978, 81, 83, 86; group shows include Nat. Collection Fine Arts, Washington, 1961-70, High Mus. Art, Atlanta, 1965, Ark. Art Ctr., Little Rock, 1966, Birmingham Mus. Art, Ala., 1967, Hirschhorn Mus. and Sculpture Garden, Washington, 1981; represented in permanent collections Hirschhorn Collection; designer fountain, Gallery of Modern Art, Fredericksburg, 1967; author: The

Handmade Furniture Book, 1981; contbr. articles to profl. jours. Fine arts panelist D.C. Commn. for Arts, 1973-79; chmn. bd. Market Five Gallery, Washington, 1978-82; bd. dirs. Franz Bader Gallery, Washington, 1981-85. Recipient 1st prize Washington Religious Arts Council, 1960, for sculpture, Little Rock, 1966, Louisville, 1968, Silver medal Audubon Soc., Washington, 1971. Mem. Guild for Religious Architects, Artists Equity Assn. (pres. D.C. chpt. 1973-75), AAUP, Am. Austrian Soc. (pres. 1968-70, exec. com.), Soaring Soc. Am. Home: 18 9th St NE Apt 406 Washington DC 20002

SCHNABEL, ROCKWELL ANTHONY, investment banking executive; b. Amsterdam, Holland, Dec. 30, 1936; came to U.S., 1957; s. Hans and Wilhelmina S.; m. Marna Belle Del Mar, 1964; children: Mary Darrin, Christy Ann, Everton Anthony. Student, Trinity Coll., Haarlem, Netherlands, 1951-56. Pres. Unilife Assurance Group S.H. Luxembourg, 1974-78; dir. Bateman Eichler, Hill Richards, Los Angeles, 1967-82, sr. v.p., 1969-82, vice chmn. bd., mem. exec. com., 1978-82; pres. Bateman Eichler Hill Richard Group, Los Angeles, 1981-83; dep. chmn. Morgan, Olmstead, Kennedy & Gardner, Inc., Los Angeles, 1983—; dir. Angeles Corp., Los Angeles, Macrodyne Industries. Fin. co-chmn. Republican Party candidates, 1982; adv. council Commn. Econ. Devel. Calif., 1982; attache Netherlands Olympic Com., 1982; dir. Los Angeles Ballet, 1982; hon. consul Republic of South Africa, 1968-81. Served with Air N.G., 1958-64. Named Comdr. Order of Good Hope South Africa, 1981; named Consul Emeritus of South Africa South Africa, 1981. Mem. Los Angeles Bond Club, Stock Exchange Club, Kappa Beta Phi. Club: Los Angeles Beach. Home: 3350 Serra Rd Malibu CA 90265 Office: Morgan Olmstead Kennedy & Gardner Inc 606 S Olive St Los Angeles CA 90014 *

SCHNACK, GAYLE HEMINGWAY JEPSON (MRS. HAROLD CLIFFORD SCHNACK), corporate executive; b. Mpls., Aug. 14, 1926; d. Jasper Jay and Ursula (Hemingway) Jepson; student U. Hawaii, 1946; m. Harold Clifford Schnack, Mar. 22, 1947; children: Jerrald Jay, Georgina, Roberta, Michael Clifford. Skater, Shipstead & Johnson Ice Follies, 1944-46; v.p. Harcliff Corp., Honolulu, 1964—, Schnack Indsl. Corp., Honolulu, 1969—, Nutmeg Corp., Cedar Corp.; ltd. ptnr. Koa Corp. Mem. Internat. Platform Soc., Beta Sigma Phi (chpt. pres. 1955-56, pres. city council 1956-57). Established Ursula Hemingway Jepson art award, Carlton Coll., Ernest Hemingway creative writing award, U. Hawaii. Office: PO Box 3077 Honolulu HI 96802 also: 1200 Riverside Dr Reno NV 89503

SCHNACK, HAROLD CLIFFORD, lawyer; b. Honolulu, Sept. 27, 1918; s. Ferdinand J. H. and Mary (Pearson) S.; m. Gayle Hemingway Jepson, Mar. 22, 1947; children: Jerrald Jay, Georgina Schnack Hankinson, Roberta Schnack Poulin, Michael Clifford. BA, Stanford, 1940, LLB, 1947. Bar: Hawaii, 1947. Dep. prosecutor City and County Honolulu, 1947-48; gen. practice with father F. Schnack, 1948-60; pvt. practice, Honolulu, 1960-86; pres. Harcliff Corp., 1961—, Schnack Indsl. Corp., 1969-73, Instant Printers, Inc., 1971-81, Koa Corp., 1964—, Nutmeg Corp., 1963—, Global Answer System, Inc., 1972-78. Pres. Goodwill Industries of Honolulu, 1971-72. Mem. ABA, Hawaii Bar Assn., Phi Alpha Delta, Alpha Sigma Phi. Clubs: Outrigger Canoe, Pacific. Lodge: Masons. Office: 817 A Cedar St PO Box 3077 Honolulu HI 96802

SCHNALL, EDITH LEA (MRS. HERBERT SCHNALL), microbiologist, educator; b. N.Y.C., Apr. 11, 1922; d. Irving and Sadie (Raab) Spitzer; A.B., Hunter Coll., 1942; A.M., Columbia U., 1947, Ph.D., 1967; m. Herbert Schnall, Aug. 21, 1949; children—Neil David, Carolyn Beth. Clin. pathologist Roosevelt Hosp., N.Y.C., 1942-44; instr. Adelphi Coll., Garden City, N.Y., 1944-46; asst. med. mycologist Columbia Coll. Physicians and Surgeons, N.Y.C., 1946-47, 49-50; instr. Bklyn. Coll., 1947; faculty Sarah Lawrence Coll., Bronxville, N.Y., 1947-48; lectr. Hunter Coll., N.Y.C., 1947-67; adj. assoc. prof. Lehman Coll., City U. N.Y., 1968; asst. prof. Queensborough Community Coll., City U. N.Y., 1967, assoc. prof. microbiology, 1968-75, prof., 1975—, adminstr. Med. Lab. Tech. Program, 1985—; vis. prof. Coll. Physicians and Surgeons, Columbia U., N.Y.C., 1974; advanced biology examiner U. London, 1970—. Mem. Alley Restoration Com., N.Y.C., 1971—; mem. legis. adv. com. Assembly of the State of N.Y., 1972. Mem. Community Bd. 11, Queens, N.Y., 1974—, 3d vice-chmn., 1987—; public dir. of bd. dirs. Inst. Continuing Dental Edn. Queens County, Dental Soc. N.Y. State and ADA, 1973—. Research fellow NIH, 1948-49; faculty research fellow, grantee-in-aid Research Found. of SUNY, 1968-70; faculty research grant Research Found. City U. N.Y., 1971-74. Mem. Internat. Soc. Human and Animal Mycology, AAAS, Am. Soc. Microbiology (council N.Y.C. br. 1981—, co-chairperson ann. meeting com. 1981-82, chair program com. 1982-83, v.p. 1984-86, pres. 1986—), Med. Mycology Soc. N.Y. (sec.-treas. 1967-68, v.p. 1968-69, 78-79, archivist 1974—, fin. advisor 1983—, pres. 1969-70, 79-80, 81-82), Bot. Soc. Am., Med. Mycology Soc. Americas, Mycology Soc. Am., N.Y. Acad. Scis., Sigma Xi, Phi Sigma. Clubs: Torrey Botanical (N.Y. State); Queensborough Community Coll. Women's (pres. 1971-73) (N.Y.C.). Editor: Newsletter of Med. Mycology Soc. N.Y., 1969-85; founder, editor Female Perspective newsletter of Queensborough Community Coll. Women's Club, 1971-73. Home: 214-06 29th Ave Bayside NY 11360

SCHNAPP, ROGER HERBERT, lawyer; b. N.Y.C., Mar. 17, 1946; s. Michael Jay and Beatrice Joan (Becker) S.; m. Candice Jacqueline Larson, Sept. 15, 1979. BS, Cornell U., 1966; JD, Harvard U., 1969; grad. Pub. Utility Mgmt. Program, U. Mich., 1978. Bar: N.Y. 1970, Calif. 1982, U.S. Dist. Ct. (so. dist.) N.Y. 1975, U.S. Dist. Ct. (no. dist.) Calif. 1980, U.S. Dist. Ct. (cen. dist.) Calif. 1982, U.S. Dist. Ct. (ea. dist.) Calif. 1984), U.S. Ct. Appeals (2d cir.) 1970, U.S. Ct. Appeals (4th and 6th cirs.) 1976, U.S. Ct. Appeals (7th cir.) 1977, U.S. Ct. Appeals (8th cir.) 1980, U.S. Supreme Ct. 1974. Atty. CAB, Washington, 1969-70; labor atty. Western Electric Co., N.Y.C., 1970-71; mgr. employee relations Am. Airlines, N.Y.C., 1971-74; labor counsel Am. Electric Power Service Corp., N.Y.C., 1974-78, sr. labor counsel, 1978-80; indsl. relations counsel Trans World Airlines, N.Y.C., 1980-81; sr. assoc. Parker, Milliken, Clark & O'Hara, Los Angeles, 1981-82; ptnr. Rutan & Tucker, Costa Mesa, Calif., 1983-84; ptnr. Memel, Jacobs, Pierno, Gersh & Ellsworth, Newport Beach, Calif., 1985-86; ptnr. Memel, Jacobs & Ellsworth, Newport Beach, 1986-87; sole practice, Newport Beach, 1987—; cons. collective bargaining Am. Arbitration Assn.; commentator labor relations Fin. News Network; lectr. Calif. Western Law Sch., Calif. State U.-Fullerton, Calif. State Conf. Small Bus.; lectr. collective bargaining Pace U., N.Y.C. N.E. regional coordinator Pressler for Pres., 1979-80. Mem. ABA (R.R. and airline labor law com., internat. labor law com.), Internat. Bar Assn., N.Y. State Bar Assn., Calif. Bar Assn., Conf. R.R. and Airline Labor Lawyers, Newport Harbor Area C. of C. Republican. Jewish. Clubs: Balboa Bay, Lincoln of Orange County, Center. Lodge: Masons. Author: Arbitration Issues for the 1980s, 1981; A Look at Three Companies, 1982; editor-in-chief Industrial and Labor Relations Forum, 1964-66; contbr. articles to profl. publs. Office: PO Box 9049 Newport Beach CA 92658

SCHNEIDER, ALAN, theatre director; b. Kharkov, Russia, Dec. 12, 1917; s. Leo Victor and Rebecka (Malkin) S.; m. Eugenie Muckle; 2 children. Dir. Theater Ctr. Juilliard Sch., N.Y.C., 1976-79; prof. drama U. Calif., San Diego, 1979—. Dir. numerous stage plays, including (by Beckett) Waiting for Godot, 1956, Endgame, 1958, Happy Days, 1961, Krapp's Last Tape, 1961, Play, 1964, Box, 1968, Quotations from Chairman Mao Tse-Tung, 1968, (by Edward Albee), Not I, 1972, That Time, 1976, Footfalls, 1976, Rockaby, 1981, Ohio Impromptu, (by Albee) American Dream, 1961, Who's Afraid of Virginia Woolf?, 1962, Tiny Alice, 1964, A Delicate Balance, 1966, (by Anderson) You Know I Can't Hear You When the Water's Running, 1967, I Never Sang For My Father, 1968, Inquest, 1970, (by Pinter) Dumbwaiter, 1962, The Collection, 1962, The Birthday Party, 1967, A Kind of Alaska, 1984, (by Edward Bond) Saved, 1970, (by Michael Weller) Moonchildren, 1971, Loose Ends, 1979, (by Gunter Grass) Uptight, 1972, (by E.A. Whitehead) Foursome, 1972, (by Elie Wiesel) The Madness of God, 1974, (by Preston Jones) The Last Meeting of the Knights of the White Magnolia, 1975, Texas Trilogy, 1976; dir. films and TV prodns. including Oedipus the King, 1956, The Life of Samuel Johnson, 1957, The Years Between, 1958, The Secret of Freedom, 1959, (by Archibald McCloud), Waiting for Godot, 1960, Film, 1964, Act Without Words II, 1965, Eh, Joe?, 1966, The Madness of God, 1975. Recipient Antoinette Perry (Tony) award, 1962, Off-Broadway (Obie) award, 1962. Office: Dept Drama U Calif Box 109 La Jolla CA 92093

SCHNEIDER, ALAN NEIL, mortgage banker, author, lawyer; b. Louisville; s. Samuel Joseph and Jennie S.; A.B., DePauw U., Greencastle, Ind., 1938; J.D., Harvard U., 1942; m. Mabel M. Pedersen, July 4, 1950; 1 dau., Karen Elizabeth. Admitted to Ky. bar, 1947; public relations dir. City of Louisville, 1947-48, adminstrv. asst. mayor, also spl. counsel, 1948-49; asst. city atty., 1950-59; pres., chmn. bd. King's Way Mortgage Co., Coral Gables, Fla., 1960—, Veritas Ins. Agy., 1960—, Omega Title Corp., 1960—, Alpha Inc., 1960—; pres. Sigma Devel. Corp.; vice chmn. bd. Pan Am. Mortgage Corp.; v.p. Pan Am. Bank; dir. Greenacre, Inc.; chief counsel Security Fin. Agy., Inc., Southeastern Mortgage Co.; adj. prof. U. Miami. Pres., Ky. Library Assn., 1957, pres. Am. Assn. Library Trustees, 1958-59; trustee Louisville Free Public Library, Red Cross Hosp., Louisville, Race Found.; bd. dirs. Fla. Soc. Prevention Blindness. Served to lt. comdr. USNR, 1941-45. Author: Ian and I. Named Outstanding Trustee, Am. Assn. Library Trustees, 1959. Mem. Am., Ky., Louisville, Internat. Bar Assns., Naval Intelligence Profls., Mortgage Bankers Am., Assn. Former Intelligence Officers, Phi Beta Kappa, Sigma Chi (Balfour award 1938). Presbyterian. Clubs: Coral Gables Athletic, Coral Gables Country; Bankers, Harvard (Miami); Spl. Forces (London); Biltmore. Office: 265 Sevilla Ave PO Box 158 Coral Gables FL 33134

SCHNEIDER, CALVIN, physician; b. N.Y.C., Oct. 23, 1924; s. Harry and Bertha (Green) S.; A.B., U. So. Calif., 1951, M.D., 1955; J.D., LaVerne (Calif.) Coll., 1973; m. Elizabeth Gayle Thomas, Dec. 27, 1967. Intern Los Angeles County Gen. Hosp., 1955-56, staff physician, 1956-57; practice medicine West Covina, Calif., 1957—; staff Inter Community Hosp., Covina, Calif. Cons. physician Charter Oak Found., Covina, 1960—. Served with USNR, 1943-47. Mem. AMA, Calif., Los Angeles County med. assns. Republican. Lutheran. Office: 224 W College Covina CA 91723

SCHNEIDER, EARL GARY, lawyer; b. Chgo., Apr. 6, 1933; s. Isadore and Doris (Shiffman) S.; m. Enid R. Levy, Aug. 29, 1954; children—Keith, Gene. J.D., Ill. Inst. Tech.-Chgo. Kent Coll. Law, 1955. Bar: Ill. 1955. Ptnr. Miller, Schneider & Galasso and predecessor, Chgo., 1957-78, Schneider & Morrison Ltd., Chgo., 1978-87, Schneider & Schneider, P.C., 1987—. Served with U.S. Army, 1955-57. Mem. ABA, Ill. Trial Lawyers Assn. Home: 3745 Bordeaux Northbrook IL 60062 Office: Schneider & Schneider PO Box 14828 Chicago IL 60614

SCHNEIDER, EBERHARD GEORG, Sovietologist; b. Grossenhain, Fed. Republic Germany, Aug. 29, 1941; s. Friedrich-Wilhelm and Hildegard (Huebner) S.; m. Marianne Erika Buettner, Mar. 31, 1967; children: Markus, Christian. Lic. philosophy, Philos. High Sch., Munich, 1966; Dr. philosophy, U. Munich, 1970. Lectr. U. Hamburg, Fed. Republic Germany, 1971-76; sr. researcher Fed. Inst. East European and Internat. Studies, Cologne, Fed. Republic Germany, 1976—. Author: Moskaus Leitlinie fuer das Jahr 2000, 1987, Sowjetunion heute, 1982, Breshnews neue Sowjetverfassung, 1978, Einheit und Gegensatz in der Sowjetphilosophie, 1978. Mem. Internat. Polit. Sci. Assn., German Assn. Fgn. Policy, Ger. Assn. for East European Studies, Assn. for German Studies, German Assn. for Polit. Sci. Roman Catholic. Office: Fed Inst for East European, and Internat Studies, Lindenbornstr 22, D-5000 Koeln 30 Federal Republic of Germany

SCHNEIDER, EDGAR WERNER, linguist; b. Kirchdorf, Austria, May 30, 1954; s. Werner Paul and Luise (Baldauf) S.; m. Jutta Kosma, Jan. 6, 1979; children: Berit, Miriam. MA, U. Graz, Austria, 1978; PhD, U. Bamberg, Fed. Republic Germany, 1981, habilitation, 1987. Asst. prof. U. Bamberg, Fed. Republic Germany, 1979-87, assoc. prof. linguistics, 1987—. Author: American Early Black English, 1981, Bibliography of Varieties of English, 1984, Variability of Lexical Meaning, 1988; contbr. articles to profl. jours. Mem. Am. Dialect Soc., Linguistic Soc. Am., Soc. European Linguistics, Anglistentag. Roman Catholic. Home: Landsknechtstrasse 92, D-8605 Hallstadt, Bavaria Federal Republic of Germany Office: U Bamberg, An Der Universitat 9, D-8605 Bamberg, Bavaria Federal Republic of Germany

SCHNEIDER, FRANKLIN RICHARD, educational administrator; b. Chelsea, Mich., May 9, 1935; s. Lewis William and Evelyn Bernice (Hall) S.; student Mich. State U., 1953-55; B.A., Linfield Coll., 1957; M.S.W., Fla. State U., 1960; Ph.D., Clayton U., 1976; m. Ruth Ann Eddy, Aug. 23, 1958; children—Daniel, Gary, Debra, Mark, David. Dir., Housing Authority Yamhill County, Oreg., 1955-58; caseworker, dir. social services Winnebago Childrens Home, Neillsville, Wis., 1960-65; exec. dir. Buckhorn Childrens Center (Ky.), 1965-67; exec. dir. Spaulding for Children, Chelsea, 1967-68; dist. rep. Alaska Dept. Health and Welfare, Bethel, 1968-69; chief social worker Bur. Indian Affairs, Bethel, 1969-73; dir. resident services rev. State of Oreg., Salem, 1976-79, dir. Clackamas region, 1979-80, mgr. sr. services div., 1979-83; chancellor World Peace U., 1983—; cons. Bethel Social Services Inc., Wetangwich Corp., bd. dirs. Sunrise New Life and Living, Inc., 1980-83; mem. exec. com. Internat. Forum Clayton U., 1976—; mem. adv. bd. Inst. for Planetary Synthesis, Switzerland, Found. for Advancement World Peace, 1985—. NIMH grantee, 1958-60.

SCHNEIDER, JENNY ELISABETH, art historian, retired museum director; b. The Hague, The Netherlands, Dec. 7, 1924; d. Hans and Suzanne (Christ) S. Ph.D., Basle U., Switzerland, 1951. Asst. Swiss Nat. Mus., Zurich, 1956-61, curator dept. textiles and costumes, 1961—, vice dir. mus., 1971-81, dir. mus., 1982-86. Author catalogues, on stained glass, textiles and costumes and their care; also articles. Mem. Internat. Com. for Mus. and Collection of Costume, Switzerland-Holland Soc. (bd. dirs.), Internat. Fedn. Univ. Women, Internat. Fedn. Bus. and Profl. Women. Office: Spiegelgasse 13, CH-8001 Zurich Switzerland

SCHNEIDER, LAZ LEVKOFF, lawyer; b. Columbia, S.C., Mar. 15, 1939; s. Philip L. and Dorothy Harriet (Levkoff) S.; m. Ellen Linda Shiffrin, Dec. 12, 1968; 1 son, David Allen. B.A., Yale U., 1961, LL.B., 1964; LL.M., NYU, 1965. Bar: D.C. 1965, N.Y. 1965, Fla. 1970. Assoc. Fulton, Walter & Duncombe, N.Y.C., 1965-67, Rosenman, Colin Kaye Petschek Freund & Emil, N.Y.C., 1967-69; assoc. Kronish, Lieb, Weiner, Shainswit & Hellman, N.Y.C., 1969-70; ptnr. Ruden Barnett McClosky & Schuster, Ft. Lauderdale, Fla., 1970-80; sole practice, Ft. Lauderdale, 1980-86; ptnr. Sherr, Tiballi, Fayne & Schneider, Ft. Lauderdale, Fla., 1987—. Mem. exec. com. Fla. regional bd. Anti Defamation League, 1972—. Mem. ABA, Fla. Bar Assn., Broward County Bar Assn. (chmn. sect. corp. bus. and banking law 1978-80). Jewish. Club: Yale (pres. 1977-79). Grad. editor Tax Law Rev., 1964-65. Office: 600 Corporate Dr Fort Lauderdale FL 33334

SCHNEIDER, NORMAN RICHARD, veterinary toxicologist; educator; b. Ellsworth, Kans., Mar. 28, 1943; s. Henry C. and Irene C. (Ney) S.; BS, Kans. State U., 1967, DVM, 1968; MS (Air Force Inst. Tech. fellow), Ohio State U., 1972; m. Karen Marjorie Nelson, July 1, 1968; 1 child, Nelson R. Commd. capt. U.S. Air Force, 1968, advanced through grades to lt. col., 1986; base veterinarian Goose AB, Labrador, Can., 1968-70; veterinary scientist/toxicologist Armed Forces Radiobiology Research Inst., Bethesda, Md., 1972-76; vet. toxicologist Aerospace Med. Research Lab., Wright-Patterson AFB, Dayton, Ohio, 1976-79; assoc. prof./vet. toxicologist dept. vet. sci. U. Nebr., Lincoln, 1979—, courtesy appointment dept. pharm. scis.U. Nebr. Med. Ctr.; chief environ. health services 155th Tactical Reconnaissance Group, Nebr. Air Nat. Guard, Lincoln, 1979—. Decorated Joint Services Commendation medal, Air Force Commendation medal, NG Disting. Service award; diplomate Am. Bd. Vet. Toxicology. Mem. Am. Coll. Vet. and Comparative Toxicology (councillor), Nebr. Vet. Med. Assn., Kans. Vet. Med. Assn., AVMA, Am. Assn. Vet. Lab. Diagnosticians, Am. Bd. Vet. Toxicology (pres. 1988-91), Assn. Ofcl. Analytical Chemists, N.G. Assn. U.S., N.G. Assn. Nebr., Alliance Air N.G. Flight Surgeons, Alliance Environ. Health Profls., Assn. Mil. Surgeons U.S., Council Agrl. Sci. and Tech., Alpha Zeta, Phi Zeta, Am. Legion, Nat. Rifle Assn., FarmHouse Fraternity. Roman Catholic. Home: Route 1 Box 70 Ceresco NE 68017 Office: Vet Diagnostic Ctr Lincoln NE 68583-0907

SCHNEIDER, RAYMOND CLINTON, architect, educator; b. Smyrna, N.Y., Dec. 10, 1920; s. George William and Helen (Carey) S.; m. Margaret Maude Pearce, Sept. 16, 1943 (dec. Aug. 3, 1982); children: Stephen Eric, Martha Anne, Pearce Clinton.; m. Ruth Brown Martsolf, Jan. 2, 1983 (div. Jan. 1986); m. Gertraude R. McMullen, May 28, 1986 (div. Sept. 1988). B.S. in Architecture, Kans. State U., 1949, M.S. in Edn, 1952; Ed.D., Stanford U., 1955. Architect firms in Salina and Manhattan, Kans., 1947-51; assoc. dir. sch. planning lab., asso. dir. W. Regional Center Ednl. Facilities Lab., also research asso., lectr. edn. Stanford U., Palo Alto, 1955-62; head personnel subsystems sect., systems tech. lab. Sylvania Corp., Mountain View, Calif., 1962-63; dir. research and planning Porter, Gogerty, Meston, San Jose, Calif., 1963-64; assoc. prof. edn. and architecture U. Wash., Seattle, 1964-78; prof. architecture and edn. U. Wash., 1978-82, prof. emeritus, 1983—; asst. to dean, 1964-73, dir. grad. program architecture, 1976-83, exhibiting artist and sculptor, 1946—, cons. in field. Author articles in field, chpts. in books. Served with AUS, 1942-46. Kellogg fellow, 1953-54; Masonite Co. fellow, 1954-55; Borg-Warner Co. fellow, 1954-55. Mem. Am. Assn. Retired Persons. Lodge: Elks. Address: 13206 47th Ave SE Everett WA 98208

SCHNELL, ROGER THOMAS, military officer; b. Wabasha, Minn., Dec. 11, 1936; s. Donald William and Eva Louise (Barton) S.; m. Barbara Ann McDonald, Dec. 18, 1959 (div. Mar. 1968); children: Thomas Allen, Scott Douglas; m. Young H. Kim, Sept. 25, 1987; children: Eunice, Candice. A in Mil. Sci., Command and Gen. Staff Coll., 1975; A in Bus. Administn., Wayland Bapt. U., 1987. Commd. 2d lt. Alaska N.G., 1959, advanced through grades to col., 1975; shop supt. Alaska N.G., Anchorage, 1965-71, personnel mgr., 1972-74, chief of staff, 1974-87; electrician Alaska R.R., Anchorage, 1955-61, elec. foreman, 1962-64; dir. support personnel mgmt. Joint Staff Alaska N.G., 1988—. Mem. Fed. Profl. Labor Relations Execs. (sec. 1974-75), Alaska N.G. Officers Assn. (bd. dirs. 1988—), Am. Legion, Amvets. Republican. Methodist. Lodge: Elks. Home: 2751 Pelican Ct Anchorage AK 99515 Office: Hdqrs Alaska NG 3601 C St Anchorage AK 99503

SCHNELLER, GEORGE CHARLES, chiropractor; b. St. Louis, Feb. 22, 1921; s. Michael Alois and Eleanora Christine (Weber) S.; m. Dorothy Virginia Doran, Mar. 6, 1943; children—George Charles, Judith Ann. D. Chiropractic, Mo. Chiropractic Coll., 1946, Ph.Chiropractic, 1946. Ordained priest Anglican Orthodox Ch., 1973. Gen. practice chiropractic, St. Louis, 1946—; chiropractic staff Lindell Hosp., St. Louis; faculty Mo. Chiropractic Coll., 1947-51, dean, 1957-61. Fellow Internat. Chiropractors Assn.; mem. Mo. Acad. Chiropractors (pres. 1970-75), Dist. One Mo. State Chiropractic Assn. (pres. 1952). Clubs: Kiwanis (past pres. Maplewood, Mo.), Moose. Home: 1131 Culverhill Dr Webster Groves MO 63119 Office: 3538 Jamieson Ave Saint Louis MO 63139

SCHNIEDERJANS, MARC JAMES, management science educator; b. Pocahontas, Ark., Oct. 8, 1950; s. Oliver H. and Florence (Schutte) S.; m. Jill Marlene Schniederjans, Aug. 13, 1971; children: Ashlyn M., Alexander J., Dara G. BS, U. Mo., 1972; MBA, St. Louis U., 1974, PhD, 1978. Program dir. St. Louis U., 1975-78; lectr. U. Mo.-St. Louis, 1976-78, asst. prof., 1979-80, U. Nebr.-Omaha, 1978-79, asst. prof. mgmt., Lincoln, 1981-85, assoc. prof., 1985—; asst. prof. U. Hawaii, Hilo, 1980-81; cons. Blue Hills Homes Corp., St. Louis, 1979—, Ralston Purina Corp., 1980—, Union div. Inds., Lincoln, 1983—. Author: (with N.K. Kwak) Managerial Applications of Operations Research, 1982; Linear Goal Programming, 1984; (with N.K. Kwak) Operations Research: Applications in Health Care Planning, 1984; Introduction to Mathematical Programming, 1987; Case Studies in Decision Support, 1987; contbr. articles to profl. jours. Mem. Am. Inst. Decision Scis., Inst. Mgmt. Scis., Ops. Research Soc. Am., Am. Prodn. and Inventory Soc. Home: 5220 S 66th Circle Lincoln NE 68516 Office: U Nebraska Dept Mgmt Lincoln NE 68588

SCHNITZER, JORDAN DIRECTOR, real estate executive; b. Portland, Oreg., May 8, 1951; s. Harold J. and Arlene (Director) S. B.A. in Lit., U. Oreg., 1973; J.D., Northwestern Sch. Law, Portland, 1976. Vice pres. Harsh Investment Corp., Portland, 1970—; owner, operator Jordan Schnitzer Properties, Portland, 1976—. Pres. U. Oreg. Mus. Art Council, Eugene, 1978-83; trustee Temple Beth Israel, 1982-88; bd. trustees, Oreg. Art. Inst., 1981-87; mem. standing com. Lewis and Clark Coll. Northwestern Sch. Law, 1982—; bd. dirs. Assocs. of Good Samaritan Hosp., Portland, 1980-83; mem. exec. bd. Columbia Pacific Council Boy Scouts Am., 1980—; trustee Oreg. Art Inst., 1981-87; mem. bus. adv. council U. Oreg., 1985—. Named an Outstanding Young Man of Am., U.S. Jaycees, 1981. Mem. Japanese Garden Soc. (v.p. 1981—, pres. Oregon chpt. 1987—), Young Pres.'s Orgn. Democrat. Jewish. Office: Jordan Schnitzer Properties 1121 SW Salmon St Portland OR 97205

SCHNITZER, MARTIN COLBY, economics educator; b. Wilmette, Ill., Aug. 20, 1925; s. Leon Wendell and Homera Almeda (Portman) S.; m. Joan Hammet Brown, June 30, 1951; children: Melanie, Meredith, Marcy. Student, U. of South, 1944-46; B.A., U. Ala., 1949, M.B.A, 1951; Ph.D., U. Fla., 1960. Asst. prof. bus. U. Ark., Fayetteville, 1955-58; asst. prof. U. Fla., Gainesville, 1958-60; prof. mgmt. Va. Poly. Inst. and State U., Blacksburg, 1964—; lectr. Inst. Econ. Planning and research, Warsaw, Poland, 1985, Oskar Lange Acad. Econs., Wroclaw, Poland, Karl Marx U., Budapest, Hungary; mem. Va. Gov's Adv. Bd. of Economists, 1978-82; mem. adv. bd. to U.S. Sec. of Commerce, 1970-72; mem. U.S. East-West Trade Commn., 1974-75, Va. Indsl. Facilities Financing Commn., 1974-76, Fulbright Selection Com., 1976, Va. Export Council, 1982—. Author: The Economy of Sweden, 1970, Comparative Economic Systems, 1971, 3d edit., 1983, 4th edit., 1987, Readings in Public Finance and Public Policy, 1972, East and West Germany: A Comparative Economic Analysis, Income Distribution, 1975, Contemporary Government and Business Relations, 1978, 2d edit., 1983, 3d edit., 1987, U.S. Business Involvement in Eastern Europe, 1980, Doing Business in Washington, 1981, International Business, 1984; editor: Va. Social Sci. Jour., 1964-68. Ford Found. grantee, 1962-63; Am. Philos. Soc. grantee, 1963-64. Episcopalian. Club: Rotary. Home: 606 Rainbow Ridge Blacksburg VA 24060

SCHNITZER, MOSHE, exporting company executive; b. Czernowitz, Israel, Jan. 21, 1921; s. Menahem and Ethel (Neumann) S.; m. Varda Reich, Aug. 13, 1946; children: Hana, Shmuel, Etty. D (hon.), Hebrew U., Jerusalem; postgrad., Bar Ilan U., Tel Aviv. Pres. Israel Diamond Exchange; dir. First Internat. Bank of Israel. Author, editor: Diamonds. Served with Israel Army. Mem. World Fedn. Diamond Bourses. Home: 78 Sharet, Tel Aviv Israel Office: care Israel Diamond Exchange, 3 Jabotinsky Rd, Ramat-Gan Israel

SCHNURMAN, ALAN JOSEPH, lawyer; b. N.Y.C., July 1, 1945; s. Albert and Ruth (Sirota) S.; m. Judith Bernstein, Mar. 31, 1974; children—Michele, David. B.S. in Acctg., Bklyn. Coll., 1967; J.D., N.Y. Law Sch., 1971. Bar: N.Y. 1972, U.S. Ct. Appeals (2d cir.) 1973, U.S. Dist. Ct. (ea. and so. dists.) N.Y. 1974, U.S. Supreme Ct. 1976. Acct. tax dept. Arthur Andersen & Co., N.Y.C., 1971-72; sole practice, N.Y.C., 1972-80; ptnr. Zalman & Schnurman, N.Y.C., 1980—. Host Lawline cable TV program; assoc. editor N.Y. State Trial Lawyers Quar., 1981. Mem. ABA, Am. Judges Assn., N.Y. State Bar Assn., Am. Trial Lawyers Assn., N.Y. State Trial Lawyers Assn. (bd. dirs. 1988—), Assn. Trial Lawyers N.Y.C. (bd. dirs. 1986—), N.Y. County Lawyers Assn., N.Y. Law Sch. Alumni Assn. (bd. dirs. 1983—). Democrat. Jewish. Home: 623 3d St Brooklyn NY 11215 Office: Zalman & Schnurman 63 Wall St New York NY 10005

SCHNURRE, WOLFDIETRICH, author; b. Frankfurt am Main, Germany, Aug. 22, 1920; s. Otto S.; m. Marina Schnurre, 1966; 1 son. Ed. Humanistisches Gymnasium. Free-lance writer, 1945—; founder-mem. Group 47, 1947; mem. Akademie fur Sprache und Dichtung, 1959. Author: (satire) Aufzeichnungen des Pudels Ali, 1951, 62; (poems) Kassiber, 1956, 64; (satirical poems) Abdenlandler, 1957; (fables) Protest im Parterre, 1957; (short stories) Eine Rechnung, die nicht aufgeht, 1958; (novel) Als Vaters Bart rot war, 1958; (novel) Das Los unserer, 1959; (short stories) Man solte dagegen sein, 1960; (documentary) Die Mauer des 13 August, 1961; (documentary) Berlin—eine Stadt wird geteilt, 1962; (short stories) Funke im Reisig, 1963; (essays) Schreibtisch unter freiem Himmel, 1964; (short stories) Ohne Einsatz kein Speil, 1964; (stories) Die Erzuhlungen, 1966; (radio plays) Spreezimmer Mobliert, 1967; (for children) Die Zwengel, 1967; (prose collection) Was ich fur mein Leben gern tue, 1968; (for children) Ein Schneemann fur den grossenBrudder 1969, Gocko, 1970, Die Sache mit den Meerschweinchen, 1970; (short stories) Schnurre Heiter, 1970; (satire) Die Wandlung des Hippipotamos, 1970; (for children) Immer mehr Meerschweinchen, 1971; (tales and verse) Der Spatz in der Hand, 1971; (for children) Wie der Koalabar wider lachen lernte, 1971, Der

Meerschweinchendieb, 1972; (prose pieces) Auf Tauchstation, 1973; (dialogue) Ich frag ja bloss, 1973; (satire) Der wahre Noah, 1974; (for children) Schnurren und Murren, 1974; (short stories) Ich brauche dich, 1976; (prose pieces) Eine schwierige Reparatur, 1976; (essay) der Schattenfotograf, 1978; (novel) Ein Unglucksfall, 1981; (essays) Gelernt ist gelernt, 1984. Served with German Army, 1939-45. Recipient Young Generation prize City of Berlin, 1958, Immermann prize, Dusseldorf, W.Ger., 1959, George Mackensen Lit. prize, 1962. Address: Prinz-Friedr-, Leopoldstrasse 33a, 1000 Berlin 38 Federal Republic of Germany *

SCHOBINGER, JUAN, archaeology educator; b. Lausanne, Switzerland, Feb. 18, 1928; arrived in Argentina, 1931; s. Jacques and Elsa (Huber) S.; m. Liliana Schickendantz, Dec. 15, 1980; children by previous marriage: Juan Cristian, Verena. Prof. History, U. Buenos Aires, 1951, PhD, 1954. Prof. anthropology Univ. Nacional de Cuyo, Mendoza, Argentina, 1956-73; prof. archaeology Univ. Nacional de Cuyo, 1956—; dir. Inst. Archaeology and Enthnology, 1956—; assessor Consejo Nacional de Investigaciones Cientificas and Tecnicas, Buenos Aires, 1969-78. Editor: La Momia del Cerro El Toro, 1966; author: Prehistoria de Sudamerica, 1969; 2d edit. 1988, Estudios de Arqueologia Sudamericana, 1982; (with C. Gradin) Cazadores de la Patagonia Y Agricultures Andinos, 1985; contbr. articles to profl. jours. Fellow Colegio de Graduados en Antropologia; mem. Internat. Assn. for Study of Prehistoric Religions (founding mem.), Internat. Com. for Rock Art, Internat. Union of Prehistoric and Protohistoric Scis. (mem. permanent council, exec. council). Home: Videla Castillo 1968, Mendoza Argentina 5500 Office: Univ Nacional de Cuyo, Inst de Arqueologia y Etnologia, PO Box 345, Mendoza Argentina 5500

SCHOCH, JACQUELINE LOUISE, university official; b. DuBois, Pa., July 17, 1929; d. Horace Gordon and Cora (Wineberg) S.; B.Sc. in Health and Phys. Edn., Pa. State U., 1951, M.Ed. in Counseling and Psychology, 1960, D.Ed. in Counseling and Psychology, 1965; cert. Inst. Ednl. Mgmt., Harvard U., 1979. Tchr. girls' phys. edn. Jr.-Sr. High Sch., Ford City, Pa., 1951-52; tchr. girl's phys. edn., acad. U.S. history DuBois Area Sr. High Sch., 1952-56, girls' guidance counselor, 1956-65; dir. guidance DuBois Area Sch. Dist., 1965-67, dir. instrn., 1967-70; asst. dir. for resident instrn. DuBois campus Pa. State U., 1970-76, asso. dir. acad. affairs, 1976—, dir. DuBois campus, 1978-83, campus exec. officer, 1983—, also mem., chmn. univ. coms., faculty senate. Instr. polit. action courses local C. of C., 1963; instr. adult swimming classes local YMCA, 1953-55; instr. continuing edn. program Pa. State U., 1967-70, also asst. prof. edn., 1970—. Cons. Appalachia project, W.Va., 1967-68; mem. evaluating teams for evaluating secondary schs. Middle States Evaluation Com., 1960-62; chair Penelec Consumer Adv. Com.; mem. Penelec Ednl. Com.; mem. commn. for women Pa. State U.; mem. adv. com. Pa. State U. Alumni Assn. Bd. dirs. DuBois area United Fund, co-chmn. fund raising campaign, 1967-68, 2d v.p., 1970—; bd. dirs. DuBois council Girl Scouts, 1954-56, Family Life Center-Luth. Services, 1972-76; treas. DuBois Ednl. Found., 1981—; bd. dirs. DuBois Area YMCA; v.p. bd. dirs. Clearfield County Area Agy. on Aging; deacon St. Peters United Ch. of Christ. Named Boss of Yr., Internat. Secs. Assn., 1977. Delta Mu Sigma, Delta Psi Omega, Iota Alpha Delta, Delta Kappa Gamma, Pi Lambda Theta, Phi Delta Kappa. Lodge: Rotary (DuBois). Office: DuBois Campus Pa State U DuBois PA 15801

SCHOCH, ROBERT MILTON, science educator, researcher, consultant; b. Washington, Mar. 30, 1957; s. Milton Ralph and Cornelia Alicia (Goetz) S.; m. Cynthia Benfield Pettit, June 11, 1983; 1 child, Nicholas Robert. B.A. in Anthropology, George Washington U., 1979, B.S. in Geology, 1979; M.S., Yale U., 1981, M.Phil., 1981, Ph.D., 1983. Curatorial asst. Peabody Mus., New Haven, 1982-83, research asst., 1983-84; asst. prof. div. sci., coll. basic studies Boston U., 1984—, asst. prof. dept. geology, 1985—; research assoc. Schiele Mus. Natural History, Gastonia, N.C., 1984—; curatorial affiliate Peabody Mus. Natural History, New Haven, 1985—; fossil collecting expdns. to many countries, 1979-84. Author: Phylogeny Reconstruction in Paleontology, 1986, Systematics, Functional Morphology and Macroevolution of the Extinct Mammalian Order Taeniodonta, 1986; editor Vertebrate Paleontology, 1984; contbr. articles to profl. jours. Grantee NSF, 1979-84. Mem. Paleontol. Soc., Soc. Vertebrate Paleontology, Geol. Soc. Am., Sigma Xi. Office: Boston U Div Sci Coll Basic Studies Boston MA 02215

SCHOCH, WILLY HEINRICH, computer company executive; b. July 7, 1944; s. Willy Heinrich and Adrienne Marie (Descloux) S.; m. Lilly Renggli, Nov. 22, 1964 (div. Feb. 1970); 1 dau., Caroline. Student U. Berne, 1963-64. Orgn. specialist various cos., Switzerland, 1964-68; orgn. cons. Interdata, Langenthal, Switzerland, 1969-71; sales mgr. Varian Data Machines, Basle, Switzerland, 1971-74; with Digital Equipment Corp., Geneva, 1974-81, sales mgr. new territory, 1977-79, dist. mgr., 1979-81; mng. dir. Tandem Computers, Zurich, 1981-87; mng. dir. Wang, Switzerland, 1987—. Mem. Swiss EDP Assn., Swiss Office Staff Assn., Swiss Am. C. of C., Swiss Comml. Assn. Home: Seeweg 20, 6300 Cham/ZG Switzerland Office: Wang AG, Talackerstrasse 7, 8152 Glattbrugg/ZH Switzerland

SCHOCHOR, JONATHAN, lawyer; b. Suffern, N.Y., Sept. 9, 1946; s. Abraham and Betty (Hechtor) S.; m. Joan Elaine Brown, May 31, 1970; children—Lauren Aimee, Daniel Ross. BA, Pa. State U., 1968; JD, Am. U., 1971. Bar: D.C. 1971, Md. 1974, U.S. Dist. Ct. D.C. 1971, U.S. Ct. Appeals (D.C. cir.) 1971, U.S. Dist. Ct. Md. 1974, U.S. Ct. Appeals (4th cir.) 1974, U.S. Supreme Ct. 1986. Assoc., McKenna, Wilkinson & Kittner, Washington, 1970-74; assoc. Ellin & Baker, Balt., 1974-84; ptnr. Schochor, Federico & Staton, Balt., 1984—; lectr. in law; expert witness to state legis. Assoc. editor-in-chief American U. Law Rev., 1970-71. Mem. ABA, Assn. Trial Lawyers Am., Am. Judicature Soc., Md. State Bar Assn. (spl. com. on health claims arbitration 1983), Md. Trial Lawyers Assn. (bd. govs. 1986-87, mem. legis. com., 1985-88, chmn. legis. com. 1986-87, sec. 1987-88, exec. com. 1987-88, v.p. 1988—), Balt. City Bar Assn. (legis. com. 1986-87, spl. com. on tort reform 1986), Bar Assn. D.C., Internat. Platform Assn., Phi Alpha Delta. Office: Schochor Federico & Staton PA 1211 St Paul St Baltimore MD 21202

SCHOCKEN, GERSHOM GUSTAV, publisher, editor; b. Sept. 1912. Ed. U. Heidelberg, London Sch. Econs. Joined staff Haaretz daily newspaper, Tel Aviv, 1937, pub., editor, 1939—; dir. Schocken Pub. House Ltd.; mem. Knesset, 1955-59. Named Internat. Editor-of-Yr., World Press Rev., 1983. Office: Haaretz Bldg, 21 Salman Schocken St Box 233, Tel Aviv Israel

SCHOECK, HELMUT, sociology educator, author; b. Graz, Austria, July 3, 1922; emigrated to U.S., 1950, naturalized, 1956; s. Stephan J. and Anna (Heigl) S.; m. Margaret Weiler, June 24, 1947; children: Natalia, Raymond, Stephanie. Student, U. Munich Med. Sch., 1941-45, U. Tuebingen, 1946-50; Dr. Phil., 1948; postdoctoral fellow sociology, Yale, 1953-54. Asst. dept. philosophy U. Munich, 1943-45; asst. to script dir. Radio Stuttgart, 1946; prof. social sci. Fairmont (W.Va.) State Coll., 1950-53; asst. prof. sociology Emory U., 1954-56, asso. prof. sociology, 1956-65; prof., dir. Inst. Sociology, U. Mainz, 1965—; vis. prof. Am. studies U. Erlangen-Nürnberg, 1964; Dir. Interdisciplinary Symposium on Culture Contact in Underdeveloped Countries Emory U., 1957; dir. symposium on Scientism and the Study of Man, 1958, on Relativism and the Study of Man, 1959, on effects psychiatric theories modern society, 1960; dir. Symposium on pvt. sector versus pub. sector, 1961. Author: Nietzsches Philosophie des Menschlich-Allzumenschlichen, 1948, Religionssoziologie, trans., 1951, Soziologie, 1952, USA: Motive und Strukturen, 1958, Was Heisst politisch unmoeglich, 1959, Umgang mit Völkern: Amerikaner, 1961, Die Soziologie und die Gesellschaften, 1964, Der Neid: Eine Theorie der Gesellschaft, 1966, Envy: A Theory of Social Behavior, New York-London, 1969, Chinese translation under the auspices of the Chinese Acadamy of Social Sciences, Beijing, 1988; Italian edit., 1974, rev. edit., 1987, Soziologisches Wörterbuch, 1969, Spanish edit., 1973, La Envidia, Buenos Aires, 1970, 1st Leistung unanstaendig, 1971, Entwicklungshilfe, 1972, Vorsicht Schreibtischtaeter, 1972, Die Lust am schlechten Gewissen, 1973, Umverteilung als Klassenkampf, 1974, L'Invidia e la Società, 1974, Geschichte der Soziologie, 1974, Das Geschäft mit dem Pessimismus, 1975, Schülermanipulation, 1976, Vermogensdeling—Aspect van Klassenstrijdë, 1977, Historia de la Sociologia, 1977, Das Recht auf Ungleichheit, 1979, Der Neid. Die Urgeschichte des Bösen, 1980, Storia della Sociologia, 1980, Der Arzt zwischen Politik und Patient, 1983, Die 12 Irrtuemer unseres Jahrhunderts, 1985, Kinderverstoerung, 1987; columnist: Internat. Med. Tribune, 1977—, Welt am Sonntag, Christ und Welt/Rheinischer Merkur; articles in field.; editor: Foreign Aid Reexamined, 1958, Central Planning and Neomercantilism, 1964, others. Fellow Am. Anthrop. Assn., Am. Sociol. Assn.; mem. Mont Pelerin Soc. Office: Univ Mainz, 6500 Mainz Federal Republic of Germany

SCHOEFFLER, RONALD WILLIAM, social services administrator; b. Gloversville, N.Y., July 4, 1949; s. William Charles and Helena Bertha (Bruse) S.; m. Vada Susan Cheshire, Aug. 25, 1974; children: Bryan Hall, John Howard, Rachel Helena. AA, Fulton-Montgomery Community Coll., 1969; BS, High Point Coll., 1971; MEd, U. N.C. at Greensboro, 1973; EdD, U. Ga., 1979. Dist. scout exec. Boy Scouts Am., Tifton, Ga., 1973-75; family housing resident mgr. U. Ga., Athens, 1976-79; asst. dir. Athens (Ga.) Community Council on Aging, Inc., 1980-81, exec. dir., 1981-86; treas. Morton Theatre Corp., 1982-84, pres., 1985-86, mem., 1981-87; program dir. Boy Scouts Am., Camp Osborn, Albany, Ga., 1974, camp dir., 1975, dist. commr. Cherokee dist., N.E. Ga. council, 1980-82, award of merit, 1981, exec. bd. N.E. Ga. council, 1982-87, chmn. Scout show N.E. Ga. council, 1985-87; exec. dir. Sr. Citizens Council Greater Augusta and Cen. Savannah River Area, Ga., Inc., 1987—, mem. community care adv. council, 1987—, area agy. on aging adv. council, 1987—; mem. del. council Nat. Inst. Sr. Ctrs., Nat. Council on Aging Inc., 1988—; mem. adv. council Augusta Resource Ctr. on Aging, 1980—; mem. Sr. Enrichment Assn. Augusta, 1987—, St. Joseph Home Health Care/Hospice Adv. Bd., 1987—; leadership devel. cons. U. Ga. Student Devel. Lab., 1976-78; exec. officer U. Ga. Family Housing Council, 1976-79; cons. and small group facilitator Program of Edn. and Career Exploration, Div. Vocational Edn., Ga. Dept. Edn., 1977-78; facilitator or co-facilitator various workshops on student devel., leadership devel, 1975-79; mem. ch. council St. Anne's Episcopal Ch., Tifton, 1975; mem. Tift County Bicentennial Com., 1974-75; mem. outreach com. and pastoral care team Emmanuel Episcopal Ch., Athens, 1980-87, mem. vestry, 1986-87; mem. Leadership Augusta, 1988—; membership chmn. Clarke County (Ga.) Dem. Com., 1980-82, sec., 1983-87; del. Ga. State Dem. Conv., 1982, 86; mem. Clarke County Dem. com., 1983-87; Dem. candidate for Ga. House Dist. 68, 1986; mem. Leadership Athens, Class of 1985; peer reviewer Nat. Home Caring Council, 1985—; founder, pres. N.E. Ga. Community Resource Council, 1981; bd. dirs. N.E. Ga. Community Resource Council, 1981-83, mem., 1981-87; mem. Ga. Social Services Adv. Council, Ga. Dept. Human Resources, 1980-87, 2nd vice chmn., 1985-86, 1st vice chmn., 1986-87; mem. Dist. X Social Services Adv. Council, 1980-87, 2nd vice chmn., 1984-86; chmn. citizens adv. bd. So. Bell-Ga., 1983-85, mem. 1983-86; mem. Selective Service bd. 15, Ga., 1981-87; loaned exec. United Way N.E. Ga., 1982; treas. Athens Area Human Relations Com., 1982-86, mem., 1981-87; founder and mem. steering com. Hospice of Athens, 1981-82, sec., 1982-83, v.p., 1983-84, pres., 1984-85. Recipient Scouter's Tng. award, Boy Scouts Am., 1970, Pro Deo Et Patria Religious award, 1964; named to Vigil, Order of Arrow, 1974—. Mem. Gerontol. Soc. Am., Ga. Gerontol. Soc. (bd. dirs. 1985—, chmn. awards com. 1986, ann. conf. com. 1982—, chmn. 1988), Nat. Eagle Scout Assn. (annual conf. planning com. 1984—, chmn. 1988), Athens Area C. of C. (conv. and visitors bur. com. 1986-87), Nat. Service Fraternity Alpha Phi Omega. Asso. editor The Viewpoint, 1976-77; contbr. articles to profl. jours. Lodge: Rotary (chmn. Athens club conf. and conv. promotion com. 1985-86, chmn. spl. project com. 1985-86, chmn. Augusta West club bull. com. 1988—)., chmn. spl. project com. 1985-86, chmn. dist. conf. com. 1982-85, found. student counselor 1983-84, mem. 1981-86). Home: 2709-G Woodcrest Dr Augusta GA 30909 Office: Sr Citizens Council Greater Augusta and Civil Service Reform Act 535 15th St Augusta GA 30901

SCHOELLER, FRANZ JOACHIM PHILIPP, German ambassador to Poland; b. Dusseldorf, July 24, 1926; s. Franz and Therese Schoeller; m. Helga Ingetraud Neul, 1956; 1 son, 1 dau. Ed. U. Paris and Cologne. Attache Fgn. Service, Bonn, 1955, 3d sec., 1957-59, 2d sec., 1963-66, minister, dep. chief protocol, 1973-75, ambassador, chief of protocol, 1975-80; served in Paris, 1956-57, Rome, 1959-61; consul, charge d'affaires, Dar-es-Salaam, 1961-63; 1st sec., Madrid, 1966-69; counsellor, Teheran, 1971-73; ambassador to Brazil, 1980-83, to Paris, 1983-87, to Warsaw, 1987— . Decorated Order of Merit (W.Ger.); KCVO; comdr. Legion d'Honneur; other decorations. Office: Embassy of Fed Rep of Germany, PO Box 1500, 5300 Bonn France

SCHOEN, CHARLES JUDD, service executive; b. Owatonna, Minn., Sept. 6, 1943; s. John Nicholas and Dorothy Georgine (Jacobson) S.; m. Birgitta Marianne Haggren, Dec. 15, 1972; 1 child, Vanja Karina. BA, U. Minn., 1965. Stockbroker Harris, Upham and Co., Mpls., 1967-70; with Litton Industries, Sydney, Australia, 1970-71; gen. mgr. Westinghouse Electric, Mpls., 1971-77; pres. Westec Security, Mpls., 1977—. Served with USN, 1966-67. Mem. Alarm Dealers Assn. (v.p.), Nat. Trade Group. Home: 2430 Northshore Dr Wayzata MN 55391 Office: Westec Security 3280 Gorham Ave S Minneapolis MN 55426

SCHOEN, MARC ALAN, pension and employee benefits executive; b. Worcester, Mass., May 30, 1938; s. A. Robert and Ruth D. (Kulin) S.; m. Joanne S. Schultz, June 24, 1962; children: Elliott, Aaron, Jennifer, Matthew. BBA, BS, U. Miami, 1965. Asst. buyer Allied Stores, Miami, Fla., 1965-66; agt. Fidelity Mut. Ins., Miami, 1966-67, Prudential Ins. Co., Miami, 1967-68; pvt. practice registered rep., agt. Miami, 1973-81; pres. Pencoa, Miami, 1981—; cons. Criterion Funds, Inc., Houston, 1983—, Hibbard Brown & Co., Inc., Greenbelt, Mo., 1987—, Wood Logan Assocs., Inc., Old Greenwich, Conn.; bd. dirs. Beagle Group-Miramar, Fla., 1987—, Integrated Capital Planning Corp., Miami, Fla. Columnist for newspapers, 1969-76, 84. Mem. So. Fla. Employee Benefits Council, N. Dade Estate Planning Council; Scoutmaster Boy Scouts Am., Miami, 1966—; exec. bd. dirs. Crouse Found. to Pub. Arts, N.Y.C., 1983—. Served with USN, 1957-62. Recipient Community Service award Prudential Ins., 1968; named Outstanding Young Man Yr., Optimists, 1967; named to Rollins Coll. Sports Hall of Fame, 1987. Mem. assoc. mem. Am. Soc. Pension Actuaries, Internat. Assn. Fin. Planners, Million Dollar Round Table (qualifying life). Lodges: Optimists, Rotary, Masons. Home: 6725 SW 90 Court Miami FL 33173

SCHOENFELD, LAWRENCE JON, jewelry manufacturing company executive, consultant; b. Los Angeles, Nov. 30, 1945; s. Donald and Trudy (Libizer) S.; Carol Sue Gard, Aug. 24, 1969. AA, Los Angeles Valley Coll., Van Nuys, Calif., 1963; BBA, Wichita State U., 1969, MSBA, 1970. Cert. tchr. (life), Calif. Asst. treas. Advance Mortgage, Los Angeles, 1970-72; v.p. ops. Unigem Internat., Los Angeles, 1972—; bd. dirs. Schoenfeld Constrn. Co., The Telcom Group, Uniorr Corp., Execucentre-West, Schoenfeld & Co., Schoenfeld Constrn. Co., Customer Ground Handling Service Corp.; co-developer Bay-Osos Mini Storage Co., San Luis Obispo, Calif.; El Mercadeo World Trade Show, Guatemala, 1986, Santiago, 1987, Bahai, 1988. Mem. Improvement Commn., Hermosa Beach., Calif. 1976-78. Served to maj. US Army Med. Service Corps, 1970-72, with res. 1972—. Mem. South Am. Travel Assn., World Trade Assn. (assoc.), Town Hall, Wichita State U. Alumni Assn. (Nat. dist. rep.). Jewish. Office: Unigem Internat 448 S Hill 12th Floor Los Angeles CA 90266

SCHOENFELD, MICHAEL P., lawyer; b. Bronx, N.Y., Oct. 17, 1935; s. Jack and Anne S.; B.S. in Acctg., N.Y.U., 1955; LL.B., LL.D., Fordham U., 1958; m. Helen Schorr, Apr. 3, 1960; children—Daniel, Steven, Tracy. Admitted to N.Y. bar, 1959, U.S. Supreme Ct., 1963; atty. Am. Home Assurance Co., N.Y.C., 1958-62; partner firm Schoenfeld & Schoenfeld, Melville, 1959—; v.p. Interstate Brokerage Corp., 1965—; partner Melville Realty Co., 1977—; legal adv. various bus. orgns. Vice pres., trustee Temple Beth David, Commack, N.Y., 1972-75; chmn. Community Action Com. of Dix Hills and Commack, 1970-72, Dix Hills Planning Bd., 1972-74; treas. Dix Hills Republican Club, 1976—; mem. Huntington (N.Y.) Zoning Bd. Appeals, 1980—, chmn., 1986—. Recipient United Jerusalem award Israel Bond Drive, 1977; City of Hope Service award; George Bacon award Fordham Law Sch. Mem. N.Y. State Bar Assn., Suffolk County Bar Assn. Home: 14 Clayton Dr Dix Hills NY 11746 Office: 60 Broad Hollow Rd Melville NY 11747

SCHOENWALD, ARTHUR ALLEN, financial adv.; b. Bklyn., Mar. 3, 1940; s. Saul Morris and Charlotte (Lipschitz) S.; B.B.A., Baruch Sch. Bus., CCNY, 1961; M.B.A. (Baruch Sch. honor scholar), U. Chgo., 1962; D.B.A. (Arthur Andersen & Co. fellow), Harvard U., 1968; m. Maxine Rapchik, Nov. 4, 1961; children—Scott M., Ellen Beth. Asst. prof. bus. adminstrn. Rutgers U., Newark, 1967-68, asso. prof., 1968-72; exec. dir. N.J. Public Utilities Commn., Newark, 1972-74; mgr. electric utilities group Salomon Bros., N.Y.C., 1974-75; pres. A.A. Schoenwald Assos., Inc., Colonia, N.J., 1975—; lectr. in field. Fin. cons. N.J. Gov.'s Commn. to Evaluate Capital Needs of N.J., 1968; mem. N.J. Gov.'s Commn. on Public Electric Power Authority, 1975, N.J. Gov.'s Econ. Recovery Commn., 1975; treas. Middlesex County (N.J.) Republican Orgn. Recipient Chgo. Control award Controllers Inst. Am., 1962; named Tchr. of Yr., Rutgers U. Grad. Sch. Bus., 1971. Mem. Fin. Mgmt. Assn., Beta Gamma Sigma, Beta Alpha Psi. Jewish. Clubs: Colonia Country, Channel, K.P., Harvard Bus. Sch. of Greater N.Y., U. Chgo. Bus. of N.Y. Home and Office: 26 Cambridge Dr Colonia NJ 07067

SCHOEPP, JEAN-PIERRE, corporate executive; b. Charleroi, Belgium, Apr. 3, 1937; s. Andre and Marie-Cecile (Daubresse) S.; m. Marie-clementine Vandroogenbroeck, June 1, 1940; children: Isabelle, Frederic, Didier. Grad. Coll. St. Michel-Brussels, 1957, postgrad. in Math., 1958; grad. Engring., U.G. Liège, 1963. Sales engr. Regulation Mesure, Brussels, 1963-73, v.p., 1973-80, pres., 1980—, pres. bd., 1981—. Mem. Union des Constructeurs et Importateurs d'Appareils Scientitiques, Médicaux et de Contrôle (pres. 1973—), Fabricants et Importateurs de Matérial de Transmission Oleó-Hydraulique et Pneumatique' (pres. 1982-83), Institut Belge de Régulation et d'Automatisme (dir. 1980—), Fédération du Commerce de l'Appareillage Electrique. Home: Ave du Kouter 240, B-1160 Brussels Belgium Office: 73 av Vandendriessche, B-1150 Brussels Belgium

SCHOFIELD, NICHOLAS JOHN, hydrologist; b. Reading, Eng., Jan. 19, 1952; s. William Edwin and Pamela Sandra (Bunce) S.; m. Anne Clover, Nov. 28, 1982; children: Timothy, James, Harrison. BS in Physics with honors, Imperial Coll., London, 1973; PhD, U. York (Eng.), 1979. Research fellow hydrology U. Leeds, Eng., 1977-78; lectr. physics Curtin U. of Tech., Perth, West Australia, 1980-83; research hydrologist Pub. Works Dept., Perth, West Australia, 1983-85, head hydrology and land use research; research hydrologist Water Authority, Perth, West Australia, 1985—. Contbr. articles to profl. jours. Fellow RAS; mem. Australian Inst. of Physics, Royal Coll. of Sci., Internat. Assn. Hydrological Scis. Home: 65 Daglish St Wembley, 6014 Perth Australia Office: Water Authority of WA, 629 Newcastle St, 6007 Perth Australia

SCHOFIELD, ROGER SNOWDEN, historical demographer, research director; b. Leeds, Yorkshire, Eng., Aug. 26, 1937; s. Ronald Snowden and Muriel Grace (Braime) S.; m. Elizabeth Mary Cunliffe, Sept. 3, 1961; 1 child, Melanie. BA, U. Cambridge, Eng., 1959, PhD, 1963. Fellow Clare Coll., Cambridge, Eng., 1962-65, 69—; asst. dir. research of U.K. Social Sci. Research Council, Cambridge, Eng., 1966-73, research unit dir. of U.K., 1974—; mem. computing and stats. com. Social Sci. Research Council, London, 1970-78; mem. Population Investigation Com., London, 1976—, treas., 1987—; mem. hist. demography com. study of population Inst. Union for Sci., London, 1983—, pres., 1987—. Co-author: The Population History of England, 1981; contbr. articles to profl. jours.; editor Population Studies, 1979—. Sherman Fairchild Disting. scholar, 1984-85. Fellow Royal Hist. Soc., Royal Stats. Soc., British Acad.; mem. Brit. Soc. for Population Studies (council 1979-87, treas. 1981-83, v.p. 1983-85, pres. 1985-87), Soc. de Demographie Historique. Home: Clare Coll, Cambridge CB2 1TL, England Office: Econ & Social Research Council, 27 Trumpington St, Cambridge CB2 1QA, England

SCHOFIELD, WILLIAM GREENOUGH, writer, retired university official; b. Providence, June 13, 1909; s. Harry Leon and Elizabeth (Smallman) S.; m. Blanche Mary Hughes, Nov. 21, 1934; children: Michael, Elinor, Peter. StudentBrown U., 1927-30, Armed Forces Staff Coll., 1960, U.S. Naval War Coll., 1964. Feature writer Providence Jour., 1936-40; columnist Boston Traveler, 1940-52, fgr. corr., Europe, Asia, Latin Am., 1946-62, chief editorial writer, fgn. news analyst, 1952-67; mgr. editorial services Raytheon Co., 1967-70; assoc. dir. public info. Boston U., 1970-74, ret.; cons. univ. public affairs, 1975-79; news reporter radio and TV, 1946-56. Founder Freedom Trail, Boston; past pres. Serra Club, Boston. Served to lt. comdr. USNR, 1942-45, now capt. (ret.) U.S. Naval Res. Recipient Achievement award Dept. Interior, 1976. Mem. Am. Newspaper Guild, Boston Press Club, Ret. Officers Assn., Nat. Def. Exec. Res., Navy League, Alpha Tau Omega. Roman Catholic. Author: Ashes in the Wilderness, 1942; The Cat in the Convoy, 1946; Payoff in Black, 1947; The Deer Cry, 1948; Seek for a Hero, 1956; Sidewalk Statesman, 1958; Destroyer 60 Years, 1962; Treason Trail, 1964; Eastward the Convoys, 1966; Freedom by the Bay, 1974; Frogmen: First Battles, 1987; others. Home: 16 Hunnewell Circle Newton MA 02158

SCHOLES, ROBERT THORNTON, physician, research adminstr.; b. Bushnell, Ill., June 24, 1919; s. Harlan Lawrence and Lura Zolene (Camp) S.; student Knox Coll., 1937-38; B.S., Mich. State U., 1941; M.D., U. Rochester, 1950; postgrad. U. London, 1951-52, U. Chgo., 1953; m. Kathryn Ada Tew, Sept. 3, 1948; 1 dau., Delia. Intern, Gorgas Hosp., Ancon, C.Z., 1950-51; lab. asst. dept. entomology Mich. State U., 1940-41; research asst. Roselake Wildlife Exptl. Sta., 1941; research assoc. Harvard U., 1953-57; served to med. dir. USPHS, 1954-71, med. officer, dep. chief health and sanitation div. U.S. Ops. Mission, Bolivia, 1954-57, chief health and sanitation div., Paraguay, 1957-60, internat. health rep. Office of Surgeon Gen., 1960-62; br. chief, research grants officer, acting assoc. dir. Nat. Inst. Allergy and Infectious Diseases, NIH, Bethesda, Md., 1962-71; pres. The Bioresearch Ranch, Inc., Rodeo, N.Mex., 1977—; cons. Peace Corps, 1961, Hidalgo County Med. Services, Inc., 1979—, N.Mex. Health Systems Agy., 1980-86, N.Mex. Health Resources, Inc., 1981—. Served to capt. USAAF, 1942-45. Commonwealth Fund fellow, 1953. Mem. AAAS, Am. Soc. Tropical Medicine and Hygiene, N.Y. Acad. Sci., Am. Pub. Health Assn., Am. Ornithologists Union, Sembot Hon. Soc. Contbr. papers to profl. publs. Home and Office: PO Box 117 Rodeo NM 88056

SCHOLTEN, KIM STANDRIDGE, accountant; b. Santa Ana, Calif., Apr. 26, 1957; d. Howard Vernon and Mary Louise (Countryman) Horner; m. Roger Odell Standridge, Jan. 7, 1978 (div. Aug. 1983); m. R. Edward Scholten, Aug. 28, 1987. BSBA, Okla. State U., 1984. CPA, Okla. Acct., Kerr-McGee Corp., Oklahoma City, 1980-82, Warren Petroleum Co., Tulsa, 1983, Cities Service Oil & Gas Corp., Tulsa, 1985—; auditor Arthur Young & Co., Tulsa, 1984-85. Mem. Am. Inst. CPA's, Okla. Soc. CPA's, Nat. Assn. Accts., Nat. Assn. Female Execs., Phi Kappa Phi, Beta Gamma Sigma, Beta Alpha Psi. Republican. Methodist. Club: Toastmasters. Avocations: singing and performing in musicals, snow and water skiing, sailing, softball. Home: 1430B E 38th Pl Tulsa OK 74105 Office: Cities Service Oil & Gas Corp PO Box 300 Tulsa OK 74102

SCHOLTENS, JOHAN, biologist, psychologist; b. Koog aan de Zaan, The Netherlands, July 8, 1953. MSc, U. Amsterdam, 1980; postgrad., U. Utrecht, Netherlands. Scientist U. Amsterdam, Netherlands, 1980—. Sec.-treas. Instn. for Help and Service by Telephone, Amsterdam, 1980—. Mem. Dutch Soc. Psychical Research. Club: Mazzo (Amsterdam). Home: Oudezijds Achterburgwal 134, 1012 DV Amsterdam The Netherlands Office: Neth Inst Brain Research, Meiberg Dreef 33, 1105 AZ Amsterdam The Netherlands

SCHOLZ, RUPERT, German government official; b. Berlin, Federal Republic of Germany, May 23, 1937; s. Ernst and Gisela (Merdas) S.; m. Helga Hoppe. LLD, U. Munich, 1966, post-doctoral degree, 1970. Prof. law Free U. Berlin, 1972-78, Munich U., 1978-81; sen. for justice Provice of Berlin, 1981-82, sen. for justice and fed. affairs, 1982-88, mem. ho. reps., 1985—; minister of def. Govt. of Fed. Republic of Germany, 1988—; mem. North Atlantic Assembly, 1982. Contbr. articles to profl. jours. Mem. Christian Dem. Union. Roman Catholic. Office: Fed Ministry of Def, D-5300 Bonn Federal Republic of Germany

SCHOLZE, DIETRICH HERMANN JOHANNES, Slavonic literature educator, editor, translator; b. Bautzen, Saxony, Germany, Sept. 8, 1950; s. Johannes Otto and Herta (Halank) S.; m. Dorothea Margarete Piatza, Feb. 18, 1981; 1 child, Karl. Diploma in Slavonic Langs., Humboldt U., Berlin, 1973; Ph.D., Acad. Scis., Berlin, 1980, habilitation, 1988. Mem. staff Acad. Scis., Berlin, 1974—; tchr. Humboldt U., Berlin, part time, 1974—. Editor: W.S. Reymont, Novellen, 1981, 2d ed., 1984; (4 vols.) J. Putrament, Ein halbes Jahrhundert. Memoiren, 1982, 1984; I. Iredynski, Leb wohl Judas, 1983. Translator: I. Iredynski, Manipulation, 1978, 2d edit., 1985. Contbr. articles to profl. jours. Mem. Vereinigung der Sprachmittler DDR. Lutheran.

SCHONHOFF, ROBERT LEE, marketing and advertising executive; b. Detroit, May 24, 1919; s. John Clement and Olympia Regina (Diebold) S.; m. Kathleen O'Hara, Dec. 24, 1971; children: Rita, Elise, Robert. Student, Wayne State U., 1940-41. Artist, J.L. Hudson, 1939-42; v.p. advt. and mktg. Dillard Dept. Stores, Little Rock and San Antonio, 1963-77; owner R.L. Schonhoff Advt. and Mktg., San Antonio, 1977-83; owner Ad Graphics, AMC Printers Inc.; co-owner New Orleans Saints football team; mem. faculty Bus. Sch., St. Mary's U., 1975-81; bd. dirs. Comml. Nat. Bank, San Antonio. Permanent deacon Roman Catholic Ch., San Antonio Diocese. Served to 1st lt. USAF, 1942-46. Mem. Am. Mktg. Assn. (founding dir. San Antonio chpt.). Clubs: Tapatio Springs Country; Josef (San Antonio). Home: 501 Hillside Dr San Antonio TX 78212 Office: 1528 Contour St Suite 101 San Antonio TX 78212

SCHOOLS, CHARLES HUGHLETTE, banker, lawyer; b. Lansing, Mich., May 24, 1929; s. Robert Thomas and Lillian Pearl (Lawson) S.; B.S., Am. U., 1952, M.A., 1958; J.D., Washington Coll. of Law, 1963; LL.D., Bethune-Cookman U., 1973; m. Rosemarie Sanchez, Nov. 22, 1952; children—Charles, Michael. Dir. phys. plant Am. U., 1952-66; owner, 1957—, Gen. Security Co., Washington, 1969—; chmn., pres. Consol. Ventures Ltd.; pres., chmn. bd. McLean Bank (Va.), 1974—, Instl. Environ. Mgmt. Services; chmn. bd. Harper & Co.; chmn., pres. Community Assos. of Va., Associated Real Estate Mgmt. Services; dir. Computer Data Systems Inc., DAC Devel. Ltd., Am. Indsl. Devel. Corp., Intercoastal of Iran; mem. Met. Bd. Trades. Pres., McLean Boys' Club; bd. dirs. D.C. Spl. Olympics, Nat. Kidney Found.; trustee Bethune Cookman Coll., Western Md. Coll., Randolph Macon Acad. Served with USAAF, 1946-47, USAF, 1947-48. Mem. Va. C. of C., Profl. Businessman's Orgn., Alpha Tau Omega. Democrat. Clubs: Georgetown of Washington, Touchdown of Washington, Univ. of Washington, Washington Golf and Country, Pisces (Washington); Halifax (Daytona Beach, Fla.); Masons. Home: 1320 Darnall Dr McLean VA 22101 Office: Consol Ventures Ltd 1340 Old Chain Bridge Rd McLean VA 22101

SCHOON, WARREN EUGENE, automotive executive; b. Ash Creek, Minn., Oct. 3, 1921; s. Jacob and Viola (Hansen) S.; m. Elizabeth Johnson, Dec. 25, 1943 (div. 1969); children: Steven, Susan, Peter, Christian, Robert; m. Marjorie Costello, Oct. 10, 1969. BA, U. Minn., 1943. Various jr. exec. positions Gen. Motors Corp., Mpls. and St. Louis, 1947-50; nat. advt. and N.Y. zone mgr., Pontiac div. Gen. Motors Corp., N.Y.C., 1957-60; ptnr. McKean and Schoon Ford, Sioux Falls, S.D., 1951-54; pres. and owner Schoon Motors, Luverne, S.D., 1960—; pres. New Chrysler Inc., Luverne, 1977—, Luverne Oil Co., 1971—; master adv. bd. dirs. Met. Fin. Corp., Fargo, N.D.; v.p., bd. dirs. Sioux Land Broadcasting, Luverne; chmn. Oldsmobile Zone Dealer Council, Mpls., 1984-85; chmn. bd. dirs. Dakota Savs. and Loan, Sioux Falls (merger Met. Fed. Bank, Fargo), 1982-86. Mayor City of Luverne, 1955-57; small bus. adv. com. U.S. Sen. R. Boschwitz, Minn., 1982—, U.S. Sen. Pressler, S.D., 1985—; adv. bd. McKennan Hosp., Sioux Falls, 1985—, pres. 1988—; bd. dirs. S. Dakota Crippled Children's Sch., 1986—; chmn. Rock County (Minn.) Reps., 1954-57, 60-70; mem. Nat. Bd. Ctr. Western Studies Augustana Coll., Sioux Falls. Served to lt. (j.g.) USN, 1943-47, PTO. Mem. Iowa-Minn. Pontiac Advt. Assn. (pres. 1970-86), U. Minn. Alumni Assn. (pres. Rochester chpt. 1974-75), Minn./S. Dakota Cadillac Dealer's Mktg. Assn. (pres. 1986—), Am. Legion, VFW, Phi Beta Kappa. Republican. Presbyterian. Club: Minnehaha Country (Sioux Falls). Lodges: Rotary (bd. dirs. Sioux Falls Downtown Club 1984-85), Masons, Shriners, Elks. Home: 1942 S First Ave Sioux Falls SD 57105 Office: Schoon Motors Cedar & Maple Luverne MN 56156

SCHOONOVER, JACK RONALD, judge; b. Winona, Minn., July 23, 1934; s. Richard M. and Elizabeth A. (Hargeisheimer) S.; student Winona State Coll., 1956-58; LL.B., U. Fla., 1962; m. Ann Marie Kroez, June 18, 1965; children—Jack Ronald, Wayne J. Bar: Fla. 1962. Since practiced in Charlotte County; atty. Charlotte County Sch. Bd., 1969-75; asst. state's atty., 1970-72; city judge, Punta Gorda, Fla., 1973-74; judge Fla. Circuit Ct., 1975-81; appellate judge, 1981—. Served with USAF, 1952-56. Mem. Am. Legion. Home: 1224 Stratton Ct W Lakeland FL 33813 Office: PO Box 327 Lakeland FL 33802

SCHOOR, HOWARD M., engineer, consultant; b. S.I., N.Y., Jan. 13, 1939; s. Samuel Edward and Sadie Diana (Garelick) S.; B.S.C.E., Lafayette Coll., 1961; postgrad. N.Y.U., 1962-63; m. Frances A. Loscoe, Dec. 14, 1973; children—Barbara, Debra. Field engr. N.Y. State Dept. Pub. Works, 1961-63; project mgr. Aurnhammer Assos., Inc., Summit, N.J., 1963-68; chief exec. officer Schoor, DePalma & Canger, Inc., cons. engrs., Manalapan, N.J., 1968—; mcpl. engr., boroughs of Keyport, Matawan, Netcong, Edgewater, Allentown, Caldwell, Franklin, Highlands, Hightstown, Hi-Nella, Madison, Odgensburg, Pomptain Lakes, Prospect Parks, Roseland, Runnemeade, Sussex, Woodlynne, twps. of Berlin, Lopatcong, Mt. Olive, Roxbury, S. Orange Village, Town of Phillipsburg, Little Egg Harbor, East Hanover, Mine Hill, Mount Olive, Vernon, Hazlet Twp. Sewerage Authority, Little Egg Harbor Mcpl. Utilities Authority, Ocean Twp. Sewerage Authority, Stafford Mcpl. Utilities Authority, Marlboro Twp. Utilities Authority, Merchantville-Pensuaken Water comm.; cons. in field; pres. Collier Found. Services, Inc. Mem. nat. fin. council Dem. Nat. com. Fellow ASCE; mem. Am. Water Works Assn., Monmouth County socs. profl. engrs., N.J. Soc. Profl. Planners, N.J. Shore Builders Assn., N.J. Builders Assn., Nat. Assn. Home Builders, N.J. Soc. Municipal Engrs., Fedn. Planning Ofcls., Am. Congress Mapping and Surveying, Water Pollution Control Fedn., Standardbred Breeders and Owners Assn. N.J. (dir.). Clubs: Broken Sound (Boca Raton), Masons. Home: 14 Colts Gait Ln Colts Neck NJ 07722 Office: 200 Route 9 N Manalapan NJ 07726

SCHOOTS, PIET JOHAN THEODORUS, librarian; b. Eindhoven, Noord-Brabant, The Netherlands, Oct. 10, 1929; s. Petrus J. and Geertruida (Sleegers) S.; m. Egidia W.J.M. Wilderbeek, May 24, 1956; children: Mirjam Ellen, Carolien Marlies. Student, St. Joris Coll., Eindhoven, 1942-47, Library Sch. G.O., The Hague, The Netherlands, 1951-52, 65-66. Library asst. N.V. Philips, Eindhoven, 1947-55; head library and info. dept. N.V. Gist-Brocades, Amsterdam, The Netherlands, 1955-74; dir. City Library of Rotterdam, The Netherlands, 1974—; dir. ad interim Maritime Mus. Prins Hendrik, Rotterdam, 1987—; bd. dirs. Internat. Bur. for Library and Info. Affairs, 1987, Adv. Body for Library and Info. Affairs, 1987; vice chmn. bd. Project Integrated Catalouguing Holland (PICA), 1986. Contbr. articles to profl. jours. Home: Vijverlaan 508, 2925 VL Krimpen aan de Ijssel The Netherlands Office: City Library of Rotterdam, Hoogstraat 110, 3011 PV Rotterdam The Netherlands

SCHOPPE, SIEGFRIED GEORG, economist, educator; b. Hoerstel, Fed. Republic of Germany, Apr. 25, 1944; s. Bernhard Hermann and Sophia Agnes (Hoffrogge) S.; m. Marianne Josephine Raters, Jan. 3, 1970; children: Christian Marten, Stephan Andreas, Anja Karen. Diploma, U. Munster, Fed. Republic of Germany, 1971, D of Polit. Research, 1973; Privatdozent, U. Hamburg, Fed. Republic of Germany, 1979. Lectr. adult edn. courses Freckenhorst, Fed. Republic of Germany, 1971-74; asst. prof. U. Hamburg, 1975-83, prof., 1983—; founder, dir. Internat. Bus. Sch., GmbH, Lippstadt, Fed. Republic of Germany, 1984—. Author: Die sowjetische Westhandelsstruktur: ein aussenhandelstheoretisches Paradoxon?, 1981; contbr. articles to profl. jours. Mem. Verein für Socialpolitik, Atlantic Econ. Soc. Roman Catholic. Office: U Hamburg, Von Melle Park 5, 2000 Hamburg 13 Federal Republic of Germany

SCHOPPMEYER, MARTIN WILLIAM, educator; b. Weehawken, N.J., Sept. 15, 1929; s. William G. and Madeleine M. (Haas) S.; m. Marilyn M. Myers, Aug. 9, 1958; children: Susan Ann, Martin William. B.S., Fordham U., 1950; Ed.M., U. Fla., 1955, Ed.D., 1962. Tchr. Fla. pub. schs., 1955-59; instr., then asst. prof. U. Fla., 1960-63; assoc. prof., then prof. edn. Fla. Atlantic U., Boca Raton, 1963-68; dir. continuing edn. Fla. Atlantic U., 1965-67; mem. faculty U. Ark., Fayetteville, 1968—; prof. edn. U. Ark., 1971—, program coordinator ednl. adminstrn., 1983—; mem. Nat. Adv. Council Edn. Professions Devel., 1973-76; exec. sec. Ark. Sch. Study Council, 1976—; evaluator instructional tng. program Nat. Tng. Fund, 1978; bd. dirs. Women's Ednl. and Devel. Inst., 1977-80, Nat. Sch. Devel. Council; mem. oversight com. S. Conway (Ark.) County Sch. Dist.; mem. state commn. to study effect of Amendment 59 to Ark. Constn. Author books, monographs, articles in field. Mem. Pres.'s council Subiaco Acad. Served with AUS, 1951-53, Korea. Recipient numerous fed. grants. Mem. NEA, Ark. Edn. Assn. (past chpt. pres.), Ark. Assn. Ednl. Adminstrs., Kappa Delta Pi, Phi Delta Kappa, Delta Tau Kappa. Roman Catholic. Lodges: Rotary; K.C. Home: 2950 Sheryl Ave Fayetteville AR 72703 Office: U Ark 244 Grad Edn Bldg Fayetteville AR 72701

SCHOR, BERL, consulting mechanical engineer; b. Krakow, Poland, Nov. 5, 1927; s. Majer and Miriam (Frankel) S.; m. Hanna Edelmann, June 2, 1957; children—Yair, Uri, David, Michael. B.E. in Mech. Engring., U. N.Z., 1952; B.Sc., 1953. Engr. Ellis, Hardie, Syminton, Ltd., Wellington, N.Z., 1951-53, Esher-Wyss A.G., Zurich, Switzerland, 1953-55; cons. engr. B. Schor & Co., Cons. Engrs., Tel Aviv, Savion, Israel, 1955—; dir. Allied Cons. Engrs., Ltd., Tel Aviv, Israel, 1975—. Mem. Israel Assn. Engr. and Architects, Israel Assn. Cons. Engrs. (pres. 1967-78, 1982-83). Jewish. Advocations: Art; photography, archeology. Home: 18 Hahermesh St, PO Box 2151, Savion 56530, Israel Office: B Schor & Co Cons Engrs Ltd, PO Box 2151 51 Simtat, Hahermesh 56530, Israel

SCHOR, ISAIAS, physician, educator; b. Buenos Aires, Nov. 7, 1925; s. Simon and Flora (Lexman) S., m. Vera Perla Zuchowiciki, Aug. 16, 1952; children: Eduardo Alberto, Carlos Marcelo. Student in gastroenteroloty, U. Pa., 1952-53; MD, U. Buenos Aires, 1954; postgrad., Acad. Med., Rome, 1970. Fellow in gastroenterology Mt. Sinai Hosp., N.Y.C., 1952-53; specialist in nutrition U. Buenos Aires, 1954-64, asst. prof. nutrition, 1964-86, prof., 1986—; head nutrition dept. Hosp. Gastroenterologia, Buenos Aires, 1971-86; prof. nutrition sci. U. Argentina de la Empresa, Buenos Aires, 1975-81; head nutrition and dietetics dept. Hosp. Clinicas, Buenos Aires, 1986—. Co-author: To Live as a Diabetic, 1985; co-editor: Nutrition, 1986. Mem. Artentine Nutrition Assn., Argentine Diabetes Assn. (pres. 1979-80), Am. Soc. Nutrition Educators, Am. Assn. Diabetes Edn., Argentine Med. Assn., Argentine Gastroent. Assn., Argentine Assn. Enteral and Parenteral Nutrition (pres. 1984-85), Argentine Assn. Food Technologists, Bockus Internat. Soc. Gastroenterology, Latin Am. Soc. Nutrition, Latin Am. Soc. Diabetes, Internat. Diabetes Fedn., Am. Soc. Parenteral and Enternal Nutrition, Inst. Food Technologists, Brasilian Soc. Parenteral and Enteral Nutrition. Office: Rodriguez Pena 1405, 1021 Buenos Aires Argentina

SCHOR, OLGA SEEMANN, mental health counselor, real estate broker; b. Havana, Cuba, Mar. 2, 1951; came to U.S., 1961; d. Olga del Carmen (Hernandez) S.; m. David Michael Schor, Apr. 22, 1979; 1 child, Andrew. A.A., Miami Dade Community Coll., 1971; B.A., U. Fla.-Gainesville, 1973; M.Edn., U. Miami, Fla., 1976; Psy.D., Nova U., 1981; cert. Bert Rodgers Sch. Real Estate, Miami, 1981, Gold Coast Sch. Real Estate, 1988; lic. real estate broker. Teaching asst. U. Fla., Gainesville, 1972-73; counselor U. Miami, Fla., 1974-79; assoc. psychotherapist Linda H. Jamrozy & Assocs., Miami, 1976-78, Interactive Systems, Miami, 1978-79; psychometrist Jackson Meml. Hosp., Miami, 1978-79; assoc. psychotherapist Behavioral Medicine Inst., Miami, 1979-85, Tony Ciminero & Assocs., Miami, 1985-86; lectr. U. Miami, 1976-78, Jackson Meml. Hosp. Sch. Nursing, Miami, 1976; real estate broker The Keyes Co. Realtor, Coral Gables, 1981—; sec./treas. bd. dirs. BODS Inc., Miami. Recipient Assoc. of Quarter award Keyes Co. Realtors, 1986. Mem. Am. Psychol. and Guidance Assn., Keyes Comml. Roundtable, Coral Gables Bd. Realtors, Dade County Mental Health Assn., Million Dollar Sales Club. Club: South Fla. Sailing Assn. (Miami). Avocations: sailing; diving; reading; running; theater; acting; tennis. Office: 357 Miracle Mile Coral Gables FL 33134

SCHORR, DAVID JAY, forensic engineer; b. Phila., Apr. 6, 1931; s. Solomon and Ida Hilda (Kramer) S.; B.S.C.E., Drexel Inst., 1954; M.S.C.E., U. Pa., 1959; m. Beverly Helen Rubin, Aug. 31, 1952; children—Alan, Michael, Steven, Devra. Diplomate Nat. Acad. Forensic Engrs. Asst. prof. engring. Villanova U., 1962-85, asst. to dean of engring., 1975-79; pres. Forensic Engring. Services and Town Engrs., both divs. DJS Assocs., 1982—; pres. Town Engrs., 1962-82; mem. Engrs. Week com. Delaware Valley, Delaware Valley Citizens Transp. Com., Pa. Engring. Found.; pres. Forensic Engring. Services, Town Engrs., Tech. Research, Multi Media Exhibits and Expert Network, all divs. of DJS Assocs. Inc. Prin. Beth Chaim Religious Sch.; mem. exploring council Boy Scouts Am. Recipient award Nat. Cancer Soc., 1974; Fed. Hwy. Adminstrn. fellow, 1979; NSF fellow, 1965; registered profl. engr., Pa., N.J., Del. Mem. Am. Acad. Forensic Scis., Am. Soc. Engring. Edn., Nat. Soc. Profl. Engrs., Inst. Transp. Engrs., Pa. Soc. Profl. Engrs., Profl. Engrs. Pvt. Practice, Blue Key, Chi Epsilon, Tau Beta Pi. Jewish. Club: Golden Slipper. Contbr. articles to profl. jours. Office: Forensic Engring Services 1603 Old York Rd Abington PA 19001

SCHOTTENSTEIN, DIANE STEINBERG, lawyer; b. N.Y.C., June 13, 1957; d. Max and Shirley (Minaker) Steinberg; m. Edwin Michael Schottenstein, Oct. 16, 1983. B.S., Cornell U., 1978; J.D., NYU, 1981, LL.M. in Taxation, 1986. Bar: N.Y. 1982, U.S. Dist. Ct. (so. and ea. dists.) N.Y. 1982, N.J. 1983, Fla. 1983,U.S. Tax Ct. 1985. Clk., N.Y. Pub. Library, N.Y.C., 1975; banking clk. Lincoln First Internat. Bank, N.Y.C., 1976; advt. asst. Fairchild Publs., N.Y.C., 1978; law clk. N.Y.C. Dept. Health Adminstrv. Tribunal, N.Y.C., 1979; law clk. Citicorp, N.Y.C., 1979-81; assoc. atty. Matays Hughes & Brown, N.Y.C., 1981-86; assoc. atty. Law Offices of Arthur I. Frankel, P.C., 1986—; intern N.Y. State Office Lt. Gov., Albany, 1977. Trustee Brooklyn Heights Synagogue, Bklyn., 1986-87. Mem. Women in Housing and Fin., Inc., Housing Services of Am., Inc. (v.p. corp. sec. 1987—), Realty Services of Am. Inc. (v.p. 1988—), Phi Kappa Phi. Jewish. Office: Law Offices of Arthur I Frankel 110 E 59th St New York NY 10022

SCHOUTEN, CEES, plastic company executive; b. Alkmaar, North Holland, Netherlands, May 20, 1927; came to Belgium, 1974; s. Johannes Adrianes and Petronella (Bakker) S.; m. Afra Catharina Leering, Apr. 23, 1954; children—Ellen, Inge, Joppe. Diploma in Civil Engring., H.T.S., Amsterdam, Holland, 1952. Registered prof. engr., Netherlands. Engr., Aramco, Netherlands, Saudi Arabia, 1953-56; chief engr. Du Pont Co., Netherlands, 1956-62; mng. dir. Dymo, Belgium, U.S.A., 1962-70; v.p. Borg-Warner Co., Netherlands, Belgium, 1973-78; exec. European-Enterprises, France, 1970-73; chief exec. officer Sep. N.V., Gent, Belgium, 1978—, also dir. Served with Dutch Army, 1948-50. Roman Catholic. Home: Astridlaan 26, 1640 Saint Genesius-Rode Belgium Office: Sep-Imco NV, Singel-20, 9000 Gent Belgium

SCHRADER, ALFRED EUGENE, lawyer; b. Akron, Ohio, Nov. 1, 1953; s. Louis Clement and Helen Maye (Eberz) S.; m. Cathy Diane Fincher, Apr. 17, 1982; children—Eric Brian, Angela Diane. B.A. in Polit. Sci. magna cum laude, Kent State U., 1975; J.D., Ohio State U., 1978. Bar: Ohio 1978, U.S. Dist. Ct. (no. dist.) Ohio 1978, U.S. Ct. Appeals (6th cir.) 1985, U.S. Supreme Ct. 1985. Dep. clk. Summit County Clk. of Cts., Akron, 1972-74; sole practice, Akron, 1978—; spl. counsel Bath Twp., Ohio, 1980—; law dir. Northampton Twp., Ohio, 1983-86, Franklin Twp., Ohio, 1984—, Twinsburg Twp., Ohio, 1981—; spl. counsel Richfield Twp., Ohio, 1983-85; consulting counsel law dept. City of Cuyanoga Falls, 1986; spl. annexation counsel Bath, Perry and Shawnee Twps., Allen County, Ohio, 1986—; spl. counsel Carlisle Twp., Lorain County, 1986-87; spl. annexation counsel Perry Twp., Lake County, Ohio, Brimfield Twp., Portage County, 1986—. Trustee Springfield Twp., Ohio, 1973—, pres., 1975, 79, 82, 88; mem. adv. com. Community Devel. Block, Summit County, 1985—, Summit County Annexation Com., Ohio, 1981-85; mem. Summit County Jail Study Commn., 1983, 84; mem. adv. bd. Springfield Schs., 1975. Mem. Akron Bar Assn. (v.p. legis. com. 1981-82), Ohio Acad. Trial Lawyers, Assn. Trial Lawyers Am., Ohio Bar Assn., Summit County Twp. assn. (exec. com. 1983—), Ohio Twp. Assn. (exec. com. 1983—), Nat. Assn. Town and Twp. Attys. (dir. Ohio chpt. 1986, sec. 1987-88). Democrat. Roman Catholic. Home: 3344 Brunk Rd Akron OH 44312 Office: Dalessio Shapiro Manes et al 441 Wolf Ledges Pkwy Suite 400 Akron OH 44311-1054

SCHRAER, ROSEMARY S. J., university chancellor; b. Ilion, N.Y., Aug. 1, 1924; d. Ulysses Sidney and Rose Katherine (Ortner) Schmidt; m. Allan Gramlick Jenkins, May 3, 1946 (dec. Aug. 13, 1947; 1 child, David; m. Harald Schraer, June 12, 1952. AB, Syracuse U., 1946, MS, 1949, PhD, 1953. Vis. research assoc. Harvard Med. Sch., Boston, Mass., 1967-68; vis. scientist Radcliffe Inst. Ind. Study, Cambridge, Mass., 1967-68; acting head dept. computer sci. Pa. State U., Univ. Park, 1973-74, assoc. dean for research, 1973-78, prof. biochemistry, 1975-86, assoc. provost, 1981-85; exec. vice chancellor U. Calif., Riverside, 1985-87, chancellor, 1987—; vis. fellow Cavendish Coll., Cambridge U., Eng., 1984-85; bd. dirs. Am. Council on Pharm. Edn., Chgo., 1988—, Accrediting Commn. for Sr. Colls. & Univs., Oakland, Calif., 1988—, Presley Inst. of Corrections Research & Tng., Sacramento, Calif., 1988; bd. visitors Southwestern U. Sch. Law, Los Angeles, 1988. Mem. Monday Morning Group, Riverside, 1987—; bd. dirs. Community Health Corp., Riverside. 1988—, Riverside Land Conservancy, 1988—. University fellow Syracuse U., 1951-52. Mem. AAUP, AAAS, Am. Chem. Soc., Am. Inst. Chemists, Am. Soc. for Cell Biology, Phi Beta Kappa. Office: Univ Calif-Riverside Office of Chancellor 900 University Ave Riverside CA 92521-4009

SCHRAGER, MINDY RAE, business executive; b. Paterson, N.J., Jan. 18, 1958; d. Julius Maxwell and Miriam (Max) S. Student Middlebury Coll., 1977, Inst. European Studies, Nantes, France, 1977-78; BA, Dickinson Coll., 1979; MBA, Babson Coll., 1981. Cons., Nolan Norton & Co., Lexington, Mass., 1981-86; mgr. sales support Logos Corp., Dedham, Mass., 1986-87; resource ctr. supr. Codex Corp., Canton, Mass., 1987—. Mem. Nat. Assn. Female Execs., Am. Mgmt. Assn. Avocations: reading, travel, music, dance. Home: 80 Walnut St Canton MA 02021

SCHRAMM, DAVID NORMAN, astrophysicist, educator; b. St. Louis, Oct. 25, 1945; s. Marvin and Betty (Math) S.; m. Melinda Holzhauer, 1963 (div. 1979); children: Cary, Brett.; m. Colleen Rae, 1980 (div. 1981); m. Judith J. Zielinski, 1986. S.B. in Physics, MIT, 1967; Ph.D. in Physics, Calif. Inst. Tech., 1971. Research fellow in physics Calif. Inst. Tech., Pasadena, 1971-72; asst. prof. astronomy and physics U. Tex., Austin, 1972-74; assoc. prof. astronomy, astrophysics and physics Enrico Fermi Inst. and the Coll., U. Chgo., 1974-77, prof., 1977—, Louis Block prof. phys. scis., 1982—, prof. conceptual founds. of sci., 1983—, acting chmn. dept. astronomy and astrophysics, 1977, chmn., 1978-84; resident cosmologist Fermilab, 1982-84; cons., lectr. Adler Planetarium; organizer numerous sci. confs.; frequent lectr. in field; bd. trustees Aspen Ctr. for Physics; pres. Big Bang in Aviation Inc. Contbr. over 200 articles to profl. jours.; co-editor: Explosive Nucleosynthesis, 1973; editor: Supernovae, 1977; assoc. editor: Am. Jour. Physics, 1978-81; co-editor: Phys. Cosmology, 1980, Fundamental Problems in Stellar Evolution, 1980, Essays in Nucleosynthesis, 1981; editor: U. Chgo. series Theoretical Astrophysics; Physics Reports, 1981—; editorial bd.: Ann. Revs. Nuclear and Particle Sci., 1976-80; columnist: Outside mag.; co-author: Advanced Stages of Stellar Evolution, 1977. Nat. Graeco-Roman wrestling champion, 1971; recipient Robert J. Trumpler award Astron. Soc. Pacific, 1974, Gravity Research Found. awards, 1974, 75, 76, 80, Humboldt award Fed. Republic Germany, 1987-88. Fellow Am. Phys. Soc., Meteoritical Soc.; mem. Nat. Acad. Sci. (elected, 1986), Am. Astron. Soc. (Helen B. Warner prize 1978, exec. com. planetary sci. div. 1977-79, sec.-treas. high energy astrophysics div. 1979-81), Am. Assn. Physics Tchrs. (Richtmeyer prize 1984), Astron. Soc. Pacific, Internat. Astron. Union (commns. on cosmology, stellar evolution, high energy astrophysics), Aircraft Owners and Pilots Assn., Am. Alpine Club, Austrian Alpine Club, Sigma Xi. Club: Quadrangle. Home: 1163 Cemetery Ln Aspen CO 81611 Office: 5640 S Ellis Ave AAC-140 Chicago IL 60637

SCHRAMM, FREDERIC BERNARD, lawyer; b. Cleve., June 3, 1903; s. A. Bernard and Flora Frederica (Leutz) S. B.S., Case Inst. Tech., 1925; J.D., George Washington U., 1931; LL.M., Western Res. U., 1955. Bar: U.S. Patent Office 1930, D.C. 1931, Ohio 1944, N.Y. 1933, Calif. 1957. Patent atty. Gen. Electric Co., Schenectady, 1925-42; ptnr. Richey & Watts, Cleve., 1942-54, Kendrick, Schramm & Stolzy, Los Angeles, 1954-60, Schramm, Kramer & Sturges, Cleve., 1960-72, Schramm & Knowles, Cleve., 1972-80; instr. Fenn Coll., 1973-74, Cleve. Marshal Law Sch., Cleve. State U., 1974-75. Mem. ABA, Cleve. Bar Assn., Am. Patent Law Assn., Cleve. Patent Law Assn., IEEE, Sigma Xi, Eta Kappa Nu, Tau Beta Pi. Clubs: Kiwanis (pres. 1987-88) (Shaker Heights, Ohio); Univ., Torch (Cleve.). Author: Handbook on Patent Disputes, 1974; contbr. articles to law jours. Office: 3570 Warrensville Center Rd Suite 201 Cleveland OH 44122

SCHRECK, NOLDI, architect; b. Zurich, Switzerland, Sept. 14, 1921; came to Mex., 1950, naturalized, 1975; s. Fritz and Helen (Tschertock) S.; m. Ruth Schuler, Sept. 5, 1953; children—Veronica, Alexis. Student of architecture and art various schs. in Switzerland, Italy and France. Architect several firms, Zurich, 1939-47; assoc. Burton A. Schutt, Architects, Beverly Hills, Calif., 1947-50; pres., owner Noldi Schreck & Assoc., Mexico City. 1950—; archtl. dir. Fed. Welfare Com., Mexico City, 1970-76, Zona Rosa Program, Mexico City; cons. Minister of Tourism, Mexico City, 1976-82; art dir. Soccer World Cup, Mexico City, 1986. Served with Swiss armed forces, 1940-47. Club: Golf Avandaro Valle de Bravo (Mex.). Lodge: Rotary. Avocations: painting; golf; soccer. Home: Hamburgo #151 1st Floor, 06600 Mexico City Mexico Office: Noldi Schreck & Assocs SC, Hamburgo #151, 06600 Mexico City Mexico

SCHREIBER, EDWARD, computer scientist; b. Zagreb, Yugoslavia, Mar. 17, 1943; came to U.S., 1956, naturalized, 1960; s. Hinko and Helen (Iskra) S.; m. Barbara Nelson, 1967 (div. 1969); m. Lea Lusia Hausler, Nov. 7, 1983. BSEE, U. Colo., Denver, 1970. Registered profl. engr. Colo.; cert. data processor. Sr. software scientist Autotrol, Denver, 1972-78; software engr. Sigma Design, Englewood, Colo, 1979-82; founder, v.p. Graphics, Info., Denver, 1982-86; pres. Schrieber Instruments, 1987—; instr. computer sci. U. Colo., Denver, 1971-72, Colo. Women's Coll., Denver, 1972-73, U. Denver, 1983. Contbr. articles on computer graphics to profl. jours. Trustee 1st Universalist Ch., Denver, 1972-78; Dem. candidate for U.S. Ho. of Reps., 1980. Served with U.S. Army, 1960-66. Mem. IEEE, Assn. for Computing Machinery, Nat. Computer Graphics Assn., Mensa. Home and Office: 7250 Eastmoor Dr #226 Denver CO 80237

SCHREIBER, HARRY, JR., management consultant; b. Columbus, Ohio, Apr. 1, 1934; s. C. Harry and Audrey (Sard) S.; B.S., Mass. Inst. Tech., 1955; M.B.A., Boston U., 1958; m. Margaret Ruth Heinzman, June 12, 1955; children—Margaret Elizabeth, Thomas Edward, Amy Katherine Schreiber Garcia. Accountant truck and coach div. Gen. Motors Corp., Pontiac, Mich., 1955; instr. Mass. Inst. Tech., 1958-62; pres. Data-Service, Inc., Boston, 1961-65; pres. Harry Schreiber Assos., Wellesley, Mass., 1965; mgr., nat. dir. merchandising Peat, Marwick, Mitchell & Co., N.Y.C., 1966-70, partner, Chgo., 1970-75; chmn. bd. Close, Martin, Schreiber & Co., 1975-82; partner Deloitte Haskins & Sells, 1983-85; chmn. bd. Harry Schreiber & Assocs., Ltd., 1985—. Staff, Work Simplification Conf. Lake Placid, N.Y., 1960-61. Served to 1st lt. AUS, 1956-58. Mem. Am. Inst. Indsl. Engrs. (chmn. data-processing div. 1964-66, chpt. v.p. 1961, 65, chmn. retail industries div. 1976-78), Com. Internat. Congress Transp. Confs., Assn. for Computing Machinery, Assn. for Systems Mgmt., Inst. Mgmt. Scis., Retail Research Soc., Retail Fin. Execs., Nat. Retail Mchts. Assn. (retail systems specifications com.), Food Distbn. Research Soc. (dir. 1972—, pres. 1974), Japan-Am. Soc. Chgo. Republican. Methodist. Clubs: MIT Faculty; Hidden Creek Country (Reston, Va.); Army and Navy (Washington); Plaza (Chgo.). Home and Office: 12137 Stirrup Rd Reston VA 22091

SCHREIER, THOMAS STEPHEN, accounting firm executive; b. St. Paul, Oct. 13, 1936; s. Mathew Henry and Sophie Marcella (Wesolawski) S.; m. Mary Rae Billstein, Oct. 21, 1961 (dec. May 1986); children—Thomas Stephen, John, Jennifer, Martin. B.A., Coll. St. Thomas, St. Paul, 1960. CPA, Minn. Staff acct. Sevenich & Co., CPA's, St. Paul, 1958-61; sr. acct. Boulay & Co., CPA's, Mpls., 1962-67; ptnr. Schreier & Mazanec, CPA's, St. Paul, 1967-71; mng. ptnr. Schreier, Heimer, Kosbab & Co., CPA's, St. Paul, 1972-87; ptnr. Schreier Kosbab, Cornell, Kahler & Co., CPA's, 1988—; cons. Bus. Furniture, Inc., Mpls., 1981—. Trustee, treas. Children's Hosp., St. Paul, 1980—; trustee St. Thomas Acad., St. Paul, 1981—; chmn. bd. dirs. Archdiocese St. Paul & Mpls., 1988—. Republican. Roman Catholic. Club: North Oaks Country (St. Paul) (v.p. 1985-87, pres. 1988—). Avocations: golf, reading, gardening. Home: 15 Lily Pond Rd Saint Paul MN 55127 Office: Schreier Heimer Kosbab & Co CPAs 3570 N Lexington Ave Saint Paul MN 55126

SCHREUDER, HEIN, research institute executive, business administration educator; b. Djakarta, Indonesia, Dec. 24, 1951; s. Hendrikus and Cornelia

G. (Kiesewetter) S.; divorced; 1 son, Hans Christiaan. M.B.A., Erasmus U., Rotterdam, Netherlands, 1976; Ph.D., Free U. Amsterdam (Netherlands), 1981. Bus. researcher Netherlands Econ. Inst., Rotterdam, 1975-76; head bus. research Econ. and Social Inst., Amsterdam, 1976-81, dir., 1981-84; prof. bus. adminstrn. Maastricht, 1984—; fellow European Inst. Advanced Studies in Mgmt., Brussels, 1981—; vis. scholar U. Wash., Seattle, 1982-83; disting. internat. lectr. Am. Acctg. Assn., 1985; pres. Ecozoek, The Dutch Found. for Pure Econ. Research, 1987-88. Author: (with Jan Klaassen) Corporate Reports, 1980; Social Responsibility, 1981; (with Jan Klaassen) Forecasting, 1982; co-editor: European Accounting Research, 1984; General Economics and Business Economics, 1985; Accounting Research and Practice, 1988. Netherlands Orgn. Advancement of Pure Research grantee, 1982; Fulbright grantee, 1982. Mem. Acad. of Mgmt., European Acctg. Assn., Am. Acctg. Assn., European Group of Orgn. Studies. Home: Gr v Waldeckstraat 35, 6212AN Maastricht The Netherlands Office: U Limburg, PO Box 616, 6200 MD Maastricht The Netherlands

SCHREYER, WILLIAM ALLEN, investment firm executive; b. Williamsport, Pa., Jan. 13, 1928; s. William L. and Elizabeth (Engel) S.; m. Joan Legg, Oct. 17, 1953; 1 dau., Drue Ann. B.A., Pa. State U., 1948. With Merrill Lynch, Inc. and predecessors, N.Y.C., 1948—; v.p. Merrill Lynch, Pierce, Fenner & Smith, Inc., N.Y.C., 1965-78, sales dir., 1969-72, met. regional dir., 1972-73; chmn. Merrill Lynch Govt. Securities, Inc., N.Y.C., 1973-76, exec. v.p. capital markets activities, 1976-78, pres., 1978-85, chmn., 1981-85, pres., chief operating officer, 1982-85; chief exec. officer Merrill Lynch & Co., N.Y.C., 1984—, chmn., 1985—, also bd dirs. various subs.; bd. dirs. N.Y. Stock Exchange, Inc., Schering-Plough Corp. Trustee Med. Center at Princeton, 1974-80, Am. Mgmt. Assns., 1979—; chmn. Sigma Phi Epsilon Ednl. Found., 1979—. Served with USAF, 1955-56. Mem. Securities Industry Assn. (gov. 1979—, vice chmn. 1978-83), Bus. Roundtable (budget task force com.), Com. of Econ. Devel. (trustee), Fgn. Policy Assn. (gov.), Ctr. for Strategic and Internat. Studies (internat. councillor). Roman Catholic. Clubs: Bond (N.Y.C.), River, Links; Saturn (Buffalo); Springdale Golf (Princeton), Nassau; Knights of Malta. Office: Merrill Lynch & Co Inc 165 Broadway New York NY 10080 *

SCHRICKX, WILLEM KAREL, English and American literature educator; b. Antwerp, Belgium, Dec. 30, 1918; s. Frans and Dorothea (Callot) S.; children: Eric, Frank. Licentiate, U. Ghent, Belgium, 1944, Doctorate, 1949, Spl. Doctor, 1956. Tchr. State Normal Sch., Ghent, 1944-47; prof. U. Ghent, 1958-85, now prof. emeritus. Author: Shakespeare, 1956, Shakespeare's Early Contemporaries, 1956, Foreign Envoys and Travelling Players in the Age of Shakespeare and Jonson, 1986. Mem. Maatschappij der Nederlandse Letterkund, Internat. Assn. Univ. Profs. English, Internat. Shakespeare Assn. Home: James Ensorlaan 28, 9820 Ghent Belgium

SCHRIEFFER, JOHN ROBERT, research institute administrator; b. Oak Park, Ill., May 31, 1931; s. John Henry and Louise (Anderson) S.; m. Anne Grete Thomsen, Dec. 30, 1960; children: Anne Bolette, Paul Karsten, Anne Regina. B.S., Mass. Inst. Tech., 1953; M.S., U. Ill., 1954, Ph.D., 1957, Sc.D., 1974; Sc.D. (hon.), Tech. U., Munich, Germany, 1968, U. Geneva, 1968, U. Pa., 1973, U. Cin., 1977, U. Tel Aviv, 1987. NSF postdoctoral fellow U. Birmingham, Eng., also; Niels Bohr Inst., Copenhagen, 1957-58; asst. prof. U. Chgo., 1958-59; asst. prof., then assoc. prof. U. Ill., 1959-62; prof. U. Pa., Phila., 1962-79; Mary Amanda Wood prof. physics U. Pa., 1964-79; Andrew D. White prof. at large Cornell U., 1969-75; prof. U. Calif., Santa Barbara, 1980—, Chancellor's prof., 1984—, dir. Inst. for Theoretical Physics,, 1984—; vis. prof. Niels Bohr Inst., summer 1960, 67, U. Geneva, fall 1963, 67; vis. prof. Stanford U., 1978. Author: Theory of Superconductivity, 1964. Guggenheim fellow Copenhagen, 1967; Recipient Comstock prize Nat. Acad. Sci.; Nobel Prize for Physics, 1972; John Ericsson medal Am. Soc. Swedish Engrs., 1976; Alumni Achievement award U. Ill., 1979; recipient Nat. Medal of Sci., 1984; Exxon faculty fellow, 1979—. Fellow Am. Phys. Soc. (Oliver E. Buckley solid state physics prize 1968), Exxon Faculty, Los Alamos Nat. Lab.; mem. Nat. Acad. Sci., Am. Acad. Arts & Scis., Am. Philos. Soc. (Nat. Medal Sci. 1985), Royal Danish Acad. Scis. and Letters. Office: Inst Theoretical Physics U Calif Santa Barbara CA 93106 *

SCHRIESHEIM, ALAN, research administrator; b. N.Y.C., Mar. 8, 1930; s. Morton and Frances (Greenberg) S.; m. Beatrice D. Brand, June 28, 1953; children: Laura Lynn, Robert Alan. B.S. in Chemistry, Poly. Inst. Bklyn., 1951; Ph.D. in Phys. Organic Chemistry, Pa. State U., 1954. Chemist Nat. Bur. Standards, 1954-56; with Exxon Research & Engring. Co., 1956-83, dir. corp. research, 1975-79; gen. mgr. Exxon engring., 1979-83; sr. dep. lab. dir. Argonne Nat. Lab., 1983-84, lab. dir., 1984—; Karcher lectr. U. Okla., 1977; Hurd lectr. Northwestern U., 1980; Rosensteil lectr. Brandeis U., 1982; Welch Found. lectr., 1987; co-chmn. bd. on chem. scis. and tech. NRC, 1980-85; mem. com. to define future role of chemistry, 1983-84; vis. com. chemistry dept. MIT, 1978-85; mem. adv. com. mech. engring. and aerospace dept. Princeton (N.J.) U., 1983-87; mem. Pure and Applied Chemistry Com.; del. to People's Republic of China, 1978; mem. U.S. nat. com. Internat. Union Pure and Applied Chemistry, 1982-85; mem. adv. com. process research and devel. Nat. Bur. Standards, 1979-83, mem. bd. assessment of programs, 1983-86; mem. magnetic fusion adv. com. Dept. Energy, 1983-86; mem. adv. com. Div. Phys. Scis. U. Chgo.; mem. DOE Energy Research Adv. Bd., 1983-85; mem. Congl. Adv. Com. on Sci. and Tech., 1985—; mem. com. on advanced fossil energy techs. NRC, 1983-85; mem. vis. coms. Stanford (Calif.) U., U. Utah, Tex. Agrl. and Mech. U., Lehigh U.; bd. govs. Argonne Nat. Lab.; mem. adv. com. on space systems and tech. NASA, 1987—; mem. nuclear engring. and engring. physics vis. com. U. Wis., Madison; mem. comml. space adv. com. U.S. Dept. of Commerce, 1988—; mem. Council of Great Lakes Govs. Regional Econ. Devel. Commn., 1987—, rev. bd. Ceompact Ignition Tokamak Princeton U., 1988—; advisor Sears Investment Mgmt. Co., 1988—; bd. dirs. Petroleum Research Fund, ARCH Venture Corp., Heico Instruments, Valley Indsl. Assn., Council on Superconductivity for Am. Competitiveness. Bd. editors: Chem. Tech.; mem. editorial bd. Research and Devel., 1988, Superconductor Industry Mag., 1988—. Mem. spl. vis. com. Field Mus. of Natural History, Chgo., 1987—; bd. dirs. LaRabida Children's Hosp. and Research Ctr., Children's Meml. Inst. for Edn. and Research. Fellow N.Y. Acad. Scis.; mem. Am. Chem. Soc. (recipient award petroleum chemistry 1969, chmn. petroleum div., councilor), Nat. Conf. Advancement Research, Am. Petroleum Inst. (com. on refinery equipment), Am. Inst. Chem. Engrs., Gas Research Inst. (research coordination council), AAAS, Sigma Xi, Phi Lambda Upsilon. Club: Cosmos (Washington); Chicago, Economic, Commercial (Chgo.). Home: 1440 N Lake Shore Dr Apt 31AC Chicago IL 60610 Office: Argonne Nat Lab 9700 S Cass Ave Argonne IL 60439

SCHROEDER, OLE, shipping concern executive; b. Oslo, Norway, May 24, 1919; s. Ole and Aagot (Schjoett) S.; m. Ruth Farstad, Apr. 28, 1945; children: Anne, Elisabeth, Cathrine, Ole Christian. Cert. edn., Comml. Sch. U., Oxford, Eng., 1939. Mng. dir. A.O. Andersen & Co. A/S, Oslo, 1955-65; mng. dir., chmn. bd. dirs. Anco Tanker Service A/S, Oslo, 1965-70; chmn. bd. dirs., shipowner Osco Group, Oslo, 1970—; chmn. bd. dirs. Opak A/S, Oslo, 1960-85, Grand Hotel A/S, Oslo, 1960-85. Clubs: Oslo Conservative, Oslo Tennis, Oslo Hoeyre, Royal Norwegian Yacht (Oslo); Hankø (Norway) Yacht; Royal Bachelors (Gøteborg, Sweden), Norske Selskab. Office: Osco Group, Hovfaret 4, 0275 Oslo 2 Norway

SCHROEDER, RITA MOLTHEN, chiropractor; b. Savanna, Ill., Oct. 25, 1922; d. Frank J. and Ruth J. (McKenzie) Molthen; m. Richard H. Schroeder, Apr. 23, 1948 (div.); children—Richard, Andrew, Barbara, Thomas, Paul, Madeline. Student, Chem. Engring., Immaculate Heart Coll., 1940-41, UCLA, 1941, Palmer Sch. of Chiropractic, 1947-49; D. Chiropractic, Cleve. Coll. of Chiropractic, 1961. Engring.-tooling design data coordinator Douglas Aircraft Co., El Segundo, Santa Monica and Long Beach, Calif., 1941-47; pres. Schroeder Chiropractic, Inc., 1982—; dir. Pacific States Chiropractic Coll., 1978-80, pres. 1980-81. Recipient Palmer Coll. Ambassador award, 1973. Parker Chiropractic Research Found. Ambassador award, 1976, Coll. Ambassador award Life West Chiropractic Coll. Mem. Internat. Chiropractic Assn., Calif. Chiropractic Assn., Internat. Chiropractic Assn. Calif., Assn. Am. Chiropractic Coll. Presidents, Council Chiropractic Edn. (Pacific State Coll. rep.). Home: 9870 N Millbrook Ave Fresno CA 93710 Office: Schroeder Chiropractic Inc 2535 N Fresno Ave Fresno CA 93703

SCHROEDER, ROBERT ANTHONY, lawyer; b. Bendena, Kans., May 19, 1912; s. Anthony and Nanon (Bagby) S.; m. Janet Manning, Nov. 21, 1936; 1 child, Robert Breathitt. LLB cum laude, U. Kans., 1937. Bar: Mo. 1937. Atty. Allstate Ins. Co., Chgo., 1937-38; assoc. Madden, Freeman, Madden & Burke, Kansas City, Mo., 1938-48; ptnr. Swofford, Schroeder & Shankland, Kansas City, 1948-59; pvt. practice law 1959-67; ptnr. Schroeder & Schroeder, 1967-84; commr. 16th Jud. Circuit, 1974-80, Appellate Jud. Commn. of Mo., 1980-86; pres., bd. dirs. Roxbury State Bank, Kans., 1954-77, chmn. bd. dirs., 1977—; chmn. bd. dirs. Roxbury Bancshares Inc., 1984—; pres. Douglas County Investment Co.; chmn. bd. dirs. Hub State Bank, 1974-82; hon. chmn. Mark Twain Bank Noland, 1982—; regional dir. Mark Twain Bancshares; sr. counsellor Mo. Bar, 1987. Author: Twenty-Five Years Under The Missouri Plan, Twenty-Five Years Experience with Merit Judicial Selection in Missouri; editorial bd.: Kan. Bar Jour, 1935-36. Hon. trustee Kansas City Art Inst.; bd. dirs. Mo. Inst. for Justice; mem. dirs. club U. Kans. Williams Ednl. Fund, 1978-81, execs. club, 1981-85, All Am. club, 1986—. Recipient Disting. Alumnus award U. Kans. Sch. Law; hon. fellow Harry S. Truman Library Inst., disting. charter fellow Kansas City Bar Found.; donor Robert A. Schroeder endowed chair for disting. prof., 1981; established Robert A. Schroeder scholarships and fellowship at U. Kans. Sch. Law.; donor Roberta Schroeder Scholarship at Midway High Sch., Kans., 1985. Fellow Am. Coll. Probate Counsel, Am. Bar Found., Kans. U. Law Soc. (trustee 1970-74); mem. ABA (Mo. chmn. membership com. 1961-65, del. 1966-70, lawyer referral com.), Mo. Bar Found. (v.p. 1965-69, pres. 1969-73), Mo. Bar Assn. (bd. govs. 1959-67), Mo. Bar (exec. com. 1963-67, pres. 1965-66, v.p., pres. found., chmn. legal edn. com. 1964-65, chmn. cts. and judiciary com. 1971-72, mem. bench and bar com. 1970-80, vice chmn. 1970-71; Pres.'s award 1972), Bar Assn. State Kans. (hon. life), Kansas City Bar Assn. (pres. 1957-58, chmn. exec. com., chmn. law day com., chmn. program com. 1968-70, chmn. prepaid legal services com. 1975-76; Achievement award 1976), Am. Judicature Soc. (bd. dirs. 1967-69), Nat. Legal Aid and Defender Assn., U. Kans. Law Alumni Assn. Greater Kansas City (past pres.), Order of Coif, Delta Tau Delta, Phi Delta Phi. Club: Mason. Office: 11324 Madison St Kansas City MO 64114

SCHROEDER, WAYNE HAROLD, administrative executive; b. Milw., Feb. 23, 1944; s. Harold and Carice (Duval) S.; m. Mary Lynn Comerford, June 16, 1971; stepchildren: Kelly, Steven; children: Phillip, Amy. AA, U. Wis., Oshkosh, 1984, BA cum laude, 1987. Draftsman Rasche Schroeder Spransy Architects, Milw., 1963-65, Shattuck Siewert Architects, Neenah, Wis., 1965-66; draftsman, engring. technician, project engr. Appleton (Wis.) Papers Inc., 1966-82, sr. project engr., 1982-84, engring. support services supr., 1984-87, adminstrv. services mgr. Research and Devel. Engring. Dept., 1987—; bd. dirs. adv. Fox Valley Technical Coll., 1985-86. Pres. Park Commn., Menasha, 1976; v.p. Tri County Ice Arena, Menasha, 1979; adv. bd. mem. Appleton Area Sch. Dist. Drafting Com., 1984-85; U. Wis. Oshkosh Acad. Council Rep., 1985-86. Mem. Internat. Facility Mgmt. Assn., Am. Inst. Design and Drafting, U. Wis. Oshkosh Alumni Assn. Home: 1268 Mayer St Menasha WI 54952 Office: Appleton Papers Inc 825 E Wisconsin Ave Appleton WI 54911

SCHROETER, KLAUS MAX PAUL, editor, literary critic; b. Königsberg, German Dem. Republic, July 3, 1931; s. Hans and Ilse (Brummund) S. PhD, U. Hamburg, 1961. Asst. editor Goethe Bibliography, Hamburg, Fed. Republic Germany, 1957-66; assoc. prof. SUNY, Stony Brook, 1966-67, prof., 1972-81; asst. editor Goethe and Klopstock Bibliography, Hamburg, 1967-69; prof. Columbia U., N.Y.C., 1969-72; gen. editor Rowohlt Publs., Hamburg, 1982—; cons. New Columbia Ency., N.Y.C., 1971-72; vis. prof. U. Hamburg, 1974-75, U. Amsterdam, The Netherlands, 1976-77. Author: Thomas Mann, 1964, Heinrich Mann, 1966, Heinrich Böll, 1982, Wolfgang Goethe, 1983. Mem. Germanistic Soc. Am. (sec. 1972-81), Goethe Soc., Thomas Mann Soc., PEN Fed. Republic Germany. Home: Abendrothsweg 26, D-2000 Hamburg 20 Federal Republic of Germany Office: Rowohlt Publs, 17 Hamburger Strasse, D-2057 Reinbek Federal Republic of Germany

SCHROETER, OTTO FERDINAND, data communications engineer; b. Elbing, Germany, Apr. 16, 1924; s. Heinrich Ferdinand and Kate Margarete (Adloff) S.; m. Gertrude Charlotte Rogosch, Sept. 27, 1949; children—Detlef Ferdinand, Jurgen Otto. Engr. Grad., H.T.L. Gauss, Berlin, 1949. Cert. telecommunciations engr., Germany, France. Various mng. positions IBM Germancy, Stuttgart, 1955-61; mgr. spl. systems IBM Europe, Paris, 1962-67; mgr. communications systems IBM Germany, 1967-71; dir., div. mgr. S.E.L. A.G., 1972-81; gen. mgr. European Data Communication Ctr., ITT Europe, Colnbrook, Eng., 1982-84; owner, cons. engr. Data Communications, Lossburg, Fed. Republic Germany, 1985—. Contbr. articles to profl. jours. Served to 2d lt. Signal Corps Germany, 1943-45. Mem. German Engring. Assn., German Assn. Data Protection and Data Security. Liberal. Lutheran. Avocations: hiking; studying German history. Home: Breuningerweg 17, D-7298 Lossburg Federal Republic of Germany

SCHROPP, JAMES HOWARD, lawyer; b. Lebanon, Pa., June 20, 1943; s. Howard J. and Maud E. (Parker) S.; m. Jo Ann Simpson, Sept. 4, 1965; children: James A., John C., Jeffrey M., Jeremy M. BA, U. Richmond, 1965; JD, Georgetown U., 1973. Bar: D.C. 1973, U.S. Supreme Ct. 1980. Asst. gen. counsel SEC, Washington, 1973-79; ptnr. Fried, Frank, Harris, Shriver & Jacobson, Washington, 1979—; adj. prof. Georgetown U., Washington, 1982-86. Mem. ABA (discovery com. litigation sect. 1984-86, tender offer litigation subcom. corp. banking and bus. law sect. 1985-86, task force Broker-Dealer Compliance Supervisory Procedures 1987—). Office: Fried Frank Harris et al 1001 Pennsylvania Ave NW Suite 800 Washington DC 20004

SCHROTH, PETER W(ILLIAM), lawyer, educator; b. Camden, N.J., July 24, 1946; s. Walter and Patricia Anne (Page) S.; m. Keven Anne Murphy, Jan. 2, 1986; children: Laura Salome Erickson-Schroth, Julia James. AB, Shimer Coll., 1966; JD, U.Chgo., 1969, M.Comp.L., 1971; S.J.D, U. Mich., 1979; postgrad. U. Freiburg (W.Ger.), Faculté Internationale pour l'Enseignement de Droit Comparé; MBA, Rensselaer Poly. Inst., 1988. Bar: Ill. 1969, N.Y. 1979, Conn. 1985. Asst. prof. So. Meth. U., 1973-77; fellow in law and humanities Harvard U., 1976-77, vis. scholar, 1980-81; assoc. prof. N.Y. Law Sch., 1977-81; prof. law Hamline U., St. Paul, 1981-83; dep. gen. counsel Equator Bank Ltd., 1984-87, v.p., dep. gen. counsel, Equator Holdings Ltd. 1987—; adj. prof. law U. Conn., 1985—, of mgmt. Rensselaer Poly. Inst., 1988—; . Mem. ABA, Am. Fgn. Law Assn., Am. Assn. Comparative Study of Law, Internat. Bar Assn., Assn. Trial Lawyers Am., Conn. Civil Liberties Union (bd. dirs.), Environ. Law Inst. (assoc.), Columbia U Peace Seminar (assoc.). Author: Foreign Investment in the United States, 2d edit., 1977; (with Stiefel) Products Liability: European Proposals and American Experience, 1981; Handbook for Practice of Comparative Law, 1983; bd. editors Am. Jour. Comparative Law, 1981-84; editor in chief ABA Environ. Law Symposium, 1980-83; contbr. articles to profl. jours. Office: Equator House 111 Charter Oak Ave Hartford CT 06106

SCHROTT, NORMAN, clinical social worker; b. N.Y.C., Jan. 26, 1938; s. Walter Quido Otto and Anna (Klein) S.; B.A. in Sociology, Cleve. State U., 1972; M.S. in Social Planning and Adminstrn. (grantee State of Ohio 1974-76), Case Western Res. U., 1976; m. Janet Ann Cupolo, July 25, 1964. Lic. Ind. Social Worker, Ohio. Adminstrv. specialist div. social services Cuyahoga County Welfare Dept., Cleve., 1972-74, foster care specialist, 1976-79, child abuse supr., 1979-80, protective services supr., 1980—. Served with U.S. Army, 1962-65. Mem. Acad. Cert. Social Workers, Nat. Assn. Social Workers, Nat. Conf. Social Welfare, Am. Public Welfare Assn., Am. Acad. Polit. and Social Scis., Nat. Audubon Soc., Am. Orchid Soc. Club: Kiwanis. Home: 25925 Lake Rd Bay Village OH 44140 Office: 3955 Euclid Ave Cleveland OH 44115

SCHUBERT, BLAKE H., corporate executive, lawyer; b. Wheeling, W.Va., Apr. 21, 1939; s. John Arnold and Esther Elizabeth (Masters) S.; m. Carol Jean Cramp, Jan. 13, 1962; children—Cheryl Lynn, Charles Bradley, Elisabeth Anne. B.A., Ohio Wesleyan U., 1961; J.D., U. Chgo., 1964. Bar: Ill. 1964, U.S. Dist. Ct. (no. dist.) Ill. 1968. Atty., Brunswick Corp., Chgo., 1964-68; asst. group counsel FMC Corp., Chgo., 1968-73; gen. counsel Dresser Tool Group, Chgo., 1973-79; chmn. Schubert Securities Corp., Oak Park, Ill., 1979-84, Inter-Am. Investments, Inc., Oak Park, 1980—; gen. ptnr. Investment Trust Ltd., St. Petersburg, Fla., 1981—, Inter-Am. Fund, Oak Park, 1982—, Inter-Am. Fund I, Oak Park, 1982-87, Inter-Am. Fund II, Oak Park, 1984—; chmn. Compath Video Corp., Oak Park, 1984-85; lectr. Am. Inst. Banking, 1965, Chgo. Inst. Fin. Studies, 1984-85. Author: The Well-Kept Secrets of Investing, 1982. Chmn., 1st United Ch. Endowment Fund, Oak Park, 1975-80, Park Forest Co-op. (Ill.), 1966-70. Recipient Bancroft-Whitney Prize U. Chgo., 1964. Mem. Ill. State Bar Assn., Chgo. Bd. Options Exchange. Home: 522 Linden Ave Oak Park IL 60302 Office: 175 W Jackson Blvd Chicago IL 60604

SCHUBERT, ELIZABETH M(AY), paralegal administrative assistant; b. Hamilton, Ohio, Sept. 10, 1913; d. A(ndreas) Gordon and Grace Symmes (Laxford) S.; B.S. in Edn. cum laude, Miami U., 1933. Sec., Beta Kappa Nat. Frat., Oxford, Ohio, 1931-38; adminstrv. asst. to dir. Ohio State Employment Service, Columbus, 1938-45, supr. procedures, 1945-47; adminstrv. asst. to pres. Schaible Co., Cin., 1948-50; paralegal adminstrv. asst. to Gordon H. Scherer, Atty.-at-Law, mem. U.S. Congress, U.S. del. to UN, U.S. rep. to exec. bd. UNESCO, Paris, 1950—. Mem. Phi Beta Kappa. Republican. Presbyn. Home: 1071 Celestial St Apt 1701 Cincinnati OH 45202 Office: 1071 Celestial St Suite 2103 Cincinnati OH 45202

SCHUBERT, MARTIN WILLIAM, investment bank executive; b. N.Y.C., Oct. 27, 1935; s. Charles and Ann (Kaplan) S.; m. Irene Ginsberg, Jan. 17, 1960 (div. July 1974); children: Lisa, Douglas, Jeffrey; m. Carol Sue Howard, Dec. 28, 1986.. BA, Bklyn. Coll., 1957; MBA, CCNY, 1962; postgrad., NYU, 1962-65. Trader Phillip Bros. (PHIBRO), N.Y.C., 1959-64; sr. v.p. Rosenthal & Rosenthal Inc., N.Y.C., 1964-82; pres. Rosenthal Internat. Ltd., N.Y.C., 1976-82; chmn., chief exec. officer European Interam. Fin. Co., N.Y.C., 1982—; bd. dirs. Singer & Friedlander Ltd., London; chmn., bd. dirs. Finex Corp., N.Y.C., 1985-87; vice chmn., bd. dirs. Trade Credit Underwriters Agy., N.Y.C., 1985-86; mng. ptnr., bd. dirs. Eurinam Capital Ptnrs., N.Y.C., 1985-86. Co-author: Pick's Currency Annual, 1963, Challenge of International Finance, 1966; contbr. numerous articles on internat. fin. to profl. jours. Mem. U.S. Council of Mex.-U.S. Bus. Com. Council of Americas, 1987—. Republican. Home: 245 E 40th St Apt 25C New York NY 10016 Office: European Interamerican Fin Corp 400 Madison Ave Suite 401 New York NY 10017

SCHUBERT, NANCY ELLEN, beauty industry executive, management consultant, franchise director; b. Chgo., June 25, 1945; d. Raymond James and Kathleen Mary (Gibbons) Nugent; m. Emil Joseph Schubert, Jan. 14, 1967; children—James Bryant, Erin Heather, Shannon Kathleen. B.F.A., Mundelein Coll., 1968. Freelance artist, Chgo., 1968; tchr. St. Pius X Sch., Lombard, Ill., 1975-76; pres., treas., dir. Super Style, Inc., Hoffman Estates, Ill., 1981—, Super Six, Inc., Glendale Heights, Ill., 1983—, N.E.S. Mgmt. Inc., Schaumburg, Ill., 1985—, Super Style III, Inc., Berwyn, Ill., 1985—; created and developed Super Style concept and system of operation; created SuperStyle logo and design trademarked in 1983. Mem. Cermak Plaza Mcht. Assn. (bd. dirs.). Republican. Roman Catholic. Avocations: licensed pilot, downhill skiing, horseback riding. Office: Super Style Inc 707 W Golf Rd Hoffman Estates IL 60194

SCHUCK, MARJORIE MASSEY, publisher, editor, authors' consultant; b. Winchester, Va., Oct. 9, 1921; d. Carl Frederick and Margaret Harriet (Parmele) Massey; student U. Minn., 1941-43, New Sch., N.Y.C., 1948, N.Y. U., 1952, 54-55; m. Ernest George Metcalfe, Dec. 2, 1943 (div. Oct. 1949); m. 2d, Franz Schuck, Nov. 11, 1953 (dec. Jan. 1958). Mem. editorial bd. St. Petersburg Poetry Assn., 1967-68; co-editor, pub. poetry Venture Mag., St. Petersburg, Fla., 1968-69, editor, pub., 1969-79; co-editor, pub. Poetry Venture Quar. Essays, Vol. I, 1968-69, Vol. 2, 1970-71; pub., editor poetry anthologies, 1972—; founder, owner, pres. Valkyrie Press, Inc. (name changed to Valkyrie Pub. House 1980), 1972—; cons. designs and formats, trade publs. and ann. reports, lit. books and pamphlets, 1973—; founder Valkyrie Press Roundtable Workshop and Forum for Writers, 1975-79; established Valkyrie Press Reference Library, 1976-80; pub., editor The Valkyrie Internat. Newsletter, 1986—; exec. dir. Inter-Cultural Forum Villanor Ctr., Tampa, Fla., 1987—; pres. Found. for Human Potentials, Inc., Tampa, 1988—; lectr. in field. Judge poetry and speech contests Gulf Beach Women's Club, 1970, Fine Arts Festival dist. 14. Am. Fedn. Women's Clubs, 1970, South and West, Inc., 1972, The Sunstone Rev., 1973, Internat. Toastmistress Clubs, 1974, 78, Beaux Arts Poetry Festival, 1983; judge Fla. Gov.'s Screenwriters Competition, 1984—. Corr.-rec. sec. Women's Aux. Hosp. for Spl. Surgery, N.Y.C., 1947-59; active St. Petersburg Mus. Fine Arts (charter), St. Petersburg Sister City Com., St. Petersburg Arts Center Assn.; mem. Orange Belt express com. 1988 Centennial Celebration for St. Petersburg, mem. Com. of 100 of Pinellas County, Inc., exec. bd., 1975-77, membership chmn., 1975-77; pub. relations chmn. Soc. for prevention Cruelty to Animals, 1968-71, bd. dirs., 1968-71, 75-77; mem. Pinellas County Arts Council, 1977-79, chmn., 1977-78; mem. grant rev. panel for lit. Fine Arts Council of Fla., 1979. Named One of 76 Fla. Patriots, Fla. Bicentennial Commn., 1976; a recipient 1st ann. People of Dedication award Salvation Army, Tampa, 1984. Mem. Acad. Am. Poets, Fla. Suncoast Writers' Confs. (founder, co-dir., lectr. 1973-83, adv. bd. 1984—), Fla. Poets Assn., Com. Small Mag. Editors and Pubs., Coordinating Council Lit. Mags., Friends of Library of St. Petersburg, Suncoast Mgmt. Inst. (exec. bd.; chmn. Women in Mgmt. 1977-78), Pi Beta Phi. Democrat. Episcopalian. Author: Speeches and Writings for Cause of Freedom, 1973. Contbr. poetry to profl. jours. Home: 8245 26th Ave N Saint Petersburg FL 33710 Office: 8245 26th Ave N Saint Petersburg FL 33710

SCHUCK, ROBERT DAVID, entrepreneur; b. Birmingham, Eng., May 20, 1948; s. Karel Wilhelm and Violet May (Condick) S.; m. Alexandra Maureen Hanley, Nov. 26, 1984; children: Louie, Maximillian. Diploma in Bus. Studies, Eng., 1966. Mgr. dept. Marks and Spencer, London, 1966-68; specialist sales 3M Co., London, 1968-69; owner restaurants, London, 1969-73, property developer, London, 1973-84, Cata Pult Catamarans, London, 1984—; dir. Gulf Investments Internat. Ltd., London 1984—, Cata Pult Craft Internat. Ltd., London 1986—, Gulf Inversiones Internat. S.A., Spain 1985—; pres. Cata Pult Catamarans Inc., Fla. 1987—. Co-designer: boat design, 1985, 86 (recipient Silkcut Nautical award, 1986). Office: Cata Pult Cataramans Inc 1323 SE 17th St Suite 101 Fort Lauderdale FL 33316

SCHUCK, VICTORIA, political science educator; b. Oklahoma City, Mar. 16, 1909; d. Anthony B. and Anna (Priebe) S. A.B. with great distinction, Stanford U., 1930, M.A., 1931, Ph.D., 1937; L.H.D. (hon.), Mt. Vernon Coll., 1980. Univ. fellow Stanford U., 1931-33, teaching asst., 1934-35, acting instr., 1935-36, instr., 1936-37; asst. prof. Fla. State Coll. Women, 1937-40; mem. faculty Mt. Holyoke Coll., 1940-77, prof. polit. sci., 1950-77; pres. Mt. Vernon Coll., Washington, 1977-80; vis. lectr. Smith Coll., 1948-49; vis. prof. Stanford U., summer 1952, vis. scholar polit. sci., 1982—; guest scholar Brookings Instn., 1967-68, summers 68, 70, Woodrow Wilson Ctr. Internat. Scholars, 1980; Prin. program analyst, planning for local bds. OPA, 1942-44; rep. Am. Polit. Sci. Assn. UN World Conf. of UN Decade for Women, Nairobi, Kenya, 1985; sponsor. Women's Fgn. Policy Council, N.Y., 1986; cons. Office Temporary Controls, 1945-47; mem. internat. secretariat UN Conf. San Francisco, 1945; mem. Mass. Commn. Interstate Coop., 1957-60, U. Mass. Bldg. Authority, 1960-68; Mass. adv. com. U.S. Commn. Civil Rights, 1962-78; cons. GAO, 1980-82; non-govtl. rep. UN Commn. on Status of Women, Vienna, Austria, 1988. Regional editor: Ency. Brit., 1958-61; co-editor and contbr.: Women Organizing: An Anthology, 1979, New England Politics, 1981; contbr. articles to profl. jours. Mem. Pres.'s Commn. Registration and Voting Participation, 1963; mem. Berkshire Community Coll. Planning Com., 1964-68, Greenfield Community Coll. Planning Com., 1965-68, Mass. Bd. Higher Edn., 1976-77; mem. Town of South Hadley Planning Bd., 1959-67, chmn., 1961-67; trustee U. Mass., 1958-65. Grantee Haynes Found., 1951-52; Grantee Asia Soc., 1971-72. Mem. Am. Polit. Sci. Assn. (sec. 1959-60, v.p. 1970-71), New Eng. Polit. Sci. Assn. (pres. 1950-51), Northeastern Polit. Sci. Assn. (pres. 1972-73), AAUW (pres. Mass. 1946-50, nat. chmn. legis. program com., bd. dirs. 1965-69), Am. Soc. Pub. Adminstrn., AAUP (pres. Mt. Holyoke 1962-64), Internat. Polit. Sci. Assn., Phi Beta Kappa, Chi Omega, Mortar Bd. (hon.). Club: Cosmopolitan (N.Y.C.). Home: 4000 Cathedral Ave NW Washington DC 20016

SCHUCKER, CHARLES, artist, educator; b. Gap, Pa., Jan. 19, 1908; s. Gabriel and Carrie (Musgrove) S.; m. Margaret Hamilton Rust, Apr. 16, 1938; children—Cheryl Chang, Carrie Schucker Gerowitz. Grad. Md. Inst. Fine and Mech. Arts, 1934. Instr. NYU, 1947-54, CCNY, 1955-56; prof.

Pratt Inst., 1956-74, emeritus, 1974—; one-man shows include: Chgo. Art Inst., 1947, Macbeth Gallery, N.Y.C. 1946, 49, 53, Passedoit Gallery, N.Y.C., 1955, 58, Howard Wise Gallery, N.Y.C., Whitney Mus. Am. Art, 1971, Max Hutchinson Gallery, N.Y.C., 1972, 74, 78, Katonah Art Gallery, 1955, 73, 78, Gallery Camino Real, Boca Raton, Fla., 1980, 81, 84, Rotunda Gallery Inaugural, Bklyn. Borough Hall, 1981, Solomon Downtown, Los Angeles, 1984; exhibited group shows including Mus. Modern Art, Bertha Schaefer Gallery, Carnegie Inst., Walker Art Ctr., Contemporary Am. Painting, Met. Mus. Art, Art in 20th Century, Phila. Acad. Fine Art, Calif. Palace Annual, Chgo. Art Inst., San Francisco Mus. Art, Whitney Mus. Am. Art, Bklyn. Mus., Amherst Coll., Contemporary Arts Ctr., SUNY-Potsdam, Hotel Stamford Plaza, Gallery Camino Real, Boca Raton, Fla., Katonah Gallery, N.Y., others; represented in permanent collections Am. Acad. Arts and Letters, Bklyn. Mus., Bklyn. Heights Library, Newark Mus., New Britain (Conn.) Mus., Whitney Mus. Am. Art, Harcourt, Brace Jovanovitch, Louisa and John I. H. Baur, Roy Neuberger, Percy Uris, Paul Ferber, Howard Wise, Woodhull Hosp., Dr. Janna Claire Collins, Archtl. Digest, Katonah Village Library, others. Recipient Henry Walters Traveling Fellowship, Guggenheim Found. Fellowship, 1953, Audubon prize for Oil Painting, 1949; Childe Hassam prize, AAAL, 1952, Bklyn. and L.I. Biennial award for Oil Painting, 1948, 50; subject of video documentary Schucker, Portrait in Color, 1986. Address: Studio 33 Middagh St Brooklyn Heights NY 11201-1339

SCHUEBELIN, PETER WALTER, food products executive; b. Bern, Switzerland, May 21, 1940; arrived in France, 1975; s. Walter and Marie (Kern) S.; m. Mirjam C. Lecher, Dec. 4, 1970; children: Diana S., Rodrigue G. Diploma in physics, U. Bern, 1964, PhD, 1967. Fellow Cern, Geneva, 1964-69; asst. physicist Brookhaven Nat. Lab., Upton, N.Y., 1969-71, assoc. physicist, 1971-74, full physicist, 1974-75; maitre of research CRN, Strasbourg, France, 1975-80; chief exec. officer Unicorn Corp., F 67270 Bossendorf, France, 1980—, Gelcorn Corp., Bossendorf, 1984—; pres. Unicorn Switzerland, CH 5524 Niederwil, 1986—. Contbr. articles to profl. jours. Served to capt. Swiss Army, 1960-69. Home and Office: S'Vierthalers, 67270 Bossendorf, Alsace France

SCHUETZ, CARY EDWARD, thermophysics engineer; b. San Diego, Dec. 6, 1953; s. Celestine Edward and Doris Marjorie (Berquist) S.; m. June Wong, Mar. 11, 1983. BS in Mech. Engring., U. Calif.-Santa Barbara, 1978. Engr., U. Calif.-Santa Barbara, 1976-78; engr./scientist McDonnell Douglas Corp., Long Beach, Calif., 1978-81; sr. engr. Northrop Corp., Los Angeles, 1981—. Mem. AIAA, Internat. Platform Assn. Designed and built thermoelectric generator, 1978; developed advanced state of the art in aircraft ice-prevention technology, 1980; formulator thermal-structural interface theory, 1985; contbr. articles on automatic computational methods for numerical heat transfer, 1982, 84. Home: 1927 N Fairview St Burbank CA 91505 Office: Northrop Corp 1 Northrop Ave 3813/82 Hawthorne CA 90250

SCHUHL, JEAN-FRANCOIS, orthopedic surgeon; b. Dijon, France, June 20, 1945; s. Lucien and Janine S.; m. Sylvie Cotonea, Dec. 17, 1971; children: Pierre, Mathieu. MD, Lyon, France, 1972. Intern Hospices Civils Clin., Lyon, 1970-76, resident, 1976-78, chief, 1976-78; orthopaedic surgeon specializing in hand surgery Red Cross Hosp., Bois-Guillaume, France, 1978—; ins. med. cons. AXA Group, Bois-Guillaume, 1980—; legal cons. Cour d'Appel, Rouen, France, 1985—; pres. med. cons. clin. Panorama du Medicin, Paris, 1985—. Contbr. articles to profl. jours. Grantee Sofcot, Paris, 1980. Mem. Soc. Europeenne Chirugie Epaule et Coude, French Orthopaedic Soc., French Hand Surgery Soc., Sport Medicine Soc., Chines-French Med. Soc. Home: 1071 Rue de l'Eglise, 76230 Bois Guillaume France Office: Hopital de La Croix Rouge, Chemin De La Breteque, 76230 Bois-Guillaume France

SCHUL, BILL DEAN, psychological administrator, author; b. Winfield, Kans., Mar. 16, 1928; s. Fred M. and Martha Mildred (Miles) S.; B.A., Southwestern Coll., 1952; M.A., U. Denver, 1954; Ph.D., Am. Internat. U., 1977; m. Virginia Louise Duboise, Aug. 3, 1952; children—Robert Dean, Deva Elizabeth. Reporter and columnist Augusta (Kans.) Daily Gazette, 1954-58, Wichita (Kans.) Eagle-Beacon, 1958-61; Kans. youth dir. under auspices of Kans. Atty. Gen., 1961-65; Kans. state dir. Seventh Step Found., Topeka, 1965-66; mem. staff Dept. Preventive Psychiatry, Menninger Found., Topeka, Kans., 1966-71; dir. cons. Center Improvement Human Functioning, Wichita, 1975—; author: (with Edward Greenwood) Mental Health in Kansas Schools, 1965; Let Me Do This Thing, 1969; (with Bill Larson) Hear Me, Barabbas, 1969; How to Be An Effective Group Leader, 1975; The Secret Power of Pyramids, 1975; (with Ed Pettit) The Psychic Power of Pyramids, 1976, Pyramids: The Second Reality, 1979; The Psychic Power of Animals, 1977; Psychic Frontiers of Medicine, 1977. Bd. dirs. Recreation Commn., Topeka, United Funds, Topeka, Adamic Inst., Trees for Life; v.p. Pegasus Way; mem. adv. bd. Clayton U. Served with USN, 1945-46. Recipient John H. McGinnis Meml. award for Nonfiction, 1972, Am. Freedom Found. award, 1966, Spl. Appreciation award Kans. State Penitentiary, 1967. Mem. Acad. of Parapsychology and Medicine, Kans. Council for Children and Youth (pres. 1965-66), Assn. for Strenghtening the Higher Realities and Aspirations of Man (pres. 1970-71), Smithsonian Inst. Club: Lions (pres. 1957). Address: Rural Route 3 Winfield KS 67156

SCHULER, ALISON KAY, lawyer; b. West Point, N.Y., Oct. 1, 1948; d. Richard Hamilton and Irma (Sanken) S.; m. Lyman Gage Sandy, Mar. 30, 1974; 1 child, Theodore. A.B. cum laude, Radcliffe Coll., 1969; J.D. Harvard U., 1972. Bar: Va. 1973, D.C. 1974, N.Mex. 1975. Assoc., Hunton & Williams, Richmond, Va., 1972-75; asst. U.S. atty. U.S. Atty's. Office, Albuquerque, 1975-78; adj. prof. law U. N.Mex., 1983-85; ptnr. Sutin, Thayer & Browne, Albuquerque, 1978-85, Montgomery & Andrews, P.A., Albuquerque, 1985-88; sole practice, Albuquerque, 1988—. Bd. dirs. Am. Diabetes Assn., Albuquerque, 1980-85, chmn. bd. dirs., 1984-85; bd. dirs. June Music Festival, 1980—, pres., 1983-85; bd. dirs. Albuquerque Conservation Trust, 1986—; chairperson Albuquerque Com. Fgn. Relations, 1984-85, sec. 1987—; mem. N.Mex. Internat. Trade and Investment Council, Inc., 1986—, sec., 1987—. Mem. Fed. Bar Assn. (coordinator), ABA, Va. Bar Assn., N.Mex. State Bar Assn. (chmn. corp., banking and bus. law 1982-83, bd. dirs. internat. and immigration law sect. 1987—), Nat. Assn. Women Lawyers, Am. Jud. Soc., Harvard Alumni Assn. (mem. fund campaign, regional dir. 1984-86, v.p. 1986—, chmn. clubs com. 1985—), Radcliffe Coll. Alumnae Assn. Bd. Mgmt. (regional dir. 1984—). Club: Harvard-Radcliffe (pres. 1980-84). Home: 632 Cougar Loop NE Albuquerque NM 87122 Office: 5700 Harper Dr NE Suite #300 PO Box 14721 Albuquerque NM 87191-4721

SCHULER, HANS, chemical engineer; b. Biberbach, Fed. Republic Germany, Dec. 24, 1950; s. Konrad and Sofie (Voelkle) S.; m. Angela Frank, 1982. Diploma in Engring., U. Stuttgart, 1975, PhD in Engring., 1982. Sci. asst. U. Stuttgart, Fed. Republic Germany, 1975-82; chem. engr. BASF A.G., Ludwigshafen, Fed. Republic Germany, 1982—. Contbr. articles to profl. jours. Recipient Heinz Maier Leibnitz prize Ministry Culture and Sci., 1985. Mem. Verein Deutscher Ingenieure, Deutsche Gesellschaft fuer Chemisches Apparatewesen Chemische Technik und Biotechnologie, Gesellschaft Verfahreustechnik und Chemie ingenieur weseu, Gesellschaft Mess-und Automatisierungstechnik. Home: Bockenheimer Strasse 10, D6700 Ludwigshafen Federal Republic of Germany

SCHULER, PHILIPPE, interior decorator; b. Lausanne, Vaud, Switzerland, July 12, 1942; m. Elfi Weitgasser: children: Patrick, Laurent. Degree, U. Lausanne, 1965. Counselor Commune of Pully, 1978—. Served with Swiss Air Force, 1966—. Recipient Prix de l'Excellence Européenne, 1988. Liberal. Roman Catholic. Lodge: Rotary (Pully). Club: Lausanne Golf. Office: Grand Chene 8, CH 1002 Lausanne Switzerland

SCHULERT, ARTHUR ROBERT, engineering company executive, chemist; b. Gladwin, Mich., Feb. 26, 1922; s. Oscar Edward and Ruth Olive (Sanford) S.; m. Ruth Barbara Darling, June 17, 1949; children—Barbara, Mark, Jean, Philip, Andrew, Peter, Timothy. B.S., Wheaton Coll., 1943; M.A., Princeton U., 1947; Ph.D., U. Mich., 1951. Research asst. Manhattan Project, Princeton, N.J., 1943-46; fellow medicine NYU, 1951-53; research assoc. Columbia U., N.Y.C., 1953-61; dir. biochemistry dept. U.S. Naval Med. Research Unit, Cairo, 1961-66; from asst. prof. to assoc. prof. Vanderbilt U., Nashville, 1961-73; pres. Environ. Sci. and Engring. Corp., Mount Juliet, Tenn., 1970—; cons. Isotopes, Inc., Westwood, N.J., 1957-61, NIH, Bethesda, Md., 1958-64. Co-author: Strontium-90 in Man, 1961, 62. Bd. dirs. Mount Juliet Christian Acad., Mount Juliet, 1981—. Fellow Am. Assn. Clin. Chemists, Am. Inst. Chemists; mem. Am. Chem. Soc., AAAS, Am. Inst. Nutrition, Nat. Speakers Assn., Sigma Xi, Phi Lambda Upsilon. Baptist. Avocations: tennis; camping. Home: 83 E Hill Dr Mount Juliet TN 37122 Office: Environ Sci and Engring Corp 1776 Mays Chapel Rd Mount Juliet TN 37122

SCHULHOF, MICHAEL PETER, electronics company executive; b. N.Y.C., Nov. 30, 1942; s. Rudolph B. and Hannelore (Buck) S.; m. Paola Nissim, Apr. 17, 1969; children: David Kenneth, Jonathan Nissim. BA, Grinnell Coll., 1964; MS, Cornell U., Ithaca, N.Y., 1967; PhD (NSF fellow), Brandeis U., 1970. Lic. comml. pilot. Am. research fellow Brookhaven Nat. Lab., Uptown, N.Y., 1969-71; asst. to v.p. mfg. CBS Records, Inc., N.Y.C., 1971-73, mem. exec. com., bd. dirs., 1987—; gen. mgr. bus. products div. Sony Corp., N.Y.C., 1973-77, v.p., 1977-78, sr. v.p., 1978-86, also bd. dirs., mem. exec. com., pres., 1987—; pres. Sony Industries, N.Y.C., 1978-86, Digital Audio Disc Corp., Terre Haute, Ind., 1986—; chmn. bd. dirs. Quadriga Art Inc., 1980—, Sony Video Software; vice-chmn., bd. dirs. Sony Corp. of Am.; dep. pres. Sony USA, Inc.; trustee Brandeis U. Bus. Sch. Com., 1986—. Contbr. articles to profl. jours. Patentee audio disc apparatus, 1986. Mem. Am. Phys. Soc. (dir. 1978), Computer and Bus. Equipment Mfrs. Assn. (dir.), Am. Radio Relay League, Aircraft Owners and Pilots Assn., Guggenhiem Mus., Whitney Mus. Clubs: Harmony, Gypsy Trail, East Hampton Tennis, Profile, Fenway Golf. Home: 1021 Park Ave New York NY 10028 Office: 9 W 57th St New York NY 10019

SCHULMAN, JOSEPH DANIEL, physician, medical geneticist, reproductive biologist, educator; b. Bklyn., Dec. 20, 1941; s. Max and Miriam (Grossman) S.; m. Carol Ann Brimberg, June 14, 1964; children: Erica N., Julie K. B.A., Bklyn. Coll., 1961; M.D., Harvard U., 1966. Diplomate Am. Bd. Pediatrics, Am. Bd. Ob-Gyn, Am. Bd. Med. Genetics. Intern, resident in pediatrics Mass. Gen. Hosp., Boston, 1966-68; clin. assoc. Nat. Inst. Arthritis and Metabolic Diseases, 1968-70; resident in obstetrics and gynecology and fellow in pediatrics N.Y. Hosp.-Cornell Med. Center, 1970-73; Gilbert and Nat. Found. fellow Cambridge (Eng.) U., 1973-74; head sect. human biochem. genetics Nat. Inst. Child Health and Human Devel., NIH, Bethesda, Md., 1974-83; dir. med. genetics program NIH, Bethesda, Md., 1979-1983; prof. ob/gyn, pediatrics, and genetics George Washington U., 1983-84, founder in vitro fertilization program; dir. Genetics & IVF Inst., Fairfax, Va., 1984—; chmn. Genetics & IVF Inst., Fairfax, 1988—; prof. human genetics, pediatrics, obstetrics and gynecology Med. Coll. Va., 1984—; with dept. ob-gyn Fairfax Hosp., 1984—. Author 3 books; contbr. numerous articles to med. jours. Served with USPHS, 1968-70, 74-83. Fellow Am. Coll. Obstetricians and Gynecologists; mem. Soc. Pediatric Research, Soc. Gynecologic Investigation, Am. Soc. Clin. Investigation, Am. Soc. Human Genetics, Phi Beta Kappa, Sigma Xi. Clubs: Harvard, Cosmos. Home: 9207 Aldershot Dr Bethesda MD 20817 Office: 3020 Javier Rd Fairfax VA 22031

SCHULSINGER, GILBERT, surgeon; b. Paris, July 8, 1928; s. Armand and Eva (Fiks) S.; m. Helen Annie Nousse, Jan. 7, 1959; children: Frank Emmanuel, Marianne Sophie. M.D., U. Paris, 1959. Med. diplomate, U. Paris. Resident, Hosps. of Paris, 1956-59; chief surgeon Hosp. of Lamantin, Martinique, 1959-60; chef de clinique Beaujon Hosp., Paris, 1961-62; pvt. practice gen. surgery, Paris, 1961—. Expert Pré La Cour d'Appel de Paris. Author: About Abnormal Pulmonary Arteries, 1959. Editor: Thoracic Traumatology, 1962. Fellow Internat. Coll. Surgeons; mem. Société des Chirurgiens de Paris (gen. sec. 1971-75). Jewish. Avocation: golf. Home: 95 rue de Courcelles, 75017 Paris France

SCHULTHEIS, EDWIN MILFORD, educator; b. N.Y.C., Apr. 15, 1928; s. Milford Theodore and Lillian May (Hill) S.; B.S., Hofstra Coll., 1950; M.B.A., N.Y. U. Grad. Sch. Bus. Adminstrn., 1958, Ed.D., Sch. Edn., 1972; m. Joan Edna Bruckner, June 23, 1956. Officer mgr., sales rep. Topton Rug Mfg. Co., N.Y.C., 1950-54; area mgr., trainer Mobil Oil Co., N.Y.C., 1954-62; coordinator nat. distributive edn. North Babylon (N.Y.) Public Schs., 1962-88; prof. bus. adminstrn. SUNY, Farmingdale, 1970—; asst. prof. edn. N.Y. U., 1973—; dir. edn. Syracuse (N.Y.) U., 1973-88; chmn. bus. mktg. and indsl. edn. depts. North Babylon (N.Y.) Pub. Schs., 1988—; test writer, cons. N.Y. State Dept. Edn., Albany, 1965—; textbook reviewer McGraw-Hill Book Co., N.Y.C., 1967-69; cons. Cornell U., 1975; dist. adviser Distributive Edn. Clubs N.Y., 1970, bd. govs., 1967-68, trustee, 1975—, chmn. dept. bus., mktg. and indsl. edn. North Babylon Pub. Schs., 1988—; mem. curriculum adv. council Suffolk County (N.Y.) Distributive Edn. Assn., 1967—; elder Presbyn. Ch., U.S.A. Named N.Y. State Tchr. of Yr., 1976; Outstanding Tchr. in N.Y. State, 1978; recipient Outstanding Service award Distributive Edn. Clubs. N.Y., Suffolk County Distributive Edn. Assn.; Tchr. Excellence award N.Y. State, 1980. Mem. Acad. Mgmt., Am. Petroleum Inst., Am. Security Council, Suffolk County Assn. Distributive Edn. Tchrs. (mem. exec. bd. 1962-74), N.Y. State (pres. 1975-78), L.I. (exec. bd. 1972-75) distributive edn. assns., N.Y. State Occupational Edn. Assn. (v.p. 1975-78), Distributive Edn. Clubs Am. (regional leader 1972-75), Phi Delta Kappa, Kappa Delta Pi, Sigma Alpha Lambda. Presbyterian (ordained ruling elder). Club: Bellport (N.Y.) Golf. Author: Modern Petroleum Marketing, 1971. Home: 10 Brendan Ave Massapequa Park NY 11762 Office: North Babylon Pub Schs North Babylon NY 11703

SCHULTHEISS, WOLFGANG W., diplomat; b. Paehl, Fed. Republic Germany, Mar. 10, 1945; s. Walther and Ingetraud (Friedrich) S.; m. Lene G. Vilsgaard; children: Christian, Michael. Degree in law, U. Bonn, Fed. Republic Germany, 1969, Doctorate, 1973; LLM, U. Va., 1972; degree in law, State of North-Rhine Westfalia, Fed. Republic Germany, 1974. With Embassy of Fed. Republic Germany, Algiers, Algeria, 1976-80; del. of Fed. Republic Germany to MBFR Talks, Vienna, Austria, 1980-83; with Ministry Fgn. Affairs, Bonn, Fed. Republic Germany, 1983-86; West German ambassador to Dominican Republic Santo Domingo, 1986—. Office: Embassy Fed Republic Germany, Mejia y Cotes 37, Santo Domingo Dominican Republic

SCHULTZ, ALVIN LEROY, internist, medical educator; b. Mpls., July 27, 1921; s. Maurice Arthur and Elizabeth Leah (Gershin) S.; m. Martha Jean Graham, Aug. 14, 1947; children—Susan Kristine, David Matthew, Peter Jonathan, Michael Graham. B.A., U. Minn.-Mpls., 1943, M.B., 1946, M.D., 1947, M.S., 1952. Diplomate: Am. Bd. Internal Medicine. Instr. medicine U. Minn.-Mpls., 1952-54, asst. prof., 1954-59, assoc. prof., 1959-65, prof., 1965-88, prof. emeritus, 1988—; asst. chief medicine Mpls. VA Hosp., 1952-54; dir. endocrine clinic U. Minn., 1954-59; dir. medicine and research Mt. Sinai Hosp., Mpls., 1959-65; chief of medicine Hennepin County Med. Ctr., Mpls., 1965-88; chmn. bd. acad. practice plan Hennepin Faculty Assocs., 1983-87; sr. v.p. med. affairs Health One Corp., 1988—. Editor: Jour. Lab. and Clin. Medicine, 1966-69, Modern Medicine, 1960—; editorial bd.: Minn. Medicine, 1965—; Data Centrum, 1984-87; contbr. articles profl. jours. Bd. dirs. Planned Parenthood of Minn., 1970-75, Hennepin County Med. Philanthropic Found., 1976—. Served to capt. AUS, 1947-49. Fellow ACP (Minn. gov. 1983-86; chmn. elect bd. govs. 1986-87, chmn. 1987-88, regent 1988—); mem. Central Soc. Clin. Research, Am. Fedn. Clin. Research, Endocrine Soc., Am. Thyroid Assn., Minn. Med. Assn. (ho. of dels. 1980-85), Minn. Assn. Pub. Teaching Hosps. (pres. 1983-84), Hennepin County Med. Soc. (dir. 1977-81, pres.-elect 1987-88, pres. 1988—). Republican. Jewish. Home: 5127 Irving Ave S Minneapolis MN 55419 Office: Health One Corp 2810 57th Ave N Minneapolis MN 55430-2496

SCHULTZ, ARTHUR WARREN, retired communications company executive; b. N.Y.C., Jan. 13, 1922; s. Milton Warren and Genevieve (Dann) S.; grad. U. Chgo.; D.Letters (hon.), Rosary Coll.; m. Elizabeth Carroll Mahan, 1949 (div. 1987); children—Arthur Warren, John Carroll (dec.), Julia Hollingsworth; m. Susan Keefe, 1988. With Foote, Cone & Belding Communications, Chgo., 1948-82, v.p., 1957-63, sr. v.p., dir., 1963-69, exec. v.p., 1969, chmn. bd., chief exec. officer, 1970-81, chmn. exec. com., chief exec. officer, 1981-82; dir. Springs Industries, Inc., Zenith Electronics Corp., Chgo. Sun-Times Co., Folger Adams Co.; Schwinn Bicycle Co. Pres. Cook County Sch. Nursing, 1963-64, Welfare Council Met. Chgo., 1965-67; mem. bus. adv. council Urban League Chgo., 1971-82; chmn. Nat. Com. to Save Am.'s Cultural Collections; mem. Pres.'s Com. on Arts and Humanities, 1984—; bd. dirs. Chgo. Crime Commn., 1965-71, Community Fund Chgo., 1966-67, Better Bus. Bur., 1970-78, Lyric Opera Chgo., 1967-77, Chgo. Council Fgn. Relations, 1977-86, Chgo. Public TV, 1978-82, Chgo. Central Area Com., 1978-82; trustee YWCA, 1962-74, Calif. Coll. Arts and Crafts, 1985-87; trustee Art Inst. Chgo., 1975—, chmn. bd., 1981-84; trustee U. Chgo., 1977—, Santa Barbara Mus. Art, 1988—. Served to 1st lt. USAAF, 1943-45. Recipient Alumni Service award U. Chgo., 1986. Mem. Am. Assn. Advt. Agys. (dir. 1968-71, 74-76, chmn. Chgo. council 1964-65, chmn. Central region 1970-71), Delta Kappa Epsilon. Episcopalian. Clubs: Chgo., Racquet (Chgo.); Commercial; Old Elm; Valley (Montecito, Calif.), Birham Wood. Home: 422 Court Place Santa Barbara CA 93108 Office: FCB Center 101 E Erie Chicago IL 60611-2897

SCHULTZ, FREDERICK H. C., physics educator, energy consultant; b. Hanks, N.D., June 11, 1921; s. Herman A. and Helvene G. (Ausl) S.; m. Lila Fay Gregory, Aug. 27, 1949; children—Michael F., Jane F., John F. Ph.B., U. N.D.-Grand Forks, 1942; M.S., U. Idaho-Moscow, 1950; Ph.D., Wash. State U.-Pullman, 1967. Instr. physics Mont. Sch. Mining, Butte, 1950-55; asst. prof. Mont. State U.-Bozeman, 1955-61; physicist U.S. Naval Ordnance Lab., Corona, Calif., summers 1957, 59, 61, 63; asst. prof. Minot (N.D.) State U., 1961-63, Wash. State U., 1963-68; prof. U. Wis.-Eau Claire, 1968—; dir. seismograph sta. U.S. Coast & Geol. Survery, Bozeman, 1955-61; dir. Summer Inst. NSF, Pullman, 1967-68; energy cons. W.C. Wis. Regional Planning Commn., Eau Claire, 1981—. Served with U.S. Navy, 1944-46. Mem. Wis. Assn. Physics Tchrs., Am. Assn. Physics Tchrs., N.Y. Acad. Sci., Optical Soc. Am., Sigma Xi. (local pres. 1979-81). Republican. Lutheran. Office: U Wis Dept Physics Eau Claire WI 54701 Home: 3834 Nimitz St Eau Claire WI 54701

SCHULTZ, GWEN MANETTE, geographer, writer, publisher; b. Milwaukee; d. Herbert A. F. and Aurelia (Nickel) S. B.A., U. Wis.-Madison, 1944, M.A., 1950. Assoc. prof. geography Wis. Geol. and Natural History Survey, U. Wis-Madison, 1969—; owner Reading Gems, Madison, 1972—; owner Hammock & Inglenook, Madison, 1981—. Author: Ice Age Lost (Council for Wis. Writers 1st place award 1975); Icebergs and Their Voyages (Council for Wis. Writers 1st place award 1976); Glaciers and the Ice Age; The Blue Valentine; The Bucky Badger Story; Wisconsin's Foundations (State Hist. Soc. of Wis. award of merit, Council for Wis. Writers award, 1986); Colorprint World Atlas. Contbr. articles, fiction, revs., poetry to mags. and profl. jours. Recipient Midwest Authors and Artists Tribute, 1979, 1st place short story award Nat. League Am. Pen Women, 1979. Mem. Friend of Libraries and Hist. Soc., Council for Wis. Writers (v.p. 1976-84), Authors Guild, Assn. Am. Geographers, AAUP, Am. Quaternary Assn., Wis. Acad. Scis., Arts and Letters, Wis. Archaeol. Soc, Friends of U. Wis. Geology Mus. (bd. dirs.), Wis. Authors and Pubs. Alliance, Wis. Council Geographic Edn., Fedn. Women's Clubs. Home: 111 W Wilson St Apt 201 Madison WI 53703 Office: Wis Geol and Natural History Survey Univ Wis Madison WI 53706

SCHULTZ, JEFFREY ERIC, optometrist; b. Cleve., Jan. 28, 1948; s. Albert I. and Lenore (Aster) S.; m. Nancy Lynne Wachs, July 5, 1970; children—Brian David, Amy Robin. B.S. in Zoology, Ohio State U., 1970, O.D., 1974, M.S. in Physiol. Optics, 1974. Lic. optometrist, Ohio, Fla. Research asst. Ohio State U. Coll. Optometry, Columbus, 1970-74, clin. instr., 1974-75; gen. practice optometry, Cleve., 1975—. Contbr. articles to profl. jours. Nikon scholar. Mem. Ohio Optometric Assn. (continuing edn. com. 1976—, chmn. sports vision com. 1977-79, Optometric Recognition award 1978), Fla. Optometric Assn., Am. Optometric Assn. (Optometric Recognition award 1980, 82—, charter mem. contact lens sect. 1982—, mem. sports vision sect. 1983—), Am. Acad. Optometry, Nat. Eye Research Found., Council Sports Vision, Vision Conservation Inst., Better Vision Inst., Ohio Contact Lens Soc., Cleve. Optometric Assn. (trustee 1985—), Beta Sigma Kappa, Phi Eta Sigma. Lodge: Masons. Avocations: philately, fine art collecting. Office: 5706 Turney Rd Garfield Heights OH 44125 also: 5395 Mayfield Rd Lyndhurst OH 44124

SCHULTZ, TERRY ALLEN, architect; b. Elmhurst, Ill., May 18, 1946; s. Clarence Frederick Theodore and Elvera Stella (Landmeier) S. BArch, U. Ill., 1970, MS, 1971; MBA, Keller Grad. Sch. Mgmt., 1980. Registered architect, Wis. Sr. project structural engr. Skidmore Owings & Merrill, Chgo., 1971-75; gen. mgr. Archtl. Engring. Cons., Arlington Heights, Ill., 1975-77; project engr. Gillum-Colaco, Chgo., 1977-79; prin. A/E Consulting, Arlington Heights, 1979—; Bd. dirs. Evang. Health Systems Corp., Oak Brook, Ill., 1978—; chmn. bd. dirs. Evang. Care Corp., Oak Brook, 1985—. Mem. bd. govs. Good Sheperd Hosp., Barrington, Ill., 1978-83; trustee Bethany Hosp., Chgo., 1980—; v.p. Good Sheperd Manor, Barrington, 1985—; pres., treas. St. John United Ch. of Christ, Arlington Heights, 1976-80. Mem. AIA, Nat. Assn. Corp. Dirs. Republican. Club: American (Hong Kong). Lodge: Lions. Home and Office: 316 E Euclid St Arlington Heights IL 60004

SCHULTZ, THEODORE WILLIAM, retired educator, economist; b. Arlington, S.D., Apr. 30, 1902; s. Henry Edward and Anna Elizabeth (Weiss) S.; m. Esther Florence Werth; children: Elaine, Margaret, T. Paul. Grad., Sch. Agr., Brookings, S.D., 1924; B.S., S.D. State Coll., 1927, D.Sc. (hon.), 1959; M.S., U. Wis., 1928, Ph.D., 1930; LL.D. (hon.), Grinnell Coll., 1949, Mich. State U., in 1962, U. Ill., 1968, U. Wis., 1968, Cath. U. Chile, 1979, U. Dijon, France, 1981; LL.D., N.C. State U., 1984. Mem. faculty Iowa State Coll., Ames, 1930-43; prof., head dept. econs. and sociology Iowa State Coll., 1934-43; prof. econs. U. Chgo., 1943-72, chmn. dept. econs., 1946-61, Charles L. Hutchinson Disting. Service prof., 1952-72, now emeritus; econ. adviser, occasional cons. Com. Econ. Devel., U.S. Dept. Agr., Dept. State, Fed. Res. Bd., various congl. coms., U.S. Dept. Commerce, FAO, U.S. Dept. Def., Germany, 1948, Fgn. Econ. Adminstrn., U.K. and Germany, 1945, IBRD, Resources for the Future, Twentieth Century Fund, Nat. Farm Inst., others.; dir. Nat. Bur. Econ. Research, 1949-67; research dir. Studies of Tech. Assistance in Latin Am.; bd. mem. Nat. Planning Assn.; chmn. Am. Famine Mission to India, 1946; studies of agrl. developments, central Europe and Russia, 1929, Scandinavian countries and Scotland, 1936, Brazil, Uruguay and Argentina, 1941, Western Europe, 1955. Author: Redirecting Farm Policy, 1943, Food for the World, 1945, Agriculture in an Unstable Economy, 1945, Production and Welfare in Agriculture, 1950, The Economic Organization of Agriculture, 1953, Economic Test in Latin America, 1956, Transforming Traditional Agriculture, 1964, The Economic Value of Education, 1963, Economic Crises in World Agriculture, 1965, Economic Growth and Agriculture, 1968, Investment in Human Capital: The Role of Education And of Research, 1971, Human Resources, 1972, Economics of the Family: Marriage, Children, and Human Capital, 1974, Distortions of Agricultural Incentives, 1978, Investing in People: The Economics of Population Quality, 1981; co-author: Measures for Economic Development of Under-Developed Countries, 1951; editor: Jour. Farm Econs., 1939-42; contbr. articles to profl. jours. research fellow Center Advanced Study in Behavioral Sci., 1956-57; recipient Nobel prize in Econs., 1979. Fellow Am. Acad. Arts and Scis., Am. Farm Econs. Assn., Nat. Acad. Scis.; mem. Am. Farm Assn., Am. Econ. Assn. (pres. 1960, Walker medal 1972), Royal Econ. Soc., Am. Philos. Soc., others. Home: 5620 Kimbark Ave Chicago IL 60637 Office: Univ of Chgo Dept of Economics 1126 E 59th St Chicago IL 60637

SCHULZ, CHARLES MONROE, cartoonist; b. Mpls., Nov. 26, 1922; s. Carl and Dena (Halverson) S.; m. Joyce Halverson, Apr. 18, 1949; children: Meredith, Charles Monroe, Craig, Amy, Jill. L.H.D. (hon.), Anderson Coll., 1963. Cartoonist St. Paul Pioneer Press, Sat. Eve. Post, 1948-49; created syndicated comic strip Peanuts, 1950; recipient Outstanding Cartoonist award Nat. Cartoonist Soc. 1956, Emmy award for children's program A Charlie Brown Christmas, CBS cartoon spl. 1966; collected cartoons pub. in book form, 1952, More Peanuts, 1954, Good Grief, More Peanuts, 1956, Good Ol' Charlie Brown, Snoopy, You're Out of Your Mind Charlie Brown, But We Love You Charlie Brown, Peanuts Revisited, Go Fly a Kite Charlie Brown, Peanuts Every Sunday, You Can Do It, Charlie Brown, Happiness is a Warm Puppy, 1962, Love is Walking Hand in Hand, 1965, A Charlie Brown Christmas, 1965, You Need Help, Charlie Brown, 1966, Charlie Brown's All-Stars, 1966, You've Had It Charlie Brown, 1969, The Snoopy Festival, 1974, many others; also author, illustrator collected cartoons pub. in book form Snoopy and the Red Baron, 1966, Snoopy and His Sopwith Camel, 1969, The Snoopy Come Home Movie Book, 1972, The

Charlie Brown Dictionary. Office: care United Feature Syndicate 200 Park Ave New York NY 10166 *

SCHULZ, PAUL, physicist; b. Rostock, Germany, Jan. 31, 1911; s. Heinrich and Marie (Bahrdt) S.; student U. Munich, U. Rostock, 1929-34; Ph.D., U. Rostock, 1934; Dr. Rer. Nat. Habil, U. Bonn, 1943; m. Irene Kerp, 1938; children—Ingrid, Beate, Gabriele. Asst. phys. inst. U. Bonn (Germany), 1935-37; head Osram Elec. Lighting Research Lab., Berlin, 1937-46; dir. Gas Discharge Research Inst., German Acad. Sci., Greifswald, 1946-49; prof. physics U. Greifswald, 1948-49; faculty U. Karlsruhe (W. Ger.), 1949—, prof., 1949—, rector (pres.), 1963-65. Recipient Elenbaas prize, 1969. Mem. Deutsche Physikalische Gesellschaft (chmn. fachausschuss fur plasma-physik 1950-60), Deutsche Lichttechnische Gesellschaft (pres. 1954-57, hon. mem. 1976—), Am. Phys. Soc., Commn. Internat. Photobiologie, Commn. Internat. de l'Eclairage, Heinrich-Hertz Soc. Mem. Evangelical Ch. Author: Elektronische Vorgange in Gasen und Festkorpern, 1968, rev. edit., 1974. Contbr. articles to profl. publs. Inventor xenon and metallhalide discharge lamps 1943, 49, patentee in field. Home: 5 Aschenbrodelweg, 7500 Karlsruhe 51 Federal Republic of Germany Office: 12 Kaiserstrasse, 7500 Karlsruhe 1 Federal Republic of Germany

SCHULZ, RAINER WALTER, computer co. exec.; b. Berlin, Jan. 29, 1942; s. Horst and Marta S.; came to U.S., 1959, naturalized, 1964; B.A. summa cum laude in Math., San Jose State U., 1964; children—Heidi, Kenneth, Kirsten. System devel. asso. IBM, San Jose, Calif., 1964-65, SDS, Santa Monica, Calif., 1965-67, U. Calif., Berkeley, 1967-70; system mgmt. asso. Stanford (Calif.) U., 1970-77; v.p. Computer Curriculum Corp., Palo Alto, Calif., 1973-81, dir., sec., 1978-81; mgr. Tandem Computers Inc., Cupertino, Calif., 1981-83; v.p. computing and info. systems Teknowledge, Palo Alto, 1983—; cons. NSF., 1974-77. Mem. Am. Electronics Assn., Conf. Bd. Republican. Lutheran. Home: PO Box 50243 Palo Alto CA 94303 Office: Teknowledge 1850 Embarcadero Rd Palo Alto CA 94303

SCHULZ, WILLIAM FREDERICK, JR., lawyer, educator; b. Urbana, Ill., Feb. 18, 1912; s. William Frederick and Christene (Beeuwkes) S.; m. Jean H. Smith, Aug. 9, 1936 (dec. 1974); 1 son, William Frederick III; m. Rose Mary Pease, June 25, 1976. AB, U. Ill., 1932, MA in History, 1934, JD, 1937. Bar: Ill. 1937, Pa. 1962. Asst. atty. gen. Ill., 1937-41; asst. public utilities counsel OPA, 1946; assoc. prof. law Stetson U., 1946-48; vis. asso. prof. law Ind. U., 1948-49; prof. law U. Pitts., 1949—. Author: Conservation Law and Administration, 1953, also articles and revs.; Editor: Adminstrv. Law Rev, 1962-74, Transp. Law Jour, 1968-75. Mem. Pa. Forest Commn. Served from 1st lt. to maj. JAGC AUS, 1941-46. Mem. Fed., Am., Ill., Pa., Allegheny County bar assns., Am. Law Inst., Am. Judicature Soc., Am. Acad. Polit. and Social Sci., Am. Soc. Legal History, Selden Soc., Order of Coif, Zeta Psi, Phi Delta Phi. Democrat. Unitarian. Home: Apt 904 220 N Dithridge St Pittsburgh PA 15213

SCHULZE-THULIN, AXEL, museum curator; b. Berlin, Apr. 7, 1938; s. Werner Schulze-T; m. Hanni Jung, Mar. 31, 1964; 1 child, Britta. PhD, U. Cologne, 1972. Curator Linden Mus., Stuttgart, Fed. Republic Germany, 1972—. Author catalogs on Plains Indians, old Peru, eskimo art, others; author: Way Without Moccasins, 1976; editor Amedian mag., 1973—. Mem. German Am. Indian Group (chmn. Stuttgart sect. 1973—), several prehistoric orgns. Lutheran. Home: Koellestrasse 11, 7000 Stuttgart 1 Baden Wurtt Federal Republic of Germany Office: Linden Mus Stuttgart, Hegelplatz 1, 7000 Stuttgart Baden Wurtt Federal Republic of Germany

SCHUMACHER, BARRY LEE, lawyer; b. Akron, Ohio, May 19, 1952; s. Lee Richard and Jane (Barry) S.; m. Judy Martha Sedlak, Dec. 7, 1974; children: John Barry, Jennifer Martha. BS in Biology, Allegheny Coll., 1974; JD, U. Denver, 1979, LLM in Taxation, 1980. Bar: Colo. 1979, U.S. Dist. Ct. Colo. 1979, U.S. Tax Ct. 1980, U.S. Ct. Appeals (10th cir.) 1982, U.S. Ct. Claims 1985. Law clk. to judge U.S. Dept. Interior, Denver, 1978; assoc. Oates, Austin, McGrath & Jordan, Aspen, Colo., 1980-82; ptnr. Wright & Schumacher, Aspen, 1982—; instr. law Colo. Mountain Coll., Aspen, Colo., 1985. Editor, Denver Law Jour., 1977-79, Denver Tax Law Jour., 1979-80. Mem. ABA (staff editor of taxation jour. 1983—), Colo. Bar Assn., Denver Bar Assn., Pitkin County Bar Assn., Phi Alpha Delta. Republican. Home: 0115 Glen Eagles Dr Aspen CO 81611 Office: Wright & Schumacher 201 N Mill St Suite 106 Aspen CO 81611

SCHUMACHER, FREDERICK RICHMOND, lawyer; b. N.Y.C., Sept. 4, 1930; s. Frederick William and Anna De Rose Elizabeth (Richmond) S.; A.B., Princeton U., 1952; J.D., Cornell U., 1957; postgrad. in law, cert. in taxation, U. So. Calif., 1959-61; m. Birte Vestel, Dec. 1, 1973; children—Anna Lisa, Frederick, Ian, Eric. Admitted to N.Y. bar, 1957, Calif. bar, 1960; assoc. firm Clark, Carr & Ellis, N.Y.C., 1957-59, firm Thelen, Marrin, Johnson & Bridges, Los Angeles, 1960-62; individual practice law, 1963—, pres. Frederick R. Schumacher, Ltd., Carlsbad, Calif. 1988 ; dir. Republic Resources, Inc.; cons. fed. and internat. taxes. Active Republican Nat. Com., 1981—. Served with USMC, 1952-54. Mem. N.Y. State Bar Assn., Calif. Bar Assn., Hunting Hall of Fame Found. (charter). Club: So. Calif. Safari. Author: International Letters of Credit, 1960. Office: 2310 Faraday Ave Carlsbad CA 92008

SCHUMACHER, JAMES DELBERT, trade corporation executive; b. Kouts, Ind., Jan. 23, 1931; s. Adolph John and Grace Marie (Hampshire) S.; m. Betty Joan McDaniel, Oct. 11, 1952; children: James D. Jr., Stephen S., Elizabeth A., Donald B., Curtis A., Aaron R., Joannah M. Student in civil engring., U. Nev. Pres. Golden Meadows Corp., Albuquerque, 1974-76; projects mgr. Kent Nowlin Constrn., Albuquerque, 1976-78; div. mgr. Armstrong Bros., Tucson, 1978-80; pres. Schumacher Constrn., Reno, 1980-82; projects mgr. Indsl. Constructors, Albuquerque, 1982-1984; pres, chief exec. officer Nev. Internat. Trade Exchange, Sparks, 1984—; bd. dirs. Mogul Corp., Albuquerque; cons. ICC Powers, Albuquerque, 1970—. Rep. state conv. del., Austin, Nev., 1960; Am. Ind. state conv. del., Tonopah, Nev., 1976, Chgo., 1976; presdl. candidate Am. Ind. Party, Sacramento, 1980. Served to sgt. USMC, 1951-54. Republican. Mormon. Office: Nev Internat Trade Exchange 1607 Greg St Reno NV 89431

SCHUMACHER, JOHN CHRISTIAN, semiconductor materials and equipment manufacturing company executive; b. Spring Valley, Ill., Feb. 8, 1935; s. Joseph Charles and Theresa Isobel (Flynn) S.; B.S., Stanford U., 1956; M.S., M.I.T., 1958; Ph.D., Stanford U., 1973; m. Brooke Schumacher; children—Jennifer Lea, Jesse Colin, Jacqueline Chanel. Research engr. Calif. Inst. Tech., 1958-60; research and teaching asst. M.I.T., 1960-62; dept. mgr. Lockheed Missile & Space Co., Sunnyvale, Calif., 1962-64, program mgr., Lockheed Research, Palo Alto, Calif., 1964-69; research asso., thesis dir. Stanford U., 1969-73; v.p. J. C. Schumacher Co., Oceanside, Calif., 1973-74, pres., 1974-76, pres., chief exec. officer, 1976-86, Diamond Cubic Corp., 1986-87; founder, pres., chief exec. officer, Custom Engred. Materials, Inc., 1987—. Chmn. Oceanside New Bus. and Industry Commn., 1976-78. Mem. Oceanside C. of C. (dir. 1974-78), Electrochem. Soc., Newcomen Soc., IEEE, AAAS, Phys. Soc. Am., Am. Inst. Chem. Engrs. Republican. Club: La Jolla Country. Patentee improved semicondr. device processing materials and equipment; low cost silicon; energy efficient photovoltaic solar cell mfg. Home: 1545 Calle Ryan Encinitas CA 92024 Office: 4039 Avenida de la Plata Oceanside CA 92056

SCHUMAN, WILLIAM HOWARD, composer, administrator, educator; b. N.Y.C., Aug. 4, 1910; m. Frances Prince, Mar. 27, 1936; children—Anthony William, Andrea Frances Weiss. BS, Columbia U., 1935, MA, 1937, MusD, 1954; pvt. study, Max Persin, Charles Haubiel, Roy Harris; MusD (hon.), Chgo. Mus. Coll., 1946, U. Wis., 1949, Phila. Conservatory Music, 1952, Cin. Coll. Music, 1953, Hartt Coll. Music, 1956, Allegheny Coll., 1961, N.Y. U., 1962, Oberlin Coll., 1963, U. R.I., 1965, Peabody Conservatory, 1971, U. Rochester, 1972; DFA (hon.), Adelphi Coll., 1963, Northwestern U., 1963, U. N.Mex., 1964, State U. N.Y., 1974; DJ (hon.), Bates Coll., 1966; LHD (hon.), Colgate U., 1960, Brandeis U., 1962, Dartmouth Coll., 1962, N.Y. U., 1962, Fordham U., 1970, Ashland Coll., 1970. Dir. chorus, mem. faculty Sarah Lawrence Coll., Bronxville, N.Y., 1935-45; dir. publs. G. Schirmer, Inc., N.Y.C., 1944-45; spl. publs. cons. 1945-52; pres. Juilliard Sch. Music, N.Y.C., 1945-62; pres. emeritus Julliard Sch. Music, 1962—; pres. Lincoln Center Performing Arts, N.Y.C., 1962-69; emeritus Lincoln Center Performing Arts, 1969—; mem. adv. com. cultural info. USIA; vice chmn. U.S. delegation UNESCO Internat. Conf. Creative Artists, Venice, Italy, 1952. Recipient numerous awards including 1st Town Hall-League of Composers award 1940, N.Y. Music Critics Circle award 1941-42, award of Merit Nat. Assn. Am. Composers and Condrs. 1941-42, 1st Pulitzer prize for music 1943, award Nat. Inst. Arts and Letters 1943, N.Y. Music Critics Circle award 1950-51, Columbia U. Bicentennial Anniversary medal 1957, 1st Brandeis U. Creative Arts award in music 1957, Citation of Merit State U. N.Y. 1963, Gold Medal Honor for music, Nat. Arts Club 1964, Ann. Composer's Award, Lancaster Symphony Orch. 1965, Brandeis medal for distinguished service to higher edn. 1965, certificate of Merit Sigma Alpha Iota 1967, Concert Artists Guild award 1967, Mark M. Horlolit prize for composition Boston Symphony Orch. 1980; prin. compositions include: (orchestral works) 10 symphonies, Three Colloquies for French horn and orch., New England Triptych, numerous others; (choral works) cantatas including A Free Song, numerous shorter works such as Carols of Death; (band works) George Washington Bridge, 1950, overture Chester, 1956; (chamber music) 4 string quartets In Sweet Music; (piano compositions) Voyage, 1953; (score for film) Steeltown; (opera) The Mighty Casey; recs. Evocation-To Thee Old Cause; prin. commns. include, Elizabeth Sprague Coolidge Found. in Library of Congress, The Koussevitzky Music Found., Inc., Dallas Symphony League, Louisville Philharmonic, Ballet Theatre, U.S. Nat. Commn. for UNESCO through Dept. of State, Andre Kostelanetz, Samuel Dushkin, St. Lawrence U., Ford Found., Chamber Music Soc. Lincoln Center, N.Y. Philharmonic (3), Boston Symphony Orch., Nat. Symphony Orch., St. Louis Symphony Orch., Broadcast Music, Inc.; composer (collaboration with Richard Purdy Wilbur) On Freedom's Ground: An American Cantata, 1985, commd. for 100th anniversary of Statue of Liberty. Chmn. bd. judges Student Composers Awards of Broadcast Music, Inc.; bd. dirs. Nat. Ednl. TV Bd.; music panel Nat. Endowment for Arts; adv. council N.C. Sch. Arts.; Dir. Koussevitzky Music Found., Walter W. Naumburg Found., Composers Forum; chmn. MacDowell Colony, Chamber Music Soc. and Film Soc. Lincoln Center. Guggenheim fellow, 1939-41; recipient Nat. Medal Arts, 1987. Fellow Nat. Inst. Arts and Letters, Am. Acad. and Inst. Arts and Letters; mem. Royal Acad. Music (hon.), others. Clubs: Century (N.Y.C.), Lotos (N.Y.C.). Office: Lincoln Ctr Performing Arts 150 W 65th St New York NY 10023 *

SCHUMANN, MAURICE, French writer, politician; b. Paris, Apr. 10, 1911; m. Lucie Daniel, 1944; 3 children. With Havas News Agy., 1932-40; chief ofcl. broadcaster BBC French Service, 1940-44; liaison officer Allied Expeditionary Forces from D-Day until liberation of Paris; mem. French Provisional Consultative Assembly, 1944-45; mem. Constituent Assembly, 1945-46, 46; chmn. Mouvement Republicain Populaire, 1945-49; dep. for Nord, Nat. Assembly, 1945, 58, 67, 68; sec. of state for fgn. affairs, 1951-54; pres. fgn. affairs com. Nat. Assembly, 1969; minister of state, Prime Minister's Office, 1962; minister of state for sci. research, 1967-68; minister of Social Affairs, 1968-69; minister of Fgn. Affairs, 1969-73; senator for Nord, 1974—, v.p. Senate, 1977—. Mem. Academie Française, 1974; recipient Grand Prix Catholique de Litterature, 1978; decorated Compagnon de la Liberation; Chevalier Legion d'honneur, Order of Leopold; Croix de Guerre. Author: (fiction) Le Rendez-vous avec Quelqu'un, 1962, Les flots roulant au Loin, 1973, La Communication, 1974, Le Concerto en Ut Majeur, 1982; (non-fiction) La Mort née de leur propre Vie, 1974; Le Vrai Malaise des Intellectuels de Gauche, 1957; Angoisse et Certitude, 1978; Un Certain 18 Juin (Prix Aujourd'hui 1980); Qui a tué le duc d'Enghien'9, 1984. Office: 53 Ave Marechal-Lyautey, 75016 Paris 16e France *

SCHUNK, DALE HANSEN, psychology educator, researcher; b. Chgo., Aug. 14, 1946; s. Elmer Charles and Mildred Augusta (Hansen) S.; m. Caryl S. Cook. B.S., U. Ill.-Urbana, 1968; M.Ed., Boston U., 1974; Ph.D., Stanford U., 1979. With NATO, Naples, Italy, 1970-74; teaching asst. Stanford U., 1975, research asst., 1975-79; prof. edn. psychology U. Houston, 1979-86, U. N.C., 1986—; ednl. cons. Spring Branch Sch. Dist., Houston, 1981—. Contbr. articles to profl. jours. Served to capt. USAF, 1968-74. Spencer Found. research grantee, 1980, 84; NSF research grantee, 1980, 85. Mem. Am. Psychol. Assn. (Early Contbns. to Ednl. Psychology award 1982), AAAS, N.Y. Acad. Sci., Am. Ednl. Research Assn., Soc. Research in Child Devel., Southwestern Psychol. Assn., S.W. Ednl. Research Assn. Home: 104 Pitch Pine Ln Chapel Hill NC 27514 Office: U NC Sch Edn Peabody Hall CB 3500 Chapel Hill NC 27599

SCHURMANN, LEO, broadcasting executive; b. Olten, Switzerland, Apr. 10, 1917; s. Leo S. and Josefine de Podesta; m. Cécile Baur, 1943. Student, U. Basle, Switzerland, LLD, 1939. Lawyer state administrn. and banks London, 1940; sr. judge 1953-74; prof. Fribourg (Switzerland) U., 1954—; vice chmn. Swiss Nat. Bank, 1974-80; gen. dir. Swiss Broadcasting Corp., 1981-87; pres. Swiss cartel commn.; mem. several fed. export commns. Founder, editor: (review) Wirtschaft und Recht; contbr. articles to profl. jours.

SCHUSSLER, THEODORE, lawyer, physician, consultant; b. N.Y.C., July 27, 1934; s. Jack and Fannie (Blank) S.; m. Barbara Ann Schussler, June 18, 1961; children—Deborah, Jonathan, Rebecca. B.A. in Polit. Sci., Bklyn. Coll., 1955; LL.B., Bklyn. Law Sch., 1958; J.D., Bklyn. Law Sch., 1967; M.D., U. Lausanne (Switzerland), 1974. Bar: N.Y. 1959, U.S. Dist. Ct. (so. and ea. dists.) N.Y. 1975, U.S. Tax Ct. 1961, U.S. Ct. Appeals (2d cir.) 1962, U.S. Supreme Ct. 1975. Clerkship and practice, N.Y.C., 1956, 58-59; legal editor tax div. Prentice-Hall, Inc., Englewood Cliffs, N.J., 1956; vol. criminal law div. Legal Aid Soc., N.Y.C., 1959; atty. legal dept. N.Y.C. Dept. Welfare, 1959-60; sole practice, N.Y.C., 1960—; sr. staff asst. IBM-Indsl. Medicine Program, 1969-70, 74-76; intern in medicine St. Vincent's Med. Center of Richmond, S.I., N.Y., 1976-77, resident emergency medicine, 1977-79, resident in gerontology, chief house physicians Carmel Richmond Nursing Home, S.I.; 1978-80; surg. rotation emergency dept. Met. Hosp. Ctr., 1979; house physician dept. medicine Richmond Meml. Hosp. and Health Ctr., 1979-80; gen. practice medicine, 1980—; attending physician, chief dept. family practice, chmn. med. care evaluation and by-laws coms., physician advisor emergency dept., mem. blood transfusion, credential's, med. records rev. emergency dept. coms., mem. exec. com. med. staff Community Hosp. of Bklyn., 1980-83; attending physician Meth. Hosp., Bklyn., 1984—; supervising emergency dept. physician, dept. ambulatory care Meth. Hosp., Bklyn., 1980-83; attending physician Kings Hwy. Hosp., 1981-88 , coordinator emergency emergency dept., 1981; Methodist Hosp., Bklyn., 1984—; clin. instr. dept. preventive medicine and community health, Downstate Med. Ctr. SUNY, Bklyn., 1981-88; clin. asst. prof. dept. of Preventive Medicine and Community Health, SUNY, 1988—; SUNY Health Service Ctr. med. dir. Mishkon JBFCS, Bklyn., 1982—; cons. in gerontology Palm Beach Home for Adults, Bklyn.; med.-legal cons. to professions of medicine and law. Served to capt. (med. corp.) USAR. Fellow Am. Coll. Legal Medicine; mem. Am. Coll. Emergency Physicians (past bd. dir. N.Y. chpt., past chmn. medico-legal com. N.Y. chpt.), Bklyn. Law Sch. Alumni Assn. (bd. dirs.), Delta Sigma Rho. Author: Torts; Jurisdiction and Practice in Federal Courts; Constitutional Law; Conflict of Laws; contbr. articles to profl. jours. Home: 760 E 10th St Apt 6H Brooklyn NY 11230 Office: 1415 Coney Island Ave Brooklyn NY 11230

SCHUSTER, EUGENE IVAN, venture capital executive; b. St. Louis, Dec. 8, 1936; s. David Theodore and Anne (Kalisher) S.; B.A., Wayne State U., 1959, M.A., 1962; postgrad. U. Mich., 1959-62, (Fulbright scholar) Warburg Inst., U. London, 1962-65, Courtauld Inst., U. London and London Sch. Econs., 1962-65; m. Barbara Zelmon, June 22, 1958 (div.); children—Joseph, Sarah, Adam. Lectr. art history Wayne State U., Detroit, 1959-62, Eastern Mich. U., Ypsilanti, 1960, Rackham extension U. Mich., 1961, Nat. Gallery, London, 1962-65; owner London Art Gallery, Detroit, 1965—; chmn. bd. Venture Funding Ltd.; chmn. bd. dirs., pres., founder Quest Biotechnology Inc., The Claridge Art Gallery, Inc.; founder, bd. dirs. Univ. Sci. Ptnrs., Inc. Recipient Distinguished Alumni award Wayne State U., 1968. Mem. Founders Soc., Detroit Inst. Arts, Detroit Art Dealers Assn., Art Appraisers Assn. Am. Home: 25425 Dennison Franklin MI 48025 Office: Venture Funding Ltd 321 Fisher Bldg Detroit MI 48202

SCHUSTER, KARL, banker; b. Kirchberg, Austria, Jan. 26, 1929; s. Franz and Mathilde (Leidinger) S.; m. Eva-Maria Smeskal, Aug. 22, 1959; 1 son, Daniel-Martin. Trainee loan sector and sphere of branches Bank fur Oberösterreich and Salzburg, Linz, Austria, 1946-63, br. mgr., 1964-66, mgr. internat. div., holder procuration, 1968-77, mng. dir. internat. div., 1977-81, mem. bd. mgmt., 1982—; supervisory bd. Telefunken Electronic GmbH, Vöcklabruck, Austria, 1982—, O.Ö. Kreditgarantiegesellschaft, Linz, 1982—, Österreichisch-Polnische Gesellschaft, Wien; mem. governing body Deutsche Handelskammer, Österreich, Wien., Kammerrat of Schweizerische Handelskammer. Clubs: Guincho (Portugal); Overseas Bankers (London). Lodge: Rotary. Office: Bank Oberosterreich Salzburg, PO Box 60 Hauptplatz 11, A-4010 Linz Austria

SCHUSTER, MARVIN MEIER, physician, researcher, educator; b. Danville, Va., Aug. 30, 1929; s. Isaac and Rosel (Katzenstein) S.; m. Lois R. Bernstein, Feb. 19, 1961; children—Roberta, Nancy, Cathy. B.A., B.S., U. Chgo., 1951; M.D., 1955. Diplomate Am. Bd. Internal Medicine. Intern Kings County Hosp., Bklyn., 1955-56; resident Balt. City Hosp., 1956-58, chief digestive disease div., resident, 1961—; Johns Hopkins Hosp., Balt., 1958-61; prof. medicine and psychiatry Johns Hopkins U. Sch. Medicine, Balt., 1976—. Author: Gastrointestinal Disorders: Behavioral and Physiological Basis for Treatment. Editor: Gastrointestinal Motility Disorders, 1981; contbr. chpts. to textbooks, articles to profl. jours.; mem. editorial bd.: Gastroenterology, 1978-81, Gastrointestinal Endoscopy, 1979-81, Psychosomatics, 1979—. Bd. dirs. Am. Cancer Soc., 1975—, pres., 1984-86; chmn. med. adv. bd. Balt. Ostomy Assn., 1966—. Recipient St. George Disting. Service award Am. Cancer Soc., 1979. Fellow ACP, Am. Psychiat. Assn.; mem. Am. Gastroent. Assn. (chmn. audiovisual com. 1975-78), Am. Soc. Gastrointestinal Endoscopy (governing bd. 1975-78), Am. Physiol. Soc., AAUP. Democrat. Jewish. Research on gastroenterology and application of biofeedback to gastrointestinal control. Home: 3101 Northbrook Rd Baltimore MD 21208 Office: Baltimore City Hosp 4940 Eastern Ave Baltimore MD 21224

SCHUSTER, PHILIP FREDERICK, II, lawyer; b. Denver, Aug. 26, 1945; s. Philip Frederick and Ruth Elizabeth (Robar) S.; m. Barbara Lynn Nordquist, June 7, 1975; children: Philip Christian, Matthew Dale. BA, U. Wash., 1967; JD, Willamette U., 1972. Bar: Oreg. 1972, U.S. Dist. Ct. Oreg. 1974, U.S. Ct. Appeals (9th cir.) 1986, U.S. Supreme Ct. 1986. Dep. dist. atty. Multnomah County, Portland, Oreg., 1972; title examiner Pioneer Nat. Title Co., Portland, 1973-74; assoc. Buss, Leichner et al, Portland, 1975-76; from assoc. to ptnr. Kitson & Bond, Portland, 1976-77; sole practice Portland, 1977—; arbitrator Multnomah County Arbitration program, 1983—. Contbr. articles to profl. jours. Organizer Legal Aid Services for Community Clinics, Salem, Oreg. and Seattle, 1969-73; dem. committeeman, Seattle, 1965-70; arbitrator arbitration program Multnomah County, 1985—. Mem. ABA, NAACP (exec. bd. 1979—). Lodge: Sertoma. Office: 1500 NE Irving Suite 540 Portland OR 97232

SCHUSTER, ROBERT PARKS, lawyer; b. St. Louis, Oct. 25, 1945; s. William Thomas Schuster and Carolyn Cornforth (Daugherty) Hathaway; 1 child, Susan Michele. A.B., Yale U., 1967; J.D. with honors, U. of Wyo., 1970; LL.M., Harvard U., 1971. Bar: Wyo. 1971, U.S. Ct. Appeals (10th cir.) 1979, U.S. Supreme Ct. 1984. Dep. county atty. County of Natrona, Casper, Wyo., 1971-73; sole practice, Casper, 1973-76; assoc. Spence & Moriarity, Casper, 1976-78; ptnr. Spence, Moriarity & Schuster, Jackson, Wyo., 1978—. Trustee U. Wyo., 1985—; polit. columnist Casper Star Tribune, 1987—. Ford Found. Urban Law fellow, 1970-71; pres. United Way of Natrona County, 1974; bd. dirs. Dancers Workshop, 1981-83. Mem. ABA, Assn. Trial Lawyers Am., Nat. Assn. of Criminal Defense Lawyers. Wyo. Trial Lawyers Assn. Home: PO Box 548 Jackson WY 83001 Office: Spence Moriarity & Schuster 265 W Pearl Jackson WY 83001

SCHUSTER, TODD MERVYN, biophysics educator, biotechnology company executive; b. Mpls., June 27, 1933; s. David Theodore and Ann (Kaluser) S.; m. Nancy Joann Mottashed, Jan. 25, 1958; 1 child, Lela Alexa. B.A., Wayne State U., 1958, M.S., 1960; Ph.D., Washington U., 1963. Research assoc. Max Planck Inst. Phys. Chemistry, Goettingen, W.Ger., 1963-66; asst. prof. SUNY-Buffalo, 1966-70; assoc. prof. U. Conn., Storrs, 1970-75, prof. biochemistry, biophysics, 1975—, dept. head, 1977-81, dir. Biotech. Ctr., 1986—; pres., founder Xenogen Inc., 1981; 88s. prof. Ind. U., Bloomington, 1975, U. Peking, People's Republic of China, 1987; McCollum-Pratt vis. prof. Johns Hopkins U., Balt., 1979-80; mem. NIH grant rev. panels, biophysics and biophys. chemistry panel, 1971-75, biomed. scis. postdoctoral fellowship panel, 1976, Sickle Cell Disease Adv. Panel, 1977; mem. biol. instrumentation rev. panel NSF, 1984—; mem. biol. facilities rev. panel NSF, 1987—, sci. and tech. ctrs. rev. panel NSF, 1988—. Contbr. research articles on rapid reaction kinetics, biopolymers, hemeprotein structure and function, virus structure and assembly to profl. jours. USPHS fellow, 1959-63, 63-66. Mem. Am. Chem. Soc., Biophys. Soc., Protein Soc., Am. Soc. Biol. Chemists, AAAS, Am. Soc. Virology. Home: 124 Waterville Rd Farmington CT 06032 Office: U Conn Dept Molecular and Cell Biology Box 125 Storrs CT 06268

SCHUTTE, PAULA MARION, information systems strategist, consultant; b. St. Paul, Oct. 29, 1941; d. Paul Maurice and Marion (McAllister) S. BA in Chemistry, Rosary Coll., River Forest, Ill., 1963; MBA, NYU, 1985. Med. research chemist Geigy Chem. Corp., Ardsley, N.Y., 1964-70; group leader, sci. systems CIBA-Geigy Corp., Ardsley, N.Y., 1970-77, mgr. sci. info., 1980-83, sr. research fellow, 1985-86, dir. end user services, 1986-87; dir. info. techs. CIBA-Geigy Corp., Ardsley, 1987—; dir. med. systems pharm. div. CIBA-Geigy Corp., Summit, N.J., 1977-80; dir. sci. info. systems pharm. div. CIBA-Geigy Corp., Summit, 1983-85; research coordinator Prism, Cambridge, Mass., 1985—; info. systems cons. St. Jude's, Thornwood, N.Y., 1985-86; adv. Pace U. Computer Sci. and Info. Systems Bd. Patentee in field. Mem. Am. Mgmt. Assn., Assn. Computing Machinery, Chem. Notation Assn. Office: CIBA-Geigy Corp 444 Saw Mill River Rd Ardsley NY 10502

SCHUTZ, JOHN ADOLPH, university dean, historian; b. Los Angeles, Apr. 10, 1919; s. Adolph J. and Augusta K. (Glueker) S. A.A., Bakersfield Coll., 1940; B.A., UCLA, 1942, M.A., 1943, Ph.D., 1945. Asst. prof. history Calif. Inst. Tech., Pasadena, 1945-53; assoc. prof. history Whittier (Calif.) Coll., 1953-56, prof., 1956-65; prof. Am. history U. So. Calif., Los Angeles, 1965—; chmn. dept. history U. So. Calif., 1974-76, dean social scis. and communication, 1976-82. Author: William Shirley: King's Governor of Massachusetts, 1961, Peter Oliver's Origin and Progress of the American Rebellion, 1967, The Promise of America, 1970, The American Republic, 1978, Dawning of America, 1981, Spur of Fame: Dialogues of John Adams and Benjamin Rush, 1980; joint editor: Golden State Series; contbg. author: Spain's Colonial Outpost, 1985, Generations and Change: Genealogical Perspectives in Social History, 1986, Making of America: Society and Culture of the United States, 1987. Trustee Citizens Research Found., 1985—. Nat. Endowment for Humanities grantee, 1971; Sr. Faculty grantee, 1971-74. Mem. Am. Hist. Assn. (pres. Pacific Coast br. 1972-73), Am. Studies Assn. (pres. 1974-75), Mass. Hist. Soc. (corr.), New. Eng. Hist. Geneal. Soc. (council 1979—), Colonial Soc. Mass. (corr.). Home: 1100 White Knoll Los Angeles CA 90012 Office: U So Calif Los Angeles CA 90089-0034

SCHUTZMAN, FRANS, hotel executive; b. Surabaja, Indonesia, Mar. 30, 1915; s. Leo and Clara (Binstock) S.; divorced; children: Peter, Pia, Clara. B on Comml. Sci., Acad. of Comml. Sci., Prague, Czechoslovakia. Mgr. Raffles Hotel, Singapore, 1950-59; gen. mgr. Nile Hotel, Cairo, 1960-61, Cavalieri Hotel, Rome, 1962-64; v.p. Europe Frank Waters Oil Co., Houston, 1965-70; gen. mgr. Hyatt Regency Toronto, Ont., Can., 1971-74; v.p., gen. mgr. UN Plaza Hotel, N.Y.C., 1974-76; gen. mgr. The Manila Hotel, 1976-87; chmn. Prestigious Hotels of Asia, 1982. Spl. ind. mem. United Way Philippines. Decorated Knight of the Papal Order by His Holiness Pope Paul VI, 1963. Mem. Am. Hotel & Motel Assn. (internat.), Hotel & Restaurant Assn. of the Philippines (bd. dirs.), Chaine Des Rotisseurs, Les Toques Blanches Philippines, Singapore Hotel Assn. Clubs: Circumnavigators Club (Manila) (pres.), Puerto Azul Beach and Country. Home: URB Sol de Mallorca, Edificio Goya F2, Palma de Mallorca, Magalluf Spain

SCHUYLER, DANIEL MERRICK, lawyer, educator; b. Oconomowoc, Wis., July 26, 1912; s. Daniel J. and Fannie Sybil (Moorhouse) S.; m. Claribel Seaman, June 15, 1935; children: Daniel M., Sheila Gordon. A.B. summa cum laude, Dartmouth Coll., 1934; J.D., Northwestern U., 1937. Bar: Ill. 1937, U.S. Supreme Ct. 1942, Wis. 1943. Tchr. constl. history Chgo. Latin Sch., 1935-37; assoc. Schuyler & Hennessy (attys.), 1937-42, ptnr., 1946-48; partner Schuyler, Richert & Stough, 1948-58, Schuyler, Stough & Morris, Chgo., 1958-76, Schuyler, Ballard & Cowen, 1976-83, Schuyler, Roche & Zwirner, P.C., 1983—; treas., sec. and controller B-W Superchargers, Inc. div. Borg-Warner Corp., Milw., 1942-46; lectr. trusts, real property, future interests Northwestern U. Sch. Law, 1946-50, asso. prof. law, 1950-52, prof., 1952-80, prof. emeritus, 1980—. Author: (with Homer F. Carey) Illinois Law of Future Interests, 1941; supplement, 1954; (with William M. McGovern, Jr.) Illinois Trust and Will Manual, 1970; supplements, 1972, 74, 76, 77, 79, 80, 81, 82, 83, 84; contbr. to profl. jours. Republican nominee for judge Cook County Circuit Ct., 1958; bd. dirs. United Cerebral Palsy Greater Chgo. Fellow Am. Bar Found.; mem. Chgo. Estate Planning Council (past pres., Disting. Service award 1977), Am. Coll. Probate Counsel (past pres.), Internat. Acad. Estate and Trust Law, ABA (past mem. ho. dels., past chmn. sect. real property, probate trust law), Chgo. Bar Assn. (past chmn. coms. on trust law and post-admission edn., past bd. mgrs.), Ill. Bar Assn. (past chmn. real estate and legal edn. sects., past bd. govs.), Wis. Bar Assn., Phi Beta Kappa, Order of Coif, Phi Kappa Psi. Clubs: Legal (Chgo.), Law (Chgo.), Chicago (Chgo.), University (Chgo.). Home: 324 Cumnor Rd Kenilworth IL 60043 Office: 3100 Prudential Plaza Chicago IL 60601

SCHUYLER, JANE, fine arts educator; b. Flushing, N.Y., Nov. 2, 1943; d. Frank James and Helen (Oberhofer) S.; BA, Queens Coll., 1965; MA, Hunter Coll., 1967; PhD, Columbia U., 1972. Asst. prof. art history Montclair State Coll., Upper Montclair, N.J., 1970; coordinator fine arts, asst. prof. York Coll., CUNY, Jamaica, 1973-77, 78-87, assoc. prof., 1988— , C.W. Post Coll., LIU, Greenvale, N.Y., 1971-73, adj. assoc. prof., 1977-78. Mem. Fine Arts Com. Internat. Women's Arts Festival, 1974-76; , 1987—, pres. United Community Democrats of Jackson Heights, 1987—. N.Y. Columbia U. Summer Travel and Research grantee, 1969. Mem. Coll. Art Assn. Am., Women's Caucus for Art, AAUP, Nat. Trust Hist. Preservation, Renaissance Soc. Am. Roman Catholic. Contbr. articles on occult and art to Cakes and Ale, 1978, Italian Quar., 1982, Secac Jour. on Italian Renaissance art, 1983, 85, Source, 1986, 87, Studies in Iconography, 1987. Author: Florentine Busts: Sculpted Portraiture in the Fifteenth Century, 1976. Sculpted Portraiture in the Fifteenth Century, 1976. Home: 35 37 78th St Jackson Heights NY 11372

SCHUYTEN, GILBERTE, mathematics educator; b. Kapellen, Belgium, Oct. 4, 1942; d. Frederik Schuyten and Irma Lathouwers; m. Rauoul Windey, Jan. 10, 1987; children: Marianne, Annick, Steven, Patrick, Luc, Annick. PhD in Math., State U. Ghent, Belgium, 1971. Assoc. prof. State U. Ghent, 1979—; dir. Educatieve Informatika, 1977—. Author: Geometry at Elementary School, 1978, 2d edit., 1979, 3d edit., 1982, The Computer, the Teacher and the Student, 1984, New Information Technologies and Software in Schools, 1986, Learning Programming at Elementary School, 1986, The Computer at the Flemish Primary Schools, 1987. Mem. Nat. Council Tchrs. Math., Internat. Fedn. Info. Processing, World Assn. Ednl. Research, Psychometric Soc., Wiskundig genootschap van Belgie. Home: Jemappesstraat 8, B9000 Ghent Belgium

SCHWAAB, RICHARD LEWIS, lawyer, educator; b. Oconomowoc, Wis., Nov. 15, 1945. B.S. in Chem. Engring., U. Wis., 1967; J.D. with honors, George Washington U., 1971, LL.M. in Internat. Law with highest honors, 1979. Bar: Va. 1971, U.S. Dist. Ct. (ea. dist.) Va. 1979, U.S. Supreme Ct. 1980, U.S. Ct. Appeals (fed. cir.) 1982. Ptnr., Stepno, Schwaab & Linn, Arlington, 1972-74, Bacon & Thomas, Arlington, 1974-78, Schwartz, Jeffery, Schwaab, Mack, Blumenthal & Evans, P.C., Alexandria, 1978—; Foley & Lardner, Schwartz, Jeffery, Schwaab, Mack, Blumenthal & Evans, Alexandria, 1988—; lectr. law George Washington U., 1978—. Max Planck Inst. Fgn. and Internat. Patent, Copyright and Competition Law fellow, 1971-72. Mem. ABA, Am. Patent Law Assn., Va. State Bar (gov. 1974-78), Am. Soc. Internat. Law, Internat. Patent and Trademark Assn., Internat. Fedn. Indsl. Property Attys., Phi Kappa Phi, Tau Beta Pi. Co-author Patent Practice, 6 vols., 1985; International Patent Law: EPC & PCT, 3 vols., 1978; Intellectual Property Protection for Biotechnology Worldwide, 1987. Contbr. articles to profl. jours. Home: 542o Masser Ln Fairfax VA 22032 Office: King St Sta 1800 Diagonal Rd Alexandria VA 22313

SCHWAB, HANS-CHRISTOPH, pharmaceutical company executive; b. Fuessen, Germany, Sept. 9, 1945; s. Paul and Hildegard (Terhaerst) S.; m. My Van Nguyen, Dec. 19, 1974. Grad., Atlantic Coll., South Wales, 1964; degree in Law, Ruhr U., Bochum, Germany, 1969, postgrad., 1970; M.B.A., Columbia U., 1972. Fin. analyst Eli Lilly & Co., Bad Homburg, Fed. Republic Germany, 1973-74, planning mgr., 1974-79, mktg. dir. E. Europe, Vienna, Austria, 1979-80, dir. market research, Bad Homburg, 1980-81, regional sales dir., 1981-82, dir. pharms., Brussels, 1982-85, dir. internat. bus. devel., Indpls., 1985-86, gen. mgr. med. instrument systems, Giessen, Fed. Republic Germany, 1986—. Mem. Rescue service Royal Nat. Lifeboat Inst., St. Donat's Castle, 1963, 64. Club: German Debating (Berlin) (pres. 1966). Home: Heinrich-Von-KleistStr 58, 6380 Bad Homburg Federal Republic of Germany Office: Lilly Medizintechnik, Teichweg 3, 6300 Giessen Federal Republic of Germany

SCHWAB, HAROLD LEE, lawyer; b. N.Y.C., Feb. 5, 1932; s. Harold Walter and Beatrice (Braverman) S.; m. Rowena Vivian Strauss, June 12, 1953; children—Andrew, Lisa, James. B.A., Harvard Coll., 1953; LL.B., Boston Coll., 1956. Bar: N.Y. 1957, U.S. Ct. Mil. Appeals 1958, U.S. Dist. Cts. (so. and ea. dist.) N.Y. 1967, U.S. Ct. Appeals (2d cir.) 1971, U.S. Supreme Ct. 1971, U.S. Dist. Ct. (no. dist.) N.Y. 1974, U.S. Ct. Appeals (D.C. cir.) 1986. Vice pres. H.W. Schwab Textile Corp., N.Y.C., 1959-60; assoc. Emile Z. Berman & A. Harold Frost, N.Y.C., 1960-67, ptnr., 1967-74; sr. ptnr. Lester Schwab Katz & Dwyer, N.Y.C., 1974—; lectr. N.Y. State Bar Assn., N.Y. County Lawyers Assn., Practicing Law Inst. Served to lt. col. USAFR. Mem. Soc. Automotive Engrs., ASTM, Assn. for Advancement of Automotive Medicine, Product Liability Adv. Council, Motor Vehicles Manufacterer's Assn., N.Y. State Bar Assn. (chmn. trial lawyers sect. 1980-81), Am. Bd. Trial Advs. (pres. N.Y. chpt. 1982-83), Fedn. Ins. Counsel (v.p. 1979-80), ABA, Assn. Bar City of N.Y., N.Y. County Lawyers Assn., Am. Trial Lawyers Assn., N.Y. State Trial Lawyers Assn., Def. Assn. N.Y. Clubs: Harvard of N.Y., Governors Island Officers, Mason. Contbr. articles to legal jours.; editor Trial Lawyers Sect. Newsletter-N.Y. State Bar Assn., 1981-84; mem. editorial bd. Jour. Products Liability, 1976—. Home: 205 Beach 142d St Neponsit NY 11694 Office: 120 Broadway New York NY 10271

SCHWAB, THOMAS-ARTHUR, surgeon; b. Basel, Switzerland, Nov. 2, 1939; s. Fritz-Ewald and Brigitte-Agnes (Krahmann) S.; m. Eva Beatrice Stürchler, June 11, 1982. Diploma in Medicine and Surgery, Basel U., 1967, D.M.S., 1969. Asst., registrar surgery Basel Univ. Clinics, 1968-70, 72-77. asst. surgery and obstetrics Albert Schweitzer Hosp., Lambarene, Gabon, 1970-71, 74; vice chief surgeon S. Giovanni Hosp., Bellinzona, Switzerland, 1977-80, 83; chief surgeon obstetrician Albert Schweitzer Hosp., 1980-82; chief surgeon Bleniese Hosp., Acquarossa, Switzerland, 1984—; chief surgeon field hosp., Beirut, Lebanon, 1976, Swiss Red Cross, Kassala, Sudan, 1979; instr. osteosynthesis, Davos, Switzerland, 1973, 83; instr. tropical surgery Tropical Inst., Basel, 1974, 75, 76. Contbr. articles to profl. jours. Served to 1st lt. Swiss Army, 1968—. Mem. Fed. Medico Helvetica, Ordine dei Medici del Cantone Ticino. Avocations: aviation; horse riding; art works collecting; boxing. Home: Via Monte Erto, Biasca 6710 Switzerland Office: Ospedale Bleniese, Acquarosa 6716,, Switzerland

SCHWABE, JOHN BENNETT, II, lawyer; b. Columbia, Mo., June 14, 1946; s. Leonard Wesley and Hazel Fern (Crouch) S. A.B., U. Mo.-Columbia, 1967, J.D., 1970. Bar: Mo. 1970, U.S. Dist. Ct. (we. dist.) Mo. 1970, U.S. Ct. Mil. Appeals 1971, U.S. Supreme Ct. 1973. Owner, prin. John B. Schwabe, II & Assocs., Columbia, 1974—, St. Louis, 1984—. Trustee, lay leader, mem. adminstrv. bd. Wilkes Blvd. United Meth. Ch., 1974-79, chmn. pastor-parish relations com., 1984-85 ; mem. Friends of Music, Columbia, 1979—, bd. dirs., 1979-81; bd. dirs. Mo. Symphony Soc., 1984-85 . Served to capt. JAGC, USAF, 1970-74. Mem. ABA, Boone County Bar Assn. (sec. 1977-79), Bar Assn. Met. St. Louis, Assn. Trial Lawyers Am., Mo. Assn. Trial Attys., Personal Injury Lawyers Assn., Lawyers Assn. St. Louis, Columbia C. of C., Am. Legion, Phi Delta Phi. Methodist. Club: Wilkes Men's (pres. 1977-79) (Columbia). Office: 314 N Broadway Marquette Bldg Suite 830 Saint Louis MO 63102

SCHWAGER, EDITH COHEN, editor; b. Trenton, N.J., Dec. 16, 1916; d. Michael and Clara (Panitch) Cohen; children—Michael J., Karen S. Exec. editor, adj. lectr., adminstrv. dir. alcoholism clinic Hahnemann Med. Coll. (now Hahnemann U.), Phila., 1966-75; dir. editorial services Dorland & Sweeney, 1976-81; freelance editor in medicine and pharms., 1981—. Fellow Am. Med. Writers Assn. (pres. chpt. 1973-77; editor jour. Med. Communications 1977-81, 83-85, chair editorial bd. AMWA Jour., 1985—. John P. McGovern Honor lectureship award 1983, Del. Valley chpt. Pres. award 1985, Swanberg award 1986), Women in Communications (Super-Communicator award 1984). Columnist, Dear Edie. Home: 4404 Sherwood Rd Philadelphia PA 19131

SCHWAN, LEROY BERNARD, artist; b. Somerset, Wis., Dec. 8, 1932; s. Joseph L. and Dorothy (Papenfuss) S.; student Wis. State U., River Falls, 1951-53, Southeastern Signal Sch., Ga., 1954; B.S., U. Minn., 1958, M.Ed., 1960, postgrad., 1961-64; postgrad. No. Mich. U., 1965, Tex. Tech. U., 1970, So. Ill. U., 1978, U. Iowa, 1980; children—David A., Mark J., William R., Catherine L., Maria E. Head art dept. Unity Pub. Schs., Milltown, Wis., 1958-61; instr. art Fridley Pub. Schs., Mpls., 1961-64; asst. prof. art No. Mich. U., Marquette, 1964-66; asst. prof. art Mankato (Minn.) State Coll., 1966-71, assoc. prof., 1971-74, tchr. off-campus grad. classes Northeast Mo. State U., John Wood Community Coll.; dir. Art Workshop Educultural Center, 1968; dir. art edn. Quincy (Ill.) Pub. Schs., 1974-78, now art tchr.; tchr. art to mentally retarded children, Faribault, Minn., Owatonna, Minn., Mankato, Lake Owasso Children's Home, St. Paul; dir. art workshops, Mankato, 1970, St. Paul, 1972, 73, 74, 75; dir. workshops tchrs. mentally retarded Mankato, 1971, Faribault, 1972, Omaha, 1972-73, Quincy, 1974, 79, 82, 84-86, asst. adj. Ill. VA Home, 1980—; one-man shows: Estherville Jr. Coll., 1968, Mankato State Coll., 1968, 71, 73, Farmington, Wis., 1970, 71, Good Thunder, Minn., 1972, Quincy, 1975, 77, 84, Mankato, Minn., 1975, Western Ill. U., 1979; exhibited in group shows: Pentagon, Washington, 1955, U. Minn., 1958, No. Mich. U., 1965, St. Cloud State Coll., 1967, Moorhead State Coll., 1967, Bemidji (Minn.) State Coll., 1967, MacNider Mus., Mason City, Iowa, 1969, 72, 73, 74, Gallery 500, Mankato, Minn., 1970, Rochester, Minn., 1972, Minn. Mus., St. Paul, 1973, Hannibal, Mo., 1976, 77-78, Quincy, Ill., 1976, 77, 85, Ill. Art Educators Show, 1984-85, Tchrs. Retirement Art Show, Springfield, Ill., 1987; producer ednl. TV series, 1964-65, also 2 shows Kids Komments, Sta. WGEM, Quincy; mural commd. Gem City Coll., 1977. Webelos leader Twin Valley council Boy Scouts Am., 1968-69. Served with Signal Corps, AUS, 1954-56. Recipient certificate of accomplishment Sec. Army, 1955, Golden Poet award, 1985, 86. Mem. Nat. Art Edn. Assn., Ill. Art Edn. Assn., Cath. Order Foresters, Am. Legion, Phi Delta Kappa. Author: Art Curriculum Guide Unity Public Schs., 1961; Portrait of Jean, 1974; Schwan's Art Activities, 1984; co-author: Bryant-Schwan Design Test, 1971, Bryant-Schwan Art Guide, 1973; contbr. articles to profl. jours., poems to Am. Poetry Assn. publs., 1984, 85. Home: PO Box 49 Star Prairie WI 54026 Office: 3000 Maine St Quincy IL 62301

SCHWANECKE, HELMUT, naval architect, marine engineer; b. Berlin, Nov. 22, 1927; s. Johannes Hans Karl and Elise Klara (Bierwas) S.; Dipl.Ing., Tech. U. Berlin, 1955, Dr.Ing., 1958; m. Ingrid Runde, Oct. 14, 1961. Br. leader Berlin Ship Model Basin, 1955-62; dept. leader Hamburg Ship Model Basin, 1962-73; asso. prof. naval architecture U. Tech., Hannover, 1972-73; prof. naval architecture Inst. Naval Architecture and Marine Engring., U. Tech., Vienna, Austria, 1973-81; mng. dir. Berlin Ship Model Basin (VWS), 1981—; mem. adv. council 18th, 19th and 20th Internat. Towing Tank Confs., del. 11th Conf., Tokyo, 12th, Rome, 13th, Hamburg and Berlin, 14th, Ottawa. Served with German Navy, 1945. Fellow Royal Inst. Naval Architects; mem. Soc. Naval Architects of Japan, Schiffbautechnische Gesellschaft e.V., Hamburg, Verband Deutscher Schiffahrts-Sachverständiger, e.V., Hamburg. Home: 35A Fasanenstrasse, D-1000 Berlin 15 Federal Republic of Germany

SCHWANHAUSSER, ROBERT ROWLAND, aerospace engineer; b. Buffalo, Sept. 15, 1930; s. Edwin Julius and Helen (Putnam) S.; m. Mary Lea Hunter, Oct. 17, 1953 (div. 1978); children—Robert Hunter, Mark Putnam; m. Beverly Bohn Allemann, Dec. 31, 1979. S.B. in Aero. Engring., MIT, 1952. V.p. aerospace systems, then exec. v.p. programs Teledyne Ryan Aero., San Diego, 1954-74, v.p. internat. requirements, 1977-79, v.p. Remotely Piloted Vehicles programs, 1979-81; pres. Condur, La Mesa, Calif., 1973-74; v.p. bus. devel. All Am. Engring., 1976-77; v.p. advanced programs Teledyne Brown Engring., Huntsville, Ala., 1981-83; pres. Teledyne CAE, Toledo, Ohio, 1983—; bd. dirs. Ohio Citizen's Bank, Toledo, 1987. Bd. dirs. Riverside Hosp., Toledo, 1985. Served to lt. USAF, 1952-54. Fellow AIAA (assoc., Outstanding Contbn. to Aerospace award 1971); mem. Assn. Unmanned Vehicle Systems (Pioneer award 1984), Nat. Mgmt. Assn. (Silver Knight of Mgmt. award 1972, Gold Knight of Mgmt. award 1987), Air Force Assn., Am. Def. Preparedness Assn., Nat. Rifle Assn., Navy League, Theta Delta Chi. Republican. Presbyterian. Clubs: Greenhead Hunting (Pine Valley, Calif.), Inverness (Toledo), Maumee River Yacht (Ohio), Gulf Shores Country (Ala.), The Crew's Nest (Ohio). Avocations: boating; hunting, skiing, golf. Home: 28765 East River Rd Perrysburg OH 43551 Office: Teledyne CAE 1330 Laskey Rd Toledo OH 43612

SCHWARTZ, CHERYL ANN, health lecturer, video and television producer, writer, actress; b. Cin., Sept. 4, 1949; d. Denny Lee and Alice Jane (Taylor) S. A.S., U. Cin., 1970, student 1967-72; student West Los Angeles Coll., 1977-79, Calif. State U.-Northridge, 1979-80, Pierce Coll., Woodland Hills, Calif., 1981-83, UCLA, 1986, U. So. Calif., 1986. Publisher, editor The Well Woman, Beverly Hills, Calif., 1980—, The Showhawk Flash, Hawaii Expressions; lectr. Internat. Toxic Shock Syndrome Network, Beverly Hills, 1980—, also founder, dir.; dir. Hawaii Express, Los Angeles, 1982; owner, mgr. C.A. Schwartz & Assocs., Beverly Hill, 1982—; producer, host. The Well Woman, Encino, 1983-84, Cheryl & Co., Santa Monica, Calif., 1984—; pres. Cheryl A. Schwartz Prodns., Beverly Hills, 1983—; cons. Nat. Women's Health Network, Washington, 1981—. Author: In the Gutter Looking at Stars, 1980; editor: The Showhawk Flash, Hawaii Expressions; exec. producer, writer Easy Does It: The Excercise Video for the Rest of Us; editor: The Showhawk Flash, Hawaii Expressions. Mem. commn. on Status of Women, Los Angeles, 1980—; bd. dirs. Womens Equal Rights Legal Def. and Edn. Fund, 1983—; vol. UCLA Med. Center 1976-80; mem. Inter-Agy. Council on Child Abuse and Neglect, Los Angeles, 1983, Wildlife Waystation, Starlight Found., So. Calif. Coalition on Battered Women, United Friends of the Children; media cons. Wild Horse Sanctuary; mem. women's aux. John Wayne Cancer Clinic; co-chmn. Olympic Women's Marathon Celebration, Los Angeles, 1984. Mem. Am. Fedn. TV and Radio Artists, ASTM, Am. Film Inst., Screen Actors Guild, Aircraft Owners and Pilots Assn., Calif. Women's Health Network, Writers Guild Am., Empire State Consumer Assn., Nat. Consumers League, Women in Show Bus., Women in Film, Women Health Internat. (resourcee). Republican. Clubs: Farkus (Beverly Hills); Los Angeles Polo, Show Hawks Flying. Office: PO Box 1248 Beverly Hills CA 90213-1248

SCHWARTZ, FREDERIC N., business executive; b. Springfield, Mass., Dec. 3, 1906; s. Michael J. and Regina (Burdick) S.; m. Eleanor Haley, 1935. A.B., Syracuse U., 1931, LL.D., 1963. Chmn. bd., pres. Bristol-Myers Co., until 1965, chmn. bd., 1965-66, chmn. exec. com., 1967-71. Served as lt. col. AUS, 1942-45. Decorated Legion of Merit, 1945. Mem. Delta Kappa Epsilon. Club: River, University (N.Y.C.). Office: 345 Park Ave New York NY 10154

SCHWARTZ, GERALD, public relations and fund raising agency executive; b. N.Y.C., June 22, 1927; s. George and Martha F. S.; student N.C. State U., 1944-45; A.B., U. Miami, 1949, B.S., 1950, postgrad., 1966-67; m. Felice P., June 25, 1950; children—Gary R., Gregg R., Wendy L. Staff writer Miami (Fla.) Herald, 1941-44; publicity dir. U.S. Army in Europe, 1946-48; editor Miami Beach Sun, 1950-51; fund raising and public relations counselor, Miami, 1952-58; press sec. to Gov. Nebr., 1959-60; exec. v.p. Bar-Ilan U., Ramat Gan, Israel, Israel, 1960-61; prin. Gerald Schwartz Agy., Miami, Fla., 1962—. Dep. chmn. Democratic Midwest Conf., 1958-60; pres. Am. Zionist Fedn. So. Fla., 1970-73, 86-88; nat. v.p. Am. Zionist Fedn., 85—; pres. Pres.'s council Zionist Orgn. Am., 1983-85; bd. dirs. Temple Emanu-El of Greater Miami, Papanicolaou Cancer Research Inst., Miami, 1962-80; vice chmn. Urban League of Greater Miami, 1983-87; vice chmn. City of Miami Beach Planning Bd., 1953-55; bd. dirs. Greater Miami Symphony, 1982-87, Miami Beach Taxpayers Assn.; pres. Civic League Miami Beach, 1985-87; nat. chmn. Friends of Pioneer Women/Na'amat, 1984—; pres. Greater Miami chpt. Assn. Welfare of Soldiers in Israel, 1983-86; chmn. City of Miami Beach Hurricane Def. Com., 1978-86; trustee South Shore Hosp. and Med. Ctr., Miami, 1987—; bd. govs. Barry U., 1985-86; chmn. Econ. Devel. Council City of Miami Beach, 1985—. Served with U.S. Army, 1944-46. Recipient Jerusalem Peace award State of Israel Bonds, 1978. Mem. Public Relations Soc. Am. (accredited; treas. So. Fla. chpt. 1962-64), Am. Public Relations Assn. (pres. chpt. 1960-61), Internat. Assn. Political Cons., Am. Assn. Polit. Cons, Nat. Assn. Fund Raising Execs. (pres. chpt. 1977-78), Miami Beach C. of C. (v.p. 1978-80, 81-84, 86-87), Lead and Ink, Theta Omicron Pi, Omicron Delta Kappa, Alpha Delta Sigma (pres. chpt. 1965-67), Zeta Beta Tau. Club: Tiger Bay (pres. 1986-88). Lodge: B'nai B'rith (pres. lodge 1964-66). Office: 600 Alton Rd Miami Beach FL 33139

SCHWARTZ, GERALD WILFRED, financial executive; b. Winnipeg, Man., Can., Nov. 24, 1941; s. Andrew O. and Lillian Arkin (Leith) S.; m. Heather Reisman, May 15, 1982; children—Carey, Jill, Andrea, Anthony. B.Commerce, U. Man., 1962, LL.B., 1966; M.B.A., Harvard U., 1970. Vice pres. Estabrook & Co., Inc., N.Y.C., 1970-73, Bear Stearns & Co., N.Y.C., 1973-77; pres., dir., mem. exec. com. CanWest Capital Corp., Winnipeg, 1977-83; pres., chief exec. officer ONEX Corp., Toronto, 1984—; chmn. bd., chmn. exec. com. Na-Churs Plant Food Co.; chmn. bd. Onex Packaging Inc.; chmn. bd. Sky Chefs Inc.; chmn. bd. Beatrice Foods, Can. Ltd.; chmn. bd. Purolator Courier Ltd., pres. Can West Advisor Ltd.; tchr. law Man. Inst. Chartered Accts., 1966-68, Estate Planning Inst. Can., 1966-68; adj. assoc. prof. dept. fin. Grad. Sch. Bus. Adminstrn., NYU, 1975-77. Bd. dirs. Toronto Arts Awards, Council for Bus. and Arts in Can., Can. Friends Tel Aviv U., Can. Soc. for Weizman Inst. Sci., Can. Council Christians and Jews, Mt. Sinai Hosp. of Toronto; mem. gov. council U. Toronto; nat. chmn. revenue com. Liberal Party of Can. Served with RCAF, 1958. Office: Commerce Ct, PO Box 153, Toronto, ON Canada M5L 1E7

SCHWARTZ, IRVING LEON, scientist, educator, physician; b. Cedarhurst, N.Y., Dec. 25, 1918; s. Abraham and Rose (Doniger) S.; m. Felice T. Nlerenberg, Jan. 12, 1946; children: Cornelia Ann, Albert Anthony, James Oliver. AB, Columbia U., 1939; MD, NYU, 1943. Diplomate: Am. Bd. Internal Medicine. Intern, then asst. resident Bellevue Hosp., N.Y.C., 1943-44, 46-47; NIH fellow physiology NYU Coll. Medicine, N.Y.C., 1947-50; Am. Physiol. Soc. Porter fellow, also Gibbs meml. fellow in clin. sci. Rockefeller Inst., N.Y.C., 1950-51, Am. Heart Assn. fellow, 1951-52, asst., then assoc., 1952-58; asst. physician, then assoc. physician Rockefeller Inst. Hosp., 1950-58; sr. scientist Brookhaven Nat. Lab., Upton, N.Y., 1958-61, research collaborator, 1961—; attending physician Brookhaven Nat. Lab. Hosp., 1958—; Joseph Eichberg prof. physiology, dir. dept. U. Cin. Coll. Medicine, 1961-65; dean grad. faculties Mt. Sinai Med. and Grad. Schs., CUNY, 1965-80, prof. physiology and biophysics, chmn. dept., 1968-79, exec. officer biomed. scis. doctoral program, 1969-72, Dr. Harold and Golden Lamport disting. prof., 1979—; dir. Ctr. Peptide and Membrane Research Mt. Sinai Med. Ctr., 1979-87; dean emeritus Mt. Sinai Grad. Sch. Biol. Scis., 1980—. Contbr. articles to sci. publs. Pres. Life Scis. Found., 1962—. Served from 1st lt. to capt., M.C. AUS, 1944-46. Fellow A.C.P.; mem. Am. Physiol. Soc., Soc. Exptl. Biology and Medicine, Am. Soc. Clin. Investigation, Am. Fedn. Clin. Research, Biophys. Soc., Endocrine Soc., Harvey Soc., Soc. for Neurosci., Am. Heart Assn., John Jay Assos. Columbia Coll., AAAS, N.Y. Acad. Sci., Sigma Xi, Alpha Omega Alpha. Home: 1120 Fifth Ave New York NY 10128 also: 9 Thorn Hedge Rd Bellport NY 11713 Office: CUNY Mt Sinai Med and Grad Schs 100th St and Fifth Ave New York NY 10029 also: Med Research Center Brookhaven Nat Lab Upton NY 11973

SCHWARTZ, JAMES PETER, real estate broker; b. Bridgeport, Conn., Oct. 30, 1919; s. Joseph and Fannie (Tischler) S.; m. Natalie Postol, Mar. 12, 1941; 1 child, Joseph William. Student Coll. Commerce New Haven, 1939-41. Reporter Bridgeport Times-Star, 1940-41; reporter, photographer Bridgeport Post, 1942-43, 45-49; pres. Jay James Inc., Fairfield, Conn., 1949-70; owner James P. Schwartz & Assocs., Fairfield, 1970—; dir. Lafayette Bank & Trust Co., 1965—, Lafayette Bancorp, 1985—. Treas. Greater Bridgeport Bd. Realtors, 1974-77, sr. v.p., 1978, pres., 1979. Contbg. editor Photog. Trade News, 1960-70. Pres. Barnum Festival Soc., 1975-76; ringmaster Barnum Festival, 1979; justice of peace, 1970—; mem. Easton (Conn.) Zoning Bd. Appeals, 1971-76; police commr., Easton, 1976—, chmn. bd. police commrs., 1986—; bd. dirs. Bridgeport div. Am. Cancer Soc., 1977—; bd. assocs. U. Bridgeport, 1962—. Served with AUS, 1943-45. Named Man of Yr. dept. sociology U. Bridgeport, 1962, Realtor of Yr. award Greater Bridgeport Bd. Realtors, 1979. Mem. Fairfield Bd. Realtors, Nat. Assn. Realtors (bd. dirs.), Conn. Assn. Realtors (treas. 1981-82, pres. 1984-85). Lodge: Masons. Home: 78 Blanchard Rd Easton CT 06612 Office: 161 Kings Hwy Fairfield CT 06430

SCHWARTZ, LEONARD JAY, lawyer; b. San Antonio, Sept. 23, 1943; s. Oscar S. and Ethel (Eastman) S.; m. Sandra E. Eichelbaum, July 4, 1965; 1 dau., Michele Fay. B.B.A., U. Tex. 1965, J.D., 1968. Bar: Tex. 1968, Ohio 1971, U.S. Dist. Ct. (no., ea., we., so. dists.) Tex., U.S. Dist. Ct. (no., so. dists.) Ohio, U.S. Dist. Ct. Nebr., U.S. Ct. Appeals (5th, 6th, 7th, 11th cirs.), U.S. Supreme Ct. 1971. Assoc. Roberts & Holland, N.Y.C., 1968-70; ptnr. Rigely, Schwartz & Fagan, San Antonio 1970-71; staff counsel ACLU of Ohio, Columbus, 1971-73; ptnr. Schwartz, Fisher, Spater, McNamara & Marshall, Columbus, 1973-77, Schwartz & Fishman, Columbus, 1977-79; elections counsel to sec. of state of Ohio, Columbus 1979-80; ptnr. Waterman & Schwartz, Austin, Tex., 1981-84; mng. dir. Schwartz, Waterman, Fickman & Van Os, P.C., Austin and Houston, 1984-85, sole practice, Austin, 1985-86; mng. dir. Schwartz & Eichelbaum, P.C., Austin, 1986—. lectr. in field. Contbr. articles to profl. jours. Recipient Outstanding Teaching Quizmaster award U. Tex. Sch. Law, 1968. Mem. ABA, Tex. Bar Assn., Travis County Bar Assn., Am. Trial Lawyers Assn., Tex. Trial Lawyers Assn., Phi Delta Phi. Jewish. Home and Office: 5800 Back Ct Austin TX 78731

SCHWARTZ, MARTIN WEBER, lawyer, investment advisory company executive, business consultant, author; b. N.Y.C., Sept. 30, 1944; s. Robert R. and Rose Weber (Caesar) S.; B.A., NYU, 1965; J.D., Bklyn. Law Sch., 1968. Bar: N.Y. 1971, U.S. Supreme Ct. 1975. Spl. agt. Customs Agy. Service U.S. Dept. Treasury, 1970-71; spl. agt. security, 1973-76; asst. dist. atty. Bronx County, City N.Y., 1971-73; sole practice, Yonkers, N.Y., 1976—; chief welfare frauds unit Dist. Atty.'s Office, N.Y.C., 1972-73; pres. Wall St. Research Corp., N.Y.C., 1982-85, MRM Corp., 1985—; Recipient Commendation Govt. Can., 1971; Commendation U.S. Atty. So. Dist. N.Y. 1971; Commendation Bronx County N.Y.C. Dist. Atty., 1972; Commendation Police Commr. City N.Y. 1973; cert. award U.S. Dept. Treasury, 1976. Mem. ABA, N.Y. State Bar Assn., Assn. of Bar of City of N.Y., N.Y. Acad. Sci. Jewish. Contbr. in field. Office: 23 Centuck Station Yonkers NY 10710

SCHWARTZ, MORTIMER LEONARD, medical educator, researcher; b. Newark, Jan. 12, 1915; s. Herman and Rose (Nusbaum) S.; m. Rene Kanengiser, Mar. 25, 1941; children—Gary, Jessica Schwartz Auerbach, Alison. M.D., Eclectic Med. Coll., Cin., 1938. Diplomate Am. Bd. Internal Medicine, Am. Bd. Cardiovascular Disease. Intern Alexian Bros. Hosp., Elizabeth, N.J., 1938-39; resident Jersey City Hosp., 1947-48; practiced medicine specializing in internal medicine and cardiovascular disease, N.J., 1940-42, 46-47, 47—; mem. faculty N.J. Med. Sch., Newark, 1958-72; prof. medicine Albert Einstein Coll. Medicine, Bronx, N.Y., 1973-77; chief cardiovascular sect. Bronx Lebanon Hosp., 1972-77; dir. medicine Mountainside Hosp., Montclair, N.J., 1977-80; prof. medicine U. Medicine and Dentistry/N.J. Med. Sch., Newark, 1966-72, 79—; dir. dept. medicine Bergen Pines County Hosp., Paramus, N.J., 1981-84. Served to maj. U.S. Army, 1942-46. Recipient Harry Gold award, 1974. Fellow ACP Am. Coll. Cardiology, Am. Coll. Chest Physicians, Council on Clin. Cardiology of Am. Heart Assn., Am. Coll. Clin. Pharmacology. Research on pharmacology. Home: 49-51 Sommer Ave Maplewood NJ 07040

SCHWARTZ, PERRY LESTER, infosystems engineer, consultant; b. Bklyn., July 29, 1939; s. Max David and Sylvia (Weinberger) S.; m. Arlene Metz, Jan. 24, 1960; 3 children. BEE, CUNY, 1957-62; MS in Indsl. Engring. and Computer Sci., NYU, 1967. Registered profl. engr., N.J.; registered profl. planner, N.J.; cert. mediator and arbitrator. Microwave engr. Airbourne Inst. Lab., Deer Park, N.Y., 1962-63, ITT Fed. Labs., Nutley, N.J., 1963-64; program mgr. Western Electric Co., N.Y.C., 1964-69; dept.

head RCA, Princeton, N.J., 1970-71; dir. engring. Warner Communications Inc., N.Y.C., 1972-74; cons. engr. Intertech Assocs., Englishtown, N.J., 1974—; adj. faculty CCNY, 1962-71, Ocean County Coll., Toms River, N.J., 1981-83, Rutgers U., New Brunswick, N.J., 1984-87. Mem. Am. Cons. Engrs. Council, Nat. Assn. Radio and Telecommunications Engrs. (sr. mem., charter mem.), IEEE (sr.), Intelligent Bldgs. Inst. Found. (steering com., trustee 1982—), Nat. Soc. Profl. Engrs., Cons. Engrs. Council N.J., Am. Arbitration Assn., Zeta Beta Tau (chpt. founder 1958). Lodge: K.P. Office: Intertech Associates 7 Plaza Nine Englishtown NJ 07726

SCHWARTZ, PETER, controller; b. Berlin, Feb. 27, 1938; s. Clemens and Edith (Wienands) S.; m. Birgit Claas, Apr. 25, 1969; children: Bettina, Martin. Degree in econs., U. Cologne, Fed. Republic Germany, 1967; postgrad., Econ. Inst. of the Iron and Steel Industry, Dusseldorf, Fed. Republic Germany, 1967-68. Asst. to bd. Rheinstahl Huettenwerke AG, Essen, Fed. Republic Germany, 1968-69; coordinator of affiliates Henkel KGaA, Dusseldorf, Fed. Republic Germany, 1969-78, fin. controller, head controlling Henkel Group, 1985—; dir. controlling div. Henkel France SA, Paris, 1979-85. Contbr. articles to profl. jours. Home: 11 Lucas-BolsStr, 4040 Neuss Federal Republic of Germany Office: Henkel KGaA, PO Box 1100, 4000 Dusseldorf Federal Republic of Germany

SCHWARTZ, PHILIP, lawyer; b. N.Y.C., June 7, 1930; s. Louis and Kate (Brodsky) S.; m. Iris M. Ballin, Nov. 28, 1953 (div. 1979); children: David, Elyse, Donna; m. Monique W. Wagner, July 26, 1982. BA, George Washington U., 1952, JD, 1959; LLM in Taxation, Georgetown U., 1961. Bar: Va. 1959, D.C. 1966, U.S. Ct. Appeals (D.C. cir.) 1966, U.S. Ct. Mil. Appeals 1966, U.S. Supreme Ct. 1966, U.S. Ct Appeals (4th cir.) 1982, U.S. Ct. Internat. Trade, 1988, N.Am. Council London Ct. Internat. Arbitration, 1988. Sr. intelligence analyst Nat. Security Agy., Washington, 1952-54, 56-63; assoc. Varoutsos, Koutoulakos & Arthur, Arlington, Va., 1963-67; ptnr. Schwartz and Ellis, Ltd., Arlington, 1968—; instr. No. Va. Life Underwriters Tng. Council, Fairfax, Va., 1974, No. Va. Paralegal Inst., Arlington, 1976; moot ct. judge George Washington U., Washington, 1976, Georgetown U., Washington, 1977; speaker, lectr. in field. Mem. Arlington County Bd. Zoning Appeals, 1972-85, Arlington County Council Human Relations, 1973; bd. dirs. Jewish Community Ctr. Greater Washington, 1975. Served with M.I., U.S. Army, 1954-56. Fellow Am. Acad. Matrimonial Lawyers (sec. 1986—, pres. U.S. chpt.), Internat. Acad. Matrimonial Lawyers; mem. ABA (chmn. family law sect. com. internat. laws and procedures 1983-86, com. fed. legislation 1986—), Internat. Bar Assn. (vice-chmn. family law div. 1984—, liaison officer to IMF), Va. Trial Lawyers Assn. (instr. 1984), Assn. Trial Lawyers Am., Va. State Bar (bd. govs. internat. law sect., liaison to ABA internat. law sect.), N.Y. State Bar Assn. (internat. law sect.), D.C. Bar, Arlington County Bar Assn. (cts. com., legis. com.), Brit. Inst. Internat. and Comparative Law, Am. Soc. Internat. Law, Inter-Am. Bar Assn., Internat. Soc. Family Law, Solicitors Family Law Assn. London (assoc.), Am. Fgn. law Assn., Internat. Law Assn., Asia-Pacific Lawyers Assn., Arlington Jaycees, Phi Epsilon Pi, Delta Phi Epsilon, Phi Delta Phi. Lodge: Kiwanis. Office: Schwartz Ellis & Sullivan Ltd 6950 N Fairfax Dr Arlington VA 22213

SCHWARTZ, RICHARD BRENTON, educator, university dean, writer; b. Cin., Oct. 5, 1941; s. Jack Jay and Marie Mildred (Schnelle) S.; m. Judith Mary Lang, Sept. 7, 1963; 1 son, Jonathan Francis. A.B., U. Notre Dame, 1963; A.M., U. Ill., 1964, Ph.D., 1967. Instr. English U.S. Mil. Acad., 1967-69; asst. prof. U. Wis.-Madison, 1969-72, assoc. prof., 1972-78, prof., 1978-81; assoc. dean U. Wis.-Madison (Grad. Sch.), 1977, 79-81; prof. English, dean Grad. Sch., Georgetown U., Washington, 1981—; mem. exec. bd. Ctr. Strategic and Internat. Studies, 1981—. Author: Samuel Johnson and the New Science, 1971, Samuel Johnson and the Problem of Evil, 1975, Boswell's Johnson: A Preface to the Life, 1978, Daily Life in Johnson's London, 1983; editor: The Plays of Arthur Murphy, 4 vols, 1979; contbr. articles to profl. jours. Served to capt. U.S. Army, 1967-69. Nat. Endowment Humanities grantee, 1970, 87; Inst. for Research in Humanities fellow, 1976; Am. Council Learned Socs. fellow, 1978-79; H.I. Romnes fellow, 1978-81. Mem. MLA, Johnson Soc. So. Calif., Am. Soc. Eighteenth-Century Studies, Council Grad. Schs., NE Assn. Grad. Schs. (exec. com. 1986—), Assn. Grad. Schs. in Cath. Univs. (exec. com. 1984—), N.Am. Confr. British Studies. Roman Catholic. Home: 4132 41st St N Arlington VA 22207 Office: Georgetown U Grad Sch Washington DC 20057

SCHWARTZ, ROBERT GEORGE, insurance company executive; b. Czechoslovakia, Mar. 27, 1928; came to U.S., 1929, naturalized, 1935; s. George and Frances (Antoni) S.; m. Caroline Bachurski, Oct. 12, 1952; children: Joanne, Tracy, Robert G. B.A., Pa. State U., 1949; M.B.A., NYU, 1956. With Met. Life Ins. Co., N.Y.C., 1949—, v.p. securities, 1968-70, v.p., 1970-75, sr. v.p., 1975-78, exec. v.p., 1979-80, vice chmn. bd., chmn. investments com., 1980-83, chmn., 1983—, also dir. parent co. and various subs.; dir. NL Industries, Inc., N.Y.C., Potlatch Corp., San Francisco, Lowe's Cos., Inc., North Wilkesboro, N.C., Kaiser Cement Corp., Oakland, Calif., R.H. Macy & Co., Inc., N.Y.C.; chmn. investment adv. com. The Christophers, Inc., 1979—. Mem. Pres.'s Export Council; trustee Com. for Econ. Devel.; bd. dirs. Greater N.Y. council Boy Scouts Am. Served with AUS, 1950-52. Recipient Alumni Achievement award NYU Grad. Sch. Bus. Adminstrn., 1981, Disting. Alumni award Pa. State U., 1983. Mem. Alpha Chi Rho. Clubs: Treasurers (Ligonier, Pa.), Seaview Country (Ligonier, Pa.), Springdale Country (Ligonier, Pa.), Laurel Valley Golf (Ligonier, Pa.); Marco Polo (N.Y.C). Office: Met Life Ins Co 1 Madison Ave New York NY 10010 other: Mobil Corp 150 E 42nd St New York NY 10017 *

SCHWARTZ, ROBERT WILLIAM, consultant; b. N.Y.C., Oct. 23, 1944; s. Edward and Bertha R. Schwartz; B.S., Cornell U., 1967; postgrad. in bus. adminstrn. SUNY, Albany, 1970; m. Gail Beth Greenbaum, Mar. 18, 1967; children—Jill, Evan. Asso., IBM, 1967-68; cons. Peat, Marwick, Mitchell & Co., Albany, 1970-71; v.p. Security Gen. Services, Inc., Rochester, N.Y., 1971-73; v.p. fin. and adminstrn. Gardenway Mfg. Co., Troy, N.Y., 1973-77; exec. v.p. United Telecommunications Corp., Latham, N.Y., 1977-79, pres., 1980-82, also dir.; pres., chief exec. officer Winsource, Inc., Albany, N.Y., 1982-85; pres., chief exec. officer Robert W. Schwartz, Inc., 1985—; dir. Caddim Corp., Union Nat. Bank, Albany; adj. prof. Rochester Inst. Tech., 1971-73. Bd. dirs. United Cerebral Palsy of Capital Dist., 1973—; trustee Newman Found., Rensselaer Poly. Inst., 1974-78, Gov. Clinton council Boy Scouts Am. Mem. Am. Mgmt. Assn., N.Am. Telephone Assn., Assn. for Systems Mgmt. Republican. Clubs: Ft. Orange; Economic, Cornell (N.Y.C.). Home and Office: 2 Myton Ln Menands NY 12204

SCHWARTZ, SANDRA, science and mathematics educator; b. N.Y.C., Jan. 25, 1932; d. Abraham and Pauline (Eisner) Wiener; divorced; children—Rachel Paula Fainman, Abby G. Schwartz. B.S. in Edn., CCNY, 1951; M.S., Rutgers U., 1952; Ph.D., Yale U., 1956. Vis. instr., dep. chmn. Columbia U., 1964-69; adj. asst. prof. Baruch Coll., N.Y.C., 1979-80; instr. Queens Coll., N.Y.C., 1980-81; adj. asst. prof. N.Y. Inst. Tech., 1979—; mem. faculty New Sch., N.Y.C., 1981—. Chmn. LWV, N.Y.C., 1961-63. Fellow Rutgers U., 1951-52, Yale U., 1952-56; research grantee AAUW, 1955-56. Mem. AAAS, Am. Astron. Soc., Planetary Soc., Nat. Space Inst. Current work: Research in radiative transfer; teacher of astronomy, astrophysics (graduate level) space science, physics, mathematics. Home: 401 E 86th St New York NY 10028

SCHWARTZ, (ELLEN) SHIRLEY ECKWALL, chemist; b. Detroit, Aug. 26, 1935; d. Emil Victor and Jessie Grace (Galbraith) Eckwall; m. Ronald Elmer Schwartz, Aug. 25, 1957; children: Steven Dennis, Bradley Allen, George Byron. B.S., U. Mich., 1957; M.S., Wayne State U., 1962, Ph.D., 1970; B.S., Detroit Inst. Tech., 1978. Asst. prof. Detroit Inst. Tech., 1973-78, head div. math. sci., 1976-78; research staff mem. BASF Wyandotte Corp., Wyandotte, Mich., 1978-81, head sect. functional fluids, 1981; staff research scientist Gen. Motors Corp., Warren, Mich., 1981—. Contbr. articles to profl. jours.; patentee in field. Corr. sec. Childbirth Without Pain Edn. Assn., 1962; corr. sec. Warren-Centerline Human Relations Council, 1968. Recipient Wilbur Deutsch Meml. award, 1987, McCuen award, 1988. Mem. Am. Soc. Lubrication Engrs. (treas. Detroit sect. 1981, pres. sect. 1982-83, dir. 1985—), Am. Chem. Soc., Tissue Culture Assn., Soc. Automotive Engrs., Mensa, Sigma Xi. Lutheran. Club: Classic Guitar Soc. Mich. Office: Gen Motors Research Labs Warren MI 48090

SCHWARTZ, VALERIE BREUER, interior designer; b. Senica, Czechoslovakia, May 13, 1912; came to U.S., 1928, naturalized, 1928; d. Jacob and Ethel (Weiss) Breuer; m. Leo Schwartz, Feb. 5, 1939; children—Catherine, Robert, William. Student States Real Gymnazium, Prague, 1925-28; Parsons N.Y. Sch. of Fine and Applied Arts, 1930-32. Cert. Am. Soc. Interior Designers. Self-employed interior designer, N.J., 1932—. Contbr. to various mags. including N.Y. Times, House & Garden, Cue Mag., Confort, Argentina; guest radio talk shows. Mem. Hadassah (life). Designed Holocaust Room, Kean Coll., N.J.

SCHWARTZ, WILLIAM, university dean, legal educator; b. Providence, May 6, 1933; s. Morris Victor and Martha (Glassman) S.; m. Bernice Konigsberg, Jan. 13, 1957; children: Alan Gershon, Robin Libby. A.A., Boston U., 1952, J.D. magna cum laude, 1955, M.A., 1960; postgrad., Harvard Law Sch., 1955-56. Bar: D.C. 1956, Mass. 1962. Prof. law Boston U., 1955—, Fletcher prof. law, 1968-70, Roscoe Pound prof. law, 1970-73, dean Sch. of Law, 1980-88, dir. Ctr. for Estate Planning, 1988—; of counsel firm Swartz & Swartz, Boston, 1973-80; counsel Cadwalader, Wickersham and Taft, N.Y.C., Washington and Palm Beach, 1988—; mem. faculty Frances Glessner Lee Inst., Harvard Med. Sch., Nat. Coll. Probate Judges, 1970, 77, 78, 79; gen. dir. Assn. Trial Lawyers Am., 1968-73; reporter New Eng. Trial Judges Conf., 1965-67; participant Nat. Met. Cts. Conf., 1968; dir. Mass. Probate Study, 1976—; of cousel Cadwalader, Wickersham and Taft, N.Y., Washington D.C. and Fla., 1988—; vice chmn. bd. UST Corp.; bd. dirs. Viacom Inc., Viacom Internat. Inc., U.S.T. Corp.; mem. legal adv. com. N.Y. Stock Exchange. Author: Future Interests and Estate Planning, 1965, 77, 81, 86, Comparative Negligence, 1970, A Products Liability Primer, 1970, Civil Trial Practice Manual, 1972, New Vistas in Litigation, 1973, Massachusetts Pleading and Practice, 7 vols, 1974-80, others.; Note editor: Boston U. Law Rev, 1954-55; property editor: Annual Survey of Mass. Law, 1960—; Contbr. articles to legal jours. Bd. dirs. Kerry Found.; trustee Hebrew Coll., 1975—, Salva Regina Coll.; rep. Office Public Info., UN, 1968-73; chmn. legal adv. panel Nat. Commn. Med. Malpractice, 1972-73; examiner of titles Commonwealth of Mass., 1964—; spl. counsel Mass. Bay Transp. Authority, 1979—. Recipient Homer Albers award Boston U., 1955, John Ordronaux prize, 1955; Disting. Service award Religious Zionists Am., 1977; William W. Treat award; William O. Douglas award. Mem. ABA, Am. Law Inst., Mass. Bar Assn. (chmn. task force tortliability), Mass. Trial Lawyers Assn., Nat. Coll. Probate Judges (hon. mem.), Phi Beta Kappa. Office: 765 Commonwealth Ave Boston MA 02215

SCHWARTZMAN, JACK, lawyer, educator, writer; b. Vinnitsa, USSR, Mar. 22, 1912; came to U.S., 1925; s. Solomon and Anna (Toporoff) S.; m. Vivian Reicher; children: Steven, Marcia, Robert. BS, CCNY, 1936; LLB, Bklyn. Law Sch., 1936, JSD, 1953; PhD, NYU, 1970. Bar: N.Y. 1938. Instr., Henry George Sch., N.Y.C., 1938-40, 46-49, 68-72, Rhodes Sch., N.Y.C., 1956-60; editor, writer Fragments Quar., Floral Park, N.Y., 1963—; prof. Nassau Community Coll., SUNY, Garden City, 1964—; sole practice, N.Y.C., L.I., 1938—; lectr. in field. Author: Rebels of Individualism, 1949; Alleged Rights to Organize Under the Soviet Constitution, 1953, The Philosophy and Politics of Paul N. Miliokov, 1970; contbr. chpts. to books and over 400 articles to profl. jours. Served to capt. AUS, 1942-46. Decorated Citation for the Army Commendation; recipient Founders Day award NYU, 1971; N.Y. State Chancellor's award for excellence in teaching SUNY, 1974. Mem. N.Y. State Bar Assn., Disting. Teaching Professorship (rev. com.), MLA, Thoreau Soc., Albert Jay Nock Soc., Council of Georgist Orgns., Univ. Profs. Acad. Order, Acad. of Polit. Sci., Found. for Econ. Edn., Albert Keith Chesterton Soc., Christopher Morley Knothole Assn., Internat. Platform Assn., N.Y. Acad. of Sci., Walt Whitman Birthplace Assn., Henry George Inst. (bd. dirs.), Walden Forever Free (bd. sponsors), Townsend Harris Assn., Pi Sigma Alpha, Phi Theta Kappa. Office: 87-16 Winchester Blvd Suite 3E Bellerose NY 11427

SCHWARZ, HANS THOMAS, linguist, language expert; b. Frankfurt, Germany, Dec. 15, 1919; s. Johann and Elisabeth (Laufer) S.; m. Alma Fischer, Oct. 15, 1944; children—Norbert, Wolfgang. Student pub. schs., Frankfurt. Adminstrv. mgr. mil. govt., Fed. Republic Germany, 1945-48; chief clk. wholesale and fgn. trade, Fed. Republic Germany, 1948-55; owner, operator Hans Th. Schwarz Translation Service, Frankfurt, 1955—, also dir. Decorated Cross of Merit 2d and 1st class (Govt. of Fed. Republic Germany); recipient Letter of Honor, Govt. of Hesse, Wiesbaden, Fed. Republic Germany, 1975. Mem. Internat. Fedn. Translators (sr. v.p., author, editor Babel bull., v.p., 1974—, Pierr-F. Caille Meml. medal, 1981), German Fedn. Translators (pres. 1974—), Inst. Linguists (Diamond Jubilee medal 1975). Home: Olbrichstrasse 53, 6 Frankfurt am Main Federal Republic of Germany

SCHWARZ, HANS-RUDOLF, mathematics educator; b. Zurich, Switzerland, Nov. 20, 1930; s. Jakob and Anna (Ochsner) S.; m. Rosmarie Hatt, May 7, 1958; 1 child, Beatrice. Diploma in math., Swiss Fed. Inst. Tech., Zurich, 1953, PhD in Math., 1957. Cert. educator Switzerland. Mathematician airplane factory Altenrhein, Switzerland, 1953-57; research asst. Swiss Fed. Inst. Tech., 1957-72; asst. prof. U. Zurich, 1972-74, assoc. prof., 1974-83, prof. mathematics, 1983—; vis. assoc. prof. Brown U., Providence, 1962-63. Author: Numerical Linear Algebra, 1968, Finite Element Method, 1980, Fortran Programs for FEM, 1981, Numerical Analysis, 1986. Mem. Swiss Math. Soc., Soc. Indsl. Applied Math., Soc. Applied Math, German Math. Soc. Office: U Zurich, Ramistrasse 74, CH-8001 Zurich Switzerland

SCHWARZ, WOLFGANG, psychologist; b. Stuttgart, Ger., Oct. 30, 1926; s. Mole and Edith (Gutstein) S.; brought to U.S., 1934, naturalized, 1940; A.B., N.Y. U., 1948, A.M., 1949, Ph.D., 1956; m. Cynthia Mae Johnson, Sept. 12, 1949 (div.); children—Amy Maria, Casey Andrew, Darcy Lynn, Priscilla Anne, Lydia Beth, Emily Jane; m. Susan Decker, 1976; children—Jaime Bartholomew, Noah. Intern, Bellevue Med. Center, N.Y., 1949-51; chief psychology Rip Van Winkle Med. Found., Hudson, N.Y., 1951-53; dir. psychology Hillcrest Med. Center, Tulsa, 1953-56, Hollywood Presbyn. Hosp., Los Angeles, 1956-58; cons. psychology Cedars Lebanon Hosp., Los Angeles, 1956-58; spl. cons. to D.C. Govt., 1959-61, NIH, Bethesda, Md., 1962-64; dir. psychol. research Mass. Dept. Mental Health, Boston and Malden, 1965-68; individual practice clin. psychology, Tulsa, 1953-56, Beverly Hills, Calif., 1956-59, Washington, 1959-63, Concord and Malden, Mass., 1963-73, Mt. Kisco, N.Y., 1973—; lectr. U. Tulsa, 1953-54, Hillcrest Med. Center, Tulsa, 1953-56, Los Angeles State Coll., 1956-57; asst. prof. Howard U., 1961; asso. prof. George Washington U., 1961-62; vis. research asst. Harvard Psychiatry, Lab., 1966-68; prof. Malden Hosp., 1968-71; cons. No. Westchester Hosp., 1974—, United Hosp., 1975—, Four Winds Hosp., 1975-80; cons. psychology Peace Corps, Mass., 1969—. Mem. exec. com. Mayor's Model City Program, Malden, 1967-68. Served with USNR, 1945-46. Recipient Founder's Day award N.Y. U., 1956, Individual award USPHS/NIH, 1960-64. Diplomate Am. Bd. Profl. Psychology. Mem. Am., N.Y., Mass. psychol. assns., Washington Soc. History of Medicine (exec. com. 1963-64), N.Y. Acad. Scis., Psi Chi, Beta Lambda Sigma. Author: A Survey of the Mental Health Facilities in the District of Columbia, 1961; also articles. Home: 81 Paulding Dr Chappaqua NY 10514 Office: 121 Smith Ave Mount Kisco NY 10549

SCHWARZBART, ROBERT MORTON, judge; b. N.Y.C., July 20, 1931; s. Hugo and Lilly (Goodfriend) S.; m. Sandra Rae Blockstein, Mar. 26, 1972. B.A., N.Y. U., 1953; J.D., Bklyn. Law Sch., 1958. Bar: N.Y. 1959, U.S. Ct. Appeals (2d and 3d cirs.) 1964. Pvt. pratice, N.Y.C., 1958-61; with NLRB, Chgo., Ill., Newark, and Washington, 1961—, atty., 1961-69, trial specialist, 1969-71, Supervisory atty., 1971-75, adminstrv. law judge, Washington, 1975—; judge Moot Ct., Seton Hall U., 1974; vis. lectr. Fairleigh Dickinson U., 1967. Served with U.S. Army, 1954-56. Recipient cert. commendation Gen. Counsel NLRB, 1973. Mem. ABA (Conf. Adminstrv. Law Judges, sects. on litigation and labor law), Fed. Adminstrv. Law Judges Conf. (exec. bd. 1977-78). Office: 1717 Pennsylvania Ave NW Washington DC 20570

SCHWARZENBACHER, GERALD, export marketing executive; b. Radenthein, Austria, Apr. 11, 1950; s. Sylvester and Inge (Ritter) S. MBA, U. Vienna, 1979. Fin. analyst Genossenschaftliche Aentralbank, Vienna, 1979-80; mktg. asst. Österr, Doka, Amstetten, Austria, 1980-82; export mgr. Ybbstaler Obstverwertung, Amstetten, Austria, 1982-85, Adler-Lackfabrik, Schwarz, Austria, 1985-87; export mktg. mgr. Österreichische Weinmarketing, Vienna, 1987—. Served with Austrian Army, 1970-77. Mem. Austrian Mktg. Assn., Austrian Brit. Assn., Austrian Am. Assn., Austrian-Latinamerica Assn. Home: Feldwed 2, 9545 Radenthein, Karnten Austria Office: Austrian Winemarketing, Gumpendorferstrabe 5, 1060 Vienna Austria

SCHWARZROCK, SHIRLEY PRATT, author, lecturer, educator; b. Mpls., Feb. 27, 1914; d. Theodore Ray and Myrtle Pearl (Westphal) Pratt; B.S., U. Minn., 1935, M.A., 1942, Ph.D., 1974; m. Loren H. Schwarzrock, Oct. 19, 1945 (dec. 1966); children: Kay Linda, Ted Kenneth, Lorraine V. Sec. to chmn. speech dept., U. Minn., Mpls., 1935, instr. in speech, 1946, team tchr. in creative arts workshops for tchrs., 1955-56, guest lectr. Dental Sch., 1967-72, asst. prof. (part-time) of practice adminstrn. Sch. Dentistry, 1972-80; tchr. speech, drama and English, Preston (Minn.) High Sch., 1935-37; tchr. speech, drama and English, Owatonna (Minn.) High Sch., 1937-39, also dir. dramatics, 1937-39; tchr. creative dramatics and English, tchr.-counselor Webster Groves (Mo.) Jr. High Sch., 1939-40; dir. dramatics and tchr.-counselor Webster Groves Sr. High Sch., 1940-43; exec. sec. bus. and profl. dept. YWCA, Mpls., 1943-45; tchr. speech and drama Covent of the Visitation, St. Paul, 1958; editor pro-tem Am. Acad. Dental Practice Adminstrn., 1966-68; guest tchr. Coll. St. Catherine, St. Paul, 1969; vol. mgr. Gift Shop, Eitel Hosp., Mpls., 1981-83; cons. for dental med. programs Normandale Community Coll., Bloomington, Minn., 1968; cons. on pub. relations to dentists, 1954—; guest lectr. to various dental groups, 1966—; lectr. Internat. Congress on Arts and Communication, 1980, Am. Inst. Banking, 1981; condr. tutorials in speaking and profl. office mgmt., 1985—. Author books (series): Coping with Personal Identity, Coping with Human Relationships, Coping with Facts and Fantasies, Coping with Teenage Problems, 1984; individual book titles include: Do I Know the "Me" Others See?, My Life-What Shall I Do With It?, Living with Loneliness, Learning to Make Better Decisions, Grades, What's So Important About Them, Anyway?, Facts and Fantasies About Alcohol, Facts and Fantasies About Smoking, Food as a Crutch, Facts and Fantasies About the Roles of Men and Women, You Always Communicate Something, Appreciating People-Their Likenesses and Differences, Fitting In, To Like and Be Liked, Can You Talk With Someone Else? Coping with Emotional Pain, Some Common Crutches, Parents Can Be a Problem, Coping with Cliques, Crises Youth Face Today; Effective Dental Assisting, 1954, (with J.R. Jensen) 6th edit., 82; (with Lorraine Schwarzrock) Workbook for Effective Dental Assisting, 1979, 6th edit., 1982, Manual for Effective Dental Assisting, 1978, 6th edit., 1982; (with Donovan F. Ward) Effective Medical Assisting, 1969, 1976; Workbook for Effective Medical Assisting, 1969, 76; Manual for Effective Med. Assisting, 1969, 2d edit., 1976; author: (with C.G. Wrenn) The Coping With series of books for high sch. students, 1970, 73, The Coping With Series Manual, 1973, 2d edit., 1984, Contemporary Concerns of Youth, 1980. Pres. University Elem. Sch. PTA, 1955-56. Fellow Internat. Biog. Assn.; mem. Minn. Acad. Dental Practice Adminstrn. (hon.), Internat. Platform Assn., Zeta Phi Eta (pres. 1948-49), Eta Sigma Upsilon.

SCHWARZSTEIN, RICHARD JOSEPH, lawyer; b. Yonkers, N.Y., July 6, 1934; s. Jack H. and Beatrice (Florman) S.; m. Ann Sanford Adsley; children: Cynthia L., Alisa J., Amy B. AB, Columbia Coll., N.Y.C., 1956; JD, Harvard U., 1959. Bar: N.Y. 1960, U.S. Dist. Ct. (ea. and so. dists.) N.Y. 1960, U.S. Ct. Appeals (2d cir.) N.Y. 1960, U.S. Dist. Ct. (cen. dist.) Calif., 1976. Clk. White & Case, N.Y.C., 1957-58; assoc. Kramer & Lans, N.Y.C., 1960-62; assoc., then ptnr. Delson & Gordon, N.Y.C., 1961-74; sole practice, Newport Beach, Calif., 1974—; lectr. George Washington U. Law Sch., U. Calif., Irvine, Calif. State U., Fullerton, Long Beach, Orange Coast Coll., U. So. Calif. Contbr. articles to profl. jours. Bd. dirs. Orange County Philharmonic Soc., 1975—, Econ. Devel. Corp. Orange County, 1983-85, Hist. and Cultural Found. Orange County, 1985—. Mem. ABA, Internat. Bar Assn., Calif. Bar Assn. (econ. and law sect. exec. com. 1977-80, exec. com., internat. practice com. 1986-87), Orange County Bar Assn. (chmn. internat. law sect. 1984—), World Trade Center Assn. Orange County (bd. dirs. 1976—, chmn. 1986—), Orange County C. of C., Am. Arbitration Assn. (nat. panel), Union Internationale des Avocats. Lodge: Rotary. Home: 441 El Bosque Laguna Beach CA 92651 Office: 1201 Dove St 6th Fl Newport Beach CA 92660

SCHWEBEL, BERNICE LOIS, educator, corporate executive; b. Hartford, Conn., Sept. 27, 1916; d. Joseph and Sara (Brewer) Davison; B.A., Russell Sage Coll., 1938; teaching cert. SUNY, 1949; M.A., NYU, 1963; m. Milton Schwebel, Sept. 3, 1939; children—Andrew, Robert. Co-founder, dir. Counseling and Placement Services for Refugees, Jewish Community Center, Troy, N.Y., 1936; social case worker Troy Orphan Asylum, 1938-39; cottage mother Pleasantville (N.Y.) Cottage Sch., 1939-40; head tchr. Birnby Nursery Sch., N.Y.C., 1945-46; tchr. kindergarten, primary grades, Valley Stream, N.Y., 1950-67; supr. student tchrs. edn. dept. Douglass Coll., Rutgers U., New Brunswick, N.J., 1973-76; v.p. ednl. programs and materials Univ. Assocs., Columbus, Ohio, 1976—; treas. Continental Land Holding, New Brunswick, 1984—. Trustee, Rutgers-Livingston Day Care Ctr., 1977-80; chmn. Rutgers-Old Queens Visitation Com., New Brunswick Tercentenary, 1979-80. Mem. Authors Guild, LWV, NOW, Women's League of Voters, Russell Sage Alumnae Assn., N.Y.U. Alumni Assn. Co-author film script Resistance to Learning, 1962; author: Student Teachers Handbook, 1979; contbr. articles to various publs. Home: 1050 George St New Brunswick NJ 08901 Office: Univ Assocs 4123 Kendra Ct S Columbus OH 43220

SCHWEBEL, MILTON, psychologist, educator; b. Troy, N.Y., May 11, 1914; s. Frank and Sarah (Oxenhandler) S.; m. Bernice Lois Davison, Sept. 3, 1939; children—Andrew I., Robert S. A.B., Union Coll., 1934; M.A., SUNY, Albany, 1936; Ph.D., Columbia U., 1949; certificate in psychotherapy, Postgrad. Center for Mental Health, 1958. Diplomate: Am. Bd. Examiners Profl. Psychology; licensed psychologist, N.Y., N.J. Reporter, radio news announcer, tchr., career counselor, labor market analyst 1936-43; asst. prof. psychology Mohawk Champlain Coll., 1946-49; asst. to prof. edn., dept. chmn., assoc. dean NYU, 1949-67; dean, prof. edn. Grad. Sch. Edn., Rutgers U., New Brunswick, N.J., 1967-77; prof. Grad. Sch. Applied and Profl. Psychology, 1977-85, prof. emeritus, 1985—; vis. prof. U. So. Calif., U. Hawaii; lectr. psychologist Postgrad. Center for Mental Health, 1958-60; cons. NIMH, U.S., state, city depts. edn., ednl. ministries Europe, Asia, UNESCO, univs. and pub. schs.; pvt. cons. psychologist and psychotherapist, 1953—. Author: The Interests of Pharmacists, 1951, (with Ella Harris) Health Counseling, 1951, Resistance to Learning, 1963, Who Can Be Educated, 1968, (with Andrew, Bernice and Carol Schwebel) Student Teacher's Manual, 1979; film Why Some Children Don't Learn, 1962; State of the Art Report: Research on Cognitive Development and Its Facilitation, 1983; editor: Behavioral Science and Human Survival, 1965, Piaget in the Classroom, 1973, Mental Health Implications of Life in the Nuclear Age, 1986, Facilitating Cognitive Development, 1986; rev. editor: Am. Jour. Orthopsychiatry, 1963-71; mem. editorial bd.: Jour. Contemporary Psychotherapy, 1965-73, Jour. Counseling Psychology, 1966-75; Jour. Social Issues, 1965-70, NYU Edn. Quar, 1969-84, Rev. of Edn, 1974—, Rutgers Profl. Psychology Rev, 1981—; editorial advisory bd.: Change in Higher Edn, 1969-74. Trustee Edn. Law Center, 1973-81; trustee Nat. Com. Employment Youth, Nat. Child Labor Com., 1967-75, Union Exptl. Colls. and Univs., 1976-78; chmn. adv. com. Nat. Com. Edn. Migrant Children, 1970-75; Pres. Nat. Orgn. for Migrant Children, 1980-85. Served with AUS, 1943-46, ETO. Postdoctoral fellow Postgrad. Center for Mental Health, 1954-56; Met. Applied Research Council fellow, 1970-71. Fellow Am. Psychol. Assn., Am. Orthopsychiatry Assn., Soc. Psychol. Study Social Issues; Jean Piaget Soc. (trustee), Am. Ednl. Research Assn., N.Y. Acad. Scis. Home: 1050 George St Apt 17-L New Brunswick NJ 08901 Office: Rutgers U Grad Sch Applied and Profl Psychology Piscataway NJ 08854

SCHWEBEL, STEPHEN MYRON, judge; b. N.Y.C., Mar. 10, 1929; s. Victor and Pauline (Pfeffer) S.; m. Louise Ingrid Nancy Killander, Aug. 2, 1972; children: Jennifer, Anna. BA in Govt. magna cum laude, Harvard U., 1950; postgrad., Cambridge (Eng.) U., 1950-51; LLB, Yale U., 1954; LLD, Bhopal (India) U., 1983. Bar: N.Y. 1955, U.S. Supreme Ct. 1965, D.C. 1976. Dir. UN hdqrs. office World Fedn. UN Assns., 1950-53; lectr. Am. fgn. policy various univs. U.S. State Dept., India, 1952; research, drafting asst. to Trygve Lie for writing of In the Cause of Peace, 1953; assoc. White & Case, N.Y.C., 1954-59; asst. prof. law Harvard U., Cambridge, Mass., 1959-61; asst. legal advisor U.S. Dept. State, Washington, 1961-66, dep. legal advisor, 1973-81; Burling prof. internat. law Sch. of Advanced Internat. Studies,

Johns Hopkins U., Washington, 1967-81, mem. adv. council Bologna Ctr., 1982-88; exec. dir. Am. Soc. Internat. Law, Washington, 1967-72; judge Internat. Ct. Justice, The Hague, The Netherlands, 1981—; spl. rep. Micronesian claims U.S. Dept. State, 1966-71; legal adviser U.S. del. 16th-20th and 4th Spl. Gen. Assemblies UN; U.S. assoc. rep. Internat. Ct. Justice, 1962, U.S. dep. agt., 1979-80, U.S. counsel, 1980; U.S. rep., chmn. U.S. del. to 1st session UN Spl. Com on Principles Internat. Law concerning friendly relations and cooperation among states, Mexico City, 1964; U.S. rep. on adv. com. UN Program Assistance in Teaching, Study, Dissemination and Wider Appreciation Internat. Law, 1966-74; U.S. counsel Franco-Am. Air Arbitration, 1978; legal adv. U.S. del. to 32d and 33d WHO Assemblies, Geneva, 1979-80; vis. prof. internat. law Australian Nat. U., Canberra, 1969; U.S. rep., chmn. del. 3d session UN Spl. Com. on Question Defining Aggression, Geneva, 1970; counselor internat. law U.S. Dept. State, 1973; U.S. rep., chmn. del. 2d and 4th sessions UNCTAD Working Group on Charter Econ. Rights and Duties of States, Geneva, 1973, Mexico City, 1974; U.S. alt. rep. UN Econ. and Social Council, Geneva, 1974; legal adviser U.S. del. Conf. Internat. Econ. Coop., Paris, 1975; mem. U.S. Tripartite Adv. Com. on Internat. Labor Standards, 1980, Internat. Law Commn., UN, Geneva, 1977-81; spl. rapporteur internat. watercourses Internat. Law Commn., UN, 1977-81, chmn. drafting com., 1978; mem. bd. arbitration Brit. Petroleum v. Iran and Nat. Iranian Oil Co., Paris, 1982-85; mem. exec. com. Commn. Study Orgn. Peace, 1948-61; adv. joint com. law internat. transactions Am. Law Inst. and Am. Bar Assn., 1959-61; nat. chmn. Collegiate Council for UN, 1948-50; pres. Internat. Student Movement for UN, 1950-51; undergrad. orator Harvard U. Commencement, 1950; mem. adv. bd. Ctr. Oceans Law and Policy U. Va., 1975-81; vice chmn. Sec. State's Adv. Com. Pvt. Internat. Law, 1978-79, chmn., 1979-81; mem. internat. adv. bd. Cambridge U. Ctr. for Research in Internat. Law, 1983—; Arbitrator and lectr. Hague Acad. Internat. Law, 1972, Cath. U., 1983, Cambridge U., 1983, U. Wash., 1985, Yale U., 1988; Otto Water Internat. Fellow, N.Y. Law Sch., 1987; Centennial Morris vis. prof. Chgo.-Kent Coll. of Law, 1988; Page Disting. vis. jurist U. Kans., 1988. Author: The Secretary-General of the United Nations, 1952, International Arbitration: Three Salient Problems, 1987; editor: The Effectiveness of International Decisions, 1971; mem. editorial bd.: Am. Jour. Internat. Law, 1967-81; chmn. editorial adv. com.: Internat. Legal Materials, 1967-73. Recipient Gherini prize Yale U. Sch. Law, 1954; Frank Knox fellow Harvard U., 1950-51. Mem. Am. Law Inst., Am. Soc. Internat. Law (exec. v.p. 1967-73, hon. v.p. 1982—), Council Fgn. Relations, Inst. de Droit Internat. ABA, Internat. Law Assn., Phi Beta Kappa. Clubs: Harvard (N.Y.C.); Athenaeum (London); Cosmos (Washington); Haagsche (The Hague, The Netherlands). Office: Internat Ct Justice, Peace Palace, 2517 The Hague The Netherlands

SCHWED, PETER, writer, retired editor and publisher; b. N.Y.C., Jan. 18, 1911; s. Frederick and Bertie (Stiefel) S.; m. Antonia Sanxay Holding, Mar. 6, 1947; children: Katharine Holding (Mrs. Eric F. Wood), Peter Gregory, Laura Sanxay, Roger Eaton. Grad., Lawrenceville (N.J.) Sch., 1928; student, Princeton, 1929-32. Asst. v.p. Provident Loan Soc. N.Y., 1932-42; with Simon & Schuster, Inc., N.Y.C., 1946-84; v.p., exec. editor Simon & Schuster, Inc., 1957-62, exec. v.p., 1962-66, pub. trade books, 1966-72, chmn. editorial bd., 1972-82, editorial chmn. emeritus, 1982-84, dir., 1966-72. Author: Sinister Tennis, 1975, God Bless Pawnbrokers, 1975, The Serve and the Overhead Smash, 1976, Hanging in There, 1977, (with Nancy Lopez) The Education of a Woman Golfer, 1979, Test Your Tennis IQ, 1981, Turning the Pages, 1984, Overtime: A 20th Century Sports Odyssey, 1987, How to Talk Tennis, 1988; compiler: The Cook Charts, 1949; editor: (with H.W. Wind) Great Stories From the World of Sports, 1958, (with Allison Danzig) The Fireside Book of Tennis, 1972; contbr. articles to periodicals. Trustee Lawrenceville Sch., 1968-72. Served to capt. F.A. AUS, World War II. Decorated Bronze Star, Purple Heart. Mem. Authors Guild, P.E.N. Democrat. Club: Century Assn. (N.Y.C.). Home: 151 W 86th St New York NY 10024

SCHWEICKART, RUSSELL L., government official, astronaut; b. Neptune, N.J., Oct. 25, 1935; s. George L. Schweickart; m. Clare Grantham Whitfield (div.); children: Vicki Louise, Russell and Randolph (twins), Elin Ashley, Diana Croom. B.S. in Aero. Engring, Mass. Inst. Tech., 1956, M.S. in Aeros. and Astronautics, 1963. Former research scientist Mass. Inst. Tech. Exptl. Astronomy Lab.; astronaut Johnson Manned Spacecraft Center, Houston, lunar module pilot (Apollo 9, 1969); dir. user affairs Office of Applications, NASA; sci. adv. to Gov. Edmund G. Brown, Jr. State of Calif., 1977-79; chmn. Calif. Energy Commn., 1979-83, commr., 1979-85; pres. Assn. Space Explorers, 1985—; cons. and lectr. in field. Served as pilot USAF, 1956-60, 61; Capt. Mass. Air N.G. Recipient Distinguished Service medal NASA, 1970, Exceptional Service medal NASA, 1974, De La Vaulx medal FAI, 1970, Spl. Trustees award Nat. Acad. TV Arts and Scis., 1969. Fellow Am. Astronautical Soc.; mem. Soc. Exptl. Test Pilots, AIAA, Sigma Xi. Club: Explorers. Office: Assn Space Explorers 3278 Sacramento St San Francisco CA 94115 *

SCHWEITZER, MIGUEL, former Chilean minister of foreign affairs, legal educator; b. Santiago, Chile, July 22, 1940; s. Miguel Schweitzer Speisky and Cora Walters; m. M. Luisa Fernandez Maynard, May 16, 1964; children—Miguel, Daniel, Macarena. Diploma, U. Chile, 1964; D. Penal Law, Roma U., 1965. Prof. penal law U. Chile Law Sch., Santiago, 1966—, researcher penal law and legal medicine, 1966-80, dir. penal scis. dept. law sch., 1974-76; Chilean del. to UN Gen. Assembly, 1975, 76, 78; ambassador on Spl. Missions, 1976 79; Chilean del to OAS, Gen. Assembly, 1976-78; Chilean ambassador to U.K., London, 1980-83; Chilean minister of fgn. affairs, 1983-84. Author: El error de Derecho en Materia Penal, 1964; Sull Elemento soggettivo nel reato di bancarotta del l'imprenditore, 1965; Prospectus for a course on the Special Part of Penal Law, 1969. Decorated Gt. Cross of Order of White Elephant (Thailand); Gwanghwa medal Diplomatic Merit Order, (Korea). Club: Prince of Wales Golf (Santiago). Office: Lawyers Office, 1040 Moneda St, Santiago Chile

SCHWEITZER, PIERRE-PAUL, retired bank executive; b. Strasbourg, France, May 29, 1912; s. Paul and Emma (Munch) S.; m. Catherine Hatt, Aug. 7, 1941; children: Louis, Juliette. Grad., univs. Strasbourg and Paris, Ecole Libre des Sciences Politiques; LL.D., Yale U., 1966, Harvard U., 1966, Leeds (Eng.) U., N.Y. U., 1968, George Washington U., 1972, U. Wales, 1972, Williams Coll., 1973. Insp. Fin. French Treasury, 1936-47; alternate exec. dir. for France IMF, 1947-48, mng. dir., 1963-73; sec. gen. Interministerial Com. European Econ. Coop., 1948-49; fin. attache embassy Washington, 1949-53; dir. treasury Ministry Fin., 1953-60; dep. gov. Bank of France, 1960-63; also chmn. exec. bd., hon. inspecteur général des finances 1974; chmn. bd. Bank Am. Internat. S.A., Luxembourg, 1974-77, Bank Petrofigaz, Paris, 1974-79, Compagnie de Participations et d'Investissements Holding S.A., Luxembourg, 1975-84, Société Financière Internationale de Participations, Paris, 1976-84, Compagnie Monégasque de Banque, Monaco, 1978-88; adv. dir. Unilever N.V. Rotterdam, 1974-84; dir. Banque Pétrofigaz; mem. supervisory bd. Robeco Group, Rotterdam, Netherlands, 1974-82. Decorated grand croix Legion of Honour, Croix de Guerre, Medaille de la Resistance. Mem. Am. Philos. Soc. Home: 19 rue de Valois, 75001 Paris France Office: Petrofigaz, 49 Ave de l'Opéra, 75002 Paris France

SCHWEITZER, THEODORE GOTTLIEB, III, United Nations administrator; b. Hannibal, Mo., Aug. 28, 1942; s. Theodore Gottlieb Jr. and Dorothy Lois (Burnett) S.; m. Wannah Mohtsang, June 18, 1976; children: Angelee, Angela. Cert. in Lang., U. Paris, 1968; BA, U. Iowa, 1970, MA, 1974. Cert. Thai Lang. Am. Alumnae Assn., Bangkok, 1976, profl. tchr., Iowa. Tchr., librarian Lewis County Schs., Ewing, Mo., 1971-73; head librarian Internat. Sch., Bangkok, 1974-76; info. officer U.S. Army, Udorn, Thailand, 1974-76; dir. media services Am. Sch., Teheran, 1976-78; refugee officer UN HCR, Geneva, 1979—; pres. Internat. Library Cons., Lewistown, 1978—; founder SEA REscue Found., Lewiston, 1981—. Author: Ted Schweitzer Story, 1985. Served with USAF, 1959-62. Recipient Award of merit SOS Boat people Com., San Diego, 1982, replica of Nobel Peace Prize, UN High Commr. for Refugees, 1981. Democrat. Baptist. Lodge: Elks. Home: 158 Arbelle St Lewistown MO 63452 Office: UN High Commr for Reguges, Palais Des Nations, Geneva Switzerland

SCHWENDENWEIN, HUGO, university dean, theologian, lawyer; b. Klagenfurt, Austria, Nov. 5, 1926; s. Hugo and Gabriele (Farny) S.; LLD, U. Vienna, 1948; D in Canon Law, U. St. Thomas, Rome, 1964. Ordained priest Roman Catholic Ch., 1954; admitted to bar, 1977; mem. faculty U. Graz, 1969—, prof. canon law, 1973—, dir. Inst. Ch. History and Canon Law, 1973-77, dean Faculty Theology, 1976-79, univ. pro-dean, 1979-80; dir. Inst. Canon Law, 1977—. Decorated Austrian Honor Cross for Sci. and Art 1st class, Gt. Honor Distinction of Styrian Gold; named Papal Chaplain (Prelat), 1982, Praelat, 1985. recipient Cardinal Innitzer prize, 1969. Mem. Internat. Soc. Family Law, Soc. Jean Bodin L'histoire comparatives des Instns., Consociatio Internat. studio Iuris Canonici promovendo, Austrian Acad. Scis. (corr. mem.), Oesterreichische Gesellschaft Kirchenrecht, Deutscher Rechtshistorikertag, Cath. Acad. Vienna, Australian Acad. Scis. (corr. mem.). Author: Priesterbildung in Umbruch des Kirchenrechts, 1970; Rechtsfragen in Kirche und Staat, 1979; Das Neue Kirchenrecht-Gesamtdarstellung, 2d edit., 1984; others. Office: 23 Schuberstrasse, A-8010 Graz Austria

SCHWEPPENHAEUSER, HERMANN KARL, philosopher, educator; b. Frankfurt, Fed. Republic Germany, Mar. 12, 1928; s. Otto and Anna (Raisch) S.; m. Gisela Cornehl, June 24, 1925; children: Sabine, Gerhard. PhD, Goethe U., 1956, PhD Habilitation, 1966. Asst. Social Research, Frankfurt, 1950-54, Inst. Philosophy, Frankfurt, 1956-60; prof. Paedagogische Hochschule, Lueneburg, Fed. Republic Germany, 1961-69; lectr. Goethe U., Frankfurt, 1966-70, hon. prof., 1971—; prof. ordinary Paedagogische Hochschule Niedersachsen, Lueneberg, 1970-78, ordinary Hochschule Lueneberg, 1978—. Author: Kierkegaards Angriff auf die Spekulation, 1967, Verbotene Frucht Aphorims, 1966, Tractanda, 1972, Vergegenwaertigungen zur Unzeit, 1986; co-editor: Walter Benjamin Gesammelte Schriften, Vol. 1-7, 1972-88. Grantee Stiftung Volkswagenwerk, Thyssen-Stiftung, Benjamin Archiv, Frankfurt, 1972-84. Roman Catholic. Home: 5 Wilhelm Raabe Str, D-2121 Deutsch Evern Federal Republic of Germany Office: Hochschule Lueneberg, Wilschenbrucher Weg 84, D-2120 Lueneberg Federal Republic of Germany

SCHWIER, PRISCILLA LAMB GUYTON, television broadcasting company executive; b. Toledo, Ohio, May 8, 1939; d. Edward Oliver and Prudence (Hutchinson) L.; m. Robert T. Guyton, June 21, 1963 (dec. Sept. 1976); children—Melissa, Margaret, Robert; m. Frederick W. Schwier, May 11, 1984. B.A., Smith Coll., 1961; M.A., U. Toledo, 1972. Pres. Gt. Lakes Communications, Inc., 1982—; vice chmn. Seilon, Inc., Toledo, 1981-83, also dir.; pres. Lamb Enterprises, Inc., Toledo, 1983—; dir. Lamb Enterprises, Inc., Toledo, 1976—. Contbr. articles to profl. jours. Trustee Wilberforce U., Ohio, 1983—, Planned Parenthood, Toledo, 1979-83; trustee Maumee Valley Country Day Sch., Toledo. Episcopal Ch., Maumee, Ohio, 1983—; bd. trustees Toledo Hosp. Democrat. Episcopalian. Home: 345 E Front St Perrysburg OH 43551 Office: 1630 Ohio Citizens Bank Toledo OH 43604

SCHWIMMER, DAVID, physician, educator; b. Gödényháza, Hungary, Dec. 8, 1913; came to U.S., 1921; s. George and Laura (Green) S.; m. Gertrude Alpha Dounn, Nov. 12, 1939; children: Betty Laura, Georgia, Mark Ian. B.S. cum laude, Lafayette Coll., 1935; M.D., N.Y. U., 1939; M.Med. Sci., N.Y. Med. Coll., 1944. Diplomate: Am. Bd. Internal Medicine. Intern Met. Hosp., N.Y.C., 1939-41; resident Met. Hosp., 1942-44; practice medicine specializing in internal medicine N.Y.C., 1944—; attending physician Flower Fifth Av. Hosp., pres. med. bd., 1970-71; attending physician Met., Bird S. Coler, Doctors, Manhattan Eye, Ear and Throat, Lenox Hill hosps.; mem. faculty N.Y. Med. Coll., 1944—, clin. prof. medicine, 1966—; cons. internist Monmouth Med. Center, Long Branch, N.J., 1950—; cons. St. Luke's Hosp., 1985—; spl. lectr. in medicine Columbia U. Coll. Physicians and Surgeons, 1980—. Author: (with Morton Schwimmer) Role of Algae and Plankton in Medicine, 1955; Contbr. to profl. jours. Research fellow N.Y. Med. Coll., 1944-51; fellow internal medicine, 1941-44. Fellow A.C.P., N.Y. Acad. Medicine, N.Y. Acad. Scis., Am. Coll. Angiology, N.Y. Cardiol. Soc.; mem. Endocrine Soc., Harvey Soc., AAAS, AAUP, Am. Soc. Internal Medicine, Royal Soc. Medicine (affiliate), Alpha Omega Alpha. Home: 764 Carrol Pl Teaneck NJ 07666 Office: 239 E 79th St New York NY 10021

SCHWINDEN, TED, governor of Montana; b. Wolf Point, Mont., Aug. 31, 1925; s. Michael James and Mary (Preble) S.; m. B. Jean Christianson, Dec. 21, 1946; children: Mike, Chrys, Dore. Student, Mont. Sch. Mines, 1946-47; B.A., U. Mont., 1949, M.A., 1950; postgrad., U. Minn., 1950-54. Owner-operator grain farm; Roosevelt County, Mont., 1954—; land commr. State of Mont., 1969-76, lt. gov., 1977-80, gov., 1981—; mem. U.S. Wheat Trade Mission to Asia, 1968. Chmn. Mont. Bicentennial Adv. Council, 1973-76; mem. Mont. Ho. of Reps., 1959, 61, Legis. Council, 1959-61, Wolf Point Sch. Bd., 1966-69, Pub. Employees Retirement System Bd., 1969-74. Served with inf. AUS, 1943-46. Decorated Combat Inf. badge. Mem. Mont. Grain Growers (pres. 1965-67), Western Wheat Assos. (dir.). Democrat. Lutheran. Clubs: Masons, Elks. Office: Office of Gov State Capitol Helena MT 59620 *

SCHWINGER, JULIAN, educator, physicist; b. N.Y.C., Feb. 12, 1918; s. Benjamin and Belle (Rosenfeld) S.; m. Clarice Carrol, 1947. A.B., Columbia U., 1936, Ph.D., 1939, D.Sc., 1966; D.Sc. (hon.), Purdue U., 1961, Harvard U., 1962, Brandeis U., 1973, Gustavus Adolphus Coll., 1975; LL.D., CCNY, 1972. NRC fellow 1939-40; research asso. U. Calif.-Berkeley, 1940-41; instr., then asst. prof. Purdue U., 1941-43; staff mem. Radiation Lab., MIT, 1943-46; staff Metall. Lab., U. Chgo., 1943; asso. prof. Harvard U., 1945-47, prof., 1947-72, Higgins prof. physics, 1966-72; prof. physics UCLA, 1972-80, Univ. prof., 1980—; Mem. bd. sponsors Bull. Atomic Sci.; sponsor Fedn. Am. Scientists; J.W. Gibbs hon. lectr. Am. Math. Soc., 1960. Author: Particles and Sources, 1969, (with D. Saxon) Discontinuities in Wave Guides, 1968, Particles, Sources and Fields, 1970, Vol. II, 1973, Quantum Kinematics and Dynamics, 1970, Einstein's Legacy, 1985; editor: Quantum Electrodynamics, 1958. Recipient C. L. Mayer nature of light award, 1949, univ. medal Columbia U., 1951, 1st Einstein prize award, 1951; Nat. Medal of Sci. award for physics, 1964; co-recipient Nobel prize in Physics, 1965; recipient Humboldt award, 1981, Monie A. Fest Sigma Xi award, 1986, Castiglione di Sicilia award, 1986, Am. Acad. of Achievement award, 1987; Guggenheim fellow, 1970. Mem. Nat. Acad. Scis., Am. Acad. Arts and Scis., Am. Phys. Soc., Royal Instn. Gt. Britain, ACLU, AAAS, N.Y. Acad. Scis. Office: Dept Physics U Calif Los Angeles CA 90024 *

SCHWINN, ROBERT JAMES, architect; b. Cedar Rapids, Iowa, Nov. 27, 1930; s. Charles S. and Mary (McCook) S.; m. Mary Philipa Lewis, July 23, 1960; children—Elizabeth Ann, Mary Catherine, Caroline Patricia, Amy Louise, Robert James. B.Arch., U. Notre Dame; M.Arch., Columbia U., 1958. Registered architect, Md. Project architect Rogers & Butler, N.Y.C., 1958-62; dir. design and engring. Carl M. Freeman Assocs., Silver Spring, Md., 1962-64; prin. Robert Schwinn AIA and Assocs., Silver Spring, 1964—. Archtl. works include: James Rouse Apt. Community Columbia, Md., 1968, Prudential High-Tech Office Park, Fairfax County, Va., 1983, Va. Planned Community, Fairfax County (NVBA award 1963), Monroe Office Bldg., Washington, 1967. Recipient Sculpture prize U. Notre Dame, 1953; Quincy Ward Boese fellow, 1957. Mem. AIA (Washington met. chpt.), Silver Spring C. of C. Roman Catholic. Home: 7200 Brookstone Ct Potomac MD 20854 Office: 3 Bethesda Metro Ctr Suite 700 Bethesda MD 20814

SCHWIPPERT, GUUSTAAF ARTHUR, electronics executive; b. Cheribon, Indonesia, Nov. 23, 1935; s. Gustav Adolf and Elisabeth Wilhelmina (Kennedy) S.; B.Sc., Tech. U., Amsterdam, 1957; M.Sc., Tech. U., Delft, 1966; m. Fokeltje Van Der Koogh, June 2, 1962; children—Bart A., Nicolien K., Hanneke M. With Figee, Haarlem, Netherlands, 1954-56, HSA Hengelo, 1956; tech. specialist Werkspoor, Amsterdam, 1957-62; research and devel. employee TNO-Central Labs., 1962-66, group leader research and devel. electronics, 1966-73, dept. dep. head, Delft, 1974-75, head dept. research and devel. electronics, 1976-81, dir. micro-electronics center, 1982-87; gen. mgr. Found. Ctrs. for Micro-electronics in the Netherlands, 1988; chmn. nat. com. for standardization of security systems: JECTC79 NL, 1979. Mem. Electronics and Radio Engrs. Netherlands, Royal Inst. Engrs., Am. Soc. Indsl. Security, Internat. Electrotech. Com. Patentee in field; contbr. articles to profl. jours. Home: 5 Dykerwaal, 2641 LH Pynacker The Netherlands Office: 97 Schoemakerstraat, PO Box 67, 2600 AB Delft The Netherlands

SCHWOB, PIERRE ROGER, software company executive; b. Los Angeles, Oct. 4, 1946; s. Robert Lucien and Mary Elizabeth (Perkins) S. HEC, Geneva U., 1966. Adminstrv. dir. Imprimerie & Editions Avenir, Geneva, Switzerland, 1971-73; mgmt. cons. Syn-cronamics, Englewood, N.J., 1974-75; pres. PRS-Program Research & Software Corp., N.Y.C., 1978—; asst. prof. NYU, 1981—; chief exec. officer Rising Star Industries, Inc., Calif., 1986. Author: The Chess Tutor: Opening Moves, 1976, How to Use Pocket Calculators, 1976, The Great Historical Documents of the World, 1977, Introduction to Computer Graphics, 1983. Served with Swiss Army, 1965-67. Mem. Am. Math. Assn., Nat. Assn. Computer Graphics, IEEE, Assn. for Computing Machinery, Swiss Assn. Tech. (pres. 1971-73), Am. Brass Chamber Music Assn. (v.p. 1982—), N.Y. Acad. Scis., Aircraft Owners & Pilot Assn., Swiss-Israel C. of C. (pres. 1970-73). Office: 257 Central Park W New York NY 10024

SCHWOERER, FRANK, publishing company executive; b. Eisenbach, Germany, Sept. 7, 1925; s. Linus and Berta (Fehrenbach) S.; m. Elisabeth K. Suemmermann, Feb. 13, 1953; children: Thomas C., Martin B. Abitur Gymnasium, Freiburg, Germany. Book pub. asst. Herder Pubs., Freiburg, 1949-51, Herder Editorial, Barcelona, Spain, 1951-52, pub., São Paulo, Brazil, 1952-61; pres. Herder and Herder, N.Y.C., 1961-72; mng. dir. Burns and Oates Ltd., London, 1967-70; Campus Verlag, Frankfurt, Fed. Republic Germany, 1972—. Home: Falkenstrasse 60, 6232 Bad Soden Federal Republic of Germany Office: Campus Verlag GmbH, Bockenheimer Landstr 100, D-6000 Frankfurt am Main Federal Republic of Germany

SCIACCA, WILLIAM WAYNE, hospital administrator; b. New Orleans, June 20, 1945; s. Thomas John and Pauline Louise Sciacca; B.A., La. State U., 1967; m. Margaret A. D'Abadie, June 11, 1983; children—William, Deborah, Mark, Scott, David, Mollie. Asst. mgr. Brennan's Restaurant, New Orleans, 1971-73; dir. dietary Hotel Dieu Hosp., New Orleans, 1973-76; dir. food service and housekeeping Tulane Med. Center Hosp. and Clinic, New Orleans, 1976—; cons. in field. CPR instr. Am. Heart Assn., New Orleans. Served to capt. U.S. Army, 1967-71. Decorated Bronze Star. Mem. Am. Soc. Hosp. Food Service Adminstrs. (pres. La. Bayou chpt. 1980-81), La. Restaurant Assn., Internat. Food Service Execs. Assn., Nat. Exec. Housekeepers Assn., Les Chefs de Cuisine de la Louisianne (trustee), Res. Officers Assn., Theta Xi. Republican. Roman Catholic. Clubs: Lions, Confederation Mondiale des Activites Subquatiques. Home: 316 28th St New Orleans LA 70124 Office: 1415 Tulane Ave New Orleans LA 70112

SCIAMMARELLA, CESAR AUGUSTO, mechanical engineer, educator, researcher; b. Buenos Aires, Argentina, Aug. 22, 1926; s. Emilio Silvio and Maria Belen (Mansilla) S.; m. Esther Elba Norbis; children: Alejandro, Eduardo, Federico. Diploma in Civil Engring, U. Buenos Aires, 1950; PhD, Ill. Inst. Tech., 1960. Prof. mech. engring. U. Buenos Aires, 1955-57, U. Fla., 1961-65, Poly. Inst. Bklyn., 1967-72; prof. Ill. Inst. Tech., Chgo., 1972—, dir. Exptl. Stress Analysis Lab.; vis. prof. Poly. Inst., Milan, Italy, 1979, U. Cagliari, Italy, 1979, Poly. Inst. Lausanne, Switzerland, 1979, U. Poitiers, France, 1980; cons. to govt., pvt. industry. Contbr. articles to profl. jours.; patentee in field. Recipient Faculty Research award Sigma Xi, 1966, Outstanding Paper award Acad. Mechanics, 1970, Hetemy award, 1983. Fellow Soc. for Exptl. Mechanics (Frocht award 1980), ASME (Disting. Services award 1972); mem. Internat. Soc. Optical Engring., ASTM, Gesellschaft für Angewandte Mathematik und Mechanik, Optical Soc. Am., Soc. Photo-optical Instrumentation Engrs. Roman Catholic. Research in optical techniques applied to stress analysis, mechanics of materials, fracture mechanics and fatigue. Home: 175 E Delaware #7008 Chicago IL 60611

ŠCIBOR-MARCHOCKI, ROMUALD IRENEUS, research scientist; b. Highland Park, Mich., Dec. 29, 1926; s. Sigismond August and Sophy L. Ŝcibor-Marchocka. B.S., Wayne State U., 1947, M.S., 1948; postgrad. Calif. Inst. Tech., U. So. Calif. Asst. physics Wayne State U., 1943-47, spl. instr., 1947-48; sr. engr. labs. div. Hoffman Radio Corp., 1949-59; design specialist Aerojet Gen. Corp. div. Gen. Tire & Rubber Co., 1959-62; sr. scientist Nortonics div. Northrop Corp., 1962-68; mem. tech. staff Jet Propulsion Lab., Pasadena, 1968-72, staff scientist, 1970-72; owner Mädchental Kennels, Baldwin Park, 1955—; with Wells Fargo Security Guard Services div. Baker Protective Services, 1973-81; tutor Mt. San Antonio Coll., 1978—, staff math. dept., 1979—; cons. in math. and computer sci., 1980—. Mem. Calavo Growers Assn., Acoustical Soc., Math. Assn., Am. Def. Preparedness Assn., Assn. Physics Tchrs., N.Y. Acad. Sci., AAAS, Nat. Rifle Assn., Free for All, Mensa, Naturist Soc., Nat. Free Lance Photographers Assn., Sigma Xi. Contbr. articles to profl. jours. Home: 15250 E Arrow Hwy Baldwin Park CA 91706

SCICLUNA, RONNIE NAZARENE, promotions manager; b. Valletta, Malta; s. Anthony Carmel and Connie (Bartolo) S.; m. Maria Dolores Pecorella, Nov. 5, 1971; children: Mark Anthony, Marie Corine, Moira Ann. Student, Coll. Arts Sci., Msida, Malta. Tour organizer Malta Steamship Co. Ltd., 1954-56, Laferla Lines Co. Ltd., 1957-59, Mifsud Bros. Co. Ltd., 1960-61; ticketing reservation supr. Malta Airlines, 1961-73; mgr. Air Malta Co. Ltd., N.Africa, 1974-77; Air Malta Co. Ltd., Egypt, 1977; sales mgr. Air Malta Co. Ltd., 1978-79, mgr. tours, 1979-81, mgr. promotions pub. relations dept., 1981—. Home: Michiko Old Railway Rd, Balzan Malta Office: Air Malta Co Ltd, Head Office, Luqa Malta

SCOFFIER, HENRI, chef, restaurant owner; b. Kpg Cham, Kampuchea, Aug. 31, 1949; arrived in France, Apr. 1970; adopted s. Jean Pierre S. Registered chef de cuisine, France. Apprentice, asst. cook La Ficelle, La Reine Chistine, Paris, 1972-75; cook Le Bistro d'Hubert, Paris, 1975-76; head cook Le Grenier sur l'eau, Paris, 1976-77; cook Jacqueline Fénix, Neuilly, France, 1977, Les Semailles, Paris, 1977; head cook Le Chardenoux, Paris, 1977-78; head cook and ptnr. Les Prejuges, Montfort-l'Amaury, France, 1978—. Recipient 16 two hats Gault & Millau Guide, 1978-87, one star Michelin Gastronomic Guide, 1982, Merite Culinaire Chevalier, 1987. Mem. Academie des Arts de la Table, Club Proper Montagné, Chambre Syndicale de l'Industrie Hôtelière & de la Restauration. Buddhist. Home: 11 rue de la Treille, 78490 Montfort L'Amaury France Office: Restaurant Les Prejuges, 18 Place Robert Brault, 78490 Montfort L'Amaury France

SCOFFIER, JEAN PIERRE, restaurant director, physician; b. Nice, France, Oct. 8, 1930; s. Louis Benoît and Marie Eléonore (Tavano) S.; adopted children: Henri, Frédéric. MD, Med. Sch., Paris, 1957. Dir. med. services Uranium de Franceville, Gabon, 1960, Cie Constr. des Batignolles, Indonesia, 1960-64, Plantation Paul Fournier, Kampuchea, 1964-70; med. dir. Far East Laboratoires Servier, France, 1971-84; owner, dir. Restaurant Les Prejuges, Montfort l'Amaury, France, 1979—. Served to lt., Med. Corps, France, 1958-60. Recipient one star Michelin Gastronomic Guide, 1982, 16 two hats Gault & Millau Guide. Mem. Academie des Arts de la Table, Club Prosper Montagné, Chambre Syndicale Industrie hôtelière & restauration. Buddhist. Home: 11 rue de la Treille, 78490 Montfort 1 Amaury France Office: Restaurant Les Prejuges, 18 Place Robert Brault, 78490 Montfort 1 Amaury France

SCOFIELD, PAUL, actor; b. Jan. 21, 1922; m. Joy Parker; 2 children. Trained London Mask Theatre Drama Sch., Birmingham Repertory Theatre 1941, 43-46; Stratford-on-Avon Shakespeare Meml. Theatre, 1946-48, Arts Theatre, 1946, Phoenix Theatre, 1947. With H.M. Tennent, 1949-56; assoc. dir. Nat. Theatre, 1970-71; has appeared in Chekhov's Seagull, Anouilh's Ring Round the Moon, Charles Morgan's The River Line, Richard II, Time Remembered, A Question of Fact, Hamlet, Power and the Glory, Family Reunion, A Dead Secret, Expresso Bongo, The Complaisant Lover, A Man for All Seasons, Stratford Festival, Ont., Can., 1961, Coriolanus, Don Armado New York, 1961-62, A Man for All Seasons London, 1962-63, King Lear, 1963, Timon, 1967, Macbeth, 1968, The Hotel in Amsterdam, 1968, Uncle Vanya, 1970, The Captain of Kopenik, 1971, Rules of the Game, 1971, Savages 1973, The Tempest, 1974, 75, Dimetos, 1976, Volpone, 1977, The Madras House, 1977, The Family, 1978, Amadeus 1979, Othello, 1980, Don Quixote, 1982, A Midsummer Night's Dream, 1982, I'm Not Rappaport, 1986-87; films: The Train, 1963, A Man for All Seasons (Oscar and N.Y. Film Critics award Moscow Film Festival and Brit. Film Acad. awards), King Lear, 1970, Scorpio, 1972, A Potting Shed, 1981, If Winter Comes, 1981, Song at Twilight 1982, Come into the Garden Maud, 1982, 1919, 1984, Anna Karenina, 1984, Mr. Corbett's Ghost, 1986, The Attic, 1987; Decorated comdr. Brit. Empire. Address: The Gables, Balcombe Sussex, England

SCOLA, ETTORE, film director, script writer; b. Treviso, Italy, 1931. Journalist humorous mags., 1954; script writer films including Il Sorpasso, 1962, Anni Ruggenti, 1962, I Mostri, 1963, Iola Conoscevo Bene, 1965; director films Se Permette Parliamo di Donne, 1964, Dramma della Gelosia, 1970, C'eravamo tanto amati, 1974, Brutti, Sprochi e Cattivi, 1976, Una Giornata Particolare, 1977, I Nuovi Mostri, 1977, La Terrazza, 1979, Ballando ballando, 1984, Maccheroni, 1984. Recipient César award, 1984. Home: Via Bertoloni L/e, I-00197 Rome Italy *

SCOON, PAUL, governor general of Grenada; b. July 4, 1935; m. Esmai Monica Lumsden, 1970; 3 stepchildren. Ed. Inst. Edn., Leeds U., Eng., B.A., M.Ed., Toronto U., Ont., Can. Tchr., Grenada Boys' Secondary Sch., 1953-67; chief edn. officer, Grenada, 1967-68, permanent sec., 1969, sec. to cabinet, 1970-72; dep. dir. Commonwealth Found., 1973-78; gov. Centre for Internat. Briefing, Farnham Castle, 1973-78; gov. gen. of Grenada, 1978—. Created Knight. Mem. Civil Service Assn. Grenada (v.p. 1968), Assn. Masters and Mistresses of Grenada (co-founder, past pres.). Office: Gov Gen House, Saint George's Grenada T 2401 *

SCOPINICH, JILL LORIE, editor, writer; b. Seattle, Dec. 7, 1945; d. Oscar John and Marcella Jane (Hearing) Younce; 1 child, Lori Jill. AA in Gen. Edn., Am. River Coll., 1969; BA in Journalism with honors, Sacramento State U., 1973. Reporter Carmichael (Calif.) Courier, 1968-70; mng. editor Quarter Horse of the Pacific Coast, Sacramento, 1970-75, editor, 1975-84; editor Golden State Program Jour., 1978, Nat. Reined Cow Horse Assn. News, Sacramento, 1983-88, Pacific Coast Jour., Sacramento, 1984-88, Nat. Snaffle Bit Assn. News, Sacramento, 1988—; mag. cons., 1975—. Bd. dirs. Carmichael, Winding Way, Pasadena Homeowners Assn., Carmichael, 1985-87. Recipient 1st pl. feature award, 1970, 1st pl. editorial award Jour. Assn. Jr. Colls., 1971, 1st pl. design award WCHB Yuba-Sutter Counties, Marysville, Calif., 1985. Mem. Am. River Jaycees (recipient speaking award 1982), Am. Horse Publs. (recipient 1st pl. editorial award 1983, 88), MENSA (bd. dirs., asst. local sec., activities dir. 1987-88, membership chair 1988—). Republican. Roman Catholic. Club: 5th Wheel Touring Soc. (Sacramento) (v.p. 1970). Home: 440 Adelma Beach Rd Port Townsend WA 98368

SCORSESE, MARTIN, film director, writer; b. Flushing, N.Y., Nov. 17, 1942; s. Charles and Catherine (Cappa) S. BS in Film Communications, NYU, 1964, MA in Film Communications, 1966. Faculty asst., then instr. film NYU, N.Y.C., 1963-70. Dir., writer: What's a Nice Girl Like You Doing in a Place Like This?, 1963, It's Not Just You, Murray, 1964, Who's That Knocking At My Door, 1968, The Big Shave, 1967-68, also documentaries; dir.: (play) The Act, 1977-78; supervising editor, asst. dir.: (film) Woodstock, 1970; assoc. producer, post prodn. supr.: (films) Medicine Ball Caravan, 1971, Box Car Bertha, 1972, Mean Streets, 1973; dir. films include Alice Doesn't Live Here Anymore, 1974, Italian American, 1974, Taxi Driver, 1976 (Grand prize), New York, New York, 1977, American Boy, 1978, Raging Bull, 1980, The King of Comedy, 1983, After Hours, 1985, The Color of Money, 1986, The Last Temptation of Christ, 1988; appeared in films Cannonball, 1976, Triple Play, 1981, 'Round Midnight, 1986; also actor, dir. film The Last Waltz, 1978. Recipient Edward L. Kingsley Found. award, 1963-64, 1st prize Rosenthal Found. awards Soc. Cinemetologists, 1964, 1st prize Screen Producer's Guild, 1965, 1st prize Brown U. Film Festival, 1965, also others; named Best Dir. Cannes Film Festival, 1986. Office: care CAA 1888 Century Park E Suite 1400 Los Angeles CA 90067 also: care United Artists 10202 W Washington Blvd Culver City CA 90230 *

SCOTT, ALAN JAMES, diplomat; b. Jan. 14, 1934; s. Harold James and Mary Phyllis Barbara Scott; m. Mary Elizabeth Ireland, 1958 (dec. 1969); 3 children; m. Joan Hall, 1971; 3 stepchildren. Student, U. Cambridge, Eng. Controller Orgn. and Establishments, 1969, Hong Kong, 1971-87; dep. chief sec. 1985-87, gov. Cayman Islands, 1987—. Pres. Fiji AAA, 1964-69, Hong Kong AAA, 1978-87. Served Brit. Army, 1952-54. Decorated CVO, 1986, CBE, 1982. Mem. Royal Commonwealth Soc. Clubs: Farmers. Office: Government House Cayman Islands BW1 also: Petraea, Claviers 83122, France *

SCOTT, BLAINE WAHAB, III, insurance executive; b. Phila., Apr. 22, 1927; s. Blaine W., Jr., and Dorothy (Fox) S.; ed. Friends' Central Sch.; m. Mary L. Howe, Nov. 14, 1964; 1 son, Robert P.; children by previous marriage—M. Kathleen, Bruce K., Sharon L., Linda, Blaine Wahab, Carol. Registered Health Underwriter. Pres., dir. World Life & Health Ins. Co. of Pa.; pres., dir. Worlco Inc., also pres., dir. all affiliates and subsidiaries; pres. Upper Merion Investment Corp.; dir. Royal Bank Pa., Gen. Devices, Inc., Agy. Rent-A-Car, Worlco Data Systems. Mem. Upper Merion Bd. Suprs., 1960-66, chmn., 1961-66; trustee Temple U., 1969-73, Valley Forge Mil. Acad. and Jr. Coll., 1978-84, 86—; dir. Valley Forge Country Convention Vis. Bur., dir. emeritus King of Prussia C. of C. Served in U.S. Army, World War II, Korea. Named one of 5 outstanding young men of commonwealth, Pa. Jr. C. of C., 1962, Republican of Yr. Upper Merion Rep. Com., 1984. Mem. VFW, Nat. Assn. Health Underwriters, Greater Delaware Valley Assn. Health Underwriters (dir.), Ins. Fedn. of Pa., Inc. (chmn. 1985 86, bd. dirs. 1964—), Greater Valley Forge Hotel Assn. (Man of the Yr. 1987). Clubs: Union League (Phila.). Home: 480 General Washington Rd Wayne PA 19087 Office: 215 W Church Rd King of Prussia PA 19406

SCOTT, BRADLEY STERLING, automotive executive; b. Santa Monica, Calif., Apr. 20, 1948; s. Milton and Jeanne Scott; m. Jillian A. Miller, May 12, 1979; children: Jilina, Sterling. BA, U. So. Calif., 1970. V.p. sales United Visuals Corp., Los Angeles, 1972-76; mgr. nat. sales Technicolor Corp., Costa Mesa, Calif., 1976-80; dir. sales Microsonics Corp., Los Angeles, 1980-81; pres., founder Los Angeles Auto Salvage, Inc., Van Nuys, Calif., 1982—; v.p., dir. Valley Auto Dismantlers Assn., Sun Valley, Calif., 1984—; adv. council dirs. U. So. Calif. Sch. of Bus. Entrepreneur Program, 1984—; owner Golden State Equipment Leasing Co. Patentee sound motion picture projection and viewing device, 1976. Mem. Young Pres. Orgn. Republican. Clubs: Los Angeles Country, Balboa Bay (Newport Beach, Calif). Office: Los Angeles Auto Salvage 7245 Laurel Canyon North Hollywood CA 91605

SCOTT, BRIAN WALTER, management consultant; b. Melbourne, Victoria, Australia, Apr. 23, 1935; s. Walter and Dorothy Ada (Ransom) S.; m. Dorothy Yvonne Allen, Aug. 15, 1959; children: David, Mark, Jennifer, Susan. B of Econs., Sydney (Australia) U., 1955; MBA, Stanford U., 1959; D of Bus. Adminstrn., Harvard U., 1963. Asst. prof. U. So. Calif., Los Angeles, 1961-62; cons. mgmt. W.D. Scott and Co. Pty. Ltd., Sydney, 1963-69, dir., 1969-74, mng. dir., 1974-79, chmn., 1979-85; dep. chmn. A.C.I. Internat. Ltd., Sydney, 1985-86, chmn., 1986-88; chmn. Mgmt. Frontiers Pty. Ltd., Sydney, W.D. Scott Internat. Devel. Cons. Pty. Ltd.; bd. dirs. ANZ Banking Corp. Ltd., Melbourne, Imagineering Tech. Ltd., Sydney. Author: Long-Range Planning in American Industry, 1965; contbr. articles on mgmt. and bus. to profl. jours. Chmn. Trade Devel. Council, Canberra, 1984—, Knox Grammar Sch., Sydney, 1981—, Australia-Asean Bus. Council, Canberra, 1980-82. Named Officer, Order of Australia. Fellow Inst. Dirs. Australia (fed. pres. 1982-86), Internat. Acad. Mgmt., Australian Inst. Mgmt., Inst. Mgmt. Cons.; mem. Trade Policy Research Ctr. (mem. council). Clubs: Royal Sydney Yacht Squadron, Am. (Sydney). Home: 2 Carnarvon Rd, Roseville, New South Wales 2069, Australia Office: Mgmt Frontiers Pty Ltd, 118 Mount St, North Sydney, New South Wales 2060, Australia

SCOTT, DANIEL WEBSTER, II, racing stable executive; b. Harrodsburg, Ky., Jan. 18, 1916; s. Harrie Burgoyne and Jenny (Baker) S.; student U.S. Naval Acad., 1934; B.S. in Commerce summa cum laude, U. Ky., 1937; m. Lucile Thornton, Oct. 21, 1939; children—Daniel Webster, Wade Thornton; m. 2d, Alice B. Hollister, Mar. 10, 1954. Jr. exec. acct. Gen. Electric Co., Bridgeport, Conn., 1937-39; owner, operator racing stable, Lexington, Ky., 1939—. Served with USN, 1942-46. Recipient Breeder of Stakes Winners award, 1973, 75, 77. Mem. Thoroughbred Club Am. (pres. 1951-52), Horsemen's Benevolent and Protective Assn. (v.p., dir. Ky. div.), Thoroughbred Breeders Ky. (dir). Democrat. Episcopalian. Home and Office: 2470 Russell Cave Rd Route 3 Lexington KY 40511

SCOTT, DAVID C., manufacturing company executive; b. Akron, Ohio, Oct. 21, 1915; m. Eudora A. Vance, 1940 (dec. May 1973); children—Sally Scott Vincent, David C. Jr.; m. Mary M. Donohue, May 23, 1975. B.S., U. Ky., 1940, D.Sc. (hon.), 1971; LL.D. (hon.), Marquette U., 1980, Brescia Coll., Owensboro, Ky., 1985. Owner Inst-Tech. Research, 1942; with Gen. Electric Co., 1945-63; mgr. power tube plant Gen. Electric Co., Schenectady, N.Y., 1954-60; gen. mgr. cathode ray tube dept. Gen. Electric Co., Syracuse, N.Y., 1960-63; v.p., group exec. Colt Industries Inc., 1963-65, exec. v.p., dir., 1965-68; pres. Allis-Chalmers Corp., Milw., 1968-69, chmn. bd., chief exec. officer, 1969-83; pres. David C. Scott Found., Inc.; chmn., dir. Siemens Power Systems, Inc.; bd. dirs. Allis-Chalmers, First Wis. Trust of Fla., Humana, Inc.; former chmn., dir. Fiat-Allis, Siemens-Allis; former dir. Am. Can., First Wis. Corp., Harris Corp., Martin Marietta Corp., The Travelers Corp.; former pres. Egypt-U.S. Bus. Council, Czech-US Bus. Council, Poland-U.S. Bus. Council; former chmn., dir. Nat. Council-U.S.-China Trade; former vice chmn. Sudan-U.S. Bus. Council; former dir. U.S.-USSR Trade and Econ. Council; former chmn. Pres.'s Export Council. Trustee Marquette U.; past trustee Thomas A. Edison Found.; bd. dirs. Rockefeller U. Devel. Council, U. Ky. Devel Council, U. Ky. Coll. Engring. Mem. U. Ky. Alumni Assn. (mem. devel. council). Home: Village of Golf FL 33436 Office: 4600 N Ocean Blvd Boynton Beach FL 33435

SCOTT, DAVID KNIGHT, physicist, university administrator; b. North Ronaldsay, Scotland, Mar. 2, 1940; married, 1966; 3 children. B.Sc., Edinburgh U., 1962; D.Phil. in Nuclear Physics, Oxford U., 1967. Research officer Nuclear Physics Lab. Oxford U., 1970-73; research fellow nuclear physics Balliol Coll., 1967-70, sr. research fellow, 1970-73; physicist Lawrence Berkeley Lab. U. Calif., 1973-75, sr. scientist nuclear sci., 1975-79; prof. physics, astronomy and chemistry Nat. Superconducting Cyclotron Lab. Mich. State U., East Lansing, 1979—, Hannah disting. prof. physics Nat. Superconducting Cyclotron Lab., 1979-86, assoc. provost, 1983-86, provost, v.p. acad. affairs, 1986—. Fellow Am. Phys. Soc.; mem. AAAS. Office: Office of the Provost Mich State U East Lansing MI 48824

SCOTT, DAVID WILLIAM, automotive company executive; b. Shillong, Assam, India, July 24, 1940; came to U.S., 1962; s. Ronald Bayne and Patricia (Cooper) S.; m. Virginia Del Crowley, Jan. 12, 1962; children: Virginia, Kelley, Tara, Meredith. BA in Polit. Sci., Southeast Mo. State U., 1967. Trainee Ford Motor Co., Dearborn, Mich., 1967-68, pub. affairs mgr. truck div., 1969-73, exec. asst., 1973-75; regional pub. affairs mgr. Ford Motor Co., Los Angeles, 1975-76; internat. pub. affairs mgr. Ford Motor Co., Dearborn, 1976-77; v.p. pub. affairs Ford of Can., Oakville, Ont., 1971-78; dir. internat. pub. affairs Ford Motor Co., Dearborn, 1978-81, dir. N. Am. pub. affairs, 1981-85, v.p. pub. affairs, 1986-88, v.p. external affairs, 1988—; trustee Ford Fund, Dearborn, 1986—, Found. Am. Communications. Mem. pub. affairs com. Nat. 4-H Council, Washington, 1983—, pvt. sector pub. affairs com. U.S. Info. Agy., Washington, 1985—; bd. dirs. Police Athletic League, Detroit, 1983-84. Mem. Pub. Relations Soc. Am. Clubs: Detroit Press, Bloomfield Hills Country, Forest Lake Country. Office: Ford Motor Co The American Rd Dearborn MI 48121

SCOTT, HENRY L., concert pianist-humorist; b. Tivoli on Hudson, N.Y., Jan. 20, 1908; s. Walter and Mary Wigram (Keeney) S.; m. Mary Bell Bard, Aug. 28, 1938; children: Barbara Bell, Henry Lawrence. Student, Syracuse (N.Y.) U., class 1930; L.H.D., Bard Coll., Annandale, N.Y., 1964. head Henry Scott Sch. Modern Piano, N.Y.C.; mem. faculty Champlin Sch., 1940-42; pres., chmn. bd. Solo Theater of Am. Corp., 1948; asst. to pres. Bard Coll., Annandale-on-Hudson, 1966. Teaching and radio, screen, stage and TV work, 1931-41; concert work, throughout U.S., 1939—, debut, Town Hall, 1941, Carnegie Hall, 1945-46, 27 transcontinental concert tours, Carnegie Hall, N.Y.C. (2), Town Hall, N.Y.C. (2), Detroit Town Hall, Kansas City Town Hall, West Point Mil. Academy (12), Akron Concert Course, Fine Arts Series, Worcester, U. Minn. (8), U. Tex. (3), U. Notre Dame (2), Miss Porters Sch., Conn. (2), St. Mark's Sch., Southborough, Mass. (5), So. Ill. U. (10), USAF Acad., 1960, Mt. Mary Coll., Milw., Emanuel Missionary Coll., Mich., Pacific Union Coll., Calif., U. So. Calif., Amherst (Mass.) U., Dartmouth Coll., Purdue U., U. N.C., U. Oreg., Med. Coll. Va., Union Coll., Lincoln, Nebr., U. N.Mex., Teaching and radio, screen, stage and TV work, Woman's Inst., Knoxville Friday Morning Musicales, Syracuse, Meml. Auditorium, Lowell, Mass., Eaton Auditorium, Toronto, Met. Opera House, N.Y.C., U. Wash., U. Utah, U. Fla. (3), U. Ga., Artists Series, San Diego, U. N.C. (3), North-Western State Coll. (7), 6th tour, Can., 1966-67, Hawaiian Islands, Saudi Arabia, 1963; guest artist various orchs. and symphonies; indsl. concerts for, General Electric Co., Eastman Kodak, IBM Corp., others, 1958-61; pioneer concert humor; now presenting humorous and ednl. lecture recitals in schs., colls., univs. and concert halls; producer, star: Concerto for Fun, 1949; introduced: Fun at the Philharmonic, 1952; guest appearance: TV show Be Our Guest, 1960; Composer: Clavichord Joe. Trustee Bard Coll., Annandale, N.Y., 1953-63, Crow Hill Sch., Rhinebeck, N.Y., 1969-70, Charleston Symphony Orch., 1971-75; trustee Charleston Concert Assn., 1971-78, pres., 1979-84; trustee, 2d v.p. Dock St. Theater, Charleston, 1981-83; founder, chmn. Stockholder Advocate Found., 1975-83, Stockholder Adv. Assn., Inc., 1976-79; investment adviser Johnson Lane Space and Smith, 1978—, St. Philips Ch.; bd. visitors Kanuga Episcopal Conf. Ctr., Henderson, N.C., 1985-88; trustee, treas. Dockside, Charleston, 1986-87. Mem. English Speaking Union (pres. Charleston 1977-79, bd. dirs. 1985-88), Rhinebeck, Dutchess County hist. socs. Republican. Clubs: Carolina Yacht (Charleston), Old Town (Charleston) (pres. 1981-82); Beach House (Sullivan's Island, S.C.) (pres. 1979-80). Home: 330 Concord St 5E Charleston SC 29401 also: Dockside Charleston SC 29401

SCOTT, HOWARD WINFIELD, JR., temporary help service company executive; b. Greenwich, Conn., Feb. 24, 1935; s. Howard Winfield and Janet (Lewis) S.; B.S., Northwestern U., 1957; m. Joan Ann MacDonald, Aug. 12, 1961; children—Howard Winfield III, Thomas MacDonald, Ann Elizabeth. With R.H. Donnelly Corp., Chgo., 1958-59; sales rep. Masonite Corp., Chgo. also Madison, Wis., 1959-61; sales rep. Manpower Inc., Chgo., 1961-63, br. mgr., Kansas City, Mo., 1963-65, area mgr., Mo. and Kans., 1964-65, regional mgr. Salespower div., Phila., 1965-66; asst. advt. mgr. soups Campbell Soup Co., Camden, N.J., 1966-68; pres. PARTIME, Inc., Paoli, Pa., 1968-74; dir. marketing Kelly Services Inc., Southfield, Mich., 1974-78; pres. CDI Temporary Services, Inc., 1978—. Served with AUS, 1957-58. Mem. Nat. Assn. Temporary Services (sec. 1970-71, pres. 1971-73, bd. dirs. 1982—), Kappa Sigma. Republican. Episcopalian. Home: PO Box 237 Paoli PA 19301 also: 1204 Annapolis Sea Colony E Bethany Beach DE 19930 Office: CDI Temporary Services Inc 10 Penn Ctr Philadelphia PA 19103-1670

SCOTT, IRENA MCCAMMON, neurophysiologist, writer; b. Delaware, Ohio, July 31, 1942; d. James Robert and Gay (Nuzum) McCammon; m. John Watson Scott, Dec. 6, 1969; 1 child, Rosa. B.Sc., Ohio State U., Columbus, 1965; M.S., U. Nev., Las Vegas, 1972; Ph.D., U. Mo., Columbia, 1976. Teaching and research asst. U. Nev., 1970-72; research asst. U. Mo., 1972-76; researcher Cornell U., 1977-78; asst. prof. biology St. Bonaventure (N.Y.) U., 1978-79; researcher Ohio State U., 1979—, Batelle Meml. Inst., 1980-86; correspondent Popular Mechanis mag., 1985—; contbr. articles to profl. jours., mags., newspapers. Vol. Ohio State U. Radio Telescope, 1981—; trustee Lewis Ctr. Meth. Ch., Ohio State U. Hosp. Grantee St. Bonaventure U. Mem. AAAS, Am. Physiol. Soc., Am. Dairy Sci. Assn., Mo. Acad. Sci., Ohio State U. Astronomy Club, Mutual Unidentified Flying Object Network (cons.). Verse Writers Guild Ohio, Olentangy Poets, Mensa (group coordinator, newsletter editor), Sigma Xi, Gamma Sigma Delta. Contbr. articles to profl. jours. Home: 6520 Bale Kenyon St Galena OH 43021 Office: Ohio State U 310 Hamilton Hall Columbus OH 43210

SCOTT, JAMES REID, business executive; b. Hamilton, Ont., Can., Sept. 25, 1931; s. John Reid and Mary E. (Leslie) S.; m. Helen Porter, Nov. 17, 1956; children—Iain Douglas, Alistair Graham, Neil Blair. With Dunlop Holding Ltd., India, Malaysia and London, 1957-77; group chief exec. Sime Darby Berhad, Kuala Lumpur, Malaysia, 1977-82; group mng. dir. Al Futtaim Group, Dubai, United Arab Emirates, 1984—. Served to lt. Seaforth Highlanders then parachute regt., 1955-57. Mem. Inst. Chartered Accts. Scotland. Conservative. Mem. Ch. of Scotland. Clubs: East India (London); Royal and Ancient Golf of St. Andrew's (Scotland). Office: Al Futtaim Group, Al Riqa Bldg PO Box 152, Dubai United Arab Emirates

SCOTT, JOHN ROLAND, oil company executive, lawyer; b. Wichita Falls, Tex., May 13, 1937; s. John Robert and Margaret Willena (Rouse) S.; m. Joan Carol Redding, Sept. 5, 1959; 1 child, John Howard. LL.B., Baylor Sch. Law, Waco, Tex., 1962. Bar: Tex. 1962, Alaska 1970, U.S. Dist. Ct. (we. dist.) Tex. 1965, U.S. Dist. Ct. Alaska 1975. Assoc. litigation sect Lynch & Chappell, Midland, Tex., 1962-65; regional atty. Atlantic Richfield Co., Midland, 1965-79; sr. atty., Anchorage, 1969-77, sr. atty., Dallas, 1977-80; v.p., assoc. gen. counsel Mitchell Energy & Devel. Corp., Houston, 1980-82; asst. gen. counsel Hunt Oil Co., Dallas., 1982-84, v.p., chief counsel, 1984—; bar examiner in Alaska, 1974-77. Mem. State Bar Tex. (lectr.), Dallas Bar Assn., ABA, Phi Alpha Delta. Republican. Clubs: Petroleum, University (Dallas). Office: Hunt Oil Co 2900 InterFirst One Bldg 1401 Elm St Dallas TX 75202

SCOTT, KERRIGAN DAVIS, investor; b. Magdalene, Fla., Sept. 26, 1941; s. Thurman Thomas and Jacqueline (Glenister) S.; children: Katherine, Stephanie, Jennifer. degree U. Va., 1964. Investor Mcht. Marine and Plantation Properties, Hilton Head Island, S.C., 1965—. Author: Aristocracy and Royalty of the World, 1983. Capt. U.S. Mcht. Marines. Mem. Million Dollar Round Table, RMS Queen Mary Hist. Soc. (founder). Episcopalian. Club: Shipyard Plantation Racquet (Hilton Head Island). Avocations: maritime subjects, Southern history, art. Home: Hilton Head Plantation 10 Windflower Ct Hilton Head Island SC 29928

SCOTT, LORRAINE ANN, association executive; b. Cleve., Dec. 14, 1947; d. Harry F. and Ann Mae (Dolecek) Dufek; m. John William Scott, Jan. 4, 1969; 1 son, Bruce. B.B.A., Dyke Coll., Cleve., 1967. Acct., Fulton, Reid & Staples, Cleve., 1967-69; acct., data control Nat. City Bank, Cleve., 1969-70; asst. treas. Independence (Ohio) Bd. of Edn. 1978-80; exec. dir. Nat. Frat. of Phi Gamma Nu, Cleve., 1980—. Mem. Am. Soc. Assn. Execs. Republican. Lutheran. Editor Phi Gamma Nu mag., 1980—.

SCOTT, SIR PETER (MARKHAM), artist, ornithologist; b. Sept. 14, 1909; s. Robert Falcon Scott and Kathleen Bruce Young; m. Elizabeth Jane Howard, 1942 (div. 1951); 1 daughter; m. Philippa Talbot-Ponsonby, 1951; 2 children. MA, U. Cambridge; student, Munich State Acad., Royal Acad. Schs., London; LLD (hon.), U. Exeter, 1963, U. Aberdeen, 1963, U. Birmingham, 1974, U. Bristol, 1974, U. Liverpool, 1984; DSc., U. Bath, 1979, U. Guelph, 1981, U. Ulster, 1987. Chmn. World Wildlife Fund Internat., 1961-82, chmn. council, 1983-85, hon. chmn., 1985—; chmn. Survival Service Commn. IUCN, 1962-81, Falkland Islands Found., 1979—; trustee emeritus World Wildlife Fund U.K., chmn. yachting com., 1947-48; internat. jury for yachting, Olympic Games, Melbourne, 1956, Naples, 1960, Tokyo, 1964; chancellor Birmingham U., 1974-83; rector Aberdeen U., 1960-63; leader ornithological expeditions to Cen. Highlands, Iceland to mark wild geese, 1951, 53, expeditions to Australiasia Galapagos Islands, Seychelles and Antarctic; represented Great Britain in Olympic Games in single-handed sailing, 1936; explored unmapped Perry River area in Can. Arctic, 1949; speaker nature feature programmes on TV. Author: Morning Flight, 1935, Wild Chorus, 1938, The Battle of the Narrow Seas, 1945, Portrait Drawings, 1949, Key to Wildfowl of the World, 1949 (Coloured Key 1958), Wild Geese and Eskimos, 1951; (with James Fisher) A Thousand Geese, 1953; (with Hugh Boyd) Wildfowl of the British Isles, 1957; (with Philippa Scott) Animals in Africa, 1962; (with the Wildfowl Trust) The Swans, 1972, Fishwatchers' Guide to West Atlantic Coral Reefs, 1972, Observations of Wildlife, 1980, Travel Diaries of a Naturalist, vol. I, 1983, vol. II, 1985, vol. III, 1987; (autobiography) The Eye of the Wind, 1961; illustrator books A Bird in the Bush, Grey Goose, Through the Air, The Snow Goose, Adventures Among Birds, Handbook of British Birds, vol. III, Waterfowl of the World, Birds of the Western Palearctic, vol. I, The Wildfowl of Britain and Europe; oil paintings exhibited at London and N.Y.C. Chmn. The Otter Trust, Inland Waterways Assn., Winston Churchill Meml. Trust; mem. council Boy Scout Assn., 1945-73. Served with Brit. mil., 1939-45. Decorated Icelandic Order of the Falcon, 1969, Comdr. Dutch Order of Golden Ark, 1976; recipient Internat. Gold badge for gliding, 1958, Internat. Diamond badge, 1963, Nat. Gliding Championship award, 1963, Cherry Kearton medal RGS, 1967, Albert Medal RSA, 1970, Bernard Tucker medal BOU, 1970, Arthur Allen medal Cornell U., 1971, Gold medal N.Y. Zoolog. Soc., 1975, Internat. Pahlavi Environment prize U.N., 1977, IUCN John Phillips medal, 1981, World Woldlife Fund 20th Anniversary Spl. award, 1981, Founder's medal, 1983, Gold medal Phila. Acad. of Natural Scis., 1983, RSPB Gold award, 1986, J.P. Getty prize, 1986. Mem. Soc. of Wildlife Artists (pres. 1964-78), Fauna and Flora Preservation Soc. (pres. 1981—), Glos Assoc. of Youth Clubs, Internat. Yacht Racing Union (pres. 1955-69), Glos Trust for Nature conservation, Brit. Butterfly Conservation Soc., Brit. Gliding Assn. (v.p., chmn. 1968-70), Inland Waterways Assn., Camping Club of Great Britain, Bristol Gliding Club. Clubs: Royal Thames Yacht, Explorers (N.Y.C.). Home: New Grounds, Slimbridge, Glos GL2, England *

SCOTT, ROBERT ALLYN, college administrator; b. Englewood, N.J., Apr. 16, 1939; s. William D. and Ann. F. (Waterman) S.; BA, Bucknell U., 1961; PhD, Cornell U., 1975; m. Phyllis Virginia Brice, Mar. 23, 1963; children—Ryan Keith, Kira Elizabeth. Mgmt. trainee Procter & Gamble Co., Phila., 1961-63; asst. dir. admissions Bucknell U., Lewisburg, Pa., 1965-67; asst. dean Coll. Arts and Scis., Cornell U., Ithaca, N.Y., 1967-69, assoc. dean, 1969-79, prof. anthropology, 1978-79; dir. acad. affairs Ind. Commn. for Higher Edn., Indpls., 1979-84; asst. commr., 1984-85; pres. Ramapo Coll. N.J., 1985—; lectr. U. Philippines, 1964-65; cons. to Sta. WSKG Public TV and Radio, 1977-79; cons. to various colls. and univs., pubs., 1966—; mem. curriculum adv. com. Ind. Bd. Edn., 1984-87 ; mem. Lilly Endowment Thinktank, 1984-86; bd. dirs. United Jersey Bank, Assn. Commerce and Industry, Hackensack (N.J.) Med. Ctr. Trustee, Bucknell U., 1976-78, First Unitarian Ch., Ithaca, 1970-73, 78-79, chmn., 1971-73, Unitarian Universalist Ch. of Indpls., 1980-85 . Served with USNR, 1963-65. Spencer Found. research grantee, 1972, Exxon Edn. Found. research grantee, 1977; recipient Prudential Found. Leader of Yr. award, 1987. Fellow Am. Anthrop. Assn.; mem. Assn. Study Higher Edn., Am. Sociol. Assn., Am. Assn. Higher Edn., Higher Edn. Colloquim (chmn. 1982-84), Bucknell U. Alumni Assn. (dir. 1971-80, pres. 1976-78), Indpls. Com. on Fgn. Relations, Phi Kappa Psi, Phi Kappa Phi. Clubs: Ithaca Yacht; Econs. of Indpls; Indian Trails. Contbr. articles to sociol., ednl. and popular publs.; author books and mongraphs; editorial bd. Cornell Rev., 1976-79; book rev. editor Coll. and Univ., 1974-78; cons. editor Change mag., 1979—; cons. editor Jour. Higher Edn., 1985—; exec. editor Saturday Evening Post book div. Curtis Pub. Co., 1982-85 . Office: Ramado Coll NJ 505 Romado Valley Rd Mahwah NJ 07430

SCOTT, ROBERT GENE, lawyer; b. Montague, Mass., Aug. 29, 1951; s. Edwin Ray and Barbara Agnes (Painchaud) S.; m. Laura Beth Williams, May 27, 1978; children: Jason Robert, Amanda Marie, Leah Beth. BS, U. Notre Dame, 1973, MS, 1975; postgrad. U. Tex. Med. Br., 1975-76; JD, U. Notre Dame, 1980. Bar: Ind. 1980, Mo. 1981, U.S. Dist. Ct. (no. dist.) Ind. 1980, U.S. Dist. Ct. (we. dist.) Mo. 1981, U.S. Patent Office 1980, U.S. Ct. Appeals (11th cir.) 1986, U.S. Ct. Appeals (8th cir.) 1987, U.S. Ct. Appeals (10th cir.) 1987. Asst. women's basketball coach U. Notre Dame, Ind., 1977-80; assoc. atty. Oltsch, Knoblock & Hall, South Bend, Ind., 1980-81; atty. Swanson, Midgley, et al, Kansas City, Mo., 1981-82; exec. adminstr. Council of Fleet Specialists, Shawnee Mission, Kans., 1982-83; atty. Levy and Craig, Kansas City, Mo., 1983—. Precinct Committeeman Johnson County Rep. Party, Kans., 1983-84. Mem. ABA, Ind. Bar Assn., Mo. Bar Assn., Kansas City Bar Assn., Kansas City Lawyers Assn. Republican. Roman Catholic. Club: Notre Dame of Kansas City (pres. 1985-86). Home: 9405 Dice Ln Lenexa KS 66215 Office: 11900 Coll Blvd 300 Metcalf Bank Bldg Overland Park KS 66212

SCOTT, ROLAND BOYD, pediatrician; b. Houston, Apr. 18, 1909; s. Ernest John and Cordie (Clark) S.; m. Sarah Rosetta Weaver, June 24, 1935 (dec.); children—Roland Boyd, Venice Rosetta, Estelle Irene. BS, Howard U., 1931, MD, 1934, DSc (hon.), 1987. Diplomate Nat. Bd. Med. Examiners, Am. Bd. Pediatrics. Gen. Edn. Bd. fellow U. Chgo., 1936-39; faculty Howard U., Washington, 1939—, prof. pediatrics, 1952-77, disting. prof. pediatrics and child health, 1977—, chmn. dept. pediatrics, 1945-73; dir. Ctr. for Sickle Cell Anemia, 1973—; chief pediatrician Freedmen's Hosp., 1947-73; professorial lectr. in child health and devel. George Washington U. Sch. Medicine, 1971-75; staff Children's Hosp., Providence Hosp., Columbia Hosp., D.C. Gen. Hosp., Washington Hosp. Center; cons. in pediatrics to NIH, hosps.; Mem. com. Pub. Health Adv. Council, 1964—, U.S. Children's Bur., 1964-70; mem. Nat. Com. for Children and Youth.;

mem. sickle cell adv. com. NIH, 1983-88. Author: (with Althea D. Kessler) Sickle Cell Anemia and Your Child, (with C.G. Uy) Guidelines For Care of Patients With Sickle Cell Disease; Editor: Procs. 1st Internat. Conf. on Sickle Cell Disease: A World Health Problem, 1979; Mem. editorial bd.: Advances in the Pathophysiology, Diagnosis and Treatment of Sickle Cell Disease, 1982, Clin. Pediatrics, 1962-80, Jour. Nat. Med. Assn, 1978; cons. editor: Medical Aspects of Human Sexuality; editorial bd.: Annals of Allergy, 1977-82, Pediatrics, 1988. Recipient Sci. and Community award Medico-Chirurgical Med. Soc. D.C., 1971, Community Service award Med. Soc. D.C., 1972, award for contbns. to sickle cell research Delta Sigma Theta, 1973, 34 years Dedicated and Disting. Service award in pediatrics dept. pediatrics Howard U., 1973, Faculty award for excellence in research, 1974, Alumni award for Service and Dedication, 1984, spl. recognition plaque for contbns. to research and edn., 1985, Ronald McDonald Children Charities award, 1987; certificate of appreciation Sickle Cell Anemia Research and Edn., 1977; Mead Johnson award D.C. chpt. Am. Acad. Pediatrics, 1978; Percy L. Julian award We Do Care, Chgo., 1979; Abraham Jacobi Meml. award AMA and Acad. Pediatrics, 1985; also plaques for work in sickle cell disease various orgns. including Columbia U. Sickle Cell Ctr., 1984, Elks, Nat. Assn. Med. Minority Educators, NIH, 1980-82. Fellow Am. Coll. Allergists (Disting. Service award 1977); mem. AMA, Am. Hematology Soc., Am. Pediatric Soc., Soc. Pediatric Research, Am. Acad. Allergy (v.p. 1966-67), Am. Acad. Pediatrics (mem. com. on children with handicaps, cons. head start program), Am. Fedn. Clin. Research, Nat. Med. Assn. (Disting. Service medal 1966), AAAS, Internat. Corr. Soc. Allergists, Assn. Ambulatory Pediatric Services, AAUP, Internat. Congress Pediatrics, Can. Sickle Cell Soc. (hon. life), Phi Beta Kappa, Sigma Xi (Percy L. Julian award Howard U. chpt. 1977), Kappa Pi, Beta Kappa Chi, Alpha Omega Alpha, others. Home: 1723 Shepherd St NW Washington DC 20011 Office: Howard U 2121 Georgia Ave NW Washington DC 20059

SCOTT, THEODORE R., lawyer; b. Mount Vernon, Ill., Dec. 7, 1924; s. Theodore R. and Beulah (Flannigan) S.; m. Virginia Scott, June 1, 1947; children: Anne Lawrence, Sarah Buckland, Daniel, Barbara Gomon. AB, U. Ill., 1947, JD, 1949. Bar: Ill. 1950. Law clk. to judge U.S. Ct. Appeals, 1949-51; sole practice Chgo., 1950—; assoc. Spaulding Glass, 1951-53, Loftus, Lucas & Hammand, 1953-58, Ooms, McDougall, Williams & Hersh, 1958-60; ptnr. McDougall, Hersh & Scott, Chgo., 1960-87; of counsel Jones, Day, Reavis & Pogue, 1987—. Served to 2d lt. USAAF, 1943-45. Decorated Air medal. Fellow Am. Coll. Trial Lawyers.; mem. ABA, Ill. Bar Assn., Chgo. Bar Assn., 7th Circuit Bar Assn. (past pres.), Legal Club Chgo., Law Club Chgo., Patent Law Assn. Chgo. (past pres.), Phi Beta Kappa. Clubs: Union League (Chgo.); Exmoor Country (Highland Park, Ill.). Home: 1569 Woodvale Ave Deerfield IL 60015 Office: 225 W Washington St Chicago IL 60606

SCOTT, TIMOTHY, research scientist; b. London, Mar. 31, 1952; s. Thomas Ronald and Eleanor Joyce (Evans) S. BSc, U. London, 1973, PhD, 1976. NATO research fellow U. So. Calif., Los Angeles, 1976-78; sr. research asst. U. Durham, Eng., 1979-81; sr. sci. officer U.K. Atomic Energy Authority, Winfrith, Dorset, Eng., 1981-85, prin. sci. officer, 1985—. Fellow Inst. Math. and its Applications; mem. Inst. Physics, Soc. Petroleum Engrs. Ch. of England. Office: UK Atomic Energy Authority, Atomic Energy Establishment, Winfrith, Dorset DT2 8DH, England

SCOTT, WILLIAM GEORGE, artist; b. Greenock, Scotland, Feb. 15, 1913; s. William John and Agnes (Murray) S.; m. Hilda Mary Lucas, May 19, 1937; children: Robert, James. Student, Belfast (Northern Ireland) Sch. Art, 1929, Royal Acad. Art, London, 1931; DrRCA (hon.), Royal Coll. Art, London, 1975; DLitt (hon.), Queens U., Belfast, 1976, Trinity Coll., Dublin, Ireland, 1977. Works exhibited Leger Gallery, 1942, 44, 46, Leicester (Eng.) Gallery, 1948, 51, Hanover (Fed. Republic of Germany) Gallery, 1953, 56, 61, 63, 65, 67, Martha Jackson Gallery, N.Y.C., 1954, 58, 73-74, Venice (Italy) Bienale, 1958, São Paulo (Brazil) Bienal, 1953, 61, Tate Gallery, 1972, 86, Gimpel Fils Galley, 1974, 76, 78, 80, 85, 87, Moos Gallery, Toronto, Can., 1975, 82, Kasahara (Japan) Gallery, 1976, Ulster Arts Council, 1979, 86, Imperial War Mus., 1981, Gimpel Weidenhofer Gallery, N.Y.C., 1983, Nat. Gallery Scotland, 1986, Mus. Modern Art, St. Ettienne, France, 1987, Victoria and Albert Mus., also Paris, N.Y., Toledo, Republic of South Africa, Can., Australia, S.Am.; contbr. (film): Every Picture Tells a Story, 1987. Decorated CBE, Royal Academician. Club: Chelsea (Eng.) Arts (hon. life). Home and Office: 13 Edith Terr, London SW10, England

SCOTT, WILLODENE ALEXANDER, library administrator; b. Ethridge, Tenn., Sept. 4, 1922; d. Jesse Cary and Maud (Goff) Alexander; B.A., George Peabody Coll. for Tchrs., 1946, B.S. in L.S., 1947, M.A., 1949, Ed.S., 1972, Ph.D., 1986; m. Ray Donald Scott, Nov. 27, 1959; 1 dau., Pamela Dean. Librarian, Sylvan Park Elem. Sch., Nashville, 1947-51, Waverly Belmont Jr. High Sch., Nashville, 1951-54, Howard High Sch., Nashville, 1954-62, Peabody Demonstration Sch., Nashville, 1962-63; librarian McCann Elem. Sch., Nashville, 1963-66; supr. instructional materials, library div. Metro Nashville-Davidson County Schs., Nashville, 1966-73, dir. instructional materials and library services, 1973-87; dir. libraries Watkins Inst., Nashville, 1987-88; lectr. Peabody Coll. Library Sch., Nashville, summers, 1950-66, 71, 72, 76, U. Tenn., Nashville Center, 1970; Tenn. rep. White House Conf., 1970. Chmn. nat. alumni fund-raising George Peabody Coll. for Tchrs., 1975-76, nat. alumni pres., 1977-78, trustee, 1976-78; bd. dirs. Friends of Music, 1977-79; mem. vis. com. bd. trustees Vanderbilt U., 1979-85. Recipient Disting. Alumni award Peabody Library Sch., 1987, Tenn. Library Assn. honor award, 1986; pub. "Experiencing Literature With Children", Elementary English, 1967, "Instructional Materials Center", Tenn. Librarian, 1969. Mem. ALA, Southeastern Library Assn. (scholarship com. 1968-70), Tenn. Library Assn. (membership chmn. 1955, 64, treas. 1977-78, honor award 1986), Tenn. Edn. Assn. (library sect. pres. 1954), Met. Nashville Edn. Assn., NEA (life), Children's Internat. Edn. Center of Nashville (charter mem.-at-large), AAUW, Woman's Nat. Book Assn. (charter mem.), DAR (organizing treas. Buffalo River chpt. 1967-69), Delta Kappa Gamma (v.p. 1984-86). Baptist. Club: Nashville Library (pres. 1952-53). Lodge: Order Eastern Star. Home: 525 Clematis Dr Nashville TN 37205 Office: Watkins Inst 601 Church St Nashville TN 37219-2309

SCOTT, WINFIELD JAMES, marketing executive; b. Worcester, Mass., Jan. 4, 1933; s. Gherald Dean and Helen L. S.; B.A., Norwich U., 1955; postgrad. Marquette U., 1961-62; m. Betty Joan Price, June 29, 1957; children—Mary Jo, Susan Elizabeth. With sales dept. Norton Co., Worcester, 1956, sales rep. Chgo. dist., 1957, sales supr. Wis. dist., 1960-71; founder, pres. The Abrasive Group, Wauwatosa, Wis., 1971—; ad hoc prof. mktg. U. Wis. Extension. Mem. Abrasive Engring. Soc. (co-gen. chmn. internat. conf.), Nat. Small Bus. Assn., Wis. Mfrs. and Commerce, Ind. Bus. Assn. Wis., Met. Milw. Assn. Commerce, Nat. Fedn. Ind. Bus. Republican. Episcopalian. Author: Modern Machine Shop, 1967. Home: 11037 W Derby Ave Wauwatosa WI 53225 Office: PO Box 13244 Wauwatosa WI 53213

SCOTTO, RENATA, soprano; b. Savona, Italy, Feb. 24, 1935; m. Lorenzo Anselmi. Studied under, Ghirardini, Merlino and Mercedes Llopart, Accademia Musicale Savonese, Conservatory Giuseppe Verdi, Milan. Debut in La Traviata, Teatro Nuevo, Milan, 1954; then joined La Scala Opera Co.; appeared with Met. Opera, N.Y.C., 1965, Convent Garden, Hamburg (Fed. Republic of Germany) State Opera, Vienna (Austria) State Opera, Nat. Theatre Munich, San Francisco Opera, Chgo. Lyric Opera, 1988; roles include: Ballo in Maschera, La Sonnambula, I Puritani, L'Elisir d'amore, Lucia di Lammermoor, La Boheme, Turandot, Otello (Verdi), Trovatore, Le Prophete, Madama Butterfly, Adriana Lecouvreur, Norma, Tosca, Manon Lescaut. Address: care Robert Lombardo Assocs 61 W 62d St Suite 6F New York NY 10023 also: care Il Teatro la Scala, via Filodrammatici 2, Milan Italy *

SCOURFIELD, EIRA J., mathematics educator; b. London. BSc, U. London; MSc, U. Exeter, Eng.; PhD, U. Glasgow, Scotland. Asst. U. Glasgow; lectr. Westfield Coll. U. London, lectr. Royal Holloway and Bedford New Coll.; mem. Inst. Advanced Study, Princeton, N.J., 1981. Contbr. articles to profl. jours. Mem. Am. Math. Soc., London Math. Soc., Edinburgh Math. Soc., Glasgow Math. Assn.

SCRAFTON, DEREK, Australian state government administrator; b. Darlington, Eng., Sept. 25, 1937; came to Australia, 1972; s. Ronald and Mary Elizabeth (Shann) S.; m. Barbara Whiteley, Aug. 13, 1963; children: Mary Elisabeth, Katherine Jean. BS, U. London, 1959, PhD, 1968. Economist railway and highway div. Ministry Transport, Ottawa, ON, Can., 1966-67, chief urban transp. devel div., 1968-69, dir. urban and regional transport, 1970-71; dir.-gen. Govt. South Australia, Adelaide, South Australia, 1972—; Commr. Australian Nat. Railways, 1980—; mem. faculty architecture and planning Adelaide U., 1974—. Contbr. articles, papers, reports to profl. jours. Mem. State Transport Authority, 1975—, City Planning Commn., Adelaide, 1982-87; bd. dirs. Internat. Ch. Trade and Industry Mission, 1985—. Fellow Royal Geographical Soc., Pub. Administrn. Inst., Australian Inst. Mgmt.; mem. Australian Transport Research Forum (chmn. 1975, 83), Internat. Union Pub. Transport. (assoc.). Clubs: Adelaide U. Soccer (pres. 1975—), Darlington Football (v.p. 1975—). Office: South Australia Dept Transport, Box 1599 GPO, 5001 Adelaide Australia

SCRAGG, THOMAS WILLIAM, librarian, historical researcher, solicitor; b. Wirral, Cheshire, Eng., Sept. 19, 1940; s. Joseph and Norah (Scragg) S.; B.A. with honours, Sch. Slavonic and E. European Studies, U. London; B.Phil., U. Liverpool; M.A., Manchester Poly. (Eng.); postgrad. King's Coll., U. London; Dipl.Lib., Manchester Library Sch.; m. Isabel Mary Thomas, Apr. 3, 1972; children—Maximian Rhys Joseph, Halcyon Rosemary Louise, Sophia Isabel Hannah, Mortimer Henry Thomas. Solicitor, Supreme Ct., 1968—; music adviser, hist. researcher, program annotator Chester Festival, 1967, 86-88, Festival in Gt. Irish Houses, 1970-81, Queen's Festival, U. Belfast, 1971, 72, Newcastle-upon-Tyne Festival, 1972-75, Portsmouth Festival, 1977-78, Dublin Festival, Royal Dublin Soc., 1979, Alfred Beit Found., 1979-81, Leeds Castle Festival, 1987, Music Assn. Ireland, others; phonographic cons., cataloguer Sir Compton MacKenzie's Jethou Record Collection, 1973-75; music library cons. Granada TV Ltd., 1973-77; librarian Knowsley Library, 1974—. Recipient Polska Spl. Corr. award, Warsaw, 1966. Fellow Royal Geog. Soc., Royal Soc. Arts, Soc. Antiquaries of Scotland; mem. Law Soc., Library Assn. (assoc.), Soc. Archivists , Royal Mus. Assn., Soc. Genealogists, Polish Inst. Arts and Scis. Am. (assoc.), Anglo-Polish Music Circle Gt. Britain (hon. v.p. 1970), E.S.U., Royal Commonwealth Soc., Fauna and Flora Preservation Soc. Author articles, festival program material; Claudio Arrau Discography, 1978, 2d edit., 1982. Home: The Woodcroft, Barnston Wirral, Cheshire England

SCREPETIS, DENNIS, consulting engineer; b. Hoboken, N.J., Feb. 12, 1930; s. George and Athanasia (Stasinos) S.; student Stevens Inst. Tech., Bklyn. Poly. Inst., Cooper Union, Rutgers U.; m. Betty Pravasilis, Sept. 17, 1960. Registered profl. engr., N.J., N.Y. Nuclear engr. Vitro Corp. Am., N.Y.C., 1957-60; project engr. Gen. Cable Corp., Bayonne, N.J., 1960-63; project mgr. AMF Atomics, York, Pa., 1963-65; sr. staff engr. nuclear div. Combustion Engring. Corp., Windsor, Conn., 1965-66; corp. engr. Standard Packaging Corp., N.Y.C., 1966-68; v.p. engring. Eastern Schokbeton, Bound Brook, N.J., 1968-74; cons. engr., Ft. Lee, N.J., 1974—; Patentee in nuclear sci. Mem. Am. Concrete Inst., Pre-Stressed Concrete Inst., Concrete Reinforcing Inst., Nat. Safety Council, Am. Nat. Standards Inst., Internat. Platform Assn., Am. Inst. Steel Constrn., ASTM, Am. Welding Soc., Concrete Industry Bd., Bldg. Ofcls. and Code Adminstrs. Soc. of Am. Mil. Engrs., Nat. Forensic Ctr., Am. Biog. Inst. Research Assn. (bd. dirs.). Greek Orthodox. Home and Office: 2200 N Central Rd Fort Lee NJ 07024

SCRITSMIER, JEROME LORENZO, lighting fixture manufacturing company executive; b. Eau Claire, Wis., July 1, 1925; s. Fredrick Lorenzo and Alvera Mary (Schwab) S.; B.S., Northwestern U., 1950; m. Mildred Joan Lloyd, June 27, 1947; children—Dawn, Lloyd, Janet. Salesman, Sylvania Elec. Products, Los Angeles, 1951-69; owner, mgr. Real Properties, 1965—; chief fin. officer Environ. Lighting for Architecture Co., Los Angeles, 1973—. Served with USAAF, 1943-46. Mem. Apt. Assn. (pres., dir. Los Angeles County). Republican. Club: Jonathan (Los Angeles). Home: 2454 N Cameron Ave Covina CA 91724 Office: 17891 Arenth St City of Industry CA 91748

SCULLI, DOMENIC, operational research educator, mathematician; b. Ferruzzano, Italy, Mar. 17, 1946; arrived in Hong Kong, 1974; s. Stefano and Paulina (Scopelliti) S.; m. Jacqueline Oi Yin Lai, June 21, 1980; 1 child, Pauline. MS in Operational Research, U. Birmingham, Eng., 1971. Operational research analyst Australian Consol. Industries, Melbourne, 1968-74; lectr. U. Hong Kong, 1974-85, sr. lectr., 1985—. Contbr. articles to profl. jours. Fellow Inst. Math. and Its Applications, Eng. Office: U Hong Kong, Pokfulam Rd, Hong Kong Hong Kong

SCULLY, JOHN ROBERT, oral and maxillofacial surgeon; b. N.Y.C., Mar. 2, 1949; s. Frank Edward and Helen Veronica (Sawyer) S.; m. Bonnie Diane Baron, Aug. 28, 1971; children: AmandaRose, John Robert Jr. B.S. Chemistry, Spring Hill Coll., 1970; D.D.S., Med. Coll. Va., 1974; M.S., U. Iowa, 1980. Diplomate Am. bd. Oral and Maxillofacial Surgery. Resident in oral and maxillofacial surgery U. Iowa, 1977-1980; pvt. practice oral and maxillofacial surgery, Asheville, 1980—; chief oral and maxillofacial surgery St. Josephs Hosp., Asheville, 1984—, Meml. Mission Hosp., 1984—; cons. Pardee Hosp., Hendersonville, N.C., 1983—. Contbr. articles to profl. jours. Served to capt. USAF, 1974-77. USAF Merit scholar, 1972-74. Fellow Am. Assn. Oral and Maxillofacial Surgery; mem. ADA, N.C. Dental Soc., Southeastern Soc. Oral and Maxillofacial Surgeons, N.C. Soc. Oral and Maxillofacial Surgeons, Health Vols. Overseas, Internat., Buncombe County Dental Soc., Asheville C. of C., Zebulon Vance Debating Soc., Internat. Platform Assn., Delta Sigma Delta. Club: Asheville Country. Avocations: music; rock and folk guitar; dance; tennis; auto racing. Home: 17 Bluebriar St Asheville NC 28804 Office: Rockcliff Place Asheville NC 28801

SCULLY, ROGER TEHAN, lawyer; b. Washington, Jan. 10, 1948; s. James Henry and Marietta (Maguire) S.; m. Martha Anne Seebach, Dec. 29, 1979. BS, U. Md., 1977; JD, Cath. U., 1980. Bar: Md. 1980, D.C. 1981, U.S. Tax Ct. 1982, U.S. Supreme Ct. 1988. V.p. Bogley Related Cos., Rockville, Md., 1971-75; law clk. to presiding justice Superior Ct. of D.C., Washington, 1979-81; assoc. Lerch, Early & Roseman, Bethesda, Md., 1981-82; gen. counsel Westwood Corps., Bethesda, 1982—; of counsel Laszlo N. Tauber, M.D., Bethesda, 1982—; cons. in real estate Order of Friar Minor, N.Y.C, 1977—; lectr. Mortgage Bankers Assn., Washington, 1984—. Mem. Pres.'s Council St. Bonaventure U., Olean, N.Y., 1986—; trustee Edmund Burke Sch., Washington, 1984—; bd. dirs. Nat. Children's Choir, Washington, 1980—, Manor Montessori Sch., Potomac, Md., 1981-84; bd. of govs. Goodwill Industries, Washington, 1987—. Recipient First Order Affiliation Order of Friars Minor, 1985; named one of Outstanding Young Men in Am., 1982. Mem. ABA, Fed. Bar Assn., Md. Bar Assn., D.C. Bar Assn., Assn. Trial Lawyers Am., Am. Judicature Soc., Selden Soc., Phi Delta Phi. Republican. Roman Catholic. Clubs: Nat. Press (Washington); Nat. Aviation (Arlington, Va.). Home: 10923 Wickshire Way Rockville MD 20852 Office: Westwood Ctr II 5110 Ridgefield Rd Suite 408 Bethesda MD 20816

SCULTHORPE, PETER JOSHUA, composer; b. Launceston, Tasmania, Apr. 29, 1929; s. Joshua and Edna (Moorhouse) S. Ed. U. Melbourne, Wadham Coll., Oxford U.; D.Litt. (hon.), Tasmania. Sr. lectr. in music U. Sydney (Australia), 1963—; reader in music, 1968; vis. prof. music U. Sussex, 1971-72; mem. various commns., including Australian Broadcasting Commn., Birmingham Chamber Music Soc., Australian Elizabethan Theatre Trust, Australian Ballet. Compositions include: The Loneliness of Bunjil, 1954; Sonatina, 1954; Violin Sonata, 1955; Irkanda I, 1955, II, 1959, III, 1960, IV, 1961; Ulterior Motifs, a musical farce and music for various revues, 1957-59; Sonata for Viola and Percussion, 1960; Orchestral Suite (from film They Found a Cave), 1962; Sonata for Piano, 1963; The Fifth Continent, 1963; String Quartet No. 6, 1965; South by five, 1965; Sun Music II, 1969; Orchestral Suite (from film The Age of Consent), 1968; Sun Music Ballet, 1968; Ketjak for orch., 1969; String Quartet Music, 1969; Love 200 for pop group and orch., 1970; The Stars Turn, 1970; Music for Japan, 1970; Rain, 1970; Dream, 1970; Rain, 1965-70; Snow, Moon & Flowers, 1971; Landscape, 1971; Stars, 1971; How The Stars Were Made, 1971; Ketjak, 1972; Koto Music, 1972; Rites of Passage, 1972; Music of Early Morning, 1974; also other works for radio, TV, theatre and film. Decorated comdr. Order Brit. Empire; recipient Composers' award Australian Council, 1975-78; Australian film award, 1980; vis. fellow Yale U., 1965-67; Fulbright scholar-in-residence, 1980. Address: 91 Holdsworth St, Wollahra, Sydney New South Wales 2025, Australia *

SCURO, JOSEPH E., JR., lawyer; b. Jersey City, Mar. 28, 1948; s. Joseph E. and Phyllis (Amato) S.; m. Cheryl K. Scuro. BA, Manhattan Coll., 1970; JD, Ohio State U., 1972. Bar: Tex., Ohio, U.S. Dist. Cts., U.S. Ct. Appeals (5th and 10th cir.), U.S. Tax Ct., U.S. Mil. Appeals, U.S. Supreme Ct. Asst. atty. gen. Ohio, 1973-81; chief legal counsel Ohio State Hwy. Patrol, 1975-81; practice law, 1973—; counsel Nicholas & Barrera, San Antonio, 1982—; atty.-counsel San Antonio Police Officers Assn.; counsel Combined Law Enforcement Assn. Tex., Alamo Heights Police Officers Assn.; Counsel Tex. Mcpl. League; police legal adviser to cities of San Marcos, New Braunfels, Balcones Heights, La Vernia, Poteet, Laredo, Dilley, Kiley, Universal City, Del Rio and others; spl. counsel on tng. San Antonio Police Dept.; counsel to Bexar County Constable's Assn.; condr. seminars. Contbr. articles on police and law enforcement to profl. jours. Bd. dirs. Nat. Hispanic Arts Endowment. Served to capt. USAF, 1970-75. Fellow Southwestern Legal Found.; mem. Tex. Bar Assn., Ohio Bar Assn., ABA, San Antonio Bar Assn., Columbus (Ohio) Bar Assn., Am. Trial Lawyers Assn., Police Exec. Research Forum, Internat. Assn. Chiefs of Police (ins. bd. advs., program), Ams. for Effective Law Enforcement (bd. advs.), Southwestern Law Enforcement Inst. (bd. advs.), Internat. Soc. Law Enforcement and Criminal Justice Instrs., Combined Law Enforcement Assn. Tex., Fed. Criminal Investigators Assn., Ohio Assn. Polygraph Examiners. Democrat. Presbyterian. Office: PO Drawer 50966 Main Place Station Dallas TX 75250

SCURRAH, MARTIN JOHN, educator; b. Hobart Tasmania, Australia, Nov. 9, 1941; s. Terence Clifton and Sheila Noreen (Carroll) S.; BEc with honors, U. Tasmania, 1964; MBA, U. Wash., 1967; PhD, Cornell U., 1972; m. Maria Isabel Mayer, July 11, 1970; children: Cecilia, Lucia, Natalia. Research assoc. Escuela de Administracion de Negocios Para Graduados, Lima, Peru, 1970-74, assoc. prof. organizational behavior, 1974-78, prof., 1978-83, dir. MA program, 1976, dir. research dept., 1977-79; social sci. cons. Ford Found., Lima, 1979-84; assoc. dir. Grupo de Estudios Para el Desarrollo, 1984—, acting dir., 1986; vis. research fellow Agrarian U., Wageningen, Netherlands, 1978, La Trobe U., Melbourne, Australia, 1985; mem. governing bd. Asociacion Antisuyo; cons. Oxford Com. for Famine Relief, UNICEF, ILO, Inter-Am. Found., NOVIB, HIVOS, CIDA, Lutheran World Relief. Recipient award social sci. research competition Ford Found., 1978. Mem. Am. Polit. Sci. Assn., Am. Sociol. Assn., Latin Am. Studies Assn., Consejo Latino-Americano Para La Autogestion, Interam. Psychol. Soc., Internat. Sociol. Assn., Assn. for Workplace Democracy. Club: Cricket and Football (Lima). Author: (with Peter S. Cleaves) Agriculture, Bureaucracy and Politics in Peru, 1980; (with Kenneth Langton, Carlos Franco) Personalidad, Poder y Participacion, 1981, (with Bruno Podesta) Experiencias Autogestionarias Urbanas en Peru y Chile, 1986; editor: Encuentro sobre Experiencias Autogestionarias, 1985, Empresas Asociativas y Comunidades Campesinas: Puno después de la Reforma Agraria, 1987; contbr. articles to profl. jours. Home: Tripoli 365, Lima Peru Office: Apartado 270002, San Isidro, Lima 27 Peru

SCUTT, DER, architect; b. Reading, Pa., Oct. 17, 1934; s. George W. and Hazel (Smith) S.; student Wyomissing Poly. Inst., 1952-54, Pa. State U., 1956-58; B.Arch. (Winchester Wirt travel fellow), M.Arch., Yale U., 1961; m. Leena Liukkonen, Feb. 18, 1967; children—Hagen, Kirsti Karina. Design ptnr. Swanke Hayden Connell & Partners, 1975-81; pvt. practice architecture, N.Y.C., 1981—; tchr. architecture Barlow Sch., Amenia, N.Y., 1964-66; vis. critic Yale U., 1982, 83; numerous radio and TV appearances on energy conservation, other subjects. Trustee The Chapin Sch., 1984—. Recipient medal AIA, 1961; Rotary Internat. fellow, 1955-56. Fellow Illuminating Engrs. Soc. (bd. mgrs. N.Y. sect. 1971-72, 74-75, v.p. 1972-73, pres. 1973-74, Disting. Service award 1976); mem. AIA (sec. N.Y. chpt. 1970-72, fin. com. 1974-78, Brunner scholarship com. 1975-76, chmn., 1976-77, N.Y. chpt. spl. com. on proposed zoning modifications 1980, 82), Archtl. League N.Y. (chmn. scholarships and award com. 1970-72, exec. com. 1970—, v.p. for architecture 1972-73, N.Y. Bldg. Congress (bd. govs., v.p. 1984—, v.p. 1985-87, treas. 1987—), U.S. Inst. Theatre Tech. (dir. 1970-72). Methodist. Contbr. articles to profl. jours.; lectr. Contbg. editor Lighting Design and Application, 1972—. Project designer, prin. works include: library Barlow Sch., Amenia, 1964, Crossroads Office Bldg., Rochester, N.Y., 1969, One Astor Plaza and Minskoff Theatre, N.Y.C., 1973, Western Union office bldg., Upper Saddle River, N.J., 1973, Equitable Life Assurance Data Center, Easton, Pa., 1973, Creative Perfumery Center, Roure Bertrand Dupont, Teaneck, N.J., 1973, retrofit, 1982, Hercules, Inc. Computer Center, Wilmington, Del., 1974, Northwestern Mut. Life Ins. Co., Milw., 1979, Barnes Group Inc. corp. hdqrs., Bristol, Conn., 1979, Grand Hyatt Hotel, N.Y.C., 1980, 520 Madison Ave., N.Y.C., 1983, Continental Center Office Tower, N.Y.C., 1983, Trump Tower, N.Y.C., 1983, St. Luke's/Roosevelt Hosp. Hand Surgery Clinic, N.Y.C., 1984, U.S. hdqrs. Hong Kong Bank, N.Y.C., 1985, 505 Park Ave. Office Bldg., N.Y.C., 1986, 100 UN Plaza Tower, N.Y.C., 1986, The Corinthian, N.Y.C., 1988, 625 Madison Ave. Office Bldg., N.Y.C., 1988, The Milan, W. 23d St., N.Y.C., 1988. Office: Der Scutt Architect 44 W 28th St New York NY 10001 also: The Milan W 23rd St New York NY 10001

SEABORG, GLENN THEODORE, chemistry educator; b. Ishpeming, Mich., Apr. 19, 1912; s. H. Theodore and Selma (Erickson) S.; m. Helen Griggs, June 6, 1942; children: Peter, Lynne Seaborg Cobb, David, Stephen, John Eric, Dianne. AB, UCLA, 1934; PhD, U. Calif.-Berkeley, 1937; numerous hon. degrees; LLD, U. Mich., 1958, Rutgers U., 1970; DSc, Northwestern U., 1954, U. Notre Dame, 1961, John Carroll U., Duquesne U., 1968, Ind. State U., 1969, U. Utah, 1970, Rockford Coll., 1975, Kent State U., 1975; LHD, No. Mich. Coll., 1962; DPS, George Washington U., 1962; DPA, U. Puget Sound, 1963; LittD, Lafayette Coll., 1966; DEng, Mich. Technol. U., 1970; ScD, U. Bucharest, 1971, Manhattan Coll., 1976; PhD, U. Pa., 1983. Research chemist U. Calif.-Berkeley, 1937-39, instr. dept. chemistry, 1939-41, asst. prof., 1941-45, prof., 1945-71, univ. prof., 1971, leave of absence, 1942-46, 61-71, dir. nuclear chem. research, 1946-58, 72-75, asso. dir. Lawrence Berkeley Lab., 1954-61, 71—; chancellor Univ. (U. Calif.-Berkeley), 1958-61, dir. Lawrence Hall of Sci., 1982—; sect. chief metall. lab. U. Chgo., 1942-46; chmn. AEC, 1961-71, gen. adv. com., 1946-50; research nuclear chemistry and physics, transuranium elements.; chmn. bd. Kevex Corp., Burlingame, Calif., 1972—; mem. Pres.'s Sci. Adv. Com., 1959-61; mem. nat. sci. bd. NSF, 1960-61; mem. Pres.'s Com. on Equal Employment Opportunity, 1961-65, Fed. Radiation Council, 1961-69, Nat. Aeros. and Space Council, 1961-71, Fed. Council Sci. and Tech., 1961-71, Nat. Com. Am.'s Goals and Resources, 1962-64, Pres.'s Com. Manpower, 1964-69, Nat. Council Marine Resources and Engring. Devel., 1966-71; chmn. Chem. Edn. Material Study, 1959-74, Nat. Programming Council for Pub. TV, 1970-72; dir. Ednl. TV and Radio Center, Ann Arbor, Mich., 1958-64, 67-70; pres. 4th UN Internat. Conf. Peaceful Uses Atomic Energy, Geneva, 1971, also chmn. U.S. del., 1964, 71; U.S. rep. 5th-15th gen. confs. IAEA, chmn., 1961-71; chmn. U.S. del. to USSR for signing Memorandum Cooperation Field Utilization Atomic Energy Peaceful Purposes, 1963; mem. U.S. del. for signing Limited Test Ban Treaty, 1963; mem. commn. on humanities Am. Council Learned Socs., 1962-65; mem. sci. adv. bd. Robert A. Welch Found., 1957—; mem. Internat. Orgn. for Chem. Scis. in Devel., UNESCO, 1980—, chmn., 1981; mem. Nat. Commn. on Excellence in Edn., Dept. Edn., 1981—. Author: (with Joseph J. Katz) Chemical Actinide Elements, 1954, 2d ed. (with Joseph J. Katz and Lester R. Morss) Vols. I & II, 1986, The Chemistry of the Actinide Elements, 1957, The Transuranium Elements, 1958, (with E.G. Valens) Elements of the Universe, 1958 (winner Thomas Alva Edison Found. award), Man-Made Transuranium Elements, 1963, (with D.M. Wilkes) Education and the Atom, 1964, (with E.K. Hyde, I. Perlman) Nuclear Properties of the Heavy Elements, 1964, (with others) Oppenheimer, 1969, (with W.R. Corliss) Man and Atom, 1971, Nuclear Milestones, 1972, (with Ben Loeb) Kennedy, Khruschev and the Test Ban, 1981; editor: Transuranium Elements: Products of Modern Alchemy, 1978; asso. editor: Jour. Chem. Physics, 1948-50; editorial adv. bd.: Jour. Inorganic and Nuclear Chemistry, 1954-82, Indsl. Research, Inc, 1967-75; adv. bd.: Chem. and Engring. News, 1957-59; editorial bd.: Jour. Am. Chem. Soc, 1950-59, Ency. Chem. Tech., 1975—, Revs. in Inorganic Chemistry, 1977—; mem. hon. editorial adv. bd.: Internat. Ency. Phys. Chemistry and Chem. Physics, 1957—; mem. panel: Golden Picture Ency. for Children, 1957-61; mem. cons. and adv. bd.: Funk and Wagnells Universal Standard Ency, 1957-61; mem.: Am. Heritage Dictionary Panel Usage Cons, 1964—; contbr. articles to profl. jours. Trustee Pacific Sci. Center Found., 1962-77; trustee Sci. Service, 1965—, pres., 1966—; trustee Am.-Scandinavian Found., 1968—, Ednl. Broadcasting Corp., 1970-72; bd. dirs. Swedish Council Am., 1976—, chmn. bd. dirs., 1978-82; bd. dirs. World Future Soc., 1969—, Calif.

Council for Environ. and Econ. Balance, 1974—; bd. govs. Am. Swedish Hist. Found., 1972—. Recipient John Ericsson Gold medal Am. Soc. Swedish Engrs., 1948; Nobel prize for Chemistry (with E.M. McMillan), 1951; John Scott award and medal City of Phila., 1953; Perkin medal Am. sect. Soc. Chem. Industry, 1957; U.S. AEC Enrico Fermi award, 1959; Joseph Priestley Meml. award Dickinson Coll., 1960; Sci. and Engring. award Fedn. Engring. Socs., Drexel Inst. Tech., Phila., 1962; named Swedish Am. of Year, Vasa Order of Am., 1962; Franklin medal Franklin Inst., 1963; 1st Spirit of St. Louis award, 1964; Leif Erikson Found. award, 1964; Washington award Western Soc. Engrs., 1965; Arches of Sci. award Pacific Sci. Center, 1968; Internat. Platform Assn. award, 1969; Prometheus award Nat. Elec. Mfrs. Assn., 1969; Nuclear Pioneer award Soc. Nuclear Medicine, 1971; Oliver Townsend award Atomic Indsl. Forum, 1971; Disting. Honor award U.S. Dept. State, 1971; Golden Plate award Am. Acad. Achievement, 1972; John R. Kuebler award Alpha Chi Sigma, 1978; Founders medal Hebrew U. Jerusalem, 1981; Henry DeWolf-Smyth award Am. Nuclear Soc., 1982, Great Swedish Heritage award, 1984, Ellis Island Medal of Honor, 1985, Vannevar Bush Award, Nat. Sci. Bd., 1988; decorated officier Legion of Honor France; Daniel Webster medal, 1976. Fellow Am. Phys. Soc., Am. Inst. Chemists (Pioneer award 1968, Gold medal award 1973), Chem. Soc. London (hon.), Royal Soc. Edinburgh (hon.), Am. Nuclear Soc., Calif., N.Y., Washington acads. scis., AAAS (pres. 1972, chmn. bd. 1973), Royal Soc. Arts (Eng.); mem. Am. Chem. Soc. (award in pure chemistry 1947, William H. Nichols medal N.Y. sect. 1948, Charles L. Parsons award 1964, Gibbs medal chgo. sect. 1966, Madison Marshall award No. Ala. sect. 1972, Priestley medal 1979, pres. 1976), Am. Philos. Soc., Royal Swedish Acad. Engring. Scis. (adv. council 1980), Am. Nat., Argentine Nat., Bavarian, Polish, Royal Swedish, USSR acads. scis., Royal Acad. Exact, Phys. and Natural Scis. Spain (acad. fgn. corr.), Soc. Nuclear Medicine (hon.), World Assn. World Federalists (v.p. 1980), Fedn. Am. Scientists (bd. sponsors 1980), Deutsche Akademie der Naturforscher Leopoldina (East Germany), Nat. Acad. Pub. Adminstrn., Internat. Platform Assn. (pres. 1981—), Am. Hiking Soc. (dir. 1979—, v.p. 1980), Phi Beta Kappa, Sigma Xi, Pi Mu Epsilon, Alpha Chi Sigma (John R. Kuebler award 1978), Phi Lambda Upsilon (hon.); fgn. mem. Royal Soc. London, Chem. Soc. Japan, Serbian Acad. Sci. and Arts. Clubs: Bohemian (San Francisco); Chemists (N.Y.C.); Cosmos (Washington), University (Washington); Faculty (Berkeley). Office: Lawrence Berkeley Lab U Calif Berkeley CA 94720 *

SEABURG, JEAN, lawyer; b. Mpls., May 3, 1935; d. Gunnar Fredrick and Lorraine Elise (Otto) Dahlstrom; m. Paul A. Seaburg, July 27, 1957 (div. Jan. 1973); children—Mark David, Gunnar Paul; m. Richard J. Lee, Feb. 24, 1984 (dec. June 1986). Student U. Minn., 1953-57; B.S.C.E., Marquette U., 1967, J.D., 1974. Bar: Wis. 1974, Minn. 1986, U.S. Dist. Ct. (ea. and we. dists.) Wis. 1974, U.S. Dist. Ct. Minn. 1986, U.S. Patent Office 1986; registered profl. engr., Wis., Minn. Engr., Howard, Needles, Tammen & Bergendoff, Milw., 1967-71; law clk. Habush, Habush & Davis, Milw., 1973-74, assoc., 1974-77, ptnr., 1977-86; assoc. James E. Olds, Ltd., Mpls., 1986—. Mem. ABA, Assn. Trial Lawyers Am., ASCE, Nat. Soc. Profl. Engrs. Lutheran. Office: James E Olds Ltd 10800 Lyndale Ave S Minneapolis MN 55420

SEADLER, STEPHEN EDWARD, business and computer consultant, social scientist; b. N.Y.C., 1926; s. Silas Frank and Deborah (Gelbin) S.; AB in Physics, Columbia U., 1947, postgrad. in atomic and nuclear physics, 1947; postgrad. in relativity, cosmology and quantum mechanics, George Washington U., 1948-50; m. Ingrid Linnea Adolfsson, Aug. 7, 1954; children—Einar Austin, Anna Carin. Legal research asst., editor AEC, Washington, 1947-51; electronic engr. Cushing & Nevell, Warner, Inc., N.Y.C., 1951-54; seminar leader, leader trainer Am. Found. for Continuing Edn., N.Y.C. 1955-57; exec. dir. Medimetric Inst., 1957-59; mem. long range planning com., chmn. corporate forecasting com., mktg. research mgr. W. A. Sheaffer Pen Co., Ft. Madison, Iowa, 1959-65; founder Internat. Dynamics Corp., Ft. Madison and N.Y.C., 1965, pres., 1965-70; orginator DELTA program for prevention and treatment of violence, 1970; founder ID Center, Ft. Madison, now N.Y.C., 1968, pres., 1968—; mgmt. cons. in human resources devel. and conflict reduction, N.Y.C., 1970-73; pres. UNICONSULT computer-based mgmt. and computer scis., N.Y.C., 1973—; speaker on decision support systems, internat. affairs and ideological arms control; author/speaker (presentation) Holocaust, History and Arms Control; originator social scis. of ideologics and computer based knowledge systems sci. of ideotopology. Instr. polit. sci. Ia. State Penitentiary, 1959-62. Served with AUS, 1944-46. Mem. Am. Phys. Soc., Am. Statis. Assn., Acad. Polit. Sci., Am. Sociol. Assn., IEEE, N.Y. Acad. Sci., Am. Mgmt. Assn. (lectr. 1963-68), Internat. Platform Assn. Unitarian. Lodges: Masons (32 deg.), Shriners. Contbr. Ideologics and ideotopology sects. to Administrative Decision Making, 1977, Societal Systems, 1978; Management Handbook for Public Administrators, 1978; also articles profl. jours. Testimony on ideological arms control in Part 4 of Senate Fgn. Relations Com. Hearings on Salt II Treaty, 1979.

SEAGA, EDWARD PHILIP GEORGE, prime minister of Jamaica, politician; b. Boston, May 28, 1930; s. Philip and Erna (Maxwell) S.; B.A., Harvard U., 1952; LL.D., U. Miami, 1981. m. Marie Elizabeth Constantine, 1965; children—Christopher, Annabella, Andrew-Marc. M.P. for West Kingston, Jamaican Parliament, 1962—; minister of Devel. and Welfare, 1962-67; minister of Fin., 1967-72; leader of the Opposition, 1974-80; prime minister of Jamaica, 1980—; former gov. World Bank, IMF, Inter-Am. Devel. Bank. Leader, Jamaica Labour Party, 1974—; founding mem. UNESCO Internat. Fund Promotion of Culture, 1971—. Decorated Grand Collar Venezuela, 198—. Gold Key award, N.Y.C., 1981; Golden Mercury award, 1981; Grand Cross Order of Merit (W. Ger.), 1981. Anglican. Author: The Development of Chidld, Revival Spirit Cults. Home: Vale Royal, Kingston Jamaica Office: Jamaica Labour Party, 20 Belmont Rd, Kingston Jamaica *

SEAH, KIM SWEE, management consultant; b. Singapore, May 15, 1947; s. Yang Sieu and Seu Tee (Oh) S.; m. Swee Neo Ong, Oct. 24, 1970; children: Winston Kok Leong, Serene Li-ling. Diploma in Bus. Adminstrn., Inst. Bus. Adminstrn., Australia, 1978. Tchr. primary sch., Singapore, 1965; clerical officer Telcommunications Dept., Singapore, 1966-70; accounts asst. K C Heng & Co., Singapore, 1971-74; dir., mgr. K C Mgmt. Cons. Pte. Ltd., Singapore, 1975—, Hong Joo Auto Ctr. Pte. Ltd., Singapore, 1987—. Recipient Pub. Service Medal award 1985. Vice-chmn. mgmt. com. Leng Kee Community Ctr., 1987—; sec. Citizen's Consultative Com., 1979—. Mem. Brit. Inst. Mgmt., Singapore Inst. Mgmt., Australian Inst. Mgmt. Clubs: Automobile Assn., Consumers' Assn. (Singapore). Home: 401 Pandan Gardens, Apt 10-01, Singapore 2260, Singapore Office: KC Mgmts Cons Pte Ltd, 35 36 Carpenter St, Suite 04-00, Singapore 0105, Singapore

SEAICH, JOHN LAIRD, physician; b. Salt Lake City, May 26, 1941; s. Eric John and Gladys (Jensen) S.; m. Ina Mae Copper, Feb. 5, 1968; children—Joseph, Jennifer, Jessica. B.S., U. Utah, 1965; M.D., Creighton U., 1969. Diplomate Am. Bd. Internal Medicine, Am. Bd. Endocrinology. Intern Riverside Gen. Hosp., Calif., 1969-70, resident in internal medicine, 1970-73; fellow in endocrinology U. Oreg., Portland, 1973-75; assoc. physician Twin Falls Clinic and Hosp., Idaho, 1975—; mem. cons. staff Magic Valley Regional Med. Ctr., Twin Falls, 1975—. Bd. dirs. Port of Hope,, Twin Falls, 1979-88. Fellow ACP; mem. Am. Diabetes Assn. (bd. dirs. Idaho affiliate 1978-84), AMA, Idaho Med. Assn., Alpha Omega Alpha. Republican. Morman. Home: 2028 Oakwood Dr Twin Falls ID 83301 Office: Twin Falls Clinic 666 Shoshone St E Twin Falls ID 83301

SEAL, MICHAEL, physicist; b. Weston Super Mare, Eng., Apr. 15, 1930; s. Carl Cyril and Ina May (Hurford) S.; m. Cynthia Ida Austin Leach, Aug. 7, 1954; children: David, Anne, Rosemary, Susan, Christopher. BA, Cambridge U., 1952, MA, 1956, PhD, 1957. Head diamond research Engelhard Industries Inc., Newark, 1959-67, tech. coordinator research and devel. div., 1965-67; dir. research Amsterdam Diamond Test and Devel. Ctr., D. Drukker & Zn. N.V., Amsterdam, 1967—; adj. dir. 1970—; bd. dirs. Dubbeldee Diamond Corp., Mt. Arlington, N.J. Contbr. articles to profl. jours. Served with RAF, 1948-49. Postdoctoral research fellow Cavendish Lab., Cambridge, 1957-59. Fellow Explorers Club, Inst. Physics of London, Mineral Soc. Am.; mem. IEEE, N.Y. Acad. Scis. (life), Am. Chem. Soc., Dutch Phys. Soc., Indsl. Diamond Assn. Am. (assoc.), Dutch Abrasives Soc. (chmn. 1977—), European Fedn. Abrasives Mfrs. (premier del. for Netherlands, chmn. diamond grains subcom. 1976—). Club: United Oxford and Cambridge Univs. Home: 5 Guido Gezelle St, 1077 WN Amsterdam The Netherlands Office: 12 Sarphatikade, 1017 WV Amsterdam The Netherlands

SEALE, CLARENCE DAVID, corporate executive; b. Bridgeton, Barbados, Dec. 11, 1937; s. Reginald Clarence and Ena Dorothy (Hill) S.; m. Margaret Anne Seale; children: Lisa, Janine, Richard, Tracey. Student, Harrison Coll., Barbados, 1947-54. Clk. Brit. West India Airways, Barbados, 1956-62; sales mgr. R.L. Seale Co. Ltd., Barbados, 1962-66, dir., 1966-71, chmn., chief exec. officer, 1971—; mem. Barbados Senate, 1981-86; chmn. Barbados Devel. Bank, 1976-86. Club: Barbados Turf (pres.). Home: Hopefield, Christ Church Barbados Office: Seale & Co Ltd RL, Tudor Bridge Bridgetown, Saint Michael Barbados

SEALY, TOM, lawyer; b. Santa Anna, Tex., Feb. 18, 1909; s. Thomas Richard and Elizabeth (Harper) S.; m. Mary Velma McCord, Jan. 16, 1936; 1 child, Nancy. LL.B., U. Tex., 1931. Bar: Tex. 1931. Practice in Midland, 1935—; mem. firm Stubbeman, McRae, Sealy, Laughlin & Browder, 1936—; hon. dir. First City Nat. Bank, Midland; past dir. First Savs. and Loan Assn., Tex. Land & Mortgage Co., Midland, Champlin Petroleum Co., Tex.-N.Mex. Ry. Co. Past mem. city council, Midland.; Past chmn. bd. regents U. Tex., past. chmn. devel. bd.; mem., former chmn. coordinating bd. Tex. Coll. and U. System; past trustee Tex. Presbyn. Found., Presbyn.-Austin Theol. Sem.; hon. trustee Southwestern Legal Found.; past chmn., dir. Tex. Research League; past pres. U. Texas Law Sch. Found., bd. govs. Midland Meml. Found., 1984—. Served to lt. col. USAAF, World War II. Recipient Disting. Alumnus award U. Tex., 1966, Outstanding Alumnus award U. Tex. Law Sch., 1970; Tom Sealy research professorship in energy law established in his honor at U. Tex. Law Sch. Atlantic Richfield Co. Fellow Am. Bar Found., Tex. Bar Founds. (50-Yr. award 1985); mem. Midland C. of C. (past pres.), Tex. Assn. Def. Counsel (past pres.), Am. Bar Assn., State Bar of Tex., Internat. Assn. Ins. Counsel, Am. Assn. Petroleum Landmen (hon.), Phi Delta Phi (hon.). Presbyn. Clubs: Midland Petroleum (past pres.), Plaza (vice chmn. bd. govs.) Headliners (Austin); Midland Country, Midland Racquet, Chaparral (Dallas); Century II (Ft. Worth); St. Anthony (San Antonio). Home: 915 Harvard St Midland TX 79701 Office: Stubbeman McRae Sealy Laughlin & Browder Two First City Ctr Suite 800 Midland TX 79701

SEAMAN, PEGGY JEAN, lawyer; b. New Orleans, Nov. 21, 1949; d. William David and Leah Catherine (Bourdet) Smith; m. Terry Noako Seaman, Dec. 22, 1970; children—Vanya Lianne, Ember Catherine. B.A., Rutgers U.-Camden, 1974; J.D., N.Y. Law Sch., 1978. Bar: N.Y. 1978, Va. 1980, U.S. Dist. Ct. Va., 1980, U.S. Dist. Ct. (so. and ea. dists.) N.Y. 1978. Assoc., Carol Lilienfeld, Esq., N.Y.C., 1978-79; gen. atty. Merit Systems Protection Bd., Office of Appeals, Washington, 1980-82, presiding ofcl., Washington regional office, Falls Church, Va., 1982-85, adminstrv. judge St. Louis regional office, 1985-87; atty., Office of Dep. Exec. Dir. for Regional Ops., Washington, 1987—. Recipient Sustained Superior Performance award Merit Systems Protection Bd., 1982, 84, Spl. Act award, 1988. Mem. ABA, Athenaeum Honor Soc., Mensa. Democrat. Home: 8302 Crown Court Rd Alexandria VA 22308 Office: Merit Systems Protection Bd 1120 Vermont Ave NW Washington DC 20419

SEAMAN, RICHARD HARPER, service executive; b. Phila., Nov. 2, 1916; s. Samuel Arthur and Isabel Curry (Gibson) S.; m. Jane Drenning, Nov. 22, 1941; children: Richard D., Cynthia Jane, Mark Cameron. Student, Wyomissing Poly. Inst., 1933-35, Pa. State U., 1936-37. Pres., chief exec. officer Berkleigh Equipment Co., Reading, Pa., 1946-54, Seaman Mill Supplies, Inc., Reading, Pa., 1954—, 200 Pa. Ave. Realty Corp., W. Reading, Pa., 1960—, S&B Leasing Co., Inc., W. Reading, Pa., 1970—; chmn. bd. ABE Berkleigh Corp., W. Reading, Pa., 1984—; pres. U.S. Mobile Energy Co., Inc., Reading, 1985—. Served as capt. Ordnance Dept., U.S. Army, 1941-46, PTO. Decorated Bronze Star, Bronze Arrowhead. Club: Young Rep. (Wyomissing, Pa.) (bd. dirs. 1948-60, pres. 1954-60). Office: Berkleigh Power Equip Co Inc 10 S 2nd Ave West Reading PA 19611

SEARBY, RICHARD HENRY, newspaper company executive, lawyer; b. July 23, 1931; s. Henry and Mary Searby; m. Caroline McAdam, 1962; 3 sons. BA (hons.), U. Oxford. Bar: London 1956, Victoria, Australia 1957. Assoc. to Chief Justice of Australia Rt. Hon. Sir Owen Dixon, 1956-59; ind. lectr. law relating to executors and trustees U. Melbourne, 1961-72; chmn. News Corp. Ltd., Australia, 1981—, News Internat. plc, U.K., 1987—; dep. chmn. Times Newspapers Holdings Ltd., 1981—; bd. dirs., chmn. S. China Morning Post, 1987—, Equity Trustees Executors and Agy. Co. Ltd., 1980—; bd. dirs. CRA Ltd., Shell Australia Ltd., Ansett Transport Industries Ltd. Chmn. Geelong Grammar Sch., 1983—. Decorated QC (Australia) 1971. Clubs: Melbourne, Australian (Melbourne). Office: 126 Kooyong Rd, Armidale, New South Wales 3143, Australia *

SEARCY, WILLIAM NELSON, lawyer; b. Moultrie, Ga., June 26, 1942; s. Floyd Hartsfield and Anna (Pidcock) S.; m. Camille Heery, June 17, 1967; 1 child, Amelia Ashburn. AB, U. Ga., 1964, JD, 1967; LLM in Taxation, Washington U., St. Louis, 1968. Bar: Ga. 1967, U.S. Dist. Ct. (so. dist.) Ga. 1970, U.S. Ct. Appeals (5th cir.) 1976, U.S. Ct. Appeals (11th cir.) 1984. Assoc. Bouhan, Williams & Levy, Savannah, Ga., 1970-73; ptnr. Brannen, Wessels, Searcy & Smith, Savannah, 1973—; bd. dirs. Citizens Bank, Cairo, Ga.; sec. Am. Fed. Savs. and Loan Assn., 1978-81; mem. adv. bd. Liberty Svgs. Bank. Pres. Chatham-Savannah Voluntary Action Ctr., Inc., 1978-80. Served to lt. col. Air N.G., 1967—. Mem. ABA (sec. spl. liaison tax com. S.E. region 1983-84, chmn. 1984-85), State Bar Ga. (chmn. sect. taxation 1983-84, mem.-at-large exec. council Young Lawyers Sect. 1975-78, chmn. conf. with Ga. Soc. CPA's 1979-81), Savannah Bar Assn. (pres. Younger Lawyers Sect. 1975-76), Am. Judicature Soc., Savannah Estate Planning Council. Clubs: Oglethorpe, Savannah Golf, Plimsoll (Savannah), Georgian (Atlanta). Office: PO Box 8002 Savannah GA 31412

SEARLE, JAMES ELMHURST, international business consultant; b. Winnipeg, Man., Can., June 13, 1929; s. James Winning and Agnes Elizabeth (Graham) S.; m. Jean Margaret McEachern, Mar. 3, 1953 (div. 1972); children: Lauraine, James, Christine, Michael; m. 2d, Judith Patricia Menzies, Mar. 9, 1974. BArch, U. Man., Winnipeg, 1951. Ptnr., Smith Carter Searle, Winnipeg, 1953-69; ptnr. Searle Wicbee Rowland, Toronto, Ont., Can., 1969-75; corp. v.p. Genstar Corp., Toronto, 1975-82; cons. Searle Cons., London, 1982—; dir. Western Foundry, Wingham, Ont., 1960—. Fellow AIA (hon.), Royal Archtl. Inst. Can. (pres. 1967); mem. Ont. Assn. Architects. Club: University (Toronto). Home: 32 Cranley Gardens #4, London SW7 3DD, England Office: J Searle Cons, 11 Church St Suite 200, Toronto, ON Canada M5E 1W1

SEARLE, PHILIP FORD, bank executive; b. Kansas City, Mo., July 23, 1924; s. Albert Addison and Edith (Thompson) S.; m. Jean Adair Hanneman, Nov. 22, 1950; 1 child, Charles Randolph. AB, Cornell U., 1949; grad. in banking, Rutgers U., 1957, 64. With Geneva (Ohio) Savs. and Trust Co., 1949-60, pres., 1959-60; pres., sr. trust officer Northeastern Ohio Nat. Bank, Ashtabula, 1960-69; pres., chief exec. officer BancOhio Corp., Columbus, 1969-75; chmn., chief exec. officer Flagship Banks, Inc., Miami, Fla., 1975-84; chmn. bd. Sun Banks, Inc., Orlando, Fla., 1984—, also bd. dirs.; mem. faculty Sch. Banking, Ohio U., 1959-70, Nat. Trust Sch., Northwestern U., Evanston, Ill., 1965-68; mem. corp. adv. com. Nat. Assn. Securities Dealers, 1981-83; v.p., mem. fed. adv. council to bd. govs. Fed. Res. System; bd. dirs. ALLTEL Corp. Co-author: The Management of a Trust Department, 1967; mem. editorial adv. bd.: Issues in Bank Regulation, 1978—. Past chmn. bd. regents Stonier Grad. Sch. Banking, Rutgers U., 1974-76, past mem. faculty. Served to capt. AUS, 1943-46, 51-52. Decorated Bronze Star; named Outstanding Citizen in Ashtabula County, 1967. Mem. Am. Bankers Assn. (bd. dirs. 1972-74, governing council), Fla. Bankers Assn. (bd. dirs. 1979-81, council 1981), Ohio Bankers Assn. (pres. 1970-71), Assn. Bank Holding Cos. (bd. dirs. 1979-81, exec. com. 1981), Fla. Assn. Registered Bank Holding Cos. (pres. 1979-81), Fla. Council 100, Fla. C. of C. (bd. dirs. 1978-82), Phi Kappa Tau. Clubs: Bay Hill, Citrus (Orlando, Fla.). Office: Sun Banks Inc Sun Bank NA Bldg 200 S Orange Ave Orlando FL 32801 also: PO Box 2848 Orlando FL 32802 *

SEARLE, RONALD, artist; b. Cambridge, Eng., Mar. 3, 1920; s. William James and Nellie (Hunt) S.; m. Monica Koenig, 1967. Ed., Cambridge Sch. Art. Author: pub. in U.S. The Female Approach, 1954, Merry England, 1957; (with Kaye Webb) Paris Sketchbook, 1958, The St. Trinian's Story, 1959, Refugees, 1960, (with Alex Atkinson) The Big City, 1958, U.S.A. for Beginners, 1959, Russia for Beginners, 1960, Escape from the Amazon, 1964, Which Way Did He Go?, 1962, From Frozen North to Filthy Lucre, 1964, Those Magnificient Men in Their Flying Machines, 1965, (with Heinz Huber) Haven't We Met Before Somewhere?, 1966, Searle's Cats, 1968, The Square Egg, 1969, Hello: Where Did All the People Go?, 1970, (with Kildare Dobbs) The Great Fur Opera, 1970, The Addict, 1971, More Cats, 1975, Zoodiac, 1978, Ronald Searle Album, 1979, The Situation is Hopeless, 1981, The Big Fat Cat Book, 1982, Winespeak, 1983, Ronald Searle in Perspective, 1985, To the Kwai-- and Back, 1986, Something in the Cellar, 1988, Ah Yes, I Remember It Well: Paris 1961-75, 1988; contbr. to New Yorker; 1st pub. work appeared in Cambridge Daily News, 1935-39; one-man exhbns. include Leicester Galleries, London, 1948, 50, 54, 57, Kraushaar Gallery, N.Y.C., 1959, Blanchini Gallery, N.Y.C., 1963, city mus. Bremen, Hannover, Dusseldorf, Stuttgart, Berlin, 1965, 3d Biennale, Tolentino, Italy, 1965, Galerie Pro Arte, Delmenhorst, Germany, Mus. Art, Bremerhaven, Germany, Galerie Münsterberg, Basle, Switzerland, Galerie Pribaut, Amsterdam, Holland, Wolfgang-Gurlitt Mus., Linz, Austria, Galerie La Pochade, Paris, 1966-71, Art Alliance Gallery, Phila., 1967, Galerie Gurlitt, Munich, 1967-76, Grosvenor Gallery, London, 1968, Galerie Obere Zaune, Zurich, 1968, Galerie Hauswedell, Baden-Baden, 1968, Galerie Brumme, Frankfurt, 1969, Konsthallen, Södertä lje, Sweden, 1969, Rizzoli Gallery, N.Y.C., 1969-81, Kunsthalle, Konstanz, 1970, Würzburg, 1970, Galerie Welz, Salzburg, 1971, Galerie Rivolta, Lausanne, 1972, Galerie Gaëton, Geneva, 1972, Bibliothè que Nationale, Paris, 1973, Galerie Würthle, Vienna, 1973, Kulterhaus Graz, Austria, 1973, 79, Galerie Rivolta, Lausanne, 1974, 78, Galerie l'Angle Aigu, Brussels, 1974, 77, Galerie Carmen Casse, Paris, 1975-77, Staatliche Museen Preussicher Kulturbesitz, Berlin, 1976, Galerie Bartsch and Chariau, Munich, 1981, Neue Galerie Wien, Vienna, 1985, 1988, Imperial War Mus., London, 1986, British Mus., London, 1986, Fitzwilliam Mus., Cambridge, 1987, Fine Arts Mus., San Francisco, 1987, others; contbr. to nat. publs., 1946—; theatre artist: Punch, 1949-61; created series of cartoons on fictitious girls sch., 1941; became: film series Belles of St. Trinian's, 1954, Blue Murder at St. Trinian's, 1957, The Pure Hell of St. Trinian's, 1960, The Great St. Trinian's Train Robbery, 1965, Wildcats of St. Trinian's, 1980; films designs include John Gilpin (Brit. Film Inst.), 1951, On the Twelfth Day, 1954 (nominated Acad. award), Energetically Yours, 1957, The Kings Breakfast, 1963, Those Magnificent Men in Their Flying Machines, 1965, Monte Carlo or Bust, 1969, Scrooge, 1970, Dick Deadeye, or Duty Done, 1975. Recipient medal Art Dirs. Club Los Angeles, 1959, medal Art Dirs. Mem. Club Phila., Pa., 1959, gold medal 3d Biennale, Tolentino, Italy, 1965, Prix de la Critique Belge, 1968, medaille de la ville d'Avignon, 1971, Prix de l' Humour S.P.H. Festival d' Avignon, 1971, Prix de l' Humour Noir Grandville France, 1971, Prix Internationale Charles Huard France, 1972, Best Advt. Illustration award Nat. Cartoonists Soc., 1988. Club: The Garrick (London). Home: care Tessa Sayle, 11 Jubilee Pl, London SW 3-3TE England Office: care John Locke Studio 15 E 76th St New York NY 10021

SEARS, MICHAEL, mathematics educator; b. Johannesburg, Transvaal, Repub. S. Africa, Aug. 17, 1947; s. Douglas Barker and Teda (De Moor) S. BSc, U. Adelaide, Australia, 1968; BSc with honors, Flinders U., Adelaide, 1969, PhD, 1972. Sr. lectr., assoc. prof., prof. U. Witwatersrand, Johannesburg, 1972-79, prof. of math., 1980—; vis. prof. U. Minn., Mpls., 1975, 79, 81, 85; head dept. applied math. U. Witwatersrand, 1979-84, acting dean faculty sci., 1986-87, dean faculty sci., 1988—. Contbr. articles to profl. jours. Research grantee Council for Scientific and Indsl. Research of South Africa continuing grants and support. Mem. Am. Math. Soc., Australian Math. Soc., South African Math. Soc. Home: 29 Brigish Dr, Johannesburg 2195, Republic of South Africa Office: U Witwatersrand, PO Wits, Johannesburg 2050, Republic of South Africa

SEARS, ROBERT LOUIS, industrial engineer; b. Oakland, Calif., Jan. 28, 1927; s. Louis Francis and Lucille (Hargreaves) S.; m. Phyllis Ann Barnes, Apr. 30, 1955; children—Stephen A., Jeffrey R., Garth E. B.S., U.S. Mil. Acad., 1952; M.S. in Indsl. Engring., Ariz. State U., 1968. Commd. 2d lt. U.S. Army, 1952, advanced through grades to col., 1972, ret. 1973; supt. emergency med. services State of Ariz., 1973-75; gen. mgr. Behavior Modification Clinic, Inc., Phoenix, 1975-78; dir. Indsl. Systems Assocs., Phoenix, 1978-80; assoc. dir. Ariz. Solar Energy Commn., Phoenix, 1980-87; program dir. Cogeneration Research Ctr. for Energy Systems Research Coll. Engring. and Applied Scis. Ariz. State U., Tempe, 1987—; pres. Robert Sears and Assocs., 1985—. Decorated Legion of Merit (2). Mem. Am. Soc. Profl. Engrs., Am. Inst. Indsl. Engrs. (sr.), Assn. Energy Engrs. (sr.) (pres. Ariz. chpt. 1986-87, bd. dirs., 1987—), Am. Solar Energy Soc., Am. Cogeneration Assn., Ariz. Cogeneration Assn. (pres. 1988—). Republican. Episcopalian. Club: Ariz. Road Racers, Greater Ariz. Bicycle Assn. (Phoenix), U.S. Masters Swimming. Contbr. articles to profl. jours.

SEATON, GEORGE LELAND, former utility company executive, civic worker; b. Sunny South, Calif., Feb. 9, 1901; s. Frank H. and Charity Jane (Lee) S.; B.S.E.E., Iowa State U., 1923; A.A. (hon.), Coll. DuPage; m. Mildred Irene Sandall, Aug. 14, 1926 (dec. Nov. 1984); children—Robert Lee, James Mann, Mary Seaton Martin. Engr., Gen. Electric Co., Ft. Wayne, Ind., 1923; with Ill. Bell Telephone Co., Chgo., 1923-66, asst. v.p., 1952-64, v.p., 1964-66, ret., 1966. Mem. Hinsdale (Ill.) Bd. Edn., 1941-47; chmn. Chgo. council Boy Scouts Am., 1958-63; chmn. exec. com. Gt. Books Found., Chgo., 1965—; treas. Disciples Div. House, U. Chgo., 1945—, mem. vis. com. U. Chgo. Div. Sch., 1977—; mem. Ill. Fair Employment Com., 1961-69; chmn. Coll. DuPage, 1966-72. Served to 2d lt. C.E., USAR, 1923-28. Recipient Silver Beaver award Boy Scouts Am., Silver Antelope award. Mem. Western Soc. Engrs., Am. Statis. Assn. Republican. Mem. Christian Ch. (Disciples of Christ). Clubs: Union League (Chgo.); Hinsdale Golf, Econ. Home: 6110 S County Line Burr Ridge IL 60521

SEAVER, JAMES EVERETT, historian, educator; b. Los Angeles, Oct. 4, 1918; s. Everett Herbert and Gertrude Lillian (Sharp) S.; m. Virginia Stevens, Dec. 20, 1940; children—Richard Everett, William Merrill, Robert Edward. A.B., Stanford U., 1940; Ph.D., Cornell U., 1946. Asst. instr. history Cornell U., 1940-42, 44-46; instr. Mich. State U., 1946-47; mem. faculty U. Kans., Lawrence, 1947—; prof. history U. Kans., 1960—, pres. faculty, 1972-74, 82-83. Author: The Persecution of the Jews in the Roman Empire, 313-438 A.D, 1952, also articles. Fulbright-Hays grantee Italy, 1953-54; Fulbright-Hays grantee Israel, 1963-64; Carnegie grantee Costa Rica, 1966-67. Mem. Am. Hist. Assn., Am. Philol. Assn., Archaeol. Inst. Am., Am. Numismatic Soc., AAUP, Am. Acad. Rome, U.S. Archives of Recorded Sound. Democrat. Episcopalian. Clubs: Alvamar Tennis, Alvamar Country. Home: 600 Louisiana St Lawrence KS 66044 Office: U Kans Dept History Lawrence KS 66045

SEAWELL, DONALD RAY, lawyer, publisher, arts center executive, producer; b. Jonesboro, N.C., Aug. 1, 1912; s. A.A.F. and Bertha (Smith) S.; m. Eugenia Rawls, Apr. 5, 1941; children: Brook Seawell Speidel, Donald Brockman. A.B., U. N.C., 1933, J.D., 1936, D.Litt., 1980; L.H.D., U. No. Colo., 1978. Bar: N.C. 1936, N.Y. 1947. With SEC, 1939-41, 45-47, Dept. Justice, 1942-43; chmn. bd., dir., pub., pres. Denver Post, 1966-81; chmn. bd., dir. Gravure West, Los Angeles, 1966-81; dir. Swan Prodns., London; of counsel firm Bernstein, Seawell, Kove & Maltin, N.Y.C., 1979—; chmn. bd., chief exec. officer Denver Ctr. Performing Arts, 1973—; ptnr. Bonfils-Seawell Enterprises, N.Y.C. Chmn. bd. ANTA, 1965—; mem. theatre panel Nat. Council Arts, 1970-74; bd. govs. Royal Shakespeare Theatre, Eng.; trustee Am. Acad. Dramatic Arts, 1967—, Hofstra U., 1968-69, Central City Opera Assn., Denver Symphony; bd. dirs., chmn. exec. com. Air Force Acad. Found., Nat. Ints. Outdoor Drama, Walter Hampden Meml. Library, Hammond Mus.; pres. Helen G. Bonfils Found., Denver Opera Found.; past chmn., mem. founding bd. Civilian/Mil. Inst. Served with AUS, World War II. Recipient Tony award for producing On Your Toes, 1983, Voice Research and Awareness award Voice Found., 1983. Clubs: Bucks (London); Players, Dutch Treat (N.Y.C.); Denver Country, Denver, Cherry Hills Country, Mile High (Denver); Garden of Gods (Colorado Springs, Colo.). Office: Denver Ctr for Performing Arts 1050-13th St Denver CO 80204

SEAY, GEORGE EDWARD, lawyer; b. Dallas, Jan. 12, 1909; s. Dero Eugene and Pauline Adrienne (Bolanz) S.; m. Mary Everman Saville, Feb. 4,

1937; children—George, John Everman, Edith. B.A., U. Tex.-Austin, 1930, LL.B., with highest honors, 1932. Bar: Tex. 1932, U.S. Ct. Appeals (5th cir.) 1941, U.S. Dist. Ct. (no. dist.) Tex. 1933, U.S. Dist. Ct. (we. dist.) Tex. 1979, U.S. Ct. Appeals (D.C. cir.) 1971. Practiced in Dallas, 1932—, ptnr. Malone Lipscomb & Seay, 1950-60, Malone, Seay & Gwinn, 1960-66, Malone Seay Gwinn & Crawford, 1967-70, Seay Gwinn Crawford & Mebus, 1970-75, Seay Gwinn Crawford Mebus & Blakeney, 1975-82; of counsel Haynes & Boone, Dallas, 1982—; chief pros. staff atty. Nuremberg Trials, 1945-46; speaker Bar Assn. Seminars, Dallas, 1947-49, 78-79. Bd. dirs. Dallas TB Assn., 1948-51, Dallas Day Nursery Assn., 1952-60; mem. bd. elders Highland Park Presbyn. Ch., 1963—. Served to lt. col. AUS, 1942-46. Mem. Southwestern Legal Found. (chmn. labor law sect. 1948-55, mem. planning com. 1970—), State Bar Tex. (chmn. labor law sect. 1952-53), Am. Coll. Trial Lawyers, Tex. Bar Found. (charter mem., fellow), ABA, Dallas Bar Assn., Fed. Bar Assn., Am. Judicature Assn., Chancellors, Order of Coif, Phi Beta Kappa, Phi Delta Phi. Republican. Presbyterian. Clubs: Dallas Country, City. Home: 5353 Montrose Dr Dallas TX 75209

SEBAHOUN, GERARD, hematologist; b. Aubagne, France, Aug. 21, 1945; s. Armand and Gladys (Pariente) S.; m. Solange Francoise Delarue, Mar. 28, 1971; children: Valerie, Pascale. MD, Med. U. Marseilles, 1968. Intern Marseilles' Hosps., 1968-72, Henri Mondor Hosp. and St. Louis Hosp., Paris, 1973-74; practice medicine specializing in hematology Marseilles, 1974—; cons. clin. hematology Institut Paoli-Calmettes, Marseilles, dir. hematology lab., 1979; prof. hematology Med. U., Marseilles, 1986. Contbr. articles to profl. publs. Mem. French Soc. Hematology, French Soc. Oncology, European Soc. Med. Oncology, Internat. Soc. Hematology. Home: Prado Parc 1, 411 Ave du Prado, 13008 Marseilles France Office: Institut Paoli Calmettes, 232 BD Ste Marguerite, 13009 Marseilles France

SEBASTIAN, PETER, former U.S. ambassador; b. Berlin, June 19, 1926; m. Harvel Huddleston, Dec. 11, 1951; 1 child, Christopher. B.A., U. Chgo., 1951; postgrad., U. d'Aix-Marseille, Nice, France, 1949, New Sch. for Social Research, N.Y.C., 1950, Nat. War Coll., 1969-70. Dir., owner cons. co., N.Y.C., 1950-57; U.S. Fgn. Service officer Dept. State, Washington, 1957-76, dep. exec. sec., 1976-77; U.S. consul gen. Dept. State, Casablanca, Morocco, 1978-80; minister, counselor Am. embassy, Rabat, Morocco, 1980-82; dir. for North Africa Dept. State, Washington, 1982-84; ambassador to Tunisia Tunis, 1984-87; ambassador-in-residence Ctr. for Strategic Internat. Studies, Georgetown U., Washington, 1987—; cons in fgn. affairs, lectr. 1988—. Contbr. poems to Osmose, 1949; author studies for Fgn. Service Inst. Served to sgt. AUS, 1944-46. Decorated Ouissam Alaouite (Morocco), numerous U.S. mil. decorations; recipient Presdl. Meritorious Service award, 1985. Mem. Am. Fgn. Service Assn., Nat. Geog. Soc. Episcopalian. Office: Ctr Strategic Internat Studies CSIS 1800 K St NW Washington DC 20006

SEBBAH, REMY GASTON, physician; b. Algiers, Algeria, Sept. 10, 1953; s. Louis Jack and Josette Anais (Mamane) S.; m. Brigitte Castelain, June 24, 1981; children: Virginie, Julie, Jérémie. Diplome d'état de Docteur en Médecine, Faculté de Médecine de Marseille, 1980, Certificat d'études complémentaires de Gériatrie, 1984. Directeur d'Enseignement Clinique Faculté de Médecine de Marseille, 1985—; instr. Médecin Généraliste, Marseille, 1980—. Mem. Union Regionale de la Formation Medicale Continue (v.p. 1987—), Coll. Provencal Médecines Généralistes Enseignants (pres. 1986—), Conseil Regional Formation Medicale Continue (sec. gen.). Office: 3 Ave Jules Cantini, 13006 Marseilles France

SEBBAS, LARS-OLAV, consulting company executive; b. Korsnäs, Finland, Dec. 2, 1936; s. Hugo and Ester Sebbas; Anita Helminen, Sept. 26, 1961; children: Leif, Nina, Niklas. MCE, Helsinki (Finland) U. Tech., 1959. Structural engr. Consulting Engrs. Holger Holmberg, Helsinki, 1960-61; engr. Imbau Spannbeton GMBH, Leverkusen, Fed. Republic Germany, 1961; structural engr. Insinööritoimisto Pentti Kaista and Co Oy, Helsinki, 1961-65; mgr. Cons. Engrs. Oy Kaista and Sebbas Ab, Helsinki, 1965-74, mng. dir., 1975-79; chmn. bd. dirs. Finnmap Oy, Helsinki, 1978-79, mng. dir., 1979—. Mem. Assn. Finnish Civil Engrs. (vice chmn. 1967-68, chmn. 1988—), Finnish Assn. Cons. Firms (bd. dirs. 1982-84, vice chmn. 1983-84), Concrete Assn. Finland, Am. Concrete Inst., Engring. Soc. Finland (vice chmn. 1977-85, chmn. 1985-87), Finnish Constructional Steelwork Assn. Ltd., Finnish Assn. Cons. Engrs., Concrete Soc. Great Britain, Internat. Assn. for Bridge and Structural Engring. Office: Finnmap Oy, PO Box 75, SF-00511 Helsinki Finland

SEBESTYÉN, ISTVÁN, computer scientist, educator, consultant; b. Budapest, Hungary, Aug. 14, 1947; arrived in Austria, 1977; s. János and Hedvig (Vadnai) S.; m. Eszter Molnár, Oct. 25, 1975; children: Adam, David Richard. MS in Elec. Engring., Tech. U. Budapest, 1970, PhD in Elec. Engring., 1974. Diplomate in elec. engring. Research asst. dept. high voltage techniques Tech. U. Budapest, 1968-70; sci. collaborator Inst. for Coordination Computer Techniques, Budapest, 1970-77; mgmt. cons. UN Indsl. Devel. Orgn., Vienna, Austria, 1977-78; scientist, research scholar Internat. Inst. Applied Systems Analysis, Laxenburg, Austria, 1978-84; systems planner, telecommunications adviser Siemens AG, Munich, 1985—; vis. prof. Tech. U. Graz, Austria, 1983-85; lectr., tchr. U. Klagenfurt, Austria, 1985—; cons. to internat. orgns. Author: Experimental and Operational East-West Computer Networks, 1983, Transborder Data Flows and Austria, 1986; mem. adv. bd. Jour. Transnat. Data Report, Washington, 1983—; contbr. over 75 articles to sci. jours. Mem. Austrian Computer Soc., Hungarian Computer Soc. Avocations: travel, sports. Home: Sollnerstrasse 10, 8000 Munich 71 Federal Republic of Germany Office: Siemens AG, Hofmannstrasse 51, 8000 Munich 70 Federal Republic of Germany

SECRETAN, LANCE H., business executive, consultant; b. Amersham, Buckinghamshire, Eng., Aug. 1, 1939; arrived in Can., 1959; s. Kenyon and Marie-Therése (Haffenden) S.; children: Sandi, Natalie. MA in Internat. Relations with distinction, U. So. Calif., 1980; PhD, London Sch. Econs. Sales mgr. J.J. Little & Ives, Toronto, 1959; analyst Toronto Stock Exchange, 1960; sales mgr. Office Overload, Toronto, 1960-67; mng. dir. Manpower Ltd., London, 1967-81; pres. The Thaler Corp., Inc., Toronto, 1981—. Author: How to be an Effective Secretary, 1972, Managerial Moxie, 1986, The State of Small Business, 1987, The Master Class, 1988. Mem. Greater London Council, 1978-80. Mem. Internat. Studies Assn., Acad. Mgmt., Royal Soc. Arts, Inst. Employment Cons., MENSA. Club: University (Toronto). Home and Office: RR #2, Alton, ON Canada L0N 1A0

SEDDOH, KOMPAVI FOFOLI, university administrator, geology educator; b. Atakpame, Togo, July 29, 1941; s. Komi and Kwamba (Djiyehoue) S.; m. Nerissa Anthony, Mar. 25, 1972; 1 child, Sena Adjoui. Licence des Sciences Naturelles, U. Dijon, France, 1965, D of Geology, 1968, Docteur d'Etat, 1973. Asst. prof. U. Dijon, 1966-74; head geology dept. U. Benin, Lome, Togo, 1974-77, prof., dir. Inst. Sci. and Edn., 1977-79; sec.-gen. Ministry of Edn.-Scientific Research, Lome, 1979-86, chaired prof., 1979—, rector, 1986—; mem. sci. com. Internat. Program Sci. Evaluation-UNESCO, Paris, 1984. Author: Guide Geologique: Bourgogne-Morran, 1973, Geology text, 1982. Mem. cen. com. Rassemblement du Peuple Togolais, 1986, exec. bd. UNESCO, 1988—. Recipient Ordre du Mond Pres. of Togo, 1981, Ordre du Palms French Minister of Edn., 1980, highest officer, 1985. Mem. Cons. Com. Univs. (chmn. 1985—), Geol. Soc. Africa, Geol. Soc. France. Roman Catholic. Home: PO Box 3680, Lome Togo Office: Univ du Benin, BP 1515, Lome Togo

SEDGWICK, RAE, psychologist, lawyer; b. Kansas City, Kans., Apr. 7, 1944; d. Charles and Helen (Timmons) Sedgwick. R.N., Bethany Sch. Nursing, 1965; B.S., U. Iowa, 1967; M.A., U. Kans., 1970, Ph.D., 1972, JD, 1986. Cert. psychologist, Kans.; bar: Kans. 1986. Med./surg., orthopedic and obstet. nurse, Iowa City, Iowa, 1965-67; with Community Mental Health Nursing, Kansas City, Kans., 1967-68; specialist Lab. Edn., Washington, 1971-72; adj. clin. staff community psychiatry, 1975-76; coordinator Health C.A.R.E. Clinic, Pa. State U., 1974-76; head grad. program in community mental health nursing and family therapy, Pa. State U., 1974-76, asst. prof., 1972-76; pvt. practice psychology, Bonner Springs, Kans., 1976—; cons. in field.; staff Bethany Med. Ctr., Kansas City, Kans., Cushing's Meml. Hosp., Leavenworth, Kans., St. John's Hosp., Leavenworth; del. Internat. Council Nurses, Frankfurt, Germany, People for People, People's Republic of China, 1982. Active Am. Heart Assn.; city councilwoman Bonner Springs, 1981—, pres. pro tem, 1983-87; mem. Kans. Internat. Women's Yr. Commn. Recipient Outstanding Young Woman award, U. Kans., Bus. and Profl. Women's Club scholar; elected to Kans. U. Women's Hall of Fame, 1987. Fellow Am. Orthopsychiat. Assn.; mem. AAAS, ABA, Kansas Bar Assn., Am. Assn. Psychiatric Services for Children, Am. Group Psychotherapy Assn. (dir.), Am. Nurses Assn., Am. Psychol. Assn., Anthrop. Assn. for Study of Play, Council of Advanced Practitioners in Psychiat. Mental Health Nursing, Kans. Psychol. Assn., Council Nurse Researchers, Sigma Theta Tau. Republican. Methodist. Club: Pilot. Author: Family Mental Health, 1980; The White Frame House, 1980; contbr. articles to profl. jours.

SEDKI, ATEF, prime minister of Egypt; b. 1930. Prof. gen. fin. Cairo U., 1958-73; cultural attaché Egyptian Embassy, Paris, 1973-80; pres. com. econ. and fin. affairs Govt. Adv. Council, 1980-85; pres. govt. audit office Arab Republic Egypt, Cairo, 1985-86, prime minister, 1986—, also minister internat. coop. Address: Office Prime Minister, Cairo Arab Republic of Egypt *

SEDKY, CHERIF, lawyer; b. Alexandria, Egypt, Dec. 10, 1943; came to U.S. 1958; s. Abdalla and Mona Frances (Smith) S.; m. Julie A. Greer, Dec. 18, 1964 (div.); children—Tarik, Mona; m. Linda M. Jackson, Dec. 26, 1987. B.A., Stanford U., 1966; J.D., Georgetown U., 1969. Bar: D.C. 1969, U.S. Ct. Appeals (D.C. cir.) 1969, U.S. Supreme Ct. 1974. Assoc. Surrey Karasik Greene & Hill, Washington 1969-71, Hill Christopher & Phillips, Washington 1971-72, 73-75; ptnr. Kirkpatrick & Lockhart and predecessor firms, Washington, 1976—; asst. gen. counsel MCI Communications Corp., Washington, 1972-73. Bd. Dirs. Arab-Am. Cultural Found., Am. Near East Refugee Aid. Mem. ABA, D.C. Bar Assn., Phi Delta Phi. Moslem. Clubs: Metropolitan, City Tavern (Washington). Office: 1800 M St NW Washington DC 20036

SEDLAK, RICHARD, naprapath; b. Berwyn, Ill., July 7, 1944; s. Richard and Alice H. (Tejcek) S. D in Naprapathy, Nat. Coll. Naprapathy, Chgo., 1966; D in Phys. Therapy, Am. Inst. of Sci., 1967; D in Chiropractic Medicine, Palmer Coll. Chiropractic Medicine, 1970; PhD (hon.), Community Ch. Coll., Wheatfield, Ind., 1979. Diplomate Nat. Bd. Chiropractic and Phys. Therapy, Diplomate Am. Bd. Phys. Therapy Examiners; bd. cert. naprapath. Phys. therapist West Suburban Hosp., Oak Park, Ill., 1964-66; pvt. practice naprapath, phys. therapist Cicero, Ill., 1970—; cons. phys. therapist Pershing Convalescent Home, Stickney, Ill., 1985—; assoc. dean Nat. Coll. Naprapathy, 1966-69, founder United Health Assn., 1976. Spl. police officer City of Cicero, 1968—. Recipient Cert. of Merit, Am. Massage Therapy Assn., 1969, Cert. of Achievement Palmer Coll. of Chiropractic Medicine, 1970, Cert. Achievement AMA, 1980. Fellow Soc. for Nutrition and Preventive Medicine; mem. Am. Naprapathic Assn., United Naprapathic Assn. (sec. 1972-73). Democrat. Roman Catholic. Home: 5537 W 24th Pl Cicero IL 60650 Office: 2137 Oak Park Ave Suite 1 Berwyn IL 60402

SEDLAK, VALERIE FRANCES, educator; b. Balt., Mar. 11, 1934; d. Julian Joseph and Eleanor Eva (Pilot) Sedlak; 1 child, Barry. AB in English, Coll. Notre Dame, Balt., 1955; MA, U. Hawaii, 1962; postgrad., U. Pa., 1982. Tchr. Sacred Heart Sch., Pensacola, Fla., 1955-56; grad. teaching fellow East-West Cultural Ctr., U. Hawaii, 1959-60; adminstrv. asst. Korean Consul Gen., Honolulu, 1959-60; tchr. Boyertown (Pa.) Sr. High Sch., 1961-63; asst. prof. English, U. Balt., 1963-69; asst. prof. Morgan State U., Balt., 1970—, sec. to faculty, 1981-83, faculty research scholar, 1982-83. Author poetry and lit. criticism. Coordinator Young Reps., Berks County, Pa., 1962-63; chmn. Md. Young Reps., 1964; election judge Baltimore County, Md., 1964-66; regional capt. Am. Cancer Soc., 1978-79; adv. bd. Our Md. Anniversary, 1984, The Living Constitution: Bicentennial of the Fed. Constitution, 1987. Fellow Morgan-Penn Faculty, 1977-79, Nat. Endowment Humanities, 1984; named Outstanding Teaching Prof., U. Balt. Coll. Liberal Arts, 1965, Outstanding Teaching Prof. English, Morgan State U., 1987. Mem. MLA, South Atlantic MLA, Coll. Lang. Assn., Coll. English Assn. (v.p. Mid.-Atlantic Group, 1987—), Women's Caucus for Modern Langs., Md. Council Tchrs. English, Md. Poetry and Literary Soc., Mid. Atlantic Writers' Assn. (founding 1981), AAUW. Roman Catholic. Club: U. Auburn. Home: 102 Gorsuch Rd Lutherville-Timonium MD 21093 Office: Morgan State U Dept English Baltimore MD 21239

SEDLOCK, JOY, psychiatric social worker; b. Memphis, Jan. 23, 1958; d. George Rudolph Sedlock and Mary Robson; m. Thomas Robert Jones, Aug. 8, 1983. AA, Ventura (Calif.) Jr. Coll., 1978; BS in Psychology, Calif. Luth. U., 1980; MS in Counseling and Psychology, U. LaVerne, 1983; MSW, Calif. State U., Sacramento, 1986. Research asst. Camarillo (Calif.) State Hosp., 1981, tchr.'s aide, 1982; sub. tchr. asst. Vertura County Sch. Dist., 1981; teaching asst. Ventura Jr. Goll., 1980-82, tchr. adult edn., 1980-84; psychiatric social worker Yolo County Day Treatment Ctr., Broderick, Calif., 1986, Napa (Calif.) State Hosp., 1986—. Mem. Nat. Assn. Social Workers, NOW (campaign 1984 presdl. election). Mem. Humanist Orgn. Ch. Home: 17 Griggs Ln Napa CA 94558 Office: Napa State Hosp Napa/Vallejo Hgwy Napa CA 49558

SEDOC, EDWIN JOHAN, Suriname government official; b. Paramaribo, Suriname, Nov. 17, 1938; married. Degree in math., U. Amsterdam. Statistician eceon. affairs dept. Ministry Fin., Paramaribo, 1971-72, 73-74, head econ. affairs dept., 1974-75; statistician eceon. affairs dept. Inst. Social Ins., 1972-73; dep. dir. Ministry Fin., 1975-80, Ministry Health, Paramaribo, 1980-81; dir. Nat. Health Service, 1981-83; with seminars MIT, Columbia U., Boston and N.Y.C., 1983-84; lectr. dept. stats. U. Fla., Gainsville, 1984-85; fin. and statis. cons. 1985-86; fin. dir. Diakonessen Hosp., 1987; minister fgn. affairs Republic Suriname, Paramaribo, 1988—; lectr. stats. Faculty Law U. Suriname, 1972-82, Inst. for Social and Econ. Studies, 1974-75, Socio-Econ. Faculty U. Suriname, 1975-82. Address: Ministry Fgn Affairs, Paramaribo Suriname *

SEEBASS, HORST ALFRED, university educator; b. Berlin, Germany, Aug. 3, 1934; s. Werner and Gertrud (Schöning) S.; m. Anita Wöstmann, Dec. 27, 1985; 6 children:. Student, Bonn U., 1954-56, Wien U., Austria, 1956-57, Göttingen U., 1957-59; doctorate, Göttingen U., 1962; habilitation, Bonn. U., 1964. Lectr. Kirchliche Hochschule Bethel, Biellefeld, Fed. Republic Germany, 1961-66; dozent Westfälische Wilhelms-U. Münster, Fed. Republic Germany, 1966-71, apl. prof., 1971-81; ordentlicher prof. Johannes Gutenberg-U. Mainz, Fed. Republic Germany, 1981—. Mem. Wissenschaftliche Gesellschaft Theologie, Deutscher Verein Erforschung Palästinas. Sozialdemokrat. Partei Deutschlands. Home: Am Hasenkamp 16, D-4544 Ladbergen Federal Republic of Germany Office: Johannes Gutenberg Univ, Saarstr 21, D 6500 Mainz Federal Republic of Germany

SEEBERT, KATHLEEN ANNE, international trade consultant; b. Chgo.; d. Harold Earl and Marie Anne (Lowery) S.; BS U. Dayton, 1971, M.A., U. Notre Dame, 1976; M.M., Northwestern U., 1983. Publs. editor ContiCommodity Services, Inc., Chgo., 1977-79, supr. mktg., 1979-82; dir. mktg. MidAm. Commodity Exchange, 1982-85; internat. trade cons. to Govt. of Ont., Can., 1985—; guest lectr. U. Notre Dame. Registered commodity rep. Mem. Futures Industry Assn. Am. (treas.). Republican. Roman Catholic. Clubs: Notre Dame of Chgo., Northwestern Mgmt. of Chgo. Office: 208 S LaSalle St Suite 1806 Chicago IL 60604

SEEDLOCK, ROBERT FRANCIS, engineering and construction company executive; b. Newark, Feb. 6, 1913; s. Frank Andrew and Mary Elizabeth (Prosner) S.; m. Hortense Orcutt Norton, Sept. 1, 1937; children—Robert Francis, Elizabeth Munsell Seedlock Morrissette, Walter Norton, Mary Marion. Student Case Inst. Tech., 1931-33; B.S., U.S. Mil. Acad., 1937; M.S. in Civil Engring., MIT, 1940; grad. Armed Forces Staff Coll., 1948, Nat. War Coll., 1958. Registered profl. engr., D.C., Pa. Commd. 2d lt. U.S. Army, 1937, advanced through grades to maj. gen., 1963; asst. to dist. engr., Pitts., 1937-39, Tulsa Aircraft Assembly Plant, 1941; regtl. exec. bn. comdr. Engr. Unit Tng. Ctr., Camp Claiborne, La., 1942; asst. theatre engr., CBI, also comdr. Burma Road Engrs., also chief engr. Shanghai Base Command, 1943-47; mem. gen. staff U.S. Army, Mem. Am. del. Far Eastern Commn., 1948-49; aide to chief staff U.S. Army, 1949, 54; mem. U.S. del. NATO Ministerial Conf., 1952-53; dep. div. engr. Mediterranean div., 1954-57; mil. asst. to asst. sec. def. for pub. affairs, 1958-62; div. engr. Missouri River, Omaha, 1962-63; sr. mem. UN Mil. Armistice Commn., Korea, 1963-64; dir. mil. personnel Office dep. chief of staff for personnel Dept. Army, 1964-66; dir. mil. constrn. Office Chief of Engrs., 1966; comdg. gen. U.S. Army Engr. Center and Ft. Belvoir, Va., and comdt. U.S. Army Engr. Sch., Ft. Belvoir, 1966-68, ret., 1968; pres. Yuba Industries, 1968-69, v.p. Standard Prudential Corp. (merged with Yuba Industries), 1969-70; v.p., dir. Petro-Chem. Devel. Co., Inc., N.Y.C., 1968-70, Petchem Constrn. Co., N.Y.C., 1968-70, Petrochem. Isoflow Furnaces, Ltd. (Can.), 1968-70; dir. constrn. and devel. Port Authority of Allegheny County, Pitts., 1970-73; assoc. Parsons, Brinckerhoff, Quade & Douglas, N.Y.C., 1973-75, mgr. So. region, 1975-77; dep. project dir. Parsons, Brinckerhoff-Tudor-Bechtel, Atlanta, 1973-77; program dir. Ralph M. Parsons Co., Washington, 1977-84; cons. engr. 1984—; dir. T.Y. Lin Intl., 1985—; chief liaison, cons. Chinese Acad. Sci. for Beijing Inst. Mgmt., 1985—; U.S. rep. to Permanent Tech. Com. Number 1 of Permanent Intl. Assn. of Navigation Congresses, 1984—; chmn. Sino-Am. Ventures, Inc., 1987—. Contbr. to mil. and engring. jours. Bd. dirs. Army and Air Force Exchange and Motion Picture Service, 1964; mem. Miss. River Commn., 1962-63, Bd. Engrs. Rivers and Harbor, 1962-63, Def. Adv. Commn. Edn., 1964; chmn. Mo. Basin Inter-Agy. Com., 1962-63; fed. rep., chmn. Big Blue River Compact Commn., 1962-63; mem. U.S. Com. on Large Dams, 1962—; exec. bd. Nat. Capital Area council Boy Scouts Am., 1967-68, Atlanta Area council, 1975-77. Decorated D.S.M., Legion of Merit with oak leaf cluster; chevalier Legion of Honor (France); 1st class, grade A medal Army, navy, air force, also spl. breast order Yun Hui (China); named Engr. of Yr., Met. Atlanta Engring. Soc., 1976; Ga. Engr. of Yr. in Govt., Ga. Soc. Profl. Engrs., 1976; recipient Silver Beaver award Boy Scouts Am., 1977. Fellow Soc. Am. Mil. Engrs. (nat. dir.); mem. ASCE (hon., aerospace div. programming council 1980-82, sec. exec. council 1982-83, chmn. 1984-85, editor Jour. Aerospace Engineering, 1986—), Assn. U.S. Army, West Point Soc. N.Y. (life), West Point Soc. Atlanta (pres. 1976), Sigma Xi, Tau Beta Pi. Roman Catholic. Clubs: Army-Navy Country (sec., chmn. bd. govs. 1952-54, 61-62) (Arlington, Va.); MIT (pres. Shanghai 1946); Met. (N.Y.C.); Oglethorpe (Savannah, Ga.), Ansley Golf (Atlanta). Office: 1133 15th St NW Suite 800 Washington DC 20005-2701

SEEFEHLNER, EGON HUGO, opera director; b. Vienna, Austria, June 3, 1912; s. Egon Ewald and Charlotte (von Kerpely-Krasso) S.; ed. Theresianum, U. Vienna, Konsularakademie. Co-founder, gen. sec. Austrian Cultural Assn., 1945; chief editor Der Turm (cultural) mag., 1945; gen. sec. Wiener Konzerthausgesellschaft, 1946-61; dep. dir. Vienna State Opera, 1954-61, gen. mgr., 1976—, interim dir., 1984-86; dir. gen. mgr. Deutsche Oper, W. Berlin, 1961-72, dir. gen., 1972-76. Roman Catholic. Decorated Comdr.'s Cross, Papal Order of Silvester; officer Ordre des Arts et des Lettres; Goldenes Ehrenzeichen für Verdienste um das Land Wien; Österreichisches Ehrenkreuz für Wissenschaft und Kunst, 1st class; Clemens Krauss Silver medal, Golden Cross of Republic of Austria, others. Office: care Staatsoper, Opernring 2, Vienna Austria *

SEEFELDER, MATTHIAS, industrial executive; b. Boos, Fed. Republic Germany, 1920. Ed. Univ. Munich. With BASF AG, 1951—, dep. mem. mng. bd., 1971-73, chmn. mng. bd., 1974-83, chmn. supervisory bd., 1983—; hon. prof. chemistry U. Heidelberg, 1974—; chmn. supervisory bd. MAN Aktiengesellschaft, 1983—. Mem. Senate of Max Planck Soc. for the Advancement of Sci., Munich; bd. dirs. German Mus.; trustee Friends of the Haus der Kunst; hon. court U. Heidelberg, Tech. U. Munich, U. Mannheim. Decorated Chevalier Légion d'Honneur, Cross of Outstanding Merit, Grand Cross with Star, Order of Merit; Gran Cruz de la Orden del Mérito (Spain). Mem. Soc. German Chemists, Fondation de la Maison de la Chimie (adminstrv. council), Acad. Scis. Mainz (corr.). Office: BASF, 6700 Ludwigshafen Federal Republic of Germany *

SEEGALL, MANFRED ISMAR LUDWIG, physicist, educator; b. Berlin, Germany, Dec. 23, 1929; s. Leonhard and Vera Antonie (Vodackova) S.; came to U.S., 1952, naturalized, 1957; m. Alma R. Sterner Clarke; 2 stepchildren—James, Mark. B.S. magna cum laude, Loyola Coll., 1957; M.S., Brown U., 1960; Ph.D., Stuttgart (Germany) Tech. U., 1965. Research engr. Autonetics Corp. div. N.Am. Aviation, Downey, Calif., 1959-61; physicist Astronautics div. Gen. Dynamics, Inc., San Diego, 1961-62; research scientist Max Planck Inst., Stuttgart, 1962-65; instr. stats. and algebra San Diego City Coll., 1966; sr. research engr. Solar div. Internat. Harvester Co., San Diego, 1967-73; research cons. in energy and pollution, San Diego, 1974-83; part-time evening instr. Mesa Coll., San Diego, 1980-81; instr. Grossmont Coll., El Cajon, Calif., 1981; sr. scientist Evaluation Research Corp., San Diego, 1981-82, RCS analyst Teledyne Micronetics, San Diego, 1983-84, sr. design specialist Alcoa Defense Systems, San Diego, 1984-87, cons. phys scis., 1987— . Mem. IEEE (sr.), Internat. Platform Assn., Calif. Parapsychology Found. (sec. research com.), Cottage of Czechoslovakia of House of Pacific Relations, Rosicrucian Order, Loyola Coll., Brown U. alumni assns. Republican. Club: San Diego Lodge AMORC. Contbr. articles on acoustics, pollution and temp. measurement methods to tech. jours.; patentee in field. Address: 8735 Blue Lake Dr San Diego CA 92119

SEEGERS, WALTER HENRY, hematology educator emeritus; b. Fayette County, Iowa, Jan. 4, 1910; s. William and Mary (Wente) S.; m. Lillian Entz, Dec. 31, 1935; 1 child, Dorothy Margaret. B.A., U. Iowa, 1931, M.S., 1932, Ph.D., 1934; D.Sc., Wartburg Coll., 1953; M.D. (hon.), Justus Liebig U., Fed. Republic Germany, 1974; D.Sc. (hon.), Med. Coll. Ohio, 1978. Research fellow U. Iowa, 1931-34, research assoc., 1934-35, 1937-42; research assoc. Antioch Coll., 1936-37; researcher Parke, Davis & Co., Detroit, 1942-45; assoc. prof. physiology Wayne State U. Coll. Medicine, 1945-46, prof., head dept. physiology, 1946-48, prof. physiology and pharmacology, 1948—, William D. Traitel prof. hematology, 1965-80, emeritus, 1980—, chmn. symposium on blood, 1950-68, dir. Thrombosis Specialized Ctr. of Research, 1972-77; prof. physiology U. Detroit, 1946-51; vis. prof. Baylor U., 1950, 52, U. Uruguay, summer, 1957; vis. scientist, lectr. Rio de Janeiro, 1963; hon. mem. faculty medicine U. Chile; lectr., exhibitor med., chem., indsl. sci. subjects; NSC vis. chair prof. Nat. Taiwan U., 1975; mem. health research facilities sci. rev. com. NIH, USPHS, 1966-70; chmn. subcom. blood coagulation NRC, 1950-53, chmn. panel on blood coagulation, 1953-57; mem. Internat. Com. on Hemostasis and Thrombosis, 1954—, Detroit Mayor's Com. Rehab. Narcotic Addicts, 1961-73; mem. sci. adv. bd. ARC, 1969-72. Author: Prothrombin, 1962; (with E.A. Sharp) Hemostatic Agents, 1948; (with J.M. Dorsey) Living Consciously: The Science of Self, 1959; (with Shirley A. Johnson) Physiology of Hemostasis and Thrombosis, 1967; Prothrombin in Enzymology, Thrombosis and Hemophilia, 1967; Blood Clotting Enzymology, 1967; John M. Dorsey Memorabilia, 1982; (with D.A. Walz) Prothrombin and other Vitamin K Proteins, 1986; contbg. author: The Enzymes. Mem. editorial bd.: Am. Jour. Applied Physiology, 1956-63, Am. Jour. Physiology, 1956-63, Circulation Research, 1954-64, Preparative Biochemistry, 1970-80, Thrombosis Research, 1972. Contbr. articles to profl. jours. Bd. regents Wartburg Coll., 1966-80; mem. bd. Ctr. Health Edn., 1961-80, pres., 1969. Co-recipient Ward Burdick award Am. Soc. Clin. Pathologists, 1940, James F. Mitchell Found. Internat. award for heart and vascular research, 1969; recipient Commonwealth Fund Spl. award, 1957, Mayo Clinic Vis. Faculty cert., 1964, Disting. Service award Lutheran Brotherhood Ins. Soc., 1967, Acad. Achievement award Probus Club, 1963, Research award Wayne chpt. Sigma Xi, 1957, Disting. Service cert. Wartburg Alumni Assn., 1959, Faculty Service award Wayne State U. Alumni, 1971, Wisdom award honor Wisdom Soc., 1970, Mich. Minuteman Gov.'s award, 1973, H.P. Smith award Am. Soc. Clin. Pathologists, 1978; Disting. Grad. Faculty award Wayne State U., 1980, Med. Sch. Disting. Service award, 1980; commendation Stritch Sch. Medicine, Loyola U., 1980. Fellow N.Y. Acad. Scis.; mem. AAAS, Am. Inst. Chemists, Am. Soc. Hematology, Am. Heart Assn., Am. Chem. Soc., Am. Soc. Biol. Chemists, Soc. Exptl. Biology and Medicine, Am. Physiol. Soc., Detroit Physiol. Soc. (hon., pres. 1948, 80), Can. Physiol. Soc., Mich. Acad. Sci., Harvey Soc. (hon.), Chilean Soc. Transfusion and Hematology (hon.), Am. Coll. Clin. Pharmacology and Chemotherapy, Engring. Soc. Detroit, N.Y. Acad. Scis. (hon. life), Med. Soc. Turkey (hon.), Hematology Soc. Turkey (hon.), Mexican Soc. Hematology (hon.), Japanese Soc. Thrombosis and Hemostasis (hon.), Phi Beta Kappa (hon.), Sigma Xi, Alpha Omega Alpha (hon.), Phi Lambda Upsilon, Alpha Chi Sigma, Phi Beta Pi (hon.). Lutheran. Clubs: Torch, Economics (Detroit). Home: 2857 Ptarmigan #5 Walnut Creek CA 94595

SEELBACH, CHARLES WILLIAM, chemist; b. Buffalo, Dec. 13, 1923; s. Charles George and Marcia (Grimes) S.; A.B., Cornell U., 1948; M.S., Western Res. U., 1952; Ph.D., Purdue U., 1955; m. Patricia O'Reilly, July 7, 1946; children—Janet, Jeanne, Paul. Group leader Ohio Research, Cleve., 1948-52; asst. sect. head Esso Standard Oil, Baton Rouge, 1956-57; sect.

head Esso Research and Engring., Linden, N.J., 1955-56, 58-63; bus. mgr. Esso Chem. Inc., N.Y.C., 1963-67; mgr. devel. USS Chems., Pitts., 1968-83; cons., 1983—. Elder Presbyn. Ch., Cranford, N.J., also trustee. Served with USMC, 1942-46. Purdue U research fellow, 1953-55. Mem. Am. Chem. Soc., Comml. Devel. Assn., Am. Mgmt. Assn., AAAS, Catalysis Soc., N.Y. Acad. Scis., Am. Oil Chemists Soc., Psi Lambda Upsilon. Patentee in field. Office: 1405 Parkview Dr Allison Park PA 15101

SEELEY, CHRISTOPHER, Japanese language educator; b. Kingston, Surrey, Eng., Oct. 23, 1948; came to New Zealand, 1977; s. Henry Stewart and Margaret (Colquitt) S.; m. Kazuko Nishibu, Mar. 11, 1976; children: Rowan Christopher, Royden Christopher. BA in Japanese with honors, U. London, 1971, PhD in Japanese Lang., 1975. Lectr. Japanese U. Canterbury, Christchurch, New Zealand, 1977-80, sr. lectr., 1981—, head dept. Asian langs., 1982—. Guest editor: Visible Lang., Vol. 18, No. 3, 1984. Recipient Profl. award Japan Found., Tokyo, 1984-85. Mem. European Assn. Japanese Studies, Assn. for Study Japanese Lang. Office: U Canterbury, Dept Asian Langs, Pvt Bag, Christchurch New Zealand

SEET, RICHARD ENG TIONG, electronics engineer; b. Singapore, Republic of Singapore, Nov. 11, 1949; s. Hong Lam and Chwee Sian (Tan) S.; m. Guek Neo, Aug. 20, 1980; children—Angeline Seet Li Ching, Elfie Seet Qin Fong. Cert., City and Guilds of London Inst. Full Tech., 1976. Service tech. Philips, Singapore, 1973-76; test engr. Intersil, Singapore, 1976-80; electronics engr. Prodn. Machine Pte, Ltd., Singapore, 1980-84; electronics maintenance engr. P.C.I., Singapore, 1984-87, Cosmotron Electronics, Singapore, 1987-88, prodn. exec. Flexible Automation System, 1988—; designer, cons. Robotics, Inc., Singapore, 1980-84. Vol. aftercare officer Singapore Anti-Narcotics Assn., 1979. Served to cpl. Singapore Air Force, 1969-73. Fellow Inst. Mgmt. Specialists U.K, IMS Cert. Info. Technol.; mem. IEEE, Assn. Computing Machinery, Am. Soc. Quality Control, Am. Soc. Metals, IEEE Nuclear and Plasma Scis. Soc., IEEE Reliability Soc., IEEE Computer Soc., Nat. Productivity Assn., Singapore Quality Reliability Assn. Home: 42 Telok Blangah Rise 10-618, Singapore 0409, Singapore

SEETHALER, WILLIAM CHARLES, international business executive, consultant; b. N.Y.C., Dec. 4, 1937; s. William Charles and Catherine Frances (Flaherty) S.; student Quinnipiac Coll., Conn., 1955-56, Ohio State U., 1956-58; BS in Bus. Adminstrn., U. San Francisco, 1977; MBA, Pepperdine U., 1982. Asst. to v.p. sales T. Sendzimir, Inc., Waterbury, Conn. and Paris, 1960-66; mgr. internat. ops. Dempsey Indsl. Furnace Co., E. Longmeadow, Mass., 1966-67; mgr. internat. sales Yoder Co., Cleve., 1967-74; mng. dir., owner Seethaler & Assocs.; owner, chief exec. officer Seethaler Internat. Ltd., Palo Alto, Calif., 1974—; ptnr. DFS Computer Assocs., San Jose, Calif., 1976—. Bd. dirs. Palo Alto Fund, 1979—, chmn., 1986—; mem. community adv. panel Stanford U., 1986—. Mem. Menlo Park C. of C., Palo Alto C. of C. (v.p. orgn. affairs 1976-77, pres. 1977-78, dir. 1975-79), Assn. Iron and Steel Engrs., Inst. Indsl. Engrs. (sr. mem.), U. San Francisco Alumni Assn., Stanford U. Alumni Assn., Pepperdine U. Alumni Assn., Assn. MBA Execs., Am. Mgmt. Assn. Clubs: Stanford Buck, Stanford Cardinal Cage, Stanford Diamond.

SEEVERS, CHARLES JUNIOR, foundation executive, psychologist; b. Seward, Nebr., May 13, 1925; s. Ferdinand Carl and Hilda Anna (Schultz) S.; m. Florine Marie Viets, June 5, 1949; children: Steven, Roger, Sandra, Jane. AA, St. John's Coll., 1945; BA, Concordia Sem., St. Louis, 1949; M.S. magna cum laude, St. Francis Coll., Ft. Wayne, Ind., 1965, postgrad., 1966; Ph.D., U. Notre Dame, 1970. Ordained to ministry Lutheran Ch., 1949; asst. pastor Immanuel Luth. Ch., Balt., 1949-50; pastor St. Paul's Luth. Ch., Kingsville, Md., 1950-57, Bethlehem Luth. Ch., Richmond, Va., 1957-63; sr. pastor Zion Luth. Ch., Ft. Wayne, 1963-66; exec. dir. Assn. for Disabled of Elkhart County, Ind., 1966-82, Aux Chandelles Found., 1982—; adj. prof. psychology and spl. edn. Ind. U., South Bend, 1972-76; speaker Pres.'s Com. on Mental Retardation 3d Internat. Congress on Prevention of Mental Retardation, Buenos Aries, Argentina, 1986; apptd. del. health psychologist Ind. People to People Internat. Study Mission to Russia, People's Republic China, 1987; 1 cons. Kans. Developmental Disabilities Div., 1972-79, Accreditation Council for Facilities for the Mentally Retarded, Chgo., 1972-80; cons. on assessment of developmentally disabled in various states, 1974—, cons., Leicester, Eng., 1974-75; mem. Ind. Gov.'s Planning and Adv. Bd. for Mental Retardation and Other Developmental Disabilities, 1973-78, chmn., 1976-78; mem. Gov.'s Preventive Health and Handicap Services Coordination Study Commn., 1987—, Devel. Disabilities Planning Council on Child Health, 1987—, No. Ind. Health Systems Agy. Central Sub-Area Adv. Council, 1976-78, vice chmn., 1977-78; cons. psycho-nutrition, 1981—; regional psychologist Youth for Understanding, 1985-87. Contbr. articles to profl. publs. Chmn. United Way Execs., Elkhart, 1971-73; bd. dirs. Mill Neck Manor Sch. for the Deaf, L.I., N.Y., 1950-57, Assn. for Retarded Citizens Ind., 1983—, No. Ind. Health Found., 1981-87; charter mem. Area Vocat. Edn. Adv. Bd., 1973-76; mem. state adv. bd. Prevention: To Be Born Well Curriculum Project, 1977-80; mem. residential services and facilities com. Nat. Assn. Retarded Citizens, 1973-78; mem. No. Ind. Developmental Disabilities Adv. Council, 1977-81, chmn., 1980-81; mem. Dept. Mental Health Multi-Disciplinary Screening Team, 1983-84; mem. bd. teenage parents adv. bd. Elkhart Community Schs., 1984-87; chmn. state policy Ind. Healthy Mothers/Healthy Babies Coalition, 1986-87; hon. chmn. Michiana Fetal Alcohol Syndrome Week, 1986. Recipient United Way Exec. of Yr. award, 1979; Eli Lilly fellow in religion and mental health Ind. U. Med. Center, Indpls., 1964-65; Recipient Liberty Bell award Elkhart Bar Assn., 1974, Outstanding Kindness award Elkhart County Assn. for Retarded, 1974, Concerned for Mankind in Our Nation award Jaycees, 1975, State of Ind. Citizen Participation award Gov.'s Voluntary Action Program. Mem. Nat. Conf. Execs. of Assns. for Retarded Children (chmn. 1974-75), Am. Psychol. Assn., Soc. Behavioral Medicine, Am. Pub. Health Assn., Nat. Fedn. Parents for Drug Free Youth, Luth. Acad. for Scholarship, Internat. Psychol. Assn., United Cerebral Palsy Am., Luth. Human Relations Assn. Am., Ctr. for Sci. in Pub. Interest, Am. Orthopsychiat. Assn., Elkhart C. of C. (bd. dirs. 1974-76), Am. Council on Drug Edn., Assn. Birth Defect Children, Healthy Mothers/Healthy Babies Coalition, Internat. Council Psychologists. Lodge: Rotary (v.p. 1986, chmn. world affairs conf. dist. 654, 1985-87, gen. chmn. dist. assembly conf. 1986-87, Gov's. award 1987, Chmn. of Yr. 1987). Home: 1744 Canterbury Dr Elkhart IN 46514 Office: PO Box 398 Bristol IN 46507

SEFERIS, JAMES CONSTANTINE, chemical engineer, educator; b. Athens, Greece, Nov. 3, 1950, came to U.S., 1968. naturalized, 1982; s. Constantine Dimitrios and Roubina L. (Georgoulis) S.; m. Anne V. Moudon, 1982; children: Louiza, Constantine T. B.S. in Chem. Engring., U. Colo., 1973; Ph.D. in Chem. Engring., U. Del., 1977. Adj. asst. prof. U. Del., Newark, 1977-78; vis. asst. prof. Drexel U., Phila., 1977; asst. prof. U. Wash., Seattle, 1977-81, assoc. prof., 1981-85, prof. chem. and polymer engring., 1985—; vis. prof. Nat. Tech. U. of Athens, 1982; adj. prof. U. Naples, Italy, 1986—; dir. U. Wash. Polymeric Composites Lab., Seattle, 1982—; cons. Boeing Co., Seattle, 1977—; cons. E.I. duPont de Nemours, Wilmington, Del., 1979—, Shell Devel. Co., 1983—, Rhone Poulenc France, 1984—, IBM, San Jose, Calif., 1986, BF Goodrich. Editor: The Role of the Polymeric Matrix in the Processing and Structural Properties of Composite Materials, 1983; Interrelations between Processing Structure and Properties of Polymeric Materials, 1984; Composite Systems from Natural and Systematic Polymers; contbr. articles to profl. jours; mem. editorial bd. Polymer Composite Jour. Recipient First Presdl. Young Investigator award NSF, 1984, Alexander von Humboldt award, 1987; named chmn. Gordon Research Conf. on Composites, 1987. Mem. Am. Inst. Chem. Engrs., Am. Chem. Soc., Am. Phys. Soc., Soc. Plastic Engrs., Soc. Advancement of Materials and Processing Engring. Club: Cosmos (Washington). Current work: High performance polymer composites; polymer physics and engring.; processing-structure-property relations of polymers and composites; thermal characterization and rate phenomena. Subspecialties: Composite materials; Polymers (materials science). Home: 1911 N 40th Seattle WA 98103

SEFIA, GABRIEL NAJOMO, oil company executive, consultant; b. Ovwian, Bendel, Nigeria, Oct. 1, 1929; s. Jaman and Yaro (Orumere) S.; m. Cecilia Ovuoromaroye Arubayi, Jan. 1, 1953; children—Ovuoroye, Mirute, Mrejiri, Akpovo, Kwaire, Brume, Ochuko, others. B.A. with honors, U. Calcutta, 1958; M.A. in Econs., Yale U., 1962. Asst. sec. Prime Minister's Office, Lagos, Nigeria, 1958-62; dep. permanent sec. Ministry of Trade, Lagos, 1963-68; sr. economist UN, Geneva, 1968-72, dir. Africa Trade Centre, Addis Ababa, 1972-74; mng. dir. Grenigas Ltd., Nigeria, 1977-79, Sedeg Ltd., Warri, Bendel, Nigeria, 1980—; dir. Grenigas Ltd., Nigerian Agrl. Bank; cons. Liquified Petroleum Gas. Contbg. author: The Marketing Board System, 1974. Contbr. to UNCTAD Documents, 1969-72. Constituency chmn. Nat. Party of Nigeria, Bendel, 1983, commr. for econ. devel. and budgeting, 1983; mem. Bendel State Devel. Fund, 1985, Udu Community Leadership Caucus, Bendel State, 1982—. Mem. Econ. Soc. Nigeria, Nigerian Inst. Mgmt. Club: Warri. Avocations: swimming; table tennis; angling. Home: No 1 Sefia Close, 3d Marine Gate, PO Box 1214, Warri, Bendel Nigeria Office: Sedeg Ltd, No 1 Udu Bridge Rd, PO Box 1214, Warri, Bendel Nigeria

SEGAL, BERNARD GERARD, lawyer; b. N.Y.C., June 11, 1907; s. Samuel I. and Rose (Cantor) S.; m. Geraldine Rosenbaum, Oct. 22, 1933; children: Loretta Joan Segal Cohen, Richard Murry. AB, U. Pa., 1928, LLB, 1931, LLD, 1969; LLD, Franklin and Marshall Coll., 1953, Temple U., 1954, Dropsie U., 1966, Jewish Theol. Sem. Am., 1977, Vt. Law Sch., 1978, Villanova U., 1980, Georgetown U., 1983; JSD, Suffolk U., 1969; DHL, Hebrew Union Coll., 1970. Bar: Pa. 1932. Mem. faculty U. Pa., 1928-35, 45-47; legal asst. Am. Law Inst., 1932-33; Am. reporter on contracts Internat. Congress of Law, Hague, Netherlands, 1932; dep. atty. gen. Commonwealth of Pa., 1932-35; co-founder Schnader, Harrison, Segal & Lewis, Phila., 1935—; chmn. Schnader, Harrison, Segal & Lewis, 1968-86; sr. ptnr. Schnader, Harrison, Segal & Lewis, Phila., 1986-88, counsel, 1988—; instr. grad. bus., govt. debating Am. Inst. Banking, 1936-39; lectr. law Franklin and Marshall Coll., 1937-38; chmn. Commn. Jud. and Congl. Salaries, U.S. Govt., 1953-55; mem. Bd. Law Examiners, Phila., 1940-46; mem. council World Peace Through Law Ctr., 1973—, also World Confs. Athens, Washington, Geneva, Bangkok, Abidjan, Manila and Cairo, chmn. first demonstration trial, Belgrade, Yugoslavia, 1971, also chmn. com. on internat. communications, world chmn. World Law Day, Madrid, 1979, Berlin, 1985; chmn. World Conf. on Peace and Violence, Jerusalem, 1979; chmn. bd. Council Legal Edn. Opportunities, 1968-71; co-chmn. Lawyers Com. Civil Rights Under Law, 1963-65; adviser Commn. Commitment, Detention and Discharge of Prisoners, 1953-55; mem. Atty. Gen.'s Nat. Com. to Study Antitrust Laws, 1953-55; exec. com. Atty. Gen.'s Nat. Conf. on Court Congestion, 1958-61; chmn. jud. nominating commn. Commonwealth of Pa., 1964-66; mem. Appellate Ct. Nominating Commn., 1973-79; standing com. on rules of practice and procedure Jud. Conf. U.S., 1959-76; mem. Nat. Citizens Com. on Community Relations, 1964-74; adv. com. U.S. mission UN, 1967-68; adv. panel internat. law U.S. Dept. State, 1967-79; mem. Adminstrv. Conf. U.S., 1968-74; chmn. nat. adv. com. on legal services OEO, 1968-74, chmn. exec. com., 1971-74; mem. U.S. Commn. Revision Fed. Ct. Appellate System, 1974-75; mem. Jud. Council Pa., 1968-71; mem. U.S. Commn. on Exec., Legis. and Jud. Salaries, 1972-73, 76-77. Editor-in-chief: Pennsylvania Banking Building and Loan Law, 3 vols., 1941; contbr. articles to law revs., other publs.; editor: The Belgrade Spaceship Trial, 1972; mem. internat. hon. bd. Ency. Judaica. Mem. Commn. on Anti-Poverty Program for Phila., 1967-71, Commonwealth Commn. on Bicentennial of U.S. Constn., 1986-87; mem. planning commn. Miracle at Phila., 1986-87; life trustee emeritus, past. exec. bd. trustees U. Pa., also bd. overseers Law Sch.; bd. govs. emeritus, past v.p., past treas. Dropsie U.; chmn. bd. Council Advancement Legal Edn., 1972-77; hon. gov. Hebrew U. Jerusalem; trustee Chapel of Four Chaplains; trustee emeritus, former exec. com. Albert Einstein Med. Ctr.; bd. dirs. NAACP Legal Def. and Ednl. Fund Found. Fed. Bar Assn.; mem. Archdiocese Leadership Com. on Edn. in Cath. Schs., 1979—; bd. dirs. So. Africa Legal Services and Legal Edn. Project, 1979—; trustee Phila. Martin Luther King, Jr. Ctr. Nonviolent Social Change, 1984—, Found. for the Commemoration of the U.S. Constn., 1986-88, Found. for U.S. Constn., 1988—. Recipient World Lawyer award World Peace through Law Ctr., 1975, Judge William H. Hastie award NAACP Legal Def. Fund, Legion Honor Gold Medallion award Chapel of Four Chaplains; co-recipient Nat. Neighbors Disting. Leadership in Civil Rights award. Fellow Am. Coll. Trial Lawyers (pres. 1964-65), ABA, Inst. Jud. Adminstrn., Am. Bar Found. (pres. 1976-78); mem. Fedn. Jewish Agys., Pa. Bar Assn., Phila. Bar Assn. (chancellor 1952, 53), Pa. Urban Affairs Ptnrship, Fed. Bar Assn. (nat. council), Assn. Bar City N.Y., Am. Arbitration Assn. (former dir.), Am. Law Inst. (1st v.p. 1976-86, treas. 1955-69, counselor emeritus), Am. Judicature Soc. (chmn. 1958-61, bd. dirs. 1956—), Council Legal Edn. for Profl. Responsibility (dir.), Fed. Jud. Conf. 3d Circuit (life), World Assn. Lawyers (pres. for Ams. 1976-86), Nat. Conf. Bar Pres., Taxpayers Forum Pa. (past pres.), Allied Jewish Appeal (past pres., hon. pres.), Legal Aid Soc. Phila. (bd. dirs.), Jewish League Israel (nat. bd.), Jewish Pub. Soc. Am. (life trustee, mem. exec. com.), Jewish Family Service (hon. dir.), Order of Coif, Tau Epsilon Rho, Delta Sigma Rho. Republican. Clubs: Socialegal, Locust, Union League, Metropolitan (Washington). Home: The Philadelphian 2401 Pennsylvania Ave Apt 19-C-44 Philadelphia PA 19130 Office: Suite 3600 1600 Market St Philadelphia PA 19103

SEGAL, DONALD HENRY GILBERT, real estate developer; b. Phila., Mar. 20, 1928; s. A. Louis and Harriet B. S.; B.S. in Econs., U. Pa., 1950; children—Susan, John. Vice pres. Sandee Constrn. Co., Brookhaven, Pa., 1951-59; pres. Segal Constrn. Co., Cinnaminson, N.J., 1959-76, Segal Assocs., Inc., Bellmawr, N.J., 1976—; chmn. bd. Hotel Devel. Assocs., 1985—; commr. Lower Merion Twp., Pa., 1972-80, pres. bd. commrs., 1974-80. Bd. dirs. Phila. All Star Forum, 1980—, Phila. Child Guidance Clinic, 1981—, Atlantic City Ballet Co., 1981—; bd. mgrs. Moore Coll. Art, 1981—. Mem. Nat. Assn. Home Builders, N.J. Builders Assn., Community Assns. Inst. Republican. Jewish. Club: Corinthian Yacht (Cape May, N.J.). Home: 422 Garden Ln Bryn Mawr PA 19010 Office: 560 Benigno Blvd Bellmawr NJ 08031 also: 1830 Maryland Ave Cape May NJ 08204

SEGAL, JEFFRY MARK, management consultant; b. Phila., Aug. 3, 1943; s. Morris and Edith (Pikus) S.; B.S. in Acctg., U. Ariz., 1965, B.S. in Area Devel., 1966, M.B.A. in Acctg., 1969; m. Marianne G. Solomon, Aug. 16, 1970; children—Jonathan Barret, Daniel Jason. Mem. staff Seidman & Seidman, 1967-68; audit sr. Hurdman & Cranstoun, Los Angeles, 1968-70; assoc. Irwin, Silberman & Assocs., Economists, New Hyde Park, N.Y., 1971-72; audit sr. McMillan, Inc., N.Y.C., 1972-73; controller Chappell Music Co., N.Y.C., 1973-75, Chgo. Tribune-N.Y. News Syndicate, Inc., N.Y.C., 1976-79, Colvac Internat. Corp., 1980-82; v.p. Cherokee Oil & Gas Exploration Corp., Woodbury, N.Y., 1982-84; pres. J.M. Segal & Co., 1985—; dir. Magna Paper Co., N.Y.C.; asst. prof. Queensborough Community Coll. C.P.A., N.Y., Calif. Mem. Am. Inst. C.P.A.s, N.Y. State, Calif. socs. C.P.A.s, Am. Acctg. Assn., C.W. Post Coll. Tax Inst., Internat. Platform Assn. Home: 9 Waydale Dr Dix Hills NY 11746

SEGAL, PAUL, architect; b. N.Y.C., Sept. 18, 1944; s. Martin E. and Edith (Levy) S.; m. Ryna Appleton, Jan. 21, 1968; 1 child, Emma I. A.B., Princeton U., 1966, M.F.A. in Architecture, 1969. Registered architect N.Y., Conn., N.J., Vt., Mass., Pa.; cert. NCARB. Designer, Skidmore Owings & Merrill, N.Y.C., 1966-67, Gruzen & Ptnrs., N.Y.C., 1968, TAMS, N.Y.C., 1969-71; ptnr. Paul Segal Assocs. Architects, N.Y.C., 1971—; design adv. bd. Formica Corp., Wayne, N.J., 1977—; adj. assoc. prof. architecture Columbia U. Mem., Mayor's Theater Adv. Council, N.Y.C., 1982—; mem. gov.'s Citizens Cultural Adv. Council, 1984—; trustee Preservation League, N.Y. State, 1984—. Recipient Design Excellence awards N.Y. State Assn. Architects, 1976, 78, 79, 81, 82. Mem. AIA (pres. N.Y. chpt. 1985-86, design excellence awards 1974, 77, 79, 81, 83, Coll. of Fellows). Avocation: sailing. Home: 1 W 72d St New York NY 10023 Office: Paul Segal Assocs Architects 119 Fifth Ave New York NY 10003

SEGAL, RONALD MICHAEL, author, editor; b. Cape Town, South Africa, July 14, 1932; s. Leon and Mary S.; m. Susan Wolff, 1962; 3 children. Ed. U. Cape Town, Trinity Coll., Cambridge U. Dir. faculty and cultural studies Nat. Union of South African Students, 1951-52; pres. U. Cape Town Council Univ. Socs., 1951; Philip Francis duPont fellow U. Va., 1955-56; founder Africa South quar., 1956; gen. editor Penguin African Library, 1961-84, Pluto Crime Fiction, 1983—. Author: (Fantasy) The Tokolosh, 1960; Political Africa: A Who's Who of Personalities and Parties, 1961; African Profiles, 1962; Into Exile, 1963; The Crisis of India, 1965; The Race War, 1966; America's Receding Future, 1968; The Struggle against History, 1971; Whose Jerusalem? The Conflicts of Israel, 1973; The Decline and Fall of the American Dollar, 1974; The Tragedy of Leon Trotsky, 1979; The State of the World Atlas, 1981; The New State of the World Atlas, 1984; editor: Sanctions Against South Africa, 1974; South West Africa: Travesty of Trust, 1967. Helped launch econ. boycott, South Africa, 1959; banned by South African govt. from all meetings, July 1959; in Eng. with Africa South in Exile, 1960-61; hon. sec. South African Freedom Assn., 1960-61; convenor Internat. Conf. on Econ. Sanctions against South Africa, 1964, Internat. Conf. on S.W. Africa, 1966. Vis. fellow Ctr. for Study Democratic Instns., Santa Barbara, Calif., 1973. Mem. The Walton Soc. (founding chmn. 1975-79, pres. 1979—). Home: The Old Manor House, Manor Rd, Walton-on-Thames Surrey, England *

SEGAL, SIMON, real estate exec.; b. Havana, Cuba, Apr. 16, 1941; brought to U.S., 1955, naturalized, 1970; s. Govsey and Julia (Getzug) S.; B.C.E., Cornell U., 1965; M.S. in Mgmt., Fla. Internat. U., 1982; M.S. in Fin., Fla., Internat. U., 1987. Owner, Simon Segal Constrn. Co., Miami Beach, 1971-75; pres. Investex Realty Corp., Miami, Fla., 1973-75, S.S. Investments, Inc., Miami, 1975-85; pres. Simar Corp. Am., Miami, 1983—. Recipient Key to City of Miami, 1974, Key to City of South Miami, 1975; registered profl. engr., Fla.; registered real estate and mortgage broker, Fla. Mem. Fla. Engring. Soc., Nat. Soc. Profl. Engrs., ASCE (sec. 1970), Cornell Soc. Engrs., Greater Miami, Cuban Am. (founder, pres. 1971), Internat. (senator) Jr. C.'s of C., Soc. Am. Mil. Engrs., Cornell U., Peekskill Mil. Acad., Fla. Internat. U. alumni assns., Beta Gamma Sigma. Home: 8905 SW 102d Ct Miami FL 33176 Office: Ingraham Bldg Miami FL 33131

SEGALL, MAURICE, retail company executive; b. Joliette, Que., Can., May 16, 1929; came to U.S., 1962; s. Jack and Adela (Segall) S.; m. Sarah Ostrovsky, Nov. 25, 1951; children: Elizabeth, Eric, Peter. B.Econs., McGill U., Montreal, Que., 1950; M.Econs., Columbia U., 1952; Hudson Bay Co. fellow, London Sch. Econs., 1953-54. Economist Canadian Fed. Govt., 1951-55; chief economist, dir. research planning and orgn. Steinbergs Ltd. of Montreal, 1955-62; dir. ops. treasury stores J.C. Penney Co., N.Y.C., 1962-70, dir. treasury stores, 1970-71; sr. v.p. Am. Express Co., N.Y.C., 1971, gen. mgr. credit card div., 1971-74; pres. Am. Express Co./Credit Card Div., N.Y.C., 1974-78; chmn., pres., chief exec. officer Zayre Corp., Framingham, Mass., 1978—; chmn. TJX Cos., Inc., Natick, Mass.; dir. Shawmut Corp., New Eng. Telephone, AMR Corp., Gen. Cinema Corp. Mem. Mass. Bus. Roundtable (bd. dirs.). Office: The TJX Cos Inc One Mercer Rd Natick MA 01760 *

SEGATTO, BERNARD GORDON, lawyer; b. Joliet, Ill., July 27, 1931; s. Bernard Gordon and Rose Mary (Fracaro) S.; m. Nancy L. Grady, May 2, 1959; children—Bernard Gordon III, Randall Wayne, Amy Margot. B.A., Beloit Coll., 1953; J.D., U. Ill., 1958. Bar: Ill. 1958. Ptnr. Barber, Segatto, Hoffee & Hines, Springfield, Ill., 1958—; dir. Rochester State Bank, Ill. Contbr. articles to profl. jours. Pres., Little Flower Sch. PTA, Springfield, 1971-73; chmn. adv. bd. Griffin High Sch., Springfield, 1974-82; nat. judge adv. Daus. Union Vets. of Civil War 1861-65, 1972-73, 75—. Served with AUS, 1953-55. Recipient Real Estate award Lawyers Title Ins. Co. of Richmond, Va., 1958. Mem. ABA, Ill. Bar Assn. (chmn. sch. law com. 1965-66, v.p. jud. adv. polls com. 1974-83), Sangamon County Bar Assn., Am. Arbitration Assn. (arbitrator), Order of Coif, Phi Delta Phi, Sigma Chi. Roman Catholic. Club: Sangamo, Island Bay Yacht (Springfield). Lodge: Rotary. Home: 2600 W Lakeshore Dr Springfield IL 62707 Office: Barber Segatto Hoffee & Hines PO Box 79 Springfield IL 62705

SEGERS, GÉRÔME PETRUS, engineer; b. Flanders, Belgium, Nov. 22, 1947; s. Jan and Rachel (Herstens) S.; m. Magda Goossens, Dec. 19, 1975; children: Caroline, Michael. B. in Civil Engring., State U., 1971. Registered profl. engr., Belgium. Mgr. sales Burroughs, Brussels, 1983-84; mgr. key accts. ICL Belgium, Brussels, 1984-85; mktg. mgr. Burroughs N.V., Brussels, 1985-86; br. mgr. Unisys N.V., Antwerp, Belgium, 1987—. Mem.C. of C. Roman Catholic. Office: Unisys NV, 2000 Antwerp Belgium

SEGISMUNDO, MYRNA DIZON, hotel and restaurant executive; b. Manila, June 4, 1955; d. Jose Roxas and Emilia (Dizon) S. BS in Hotel and Restaurant Adminstrn., U. Philippines, 1977. Security safe supr. Waldorf-Astoria, N.Y.C., 1977-78; room clk. St. Moritz on-the Park, N.Y.C., 1978-79; asst. coffee shop mgr. Sheraton Ctr., N.Y.C., 1979-80; mgr. catering and banquet dept. Philippine Village Hotel, Manila, 1980-82; asst. mgr. dept. food and beverage Manila Hilton Internat., 1982-84; gen. mgr. Sign of the Anvil, Manila, 1984—. Mem. Hotel and Restaurant Assn. Philippines. Home: 2574 Taft Ave Malate, Manila Philippines Office: Sign of the Anvil, PCIBank Tower 1 2d Floor, Makati Ave, Metro Manila Philippines

SEGRE, EMILIO, physicist, educator; b. Tivoli, Rome, Italy, Feb. 1, 1905; came to U.S., 1938, naturalized, 1944; s. Giuseppe and Amelia (Treves) S.; m. Elfriede Spiro, Feb. 2, 1936 (dec. Oct. 1970); children: Claudio, Amelia, Fausta; m. Rosa Mines, Feb. 12, 1972. Ph.D., U. Rome, 1928; Dr. honoris causa, U. Palermo, Italy, Gustavus Adolphus Coll., St. Peter, Minn., Tel Aviv U., Hebrew Union Coll., Los Angeles, U. Genova, Italy. Asst. prof. U. Rome, 1932-36; dir. physics lab. U. Palermo, Italy, 1936-38; research asst. U. Calif.-Berkeley, 1938-43, prof. physics, 1945-72, emeritus, 1972—, group leader Los Alamos Sci. Lab., 1943-46; hon. prof. San Marcos U., Lima; vis. prof. U. Ill., Purdue U.; prof. physics U. Rome, 1974-75. Recipient Hofmann medal German Chem. Soc., Cannizzaro medal Accad. Lincei; Nobel prize in physics, 1959; decorated great cross merit Republic of Italy; Rockefeller Found. fellow, 1930-31; Guggenheim fellow, 1959; Fulbright fellow. Fellow AAAS, Am. Phys. Soc.; mem. Nat. Acad. Scis., Am. Philos. Soc., Am. Acad. Arts and Scis., Heidelberg Akademie Wissenschaften, European Phys. Soc., Acad. Scis. Peru, Soc. Progress of Sci. (Uruguay), Società Italiana di fisica, Accad. Naz. Lincei (Italy), Accad. Naz. XL (Italy), Indian Acad. Scis. Bangalore, others. Home: 3802 Quail Ridge Rd Lafayette CA 94549 Office: Dept Physics U of California Berkeley CA 94720

SEGRE, MICHAEL, science historian, educator; b. Rome, Nov. 11, 1950; s. Vittorio and Rosetta (Bauducco) S.; m. Malka Aranowicz, Sept. 3, 1985; children: Marco, Amos. BSc, Hebrew U., Jerusalem, 1974, MSc, 1979, PhD, 1983. Postdoctoral fellow Tel Aviv U., 1982-84; Wissenschftlicher Asst. Munich U., 1987—; vis. scholar Deutsche Copernicus Forschungsstelle, Munich, 1986-87. Contbr. articles to profl. jours. Grantee Italian Fgn. Ministry, Pisa, 1978-79; fellow Scuola Normale Superiore, Pisa, 1979-82. Mem. Deutsche Gesellschaft für Geschichte der Medizin. Office: Deutsches Mus, 8000 Munich 26 Federal Republic of Germany

SEGURA, OLIVERIO OCTAVIO, ophthalmologist, educator; b. Cebu, Philippines, Jan. 18, 1933; s. Valeriano Segura and Encarnacion (Rodis) Veloso; m. Lucia Macaraig Reyes, Mar. 17, 1962; children: Jacinto, Dennis, Sofia, Peter, Alice. Diplomate Otolarngology, ophthalmology. Chief resident in otolarnygology UP-PGH Med. Ctr., Manila, Philippines, 1960-61; sr. resident Dept Eyes, Ear, Nose, Throat Cebu Velez Gen. Hosp., Philippines, 1963-66; chmn. dept. eyes, ear, nose, throat Andres Soriano Jr. Med. Ctr., Toledo City, Philippines, 1967-84; asst. med. dir. Andres Soriano Jr. Med. Ctr., Toledo City, 1975-80; asst. dir. health and hosp. services Atlas Consolidated Mining and Devel. Corp., Toledo City, 1981-84; chmn. dept. eyes, ear, nose, throat Cebu Drs. Coll. of Medicine, Cebu, 1980-83, asst. prof., 1984-85, prof. II, 1986—; cons. Cebu Drs. Hosp., 1980—, Chong Hua Hosp., Cebu, 1985—, Atlas Mining Hosp., 1985—, Timex, Philippines, Mactan, Cebu, 1987—. Fellow Philippine Bd. Ophthalmology, Otolaryngology, Philippine Coll. of Surgeons (councilor 1983, bd. dirs. 1987), Philippine Occupational and Indsl. Med. Assn.; mem. Assn. of Surgeons of SE Asia. Lodge: Rotary. Home: 443 Gorordo Ave, Cebu Philippines Office: Cebu Drs Hosp, Osmeña Blvd, Cebu Philippines

SEHEULT, MALCOLM MCDONALD RICHARDSON, solicitor, barrister, author, educator; b. Port of Spain, Trinidad, July 18, 1949; s. Errol Andre and Laura (Laltoo) S.; m. Robin Lynn Montanye; children: Kristie, Julie, Laura, Aimée. BA in Sociology magna cum laude, U. Toronto, 1971, BEd, 1972, MA, 1973; LLB, U. Toronto, Ottawa, 1976; JD, Kensington U., 1988. Bar: Ontario, Can. 1978, N.Y. 1987; cert. tchr., Toronto, Can. Sole practice Toronto, 1978-85; assoc. Outerbridge, Barristers & Solicitors, Mississauga, Can., 1985-86, Don & Brown, Mississauga, 1986—; lectr. numerous profl. and community groups and orgns. Producer, editor Where Is Tomorrow?, 1969; editor Ottawa Law Rev.; also articles. Mem. Justice for Children, Vanier Inst. of Family, Ont. Sch. Tchrs. Fedn.; bd. dirs. North York Branson Hosp. Mem. ABA, N.Y. State Bar Assn., Can. Bar Assn., Assn. Trial Lawyers Am., Law Soc. Upper Can., Medico-Legal Soc., Lawyers Club, Can. Civil Liberties Union, Royal Soc. Arts (fellow 1979), Mensa

Internat., Can. Sociology and Anthropology Assn., Nat. Directory Sociology of Edn. and Ednl. Sociology, Am. Philatelic Soc., Phi Kappa Phi. Home: 25623 State St Loma Linda CA 92354 Address: 2638 Victoria Park Ave, Willowdale, ON Canada M2J 4A6

SEHGAL, AMAR NATH, sculptor; b. Campbellpur, West Pakistan, Feb. 5, 1922; s. Ram Asra Mal and Parmeshwari Devi; m. Shukla Dhawan, 1954; 2 children. Ed. Punjab U., Govt. Coll., Lahore, and NYU; M.A. Hon. art cons. to Ministry Community Devel., Govt. India, 1955-66; participant Scupture Biennale, Musee Rodin, Paris, 1966, UNESCO Conf. on role of art in contemporary soc., 1974; organizer Internat. Children's Art Workshop, UNESCO, Paris, 1979. One-man shows: N.Y., 1950-51, Paris, 1952, East Africa, India, (retrospectives) Nat. Gallery Modern Art, New Delhi, 1972, City Hall, Ottawa, Ont., Can., 1975, Aerogolf, Luxembourg, 1975, India House, N.Y.C., 1976, Rathaus, Fransheim, W.Ger., 1977, Frankfurt Airport, 1977, Neustadt, 1978, Brenners Park, Baden-Baden, 1979, Luxembourg, 1980; group shows: Dubai, Abu Dhabi, 1980, Jeddah, 1981, Chaux de Fond, Switzerland, 1982; represented in permanent collections: Vigyan Bhawan (India's Internat. Conf. bldg.), White House, New Delhi Airport, also in Jerusalem, Vienna, Paris, Berlin, Antwerp, Luxembourg, Conn., New Delhi; works include: Voice of Africa (Ghana), 1959, A Cricketer, 1961, Mahatma Gandhi, Amritsar, To Space Unknown bronze, 1963, Conquest of the Moon bronze, 1969, Anguished Cries bronze monument, 1971, Gandhi monument, 1971, Monument to Aviation, 1972, Rising Spirit, 1978; sculpture exhbns., Belgarde, 1964, Musee d'Art Moderne, Paris, 1965, Pauls-kirche Frankfurt, 1965, Haus am Lutzoplatz West Berlin, 1966, Musees Royaux D'Art et Histoire, Brussels, 1966, Musee Etat Luxembourg, 1966, Wiener Secession, Vienna, 1966, Flemish Acad. Arts, 1967, Tokyo Internat. Fair, 1973, others; author: Arts and Aesthetics; Organising Exhibitions in Rural Areas; (poetry) Der Innere Rhythmus, 1975; Folio of Graphics, 1981. Recipient Sculpture award Lalit Kala Acad., 1957, Pres.'s award (donated to Prime Minister Nehru during Chinese invasion), 1958. Home: J-23 Jangpura Extension, New Delhi 110014, India *

SEHNKE, ERROL DOUGLAS, geologist; b. Superior, Wis., Mar. 14, 1943; s. Henry Herman and Athlyn Marion (Westlund) S. B.S., U. Wis., 1965; M.S., U. Mich., 1969. Jr. geologist Aluminum Co. of Am., Phoenix, 1971-72, exploration mgr. Alcoa-Fairview Mining, Derbyshire, Eng., 1972-74, project geologist Alcoa-Cimca, San Jose, Costa Rica, 1974-77, sr. geologist Alcoa-Chelsea Properties, Phoenix, 1977-80, staff geologist Alcoa-Suralco, Moengo, Suriname, 1980-83, projects mgr. Alcoa-Western Mining Ltd., Rio de Janiero, Brazil, 1983-86; cons. Superior, Wis., 1986—. Mem. Soc. Mining Engrs. of AIME, Geol. Soc. Am., Am. Soc. Photogrammetry. Home: 6122 John Superior WI 54880 Office: PO Box 3007 Superior WI 54880

SEHORN, MARSHALL ESTUS, music industry executive; songwriter; b. Concord, N.C., June 25, 1934; s. William Thomas and Bertha (Mesmer) S.; m. Barbara Ann Darcy, May 11, 1974. B.S. in Agr., N.C. State Coll., 1957; B.A. in Music, Belmont Coll., 1981, Council Devel. of French in La., 1983. Owner, operator comml. farm, Concord, 1957-58; producer, co-owner Fury/Fire Records, N.Y.C., 1958-63; producer EMI, London, 1963-64; pres., co-owner Marsaint/Sansu Enterprises, New Orleans, 1965—; sec., co-owner Sea-Saint Studio, New Orleans, 1972—; pres. Jefferson Jazz, New Orleans, 1980—. Producer: (recording) Kansas City (gold record 1959), 1959; co-producer: (recording) Lady Marmalade (gold record 1974), 1974; pub.: (song) Southern Nights (Broadcast Music, Inc. award 1977), 1975; exec. producer: (album) Elvis Live at La. Hayride, 1983. Presdl. appointee Civil Rights Com., Washington, 1961; mem. NAACP, New Orleans, 1965—; gov.'s appointee La. Music Commn., Baton Rouge, 1981—; presdl. appointee Anti-Piracy Commn., Washington, 1981-85. Named Record Man of Yr., Am. Record Mfg. and Distbrs. Assn., 1961, Producer of Yr., 1961; recipient Outstanding Service award Gov. of La., 1979, 82; Outstanding Music Contbn. award Mayor of New Orleans, 1982. Mem. Broadcast Music Inc., Am. Songwriters Assn. (cons., Merit award), Am. Fedn. Musicians, Recording Engrs. Assn., New Orleans C. of C., Ducks Unltd. (Slidell, La.). Republican. Methodist. Clubs: Bass Anglers Am. (New Orleans) (life). Avocations: boating; fishing; songwriting; hunting; art collecting. Home: 10136 Idlewood Pl River Ridge LA 70123 Office: Sea-Saint Recording Studio 3809 Clematis Ave New Orleans LA 70122

SEIBEL, ERWIN, oceanographer, educator; b. Schwientochlowitz, Germany, Apr. 29, 1942; came to U.S., 1952. BS, CCNY, 1965; MS, U. Mich., 1966, PhD, 1972. Asst. research oceanographer U. Mich., Ann Arbor, 1972-75, assoc. research oceanographer, 1975-78, asst. dir. sea grant, 1975-78; environ. lab dir. San Francisco State U., 1978-81, chmn. dept. geoscis., 1988—; sr. scientist cruises U. Mich., 1971-78; mem. sea grant site rev. teams Nat. Sea Grant Program, Washington, 1978—; bd. govs. Moss Landing Marine Labs., Calif., 1981—; mem. adv. com. Ctr. Advancement Mercantile Spacefaring; exec. sec. Oceans 83 Marine Tech. Soc., IEEE, San Francisco, 1982-83; co-ordinator Symposium for Pacific AAAS El Nino Effect, 1983-84; dir. environ. monitoring nuclear power plant, 1972-78. Contbr. articles to profl. jours.; developer photogrammetric technique for continuous shoreline monitoring, 1972-78. Advisor MESA program for Minority Students, San Francisco area, 1981-88; vol. San Francisco Bay Area council Girl Scouts U.S., 1982-86. Served to capt. U.S. Army, 1967-71, Vietnam. Grantee Am. Electric Power Co., 1972-78, Gt. Lakes Basin Commn., 1975-76, Calif. Div. Mines and Geology, 1986—. Recipient Exceptional Merit Service award San Francisco State U., 1984. Fellow AAAS, Calif. Acad. Scis., Geol. Soc. Am.; mem. N.Y. Acad. Scis., Am. Geophys. Union, Marine Tech. Soc. (pres. San Francisco Bay chpt. 1982-83), U. Mich. Alumni Assn., Gold Key (hon.), Sigma XI (pres. San Francisco State U. chpt. 1982-84). Office: San Francisco State U Office Dean Undergrad Studies 1600 Holloway Ave San Francisco CA 94132

SEIBEL, GEORGE HENRY, JR., retired ammunition specialist; b. Centralia, Ill., Apr. 21, 1921; s. George Henry and Marie Sophia (Johnson) S.; student Greer Coll., Chgo., 1939-41, also numerous mil. schs.; m. Estelle Lucille Gulley, Oct. 24, 1948; children—Lorita Joeann, Georgeania Marie, Clifford George, Henry Curtis. Enlisted U.S. Army Air Corps, 1939, advanced to sgt. U.S. Air Force, 1954; ret., 1962; various positions in county and state govt., 1962-66; civilian with U.S. Army, 1966—, surveillance insp. ammunition Blue Grass Army Depot, Richmond, Ky., 1971-73, chief chem. def. team Anniston (Ala.) Army Depot, 1973-79; chief surveillance 193d Inf. Brigade and So. Command, Panama, 1979-81; ret. 1982; cons. in field. Mem. bd. Valier (Ill.) High Sch., 1963-64, Valier Grade Sch., 1963-64; city water and road commr., Valier, 1964. Decorated numerous area ribbons, letters of appreciation and commendation. Mem. Pearl Harbor Survivors Assn. (life), Am. Def. Preparedness Assn., Am. Security Council (nat. adv. bd.), USAF Sgts. Assn., Nat. Hist. Soc., Early Am. Soc., AIAA, Am. Fedn. Govt. Employees. Clubs: USAF Non-Commnd. Officers, Elks. Inventor electronics devices. Home: 607 Briarwood Ave Oak Ridge Estates Eastaboga AL 36260

SEIBERLICH, CARL JOSEPH, retired naval officer; b. Jenkintown, Pa., July 4, 1921; s. Charles A. and Helen (Dolan) S.; m. Trudy Germi, May 29, 1952; children: Eric P., Heidi M., Curt A. B.S., U.S. Mcht. Marine Acad., 1943; grad., Armed Forces Staff Coll., 1959. Commd. ensign U.S. Navy, 1943, advanced through grades to rear adm., 1971; designated naval aviator 1947, carrier ops. Heavier-than-Air, Lighter-than-Air and helicopters; comdg. officer Airship ZPM-1, 1949, Air Anti-Submarine Squadron 26, 1961, U.S.S. Salamonie, 1967, U.S.S. Hornet, 1969; dir. recovery astronauts Apollo 11 and 12 lunar missions, 1969; comdr. anti-submarine warfare group 3 Flagship U.S.S. Ticonderoga, 1971; comdr. task force 74 Viet Nam Ops., 1972; asst. dep. chief naval ops. for air warfare Navy Dept., 1975-77; dep. chief naval personnel 1977-78; comdr. Naval Mil. Personnel Command, 1978-80; with VSE Corp., 1980-82; pres. U.S. Maritime Resource Ctr.; dir. mil. program Am. Pres. Lines, 1983—. Vice pres. Naval Aviation Mus. Found.; active Boy Scouts Am. Decorated Legion of Merit (6), Air medal; recipient Harmon Internat. trophy for devel. 1st variable depth towed sonar, 1951. Mem. AIAA, Am. Soc. Naval Engrs., Am. Helicopter Soc., U.S. Naval Inst., U.S. Naval Sailing Assn. (commodore 1979), Am. Angus Assn., Order Daedalians, Tailhook Assn., Navy Helicopter Assn., Naval Airship Assn., U.S. Mcht. Marine Acad. Alumni Assn., Assn. Naval Aviation, Am. Legion, Delta Sigma Pi. Clubs: N.Y. Yacht, Capital Yacht, Nat. Space. Home: Seagate Farm 1510 Loudoun Dr Haymarket VA 22069 Office: Am Pres Lines 1101 17th St NW Suite 400 Washington DC 20036

SEIBERT, PETER FRANZ, German literature educator; b. Weiskirchen, Saarland, Fed. Republic Germany, June 27, 1948; s. Joseph Peter and Clara (Fett) S.; m. Angela Dencker; 1 child, Julian Philipp. MA, U. Bonn, Fed. Republic Germany, 1973; PhD, U. Siegen, Fed. Republic Germany, 1977; Habilitation, U. Siegen, 1987. Asst. prof. U. Siegen, 1978-88, prof. German lit., 1988—. Author: Aufstandsbewegungen in der Reimliteratur, 1978; co-editor Dramaturgie der sechziger Jahre, 1974; contbr. articles to profl. jours. Office: U Gesamthochschule Siegen, Adolf Reichweinstr. 5900 Siegen Federal Republic of Germany

SEIDEL, SELVYN, lawyer, legal educator; b. Longbranch, N.J., Nov. 6, 1942; s. Abraham and Anita (Stoller) S.; m. Deborah Lew, June 21, 1970; 1 child, Emily. B.A., U. Chgo., 1964; J.D., U. Calif.-Berkeley, 1967; Diploma in Law, Oxford U., 1968. Bar: N.Y. 1970, U.S. Dist. Ct. (so. and ea. dists.) N.Y. 1970, D.C. Ct. Appeals, 1982. Ptnr. Latham & Watkins, N.Y.C., 1984—; adj. prof. Sch. Law, NYU, 1974-85; instr. Practicing Law Inst., 1980-81, 84. Mem. ABA, New York County Bar Assn., N.Y.C. Bar Assn. (mem. fed. cts. com. 1982-85), Boalt Hall Alumni Assn. (bd. dirs. 1980-82). Contbr. articles to profl. jurs. Club: Union League. Home: 110 Riverside Dr New York NY 10024 also: North St Lichfield CT 06759 Office: 885 3d Ave New York NY 10022

SEIDEN, HENRY, advertising agency executive; b. Bklyn., Sept. 6, 1928; s. Jack S. and Shirley (Berkowitz) S.; m. Helena Ruth Zaldin, Sept. 10, 1949; children: Laurie Ann, Matthew Ian. B.A., Bklyn. Coll., 1949; M.B.A., CCNY, 1954. Trainee Ben Sackheim Advt. Agy., 1949-51; nat. promotion mgr. N.Y. Post Corp., 1951-53; promotion mgr. Crowell-Collier Pub. Co., Inc., 1953-54; copy group head Batten, Barton, Durstine & Osborn, Inc., 1954-60; v.p., creative dir. Keyes, Madden & Jones, 1960-61; sr. v.p., assoc. creative dir. McCann-Marschalk, Inc., 1961-65, chmn. plans bd., 1964-65; creative dir., dir., prin. Hicks & Greist, Inc., N.Y.C., 1965—, sr. v.p., 1965-74, exec. v.p., 1974-83, chief operating officer, 1983—, pres., 1986—; chief exec. officer Ketchum/Hicks & Greist Inc., 1987—; Guest lectr. Bernard M. Baruch Sch. Bus. and Pub. Adminstrn., Coll. City N.Y., 1962—, Baruch Coll., CCNY, 1969—, New Sch. Social Scis., 1968, 72, 73, Sch. Visual Arts, 1979, 80—, Lehman Coll., CCNY, 1980—, Ohio U., 1981, Newhouse Grad. Sch., Syracuse U., 1981, NYU, 1983; cons. pub. relations and communication to mayor of New Rochelle, N.Y., 1959—, also; marketing dept. Ohio State U.; Cons. to pres. N.Y.C. City Council, 1972-73, to Postmaster Gen. U.S., 1972-74; communications adviser to Police Commr. N.Y.C., 1973—; bd. dirs. Transmedia Network Inc., 1988—, Cancer Research and Treatment Fund Inc., 1988—. Author: Advertising Pure and Simple, 1976; Contbg. editor: Madison Ave. mag, 1966—, Advt. Age, Mag. Age; guest columnist: N.Y. Times, 1972. Vice commr. Little League of New Rochelle.; Bd. dirs. Police Res. Assn. N.Y.C., 1973—; bd. dirs., exec. v.p. N.Y.'s Finest Found., 1975—. Recipient award Four Freedoms Found., 1959, award Printers Ink, 1960, promotion award Editor and Publisher, 1955, Am. TV Commls. Festival award, 1963-69, Effie award Am. Marketing Assn., 1969, 70, award Art Directors Club N.Y., 1963-70, award Am. Inst. Graphic Arts, 1963, Starch award, 1969; spl. award graphic art lodge B'nai B'rith Greater N.Y., 1971, 87. Mem. A.I.M. (asso.), Nat. Acad. TV Arts and Scis., Advt. Club N.Y. (exec. judge Andy awards, award 1963-65), Advt. Writers Assn. N.Y. (Gold Key award for best newspaper and mag. advts. 1962-64), Copy Club (co-chmn. awards com., Gold Key award for best TV comml. 1969), Alpha Phi Omega. Home: 1056 Fifth Ave New York NY 10028 Office: 220 E 42d St New York NY 10017

SEIDEN, RICHARD STEVEN, interior designer; b. Albany, N.Y., May 7, 1938; s. Henry Wallace and Beatrice (Olshein) S.; m. Roberta Cohen, Apr. 3, 1960; children—Terri B., Sharon L., Melinda B. Grad. Interior Design, N.Y. Sch. Interior Design, 1959. Interior designer Sharlet Furniture, Latham, N.Y., 1962-67; design dir. Concord House, Schenectady, 1967-74; owner R.S.I. Interiors, Albany, N.Y., 1974—; pres. Seiden Realty. Pres. Colonie Village PTA, 1968; dir. B'nai Brith Parkview Home, 1986—; adv. interior design program Jr. Coll. Albany; co-chmn. adv. network interior design Capitol Dist. Psych. Ctr. Mem. Nat. Soc. Interior Designers (sec.-treas. 1968-74), Internat. Soc. Interior Designers, Am. Soc. Interior Designers (bd. dirs.). Democrat. Jewish. Clubs: Automobilists of Hudson Valley, Antique Auto Am. Lodges: Elks, B'nai B'rith (v.p. Gideon lodge), K.P. Home: 164 Vly Rd Schenectady NY 12309 Office: RSI 238 N Allen St Albany NY 12206

SEIDENSTICKER, EDWARD GEORGE, Japanese language and literature educator; b. Castle Rock, Colo., Feb. 11, 1921; s. Edward George and Mary Elizabeth (Dillon) S. B.A., U. Colo., 1942; M.A., Columbia U., 1947; post-grad., Harvard U., 1947-48. With U.S. Fgn. Service, Dept. State, Japan, 1947-50; mem. faculty Stanford U., 1962-66, prof., 1964-66; prof. dept. Far Eastern langs. and lit. U. Mich., Ann Arbor, 1966-77; prof. Japanese Columbia U., 1977-85, prof. emeritus, 1986—. Author: Kafu The Scribbler, 1965, Japan, 1961, Low City, High City, 1983; Translator: (by Murasaki Shikibu) The Tale of Genji, 1976. Served with USMCR, 1942-46. Decorated Order of Rising Sun Japan; recipient Nat. Book award, 1970; citation Japanese Ministry Edn., 1971; Kikuchikan prize, 1977; Goto Miyoko prize, 1982; Japan Found. prize, 1984; Tokyo Cultural award, 1985. Mem. Am. Oriental Soc., Assn. for Asian Studies.

SEIDL, JOHN MICHAEL, oil company executive; b. Milw., Mar. 24, 1939; s. Lawrence E. and Dorothy (Gilbert) S.; m. Madelyn S., July 7, 1962; children: Michele A., John D., Sarah C. BS, U.S. Mil. Acad., 1961; MBA, Harvard U., 1966, Ph.D., 1969. Commd. capt. U.S. Air Force, 1961-71; pres. Natomas N. Am., Houston, 1981-83; sr. v.p. Houston Natural Gas, 1984-85; exec. v.p. Enron Corp. (formerly HNG Internorth PL Co), Houston, 1985-86; pres., chief operating officer HNG Internorth (now known as Enron Corp.), Houston, 1986—; chmn. HNG Interstate P L Co, Houston, from 1985. Author: Politics American Style, 1972. Contbr. articles to profl. jours. Bd. dirs. Houston Ballet Found., Alley Theatre, Soc. Performing Arts. Served to capt. USAF, 1961-71. Mem. Young Pres.' Orgn., Ind. Petroleum Assn. Am. Clubs: Ramada (Houston), Petroleum. *

SEIDLER, EDOUARD A., journalist, consultant; b. Brno, Czechoslovakia, Mar. 23, 1932; s. Oscar and Helene (Lustig) S.; m. Rhoda Madden, Oct. 20, 1958; children: Catherine, Marianne. Diploma, Inst. D'Etudes Polits., Paris, 1953; MBA, UCLA, 1954. Cons. S.J. Capelin Assocs., N.Y.C., 1957-60; with L'Equipe newspaper, Paris, 1960-84, successively editor, editor in chief, mng. editor, pub.; cons. to mgmt., editorialist L'Action Automobile mag., Paris, 1985—; corr. to various fgn. publs. Author, editor numerous books; producer French TV, 1961-72, 87—. Served to lt. French Air Force, 1954-57. Decorated Knight of French Legion of Honor, Officer Nat. Order of Merit (France); recipient numerous profl. awards. Mem. Guild Motoring Writers (London), Assn. Française de la Presse Automobile. Clubs: Racing of France, Automobile of France (Paris). Home: 104 rue Brancas, 92310 Sevres France

SEIDLER, FRANZ WILHELM, history educator, writer; b. Wigstadtl, Moravia, Germany, Mar. 2, 1933; s. Franz J. and Maria (Kaschuba) S.; m. Renate E. Guetgemann, Apr. 18, 1962; children—Martin, Stefan, Daniel, Christof. M.A., D.Phil., U. Munich., 1955, Ph.D., 1956. Tchr. secondary schs. Wagenburg Coll., Stuttgart, 1956-59; dep. headmaster NCO Coll., Cologne, 1959-63; ednl. adviser Ministry of Def., Bonn, 1963-67; acad. dir. Officers Acad., Munich, 1967-73; prof. mil. history Bundeswehr U., Munich, 1973—. Author: Deutsche Sanitaetsfuehrung, 1977; Frauen zu den Waffen, 1978; Blitzmaedchen, 1979, Militaerkarikatur, 1982, Friendenssicherung, 1983; Fritz Todt Biography, 1986; Organization Todt in WWII, 1987. Mem. exec. com. Christian Democratic Union, 1956-60, election com., Cologne, 1960-67. Mem. Nat. Hist. Assn., Inter Univ. Seminar on Armed Forces and Society, Internat. Sociol. Assn. Roman Catholic. Home: Guttenbrunner Weg 28, D-8000 Munich 82 Federal Republic of Germany Office: Universitaet der Bundeswehr, Heisenbergweg 39, D-8014 Neubiberg Federal Republic of Germany

SEIDLER, HARRY, architect, educator; b. Vienna, Austria, June 25, 1923; s. Max and Rose S.; m. Penelope Evatt, 1958; 2 children. Ed. Cambridge Tech. Sch., U. Man., Harvard U., Black Mountain Coll.; M.Arch.; studied with Walter Gropius, Harvard U., 1946; student Josef Albers, Black Mountain Coll., 1946. Chief asst. Marcel Breuer, N.Y.C., 1946-48; prin. architect Harry Seidler and Assocs., Sydney, Australia, 1948—; Thomas Jefferson prof. architecture U. Va., 1978—; vis. prof. Harvard U., 1976-77, U. New South Wales, 1980, U. Sydney, 1984. Maj. works: housing units in Australia, urban redevel. Australia Sq., Sydney, 1962-66, Commonwealth Trade Office Complex, Canberra, Australia, 1970-72, High Rise Apts., Acapulco, 1970, M.L.C. Ctr., Martin Pl., Sydney, 1972-75, Australian Embassy, Paris, 1974-76, Hong Kong Club and Office Bldg., 1980-84; author: Houses, Interiors and Projects, 1949-54; Harry Seidler, 1955-63; Architecture in the New World, 1974; Australian Embassy, Paris, 1979; Two Towers, Sydney, 1980. Decorated Companion of the Order of Australia, 1987, Order Brit. Empire; recipient Wilkinson award, 1965, 66, 67, Sir John Sulman medal, 1951, 67, 81, 83, Civic Design award, 1967, 81, Sir Zelman Cowen Nat. award, 1987, Fellow AIA (hon.; Pan Pacific citation 1968), Royal Australian Inst. Architects (life; Gold medal 1976), Australia Acad. Tech. Scis.; mem. Academie D'Architecture Paris, Academician Internat. Acad. Architecture. Home: 2 Glen St, Milsons Point, NSW 2061 Australia also: 13 Kalang Ave, Killara, NSW 2071 Australia

SEIERUP, JENS-CHRISTIAN, information engineer; b. Mar. 21, 1939. Student, Tech. Coll., Aalbong, Denmark, 1963. Asst. engr. Dept. Hydraulic Engring., Hamstholm, Denmark, 1964-69; chief supr. Contact Bldg. Soc., Aarhus, Denmark, 1969-75, Asmussen of Weber, Westmanager Island, Denmark, 1975-76, Globe Bldg. Soc., Saby, Denmark, 1976-78, Saudi Comet, Alkobar, Saudi Arabia, 1978-79; asst. info. engr. Aalborg Postland, 1979-81, chief info. engr., 1981—; state dir. of libraries Denmark, 1985—. Mem. Soc. Engrs. Denmark, Soc. Tech. Info., On-line Users Group Danish. Office: Aalbong Portland, Rordalsvej 44, PO Box 165, 9100 Aalborg Denmark

SEIFER, ARNOLD DAVID, engineer; b. Newark, Apr. 22, 1940; s. Abe W. and Bessie R. (Coopersmith) S. BS in Math, Rensselaer Poly. Inst., 1962, MS, 1964, PhD, 1968. Research specialist Gen. Dynamics Corp., Groton, Conn., 1967-73; sr. staff mathematician Applied Physics Lab., Laurel, MD., 1973-76; sr. staff engr. Emerson Electric Co., St. Louis, 1976-80; prin. engr. Raytheon Co., Wayland, Mass., 1980—. Contbr. sci. papers to profl. jours. Mem. IEEE (sr.), Soc. Indsl. and Applied Math., Sigma Xi. Home: 66 Dinsmore Ave Apt 606 Framingham MA 01701 Office: Raytheon Co Equipment Devel Labs 430 Boston Post Rd Wayland MA 01778

SEIFERT, CHRISTIAN, electronic company executive; b. Berlin, June 21, 1943; s. Hans-Walter and Ingeborg (Holtz) Seifert; m. Brigitte Breitbarth, Feb. 25, 1966; 1 son, Markus Francis. Engr., Enging. Sch., El Paso, 1966. Chief instr., German Air Force, El Paso, Tex., 1966-69; mgr. new products MDS, Cologne, 1971-74; v.p. NAVSAT, Bonn, 1975-77; dir. Sperry, Frankfurt, 1977-81; dir. Standard Electric Lorenz, Stuttgart, 1981—; dir. Air Space Mgmt. Systems, Brussels, 1982-85, vice chmn. bd., 1985, chmn., 1986—; mem. adv. bd. U.S. German Industry Relation Adv. and Cons. Venture, 1984—. Contbr. articles to profl. jours. Chmn. econ. bd. Christian Democratic Union, Siegburg, 1979—, vice chmn. personnel bd., 1979—, mem. city council, 1979—. Hon. citizen El Paso City Council, 1964. Mem. Armed Forces Communications and Electronics Assn., Fernmeldering. Clubs: Flying (Bonn), Clausewitz Gesellschaft (Fed. Republic Germany).

SEIFERT, JOSEF M.M., philosopher; b. Seekirchen, Austria, Jan. 6, 1945; s. Eduard and Edith (Schuchter) S.; m. Mary K. Heyne, Dec. 27, 1972; children: Maria Gabriel, Katharina, Raphaela, Johannes. PhD, U. Salzburg, 1969; Habilitation PhD, U. Munich, 1975. Asst. prof. U. Salzburg, Austria, 1969-72; asst. prof. U. Dallas, Irving, Tex., 1972-76, assoc. prof., 1976-81; prof., dir. PhD program Internat. Acad. of Philosophy, Irving, 1980-85; prof. philosophy, rector Internat. Akademie für Philosophie im Fürstentum Liechtenstein, Schaan, 1985—; chmn. grad. philosophy program U. Dallas, Irving, Tex., 1973-80. Author: Erkenntnis Obj. Wahrheit, 1976, Was ist und was Motivert Eine Sittliche Handlung?, 1976, Das Leib-Seele-Problem, 1982, Back To Things In Themselves, 1987, Essere e Persona, 1988, Schachphilosophie, 1988; editor internat. jour. Aletheia. Mem. Am. Philos. Assn., Am. Cath. Philos. Assn., Amis Gabriel Marcel, D. Gesellschaft für Phänomenol, Dietrich von Hildebrand Gesellschaft. Roman Catholic. Home: Dorfstr 73, FL-9491 Ruggell Liechtenstein Office: Internat Acad Philos, Obergass 75, FL-9494 Schaan Liechtenstein

SEIFERT, KARL HEINZ, psychology educator, researcher; b. Ilsenburg, Fed. Rep. Germany, July 2, 1928; came to Austria, 1970; s. Paul and Erna (Rietzschel) S.; m. Ingeborg Schueler, Dec. 28, 1957; 1 child, Angelika. Diplom-Psychologist, U. Heidelberg, Fed. Rep. Germany, 1953, Ph.D., 1957, Habilitation, 1967. Lic. psychologist. Asst. Paedagogik Hochschule, Heidelberg, 1958-64, lectr., 1964-69; prof. U. Mainz, Fed. Rep. Germany, 1969-70, U. Linz, Austria, 1970—, head Institut fuer Paedagogik und Psychologie, 1971-81, 85—. Author: Lehrerverhaltens-training, 1979, Einstellungen geg. Korperbehinderten, 1981. Editor, author (handbook), Handbuch der Berufspsychologie, 1977. Contbr. articles to sci. jours. Recipient Austrian-Am. Ednl. Commn. Fulbright research award, U.S., 1985; hon. fellow U. Minn. Mem. German Psychol. Assn., Internat. Assn. Applied Psychology, Austrian Assn. Pedagogics. Office: Johannes Kepler Universaet, Inst Paedagogik Psychologie, A-4040 Linz Austria

SEIFERT, THOMAS LLOYD, lawyer; b. Boston, June 6, 1940; s. Ralph Frederick and Hazel Bell (Harrington) S.; m. Ann Cecelia Berg, June 19, 1965. B.S. cum laude, Ind. U., 1962, J.D. cum laude, 1965. Bar: Ill. 1965, Ind. 1965, N.Y. State 1979. Assoc. law firm Keck, Mahin & Cate, Chgo., 1965-67; atty. Essex Group, Inc., Ft. Wayne, Ind., 1967-70, Standard Oil Co. (Ind.), Chgo., 1970-73; assoc. gen. counsel, asst. sec. Canteen Corp., Chgo., 1973-75; sec., legal counsel The Marmon Group, Inc. (and predecessor cos.), Chgo., 1975-78; v.p., gen. counsel, sec. Hanson Industries, Inc., N.Y.C., 1978-82; sr. v.p. law, chief fin. officer Petrie Stores Corp., N.Y.C., 1982-83; mem. firm Finley, Kumble, Wagner, Heine, Underberg, Manley, Myerson & Casey, N.Y.C., 1983-88, Paul, Weiss, Rifkind, Wharton & Garrison, N.Y.C., 1988—. Note editor: Ind. Law Jour, 1964-65. Mem. Am. Soc. Corp. Secs., ABA (mem. bus. com.), Assn. of Bar of City of N.Y., Phi Delta Phi, Order of Coif, Beta Gamma Sigma, Sigma Nu. Home: 800 Fifth Ave New York NY 10021 Office: Paul Weiss Rifkin et al 1285 Avenue of the Americas New York NY 10019

SEIGLER, MICHAEL EDWARD, lawyer; b. Tallahassee, Oct. 14, 1948; s. Claude Milo and Roberta Bradford (Whitfield) S.; m. Janet Cummings, Feb. 19, 1971; children: Kelly Elizabeth, Megan Whitfield. A.A., Lake Sumter Community Coll., 1968; B.S., Fla. State U., 1970, M.S., 1974; J.D., Atlanta Law Sch., 1980. Bar: Ga. Cert. tchr., librarian. Tchr., Sumter Correctional Inst., Bushnell, Fla., 1970-73; asst. library dir. Leesburg Pub. Library (Fla.), 1974-75, library dir., 1975-77; library dir. Atlanta Law Sch., 1979-81; atty. Brooks & Brock, Marietta, Ga., 1981-83; librarian Port Charlotte Pub. Library (Fla.), 1983-84; assoc. Brooks & Brock, Marietta, Ga., 1985, Brock & Barr, Marietta, 1985-86; Brock & Clay, 1987; judge pro hoc vice State Ct. of Cobb County, 1986. Contbr. articles to jours. Vol. worker ACLU, Atlanta, 1979; mem. Fla. State U. Library Com., Tallahassee, 1974, Children's Program Com., Port Charlotte, 1983, Port Charlotte Cultural Ctr. Adv. Com., 1984—; mem. Cobb County Dem. Exec. Com., 1986—; exec. com. Cobb Christmas, 1986-87. Named Tchr. of Yr., Sumter Correctional Inst., 1973. Mem. Nat. Library Assn. (com. chmn. 1975-76), Fla. Library Assn. (caucus chmn. 1976-77), ABA, Cobb County Bar Assn. (com mem.), Atlanta Law Sch. Alumni Assn. (treas. 1986—), Fla. State U. Alumni Assn. (life), Mensa (sec 1987—, pres. Ga. chpt. 1988—). Democrat. Episcopalian. Lodges: Masons (sr. steward Gate City Lodge 2), Scottish Rite, Shriners. Home: 3023 Bay Berry Dr Marietta GA 30060 Office: Brock & Clay 30 S Park Sq Marietta GA 30060

SEIGNORET, SIR CLARENCE HENRY AUGUSTUS, President of the Commonwealth of Dominica; b. Roseau, Dominica, Feb. 25, 1919; s. Clarence Augustus and Violet (Riviere) S.; m. Judith Laronde, Apr. 4, 1950; children—Joseph Phillip, Gilbert Karol Theodore. Student Balliol Coll., Oxford U. Civil servant Govt. Dominica, Roseau, 1936-77, permanent sec., 1956-67, sec. to cabinet, head Civil Service, 1967-77, now pres. of Dominica, Roseau; exec. sec. Dominica Assn. Industry and Commerce, Roseau, 1979-83. Decorated officer Order Brit. Empire, Knight grand cross Order of Bath, Collar of the Order of the Liberator. Office: Office of President, Morne Bruce, Roseau Commonwealth of Dominica

SEIKKALA, SEPPO ANTERO, mathematics educator; b. Oulu, Finland, May 24, 1946; s. Antti and Vieno (Aspegren) S.; m. Anna-Riitta Pyykkö, Aug. 15, 1970; 1 child, Annamari. MS, U. Oulu, 1972, PhD, 1978. Asst. U. Oulu, 1974-78, assoc. prof. math., 1978—; researcher U. Tex., Arlington, 1984, Finnish Acad., Arlington, 1986. Contbr. math. articles to acad. jours. Served to lt. inf. Finnish army, 1965-66. Mem. Am. Math. Soc., Finnish Math. Soc. Office: U Oulu, Sect Math, Linnanmaa, 90 570 Oulu Finland

SEIPP, WALTER, banker, corporate executive; b. Langen, Germany, Dec. 13, 1925; m. 1954; 2 children. Law student U. Frankfurt am Main; Assesor, Ph.D., 1953. With Deutsche Bank AG, 1951-74, exec. v.p., 1970-74; mem. mng. bd. Westdeutsche Landesbank Girozentrale, 1974-77, vice chmn., 1978-81; chmn. mng. bd. Commerzbank AG, 1981—; chmn. supervisory bd. Berliner Commerzbank AG, Karstadt AG, Essen, Rheinische Hypothekenbank AG, Frankfurt, W.Ger., Commerz Internat. Capital Mgmt. GmbH, Frankfurt; chmn. adminstrn. bd. Commerzbank (South East Asia) Ltd., Singapore, Commerzbank Internat. S.A., Luxembourg, Commerzbank (Schweiz) AG, Zurich, Commerzbak Capital Markets Corp., N.Y.C., Commerz Securities Co. Ltd., Tokyo; mem. supervisory bd. Allianz Versicherungs-AG, Munich, Daimler Benz AG, Stuttgart, Standard Elektrik Lorenz AG, Stuttgart, Vereinigte Industrie-Unternehmungen AG, Bonn, Hochtief AG, Essen, Linde AG., Wiesbaden, MAN AG, Munich, Thyssen AG, Duisburg, Bayer AG, Leverkusen, others; mem. bd. mng. dirs. Bundesverband deutscher Banken e.V., Cologne. Office: Commerzbank Aktiengesselschaft, Neue Mainzer Strasse 32-36, 6000 Frankfurt am Main Federal Republic of Germany

SEIREG, ALI A(BDEL HAY), mechanical engineer; b. Arab Republic of Egypt, Oct. 26, 1927; came to U.S., 1951, naturalized, 1960; s. Abdel Hay and Aisha Seireg; m. Shirley Marachowsky, Dec. 24, 1954; children: Mirette Elizabeth LaFollette, Pamela Aisha. B.Sc. M.E., U. Cairo, 1948; Ph.D., U. Wis., 1954. Lectr. Cairo U., 1954-56; staff adv. engr. Falk Corp., Milw., 1956-59; assoc. prof. theoretical and applied mechanics Marquette U., 1959-64, prof., 1964-65; prof. mech. engring. U. Wis., Madison, 1965—; Ebaugh Prof. U. Fla., Gainesville, 1986—; cons. industry, ednl. and govt. agys.; chmn. U.S. council Internat. Fedn. Theory of Machines, 1974—; co-chmn. 5th World Congress of Theory of Machines, 1979. Author: Mechanical Systems Analysis, 1969; editor: Computers in Mechanical Engineering; editor-in-chief: SOMA, Engineering for the Human Body, 1986—; contbr. numerous articles to profl. jours. Fellow ASME (Richards Meml. award 1973, Machine Design award 1978, chmn. div. design engring. 1977-78, chmn. computer tech. 1978-81, mem. policy bd. communications 1978-80, mem. policy bd. gen. engring. 1979-80, chmn. Century II Internat. Computer Tech. Conf. 1980, founding chmn. computer engring. div. 1980-81, v.p. systems and design 1981-85, sr. v.p., chmn. council on engring. 1985—, pres. Gen. Research Inst. 1984—), Am. Soc. Engring. Edn. (George Westinghouse award 1970), Soc. Exptl. Stress Analysis, Am. Gear Mfg. Assn. (E. P. Connell award 1974), Automation Research Council; mem. Chinese Mech. Engring. Soc. (hon.). Home: 219 DuRose Terr Madison WI 53705 Office: 1513 University Ave Madison WI 53706

SEITH, ROBERT THEODORE, management consultant; b. Racine, Wis., Aug. 12, 1926; s. Theodore Lewis and Ruth (Cleaver) S.; B.S. in Chem. Engring., Purdue U., 1949; cert. mgmt. cons. Inst. Mgmt. Cons.; m. Ruth Marilyn Sievert, Oct. 12, 1946; children—Michael Robert, Deborah Lynn, Elizabeth Jane. With Mosinee Paper Mills Co. (Wis.), 1949-69, successively research chemist, dir. product devel., sales mgr., 1957-61, v.p. marketing, 1961-69, exec. v.p. Celluponic System, Inc., 1962-69; v.p. marketing, paper div. Gulf States Paper Corp., 1969-77; mgmt. cons., 1977—; pres. R.M. Assocs. Inc., 1983—, Arma Ltd., 1981—; dir. Bag West Paper Co., 1965-69; dir. Shuld Mfg. Co. Active Children's Service Soc. Wis., Wis. Assn. for Mental Health. Co-chmn. Republican party Marathon County, 1953. Served with AUS, 1944-46. Mem. Def. Supply Assn. (dir., past pres. Midwest), Salesmens Assn. Paper Industry (v.p. Wis. div. 1962-63, nat. pres. 1966—), Am. Paper Inst. (bd. govs.), Am. Legion, Bleached Converting Assn. (dir.), Kraft Paper Assn. (exec. com. 1960, mem. research and devel. com.), Ala. World Trade Assn., Assn. Mgmt. Cons., Am. Legion, Sigma Phi Epsilon. Episcopalian. Mason, Lion (pres. 1953-54). Author various articles profl. jours. Patentee in field. Home: 808 Indian Hills Dr Tuscaloosa AL 35401 Office: 512-514 Alabama Federal Bldg Tuscaloosa AL 35401

SEITSCHEK, VIKTOR RUDOLF, mechanical engineer, manufacturing executive director; b. Loosdorf, Austria, July 25, 1943; s. Viktor and Anna (Tilge) S.; m. Christa Köck, July 15, 1967; children: Thomas, Andreas. Degree in mech. engring., Tech. U., Vienna, 1962. Cert. quality assurance engr. Mgr. quality assurance Vogel Pumps, Stockerau, Austria, 1962-68; mem. sr. exec. staff Brown Boveri, Baden, Switzerland, 1968-78; exec. group v.p. Engel Machinery Co., Schwertberg, Austria, 1978—. Author: Qualitätssicherungsorganisation, 1981, Qualitätssicherungssyteme, 1985; contbr. articles to profl. jours. Mem. European Orgn. for Quality (ofcl. rep. for Austria 1979—), German Assn. for Quality, Austrian Assn. for Quality (exec. v.p., bd. dirs. 1978—), Am. Soc. for Quality Control (sr.). Home: Magdalenastrasse 20, A-4040 Linz Austria

SEITZ, ANNE MARIE, sociology educator; b. Munich, June 30, 1939; arrived in Australia, 1959; d. Karl Joseph Lipp and Katharina (Grad) Lipp Sturm; m. Anton Seitz (div. 1981); children: Irmgard, Eric, Robert. Diploma in Pharmacology and SBA, Pharm. Coll. Munich, 1957; BA with first class honors, Monash U., 1980. Tutor, lectr. Monash U., Melbourne, Australia, 1980-85; research fellow Australian Inst. Multicultural Affairs, Melbourne, 1986; lectr. La Trobe U., Melbourne, 1986-87, Swinburne Inst. Tech., Melbourne, 1987—; cons. Dept. Immigration and Ethnic Affairs, Melbourne, 1987. Co-author: Essay Writing in the Social Sciences, 1986; contbr. articles to profl. publs. Dep. convenor Victoria Women's Consultative Council, Melbourne, 1987—; convenor Victoria Ethnic Communities Council, 1984-88, chairperson women's com. Commonwealth scholar, Australia Dept. Edn., 1980; grantee Monash U., 1986. Mem. Australian Social Research Assn., Australian and N.Z. Assn. for Advancement of Sci., Internat. Sociol. Assn., Soc. Feminism in Social Theory (founding mem.), Australian Fedn. U. Women, Assn. for Can. Studies in Australia and New Zealand, Assn. German Speaking Communities (pres. 1988, com. mem. 1985-87), Council of Australian Postgrad. Assns. (pres. 1986, 87), Affirmative Action Tng. Inc. (bd. dirs. 1988). Home: 9 Cornell St, Camberwell, Victoria 3124, Australia Office: Swinburne Inst Tech, Victoria 3122, Australia

SEITZ, HOWARD ALEXANDER, lawyer; b. Bklyn., Nov. 14, 1907; s. Louis A. and Elizabeth A. (Ternan) S.; m. Mary V. Cunningham, Sept. 7, 1933; children: Mary Virginia Seitz Gallagher, Howard G. A.B., Fordham U., 1930; LL.B., Columbia U., 1933. Bar: N.Y. 1934, Fla. 1978. Practiced in N.Y.C., 1934—; mem. Paul, Weiss, Rifkind, Wharton & Garrison, 1943-78, counsel, 1978—. Chmn. Cardinal's Task Force on Aging, 1977-82; chmn. N.Y. State Catholic Conf. Commn. on Elderly, 1983-87; bd. dirs. Bklyn. Bur. Community Service, Community Council Greater N.Y., Inner City Scholarship Fund, Inc. Decorated knight of Malta, knight Holy Sepulchre. Mem. ABA, N.Y. State Bar Assn., Fla. Bar, Assn. Bar City N.Y. Roman Catholic. Clubs: Apawamis; Lost Tree. Home and Office: 11392 Turtle Beach Rd North Palm Beach FL 33408 Office: 1285 Avenue of the Americas New York NY 10019

SEITZ, LAURA RUTH, graphic design company executive; b. Detroit, Nov. 29, 1951; d. John Calvin and Charlotte Mary (Collins) S. Student Western Mich. U., 1969-72, Los Angeles Mcpl. Art Galleries, 1975-78, UCLA, 1978. Clothing designer, dressmaker Moonshadow Designs, Ann Arbor and Los Angeles, 1974-77; sales coordinator Edwards Bros. Inc., Ann Arbor, 1973-74; sec. Maher Elen Advt., Los Angeles, 1976-79; account exec., 1979-80, account supr., 1980-81; sales mgr. Sojourn Design Group, Pico Rivera, Calif., 1981-82; dir. sales and mktg. John Anselmo Design Assocs., Santa Monica, Calif., 1982-83, owner O'Mara-Seitz Design Group, Santa Monica, 1983-87; mktg. cons., 1987—; freelance copywriting, lectr. Mem. task force NOW, 1977; mem. Olympics Steering Com., Muscular Dystrophy Assn., 1979; mem. Superwalk Steering Com., March of Dimes, 1981. Mem. Los Angeles Ad Club, Nat. Assn. Female Execs., Internat. Assn. Bus. Communicators, Graphic Artists Guild, Mktg. Assn. Calif. Office: 2036 6th St Santa Monica CA 90405

SEKEBA, DRAKE SIMWOGERERE, newspaper editor; b. Kampala, Uganda, Oct. 3, 1944; s. Nehemia Semakula Batume and Eriosi (Kabejja) Numagaanyi; m. Margaret Nakayiza, May 12, 1973; children: Monica, Linda, Miranda, Amanda. Trainee reporter Sekanyolya newspaper, Kampala, 1965-66; account exec. Uganda Outdoor Advt. Ltd., Kampala, 1968-70; sub-editor The People Newspaper Ltd., Kampala, 1970-72; account exec. Publicity Services Ltd., Kampala, 1972-74; editor The Star newspaper, Kampala, 1981—; bd. dirs. Shield Publs., Kampala. Lodge: Rotary. Home: Lukuci-Makindye, Kampala Uganda Office: The Star/Ngabo Newspapers, POB 9362, Kampala Uganda also: PO Box 1708, Kampala Uganda

SEKELJ, LASLO IMRE, sociologist; b. Subotica, Yugoslavia, Aug. 4, 1949; s. Imre Aron and Maria Imre (Löbl) S. BA in Polit. Sci., U. Belgrad, Yugoslavia, 1972, BA in Philosophy, 1974; MA in Sociology, U. Zagreb, Yugoslavia, 1977, PhD in Sociology, 1984. Asst. Inst. Labour Movement, Belgrad, Yugoslavia, 1974-76; asst. prof. Faculty of Law, Novi Sad, 1977-85; chief researcher U. Belgrad Ctr. Philosophy and Social Theory, Yugoslavia, 1985—. Author: Anarchism, 1982, 87, Communism and State, 1988; editor: Criticism of Bolshevism, 1987, Social Movements and Political System in Hungary. Mem. Yugoslav Sociol. Assn., Internat. Sociol. Assn., World Future Studies Fedn., Internat. Communal Studies Assn. Office: U Beograd Ctr Philosophy and Social Theory, 11000 Narodnog Fronta 45 Yugoslavia

SEKIGUCHI, TAIJI, engineer; b. Tokyo, Apr. 13, 1931; s. Toyozo and Hideko (Ichiba) S.; m. Midori Okura, Mar. 30, 1958; children: Atsuko, Seiichiro. B in Engring., Tokyo U., 1954. Chief platemaking Tosho Printing Co., Ltd., Numazu, Japan, 1959-64; chief of tech. devel. Tosho Printing Co., Ltd., Tokyo, 1964-70; mgr. system engring Sha-ken Co., Ltd., Tokyo, 1970-75, chief tech. coordinator, 1975—. Author (with others): The Japanese Character, 1985. Mem. Japanese Soc. Printing Sci. and Tech., Info. Processing Soc. Japan. Home: 7-33-2, Negishidai, 351 Asaka, Saitama Japan Office: Sha-ken Co Ltd, 2-26-13, Minamiotsuka, 170 Toshima-ku, Tokyo Japan

SEKIGUCHI, YOSHI, graphic designer, visual communicator; b. Yokosuka, Japan, Apr. 15, 1931; came to U.S., 1964; s. Tatsuji and Ume (Fukuda) S.; diploma with honors, Tamagawa Comml. Art Coll., 1953; postgrad. Art Inst. Chgo., 1965-66; m. Yoshiko Nakajima, Dec. 19, 1959; children—Risa, Chika, Juri. Art. dir. Staff, Inc., Tokyo, 1955-64, Medalist Publs., Chgo., 1964-65; asst. prodn. dir. Nobart, Inc., Chgo., 1965-69; art dir. Cahners Pub. Co., Chgo., 1969-71, Playboy Clubs Internat., Chgo., 1971-75; pres., owner Rising Sun Design, Design I, Build Your Own Legend, Ltd., SOHZOH Creations Ltd., Highland Park, Ill., 1975—; cons. graphic dir. Conflict Resolution Movement. Recipient Internat. Calendar Design award, 1964; Nat. Christmas Seal design award, 1967; Jesse H. Neal Editorial Achievement awards, 1970, 80; Soc. Publ. Designers ann. awards, 1971, 72; Communication Art Mag. ann. award 1975, 81; N.Y. One Show award, 1976; Type Dirs. Club ann. awards, 1976, 77; N.Y. Art Dirs. Club ann. award, 1978, 82. Mem. Artists Guild Chgo., Japanese C. of C. and Industry Chgo. Author: Inside Design, Japanese and English edits. contbr. articles to U.S. and Japanese profl. jours. Home and Office: 437 Marshman St Highland Park IL 60035

SEKIMOTO, TADASHIRO, electronics company executive; b. Kobe, Japan, Nov. 14, 1926; s. Taichiro and Tomi (Katayama) S.; B.S. in Physics, U. Tokyo, 1948, D.Engring., 1962; m. Mayako Mori, Apr. 16, 1956; children: Masakazu, Sumito, Misako. With Nippon Electric Co., Ltd., 1948-65, 67—, dir., 1974—, assoc. sr. v.p., then sr. v.p., 1974-78, exec. v.p., 1978-80, pres., 1980—, also acting dir. subsidiaries; mgr. communications process lab. COMSAT, 1965-67; vice chmn. Japan Assn. Corp. Execs.; chmn. Space Activities Promotion Council, New Bus. Conf. Recipient Japanese Govt. prize, 1976. Fellow IEEE; mem. Inst Electronics and Communications Engrs. Japan, Inst. Elec. Engrs. Japan, Acoustical Soc. Japan, Info. Processing Soc. Japan, Ops. Research Soc. Japan. Buddhist. Author, patentee in field. Home: 14-9 Nishikata 2-chome, Bunkyo-ku, Tokyo 113 Japan Office: NEC Corp, 33-1 Shiba, 5-Chome, Minato-ku, Tokyo 108 Japan *

SEKINE, SHIGERU, chemical company executive; b. Tokyo, Dec. 15, 1948; s. Masami Sekine and Kazuko Odashima; m. Toshiko Shibano. BA, Aoyamagakuin U., Tokyo, 1971; Diploma, Keio U. Bus. Sch., Tokyo, 1972; MA in Internat. Bus. Studies, U. S.C., 1977. Lending officer asst. Bank Am. NT & SA, Tokyo, 1972-75; pres. Nikko Chemicals Co. Ltd., Tokyo, 1977—. Home: 3-5-16-305 Shimachi Setagaya-Ku, 154 Tokyo Japan Office: Nikko Chemicals Co Ltd, 1-4-8 Bakurocho Nihon Bashi, 103 Tokyo Japan

SEKULA, EDWARD JOSEPH, JR., financial executive; b. Brandonville, Pa., Sept. 2, 1937; s. Edward Joseph and Dorothy May (Fritz) S.; B.S. in B.A., Pa. State U., 1961; m. Carol Lee Helton, July 13, 1963; 1 child, David. Dep. fin. officer Aberdeen Proving Ground, Md., 1961-63; with Peat, Marwick, Mitchell & Co., N.Y.C., 1963-77; corp. controller N.Y.C. Health & Hosp. Corp., 1977-78; dir. fin. Mt. Sinai Med. Center, N.Y.C., 1979-82; chief fin. officer Vis. Nurse Service N.Y., N.Y.C., 1982-86, Wallkill Valley Gen. Hosp., 1986—; sec.-treas. Planning Assistance Inc., N.Y.C., 1978—. Mem. parish council of deacons Abiding Peace Luth. Ch., 1972—; cubmaster, com. chmn., Webelos leader Cub Scouts Am., 1974-78; scoutmaster Troop 186, Boy Scouts Am., 1978-85, asst. dist. commr. ; vol. fireman Netcong Fire Co. 1, 1974—; co-treas. Lenape Valley Regional High Sch. Band Parents Assn., 1981-83. Served with U.S. Army, 1961-63; capt. Res. (ret.). Recipient Dist. Award of Merit, Boy Scouts Am. Mem. Hosp. Fin. Mgmt. Assn., Home Care Assn., Am. Inst. C.P.A.s, N.Y. Soc. C.P.A.s, Beta Alpha Psi, Phi Kappa Tau. Republican. Lutheran. Clubs: Muskanetcong Fishing, Trout Unltd., Rotary. Home: 39 Amendola Dr Netcong NJ 07857 Office: 20 Walnut St Sussex NJ 07461

SEKULIC, ANTE, educator; b. Tavankut/Subotica, Yugoslavia, Nov. 16, 1920; s. Sime and Julka (Pavlic) S.; Secondary Sch. degree U. Zagreb, 1945, Sc.D., 1947; m. Ruza Crnkovic, Aug. 24, 1954; 1 child, Ante. Secondary sch. tchr., 1946-67; dep. dir. secondary sch., Delnice, Yugoslavia, 1959-66; prof., chmn. dept. Slavic langs. Rijeka U., 1969-72; author, lectr., cons., 1972—; author: Zvona bjeline, 1947; Hrvatski realizam, 1957; Knjizevnost backih Hrvata, 1970; Drevni Bac, 1978; Tragom franj. ljetopisa u Suboticí, 1978; Narodni zivot i obicaji backih Bunjevaca, 1981, Marijanske pobožnosti podunavskih Hrvata, 1985, Remete, 1986, Bački Bunjevci i Šokci, 1988, others. Recipient award Matica suboticka, 1940. Mem. Philol. Soc. Croatia, Soc. Croatian Authors, also others. Home and Office: 133 Vlaska, 4100 Zagreb Yugoslavia

SELA, MICHAEL, immunologist, chemist; b. Tomaszow, Poland, Mar. 6, 1924; came to Israel, 1941; s. Jakob and Roza (Aleskowski) Salomonowicz; m. Sara Kika, Nov. 25, 1976; 1 child, Tamar; m. Margalit Liebmann, June 20, 1948 (dec. Jan. 1975); children—Irit, Orlee. Grad. Ecole de Chimie, U. Geneva, 1947; M.Sc., Hebrew U., Jerusalem, 1946, Ph.D., 1954; Doctor honoris causa, U. Bordeaux II, 1985, National Autonomous U. Mex., 1985. Mem. faculty Weizmann Inst. Sci., 1950—, head dept. chem. immunology, 1963-75, v.p., 1970-71, dean faculty biology, 1970-73, bd. govs., 1970—, pres., 1975-85, dep. chmn. bd. govs., 1985—; W. Garfield Weston prof. immunology, inst. prof., 1985; vis. scientist NIH, Bethesda, Md., 1956-57, 60-61; vis. prof. molecular biology U. Calif., Berkeley, 1967-68, dept. medicine Tufts U., Boston, 1986-87, dept. biology MIT, Cambridge, Mass., 1986-87, vis. prof. pathology faculty of medicine, Harvard U., Cambridge, 1986-87; scholar-in-residence Fogarty Internat. Ctr., Bethesda, 1973-74; pres. Internat. Union Immunol. Socs., 1977-80; chmn. sci. adv. com. European Molecular Biology Lab., 1978-81; chmn. Council European Molecular Biology Orgn., until 1979; mem. adv. com. on med. research WHO, also spl. program for research and tng. in tropical diseases, 1979-81; mem. council Paul Ehrlich Found., Frankfurt, 1980—, adv. bd. Tables Rondes Roussel UCLAF, France, 1980—; mem. sci. com. bd. Institut Scientific Roussel Italia; mem. external rev. com. U.S.-Israel Binat. Agrl. Research and Devel. Fund, 1987; mem. intern guidance panel Israel Inst. for Gifted Children, 1987; mem. scientific counsel Internat. Inst. Cellular and Molecular Pathology, Brussels, 1980-83. Recipient numerous awards including Israel prize in natural scis., 1959; Rothschild prize in chemistry, 1968; Emil von Behring prize, 1973, Otto Warburg medal German Soc. Biol. Chemistry, 1968, Gairdner Found. internat. award 1980, prix de l'Institut de la Vie, 1984, prix Jaubert, Faculty of Sci., Univ. Geneva, 1986, Comdr.'s Cross of Order of Merit award Fed. Republic Germany, 1986, l'Ordre de la Legion d'Honneur, France, 1987. Mem. Max Planck Soc. (fgn.), Am. Acad. Arts and Scis. (fgn. hon.), Israel acad. Scis. and Humanities, Pontifical Acad. Scis., Nat. Acad. Scis. U.S. (fgn. assoc.), Am. Soc. Biol. Chemists (hon.), Scandinavian Soc. Immunology (hon.), Am. Assn. Immunologists (hon.), French Soc. Immunology (hon.), Chilean Soc. Immunology, Internat. Council Scientific Unions (nat.). Editor: The Antigens, 6 vols.; mem. editorial bds. including European Jour. Immunology, Asian Pacific Jour. Allergy and Immunology, Exptl. and Clin. Immunogenetics, Critical Revs. Biochemistry, Receptor Biology Revs., Handbook of Biochemistry and Molecular Biology, The FASEB Jour., Encyclopedia of Human Biology; contbr. over 500 articles to profl. jours. Office: Weizman Inst of Sci, PO Box 26, Rehovot Israel

SELBERG, INGRID MARIA, publisher; b. Princeton, N.J., Mar. 13, 1950; d. Atle and Hedvig (Liebermann) S. BA, Columbia U.l, N.Y.C., 1971. Editor Collins Pub., London, 1978-84; editorial dir. Bantam UK, London, 1984-85; pub. William Heinemann, London, 1986—; also pub. Methven Children's Books, London. Author: Trees and Leaves, 1977, Our Changing World, 1981, Our Hidden World, 1983. Office: Heinemann Young Books, Michelin House 81 Fulham Rd, London SW3 6RB, England

SELBERHERR, SIEGFRIED, microelectronics educator, researcher, consultant; b. Klosterneuburg, Austria; Aug. 3, 1955; s. Johannes and Josefine (Henninger) S.; m. Margit Leonhard, Oct. 12, 1979; children—Andreas, Julia. Dipl. Ing. Tech. U., Vienna, Austria, 1978, Dr. techn., 1981, venia docendi, 1984. Research assoc. Tech. U. Vienna, 1978-79, asst. prof. microelectronics, 1979-84, prof. computer-aided design, 1984-88, dean microelectronics, 1988—; cons. to bus. and industry. Author: Analysis and simulation of Semicondr. Devices, 1984. Editor: Jour. Transactions of the Soc. for Computer Simulation, 1983—, Jour. Electrosoft, 1986—, Jour. Mikroelektronik, 1988; book series Computational Microelectronics, 1985—. Contbr. articles to profl. jours. Recipient Dr. Ernst Fehrer award Tech. U. Vienna, 1983, Heinz Zemanek award, 1988, Dr. Herta Firnberg Fed. award. Mem. IEEE (sr.), Assn. Computing Machinery, Soc. Indsl. and Applied Math., Nachrichtentechnische Gesellschaft (award 1985). Home: Fasanstrasse 1, A 3430 Tullh Austria Office: Tech U Vienna, Gusshausstrasse 27-29, A 1040 Vienna Austria

SELBY, MICHAEL DAVID, financial and business consultant; b. Rochester, N.Y., May 11, 1954; s. Bernard and Norine (Chatman) S.; m. Windrati Pramono, Nov. 15, 1977; children: Jaclyn, Elizabeth. BA in Polit. Sci., George Washington U., 1973, MA in Internat. Relations, 1974. Mgr. internat. projects group Sci. Radio Systems, Rochester, 1974-76; fin. advisor ANTARA (Indonesian Nat. Press Agy.), Jakarta, Indonesia, 1977-82; mng. ptnr. Bus. Adv. Group, Jakarta and Singapore, 1983—; fin., project adv. to minister, Ministry Def., Jakarta, 1976-78; fin. advisor to v.p. of Indonesia, 1976-79, Directorate Gen. Tourism, Jakarta, 1976-80; advisor Directorate Gen. Domestic Monetary Affairs, Indonesia, 1980-85; bd dirs. Airfast Indonesian Airlines, Internat. Capital Corp. Bank Ltd., Siam Citizens Leasing Ltd., Bangkok, Siam Motors Corp., Bangkok. Author: Financial Development of the Indonesian Tobacco Industry, 1981; contbr. articles on credit analysis and debt. restructuring to profl. publs. Nat. Merit scholar, 1970. Mem. Am. C. of C., Young Pres. Orgn. Clubs: American (Jakarta); Royal Bangkok Sport. Office: Bus Adv Group, Kuningan Plaza Suite 34, North Tower J1 HR Rasuna, Said C11-14, Jakarta Indonesia

SELDEN, RAMAN, English literature educator; b. London, Dec. 31, 1937; s. Atma Chuharmal and Phyllis Ruby (Planten) Ramchandani; m. Margaret Jane Twemlow, 1978; children from previous marriage: Paul Daniel, William Matthew. BA in Classics, Univ. Coll., London, 1960; BA in English, Birkbeck Coll., London, 1965, PhD, 1971. Lectr. Portsmouth Poly., Hampshire County, Eng., 1965-71; from lectr. to sr. lectr. Durham (Eng.) U., 1972-85; prof. English Lancaster U., Lancashire, Eng., 1986—. Author: English Verse Satire, 1978, Criticism and Objectivity, 1984, A Reader's Guide to Contemporary Literary Theory, 1985, Dryden's Absalom and Achitophel, 1986; co-editor: The Poems of John Oldham, 1987, The Theory of Criticism...A Reader, 1988; mem. editorial bd. 17th Century, 1986—; joint editor Longman 'Critical Reader' Series. Office: Lancaster U, English Dept Bowland Coll, Lancaster LA1 4YT, England

SELDITCH, ALAN DANIEL, industrial engineer; b. Phila., Sept. 8, 1926; s. Jacob and Sarah Molly (Simons) S.; m. Betty Elaine Simpson, Sept. 29, 1974 (div. 1982); children—Gretchen, Edward, Michael, Ronald, Kimberly. Student St. Lawrence U., 1944-46; B.S., U. So. Calif., 1948; postgrad. Los Angeles City Coll., LaSalle U.; M.S., Heed U., 1979, Ph.D., 1982. Registered profl. engr., Calif., Environ. Assessor, Calif.; cert. profl. methods engr. Chief projects and engring., pres. Sigma Assocs., Los Angeles, 1950-57; chief indsl. and project engr. Semco, Sweet & Mayers, Los Angeles, 1957-61; mgr. indsl. engring. and plant maintenance Rexall Drug & Chem. Co., 1962-65; regional cons. mgr. H.B. Maynard & Co., Sherman Oaks, Calif., 1965-69; asst. to pres. P.O.P. Systems/ISI, Santa Ana, Calif., 1970-72; mgr. facilities and corp. planning Systems Resource Recovery/System Assos., Long Beach, Calif., 1972-75; gen. mgr. Flowtrace, Los Angeles, 1975-79; mgr. energy/environ. Signetics, Sunnyvale, Calif., 1977-83; pres. A.D. Selditch & Assos., San Jose, Calif., 1977—. Contbr. articles to profl. jours. Served with USNR, 1944-46. Maynard Research Inst., 1969. Mem. AAAS, Am. Inst. Indsl. Engrs., Am. Public Works Assn., Am. Soc. Mgmt., ASME, Am. Soc. Metals, Am. Soc. Standards, Assn. Energy Engrs., Calif. Soc. Profl. Engrs., Govtl. Refuse Collection and Disposal Assn., Internat. Material Mgmt. Soc. (cert. in material mgmt. and handling), IEEE, Inst. Solid Wastes, Los Angeles Forum Solid Waste Mgmt., Mgmt. Inst. Los Angeles, Methods, Time-Measurement Assn. for Standards and Research (cert.), Nat. Assn. Solid Waste Mgmt., Nat. Soc. Profl. Engrs. Republican. Jewish. Home and Office: 6267 #E Joaquin Murieta Newark CA 94560

SELF, JAMES MAURICE, research chemist, consultant; b. Syracuse, Mo., Aug. 4, 1937; s. James Francis and Opal Irene (Lusk) S.; m. Penny Love Boggs (div. Feb. 1974); children—Pamela, James E., Deborah; m. Lynda Hall, Dec. 11, 1979; 1 stepchild, Johhnna. B.S., Central Mo. State U., 1959; M.S., Ph.D., Oreg. State U., 1964. Sales research chemist E.I. duPont de Nemours, Wilmington, Del., 1966-72; research fellow Mellon Inst., Pitts., 1972-76; tech. dir. Tanner Chem. Co., Greenville, S.C., 1976-82; cons. ABCO Industries, Spartanburg, S.C., 1983-84, research chemist, 1984—; cons. Southeastern Chem., Lenoir, N.C., 1983-84. Contbr. articles to profl. publs. Patentee in field. Officer, Wilmington Civic Assn., 1968-72; mem. dist. com. Boy Scouts Am., 1969-72; pres. local PTA, Wilmington, 1967-72, Pitts., 1972-75; coach Pebble Creek Swim Club, 1976-79. Mem. Am. Chem. Soc., Research Soc. Am., Soc. Plastics Industry. Democrat. Baptist. Current work: Polymerization catalyst, polymer extension and forming, coupling agents for polymer reinforcements. Subspecialties: Composite materials; Inorganic chemistry.

SELF, JOSEPH MORRISON, investment banker; b. Clinton County, Pa., Apr. 23, 1929; s. Luther Esther and Annie (Bettini) S.; m. Anne Gore-Browne Higgins, Oct. 21, 1961; children—John Higgins, Elizabeth Laird, Paul Schoolfield. A.B., Duke U., 1953; M.B.A., Columbia U., 1959. Chartered fin. analyst. Vice pres. Union Service Corp., N.Y.C., 1959-69, Morgan Stanley & Co., N.Y.C., 1969-76; mng. dir. Wm Sword & Co., Inc., Princeton, N.J., 1976—. Mem. investment adv. commn. Diocese of N.J., Trenton, 1981-87; warden St. John on Mountain, Bernardsville, N.J., 1977-79, vestry, 1964-75; trustee Peck Sch., Morristown, N.J., 1973-79; assoc. vestry St. Bartholomew's Ch., N.Y.C., 1963-65. Served to lt. col., USMCR 1951-73, active duty 1953-57. Mem. Inst. Chartered Fin. Analysts. Republican. Episcopalian. Clubs: Somerset Hills Country (Bernardsville); Univ. (N.Y.C.). Home: Post Rd Bernardsville NJ 07924 Office: Wm Sword & Co Inc 22 Chambers St Princeton NJ 08542

SELFRIDGE, CALVIN, lawyer; b. Evanston, Ill., Dec. 20, 1933; s. Calvin Frederick and Violet Luella (Bradley) S. BA, Northwestern U., 1956; JD, U. Chgo., 1960. Admitted to Ill. bar, 1961; trust officer Continental Ill. Nat. Bank & Trust Co. Chgo., 1961-71; individual practice law, Chgo., 1972-76; mem. firm Howington, Elworth, Osswald & Hough, Chgo., 1976-79; individual practice law, 1979—; pres., dir. Des Plaines Pub. Co., Northwest Newspapers Corp. Pres., bd. dirs. Scholarship Fund Found., 1965—; trustee Lawrence Hall Sch. for Boys, 1982—; mem. Soc. Colonial Wars. Served with AUS, 1959. Mem. Chgo., Am., Ill. bar assns., Law Club Chgo., Legal Club Chgo., Chi Psi, Phi Delta Phi. Republican. Congregationalist. Clubs: Attic (gov., sec., pres.), Univ. Racquet (Chgo.); Balboa (Mazatlan, Mexico); Indian Hill Country (Winnetka, Ill.). Home: 1320 N State Pkwy Chicago IL 60610 Office: 135 S LaSalle St Suite 2120 Chicago IL 60603

SELIG, DANIEL ALFRED, allergist; b. Colmar, Alsace, France, May 15, 1942; s. Alfred Michel and Marguerite (Hilfiger) S.; m. Françoise Haumesser, Dec. 1, 1967; 1 child, Catherine. MD, U. Strasbourg, 1975, Diploma Allergology, 1975. Practice medicine specializing in allergies Colmar, 1976—. Home: 17 Rue Wilson, 68000 Colmar France Office: 11 Rue des Bains, 68000 Colmar France

SELIG, KARL-LUDWIG, educator; b. Wiesbaden, Germany, Aug. 14, 1926; naturalized, 1948; s. Lucian and Erna (Reiss) S. B.A., Ohio State U., 1946, M.A., 1947; postgrad., U. Rome, Italy, 1949-50; Ph.D., U. Tex., 1955. Asst. prof. Romance langs. and lit. Johns Hopkins U., Balt., 1954-58; assoc. prof. U. N.C., Chapel Hill, 1958-61, U. Minn., Mpls., 1961-63; vis. prof. U. Tex., Austin, 1963-64, prof. Romance langs. and lit., 1964-65; Hinchliff prof. Spanish lit. Cornell U., Ithaca, N.Y., 1965-69; dir. grad. studies in Romance lit. Cornell U., Ithaca, 1966-69; prof. Spanish lit. Columbia U., N.Y.C., 1969—; vis. prof. U. Munich, Germany, 1963, 64, U. Berlin, Germany, 1967; cons. prof. Ohio State U., Columbus, 1967-69; vis. lectr. U. Zulia, Maracaibo, Venezuela, 1968; dir. summer seminar NEH, 1975, cons., 1975-77; vis. scholar Ga. U. System, 1977; vis. research scholar Fondation Hardt, Vandoeuvres, Switzerland, 1959; mem. com. grants-in-aid Am. Council Learned Socs., 1969-73; chmn. Comparative Lit. Program and Colloquia, Columbia Coll., 1974-88. Author: The Library of Vincencio Juan de Lastanosa, Patron of Gracián, Geneva, 1960, also numerous articles, revs.; editor: (Thomas Blundeville) of Councils and Counselors, 1963, (with A. G. Hatcher) Studia Philologica et Litteraria in Honorem L. Spitzer, 1958, (with J. E. Keller) Essays in Honor of N. B. Adams, 1966, (with R. Brinkmann) Theatrum Europaeum. Festschrift E. M. Szarota, 1982, (with S. Neumeister) Theatrum Mundi Hispanicum, 1986, (with R. Somerville) Florilegium Columbianum: Essays in Honor of Paul Oskar Kristeller, 1987; assoc. editor Modern Lang. Notes, 1955-58; mng. editor Romance Notes, 1959-61; editor: U. N.C. Studies in Comparative Lit, 1959-61, Bull. Comediantes, 1959-64, assoc. editor 1964-68, 79—; co-editor Yearbook of Comparative Lit., Vol. IX, 1960; editorial bd. Colección Támesis, London, 1962-79, Romanic Rev., 1969—, Teaching Lang. Through Lit, 1978—; assoc. editor Hispania, 1969-74, Ky. Romance Quar, 1973-85; gen. editor Revista Hispánica Moderna, 1971-86; mem. nat. adv. bd. MLA Internat. Bibliography, 1978—; editorial bd. Yale Italian Studies, 1976-80. Recipient Mark Van Doren award Columbia, 1974; fellow Fulbright Found., Rome, 1949-50, Newberry Library, 1958, Folger Shakespeare Library, 1959, 63, Belgian Am. Ednl. Found., 1961-62, Mediaeval and Renaissance Inst. Duke U., 1978; Fulbright research scholar Utrecht, The Netherlands, 1958-59; vis. research scholar Herzog August Bibliothek Wolfenbüttel, Fed. Republic Germany, 1979—. Mem. MLA (sec., then chmn. Romance sect. 1965-66, chmn. comparative lit. 1973), Am. Friends of Herzog August Bibliothek (bd. dirs.), Internat. Assn. Hispanists, Am. Comparative Lit. Assn., Coll. Art Assn., Acad. Lit. Studies, Phi Beta Kappa (hon.). Home: 30 E 37th St New York NY 10016

SELIG, LEON MORANGE, educator; b. New Rochelle, N.Y., Apr. 19, 1933; arrived in France, 1987; s. Ivan and mary Marguerite (Morange) S.; m. Marion Frances Joubin, Sept. 9, 1961 (div. 1974); children: Marea Liane, David Francis. BA, Wesleyan U., 1955; MBA, INSEAD, Fontainebleau, France, 1962; cert., Inst. d'Etudes Politiques, Paris, 1976; postgrad., U. Lyon (France) III, 1986—. Asst. to pres. interstate div. Burlington Industries, N.Y.C., 1955-61; fgn. service officer U.S. Dept. State, Washington, 1961-63; pres., gen. mgr. Patrons et Periodiques Internat. S.A., Paris, 1964-71; gen. mgr. Jayfran Enterprises Ltd., Toronto, Ont., Can., 1971-73; v.p., mgr. Internat. Flavors & Fragrances S.A., Paris, 1974-76; dir. internat. relations Mayor's Office N.Y.C., 1976-78; assoc. dean, prof. Pace U., N.Y.C., 1978—; vis. prof. Group Ecole Supérieure de Commerce de Lyon, 1987; dir. exec. edn. INSEAD, Fontainebleau, 1987—; v.p., bd. dirs. Selgreen Found., N.Y.C., 1975—; bd. dirs. Inst. Can.-U.S. Bus. Studies, N.Y.C., Inst. Brazilian Am. Bus. Studies, N.Y.C. Served to capt. U.S. Army, 1957-59. Mem. Fin. Women's Assn. N.Y., Women's World Banking N.Y. (mktg. research com.). Clubs: Polo, Automobile, Cercle de l'Union Interalliée, Maxim's Bus. (Paris). Office: INSEAD, 77305 Fontainebleau Cedex, France

SELIG, OURY LEVY, port financial consultant; b. Galveston, Tex., Sept. 24, 1924; s. Andrew Lionel and Freda (Schreiber) S.; m. Miriam Claire Pozmantier, Aug. 22, 1948; children: Michael, Debra, Madeline, James. BBA, U. Tex., 1949, postgrad., 1950; postgrad., U. Houston, 1953-56. Asst. bus. adminstr. of hosp. U. Tex. Med. Br., Galveston, 1952-54; acct. Port of Galveston, 1954-57, asst. auditor, 1957-64, asst. to gen. mgr., 1964-69, dir. fin. and adminstrn., 1966-74, dep. exec. dir., 1974-88. Exec. bd. Bay Area council Boy Scouts Am., Galveston, 1963—; bd. dirs. Galveston County Jewish Welfare Assn., 1982-84. Served as sgt. USAF, 1943-46. Recipient Nehemiah Gitelson award, Alpha Epsilon Pi, 1948, Silver Beaver award Boy Scouts Am., 1968, Shofar award, Boy Scouts Am., 1968, Disting. Service award, Galveston Jaycees, 1968. Mem. Am. Assn. Port Authorities (chmn. fin. com. 1972-76, chmn. risk mgmt. com. 1981-85, vice chmn. task force on tax reform 1985-86) Tex. Water Conservation Assn. (pres. 1979-80), Govt. Fin. Officers Assn., Risk and Ins. Mgmt. Assn., Pub. Risk and Ins. Mgmt. Assn., Gulf Intracoastal Canal Assn., Nat. Waterways Conf., Galveston Hist. Found., Sierra Club, Friar Soc. Democrat. Lodge: B'nai B'rith (pres. Tex. State Assn. 1960-61, local club 1958-59). Home and Office: 11 Colony Park Circle Galveston TX 77551

SELIGMAN, RAPHAEL DAVID, lawyer; b. Dublin, Ireland, Nov. 29, 1919; s. Ephraim and Esther (Wigoder) S.; B.A., Trinity Coll., U. Dublin, 1939, LL.B., 1940, M.A., 1960; m. Lorna Duke, Aug. 19, 1962; children—Arthur, Helene, Edgar. Admitted solicitor Supreme Ct. of Ireland, 1942; practiced in Dublin, 1942-57; internat. legal cons., Nassau, Bahamas, 1957-67; stipendiary magistrate, circuit justice, Nassau, 1962-67; admitted to Bahamas bar, 1967; of counsel firm Seligman, Maynard & Co., Nassau, 1967-86, Graham, Thompson & Co., 1986—; dir. Commodore Internat. Ltd., numerous Bahamian cos. Author (with Pine and Whoriskey) The Tax and Business Benefits of The Bahamas; contbr. articles to legal jours. Hon. consul gen. of Israel in Bahamas, 1974—. Fellow Inst. Dirs. (London); mem. Internat., Bahamas bar assns., Inc. Law Soc. Ireland. Lodge: Masons (33 deg., Supreme Council of Israel, dist. grand master Bahamas and Turks, Grand Lodge of Eng., past grand sr. deacon Grand Lodge of Ireland, mem. Mahi Shrine Miami); Clubs: Lyford Cay, Royal Nassau Sailing; Naval and Mil. Home: PO Box N7776, Lyford Cay, Nassau The Bahamas Office: Sassoon House, Shirley St PO Box N272, Nassau The Bahamas

SELIGSON, M. ROSS, psychologist; b. Balt., May 18, 1949; s. Joseph Jerome and Dorothy G. (Greenfeld) S. B.A., U. Md., 1971; Ed.M., Loyola Coll., Balt., 1975; Ph.D., Calif. Sch. Profl. Psychology, 1979. Lic. psychologist, Fla. Clin. psychology intern Long Beach (Calif.) Neuropsychiat. Inst. and Hosp., 1975-76, Orange Coast Coll. Student Health Ctr., Costa Mesa, Calif., 1976-77; psychology field trainee sect. on legal psychiatry UCLA, 1977-78; clin. psychologist Logansport (Ind.) State Hosp. (Isaac Ray Unit), 1978-80, South Fla. State Hosp., Hollywood, 1980-83, Counseling Affiliates, Inc., Ft. Lauderdale, 1981—; chmn. exec. com. Av-Med. Health Plan, Miami, 82 clin. dir. North Miami Community Mental Health Ctr.; AIDS educator to gen. public; staff writer Women's Issues, Ft. Lauderdale, 1982; mem. adj. faculty Barry U., 1982, Nova U., 1982-83; guest appearances include Factline, Selkirk TV Cable Sta., also radio programs. Contbr. articles to profl. jours. Mem. North Area Adv. Bd. of Regional Mental Health Team of Newport Beach, Costa Mesa and Irvine, Calif., 1976. Calif. Sch. Profl. Psychology scholar, 1976; recipient cert. of appreciation Am. Bus. Women's Assn., 1982. Mem. Wash. Area Counsel on Alcohol and Drug Abuse, Calif. Psychol. Assn., Am. Psychol. Assn., Fla. Psychol. Assn. (Broward County rep.), Fla. Assn. Practicing Psychologists, Broward County Psychol. Assn. (mem exec. com., pres., founder). Democrat. Jewish. Research on psychol. adjustment, social history factors and tng. performance measures as predictors of suicide prevention. Office: Counseling Affiliates Inc 2901 Stirling Rd Suite 200 Fort Lauderdale FL 33312

SELKIRK, KEITH EDWARD, mathematician; b. Wirral, Merseyside, Eng., Jan. 28, 1936; s. Cyril and Bertha Mabel (Jones) S.; m. Jennifer Anne Birch, July 29, 1961; children: Stephen, Katherine, Timothy. BA, Oxford U., Eng., 1960, MA, 1964; PhD, Nottingham U., Eng., 1984. Tchr. Bedford (Eng.) Sch., 1960-65; head dept. Croesyceiliog Grammar Sch., Cwmbran, Gwent, Eng., 1965-71; lectr. Nottingham (Eng.) U., 1971-86, sr. lectr., 1986—. Author: Pattern and Place, 1982, Teaching Mathematics, 1984; contbr. articles to profl. and scholarly jours. Named Fell Exhibitioner and Honorary Scholar Christ Ch., Oxford, 1958. Mem. Math. Assn., Assn. Tchrs. of Math., Assn. Univ. Math. Edn. Tchrs. (sec. 1978-81, chmn. 1982-85). Anglican. Home: 32 Moor Ln, Bunny NG11 6QX, England Office: Nottingham Univ, University Park, Nottingham NG7 2RD, England

SELL, ALAN PHILIP FREDERICK, theologian; b. Farncombe, Eng., Nov. 15, 1935; s. Arthur Philip and Freda Marion (Bushen) S.; m. Karen Elisabeth Lloyd, Aug. 1, 1959; children: Bridget Rebecca Karen, Judith Bronwen Amanda, Jonathan Patrick Alan. BA, U. Manchester, Eng., 1957, BD, 1959, MA, 1961; PhD, U. Nottingham, Eng., 1967; DD, Ursinus Coll., 1988. Ordained United Reformed Ch., 1959. Minister various Congl. Chs., Eng., 1959-68; lectr. West Midlands Coll. of Higher Edn., Eng., 1968-83; theological sec. World Alliance of Reformed Chs., Geneva, 1983-87; prof., chair Chrsitian Thought U. Calgary, Alta., Can., 1988—; sec. youth and edn. Worcestershire Congl. Chs., 1966-68; pres. Worcester and Dist. Free Ch. Fed. Council, 1966-67; chmn. West Midlands Provincial Dept. World Ch. and Mission, 1977-83; mem. Doctrine and Worship Com., United Reformed Ch., 1979-83; dir. tng. auxiliary ministry, 1980-83. Author: Alfred Dye, Minister of the Gospel, 1974, Robert Mackintosh: Theologian of Integrity, 1977, God Our Father, 1980, The Great Debate: Calvinism, Arminianism and Salvation, 1982, Church Planting: A Study of Westmorland Nonconformity, 1986, Theology in Turmoil: The Roots, Course and Significance of the Conservative-Liberal Debate in Modern Theology, 1986, Saints: Visible, Orderly and Catholic. The Congregational Idea of the Church, 1986, Defending and Declaring the Faith: Some Scottish Examples 1860-1920, 1987, The Philosophy of Religion 1875-1980, 1988, Christ, The Spirit and the Church, 1989; contbr. articles to profl. jours. Councillor Sedbergh Rural Dist. Council, Yorkshire, Eng., 1962-64. Recipient Gunning prize Victoria Inst., 1981. Fellow Royal Hist. Soc., Royal Soc. Arts, Soc. Antiquaries of London; mem. Soc. for the Study of Theology (mem. com. 1984-87), Soc. Tchrs. Speech and Drama, Brit. Fedn. Music Festivals (adjuicator). Office: U Calgary, Dept Religious Studies, 2500 University Dr NW, Calgary, AB Canada T2N 1N4

SELLARS, VICTOR CAROL GENE, lawyer; b. Dallas, Nov. 30, 1929; s. Rod and Vera (Arnold) S.; m. Barbara Brown, Aug. 28, 1954; 1 son, Glenn S. BBA, U. Tex., Austin, 1958; JD, Baylor U., 1961. Bar: Tex. 1961, U.S. Dist. Ct. (no. dist.) Tex. 1964. Ptnr., Sellars, Terry and Fuller, Dallas County, Tex., 1961-65; atty. advisor Fed. Nat. Mortgage Assn., Dallas, 1965-69, asst. regional counsel, 1969-73, regional counsel Southwestern region, 1973-79, ret., 1979; real estate, oil and gas investor, 1979—. Served to 1st lt. USAF, 1950-55; Korea. Mem. Tex. Bar Assn.

SELLECK, FREDERIC THOMPSON, chemical engineer; b. Loma Linda, Calif., June 7, 1924; s. Willard Martineau and Florence Elizabeth (Broderick) S.; m. Phyllis Mildred MacDowell, July 12, 1952; children—Pamela L. Selleck-Holderman, Jeffrey MacDowell. B.S. in Applied Chemistry, Calif. Inst. Tech., 1949. Research engr. Standard Perlite Corp., Pasadena, Calif., 1949-50; staff research asst. Chem Engring. Lab., Calif. Inst. Tech., Pasadena, 1950-53; sr. research engr. Fluor Corp., Whittier, Calif., 1953-60; supervising process engr. Fluor E & C, Inc., Los Angeles, 1960-82; dir. process methods and data Fluor Engrs., Inc., Irvine, Calif., 1982-87, cons. 1987—; pres., bd. chmn. Fluid Properties Research, Inc., Okla. State U., Stillwater, 1973-83; vis. lectr. U. So. Calif. and others. Author, editor (with others): API-RP37 Monograph II, 1955; 5 books, numerous papers; contbr. articles to profl. jours.; reviewer Jour. Chem. Engring., Data, Jour. Am. Inst. Chemical Engrs. Patentee process of separating acid gases from hydrocarbons. Served with U.S. Army, 1942-46, ETO. Mem. Am. Chem. Soc., Am. Inst. Chem. Engrs. (chmn. awards and honors com.), Inst. for Advancement in Engring. (outstanding engr. award 1986), Calif. Inst. Tech. Alumni Assn. (pres., bd. chmn.), Sigma Xi. Republican. Unitarian. Home: 14304 Bronte Dr Whittier CA 90602 Office: Fluor Engrs Inc Advanced Tech Div 3333 Michelson Dr Irvine CA 92730

SELLERS, GREGORY JUDE, physicist; b. Far Rockaway, N.Y., June 20, 1947; s. Douglas L. and Rita R. (Dieringer) S.; m. Lucia S. Kim, Nov. 26, 1983. A.B. in Physics, Cornell U., 1968, M.S., U. Ill., 1970, Ph.D., 1975. Sr. scientist B-K Dynamics, Inc., Rockville, Md., 1974-76; with Allied-Signal Corp., Morristown, N.J., 1976—, applications physicist, 1977—, product supr. amphenol fiber optic product, 1985—; dir. Thermo-Tek, Inc., Madison, N.J. Mem. AAAS, Am. Phys. Soc., IEEE. ESubspecialties: Fiber Optics; Polymers; Materials. Current work: Development and commercialization of fiber optic products; development of applications for polymeric materials and glassy metals in the electrical and electronics arena. Co-inventor adhesive bonding metallic glass, electromagnetic shielding, testing of thermal insulation, amorphous antipilferage marker, amorphous spring-shield. Home: 7S 515 Oak Trails Dr Naperville IL 60540 Office: Amphenol Fiber Optic Products 1925 Ohio St Lisle IL 60532

SELLMAN, WAYNE STEVEN, industrial psychologist; b. Texarkana, Tex., Aug. 30, 1940; s. Albert Clay and Irene Lois (Baird) S.; B.A., Tex. A&M U., 1962, M.A., 1963; Ph.D., Purdue U., 1968; diploma in nat. and internat. security, Harvard U., 1986; m. Elaine Elizabeth Seedle, June 1, 1963; children—Christine Lynn, Margaret Elaine. Commd. 2d lt., U.S. Air Force, 1962, advanced through grades to maj., 1974; research psychologist 3320th Retraining Group, Amarillo AFB, Tex., 1963-65; chief test rev. sect. Air Force Human Resources Lab., Lackland AFB, Tex., 1968-69; research psychologist Lowry AFB, Colo., 1969-72; exchange officer Royal Australian Air Force, Melbourne, 1972-74; chief Air Force personnel testing Air Force Mil. Personnel Center, Randolph AFB, Tex., 1974-78; ret., 1980; dir. testing Dept. Def., Washington, 1980-84, dir. accession policy, 1984—; lectr. St. Mary's U., San Antonio, Tex., 1968-69, Our Lady of Lake Coll., San Antonio, 1968-69, U. Colo., Boulder, 1970-71, Tex. Luth. Coll., Seguin, 1976-77. Mem. adv. com. Nat. Gen. Ednl. Devel. program, Washington, 1981-86. Recipient Cert. of Merit Dept. Def., 1975. Mem. Am. Psychol. Assn., Am. Ednl. Research Assn., Nat. Council Measurement in Edn., Phi Kappa Phi, Psi Chi, Phi Eta Sigma, Phi Delta Kappa. Methodist. Club: Masons. Contbr. articles to profl. publs. Home: 7511 Bellefield Ave Fort Washington MD 20744 Office: OASD (FM&P) The Pentagon Washington DC 20301

SELLS, HAROLD E., retail company executive; b. Ozark, Ark., 1928; married. Various operational, mktg. positions Kinney Shoe Corp., 1945-65, pres. Real Estate div., 1965-74; with F.W. Woolworth Co., N.Y.C., 1974—, v.p. real estate, 1974-80, sr. v.p. corp. devel., 1980-81, sr. v.p. internat. ops., property devel., 1982, pres., chief operating officer, 1983-87, chmn., chief exec. officer, 1987—, also bd. dirs.; bd. dirs. Bank of N.Y., Centennial Ins. Co., Atlantic Reins. Co.; trustee Atlantic Mut. Ins. Co. Office: FW Woolworth Co 233 Broadway New York NY 10279

SELLS, HAROLD ROBERT, petroleum engineer; b. Effingham, Kans., June 26, 1917; s. William H. and Bertha E. (McPhilimy) S.; m. Alice Plunkett Starbuck, June 25, 1978; 1 child, Jo Jo Starbuck. B.S. in Petroleum Engring., Kans. U., 1940; M.B.A., Columbia U., 1953. Registered profl. engr., Tex. Petroleum engr. Kerr-McGee Corp., Oklahoma City, 1940-42, Sohio Petroleum Corp., Oklahoma City, 1947-50; instr. Kans. U., Lawrence, 1946-47; cons. engr. Amstutz & Yates, Wichita, Kans., 1950-51; petroleum engr. Rockefeller Bros., N.Y.C., 1953-59; pres. Sells Cons. Services, N.Y.C., 1959-79; geothermal engr. San Diego Gas & Electric, 1979-87; ind. cons., Las Vegas, 1987— . Served to lt. comdr. USN, 1942-46. Bronfman fellow, 1952. Mem. NSPE, Soc. Petroleum Engrs. (tech. editor; sr. mem.), Am. Assn. Petroleum Geologists, Geothermal Resources Council, Tau Beta Pi, Sigma Tau, Beta Gamma Sigma, Kappa Sigma. Republican. Presbyterian. Lodges: Masons (32 deg.), Shriners, Elks. Home and Office: 5025 Pacific Grove Dr Las Vegas NV 89130

SELLS, SAUL B., research psychologist, educator, consultant; b. N.Y.C., Jan. 13, 1913; s. Maxwell I. and Dora B. S.; m. Helen Francis Roberts, July 2, 1939 (dec.). A.B., Bklyn. Coll., 1933; Ph.D., Columbia U., 1936; D.Sc. (hon.), Tex. Christian U., 1983. Research asst., instr. edn. research Tchrs. Coll., Columbia U., N.Y.C., 1934-36; instr. psychology Columbia U., N.Y.C., 1935-37; research assoc. Bd. Edn., N.Y.C., 1935-40; lectr. in psychology Grad. Sch., Bklyn. Coll., 1936-37; research analyst Pub. Work Reserve, Washington, 1940-41; chief statistician Office Price Adminstrn., Washington, 1941-46; asst. to pres. A.B. Frank Co., San Antonio, 1946-68; prof., head dept. med. psychology U.S. Air Force Sch. Aerospace Medicine, Randolph AFB, Tex., 1948-58, cons., 1959-62; adj. prof. Trinity U., San Antonio, 1949-55; vis. prof. U. Tex., Austin, 1950-51, Tex. A&M U., College Station, 1984—; prof. psychology Tex. Christian U., Fort Worth, 1958-62, research prof., dir. inst. behavioral research, 1962-83, research prof. emeritus, 1983—; pres. IBR Assocs., 1984—; cons. Nat. Ctr. Health Stats., Washington, 1965-70; mem. research career award com. Nat. Inst. Gen. Med. Sci., NIH, Washington; chmn. personality soc. U.S. Office Edn., Washington; research cons. Am., Eastern Pan Am., Trans World, Pan Am, U.S. Air, Fed. Express, COMAIR, other airlines, 1960—; cons.-reviewer VA, Washington, 1981—, NSF, Washington, 1975—, Can. Sci. Council, Ottawa, 1980-81; pres. Psychology Press, Inc., Brandon, Vt., 1963-68; cons. WHO, Geneva, Switzerland, 1976; mem. Gov.'s Council on Drug Abuse, Austin, Tex., 1980—; mem. adv. com. on research Div. Mental Health and Devel. Disorders, State of Ill., Chgo., 1981—; bd. dirs. Commodore Savs. Assn., Dallas. Cons. editor Psychol. Bull., 1955-58, Jour. Clin. Psychology, 1960—, Psychology in Schs., 1963—; editor Behavioral Research Monographs, 1962—; mng. editor, assoc. editor Multivariate Behavioral Research, 1966—. Chmn. Tarrant County Heart Assn., Fort Worth; mem. Bexar County Mental Health Assn., San Antonio. Recipient Commendation for Meritorious Civilian Service U.S. Air Force, 1955, Pace Setter award Nat. Inst. Drug Abuse, 1978, Appreciation award, Meritorious Service award Tex. Commn. Alcohol and Drug Abuse, 1986. Fellow Am. Psychol. Assn. (pres. mil. div. 1970), Aerospace Med. Assn. (Longacre award 1956), AAAS; mem. Am. Astronautical Soc. (sr.), Soc. Multivariate Exptl. Psychology (pres. 1964), Am. Ednl. Research Assn., Psychometric Soc., Am. Statis. Assn., Soc. Psychol. Study Social Issues, Southwestern Psychol. Assn. (pres.), Tex. Psychol. Assn. (pres.), Southwest Research Inst. Sigma Xi. Current work: Application of psychology to behavioral problems involving individual and organizational measurement, personnel selection, personality measurement, organizational climate, management strategies, drug and alcohol abuse, air traffic control, aviation space travel and related areas. Subspecialties: Behavioral psychology; Ecology (environmental science). Office: Tex Christian U 2800 University Blvd PO Box 32902 Fort Worth TX 76129

SELM, ROBERT PRICKETT, architectural engineer; b. Cin., Aug. 9, 1923; s. Frederick Oscar and Margery Marie (Prickett) S.; m. Rowena Imogene Brown, Nov. 25, 1945 (div. Jan. 1975); children: Rosalie C. Selm Pace, Linda R. Selm Partridge, Robert F., Michael E.; m. Janis Claire Broman, June 24, 1977. BS in Chem. Engring., U. Cin., 1949. Enlisted U.S. Army, 1943; advanced through grades to sgt. U.S. Army, CBI Marianas, 1943-46; commd. capt. U.S. Army, 1949, resigned, 1954; design engr. Wilson & Co., Salina, Kans., 1954-67, gen. ptnr., 1967-81, sr. ptnr., 1981—; ptnr. in charge Wilson Labs., Salina, Kans., 1956—, chmn. bd. dirs. Contbr. articles to profl. jours.; patentee in field. Named Engr. of Yr. Kans. Engring. Soc., Topeka, 1986. Fellow Am. Inst. Chem. Engrs.; mem. Am. Chem. Soc., NSPE (state chmn. environ. resource com.), Am. Water Works Assn., Water Pollution Control Fedn., Am. Acad. Environ. Engrs. (diplomate). Republican. Episcopalian. Clubs: Petroleum (Wichita, Kans.); Salina Country (pres. 1986). Lodges: Elks, Shriners. Home: 135 Mt Barbara Rd Salina KS 67401 Office: Wilson & Co 631 E Crawford Salina KS 67402-1640

SELTZER, JEFFREY LLOYD, lawyer, investment banker; b. Bklyn., July 27, 1956; s. Bernard and Sue (Harris) S.; m. Ana Isabel Sifre, Aug. 24, 1985; 1 child, Ian Alexander. BS in Econs. cum laude, U. Pa., 1978; JD, Georgetown U., 1981. Bar: N.Y. 1982. Assoc. Austrian, Lance & Stewart, N.Y.C., 1981-85; assoc. gen. counsel, asst. v.p. Shearson Lehman Bros. Inc. (now Shearson Lehman Hutton Inc.), N.Y.C., 1986; sr. v.p., dir. swap fin. adminstrn. Shearson Lehman Hutton Inc., N.Y.C., 1986—. Author: The U.S. Greeting Card Market, 1977, Starting and Organizing a Business, 1984, Swap Risk Management: A Primer, 1988. Mem. nat. adv. council U.S. Small Bus. Adminstrn., Washington, 1982-87; mem. small bus. adv. council Rep. Nat. Com., Washington, 1984—; advisor New Yorkers for Lew Lehrman, N.Y.C., 1981-82; policy analyst Reagan-Bush com., Arlington, Va., 1980. Named one of Outstanding Young Men Am., 1981, 87. Mem. ABA, Republican Nat. Lawyers Assn., Federalist Soc. Home: 45 W 60th St #21J New York NY 10023 Office: Shearson Lehman Hutton Inc Am Express Tower World Financial Ctr New York NY 10285-1200

SELTZER, VICKI LYNN, physician; b. N.Y.C., June 2, 1949; d. Herbert Melvin and Marian Elaine (Willinger) S.; m. Richard Stephen Brach, Sept. 2, 1973; children: Jessica Lillian, Eric Robert. BS, Rensselaer Poly. Inst., 1969; MD, NYU, 1973. Diplomate Am. Bd. Ob-Gyn, Intern, Bellevue Hosp., N.Y.C., 1973-74, resident in Ob-Gyn, 1974-77; fellow gynecol. cancer Am. Cancer Soc., N.Y.C., 1977-78, Meml. Sloan Kettering Cancer Ctr., N.Y.C., 1978-79; assoc. dir. gynecol. cancer Albert Einstein Coll. Medicine, N.Y.C., 1979-83; assoc. prof. Ob-Gyn, SUNY, Stony Brook, N.Y.C., 1983—; dir. Ob-Gyn, Queens Hosp. Ctr., Jamaica, N.Y., 1983—, pres. med. bd., 1986—. Author: Every Woman's Guide to Breast Cancer, 1987; mem. editorial bd. Women's Life mag., 1980-82; contbr. articles to profl. jours. Chmn. health com. Nat. Council Women, N.Y.C., 1979—; mem. Mayor Beame's Task Force on Rape, N.Y.C., 1974-76; bd. govs. Regional Council Women in Medicine, 1985—; chmn. Council on Resident Edn. in Ob-Gyn, 1987—. Galloway Fund fellow 1975; recipient citation Am. Med. Women's Assn., 1973, Nat. Safety Council, 1978, Achiever award Nat. council Women, 1985, Achiever award L.I. Ctr. Bus. and Profl. Women, 1987. Fellow N.Y. Obstet. Soc., Am. Coll. Ob-Gyn (gynecol. practice com. 1981); mem. Women's Med. Assn. (v.p. N.Y. 1974-79, editorial bd. jour. 1985—), Am. Med. Women's Assn. (com. chmn. 1975-77, 78-79, editorial bd. jour. 1986—), N.Y. Cancer Soc., NYU Med. Alumni Assn. (bd. govs. 1979—, v.p. 1987—), Alpha Omega Alpha. Office: OB Gyn Queens Hosp Ctr 82-68 164th St Jamaica NY 11432

SELWYN, SYDNEY, microbiology educator; b. Leeds, Eng., Nov. 7, 1934; s. Louis and Ruth (Skibben) S.; B.Sc., Edinburgh U., 1958, M.B. Ch.B., 1959, M.D., 1966; m. Flora Schmerling, July 14, 1957; children—Alan, Miriam, Barry, Jonathan. Resident physician Edinburgh City Hosp., 1959-60; research fellow med. microbiology Edinburgh U., 1957-58, lectr. clin. bacteriology, 1962-66; prof. bacteriology, med. cons. WHO, Baroda U., India, 1966-67; reader med. microbiology London U., 1967-79, prof. Charing Cross and Westminster Med. Sch., 1979—; cons. microbiologist Westminster Hosp., London, 1967—, Charing Cross Hosp., 1983—; adv. smallpox Brit. Dept. Health. Carnegie Trust fellow, 1960, Nat. Polio Fund fellow, 1961-62; recipient Wellcome Trust medal and prize, 1964; Peel Med. Research award, 1970. Fellow Royal Coll. Pathologists, Inst. Biology, Faculty of History and Philosophy of Medicine (pres.); mem. Assn. Clin. Pathologists, European Soc. Dermatol. Research, Brit. Soc. History of Medicine (hon. sec.), Harveian Soc. London (v.p.), Royal Soc. Medicine (v.p. pathology), Royal Instn. Gt. Brit., Worshipful Soc. Apothecaries London (Liveryman). Author: The Beta-lactam Antibiotics: Penicillins and Cephalosporins in Perspective, 1980; contbr. chpts. to med. books, articles to profl. jours. Home: 27 Brancaster Ln, Purley, Surrey CR2 1HJ, England Office: Charing Cross and Westminster Med Sch, Fulham Palace Rd, London W6 8RF, England

SELZER, ARTHUR, cardiologist, educator; b. Lwow, Poland, July 3, 1911; came to U.S., 1938, naturalized, 1943; s. Martin and Janina (Lam) S.; m. Jadwiga Winkler, July 31, 1936; children: Martin Arthur, Peter Michael. M.D., U. Cracow, 1936; postgrad., U. London, 1936-38. Intern Univ. Hosp. Lwow, 1935-36; vol. asst. Hammersmith Hosp., also Nat. Heart Hosp., London, 1936-38; practice medicine specializing in cardiology San Francisco, 1941-59, cons. in cardiology, 1959—; mem. faculty Stanford U. Med. Sch., 1941—, clin. prof. medicine, 1957-76, emeritus, 1976—; mem. faculty U. Calif. Med. Sch., San Francisco, 1960—, clin. prof. medicine, 1960—; mem. staff Presbyn. Hosp., San Francisco, 1959—, chief cardiology, 1959-84; chmn. San Francisco Community Chest Health Council, 1953-55. Author: The Heart: Its Functions in Health and Disease, 1965, Principles of Clinical Cardiology, 1975, 83; also articles. Fellow Am. Coll. Cardiology; master ACP; mem. Calif. Acad. Medicine (pres. 1972-73). Home: 5 Greenview Ln Hillsborough CA 94010 Office: Pacific Presbyn Med Ctr Clay and Buchanan Sts San Francisco CA 94115

SEMEDO, JULIO, Guinea-Bissau government official; b. Mansoa, Guinea-Bissau, Apr. 12, 1942; married; 1 daughter. Ambassador extraordinary, plenipotentiary permanent rep. to UN Guinea-Bissau, 1974-75, ambassador extraordinary, plenipotentiary to Portugal, 1975-78; dir. gen. Ministry Fgn. Affairs, 1978-80, sec. gen., 1980-81; counselor Supreme Tribunal of Justice, 1981; sec. gen. Council of Ministers, 1982-84; minister fgn. affairs Guinea-Bissau, 1984—; mem. cen. com. Partido Africano da Independencia da Guine e Cabo Verde, 1984—; mem. State Council, 1984—. Address: Ministry Fgn Affairs, Bissau Guinea-Bissau *

SEMELAS, ALFREDO ARROYO, construction company executive; b. Madrid, Oct. 2, 1921; s. Gabriel and Josefa (Arroyo) S.; m. Blanca Ledesma, Dec. 1, 1950; children: Eloisa, Gabriel, Ignacio, Blanca, Alfredo, José, Mercedes, Javier, Isabel, Jaime. French Bachelor, Janson de Sailly, Paris, 1939; Spanish Bachelor, Instituto San Isidro, Madrid, 1939; Civil Engr., Escuela de Caminos, Madrid, 1945; Scholarship, Del Amo Found., 1948; D.Engr., Escuela de Caminos, Madrid, 1960. Civil engr. Ministerio O.P., Madrid, 1948-50; mng. dir. Prepakt Ibérica SA, Madrid, 1950—; pres. Pilsa, Luxemburg, 1960—; dir. Los Remedios SA, Madrid, 1951—, Rheax Españ ola SA, Madrid, 1956—, Tagarral SA, Madrid, 1972—; pres. Previsa, Madrid, 1987—. Translator: Hydraulics (H. Rouse); contbr. articles in field to profl. jours.; patentee in field. Fellow ASCE (life); mem. Colegio Ingenieros Caminos, Instituto Ingenieros Civiles. Roman Catholic. Clubs: Club 24, Real Automovil (Madrid). Home: Av Pio XII 57, 28016 Madrid Spain Office: Previsa, Rafael Salgado 3, 28036 Madrid Spain

SEMERENA, PIERRE, automobile corporation executive; b. June 20, 1927; married; 3 children. D.Bus., Hautes Etudes Commmerciales, Paris, 1949. Various positions Renault, 1950-78; mgr. Renault Brazil, until 1978, dir. mktg. Latin Am., until 1978; mng. dir. Renault Spain, until 1978; v.p. Renault Internat. Automobile Div., 1978-80; v.p. planning and control Renault Automobile Ops., 1982; pres., chief exec. officer Renault Vehicules Industriels, 1982-84; chief exec. officer Renault Automobile Div., 1984-85; exec. v.p. Renault, 1985; dir. Am. Motors Corp., Southfield, Mich., 1980-82, chmn. bd., 1985—. Office: Am Motors Corp 27777 Franklin Rd Southfield MI 48034 *

SEMKOW, JERZY STANISLAW (GEORG), conductor; b. Radomsko, Poland, Oct. 12, 1928; came to U.S., 1975; s. Aleksander and Waleria (Sienczak) S. Student, U. Cracow, Poland, 1946-50; grad., Leningrad Mus. Conservatoire, USSR, 1951-55. Asst. condr. Leningrad Philharm. Orch., 1954-56, Bolshoi Opera and Ballet Theater, Moscow, 1956-58, artistic dir., prin. condr. Warsaw (Poland) Nat. Opera, 1959-62, permanent condr. Danish Royal Opera, Copenhagen, 1966-70, music dir., prin. condr. St. Louis Symphony Orch., 1975-79; music dir. Orchestra Sinfonica della RAI, Rome, 1979-82; artistic advisor, prin. condr. Rochester Philharm. Orch., 1985—; guest condr. Vienna Symphony Orch., Suisse Romande Orch., Orchestre de Paris, London Philharm., Madrid Symphony Orch., orchs. in Berlin, Milan, and others in U.S., including N.Y. Philharm., Boston Symphony, Chgo. Symphony, Cleve. Symphony Orch. and others; condr. at numerous festivals; 1st complete rendition of the original Mussorgsky version of opera Boris Godunov with Polish Nat. Radio and TV Orch., honored with 5 internat. awards. Decorated Great Order Commandoria Polonia Restituta; recipient Polish Radio award, 1965, Polish Nat. Radio and TV ann. Award of First Degree Deutschen Schallplatten Preis, Ger., Premio Discográfico Italiano Italy, Grand Prix des Discophiles France; Grammy award nomination for Best Opera Rec. Mem. Respighi Soc. Bologne (hon.). Address: care ICM Artists Ltd 40 W 57th St New York NY 10019 also: Rochester Philharm Orch 108 East Ave Rochester NY 14604 *

SEMLER, JERRY D., insurance company executive; b. Indpls., 1937; m. Rosemary Semler; children: Mary, Jack, Kristin, Kimberly, Michael, Jeffrey, Sally. B.S., Purdue U., 1958. CLU; registered health underwriter. With Am. United Life Ins. Co., Indpls., 1959—, pres., 1980-84, pres., chief operating officer, 1984—, dir. Bd. dirs. United Way Cen. Ind., Indpls. Conv. and Visitors Bur., Marion County Assn. for Retarded Citizens; chmn. bd. Ctr. for Leadership Devel. Inc.; mem. exec. com. Ind. Repertory Theatre; mem. Purdue U. Pres.'s Council, immediate past chmn.; mem. dean's adv. council Purdue U. Krannert Sch. Mgmt.; bd. dirs., past. pres., hon. chmn. "500" Festival Assocs., vice chmn. bd., 1986, chmn. bd., 1987; bd. dirs., past pres. Mus. Indian Heritage; bd. advisors Ind. Sch. Medicine. Served with U.S. Army. Mem. Health Ins. Assn. Am. (bd. dirs.), Am. Coll. Life Underwriters, Nat. Assn. Life Underwriters, Million Dollar Round Table (life), Ind. State C. of C., Alpha Tau Omega. Roman Catholic. Office: Am United Life Ins Co 1 American Sq PO Box 368 Indianapolis IN 46206

SEMONES, JAMES KING, sociology educator, human resource consultant, author; b. Bristol, Va., Nov. 10, 1948; s. James Hogue and Nelwyn (King) S.; m. Phyllis Kay Hicks, Apr. 20, 1968. BS, East Tenn. State U., 1971, MA, 1972; EdD, U. North Tex. (name formerly North Tex. State U.), 1983. Instr. sociology Jacksonville State U., Ala., 1972-74, El Paso Community Coll., Tex., 1975-81, San Jacinto Coll., Houston, 1984—; human resource cons. Xerox Corp., Am. Heart Assn.; tng. cons. Gibralter Savings, Irving, Tex., Pub. Service Co. Okla., Tulsa. Author: Introductory Sociology: A Core Text, 1977, Bruce Marshall: The Man and His Legacy, 1988; (with others) Key Issues in Higher Education and Society, 1983, Adult Education: Theory and Practice, 1984. Editor: (with others) Adult Learning and Program Development, 1983. Contbr. articles to profl. jours. and book chpts. Mem. Profl. Assn. Coll. Educators (pres. 1979-80), Tex. State Tchrs. Assn., NEA, So. Sociol. Soc., Am. Soc. Tng. and Devel., Phi Kappa Phi, Pi Gamma Mu, Alpha Kappa Delta, Phi Delta Kappa. Presbyterian. Avocations: antiques, art, photography, travel. Home: 7607 Heather Row Houston TX 77044 Office: San Jacinto Coll Div Social Behavioral Scis N Campus 5800 Uvalde Houston TX 77049-4589

SEMONIAN, ROBERT ALEXANDER, energy and lighting consultant; b. Boston, May 17, 1939; s. Leon Astor and Veron (Agojian) S. BBA, U. Miami, Fla., 1964. Editor The Miami Sunlight, 1962-64; adminstr. cost acctg. Raytheon Co., Bedford, Mass., 1964-68; acct. corp. staff L.F.E. Corp., Boston, 1968-70; cons. Watertown, Mass., 1970-73; mktg. rep. Cenebal Corp., Dedham, Mass., 1973-75; energy/lighting cons. No. Am. Philips Corp., Boston, 1975—; dir. Communications Engring. Inc., Cambridge, Mass., 1972—, Systems and Analytical Scis., Bedford, 1981—; advisor to newspaper The Impartial Observer, 1985. Exec. dir. Mass. Conservative Caucus, Marlborough, Mass., 1984—, membership chmn., 1984, program chmn., 1983; chmn. Watertown Rep. Town Com., Mass., 1980-88, advisor, 1972-88, vice chmn., 1968-72; trustee Cambridge Emergency Relief Trust, 1972—; treas. Reps. for Middlesex County, Weston, Mass., 1972—; treas. Armenian-Am. Rep. Club Mass., Watertown, 1972—, Conservation Commn., Watertown, 1966-69, treas. Reagan Dinner, Waltham, Mass., 1975, Boxborough, Mass., 1977; Mass. chmn. Nat. Conservative Alliance, Waterloo, Iowa, 1985—, Am. Freedom Coalition Mass., Peabody, 1987—; treas. Greater Boston Young Rep. Club, 1968, v.p., 1969-70; mem. exec. com. Mass. Reagan for Pres. Com., 1975-76, state nationalities chmn., 1979-80, state vice chmn., 1979-80, exec. com., 1979-80; del. Rep. Nat. Conv., Detroit, 1980, Dallas, 1984, New Orleans, 1988; mem. Watertown Town Mtg., 1965-75; state committeeman Mass. Rep. State Com., Boston, 1972-80, dep. chmn., 1972-80, heritage chmn., 1972-80, exec. com., 1972-80; del. Mass. Rep. Conv., 1972, 74, 78, 82, 86, chief page, 1974; Mass. state nationalities co-chmn. Reagan/Bush Com., Mass., 1980; Watertown chmn. Reagan/Bush Com., 1980, 84, State Legislators Conf., Scottsdale, Ariz., 1985, Washington, 1986, World Media Conf., 1986; Am. Leadership Conf., Washington; state chmn. Robertson for Pres., 1988; co-chmn. East Coast Conservative PAC, Marlborough, 1986—; mem. Appalachian Nat. Scenic Trail Commn., Harpers Ferry, W.Va., 1986—; dir. Watertown Better Govt. Assn., 1966—, World Info. Network/N.E. Team, Vernon. N.H., 1986—. Recipient Service award N.Am. Philips Corp., 1978; hon. Lt. Col. Aide-de-Camp in Ala. State Militia, 1986. Mem. Am. Policy Adv. Council (treas., exec. com. 1983—), Fed. Emergency Mgmt. Agy. (Nat. Def./Exec. Res. 1982—), U. Miami Alumni Assn., Armenian Students Assn. (nat. v.p. 1971-72, pres. Boston br. 1970-71, 77-78), Delta Sigma Pi. Mem. Armenian Apostolic Ch. Lodge: Masons. Avocation: politics. Home: 11 Howe St Watertown MA 02172

SEMPLE, MURIEL V., retired educator, civic worker; b. Bklyn., Aug. 22, 1915; d. Michael James and Jennie Anne (Maguire) Campion; m. Robert L. Semple, Apr. 19, 1944 (dec. 1977); children—Edmund Campion, Susan Jane, Robert Louis, Michael James Semple. B.A., St. Joseph's Coll., Bklyn., 1937; M.D.H., Columbia U., 1939; M.S. in Edn., New Paltz State Coll., N.Y., 1961. Cert. tchr. N.Y., dental hygienist N.Y., cert. tchr. Fla. Dental hygienist Raymond M. Bristol, DDS, N.Y.C., 1939-42; tchr. dental hygiene Elwood Schs., N.Y., 1957; elem. tchr. Huntington, Port Jefferson, Copiague Schs., N.Y., 1957-80; vol. Citizen Crime Watch, Boca Raton, Fla., 1983-88, Covenant House, Fort Lauderdale, Fla., 1985-88; vol., resource person in field. Sec., Maidstone Park Springs Civic Assn., East Hampton, N.Y., 1970-72, Boca Towne Centre Owners Assn., 1982-83; mem. St. Joan of Arc Ch., St. Joan of Arc Guild, 1984-88. Mem. Columbia U. Sch. Dentistry Alumni Assn., NEA, N.Y. State Tchrs. Assn.; mem. AAUW, S. Huntington PTA (Tchr. of Yr. 1980). Republican. Roman Catholic. Clubs: Royale Woman's (corresponding sec. 1988, editor newsletter 1985, rec. sec. 1986—, chmn. Irish sweepstakes Irish Country Fair, 1988) (Boca Raton), Boca Raton Garden, Boca Raton Hist. Soc.

SEN, AMARTYA KUMAR, economist; b. Santiniketan, India, Nov. 3, 1933; s. Ashutosh and Amita Sen; B.A., Calcutta U., 1953; B.A., Cambridge U., 1955, Ph.D., 1958; D.Litt. (hon.), U. Sask., 1979, Visva-Bharati U., 1983, U. Essex, 1984; D.Sc. (hon.), U. Bath, 1984. Prof. econs. Jadavpur U., Calcutta, 1956-58; fellow Trinity Coll., Cambridge U., 1957-63; prof. econs. Delhi U., 1963-71, London Sch. Econs., 1971-77; prof. econs. Oxford U., 1977-80, Drummond prof. polit. economy, 1980—; vis. prof. U. Calif., Berkeley, 1964-65; vis. prof. Harvard U., 1968-69, prof. econs. and philosophy, 1987—; Andrew D. White prof.-at-large Cornell U., Ithaca, N.Y., 1978-84; chmn. expert group role advanced skill and tech. UN, 1967; hon. fellow Inst. Social Studies, The Hague, Inst. Devel. Studies, U. Sussex, London Sch. Econs., U. London. Fellow Brit. Acad., Econometric Soc. (past pres.); fgn. hon. mem. Am. Acad. Arts and Scis.; mem. Am. Econ. Assn. (hon.), Indian Econ. Assn., Royal Econ. Soc. (council), Indian Econometric Conf., Devel. Studies Assn. (past pres.). Author: Choice of Techniques, 1960; Collective Choice and Social Welfare, 1970; Growth Economics, 1970; On Economic Inequality, 1973; Employment, Technology and Development, 1975; Poverty and Famines: An Essay on Entitlement and Deprivation, 1981; Utilitarianism and Beyond, 1982; Choice, Welfare and Measurement, 1982; Resources, Values and Development, 1984; Commodities and Capabilities, 1985, One Ethics and Economics, 1987, The Standard of Living, 1987; also articles. Home: 19 Lawford, London NW5 2LH, England Office: Harvard U Cambridge MA 02138 *

SEN, RATHINDRA NATH, professor, researcher; b. Calcutta, Bengal, India, Sept. 15, 1933; arrived in Israel, 1968; s. Upendra Nath and Mukul S.; m. Alice Gourevitch; children: Itay Arjun, Noa Mandovi. BS, Delhi (India) U., 1952, MA, 1954; PhD, Hebrew U., Jerusalem, 1963. Researcher U. Naples (Italy), 1963-66; research assoc. U. Wisc., Milwaukee, 1966-67; vis. asst. prof. U. Wisc., 1967-68; sr. lectr. Technion Israel Inst. of Tech., Haifa, 1968-72; vis. prof. U. Geneva, Switzerland, 1972-73, U. Goettingen, Fed. Republic of Germany, 1973-74; assoc. prof. Ben Gurion U., Beer Sheva, Israel, 1975—. Editor: Statistical Mechanics and Field Theory, 1972; contbr. numerous articles to profl. jours. Recipient Gauss Professorship Goettingen Acad. of Scis., 1984, 86. Mem. Am. Math. Soc., Internat. Assn. for Math. Physics. Home: Hebrew Sinai 1, Beer Sheva 84730, Israel Office: Ben Gurion U, PO Box 653, Beer Sheva 84105, Israel

SENDAX, VICTOR IRVEN, dentist, implant magnetics researcher; b. N.Y.C., Sept. 14, 1930; s. Maurice and Molly R. S.; m. Deborah deLand Cobb, Dec. 17, 1969 (div. June 1976); 1 dau., Jennifer Reiland; m. Marcia Ayer Pearson, Dec. 13, 1986. B.A., NYU, 1951, D.D.S., 1955; postgrad., Harvard U. Sch. Dental Medicine, 1969-72. Commr. N.Y. State Dental Service Corp., 1969-73; pres. BioDental Research Found., Inc., N.Y.C., 1975—, Victor I. Sendax, D.D.S., P.C., N.Y.C., 1972—, Sendax Dental Implant Magnetics Inc., 1985—; adj. assoc. prof. implant prosthodontics Columbia U. Sch. Dental and Oral Surgery, N.Y.C., 1974—; dental implant research adv. com. Nat. Inst. Dental Research, HHS; cons. Juilliard Sch. Voice and Drama, N.Y.C., 1972—, Vocal Dynamics Lab., Lenox Hill Hosp., N.Y.C., 1970—; founder Sendax Seminars on coated dental implants. Author: Magnetic Dental Implants, 1987; mem. editorial bd.: Oral Implantology, 1979—; patentee in field. Bd. dirs. City Ctr. Music and Drama, Inc. div. Lincoln Ctr. Performing Arts, N.Y.C., 1966-75; mem. adv. bd. Amagansett (N.Y.) Hist. Assn., 1969—; trustee Leukemia Soc. Am., N.Y.C., 1967; bd. dirs. Schola Cantorum, 1980—, Soc. Asian Music, 1965-76. Served to capt. Dental Corps USAF, 1955-57. Recipient Spl. Recognition Am. Fund Dental Health, 1981—. Fellow Am. Coll. Dentists, Internat. Coll. Dentists, Am. Acad. Implant Dentistry (pres. 1981); mem. ADA (ho. of dels. 1969), Am. Assn. Dental Schs. (chmn. spl. interest group implant prosthodontics), Acad. of Osseointegration, Royal Soc. Medicine Gt. Britain, Am. Prosthodontic Soc., Am. Equilibration Soc., Am. Analgesia Soc., Fedn. Dentaire Internat., Am. Assn. Dental Research (implant group), Internat. Assn. Dental Research, N.Y. Acad. Scis., Japan Soc., Sigma Epsilon Delta. Club: Players (N.Y.C.). Home: 70 E 77th St Apt 6A New York NY 10021 Office: Victor I Sendax DDS PC 30 Central Park S Suite 14B HA Dental Implant Condominium New York NY 10019

SENDJAJA, JOHANES ERWIN, machinery company executive; b. Surabaya, Jawa Timur, Indonesia, Oct. 28, 1947; s. Then Siong and Djioen Jin (Tan) Joeng; m. Juliani Sukowirjo, June 15, 1950; children: Sisca Damayanti, Hans William. Degree in Engring., Gajah Mada U., Yogyakarta, Indonesia, 1973. Sales exec. Carrier cen. dept. P.T. Mansyur Engring., Surabaya, Indonesia, 1973-74; sales mgr. tech. products P.T. Berca Indonesia/Sales Div., Surabaya, 1974-77; mng. dir., chief exec. officer P.T. Bukit Jaya Abadi Group, Surabaya, 1977—; bd. dirs. PT Catur Bakti Abadi, Surabaya, PT, Trijaya Abadi, Surabaya; commr. PT Duta Bisma Perkasa, Jakarta, PT. Bukit Baja Abadi, Surabaya. Home: Jl Dharmahusada Indah, Utara III/85, Surabaya Indonesia Office: PT Bukit Jaya Abadi, Jl Kedung Tarukan 122, 60002 Surabaya Indonesia

SENDOV, BLAGOVEST HRISTOV, mathematician, educator; b. Asenovgrad, Plovdivska, Bulgaria, Feb. 8, 1932; s. Hristo Stoev and Marushka (Blagova) S.; children from previous marriage: Marushka, Ana; m. Anna Marinova, July 4, 1951; 1 child, Blagovest. PhD in Math., Sofia (Bulgaria) U., 1964; DSc in Math., Moscow U., 1967, LHD (hon.), 1977. Prof. math. Sofia U., 1968, rector, 1973-79; v.p. Bulgarian Acad. Scis., 1981-88, pres., 1988—; pres. Com. for Sci., Sofia, 1976—. Mem. parliament Nat. Assembly, Sofia, 1975-88. Recipient Dimitrov's prize Bulgarian Govt., 1969. Mem. Am. Math. Soc., Bulgarian Math. Union., Internat. Assn. Univs. (hon. pres. 1985—).

SENDSTAD, ERLING, biologist; b. Ringsaker, Norway, Oct. 24, 1948; s. Lennart and Oddrun (Stenset-Moe) S. Cand. real, U. Trondheim, 1975. Research asst. U. Trondheim, 1975-78; scientist SINTEF, Trondheim, 1978-83, asst. div. mgr., 1983-84, div. mgr., 1984-85; head research Dyno Industries, Oslo, 1986—. Contbr. articles to profl. jours. Avocations: outdoor life, hunting. Home: Ole Messelts v 182 A, 0676 Oslo Norway Office: Dyno Industries, Box 160, N-2001 Lillestroem Norway

SENG, MINNIE ANNA, librarian, editor; b. Muskegon, Mich., Nov. 30, 1909; d. Edward and Ella Barbara (Pattie) S.; student Muskegon Community Coll., 1927-29; A.B., U. Mich., 1932, A.B. in Library Sci., 1935, M.A. in Library Sci., 1943. Asst. med. librarian U. Iowa, 1935-39; cataloger Bay City (Mich.) Pub. Library, 1939-40; order librarian Mich. Technol. U., Houghton, 1940-42; continuations cataloger U. Ark., 1943-44; head cataloger Calif. State U., Fresno, 1944-59; editor Edn. Index, H.W. Wilson Co., Pubs., Bronx, N.Y., 1959-66; head cataloger St. Ambrose Coll., Davenport, Iowa, 1967-72; periodicals librarian Frostburg (Md.) State U., 1972-74; ret., 1974. Mem. Am. Hort. Soc., AAUW. Democrat. Mem. Christian Ch. Home: 110 S Broadway Townhouse Q Frostburg MD 21532

SENGER, LESLIE WALTER, environmental consultant; b. Buffalo, June 8, 1945; s. Walter and Clara Mary (Jakubiak) S. BA, UCLA, 1967, MA, 1969, PhD, 1972. Research geographer U. Calif., Santa Barbara, 1970-73; cons. Dames & Moore, Santa Barbara, 1973—. Co-editor: Remote Sensing: Techniques for Environmental Analysis, 1974; contbr. numerous articles to profl. jours. Mem. AAAS, Assn. Am. Geographers (honoraria cons. 1968-70), Am. Soc. Phogrammetry. Home: 831 Cliff Dr #B-1 Santa Barbara CA 93109 Office: Dames & Moore 175 Cremona Dr Santa Barbara CA 93117

SENGUPTA, INDRA NARAYAN, information scientist, scientometrist; b. Dighirpar Kotwalipara, Bengal, India, May 1, 1931; s. Ramani Mohon and Labanya Prova Sengupta; m. Parijat Ray, Aug. 8, 1964; children: Sagar, Sabyasachi. BS, Calcutta U., India, 1951, MS, 1955, PhD, 1983; PhD, Karnataka U., India, 1984. Sr. sci. asst. Indian Inst. of Biochemistry and Exptl. Medicine, Calcutta, 1959-68; sr. documentation officer Nat. Chem. Lab., Pune, India, 1968-69; scientist B Indian Inst. Exptl. Medicine, Calcutta, 1969-73; dep. director documentation Research Designs and Standards Orgn., Lucknow, India, 1973-75; scientist C Indian Inst. of Chem. Biology, Calcutta, 1976-80, scientist EI, 1981-85, scientist EII, 1986—; scientist-in-charge library and documentation Indian Inst. Chem. Biology, 1976—; mem. faculty council for postgrad. studies in Edn., Journalism, and Library Sci., Calcutta U., 1987—; mem. adv. bd. Library Sci, Info. Sci.; Cen. Drug Research Inst., Lucknow, 1985—, Indian Statis. Inst., Calcutta, 1984—; faculty mem. several Indian univs., 1975—; cons. in field; mem. FID Conm. for Informetrics. Author: Bibliometric Research, 1988; co-editor: Bibliometric Studies: Current Information, 1986; assoc. editor Scientometrics and Internat. jour., 1977—; contbr. more than 65 articles to profl. jours. Recipient Ranganathan-Kaula medal. Mem. Indian Library Assn., Indian Assn. Spl. Libraries and Info. Ctrs., Indian Med. Library Assn., Soc. for Info. Sci., Indian Techno-Sci. Libraries and Info. Scientist's Assn., Indian Assn. for Tchrs. of Library and Info. Sci. (pres. documentation group), Soc. for Info. Sci. (mem. exec. com., Recipient Fellow Soc. for Info. Sci.). Home: Block I Flat 9B, 59 Lake Rd, Calcutta 700029, India Office: Indian Inst of Chem Biology, 4 Raja S C Mullick Rd, Calcutta 700032, India also: 43A G T Rd Jhilbangan, P O Serampore, Dt Hooghly India

SENGUPTA, SUBIR, orthopedic surgeon, educator; b. Calcutta, Bengal, India, Jan. 2, 1934; arrived in Malaysia, 1966; s. Ramesh Chandra and Usha (Roy) S.; m. Supti Choudhury, July 30, 1960; 1 child, Shampa. B in Medicine and BS, U. Calcutta, 1957. Lectr. Faculty Medicine, Dept. Orthopaedic Surgery U. Malaya, Kuala Lumpur, Malaysia, 1966-74, assoc. prof., 1975—; cons. Univ. Hosp., Kuala Lumpur, 1975—. Fellow Royal Coll. Surgeons; mem. Soc. Internat. Chirurgie Orthopaedic & Trauma, Western Pacific Orthopaedic Assn. (Malysian del. 1970), Assn. South East Asian Nations Orthopaedic Assn., Malaysian Orthopaedic Assn. (sec. 1967, treas. 1972). Hindu. Office: Dept Orthopaedic Surgery, Univ Malaya, Kuala Lumpur Malaysia

SENIOR, GRAHAME, advertising agency executive; b. Huddersfield, Yorkshire, Eng., Oct. 21, 1944; s. Raymond and Evelyn (Wood) S.; m. Prudence Elisabeth Holland, July 10, 1965; children: Claire Elisabeth, Adam Michael, Charlotte Elisabeth. Student pub. schs., Almondaury, Eng. Mgmt. trainee Royal Ins. Group, Liverpool, Eng., 1961-64; writer Vernons Orgn., Liverpool, 1964-66; devel. writer Osborne Peacock Agy., Manchester, Eng., 1966-67; copy chief Royos Advt. Agy., Manchester, 1967-69; creative dir. Brunnings Liverpool Advt., 1969-77; mng. dir. Brunnings Group, London, 1977-78, Brunnings Overseas, U.S., Europe, 1978-79; joint chmn., mng. dir. Senior King Ltd., London, 1979—; bd. dirs., chmn. Michael Kann Film Assocs., London. Author; (play) Running Down Man, 1971; dir. Served with Royal Engrs. Brit. Army Parachute Squadron Res., 1962-64. Mem. Inst. Practioners in Advt., Inst. Mktg., Chartered Ins. Inst., Ins. Dirs. Conservative. Anglican. Club: RAC (Pall Mall). Office: Senior King Ltd, 14/15 Carlisle St, London W1V 5RE, England

SENIOR, RICHARD JOHN LANE, textile rental services executive; b. Datchet, Eng., July 6, 1940; came to U.S., 1972, naturalized, 1977; s. Harold Denis Senior and Jane Lane Dorothy (Chadwick) Senior Rigg; B.A., Oxford U., 1962; M.I.A., Yale U., 1964; m. Diana Morgan, Dec. 19, 1966; children—Alden, Alicia, Amanda. Mgmt. cons. McKinsey & Co., Inc., London and Chgo., 1967-74; pres., chief exec. officer Morgan Services, Inc., Chgo., 1974—. Pres. bd. trustees Latin Sch., Chgo., 1979-83. Mem. Textile Rental Services Assn. Am. (pres. 1983-85, dir. 1978-86, mem. exec. com.). Clubs: Racquet (bd. govs. 1983—), Chicago, Glen View, Econ. Home: 1420 Lake Shore Dr Chicago IL 60610 Office: Morgan Services Inc 222 N Michigan Ave Chicago IL 60601

SENN, CHARLES LIESTER, environmental consultant, sanitary engineer. B.S.C.E., U. Wis., Milw. and Madison, 1932; postgrad. in pub. health, U. Minn., 1937; M.S. in Pub. Adminstrn., U. So. Calif., 1952. Registered civil engr., Calif. registered sanitarian, Calif. cert. milk insp., Calif. registered profl. engr., Tex., Wis. Lab. asst. U. Wis.-Milw., 1928-29, U. Wis., Madison, 1929-30; chief survey party, constrn. engr. Wis. Hwy. Commn., 1932-36; dist. san. engr. Wis. Health Dept., 1936-39; san. engr., chief san. inspection Milw. Health Dept., 1939-43; environ. health dir. Los Angeles City Health Dept., 1943-64, environ. sanitation cons., 1964-67; mem. pub. health faculty UCLA, 1946-77, dir. grad. environ. health mgmt. program, 1967-76; prof. environ. health U. Calif.-Northridge, 1966-73; pres. Senn Environ. Cons. Assocs., Inc., 1970—; lectr. Sch. Medicine U. So. Calif., 1946-75; mem. Calif. Adv. Com. on Sanitarian Registration; mem. environ. health adv. com. Calif. Dept. Pub. Health; vis. prof. Zagazig U., Egypt, 1983; chmn. expert com. on appraisal of hygienic quality of housing WHO, 1966, prin. cons. World Health Assembly, Geneva, 1967; pub. health specialist and engring. coordinator Market Town Project, Jafna, Sri Lanka, 1982. Contbr. articles to profl. publs. Recipient plaque of appreciation Pollution Control Assn. of Philippines, 1985; Senn award established in his honor Calif. Environ. Health Assn., 1981. Fellow Am. Pub. Health Assn. (governing council 1940-72, chmn. program area com. on housing and health 1967-72, tech. devel. bd. 1967-72, chmn. Environ. Sect. 1950), ASCE (chmn. com. pub. health activity 1959-64); mem. Am. Waterworks Assn., Conf. Local Environ. Health Adminstrs. (chmn. 1946-49, editor newsletter 1967-82 Spl. plaque), Nat. Environ. Health Assn. (chmn. com. on-site wastewater mgmt. 1981-83, Presdl. citation, Hancord award 1985), Nat. Sanitation Found. (council pub. health cons. 1946-70, chmn. joint com. on equipment and food equipment standards 1957-75 Walter Snyder award with Nat. Environ. Health Assn.), AAAS, Internat. Assn. Plumbing and Mech. Ofcls.; mem. Calif. Conf. Local Environ. Health Dirs. (chmn. 1946, hon. life mem.), So. Calif. Met. Area Environ. Dirs. (founding, chmn. 1979-80), So. Calif. Pub. Health Assn. (pres. 1950-51), Sigma Xi, Delta Omega. Home and Office: 5522 Atlas St Los Angeles CA 90032

SENSI, GUISEPPE MARIA CARDINAL, Cardinal; b. Cosenza, Italy, May 27, 1907; s. Francesco and Melania (Andreotti Loria) S. Ed. Lateran U., Rome. Ordained priest Roman Cath. Ch., 1929; elevated to Sacred Coll. Cardinals, 1976. Diplomatic service for the Holy See, 1934-76; ordained titular archbishop of Sardes, 1955; apostolic nuncio to Costa Rica, 1955; apostolic. del. to Jerusalem, 1956-62; nuncio to Ireland, 1962-67, Portugal, 1967-76; Hon. mem. Acad. Consentina. Address: 16 Piazza S Calisto, 00153 Rome Italy *

SENSOR, MARY DELORES, hospital official, consultant; b. Erie, Pa., July 20, 1930; d. Sergie Pavl Malinowski and Leocadia Mary Francis (Machalinski) Harner; m. Robert Louis Charles Sensor, Apr. 21, 1945; children—Robert Louis Paul, Stephen Maxmillian Augustus, Therese Blaze, Katryn Anne. Student in Pre-Medicine, Gannon U., 1968-72, M.S. in Health Care Adminstrn., 1986; B.S. in Hosp. Adminstrn., Daemon Coll., 1972. Intern in hosp. adminstrn. Harvard U., Boston, 1972; dir. med. records St. Mary Hosp., Langhorne, Pa., 1972-74, Moses Taylor Hosp., Scranton, Pa., 1975-77, Erie County Geriatric Ctr., Fairview, Pa., 1977-82; dir. utilization rev. Millcreek Community Hosp., Erie, Pa., 1983—; bd. dirs. Christian Health Care Ctr., Erie, 1983-84; cons. prof. in-hosp. adminstrn. and med. records U. Pitts. and Temple U., 1972-74; contbr. paper 6th World Congress Automated Med. Data, Washington; presenter paper, Computer Adaption of SNOMed to DRG Assignment, to 12th Annual Symposium on Computer Application in Med. Care, Washington., Bd. dirs St. John Kanty Prep. Sch., Erie, 1970-71, pres. Ladies Aux., 1970-71. Mem. Am. Med. Rec. Assn., Pa. Med. Record Assn., NW Pa. Med. Record Assn. (sec. treas. 1982-84), Nat. Assn. Quality Assurance Profls., Pa. Assn. Quality Assurance Profls. Roman Catholic. Club: Siebenburger Singing Soc. Avocations: Profl. classical dancing; researcher early man's migration patterns; gourmet cooking; collecting jazz. Home: 3203 Regis Dr Erie PA 16510

SENTER, ROGER CAMPBELL, hotel company executive; b. Manchester, N.H., Apr. 21, 1932; s. Kenneth Lee and Beatrice (Campbell) S. B.A., Boston U., 1954, LL.B., 1956. Mem. grad. student tng. program Westinghouse Co., Pitts., 1956-59; asst. mgr. recruiting Semi-Condr. div.

Raytheon Co., Boston, 1959-61; founder McGovern, Senter & Assocs., Inc., Boston, 1961; v.p. McGovern, Senter & Assocs., Inc., 1961-65; dir. recruiting ITT World Hdqrs., N.Y.C., 1965-70; sr. v.p., dir. adminstrn. Sheraton Corp., Boston, 1970—; also dir. Sheraton Corp.; bd. dirs. Am. Hotel Found., Bay Tower Restaurants Inc. Bd. dirs. Mass. Mental Health Assn. Mem. Am. Hotel and Motel Assn., Hotel Sales Mgmt. Assn. (pres.), Nat. Assn. for Corp. and Profl. Recruiters (pres., dir.). Clubs: Corinthian Yacht (Marblehead, Mass.); Quechee (Vt.). Office: The Sheraton Corp 60 State St Boston MA 02109

SENTER, WILLIAM JOSEPH, publishing company executive; b. N.Y.C., Dec. 4, 1921; s. Joseph and Sarah (Greenglass) S.; m. Irene Phoebe Marcus, Aug. 3, 1952; children: Adam Douglas, Caren Amy. B.B.A., CCNY, 1947. Chmn. bd., mng. editor Deadline Data, Inc., N.Y.C., 1962-66; pres. Unipub, Inc. (merged with Xerox Corp. 1971), N.Y.C., 1966-72; v.p. planning and devel. Xerox Info. Resources Group (includes AutEx Systems, R.R. Bowker Co., Ginn & Co., Univ. Microfilms Internat., Unipub Inc., Xerox Edn. Publs., Xerox Learning Systems, Xerox Computer Services), Greenwich, Conn., 1973-74; v.p. info. pub. Xerox Info. Resources Group, Greenwich, 1974-75; pres. Xerox Info. Resources Group, 1976-80, chmn., 1980-86; v.p. Xerox Corp., Stamford, Conn., 1978-86; pres. R.R. Bowker Co., N.Y.C., 1974-75. Served with U.S. Army, 1942-46. Mem. Assn. Am. Pubs. (dir. 1978-81), Info. Industry Assn. (dir. 1980-83). Office: Box 364 Cos Cob CT 06807

SEPPALA, MARKKU TAPIO, gynecologist, obstetrician, educator; b. Helsinki, Finland, May 16, 1936; s. Aate Ensio and Annikki (Partanen) S.; m. Maija Leena Peltonen, Aug. 26, 1961; children—Jussi Markku P., Kalle Thomas. MD, U. Helsinki, 1964, Dr.Med.Sci., 1965. Intern, dept. surgery Univ. Central Hosp., Helsinki, 1964, resident, 1965; practice medicine, specializing in ob-gyn, Helsinki, 1969—; adminstrv. head dept. ob-gyn, U. Central Hosp. of Helsinki, 1983-84, 87—; asst. prof. U. Helsinki, 1970, assoc. prof., 1976, prof. ob-gyn, 1979—. Editor, Acta Endocrinologica, 1981-85, Acta Obstetrica et Gynecologica Scandinavica, 1983—, Placental Proteins, 1982—; guest editor Annals of N.Y. Acad. Sci., 1984; assoc. editor Obstetrical and Gynecol. Survey, 1981—, Tumor Biology, 1986—; editorial bd. Human Reproduction, 1986—, Archives of Gynecology, 1987—, Internat. jour. Gynecology and Obstetics. Bd. dirs. Cancer Soc. Finland, 1982; congress pres. III World Congress of In Vitro Fertilization and Embryo Transfer, 1984, XIV meeting Internat. Soc. Oncodevel. Biology and Medicine, 1986. Recipient Matti Ayrapaa prize, Finnish Med. Soc. DuoDecim, 1981; Wissenschafts prize, Deutscheprechende Professoren, Luzern, Switzerland, 1971. Fellow N.Y. Acad. Sci.; mem. Internat. Soc. Oncodevelopmental Biology and Medicine (dir.), Population Council N.Y. (bd. trustees), Finnish Med. Found. (bd. trustees), European Assn. Gynaecologists and Obsteticians (sec. gen. 1985-88), Internat. Fedn. Gynecology and Obsetics(exec. bd.). Lutheran. Address: Pihlajatie 20B 15, 00270 Helsinki 27 Finland

SEPPINEN, JUKKA TAPANI, Finnish diplomat, civil servant; b. Helsinki, Finland, Oct. 24, 1945; s. Aleksanteri and Sointu Annikki (Kinnunen) S.; m. Harriet Solveig, Apr. 25, 1969 (div. Aug. 1982); children: Eerika, Pauli, Jutta; m. Tuija Merja, Nov. 2, 1985. LL.M., Helsinki U., 1969, M.Polit. Sci., 1975; diploma Ecole Nationale d'Administration, Paris, 1978. Attaché, Ministry Fgn. Affairs, Helsinki, 1970-71; attaché Finnish Embassy, Copenhagen, 1971-73, 2d sec., Sofia, Bulgaria, 1973-75, 1st sec., Paris, 1978-80, counsellor, London, 1983-84; counsellor Ministry Fgn. Affairs, Helsinki, 1984-87; sec. gen. Ruotsinsalmi, City of Kotka, 1987—; dep. gov. Abira, U.S.A.; columnist Kymen Sanomat. Chmn., Union Functionaries in Ministry Fgn. Affairs, 1976-77, Assn. Former Finnish Students in Ecole Nationale d'Administration, 1985—. Served with inf. Finnish Army, 1965. Decorated knight 1st class Order of Lion (Finland), 1979. Fellow Internat. Biog. Assn., England. Lutheran. Clubs: Suomen Latu, Paasikiviseura (Helsinki). Avocations: music; literature; trekking; hunting. Office: City Hall, PL 205, 48101 Kotka Finland

SEPULVEDA AMOR, BERNARDO, diplomat, legal educator; b. Mexico D.F., Mexico, Dec. 14, 1941; s. Bernardo and Margarita S.; m. Ana Yturbe, Oct. 24, 1970; children: Santiago, Pablo, Bernardo. B.A. magna cum laude, U. Mexico, 1964; M.Internat. Law, Cambridge U., 1966; D honoris causa, U. San Diego, 1982. Dep. dir. gen. for legal affairs Sec. of Presidency Govt. Mexico, 1968-70, dir. fgn. investment program Sec. of Treasury, 1971-75, sec. internat. affairs, sec. of treasury, 1976-81; prin. advisor internat. affairs to Ministry Planning and Budget Govt. Mexico, Washington, 1981; minister fgn. affairs Govt. Mexico, Mexico City, 1982—; sec. internat. affairs Instn. Revolutionary Party, Mexico City, 1981-82; prin. advisor affairs to Instrn. Revolutionary Party Presdl. Candidate Miguel de la Madrid, 1981-82. Author: Foreign Investment in Mexico, 1973, Transnational Corporation in Mexico, 1974, A View of Contemporary Mexico, 1979, Planning for Development, 1981. Mem. Instituto Hispano-Luso Americano de Derecho Internat., Am. Soc. Internat. Law. Office: Ministry of Fgn Affairs, Flores Magon 1, Mexico City Mexico 06995 *

SEQUELA, JACQUES, advertising agency executive; b. Paris, Feb. 23, 1934; s. Louis and Simone (Le Forestier) S.; m. Anne Marie Dubois Dumee; m. Sophie Seguela, Mar. 22, 1978; children: Tristan, Sara, Lola. PharmD, Montpellier U., 1965. Reporter Paris-Match Mag., 1959-60; copywriter Axe-Publicité, Paris, 1965; with Roux Seguela, Paris, 1969; pres. Goupe Roux Seguela Cayzac & Goudard, Paris, 1976—. Author: La Terre en rond, 1960, Don't Tell My Mother I Work in an Ad Agency, 1979, Hollywood Washes More White, 1982, Son of Ad, 1984, Cache Cache PUb, 1986. Recipient Gold medal ad compaign for A.F.M.E., Internat. Festival of N.Y., 1986. Mem. Association Francaise pour la maîtrise de l'énergie, French Energy Saving Com. Office: Roux Seguela Cayzac & Goudard, 99 quai du Pdt F Roosevelt, 92136 Issy les Moulineaux France

SERCHUK, IVAN, lawyer; b. N.Y.C., Oct. 13, 1935; s. Israel and Freda (Davis) S.; children: Camille, Bruce Mead, Vance Foster. BA, Columbia U., 1957, LLB, 1960. Bar: N.Y. 1961, U.S. Dist. Ct. (so. dist.) N.Y. 1963, U.S. Ct. Appeals (2d cir.) 1964, U.S. Tax Ct. 1966. Law clk. to judge U.S. Dist. Ct. (so. dist.) N.Y., 1961-63; assoc. Kaye, Scholer, Fierman, Hays & Handler, 1963-68; dep. supt., counsel N.Y. State Banking Dept., N.Y.C. and Albany, 1968-72; mem. Berle & Berle, 1972-73; spl. counsel N.Y. State Senate Banks Com., 1972; mem. Serchuk & Siwek, White Plains, N.Y., 1974; sr. ptnr. Serchuk Wolfe & Zelermyer, White Plains, 1976—; lectr. Practising Law Inst., 1968-71; bd. dirs. United Orient Bank, N.Y.C. Mem. Assn. Bar City of N.Y., N.Y. State Bar Assn. Home: Mead St Waccabuc NY 10597 Office: 81 Main St White Plains NY 10601

SERE, JOUKO EMIL, business executive; b. Uskela, Finland, Feb. 12, 1927; s. Emil and Alina (Weikkolin) S.; m. Helena Mattila, 1952; children—Merja, Hanna. Dipl. Ing., Helsinki U. of Tech., 1955. With Rauma-Repola Oy, 1963—, mgr., 1970, dir. Rauma works, Finland, 1970-73, v.p., Helsinki, Finland, 1973-76, pres., 1976-84, vice chmn. bd., 1984—, also dir.; dir. various indsl. cos., Finland. Decorated Title of Vuorineuvos, Pres. of Finland. Office: Rauma-Repola Oy, Snellmanink 13, 00170 Helsinki Finland

SERENA, GIANNI, prefab company executive; b. Vedelago, Treviso, Italy, July 15, 1932; s. Piero and Anna (Doro) S.; m. Teresita Spinelli, Jan. 6, 1957; children: Giampiero, Cristina, Luca, Alberto. B Chemistry, U. Padova, Italy, 1957. Chemist various cos., Treviso, 1957-58; mng. dir. Serena Prefabricati Spa, Albaredo, Treviso, 1960-75, pres., 1975—. Inventor in field. Mem. Conexport Treviso (v.p. 1982-87), Assn. Italiana Prefab. Lodge: Rotary. Office: Serena Prefabbricati, Viale Stazione 86, 31030 Albaredo, Treviso Italy

SERINGE, RAPHAEL JULIEN, pediatric surgeon, educator; b. Paris, Oct. 3, 1942; s. Philippe and Gilberte (Gillet) S.; m. Hélène Milsant, Feb. 26, 1970; children: Sophie, Mathilde, Elise. Intern Hosp. de Paris, 1965-71, chief of surgery clinic, 1971-76; prof., head pediatric orthopedics dept. Hosp. St. Vincent de Paul, Paris, 1977—. Contbr. articles to med. publs. Mem. French Orthopaedic Soc., Surg. Pediatric Soc. Roman Catholic. Office: Hosp St Vincent de Paul, 74 Ave Denfert-Rochereau, 75674 Paris France

SERKIN, RUDOLF, pianist; b. Eger, Bohemia, Mar. 28, 1903; s. Mordko Serkin and Augusta (Schargl) S.; m. Irene Busch; children: Ursula, Elisabeth, John, Peter, Judith, Marguerite. Studied piano with Richard Robert, studied composition with J. Marx and Arnold Schoenberg; MusD, Curtis Inst. Music, Williams Coll., Temple U., U. Vt., Oberlin (Ohio) Coll., U. Rochester, Harvard U., 1973, Marlboro Coll.; MusD (hon.), New Eng. Conservatory Music, 1985. Apptd. dept. piano Curtis Inst. Music, Phila., 1939-75, dir., 1968-75; artistic dir., pres. Marlboro Music Sch. and Festival, Vt.; former mem. Nat. Council on Arts, Carnegie Commn. Report. European concert debut as guest artist with Vienna Symphony Orch., 1915; began concert career in solo, concerto and chamber music recitals, Europe, 1920; appeared with Adolf Busch in series of sonatas for violin and piano, with Busch Chamber Players in the Bach suites and Brandenburg concertos; debut in Am., Coolidge Festival, Washington, 1933; launched concert career in U.S. with N.Y. Philharm. under Toscanini, 1936; played a series of Mozart and Beethoven, with Nat. Orch. Assn., 1937; with Adolf Busch; played complete series of Beethoven piano and violin sonatas, N.Y.C., 1938; has made ann. concert tours in U.S. since, 1934; frequent participant Casals Festival, 1950—. Decorated grand officiale del Ordina, Orden pour le Merite (Fed. Republic of Germany), Cross of Honor for Scis. and Artist (Austria), comdr's. cross Icelandic Order of Falcon; recipient Presdl. medal of freedom, 1963, Honors medal Kennedy Ctr., 1981, Ernst von Siemens Musikpreis, 1978, Nat. medal of arts, 1988. Fellow Am. Acad. Arts and Scis.; mem. Acad. Nationale di Santa Cecilia (Rome) (hon.), Verein Beethoven Haus (Bonn), Neue Bachgesellschaft (Bonn), Philharm. Symphony Soc. N.Y., Am. Philos. Soc., Riemenschneider Bach Inst. Home: RFD 3 Brattleboro VT 05301 Office: care Herbert Barrett Mgmt 1776 Broadway New York NY 10019 *

SERLIPPENS, ROBERT AL, lawyer; b. Monceau, Hainaut, Belgium, June 13, 1926; came to Zaire, 1960; s. Camille Leon and Mathilde Marie (Meunier) S.; m. Teresa Marie Vanderbeck, July 25, 1945; children: Colette Marie, Monique Paulette. LLD, U. Brussels, 1951, M of Notary, 1977. Bar: Nivelles 1951, Kinshasa 1962. Sole practice Nivelles, Belgium, 1951-62, Kinshasa, Zaire, 1962—. Mem. Union Internat. Avocats, U.S. Trademark Assn., Asia Pacific Lawyers Assn., League Internat. Creditors. Office: PO Box 2639, Kinshasa Zaire

SERNA, FRANCISCO JAVIER, civil engineer; b. Mexico City, Dec. 3, 1925; s. Oscar and Belem (Baylor) S.; student Nat. U. Mex., 1941-43; BSCE, Tex. A&M U., 1947; m. Margarita Cervantes, Aug. 18, 1951; children—Maria Cristina, Francisco Javier. Pres., Constructora Franser S.A., 1956—, Ingenieros y Arquitectos Consultores, 1965—, Aditec SA de CV, 1970—, INARCO S.A., 1972—, INARCO Eduvision, 1973—, Franina SA de CV, 1980—, INARCO Internacional, 1981—, Edificio San Rafael SA, 1981—, San Miguel Chapultepec SA, 1983—, Cerniser SA de CV, 1983—, Serfran S.A., 1984—; lectr. engring. doctorate div. U. Mex., 1960-70; lectr. U. Guanajuato, others; ASCE tech. lectr. Civil Engring. Coll. of Guatemala; cons. Dept. Environment, London, 1963-68; prof. U. Chile, 1967; cons. Fgn. Bldg. Office, Washington, 1976-71, Secretaria de Asentamientos Humanos y Obras Publicas, 1977-80. Coordinator Christian Family Movement, 1960-65; bd. govs. Am. Brit. Cowdray Hosp., Mexico City, 1965—, pres., 1977-78; pres. Council Past Pres. ABC Hosp., Mexico City. Mem. Asociacion de Ingenieros y Arquitectos de Mexico, Consejo Mexicano de Gerencia Profesional (pres. 1964), Sociedad Mexicana de Ingenieria Sismica, ASCE (pres. Mex. sect. 1979-81, internat. dir. 1983-86), Nat. Chamber Cons. Mex. (exec. commn.). Clubs: University (dir. 1958-60), Industrial. Lodge: Rotary (dir. 1984-85). Author publs. in field. Home: 126-4 F Berenguer, 11000 Mexico City Mexico

SERNETT, RICHARD PATRICK, publishing company executive, lawyer; b. Mason City, Iowa, Sept. 8, 1938; s. Edward Frank and Loretta M. (Cavanaugh) S.; m. Janet Ellen Ward, Apr. 20, 1963; children: Susan Ellen, Thomas Ward, Stephen Edward, Katherine Anne. BBA, U. Iowa, 1960, JD, 1963. Bar: Ill. 1965. With Scott, Foresman & Co., Glenview, Ill., 1963-80, house counsel, asst. sec., 1967-70, sec., legal officer, 1970-80; with SFN Cos. Inc., Glenview, Ill., 1980—, v.p. law, sec., 1980-83, sr. v.p., sec., gen. counsel, 1983-86, exec. v.p. and gen. counsel, 1986—; mem. adv. panel on internat. copyright U.S. Dept. State, 1972-75; bd. dirs. Iowa State U. Broadcasting Corp. Mem. ABA (chmn. copyright div. sect. patent, trademark and copyright law 1972-73), Ill. Bar Assn. (chmn. copyright law com. 1978-79), Chgo. Bar Assn., Am. Patent Law Assn. (chmn. copyright matters com. 1972-73, bd. mgrs. 1981-84), Patent Law Assn. Chgo. (chmn. copyright com. 1972-73, 77-78, bd. mgrs. 1979-81), Copyright Soc. U.S.A. (trustee 1972-75, 77-80), Am. Judicature Soc., Am. Soc. Corporate Secs., Assn. Am. Pubs. (chmn. copyright com. 1972-73, vice chmn. 1973-75), Phi Delta Phi, Phi Kappa Theta. Clubs: Met. (Chgo.); North Shore Country (Glenview, Ill.); Eagle Ridge Country (Galena, Ill.). Home: 2071 Glendale Ave Northbrook IL 60062 Office: 1900 E Lake Ave Glenview IL 60025

SEROK, SHRAGA, psychologist, educator; b. Ostrolenka, Poland, Apr. 10, 1929; came to Israel, 1949; s. Eliezer David and Chaya (Shafran) Serok; m. Frieda Novick, Oct. 11, 1955; children—Varda, Liora, Sigal. Diploma Social Work, Tel Aviv Sch. Social Work, 1956; B.A. in Psychology, Tel Aviv U., 1967, postgrad., 1969-71; Ph.D., Case Western U., 1975. Diploma gestalt therapist Gestalt Inst. Cleve., 1975. Youth probation officer, supr. Israeli Govt., Tel Aviv, 1956-70; lectr. Tel Aviv U., 1975—, dir. Faye Ratner Gestalt Program, 1982—; lectr. Ben Gurion U., Beer Sheva, 1982—; pvt. practice psychotherapy, Rishon Lezion, 1975—; cons. group dynamics Israeli Def. Forces, 1975-82; instr. Inst. Productivity Tel Aviv, 1967-72; expert supervision ctrativity and human potential in couples. Author: Human Potential Challenge, 1984; contbr. articles to profl. jours. Mem. Israeli Union Social Workers, Israeli Assn. Psychotherapy, Am. Pschol. Assn., Cert. Cons. Inernat. Office: Ben Gurion U Negev, Dept Social Work, Beer Sheva 81405, Israel

SEROTA, NICHOLAS ANDREW, art gallery director; b. Apr. 27, 1946; s. Stanley and Beatrice Serota; m. Angela Mary Beveridge, 1973; 2 children. BA, Cambridge (Eng.) U., 1968; MA, Courtauld Inst. Art, London, 1970. Regional art officer, organizer exhibitions Arts Council Gr. Britain, 1970-73; dir. Mus. Modern Art, Oxford, Eng., 1973-76, Whitechapel Art Gallery, London, 1976-88, Tate Gallery, London, 1988—; mem. fine arts adv. com. Brit. Council, 1976—; mem. adv. com. Carnegie Internat. Pitts., 1985, 88. Trustee Pub. Art Devel. Trust, 1983-87. Office: Tate Gallery, Millbank, London SW1P 4RG, England

SERRA, ROBERTO, research scientist and administrator; b. Bologna, Emilia-Romagna, Italy, May 16, 1952; s. Alcide Serra and Marika Vuga; m. Elena Tenze, Dec. 23, 1978; children: Francesca, Eleonora. Laurea in Fisica, U. Bologna, Italy, 1977. Postdoctoral fellow dept. physics U. Bologna, Italy, 1978; application engr. digital signal analysis Hewlett-Packard, Milan, Italy, 1978-79; research assoc. TEMA (ENI Group), Bologna, 1979-82, research group mgr. math. modeling group, 1982-85, div. mgr. complex systems div., 1986—; research coordinator massively parallel systems ENIDATA (ENI Group), Bologna, 1987—. Co-author: Introduction to the Physics of Complex Systems, 1986, Tra Ordine E Caos, 1986. Recipient Guglielmo Marconi medal Cavalieri del Lavoro, 1979. Mem. Soc. Indsl. and Applied Math., Soc. Italiana per La Ricerca Sui Sistemi (bd. dirs.), soc. Gen. Systems Research, World Wildlife Fund. Home: Via S Gaetanino 245, 48100 Ravenna, Emilia Romagna Italy Office: TEMA (ENI Group), Via Aldo Moro 38, 40127 Bologna, Emilia Italy

SERRAF, LUC ELYSÉE, editor, publisher; b. Alger, Algeria, Sept. 9, 1936; s. David Marcel and Anaïs (Darmon) S.; m. Monique Brouck, 1962 (div. 1980); children: Anne, Hugues, Pierre-Yves; m. Marie-Jane Virrion, May 1983; children: Benoît, Anaïs. Degree in Bus., Sch. of Commerce, Algeria; degree, Sch. Beaux-Arts, Algeria; degree in Design, Algeria; degree in Music, Music Conservatory, Algeria. Painter, sculptor freelance, 1960—; dir. Agy. Havas, Constantine, Algeria, 1961, Lorient, France, 1962, Vannes, France, 1962-64; publicity chief Agy. Havas, Marseille, France, 1964-66; dir. Groupe Panorama, Marseille, 1966-73; pub. La Cote des Arts, Marseille, 1973—; dir. art gallery Marseille, 1977-84; dir. sch. and art gallery, 1987—. Author (play): L'Expulsion, 1981; editor: De La Cote des Arts, 1979. Served with the French army, 1958-60. Recipient War Medal of Algeria, Keeping of Order, Commemorative War Medal, 1960, Merite et Dévovement Francais from the French Pres., 1982, Arts, Scis., and Letters award, also numerous art awards and prizes. Mem. Spl. Press Syndicate, French Copyright (v.p. 1981), Inter-Arts. Lodge: B'nai Brith (sec. 1980-84).

SERRANO, FERNANDO PIRES, electronics importing company executive; b. Lisbon, Portugal, Feb. 9, 1924; s. Ruy and Virginia (Pires) S.; m. Maria Cristina Figueiredo, Feb. 14, 1948 (div. 1970); children: Pedro, Jose Eduardo, Anacristina. Chartered acct., Comml. Inst., 1944. Clk. Bank of London, Lisbon, 1945-46; order service asst. Gen. Electric Portugal, Lisbon, 1946-50, order service mgr., 1950-57; office mgr. Telectra SA, Lisbon, 1957-68, asst. dir., 1968-70, v.p., 1970-76, chief exec. officer, pres., 1976—. Served to sgt. cadet, arty., 1944-45. Christian-Democrat. Office: Telectra SA, Rua Rodrigo Da Fonseca 103, 2750 Lisbon Portugal

SERRANO, GUSTAVO MARCOS, accountant; b. Santiago, Chile, Oct. 7, 1927; s. Mariano Serrano and Maria Mahns; m. Delia Teresa Gildemeister; children: Gustavo, Cecilia, Francisco, Catalina, Teresita, Matias. Degree in Acctg., Comml. Sch. Santiago, 1947; LLB, Cath. U., Santiago, 1954. Bar: City of Santiago, 1955. Atty. Anaconda Corp., Santiago, 1954-60; mgr. Price Waterhouse, Santiago, 1960-62, ptnr., 1962-88; dep. sr. ptnr., adminstrv. ptnr. for S.Am. Price Waterhouse, 1983-88; prof. law Cath. U., Diego Portales U., Santiago. Author: (with others) Ley de Impuesto a la Renta, 1969. Recipient Chile Adminstrv. Enterprises prize, 1976. Mem. Colegio de Abogados, Colegio de Contadores, Internat. Fiscal Assn., Internat Inst. of Pub. Fin., Inst. Chileno Derecho Tributario (v.p. 1967-68). Clubs: Unión, Prince of Wales Country (pres. 1979-80); Golf (Los Leones). Home: Hernando de Aguirre 1025, Santiago Chile

SERRA Y SERRA, NARCISO, Spanish minister of defense; b. Barcelona, Spain, May 30, 1943; m. Conxa Villalba Ibanez. Grad. in Econs., U. Barcelona, 1965; postgrad. London Sch. Econs., doctorate Autonomous U., 1973. Asst. lectr. in econs. U. Barcelona, 1965; mem. faculty Autonomous U., 1972; prof. U. Seville (Spain), 1976; prof. Autonomous U., Barcelona, 1976; councillor for territorial policy and pub. works Catalan Generalitat, 1977-79; mayor City of Barcelona, 1979-82; minister of def. Govt. Spain, Madrid, 1982—. Office: Gabinete Tecnico del Ministro, de Defensa, Romero Robledo 8, Madrid 8 Spain *

SERRES, MADELEINE, physician; b. Mazères, France, Jan. 3, 1943; d. Elie and Georgette (Audabram) S.; m. Lamazouade, Apr. 13, 1965; children: Anne, FranÇois, Olivier. D Lauréat, Acad. Nat. Medecine, Paris, 1977. Practice medicine Cabinet Medical, Tarbes, France; chef medecin Cir. Paul Armagnac, Nogaro, France, 1978—. Mem. Ministere Jeunesse et Sport. Home: 8 Beraldi, 65000 Tarbes France Office: Cabinet Medical, 8 Street Beraldi, 65000 Tarbes France

SERRES, PATRICK, plastic surgeon, laser researcher; b. Tours, France, Aug. 7, 1945; s. Henri and Simone (Ballon) S.; m. Josette Reaud Epouse, Oct. 4, 1969; children—Frederic, Ludovic, Cedric, Magali. Baccalaureat, U. Bordeaux, 1961; M.D., U. Paris, 1975. Resident U. Paris; practice medicine specializing in plastic and reconstructive surgery, Frejus, 1975—. Patentee argon laser in plastic surgery. Fellow Ancien Interne des Hopitaux de Paris. Lodge: Lions (pres. 1981). Avocation: diving. Office: 601 Blvd de la Mer, 83600 Frejus France

SERSTOCK, DORIS SHAY, microbiologist, educator; civic worker; b. Mitchell, S.D., June 13, 1926; d. Elmer Howard and Hattie (Christopher) Shay; B.A., Augustana Coll., 1947; postgrad. U. Minn., 1966-67, Duke U., summer 1969, Communicable Disease Center, Atlanta, 1972; m. Ellsworth I. Serstock, Aug. 30, 1952; children—Barbara Anne, Robert Ellsworth, Mark Douglas. Bacteriologist, Civil Service, S.D., Colo., Mo., 1947-52; research bacteriologist U. Minn., 1952-53; clin. bacteriologist Dr. Lufkin's Lab., 1954-55; chief technologist St. Paul Blood Bank of ARC, 1959-65; microbiologist in charge mycology lab. VA Hosp., Mpls., 1968—; instr. Coll. Med. Scis., U. Minn., 1970-79, asst. prof. Coll. Lab. Medicine and Pathology, 1979—. Mem. Richfield Planning Commn., 1965-71, sec., 1968-71. Fellow Augusta Coll.; named to Exec. and Profl. Hall of Fame; recipient Alumni Achievement award Augustana Coll., 1977; Superior Performance award VA Hosp., 1978, 82; Golden Spore awardsMycology Observer, 1985, 87. Mem. Am. Soc. Microbiology, N.Y. Acad. Scis., Minn. Planning Assn. Republican. Lutheran. Clubs: Richfield Women's Garden (pres. 1959), Wild Flower Garden (chmn. 1961). Author articles in field. Home: 7201 Portland Ave Richfield MN 55423 Office: VA Hosp Minneapolis MN 55417

SERVAN-SCHREIBER, JEAN-JACQUES, engineer, author; b. Paris, Feb. 13, 1924; s. Emile and Denise (Bresard) Servan-S.; grad. Ecole Polytechnique, Paris, 1947; children: David, Emile, Franklin, Edouard. Journalist, fgn. affairs editor newspaper Le Monde, Paris, 1948-53; pres.-gen. mgr. pres. Groupe Expres, mags. L'Express, 1953-73; mem. nat. Parliament from Nancy; pres. Radical Party; pres. Lorraine region 1970-79; founder, 1979, chmn. Groupe de Paris (Europe, Japan, Arabia); chmn. World Center for Informatics and Human Resources, Paris, 1982-85; chmn. internat. com. Carnegie-Mellon U., Pitts., 1985. Served as fighter pilot Free French Forces, World War II. Decorated Cross of Mil. Valor. Author: Lieutenant in Algeria, 1957, The American Challenge, 1967, The Radical Manifesto, 1971, Regional Power, 1972, The World Challenge, 1981, The Choice of the Jews, 1988. Office: International Ctr 623 Morewood Ave Pittsburgh PA 15213

SERWY, ROBERT ANTHONY, accountant; b. Chgo., Mar. 26, 1950; s. Anthony J. and Bernice (Zubek) S.; m. Margaret A. Smejkal, Aug. 12, 1972; children: Karen, Steven. BS in Engring., U. Ill., 1972; M Mgmt., Northwestern U., 1974. Mgr. cons. Arthur Andersen & Co., Chgo., 1974-83; dir. fin. planning Teepak, Inc., Oak Brook, Ill., 1983-85; sr. mgr. cons. Peat Marwick & Mitchell, Chgo., 1985-86; dir. cons. Warady & Davis, Lincolnwood, Ill., 1986—. F.C. Austin scholar, 1972. Mem. Am. Inst. CPA's, Ill. CPA Soc. Roman Catholic. Home: 721 Valley Rd Lake Forest IL 60045 Office: Warady & Davis 7383 N Lincoln Ave Lincolnwood IL 60646

SESSA, WILLIAM LAWRENCE, journalist, state official; b. Pitts., Nov. 21, 1947; s. Lawrence Joseph and Mary (Summers) S.; children by previous marriage—Rebecca Lynn, Sara Lynn; m. Sheila Dee Marsee, Dec. 20, 1981. B.S. in Journalism, Calif. State U.-Sacramento, 1969; A.A., American River Coll., 1967; postgrad. NYU, 1976-79. Communications advisor Air Resources Bd., Sacramento, 1979-84; press sec., communication dir. Calif. Office Environ. Affairs, Sacramento, 1983—; contbg. editor Pacifica Pub. Co., Los Angeles, 1987—, Lopez Pub. Co., Alexandria, Va., 1979—. Mem. State Info. Officers Council (pres. 1978-79). Democrat. Club: Sacramento Press (bd. dirs. 1981—, chmn. scholarship com. 1982—). Office: Calif Air Resources Bd PO Box 2815 Sacramento CA 95812

SESTINA, JOHN E., financial planner; b. Cleve., Mar. 17, 1942; s. John J. and Regina Sestina; B.S., U. Dayton, 1965; M.S. in Fin. Service, Am. Coll, 1982; m. Mary Barbara Jezek, Dec. 20, 1970; 1 dau., Alison. Cert. fin. planner, chartered fin. cons. With Sestina, Budros and Ruhlin, Inc., Columbus, Ohio, 1967—. Mem. Soc. Ind. Fin. Advisers (past pres., Fin. Planner of Yr. award 1982), Internat. Assn. Fin. Planners, Nat. Assn. Personal Fin. Advisors (pres.), Inst. Cert. Fin. Planners. Author: Complete Guide to Professional Incorporation, 1970; contbr. articles to profl. jours.; contbr. weekly fin. planning segment AM Columbus, WOSU-AM, 1979—. Office: 3726 Olentangy River Rd Columbus OH 43214

SESVOLD, RONALD LOUIS, business service company executive; b. Clarkston, Mich., Jan. 14, 1941; s. William and Thelma Yvonne (Mou Feis) S.; children: Mark Joel, Terry Scott, Chad Louis. BBA, Ea. Mich. U., 1967; BSBA, Cleary Coll., DSc in Bus. Adminstrn. (hon.). Dir. faculty and student affairs Ea. Mich. U., Ypsilanti, 1966-68; mgr. retail advt. Oakland (Mich.) Press, 1968-71; gen. mgr. Tel-Twelve Mall, Southfield, Mich., 1971-78; dir. shopping ctrs. and pub. affairs Ramco-Gershenson, Inc., Farmington Hills, Mich., 1979—; v.p. spl. projects and pub. affairs Ramco-Gershenson, Inc., Farmington Hills, 1984—; mem. faculty, chair Mich. conv., mem. admissions com., mem. governing bd. Council Shopping Ctrs., 1972. Contbr. articles to trade publs. Vice chmn. United Fund North Oakland County, 1969-70; v.p. Union Lake Shore Assn., 1973-85, Spl. Projects and Pub. Affairs, 1984—, pres., 85—; bd. dirs., pres. Southfield Arts Council, 1974; trustee Cleary Coll., 1975-77, treas., 1976; chmn. Oakland County Week,

1975—, Southeastern Mich. Week, 1977—, Mich. Week, 1982; bd. govs. Greater Mich. Found., 1977—; founder Greater West Bloomfield Council for Arts, 1977, Lakes Area Council for Arts, 1977-79; chmn. adv. council LWV, 1979-81; mem. career, vocat. and placement adv. council Southfield Pub. Schs., 1980-81; bd. dirs. Lake Orion Stadium Elem. Sch., 1980-81, pres., 1981-82; bd. dirs. Union Lake Subdiv. Property Owners Assn., 1973—, pres., 1974, 76, 79, 85, 86, 87, Oakland County Traffic Improvement Assn., 1973—, Oakway Symphony, 1974-84, West Bloomfield Symphony, 1976-78; treas. Walled Lake Schs. Bd. Edn. 1984-85; pres. Union Lake Shores Assn. 1973-84, Union Lake Subdivision Property Owners Assn., 1973, 76, 79, 86—; treas. Walled Lake Cen. High Sch. PTSA 1987-88. Mem. Southfield C. of C. (bd. dirs. 1973-76, v.p. 1974), Spirit of Detroit Assn. (commodore 1978), Ea. Mich. U. Alumni Assn. (pres. 1976). Lodge: Civitan. Home: 7860 Barnsbury St Union Lake MI 48085 Office: 27600 Northeastern Hwy Suite 200 Southfield MI 48034

SETH, NAVEEN KUMAR, food products executive; b. Lahore, Pakistan, Oct. 26, 1935; s. Surendra Nath and Phoolwati Seth; m. Veena Sahi, Nov. 29, 1964; children: Navneet, Shalini. MA, Christ Ch. Kanpur, India, 1957; LLB, Dayanand Law Coll., Kanpur, 1958. Mgr. factory Tarzan Hoisery Pvt. Ltd., Kanpur, 1954-59; supr. sales Hindustan Lever, Ltd., Bombay, India, 1959-62; mgr. territory sales Indo-Burma Petroleum Co. Ltd., Calcutta, India, 1962-69; gen. mgr. Ajrondha Ice Factory, 1969-70; v.p. Kwality Frozen Foods Pvt. Ltd., Bombay, 1970—; mng. dir. Yankee Doodle Food and Ice Cream, Bombay, Ghai Mgmt. and Consultancy Services Ltd., Bombay; bd. dirs. GL Hotels, Bombay, Indo-Mark Dairy Equipment. Mem. Internat. Assn. Ice Cream Mfrs., Internat. Assn. Food and Sci.Technologists, Indo Am. C. of C., All India Mgmt. Assn., Bombay Mgmt. Assn., Am. Mgmt. Assn. Clubs: Diners, Nat. Sports of India. Home: 138B Madhuban Bldg, World Hill Rd, Bombay 400018, India Office: Kwality Frozen Foods Pvt Ltd, 254C Dr Annie Besant Rd, Worli, Bombay 400025, India

SETHI, RAMESH KUMAR, corporate finance executive; b. Nairobi, Kenya, Dec. 27, 1943; came to U.K., 1965; s. Pyare Lal and Shanti Devi (Bhalla) S.; m. Suresh Kumari Parmar, Oct. 7, 1965; children—Ashwin Kumar, Sunita, Punam, Rajesh Atul. Cons. Mgmt. Acct. Sr. asst. auditor Midlands Electricity Bd., Birmingham, U.K., 1966-67; sr. auditor S. Wales Electricity Bd., Cardiff, U.K., 1967-70; cost acct. Anglo Am. Corp., Chingola, Zambia, 1970-73; systems auditor Forward Trust Group Ltd., Birmingham, 1973-79, audit mgr., 1979-81, chief internal auditor, 1981-86; div. dir. audit, 1986-87; head of internal audit, U.K. Banking, Midland Bank, 1987-88; fin. dir. Halfords, Ward White Retail U.K. Ltd., 1988—. Contbr. articles to profl. publs. Fellow Chartered Inst. Mgmt. Accts. accredited, dist. exec. com. 1979-85), chartered Assn. Cert. Accts., Inst. Chartered Secs. and Adminstrs. (chartered sec.), Inst. Mgmt. Services (chmn. Birmingham dist. 1979-82); mem. Brit. Inst. Mgmt., Inst. Internal Auditors (mem. U.K. council 1982-84, dist. chmn. 1982-83), Assn. Internat. Accts. (hon. sec. Midlands region 1974-85), Orgn. Methods Soc. Zambia (founder 1970, chmn. 1970-73), Civil Justice Assn. (pres. 1965), Chingola Hindu Assn. (hon. sec. 1972), Shri Geeta Bhawan Mandir (life mem.; hon. auditor 1975—), Greenlands Assn. of Henley Mgmt. Coll. (life). Hindu. Club: Edgbaston Priory. Home: 9 Woodbourne Rd Edgbaston, Birmingham B15 3QJ England Office: Halfords, Icknield Street Dr, Washford West,, Redditch, Worcestershire B98 0DE, England

SETHNESS, CHARLES HENRY, JR., food company executive; b. Chgo., July 30, 1910; s. Charles Henry and Mabel Anna (Pehlke) S.; student U. Ill., 1928-31; m. Mary G. Buckley, Feb. 12, 1938; children—Mary B. Arnold, Charles B., Daniel B., Henry B. With Sethness Products Co., Chgo., 1931—, shipping clk., 1931-33, salesman, 1933-36, pres., 1936—; dir., sec.-treas. Food Concentrates, Inc., Woodbridge, N.J., 1965—; past dir. Chgo. Bank Commerce. Past trustee Latin Sch. Chgo.; past dir. Chgo. Maternity Center, 1500 Lake Shore Dr. Bldg. Corp. Mem. Phi Delta Theta. Clubs: Casino, Saddle and Cycle, Tavern; Capitol City, Piedmont Driving (Atlanta). Home: 1500 Lake Shore Dr Chicago IL 60610 Office: 2367 Logan Blvd Chicago IL 60647

SETTERGREN, INGEMAR, veterinary medicine educator; b. Skovde, Sweden, Oct. 8, 1922; s. Leonard Johannes and Hedvig Elisabeth (Schaerling) S.; m. Elsa-Britta Berglund, Aug. 13, 1949 (div. 1971); children—Barbro Gerda Margareta, Bo Ingemar. D.V.M., Royal Vet. Coll., Stockholm, 1949, Ph.D., 1964. Diplomate Theriogenology, U.S.A. Asst. prof. vet. medicine Royal Vet. Coll., Stockholm, 1950-55, assoc. prof., 1955-65; now prof. Coll. Vet. Medicine, Uppsala, Sweden; vis. prof. Cornell U., 1969-70, 74-75; FAO expert UN, India, 1964-65, Thailand, 1968-69. Contbr. articles to profl. jours. Mem. Swedish Vet. Assn., Soc. Study Fertility, Am. Soc. Theriogenologists. Office: Coll Veterinary Medicine, KC Ultuna, 75007 Uppsala Sweden

SETTIS, SALVATORE, archaeologist, art historian; b. Rosarno, Italy, June 11, 1941; s. Rocco and Carmela (Megna) S.; m. Chiara Frugoni, Dec. 9, 1965 (div. 1982); children: Silvano, Andrea, Marta; m. Maria Michela Sassi, Jan. 4, 1984. Grad., U. Pisa, Italy, 1963; PhD, Scuola Normale Superiore, Pisa, 1965. Asst. prof. U. Pisa, 1965-69; lectr. 1969-75, prof., 1976-84, dean Faculty Letters and Philosophy, 1978-81; prof. Scuola Normale Superiore, Pisa, 1984—, dean Faculty Letters and Philosophy, 1986—. Author: La Tempeftas Interpretata, 1978. Office: Scuola Normale Superiore, Piazza dei Cavalieri 7, 56100 Pisa Italy

SETTON, KENNETH M., historian, educator; b. New Bedford, Mass., June 17, 1914; s. Ezra and Louise (Crossley) S.; m. Josephine W. Swift, Sept. 11, 1941 (dec. Aug. 1967); 1 son, George Whitney Fletcher; m. Margaret T. Henry, Jan. 4, 1969 (dec. Mar. 1987). A.B., Boston U., 1936, Litt.D. (hon.), 1957; postgrad., U. Chgo., 1936, Harvard U., 1939-40; A.M., Columbia U., 1938, Ph.D., 1941; Dr. Phil. h.c., U. Kiel, Germany, 1979. Instr. classics, history Boston U., 1940-43; assoc. prof. European history U. Man., Can., 1943-45; prof., head dept. history U. Man., 1945-50; Henry C. Lea assoc. prof. medieval history, curator Lea Library, U. Pa., Phila., 1950-53, Lea prof. history, 1953-54, Lea prof. history, dir. libraries, 1955-65, Univ. prof. history, 1962-65; prof. history Columbia U., 1954-55; William F. Vilas research prof. history, dir. Inst. Research in Humanities, U. Wis., 1965-68; prof. history Inst. Advanced Study, Princeton, N.J., 1968—; vis. lectr. medieval history Bryn Mawr (Pa.) Coll., 1952-53; research fellow Gennadius Library, Am. Sch. Classical Studies, Athens, Greece, 1960-61; mem. exec. and mng. coms. Am. Sch. Classical Studies, Athens. Author: Christian Attitude Towards the Emperor in the Fourth Century, 1941, 2d edit., 1967, Catalan Domination of Athens, 1311-1388, 1948, rev. edit., 1975, (with Henry R. Winkler) Great Problems in European Civilization, 1954, 2d edit., 1966, Europe and the Levant in the Middle Ages and the Renaissance, 1974, Athens in the Middle Ages, 1975, Los Catalanes en Grecia, 1975, The Papacy and the Levant, 1204-1571, vol. I, 1976, vol. II, 1978, vols. III-IV, 1984; contbr. articles to jours.; editor-in-chief: History of the Crusades, 6 vols., 1969-88. Guggenheim Meml. fellow Greece, Italy, 1949, 50; Decorated Gold Cross Order George I, Greece; recipient Premi Catalonia Barcelona, 1976; Prix Gustave Schlumberger Paris, 1976; John Gilmary Shea prize Washington, 1979. Fellow Mediaeval Acad. Am. (pres. 1971-72, Haskins medal 1980), Soc. Macedonian Studies (hon.), Am. Acad. Arts and Scis.; mem. Am. Philos. Soc. (John Frederick Lewis prize 1957, 84, v.p. 1966-69, 85—), Am. Hist. Assn., Inst. Catalan Studies (corr.), Phi Beta Kappa. Episcopalian. Office: Institute for Advanced Study Princeton NJ 08540

SETZER, HERBERT JOHN, chemical engineer; b. N.Y.C., Oct. 23, 1928; s. Leo and Barbara (Hafner) S.; BChemE, CUNY, 1951; MChemE, NYU, 1958; m. Elizabeth Bernadette Curran, May 30, 1957; children: Stephen Lawrence, Robert Drew, John Herbert, Brian Edmund. Engr. U.S. Army Ordnance Corps, Redstone Arsenal, Huntsville, Ala., 1955-57; research asst. NYU, N.Y.C., 1958-61; research engr. Internat. Fuel Cells (joint venture United Technologies Corp., Hartford, Conn. and Toshiba Corp., Tokyo), 1962—. Holder 19 U.S. patents chem. processing and hydrogen generation, other patents in Can., Europe, Africa, Asia, Australia; contbr. tech. papers in field to pubis. Chmn. troop com. Long Rivers council Boy Scouts Am., 1971-81, com. mem., 1973-81. Served with U.S. Army, 1951-56. Recipient Mason award, NYU, 1962; Spl. award United Technologies Corp., 1980. Mem. Catalyst Soc. New Eng., Sigma Xi. Roman Catholic. Club: Elks. Home: 17 Virginia Dr Ellington CT 06029 Office: PO Box 109 South Windsor CT 06074

SEUREN, PIETER ALBERT MARY, philosophy educator; b. Haarlem, The Netherlands, July 9, 1934; s. Johannes and Catharina (Schavemaker) S. Doctorandus, Amsterdam U., The Netherlands, 1958; PhD, Utrecht U., The Netherlands, 1969. Lectr. linguistics Cambridge U., Eng., 1967-70, Oxford U., Eng., 1970-74; prof. philosophy of lang. Nijmegen U., The Netherlands, 1974—. Author: Operators and Nucleus, 1969; Discourse Semantics, 1985; contbr. articles to profl. jours. Mem. Linguistic Soc. Am., Linguistics Assn. Great Brit., Societas Linguistica Europea, Soc. Caribbean Linguistics. Office: Nijmegen U, Philosophy Inst PO Box 9108, 6500 HK Nijmegen The Netherlands

SEVAGIAN, ARAM HAIG, chemist; b. Mattapan, Mass., May 10, 1932; s. Haig Ohanes and Surpoohy Terzian Tarbassian S.; student Northeastern U., 1949-54; B.S. with honors, Suffolk U., 1960, M.A. in Edn. (fellow), 1962; postgrad. (NSF grantee) Trinity U., San Antonio, 1968. With E & F King Corp., Norwood, Mass., 1952-53; indsl. diamond dust researcher Raytheon Mfg. Co., Waltham, Mass., 1953-54; chem. analyst Petrochem. div. Nat. Research Corp., Cambridge, Mass., 1957-58; instr. chemistry and physics lab. Suffolk U., Boston, 1959-60, instr. grad. chemistry lab., 1960-62, lectr. chemistry, 1962-66; tchr. chemistry and physics Westwood (Mass.) High Sch., 1960-63, Braintree (Mass.) High Sch., 1963—; cons. on drug identification and chemistry coordinator, 1972-86. Mem. Citizens Com. Right to Keep and Bear Arms. Served with U.S. Army, 1955-57. Life mem. NEA, Mass. Tchrs. Assn., AAAS, Nat. Sci. Tchrs. Assn., U.S. Naval Inst., U.S. Chess Fedn., Mass. Chess Assn., Nat. Rifle Assn., Mass. Rifle and Pistol Assn., GOAL, Am. Def. Preparedness Assn., Internat. Benchrest Shooters, Nat. Bench Rest Assn.; mem. Am. Chem. Soc. (div. chem. educators), Am. Inst. Physics, Am. Assn. Physics Tchrs., Braintree Edn. Assn., Norfolk County Tchrs. Assn., Mass. Assn. Sci. Tchrs., N.E. Assn. Chemistry Tchrs., Japanese Sword Soc. (life), Am. Legion, Amvets. U.S. Mem. Armenian Apostolic Ch. Clubs: Braintree Rifle and Pistol (dir. jrs. 1974—), Masons. Office: Braintree High Sch 128 Town St Braintree MA 02184

SEVAT, JACQUES JEAN, ophthalmologist; b. Vanves, France, Feb. 8, 1928; s. Jean and Marie-Louise (DuMontet) S. MD, Universite de Paris, 1957, cert. opthalmology, 1958, cert. aeronautic medicine, 1965. Intern Hosps. in the Paris region, 1953-56; practice medicine specializing in opthalmologie 1959—; chief opthalmology Hopital de Longjumeau, France, 1962—; expert in medicine Aviation Civile, expert judiciaire preés la Cour d'Appel de Paris, 1978; elected council l'Ordre des Medecins, Essonne, France, 1978-81. Recipient Commemorative medal Arme Francaise Nationale, 1957; named hon. capt. Arme Francaise, 1978. Mem. Societe Francaise d'Opthalmologie, Coll. Opthalmologiste des Hopitaux de la Region Parisienne, Comite de Lutte Contre le Glaucome. Home: 167 Ave Gabriel Peri, 91700 Sainte Genevieve des Bois France Office: Hopital de Longjumeau, 91700 Longjumeau France

SEVER, SHMUEL, library director; b. Galatz, Romania, Jan. 16, 1933; arrived in Israel, 1948; s. Menahem and Betty (Herskovitz) S.; m. Irene Bassin, Nov. 27, 1956; children: Oded, Yuval, Aviv. BA in History and Polit. Sci., Hebrew U., Jerusalem, 1956, MLS, 1957; MA, U. Chgo., 1968, PhD, 1975. Serials cataloguer, reference librarian Jewish Nat. and U. Library, Jerusalem, 1954-59; head librarian Israel Atomic Energy Commn., Nahal-Soreck, 1959-61; dir. libraries Nat. and U. Inst. Agr., Rehovot, Israel, 1961-68; exec. sec., lectr. Grad. Library Sch. Hebrew U., Jerusalem, 1968-69; dir. library, prof. library sci. U. Haifa, Mt. Carmel, Israel, 1969—; advisor library sect. of Ministry of Edn., 1966-78; mem. Israeli Standing Com. Nat. and U. Libraries, 1975-78; mem. Israeli sect. Standing Conf. on Nat. and U. Libraries; mem. subcom. on libraries of the Univ. Grants Com.; vis. prof. various Am. univs. Contbr. articles to profl. jours. Trustee Ctr. Pub. Libraries, Israel, 1975—. Grantee Ruth Kahn-Eber Fund, 1970. Mem. Israel Library Assn., ALA (lectr. Carl Milam tour), Israel Soc. Spl. Libraries & Info. Ctrs.; Council for Pub. Libraries. Home: 3 Biram St, Haifa 34986, Israel Office: Univ Haifa Library, Mount Carmel, Haifa 31999, Israel

SEVERAID, RONALD HAROLD, lawyer; b. Berkeley, Calif., July 13, 1951; s. J. Harold and Irene Ann (Clark) S.; m. Peggy R. Chappus. B.A., U. Calif.-Davis, 1973; J.D., Georgetown U., 1977. Bar: Calif. 1977, D.C. 1979, U.S. Dist. Ct. (ea. and cen. dists.) Calif. 1977. Assoc. Kindel & Anderson, Los Angeles, 1977-79; exec. v.p., gen. counsel Pacific Mktg. Devel., Sacramento, 1979-80, pres., 1980-81; sec. Aaron-Ross Corp., Glendora, Calif., 1983-84; sole practice, Sacramento, 1979-84; sr. atty. Severaid & Seegmiller, Sacramento, 1984—. Co-editor Internat. Cts. of Justice Opinion Briefs, 1978; sr. topics editor Law and Policy in Internat. Bus., 1975-76; contbr. articles to profl. jours. Asst. sec. Internat. Relations Sect.-Town Hall, Los Angeles, 1978-79; pres. Pacifica Villas Homeowners Assn., 1978-79. Mem. ABA, Calif. State Bar Assn., Sacramento County Bar Assn., Community Assns. Inst., Calif. Trustees Assn. Republican. Roman Catholic. Office: Severaid & Seegmiller 601 University Ave Suite 125 Sacramento CA 95825

SEVERINGHAUS, WILLIAM DANIEL, environmental biologist; b. Ithaca, N.Y., Sept. 15, 1942; s. Charles William and Ethel (Long) S.; m. Mary Catherine Charles, May 27, 1976; children—William Joseph, Steven Nathaniel. A.A.S., Onondaga Community Coll., 1965; B.S., Lambuth Coll., 1968; M.S., Memphis State U., 1969; Ph.D., U. Ill., 1976. Ecologist USA-Constrn. Engring. Research Lab., Champaign, Ill., 1976—; alt. mem. Dept. Def. Natural Resources Group Com., 1983—; research assoc. U. Ill. Mus. Natural History. Contbr. articles to profl. jours., presentations to profl. societies. Officer, Illini Statesmen Soc. Preservation and Encouragement of Barber Shop Singing in Am. (pub. relations officer of yr., 1988), Champaign, 1984-85. Recipient Cert. Appreciation, Vol. Action Ctr., 1983, 84, 85, 86; named Researcher of Yr., USA-CERL, 1983, Ill. Dist. Pub. Relations Officer of Yr., 1985, 86, 87, ; Barber of Yr. Champaign chpt., 1986. Mem. Am. Soc. Mammalogists (chmn. resolutions com. 1982-83, poster award winner 1984), Ecol. Soc. Am. (sr. ecologist, appeals com. bd. profl. cert. 1984—), Am. Soc. Naturalists, Soc. Study Evolution, Soc. Systematic Zoology, Tenn. Acad. Sci. Current work: Applications of ecological principles to environmental preservation, conservation, and management of distrubed lands. Home: RR5 Box 3 Mahomet IL 61853

SEVILLYA, NAOMI, small business owner; b. Tel Aviv, Nov. 29, 1953; d. David and Rivka (Meshulam) S. Student, Ben Gurion U., Beer Sheva, 1974-77, Hebrew U., Jerusalem, 1978-81. Mgr. David Furniture, Tel Aviv, 1980—. Served as sgt. Israel Army, 1972-73. Home: 50 Dizengoff, Tel Aviv 64332, Israel Office: David Furniture, 62 Herzel St, Tel Aviv 66887, Israel

SEVRIN, ROBERT, geography educator; b. Tamines, Belgium, Apr. 25, 1920; s. Camille and Ida (Gutknecht) S.; m. èl Philomène Chapelle, Apr. 8, 1943; children: Pierre, Michelle, Françoise. B in Geog. Sci., State U. Liège, Belgium, 1942, D in Geog. Sci., 1953. Cert. secondary tchr. Tchr. Athénée Royal, Tournai, Belgium, 1942-56, 57-75; head Inst. Recherche Économique Hainaut, Mons, Belgium, 1956-57; tchr. Acad. Beaux Arts, Tournai, 1954-82, Inst. Provincial d'Enseignement Tech. du Tournaisis, Tournai, 1961-77; prof. Catholic Faculties, Lille, France, 1968-88; cons. in field. Contbr. more than 170 published works. Corresponding mem. Commn. Royale des Monuments, Mons, 1977—. Recipient Chevalier Ordre de Leopold award Ministry of Nat. Edn., Brussels, 1972. Fellow Soc. Royale Belge Geog. (cen. com. mem.), Soc. Geog. Lille (enquiry com. mem.), Soc. Royale Histore Archéologie Tournai, Soc. Arts, Lettres, Scis. Hainaut, Soc. Geog. Liège. Home: Ave Elisabeth 69, B7500 Tournai, Hainaut Belgium Office: Facultés Catholiques de Lille, 60 Blvd Vauban, BP109 F59076 Lille Cedex France

SEWARD, GEORGE CHESTER, lawyer; b. Omaha, Aug. 4, 1910; s. George Francis and Ada Leona (Rugh) S.; m. Carroll Frances McKay, Dec. 12, 1936; children: Gordon Day, Patricia McKay (Mrs. Dryden G. Liddle), James Pickett, Deborah Carroll (Mrs. R. Thomas Coleman). BA, U. Va., 1933, LLB, 1936. Bar: Va. 1935, N.Y., Ky., D.C., U.S. Supreme Ct. With Shearman & Sterling, N.Y.C., 1936-53, Seward & Kissel, N.Y.C., 1953—; Mem. legal adv. com. N.Y. Stock Exchange, 1984-87. Author: Basic Corporate Practice; Seward and Related Families; co-author: Model Business Corporation Act Annotated. Trustee Edwin Gould Found. for Children; mem. U. Va. Arts and Scis. Council. Fellow Am. Bar Found. (chmn. model corp. acts com. 1956-65); mem. Internat. Bar Assn. (founder, chmn. bus. law sect. 1969-74, hon. life pres. assn., also hon. life pres. sect.), ABA (chmn. sect. corp. banking bus. law 1958-59, chmn. sect. com. corp. laws 1952-58, chmn. sect. banking com. 1960-61, mem. ho. of dels. 1959-60, 63-74), Am. Law Inst. (mem. joint com. with Am. Bar Assn. on continuing legal edn. 1965-74), Cum Laude Soc., Raven Soc., Order of Coif, Phi Beta Kappa Assos. (pres. 1969-75), Phi Beta Kappa, Theta Chi, Delta Sigma Rho. Clubs: Down Town Assn., Knickerbocker, N.Y. Yacht (N.Y.C.); Univ. (Chgo.); Met. (Washington); Bohemian (San Francisco); Scarsdale Golf, Shelter Island Yacht (N.Y.), Gardiner's Bay Country. Home: 48 Greenacres Ave Scarsdale NY 10583 also: Ram Head Shelter Island NY 11964 Office: Seward & Kissel Wall St Plaza New York NY 10005 also: 818 Connecticut Ave Washington DC 20006

SEWARD, JOHN EDWARD, JR., insurance company executive; b. Kirksville, Mo., June 12, 1943; s. John Edward and Ruth Carol (Connell) S.; B.S. in Fin., St. Joseph's Coll., 1968; children—Mitch, Justina. Mgr. acctg. services Guarantee Res. Life Ins. Co., Hammond, Ind., 1964-69; asst. controller Gambles Ins. Group, Mpls., 1969-71, N.Am. Cos., Chgo., 1971-73; pres., dir. mem. exec. com. Home & Auto. Ins. Co., Chgo., 1975-83; pres. and chief exec. officer, dir., mem. exec. com. Universal Fire & Casualty Ins. Co., 1983—; Park Lane Ins. Agy., Bd. dirs. Calumet Council Boy Scouts Am., 1979-85, Teddy Bear Club for Shriners Hosp., 1979-81, Chgo. Baseball Cancer Charities, 1981—. F.L.M.I., C.L.U., C.P.C.U. Home: 9549 Prairie Ave Highland IN 46322 Office: 730 W 45th St Munster IN 46321

SEWELL, CHARLES ROBERTSON, geologist, exploration company executive; b. Malvern, Ark., Feb. 7, 1927; s. Charles Louis and Elizabeth (Robertson) S.; m. Margaret Helen Wilson, Dec. 26, 1953 (dec. July 1985); children—Michael Stuart, Charles Wilson, Marion Elizabeth; m. Louise T. Worthington, Nov. 29, 1985. B.S., U. Ark.-Fayetteville, 1950; M.A., U. Tex.-Austin, 1955, postgrad., 1961-64. Registered geologist, Calif., Ariz. Well logging engr. Baroid, Houston, 1950; asst. metallurgist Magcobar, Malvern, Ark., 1951; geologist Socony-Mobil Petroleum Co., Roswell, N.Mex., 1955; sr. geologist Dow Chem. Co., Freeport, Tex., 1956-61; spl. instr. U. Tex., Austin, 1962-65; pvt. practice cons. geologist, Austin, 1962-65; dist. geologist, mgr. Callahan Mining Corp., Tucson, 1965-68; owner, cons. geologist Sewell Mineral Exploration, worldwide, 1968—. Contbr. articles to profl. jours. Elder, Presbyn. Ch., Tucson, 1973—. Served with USN, 1944-46, 51-53. NSF grantee, 1962-64, 63. Mem. AIME, Ariz. Geol. Soc., Mining Club Southwest (bd. govs. 1982-86, pres. 1984), Colo. Mining Assn., Sigma Xi. Republican. Lodge: Masons. Discoverer/co-discoverer numerous metallic and non-metallic ore deposits. Home and Office: 260 S Sewell Pl Tucson AZ 85748

SEWELL, WILLIAM GEORGE, III, electronics engineer; b. Roanoke, Va., Dec. 14, 1950; s. William George Jr. and Elizabeth Marie (Morrison) S.; m. Verna Landry, Aug. 25, 1970 (div. 1974); children—Ronald Allen, Bryan Joseph; m. 2d, Colleen Rose Gaynor, May 15, 1981. B.S. in Engring., U. Ill.-Chgo., 1980; Ph.D., Universal Life U., Modesto, Calif., 1981. Electronic technician 928 Airlift Group, Chgo., 1972-74; with FAA, Chgo., 1974-85, staff engr., Wheeling, Ill., 1980-82, regional nav. and landing systems engr., Chgo., 1982-85; with FAA, Washington, 1985-87; with Jerry Thompson & Assocs., Kensington, Md., 1987-88; v.p. Navcom Systems, Inc., 1988—; cons. engr. W.G. Sewell & Assocs., Internat., Niles, Ill., 1981—; mgr. navigation systems VHF Direction Finder Program, 1985-87. Mem. Chgo. Council Fgn. Relations, 1976-80. Served with USAF, 1970-72. Decorated Viet Nam Service medal. Recipient 1st Prize Am. Soc. Electro-Surgery, 1982. Mem. IEEE, Antennas and Propagation Soc., Microwave Theory and Techniques Soc., Aerospace and Electronic Systems Soc., Soc. Automotive Engrs., Aircraft Owners and Pilots Assn., Exptl. Aircraft Assn., Air Traffic Control Assn. Inventor high speed turn control for land vehicles, 1980; contbr. tech. articles to profl. publs. Office: 10563 Metropolitan Ave Kensington MD 20895

SEXAUER, ARWIN F.B. GARELLICK, librarian, poet, editor; b. Richford, Vt., Aug. 18, 1921; hon. diploma in arts and letters, Athens, Greece, 1979; D.Litt. (hon.), World U., World Acad. Arts and Letters, 1982; hon. diploma arts and letters Accademia Internazionale, Italy, 1982; m. Charles D. Bashaw, 1942 (dec.); children—Dawn Bashaw Mennucci, Alson C. Bashaw; m. 2d, Jack L. Garellick, 1963 (dec.); m. 3d, Howard T. Sexauer, 1979 (dec.). Asst. librarian Kellogg-Hubbard Library, Montpelier, Vt., 1966-73, head librarian, 1974-76; editor Vt. Odd Fellow mag., 1959-70; author: (book of poetry) Remembered Winds, 1963; poems in numerous anthologies; lyricist, monologist. Co-founder Music Mission Inc., 1963; past pres. United Meth. Ch. Women, Franklin County Pomona Grange, PTA; past v.p. Vt. 4-H Council; youth leader 4-H. Recipient numerous awards, including George Washington Honor medals, 1957, 59, 73, ASCAP Popular Panel awards (13), 1967-78, 82, citation, 1982; Richard Rodgers Music Found. award, Grand Ole Opry Trust Fund award, Dr. Arthur Hewitt Meml. award religious poetry, Virgilio-Mantegna medal, 1982; 2 spl. merit citations for poetry, 1982; spl. citation for poetry Internat. Congress Poets, 1982, numerous others. Fellow Internat. Acad. Poets (life), Anglo-Am. Acad. (hon.); mem. Accademia Leonardo da Vinci (diploma di benemerenza, diploma of honor The Glory, poet award, hon. rep.), World Poetry Soc. Intercontinental (disting. service citation, Vt. state rep.), Hellenic Writer's Club (life), Dr. Stella Woodall Poetry Soc. Internat., Calif. Fedn. Chaparral Poets, Poetry Soc. Vt., Gospel Music Assn., ASCAP, Vt. Library Assn., Internat. Press Assn., numerous others. Club: Rebekah (past noble grand). Poems, songs, other artifacts at Gleeson Library, U. San Francisco.

SEXTON, RICHARD, lawyer, diversified manufacturing company executive; b. Madison, Wis., 1929; s. Joseph Cantwell and Eleanor Carr (Kenny) S.; m. Joan Fleming, 1957; children: Molly, Joseph, Lucy, Michael, Ann, Katherine. Student, Amherst Coll., 1947-49; B.S., U. Wis., 1951; LL.B., Yale U., 1958. Bar: N.Y. 1959, U.S. Supreme Ct. 1968. Assoc. firm Sullivan & Cromwell, N.Y.C., 1958-64; with SCM Corp., N.Y.C., 1964-86; asst. counsel SCM Corp., 1964-67, div. gen. counsel Smith-Corona Marchant div., 1967-72, v.p., gen. counsel parent co., 1972-86, sec., 1977-86. Served to lt. (j.g.) USNR, 1951-55. Mem. Assn. Bar City N.Y., ABA, U.S. C. of C. (com. on antitrust policy). Club: Yale. Home: 532 3d St Brooklyn NY 11215 Office: 230 Park Ave Suite 1635 New York NY 10169

SEYAL, ABDUL RASHID, physician; b. Multan, Pakistan, Aug. 30, 1939; d. Seth Haji Allah and Aisha (Allah) Bakhsh; m. Zahida Nazli Seyal, Oct. 25, 1965; 1 child, Jodat M. MBBS, Nishtar Med. Coll., Multan, 1961; MD, Hosp. Western Toronto, 1975. Physician Seyal Clinic, Multan, 1962-68; med. dir. 25 Bed Indoor Hosp., Multan, 1968-75; clin. asst. Toronto Western Hosp., 1975-76; med. dir. Seyal Med. Ctr., Multan, 1986—; pres. Shah Rukni-Alam Med. Ctr., Multan, 1978—; speaker in field. Contbr. articles to profl. jours. Contbr. plans to rural health program. Mem. Pakistan Med. Assn. (life), Egyptian Cardiac Soc. (life), Am. Assn. Physicians and Surgeons, Am. Heart Assn., Am. Acad. Environ. Medicine. Office: Seyal Med Ctr, Off LMQ Road, PO Box 155, Multan Pakistan

SEYDEL, RÜDIGER ULRICH, mathematics educator; b. Cochstedt, Germany, June 15, 1947; s. Joachim and Charlotte (Hermann) S.; m. Friederike Gudrun Böltz, Apr. 25, 1975; children: Reinhard, Roland. PhD, Tech. U. Munich, 1977, Habilitation, 1982. Acad. asst. Tech. U. Munich, 1974-85; vis. assoc. prof., lectr. SUNY, Buffalo, 1983-85; prof. applied math. U. Würzburg, Fed. Republic Germany, 1985—. Author: Vom Regenbogen zum Farbfernsehen, 1986, From Equilibrium to Chaos, 1988; editor: Bifurcation: Analysis, Algorithms, Applications, 1986; contbr. articles to profl. jours; writer, dir. Vibration of a Duffing Oscillator, 1985. Research fellow Humboldt Found., 1983-85. Mem. Soc. Indsl. and Applied Math., Gesellschaft Angewandte Mathematik und Mechanik.

SEYDEL, SCOTT O'SULLIVAN, chemical company executive; b. Atlanta, Mar. 29, 1940; s. John Rutherford and Jane (Reynolds) S.; m. Ruth Clark, Apr. 20, 1985; children—John Rutherford II, Rosina Marie, Lael Elizabeth, Scott O'Sullivan, Howard Clark. Student Ga. Inst. Tech., 1959-62, U. Ga. Sch. Journalism, 1962-63; student bus. adminstrn. N. Tex. State U., 1963. With Tex. Textile Mills, Inc., McKinney, 1963-64; personnel dir. 1965 Corp., AZS Corp., Atlanta, 1965, pub. relations dir., 1966, asst. v.p., 1967, asst. exec. v.p., 1968, corp. dir., 1968-71, v.p. diversification, dir. internat. activities, 1969-70; pres. Seydel Cos., Atlanta, 1970—; v.p., dir. SICHEM, Ghent, Belgium, 1975-78, SICO South Africa, Durben, South Africa, 1975—, Siven, S.A., Caracas, Venezuela, 1971—, Quatic Soc., Inc., Atlanta, 1978-84; v.p., treas. European Homes Ltd., Atlanta; chmn. Ednl. Solutions, Inc.; dir. Seydel Peruana, S.A.; dir. Guatemala, Sifin Oy, Aanakoski, Finland, Anilinas

Argentinas div. SEYCO, Buenos Aires, Inpal, S.A., Rio de Janeiro, Seydel Peruana, Lima. Contbr. articles to profl. jours. Bd. dirs. Coll. Internat. Bus., Ga. State U., Atlanta Lung Assn.; bd. dirs., mem. exec. com. Inst. for Internat. Edn.; bd. dirs. Met. Atlanta YMCA; dir. Atlanta Triad Edn. Consortium; chmn. bd. advs. Ga. World Congress Inst., 1981-83; trustee Atlanta Internat. Sch. Fellow Am. Assn. Textile Chemists and Colorists; mem. Internat. Council for Textile Technologists (dir. 1957—, sec. 1971-88), So. Textile Assn., Atlanta Assn. Internat. Edn. (dir.), U.S. C. of C. (exec. res. com., export council), Atlanta Benedicts (v.p. 1972, dir. 1971-73), Atlanta Carribean Trade Orgn. (bd. dirs.), Chi Phi. Clubs: Atlanta Commerce, Piedmont Driving (Atlanta). Lodge: Rotary. Home: 2700 Habersham Rd NW Atlanta GA 30305 Office: Seydel Cos 4200 Northside Pkwy NW Atlanta GA 30327

SEYMOUR, JEFFREY ALAN, governmental relations consultant; b. Los Angeles, Aug. 31, 1950; s. Daniel and Evelyn (Schwartz) S.; m. Valerie Joan Parker, Dec. 2, 1973; 1 child, Jessica Lynne. AA in Social Sci., Santa Monica Coll., 1971; BA in Polit. Sci., UCLA, 1973, M Pub Adminstrn., 1977. Councilmanic aide Los Angeles City Council, 1972-74; county supervisor's sr. dep. Los Angeles Bd. Suprs., 1974-82; v.p. Bank of Los Angeles, 1982-83; prin. Jeffrey Seymour & Assocs., Los Angeles, 1983-84; mem. comml. panel Am. Arbitration Assn., 1984—; Chmn. West Hollywood Parking Adv. Com., Los Angeles, 1983-84, chmn. social action com. Temple Emanuel of Beverly Hills., 1986, bd. dirs. 1988—; mem. Pan Pacific Park Citizens Adv. Com., Los Angeles, 1982—; bd. dirs. William O'Douglas Outdoor Classroom, Los Angeles, 1981—; exec. sec. Calif. Fedn. Young Democrats, 1971; mem. Calif. Dem. Cen. Com., 1979-82; pres. Beverlywood-Cheviot Hills Dem. Club, Los Angeles, 1978-81; co-chmn. Westside Chancellor's Assocs. UCLA; mem. Los Angeles Olympic Citizens Adv. Com.; mem. liaison adv. commn. with city and county govt. for 1984 Olympics, 1984; v.p. community relations metro region, Jewish Fedn. Council of Los Angeles, 1985-87, co-chmn. urban affairs commn., 1987—; mem. platform on world peace and internat. relations Calif. Dem. Party, 1983; pres. 43d Assembly Dist. Dem. Council, 1975-79; arbitrator Better Bus. Bur., 1984—. Recipient Plaques for services rendered Beverlywood Cheviot Hills Dem. Club, Los Angeles, 1981, Jewish Fedn. Council Greater Los Angeles, 1983; Certs. of Appreciation, Los Angeles Olympic Organizing Com., 1984, County of Los Angeles, 1984, City of Los Angeles, 1987; commendatory resolutions, rules com. Calif. State Senate, 1987, Calif. State Assembly, 1987, County of Los Angeles, 1987, City of Los Angeles, 1987. Mem. Am. Soc. Pub. Adminstrn., Am. Acad. Polit. and Social Scis., Town Hall of Calif., So. Calif. Planning Congress, Bldg. Industry Assn. So. Calif., Greater Los Angeles C. of C., UCLA Alumni Assn. (govtl. affairs steering com. 1983—). Office: Morey/Seymour and Assocs 12424 Wilshire Blvd Suite 1050 Los Angeles CA 90025-1044

SEYMOUR, LYNN, ballet dancer; b. Wainwright, Alta., Mar. 8, 1939; d. E.V. Springett; m. Colin Jones, 1963 (div. 1974); 3 children; m. Philip Pace, 1974; m. Vanya Hackel, 1983. Ed. Royal Ballet Sch.; grad. into Royal Ballet, 1957. Promoted to soloist rank, Royal Ballet, 1958, to prin., 1958; joined Deutsche Oper, Berlin, 1966; guest artist Royal Ballet, 1970-78; artistic dir. Ballet Bayerische Staatsoper, 1978-79; guest artist with other cos. including Alvin Ailey. Ballets include The Burrow, 1958, Swan Lake, 1958, Giselle, 1958, The Invitation, 1960, The Two Pigeons, 1961, Symphony 1963, Romeo and Juliet, 1964, Anastasia, 1966, Dances at a Gathering, The Concert, The Seven Deadly Sins, Flowers, 1972, Shukumei, The Four Seasons, 1975, Side Show, Rituals, 1975, Manon Lescaut, 1976, A Month in the Country, 1976, Mayerling, 1978, Manon, 1978, Choreography for Rashomon, 1976, The Court of Love, 1977, Intimate Letters, 1978, Mae and Polly, Boreas, 1980, Tattooed Lady, 1980, Wolfy, the Ballet Rambert, 1987. Author (with Paul Gardner): Lynn, 1984. Recipient Evening Standard Drama award, 1977. Office: Artistes in Action, 16 Balderton St, London W1Y 1TF, England also: Bayerische Staatsoper, Max-Joseph-Platz 2, 8000 Munich Federal Republic of Germany *

SEYMOUR, RAYMOND B(ENEDICT), chemistry educator, chemical engineer; b. Boston, July 26, 1912; s. Walter A. and Marie E. (Doherty) S.; m. Frances B. Horan, Sept. 16, 1936; children: David Ray, Susan Seymour Smith, Peter, Phillip Alan. BS, U. N.H., 1933, MS, 1935; PhD, U. Iowa, 1937. Registered profl. engr., Tex., Ohio. Instr. chemistry U. N.H., Durham, 1933-35, U. Iowa, Iowa City, 1935-37; research chemist Goodyear Tire & Rubber Co., Akron, Ohio, 1937-39; chief chemist Atlas Mineral Products div. Electric Storage Battery Co., Mertztown, Pa., 1939-41, exec. v.p., gen. mgr., tech. dir., 1949-54, pres., also bd. dirs., 1954-55; research group leader Monsanto Co., Dayton, Ohio, 1941-45; dir. research U. Chattanooga, 1945-48, Johnson & Johnson, New Brunswick, N.J., 1948-49; pres., tech. dir. Loven Chem. of Calif., 1955-58; pres. Corrosion Resistant Products, Inc., 1956-57; pres., chmn. bd. Alcylite Plastics & Chem. Corp., 1958-60; prof. chemistry, chmn. sci. div. Sul Ross State U., 1959-64; assoc. chmn. chemistry dept. U. Houston, 1964-66, coordinator polymer chemistry, 1964-76, assoc. prof. chemistry, 1964-69, prof., 1969-76, prof. emeritus, 1976—, assoc. dir. research, 1966-68; adj. prof. polymer sci. U. So. Miss., Hattiesburg, 1974-76, disting. prof., 1976—; cons. edn. AID, U.S. Dept. State, East Pakistan, 1968; dir. NSF Inst., 1965; Nat. Acad. Scis. vis. prof. fgn. countries, 1976-79; plenary speaker Plastec, Internat., Zagreb, Yugoslavia, 1986, Plastique Modernos, Madrid, 1987; U.S. del. Internat. Union Pure and Applied Chemistry, Jerusalem, 1987; chmn. Experimat 87, Bordeaux, 1987, Engring. Polymer Source Book, 1988. Author numerous books including: Polymer Chemistry: An Introduction, 1981, History of Polymer Chemistry, 1981, Plastics vs. Corrosives, 1982, Marcomolecular Solutions, 1982Structure-Property Relationships in Polymers, 1983, History of Polyolefins, 1985, Pioneers in Polymer Science: Selected Biographies, 1986, Advances in Polyolefins, 1986, Origin and Development of High Performance Polymers, 1986, Polymers for Engineering Applications, 1987, Origin and Development of Polymer Composites, 1987, Polymer Chemistry: An Introduction, 1987, New Advances in Polyolefins, 1987, Applications of Polymers, 1987, Engineering Polymers Sourcebook, 1987, Eminent Polymer Scientists, 1987, Applications of Polymers, 1987, Polymer Composites, 1987, Giant Molecules, 1988; contbr. articles to profl. jours.; patentee in field. Recipient Western Plastics award, 1960; Teaching Excellence award U. Houston, 1975, Catalyst Excellence in Teaching award Chem. Mfrs. Assn., 1976, So. Chemists award, 1981, Silver placque Plasticos Modernos, 1987; elected to Western Plastics Hall of Fame, 1981; named Outstanding Scientist in Miss., 1986; named to Internat. Plastics Hall of Fame, 1988. Fellow AAAS, Am. Inst. Chemists (honor scroll 1980, Chemist Pioneer award 1985), Tex. Acad. Sci.; mem. Am. Inst. Chem. Engrs., Am. Chem. Soc. (Southeastern Tex. ann. award 1972, Charles Herty award 1985), Soc. Plastics Industry, Nat. Assn. Corrosion Engrs., Am Soc. Oceanography, AAUP, Soc. Plastics Engrs. (internat. edn. award 1982), Plastics Pioneers Assn., Miss. Acad. Sci., Sigma Xi, Phi Kappa Phi, Alpha Chi Sigma, Gamma Sigma Epsilon. Club: Hattiesburg Country. Lodge: Rotary. Home: 111 Lakeshore Dr Route 10 Hattiesburg MS 39402

SEYMOUR, ROBERT KENNETH, architect; b. Detroit, Nov. 27, 1948; s. Kenneth John and Ann Margaret (Nikolits) S. BArch magna cum laude, U. Detroit, 1973, MArch, 1974. Draftsman W.P. Lindhout, Livonia, Mich., 1965-66; draftsman, designer Architects Assocs., Southfield, Mich., 1970-71, 73; designer Hubble, Roth & Clark, Bloomfield Hills, Mich., 1971-72; designer, job capt. Clark W. Corey, Westland, Mich., 1973; cons. designer Cement Enamel Devel., Redford, Mich., 1973-74; prin. Robert K. Seymour, Architect, Livonia, 1975—. Author: Hill House Documentation, 1978. Archtl. advisor Hist. Commn., Livonia, 1976-81; chmn. Detroit United Railway Sta. Restoration Com., Livonia, 1977-79; chmn. Hist. Preservation Commn., Livonia, 1978-80; adv. Bldg. Trades Adv. Com., Livonia, 1980—. Recipient Mayor's proclamation City of Livonia, 1982, cert. of honor Am. Soc. Body Engrs., Detroit, 1966, Design award City of Southfield (Mich.), 1987. Mem. AIA, Mich. Soc. Architects, Assn. for Preservation Tech., Nat. Council Archtl. Registration Bds. (cert.), Livonia Hist. Soc. (Heritage award 1984), Blue Key (life). Club: 1st Pa. Regiment (Livonia) (founder, pres. 1974-83). Avocations: hunting, fishing, wood carving, photography.

SFAR, RACHID, former prime minister of Tunisia; b. Mahdia, Tunisia, Sept. 22, 1933. Grad., Inst. Higher Studies, Tunisia, Nat. Sch. Taxation, Paris. Inspector of taxation Ministry of Fin., Tunisia, then prin. insp., 1960-65, dir.-gen. Nat. Adminstrn. of Tobacco and Matches, Tunisia, 1965-69, dir. taxation Ministry of Fin., 1969-71, sec.-gen. Ministry Nat. Edn., 1971-73, sec.-gen. Ministry of Fin., 1973-77, minister of industry, mines and energy, 1977-79, minister nat. defense, 1979-80, minister pub. health, 1980-83, minister nat. economy, from 1983, prime minister of Tunisia 1986-1987. Mem. Central Com., Social Democratic Party, from 1979; mem. Polit. Bur., 1979—, treas., 1979—, dep., 1979—. Decorated Comdr., Order of Independence, Order of the Republic. Address: care Office of Prime Minister, Tunis Tunisia *

SFEIR, SAMI G., advertising director; b. Beirut, Lebanon, Jan. 5, 1946; arrived in France, 1976.; s. Georges and Nadia (Oquet) S.; m. Aimee Azar Sfeir, Oct. 2, 1976; children: Samy Eric, Najy Stephane, Antoine Taymour. Degree in Philosophy, Notre Dame Jamhour, Beirut, 1965; lic. Law and Polit. Sci., U. St. Joseph, Beirut, 1969. Sales exec. Editions Orientales, Beirut, 1969-72; gen. mgr. Impact Visuel, Beirut, 1972-76; advt. dir. Al Mostakbal, Paris, 1976-83; mng. dir. Media-Links, Paris, 1983—. Mem. Internat. Advt. Assn. Office: Media-Links, 36 rue Washington, 75008 Paris France

SGALL, PETR, linguist, educator; b. Budějovice, Czechoslovakia, May 27, 1926; s. Oskar Sgall and Ružena (Hüblová) Sgallová; m. Eva Zahelová, 1950 (div. 1952); 1 child, Ivan; m. Květuše Hofbauerová, 1958; children: Jiří, Alena. PhD, Charles U., Prague, Czechoslovakia, 1949, CSc, 1955, DrSc, 1966. Asst. prof. Charles U., 1949-61, vice dean faculty of philosophy, 1959-61, assoc. prof., 1961-62, vice dean faculty of math. and physics, 1963-64, sr. research worker, 1962-67, research prof., 1967—. Author: Infinitive im Rigveda, 1958; author (with others): Functional Approach to Syntax, 1969, Topic, Focus and Generative Semantics, 1973, Meaning of Sentence, 1986. Mem. Soc. Linguistica Europaea, Czechoslovak Linguistic Soc., Czechoslovak Cybernetic Soc., Czechoslovak Union of Mathematicians and Physicists. Home: Dimitrovo n 24, 17000 Prague 7 Czechoslovakia Office: Charles Univ Faculty Math & Physics, Malostranskén 25, 11800 Prague 1 Czechoslovakia

SGARLATA, FRANCESCO, crystallography educator, researcher; b. Ramacca, Sicily, Italy, July 25, 1926; s. Giuseppe and Anna (Scuderi) S.; m. Aurelia Urso, Apr. 26, 1963; children—Anna, Elisabeth, Monica. Dr. Physics, U. Rome, 1949. Asst. prof. crystallography U. Palermo, Italy, 1950-58; asst. prof. U. Rome, 1958-70, prof., 1970—. Roman Catholic. Office: Inst Mineralogy Univ, Piazza A Moro 2, 00185 Rome Italy

SGHIBARTZ, CRISTIAN MARIUS, chemical company executive; b. Mihailesti, Romania, Sept. 8, 1950; arrived in Eng., 1971; s. Ion and Maria (Panaitopol) S.; m. Evelyn See, Jan. 12, 1978; 1 child, Cristina Amanda. BSc with honors, Imperial Coll., London, 1974; PhD, King's Coll., 1977. Project leader Internat. Paint Co. Ltd., Felling, Eng., 1978-83; mgr. research and devel. Jotun Marine Coatings Co., Sandefjord, Norway, 1983-86; mgr. group research and devel. and bus. RTZ Chems. Ltd., London, 1986—; lectr. in over 25 countries. Contbr. articles to profl. jours.; patentee in field. Fellow Royal Soc. Chemistry (chartered). Home: 1 Saint Crispins Close, Hampstead, London NW3 2QF, England Office: RTZ Chems Ltd, 33 Ashley Pl, London SW1P PLS, England

SGORBATI, GIOVANNI, electromechanical company executive; b. Stradella, Pavia, Italy, Aug. 3, 1925; s. Vittorio and Rosa (Trespidi) S.; m. Lidia Colombo; children: Giuseppe, Marina, Alessandro, Roberto. Grad., Radio Technique Inst., Milan, 1945; MBA, Poly. Univ., Milan, 1965. Designer Compagnia Gen. Elettricità, Milan, 1942-60, engring. mgr. elec. projects, 1960-70, mgr. def. elec. bus., 1970-72, gen. mgr. def. system dept., 1972-76; mng. dir. Savigliano, Turin, 1976—; instr. Gen. Electric Co./Fin. Mgmt. program, Milan, 1970-73. Patenteein field. Named Cavaliere della Repubblica, Pres. Italian Republic, Rome, 1973; recipient Commendatore al merito dell Repubblica, Italian Presidence Bd. Minstry, Rome, 1981. Office: Soc Nazionale Officine Savigliano, Corso Mortara N 4, 10149 Turin Italy

SHACKELFORD, GEORGE GREEN, historian, educator; b. Orange, Va., Dec. 17, 1920; s. Virginius Randolph and Peachy Gasoigne (Lyne) S.; m. Grace Howard McConnell, June 9, 1962. B.A., U. Va., 1943, M.A., 1948, Ph.D., 1955; postgrad., Columbia U., 1949-51; cert., Attingham, Eng., 1957. Asst. prof. history Birmingham So. Coll., Ala., 1948-49; research fellow Va. Hist. Soc., Richmond, 1951-53; instr. Va. Poly. Inst. and State U., Blacksburg, 1954-55; asst. prof. history Va. Poly. Inst. and State U., 1955-58, assoc. prof., 1958-68, prof., 1968—; cons. hist. mgmt. Westmoreland Davis Meml. Found., Leesburg, Va., 1967-73, 77—. Author: George Wythe Randolph and the Confederate Elite, 1988; editor: Monticello Assn. Collected Papers, Vol. I, 1965, Vol. 2, 1984; co-editor Va. Social Sci. Jour., 1967-68; contbr. articles in field to profl. jours. Served to lt. USNR, 1943-49. Recipient award Va. soc. Am. Inst. Architects for Historic Preservation, 1985. Mem. Am. Hist. Assn., English Speaking Union (pres. SW Va. br. 1979), Nat. Trust Historic Preservation (bd. advs. 1976-79), Assn. Inst. Early Am. History and Culture, Attingham Assos., Assn. Preservation Va. Antiquities (dir. 1960-64, 67-77), Monticello Assn. (pres. 1969-71), So. Hist. Assn., Va. Hist. Assn., Soc. Archtl. History. Democrat. Episcopalian. Clubs: Farmington Country (Charlottesville, Va.); Shenandoah (Roanoke, Va.); Univ. (Blacksburg, Va.). Home: Box 219 301 Wall St Blacksburg VA 24063 Office: Va Poly Inst and State U Dept History Blacksburg VA 24061

SHACKELFORD, SCOTT ADDISON, air force officer, chemist; b. Long Beach, Calif., Aug. 11, 1944; s. Richard Walter and Phyllis Marian (Pearson) S.; m. Alpha Marilyn Coon, Aug. 23, 1969; children—Laura DeAnna, Vicki LeAnna. Student Colo. State U., 1962-64; B.A., Simpson Coll., 1964-66; M.A., No. Ariz. U., 1968; Ph.D., Ariz. State U., 1973. Second lt. U.S. Air Force, 1972, advanced through grades to major, 1988; research chemist F.J. Seiler Research Lab., U.S. Air Force Acad., Colo., 1972-74, research group chief, 1974-77,instr., asst. prof. dept. chemistry and biol. scis., 1977-78; lang. student Nat. Def. Lang. Inst., Monterey, Calif., 1978; exchange scientist DFVLR-Institut fuer Chemische Antriebe und Verfahrenstechnik, Hardthausen A.K., Fed. Republic Germany, 1978-80; research sect. chief Air Force Rocket Propulsion Lab., Edwards AFB, Calif., 1980-84; research liaison officer European Office Aerospace Research and Devel., London, 1984-87; dir. Aerospace Research Liaison, 1986-88; sr. scientist F.J. Seiler Research Lab. USAF Acad., Colo., 1987—; sec. Tri-Services Joint Tech. Coordinating Group/Munitions Devel./Working Party for Explosives, Washington, 1975-77; lab. research task mgr. to Air Force Office Sci. Research, Washington, 1981-84, 88—; nat. propellant survey cons., 1981-82; mem. sci. adv. com. Simpson Coll., Indianola, Iowa, 1983-87; mem. Jannaf combustion sub-com. Chem. Combustion Kinetics, 1988—. Contbr. articles to profl. publs. Patentee in field. Co-mgr. Tee Ball Youth Baseball Team, Fort Collins, Colo., 1964; asst. coach Am. Legion Summer Baseball Team, Pacifica, Calif., 1967, 68; Sunday school tchr. Village Christian Ch., Colorado Springs, Colo., 1975-77; adult class leader Base Protestant Chapel, Edwards, Calif., 1984. Recipient Research and Devel. award U.S. Air Force Chief-of-Staff, 1982, Alumni Achievement award Simpson Coll. Alumni Assn., 1985. Mem. Am. Chemical Soc. (fluorine div.). Mem. Disciples of Christ. Ch. Current work: In-situ mechanistic studies of thermochemical decomposition and combustion processes with deuterium isotope effects, polynitroaliphatic synthesis, selective organic fluorination with xenon difluoride. Subspecialties: Organic chemistry; Condensed Phase Reaction Mechanisms. Home: 2134 Wildwood Dr Colorado Springs CO 80918

SHACKLE, GEORGE LENNOX SHARMAN, economist, educator; b. Cambridge, Eng., July 14, 1903; s. Robert Walker and Fanny (Sharman) S.; B.A., U. London, 1931, Ph.D., 1937; D.Phil., U. Oxford, 1940; D.Sc. (hon.), New U. Ulster, 1974; D.Social Sci. (hon.), U. Birmingham (Eng.), 1978, U. Strathclyde, 1988; m. Gertrude Susan Rowe, Mar. 14, 1939 (dec. Apr. 1978); children—Robert Richard, Caroline; m. Catherine Squarey Gibb, Jan. 30, 1979. Mem. Sir Winston Churchill's statis. br. Brit. Admiralty and Cabinet Office, 1939-45, mem. econ. sect. Cabinet Office, 1945-50; reader econ. theory U. Leeds (Eng.), 1950-51; Brunner prof. econ. sci. U. Liverpool (Eng.), 1951-69; vis. prof. Columbia U., 1957-58; vis. prof. econs. U. Pitts., 1967, vis. prof. philosophy, 1967; Brit. Acad. Keynes lectr., 1976. Fellow Brit. Acad., History of Econs. Soc. (disting. fellow 1985); mem. Brit. Assn. for Advancement Sci. (pres. econs. sect. 1966), Royal Econ. Soc. (mem. council 1955-69). Author: Expectations, Investment and Income, 1938; Expectation in Economics, 1949; Mathematics at the Fireside, 1952; Uncertainty in Economics, 1955; Time In Economics, 1958; Economics for Pleasure, 1959; Decision, Order and Time, 1961; A Scheme of Economic Theory, 1965; The Nature of Economic Thought, 1966; The Years of High Theory, 1967; Expectation, Enterprise and Profit, 1970; Epistemics and Economics, 1972; An Economic Querist, 1973; Keynesian Kaleidics, 1974; Imagination and the Nature of Choice, 1979, Business, Time and Thought, 1988. Home: Rudloe Alde House Dr, Aldeburgh, Suffolk IP15 5EE, England

SHACKLETON, BRYAN, engineering company director; b. Doncaster, Yorkshire, Eng., July 11, 1933; s. Frank and Hetty (Roberts) S.; m. Bernadette Eugenie Ritchie, Oct. 1987; children: Ian Craig, Robert Ritchie, Ryan Michael. Mem. Inst. Mech. Engrs. Stockport Coll. Tech., 1957. Chartered engr. apprentice engr. Simon Engring. Ltd., Stockport, Cheshire, 1949-54; design draughtsman, 1956-59, tech. engr., 1959-63; tech. sales engr., sales mgr. R.W. Transmissions Ltd., Newcastle, Northumberland, Eng., 1963-66; mng. dir. Shackleton Engring. (UK) Ltd., Stockport, Cheshire, 1966-87; bd. dirs. Babcock Gears Ltd., Bolton, 1987—. Recipient Queen's award Queen's Awards Office, 1981, 82, Endeavour award Metro. Borough of Stockport, 1978. Fellow British Inst. Mgmt.; mem. Inst. Mech. Engrs. Mem. Ch. Eng. Club: Reddish Vale Golf (Stockport) (capt. 1973-74; 79-80). Inventor screw jacks, height adjusting units. Office: Babcock Gears Ltd, Albion Works, Waterloo St, Bolton BL1 8HW, England

SHACKLETON, RICHARD JAMES, lawyer; b. Orange, N.J., May 24, 1933; s. S. Paul and Mildred W. (Welsh) S.; m. Katharine L. Richards, June 16, 1956; children: Katharine Margaret, Julia Anne, Forrest Maxwell. Student Kalamazoo Coll., 1957; JD, Rutgers U., 1961. Bar: N.J. 1961, U.S. Dist. Ct. N.J., U.S. Dist. Ct. (ea. dist.) Va., N.Y. 1982, U.S. Dist. Ct. (so. dist.) N.Y., U.S. Ct. Appeals (3d and 4th cirs.), U.S. Supreme Ct. Ltd. atty. Berry Whitson & Berry, 1961; practice, Ship Bottom, N.J., 1961—; sr. ptnr. Shackleton, Hazeltine & Dasti, Ship Bottom, 1965—; dir. Citizens State Bank of N.J., Forked River. Pres., Beach Haven Inlet Taxpayers Assn., 1958-68; pres. Ocean County Vis. Homemakers Assn., 1966-72. Mem. Am. Trial Lawyers Assn., Am. Judicature Soc., ABA, N.J. Bar Assn., N.Y. Bar Assn., Ocean County Bar Assn., Essex County Assn., Ocean County Lawyers Club, Henryville Conservation Club (chmn. bd.), Henryville Flyfishers Club (pres.), Phila. Gun Club. Republican. Clubs: Seaview Country (Absecon, N.J.); Tuscarora. Home: 5614 West Ave Beach Haven NJ 08008 Office: 22d St and Long Beach Blvd Ship Bottom NJ 08008

SHAD, JOHN, diplomat, investment banker; b. Brigham City, Utah, June 27, 1923; s. John Sigsbee and Lillian (Rees) S.; m. Patricia Pratt, July 27, 1952; children: Leslie Anne, Rees Edward. BS cum laude, U. So. Cal., 1947; MBA, Harvard U., 1949; LLB, NYU, 1959; LD (hon.), Rochester U., 1987. Security analyst, account exec., investment banker 1949-62; with E.F. Hutton Group Inc. and E.F. Hutton & Co., Inc., 1963-81, v.p. to vice chmn. bd.; chmn. SEC, Washington, 1981-87; ambassador to The Netherlands 1987—; bd. dirs. Figgie Internat. Inc., Scudder Duo-Vest, Inc., Sheller-Globe Corp., Katy Industries, Inc., Kaufman & Broad, Inc., Triangle-Pacific Corp., also others; faculty N.Y. U. Grad. Sch. Bus. Adminstrn., 1961-62; mem. fin. adv. panel Nat. R.R. Passenger Corp. (Amtrack), 1970-75; speaker, writer on fin. markets, corp. fin. and mergers. Author: How Investment Bankers Appraise Corporations, Financial Realities of Mergers and others. Chmn. Reagan-Bush N.Y. Fin. Com., 1980. Served to lt. (j.g.) USNR, 1943-46. Recipient Bus. Statesman of Yr. award Bus. Sch. Club Harvard U., 1988, Investment Banker of Year award Fin. mag., 1972, Brotherhood award NCCJ, 1981 and other awards. Mem. Navy League, Beta Gamma Sigma, Phi Kappa Phi, Alpha Kappa Psi. Clubs: University (N.Y.C.), Harvard Business School (N.Y.C., named Bus. Statesman Yr., 1988), India House (N.Y.C.); Metropoliton (Washington), Greenwich Country, Chevy Chase Country. Office: American Embassy The Hague APO New York NY 09159

SHAFFER, ANITA MOHRLAND, educator, counselor; b. Racine, Wis., Apr. 5, 1939; d. Milton Arthur and Gudrun Amanda (Sundvoll) Stoffel; m. Ronald Dean Williams, June 24, 1987. BS magna cum laude, U. Wis.-Madison, 1961; MEd, U. Wash., 1966; postgrad. Ariz. State U., 1971-76. Cert. in elem. edn., social sci. secondary edn., spl edn., Tex., Ariz.; lic. profl. counselor, Tex.; diplomate Internat. Acad. Behavioral Medicine, Counseling and Psychotherapy. Tchr. Racine Unified Dist. 1, 1961-63, Edmonds Sch. Dist. 15, Alderwood Manor, Wash., 1963-70; tchr. Ariz. Dept. Corrections, Phoenix, 1971-77; tchr. spl. edn. Pasadena Ind. Sch. Dist. (Tex.); 1977-78, spl. edn. counselor, 1978—. Mem. Am. Assn. Counseling and Devel., Am. Mental Health Counselors Assn., Am. Sch. Counselor Assn., Tex. Assn. Counseling and Devel., AAUW, Nat. Assn. Female Execs., Mus. Fine Arts Houston (patron), Beta Sigma Phi, Pi Lambda Theta. Home: 260 El Dorado Blvd Apt 801 Webster TX 77598 Office: Pasadena Ind Sch Dist Spl Services 3010 Bayshore Dr Pasadena TX 77502

SHAFFER, EDWARD HARRY, economics educator; b. Pitts., Jan. 26, 1923; s. Meyer J. and Sylvia (Bubligoff) S.; m. Florence Schll, Feb. 28, 1959; children—Martha, Paul. B.A., U. Mich., 1948, M.A., 1949; Ph.D., Columbia U., 1966. Asst. prof. Western Wash. State Coll., Bellingham, Wash., 1965-68; asst. prof. Occidental Coll., Los Angeles, 1966-70; prof. econs. U. Alta., Edmonton, Can., 1970-88; prof. emeritus, 1988—. Author: The Oil Import Program, 1968; The United States and Control of World Oil, 1983; Canada's Oil and The American Empire, 1983. Served with AUS, 1943-46. Columbia U. Presidents fellow, 1964; Dept. Energy, Mines & Research grantee, 1971, 78. Mem. Am. Econ. Assn., Can. Econs. Assn., Western Econ. Assn., Assn. Evolutionary Econs., Indsl. Orgn. Soc. Avocations: photography; bicycling. Home: 522 Moberley Rd #705, Vancouver, BC Canada V5Z 4G4 Office: Univ Alta, Dept Econs, Edmonton, AB Canada T6G 2H4

SHAFFER, HOWARD JEFFREY, clinical psychologist, consultant, researcher, educator; b. Boston, Sept. 1, 1948; s. Milton and Ruth Ann (Weiner) S.; m. Linda Marie Andrews; children: David Andrew, Paige Meredith. B.A., U. N.H., 1970; M.S., U. Miami, Coral Gables, Fla., 1972, Ph.D., 1974. Lic. psychologist, Mass., N.H.; registered psychologist Nat. Register Health Service Providers in Psychology, 1982. Research dir. Psycho-Social Rehab. Ctr. Dade County (Fla.), Inc., 1974-75; clin. dir. Project Turnabout, Inc., Hingham, Mass., 1975-78, East Boston (Mass.) Drug Rehab. Clinic, 1976-77; dir. spl. consultation and treatment program for women Judge Gould Inst. Human Resources, Inc., Worcester, Mass., 1977-78; dir. narcotics treatment program Drug Problems Resource Center, dept. psychiatry Harvard Med. Sch. at Cambridge (Mass.) Hosp. and North Charles Found. for Tng. and Research, 1978-82, Ctr. for Addition Studies Harvard Med. Sch. and The Cambridge Hosp., 1986—; chief psychologist N. Charles. Inst. for the Additions, 1983—; mem. adj. faculty U. Miami, 1974; mem. clin. faculty Barry Coll., 1974-75; mem. field faculty Lone Mountain Coll., 1974-75; teaching cons. U. Lowell, 1975-76; clin. assoc. prof. counseling psychology Boston U., 1976-78; instr. psychology dept. psychiatry Harvard Med. Sch. at Cambridge Hosp., 1978-81, asst. prof. psychology, 1982—; mem. faculty Mass. Psychol. Center, Boston, 1980; mem. council on marijuana and health 1981-85; mem. adv. bd. and faculty Northeastern Comprehensive Service Inst., Danvers, Mass., 1983-85; mem. field faculty Grad. Sch. Psychology and Counseling, Lesley Coll., 1983—; chief psychologist North Charles Inst. for Addictions, 1982—; mem. spl. study sect. NIH and Nat. Cancer Inst., 1984—; dir.Ctr. for Addiction Studies, Harvard Med. Sch., 1986—. Contbr. articles, revs., abstracts to profl. publs., presentations in field; editor: a book about drug issues Myths and Realities, 1977, (with M. E. Burglass) Classic Contributions in the Addictions, 1981 (alt. main selection Behavioral Sci. Book Club 1981); The Addictive Behaviors, 1985; (with H. Milkman) Addictions: Multidisciplinary Perspectives and Treatments, 1984; (with S. Jones) Quitting Cocaine: The Struggle Against Impulse, 1988; assoc. editor Jour. Substance Abuse Treatment, 1984—; assoc. editor: Psychology of Addictive Behavior, 1982—; guest editor: spl. issue Advances in Alcohol and Substance Abuse, 1983; mem. editorial rev. bd.: Jour. Psychoactive Drugs, 1981—, Advances in Alcohol and Substance Abuse, 1982—. Mem. Andover (Mass.) Substance Abuse Com., 1982. Recipient 1st place award U. N.H. Undergrad. Conf. for Psychol. Research, 1969. Mem. Am. Psychol. Assn., AAAS, Soc. Psychologists in Addictive Behavior, Boston Computer Soc., Psi Chi, Phi Kappa Phi. Democrat. Jewish. Clubs: Harvard (Boston). Research on cognitive, behavioral, and psychodynamic factors associated with substance use and abuse, social psychology of psychotherapy; philosophy of sci. Home: 171 Summer St Andover MA 01810 Office: Harvard U Med Sch Dept Psychiatry 1493 Cambridge St Cambridge MA 02139

SHAFFER, JOHN WHITCOMB, psychologist, consultant; b. Harrisburg, Pa., Jan. 6, 1932; s. William Andrew and Annie Martha (Lauffer) S.; B.S., Pa. State U., 1953, M.S., 1954, Ph.D., 1957; m. Sandra Miriam Slifkin, Jan.

30, 1953; children—Jeffrey Brian, Clifford Alan. Instr. to asso. prof. med. psychology Johns Hopkins U. Sch. Medicine, Balt., 1957—; cons. in Balt., Friends Med. Sci. Research Center, Inc., 1960—, Social Security Adminstrn., 1965—, Md. Dept. Mental Hygiene, 1967—; pvt. practice research cons., Balt.; mem., chmn. Md. Bd. Examiners of Psychologists, 1968-71; investigator, co-investigator govt. and pvt. behavioral and med. scis. research. Lic. psychologist, Md. Mem. Am. Statis. Assn., Am. Psychol. Assn., Md. Psychol. Assn. Episcopalian. Author, co-author sci. articles in books, nat., internat. sci. and profl. jours. Home and Office: 406 Crosby Rd Baltimore MD 21228

SHAFFER, PETER LEVIN, playwright; b. Liverpool, Eng., May 15, 1926; s. Jack and Reka (Fredman) S. B.A., Cambridge U., Eng., 1950. Conscript coal mines, Eng., 1944-47; music critic Time and Tide, 1961-62. Author: Five Finger Exercise, 1958 (N.Y. Drama Critics Circle award 1960), The Private Ear and the Public Eye, 1963, The Royal Hunt of the Sun, 1964, Black Comedy, 1965, The Battle of Shrivings, 1970, Equus, 1973 (Antoinette Perry award, Drama Critics award), Amadeus, 1979 (Evening Standard Drama award, London Drama Critics award, Antoinette Perry award, Acad. award for best adapted screenplay 1985), Lettice and Lovage, 1987, (films) Amadeus, 1984, Yonadab, 1985, (TV plays) The Prodigal Father, 1955, The Salt Land, 1955, Balance of Terror, 1957. Recipient Drama award Evening Standard, 1958, 79. Mem. Dramatists Guild (Commdr. of the Order of the Brit. Empire award 1987). Club: Garrick (London). Address: 173 Riverside Dr New York NY 10024

SHAFFER, RONALD LOWREY, broadcasting executive; b. Hutchinson, kans., Feb. 13, 1951; s. Frederick I. Jr. and June Louise (Lowrey) S.; m. Brenda Gay Miller, July 7, 1973; children: Stephanie Anne, Christopher Toban. BS, U. Kans., 1973. V.p. Shaffer Oil & Gas Co., Hutchinson, 1973-76; exec. v.p. Kans. Crude Inc., Hutchinson, 1976-78, pres., 1978-85; chmn. bd. Consolidated Communications Network, Inc., Hutchinson, 1986—; bd. dirs. Mar-wa-ka Broadcasting Co., Lawrence, Dimension Fin. Corp., New Caanan, Conn., Traditional Bldgs., Inc., Hutchinson, Kan-Cal Spyglass Hills, Inc., San Francisco and Hutchinson. Fund raiser YMCA, Boy Scouts Am., Am. Cancer Soc., 1973—. Named one of Outstanding Young Men Am., 1984. Mem. Nat. Assn. Broadcasters, Kans. Ind. Oil and Gas Assn. Democrat. Presbyterian. Clubs: Prairie Dunes Country (Hutchinson), Biltmore Country (Phoenix). Office: Consolidated Communications Network Inc 200 Wolcott Bldg Hutchinson KS 67501

SHAFI, YOUSIF M., government official; b. Taif, Saudi Arabia, Oct. 15, 1952; s. Mohammad H. Shafi and Fatimah Orainan; m. Mohammad Khushaiban Badriah, July 14, 1983; children: Mohammad, Fatimah. B.S. in Elec. Engring., Weber State Coll., Utah, 1979. Mgr., SAFE, Taif and Jeddah, Saudi Arabia, 1979-81; sec. gen. Taif C. of C. and Industry, 1981—; dir. Al-Rawdhah Kindergarten, Taif, 1985—. Home: Karwa, Taif Saudi Arabia Office: Taif C of C and Industry, PO Box 1818, Taif Saudi Arabia Other: Al Rawdhah Kindergarten, PO Box 2244, Taif Saudi Arabia

SHAFTAN, BERNICE, fashion design studio executive; b. N.Y.C.; d. Samuel David and Hannah Shirley (Averick) Miller; m. Gerald Wittes Shaftan, May 28, 1956; children—Richard Keith, Susan Debra. Student Art Students League, 1948-50. Designer Carlisle Shoe Co., N.Y.C., 1950-52; dir. design, fashion dir. Hamilton Shoe Co., St. Louis and N.Y.C., 1952-57; pres. Bernice Shaftan Designs Ltd., N.Y.C., 1957—; cons. mktg. dir. Carr Leather Co., Lynn, Mass., 1978—; cons., interior design Hotel Montalembert, Paris, 1976—; cons. design dir. I.T.I., Bologna, Italy, The Portuguese Trade Co., N.Y. and Portugal. Contbr. articles to profl. jours. Mem. county com. Conservative Party, N.Y. County, 1982-84. Recipient shoe design award Tanners Council Am., 1964. Mem. Color Assn., Internat. Platform Assn., Fashion Group, Inc., Shoe Women Execs., Inc., (pres. 1969-70, chmn. bd. dirs. 1970-71), Footwear and Accessories council (pres. 1980-82, chmn. bd. dirs. 1982-84, bd. dirs., Named Woman of Yr. 1987), Nat. Arts Club, Gramercy Park Assn., Brookdale Hosp. Jr. League. Avocations: skiing; painting; ballet. Home: Apt 11A-60 Gramercy Park New York NY 10010 Office: Bernice Shaftan Designs Ltd Apt Penthouse A-D 60 Gramercy Park North New York NY 10010

SHAH, AMRITLAL JIVRAJ, textile and clothing industry executive; b. Mombasa, Kenya, Nov. 6, 1941; s. Jivraj Devraj and Vejiben Shah; m. Manjula Amritlal, Oct. 23, 1967; children—Reshma, Amar. B.Com., Sydenham Coll. Commerce and Econs., Bombay U., 1963. Trustee, Nat. Provident Fund, Dar Es Salaam, Tanzania, 1975-79; vice chmn. Tanzania Soc. for the Deaf, Dar Es Salaam, 1974 84; vice chmn. Assn. Tanzania Employer, Dar Es Salaam, 1969—, chmn., 1987—; mng. dir. Garments Mfrs. Ltd., Dar Es Salaam, 1966—, Polyknit Textile Industries Ltd., Dar Es Salaam, 1977—. Fellow Inst. Dirs.; mem. Brit. Inst. Mgmt. Lodges: Guiding Star; Rotary (dist. gov.). Home: 15 Ocean Rd, PO Box 2358, Dar Es Salaam Tanzania Office: Garments Mfrs Ltd, 62 Migeyo Rd, Dar Es Salaam Tanzania

SHAH, APOORVA SHANTILAL, steel tube company executive; b. Ahmedabad, Gujarat, India, Apr. 14, 1939; s. Shantilal Mangaldas and Vasantben Shantilal (Maniben) S.; m. Karuna Apoorva Anubhai, Jan. 20, 1964; children—Chintan, Tejal. B.S., St. Xavier's Coll., 1960. Dir. Gujarat Steel Tubes Ltd., Ahmedabad, 1968-69, mng. dir., 1970—, chmn., 1977—; chmn. Neeka Tubes Ltd., Ahmedabad, 1974—; dir. Lucky Agencies, Ahmedabad, 1981—. Mem. Internat. Tube Assn. (internat. adv. com.), Confedn. Indian Engring. Industry (exec. council 1979-85, Western regional com. 1979—), Engring. Export Promotion Council (western regional com. 1979—), Gujarat C. of C. and Industry (exec. com. 1986—). Clubs: Gujarat Table Tennis (pres. Ahmedabad 1982-84), Ahmedabad Gymkhana (hon. treas. 1983-84). Avocations: reading; social activities; tennis; yoga. Home: Near Police Hdqtrs, Shahibag, Ahmedabad, Gujarat 380004, India Office: Gujarat Steel Tubes Ltd, Bank of India Bldg Bhadra, Ahmedabad, Gujarat 380001, India

SHAH, CHANDRAKANT PADAMSHI, medical educator, health consultant; b. Limbdi, India, Apr. 7, 1936; came to Can., 1965; s. Padamshi Jasraj and Surajben Padamshi Shah; m. Sudha Jayantilal Parekh, July 10, 1966; children: Sunil Steven, Rajiv Robert. MBBS, Gujarat Univ., 1961; diploma Am. Bd. Pediatrics (Chgo.), 1964; MRCP, DCH, Royal Coll. Physicians and Surgeons (Glasgow), 1965; FRCP, Royal Coll. Physicians and Surgeons (Can.), 1967; MS in Hygiene, Harvard Sch. Pub. Health (Boston), 1974. Asst. prof. pediatrics U. B.C., Vancouver, 1967-69; med. dir. Children's Aid Soc. Vancouver, 1970-72; assoc. prof. preventive medicine and biostats U. Toronto, 1972-80, dir. residency program community health, 1976-88, prof. health adminstrn., 1980—, preventive medicine and biostats, 1980—, prof. pediatrics, 1972—, prof. family and community medicine, 1988—, prof. faculty social work, 1982—; pepediatric cons. Hosp. Sick Children, Toronto, 1972—, Sioux Lookout Zone, Ont., Can., 1974. Contbr. articles to profl. jours. Nat. Health grantee, 1967-68, 68-70, 69-71, 70-72, 70-73, 71-74, 71-74, 73-74; Children's Hosp. grantee, 1969; P.S.I. Found. grantee, 1975-76, 75-76, 80, 85-85; Hosp. Sick Children Found. grantee, 1976-77, 76-79, 80-82, 83-86; Health Activities Summer Employment Program Students grantee; Faculty Medicine Summer Student Scholarship, 1982. Mem. Can. Med. Assn., Ont. Med. Assn., Can. Pub. Health Assn., Can. Assn. Tchrs. Social and Preventive Medicine (sec.-treas. 1980-82), Can. Pediatric Soc. Avocations: hiking; classical music; writing poems. Home: 31 Newgate Rd, Toronto, ON Canada M6B 3G6 Office: U Toronto, Dept Preventive Medicine, and Biostatistics, 12 Queens Park Crescent W, Toronto, ON Canada M5S 1A8

SHAH, NATVERLAL JAGJIVANDAS, cardiologist; b. Godhra, Gujarat, India, Aug. 3, 1926; s. Jagjivandas Purshottamdas and Mahalaxmi (Jagjivandas) S.; m. Sundri Choitram Malkaney, Mar. 15, 1956; children—Sailesh N., Sarina N. M.D., U. Bombay, 1954. Med. registrar, sr. med. tutor Cardiology King Edward Meml. Hosp., Bombay, 1954-56; hon. assoc. physician Gokuldas Tejpal Hosp., also hon prof. medicine Grant Med. Coll., Bombay, 1959-74; hon. physician and cardiologist, head ICC unit, mobile coronary CCU, exercise stress test Bombay Hosp., 1960—; patron 2d Internat. Conf. on Hypertension, 1985. Author: A Handbook of Endocrine Disorders, 1960; Prevent a Heart Attack, 2d edit., 1977; An Approach to Electrocardiography, 3d edit., 1978; Heart-Before, During, After, 1984; Advanced Electrocardiography, 1986; Clinical Electrocardiography, 1988. Contbr. articles to profl. jours. Hon. spl. exec. magistrate Govt. of Maharashtra, 1980—. Mem. Internat. Congress Hypertension (pres. 1977), Cardiol. Soc. Indian (chmn. Bombay br. 1977-78), Internat. Conf. Advances Internat. Medicine (v.p.), Internat. Conf. Prevention Heart Disease and Cardiac Rehab. (v.p. 1978), Nat. Council Hypertension (pres., founder 1978-81), Nat. Soc. Prevention Heart Disease and Rehabilitation (pres. 1988—). Clubs: Wellingdon Sports, Nat, Sports (Bombay). Home: 4/D Ananta, Rajaballi Patel Rd, Bombay 400026, India Office: Med Research Centre, New Marine Lines, Bombay 400020, India

SHAH, RAMESH PREMCHAND, entrepreneur; b. Bardoli, Gujarat, India, Feb. 24, 1937; came to U.S., 1959; s. Premchand L. and Mangiben P. S.; m. Jaya B. Patel, Aug. 21, 1966; children: Baiju, Bella. BE, U. Bombay, 1959; MSEE, U. Ill., 1960; MBA, Marquette U., 1965. Pres. Alpha Devel. Corp., Mentor, Ohio, 1976—; chief exec. officer, v.p. Computer Resources, Cleve., 1986—, also bd. dirs.; bd. dirs. ALFA Rhythms Pvt. Ltd., Bombay, Trans Datacom Pvt. Ltd., Bombay; ptnr. Elektrotek System Industries, Bombay, 1984—; chmn. New Ventures Mgmt. Lake Erie Coll., Painesville, Ohio, 1976-82. Mgr. Greater Cleve. Growth Assn., 1973-76. Mem. Cleve. Engring. Soc. (chmn. tech. edn. sect. 1974-76). Hindu. Office: Alpha Profl Bldg 8925 Mentor Ave Mentor OH 44060

SHAH, SAIYID MASROOR, med. physicist; b. Rampur, India, Jan. 8, 1938; came to U.S., 1974; s. Syed Maqsood and Noor Jehan (Ali) S.; m. Janice Moore, Aug. 8, 1970. Ph.D., Tex. Tech. U., 1970. Lectr. in physics SRA/DJ Colls., Karachi, 1958-64; asst. prof. physics U. Karachi, 1970-72; assoc. prof. physics Baluchistan U. Quetta, 1972-73; fgn. research fellow Sophia U., Tokyo, 1973-74; postdoctoral research fellow physics M.D. Anderson Hosp., Houston, 1976; med. physicist Rosewood Hosp., Houston, 1976-83, St. Mary's Med. Ctr., Evansville, Ind., 1984—; cons., instr. continuing edn. program, 1976—. Contbr. articles to profl. jours. Japan Soc. for Promotion of Sci. Fgn. Research fellow, 1973; Fulbright Travel scholar, 1964; recipient Am. Friends of Middle East Hon. Mention award, 1969. Mem. Assn. Physicists in Medicine. Muslim. Subspecialties: Medical physics; Atomic and molecular physics. Current work: Radiation physics; cancer treatment planning; radiation safety; cancer treatment plan optimization for high energy radiation beams, quality control, dosimetry, radiation safety. Home: PO Box 5234 Evansville IN 47715 Office: St Mary's Med Ctr 3700 Washington Ave Evansville IN 47750

SHAH, SHĀ SHĀNK JAYANTILAL L., chemical engineer; b. Ahmedabad, Gujarat, India, Feb. 28, 1957; s. Jayantilal L. and Jaya J. Shah; m. Ranna Shashank, Jan. 12, 1961; 1 child, Aarohi Shashank. BE in Chemistry, L.D. Coll. Engring., Ahmedabad, 1979. Trainee engr. chem. div. Calico Mills, Ahmedabad, 1979-80; chem. engr. Maize Products Ltd., Ahmedabad, 1980-81; chief exec. officer Aarohi Chemwax, Ahmedabad, 1983—; chief exec. officer, mng. dir. Aarohi Motors, Ahmedabad, 1985—; mng. dir. Aarohi Motors, Ahmedabad, 1985; bd. dirs. Perfect Agys., Ahmedabad. Mem. exec. com. Youth Hostel Assn. India, Ahmedabad, 1981-82. Mem. Ahmedabad Mgmt. Assn. (life), Indian Instn. Chem. Engrs. Clubs: Rajpath Ltd., Rifle Ltd. (Ahmedabad). Lodge: Lions (pres. 1978-79, chmn. 1980-81, Community Betterment award 1980-81). Office: Aarohi Motors Ltd, 1 Laxmi Estate NH #8 Narol, Ahmedabad, Gujarat 382 405, India

SHAH, SHIRISH KALYANBHAI, educator; b. Ahmedabad, India, May 24, 1942; came to U.S., 1962, naturalized, 1974; s. Kalyanbhai T. and Sushilaben K. Shah; B.S. in Chemistry and Physics, St. Xavier's Coll., Gujarat U., 1962; PhD in Phys. Chemistry, U. Del., 1968; cert. in bus. mgmt. U. Va., 1986; PhD in Cultural Edn. (hon.) World Univ. West, 1986; m. Kathleen Long, June 28, 1973; 1 son, Lawrence. Asst. prof. Washington Coll., Chestertown, Md., 1967-68; dir. quality control Vita Foods, Chestertown, 1968-72; asst. prof., asso. prof. sci., adminstr. food, marine sci. and vocat. programs Chesapeake Coll., Wye Mills, Md., 1968-76; asso. prof., prof. sci., chmn. dept. tech. studies Community Coll. of Balt., 1976—, chmn. computer systems and engring. techs., 1982—; mem. Balt. City Adult Edn. Adv. Com., 1982—; chmn. Coll. wide computer user com., 1985—; permanent mem. Republican Senatorial Com. Mem. com. Am. Lung Assn., 1971-80; mem. Congl. Adv. Com., 1983. Fellow Am. Inst. Chemists; mem. IEEE, Am. Chem. Soc., Data Processing Mgmt. Assn., Nat. Environ. Tng. Assn., Nat. Sci. Tchrs. Assn., Am. Vocat. Assn., Am. Tech. Edn. Assn., Am. Fedn. Tchrs., Md. State Tchrs. Assn., Md. Assn. Community and Jr. Colls. (v.p. 1977-78, pres. 1978—), Sigma Xi, Iota Lambda Sigma Nu. Roman Catholic. Contbr. articles on sci. and tech. to profl. jours. Home: 5605 Purlington Way Baltimore MD 21212 Office: Community Coll Balt Harbor Campus Baltimore MD 21202

SHAH, SUNIL NARSHI, management executive; b. Kisumu, Nyanza, Kenya, July 26, 1953; s. Narshi Punja Lakhtir and Kanchan (Narshi) S.; m. Shakuntala Sunil, Apr. 29, 1979; children: Sajni, Savan. Grad. high sch., Kisumu. Exec. dir. United Millers Ltd., Kisumu, 1977—. Hindu. Club: Nyanza (Kisumu) (golf capt.). Office: United Millers Ltd, PO Box 620, Kisumu Kenya

SHAH, SYED ASLAM, surgeon; b. Karachi, Sind, Pakistan, Sept. 10, 1953; s. Syed Mustafa Shah and Farhati Bano; m. Rehana Shaheen Aslam, July 31, 1984; 1 child, Maimoona Aslam. BS in Medicine, Dow Med. Coll., Karachi, 1976. Med. officer Cen. Govt. Ployclinic, Islamabad, Pakistan, 1977-78, intern then resident, 1979-81, registrar in surgery, 1978-84, sr. registrar, 1984-85; surg. specialist Cantonment Gen. Hosp., Rawalpinidi, Pakistan, 1985-86; surgeon Pakistan Inst. Med. Scis., Islamabad, 1986—. Editor brochures med. symposium and pediatric conf., 1984, 86. Fellow Coll. Physicians and Surgeons; mem. Pakistan Med. Assn., Soc. Surgeons. Home: 1514-C, Street 40, G-6/1-3 Islamabad Pakistan Office: Pakistan Inst Med Scis, G-8/3 Islamabad Pakistan

SHAH, ZAFARYAB ALI, medical tools company executive; b. Bignoor, Pakistan, June 8, 1942; s. Syed Mehfooz and Umbrun-Nisa (Syeda Umrun) Ali Shah; m. Musarat Zafaryab, May 26, 1975; 1 child, Um-E-Saleha. B of Engring., Dawood Engring. Coll., Karachi, 1968. Design/prodn. engr. Telephone Industries of Pakistan, Haripur Hazara, 1969-76; sr. planning engr. Telephone Industries of Pakistan, 1976-81, safety engr., 1974-81; prodn. engr. Accuray Surgs. Ltd., Sialkot, Pakistan, 1981-85; factory mgr. Accuray Surgs. Ltd., 1985—; engring. cons. Cen. Engring. div. Lakson Group of Cos., Karachi, 1982—; Al-Kamal Group of Industries, 1986—. Hon. mem. cen. body Tehrik-E-Istaqlal Party, Pakistan, 1973-78. Mem. Am. Soc. Metals, Pakistan Engring. Council Islamabad, Sialkat C. of C., Surg. Instruments Mfrs. Assn. Pakistan Muslim League. Club: T & T Colony. Office: Accuray Surgs Ltd, 71A SIE, Sialkot Pakistan

SHAHANEY, RAM JAVHERMAL, manufacturing executive; b. Hyderabad, Sind, India, Oct. 29, 1930; s. Javhermal Tahilram and Gomibai Shahani; m. Sunita Keswani, Oct. 3, 1984. BS in Engring., Imperial Coll. Sci. and Tech., London, 1950. With Jessop & Co., Ltd., Calcutta, India, 1953-78, mng. dir., 1972-75; chmn., mng. dir. Ashok Leyland, Ltd., Madras, India, 1975-78. Fellow Indian Inst. Welding; mem. City and Guilds Inst. London (assoc.), Brit. Inst. Mgmt. (companion). Clubs: Madras; Calcutta, Bengal (Calcutta). Home: #6 Boat Club Rd 2d Ave, Madras, Tamil Nadu 600028, India Office: Ashok Leyland Ltd, 19 Rajaji Salai, Madras, Tamil Nadu 600001, India

SHAHARIR, BIN MOHAMAD ZAIN, mathematics educator; b. Pasir Putih, Kelantan, Malaysia, Jan. 1, 1948; s. Mohamad Zain and Azizah Mamat; m. Miskiah Ahmad; children—Syahrul Sazli, Syahrul Sazliyana, Syahrul Sazlida, Syahrul Syazwani. B.Sc. with honors, LaTrobe and Syazwan U., Australia, 1970, Ph.D. in Applied Math., 1974. Head math. dept. U. Kebangsaan Malaysia, Kuala Lumpur, 1975-79, assoc. prof., 1978-82, prof., 1983—, dir. Ctr. Quantitative Studies, Bangi, 1984-85, dep. vice-chancellor, 1986—; cons. Malaysian Lang. Planning Ctr., Kuala Lumpur, 1977—. Author: The Role of Mathematics in Industry, 1979; Planning via Mathematics, Elementary Linear Programming, 1980; Elementary Mathematics and Its Applications in Life and Medical Sciences, 1982; The Role and the Policy of Mathematics Education in Malaysia, 1984; Series and Its Applications in Differential Equations, 1985; Some Elementary Problems in Life and Medical Sciences: A Mathematical Approach and Its Solutions, 1985; A Note on Techniques of Integration of a Single Variable Function, 1985; Advanced Linear Programming, 1985; Fourier Transformation and Its Applications, 1985; Introduction to History and Philosophy of Science, 1987; translator: Impact of Science on Society (Bertrand Russell), 1980, Science and Sociology of Knowledge (Mulkay); contbr. articles to profl. jours.; chief editor sci. bull. Suara Sains, 1985, Asasains, 1984—. Vice-pres. Assn. Tchrs. and Parents, 1982. Assoc. fellow Inst. Math. and Its Applications (U.K.); mem. Inst. Physics Malaysia, Malaysian Math. Soc. (v.p. 1980-81), Malaysian Islamic Sci. Acad. (v.p. 1980-84, pres. 1985-86, sec. gen. 1986—). Avocations: soccer, writing, reading. Home: No 11 Jalan 3/4, Bandar Baru Bangi, Selangor Malaysia Office: U Kebangsaan Malaysia, Vice Chancellor Office, Bandar Baru Bangi, Selangor Malaysia

SHAHNAVAZ, HOUSHANG, ergonomics educator; b. Tehran, Iran, Mar. 12, 1936; arrived in Sweden, 1980; s. Mohamad Nasser Shahnavaz; m. Azita Shahnavaz; children: Rasmy-Nive, Shadi. Diploma in Mech. Engring., Darmstadt, 1966; MSc in Ergonomics, Birmingham (Eng.) U., 1973, PhD in Ergonomics, 1976. Tech. dir. Tehran Opera House, 1966-68, asst. prof., 1977-80; lectr. Tehran Tech. U., 1968-73; research fellow Birmingham U., 1976-77; acting prof. indsl. ergonomics LuleÅ (Sweden) U., 1980—, dir. Ctr. for for Ergonomics of Developing Countries, 1983—; head coordinating dept. Royal Commn., Tehran, 1978; cons. ergonomics WHO, Internat. Labour Office and World Bank. Spl. editor Internat. Jour. Indsl. Ergonomics, Internat. Jour. Applied Ergonomics; contbr. numerous articles to profl. jours. Fellow Ergonomics Soc.; mem. Human Factors Soc., Internat. System Safety Soc., S.E. Asian Ergonomics Soc., Nordiska Ergonomisällskapet. Office: Lulea U, Dept Ergonomics, 951-87 Lulea Sweden

SHAIFER, NORMAN, communications executive; b. Bklyn., Oct. 28, 1931; s. Abe and Rose (Cohen) S. Student, Coll. City N.Y., 1949-52. Founder, pres. Custom Communications Systems, Inc., S. Hackensack, N.J., 1962—; publisher Priest Forum mag., 1968—; pres. Heritage Arts Ltd., Brit. Nat. Trust Collection; mem. bd. Mgmt. Decision Lab. Grad. Sch. Bus. Adminstrn. N.Y. U.; cons. to pub. and printing industry orgns.; cons. on communications and organizational and fund-raising to various non-profit orgns. including ARC. Author: John Paul II, a Son of Poland. Pres. Heritage Arts Ltd. Brit. Nat. Trust Collection, bd. dirs. Royal Oak Found., Inc. Served in U.S. Army, 1952-54. Mem. GraphicArts Tech. Found., Soc. Photog. Scientists and Engrs., Guild for Religious Architecture.

SHAIKH, SIKANDER AHMED, executive chef; b. Solapur, Maharashtra, India, May 26, 1950; s. Ahmed Mohomed and Kamarunissa Ahmed Shaikh; m. Farzana Sikander Shaikh, Nov. 21, 1975; children: Shebaz, Durrain, Aafreen. Degree in Applied Nutrition, Hotel Mgmt., Catering Tech., Bombay, 1972; student, Culinary Inst. Am., 1981. Chef trainee Taj Inrercontinental, Bombay, 1972-73, jr. sous chef, 1973-74, sr. sous chef, 1974-76, chef, 1977-83; exec. chef West End Hotel, Bangalore, India, 1984—; designer kitchen plan West End Hotel, Bangalore, 1987-88; designer kitchen plan Savoy Hotel, Ooty, India, 1987-88. Islamic. Home: Niveditha 15, Miller Tank Bund RD, Bangalore Karnataka India 560 052 Office: West End Hotel, Race Course Rd, Bangalore India 560 001

SHAIN, IRVING, chemical company executive; b. Seattle, Jan. 2, 1926; s. Samuel and Selma (Blockoff) S.; m. Mildred Ruth Udell, Aug. 31, 1947; children—Kathryn A., Steven T., John R., Paul S. B.S. in Chemistry, U. Wash., 1949, Ph.D. in Chemistry, 1952. From instr. to prof. U. Wis., Madison, 1952-75, vice chancellor, 1970-75, chancellor, 1977-86; provost, v.p. acad. affairs U. Wash., Seattle, 1975-77; v.p., chief scientist Olin Corp., Stamford, Conn., 1987—, also bd. dirs.; mem. tech. adv. group Johnson Controls, Inc., Milw., 1980—; bd. dirs. Olin Corp., Stamford, Conn., Univ. Research Park Inc., Madison, 1984-86. Contbr. articles on electroanalytical chemistry to profl. jours. Bd. dirs. Madison Gen. Hosp., 1972-75; mem. Wis. for Research Inc., Madison, 1983-86; v.p. Madison Community Found., 1984-86. Served with U.S. Army, 1943-46, PTO. Fellow AAAS; mem. Am. Chem. Soc., Electrochem. Soc., Internat. Soc. Electrochemistry, Phi Beta Kappa, Sigma Xi, Phi Kappa Phi. Home: 224 Blackberry Dr Stamford CT 06903 Office: Olin Corp 120 Long Ridge Rd Stamford CT 06903

SHAINIS, MURRAY JOSEPH, management consultant; b. N.Y.C., June 9, 1926; s. Henry and Lena (Edelman) S.; m. Hilda Gertler, June 28, 1953; children: Daniel, Julie, Janet. BEE, CCNY, 1949; MME, Poly. Inst. N.Y., 1957, MS in Mgmt., 1970. Registered profl. engr., N.Y. Mgr. quality control, production control mgr., production engr. Presto Recording Corp., Paramus, N.J., 1949-55; staff mgmt. engr. Mergenthaler Linotype, Bklyn., 1955-57; asst. dir. electronics Fairchild Electronics, Syosset, N.Y., 1957-59; mgr. ops. Advanced Devel. Lab., Westbury, N.Y., 1959-62; mgr. engring. Gen. Instrument, Hicksville, N.Y., 1962-69; pres. Murray J. Shainis, Inc., Beechhurst, N.Y., 1969—. Author: Engineer as Manager, 1972, Office Furniture Industry, 1974, Engineering Management, 1976, Operations Managers Desk Book, 1982. Served with USN, 1943-46, ETO, PTO. Mem. Engring. Mgmt. Soc., Soc. Profl. Mgmt. Cons., Inst. Mgmt. Cons. (cert.), IEEE (sr.). Home: PO Box 730 Sheffield MA 01257 Office: 157-11 9th Ave Beechhurst NY 11357

SHAKAGORI, FUMIO, design printing company executive; b. Osaka, Japan, Aug. 8, 1948; s. Yahichi and Yssue (Yoshida) S.; m. Harue Yamane, May 15, 1982; children: Masao, Rie. B in Econs., Kinki U., Osaka, 1987. Mgr. Daiwa Co. Ltd., Osaka, 1987—. Clubs: Bokai Yacht (Kobe, Japan), Shorinji Kenpo (Osaka). Home: 2-6-20 Chuo Jotoku, Osaka 536, Japan Office: Daiwa Co Ltd, 1-4-57 Shigita Jotoku, Osaka 536, Japan

SHAKELY, JOHN (JACK) BOWER, foundation executive; b. Hays, Kans., Jan. 9, 1940; s. John B. and Martha Jean (Gaston) S.; 1 son, Benton. B.A., U. Okla., 1962. Vol. Peace Corps., Costa Rica, 1963-64; editor publs. Dept. Def., 1967-68; dir. devel. U. Okla., 1968-70, Resthaven Mental Health Ctr., Los Angeles, 1970-74; pres. Jack Shakely Assocs., Los Angeles, 1974-75; sr. adv. Grantsmanship Ctr., Los Angeles, 1975-79, Council on Founds., Washington, 1979; pres. Calif. Community Found., Los Angeles, 1980—; lectr. in field. Bd. dirs. Coro Found., Los Angeles, 1982-85; bd. dirs. So. Calif. Assn. Philanthropy, 1980—, Calif. Hist. Soc., 1985—. Served to 1st lt. U.S. Army, 1965-68. Decorated Army Commendation medal. Democrat. Office: Calif Community Found 3580 Wilshire Blvd Suite 1660 Los Angeles CA 90010

SHAKESPEARE, FRANK, ambassador; b. N.Y.C., Apr. 9, 1925; s. Francis Joseph and Frances (Hughes) S.; m. Deborah Anne Spaeth, Oct. 9, 1954; children: Mark, Andrea, Fredricka. B.S., Holy Cross Coll., 1945; D.Eng. (hon.), Colo. Sch. Mines, 1975; D.C.S. (hon.), Pace U., 1979; LL.D., Del. Law Sch., 1980, Sacred Heart U., 1985. Formerly pres. CBS-TV Services; sr. v.p. CBS-TV Network; exec. v.p. CBS-TV Stas.; dir. USIA, 1969-73; exec. v.p. Westinghouse Electric Corp., 1973-75; pres. RKO Gen. Inc., N.Y.C., 1975-85, vice chmn., 1983-85; U.S. ambassador to Portugal Lisbon, 1985-87; U.S. ambassador to The Holy See Vatican City, 1987—. Chmn. Heritage Found., 1975-85; chmn. Radio Free Europe/Radio Liberty, Inc., 1976-85. Served to lt. (j.g.) USNR, 1945-46. Club: Union League. Home: Villa Richardson, Via Giacoma Medici, 11 Rome Italy *

SHAKHMUNDES, LEV, mathematician; b. Leningrad, USSR, Dec. 29, 1933; came to Can., 1975; s. Yudel and Alexandra (Voitsekhovskaya) S. MS., Leningrad U., 1957; Ph.D., Leningrad Poly. Inst., 1965. Engr., research assoc., cons., various instns., Leningrad, 1957-74; research asst. U. Toronto, 1976-78; sr. cons. systems analyst Union Gas Ltd., Chatham, Ont., 1978—; head pvt. investment co., Chatham, 1978—. Coauthor: Economic Efficiency of Capital Expenditures (in Russian), 1969; contbr. articles to Soviet periodicals; patentee Ministry Sci. and Tech. USSR. Mem. Assn. Profl. Engrs. Ont., Canadian Econs. Assn., Am. Econs. Assn. Avocations: Sports. Home: PO Box 383, Chatham, ON Canada N7M 5K5

SHAKIR, NAEEM, automotive management company executive; b. Lahore, Punjab, Pakistan, Jan. 1, 1939; s. Mohammad Ebrahim and Hamidah (Begum) S.; m. Lynda Symeena, Dec. 20, 1970; children: Tariq Jamil, Farah Yasmine. BA, York U., Toronto, Ont., Can., 1976; diploma in mktg. (hon.), Rayerson Poly. Inst., Toronto, 1969. Sales mgr. Haroon Industries Ltd., Karachi, Pakistan, 1960-66; mktg. exec. Chrysler Can. Ltd., Toronto, 1966-77; gen. mgr. Galadari Automotive Group, Dubai, United Arab Emirates, 1977—. Mem. Ford Middle East Dealers Assn. (sec. 1987), Am. Bus. Council of Dubai. Home: 123/108 Saluddin Rd, Dubai United Arab

Emirates Office: Galadari Automobiles Ltd, PO Box 8494, Dubai United Arab Emirates

SHALALA, DONNA EDNA, political scientist, educator; b. Cleve., Feb. 14, 1941; d. James Abraham and Edna (Smith) S. AB, Western Coll., 1962; MSSC, Syracuse U., 1968, PhD, 1970; 12 hon. degrees, 1981-88. Vol. Peace Corps, Iran, 1962-64; asst. to dir. met. studies program Syracuse U., 1965-69; instr. asst. to dean Syracuse U. (Maxwell Grad. Sch.), 1969-70; asst. prof. polit. sci. Bernard M. Baruch Coll., U. City N.Y., 1970-72; assoc. prof. politics and edn. Tchrs. Coll. Columbia U., 1972-79; asst. sec. for policy devel. and research HUD, Washington, 1977-80; prof. polit. sci., pres. Hunter Coll., CUNY, 1980-88; prof. polit. sci., chancellor U. Wis., Madison, 1988—. Author: Neighborhood Governance, 1971, The City and the Constitution, 1972, The Property Tax and the Voters, 1973, The Decentralization Approach, 1974. Gov. Am. Stock Exchange, 1981-87; trustee TIAA, 1985—, Com. Econ. Devel., 1982—; bd. dirs. Inst. Internat. Econs., 1981—, Children's Def. Fund, 1980—, Am. Ditchley Found., 1982—, Spencer Found., 1988—. Ohio Newspaper Women's scholar, 1958; Western Coll. Trustees scholar, 1958-62; Carnegie fellow, 1966-68; Nat. Acad. Edn. Spencer fellow, 1972-73; Guggenheim fellow, 1975-76. Mem. Am. Polit. Sci. Assn., Am. Soc. Public Adminstrn., Nat. Acad. Public Adminstrn., Council Fgn. Relations, Nat. Acad. Edn. Office: U Wis-Madison 158 Bascom Hall 500 Lincoln Dr Madison WI 53706

SHALHOUB, MICHAEL See **SHARIF, OMAR**

SHALITA, ALAN REMI, dermatologist; b. Bklyn., Mar. 22, 1936; s. Harry and Celia; m. Simone Lea Baum, Sept. 4, 1960; children: Judith and Deborah (twins). A.B., Brown U., 1957; B.S., U. Brussels, 1960; M.D., Bowman Gray Sch. Medicine, 1964. Intern Beth Israel Hosp., N.Y.C., 1964-65; resident dept. dermatology N.Y. U. Med. Center, 1967-68, NIH tng. grant fellow dept. dermatology, 1968-70, instr. dermatology, 1970-71, asst. prof., 1971-73; asst. prof. dermatology Columbia U. Coll. Physicans and Surgeons, 1973-75; assoc. prof. medicine, head div. dermatology SUNY Downstate Med. Center, Bklyn., 1975-79; prof. medicine, head div. dermatology SUNY Downstate Med. Center, 1979-80, prof. and chmn. dept. dermatology, 1980—, asst. dean, 1977-83, acting dean Queen's campus, 1983-84; asst. attending in dermatology Univ. Hosp., N.Y.C., 1970-73, Bellevue Hosp. Center, 1970-73, Manhattan VA Hosp., 1972-74, Presbyn. Hosp., 1973-75; dir. dermatology services State Univ. Hosp., Bklyn., 1975-86, pres. 1986—; dir. Kings County Hosp. Center, 1975—; cons. dermatology Bklyn. VA Hosp., 1975—; chief dermatology Brookdale Med. Center, 1977—. Contbr. articles in field to med. jours. Pres. Temple Shaaray Tefilay, N.Y.C., 1982-86 . Served to lt. M.C. USNR, 1965-67. Recipient Surg. and Pediatric awards Beth Israel Hosp., N.Y.C., 1965; Spl. fellow NIH, 1970-73. Mem. Am. Acad. Dermatology (dir. 1983-87), Soc. Investigative Dermatology, Dermatology Found. (former trustee), Am. Dermatol. Assn., AMA, N.Y. Acad. Scis., A.C.P., Nat. Program Dermatology, Am. Soc. Dermatol. Surgery (past dir.), AAAS, Internat. Soc. Tropical Dermatology, N.Y. State Med. Soc., Soc. Cosmetic Chemists, N.Y. Acad. Medicine (sec. sect. on dermatology and syphilology 1981-82, chmn. sect. 1982-83), Dermatol. Soc. Greater N.Y. (pres. 1980-81), N.Y. State Dermatol. Soc. (past dir.). Republican. Home: 70 E 77th St New York NY 10021 Office: 450 Clarkson Ave Brooklyn NY 11203

SHALLOWAY, DAVID IRWIN, molecular biologist; b. Miami, Fla., Apr. 6, 1948; s. Charles Leon and Bette (Sir) S.; m. Carolyn Renee Fink, Dec. 24, 1977 (div. Aug. 1983); m. Kelly Lynn Morris, June 30, 1985. S.B., MIT, 1969; M.S., Stanford U., 1970; Ph.D., MIT, 1975. Research assoc. Lab. for Nuclear Studies, Cornell U., Ithaca, N.Y., 1975-77; NIH research fellow in microbiology and molecular genetics Sidney Farber Cancer Inst., Harvard Med. Sch., Boston, 1977-81; asst. prof. molecular biology Pa. State U.-State College, 1982-87, assoc. prof., 1987—. Contbr. articles to profl. jours. Mem. Union Concerned Scientists, Hunger Project. Fellow Danforth Found., 1969, Woodrow Wilson Found., 1969, NSF, 1969, Am. Cancer Soc., 1977; recipient Jr. Faculty Research award Am. Cancer Soc., 1983, Research Career Devel. award NIH, 1987; grantee: Nat. Cancer Inst., 1982, Am. Cancer Soc., 1982, March of Dimes, 1983, Nat. Cancer Inst., 1985, 88. Mem. AAAS, Am. Soc. Microbiologists. Democrat. Jewish. Home: RD 2 Box 575 Port Matilda PA 16870 Office: Pa State U 406 S Frear St University Park PA 16802

SHALLWANI, PIR MUHAMMAD V., physician; b. Hyderabad, Pakistan, Mar. 12, 1926; s. Wali Muhammad and Najabhai S.; m. Badrunnisa Shallwani, Mar. 21, 1957; children: Nasreen, Shahnaz, Zulfiqar Ali, Iftikhar Ali. B in Medicine and Surgery, Dow Med. Coll., Karachi, Pakistan, 1955; D in Tropical Medicine and Hygiene, London Sch. of Hygiene and Tropical Medicine, 1961; MS, Royal Soc. Health, London, 1962. Med. officer of health Mcpl. Corp., Hyderabad, Pakistan, 1956-68; med. officer Sui Gas Transmission Co., Ltd., Hyderabad, Pakistan, 1960-64, Trading Corp. of Pakistan, Hyderabad, Pakistan, 1974-80. Editorial bd. jour. The Doctor, Karachi, 1975-80; contbr. articles to profl. jours. Mem. Pakistan Med. Assn. (v.p. Sind zone 1969-72, v.p. Hyderabad 1973-75). Moslem. Club: Hyderabad Gynkhana. Home: 142-E Unit #6 Latifabad, Sind Hyderabad Pakistan Office: Prince Aly Rd, Hyderabad Sind Pakistan

SHALOWITZ, ERWIN EMMANUEL, civil engineer; b. Washington, Feb. 13, 1924; s. Aaron Louis and Pearl (Myer) S.; m. Elaine Mildred Langerman, June 29, 1952; children—Ann Janet, Aliza Beth, Jonathan Avram. Student, U. Pa., U. Notre Dame, 1944-45; B.C.E., George Washington U., 1947, postgrad., 1948-49; grad. soil mechanics, Cath. U., 1951; M.A. in Pub. Adminstrn. (fellow U.S. Civil Service Commn.), Am. U., 1954. Registered profl. engr., Washington. Engr. Klemitt Engring. Co., N.Y.C., 1947; with cons. firm Whitman, Requardt & Assos., Balt., 1947-48; chief structural research engr., head def. research sect., project officer and tech. adviser for atomic tests Bur. Yards and Docks, Dept. Navy, Washington, 1948-59; supervisory gen. engr. spl. asst. for protective constrn. programs, project mgr. for bldg. systems, chief research br., chief mgmt. information, chief contracting procedures and support Pub. Bldgs. Service, Gen. Services Adminstrn., Washington, 1959—; chmn. fed. exec. tng. program U.S. Civil Service Commn., 1950; fallout shelter analyst Dept. Def.; mem. Nat. Evaluation Bd. Architect-Engr. Selections; mem. standing com. on procurement policy Nat. Acad. Sci. Bldg. Research Adv. Bd. and Interagency Com. on Procurement Curriculum Rev.; coordinator pub. bldgs. design and constrn. Small Bus. Program and Minority Enterprise and Minority Subcontracting Programs. Contbr. articles profl. jours. Served to engring. officer USNR, 1944-46. Recipient Commendable Service award GSA, 1968, Outstanding Performance recognition, 1976, 77, 79, 87; cash award, 1977, 79, 87; recipient Engr. Alumni Achievement award George Washington U., 1985. Fellow ASCE, Am. Biog. Inst.; mem. Soc. Advancement Mgmt., Soc. Am. Mil. Engrs., Sigma Tau, Pi Sigma Alpha. Jewish. Home: 5603 Huntington Pkwy Bethesda MD 20814 Office: 19th and F Sts NW Washington DC 20405

SHAMBAUGH, STEPHEN WARD, lawyer; b. South Bend, Ind., Aug. 4, 1920; s. Marion Clyde and Anna Violet (Stephens) S.; m. Marilyn Louise Pyle; children—Susan Wynne Shambaugh Hinkle, Kathleen Louise Shambaugh Thompson. Student San Jose State Tchrs. Coll., 1938-40, U. Ark., 1951; LL.B., U. Tulsa, 1954. Bar: Okla. 1954, Colo. 1964. Mem. staff Reading & Bates, Inc., Tulsa, 1951-54; v.p., gen. mgr., legal counsel Reading & Bates Drilling Co. Ltd., Calgary, Alta., Can., 1954-61; sr. ptnr. Bowman, Shambaugh, Geissinger & Wright, Denver, 1964-81; sole practice, Denver, 1981—; dir., fin. counsel various corps. Served to col. USAF ret. Mem. ABA, Fed. Bar Assn., Colo. Bar Assn., Okla. Bar Assn., Denver Bar Assn., P-51 Mustang Pilots Assn., Phi Alpha Delta. Clubs: Spokane; Petroleum of Bakersfield (Calif.); Masons, Shriners, Elks.

SHAMIR, YITZHAK, Israeli politician; b. (as Yitzhak Jazernicki) 1915, Poland; married; 2 children; ed. Hebrew Secondary Sch., Bialystok, attended Warsaw Univ. Law Sch. and Hebrew Univ. of Jerusalem; mem. Irgun Zvai Leumi (Jewish mil. org.) 1937, then a founder and leader of Lohamei Herut Yisrael (Stern Group) 1940-41; arrested by British Mandatory Authority 1941, 1946 (exiled to Eritrea); given political asylum in France, returned to Israel 1948; ret. from polit. activity until 1955; Sr. post Civil Service 1955-65; mng. dir. several business concerns 1965—; mem. Herut Movement 1970—, chmn. exec. com. 1975—; mem. Knesset 1973—, Speaker 1977-80; minister of fgn. affairs 1980-83, 84-86, prime minister, Sept. 1983-84, 86—, vice prime minister 1984-86, now also minister of interior. Address: Office of Prime Minister, Hakirya, Kaplan St, Jerusalem Israel

SHAMMA', MAHMOUD ZUHEIR, electronics company executive; b. Amman, Jordan, July 22, 1953; s. Zuheir Mahmoud and Haifa Mahmoud (Kanawati) S.; m. Nisrine Hisham Shawwa, Jan. 1, 1984; children: Nadine, Zuheir. Degree, Swansea Coll., Eng., 1973; B in Elec. Engring., Bristol U., Eng., 1976. Engr. Shlumberger, France, 1976-77; electronics instr. Alia, Royal Jordanian, Amman, 1977-78; mgr. Shamma' & Ghishan Engring., Amman, 1978-82; mng. dir. Sound & Security Engring. Co., Amman, 1982-86; chief exec. officer Sound & Security Engring. Co., 1986—; founder, bd. dirs. Arab Elec. Industries, Amman. Mem. IEEE (assoc.), Jordan Inst. Engrs. Home and Office: Sound & Security Engring Co, PO Box 9881, Amman Jordan

SHAMSUDHEEN, K. V. (KARAPPAM VEETTIL), investment consultant; b. Chavakkad, S. India, Nov. 2, 1946; s. Aboobacker Ahmed and Nafeessu Umma; married; children: Sameesh, Shamil. BA in Commerce, Kerala U., 1968. Rep. Unit Trust of India, Sharjah, 1979—. Pres. Overseas Indian Investors Forum, Sharjah, 1984—; active anti-smoking and anti-drug campaigning. Mem. Indian Assn. Sharjah (gen. sec. 1982-83). Office: Unit Trust of India, PO Box 940, Sharjah India

SHAMUYARIRA, NATHAN MARWIRAKUWA, government official; b. Sept. 29, 1930; married; 1 daughter. Student, Waddilove Inst., Zimbabwe; degree in polit. sci., Princeton (N.J.) U. Tchr. various schs; then reporter African Newspapers, 1953, editor-in-chief, 1959-62; editor Daily News, 1956; founding mem. Zimbabwe African Nat. Union, sec. for external affairs, 1968-71; dir. edn. dept. Zimbabwe African Nat. Union, Mozambique, 1977; then adminstrv. sec. Zimbabwe African Nat. Union, administrv. sec. election directorate, 1980; researcher Oxford (Eng.) U.; lectr. polit. sci. U. Dar es Salaam, Tanzania; then minister info., posts an telecommunicaiotns Govt. of Zimbabwe, now minister fgn. affairs. Author: Crisis in Rhodesia; contbr. articles to various jours. Office: Ministry of Fgn Affairs, Harare Zimbabwe *

SHANE, DEBORAH LYNNE, broadcasting executive; b. Chgo., Mar. 24, 1950; d. Raymond and Francine Shane; student Bradley U., 1967-68; B.A., U. Miami, 1971, Ph.D., 1977. Performer, Theatre on the Lake, Chgo., summer 1967; asst. programming dir., disk jockey, audio engr. WRBU-AM, Peoria, Ill., 1967-68; asst. sta. mgr., audio engr. WTVP-TV, Peoria, 1967-68; performer, tech. adviser Ring Theatre Childrens Theatre Touring Co., Miami, Fla., 1968; asst. producer, dir. pub. affairs and childrens programming Learning Ladder, WPLG-TV, Miami, 1969-70; asst. programming dir. WINZ-AM, Miami, 1970-71; Midwest office mgr., dir. pub. relations and communications Gulf Leasing Corp., Chgo., 1971-72; comedy scriptwriter, guest performer Bozo's Circus, WGN-TV, Chgo., 1973-75; freelance writer, producer, dir. and performer for radio, television, films and theatre, Chgo., 1975-77; co-hostess, writer-producer television show Self Discovery from A to Z, WLRN-TV, Miami, 1977; v.p. broadcast and communications div. Asso. Leasing Internat. Corp., Ft. Lauderdale, Fla., 1977—; cons. Miami and S.E. Fla. area U.S. Inst. Theatre Tech.; guest author Lighting Dimensions mag.; guest author Backstage Mag.; asst. instr. U. Wis. Summer Speech Inst. Press coordinator Gov. Askew's Sunshine Amendment Day, Miami, 1976. Recipient B'nai B'rith Woman of Year award for pub. service to Greater Chgo. Met. Community, 1974; judge 17th Ann. Chgo. Emmy awards, 1975, 11th ann. Fla. Hosp. Pub. Relations awards, 1978; awarded Key to City of Miami Beach, 1979. Mem. Am. Women in Radio and TV (membership chmn., dir., 1976, pres. chpt. 1977-80, mem Speakers Bur. 1971—), AFTRA, Soc. Motion Picture and TV Engrs., Fla. Motion Picture and TV Assn. (rec. sec., dir., com. chmn. state bd.), Nat. Acad. TV Arts and Sci. (bd. govs.), Women in Communications, Playwrights Center (charter), Chgo. Women in Broadcasting (Spl. award for promoting better children's programming 1973, Radio and TV appreciation award 1978, 79), Panhellenic Assn. Ft. Lauderdale, Women's Fla. Assn. Broadcasters (pres. 1978-83), U. Miami Young Alumni Assn., Nat. Thespians Troupe 113 (life), Am. Soc. Notaries, Ft. Lauderdale/Broward County C. of C., Delta Zeta (Outstanding Alumni Recognition award 1977), Sigma Phi Epsilon (pres. Little Sisters Orgn.). Jewish. Clubs: B'nai B'rith Women (Chaverim chpt.); Cricket of Miami; Woodlands Country. Writer, hostess 24 episodes Self Discovery television talk show, 1976-77; writer, star 20 shows Debbie and Friends, 1973-74; screenplay collaborator The Eddie Faye Story. Office: Associated Leasing Internat Corp Trafalgar Plaza I Suite 219 5300 NW 33d Ave Fort Lauderdale FL 33309

SHANE, LEONARD, savings and loan executive; b. Chgo., May 28, 1922; s. Jacob and Selma (Shayne) S.; m. Marjorie Cynthia Konecky, Jan. 14, 1941; children: Judith Shane Shenkman, Marsha Kay Shane Palmer, William Alan, Shelley Rose Shane Asidon. Student, U. Chgo., 1939-41, Ill. Inst. Tech., 1941-42. Writer-editor UPI, 1942-44; cons. indsl. areas 1944-46; writer-rancher Tucson, 1946-48; writer-producer ABC, Los Angeles, 1948-49; owner cons. agency Los Angeles, 1949-64; chmn. bd., dir., chief exec. officer Mercury Savs. and Loan Assn., Huntington Beach, Calif., 1964—. Chmn. United Jewish Welfare Fund of Orange County, 1972-73; pres. Western region, mem. internat. bd. govs. Am. Assos. Ben Gurion U., Israel; pres. Los Angeles Recreation and Park Commn., 1960-63, Jewish Fedn. Council of Orange County, 1973-74; trustee Ocean View Sch. Dist., 1970-72, City of Hope, 1968—. Mem. U.S. League Savs. Instns. (vice chmn. 1981-82, chmn. 1982-83, legis. chmn. 1987—), Calif. Savs. and Loan League (dir. 1969-73, v.p. 1979-80, pres. 1980-81), Phi Sigma Delta. Clubs: Big Canyon Country, Masons, Shriners. Office: Mercury Savs and Loan Assn 7812 Edinger Ave Huntington Beach CA 92647

SHANE, WILLIAM WHITNEY, astronomer; b. Berkeley, Calif., June 3, 1928; s. Charles Donald and Mary Lea (Heger) S.; B.A., U. Calif., Berkeley, 1951, postgrad., 1953-58; Sc.D., Leiden U. (Netherlands), 1971; m. Clasina van der Molen, Apr. 22, 1964; children—Johan Jacob, Charles Donald. Research asso. Leiden (Netherlands) U., 1961-71, sr. scientist, 1971-79; prof. astronomy, dir. Astron. Inst., Cath. U. Nijmegen, Netherlands, 1979—; mem. astronomy chamber Assn. Dutch Univs.; dir. J. C. Kapteyn Fund, Pastor Schmeitz Found. Served with USN, 1951-53. Mem. Internat. Astron. Union (commns. 33, 34), Am. Astron. Soc., Astron. Soc. Netherlands, Astron. Soc. of the Pacific, AAAS, Phi Beta Kappa. Research on structure and dynamics of galaxies, radio astronomy. Home: Postbus 43, 6580 AA Malden The Netherlands Office: Katholieke U Sterrenkundig Instituut, Toernooiveld, 6525 ED Nijmegen The Netherlands

SHANFARI, SAID AHMED AL, Omani minister of petroleum and minerals, businessman; b. Salalah, Sultate of Oman, 1939. Student in Dhofar and Saudi Arabia. With Arabian-Am. Oil Co. (Aramco), Saudi Arabia, 1954-59; dir. several businesses in Salalah; Omani minister of agr., fisheries, petroleum and minerals, 1974-79, minister of petroleum and minerals, 1979—. Address: Ministry of, Petroleum and Minerals, Muscat Oman *

SHAN FOO, CHENG, city administrator, educator; b. Amoy, Fuken, China, Oct. 10, 1927; s. Kong-Sei and Bo-Lean (Chen) C.; m. Ong Lee-Yea, Oct. 28, 1959; children—Chi-Lan, Chi-Hui, Chi-Feng, Chi-Chung. LL.B., Nat. Amoy U., 1949; LL.B., Nat. Chung Shin U., Taipei, 1950; LL.M., Coll. of Taiwan Provincial Inst. Pub. Adminstrn., 1951. Bar: Taipei 1950. Sec. Oversea Chinese Affairs Com., Taipei, Taiwan, 1951-54; editor-in-chief Chung Shin Daily News, Singapore, 1954-56; sec.-in-chief Taipei City Govt., 1956-63, dir. Taipei Bus. Adminstrn., 1963—; prof. Tamkang U., Taipei, 1964—. Author: A Comparative Study of Parliamentary Systems, 1951; An Introduction to Local Administration, 1952; Organization and Management of Business, 1966; Public Finance, 1969; Computerization of City Business Management, 1971; Modern Economic and Finance Rev., 1985. Mem. China Road Fedn., Oversea Chinese Inst. Assn. (com.), Taipei Bus. Assn. (com.). Office: Taipri City Bus, 5 Papin Rd, Taipei 100, Republic of China

SHANK, CLARE BROWN WILLIAMS, political worker; b. Syracuse, N.Y., Sept. 19, 1909; d. Curtiss Crofoot and Clara Irene (Shoudy) Brown; m. Frank E. Williams, Feb. 18, 1940 (dec. Feb. 1957); m. Seth Carl Shank, Dec. 28, 1963 (dec. Jan. 1977). B.Oral English, Syracuse U., 1931. Tchr. 1931-33, merchandising exec., 1933-42; Pinellas County mem. Rep. State Com., 1954-58; life mem. Pinellas County Rep. Exec. Com.; exec. com. Fla. Rep. Com., 1954-64; Fla. committeewoman Rep. Nat. Com., 1956-64, mem. exec. com., 1956-64, asst. chmn. and dir. women's activities, 1958-64; alt., mem. exec. arrangements com., major speaker Rep. Nat. Conv., Chgo., 1960; alt., program and arrangement coms. Rep. Nat. Conv., 1964. Pres. St. Petersburg Women's Rep. Club, 1955-57; Mem. Def. Adv. Com. on Women in Services, 1959-65; trustee St. Petersburg Housing Authority, 1976-81. Recipient George Arents medal Syracuse U., 1959; citation for patriotic civilian service 5th U.S. Army and Dept. Def. Mem. AAUW, Gen. Fedn. Women's Clubs, DAR, Colonial Dames 17th Century, Fla. Fedn. Women's Clubs (dist. pres. 1976-78), Zeta Phi Eta, Pi Beta Phi (nat. officer 1945-48). Methodist. Clubs: Woman's (St. Petersburg) (pres. 1974-76), Yacht (St. Petersburg). Home: 1120 North Shore Dr NE Apt 901 Saint Petersburg FL 33701

SHANK, ROXANNE CRYSTAL, insurance professional; b. Edmonton, Alta., Can., June 25, 1954; d. Clarence Rosario and Rosalind Juliana (Benz) S.; m. John Scott Bradley, May 1, 1980 (div. Mar. 1985); m. Murray Phillip William Kammer, Nov. 22, 1986. BA with honors, Brock U., St. Catherines, Ont., Can., 1975, MA, 1976; postgrad., McMaster U., Hamilton, Ont., 1976-80. Asst. prof. philosophy Ryerson Poly. Inst., Toronto, Ont., 1979-81; field rep. Boiler and Inspection Ins. Co., Toronto, 1981-83; mgr. boiler and machinery dept. Chubb Ins. Co. Can., Toronto, 1983—; rep. to Internat. Engring. Confs., Toronto, 1983—; presenter in field. Mem. Ins. Inst. Can. (assoc.), Can. Boiler and Machinery Underwriters Assn. (exec. bd. 1983—), Toronto Bd. Trade, Toronto Bus. and Profl. Womens Club (2d v.p. 1985-86, 1st v.p. 1986-87, pres. 1987-88). Roman Catholic. Home: 209 Waverley Rd, Toronto, ON Canada M4L 3T4 Office: Chubb Ins Co, 26 Wellington St E, Toronto, ON Canada M5E 1S2

SHANKAR, RAMSEWAK, president of Suriname; b. Nickerie, Suriname, Nov. 6, 1937; m. Gisela Prabhawatie Sewsahai. Student, U. Agr., Wageningen, Suriname, Inst. for Social Studies. With Bur. Nat. Devel., Suriname, 1962-63; minister agr., animal husbandry and fisheries Suriname, 1965-69; minister justice and police May Caretaker Cabinet, 1969; minister agr., animal husbandry and fisheries Sedney Cabinet, 1969-71; dir. Found. for Mech. Agr. in Suriname, Wageningen, 1971-81; agrarian advisor Surinaamsche Bank N.V., 1981—; dir. Nickerie Agrl. Co. and Nickerie Rice Industry, Suriname, 1987—; pres. of Suriname Paramaribo, 1988—. Address: Office of the President, Paramaribo Suriname *

SHANKAR, RAVI, sitar player, composer; b. Apr. 7, 1920. Studied under Ustad Allauddin Khan of Maihar; trained in Guru-Shishya tradition; pupil of Ustad Allauddin Khan, 1938. Solo sitar player; former dir. music All India Radio, also founder Nat. Orch.; founder, dir. Kinnara Sch. Music, Bombay, 1962—, Kinnara Sch. Music, Los Angeles, 1967; many recordings of traditional and exptl. variety in India, U.K., U.S.A., including Tana Mana, 1987; concert tours in Europe, U.S.A., The East; vis. lectr. U. Calif., 1965; appeared in film Raga, 1974; fellow Sangeet Natak Akademi 1976; responsible for music and choreography for ASIAD, 1982. Recipient Deshikottam award, 1982; Silver Bear of Berlin; award of Indian Nat. Acad. Music, Dance and Drama, 1962; award of Padma Bhushan 1967, Padma Vibushan, 1981, Internat. Music Council UNESCO award, 1975; elected to the Rajya Sabha, India, 1986. Film scores: Pather Panchali, The Flute and the Arrow, Nava Rasa Ranga, Charly, Gandhi, and many musical compositions including Concerto for Sitar No. 1 1971, No. 2, 1981, and numerous rajas and talas; author: My Music, My Life, 1969, Rag Anurag (Bengali). Office: care Basil Douglas Artists Mgmt, 8 Saint Georges Terr, London NW1 8XJ, England

SHANKLIN, DOUGLAS RADFORD, physician; b. Camden, N.J., Nov. 25, 1930; s. John Ferguson and Muriel (Morgan) S.; student Wilson Tchrs. Coll., 1949; A.B. in Chemistry, Syracuse U., 1952; M.D., SUNY, Syracuse, 1955; m. Virginia McClure, Apr. 7, 1956; children—Elizabeth, Leigh, Lois Virginia, John Carter, Eleanor. Intern in pathology Duke U., 1955-56, resident, 1958; resident in pathology SUNY, Syracuse, 1958-60; practice medicine specializing in pathology, Gainesville, Fla., 1960-67, 78-83; mem. faculty U. Fla., 1960-67; prof. pathology, ob-gyn U. Chgo., 1967-78; pathologist-in-chief Chgo. Lying-In Hosp., 1967-78; prof., vice chmn. dept. pathology U. Tenn.-Memphis, 1983—; vis. prof. U. Okla., 1967, Duke U., Mich. State U., 1969, Leeds U., Dundee U., Karolinska, 1974, Leeds U., 1978, 85, Emory U., 1980, London U., Edinburgh U., 1981, 85, U. Brit. Coll., 1987; jr. investigator Marine Biol. Lab., Woods Hole, Mass., 1951-54, sr. investigator, 1966—, mem. corp., 1970—; chmn. nat. adv. com. W-I-C evaluation U.S. Dept. Agr., 1979-86; lectr. Coll. Law U. Fla., 1963-67, 77-83; cons. Pan Am. Health Orgn., 1973—; sr. cons. Santa Fe Found., 1976-79, exec. dir., 1979-83; course dir. Center Continuing Edn., U. Chgo., 1980-82. Trustee Coll. Light Opera Co., Falmouth, Mass., 1970—, Hippodrome Theatre, Gainesville, 1975-83. Served with M.C., USNR, 1956-58. Recipient Best Basic Sci. Teaching award U. Fla., 1967; named freeman citizen of Glasgow, 1981. Mem. Am. Assn. Pathologists, Soc. Pediatric Research, Soc. Exptl. Pathology, Internat. Acad. Pathologists, So. Soc. Pediatric Research, So. Med. Assn., N.Y. Acad. Scis., Am. Coll. Ob-Gyn, Internat. Soc. Gynecologic Pathologists, Council Biology Editors, AAAS, Royal Soc. Medicine (London), Coll. Physicians and Surgeons Costa Rica, AMA, Tenn. Med. Assn., Pediatric Pathology Club (sec.-treas. 1970-75, pres. 1981-82), Phi Beta Kappa. Sigma Xi. Author: Syllabus for Study of Gynecologic-Obstetric-Pediatric Disease, 1961; Diseases of Woman, Pregnancy, Child, 1964; Maternal Nutrition and Child Health, 1979; Tumors of Placenta and Cord, 1984; editor: Interscience Devel. Disorders, 1971-80; asso. editor Jour. Reproductive Medicine, 1968-70, 79—, editor in chief, 1970-75; contbr. articles to profl. jours. Home: 1238 NW 18th Terr Gainesville FL 32605 Office: 134 Grove Park Circle Memphis TN 38117

SHANKS, HERSHEL, lawyer, publisher, editor; b. Sharon, Pa., Mar. 8, 1930; s. Martin and Mildred (Freedman) S.; m. Judith Alexander Weil, Feb. 20, 1966; children: Elizabeth Jean, Julia Emily. B.A., Haverford (Pa.) Coll., 1952; M.A., Columbia, 1953; LL.B., Harvard, 1956. Bar: D.C. 1956. Trial atty. Dept. Justice, 1956-59; pvt. practice Washington, 1959-88; partner firm Glassie Pewett, Beebe & Shanks, 1964-88; editor Bibl. Archaeology Rev., Washington, 1975—; pres. Bibl. Archaeology Soc., 1974—, Jewish Ednl. Ventures Inc. Author: The Art and Craft of Judging, 1968, The City of David, 1973, Judaism in Stone, 1979; also articles.; co-editor: Recent Archeology in the Land of Israel, 1984; editor Ancient Israel, 1988, Bible Rev., 1985—; editor, publisher Moment mag., 1987—. Mem. Am., Fed., D.C. bar assns., Am. Schs. Oriental Research, Phi Beta Kappa. Clubs: Nat. Lawyers (Washington); Nat. Press. Home: 5208 38th St NW Washington DC 20015 Office: Biblical Archaeology Review 3000 Connecticut Ave NW Suite 300 Washington DC 20008

SHANKS, LORNA EVELYN, marketing manager; b. Johannesburg, South Africa, May 24, 1938; came to U.S., 1968; d. Andrew Cunningham Shanks and Elizabeth Comfort (Bailie) Challinor. Diploma in graphic design Witwatersrand Tech. Coll., Johannesburg, 1959; postgrad. Ravensbourne Coll. Art and Design, Bromley, Eng., 1965. Graphic designer Henrion Design Assocs., London, 1965, Corning Glass Works, N.Y., 1971-73; cons. graphics White House/Nat. Endowment for Arts, Washington, 1973-74; mktg. mgr. Mergenthaler Linotype Co., Plainview, N.Y., 1975-78; dir. Internat. Typeface Corp., N.Y.C., 1979-82; mktg. mgr. Xerox Corp., El Segundo, Calif., 1983—; guest lectr. Pratt Inst., 1981, Smithsonian Instn., 1981, MIT, 1980, R.I. Sch. Design, 1980, AAUW, 1972. Mem. Am. Inst. Graphic Arts (bd. dirs. 1979-82), Type Dirs. Club. Office: Xerox Corp 701 S Aviation Blvd El Segundo CA 90245

SHANKS, STEPHEN RAY, engineer; b. San Antonio, Tex., Nov. 1, 1956; s. Leroy and Jane Adams (Coats) S.; m. Vickie Lynn Morrow, Aug. 6, 1977; 1 child, Erin Monette. Student pub. schs., Corpus Christi, Tex. Engring. technician Gulf Coast Testing Lab., Inc., Corpus Christi, part-time, 1971-75, full-time, 1975-78; projects mgr., quality control adminstr. Shilstone Engring. Testing Lab. div. Profl. Service Industries, Tex. and La., 1978-86; div. mgr. constrn. services Bhate Engring. Corp., southeastern U.S., 1987—. Author: Procedures and Techniques for Construction Materials Testing, 1978, Inspection and Testing of Asphaltic Concrete, 1979, Concrete Barges: Construction and Repair Techniques, 1984, Management and Marketing Strategies for Branch Offices with Rural Influences, 1985, How to Improve Profitability and Increase the Quality of Services, 1986; editor: (lit. mag.) Viva!, 1975; contbr. articles to profl. jours. Mem. ASTM, Am. Soc. for Nondestructive Testing, Am. Concrete Inst., Am. Mgmt. Assn., Am.

Welding Soc., Constrn. Specifications Inst., Constrn. Mgmt. Assn. Am. Democrat. Episcopalian. Lodge: Rotary. Home: 4660 Wooddale Ln Pelham AL 35124 Office: 5217 5th Ave S Birmingham AL 35212

SHANMAN, JAMES ALAN, lawyer; b. Cin., Aug. 1, 1942; s. Jerome D. and Mildred Louise (Bloch) S.; m. Marilyn Louise Glassman, June 11, 1972; 1 child, Ellen Joan. BS, U. Pa., 1963; JD, Yale U., 1966. Bar: N.Y. 1967, U.S. Supreme Ct. 1971, U.S. Ct. Mil. Appeals 1971, U.S. Ct. Appeals (2d cir.) 1972, U.S. Dist. ct. (so. and ea. dists.) N.Y. 1972, U.S. Ct. Internat. Trade, 1976, U.S. Ct. Appeals (fed. cir.), 1987. Assoc. Cahill Gordon & Reindel, N.Y.C., 1971-74, Freeman, Meade, Wasserman, Sharfman & Schneider, N.Y.C., 1974-76; assoc. Sharfman, Shanman, Poret & Siviglia, P.C., N.Y.C., 1976—; speaker on reins. law topics. Served to capt. USAF, 1966-71. Mem. ABA, N.Y. State Bar Assn., Assn. Bar City N.Y. (com. on ins. law, 1985—), Am. Arbitration Assn. (comml. panel arbitrators), Air Force Assn. Club: Lotos. Office: 1370 Ave of Americas New York NY 10019

SHANMUGAN, SUPPIAH, orthopedic surgeon; b. Tamilnadu, India, May 7, 1949; s. Shanmugam and Alagammai; m. Bishan Khor; children: Sumithra, Surendran. Grad., St. Joseph's Coll., Trichy, India, 1969; MBBS, Madurai Med. Coll., India, 1976; diploma in underwater medicine, HMAS Penguin, Sydney, Australia, 1981; MS in Orthopaedics, U. Kebangsaan, Malaysia, 1987. Trainee housemanship Seremban (India) Gen. Hosp., 1977-78; med. officer surg. dept. Dist. Hosp. Kuala Pilah, Negeri Sembilan, India, 1977-80; trainee dept. orthopaedics U. Kebangsaan, Malaysia, 1982-86; orthopaedic surgeon Kinrara Army Hosp., Malaysian Armed Forces, Kuala Lumpur, 1987—. Served to maj. Malaysian Army, 1979—. Mem. Malaysian Med. Assn. Hindu. Home: 383 Jalan B10, Taman Melawati, Kuala Lumpur 53100, Malaysia Office: Malaysian Armed Forces, 95 Kinrara Army Hosp, Jalan Puchong, Kuala Lumpur 50634, Malaysia

SHANNON, DAVID THOMAS, theological seminary official; b. Richmond, Va., Sept. 26, 1933; s. Charlie Lee and Phyllis (Gary) S.; m. Shannon P. Averett, June 15, 1957; children—Vernitia Averett, Davine Belinda S. Sparks, David Thomas Jr. B.A., VA. Union U., 1954, B.D., 1957; S.T.M., Oberlin Grad. Sch. Theology, 1959; D. Min., Vanderbilt U., 1974; D.D. (hon.), U. Richmond, 1983; Ph.D., U. Pitts., 1975. Pastor Fair Oaks (Va.) Bapt. Ch., 1954-57; student asst. Antioch Bapt. Ch., Cleve., 1957-59; grad. asst. Oberlin (Ohio) Grad. Sch. Theology, 1958-59; univ. pastor Va. Union U., Richmond, 1960-61, lectr. humanities and history, 1959-69; pastor Ebenezer Bapt. Ch., Richmond, 1960-69; eastern dir. Christian Higher Edn. Services Am. Bapt. Bd. Edn. and Publ., Valley Forge, Pa., 1969-71; vis. prof. St. Mary's Sem. Urban Tng. Program, Cleve., 1969-72; assoc. prof. religion and dir. minority studies Bucknell U., Lewisburg, Pa., 1971-72; dean faculty Pitts. Theol. Sem., 1972-79; Bibl. scholar Hartford (Conn.) Sem. Found., 1979; pres. Va. Union U., Richmond, 1979-85; vice pres. for acad. services, dean faculty Interdenominational Theol. Ctr., Atlanta, 1985—; co-chmn. internat. dialogue Secretariat of Roman Catholic Ch. Bapt., Rome and Washington, 1983—; co-chmn. task force on witnessing apostolic faith World Council of Chs., Geneva, 1984—; mem. faith and order commn. Nat. Council of Chs., N.Y.C., 1984; mem. commn. on doctrine and inter-ch. cooperation Bapt. World Alliance, Washington, 1980—; bd. dirs. Presbyn. Sch. Christian Edn., Richmond, 1985; mem. commn. on accreditation Assn. Theol. Schs., Vandalia, Ohio, 1985—; bd. dirs. Urban Tng., Atlanta, 1985—; mem. Deans and Registrars Atlanta U. Ctr., 1985—. Author: Studies in the Life and Works of Paul, 1961; Old Testament Experience of Faith, 1977; contbr. articles to profl. jours., chpts. to books. Life mem. NAACP, N.Y., 1950. Named Man of Yr., NCCJ, 1981. Mem. Am. Assn. Higher Edn., Am. Acad. Religion, Soc. for Study of Black Religion, Soc. Bibl. Lit., Alpha Kappa Mu, Phi Beta Sigma. Home: 3640 Rolling Green Ridge SW Atlanta GA 30331 Office: Interdenominational Theol Ctr 671 Beckwith St SW Atlanta GA 30314

SHANNON, WILLIAM NORMAN, III, food service executive, marketing educator; b. Chgo., Nov. 20, 1937; s. William Norman Jr. and Lee (Lewis) S.; m. Bernice Urbanowicz, July 14, 1962; children: Kathleen Kelly, Colleen Patricia, Kerrie Ann. BS in Indsl. Mgmt., Carnegie Inst. Tech., 1959; MBA in Mktg. Mgmt., U. Toledo, 1963. Sales engr. Westinghouse Electric Co., Detroit, 1959-64; regional mgr. Toledo Scale, Chgo., 1964-70; v.p. J. Lloyd Johnson Assoc., Northbrook, Ill., 1970-72; mgr. spl. projects Hobart Mfg., Troy, Ohio, 1972-74; corp. v.p. mktg. Berkel, Inc., La Porte, Ind., 1974-79; gen. mgr. Berkel Products, Ltd., Toronto, Can., 1975-78; chmn. Avant Industries, Inc., Wheeling, Ill., 1979-81; chmn., pres. Hacienda Mexican Restaurants, Mishawaka, Ind., 1978—; chmn. Hacienda Franchising Group, Inc., South Bend, Ind., 1987—, Ziker Shannon Corp., South Bend, Ind., 1982-88; assoc. prof. mktg. Saint. Mary's Coll., Notre Dame, Ind., 1982—, London Program Faculty, 1986. Co-author: Laboratory Computers, 1971; contbr. articles to profl. jours. V.p. mktg. Jr. Achievement, South Bend, Ind., 1987—; pres. Small Bus. Devel. Council, South Bend., 1987—; bd. dirs. Ind. Small Bus. Council, Indpls., Mental Health Assn., South Bend, 1987—; chmn. bd. trustees, Holy Cross Jr. Coll., Notre Dame, Ind., 1987—; chmn. St Joseph County Higher Edn. Council, 1988—. Named Small Bus. Person of Yr., City of South Bend, 1987, Small Bus. Advocate of Yr., State of Ind., 1987. Mem. Am. Mktg. Assn. (chmn. Mich./Ind. chpt., pres. 1985-86), Ind. Inst. New Bus. Ventures (mktg. faculty 1987—), Michiana Investment Network (vice chmn. 1988—), SBA (adminstrn. adv. council 1988—, contbg. editor Our Town Michiana mag. 1988—), South Bend C. of C. (bd. dirs. 1987—), Assn. for Bus. Communication (nat.conf. program chmn. 198—). Roman Catholic. Club: University of Notre Dame (vice chmn.). Lodge: Rotary. Home: 2920 S Twyckenham South Bend IN 46614 Office: Saint Mary's Coll Notre Dame IN 46556

SHANON, BENNY MICHAEL, university educator; b. Tel Aviv, Dec. 28, 1948; s. Eliahu and Naomi (Schneior) S. BA, Tel Aviv U., 1971; MA, Stanford U., 1974, PhD, 1974. Spl. lectr. MIT, 1974-76; lectr., sr. lectr. Hebrew U., Jerusalem, 1976—; vis. assoc. prof. Cornell U., Ithaca, 1984; assoc. prof. Swarthmore Coll., 1986. Fulbright fellow, 1971-74. Home: 21 Ephrata, Jerusalem Israel Office: Dept Psychology, Hebrew U, Jerusalem Israel

SHANOR, LELAND, botanist, educator; b. Butler, Pa., July 21, 1914; s. Paul Lel and Marion (McCandless) S.; m. Mary Williams Ward, June 20, 1940; children—Charles Algernon, Paul Leland II. A.B., Maryville Coll., 1935; M.A., U. N.C., 1937; Ph.D., 1939; D.Sc. (hon.), Ill. Wesleyan U., 1961. Asst. biology Maryville Coll., 1933-35; grad. asst., teaching fellow botany U. N.C., 1935-39; fellow U. N.C. (Highlands Lab.), summer 1937; dir. Highlands Mus. Natural History, summer 1939; instr. botany Clemson Coll., 1939-40; instr. botany U. Ill., 1940-43, asst. prof., 1946-48, asso. prof., 1948-51, prof., 1951-56, curator mycol. collections, 1948-56; prof. botany Fla. State U., 1956-63, head dept. biol. sci., 1956-62; dean div. advanced studies Fla. Inst. for Continuing Univ. Studies, 1962-65; prof. U. Fla., Gainesville, 1965-85, prof. emeritus, 1985—; chmn. dept. botany U. Fla., 1965-73; Sect. head div. sci. personnel and edn. NSF, 1964, dir. div. undergraduate edn. in sci., 1965; pathologist Dept. Agr., 1943-44; research mycologist OSRD, George Washington U., 1944-45; research asso. Johnson Found. U. Pa., Panama C.Z. Lab., 1946; mem. adv. com. C.Z. Biol. Area, 1954-66; mem. sci. adv. com. Ill. Wesleyan U., 1956-85; mem. sci. adv. com. Inter-Inst. Commn. on Nuclear Research, 1957-63, sec., 1957-58, chmn., 1958-59; cons. div. sci. personnel and edn. NSF, 1960-63; mem. sci. adv. com. Fairchild Tropical Garden, 1966-84, trustee, 1971-80. Editorial bd.: Ill. Biol. Monographs, 1948-56; chmn., 1953-56; editorial bd.: MYCOLOGIA, 1961-70; Contbr. articles to profl. pubs. Treas. 2d Internat. Mycol. Congress, 1977; adv. com. Southeastern Plant Environment Labs., 1968-73; Bd. govs. Center for Research in Coll. Instrn. Sci. and Math., 1967-70, sec., 1968, chmn., 1970; trustee Highlands Biol. Sta., 1956—, pres. bd., 1958-63. Recipient Alumni citation Maryville Coll., 1965; Merit citation Highlands Biol. Sta., 1964; Guggenheim fellow, 1951-52. Fellow A.A.A.S.; mem. Bot. Soc. Am. (chmn. south-eastern sect. 1966), Mycol. Soc. Am. (sec.-treas. 1951-53, editor newsletters 1950-53, pres. 1954, councilor 1955-57), Ill. Acad. Sci. (sec. 1949-51, councilor 1951-53, pres. 1955), Assn. Southeastern Biologists (treas. 1962-65, v.p. 1970-71, pres. 1972-73), Nature Conservancy, Explorers Club, Sigma Xi, Phi Sigma, Gamma Sigma Delta. Clubs: Torch (pres. local 1980-81); Turkey Creek Golf and Racquet (Alachua, Fla.); Rotary. Home: 2816 NW 21st Ave Gainesville FL 32605

SHANTARAM, VANKUDRE, movie director, producer, actor; b. Nov. 18, 1901; student Kolhapur High Sch. Founder, mem. Prabhat Film Co., Poona; former chief producer Govt. India Films Div.; mem. Censor Bd., Film Adv. Bd., Film Enquiry Com.; dir., producer numerous films, including King of Ayodhya, Chandrasena, Duniya-na-mane, Shakuntala, Ramjoshi, Amar Bhoopali, Jhanak Jhanak Payal Baaje, Do Ankhen Barah Haath. Recipient Berlin Gold Bear award. Internat. Catholic award, Hollywood Fgn. Press award. Address: Rajkamal Kalamandir Pvt Ltd, Parel, Bombay 12 India *

SHANTI, WAEL MOHAMED, engineer; b. Qalgilia, Jordan, Feb. 12, 1946; s. Mohamed Darwish Shanti and Amina Musa Tayeh; m. Amira Ramzia Vezovic, Nov. 28, 1969; children—Raji, Ruba. BSc in Mech. Engring., Univ. Sarajevo (Yugoslavia), 1970. Mech. engr. S.A.C. Co., Das-Island, United Arab Emirites, 1972-74, project mgr., 1974-79; constrn. mgr. E.M. In. Co., Amman, Jordan, 1980-83; gen. mgr., pres. Electro Mech. Engring. Group, Amman, 1983—; del. to 3d World Advt. Congress, Beijing, 1987. Recipient 3d Arab Trophy, Geneva, 1986, Internat. award for Technol. Innovation, London, 1986. Mem. Jordan Engrs. Assn., Jordan Contractors Assn., Jordan Industries Assn., Jordan Traders Assn., Internat. Traders Leader Club. Avocations: books, sports. Home: PO Box 926510, 7th Circle, Amman Jordan Office: Electro-Mech Engring Group Co, PO Box 926510, Amman Jordan

SHAO, OTIS HUNG-I, corporate executive; b. Shanghai, China, July 18, 1923; came to U.S., 1949, naturalized, 1956; s. Ming Sun and Hannah (Chen) S.; m. Marie Sheng, Apr. 2, 1955. B.A., St. John's U., 1946; M.A., U. Colo., 1950; Ph.D., Brown U., 1957. From instr. to prof. polit. sci. Moravian Coll., Bethlehem, Pa., 1954-62; asso. prof., then prof. polit. sci. Fla. Presbyn. Coll., St. Petersburg, 1962-68; prof. internat. politics, dean (Grad. Sch., U. Pacific), 1968-74; dir. Pub. Affairs Inst., 1969-74; provost Callison Coll., 1974-76; dean faculty, v.p. Occidental Coll., 1976-78; asso. exec. dir. sr. commn. Western Assn. Schs. and Colls., 1978-80; v.p., dean Hawaii Loa Coll., 1980-85; pres. Sheng Shao Enterprises Calif., 1985—; Mem. grad. students relations com. Council Grad. Schs. U.S., 1970-73; mem. exec. council undergrad. assessment program Ednl. Testing Service, 1978-80. Contbr. articles to profl. jours. Chmn. bd. dirs. Fgn. Policy Assn. Lehigh Valley, 1961-62; bd. dirs. World Affairs Council, San Joaquin County, 1969-77; trustee Inst. Med. Scis., Pacific Med. Center, San Francisco, 1968-72, optical scis. group of Profl. and Pub. Service Found., 1969-72; Resident fellow Harkness House, Brown U., 1953-54, Danforth Assn., 1958-85. Recipient Distinguished Service award Fgn. Policy Assn. Lehigh Valley, 1962. Mem. AAUP (pres. Fla. Presbyn. Coll. chpt. 1965-66), Am. Assn. Higher Edn., Rho Psi, Tau Kappa Epsilon. Democrat. Presbyn. Home: 3143 Rutledge Way Stockton CA 95209

SHAO, SHIU, financial executive; b. Taipei, Taiwan, Rep. of China, Nov. 13, 1951; came to U.S., 1975; s. Chi-Ching and Tintz (Yu) S.; m. Misara Chan. B.S. in Physics, Chan Yuan U., 1973; M.B.A. in Fin., U. Pitts., 1977. Programmer analyst Standard Brands, Inc., Burlingame, Calif., 1977-78; acctg. analyst Watkins Johnson Co., Palo Alto, Calif., 1978-81; controller Oromeccanica Inc., Burbank, Calif., 1981-82; v.p. fin., chief fin. officer Oroamerica, Inc., Burbank, 1982—; dir. Am. Internat. Chain Co., Emex Corp. Author: Financial Credit Line Tie to Commodity Index for Precious Metals Industries, 1982. Jr. Achievement advisor, Santa Clara County, Calif., 1979. Served to 2d lt. Chinese Marine Corps, 1973-75. Mem. Nat. Assn. Accts. Home: 250 W Fairview Ave #308 Glendale CA 91202 Office: Oroamerica Inc 443 N Varney St Burbank CA 91502

SHAPERO, DONALD CAMPBELL, physicist, government official; b. Detroit, Apr. 17, 1942; s. Donald Mayer and Lillian Emily (Campbell) S.; m. Diana B. Berner, Dec. 17, 1969 (div.); 1 child, Stephen B.; m. Linda J. Ravdin, Sept. 8, 1985; 1 child, Daniel R. B.S., MIT, 1964, Ph.D., 1970. Thomas J. Watson fellow IBM Corp., Yorktown Heights, N.Y., 1970-72; asst. prof. physics Am. U., Washington, 1972-73, Catholic U., 1973-75; exec. dir. Energy Research Adv. Bd. U.S. Dept. Energy, Washington, 1978-79; sr. staff officer Nat. Acad. Scis., Washington, 1975-78, spl. asst. for program coordination, 1979-82, staff dir. bd. physics and astronomy, 1982—; exec. sec. com. effects on multiple nuclear weapon detonations Nat. Acad. Scis.-NRC, Washington, 1975-76, exec. sec. geophys. data panel, 1976, exec. sec. panel to assess nat. need for facilities dedicated to prodn. synchrotron radiation, 1976, sr. staff officer geophys. study com., 1976-78; dir. com. sci. and pub. policy nuclear risk survey Nat. Acad. Sci., 1976-78, sr. staff officer for five yr. outlook sci. and tech., 1979-82, sr. staff officer workshop sci. instrumentation, 1982; staff dir. physics survey Physics Throught the 1990's, 1982-86, materials sci. and engring. study, 1985—. Contbr. sci. articles to profl. publs. Vice pres. Bethesda Jewish Congregation, 1983-84, pres. 1984. NSF fellow, 1964-68; Cottrell Research grantee, 1975. Mem. Am. Phys. Soc. Home: 7537 Heatherton Ln Potomac MD 20854 Office: Nat Acad Scis 2101 Constitution Ave Washington DC 20418

SHAPERO, HARRIS JOEL, pediatrician; b. Winona, Minn., Nov. 22, 1930; s. Charles and Minnie Sara (Ehrlichman) S.; m. Byong Soon Yu, Nov. 6, 1983; children by previous marriage: Laura, Bradley, James, Charles. A.A., UCLA, 1953; B.S., Northwestern U., 1954, M.D., 1957. Diplomate and cert. specialist occupational medicine Am. Bd. Preventive Medicine; cert. aviation medicine FAA. Intern, Los Angeles County Harbor Gen. Hosp., 1957-58, resident in pediatrics, 1958-60, staff physician, 1960-64; attending physician Perceptually Handicapped Children's Clinic, 1960-63; disease control officer for tuberculosis, Los Angeles County Health Dept., 1962-64; practice medicine specializing in pediatrics and occupational medicine, Cypress, Calif., 1965-85; pediatric cons. Los Angeles Health Dept., 1963-85, disease control officer sexually transmitted diseases, 1984-85; pediatric cons. Bellflower Clinic, 1962-85; emergency room dir. AMI, Anaheim, Calif., 1968-78; mem. med. staff Anaheim Gen. Hosp., Beach Community Hosp., Norwalk Community Hosp.; courtesy staff Palm Harbor Gen. Hosp., Bellflower City Hosp.; pediatric staff Hosp. de General, Ensenada, Mex., 1978—; primary care clinician Sacramento County Health, 1987-88; pvt. practice medico-legal evaluation, 1987-88; founder Calif. Legal Evaluation Med. Group; health care provider, advisor City of Anaheim, City of Buena Park, City of Cypress, City of Garden Grove, Cypress Sch. Dist., Magnolia Sch. Dist., Savanna Sch. Dist., Anaheim Unified Sch. Dist., Orange County Dept. Edn.; pediatric and tuberculosis cons. numerous other orgns.; FAA med. examiner, founder Pan Am. Childrens Mission. Author: The Silent Epidemic, 1979. Named Headliner in Medicine Orange County Press Club, 1978. Fellow Am. Coll. Preventive Medicine; mem. Los Angeles County Med. Assn., Los Angeles County Indsl. Med. Assn., Am. Coll. Emergency Physicians, Los Angeles County Pediatric Soc., Orange County Pediatric Soc., Am. Pub. Health Assn., Mex.-Am. Border Health Assn. Republican. Jewish. Avocations: antique books and manuscripts, photography, graphics, beekeeper. Home: 127 N Hamilton Dr #1 Beverly Hills CA 90211 Office: Beverly Hills Multispecialty Med Group 1125 S Beverly Dr Los Angeles CA 90035

SHAPIRO, ALLAN EDGAR, lawyer; b. N.Y.C., Oct. 1, 1927; s. Jacob Jerome and Dorothy (Cohen) S.; m. Yona Baratz, Oct. 26, 1956; 1 child, Rôn. BA, Yale U., 1947; LLB, Harvard U., 1950. Bar: N.Y 1950. Lectr. in law Tel-Aviv U., 1967-74, Haifa (Israel) U., 1973—; mem. Kibbutz Degania Aleph, Emek Hayarden, Israel, 1955—; research fellow Inst. for Kibbutz Research U. Haifa, 1985—. Contbr. articles to profl. jours. Grantee Sacher Inst. Hebrew U. Faculty Law, 1986. Home and Office: Kibbutz Degania Aleph, Emek Hayarden Israel

SHAPIRO, AVRAHAM, rabbi; b. Jerusalem, Israel, 1918. Faculty, Merkaz Harav Yeshiva, Israel for 30 years, dir., 1981—; Chief Rabbi Ashkenazic Community of Israel, 1983—. Address: Rabbinate Ashkenazi Community, Jerusalem Israel *

SHAPIRO, BENJAMIN LOUIS, lawyer; b. N.Y.C., June 5, 1943; s. Leonard and Henrietta (Cohen) S.; m. Madeleine Fortin, May 28, 1968 (div. Oct. 1982); m. Carol Ann McLaughlin, May 18, 1986. B.A., L.I. U., 1966; J.D., New Eng. Law Sch., 1972; LL.M., NYU, 1973. Bar: Mass. 1975, U.S. Dist. Ct. Mass. 1975, U.S. Ct. Appeals (1st cir.) 1975. Ct. planner Gov.'s Commn. on Adminstrn. of Justice, Montpelier, Vt., 1973-74; staff atty. Nat. Ctr. for State Cts., Boston, 1974-76; regional counsel U.S. Dept. Justice Law Enforcement Assistance Adminstrn., Boston, 1976-77; ct. specialist, 1977-80, exec. asst. to adminstr., 1980-81; atty. advisor U.S. Dept. Justice, Office Justice Assistance, Washington, 1981-82, program mgr., dep. asst. adminstr. Office Juvenile Justice and Delinquency Prevention, 1982—. Asst. editor-in-chief New Eng. Law Rev. Chmn. host com. Nat. Salute to Vietnam Vets., v.p. D.C. Chpt. Vietnam Vets. Am., 1982; presenter Internat. Symposium on Seriously Troubled Youth, Princeton U., 1986. Served with U.S. Army, 1966-69. Mem. ABA (mem. victims com. criminal justice sect.). Democrat. Jewish. Home: 801 S Pitt St Apt 326 Alexandria VA 22314 Office: US Dept Justice Juvenile Justice and Delinquency Prevent 633 Indiana Ave NW Washington DC 20351

SHAPIRO, DANIEL MURRY, lawyer, ophthalmologist; b. N.Y.C., Feb. 28, 1926; s. Rubin and Laura (Balton) S.; m. Olga Werchola, Apr. 14, 1981; children—Robert, Suzanne, Stephen. BA, George Washington U., 1948, MA, 1949; MD, U. Lausanne, Switzerland, 1957; J.D., Bklyn. Law Sch., 1977. Bar: N.Y. 1978, Pa. 1984, La., U.S. Dist. Ct. (ea. and so. dists.) N.Y. 1978, U.S. Ct. Appeals (5th cir.) . Assoc. Gair, Gair & Conason, N.Y.C., 1977-81, Fuchsberg & Fuchsberg, N.Y.C., 1981-82; ptnr. Katz, Katz, Shapiro & Brand, N.Y.C., 1982-83, Shapiro, Baines & Saesto, N.Y.C., 1983-87, Shapiro & Baines, 1988—; clin. asst. prof. community health NYU, N.Y.C., 1978—. Editor Trial Lawyers Quar., 1981-84, Med. Malpractice Reporter, 1981-86, Med. Malpractice, 1983. Mem. ABA, Assn. Trial Lawyers Am., Pa. Bar Assn., N.Y. State Trial Lawyers, Met. Womans Bar Assn. (bd. trustees), Pike County Bar Assn., Assn. Bar N.Y., AMA, Acad. Ophthalmology, N.Y. County Lawyers Assn., N.Y. State Med. Soc., Bronx County Med. Soc. Patentee in field. Home: 48 Laurel Cove Rd Laurel Hollow NY 11771 Office: Shapiro Baines & Saasto 55 Mineola Blvd Mineola NY 11501

SHAPIRO, EDWARD MURAY, dermatologist; b. Denver, Oct. 6, 1924; s. Isador Benjamin and Sara (Berezin) S.; student U. Colo., 1941-43; A.B. with honors, U. Tex., 1948, M.D., 1952; m. Ruth Young, Oct. 14, 1944; children—Adrian Michael, Stefanie Ann. Intern, Jefferson Coll. Medicine Hosp., Phila., 1952-53; resident in dermatology U. Tex. Med. Br., Galveston, 1953-55; resident in dermatology Henry Ford Hosp., Detroit, 1955-56, asso. in dermatology div. dermatology, 1956-57; clin. instr. dermatology Baylor U. Coll. Medicine, Houston, 1957-68, assoc. clin. prof., 1968—; staff Jefferson Davis Hosp., Houston, 1958—; active staff Pasadena (Tex.) Gen. Hosp., 1958—, Pasadena Bayshore Hosp., 1962—, Southmore Hosp., Pasadena, 1958—. Served with USAAF, 1943-46. Henry J. N. Taub research grantee, 1958-60; diplomate Am. Bd. Dermatology. Fellow Am. Acad. Dermatology; mem. AMA, Tex. Med. Assn., Tex. Dermatol. Soc. (pres.-elect 1988), South Cen. Dermatol. Assn. (bd. dirs. 1987—), Harris County Med. Assn. (pres. S.E. br. 1968-69), Houston Dermatology Assn., Houston Art League, Gulf Coast Art Soc., Am. Physicians Art Assn. Jewish. Clubs: B'nai B'rith, Rotary. Contbr. articles in field to med. jours. Home: 2101 S Houston Rd Pasadena TX 77502 Office: 1020 S Tatar St Pasadena TX 77506

SHAPIRO, ELI, business consultant, educator, economist; b. Bklyn., June 13, 1916; s. Samuel and Pauline (Kushel) S.; m. Beatrice Ferbend, Jan. 18, 1946; children—F. Stewart, Laura J. A.B., Bklyn. Coll., 1936; A.M., Columbia U., 1937, Ph.D., 1939. Instr. Bklyn. Coll., 1936-41; research asso. Nat. Bur. Econ. Research, 1938-39, cons., 1939-42, research staff, 1955-62; asst. prof. fin. U. Chgo., 1946-47, asso. prof., 1948-52, prof., 1952; prof. fin. Mass. Inst. Tech., 1952-61; asso. dean Mass. Inst. Tech. (Sch. Indsl. Mgmt.), 1954-58, Alfred P. Sloan prof. mgmt., 1976-84, prof. emeritus, 1984—; prof. fin. Harvard Bus. Sch., 1962-70, Sylvan C. Coleman prof. fin. mgmt., 1968-70; chmn. fin. com., dir. Travelers Ins. Cos., Hartford, Conn., 1971-77; vice chmn. bd., dir. Travelers Ins. Cos., 1976-78; chmn. bd. Mass. Co., 1971-72; pres. Nat. Bur. Econ. Research, 1982-84; chmn. bd. Fed. Home Loan Bank Boston; trustee Wells Fargo Mortgage and Equity Trust, Putnam Funds; econ. analyst div. monetary research U.S. Dept. Treasury, 1941-42; economist research div. OPA, 1941-42; staff cons. Com. Econ. Devel., 1950-51, mem. research adv. com., 1961-64, 69—, project dir., 1966-69; cons. to sec. treasury; mem. enforcement commn. WSB, 1952-53; cons. Inst. Def. Analyses; dep. dir. Research Com. on Money and Credit, 1959-61; bd. dirs. Reece Corp., Commonwealth Mortgage Co. Author: (with others) Personal Finance Industry and Its Credit Standards, 1939, (with Steiner) Money and Banking, 1941, Development of Wisconsin Credit Union Movement, 1947, Money and Banking, 1953, (with others), 1958, (with D. Meiselman) Measurement of Corporate Sources and Uses of Funds, 1964, (with others) Money and Banking, 1969, (with Wolf) The Role of Private Placement in Corporate Finance, 1972; Editor: (with W.L. White) Capital for Productivity and Growth, 1977. Served from ensign to lt. USNR, 1942-46. Recipient Econ. Dept. award Bklyn. Coll., 1936, Honors Day award for distinguished alumni, 1949. Fellow Am. Acad. Arts and Scis.; mem. Nat. Bur. Econ. Research (pres.), Am. Econ. Assn., Council Fgn. Relations, Am. Fin. Assn. Home: 180 Beacon St Boston MA 02116

SHAPIRO, GEORGE M., lawyer; b. N.Y.C., Dec. 7, 1919; s. Samuel N. and Sarah (Milstein) S.; m. Rita V. Lubin, Mar. 29, 1942; children: Karen Shapiro Spector, Sanford. B.S., LIU, 1939; LL.B. (Kent scholar), Columbia U., 1942; LL.D. (hon.), L.I. U., 1986. Bar: N.Y 1942. Mem. staff gov. N.Y. 1943-51, counsel to gov., 1951-54; partner firm Proskauer, Rose, Goetz & Mendelsohn, N.Y.C., 1955—, mem. exec. com., mng. ptnr., 1974-84; pres. Edmond de Rothschild Found., 1964—; dir. Bank of Calif., 1973-84; counsel, majority leader N.Y. Senate, 1955-59; counsel N.Y. Constl. Revision Commn., 1960-61. Chmn. council State U. Coll. Medicine, N.Y., 1955-71; mem. Gov.'s Com. Reapportionment, 1964, Mayor's Com. Jud. Selection, 1966-69; chmn. Park Ave. Synagogue, 1973-81. Served with USAAF, 1943-45. Mem. Council on Fgn. Relations. Club: Harmonie. Home: 1160 Park Ave New York NY 10128 Office: 300 Park Ave New York NY 10022

SHAPIRO, HAROLD TAFLER, university president, economist; b. Montreal, Que., Can., June 8, 1935; s. Maxwell and Mary (Tafler) S.; m. Vivian Bernice Rapoport, May 19, 1957; children: Anne, Marilyn, Janet, Karen. B.Comm., McGill U., Montreal, 1956; Ph.D. in Econs. (Harold Helm fellow, Harold Dodds sr. fellow), Princeton U., 1964. Asst. prof. econs. U. Mich., 1964-67, assoc. prof., 1967-70, prof., 1970-76, chmn. dept. econs., 1974-77, prof. econs. and pub. affairs, from 1977, v.p. acad. affairs, 1977-79, pres., 1980-87; research adv. Bank Can., 1965-72; prof. econ. and pub. policy, pres. Princeton U., 1988—; dir. Unisys Corp., Kellogg Co., Dow Chem., mem. tech. adv. council Ford Motor Co., 1985—, bd. of trustees Univs. Research Assn., 1988—, Interlochen Ctr. for the Arts, 1988—. Trustee Alfred P. Sloan Found., 1980—; chmn. Spl. Presdl. Com., The Research Libraries Group, 1980—; mem. Gov.'s High Tech. Task Force, Mich., 1980-87; mem. Gov.'s Commn. on Jobs and Econ. Devel. (Mich.), 1983-87; mem. Nat. Acad. Scis. Council of Govt.-Univ.-Industry Research, 1984-87 ; mem. Carnegie Commn. on Coll. Retirement, 1984-86, mem. Exec. Com. Assn. Am. Univs., 1985—, N.J. Commn. on Sci. and Tech., 1988—. Recipient Lt. Gov.'s medal in commerce McGill U., 1956. Fellow Mich. Soc. Fellows (sr.). Office: Princeton U 1 Nassau Hall Princeton NJ 08544

SHAPIRO, HARVEY ALLAN, environmental planner, educator; b. Toledo, Apr. 21, 1941; arrived in Japan, 1970; s. Meyer and Mary (Goodman) S.; m. Fukiko Nakao; children: Mina Lorine, Mona Rose-Ann. BArch, U. Detroit, 1965; M in Regional Planning., U. Pa., 1970. Prof. environ. planning Osaka (Japan) Geijutsu U., 1971—; ptnr., cons. Regional Planning Team, Inc., Tokyo, 1974—; lectr. Kobe (Japan) U., 1976-84, Osaka Indsl. U., Neyagawa, Japan, 1984-86, Nara (Japan) U., 1986—; planning advisor Taishi (Japan) City Council, 1985-87; provisional chmn. Asia-Pacific Environ. Planning Subcommn., Internat. Union for Conservation of Nature and Natural Resources, Kyoto, Japan, 1986—; cons. RPT Assocs., Inc., Tokyo, 1974—; project mem. Environ. and Policy Inst., Honolulu, 1987—. Author: (with others) Landscape Synthesis, 1983; contbr. articles to profl. jours., 1975—. Concertmaster Forum Orch., Kyoto, 1987—. Served as 1st lt. U.S. Army, 1966-68, Vietnam. Mem. Internat. Geog. Union, Pacific Sci. Assn., World Future Soc., Internat. Union for Conservation Nature (mem. sustainable devel. commn.), Japan Environment Soc., Japan Coastal Zone Soc. Office: Osaka Geijutsu U, Minami-Kawashi Gun, Kannan-cho Higashiyama, Osaka 585, Japan

SHAPIRO, ISADORE, material scientist, consultant; b. Mpls., Apr. 25, 1916; s. Jacob and Bessie (Goldman) S.; B. Chem. Engring. summa cum laude, U. Minn., 1938, Ph.D., 1944; m. Mae Hirsch. Sept. 4, 1938; children—Stanley Harris, Jerald Steven. Asst. instr. chemistry U. Minn., 1938-41, research fellow, 1944-45; research chemist E. I. duPont de Nemours and Co., Phila., 1946; head chem. lab. U.S. Naval Ordnance Test Sta., Pasadena,

Calif., 1947-52; dir. research lab. Olin-Mathieson Chem. Corp., 1952-59; head chemistry Hughes Tool Co., Aircraft div., Culver City, Calif., 1959-62; pres. Universal Chem. Systems Inc. 1962—, Aerospace Chem. Systems, Inc., 1964-66; dir. contract research HITCO, Gardena, Calif., 1966-67; prin. scientist Douglas Aircraft Co. of McDonnell Douglas Corp., Santa Monica, Calif., 1967; prin. scientist McDonnell Douglas Astronautics Co., 1967-70; head materials and processes AiResearch Mfg. Co., Torrance, Calif., 1971-82, cons., 1982—. Rater U.S. Civil Service Bd. Exam., 1948-52. Served 1st lt. AUS, 1941-44. Registered profl. engr., Calif. Fellow Am. Inst. Chemists, Am. Inst. Aeros and Astronautics (asso.); mem. AAAS, Am. Ordnance Assn., Am. Chem. Soc., Soc. Rheology, Soc. Advancement Materials and Process Engring., Am. Inst. Physics, AIM, Am. Phys. Soc., N.Y. Acad. Sci., Am. Assn. Contamination Control, Am. Ceramic Soc., Nat. Inst. Ceramic Engrs., Internat. Plansee Soc. for Powder Metallurgy, Sigma Xi, Tau Beta Pi, Phi Lambda Upsilon. Author articles in tech. publs. Patentee, discoverer series of carborane compounds. Home: 5624 W 62d St Los Angeles CA 90056

SHAPIRO, JOAN ISABELLE, laboratory administrator, nurse; b. Fulton, Ill., Aug. 26, 1943; d. Macy James and Frieda Lockhart; m. Ivan Lee Shapiro, Dec. 28, 1968; children—Audrey, Michael. R.N., Peoria Methodist Sch. Nursing, Ill., 1964. Nurse, Grant Hosp., Columbus, Ohio, 1975-76; nurse Cardiac Thoracic and Vascular Surgeons Ltd., Geneva, Ill., 1977—, mgr. non-invasive lab., 1979—; owner, operator Shapiro's Mastiff's 1976-82; sec.-treas. Sounds Services, 1976—, Mainstream Sounds Inc., 1980-84; co-founder Cardio-Phone Inc., 1982—; co-founder Edgewater Vascular Inst., 1987—; v.p., dir. Computer Specialists Inc., 1986—. Mem. Soc. Non-invasive Technologists, Soc. Peripheral Vascular Nursing (community awareness com. 1984—), Kane County Med. Soc. Aux. (pres. 1983-84, adviser, 1984-85). Lutheran. Office: Cardiac Thoracic and Vascular Surgeons Ltd PO Box 564 Geneva IL 60134

SHAPIRO, MILTON STANLEY, lawyer; b. N.Y.C., May 9, 1922; s. Philip and Lena (Cohen) S.; m. Beatrice Leibowitz, June 9, 1946; children—Susan Shapiro Levkoff, Philip J. B.A., Bklyn. Coll., 1942; LL.B. cum laude, NYU, 1948. Admitted to N.Y. bar, 1948, U.S. Supreme Ct. bar, 1961; asso. firm Bernheimer & Zucker, N.Y.C., 1948-55; individual practice law, N.Y.C., 1955-65; partner firm Zucker, Weiden & Shapiro, N.Y.C., 1965-73, Shapiro, Weiden & Mortman, 1973-75, Kuh, Shapiro, Goldman, Cooperman & Levitt, N.Y.C., 1975-78, Shapiro, Mortman & Schwartz, p.c., 1978-85, Shapiro, Mortman, Schwartz & Greene, 1986-87, Shapiro & Schwartz, 1987—; dir. Chelsea Town Co., Apex Resources, Inc., Chadlin Enterprises, Inc., Mayflower Studios, Ltd., Amanuensis Ltd., Marcom Telecommunications, Inc., Ohio Match Co., others; del. World Zionist Congress. Pres., Nirvana Gardens Civic Assn., Great Neck, N.Y., 1962-65; vice chmn. 29th-30th St. Community Council, 1964—; bd. dirs. Vocal Arts Found., N.Y.C., United Israeli Appeal, Inc.; chmn. Am. Zionist Fund, 1985-86. Served with USAAF, 1942-45. Recipient Brandeis award Zionist Orgn. Am., 1981; hon. Ky. col. Mem. Assn. Bar City N.Y., Am. Bar Assn., N.Y. State Bar Assn., Zionist Orgn. of Am. (nat. pres. 1986—), Am. Israeli Pub. Affairs Com. (exec. bd.). Jewish. Clubs: KP; Muttowntown Golf and Country (East Norwich, N.Y.); Banyan Golf (Palm Beach, Fla.); Governor's (West Palm Beach, Fla.). Mem. Law Rev. N.Y. U., 1947-48. Home: 799 Park Ave New York NY 10021 Office: 800 3d Ave New York NY 10022

SHAPIRO, NELSON HIRSH, lawyer; b. Washington, Feb. 3, 1928; s. Arthur and Anna (Zenitz) S.; m. Helen Lenora Sykes, June 27, 1948; children—Ronald Evan, Mitchell Wayne, Jeffrey Mark, Julie Beth. B.E.E., John Hopkins U., 1948; J.D., George Washington U., 1952. Bar: D.C. 1952, Va. 1981. Patent examiner U.S. Patent Office, 1948-50; patent advisor U.S. Signal Corps, 1950-52; mem. Shapiro & Shapiro, Arlington, Va., 1952—. Mem. ABA, Am. Patent Law Assn., Bar Assn. D.C., Order of Coif, Tau Beta Pi. Patentee; contbr. articles to legal publs. and Ency. of Patent Practice and Invention Management, 1964. Home: 7001 Old Cabin Ln Rockville MD 20852 Office: Shapiro and Shapiro 1100 Wilson Blvd Suite 1701 Arlington VA 22209

SHAPIRO, RICHARD STANLEY, physician; b. Moline, Ill., June 11, 1925; s. Herbert and Esther Dian (Grant) S.; B.S., St. Ambrose Coll., 1947; B.S. in Pharmacy, U. Iowa, 1951, M.S. in Preventive Medicine and Environ. Health, 1951, M.D., 1957; m. Arlene Blum, June 12, 1949; children—Michele Pamela, Bruce Grant, Gary Lawrence; m. 2d, Merry Lou Cook, Oct. 11, 1971. Pharmacist, Rock Island, Ill., 1951-53; research asst. U. Iowa Coll. Medicine, Iowa City, 1950-51, 53-57; practice medicine specializing in allergy, Beverly Hills, Calif., 1958-62, Lynwood, Calif., 1962—; attending physician Good Hope Found. Allergy Clinic, Los Angeles, 1958-62, Cedars of Lebanon Hosp., Hollywood, Calif., 1959-68, U. So. Calif.-Los Angeles County Med. Center, 1962—; physician St. Francis Hosp., Lynwood, 1962—; assoc. clin. prof. medicine U. So. Calif., 1978-84, emeritus, 1984—. Bd. dirs. Westside Jewish Community Center, 1961-65, Camp JCA, 1964-65. Served with USNR, 1943-45; PTO. Diplomate Am. Bd. Allergy and Immunology. Fellow Am. Geriatric Soc., Am. Coll. Allergy, Am. Assn. Clin. Immunology and Allergy; mem. Am. Soc. Tropical Medicine and Hygiene, Am. Acad. Allergy, Los Angeles Allergy Soc., AMA, Calif., Los Angeles County med. assns., West Coast Allergy Soc., AAAS, Am., Calif. socs. internal medicine, Calif. Soc. Allergy, Am. Heart Assn., Sierra Club, Sigma Xi. Jewish. Mason; mem. B'nai B'rith. Contbr. articles to profl. jours. Office: 11411 Brookshire Ave Downey CA 90241

SHAR, MARCUS Z., lawyer; b. Columbus, Ohio, May 14, 1951; s. Farrell K. and Adeline (Thall) S.; m. Gwen Ellen Abrams, Aug. 13, 1972; children—Jonathan Carrie, Debra Erin, David Eric, Helaine Beth. B.A., Ohio State U., 1973; J.D., U. Md., 1976. Bar: Md. 1976, U.S. Dist. Ct. Md. 1976, U.S. Bankruptcy Ct. Md. 1984. Assoc. Peter G. Angelos, Balt., 1976-79; sr. ptnr. Bierer & Shar P.A., Balt., 1979—; mem. faculty Nat. Coll. Trial Advocacy, Washington, 1983—; med. malpractice corr. Md. Daily Record, Balt., 1984—; lectr. profl. assns. Author: Medical Malpractice Law of Maryland. Contbr. articles to legal jours., model pleadings to legal treatises. Mem. youth commn. Union of Orthodox Congregations of Am., Atlantic Seaboard Region, 1978; mem. adv. com. Nat. Conf. Synagogue Youth, Atlantic Seaboard Region, 1979; mem. adv. com. Project Yedid, Balt., 1983-84; bd. govs. Union of Orthodox Congregations, 1985. Recipient cert. merit Moot Ct., U. Md. Sch. Law, 1974. Mem. Balt. City Bar Assn., Md. State Bar Assn. (com. 1984), Md. Trial Lawyers Assn. (bd. govs. 1985—), Assn. Trial Lawyers Am. (com. 1981, 84). U. Md. Law Sch. Alumni Assn. Democrat. Jewish. Home: 2506 Shelleydale Dr Baltimore MD 21209 Office: Bierer & Shar PA 926 Saint Paul St Baltimore MD 21202

SHARA, FAROUK AL- See AL-SHARA, FAROUK

SHARAN, MITHILA BIHARI, psychology educator; b. Muzaffarpur, Bihar, India, Jan. 10, 1943; s. Sita Ram Sah and Dhanwanti Devi; m. Savita Prasad, June 6, 1966; children—Alok, Avinash, Gouri. B.A. with honors, U. Bihar, 1962, M.A. in Psychology, 1964; Ph.D in Psychology, Patna U., Bihar, 1974. Lectr. in psychology Patna Coll., 1965-66, T.N.B. Coll., Bhagalpur, Bihar, 1966-75; asst. prof. Indian Inst. Tech., Kharagpur, West Bengal, India, 1975-84, prof. psychology, 1984—, head humanities and social scis. dept., 1985-88. Author: A Study of Role Conflict and Its Influence on Role Performance, 1977. Contbr. articles to profl. jours. Mem. Indian Sci. Congress, Indian Psychol. Assn. Lodges: Rotary. Avocations: writing; magic. Office: IIT Dept Humanities and Social Scis, Midnapur, Kharagpur, West Bengal 721302, India

SHARE, RICHARD HUDSON, lawyer; b. Mpls., Sept. 6, 1938; s. Jerome and Millicent S.; m. Carolee Martin, 1970; children: Mark Lowell, Gregory Martin, Jennifer Hillary, Ashley. B.S., UCLA, 1960; J.D., U. So. Calif., 1963. Bar: Calif. Sup. Ct. 1964, U.S. Dist. Ct. (cen. and so. dists.) Calif., U.S. Supreme Ct. 1974. Field agt. IRS, 1960-63; mem. law div., asst. sec. Avco Fin. Services, 1963-72; founder Frandzel and Share, ptnr. predecessor firm Foonberg and Frandzel, Los Angeles, Calif., 1972—; lectr. in field. Mem. Calif. Bankers Assn., Fin. Lawyers Assn. Clubs: Rivera Tennis, Pacific Palisades. Office: 6500 Wilshire Blvd 17th Floor Los Angeles CA 90048 also: Fed Res Bank Bldg 101 Market St San Francisco CA 94105 also: 18300 Von Karman Ave Irvine CA 92715 Also: 2310 Tulane St Suite 300 Fresno CA 93721

SHARETT, ALAN RICHARD, lawyer; b. Hammond, Ind., Apr. 15, 1943; s. Henry S. and Frances (Givel) Smulevitz; children—Lauren Ruth, Charles Daniel; m. Sarah Rebecca Gaber, June 6, 1987. Student Ind. U., 1962-65; J.D., DePaul U., 1968. Bar: N.Y. 1975, Ind. 1969, U.S. Ct. Appeals (2d cir.) 1975, U.S. Ct. Appeals (7th cir.) 1974, U.S. Supreme Ct. 1973. Assoc. Call, Call, Borns & Theodoros, Gary, Ind., 1969-71; judge protem Gary City Ct., 1970-71; environ. dep. prosecutor 31st Jud. Circuit, Lake County, Ind., 1971-75; mem. Cohan, Cohan & Smulevitz, 1971-75; judge pro tem Superior Ct., Lake County, Ind., 1971-75; professorial dir. NYU Pub. Liability Inst., N.Y.C., 1975-76; asst. atty. gen. N.Y. State, N.Y.C., 1976-78; sole practice, Flushing, N.Y., 1980-82, Miami Beach, Fla., 1982—; chmn. lawyers panel for No. Ind., ACLU, 1969-71; mem. Nat. Dist. Attys. Assn., 1972-75, mem. environ. protection com. Recipient Honors award in medicolegal litigation Law-Sci. Acad. Am., 1967. Mem. ABA, Assn. Bar City N.Y., N.Y. County Lawyers Assn. (com. on fed. cts. 1977-82), Am. Judicature Soc., Assn. Trial Lawyers Am., N.Y. State Trial Lawyers Assn., N.Y. State Bar Assn., Ind. State Bar Assn., Queens County Bar Assn., Am. Acad. Poets. Democrat. Contbr. articles to profl. jours. Address: 3100 Collins Ave Miami Beach FL 33140

SHARFMAN, HERBERT, judge; b. Northampton, Pa., July 29, 1909; s. Meyer and Minnie (Caplan) S.; m. Dorothy Muriel Cohen, Feb. 8, 1932; children—Richard M., Jo-Ellen Crews. A.B., U. Pa., 1930; LL.B., Columbia U., 1933. Bar: Pa. 1933, U.S. Dist. Ct. (ea. dist.) Pa. 1935, U.S. Supreme Ct., 1945. Sole practice, Lehigh and Northampton Counties, Pa., 1933-44; atty.-adv. pub. utilities br. OPA, Washington, 1944-46, FCC, Washington, 1946-52; adminstrv. law judge FCC, Washington, 1952-74, Postal Rate Commn. Washington, 1974-76, part-time adminstrv. law judge, 1976—. Mem. ABA, Pa. State Bar Assn., Lehigh County Bar Assn. Jewish. Home: 162 W Center Ave Sebring FL 33870

SHARIF, OMAR (MICHAEL SHALHOUB), actor; b. Alexandria, Egypt, Apr. 10, 1932; s. Joseph and Claire (Saada) Shalhoub; m. Faten Hamama, Feb. 5, 1955; 1 son, Tarek. Attended, Victoria Coll., Cairo. Appeared in: numerous Egyptian, French and Am. films, including Lawrence of Arabia, 1962 (Golden Globe award for best supporting actor), Behold a Pale Horse, 1964, The Fall of the Roman Empire, 1964, Genghis Khan, 1965, The Yellow Rolls Royce, 1965, Doctor Zhivago, 1966 (Golden Globe award best actor), Night of the Generals, 1967, More Than a Miracle, 1967, Funny Girl, 1968, Mayerling, 1969, Che!, 1969, MacKenna's Gold, 1969, The Horsemen, 1970, The Last Valley, 1971, The Burglars, 1972, The Tamarind Seed, 1974, The Mysterious Island of Captain Nemo, 1974, Juggernaut, 1974, Funny Lady, 1975, Crime and Passion, 1975, Ashanti, 1979, Bloodline, 1979, Oh Heavenly Dog, 1980, The Baltimore Bullet, 1980, Top Secret, 1984; TV miniseries Peter the Great, 1986, Anastasia: The Mystery of Anna, 1986. Author: The Eternal Male, 1977; author syndicated columns on bridge. Office: William Morris Agy care Ames Cushing 151 El Camino Blvd Beverly Hills CA 90212 also: care William Morris Agy, 147 Wardour St, London WL England *

SHARIF-EMAMI, JAFAR, former prime minister of Iran; b. Tehran, Iran, Sept. 8, 1910; s. Haji Mohammad Hossein and Banu (Kobra) Sharif-E.; m. Eshrat Moazzami, Nov. 16, 1946; children: Shirin, Simin, Ali. Ed., Reichsbahn Zentralschule, Brandenburg, Germany, Statens Tekniskaskolan, Boras, Sweden; Dr.H.C., Seoul U., 1978. Joined Iranian State Rys., 1931, tech. dep. gen. dir., 1942-46; chmn., mng. dir. Ind. Irrigation Corp., 1946-50, gen. dir., 1950-51; undersec. to Minister Roads and Communications, 1950-51, minister roads and communications, 1951; mem. Senate of Iran from Tehran, 1955-57, 63—, pres. senate house, 1963-78; pres. 3d Constituent Assembly, 1967; minister industries and mines 1957-60, pres. chamber industries and mines, 1962-67, prime minister of Iran, 1960-61, 78—; dep. custodian Pahlavi Found., 1962-78; pres. chamber of industries and mines, 1962-67; chmn. bd. Indsl. and Mining Devel. Bank, 1963-78. Mem. high council Plan Orgn., 1951-52, mng. dir., chmn. high council, 1953-54; pres. 22d Internat. Conf. Red Cross, 1973; bd. dirs. Royal Orgn. Social Services, 1962-78; trustee Pahlavi U., Shirz, 1962-78, Nat. U., Tehran, 1962-78, Aria Mehr Tech. U., 1965-78, Queen Pahlavi's Found., 1966-78; bd. founders Soc. Preservation Nat. Monuments, 1966-78. Decorated 1st grade Order Taj, Iran; decorated 3d and 1st grade Order Homayoon, Iran, 1st grade Order Social Services, Iran, 1st grade Order Land Reform, Iran, 1st grade Order Labour, Iran, 1st grade Order Cooperative, Iran, 1st grade Order Coronation, Iran, 1st grade Order 25th Shahrivar, Iran, 1st grade Order of Celebration 2500th Anniversary Founding of Persian Empire by Cyrus the Great, Iran, chevalier de Grand Croix Italy, das Gross-Kreux Verdienstorden Germany, grand officer Legion of Honor, France, grand cross Legion of Honor, France, Stora Korset av Kingl. Nordstjarneoden Sweden, grand cross Order de la Courone, Belgium, grand cordon Order Leopold, Belguim, Das Grosse Golden Ehrenzelchen am Bande Austria, Order St. Michael and St. George U.K., Order Sacred Treasure 1st grade Japan, Order of Rising Sun 1st grade Japan, Tudor Vladimirescu 1st grade Romania, knight grand cross Most Exalted Order of White Elephant 1st grade, Thailand, Alesteghlal 1st grade Tunisia, Den Kgl. Norske St. Olavs Orden 1st grade Norway, Order of Danbrok 1st grade Denmark, Order Al-Arsh 1st grade Morocco, Order Jugoslovenske Zvenzde Za Lentom Yugoslavia, Krzyz Wielki Order Odrodzenia Polski Poland, Di-Peliharakan Allah Panckuan Necara Malaysia, grand condon Order Menelik Second, Ethiopia, Order of Banner of Hungarian Peoples Republic 1st grade, Ghaede Azam Pakistan, 1st grade Veshahol Malek Abdol-Aziz Saudi Arabia, Order Nile 1st grade Egypt, Grand Croix Ordre du Merite Senegal, Esteghlal Qatar. Fellow ASCE; mem. Red Lion and Sun (dir 1963, dep. chmn. 1966-78), Internat. Bankers Assn. (pres. 1975), Iranian Engrs. Assn. (pres. 1966-78).

SHARIFY, NASSER, librarian, educator, author; b. Tehran, Iran, Sept. 23, 1925; came to U.S., 1953, naturalized, 1972; s. Ebrahim and Eshrat (Saghafy) S.; m. Homayoun Taslimy, June 14, 1950 (div. 1978); children: Shareareh, Shahab. Licencie es Lettres, U. Tehran, 1947; M.S., Columbia U., 1954, Dr. L.S., 1958. Editorial staff Teheran jours. Rah-e Now, Jahan-e Now, Saba, Jonb va Jush, 1943-51; translator, announcer All India Radio, 1948-49; librarian, dep. dir. Library of Parliament Iran, Tehran, 1949-53; cataloger Library of Congress, 1954-55; program asst. libraries devel. sect. UNESCO, Paris, 1959-61; acting chief servicing sect. Dept. Edn., 1962-63; dir. gen. Ministry Edn., Tehran, 1961-62; asst. prof. library and info. scis. and internat. edn. U. Pitts., 1963-66; founder, dir. Internat. Library Info. Center, 1964-66; vis. lectr. SUNY Albany Sch. Library Sci., summer, 1966; dir. internat. librarianship and documentation, internat studies and world affairs SUNY, Oyster Bay, 1966-68; lectr., instr. Sch. Library Sci., U. Okla., 1969; dean, prof. grad. sch. library and info sci. Pratt Inst., Bklyn., 1968-87, chmn. inst. research council, 1971—, disting. prof., dean emeritus sch. computer, info. and library scis., 1987—; pres. B.E.L.T., Inc., internat. planning cons., 1981—; Dir. Grad. Library Tng. Program, UNESCO Mission, Nat. Tchrs. Coll., Tehran, 1960; Iran's Ofcl. del. to UNESCO Conf. Ednl. Pubs., Geneva, 1961, SE Asia Edn. Secs. Conf., Murree, Pakistan, 1961, Internation Conf., on Cataloging Prins., Paris, 1961, CENTO Library Devel. Conf., Ankara, Turkey, 1962; chmn. standing com. for preparation reading materials for new literates UNESCO, Tehran, 1961-62; mem. AID Mission, Turkey, Pakistan, 1966; dir. Conf. on Internat. Responsibility Coll. and Univ. Librarians, Oyster Bay, 1967; U.S. del. 33d Conf. and Internat. Congress on Documentation, Tokyo, 1967; ALA del. UN Conf. on Non-Govtl. Orgn., 1969; cons. U.S. AID, Conf. on Book Devel., 1967; mem. adv. bd. Ency. Library and Info. Scis., 1969—; chmn. Pre-Am. Library Assn. Conf. Inst. on Internat. Library Manpower, Edn. and Placement in N.Am., Detroit, 1970; mem. Am. del. Internat. Fedn. Library Assn. Conf., Liverpool, Eng., 1971, Budapest, 1972, Grenoble, France, 1973, Washington, 1974, Brussels, 1977, Montreal, 1982, Chgo., 1985; bldg. cons. Learning Resources Center, Nat. Tchrs. Coll., Iran, 1972-73, cons. campus planning, 1972-73; UNESCO cons. missions to plan and evaluate Nat. Sch. Info. Sci., Morocco, 1973-74, 79-81; chmn. Conf. on Orgn. and Control of Info for Islamic Research, 1982; chmn. bd. cons. to Nat. U. Iran, 1974-75, Pahlavi Nat. Library of Iran, 1975-77. Author: cataloging of Persian works Including Rules for Transliteration Entry and Description, 1959, Book Production, Importation and Distribution in Iran, Pakistan and Turkey, 1966; Beyond the National Frontiers: The International Dimension of Changing Library Education for a Changing World, 1973; The Pahlavi National Library of the Future, 17 vols., 1976; other books; contbr. to Ency. of Library and Info. Sci., 1969, ALA World Ency. Library and Info. Services, 1980, 86, library jours., 1973—, Bookmark, 1972; contbr. poetry to various jours., 1947-51, 67, lyrics to Iranian motion pictures and recs., 1948-52; Contbr. to: film script for motion picture Morad, 1951-52. Trustee Bklyn. Public Library, 1970-82; pres. Maurice F. Tauber Found., 1981—. Mem. ALA (chmn. com. equivalencies and reciprocity 1966-71, mem. UNESCO panel, mem. nominating com. 1970-71, chmn. Pakistan and Middle East Resource panels, internat. library edn. com., mem. com. internat. library schs. div. library edn. 1968-72, coordinator country resources panels, internat. library edn. com. library edn. div. 1973-78), N.Y. Library Assn. (dir. library edn. sect. 1969-72), Pub. Library Assn. (task force on internat. relations 1981-86), Am. Assn. Library Schs. (chmn. govtl. relations com., 1984-88), Am. Soc. Info. for Sci., Spl. Librarian Assn., Internat. Fedn. Library Assns. (adv. group library edn. 1971-73, v.p. library schs. sect. 1973-77), Assn. des Bibliothécaires Français. Home: 252 Jericho Turnpike Westbury NY 11590 Office: 200 Willoughby Ave Brooklyn NY 11205

SHARLOW, THELMA FACEMIRE JACOBS, insurance agent; b. Centralia, W.Va., June 20, 1929; d. Guy Willard Facemire and Florence (Brady) Facemire Chasonis; m. Arthur F. Jacobs, Jr., Mar. 16, 1948 (dec. 1975); children: Betty Lou, Colleen, Randy, Arthur F. III. Student ins. courses Keene State Coll. (N.H.) Herd classification dept. Holstein-Friesian, Brattleboro, Vt., 1948-67, indexer, 1963-67; supr. comml. lines Richards, Inc., Brattleboro, 1967—. Mem. Nat. Assn. Ins. Women (past del. regional conv., bd. dirs., 2d v.p. So. Vt. and So. N.H.), Cert. Profl. Ins. Women. Baptist. Club: Evening Star Grange (Dummerston, Vt.). Home: 464 Western Ave Brattleboro VT 05301 Office: Richards Gates Hoffman & Clay 25 Harris Pl Brattleboro VT 05301

SHARMA, KRISHAN KUMAR, computer company executive, physicist; b. Paprola, Himachal Pradesh, India, Oct. 20, 1936; came to Eng., 1968, naturalized, 1978; s. Khazana Ram and Kirpi Devi S.; m. Veronica Ann Edge, June 16, 1964; children: Ravi, Priya. B.Sc. in Physics with honors, Delhi U., 1959; M.Sc. in Physics, Nagpur U., India, 1968. Sci. asst. India Meteorol. Dept., 1959-68; research asst. U. Lancaster, Eng., 1969-70; engr. Internat. Computer Ltd., Kidsgrove, Stoke-on-Trent, Eng., 1971-77, prin. engr., 1977-81, sr. mgr. printed cir. test assemblies, 1982-87, ret., 1987; fine art, antigue dealer, Stoke-on-Trent, 1987—; cons., non-exec. dir. U.K. (Cyprus) Fire Ltd.; bus. exec., mng. dir. Export-Import Products U.K. Author: Stress in High Technical Society; contbr. research articles to India Meteorol. Jour. Research, 1964-68. Hindu. Avocations: research in old oil paintings; chess; stock market studies; camping; homeopathy. Home: 13 Acacia Dr, Sandbach Cheshire CW 11 9ER England

SHARMA, SHAIL KUMARI, biochemist, educator; b. Bareilly, India, June 1, 1935; s. Devi Charan and Radha Devi Sharma. MS, Agra U., Bareilly, 1956; PhD in Biochemistry, McGill U., Montreal, Can., 1963. Prof., head dept. biochemistry All India Inst. Med. Scis., New Delhi, 1985—. Mem. editorial bd.: Molecular and Cellular Biochemistry, 1987—, Jour. Bioscis., 1987—; contbr. articles to profl. jours. Life mem. Bd. Control, Bareilly Coll. Fogarty internat. fellow NIH, Bethesda, Md., 1973-75. Mem. Internat. Soc. Neurochemistry, Internat. Brain Research Orgn., Internat. Narcotic Research Conf., Internat. Soc. Biomed. Research on Drug Dependence. Office: All India Inst Med Scis, 29 Darzi Chouk, Bareilly 243003, India

SHARMA, SHANKAR DAYAL, Indian government official, lawyer; b. Aug. 19, 1918. Ed., Lucknow U., Cambridge U., Lincoln's Inn. Practice law 1942—; mem. All India Congress Com., 1950—, pres., 1972-74; gen. sec. Indian Nat. Congress, 1968-72; mem. Lok Sabha, 1971-77; minister communications India, New Delhi, 1974-77; gov. Andhra, India, until 1985, Punjab, India, 1985-86; v.p. India, New Delhi, 1987—. Address: Office Vice Pres, New Delhi India *

SHARON, ARIEL, Israeli minister; b. Kfar Malal, nr. Tel Aviv, 1928; student Hebrew U., 1952-53, Staff Coll., Camberley (U.K.), 1957-58, Tel Aviv U., 1966; married; 2 children. Joined Israeli Def. Forces; instr. Jewish Police units, 1947; platoon comdr. Alexandroni Brigade; regimental intelligence officer, 1948; co-comdr., 1949; comdr. Brigade Reconnaissance unit, 1949-50; intelligence officer Cen. Command and Northern Command, 1950-52; founder, head spl. 101 unit until 1957; tng. comdr. Gen. Staff, 1958; comdr. Inf. Sch., 1958-69; comdr. Armoured Brigade, 1962; head staff Northern Command, 1964; head Brigade Group during Six-Day War, 1967; resigned from Israeli Army, 1973; recalled as comdr. cen. sect. of Sinai Front during Yom Kippur War, 1973; mem. Israeli Knesset, 1973-74, 77—; adv. on security affairs to Prime Minister Rabin, 1975-76; founder Shlomzion Party, 1977, merged with Herut Party faction of Likud bloc, 1977; minister of agr., 1977-81; minister of def., 1981-83, minister without portfolio, 1983-84, minister of industry and commerce, 1984—. Office: Ministry of Industry, and Commerce, Jerusalem Israel *

SHARON, ERNST SHIMON, oil company auditor; b. Vienna, Austria, Jan. 20, 1923; came to Israel, 1938; s. Joseph and Sally (Lumer) Schenk; m. Rose Shoshana Helfant, Feb. 5, 1946; children—Dafna, Yael-Anat. B.Sc. in Econs. with honors, U. London, 1958. Chief budget officer Municipality of Haifa, Israel, 1950-58, city treas., 1958-64; sr. exec. Dagon Indsl. Corp., Haifa, 1964-75; dir. internal audit Oil Refineries Ltd., Haifa, 1975—; regional dir. Jewish Nat. Fund (KKL), Fed. Republic Germany, 1979-83; lectr. on local govt., pub. fin., internal auditing, budgeting. Contbr. articles to profl. jours. Mem. exec. com. Haifa Mcpl. Theater, 1961-78; bd. dirs. Haifa Symphony Orch., 1960-74, Petrochemical Industries, 1985—. Served with Brit. Army, 1942-46; capt. Israeli Def. Army, 1948-50. Mem. Inst. Internal Auditors. Jewish. Lodges: Lions (v.p.), B'nai B'rith. Home: 33 Hatishbi St, Haifa 34526, Israel Office: Oil Refineries Ltd, PO Box 4, Haifa Israel

SHARON, TIMOTHY MICHAEL, physicist; b. Portsmouth, Va., Aug. 21, 1948; s. Lester Clark and Ruth May (Banister) S.; student Santa Ana Coll., 1966-68; B.A., U. Calif.-Irvine 1970, M.A., 1972, Ph.D., 1976; m. Carla Deon Colley, Dec. 17, 1977. Jr. specialist solid state theory U. Calif.-Irvine, 1976, research asst. radiation physics Med. Center and Sch. Medicine, 1976-77, cons. to attending staff Research and Edn. Found., 1976-77; mktg. physicist Varian Assos., Irvine, 1977-78; prin. engr., program mgr. Spectra Research Systems, Newport Beach, Calif., 1977-82; v.p. Brewer-Sharon Corp., Newport Beach, 1981-86, Micor Instruments, Inc., Irvine, Calif., 1983-86; pres., chief exec. officer Medelec Instruments Co., Inc., Newport Beach, 1986-88; pres. Pacific Crest Enterprises, El Toro, Calif., 1988; adj. faculty physics and engring. Columbia Pacific U., San Rafael, Calif., 1981-87; dean Sch. Engring., Newport U., Newport Beach, Calif., 1983-87; mem. adv. panel on pub. Am. Inst. Physics, 1974-75. Brython P. Davis univ. fellow, 1973-74. Mem. AAAS, Am. Phys. Soc., Brit. Interplanetary Soc. (asso. fellow), Am. Assn. Physicists in Medicine, IEEE, Assn. Advancement Med. Instrumentation, Smithsonian Instn., Am. Film Inst., Nat. Hist. Soc., Nat. Geog. Soc., Festival of Arts Laguna Beach, Mensa, Intertel, Sigma Pi Sigma, Phi Theta Kappa, Alpha Gamma Sigma. Clubs: Acad. Magical Arts, Magic Island, Club 33. Contbr. articles to profl. jours. Office: 21081 Paseo Verdura El Toro CA 92630

SHARP, DOUGLAS RICE, theological educator; b. Monte Vista, Colo., Mar. 1, 1949; s. William Edward and Pauline Marie (Settle) S.; B.A., William Jewell Coll., 1971; M.Div., Am. Bapt. Sem. of West, 1975; Ph.D., Grad. Theol. Union, 1987; m. Linda K. Sharp; children—Michelle Lynn, Jason Douglas; m. 2d Linda Kay, July 30, 1983. Ordained to ministry Am. Baptist Ch., 1975; pastor Immanuel Chapel, South Fork, Colo., 1971; chaplain VA Hosp., La Jolla, Calif., 1972; asso. minister 1st Bapt. Ch., San Diego, 1973; adminstrv. asst. to v.p. Am. Bapt. Sem. of West, Berkeley, Calif., 1973-74, assoc. dir. field edn., 1974-75, dir. field edn., 1975-84, instr. theology, 1977-84, registrar, 1977-84; registrar, dir. admissions asst. prof. Christian Theology No. Bapt. Theol. Sem., 1985—; minister edn. Ch. of Valley, San Ramon, Calif., 1977-79. Recipient Clairborne M. Hill award Am. Bapt. Sem. of West, 1975; Pulliam scholar, 1975, 76; Order of Eastern Star grantee, 1975. Mem. Minister's Council Am. Bapt. Chs. U.S.A., Assn. for Theol. Field Edn., Assn. for Profl. Edn. for Ministry, Am. Soc. Ch. History, Am. Acad. Religion, Soc. Bibl. Lit. Democrat. Club: Masons. Research in 19th and 20th century reformed theology. Home: 465 Raintree Ct #1D Glen Ellyn IL 60137 Office: No Bapt Theol Sem 660 E Butterfield Rd Lombard IL 60148

SHARP, ERIC, business executive; b. Aug. 17, 1916; s. Isaac and Martha Sharp; m. Marion Freeman, 1950; 2 children. B.S. in Econs. with honors, London Sch. Econs. Prin., Ministry of Power, 1948; U.K. del. Coal and

Petroleum Com. of OEEC, 1948-50; vice chmn. Electricity Com., OEEC, 1951-54; sec. to Herbert Com. of Inquiry into Electricity Supply Industry, 1955-56; with Brit. Nylon Spinners Ltd., 1957-64; dir. ICI Fibres Ltd., 1964-68; mem. bd. Monsanto Europe, 1969; mem. mgmt. bd. Monsanto Europe, 1970-72, dep. chmn., 1973-74, chmn., 1975-81, Monsanto Ltd.; chmn. Polyamide Intermediates Ltd., 1975-81; chmn. Chem. Industry Safety and Health Council, 1977-79; pres. Chem. Industries Assn., 1979-80; chmn. Cable & Wireless p.l.c., 1980—, chief exec. officer, 1981—; part-time mem. London Electricity Bd., 1969-78; mem. EDC for Chem. Industry, 1980-82, Central Electricity Generating Bd., 1980-86. Avocations: music; wine; gardening. Address: care Cable and Wireless Ltd, Mercury House, Theobalds Rd, London WC1, England *

SHARP, HOWARD EDWARD, shipping industry executive; b. Myrtleford, Victoria, Australia, Aug. 23, 1943; s. Sidney Herbert and Helen Mary (Vuillerman) S.; m. Patricia Ann Batcheldor, Nov. 23, 1971; children: Joanna Louise, Andrew James. BS, Melbourne U., 1965, BA in Econs. and Fin., 1971. Research chemist Monsanto Chems., Melbourne and Sydney, 1965-68; product mktg. mgr. Union Carbide, Sydney, 1968-79; devel. mgr. Permutit Australia, Sydney, 1979-81; nat. mktg. mgr. Union Bulkships, Sydney, 1981—. Served as lt. Royal Australian Navy, 1976—. Fellow Australian Inst. of Mgmt. (assoc.); mem. Royal Australian Chem. Inst. (assoc.). Roman Catholic. Clubs: Balmoral Beach Country, Naval and Mil. of Melbourne. Office: Union Bulkships, TNT Tower 1, Lawson Sq, Redfern NSW 2016, Australia

SHARP, J(AMES) FRANKLIN, investments manager and educator; b. Johnson County, Ill., Sept. 29, 1938; s. James Albert and Edna Mae (Slack) S. B.S. in Indsl. Engring., U. Ill., 1960; M.S., Purdue U., 1962, Ph.D., 1966, cert. mgmt. acctg., 1979. Chartered fin. analyst, 1980. Asst. chmn. fin. dept. Pace U. Grad. Sch. Bus., N.Y.C., 1987—; asst. prof. engring., econs. Rutgers U., New Brunswick, N.J., 1966-70; assoc. prof. NYU Grad. Sch. Bus., N.Y.C., 1970-74; supr. bus. research AT&T, N.Y.C., 1974-77, dist. mgr. corp. planning, 1977-81, dist. mgr. fin. mgmt. and planning, 1981-85; prof. fin. Grad. Sch. Bus., Pace U., N.Y.C., 1975—; asst. chmn. dept. fin. Pace U. Grad. Sch. Bus., N.Y.C., 1987—; speaker, moderator meetings, 1965—, cons. sharp investment mgmt., 1967—. Contbr. numerous articles to profl. publs.; corr.: Interface, 1975-78; fin. editor: Planning Rev., 1975-78. Mem. N.Am. Soc. Corp. Planning (treas. 1976-77, bd. dirs. at large 1977-78), Inst. Mgmt. Sci. (chpt. v.p. acad. 1973-74, chpt. v.p. program 1974-75, chpt. v.p. membership 1975-76, chpt. pres. 1976-77), Internat. Affiliation Planning Socs. (council 1978-84), N.Y. Soc. Security Analysts (CFA Rev. 1985—), Ops. Research Soc. Am. (pres. corp. planning group 1976-82), Theta Xi. Republican. Home: 315 E 86th St New York NY 10028 Office: Pace Univ W 440 Pace Plaza New York NY 10038

SHARP, JAN, film producer, writer, director; b. Melbourne, Australia, May 16, 1946; s. John Henry and Ruby (Peacock) S.; children: Alice Lodge, Lucia Noyce. BA, Melbourne U., 1968. Prodn. asst. Film Australia, Sydney, 1969-71, film dir., 1974-78, producer, 1978-80; program officer Australian Broadcasting Commn., Sydney, 1971-74; producer, owner, mgr. Laughing Kookaburra Prodns., Sydney, 1980—. Writer, exec. producer feature film Shadows of the Peacock, 1986; producer feature film The Good Wife, 1986. Recipient documentary award Australian Film Inst., 1978. Office: Laughing Kookaburra Prodns, 92 Surrey St, Potts Point NSW 2011, Australia

SHARP, MARGERY, author; m. G. L. Castle, 1938. B.A. in French with honors, London U. Author: Rhododendron Pie; Fanfare for Tin Trumpets; The Flowering Thorn; Four Gardens; The Nymph and the Nobleman; Sophy Cassmajor; (play) Meeting at Night; The Nutmeg Tree, 1937 (play, U.S., 1940, Eng., 1941, filmed as Julia Misbehaves, 1948); The Stone of Chastity, 1940; Cluny Brown, 1944 (filmed 1946); Britannia Mews, 1946 (filmed 1949); The Foolish Gentlewoman, 1948 (play, London, 1949); Lise Lillywhite, 1951; The Gipsy in the Parlour, 1953; The Tigress on the Hearth, 1955; The Eye of Love, 1957; The Rescuers, 1959; Something Light, 1960; Martha in Paris, 1962; Martha, Eric and George, 1964; The Sun in Scorpio, 1965; in Pious Memory, 1968; Rosa, 1969; The Innocents, 1971; The Faithful Servants, 1975; books for children: Miss Bianca, 1962; The Turret, 1964, U.S. edit., 1963; Miss Bianca in the Salt Mines, 1966; Lost at the Fair, 1967; Miss Bianca in the Orient, 1970; Miss Bianca in the Antarctic 1971; Miss Bianca and the Bridesmaid, 1972; The Magical Cockatoo, 1974; The Children Next Door, 1974; Bernard the Brave, 1976; Summer Visits, 1977; short stories: The Lost Chapel Picnic, 1973. Office: care William Heinemann Ltd, 10 Upper Grosvenor St, London W1X 9PA, England also: 32 Crag Path, Aldenburgh Suffolk, England *

SHARP, THOMAS ROGERS, lawyer; b. Monte Vista, Colo., Dec. 5, 1944; s. W. Edward and Pauline Sharp; m. Sandra J. Sharp, Aug. 12, 1967; children—Thomas R., Daniel, Brian, Rebecca. A.B. magna cum laude, William Jewell Coll., Liberty, Mo., 1966; J.D. magna cum laude, U. Denver, 1969. Bar: Colo. 1969, Mo. 1970. Law clk. to judge U.S. Ct. Appeals (8th cir.), 1969-70; assoc. Bryan, Cave, McPheeters & McRoberts, St. Louis, 1970; assoc. Holme Roberts & Owen, Denver and Steamboat Springs, Colo., 1972-75; ptnr. Sharp and Black, 1975-86; ptnr., Sharp and Casson, 1986—; dir. United Bank of Steamboat Springs, Fish Creek Water and Sanitation Dist., 1974—, Upper Yampa Water Conservancy Dist., 1978—, Colo. Water Resources and Power Devel. Authority, 1981— (chmn. 1987-88), Steamboat Springs Sch. Dist., 1984—. Served with U.S. Army, 1970-72. Mem. Colo. Bar Assn. (bd. govs. 1978-80, v.p. 1988—), Mo. Bar Assn. Routt County Bar Assn. (pres. 1975-76). Democrat. Club: Kiwanis (pres. 1982-83). Real property. Home: 60 Highland Dr PO Box 2055 Steamboat Springs CO 80477 Office: 401 Lincoln Ave PO Box 4608 Steamboat Springs CO 80477

SHARP, WILLIAM WHEELER, geologist; b. Shreveport, La., Oct. 9, 1923; s. William Wheeler and Jennie V. (Benson) S.; m. Marsha Simpson, 1948 (div.); 1 child, John E.; m. Rubylin Slaughter, Aug. 15, 1958; children: Staci Lynn, Kimberly Cecile. BS in Geology, U. Tex., Austin, 1950, MA, 1951. Geol. Socony-Vacuum, Caracas, Venezuela, 1951-53; surface geol. chief Creole, 1953-57; dist. devel. geologist, expert geol. witness, coll. recruiter, research assoc. ARCO, 1957-85; discovered oil and gas at Bayou Boullion, Bayou Sale, Jeanerette, La. Author/co-author geol. and geophys. publs. Past dir., past chmn. U.S. Tennis Assn. Tournaments, Lafayette; pres. Lafayette Tennis Adv. Com., 1972. Served as sgt. USAF, 1943-46, PTO. Winner and finalist more than 75 amateur tennis tournaments including Confederate Oil Invitational, Gulf Coast Oilmen's Tournament, So. Oilmen's Tournament, Tex.-Ark.-La. Oilmen's Tournament; named Hon. Citizen of New Orleans, 1971. Mem. Dallas Geol. Soc., Lafayette Geol. Soc. (bd. dirs. 1973-74), Am. Assn. Petroleum Geologists, Am. Legion, Appaloosa Horse Club, Palomino Horse Breeders Am. Republican. Methodist. Avocations: sports, music, breeding and training Appaloosa and Palomino horses.

SHARPE, JOHN HENRY, member Parliament Bermuda, minister labour and home affairs; b. Bermuda, Nov. 8, 1921; s. Harry and Jessie Elizaebth (White) S.; grad. Mt. Allison Comml. Coll., N.S., Can.; m. Eileen Margaret Morrow; children—John, Kathleen. Chmn. bd. Purvis Ltd., mfrs. reps., Hamilton, Bermuda, 1978—, chmn. bd., 1978—; mem. Parliament for Warwick West, 1963—; mem. Def. Bd., Planning Bd., Police Liaison Commn., Race Relations Council and various coms. Ho. of Assembly; mem. Bermuda delegation Constl. Conf., London, 1966; minister of fin., 1968-75; premier, 1975-77; minister of transport, 1980; minister sea and air, 1981; minister labourand home affairs, 1982—. Past pres. Bermuda Athletic Assn.; past chmn. Warwick Parish Vestry; churchwarden St. Mary's Anglican Ch., Bermuda. Served with RCAF, 1943-45. Created knight bachelor, 1977; decorated comdr. Order Brit. Empire. Mem. Bermuda War Vets. Assn. Mem. Umited Party Bermuda. Clubs: Royal Hamilton Dinghy, Royal Bermuda Yacht, Coral Beach and Tennis. Office: Purvis Ltd, Ministry of Labour and Home Affairs, Hamilton Bermuda

SHARPTON, THOMAS, physician; b. Augusta, Ga., July 15, 1949; s. Thomas and Elizabeth (Dozier) S. BA, Northwestern U., 1971; MS, Stanford U., 1973, MD, 1977. Intern Martinez (Calif.) VAMC, 1977-78, resident, 1978-80; mem. staff Kaiser Permanente Med. Group, Oakland, Calif., 1980—; cons. Berkeley (Calif.) Free Clinic, 1977—; chmn. peer review Kaiser Permanente Med. Group, Oakland, 1985-86. Mem. Alameda County Profl. Adv. Com., Oakland, 1984—, Alameda County AIDS Task Force, Oakland, 1985—. Mem. ACP, Mensa, Sigma Pi Sigma, Phi Beta Kappa. Democrat. Club: Phi Beta Kappa of No. Calif. Office: Kaiser PMG 280 W MacArthur Blvd Oakland CA 94611

SHARQ, MOHAMMAD HASSAN, prime minister of Afghanistan. Ambassador Afghanistan to India, until 1988; prime minister Afghanistan, 1988—. Address: Office of Prime Minister, Kabul Afghanistan *

SHARQAWY, ABDEL RAHMAN, lawyer; b. United Arab Emirates, 1920. LLB, Cairo U. Sole practice 1943-45; solicitor Ministry Edn., 1945-46; lit. editor Ash-Sha'b, Al Goumhouriya; editor At-Tah'a, Tomorrow mag.; counselor Ministry of Culture and Guidance, Cairo, 1964—. Author: (novels) The Earth, 1954, Empty Hearts, 1955, Back Streets, 1958, The Peasant; (short stories) Little Dreams, 1956; Muhammad, a Prophet of Freedom, 1962, Aly The Imam of the Pious, The Fifth Caliph, Omar Ibn El-Khattab, others; (poetic dramas) An Algerian Tragedy, 1962, Mahran the Cavalier, 1965, The Red Eagle, Al Hussein: The Rebel, Al Hussein: The Martyr, The Statue of Liberty, Accra My Homeland, Orabi, The Peasant Leader. Recipient State Prize of Merit, 1974. Home: 48 Giza St, Dokki, Cairo Arab Republic of Egypt

SHARTLE, STANLEY MUSGRAVE, civil engineer, land surveyor; b. Brazil, Ind., Sept. 27, 1922; s. Arthur Tinder and Mildred C. (Musgrave) S.; m. Anna Lee Mantle, Apr. 7, 1948 (div. 1980); 1 child, Randy. Student Purdue U., 1947-50. Registered profl. engr., land surveyor, Ind. Chief dep. surveyor Hendricks County, Ind., 1941-42; asst. to hydrographer Fourteenth Naval Dist., Pearl Harbor, Hawaii, 1942-44; dep. county surveyor Hendricks County (Ind.), Danville, 1944-50, county engr., surveyor, 1950-54, county hwy. engr., 1975-77; staff engr. Ind. Toll Rd. Commn., Indpls., 1954-61; chief right of way engring. Ind. State Hwy. Commn., Indpls., 1961-75; owner, civil engr. Shartle Engring., Stilesville, Ind., 1977—; right of way engring. cons. Gannett Fleming Transp. Engrs., Inc., Indpls., 1983—; part-time lectr. Purdue U. for Ind. State Hwy. Commn., 1965-67. Author: Right of Way Engineering Manual, 1975, Musgrave Family History, 1961, Shartle Genealogy, 1955; contbr. tech. articles in sci. jours. Ex-officio mem., charter mem. exec. sec. Hendricks County (Ind.) Plan Commn., 1951-54. Recipient Outstanding Contbn. award Hendricks County Soil and Water Conservation Dist., 1976. Mem. Am. Congress Surveying and Mapping (life), Nat. Soc. Profl. Surveyors, Ind. Soc. Profl. Land Surveyors (charter, bd. dirs. 1979), Nat. Geneal. Soc. (Quarter Century club), Ind. Toll Road Employees Assn. (pres. 1959-60), The Pa. German Soc. Republican. Avocations: astronomy, genealogy, geodesy. Home and Office: Shartle Engring Rural Route 1 Box 33 Stilesville IN 46180

SHARWOOD, GORDON ROBERTSON, bank executive; b. Montreal, Que., Can., Feb. 26, 1932; s. Robert W. and Joan M.H. S.; m. Sandra Shaw; children: Robert, Brian, Alexandra. BA in Philosphy (hon.), McGill U., Montreal, Que., Can., 1953; BA, MA in Jurisprudence, Oxford (Eng.) U., 1955; postgrad., Harvard U., 1961-62. With Can. Imperial Bank of Commerce, various, 1956-62; asst. gen. mgr. Can. Imperial Bank of Commerce, Toronto, Ont., Can., 1962-63, regional gen. mgr., 1963-66, dep. chief gen. mgr., 1966-68, chief gen. mgr., 1968-69; pres., chmn. Acres, Ltd., 1971-74, Guaranty Trust Co. of Can., 1974-76; founder, chmn. bd. First Choice Can. Communications, 1981-82; pres. Sharwood and Co., Toronto, 1982—; Bd. dirs. Dover Industries Ltd., Toronto, Family TRust Corp., Toronto, Can. Pacific Express and Transport Ltd., Toronto, Jacobs-Suchard Can., Union Drawn Steel Co. Ltd., Hamilton, Meridian Techs. Inc., Toronto, Climate MAster Inc., Can.; trustee Real Property Trust of Can. Mem. Can. Assn. of Family Enterprise (chmn., founder). Clubs: Toronto Golf; Badminton and Racquet (Toronto). Office: Sharwood and Co, 8 King St E, Suite 300, Toronto, ON Canada M5C 1B5

SHARWOOD SMITH, MICHAEL ANTHONY, linguist, educator; b. Cape Town, Republic of South Africa, May 22, 1942; s. Bryan Evers and Winifred Joan (Mitchell) S.; m. Ewa Maria Wróblewska, July 1, 1972; children: Kirsty, Ania. MA in French and German with honors, St. Andrew's U., Scotland, 1966; diploma applied linguistics, Edinburgh (Scotland) U., 1970; PhD in Lingustics, A. Mickiewicz U., Poznan, Poland, 1974. Lectr. Ctr. Pédagogique Régional, Montpellier, France, 1966, Brit. Ctr., Volksuniversitet, Sweden, 1967-69; sr. lectr. Brit. Council, A. Mickiewicz U., 1970-74; assoc. prof. linguistics U. Utrecht, The Netherlands, 1974—; chair conf., organizer Language Acquisition Research Symposia, Utrecht, 1984—. Author: Aspects of Future Reference in a Pedagogical Grammar of English, 1977; editor, author: Crosslinguistic Influence in Second Language Acquisition, 1986, Grammar and Language Teaching, 1988; founding editor: Interlanguage Studies, Utrecht, 1976-85, Second Language Research, London, 1985—; contbr. 93 articles to profl. publs. Mem. Dutch Sci. Found. (project supr. 1980-84, 87—). Anglican. Office: Rijksuniversiteit Utrecht, KR Nieuwegracht 46, 3512 HJ Utrecht The Netherlands

SHASH, MOHAMED EL-TAHER, ambassador; b. Sharkia, Egypt, Nov 3, 1929; s. Amin Shash and Munira El-Moselhi; m. Jaylane Abdel Kerim; children—Mai, Dina. Student Fouad I Univ., 1946-50, LLB, Cairo Univ., 1963-64, Ein Shams Univ., 1964-65. Substitut de Parquet, 1950-54, diplomat with fgn. affairs, 1954—, ambassador in Peru, 1975-79, legal advisor under sec. fgn. affairs, 1979-82; ambassador to Austria, permanent rep. of Egypt to UN, UNIDO, IAEA, 1982-86; chmn. IAEA Bd. Govs., 1984-85. Contbr. articles to internat. law jours. Recipient Egyptian Order of Merit; Egyptian Order of Republic; Grand Crux del Sol Peru, 1979; Commandatori of Italy, 1969. Office: Embassy of Arab Republic Egypt, Gallmeyergasse 5, 1190 Vienna Austria also: Ministry of Fgn Affairs, Office Asst Fgn Minister, Cairo Egypt

SHASSERE, JUNE KNIGHT, public relations and fund-raising consultant; b. Chgo., Apr. 22, 1940; d. John and Mary Alice (Rudisel) Knight; B.S., Ind. State U., 1962; M.A., Ball State U., 1976; m. William Glenn Shassere, July 27, 1963. Tchr. high sch. journalism and English in Ind., 1962-64; newspaper reporter, Plymouth, Ind., 1964-66; editor U. Notre Dame, 1966-68; dir. public relations and devel. Culver Mil. Acad., St. Mary's Acad., also Ladywood-St. Agnes Sch., Goodwill Industries Found., 1968-88; dir. public info. Ind. Office Manpower Devel., 1974-76; ind. public relations cons., 1972—; staff assoc. Ind. U., 1977-80, dir. women in politics project, 1977-81, assoc. faculty, 1981-82; vis. lectr. communications Purdue U., 1978-80; mem. Ind. Gov.'s Commn. Status Women, 1973-75; program leader, tng. cons. in field. Active fund raising; 75th anniversary chmn. Ind. Soc. to Prevent Blindness, bd. dirs., 1984-87; com. mem. 1987 Pan-Am. Games; bd. dirs. Indpls. YWCA, 1982-83; pres. Ind. Ptnrs. of the Ams., 1986-87. Named Outstanding Woman, Ind. Women's Polit. Caucus, 1979; Kellogg Found. fellow, 1984-86; recipient Jefferson award 1988, Sagamore of the Wabash 1987. Mem. Pub. Relations Soc. Am., LWV, Ind. Soc. Public Adminstrn. (chmn. conf. 1979), Ind. Soc. Fund Raising Execs. (dir., officer 1982-84), Ind. Hist. Soc., Northumberland and Durham Family History Soc., Aberdeen and Northeast Scotland Family History Soc., Bradford County Hist. Soc. (Pa.), Vigo, Decatur and Sullivan Counties Hist. Soc., Anglo-Scottish Family History Soc., Sigma Delta Chi (dir.). Author tng. guides in field; editor: Women in Politics: Practical Hints for Candidates and Campaigners, 1978, Development of Downtown Terre Haute, Indiana: A Feasible Strategy, 1977, The Role of Women on Indiana Newspapers 1876-1976, 1977, Running Winning Leading: Public Leadership Development for Women, 1980. Home: 4491 Washington Blvd Indianapolis IN 46205

SHASTRI, VAGISH (BHAGIRATH PRASAD TRIPATHI), research institute director; b. Bilaia, India, July 24, 1934; s. Yamuna Prasad and Parvati Devi (Tiwari) Tripathi; Acharya, 1959; m. Kanti Pathak, June 12, 1959; children: Vachaspati, Vastoshpati Shastri, Ashapati Shastri. PhD, Vidyavaridhi, 1964; German diploma, 1965; DLitt, Vachaspati, 1969. Tchr. Bharatiya Sahitya Vidyalaya, 1956-59; tchr. Paninian grammar Teekamani Sanskrit Coll., Varanasi, India, 1959-64; publ. officer, sub-editor Saraswati Sushama, V. Sanskrit Varsity, 1964; research asst. V. Sanskrit U., Varanasi, 1968-70; dir. research inst., editor Saraswati Sushama, Sampurnanand Sanskrit U., Varanasi, 1970—; chmn. Press Samiti; founder, pres. Yogic Voice Consciousness Inst. Univ. Grants Commn. sr. research fellow, 1964-67; grantee Panini Dhatupatha Samiksha, 1965. Mem. Bharaiya Anusandhana Sansthana, Smarika Nivedita Shiksha Sadana (chmn.). Author: Krishakanam Nagapashah (radio play), 1958, Kathasamvartika, 1959, Bundelkhand Ki Prachinata, 1965, Paniniya Dhatupatha Samiksha, 1965, Taddhitántah Kechana Shabdah, 1967, Anusandhana Paddhatih, 1969, Tolstoy Kathasaptakam, 1970, Bharata Men Sanskrit Ki Anivaryata Kyon, 1977, Dhatvartha Vijnanam, 1980, An Easier and Scientific Method to Learn Sanskrit Language, 1982, Ganga-stavana-Chayanika, 1982, Shiva-stavana-Chayanika, 1984, Narma-saptashati (Sanskrit satires), 1984, Gypsy Languages, 1986; inventor Sanskrit Mnemonic Method, 1980. Home: B 3/115 Shivala, Varanasi 221001, India Office: Sampurnanand Sanskrit U, Varanasi 221002, India

SHATTUCK, BARBARA ZACCHEO, investment banker; b. New Rochelle, N.Y., Dec. 25, 1950; d. John Nicholas and Mary-Jane (Haller) Zaccheo; m. John Garrett Shattuck (div.); m. Arthur M. Dubow. AB, Conn. Coll., 1972; postgrad. NYU Sch. Bus., 1974-75. Bond analyst Standard & Poor's, N.Y.C., 1972-76; assoc. Blyth, Eastman Dillon & Co., N.Y.C., 1976; v.p. Goldman, Sachs, N.Y.C., 1976-82; ptnr. Cain Bros, Shattuck & Co., N.Y.C., 1982—; speaker Practicing Law Inst., Am. Hosp. Assn. Fundraiser Mondale for Pres., N.Y.C., 1983-84, mem. nat. fin. com. Dukakis for Pres.; bd. dirs. Seltzer Found.; mem. friends of collection com. Parrish Art Mus., Southampton, N.Y. Mem. Women's Econ. Round Table. Democrat. Episcopalian. Club: India House (N.Y.C.).

SHAUGHNESSY, JAMES MICHAEL, lawyer; b. Rockville Centre, N.Y., Feb. 1, 1945; s. James Gregory and Frieda Louise (Brosche) S.; m. Linda Ann Bonfiglio, Aug. 17, 1968; m. 2d, Kari Marie Thoring, Nov. 19, 1977; children—Brendan Michael, Megan Ann. B.A., Adelphi U., 1967; J.D., NYU, 1969. Bar: N.Y. 1970, U.S. Dist. Ct. (so. and ea. dists.) N.Y. 1971, U.S. Ct. Appeals (2d cir.) 1974, Calif. 1977, U.S. Dist. Ct. (so. dist.) Calif. 1977, U.S. Ct. Appeals (9th cir.) 1977, U.S. Ct. Appeals (5th cir.) 1983, U.S. Supreme Ct. 1979, U.S. Dist. Ct. (no. dist.) N.Y. 1982, N.J. 1983, U.S. Dist. Ct. N.J. 1983, U.S. Tax Ct. 1983, U.S. Dist. Ct. (we. dist.) N.Y. 1987. Assoc. Casey, Lane & Mittendorf, N.Y.C., 1969-76, ptnr., 1976-82; ptnr. Haythe & Curley, N.Y.C., 1982-87, Windels, Marx, Davies & Ives, N.Y.C., 1987—. Served with N.Y. N.G., 1969-70. Recipient Benjamin F. Butler award Sch. Law NYU, 1969. Mem. ABA, Assn. Bar City of N.Y., N.Y. State Bar Assn., Fed. Bar Council, N.J. State Bar Assn. Republican. Roman Catholic. Office: Windels Marx Davies & Ives 156 W 56th St New York NY 10019

SHAUNNESSY, GEORGE DANIEL, medical company executive; b. Joliet, Ill., Apr. 15, 1948; s. Daniel Joseph and Florence Elizabeth (Dunfee) S.; m. Martha Ann Waibel, Sept. 20, 1975; children: Katherine Erin, Daniel Joseph, Ellen Frances. BS in Indsl. Adminstrn., St. Louis U., 1970; MHA, Xavier U., Cin., 1973. With Hosp. Affiliates Internat., Inc., Nashville, 1973-80, regional dir., Miami, 1977-78, v.p. subs. Hosp. Affiliates Mgmt. Corp., 1978-79, v.p. hosp. ops. Southeast Group, Atlanta, 1979-80; v.p. hosp. ops. Charter Med. Corp., Macon, Ga., 1980-86; sr. v.p. hosp. ops., 1986-87; pres. Foster Med. Corp., Phila., 1987-88; pres. Nat. Healthcare Inc., Atlanta, 1988—, also bd. dirs.; trustee, officer, dir. numerous hosps. Home: 130 Grogran's Lake Dr Dunwoody GA 30350

SHAVIT, MORDECHAI, electronics executive; b. Jerusalem, June 20, 1929; s. David and Aliza (Brande) Weissenstern; m. Esther Shavit/Boger, Oct. 9, 1966; children—David, Gideon. B.S.E.E., MIT, 1953, M.S.E.E., 1956. Mem. tech. staff Fairchild Semiconductro Inc., Palo Alto, Calif., 1959-61; v.p., founder Signetics, Sunnyvale, Calif., 1961-65; v.p. Elta Electronic Ind., Ashdod, Israel, 1965-70; gen. mgr. Monsel, Ltd., Haifa, Israel, 1970-74; v.p. Elbit Computers, Ltd., Haifa, 1974-79; gen. mgr. Lambda Electronics, Ltd., Karmiel, Israel, 1979—. Inventor in field; contbr. articles to profl. jours. Served with Israeli Air Force, 1948-50. Mem. IEEE (chmn. Israel sect. 1976-79). Home: 27 Alexander Yanai, Haifa 34816, Israel Office: PO Box 500, Karmiel 20100, Israel

SHAW, ALAN ERIC, federal official, actor; b. Bklyn., Sept. 6, 1948; s. Eric Paul and Helen (Pochynok) S. A.A. cum laude, Skyline Coll., 1972; B.A. magna cum laude, San Francisco State U., 1975; M.B.A. magna cum laude, Golden Gate U., 1978. Draftsman, printer Coen Co., Burlingame, Calif., 1970-75; mgmt. intern HHS, San Francisco, 1975-78; sr. budget analyst Office Hearings and Appeals, Arlington, Va., 1978-80; fin. mgr. and adminstr. officer White House, Washington, 1980-84; assoc. dir. for adminstrn. Minerals Mgmt. Service, Los Angeles, 1985—; pvt. practice cons., San Francisco, 1977-78, Washington, 1978-80. Actor ABC film documentary: Saving of the President, 1982 (winner 11 maj. internat. awards); actor various theatre and TV performances, 1979—. Served with U.S. Army, 1968-70, Vietnam. Decorated Vietnamese Cross of Gallantry with Palm, Bronze Star and other various decorations. Recipient Achievement award, Exec. Office of Pres., 1981, Presdl. letter of commendation, 1983. Mem. AFTRA, Assn. M.B.A. Execs., Golden Gate U. Alumni Assn., Am. Mgmt. Assn., Am. Film Inst., Screen Actors Guild, Beta Gamma Sigma. Home: PO Box 17541 Los Angeles CA 90017 Office: Minerals Mgmt Service 1340 W 6th St Suite 100 Los Angeles CA 90017

SHAW, ANTHONY RAYMOND, JR., research company executive; b. N.Y.C., Dec. 26, 1942; s. Anthony Raymond and Isabelle Leone (Bisson) S.; m. Diane Lynn Tomason, Nov. 1986; children: Amy, Anthony Raymond III (dec.), Danielle, Devon; 1 stepdaughter, Devon Young. B.A. cum laude, St. John's Sem. Coll., Boston, 1964; postgrad. Loyola U., Chgo., 1970-71, Rutgers U., 1975, Brookings Instn., 1987-88. Positions in personnel, purchasing and service ops. AT&T Bell Labs., Chgo., Denver and N.J., 1969-77, head adminstrn. network planning div., Holmdel, N.J., 1977-81, mgr. adminstrn. personnel services, 1981-85, dir. research and devel. security and spl. projects, Whippany, N.J., 1986—. Sgt. Westfield (N.J.) Spl. Police Force. Served to capt. USMC, 1965-69. Decorated Purple Heart. Recipient Keyman award N.J. Jaycees, 1980. Mem. Brookings Instn., Am. Soc. Indsl. Security, Nat. Classification Mgmt. Soc. Republican. Roman Catholic. Club: Warinanco Hockey. Author: Low/High Altitude Instrument Approach Procedures, 1969. Office: Bell Labs Whippany Rd Whippany NJ 07981

SHAW, ARACELIS GOBERNA, educator; b. Pinar del Rio, Cuba, June 22, 1922; came to U.S., 1948, naturalized, 1955; d. Jose B. and Eloisa (Santiuste) Goberna; B.S., B.L., Inst. Pinar del Rio, 1941; Ph.D. and Letters, U. Havana, 1948; M.A., U. Fla., 1957; m. Steven J. Shaw, June 8, 1952. Instr., Berlitz Sch. Langs., Miami, Fla., 1949-52, N.Y.C., 1952-54; research asst. U. Fla., 1955-57; mem. faculty Columbia (S.C.) Coll., 1957—, prof. Spanish, 1963-88, chmn. dept. fgn. langs., 1962—, head Intercultural and Lang. Center, 1977-87; dir. lang. workshops, cons. in field. Pres. S.C. chpt. Partners of Americas, 1975-78, 81-87 exec. dir. 1987—. Recipient Cervantes award, 1976, S.C. Bicentennial award, 1976; Am. Express award for excellence in internat. volunteerism, 1983. Mem. Am. Assn. Tchrs. Spanish and Portuguese (pres. S.C. chpt. 1973-74), Southeastern Conf. Latin Am. Studies, Sigma Delta Pi. Roman Catholic. Club: Columbia Coll. Internat. Author: (for TV) El Espanol Paso a Paso, 1969; also workbooks, lab. manuals. Home: 4832 Forest Ridge Ln Columbia SC 29206 Office: Columbia Coll Ptnrs of the Americas Columbia SC 29203

SHAW, DAVID ANTHONY, lawyer; b. Gary, Ind., July 31, 1948; s. James Anthony and Martha Fay (McCulloch) S.; m. Kathy Louise McCullough, June 11, 1971; children—Amanda Louise, Jason Anthony. BS, Ind. U., 1970, JD, 1973. Bar: Ind. 1973, D.C. 1974, U.S. Dist. Ct. (so. dist.) Ind. 1973, U.S. Dist. Ct. D.C. 1974, U.S. Ct. Claims 1977, U.S. Ct. Mil. Appeals 1973, U.S. Tax Ct. 1974, U.S. Ct. Appeals (D.C. cir.) 1974, U.S. Ct. Appeals (4th cir.) 1976, U.S. Ct. Appeals (5th cir.) 1976, U.S. Ct. Appeals (10th cir.) 1976, U.S. Supreme Ct. 1976. Atty. appellate div. U.S. Army, Washington, 1973-75, litigation div., 1975-76; spl. asst. U.S. atty. Dept. Justice, Washington, 1976-77; counsel Senate Select Com. on Intelligence, Washington, 1977-81; exec. v.p. Software div. Gould, Inc., Urbana, Ill., 1981-84; ptnr. Eastham & Shaw, Washington, 1985—; mng. dir. New Venture Devel. Corp., 1985—, Venture Lease Inc., 1985—; v.p. Triad Leasing Corp., 1985—; mng. ptnr. Kimberly, Brunell & Lehman, Inc., 1986—; exec. v.p. The Jefferson Group, Inc.; advisor, dir. various cos. Contbr. articles to profl. publs. Chmn. bd. Devel. Services Ctr., Champaign, Ill., 1983—. Served to capt. U.S. Army, 1973-77. Mem. ABA, Fed. Bar Assn., D.C. Bar Assn., Ind. Bar Assn. Home: 10117 New London Dr Potomac MD 20854 Office: Eastham & Shaw 1024 Thomas Jefferson St NW Suite 145 Washington DC 20007

SHAW, DENNIS FREDERICK, library director, chartered physicist; b. Teddington, Middlesex, Eng., Apr. 20, 1924; s. Albert and Lily Florence (Hill) S.; m. Joan Irene Chandler, June 25, 1949; children—Peter James, Margaret Denise, Katherine Joan, Deborah Mary. B.A. in Physics, U.

Oxford, 1945, M.A., 1950, D.Phil. Nuclear Physics, 1950. Sr. research officer Oxford U., Eng., 1950-75, tutor in physics Keble Coll., 1956-75, professorial fellow, 1977—, keeper of sci. books, 1975—; vis. scientist CERN, Geneva, 1960-61; vis. prof. U. South Tenn., 1974; sec. Internat. Assn. Tech. Univ. Libraries, 1983-85, pres. 1986—; mem. Home Officer Sci. Adv. Council, London, 1966-78; mem. Home Def. Sci. Adv. Com., London, 1978—; mem. Hebdomadal Council, Oxford U., 1980—. Contbr. articles to profl. jours. Almoner, Christ's Hosp., London, 1980—; mem. Oxford City Council, 1963-67. Decorated Comdr. Brit. Empire, 1974. Fellow Inst. Physics, Zool. Soc.; mem. Am. Inst. Physics, N.Y. Acad. Sci. Anglican, Internat. Fedn. Library Assns. (chmn. Sci. Tech. Libraries sect. 1987—). Club: Oxford and Cambridge. Home: 29 Davenant Rd, Oxford OX2 8BU, England Office: Radcliffe Sci Library, Parks Rd, Oxford OX1 3QP, England

SHAW, EDWARD JAMES, physician; b. N.Y.C., Oct. 22, 1914; s. Samuel Johnson and Adele (Herndon) S.; B.A., Columbia U., 1934; M.D., Yale U., 1937; m. Huguette Adele Herman, Apr. 19, 1965; children—Edward James, Emily K., Barbara A. Intern Bellevue Hosp., N.Y.C., 1937-38, resident surgery, 1938-39; resident surgery N.Y. Postgrad. Med. Sch. and Hosp., N.Y.C., 1939-41; chief surg. services U.S. Army Sta. Hosp., Plattsburg Barracks, N.Y., 1941-42, chief gen. surg. sect. 69th Sta. Hosp., North Africa, 1942-44, comdg. officer and chief surgeon 16th Sta. Hosp., Wiesbaden, Ger., 1945-46; chief resident surgery New Rochelle (N.Y.) Hosp., 1946-47; practice medicine specializing in gen. surgery, New Rochelle, 1947-52; chief resident surgery Lawrence and Meml. Hosp., New London, Conn., 1952-53; chief resident and surgery resident Doctors Hosp., N.Y.C., 1953-54, attending surgeon, 1954-65; practice medicine specializing in gen. surgery, N.Y.C., 1954-65, St. Louis, 1965-67; chief surgeon Sutter Clinic, St. Louis, 1967-71; practice medicine specializing in surgery and occupational medicine, St. Louis, 1971—; mem. surg. staffs Luth. Hosp., St. Louis, Incarnate Word Hosp., St. Louis, St. Elizabeth Hosp., Granite City; asst. clin. prof. N.Y. Med. Coll., N.Y.C., 1954-65; asst. attending surgeon Flower Fifth Ave. Hosp., N.Y.C., 1954-65; assoc. attending surgeon Met. and Bird S. Coler hosps., N.Y.C., 1954-65; pres. Shaw Surg. Clinic, St. Louis and Granite City, 1975-85; mem. N.Y.C. and Bklyn. regional com. Trauma, 1955-67. Served with AUS, 1941-44, U.S. Army, 1944-46. Diplomate Am. Bd. Surgery, Am. Bd. Abdominal Surgery. Fellow ACS, Southwestern Surg. Congress, Internat. Coll. Surgeons, St. Louis Soc. Colon and Rectal Surgeons, N.Y. Acad. Medicine; mem. Am. Soc. Colon and Rectal Surgeons, Am. Occupational Med. Assn., Am. Geriatrics Soc., Central States Soc. Occupational Medicine, Aerospace Med. Assn., Pan Am. Med. Assn., St. Louis Met. Med. Assn. (del. to Mo. Med. Assn. 1978-83), Mo. Med. Assn., AMA, Mo. Surg. Soc., Assn. Mil. Surgeons U.S., N.Y. Acad. Gastroenterology. Club: Yale of St. Louis. Home: 3105 Longfellow Blvd Saint Louis MO 63104 Office: Barnes Sutter Healthcare Inc 819 Locust St Saint Louis MO 63101

SHAW, GRACE GOODFRIEND (MRS. HERBERT FRANKLIN SHAW), publisher, editor; b. N.Y.C.; d. Henry Bernheim and Jane Elizabeth (Stone) Goodfriend; m. Herbert Franklin Shaw; 1 son, Brandon Hibbs. Student, Bennington Coll.; BA magna cum laude, Fordham U., 1976. Reporter Port Chester (N.Y.) Daily Item; editorial coordinator World Scope Ency., N.Y.C.; assoc. editor Clarence L. Barnhart, Inc., Bronxville, N.Y.; free-lance writer for reference book; editing supr. World Pub. Co., N.Y.C., 1965-68; mng. editor World Pub. Co., 1968-69, sr. editor, 1969; mng. editor Peter H. Wyden Co., N.Y.C., 1969-70; assoc. editor Dial Press, N.Y.C., 1971-72; sr. editor Dial Press, 1972, David McKay Co., N.Y.C., 1972-75, Grosset & Dunlap, 1975-77; chief editor Today Press, 1977-79; sr. editor, coll. dept. Bobbs-Merrill, N.Y.C.; mng. editor Bobbs-Merrill, exec. editor trade div., 1979-80, pub., 1980-84; mng. editor Rawson Assocs. div. Macmillan Pub., 1985—. Club: Overseas Press (bd. dirs. 1984-88, chmn. fgn. policy book awards 1983-87). Home: 85 Lee Rd Scarsdale NY 10583 Office: 866 3d Ave New York NY 10022

SHAW, JACK ALLEN, communications company executive; b. Auburn, Ind., Jan. 1, 1939; s. Marvin Dale and Vera Lucille (Harter) S.; m. Martha Sue Collins, May 14, 1940; 1 child, Mark Allen. B.S.E.E., Purdue U., 1962. Project engr. Hughes Aircraft Co., El Segundo, Calif., 1962-69; dir. program mgmt. ITT Space Communications, Ramsey, N.J., 1969-74; v.p., corp. devel. Digital Communications Corp., Gaithersburg, Md., 1974-78, exec. v.p., chief operating officer, Germantown, Md., 1978-81, pres. chief exec. officer, 1981-84, pres., chief exec. officer M/A-com Telecommunications div., 1984-87, also bd. dirs. 1978—, Hughes Network Systems Inc., Germantown, 1987—; bd. dirs. DCC Ltd., Milton Keyes, Eng. Vice chmn. United Fund Campaign Montgomery County, 1982 . Mem. IEEE. Republican. Clubs: Lakewood Country, Aspen Hill Racquet. Home: 11504 Lake Potomac Dr Potomac MD 20854 Office: Hughes Network Systems Inc 11717 Exploration Ln Germantown MD 20874

SHAW, JEANNE OSBORNE, editor, poet; b. Stone Mountain, Ga., June 1, 1920; d. Virgil Waite and Daisy Hampton (Scruggs) Osborne; B.A., Agnes Scott Coll., 1942; m. Harry B. Shaw, Dec. 10, 1982; children—Robert Allan Gibbs, Marilyn Osborne Gibbs. Mem. editorial staff Atlanta Constitution, 1942; feature writer New London (Conn.) Day, 1943; book reviewer Atlanta Constitution, 1940-42, Atlanta Jour., 1945-48; poetry editor Banner Press, Emory U., 1957-59; book editor Georgia Mag., Decatur, 1957-73. Pres., Newton class Druid Hills Baptist Ch., 1973-74, dir. ch. tng., 1978-79. Recipient Robert Martin, Burke, Otto, in praise of poetry awards N.Y. Poetry Forum, 1973, 79, 81; Westbrook award Ky. Poetry Soc., 1976; Ariz. award Nat. Fedn. State Poetry Socs., 1981. Mem. Ga. Writers Assn. (lit. achievement award 1971), Poetry Soc. Ga. (John Clare prize 1955, Katharine H. Strong prize 1975, Eunice Thomson prize 1976, Jimmy Williamson prize 1977, Capt. Frank Spencer prize 1985, 88, Conrad Aiken prize, 1987, 88), Atlanta Writers Club (pres. 1949-50, named Aurelia Austin Writer of Year in poetry 1971, Wyatt award 1986), Ga. State Poetry Soc. (Traditional award 1984, Cole and Ledford award 1986, Goreau award, 1987), Phi Beta Kappa. Author: The Other Side of the Water (Author of Year in Poetry award Dixie Council of Authors and Journalists), 1970; Unravelling Yarn, 1979; co-author: Noel! Poems of Christmas, 1979; They Continued Steadfastly, History of Druid Hills Baptist Church, 1987; author: Faithbuilders, 1982-84; contbr. poems to mags. Home: 809 Pinetree Dr Decatur GA 30030

SHAW, KENNETH ALAN, university system president; b. Granite City, Ill., Jan. 31, 1939; s. Kenneth W. and Clara H. (Lange) S.; m. Mary Ann Byrne, Aug. 18, 1962; children: Kenneth William, Susan Lynn, Sara Ann. BS, Ill. State U., Normal, 1961; EdM, U. Ill., Urbana, 1963; PhD, Purdue U., 1966; DHL, Towson State, 1979, Ill. Coll., 1986, Ill. State U., 1987. Tchr. history, counselor Rich Twp. High Sch., Park Forest, Ill., 1961-63; residence hall dir., instr. edn. Ill. State U., 1963-64; counselor Office Dean of Men, Purdue U., 1964-65, Office Dean of Men, Purdue U. (Office Student Loans), 1965-66; asst. to pres., lectr. sociology Ill. State U., 1966-69; v.p. acad. affair, dean Towson State U., Balt., 1969-76; pres. So. Ill. U., Edwardsville, 1977-79; chancellor so. Ill. U. System, Edwardsville, 1979-86; pres. U. Wis. System, Madison, 1986—; mem. cost containment com. State Higher Edn. Exec. Officers. Chmn. McLean County United Community Services Fund Drive, 1967; chmn. edn. com. Balt. chpt. NCCJ; mem. Baltimore County Task Force on Edn., 1975-77, Ill. Gov.'s Task Force Math. and Sci., 1983-84, Ill. Gov.'s Commn. on Sci. and Tech., 1982-86; Wis. Gov.'s Task Force on Biotech., 1986, Bd. Competitive Wis., 1986—; bd. govs. Ill. Council Econ. Edn., 1983-86; governing bd. St. Louis Symphony Soc., 1977-78, St. Louis Regional Commerce and Growth Assn., 1978-80; bd. govs. Ill. Council Econ. Edn., 1983-86, Competitive Wis., 1986—, Forward Wis., 1988—; adv. U.S. Peace Corp.; trustees Council for Advance and Support of Edn., 1988—. recipient Young Leader in Edn. award, 1980, Citizen of Yr. award, So. Ill. Inc., 1985, Silver Anniversary award NCAA, 1986, Coaches Silver Anniversary award Nat. Assn. of Basketball, 1986; named to Ill. Basketball Hall of Fame, 1983. Mem. Am. Assn. State Colls. and Univs. (external relations com. 1986—), Am. Council Edn. (chmn. com. on minorities in higher edn. 1987), Assn. Governing Bds. Project on Strategic Indicators (cost containment com.), Am. Sociol. Assn., Am. Higher Edn. Assn., Phi Delta Kappa, Pi Gamma Mu. Office: U of Wis System 1720 Van Hise Hall 1220 Linden Dr Madison WI 53706

SHAW, MADELINE READ, machine tool company executive; b. Saginaw, Ala., July 16, 1910; d. Thomas H. and Eleanor (Satterwhite) Read; student U. Ala., 1919-22; m. Ralph M. Shaw Jr., June 15, 1927. 1 child Mary Eleanor Shaw Carretta (dec.). Tchr., Stafford Sch., Tuscaloosa, Ala., 1922-24; pvt. tchr. music, Gorgas, Ala., 1924-25; organist Paramount Publix Co., Miami, Fla. and N.Y.C., 1925-27; with Pedrick Tool & Machine Co., Riverton, N.J., 1939—, v.p. fin., 1940-79, pres., 1979—. Republican. Episcopalian. Club: Cosmopolitan (Phila). Home: Shawnee Hall Beverly NJ 08010 Office: 1518 Bannard St Riverton NJ 08077

SHAW, MELVIN ROBERT, lawyer, public affairs consultant, educator; b. Bklyn., Nov. 23, 1948; s. Arthur and Pearl (Gutterman) S. B.A. in Polit. Sci., L.I. U., 1970; M.P.A., U. Ill., 1972; Let.D., London Inst. Applied Research, 1973; LL.D. (hon.), Roman Coll., Rome, 1974; B.S. in Law, Western State U., 1984, J.D., 1984; M.A. in Human Behavior, Nat. U., 1985; M.S. in Mgmt., NYU, 1988; postgrad. in health law, DePaul U. Bar: Ind. 1985, U.S. Dist. Ct. (no. and so. dist.) Ind. 1985, U.S. Dist. (no. dist.) Calif. 1985, U.S. Dist. Ct. (ea. dist.) Wis. 1985, U.S. Dist. Ct. Hawaii 1985, U.S. Ct. Appeals (3d, 5th, 7th, 9th, D.C., fed. cirs.) 1985, U.S. Ct. Internat. Trade 1985, U.S. Ct. Mil. Appeals 1985, U.S. Ct. Claims 1985, U.S. Tax Ct. 1985, U.S. Supreme Ct. 1988. Exec. asst. N.Y. State Senate, Albany, 1969-71; polit. cons. Kirson & Shaw, Ltd., N.Y.C., 1972-76; pres. Master Pubs., Inc., Chgo., 1976-80; lectr. Inst. for Internat. Affairs, Washington, 1978—; sr. ptnr. Littlejohn & Shaw Assocs., N.Y.C., Chgo., San Diego, 1980-85; gen. ptnr. Shaw, Smith Schimek and Rosenfeld, Indpls., South Bend, Ind., San Diego, N.Y.C., Phila., 1985—; instr. law Calif. Community Colls., 1985—; dir. Hudson Industries, San Diego, Master Communications, N.Y.C., Inst. for Internat. Affairs, 1979—. Contbr. articles to profl. jours. Editor Internat. Relations Jour., 1982. Active Am. Jewish Com., Jewish Nat. Fund, Dem. Nat. Com. Mem. ABA, Fed. Bar Assn., Ind. State Bar Assn., N.Y. State Bar Assn., San Diego County Bar Assn., Am. Soc. Internat. Law, (chpt. pres. 1983—), Assn. Trial Lawyers of Am., Am. Judicature Soc., Am. Arbitration Assn., Am. Soc. Communications and Media Execs., Nat. Mgmt. Execs., Am. Polit. Sci. Assn., ACLU, Delta Theta Phi. Clubs: N.Y. Pub. Relations, N.Y. Publicity, Amnesty Internat., Chgo. Pub. Relations. Democrat. Jewish. Lodges: Odd Fellows, B'nai B'rith. Office: Shaw Smith et al 3925 N College Ave Indianapolis IN 46205

SHAW, PATRICK, architect; b. Chgo., June 29, 1933; s. Alfred Phillips and Rue (Winterbotham) S.; student Middlesex Sch., Concord, Mass., 1947-51; A.B., Harvard U., 1958, postgrad., 1958-61; m. Joanne Nagel, Jan. 19, 1968 (div. Jan. 1978); children—Sophia Neoma, Alfred Michael. With various archtl. firms, 1960-65; pres. Shaw & Assocs., architects, Chgo., 1965—. Bd. dirs., sec. Greater N. Michigan Ave. Assn. Chgo., chmn. zoning com.; aux. bd. Art Inst. Chgo. Served with U.S. Army, 1952-54. Mem. A.I.A., Modern Poetry Assn. (pres.), Chgo. Hist. Soc. Clubs: University, Arts, Tavern, Racquet (Chgo.). Prin. works include Campus Center and Residence Hall at Loyola U., Chgo., Main P.O. Bldg., Springfield, Ill., Mid-Continental Plaza office bldg., Chgo., Commerce Plaza Office Bldgs., Oak Brook, Ill., Truman Coll. Multi-Use Facility, Chgo., Drake Hotel and office bldg., Oak Brook, Chgo. Bd. Trade addition, Presidents Plaza Office Bldgs., Mid-Am. Plaza, Oak Brook, Santa Fe hdqrs., Topeka, 5215 Old Orchard Rd., Skokie, Ill., Mid Am. Ctr., Oakbrook Terrace, Ill., Burroughs Ctr., Lombard, Ill., Imperial Pl., Lombard, Park Place of Naperville, Ill., 190 S. Lasalle St., Chgo. (with Philip Johnson), 35 W. Wacker Dr., Chgo. (with Kevin Roche), Corp. 500, Deerfield, Ill., Dearborn Ctr., Lombard, Embassy Plaza, Schaumburg, Ill., 100 Corp. N., Bannockburn, Ill., NW Point Office Bldg., Elk Grove Village, Ill., 191 W Madison (with Caesar Pelli), AMA World Hdqrs. (with Caesar Pelli), Union Pacific Officer Bldg. Naperville, Ill, Chatham Ctr., Schaumburg, Ill, Corp. 500, Phase 1 and Phase 2 Naperville, others. Home: 1209 N Astor St Chicago IL 60610 Office: 55 E Monroe St Chicago IL 60603

SHAW, RICHARD JOHN GILDROY, insurance executive; b. Southampton, Eng., June 7, 1936; s. Edward Philip and Mary Elizabeth (Tanner) S.; m. Yvonne Kathleen Maskell; 1 child, Rupert Henry Gildroy. Ins. assoc. J.H. Minet & Co., Ltd., London, 1957-66; asst. dir. H.J. Symons, London, 1967-70; dep. chmn. C.E. Heath & Co., Ins. Broking Ltd., London, 1970-79; chmn. C.E. Heath & Co. Latin Am., Ltd., London, 1979—; chief exec. officer Lowndes Lambert Group, Ltd., London, 1979—. Mem. Ch. of England. Clubs: Portland (London); Sunningdale (Ascot, Eng.); Golf (Berkshire, Eng.). Home: 18 Phillimore Gardens, W8 7QE London England Office: Lowndes Lambert Group Ltd, Lowndes Lambert House, 53 Eastcheap, EC3P 3HL London England

SHAW, RICHARD MELVIN, gemologist, gold company executive; b. Los Angeles, Jan. 14, 1947; s. Melvin and Harriet Louise (Hammond) S.; m. Deanna Lee Revel, Mar. 9, 1968 (div. 1973); 1 child, Katharine Lillian; m. Janet Lynne Gribble, Dec. 31, 1981; 1 child, Jacquelyn Louise. Student Los Angeles Valley Coll.-Van Nuys, 1965-67; grad. Gemological Inst. Am., 1976. Design coordinator Foxy Jon's Smokehouse Cabins, Inc., Los Angeles, 1968-71; Pantera specialist, used car mgr. Bricker Lincoln-Mercury, Los Angeles, 1971-74; designer Melvin Shaw & Assos., Santa Monica, Calif., 1974-76; instr. Gemological Inst. Am., Santa Monica, 1976-79, dir. research and devel., 1979-82; ptnr., dir. sales and mktg. Northwest Gold Mktg., Woodland Hills, Calif., 1982-83; exec. v.p. Nat. Gold Distbr., Ltd., Canoga Park, Calif., 1983-86; pres., chief exec. officer Campbell Shaw, Inc., 1987—; founder, chief exec. officer Campbell-Shaw, Inc., Woodland Hills, 1986—. Developer, designer Diamond Pen instrument. Mem. Los Angeles County Mus. Alliance, Mineral. Soc. So. Calif., Nat. Assn. Underwater Instrs., Instrument Soc. Am.

SHAW, SEN-YEN, mathematician, educator; b. Nantou, Taiwan, Mar. 26, 1945; s. Jeng-Li and Rei-Urh (Liu) S.; m. Tsui Yueh Chen, Dec. 18, 1974; children—Alice, Ting-Wen. B.S., Fu-Jen U., Taiwan, 1967; M.A., U. Ill. at Chgo., 1972, Ph.D., 1977. Assoc. prof. Nat. Central Univ., Chung-Li, Taiwan, 1977-82, prof. math., 1982—, head dept. Math., 1987—; vis. scholar Stanford Univ., Palo Alto, Calif., 1984-85. Contbr. articles to profl. jours. Recipient Sun Yat-sen prize, 1985. Mem. Math. Soc. Republic of China, Am. Math. Soc. Home: F3, 6-1, Lane 36, Hoping E Rd, Sec 2, Taipei, Taiwan Republic of China Office: Nat Cen U, Dept Math, 320 Chung-Li Republic of China

SHAW-JACKSON, HAROLD NICHOLAS, coal company executive; b. Springs, South Africa, Jan. 13, 1942; came to Belgium, 1978; s. Harold Shaw and Doreen Edna (Woolley) J.; m. Beatrice Valerie Marie Dondelinger, May 6, 1965; children—Flavia, Chloe, Catherine, Philippe. Founder, mng. dir. Fibreglass Devel. Co., Johannesberg, South Africa, 1963—, Jackson's Fibreglass Pty. Ltd., Johannesburg, 1964—; mng. dir. H.N.S. Jackson Athracite Pty. Ltd., Johannesburg, 1974—; dir. Rauli Kohlen Ag, Zug, Jackson Shipping and Coal SA, Brussels. Clubs: Chevaliers du Tastevin, Rand (Johannesburg). Home: 11 Chemin de la Brire, 1328 Ohain, Brussels Belgium

SHAWSTAD, RAYMOND VERNON, computer specialist; b. Brainerd, Minn., Mar. 17, 1931; stepson Klaas Ostendorf, s. Ruth Catherine Hammond; student West Coast U., 1960-62, UCLA Extension, 1966-81, Liberal Inst. Natural Sci. and Tech., 1973-83, Free Enterprise Inst., 1973-83. Salesman, Marshalltown, Iowa, 1952-53; asst. retail mgr. Gamble-Skogmo, Inc., Waverly, Iowa, 1953-54, retail mgr., Iowa Falls, 1954-57; sr. programmer County of San Bernardino (Calif.), 1958-64; info. systems cons. Sunkist Growers, Inc., Van Nuys, Calif., 1965-75, sr. systems programmer, 1975—; univ. extension instr. UCLA, 1980-81; propr., artificial intelligence researcher Lang. Products Co., Reseda, Calif., 1980—; propr., fin. planner Pennyseed Mgmt. Co., Reseda, 1987—; cons., tchr. in field, 1961-63. Vol. VA Hosp., 1983-87; bedside music therapist Vets. Adminstrn., 1983-87; musician Project Caring, 1983-87; rep. U.S. Senatorial Bus. Adv. Bd., Calif., 1988—. Fellow Internat. Biog. Assn.; mem. Assn. Computing Machinery, Bus. Data Processing and Software Engring., Assn. Systems Mgmt., Data Processing Mgmt. Assn. (cert.), Los Angeles VM User Group, Am. Def. Preparedness Assn., Res. Officers Assn., Jewish Vegetarian Soc., U.S. Naval Assn., Am. Math. Soc., Aircraft Owners and Pilots Assn., Math. Assn. Am. Author numerous software programs; editor VM Notebook of GUIDE Internat. Corp., 1982—. Lodge: B'nai B'rith. Home: PO Box 551 Van Nuys CA 91408 Office: PO Box 1667 Reseda CA 91335

SHAY, ROBERT MICHAEL, manufacturing company executive, consultant; b. Phila., Sept. 14, 1936; s. Harry and Bertha (Shaivitz) S.; m. Elaine Lee Rosenthol-Kushner, June 8, 1956; children: Susan, Lauri, Robert Michael Jr., Heather. BS in Econs., U. Pa., 1958, JD, 1961. Bar: Pa. 1962, U.S. Supreme Ct. 1962. Pres. Nat. Crematory Corp., 1987—; chief operating officer, sec., treas. Montefiore Cemetery Co., Phila., 1952-88, pres. 1988—; dir., sec., treas. Metachron Research Corp., Phila., 1955-59; assoc. Fox, Rothschild, O'Brien & Frankel, Phila., 1961-74, ptnr., 1973; treas., dir. Forest Hills Cemetery Corp., Phila., 1964-83; chmn. bd., chief exec. officer, officer, dir. various operating subs. Morlan Internat., Inc. and its domestic and fgn. subs., Phila., 1969-83; chmn. bd. Superior Holding Corp., Cleve., Bike-O-Matic, Ltd., Internat. and Commerce Bank, Phoenix; chmn. bd., chief exec. officer Terraplex Corp. and subs., Phila., 1983—; chmn. bd., chief exec. officer Regal Corrugated Box Co., Inc., 1986—, also bd. dirs.; dir. Am. Cemetery Services, Inc., 4-U Corp., also various fin. corps.; lectr. Am. Coll. Life Underwriters, Bryn Mawr, Pa.; cons. in health care field. Contbr. articles to profl. publs. Shelter mgr., mem. Abington CD and Race Network, Pa., 1960-61; co-leader Sawmill Hill council Boy Scouts Am., 1974; co-pres. Huntingdon Jr. High Sch. PTO, Abington, 1973-74; fin. chmn. Coyle for State Rep. Com., Abington, 1978, Swan for State Rep. Com., Abington, 1980, Greenleaf for State Senate Com., Abington, 1982, 86; co-fin. chmn. Fox for State Rep. Com., Abington, 1984, 86; alt. del. Rep. Nat. Conv., 1988; chmn. Century Club, Abington Twp. Rep. Orgn., 1983-86; chmn. bd. dirs. Contemporary Opera Co. Am., Phila., 1983-84; bd. dirs. Mann Music Ctr., Phila., 1975—, Nat. Mus. Am. Jewish History, Phila., 1982-84, Am. com. Phila. br. Shaare Zedek Hosp., 1982—; bd. dirs., sec. Phila. br. Am. Friends of Haifa U., 1982-86, pres., 1986—, also bd. dirs.; treas., trustee Abington Free Library, 1981—. Mem. ABA, Young Pres. Orgn., World Bus. Council, Phila. Pres. Orgn., Am. Cemetery Assn. (bd. dirs. 1979-81, chmn. spring conf. 1982), Cemetery Consumer Service Council (pres. 1982-83), Keystone State Assn. Cemeteries, Cemetery Assn. Greater Phila. and Vicinity, Md. Cemetery Assn., Nat. Assn. Cemeteries, Casket Mfrs. Assn., Jewish Cemeteries Assn. Greater Phila. and Vicinity (pres. 1967), Cremation Assn. N.Am., Tech. Assn. Pulp and Paper Industry, Aircraft Owners and Pilots Assn., Beta Gamma Sigma, Beta Alpha Psi. Avocations: travel, swimming, reading. Home: 1326 Panther Rd Rydal PA 19046 Office: Terraplex Corp Church Rd and Borbeck St Philadelphia PA 19111

SHCHEDRIN, RODION KONSTANTINOVICH, composer; b. Moscow, Dec. 16, 1932; s. Konstantin Michailovich and Konkordia Ivanovna (Ivanova) S.; grad. Moscow Consezvatoire, 1955; m. Maya Plisetskaya, Oct. 2, 1958. Composer: operas: Not Love Alone, 1961, Dead Souls, 1976; ballets: The Humpbacked Horse, 1955, Carmen Suite, 1967, Anna Karenina, 1972, The Sea-Gull, 1980, Self-portrait; 2 symphonys, 2 concerto for orch., 3 piano concertos, 24 preludes and fugues for piano, music for organ and wind instruments. Recipient State prize of the USSR, Lenin prize; named People's Artist of the USSR. Mem. Bayerische Akademie der Schonen Kunste, Akademie der Kunste (E.Ger.), Am. Liszt Soc. Home: 25/g app 31, Gozky, Moscow USSR Office: Union of USSR Composers, ul Nezhdanovoi 8/10, Moscow USSR *

SHEA, BERNARD CHARLES, pharmaceutical company executive; b. Bradford, Pa., Aug. 7, 1929; s. Bernard and Edna Catherine (Green) S.; m. Marilyn Rishell, Apr. 12, 1952; children—David Charles, Melissa Leone. B.S. in Biology, Holy Cross Coll., Worcester, Mass. Dir. mktg. Upjohn Co., Kalamazoo, Mich., 1954-80; pres. Pharm. div. Pennwalt Corp., Rochester, N.Y., 1980-86; v.p. Health div. Pennwalt Corp., Phila., 1986, sr. v.p., 1987—. Served to lt. (j.g.) USN, 1951-54, Korea. Office: Pennwalt Corp Corp Hdqrs 3 Pkwy Philadelphia PA 19102

SHEAHAN, ROBERT EMMETT, lawyer, management labor and employment consultant; b. Chgo., May 20, 1942; s. Robert Emmett and Lola Jean (Moore) S. BA, Ill. Wesleyan U., 1964; JD, Duke U., 1967; MBA, U. Chgo., 1970. Bar: Ill. 1967, La. 1975, N.C. 1978. Vol. VISTA, N.Y.C., 1967-68; trial atty. NLRB, Milw. and New Orleans, 1970-75; ptnr. Jones, Walker, Waechter, Poitevent, Carrere & Denegre, New Orleans, 1975-78; sole practice, High Point, N.C., 1978—; cons., tchr. Robert Pearlman & Assocs. Author: Employees and Drug Abuse: An Employer's Handbook; contbg. author: The Developing Labor Law, 1975—; editor: The World of Personnel; contbg. editor: Employee Testing and the Law. Bd. dirs. High Point United Way, 1979-83; mem. congressional action com. High Point C. of C., 1979—. Mem. ABA, N.C. Bar Assn., High Point Bar Assn., Ill. Bar Assn., La. Bar Assn. Republican. Roman Catholic. Clubs: Sedgefield (N.C.) Country; String and Splinter (High Point). Home: 101 Bellwood Ct Jamestown NC 27282 Office: Eastchester Office Ctr 603-B Eastchester Dr High Point NC 27260

SHEAR, NATHANIEL, physicist; b. Bklyn., Dec. 20, 1908; s. Victor Jacob and Henrietta Leah (Robinson) S. A.B. with honors, Columbia U., 1930, M.A., 1932. Physicist U.S. Navy, Civil Service, Washington, Phila., Lakehurst, N.J., 1937-44; research physicist div. war research Columbia U., N.Y.C., 1944-46; ops. research analyst MIT Ops. Evaluation Group, U.S. Navy, Washington, 1946-48; physicist Bur. Ships, U.S. Navy, Washington, 1948-51; cons. physics, Alexandria, Va., 1951-60; cons. physicist U.S. Naval Research Lab., Washington, 1954-60; physicist Emerson Research Lab., Silver Spring, Md., 1960-62; sr. physicist Johns Hopkins U. Applied Physics Lab., Laurel, Md., 1962-66; cons. in physics, Silver Spring, Md., 1966-69; ops. research analyst Def. Spl. Projects Group, Washington, 1969-72; retired, 1972. Author sci. reports for U.S. Navy. Mem. Va. Acad. Sci., Ops. Research Soc. Am., Am. Phys. Soc., U.S. Naval Inst., Phi Beta Kappa. Subspecialties: Operations research (mathematics); Oceanography. Current work: research on elecromagnetic propagation in the ocean; statis. analyses of price variations of selected stocks. Home: 1401 Blair Mill Rd Apt 612 Silver Spring MD 20910

SHEAR, THEODORE LESLIE, JR., archaeologist, educator; b. Athens, Greece, May 1, 1938; s. Theodore Leslie and Josephine (Platner) S.; m. Ione Doris Mylonas, June 24, 1959; children: Julia Louise, Alexandra. AB summa cum laude, Princeton U., 1959, MA, 1963, PhD, 1966. Instr. Greek and Latin Bryn Mawr Coll., 1964-66, asst. prof., 1966-67; asst. prof. art and archaeology Princeton U., N.J., 1967-70, assoc. prof., 1970-79, chmn. program in classical archaeology, 1970-85, assoc. chmn. dept. art and archaeology, 1976-78, 82-83, prof. classical archaeology, 1979—; prof. archaeology Am. Classical Studies, Athens; mem. mng. com. Am. Sch. Classical Studies, Athens, 1972—; mem. archaeol. expdns. to Greece and Italy, including Mycenae, 1953-54, 58, 62-63, 65-66, Eleusis, 1956, Perati, 1956, Corinth, 1960, Morgantina, Sicily, 1962; mem. Ancient Agora of Athens, 1955, 67, field dir., 1968—; trustee William Alexander Procter Found., 1982—, Princeton Jr. Sch., 1983—. Author: Kallias of Sphettos and the Revolt of Athens in 286 B.C., 1978; contbr. articles to profl. jours. White fellow Am. Sch. Classical Studies, 1959-60. Mem. Archaeol. Inst. Am., Am. Philol. Assn., Coll. Art Assn., Phi Beta Kappa. Republican. Episcopalian. Clubs: Century Assn. (N.Y.C.); Nassau (Princeton); Princeton (N.Y.C.); Hellenic Yacht (Piraeus, Greece). Home: 87 Library Pl Princeton NJ 08540

SHEARER, HUGH LAWSON, Jamaican deputy prime minister and minister of foreign affairs and foreign trade; b. Martha Brae, Trelawny, Jamaica May 18, 1923; ed. St. Simon's Coll.; LL.D. (hon.), Howard U., 1968 Journalist, editorial staff Jamaica Worker, 1941-47; mem. Kingston and St. Andrew Corp. Council, 1947-51; mem. Jamaican Ho. of Reps., 1955-59; mem. Legis. Council (now Senate), 1961-66; minister without portfolio and leader of govt. bus. in Senate, 1962-67; dept. chief mission Jamaican del. to UN, 1962-67; mem. Jamacian Ho. of Reps., from 1967, minister of external affairs, 1967-72, prime minister, 1967-72, mem. privy council, 1969—, leader of the opposition, 1972-74, dep. prime minister, minister of fgn. affairs and fgn. trade, 1980—; mem. Bustamante Indsl. Trade Union, 1941—, asst. gen. sec., 1947-53, island supr., 1953-60, v.p., 1960-77, pres., 1977—; leader Jamaican Labor Party, 1967-74; Jamaican rep. Non-Aligned Movement, from 1981; Jamaican del. Commonwealth Heads of Govt. Conf., 1969, 71, 83; mem. African, Caribbean and Pacific Council of Ministers, from 1984, pres., 1984; mem. CARICOM Council of Ministers. Decorated 1st class Order of Francisco de Miranda, Govt. of Republic of Venezuela. Office: Office of Deputy Prime Minister, Kingston Jamaica *

SHECKTOR, ANDREW MARK, manufacturing executive; b. Phila., Oct. 11, 1956; s. Fred K. and Maria (Caporale) S.; m. Hillary Ann Bunks, Sept. 21, 1980; children: Robyn Marie, Francine Dyan. BEE, Drexel U., 1980; student Temple U., 1978-80. Ptnr., pres. Shecktor Ent., Inc., Centre Square, Pa., 1974—; computer cons. Computer Alternatives, Inc., 1976—, Data Systems, Inc., 1983—; bus. specialist Bus. Investment Group, Huntington,

Valley, Pa., 1984-85; diagnostic equip. cons. Cor Monitor, Inc., Norristown, 1978—, Selmedic Inc., 1984-88. Author, editor, Electronic Weaponry, 1982—. Mem. Barren Hill Vol. Fire Co., Lafayette Hill, Pa., 1975—; asst. chief Greater Phila. Search and Rescue, 1979—. Mem. Diversified Investor Group, North Pa. C. of C. Republican. Quaker. Clubs: Lehigh Valley Amateur Astronomers Assn. Address: Shecktor Enterprises Inc 1750 Skippack Pike #509 Center Square PA 19422

SHEEDER, WILLIAM BENJAMIN, university dean; b. Elmira, N.Y., Jan. 21, 1938; s. Fred and Amy Sheeder; children: Lynn, Traci A.B. in Philosophy, Ottawa (Kans.) U., 1960; M.A. in Human Relations, Ohio U., Athens, 1966. Mem. faculty Ohio U., 1961-65, assoc. dir. Baker U. Ctr., 1962-64, asst. to dean Coll. Arts and Scis., 1964-66; mem. adminstrn. U. Miami, Coral Gables, Fla., 1966—, dir. student activities Student Union, 1968-73, v.p., sec. Univ. Rathskeller, Inc., 1972—, asst. v.p. student affairs, 1973—, dean students, 1976—; pres. Sheeder Enterprises, Inc., 1982—; v.p. Sta. WVUM, Inc., 1987—. Active Dade County Wesley Found., treas., 1971-73, chmn. bd. dirs., 1973-77; mem. work area higher edn. and campus ministry Fla. conf. Council Ministries, United Methodist. Ch., 1976-80, 81—. Mem. Assn. Coll. Unions (enrichment chmn. 1975), Nat. Assn. Student Personnel Adminstrs., Nat. Orientation Dirs. Assn., Am. Assn. Higher Edn., Am. Assn. for Counseling and Devel., Am. Coll. Personnel Assn., Iron Arrow, Sigma Alpha, Omicron Delta Kappa, Phi Delta Kappa, Phi Kappa Epsilon, Omega, Phi Mu Alpha, Zeta Beta Tau (adj. brother 1971—). Author articles. Address: Office Dean Students Univ Miami Coral Gables FL 33124

SHEEHAN, PETER WINSTON, psychology educator, researcher; b. Sydney, Australia, Dec. 8, 1940; s. John Dominic and Frances Mary (Quinn) S.; m. Mary Christina Tutt, Dec. 14, 1963; children—Grania Rachael, Madoc Emmanuel. B.A. with honours, U. Sydney, 1961, Ph.D., 1965. Research assoc. Pa. Hosp., Phila., 1965-67; asst. prof. CUNY, 1967-68; from lectr. to sr. lectr. U. New Eng., Armidale, Australia, 1968-73; prof. U. Queensland, Brisbane, Australia, 1973—; dir. research U. Queensland, 1987—; chmn. Australian Research Grants Scheme, Canberra, 1983-85. Co-author: Methodologies of Hypnosis, 1976, Hypnosis and Experience (Arthur Shapiro award 1983), 1982; editor: The Function and Nature of Imagery, 1972, Australian Jour. Psychology, 1986—; assoc. editor Internat. Jour. Clin. and Exptl. Hypnosis, 1981—; editorial bd. Jour. Abnormal Psychology, 1979—. Dep. chmn. Commonwealth Films Bd. Rev., Sydney, 1985, chmn., 1986—. Recipient Henry Guze award Soc. Clin. and Exptl. Hypnosis; best Research Publ. in Hypnosis grantee, 1971, 81, 82, 84. Fellow Australian Psychol. Soc., Am. Psychol. Assn., Acad. Social Scis. Australia. Roman Catholic. Avocation: film appreciation and evaluation. Home: 25 Glenfield St, Hill End, Queensland 4101, Australia Office: U Queensland Dept Psychology, St Lucia, Brisbane 4067, Australia

SHEEHY, JOHN PATRICK, architect; b. Hibbing, Minn., Jan. 19, 1942; s. Justin Patrick and Vivian (Naeseth) S.; m. Katherine L. Kaliher, July 11, 1964 (div.); 1 son, James. B.Arch., U. Minn., 1966; M. Arch., MIT, 1967. Registered architect, Mass., Colo., Tex. Sr. designer Skidmore Owings & Merrill, Chgo., 1965-66; architect Harry Weese & Assocs., Chgo., 1967-68; sr. architect Hugh Stubbins & Assocs., Cambridge, Mass., 1968-69; prin., ptnr. Architects Collaborative Inc., Cambridge, 1969—; design critic Boston Archtl. Ctr., 1966—; guest lectr. Calif. State U.-Pomona, 1983-84; lectr. Smithsonian Instn., Washington, 1979, Walker Art Ctr., Mpls., 1983. Architect Johns-Manville World Hdqrs., Denver (AIA award 1979), 1976, Nat. Shawmut Bank Bldg., Boston, Cyprus Govt. Ctr. (2d place award), 1972, Copley Place Complex, Boston, Govt. Services Ins. System Hdqrs., Manila, 1978, Arab Investment Bldg., Saudi Arabia, 1979, Bering Office Tower, Houston, 1980, Beechwood Office Complex, Cleve., 1982, Kuala Lumpur Mixed-Use Project, 1983, Reston Office Bldg., Va., 1984, Liberty Ctr. mixed-use devel., Pitts., 1985, Union Sq., San Francisco, 1985, 86—, Tyson's II Office Complex, Washington D.C. Sponsor, Architects for Gov. Dukakis, Boston, 1982. Recipient Hon. Mention Paris prize Nat. Inst. Archtl. Edn., 1964; Avlon scholar MIT, 1966. Mem. AIA (honor award 1979), Boston Soc. Architects (honor award 1978, Rotch Travelling scholar 1971, Boston Export award 1978), Archtl. League of N.Y., Alpha Rho Chi (v.p. Mpls. 1963-64). Home: 65 E India Row Suite 26-B Boston MA 02110 Office: The Architects Collaborative Inc 46 Brattle St Cambridge MA 02138

SHEEHY, PATRICK, manufacturing company executive; b. Sept. 2, 1930; s. Sir John Francis Sheehy and Jean Newton Simpson; m. Jill Patricia Tindall, 1964; 2 children. Grad., Ampleforth Coll., Yorkshire, Eng.; LHD (hon.), Va. Union U., 1985. Joined Brit.-Am. Tobacco Co., 1950, sales mgr., Nigeria, 1953-57, mktg. dir., Jamaica, 1957-61, mktg. advisor, Barbados, 1962-67, gen. mgr., Holland, 1967-70, bd. dirs., 1970-76, chmn. bd. dirs., 1976-81; vice chmn. B-A-T Industries, London, 1981-82, chmn. bd. dirs., 1982—; now also chmn., dir. Batus, Inc., Louisville; chmn. B-A-T Fin. Services, London, 1985—; bd. dirs. Eagle Star, London, Brit. Petroleum, London. Served to 2d lt. Irish Guards, 1948-50. Mem. Confedn. Brit. Industry (task force on urban regeneration), Trade Policy Research Ctr., Action Com. for Europe. Avocations: golf, reading. Office: Batus Inc 2000 Citizens Plaza Louisville KY 40202

SHEETS, MILLARD OWEN, artist; b. Pomona, Calif., June 24, 1907; s. John Jasper and Millie (Owen) S.; m. Mary Baskerville, Apr. 25, 1930; children: Millard Owen, Carlyn Owen Towle, David, John Anthony. Student, Chouinard Sch. Art, 1929; M.F.A. Hon., Otis Art Inst., Los Angeles, 1963; LL.D. Hon., Notre Dame U., 1964; D.F.A. (hon.), Otis-Parsons Inst. Design, New Sch. Social Research, 1984. Dir. art dept. Scripps Coll., Claremont, Calif., 1932-55; dir. art dept. grad. sch. Scripps Coll., 1938-55; dir. Los Angeles County Art Inst. (now Otis Parson Art Inst.), 1953-59; pres. Millard Sheets Designs, Inc., Claremont, 1954—; artist, war corr. Life Mag., India-Burma, 1943-44; mem. U.S. Dept. State Specialist program, Turkey-Russia, 1960-61; guest U.S. Mus. Dirs., W.Ger., 1958; mem. conf. on humanities Am. Council Learned Soc., Corning, N.Y., 1951; works include Library Tower Christ the Tchr., U. Notre Dame, 1964; works include mosaic dome and chapel Nat. Shrine, Washington, 1968, 70; works include mosaic facade Detroit Pub. Library, 1960; works include two tile murals-facade Los Angeles City Hall E, 1972; one man shows U.S. and abroad. Author: Your Drawing is a Measure of Your Mind, 1983, subject: Milard Sheets: One - Man Renaissance, 1983; murals include Rainbow Tower, Honolulu, numerous bldgs., Calif., Tex., 17 USAF tng. schs. Recipient Grand award Artists Guild of Chgo., 1951; recipient award for contbn. to profession Am. Inst. Bldg Design, 1964, Cert. of Achievement Bicentennial City of Los Angeles, 1981; named Guest of Honor Internat. Watercolor Exhbn., Art Inst. Chgo., 1938. Mem. NAD, Nat. Watercolor Soc. (pres. citation distinctive achievements), Calif. Watercolor Soc., Am. Watercolor Soc. (Dolphin medal 1986), San Diego Watercolor Soc. Office: Kennedy Galleries 40 W 57th St New York NY 10019

SHEETZ, RALPH ALBERT, lawyer; b. Dauphin County, Pa., June 13, 1908; s. Harry Wesley and MaNora (Enders) S.; m. Ruth Lorraine Bender, May 19, 1938; 1 son, Ralph Bert. Ph.B., Dickinson Coll., 1930; J.D., U. Ala., 1933. Bar: Pa. 1934, U.S. Dist. Ct. (mid. dist.) Pa. 1944. Solicitor, East Pennsboro Twp., Pa., 1937-53, Peoples Bank of Enola (Pa.), 1935-75; atty. Lawyers Title Ins. Corp., Richmond, Va., 1956—, Commonwealth Land Title Ins. Co., Phila., 1957—; atty. Employees Loan Soc., 1966-76. Ofcl. Appeal Area no. 4, SSS, Pa., assoc. legal adviser to Draft Bd. No. 2, adviser to registrants to Local Bd. No. 55, Harrisburg, Pa., 1974—; counselor Camp Kanestake, Huntingdon County, Pa., Methodist Ch.; treas., atty. Enola Boys Club, from 1950; pres. East Pennsboro Twp. PTA, 1951-52; atty. hon. mem. Citizens Fire Co. No. 1, Enola, 1951; sec., treas. West Shore Regional Coordinating Com., Cumberland County, 1956-66; mem. bd. adjustments East Pennsboro Twp., 1959, chmn., 1959, mem. planning commn, 1956-59, vice-chmn., mem. zoning commn., 1958, chmn., 1959; mem. East Pennsboro Twp. Republican Club, from 1936. Recipient numerous awards and honors from Pres. of U.S. for service to SSS; Order of the Silver Trowel, Council of Anointed Kings Commonwealth of Pa., Altoona, 1948. Mem. Dauphin Bar Assn. (social com. 1934—), Cumberland County Bar Assn., Pa. Bar Assn., ABA. Clubs: Tall Cedars of Lebanon (historian Harrisburg Forest No. 43 1980—, exec. com.), Shriners, Masons (York cross of honor), K.T. (comdr. 1946).

SHEFF, HONEY A., clinical psychologist, educator; b. Bklyn., Nov. 24, 1954; d. Herbert Jack and Helene Ida (Susman) Mendelson; m. Michael Robert Sheff, May 30, 1976; BA summa cum laude, Queens Coll., CUNY, 1975; MA, SUNY-Stony Brook, 1978, PhD, 1981. Lic. clin. psychologist. Psychologist Callier Ctr. for Communication Disorders, U. Tex., Dallas, 1981-83; pvt. practice clin. psychology cons., Dallas, 1983—, TV and radio appearances, Dallas, 1983—; lectr. U. Tex., Dallas, 1982—, clin. instr. psychology, dept. psychiatry U. Tex. Health Sci. Ctr. Southwestern Med. Sch., Dallas, 1983-86; clin. asst. prof. in psychology, 1986—; mem. Allied Health Profls. Staff, Green Oaks Hosp., Dallas, 1988—; guest lectr. dept. emergency med. services U. Tex. Health Sci., Southwestern Med. Sch., Dallas, 1985—, also cons. research project dept. psychiatry; cons. psychologist McKinney Job Corps Ctr., Tex., 1984-86; presenter, workshop leader, tng. on family violence, Tex., N.Y. and N.H., 1977—; liaison com. Mental Health Assn. Dallas County and Mental Health Assn. Collin County; mem. profl. adv. bd. Dallas Ind. Sch. Dist. Psychol. Services, 1988—. Chmn. Dallas County Mental Health-Mental Retardation Ctr. task force to rev. services to children and adolescents, 1985; chmn. Profl. Adv. Com. on Child and Adolescent Services, Dallas County Mental Health-Mental Retardation Ctr., 1986—; founding mem. Parents Helping Parents Task Force, 1982-85; project designer Adolescent Mental Health Needs Dallas County, 1984; co-author jour. article, paper for profl. conf. (now chpt. in book). Charter mem. Parker Vol. Fire Dept., Tex., 1982—, sec.-treas., 1983-85. Recipient Robert S. Woodworth medal for excellence in psychology, Queens Coll., CUNY, 1975; commendation dept. psychology SUNY-Stony Brook, 1977, spl. recognition and award Dallas County Rape Crisis and Child Sexual Abuse Ctr. for Service to Community, 1985; . Mem. Am. Psychol. Assn., Tex. Psychol. Assn., Dallas Psychol. Assn. (pub. forum 1984), Nat. Register of Health Service Providers in Psychology, Mental Health Assn. Dallas County (mem., chmn. coms., award 1985, elected to bd. dirs.), Nat. Council Family Relations, Tex. Council Family Violence, Internat. Soc. Prevention Child Abuse and Neglect, Phi Beta Kappa. Democrat. Jewish. Avocations: Horseback riding; knitting and needlepoint; reading. Office: Stone Tower 13760 Noel Rd Suite 805 Dallas TX 75240

SHEFF, JAMES ROBERT, nuclear and energy engineering educator; b. Colorado Springs, Colo., Nov. 5, 1936; s. Robert Lee and Jessie Marie (Leathers) S.; m. Linda Anne Smith, June 7, 1959 (div. June 1973) m. Linda M. Edgerly, June 29, 1984; children—Robert Benjamin, Nancy Elizabeth (dec.), Natalie Joy, Matthew Garner; 1 stepchild, Robbin Alley. B.S.Ch.E., U. Colo., Boulder, 1959; M.S., U. Wash.-Seattle, 1962, Ph.D., 1965; post-grad., Columbia Basin Coll., 1976. Registered profl. engr., Wash. Chem. engr. Gen. Electric Co., Richland, Wash., 1959-60; sr. research engr. Battelle N.W., Richland, 1965-70, WADCO (Westinghouse subs.), 1970-71; sr. research scientist Battelle-N.W., Richland, 1971-77; prof. nuclear and energy engrng. U. Lowell, Mass., 1977—; pres., cons. Desert Ventures, Richland, Wash., 1973-77, Ventures in Energy, Lowell, Mass., 1977-81; cons. Gen. Pub. Utilities-Three Mile Island, Harrisburg, Pa., 1981-85; pres., cons. Lowell (Mass.) Tech. Assocs., 1982—; vis. cons. Instituto National de Investigaciones Nucleares, Mexico City, 1985-86; cons. Pilgrim Nuclear Plant, 1987. Contbr. articles in field to profl. jours. Mem. Mass. Voice of Energy, Boston, 1977-80. U.S. Dept. Energy grantee, 1977. Mem. Am. Nuclear Soc., Soc. Profl. Well Log Analysts, N.Y. Acad. Scientists, Sigma Xi, Tau Beta Pi, Phi Lamba Upsilon. Club: Toastmasters (Richland, Wash.) (pres. 1965-70). Subspecialties: Nuclear engineering; Wind power. Current work: Nuclear, wind and geothermal engineering topics, rad waste disposal, reactor physics, windmill design theory, geothermal theory. Home: PO Box 811 Lowell MA 01853 Office: U Lowell 226 Engring Bldg Lowell MA 01854

SHEFFIELD, ELIZABETH, university lecturer; b. London, Feb. 6, 1954; d. Donald Victor and Lilian Kate Mary S. BSc in Botany 1st class with hons., Goldsmiths Coll., 1975; PhD, London U., 1978. Lectr. botany Birkbeck Coll., London, 1977-81; research asst. Univ. Coll., London, 1978-79; lectr. U. Manchester, Eng., 1981-88, sr. lectr., 1988—. Contbr. 41 articles to profl. jours. Scholar Sci. and Engring. Research Council, 1982-84, instant award, 1983, studentship, 1987; research assistantship Nuffield Found., 1984, 85, 87, grad. assistantship, 1986; NATO scholar, 1985-87, 87—; Natural Environ. Research Council CASE studentship, 1983, 86, 88,; travel grantee Royal Soc., 1983, 85. Fellow Linnaean Soc.; mem. Pteridological Soc. Office: Manchester Univ Cell and Structural Biology Dept, Oxford Rd, Manchester M13 9PL, England

SHEFFIELD, LESLIE FLOYD, agricultural educator; b. Orafino, Nebr., Apr. 13, 1925; s. Floyd L. and Edith A. (Presler) S.; B.S. with high distinction in Agronomy, U. Nebr., 1950, M.S., 1964; postgrad. U. Minn., summer 1965; Ph.D., U. Nebr., 1971; m. Doris Fay Fenimore, Aug. 20, 1947; children—Larry Wayne, Linda Faye (Mrs. Bernard Eric Hempelman), Susan Elaine (Mrs. Randy Thorman). County extension agt. Lexington and Schuyler, Nebr., 1951-52; exec. sec. Nebr. Grain Improvement Assn., 1952-56; chief Nebr. Wheat Commn., Lincoln, 1956-59; exec. sec. Great Plains Wheat, Inc., market devel., Garden City, Kans., 1959-61; asst. to dean Coll. Agr., U. Nebr. at Lincoln, 1961-66, supt. North Platte Expt. Sta., 1966-71, asst. dir. Nebr. Coop. Extension Service, Nebr. Agrl. Expt. Sta., Lincoln, 1971-75, asst. to vice chancellor Inst. Agr. and Natural Resources, 1975-84, also extension farm mgmt. specialist and assoc. prof. agrl. econs., 1975—; v.p. U. Nebr. Found., 1982-86; sec.-treas. Circle 4S-L Acres, Wallace, Nebr., 1973-87. Cons. econs. of irrigation in N.D., Minn., S.D. and Brazil, 1975, Sudan, Kuwait and Iran, 1976, People's Republic of China, 1977, 81, Can., 1977, 78, 79, 80, Mex., 1978, 79, Argentina, 1978, Hong Kong, 1981, Japan, 1981, Republic of South Africa, 1985. Served with U.S. Army, 1944-46; ETO. Recipient Hon. State Farmer award Future Farmers Am., 1955, Hon. Chpt. Farmer award, North Platte chpt., 1973; fellowship grad. award Chgo. Bd. Trade, 1964; Agrl. Achievement award Ak-Sar-Ben, 1969; NASA research grantee, 1972-77; Citizen award U.S. Dept. Interior Bur. Reclamation, 1984; Pub. Service award for contbns. to Nebr. agr. Nebr. Agribus. Club, 1984. Mem. Am. Agrl. Econs. Assn., Am., Nat., Nebr. (Pres.'s award 1979) water resources assns., Nebr. Irrigation Assn., Nebr. Assn. Resource Dists., Am. Soc. Farm Mgrs. Rural Appraisers, Orgn. Profl. Employees of U.S. Dept. Agr., Lincoln C. of C. (chmn. agrl. com. 1974-77), Gamma Sigma Delta, Alpha Zeta. Club: Rotary (dir. 1965-66). Editor: Procs. of Nebr. Water Resources and Irrigation Devel. for 1970's, 1972; contbg. editor Irrigation Age Mag., St. Paul, 1974—. Contbr. articles to various publs. Home: 3800 Loveland Dr Lincoln NE 68506 Office: U Nebr-Lincoln 223 Filley Hall Lincoln NE 68583

SHEFRIN, HAROLD (HERSH) MARVIN, economist, educator, consultant; b. Winnipeg, Man., Can., July 27, 1948; came to U.S., 1974, s. Samuel and Clara Ida (Danzker) S.; m. Arna Patricia Saper, June 28, 1970. B.Sc. with honors, U. Man., Winnipeg, 1970; M.Math., U. Waterloo, Can., 1971; Ph.D., London Sch. Econs., 1974. Asst. prof. econs. U. Rochester, N.Y., 1974-79; asst. prof. U. Santa Clara, Calif., 1979-80, assoc. prof., 1981, chmn. econs., 1983—, full prof., 1986—; cons. Nuclear Regulatory Commn., U.S. Dept. Energy, Livermore, Calif., 1979-82, Syntex Corp., Palo Alto, Calif., 1983—. Contbr. articles to profl. jours. Mem. Am. Econ\Assn., Econometric Soc., Western Econ. Assn., Western Fin. Assn., Fin. Mgmt. Assn., Am. Profs. for Peace in the Mid. East., European Fin. Assn., Internat. Assn. Math. Modeling. Jewish. Co-developed econ. theory of self control, behavioral finance; contbr. econ. theory of uncertainty, and consumer aggregation. Office: Santa Clara U Dept Econs Santa Clara CA 95053

SHEFTEL, ROGER TERRY, banking, leasing company executive; b. Denver, Sept. 10, 1941; s. Edward and Dorothy (Barnett) S.; B.S. in Econs., U. Pa., 1963; m. Phoebe A. Sherman, Sept. 7, 1968; children—Tisha B., Ryan B. Comml. lending officer Provident Nat. Bank, Phila., 1963-65; asst. to pres. Continental Finance Corp., Denver, 1965-68; v.p. Eastern Indsl. Leasing Corp., Phila., 1968-71, exec. v.p., dir., 1971-73; exec. v.p., dir. HBE Leasing Corp., Phila., 1971-73; pres., dir. Zebley & Strouse, Inc., Phila., 1973-75; dir. Kooly Kupp, Inc., Boyertown, Pa., 1974-77, pres., dir., 1977; prin. Trivest, Phila., 1973-77; pres. Trivest, Inc., Phila., 1977-78, 1670 Corp., mgmt. cons.'s, 1978-82; pres. Am. Cons. Group, Inc., 1982-83; exec. v.p., dir. Argus Research Labs., Inc., 1982-83; pres. Leasing Concepts, Inc., 1983—. Mem. bd. organized classes, exec. com. U. Pa. Mem. Am. Assn. Equipment Lessors, Eastern Assn. Equipment Lessors (bd. dirs.), Western Assn. Equipment Lessors, Kite and Key Soc. Clubs: Nantucket Yacht; Friars. Lodge: Rotary. Home: 414 Barclay Rd Rosemont PA 19010

SHEFVELAND, KENNETH MARTIN, data processing executive; b. Spokane, Wash., Dec. 3, 1947; s. Harvey Norman and Jane Marie (Stirn) S.; m. Janet Elaine Ebaugh, Sept. 16, 1973 (div. July 1975); m. Linda Louise Ernst, June 18, 1977; 1 child, Henry Freymueller Shefveland. Student Everett Community Coll., 1966-67, U. Md., London, 1969-70; A.A., Shoreline Community Coll., 1973; B.B.A., U. Wash., 1975. Ops. supr. N.W. Data Systems, 1975-77; systems analyst Seafirst Bank, Seattle, 1977-78, prodn. control mgr., 1978-79, ops. support mgr., 1979-80, computer ops. v.p., mgr., 1980-85; dir. data processing services Pay 'n Save Corp., Seattle, 1985-86; dir. mgmt. info. techs. Seattle Holdings Corp., 1986-87; v.p., chief operating officer InfoTech Corp., Seattle, 1987—. Vice chmn. registration com. Seafair Boat Club, Seattle, 1978; fire marshal Snohomish County Fire Protection Dist. 7, 1979 fire investigator Snohomish County Arson Task Force, Everett, Wash., 1984; dep. sheriff Snohomish County, 1984. Served with USAF, 1967-71. Recipient Firefighter of Yr. award Snohomish County Fire Protection Dist. 7, 1981, 85. Mem. Phi Theta Kappa, Alpha Kappa Psi. Congregationalist. Office: InfoTech Corp 1511 6th Ave Seattle WA 98101

SHEIKH, ABBAS ALI, physician; b. Shikarpuk, Sind, Pakistan, Feb. 9, 1928; s. Shaikh Sadik and Shaikh (Hakim) Sadik Ali; m. Sultan Abbas, Oct. 10, 1955; children: Asghar, Ghazala, Abrar. B in Medicine and Surgery, Dow Med. Coll., Karachi Pak, Pakistan, 1953. Physician Abbas Clinic, Jacobabad, Pakistan, 1955—. Mem. Pakistan Med. Assn. (founder 1958, pres. 1987—). Home: Kamora Ln, Sind Jacobabad Pakistan

SHEIKH, MOHAMMAD LATIF, physician; b. Lahore, Punjab, Pakistan, Oct. 18, 1931; s. Abdul Rahman and Sardar Begum Sheikh; married; 2 children. MBBS, King Edward Med. Coll., Lahore, 1955. Asst. surgeon Pakistan Rys., Lahore, 1955-58; with med. office Telephone & Telegraph Dept., Lahore, 1969-84, Mechanised Constrn. Pakistan, Lahore, 1974-80; gen. practice medicine Lahore, 1980—; med. advisor Pakistan Oxygen Ltd., Nespak Ltd., State Life Ins., United Bank. Mem. Pakistan Med. Assn. Home: 79 B-1 Gulberg III, Lahore, Punjab Pakistan Office: Latif Clinic, Soekarno Bazar Moghalpura, Lahore, Punjab Pakistan

SHEIKH, MUHAMMAD SANAULLAH, physician; b. Lahore, Punjab, Pakistan, Jan. 13, 1935; s. Muhammad Jahangir S.; m. Shahnaz Sheikh, Nov. 13, 1965; children: Moazam, Uzma, Mukarram, Azam. B in Medicine and Surgery, King Edward Med. Coll., Lahore, 1957. With venereology and dermatology depts., Mayo Hosp., Lahore, Pakistan, 1957-58; gen. practice medicine Lahore, Pakistan, 1958—; cons. family physician various banks, ins. cos., and businesses, 1960—. Artistic metalwork etchings displayed permanent exhibit Lahore Mus., 1974—. Mem. Pakistan Med. Assn. (exec. com. 1959-74, 84—, cen. councillor 1965-67, joint sec. 1959-61, fin. sec. 1965-67, sec. editorial sect. 1961-63), Coll. Family Medicine (founder 1981—). Moslem. Club: Cosmopolitan (Lahore, Pakistan). Lodge: Lions. Home: 229-H Ferozepur Rd, Lahore Pakistan Office: 45 Fleming Rd, Lahore Pakistan

SHEIMAN, RONALD LEE, tax lawyer; b. Bridgeport, Conn., Apr. 26, 1948; s. Samuel Charles and Rita Doris (Feinberg) S.; m. Deborah Joy Lovitky, Oct. 16, 1971; children—Jill, Laura. B.A., U. Mich., 1970; J.D., U. Conn., 1973; LL.M. in Taxation, NYU, 1974. Bar: Conn. 1973, U.S. Ct. Appeals (2d cir.) 1975, U.S. Dist. Ct. Conn. 1975, U.S. Tax Ct. 1975, U.S. Supreme Ct. 1977, D.C. 1978, N.Y. 1981. Sr. tax atty. Office of Regional Counsel, IRS, Phila., 1974-78; sole practice, Westport, Conn., 1978—. Adv. bd. Early Childhood Resource and Info. Ctr., N.Y. Pub. Library, N.Y.C., 1984. Mem. ABA, Fed. Bar Assn., Conn. Bar Assn., Westport Bar Assn. Home: 128 Random Rd Fairfield CT 06432 Office: 1804 Post Rd E Westport CT 06880

SHEINBAUM, STANLEY K., economist; b. N.Y.C., June 12, 1920; m. Betty Warner, May 29, 1964; 4 children. AB in Far East History summma cum laude, Stanford U., 1949, postgrad., 1949-53. Mem. faculty dept. econs. Stanford (Calif.) U., 1950-53, Mich. State U., East Lansing, 1955-60, U. Calif., Santa Barbara, 1963; Pres. Fairtree Enterprises, 1980—. cons. in econs. Ency. Brit., 1961-64, Calif. State Commn. Manpower and Tech., 1963-65; cons. fiscal policy Govt. South Vietnam, Saigon, 1957-59; cons. on Vietnam Spl. Ops. Research Office, Am. U., Washington, 1958-59; sr. fellow Ctr. for Study of Dem. Instns., Santa Barbara, 1960-70; v.p. Warner Ranch, Inc., Los Angeles, 1965-69, Warner Industries, Inc., Los Angeles, 1968-73; cons. editor, Ramparts, 1965073; mem. editorail bd. Democracy periodical, 1981-84; publisher New Perspectives Quarterly, 1985. Dem. candidate Congress from Santa Barbara and Ventura, 1966-68; bd. govs. Calif. Dem. Council, 1968-72; del. Dem. Nat. Conv., 1968-72; So. Calif. fin. chmn. McGovern presdl. campaign, 1972; exec. dir. Com. to Improve Tchr. Edn.; bd. dirs. Council on Econ. Priorities, N.Y.C., 1970-75, Com. for Pub. Justice, 1972—, Bill of Rights Found., N.Y., 1973—, Ctr. for Law in the Pub. Interest, Los Angeles, 1976—, Am. Jewish Com., Los Angeles, 1977—, People for the Am. Way, Washington, 1980—; organizer, coordinator legal def. team Pentagon Papers Trial, Los Angeles, 1971-73; mem. ACLU Nat. Adv. Council, N.Y.C., 1974—; chmn. bd. dirs. ACLU Found. So. Calif., Los Angeles, 1973—; founder, bd. dir. Energy Action Com., Washington, 1975-82; mem. ofcl. salaries authority City of Los Angeles, 1976-78; chmn. Clarence Darrow Found., 1977—; commr. Calif. Postsecondary Edn. Commn., 1978-80; bd. dirs. Presidio Savs. & Loan Assn. Santa Barbara, 1964-69, Music Ctr. Dance Assn., Los Angeles, 1978-85, chmn. 1979-85, Helsinki Watch and Am. Watch, N.Y. and Los Angeles, 1981—; trustee Fedn. Am. Scientists Fund, Washington, 1979—, Internat. Ctr. Peace in Mid. east, Tel Aviv, Israel, 1982—; mem. adv. bd. Breast Ctr., Valley Med. Ctr., Van Nuys, Calif., 1979, Calif. Common Cause, Los Angeles, 1986—; regent U. Calif., 1977—, vice-chmn., 1983-84; founder Legal Def. Ctr. Santa Barbara, 1970—. Fulbright fellow, Paris, 1953-55, fellow Hoover Inst., Stanford U., 1955—, fellow Scientist Inst. for Pub. Info., N.Y., 1977-82. Mem. Phi Beta Kappa, Phi Eta Sigma. Home: 345 N Rockingham Ave Los Angeles CA 90049

SHEKHAR, CHANDRA, president of Janata Party, India; b. Ballia, Uttar Pradesh, India, July 1, 1927. M.S. in Polit. Sci., Allahabad U., India. Sec. Dist. Socialist Party, Ballia; joint sec. Uttar Pradesh State Socialist Party; gen. sec. Uttar Pradesh State Socialist Party, 1955; gen. sec. Congress Parliamentary Party, 1967-77; elected Lok Sabha seat, 1977, reelected, 1980—; pres. Janata Party, 1977—. Author: Meri Jail Diary; Dynamics of Social Change. Editor weekly Young Indian. Office: Janata Party, 7 Jantar Mantar Rd, New Delhi India *

SHEKHAWAT, PRAHLAD SINGH, political scientist; b. Jaipur, Rajasthan, India, Mar. 24, 1951; s. Sumer Singh and Brij Kanwar Shekhawat. BA, Rajasthan Coll., 1970; MA, U. Rajasthan, 1972; MA in Devel. Studies, Inst. Social Studies, The Hague, Netherlands, 1985. Lectr. dept. polit. sci. U. Rajasthan, Jaipur, 1974-75; research assoc. Indo-Dutch project on Alternatives in Devel., The Hague, 1982-86, Inst. Devel. Studies, Jaipur, 1987—; coordinator Peoples Union Civil Liberties, Rajasthan, 1970—; cons. Rural Devel. Awareness Com., Jaipur, 1986—. Author: Development, Ecology and Culture, 1988; contbr. articles to research jours, also poems. Home: F174 Gautum Marg, Ashok Nagar, Jaipur Rajasthan 302001, India Office: Inst Devel Studies, B124 Mangal Marg Bapu Nagar, Jaipur Rajasthan 302001, India

SHEKHTER, MARK SEMENOVICH, psychologist; b. Moscow, Nov. 9, 1929; s. Semen D. and Klara A. (Topolynskaya) S.; m. Eugenie D. Abramkina, Sept. 12, 1941; 1 child, Leonid M. Grad., Moscow U., 1953; D Psychology, Gen. Pedagog. Psychol. Research Inst., Moscow, 1981. Research worker Inst. Defectology Acad. Pedagog. Sci., Moscow, USSR, 1960-62; prof., sr. worker Research Inst. Gen. and Pedagog. Psychology, Moscow, 1962—. Author: Psychological Problems of Recognition, 1967, Vision Recognition: Regularities and Mechanisms, 1981; contbr. articles to prof. publs. Mem. Psychol. Soc. USSR. Office: Inst Gen Pedagog Psychology, Karl Marx, Ave 20B, 103 009 Moscow USSR

SHELBY, JAMES STANFORD, cardiovascular surgeon; b. Ringgold, La., June 15, 1934; s. Jesse Audrey and Mable (Martin) S.; student La. Tech. U., 1952-54; M.D., La. State U., 1958; m. Susan Rainey, July 15, 1967; children—Bryan Christian, Christopher Linden. Intern, Charity Hosp. La., New Orleans, 1958-59, resident surgery and thoracic surgery, 1959-65; fellow cardiovascular surgery Baylor U. Coll. Medicine, Houston, 1965-66; practice medicine specializing in cardiovascular surgery, Shreveport, La., 1967—; mem. staff Schumpert Med. Center, Highland Hosp., Willis-Knighton Med. Ctr.; assoc. prof. surgery La. State U. Sch. Medicine, Shreveport, 1967—. Served with M.C., AUS, 1961-62. Diplomate Am. Bd. Surgery, Am. Bd. Thoracic Surgery. Mem. Am. Coll. Cardiology, AMA, Soc. Thoracic Surgeons, Am. Heart Assn., Southeastern Surg. Congress, So. Thoracic Surg. Assn. Home: 6003 East Ridge Dr Shreveport LA 71106 Office: 2751 Virginia Ave Shreveport LA 71103

SHELBY, RICHARD CRAIG, U.S. senator, former congressman; b. Birmingham, Ala., May 6, 1934; s. O.H. and Alice L. (Skinner) S.; m. Annette Nevin, June 11, 1960; children: Richard Craig, Claude Nevin. A.B., U. Ala., 1957, LL.B., 1963. Bar: Ala. 1961, D.C. 1979. Law clk. Supreme Ct. of Ala., 1961-62; practice law Tuscaloosa, Ala., 1963-79; prosecutor City of Tuscaloosa, 1964-70; spl. asst. atty. gen. State of Ala., 1969-70; U.S. magistrate No. Dist. of Ala., 1966-70; mem. Ala. State Senate, 1970-78, 96th-99th Congresses from 7th Ala. dist., 1979-87, Energy and Commerce Com., Vets. Affairs Com.; U.S. senator from Ala., 1987—; mem. Armed Services Com., Banking Com., Housing and Urban Affairs Com., Spl. Com. on Aging. Active Boy Scouts Am.; pres. Tuscaloosa County Mental Health Assn., 1969-70; bd. govs. Nat. Legis. Conf., 1975-78; mem. exec. com. Ala. State Dem. Party. Mem. ABA, Ala. Bar Assn., Tuscaloosa County Bar Assn., D.C. Bar Assn. Democrat. Presbyterian. Club: Exchange. Home: 1414 High Forest Dr N Tuscaloosa AL 35406 Office: US Senate 313 Hart Senate Bldg Washington DC 20510 *

SHELDON, MICHAEL GRAHAM, physician; b. Evesham, Eng., Mar. 14, 1941; s. Murray Fosbrook and Gladys (Evans) S.; m. Jennifer Christine White, Oct. 1, 1966; children—Matthew, Polly, Barnaby, Toby. M.B., B.S., London U., 1964. Surg. registrar Harefield Hosp., Middlesex, Eng., 1966-67; research registrar St. Thomas' Hosp., London, 1967-68; med. asst. Horton Hosp., Banbury, Eng., 1971-73; gen. practice medicine, Banbury, 1973-79; sr. lectr. Nottingham U., Eng., 1979-85; med. missionary Youth With a Mission, Nuneaton, Eng., 1985—; cons. Trent Regional Health Authority; temporary advisor WHO; past chmn. research com. WONCA. Editor: Decision Making in General Practice, 1985; Trends in General Practice Computing, 1985. Contbr. articles to profl. jours. Fellow Royal Coll. Gen. Practitioners (council 1983—, Upjohn prize 1975, Stanning fellow 1976, Butterworth medal 1981); mem. Brit. Computer Soc., World Orgn. Nat. Colls. and Acads. Gen. Practice (chmn. research com. 1983-85), Irish Coll. Gen. Practice. Avocations: gardening; evangelism. Office: c/o Youth With a Mission, The King's Lodge Watling St, Nuneaton CV10 0TZ, England

SHELDON, NANCY WAY, management consultant; b. Bryn Mawr, Pa., Nov. 10, 1944; d. John Harold and Elizabeth Semple (Hoff) W.; m. Robert Charles Sheldon, June 15, 1968. BA, Wellesley Coll., 1966; MA, Columbia U., 1968, M in Philosphy, 1972. Registered pvt. investigator, Calif. Mgmt. cons. ABT Assocs., Cambridge, Mass., 1969-70; mgmt. cons. Harbridge House, Inc., 1970-79, Los Angeles, 1977-79, v.p., 1977-79; mgmt. cons., pres. Resource Assessment, Inc., 1979—; ptnr., real estate developer Resource Devel. Assocs., 1980—; ptnr. Anubis Group, Ltd., 1980—. Author: Social and Economic Benefits of Public Transit, 1973. Contbr. articles to profl. jours. Columbia U. fellow, 1966-68; recipient Nat. Achievement award Nat. Assn. Women Geographers, 1966. Mem. Am. Mining Congress, Am. Inst. Mining, Metall. and Petroleum Engrs., Nat. Wildlife Fedn., Nat. Audubon Soc., Nature Conservancy, World Wildlife Fund (charter mem.), Nat. Assn. of Chiefs of Police, Grad. Faculties Alumni Assn. Columbia U., DAR, Am. Wildlife Soc., Air Pollution Control Assn., East African Wildlife Soc. Club: Wellesley (Los Angeles). Office: Resource Assessment Inc 1431 Washington Blvd Suite 2811 Detroit MI 48226

SHELDON, STEPHEN, osteopathic pediatrics educator, researcher; b. Miami Beach, Fla., Nov. 4, 1947; s. Murray M. and Sally (Lee) S.; m. Eugenia Edwina Korona, Dec. 5, 1976; children: David Patrick, Susan Victoria. BS, U. Fla., 1969; DO, Chgo. Coll. Osteo. Medicine, 1975. Diplomate Am. Bd. Physicians and Surgeons, Am. Bd. Pediatrics. Resident in pediatrics Rush-Presbyn.-St. Luke's Med. Ctr., Chgo., 1975-78, chief pediatric resident, 1977-78, coordinator pediatric residency, 1978-80, dir. pediatric residency, 1980-83; dir. pediatric research Mt. Sinai Hosp. Med. Ctr., Chgo., 1983-85; chmn. dept. pediatrics Chgo. Coll. Osteo. Medicine, 1985—; cons. pediatrician Rush-Presby.-St. Lukes Med. Ctr., 1983—, Mt. Sinai Hosp. Med. Ctr., 1980—, Christ Hosp., Oak Lawn, Ill., 1980—; vis. faculty U. Ill. Coll. Dentistry, Chgo., 1982—. Author: Pediatric Differential Diagnosis, 1979, 2d edit. 1986, Manual of Practical Pediatrics, 1981, Diagnosis and Management of the Hospitalized Child, 1984. Fellow Am. Acad. Pediatrics (cert. merit 1985); mem. AMA, Am. Osteo. Assn. (research grantee 1986), Ambulatory Pediatric Assn. Office: Chgo Coll Osteo Medicine 5200 S Ellis Ave Chicago IL 60615

SHELDON, THOMAS DONALD, educator; b. Canastota, N.Y., July 15, 1920; s. Harry Ellsworth and Sadie Joyce (McNulty) S.; m. Helen Elizabeth Kyser, Aug. 29, 1942; children: Thomas, Paul, Edward, Patricia, Curtis, Roberta, Kevin. B.S., Syracuse U., 1942, M.S., 1949, Ed.D., 1958; grad., USAF Air War Coll., 1972. Tchr. sci., coach Split Rock (N.Y.) High Sch., 1942-43; tchr. sci., coach, vice prin., prin. Minoa (N.Y.) High Sch., 1946-59; prin., asso. supt. Hempstead (N.Y.) High Sch., 1959-63; supt. schs. Hempstead Public Schs., 1963-68; supt. Balt. City Schs., 1968-71; dep. commr. N.Y. State Edn. Dept., Albany, 1971-77; pres. Utica Coll. of Syracuse U., 1977-82; interim pres. Mohawk Valley Community Coll., 1983; then interim pres. Onondaga Community Coll., 1984, now hon. pres. emeritus; prof. ednl. adminstrn. Syracuse U., N.Y., 1983-85; supt. Sewanhaka Central High Sch. Dist., 1985-86; exec. dir. Syracuse U. Relations, N.Y.C., 1987—. Co-author and editor various N.Y. State Regents publs., 1971-76. Served with U.S. Army, 1943-46; Served with USAF, 1961-62, Berlin; to brig. gen. Air N.G. 1955-76. First recipient Outstanding Grad. award Syracuse U. Sch. Edn., 1977; recipient Outstanding Md. Educator award Md. State Council PTA's, 1969; Disting. Am. Educator award Freedoms Found., 1966; Conspicuous Service medal N.Y. State Gov., 1976; N.Y.C. Psal medal, 1978; named to Balt. Afro-Am. Honor Roll, 1970. Mem. Am. Assn. Sch. Adminstrs., N.Y. State Council Chief Sch. Dist. Adminstrs., N.Y. State PTA (hon. life), Md. PTA (hon. life), Utica C. of C. (dir.), Air Force Assn., Militia Assn. N.Y., N.Y. State Coaches Assn. (pres. 1957), Am. Legion, Phi Delta Kappa. Clubs: Lions (hon. (life).

SHELESKI, STANLEY JOHN, accountant, comptroller, consultant; b. Harleigh, Pa., Feb. 20, 1931; s. Stanley Joseph and Agnes Rose (Yeshmond) S.; m. Sandra Lee Atkins. BS in Fin. Acctg., Rider Coll., 1958. Treas., mgr. United Savs. and Loan, Trenton, N.J., 1958-62; mgr. acctg. dept. Allstates Engring. Co., Trenton, 1962-85, asst. treas., asst. sec., comptroller, 1985—; v.p. fin. Allstates Design and Devel. Co., Trenton, 1988—; bd. dirs. Allstates Credit Union, Trenton, 1966—, treas. and gen. mgr. Allstates Credit Union, 1968—. Planner Jr. C. of C., Trenton, 1959. Served to sgt. USMC, 1952-54, Korea. Mem. Nat. Assn. Accts., Ewing Bus. Assn. (treas. 1959-62). Republican. Roman Catholic. Lodge: North Star Club (v.p. 1953-58).

SHELL, KURT LEO, research center administrator, political science educator emeritus; b. Vienna, Austria; s. Josef and Eugenie (Wulkan) S.; m. Enid V.M. Cox, 1943 (div. 1963); m. Ingrid Evelyn Herzog, 1965; 1 child, Karin Jennifer. BS, Columbia U., 1948, MA, 1949, PhD, 1955; Dr. honoris causa, U. Southampton, Eng., 1985. Lectr. Columbia U., N.Y.C., 1950-56; asst. prof. SUNY, Binghamton, 1956-58, 1958-61, assoc. prof., 1964-66, prof. polit. sci., 1966-67; prof. U. Frankfurt, Fed. Republic Germany, 1967-86; dir. Ctr. N.Am. Research, Frankfurt, 1979—; research assoc. Inst. Polit. Sci., Free U., Berlin, 1961-64. Author: Transition of Austrian Socialism, 1962, Bedrohung und Bewährung, 1965, Das politische System der USA, 1975, Liberal-demokcratische Systeme, 1981, Der amerikanische Konservatismus, 1986. Served with U.S. Armed Forces, 1942-46. Grantee Columbia U., 1955, Volkswagen-Stiftung, 1981-84. Mem. Deutsche Vereinigung für politische Wissenschaft, Deutsche Gesellschaft für Amerikastudien. Office: Zentrum Nordamerikaforshung, Freiherr vom Stein Strasse 24-26, D-6000 Frankfurt, Main Federal Republic of Germany

SHELL, OWEN G., JR., banker; b. Greenville, S.C., June 19, 1936; s. Owen and Katherine S.; m. Mary Ruth Trammell, Aug. 9, 1980; children: Katherine Sloan, Mary Carroll, Robert Owen, James Walker. B.S., U. S.C., 1960; post grad., Stonier Grad. Sch. Banking, 1971; grad., Advanced Mgmt. Program, Harvard U., 1979. Tech. supt. Deering-Milliken, Inc., 1962-63; v.p. Citizens & So. Nat. Bank S.C., Columbia, 1968-71; sr. v.p. Citizens & So. Nat. Bank S.C., 1971-74, exec. v.p., 1974-79; pres., dir., chief exec. officer First Am. Nat. Bank, Nashville, 1979-86; vice chmn. bd., dir. First Am. Corp., 1979-86; pres., chief exec. officer Sovran Fin. Corp./Cen. South, Nashville, 1986—, Sovran Bank/Cen. South, Nashville, 1986—; dir. Nashville br. Fed. Res. Bank of Atlanta, 1986—; dir. Engineered Custom Plastics Corp., 1972-80, Sloan Constrn. Co., 1972-81; dir. Nashville br. Fed. Res. Bank of Atlanta. Active Tenn. Performing Arts Found., Middle Tenn. council Boy Scouts Am., Girl Scouts U.S., Cumberland Valley Girl Scout Council, Owen Grad. Sch. Mgmt. Served to maj. USAF, 1960-64. Mem. Assn. Res. City Bankers, Nashville Area C. of C., Kappa Alpha, Omicron Delta Kappa. Presbyterian. Clubs: Rotary, Cumberland, Belle Meade Country. Home: 4412 Chickering Ln Nashville TN 37215

SHELLEY, EDWIN FREEMAN, engineer, university official; b. N.Y.C., Feb. 19, 1921; s. Robert and Jessie (Sinick) S.; A.B., Columbia Univ., 1940, BSEE, 1941; postgrad. Harvard U., 1957; ScD (hon.) Nova U., 1984; m. Florence Dubroff, Aug. 29, 1941; children—William, Carolyn. Exptl. flight test engr. Curtiss-Wright Corp., Propeller div., Caldwell, N.J., 1941-47; cons. electronics Wilson Mech. Instrument Co., N.Y.C., 1945-47, Bridgeport, Conn., 1945-47; pres., chief engr. Am. Chronoscope Corp., Mt. Vernon, N.Y., 1948-50; spl. cons. Mercury Totalizator Co., Inc., N.Y.C., 1949-50; co-founder, v.p., gen. mgr. Bulova Research & Devel. Labs., Inc., Flushing, N.Y., 1950-57; dir. advanced programs U.S. Industries, Inc., N.Y.C., 1957-60, v.p., 1960-64; pres. U.S. Industries Robodyne Div., 1958-60; pres. E.F. Shelley & Co., Inc., 1965-71, chmn. bd., 1971-75; dir. Center for Energy Policy and Research, N.Y. Inst. Tech., Old Westbury, 1975—. Past pres. Nat. Council on Aging. Trustee N.Y. Inst. Tech.; trustee Nova U., Ft. Lauderdale, Fla., 1970-85; bd. dirs. Center for Community Change, Inst. Responsive Edn.; adv. bd. N.Y. State Legis. Commn. Sci. and Tech. Mem. IEEE (sr.), Am. Phys. Soc., Am. Inst. Aeros. and Astronautics, AAAS, N.Y. Acad. Scis., Newcomen Soc. in N.Am. Patentee in field. Home: 339 Oxford Rd New Rochelle NY 10804 Office: NY Inst Tech Old Westbury NY 11568

SHELLEY, GABRIEL CHARLES, management consultant; b. Budapest, Hungary, Dec. 11, 1950; arrived in Can., 1957; s. Charles I. and Judith R. (Kartal) S.; m. Jennifer A. Robinson, Sept. 2, 1972; children: Paul A., David J. BS, Queen's U., Kingston, Can., 1972; MBA, York U., Toronto, Can., 1980. Process engr. DuPont Ltd., Kingston, Ont., 1972-74; mgr., indsl. engr. Dominion Stores Ltd., Toronto, Ont., 1974-76; mgr. Kearney Mgmt. Cons., Toronto, 1976-78; prin. Stevenson & Kellogg, Toronto, 1978-80; mng. ptnr. Stevenson, Kellogg, Ernst & Whinney, Edmonton, Alta., 1980—. Contbr. articles to profl. jours. Bd. dirs. Nexus Theatre, Edmonton, 1985-86. Recipient award Purchasing Mgmt. Assn., Toronto, 1979. Mem. Assn. Profl. Engrs., Inst. Mgmt. Cons. (bd. dirs. 1984-86), Council Logistics Mgmt. Office: Stevenson Kellogg Ernst & Whinney, 2800 Canada Trust Tower, Edmonton, AB Canada T5J 0H8

SHELLEY, RULON GENE, manufacturing company executive; b. 1924; s. John Franklin and Linda Marie (Gutke) S.; m. Theora Whiting, June 21, 1946; children: Dennis, Kenneth, Ronald, Patricia. BSEE, U. Ariz., 1948; MS, MIT, 1949. Chief engr. aerospace div. N.Am. Aviation, 1949-61; v.p. Tamar Electronics Inc., 1961-64; with Raytheon Co., Lexington, Mass., 1964—, from mgr. Santa Barbara Ops. to v.p. gen. mgr. equipment div., 1964-78, v.p. gen. mgr. group exec. equipment div., 1978-79, sr. v.p. group exec., 1979-86, pres., 1986—, also bd. dirs.; bd. govs. AIA, Washington, 1986—; bd. trustees Nat. Security and Internat. Affairs, Washington, 1986—. Served to 2d lt. A.C., U.S. Army, 1943-46. Mem. Assn. Old Crows, Air Force Assn., Am. Defense Preparedness Assn., Assn. U.S. Army, Nat. Space Club, Navy League U.S., Tau Beth Pi. Office: Raytheon Co 141 Spring St Lexington MA 02173

SHELLHASE, LESLIE JOHN, social work educator; b. Hardy, Nebr., Jan. 12, 1924; s. John Clayton and Sanna Belle (Muth) S.; m. Fern Eleanor Kleckner, June 8, 1948; children: Jeremy Clayton, Joel Kleckner. Student, U. Calif.-Berkeley, 1943-44; A.B., Midland Coll., 1947; M.S.W., U. Nebr., 1950; D.Social Work, Catholic U. Am., 1961. Lic. social worker, Ala. Parole supr. Child Welfare, Omaha, 1948-49; psychiat. social work intern Letterman Gen. Hosp. San Francisco, 1950-51; commd. 2d lt. U.S. Army, 1949, advanced through grades to lt. col., 1966; chief social worker (6th Inf. Div.), Ft. Ord, Calif., 1952-55; chief med. social worker Walter Reed Gen. Hosp. Washington, 1955-57, research investigator Walter Reed Inst. Research, 1957-63; head social work faculty Med. Field Service Sch., Ft. Sam Houston, Tex., 1963-66; chief sociologist U.S. Army, Washington, 1966-68; prof. Sch. Social Work, U. Ala., University, 1968—; pvt. practice social work 1968—; dir. tour, interpreter to surgeon gen. Belgium Armed Forces, 1961; lectr. Catholic U. Am., 1961-63, 66-68; research dir. Jewish Social Service Fedn., San Antonio, 1963-66; rep. to internat. social and behavioral scis. community Dept. Army, 1966-68; cons. Family Service Assn. Am., 1969—; mem. expert group on social welfare UN, 1975—; mem. Internat. Relations Forum, 1981—; research fellow U. Exeter, 1981-82; mem. social work tng. com. NIMH, 1983—; condr. workshops. Author: The Group Life of the Schizophrenic Patient, 1961, Bibliography of Army Social Work, 1962; book rev. editor: Social Perspectives, 1979-83; editorial reviewer Social Work Papers, editorial bd., 1986—; contbr. articles on social and behavioral sci. to nat. and internat. profl. jours. and chpts. to books. Bd. dirs. Crisis Intervention Center; bd. dirs., chmn. Soc. for Crippled Children and Adults; chmn. bd. social ministry So. Dist. Lutheran Ch. Served with inf. U.S. Army, 1942-46. Decorated Legion of Merit, Bronze Star, Purple Heart; recipient letters of commendation from Pres., 1968, letters of commendation from Surgeon Gen., 1961. Fellow Am. Sociol. Assn.; mem. Nat. Assn. Social Workers (mem. nat. task force on ethics 1976-79, chmn. 1976-77, dir. 1963-66), Council Social Work Edn., Nat. Conf. Social Welfare, Acad. Cert. Social Workers, Brit. Sociol. Assn., Brit. Assn. Social Workers, ACLU, Am. Vets Com., Ret. Officers Assn., Pershing Rifles, Hastings Soc., Blue Key, So. Sociol. Soc. Democrat. Home: 3823 Somerset Pl Tuscaloosa AL 35405 Office: Box 1935 Tuscaloosa AL 35487-1935

SHELNUTT, ROBERT CURTIS, manufacturing company administrator; b. Shawmut, Ala., Sept. 2, 1928; s. Curtis Lee and Odell (Campbell) S.; B.S. in Chemistry, U. Ga., 1954; M.B.A., Pepperdine U., 1981; m. Faye Mahan; children—Robert Curtis, Susan Elaine. With Am. Enka Co., Lowland, Tenn., 1954-79, gen. tech. supr. chem., spinning and finishing depts., 1969-71, tech. mgr. rayon filament plant, 1971-75, tech. mgr. rayon staple plant, 1975-76, energy and devel. mgr. rayon staple plant, 1976-77, energy and devel., mgr. Tenn. ops., 1977-79; gen. mgr. chem. ops. Chatsworth div. Organon Teknika Corp., Chatsworth, Calif., 1979-81, dir. mfg. and chem. engring. research and devel., Oklahoma City, 1981-82, dir. quality assurance and chem. activities, 1982—. Served with USAF, 1946-49. Mem. Am. Chem. Soc., Am. Mgmt. Assn. Republican. Baptist. Clubs: Masons, Shriners. Home: 9105 Pebble Ln Oklahoma City OK 73132 Office: Organon Teknika Corp 5300 S Portland Oklahoma City OK 73119

SHELTON, WILLIAM CHASTAIN, retired government statistician; b. Athens, Ga., May 5, 1916; s. William Arthur and Effie Clyde (Landrum) S.; m. Helen Higgins, Dec. 17, 1938; children: Stuart H., Terry Ann Shelton Coble, Jean R. Shelton Jaffray, Alvic C. AB, Princeton U., 1936; postgrad. U. Chgo., 1937-38. Economist, statistician Fed. Govt., Washington, 1936-48; chief stats. sect. USRO-Marshall Plan, Paris, France, 1948-55; mgr. bus. research Fla. Devel. Com., Tallahassee, 1956-60; asst. com. foreign labor Bur. Labor Stats., Washington, 1960-75; spl. asst. statis. policy div. Office Mgmt. and Budget, 1975-77. Author: (with Joseph W. Duncan) Revolution in U.S. Government Statistics, 1926-76, 1978; contbr. articles to profl. jours. Mem. Am. Statis. Assn., Washington Soc. Investment Analysts, Nat. Economics Club, Soc. History in Fed. Govt., Sigma Xi, Phi Beta Kappa. Republican. Presbyterian. Home: 8401 Piney Branch Rd Silver Spring MD 20901

SHEMER, ISAAC MOSHE, accountant; b. Tel Aviv, Aug. 25, 1924; s. Alter Shneur Zalman and Shoshana Sara (Keidan) Shmerling; m. Aviva Goldwasser, Sept. 3, 1948; children: Ehud, Assaf, Vered. Student, Tel Aviv U., 1971-72, Everymen's U., Tel Aviv, 1979—. CPA, Israel. Staff mem. Kesselman & Kesselman, Tel Aviv, 1941-53, ptnr., 1953-64, sr. ptnr., 1965—, chmn., 1984—. Contbr. articles to profl. jours. Chmn. Akim Israel Assn. for Rehab. Mentally Retarded Persons, 1965-69, 73; mem. exec. council, hon. treas. Internat. League Socs. for Mentally Handicapped Persons, 1968-76. Served with Israeli Def. Forces, 1947-49. Mem. Israel Inst. CPA's (council, hon. treas. 1959-63, 84-86). Club: Tel Aviv Country. Home: 17 Kish, Ramat Gan 52-312, Israel Office: Kesselman & Kesselman, 37 Montefiore St, Tel Aviv 65-201, Israel

SHEMORRY, CORINNE JOYNES, marketing executive; b. Rolla, N.D., Jan. 24, 1920; d. William H. and Edna Ruth (Conn) Joynes; children: Gay, Jan. Publisher, Williston (N.D.) Plains Reporter, 1953-78; mktg. dir. Williston Credit Union, 1979—; journalist, lectr., cons., author, reporter. Recipient numerous awards in journalism on state and nat. level, including Outstanding Woman in Journalism in N.D., 1987, 1st Place Golden Mirror award Credit Union Nat. Assn. Mem. N.D. Press Assn., N.D. Press Women (past pres.), Nat. Press Women, Williston C. of C., Nat. Assn. Female Execs., Fin. Mktg. Assn. (charter), Sigma Delta Chi. Mem. United Ch. Club: Bus. and Profl. Women's (past pres.). Home: 210 E 14th St PO Box 1030 Williston ND 58801

SHEN, CHANG HUAN, state official, diplomat; b. Kiangsu, China, Oct. 16, 1913; s. Chu Shan Shen and Feng Yi Chow; m. Helen Lay; 1 child. BA, Kuanghua U., Shanghai, China, 1933; MA, U. Mich., 1937; LLD (hon.), Yonsei U., 1961. Prof. Nat. Sun Yat-Sen U., Canton, China, 1937-40; counsel Chinese Expeditionary Forces, 1943-45; personnel sec. to Pres. Chiang Kai-Shek Chungking, China, 1945-48; dir. Govt. Info. Office, Nanking, China, 1949; govt. spokesman Exec. Yuan, Taipei, Republic of China, 1950-53; ambassador Spanish Embassy, Madrid, 1959-60, Holy See, Vatican City, 1966-69, Thai Embassy, Bangkok, 1969-72; vice minister Ministry Fgn. Affairs, Taipei, 1953-59, minister, 1960-66, 72-79; sec.-gen. Nat. Security Council, Taipei, 1979-84, President's Office, Taipei, 1984—. Contbr. papers, speeches in field. Served to brig. gen. Chinese mil., 1943-45, CBI. Mem. Kuomintang Party. Office: President's Office, 122 Chungking S Rd, Sec 1, Taipei Republic of China

SHEN, CHIA THENG, former steamship company executive, religious institute official; b. Chekiang, China, Dec. 15, 1913; came to U.S., 1952, naturalized, 1964; s. Foo Sheng and Wen Ching (Hsai) S.; m. Woo Ju Chu, Apr. 21, 1940; children: Maria May Shen Jackson, Wilma Way Shen George, David Chuen-Tsing, Freda Foh. B.E.E., Chiao Tung U., 1937; Litt.D. (hon.), St. John's U., 1973. With Central Elec. Mfg. Works, China, 1937-44; factory mgr. Central Elec. Mfg. Works, 1942-44; dep. coordinating dept. Nat. Resources Commn., Govt. of China, 1945-47; pres. China Trading and Indsl. Devel. Corp., Shanghai, 1947-49; mng. dir. China Trading & Indsl. Devel. Co. Ltd., Hong Kong, 1949-53; with TransAtlantic Financing Corp., 1954-62, pres., 1958-62; pres. Pan-Atlantic Devel. Corp., N.Y.C., 1955-70; with Marine Transport Lines Inc., N.Y.C., 1958-70; sr. v.p. Marine Transport Lines Inc., 1964-70; with Am. Steamship Co., Buffalo, 1967-80; chmn. bd., chief exec. officer Am. Steamship Co., 1971-80. Trustee Inst. Advanced Studies World Religions, N.Y., 1970—, chmn. bd., chief exec. officer, 1970—, pres., 1970-84; trustee China Inst. in Am., N.Y.C., 1963—, vice chmn., 1970-79, chmn., 1979-80, mem. exec. com., 1963-84; trustee, v.p. Buddhist Assn. U.S., N.Y.C., 1964—. Mem. Chinese Inst. Engring. Home and Office: 131 Tekening Dr Tenafly NJ 07670

SHEN, DALI, language educator; b. Yanan, Shaanxi, People's Republic China, Apr. 9, 1938; s. Shen Xi and Song Ying; m. Liu Fongyun, 1962; 1 child, Shen Xiasong, Shen Xiaorong. Diplômé de, Beijing U., 1962. Prof. langs. Beijing Fgn. Langs. Inst., 1964-78; translator UNESCO, Paris, 1978-81, réviseur, 1985—; envoyé Chine au Colloque Internat., Geneva, 1984-85. Author: (novel) The Humble Violet, 1983, The Children of Yenan, 1985, Les Lys Rouges, 1987; (play) La Flûte des Titans, 1987. Mem. Assn. des Écrivains de Chine, Conseil Sci. de l'Inst. de Recherches sur La Lit. Étrangère L'Université des Langs. Étrangères Beijing, Conseil Assn. des Traducteurs de Pekin. Address: Beijing Fgn Langs Inst, Beijing Peoples Republic China

SHEN, SIN-YAN, physicist, energy specialist; b. Singapore, Nov. 12, 1949; came to U.S., 1969, naturalized, 1984; s. Shao-Quan and Tien-Siu (Chen) S.; m. Yuan-Yuan Lee, Aug. 4, 1973; children—Jia, Jian. B.Sc. U. Singapore, 1969; M.S. Ohio State U. 1970, Ph.D., 1973. Instr. math. U. Singapore, 1969; asst. prof. physics Northwestern U., Evanston, Ill., 1974-77; faculty assoc. Argonne Nat. Lab., Ill., 1974-77, scientist, 1977-83; sr. research leader, 1983—; meeting series reviewer NSF, Washington, 1981—; coordinator Tech. Rev., Argonne, Atlanta, Phoenix, Portland (Oreg.), 1983—; advisor Internat. Energy Agy, 1986—, SUPCON Internat., 1986—, Nat. Geographics, 1986—; prof. Chinese Acad. Forestry, 1986—; mem. panel on biol. diversity Nat. Acad. Scis., Smithsonian Instn., 1986. Author: Superfluidity, 1982. Patentee molten liquids, 1974, 1980. Contbr. articles prof. jours. Fulbright scholar U.S. State Dept, 1969; merit scholar Govt. Singapore, 1967; adv. Ency. Brit., 1983—. Mem. AAAS, Am. Phys. Soc., Ops. Research Soc. Am., Acoustical Soc. Am., Chinese Music Soc. N.Am. Current work: Renewable energy and materials techs.; indsl. sonic techs.; energy policy, planning and economics; acoustics. Home: 2329 Charmingfare Woodridge IL 60517

SHEN, YAO TIAN, mathematics educator; b. Tianjin, Peoples Republic of China, Oct. 15, 1938; s. Yuxin (Yoashing Sheng) and Huijun (Zhou) S; m. Meizhi Chen, July 27, 1972; 1 child, Yuanyi. BS, U. Fudan, Shanghai, Peoples Republic of China, 1961. Assoc. prof. U. Sci. Tech. of China, Hefei, 1978-86; prof. South China Inst. Tech., Guangzhou, 1986—. Contbr. articles to profl. jours. Mem. Am. Math. Society, Math. Review. Office: South China Inst Tech, Dept Applied Maths, Guangzhou Peoples Republic of China

SHEN, ZUHE, mathemathics educator, researcher; b. Nanchang, JiangXi, People's Republic of China, May 3, 1933; s. HanQin Shen and JueLu Zhang; m. Yunhua Liu, May 1, 1961; 1 child, Jian. MS, Nanjing U., 1959. Lectr., research asst. Nanjing U., People's Republic of China, 1959-83, assoc. prof., 1983-85, prof., 1985—; also vice-chmn. math. dept. Nanjing U., 1985—; vis. scholar U. Wis., Madison, 1979-81; vis. prof. Freiburg U., Fed. Republic Germany, 1988—; Author: Academic Press, 1978; contbg. editor Jour. Computational Mathematics, 1987; contbr. articles to profl. jours. Recipient Excellent Educator award JiangSu Province, Nanjing, 1985. Mem. Chinese Math. Soc., Am. Math. Soc., Soc. Chinese Operational Research. Home: #3 Xikong Rd Apt 13 Rm 205, Nanjing, Jiangsu People's Republic of China Office: Nanjing U Math Dept, #2 Hankou Rd, Nanjing, JiangSu People's Republic of China Address: Albert-Ludwigs U, Inst Angewandte Math, Hermann-Herder Strasse 10, 7800 Freiburg Germany

SHENK, JOHN HENRY, engineering company executive; b. Junction City, Kans., Dec. 19, 1939; s. Henry Arthur and Katherine Phobe (Frick) S.; B.S.B.A., U. Kans., 1963, B.S.C.E., 1963. Constrn. engr. Dupont Corp., Seaford, Del., 1963; engring. supt. Tumpane Co., Sinop, Turkey, 1965-67; with Pacific Architects and Engrs., Inc. and subs., 1967—, v.p. PAE, Bangkok, Thailand, 1971-72, v.p. S.E. Asia, Pacific Architects and Engrs., Inc., Bangkok, 1972-80, sr. v.p. Pacific Architects and Engrs., Inc., 1980-87; dir. PAE Internat., PAE (Thailand) Co. Ltd., Pacific Architects and Engrs. Co., Ltd., Pacific Services Co. Ltd., PAE (Singapore) Pte. Ltd., Maenning Corp., Syalin PAE Sdn. Bhd., Service Systems PTE Ltd., Heavylift Internat. B.V., Active Corp., Rand B Corp.; mng. dir. Nus Antara Pacific Ltd., Soon Pacific Ltd., Facilities Engring. Cons. Ltd., PAE (Thailand) Co., Ltd. (pres. 1987) Hong Kong, PAE Constrn. Co., Ltd. (pres. 1987). Served to 1st lt. C.E., U.S. Army, 1963-65. Decorated Army Commendation medal, Army Commendation medal with oak leaf cluster (U.S.); for pub. service (Thailand). Mem. ASCE, Soc. Am. Mil. Engrs., Delta Upsilon (Man of Yr. 1961). Home: 39 Pongsrichan Sapenkwai, Suthisarn, Bangkok Thailand Office: Sinkahakarn Bldg, 55 Rachadapisek Rd 6th Floor, Bangkok Thailand

SHENNAN, JOSEPH HUGH, historian, educator, academic administrator; b. Liverpool, Eng., Mar. 13, 1933; s. Hugh Cringle and Mary Catherine (Jones) S.; m. Margaret King Price, Aug. 23, 1958; children: Andrew, Robert, Christopher. BA in History with 1st class honors, U. Liverpool, Eng.; PhD, U. Cambridge, Eng. Lectr. U. Liverpool, 1960-65; sr. lectr, reader U. Lancaster, Eng., 1965-74; prof. European studies U. Lancaster, 1974-79, prof. European history, 1979—, pro-vice chancellor, 1984—. Author: The Parlement of Paris, 1968, Government and Society in France, 1969, Origins of the Modern European State, 1974, Philippe, Duke of

Orleans, 1979, Liberty and Order in Early Modern Europe, 1986; founder, editor: European Studies Review, 1971-79; adv. editor: European History Quar., 1979—. Fellow: Royal Hist. Soc. Roman Catholic. Club: Lancaster Golf Country. Home: Bull Beck House, Four Acres Brookhouse, Lancaster LA2 9JW, England Office: Univ Lancaster, Dept History Bailrigg, Lancaster, LA1 4YG England

SHENOUDA, ANBA, III, Egyptian ecclesiastic; b. Cairo, Aug. 3, 1923; B.A., Cairo U.; B.D., Coptic Orthodox Theol. Coll. Theol. tchr. and writer; former Bishop and prof. theology Orthodox Clerical Coll., Cairo; 1st chmn. Assn. of Theol. Colls. in the Near East; 117th Pope of Alexandria and Patriarch of the See of St. Mark of Egypt, the Near East and All Africa (Coptic Orthodox Church), 1971-81, 85—; removed from post by Pres. Sadat and banished to desert monastery Wadi Natroun, Sept. 1981, released Jan. 1985. Address: Coptic Orthodox Patriarchate, Anba Ruess Bldg Ramses St, Abbasiya, Cairo Egypt *

SHEPARD, ALAN BARTLETT, JR., astronaut, real estate developer; b. East Derry, N.H., Nov. 18, 1923; s. Alan Bartlett and Renza (Emerson) S.; student Admiral Farragut Acad., 1940; B.S., U.S. Naval Acad., 1944; grad. Naval War Coll., 1958; M.S. (hon.), Dartmouth Coll.; D.Sc. (hon.), Miami U.; m. Louise Brewer, Mar. 3, 1945; children—Laura, Juliana. Commd. ensign U.S. Navy, 1944, advanced through grades to rear adm., 1971; designated naval aviator, 1947; assigned destroyer U.S.S. Cogswell, Navy Test Pilot Sch., Pacific, World War II, Fighter Squadron 42, 1947-49, aircraft carriers in Mediterranean, 1947-49; with U.S. Navy Test Pilot Sch., 1950-53, 55-57; took part in high altitude tests, expts. in test and devel. in-flight refueling system, carrier suitability trials of F2H3 Banshee, also trials angled carrier deck ops. officer Fighter Squadron 193, Moffett Field, Calif. and in carrier U.S.S. Oriskany, Western Pacific, 1953-55; test pilot for F3H Demon, 1956, F8U Crusader, 1956, F4D Skyray, 1955, F11F Tigercat, 1956; project test pilot F5D Skylancer, 1956; instr. Naval Test Pilot Sch., 1957; aircraft readiness officer staff Comdr.-in-Chief, Atlantic Fleet, 1958-59; joined Project Mercury man in space program NASA, 1959; first Am. in space May 5, 1961; chief of astronaut office, 1965-74; selected to command Apollo 14 Lunar Landing Mission, 1971, became 5th man to walk on moon, hit 1st lunar golf shot; ret., 1974; ptnr. Mariner Interests, Houston, 1974; pres. Seven Fouteen Enterprises, 1986; ptnr., chmn. Marathon Constrn. Co., Houston, 1974-77; former pres. Windward Coors Co., Deer Park, Tex., 1974; apptd. by Pres. as del. to 26th Gen. Assembly UN, 1971. Decorated D.S.M., D.F.C., Presdl. unit citation, NASA Disting. Service medal, Congressional Medal of Honor, 1978; recipient Langley medal Smithsonian Instn., 1964. Fellow Soc. Exptl. Test Pilots; mem. Order Daedlians, Soc. Colonial Wars. Clubs: Lions, Kiwanis, Rotary. *

SHEPARD, CHARLES VIRGIL, human resource executive; b. Springfield, Ill., Nov. 14, 1940; s. Charles Woodrow and Catherine Elizabeth (Vlakovich) S.; B.A. in Bus. Adminstrn. and Econs., 1962; postgrad. U. Ill., Urbana, 1966-72; M.B.A., Sangamon State U., 1972; m. Judy A. Wells; children—Cynthia Lynn, Kimberly Lynn. With Allis-Chalmers Corp., Springfield, 1962-73, supr. employee benefits, 1962-67, adminstrv. asst., 1967-68, mgr. personnel services, 1968-70, mgr. orgn. planning and devel., 1970-72, mgr. indsl. relations, 1972-73; mem. corp. indsl. relations staff Rockwell Internat. Corp., Dallas, 1973, dir. indsl. relations, 1973-74, group dir. personnel, 1974-76, v.p. personnel, 1976-77, staff v.p. electronics personnel, 1977-78, corp. staff v.p. employee relations, 1978-80, v.p. electronic operations and human resources Gen. Industries, 1980-81, v.p. human resources, 1981—. Mem. Adv. Council Amigos de Ser, 1976—; mem. adv. bd. Richland Coll., 1975-76; bd. dirs. Jr. Achievement, 1981—, Dallas Theater Center, Pitts. Public Theatre, 1979—, Dallas Opera, 1982—, TACA, 1982, Boy Scouts Am., 1982—. Mem. Electronic Industries Assn. (indsl. relations council), Am. Soc. Personnel Adminstrn., Dallas C. of C. (dir. 1974-76). Republican. Methodist. Club: Masons. Home: 6122 Warm Mist Lane Dallas TX 75248 Office: Rockwell Internat Dallas TX 75207

SHEPARD, EARL ALDEN, government official; b. Aurora, Ill., Sept. 30, 1932; s. Ralph George and Marcia Louise (Phelps) S.; A.S. magna cum laude in Bus. Adminstrn. (fed. and local govt. employee scholar), Southeastern U., 1967, B.S. magna cum laude in Bus. Adminstrn., 1969; M.B.A. (Ammunition Procurement Supply Agy. fellow), U. Chgo., 1974; m. Carolyn Mae Borman, Sept. 1, 1959; 1 son, Ralph Lyle. Chief program budget div. U.S. Army Munitions Command. Joliet, Ill., 1971-73; comptroller, dir. adminstrn. U.S. Navy Pub. Works Center, Gt. Lakes, Ill., 1973-77; dep. comptroller U.S. Army Electronics Command/U.S. Army Communications Electronics Materiel Readiness Command, Ft. Monmouth, N.J., 1977-79; dir. resource mgmt., comptroller, dir. programs U.S. Army White Sands Missile Range, N.Mex., 1979—; bd. dirs. 1st Nat. Bank Dona Ana County, 1987—; adv. com. Rio Grande Bancshares/First Nat. Bank of Dona Ana County, 1983-84. Bd. govs., Southeastern Univ. Ednl. Found., 1969-71; chmn. fin. com. No. Va. Assn. for Children with Learning Disabilities, 1966-67, treas., 1968-70; pres. West Long Branch (N.J.) Sports Assn., 1979. Mem. Assn. U.S. Army, Am Soc Mil Comptrollers, Assn. Govt. Accts., Fed. Mgrs. Assn. Republican. Home: 2712 Topley Ave Las Cruces NM 88005 Office: Attention: STEWS-RM White Sands Missile Range NM 88002

SHEPARD, ROBERT KIGHT, computer systems company executive; b. Ft. Bragg, N.C., June 21, 1943; s. Corey Robert and Edwina (Kight) S.; m. Beverly Jane Wehking, June 5, 1967; children: Benjamin David, Emily Gail, Diana Corinne, Bethany Lucinda. BA in Physics, Rice U., 1964; postgrad., U. Houston, 1964-68. Med. physicist VA Hosp., Houston, 1964-68; programmer, analyst McMaster U., Hamilton, Ont., Can., 1968-72, sr. systems analyst, 1972-76, coordinator computing services, 1976-82, mgr. distributed computing, 1982-86, dir. computing devel., 1986-87; pres. Shepard Computing Enterprises, Ancaster, Ont., 1987—; chmn. Task Force on Office Automation, Hamilton, 1985; sec. faculty of sci. computing com. McMaster U., 1983-87, systems architect campus wide Ethernet, 1986-87. Author various computer software. Bd. dirs. Camp NeeKauNis, Waubashene, Ont., 1977-87. Jesse Jones scholar, 1960-64. Mem. Assn. Computing Machinery, IEEE. Home and Office: Shepard Computing Enterprises, 374 Philip Pl, Ancaster, ON Canada L9G 3G8

SHEPHARD, ROBERT ADRIAN, pharmacologist, lecturer; b. Ipswich, Suffolk, Eng., Nov. 12, 1955; s. Basil Robert and Doreen (Wilson) S.; m. Shan Thomas, Aug. 23, 1980. BS in Pharmacology, U. Leeds, Eng., 1976; MS in Psychology, U. Birmingham, Eng., 1978, PhD in Psychology, 1980. Lectr. Ulster Poly. U., Belfast, Ireland, 1980-84; lectr. psychology U. Ulster, Belfast, 1984—. Contbr. articles to profl. jours. Mem. Brit. Psychol. Soc. Office: U Ulster, Shore Rd, Belfast BT37 0Q1B, Northern Ireland

SHEPHERD, JOHN CALVIN, lawyer; b. Memphis, June 27, 1925; s. Calvin and Beatrice (Newton) S.; m. Bernice Hines, Sept. 4, 1948; children: J. Michael, William N. Student, Ill. Coll., 1946-48, LLD (hon.), 1979; JD, St. Louis U., 1951; LLD (hon.), No. Ohio U., 1984. Bar: Mo. 1951, Ill. 1962. Assoc. Sievers, Reagan & Schwartz, St. Louis, 1951-53, Haley & Frederickson, St. Louis, 1953-54; ptnr. Evans & Dixon, St. Louis, 1955-70, Coburn, Croft, Shepherd & Herzog, St. Louis, 1970-79; chmn. bd., chief exec. officer Shepherd, Sandberg & Phoenix P.C., St. Louis, 1979—; chmn. Gov.'s Commn. on Liability Ins., State of Mo., 1986-87. Chmn. bd. overseers Hoover Instn., Stanford, Calif., 1986—; bd. dirs. Mcpl. Theatre Assn. St. Louis, Barnes Hosp., St. Louis. Served with USMC, 1943-46, PTO. Recipient Disting. Alumnus award Ill. Coll., 1965, Alumni Merit award St. Louis U., 1970; named Hon. Master Bench, Middle Temple. Fellow Am. Bar Found., Am. Coll. Trial Lawyers, Internat. Acad. Trial Lawyers; mem. ABA (state del. to Ho. Dels. 1968-73, assembly del. 1974-78, chmn. Ho. Dels. 1978-80, pres. 1984-85), Bar Assn. St. Louis (pres. 1963), Internat. Soc. Barristers, Am. Law Inst., Law Soc. Eng. and Wales (hon.), Phi Beta Kappa. Republican. Roman Catholic. Clubs: Met. (Washington); Noonday, St. Louis, Mo. Athletic, Bellerive Country (St. Louis). Lodge: Knights of Malta. Home: 20 Bellerive Country Club Grounds Saint Louis MO 63141 Office: Shepherd Sandberg & Phoenix PC 1 City Centre Suite 1500 Saint Louis MO 63101

SHEPHERD, JOHN MICHAEL, lawyer; b. St. Louis, Aug. 1, 1955; s. John Calvin and Bernice Florence (Hines) S.; m. Deborah Tremaine Fenton, Oct. 10, 1981; 1 child, Elizabeth White. BA, Stanford U., 1977; JD, U. Mich., 1980. Bar: Calif. 1981, U.S. Dist Ct. (no. dist.) Calif. 1981. Assoc. McCutchen, Doyle, Brown & Enersen, San Francisco, 1980-82; spl. asst. to asst. atty. gen. U.S. Dept. Justice, Washington, 1982-84, dep. asst. atty gen., 1984-86; assoc. counsel to The President The White House, Washington, 1986-87; sr. dep. comptroller of the currency Dept. Treasury, Washington, 1987—. Asst. dir. policy Reagan-Bush Presdl. Transition Team, Washington, 1980-81; bd. dirs. Reagan Dep. Asst. Secs., Washington, 1985—, Am. Judicature Soc., 1987—. Named one of Outstanding Young Men Am., U.S. Jaycees, 1984; Wardack Research fellow Washington U., 1976. Mem. ABA (council internat. law and practice sect. 1984-86, banking law com. of bus. law sect. 1983—, standing com. on law and nat. security 1984—, chmn. internat. consumer fin. transactions com.), Bar Assn. D.C. (internat. law com.), Am. Judicature Soc. (1987—). Club: University (N.Y.). Home: 5318 Blackstone Rd Bethesda MD 20816 Office: Office Comptroller of Currency 490 L'enfant Plaza SW Washington DC 20219

SHEPHERD, JUDY CARLILE, retired government and communication official; b. Kansas City, Mo.; d. John Mercer and Mary Almeda (Chapin) Ellis; student Okla. State U., Tulsa U.; B.A., Am. U., Washington, 1960; m. Joseph Elbert Shepherd; 1 son from previous marriage, John Philip Carlile. Chief probation officer Tulsa County Ct., 1947-50; real estate broker United Farm Agy., 1952-58; bldg. fund campaign mgr. AAUW, Washington, 1958-59; govt. and public relations ofcl. Nat. Counsel Assos., Washington, 1959-61; congressional liaison Dept. Agr., Washington, 1961-65; public info. officer OEO, 1965-70, spl. asst. to dep. dir. ops. Head Start, elderly, Indian and migrant programs, 1970-73; dir. public relations Nat. Assn. Social Workers, Washington, 1973-74; social sci. analyst Congressional Research Service, Library Congress, Washington, 1976-85. Author: The Statutory History of the United States Capitol Police Force, 6 vols., 1985. Pres. bd. govs. Agr. Symphony Orch., 1961-64; bd. dirs. ARC, Boy Scouts Am., 1948-50; bd. dirs. Little Theatre, 1956-57. Recipient 1st place Fed. Editors Blue Pencil award, 1967; cert. humanist counselor. Mem. Nat. Press Club, Public Relations Soc. Am., Nat. Assn. Govt. Communicators, Am. Humanist Assn., Assn. Humanistic Psychology, Am. U. Alumni Assn., Okla. State Soc., Mo. State Soc., Ark. State Soc., Library Congress Profl. Assn., Humanist Assn. Nat. Capital Area (pres. 1977-78), Nat. Congress Am. Indians, DAR, Am. Soc. Access Profls. (charter). Club: Woman's Nat Democratic. Coordinator, Am. Discovers Indian Art exhibit, Smithsonian Instn., 1967.

SHEPHERD, MARK, JR., retired electronics company executive; b. Dallas, Jan. 18, 1923; s. Mark and Louisa Florence (Daniell) S.; m. Mary Alice Murchland, Dec. 21, 1945; children: Debra Aline (Mrs. Rowland K. Robinson), MaryKay Theresa, Marc Blaine. B.S. in Elec. Engring, So. Meth. U., 1942; M.S. in Elec. Engring, U. Ill., at Urbana, 1947. Registered profl. engr., Tex. With Gen. Elec. Co., 1942-43, Farnsworth TV and Radio Corp., 1947-48; with Tex. Instruments, Dallas, 1948—, v.p., gen. mgr. semicondr.-components div., 1955-61, exec. v.p., chief operating officer, 1961-66, pres., chief operating officer, 1967-69, pres., chief exec. officer, 1969-76, chmn. bd. dirs., chief exec. officer, 1976-84, chmn. bd. dirs., chief corp. officer, 1984-85, chmn., 1985-88, also bd. dirs.; bd. dirs. First RepublicBank Corp., USX Corp.; mem. internat. council Morgan Guaranty Trust Co.; mem. adv. com. for trade negotiations Office U.S. Trade Reps. Mem. U.S.-Japan Bus. Council; U.S. Korea Bus. Council, trustee So. Meth. U.; hon. trustee Com. for Econ. Devel., Am. Enterprise Inst. Pub. Policy Research; councillor Conf. Bd.; mem. Bus. Council, Dallas Citizens Council. Served to lt. (j.g.) USNR, 1943-46. Fellow IEEE; mem. Soc. Exploration Geophysicists, Council on Fgn. Relations, Nat. Acad. Engring., Sigma Xi, Eta Kappa Nu. Office: Tex Instruments PO Box 655474 MS 236 Dallas TX 75265

SHEPHERD, MARY PATRICIA, cardiothoracic surgeon; b. London, July 4, 1933; d. George Raymond and Florence May (Savile) S. M.B.B.S., Royal Free Hosp. Sch. Medicine, London, 1957; 1947; M.S., London U., 1972. Preregistration appointments Royal Free Hosp. and assoc. hosps., London, 1957-58, registrar in gen. surgery Royal Free Hosp., 1960-63; registrar, then sr. registrar in cardiothoracic surgery Harefield Hosp., Middlesex, Eng., 1963-68; cons. cardiothoracic surgeon, 1968-81, sr. cons., 1981-85. Author: The Heart of Harefield, 1990; contbr. articles, chpts. to profl. publs. Mem. bd. visitors Her Majesty's Prisons, Wormwood Scubs Prison, London, 1977-83; trustee Dorothea Kerslake Charitable Found., London, 1979-85. Julia Ann Hornblower Cock grad. scholar Royal Free Hosp., 1957; research fellow Hosp. for Sick Children, Toronto, Ont., Can., 1966-67. Fellow Royal Coll. Surgeons (Edinburgh), Royal Coll. Surgeons (Eng.) (Hunterian prof. 1969); mem. Brit. Med. Assn., Royal Free Hosp. Sch. Med., Soc. Thoracic and Cardiovascular Surgeons Eng. and Ireland, Brit. Thoracic Soc., Med. Women's Fedn., Old Student's Assn. Royal Free Hosp. (past sec.), Nat. Council Women. Mem. Ch. of England. Avocations: philately; writing; travel; painting. also: 33 Sleeper St Apt 107 Boston MA 02210

SHEPHERD, ROY JAMES, III, credit card company sales executive; b. Jacksonville, Fla., Dec. 27, 1942; s. Roy James, II and Willie Martha Marion (Griffith) S.; student Ohio State U., 1960, Rio Grande (Ohio) Coll., 1962-63; m. Patricia Ann Taggart, Nov. 1, 1980. Area mgr. Massey Ferguson, Ltd., Lansing, Mich., 1970-72; ordinary agt. Prudential Ins. Co., Columbus, Ohio, 1972-76, brokerage mgr., 1976-77; ptnr. Davis Agy., Pomeroy, Ohio, 1977-78; owner, operator Arlington Ins. Service, Columbus, 1978-84; owner, prin. Canterbury Fin. Strategies, 1985-86; assoc. dir. Ward, Dreshman & Reinhardt, Inc., 1987-88; salesman, Am. Express Co., 1988—; cons. Minority Devel. Corp., Inc.; composer gospel music. Served with Army N.G., 1964-85. Decorated Army Commendation Medal; recipient DeMolay Cross of Honor; named Outstanding Sales Underwriter, also recipient Nat. Quality award Nat. Assn. Life Underwriters; named hon. Ky. Coll. Mem. Profl. Ins. Agts. Assn. Am., Nat. Assn. Life Underwriters, Ins. Econs. Soc. Am., Enlisted Assn. Army N.G., Amvets. Episcopalian. Clubs: Masons, Odd Fellows. Playwright: (with others) Life of Christ, 1982. Home: 5687 Brinkley Ct Columbus OH 43235 Office: American Express Co PO Box 20204 Columbus OH 43220

SHEPHERDSON, JOHN CEDRIC, mathematics educator; b. Huddersfield, Yorkshire, Eng., June 7, 1926; s. Arnold and Elsie (Aspinall) S.; m. Margaret Smith, July 5, 1957; children: David, Jane, Judith. BA, U. Cambridge, Eng., 1946, MA, 1951, ScD, 1981. Asst. experimental officer Nat. Phys. Lab., London, Eng., 1946; asst. lectr. U. Bristol, Eng., 1946-49, lectr., 1949-55, reader, 1955-63, prof. pure math., 1966-77, H.O. Wills prof. math., 1977—. Contbr. articles to profl. jours.; mem. editorial bd. Zeitschrift für Math. Logik, 1955—, Jour. Computer and Systems Scis., 1966—, Archiv für Math Logik, 1972-87. Fellow Inst. Math. and Its Applications; mem. London Math. Soc. (mem. editorial bd., 1970-77), Am. Math. Soc., Assn. for Symbolic Logic, Math. Assn. Mem. Social Democratic Party. Clubs: Bristol Corinthian Yacht (Somerset), Avon Boardsailing (Bristol), Fell and Rock Climbing. Home: Oakhurst North Rd, Leigh Woods, Bristol, Avon BS8 3PN, England Office: Bristol U, Sch Math, Bristol BS8 1TW, England

SHEPLEY, LEWIS CLARK, telecommunications consultant, telephone engineer; b. Mpls., Dec. 16, 1921; s. Lewis Cass and Mary Josephine (Clark) S.; m. Doris M. Brun, Apr. 20, 1946; children—Nancy L. Price, L. John, Joel C., Robin Paul, Doreen C. Craig, David M. B.A. in Speech, Hamline U., 1942, Telephone engr. N.W. Bell Telephone Co., St. Paul, Pine City, Mpls. and St. Cloud, Minn., 1946-59, U.S. Air Force, Midwest City, Okla., 1959-65, NASA Kennedy Space Ctr., Fla., 1965-67; communciation specialist Rural Elec. Adminstrn., Washington, 1979-82; telecommunications cons. U.S. Army Corps Engrs., Dhahran, Saudi Arabia, 1982-84; telephone engr. Aramco, Abqaiq, Saudi Arabia, 1984-85; adminstr. pension and welfare funds Motion Picture Machine Operators Union local 224, Washington, 1978-82. Served to lt. comdr. USNR, 1950-52, Korea, 1942-46, P.T.O. Mem. Nat. Assn. Radio Telecommunications Engrs. (charter), Armed Forces Communications Electronics Assn., Soc. Am. Mil. Engrs., Am. Legion. Republican. Mormon. Avocations: genealogy; model railroads; photography. Home: 6532 Cedar Ln Falls Church VA 22042

SHEPPARD, POSY (MRS. JOHN WADE SHEPPARD), social worker; b. New Haven, Aug. 23, 1916; d. John Day and Rose Marie (Herrick) Jackson; m. John W. Sheppard, May 16, 1936; children—Sandra S. (Mrs. Allan Gray Rodgers), Gail G. (Mrs. S. Stinor Gimbel), Lynn S. (Mrs. William Muir Manger), John W. Student, Vassar Coll., 1938. Vol. field cons. Conn. A.R.C., 1955-60; vice chmn. bd. govs. Am. Nat. Red Cross, 1962-66; rep. League Red Cross Socs. to UN, 1957-80, Am. Nat. Red Cross to com. internat. social welfare Nat. Social Welfare Assembly, 1957-61; chmn. Non-Govtl. Orgn. Com. for UNICEF, 1963-64, 71-73; chmn. Non-Govtl. Orgn. Com. exec. com. for Office Pub. Information, UN, 1964-66; pres. conf. non-govtl. orgns. in consultative status with UN Econ. and Social Council, 1966-69. Nat. Inst. Social Scis., Am. Soc. Polit. and Social Sci., Soc. Internat. Devel., Nat. Soc. Colonial Dames, Descs. Signers of Declaration Independence. Clubs: Field of Greenwich, Round Hill. Home: 535 Lake Ave Greenwich CT 06830

SHEPPARD, RONALD JOHN, business education administrator; b. New Rochelle, N.Y., Apr. 13, 1939; s. Lester John and Louise Marie (Cox) S.; B.S., Rensselaer Poly. Inst., 1961; M.S., Howard U., 1962, Ph.D., 1965; M.B.A., Rochester Inst. Tech., 1974; student Detroit Coll. Law; m. Shirly Christine Saddler, June 8, 1963; children—Jeffrey Brandon, Mark Justin. Systems analyst RCA, Moorestown, N.J., 1965-66; mgr. strategic planning Booz Allen Hamilton, Inc., Washington, 1966-69; program mgr. space research Teledyne Brown Engring. Co., Huntsville, Ala., 1969-71; planning mgr., asst. group program mgr. Xerox Corp., Rochester, N.Y., 1971-77; later with Gen. Motors Corp., Warren, Mich.; now dir. Ctr. Bus. and Industry, U. Toledo; cons. Rensselaer Human Dimensions Center, 1975—; coll. student adviser Keuka Coll., 1975--; vis. faculty So. U., 1975, Empire State Coll., 1975-76, Rochester Inst. Tech., 1974-75. Pres., Rochester Montessori Sch. Bd., 1975-76; bd. dirs. Easter Seal Soc., Rochester Better Contractors Bur. NDEA fellow, 1962-64, Howard U. Trustee fellow, 1964-65, NATO fellow U. Newcastle, Eng., 1964; recipient K.B. Weissman Meml. Found. Human Relations award, 1957. Mem. Am. Mktg. Assn., Assn. Masters in Bus. Adminstrn. Execs., Nat. Black Masters Bus. Adminstrn. Assn. Democrat. Methodist. Clubs: Rensselaer Alumni, Rotary, Univ. of Rochester, Cornell of N.Y., Shriners. Home: 2401 Parliament Sq Toledo OH 43617 Office: U Toledo Ctr Bus and Industry 2801 W Bancroft St Toledo OH 43606

SHEPPARD, WALTER LEE, JR., chemical engineer, consultant; b. Phila., June 23, 1911; s. Walter Lee and Martha Houston (Evans) S.; m. Dorothy Virginia Cosby Vanderslice, Oct. 17, 1942 (div. Mar. 1947); m., Boudinot Atterbury Oberge Kendall, Mar. 24, 1953; stepchildren: Charles H. Kendall Jr., John Atterbury Kendall; BChem, Cornell U., 1932; MS, U. Pa., 1933. Control chemist various cos., 1933-35; advt. writer N.W. Ayer & Son, 1936-37; asst. to editor The Houghton Line, 1937-38; salesman Atlas Mineral Products, 1938-47; plant mgr., cons. engr. Tanks & Linings, Ltd., Droitwich, Eng., 1948-49; sales engr., dist. mgr. ElectroChem. Engring. & Mfg., and successor cos., 1949-68; field sales mgr. Corrosion Engring. div. Pennwalt Corp., Phila., 1968-76; pres. C.C.R.M., Inc.; cons. on chemically resistant masonry, 1976—; profl. genealogist, 1936—; ordained deacon Liberal Catholic Ch., 1954, priest, 1955. Dir. displaced persons camps UNRRA, also staff Chief of Mission, Vienna, Austria, 1945-46. Founding trustee Bd. Cert. Genealogists, 1965-82, pres., 1969-78, chmn., 1978-79. Served to maj. U.S. Army, 1941-45; lt. col. Res. (ret.). Registered profl. engr., Del., Calif.; diplomate Am. Acad. Environ. Engrs. Fellow Am. Soc. Genealogists (sec. 1958-61, 66-67, v.p. 1967-70, pres. 1970-73), Nat. Geneal. Soc., Pa. Geneal. Soc.; mem. Welcome Soc. (pres. 1969-76), Illegitimate Sons and Daus. of Kings and Queens of Britain (founder, sec. 1950-68, pres. 1968-88), Flagon and Trencher Soc. (co-founder, pres. 1967-73), Nat. Assn. Corrosion Engrs. (cert. competence in corrosion engring.; chmn. Phila. sect. 1962), Nat. Soc. Profl. Engrs., ASTM (membership sec. 1975-83, C-3 com.), Am. Acad. Environ. Engrs., New Eng. Historic Geneal. Soc., Nat. Geneal. Soc. (contbg. editor quar.), Geneal. Soc. Pa., Soc. Genealogists (London), Yorkshire Archeol. Soc., Savoy Co., Gilbert and Sullivan Soc. (founder, pres. Phila. br. 1957-63), Phi Kappa Psi (nat. v.p. 1964-68, pres. 1968-70), Sovereign Order St. John of Jerusalem, Mil. Order Fgn. Wars, Mayflower Descs., Order of Three Crusades, Order of the Crown of Charlemagne in Am., Alpha Chi Sigma. Author: Ancestry and Descendants of Thomas Stickney Evans and Sarah Ann Fifield, his wife, 1940; Chemically Resistant Masonry, 1977, 2d edit., 1982; Ancestry of Edward Carleton and Ellen Newton, His Wife, 1978; author, editor: Corrosion and Chemical Resistant Masonry Materials Handbook, 1986; editor: Ships and Passengers; Ancestral Roots of 60 New England Colonists, 6th edit., 1988; Magna Charta Sureties, 3d edit., 1979; contbg. editor Am. Genealogist, 1941-79, Nat. Geneal. Quar., 1961—; mem. publs. com. Pa. Geneal. Mag., 1960-76; contbr. articles on corrosion resistant masonry constrn. to profl. jours. Home and Office: 923 Old Manoa Rd Havertown PA 19083

SHEPPERD, JOHN BEN, insurance, banking and petroleum consultant; b. Gladewater, Tex., Oct. 19, 1915; s. Alfred Fulton and Berthal (Phillips) S.; m. Mamie Strieber, Oct. 6, 1938; children: Alfred Lewis, John Ben, Marianne and Suzanne (twins). LL.B., U. Tex., 1941; LL.D. (hon.), North Tex. State Coll., 1951, Chapman Christian Coll., Los Angeles, 1953, Southwestern U., 1955. Bar: Tex. 1941. Sec. State of Tex., 1950-52, atty. gen., 1952-56; ptnr. Shepperd and Meacham, Pub. Relations Cons., Shepperd and Rodman, Attys.; dir. Tex. Commerce Bank-Odessa, First State Bank-Gladewater, Blue Cross-Blue Shield, Dallas. Author: The President's Guide to Club and Organizations Management and Meetings. Former mem., chmn. Tex. Econ. Devel. Commn., Tex. Civil War Centennial Commn., Tex. Hist. Commn., Tex. Arts Commn.; mem. Tex. State Library and Archives Commn. Mem. Nat. Assn. Attys. Gen. (pres. 1956), W. Tex. C. of C. (pres. 1966), Tex. Jaycees (pres. 1941), U.S. Jaycees (pres. 1947). Democrat. Mem. Christian Ch. Home: 3107 Windsor Dr Odessa TX 79762 Office: 1208 Tex Commerce Bank Bldg Odessa TX 79761

SHEPPERSON, GEORGE ALBERT, historian, educator; b. Peterborough, East Anglia, Eng., Jan. 7, 1922; s. Albert Edward and Bertha Agnes (Jennings) S.; m. Joyce Irene Cooper, Dec. 31, 1952; 1 child, Janet Catherine. BA, U. Cambridge, Eng., 1942, MA, 1947; D. (hon.), U. York, Eng., 1987. Cert. edn., 1948. Various teaching positions U.S., Uganda, Can., etc., 1948-69; prof. commonwealth and Am. history U. Edinburgh, Scotland, 1963-86, prof. emeritus, 1987—; vis. scholar Harvard U., 1986-87. Author: David Livingstone and the Rovuma, 1964; co-author: (with Thomas Price) Independent African, 1958; co-editor (with John Hargreaves) Oxford Studies in African Affairs, 1969-85; contbr. articles to profl. jours. Mem. governing body Scottish Nat. Meml. to David Livingstone, Blantyre, 1980-88. Served to capt. British Army, 1942-46. Mem. Marshall Aid Commemorative Commn., Commonwealth Inst. Scotland (gov. 1973—), St. Andrew Soc. Edinburgh (pres. 1970-73), British Assn. Am. Studies (pres. 1971-78), British Assn. Can. Studies (v.p. 1977), African Studies Assn. of U.K. Episcopalian. Home: 23 Ormidale Terr, Edinburgh EH12 6D4, Scotland

SHER, ANWER QAYUM, investment banker; b. Quetta, Pakistan, Aug. 8, 1954; s. Abdul Qayum and Amita Sher; m. Arifa Qayum, Jan. 7, 1979; children: Aadil, Ali. BA in Polit. Sci., Punjab U., 1974; MSc in Internat. Relations, Quaid-E. Azam U., 1976. Research assoc. Inst. Strategic Studies, Pakistan, 1975-76; officer Bank Credit and Commerce Internat., Lahore, Pakistan and Abu Dhabi, United Arab Emirates, 1976-83; sr. officer mktg. Bank Credit and Commerce (Emirates), Abu Dhabi, 1983-84, mgr. main br., 1984-85, mgr. corp. bus. and treasury, 1985—. Author: Handbook of Import and Export, 1981, Capital Markets Report weekly. Vol. Internat. Com. Red Cross, Pakistan, 1972. Office: Bank Credit & Commerce, Corniche BCC Bldg Box 3865, Abu Dhabi United Arab Emirates

SHERANI, RAIS-UD-DIN KHAN, management and engineering consultant; b. Bareilly, Pakistan, Nov. 29, 1921; d. Muhammad Nazir and Fatima Begum (Fatima) Khan; m. Rehana Sherani, Dec. 25, 1942; children: Tasnim, Mrs. Shaista Nizam Quraishi, Mrs. Yasmin Nafis Hashmi, Mrs. Shaheen Nusrat, Salim, Farzana Rashid. BA, Bareilly Coll., 1944; MA, Agra U., India, 1946. Diplomate Pakistan Inst. Engrs. Liaison officer Indian Army, New Delhi, 1944-47; staff officer Pakistan Army, Rawalpindi, 1947-49; mem. staff and command Armoured Corps Pakistan Army, Risalpur, Nowshera, 1949-57, Cantonments, 1961-62; gen. staff officer Pakistan Army, Karachi, Pakistan, 1957-61; ret. Pakistan Army, 1961; gen. mgr. Pakistan Internat. Airlines, Karachi, 1962-81; pres. SAL Internat. Mgmt. and Engring. Cons., Karachi, 1981—; exec. cons. Aviation Mgmt. Adv. System, Karachi, 1981—. Author: The Universal Model of Management; In Search of Peace; America-The Hope of Mankind; Intensive Management Development Plans; A Systematic Approach to Effective Rostering and Scheduling; Management by Objective and Appraisal by Results; Techniques of Problem Solving and Decision Making; Creative Thinking; Job Analysis and Job Evaluation; Effective Planning for Successful Management; Value Analysis/Value Engineering/Value Management; Work Simplification and Methods Engineering for Greater Profitability; The Universal Principles of States and Administrative Science; Financial Management for All; contbr. articles to profl. jours. Pres. Pakistan Youth Assn., 1947; chmn. Internat. Quranic Research Assn., 1987. Decorated War medal (India); Independence medal (Pakistan). Fellow Brit. Inst. Mgmt.; mem. Chartered Inst. Transport London, Soc. Am. Value Engrs., Am. Mgmt. Assn., Inst. Indsl. Engrs. U.S.A., Nat. Assn. Cons. of Pakistan (governing party mem.). Moslem. Clubs: Services, Karachi; Rawalpindi. Lodge: Rotary. Home: 68-F/2 PECHS, Karachi 2916, Pakistan Office: SAL Internat Airlines, PO Box 3188, Karachi 029, Pakistan

SHERAR, JOSEPH WILLIAM, insurance broker, investor; b. Fresno, Calif., Sept. 27, 1930; s. Joseph William Garland and Verna Irene (Kneeland) S.; BS, U.S. Naval Acad., 1952; JD, Loyola U., New Orleans, 1965; m. Nancy Barr Gooch, Nov. 6, 1954 (div. 1988); children: Deirdra Clarisse, William Gooch, David Kneeland (dec.), Lynne Fox. Commd. ensign USN, 1952, advanced through grades to lt., 1958; destoyer officer, 1952-53; naval aviator, 1954; landing signal officer, 1956-57; aide to Vice Adm. James Thatch, Com Huk Lant, 1958; flight instr. Saufley Naval Air Sta., Pensacola, Fla., 1958; ret., 1965; trainee Marine Office Am., 1958-59; marine broker Hardin and Ferguson, 1959-61; radar instr. U.S. Maritime Adminstrn., New Orleans, 1961-62; chmn. Ingram-Armistead & Co. SPA, Milan, Italy, 1976-78, Corroon & Black, Inc., New Orleans, 1979; pres. Sherar, Cook & Gardner, Inc., Metairie, La., 1979-88, Sailing Sales Inc., New Orleans, 1972-84, Cathay Trading Corp., 1981-87, Altair Ins. Co. Ltd., 1981-84; mng. partner Severn Assos., 1981-88; lectr. and seminar chmn. in field; underwriting mem. Lloyd's of London. Edn. chmn. YPO, Rio de Janeiro, Brazil; trustee U.S. Naval Acad. Sailing Found. Inc.; chmn. Fales adv. com. U.S. Naval Acad.; chmn. aviation com. C. of C. New Orleans, 1975-79. Mem. Young Pres.'s Orgn. (chmn. La. chpt. 1978-79), U.S. Naval Acad. Alumni Assn. (pres. New Orleans chpt. 1963), SAR, Colonial Wars Soc. La. (treas. 1978-79), Delta Theta Phi (life mem.). Clubs: Cruising Am., Royal Ocean Racing London (life), Naval Acad. Sailing Squadron (life), Storm Trysail, N.Y. Yacht, So. Yacht, Lloyd's Yacht (London); The Corinthians, Essex (pres. 1971-72), Bienville. Contbr. articles to profl. jours. Office: 2325 Severn Ave Metairie LA 70001

SHERBELL, RHODA, painter, sculptor; b. Bklyn.; d. Alexander and Syd (Steinberg) S.; m. Mervin Honig, Apr. 28, 1956; 1 dau., Susan. Student, Art Students League, 1950-53, Bklyn. Mus. Art Sch., 1959-61; also; pvt. study art, Italy, France, Eng., 1956. Cons., council mem. Emily Lowe Gallery, Hofstra U., Hempstead, N.Y., 1978, pres., 1980-81, life mem. bd. friends, pres. bd. trustees; tchr. Mus. Modern Art, Nat. Acad. Design, Art Students League, N.Y.C.; instr. Mus. Modern Art, N.Y.C., 1956, Art Students League, N.Y.C., 1988, Nat. Acad. Design Art Sch., N.Y.C., 1988. Exhibited one-woman shows Country Art Gallery, Locust Valley, N.Y., Bklyn. Mus. Art Sch., 1961, Adelphi Coll., A.C.A. Galleries, N.Y.C., 1967, Capricorn Galleries, Rehn Gallery, Washington, 1968, Gallery Modern Art, N.Y.C., 1969, Morris (N.J.) Mus. Arts and Scis., 1980, Bergen Mus. Arts and Scis., N.J., 1984, William Benton Mus., Conn., 1985, Palace Theatre of the Arts, Stamford, Conn., Bronx Mus. Arts, 1986; one-woman retrospective at N.Y. Cultural Ctr., 1970, Nat. Arts Collection, Washington, 1970, Montclair Mus. of Art, 1976, Nat. Art Mus. of Sport, 1977, Jewish Mus. of N.Y.C., 1980, Black History Mus., 1981, Queens Mus., 1981, 82, Nat. Portrait Gallery, Washington, 1981, 82, Bronx Mus., N.Y., Bklyn. Mus., Mus. Modern Art, N.Y.C., Country Art Gallery, Port Washington Library, Nat. Mus. Am. Art, The Smithsonian Instn., 1982, Nat. Acad. Design, N.Y.C., 1984, Castle Gallery Mus., N.Y.C., 1987, Emily Lowe Mus., N.Y.C., 1987; exhibited group shows Downtown Gallery, N.Y.C., Maynard Walker Gallery, N.Y.C., F.A.R. Gallery, N.Y.C., Provincetown Art Assn., Detroit Inst. Art, Pa. Acad. Fine Arts, Bklyn. and L.I. Artists Show, Old Westbury Gardens Small Sculpture Show, Audubon Artists, NAD, Allied Artists, Heckscher Mus., Nat. Art Mus. Sports, Mus. Arts and Scis., Los Angeles, Am. Mus. Natural History, Post of History Mus., 1987, Caslte Gallery Mus., N.Y.C., 1987, Emiloy Lowe Mus., N.Y., 1987, Bronx Mus. Arts, 1987, Chgo. Hist. Soc., Mus. of Modern Art, N.Y.C., 1988, Sands Point Mus., L.I., NAD, others; represented permanent collections, Stony Brook Hall of Fame, William Benton Mus. Art, Colby Coll. Mus., Oklahoma City Mus., Montclair (N.J.) Mus., Schonberg Library Black Studies, N.Y.C., Albany State Mus., Hofstra U., Bklyn. Mus., Colby Coll. Mus., Nat. Arts Collection, Nat. Portrait Gallery, Smithsonian Instn., Baseball Hall of Fame Cooperstown, N.Y., Nassau Community Coll., Hofstra U. Emily Lowe Gallery, Art Students League, Jewish Mus., Queens Mus., Black History Mus., Nassau County Mus., Stamford Mus. Art and Nature Ctr., Jericho Pub. Library, N.Y., African-Am. Mus., Hempstead, N.Y., 1988; also pvt. collections, TV shows, ABC, 1968, 81; ednl. TV spl. Rhoda Sherbell-Woman in Bronze, 1977; important works include Seated Ballerina, portraits of Aaron Copland, Eleanor Roosevelt, Variations on a Theme (30 works of collaged sculpture), 1982-86; appeared several TV shows; guest various radio programs; contbr. articles to newspapers, popular mags. and art jours. Council mem. Nassau County Mus., 1978, trustee, 1st v.p. council; asso. trustee Nat. Art Mus. of Sports, Inc., 1975—; cons., community liaison WNET Channel 13, cultural coordinator, 1975-83; host radio show Not for Artists Only, 1978-79; trustee Women's Boxing Fedn., 1978. Recipient Am. Acad. Arts, Letters and Nat. Inst. Arts and Letters grant, 1960; Louis Comfort Tiffany Found. grant, 1962; Alfred G. B. Steel Meml. award Pa. Acad. Fine Arts, 1963-64; Helen F. Barnett prize NAD, 1965; Jersey City Mus. prize for sculpture, 1961; 1st prize sculpture Locust Valley Art Show, 1966, 67; Ann. Sculpture prize Jersey City Mus.; Bank for Savs. 1st prize in sculpture, 1950; Ford Found. purchase award, 1964; MacDowell Colony fellow, 1976; 2 top sculpture awards Mainstreams 77; Cert. of Merit Salmagundi Club, 1978; prize for sculpture, 1980, 81; award for sculpture Knickerbocker Artists, 1980, 81; top prize for sculpture Hudson Valley Art Assn.,1981; Sawyer award NAD, 1985; Gold medal of honor Audubon Artists, 1985; Ford Found. grantee, 1964. Fellow Nat. Sculpture Soc.; mem. Nat. Arts Club, Sculpture Guild (dir.), Nat. Assn. Women Artists (Jeffery Childs Willis Meml. prize 1978), Allied Artists Soc. (dir.), Audubon Artists (Greta Kempton Walker prize 1965, Chaim Gross award, award for disting. contbr. to orgn. 1979, 80, Louis Weskeem award; dir.), Woman's Caucus for Art, Coll. Art Assn., Am. Inst. Conservation Historic and Artistic Works, N.Y. Soc. Women Artists, Artists Equity Assn. N.Y., Nat. Sculpture Soc., Internat. Platform Assn., Profl. Artists Guild L.I., Painters and Sculptors Soc. N.J. (Bertrum R. Hulmes Meml. award), Am. Watercolor Soc. (award for disting. contbn. to orgn.), Catharine Lorillard Wolfe Club (hon. mention 1968). Home: 64 Jane Ct Westbury NY 11590

SHERBURNE, PAUL VERNON, association executive; b. Menomonie, Wis., Jan. 2, 1948; s. Marvin Dale and Irene Ann (Steinbring) S.; m. Patricia Jo Armstrong, Sept. 23, 1977; children: Andrew Armstrong, Nina Armstrong. B.A., Macalester Coll., 1974; cert. of completion, Humphrey Inst., U. Minn., 1982. Photographer St. Paul, 1972-76; program dir. World Press Inst., St. Paul, 1976-80, exec. dir., 1980-87; founder, pub., Topic mag., 1982-85; pres. The Travelers' Soc., 1987—. Home: 1283 Dayton Ave Saint Paul MN 55104 Office: The Travelers' Socute PO Box 2846 Loop Sta Minneapolis MN 55402

SHERIDAN, ALFRED PATRICK STANISLAUS, development corporation executive; b. Barnsley, Yorkshire, Eng., Dec. 5, 1926; arrived in Zimbabwe, 1980; s. John Brady and Eva (Moran) S.; m. Ellerie Priscilla Aldridge, Apr. 19, 1949 (dec. Apr. 1968); children: Maj Anthony John, Richard Dermuid, Philippa Jane; m. Penelope Ann Wallis, May 29, 1969; children: Simon Bennet, Michael Patrick. BA, Trinity Coll., Dublin, Ireland, 1951; LLB, Kings Inn, Dublin, 1951; postgrad., London Sch. Econs., Sch. Oriental and African Studies, 1951-52. Dist. commr. Uganda Civil Service, 1952-63; farmer Ireland, 1963-69; adminstr. Royal Instn. Chartered Surveyors in Ireland, Dublin, 1969-71; AG permanent sec., chief lands officer Kaduna Civil Service, Nigeria, 1971-79; chief exec. officer Inst. Bus. Devel., Zimbabwe, 1980-83; dep. gen. mgr. Small Enterprises Devel Co., Zimbabwe, 1984—; cons. Cath. Devel. Commn., Harare, Zimbabwe, 1983-84. Author, editor Inst. Bus. Devel. mag., 1980-83. Supr. Ind. elections, Zimbabwe, 1980; observer Commonwealth team for Uganda elections, 1980. Served to lt. inf. Indian Army, 1944-47. Recipient Independence medal Uganda, 1963, Independence medal Zimbabwe, 1980, Zimbabwe medal Eng., 1980. Clubs: New, Borrowdale Country (trustee, com.) (Harare). Office: Small Enterprises Devel Co, Angwa St, Harare Zimbabwe

SHERIDAN, BRIAN JAMES, airline executive; b. Limerick, Ireland, Feb. 29, 1944; s. James and Margaret (O'Connor) S.; m. Catherine Theresa Conway, Oct. 21, 1967; children: Edel, Aisling. Diploma in prodn. mgmt., Irish Mgmt. Inst. Asst. buyer AER Lingus, Dublin, Ireland, 1962-64, buyer, 1965-66, sr. buyer, 1967-70, materials systems analyst, 1971-73, asst. to purchasing supt., 1974-79, mgr. tech. purchasing, 1979—. Co-author, editor (booklet) A New Approach to Financing Home Mortgages, 1972. Mem. Assn. European Airlines (vice chmn. purchasing working group 1985-86, chmn. 1986—), Assn. Combined Residents Assn. (chmn. mortgages com. 1971-72). Progressive Democrats. Roman Catholic. Office: AER Lingus, Tech Purchasing, Dublin Airport Ireland

SHERIDAN, PATRICK MICHAEL, finance company executive; b. Grosse Pointe, Mich., Apr. 13, 1940; s. Paul Phillip and Frances Mary (Rohan) S.; m. Diane Lorraine Tressler, Nov. 14, 1986; children: Mary, Patrick, Kelly, Kevin, James. B.B.A., U. Notre Dame, 1962; M.B.A., U. Detroit, 1975. Acct. Peat, Marwick, Mitchell & Co., Detroit, 1962-72, audit mgr., 1969-72; exec. v.p. fin. Alexander Hamilton Life Ins. Co., Farmington, Mich., 1973-76; sr. v.p. ops. Sun Life Ins. Co. Am., Balt., 1976-78, exec. v.p., 1978-79; pres. Sun Ins. Services, Inc., 1979-81; pres., chief exec. officer Am. Health & Life Ins. Co., Balt., 1981-85; chief exec. officer Gulf Ins. Co., 1985-86; sr. v.p., chief fin. officer Comml. Credit Co., 1985-86, sr. v.p. audit, 1987; exec. v.p., chief fin. officer The Associated Group, Indpls., 1987—. Republican candidate for U.S. Congress, 1972; past pres. Charlesbrooke Community Assn.; past v.p. Jr. Achievement of Met. Balt., 1984-85; bd. dirs. Goodwill Industries of Balt., 1986; bd. govs. Served to capt. AUS, 1963-65. Recipient various Jaycee awards. Fellow Life Mgmt. Inst.; mem. Am. Mgmt. Assn. (pres.'s assn.), Am. Inst. C.P.A.s, Mich. Assn. C.P.A.s, Md. Assn. C.P.A.s, Am. Soc. C.L.U.s, U.S. Jaycees (treas. 1973-74), Mich. Jaycees (pres. 1971-72), Detroit Jaycees (pres. 1968-69), Balt. C. of C. (bd. dirs.), Mensa. Clubs: Notre Dame (Balt., Indpls.); Indpls. Athletic.

SHERIDAN, PHILIP HENRY, pediatric neurologist; b. Washington, June 29, 1950; s. Andrew James and Mildred Adele (Stohlman) S.; m. Margaret Mary Williams, Oct. 3, 1987; 1 child, Gerard Andrew. BS magna cum laude, Yale U., 1972; MD cum laude, Georgetown U., 1976. Diplomate Am. Bd. Pediatrics, Am. Bd. Psychiatry and Neurology, Am. Bd. Qualification in Electroencephalography. Resident in pediatrics Children's Hosp. Phila., 1976-79; fellow in pediatric neurology Hosp. of U. Pa., Phila., 1979-82; med. staff fellow NIH, Bethesda, Md., 1982-84, neurologist, epilepsy br. Nat. Inst. Neurol. and Communicative Disorders and Stroke, 1984—, health scientist adminstr., guest worker researcher, 1984—; cons., lectr. Nat. Naval Med. Ctr., Bethesda, 1984—; commdr. U.S. Pub. Health Service. Contbr. articles on clin. and research neurology to med. jours. Vol. neurologist Bur. Crippled Children, Fairfax, Va., 1984—. Fellow Am. Acad. Pediatrics (neurology sect.); mem. Am. Acad. Neurology, Child Neurology Soc. (ethics com.), Soc. for Neurosci., Am. Epilepsy Soc. (invited book reviewer), Alpha Omega Alpha. Roman Catholic. Current work: Understanding the neurobiological basis for and improving the clinical management of epilepsy and related paroxysmal disorders. Subspecialties: Neurology; Pediatrics. Office: NIH Fed Bldg Room 114 Bethesda MD 20892

SHERIDAN, RICHARD BERT, economics educator; b. Emporia, Kans., Feb. 10, 1918; s. Bert and Olive Nancy (Davis) S.; m. Audrey Marion Porter, Oct. 18, 1952; children—Richard David, Margaret Anne. B.S., Emporia Kans. State U., 1940; M.S., U. Kans., 1947; Ph.D., London Sch. Econs. and Polit. Sci., 1951. Instr. to assoc. prof. U. Kans., Lawrence, 1947-62, prof. econs., 1963—; external examiner U. W.I., Kingston, Jamaica, 1964-74; vis. prof. Coll. V.I., St. Thomas, 1971, U. West Indies, St. Augustine, Trinidad, 1987. Author: Economic History of South Central Kansas, 1956, Chapters in Caribbean History, 1970, Sugar and Slavery, 1974, Doctors and Slaves, 1985; contbr. articles to profl. jours; cons. editor: Jour. Caribbean History, 1971—. Served to lt. USNR, 1942-46. Royal Hist. Soc. fellow, 1988; recipient Article award N.C. Bicentennial Contest, 1976; Fulbright scholar U. W.I., 1962-63; grantee NIH, Nat. Library Medicine, 1973. Mem. Econ. History Assn., Econ. History Soc., Agrl. History Soc., Assn. Evolutionary Econs. Democrat. Congregationalist. Home: 1745 Louisana St Lawrence KS 66044 Office: U Kans Dept Econ Lawrence KS 66045

SHERIDAN, THOMAS BROWN, engineering and applied psychology educator, researcher consultant; b. Cin., Dec. 23, 1929; s. Mahlon Brinsley and Esther Anna (Brown) S.; m Rachel Briggs Rice, Aug. 1, 1953; children—Paul Rice, Richard Rice, David Rice, Margaret Lenore. B.S., Purdue U., 1951; M.S., UCLA, 1954; Sc.D., MIT, 1959. Registered profl. engr., Mass. Asst. prof. mech. engring. MIT, Cambridge, 1959-65, assoc. prof., 1965-70, prof., 1970-78, prof. engring. and applied psychology, 1978—; lectr. U. Calif.-Berkeley, Stanford U., 1968; vis. prof. U. Delft, Netherlands, 1972; chmn. com. human factors, mem. com. aircrew-vehicle interaction NRC; mem. adv. com. on applied phys., math. and biol. scis. NSF; mem. life scis. adv. com., study group on robotics, oversight com. flight telerobotic servicer NASA; mem. task force on appropriate tech. U.S. Congress Office Tech. Assessment; mem. study sect. accident prevention and injury control NIH; mem. Def. Sci. Bd. Task Force on Computers, Tng. and Gaming, Nuclear Regulatory Commn. on Nuclear SAfety Research Review Com. Co-author: Man Machine Systems, 1974; editor: (with others) Monitoring Behavior and Supervisory Control, 1976; assoc. editor Automatica, 1982—; mem. editorial adv. bd. Tech. Forecasting and Social Change, Computer Aided Design, Advanced Robotics, and Robotics and Computer Integrated Mfg. Served to 1st lt. USAF, 1951-53. Fellow IEEE (pres. Systems, Man and Cybernetics Soc. 1974-76), Human Factors Soc. (Paul M. Fitts award 1977). Democrat. Mem. United Ch. of Christ. Office: Mass Inst Tech 77 Massachusetts Ave Cambridge MA 02139

SHERIF, MAHMOUD MOHAMED, FAO official; b. Alexandria, Egypt, Feb. 25, 1930; s. Mohamed Ahmed and Atiat (El-Hussainy) S.; m. Siham Abdel-Fattah El-Amir, Aug. 3, 1933; children—Mohamed, Maha, Ahmed. B.S., Alexandria U., 1951, M.S., 1959, Ph.D., Iowa State U., 1965. Prof. agrl. econs. Alexandria U., Egypt, 1966-78; dir. projects and ops. Arab Authority for Agrl. Investment and Devel., Khartoum, Sudan, 1978-85, acting dir. fin., 1983-85; dir. Joint Econ. and Social Commn. for Western Asia, FAO Agr div., Baghdad, Iraq, 1985—. Mem. council agrl. devel. Fed. Ministry Sci. Research, Cairo, 1969-71, council for livestock research Acad. Sci. Egypt, 1970-75; mem. permanent Com. on Rice Research Cairo, 1971-75. Author: Egyptian Agriculture, 1967; Principles of Economics (Micro), 1969, Principles of Economics (Macro), 1971. Govt. Egypt. scholar, 1961-65. Mem. Assn. Egyptienne de l'Economie Politique, Statistique et Legislation, Assn. Agrl. Economists, Syndicate Agriculturists. Moslem. Club: Alexandria Sporting. Avocations: piano; painting; tennis. Home: 19 Syria St, Rushdy, Alexandria Arab Republic of Egypt Office: UN Econ Social Commn Western Asia, PO Box 27, Baghdad Iraq

SHERIF, MOSTAFA HASHEM, engineer, educator; b. Cairo, Sept. 6, 1950, came to U.S., 1975; s. Said Gabr Sherif and Fateia Draz. B.Sc., Cairo U., 1972, M.Sc., 1975; Ph.D., UCLA, 1980. Teaching and research asst. Cairo U., 1972-75; research asst. Tex. Tech. U., Lubbock, 1975-76; teaching fellow UCLA, 1978-80; sr. systems engr. Recognition Systems, Van Nuys, Calif., 1981-82; cons., Los Angeles, 1982-83; mem. tech. staff AT&T Bell Labs., Holmdel, N.J., 1983—. Contbr. numerous articles to profl. jours. Mem. IEEE , AAAS, Sigma Xi. Moslem. Current work: Software Engrs. Packet switching; computer communications; myoelectric signal processing; Box and Jenkins analysis. Home: 60 Beaumont Ct Tinton Falls NJ 07724

SHERMAN, HUNTER B., clergyman, educator; b. Long Beach, Calif., Aug. 30, 1943; s. Hunter B. and Mary Rawls (French) S.; B.A., Calif. State U., Long Beach, 1965; postgrad. Bapt. Bible Coll., 1965-66; M.Div., Talbot Theol. Sem., 1970; Ph.D., Calif. Grad. Sch. Theology, 1976; m. Louisa Ann Stahl, June 27, 1964; children—Whitnae Nicolle, Garrett Hunter. Prof., Bapt. Bible Coll., Springfield, Mo., 1970—, chmn. Bible dept., 1975-78, acad. dean, 1979-83; pastor Bellview Bapt. Ch., Springfield, 1983—. Mem. Soc. Bibl. Lit., Am. Assn. Collegiate Registrars, Am. Schs. Oriental Research, Israel Exploration Soc., Oriental Inst. U. Chgo. Author: Must Babylon Be Rebuilt, 1970; The Biblical Concept of Babylon, 1976. Recipient Audrey Talbot Meml. award Talbot Theol. Sem., 1970. Office: 628 E Kearney St Springfield MO 65802

SHERMAN, JEFFREY DENNIS, banker; b. London, July 10, 1955; s. H. Arnold Sherman and Esme Temple.; m. Margaret Ann Black, Aug. 20, 1978; 1 child, Daniel Morris. B in Commerce, U. Toronto, 1977; MBA, York U., 1983. Staff acct. Clarkson Gordon, Toronto, Ont., 1977-81; mgr. audit Clarkson Gordon, Toronto, 1981-83; corp. controller NEI Can. Ltd., Toronto, 1983-85; sr. mgr. Woods Gordon, Mergers & Acquisitions Group, Toronto, 1985-87; mgr. treasury insp. Toronto-Dominion Bank, 1987—; course dir. York U., Toronto, 1984—; lectr. Law Soc. Upper Can., 1980-87. Author: Migration-Canada, 1985; contbr. articles to profl. jours. Mem. Inst. Chartered Accts. Ont. (seminar leader), Can. Inst. Chartered Accts., Can. Tax Found.

SHERMAN, JOSEPH VINCENT, cons. economist, writer; b. Beacon, N.Y., Dec. 18, 1905; s. Joseph Francis and Catherine Adele (Killeen) S.; A.B., Columbia Coll., 1928; m. Viola Signe Maria Lidfeldt, Nov. 18, 1944. Mgr. investment dept. Nat. Newark & Essex Banking Co., Newark, 1929-36; statistician Case, Pomeroy & Co., N.Y.C., 1936-38; v.p. Econ. Analysts, Inc., N.Y., 1938-42; asso. Herbert R. Simonds, cons. engr., 1943-45. Served with AUS, 1942-43. Mem. AAAS, Am. Econ. Assn., Am. Statis. Assn. Author: Research as a Growth Factor in Industry, 1940; The New Plastics, 1945; Plastics Business, 1946; The New Fibers, 1946. Contbr. to Barron's Nat. Business and Financial Weekly and various other pubs., 1939—. Home: 160 Columbia Heights Brooklyn NY 11201 Office: 280 Broadway New York NY 10007

SHERMAN, MARTIN, entomologist; b. Newark, Nov. 21, 1920; s. Louis and Anna (Norkin) S.; m. Ruth Goldsmith, Sept. 25, 1943 (div. Nov. 1975); children: Laurel Deborah Sherman Englehart, Susan Sherman Kitakis. B.S., Rutgers U., 1941, M.S., 1943; Ph.D., Cornell U., 1948. Research fellow in entomology Rutgers U., 1941-43; research asst. Cornell U., 1945-48; entomologist Beech-Nut Packing Co., Rochester, N.Y., 1948-49; mem. faculty U. Hawaii, Honolulu, 1949—; prof. entomology U. Hawaii, 1958-86, prof. emeritus entomology, 1986—; Fulbright scholar U. Tokyo, 1956-57, Royal Vet. and Agrl. Coll. of Denmark, 1966; vis. prof. Rutgers U., 1973. Editorial bd.: Pacific Sci, 1962-66, Jour. Med. Entomology, 1968-72. Served to 1st lt. USAAF, 1943-45. Fellow Am. Inst. Chemists; mem. Entomol. Soc. Am. (gov. bd. 1974-77, pres. Pacific br. 1970), Am. Chem. Soc., Soc. Toxicology, Soc. Environ. Toxicology and Chemistry, Am. Registry Profl. Entomologists, Japanese Soc. Applied Entomology and Zoology, Hawaiian Entomology Soc. (pres. 1969-70), Internat. Soc. for Study Xenobiotics, Sigma Xi, Delta Phi Alpha, Phi Kappa Phi, Gamma Sigma Delta. Club: Torch. Address: 1121 Koloa St Honolulu HI 96816

SHERMAN, SAUL LAWRENCE, lawyer, government official; b. N.Y.C., Sept. 5, 1926; s. Louis and Hannah Jean (Auerbach) S.; m. Carol Esberg, Nov. 12, 1964 (dec. 1972); children: Kate M., William Benjamin; m. Judith Shonkoff, June 5, 1977. Grad., Fieldston Sch., 1943; S.B. magna cum laude, Harvard U., 1946, J.D. cum laude, 1949. Bar: N.Y. 1949, D.C. 1964, also U.S. courts. With U.S. Fgn. Service, Frankfurt, Fed. Republic of Germany, 1949-51, London, 1951-52; assoc. Lord, Day & Lord, N.Y.C., 1952-62; ptnr. Rivkin Sherman & Levy (and predecessor firms), N.Y.C., 1962-84, Schnader, Harrison, Segal & Lewis, N.Y.C., 1984-87; sole practice N.Y.C., 1987—; exec. sec. U.S. affiliate Internat. Commn. Jurists, 1962-66; U.S. mem. Bd. Validation German Dollar Bonds, 1962—; adv. on multilateral trade agreements U.S. Dept. Commerce, 1978-80; mem. U.S. Trade Representative industry adv. com. on customs and trade matters, 1980-86; adv. working party on customs valuation Internat. C. of C., Paris, 1979—; lectr. internat. trade to profl. and bus. groups. Author: (with H. Glashoff) Commentary on the GATT Customs Valuation Code, 2d edit., 1988; contbr. articles to profl. jours. Served with USNR, 1944-45. Mem. ABA, Am. Soc. Internat. Law, N.Y. State Bar Assn. (exec. com., internat. law and practice sect.), Assn. Bar City N.Y. (com. on internat. trade 1984—, chmn. 1987—), Customs and Internat. Trade Bar Assn. (bd. dirs. 1972-81), Am. Assn. Exporters and Importers (bd. dirs. 1974-88, trade policy com., chmn. com. on U.S.-Can. free trade agreement), Phi Beta Kappa. Home: 4920 Arlington Ave Riverdale NY 10471 Office: 750 3d Ave New York NY 10017

SHERR, SOL, infosystems specialist; b. N.Y.C., Mar. 23, 1918; s. Isidor and Louise (Newfield) S.; m. Claire Ginsberg, May 9, 1942; children—Richard J., Deborah Ann Sherr-Ziarko. B.A., NYU, 1947, M.S. in Physics 1956. Assoc. chief engr. Gen. Precision Co., Pleasantville, N.Y., 1951-62; v.p. Spaceonics, Scarsdale, N.Y., 1962-63; sr. research sect. head Sperry Gyroscope, Lake Success, N.Y., 1964-68; mgr. display plan Hazeltine Corp., Greenlawn, N.Y., 1968-70; chief scientist North Hills Electric Co., Glen Cove, N.Y., 1970-82; pres. Westland Electronics Ltd., Hartsdale, N.Y., 1983—; lectr. U. Wis.-Milw., 1967—, George Washington U., 1978-82, Tech. Transfer, London, 1984; cons. Frost & Sullivan, N.Y.C., 1981—. Author: Fundamentals of Display Systems Design, 1970; Electronic Displays, 1979; Video and Digital Electronic Displays, 1982; editor: Computer Graphics: Technology and Applications, 1986—. Fellow Soc. Info. Display (v.p. 1966-67; editor Proc. 1978—, chmn. standards com. 1968-78); mem. IEEE (life). Democrat. Jewish. Home and Office: Westland Electronics Ltd PO Box 84 Murdock St Old Chatham NY 12136

SHERRARD, MICHAEL DAVID, lawyer; b. London, June 23, 1928; s. Morris and Ethel (Werbner) S.; m. Shirley Bagrit, Nov. 19, 1927; children: Nicholas, Jonathan. LLB, King's Coll., London, 1949. Mem. Hon. Soc. of Middle Temple, London, 1949, Queen's Counsel, London, 1968; Recorder Crown Ct., London, 1974; Master of Bench Middle Temple, London, 1977—; mem. of council, exec. of justice Internat. Commn. of Jurists; chmn. pub. inquiry into Normansfield Hosp., London, 1977, 78; inspector into London Capital Group Ltd. Dept. of Trade, London, 1976, 77. Mem. Assn. of the Bar of City of N.Y., Oriental art. Club: Oriental (London). Office: 2 Crown Office Row, Temple, London EC4Y 7HJ, England

SHERRATT, GERALD ROBERT, college president; b. Los Angeles, Nov. 6, 1931; s. Lowell Heyborne and Elva Genevieve (Lamb) S. B.S. in Edn., Utah State U., 1953, M.S. in Edn. Adminstrn., 1954; Ph.D. in Adminstrn. Higher Edn., Mich. State U., 1975. Staff assoc. U. Utah, Salt Lake City, 1961-62; dir. high sch. relations Utah State U., Logan, 1962-64, asst. to pres., 1964-77, v.p. for univ. relations, 1977-81; pres. So. Utah State Coll., Cedar City, 1982—; dir. Honeyville Grain Inc., Utah; mem. council pres. Utah System Higher Edn., 1982—; chmn. bd. Utah Summer Games, Cedar City, 1984—; chmn. pres.'s council Rocky Mountain Athletic Conf., Denver, 1984-85. Author hist. pageant: The West: America's Odyssey, 1973 (George Washington Honor medal 1973). Chmn. Festival of Am. West, Logan, Utah, 1972-81; chmn. bd. Utah Shakespearean Festival, Cedar City, 1982-86. Served to 1st. lt. USAF, 1954-57. Recipient Editing award Indsl. Editors Assn., 1962, Robins award Utah State U., 1967, Disting. Alumnus award Utah State U., 1974. Mem. Am. Assn. State Colls. and Univs., Cache C. of C. (bd. dirs. 1980-82), Utah N.G. (hon. col. corps), Phi Kappa Phi, Phi Delta Kappa, Sigma Nu (regent 1976-78). Mormon. Lodge: Rotary. Home: 331 W 200 S Cedar City UT 84720 Office: So Utah State Coll 351 W Center Cedar City UT 84720

SHERREN, ANNE TERRY, chemistry educator; b. Atlanta, July 1, 1936; d. Edward Allison and Annie Ayres (Lewis) Terry; m. William Samuel Sherren, Aug. 13, 1966. B.A., Agnes Scott Coll., 1957; Ph.D., U. Fla.-Gainesville, 1961. Grad. teaching asst. U. Fla., Gainesville, 1957-61; instr. Tex. Woman's U., Denton, 1961-63, asst. prof., 1963-66; research participant Argonne Nat. Lab., 1973-80; assoc. prof. chemistry N. Central Coll., Naperville, Ill., 1966-76, prof., 1976—. Clk. of session Knox Presbyn. Ch., 1976—, ruling elder, 1971—. Mem. Am. Chem. Soc., Am. Inst. Chemists, AAAS, AAUP, Ill. Acad. Sci., Sigma Xi, Delta Kappa Gamma, Iota Sigma Pi (nat. pres. 1978-81, nat. dir. 1972-78). Presbyterian. Contbr. articles to field to profl. jours. Office: N Central Coll Naperville IL 60566

SHERRICK, DANIEL NOAH, building materials manufacturing holding company executive; b. Greenup, Ill., Mar. 28, 1929; s. Conrad Donovan and Helen Lorene (Neeley) S.; m. Dora Ann Moore, Aug. 11, 1957; children: Renata Ann Sherrick McBride, Sherrie Dee Sherrick Sierra. B.S. in Edn., Eastern Ill. U., Charleston, 1956. Owner Midwest Ins. Agy., Greenup, 1956-60; supt. agys. Midwest Life Ins. Co., Lincoln, Nebr., 1960-62; asst. v.p. Gulf Life Ins. Co., Jacksonville, Fla., 1962-71; pres. Bank of Carbondale, Ill., 1971-74, Prescription Learning Corp., Springfield, Ill., 1974-76; exec. v.p. Imperial Industries, Inc., Miami Lakes, Fla., 1976-88, pres., chief exec. officer, 1988—. Pres. Alderman Park Civic Assn., Jacksonville, 1968, Heritage Hills Home Owners Assn., Carbondale, 1973; bd. dirs. Miami Lakes Bus. Assn. Served with USAF, 1948-52. Mem. Miami Lakes Bus. Assn. (bd. dirs.), Am. Legion, VFW. Mem. United Ch. of Christ. Lodges: Masons; Scottish Rite; Elks. Home: 14420 Lake Candlewood Ct Miami Lakes FL 33016 Office: Imperial Industries Inc 8550 NW South River Dr Miami FL 33166

SHERRILL-EDWARDS, IVA, communications company executive, professional development consultant, columnist; b. Little Rock, Aug. 18, 1937; d. Leroy and Beulah (Wardlow) Sherrill; m. John Moses Edwards, May 19, 1956 (div. Jan. 1979); children—Delmonte, Dennis, Tina Marie. B.A., The Union, Cin., 1985. Service rep. Cin. Bell, 1968-79, customer advisor, 1979-81, facilities coordinator, 1981—; instr. Discovery Learning Ctr., Cin., 1985—; image cons. Iva S. Edwards Cons., Cin., 1984—; producer cable TV show and talk show host. Com. mem. allocations Community Chest, Cin., 1986. Mem. Nat. Assn. Female Execs. (network dir. 1985), Am. Bus. Women Assn. (com. mem. 1985). Republican. Mem. African Methodist Episcopal Ch. Avocations: tennis; swimming; reading; traveling. Office: Iva Sherrill-Edwards & Assocs PO Box 37555 Cincinnati OH 45222

SHERRY, GEORGE LEON, political science educator; b. Lodz, Poland, Jan. 5, 1924; came to U.S., 1939, naturalized 1945; s. Leon G. and Henrietta (Mess) S.; m. Doris H. Harf, Mar. 6, 1947; 1 child, Vivien Gail Sherry Greenberg. BA summa cum laude, CCNY, 1944; MA, Columbia U., 1951, MA, cert. Russian Inst., 1955, PhM, 1959. Reporter, radio news writer The N.Y. Times, N.Y.C., 1944-46; editor, interpreter, then sr. interpreter UN, N.Y.C., 1946-59, from polit. officer to dir. and dep. to under sec.-gen. for spl. polit. affairs, 1959-83; polit. advisor to missions Congo, Cyprus, India and Pakistan, 1962-66; asst. sec.-gen. for spl. polit. affairs UN, N.Y.C., 1984-85; Stuart Chevalier prof. diplomacy and world affairs Occidental Coll., Los Angeles, 1985—; dir. Occidental at-the-UN program, N.Y., 1986—; U.S. del. staff Dartmouth Soviet-Am. confs., 1961—; assoc. seminar on problem of peace Columbia U., N.Y.C. Mem. editorial adv. bd. Polit. Sci. Quar., N.Y.C., 1973—; contbr. articles and revs. to profl. jours. UN Inst. for Tng. and Research sr. fellow, 1985—. Mem. Council on Fgn. Relations, Acad. Polit. Sci., Internat. Studies Assn., Phi Beta Kappa. Democrat. Home: 185 E 85th St New York NY 10028

SHERRY, NEIL, advertising executive; b. Chadderton, Eng., May 7, 1947; s. Ronald and Nellie (Warwick) S.; m. Margaret Helen Wolfenden, Dec. 14, 1968; children: Thomas Neil, Elizabeth Margaret, Helen Catherine. Artist Crane Wood, Manchester, Eng., 1966-68; art dir. Farmer Advt., Manchester, 1968-69; group head Brunning Advt. Group, Manchester, 1969-75; creative dir. Stowe & Bowden, Manchester, 1975-79; dir., creative dir. Brockie Haslam, Manchester, 1979-83; dir. Ingham Middleton Dicks Maud Ltd., Manchester, 1983-85, Baglow Harris Sherry, Salford, Eng., 1985-86, Baglow Sherry & Ptnrs. Ltd., Salford, 1986—. Fellow Inst. of Dirs. Office: Baglow Sherry & Ptnrs Ltd, 32/33 Crescent, Salford Manchester M54PF, England

SHERWAN, ROY GLENN, travel agency executive; b. St. Louis, Aug. 19, 1930; s. August Carl and Florence (Worth) S.; student Spencerian Coll., Milw., 1949; m. Carol Lee Sorenson, Nov. 10, 1951; children—Scott, Kimberly. Adminstrv. asst. Wis. N.G., Whitefish Bay, 1949-50; teller Home Savs. Bank, Milw., 1951-52; sales corr. Centralab div. Globe Union Co., Milw., 1952-54; sales rep. Am. Airlines, Milw. and Chgo., 1954-70; pres. 1st Maine Travel Agy., Des Plaines, Ill., 1970-85, also chmn. bd. Mem. United Air Lines Travel Agts. Council, Eastern Air Lines Travel Agts. Adv. Bd., Norwegian Caribbean Lines Agts. Council. Bd. dirs. United Way of Des Plaines, 1982-85, gen. chmn., 1983-84, 84-85, v.p., 1985-86, pres. 1986-87. Served to capt. U.S. Army, 1951-52, 61-62. Mem. Am. Soc. Travel Agts.(bd. dirs. midwest chpt.1986—, v.p. midwest chpt. 1988—), Assn. Bank Travel Burs., Chgo. Bon Vivants, Pacific Area Travel Assn., Chinese Passenger Club Chgo., Des Plaines C. of C. (dir. tourism 1984-85, bd. dirs. 1986-87). Presbyterian. Clubs: Elks, Bus. Breakfast (pres. 1976), Rotary (dir. Des Plaines 1978, 79-81). Home: 700 Graceland Ave Des Plaines IL 60016 Office: 728 Lee St Des Plaines IL 60016

SHERWOOD, JAMES BLAIR, marine leasing and shipping company executive; b. New Castle, Pa., Aug. 8, 1933; s. William Earl and Florence (Balph) S.; m. Shirley A.M. Cross, Dec. 31, 1977; stepchildren—Charles N.C. Sherwood, Simon M.C. Sherwood. B.A., Yale U., 1955. Mgr. French ports U.S. Lines Inc., LeHavre, France, 1959-62; asst. gen. freight traffic mgr. U.S. Lines Inc., N.Y.C., 1962-63; gen. mgr. CTI Inc., N.Y.C., 1963-65; pres. Sea Containers Ltd., London, 1965—; chmn. Brit. Ferries Ltd., 1984—, Orient-Express Hotels Inc., 1987—; dir. Through Transit Marine Mut. Assurance Assn., Hamilton, Bermuda, Venice Simplon-Orient Express Ltd., London, Hotel Cipriani S.P.A., Venice, Italy; v.p. Transport Trust, London, Eng. Author: James Sherwood's Discriminating Guide to London, 1975, rev. edit., 1977. Curator Transylvania U., Lexington, Ky., 1980—, bd. dirs. Peggy Guggenheim Mus., Venice, Italy, 1983—, Mus. Modern Art, Oxford, Eng., 1987—. Episcopalian. Clubs: Pilgrims, Hurlingham, Mark's, Annabel's, Harry's Bar (London). Home: Hinton Manor, Hinton Waldrist Oxfordshire England Office: Sea Containers Ltd, 20 Upper Ground, London England

SHERWOOD, (PETER) LOUIS, supermarket executive; b. London, Oct. 27, 1941; came to U.S., 1979; s. Peter and Mervyn (De Toll) S.; m. Nicole Dina, Aug. 22, 1970; children: Christopher, Anne, Isabelle. B.A., Oxford U., 1963, M.A., 1966; M.B.A. (Harkness fellow), Stanford U., 1965. Fin. planning officer Morgan Grenfell & Co. Ltd., London, 1965-68; gen. mgr. Melias Ltd., Welwyn Garden City, Eng., 1969-72; dir. Anglo-Continental Investment & Fin. Co. Ltd., London, 1973-79; chmn., chief exec. officer Maidenhead Investments, London, 1977-79; sr. v.p. Grand Union Co., Elmwood Park, N.J., 1979-85; pres. Gt. Atlantic & Pacific Tea Co. Inc., Montvale, N.J., 1985—. Office: Great Atlantic & Pacific Tea Co Inc 2 Paragon Dr Montvale NJ 07645

SHERWOOD, WILLIAM JAMES, JR., dentist; b. Chgo., Apr. 26, 1942; s. William James and Julia Parker (Bowen) S.; m. Beverly Virginia Stanley, Sept. 25, 1971; 1 child, Mary Elizabeth. D.D.S., U. N.C.-Chapel Hill, 1967. Lic. dentist, N.C. Practice gen. dentistry, Raleigh, N.C., 1968-76, O'Berry Ctr. for Retarded, Goldsboro, N.C., 1976-78; gen. dentist Aramco Dental Services, Abqaiq, Saudi Arabia, 1978-80, supr. dental services, 1980-86, chief dist. dental services, Dhahran, 1986—. Bd. dirs. Raleigh Jaycees, 1969. Mem. ADA, N.C. Dental Soc., Federation Dentaire Internationale. Republican. Presbyterian. Avocations: antiques, reading, painting, swimming. Home: Box 2710, Dhahran 31311, Saudia Arabia Office: Box 102, Dhahran 31311, Saudi Arabia

SHESTACK, JEROME JOSEPH, lawyer; b. Atlantic City, N.J., Feb. 11, 1925; s. Isidore and Olga (Shankman) S.; m. Marciarose Schleifer, Jan. 28, 1951; children: Jonathan Michael, Jennifer. A.B., U. Pa., 1944; LL.B., Harvard U., 1949. Bar: Ill. 1950, Pa. 1952. Teaching fellow Northwestern U. Law Sch., Chgo., 1949-50; asst. prof. law, faculty editor La. State Law Sch., Baton Rouge, 1950-52; dep. city solicitor City of Phila., 1952, 1st dep. solicitor, 1952-55; ptnr. Schnader, Harrison, Segal & Lewis, Phila. and Washington, 1956—; adj. prof. law U. Pa. Law Sch., 1956; U.S. rep. to UN Human Rights Commn., 1979-80; U.S. del. to Econ. and Soc. Council UN, 1980; pres. Internat. League Human Rights, 1972—; bd. dirs., sec. Internat. Com. Jurists Am.; chmn. Lawyers Com. Internat. Human Rights, 1979-80; mem. nat. adv. com. legal services OEO, 1965-72; bd. dirs., mem. exec. com. Lawyers Com. Civil Rights Under Law, Washington, 1963—. Editor: (with others) Rights of Americans, 1971, Human Rights, 1979. Mem. fin. com. Dem. Nat. Com., 1975—; bd. dirs. Fedn. Jewish Agys., 1962—; bd. overseers Jewish Theol. Soc. Am., 1968—; bd. govs. Hebrew U., 1969—; chmn. bd. dirs. Am. Poetry Ctr., 1986—; trustee Free Library of Phila., 1986—. Served with USNR, 1943-46. Fellow Am. Bar Found.; mem. ABA (nomination com., mem. ho. dels. 1971-73, 77—, chmn. numerous coms.), Am. Law Inst., Am. Coll. Trial Lawyers, Jewish Pub. Soc. (pres. 1973-76, trustee 1955—), Nat. Legal Aid and Defender Assn. (dir., mem. exec. com. 1970-80), Order of Coif. Clubs: Harvard, Varsity (Phila.). Home: Parkway House 2201 Pennsylvania Ave Philadelphia PA 19130 Office: Schnader Harrison Segal & Lewis 1600 Market St Suite 3600 Philadelphia PA 19103

SHETH, AJIT VANDRAVAN, advertising executive, composer; b. Bombay, Sept. 19, 1932; s. Vandravan Gordham and Prabha Vandravan (Prabha Shah) S.; m. Nirupama Ajit, Feb. 5, 1957; children: Abhijit, Falguni. BA in Commerce, Sydenham Coll., Bombay, 1954. Fin. journalist Comml. Info. Bur., Bombay, 1957; mng. dir. Adroit Group of Cos., Bombay, 1967—. Author: Anthology on Indian Musician and Playback Singer, Pankaj Mullick, 1981.; producer Amrita. sec. Performing Arts-Bharatiya Vidya Bhavan, Bombay, 1957—; founder dir. Pankaj Mullick Music Research Found., Bombay, 1978—; chief exec. Music T.V. (India) Ltd., Bombay, 1986. Recipient hon. citation in contemporary music Baroda Sch. of Music, 1987. Mem. Audit Bur. Circulations, Internat. Communications Industries Assn., Assn. for Multi-Image Internat., Audio Visual Producers Assn., Advt. Agys. Assn. of India (Excellence in Advt. award 1975 79 81 83 86), Radio and T.V. Advt. Practitioners' Assn. of India Ltd. (Cert. Merit 1980 82 86), Advt. Club Bombay, Comml. Artists Guild (Cag Silver award 1978), Printing Assn. of Fed. Republic Germany (Excellence in Printing award 1982). Lodges: Rotary, Lions. Home: Ajit Villa Laburnum Rd Gamdevi, Bombay Maharashtra 400 007, India Office: Adroit Advt and Mktg Pvt Ltd, Ismail Bldg Flora Fountain, Bombay Maharashtra 400 023, India

SHETTY, TARANATH, neurologist, educator; b. Mangalore, India, Apr. 29, 1938; s. Shankar and Bhavani S.; m. Urmila Shetty, Dec. 1972; children—Neeta, Teena, Geema. M.B.B.S, Madras U., 1962; M.D., Lucknow U., 1965. Diplomate Am. Bd. Pediatrics, Am. Bd. Neurology with Spl. Competence in Child Neurology. Am. Bd. Electroencephalography. Resident in pediatrics Children's Hosp. Med. Ctr., Boston, 1967-68, fellow in neurology, 1968-69; research fellow in neurology Harvard U., 1968-69, teaching fellow, 1971-72; resident in neurology Boston City, Hosp., 1969-72; instr. Brown U., Providence, 1973-74, asst. prof., 1974-79, clin. assoc. prof., 1979—; dir. pediatric neurology R.I. Hosp., Providence, 1976—. Fellow Am. Acad. Neurology, Royal Coll. Physicians Can.; mem. Child Neurology Soc. Hindu. Club: University (Providence). Home: 80 Clarendon Ave Providence RI 02906 Office: 120 Dudley St Providence RI 02905

SHEU, FONG SHYONG, obstetrician; b. Tsaotun Nantou, Taiwan, Aug. 13, 1943; parents Jin Bei and Zoon (Hung) S.; m. Chiun Chu Hung Sheu, Oct. 27, 1973; children: Kai Yu, Kai Lun. B, Chung Shan Med. and Dental Coll., Taichung City, Taiwan, 1984. Tchr. Chung Yuan Elem. Sch., Tsaotun, Nantou, 1962-67; intern Chung Shan Meml. Hosp., Taichung City, Taiwan, 1971-72; resident in surgery Chern-Chin Gen. Hosp., Taichung City, 1973-75; resident Shei-Ho Gen. Hosp., Yuan Lin, Chung Hua, Taiwan, 1975-77; provincial Chung Shin Hosp., Taichung City, 1977-79; practice medicine Tye-Ann Ob-Gyn Hosp., Tsaotun, Nantou, 1979—; exec. mem. Tsaotun Elem. Sch. parent Assn., 1981—; com. mem. Tsaotun County Sanitary Assn., 1982—. Com. mem. Victor High Sch. Parents Assn., Taichung City, 1986—. Served with Taiwan Army, 1972-73. Recipient Outstanding Achievement on Family Planning award Taiwan Provincial Family Planning Research Ctr., Taichung City, 1982, 84. Mem. Assn. Ob-Gyn Republic China, Med.Assn. Republic China, Assn Laser Republic China, Assn. Ultrasound Republic China. Home: 608 Chung Xeng Rd, Tsaotun 54203, Republic of China Office: Tye-Ann Ob-Gyn Hosp, 608 Chung Xeng Rd, Tsaotun 54203, Republic of China

SHEVARDNADZE, EDUARD AMVROSIYEVICH, minister of foreign affairs of Soviet Union; b. Mamati Lanchkhutsky Raion, Georgia, Jan. 25, 1928; m. Nanuli Shevardnadze; children: Manana, Paata. Grad. Republican Party Sch. of Cen. Com., Communist Party of Georgia, 1951, Kutaisi Pedagogical Inst., 1959. Joined Communist Party Soviet Union, 1948; Komsomol and party work, 1948-56; 2d sec. Cen. Com., Georgian Komsomol, 1956-57, 1st sec., 1957-61; mem. Cen. Com., Georgian Communist Party, 1960—, candidate mem. Bur. of Cen. Com., 1960-61, mem. Politburo, 1972—, 1st sec., 1972-85; 1st sec. Mtskheti Raion Com., 1961-63, Pervomaisky Raion Com., Tbilisi City, Communist Party of Georgia, 1963-64, 1st dep. minister for Protection of Pub. Order, 1961-65, minister (renamed Ministry of Internal Affairs 1968) 1965-72; 1st sec. Tbilisi City Com. of Cen. Com., Communist Party of Georgia, 1972; mem. Cen. Com. of Communist Party Soviet Union, 1976—, candidate mem. Politburo, 1978-85, mem. 1985—; dep. to USSR Supreme Soviet, 1978—, minister of fgn. affairs, 1985—. Decorated Order of Lenin (5), Order of Red Banner of Labour, Hero of Socialist Labour, 1981 (2), others. Address: Ministry of Fgn Affairs, The Kremlin, Moscow USSR *

SHEVCHENKO, VALENTINA SEMENOVNA, Soviet government official; b. Krivoy Rog, Ukraine, USSR, 1935. Sec. cen. com. Ukrainian Komsomol, 1962-69; mem. cen. com. Ukrainian Communist Party, 1976—; minister edn. Ukranian Soviet Socialist Republic, Kiev, USSR, 1972-75; chair Presidium of the Ukrainian Soc. of Friendship and Cultural Relations with Fgn. Countries, 1972-75; dep. chair Presidium of the Ukrainian Soviet Socialist Republic Supreme Soviet, Kiev, 1975-85, chair, 1985—, now pres.; vice chair Presidium of Supreme Soviet USSR, 1985—. Decorated Order of the Oct. Revolution, Order of the Red Banner of Labour, Order of People's Friendship. Address: Supreme Soviet Ukrainian SSR, Kiev Ukraine, USSR *

SHEYNIN, OSCAR BORISOVITCH, engineer, mathematician; b. Moscow, Nov. 29, 1925; s. Boris Abramovitch and Sophie Alexandrovna (Cohan) S.; m. Ida Semenovna Blostein, Oct. 14, 1956; 1 child, Michael. Student, Moscow Inst. Geodesy, Air Survey and Cartography, 1946-51, Moscow State U., 1953-59, Inst. History Natural Sci. and Tech., Moscow, 1967. Subeditor jour. Astronomy and Geodesy, Moscow, 1960-65; asst. prof., docent, chair math. Plekhanov Inst. Nat. Economy, Moscow, 1965-78; researcher Moscow, 1979—; instr. geodesy topographical tech. sch., instr. math. secondary sch. Contbr. articles to scholarly jours., chpt. in book; referee jours. Mem. Internat. Statis. Inst. Home: Mishin St 12, Flat 35, Moscow 125083, USSR

SHIAU, CHUEN HER, marine engineer; b. Republic of China, Oct. 17, 1937; came to U.S., 1969, naturalized, 1978; s. Lung Tan and Lu T. (Lin) S.; m. Shing Lien Wang, July 3, 1959; children: Hui Chen, Hui-Lin, Hui-Wen, Hui-Jen. B of Engring., Taiwan Nat. Coll. Marine and Oceanic Tech., 1959; M of Engring., U. Minn., 1971. Instr. Taiwan Maritime Coll., 1961-65; chief ship repair sect. Taiwan Shipbldg. Corp., 1965-69; mech. marine engr. Fraser Shipyard, Inc., Superior, Wis., 1971-75; repair supt. Exxon Internat. Co., Florham Park, N.J., 1975-79, sr. marine design engr., 1979-82, ops. supt., 1982-85; sr. engr. Am. Systems Engring. Corp., Virginia Beach, Va., 1986-88; mech. engr. Mil. Sealift Command Atlantic, Bayonne, N.J., 1988—. Served to ensign Republic of China Navy. Mem. Soc. Marine Port Engrs., Chinese Inst. Engrs., Internat. Platform Assn., Soc. Naval Architects and Marine Engrs. Office: Mil Ocean Terminal Bldg 42 Bayonne NJ 07002-5399

SHIBAZAKI, KIKUO, public affairs consultant; b. Tokyo, Sept. 9, 1928; s. Uhachi and Tomi S.; LL.M., Chuo U., Tokyo, 1953; m. Sumiko Kojima, Oct. 3, 1957; children—Ula, Yoshio. Writer/editor The Yomiuri Shimbun, Tokyo, 1953-62; public affairs mgr. Esso Standard Sekiyu K.K., Tokyo, 1962-70, public relations advisor Esso Eastern, Inc., Houston, 1976-78, public affairs cons., Tokyo, 1979-80; environ. conservation advisor Exxon Corp., N.Y.C., 1971-73; dir. corp. communication The Daiei, Inc., Osaka, Japan, 1981-83; public affairs cons., Tokyo, 1983—. Mem. Public Relations Soc. Am., Internat. Bus. Communicators Assn., Japan-Am. Soc., Mem. Christian Ref. Ch. of Japan. Club: Fgn. Corrs. Japan (Tokyo). Home: 1-7-6 Yamanone, 408 Zushi, Kanagawa 249, Japan Office: 4-15-29 Mita 425, Minato-ku, Tokyo 108, Japan

SHIBOLET, SHLOMO, internist, educator; b. Malang, East Java, Indonesia, Apr. 26, 1927; s. Wolf and Klaartje (Visser) Schyveschuurder; m. Orna Zusman, Jan. 7, 1957; children: Hamutal, Dana, Omer, Assaf, Ariel. Med. Doctorandus, Mcpl. Med. Sch., Amsterdam, The Netherlands, 1951; MD, Hadassah Med. Sch., Jerusalem, 1955. Intern Sheba Hosp., 1955-57, resident, 1957-62; house physician Sheba Med. Ctr., Israel, 1962-65, sr. physician, 1965-69; vis. scientist NIH, Bethesda, Md., 1969-71; dep. head internal med. Sheba Med. Ctr., Israel, 1971-75; head dept. internal med. Ichilov Hosp., Tel Aviv, Israel, 1975—; prof. internal med. Tel Aviv U., 1978—; head physician Rehab. Dept. Treasury of State, Tel Aviv, 1982—; bd. dirs. Treasury Dept., Tel Aviv. Served to lt. col. Israeli mil., 1955-62, 1969-75. Mem. Internat. Soc. Internal Medicine, Israel Soc. Internal Medicine, Am. Soc. Bone and Mineral Research. Jewish. Office: Ichilov Hosp, 6 Weizmann St, Tel Aviv 64239, Israel

SHICK, RICHARD ARLON, college dean; b. DuBois, Pa., July 17, 1943; s. Arlon Elmer and Melva Elizabeth (Bartell) S.; m. Linda B. Shick; children—Richard Arlon, Charles, Elizabeth. BS, SUNY-Buffalo, 1966, MBA, 1968, PhD, 1972. Asst. prof. banking and fin. U. Ga., Athens, 1970-75; assoc. prof. fin. St. Bonaventure U. (N.Y.), 1975-78, chmn. fin. dept., 1975-78, acting chmn. mktg. dept., 1976-78; assoc. prof. fin. Canisius Coll., Buffalo, 1978—, dean Sch. Bus. Adminstrn., 1979—; also cons. Mem. editorial bd. Jour. Bus. Research, 1973-76, Jour. Fin. Research, 1977-81, Jour. Econs. and Bus., 1984—; mem. editorial bd. Fin. Rev., 1976-87, editor for fin. edn., 1981-82; contbr. articles to acad. jours. Chmn. mayor's rev. com. Buffalo Bd. of Edn., 1981-82; mem. Philharm. Steering Com., Buffalo, 1983—. NDEA fellow, 1966-68; U.S. Savs. and Loan League grantee, 1974; St. Bonaventure U. grantee, 1976. Mem. Am. Fin. Assn., Eastern Fin. Assn., Southwestern Fin. Assn., So. Fin. Assn., Western Fin. Assn., Am. Mgmt. Assn., Assn. Jesuit Colls. and Univs. Deans of Bus. Schs. (treas. 1983-84, v.p. 1985-89, pres. 1987-88), Middle Atlantic Assn. Colls. and Schs. Bus. Adminstrn. (v.p. 1985-86, pres. 1986-87), Am. Assembly of Collegiate Schs. of Bus., Beta Gamma Sigma, Alpha Kappa Psi, Di Gamma. Republican. Clubs: Buffalo Yacht, The Buffalo; Town of Jamestown (N.Y.). Home: 443 Cottonwood Dr Williamsville NY 14221 Office: Canisius College 2001 Main St Buffalo NY 14208

SHICKLE, PAUL EUGENE, educator; b. Bloomington, Ill., Aug. 29, 1927; s. Benjamin Wilson and Eathel Delores (Rowe) S. B.S., Ill. State U., 1949. Cert. secondary tchr., Calif. Tchr. San Marino Unified Sch. Dist., Calif., 1956—, head fgn. lang. dept., 1967—. Mem. performing arts council Music Ctr. Los Angeles County. Mem. Soc. Indian Pioneers, Filson Club, Calif. Classical Assn. (pres. so. sect. 1981-82), Modern and Classical Assn. So. Calif., Am. Council Study Fgn. Lang., Calif. Humanities Assn., Am. Acad. Religion, Nat. Tchrs. Assn., Calif. Tchrs. Assn., Assn. for Supervision and Curriculum Devel., Am. Classical Assn., Am. Acad. Polit. and Soc. Sci., Am. Acad. Polit. Sci., Am. Council for Arts, Ams. United for Separation Ch. and State, Ind. Hist. Soc., Bibl. Archaeology Soc., Calif. Assn. Supervision and Curriculum Devel., Am. Film Inst., Va. Geneal. Soc., Ky. Geneal. Soc., N.Am. Conf. Brit. Studies, History Sci. Soc., Oceanic Soc., Nelson County (Ky.) Hist. Soc., Smithsonian Assocs., Nat. Trust for Historic Preservation, Met. Mus. Art (nat. assoc.), Met. Opera Guild, Asia Soc., Zionist Orgn. Am., ACLU, Amnesty Internat., Ctr. for Study of Presidency, Clan Fraser Soc. North Am., Archeol. Inst. Am., Va. Country Civil War Soc., Nat. Park and Conservation Assn., UN Assn. of U.S., Soc. French Hist. Studies, Am. Com. for Irish Studies, Conf. Group for Cen. European History. Republican. Roman Catholic. Home: 2115 Leafwood Ln Arcadia CA 91006 Office: San Marino Unified Sch Dist 2701 Huntington Dr San Marino CA 91008

SHIEH, NARN-RUEIH, mathematician; b. Taipei, Republic of China, Oct. 6, 1950; s. J.S. and P.Z. (Chiang) S.; m. Mei-Ing Lu Shieh; children: Jing-Bey, Jing-Hua. BS, Nat. Taiwan Normal U., 1974; PhD, Nat. Taiwan U., 1980. Assoc. prof. Nat. Taiwan U., Taipei, 1973-87; vis. prof. La. State U., Baton Rouge, 1986-87; prof. Nat. Taiwan U., Taipei, 1987—. Contbr. articles to profl. jours. Mem. Chinese Math. Soc., Am. Math. Soc. Home: Wen-chou St Lane 68, #4 5th Floor, Taipei Republic of China Office: Nat Taiwan U, Dept Math, Taipei Republic of China

SHIELDS, FRANK COX, merchant banker, stockbroker, economist; b. Dublin, Ireland, Sept. 10, 1944; s. Joseph Francis and Alice (Cox) S.; m. Elizabeth Kinross, Oct. 9, 1971; children—Henrietta Olivia, Oliver Elliot Maxwell, Alexander Sheridan Grant. A.B. with honors, Harvard Coll., 1966; M.B.A., Wharton Grad. Sch., U. Pa., 1969. Mem. research staff London Sch. Econs., 1969-71; stockbroker Cazenove & Co., London, 1971-73, Grieveson, Grant & Co., London, 1973-78; mcht. banker European Banking Co. Ltd., London, 1978-85, EBC Amro Bank Ltd., 1985-86; sr. rep. Maruman Securities Co., Ltd., London, 1987—, dir., gen. mgr., 1987—; econ. cons. Oesterreichische Kontrollbank Aktiengesellschaft, Vienna, Austria, 1979-83; bd. dirs., gen. mgr. Maruman Securities (Europe) Ltd., London, 1987—. Club: Buck's (London). Home: 24 Church Row, Hampstead, London NW3, England Home: Piso Atico, Edificios Altamar Cap de Ras, Llansa, Gerona Spain Office: Maruman Securities Ltd(Europe), 1 Liverpool St, London ECM2M 7NH, England

SHIELDS, JAMES GERARD, French educator; b. Baillieston, Strathclyde, Scotland, Feb. 23, 1957; s. John and Lena (Boyle) S. MA in French and Hispanic studies with honors, Glasgow U., Scotland, 1979. Postgrad. researcher Glasgow U., 1979-83; lectr. U. Caen, Normandy, France, 1983-84; lectr. French Aston U., Birmingham, Eng., 1984—; sr. residence tutor Aston Univ. Village, Handsworth, Birmingham, 1984—; tutor Glasgow Univ., 1979-80; tchr. Reid Kerr Coll., Paisley, Scotland, 1980-81; interpreter Cen. Sch. Langs., Glasgow, 1979-82, Strathclyde (Scotland) Regional Council, 1980-83. Contbr. articles to profl. jours. Various student awards Glasgow Univ., 1975-76, Faculty Arts award Glasgow Univ. 1979-82, Major Studentship award Scottish Edn. Dept., 1979-82, Carnegie Trust Research award, 1982-83. Mem. Assn. Principals Wardens, Assn. Study Modern Contemporary France, Stendhal Club. Office: Aston Univ, Dept Modern Langs, Aston St, Birmingham B4 7ET, England

SHIELDS, LLOYD NOBLE, lawyer; b. Longview, Tex., Dec. 11, 1951; s. Lloyd Leon and Carolyn Lynch (Noble) S.; m. Lynn Ellen Hufft, June 15, 1974; children—Carolyn Elise, Ellen Lynch, Audrie Menville. B. Arch., Tulane U., 1974, J.D., 1977. Bar: La. 1977, U.S. Dist. Ct. (ea., we. and mid. dists.) La., U.S. Ct. Appeals (5th cir.) 1978, U.S. Patent Office 1981. Law clk. Civil Dist. Ct., New Orleans, 1977-78; assoc. Deutsch, Kerrigan & Stiles, New Orleans, 1978-79; ptnr. Simon, Peragine, Smith & Redfearn, New Orleans, 1979—; instr. New Orleans Bar Review, Inc., 1980—, Loyola U. Law Sch., 1987—. Bd. dirs. Preservation Resource Ctr., New Orleans, 1983—, pres. 1986-88; pres. Operation Comeback Inc. 1988—. Mem. ABA (chmn. automobile law com. torts and ins. practice sect. 1984-85), Am. Arbitration Assn. (constrn. industry panel). Presbyterian. Office: Simon Peragine Smith & Redfearn 3000 Energy Ctr New Orleans LA 70163

SHIELY, JOHN STEPHEN, lawyer; b. St. Paul, June 19, 1952; s. Vincent Robert and Mary Elizabeth (Hope) S.; m. Helen Jane Pauly, Aug. 29, 1981; children: Michael, Erin. BBA in Acctg., U. Notre Dame, 1974; JD, Marquette U., 1977. Bar: Wis. 1977, U.S. Dist. Ct. (ea. and we. dists.) Wis. 1977. Sr. assoc. Arthur Andersen & Co., Milw., 1977-79l; assoc. Hughes Hubbard & Reed, N.Y.C. and Milw., 1979-83; asst. sec. Allen-Bradley Co., Milw., 1983-86; asst. gen. counsel Rockwell Internat. Corp., Milw. and Pitts., 1985-86; gen. counsel Briggs & Stratton Corp., Milw., 1986—; adj. lectr. in law Marquette Univ., Milw., 1986-87. Vice chmn. St. Charles Boys' Home, Milw., 1978—; mem. planned giving com. Arthritis Found., Milw., 1980-86; chmn. Wauwatosa (Wis.) Bd. Tax Rev., 1984-87. Mem. Wis. Bar Assn., Am. Corp. Counsel Assn. (pres., bd. dirs. Wis. chpt. 1984—), Assn. for Corp. Growth (sec., bd. dirs. Wis. chpt. 1987—). Home: 15270 Briaridge Ct Elm Grove WI 53122 Office: Briggs & Stratton Corp PO Box 702 Milwaukee WI 53201

SHIER, JEROME BAER, paint and home decorating chain executive; b. N.Y.C., Apr. 15, 1918; s. David and Stella (Schilder) S.; student CCNY, 1936-37, N.Y. U., 1937-38; m. Mildred Siver, June 20, 1940; children—Ferne Diane Shier Mitchell, Iris Gail Shier Bodnar. With R.H. Macy & Co., N.Y.C., 1936-49; operating v.p. Gertz, LI., 1949-65; mng. dir. Garbers of S.I., 1965-67; exec. v.p., chief operating officer Martin Paint Stores, Jamaica, N.Y., 1967—; dir. security mgmt. John Jay Sch. Criminal Justice; mem. adv. council Center Labor and Indsl. Relations. Pres. Nassau County (N.Y.) Police Res. Assn.; bd. dirs. N.Y. Finest Found., N.Y. State Troopers Found.; bd. overseers N.Y. Inst. Tech.; flag officer Jewish Inst. Nat. Security Affairs. Recipient Pres.'s award to Store Mgr. Yr. Allied Stores Corp., 1956-57; Heritage award L.I. Found. Edn., 1979; Man of the Yr. award Nassau Civic Club, 1981; Nat. Youth Services award B'nai B'rith, 1984, nat. trustee, 1987; Disting. Patriot award Council Inter-Am. Security, 1986. Mem. Am. Acad. Profl. Law Enforcement, Internat. Narcotics Enforcement Officers Assn Inc. Home: 2588 Saw Mill Rd North Bellmore NY 11710 Office: 182-20 Liberty Ave Jamaica NY 11432

SHIGEMATSU, TSUNENOBU, analytical chemist, educator; b. Ehime-Ken, Japan, Dec. 28, 1916; s. Tasaburo and Misao S.; M.S., Kyoto U., 1940, D.Sc., 1952; m. Takako, Aug. 1, 1944; children—Toshihi-ko, Tatsuhiko. Lectr., Faculty of Engring., Kyoto U., 1950-52, asso. prof. Faculty of Sci., 1952-57, prof. Inst. Chem. Research, 1957-80, prof. emeritus, 1980—, dir. Inst., 1976-78; prof. gen. edn. Kinki U., Higashi, Osaka, 1980—. Mem. Japan Soc. Analytical Chemistry (award 1965), Soc. Sea Water Sci. (award 1973), Chem. Soc. Japan, Geochem. Soc. Japan, Kinki Soc., Atomic Energy Soc. Japan, Japan Health Physics Soc. Research in partition of trace elements between two phases and their application to analytical chemistry, radiochemistry and marine chemistry. Home: 81-2 Tohyama Momoyama-cho, Fushimi-ku, Kyoto 612, Japan Office: Kinki U, Kowakae, Higashi-Osaka 577, Japan

SHIH, J. CHUNG-WEN, educator; b. Nanking, China; came to U.S., 1948, naturalized, 1960; d. Cho-kiang and Chia-pu (Fang) S. B.A., St. John's U., Shanghai, 1945; M.A., Duke U., 1949, Ph.D., 1955. Asst. prof. English Kings Coll. N.Y., 1955-56; asst. prof. U. Bridgeport, Conn., 1956-60; postdoctoral fellow East Asian Studies Harvard, 1960-61; asst. prof. Chinese Stanford, 1961-64; asso. prof. Chinese Pomona Coll., 1965-66; asso. prof. George Washington U., 1966-71, prof., chmn. dept. East Asian langs. and lit., 1971—. Author: Injustice to Tou O, 1972, the Golden Age of Chinese Drama: Yuan Tsa-chu, 1976, Return from Silence: China's Writers of the May Fourth Tradition, 1983. Bd. dirs. Sino-Am. Cultural Soc., Washington, 1971-80. AAUW fellow, 1964-65; Social Sci. Research Council fellow, 1976-77; grantee Nat. Endowment Humanities, 1979-80; sr. scholars exchange program Nat. Acad. Sci., China, spring 1980. Mem. Assn. Asian Studies, Am. Council Fgn. Lang. Tchrs., Chinese Lang. Tchrs. Assn. (chmn. exec. bd. 1976-78). Home: Apt 602-S 2500 Virginia Ave NW Washington DC 20037 Office: Dept East Asian Langs and Lit George Washington U Washington DC 20052

SHIKARA, IZZALDIN ABBAS, neurologist, physician, educator; b. Baghdad, Iraq, July 1, 1929; s. Abbas Bakir and Maryam Husain (Shikara) S.; m. Anisa Yeusif Shikara, Jan. 1, 1961; children: Zaineb, Ali, Amina, Akeel, Aliaa. MB, M in Surgery, Med. Coll., Baghdad, 1953; D in Tropical Medicine, Sch. Tropical Medicine, London, 1960. Physician Ministry of Health, Baghdad, 1954-63; tchr., head dept. medicine U. Mosul, Iraq, 1964-78; head dept. neurology U. Baghdad, 1978-80; cons. physician, neurologist Baghdad, 1980—; founder Med. Ctr. and Intensive Care Unit, Mosul Teaching Hosp., 1972-76. Author: Diseases of the Nervous System, 1984; contbr. chpts to books; contbr. articles to profl. jours. Fellow Royal Coll. Physicians, (London, Edinburgh, Glasgow), Royal Soc. Medicine, London Soc. Medicine; mem. Arab Fedn. Neurol. Scis. Found. (pres.). Home: PO Box 28068 Dawoodi, Baghdad Iraq Office: Al Sameen Bldg, Saadoon St, Nasr Sq, Baghdad Iraq

SHIKIKO, SAITOH, architect; b. Tochigi, Kanto, Japan, June 13, 1944; parents: Kiyoshi Inoue and Mie Inoue; m. Masasuke Saitoh, Dec. 5, 1969. BArch, Hosei U., 1968. Registered architect, Japan. Architect Shigeru Aoki & Assocs., 1968—; asst. prof. architecture Hosei U., 1972—; pres. Shiki Architect & Assocs., Tokyo, 1978—; dir. Project of Alsace Village, Ito, Japan, 1986—. Prin. works include: Hangar for 747 Jumbo Jet, Tokyo, 1972, United Calif. Bank, Tokyo, 1975, Ch. of Immanuel in Tokyo, 1980. Mem. Archtl. Inst. of Japan, Japan Inst. of Architects, Forum On Sci. Clubs: Taiyo (Shizuoka). Home: 41-17 2 Nishi, Kunitachi City, Tokyo 186, Japan Office: Shiki Architect and Assocs, 41-17 2 Nishi, Kunitachi City, Tokyo 186, Japan

SHIM, SANG KOO, state mental health official; b. Tokyo, Japan, Oct. 1, 1942; came to U.S., 1968; s. Sang Taek and Kum Ryon (Bae) S.; m. Jae Hee Lee, July 12, 1972; children: Tammy, David. BS, Seoul Nat. U., Korea, 1967; MBA, No. Ill. U., 1970; MS, U. Wis., 1975. CPA, Ill. Acct. Vaughn Mfg. Co., Chgo., 1970-72, Stewart-Warner Corp., Chgo., 1972-73; fin. cons. Cen. Acctg. Assn., New Baden, Ill., 1977-79; auditor Ill. Dept. Mental Health, Springfield, 1980-82, chief fiscal officer, 1983—. Treas. Korean Assn. Greater St. Louis, 1982. Mem. Ill. CPA Soc., Assn. Govt. Accts. Home: 5 Settlers Ln Springfield IL 62707 Office: Ill Dept Mental Health Office of Mgmt and Budget 401 S Spring St Springfield IL 62706

SHIMADA, HIDEO, mining company executive; b. Tokyo, Mar. 29, 1926; s. Yoshiji and Kou (Yamanaka); m. Hiroko Hori, Nov. 30, 1959; children: Akiko, Tomoko. LLB, Tokyo U., 1948; completed advanced mgmt. program, Harvard Bus. Sch., 1977. With Marunouchi Trading Co., Tokyo, 1949-52, Fuji Trading Co., Tokyo, 1952-54; with Mitsubishi Corp., 1954-84, Santiago, Chile, 1961-64, New Delhi, 1969-72, London, 1972-74; dir., v.p., gen. mgr. coordination dept. Mitsubishi Internat. Corp., N.Y.C., 1978-82; gen. mgr. coordination dept. Mitsubishi Corp., Osaka, Japan, 1982-83; rep. Tokyo liaison office Mitsubishi Devel. Proprietary, Ltd., Tokyo, 1983—; pres. B & H Corp., N.Y., 1980-82. Contbr. articles to profl. jours. Buddhist. Home: 2-20-23 Nishiogi-kita, Suginami-ku, Tokyo 167, Japan

SHIMAZAKI, YASUHISA, cardiac surgeon; b. Kagoshima, Japan, Feb. 19, 1946; s. Hisashi and Sumiko (Tsukada) S.; m. Yuko Inomata, Oct. 10, 1987; children: Taisuke John, Kyosuke. MD, Osaka U., 1970, DMS, 1987. Resident in surgery Osaka U. Hosp., 1970-77; asst. Osaka U. Med. Sch., 1977-82, sr. assoc., 1986—; Graham Traveling Fellow Am. Assn. for Thoracic Surgery, Birmingham, Ala., 1982-83; cardiovascular surgery fellow U. Ala., Birmingham, 1983-84; staff surgeon Osaka Boshi Ctr. Hosp., Sakai, 1984-86. Mem. Japan Assn. Thoracic Surgery, Japan Assn. Pediatric Surgery. Home: 1-9-21 Inaba, Higashiosaka 578, Japan Office: Osaka U Med Sch, Fukushima,, Fukushima-ku,, 553 Osaka Japan

SHIMEALL, WARREN GLEN, lawyer; b. Topeka, Nov. 13, 1925; s. Glen Woodard and Pearl Agnes (Thoroughman) S. Student, U. Tulsa, 1943, George Washington U., 1947; JD, U. Okla., 1950; grad., USMSRTA Acad., Boston, 1944; postgrad., Harvard U., 1979. Bar: Okla. 1950, Korea 1952, Japan 1954, U.S. Ct. Internat. Trade 1971, U.S. Ct. Mil. Appeals 1980. Assoc. Leon I. Greenberg, Tokyo, 1954-59; ptnr. Bushell & Shimeall, Tokyo, 1959-74, Welty & Shimeall, Tokyo, 1974-79; sr. ptnr. Welty, Shimeall & Kasari Internat. Law and Patents, Tokyo, 1979—; pres. Fast Food Y.K., Tokyo, 1982—; pres. Japan Pizza Co., Roman Meal Co., Japan, Suntown Co. Ltd., Hong Kong; pres., pub. Japan TV Guide. Pres. Tokyo Union Ch. Shuyko Hojin, TUC Found., Dela; co-founder, dir. Clark Hatch Athletic Ctr., Seoul, Republic of Korea, 1971—. Served to col. U.S. Army, 1951-82. Mem. Am. C. of C.-Japan, Am.-Japan Soc., Asiatic Soc. Japan, Japan-Am. Soc. Legal Studies, Internat. House Japan, Tokyo Dai-Ni Bar Assn., ABA, Okla. Bar Assn., Japan Bar Assn., Assn. U.S. Army, Navy League, U.S. Naval Inst., VFW, Mil. Order World Wars, Res. Officers Assn., Phi Delta Phi. Clubs: Tokyo, Fgn. Corrs., American; Commodore (Washington). Lodges: Masons (master Tokyo club 1985-87), Order Rose Croix (past wise master), Grand Lodge Japan (grand orator 1987). Office: Welty Shimeall & Kasari, New Otemachi Bldg 450, 1-2-1, Otemachi Tokyo 100, Japan

SHIMER, DANIEL LEWIS, corporate executive; b. San Angelo, Tex., July 30, 1944; s. Lewis V. and Mary A. (Slick) S.; divorced. BS in Acctg. and Mktg., Ind. U., 1972; postgrad., Loyola U., New Orleans, 1977. CPA. Sr. acct. Peat, Marwick, Mitchell & Co., Indpls., 1973-75; corp. audit mgr. Lykes-Youngstown Corp., New Orleans, 1975-76, dir. working capital, 1976-77, asst. treas., 1977-78; asst. treas. LTV Corp., Dallas, 1978-79; v.p. fin. Stoller Chem. Co., Houston, 1979-81, Petro-Silver, Inc., Denver, 1981-83; v.p., treas. FoxMeyer Corp., Denver, 1983-86, CoastAmerica Corp., Denver, 1986—; bd. dirs. Petro-Silver, Inc., Denver. Mem. Am. Inst. CPA's, Nat. Assn. of Corp. Treas., Colo. Cash Mgmt. Assn., Multiple Sclerosis Soc. Colo. (dir.), Cherry Creek Commerce Assn. (bd. dirs.). Roman Catholic. Home: 445 N Clarkson Denver CO 80218 Office: Coast Am Corp 501 S Cherry St #1100 Denver CO 80222

SHIMIZU, NORIHIKO, consulting company executive; b. Kamiosaki, Japan, Apr. 1, 1940; s. Shirokichi and Itsuko (Gohko) S.; m. Hinako Miyazaki, Dec. 18, 1970; children—Daijo, Hironobu. B.A., Keio U., Tokyo, 1963; M.B.A., Stanford U., 1967. Mem. staff Tokio Marine & Fire Ins. Co., Tokyo, 1963-67; cons. Boston Cons. Group, Inc., 1967-69, mng. dir., Tokyo, 1970-74, v.p., dir., 1970-87; pres. Shimizu & Co., Inc., 1987— ; adviser Japan Devel. Bank, 1969-73; lectr. Sophia U., Tokyo, 1969-73; vis. lectr. UCLA, 1974. Author: (with others) Japanese Management, 1970; editor: (with others) Business Strategy, 1970. Recipient award Sophia U., 1956. Mem. New Mgmt. Club (v.p.), Bus. Research Inst., Stanford Alumni Assn. Japan (trustee), Stanford Bus. Sch. Alumni Assn. Japan (pres.). Office: 601C 6th floor, 39 Mori Bldg 2-4-5 Azabudai, Minato-ku Tokyo 106, Japan

SHIMMEL, ROBERT GILHAM, dermatologist; b. Jackson, Mich., Feb. 23, 1930; s. Earl Clinton and Alta Stewart (Reid) S.; m. Janice Marie Evely, Oct. 12, 1957; children—Anne E., Thomas R., Amie S., Elizabeth A. B.A., Albion Coll., 1951; D.O., Chgo. Coll. Osteopathic Medicine, 1955. Diplomate Am. Osteo. Bd. Dermatology. Intern Chgo. Osteo. Hosp., 1955-56; dermatology preceptor Chgo. Osteo. Hosp., 1956-59; pvt. practice dermatology, Riverview, Mich., 1959—; cons. Riverside Osteo. Hosp., Trenton, Mich., 1959—; clin. prof. Mich. State U. Coll. Osteo. Medicine, Lansing, 1972—. Diplomate Nat. Bd. Examiners for Osteo. Physicians and Surgeons. Fellow Am. Osteo. Coll. Dermatology (pres. 1963-64, sec. 1969-74); mem. Am. Osteo. Assn., Mich. Osteo. Soc. Dermatologists (pres. 1969-70), Mich. Assn. Osteo. Physicians and Surgeons, Inc., Acad. Dermatology, Wayne County Osteo. Assn. Republican. Presbyterian. Avocation: running. Home: 19891 Parke Ln Grosse Ile MI 48138 Office: 17171 Fort Box 2070 Riverview MI 48192

SHIMMIN, JOHN ALLEN, museologist, archaeologist; b. Detroit, Mar. 29, 1946; s. George Allen and Gertrude (Reeve) S. B.A., Mich. State U., 1975. Artist/cartographer Mich. State U., East Lansing, 1975-76; archaeol. field supr. Mackinac Island State Park Commn., Mich., 1976-79; pres. Archaeographic, Royal Oak, Mich., 1978-82; geophys. data analyst Gold Fields Mining Corp., Denver, 1983—; exec. dir. Archaeographic, Denver, 1982—; archaeol. investigator Western U.S. and Mich.; creator displays for pub. and pvt. mus.; lectr. in field. Illustrator: An Archaeological Inventory and Evaluation of the Sleeping Bear Dunes National Lakeshore, Leelanau and Benzie Counties, Michigan, 1976; The Garfield Orbit, 1978; also numerous other maps and illustrations for profl. jours. Contbr. various articles. Recipient 1st place drawing show Kent State U., 1965-67. Mem. Internat. Platform Assn., Archaeol. Inst. Am., Delta Tau Delta. Presbyterian. Address: 411 Ogden St Denver CO 80218

SHIMOJI, KOKI, physician, educator; b. Tarama, Japan, Nov. 21, 1935; s. Kochu and Eiko Shimoji; m. Yoko Sano, Jan. 9, 1972; children—Yuko, Kaoru. M.D., Kumamoto U. (Japan), 1960; D. Med. Sci., Kyoto U. (Japan), 1965. Intern Kumamoto U. Hosp., 1960-61; instr. Kyoto U., 1965-66; asst. prof. Kumamoto U., Japan, 1966-68, assoc. prof., 1968-73; assoc. prof. Tokyo Med. and Dental U., 1973-74; prof., chmn. Niigata U. (Japan), 1974—. Author: Neuroanesthesia, 1972; contbr. articles to profl. jours. Mem. Japan Soc. Anesthesiologists (councillor; most disting. paper award 1965), Japan Soc. EEG and EMG (councillor), Japan Soc. Acute Medicine (councillor), Japan Soc. Pain Clinic (pres. 1982-83), Japan Med. Assn. (clinical application spinal cord potential award 1983), Internat. Brain Research Orgn., Internat. Assn. Study Pain. Buddhist. Home: 1-757 Asahi-Machi, Niigata 951, Japan Office: Niigata U Sch Medicine, Asahi-Machi, Niigata 951, Japan

SHIMP, LAWRENCE ALBERT, research chemist; b. Phila., Nov. 17, 1949; s. Hans George and Lydia (Bacon) S. BA, Northwestern U., 1971; PhD, MIT, 1976. Postdoctoral research assoc. U. Tex., Austin, 1976-77, Argonne (Ill.) Nat. Lab., 1977; research chemist FMC Corp., Princeton, N.J., 1977-85; prin. scientist Coors Biomed. Co., Lakewood, Colo., 1985-88; project mgr. Cobe Labs., Inc., Arvada, Colo., 1988—. Contbr. articles to profl. jours.; inventor tetramethylpentane blood substitutes, others. Fellow Am. Inst. Chemists; mem. Am. Chem. Soc., N.Y. Acad. Scis., Sigma Xi. Home: 7470 Terry Ct Golden CO 80403 Office: Cobe Labs Inc 14401 W 65th Way Arvada CO 80004

SHIN, BU YONG, transportation executive; b. Seoul, Republic of Korea, Jan. 15, 1943; s. Ji-Bom Shin and Yang-Ok Lee; m. Hae-Jin Byon, May 30, 1970; 1 child, Yong-Yee. BSc, Seoul Nat. U., 1964; MA, U. Toronto, Ont., Can., 1973, PhD, 1981. Planning engr. Korea Cons. Engrs. Co., Seoul, 1967-69; transp. engr. Read, Voohees & Assocs., Toronto, Can., 1971-74; transp. engr. N.D. Lea & Assocs., Toronto, Can., 1975-76, transp. cons., 1976-81; dir. Transport System Research G. KAIST, Seoul, Republic of Korea, 1981-86; v.p. Korea Transport Inst., Seoul, 1986—; lect. McMaster U., Hamilton, Ont., Can., 1976-78. Patentee in field. Served as cpl. engineers Korean army, 1964-67. Fellow Rd. and Transp. Assn. Can.; mem. Korea Inst. Transp. Engrs., Assn. Profl. Engrs. Korea (cert.), Inst. Transp. Engrs., Assn. Profl. Engrs. Ont. (cert.), Japan Soc. Traffic Engrs. Home: 574-9 Suyuo-dong, Tobong-ku, Seoul Republic of Korea Office: Korea Transport Inst, 61 Youido-dong, 150 Seoul Republic of Korea

SHINDO, SADAKAZU, manufacturing executive; b. Kure City, Hiroshima Prefecture, Japan, Mar. 4, 1910; s. Tokuichi and Fuji Shindo; m. Eiko Higashii, 1964; 2 children. grad. Kyushu U., 1933. Former pres. Mitsubishi Electric Corp., Tokyo, chmn., 1980—. Recipient Medal of Honor with Blue Ribbon, 1974. Home: 36-8-101 Yoyagi, 3-chome, Tokyo 151 Japan Office: Mitsubishi Electric Corp, 2-3 Marunouchi, 2-chome Chiyoda-ku, Tokyo 100 Japan *

SHINE, JOHN, molecular geneticist; medical researcher; b. Brisbane, Australia; July 3, 1946; came to U.S., 1984; s. Patrick and Molly Gertrude (Hoare) S.; m. Kathleen Mary Morgan, Feb. 15, 1969; children—Rebecca Kathleen, Michael Patrick. B.Sc. with honors, Australian Nat. U., 1972, Ph.D., 1975. Research fellow Molecular Biology Unit Australian Nat. U., Canberra, 1978-80, fellow dept. genetics, 1980-83, sr. fellow dept. genetics, 1983-87 , assoc. dir. Centre Recombinant DNA Research, 1983-87 ; adj. prof. medicine U. Calif.-San Francisco, 1985-87 ; v.p. research and devel. Calif. Biotech. Inc., Mountain View, 1984-86; pres., chief sci. officer, 1986-87, prof. molecular biol. U. N.S.W., 1987— ; cons. Agrigenetics Corp., Boulder, 1982-84, Calif. Biotech. Inc., 1982-84; dir. Biotech. Research Ptnrs., Mountain View, 1984—, dep. dir. Garvan Inst. Med. Research, Australia, 1987—; chmn. Pacific Biotech. Ltd., 1987— . Editor Molecular Biology and Medicine, DNA. Patentee; contbr. articles to profl. jours. Recipient Boehringer-Mannheim medal Australian Biochem. Soc., 1980; Gottschalk medal disting. research in biol. med. sci. Australian Acad. Sci., 1982. Current work: Molecular genetics and molecular neurobiology-hypertension and molecular biology of cardiovascular disease. Subspecialties: Molecular biology; Genetics and genetic engineering (medicine).

SHINER, ADRIAN JAMES, electronics engineer; b. Bristol, Eng., May 1, 1947; s. James Henry and Betty (Alway) S.; m. Joyce Margaret Day, July 29, 1972; children: Ruth, Naomi. BS, Bath (Eng.) U., 1970. Design engr. Brit. Aircraft Corp., Bristol, Eng., 1970-73; design and devel. engr. Automatic Handling, Bristol, 1973-81; project engr. Kone Oy, Hyninkää, Finland, 1982-84; asst. test. mgr. Kone Marryat Scott, London, 1984-85, product support mgr., 1985—. Patentee in field. Mem. Inst. Elec. Engrs. Home: 60 Pennine Way, Farnborough Hampshire, England GU14 9JA Office: Kone Lifts Ltd, Wellington Rd S, Hounslow, Middlesex TW4 5JN, England

SHINFUKU, NAOTAKE, psychiatrist, research counselor; b. Kagoshima, Japan, Mar. 2, 1914; s. Sukenoshin and Yuki (Nakano) S.; m. Makiko Shigetomi, Nov. 20, 1942; 1 child, Naotaka. Medicinae doctor, Kyushu U., Fukuoka, 1937, M.D., 1947. Asst., Taihoku U., Formosa, 1940-45; vice dir. Prefectural Mental Hosp., Fukuoka, 1951-52; asst. prof. Tottori U., Yonago, Japan, 1952-56; prof. and dir. dept. psychiatry Faculty Medicine, 1956-66; prof., dir. dept. psychiatry Jikei U. Sch. Medicine, Tokyo, 1966-79; counselor Tokyo Met. Inst. Gerontology, 1979—, Life Planning Ctr., Tokyo, 1977—. Author: Clinical Psychiatry of the Aged, 1969, Masked Depression, 1978, Textbook of Modern Psychiatry, 1979; editor-in-chief Japanese Jour. Psychotherapy, 1978—. Mem. Japanese Assn. Psychosomatic Medicine (hon.; pres. 1973-74) Japanese Med. Soc. Alcohol Studies (pres. 1973-74), Japanese Soc. Traffic Sci.; collaborative mem. WHO Depression Study. Home: 6-1-22 Okusawa, Setagaya-ku, Tokyo 158 Japan Office: Inst of Gerontology, 35-2 Sakae-cho, Itabashi-ku, Tokyo 173 Japan

SHINN, ALLEN MAYHEW, retired naval officer, business executive; b. Niles, Calif., June 6, 1908; s. Joseph Clark and Florence Maria (Mayhew) S.; m. Sevilla Hayden Shuey, June 20, 1936; children: Allen Mayhew, James Washburn, Jonathan Hayden. B.S., U.S. Naval Acad., 1932; grad., Nat. War Coll., 1953. Commd. officer USN, 1932, advanced through grades to vice adm.; served in battleships, 1932-36; naval aviator 1937, served in various fleet aircraft squadrons, comdr. 3, also comdr. attack carrier air group, 1944-45; served on various staffs; comdr. 2 carriers USS Saipan, 1956, USS Forrestal, 1958; comdt. midshipmen U.S. Naval Acad., Annapolis, Md., 1956-58; comdr. Anti-Submarine Warfare Carrier Task Group, 1960-61, Attack Carrier Task Force, 1963-64; chief Bur. Naval Weapons, Washington, 1964-66; comdr. Naval Air Force Pacific Fleet, 1966-70; ret. 1970; chmn. bd. Harvard Industries, Inc., 1970-71, All-Am. Industries, 1973-78; pres. Internat. Controls Corp., 1973-78, dir., 1973-79; dir. Loral Corp., 1973—, Pennzoil Co., 1970—; Bd. dirs. Navy Mut. Aid Assn., 1962-66; bd. editorial control U.S. Naval Inst., 1964-66; bd. mgrs. Navy Relief Soc., 1962-64; pres. Naval Acad. Athletic Assn., 1956-58, North Water St. Corp., Edgartown, Mass., 1948-50. Trustee Longfellow Sch. Boys, Bethesda, Md., 1950-53. Mem. Soc. Mayflower Descendants., Delta Tau Delta. Republican. Unitarian. Clubs: Cosmos, N.Y. Yacht, Edgartown Yacht. Home: 100 Thorndale Dr San Rafael CA 94903 also: Edgartown MA 02539

SHINN, ARTHUR FREDERICK, clinical pharmacist, business executive, educator; b. N.Y.C., May 23, 1945; s. A. Frederick and Eleanor (McDonald) S.; m. Margaret See, Aug. 12, 1978; children: Jeffrey, Kara Nicole, Caitlin Jennifer. BS, L.I. U. Bklyn. Coll. Pharmacy, 1968; PharmD, U. Mich., 1972. Lic. pharmacist, Tenn., Mo., Mich. Supr., dir. drug info. ctr. William Beaumont Hosp., Royal Oak, Mich., 1972-76; asst. prof., dir. clin. pharmacy Wayne State U., Detroit, 1972-76; asst. prof., dir. drug info. ctr. St. Louis Coll. Pharmacy, 1976-78; mgr. profl. relations med. dept. Beecham Labs., Bristol, Tenn., 1978-82; med. dir., exec. v.p. Profl. Drug Systems, St. Louis, 1982—, also bd. dirs.; adj. assoc. prof. family practice Quillen Dishner Sch. Med., Johnson City, Tenn., 1979-82; staff cons. clin. pharmacology Faith Hosp., Creve Coeur, Mo., 1983—; bd. dirs. Trimel Corp., Toronto, Ont., Can. Editor: Evaluations of Drug Interactions, 1985; cons. clin. editor: Mosby's Pharmacology in Nursing, 1986; contbr. numerous articles to profl. jours. Fellow NIH, 1968. Mem. Am. Coll. Clin. Pharmacy, Am. Pharm. Assn., Am. Soc. Hosp. Pharmacists, Drug Info. Assn., Rho Chi, Iota Mu Pi. Home: 630 Clover Trail Dr Chesterfield MO 63017 Office: Profl Drug Systems Inc 2388 Schuetz Rd Suite A56 Saint Louis MO 63146

SHINN, DAVID HAMILTON, diplomat; b. Yakima, Wash., June 9, 1940; s. Guy Wilson and Ada Louise (Gelvin) S.; m. Judy Karen Rolfe, Sept. 9, 1961; children: Steven Hamilton, Christopher Rolfe. AA, Yakima Valley Coll., 1960; BA, George Washington U., 1963, MA, 1964, PhD, 1980; cert. African studies, Northwestern U., Evanston, Ill., 1969. With U.S. State Dept., 1964—; rotational officer U.S. Embassy, Beirut, Lebanon, 1964-66; polit. officer Nairobi, Kenya, 1967-68; desk officer East African affairs Washington, 1969-72; polit. officer Dar es Salaam, Tanzania, 1972-74; dep. chief of mission Nouakchott, Mauritania, 1974-76; dep. coordinator state and local govt. Washington, 1978-81; dep. chief of mission Yaounde, Cameroon, 1981-83, Khartoum, Sudan, 1983-86; U.S. ambassador Ouagadougou, Burkina Faso, 1987—. Recipient Superior Honor award State Dept., 1980, 85. Mem. Internat. Studies Assn., Am. Fgn. Service Assn., Am. Philatelic Soc. Methodist. Office: Dept of State US Ambassador to Burkina Faso Washington DC 20520

SHINODA, MASAHIRO, film director; b. Gifu City, Japan, Mar. 9, 1931; s. Toshiji and Hama (Kawamura) S.; grad. Waseda U., 1953; m. Shima Iwashita, Mar. 3, 1967; 1 child, Mai. Asst. dir. Shochiku Co., Ltd., 1953-59; dir. films including: Pale Flower, 1964, The Assassin, 1964, Samurai Spy, 1965, Beauty and Sorrow, 1965, Punishment Island, 1966, One Way Ticket, 1966, Clouds at Sunset, 1967, Double Suicide, 1968, The Scanda-lous Adventure of Himiko, Buraikan, 1970, Silence, 1971, Himiko, 1974, Under the Blossoming Cherry Trees, 1975, The Ballade of Orin, 1977, Demon Pond, 19779, Mac Arthur's Children, 1983 (Blue Ribbon Houston Internat. Film Festival, 1984), Gonza the Spearman, 1985 (Silver Bear award Berlin Film Festival, 1986). Recipient Spl. Jury prize Adelaide Internat., 1971; award Asia Film Festival, Sydney, 1978. Mem. Dirs. Guild Japan. Home: 1-11-13 Kita-Senzoku, Ota-ku, Tokyo 145, Japan

SHINOZUKA, MASANOBU, civil engineer, educator; b. Tokyo, Dec. 23, 1930; s. Akira and Kiyo S.; came to U.S., 1957, naturalized, 1971; B.S., Kyoto (Japan) U., 1953, M.S., 1955; Ph.D., Columbia U., 1960; m. Fujiko Sakamoto, Oct. 25, 1954; children—Rei, Naomi, Megumi. Research asst. civil engring. Columbia U., N.Y.C., 1958-61, asst. prof., 1961-65, asso. prof., 1965-69, prof., 1969—, Renwick prof., 1977-88; prof. Princeton U., 1988—; vis. scholar N.C. State U., Raleigh, 1967-68; pres. Modern Analysis Inc., Ridgewood, N.J., 1972—; co-chmn. 2d Internat. Conf. on Structural Safety and Reliability, 1978, 3d, 1981, 4th, 1985, also co-editor Proc. of 2d, 3d and 4th confs. cons. in field. NSF grantee, 1968—. Mem. Nat. Acad. Engring., ASCE (Walter L. Huber prize 1972; State-of-the-Art of Civil Engring. award 1973, Alfred M. Freudenthal medal 1978, Nathan M. Newmark medal 1985, Moisseiff award, 1988), ASME, AIAA, Japan Soc. Civil Engrs., Sigma Xi. Editor: Reliability Approach in Structural Engineering, 1975; co-editor Proc. ASCE Symposium on Probabilistic Methods in Structural Engring., 1981. Home: 15 Andrews Ln Princeton NJ 08540 Office: Princeton U E232 Engring Quad Princeton NJ 08544

SHINTO, HISASHI, Japanese telecommunications company executive; b. Fukuoka Prefecture, Japan, July 2, 1910; s. Yasuhide and Michiyo S.; m. Michiko Kushiro, 1936; 4 children.BS Kyushu Imperial U., 1934, PhD, 1958. With Harima Shipbuilding & Engring. Co., Ltd., 1934, Nat. Bulk Carriers Corp., Kure Yard, 1951; mng. dir. Ishikawajima-Harima Heavy Industries, Ltd. (IHI), div. mgr. shipbuilding div., 1960, exec. v.p. IHI, 1964, pres., 1972-79, counsellor, 1979-80; pres. Shipbuilders Assn. Japan, 1977-79; mng. dir. Japan Ship Exporters Assn., 1979-80; counsellor Transp. Technics, Ministry of Transp., 1979-83; pres., commr., mem. council mgmt. com. Nippon Telegraph and Telephone Pub. Corp. (NTT), 1981, pres., chief exec. officer, 1985—; dir. Tokyo Shibaura Electric Co. Ltd. (Toshiba), 1966—. Recipient medal of honor with blue ribbon; Legion d' Honner. Avocations: golf; photography. Address: NTT Head Office I-chome, 1-6 Uchisawai-cho, Chiyoda-ku, Tokyo 100, Japan

SHINZO, MATSUOKA, steel company executive; b. Hikari, Yamaguchi, Japan, Sept. 15, 1923; s. Yousuke and Ryoko (Shin) M.; m. Haruko Kachoo, July 7, 1965. BA in Juris Prudence, Kyoto (Japan) U., 1935. Exec. v.p. Union Pipe Inc., N.Y.C., 1960-64; chmn., pres. Sumitomo Metal Am. Inc., N.Y.C., 1974-80; exec. dir. Sumitomo Metal Industries Ltd., Tokyo, 1980-83, exec. mng. dir., 1983-86, exec. sr. mng. dir., 1986—, exec. advisor, 1988—; bd. dirs. Tubemakers of Australia Ltd., Sydney; vice chmn. Productora Mexicana de Tuberia, Mex. Home: 705 19 40 Akasaka 6 Chome, Minato ku, Tokyo 107, Japan Office: Sumitomo Metal Industries Ltd, OTE Ctr Bldg, 1 3 Otemachi 1 chome, Chiyoda ku, Tokyo 100, Japan

SHIN-ZOULEK, YOON SOOK, biochemist, researcher; b. Seoul, Aug. 5, 1946; came to Ger., 1975; d. Jung Sik and Chung Ja (Kwon) S.; m. Karl Ulrich Buhring, Aug. 15, 1974 (div. June 1980); m. 2d, Gert Zoulek, July 11, 1980. B.S., U. Seoul, 1968, Pharmacist, 1968; Ph.D., U. Calif.-Berkeley, 1972. Teaching asst. U. Calif., 1970-72, research asst., 1968-72; research assoc. U. Calif.-Berkeley and U. Rochester, N.Y., 1975—; Wissenschaft asst. U. Munich, Fed. Republic Germany, 1975—. Contbr. articles in field to profl. jours. Deutsche Forschunge Gemeinschaft grantee, 1975-79. Mem. N.Y. Acad. Scis., Korean Scis. and Engrs. Assns. in Europe (sec., gen.), European Soc. Pediatric Research, Soc. Inborn Errors of Metabolism, Sigma Xi. Office: Univ Munich Kinderklinik, Lindwurmstr 4, 8000 Munich 2 Federal Republic of Germany

SHIOKAWA, YOSHITO, soft drink company executive; b. Kita-Kyushu, Fukuoka, Japan, Jan. 22, 1931; s. Yahachiro and Kimi (Ohto) S.; m. Michiko Ayano, Mar. 1, 1936; children: Hiroyoshi, Naoko. B in Fisheries, Tokyo U. of Fisheries, 1955. Staff Inaba Foods Co. Ltd., Ibara-gun, Shizuoka, Japan, 1955-56; staff Calpis Food Industry Co. Ltd., Tokyo, 1956-71, mgr. research lab., 1971-77, mgr. Okayama plant, 1977-83, dir., 1983-85, sr. mng. dir., 1985—. Mem. Japan Health Food Assn. Office: Calpis Food Industry Co Ltd, 20-3 2-chome Ebissu-Nishi, Shibuya-ku, Tokyo 150, Japan

SHIPLEY, SHIRLEY DAHL, oil company executive; b. Orange, N.J., Oct. 17, 1932; d. Conrad George and Sylvia Marion (Gronquist) D.; B.S., Cedar Crest Coll. Allentown, Pa., 1954; m. William Stewart Shipley II, July 2,

1955; children—William Stewart III, Linda Ann, Elizabeth Marion. Tchr., Radnor Twp. (Pa.) Schs., 1954-55, Sarasota County (Fla.) Schs., 1955-56; adminstrv. v.p. Shipley Oil Co., Inc., York, Pa., 1977—. Pres., York Suburban Sch. Dist. Bd., 1973-79; bd. dirs., co-chmn. York Country Day Sch., York County Library System, York County Mental Health Center, Greater York, Inc., United Community Services, York County Literacy Council, ARC, Women's Assn. York Symphony Orch., York Found.; pres. Childrens Home; trustee, mem. exec. com. York Coll. of Pa., 1972—; mem. York, Franklin and Adams County Intermediate Unit Sch. Bd. pres. Jr. League York, 1967-69; nat. bd. dirs. Assn. Jr. Leagues, 1970-72; mem. Pa. adv. council U.S. Commn. Civil Rights; trustee York Coll. Pa. Mem. Pa. Petroleum Assn., Petroleum Marketers Assn. Am. Republican. Presbyterian. Home: 1000 Clubhouse Rd York PA 17403 Office: 550 E King St PO Box 946 York PA 17405

SHIPLEY, WALTER VINCENT, banker; b. Newark, Nov. 2, 1935; s. L. Parks and Emily (Herzog) S.; m. Judith Ann Lyman, Sept. 14, 1957; children: Barbara, Allison, Pamela, Dorothy, John. Student, Williams Coll., 1954-56; BS, NYU, 1960. With Chem. Bank, N.Y.C., 1956—, exec. v.p. in charge internat. div., 1978-79, sr. exec. v.p., until 1981, pres., 1982-83; chmn. bd. Chem. Banking Corp., N.Y.C., 1983—, Chem. N.Y. Corp., N.Y.C., 1983—; bd. dirs. Champion Internat. Corp., NYNEX Corp. Bd. dirs. Japan Soc., Lincoln Ctr. for Performing Arts Inc., N.Y. City Partnership Inc., Goodwill Industries Greater N.Y. Inc., United Way Tri-State; mem. bd. trustees Cen. Park Conservancy, NYU. Mem. N.Y. C. of C. and Industry (bd. dirs.), The Bus. Council, Bus. Roundtable, Council Fgn. Relations, English Speaking Union, Pilgrims of U.S. Clubs: Links; Augusta Nat. Golf; Baltusrol Golf (Springfield, N.J.); Blind BrookGolf. Office: Chem Bank 277 Park Ave New York NY 10172

SHIPMAN, MARK SAMUEL, lawyer; b. Hartford, Conn., Apr. 16, 1937; s. Paul David and Reeva (Joseph) S.; m. Sonia S. Sosensky, Aug. 28, 1960; children—Paul, Lawrence, William. B.A., U. Conn. Hartford, 1959, LL.B., 1962. Bar: Conn. 1962, U.S. Dist. Ct. Conn. 1963, U.S. Ct. Appeals (2d cir.) 1967, U.S. Supreme Ct. 1973. Assoc. Schatz & Schatz, Hartford, 1962-64; asst. state's atty. State of Conn., 1964-66; ptnr. Schatz & Schatz, Ribicoff & Kotkin, Hartford, 1967—. Mem. Greater Hartford Transp. Dist., 1973-86, chmn., 1978-86; mem. council Town of Newington (Conn.), 1966-68, 73-75; mem. Bd. of Edn., Newington, 1979-81; town atty., Newington, 1975-77, 81-86; sec., vice-chmn. state commn. Med. Legal Investig, 1986—; chmn. Charter Rev. Commn., Newington, 1969, 71; mem. adv. bd. Downtown Council, chmn. Transp. Com., 1986—. Mem. ABA, Conn. Bar Assn., Hartford County Bar Assn., Assn. Trial Lawyers Am., Conn. Trial Lawyers Assn., Am. Acad. Forensic Sci. (chmn. juris sect. 1977, exec. com. 1980-83, v.p. 1983-84), Nat. Def. Lawyers Assn. Democrat. Jewish. Clubs: Lions, Tumblebrook Country, Masons. Home: 83 Kenmore Rd Bloomfield CT 06002 Office: 90 State House Sq Hartford CT 06103

SHIR, JAY, Writer, educator, musician; b. Spartanburg, S.C., Dec. 29, 1946; s. Jackson Holt Birdsong and Rachel Walker (Persons) B.; m. Nomi Erteschik (div. 1979); children—Tamar, Dafna; m. Zohara Belorai, 1987. B.A., Antioch Coll., 1969; M.A., Boston U., 1973; Ph.D., Hebrew U., Jerusalem, Israel, 1977. Composer, conductor music for legitimate stage, Montreal, Que., Can., and Boston, 1969-73; lectr. dept. lit. Ben-Gurion U. of the Negev, Beer-Sheva, Israel, 1975-84; free-lance writer and musician, Jerusalem, 1984—; voice instr. Hebrew Union Coll., Jerusalem; assoc. editor Tel Aviv Rev., guest lectr. in field. Composer scores for He Who Gets Slapped, The Exception and the Rule, A Day in the Death of Joe Egg, Alice in Wonderland; conductor Threepenny Opera; drama critic The Nation, Israel; poems published in U.S., France, Israel; soloist, Jerusalem Opera Theatre, Jerusalem Symphony Orch.; contbr. articles to profl. jours. Nat. Merit scholar, 1964-69; Ben-Gurion U. grantee, 1978-83; Govt. of Israel scholar, 1974-75. Avocations: painting, hiking, swimming. Home: PO Box 8558, Jerusalem Israel

SHIRAI, IKUMA, architect; b. Tokyo, June 6, 1944; s. Seiiti and Teruko (Kawamura) S.; m. Tizu Yanagisawa; children: Ryoh, Jyoh. BA, Internat. Christian U., Tokyo, 1966; postgrad., Freie U., Berlin, 1971, Staatliche Hochschule Bildende Künstein, Berlin, 1973. Asst. architect Shirai Seiiti Archtl. Inst., Tokyo, 1973-83, mgmt. architect, 1983—. Prin. works include Sekisui-kan Art Mus., 1981, Keika-no-ie residential home, 1983, Jupiter Bldg., 1988; editor: Shirai Seiiti Study, 1975-83; author: Complete Works of Shirai Seiiti, 1987. Home: Ehara-cho 2-31 Nakano-ku, Tokyo Japan

SHIRATORI, REI, political science educator; b. Taipei, Taiwan, Aug. 26, 1937; s. Katsuyoshi and Mitsu (Wada) S.; m. Rieko Nishikawa, Jan. 5, 1965; children—Hiroshi, Yuki. B.A., Waseda U., Japan, 1960, M.A., 1962; postgrad. Pembroke Coll., Oxford U., Eng., 1963-64. Lectr. polit. sci. Dokkyo U., Japan, 1967-70, assoc. prof., 1970-75; prof. polit. sci., 1975-87, prof. emeritus, 1987—; prof. dept. polit. sci. and econs. Tokai (Japan) U., 1987—, dean dept., 1988—, dir. Inst. Social Sci., 1988—; fellow W. Wilson Ctr., Smithsonian Instn., Washington, 1978-79; prof. dept. govt., dir. Centre for Study Contemporary Japan, U. Essex, Colchester, Eng., 1984-88; dir. Inst. for Polit. Studies in Japan, Tokyo, 1973-87, chmn. bd. dirs., 1987—. Author: (in Japanese) Political Development, 1968, Public Opinion, Election and Politics, 1972; editor: (in Japanese) History of Japanese Cabinet, 3 vols., 1981; (in English) Japan in the 1980s, 1982. Mem. Japan Polit. Sci. Assn. (mem. council 1977-79, 81-83), Japan Peace Studies Assn. (v.p. 1976-80), Japan Election Studies Assn. (mem. council 1981—). Avocations: violin, swimming. Office: Tokai U 1117, Dept Polit Sci and Econs, Kitakaname, Hiratsuka-shi, Kanagawa-ken 259-1, Japan

SHIRAWI, YOUSUF AHMED, Bahrain government official; b. Muharraq, Bahrain, Mar. 10, 1927; s. Ahmed Shirawi; m. May Al Arrayed; 6 children. BA in Chemistry, Am. U., Beirut, 1950; ARTC, Glasgow, Scotland, 1955. Dir. edn. Ministry of Edn., Govt. of Bahrain, 1955-57, adminstrv. council, 1957-63, dir. oil Ministry Devel. and Engring., 1963-67, dir. devel., 1967-70, minister for devel. and engring., 1970-75, minister devel. and industry, 1975—, acting minister of state for cabinet affairs, 1982—; chmn. bd. Bahrain Petroleum Co., Aluminum Bahrain, Bahrain Nat. Oil Co.; chmn. exec. com. Gulf Air Co. Vice chmn. Arab Thought Forum. Mem. Gulf Coop. Council (ministerial oil and indsl. coms.). Muslim. Avocation: astronomy. Home: PO Box 235, Manama Bahrain Office: Ministry of Devel and Industry, PO Box 1435, Manama Bahrain

SHIRCLIFF, JAMES VANDERBURGH, restaurant executive; b. Vincennes, Ind., Dec. 11, 1938; s. Thomas Maxwell and Martha Bayard (Somes) S.; A.B., Brown U., 1961; postgrad. U. Va., 1963-64; m. Sally Anne Hoing, June 20, 1964; children—Thomas, Susan, Anne, Catherine, Caroline. Asst. gen. mgr. Pepsi Cola Allied Bottlers, Inc., Lynchburg, Va., 1964-65; gen. mgr. First Colony Canners, Inc., Lynchburg, 1965-66; v.p., divisional coordinator Pepsi Cola Allied Bottlers, Inc., Lynchburg, 1966-68, v.p., dir. personnel, 1968-70; v.p., gen. mgr. GCC Beverages, Inc., Lynchburg, 1970-74, group v.p. Va., 1974-75; corp. v.p. Gen. Cinema Corp., Beverage Div., Lynchburg, 1976-77; owner/mgr. WLLL-AM, WGOL-FM, Lynchburg, 1977-86; pres. Jamarbo Corp., 1977—; pres. Swensen's of Va., Inc., mem. exec. com. Swensen's owners council; presdl. interchange exec., 1975-76; exec. dir. Nat. Indsl. Energy Council, Dept. Commerce, Washington, 1975-76. Vice pres. JOBS, Lynchburg, 1970; dir. Central Va. Health Planning Council, 1974-75; mem. Govs. Indsl. Energy Adv. Council, 1976—; dir. Piedmont council, Boy Scouts Am., 1972-73; mem. City of Lynchburg Keep Lynchburg Beautiful Commn., 1974-75, chmn. emergency planning bd., 1974-75, chmn. overall econ. planning council, 1977—; bd. dirs. Lynchburg Broadway Theatre, 1973-75, Acad. Music, 1973-74, United Fund, Lynchburg, 1966-67, Central Va. Industries, 1971-72, Va. Public Telecommunications Council; chmn. campaign United Way, 1982, pres., 1983; chmn. Citizens for a Clean Lynchburg; campaign chmn. United Way of Central Va.; trustee Va. Episc. Sch.; mem. pres.' council Randolph-Macon Women's Coll.; mem. Va-Israel Commn. Served to lt. (j.g.), USN, 1961-63. Recipient Cloyd Meml. award for outstanding service, Greater Lynchburg C. of C., 1975; Va. Soft Drink Assn. citation, 1970, 73, 74; NCCJ Brotherhood Citation; Public Service award Radio-TV Commn. of So. Bapt. Conv. Mem. Va. C. of C. (dir. 1976-79), Greater Lynchburg C. of C. (dir., v.p. 1973-74, chmn. community appearance task force 1977-79), Va. Soft Drink Assn. (pres. 1973-74), Va. Pepsi Cola Bottlers Assn. (pres. 1970-73), Nat., Va. (dir. 1974, pres. 1985-86) assns. broadcasters, Lynchburg Advt. Club (v.p.), Va. AP Broadcasters Assn. (pres.), Lynchburg Fine Arts Center (pres.). Roman Catholic. Clubs: Mensa (N.Y.); Commonwealth (Richmond, Va.); Farmington Country (Charlottesville, Va.); Army-Navy (Washington); Oakwood Country (Lynchburg); Piedmont (Lynchburg); Navy League, Galliard, Visa Yacht, Pelican Point Yacht. Lodge: Rotary (pres., Paul Harris fellow 1982, dist. gov. 1986-87). Home: 3525 Otterview Pl Lynchburg VA 24503

SHIRCLIFF, ROBERT THOMAS, mgmt. cons.; b. Vincennes, Ind., May 20, 1928; s. Thomas Maxwell and Martha (Somes) S.; B.S., Ind. U., 1950; m. Carol Reed, May 9, 1953; children—Laura Reed Shircliff Howell, Elizabeth Somes. Vice pres., gen. mgr. Pepsi-Cola Bottling Co., Bloomington, Ind., 1950-55, v.p., treas., Charleston, W.Va., 1955-63, pres. co. Savannah, Ga.; pres. Pepsi-Cola Allied Bottlers, Inc., Jacksonville, Fla., 1963-72; pres. Nat. Pepsi-Cola Bottlers Assn. 1971-72, Robert T. Shircliff and Assos., Inc., mgmt. cons.; pres. Burrows Broadcasting, Inc., 1977-84; chmn. bd. The Jamarbo Corp., 1972-87, Shoney's Inc. Chmn. bd. Duval County chpt. ARC, 1969-70; trustee Cummer Mus. Found., chmn., 1984—; pres. Speech and Hearing Clinic, Jacksonville; bd. dirs. YMCA, North Fla. Heart Assn.; chmn. bd. dirs., community bd. St. Vincent's Med. Ctr., 1986—; pres. St. Vincents Found., 1983-85; bd. dirs. United Fund, pres., 1977; trustee, chmn. Jacksonville U.; chmn. Jacksonville Community Found.; trustee Jacksonville Community TV (WJCT). Recipient top mgmt. awards SMEJ, 1973, NCCJ Brotherhood award, 1977; named Jacksonville's Outstanding Citizen, 1983. Mem. Jacksonville C. of C. (pres. 1977), Sovereign Mil. Order Malta, Sigma Alpha Epsilon. Clubs: River (pres. 1979), Timuquanna Country, University; Ponte Vedra (Jacksonville); Fla. Yacht, Plantation, Commodores' League. Lodge: Rotary (pres. W. Jacksonville 1970, dist. gov. 1975-76). Home: 4918 Prince Edward Rd Jacksonville FL 32210 Office: 2529 Gulf Life Tower Jacksonville FL 32207

SHIRE, HAROLD RAYMOND, legal educator, author; b. Denver, Nov. 23, 1910; s. Samuel Newport and Rose Betty (Herrmann) S.; m. Cecilia Goldhaar, May 9, 1973; children: Margaret, David, Donna, Darcy, Esti. M.B.A., Pepperdine U., 1972; LL.D. (hon.), 1975; J.D., Southwestern U., Los Angeles, 1974; M.Liberal Arts, U. So. Calif., 1977; Ph.D. in Human Behavior, U.S. Internat. U., San Diego, 1980. Bar: Calif. 1937, U.S. Dist. Ct. (so. dist.) Calif. 1939, U.S. Supreme Ct. 1978. Dep. dist. atty. Los Angeles County, Calif., 1937-38; asst. U.S. atty. So. Dist. Calif., Los Angeles and San Diego, Justice Dept., 1939-42; sole practice, Los Angeles, 1946-56; pres., chmn. bd. Gen. Connectors Corp., U.S. and Eng., 1956-73; prof. mgmt. and law Pepperdine U., Malibu, Calif., 1974-75, U.S. Internat. U., San Diego, 1980-83; dir. Bestobell Aviation, Eng., 1970-74. Advisor U. S.C. Gerentology, Andrus Sch., pre-retirement tng., 1976-80; bd. dirs. Pepperdine U., 1974-80; nat. bd. govs. Union Orthodox Jewish Congregations Am., 1973—. Served with U.S. Army, 1942-46. Author: Cha No Yu and Symbolic Interactionism: Method of Predicting Japanese Behavior, 1980; The Tea Ceremony, 1984. Patentee aerospace pneumatics; invented flexible connectors. Decorated chevalier du vieux moulin (France); companion Royal Aero. Soc. (U.K.), recipient Tea Name Grand Master Soshitsu Sen XV Urasenke Sch., Kyoto, Japan, 1976. Mem. Am. Legion (service officer). Republican. Office: PO Box 1352 Beverly Hills CA 90213

SHIREK, JOHN RICHARD, savings and loan executive; b. Bismarck, N.D., Feb. 5, 1926; s. James Max and Anna Agatha (Lala) S.; student U. Minn., 1944-46; B.S. with honors, Rollins Coll., 1978; m. Ruth Martha Lietz, Sept. 22, 1950; children: Barbara Jo (Mrs. James A. Fowler), Jon Richard, Kenneth Edward. Sports editor Bismarck (N.D.) Tribune, 1943-44; with Gate City Savs. and Loan Assn., Fargo, N.D., 1947-65, v.p., dir., 1960-65; exec. v.p., dir. 1st Fed. Savs. and Loan Assn., Melbourne, Fla., 1966-70; pres., dir. 1st Fed. Savs. and Loan Assn., Cocoa, Fla., 1970-82; exec. v.p., dir. The First, F.A. (formerly 1st Fed. Savs. and Loan Assn. of Orlando), 1982—; interim pres. Freedom Savs. and Loan Assn., Tampa, Fla., 1987-88; trustee Savs. & Loan Found., Inc., 1980-84; dir. Fin. Trans. Systems, Inc., Magnolia Savs. Corp., 1st Cocoa Corp., Magnolia Realty Co., 1982. Chmn., dir. United Fund, Fargo, N.D., 1962-65; dir., exec. bd. mem. Boy Scouts Am., 1960-70, mem. adv. bd. Central Fla. council, 1983-85, exec. bd., 1985—; bd. assos. Fla. Inst. Tech., founding pres., 1968; moderator St. Johns Presbytery, 1979, chmn. coordinating council, 1980-81; moderator Synod of Fla., 1983;mem. adv. bd. Brevard Art Center and Mus., 1980-82; bd. dirs., founding chmn. devel. council Holmes Regional Med. Center, Melbourne, 1981-84; bd. dirs. Orlando Regional Med. Ctr. Found., 1982-85; mem. fin. com. Mayor's Task Force on Housing, 1983-84; chmn. spl. com. on Nat. Council Chs./World Council Chs. relations Presbyn. Ch. in U.S.A., 1983-86; pres. Ecumenical Ctr. Inc., Orlando, 1985—. Served to lt. (j.g.) USN, World War II. Mem. Fla. Savs. and Loan League (past dir.), Fla. Savs. and Loan Services (past dir.), Savs. and Loan Found. (state membership chmn. 1976), Fla. Savs. and Loan Polit. Action Com. (dir. 1976-82), U.S. Savs. and Loan League (chmn. advt. and pub. relations com. 1969-70), Downtown Melbourne Assn. (past pres.), Beta Theta Pi, Omicron Delta Epsilon. Republican. Clubs: Cocoa Country, Cocoa Rotary (pres. 1979); Sapphire Lake Country (N.C.); Orlando Rotary, Rio Pinar Country, University; Citrus (Orlando), Masons, Shriners, Elks. Office: PO Box 2073 Orlando FL 32802

SHIRILAU, MARK STEVEN (SHIREY), utilities executive; b. Long Beach, Calif., Dec. 13, 1955; s. Kenneth Eugene and Marjorie Irene (Thorvick) Shirey. BSEE, U. Calif., Irvine, 1977, MS Bus. Adminstrn., 1980; M in Engring., Calif. Poly. State U., 1978; Diploma in Theology, Episc. Theol. Sch., Claremont, Calif., 1984; MA in Religion, Sch. Theology at Claremont, 1985; PhDEE, U. Calif., Irvine, 1988. Ordained priest Ecumenical Cath. Ch., 1987. Grad. asst. Electric Power Inst., 1977-78; pres., chief exec. officer M.S.E., Santa Ana, Calif., 1977—; adminstrv. mgr. EECO Inc., Santa Ana, Calif., 1979-83; fin. engr. So. Calif. Edison Co., Rosemead, 1983-84, conservation engr., 1984-85, conservation supr., 1985—; part-time instr. Santa Ana Coll., 1982-84; lectr. engring. West Coast U., Orange, Calif., 1984—. Pastor St.John's Ecumenical Cath. Ch., Santa Ana. Mem. IEEE, Eta Kappa Nu. Democrat. Author: Triune Love: An Insight into God, Creation, and Humanity, 1983. Home: 2302 W Adams St Santa Ana CA 92704 Office: 2244 Walnut Grove Ave Rosemead CA 91770

SHIRLEY, ROBERT PRESTON, lawyer; b. Ft. Worth, Nov. 14, 1912; s. James Preston and Nevra (Boykin) S.; m. Elizabeth Hodgson, Nov. 13, 1936; children—Susan E. Shirley Eckel, Carolyn D. Shirley Wimberly, Sarah J. Shirley-White. Student Tex. Christian U., 1928-30; LLB, U. Tex., 1933. Bar: Tex. 1933. Ptnr. Boykin, Ray & Shirley, Ft. Worth, 1933-36; assoc. prof. law U. Tex., Austin, 1936-40; ptnr. Kelley & Looney, Edinburg, Tex., 1940-41, Holloway, Hudson & Shirley, Ft. Worth, 1945-47, Mills, Shirley, McMicken & Eckel, Galveston, Tex., 1947-86, Mills, Shirley, Eckel & Bassett, 1986—; ret. chmn. bd. First Republic Bank, Galvestin, N.A.; bd. dirs. Am. Indemnity Co., Am. Fire & Indemnity Co., Tex. Gen. Indemnity Co. Mem. U. Tex. Devel. Bd., Austin, chmn., 1965-66, 66-67; mem. devel. bd. U. Tex. Med. Br., Galveston, 1967—; Chmn. Galveston Charter Rev. Commn., 1968, 72, mem., 74, 1970; mem. Planning Commn. City of Galveston, 1961-69; mem. Tex. Constl. Revision Commn., 1973—; mem. Gov.'s Task Force on Higher Edn., 1981; bd. dirs., exec. v.p. Sealy & Smith Found. for John-Sealy Hosp., Galveston; bd. dirs. U. Tex. Found., Pres., 1970-72; life trustee, pres. U. Tex. Law Sch. Found.; trustee Mary Hardin Baylor Coll., Belton, Tex., 1974-78. Served from 2d lt. to lt. col., AUS, 1942-45; CBI. Fellow Am. Coll. Trial Lawyers, Am. Coll. Probate Counsel, Am. Bar Found., Tex. Bar Found. (Outstanding 50-yr. Lawyer 1983); mem. Tex. Assn. Def. Counsel (pres. 1963-64), Galveston County (pres. 1954-55), ABA, State Bar Tex. (com. adminstrn. justice 1952-72), Internat. Assn. Ins. Counsel, Assn. Ins. Attys., Order of Coif, Phi Delta Phi, Phi Kappa Psi. Club: Galveston Arty. Home: 39 Colony Park Circle Galveston TX 77551 Office: 2228 Mechanic Galveston TX 77550

SHIVELY, JOHN TERRY, business executive; b. Middletown, N.Y., July 1, 1943; s. Marvin Rathfelder and Esther (Manning) Westervelt; adopted child, Harold Eugene Shively; B.A., U. N.C., 1965. Vol. worker VISTA, Bethel, Yakutat, and Fairbanks, Alaska, 1965-68; health planner Greater Anchorage Area Community Action Agy., 1968-69; health cons. Alaska Fedn. Natives, Anchorage, 1969; dep. dir. Rural Alaska Community Action Program, Anchorage, 1969-70, exec. dir., 1971-72; exec. v.p. Alaska Fedn. Natives, Anchorage, 1972-75; v.p. ops. NANA Regional Corp., Kotzebue, Alaska, 1975-77, NANA Devel. Corp., Anchorage, 1977-82, sr. v.p., 1982-83; chief of staff to gov. of Alaska, 1983-85; cons. bus. and govt., 1985-86; sr. v.p. NANA Regional Corp., Inc., 1986—; chmn., chief exec. officer United Bar Corp., United Bank Alaska, 1987—; chmn. Alaska State Bd. Game, 1983-84. dir. Unicorp. Inc., United Bank of Alaska, NANA Oilfield Services. Mem. Greater Anchorage Area Comprehensive Health Plan Council, 1969-75, chmn., 1969-75; founding mem. bd. dirs. Alaska Pub. Interest Research Group, 1974-75, 86—; mem. Gov.'s Rural Affairs Council, 1971-76, Gov.'s Manpower Commn., 1971, Greater Anchorage Health Bd., 1969-75, Alaska Pipeline Edn. Com., 1973-74; bd. regents U. Alaska, 1979-83. Mem. Alaska Fedn. Natives. Democrat. Episcopalian. Home: PO Box 101758 Anchorage AK 99510 Office: NANA Regional Corp 4706 Harding Dr Anchorage AK 99503

SHIVJI, ISSA GULAMHUSSEIN, law educator; b. Kilosa, Morogoro, Tanzania, July 15, 1946; s. Gulamhussein Esmail and Mariam Jivraj (Bawa) S.; m. Parin Jaffer Virji, Oct. 1, 1976; 1 child, Natasha. LLB with hons., U. East Africa, 1970; LLM, U. London, 1971; PhD, U. Dar Es Salaam, Tanzania, 1982. Advocate High Ct. Tanzania, Tanzania Ct. Appeals. With U. Dar Es Salaam, 1970—, prof. law, 1986—, head dept. legal theory, 1985—; chmn. Tanzania Breweris Ltd.; vis. research prof. Coll. Mex., 1982; vis. prof. law U. Zimbabwe, 1988. Mem. Tanzania Law Soc. (legal aid com. 1977—). Office: U Dar Es Salaam, 35093 Dar Es Salaam Tanzania

SHIVLER, JAMES FLETCHER, JR., retired civil engineer; b. Clearwater, Fla., Feb. 17, 1918; s. James Fletcher and Estelle (Adams) S.; m. Katherine Lucille Howlett, Feb. 2, 1946; children: James Fletcher, Susan (Mrs. William J. Schilling). B.C.E., U. Fla., 1938, M.S., 1940. Registered profl. engr., Fla., Ga., N.C. Mem. engring. faculty U. Fla., 1940-41; with Reynolds, Smith & Hills Architects-Engrs.-Planners, Inc. (formerly Reynolds, Smith & Hills, architects and engrs.), Jacksonville, Fla., 1941-88, partner, 1950-69, pres., 1970-88, chmn. bd., 1983-88; partner Lewis-Eaton Partnership (Architects-Engrs. & Planners), Jackson, Miss., 1969—; dir. Fla. Nat. Banks of Fla., Inc. Mem. Fla. Bd. Engr. Examiners, 1964-70, v.p., 1964-65, pres., 1965-70. Served to lt. j.g. USNR, 1943-46. Recipient Outstanding Service award Fla. Engring. Soc., 1971, Disting. Alumnus award U. Fla., 1972, citation for service to constrn. industry Engring. News Record, 1973. Fellow ASCE (pres. Fla. sect. 1952), Am. Cons. Engrs. Council, Fla. Engring. Soc. (pres. 1960-61); mem. Nat. Soc. Profl. Engrs. (pres. 1972-73, Meritorious Service award 1981), Am. Assn. Engring. Socs. (chmn. engring. affairs council 1982-83), Fla. C. of C. (dir.-at-large 1971—), Jacksonville Area C. of C., Tau Beta Pi. Presbyterian. Clubs: Jacksonville Exchange, University, Deerwood, Florida Yacht, Jacksonville Power Squadron. Home: 8191 Hollyridge Rd Jacksonville FL 32256

SHLAUDEMAN, HARRY WALTER, ambassador; b. Los Angeles, May 17, 1926; s. Karl Whitman and Florence (Pixley) S.; m. Carol Jean Dickey, Aug. 7, 1948; children: Karl Frederick, Katherine Estelle, Harry Richard. B.A., Stanford U., 1952. Joined U.S. Fgn. Service, 1955; vice consul Barranquilla, Colombia, 1955-56; polit. officer Bogotá, Colombia, 1956-58; assigned lang. tng. Washington, 1958-59; consul Sofia, Bulgaria, 1960-62; chief polit. sect. Santo Domingo, Dominican Republic, 1962-64; officer charge Dominican Affairs State Dept., 1964-65; asst. dir. Office Caribbean affairs, 1965-66; sr. seminar fgn. policy State Dept., 1966-67; spl. asst. to sec. state 1967-69; dir. INR/RAR, 1969; dep. chief of mission, counselor of embassy Santiago, Chile, 1969-73; dep. asst. sec. state for Inter-Am. affairs, Washington, 1973-75; ambassador to Venezuela 1975-76; asst. sec. state for Inter-Am. affairs, 1976-77; ambassador to Peru Lima, 1977-80; ambassador to Argentina 1980-83; exec. dir. Nat. Bipartisan Commn. on Central Am., 1983-84; spl. ambassador to Central Am. 1984-86; U.S. Ambassador to Brazil Brasilia, 1986—. Served with USMCR, 1944-46. Recipient Disting. Honor award Dept. State, 1966. Mem. Phi Gamma Dalta. Club: Bethesda (Md.) Country. Office: US Ambassador's Office, Avenida das Nacoes, Lote 3, Brasilia Brazil

SHMUKLER, STANFORD, lawyer; b. Phila., June 16, 1930; s. Samuel and Tessye (Dounne) S.; m. Anita Golove, Mar. 21, 1951; children—Jodie Lynne Shmukler Girsh, Joel Mark, Steven David. B.S. in Econs., U. Pa., 1951, J.D., 1954. Bar: D.C. 1954, Pa. 1955; U.S. Ct. Appeals (2d cir.), 1959, U.S. Supreme Ct. 1959, U.S. Ct. Appeals (3d cir.), 1960, U.S. Ct. Claims, 1966, U.S. Tax Ct., 1966, U.S. Ct. Mil. Appeals 1966. Atty., U.S. Bur. Pub. Roads, 1954-55, cons., 1955-57; sole practice, Phila., 1955—; lectr. Temple U. Law Sch., 1975-78; mem., past sec., exec. dir. crminal procedural rules com. Pa. Supreme Ct., 1971-87; mem. lawyers adv. com. Ct. Appeals for 3d cir., 1977-80; selection com. Criminal Justice Act Panel, 1979-84. Bd. dirs. Ecumenical Halfway House, 1967-71. Served to col. JAGC, USAR, from 1955 (ret.). Recipient Phila. Bar Assn. Criminal Justice Sect. award, 1972; Legion of Honor, Chapel of the Four Chaplains, 1983. Mem. ABA, Pa. Bar Assn., Phila. Bar Assn. (bd. govs. 1971-73, past chmn. criminal justice com. and mil. justice com.), Fed. Bar Assn. (co-chmn. criminal law com. Phila. chpt.), Pa. Trial Lawyers Assn. Democrat. Jewish. Lodges: Justice Lodge, B'nai B'rith. Contbr. articles to profl. jours. Home: 1400 Melrose Ave Melrose Park PA 19126 Office: 24th Floor Packard Bldg 15th and Chestnut Sts Philadelphia PA 19102

SHOAFSTALL, EARL FRED, entrepreneur, consultant; b. Des Moines, Jan. 26, 1936; s. Ralph Paul and Josephine E. (Carnes) S.; m. Sharon I. Vannoy, Mar. 21, 1962 (div. 1980); children: Michael E., Angela R.; m. Carlene Christenson, Dec. 11, 1980. BA, MBA, Drake U., 1962. Enlisted USAF, Des Moines, 1954; advanced through grades to sgt. USAF, 1961, resigned, 1962; underwriter Hawkeye Security Ins., Des Moines, 1962-65; mgr., owner B & B Transfer and Storage Inc., West Des Moines, Iowa, 1965—; cons., owner B & B Mini Storage Inc., West Des Moines, 1975—, Iowa Truck Driving Sch., West Des Moines, 1976—, Great Expectations Salon, West Des Moines, 1978—. Inventor pressure gage, control valve for air and liquid. Republican. Club: Des Moines Golf and Country. Lodges: Masons (32 degree), Shriners. Home: 103 W Ridge Dr West Des Moines IA 50265 Office: B & B Transfer and Storage Inc 536 S 19th West Des Moines IA 50265

SHOCKEY, THOMAS EDWARD, retired real estate executive, engineer; b. San Antonio, Aug. 17, 1926; s. Verlie Draper and Margaret Ruth (Shuford) S.; BS (Davidson fellow Tau Beta Pi), Tex. A&M U., 1950; postgrad. St. Mary's U., 1964, San Antonio Coll., 1972, Pacific Western U., 1981; m. Jacqueline McPherson, June 4, 1949; children—Cheryl Ann, Jocelyn Marie, Valerie Jean. With Petty Geophys. Survey, summers 1947-49, J.E. Ingram Equipment Co., 1950-51; co-owner, archtl. engr., realtor Moffett Lumber Co., Inc., San Antonio, 1952-76; cons. gen. contracting, gen. real estate, 1944—, retailer wholesale bldg. material, 1951—, v.p., 1959—; real estate counselor, appraiser, 1972—; real estate appraiser Gill Appraisal Service, San Antonio, 1977—; comml. loan appraiser, underwriter, analyst Gill Savs. Assn., Gill Cos., San Antonio, 1979; chief appraiser, underwriter, architect, engr., insp. Gill Cos., 1981, v.p., 1981-87, ret., 1987. Served with inf. Signal Corps, U.S. Army, 1944-46; ETO. Mem. San Antonio C. of C., Nat. Lumber Dealers, Nat. Home Builders, Nat. Real Estate Bd., Nat. Inst. Real Estate Brokers, Internat. Soc. Real Estate Appraisers, Tex. Assn. Real Estate Insps., Real Estate Appraisers Tex., Nat. Assn. Rev. Appraisers and Mortgage Underwriters, Internat. Inst. Valuers, Internat. Platform Assn. Home: Star Route Box 87 Mico TX 78056

SHOCKLEY, THOMAS DEWEY, electrical engineering educator; b. Haynesville, La., Nov. 2, 1923; s. Thomas Dewey and Inez (Hudson) S.; m. Willie Belle Austin, Feb. 13, 1947; children: Dianne, Cecilia. B.S. in Elec. Engring, La. State U., 1950, M.S. in Elec. Engring, 1952; Ph.D., Ga. Inst. Tech., 1963. Instr. La. State U., 1950-53; aerophysics engr. Gen. Dynamics, 1953-56; research engr., asst. prof. Ga. Inst. Tech., 1956-63; assoc. prof. U. Ala., 1963-64; prof. U. Okla., 1964-67; prof., chmn. dept. elec. engring. Memphis State U., 1967-83; pres. SSC, Inc., Germantown, Tenn., 1978—, chmn. bd., 1981—; system cons. ITT, Md. Co., State Farm Fire & Casualty Co., Aetna Ins. Cos., CNA Ins. Co. Mem. elec. code panel, Shelby County, Tenn., 1978-84; mem. Memphis-Shelby County Appeals Bd., 1984—. Served with AUS, 1942-46, 1950. Mem. IEEE (treas. Memphis sect. 1970-71, sec. 1971-72, vice chmn. 1972-73, chmn. 1973-74, Centennial medal 1984), Nat. Soc. Profl. Engrs., Tenn. Soc. Profl. Engrs., Nat. Fire Protection Assn. (com. 110), Sigma Xi (chpt. pres. 1969-71), Phi Kappa Phi (chpt. pres. 1973-74, 84-85). Home: 1526 Poplar Estates Pkwy Germantown TN 38038 Office: Memphis State U Memphis TN 38111

SHOCKLEY, WILLIAM BRADFORD, physicist, emeritus educator; b. London, Feb. 13, 1910; (parent Am. citizens); s. William Hillman and May (Bradford) S.; m. Jean A. Bailey, 1933 (div. 1955); children: Alison, William Alden, Richard Condit; m. Emmy Lanning, 1955. B.S., Calif. Inst. Tech., 1932; Ph.D., M.I.T., 1936; Sc.D. (hon.), Rutgers U., 1956, U. Pa., 1955, Gustavus Adolphus Coll., Minn., 1963. Teaching fellow M.I.T., 1932-36; mem. tech. staff Bell Telephone Labs., 1936-42, 45, became dir. transistor physics research, 1954; dir. Shockley Semicondr. Lab.; pres. Shockley Transistor Corp., 1958-60; cons. Shockley Transistor unit Clevite Transistor, 1960-65; lectr. Stanford U., 1958-63, Alexander M. Poniatoff prof. engring. sci. and applied sci., 1963-75, prof. emeritus, 1975—; exec. cons. Bell Telephone Labs., 1965-75; dep. dir. research, weapons systems evaluation group Dept. Def., 1954-55; expert cons. Office Sec. War, 1944-45; vis. lectr. Princeton U., 1946; vis. prof. Calif. Inst. Tech., 1954-55; sci. adv., policy council Joint Research and Devel. Bd., 1947-49; sr. cons. Army Sci. Adv. Panel.; Dir. research Anti-submarine Welfare Ops. Research Group USN, 1942-44. Author: Electrons and Holes in Semiconductors, 1950, (with A.A. Gong) Mechanics, 1966; editor: Imperfections of Nearly Perfect Crystals, 1952. Recipient medal for Merit; Air Force Assn. citation of honor, 1951; U.S. Army cert. of appreciation, 1953; co-winner (with John Bardeen and Walter H. Brattain) Nobel Prize in Physics, 1956; Wilhelm Exner medal Oesterreichischer Gewerbeverein Austria, 1963; Holley medal ASME, 1963; Calif. Inst. Tech. Alumni Disting. Service award, 1966; NASA cert. of appreciation Apollo 8, 1969; Public Service Group Achievement award NASA, 1969; named to Inventor's Hall of Fame, 1974; named to Calif. Inventor's Hall of Fame, 1983. Fellow AAAS; mem. Am. Phys. Soc. (O.E. Buckley prize 1953), Nat. Acad. Sci. (Comstock prize 1954), IEEE (Morris Liebmann prize 1952, Gold medal, 25th anniversary of transistor 1972, Medal of Honor 1980), Sigma Xi, Tau Beta Pi. Home: 797 Esplanada Way Stanford CA 94305

SHODA, TATSUO, banker; hon. chmn., Nippon Credit Bank, Ltd., Tokyo, Japan. Office: Nippon Credit Bank Ltd 13-10, Kudan-kita 1 chome chiyoda-ku, Tokyo 102, Japan

SHOEMAKER, HAROLD LLOYD, infosystem specialist; b. Danville, Ky., Jan. 3, 1923; s. Eugene Clay and Amy (Wilson) S.; A.B., Berea Coll., 1944; postgrad. State U. Ia., 1943-44, George Washington U., 1949-50, N.Y. U., 1950-52; m. Dorothy M. Maddox, May 11, 1947. Research physicist State U., Ia., 1944-45, Frankford Arsenal, Pa., 1945-47; research engr. N.Am. Aviation, Los Angeles, 1947-49, Jacobs Instrument Co., Bethesda, 1949-50; asso. head systems devel. group The Teleregister Corp., N.Y.C., 1950-53; mgr. electronic equipment devel. sect., head planning for indsl. systems div. Hughes Aircraft Co., Los Angeles, 1953-58; dir. command and control systems lab. Bunker-Ramo Corp., Los Angeles, 1958-68, v.p. Data Systems, 1968-69, corp. dir. data processing, 1969-75; tech. staff R & D Assocs., Marina Del Rey, Calif., 1975-85; info. systems cons., 1985—. Served with AUS, 1945-46. Mem. IEEE. Patentee elec. digital computer. Home: PO Box 3385 Granada Hills CA 91344

SHOEMAKER, ROBERT LEWIS, optometrist; b. Elkhart, Ind., Dec. 22, 1928; s. W. Albert and Annetta (Wilson) S.; m. Alice Marie Amick, Aug. 7, 1954; children—Mark Amick, Scott Robert. Student DePauw U., 1946-48, Ind. U., 1948-49; O.D., Pa. Coll. Optometry, 1953. Diplomate Nat. Bd. Optometry. Cons. Wayne Twp. Sch. System, Indpls., 1970-73, Warren Twp. Sch. System, 1972-73, Ind. Dept. Pub. Instrn., 1974-84, Ind. Boy's Sch., Ind. Dept. Correction, Indpls., 1972-86; guest lectr. Butler U., Ind. U., Ind. Central Coll., 1972-80, U. Ill., Bradley U., Congress European Optometric Socs., Paris, 1975. Mem. editorial council Jour. Optometric Vision Therapy, 1970-72. Contbr. articles to profl. jours. Bd. dirs. Prisoners Aid By Citizens' Effort, Indpls., 1968-72, Meridian St. Methodist Ch., 1982—. Served as cpl. U.S. Army, 1953-55. Named Optometrist of Yr., 1970—. Fellow Am. Acad. Optometry (pres. Ind. chpt. 1979-81); mem. Coll. Optometrists in Vision Devel. (bd. dirs. 1971-73). Republican. Avocation: photography. Home: 7204 Harbour Isle Indianapolis IN 46240 Office: 6214 N Broadway Indianapolis IN 46220

SHOEMAKER, VAUGHN, cartoonist, painter, lecturer; b. Chgo., Aug. 11, 1902; s. William Henry and Estella Jane (Vaughn) S.; m. Evelyn Marian Arnold, July 3, 1926; 1 son, Vaughn Richard, Jr. Ed. grammar sch. and Bowen High Sch.; ed., Art Inst. Chgo., Chgo. Acad. Fine Arts; Litt.D. (hon.), Wheaton Coll. (Ill.), 1945. With art dept. Chgo. Daily News, 1922, chief cartoonist, 1925-52; editorial cartoonist N.Y. Herald Tribune, 1956-61, 70; became chief cartoonist Chgo. Am. and Chgo. Today, 1961-71; creator John Q. Public, 1930; syndicated Des Moines Register and Tribune, Nat. Newspaper syndicate, Chgo. Tribune, N.Y. News, 1930-71; instr. Chgo. Acad. Fine Arts, 1927-42. Author: The Best of Shoemaker Cartoons, 7 books, 1938-66; Permanent Editorial Cartoon Collection, Huntington Library, San Marino, Calif.; Permanent Editorial Cartoon Collection, Syracuse (N.Y.) U., U. Mo., Wheaton (Ill.) Coll.; one-man water color exhbn., Obrien Galleries, Chgo., 1935, 36, Marshall Field Galleries, 1938, one-man oil exhbn., Masters Gallery, Carmel, Calif., 1973, El Prado Gallery, Sedona, Ariz., 1984; first telecasting of cartoons in Chgo., Sta. W9XAP, 1930; TV shows Over Shoemaker's Shoulder, WBKB, NBC, ABC, 1949-50. Awarded Pulitzer prize in cartooning, 1938, 47; Nat. Headliner's award Atlantic City, 1943; Nat. Safety Council Grand award, 1946, 49; Outstanding Achievement award, 1952, 53, 58; Sigma Delta Chi awards, 1945, 50; Freedom Found. Gold medals Valley Forge, 1949 through 1969; Christopher Gold Medal award, 1957; Lincoln Nat. Life Found. awards, 1955, 66, 68. Mem. Christian Bus. Men's Com., The Gideons; mem. Nat. Cartoonist Soc. N.Y., Assn. Am. Editorial Cartoonists, Soc. Western Artists San Francisco, Sigma Delta Chi. Clubs: Palette and Chisel Acad. Fine Art (Chgo.) (hon.), Ill. Athletic (Chgo.), Jackson Park Yacht (Chgo.) (dir. 1948), Great Lakes Cruising (Chgo.) (commodore 1949), Chgo. Press (Chgo.), Chgo. Headline (Chgo.); San Francisco Press (San Francisco), Marine's Memorial (San Francisco); National Press (Washington, D.C.). Home: Drawer V Carmel CA 93921

SHOHET, NORMAN H., financial consultant; b. Jersey City, Feb. 28, 1926; s. Leon A. and Rose S.; B.B.A. in Acctg., CCNY, 1954; C.L.U., Am. Coll., 1971; registered investment advisor; m. June Brook; children—Michael B., Robert L. Controller, J. J. Little & Ives Pub. Co., N.Y.C., organizer, gen. mgr. Canadian subs., 1959-60; with Fin. Mgmt. Co., Garden City, N.Y., 1961—, employee benefit specialist and pension cons., 1965—, profl. counselor tax advantaged planning qualified plans and group programs, 1968—, fin. planner, cons. for corp. profl. and personal clients, 1975—; chmn., pres. Republic Pension Services, Inc., 1983—, Fin. and Investment Services Co. C.L.U. instr. Hofstra U.; adj. asst. prof. Nassau Community Coll., 1978—, Suffolk County Community Coll., 1980—; guest lectr. fin. mgmt. seminars, 1980-82. Founder, organizer Cub Scout Troop, Boys Scouts Am., chmn., 1969-72; bd. dirs. North Shore Jewish Center, Port Jefferson, N.Y., 1970-81; fin. v.p., chmn. bd. trustees, 1977-79. Served with USN, 1944-46. Named to New Eng. Life Ins. Co. Hall of Fame; recipient Nat. Quality awards. Mem. Am. Soc. C.L.U.s, Nat. Assn. Life Underwriters (both Nassau chpts.), Nat. Assn. Security Dealers (registered broker), Am. Philatelic Soc., Soc. of Philatelic Ams., Bur. Issues Assn., Nat. Assn. Accts. (past dir. N.Y. chpt.), Jewish War Vets. Club: KP (founding mem. Smithaven Lodge, chancellor comdr. 1973-74. Office: 20 Broadhollow Rd Melville NY 11747

SHOHOJI, TAKAO, statistician; b. Kure, Japan, Jan. 1, 1938; d. Mitsuto and Takeko (Ishida) S.; m. Yoshie Nagasawa, May 25, 1967; children—Takashige, Mio. B.A., Hiroshima U., 1962, M.A., 1965; Ph.D., NYU, 1972. Analytic statistician Atomic Bomb Casualty Commn., Hiroshima, 1965-72; research scientist NYU Med. Ctr., 1968-72; asst. prof. Hiroshima U., 1972-74, acting head computing ctr., 1972-78, head lab computing ctr., 1978-80, assoc. prof., 1974-85, prof., 1985—; sr. cons. Kure Nat. Hosp. (Hiroshima), 1982—, Senogawa Hosp., Hiroshima, 1966—. Contbr. articles to profl. jours. Recipient Toyota Found. award, 1982, Founders Day award NYU, 1973. Mem. Japan Math. Soc., Japan Statis. Assn. (council 1988—), Chugoku Newmedia Assn. (chmn. 1987—), Japanese Soc. Applied Statis. (council 1986—), Biometric Soc., Am. Statis. Assn., Internat. Statis. Inst., Japanese Soc. Co. Statis. Assn. (council 1987—, assoc. editor 1987—), Biometric Soc. Japan (sec. 1986—, counselor 1982—). Club: Gehnan Tennis. Home: 10-46, 2 chome Shimizu, Kure 737, Japan Office: Hiroshima U Faculty Integrated Arts Scis, 1-1-89 Higashi-senda-machi, Hiroshima 730, Japan

SHOLLENBERGER, SYDNI (SYDNEY) ANN CRAWFORD, author, publicist; b. Cleve., June 23, 1940; d. Charles Burger and Carolyn Louise (Hull) Crawford; B.A., Allegheny Coll., 1962; m. Lewis W. Shollenberger, Jr., Aug. 18, 1962. Public info. officer and editor Space News Roundup, NASA, Houston, 1970-72. mng., editor Travel Publs., Am. Automobile Assn., Washington, 1972-74; free lance journalist, publicist, 1974-84; adminstrv. asst. for community relations Walnut Creek (Calif.) Sch. Dist., 1984-87; public relations cons., 1988—; Publicity dir. Falls Church Bicentennial Commn., 1976-81; bd. dirs. Falls Church Village Preservation and Improvement Soc.; publicity co-chmn. Falls Church Citizens for a Better City, 1978, fin. chmn., 1982 docent Cherry Hill Farm; pres. Broadmont Citizens Assn., 1978-79; press cons. Fisher for Congress campaign, 1978, 80; chmn. Falls Church Adv. Bd. on Parks and Recreation 1979-83; community relations coordinator Fairfax County Reentry Women's Employment Center; sec. Welcome to Washington Internat. Club, 1978-80. Mem. Pub. Relations Soc. Am., Nat. Fedn. Press Women, Capital Press Women (v.p. 1976-78), Nat. Sch. Pub. Relations Assn., Washington Edn. Press Assn., Calif. Sch. Pub. Relations Assn. Club: Capital Speakers (class pres. 1977, chpt. 3 pres. 1980-81); Commonwealth (San Francisco). Home: 3221 Sugarberry Ln Walnut Creek CA 94598

SHOMER, ROBERT BAKER, employee benefit consultant; b. Lakewood, Ohio, Aug. 26, 1943; s. John Edward and Margaret Jeannette (Yeager) S.; BA in Psychology, Cen. Wash. State U., 1966; m. Phyllis B. Newman, Apr. 25, 1985; children: Adam. Jessica, Jaclyn. Brokerage Supr. Aetna Life and Casualty Co., San Francisco, 1971-73; regional dir. Hartford Variable Annuity Co., 1973-75; dir. deferred compensation dept. Galbraith & Green, Inc., Tempe, Ariz., 1976-79, v.p., 1980-82; sr. v.p. Fred S. James, 1983-86; exec. v.p. mktg./nat. accounts Alta Health Strategies, Inc., Salt Lake City, 1986—. Served as capt. USAF, 1967-71. Home: 9733 S Quail Ridge Rd Sandy UT 84092 Office: Alta Health Strategies Inc 2614 S 1935 W Salt Lake City UT 84119

SHONK, ALBERT DAVENPORT, JR., publishers representative; b. Los Angeles, May 23, 1932; s. Albert Davenport and Jean Spence (Stannard) S.; B.S. in Bus. Adminstrn., U. So. Calif., 1954. Field rep. Los Angeles Examiner, 1954-55, asst. mgr. mktg. div. 1955-56, mgr., 1956-57; account exec. Hearst Advt. Service, Los Angeles, 1957-59; account exec., mgr. San Francisco area Keith H. Evans & Assos., 1959-65; owner, pres. Albert D. Shonk Co., Los Angeles, 1965—; pres., Signet Circle Corp., Inc., 1977-81, dir., 1962-81, hon. life dir., 1977-86. Bd. dirs., sec., 1st v.p. Florence Crittenton Services of Los Angeles, exec. v.p., 1979-81, pres., 1981-83, chmn. bd., 1983-85, hon. life dir., 1986—; founding chmn. Crittenton Assos. Recipient Medallion of Merit Phi Sigma Kappa, 1976, Founders award, 1961. Mem. Advt. Club Los Angeles, Bus. and Profl. Advt. Assn., Pubs. Rep. Assn. of So. Calif., Nat. Assn. Pubs. Reps. (past v.p. West Coast 1981-83), Jr. Advt. Club Los Angeles (hon. life; dir., treas., 1st v.p.), Trojan Club, Skull and Dagger, Inter-Greek Soc. (co-founder, hon. life mem. and dir., v.p. 1976-79, pres. 1984-86), Phi Sigma Kappa (dir. grand council 1962-70, 77-79, grand pres. 1979-83, chancellor 1983-87, court of honor , life, trustee, v.p. meml. found. 1979-84, pres. 1984, trustee pres. Phi Sigma Kappa found. 1984—), Alpha Kappa Psi. Home: 3460 W 7th St Los Angeles CA 90005 Office: 3156 Wilshire Blvd Los Angeles CA 90010

SHONS, ALAN RANCE, plastic surgeon, educator; b. Freeport, Ill., Jan. 10, 1938; s. Ferral Caldwell and Margaret (Zimmerman) S.; A.B., Dartmouth Coll., 1960; M.D., Case Western Res. U., 1965; Ph.D. in Surgery, U. Minn., 1976; m. Mary Ella Misamore, Aug. 5, 1961; children—Lesley, Susan. Intern, U. Hosp., Cleve., 1965-66, resident in surgery, 1966-67; research fellow transplantation immunology U. Minn., 1969-72; resident in surgery U. Minn. Hosp., 1972-74; resident in plastic surgery NYU, 1974-76; asst. prof. plastic surgery U. Minn., Mpls., 1976-79, assoc. prof., 1979-84, prof., 1984; dir. div. plastic and reconstructive surgery U. Minn. Hosp., St. Paul Ramsey Hosp., Mpls. VA Hosp., 1976-84; cons. plastic surgery St. Louis Park Med. Center, 1980-84; prof. surgery Case Western Res. U., Cleve., 1984—; dir. div. plastic and reconstructive surgery Univ. Hosps. Cleve., 1984—. Served to capt. USAF, 1967-69. Diplomate Am. Bd. Surgery, Am. Bd. Plastic Surgery. Fellow ACS (chmn. Minn. com. on trauma); mem. Am. Soc. Plastic and Reconstructive Surgeons, Am. Assn. Plastic Surgeons, Minn. Acad. Plastic Surgeons (pres. 1981-82), AMA, Soc. Head and Neck Surgeons, Am. Assn. Surgery Trauma, Transplantation Soc., Plastic Surgery Research Council, Am. Soc. Aesthetic Plastic Surgery, Am. Soc. Maxillofacial Surgeons, Am. Assn. Immunologists, Soc. Exptl. Pathology, Am. Burn Assn., Am. Cleft Palate Assn., Am. Soc. Nephrology, Assn. Acad. Surgery, Pan Am. Med. Assn., Central Surg. Assn., Ohio State Med. Assn.,Sigma Xi. Office: 2074 Abington Rd Cleveland OH 44106

SHORE, MICHAEL ALLAN, lawyer, accountant; b. Cleve., Dec. 6, 1931; s. Herman and Genevieve Elizabeth (Cohen) S.; m. M. Kay Shore; children: Debbie E., Steven J. BS in Econs., U. Pa., 1953, JD, Cleve. State U., 1959, postdoctoral studies Sch. Law, Case Western Res. U. Bar: Ohio, U.S. Supreme Ct. CPA, Ohio, N.Y. Prin. Michael A. Shore Co., L.P.A., Cleve.; pres., ptnr. Shore, Shirley & Co., CPA's, Cleve.; dir. various corps.; lectr. taxation Case Western Res. U., Cleve.; acting judge Shaker Heights Municipal Ct., 1983—; arbitrator Am. Arbitration Assn. Served with U.S. Army, 1953-55. Mem. Ohio Bar Assn., Cleve. Bar Assn., Am. Assn. Atty.-CPA's, Am. Inst. CPA's. Republican. Jewish. Lodge: Masons. Office: 23200 Chagrin Blvd Cleveland OH 44122

SHORR, NORMAN, chemical engineer; b. Pitts., Mar. 25, 1917; s. Benjamin and Ida S.; Ph.D., Calif. Western U., 1977; m. Pearle V. Gawlowski, Feb. 13, 1943. Sr. devel. engr. Goodyear Aircraft Corp., Akron, Ohio, 1953-55; sr. engring. assoc. PPG Industries Inc., Pitts., 1955-76; sr. staff engr. Polycom Huntsman, Inc., Washington, Pa., 1985—. cons. mil. engr., Mt. Lebanon, Pa., 1976—; cons. engr. Polycom, Inc., 1979—; staff engr. Polycom Huntsman Inc., Donora, Pa., 1979—. Served with USNR, 1940. Registered profl. engr., Pa., Ohio, Fla. Mem. Am. Def. Preparedness Assn., Soc. Am. Mil. Engrs. Research transparent armor, aircraft glazing, plastics; patentee in field. Home: 200 Buchanan Pl Mount Lebanon PA 15228

SHORR, RONALD PHILIP, investment analyst; b. Chgo., Mar. 28, 1937; s. Ralph Louis and Babette Josephine (Zucker) S.; children—David Baker, Scott Alden. B.A., U. Mich., 1958; M.B.A., Harvard U., 1961; postgrad. Columbia U., 1965-66. Investment adviser, N.Y.C., 1961-63; with Hardy & Co., 1963-64, Roth, Gerard & Co., 1964-69; exec. v.p. Minbanco Corp., 1969-71; v.p. Dean Witter & Co., 1971-74; v.p. E.F. Hutton & Co., N.Y.C., 1974-79; 1st v.p. Blyth Eastman Dillon & Co., 1979; assoc. dir. Bear Stearns & Co., 1979. Contbr. chpt. to Economics of the Mineral Industries, 1976. Served with U.S. Army, 1959-60. Chartered fin. analyst. Mem. Am. Inst. Mining Engrs., N.Y. Soc. Security Analysts, Non-ferrous Metals Group, Steel Analysts Group. Home: 401 E 88 St New York NY 10128 Office: Bear Stearns & Co 245 Park Ave New York NY 10167

SHORS, SUSAN DEBRA, lawyer; b. Detroit, Nov. 23, 1954; d. Clayton Marion and Arlene Lois (Towle) S.; m. Brian F. Connors. B.A., Pitzer Coll., 1976; J.D., Golden Gate U., 1984. Bar: Calif. Extern, Calif. Supreme Ct., San Francisco, 1983; research atty. Calif. Ct. Appeal, San Francisco, 1984-85; appellate atty., San Francisco, 1985—; cons. Nob Hill Neighbors, San Francisco, 1982-86. Sr. editor Golden Gate Law Rev. Notes and Comments, 1985; mem. editorial bd. Barrister's Club Mag., 1986—. Atty. Lawyers Com. for Urban Affairs/Asylum Project, San Francisco, 1986. Mem. ABA, Calif. Bar Assn., Calif. Women Lawyers, Bar Assn. San Francisco (mem. appellate com. 1986—), ACLU, Nat. Assn. Criminal Def. Lawyers. Democrat. Office: Law Offices 2500 Clay St San Francisco CA 94115

SHORT, BYRON ELLIOTT, engineering educator; b. Putnam, Tex., Dec. 29, 1901; s. Samuel W. and Florence Gertrude (Sublett) S.; m. Mary Jo Fitzgerald, June 1, 1937; children: Mary Aileen (Mrs. James L. Gauntt), Byron Elliott, Jr. B.S., U. Tex., 1926, M.S., 1930; M.M.E., Cornell U., 1936, Ph.D., 1939. Cadet engr. Tex Co., summers 1926-27, mech. engr., summers 1928-30; instr. U. Tex., 1926-29, asst. prof., 1929-36, charge heat-power, fluid mechanics lab., 1930-65, mech. engr., summers 1932-36, 40, asso. prof., 1936-39, prof. mech. engring., 1939-73, prof. emeritus, 1973—, chmn. dept., 1945-47, 51-53; acting dean U. Tex. (Coll. Engring.), 1948-49; teaching fellow Cornell, 1935-36; cons. Oak Ridge Nat. Lab., research participant, 1956, 57. Author: Flow, Measurement and Pumping of Fluids, 1934, Engineering Thermodynamics, (with H.L. Kent, B.F. Treat), 1953, Pressure Enthalpy Charts, (with H.L. Kent and H.A. Walls), 1970; Editor: Design Volume, Am. Soc. Refrigerating Engrs. Databook, 10th edit; Contbr. articles to engring. jours. Fellow ASME (chmn. Tex. sect. 1938-39, mem. heat transfer and power test code com.); life mem. ASHRAE (asso. editor Databook 1953, 55), Am. Soc. Engring. Edn., Huguenot Soc. Am. (state pres. 1983-85), SAR, Sigma Xi, Tau Beta Pi, Phi Kappa Phi, Pi Tau Sigma. Club: Mason (33 deg., K.T., Shriner). Home: 502 E 32d St Austin TX 78705

SHORT, KENNETH RICHARD MACDONALD, history educator, researcher; b. Woodbury, N.J., Feb. 16, 1936; went to Eng., 1967; s. Donald William and Naomi Bell (Shoares) S.; m. Mary Jane Tharp, Sept. 3, 1960; children—Douglas MacDonald, Donald William II. B.A. with honors in History, Dickinson Coll., 1957; M.A., U. Rochester, 1960, Ed.D., 1970; B.D., Colgate Rochester Div. Sch., 1960; D.Phil., U. Oxford (Eng.), 1972. Chmn. dept. history Lakeland Coll., Sheboygan, Wis., 1962-65; assoc. librarian Colgate Rochester (N.Y.) Div. Sch., 1965-67; tchr. history Matthew Arnold Sch., Oxford, 1968-70; sr. lectr. in history Westminster Coll., Oxford U., 1970—; vis. research prof. Ctr. for Interdisciplinary Research, U. Bielefeld (W.Ger.), 1978-79; dir. Oxford Hist. Microforms, 1982—; cons. in field; conf. organizer Rockefeller Found., Bellagio, Italy, 1982, Freedoms Found., Valley Forge, 1984. Author: The Dynamite War: Irish American Bombers in Victorian Britain, 1979; editor: Feature Films as History, 1981; Film and Radio Propaganda in World War II, 1983; editor microfiche: World War II in American Newsreels: A Documentary History, 1985; Western Broadcasting Over the Iron Curtain, 1986; co-editor: Hitler's Fall—The Newsreel Witness, 1988; gen. editor: A History of the Cinema—A Microfiche Library, 1986; editor, founder Hist. Jour. Film, Radio and TV, 1980—. Fulbright scholar U. Southampton (Eng.), 1960-61; NDEA fellow U. Rochester, 1965-67. Mem. Am. Hist. Assn., Brit. Film Inst., Brit. Univs. Film and Video Council (instl. rep. 1974—), Interuniv. History Film Consortium (exec. com. 1981—), Internat. Assn. for Audio-Visual Media in Hist. Research and Edn. (sec. gen. 1979-85, treas. 1985—). Home: 8310 Deer Falls Dr Kingwood TX 77345 Office: U Houston Sch of Communication 4800 Calhoun Rd Houston TX 77004

SHORT, KEVIN MICHAEL, financial consulting company executive; b. Louisville, Sept. 5, 1956; s. Michael Smith and Carolyn (Lockard) S.; m. Patti Anne Cannon, May 31, 1980; children: Brittney Lauren, Jennifer Anne. V.p. Security Research Assocs., St. Louis, 1978-80; pres. Clayton Fin. Group, St. Louis, 1980—. Bd. dirs. Bd. Edn. St. Louis Archdiocese, 1985—, found. bd., 1985—, treas., 1986—; active Leadership St. Louis, 1987—, Pres.'s Club Regional Commerce and Growth Assn., 1988—. Mem. Nat. Soc. Pub. Accts., Ind. Accts. Soc. Mo., Leadership St. Louis. Roman Catholic. Club: Clayton (St. Louis).

SHORT, ROBERT STUART, historian, educator; b. Croydon, Surrey, Eng., May 13, 1938; s. Charles Stanley and Edith Audrey (Pulford) S.; m. Virginia Ann Page, June 25, 1965; children: Octavia Alice, Lucien Pulford. BA, MA, Cambridge U., 1960; PhD, U Sussex, Brighton, Eng., 1965. Asst. lectr. dept. Politics U. Hull, Eng., 1967; lectr. to sr. lectr. U. East Anglia, Norwich, Eng., 1967—. Author: Paul Klee, 1979, Dada and Surrealism, 1980; co-author: (with Roger Condinal) Surrealism: Permanent Revelation, 1970, (with Peter Webb) Hans Bellmer, 1985. Chmn. Norfolk Contemporary Art Soc., 1985—. Mem. Labor Party. Home: 5 St Giles Terr, Norwich, Norfolk NR2 1NS, England Office: U E Anglia, Sch Modern Lang and, European Studies, Norwich NR4 7TJ, England

SHORT, SKIP, lawyer; b. N.Y.C., July 13, 1951; s. Albert Joseph and Gertrude B. (Johnson) S. B.A., Fordham Coll., 1972; J.D., Georgetown U., 1975. Bar: N.Y. 1976, U.S. Dist. Ct. (ea. dist.) N.Y. 1976, U.S. Dist. Ct. (so. dist.) N.Y. 1978, D.C. 1979, U.S. Ct. Appeals (1st cir.) and D.C. Cir. 1983, U.S. Supreme Ct. 1984. Assoc. Russakoff & Weiss, Bklyn., 1975-76; sole practice, N.Y.C., 1976-79; ptnr. Short & Billy, N.Y.C., 1979—; cons. ins. seminars, 1978—; arbitrator N.Y. Civil Ct., 1981—; adminstrv. law judge N.Y. Environ. Control Bd., 1980-82; arbitrator Am. Arbitration Assn., N.Y.C., 1981—, U.S. Dist. Ct. (ea. dist.) N.Y., 1986—; spl. master N.Y. Supreme Ct., 1988—. Spl. envoy Internat. Human Rights Found., 1986-87. Author: First Party Claims, 1979; co-author: First Party Claims Under the New York Comprehensive Automobile Reparations Act, 3d edit., 1984. Mem. N.Y. State Bar Assn., N.Y. County Lawyers Assn. Office: Short & Billy 217 Broadway New York NY 10007

SHORT, STEPHANIE DORIS, physiotherapist, sociologist; b. Sydney, New South Wales, Australia, Jan. 1, 1956; d. Donald Wheeler Short and Ruth (Clucas) Hawkshaw. Diploma in physiotherapy, Cumberland Coll. Health Scis., 1977; BA with honors, U. New South Wales, Australia, 1983; MS in Econ., U. London, Eng., 1984. Registered physiotherapist. Physiotherapist The Royal Prince Alfred Hosp., Sydney, New South Wales, Australia, 1977; lectr. sociology U. Wollongong, New South Wales, 1986—. Contbr. articles to profl. jours. Founder Women in Sci. and Health, Wollongong, 1986; mem. Women in Sci Enquiry Network, Soc. for Social Responsibility in Engring, Migrant Health Action, Cancer Info. and Support Soc., Wollongong Women's Ctr., Illawarra Migrant Resource Ctr. Commonwealth scholar, 1983-85; Sir John Gellibrand Meml. scholar, 1984. Office: U Wollongong Dept Sociology, PO Box 1144, Wollongong, NSW 2500, Australia

SHORTAL, TERENCE MICHAEL, systems company executive; b. St. Louis, Oct. 13, 1937; s. Harold Leo and Catherine Margaret S.; B.S. in Elec. Engring., U. Mo., 1961; M.S., U.S. Naval Postgrad. Sch., 1966; grad. program execs., Carnegie-Mellon U., 1979; m. Linda Margaret Elias, May 29, 1965; children—Jennifer Meer, Bradley Alexander. Commd. ensign U.S. Navy, 1961, advanced through grades to capt., 1980; service in Vietnam; asst. officer in charge Engring. Duty Officer Sch., Vallejo, Calif., 1974-77; ship engring. mgr. AEGIS shipbldg. project Naval Sea Systems Command, Washington, 1977-79, tech. dir. DDGX Project, 1979-81; ret., 1981; v.p., dir. Kastle Systems Inc., 1981—. Trustee, pres. bd. dirs., Cathedral Choral Soc., Washington; mem. of vestry St. John's Episcopal Ch., McLean, Va.; pres. bd. dirs. Langley Sch., McLean. Decorated Meritorious Service medal (2), Navy Commendation medal (2). Mem. Am. Soc. Naval Engrs. (Flagship Sect. award 1979), IEEE (br. award 1961), Assn. Energy Engrs., Sigma Xi, Phi Kappa Theta. Club: Langley (McLean, Va.). Home: 858 Canal Dr McLean VA 22102 Office: 1501 Wilson Blvd Arlington VA 22209

SHORTER, WALTER WYATT, forest products executive; b. 1932; B.S. in Chemistry, Va. Mil. Inst., 1953; M.S. in Pulp and Paper Tech., U. Maine, 1957; married. With Union Camp Corp., 1957-78, v.p., resident mgr., until 1978; pres. Mac Millan Bloedel Inc., Pine Hill, Ala., 1978—, also dir.; dir. First Ala. Bank of Montgomery, First Ala. Bancshares, Inc., N.A., Jenkins Brick Co., Fourdrinier Kraft Bd. Group. Bd. visitors Duke U. Sch. Forestry; mem. Govs. Agrl. Emphasis com. Ala.; trustee Huntingdon Coll. Served to capt. USMC, 1953-58. Mem. Paper Industry Mgmt. Assn. (past pres., now trustee), Bus. Council of Ala. (dir.), Am. Paper Inst. (dir.), Ala. Alliance Bus. and Industry (chmn.), Ala. Council Econ. Edn. Office: MacMillan Bloedel Inc Hwy 10 Pine Hill AL 36769

SHOSHAN, ZVI, industrial research company executive; b. N.Y.C., Mar. 4, 1939; arrived in Israel, 1957; s. Joseph and Lila (Selicoff) S.; m. Michal Mark, Mar. 17, 1968 (div. May 1979); children: Yonit, Efrat; m. Yaffa Tikotzky, Mar. 24, 1985. BSc in Engring. cum laude, Technion U., Haifa, Israel, 1974. Cert. engr., Israel. Enlisted Israel Defense Forces, 1957, commd., 1960, advanced through grades to Col., 1979, retired, 1983; project cons. Clal-Industries-Neta, Israel, 1983-85; v.p. mktg. Innovative Milit. Techs., Inc., N.Y.C., 1985-86; gen. mgr. Ramot-U. Authority for Applied Research and Indsl. Devel. Ltd., Tel Aviv, 1986—. Mem. Engrs. Assn. Jewish.

SHOSTAKOVICH, MAXIM DMITRIYEVICH, symphonic conductor; b. Leningrad, USSR, May 10, 1938; came to U.S., 1981; s. Dmitri Dmitriyevich and Nina (Varzar) S.; 1 child, Dmitri. Student, Leningrad Conservatory, 1961-62, Moscow Conservatory, 1963; DFA, U. Md., 1982. Asst. condr. Moscow Symphony Orch., 1963-66, Moscow State Symphony Orch., 1966-69; prin. condr., artistic dir. Orch. Radio and TV USSR, Moscow, 1971-81; mus. advisor Hartford Symphony Orch., Conn., 1985—; prin. guest condr.

Hong Kong Philharm., 1982—; music dir. New Orleans Symphony Orch., 1986—. Debut London Philharm. Orch., 1968; toured Can., U.S., Mex. with USSR State Symphony Orch., 1969; guest condr., Europe, N.Am., Japan and Australia; pianist including Piano Concerto No. 2; rec. father's ballet compositions including Bolt, The Age of Gold, suites, music for films Zoya, Pirogov with Bolshoi Theater Orch., Shostakovich Symphonies; recs. EMI, Philips, Chandos including Shostakovich's Violin Concerto No. 1, Shostakovich's Symphony No. 5, Suite on Verses of Michelangelo, 1971, 77, Piano Concerti Nos. 1 and 2 rec. with Philips Shostakovich's Cello Concerti, 1984. Recipient Outstanding Performance for Arts award Combo Fund Campaign, 1982. Mem. Concert Artists Guild, Great Artists Series NYU (exec. bd. Gallatin div. N.Y.C.). Home: 309 Florida Hill Rd Ridgefield CT 06877 Office: care Columbia Artists Inc 165 W 57th St New York NY 10019 also: New Orleans Symphony Orch 212 Loyola Ave Suite 500 New Orleans LA 70112 *

SHOUB, EARLE PHELPS, chemical engineer; b. Washington, July 19, 1915; B.S. in Chemistry, Poly. Inst. Bklyn., 1938, postgrad., 1938-39; m. Elda Robinson; children—Casey Louis, Heather Margaret Shoub Dills. Chemist, Hygrade Food Products Corp., N.Y.C., 1940-41, Nat. Bur. Standards, 1941-43; with U.S. Bur. Mines, 1943-70, chief div. accident prevention and health, Washington, 1963-70; dep. dir. Appalachian Lab. Occupational Respiratory Diseases, Nat. Inst. Occupational Safety and Health, Morgantown, W.Va., 1970-77, dep. dir. div. safety research, 1977-79; mgr. occupational safety, indsl. environ. cons., safety products div. Am. Optical Corp., Southbridge, Mass., 1979, cons., 1979—; asso. prof. dept. anesthesiology W.Va. U. Med. Center, Morgantown, 1977-82, prof. Coll. Mineral and Energy Resources, 1970-79. Recipient Disting. Service award Dept. Interior and Gold medal, 1959. Registered profl. engr.; cert. safety profl. Fellow Am. Inst. Chemists; mem. Am. Indsl. Hygiene Assn., Vets. of Safety, AIME, Am. Soc. Safety Engrs., Nat. Fire Protection Assn., Nat. Soc. Profl. Engrs., Am. Conf. Govtl. Indsl. Hygienists, Internat. Soc. Respiratory Protection (pres.), ASTM, Am. Nat. Standards Inst., Sigma Xi. Methodist. Contbr. articles to profl. jours. and texts. Home: Apt 202C 5850 Meridian Rd Gibsonia PA 15044-9605

SHOUP, CARL SUMNER, economist; b. San Jose, Calif., Oct. 26, 1902; s. Paul and Rose (Wilson) S.; m. Ruth Snedden, Sept. 27, 1924; children: Dale, Paul Snedden, Donald Sumner. A.B., Stanford U., 1924; Ph.D., Columbia U., 1930; Ph.D. (hon.), U. Strasbourg, 1967. Mem. faculty Columbia U., 1928-71; dir. Internat. Econ. Integration Program and Capital Tax Project, 1962-64; Editor Bull. Nat. Tax Assn., 1931-35; staff mem. N.Y. State Spl. Tax Commns., 1930-35; tax study U.S. Dept. Treasury, June-Sept. 1934, Aug.-Sept. 1937, asst. to sec. Treasury, Dec. 1937-Aug. 1938, research cons., 1938-46, 62-68; interregional adviser, tax reform planning UN, 1972-74; sr. Killam fellow Dalhousie U., 1974-75; staff Council of Econ. Advisers, 1946-49; dir. Twentieth Century Fund Survey of Taxation in U.S., 1935-37, Fiscal Survey of Venezuela, 1958, Shoup Tax Mission to Japan, 1949-50, Tax Mission to Liberia, 1969; co-dir. N.Y.C. finance study, 1950-52; pres. Internat. Inst. Pub. Finance, 1950-53; cons. Carnegie Ctr. for Transnat. Studies, 1976, Harvard Inst. for Internat. Devel., 1978-83, Venezuelan Fiscal Commn., 1980-83, Jamaica Tax Project, 1985, World Bank Value-Added Tax Study, 1986-87, Duke U. Tax Missions Study, 1987-88; vis. prof. Monash U., 1984. Author: The Sales Tax in France, 1930, (with E.R.A. Seligman) A Report on the Revenue System of Cuba, 1932, (with Robert M. Haig and others) The Sales Tax in the American States, 1934, Facing the Tax Problem, 1937, (with Roswell Magill) The Fiscal System of Cuba, 1939, Federal Finances in the Coming Decade, 1941, Taxing to Prevent Inflation, 1943, Principles of National Income Analysis, 1947, (with others) Report on Japanese Taxation, 1949, The Fiscal System of Venezuela, 1959, Ricardo on Taxation, 1960, The Tax System of Brazil, 1965, Federal Estate and Gift Taxes, 1966, Public Finance, 1969 (transl. into Japanese 1974, Spanish 1979), (with others) The Tax System of Liberia, 1970; Editor: Fiscal Harmonization in Common Markets, 1966. Decorated Order Sacred Treasure (Japan). Disting. fellow Am. Econ. Assn.; mem. Nat. Tax Assn. (pres. 1949-50, hon. mem.). Address: Rural Rt 1 Box 303 Center Sandwich NH 03227

SHOWS, CLARENCE OLIVER, dentist; b. nr. Brantley, Ala., Oct. 17, 1920; s. John Oliver and Cora (Nichols) S.; student Wis. State Coll., 1946-47; D.D.S., Northwestern U., 1951; m. Rita Silverman Orenstein, Nov. 25, 1987; children from previous marriage: Toni Cherie, Kristin Clare Shows Ball, Bradley Scott, Gregory Norman, Jeffery Ryan. Individual practice dentistry, Valparaiso, Fla., 1951-53, Pensacola, 1953—. Mem. Pensacola Art Assn.; past pres. Escambia County unit Am. Cancer Soc., now bd. dirs. Fla. unit, also hon. life mem.; mem. Eagle Scout Bd. Rev., Escambia County; sec. Gulf Breeze Vol. Fire Dept. Served with USCG, 1939-46. Fellow Royal Soc. Health, Internat. Coll. Dentists, Internat. Acad. Gen. Dentistry, Am. Coll. Dentists; mem. Am. Acad. Gen. Dentistry (master, past pres. Fla. unit), Internat. Orthodontic Assn., Internat. Acad. Preventive Medicine, Am. Orthodontic Soc., Gulf Breeze C. of C. (past pres.), Fla. Soc. Dentistry for Children (past pres.), Acad. Gen. Dentistry, ADA, AAAS, Am. Profl. Practice Assn., L.D. Pankey Dental Found., Fedn. Dental Internat., Am. Assn. Clin. Hypnosis, Northwestern U. Alumni Assn., Navy League (life), G.V. Black Soc. (life), Pensacola Jr. Coll. Found. (life), Psi Omega. Presbyterian (elder). Clubs: Masons, Shriners, Jesters, Elks; Pensacola (pres.), Exchange. Home: 516 Navy Cove Blvd Gulf Breeze FL 32561 Office: 3090 Navy Blvd Pensacola FL 32505

SHRESTHA, BUDDHI MAN, scientist, cariologist, pathologist, pedodontist; b. Chainpur Bazar, Sankhuwa Sabha, Nepal, Sept. 28, 1936; came to U.S., 1973; naturalized U.S. citizen; s. Lok Man and Subhadra Devi Shrestha. B.D.S., Panjab (India) U., 1963; M.S. in Dental Sci., U. Rochester, 1970; Ph.D. in Pathology, U. Rochester, 1980. Cert. pedodontics, clin. intern. Dental surgeon Dept. Health Services, Govt. of Nepal, 1965-73; research assoc. Eastman Dental Ctr. Rochester, N.Y., 1973-74; postdoctoral fellow U. Rochester, 1975-80; scientist, cariologist Oral Health Research Ctr. Sch. Dentistry, Fairleigh Dickinson U., Hackensack, N.J., 1981-82, adj. assoc. prof. pathology, 1982-85, dir. div. nutrition and cariology, 1982-85; part-time clin. assoc. prof. oral medicine Coll. Dentistry NYU, N.Y.C., 1982-85; mem. adv. com. on nutrition edn. in profl. schs. N.Y. Acad. Medicine, 1982—; cons. pedodontist Anthony L. Jordan Health Ctr., Rochester, N.Y., 1985—; cons. pathologist Fairleigh Dickinson U. Sch. Dentistry, Hackensack, 1985—, pedondist, Lakeside Meml. Hosp., Brockport, N.Y., 1986—. Dental scholar Colombo Plan, 1959-63; research fellow Eastman Dental Ctr., 1968-70; postdoctoral fellow NIH, U. Rochester, 1975-78. Mem. Nepal Med. Assn. Biratnagar Br. (hon. joint sec. 1965-67), Nepal Dental Soc. (founding, hon. exec. sec. 1971-73), Internat. Assn. Dental Research, European Orgn. Caries Research (sr.), Am. Assn. Dental Research. Club: Lake Shore Country. Patentee method of coating teeth with a durable glaze; inventor UV method for detection and scoring of rat caries. Home: 22 Belmeade Rd Rochester NY 14617 Office: Anthony L Jordan Health Ctr 82 Holland St Rochester NY 14605

SHRESTHA, MARICH MAN SINGH, prime minister Nepal. Prime minister, minister of def. Kathmandu, Nepal, 1986—. Address: Office of Prime Minister, Kathmandu Nepal *

SHREVE, GENE RUSSELL, law educator, consultant; b. San Diego, Aug. 6, 1943; s. Ronald D. and Hazel (Shepherd) S.; m. Marguerite Russell, May 26, 1973. A.B. with honors, U. Okla., 1965; LL.B. Harvard U., 1968, LL.M., 1975. Bar: Mass. 1969, Vt. 1981, U.S. Dist. Ct. (no. dist.) Tex. 1969, U.S. Dist. Ct. Mass. 1970, U.S. Ct. Appeals (1st cir.) 1971, U.S. Dist. Ct. Vt. 1976. law clk. U.S. Dist. Ct., Dallas, 1969-70; assoc. prof. Vt. Law Sch., Royalton, 1975-81; vis. assoc. prof. George Washington U., Washington, 1981-83; assoc. prof. law N.Y. Law Sch., N.Y.C., 1983-84, prof., 1984-87; vis. prof. law Ind. U., Bloomington, 1986, prof., 1987—; appellate atty. and state extradition hearing examiner Office of Mass. Atty. Gen., 1968-69; ; staff and supervising atty. Boston Legal Assistance Project, 1970-73; cons. Conn. Bar Examiners, Hartford, 1978—, Vt. Bar Examiners, Montpelier, 1980; reporter Speedy Trial Planning Group, U.S. Dist. Ct., Montpelier, 1976-77. Contbr. numerous articles to legal jours. Mem. Am. Arbitration Assn. Democrat. Episcopalian. Office: Ind U Sch of Law Bloomington IN 47405

SHRIER, ADAM LOUIS, energy company executive; b. Warsaw, Poland, Mar. 26, 1938; came to U.S., 1943, naturalized, 1949; s. Henry Leon and Mathilda June (Czamanska) S.; m. Diane Kesler, June 10, 1961; children: Jonathan, Lydia, Catherine, David. B.S., Columbia U., 1959; M.S. (Whitney fellow), M.I.T., 1960; D.Engr. and Applied Sci. (NSF fellow), Yale U., 1965; postdoctoral visitor, U. Cambridge, Eng., 1965-66; J.D., Fordham U., 1976. With Esso Research & Engring. Co., Florham Park and Linden, N.J., 1963-65, 66-72; head. environ. scis. research area Esso Research & Engring. Co., 1969-72; coordinator pollution abatement activities, tanker dept. Exxon Internat. Co., N.Y.C., 1972-74; project mgr., energy systems Exxon Enterprises Inc., N.Y.C., 1974-75; mgr. solar energy projects Exxon Enterprises Inc., 1975-77, pres. solar thermal systems div., 1977-81; corp. planning cons., sec. new bus. investments Exxon Corp., N.Y.C., 1981-82; mgr. industry analysis Exxon Internat. Co., N.Y.C., 1983-86, mgr. policy and planning, 1986—; dir. Solar Power Corp., North Billerica, Mass., Solar Power, Ltd., London, Daystar Corp., Burlington, Mass.; adj. lectr. chem. engring. Columbia U., N.Y.C., 1967-69; industry adv. bd. Internat. Energy Agy., 1984—, Energy and Environ. Policy Ctr., Harvard U., 1986—, Internat. Energy Program, Johns Hopkins U., 1987—. Contbr. articles to profl. jours. Mem. Am. Inst. Chem. Engrs., Am. Chem. Soc., AAAS, N.Y. Acad. Scis., Am. Inst. Energy Economists, Am. Bar Assn., Sigma Xi, Tau Beta Pi, Phi Lambda Upsilon. Club: United Oxford and Cambridge (London). Home: 543 Park St Upper Montclair NJ 07043 Office: Exxon Co Internat 200 Park Ave Florham Park NJ 07932

SHRIER, DIANE KESLER, psychiatrist; b. N.Y.C., Mar. 23, 1941; d. Benjamin Arthur and Mollie (Wortman) Kesler; B.S. magna cum laude in Chemistry and Biology (Regents scholar 1957-61), Queen's Coll., CUNY, 1961; student Washington U. Sch. Medicine, St. Louis, 1960-61; M.D., Yale U., 1964; m. Adam Louis Shrier, June 10, 1961; children—Jonathan Laurence, Lydia Anne, Catherine Jane, David Leopold. Pediatric intern Bellevue Hosp., N.Y.C., 1964-65; psychiat. resident Albert Einstein Coll. Medicine-Bronx (N.Y.) Mcpl. Municipal Hosp. Center, 1966-68, child psychiatry fellow, 1968-70; staff cons. Family Service and Child Guidance Center of the Oranges, Maplewood, Milburn-Orange, N.J., 1970-73, cons., 1973-79; pvt. practice, Montclair, N.J., 1970—; cons. Community Day Nursery, E. Orange, 1970-79, Montclair State Coll., 1976-78; psychiat. cons. Bloomfield (N.J.) public schs., 1974-75; clin. instr. Albert Einstein Coll. Medicine, 1970-73; clin. asst. prof. psychiatry U. Medicine and Dentistry N.J., 1978-82, clin. assoc. prof., 1982—. Trustee, Montessori Learning Center, Montclair, 1973-75. Diplomate Am. Bd. Psychiatry and Neurology. Fellow Am. Psychiat. Assn., Am. Orthopsychiat. Assn., Acad. Child Psychiatry; mem. Tri-County Psychiat. Assn. (exec. com., rec. sec. 1977-78, 2d v.p. 1978-79, 1st v.p. 1979-80, pres. 1977-81), N.J. Psychiat. Assn. (councillor 1981-84), Phi Beta Kappa. Contbr. articles to med. jours. Address: 543 Park St Upper Montclair NJ 07043

SHROFF, FALI JAMSEDJI, neurosurgeon; b. Hong Kong, Nov. 25, 1934; s. Jamsedji H. and Soona J. Shroff; m. Trity Fali Baria, Nov. 29, 1960. MBBChir, Bomba U., India, 1957. Diplomate Scotland Bd. Neurosurgery. Registrar Nat. Health Service, Newcastle, 1961-71; sr. med. officer Hong Kong Govt., 1972-76; practice medicine specializing in cons. neurosurgery Hong Kong, 1976—. Recipient cert. of merit Dictionary Internat. Biography, 1986. Fellow Royal Coll. Surgeons (Edinburgh); mem. Royal Commonwealth Soc. (council mem. 1983—). Lodge: Kiwanis (pres. 1986-87). Office: 18 Ice House St, Hong Kong Hong Kong

SHROFF, FIROZ SARDAR, real estate developer; b. Karachi, Pakistan, Feb. 27, 1950; s. Sardar Mohammad Shroff and Kulsum (Bano) Dhanji; m. Munira Firoz, Oct. 27, 1977; children: Khurram, Sara, Ally. Grad. high sch., Nairobi, Kenya. Apprentice, duty incharge Empire Investment Ltd., Nairobi, 1966-67; asst. mgr. to mgr. Trade Aids Inc., Karachi, 1967-69, asst. gen. mgr., 1969-72; gen. mgr. Canorient Overseas Distbrs. Ltd., London, 1972-74; dir., gen. mgr. Westland Securities Ltd., Nairobi, 1974-75; dep. mng. dir. Sasi Ltd., Karachi, 1975-78; dir. internat. expansion Sasi Group Cos., Karachi, 1978-80, mng. dir., 1984—; dir. operation Key Internat. S.A., London, 1980-84; participant Nat. Book Devel. Council, Singapore, 1980, Arthur D. Little Mgmt. Edn. Inst. and Pakistan Inst. Mgmt., 1986; trustee Sasi Found., Karachi, 1985. Recipient Cert. Recognition Asia-Pacific Real Estate Congress, 1987. Mem. Pakistan Pubs. and Booksellers Assn. (copyright com. 1975-80), Internat. Real Estate Fedn., Assn. Builders and Developers (convenor 1985), Internat. Real Estate Inst. (chpt. head 1986), Inst. Dirs., Pakistan C. of C. and Industry, United Coop. Credit Soc. (bd. dirs. 1977-79), Property Cons. Soc., Internat. Airline Passengers Assn. Muslim. Clubs: Karachi Golf; Def. Lodge: Rotary. Office: Sasi Group Cos, Sasi Towers, Zaibunnisa St, Karachi Pakistan

SHRUM, SAMUEL HOPKINS, construction company executive; banker; b. Dayton, Va., June 19, 1912; s. George Edgar and Annie (Rolston) S.; B.S., Va. Poly. Inst., 1933; postgrad. Westminster Choir Coll., 1938; m. Evelyn L. Vaughan, June 14, 1941; children—Edgar Vaughan, Marilyn Ann. Partner, George E. Shrum & Son, masonry contractors, 1933-42; prodn. engr. Newport News Shipbldg. & Drydock Co., 1942-45; exec. v.p., gen. mgr. treas., dir. Nielsen Constrn. Co., Harrisonburg, Va., 1945-61, pres., 1961-73, chmn. bd., chief exec. officer, 1974-75; dir. Rockingham Nat. Bank, chmn. bd., 1981-84; dir., exec. v.p. Alexandria Prestressed Concrete Co., Inc. 1961; exec. v.p., gen. mgr. Shen Valley, Inc. 1964-67, also dir.; sec.-treas., gen. mgr. of Valley Developers, Inc., 1964-70, also dir.; chmn. Rockingham Area bd. Dominion Bank Shenandoah Valley, 1984—. Chmn. Capitol Stock Com., vice chmn. bldg. com.; mem. Rockingham Devel. Corp.; mem. steering com., publicity chmn. Bridgewater Coll. Crusade for Excellence; mem. com. on nominations Presbytery of Lexington; pres. Sunnyside Presbyn. Home, 1967-71, 72—; mem. Nat. Right of work Com., Washington; mem. state adv. council for vocational edn. Commonwealth of Va., 1971-74. Trustee, asst. treas. Sunnyside Presbyn. Home, 1952, bd. dirs., chmn. finances; bd. dirs. Va. Found. Archtl. Edn., Inc.; trustee v.p. Massanetta Springs Bible Conf., 1953-58; mem. Harrisonburg Downtown Devel. Com., 1975-80; mem. Indsl. Devel. Authority Rockingham County (Va.), 1979—; chmn., Westminster Fellowship, Campus Christian Life Com., 1959-65; chmn. coordinating com. Homes for Aging, Synod of Va., 1968-70; trustee Presbyn. Nursing Homes, Inc.; adv. council Sch. Bus., James Madison U., Harrisonburg, 1978-81; bd. dirs. Valley Outreach for Christ, 1984—; pres. Sonshine Ministries, Inc., 1985—. Named Va. Constrn. Man of Year, 1970; recipient Nations 1st Nat. Bus. Day award, Bus. Man of Year award, 1975; Samuel H. Shrum Excellence award named in his honor James Madison U., 1985. Mem. Engrs. Soc., Nat. Small Bus. Men's Assn., Nat. Labor-Mgmt. Found., Harrisonburg-Rockingham C. of C., Va. C. of C., Vocat. Indsl. Clubs Am. (hon. life mem.), Shenandoah Valley, Inc., Asso. Gen. Contractors (v.p., dir. Va., mem. nat. com. emergency planning, pres. Va. br. 1969-70, nat. membership com. 1968-80, nat. manpower com. 1969-80), Va. Assn. Non-Profit Homes for Aging (trustee 1982). Presbyn. (past deacon, mem. of session, 1946—, moderator Shenandoah Presbytery 1982). Mason, Rotarian (pres. 1967-68, dir. Harrisonburg). Home: Sunnyside Village Harrisonburg VA 22801 Office: Sunnyside Presbyn Home PO Box 928 Harrisonburg VA 22801

SHUB, HARVEY ALLEN, surgeon; b. Bklyn., Oct. 28, 1942; s. Irving and Sara (Levin) S.; m. Susan Jayne Smith, Dec. 26, 1970; children—Carolyn, Todd. Student, NYU, 1960-61, 1964-65; B.S. in Zoology, Physics, U. Miami, 1964; M.D., U. Rome, Italy, 1971. Diplomate Am. Bd. Colon and Rectal Surgery. Intern, Beth Israel Med. Ctr., N.Y.C., 1971-72, resident in surgery, 1972-76; fellow in colon and rectal surgery, Muhlenberg Hosp., Plainfield, N.J., 1976-77; practice medicine specializing in colon and rectal surgery, Orlando, Fla., 1977—; chmn. dept. surgery Fla. Hosp., 1988—; mem. staff Winter Park Meml. Hosp., Orlando Regional Med. Ctr., Lucerne Gen. Hosp., South Seminole Community Hosp.; clin. asst. prof. dept. family medicine U. South Fla., Tampa, 1982—. Chmn. pub. edn. com. Am. Cancer Soc. Orange County 1982—. Served to capt. M.C., USAR, 1971-77. Recipient Physician's Recognition award, AMA, 1976, 79, 81, 83, 87. Fellow ACS, Am. Soc. Colon and Rectal Surgeons, Internat. Coll. Surgeons, Southeastern Surg. Congress, Internat. Soc. Colon and Rectal Surgeons, Am. Soc. for Laser Medicine and Surgery; mem. AMA, So. Med. Assn., Fla. Med. Assn. (council splty. medicine), Orange County Med. Assn., Piedmont Soc. Colon and Rectal Surgeons, Orange County Ostomy Assn. (med. adviser), Fla. Soc. Colon and Rectal Surgeons (sec.-treas. 1980-82, pres. 1983-84), Am. Soc. Gastrointestinal Enodoscopy, Internat. Soc. Univ. Colon and Rectal Surgeons, Am. Soc. Laser Medicine and Surgery, Soc. Am. Gastrointestinal Endoscopic Surgeons. Consulting editor Jour. Fla. Med. Assn.; contbr. articles to profl. jours. Home: 1224 Roxboro Rd Longwood FL 32750 Office: 308 Groveland St Orlando FL 32804

SHUBEROFF, OSCAR JULIO, university administrator; b. Buenos Aires, July 17, 1943; s. Pablo Shuberoff and Jaica Malitz; m. Angelita Luna Sirolli; children: Pablo Alfredo, Diego Leandro, Amalia Ines. Degree in Ciencias Econs., U. Buenos Aires, 1968. Pres. Empryser Aedes SA, Buenos Aires, 1976-88; assoc. prof. U. Buenos Aires, 1972-82, dean of the faculty of Ciencias Econs., 1984-86; chaired prof. U. Lomas de Zamora, Argentina, 1985—; rector U. Buenos Aires, 1986—. Author: Organizing and Administration, 1972; contbr. articles to profl. jours. Sec.-gen. Argentine Fedn. of Econs. Grads., 1982; del. Com. Radical Civic Union-Capital, 1986. Home: Rivadaria 4658, 9-A, Buenos Aires Argentina Office: Universidad de Buenos Aires, Calle Viamonte 430, 1053 Buenos Aires Argentina

SHUBIN, HARRY, internist; b. Phila., Mar. 17, 1914; s. Sam and Hannah (Pisner) S.; B.S., Temple U., 1933, M.D., 1937; m. Celia Fierman, July 8, 1938; children—Charles I., Elliot B. Intern Frankford Hosp., Phila., 1937-38; resident Rush Hosp., Phila., 1938-41, chief vis. physician, 1941-58; practice medicine specializing in internal medicine, pulmonary diseases and occupational medicine, Phila., 1938—; vis. physician Phila. Gen. Hosp., 1944-72, also chmn. dept. pulmonary diseases, 1950-59, pres. med. staff No. div., 1956-58; med. dir., adminstr. Center City Hosp., Phila., 1969-81; med. dir., ADVATEC Pulmonary Lab., med. advisor SSI. Cons., HEW, State of Pa. Mem. exec. com. South Phila. High Sch., 1950—. Bd. dirs. Oak Lane Day Sch., Blue Bell, Pa. Recipient Selective Service medal SSS, 1944. Fellow Royal Coll. London, Am. Coll. Chest Physicians (emeritus 1982), Am. Acad. Med. Adminstrs. (nat. sec., diplomate 1987, Merit award), Am. Pub. Health Assn., Am. Acad. Psychosomatic Medicine; mem. A.C.P. (life mem.), Royal Soc. Health, Am. Trudeau Soc., AAAS, Am. Geriatric Soc., Am. Coll. Health Care Adminstrs., AMA, World Med. Assn. (founder), Am. Acad. Tb Physicians (pres. 1948-50), 50th Ward Community Ambulance Assn. (med. adviser), Asbestos Victims Edn. and Info. (co-chmn. co-founder). Lodges: Lions, Masons (32 deg.). Contbr. articles to profl. jours. Home: 1810 Rittenhouse Sq Philadelphia PA 19103 Office: 1829 Pine St Philadelphia PA 19103

SHUE, WILLIAM ALBRIGHT, retired administrative law judge; b. Fall River, Mass., May 18, 1921; s. Harden Albright and Anna Marie (Blake) S.; m. Ruth E. Kennedy, June 21, 1952 (dec. 1964); children—William Albright, Robert Blake, Judith Shue; m. 2d Gerda Lindenberg, Dec. 14, 1982. A.B., Harvard U., 1947; J.D., Boston Coll., 1949. Bar: Mass. 1950. Spl. asst. atty. gen. Commonwealth of Mass., 1969-73; adminstrv. law judge ICC, Washington, 1975-86. Served with U.S. Army to 1st lt., 1943-46, ETO; res. to col., 1946-74. Decorated Army Commendation medal. Mem. Boston Bar Assn., Fed. Adminstrv. Law Judges Conf. Home: 4024 Ellicott Saint Alexandria VA 22304

SHUEBROOK, RONALD LEE, artist, educator; b. Fort Monroe, Va., July 29, 1943; s. George Albert and Ruth Ellen (Nowling) S.; m. Frances Gallagher, Mar. 2, 1968; children—Paul David, Meghan Sara. B.S. in Art Edn., Kutztown State Coll., 1965, M.Edn., 1969; postgrad. Haystack Mountain Sch. Crafts, 1965, 67; M.F.A., Kent State U., 1972. Instr. at U. Saskatchewan, Saskatoon, Can., 1972-73; asst. prof. Acadia U., Wolfville, N.S., Can., 1973-77; assoc. prof., coordinator art Edn. York U., Downsview, Ont., Can., 1977-79; assoc. prof. of studio N.S. Coll. Art and Design, Halifax, Can., 1979-80, chmn. studio div., 1980-83, assoc. prof., coordinator painting and drawing, 1983-85, assoc. prof., 1985-87; exec. dir. Ottawa (Ont.) Sch. Art, 1987-88; chmn. dept. fine art, U. Guelph, Ont., 1988— vis. artist, lectr. numerous art depts. and galleries across Can., 1974—; mem. visual arts awards juries Can. Council, Ottawa, 1977—; curriculum cons. Acadia U., Wolfville, N.S., Bishop's U, Lennoxville, Quebec, 1984. Contbr. articles to profl. jours., essays to catalogues. Exhibited in one-man shows; represented in numerous public and pvt. collections. Mem. founding exec. com. Visual Arts N.S., Halifax, 1975-77, chmn., 1986-87; mem. N.S. Art Bank Com., Dept. of Culture, N.S., Halifax, 1975-77; mem. task force for art history in pub. schs. N.S. Dept. Edn., Halifax, 1975; bd. dirs. Eye Level Gallery, Halifax, 1977, 81-83, Art Gallery N.S., 1986-87. Fellow Fine Arts Work Ctr., 1969-70, MacDowell Colony, 1981; Can. Council grantee, 1980, 81, 83, 85. Mem. Can. Assn. Univ. Tchrs., Visual Arts N.S. (hon.), Univ. Art Assn. Can., Faculty Assn. N.S. Coll. Art and Design (pres. 1984-85). Home: 27-C Barber Ave, Guelph, ON Canada N1H 5E6 Office: U Guelph, Chmn Dept Fine Art, Guelph, ON Canada N1G 2W1

SHUG, AUSTIN LEO, biochemist, researcher, educator, consultant; b. Paterson, N.J., July 23, 1925; s. Leo Austin and Alice (Fiederlein) S.; m. Kathryn Jean Snyder, Sept. 24, 1955; children—Barbara, Mary, Leo. B.S., U. Tenn., 1951, M.S., 1952; Ph.D., U. Wis., 1958. Postdoctoral fellow U. Ind., Bloomington, 1957-59; research assoc. Enzyme Inst. U. Wis., Madison, 1959-60; chemist, prof. neurology dept. U. Wis. and VA Hosp., Madison, 1961—; chemist NIH, Bethesda, Md., 1960-61; part time lab. dir. Metabolic Analysis Labs., Inc., Madison, 1981—; cons. Sigma-Tau Chem. Co., Rome, Italy, 1977—. Contbr. chpts. to books, articles to profl. jours. Served with USN, 1943-46. Grantee NIH, 1975-81, 81—, VA, 1961—, Muscular Dystrophy Research Assn., 1982-83. Fellow Am. Inst. Chemists; mem. Am. Soc. Biol. Chemists, Fedn. Am. Socs. for Exptl. Biology, Sigma Xi, Phi Lambda Upsilon. Democrat. Roman Catholic. Home: 1201 Shorewood Blvd Madison WI 53705 Office: VA Hosp 2500 Overlook Terr Madison WI 53705

SHUGAN, STEVEN MARK, marketing educator; b. Chgo., Apr. 21, 1952; s. David Lester and Charlotte Rose Shugan; m. Irene H. Ginter, Dec. 16, 1973; children: Adam Joshua, Elliot Hillel. BS in Chemistry, So. Ill. U., 1973, MBA, 1974; PhD in Managerial Econs. and Decision Scis. (fellow), Northwestern U., 1978. Lectr. Grad. Sch. Mgmt., Northwestern U., Evanston, Ill., 1975-76; asst. prof. bus. adminstrn. Grad. Sch. Mgmt., U. Rochester (N.Y.), 1977-79; asst. prof. mktg. Grad. Sch. Bus., U. Chgo., 1979-82, assoc. prof., 1982-87, prof., 1987—; chmn., organizer sessions numerous nat. confs., 1979—; cons. various cos., 1976—; chmn. Mktg. Sci. Conf., 1983; pres. Coll. Mktg., The Inst. of Mgmt. Scis. Mem. Am. Mktg. Assn., Ops. Research Soc. Am., Assn. for Consumer Research, Inst. Mgmt. Scis., Am. Statis. Assn. Contbr. articles and revs. to profl. jours., chpts. to books; assoc. editor Mgmt. Sci.; mem. editorial bd. Mktg. Sci. Jour., 1985—. Office: U Chgo Grad Sch Bus Chicago IL 60637

SHUGGI, GABY GEORGE, pharmaceutical company executive; b. Omdurman, Khartoum, Sudan, Dec. 3, 1947; s. George F. and Josephine (Hallak) S.; m. Eleonore Therese Okosdinossian, Mar. 3, 1973; 1 child, Rania. B.Sc., U. Khartoum, 1969. Med. rep. Upjohn Internat. Inc., Khartoum, Sudan, 1969-73, sr. rep. 1973-75, sales mgr. E. Africa, 1975-78, mgr. E. Africa, Nairobi, Kenya, 1978-85, mktg. planning mgr., Africa, Brussels, Belgium, 1985-86, mkt. planning mgr. Middle East, 1986—; mem. Am. Bus. Com., Khartoum, 1975-78, Nairobi, 1982-85. Mem. Kenya Assn. Pharm. Ind. (mem. exec. com. 1979-85, cert. 1985). Clubs: Catholic Young Men Soc., American (Khartoum). Avocations: tennis, do-it-yourself activities, reading, model trains, stamp collecting. Office: Upjohn Export Adminstrn, 10-Rue de Geneva, 1140 Brussels Belgium

SHUKLA, CHANDRAKANT, mgmt. cons.; b. Jambusar, India, Dec. 8, 1922; s. Manishanker and Hiralaxmi Shukla; M.A., Bombay U., 1942; B.A., Oxford (Eng.) U., 1945; Ph.D., U. London, 1952; m. Manoo Keshwani, Jan. 26, 1960; children—Oorjit, Yashaswini, Prashma. Mem. faculty Baroda U., 1952-60, prof. English lang. and lit., 1956-60, dean Faculty Arts, 1959-60, editor univ. research, 1952-60; chief human, indsl. and public relations and orgnl. devel. div. Mukand Iron and Steel Works Ltd., Bombay, 1961-71; mng. dir. Acropolis: Centre Mgmt. Services, Bombay, 1971—; mem. vis. faculty Bankers Tr. Instns.; cons. in field. Founder, 1964, since pres. Indian Centre for Encouraging Excellence; bd. dirs. Indian Drama Acad.; pres. Premanand Lit. Soc. Mem. Indian Assn. Trainers and Mgmt. Cons. Club: Royal Bombay Yacht. Home: 1 Oorjit Saibaba Rd, Santa Cruz W, Bombay 400 054, India Office: 28-A Nariman Bhavan, Nariman Point, Bombay 400 021 India

SHUKMAN, SOLOMON JOSEPH, artist; b. Bobr, Minsk, USSR, July 5, 1927; came to U.S., 1974, naturalized, 1980; s. Joseph Solomon Shukman and Eugenia (Aaron) Shukman Golden; m. Ludmila N. Berman, Nov. 14, 1954; children—Janna, Roman. Student, Coll. of Fine Arts and Theatre, Moscow, 1946-49, Stroganof Inst. of Art, Moscow, 1949-52. Dep. adviser artistic councils Artists Found. of USSR, 1952-74; painter frescoes and murals for internat. exhibits; also artist in graphics, painting, drawing and lithography; mem. of Union of Soviet Artist Internat. Exhibits, 1963-74. One man shows include Denver, 1974, Transam. Pyramid, San Francisco, 1975, Los Altos, Calif., 1976, 80, Nathan Gallery, San Francisco, 1977, Pantheon Gallery, San Francisco, 1978, Magnes Mus., Berkeley, Calif., 1979-80, Internat. Art-Expo, N.Y.C., 1985, Los Angeles, 1985, JBM Gallery, San Francisco, 1985, Koret Gallery, Palo Alto, Calif., 1985, Civic Arts Gallery, Walnut Creek, Calif., 1986; exhibited in group shows N.Y.C., 1956, Paris, 1959, Brussels, 1961, Warsaw, Poland, 1964, Progue, 1967, Ehrfort, German Democratic Republic, 1969, also at Sokolnike, Moscow; represented in permanent collections Nathan Gallery, Pantheon Gallery, Magnes Mus., Godfrey Gallery; also numerous pvt. collections. Contbr. articles to profl. jours. Subject of numerous newspaper and mag. articles; works pub. in Print World Directory, 1985. Mem. Graphic Arts Council of Achenbach Found. for Graphic Arts, Internat. Soc. Artists, World Prints Council, Ctr. for Visual Arts. Democrat. Jewish. Home: SoloArt Studio PO Box 1337 Menlo Park CA 94026

SHULA, ROBERT JOSEPH, lawyer, medical clinic executive; b. South Bend, Ind., Dec. 10, 1936; s. Joseph Edward and Bertha Mona (Buckner) S.; m. Gaye Ann Martin, Oct. 8, 1978; children: Deirdre Regina, Robert Joseph II, Elizabeth Martin. BS in Mktg., Ind. U., 1958, JD, 1961. Bar: Ind. 1961; Diplomate Ind. Def. Trial Counsel. Ptnr. Bingham Summers Welsh & Spilman, Indpls., 1965-82, sr. ptnr., 1982—; mem. faculty Nat. Inst. Trial Advocacy; guest lectr. Brit. Medicine and Law Soc., 1979, Ind. U. Sch. Law; medico-legal lectr. Ind. U. Schs. Medicine, Dentistry, and Nursing. Bd. dirs. Arts Insight, Indpls.; pres. Oriental Arts Soc., Indpls., 1975-79, Meridian Women's Clinic, Inc., Indpls.; trustee Indpls. Mus. Art, 1975-78, life trustee, 1984—; bd. dirs Ind. Repertory Theatre, Indpls., 1982—, chmn. bd., pres., 1985—; v.p., bd. dirs. Flanner House of Indpls., Inc., 1977—. Served to maj. JAGC, USAFR, 1961-65. Mem. ABA, Fed. Bar Assn., Ind. State Bar Assn., Indpls. Bar Assn., Bar Assn. 7th Fed. Circuit, Assn. Trial Lawyers Am., Am. Law Inst. Democrat. Episcopalian. Clubs: Indpls. Athletic, Woodstock Country. Home: 4137 N Meridian St Indianapolis IN 46208 Office: Bingham Summers Welsh & Spilman One Indiana Sq 2700 Ind Tower Indianapolis IN 46204

SHULMAN, VALERIE LOWITZ, development, evaluation administrator; b. N.Y.C., Mar. 22, 1940; d. Meyer Martin and and Gertrude (Alboum) Lowitz; m. Morris Shulman, Aug. 13, 1961; children—Michael, Joyce Anne, Carolyn. B.S. in English, Upsala Coll., 1960; M.S. in Counseling and Spl. Services, Seton Hall U., 1965; Ph.D., Fordham U., 1978; postgrad., U. Geneva, 1978. Tchr. spl. edn. Newark Bd. Edn., 1960-65; instr. dept. counseling and spl. services Seton Hall U., 1965-70; pres. Shulman Assocs. Mgmt. Cons., South Orange, N.J., 1972—, also Paris, from 1975; ptnr. Writers and Researchers, Inc., Short Hills, N.J.; mem. World Trade Ctr., Paris and N.Y.C.; tchr. corps consortium coordinator Fordham U., CUNY, NYU, 1978-80; dir. spl. projects Fordham U., 1979-81; campus dean, Fordham U., Caguas, P.R.; asso. dir. Fordham U.-U. Geneva, Piaget Inst., N.Y.C. and Geneva, 1979—; cons. P.R. Jr. Coll., Met. Coll., U. Turabo, 1981—; lectr. in field. Sr. editor: The Future of Piagetian Theory; The Neo-Piagetians, 1984; Humor in Industry, 1984; Overlap-Analysis, 1984; (with R. Moss) Excellence in Service Programs for the Food Service Industry; (with A. Lerman and P. Buchak) Facilitating Employment Through a Consortium in New York, 1986. Mem. budget com. Village South Orange, N.J., 1971-75, 1978-80; trustee Village South Orange, 1975-77. Recipient Dissertation of Yr. award, Phi Delta Kappa, 1978; numerous grants. Mem. Am. Soc. Curriculum Devel., Assn. French Speaking Psychologists, Am. Ednl. Research Assn., Assn. Bilingual Educators, Am. C. of C. in France (quar. contbr. to jour.), Piaget Soc., Phi Delta Kappa, Kappa Delta Pi. Club: Altrusa. Address: 7 Rue Leroux, 75016 Paris France

SHULTIS, ROBERT LYNN, educator, retired association executive; b. Kingston, N.Y., June 30, 1924; s. Albert H. and Dorothy Elizabeth (Jenkins) S.; m. Bernice Elizabeth Johnson, Jan. 20, 1946; 1 son, Robert Lee. B.S., Columbia Univ. Sch. Bus., 1949, postgrad., 1949-51. Staff acct. Price Waterhouse, N.Y.C., 1949-52; credit. mgr., controller Organon, Inc., West Orange, N.J., 1952-68; v.p., treas., chief fin. officer Arwood Corp., Rockleigh, N.J., 1968-72; v.p., controller Technicon, Tarrytown, N.Y., 1972-80; exec. dir. Nat. Assn. Accountants, N.Y.C., 1980-86; faculty, exec. dir. Ctr. for Exec. Devel. Coll. William & Mary, Williamsburg, Va., 1987—; instr. Rutgers Univ., 1964-74, Fairleigh Dickinson U., 1967-68; mem. Fin. Acctg. Standards Adv. Council, 1981-86. Author: Improving Communications Skills of Accountants, 1988; columnist Jour. Bank Acctg. and Auditing; series editor, John Wiley, Inc., 18 vols. on systems and controls for fin. mgmt.; contbr. articles to profl. jours. Bd. advs. U. Fla. Sch. Accountancy, James Madison U. Sch. Accountancy. Served with USAF, 1943-45. Decorated Presdl. Unit Citation. Mem. Fin. Execs. Inst., Assn. Systems Mgmt., Nat. Assn. Accts., Am. Acctg. Assn., Ross Inst. Acctg. Research.; Beta Alpha Psi (adv. forum). Club: Met. (N.Y.C.).

SHULTS, ROBERT LEE, real estate executive, airline executive; b. Helena, Ark., Feb. 23, 1936; s. Albert and Mary Shults; m. Belinda Housley, Aug. 21, 1965; children: Catherine Ann, Robert L. BS in Acctg. magna cum laude, U. Ark.-Fayetteville, 1961. CPA, Ark. Mgr., Arthur Andersen & Co., Memphis, 1961-70; exec. v.p. Allied Telephone Co., Little Rock, 1970-80; chmn. bd. Scheduled Skyways, Inc., Little Rock, 1980-85, chmn. bd., chief exec. officer, Fin. Ctr. Corp., Little Rock, 1980—, cons. Alltel Corp., Little Rock, 1980—; dir. Fin. Ctr. Corp., Air Midwest Inc.; past chmn. bd. Regional Airline Assn., Washington, 1984. Bd. dirs. Ark. Children's Hosp., 1985—, Am. Cancer Soc., Little Rock, 1976—, Inst. Pub. Utilities, Mich. State U., 1976-80; mem. Ark. Arts Ctr.; chmn. bd. trustees Trinity Cathedral, 1982—. Served with USMC, 1956-58. Recipient Pres.'s citation, U.S. Ind. Telephone Assn., 1978, 80. Mem. Am. Inst. CPA's, Fin. Execs. Inst., Nat. Assn. Accts., Mo. Bd. Accts., Tenn. Bd. Accts., Met. Little Rock C. of C. Episcopalian. Clubs: Little Rock, The Capital, Summit, Little Rock Country. Lodge: Rotary. Office: Fin Ctr Corp PO Box 56350 Little Rock AR 72215

SHULTZ, EMMET LAVEL, oil company executive; b. Blackfoot, Idaho, Apr. 23, 1934; s. Emmet Franklin and Alba Elizabeth (Larsen) S.; m. Joan C. Kirby, Nov. 7, 1953; children: Joanne M., Jeanette G.; m. Marilyn Barney, Aug. 4, 1978. Asst. to pres. Flying Diamond Corp., Salt Lake City, 1973-74; pres., also bd. dirs. Shuhart Industries, Inc., Salt Lake City, 1974-75; v.p. Hunstman Chem. and Oil Corp., Salt Lake City, 1975-76; exec. v.p. Huntsman Coal Corp., Salt Lake City, 1975-76; pres., chmn. bd. Gulf Energy Corp., Salt Lake City, 1976—, Channel Energy Corp., 1983—, Kita Corp., 1985—. Bd. Dirs. Ballet West, 1980-83, Utah Symphony, 1980-83. Served with USN, 1952-56. Republican. Office: Kita Corp 144 S 500 E West Valley City UT 84119

SHULTZ, GEORGE PRATT, U.S. secretary of state; b. N.Y.C., Dec. 13, 1920; s. Birl E. and Margaret Lennox (Pratt) S.; m. Helena M. O'Brien, Feb. 16, 1946; children: Margaret Ann, Kathleen Pratt Shultz Jorgensen, Peter Milton, Barbara Lennox Shultz White, Alexander George. BA in Econs., Princeton U., 1942; PhD in Indsl. Econs., M.I.T., 1949; hon. degrees, U. Notre Dame, Loyola U., U. Pa., U. Rochester, Princeton U., Carnegie-Mellon U., Baruch Coll., N.Y.C. Mem. faculty M.I.T., 1946-57, assoc. prof. indsl. relations, 1955-57; prof. indsl. relations Grad. Sch. Bus., U. Chgo., 1957-68, dean sch., 1962-68; fellow Ctr. for Advanced Studies in Behavioral Scis., 1968-69; U.S. sec. labor 1969-70; dir. Office Mgmt. and Budget, 1970-72; U.S. sec. treasury, also asst. to Pres., 1972-74; chmn. Council on Econ. Policy, East-West Trade Policy com.; exec. v.p. Bechtel Corp., San Francisco, 1974-75, pres., 1975-80; also dir.; pres. Bechtel Group, Inc., 1981-82; prof. mgmt. and pub. policy Stanford U., 1974-82; chmn. Pres. Reagan's Econ. Policy Adv. Bd.; U.S. sec. of state 1982—; former dir. Gen. Motors Corp., Dillon, Read & Co., Inc. Author: Pressures on Wage Decisions, 1950, The Dynamics of a Labor Market, 1951, Labor Problems: Cases and Readings, 1953, (with T.A. Whisler) Management Organization and the Computer, 1960, (with Arnold R. Weber) Strategies for the Displaced Worker, 1966, Guidelines, Informal Controls and the Market Place, 1966, (with A. Rees) Workers and Wages in the Urban Labor Market, 1970, (with Kenneth W. Dam) Economic Policy Beyond the Headlines, 1978; also articles, chpts. in books, reports. Served to capt. USMCR, 1942-45. Mem. Am. Econ. Assn., Indsl. Relations Research Assn. (pres. 1968), Nat. Acad. Arbitrators. Office: Dept of State 2201 C St NW Washington DC 20520 *

SHULTZ, JOHN DAVID, lawyer; b. Los Angeles, Oct. 9, 1939; s. Edward Patterson and Jane Elizabeth (Taylor) S.; m. Joanne Person, June 22, 1968; children—David Taylor, Steven Matthew. Student Harvard Coll., 1960-61; B.A., U. Ariz., 1964; J.D., Boalt Hall, U. Calif.-Berkeley, 1967. Bar: N.Y. 1968, Calif. 1978. Assoc. Cadwalader, Wickersham & Taft, N.Y.C., 1968-77; ptnr. Lawler, Felix & Hall, Los Angeles, 1977-83 , mem. exec. com., chmn. planning com., co-chmn. recruiting and hiring com.; ptnr. Morgan, Lewis & Bockius, Los Angeles, 1983—, mem. ptnr. lateral entry com., mgmt. com., profl. evaluation com., practice devel. com., chmn. recruiting com.; sec., counsel Copy Tech., Inc., 1971-73; trustee St. Thomas Ch., N.Y.C., 1969-72, Shore Acres Point Corp., Mamaroneck, N.Y., 1975-77; mem. adv. bd. Internat. and Comparative Law Center, Southwestern Legal Found., 1981—. Mem. Republican Nat. Com. Mem. Assn. Bar City N.Y., State Bar Calif., N.Y. State Bar Assn., ABA, Phi Delta Phi, Sigma Chi. Episcopalian. Club: University (Los Angeles). Office: Morgan Lewis & Bockius 801 S Grand Ave 22d Fl Los Angeles CA 90017-3189

SHULTZ, SUSAN KENT FRIED, executive search and international business consultant; b. N.Y.C., Mar. 25, 1943; d. L. Richard and Jane (Kent) Fried; B.A. in Govt. and Econs., U. Ariz., 1964; postgrad. in internat. affairs George Washington U., 1967. Congl. legis. asst., 1964-68; campaign and press dir. various polit. campaigns, 1968-78; public relations cons., 1974-81; contbr. editor Phoenix mag., 1973—; pres. Susan Shultz and Assos., exec. search cons., Paradise Valley, Ariz., 1981—, Assoc. Exec. Search Cons.; assoc. Morgan & Ptnrs. Exec. Search, Europe, Lamay Assoc. Recruiters Conn.; writer Beverly Hills Diet and sequel, 1981-82. Republic Nat. Conv., 1964, 68, 80; charter mem. Charter 100, 1980; charter class mem. Valley Leadership, 1980; membership chmn. Village 5 Phoenix Planning Com., 1980; del. White House Conf. Small Bus., 1986. Mem. Phoenix Com. Fgn. Relations (exec. com.), Nat. Assn. Corporate Dirs., Ariz. Dist. Export Council Jr. League of Phoenix. Episcopalian. Address: 6001 E Cactus Wren Rd Paradise Valley AZ 85253

SHUMAN, R(OBERT) BAIRD, writer, educator; b. Paterson, N.J., June 20, 1929; s. George William and Elizabeth (Evans) S. A.B. (Trustees scholar), Lehigh U., 1951; M.Ed., Temple U., 1953; Ph.D. (Univ. scholar), U. Pa., 1961; cert. in philology, U. Vienna, Austria, 1954. Tchr. Phila. Pub. Schs., 1953-55; asst. instr. English U. Pa., 1955-57; instr. humanities Drexel U., Phila., 1957-59; asst. prof. San José (Calif.) State U., 1959-62; asst. prof. English Duke U., 1962-63, asso. prof., 1963-66, prof. edn., 1966-77; prof. English, dir. English edn. U. Ill., Urbana-Champaign, 1977-85; dir. freshman rhetoric U. Ill., 1979-84, coordinator Univ. Assos. in Rhetoric Program, 1978-84; vis. prof. Moore Inst. Art, 1958, Phila. Conservatory Music, 1958-59, Lynchburg Coll., 1965, King Faisal U., Saudi Arabia, 1978, 81, Bread Loaf Sch. English, Middlebury Coll., 1980, East Tenn. State U., Johnson City, 1980, Olivet Nazarene Coll., 1986, 88, U. Tenn., Knoxville, 1987. Author: Clifford Odets, 1962, Robert E. Sherwood, 1964, William Inge, 1965, Strategies in Teaching Reading: Secondary, 1978, (with Robert J. Krajewski) The Beginning Teacher: A Guide to Problem Solving, 1979, Elements of Early Reading Instruction, 1979; editor: Nine Black Poets, 1968, An Eye for an Eye, 1969, A Galaxy of Black Writing, 1970, Creative Approaches to the Teaching of English: Secondary, 1974, Questions English Teachers Ask, 1977, Educational Drama for Today's Schools, 1978, Education in the 80's—English, 1980, The Clearing House: A Closer Look, 1984, The First R: Strategies in Early Reading Instruction, 1987; exec. editor: The Clearing House, 1976—; cons. editor: Poet Lore, 1977—, Cygnus, 1978—, Jour. Aesthetic Edn., 1978-82; contbg. editor: Reading Horizons, 1975-85; editor: monthly column The Clearing house, poetry editor; editor: quar. column Reading Horizons, 1975-85. NEH researcher Trinity Coll., Dublin, Ireland, 1985. Mem. Nat. Council Tchrs. English (evaluator ERIC Clearing House, com. on alt. careers for English Profls.), Internat. Council Edn. of Tchrs., Ill. English Tchrs. Assn., AAUP, Conf. English Edn. (exec. com. 1976-79), Internat. Reading Assn. (coordinator symposium on cultural literacy 1988), MLA, Internat. Assn. Univ. Profs. English, Nat. Soc. Arts and Humanities, Nat. Soc. Study Edn., Am. Fedn. Tchrs., ACLU. Democrat. Home: Box 1687 Champaign IL 61820 Office: U Ill 208 English Bldg 608 S Wright St Urbana IL 61801

SHUMATE, CHARLES ALBERT, physician; b. San Francisco, Aug. 11, 1904; s. Thomas E. and Freda (Ortmann) S.; B.S., U. San Francisco, 1927, H.H.D., 1976; M.D., Creighton U., 1931. Pvt. practice dermatology, San Francisco, 1933-73, ret., 1973; asst. clin. prof. dermatology Stanford U., 1956-62; pres. E Clampus Vitus, Inc., 1963-64; hon. mem. staff St. Mary's Hosp. Mem. San Francisco Art Commn., 1964-67, Calif. Heritage Preservation Commn., 1963-67; regent Notre Dame Coll. at Belmont, 1965-78, trustee, 1977—; pres. Conf. Calif. Hist. Socs., 1967; mem. San Francisco Landmarks Preservation Bd., 1967-78, pres., 1967-69; trustee St. Patrick's Coll. and Sem., 1970-86. Served as maj. USPHS, 1942-46. Decorated knight comdr. Order of Isabella (Spain); knight Order of the Holy Sepulchre, knight of St. Gregory, knight of Malta. Fellow Am. Acad. Dermatology; mem. U. San Francisco Alumni Assn. (pres. 1955), Calif. Book Club (pres. 1969-71), Calif. Hist. Soc. (trustee 1958-67, 68-78, pres. 1962-64), Soc. Calif. Pioneers (dir. 1979—). Clubs: Bohemian, Olympic, Roxburghe (pres. 1958-59) (San Francisco); Zamorano (Los Angeles). Author: Life of George Henry Goddard; The California of George Gordon, 1976, Jas. F. Curtis, Vigilante, 1988, Francisco Pacheco of Pacheco Pass, 1977; Life of Mariano Malarin, 1980; Boyhood Days: Y. Villegas Reminiscences of California 1850s, 1983, The Notorious I.C. Woods of the Adams Express, 1986. Home: 1901 Scott St San Francisco CA 94115 Office: 490 Post St San Francisco CA 94102

SHUMATE, DOROTHY LEE, pharmacist; b. Oak Hill, W.Va., Feb. 4, 1956; d. Garland Lee and Betty Alice (Perry) Pugh; m. David Keith Shumate, Mar. 14, 1981; 1 child, John David. Student Concord Coll., 1974-76; B.S. in Pharmacy, W.Va. U., 1979. Registered pharmacist. Pharmacist, Rural Acres Pharmacy, Beckley, W.Va., 1979-81, Beckley Hosp., 1979, Fairway Drug, Addison, Ill., 1981-82, Martin Ave. Pharmacy, Naperville, Ill., 1982-85, Pulaski (Va.) Drugs, 1985-87, SuperX Drugs, Pulaski, 1987—; Mem. Am. Pharm. Assn., Va. Pharm. Assn., AAUW, Rho Chi, Gamma Beta Phi, Alpha Chi, Lambda Kappa Sigma. Republican. Mem. Ch. of the Brethren. Avocations: ping pong, piano, organ, racquetball. Home: Rt 2 Box 8 1747 Newbern Rd Pulaski VA 24301

SHUMATE, JOHN PAGE, diplomat; b. El Paso, Tex., Sept. 18, 1934; s. John Page and Elizabeth (McWilliams) S.; m. Caroline Taylor, June 16, 1978. B.A. in Polit. Sci., UCLA, 1956; M.A. in Internat. Relations, U. So. Calif., 1970. Counsellor of Embassy, U.S. Embassy, Quito, Ecuador, 1970-72; dir. exec. tng. Fgn. Service Inst., Washington, 1972-75; dir. U.K. Affairs, Dept. State., 1975-78, exec. dir. Bur. Ednl. and Cultural Affairs, 1978-80, exec. dir. Bur. Adminstrn., Washington, 1981-84; staff dir. Sec. of State's Adv. Panel on Overseas Security, 1984-85; exec. v.p. Am. Fgn. Service Protective Assn., 1986—; co-pres. U.S.-Mexico Cultural Commn. com., 1978-80. Recipient Superior Honor award U.S. Dept. State., 1981; Phi Kappa Phi Cert. of Honor, 1970. Mem. Am. Fgn. Service Assn., Phi Kappa Phi. Clubs: Ft. Meyer Officers, Fgn. Service, Dacor Bacon House, Bethany West Tennis. Office: Am Fgn Service Protective Assn 512 22d St NW Washington DC 20037

SHUMWAY, FORREST NELSON, corporation executive, lawyer; b. Skowhegan, Maine, Mar. 21, 1927; s. Sherman Nelson and Agnes Brooks (Mosher) S.; m. Patricia Ann Kelly, Aug. 12, 1950; children: Sandra Brooks, Garrett Patrick. Student, Deerfield (Mass.) Acad., 1943-45; B.A., Stanford U., 1950, LL.B., 1952; LL.D. (hon.), U. So. Calif., 1974, Pepperdine U., 1978. Bar: Calif. 1952. Staff Office County Counsel, Los Angeles, 1953-57; sec. Signal Oil & Gas Co., Los Angeles, 1959-61, gen. counsel, 1961-64, group v.p. operations, 1963-64, pres., 1964-68; pres., chief exec. officer The Signal Cos., 1968-80, chmn. bd., chief exec. officer, 1980-85; vice chmn. Allied-Signal Inc., 1985—, also bd. dirs.; dir. Transamerica Corp., First Interstate Bancorp, Am. Pres. Cos. Ltd., Clorox Co. Trustee U. So. Calif. Served to 1st lt. USMCR, 1945-46. Mem. ABA, State Bar Assn. Calif., Phi Delta Theta. Clubs: Cypress Point (Pebble Beach, Calif.); California (Los Angeles); Newport Harbor Yacht (Newport Beach, Calif.); Tuna (Avalon, Calif.); Bohemian (San Francisco); San Diego Yacht, La Jolla Country. Lodges: Masons, Shriners. Office: 11255 N Torrey Pines Rd La Jolla CA 92037-1059

SHURICK, EDWARD PALMES, television executive, rancher; b. Duluth, Minn., Dec. 15, 1912; s. Edward P. and Vera (Wheaton) S.; m. F(lossie) Dolores Pipes, Aug. 1, 1933; children—Patricia Annette (Mrs. Robert Dube), Sandra Sue Shurick Dryden, Linda Jean (Mrs. James Elsea), Edward P. III. Student, U. Minn., 1932-33; B.A. in Econs, U. Mo., 1946. Gen. sales mgr. Intermountain Network, Salt Lake City, 1937-41; advt. mgr. sta. KMBC, Kansas City, Mo., 1941-47; research mgr. Free & Peters, N.Y.C., 1947-49; v.p. CBS TV, N.Y.C., 1949-57; exec. v.p. Blair TV, N.Y.C., 1957-62; chmn., treas. H-R TV, N.Y.C., 1962-76; dir. Seltel, Inc., N.Y.C.; v.p., owner Sta. KXXX-AM-FM, Colby, Kans., 1963-84; v.p. treas. H-R Rep. Cos., 1970-73; pres. S&S Enterprises, Charlottesville, Va., 1959—, S & S Ranch Corp., Aspen, Colo., 1965-82; mem. bd. Chgo. Internat. Live Stock Expn., 1972-76. Author: First Quarter-Century of American Broadcasting, 1946. Pres. Shurick Research Found., Bridgewater, 1959-72; v.p. Internat. Radio and TV Found., N.Y.C., 1964-73. Recipient Alumnus award U. Mo. at Kansas City, 1968; ordre du merit for contbns. to agr. Govt. France, 1970; Ordre du Charolais Francais, 1971. Mem. Internat. Radio and TV Soc. N.Y. (pres. 1967-69), Am. Internat. Charolais Assn. (pres. 1968-69), Colonial Charolais Breeders (dir. 1967-71), World Fedn. Charolais (pres. 1973-74), Broadcast Pioneers, Am. Nat. Cattlemen's Assn. (tax com. 1968-76), Internat. Wine and Food Soc. (bd. dirs. 1985—). Episcopalian (lay reader). Clubs: Masons (32 deg.), Shriners (Kansas City, Mo.); Windemere (Eleuthera, The Bahamas); Bear Lakes Country (West Palm Beach, Fla.). Home: 2393 Saratoga Bay Dr West Palm Beach FL 33409 Office: Star Rt Box 15 Tapoco NC 28780

SHURN, PETER JOSEPH, III, lawyer; b. Queens, N.Y., Aug. 30, 1946; s. Peter J. Jr. and Vivienne M. (Tagliarino) S.; m. Ingrid Kelbert; children—Steven Douglas, Vanessa Leigh, David Michael. B.S.E.E. magna cum laude, Poly. Inst. Bklyn., 1974; J.D. magna cum laude, New Eng. Sch. Law, 1977; LL.M. in Patent and Trade Regulation Law, George Washington U., 1981. Bar: N.C., 1977, Va., 1979, Tex., 1982. Research scientist GTE Labs., 1965-77; sole practice, Raleigh, N.C., 1977-78; asso. Burns, Doane, Swecker & Mathis, Alexandria, Va., 1978-80; tech. advisor to judge U.S. Ct. Appeals (fed. cir.), 1980-81; ptnr. Arnold, White & Durkee, Houston, 1981—; adj. prof. South Tex. Coll. Law, 1984—. Served with U.S. Army, 1966-68; Korea. Mem. ABA, Houston Bar Assn., Am. Patent Law Assn. (Robert C. Watson award 1981), Houston Patent Law Assn., Assn. Trial Lawyers Am., IEEE, Sigma Xi. Contbr. articles to legal jours. Office: PO Box 4433 Houston TX 77210

SHURSKY, STANLEY JAMES, marine engineer; b. Liberty, N.Y., Mar. 21, 1952; s. Andrew Stanley and Ruth Mabel (Huschke) S.; m. Joanne Audre Schneider, May 31, 1981. B.S.C.E., MIT, 1974, M.S. in Ocean Engring., 1975. Project engr. Raytheon Co., Portsmouth, R.I., 1975-78; sr. analyst Systems Cons. Inc., Middletown, R.I., 1978-79, Arcon Corp., Waltham, Mass., 1979-81; scientist Bolt, Beranek & Newman Inc., Newport, R.I., 1981-85; cons. WPL, Inc., 1985-86; pres. Brass Rat Software, Inc, 1987—. Mem. IEEE, Soc. Naval Architects and Marine Engrs., Council Internat. Visitors (Newport), Beta Theta Pi. Roman Catholic. Club: Goat Island Yacht (Newport). Home: 1336 Salem St North Andover MA 01845 Office: 1336 Salem St North Andover MA 01845

SHURTLEFF, LEONARD GRANT, U.S. ambassador; b. Boston, June 4, 1940; s. Leonard Francis and Mary Frances (Cornish) S.; m. Christine Morrissette, Dec. 8, 1967. BA in History cum laude, Tufts U., 1962; student, Maxwell Sch., Syracuse, N.Y., 1962; student African Areas Studies, U. Chgo., 1969-70. With fgn. service Dept. State, 1962—; fgn. service officer gen. Am. Embassy, Caracas, Venezuela, 1963-65; polit. officer Am. Embassy, Freetown, Sierra Leone, 1965-67; intelligence analyst Bur. Intelligence and Research, Dept. State, Washington, 1967-69; prin. officer, consul Am. Consulate, Douala, Cameroon, 1970-72; dep. chief of mission Am. Embassy, Nouakchott, Mauritania, 1972-74; spl. asst. to ambassador Am. Embassy, Bogota, Colombia, 1975-77; alt. dir. Office of Inter-African Affairs, Washington, 1977-79; dep. dir. Office Cen. Africa Affairs, Washington, 1979-81; dep. exec. dir. Bur. African Affairs, Washington, 1981-83; dep. chief of mission (minister counselor) Am. Embassy, Monrovia, Liberia, 1983-86; mem. Sr. Sem. on Nat. and Internat. Affairs, Dept. State, Washington, 1986-87; A.E. and P. Am. Embassy, Brazzaville, Peoples Republic of Congo, 1987—. Recipient Meritorious Hon. award, 1969, Equal Employment Opportunity award, 1983, Superior Hon. award, 1986 U.S. Dept. State. Mem. World Affairs Council, U.S. Naval Inst., Am. Fgn. Service Assn., Demolay AmFornSerivce Assn., Alpha Tau Omega. Home: Meredith NH 03253 Office: American Embassy, Brazzaville Peoples Republic of the Congo

SHUSTERMAN, NATHAN, underwriter, financial consultant; b. Montreal, Que., Can., Aug. 27, 1927; came to U.S., 1950; s. Aaron and Annie (Nulman) S.; m. Norma Thalblum, Jan. 1950; children: Mark D., Claudia S. Student, Sir George Williams Coll., Montreal, 1944-47; grad. N.Y. Inst. Fin. CLU, chartered fin. cons. Retailing mgr. Jefferson Stores, Miami, Fla., 1950-65; gen. agt. Protective Life Ins. Co., Miami, 1965—, also chmn. agts. adv. com.; fin. and estate planning cons.; pres. Am. Fin. Counseling Corp., Miami; instr. in estate and tax planning Am. Coll., Bryn Mawr, Pa., 1972—, U. Miami, Coral Gables, Fla., 1972—; registered rep. Protective Equity Services Inc. Mem. North Dade- South Broward Estate Planning Council. Named Man of Yr., Gen. Agts. and Mgrs. Assn., Miami, 1965-67. Mem. Million Dollar Round Table (life), Top of Table, Assn. Advanced Life Underwriting, Am. Soc. CLU's and Chartered Fin. Cons. (past pres. Miami chpt.), Nat. Assn. Life Underwriters (Nat. Sales Achievement award, Nat. Quality award), Fla. Assn. Life Underwriters, Miami Assn. Life Underwriters, Internat. Assn. Fin. Planners, Am. Soc. Pension Actuaries (assoc.), Internat. Platform Assn. Club: Optimists (pres. 1971) (North Miami Beach, Fla.). Lodges: Masons, Shriners, B'nai B'rith (pres. 1950) (Miami). Home: 2320 NE 196th St North Miami Beach FL 33180 Office: Am Fin Counseling Corp 16121 NE 18th Ave North Miami Beach FL 33162

SHUTTLEWORTH, ANNE MARGARET, psychiatrist; b. Detroit, Jan. 17, 1931; d. Cornelius Joseph and Alice Catherine (Rice) S.; A.B., Cornell U., 1953, M.D., 1956; m. Joel R. Siegel, Apr. 19, 1959; children—Erika, Peter. Intern, Lenox Hill Hosp., N.Y.C., 1956-57; resident Payne Whitney Clinic-N.Y. Hosp., 1957-60; practice medicine, specializing in psychiatry, Maplewood, N.J., 1960—; cons. Maplewood Sch. System, 1960-62; instr. psychiatry Cornell U. Med. Sch., 1960; mem. Com. to Organize New Sch. Psychology, 1970. Mem. AMA (Physicians Recognition award 1975, 78, 81, 84, 87), Am. Psychiat. Assn., Am. Med. Women's Assn., N.Y. Acad. Scis., Acad. Medicine N.J., Phi Beta Kappa, Phi Kappa Phi. Home: 46 Farbrook Dr Short Hills NJ 07078 Office: 2066 Millburn Ave Maplewood NJ 07040

SHUZO, FURUSAKA, professor of architecture; b. Japan, July 20, 1951. B of Engring., Kyoto (Japan) U., 1974, D of Engring., 1986. Engr. Shimizu Constrn. Co., Tokyo, 1974-76; instr. Dept. Architecture Kyoto U., 1976-87, assoc. prof., 1987—. Author: Maintenance System for Wooden House, Modern Housing, Economic Evaluation Method for Maintenance and Reliability, 1986. Mem. Archtl. Inst. of Japan. Home: 23-201, 2-9 Ohharano, Nishisakaidani Nishigyo-ku, Kyoto 610-11, Japan Office: Kyoto U Dept Architecture, Yoshida-Honmachi Sakyo-ku, Kyoto 606, Japan

SHYERS, LARRY EDWARD, mental health counselor, educator; b. Middletown, Ohio, Aug. 16, 1948; s. Edward and Ruth Evelyn (Davis) S.; m. Linda Faye Shearon, July 31, 1970; children—Jami Lynn, Karen Lindsey. B.A., David Lipscomb Coll., Nashville, 1970; M.A., Stetson U., DeLand, Fla., 1973; M.Ed., U. Central Fla., 1981; postgrad. U. Fla., 1981-88. Lic. mental health counselor, Fla.; nat. cert. counselor. Ordained to ministry nondenominational Ch. of Christ, 1969; minister Ch. of Christ, Ocala, Fla., 1970-75, Mt. Dora, Fla., 1975-80; tchr. Christian Home and Bible Sch., Mt. Dora, 1970-77, dir. guidance, 1977-86; pvt. practice individual and family counselor, Mount Dora, Fla., 1980—; appointed to state regulatory bd. for clin. social work, marriage, family therapy, mental health counseling, 1987—, vice-chmn.; adjunct prof. Nova U., 1986—; mem. individual manpower tng. system bd. Vocat.-Tech. Sch., Eustis, 1984-87; adj. prof. psychology St. Leo Coll., 1985—; mem. adv. bd. U.S. Achievement Bd., 1983—; cons. in field. Dir. edn. Mt. Dora Ch. of Christ, 1983-86. Mem. Fla. Mental Health Counselors Assn. (chmn. award and profl. devel. coms. 1985, chmn. govt. relations com., pres. 1986-87), Am. Assn. Counseling and Devel., Am. Mental Health Counselors Assn. (govt. relations com. 1987—, chmn. 1988—), Am. Assn. Profl. Hypnotherapists, Internat. Acad. Profl. Counselors and

Psychotherapists, Coalition of Psychol. Services Providers, Lake Sumter Assn. for Counseling and Devel. (Pres. 1987-88), Mount Dora C. of C. (mem. youth com. 1984), Kappa Delta Pi, Pi Lambda Theta, Chi Sigma Iota. Republican. Lodge: Kiwanis. Avocations: amateur radio, target shooting. Office: 501 Hwy 19 A Suite 5 Mount Dora FL 32757-2204

SIA, TIONG-GAM, plastic surgeon; b. Phillipines, July 8, 1929; s. Sia, Giap-Long Siok-Tee (Tiu) S.; m. Esperanza Go, June 12, 1966; children: Frederick, Kendrick, Charmaine. AA, U. Santo Thomas, 1951, MD, 1956. Intern Mt. Sinia Hosp., Chgo., 1956-57; resident U. Okla., Oklahoma City, 1957-59, U. Rochester, N.Y., 1959-61; residency in plastic surgery Roswell Park Meml. Inst., Buffalo, N.Y., 1961-62; house officer plastic surgery Leasone Hosp., Cheshire, England, 1963-64; registrar in plastic surgeon Ballochmyle Hosp., Aryshire, Scotland, 1963-64; practice medicine specializing in reconstructive plastic surgery Met. Hosp., Manila, 1964—; head plastic surgery section Met. Hosp., Manila, 1964—, Chinese Gen. Hosp., Manila, 1964—. Perfomed free surgery for poor, 1964—. Recipient cert. of Appreciation for free harelip operations for poor Office of Civil Relations Armed Forces Philippines, 1975. Fellow Philippine Assn. Plastic Surgeons; mem. British Assn. Plastic Surgeons, Internat. Soc. Aesthetic Plastic Surgery, Internat. Soc. Plastic and Reconstructive Surgery, Asian-Pacific Assn. Plastic Surgeons (pres. 4th Congress), Philippines Med. Assn., Philippines Coll. SUrgeons, Filipino-Chinese Med. Soc. Office: Met Hosp, 1357 G Masangkay St, Manila Philippines

SIAD BARRE, MOHAMED, president Somalia; b. Lugh dist. Upper Juba region, Somalia, 1921; ed. pvt. schs. Mogadishu, Mil. Acad., Italy, Sch. Politics and Adminstrn.; married; 20 children. With Police Force under Brit. adminstrn. Somalia, later chief insp., 1941-50; commd. 2d lt. under Italian trusteeship, col. on founding of Somali Nat. Army, 1960, advanced through grades to maj. gen., 1966; vice comdt. Somali Nat. Army, 1960-65, comdt., 1966-69; pres. Supreme Revolutionary Council Somalia, 1969-76; chmn. Orgn. African Unity, 1974-75; chmn. Council of Ministers, 1976—; sec.-gen. Somali Socialist Revolutionary Party, 1976—; pres. Somalia, 1980—. Author: The Philosophy of Samali Revolution. *

SIALOM, SEDAT SAMI, advertising executive; b. Istanbul, Turkey, Dec. 14, 1940; s. Elie Guy and Sarah (Barzilay) S.; M in Econs., Istanbul U., 1961; Technicien en Publicite, Ecole Superieure Technique de Puplicite, Brussels, 1963; 1 child from previous marriage, Sandy; m. Cana Lakse, Mar. 3, 1985; 1 child, Selin. Account exec. Bodden Et Dechy S.A., Brussels, Belgium, 1962-63, D.T.V., London, 1963-64; account dir., group dir. Client Contract dir. Grafika-Maya A.S., Istanbul, Turkey, 1964-70, vice chmn., 1970-73, chmn., 1973—; cons. in field. Served with Turkish Navy, 1960-61. Recipient Rizzoli award, 1972. Mem. Internat. Advt. Assn., Turkish Advt. Assn., Turkish Mgmt. Assn., Internat. C. of C. Office: 2 Boyokdere, Istanbul Turkey

SIBILLE, EMMANUEL MICHEL, mathematician, computer scientist; b. Mulhouse, France, Apr. 3, 1950; s. Alphonse and Marie Odette (Robert) S.; m. Brigitte Poupard, Oct. 31, 1974; children: Léonard, Pauline, Elisabeth, Marie-Hélène. Agrégation de Math., Ecole normale supèrieure de Saint-Cloud, France, 1974; Doctorate in Math. Logic, Univ. Paris, 1982, D.E.A. in Computer Sci., 1984. Prof. agrégé Ministère Edn. Nat., Suresnes, France, 1974-85; ingenieur prin., chef du service d'études avancées et d'intelligence artificielle THOMSON-SYSECA, Thomson Informatique, Saint-Cloud, France, 1985-86; expert chargé de mission THOMSON-CSF, 1986-88; head artificial intelligence and advanced studies dept. THOMSON-SYSECA, 1987—. Cons. ESPRIT projects Commn. European Communities, 1988—. Contbr. articles to profl. jours. Mem. Am. Math. Soc. Roman Catholic. Home: 17ter rue Rouget de l'Isle, 92800 Puteaux France

SIBLEY, JAMES ASHLEY, JR., museum director educator; b. Shreveport, La., Oct. 21, 1916; s. James Ashley and Lucian Katherine (Hammond) S.; B.A., Centenary Coll., 1940, postgrad., 1941-53; M.Ed., La. State U., 1963; m. Zilda Pickett, Feb. 7, 1957 (dec. Jan. 1961); m. Anna May Switzer, Feb. 1, 1963 (dec. Mar. 1975). Asst. mgr. Sibley's Hardware and Variety Stores, 1935-41; farmer, Shreveport, 1941-45; tchr. sci., phys. edn. supr. Lab. Sch., Centenary Coll., Shreveport, 1941-42; tchr. pub. schs., Shreveport, 1942-44, Baton Rouge, 1958-71; dir. VITAL Career Info. Center, La. Dept. Edn., Baton Rouge, 1971-76; dir. Grindstone Bluff Mus. and Environ. Edn. Center, La. Landmark, Shreveport, 1976—; ednl. cons., 1976—; asst. instr. anthropology course on Caddo Indians, Centenary Coll., 1983-84; tchr. archaeology course acad. in term program Caddo Parish Sch.; personnel technician, examiner La. Civil Service Dept., Baton Rouge, 1944-48; employment counselor, test technician La. Employment Service, Shreveport, 1948-57; ednl. cons. Gulf S. Research Inst.; coordinator cultural resources Unit Project for humanities East Baton Rouge Parish Sch. Bd.; coordinator La. Arts and Sci. Center Planning Project, East Baton Rouge Parish Schs. Mem. econ. council East Baton Rouge Parish Sch. Bd., 1963-64; cons. sect. elementary sci. and social studies Assn. Childhood Edn. Internat., 1963-64; exec. asst. region 7, La. Jr. Acad. Scis., 1963-64, La. Social Studies Fair, 1972-76; adviser La. Indian edn. sect. Nat. Conf. on Employment Am. Indian; cons. La. Indian Cultural Heritage Ednl. Enrichment Program, 1975, La. studies project Caddo Parish Sch. Bd., 1981. Past mem. bd. dirs. Found. for Hist. La. Co-founder, sponsor Jr. Archeol. Soc., Inc., Meml. Mus. and Library Fund. Recipient Merit award for outstanding service to public La. chpt. Internat. Assn. Personnel in Employment Security, 1952; La. Historic Preservation award; La. Gov.'s award service to archeology, 1982; Patron Gold Tag award Shreveport Theater Art Guild, 1985; donor site for Ch. of Holy Cross Mission and Retreat Ctr./Research Ctr., 1985-86. Mem. Nat. Social Studies Council (pres. East Baton Rouge Parish chpt. 1964-65), Assn. Supervision and Curriculum Devel., La. Hist. Soc., La. Geneal. and Hist. Soc., Am., La. (exec. com., bd. 1972-73) personnel and guidance assns., Nat. Vocat. Guidance Assn., (del.), La. Guidance Assn., Nat. Sci. Tchrs. Assn., Archeol. Inst. Am., Soc. for Am. Archeology, La. Acad. Scis., La. Tchrs. Assn., La. Sch. Counselors Assn., Soc. Hist. Archaeology, La., La. Sci. tchrs. assns., Am. Assn. Mus., La. Assn. Mus., Am. Assn. for Counseling and Devel., La. Assn. for Counseling and Devel., La. Vocat. Guidance Assn. (pres. 1971-73), Nat. Trust for Hist. Preservation, Am. Anthrop. Assn., Nat., La. ret. tchrs. assns., La. Hist. Assn. No. La. Hist. Assn. (charter, past pres., cert. of appreciation 1985), La. Archaeol. Soc. (charter mem. N.W. chpt.), Ark., Okla., La. (past dir.), Tex. archeol. socs., Historic Preservation Shreveport, Am. Mus. Natural History, Am. Folklore Soc., Smithsonian Assos., Nat., La. wildlife fedns., Nat., La. recreation and park assns., Phi Delta Kappa, Psi Chi (charter mem. L.S.U. chpt.). Episcopalian (past treas. and vestryman); land donor to Ch. of Holy Cross. Author: Louisiana's Ancients of Man, 1967; The Junior Archeological Society, 1967; Geology of Baton Rouge and Surrounding S.E. La. Area, 1972; Grindstone Bluff, Sibleyshire, La. Landmark, 1975, others. Editor: Cultural Heritage of East Baton Rouge Parish, 1969; Handbook of Vital Career Information Center; The Development and Use of Behavioral Objectives, 1970; Cultural Heritage of Old Revenue Plantation, Carville, La., 1975. Contbr. articles to profl. publs. Address: PO Box 7965 Shreveport LA 71107

SIBLEY, MARK ANDERSON, ophthalmologist; b. Daytona Beach, Fla., Sept. 15, 1950; s. John Rheney and Alyce K. (McDonald) S.; m. Sue Ellen White, Jan. 27, 1978; children: Paul Anderson, Laura Katherine. AA, Daytona Beach Jr. Coll., 1970; BA, U. Fla., 1972; MD, Meharry Med. Coll., Nashville, 1976. Diplomate Nat. Bd. Med. Examiners, Am. Bd. Ophthalmology. Intern, Orlando Regional Med. Ctr., Fla., 1976-77; resident U. Ala., 1977-80; fellow Eye Found. Hosp., Birmingham, Ala., 1980; ophthalmologist Suncoast Med. Clinic, St. Petersburg, Fla., 1980—; chief med. staff Sunbay Hosp., 1983-85, staff ophthalmologist, 1980—; mem. staff Bayfront Hosp., 1980—, St. Anthony's Hosp., 1980—; asst. clin. prof. U. South Fla., Tampa, 1982—. Contbr. articles to profl. jours. Med. advisor Fla. Soc. Prevent Blindness, Tampa, 1981—; mem. Physician Edn. Network, St. Petersburg, 1981—; bd. dirs. Am. Diabetes Assn., Pinellas County, Fla., 1982—; bd. dirs. Suncoast Med. Clinic, 1984—, also mem. exec. com. Founding mem., v.p. OPTIC Found., 1987—. Recipient Blue Key award U. Fla., 1970, Physician Recognition, AMA, 1982, 85, 88. Fellow ACS, Am. Acad. Ophthalmology; mem. Fla. Soc. Ophthalmology (pub. relations com. 1981—, sec.-treas. 1986, pres. elect 1987-88, pres. 1988—), Am. Soc. Contemporary Ophthalmology (Cert. Advanced Studies award 1982, 85), Fla. Med. Soc., Am. Intraocular Implant Soc. Republican. Roman Catholic. Avocations: biking; fishing. Office: Suncoast Med Clinic 700 6th St S Saint Petersburg FL 33701

SICARD, PAUL, television editor; b. Paris, Mar. 2, 1959; s. Michel and Nicole (Alihu) S.; m. Edith Guillou, July 11, 1987. Grad., Audiovisual Dir. Superior Sch., Paris, 1981. Chief editor Army Video Ctr., Paris, 1981-83; chief editor Aquitaine, Midi Pyrenées French TV Channel 3 (FR3), Bordeaux and Toulouse, France, 1983-86; chief editor Midi-Pyrenées, Nord, Rhone Alpes French TV Channel 3 (FR3), Toulouse, Lille and Lyon, France, 1986—; instr. French TV Channel 3 formation, Paris, 1986-87. Author: Computerized Editing, 1987. Served as sgt. French Army, 1981-82. Recipient Spl. price Soc. Photographique de France, 1978. Mem. Soc. Broadcast Engring. Home: 7 rue de la Tannerie, 31400 Toulouse France

SICILIANO, ROCCO CARMINE, business executive, lawyer; b. Salt Lake City, Mar. 4, 1922; s. Joseph Vincent and Mary (Arnone) S.; m. Marion Stiebel, Nov. 8, 1947; children: Loretta, A. Vincent, Fred R., John, Maria. B.A. with honors, U. Utah, 1944; LL.B., Georgetown U., 1948. Bar: D.C. bar 1949. Legal asst. to bd. mem. NLRB, Washington, 1948-50; asst. sec.-treas. Procon Inc., Des Plaines, Ill., 1950-53; asst. sec. labor charge employment and manpower Dept. Labor, Washington, 1953-57; spl. asst. to Eisenhower for personnel mgmt., 1957-59; ptnr. Wilkinson, Cragun & Barker, 1959-69; pres. Pacific Maritime Assn., San Francisco, 1965-69; undersec. of commerce Washington, 1969-71; pres., chmn. bd., chief exec. officer Ticor, Los Angeles, 1971-84; chmn., exec. com. Ticor, 1984-85; of counsel Jones, Day, Reavis & Pogue, 1984-87; chmn. bd., chief exec. officer Am. Health Properties, Inc., 1987-88, bd. dirs., 1987—; dir. Pacific Enterprises, Am. Med. Internat., United TV, Inc.; mem. Fed. Pay Bd., 1971-73; trustee J. Paul Getty Trust. Vice chmn., bd. dirs. Los Angeles Philharm. Assn.; past chmn. Calif. Bus. Roundtable; trustee Com. for Econ. Devel.; Co. chmn. Calif. Commn. on Campaign Financing. bd. dirs. Mus. Contemporary Art; mem. adv. council Johns Hopkins Sch. Advanced Internat. Studies. Served with AUS, 1943-46; 1st lt., 10th Mountain Div. Italy; personnel officer G-1, Hdqrs., U.S. Forces Austria. Decorated Combat Infantryman Badge, Bronze Star, Army Commendation Ribbon U.S.; Order Merit Italian Republic. Mem. ABA, Nat. Acad. Pub. Adminstrn., Nat. Commn. on Pub. Service. Clubs: Met. (Washington); California (Los Angeles). Home: 612 N Rodeo Dr Beverly Hills CA 90210

SICOLI, MARY LOUISE CORBIN, psychologist, educator; b. Delaware County, Pa., Nov. 15, 1944; d. C.M. Lewis and Lucille (Weber) Corbin; m. Thomas Sicoli, Aug. 27, 1967; children—Michael, Kathryn Francesca. B.S. (Hannah Kent Schoff scholar), West Chester U., 1966, M.S., 1974; M.S. (grad. fellow), U. Wis., Madison, 1967; Ph.D., Bryn Mawr Coll., 1977. Music tchr. supr. Unionville-Chadds Ford Sch. Dist., 1967-70; supr. student tchrs. Rosemont (Pa.) Coll., 1976-78; assoc. prof. psychology, campus psychologist Cabrini Coll., Radnor, Pa., 1974—, also coordinator psychol. services; cons. Children's Services Southeastern Pa., 1974-80; supr. doctoral interns in psychology Bryn Mawr Coll., 1979-86. Contbr. articles to profl. jours. Founding mem. bd. dirs. Maternal Support System Chester County, 1981—; mem. Citizens Action for Better TV, 1981—. Recipient Legion of Honor, Chapel for Four Chaplains, 1980, Christian and Mary Lindback award for disting. coll. teaching, 1984. Fellow Pa. Psychol. Assn. (founder campus psychologist network); mem. Am. Psychol. Assn., Eastern Psychol. Assn., AAUP, Jean Piaget Soc., Assn. for Moral Devel., Kappa Delta Pi, Psi Chi, Delta Epsilon Sigma. Home: 404 Darlington Dr Westchester PA 19380 Office: Cabrini Coll Dept Psychology Radnor PA 19087

SIDABUTAR, HASIHOLAN, automotive executive; b. Tarutung, Tapanuli, Indonesia, Feb. 13, 1938; s. Wismar and Rustina (Siahaan) S.; m. Isabella R. Tobing, Sept. 16, 1953; children: Daniel Hasiando, Wilfred Halasanta, Rosabella Siholina, Manuel P. Haholongan. Degree in mech. engring., Bandung (Indonesia) Inst. Tech., 1961; cert. exec. edn., Harvard U., 1980. Head inspection group Stanvac Oil Refinery, Sei Gerong, Indonesia, 1961-64; mgr. tech. dept. Permorin, Jakarta, Indonesia, 1965-70; dir. tech. dept. P.T. New Marwa 1970 Motors, Jakarta, 1970-73; dir. ops. P.T. Krama Yudha Ratu Motor, Jakarta, 1974-77, pres., 1981-84, advisor, 1984—, also bd. dirs.; pres. P.T. Krama Yudha Surabaya Mojopahit Motors, Surabaya, 1978-81; dir. P.T. Krama Yudha, Jakarta, 1984-86, exec. v.p., 1986—; exec. v.p. P.T. Colt Engine Mfg., Jakarta, 1984-87; lectr. Christian U. Indonesia, Jakarta, 1966-67; chmn. gen. com. 3d Internat. Pacific Conf. on Automotive Engring., 1984-85; comissary P.T. Mitsubishi Krama Yudha Motors and Mfg., Jakarta, 1984-87, v.p., 1988—; advisor Indonesian Automotive Mfr. Assns., Jakarta, 1985-87. Mem. Soc. Automotive Engrs. Indonesia (bd. dirs. 1977-84, exec. v.p. 1984—), Internat. Fedn. Automotive Engring. Soc. (council mem. 1985—). Mem. Christian Ch. (Disciples of Christ). Club: Cinere Country (Jakarta). Home: JL Tebet Barat #660, 12810 Jakarta, Selatan Indonesia Office: PT Krama Yudha, JL Warung Buncit Raya #43, 12760 Jakarta Indonesia

SIDAWAY-WOLF, DAPHNE MERCEDES, food processing engineer; b. Montreal, Quebec, Can., Oct. 14, 1955; d. George Gilbert and Margaret Nancy Lydia (Dawson) S.; m. Harald Wolf, May 4, 1981; 1 child, Astrid Lydia. Baccalaureat maths et physique, Lycee Bellevue Toulouse, France, 1974; baccalaureat, Dawson Coll., Montreal, 1974-75; BS Agrl. Engring., McGill U., Montreal, 1980; MSc, McGill U., 1984; PEng, Ont. Can., 1984. Computing cons. agrl. engr. dept. McGill U., Montreal, 1980-81; lectr. food engring. McGill U., 1981; energy engr. Engring. and Stat. Research Centre Agrl. Can., Ottawa, Ont., 1982-85, food processing engr., 1985-87; processing devel. engr. Food Devel. Div. Agrl. Can., Ottawa, 1987—; pres. Allegra Mgmt. Co., Ottawa, 1984—; sec. Food Process Engring. Interest Group, 1987—; exec. Ottawa sect. Can. Inst. Food Sci. and Tech., 1985-88, mem. energy subcom. Can. Com. on Food, Ottawa, 1985—. Author: Computerized Housing Priority System User Manual, 1985, Optimization of Continuous Sterilization of Fluid Foods, 1984; contbr. articles to profl. jours. Recipient Agrl. Engring. Dept. scholar McGill U., 1980. Mem. Assn. Profl. Engrs. of Ont., Can. Soc. Agrl. Engrs., Am. Soc. Agrl. Engrs., Can. Inst. Food Sci. and Tech., Women in Sci. and Engring. Club: LaLeche League (Ottawa). Home: 34 Woodmount Crescent, Ottawa, ON Canada K2E 5R1 Office: Food Devel Div Agrl Can, 930 Carling Ave, Ottawa, ON Canada K1A 0C5

SIDDHARTHAN, NATTERI SRINIVASAN, economist educator; b. Madras, India, Jan. 29, 1945; parents: Natteri Sundaramier and Parvati (Seethapathy) Srinivasan; m. Meera Viswanathan, Aug. 23, 1971; children: Rahul, Advaith. BA, U. Madras, 1964, MA, 1966; PhD, U. Delhi, India, 1972. Research assoc. Inst. Econ. Growth, Delhi, 1971-75, reader in econs., 1975-81, prof. econs., 1981—; cons. Econ. Adv. Council Prime Minister India, Delhi, 1986-87; mem. planning council Commn. Panel Indsl. Economists Govt. India, 1986—. Author: Conglomerates and Multinationals, 1981; contbr. articles to internat. jours. Mem. Royal Econ. Soc., Indian Econometric Soc. (life). Home and Office: Inst Econ Growth, A-12 Univ Enclave, New Delhi 110 007, India

SIDDHI SAVETSILA, deputy prime minister, minister of foreign affairs of Thailand; b. Jan. 7, 1919. Degree in Engring., Chulalongkorn U.; B.S. in Metallurgy, MIT, M.S. in Metallurgy. Commd. officer Royal Thai Air Force; mem. Nat. Assembly of Thailand, Bangkok, after 1973; mem. Nat. Adminstrv. Reform Council, Bangkok, after 1976; mem. Ho. of Reps., Parliament of Thailand, Bankok; minister of Prime Minister's Office, minister fgn. affairs, 1980—, dep. prime minister, from 1986; adviser Royal Thai Air Force; sec. gen. Nat. Security Council, Bangkok, 1974-80. Office: Ministry of Fgn Affairs, Dep Prime Minister, Bangkok Thailand *

SIDDIQI, MOHAMMED RAZIUDDIN, retired mathematics educator; b. Hyderabad, Pakistan, Jan. 2, 1908; s. Mohammad Muzaffarudin and Amatullah Begum S.; m. Khurshid Jahan, Nov. 1938; children: Toufiq Aliuddin, Farida, Shirin Tahir-Kheli; saeeda Idris. BA, Osmania U., Hyderabad, 1925; DSc (hon.), Osmania U., 1942; PhD, Leipzig U., Germany, 1931. Prof., dir. research Osmania U., 1931-48, vice-chancellor, 1948-49; prof. research Peshawar (Pakistan) U., 1950-53, vice-chancellor, 1953-58; prof. emeritus Atomic Energy Commn., 1958—; mem. for research Atomic Energy Commn., Karachi, Pakistan, 1958-59; vice-chancellor Sind U., Hyderabad, 1959-64; head Sci. and Tech.Research div. Govt. of Pakistan, 1964-66; vice-chancellor U. Islamabad, Pakistan, 1964-72; prof. emeritus Quaid-i-Azam U., Islamabad, 1980—; disting. vis. prof. Midwest Univs. Consortium, U.S., 1973-74. Author more than 5 sci. and tech. books, 1937-77; contbr. 30 articles to profl. jours. Chmn. Inter-Univ. Bd. Pakistan, 1957, 62, 72. Recipient Star of Distinction Pres. of Pakistan, 1960, Grosse Verdienst Kreuz, Pres. of Fed. Republic Germany, 1962, Crescent of Order of Merit, Pres. of Pakistan, 1981. Fellow Indian Acad. Sci. (v.p. 1934—), Indian Nat. Sci. Acad. (mem. council 1937—), Pakistan Acad. Scis. (pres. 1960-67, 84-86, sec. gen. 1968-84). Home: 2 Hill Rd F-7/3, Islamabad Pakistan Office: care Pakistan Acad of Sci, Constitution Ave G-5, Islamabad Pakistan

SIDDIQI, MOHAMMED SHAHID, structural engineer; b. Karachi, Sind, Pakistan, Nov. 16, 1958; s. Mohammed Iqbal and Alia (Mazhary) S.; m. Alam Khalida, Feb. 14, 1985; 1 child, Mohammed Junaid. BE, N.E.D. U. Engring. and Tech., Karachi, 1980. Registered profl. engr. Engring. trainee Mushtaq and Bilal cons. engrs., Karachi, 1979-80, structural engr., 1980-81; structural engr. Nes-Pak Ltd., Karachi, 1981-85, sr. structural engr., 1985—; external examiner N.E.D. U. Engring. and Tech., Karachi, 1982-84, Dawood Engring. Coll., Karachi, 1984. Mem. Am. Concrete Inst., Inst. Engrs. Pakistan, Pakistan Engring. Council, Assn. Cons. Structural Engrs. (mem. organizing com. seminars 1981—). Sunni-Muslim. Club: Jr. Citizens (Karachi). Avocations: stamp and coin collecting, badminton, tennis. Home: 78-E-6 PECHS, Karachi Pakistan 816 Office: Nes-Pak Ltd, PNSC Bldg 9th Floor, Mt Khan Rd, Karachi Pakistan 5772

SIDDIQUI, ABDUL GHANI, surgeon, educator; b. Sehwan, Dadu, Pakistan, Mar. 30, 1934; s. Sadar Din and Hidayat (Khatoon) S.; m. Razia Allahditta Soomro; children: Faisal, Faud, Filza. MBBS, Dow Med. Sch., Karachi, Pakistan, 1957. House officer Jinnah Postgrad. Med. Ctr., Karachi, 1958-59, registrar, 1959-64, sr. registrar, 1964-67; asst. prof. surgery Liaquat Med. Coll., Jamshoro, Pakistan, 1967-72, prof., 1972-88; prof. surgery Dow Med. Coll., Karachi, 1988—; chief med. edn. Liaquat Med. Coll., Jamshoro, 1975—; staff Nat. Tchrs. Tng. Ctr., Govt. Pakistan, Karachi, 1980—; provincial coordinator Ctr. Med. Edn., 1980—; dean faculty med. Sind U., Jamshoro, 1986—. Author: Lecture Notes on Oesophagus, 1974, Lecture Notes on Stomach, 1975, Lecture Notes on Liver, 1978, Lecture Notes on Undergraduates Surgery, 1978, Lecture Notes on Selected Topics Surgery I, 1977, II, 1981, Test Yourself in Surgery, 1980, Multiple Choice Question in Surgery, 1976, Physical Signs in Surgery, 1980. Commonwealth fellow, 1961-62, WHO fellow, Eng., 1974-75, Iran, 77, Sudan, 78. Fellow Royal Coll. Surgeons; mem. Coll. Physicians and Surgeons Pakistan (examiner), Pakistan Med. and Dental Council (inspector for med. colls., univs.). Muslim. Home: 42 Defence Officers Colony, Hyderabad Pakistan Office: Liaquat Med Coll, Univ Campus, Jamshoro Pakistan

SIDDIQUI, MIDHAT SULTAN, construction engineering executive, consultant; b. Muradabad, India, Aug. 1, 1937; s. Sultan Ahmed and Sabra Sultan (Sabra) S.; m. Ashraf Siddiqui, Nov. 6, 1966; children—Samira, Ahmad, Emad Ahmad, Asma Ahmed. B.C.E., U. Karachi, Pakistan, 1957; M.S. in Structural Engring., U. Minn., 1960. Structural engr. Ammann & Whitny, N.Y.C., 1960-62, The H.K. Ferguson Co., San Francisco, 1962-64; Stone & Webster Corp., Toledo, 1964-66; project mgr. Fredric R. Harris, Karachi, 1966-73; pres. Agro-Fisheries Ltd., Karachi, 1973—; managing dir. M.S. Assocs. Ltd., Karachi, 1975—; cons. Asian Devel. Bank, Manila, 1978-82, Kohistan Devel. Bd., Pakistan, 1981-84. Contbr. articles to tech. jours. Fellow Inst. Engrs.; mem. Pakistan Engring. Council (lic. cons. engr., registered profl. engr.), Master Plan Dept. Govt. Pakistan (lic. structural engr.). Club: Karachi Gymkhana. Avocation: lawn tennis. Home: 164 H PECHS-3, Karachi-29 Pakistan Office: Agro-Fisheries Ltd, Seaview Bldg 40, Defense Phase 5, Karachi Pakistan

SIDENBLADH, ERIK, journalist; b. Stockholm, Mar. 22, 1946; s. Karl and Ann-Marie (Almquist) S.; m. Eva Bonnier, Jan. 5,1978; children: Samuel, Isak, Daniel. BA, U. Uppsala, Sweden, 1968. Reporter Svenska Dagbladet, Stockholm, 1972-83; reporter VI Mag., Stockholm, 1983-87, Svenska Dagbladet, Stockholm, 1987—. Author: Vattenbarn, 1982, Water Babies, 1984. Office: Svenska Dagbladet, Ralambsvagen 7, S-105 17 Stockholm Sweden

SIDOTI, RAYMOND BENJAMIN, violinist, educator; b. Cleve., Aug. 21, 1929; s. Joseph and Carmella (Alletto) S.; Mus. B., Cleve. Inst. Music, 1951, Mus. M., 1954; postgrad. (Fulbright fellow) Santa Cecilia, Rome, 1957-58; D. Musical Arts, Ohio State U., 1972; m. Mary Sue Lawrence, June 14, 1971. Concert soloist and chamber musician, U.S., Europe, 1958—; chmn. string dept. Baylor U., 1972-73; coordinator strings, first violin Shiras String Quartet, No. Mich. U., 1973-75; prof. violin, coordinator chamber music Stephens Coll., 1975-79; prof. violin, condr. Capital U., 1979-82; prof. violin, condr. Augustana Coll., 1982—; mem. faculty, soloist, concertmaster orch. Rome Festival Inst., summers 1973, 76, 77; State Dept. grantee Western Europe tours, 1959-68; concertmaster of chamber and festival orchs. Mo. Symphony Soc., 1977-78. Served with U.S. Army, 1951-53. S.D. Arts Council grantee, 1983-85. Mem. Coll. Music Soc., Cleve. Fedn. Musicians, Am. String Tchrs. Assn., S.D. String Tchrs. Assn. (pres. 1984), Pi Kappa Lambda. Author: The Violin Sonatas of Bela Bartok: An Epitome of the Composer's Development, 1972. Home: 218 Newburg Ave Baltimore MD 21228

SIDWELL, ELI ROSCOE, JR., real estate broker; b. Casey, Ill., Nov. 22, 1932; s. Eli Roscoe Sr. and Opal (Howe) S.; m. Laura Ann Gray, June 29, 1958; children: Melanie Ann, Eli R. III, Jamie Leann. BS in Edn., Eastern Ill. U., 1958. Cashier Coles County Nat. Bank, Charleston, Ill., 1961-66; from asst. dir. to dir. Embarra River Basin Agy., Greenup, Ill., 1966-67; salesman Leland Hall real Estate, Charleston, 1967-77; broker, prin. Eli Sidwell & Assoc., Charleston, 1977—; pres. Coles County Bd. Realtors, Charleston, 1975. Chmn. Citizens for Jim Edgar for State Rep., 1974, 76, 78, 80; pres. Jefferson Sch. PTA, 1978; mem. steering com. to Re-elect Rep. Harry "Babe" Woodyard, 1980, chmn. 1982; mem. State of Ill. Balance of State Planning Council, Coles County Bd. Dist. 10, 1982, chmn. pro tem, 1984, chmn. 1986—; bd. dirs. Charleston Community Theatre, 1963-64, v.p., 1965; bd. dirs. Charleston Area Econ. Devel. Found., 1986—; bd. dirs. Eastern Ill. Found., 1965-75, mem. dean's adv. bd. Eastern Ill. U.sch. bus., 1987; bd. dirs. East Cen. Ill. Devel. Corp., 1987—; mem. dean's adv. bd. Eastern Ill. U. Lumpkin Sch. Bus., 1985—, chmn. 1988; adminstrv. bd. dirs. Charleston Wesley United Meth. Ch., meml. chmn., 1981—, stewardship and fin. chmn., 1985, bd. trustees, 1988. Recipient Glen Hesler award Eastern Ill. U., 1987; named one of Outstanding Young Men Am., Charleston Jaycees, 1967, Disting. Alumnus Lumpkin Sch. Bus., 1987. Mem. Nat. Assn. Realtors, Ill. Assn. Realtors, Charleston C. of C. (bd. dirs., treas. 1964, Small Bus. of Yr. 1987, Citizen of Yr. 1987), Sigma Pi (treas. 1976-78, 80-82, sec. 1978-80, v.p. 1982-84, pres. 1984-86, past pres. 1986—). Republican. Club: Eastern Ill. U. Panther (pres. 1982). Home: Rural Rt 4 Box 29 Charleston IL 61920 Office: Eli Sidwell & Assoc 409 Buchanan St Charleston IL 61920

SIEBERT, MURIEL, business executive, former state official; b. Cleve.; d. Irwin J. and Margaret Eunice (Roseman) Siebert; student Western Res. U., 1949-52; D.C.S. (hon.), St. John's U., St. Bonaventure U., Molloy Coll., Adelfi St. Francis Coll., Mercy Coll. Security analyst Bache & Co., 1954-57; analyst Utilities & Industries Mgmt. Corp., 1958, Shields & Co., 1959-60; partner Stearns & Co., 1961, Finkle & Co., 1962-65, Brimberg & Co., N.Y.C., 1965-67; individual mem. (first woman mem.) N.Y. Stock Exchange, 1967; chmn., pres. Muriel Siebert & Co., Inc., 1969-77; trustee Manhattan Savs. Bank, 1975-77; supt. banks, dept. banking State of N.Y., 1977-82; dir. Urban Devel. Corp., N.Y.C., 1977-82, Job Devel. Authority, N.Y.C., 1977-82, State of N.Y. Mortgage Agy., 1977-82; chmn., pres. Muriel Siebert & Co., Inc., 1983—; assoc. in mgmt. Simmons Coll.; mem. adv. com. Fin. Acctg. Standards Bd., 1981; guest lectr. numerous colls. Mem. women's adv. com. Econ. Devel. Adminstrn., N.Y.C.; trustee Manhattan Coll.; v.p., mem. exec. com. Greater N.Y. Area council Boy Scouts Am.; mem. N.Y. State Econ. Devel. Bd., N.Y. Council Economy; bd. overseers NYU Sch. Bus., 1984; bd. dirs. United Way of N.Y.C.; trustee Citizens Budget Commn.; mem. bus. com. Met. Mus. Recipient Spirit of Achievement award Albert Einstein Coll. Medicine, 1977; Women's Equity Action League award, 1978; Outstanding Contbns. to Equal Opportunity for Women award Bus. Council of UN Decade for Women, 1979; Silver Beaver award Boy Scouts Am., 1981; Elizabeth Cutter Morrow award YWCA, 1983; Emily Roebling award Nat. Women's Hall of Fame, 1984; NOW Legal Def. and Edn. Fund award, 1981.

Clubs: River, Doubles, Nat. Arts, Economic (N.Y.C.). Home: 435 E 52d St New York NY 10022 Office: 444 Madison Ave New York NY 10022

SIEDZIKOWSKI, HENRY FRANCIS, lawyer; b. Chester, Pa., Dec. 27, 1953; s. Henry W. and Virginia (Szymanski) S. BA cum laude, Juniata Coll., 1975; JD magna cum laude, Villanova U., 1979. Bar: Pa. 1979, U.S. Dist. Ct. (ea. dist.) Pa. 1979, U.S. Ct. Appeals (3d cir.) 1979, U.S. Ct. Appeals (8th cir.) 1981, U.S. Dist. Ct. (we. dist.) Pa. 1986. Assoc. Dilworth, Paxson, Kalish & Kauffman, Phila., 1979-86; ptnr. Baskin, Flaherty, Elliot & Mannino P.C., Phila., 1986—; mem. hearing com. Disciplinary bd., Supreme Ct. Pa., 1985—. Mem. ABA (chmn. Lanham act subcom. of bus. torts com. of litigation sect. 1986—, rotating editor Newsletter of Anti-trust, sect. franchise com.), Pa. Bar Assn., Phila. Bar Assn. (chmn. subcom. disiplinary rules for profl. responsibility com. 1984—). Democrat. Roman Catholic. Office: Baskin Flaherty Elliot & Mannino PC 3 Mellon Bank Ctr 18th Fl Philadelphia PA 19102

SIEFF OF BRIMPTON, BARON (MARCUS JOSEPH SIEFF), business executive; b. Manchester, Eng., July 2, 1913; s. Lord Sieff and Rebecca (Marks) S.; B.A., Corpus Christi Coll., Cambridge (Eng.) U., hon. fellow, 1975; m. Rosalie Fromson, 1937 (dissolved 1947); 1 child; m. Elsa Florence Gosen, 1951 (dissolved 1953); m. Brenda Mary Beith, 1956 (dissolved 1962); 1 child; m. Pauline Lily Spatz Moretzki, 1963; 1 child. With Marks & Spencer p.l.c., London, 1935—, vice chmn., 1965-71, dep. chmn., 1971-72, chmn., 1972-84, hon. pres. 1985 ; mem. Brit. Nat. Export Council, 1965-71; chmn. Export Com. for Israel, 1965-68, 1st Internat. Bank of Israel Fin. Trust, 1983—, The Independent, 1986; dir. N.M. Rothschild & Sons, 1983—. Hon. pres. Joint Israel Appeal; v.p. Policy Studies Inst.; trustee Nat. Portrait Gallery, 1986. Served to col. Royal Arty., 1939-45. Decorated knight Order Brit. Empire, 1971; recipient Hambro award, named Businessman of Yr., 1977, Retailer Yr. award NRMA-USA, 1982; recipient AIMS nat. free enterprise award, 1978, B'nai B'rith Internat. Gold medallion, 1983. Mem. Anglo Israel C. of C. (pres.). Author: (autobiography) Don't Ask the Price, 1987. Office: Marks and Spencer plc, Michael House Baker St, London W1A 1DN, England

SIEGAL, MICHAEL, psychologist, researcher; b. Toronto, Ont., Can., Mar. 30, 1950; s. Henry and Sonia Lily (Goldbaum) S.; m. Sharon Esther Winocur, Sept. 9, 1973; 1 child, Susanna. BA with honors, McGill U., Montreal, Quebec, 1972; EdM, Harvard U., 1973; PhD, Oxford U., 1977. Vis. prof. U. B.C., Vancouver, 1978-79; lectr. U. Queensland, Brisbane, 1979-82, sr. lectr., 1983-87, reader, 1988—; vis. prof. U. B.C., 1978-79, sr. lectr. 1983-87, reader, 1988—. Author: Fairness in Children, 1982, Children, Parenthood and Social Welfare, 1985, Appreciating Children: Expiriments in Cognitive and Social Development, 1988; contbr. articles to profl. jours. Doctoral fellow Can. Council, 1974-77. Mem. Australian Psychol. Soc. (Early Career award 1983), Internat. Soc. for Study of Behavioral Devel., Soc. Research in Child Devel., Internat. Soc. for Study of History of Behavioral Scis., Soc. for Psychol. Study of Social Issues. Office: U Queensland, Dept Psychology, 4067 Saint Lucia, Queensland Australia

SIEGBAHN, KAI MANNE BÖRJE, physicist, educator; b. Lund, Sweden, Apr. 20, 1918; s. Manne and Karin (Hogbom) S.; B.S., 1939; Licentiate of Philosophy, 1942; Ph.D., U. Uppsala, 1944; D.Sc. honoris causa, U. Durham, 1972, U. Basel, 1980, U. Liege, 1980, Upsala, Coll., 1982, U. Sussex, 1983; m. Anna-Brita Rhedin, May 23, 1944; children: Per, Hans, Nils. Research assoc. Nobel Inst. Physics, 1942-51; prof. physics Royal Inst. Tech., Stockholm, 1951-54; prof., head physics dept. U. Uppsala (Sweden), 1954-84. Recipient Lindblom Prize, 1945; Bjorken Prize, 1955, 77; Celsius medal, 1962; Sixten Heyman award, 1971; Harrison Howe award, 1973; Maurice F. Hasler award, 1975; Charles Frederick Chandler medal, 1976; Torbern Bergman medal, 1979; Nobel Prize, 1981; Pitts. award spectroscopy, 1982; Röntgen medal, 1985, Fiuggi award, 1986, Humboldt award, 1986. Mem. Royal Swedish Acad. Sci., Royal Swedish Acad. Engring. Scis., Royal Soc. Sci., Royal Acad. Arts and Sci. Uppsala, Royal Physiographical Soc. Lund, Societas Scientairum Fennica, Norwegian Acad. Sci., Royal Norwegian Soc. Scis. and Letters, Am. Acad. Arts and Scis. (hon.), Comite des Poids et Mesures, Internat. Union Pure and Applied Physics (pres. 1981-84), Pontifical Acad. Scis., Nat. Acad. Scis. (fgn. assoc.). Author: Beta and Gamma-Ray Spectroscopy, 1955; Alpha, Beta and Gamma-Ray Spectroscopy, 1965; ESCA-Atomic, Molecular and Solid State Structure Studies by Means of Electron Spectroscopy, 1967; ESCA Applied to Free Molecules, 1969.

SIEGEL, ABRAHAM J., economics educator, academic administrator; b. N.Y.C., Nov. 6, 1922; s. Samuel J. and Dora (Drach) S.; m. Lillian Wakshull, Dec. 22, 1946; children: Emily Jean Siegel Stangle, Paul Howard, Barbara Ann Pugliese. B.A. summa cum laude, CCNY, 1943; M.A., Columbia U., 1949; Ph.D., U. Calif., Berkeley, 1961. Instr. dept. econs. CCNY, 1947-49; research economist Inst. Indsl. Relations, U. Calif., Berkeley, 1952-54; instr. dept. econs. M.I.T., Cambridge, 1954-56, asst. prof., 1956-59, assoc. prof., 1959-64, prof. dept. econs. Sloan Sch. Mgmt., 1964—, assoc. dean Sloan Sch. Mgmt., 1967-80, acting dean, 1980-81, dean, 1981-87; spl. lectr. Trade Union Program, Harvard U., 1961-64; vis. prof. Brandeis U., 1956-60; vis. prin. mem. div. Internat. Inst. Labour Studies, Internat. Labor Office, Geneva, 1964-65; assoc. staff dir. Com. Econ. Devel., Study Group on Nat. Labor Policy, 1960-61; trustee, chmn. adminstrv. com. M.I.T. Retirement Plan for Staff Mems., 1970—. Co-author: Industrial Relations in the Pacific Coast Longshore Industry, 1956, The Public Interest in National Labor Policy, 1961, The Impact of Computers on Collective Bargaining, 1969, Unfinished Business: An Agenda for Labor, Management and the Public, 1978. Bd. dirs. Whitehead Inst. Biomed. Research Analysis Group, Inc.; Adams Russell Electronics; Internat. Data Group; mem. adv. internat. adv. group Inst. for Applied Systems Analysis, Laxenburg, Austria; mem. Framingham Sch. Com., South Middlesex Regional Dist. Vocat. Sch. Com., 1968-71. Served with USAF, 1943-46. Mem. Am. Econ. Assn., Indsl. Relations Research Assn., Nat. Acad. Arbitrators, Am. Arbitration Assn. (mem. neutrals panel), Inst. Mgmt. Scis. Bus. Roundtable (exec. com.), Nat. Edn. Panel, Nat. Public Employment Disputes Settlement Panel, Panel for New Eng. Plan for Public Service Dispute Settlement, Phi Beta Kappa. Clubs: Comml, St. Botolph's. Home: 112 Gardner Rd Brookline MA 02146 Office: MIT Sloan Sch Mgmt 50 Memorial Dr Cambridge MA 02139

SIEGEL, ALAN MICHAEL, communications and design consultant; b. N.Y.C., Aug. 26, 1938; s. Eugene and Ruth S.; m. Gloria Fern Mendel, Nov. 6, 1965; 1 dau., Stacey Ruth. B.S., Cornell U., 1960. Account exec., sec. new products devel. group Batten, Barton, Durstine and Osborn, N.Y.C., 1964-67; account exec. Ruder & Finn Inc., N.Y.C., 1967-68, Sandgren & Murtha Inc., N.Y.C., 1968-69; chmn., chief exec. officer Siegel & Gale Inc., N.Y.C., 1969—; adj. asso. prof. Fordham U. Sch. Law; adj. asso. prof., co-dir. Communications Design Center, Carnegie-Mellon U.; mem. exec. com. document design project Nat. Inst. Edn., Cornell U. Council; pres. adv. council Coll. Architecture Arts and Planning Cornell U. Co-author: Simplified Consumer Credit Forms; Drafting Documents in Plain English, 1979, Writing Contracts in Plain English, 1981; mem. editorial bd.: Info. Design Jour.; contbr. articles to profl. jours., also speechwriter. Bd. dirs. Paul Taylor Dance Co., Design Mgtmt. Inst. Served to 1st lt. arty. U.S. Army, 1961-62. Mem. Soc. Consumer Affairs Profls. in Bus., Internat. Assn. Bus. Communicators, Am. Bus. Communication Assn., Am. Inst. Graphic Arts, Assn. Profl. Design Firms, Indsl. Communications Council, Authors Guild. Clubs: N.Y. Athletic, University. Office: Siegel & Gale Inc 1185 Ave of Americas New York NY 10036

SIEGEL, EVAN BENNETT, toxicologist, pharmacologist; b. Bronx, N.Y., May 28, 1948; s. Charles Gustav and Leona Caroline (Kern) S.; student Colby Coll., summer 1964; BS, Bucknell U., 1969; MS (USPHS fellow), Rutgers U., 1970, MPhil., 1972, PhD, 1975; postgrad. (Weinberger fellow) U.N.C., Chapel Hill, 1974-77; m. Jean Louise Strand, Mar. 28, 1987. Grad. fellow dept. environ. sci. Rutgers U., 1969-70; summer radiol. health fellow Brookhaven Nat. Lab., 1970; cancer research trng. fellow Waksman Inst. Microbiology and Rutgers U. Med. Sch., 1970-74; sr. scientist, coordinator cellular and genetic toxicology Northrop Services, Inc., Research Triangle Park, N.C., 1977-78; toxicologist FDA, Washington, 1978-80; sci. affairs assoc. Proprietary Assn., Washington, 1980-84, dir. pharmacology and toxicology, 1984-87; staff toxicologist Calif. State Dept. of Health Services, 1987-88, chief Spl. Sevices, Food and Drug Br., 1988—. V.p. PTA, Wilde Lake Middle Sch., Columbia, Md., 1981-82, pres., 1982-85. Mem. Am. Soc. Microbiology, N.Y. Acad. Scis., AAAS, Tissue Culture Assn., AAUP, Am. Soc. for Photobiology, Drug Info. Assn., Regulatory Affairs Profl. Soc., Calif. Assn. Profl. Scientists. Club: Univ. (Washington). Home: 420 Pimlico Dr Walnut Creek CA 94596

SIEGEL, HERBERT JAY, communications executive; b. Phila., May 7, 1928; s. Jacob and Fritzi (Stern) S.; m. Ann F. Levy, June 29, 1950; children: John C., William D. B.A., Lehigh U., 1950. Sec., dir. Official Films, Inc., N.Y.C., 1950-55; v.p., dir. Bev-Rich Products, Inc., Phila., 1955-56, Westley Industries, Inc., Cleve., 1955-58, Phila. Ice Hockey Club, Inc., 1955-60; chmn. bd. Fort Pitt Industries, Inc., Pitts., 1956-58, Seeburg Corp., 1958-60, Centlivre Brewing Corp., Ft. Wayne, Ind., 1950—, Baldwin-Montrose Chem. Co.; chmn. United TV, Inc., 1982—, chief exec. officer, 1983—; pres. Gen. Artists Corp., 1963-65; chmn. bd., pres. Chris-Craft Industries, Inc., 1967—; dir. Baldwin Rubber Co., Pontiac, Mich., Mono-Sol Corp., Gary, Inc., Piper Aircraft Corp., 1967-77; Warner Communications, Inc., 1984—. Bd. dirs. Phoenix House, 1978-81, United TV, Inc., 1981—; bd. advisors Vets. Bedside Network, 1980—; v.p. Friars Nat. Assn. Found., 1980—; trustee Blair Acad., 1985 . Club: Friars. Home: 190 E 72nd St New York NY 10021 Office: Chris-Craft Industries Inc 600 Madison Ave New York NY 10022

SIEGEL, JEFF ALAN, linguist; b. Chgo., Nov. 3, 1945; s. Owen R and Shirlie (Ruskin) S. BA, Cornell U., 1967; MA, U. Hawaii, 1973; diploma in Hindi, Delhi (India) U., 1974; PhD, Australian Nat. U., Canberra, 1985. Tchr. Togo Bhartia Sch., Nadi, Fiji, 1970, Nadi Secondary Sch., 1970; sr. lectr. Papua New Guinea U Tech., Lae, 1976-81; research scholar Australian Nat. U., Canberra, 1982-84; fellow Pacific languages unit U. South Pacific, Vila, Vanatu, 1985-87; lectr. in Linguistics U. New England, Armidale, New South Wales, Australia, 1988—; advisor Komiti Blong Bislama, Vila, 1986. Author: Say It in Fiji Hindi, 1977, Tradional Bridges of Papua New Guinea, 1981, Language Contact in a Plantation Environment: A Sociolinguistic History of Fiji, 1987. Mem. Australian Linguistic Soc. Office: Univ of New England, Linguistics Dept, Armidale, New South Wales 2351, Australia

SIEGEL, JEFF K., financial analyst; b. Washington, Dec. 11, 1958; s. Stanley Ernest and Mildred Siegel. BS in Indsl. Engring., Va. Poly. Inst., 1981; MBA in Fin., George Washington U., 1987. Indsl. engr. Koppers Co., Balt., 1981-82; electric system engr. Potomac Electric Power Co., Washington, 1982-86; retail, restaurant, hotel/gaming equity analyst Donaldson, Lufkin, & Jenrette, Pershing Div., N.Y.C., 1987—. Bd. dirs. Terrace Townhouses of Beverly Hills, Alexandria, Va., 1985-87; vol. algebra tutor Higher Achievement Program, Washington, Suitland High Sch. tutoring program representing Potomac Electric Power Co., 1986. Mem. Am. Inst. Indsl. Engrs., Pa. Electric Ops. Improvement Com., Assn. MBA Execs., Merchandising Analysts Group, Retail Analysts Group. Clubs: Athletic Singles (Falls Church, Va.), Ski Club of Washington, Va. Tech. Alumni (Capitol City chpt.), George Washington U. Alumni Assn. Avocations: chess; investing; tennis; physical fitness; various other athletics. Home: 4 Lincoln Ave Staten Island NY 10306 Office: Donaldson Lufkin & Jenrette Pershing Div 120 Broadway New York NY 10271

SIEGEL, LYNNE ELISE MOORE, lawyer; b. Sterling, Colo., Sept. 28, 1957; d. James Hamilton and Mabel Louise (White) Moore. B.A. in Liberal Arts, Colo. Coll., 1979; J.D., U. Denver, 1983. Bar: Colo. 1983. Law clk. Dailey, Goodwin et al, Aurora, Colo., 1980-81; asst. to prof. U. Denver, 1981; law clk. Gorsuch, Kirgis et al, Denver, 1982; summer assoc. Kirkland & Ellis, Denver, 1982; intern to presiding justice Denver Dist. Ct., 1983; assoc. Montgomery, Little, Young, Campbell & McGrew, Denver, 1983-88; law clk. to presiding judge, Colo. Ct. Appeals, 1988—. Past bd. dirs. Colo. Women's Employment and Edn., Inc.; bd. dirs. Colo. Spl. Olympics, Jr. League of Denver, Inc. Contbr. articles to profl. jours, chpts. to book. Denver Panhellenic scholar, 1977. Mem. ABA, Colo. Bar Assn., Kappa Alpha Theta (Founders' Meml. scholar). Home: 765 Lafayette St Denver CO 80218

SIEGEL, MARK JORDAN, lawyer; b. Dallas, Feb. 22, 1949; s. Jack H. and Zelda (Sikora) S. BS in Psychology, North Tex. State U., 1972; JD, South Tex. Coll. Law, 1977. Bar: Tex. 1977, U.S. Dist. Ct. (no. dist.) Tex, 1980, U.S. Ct. Appeals (11th and 5th cirs.) 1982, U.S. Supreme Ct. 1982. Sole practice, Dallas, 1977-87; bd. dirs. Intercontinental Bank, San Antonio, Scotch Corp., Dallas. Sponser Civil Justice Found. Mem. N. Dallas 40. Named one of Outstanding Young Men Am., 1985, 86. Mem. Tex. Trial Lawyers Assn., Dallas Trial Lawyers Assn., Assn. Trial Lawyers Am. Office: 3607 Fairmount St Dallas TX 75219

SIEGEL, MICHAEL ELLIOT, physician, educator, researcher; b. N.Y.C., May 13, 1942; s. Benjamin and Rose (Gilbert) S.; m. Marsha Rose Snower, Mar. 20, 1966; children—Herrick Jove, Meridith Ann. A.B., Cornell U., 1964; M.D., Chgo. Med. Sch., 1968. Diplomate Nat. Bd. Med. Examiners. Intern Cedars-Sinai Med. Ctr., Los Angeles, 1968-69; resident in radiology, 1969-70; NIH fellow in radiology Temple U. Med. Ctr., Phila., 1970-71; NIH fellow in nuclear medicine Johns Hopkins U. Sch. Medicine, Balt., 1971-73, asst. prof. radiology, 1972-76; assoc. prof. radiology, medicine U. So. Calif., Los Angeles, 1976—; dir. div. nuclear medicine, 1982—; dir. Sch. Nuclear Medicine, Los Angeles County-U. So. Calif. Med. Ctr., 1976—; dir. div. nuclear medicine Kenneth Norris Cancer Hosp. and Research Ctr., Los Angeles, 1983—; dir. nuclear medicine, cons. Orthopaedic Hosp., Los Angeles, 1981—; cons. Intercommunity Hosp., Covina, Calif., 1981—, Rancho Los Amigos Hosp., Downey, Calif., 1976—. Author: Textbook of Nuclear Medicine, 1978, Vascular Surgery, 1983, and numerous others textbooks; editor: Nuclear Cardiology, 1981, Vascular Disease: Nuclear Medicine, 1983. Coach Little League, Beverly Hills; mem. Maple Ctr., Beverly Hills. Served as maj. USAF, 1974-76. Mem. Soc. Nuclear Medicine (sci. exhbn. com. 1978-79, program com. 1979-80, Silver medal 1975), Am. Coll. Nuclear Medicine (sci. investigator 1974, 76, nominations com. 1980, program com. 1983), Radiol. Soc. N.Am., Soc. Nuclear Magnetic Resonance Imaging. Lodge: Friars So. Calif. Research on devel. of nuclear medicine techniques to: evaluate cardiovascular disease and diagnose and treat cancer, devel. of nuclear magnetic resonance (NMR) as a clinical imaging; inventor pneumatic radiologic pressure system. Office: U So Calif Med Ctr PO Box 693 1200 N State St Los Angeles CA 90033

SIEGEL, MILTON P., international executive, educator, health foundation executive, management consultant; b. Des Moines, July 23, 1911; s. Barney and Sylvy (Levinson) S.; m. Rosalie Rosenberg, May 25, 1934; children: Betsy Lee, Larry (dec.), Sally (dec.). Ed., Drake U., Des Moines. Dir. finance, statistics Iowa Emergency Relief Adminstrn., also treas.; Iowa Rural Rehab. Adminstrn., 1933-35; regional finance and bus. mgr. Farm Security Adminstrn., U.S. Dept. Agr., 1935-41, chief fiscal officer, 1942-44; asst. treas., dir. Office for Far East, UNRRA, 1944-45; asst. dir. fiscal br. prodn. and marketing adminstrn. U.S. Dept. Agr., 1945-47; asst. dir.-gen. WHO, 1947-71; prof. internat. health Sch. Pub. Health, U. Tex. Health Scis. Center, Houston, 1971-75; health mgmt. cons. Imperial Govt. of Iran, Nat. Health Ins. Orgn., 1975-76; sr. cons. to adminstr. UN Devel. Program, 1976-77; chmn. bd. trustees Mgmt. Planning Systems Internat., Inc., 1977—; pres., chief exec. officer Fedn. World Health Founds, 1978—; prof. internat. health, mgmt. and policy scis. U. Tex. Health Scis. Ctr., 1988—; mem. permanent scale contbns. commn. League Red Cross Socs., 1967-81; sr. mgmt. scientist Children's Nutrition Research Center, Baylor Coll. Medicine, Houston, 1979-80; cons. U. N.C., Chapel Hill, 1970, Carolina Population Center, 1970; vis. prof. U. Mich., 1967; awarded acad. chair U. Tex. Health Sci. Ctr., Houston, 1984. Chmn. bd. trustees World Health Found. U.S.A., 1976—. Recipient Sam Beber award, 1960. Mem. Am. Public Health Assn. Home: 2833 Sackett Houston TX 77098 also: 1 Rue Viollier, CH-1207 Geneva Switzerland

SIEGEL, PAUL, lawyer; b. Troy, N.Y., May 7, 1938; s. Benjamin and Mary (Silverman) S.; m. Elaine Beverly Kramer, May 19, 1973 (div. 1979); 1 child, Mark Aron. B.S. in Physics magna cum laude, U. Miami, 1958, LL.B. cum laude, 1962. Bar: Fla. 1963, D.C. 1964, U.S. Supreme Ct. 1967, U.S. Ct. Appeals (5th cir.) 1967, U.S. Ct. Appeals (11th cir.) 1982. Cert. civil trial lawyer Fla. Bar. Mem. gen. counsel's office AEC, Washington, 1962-65; ptnr. Sinclair, Louis, Siegel, Heath, Nussbaum & Zavertnik, P.A., Miami, Fla., 1972—. Editor-in-chief, exec. editor U. Miami Law Rev. Chmn. bd. dirs. Alliance Francaise of Dade County, 1983-87; pres. Pro-Mozart Soc. Greater Miami, 1984—. Home: 235 E San Marino Dr Miami Beach FL 33139 Office: Sinclair Louis Siegel Heath Nussbaum & Zavertnik PA 11 25 Alfred I duPont Bldg Miami FL 33131

SIEGEL, ROBERT J., industry communications official; b. N.Y.C., Feb. 26, 1929; s. Hiram and Regina (Goldstein) S.; B.S. in Econs., Marietta Coll., 1950; m. Gonnie McClung, Jan. 8, 1953; children—William Laird, Richard Joseph. With copy desk N.Y. Times, 1951-53; asso. editor Lorain (Ohio) Jour., 1953-56; reporter, Cleve. Press, 1956-61; with IBM, Armonk, N.Y., 1961—, data processing div. press relations mgr., corp. info. mgr., corp. public affairs mgr., corp. mgmt. communications mgr., 1979—, dir. info., dir. internal communications. Mem. Nat. Press Club, Overseas Press Club, Deadline Club of N.Y., Sigma Delta Chi. Home: Cedar Hill Rd Bedford NY 10506 Office: IBM Old Orchard Rd Armonk NY 10504

SIEGELE, ULRICH, musicologist; b. Stuttgart, Fed. Republic Germany, Nov. 1, 1930; m. Leonore Wenschkewitz, 1971. PhD, U. Tuebingen, Fed. Republic Germany, 1957. Lectr. in musicology U. Tuebingen, 1965-71, prof., 1971—. Author books and articles on compositional techniques, J.S. Bach, serial music. Home: Ursrainer Ring 101, 7400 Tuebingen 1 Federal Republic of Germany Office: U Tuebingen-Inst Musicology, Mohlstrasse 54, 7400 Tuebingen 1 Federal Republic of Germany

SIEGER, HERMANN WALTER, collectors' stamps company executive; b. Schwab, Gmund, Germany, Apr. 6, 1928; s. Hermann Ernest and Selma Hulda (Fritzsche) S.; ed. public schs.; m. Gisela Maria Mangold, Nov. 1, 1944; children: Gunter-Martin-Hermann, Eva-Maria, Christine-Renate-Maria. Owner, mgr. Hermann W. Sieger, Lorch/Wurttemberg, W. Ger., 1949-54, Hermann E. Sieger, Lorch Wurttemberg, 1954—, Feldkirch, Austria, 1975—, Nendeln, Ftm. Liechtenstein, 1985; cons. to fgn. postal authorities on planning of stamp edits.; holder ofcl. philatelic service U.S. Postal Adminstrn. Germany, Papua-New Guinea, USSR, Czechoslovakia, Poland, Japan. Mem. dist. mng. bd. German Red Cross, Schwab.Gmund; mem. curatory Hermann Oberth Gesellschaft, Hannover, W. Ger.; hon consul Republic of Paraguay in Stuttgart, W. Ger., 1977—. Recipient Hermann Oberth medal Hermann Oberth Gesellschaft, 1971, Ring of Wernher von Brau, gold medal Fedn. Internat. des Societes Aerophilateliques, 1972; badge of honor German Red Cross, 1979. Mem. Soc. Philaticians, Internat. Soc. Balloon Post Specialists, Philatelic Press Club, Am. Topical Assn., Space Topics Student Group, Am. Stamp Dealers Assn., Internat. Fedn. Stamp Dealers Assns., Philatelic Traders Soc. LTT, Société Aerophilatelique Belge, Association Internationale des Experts Philateliques-APHV, Am. Airmail Soc. BDPH, Association Internationale des Journalistes Philateliques, Brit. Airmail Soc., Academie d'Aerophilatelie, Internat. Aero Philatelic Club (hon.), European Aero Philatelic Club (hon.). Clubs: Deutsche Gesellschaft für Raketentechnik und Raumfahrt, others. Editor Sieger-Post, 1954—, also co. catalogue. Office: 32-34 Venusberg Lorch, 7073 Wurttemberg Federal Republic of Germany

SIEGHART, PAUL, international jurist, arbitrator; b. Feb. 22, 1927; s. Ernest Alexander and Marguerite S.; m. Rosemary Aglionby, 1954 (dec. 1956); children: Alister, Matilda; m. Felicity Ann Baer, 1959; children: William, Mary Ann. Bar: Eng., 1953. Author: Slaughterhouses (with others), 1960, Privacy and Computers, 1976, The International Law of Human Rights, 1983, The Lawful Rights of Mankind, 1985, The World of Science and the Rule of Law (with others), 1986; editor: Chalmers' Sale of Goods, 13th edit., 1957, 14th edit., 1963, Microchips With Everything, 1982; contbr. articles to legal and sci. jours. Gov. Brit. Inst. Human Rights, 1974—; bd. trustees The Tablet Trust, London, 1976—, Monteverdi Trust, London, 1980—, Tavistock Clinic Found., London, 1982—; mem. Home Office Data Protection Com., London, 1976-78, Groupe de Bellerive, Geneva, 1977—, Council Catholic Union Gt. Britain, 1981—; chmn. Exec. Com. Justice, Brit. sect. Internat. Commn. Jurists, London, 1978—, European Human Rights Found., London, 1986—; founder Council Sci. and Soc. (vice-chmn. 1972-78); hon. vis. Prof. of Law King's Coll. U. London, 1986—. Fellow Royal Soc. Arts, Chartered Inst. Arbitrators. Clubs: Brook's, Bar Yacht (London). Home: 6 Grays Inn Sq, London WC1R 5AZ, England

SIEGLER, HOWARD MATTHEW, physician, surgeon; b. N.Y.C., May 26, 1932; s. Samuel Lewis and Shirley Kendall (Matthews) S.; m. Toinette Andrau, Dec. 1, 1953 (dec. 1984); children: Samuel Lewis, Karel Lynn, Jacqueline Andrau (dec.), Todd Bradford. B.S. in Biochemistry, Hofstra U., 1951; postgrad., Yale U., 1952; M.B., Ch.B., St. Andrews U., 1958; M.D., N.Y. Med. Coll., 1965. Intern N.Y. U. Med. Center, N.Y.C., 1965, New Rochelle (N.Y.) Hosp., 1966-67; asst. to dean U. Tex., Southwestern Med. Sch., Dallas, 1967-68; sr. fellow dept. phys. medicine Baylor Coll., Houston, 1968-69; resident family practice program Meml. Bapt. Hosp., Houston, 1971; gen. practice medicine Houston, 1971, 72—; clin. fellow in obstetrics and gynecology St. Lukes Episcopal Hosp., Houston, 1971-72; dir., sr. cons. Houston Comprehensive Gen. Clinic, Tex. Med. Ctr.; mem. staff St. Lukes Episcopal Hosp., 1972—, St. Joseph's Hosp., St. Anthony's Med. Ctr., Tex. Children's Hosp.; v.p., dir. Infusion Therapy Service, Santa Monica; cochmn. Muscular Dystrophy Soc., 1964-65; cons. div. disability determination Tex. Rehab. Commn., 1973; med. cons. Home Health Care of Am.; dir. West Belt III Ltd., Heritage Sq., Ltd., San Antonio, Garth 82, Ltd., Caroline Bldg., Ltd., John Martin Inc., others. Active Assn. To Help Retarded Children, 1965-76; chmn. sr. div. Protestant Charities N.Y., 1964-65; assoc. trustee Kinkaid Sch., Houston, 1972-77, Rice U.; trustee Houston Tilliston Coll., Houston Internat. U.; mem. steering com. for excellence Tex. So. U. Served to col. USAR; maj. Army N.G.; Col., aide-de-camp Gov. of La., Gov. of Miss., Gov. of Tenn. lt. col., aide-de-camp Gov. of Ala. Honored for expertise in field of cardiovascular stress Internat. Soc. Cardiology, 1978. Fellow Royal Soc. Health, Royal Soc. Medicine (London); mem. Am. Fertility Soc., Am. Geriatric Soc., AAAS, N.Y. Acad. Scis. (life), Am. Diabetes Assn., Am. Social Health Assn., Am. Soc. Bariatrics, Christian, So. med. assns., Am. Med. Soc. Alcoholism, Am. Assn. Gynec. Laparoscopists, Am. Soc. Contemporary Medicine and Surgery, Tex. Acad. Family Physicians, Am. Coll. Nutrition, Denton A. Cooley Cardiovascular Surg. Soc., Harris County Acad. Medicine, Harris County Med. Soc., Internat. Acad. Preventive Medicine, Internam. Coll. Physicians and Surgeons, Am. Coll. Gen. Practice, Am. Coll. Medicine, Am. Soc. Contemporary Medicine and Surgery, Universal Intelligence Data Bank of Am., Tex. Assn. Disability Examiners, Internat. Platform Assn., Phi Chi. Episcopalian. Home: 1 Longfellow Ln Houston TX 77005 Office: Suite 1020 Hermann Profl Bldg 6410 Fannin St Houston TX 77030

SIEGRIST, JOHANNES, sociologist, educator; b. Zofingen, Switzerland, Aug. 6, 1943; arrived in Fed. Republic of Germany, 1964; s. Adolf and Margarete (Merz) S.; m. Karin Ochsenreither, Feb. 1982; children: Annette, Esther-Claire. MA, U. Freiburg, Fed. Republic of Germany, 1967, PhD, 1969, habilitation, 1973. Prof. and dir. dept. medicine, sociology Med. Sch., U. Marburg, Fed. Republic of Germany, 1973—, assoc. dean, 1985-87; vis. prof. Inst. Advanced Studies, Vienna, 1976-78, Johns Hopkins U., Balt., 1981; advisor World Health Orgn., Copenhagen, 1985—. Author various books and sci. articles; co-editor and editor various sci. jours. Mem. European Soc. Med. Sociology (pres. 1987), Internat. Coll. Psychosomatic Medicine (chmn. com. on epidemiology 1983—), German Coll. Psychosomatic Medicine (Roemer award 1979). Avocation: chamber music. Home: Schlehdornweg, D-3550 Marburg Federal Republic of Germany Office: U Marburg, Bunsenstrasse 2, 3550 Marburg Federal Republic of Germany

SIEKMANN, DONALD CHARLES, accountant; b. St. Louis, July 2, 1938; s. Elmer Charles and Mabel Louise (Blue) S.; m. Linda Lee Knowles, Sept. 10, 1966; 1 child, Brian Charles. BS, Washington U., St. Louis, 1960. CPA, Ohio, Ga. Ptnr., practice dir. Arthur Andersen & Co., Cin., 1960—. Columnist Cin. Enquirer, 1983-86, Gannett News Services, 1983-86; editor "Tax Clinic" column Tax Advisor mag., 1974-75. Mem. bd. Cin. Zool. Soc., 1985—, also chmn. 1984-88; officer, bd. dirs. Cin. Found. for Pub. TV, 1984—, Cin. Symphony Orch., 1973-85, Cin. Ballet Co., 1973-78, Cin. Theatrical Assn., Atlanta Opera, 1988—. Served with U.S. Army, 1961. Mem. Am. Inst. CPA's, Ohio Soc. CPA's, Cin. Estate Planning Council. Lutheran. Club: Cin. Country (trustee 1983-88), Atlanta. Lodge: Optimists (pres. Queen City chpt. 1986). Home: 610 Blue Teal Ct Atlanta GA 30327 Office: Arthur Andersen & Co 133 Peachtree St Atlanta GA 30303

SIEKMANN, REM OWEN, engineer; b. Grosse Pointe Farms, Mich., Dec. 15, 1954; s. Harold John and Joan Hoffman (Henritzy) S.; m. Kathleen Eleanor Lake, Jan. 20, 1979; children: Sarah Lake, Katherine O'Neill. BSE cum laude, Duke U., 1976; MBA, U. Chgo., 1983. Registered profl. engr. Mfg. devel. engr. Baxter Travenol Labs., Deerfield, Ill., 1976-78, sr. devel. engr., 1978-79, prin. engr., 1979-80, dir. spl. projects, 1987—; project engr. Am. Covertors div. Am. Hosp. Supply Corp., Evanston, Ill., 1980-83; new product planning mgr. Am. Hosp. Supply Corp., 1983-84, sr. bus. analyst, 1984-85, mgr. bus. devel., 1985-86; sr. bus. assoc. Baxter Travenol Labs., 1986; spl. project dir. Busken Bakery, 1987—. Patentee in field. Patroller Nat. Ski Patrol System, 1969—. Mem. Inst. Environ. Sci., Nat. Soc. Profl. Engrs., ASTM (contbr. F01.10 subcom. 1981-84). Presbyterian. Home: 7060 Mt Vernon Ave Cincinnati OH 45227 Office: Busken Bakery 2675 Madison Rd Cincinnati OH 45208

SIERLES, FREDERICK STEPHEN, psychiatrist, educator; b. Bklyn., Nov. 9, 1942; s. Samuel and Elizabeth (Meiselman) S.; m. Laurene Harriet Cohn, Oct. 25, 1970; children: Hannah Beth, Joshua Caleb. AB, Columbia U., 1963; MD, Chgo. Med. Sch., 1967. Diplomate Am. Bd. Psychiatry and Neurology. Intern Cook County Hosp., Chgo., 1967-68; resident in psychiatry Mt. Sinai Hosp., N.Y.C., 1968-69, 1969-71, chief resident, 1970-71; staff psychiatrist U.S. Reynolds Army Hosp., Ft. Sill, Okla., 1971-73; assoc. attending psychiatrist Mt. Sinai Hosp., Chgo., 1973-74; instr. psychiatry Chgo. Med. Sch., North Chicago, 1973-74, dir. undergrad. edn. in psychiatry, 1974—, asst. prof., 1974-78, assoc. prof., 1978-88—, prof., 1988—; chmn. ednl. affairs com., 1983-85, 86—; cons. psychiatry Cook County Hosp., 1974-79, St. Mary of Nazareth Hosp., 1979-84; chief Mental Health Clinic, North Chicago VA Hosp., 1982-85, chief psychiatry service, 1983-85. Author: (with others) General Hospital Psychiatry, 1985, Behavioral Science for the Boreds, 1987; editor: Clinical Behavioral Science, 1982; contbr. articles to profl. jours. Served to maj., M.C., U.S. Army, 1971-73. Recipient Ganser Meml. award Mt. Sinai Hosp., 1970; named Prof. of Yr., Chgo. Med. Sch., 1977, 80, 83; N.Y. State Regents scholar, 1959-63; NIMH grantee, 1974-83, Chgo. Med. Sch. grantee, 1974-83. Fellow Am. Psychiat. Assn.; mem. Ill. Psychiat. Soc. (fellowship com. 1985—), Assn. Interns and Residents Cook County Hosp., Assn. Dirs. Med. Student Edn. in Psychiatry (exec. council 1985—, chmn. program com. 1987—), Nat. Assn. VA Physicians (sec.-treas. North Chgo. chpt. 1984-85), Alpha Omega Alpha, Phi Epsilon Pi. Office: Chgo Med Sch 3333 Green Bay Rd North Chicago IL 60064

SIERRA, LINDA JIMENEZ, dentist; b. McAllen, Tex., Apr. 26, 1949; d. Luis and Alicia (Flores) Jimenez; m. Angel Sierra, Oct. 2, 1971; children—Louis, Tommy, Andrew. A.A., Del Mar Jr. Coll., Corpus Christi, 1969; B.A., U. Tex., 1971; D.D.S., U. Tex.-Houston, 1978. High sch. tchr. Escuela Internat. de Caracas, Venezuela, 1972; jr. high sch. tchr. Houston Ind. Sch. Dist., 1975; gen. pratice dentistry, Pasadena, Tex., 1978—; chair dental staff Humana Southmore Hosp., Pasadena, 1983-84, 87-88; vice-chair dental staff Bayshore Hosp., Pasadena, 1985-86, chmn., 1986-87. Active Sam Rayburn High Sch. Band Boosters, Jensen Elem. Sch. PTA; tchr. Sunday sch. St. Pius V Cath. Ch. Mem. ADA, Tex. Dental Assn., Houston Dental Soc., Acad. Gen. Dentistry, Pasadena C. of C. Roman Catholic. Avocations: gardening, bicycling, aerobics, swimming. Office: 4221 Vista Rd Pasadena TX 77504

SIEVEKING, VINCENT JAN, publishing house executive; b. Hamburg, W. Germany, Apr. 5, 1938; s. Wilhelm Georg and Susanne Camilla (Heymann) S.; m. Edda Johanna Kuepper, Apr. 14, 1978; 1 dau., Johanna Camilla. M.A., U. Hamburg, 1965. Editor, Langenscheidt KG, Berchtesgaden, W. Ger., 1965-66; editor Wilhelm Fink Verlag, Munich, 1966-74; editor Felix Meiner Verlag, Hamburg, 1974-77; dir. medpharm. Verlag GMBH, Wiesbaden, 1981—; bd. dirs. Franz Steiner Verlag, Stuttgart,1977—, Wissenschaftliche Verlagsgesellschaft, Stuttgart, Deutscher Apotheker Verlag, Stuttgart, S. Hirzel Verlag, Stuttgart, 1986—. Translator: Book on Tchekhov (P.M. Bicilli), 1966; contrb. translations of articles to profl. jours. Vice pres. Helmuth von Glasenapp Stiftung, Wiesbaden, 1977—. Office: F Steiner Verlag Wiesbaden GMBH, Birkenwaldstrasse 44, PF 10 15 26, D-7000 Stuttgart 1 Federal Republic of Germany

SIGEL, MARSHALL ELLIOT, financial consultant; b. Hartford, Conn., Nov. 25, 1941; s. Paul and Bessie (Somer) S. BS in Econs., U. Pa., 1963; JD, U. Miami, 1982, LLM in Taxation, 1983. Exec. v.p. Advo-System div. KMS Industries, Inc., Hartford, 1963-69, pres., 1969-72; pres. Ad-Type Corp., Hartford, 1963-69, Ad-Lists, Inc., Hartford, 1963-69; fin. cons. Hartford, 1972-83, Boca Raton, Fla., 87—; atty., 1983-87; bd. dirs. Boca Raton First Nat. Bank. Bd. dirs. Hebrew Acad. of Hartford; trustee South County Jewish Community Found. Clubs: 100 of Conn.; 200 (Miami); City, Boca West. Home and Office: PO Box 273408 Boca Raton FL 33427

SIGETY, CHARLES EDWARD, lawyer, health care executive; b. N.Y.C., Oct. 10, 1922; s. Charles and Anna (Toth) S.; m. Katharine K. Snell, July 17, 1948; children: Charles, Katharine, Robert, Cornelius, Elizabeth. B.S., Columbia U., 1944; M.B.A. (Baker scholar), Harvard U., 1947; LL.B., Yale U., 1951. Bar: N.Y. State 1952, D.C. 1958. With Bankers Trust Co., 1939-42; instr. adminstrv. engring. Pratt Inst., 1948; instr. econs. Yale U., 1948-50; vis. lectr. accounting Sch. Gen. Studies, Columbia U., 1948-50, 52; rapporteur com. fed. taxation for U.S. council Internat. C. of C., 1952-53; asst. to com. fed. taxation Am. Inst. Accountants, 1950-53; vis. lectr. law Yale U., 1952; law practice N.Y.C., 1952-67; pres., dir. Video Vittles, Inc., N.Y.C., 1953-67; dep. commr. FHA, 1955-57; of counsel Javits and Javits, 1959-60; 1st asst. atty. gen. N.Y., 1958-59; dir., mem. exec. com. Gotham Bank, N.Y.C., 1961-63; dir. N.Y. State Housing Finance Agy., 1962-63; pres., exec. adminstr. Florence Nightingale Health Center, N.Y.C., 1965-85; chmn. bd. Profl. Med. Products, Inc., Greenwood, S.C., 1982—; professorial lectr. Sch. Architecture, Pratt Inst., N.Y.C., 1962-66; mem. Sigety Assocs. (cons. in housing mortgage financing and urban renewal), 1957-67; Housing cons. Govt. Peru, S.Am., 1956. Bd. dirs., sec., v.p., treas. Nat. Council Health Centers, 1969-85; bd. dirs. Am.-Hungarian Found., 1974-76; trustee Cazenovia (N.Y.) Coll., 1981-87; bd. visitors Lander Coll., U. S.C., Greenwood, 1982-84; mem. fin. com. World Games, 1989, Karlsruhe, Fed. Republic of Germany, Confrerie des Chevaliers du Tastevin, Confrerie de la Chaine des Rotisseurs, Wine and Food Soc. Served to lt. (j.g.) USNR, 1943-47. Mem. ABA, N.Y. County Lawyers Assn., Am. Hosp. Assn., Harvard Bus. Sch. Assn. (exec. council 1966-69, area chmn. 1967-69), Confrerie des Chevaliers du Tastevin, Confrerie de la Chaine des Rotisseurs, Wine and Food Soc., Wednesday 10, Alpha Kappa Psi, Phi Delta Phi. Presbyterian. Clubs: Yale (N.Y.C.), Harvard Bus. Sch. (N.Y.C.) (pres. 1964-65, chmn. 1965-66, dir. 1964-70), Harvard (N.Y.C.); Metropolitan (Washington). Home: 2600 S Ocean Blvd Boca Raton FL 33432 Office: Profl Med Products PO Box 3288 Greenwood SC 29648

SIGLER, ANDREW CLARK, forest products company executive; b. Bklyn., Sept. 25, 1931; s. Andrew J. and Eleanor (Nicholas) S.; m. Margaret Romefelt, June 16, 1956; children: Andrew Clark, Patricia, Elizabeth. A.B., Dartmouth, 1953; M.B.A., Amos Tuck Sch., 1956. With Champion Papers Co., Hamilton, Ohio, 1957—; pres. Champion Papers div. Champion Internat. Corp., 1972, exec. v.p., dir. parent co., 1972-74, pres., chief exec. officer, Stamford, Conn., 1974-79, chmn. bd., chief exec. officer, 1979—; dir. Bristol-Myers, Chem. Bank, Gen. Electric Co. Served from 2d lt. to 1st lt. USMCR, 1953-55. Office: Champion Internat Corp 1 Champion Plaza Stamford CT 06921

SIGMON, JACKSON MARCUS, lawyer; b. Bethlehem, Pa., Apr. 15, 1918; s. William Louis and Jeanette (Marcus) S.; AB, U. Pitts., 1938; MA, Fletcher Sch. Internat. Law and Diplomacy, 1939; LLB, Duke U., 1942; student Balliol Coll., Oxford U. 1945; m. Ruth Friedman, Aug. 22, 1948; children: Mark, Hilary, Jill, Jan, William, Erica. Bar: Pa. 1943, U.S. Dist. Ct. (ea. dist.) 1946, U.S. Dist Ct. (mid. dist.) 1946; ptnr. Sigmon & Sigmon and predecessors, Bethlehem, 1946—; spl. dep. atty. gen. Pa., 1951-55, 63-72, asst. City of Bethlehem, city solicitor, 1962-65. Bethlehem rep., adv. bd. Northampton County com., Republican Party, 1956-85; spl. trial counsel City of Bethlehem, 1983—, Bethlehem Twp., Borough of Freemansburg, 1983—; counsel Northampton County Rep. Com., 1957-85; Rep. state committeeman, 1958-72, del. to Ann. Jud. Conf. of 3rd Cir. Ct. of Pa. Served from pvt. to 1st lt. AUS, 1942-46. Decorated Bronze Star, Croix de Guerre; recipient Community Leader of Am. commendation, 1969, 72. Mem. ABA, Pa. Bar Assn. (state bd. censors, ho. of dels., bd. govs., exec. grievance com., eastern dist. Pa. del. to jud. conf. of 3d cir.), Pa. Soc. Am. Legion, DAV, B'rith Sholom, Zionist Orgn. Am., Pi Lambda Phi, Pi Sigma Alpha. Sigma Kappa Phi. Club: Union League (Phila.). Lodge: Masons (32 deg.) Home: 3464 Mountainview Circle Bethlehem PA 18017 Office: 146 E Broad St Bethlehem PA 18018

SIGMUND, PETER, physics researcher and educator; b. Karlsruhe, Fed. Republic Germany, Apr. 5, 1936; s. Paul R. and Anne L. (Schmelzle) S.; m. Erna Pia Bork. Diploma in physics, U. Göttingen, Fed. Republic Germany, 1959; PhD, Tech. U., Aachen, Fed. Republic Germany, 1962. Research fellow Atomic Energy Commn., Risö, Denmark, 1962-64; lectr. U. Aarhus, Denmark, 1964-65, 69-70; scientist Kernforschunganlage, Jülich, Fed. Republic Germany, 1965-69; vis. scientist Argonne (Ill.) Nat. Lab,, 1967-69; lectr. U. Copenhagen, 1971-78; prof. U. Odense, Denmark, 1977—; cons. in field. Editor Physica Scripta, 1986—; contbr. numerous articles to profl. jours. Senator Odense U., 1982—; pres. Soc. Contemporary Music, 1982-86. Fellow Royal Danish Acad. Scis. and Letters, 1988, Argonne Nat. Lab.; recipient Dannin award Dannin Com., Copenhagen, 1982, Medard B. Welch award Am. Vacuum Soc., 1988. Mem. Danish Sci. Research Council, Danish Phys. Soc. (pres. 1987—), Danish Soc. Nat. Scis., Internat. Union of Pure and Applied Physics (Danish nat com.). Office: Odense U, Campusvej 55, 5230 Odense M Denmark

SIGMUNDSSON, GUNNLAUGUR MAGNUS, financial company executive; b. Reykjavik, Iceland, June 30, 1948; s. Sigmundur Jonsson and Nanna Gunnlaugsdottir; m. Sigridur Sigurbjörnsdottir, Aug. 25, 1973; children: Sigmundur, Sigurbjörn, Nanna. MBA, Iceland U., Reykjavik, 1974; student, Internat. Monetary Fund Inst., Washington, 1976. Advisor Ministry Fin., Iceland, 1974-78, chief div., 1978-82; asst. The World Bank, Washington, 1982-84; mng. dir. Econ. Devel. Inst., Iceland, 1985, Icelandic Fin. Investment, Iceland, 1986—. Chmn. Prog. Dem. Econ. Com., Iceland, 1987. Mem. Icelandic-Am. Assn. Washington D.C., (vice chmn. 1983-84). Lutheran. Home: Thverasel 20, 109 Reykjavik Iceland Office: Icelandic Fin Investment, Sudurlandsbraut 22, 108 Reykjavik Iceland

SIGOLOFF, SANFORD CHARLES, retail executive; b. St. Louis, Sept. 8, 1930; s. Emmanuel and Gertrude (Breliant) S.; m. Betty Ellen Greene, Sept. 14, 1952; children: Stephen, John David, Laurie. B.A., UCLA, 1950. Cons. AEC, 1950-54, 57-58; gen. mgr. Edgerton, Germeshausen & Grier, Santa Barbara, Calif., 1958-63; v.p. Xerox Corp., 1963-69; pres. CSI Corp., Los Angeles, 1969-70; sr. v.p. Republic Corp., Los Angeles, 1970-71; chief exec. officer Kaufman & Broad, Inc., Los Angeles, 1979-82; chmn., pres., chief exec. officer Wickes Cos. Inc., Santa Monica, 1982—. Contbr. articles on radiation dosimetry to profl. jours. Bd. govs. Cedars-Sinai Hosp. Served in USAF, 1954-57. Recipient Tom May award Nat. Jewish Hosp. and Research Ctr., 1972. Mem. AAAS, Am. Chem. Soc., AIAA, Am. Nuclear Soc., IEEE, Radiation Research Soc. Office: Wickes Cos Inc 3340 Ocean Park Blvd Santa Monica CA 90405 *

SIGUION-REYNA, LEONARDO, lawyer, business executive; b. Dagupan City, Philipines, Apr. 18, 1921; s. Lamberto and Felisa (Tiongson) S.; m. Armido Ponce-Enrile, Nov. 24, 1951; children: Monica, Leonardo, Carlos. Student, Ateneo de Manila, 1937-41; LLB, U. Santo Tomas, Manila, 1946-48. Bar: Philippines, 1948. Assoc. firm Perkins and Ponce Enrile, Manila, 1953-56; ptnr. Ponce Enrile, Siguion Reyna, Montecillo & Belo, Manila, 1956-67; sr. ptnr. Siguion Reyna, Montecillo, and Ongsiako, Makati Metro Manila, 1967—; chmn. bd. Phimco Industries, Inc., Manila, Sandvick Philippines, Inc., Skanfil Shipping Corp., Communication Found. for Asia, Electrolux Mktg. Corp., vice chmn. Sunripe Dessicated Coconuts Inc., Columbus Indsl. (HK) Ltd.; pres. Electronic Tele. Systems Industries, Inc., Foremost Wood Products, Manila Meml. Park Cemetary, Inc., Zamboanga Rubber Corp., Philippine Global Communications, Inc., Valmora Investment & Mgmt. Corp.; dir. Asian Savs. Bank, BA Fin. Corp., Complex Electronics Corp., Consultasia Mgmt. Services, Inc., Crismida Realty Corp., Dole Philippines, Inc., Electrolux Philippines, Inc., Filflex Indsl. & Mfg. Corp., First Pacific Capital Corp., Goodyear Philippines, Inc., Indsl. Realties, Inc., Investment & Capital Corp. of the Philippines, Perafilms, Inc., Philippine Refining Co., Inc., Rizal Comml. Banking Corp., Rubicon, Inc., Stal-Astra Refrigeration, Inc. Decorated Order of White Elephant (Thailand). Mem. Philippine Bar Assn., Philippine Brit. Soc., Casino Español de Manila. Roman Catholic. Clubs: Manila Yacht, Manila Polo. Lodge: Rotary. Home: No 7 Tangile Rd/North Forbes, Makati Metro Manila Philippines Office: 5th Floor Soriano Bldg, Ayala Ave, Makito Metro Manila Philippines

SIGURDARDOTTIR, JOHANNA, Iceland government official; b. Oct. 4, 1942; m. Thorvaldur Steinar Johannesson. Grad., Comml. Coll. Iceland, 1960. Stewardess Loftleidir, Iceland, 1962-71; clk. Kassagerd Reykjavikur, Iceland, 1971-78; M.P. Iceland, Reykjavik, 1978—, minister social affairs, 1987—; mem. leadership com. Icelandic Air Hostesses Union, 1966-69, Reykjavik Shop and Workers Union, 1976-83, mem. Social Security Bd., 1978—, chmn., 1979-80. Address: Ministry Social Affairs, Reykjavik Iceland *

SIGURDSSON, JON, government official; b. Isafjordur, Iceland, Apr. 17, 1941; s. Sigurdur Gudmundsson and Kristin Gudjona (Gundmundsdotter) G; m. Laufey Thorbjarnardottir, Aug. 26, 1962; children: Thorbjorn, Sigurdur Thor, Abnna Krisitn, Rebekka. Grad. in econs., stats., U. Stockholm, 1964; MS in Econs., London Sch. Econs. and Polit. Sci., 1967. Economist Econ. Inst. Iceland, 1964-67, chief econ. div., 1967-70, dir. econ. research, 1970-71; chief econ. research div. Econ. Devel. Inst., 1972-74; mng. dir. Nat. Econ. Inst., 1974—; mem. Althing (Parliament), minister Commerce, Minister Justice and Eccles. Affairs Iceland, 1987—; Iceland rep. to econ. and devel. rev. com. OECD, 1970—; alt. gov. IMF for Iceland, assoc. joint IBRD/IMF devel. com., 1974—; exec. dir. for Nordic countries in IMF Exec. Bd., 1980-83; adviser to Icelandic govt., 1974-80, 83-86; bd. dirs. Nordic Investment Bank, Helsinki, 1976—, chmn. bd., 1984-86. Contbr. articles to econ. jours. Candidate Social Dem. Party, Reykjavik, Iceland, 1987—. Lutheran. Home: Selbraut 15, 170 Seltjarnarnes Iceland Office: Ministry Commerce, Arnarhvoll, 101 Reykjavik Iceland

SIGURDSSON, THORDUR BALDUR, data processing executive; b. Reykjavik, Iceland, July 9, 1929; s. Sigurdur and Olafia (Hjaltested) Thordarson; m. Anna Hjaltested, Nov. 30, 1951; children—Magnus, Bjoern, Sigurdur, Anna, Ingveldur, Olafur, Katrin. Grad., Comml. Coll. Iceland, 1949; postgrad. U. Iceland, 1949-52. Chief acct. Icelandic State Land Reclamation, Reykjavik, 1947-72; mng. dir. Raftaekjaverzlunin Ltd., 1959-65; EDP mgr. Agrl. Bank of Iceland, Reykjavik, 1972-77, br. mgr., Stykkisholmur, 1974-75; tchr. math. Vogaskoli, Reykjavik, 1966-71; mng. dir. Icelandic Banks Data Ctr., Reykjavik, 1977—, dir. adv. bd., 1973-77. Editor Verzlunarskolabladid, 1947, Studentabladid, 1949, Ithrottabladid, 1967-68, Vestryman, Langholt Parish, Reykjavik, 1969-76. Recipient Gold Emblem, Athletic Union Iceland, 1968, Iceland Sports Fedn., 1972; Ace-Emblem, Athletic Union Iceland, 1967. Club: Reykjavik Football (Emblem Gold/Laures 1974). Home: Langholtsvegur 179, 104 Reyjavik Iceland Office: Icelandic Banks Data Ctr, Kalkofnsvegur 1, 150 Reykjavik Iceland

SIH, JULIUS WEI WU, engineer; b. Shanghai, China, July 2, 1922; came to U.S., 1947, naturalized, 1956; s. C.C. and Y.F. (Dai) S.; m. Susan D. Wang, Aug. 30, 1950; children: Jeanette, Daniel. B.S., Nat. Chekiang U., 1944; M.S. in Engring, U. Mich., 1948; doctoral candidate, N.Y.U., 1952. Cons. engr. major projects for cons. engring. firms in N.Y.C. and Chgo., 1948-59; chief structural engr. Chgo. Fed. Center Architects, 1959-65; pres. J.W. Sih & Assocs., Inc. (architects and engrs.), Chgo., 1965—. Contbr. articles to profl. jours.; projects include Community Hosp., numerous Ill. State regional office bldgs., indsl. facilities New Loop Coll. for, City Colls. Chgo., Orr High Sch, Lawndale High Sch, Chgo., 6th Dist. Circuit Ct. Bldg (SARA award), Ill., Rosemont Terminal Facilities, CTA-O'Hare Extension Project, CTA Addison Sta. Project, Lake Shore Drive Project, CTA Howard Expansion Project, Chgo., 3d Dist. Cir. Ct. Bldg., 5th Dist. Cir. Ct. Bldg. Chmn. Citizens Com. on Sr. Coll. Fellow ASCE; mem. Am. Concrete Inst., Internat. Soc. Soil Mechanics and Found. Engring., Internat. Assn. Bridge and Structural Engrs., Nat. Assn. Profl. Engrs., Am. Inst. Steel Constrn., Ill. Soc. Profl. Engrs. Clubs: Union League (Chgo.). Home: 608 Earlston Rd Kenilworth IL 60043 Office: 35 E Wacker Dr Chicago IL 60601

SIHANOUK, PRINCE NORODOM (HIS ROYAL HIGHNESS PRINCE NORODOM SIHANOUK), government official Cambodia (now Kampuchea); b. Oct. 31, 1922; s. Norodom Suramarit and Kossamak Neareath; studied in Saigon, Viet-Nam, Paris. Elected King of Cambodia (now Kampuchea), 1941, abdicated, 1955, prime minister, minister fgn. affairs, 1955-57, elected head state, 1960, deposed, 1970, restored as head state when Royal Govt. Nat. Union Cambodia overthrew Khmer Republic, 1975, resigned, 1976; permanent rep. to UN, 1956, spl. envoy of Khmer Rouge to UN, 1979; formed Nat. United Front for an Ind. Kampuchea, 1981; head of state in exile of Govt. of Democratic Kampuchea, 1982-87, 88—. Head Popular Socialist Community, 1955-70. Author: (with Wilfred Burchett) My War With the C.I.A., 1973; War and Hope: The Case for Cambodia, 1980; Bitter and Sweet Remembrances, 1981; producer film: Le Petit Prince. Office: Mission of Dem Kampuchea to UN 747 Third Ave 8th Floor New York NY 10017 *

SIHARE, LAXMIPRASAD, museum director; b. Mandla, India, May 1, 1933; s. Chaturbhuj and Dulari Bai Sihare; m. Shyamlata Singhania; 1 child, Vasundhara. MA in Polit. Sci., Robertson Coll., Jabalpur, India, 1956; MA in Art Criticism, M.S. Univ. Baroda, India, 1959, postgrad. diploma in museology, 1961; PhD, NYU, 1967; D (hon.), Fairleigh Dickinson U., 1975. Cons. Internat. Council Mus. Modern Art, N.Y.C., 1967-68; cons., dir. Berla Acad. Art and Culture, Calcutta, India, 1968-69; exec. dir. Nat. Gallery Modern Art, New Delhi, India, 1971-84; gen. dir. Nat. Mus., New Delhi, 1984—. Contbr. articles to profl. jours. Honored by Govt. of India as Padma Bhushan, 1984. Club: Indian Internat. Center. Home: 33 Prithviraj Rd, Flat 7B, New Delhi 110003, India Office: Nat Mus of India, Janpath, New Delhi 110011, India

SIKAND, LAKHINDER S., can manufacturing company executive; b. Quetta, Baluchistan, Pakistan, June 18, 1935; came to Nigeria, 1982; s. Bhagwant K. and Durga D. (Singh) S.; m. Harjeet Gyani, Dec. 16, 1965; children: Parveen, Shivinder, Maya. Cert. in Mech. Engring., Coll. Tech., Coventry, Eng., 1956. Dir. Metal Box India, Ltd., Calcutta, 1957-79; bus. devel. mgr. Continental Can Internat. Corp., Windsor Berkshire, Eng., 1980-82; mng. dir. Continental Can Nigeria, Ltd., Lagos, 1982—. Fellow Inst. Dirs. U.K., Brit. Inst. Mgmt.; mem. Inst. Mech. Engrs. U.K., Am. Mgmt. Assn. Sikh. Club: Met. (mgmt. com. 1986) (Lagos). Office: Continental Can Internat Corp, Coburg House, Sheet St, Windsor Berkshire SL4 1BG, England

SIKER, EPHRAIM S., anesthesiologist; b. Port Chester, N.Y., Mar. 24, 1926; s. Samuel S. and Adele (Weiser) S.; m. m . Eileen Mary Bohnel, Aug. 5, 1951; children—Kathleen Ellen, Jeffrey Stephen, David Allan, Paul William, Richard Francis. Student, Duke U., 1943-45; M.D., N.Y.U., 1949. Diplomate: Am. Bd. Anesthesiology (dir. 1971—, sec.-treas. 1974-82, pres. 1982-83) Nat. Bd. Med. Examiners. Intern Grasslands Hosp., Valhalla, N.Y., 1949-50, resident in anesthesia, 1950; resident dept. anesthesiology Mercy Hosp., Pitts., 1952-53; assoc. dir. dept. Mercy Hosp., 1955-62, chmn., 1962—; practice medicine, specializing in anesthesiology Pitts., 1954—; courtesy staff St. Clair Meml. Hosp., Pitts., 1954—; dir. anesthesia services Central Med. Pavilion, Pitts., 1973—; cons. staff St. Margaret Meml. Hosp., 1962—; pres. Pitts. Anesthesia Assos., Ltd., 1967—; clin. prof. dept. anesthesiology U. Pitts. Sch. Medicine, 1968—; mem. exec. com. Am. Bd. Med. Spltys., 1978-81; Exchange cons. Welsh Nat. Sch. Medicine, Cardiff, 1955-56; mem. Pa. Gov.'s Commn. on Profl. Liability Ins., 1968-70; mem. adv. panel U.S. Pharmacopeia, 1970-76; mem. am. acupuncture anesthesia study group of Nat. Acad. Scis. to Peoples Republic China, 1974; mem. adv. com. on splty. and geog. distbn. of physicians Inst. Medicine, Nat. Acad. Scis., 1974-76; trustee Ednl. Council for Fgn. Med. Grads., 1980-82, Mercy Hosp. Found., 1983—; bd. dirs., sec. Anesthesia Patient Safety Found., 1985—. Author: (with F.F. Foldes) Narcotics and Narcotic Antagonists, 1964; sect. on narcotic: (with F.F. Foldes) numerous other publs. in med. lit. Ency. Brittanica. Served to lt. M.C. USNR, 1950-52. USPHS postdoctoral research fellow, 1954; hon. fellow faculty anaesthetists Royal Coll. Surgeons, Eng., 1974; hon. fellow faculty anesthetists CoH. Medicine South Africa, 1983; recipient Hippocratic award Mercy Hosp., 1982. Fellow Royal Coll. Surgeons Ireland; mem. Am. Soc. Anesthesiologists (pres. 1973—, dir., Disting. Service award 1984), AMA (alternate del. 1962), Pa., Allegheny County med. socs., Pa. Soc. Anesthesiologists (pres. 1965, disting. service award 1986), Royal Soc. Medicine (Eng.), Pitts. Acad. Medicine, Am. Coll. Anesthesiologists (gov. 1969-71), World Fedn. Socs. Anesthesiologists (chmn. exec. com. 1980-84, v.p. 1984-88), Assn. Anesthesia Program Dirs. (pres. 1987—). Home: 185 Crestvue Manor Dr Pittsburgh PA 15228 Office: 1400 Locust St Pittsburgh PA 15219

SIKLOS, ANDREW, historian, educator; b. Budapest, Hungary, Oct. 28, 1922; s. Fernando and Elizabeth (Mautner) S.; m. Elisabeth Vincze (Andrew), Aug. 30, 1952; children: Edit Vincze, Susanne. D in Hist. Sci., U. Budapest, 1946. Councillor Inst. for Labour History, Budapest, 1945-53; prof. Eötvös Loránd Univ. Faculty Letters, Budapest, 1953—. Author: Ungarn 1918-1919, 1979, Revolution in Hungary and the Dissolution of the Multi-National State, 1918, 1987. Home: V Merleg u 12 IV 2, 1051 Budapest Hungary Office: Eötvös L Univ Fac Letters, V Pesti Bu 1, 1052 Budapest Hungary

SIKORA, EUGENE STANLEY, engineer; b. Duquesne, Pa., July 21, 1924; s. Adam Joseph and Helen (Pietrowska) S.; student Okla. Bapt. U., 1943-44; B.S. in Indsl. Engring., U. Pitts., 1949; C.E., Carnegie Inst. Tech., 1951; m. Corinne Mary Coliane, Sept. 7, 1946; children—Karyn Ann, Leslie Ann. Bridge design engr. Gannett, Fleming, Corddry & Carpenter, Pitts., 1949-50; structural designer Rust Engring. Co., Pitts., 1950-51, chief field engr., 1951-52, asst. project engr.; project engr. Frank E. Murphy & Assos., Bartow, Fla., 1952-55; v.p. Wellman-Lord Engring. Co., Lakeland, Fla., 1955-61; pres. Gulf Design Co., Lakeland, 1961-74, chmn. Lakeland Constrn., 1974-85; pres. Witcher Creek Coal Co., Belle, W.Va., 1979—; ptnr. Gulf Atlantic Mgmt. Assocs., Lakeland, Maingatea Mall Assocs., 1985—; chmn. Horizon Constrn. & Devel. Inc., 1974—; dir. Eldorado Resources Corp., Reno. Bd. dirs. Polk County Mus. Art. Served with USAAF, 1943-45. Mem. Nat. Soc. Profl. Engrs., Am. Inst. Mining, Metall. and Petroleum Engrs., Am. Mgmt. Assn., Am. Inst. Chem. Engrs., Am. Inst. Indsl. Engrs., Fla. Engring. Soc., Lakeland C. of C. (dir.). Democrat. Episcopalian. Home: 1400 Seville Pl Lakeland FL 33803 Office: One Lone Palm Pl Lakeland FL 33801

SILANE, MICHAEL FRANCIS, vascular surgeon, surgery educator; b. N.Y.C., May 9, 1943; s. Roy and Louise (Murano) S.; m. Margaret Welles Barber, June 11, 1977; children—Jennifer, Carolyn. B.S., Georgetown U., 1965, M.D., 1969. Diplomate Am. Bd. Surgery; Cert. Spl. Competence in Gen. Vascular Surgery. Intern, Cornell-N.Y. Hosp., N.Y.C., 1969-70, resident, 1970-72, 74-76; instr. in surgery Cornell Med. Sch., N.Y.C., 1975-76; clin. instr. U. Calif., San Francisco, 1977-78; fellow Harvard Med. Sch., Boston, 1978-79; asst. prof. surgery Cornell Med. Sch., N.Y.C., 1976-84, assoc. prof., 1984—; cons. Meml. Hosp., N.Y.C., 1984-85, assoc. attending surgeon, 1985—. Contbr. articles to profl. jours. and chpts. to books. Served to lt. commdr. USNR, 1972-74. N.Y. State Engring. scholar, 1961; NIH fellow, 1978. Fellow Am. Coll. Surgeons; mem. Internat. Cardiovascular Soc., Assn. Acad. Surgeons, N.Y. Regional Vascular Soc., Eastern Regional Vascular Soc., N.Y. Cardiovascular Soc., N.Y. Surg. Soc., Alpha Omega Alpha. Roman Catholic. Club: Pelham Country (N.Y.). Avocations: skiing, computers, golf, tennis. Office: Cornell Med Sch 525 E 68th New York NY 10021

SILAS, CECIL JESSE, petroleum company executive; b. Miami, Fla., Apr. 15, 1932; s. David Edward and Hilda Videll (Carver) S.; m. Theodosea Hejda, Nov. 27, 1965; children—Karla, Peter, Michael, James. BSChemE, Ga. Inst. Tech., Atlanta, 1953. With Phillips Petroleum Co., Bartlesville, Okla., 1953—; mng. dir. natural resource group Europe/Africa London, 1974-76; v.p. natural resource group gas and gas liquids Bartlesville, 1976-78, sr. v.p. natural resource group, 1978-80, exec. v.p. natural resource group, 1980-82, pres., chief operating officer, 1982-85, chmn., chief exec. officer, 1985—; dir. First Nat. Bank, Tulsa. Bd. dirs. Jr. Achievement, Stamford, Conn., Regional Med. Devel. Found., Bartlesville, Business-Industry Polit. Action Com., Washington, Okla. Research Found., Oklahoma City, TARGET-Drug Prevention div. Nat. Fedn. High Schs., Boys Clubs Am., N.Y.C.; trustee U. Tulsa, Ga. Tech. Found. Inc., Atlanta; trustee Frank Phillips Found., Bartlesville, Okla. Served to 1st lt. Chem. Corps AUS, 1954-

56. Decorated comdr. Order St. Olav (Norway). Mem. Conf. Bd., Am. Petroleum Inst. (bd. dirs.), Bartlesville Area C. of C. (trustee). Office: Phillips Petroleum Co 18 Phillips Bldg Bartlesville OK 74004

SILBAUGH, PRESTON NORWOOD, savings and loan consultant, lawyer; b. Stockton, Calif., Jan. 15, 1918; s. Herbert A. and Della Mae (Masten) S.; m. Maria Sarah Arriola; children—Judith Ann Freed, Gloria Stypinski, Ximena Carey Braun, Carol Lee Morgan. A.B. in Philosophy, U. Wash., 1940; J.D., Stanford U., 1953. Bar: Calif. With Lockheed Aircraft Corp., 1941-44, Pan Am. World Airways, 1944, Office Civilian Personnel, War Dept., 1944-45; engaged in ins. and real estate in Calif., 1945-54; mem. faculty Stanford Law Sch., 1954-59, asso. prof. law, 1956-59, asso. dean, 1956-59; chief dep. savs. and loan commnr. for Calif., 1959-61, bus. and commerce adminstr., dir. investment, savs. and loan commr., mem. gov.'s cabinet, 1961-63; dir. Chile-Calif. Aid Program, Sacramento and Santiago, 1963-65; chmn. bd. Beverly Hills Savs. & Loan Assn., Calif., 1965-84; dir. Wickes Cos., Inc.; chmn. bd., pres. Simon Bolivar Fund, Del Mar, Calif.; of counsel firm Miller, Boyko & Bell, San Diego. Author: The Economics of Personal Insurance, 1958; also articles. Mem. pres.'s real estate adv. com. U. Calif., 1966—; mem. Beverly Hills Pub. Bldg. Adv. Com., 1970—. Served with USMCR, 1942-43. Mem. ABA, San Diego County Bar Assn., Soc. Internat. Devel., U.S., Nat., Calif. Savs. and Loan Leagues, Inter-Am. Savs. and Loan Union, Internat. Union Building Socs., U. Wash., Stanford Alumni Assns., Calif. Aggie Alumni Assn., Order of Coif, Phi Alpha Delta. Clubs: Commonwealth (San Francisco), Town Hall (Los Angeles). Home: Costenera del Sur, Zapallar Chile

SILBER, MAURICE, artist, painter; b. Bklyn., Apr. 12, 1922; s. Leiser and Sylvia (Ehrlich) S.; student Pratt Inst., 1940, Cooper Union, 1940-42, Art Students League, 1945, Queen's Coll., Empire State Coll., SUNY, 1979-81, M.A., NYU, 1984; m. Lillian Lowy, Dec. 23, 1950; children—Roger, Rona. Designer, modelmaker fine jewelry Select Jewelry Co., N.Y.C., 1945-46; founder Jewel Arts Inc., N.Y.C., 1947, pres., 1947-69, exec. v.p. (Jewel Arts Inc. purchase by Jewelcor Inc.), 1969-71; founder Maurice Silber, Inc., 1972-75. Exhibited paintings in one-man shows: Casa de Portugal, N.Y.C., 1971, Salmagundi Club, N.Y.C., 1974, Soc. Illustrators, 1972, 75, Instituto Hondureno de Cultura Interamericana, Teguiciagalpa, Honduras, 1978, Empire State Coll., SUNY, 1981, Teatro Nacional, San Jose, Costa Rica, 1977, 78, 79, 80, 81, 83, East Hampton Hist. Soc., Marine Mus., L.I., 1980, French Cultural Ctr., 1983, Knickerbocker Artists, N.Y.C., 1980, 81, 82, Gallery 80, NYU, 1984, Wanamaker, Gallery of Centro-Cultural Costarricense Norteamericano, San Jose, Costa Rica, 1975, 76, 84, Echandi Gallery of Museo d'Arte de Costa Rica, 1986; exhibited in group shows: Malverne Art Assn. Annual, 1974, Soc. Illustrators, N.Y.C., 1973, 74, 75, 78, Hudson Valley Art Assn., 1975, Genesis Gallery, N.Y.C., 1978, World Trade Ctr., N.Y.C., 1979, Nat. Art League Ann., 1977, 79, Artists Equity, N.Y.C., 1977, Hobe Sound Gallery, Fla., 1977, 78, St. John's U., 1979, Long Beach (N.Y.) Mus., 1979, Am. Artists Profl. League Grand Nat., 1979, Port Washington Ann., N.Y.C., 1975, Salmagundi Club, 1971-87, Pacem in Terris Gallery, N.Y.C., 1975, Nat. Art League, 1977-78, Am. embassy, San Jose, 1978, Allied Artists Am., 1981, Fordham U., 1982, Alliance Queens Artists, 1984, Chung Cheng Gallery, St. John's U., N.Y., 1984, Guild Hall, East Hampton, N.Y., 1985; represented in permanent collections: East Hampton Hist. Soc., Marine Mus., Teatro Nacional, San Jose, Nat. Park Service, USAF Art Collection, USN Collection, Alianza France, San Jose, numerous others; vis. prof. U. Costa Rica, 1984, Queensboro Community Coll.; condr. workshops. Served with USAAF, 1942-45; ETO. Decorated Air medal with 6 oak leaf clusters; recipient various awards, including 1st prize and specially created award for dramatic value Am. Inst. of City N.Y., 1939; E. W. Graham Meml. award Washington Sq., 1976; Anco award, 1978; others. Mem. Salmagundi Club (admissions chmn. 1975-76, jury of awards 1976-77, art com. 1978), Soc. Illustrators, Nat. Art League, Am. Artists Profl. League, Artists Equity, Artists Fellowship, Long Beach Art Assn., Knickerbocker Artists (Anco award 1977), Am. Soc. Marine Artists. Patentee; designer chess pieces. Office: 183-07 69th Ave Fresh Meadows NY 11365

SILBERBERG, DONALD H., neurologist; b. Washington, Mar. 2, 1934; s. William Aaron and Leslie Frances (Stone) S.; m. Marilyn Alice Damsky, June 7, 1959; children—Mark, Alan. M.D., U. Mich., 1958; M.A. (hon.), U. Pa., 1971. Intern Mt. Sinai Hosp., N.Y.C., 1958-59; clin. assoc. in neurology NIH, Bethesda, Md., 1959-61; Fulbright scholar Nat. Hosp., London, 1961-62; NINDB spl. fellow in neuro-ophthalmology Washington U., St. Louis, 1962-63; assoc. neurology U. Pa., 1963-65, asst. prof., 1965-67, assoc. prof., 1967-71, prof., 1971-73, acting chmn. dept., 1973-74, prof., vice chmn. neurology, 1974-82, chmn., 1982—; inpatient staff Hosp. U. Pa.; cons. Children's Hosp., both Phila. Editorial bd.: Annals of Neurology; contbr. articles to profl. jours., abstracts, chpts. in books. Recipient grants in study of multiple sclerosis. Mem. Am. Acad. Neurology, Am. Assn. Neuropathologists, Am. Neurol. Assn. (council), Am. Soc. Neurochemistry, Assn. Research in Nervous and Mental Disease, Coll. Physicians Phila., Internat. Brain Research Orgn., Internat. Soc. Devel. Neuroscis., Internat. Soc. Neurochemistry, John Morgan Soc. U. Pa. (pres. 1974-75), N.Y. Acad. Scis., Nat. Multiple Sclerosis Soc. (exec. com. med. adv. bd.), Assn. Univ. Profs. Neurology (v.p.), Phila. Neurol. Soc. (pres. 1978-79), Soc. Neurosci., Alpha Omega Alpha. Office: Dept of Neurology Hospital of the University of Pennsylvania Philadelphia PA 19104

SILBERMAN, H. LEE, public relations executive; b. Newark, Apr. 26, 1919; s. Louis and Anna (Horel) S.; m. Ruth Irene Rapp, June 5, 1948; children: Richard Lyle, Gregory Alan, Todd Walter. B.A., U. Wis., 1940. Radio continuity writer Radio Sta. WTAQ, Green Bay, Wis., 1940-41; reporter Bayonne (N.J.) Times, 1941-42; sales exec. War Assets Adminstrn., Chgo., 1946-47; copy editor Acme Newspictures, Chgo., 1947; reporter, editorial writer Wichita (Kans.) Eagle, 1948-55; reporter Wall St. Jour., N.Y.C., 1955-57; banking editor Wall St. Jour., 1957-68; 1st v.p., dir. corporate relations Shearson-Hamill & Co., N.Y.C., 1968-74; N.Y. corr. Economist of London, 1966-72; contbg. editor Finance mag., 1970-74, editor in chief, 1974-76; v.p., dir. Fin. Services Group, Carl Boyir & Assos., Inc., N.Y.C., 1976-78, sr. v.p., 1978-80, exec. v.p., 1981-86; sr. counselor Hill & Knowlton, Inc., N.Y.C., 1986—. Contbr. articles to profl. jours. Served to capt. C.E. AUS, 1942-46. Recipient Loeb Mag. award U. Conn., 1965; Loeb Achievement award for distinguished writing on fin. Gerald M. Loeb Found., 1968. Mem. N.Y. Fin. Writers Assn., Deadline Club N.Y., Overseas Press Club, Soc. Profl. Journalists, Sigma Delta Chi, Phi Kappa Phi, Pub. Relations Soc. Am., Zeta Beta Tau, Phi Sigma Delta. Republican. Home: 80 Miller Rd Morristown NJ 07960 Office: 420 Lexington Ave New York NY 10017

SILBERNAGL, ARMIN, fine art company executive, art expert; b. Milano, Italy, June 18, 1935; s. Josef and Costanza (Bordogna) S. Ph. Doc. in Art, Univ. Bologna (Italy), 1982. Mng. dir. Arsitalia, Milano, 1959—. Served with Italian Army, 1955-57. Roman Catholic. Avocation: martial arts. Home: Via San Vittore 8, 20123 Milano Italy Office: Via San Vittore, 20123 Milan Italy

SILER, TODD LAEL, visual artist, researcher, lecturer; b. Long Island, N.Y., Aug. 21, 1953; s. Bernard O. Siler and Gloria (Kates) Haberman. BA, Bowdoin Coll., 1975; MS in Visual Studies, MIT, 1981, PhD in Psychology and Art, 1986. Hon. research affiliate Ctr. for Advanced Visual Studies MIT, 1981-83, vis. artist Computer-Aided Design Lab. Dept. Mech. Engring., 1986-88. Author: Cerebreactors, 1981, The Biomirror, 1983, The Art of Thought, 1987, Neurocosmology, 1985, Metaphorms: Forms of Metaphor, 1988; patentee in field; one man shows include Gallery Takagi, Nagoya, Japan, 1983, Ronald Feldman Fine Arts Gallery, N.Y.C., 1981, 83, 87, Compton Gallery, MIT, 1983, Galerie France Morin, Montreal, Que., Can., 1982, MIT Mus. and Hist. Collections, Cambridge, 1982; exhibited in group shows O.K. Harris Gallery, N.Y.C., 1978, Ars Electronica Internat. Brucknerfestes, Linz and Munich, 1982, Musee D'Art Moderne De La Ville De Paris, 1982, Mcpl. Art Gallery, Los Angeles, 1985, Festival Steirischer Herbst, Graz, Austria, 1985, Hokin Gallery, Miami, Fla., 1985, Chrysler Mus., Norfolk, Va., 1984, Queensboro Community Coll., CUNY, 1984, Sao Paulo Biennale, 1985, Ctr. Internat. D'Art Comtemporain, Montreal, 1986, others; vis. artist MIT, 1986-88; represented in numerous pub. and pvt. collections. Recipient Innovative Design Fund award N.Y.C., 1984; Fulbright fellow, India, 1985-86, IBM Thomas J. Watson fellow, Paris, 1975-76; William Zorach Painting scholar, 1972, painting fellow Mass. Artists Found., 1987; Council for Arts grantee MIT, 1979, 83, 87, 88; hon. research affiliate Ctr. for Advanced Visual Studies MIT, 1981-83. Office: MIT Ctr Advanced Visual Studies 40 Massachusetts Ave Cambridge MA 02139

SILES ZUAZO, HERNAN, former president of Bolivia; b. 1914. Grad., U. San Andres. Practice law, La Paz, Bolivia, 1939; M.P. for La Paz, 1943-46; in exile in Argentina and Chile, translator U.S. News agys., 1946-51; candidate v.p., Bolivia, 1951; leader revolution, 1952; v.p. Bolivia, 1952-56, pres., 1956-60, 82-85; ambassador to Uruguay, 1960-63, Spain, 1963-64; in exile, 1964-78. Pres. Movimiento Nacionalista Revolucionario-Izquierdo, 1978—. Address: care of Movimiento Nacionalista, Revolucionario-Izquirerdo, La Paz Bolivia *

SILETS, HARVEY MARVIN, lawyer; b. Chgo., Aug. 25, 1931; s. Joseph Lazarus and Sylvia (Dubner) S.; m. Elaine Lucy Gordon, June 25, 1961; children: Hayden Leigh, Jonathan Lazarus (dec.), Alexandra Rose. B.S. cum laude, DePaul U., 1952; J.D. (Frederick Leckie scholar), U. Mich., 1955. Bar: Ill. 1955, N.Y. 1956, U.S. Supreme Ct. 1959, U.S. Ct. Appeals (2d, 5th, 6th, 7th and 11th cirs.), U.S. Tax Ct., U.S. Ct. Mil. Appeals, U.S. Dist. Ct. (no. dist.) Ill. Assoc. Paul, Weiss, Rifkind, Wharton & Garrison, N.Y.C., 1955-56; asst. atty. U.S. Dist. Ct. (no. dist.) Ill., 1958-60; chief tax atty. U.S. atty. No. Dist. Ill., Chgo., 1960-62; ptnr. Harris, Burman & Silets, Chgo., 1962-79; firm Silets & Martin, Ltd., Chgo., 1979—; asst. advance tng. program IRS, U. Mich., 1952-53; law lectr. advance fed. taxation John Marshall Law Sch., 1962-66; adj. prof. taxation Chgo.-Kent Coll. Law, 1985—; gen. counsel Nat. Treasury Employees Union, 1968—; mem. Chgo. Crime Commn., 1975—; mem. adv. com. tax litigation U.S. Dept. Justice, 1979-82; mem. Tax Reform Com., State of Ill., 1982-83; mem. Speedy Trial Act Planning Group U.S. Dist Ct. (no. dist.) Ill., 1976-78; lectr. in field. Contbr. articles to profl. jours. Trustee Latin Sch., Chgo., 1970-76, Rodfei Zedek; mem. Gov.'s Commn. Reform Tax Laws, Ill. 1982-83. Served with AUS, 1956-58. Fellow Am. Coll. Trial Lawyers (chmn. com. on fed. rules of criminal procedure 1982—), Am. Coll. Tax Counsel, Internat. Acad. Trial Lawyers; mem. Bar Assn. 7th Fed. Cir. (chmn. com. criminal law and procedure 1972-82, bd. govs. 1983-86, sec. 1986—, 2nd v.p., 1988—), (fellow) Internat. Acad. Trial Lawyers, ABA (active various coms.), Fed. Bar Assn. (bd. dirs. 1971—, pres. 1977-78, v.p. 1976-77, sec. 1975-76, treas. 1974-75, active various coms.), Fed. Cir. Bar Assn. (jud. selection com. 1985—, tax appeals com. 1985—), Chgo. Bar Assn. (tax com. 1958-66, com. devel. law 1966-72, 78—, com. fed. taxation 1968—, com. evaluation candidates 1978-80), Am. Bd. Criminal Def. Lawyers, Chgo. Soc. Trial Lawyers, Decalogue Soc. Lawyers, BAr Assn. City of N.Y., Nat. Assn. Criminal Def. Lawyers, Ill. Soc. Trial Lawyers, Phi Alpha Delta, Pi Gamma Mu. Clubs: Standards, Chgo., Cliff Dwellers (Chgo.), Biltmore Country, Law of City of Chgo. Office: Silets & Martin Ltd 15th Floor 140 S Dearborn St Chicago IL 60603

SILIN, ANATOLY ALEXANDROVICH, international labor official; b. Moscow, May 19, 1929; arrived in Switzerland, 1982; s. Alexandr Gheorghievich and Vera Petrovna (Kulakova) S.; m. Svetlana Konstantinovna Leonova; 1 child, Kirill. Diploma in Internat. Law, State Internat. Relations Inst., Moscow, 1952. Consular sec. Soviet Embassy, Bucharest, Romania, 1952-56, third sec., 1959-63; first sec. Soviet Embassy, Kinshasa, Zaire, 1977-80; attache Ministry Fgn. Affairs, Moscow, 1956-59, counselor, 1971-77, 80-82; internal official Br.-Internat. Labor Office, Moscow, 1963-67; profl. official Secretariat-Internat. Labour Office, Geneva, Switzerland, 1967-70, sr. official, 1982—. Author several research studies. Mem. CPSU Party. Office: Internat Labour Office, 4 Rue Des Morillons, 22 Geneva CH 1211, Switzerland

SILKIN, JON, poet, writer, editor; b. London, Dec. 2, 1930; s. Joseph and Dora (Rubenstein) S.; m. Lorna Tracy, Mar. 9, 1974; 4 children. Ed. Wycliffe Coll., 1940-45, Dulwich Coll., 1945-47; B.A. in English with 1st class honors, Leeds U., 1962. Founder, editor Stand Mag., London, 1952—; vis. tchr. Writer's Workshop, U. Iowa, Iowa City, 1968-69, Coll. of Idaho, Caldwell, 1978, Mishkenot Sha'ananim (Jerusalem), 1980; vis. lectr. Denison U., Granville, Ohio, 1968; vis. writer U. Sydney (Australia), 1974; Bingham vis. poet U. Louisville, 1981; poet-in-residence U. Cin., 1983; works include: Out of Battle: Poets of the First World War, 1972, 79, Penguin Book of First World War Poetry, 1979, The Psalms with Their Spoils, 1980, Selected Poems, 1980, 88; The Penguin Book of First World War Prose, 1988; Gurney, a May in Verse, 1985; The Ship's Pasture, 1986. Gregory fellow, 1958-60, C. Day Lewis fellow, 1976-77; recipient Geofrey Faker award 1966. Fellow Royal Soc. of Lit. Home: 19 Haldane Terr, Newcastle-upon-Tyne NE2 3AN, England

SILL, ALEXIS MATTOS, computer company executive; b. Rio de Janeiro, Apr. 15, 1949; came to U.S., 1956, naturalized, 1960; s. Bev Arthur and Gigi Lino (Mattos) S.; m. Sandra Sarah Ann Heaslip, Aug. 24, 1974; children: Courtney Jane, Alexis Ryan, Colin George. Student Golden Gate U., San Francisco. Sales mgr. United Calif. Bank, San Francisco, 1971-77; sales exec. Automatic Data Processing, Inc., San Francisco, 1977-84;nat. sales mgr. Digital Research, Inc., Palo Alto, Calif., 1984—; pres. Mega Distbg., Sausalito, Calif. Served with USMCR, 1969-71. Republican. Home: 40 Hillside Ave San Rafael CA 94901 Office: Digital Research Inc 4401 Great America Pkwy Suite 200 Santa Clara CA 95054

SILL, GERALD DE SCHRENCK, hotel corp. exec.; b. Czechoslovakia, Dec. 11, 1917; s. Edward and Margaret (Baroness von Schrenck-Notzing) S.; B.S., Budapest Tech. U., 1942; m. Maria Countess Draskovich, May 11, 1946; children—Susan, Gabrielle. Came to U.S., 1948, naturalized, 1953. With econs. div. U.S. Hdqrs., Vienna, Austria, 1945-48; exec. hotel positions N.Y.C., 1948-52; managerial positions with Hilton Hotel Corp., 1953-61; exec. v.p. Houston Internat. Hotels, Inc., 1961-72, pres., chief exec. officer, 1972-84, chmn. bd., 1984-86; sr. chmn. bd. Preferred Hotels Worldwide; dir. Tex. Commerce Med. Bank, Houston, regional bd. dirs., mem. Silver Fox Advisors, Inc.; pres. GdSS Mgmt. and Cons. Inc., The Warwick Hotel, Houston. Clubs: Warwick (pres.), River Oaks Country (Houston). Home: 2227 Pelham Dr Houston TX 77019 Office: The Warwick 5701 Main St Box 1379 Houston TX 77251

SILLING, CYRUS EDGAR, JR., management consulting company executive; b. Charleston, W.Va., June 29, 1923; s. Cyrus Edgar and Marian Lillian (Reddington) S.; m. Margaret Gertrude Moore, Mar. 28, 1948; children—Linda Louise, Stephen Marc, Michael Andrew, Elizabeth Ann, Rebecca Caroline. B.S. in Chem. Engring., Carnegie Mellon U., 1944, postgrad., 1946-47. Registered profl. engr., W.Va. Prodn. supr. Hercules Powder Co., Parlin, N.J., 1947-50; mktg. mgr. Ohio Apex div. FMC, Nitro, W.Va., 1950-53; exec. asst. to v.p. research and devel. Am. Viscose Co., Phila., 1954-57; pres. Com-Dev Inc., Media, Pa., 1957—. Served to lt. (j.g.) U.S. Maritime Service, 1945-46. Mem. Am. Chem. Soc., Am. Inst. Chem. Engrs., Soc. Plastic Engrs., Chem. Mktg. Research Assn., Comml. Devel. Assn., Am. Ceramics Soc. Republican. Home: 697 Lenni Rd Aston PA 19014 Office: Com-Dev Inc 101 State Rd Media PA 19063

SILLITOE, ALAN, writer; b. Nottingham, Eng., Mar. 4, 1928; s. Christopher Archibald and Sylvina (Burton) S.; ed. Nottingham schs.; m. Ruth Fainlight, Oct. 19, 1959; 1 son, David Nimrod; 1 adopted dau., Susan. Employed in factory, 1942-46; served as radio operator RAF, 1946-50; engaged in writing, 1950—. Author: (novels) Saturday Night and Sunday Morning, 1958; The General, 1960; Key to the Door, 1961; The Death of William Posters, 1965; A Tree on Fire, 1967; A Start in Life, 1970; Travels In Nihilon, 1971; Raw Material, 1972; Flame of Life, 1974; The Widower's Son, 1976; The Storyteller, 1979; Her Victory, 1982; The Lost Flying Boat, 1983; Down From the Hill, 1984; Life Goes On, 1985; Out of the Whirlpool, 1988; (essays) Mountains and Caverns, 1975; (stories include) The Loneliness of the Long Distance Runner, 1959; The Ragman's Daughter, 1963; Guzman, Go Home, 1968; Men, Women and Children, 1973; The Second Chance, 1981; (poems) The Rats, 1960; A Falling Out of Love, 1964; Love In The Environs of Voronezh, 1968; Storm and Other Poems, 1974; Snow on the North Side of Lucifer, 1979; Sun Before Departure, 1984; Tides and Stone Walls, 1985; (travel) Road to Volgograd, 1964, (with David Sillitoe) Nottinghamshire, 1986; (with Fay Godwin) The Saxon Shore Way, 1983; (juvenile) The City Adventures of Marmalade Jim, 1967; Big John and the Stars, 1977; The Incredible Fencing Fleas, 1978; Marmalade Jim on the Farm, 1979; Marmalade Jim and the Fox, 1984; (plays) (with Ruth Fainlight) All Citizens are Soldiers, 1969; This Foreign Field, 1970; Three Plays, 1978. Address: 14 Ladbroke Terr, London W11 England

SILLS, BEVERLY (MRS. PETER B. GREENOUGH), opera company director, coloratura soprano; b. Bklyn., May 25, 1929; d. Morris and Sonia (Bahn) Silverman; m. Peter B. Greenough, 1956; stepchildren: Lindley, Nancy, Diana; children: Meredith, Peter B. Grad. pub. schs.; student voice, Estelle Leibling; student piano, Paolo Gallico; student stagecraft, Desire Defrere; hon. doctorates, Harvard U., NYU, New Eng. Conservatory, Temple U. Gen. dir. N.Y.C. Opera, 1979-88; radio debut as Bubbles Silverman on Uncle Bob'sRainbow House, 1932; appeared on Major Bowes Capitol Family Hour, 1934-41, on Our Gal Sunday; toured with Shubert Tours, Charles Wagner Opera Co., 1950, 51; operatic debut Phila. Civic Opera, 1947; debut, N.Y.C. Opera Co. as Rosalinda in Die Fledermaus, 1955; debut San Francisco Opera, 1953; debut La Scala, Milan as Pamira in Siege of Corinth, 1969, Royal Opera, Covent Garden in Lucia di Lammermoor, London, 1971, Met. Opera, N.Y.C., 1975, Vienna State Opera, 1967, Teatro Fenice in La Traviata, Venice; appeared Teatro Colon, Buenos Aires; recital debut Paris, 1971, London Symphony Orch., 1971; appeared throughout U.S., Europe, S. Am. including Boston Symphony, Tanglewood Festival, 1968, 69, Robin Hood Dell, Phila., 1969; title roles in: Don Pasquale, Norma, Manon, Louise, Tales of Hoffmann, Daughter of the Regiment, The Magic Flute; ret. from opera and concert stage, 1980; numerous TV spls; author: Bubbles-A Self-Portrait, 1976, autobiography Beverly, 1987. Nat. chmn. March of Dimes' Mothers' March on Birth Defects; chmn. bd. Nat. Opera Inst.; cons. to council Nat. Endowment for the Arts; bd. dirs. N.Y.C. Opera. Recipient Handel medallion, 1973, Pearl S. Buck Women's award, 1979, Emmy award for Profiles in Music, 1976, Emmy award for Lifestyles with Beverly Sills, 1978, Medal of Freedom, 1980. Office: NYC Opera NY State Theater Lincoln Ctr New York NY 10023 *

SILVA, HENRIQUEZ RAUL CARDINAL, former archbishop of Santiago de Chile; b. Talca, Chile, Sept. 27, 1907. LLD (hon.), U. Notre Dame. Ordained priest Roman Catholic Ch., 1938; ordained bishop of Valparaiso, 1959; archbishop of Santiago de Chile, 1961-84, elevated to cardinal, 1962, Archbishop of Santiago de Chile; titular ch., St. Bernard (Alle Terme). Recipient Latin Am. Jewish Conf. Human Rights prize, 1972, UN prize, 1978. Mem. Commn.: Revision of Code of Canon Law. Office: Palacio Arzobispal, Casilla 30-D, Santiago Chile *

SILVA, RUTH CARIDAD, political scientist; b. Lincoln, Nebr.; d. Ignatius Dominic and Beatrice (Davis) S. BA, U. Mich., 1943, MA, 1943, PhD, 1948. Instr. Wheaton Coll., Norton, Mass., 1946-48; faculty Pa. State U., University Park, 1948—, prof. polit. sci., 1959—; Fulbright prof. polit. sci. Cairo U., 1952-53; vis. prof. Hunter Coll., N.Y.C., 1958, John Hopkins U., 1965; spl. cons. U.S. Dept. Justice, 1957, N.Y. State Constn. Commn., 1959-60, Pa. State Constn. Commn., 1967-68; mem. Pres.'s Commn. Post Secondary Edn., 1972-73. Author: Presidential Succession, 1951, Legislative Apportionment in New York, 1960; Rum, Religion and Votes: 1928 Re-examined, 1962; co-author: American Government, Democracy and Liberty in Balance, 1976; contbr. articles in field to profl. jours. Mem. Am. Polit. Sci. Assn. (past sec., chmn. com. status of women in profession 1972-73, v.p. 1972-73), Acad. Polit. Sci., AAUP (chmn. com. relation of govt. to higher edn. 1964-68), Nat. Municipal League, Phi Kappa Phi, Chi Omega. Republican. Roman Catholic. Clubs: University; U. Mich. Pres.'s (Ann Arbor). Home: 801 Southgate D Apt B-4 State College PA 16801

SILVER, BARNARD STEWART, mechanical engineer, consultant; b. Salt Lake City, Mar. 9, 1933; s. Harold Farnes and Madelyn Cannon (Stewart) S.; B.S. in Mech. Engring., MIT, 1957; M.S. in Engring. Mechanics, Stanford U., 1958; grad. Advanced Mgmt. Program, Harvard U., 1977; m. Cherry Bushman, Aug. 12, 1963; children—Madelyn Stewart, Cannon Farnes. Engr. aircraft nuclear propulsion div. Gen. Electric Co., Evandale, Ohio, 1957; engr. Silver Engring. Works, Denver, 1959-66, mgr. sales, 1966-71; chief engr. Union Sugar div. Consol. Foods Co., Santa Maria, Calif., 1971-74; directeur du complexe SODESUCRE, Abidjan, Ivory Coast, 1974-76; supt. engring. and maintenance U and I, Inc., Moses Lake, Wash., 1976-79; pres. Silver Enterprises, Moses Lake, 1971-88, Silver Energy Systems Corp., Moses Lake, 1980—; pres., gen. mgr. Silver Chief Corp., 1983—; pres. Silver Corp., 1984-86, Silver Pubs., Inc., 1986—; v.p. Barnard J. Stewart Cousins Land Co., 1987-88; instr. engring. Big Bend Community Coll., 1980-81. Explorer adviser Boy Scouts Am., 1965-66, chmn. cub pack com., 1968-74, chmn. scout troop com., 1968-74, vice chmn. Columbia Basin Dist., 1986—; pres. Silver Found., 1971-84, v.p., 1984—; ednl. counselor MIT, 1971-88; pres. Chief Moses Jr. High Sch. Parent Tchr. Student Assn., 1978-79; missionary Ch. of Jesus Christ of Latter-day Saints, Can., 1953-55, W. Africa, 1988—; 2d counselor Moses Lake Stake Presidency, 1980-88; bd. dirs. Columbia Basin Allied Arts, 1986-88. Served with Ordnance Corps, U.S. Army, 1958-59. Decorated chevalier Ordre National (Republic of Ivory Coast); registered profl. engr., Colo. Mem. ASME, Assn. Energy Engrs., AAAS, Am. Soc. Sugar Beet Technologists, Internat. Soc. Sugar Cane Technologists, Am. Soc. Sugar Cane Technologists, Sugar Industry Technicians, Nat. Fedn. Ind. Bus.; Utah State Hist. Soc. (life), Mormon Hist. Assn., Western Hist. Assn., Univ. Archeol. Soc. (life), Sigma Xi (life), Pi Tau Sigma, Sigma Chi, Alpha Phi Omega. Republican. Mormon. Lodge: Kiwanis. Home: 4391 S Carol Jane Dr Salt Lake City UT 84124 Office: Silver Chief Corp Route 32 86 Easy St Moses Lake WA 98837 also: Silver Energy Systems Corp 140 W Moore Ave Hermistone WA 98837

SILVER, DAVID, financial institute executive, lawyer; b. N.Y.C., Jan. 27, 1931; s. Sol and Fannie (Stein) S.; m. Meryl Young, Sept. 14, 1952; children: Daniel, Matthew, Joshua. B.A., CCNY, 1953; LL.B. cum laude, Harvard U., 1958. Bar: N.Y. 1958, D.C. 1979. Pvt. practice law N.Y.C., 1960-61; spl. counsel SEC, Washington, 1961-65; gen. counsel Investors Planning Corp., N.Y.C., 1965-66; asst. counsel Investment Co. Inst., Washington, 1966-69; gen. counsel Investment Co. Inst., 1969-77, pres., 1977—; cons. securities regulation Govt. of India, 1964. Served with U.S. Army, 1953-55. Mem. Fed. Bar Assn. (exec. council securities com., past chmn. investment co. com.). Home: 5505 Mohican Rd Bethesda MD 20816 Office: 1600 M St NW Washington DC 20036

SILVER, FRANCIS, 5TH, environmental engineer; b. Martinsburg, W.Va., Jan. 4, 1916; s. Gray and Kate (Bishop) S.; student Va. Military Inst., 1933-34; B.E. in Gas Engring., Johns Hopkins U., 1937; m. J. Nevelyne Wyndham, Dec. 31, 1965 (dec.). With Standard Lime & Stone Co., Millville, W.Va., 1937-42; plant engr., Fairchild Aircraft, Hagerstown, Md., 1951-57, Boeing Aircraft, Renton, Wash., 1957; cons. environ. engr., boundary surveyor, Martinsburg, 1960—. Surveyor of lands, Berkeley County, 1964—; dir. Berkeley County Hist. Soc., 1967—; bd. trustees City Hosp., 1971—, pres., 1977-78. Served with U.S. Army, 1942-46. Registered profl. engr. W.Va. Fellow Royal Soc. Health; mem. AAAS, Am. Chem. Soc., ASME, Nat. Soc. Profl. Engrs., Air Pollution Control Assn., Am. Pub. Health Assn., Am. Acad. Environ. Engrs., Soc. Clin. Ecology (Jonathan Foreman award 1982), Am. Congress on Surveying and Mapping, W.Va. Assn. Land Surveyors, (pres. 1973-75), N.Y. Acad. Sci., Sigma Xi. Democrat. Presbyterian. Contbr. chpts. to books. Home: 203 E Burke St Martinsburg WV 25401 Office: Berkeley County Ct House Martinsburg WV 25401

SILVER, GEORGE, metal trading and processing company executive; b. Warren, Ohio, Dec. 17, 1918; s. Jacob and Sophie (Bradlyn) S.; m. Irene Miller, Aug. 5, 1945. Student U. Ala., 1938; BA, Ohio U., 1940, postgrad. law sch., 1940-41; grad. Adj. Gen. Sch., 1944. Pres., Riverside Indsl. Materials, Bettendorf, Iowa, 1947-70, Metalpel subs. Continental Telephone Co., Bettendorf, 1970-71, Riverside Industries Inc., Bettendorf, 1971—; now pres. Scott Resources Inc., Davenport, Iowa; founder Iowa Steel Mills (name changed to North Star Steel), Cargill and Wilton. Contbr. articles to profl. jours. Mem. Nat. UN Day Com., 1975-83. Served to capt. AC, U.S. Army, 1941-46, 50-51; Korea. Mem. Nat. Assn. Recycling Industries (co-chmn. nat. planning com., bd. dirs.), Copper Club, Paper Stock Inst. Am. (mem. exec. com.), Bur. Internat. de la Recuperation (chmn. adv. com.), Mining Club N.Y.C., Phi Sigma Delta. Republican. Jewish. Clubs: Outing, Hatchet Men's Chowder and Protective Assn., Rock Island Arsenal Officer's, Chemist (N.Y.C.), Crow Valley Country. Lodge: Elks (Davenport). Office: Scott Resources PO Box 3728 Davenport IA 52808

SILVERBERG, STUART OWEN, physician; b. Denver, Oct. 14, 1931; s. Edward M. and Sara (Morris) S.; B.A., U. Colo., 1952, M.D., 1955; m. Joan E. Snyderman, June 19, 1954 (div. Apr. 1970); children—Debra Sue Owen, Eric Owen, Alan Kent; m. 2d, Kay Ellen Conklin, Oct. 18, 1970 (div. Apr. 1982); 1 son, Cris S.; m. 3d, Sandra Kay Miller, Jan., 1983. Intern Women's Hosp. Phila., 1955-56; resident Kings County Hosp., Bklyn., 1958-62; practice medicine specializing in obstetrics and gynecology, Denver, 1962—; mem. staff Luth. Hosp., Rose Med. Ctr., St. Josephs Hosp., Denver; mem. staff St. Anthony Hosp., chmn. dept. obstetrics and gynecology, 1976-77, 86-87; clin. instr. U. Colo. Sch. Medicine, Denver, 1962-72, asst. clin. prof., 1972-88, assoc. clin. prof., dir. gynecol. endoscopy and laser surgery, 1988—; v.p. Productos Alimenticos, La Ponderosa, S.A.; dir., chmn. bd. Wicker Works Video Prodns., Inc.; cons. Ft. Logan Mental Health Center, Denver, 1964-70; mem. Gov.'s Panel Mental Retardation, 1966; med. adv. bd. Colo. Planned Parenthood, 1966—, Am. Med. Center, Spivak, Colo., 1967—; med. dir. Health Care United, Denver, 1988—. Mem. Colo. Emergency Resources Bd., Denver, 1965—. Served to maj. AUS, 1956-58; Germany. Diplomate Am. Bd. Obstetrics and Gynecology. Fellow Am. Coll. Obstetricians and Gynecologists, ACS; mem. Am. Internat. fertility socs., Colo. Gynecologists and Obstetricians Soc., Hellman Obstet. and Gynecol. Soc., Colo. Med. Soc., Clear Creek Valley Med. Soc. (trustee 1978, 80, 87), Phi Sigma Delta, AMA, Flying Physicians Assn., Aircraft Owners and Pilots Assn., Nu Sigma Nu, Alpha Epsilon Delta. Jewish. Mem. editorial rev. bd. Colo. Women's Mag.; editor-in-chief Physicians Video Jour., 1984—. Office: 8407 Bryant St Westminster CO 80030

SILVERMAN, ALBERT A., lawyer, manufacturing company executive; b. Copenhagen, Oct. 14, 1908; came to U.S., 1909, naturalized, 1921; s. Louis and Anna (Mendelsohn) S.; m. Gertrude Adelman, 1929 (div. 1934); 1 child, Violet (Mrs. Robert Blumenthal); m. Florence Cohen, Aug. 5, 1939 (dec. 1966); m. Francie Seifert, Oct. 1, 1975. Student, Northwestern U., 1929-34; AA, Cen. YMCA Coll., Chgo., 1936; JD, Loyola U., Chgo., 1940. Bar: Ill. 1940, Wis. 1959, U.S. Supreme Ct. 1960. With Cen. Republic Bank & Trust Co., Chgo., 1926-32; sec.-treas. Cen.-Ill. Co., 1932-42; sec. Republic Drill & Tool Co., 1942-44; asst. to treas. Hansen Glove Corp., Milw., 1944-45; v.p. Vilter Mfg. Corp., Milw., 1945-49, pres., 1949-88, chmn., chief exec. officer, 1988—, also bd. dirs., chief legal counsel; bd. dirs., pres. Vilter Found., Inc.; mem. council Marquette U. Engring. Sch., 1974—. bd. dirs. Albert J. and Flora H. Ellinger Found., 1974—. Named Man of Year Milw. chpt. Unico Nat., 1967; recipient Francis J. Rooney-St. Thomas More award Loyola U. Law Sch., Chgo., 1974, Community Relations award Milw. police chief, 1974, Antonio R. Rizzuto Gold Medal award Unico Nat. Mem. ABA, Wis. Bar Assn., Milw. Bar Assn., Chgo. Bar Assn., ASHRAE, Master Brewers Assn. Am., Zool. Soc. Milw. County, Loyola U. Alumni Assn., Beta Gamma Sigma. Jewish. Clubs: Tripoli Country, Milw. Athletic, Milw. Press (Knight of Bohemia award 1979, Headliner award 1981), Wis. Lodges: Masons (32 deg.), Shriners. Office: 2217 S 1st St Milwaukee WI 53207

SILVERMAN, ARNOLD BARRY, lawyer; b. Sept. 1, 1937; s. Frank and Lillian Lena (Linder) S.; m. Susan L. Levin, Aug. 7, 1960; children: Michael Eric, Lee Oren. B. Engring. Sci., Johns Hopkins U., 1959; LL.B. cum laude, U. Pitts., 1962. Bar: U.S. Dist. Ct. (we. dist.) Pa. 1963, Pa. 1964, U.S. Patent and Trademark Office 1965, U.S. Supreme Ct. 1967, Can. Patent Office 1968, U.S. Ct. Claims 1975, U.S. Ct. Appeals (3d cir.) 1982, U.S. Ct. Appeals (fed. cir.) 1985. Patent atty. Alcoa, New Kensington, Pa., 1962-67, 68-72, sr. patent atty., 1972-76; ptnr. Price and Silverman, Pitts., 1967-68; v.p., gen. patent counsel Joy Mfg. Co., Pitts., 1976-80; ptnr. Murray Silverman & Keck, Pitts., 1980-81, Buell, Blenko, Ziesenheim & Beck, Pitts., 1984, Eckert, Seamans, Cherin & Mellott, Pitts., 1984—; spl. asst. atty. gen. State of W.Va., 1985—; spl. counsel patents U. Pitts., 1975—; speaker on patents, trademarks, copyright, computer law. Contbr. articles to profl. jours. on intellectual property law and computer law. Mem. Churchill CSC (Pa.), 1967—, chmn., 1975—; mem. Pitts. law com. Anti-Defamation League, 1981—, regional adv. bd., 1982—, co-chmn. Pitts. region ann. dinner, 1983, mem., chmn. by-laws com., 1983; bd. govs. Slippery Rock U. Found., 1985—; Pitts. steering com. MIT Enterprise Forum, 1986-87. Served with U.S. Army, 1963-64. Recipient Cert. of Recognition Project on Pub. Policy and Tech. Transfer of Council of Ams. and Internat. C. of C. Joint Com. on Tech. Transfer, 1978; Univ scholar U. Pitts., 1960-62. Mem. ABA, Allegheny County Bar Assn. (chmn. pub. relations com. 1978-80, vice-chmn. intellectual property sect. 1981-83 chmn.), Pitts. Patent Law Assn. (chmn. pub. relations com., 1968-69, chmn. patent laws com., 1970-72, chmn. nominating com., 1973, chmn. legis. action com., 1972-75, bd. mgrs. 1974-88, newsletter editor 1974-77, sec.-treas. 1976-84, v.p. 1984-85, pres. 1985-86), Am. Intellectual Property Law Assn., U.S. Trademark Assn. (chmn. task force on advt. agys. 1981), D.C. Bar Assn., Pa. Bar Assn., Nat. Assn. Coll. and Univ. Attys., Am. Chem. Soc., ASME, Licensing Execs. Soc., Brit. Inst. Chartered Patent Agts. (fgn. mem.), Johns Hopkins U. Alumni Assn. (chmn. publicity com. 1963-66, exec. com. 1966-87, v.p. 1969-70, pres. 1971-72), U. Pitts. Gen. Alumni Assn., U. Pitts. Law Alumni Assn., Robert Bruce Soc., Golden Panthers, Stratford Community Assn. (v.p. 1966-67, gov. 1966-70, pres. 1967-68), Mensa (charter fellow lawyers in Mensa 1978—, nat. assoc. counsel patents and trademarks copyrights 1980-82, inventors' spl. interest group 1980-86), Intertel (treas. Pitts. Forum 1983—), Order of Coif, Tau Epsilon Rho, Psi Chi. Republican. Jewish. Clubs: Churchill Valley Country, Duquesne, Downtown of Pitts. (sec. and bd. dirs. 1985-87). Home: 221 Thornberry Dr Pittsburgh PA 15235 Office: 600 Grant St 42d Floor Pittsburgh PA 15219

SILVERMAN, NEIL IRWIN, obstetrician, gynecologist; b. N.Y.C., June 17, 1933; s. Mac and Florence (Kessman) S.; B.A., Dickinson Coll., 1954; M.D., U. Basel (Switzerland), 1960; m. Barbara Lee Frischman, Feb. 20, 1955; children—Sara Beth, David Sheldon. Rotating intern Kings County Hosp., Bklyn., 1961, research fellow in ob-gyn., 1962; resident in ob-gyn. Hahnemann Med. Coll. & Hosp., Phila., 1964-67, clin. sr. instr., 1966-70, clin. assoc. prof., 1970—; practice medicine specializing in ob-gyn., 1980-83; chmn. dept. gynecology Taylor Hosp.; mem. staff Crozer-Chester Hosp.; med. dir., pres. Reproductive Health and Counseling Ctr., Chester, Pa. Served to capt. M.C., U.S. Army, 1962-64. Diplomate Am. Bd. Ob-Gyn. Fellow Am. Coll. Ob-Gyn., Royal Coll. Ob-Gyn. (assoc.); mem. Am. Fedn. State Med. Bds., AMA, Pa. Med. Soc., Delaware County Med. Soc., Pan-Am. Med. Assn., Royal Coll. Medicine, Leica Hist. Soc. Am. Democrat. Jewish. Clubs: Jaguar, Jaguar Drivers. Home: 2 Nicole Dr Media PA 19063 Office: 204 E Chester Pike Ridley Park PA 19078

SILVERMAN, SAM MENDEL, physicist, lawyer; b. N.Y.C., Nov. 16, 1925; s. Moshe Aaron and Gitel (Korenbaum) S.; B.Ch.E., CCNY, 1945; Ph.D., Ohio State U., 1952; J.D., Suffolk U., 1982; m. Jacqueline Greenberg, Sept. 12, 1948 (div. Apr. 1965); children—Ann, William, Nancy; m. 2d, Phyllis Rolfe, June 26, 1966; children—Gila, Aaron. Bar: Mass. 1982, N.Y. State 1983, U.S. Ct. Appeals (1st cir.) 1982, U.S. Dist. Ct. Mass. 1982, U.S. Supreme Ct. 1986. Assoc. Ohio State U., Columbus, 1952-55; asst. prof. chem. physics U. Toledo, 1955-57; research physicist Air Force Cambridge Research Labs. (named changed to Air Force Geophysics Lab. 1975), Bedford, Mass., 1957-80, chief polar atmospheric processes br. and dir. geopole obs., 1963-74, cons., 1980—; vis. research assoc. Queens U., Belfast, 1963-64; vis. prof. Osmania U., Hyderabad, India, 1965-66; mem. adv. bd. Inst. Space and Atmospheric Studies, U. Sask. (Can.), 1965-69; sr. research physicist Boston Coll., 1981—; co-chmn. interdivisional commn. history Internat. Assn. Geomagnetism and Aeronomy, 1987—. Mem. Town Meeting Lexington (Mass.), 1973-79, 84—. Served with USAAF, 1945-46. Fellow Am. Phys. Soc., Explorers Club; mem. Am. Geophys. Union (editor, History of Geophysics newsletter), Internat. Assn. Geomagnetism and Aeronomy (co-chmn. intradivisional commn. History). Contbr. articles to profl. jours. Home: 18 Ingleside Rd Lexington MA 02173

SILVERN, LEONARD CHARLES, engineering executive; b. N.Y.C., May 20, 1919; s. Ralph and Augusta (Thaler) S.; m. Gloria Marantz, June 1948 (div. Jan. 1968); 1 son, Ronald; m. 2d, Elisabeth Beeny, Aug. 1969 (div. Oct. 1972); m. Gwen Taylor, Nov. 1985. B.S. in Physics, L.I. U., 1946; M.A., Columbia U., 1948, Ed.D., 1952. Tng. supr. U.S. Dept. Navy, N.Y.C., 1939-49; tng. dir. exec. dept. N.Y. Div. Safety, Albany, 1949-55; resident engring. psychologist Lincoln Lab., M.I.T. for RAND Corp., Lexington, 1955-56; engr., dir. edn., tng., research labs. Hughes Aircraft Co., Culver City, Calif., 1956-62; dir. human performance engring. lab., cons. engring. psychologist to v.p. tech. Northrop Norair, Hawthorne, Calif., 1962-64; prin. scientist, v.p., pres. Edn. and Tng. Cons. Co., Los Angeles, 1964-80, Sedona, Ariz., 1980, pres. Systems Engring. Labs. div., 1980—; cons. hdqrs. Air Tng. Command USAF, Randolph AFB, Tex., 1964-68, Electronic Industries Assn., Washington, 1963-69, Edn. Research and Devel. Center, U. Hawaii, 1970-74, Center Vocat. and Tech. Edn., Ohio State U., 1972-73, Council for Exceptional Children, 1973-74, Canadore Coll. Applied Arts and Tech., Ont., Can., 1974-76, Centro Nacional de Productividad, Mexico City, 1973-75, N.S. Dept. Edn., Halifax, 1975-79, Aeronutronic Ford-Ford Motor Co., 1975-76, Nat. Tng. Systems Inc., 1976-81, Nfld. Public Service Commn., 1978, Legis. Affairs Office of U.S. Dept. Agr., 1980, Rocky Point Techs., 1986; adj. prof. edn., public adminstrn. U. So. Calif. Grad. Sch., 1957-65; vis. prof. computer scis. U. Calif. Extension Div., Los Angeles, 1963-72. Dist. ops. officer, disaster communications service Los Angeles County Sheriff's Dept., 1973-75, dist. communications officer, 1975-76; bd. dirs. SEARCH, 1976—; mem. adv. com. West Sedona Community Plan of Yavapai County, 1986-88; councilman City of Sedona, 1988—. Served with USNR, 1944-46. Registered profl. engr., Calif. Mem. IEEE (sr.), Am. Psychol. Assn., Am. Radio Relay League (life), Friendship Vets. Fire Engine Co. (hon.), Soc. Wireless Pioneers (life), Quarter Century Wireless Assn. (life), Sierra Club, Sedona Westerners., Assn. Bldg. Coms. (chmn. bd. dirs. Sedona chpt., 1986—), Nature Conservance, Ariz. Ctr. Law in Pub. Interest. Contbg. editor Ednl. Tech., 1968-73, 81-85; reviewer Computing Revs., 1962—. Contbr. numerous articles to profl. jours. Office: PO Box 2085 Sedona AZ 86336

SILVERSTONE, LEON MARTIN, pedodontist, cariologist, educator; b. London, May 21, 1939; came to U.S., 1976; s. Jack Stanley and Sadie (Osen) S.; m. Susan Petyan, Dec. 20, 1964; children: Samantha, Ruth, Mark. Student, Queen Mary Coll., London, 1958-59; L.D.S., U. Leeds, U.K., 1963, B.Ch.D., 1964, D.D.Sc., 1971; L.D.S., Royal Coll. Surgeons, Eng., 1964; Ph.D., U. Bristol, Eng., 1967; postgrad., U. London, 1969-76. House surgeon Leeds Dental Hosp., Eng., 1963-64; research fellow Med. Research Council Unit, Bristol Dental Sch., 1964-67; lectr. in dental surgery U. Bristol, 1967-68; sr. lectr. in child dental health Med. Coll., London Hosp., 1969-75, reader in preventive and pediatric dentistry, 1975-76; cons. London Hosp., 1973-76; vis. Lasby prof. Dental Sch. U. Minn., Mpls., 1974-75; prof., head div. cariology Dows Inst. Dental Research, Coll. Dentistry, U. Iowa, Iowa City, 1976-82; assoc. dean for research Dental Sch. U. Colo. Health Scis. Ctr., Denver, 1982—; dir. Oral Scis. Research Inst. U. Colo. Health Scis. Ctr., 1986—; cons. Pan Am. Health Orgn., 1973—; cons. dental research VA, 1978—; mem. study sect. and program adv. com. NIH/Nat. Inst. Dental Research, 1976—, chmn. subcom. on dental caries, 1982—. Mem. editorial bd. Lanis Research, 1976-86; contbr. chpts. to books, articles in field to profl. publs. Recipient A.B. Bofors prize in child dental health, 1971, ORCA-ROLEX research prize, 1973, Disting. award in Child Dental Health, 1981; NIH/Nat. Inst. Dental Research research grantee, 1976—. Mem. European Orgn. Caries Research (mem. bd., sci. councillor 1971—, pres. 1977-79), Internat. Assn. Dental Research (pres. cariology group 1982—, Disting. Scientist award 1984), Am. Assn. Dental Research (pres. cariology group chpt. 1982-83, chmn. publs. com. 1985—), Brit. Dental Assn., Internat. Assn. Dentistry for Children (exec. com. 1972-79, jour. editor 1971-79), AAAS, Soc. Exptl. Biology and Medicine, Space Medicine Com., AAUP, Am. Acad. Pedodontics, Sigma Xi. Home: 1300 S Potomac St #110 Aurora CO 80012 Office: U Colo Health Scis Ctr Campus Box C286 4200 E 9th Ave Denver CO 80262

SILVESTRI, UMBERTO, telecommunications and electronics holding company executive; b. Rome, Sept. 17, 1932; Diploma in English, Davies's Sch., Cambridge, Eng., 1953; grad. in law, U. Rome, 1955; grad. in polit. scis. U. Turin, 1960. Mem. staff operating dept. Brit. European Airways, Rome, 1952-54, acctng. dept. Linee Aeree Italiane, Rome, 1954-57, comml. and internat. relations dept., Alitalia, 1957-58; with STET, Società Finanziaria Telefonica, Rome, 1958-73, 76—, vice gen. mgr., 1976-82, gen. mgr., sec. gen., 1982—; vice gen. mgr. Societe Italiana per l'Esercizio Telefonico, Rome, 1974-75. Author: Una vita lontana, 1976; Il mondo dei saggi, 1979; La russa inglese, 1983. Served to 2d lt. Italian Air Force, 1955-56. Mem. Amnesty Internat., Mem. cons. com. INSEAD Bus. Sch., Fontainebleau, 1977, Johns Hopkins U., Bologna Center, 1983. Mem. Elettronica San Giorgio SpA (vice chmn.), Società Italiana per l'Esercizio Telefonico (exec. com., dir.), Società Italiana Telecomunicazioni S pA (exec. com.), Centro Studi e Laboratori di Telecomunicazioni SpA (dir.), Società Mutua di Assicurazioni (dir.), Scuola Superiore Guglielmo Reiss Romoli (dir.), Associazione Sindacale Intersind (dir.), Istituto per la Formazione e l'Aggiornamento Professionale, Société Financiere pour les Télécommunications et l'Electronique, SELENIA (pres. 1987), CEDEP, LUISS Univ. Office: Selenia SpA, Via Tiburtina 1231, 00131 Rome Italy

SILVIA, HER MAJESTY THE QUEEN OF SWEDEN, Queen of Sweden; b. Heidelberg, Fed. Republic of Germany, Dec. 23, 1943; came to Sweden, 1976; d. Walther and Alice (de Toledo) Sommerlath; m. Carl XVI Gustaf His Majesty the King of Sweden, June 19, 1976; children: Victoria, Carl Philip, Madeleine. Cert. as Spanish interpreter Sprachen-Dolmetsch Inst., München, Fed. Republic Germany, 1969. Chief hostess organizing com. Olympic Games, München, 1971-72; dep. head of protocol organizing com. Olympic Games, Innsbruck, Austria, 1973-76. Named Hon. Pres. Swedish Athletic Assn., 1977. Mem. Royal Wedding fund (pres. 1976—). Home and Office: Royal Palace, Stockholm Sweden

SIM, PENG CHOON, manufacturers representative; b. Singapore, Dec. 20, 1932; s. Ban Chye and Lian Keow (Koh) S.; sr. Cambridge cert. Anglo Chinese Sch., Ipoh, 1951; m. Alice Chong Swee Kheng, Nov. 21, 1958; children—Rita, Koon Weng, Grace, Su-San. Storekeeper, Barlow & Co., Ltd., Kuala Lumpur, Malaysia, 1952; med. rep. Allen & Hanburys, Ltd., Singapore, 1953-56; mng. dir. H. Rogers & Co., Ltd., Kuala Lumpur, 1957-63; chmn., mng. dir. Polychem (M) Sdn. Bhd., Kuala Lumpur, 1967—, N.P. King Pte., Ltd., Singapore, 1970—, N.P. King (HK), Ltd., Hong Kong, 1970—; dir. Sri Timor Oilfield Supplies & Equipment Sendirian Berhad. Vice chmn. Kwan Inn Teng Found., Petaling Jaya, Malaysia, 1980-81; dir. Selangor Tung Shin Hosp., Kuala Lumpur, 1981—, Malaysian Carbon Sdn Bhd. Port Dickson, Selangor, 1988. Buddhist. Office: 7500 A Beach Rd, #10-303/305 The Plaza, Singapore 0719, Singapore

SIM, STEPHEN SZE HIAN, advertising executive; b. Singapore, Jan. 29, 1954; arrived in Eng., 1956.; s. Soon Seng and Siew (Lan) S.; m. Jane Frances Stimson; children: Rachel Li Ming, Theresa Li Hsa, Jonathan Juen Fa, Nicholas Juen Wen. Student, Westminster City Coll., 1965-70. Prodn. control exec. J. Walter Thompson, London, 1972-75; prodn. exec. Golley Slater, London, 1975-78; progress controller Saatchi, Saatchi Garland Compton, London, 1978-81; prodn. mgr. RPG, Gloucester, Eng., 1981-84, Target Advt., Cheltenham, 1984—. Home: 213 Stroud Rd, Gloucester GL1 5JU, England

SIMAPICHAICHETH, PRATAK, real estate developer, researcher, valuer; b. Bangkok, Thailand, June 6, 1941; s. Hui and Lang Simpichaicheth; married; 1 child, Weeratos. B.Econ., Thammasat U., Bangkok, 1961; MBA, Victoria U., Wellington, New Zealand, 1964. Dir. DTEC Lang. Inst., Ministry of Nat. Devel., Bangkok, 1966-72; mgr. Trok Chan br. Thai Mil. Bank, Bangkok, 1972-77; mng. dir. Bangkok Friendship Credit Foncier, 1977-81; pres. Krung Thai Health Ins. Co., Bangkok, 1981; former chmn., chief exec. officer Thai Engring. & Mgmt., Bangkok, Thai Real Estate Co., Bangkok; chmn., chief exec. officer Town Home Co., Bangkok, 1981—; bd. dirs. Thai Exim Co. Ltd., Bangkok, Group of Thai Cons. Co., Bangkok; cons. Padco Bangkok Land Study; chmn. Suan-Bangkhen Community Co-op. Bangkok; mem. study team Applied Research for Thai Govt., 1981. Bd. dirs. Indsl. Authority of Thailand, Bangkok, Econ. sect. Nat. Research Council, Bangkok, Chulalongkorn U. Social Research Inst.; mem. Nat. Housing Policy Com., Bangkok. Mem. Credit Foncier Trade Assn. (charter pres. 1975-77), Asean Assn. Planning and Housing (council mem. 1982—), AAPH (hon. treas.), Asean Valuers Assn. (hon. sec.-gen.), Thai Real Estate Assn. (v.p.). Lodge: Rotary (pres. Bangkok chpt. 1986-87). Home: 1236 Soi 43 Klongchan, Bangkok Thailand 10240 Office: Thai Real Estate Co Ltd, 32/13-15 Asoke Rd, Bangkok 10110, Thailand

SIME, DAVID, investment banker; b. Bklyn., Mar. 1, 1931; s. David and Maybelle Ottilie (Mader) S.; B.A., Wesleyan U., Middletown, Conn., 1953; student U. Edinburgh (Scotland), 1952; M.B.A., Babson Coll., 1960; m. Joann Pacino, Feb. 4, 1963; children—Debra Ann, Pamela Jeanne, Dana Evelyn. With Mfrs. Hanover Trust Co., N.Y.C., 1960-74, asst. v.p., 1968-72, v.p., 1972-74; v.p. fin. Universal Natural Resources, Ltd., Beirut, Lebanon, 1974-76; asso. First Fla. Holding Corp., Pompano Beach, 1977; dir. corp. devel. Thiokol Corp., Newtown, Pa., 1977-81; chmn. bd. Growth Ventures, Inc., Washington Crossing, Pa., 1981—; chmn. bd. Tigerville Service, Inc., 1966-78. Served with U.S. Army, 1954-58. Recipient Brotherhood award N.Y.C. Black Chs., 1973. Mem. Newcomen Soc. N.Am., Assn. Corp. Growth (sec. N.Y. 1976-77). Republican. Editor: Directory of Business Opportunities, 1968-71. Home: 17 Bailey Dr Buckland Valley Farms Washington Crossing PA 18977 Office: Hdqrs Complex 1077-6 River Rd Washington Crossing PA 18977

SIMENON, GEORGES, novelist; b. Liege, Belgium, Feb. 13, 1903; s. Desire and Henriette (Brull) S.; grad. Coll. Saint-Servais, Liege, 1917; m. Regine Renchon (div.); m. 2d, Denise Ouimet, June 22, 1950; children—Marc, Jean, Marie-Georges, Pierre. Novelist, Paris, 1921—; creator character Supr. Maigret, 1929, writer 80 novels about the character; author more than 200 novels under 17 different pseudonyms, 80 Maigret novels and 131 non-detective novels; works translated into 55 langs.; 50 novels adapted into films; non-fiction works include When I was Old; Letter to my Mother, 1974; Mé moires Intimes, 1981; 21 vols. daily recs. of thoughts, memoirs, souvenirs. Address: 12 Ave des Figuiers, 1007 Lausanne Switzerland

SIMENSEN, BJORN ERIK, opera administrator; b. Lillehammer, Norway, June 28, 1947; s. Steinar and Astrid (Sand) S.; m. Gerd Hanssen, June 25, 1977; 1 child, Bjorn Martin. Journalist Sunnmorsposten, Aalesund, Norway, 1966-73; head cultural office Sandefjord Mcpl., 1973-80; gen. mgr. Gothenburg Symphony Orch., Sweden, 1980-84, Norwegian Opera, Oslo, 1984—. Office: Den Norske Opera, Storgat 23 C, 0184 Oslo Norway

SIMEON NEGRIN, ROSA ELENA, Cuban physician, educator; b. Havana, June 17, 1943; married; 1 child. M.D., U. Havana, 1973. Chief dept. virology Nat. Ctr. Scientific Research, 1970-75, mem. scientific commn., 1970-75, scientific council, 1971-73, chief microbiol. div., 1974-76, pres. agrl. br., 1975-81; pres. scientific council Nat. Ctr. Agrl. Health, 1976-81, agrl. br., 1977-81; mem. Assessor Council, 1981-83, agrl. br., 1981-85; dir. CENSA, 1985; pres. Acad. Scis., Cuba, 1985; prof., lectr., cons. in veterinary medicine including Nat. Ctr. Animal Health. Contbr. articles to profl. jours. Recipient Anniversary medal U. Havana, 1980; France medal U. D'Alfort, 1980; medal of merit, Czechoslovakia, 1981; medal Agrl. Syndicat of Czechoslovakia, 1983; Order of Marianna Grajales, 1985. Address: Academia de Ciencias de Cuba, Industria y San Jose, Zona 2, Havana Cuba

SIMES, NATHAN PARKER, investment management company; b. Tokyo, Dec. 17, 1952; s. Stephen Hardy Simes and Sachiko (Nakamura) Abe; m. Shizuko Egashira, Nov. 23, 1979; 1 child, Thomas Hardy. BS, U.S. Internat. U., San Diego, 1976; MBA, Harvard U., 1981. Export clk. Matsukawa & Assocs., Los Angeles, 1976-77; customer service clk. Kintetsu World Express, Los Angeles, 1977, supr. customer service, 1978, account exec., 1978, mgr. sales, 1979; fin. analyst Beckman Instruments, Fullerton, Calif., summer 1980; research analyst Capital Group, Los Angeles, 1981-85; v.p. research Capital Group, Tokyo, 1985-87, v.p. mktg., 1987—. Mem. Internat. Soc. Fin. Analysts (founding mem. 1986—), Assn. Investment Mgmt. Sales Execs. Club: Harvard (Tokyo). Office: Capital Internat KK, 1-1-7 Uchisaiwaicho Chiyoda-ku, Tokyo 100, Japan

SIMINI, JOSEPH PETER, accountant, financial consultant, author, former educator; b. Buffalo, Feb. 15, 1921; s. Paul and Ida (Moro) S.; B.S., St. Bonaventure U., 1940, B.B.A., 1949; M.B.A., U. Calif.-Berkeley, 1957; D.B.A., Western Colo. U., 1981; m. Marcelline McDermott, Oct. 4, 1968. Insp. naval material Bur. Ordnance, Buffalo and Rochester, N.Y., 1941-44; mgr. Paul Simini Bakery, Buffalo, 1946-48; internal auditor DiGiorgio (Fruit) Corp., San Francisco, 1950-51; tax accountant Price Waterhouse & Co., San Francisco, 1953; sr. accountant Richard L. Hanlin, C.P.A., San Francisco, 1953-54; prof. accounting U. San Francisco, 1954-79, emeritus prof., 1983—; mem. rev. bd. Calif. Bd. Accountancy, 1964-68. Mem. council com. Boy Scouts Am., Buffalo, San Francisco, 1942-65, Scouters Key, San Francisco council; bd. dirs. United Bay Area Fund Drive, U. San Francisco, 1960, Nat. Italian Am. Found., Washington, 1979—. Served to ensign USNR, 1944-46. Recipient Bacon-McLaughlin medal St. Bonaventure U., 1940, Laurel Key, 1940; Outstanding Tchr. award Coll. Bus. Adminstrn., U. San Francisco, 1973; Disting. Tchr. award U. San Francisco, 1975, Joseph Peter Simini award, 1977. Crown Zellerbach Found. fellow, 1968-69; Gold Medal Associazione Piemontese nel Mondo, Turin, Italy, 1984; decorated Knight Order of Merit, Republic of Italy, 1982. C.P.A., Calif. Mem. Am. Inst. C.P.A.s, Calif. Soc. C.P.A.s (past chmn. ednl. standards, student relations com. San Francisco chpt.), Nat. Assn. Accts. (past pres. San Francisco chpt.), Am. Acctg. Assn., Am. Mgmt. Assn. (lectr. 1968-78), Am. Arbitration Assn. (comml. arbitrator), Delta Sigma Pi (past pres. San Francisco alumni club), Beta Gamma Sigma. Roman Catholic. Clubs: Il Cenacolo (past pres.), Toastmasters (pres. Magic Word). Lodges: K.C., Rotary. Author: Accounting Made Simple, 1967, 2d rev. edit., 1987; Cost Accounting Concepts for Nonfinancial Executives, 1976; Become Wealthy! Using Tax Savings and Real Estate Investments, 1982. Tech. editor, Accounting Essentials, 1972. Patentee Dial-A-Trig and Verbum Est card game. Home: 977 Duncan St San Francisco CA 94131 Office: PO Box 31420 San Francisco CA 94131

SIMIS, THEODORE LUCKEY, information technology executive; b. N.Y.C., June 17, 1924; s. Theodore William Ernest and Helen (Luckey) S.; m. Laura Cushman Ingraham, Sept. 8, 1946; children—Nancy Simis Ricca, Theodore Steven, Karen Simis Woods, June Simis Sobocinski. B.S., NYU, 1950, M.B.A., 1952. With Bell System, 1941-79; various positions, then asst. v.p. AT&T, 1941, 62-64, 68-69, 70-79; various positions, then v.p. N.Y. Telephone Co., 1946-52, 65-67; various positions, then v.p. ops. N.J. Bell Telephone Co., 1952-62, 69-70; sr. v.p. E.F. Hutton, Sarasota, Fla., 1982-87; pres. Pvt. Transatlantic Telecommunication System Inc., McLean, Va., 1987—; dir. Internat. Mobile Machine Corp., Phila. and Washington, Suncoast Communication Inc., Sarasota; pres., dir. Tel-Optic, Washington; dir., vice chmn. XMX Corp., Burlington, Mass.; vis. Nieman fellow Harvard U., 1977. Mem. Republican Nat. Com., 1981—. Served to 1st lt. U.S. Army, 1942-53, ETO. Mem. N.Y. Acad. Scis., U.S. C. of C. Lutheran. Club: NYU (bd. dirs. 1960—). Home: 6025 Manasota Key Rd Englewood FL 33533 Office: Pvt Transatlantic 8200 Greensboro Dr McLean VA 22102

SIMIU, EMIL, structural engineer; b. Bucharest, Romania, Apr. 8, 1934; came to U.S., 1963; s. Bernhard and Sophie (Finkelstein) S.; BS, Faculty Civil Engring., Bucharest, 1956; MS, Bklyn. Poly. Inst., 1968; PhD, Princeton U., 1971; m. Devra Beck, Dec. 29, 1970; children: Erica-Ann, Michael-Paul. Project engr. Project-Bucharest, 1956-62; structural engr. Bechtel Corp., San Francisco, 1964-65, Ammann & Whitney N.Y.C., 1965-68; research engr. Nat. Bur. Standards, Washington, 1973-88. Recipient Fed. Engr. of Yr. award, 1984; Nat. Bur. Standards-NRC postdoctoral research assoc., 1971-73; Nat. Bur. Standards fellow, 1988—. Mem. ASCE, Sigma Xi. Author: (with R.H. Scanlan) An Introduction to Wind Engineering, 1978, 2d edit., 1986, Russian transl., 1984. Home: 6031 Valerian Ln Rockville MD 20852 Office: Ctr for Bldg Tech Nat Engring Lab Nat Bur Standards Gaithersburg MD 20899

SIMMONDS, KENNEDY ALPHONSE, prime minister of St. Christopher and Nevis; b. Apr. 12, 1936; s. Arthur Simmonds and Bronte Clarke. Ed. U. West Indies. Intern Kingston Pub. Hosp., Jamaica, 1963; registrar in internal medicine Princess Margaret Hosp., Bahamas, 1966-68; resident in anesthesiology, Pitts., 1968-69; pvt. practice medicine, St. Kitts and Anguilla, 1964-66, St. Kitts, 1969-80; founder mem. People's Action Movement, 1965, pres., 1976; mem. Parliament, 1979; premier, 1980-83; minister of home and external affairs, trade, devel. and industry, 1980-84, minister of fin., home and fgn. affairs, 1984; prime minister of St. Christopher and Nevis, 1983—, minister of external affairs and fin., 1988 . Fellow Am. Coll. Anesthesiologists. Address: Office of the Prime Minister, Basseterre, Saint Kitts West Indies *

SIMMONDS, KENNETH, management educator; b. Christchurch, N.Z., Feb. 17, 1935; s. Herbert Marshall and Margaret (Trevurza) S.; m. Nancy Miriam Bunai, June 19, 1960; children—John, Jane, Peter. B.Com., U. N.Z., 1956, M.Com. with 1st class hons., 1960; D.B.A., Harvard U., 1963; Ph.D., London Sch. Econs., 1965; M.G.C.E. (hon.), U. Guipuzcoa, Spain, 1974.

Clk., Guardian Trust Co., Wellington, N.Z., 1950-53; asst. co. sec. Gordon & Gotch Ltd., Wellington, 1953-55; chief acct. William Cable Ltd., Wellington, 1955-59; cons. Arthur D. Little Inc., Cambridge, Mass., 1959-60; cons. Harbridge House, Inc., Boston, 1962-64; asst. prof. internat. bus. Ind. U., Bloomington, 1964-66; prof. mktg. U. Manchester, Eng., 1966-69; Ford Found. prof. internat. bus. U. Chgo., 1974-75; prof. mktg. and internat. bus. London Grad. Sch. Bus., 1969—; mktg. advisor Internat. Pub. Corp., 1967-78; dir. Brit. Steel Corp., 1970-72, E. Midland Allied Press Plc., 1981—; chmn. Planners Collaborative, 1985—; dir. MIL Research Group Plc., 1986—; gov. London Bus. Sch., 1980-86. Author: International Business and Multinational Enterprises, 1973, 4th edit. 1988; Case Problems in Marketing, 1973; Strategy and Marketing, 1982, 2d edit., 1986; Short MArketing Cases, 1987. Mem. The Textile Council U.K., 1968-70; com. mem. Social Sci. Research Council U.K., 1971-72; com. mem. Confedn. Brit. Industry, 1971-74; mem. Elec. Engring. Econ. Devel. Com. U.K., 1982-86. Fulbright scholar, 1959; Smith Mundt scholar, 1959; U. N.Z., traveling scholar, 1960; Ford Found. fellow, 1961; Drapers Co. lectr., 1975; Inter-U. Council fellow, 1978; Social Sci. Research fellow, 1980; Croucher Found. fellow, 1983. Fellow N.Z. Soc. Accts., Inst. Chartered Secs. and Adminstrs., Chartered Inst. Cost and Mgmt. Accts., Inst. Mktg., Acad. Internat. Bus.; mem. N.Z. Inst. Cost and Mgmt. Accts., Am. Econ. Assn., Am. Mktg. Assn., Internat. Advt. Assn. Office: London Bus Sch, Regents Park, London NW1 4SA, England

SIMMONDS, KENNETH ROYSTON, law educator, consultant; b. Watford, Eng., Nov. 11, 1927; s. Frederick John and Alice (Coxhill) S.; m. Gloria Mary Tatchell, July 26, 1958; children: Caroline Jane, Jeremy Kenneth. BA with hons., U. Oxford, Eng., 1951; MA, D. of Philosophy, U. Oxford, 1955. Mem. law faculty U. Wales, U. Liverpool, Queens U. of Belfast, Eng., 1954-63; dep. dir. Brit. Inst. Internat. Comparative Law, London, 1963-65, dir., 1965-76, hon. dir., 1976-82; prof. internat. law U. London, Queen Mary Coll., 1976—, dean faculty of laws, 1980-84; Gresham prof. law City of London, 1986—; Mem. law adv. com. The Brit. Council, 1966-86; vis. prof. McGill U. Sch Law, Montreal, Can., 1963, U. Wyoming, 1969, Free U. Brussels, 1972-73, Free U. Amsterdam, 1980—; named Klein disting. vis. prof. No. Ky. U., 1985, Florence Thelma Hall Centennial vis. prof. U. Tex., Austin, 1986-87. Gen. editor: The International and Comparative Law Quarterly, 1966-86; co-editor: The Common Market Law Rev., 1967—; mem. editorial bd., British Yearbook of Internat. Law., 1966—, The Internat. Lawyer, 1987—; contbr. over 100 articles to internat. profl. jours. Decorated Chevalier de l'Ordre Nat. de Merite France, 1973, Commdrs. Cross of the Order of Merit Fed. Republic Germany, 1983; recipient Carl H. Fulda award U. Tex., 1987. Mem. U.K. Nat. Com. Comparative Law (sec. 1959-66, chmn. 1973-76), Internat. Assn. Comparative Law (pres. 1975-76). Home: The Oast Barn Bells Forstal, Throwley near Faversham, Kent ME13 OJS, England Office: Queen Mary Coll, Univ London Law Dept, London E1 4NS, England

SIMMONS, BRADLEY WILLIAMS, pharmaceutical company executive; b. Paterson, N.J., Apr. 16, 1941; s. John Williams and Grace Law (Van Hassel) S.; m. Diane Louise Simmons, June 6, 1964 (div. May 1986); children: Susan, Elizabeth, Jonathan; m. Cheryl Lynne Westrum, Aug. 16, 1987. AB, Columbia U., 1963, BSChemE, 1964; MBA, NYU, 1974. Chem. engr. Pfizer, Inc., N.Y.C., 1969-73, analyst, 1973-76, dir. planning, 1976-79; dir., bus. analysis Bristol-Myers, N.Y.C., 1979-82, v.p., 1982-85; pres. Oncogen, Seattle, 1985—; adj. prof. Farleigh Dickinson U., Teaneck, N.J., 1974-84. Council mem. borough of Allendale, N.J., 1977-82; mem. Bergen County (N.J.) com., 1974-82. Served to lt. USN, 1964-69, Vietnam. Republican. Mem. Unity Ch. Home: 700 Crockett Pl #402 Seattle WA 98109 Office: Oncogen 3005 1st Ave Seattle WA 98121

SIMMONS, CARL KENNETH, cooperative executive; b. Kingman, Ind., Dec. 5, 1914; s. Claud Elmer and Sylvia Ethyl (Myers) S.; grad. exec. devel. program Ind. U., 1959; m. Allice Lucille Weaver, Dec. 16, 1939; 1 child, Erma Jane (Mrs. Thomas Stephen Barlow). Petroleum dept. mgr. Fountain County Coop., Veedersburg, Ind., 1936-40; dist. mgr. Ind. Farm Bur. Coop., Indpls., 1946-47; treas., mgr. Delaware County Coop., Muncie, 1940-46, 48-86; emeritus gen. mgr., treas. 1986—. Mem. Mayor's Citizens Com. Muncie, 1962; bd. dirs. Delaware County Airport Authority, 1972—, pres., 1983—. Mem. Ind. Flying Farmers. Lodge: Masons (32 degree). Club: Muncie Rifle. Home: 225 E Centennial St Muncie IN 47303 Office: 2101 N Granville Ave Muncie IN 47305

SIMMONS, CAROLINE THOMPSON, civic worker; b. Denver, Aug. 22, 1910; d. Huston and Caroline Margaret (Cordes) Thompson; AB, Bryn Mawr Coll., 1931; MA (hon.) Amherst Coll.; m. John Farr Simmons, Nov. 11, 1936; children: John Farr (dec.), Huston T., Malcolm M. Chmn. women's com. Corcoran Gallery Art, 1965-66; vice chmn. women's com. Smithsonian Assos., 1969-71; pres. Decatur House Council, 1963-71; mem. bd. Nat. Theatre, 1979-80; trustee Washington Opera, 1955-65; bd. dirs. Fgn. Student Service Council, 1956-79; mem. Washington Home Bd., 1955-60; bd. dirs. Smithsonian Friends of Music, 1977-79; commr. Nat. Mus. Am. Art, 1979—; mem. Folger com. Folger Shakespeare Library, 1979-86, trustee emeritus, 1986— (recipient award for eminent service, 1986); mem. Washington bd. Am. Mus. in Britain, 1970—; bd. dirs. Found. Preservation of Historic Georgetown, 1975—; trustee Marpat Found., 1987—, Amherst Coll., 1979-81, Dacor-Bacon House Found.; v.p. internat. council Mus. Modern Art, N.Y.C., 1978—; mem. council Phillips Collection, 1982—; bd. dirs. Alliance Francaise. Mem. Soc. Women Geographers. Presbyterian. Clubs: Sulgrave, Chevy Chase. Address: 1508 Dumbarton Rock Ct Washington DC 20007

SIMMONS, CLINTON CRAIG, human resources executive; b. Cleve., Nov. 25, 1947; s. Benjamin F. and Catharin (Thornton) R.; m. Cheryl LeRoy, June 16, 1973; 1 child, Eric. BBA, Miami U., Oxford, Ohio, 1969; grad. quality mgmt. course Winter Park, Fla., 1986. Cert. quality edn. system instr. Specialist employee and community relations Euclid Lamp Plant, Gen. Electric Co., Cleve., 1970-75; employee and indsl. relations rep. Bailey Controls Co., Wickliffe, Ohio, 1975-78; mgr., coll. recruiting Gen. Tire and Rubber, Akron, Ohio, 1978-81, profl. staffing coordinator, 1981-82; regional human resource mgr. Gilbane Bldg. Co., Cleve. 1982-86, human resource mgr. Western regions, 1987—. Past chmn. orgn. and extension com. Newton D. Baker Dist., Greater Cleve. council Boy Scouts Am., 1970-71; mem. Human Resource Com. for Greater Cleve. United Way. Bd. Edn. commr. Villa Angria Acad., Cleve., 1983—, pres., 1986-88 (U.S. Edn. Dept. award 1987); founder, advisor Explorer Post, Gilbane Bldg. Co., Cleve., 1984-88; asst. v.p., dir. human resources St. Alexis Hosp. Med. Ctr., Cleve., 1988—; mem. adv. bd. Cath. Social Services Cuyahoga County; mem. urban regional bd. Cath. Edn. Cleve., 1986; trustee Maratia Montessori Sch, Harambee Services Orgn. Cleve., 1987—. Recipient commendation Nat. Alliance of Bus., Akron, 1979, Community Service award WJW-Northwest Orient Airlines, 1975. Mem. Cleve. Employee's Equal Opportunity Assn., Am. Soc. Personnel Adminstrn., Mid-West Coll. Placement Assn. (chmn. rubber industry com. 1979-81), Ctr. for Human Services (v.p., trustee), Indsl. Relations Research Assn., NAACP, Urban League of Cleve., Greater Cleve. Hosp. Assn. (pension and benefits coms.), Alpha Phi Alpha. Democrat. Roman Catholic. Home: 24400 Emery Rd Warrensville Heights OH 44128 Office: St Alexis Hosp Med Ctr 5163 Broadway Cleveland OH 44127

SIMMONS, DAVID ROY, ethnologist, writer; b. Aukland, New Zealand, Sept. 6, 1930; s. Wilfred Henshall and Mabel Clair (Bedingfield) S.; m. Winifred Mary Harwood, Aug. 6, 1955; children: Christopher, Nigel. Diploma, Sorbonne U., Paris, 1953; diploma in Celtic studies, U. Rennes, Britanny, France, 1954; BA, U. Auckland, 1960, MA, 1962. Tchr. Dept. Edn., Auckland and Wellington, New Zealand, Bedford, Eng., 1955, Auckland, 1956-58, 60-61; asst. keeper in Anthropology Otago Mus., Dunedin, New Zealand, 1962, keeper in Anthropology, 1963-67; ethnologist Auckland Inst. and Mus., 1968-77, asst. dir., 1978-85. Author: The Great New Zealand Myth, 1976, Catalogue of Maori Artifacts in the Museums of Canada and the U.S.A., 1982, Whakairo: Maori Tribal Art, 1985 Ta Moko: The Art of Maori Tattooing, 1986, Iconography of New Zealand Maori Religion, 1986 (with others) The Art of the Pacific, 1982; contbr. numerous articles to profl. jours., 1959—. Mem. Auckland Inst. and Mus. (life), Royal Soc. New Zealand (life), Polynesian Soc. (council mem. 1979-85, Elsdon Best Meml. medal 1982, M.B.E. 1985). Home and Office: 12 Minto Rd, Remuera, Auckland 5, New Zealand

SIMMONS, EMMETT BRYSON, III, actor; b. Chgo., Apr. 6, 1953; s. Jimmy Bryson and Shirley (Edwards) S. B.S., Ill. State U., 1977; cert. Performing Arts Soc. Los Angeles, 1979, KIIS Broadcasting Profl. Workshop, 1980. Acct., Continental Bank, Chgo., 1970; newspaper columnist, radio-TV performer Ill. State U., 1971-75; urban devel. officer City of Bloomington, Ill., 1977-78; columnist Voice Newspaper, Ill., 1971-78; therapeutic house counselor Kaleidescope Inc., 1974; acctg. asst./staff talent CBS-TV Network, Los Angeles, 1978-81; adminstrv. asst./actor Columbia Pictures Industries, Inc., Hollywood, Calif., 1981—. Del. Nat. Black Polit. Convs., 1972-76; mem. P.U.S.H., Urban League, NAACP, SCLC, CORE. Mem. AFTRA. Home: 3221 W 109th St Inglewood CA 90303 Office: 2901 W Alameda Blvd Burbank CA 91505

SIMMONS, JOHN DEREK, securities analyst; b. Essex, Eng., July 17, 1931; s. Simon Leonard and Eve (Smart) S.; B.S., Columbia, 1956; M.B.A., Rutgers U., 1959; postgrad. N.Y.U., 1959-62; m. Rosalind Wellish, Mar. 5, 1961; children—Peter Lawrence, Sharon Leslie. Came to U.S., 1952. Chief cost accountant Airborne Accessories, Hillside, N.J., 1952-57; sr. cost analyst Curtiss-Wright Corp., Wood Ridge, N.J., 1957; sr. financial analyst internat. group Ford Motor Co., Jersey City, N.J., 1958-60; research asso. Nat. Assn. Accountants, N.Y.C., 1960-64; asst. to v.p. finance Air Reduction Co., Inc., 1965-67; mgr. corporate planning Anaconda Wire & Cable Co., N.Y.C., 1968; ind. financial cons., 1968-71; asso. cons. Rogers, Slade and Hill, Inc., N.Y.C., 1969-71; v.p., security analyst, economist Moore & Schley, Cameron & Co. (name now changed to Fourteen Research Corp.), 1972-81; v.p., security analyst Merrill Lynch Capital Markets, N.Y.C., 1981-88; security analyst Arnhold and S. Bleichroeder, Inc., N.Y.C., 1988—; lectr. profl. socs. and confs.; Lecturer Econs., mgmt., polit. sci. Rutgers U., 1957-64. Served to 1st lt. Brit. Army, 1950-52; granted personal coat of Arms By Queen Elizabeth II: manorial Lord of Ash., Suffolk, Eng. Mem. Am. Econ. Assn., Assn. Managerial Economists, Royal Econ. Soc., N.Y. Soc. Security Analysts. Contbr. articles on econs. of underdeveloped nations, polit. sci., mgmt., finance to U.S. and fgn. profl. and sci. jours. Home: 360 E 72d St New York NY 10021 Office: 45 Broadway New York NY 10006

SIMMONS, SAMUEL WILLIAM, retired public health official; b. Benton County, Miss., June 5, 1907; s. Britt L. and Ida E. (Pegram) S.; B.Sc. with honors, Miss. State U., 1931; A.M., George Washington U., 1934; Ph.D., Iowa State U., 1938; m. Lois Grantham, Aug. 5, 1928; children—Samuel William, Grant P. With U.S. Dept. Agr., Bur. Entomology, 1931-44; with USPHS, 1944-71, scientist to scientist dir., dir. Carter Meml. Lab., 1944-47, chief tech. devel. br., 1947-53, chief tech. br. communicable disease center 1953-66; chief pesticides program Nat. Ctr. for Disease Control, Atlanta, 1966-68; dir. div. pesticide community studies FDA, 1968-71; dir. div. pesticide community studies EPA, 1971-72, ret.; vis. lectr. tropical pub. health Harvard U., 1952-67; assoc. preventive medicine and community health Emory U., 1957-72; USPHS rep. Fed. Com. on Pest Control. Recipient Alumni Achievement award George Washington U., 1946, Alumni Centennial Citation award Iowa State U., 1958, Disting. Service medal USPHS, 1965, William Crawford Gorgas medal Assn. Mil. Surgeons U.S., 1968, Disting. Career award EPA, 1972. Hon. cons. Army Med. Library, 1940-53; adv. bd. Inst. Agrl. Medicine, U. Iowa Sch. Medicine, U.S.-Japan Com. on Sci. Cooperation. Diplomate Am. Bd. Microbiology. Fellow Am. Soc. Tropical Medicine and Hygiene (councilor 1953), Chem. Spltys. Mfrs. Assns. (interdepartmental com. pest control, subcom. vector control inter-agy. com. water resources, chmn. 1964-66), U.S.-Mex. Border Health Assn., WHO (chmn. com. on pesticides 1951, 56, 57), AMA (com. on insecticides 1950-59, com. on toxicology 1960), Research Soc. Am., Entomol. Soc. Am., Nat. Malaria Soc. (sec.-treas. 1951), Nat. Environ. Health Assn., Agrl. Research Inst., Am. Mosquito Control Assn., Armed Forces Pest Control Bd., Nat. Research Council, Nat. Assn. Watch and Clock Collectors (fellow, nat. dir. 1979-83, mem. awards com.), Sigma Xi, Phi Kappa Phi, Gamma Sigma Delta, Los Hidalgos. Contbr. over 80 articles to profl. jours.; editor and co-author: The Insecticide DDT and Its Significance, vol. II; contbr. to Human and Veterinary Medicine, 1959; author: (genealogies) Descendants of John Simmons of North Carolina, 1760, 1979, Samuel W. Simmons: An Autobiography, 1979; The Pegrams of Virginia and Descendants, 1688-1984, 1985. Home: 2050 Blackfox Dr NE Atlanta GA 30345

SIMMONS, TED CONRAD, writer; b. Seattle, Sept. 1, 1916; s. Conrad and Clara Evelyn (Beaudry) S.; student U. Wash., 1938-41, UCLA and Los Angeles State U., 1952-54, Oxford (Eng.) U., 1980; m. Dorothy Pauline Maltese, June 1, 1942; children—Lynn, Juliet. Drama critic Seattle Daily Times, 1942; indsl. writer, editor Los Angeles Daily News, 1948-51; contbr. Steel, Western Metals, Western Industry, 1951—; past poetry dir. Watts Writers Workshop; instr. Westside Poetry Center; asst. dir. Pacific Coast Writers Conf., Calif. State Coll. Los Angeles. Served with USAAF, 1942-46. Author: (poetry) Deadended, 1966; (novel) Middlearth, 1975; (drama) Greenhouse, 1977, Durable Chaucer, 1978, Rabelais and other plays, 1980, Dickeybird, 1981, Alice and Eve, 1983, Deja Vu, Deja Vu, 1986, The Box, 1987; writer short story, radio verse; book reviewer Los Angeles Times; contbr. poetry to The Am. Poet, Prairie Wings, Antioch Rev., Year Two Anthology; editor: Venice Poetry Company Presents, 1972.

SIMMS, DAVID JOHN, mathematics educator; b. Sankeshwar, India, Jan. 13, 1933; s. John Gerald and Eileen Mary (Goold-Verschoyle) S.; m. Anngret Erichson, July 16, 1965; children—Brendan Peter, Daniel Paul, Ciaran Knut. B.A., U. Dublin, 1955, M.A., 1958; Ph.D., U. Cambridge, Eng., 1960. Asst. in math., U. Glasgow, Scotland, 1958-60, lectr. in math., 1960-64; instr. math., Princeton U., N.J., 1962-63; lectr. pure math., Trinity Coll., U. Dublin, Ireland, 1964-73, fellow, 1972—, assoc. prof. pure math., 1973—; vis. prof. math., U. Bonn, Germany, 1966-67, 72-73, 78-80. Author: Lie Groups and Quantum Mechanics, 1968; (with others) Lectures on Geometric Quantization, 1976. Mem. Royal Irish Acad. (v.p. 1983-84, 87-88). Office: Sch Math U Dublin, Trinity Coll, Dublin 2 Ireland

SIMMS, JAMES ROBERT, physicist; b. Vinita, Okla., Dec. 5, 1924; s. Paul Otto and Meda (Hall) S.; m. Pauline Sue Blackwell, Aug. 12, 1950 (dec. 1969); 1 child, Suzanne Marie; m. Lanita Jayne Thiessen, Nov. 30, 1974 (dec. 1987). BS in Engring. Physics, U. Okla., 1950. Registered profl. engr., Md. Electronic engr. The Martin Co., Balt., 1950-56; systems engr. The Martin Co., Denver, 1956-61; mgr. electronics and systems engring. Fairchild, Hagerstown, Md., 1961-63; sr. tech. staff ITT Intelcom, Baileys Cross Roads, Va., 1963-67; program mgr. Systems Research Corp., Washington, 1967-70, dir. ops., 1970-71; program mgr. Gen. Elec., Valley Forge, Pa., 1971-73; cons. pvt. practice, Clarksville, Md., 1973-75; sr. assoc. Booz, Allen & Hamilton, Bethesda, Md., 1975-83; pres. Simms Industries Inc., Clarksville, 1983—; dir. Electronic Learning Facilitators, Bethesda, 1984. Author: A Measure of Knowledge, 1971, The Limits of Behavior: A Quantitative Social Theory, 1983. Contbr. articles to profl. jours. Inventor correlation missile guidance system. Bd. dirs. So. Howard County Democratic Club, Md., 1980-83, pres., 1979; county coordinator Com. to Elect Congresswoman Byron, 1978, 80, 82. Served with USN, 1943-46. Mem. IEEE, Soc. Gen. Systems Research, Am. Soc. Cybernetics, World Future Soc., Cherokee Nation of Okla. Methodist. Current work: Quantitative casual methodologies and theories in behavioral, social and political science; technology forecasting and assessment; communications; information systems; design of organizations; systems research and analysis. Subspecialties: Systems engineering; Information systems (Information science). Office: Simms Industries Inc 7413 Meadow View Circle Clarksville MD 21029 also: Cen Fla Research Park 12424 Research Pkwy Suite 305 Orlando FL 32826 also: Oak Manor Office Park Rt 206 PO Box 640 Dahlgren VA 22448

SIMMS, LEROY ALANSON, newspaper executive; b. Emelle, Ala., Sept. 17, 1905; s. John Thomas and Minnie Epes (Thomas) S.; m. Virginia Hammill, June 30, 1926 (dec.); m. Martha Alice Holliman, May 17, 1969; 1 dau., Lucie Grey Simms Grubbs (dec.). Student, U. Ill., 1924-25; L.H.D. (hon.), U. Ala., 1982. Reporter, Birmingham (Ala.) News, 1924-26; Reporter Tampa (Fla.) Morning Tribune, 1926-27; city editor Birmingham Post, 1927-28, mng. editor, 1929-31; asst. editor Newspaper Enterprise Assn., Cleve., 1931-32; day editor AP, Birmingham bur., 1933-38, Ala. corr., 1938-58; mng. editor Birmingham News, 1959-61; editor Huntsville (Ala.) Times, 1961-86, v.p., dir., 1963—, pub., 1964-85, chmn. bd., 1985—; v.p. Huntsville Indsl. Expansion Com. 1966-70, pres., 1970-71. Author: Road to War: Alabama Leaves the Union, 1960. Mem. Am., So. newspaper pubs. assns., Ala. Press Assn. (dir. 1964-66), Ala. A.P. Assn. (pres. 1965-66), Am. Soc. Newspaper Editors, C. of C. (dir.), Sigma Delta Chi (chmn. Ala. 1960), Theta Chi. Clubs: Rotarian, Huntsville Country, Heritage. Office: Huntsville Times Memorial Pkwy Huntsville AL 35807

SIMMS, NORMAN TOBY, humanities educator; b. Bklyn., July 4, 1940; arrived in New Zealand, 1970; s. Louis Maurice and CLaire (Herman) S.; m. Martha Kellerman, Nov. 25, 1965; children: Meliors Ruth, David Gawain. BA, Alfred (N.Y.) U., 1958-62; MA, Washington U., 1964, PhD, 1969. Lectr. U. Man., Winnipeg, 1966-69, asst. prof., 1969-70; sr. lectr. Waikato U., Hamilton, New Zealand, 1970—. Author: Runic Characters, 1986, Guide for the Perplexed, 1986, Silence and Invisibility, 1986; translator: Destinations, 1985. Fellow Inst. Eminescu; mem. New Zealand-Romanian Cultural Soc. (founder, sec. 1973), Folklore Soc., Council Nat. Lits. (adv. 1980), New Zealand Assn. Study Jewish Civilization (founder, exec. 1985). Jewish. Office: Outrigger Publishers Ltd, PO Box 1198, Hamilton New Zealand

SIMOENS, MARK HENRI, financial company executive; b. Kortryk, Flanders, Belgium, Oct. 22, 1950; m. Dierick Veerle; 1 child, Adinda. BS in Comml. Engring., Louvain U., Leuven, Belgium, 1973, MBA (hon.), 1978. Asst. controller Scott Paper Co., Bornem, Belgium, 1974-78; fin. exec. Med. Ctr., Kortryk, 1978-81; exec. dir. J. Deblaere, M. Simoens & Co., Kortryk, 1982-86, M. Simoens & Co., Kortryk, 1987—. Home: Doorniksesteenweg 200, 8500 Kortkyk Belgium Office: Kennedypark 29 B, 8500 Kortryk Belgium

SIMOENS, YVES, educator; b. Kinshasa, Zaire, May 10, 1942; arrived in Belgium, 1979; s. Gustave and Paula (Beukelaers) S. Maîtrise de lettres modernes, Faculté des Lettres, France, 1970; doctorate en Scis. Bibliques summa cum laude, Inst. Biblique Pontifical, Rome, 1980. Prof. Inst. d'Etudes Théologiques, Brussels, Belgium, 1979—. Contbr. articles to profl. jours. Mem. Comité de rédaction de la Nouvelle Revue Théologique. Home: Rue du College Saint-Michael 60, 1150 Brussels Belgium

SIMON, ARTHUR JAMES, plastics company executive; b. Bklyn., Feb. 12, 1927; s. Harry and Helen (Cline) S.; B.A., U. Ala., 1947; postgrad. Oxford U., 1947-48; M.B.A., U. Pa., 1949; m. Barbara Colby, July 11, 1955; children—Casey, Meri. Vice pres. Closure Research Assocs., Rutherford, N.J. 1950-62; dir. StaZon Fastener, Inc., N.Y.C., 1962-65; pres. Tho-Ro Products, Inc., Carlstadt, N.J., 1965—, Vistas in Plastics, Ltd., V.I., 1966-86, Eagle Button Co., East Rutherford, 1969—, Koala-T Classics, Paramus, N.J., 1978—, Calba Corp, Tancin, Pa., 1970—, Eagle Closure Corp., N.Y.C., 1971—; chief exec. officer Sir Steve Mfg. Corp., Clifton, N.J., 1972-85; chmn. F.A.C.T., Inc., Swarthmore, Pa., 1971—; pres. Forum for Advanced Closure Tech. Vice pres. Riverdale (N.Y.) Community Council, 1968-69; mem. Philanthropic 50 Assn.; v.p. Riverdale Little League, 1966-70. Served to capt. AUS, 1945-48, ETO. Decorated Bronze Star; recipient Cert. of Appreciation, City of N.Y., 1962. Mem. Am. Inst. Mgmt. (exec. council), Adminstrv. Mgmt. Soc. (regional v.p.), League of Presidents (bd. govs.), Soc. Plastics Industry, U. Ala. Alumni Assn. (pres. N.Y. chpt. 1987—), Phi Beta Kappa, Phi Eta Sigma. Clubs: New (Union, N.J.), B and T (New Rochelle, N.Y.); The New (Mountainside, N.J.); Quest Group (Ramsey, N.J.). Home: 89 Andrea Ln Westwood NJ 07675 Office: Eagle Button Co Inc 415 14th St Carlstadt NJ 07072

SIMON, BRADLEY ALDEN, librarian; b. Meriden, Conn., Mar. 9, 1929; s. Walter Henry and Rachel (Wetherbee) S.; student Shenandoah Coll., 1947-48; B.S., So. Conn. State Coll., 1951; M.S., Fla. State U., 1955; postgrad. U. Miami (Fla.), 1956-57, Ariz. State U., Tempe, 1965-66. Extension librarian, Ft. Meade, Md., 1955-56; base librarian Homestead AFB, Fla., 1956-57; asst. dir. libraries Pub. Library Charlotte and Mecklenburg County (N.C.), 1957-61; dir. libraries Volusia County Pub. Libraries, Daytona Beach, Fla., 1961-64; library cons. M. Van Buren, Inc., Charlotte, N.C., 1964; head librarian Central Piedmont Community Coll., Charlotte, 1964-65; cons. Colo. State Library, 1965-66; coordinator Ariz. Library Survey, Ariz. State U., 1966; library dir. Scottsdale (Ariz.) Pub. Library, 1966-71; city librarian Pomona (Calif.) Pub. Library, 1971-77, Newport Beach (Calif.) Pub. Library, 1977-78, Chula Vista (Calif.) Public Library, 1978—; exec. dir. Southeastern Pub. Library Sytem Okla.; cons. on bldg. and adminstrn. various libraries, Calif., N.C., Fla., Colo., Ariz.; pres. Pub. Library Film Circuit. Mem. Scottsdale Fine Arts Commn., 1966-71; adminstrv. council Met. Coop. Library System, Los Angeles. Served with Intelligence Service, USAF, 1951-53. Recipient John Cotton Dana Library Pub. Relations award, 1974, 75, 76; Hometown Builder award, 1975. Mem. ALA (bd. dirs. Pub. Library Assn. 1975-79), Ariz. (pres. pub. libraries sect. 1969-70), Calif., Southwestern library assns., Pub. Library Execs. So. Calif. (pres. 1975-76), Library Automation, Research and Cons. Assn. (steering com. 1969-71), Royal Arcanum, Nat. Mgmt. Assn., Pomona Municipal Mgmt. Assn. (dir.), Newport Harbor Art Mus., Newport Harbor C. of C., Pub. Library Dirs. (chmn. council Okla. 1987-88), Pomona Valley Hist. Soc., Kappa Delta Phi. Presbyterian. Club: Rotary. Contbr. articles to profl. jours. Home and Office: PO Box 783 McAlester OK 74502

SIMON, CHARLES KENNETH, corp. exec.; b. N.Y.C., Apr. 7, 1918; s. Herbert M. and Belle J. (Simon) S.; B.S., U. Pa., 1939; postgrad. N.Y. U., Pratt Inst.; m. Liane Nau, July 30, 1966; children—Charles Kenneth, Eric Nau, Lilia Nau. Exec., Brewster Aircraft, 1940-41, York Aircraft Co., 1941-43, Aerojet Gen. Corp., 1959-62; designer, creater Advanced Decision Data System, 1957—; mgmt. scientist, pres. Mgmt. Methods Corp., Sacramento and San Diego, 1962—; pres., mng. dir. Mgmt. Research Found., San Francisco and Coronado, Calif., 1975—; pres., chmn. bd. Cal-Colombian Mines Ltd.; pres. Rio Magui Mining Co. Inc.; chmn. bd. Computer Mgmt. Corp., Salt Lake City, 1970—; bd. dirs. Automated Ct. Systems, San Diego, 1976—; cons. Dept. Def., aerospace industry, 1943—; mem. teaching staff U. Calif., 1960-62. Served with USNR, 1944-46. Decorated Bronze Star. Mem. Ops. Research Soc., Inst. Mgmt. Sci., Am. Ordnance Soc., Air Force Assn., Am. Mgmt. Assn. Home: 5311 Park Place Circle Boca Raton FL 33486 Office: 44 Montgomery St Suite 500 San Francisco CA 94104 also: 31 Ocean Reef Plaza North Key Largo FL 33037

SIMON, CLAUDE, writer; b. Tananarive, Madagascar, Oct. 10, 1913; s. Antoine and Suzanne (Denamiel) Simon. Ed. Coll. Stanislas, Paris; La chevelure de Bernice, 1983, 85. Author: Le tricheur 1945, La corde raide, 1947, Gulliver, 1952, Le Sacre du printemps, 1954, Le Vent, 1957, L'herbe, 1958, La route des Flandres, 1960, Le palace, 1962, Historie 1967, Prix Medicis for Histoire, 1967, La Bataille de Pharsale, 1969, Les Corps Conductuers, 1971, Triptyque, 1973, Les Géorgiques, 1981; Nobel prize for literature. Address: Editions de Minuit, 7 rue Bernard-Palissy, 75006 Paris France

SIMON, GERALD AUSTIN, management consultant; b. N.Y.C., Aug. 19, 1927; s. William and Ray (Goldberg) S.; B.B.A., CCNY, 1950; M.B.A., Harvard U., 1956, postgrad. research fellow, 1956-58; m. Margaret Cornwall, Dec. 1979; 1 son by previous marriage, Dana Alexander; 6 stepchildren. With various advt. firms, Phila., N.Y.C., Providence, 1950-54; research asst., Ford Found. doctoral research fellow Harvard U. Bus. Sch., 1956-58; vis. lectr. Northwestern U., Evanston, Ill., 1958-59; mng. dir. Cambridge Research Inst., 1959-79; pres. Gerald Simon & Assocs., Inc., Berkeley, Calif., 1979—. Served with USNR, 1945-46. Fellow Inst. Mgmt. Cons. (founding mem., past dir.); mem. Assn. Cons. Mgmt. Engrs. (past dir.), Harvard U. Bus. Sch. Assn. (exec. council, past dir.), Assoc. Harvard Alumni (past dir.), The Planning Forum . Clubs: Harvard (N.Y.C., Boston), Harvard U. Faculty; U. Calif. at Berkeley Faculty, World Trade (San Francisco). Co-editor: Chief Executives Handbook, 1976; chmn. editorial bd. Jour. Mgmt. Cons.

SIMON, HERBERT A(LEXANDER), social scientist; b. Milw., June 15, 1916; s. Arthur and Edna (Merkel) S.; m. Dorothea Pye, Dec. 25, 1937; children: Katherine S. Frank, Peter Arthur, Barbara. A.B., U. Chgo., 1936, Ph.D., 1943, LL.D., 1964; D.Sc., Case Inst. Tech., 1963, Yale U., 1963, Marquette U., 1981, Columbia U., 1983, Gustavus Adolphus U., 1984, Mich. Tech. U., 1988; Fil. Dr., Lund U., Sweden, 1968; LL.D., McGill U., 1970, U. Mich., 1978, U. Pitts., 1979; LLD., U. Paul Valery, 1984; Dr. Econ. Sci., Erasmus U. Rotterdam, Netherlands, 1973, Duquesne U., 1988; D.SC. and LHD, Ill. Inst. Tech., 1988. Research asst. U. Chgo., 1936-38; staff mem. Internat. City Mgrs.' Assn.; also asst. editor Pub. Mgmt. and

Municipal Year Book, 1938-39; dir. adminstrv. measurement studies Bur. Pub. Adminstrn., U. Calif., 1939-42; asst. prof. polit. sci. Ill. Inst. Tech., 1942-45, asso. prof., 1945-47, prof., 1947-49; also chmn. dept. polit. and social sci. 1946-49; prof. adminstrn. and psychology Carnegie-Mellon U., Pitts., 1949-65, Richard King Mellon univ. prof. computer scis. and psychology, 1965—, head dept. indsl. mgmt., 1949-60; asso. dean Grad. Sch. Indsl. Adminstrn., 1957-73, trustee, 1972—; cons. to Internat. City Mgrs. Assn., 1942-49, U.S. Bur. Budget, 1946-49, U.S. Census Bur., 1947, Cowles Found. for Research in Econs., 1947-60; cons. and acting dir. Mgmt. Engring. br. Econ. Cooperation Adminstrn., 1948; Ford Distinguished lectr. N.Y. U., 1959; Vanuxem lectr. Princeton, 1961; William James lectr. Harvard, 1963, Sigma Xi lectr., 1964, 76-78, 86; Harris lectr. Northwestern U., 1967; Karl Taylor Compton lectr. MIT, 1968; Wolfgang Koehler lectr. Dartmouth, 1975; Katz-Newcomb lectr. U. Mich., 1976; Carl Hovland lectr. Yale, 1976; Ueno lectr., Tokyo, 1977; Gaither lectr. U. Calif., Berkeley, 1980; Camp lectr. Stanford U., 1982; Gannon lectr. Fordham U., 1982; Oates vis. fellow Princeton U., 1982; Marschak lectr. UCLA, 1983; Auguste Comte lectr. London Sch. Econs., 1987; hon. prof. Tianjin (China) U., 1980, Beijing (China) U., 1986; hon. research scientist Inst. Psychology, Chinese Acad. Scis., 1985; chmn. bd. dirs. Social Sci. Research Council, 1961-65; chmn. div. behavioral scis. NRC, 1968-70; mem. President's Sci. Adv. Com., 1968-71; cons. bus. and govtl. orgns. Author or co-author: books relating to field, including Administrative Behavior, 1947, 3d edit., 1976, Public Administration, 1950; Models of Man, 1956, Organizations, 1958, New Science of Management Decision, 1960, rev. edit., 1977, The Shape of Automation, 1965, The Sciences of the Artificial, 1968, 2d edit., 1981, Human Problem Solving, 1972, Skew Distributions and Business Firm Sizes, 1976, Models of Discovery, 1977, Models of Thought, 1979, Models of Bounded Rationality, 1982, Reason in Human Affairs, 1983, Protocol Analysis, 1984, Scientific Discovery, 1987. Chmn. Pa. Gov.'s Milk Inquiry Com., 1964-65. Recipient adminstrs. award Am. Coll. Hosp. Adminstrs., 1957; Frederick Mosher award Am. Soc. Pub. Adminstrn., 1974; Alfred Nobel Meml. prize in econ. scis., 1978; Dow-Jones award, 1983; scholarly contbns. award Acad. Mgmt., 1983; Nat. Medal of Sci., 1986, Pender award U. Pa., 1987; gold medal Am. Psychol. Found., 1988; Fiorino d'Oro City of Florence, Italy, 1988. Distinguished fellow Am. Econ. Assn. (Ely lectr. 1977); fellow Econometric Soc., AAAS, Am. Acad. Arts and Scis., Am. Psychol. Assn. (Disting. Sci. Contbn. award 1969), Am. Sociol. Soc., Inst. Mgmt. Scis. (life, v.p. 1954); mem. N.Y. Acad. Scis. (hon.), Jewish Acad. Arts Scis., Am. Polit. Sci. Assn. (James Madison award 1984), Assn. for Computing Machinery (A.M. Turing award 1975), Nat. Acad. Scis. (mem. com. sci. and pub. policy 1967-69, 82-89, chmn. com. air quality control 1974, chmn. com. behavioral scis. NSF 1975-76, mem. council 1978-81, 83-86, chmn. com. scholarly communication with PRC, 1983-87 co-chmn. com. behavioral sci. in nuclear disarmament, 1986—), Soc. Exptl. Psychologists, Am. Philos. Soc., IEEE (hon.), Royal Soc. Letters (und) (fgn. mem.), Orgnl. Sci. Soc. (Japan) (hon.), Yugoslav Acad. Scis. (fgn.), Brit. Psychol. Assn., Phi Beta Kappa, Sigma Xi (Procter prize 1980). Democrat. Unitarian. Clubs: Cosmos (Washington); University (Pitts.). Office: Carnegie-Mellon Univ Dept of Psychology Schenley Park Pittsburgh PA 15213

SIMON, HERMANN J., marketing educator; b. Hasborn, Fed. Republic of Germany, Feb. 10, 1947; m. Cecilia Sassong, July 8, 1949; children: Jeannine, Patrick J. Degree, U. Bonn, 1976. Asst. prof. U. Bonn, 1973-78; visiting fellow MIT, Cambridge, 1978-79; prof. U. Bielefeld, Fed. Republic of Germany, 1980—; scientific dir. USW German Mgmt. Inst., Cologne, 1985-88; vis. fellow, prof. INSEAD, France, Keio U., Tokyo, 1983, Stanford U., 1988; chmn. UNIC GmbH, Bonn, 1985—; mem. supervisory bd. Kodak AG, Sttutgart. Author: Price Management, 1982, Goodwill, 1985, Price Management, 1988; editor Markerfolg in Japan, 1986. Served with German Air Force, 1967-88. Bower Found fellow Harvard U., 1988-89. Mem. European Mktg. Acad. (pres. 1984-86). Roman Catholic. Home: Peter Moll Weg 6, D-5330 Koenigswinter 41 Federal Republic of Germany Office: Universitaet, D-4800 Bielefeld Federal Republic of Germany

SIMON, H(UEY) PAUL, lawyer; b. Lafayette, La., Oct. 19, 1923; s. Jules and Ida (Rogere) S.; m. Carolyn Perkins, Aug. 6, 1949; 1 child, John Clark. B.S., U. Southwestern La., 1943; J.D., Tulane U., 1947. Bar: La. 1947; CPA, La., 1947. Sole practice New Orleans, 1947—; asst. prof. advanced acctg. U. Southwestern La., 1944-45; staff acct. Haskins & Sells, New Orleans, 1945-53, prin., 1953-57; ptnr. law firm Deutsch, Kerrigan & Stiles, 1957-79; founding sr. ptnr. law firm Simon, Peragine, Smith & Redfearn, 1979—. Author: Louisiana Income Tax Law, 1956, Changes Effected by the Louisiana Trust Code, 1965, Gifts to Minors and the Parent's Obligation of Support, 1968, Deductions—Business or Hobby, 1975, Role of Attorney in IRS Tax Return Examination, 1978; assoc. editor: The Louisiana CPA, 1956-60; bd. editors Tulane Law Rev., 1945-46; estates, gifts and trusts editor The Tax Times, 1986-87. Mem. ABA (mem. tax sect. com. ct. procedure 1958—), La. Bar Assn. (com. on legislation and adminstrv. practice 1966-70), New Orleans Bar Assn., Inter-Am. Bar Assn., Internat. Bar Assn. (com. on securities issues and trading 1970—), Am. Judicature Soc., Am. Inst. CPA's, Am. Assn. Atty.-CPA's, Soc. La. CPA's, New Orleans Assn. Notaries, Tulane Alumni Assn., New Orleans C. of C. (council 1952-66), New Orleans Met. Area Com., Council for Better La., NYU Tax Conf.-New Orleans (co-chmn. 1976), Tulane Tax Inst. (program com. 1960—), La. Tax Conf. (program com. 1968-72), Bur. Govtl. Research, New Orleans Bd. Trade, Pub. Affairs Research Council, Internat. Platform Assn., Met. Crime Commn., Phi Delta Phi (past pres. New Orleans chpt.), Sigma Pi Alpha. Roman Catholic. Clubs: Young Men's Bus., (legislation com.), Petroleum, City, Press, Toastmasters Internat., New Orleans Country, International House (dir. 1976-79, 82-85), Pendennis, World Trade Ctr. (dir. fin. com. 1985-86) (New Orleans). Office: Energy Centre 30th Floor New Orleans LA 70163

SIMON, JACQUELINE ALBERT, political scientist, journalist; b. N.Y.C.; d. Louis and Rose (Axelroad) Albert; B.A. cum laude, NYU, M.A., 1972, Ph.D., 1977; m. Pierre Simon; children—Lisette, Orville. Adj. asst. prof. Southampton Coll., 1977, 79—; mng. editor Point of Contact, N.Y.C., 1975-76; assoc. editor, U.S. bur. chief Politique Internationale, Paris, 1979—; research assoc. Inst. French Studies, N.Y. U., N.Y.C., 1980—, asst. prof. govt., 1982-83; cons., 1977—; assoc. Inst. on the Media for War and Peace; frequent appearances French TV and radio. Contbg. editor Harper's, 1984—. Bd. dirs. Fresh Air Fund. 1974. Mem. Ams. for Democratic Action, Nat. Acad. Sci., Am. Polit. Sci. Assn., French-Am. Soc., Phi Beta Kappa. Contbr. articles to profl. jours. Home: 988 Fifth Ave New York NY 10021

SIMON, JAMES LOWELL, lawyer; b. Princeton, Ill., Nov. 8, 1944; s. K. Lowell and Elizabeth Ann (Unholz) S.; m. Deborah Ann Wolf, Dec. 27, 1966; children: Heather Lyn, Brandon James. Student, U. Ill., 1962-63; BSEE magna cum laude, Bradley U., 1967; JD with honors, 1975. Bar: Fla. 1975, U.S. Dist. Ct. (mid. dist.) Fla. 1976, U.S. Ct. Appeals (11th cir.) 1981, U.S. Patent Office 1983. Engineer Pan Am. World Airways, Cape Kennedy, Fla., 1967-68; assoc. Akerman, Senterfitt & Eidson, Orlando, Fla., 1975-80; ptnr. Bogin, Munns, Munns & Simon, Orlando, 1980-87, Holland & Knight, 1987—. Active Seminole County Sch. Adv. Council, Fla., 1981—, Forest City Local Sch. Adv. Com., Altamonte Springs, Fla., 1981-84, Code Enforcement Bd., Altamonte Springs, 1983-84, Central Bus. Dist. Study com., Altamonte Springs, 1983-85, Rep. Council of '76, Seminole County, 1982-87. Served to capt. USAF, 1968-72. Named one of Outstanding Young Men in Am., 1981. Mem. ABA, Orange County Bar Assn. (jud. relations com. 1982-83, fee arbitration com. 1983—), Phi Kappa Phi, Tau Beta Pi, Sigma Tau, Eta Kappa Nu. Republican. Mormon. Home: 620 Longmeadow Circle Longwood FL 32779 Office: Holland & Knight 800 N Magnolia Ave Penthouse A Orlando FL 32802

SIMON, JEAN CLAUDE, computer sciences educator, physicist, researcher; b. Paris, Sept. 10, 1923; s. Jules G. and Yvonne P. (Appert) S.; m. Arlette Gaillet, 1948 (div. 1951); children: Dominique, Catherine; m. Françoise Hutteau D'Origny, Nov. 21, 1969. Lic. Math., U. Paris Sorbonne, 1950, D in Scis., 1951. With Compagnie Générale Télégraphie Sans Fil, Paris, 1949-67, head lab., 1952-57, dir. sci., 1957-63, advisor to pres., 1963-67; vis. prof. Faculté des Scis., Paris, 1967-69; prof. computer scis. U. Pierre and Marie Curie, 1969-81; disting. prof. U. Paris Pierre and Marie Curie, 1981—; cons. to French industries; dir. Ctr. Calcul Interuniv. de la Region Parisienne, 1984-87; pres. Ctr. Culturel de Bonas, France. Recipient Acad. Scis. prize 1952, 85, Grand Prix des Techniques City of Paris, 1978; named Officier de la Legion d'Honneur, Etat Français, 1980; hon. fellow Honda Found., 1986. Mem. Internat. Assn. for Pattern Recognition (pres. 1982-84, chmn. 8th internat. conf. 1986). Roman Catholic. Home: 10 Rue de l'Université, 75007 Paris France Office: U Marie and Pierre Curie, Inst Progammation, 4 Pl Jussieu, 75007 Paris France

SIMON, JOHN BERN, lawyer; b. Cleve., Aug. 8, 1942; s. Seymour Frank and Roslyn (Schultz) S.; m. Lynda Lou Cohn, Aug. 11, 1966; children: Lindsey Helaine, Douglas Banning. B.S., U. Wis.-Madison, 1964; J.D., DePaul U., 1967. Bar: Ill. 1967. Asst. U.S. atty. U.S. Justice Dept., Chgo., 1967-70; dep. chief civil div. U.S. Justice Dept., 1970-71, chief civil div., 1971-74; spl. counsel to dir. Ill. Dept. Pub. Aid, Chgo., 1974-75; legal cons. to Commn. on Rev. of Nat. Policy Toward Gambling, Chgo., 1975-76; ptnr. firm Friedman and Koven, 1975-85, mem. exec. com., 1983-85; ptnr. firm Jenner and Block, 1986—; spl. cons. to adminstr. Drug Enforcement Adminstrn. Dept. Justice, 1976-77; counsel to Gov.'s Revenue Study Commn. on Legalized Gambling, 1977-78; spl. counsel Ill. Racing Bd., 1979-80; lectr. tng. seminars and confs.; instr. U.S. Atty. Gen.'s Advocacy Inst., Washington, 1974; lectr. Nat. Conf. Organized Crime, Washington, 1975, Dade County Inst. Organized Crime, Ft. Lauderdale, Fla., 1976; faculty Cornell Inst. Organized Crime, Ithaca, N.Y., 1976, judge Miner Moot Ct. competition Northwestern U., 1971-73; mem. law council DePaul U., 1974-83, pres. law alumni bd., 1984-85, chmn., 1975-79; adj. prof. DePaul U. Coll. Law, 1977-81; faculty Practising Law Inst., Chgo., 1984. Contbr. articles to profl. jours. Bd. dirs. Community Film Workshop of Chgo., 1977—; bd. dirs. Friends of Glencoe Parks, 1977-78, sec., 1978-79; mem. nominating com. Glencoe Sch. Bd., 1978-81, chmn. rules com., 1980-81; pres. Glencoe Hist. Soc., 1979-82; mem. Glencoe Zoning Bd. Appeals, Zoning Commn., Sign Bd. Appeals, 1981-86, chmn., 1984-86; mem. Ill. Inaugural Com., 1979, 83, 87; bd. dirs., mem. exec. com. Chgo. World's Fair Authority, 1983-85; mem. Chancery div. task force Spl. Commn. on Adminstrn. of Justice in Cook County, 1985—. Recipient Bancroft-Whitney Am. Jurisprudence award, 1965, 66. Mem. ABA (com. on liaison with the judiciary 1983-84), Fed. Bar Assn., Ill. Bar Assn., Chgo. Bar Assn. (fed. civil procedure com. 1979, chmn. 1985-86, bd. mgrs. 1987—), Ill. Police Assn., Ill. Sheriffs Assn., U.S. Treasury Agts. Assn., DePaul U. Alumni Assn. (pres. 1985-86, chmn. spl. gifts com. campaign for DePaul). Club: Standard. Office: Jenner & Block One IBM Plaza Chicago IL 60611

SIMON, KENNETH CYRIL, lawyer; b. Johannesburg, Republic South Africa, Jan. 27, 1917; s. Bertram Cecil and Clara Horner (Nicholson) S.; Attorneys Admission Part II, 1939; m. Phyllis La Grange, Sept. 16, 1944; children—Rawdon John, Robyn Anne. Ptnr. firm Dumat Pitts & Blaine (now Webber Wentzel), Johannesburg, 1946—; dir. Tower Bldg. Soc., 1948-60; dir. Revlon SA (Pty) Ltd., Pirelli Gen. Cables (SA) (Pty) Ltd., Berk Pharms. (S.A.) (Pty) Ltd., Racal Fin. (Pty) Ltd., Racal Acoustic Services (Pty) Ltd., Racal Acoustics (Pty.) Ltd., Agport (Pty.) Ltd. Served with South African M.C., 1940-45. Decorated Africa Star with 8th Army clasp, War medal, Africa Service medal. Anglican. Clubs: Rand, Wanderers, Sappers. Home: 42 Oaklands Rd, Johannesburg 2192, Republic of South Africa Office: 60 Main St, Johannesburg 2001, Republic of South Africa

SIMON, LORENA COTTS, music educator, composer, poet; b. Sherman, Tex., Jan. 16, 1897; d. George Godfrey and Willie (Jones) Cotts; student Am. Conservatory, summer 1938, Juilliard Music Sch., summer 1939; diploma Sherwood Music Sch., 1941; LittD (hon.), Internat. Acad. Leadership, Quezon City, Philippines; LHD (hon.), No. Pontificial Acad., Malmo, Sweden, 1969; MusD (hon.), St. Olav's Acad., Sweden, 1969; m. Samuel C. Simon, Nov. 6, 1918 (dec.). Tchr. violin, piano, theory and harmony, Port Arthur, Tex., 1919—. Organizer, dir. Schubert's Violin Choir, Port Arthur, 1919-55. Named Poet Laureate of Tex. 1961; Poet Laureate of Magnolia Dist., 1962-64; Poet Laureate of Port Arthur, 1962—; recipient gold plaque Tex. Fedn. Women's Club, 1962, spl. award 1st place in poetry and music Tex. heritage dept., 1963; medal of merit and diploma of merit Centro Studi Scambi Internat., Rome, Italy, 1965; Gold medal award, and hon. poet laureate-musician United Poets Laureate Internat., 1966, named Cath. Lady of Humanity, 1977; decorated Equestrian Order of Holy Sepulchre, 1981; inducted into Knights and Ladies of the Holy Sepulchre, Pope John II, 1982, Nat. Guild of Piano Tchrs.' Hall of Fame, 1986, Southeast Tex. Women's Hall of Fame, 1987; recipient Greatness and Leadership award U. Manila, 1967; Silver medal, Gold medal, Diploma Centro Studi E Scambi—Internazionali, 1967; Gold Laurel Wreath, Gold medal, Karte of Award, 1966; named to International Poets' Hall of Fame, 1969, named most outstanding woman internationally Congress of Doctors, Quezon City, Philippines, 1969; named Cath. Poet Laureate of World, 1967. Mem. Nat., Tex. press women's assns., Nat. Council Cath. Women, Nat. Guild Piano Tchrs. (charter mem.; adjudicator), Am. Coll. Musicians (adjudicator), Internat. Guild Library, Am. Poetry League, Poets Soc. Tex. (critic judge), Am. Poets Fellowship Soc. Corp., UN Assn. U.S.A., Alpha Delta Kappa. Clubs: Writers' (pres. 1963-64), Symphony. Author: The Golden Keys, 1958; From My Heart (1st place award Ann. Poetry Writers Contest of Tex. Press Women's Assn. 1961), 1959; Children's Story Hour (1st place award Nat. Fedn. Press Women's Ann. Writers' Contest 1962), 1960. Songs pub. include: Live Expectantly, 1962, In Search for Growth, 1963, Freedom's Light, 1963, What Can I Do for Jesus, 1963, I Was a Star, I Was a Lamb, I Was a Donkey; organ piece Mediation, 1967. Chmn. spl. editorial com. World Poets Laureate Anthology, 1969-70. Donor funds for constrn. of 9 churches in Africa. Home: 411 5th Ave Port Arthur TX 77642

SIMON, MURRAY, educator; b. N.Y.C., July 3, 1925; s. Max and Sarah (Markman) S.; m. Juana Romero; children—Wendy Marcia Zlotlow, Michael C., Barbara Ann, Viviana, Alexandra, Sarah. B.A., NYU, 1948, M.A., 1950, Ph.D., 1965. Office and export mgr. Queensboro Steel Corp., Wilmington, N.C., 1950-54; tchr. Topsail Sch., Hampstead, N.C., 1954-55, Lake Forest Sch., Wilmington, 1955-56; tchr., chmn. dept. social studies Hawthorne Jr. High Sch., Yonkers, N.Y., 1956-63, adminstrv. asst. Sch. Edn. NYU, N.Y.C., 1963-64; asst. to supt. schs. Ramapo Central Schs., Suffern, N.Y., 1964-65; dir. evening and extension div. Rockland Community Coll., Suffern, 1965-67, acad. dean, 1967-70; ednl. adviser U. Okla. project U. del Valle, Cali, Colombia, 1970-71, ednl. cons., 1971-74; AID adviser Colombian Ministry Edn., Bogota, 1974-77, ednl. cons., Dominican Republic, 1977, ednl. advisor Bolivian Ministry Edn., 1977-80, ednl. cons., El Salvador, 1980-81, cons. rural ednl. adminstrn., Domincan Republic, 1981, sr. planning officer Botswana Ministry Edn., Gaborone, 1981-84; ednl. cons. AID, Liberia, 1984-87, sabbatical, 1987-88; evaluator Community Devel. Projects, Bolivia, 1988; ednl. advisor, Guatamala, 1988—. Author: Education in Botswana: An Educational Guide, 1982. Chmn. bd. Tour de Force Repertory Company. Served with AUS, World War II. Deocrated Purple Heart. Mem. Assn. Curriculum Devel., Comparative and Internat. Edn. Soc., Internat. Council on Edn. for Teaching, D.A.V., Phi Delta Kappa. Home: PO Box 789 Housatonic MA 01236

SIMON, PAUL, senator, educator, author; b. Eugene, Oreg., Nov. 29, 1928; s. Martin Paul and Ruth (Troemel) S.; m. Jeanne Hurley, Apr. 21, 1960; children: Sheila, Martin. Student, U. Oreg., 1945-46, Dana Coll., Blair, Nebr., 1946-48; 27 hon. degrees. Pub. Troy (Ill.) Tribune, 1948-66, and other So. Ill. weeklies; mem. Ill. Ho. of Reps., 1955-63, Ill. Senate, 1963-69; lt. gov. Ill. 1969-73; fellow John F. Kennedy Inst. Politics Harvard, 1972-73; prof. public affairs reporting Sangamon State U., Springfield, Ill., 1973; mem. 94th-98th Congresses from 24th Dist. Ill.; U.S. Senator from Ill. 1985—. Author: Lovejoy: Martyr to Freedom, 1964, Lincoln's Preparation for Greatness, 1965, A Hungry World, 1966, You Want to Change the World, So Change It, 1971, The Tongue-Tied American, 1980, The Once and Future Democrats, 1982, The Glass House, Politics and Morality in The Nation's Capitol, 1984, Beginnings, 1986, Let's Put America Back to Work, 1986; (with Jeanne Hurley Simon) Protestant-Catholic Marriages Can Succeed, 1967; (with Arthur Simon) The Politics of World Hunger, 1973. Bd. dirs. Dana Coll. Served with CIC, AUS, 1951-53. Recipient Am. Polit. Sci. Assn. award, 1957; named Best Legislator 7 times. Mem. Luth. Human Relations Assn., Am. Legion., VFW, NAACP, Urban League. Lutheran. Office: 462 Dirksen Senate Bldg Washington DC 20510 *

SIMON, WILLIAM HENRY, information specialist; b. New Haven, Dec. 26, 1928; s. Henry Charles and Florence (Shaw) S.; A.A., Jr. Coll. Commerce, New Haven, 1948; B.A., U. Bridgeport, 1950; M.S. in L.S., Columbia, 1955; M.B.A., Western New Eng. Coll., 1964; m. Dorothy Elaine Beckett, Oct. 1, 1955; children—Stephen Eric, William Edward. Circulation desk asst. Sterling Meml. Library, Yale U., New Haven, 1951-52; profl. asst. bus. and technology dept. Bridgeport Public Library, Bridgeport, Conn., 1955-56; chief librarian New Haven Research Library Olin-Mathieson Chem. Corp., New Haven, 1956-61; tech. info. supr. Nuclear Power Systems, Combustion Engring., Inc., Windsor, Conn., 1961, mgr. info. and adminstrv. services, 1961-85, library, records mgmt cons., 1985—; research mgr. Miller, Starrett, West and Assos., Inc., mgmt. cons. and research firm, Hartford, 1961-62. Mem. Conn. adv. com. Inter-Library Coop., 1967-68; sub. chmn. adv. com. Conn. Public Library Standards, 1967-68; bd. dirs. Capitol Region Library Council, 1970-73. Chief merit badge counselor, dist. tng. chmn. Metacomet dist. Long Rivers council Boy Scouts Am., asst. dist. commr., vigil honor mem. Order of Arrow, Nat. Eagle Scout Assn. Publicity chmn. Windsor Republican Com., mem. Windsor Town Com.; justice of peace, 1965-73; chmn. bd. dirs. Windsor Public Library, 1969-74; vice-chmn. Windsor Red Cross Drive, 1962. Recipient Gen. Scholar, Sch. Library Sci., Columbia U., 1955; Wood Badge, Boy Scouts Am., 1972, Merit award, 1974. Mem. Nat. Micrographics Assn. (dir. chpt. 1979-80), Assn. Records Mgrs. Adminstrs., Assn. Conn. Library Bds. (chmn. public relations and publicity com., del.), Yale Library Assos., Am. Library Assn., Conn. Library Assn., Nat. Rifle Assn. (instr.), Nuclear Records Mgmt. Assn. (publs. chmn. 1977-79, adv. bd. 1980-84, charter mem.), NOW, Alpha Phi Omega, Beta Phi Mu. Episcopalian. Clubs: Masons (32 degree), Elks (chmn. youth activities com.), Green Mountain. Home: 17 Priscilla Rd Windsor CT 06095

SIMONDS, ROBERT BRUCE, business executive; b. Seattle, Mar. 30, 1939; s. William, Jr. and Charlotte Mary (Jewell) S.; student Long Beach (Calif.) City Coll., 1957-59, Long Beach State Coll., 1959-61; m. Loretta Frances Fota, Nov. 18, 1961; children—Robert Bruce, Cynthia Suzanne, Christina Michelle. Engr. adminstr. N. Am. Rockwell, Inc., Downey, Calif., 1962-65; dealer, gen. mgr. Mike Salta Pontiac, Inc., Honolulu 1966-74; dealer, gen. mgr. Westward Pontiac, Inc., Phoenix, 1974-79, pres., owner, Bob Simonds Pontiac Inc., Phoenix, 1979-87 ; dealer council chmn. for Southwest, Am. Honda Motor Co., Inc., 1982-87 ; chmn. bd. Bob Simonds Corp., Scottsdale, 1987—. Bd. dirs. Hawaii Found. Lupus Research, 1972-73, Valley Big Bros., 1981—, Silent Witness, 1982—, Phoenix Meml. Hosp. Found., 1982, Florence Crittenton Found., 1983-87, Tumbleweed, 1984-87 ; pres. Phoenix Pub. Safety Found., 1985-88; mem. Fiesta Bowl Golf Classic Com., Phoenix, 1985, Fiesta Bowl Football Com., Phoenix, 1986; founding mem. Lavere Meml. Found., Evanston, Ill., 1983; regional vice chmn. United Way, 1982; trustee No. Ariz. U., Flagstaff, 1987—; bd. dirs. Samaritan Med. Found., Phoenix, 1987—; bd. govs. Standard Register Turquoise Classic, Phoenix, 1987—; chmn bd. dirs. Jet Lease Inc. Crystal Lake, Ill., 1988, Simonds Investments, Scottsdale, 1987—; mem. Citizens Bond Com., Phoenix, 1986-87. Served as officer inf., USAR, 1964-68. Decorated Medal for Valor with pendant; recipient Time Magazine Dealer award nomination for State of Ariz., 1983-83; community Service award Silent Witness, 1985, Friends of Phoenix award, 1986, Bus. Appreciation Week award, Phoenix, 1987, Florence Crittenton Cup award, Phoenix, 1987, numerous letters appreciations, service awards; named Outstanding Philathropist, State of Ariz., 1986. Mem. Ariz. Automobile Dealers Assn., Pontiac Dealer Council, Valley Pontiac Dealers Advt. Assn. (pres. 1982-83), Valley Honda Dealers Advt. Assn. (pres. 1982-83), Ariz. Automobile Dealer Group Trust (trustee 1984-87), Greater Phoenix Automobile Dealers Assn. (bd. dirs., vice chmn.), Ariz. C. of C., 100 Club, Better Bus. Bur. Ariz., Sigma Alpha Epsilon. Republican. Roman Catholic. Clubs: Phoenix Country; Waialae Country (Honolulu); Old Course and Country (St. Andrews, Scotland), Gainey Ranch Golf, Troon Golf and Country (Scottsdale). Home: 4548 E Oregon Ave Phoenix AZ 85018 Office: 6900 E Camelback Rd Suite 440 Phoenix AZ 85251

SIMONELLI, CHARLES FRANCIS, business executive; b. Bklyn., May 28, 1925; s. Charles and Catherine (Simonelli) S.; m. Rose Mary Strafaci, Oct. 26, 1961; children—Angela C., Donna C. With Universal Pictures Co. Inc., 1945-62, asst. to pres., 1959-62; v.p. Technicolor Inc., 1963-66, exec. v.p., 1966-68; past dir., mem. finance com.; dir., chmn. exec. com. Thompson Starrett, 1954-56, chmn. bd., 1956-57; dir., mem. exec. com. Superior Tool and Die Co., 1956-57, Bethelem Machine and Foundry, 1956-57; chmn. mgmt. com. Bib Corp., 1956-57; exec. v.p., dir. Nat. Industries, Inc., Louisville, 1968-70; pres. Nat. Industries, Inc., 1970-72; also dir. numerous subsidiaries; sr. v.p., also dir. REA Holding Corp., 1972-74; exec. v.p., chief adminstrv. officer, dir. Nat. Bulk Carriers, Inc., Princess Properties Internat. Ltd., Am. Hawaiian Steamship Co., 1974-77; mng. dir., chief exec. officer Numinter BV, 1977-79; chmn., chief exec. officer, dir. Simstra Ltd.; chmn., dir. Resource Recovery Systems, Inc.; chmn., mem. exec. com. Satcorp, Inc., Movielab, Inc., 1981 86; dir. Transmedia Network, Inc. Del. Democratic Nat. Conv., 1952. Club: N.Y. Athletic (N.Y.C.). Home: 291 Chestnut Hill Rd Stamford CT 06903

SIMONIAN, SIMON JOHN, surgeon, educator; b. Antioch, French Ter., Apr. 20, 1932; came to U.S., 1965, naturalized, 1976.; s. John Simon and Marie Cecile (Tomboulian) S.; m. Arpi Ani Yeghiayan, July 11, 1965; children: Leonard Armen, Charles Haig, Andrew Hovig. MD, U. London, 1957; BA with honors, St. Edmund Hall, U. Oxford, Eng., 1964; MA, U. Oxford, Eng., 1969; MSc, Harvard U., 1967, Sc.D., 1969. Diplomate: Am. Bd. Surgery. Intern Univ. Coll. Hosp., London, 1957; intern Edinburgh (Scotland) Royal Infirmary, 1957-58, resident, 1961-62; clin. clk. Nat. Hosp. London, 1958; resident Edinburgh Western Gen. Hosp., 1958-59, Birmingham Accident and Burns Hosp., U. Birmingham, Eng., 1959-60; demonstrator dept. anatomy Edinburgh U., 1960-61; research fellow in pathology Harvard U., Boston, 1965-68; resident in surgery Boston City Hosp., 1970-74; dir. surg. immunology, asst. in surgery Brigham and Womens Hosp., Boston, 1968-70; attending surgeon in transplantation and gen. surgery services U. Chgo. Hosp. Med. Ctr., 1974-78; instr., assoc. in surgery Harvard Med. Sch., 1968-70, vis. prof., 1982; asst. prof. surgery, mem. com. immunology U. Chgo., 1974-78; head div. renal transplantation Hahnemann U. Sch. Medicine, 1978-87, prof. surgery, 1978—, chmn. Transplantation Com., 1983—; lectr. in field.; vis. prof. Vanderbilt U., 1968, UCLA, 1977, U. Cambridge, 1977, Karolinska Inst., 1977, U. Stockholm, 1977, Med. Coll. Pa., 1980, 81, 85, U. Pa., 1981, 85, U. Athens, 1981, U. London, 1981, Tufts U., 1982, U. Oxford, 1982, U. Edinburgh, 1982; cons. in gen. surgery City of Phila.; Jonathan E. Rhoads annual orator Phila. Acad. of Surgery, 1984. Co-author: Manual of Vascular Access Procedures, 1987; cons. to editorial bd. Dateline: Issues in Transplantation; mem. editorial bd. Phila. Medicine, Transpalntation Jour., Transplantation Proceedings; contbr. articles to profl. jours. and books; appeared in med. movie, Giving. Co-founder Armenian Youth Soc., Eng., 1953, pres., 1953-54; Armenian Studies program U. Chgo., 1975; bd. govs. Friends Sch., London, 1964-65; Mass. del. Armenian Assembly, Washington, 1970-74. Nairn scholar, 1949-52; Middlesex scholar, 1952-57; recipient Suckling prize, 1957, Brit. Med. Research Council award, 1962-64, NIH award, 1965-70, Alt prize, 1973, Thompson award, 1974-77, Johnson award, 1975-77, Presdl. Medal of Merit, 1982, Kabakjian award Armenain Student Assn. Am., 1986; named outstanding new citizen of Dept. Justice, Washington, 1976-77. Fellow Royal Coll. Surgeons Edinburgh, A.C.S., Phila. Acad. Surgery; mem. AAAS, Royal Coll. Surgeons of Eng., Nat. Assn. Armenian Studies and Research, Am. Armenian Med. Assn. (co-founder 1972, treas. 1972-74), Armenian Med. and Dental Assn. Greater Phila. (co-founder 1983, pres. 1983-85, Outreach award 1986), Assn. Acad. Surgery, Transplantation Soc. (editorial bd. 1968-70, membership com. 1980-82), Am. Fedn. Clin. Research, N.Y. Acad. Scis., Am. Soc. Transplant Surgeons (founding mem. 1974, chmn. immunosuppression study com. 1974-77, membership com. 1985-87), Phila. Acad. Scis. (co-chmn. membership com. 1980—), Greater Delaware Valley Soc. Transplant Surgeons (councillor 1978-80, 85—, pres. elect 1980-82, pres. 1982-85), Phila. County Med. Soc. (rep. City Ctr. br. 1981-83, pres. 1984, bd. dirs. 1985-87, chmn. long range planning com. 1986—), Pa. Med. Soc., AMA, Am. Technion Soc., Am. Soc. Artificial Internal Organs, European Soc. Organ Transplant, Oxford and Cambridge Soc. of Phila., Internat. Cardiovascular Soc., End Stage Renal Disease Network 24 (mem. med. rev. bd. 1986-87), AAUP, Sigma Xi. Clubs: Harvard (Phila.), Med. (Phila.). Office: Hahnemann U Broad & Vine Philadelphia PA 19102-1192

SIMONIN, MARIE-JEANNE, physician; b. Marseille, France, Sept. 29, 1950; d. Jean and Marie-Louise (Ducret) S. MD, Faculty Medicine, Marseille, 1978. Resident in endocrinology Cabinet, Clinique de Marignane, France, 1978; practice medicine specializing in endocrinology Marignane, France. Mem. Fedn. Française de Ski Nau. Roman Catholic. Home: les

Alizes Montee de la Grotte, 13620 Carry le Rouet France Office: Cabinet, 7 Blvd de la Liberation, 13700 Marignane France

SIMONIS, ADRINAUS J. CARDINAL, cardinal Roman Catholic Church; b. Lisse, Rotterdam, The Netherlands, Nov. 26, 1931. ordained 1957. Consecrated bishop Rotterdam, 1971; archbishop Utrecht, 1983; proclaimed cardinal 1985. Address: Aatsbisdom BP 14019, 3508 SB Utrecht The Netherlands *

SIMONOV, YURI IVANOVICH, conductor; b. Saratov, USSR, Mar. 4, 1941; ed. Leningrad Conservatoire. Condr., Kislovodsk Philharmonic Soc., 1967-69; condr. State Bolshoi Opera and Ballet Theatre, Moscow, USSR, 1969-70, chief condr., 1970-87, head Maly Symphony Orch., 1987—, condr. operas The Marriage of Figaro, Aida, Boris Godunov, Prince Igor, Pskovityanka, Ruslan and Ludmila, Rusalka, Queen of Spades, Eugene Onegin, Carmen, Madame Butterfly, Traviata, Tosca, also condr. ballets Anna Karenina, Carmen Suite (Scheolzin), Requiem (Verdi); vis. condr. France, Italy, German Democratic Republic, U.S., Mexico, Japan, Denmark, Sweden, Austria, W. Germany, Spain, Czechoslovakia, Hungary. Named Laureate of 2d USSR Competition of Condrs., Moscow, 1966; recipient 1st prize 5th Internat. Competition Condrs., Santa Cecilia Acad., Rome, 1968. Address: Bolshoi State Acad Theatre, 1 Ploshchad Sverdlova, Moscow USSR *

SIMONS, ELLEN ANN, advertising executive; b. N.Y.C., Dec. 26, 1941. Cert. of completion, Sch. Visual Arts, N.Y., 1961-63; student, Adelphi Coll., 1959-61. Sr. copy writer Della Femina Travisano, N.Y., 1968-70; copy supr. DKG, Inc., N.Y., 1970-73; pres., creative dir. Simons, Madden & Ptnrs., Honolulu, 1975-79; v.p., assoc. creative dir. Foote Cone Belding/L.A., Los Angeles, 1980-81; assoc. creative dir. Saatchi & Saatchi Compton, N.Y., 1982-85; pres., creative dir. Manhattan Advt., Inc., Sugar Loaf, N.Y., 1985-88, Drackett & Lavidge, Phoenix, 1988—. Recipient The Merit award The Copy Club, 1968, Distinctive Merit award Art Dirs. Club of N.Y., 1970, Award of Excellence, Ad Infinitum 1, 1972, Cert. of Merit award, Ad Infinitum 4, 1974.

SIMONS, PETER MURRAY, philosopher, educator; b. Westminster, London, Eng., Mar. 23, 1950; arrived in Austria, 1980; s. Jack and Marjorie Nita (Brown) S.; m. Susan Jane Walker, July 21, 1973; children: Rupert, Rebecca. BSc in Math. with honors, U. Manchester, Eng., 1971, MA in Philosophy, 1973, PhD in Philosophy, 1975. Asst. librarian U. Manchester, 1975-77; lectr. in philosophy Bolton Inst. Tech., Eng., 1977-80; lectr. in philosophy U. Salzburg, Austria, 1980-86, reader in philosophy, 1986—, venia docendi (habilitation) in philosophy, 1986. Author: Parts: A Study in Ontology, 1987; co-editor: Das Naturrecht heute u. morgen, 1983; mem. editorial bd. History and Philosophy Logic, 1984—, Philos. and Phenomenological Research, 1984—, (series) Primary Sources in Phenomenology, 1985—, Brentano-Studien, 1988—; reviewer Math. jours. Mem. Am. Philos. Assn., Austrian Philos. Soc. Office: U Salzburg Inst for Philosophy, Franziskanergasse 1, A-5020 Salzburg Austria

SIMONSEN, PALLE, minister of finance Denmark; b. Sall, East Jutland, Denmark, May 6, 1933; s. Skipper and Julie (Kanne) S.; m. Kirsten Krog, Jan. 10, 1960; 3 children. Engaged in pvt. enterprises, 1963-70; gen. mgr. DCK Internat. A/S, 1968-70; mng. dir. Civil Def. Assn., Denmark, 1970-82; M.P. 1968-75, 77—; minister for social affairs, 1982-84, minister of fin., 1984—. Chmn., Parliamentary Social Welfare Com., 1974-75, Def. Com., 1977-82, mem. Fin. Com., 1977-82; chmn. Conservative Party (of the Isles), 1975-81, dep. chmn., 1975-81, polit. spokesman Folketing, 1981-82. Mem. of the Radio Council, 1974-82, dep. chmn., 1982. *

SIMONSON, MICHAEL, lawyer, judge; b. Franklin, N.J., Feb. 5, 1950; s. Robert and Eleanor (Weiss) S. BA, U. Ariz., 1973; JD, Southwestern U., Los Angeles, 1976; LLM in Taxation, Washington U., St. Louis, 1978. Bar: Ariz. 1977, U.S. Dist. Ct. Ariz. 1979, U.S. Tax Ct. 1978. Bailiff, law clk. Superior Ct. Maricopa County Div. 2, Phoenix, 1976-77; sole practice, Scottsdale, Ariz., 1978-79; ptnr. Simonson, Groh, & Lindteigen, Scottsdale, 1979-81, Simonson & Preston, Phoenix, 1984-86, Simonson, Preston & Arbetman, 1986-87, Simonson & Arbetman, 1987—; judge pro tempore Mcpl. Ct., City of Phoenix, 1984—; adj. prof. Ariz. State U Coll. Bus., Tempe, 1984—, Coll. for Fin. Planning, Denver, 1984—, Maricopa County Community Colls., 1984—, Western Internat. U., Phoenix, 1984—, Ottawa U., 1987—; prof. law Univ. Phoenix, 1985—, area chmn. legal studies, 1986—. Mem. Maricopa County Foster Child Care Rev. Bd. No. 17, 1978-81; pres. Camelback Mountainview Estates Homeowners Assn., 1980-81, Congregation Tiphereth Israel, 1979-81. Co-author: Buying and Selling Closely Held Businesses in Arizona, 1986, Commercial Real Estate Transactions, 1986. Mem. ABA (taxation sect., various coms.), State Bar Ariz. (cert. specialist in tax law), Maricopa County Bar Assn., Cen. Ariz. Estate Planning Council. Democrat. Jewish. Club: Nucleus. Lodge: Masons. Office: Simonson & Arbetman 4645 N 32d St Suite 200 Phoenix AZ 85018

SIMONSON, SUSAN KAY, hospital administrator; b. LaPorte, Ind., Dec. 5, 1946; d. George Randolph and Myrtle Lucille (Opfel) Menkes; m. Richard Bruce Simonson, Aug. 25, 1973. BA with honors, Ind. U., 1969; MA, Washington U., St. Louis, 1972. Perinatal social worker Yakima Valley Meml. Hosp., Yakima, Wash., 1979-81, dir. social service, 1982—, dir. patient support and hospice program, 1981—; Spanish instr. Yakima Valley Coll., Yakima, Wash., 1981—; pres. Yakima Child Abuse Council, 1983-85; developer nat. patient support program, 1981. Contbr. articles to profl. jours. Mem. Jr. League, Yakima; mem. adv. council Robert Wood Johnson Found. Rural Infant Health Care Project, Yakima, 1980, Pregnancy Loss and Compassionate Friends Support Groups, Yakima, 1982—, Teen Outreach Program, Yakima, 1984—. Recipient NSF award, 1967, discharge planning program of yr. regional award Nat. Glassrock Home Health Care Discharge Planning Program, 1987; research grantee Ind. U., 1968, Fulbright grantee U.S. Dept. State, 1969-70; Nat. Def. Edn. Act fellowship, 1970-73. Mem. AAUW, Soc. Med. Anthropology, Soc. Hosp. Social Work Dirs. of Am. Hosp. Assn., Nat. Assn. Perinatal Social Workers, Nat. Assn. Social Workers, Phi Beta Kappa. Office: Yakima Valley Meml Hosp 2811 Tieton Dr Yakima WA 98902

SIMONTON, GAIL MAUREEN, lawyer; b. Ripley, Tenn., July 5, 1951; d. William Christopher and Elizabeth Jane (Butler) S. Student Centre Coll., Danville, Ky., 1969-71, Alliance Francaise, 1971, Institut Americain U., Avignon, France, 1971-72; BA, U. Tenn.-Martin, 1975; JD, U. Tenn.-Knoxville, 1977. Bar: Tenn. 1978. Intern, Bur. Ednl. and Cultural Affairs, U.S. Dept. State, Washington, 1973; law clk. to judge Tenn. Ct. Criminal Appeals, Covington, 1977-79; assoc. firm Thomason, Crawford & Hendrix, Memphis, 1979-82; asst. sec., staff atty. Guardsmark, Inc., Memphis, 1982-85; exec. dir., gen. counsel Com. of Nat. Security Cos., Inc., Memphis, 1985—. Research editor Tenn. Law Rev., 1976-77. Treas., bd. dirs. Covington Little Theater, 1977-78; youth league referee Covington Area Soccer Assn., 1978; participant Leadership Memphis, 1986-87. Mem. ABA, Memphis and Shelby County Bar Assn. (dir. young lawyers sect. 1983), Tenn. Bar Assn., Tenn. Fedn. Bus. and Profl. Women (nominations chmn. 1981-82, legis. chmn. 1983-84, TFBPW/PAC chmn. 1984-85, West II Dist. dir. 1985-86, fedn. chmn. 1986-87), Am. Soc. Indsl. Security, Raleigh Bus. and Profl. Women (pres. 1983-84). Home: 16 S Edgewood St Memphis TN 38104 Office: Com Nat Security Cos Inc 2670 Union Ext'd Suite 514 Memphis TN 38112

SIMPICH, GEORGE CARY, investment banker; b. Washington, June 25, 1923; s. Frederick and Margaret (Edwards) S.; 1 dau., Juliet Elizabeth. Mem. advt. staff Washington Post, 1945-47, Nat. Geog. Mag., 1947-49; with Young & Rubicam Advt. Agy., 1949-51; with Davidson & Co., 1951-56; div. mgr. Fin. Programs, Inc., Washington, 1956-61; investment cons. O'Boyle, Hearne & Fowler, Ltd., Washington, 1961-66; with various investment banking firms, 1966—; now 1st v.p. Janney Montgomery Scott, mem. N.Y. Stock Exchange, Washington. Served as pilot USAAC, 1943-45. Mem. N.Y. Economists Club, Mcpl. Fin. Forum, Bond Club. Clubs: Del Ray, Nat. Press. Republican. Episcopalian (vestryman). Home: 3210 Wisconsin Ave NW Apt 110 Washington DC 20016 Office: 1225 23d St NW Washington DC 20037

SIMPKINS, FREDA, cable television owner, educator; b. Glen Alum, W.Va., Aug. 12, 1944; d. Orville Curtis Baisden and Gertrude (Kennedy) B.; m. Andrew Charles Simpkins, Mar. 20, 1971 (dec. Apr. 1976). B.A., Marshall U., 1968. Tchr. Mingo County Bd. Edn., Williamson W.Va., 1965—, prin., 1970-71; cable TV owner A & F TV Cable, Meador, W.Va., 1974—. Mem. Community Antenna TV Assn., W.Va., Cable TV Assn., NEA, W.Va. Edn. Assn. (faculty rep. 1982—). Democrat. Mem. Ch. of Christ. Home: PO Box 40-C Meador WV 25682 Office: A&F TV Cable PO Box 40-C Meador WV 25682

SIMPSON, ALAN KOOI, U.S. senator; b. Cody, Wyo., Sept. 2, 1931; s. Milward Lee and Lorna (Kooi) S.; m. Ann Schroll, June 21, 1954; children—William Lloyd, Colin Mackenzie, Susan Lorna. B.S., U. Wyo., 1954, J.D., 1958; L.L.D. (hon.), Calif. Western Sch. of Law, 1983, Colo. Coll., 1986, Notre Dame U., 1987. Bar: Wyo. 1958, U.S. Supreme Ct. 1964. Asst. atty. gen. State of Wyo., 1959; city atty. City of Cody, 1959-69; partner firm Simpson, Kepler, Simpson & Cozzens (and predecessor), Cody, Wyo., 1959-78; mem. Wyo. Ho. of Reps., 1964-77, majority whip, 1973-75, majority floor leader, 1975-77, speaker pro tem, 1977; legis. participant Eagleton Inst. Politics, Rutgers U., 1971; mem. U.S. Senate from Wyo., 1978—, asst. majority leader, 1985-87, asst. minority leader, 1987—, ranking minority mem. vets. affairs com., ranking minority mem. nuclear regulation subcom., ranking minority mem. subcom. on immigration and refugee policy; guest lectr. London exchange program Regent's Coll., London, 1987. Formerly v.p., trustee N.W. Community Coll., Powell, Wyo., 1968-76; trustee Buffalo Bill Hist. Ctr., Cody; trustee Grand Teton Music Festival, Gottsche Found. Rehab. Ctr., Thermopolis, Wyo.; del. Nat. Triennial Episcopal Ch. Conv., 1973, 76. Recipient Nat. Assn. Land Grant Colls. Centennial Alum award U. Wyo., 1987. Mem. Wyo. Bar Assn., Park County Bar Assn., Fifth Jud. Dist. Bar Assn., Am. Bar Assn., Assn. Trial Lawyers Am., U. Wyo. Alumni Assn. (pres. 1962, 63, Disting. Alumnus award 1985), VFW (life), Am. Legion, Amvets. (Silver Helmet award). Lodges: Eagles, Elks, Masons (33 deg.), Shriners, Rotary (pres. local club 1972-73). Office: US Senate 261 Dirksen Senate Bldg Washington DC 20510 *

SIMPSON, ALFRED HENRY, retired judge; b. Dundee, Angus, Scotland, Oct. 29, 1914; s. John Robertson and Mary (Hendry) S.; m. Hilda Corson Rodgers, Dec. 30, 1941; 1 child, Velleda Hilda Corson. M.A., St. Andrews U., Scotland, 1935; LL.B., Edinburgh U., Scotland, 1938. Solicitor, 1938. Bar: Scotland, 1952, N.S.W., Australia 1967. Legal sec. British Mil. Adminstrn., Cyrenaica, 1946-48; law officer, crown counsel, Singapore, 1948-56; high ct. judge, Ghana, 1957-61, Sarawak-Sabah, Malaysia, 1962-65; judge, chief justice, Nairobi, Kenya, 1967-85; chmn. Council Legal Edn. Jud. Service Commn., Kenya, 1982-85; patron Inst. Arbitrators, Kenya, 1984-85. Editor: Laws of Singapore, 1955. Served to maj. Royal Army Service Corps, 1941-45. Named Knight Bachelor, Her Majesty Queen Elizabeth, 1985. Mem. Faculty Advocates Scotland, N.S.W. Bar. Episcopalian. Clubs: Royal Commonwealth Soc. (London); Royal Canberra Golf (Australia). Avocation: golf. Home: 23 Downes Pl Hughes, 2605 Canberra Australia

SIMPSON, ANDREA LYNN, energy company communications executive; b. Altadena, Calif., Feb. 10, 1948; d. Kenneth James and Barbara Faries Simpson; m. John R. Myrdal, Dec. 13, 1986. B.A., U. So. Calif., 1969, M.S., 1983; postgrad. U. Colo., Boulder, 1977. Asst. cashier United Calif. Bank, Los Angeles, 1969-73; asst. v.p. mktg. 1st Hawaiian Bank, Honolulu, 1973-78; v.p. corp. communications Pacific Resources, Inc., Honolulu, 1978—. Bd. dirs. Kapiolani Women's and Children's Hosp., 1988—, Hawaii Heart Assn., 1978-83, Child and Family Services, 1984-86 , Council of Pacific, Girl Scouts U.S.A., 1982-85, Arts Council Hawaii, 1977-81; trustee Hawaii Loa Coll., 1984-86; commr Hawaii State Commn. on Status of Women, 1985-87. Bd. dirs. Honolulu Symphony Soc., 1986—; active Jr. League of Honolulu. Named Outstanding Young Person of Hawaii, Hawaii Jaycees, 1978; Panhellenic Woman of Yr., Hawaii, 1979; Outstanding Woman in Bus., Hawaii YWCA, 1980; Outstanding Young Woman of Hawaii, Girl Scouts Council of the Pacific, 1986, Hawaii Legis., 1980. Mem. Am. Mktg. Assn., Pub. Relations Soc. Am. (bd. dirs. Honolulu chpt. 1984-865, Silver Anvil award 1984), Pub. Utilities Communicators Assn. (Communicator of Yr. 1984), Honolulu Advt. Fedn. (Advt. Woman of Yr. 1984), U. So. Calif. Alumni Assn. (bd. dirs. Hawaii 1981-83), Alpha Phi (dir. Hawaii). Clubs: Outrigger Canoe, Pacific, Jr. League. Office: Pacific Resources Inc PO Box 3379 Honolulu HI 96842

SIMPSON, JACK BENJAMIN, medical technologist, business executive; b. Tompkinsville, Ky., Oct. 30, 1937; s. Benjamin Harrison and Verda Mae (Woods) S.; student Western Ky. U., 1954-57; grad. Norton Infirmary Sch. Med. Tech., 1958; m. Winona Clara Walden, Mar. 21, 1957; children—Janet Lazann, Richard Benjamin, Randall Walden, Angela Elizabeth. Asst. chief med. technologist Jackson County Hosp., Seymour, Ind., 1958-61; chief med. technologist, bus. mgr. Mershon Med. Labs., Indpls., 1962-66; founder, dir., officer Am. Monitor Corp., Indpls., 1966-77; pres. Global Data, Inc., Ft. Lauderdale, Fla., 1986—; mng. partner Astroland Enterprises, Indpls., 1968—, 106th St. Assocs., Indpls., 1969-72, Keystones Ltd., Indpls., 1970-82 Delray Rd. Assoc., Ltd., Indpls., 1970-71, Allisonville Assocs. Ltd., Indpls., 1970-82, Grandview Assocs. Ltd., 1977—, Rucker Assocs., Ltd., Indpls., 1974—; mng. ptnr. Raintree Assocs., Ltd., Indpls., 1978—, Westgate Assocs., Ltd., Indpls., 1978—; pres., dir. Topps Constrn. Co., Inc., Bradenton, Fla., 1973—, Acrouest Corp., Asheville, N.C., 1980—; dir. Indpls. Broadcasting, Inc.; founder, bd. dirs. Bank of Bradenton, 1986—. Mem. Am. Soc. Med. Technologists (cert.), Indpls. Soc. Med. Technologists, Ind. Soc. Med. Technologists, Am. Soc. Clin. Pathologists, Royal Soc. Health (London), Internat. Platform Assn., Am. Mus. Natural History. Republican. Baptist. Clubs: Columbia of Indpls.; Harbor Beach Surf, Fishing of Am., Marina Bay (Fort Lauderdale, Fla.). Lodge: Elks.

SIMPSON, JOHN NOEL, hospital administrator; b. Durham, N.C., Feb. 27, 1936; s. William Hays and Lucile (McNab) S.; A.B., Duke U., 1957; M.H.A., Med. Coll. Va., 1959; m. Virginia Marshall, June 27, 1959; children—John Noel, William M. Assoc. adminstr. Richmond (Va.) Meml. Hosp., 1970-74, sr. v.p., adminstr., 1974-77, exec. v.p., 1977-80, pres., 1980-85; preceptor Sch. Health Adminstrn., Duke U. and Med. Coll. Va.; chmn. Sun Health, Inc., 1985-87; Vice-chmn. Med./Bus. Coalition, 1981-83; pres. Health Corp. of Va., 1985—; participant Leadership Met. Richmond. Served with Med. Service Corps, U.S. Army, 1959-62. Fellow Am. Coll. Hosp. Adminstrs. (Council of Regents 1976-82, Edgar C. Hayhow award 1976); mem. Va. Hosp. Assn. (dir. 1974-86, pres.-elect, chmn. 1984-85), Met. Richmond C. of C. (bd. dirs.). Republican. Presbyterian. Home: 1503 Willingham Rd Richmond VA 23233 Office: 1300 Westwood Ave Richmond VA 23227

SIMPSON, PHILIP FRANCIS, educator, consultant, writer; b. London, May 13, 1923; s. Ben Philip and Grace Frances (Freethy) S.; m. Christine Mary Dexter, Sept. 19, 1972; children: Phippa Ann, Ben Colin. Cert. in spl. edn., U. Manchester, Eng., 1955; MEd, U. Newcastle, Eng., 1971. Cert. tchr., Eng. Sr. research fellow in edn. U. Newcastle, 1968-71; course dir. spl. edn. Polytech U., Leeds, Eng., 1971-74; advisor in spl. edn. Leeds City Corp., 1975-82; dir. Spl. Edn. Cons., Halifax, Eng., 1982. Editor, contbr. book Proceedings of 1975 Annual Conference of the National Council for Special Education, 1976. Mem. nat. mgmt. com. Nat. Assn. Mental Health, London and nationwide, 1986. Served to lt. RAF, 1941-46. U. Newcastle grantee, 1968. Mem. Nat. Council Spl. Edn. (hon. life, jour. editor 1974-82, cons.), Guild Tchrs. Backward Children (gen. sec. 1967-74), European Assn. Spl. Edn. (Brit. rep. 1968-74). Club: Aircrew Assn. Home: Cedar Royd, 5 the Ings, Lightcliffe, Halifax England HX3 8XF

SIMPSON, RICHARD KENDALL, JR., physician, surgeon, researcher; b. Atlanta, Sept. 10, 1953; s. Richard Kendall and Juliet Hodges (Rowsey) S.; m. Martha Anne Baucom, Sept. 22, 1984. BA, Coker Coll., 1975; PhD, Med. U. S.C., 1980, MD, 1982; postgrad. Warnborough Coll., Oxford, Eng., 1974. Diplomate Nat. Bd. Med. Examiners. Teaching asst. dept. physiology Med. U. S.C., Charleston, 1976-80, research assoc., 1980-83, intern neurology, 1982-83; resident neurosurgery dept. neurosurgery Baylor Coll. Medicine, Houston, 1983-89; cons. Spinal Cord Injury Research, Charleston, S.C., 1980-83. Author: Peripheral Nerve Fiber Group and Spinal Corp Pathway Contributions to the Somatosensory Evoked Potential, 1980. ACS scholar, 1986-88; recipient Physician Recognition award, 1986. Mem. Am. Med. Polit. Action Com., 1983. Watson fellow Coker Coll., 1974. Mem. AMA, Am. Physiol. Soc., Soc. Neurosci., Digital Equipment Computer Users Soc., N.Y. Acad. Sci., Sigma Xi, Alpha Omega Alpha, Houston Neurol. Soc., S.C. Acad. Sci. Episcopalian. Home: 5540 Aspen St Houston TX 77081 Office: Baylor Coll Medicine Dept Neurosurgery One Baylor Plaza Houston TX 77030

SIMPSON, ROBERT ALEXANDER, language professional; b. Liverpool, Eng., Dec. 18, 1952; s. John Alexander and Christine Elizabeth (Cope) S.; m. Isabel Calvo Vera, Aug. 5, 1979 (div. July 1985); 1 child, Andrea Laura. BA, U. Oxford, Eng., 1975; diploma in Spanish, Inst. Linguistics, 1980. Dir. studies Inlingua Sch., Santander, Spain, 1979-80; cons. Exec. Lang. Ctr., Yorkshire, Eng., 1980—; materials, resource mgr. Exec. Lang. Ctr. Ltd., Yorkshire, 1981—. Office: Exec Lang Ctr, 8 St Peter's Grove, Yorkshire Y03 6AQ, England

SIMPSON, ROBERT WILFRED LEVICK, composer; b. Leamington, Warwicks, Eng., Mar. 2, 1921; s. Robert Warren and Helena Hendrika (Govaars) S.; D.Mus., Durham U., 1951; m. Bessie Fraser, 1946 (dec. 1981); m. 2d Angela Musgrave, 1982. Music producer BBC, 1951-80; composer 10symphonies, 2 concertos for piano and violin, 12 string quartets. Recipient Carl Nielsen gold medal, Denmark, 1956; also Bruckner Medal of Honor. Mem. ISM. Author: Carl Nielsen, Symphonist, 1952, 2d edit. 1979, The Essence of Bruckner, 1966; editor: The Symphony, from 1966; contbr. articles in field to profl. publs. Home: Siochâin, Killelton Nr Camp, Tralee County Kerry, Ireland

SIMPSON, RUSSELL GORDON, lawyer; b. Springfield, Mass., May 22, 1927; s. Archer Roberts and Maude Ethel (Gordon) S.; married, Sept. 11, 1954; children: Barbara G., Elisabeth Pires-Fernandes, Helen Blair Simpson Tyler. B.A., Yale U., 1951; J.D., Boston U., 1956; postgrad., Parker Sch. Internat. Law, 1962. Advt. mgr. Burden Bryant Co., Springfield, 1951-53; assoc. Goodwin, Procter & Hoar, Boston, 1956-64, ptnr., 1965-87; sr. advisor to pres. The Experiment in Internat. Living, Brattleboro, Vt., 1988—; hon. consul New Eng. of Bolivia, 1958-82; mem. spl. com. to revise Mass. Corrupt Practices Act, 1961-62; dir. Fishery Products, Inc., Bolsa Corp., Haskell Investment Corp. Author: The Lawyer's Basic Corporate Practice Manual, 1971, rev. edit., 1978, 84, 87. Bd. overseers Boston U. Sch. Mgmt., 1969-74; mem. exec. com. Sch. Law Boston U., 1978—; mem. Mass. Rep. Com., 1959-67, exec. com., 1959-67, chmn., 1962-67; del. Rep. Nat. Conv., 1964, exec. dir. Mass. Del. Rep. Nat. Conv., 1968; state convs., 1960, 62, 64, 66, 67, 70; vice chmn. Milton Rep. Town Com., 1970-71; mem. Milton Town Meeting, 1978-87; mem. Milton Town Warrant Com., 1976-80, chmn., 1978-80; adv. com. ambulatory care service Beth Israel Hosp., 1969-71; bd. dirs. Greater Boston Arts Fund, Inc., 1983-87; Milton Hosp., Mass., 1983-86; Met. Boston Area Planning Council, 1969-75; mem. Milton Town Warrant Com., 1976-80, chmn., 1978-80; mem. adv. com. Mass. Mediation Service, 1986-87; Served with USN, 1945-46. Named Outstanding Young Man of Greater Boston, 1963. Fellow Am. Bar Found., Mass. Bar Found.; mem. Mass. Bar Assn. (chmn. banking and bus. law sect. 1980-83, bd. dels., exec. com. 1983-87, v.p. 1985-87), ABA (corp. banking and bus. law sect., com. on law firms, co-chmn. com. on law firm governance, panel on corp. law ednl. programs), Boston Bar Assn., World Affairs Council, Ambassadors Club. Clubs: The Country (Brookline, Mass.), Edgartown Yacht (Mass.), Edgartown Reading Room, Golf (Edgartown), Edgartown, Squibnocket Assocs. (Martha's Vineyard, Mass.), Jupiter Island (Hobe Sound, Fla.), Bay (Boston), Yale (N.Y.C.). Home: Box 657 Brattleboro VT 05301 Office: Experiment in Internat Living Kipling Rd Brattleboro VT 05301

SIMPSON, WADE BLAND, international foods company executive; b. Big Spring, Tex., Sept. 11, 1937; s. James Bland Simpson and Modesta (Good) Stokes; m. Patricia McDaniel, Feb. 17, 1963 (div. 1963). BA, Tex. Christian U., 1959; postgrad. Sch. Law, U. Tex., Austin, 1965-66. Account exec. Rauscher, Pierce, Midland, Tex., 1962-65; owner Regalos, Inc., Austin, 1966-72; real estate agt. Swearingen, Austin, 1972-74; ptnr. Simpson-Mann, San Angelo, Tex., 1974—; pres. Tex. Pecan & Gourmet Co., 1986—; dir. Permian Basin Petroleum, Midland, 1980-82. Vestryman, Emmanuel Episcopal Ch., San Angelo, 1981-83; sec., treas., dir. San Angelo Fine Arts Council, 1981-82; bd. dirs. Fine Arts Mus., San Angelo, 1981-84, Palmer Drug Abuse Program, 1982, West Tex. Rehab.; trustee U. South Sewanee, Tenn. Served with USAF, 1959-60. Mem. Ind. Petroleum Assn. Am. (nat. energy com. 1980-84), Am. Assn. Petroleum Landmen, West Tex. Oil and Gas Assn., San Angelo Geol. Assn. (sec. treas. 1981-82), West Geol. Soc. Republican. Home: 2805 Dena Dr San Angelo TX 76904 Office: Simpson-Mann PO Box 1432 San Angelo TX 76902 also: Tex Pecan & Gourmet Co San Angelo TX 76902

SIMPSON, WILLIAM KELLY, Egyptologist, curator, educator; b. N.Y.C., Jan. 3, 1928; s. Kenneth Farrand and Helen L.K. (Porter) S.; m. Marilyn E. Milton, June 19, 1953; children: Laura Knickerbacker Simpson Thorn, Abby Rockefeller Simpson Mydland. B.A., Yale U., 1947, M.A., 1948, Ph.D., 1954. Asst. in Egyptian art Met. Mus. Art, 1948-54; research fellow Center Middle East Studies, Harvard U., 1957-58; mem. faculty Yale U., New Haven, 1958—; prof. Egyptology Yale U., 1965—, chmn. dept. Near Eastern langs., 1966-69; curator Egyptian and ancient Near Eastern art Mus. Fine Arts, Boston, 1970-86; partner Kin and Co., 1967-69, Venrock, 1970—; dir. editor of papers Penn-Yale Archaeol. Expdn. to Egypt, 1960—; mem. adv. council fgn. currency program Smithsonian Instn., 1966-69. Author: Papyrus Reisner I-Records of a Building Project, 1963, Hekanefer and the Dynastic Material from Toshka, 1963, Papyrus Reisner II-Accounts of the Dockyard Workshop, 1965, Papyrus Reisner III: Records of a Building Project in the Early Twelfth Dynasty, 1969, The Terrace of the Great God at Abydos, 1974, The Mastabas of Qar and Idu, 1976, The Offering Chapel of Sekhem-ankh-ptah, 1976, (with others) The Ancient Near East, A History, 1971, The Literature of Ancient Egypt, 1972, The Mastaba of Queen Mersyankh III, 1974. Trustee Am. Sch. Classical Studies, Athens, Am. U. in Cairo; mem. internat. council Mus. Modern Art, N.Y.C.; pres. Wrexham Found., 1965-67. Fulbright fellow Egypt, 1955-57; Guggenheim fellow, 1965. Mem. Am. Oriental Soc., Am. Philos. Soc., Archaeol. Inst. Am., Internat. Assn. Egyptologists, Egypt Exploration Soc., Soc. française d'egyptologie, German Archaeol. Inst., Foundation egyptologique Reine Elisabeth. Clubs: Century (N.Y.C.), Met. Opera (N.Y.C.), University (N.Y.C.), Union (N.Y.C.); Union Boat (Boston); Bedford (N.Y.); Golf and Tennis. Home: RD 1 Box 327 Katonah NY 10536

SIMPSON, WILLIAM RUSSELL, foundation executive; b. Appleby, England, Sept. 19, 1922; s. Alfred Gray and Jane (Hudspeth) S.; m. Liliana Brandão, Dec. 8, 1955; children—James, Henry, Edward. B. Commerce with distinction, U. Durham, Eng., 1947. Chief acct. Robert Hudson Ltd., Angola, 1950-53, Casa Americana, Angola, 1954-57; mgr. Price Waterhouse & Co., Lisbon, Portugal, 1957-59; fin. dir. Gulbenkian Found., Lisbon, 1959-86; dir. investments, 1987—. Served as flight lt. RAF, 1942-46. Fellow Inst. Chartered Accts. in Eng. and Wales, Royal Geog. Soc. Home: Sete Vistas, Galamares Sintra Portugal Office: Gulbenkian Found, Avenida de Berna, Lisbon Portugal

SIMS, EUGENE RALPH, JR., industrial engineer; b. N.Y.C., Oct. 12, 1920; s. Eugene Ralph and Rose (Simmons) S.; B. Adminstrv. Engring., N.Y. U., 1947; M.B.A., Ohio U.; m. Ethel Jane Smith, June 8, 1945; children—Pamela Jeanne, Gary Wardner, Phyllis Anne. Tool and instrument maker Sperry Gyroscope Co., N.Y.C., 1939-43; research test engr. N.Y. U., 1947; cons. indsl. engr. Drake, Startzman, Sheahan, Barclay, Inc., N.Y.C., 1947-49; plant mgr. Lit Bros. Warehouse & Furniture Plant, Phila., 1949-50; project indsl. engr. Jeffrey Mfg. Co., Columbus, Ohio, 1950-51; prin. indsl. engr., mgmt. ops. research Battelle Meml. Inst., Columbus, 1951-54; corp. materials handling engr. Anchor Hocking Glass Corp., Lancaster, Ohio, 1954-56; chief indsl. engr., asso. Alden E. Stilson & Assocs. Ltd., Columbus, 1956-58; pres. E. Ralph Sims, Jr. & Assocs., Inc. (name changed to The Sims Cons. Group, Inc.), Lancaster, 1958-86, chmn., 1986—; pres. Fairhill Devel. Co., Lancaster, 1959—; assoc. prof. Ohio U., Athens, 1985—; Dist. commr. Central Ohio council Boy Scouts Am., 1954-56; past mem. adv. council Ohio Tech. Services Program; past mem. Bd. Zoning Appeals Lancaster; command pilot/maj. CAP. Served as 1st lt. USAAF, 1943-46. Registered profl. engr., Ohio, Wis., N.Y., Pa., Calif., Mass., Ind.; chartered engr., U.K. Fellow Inst. Indsl. Engrs., Fellow Brit. Inst. M.E.; mem., ASME (fellow, life mem.), Inst. Mgmt. Cons. (founding mem., past dir.), Assn. Mgmt. Cons. (pres. 1975-76), Nat. Soc. Profl. Engrs., Air Force Assn. (charter mem.), Psi Upsilon. Clubs:

N.Y. U., Minn. Press, Masons (32 deg.), Shriners. Author: Euphonious Coding, 1967; Planning and Management of Material Flow, 1968; Contemporary Comment in Retrospect, 1973; contbg. editor: Production Handbook, 1958; Materials Handling Handbook, 1958, 84; Handbook of Business Adminstrn., 1967; Ency. Profl. Mgmt., 1978; Handbook of Industrial Engineering, 1982; The Distribution Handbook, 1984, The Warehouse Management Handbook, 1988; contbr. articles to trade jours. Home: 114 Luther Ln Lancaster OH 43130 Office: Ohio U 282 Stocker Ctr Athens OH 45701

SIMS, GRAHAM RICHARD, academic administrator; b. London, Jan. 12, 1950; s. Geoffrey Donald and Pamela Audrey (Richings) S.; m. Cecilia Mary Colville, July 26, 1975; children: Elizabeth Clare, Katherine Anne, Andrew James. BA in German with honors, U. Durham, Eng., 1973, Post Grad. Cert. Edn., 1974. Asst. master Worksop Coll., Notts, 1974-78; head langs., second master Yarm Sch., Cleveland, Eng., 1978-86; headmaster St. George's Coll., Buenos Aires, 1986—; examiner Oxford and Cambridge Examination Bd., Eng., 1980-86, Joint Matriculation Bd., Manchester, Eng., 1980-86, Associated Examining Bd., Eng., 1980-83. Author: Viel Spass, 1987. Lay reader Ch. of Eng., 1975—. Mem. MLA. Home and Office: St George's Coll, 1878 Quilmes, CC2 Buenos Aires Argentina

SIMS, PHILLIP LECIL, personnel director, consultant; b. Birmingham, Ala., Dec. 28, 1958; s. Lecil and Billie (Hayes) S.; m. Lisa J. Eilers, July 18, 1987. BBA, Troy State U., 1981. Asst. mgr. F.W. Woolworth Co., Fairfield, Ala., 1980-81; mgmt. trainee Graybar Electric, Houston, 1982-84; job developer, counselor S.E.R.-Dept. Labor, Dayton, Tex., 1984; dir. purchasing Exposaic Wire Co., Dayton, 1984-85, dir. personnel, 1984-88; city administrator City Anahuac, Tex., 1988—; cons. Sims Enterprises, Liberty, Tex., 1982—; prin. Federated Tax Service, Lioberty, 1987—. Del. Tex. Rep. Party, Liberty County, 1984, 86, 88; chmn. Liberty County Muscular Dystrophy Assn., 1987, Liberty County United Way, 1987; pres. student adv. bd. Jefferson County Bd. Edn., 1976-77; minister music, youth North Main Bapt. Ch., Liberty, 1987; coordinator Gordon for U.S. Congress, Liberty County, 1986; co-chmn. Liberty County Bush for Pres. Com., 1988; mem. Valley Players Theatrical Guild, 1987—, Troy State U. Lyceum and Assembly Com., Ingall's Nomination Bd., Student Govt. Assn., Interfraternity Council (also dir. pub. relations), Bus. Sch. Student Adv. Bd., econ. devel. com. Liberty-Dayton, Tex., Nat. Wildlife Fedn., Environ. Def. Fund; rep. Ala. Student Coalition, 1981; substaining mem. endowment, Boy Scouts Am., 1987; hon. lt. col. aide-de-camp Ala. State Militia. Named Outstanding Employer in Houston/Galveston, 1987, Outstanding Employer in Liberty County Tex. Rehabilitation Commn., 1987, Outstanding Employer of the Handicapped, 1987, Hon. lt. col. Ala. State Militia, 1980. Mem. Am. Mgmt. Assn., Tex. Salary Assn., Tex. Assn. Bus., Tex. Bus. Council, Tex. Safety Assn., Liberty-Dayton C. of C. (co-chmn. existing bus. com.), Dayton Jaycees (pres. 1985, bd. chmn. 1986, chmn. indsl. devel. com. on existing bus. 1987), Amateur Softball Assn., Umpire Assn. of Amateur Softball Assn., Delta Sigma Pi (pres. Troy State U. chpt.), Delta Chi. Republican. Baptist. Lodge: Kiwanis (pres. 1984). Home: 2530 Edgewood Liberty TX 77575 Office: 504 Beaumont Ave PO Box 896 Anahuac TX 77514

SIMS, ROBERT MCNEILL, educational administrator, soccer coach; b. Birmingham, Ala., Mar. 25, 1928; s. Edwin Webb and Margaret Pauline (McNeill) S.; BS, Birmingham-So. Coll., 1950; MA, U. Ala., 1951; postgrad. U. N.C., U. Denver, Hope Coll., Emory U.; m. Marie Ficklen Newton; children: Robert Clayton, Kevin McNeill, Boyce Griffin. Chemistry tchr. Riverside Mil. Acad., Gainesville, Ga., 1951-52, 54-57, Tuscaloosa (Ala.) High Sch., 1952-54; dir. admissions and fin. aid, chmn. sci. dept., head soccer coach Westminster Sch., Atlanta, 1957—; sci. cons. Coll. Bd.; chmn. ACS Adv. Test Com., 1986—; soccer coordinator Ga. High Sch. Assn., 1966—; mem. soccer rules com. Nat. Fedn. State High Sch. Assns., 1970-76, 83-87; coach 1st nat. All-Star soccer game, West Point, N.Y., 1984. Mem. choir Peachtree Rd. United Meth. Ch., 1957—, mem. adminstrv. bd., 1978—; mem. adminstrv. bd. Northside YMCA, 1976—. Named Atlanta STAR Tchr., 1963, 68; Nat. Tchr.-of-Yr., DuPont award, 1968; Outstanding Educator, Oglethorpe U., 1976; Nat. Soccer Coach-of-Yr., High Sch. Athletic Coaches Assn., 1975; Southeast Soccer Coach of Yr., Nat. Soccer Coaches Assn., 1981, 83; Ga. High Sch. Soccer Coach of Yr., Ga. Athletic Coaches Assn., 1983. Mem. Am. Chem. Soc. (chmn. Ga. sect. 1970), Am. Inst. Chemists (chmn. Ga. sect. 1972), Assn. Supervision and Curriculum Devel., AAAS, Atlanta Amateur Soccer League (pres. 1982-83), Nat. Soccer Coaches Assn. Am. Democrat. Club: Pine Hills Civic. Office: Westminster Sch 1424 W Paces Ferry Rd NW Atlanta GA 30327

SIMSON, DANIEL, mathematics educator, researcher; b. Zajaczkowo, Poland, Jan. 18, 1942; s. Stefan and Zofia (Wicichowska) S.; m. Sabina Mielcarek, May 4, 1963. MS, Nicholas Copernicus U., Torun, Poland, 1966, D of Math., 1970, habilitation, 1974. Asst. Inst. Math., Nicholas Copernicus U., 1966-70, adj. instr., 1970-75, docent, dir., 1975-87, prof., 1987—; vis. prof. U. Sao Paulo, Brazil, 1978, Nat. Autonomus U. Mex., Mexico City, 1978, 87, U. L'Aquila, Italy, 1982, U. Tsukuba, Japan, 1982-83, U. Paderborn, Fed. Republic of Germany, 1983, 86. Contbr. and reviewer math. jours. Mem. Am. Math. Soc., Polish Math. Soc., Polish Acad. Scis. (mem. math. com. 1984—). Home: Mickiewicza 83B M3, 87100 Torun Poland Office: Nicholas Copernicus U Inst Math, Chopina 12/18, 87100 Torun Poland

SIN, JAIME LACHICA CARDINAL, archbishop of Manila; b. New Washington, Aklan, Philippines, Aug. 31, 1928; s. Juan C. and Maxima R. (Lachica) S.; B.S. in Edn., Immaculate Conception Coll., 1959; LL.D. (hon.), Adamson U., 1975, Angeles U., 1978; S.T.D. (hon.), U. Santo Tomas, 1977; L.H.D. (hon.), De La Salle U., 1975; LLD (hon.), Adamson U., 1975. Ordained priest Roman Cath. Ch.; missionary priest Diocese of Capiz, Philippines, 1954-57; first rector St. Pius X Sem., Roxas City, 1957-67; domestic prelate of Pope John XXIII, 1960; titular bishop of Obba, from 1967; aux. bishop of Jaro, from 1967; apostolic adminstr. Sede Plena, archdiocese of Jaro, from 1970; titular archbishop of Massa Lubrense; met. archbishop of Jaro, from 1972; met. archbishop of Manila, Philippines, 1974—; elevated to Sacred Coll. of Cardinals, 1976; pres. Cath. Bishops' Conf. of the Philippines, 1977; mem. Sacred Congregation for Cath. Edn., 1978—, Sacred Congregation for the Evangelization of Peoples, 1978—; participant Conclave, The Vatican, 1978. Recipient numerous awards and citations, latest being: Real Academia de la Lengua Españ ola award, 1978; Ayuntamiento de Palma de Mallorca, Españ a, award, 1978; Disting. and Meritorious Service award Am. Legion Aux., 1979; Outstanding Citizen's award Manila, 1979. Mem. Synod of Bishops. Author: The Revolution of Love, 1972; The Church Above Political Systems, 1973; A Song of Salvation, 1974; Unity in Diversity, 1974; The Future of Catholicism in Asia, 1978; Christian Basis of Human Rights, 1978; Separation, Not Isolation, 1978; Slaughter of the Innocents, 1979. Home: Villa San Miguel Shaw Blvd, Mandaluyong, Metro Manila Philippines

SINANOGLU, PAULA ARMBRUSTER, social work educator, director; b. N.Y.C., June 30, 1935; d. William and Anna Bertha Armbruster; B.A., U. Conn., 1956, M.S.W., 1974; M.A., Yale U., 1964; children—K. Levni, Elif-Lale A., Murat H. Intelligence analyst Nat. Security Agy., Washington, 1956-62; clin. instr. social work Yale Child Study Center, Sch. Medicine, Yale U., New Haven, Conn., 1974-80, clin. asst. prof., 1980—, dir. social work tng., 1984—, dir. outpatient services, 1985—; fellow Pierson Coll., Yale Coll., 1976—; assoc. project dir. HEW tng. grant, asst. prof. residence U. Conn. Sch. Social Work, West Hartford, 1979-80; Johnson Wax fellow, vis. prof. U. Surrey (Eng.), 1984. Chmn. regional adv. council Conn. Dept. Children and Youth Services, also chmn. chmns. regional adv. councils. Mem. Nat. Acad. Social Work (sec. Conn. chpt.), Conn. Soc. Clin. Social Work, Nat. Assn. Social Workers, Acad. Cert. Social Workers, Council Social Work Edn., Mory's Assn., AAUP. Club: Yale (N.Y.C.). Author, editor works in field. Clubs: Yale (N.Y.) (New Haven).. Office: Yale Child Study Ctr 230 S Frontage Rd New Haven CT 06510

SINATRA, FRANK (FRANCIS ALBERT SINATRA), singer, actor; b. Hoboken, N.J., Dec. 12, 1915; s. Anthony and Natalie (Garaventi) S.; m. Nancy Barbato, Feb. 4, 1939 (div.); children—Nancy, Frank Wayne, Christine; m. Ava Gardner (div.); m. Mia Farrow, 1966 (div.); m. Barbara Marx, 1976. Student, Demarest High Sch., Hoboken, Drake Inst.; hon. doctorate, Stevens Inst. Tech., Hoboken, 1985. Sang with sch. band and helped form sch. glee club; worked after sch. on news truck of Jersey Observer; copy boy on graduation with sports div. covering coll. sports events (won first prize on Maj. Bowes Amateur Hour, touring with co. for 3 months); sustaining programs on 4 radio stas. and in Rustic Cabin, N.J., toured with Harry James Band, then Tommy Dorsey's, solo night club and concert appearances; starred on radio program Lucky Strike Hit Parade; appeared in motion pictures From Here to Eternity (Acad. award as best supporting actor 1953), Las Vegas Nights, 1946, Ship Ahoy, 1942, Miracle of the Bells, 1948, Kissing Bandit, 1949, Take Me Out to the Ball Game, 1949, Higher and Higher, 1942, Step Lively, 1944, Anchors Aweigh, 1945, It Happened in Brooklyn, 1947, Guys and Dolls, 1956, Not as a Stranger, 1955, The Tender Trap, 1955, The Man With the Golden Arm, 1955, Johnny Concho, 1956, The Pride and the Passion, 1957, Pal Joey, 1957, Some Came Running, 1959, Never So Few, 1960, Can-Can, 1960, Oceans 11, 1960, Pepe, 1960, The Devil at 4 O'Clock, 1961, The Manchurian Candidate, 1962, Come Blow Your Horn, 1963, None But the Brave, 1964, Assault on a Queen, 1965, Von Ryan's Express, 1966, Tony Rome, 1966, Lady in Cement, 1967, The Detective, 1968, Dirty Dingus McGee, 1970; actor, producer motion picture The First Deadly Sin, 1980, TV movie Contract on Cherry Street, 1977; hit songs include Night and Day, 1943, Nancy, 1945, Young at Heart, 1954, Love and Marriage, 1955, The Tender Trap, 1955, How Little We Know, 1956, Chicago, 1957, All the Way, 1957, High Hopes, 1959, It Was a Very Good Year, 1965, Strangers in the Night, 1966, My Way, 1969, (with Nancy Sinatra) Somethin Stupid, 1969; albums include Songs for Swingin' Lovers, 1956, Come Dance With Me, 1959, Come Fly With Me, 1962, Moonlight, 1966, Greatest Hits, 1968, My Way, 1969, Greatest Hits, Volume 2, 1970, L.A. is My Lady, 1984. Recipient Spl. Oscar award Acad. Motion Picture Arts and Scis., 1945, Sylvania TV award, 1959, Grammy awards for album of yr., 1959, 65, 66, best vocalist, 1959, 65, 66, rec. of yr., 1966, Peabody and Emmy awards, 1965, Jean Hersholt award Acad. Motion Picture Arts and Scis., 1971, Golden Apple award as male star of yr. Hollywood Women's Press Club, 1977, Humanitarian award Variety Clubs Internat., 1980, Cross of Sci. and the Arts, Austria, 1984, Presdl. Medal of Freedom, 1985, Kennedy Ctr. honor, 1986, Life Achievement award NAACP, 1987. Club: Friars (abbot). Office: care Nathan Golden 8501 Wilshire Blvd Suite 250 Beverly Hills CA 90211 other: Sinatra Enterprises Goldwyn Studios 1041 N Formosa Los Angeles CA 90046 *

SINCLAIR, HUGH M(ACDONALD), medical research institute administrator; b. Edinburgh, Scotland, Feb. 4, 1910; s. Hugh Montgomerie and Rosalie Sybil (Jackson) S. B.Sc., Oxford U. (Eng.), 1933, M.A., 1936, D.M., 1939, postgrad. Univ. Coll. Hosp., London, 1934-37; D.Sc. (hon.), Baldwin-Wallace Coll., 1968. Lectr. in biochemistry Oxford U., 1937-47, fellow Magdalen Coll., 1937—, dir. Oxford Nutrition Survey, 1942-47; dir. lab. human nutrition, 1951-58; dir. Internat. Inst. Human Nutrition Sutton Courtenay, Abingdon, Oxon, Eng., 1972—; hon. nutrition cons. as brig. Control Commn. for Germany, 1945-47. Author: Nicholl's Tropical Nutrition, 1961; Metabolic and Nutritional Eye Disorders, 1968; Hutchison's Food and Principles of Nutrition, 1969; editor: Internat. Ency. Food and Nutrition, 1969—. Decorated medal of Freedom with silver palms (U.S.); Order Orange Nassau (Netherlands); Fellow Royal Coll. Physicians, Royal Soc. Medicine, Royal Soc. Chemistry, Inst. Biology; mem. Physiol. Soc. (hon. treas. 1954-61), Am. Inst. Nutrition. Liberal. Clubs: Athenaeum, Marylebone Cricket (London). Home and Office: Internat Inst HumanNutrition, Lady Place High St, Abingdon, Oxon OX14 4AW, England

SINCLAIR, KEITH VAL, modern languages educator; b. Auckland, New Zealand, Nov. 8, 1926; s. Valentine Leslie and Coral Dorothy (Keith) S. MA, Victoria U., Wellington, New Zealand, 1949, LittD, 1974; PhD, U. Paris, 1954; DPhil, Oxford (Eng.) U., 1960, LittD, 1986. Lectr., then sr. lectr. Australian Nat. U., Canberra, 1955-62; assoc. prof. U. Calif., Davis, 1963-64; assoc. prof., sr. lectr. U. Sydney, Australia, 1964-71; vis. prof. Northwestern U., Evanston, Ill., 1971; prof. modern langs. U. Conn., Storrs, 1972-79; prof., head dept. modern langs. James Cook U., Townsville, Australia, 1979—, chmn. Acad. Bd., 1981-85. Author: Melbourne Livy, 1961, Treasures Ballarat Art Gallery, 1968, Descriptive Catalogue of Medieval Manuscripts in Australia, 1969, Tristan de Nanteuil, 1971, 2d vol., 1983, Prieres en ancien francais, 1978, 2d vol., 1987, French Devotional Texts of the Middle Ages, 1979, 3d vol., 1987. Decorated Officer of Nat. Order of Merit, Australia, France and Italy, Officer of Acad. Palms France, Officer of Order of Crown, Belgium, Cross of Merit, Knight of Sovereign Order of St. John Jerusalem. Fellow Soc. Antiquaries, Australian Acad. Humanities (charter sec. 1969-72); mem. Australian and New Zealand Medieval Assn. (charter sec. 1967-72), Medieval Acad. Am., Australasian Univs. Lang. and Lit. Soc. Office: James Cook U, Townsville 4811, Australia

SINCLAIR, RICHARD B., school system adminstrator; b. Chgo., Jan. 12, 1936; s. Barney Michael and Harriet (Kowalczyk) Kamowski; m. Barbara Ann Sturomski, June 30, 1958; children: René Janean, Suzanne Lea, Lisa Corryn, Samantha Beth. BS, Chgo. State U., 1966; MA, Roosevelt U., 1968; EdD, No. Ill. U., 1974. Tng. dir. North Am. Rockwell, Chgo.; asst. prin. Nathan Hale Sch., Schaumburg, Ill.; asst. prof. Voldosta (Ga.) State U.; cons. Posen (Ill.)-Robbins Sch. Dist., dir. state and fed. programs, adminstrv. asst., bus. mgr., supt. of schs.; bd. dirs. Moraine Valley Credit Union, Palos Hills, Ill. Author 42 booklets. Bd. dirs. Trans Allied Med. Edn. Service, Homewood, Ill., 1984—, Eisenhower Spl. Edn. Program, Alsip, Ill., 1984—. Named Those Who Excell Gov. Ill., 1986. Mem. Nat. Assn. Sch. Adminstrs., Ill. Assn. Sch. Adminstrs., Bremen Assn. Sch. Adminstrs., Supts.' Roundtable of Ill., Internat. Show Car Assn., Phi Delta Kappa. Clubs: Willow Basin Yacht (Colon, Mich.) (pres. 1986—), Internat. Show Car Assn. (Detroit). Home: 6331 N Normandy Chicago IL 60631 Office: Sch Dist 143 1/2 14025 Harrison Posen IL 60469

SINCLAIR, ROBERT EWALD, physician, educator; b. Columbus, Ohio, Jan. 19, 1924; s. George Albert and Bertha Florence (Ewald) S.; m. Mary Almira Underwood, Mar. 31, 1945; children: Marcia Ann, Bonnie Sue. BA, Ohio State U., 1948, MD, 1952. Licensed physician, Ohio, Colo., Ala., Kans. Intern, Mt. Carmel Hosp., Columbus, 1952-53; resident in neurology and psychiatry Columbus State Hosp., 1964-66, chief psychiatric resident adolescent unit, 1965-66; pvt. practice medicine, Columbus, 1953-57, Granville, Ohio, 1957-64; dir. student health service, prof. health edn., team physician Denison U., 1957-64; dir. student health service, prof. health edn., team physician U. Cin., 1966-70; dir. Lafene Student Health Ctr. and U. Hosp., team physician Kans. State U., Manhattan, 1970-80; dir. Russell Student Health Ctr. and Hosp., and prof. medicine U. Ala., University, 1980—; physician Westinghouse Electric Corp., Columbus, 1953-57; asst. zone chief Civilian Def., Columbus, 1954-57; mem. Licking County Bd. Health, Ohio, 1958-59. Bd. dirs. social health com. Cin. and Hamilton County, Ohio, 1967-70, drug abuse and edn. com., 1968-70. Served with USNR, 1943-46. Mem. AMA, Ohio Med. Soc., Kans. Med. Soc., Ala. Med. Soc., Columbus Acad. Medicine, Licking County Med. Soc. (Ohio), Riley County Med. Soc. (Kans.), Tuscaloosa County Med. Soc., Nat. Athletic Trainers Assn., Ohio Coll. Health Assn. (editor Newsletter 1968-70, pres. 1970-71), Central Coll. Health Assn. (pres. 1972-73), So. Coll. Health Assn. (pres. 1986), Delta Tau Delta (faculty advisor), Nu Sigma Nu, Nu Sigma Nu Alumni Assn. (pres. 1953-54). Lodges: Kiwanis, Rotary. Home: 1 Rollingwood Tuscaloosa AL 35406 Office: U Ala Russell Student Health Ctr Tuscaloosa AL 35487

SINCLAIR, VIRGIL LEE, JR., lawyer, writer; b. Canton, Ohio, Nov. 10, 1951; s. Virgil Lee and Thelma Irene (Dunlap) S.; m. Judy Ann Montgomery, May 26, 1969 (div. Mar. 1980); children: Kelly, Shannon. BA, Kent State U., 1973; JD, U. Akron, 1976; postgrad. Case Western Res. U., 1979. Adminstr. Stark County Prosecutor's Office, Canton, 1974-76; mem. faculty Walsh Coll., Canton, 1976-78; asst. pros. atty. Stark County, Canton, 1976-77; ptnr. Amerman Burt Jones Co. LPA, Canton, 1976—; legal adviser Mayor's Office, City of North Canton, Ohio, 1978-79; referee Stark County Family Ct., Canton, 1981; spl. referee Canton Mcpl. Ct., 1985-86. Author: Law Enforcement Officers' Guide to Juvenile Law, 1975, Lay Manual of Juvenile Law, 1976; editor U. Akron Law Rev.; contbr. to Ohio Family Law, 1983, also articles to profl. jours. Mem. North Canton Planning Comm., 1979-82; bd. mgrs. North Canton YMCA, 1976—, Camp Tippecanoe, Ohio, 1981—; profl. adviser Parents Without Partners, 1980—; spl. dep. Stark County Sheriff Dept., 1983—; trustee Palace Theatre Assn., Canton, 1982—. Recipient Disting. Service award U.S. Jaycees, 1984. Mem. ABA, Ohio Bar Assn., Stark County Bar Assn. (lectr. 1984), Ohio Trial Lawyers Assn., Assn. Trial Lawyers Am., Nat. Dist. Attys. Assn., Delta Theta Phi (bailiff 1976; nat. key winner 1975-76), Jaycees. Republican. Methodist. Lodge: Elks. Home: 6069 Paris Ave NE Louisville OH 44641

SINCLAIR, WILLIAM DONALD, church official; b. Los Angeles, Dec. 27, 1924; s. Arthur Livingston and Lillian May (Holt) S.; B.A. cum laude, St. Martin's Coll., Olympia, Wash., 1975; postgrad. Emory U., 1978-79; m. Barbara Jean Hughes, Aug. 9, 1952; children—Paul Scott, Victoria Sharon. Commd. 2d lt. USAAF, 1944, advanced through grades to col., USAF, 1970; service in Italy, Korea, Vietnam and Japan; ret., 1975; bus. adminstr. First United Methodist Ch., Colorado Springs, Colo., 1976-85; bus. adminstr. Village Seven Presbyn. Ch., 1985-87; bus. adminstr. Sunrise United Meth. Ch., 1987—; vice-chmn. council fin. and adminstrn. Rocky Mountain conf. United Meth. Ch., U.S.A., 1979-83. Bd. dirs. Chins-Up Colorado Springs, 1983—, Pikes Peak Performing Arts Ctr., 1985—, Pioneers Mus. Foundn., 1985—. Decorated Legion of Merit with oak leaf cluster, D.F.C. with oak leaf cluster, Air medal with 6 oak leaf cluster, Dept. Def. Meritorious Service medal. Fellow Nat. Assn. Ch. Bus. Adminstrs. (nat. dir., regional v.p., v.p. 1983-85, pres. 1986-87, Ch. Bus. Adminstr. of Yr. award 1983), Colo. Assn. Ch. Bus. Adminstrs. (past pres.), United Meth. Assn. Ch. Bus. Adminstrs. (nat. sec. 1978-81), Christian Ministries Mgmt. Assn. (dir. 1983-85), USAF Acad. Athletic Assn. Clubs: Colorado Springs Country, Plaza. Lodge: Rotary (pres. Downtown Colorado Springs club 1985—), Order of Daedalians. Home: 3007 Chelton Dr Colorado Springs CO 80909 Office: 420 N Nevada Ave Colorado Springs CO 80903

SINDBERG, PAULA ANN, accountant, lawyer; b. Torrance, Calif., Jan. 22, 1952; arrived in Switzerland, 1986; d. John William and Ajor-Helyn Paula (Schmidt) Johnson. AB in Polit Sci. and Econs., Stanford U., 1974; JD summa cum laude, U. Santa Clara, 1977; postgrad. in Acctg., Salisbury State Coll., 1981-83. Bar: Calif. 1977, U.S. Ct. Appeals (9th cir.) 1977; CPA, Oreg. 1986. Law clk. to Justice Mathew O. Tobriner Calif. Supreme Ct., San Francisco, 1977; assoc. Orrick, Herrington, Rowley & Sutcliffe, San Francisco, 1977-78; tax cons. Johnson & Johnson, CPA's, Redondo Beach, Calif., 1981-82; tax and fin. cons. Salisbury, Md., 1983; tax snr. Arthur Andersen & Co., Portland, Oreg., 1983-86; tax mgr. Arthur Andersen & Co., Zurich, Switzerland, 1986-87; tax mgr. Arthur Andersen AG, Zurich, Switzerland, 1987—, dir. U.S. tax practice, 1987—; cons. Assn. Oreg. Archaeologists, Portland, 1985-86; lectr. civic and profl. orgns. on tax and fin. topics. Contbr. articles to profl. jours. Scheduling coordintor Lowenstein for Congress, N.Y.C., 1972; publicity chmn. Ira Brown for Superior Ct., San Francisco, 1978; treas. Columbia Rediviva Soc., Portland, 1985-86; cons. Cultural Heritage Found., Portland, 1986—. Recipient Sells award Am. Inst. CPA's, 1983. Mem. Am. Tax Inst., Nat. Assn. Accts., Calif. Bar Assn. Republican. Home: Oberdorfstrasse 25, 8820 Waedenswil Switzerland Office: Arthur Andersen AG, Lavaterstrasse 93, 8027 Zurich Switzerland

SINDERMAN, ROGER WILLIAM, health physicist; b. West Olive, Mich., May 4, 1942; s. William August and Marta Marie (Beck) S.; B.S. in Engring. (Dupont fellow), U. Mich., 1964; M.S. in Health Physics (USPHS fellow), 1965; M.P.H. in Radiation Biology (USPHS fellow), 1966; m. Christine Kubiak, May 30, 1964 (div. Jan. 1985); children—Christian, Heidi; m. Melanie June Lathwell, May 4, 1985. Asso. engr., gen. engr. nuclear ops. dept. Consumers Power Co. Big Rock Nuclear Plant, Charlevoix, Mich., 1966-68, health physicist, plant health physicist, environ. health physicist, Jackson, Mich., 1968-80, dir. radiol. services, Jackson, 1980-84, dir. nuclear services, 1984—. Mem. Health Physics Soc. Author tech. papers in field. Home: 4403 Maple Lane Rd Rives Junction MI 49277 Office: 1945 W Parnall Rd Jackson MI 49201

SINDERMANN, HORST, government offical. German Democratic Republic; b. Dresden, Ger., Sept. 5, 1915; married, 2 children. Mem. Communist Union of Youth, Saxony, 1929; polit. imprisonment, 1934-45; chief editor Volksstimme, Chemnitz; chief editor Press Service of Sozialistische Einheitspartei Deutschlands; chief editor dist. paper Freiheit, Halle/Saale, E. Ger.; mem. staff Central Com., Sozialistische Einheitspartei Deutschlands, 1954-63, candidate mem., 1959-63, 1st sec. dist. council, 1963-71, mem., 1963—; candidate mem. Politburo, 1963-67, mem., 1967—; 1st dep. chmn. German Democratic Republic Council Ministers, 1971-73, chmn., 1973-76; vice chmn. Council of State, 1976; mem. Volkskammer, 1963—, pres., 1976—. Decorated Order Karl Marx, Vaterländischer Verdienstorden in silver and gold (2), others. Address: Volkskammer, Office of President, Berlin German Democratic Republic *

SINDONA, MARCO, electronics company executive, consultant; b. Milan, Italy, Apr. 8, 1952; s. Michele and Caterina (Cilio) S. B.S. in Bus. Econs., Milan U., also M.A. in Econs.; Ph.D. in Econs., Edinburgh, U. (Scotland). Vice pres. F.I.M.A.C., Milan, 1977-79, Perotti & Co., Milan, 1979-80; chmn. Electrotel, Milan, 1981—; internat. fin. cons. Author: Exchange-Rate Determination in Open Economies, 1977; The Role of the Public Sector, 1979; A Non-Monetarist Approach to the Balance of Payments, 1981, Come Prendere in Oiro Gli Idioti E Vivere Felici, 1987. Treas. Partito Radicale, Milan, 1977-78, polit. sec., 1979, fed. com., Rome, 1980. Co-winner Nobel Prize in Econs., 1985. Home: C Porta Vittoria 18, 20122 Milan Italy Office: Electrotel-Teledur, V Gargano 50, 20139 Milan Italy

SINGER, HANS, trading and contracting company executive; b. Berwang, Tyrol, Austria, July 17, 1928; s. Hans and Irma (Weber) S.; B.Commerce, Hochschule fuer Welthandel, Vienna, Austria, 1952, D.Econs., 1953; m. Gisela Kraft, Dec. 29, 1958; children—Hans-Guenter, Christiane. With Ferrostaal AG, Essen, W. Ger., 1954—, ordinary bd. mem. for div. export capital goods, 1968-75, exec. v.p., 1975-76, pres., 1976—; v.p. Man AG, Munich, Fed. Republic Germany; mem. supervisory bd. Bayerische Hypotheken und Wechsel-Bank A.G., Munich, W.Ger., DSD-Dillinger Stahlbau GmbH, Saarlouis, W. Ger., Deutsch-Suedamerikanische Bank AG, Hamburg, W. Ger., Flender Werft AG, Luebeck, W. Ger., MAN B&W Diesel A/S, Copenhagen, Denmark, MAN Roland Druckmaschinen AG, Offenbach am Main, Fed. Republic Germany. Pres. C. of C. Essen. Roman Catholic. Club: Rotary (Muelheim-Ruhr, W. Ger.). Office: Hohenzollernstrasse 24, 4300 Essen 1 Federal Republic of Germany

SINGER, ISAAC BASHEVIS, writer; b. Radzymin, Poland, July 14, 1904; came to U.S., 1935, naturalized, 1943; s. Pinchos Menachem and Bathsheba (Zylberman) S.; m. Alma Haimann, Feb. 14, 1940; 1 son, Israel. Student, Rabbinical Sem., Warsaw, Poland, 1920-27; D.H.L. (hon.), Hebrew Union Coll., Los Angeles, 1963; Litt.D. (hon.), L.I. U., 1979. With Hebrew and Yiddish publs. in, Poland, 1926-35, Jewish Daily Forward, N.Y.C., 1935—. Author: Satan in Goray, 1935, The Family Moskat, 1950, Gimpel The Fool, 1957, The Magician of Lublin, 1960, The Spinoza of Market Street, 1961, The Slave, 1962, Short Friday, 1964, In My Father's Court, 1966, The Manor, 1967, The Seance, 1968, The Estate, 1969, A Friend of Kafka, 1970, Enemies, A Love Story, 1972, A Crown of Feathers, 1973, Passions, 1976, A Young Man in Search of Love, 1978, A little Boy in Search of God, Shosha, 1978, Old Love, 1979, Lost in America, 1981, The Collected Stories of Isaac Bashevis Singer, 1982, The Golem, 1982, Yentl, the Yeshiva Boy, 1983, Love and Exile, 1984, The Image and Other Stories, 1985, The Death of Methuselah and Other Stories, 1988; also books for children including A Day of Pleasure, 1970 (Nat. Book award), Stories for Children, 1987; appearance in PBS prodn. American Masters: Isaac in America, 1987. Recipient Epstein Fiction award, 1963, Playboy award for best fiction/short story, 1967, Poses Creative Arts award, 1970, Nat. Book awards, 1970, 74, Nobel Prize for lit., 1978, Handel medallion, 1986. Fellow Jewish Acad. Arts and Scis., Nat. Inst. Arts and Letters, Polish Inst. Arts and Scis. in Am.; mem. Am. Acad. Arts and Scis. Club: PEN (N.Y.C.). Office: care Farrar Straus & Giroux Inc 19 Union Sq W New York NY 10003 *

SINGER, JACQUES MAURICIU, physician, microbiologist; b. Bucharest, Romania, Mar. 1, 1914; came to U.S., 1955, naturalized, 1963; s. Mauriciu and Frederica (Wechsler) S.; m. Renee Schonfeld, Jan. 22, 1949. M.D., Faculty of Medicine, U. Bucharest, 1939; postgrad. in Microbiology, Cantacuzino Inst., U. Bucharest, 1944-47. Diplomate: Am. Bd. Microbiology. Intern and resident Caritas and Noua Maternitate Hosp., Bucharest, 1937-39; attenting Caritas and Noua Maternitate Hosp., 1942-44; head dept. microbiology Iubirea de Oameni Hosp., Bucharest, 1944-47, Afula Hosp., Israel, 1948-49, Rambam Govt. Hosp., Haifa, Israel, 1949-55; research asst.

and asso. Mt. Sinai Hosp., N.Y.C., 1955-59; resident Neustater Convalescent Home Mt. Sinai Hosp., 1955-59; clin. asso. prof. medicine Downstate Med. Center, N.Y., 1959-61; head dept. microbiology and immunology Montefiore Med. Ctr., Bronx, 1982—; prof. pathology Albert Einstein Coll. Medicine, Bronx, 1976—; staff N. Central Bronx Hosp., 1978—. Contbr. articles on immunology and microbiology to profl. jours. Arthritis Rheumatism Found. fellow, 1959-64. Fellow N.Y. Acad. Medicine; mem. AMA, Bronx County Med. Soc., Arthritis and Rheumatism Found., Nat. Com. on Clin. Lab Standards (subcom. on standardization), Am. Soc. Microbiology. Home: 11 Lewis Pl New Rochelle NY 10804 Office: Montefiore Med Center Bronx NY 10467

SINGER, JOSEPH HOWARD, public relations executive; b. San Francisco, Dec. 5, 1922; s. Jack and Julia (Sullivan) S.; B.A. cum laude, Stanford U., 1950, M.A., 1951; m. Jacqueline Yvonne Auliac, Jan. 14, 1947; 1 dau., Patricia Jacqueline. Staff corr. Internat. News Service, Paris, 1951-53, Berlin bur. chief, 1953-56, chief diplomatic corr., Washington, 1956-57; Washington mgr. public relations Reynolds Metals, Washington, 1958-60, eastern public relations mgr., N.Y.C., 1960-63; dir. public relations Geigy Chem. Corp., Ardsley, N.Y., 1963-66; asst. public relations dir. Gen. Foods, 1966-72, dir. public relations, White Plains, N.Y., 1972-75; corp. dir. pub. relations Am. Hoechst Corp., Somerville, N.J., 1975-87; corp. dir. pub. relations Hoechst Celanese Corp., Somerville, 1987-88; pres., chief exec. officer Crisiscom, Short Hills, N.J., 1988—. Bd. govs. USO, 1967-80, nat. v.p., 1969-80; chmn. journalism adv. bd. Coll. White Plains, 1970-74. Bd. dirs., v.p. Travelers Aid Internat. Social Services Am. Served to 1st lt. Mil. Police Corps, AUS, 1943-48; ETO. Mem. Calorie Control Council (chmn. public relations com. 1969-74), Packaging Inst. U.S.A. (chmn. public affairs adv. com. 1970-74), Am. Chem. Soc. (pub. relations com. 1984—), Am. Importers Assn. (chmn. public relations com.), Public Relations Soc. Am. (pres. Westchester County chpt. 1971-72), Nat., Overseas press clubs, Delta Phi Epsilon. Home: 275 Hobart Ave Short Hills NJ 07078 Office: Crisiscom Short Hills NJ 07078

SINGER, NIKI, public relations company executive; b. Rochester, N.Y., Sept. 10, 1937; d. Goodman A. and Evelyn (Simon) Sarachan; B.A. cum laude, U. Mich., 1959; m. Michael J. Sheets, 1973; children—Romaine Kitty, Nicholas Simon Feramorz. Mgr. advt. sale promotion Fairchild Publs., N.Y.C., 1959-67; account exec., account supr. Vernon Pope Co., N.Y.C., 1967-69, v.p., 1969-71; pres. Niki Singer, Inc., N.Y.C., 1971—. Mem. Les Dames d'Escoffier, Am. Inst. Wine and Food. Home: 1035 Fifth Ave New York NY 10028 Office: 400 Madison Ave New York NY 10017

SINGER, STANLEY THOMAS, JR., engineering administrator; b. Detroit, June 29, 1933; s. Stanley Thomas and Agnes Frances (Maciejewski) S.; m. Iris Josephine Bandmann, Nov. 12, 1960; children: Stanley Thomas III, Eric Herms. BBA, U. Detroit, 1966; MA Cen. Mich. U., 1977. Tool designer Gen. Motors Corp., Detroit, 1951-55, prodn. engr., 55-62; prodn. engr. Ford Motor Co., Utica, Mich., 1962-64, research engr., 1964-67, engring. mgr., Dearborn, 1967—, mgr. quality assurance, 1986. Mem. exec. bd. Detroit Area Council Boy Scouts of Am., 1967—, mem. East Cen. region exec. bd.; trustee Greater Detroit Cath. Youth Orgn.; mem. Macomb County Community Relations Com. Recipient Silver Beaver award Boy Scouts Am., 1984, St. George Emblem, Cath. Ch., 1984, Ed Crowe award for service to youth, 1986. Mem. Soc. Automotive Engrs., Engring. Soc. of Detroit, Soc. Mfg. Engrs., Am. Soc. Quality Control, Delta Sigma Pi. Republican. Roman Catholic. Clubs: Detroit Yacht, Hillcrest Country. Lodge: K.C. Avocations: skiing, flying, boating.

SINGH, AMARENDRA NARAYAN, psychiatrist, cardiologist; b. Gulni, Bihar, India, Aug. 16, 1935; came to Can., 1970; s. Gaya Prasad and Bimala (Singh) S.; m. Gertraud M. Singh, Apr. 23, 1969; children: Sheila Kumari, Rajendra Narayan. BSc, Bihar U., India, 1955; MBBS, Bihar U., 1961; FRCP, Royal Coll. Physicians and Surgeons, Canada, 1972; FRC Psychiat., Royal Coll. Psychiatrists, London, 1981. Fellow Royal Coll. Physicians, Royal Coll. Psychiatrists. Intern Darbanga Med. Coll. Hosp., 1961-62; sr. house officer Inst. Neurology Queen Sq. U. London, 1963-64; jr. officer Roundway Hosp. U. Bristol, England, 1964-65; fellow in Medicine Royal Post Grad. Med. Sch. Hammersmith Hosp., London, 1965-66; registrar in EEG and psychiat. dept. psychiat. Burden Research Inst. and Barrow Hosp., Bristol, 1966-67; registrar dept. psychiat. Barrow Hosp., Bristol, 1967-68; sr. registrar in psychiat. Powick Hosp. Burmingham U., Eng., 1969-70; sr. psychiatrist Regional Psychiatric Ctr. Prince Albert, Sask., Can., 1970-71; dir. med. NE Regional Mental Health Ctr., South Porcupine, Ont., Can., 1971-72; dir. program Hamilton Psychiat. Hosp. McMaster U. Med. Ctr., Ont., Can., 1972—; dir. Adverse Reaction and Fennell Program, Hamilton; pres. 2nd Asian Congress Internat. Coll. Psychosomatic Medicine, 1986-88. Author: Depression, Recognition and Diagnosis, 1977, Depression Treatment Book 2, 1977, Depression Mixed Syndromes and Treatment, 1978, Depression, Hysterical Neurosis, Phobic and Obsessive Compulsive Disorders Book 4, 1980, Challenging Case Studies in Depression, 1979; contbr. articles in field to profl. jours. Recipient Queens Scholarship, 1967, Morris Hallet award, 1962; also many grants and fellowships in psychopharmacology and medicine. Mem. Internat. Coll. Psychosomatic Medicine (fellow), World Med. Assn., British Med. Assn., Can. Med. Assn., Internat. Assn. Suicide Prevention (fellow), Internat. Council Scientific Devel., World Psychiat. Assn. (treas. forensic psychiat. sect. 1977-86, nomenclature and classification sect. 1978-85). Hindu. Home: 7 Rhodes Ct, Dundas, ON Canada L9H 5R5 Office: Hamilton Psychiat Hosp, Box 585, Hamilton, ON Canada L8N 3K7

SINGH, ARTAJ, leader, physician; b. Patna, Bihar, India, June 13, 1960; arrived in Can., 1971; s. Ishar and Mahinder (Dhodi) S.; m. Judith M. Willoughby, July 30, 1983. BA, McMaster U., 1982, MD, 1985. Intern McMasterU. Med. Ctr., Hamilton, Ont., Can., 1986-87; practice family and emergency medicine 1988—; bd. dirs. Caleb Project, Pasadena, Calif., Spectrum Production, IVCF, Toronto, Student Mission Impact, Atlanta, Op. Mobilization Can., Hamilton, also v.p. Researcher, editor: Canadian Short-Term Missions Handbook, 1984. Dir. Southern Ont. Youth Missions Conf., Hamilton, 1982-83; founder, exec. dir. Student Mission Advance, Hamilton, 1984-85; coordinating dir. Vision 2000 Can. Nat. Task Force on Evangelism, Toronto, Ont., 1987—; initiator, dir. Can. Consul on Recruitment for Missions, 1987-88; 1st vice chmn. Golden Horseshoe, Billy Graham Crusade, 1989. Mem. Ont. Med. Assn. Office: #2-160 Centennial Pkwy, Hamilton, ON Canada L8E-1H9

SINGH, DADHIBAL, accountant; b. Suva, Fiji, June 18, 1941; s. Gulab and Dilraji Singh; m. Mangamma Pansaiya, Dec. 19, 1964; children—Devesh Deepak, Kushmanda Jyotsna. Sr. Cambridge Sch. cert., Indian High Sch., 1959. Asst. examiner Auditor Gen.'s Office, Suva, 1960-66, examiner, 1967-69, 1972-74, sr. examiner, 1975-80, auditor, 1980-83; bank officer Nat. Bank of Fiji, Suva, 1969-72, accounts supr., 1985-86, acct. fin., 1986-88, chief acct., 1988—; fin. officer Fiji Pub. Service Assn., Suva, 1983-85; exec. sec. Investment Co-op Ltd., Fiji Pub. Service Assn., 1983-85, sec. edn. com., 1983-85, sec. sports com., 1983-85. V.p. Moti St. and Environs Neighborhood Support Group, 1988—; treas commr. So. div. Police Crime Prevention Assn., 1988. Mem. Inst. Internal Auditors (gov. Fiji chpt. 1982, v.p. 1983, v.p. EDP com. 1982-83, chmn. program com. 1983, chmn. social com. 1982-83, pres. 1985-86). Hindu. Home: 27 Tawake St, GPO Box 12401, Suva Fiji Office: Nat Bank Fiji, GPO Box 1166, Suva Fiji

SINGH, GURMEET MOHINDER PAL, child development educator; b. Ludhiana, Punjab, India, Mar. 5, 1955; d. Sobha Singh and Sunder Kaur (Baweja) Arora; m. Mohinder Pal Singh, Apr. 7, 1982; children: Harmohit, Pulkit. B in Home Sci., Punjab Agrl. U., 1974; M in Child Devel., Faculty of Home Sci., Maharaja Sayaji U., India, 1976. Dist. officer child welfare Indian Council for Child Welfare, Karnal, 1976-77; extension assoc. dept. child devel. Punjab Agrl. U., Ludhiana, 1977-80, asst. prof., 1980—, coordinator lab. nursery sch. dept. child devel., 1983-86; advisor Home Sci. Assn., 1985—; examiner univs., Baroda, India, 1985—. Author: Pregnancy-The Beginning Of, 1986; co-editor Tomorrow's Hope, 1979—. Assn. Commonwealth Univs. scholar, 1987—. Mem. Child Devel. Soc. (sec. 1977-80), Indian Assn. Presch. Edn. (life), Indian Soc. Extension Edn. Office: Punjab Agrl U, Coll Home Sci, Dept Child Devel, Ludhiana 141004, India

SINGH, JAMUNA SHARAN, ecology educator; b. Allahabad, India, Dec. 26, 1941; s. Vishwambher Sharan and Chandrakali Devi Singh; m. Tripura Singh, May 7, 1960; children: Atul, Hema, Anupa, Anuj. MS, U. Allahabad, 1959; PhD, Banaras Hindu U., Varanasi, India, 1967. Lectr. ecology Kurukshetra (India) U., 1968-71; research scientist Colo. State U., Fort Collins, 1971-74; reader ecology Sch. Planning, New Delhi, India, 1975-76, Kumaun U., Naini Tal, India, 1976-84; prof. botany, ecological scis. Banaras Hindu U., Varanasi, 1984—; mem. Nat. Man and the Biosphere Com. Indian Govt., New Delhi, 1984-87, Himalayan Eco-devel. Research Com., 1985—, Spl. Com. for Geosphere-Biosphere Program Internat. Council Sci. Unions, Paris, 1987—. Author numerous research papers in field; chief editor Tropical Ecology, 1984—; editor: Environmental Regeneration in the Himalaya, 1985. Active Nat. Sci. Com., Indian Nat. Scis. Acad., 1988—, planning Commn., Indian Govt., 1988—; steering group on enviroment, forest, and wastelands devel. Recipient S.S. Bhatnagar Prize Council Sci. and Indsl. Research, New Delhi, 1980, Pitamber Pant award New Delhi Dept. Environment, 1984, Pranavanand award Univ. Grants Commn., 1985. Fellow Indian National Scis. Acad., Indian Acad. Scis., Internat. Soc. for Tropical Ecology, Cen. Himalayan Environ. Assn. Home: Banaras Hindu Univ, Old D/4 Jodhpur Colony, Varanasi, Uttar Pradesh 221005, India Office: Banaras Hindu U, Dept Botany, Varanasi, Uttar Pradesh 221005, India

SINGH, KHUSHWANT, author, free-lance journalist, former member Indian parliament; b. Hadali, Punjab, India, Feb. 2, 1915; s. Sobha Singh and Veeran Bai; m. Kaval Malik; 2 children: Rahul, Mala. Ed. Govt. Coll., Lahore; King's Coll. and Inner Temple, London. Practiced law High Ct., Lahore, India, 1939-47; commd. officer Indian Ministry of External Affairs, 1947; press attache, Can., then pub. relations officer, London, 1948-51; A.I. Radio, 1951-53; UNESCO, Paris, 1954-56; founder, editor Yojana, 1956-58; M.P. 1980-86; editor in chief The Hindustan Times, Contour, New Delhi, from 1980; vis. lectr. Oxford U., Princeton U., Swarthmore Coll., numerous other colls. and univs.; led Indian delegation to Writers' Conf., Manila, 1965; guest speaker Montreal Expo. '67; editor The Illustrated Weekly of India, 1969-79, Nat. Herald, Delhi, 1978-79, Hindustan Times, New Delhi, 1980-83; chief-editor New Delhi, 1979-80; Author: Mark of Vishnu, 1949; The Sikhs, 1951; Train to Pakistan, 1954 (Grove Press award); Sacred Writings of the Sikhs, 1960; I Shall not hear the Nightingale, 1961; Umrao Jan Ada—Courtesan of Lucknow (trans.), 1961; History of the Sikhs (2 Vols.): Ranjit Singh: Maharaja of the Punjab, 1962, Fall of the Sikh Kingdom, 1962; The Skeleton (trans.), 1963; Land of the Five Rivers (trans.), 1964; Khushwant Singh's India, 1969; Indira Gandhi Returns, 1979; Editor's Page, 1980; Iqbal's Dialogue with Allah (trans.), 1981; Homage to Guru Gobind Singh: Hymns of Nanak The Guru; Delhi—A Profile, 1982, The Sikhs, 1984; Punjab Tragedy (with Kuldip Nayar) 1984, History of the Sikhs 1769-1839 Vol. I, 1962, 1839-Present Day Vol. II, 1965 (commd. by Rockefeller Found. and Muslim U., Aligarh); The Sikhs Today: Their Religion, History, Culture, Custom, and Way of Life, 1985; contbr. numerous articles to New York Times, The Observer, New Statesman, Harpers, Evergreen Rev., London Mag., many others; contbr. all material on Sikhism to Ency. Brittanica; numerous appearance TV and radio, including BBC, CBC, All India Radio. Recipient Mohan Singh award. Avocation: bird watching. *

SINGH, KOTHARI BIJAY, accountant; b. Sept. 2, 1928; m. Smt. Puspa, Feb. 16, 1951; 1 child, Amitav. B in Commerce, Calcutta (India) U., 1948, MA, 1951. Chartered acct., India. Sr. ptnr. Kothari & Co., Chartered Accts., Calcutta and Bombay, 1951—; lectr. internat. confs.. Author numerous pamphlets and booklets on acctg.; mem. editorial bd. Chartered Accts. and Fin. and Commerce; contbr. articles to profl. jours. Justice of Peace, India; port commr. West Bengal (India) adv. com.; mem. Telephone adv. com., Calcutta Electric Supply consultative com.; trustee Kothari Lok Kalyan Trust. Mem. Inst. Chartered Accts. (cen. council, 1967-71), Consumer's Assn. (pres.), Assn. Co. Secs., Execs. and Advisers Calcutta (pres. 1967-68), Merchants C. of C. (pres. 1968-70, trustee). Clubs: Calcutta, India Internat. Ctr., New Delhi. Lodge: Lions (pres. Calcutta chpt. 1968-69). Address: 8-E Neelkanth Apts 26-B, Camac St, Calcutta 700016, India

SINGH, MAHENDRA PRATAP, electrical equipment manufacturing company executive; b. Allahabad, India, Aug. 23, 1950; s. Rajendra Prasad and Shanti Singh; m. Usha Rani Singh, July 16, 1977; children—Niharika, Namita, Deepti. B.S, Indian Inst. Tech., Kanpur, 1971; M.S., Case Western Res. U., 1974; M.B.A., U. Ill., 1976. Registered profl. engr., Wis. Research asst. Case Western Res. U., Cleve., 1971-73; research asst. dept. econs., survey research lab. U. Ill.-Champaign, 1974-75; mgr. application engring. AFL Industries, West Chicago, Ill., 1976-79; product mgr. Dana Corp., Elgin, Ill., 1979-80, Reliance Electric Co., Greenville, S.C., 1980—. Tech. reviewer Am. Soc. Heating, Refrigerating and Air-Conditioning Engrs. Jour.; contbr. numerous articles to profl. lit.; patentee control for variable speed drives. NASA research grantee, 1972-73; EPA research grantee, 1974. Mem. ASHRAE, ASME, Am. Mktg. Assn., Mensa. Club: Toastmasters (pres.). Home: 814 Plantation Dr Simpsonville SC 29681 Office: Reliance Electric Co PO Box 499 Greenville SC 29602

SINGH, MUKHTAR, chemist, educator; b. Aligarh, India, Jan. 22, 1941; s. Singh Ved Ram and Sharwati Devi. M of Sci. in Phys. Chemistry, Agra (India) U., 1962, PhD in Phys. Chemistry, 1969, D of Sci. in Phys. Chemistry, 1986. Lectr. in chemistry Agra Coll., 1962-82, assoc. prof., 1982—, research guide, PhD candidate supr., 1973, prin., 1985. Contbr. over 150 articles to sci. jours. Grantee Uttar Pradesh State, 1974, Council Sci. and Indsl. Research, 1980. Fellow Indian Chem. Soc. (life), Electro Chem. Soc. India (life), Indian Sci. Congress Assn. Club: Agra Coll. Staff. Home: 5 Huntley House, MG Rd, Agra, Uttar Pradesh 282010, India Office: Agra Coll, Chemistry Dept, Agra, Uttar Pradesh 282002, India

SINGH, NAGENDRA, presiding justice International Court of Justice, university official; b. Dangarpur, Rajasthan, Mar. 18, 1914. BA, Agra U., 1934; MA, Cambridge U., 1938, LLD, 1965; MA, Dublin U., BLitt, 1955, LLD; DSc in Law, U. Moscow, 1964; DCL, U. Delhi, 1966; DLitt, U. Bihar, 1955; DPhil, U. Calcutta, 1958; LLD (hon.), U. Bhopal, 1973, U. Kurukshetra, 1975, U. Jodhpur, 1976, U. Guru Nanek, 1977, U. Punjab, 1978, U. Rajasthan, 1982, U. Peking (Bejing), I. Cordoba, Freedom of the City of Salta, Argentina, 1987. Called to bar, 1942. Dist. magistrate, collector Madhya Pradesh, India, 1938-46; joint sec. Def. Ministry, India, 1946-56; mem. Constituent Assembly of India, 1947-48; regional commr. Ea. States, India, 1948; with Imperial Def. Coll., London, 1950; dir. gen. shipping Indian Ministry Transport, 1956-64, sec., 1964-65; spl. sec. Ministry Info. and Broadcasting India, New Delhi, 1964; sec. to Pres. India, 1966-72; chief election commr. to Govt. India, 1972, Padma Vibhushan, 1973; chancellor U. Goa, 1985—; judge ad hoc Internat. Ct. of Justice, The Hague, The Netherlands, 1972, judge, 1973—, v.p., 1976-79, pres., 1985—; justice of peace, Bombay, 1958; constl. adviser to Govt. Bhutan, 1970; numerous internat. activities, including pres. Assembly of Inter-Govtl. Maritime consultative Orgn., London, 1963-65, rep. of India to UN Gen. Assembly, 1966, 69, 71, pres. maritime session ILO, Geneva, 1970; numerous legal activities, including v.p. Brussels diplomatic confs. on maritime law, 1961, 67, mem. Permanent Ct. of Arbitration, The Hague, 1967—, judge Ct. Arbitration for Sports of Internat. Olympic Com., 1983; mem. UN World Commn. on Environment and Devel., 1984; mem. UNESCO Commn. of India, 1984; mem. bur. Internat. Acad. Human Rights, Paris, 1985; lectr. Author: Commercial Law of India, 1975; Bhutan, 1978; Maritime Flag and International Law, 1978, numerous others; also numerous articles in law jours. in India and abroad. Named hon. master of bench, Grays Inn, London, 1975; accorded rank of ambassador, 1972; fellow St. John's Coll., Cambridge U., Eng., 1974. Fellow World Acad. Art and Sci., Brit. Acad.; mem. Inst. Internat. Law, Internat. Law Assn. (exec. council), Am. Soc. Internat. Law (hon.), Internat. Inst. for Unification Pvt. Law (governing council 1963), Inst. Pub. Internat. Law (curatorium) (Greece), Indian Inst. Constl. and Parliamentary Studies (exec. council), Indian Soc. Internat. Law (pres.), Maritime Law Assn. India (pres.), Nat. Labour law Assn. India (pres.), Indian Law Inst. (v.p. 1984), World Assn. of Judges (pres. 1987, World Justice award 1987). Office: Internat Ct of Justice, Peace Palace, 2517 KJ The Hague The Netherlands

SINGH, NIRBHAY NAND, psychology educator, researcher; b. Suva, Fiji, Jan. 27, 1952; came to N.Z., 1970; s. Shiri Ram and Janki Kumari (Singh) S.; m. Judy Daya, May 17, 1973; children—Ashvind Nand, Subhashi Devi. Ph.D., U. Auckland, N.Z., 1978. Sr. clin. psychologist, head psychology dept. Mangere Hosp. and Tng. Sch., Auckland, 1976-81; assoc. in clin. psychology U. Auckland, 1977-80; lectr. psychology U. Canterbury, Christchurch, N.Z., 1981-82, sr. lectr. psychology, 1983-87; sr. research scientist Ednl. Research and Services Ctr., De Kalb, Ill., 1987—; cons. Project MESH, U. Otago, Dunedin, N.Z., 1982-87, external examiner, diploma in edn., 1982-87; cons. Kimberley Hosp. and Tng. Sch., Levin, N.Z., 1984-87; cons. adv. com. tng. officers Dept. Health, Wellington, 1984-87; cons. curriculum adv. com. Vol. Welfare Agy. Tng. Bd., Wellington, 1984-87; cons. spl. edn. adv. com. Christchurch Tchrs.' Coll., 1986-87. Co-author: I Can Cook. Editor: Mental Retardation in New Zealand: Research and Policy Issues, 1983; Mental Retardation in New Zealand: Provisions, Services and Research, 1985; Exceptional Children in New Zealand, 1987, Psychopharmacology of the Developmental Disabilities, 1988; contbr. chpts. to books; editorial bd. numerous jours. Winifred Gimblett scholar 1974; Med. Research Council postgrad. scholar, 1975-76; Erskine fellow U. Canterbury, 1984. Fellow Behavior Therapy and Research Soc.; life mem. N.Z. Assn. Tchrs. Mentally Handicapped; mem. Am. Assn. Mental Deficiency, Assn. Severely Handicapped, N.Z. Psychol. Soc., Assn. Child Psychology and Psychiatry, Assn. Advancement Behavior Therapy, Soc. Advancement Behavior Analysis, N.Z. Assn. Sci. Study Mental Deificiency (pres. 1984-87), N.Y. Acad. Scis., Behavior Analysis Soc. of Ill. Avocations: squash, racquetball. Office: Ednl Research Services Ctr 425 E Fisk Ave DeKalb IL 60115

SINGH, PASHUPATI NATH, human relations executive; b. Bihar, India, Jan. 29, 1941; s. Biswanath and Tija Devi Singh; m. Chandrakanta Singh; children: Sanjay, Sunita, Anita. BS in Engring., Indian Sch. Mines, 1963; M of Mgmt., Asian Inst. Mgmt., Manila, 1975; PhD, Bajaj Inst. Mgmt., 1981. Mgr. tng. and devel. Indian Oil Corp., Bombay, 1963-80; mgr. manpower devel. Voltas Ltd., Bombay, 1981—. Author: Training for Management Development, 1985, Developing Entrepreneurship for Economic Growth, 1986; editor: Profile of an Asian Manager, 1981, Oil Industry in India--Its Achievements and Challenges Ahead, 1986. Recipient Imm Cinni Fan award Inst. Mktg. Mgmt., 1980; named Rukmini Thread Mktg. Communicator Inst. Mktg. Mgmt., 1984. Mem. Bombay Mgmt. Assn. (pres. 1987-88), Forum Asian Mgrs. (pres. 1980—), Indian Soc. Tng. and Devel. (past pres., Tarneja award 1975), Internat. Fedn. Tng. and Devel. Orgns. (bd. dirs. 1987—). Home: 101 Blue Haven Nehru Rd, Santacruz East, Bombay, Maharashtra 400055, India Office: Voltas Ltd, 19 J N Heredia Marg, Ballard Estate, Bombay, Maharashtra 400038, India

SINGH, RAJENDRA, electrical engineering educator, researcher; b. Saharanpur, India, July 13, 1946; came to U.S., 1979; s. Kartar Singh and Savitri Devi; m. Reeta Sinha, Aug. 15, 1976; children: Rupalika, Rupangini. B.S. in Physics, Agra U., India, 1965; M.S. in Electronics, Meerut U., India, 1968; M.S. in Super Conductivity, Dalhousi U., Can., 1974; Ph.D. in Solar Cells, McMaster U., Can., 1979. Lectr. Meerut U., India, 1968-73; vis. asst. prof. U. Waterloo, Ont., Can., 1979; vis. asst. prof. Colo. State U., Ft. Collins, 1979-80; sr. research scientist Energy Conservation Devices, Troy, Mich., 1980-82; assoc. prof. elec. engring. and computer sci. U. Okla., Norman, 1982-86, prof. elec. engring. and computer sci., 1986—; cons. Howard U., Washington, 1978-79, Arco Solar, Inc., Chatsworth, Calif., 1983-86. Patentee; contbr. articles to profl. jours. Vol. Can. Red Cross, Hamilton, 1977-79. Recipient Faculty Excellence award U. Okla., 1983-84, award Outstanding Instrn. and Service, 1984, Young Faculty Devel. award, 1984, 85, Engring. Excellence award, 1987, 88. Mem. IEEE (sr., Disting. Lectr. award 1983, Disting. Technologist 1987). Hindu. Current work: High speed semiconductors and superconducting electronics, solar cells, nuclear detectors, superconductivity computers. Subspecialties: Microelectronics; Microchip technology (materials science). Home: 514 Midland Dr Norman OK 73072

SINGH, SARDAR BUTA, Indian government official; b. Mustafapur, Punjab, India, Mar. 21, 1934; s. Sardar Bir S. Grad., Lyallpur Khalsa Coll., Jalandhar, India; postgrad., Guru Nanak Khalsa Coll., Bombay. Mem. Lok Sabha, 1962, 67, 71, 80, 84; union dep. minister for railways India, New Delhi, 1974-76, union dep. minister for commerce, 1976-77, minister state in ministry shipping and transport, 1980-81, minister supply and rehab., 1981-82, minister sports, 1982-83, cabinet minister in charge of parliamentary affairs, sports, work and housing, 1983-84, minister agr. and rural devel., 1984-86, minister home affairs, 1986—. Mem. Amateur Athletic Fedn. India (life pres.), India Rural Labour Fedn. (organizing sec. 1974). Home: 16 Ashoka Rd, New Delhi 110001, India Office: Ministry Home Affairs, New Delhi India *

SINGH, SHILDENDRA KUMAR, diplomat; b. Agra, India, Jan. 24, 1932; s. Thakur Jaipal and Surendrawati (Singh) S.; m. Manju Gupta; children: Shashank, Kanishka. MA in History, Agra (India) U.; student, Cambridge U., Eng. Third sec. and OSD Ministry of External Affairs, New Delhi, 1959-62; first sec. Permanent Mission of India to UN, N.Y.C., 1962-67; sec., dir. Ministry of External Affairs, New Delhi, 1967-68, dir., joint sec. external publicity, ofcl. spokesman, 1969-74; third sec. Embassy of India, Tehran, Iran, 1957-59; ambassador to Lebanon Embassy of India, Beirut, 1974-77; ambassador to Afghanistan Embassy of India, Kabul, 1977-79; ambassador to Austria Embassy of India, 1982-85, ambassador to Pakistan, 1985—; additional sec., mem. external affairs UN, N.Y.C., 1979-82. Contbr. articles and research papers to profl. jours. Clubs: Gymkhana (New Delhi), Golf; Islamabad; Oxford & Cambridge Univ. Home: House No 17 St 19, Shalimar Pakistan Office: Embassy of India, 483-F Sector G-6/4, Islamabad Pakistan

SINGH, SHIVA PUJAN, microbiologist, educator; b. Tulsipur Majha, Gonda, India, July 15, 1947; came to U.S., 1971, naturalized, 1977; s. Ram Bahadur and Dukhana (Devi) S.; m. Patricia Ann Gangloff, Sept. 12, 1973; children—Suman R., Raj K. B.S., Pant U., Pantnagar, India, 1969, M.S., 1971; Ph.D., Auburn U., 1976. Grad. asst. Pant U., 1969-71, Auburn U., 1971-75; research assoc. Tuskegee Inst., 1976; acting head gen. biology Ala. State U., 1978, asst. prof., 1976-82, assoc. prof. biology, 1982-84, assoc. prof. biology and coordinator biomed. research, 1984-86, prof. biology, dir. Sci. research, 1986—. Argonne Nat. Lab. Faculty Research Fellowship awardee, 1979; NIH grantee, 1984—; Ala. Research Inst. grantee, 1985-86; Univ. Merit scholar, 1967-69; Indian Council Research scholar, 1969-71; recipient Vice-Chancellor's Gold Medal, 1970; named Outstanding Young Man of Am., 1983. Mem. AAAS, Am. Soc. Microbiology, Indian Microbiologists Assn. Am. (pres. 1987-88), Ala. Acad. Sci. Democrat. Hindu. Contbr. articles to profl. jours. Home: 6636 Hollis Dr Montgomery AL 36117 Office: Ala State U 915 S Jackson St Montgomery AL 36195

SINGH, ZAIL, former president of India; b. Sandhwan, Faridkot, Punjab, India, May 5, 1916; s. Kishan and Ind (Kaur) S.; m. Pardan Kaur Singh; 1 son, 3 daus. Holds title Giani (scholar). Leader, movement against autocratic rule in Punjab states; arrested at Faridkot, 1938; founder Faridkot State Congress and launcher Nat. Flag Movement, 1946; formed parallel Govt. in Faridkot State, 1948; pres. State Praja Mandal, 1946-48; revenue minister Patiala and East Punjab States Union (PEPSU) Govt., 1948-49, minister pub. works and agrl., 1951-52; pres. PEPSU Pradesh Congress Com., 1955-56; mem. Rajya Sabha, 1956-62, Punjab Assembly, 1962; minister of State, pres. Punjab Pradesh Congress Com., 1966-72; chief minister of Punjab, 1972-77; pres. Punjab Coop. Union; minister of home affairs, 1980-82, pres. of India, New Delhi, 1982-87. Address: Office of the President, Rashtrapti Bharan, New Delhi 110004 India *

SINGHAL, RAMESH CHAND, textile company executive; b. Ludhiana, Punjab, India, May 5, 1935; s. Fakir Chand and Hukam (Devi) S.; m. Veena Dhingra; children: Renuka, Radhika. BSc, Punjab U., 1957, MA, 1959; postgrad. diploma in textiles, Huddersfield Sch., Eng., 1961. Mktg. officer ICI Group Cos., Bombay, 1964-68, sect. mgr. mktg., 1968-73, sect. mgr. tech service, 1973-78, mgr. customer service, 1978-82; gen. mgr. devel. Orkay Silk Mills Ltd., Bombay, 1983-86, exec. v.p., 1986-87, dir. projects, 1987—; cons. Common Wealth Secretariat, London, 1984. Clubs: Bombay Gymkhana, Willingdon Sports. Home: 2-A Woodlands, 67 Peddar Rd, Bombay 400 026, India Office: Orkay Silk Mills Ltd, 178 Backbay Reclamation, 400 020 Bombay India

SINGHANIA, YADUPATI, corporate executive; b. Kanpur, India, Sept. 29, 1953; s. Gaur Hari and Sushila Singhania; m. Kavita Goenka, Feb. 13,

1979. B in Civil Tech., Indian Inst. Tech., Kanpur, 1976. Bd. dirs. JK Synthetics Ltd. and numerous affiliated cos., Kanpur. Mem. Yong Pres. Orgn. N.Y., Mcht. C. of C., Cement Mgf. Assn. Club: Cownpole (Kanpur). Lodge: Rotary. Home: Ganga Kuti 11 Cantt, Kanpur India Office: JK Synthetics Ltd, Kalpi Rd, Kanpur 208012, India

SINGLETON, CHARLES EDWARD, public relations executive, pastor; b. Tallulah, La., Jan. 26, 1950; s. Isaac Sr. and Pearl Beatrice (Dexter) S.; m. Charlyn Michelle Palmer, Jan. 27, 1973; children: Charles Mark, Christopher Courtland, Cory Christian, Carey Palmer. BS, So. Ill. U., 1971; MA, Cin. Grad. Sem., 1972. Recruiter Expo '72, Dallas, 1971-72; dir. Campus Crusade, San Bernardino, Calif., 1971-74; pastor Loveland Ch., Fontana, Calif., 1974—; pres. Harambee, Ontario, Calif., 1974—; ltd. ptnr. So. Garvey Med. Bldg., Pomona, Calif, 1986—; chapel speaker Los Angeles Rams, 1973—; adj. prof. Internat. Grad. Sch., San Bernardino, 1984—; cons. Fontana Unit Schs., 1986—; speaker, lectr. Author articles and books. Founder, chmn. BARAC (African relief orgn.), Pasadena, 1983; pres. Agape Acad., Ontario, 1985. Democrat. Baptist. Clubs: Holiday (Montclair, Calif.); Men's (Fontana). Home: 19689 Kauri Ave Rialto CA 92376 Office: Harambee 16888 Baseline Ave Fontana CA 92335

SINGLETON, GWYNNETH MARION, political scientist; b. Lower Hutt, New Zealand, May 27, 1943; d. Archibald and Violet (Jones) Montgomery; m. Lester Singleton, Aug. 24, 1968; children: David, Mark. BA with hons., Australian Nat. U., Canberra, 1984. Info. officer New Zealand High Commn., Canberra, 1968-71; research scholar Australian Nat. U., Canberra, 1985—. Contbr. articles to profl. jours. Mem. Royal Australian Inst. Pub. Adminstrn., Australian Polit. Studies Assn. Club: Nat. Press. Home: 8 Abbott St, Yarralumla, Canberra 2600, Australia

SINHA, ASHOK KUMAR, electronics company executive, researcher; b. Patna, India, Feb. 23, 1944; s. Kedar Nath and Shanti (Prasad) S.; m. Rekha Verma, Feb. 19, 1969; children: Gita Anjali, Anoop Kumar. BE, Indian Inst. Scis., 1964; PhD, Oxford U., 1966. With tech. staff AT&T Bell Labs, Murray Hill, N.J., 1970-76; group supr. AT&T Bell Labs., Murray Hill, N.J., 1976-82, dept. head, 1982-84; dept. head AT&T Bell Labs., Allentown, Pa., 1984-88; v.p., mfg. process devel. Sematech Consortium, Austin, Tex., 1988—; v.p. mfg. process devel.SEMATECH Consortium, Austin, Tex., 1988—; com. mem. Nat. Materials Adv. Bd., Washington, 1983-84. Contbr. over 80 articles to profl. jours.; holder over 18 patents. Mem. IEEE (sr., assoc. editor IEEE Jour. Semiconductor Mfg.), Electrochem. Soc. (div. editor 1979-80, Callinan award for Outstanding Contbrn. to Dielectrics and Insulation Sci., 1985). Home: 2281 Bishop Rd Allentown PA 18103 Office: AT&T Bell Labs 555 Union Blvd Allentown PA 18103 also: Sematech 2706 Montopolis Dr Auwtin TX 78741

SINHA, ATIN KUMAR, aerospace engineer; b. Calcutta, India, Sept. 10, 1948; came to U.S., 1979; s. Gobinda Chandra and Sheela (Mitra) S.; m. Shukla Ghosh, May 13, 1975. BME with honors, Jadavpur U., Calcutta, 1970; MAeroE, Indian Inst. Sci., Bangalore, 1973; PhD in Aerospace Engring., U. Tenn., 1984. Engr. Indian Space Research Orgn., Trivandrum, 1973; scientist Nat. Aero. Lab., Bangalore, 1973-79; engr. Gates Learjet Corp., Wichita, Kans., 1984-85; sr. engr. Garrett Engine div. Allied Signal Aerospace Co. (formerly Garrett Turbine Engine Co.), Phoenix, 1985—. Contbr. articles to profl. jours. Mem. AIAA, Sigma Xi (assoc.). Home: 915 W Diamond Dr Tempe AZ 85283 Office: Garrett Turbine Engine Div Allied Signal Aerospace 111 S 34th St M/S 93-364 503-4T Phoenix AZ 85010

SINHA, JNANENDRA PRASAD, publisher; b. West Bengal, India, Sept. 1, 1923; s. Dhirendra Prasad and Savitri (Ghosh) S.; M.A., Calcutta U., 1953, M.A. (Com.), 1949; m. Prakriti Mitra, Aug. 16, 1959; 1 child, Snehamoy. Founding partner Sci. Book Agy., Calcutta, from 1954; founder, dir. Prasun Engring. Works Ltd., Calcutta; founding dir. S.P. Sinha & Co. Ltd., Calcutta. Mem. Internat. Soc. Krishna Consciousness (life), Indian Life Saving Soc./Anderson Club, Publishers Assn. West Bengal, Indo-German C. of C., Indo-Am. Soc., Fedn. Pubs. and Booksellers Assns. in India, Am. Booksellers Assn. Home: 49/13 Hindusthan Park, Calcutta, West Bengal 700029, India Office: 56-D Mirza Ghalib St, Calcutta, West Bengal 700016, India

SINK, JOHN DAVIS, university executive, scientist; b. Homer City, Pa., Dec. 19, 1934; s. Aaron Tinsman and Louella Bell (Davis) S.; m. Nancy Lee Hile, Nov. 9, 1956 (dec. Aug. 1961); 1 child, Lou Ann. (dec. Aug. 1961); m. Claire Kaye Huschka, June 13, 1964 (div. Feb. 1987); children: Kara Joan, Karl John. B.S. in Animal/Vet. Sci., Pa. State U., 1956, M.S. in Biophysics/Animal Sci., 1960, Ph.D. in Biochemistry/Animal Sci., 1962; Ed.D. in Higher Edn., U. Pitts., 1986. Adminstrv. officer, spl. asst. to sec. agr. State of Pa., Harrisburg, 1962; prof., group leader dept. food, dairy and animal sci. Inst. Policy Research and Evaluation, Pa. State U., University Park, 1962-79; pres. Collegian, Inc., 1971-72; joint planning and evaluation staff officer Sci. and Edn. Adminstrn., U.S. Dept. Agr., Washington, 1979-80; prof., chmn intercoll. program food sci. and nutrition, interdivisional program agrl. biochemistry and div. animal and vet. scis. W.Va. U., Morgantown, 1980-85; pres., chief exec. officer Pa. State U.-Uniontown, 1985—; exec. asst., naval rep. to gov. and adj. gen. State W.Va., Charleston, 1981-84; cons. Allied Mills, Inc., Am. Air Lines, Am. Home Foods, Inc., Apollo Analytical Labs., Armour Food Co., Atlas Chem. Industries, others. Mem. nat. adv. bd. Am. Security Council, 1981—; mem. nat. adv. council Nat. Commn. Higher Edn. Issues, 1980-82; bd. dirs. W.Va. Cattleman's Assn., 1981-83, W.Va. Poultry Assn., 1980-83, Pembroke Welsh Corgi Club Am., 1980-83, Penn State Stockmen's Club, 1969-71, Greater Uniontown Indsl. Fund, 1986—; Fayette County Econ. Devel. Council, 1985—, Westomreland-Fayette council Boy Scouts Am., 1986—. Served to capt. USNR, 1956-86, ret. Decorated Army commendation medal; recipient Nat. Merit Trophy award Nat. Block and Bridle Club, 1956; W.Va. Disting. Achievement medal; Disting. Leadership award Am. Security Council Found., 1983. Pa. Meat Packers Assn. scholar, 1958-62; hon. fellow in biochemistry U. Wis., 1965-65; NSF postdoctoral fellow, 1964-65; Darbaker prize Pa. Acad. Sci., 1967. Fellow Am. Inst. Chemists, AAAS, Inst. Food Technologists; mem. Am. Meat Sci. Assn. (pres. 1974-75), Pa. Air N.G. Armory (trustee 1968-80), Pa. Acad. Sci., U.S. Naval Inst., Naval Res. Assn., Navy League U.S., Res. Officers Assn., Armed Forces Communications and Electronics Assn., Acad. Polit. Sci., Am. Assn. Higher Edn., Am. Assn. Univ. Adminstrs., Am. Chem. Soc., Biophys. Soc., Am. Soc. Animal Sci., Inst. Food Technologists, Soc. Research Adminstrs., North Fayette C. of C. (bd. dirs. 1986—), Alpha Zeta, Omicron Delta Kappa, Gamma Sigma Delta, Sigma Xi, Phi Lambda Upsilon, Gamma Alpha, Phi Tau Sigma, Phi Sigma, Phi Delta Kappa, Pi Sigma Phi. Republican. Methodist. Lodges: Rotary (sec. State College 1969-71), Elks, Internat. Assn. of Turtles. Author: The Control of Metabolism, 1974; contbr. numerous articles to profl. publs. Home: PO Box 621 Perryopolis PA 15473 Office: Pa State U PO Box 519 Uniontown PA 15401

SINNEMAKI, ULLA ULPUKKA, nurse, educator; b. Antrea, Finland, Sept. 11, 1928; d. Otto William and Kaisa Viola (Jappinen) Spjut; m. Maunu Matti J. Sinnemaki, June 12, 1949 (div. Feb. 1968); children—Markku Taneli, Sirkka Astrid. B.A., NYU, 1972; B.S., SUNY-Stony Brook, 1976; M.Ed., McNeese State U., 1978, Ed.S., 1979, M.Ed., 1981. R.N., N.Y., La., Tex. Field interviewer Bur. Census, N.Y.C., 1973-75; Operating room asst. St. Charles Meml. Hosp., N.Y.C., 1965-72; staff nurse Lake Charles Meml. Hosp., La., 1976-77; head nurse South Cameron Hosp., Cameron, La., 1977-80, dir. nursing, 1983-84; staff nurse Humana Hosp., Oakdale, La., 1984, Lake Charles, La., 1987—. Translator books, articles from English to Finnish, 1961—; designer rya rugs. Mem. Com. 1000 Baton Rouge, 1983. Mem. Nat. League Nursing, Am. Nurses Assn., Assn. Ednl. Communictions and Tech., Assn. Supervision and Curriculum Devel., Nat. Assn. Female Execs. Democrat. Lutheran. Avocations: gardening; music; photography. Address: 332 W State St Lake Charles LA 70605

SINNER, GEORGE ALBERT, governor of North Dakota, farmer; b. Fargo, N.D., May 29, 1928; s. Albert and Katherine (Wild) S.; m. Elizabeth Jane Baute, Aug. 10, 1951; children: Robert, George, Elizabeth, Martha, Paula, Mary Jo, Jim, Jerry, Joe, Eric. BA in Philosophy, St. Johns U., St. Cloud, Minn., 1950. Farmer Sinner Bros. and Bresnahan, Casselton, N.D., 1952—; mem. N.D. Senate, 1962-66, N.D. Ho. of Reps., 1982-84; chmn. fin. and tax com., 1983; gov. State of N.D., Bismarck, 1985—; founder N.D. Crops Council, Fargo, 1978-83; U.S. del. Inter-Am. Food and Agrl. Conf., 1966; founder, chmn. N.D. Crops Council, Fargo, 1978-83; chmn. No. Crops Inst. Council, Fargo, 1980-83, Interstate Oil Compact Commn., 1986—. Candidate for U.S. Congress, 1964; chmn., co-founder bd. dirs. Southeast Region Mental Health and Retardation Clinic, Carrington, N.D., 1964-66; mem. N.D. Broadcasting Council, 1968-73, N.D. Bd. Higher Edn., Bismarck, 1966-75, chmn. 1970; del. N.D. Constl. Conv., Bismarck, 1972; mem. Casselton Planning and Zoning Commn., 1982-85; co-founder bd. dirs. Tri-Coll. Univ. Bd., Fargo/Moorhead, N.D., 1970-84; chmn. Interstate Oil Compact Commn., 1986—. Served as pvt. USNG, 1950-51. Recipient Diversified Family award Fargo Rotary, 1960, Agrl. award N.D. State U., 1974, L.B. Hartz Profl. Achievement award Moorhead (Minn.) State U., 1982. Mem. Nat. Gov.'s Assn., N.D. Cattle Feeders' Assn. (farm prodn.), Red River Valley Sugarbeet Growers Assn. (pres. bd. dirs. 1975-79), Greater N.D. Assn. (bd. dirs. 1981), N.D. Farm Bur. (farm prodn.), N.D. Wheat Producers (farm prodn.), N.D. Crop Improvement Assn. (farm prodn.), N.D. Stockmen's Assn. (farm prodn.), Am. Soybean Assn. (farm prodn.), N.D. Barley Council (farm prodn.), N.D. Farmers Union (farm prodn.), Am. Legion. Democrat. Roman Catholic. Club: Casselton Community (pres. 1969). Office: Governor's Office State Capitol Bismarck ND 58505

SINNINGER, DWIGHT VIRGIL, research engineer; b. Bourbon, Ind., Dec. 29, 1901; s. Norman E. and Myra (Huff) S.; student Armour Inst., 1928, U. Chgo., 1942, Northwestern U., 1943; m. Coyla Annetta Annis, Mar. 1, 1929; m. 2d, Charlotte M. Lenz, Jan. 21, 1983. Electronics research engr. Johnson Labs., Chgo., 1935-42; chief engr. Pathfinder Radio Corp., 1943-44, Rowe Engring. Corp., 1945-48, Hupp Electronics Co. div. Hupp Corp., 1948-61; dir. research Pioneer Electric & Research Corp., Forest Park, Ill., 1961-65, Senn Custom, Inc., Forest Park and San Antonio, 1967—. Registered profl. engr., Ill. Mem. IEEE, Instrument Soc. Am., Armed Forces Communications Assn. Holder several U.S. patents. Address: PO Box 982 Kerrville TX 78028

SINNOTT, ROSE MARIE YUPPA, real estate agent; b. Cliffside Park, N.J., Oct. 4, 1936; d. Maurice P. and Jeannette Frances (Cincotta) Yuppa; B.A., Marymount Coll., Tarrytown, N.Y., 1958; postgrad. U. London, Columbia U.; grad. Realtors Inst.; m. John P. Sinnott, May 30, 1959; children—James, Jessica. Cert. residential specialist. Tchr. jr. high sch. English, N.Y.C., 1959; freelance writer, 1967—; mem. New Providence (N.J.) Zoning Bd. Adjustment, 1966-70, vice chmn., 1970-73; pres. Sinnott & Bournique, Inc., public relations, Summit, N.J., 1973-81; mem. Bd. Chosen Freeholders Union County (N.J.), 1974-82, chmn. bd., 1981; trustee Union County Econ. Devel. Corp., 1976-80; surrogate Union County Regional Health Council, 1982. Chmn. New Providence Heart Fund, 1967, Union County Heart Fund, 1974-79, Union County Mother's March of Dimes, 1978-80; Republican mcpl. committeewoman, 1972. Mem. LWV (N.J. moderator 1966—), AAUW, Bus. and Profl. Women's Club, Catholic Daus. Am. (past grand regent). Club: Soroptimist Internat. Author monthly newspaper column, also articles. Home: 2 Blackburn Pl Summit NJ 07901 Office: Burgdorff Realtors 785 Springfield Ave Summit NJ 07901

SINOWATZ, FRED, former chancellor of Austria, politician; b. Neufeld a. d. Leitha, Feb. 5, 1929; 2 children. Dr. phil., U. Vienna, 1953. Entered in service of Burgenland Govt., 1953; mem. Burgenland Landtag (provincial assembly), 1961-66, pres., 1964; landesrat (councillor of provincial govt.), 1966-71; mem. National Austria (nat. council), 1971-83; fed. minister edn. and arts Austria, 1971-83; vice chancellor, 1981-83, fed. chancellor, 1983-86. Provincial party sec. Austrian Socialist Party (SPO) in Burgenland, 1961, chmn. SPO, 1983-88. Decorated Grand Gold Badge of Honor with ribbon, Grand Badge of Honor, Comdr.'s Cross of Province of Burgenland, Grand Officer's Cross. Office: care Socialist Party Austria, Löwelstr 18, 1014 Vienna Austria

SINSHEIMER, WARREN JACK, lawyer, electronic equipment company executive; b. N.Y.C., May 22, 1927; s. Jerome William and Elizabeth (Berch) S.; m. Florence Dubin, Mar. 30, 1950; children: Linda Ruth, Ralph David, Alan Jay, Michael Neal. Student, Ind. U., 1943-47; J.D. cum laude, N.Y. Law Sch., 1950; LL.M., NYU, 1957; M.Phil., Columbia U., 1977. Bar: N.Y. bar 1950. Ptnr. Sinsheimer, Sinsheimer & Dubin, N.Y.C., 1950-78, Satterlee & Stephens, N.Y.C., 1978-86, Patterson, Belknap, Webb & Tyler, N.Y.C., 1986—; pres. Plessey, Inc., N.Y.C., 1956-70, chmn., chief exec. officer, 1970—; dir. overseas ops. and devel. The Plessey Co., Ltd., Ilford, Essex, Eng., 1969-70, now dep. chief exec., dir.; dir. Plessey, Inc.; dir. Exide Electronics Group, Inc. Chmn. Com. of 68, 1964-67; Mem Westchester County Republican Com., 1956-73; chmn. Nat. Scranton for Pres. Com., 1964; mem. N.Y. State Assembly, 1965-66; Bd. visitors Wassaic State Sch., 1962-64. Served with USNR, 1944-45; with USAF, 1950-52. Mem. Am. Bar Assn., Assn. Bar City N.Y., Torch and Scroll, Zeta Beta Tau. Jewish. Clubs: Beach Point (Mamaroneck, N.Y.); Harmonie (N.Y.C.); Century (Purchase, N.Y.). Home: 22 Murray Hill Rd Scarsdale NY 10583 Office: 30 Rockefeller Plaza New York NY 10112

SINYARD, NEIL RICHARD, film critic; b. Hull, North Humberside, Eng., Sept. 2, 1945; s. Richard and Florence Elsie (Field) S.; m. Lesley Bonham; Aug. 7, 1976; 1 child, Natalie. BA in Lit. with honors, U. Hull, Eng., 1967; MA in Comparative Lit., U. Manchester, Eng., 1968. Lectr. lit. U. Birmingham, Eng., 1969-73, lectr. film, lit., 1983—; sr. lectr. film and literature West Midlands Coll. Higher Edn., Walsall, Eng., 1974-83; freelance film critic, writer Eng., 1983—; lectr. in lit. programming cons. The Open U., Milton Keynes, Eng., 1974-79; dep. film critic Sunday Telegraph, London, 1981-86, lectr. in film Extra-Mural Dept., Birmingham, Eng., 1980-86. Author: Filming Literature, 1986, The Films of Alfred Hitchcock, 1986, The Films of Steven Spielberg, 1987, The Films of Woody Allen, 1987. Home: 4 Railway St, Leyland PR5 2XB, England

SIPPEL, WILLIAM LEROY, lawyer; b. Fon du Lac, Wis., Aug. 14, 1948; s. Alfonse Aloysious and Virginia Laura (Weber) S.; m. Barbara Jean Brost, Aug. 23, 1970; children: Katharine Jean, David William. BA, U. Wis., JD. Bar: Wis. 1974, U.S. Dist. Ct. (we. dist.) Wis. 1974, Minn. 1981, U.S. Dist. Ct. Minn. 1981, U.S. Ct. Appeals (10th cir.) 1984, U.S. Ct. Appeals (8th cir.) 1985. Research assoc. dept. agrl. econs. U. Wis., Madison, 1974-75; counsel monopolies and comml. law subcom. Ho. Judiciary Com., Washington, 1975-80; spl. asst. to asst. gen. antitrust div. U.S. Dept. of Justice, Washington, 1980-81; from assoc. to ptnr. Doherty, Rumble & Butler, Mpls. and St. Paul, Minn., 1981—. Co-author: The Antitrust Health Care Handbook, 1988. Mem. program com. Minn. World Trade Assn., Mpls., St. Paul, 1985-86, bd. dirs., 1986, Minn. Served with USAR, 1971-77. Mem. Minn. Bar Assn. (co-chmn. antitrust sect. 1986-88, internat. law sect. 1985-86, sect. council 1986—), Nat. Council of Farmer Coops. (legal tax and acctg. com. 1984—), Phi Beta Kappa. Democrat. Roman Catholic. Home: 1448 Pinewood Dr Woodbury MN 55125 Office: Doherty Rumble & Butler PA 2800 Minnesota World Trade Ctr Saint Paul MN 55101

SIPPY, RODNEY EDWARD, dentist; b. Chgo., Feb. 2, 1934; s. Everett Tunis and Helen Marie (Rydell) S.; student Purdue U., 1952-54; B.S., U. Ill., 1956, D.D.S., 1960; m. Marilyn Joyce Landis, June 13, 1954 (dec. June 1971); children—Deborah Lynn, Linda Darlene; m. 2d, Polly Palmer Lloyd, Apr. 13, 1974; children—William Joseph, Mellisa Palmer. Practice dentistry, LaGrange, Ill., 1960—; mem. attending staff Community Meml. Gen. Hosp., 1966—, sec. dental staff, 1962-65, chmn. dental staff, 1965-77; mem. staff Hinsdale San., 1968-70; chief dental service Suburban Cook County Tb Sanatorium, 1961-70; clin. instr. dept. prosthetics U. Ill. Coll. Dentistry, 1960-61; adviser Tri-County Dental Assts. Soc., Oak Brook, Ill., 1968-69, 73-74, dental asst. program Morton Coll., 1974-77; Fellow Royal Soc. Health, Am. Coll. Dentists, Am. Acad. Gen. Dentistry, Internat. Coll. Dentistry; prin. RPS Industries; owner La Grange Prosthetic Lab.; cons. Manor Care Nursing Center, Hinsdale, Ill.; chief dentist med. staff Medinah Temple, 1978-80. mem. Am. Dental Assn., Ill., Chgo., West Suburban (pres. 1977-78) dental socs., Am. Acad. Dental Group Practice, Am. Assn. Hosp. Dental Chiefs, Am. Orthodontic Soc., Internat. Acad. Orthodontics (dir. central sect. 1966-68), Pierre Fauchard Acad., Am. Soc. Preventive Dentistry, Fedn. Dentaire Internationale, U. Ill. Alumni Assn. (dir. 1967-71, pres. 1974-75), Far West Study Club, West Suburban C. of C., Art Inst. Chgo., Mus. Contemporary Art, Delta Sigma Delta. Republican. Clubs: Mason (32 deg.), Shriners, Illini, Progressive (sec. 1970-71, treas. 1968-69, pres. 1974-75); Plaza (Chgo.). Home: 1324 Laurie Ln Burr Ridge IL 60521 Office: 4727 Willow Springs Rd LaGrange IL 60525

SIRACUSA, ANGELO JOHN, association executive; b. San Francisco, Mar. 26, 1930; s. Louis and Grace Giansiracusa; B.A. in Polit. Sci., U. Santa Clara; B.S. in Bus. Adminstrn., U. Calif., Berkeley. Asst. mgr. San Mateo County (Calif.) Devel. Assn., 1958-61; gen. mgr. Fremont (Calif.) C. of C., 1962-65; v.p. Bay Area Council, San Francisco, 1966-72, pres., 1972—; dir. Am. Ind. Devel. Council, 1971-74; v.p., dir. Calif. Ind. Devel. Exec. Assn., 1968-74; dir. Real Estate Research Council No. Calif., 1968-70, Environ. Info. Clearinghouse, 1972-73, Diametrics-Decisions Info. and Analysis, 1980-81, San Francisco Econ. Devel. Corp., 1987—, Californians for Better Trans., 1987—; mem. steering com. St. Mary's Coll. Exec. Symposium, 1973—, chmn., 1975-76; mem. Gov. Calif.'s Manpower Policy Task Force, 1972-73; mem. adv. com. Calif. Office of Bus. and Ind. Devel., 1980-85; mem. San Francisco Mayor's Econ. Adv. Council, 1979-82; community adv. Jr. League San Francisco, 1976-80; mem. regional planning com. Assn. Bay Area Govts., 1978—, chmn. econ. devel. adv. com., 1979-82, mem. environ. mgmt. task force, 1977-78, mem. ind. siting task force, 1977-78; mem. steering com. San Francisco Forum, 1977-78; mem. devel. regulations council Urban Land Inst., 1979-86; mem. Met. Transp. Commn., 1986—; chmn. Bay Area Coalition for Transp., 1983—; mem. Bay Planning Coalition, 1983; mem. steering com. Bay Area and the World; mem. San Francisco Bay Conservation and Devel. Commn., 1983—, San Jose Econ. Devel. Bd., 1988—; mem. policy adv. bd. Ctr. for Real Estate & Urban Econs. U. Calif. at Berkeley, 1988—; bd. dirs. KQED, pub. TV, 1982—, Californians for Housing, 1982-86, Bridge Housing Corp., 1983—; bd. regents U. Santa Clara, 1981—, now chmn.; trustee Am. Ind. Devel. Council Edn. Found., 1968-69, Jr. Statesman Found., 1984-86; mem. adv. council U. San Francisco Sch. Bus. Adminstrn., 1973-77; bd. dirs. Santa Clara U. Alumni Council, 1973-76, San Francisco Devel. Fund, 1979-85, Coro Found., 1979-82, Big Sisters, Inc., San Francisco, 1980-81, Center for Collaborative Problem Solving, 1982-83; mem. planning div. com. United Way of Bay Area; adv. bd. Sch. Adminstrn., U. San Francisco; adv. panel Edn. Consortium for Productive Conflict, 1982—. Served with USAF, 1953-57. Mem. Soc. Indsl. and Office Realtors, No. Calif. Soc. Assn. Execs., Bus. Leadership Task Force, Am. Soc. Assn. Execs., Calif. Bus. Roundtable, Bay Area Public Affairs Council, San Francisco Planning and Urban Research Assn., Lambda Alpha. Republican. Clubs: Marin Tennis; San Francisco Tennis, World Trade, Commonwealth (San Francisco). Home: 213 Stanford Ave Mill Valley CA 94941 Office: Bay Area Council 847 Sansome St San Francisco CA 94111

SIRC, LJUBO, economist, educator; b. Kranj, Slovenia, Yugoslavia, Apr. 19, 1920; came to Eng., 1956; s. Franjo and Zdenka (Pirc) S.; m. Susan Powell, Sept. 16, 1976; 1 child, Nadia. Bachelor in Law, U. Ljubljana, Yugoslavia, 1943; D in Econs., Fribourg U., Switzerland, 1961. Dep. head Press Office, Ljubljana, 1945; monitor BBC Monitoring Service, Reading, Eng., 1957-58; lectr. U. Dhaka, Bangladesh, 1960-61; researcher Inst. Econ. Affairs, London, 1961-62; lectr. U. St. Andrews, Dundee, Scotland, 1962-65, U. Glasgow, Scotland, 1965-83; dir. Ctr. for Research into Communist Econs., London, 1983—; vis. scholar Centre National de la Rechesche Scientitigue, Paris, Frankfurt, Stanford, 1978-79. Author: Nonsense and Sense, 1968, Economic Devolution In Eastern Europe, 1969, Yugoslav Economy Under Self-Management, 1979; contbr. articles on internat. econs. to profl jours. Chmn. Yugoslav Democratic Encounters, 1980—; active Yugoslav Democratic Alternative; served as polit. prisoner, Yugoslavia, 1947-54. Served with Yugoslav army, 1944-45. Research grantee FAZIT Stiftung, Frankfurt, 1979, Earhart Found., Ann Arbor, Mich., 1979, 87. Mem. Mont Pelerin Soc., Scottish Econ. Soc., Sudosteuropa-Gesellschaft, Liberal Internat. Home: 41A Westbourne Gardens, Glasgow G12 9XQ, Scotland Office: Ctr Research Communist Economies, 2 Lord North St, London SW1P 3LB, England

SIREN, HEIKKI, architect; b. Helsinki, Oct. 5, 1918; s. Prof. J.S. and Sirkka S.; m. Kaija Siren, 1944; 2 sons, 2 daus. With Kaija Siren, Arkkitehtitoimisto Kaija & Heikki Siren, 1949—; mem. Finnish Acad. Tech. Scis. Works include: Little Stage of Nat. Theatre, Helsinki, 1954, Concert House, Lathi, 1954, Chapel in Otaniemi, 1957; Church in Orivesi, 1960, Office Bldgs., Helsinki, 1965, Housing Area in Boussy St Antoine, Paris, 1970, 'Round Bank' Kop, Helsinki, Bruckherhaus Concert Hall, Linz, Austria, 1974, Golf complex, Karuizawa, Japan, 1974, Golf Club, Onuma, Hokkaido, Japan, 1976, Reichsbrücke, Vienna, Conf. Palace, Baghdad, Iraq, others. Subject of Kaija and Heikki Siren, Architects, 1976. Recipient Hon. Citation and medal Sao Paulo Biennal, 1957; medal, 1961; hon. citation 'Auguste Perret' Union Internat des Architects, 1965; prof h.c., 1970; Officier Ordre nat. du Merite, 1971; SLK (Finland), 1974; Grand Silver Order of Austria, 1977; Camillo Sitte Prize, Vienna, 1979; Grande Medaille d'Or d'Académie d'Architecture, Paris, 1980; Archtl. Prize State of Finland, 1980; Grand Golden Order, City of Vienna, 1982. Home: Lounaisväylä 8A, 00200 Helsinki 20 Finland

SIREN, KATRI ANNA-MAIJA HELENA, architect; b. Kotka, Finland, Oct. 23, 1920; d. Gottlieb and Alma Lylli (Maljanen) Tuominen; m. Heikki Siren, Feb. 22, 1944; children—Kirsi Siren Aropaltio, Sara Siren Popovits, Jukka, Hannu. Degree in architecture, Univ. Tech. (Helsinki), 1948. Owner Siren Architects, Helsinki, 1949—. Exhibitions of architecture in Finland and abroad; contbr. articles to profl. jours. Bd. dirs. Found. Research Allergic Diseases, Helsinki, 1960—, chmn., 1971-79. Recipient Honorable mention and medal for theatre bldgs. Sao Paulo IV Biennale, 1957; medal and diploma for ch. bldgs, Sao Paulo VI Biennale, 1961; Auguste Perret hon. mention Union Internat. des Architectes, 1965; Grand Silver Order of Austria with star, 1977; Archtl. prize State of Finland, 1980; La Grand Medaille d'Or de l'Academie d'Architecture, Paris, 1980; Finnish Cultural Found. prize, 1984; decorated Officer of Order of Finnish White Rose, 1980. Mem. Finnish Architects Assn., L'Acad. d'Architecture (corr. mem.), F.A.I.A. (hon.). Office: Lounaisväylä 8A, 00200 Helsinki 20 Finland

SIRI, GIUSEPPE CARDINAL, religious administrator; b. Genoa, May 20, 1906; s. Nicolo Siri and Giulia Bellavista. Ed. Episcopal Sem., Genoa and Pontifical Gregorian U., Rome. Ordained priest, Roman Cath. Ch., 1928. Consecrated bishop; elevated to Sacred Coll. of Cardinals, 1953; Titular Bishop of Livias, 1944; archbishop of Genoa, 1946-87; proclaimed cardinal 1953; pres. Episcopal Dir. Com., Italian Cath. Action, Episcopal Conf. of Italy (C.E.I.), 1959-61; chmn. Italian Episcopal Conf., 1955-65; Apostolic adminstr. of Bobbio, 1983—; mem. Sacred Congregations of Sacraments of the Council and of Seminaries and Univs. of Study. Author: Corso di Teologia per Laici, 1942, La Strada passa per Cristo, 1985, Getsemani, Riflessioni sul Movimento teologico contemporaneo, 1980, La giovinezza della Chiesa, 1983, Il primato della verita, 1984. Home: Palazzo Arcivescovile, Piazza Matteotti 4, 16123 Genoa Italy *

SIRIGNANO, WILLIAM ALFONSO, aerospace and mechanical engineer, educator; b. Bronx, N.Y., Apr. 14, 1938; s. Anthony P. and Lucy (Caruso) S.; m. Molly Van Leeuwen, Oct. 29, 1966 (div. 1975); 1 child, Monica Ann; m. Lynn Haisfield, Nov. 26, 1977; children: Jacqueline Hope, Justin Anthony. B.Aero.Engring., Rensselaer Poly. Inst., 1959; Ph.D., Princeton U., 1964. Mem. research staff Guggenheim Labs., aerospace, mech. scis. dept. Princeton U., 1964-67, asst. prof. aerospace and mech. scis., 1967-69, assoc. prof., 1969-73, prof., 1973-79, dept. dir. grad. studies, 1974-78; George Tallman Ladd prof., head dept. mech. engring. Carnegie-Mellon U., 1979-85; dean Sch. Engring., U. Calif.-Irvine, 1985—; cons. industry and govt., 1966—; mem. emissions control panel Nat. Acad. Scis., 1971-73; lectr. and cons. NATO adv. group on aero. research and devel., 1967, 75, 80; chmn. nat. and internat. tech. confs.; chmn. acad. adv. council Indsl. Research Inst., 1985—; mem. space applications adv. com. NASA, 1985—. Assoc. editor: Combustion Sci. and Tech, 1969-70; tech. editor Jour. Heat Transfer, 1985—; contbr. articles to nat. and internat. profl. jours., also research monographs. United Aircraft research fellow, 1973-74. Fellow AIAA; mem. Combustion Inst. (treas. internat. orgn. and chmn. Eastern sect.), Soc. Indsl. Applied Math., ASME. Home: 3 Gibbs Ct Irvine CA 92715 Office: Sch Engring U Calif Irvine CA 92717

SIRISUMPAN, TIENCHAI, military officer; b. Bangkok, Mar. 19, 1925; s. Chamras and Chalong Sirisumpan; m. Khun-Ying Praparnsit, Mar. 12, 1948; children: Sittichai, Sunanta, Wutthichai, Sajeechan. Grad., St. Cabriel's Coll., Bangkok; cert., Culachomklao Royal Mil. Acad., Bangkok, 1942; grad., Command and Staff Coll., U.S., 1947, Nat. Def. Coll., Bangkok. Platoon leader 1st Infantry Regiment King's Guard, Bangkok, 1943; comdr. Airborne Bn., Lopburi, Thailand, 1957; mil. attaché Jarkata, Thailand and

Indonesia, 1964-66; comdg. gen. Army Spl. Warfare Ctr., Lopburi, 1972; dep. comdr. 4th Area, South Thailand, 1977; comdg. gen. Territorial Def. Dept., Bangkok, 1980; asst. comdr.-in-chief Royal Thai Army, Bangkok, 1982, dep. comdr.-in-chief. Senator Govt. Bangkok; vice chair Olympic Com. Thailand, Bangkok; chmn. bd. State Ry. Thailand, Bangkok; leader Rassadorn Party, Bangkok; M.P. Lopburi province, 1986, Dep. Prime Minister, 1986. Decorated Bronze Star, Knight Grand Cordon of Most Exalted Order of White Elephant, Knight Grand Cordon of Most Noble Order of Crown of Thailand. Clubs: Royal Sports of Bangkok, Army Golf. Home: 38 Soi Prachanimit Pradipat Rd, Bangkok Thailand Office: Govt House, Bangkok Thailand

SIROTKO, THEODORE FRANCIS, priest, army officer; b. Muskegon, Mich., Oct. 5, 1936; s. Theodore Felix and Dorothy Mary (Bray) S.; m. Phyllis Anne Bourziel, May 5, 1962; children: Mary Anne, Kathleen, Stephen, Michael. BS, Ferris State Coll., 1958, MDiv; D in Ministry, San Francisco Theol. Sem., 1982; MSA, U. Notre Dame, 1982. Ordained to ministry Episcopal Ch., 1965. Vicar St. Matthew Ch., Sparta, Mich., 1965-68; rector St. Mark Parish, Howe, Ind., 19689-70; sr. chaplain Howe Mil. Sch., 1968-70; commd. U.S. Army, 1970, advanced through grades to lt. col., 1985; chaplain U.S. Army, 1970—; chief parish/profl. devel. U.S. Army, Europe, 1982-85; chief pastoral ministry and counselling U.S. Army Chaplain Ctr. and Sch., Fort Monmouth, N.J., 1985-88, asst. dir. dept. mil. history, 1988—. Bd. dirs. LaGrange County Mental Health Assn., Ind., 1969-70, Sch. Opportunity, LaGrange, 1969-70. Decorated Bronze Star with 1 bronze oak leaf cluster, Air medal with 2 bronze oak leaf clusters, Meritorious Service medal with 1 bronze oak leaf cluster Mem. Mil. Chaplains Assn., Evang. and Cath. Mission, Order St. Benedict. Mem. U.S. Army Chaplain Mus. Assn. (bd. dirs. 1986—). Home: 164 St Nicholas Ave Lakewood NJ 08701 Office: US Army Chaplain Ctr and Sch Fort Monmouth NJ 07703

SIRTORI, CARLO, oncologist, pathologist, educator; b. Milano, Italy, Jan. 12, 1912; s. Cesare and Maria (Spinelli) S.; m. Antonia Biancardi, Dec. 22, 1941; children—Cesare R., Isabella, Elena. Grad. Med. Surgery, U. Milan, 1937; Specialist Cardiology, U. Paris, 1938; Specialist Radiology, U. Milan, 1939, Specialist Pneumology, 1940; Laurea Honoris Causa, Karolinska Inst.-Stockholm, 1975. Asst., Inst. Pathology and Anatomy, U. Milan, 1938-40; sr. asst. Pathology and Anatomy div. Nat. Cancer Inst., Milan, 1940-46; lectr. pathology, anatomy and histology U. Pavia, 1941; dir. pathology, anatomy and histology div. Nat. Cancer Inst. Milan, 1946-68; gen. sci. dir. G. Gaslini Ped. Inst., Genova, Italy, 1968-82; chmn. Fondazione Carlo Erba, Milano, 1959-84, sci. dir., 1984-87, dir. emeritus, 1987—; pres. SOCREA Sci. and Research Soc., 1987—; sci. dir. Centro Benessere CIGA, Stresa, 1985—; cancer expert WHO, Geneva, 1958-82; editor-in-chief Gazzetta Sanitaria, Milano and Gaslini, Genova, 1959-82, Prevenire, 1987—. Patentee in field. Author: Cancer of the Uterus, 1963; Terapia Medica Tumori, 1953; Nuova Prevenzione Antisenile, 1984, Vincere la Vita, 1986, others. Contbr. articles to profl. jours. Recipient Famel prize in cardiology U. Paris, 1937; Maurice Goldblatt Cytol. award Internat. Acad. Cytology, 1964; Madonnina Internat. award Comune Milano, 1965; Cruzeiro do Sul (Brazil), 1972; Grande Ufficiale al Merito, (Italy), 1982. Mem. Am. Assn. Cancer Research, N.Y. Acad. Sci., Armed Forces Inst. Pathology (Washington) (hon.), Internat. Acad. Cytology (hon. fellow). Home: Via Cino del Duca 8,, 20122 Milano Italy Office: SOCREA, Via Cino Del Duca 8, 20122 Milano Italy

SISK, DANIEL ARTHUR, lawyer; b. Albuquerque, July 12, 1927; s. Arthur Henry and Myrl (Hope) S.; m. Katharine Banning, Nov. 27, 1954; children: John, Sarah, Thomas. B.A., Stanford U., 1950, J.D., 1954. Bar: N.Mex. 1955, Calif. 1954. Assoc. firm Simms & Modrall, 1954-59; ptnr. firm Modrall, Sperling, Roehl, Harris & Sisk, Albuquerque, 1959-70, 71—; justice N.Mex. Supreme Ct., Santa Fe, 1970; Chmn. bd. Sunwest Fin. Services, Inc., Albuquerque, 1975—. Pres. Legal Aid Soc., Albuquerque, 1960-61; trustee Sandia Sch., 1968-72, Albuquerque Acad., 1971-73, A.T. & S.F. Meml. Hosps., Topeka, 1966-82; bd. dirs. N.Mex. Sch. Banking Found., 1981—. Served with USNR, 1945-46, PTO; to capt. USMCR, 1951-52, Korea. Mem. N.Mex. Bar Assn., Albuquerque Bar Assn. (dir. 1962-63), ABA, State Bar Calif. Presbyn. (elder). Office: Sunwest Bldg 500 4th St NW PO Box 2168 Albuquerque NM 87102

SISSON, BETTY, real estate broker; b. Burbank, Calif., Apr. 21, 1934; d. Harvey Orville and Isabel Marion (Melville) Angermeir; student public schs., Burbank; children—James Harvey, William Frank. Sales asso. Rich Port Realtors, Oak Brook, Ill., 1971-76, sales mgr., 1976-78, v.p., 1978-83; exec. v.p. Am. Growth Real Estate Corp., Oak Brook, 1979-80, The Midwest Club, Oak Brook, 1980-83, Selected Properties, Inc., Oak Brook, 1983-85, Pringley & Booth, Inc., Chgo., 1985—, Ambriance! Inc., Burr Ridge, Ill., 1987—. Mem. Nat. Assn. Realtors, Realtors Nat. Mktg. Inst., DuPage Bd. Realtors, Oak Brook Assn. Commerce and Industry. Republican. Club: Internat. Chgo. Home: 1405 Burr Ridge Club Burr Ridge IL 60521

SISSON, CHARLES HUBERT, poet; b. Bristol, England, Apr. 22, 1914; s. Richard Percy and Ellen Minnie (Worlock) S.; m. Nora Gilbertson, Aug. 19, 1937; children: Janet Louth, Hilary Cook. BA in Philosophy and Eng. Lit. with honors, U. Bristol, England, 1934; postgrad., U. Berlin, 1934-35, U. Sorbonne, Paris, 1935-36; DLitt (hon.), U. Bristol, 1980. With Dept. Employment Ministry Labour, London, 1937-62, under sec., 1962-72. Author essays, poems; translator The Aeneid of Virgil, 1986. Served with Brit. Army, 1942-45, India. Fellow Royal Soc. Lit. Anglican. Home: Moorfield Cottage, The Hill Langport, Somerset TA10 9PU, England

SISSON, EVERETT ARNOLD, industrial developer, executive; b. Chgo., Oct. 24, 1920; s. Emmett B. and Norma (Merbitz) S.; m. Betty L. DeGrado, Apr. 7, 1984; children: Nancy Lee Sisson Rassbach, Elizabeth Anne Sisson Levy. A.B., Valparaiso U., 1942. Sales mgr. Ferrotherm Corp., Cleve., 1946-51, Osborn Mfg. Co., Cleve., 1951-56; dir. sales Patterson Foundry & Machine Co., East Liverpool, Ohio, 1956-58; mgr. sonic energy products Bendix Corp., Davenport, Iowa, 1958-60; pres., chief exec. officer, dir. Lamb Industries, Inc., Toledo, 1960-65, Lehigh Valley Industries, Inc., N.Y.C., 1965-66, Am. Growth Industries, Inc., Chgo., 1966—, Workman Mfg. Co., Chgo., 1966-69, Am. Growth Devel. Corp., Chgo., 1968—; chmn. bd., chief exec. officer G.F.I. Inc., 1976-87; pres. Peru Properties, Inc., Oak Brook, 1976-87; chmn. bd., chief exec. officer Pringle & Booth, Inc., Chgo., 1986—; dir. Century Life of Am., Waverly, Iowa, Telco Capital Corp., Hickory Furniture Co., N.C., Sunstates Corp., Raleigh, N.C., Century Life Ins. Co., Waverly, Iowa, Indiana Fin. Investors Inc., Indpls., Acton (Mass.) Corp.; trustee Wis. Real Estate Investment Trust, 1980—. Pres. council, Mayfield Heights, Ohio, 1952-57; adviser to bd. trustees Valparaiso (Ind.) U., 1960-69; bd. regents Calif. Lutheran Coll., 1968—, fellow, 1969. Served Pres. capt. USAAF, 1943-46. Mem. Am. Mgmt. Assn., Cleve. Engring. Soc., President's Assn., Tau Kappa Epsilon. Clubs: Burr Ridge, Gt. Lakes Yachting, Ocean Reef. Home: 1405 Burr Ridge Club Burr Ridge IL 60521 Office: Am Growth Group Inc 1550 Spring Rd Oak Brook IL 60521

SISSON, ROBERT F., photographer, writer, lecturer; b. Glen Ridge, N.J., May 30, 1923; s. Horace R. and Frances A. S.; m. Patricia Matthews, Oct. 15, 1978; 1 son by previous marriage, Robert F.H.; 1 stepson, James A. Matthews. With Nat. Geographic Soc., Washington, 1942—, chief nat. sci. photographer, 1981-88. Photographer one-man shows, Nat. Geog. Soc., Washington, 1974, Washington Press Club, 1976, Berkshire (Mass.) Mus., 1976, Brooks Inst., Santa Barbara, Calif., 1980, Corcoran Gallery, 1988, permanent collections, Mus. Art, N.Y.C. Recipient 1st prize for color photograph White House News Photographers Assn., 1961; recipient Canadian Natural Sci. award, 1967. Fellow Biol. Photographers Assn.; mem. Biol. Photog. Assn. (awards for color prints 1967), Nat. Audubon Soc., Nat. Geog. Soc., Nat. Wildlife Fedn., Soc. Photog. Scientists and Engrs., N.Y. Acad. Scis., Sigma Delta Chi.

SIT, HONG CHAN, minister; b. St. Louis, Nov. 25, 1921; s. Gan and Ying Foon (Wong) S.; m. Amy Wang, June 16, 1949; children—David, Daniel, Estelle Joy, Mary. BS summa cum laude, U. Ill., 1943; BD, Faith Theol. Sem., 1950, STM, 1950; ThD, No. Bapt. Theol. Sem., 1957. Ordained to ministry Blue Ch., Springfield, Pa., 1950. Missionary China Inter-Varsity Fellowship, Shanghai, 1947; pastor Chinese Evang. Ch., N.Y.C., 1950-51, Chinese Bapt. Ch., Houston, 1953-56, Grace Chapel, 1956—. Pres. Chinese Fgn. Missionary Union, 1974—, Chinese Full Gospel Fellowship Internat., Hong Kong, 1983—. Author: Your Next Step With Jesus, 1977. Contbr. articles to profl. jours. Mem. Phi Beta Kappa, Phi Lambda Upsilon. Office: Grace Chapel 1055 Bingle Rd Houston TX 77055

SITA, MICHAEL JOHN, pharmacist, educator; b. St. Louis, Apr. 28, 1953; s. Julianne Gail Sita; m. Nora Ann Dillon, June 1, 1974; children: Michael John, Paul Thomas, Julianne Joyce. BS, St. Louis Coll. Pharmacy, 1976; MBA, So. Ill. U., 1983. Registered pharmacist, Mo., Ill. Staff pharmacist Luth. Med. Ctr., St. Louis, 1976-78, asst. chief pharmacist, 1978-81, adminstrv. coordinator pharmacy services, 1981-85; dir. pharmacy services Jefferson Meml. Hosp., 1985—; instr. St. Louis Coll. Health Careers, 1983-86; adj. clin. instr. pharmacy St. Louis Coll. Pharmacy, 1980—; relief pharmacist Dolgins Apothecary, St. Louis, 1976-86, Best Pharmacy, 1986-88. Author/editor Pharmacy Capsule quar., 1977-85. Mem. St. Louis Soc. Hosp. Pharmacists (treas. 1985-87, pres. 1988—), Mo. Soc. Hosp. Pharmacists, Am. Soc. Hosp. Pharmacists, Am. Pharm. Assn., Am. Soc. Parenteral and Enteral Nutrition, Hosp. Assn. Met. St. Louis (chmn. pharmacy tech. adv. com. 1985-86). Avocations: carpentry, rehabbing. Home: 6325 Pernod Ave Saint Louis MO 63139 Office: PO Box 350 Crystal City MO 63019

SITOMER, KENNETH MARK, apparel company executive; b. N.Y.C., Sept. 12, 1946; s. Harry and Beatrice (Katz) S.; BA, CCNY, 1968, MBA, 1974. Pres. Ernst and Whinney, CPA's, N.Y.C., 1969-70, Mann Judd Landau, CPA's, N.Y.C., 1970-74; chief exec. officer Bidermann Industries (parent Co. Calvin Klein Menswear, Ralph Lauren Womenswear, Yves St. Laurent, Daniel Hechter and Jean Paul Germain, Karl Lagerfeld), N.Y.C., 1974—, pres., 1977—. Served with U.S. Army, 1969. CPA, N.Y. Mem. Am. Inst. CPA's, N.Y. State Soc. CPA's, Young Pres. Orgn. Home: 303 E 57th St New York NY 10022

SITRUK, JOSEPH, rabbi; b. Tunis, Tunisia, Oct. 16, 1944; came to France, 1958; s. Jacques and Emma (Portugais) S.; m. Danielle Azoulay, Dec. 19, 1965; children: Rebecca, Yakou, Hanel, Eliaou, Sarah, Efrain, Isaac, Esther. Chief rabbi of France Paris. Office: Consistoire Cen, 17 rue St Georges, 75009 Paris France

SITSEN, JOHANNES M. A., pharmacologist; b. Amsterdam, The Netherlands, Jan. 10, 1944; s. Adriaan W. and Johanna M.C.C. (Feenstra) S.; m. Gusta G. Denee, Feb. 16, 1968; children: Martijn, Elske, Michiel, Jojanneke, Peter, Annelot. Pharmacist, State U. of Utrecht, The Netherlands, 1962-70, PhD, 1970-72, MD, 1974-80, pharmacologist, 1980-83, internal medicine, 1983-85. Cert. pharmacist, The Netherlands, pharmacologist, The Netherlands. Ind. pharmacist Harderwijk, The Netherlands, 1975-80; clin. pharmacologist Acad. Hosp., Utrecht, The Netherlands, 1983-85; med. advisor Organon Internat. BV, Oss, The Netherlands, 1985-87, head sect. CNS active drugs research, med. research devel. unit, 1987—; dir. BM&E/STV Engrs., Zaltbommel, Netherlands, Pitts., 1987—. Editor: Pharmacology and Endocrinology of Sexual Function, 1988; contbr. articles to profl. jours. Mem. British Pharmacological Soc., N.Y. Acad. Scis. Served with Royal Navy, 1972-74. Lodge: Rotary (pres. 1987-88). Home: Wilhelminalaan 6, 3851 XW Ermelo The Netherlands Office: Organon Internat BV, Kloosterstraat 6 PO Box 20, 5340 BH Oss The Netherlands

SIU, WINSTON WING YAN, holding company executive; b. Hong Kong, Oct. 11, 1951; s. Hom Sum and Kitty (Szeto) S.; 1 child, Wilson. BS, Stanford U., 1973, MS, 1976. Mgr. On Lee & Co., Hong Kong, 1978-81; mng. dir. On Lee Siu Constrn., Ltd., Hong Kong, 1981-86, On Lee Siu Holdings Ltd., Hong Kong, 1986—. Mem. campaign com. Community Chest Hong Kong, 1978—. Fellow Soc. Builders (council 1982—); mem. ASCE, Young Pres. Orgn. (Hong Kong local chmn. 1987-88, bd. dirs. 1988—, area. v.p. Transpac region 1988—). Club: Stanford (pres. Hong Kong 1980). Lodge: Rotary. Office: On Lee Siu Holdings Ltd, 1303 Pacific House, 20 Queen's Rd Central, Hong Kong Hong Kong

SIVRAJ, K. NANJAPPA, finance executive; b. Tumkur, Karnataka, India, Mar. 23, 1951; s. Nanjappa and Siddamma Sivraj; m. S. Vishalakshi, Nov. 30, 1975; 1 child, Anil B. Suraj. BS, U. Mysore, Tumkur, 1970; MA, U. Karnataka, 1974. Sci. tchr. SSR Secondary Sch., Tumkur, 1970-73; prin. Sanskrit Coll., Tumkur, 1973-75; gen. mgr. Udyog Pvt. Ltd., Bangalore, India, 1975-77; pub. relations exec. H.M.T. (Hindustan Machine Tools) Ltd., Tumkur, 1977-83; mng. dir. Adlibs Ltd., Tumkur, 1983—; trustee Swamy Shivakumara Ednl. Found., Tumkur, 1983. Editor Siddaganga mag., 1970-75; mng. editor Lokavani newspaper, 1975-77; advisor New Views newspaper, 1987—. Gov. Citizen Forum for Cleanliness, Tumkur, 1970-75; gen. sec. United Students' Assn., Tumkur, 1973-75; mem. Indian Council for Child Edn., New Delhi, 1986—. Recipient Editing award Tumkur Nagarika Samiti, 1977. Mem. Pub. Relations Soc., Indian Plastics Inst., Adclub India, Inst. Chartered Fin. Analysis (cert.), Jaycees Internat. (pres. 1970—, speaking award 1975). Mem. Congress Party. Hindu. Office: ADLIBS Ltd, BH Rd, Tumkur, Karnataka 572 101, India

SIWICKI, FLORIAN, minister of defense of Poland; b. Luck, Poland, Jan. 10, 1925. Grad. Polish officers' Sch., Ryazan, 1943, Gen. Staff Acad. of USSR, 1956. Worked in USSR, 1940-43, Red Army, 1943; vol. Tadeusz Kosciuszko First Inf. Div., 1943; comdr. sub-unit, lectr. Tadeusz Kosciuszko Inf. Officers' Sch.; worked in central insts. of Ministry of Nat. Def., comdr. different tactical units; Mil., Air and Naval attache of Embassy in People's Republic of China, 1961-63; chief of staff Silesian Mil. Dist., 1963-68, dist. comdr., 1968-71; 1st dep. chief gen. staff Polish Armed Forces, 1971-73; chief gen. staff vice-minister Nat. Defence, 1973-83, Minister Nat. Defence, 1983—; mem. Mil. Council of Nat. Salvation, 1981-83; Gen. of Army, 1984; mem. Polish Workers' Party, 1945-48; mem. Polish United Workers' Party, 1948—, dep. mem. Central Com., 1969-75, mem., 1975—, alt. mem. Polit. Bur. Central Com., 1981-86, mem., 1986—; dep. to Seym, 1976—. Recipient Order of Builders of People's Poland, Order of Banner of Labour (1st and 2d class), Order of Lenin, 1984, Grunwald Cross (1st class), other Polish and fgn. mil. decorations. Office: Ministerstwo Obrony Narodowej, 00-909 Warsaw Poland

SIX, JAN PIETER HENRIK, insurance company executive; b. Utrecht, The Netherlands, Dec. 28, 1948; s. Pieter Diederik and Anna Henriette (Van Aerssen Beyeren Van Voshol) S.; m. Elisabeth Johanna Drost, Oct. 6, 1973; children: Diederik, Florentine, Pieter. LLM, U. Utrecht, 1973. Mem. staff Nog/De Jong, Amsterdam, The Netherlands, 1973-78, v.p., 1978-83; v.p. Interpolis, Tilburg, The Netherlands, 1983—; bd. dirs. Orgn. Legal Assistance Insurers, The Hague, 1981-83, Orgn. Environ. Impairment Liability Insurers, Amsterdam, 1984—. Author: Effective Presentations, 1984. Treas. Young Liberals, Utrecht, 1969-71; bd. dirs. Kindergarten, Vreeland, 1980-83; pres. Red Cross, Loenen, 1982-83. Named Senator Jaycees Internat., Coral Gables, Fla., 1985. Mem. Jaycees The Netherlands (gen. legal counsel 1983-85, dir. internat. affairs 1986-87, rep. to ICC The Netherlands, Pres. award 1984). Liberal. Office: NV Interpolis, Conservatoriumlaan 15, 5037 DM Tilburg The Netherlands

SIZEMORE, DEBORAH LIGHTFOOT, writer, editor; b. Lamesa, Tex., Mar. 18, 1956; d. Glenn Billy and Francis Earlene (Cable) Lightfoot; m. O.E. Gene Sizemore, June 19, 1981. B.S. in Agrl. Journalism summa cum laude, Tex. A&M U., 1977. Writer, Tex. Agrl. Extension, College Station, 1976-77; copy editor Abilene Reporter-News (Tex.), 1978; customer service rep. Motheral Printing Co., Ft. Worth, 1978-79; prodn. coordinator Graphic Arts, Inc., Ft. Worth, 1980-81; writer, editor, Crowley, Tex., 1981—; agrl. writer, editor Boy Scouts Am., Irving, Tex., 1981—; contbg. editor Dairymen's Digest, Arlington, Tex., 1981—. Longhorn Scene, Ft. Worth, 1982-84; writer, photographer Harvest Times, Dallas, 1983-84; Simbrah World, Ft. Worth, 1985-87; contbg. editor Lone Star Horse Report, Ft. Worth, 1985—; contbr. photographs to mags.; contbr. articles mags. Women's issues chmn., v.p. membership, pub. info. officer, newsletter editor AAUW of Tarrant County, 1981-86; organizer nat. security pub. debate, Ft. Worth, 1983. Recipient Sr. Merit award in Agrl. Journalism, Tex. A&M U., 1978, Thomas S. Gathright Acad. Excellence award, 1976, Cert. of Merit, Livestock Publs Council, 1984, 86, 2d place Nonfiction Book award Tex.-Wide Writers' Competition, 1988. Mem. Nat. Writers Club, Western Writers Am., Am. Agrl. Editors Assn., Am. Agri-Women, Phi Kappa Phi, Gamma Sigma Delta. Club: Ft. Worth A&M. Office: 19 Frazier Ln Crowley TX 76036

SIZEMORE, HIRAM, JR., psychiatrist; b. Mullens, W.Va., Mar. 27, 1924; s. Hiram and Ruby Alice (Trent) S.; B.S., U. Mo., 1947, M.D., Washington U., 1949; m. Gisela Walter, Dec. 13, 1952 (div.); 1 dau., Angelika. Intern, Walter Reed Gen. Hosp., Washington, 1949-50; county health officer Boone County (W.Va.), 1956-57; practice medicine, Shepherdstown, W.Va., 1958-68; resident in psychiatry U. Va. Hosp., Charlottesville, 1968-71; practice medicine specializing in psychiatry, Shepherdstown, 1971—; cons. psychiatrist Allegheny County Health Dept., Brooke Lake Psychiat. Center, Hagerstown, Md., VA Center, Martinsburg, W.Va.; mem. staff Walter Reed Army Med. Center, Washington. Mem. City Council Shepherdstown, 1963-65. Served to capt. M.C., AUS, 1950-52; col. M.C., USAR. Diplomate Am. Bd. Psychiatry and Neurology. Mem. AMA, W.Va. Med. Assn., Am. Psychiat. Assn., Va. Neuropsychiat. Assn., Eastern Panhandle Med. Soc. W.Va. (pres. 1971-75). Lutheran. Home: Box 996 Route 1 Shepherdstown WV 25443 Office: Route 11 Shepherdstown WV 25443

SJOSTEDT, LARS EDVARD, transportation educator, consultant; b. Stockholm, May 4, 1939; s. Lennart Gustav and Signe Maria (Borrie) S.; m. Gerda Ingrid Aronsson, June 22, 1962; children—Mikael, Maria. B.S., Royal Inst. Tech., Stockholm, 1963, M.S., 1968, D.Sc., 1971. Research engr. Nat. Def. Research Inst., Stockholm, 1962-64, Nat. Rd. Research Inst., Stockholm, 1964-66; research asst. Royal Inst. Tech., 1966-68; chief engr. Swedish State Rys., Stockholm, 1968-78; mgr. applications United Stirling, Malmo, Sweden, 1978-80; prof. transp. Chalmers U. of Tech., Gothenburg, Sweden, 1980—; Swedish team leader Future of the Automobile, Internat. Research Program, 1980-84; bds. dir. Kalmar Verkstads AB, Kalmar Lagab AB, Kalmar Tellus, Sweden, 1980-87; bd. dirs. VBG Producleter AB, 1988—. Author: (with others), editor: High Speeds in Swedish Rail Passenger Service, 1969; author: (with others) Cities in Cooperation, 1973; contbr. articles to profl. jours. Mem. Sci. Council of Incentive Group, Stockholm, 1982—;. bd. dirs. Gothenburg Ctr. of Transp. and Traffic, 1986—. Royal Inst. Tech. Travel scholar, U.S., 1969; Agy. for Tech., Indsl. and Econ. Coop. scholar, 1974. Fellow Royal Swedish Acad. Engring. Scis.; mem. Swedish Transport Research Commn. (bd. dirs. 1981—), Swedish Assn. Traffic Engrs., Swedish Assn. Transp. Engrs., Swedish Assn. Engring. Physicists. Lutheran. Home: Bergsprangaregatan 8 B, S-41259 Gothenburg Sweden Office: Chalmers Univ of Tech, Dept Transp and Logistics, 41296 Gothenburg Sweden

SJOSTROM, MARIANNE BIRGIT CHRISTINA, television editor; b. Lund, Sweden, June 16, 1942; d. Johan Herman and Birgit Christina (Lindblad) Vigre; m. Olof Carl Sjostrom, Oct. 16, 1965; children: Carl, Louise. Grad., Am. High Sch./Armijo Joint Union High Sch., Fairfield, Calif., 1960, Lunds Privata Elementarskola, 1962; cert. journalism, U. Stockholm, 1981. Fgn. editor (news show) "Rapport" Channel 2 Swedish TV, Stokholm, 1981—. Editor Seven Days mag., 1983. Mem. Community Regional Council, Gothenburg, Sweden, 1978-80. Mem. Swedish Union Journalists, Internat. Fedn. Journalists. Lutheran. Home: 51 Strandvägen 49, 11523 Stockholm Sweden

SKADBURG, NORMAN DEAN, banker; b. Clarion, Iowa, Oct. 27, 1947; s. Percy Melvin and Ina Mae (Spangler) S.; m. Erma Louise Johnson, Dec. 29, 1968; children—Julie Ann, Jill Kristine. B.S., Iowa State U., 1969, M.S., 1971; diploma Iowa Sch. Banking, U. Iowa, 1976, Commercial Lending Sch., U. Okla., 1979, Grad. Sch. Banking, U. Wis., 1983. Vocat. agr. instr. Williamsburg Community Schs., Iowa, 1969-71; v.p. Farmers Trust & Savs. Bank, Williamsburg, 1971-75; v.p. Poweshiek County Nat. Bank, Grinnell, Iowa, 1975-81; pres. Farmers State Bank, Stanhope, Iowa, 1984-87, First State Bank, Webster City, Iowa, 1981—; dir. Ankeny State Bank, Iowa, Iowa Bankers Ins. Services, Inc., Des Moines, 1984—. V.p. Webster City Devel. Corp., 1982-85, pres., 1985-87, treas. Trinity Luth. Ch., 1983-86; sec. Williamsburg Community Devel. Corp., 1973-75; trustee Grad. Sch. Banking at Colo., 1986—. Recipient Key Man award Williamsburg Jaycees, 1974; Gov.'s Leadership award Iowa Community Betterment Program, State of Iowa, 1980; named Outstanding Young Alumnus, Iowa State U., Ames, 1981. Mem. Am. Bankers Assn., Nat. Ind. Bankers Assn., Am. Inst. Banking (v.p., dir. 1972-75, top student 1973), Iowa Ind. Bankers Assn., Iowa Bankers Assn. (dir. 1984-86), Iowa State U. Alumni Assn. (honors and awards com. 1986-87, bd. dirs. 1988—), Grinnell C. of C. (pres. 1980), Webster City C. of C. (pres. 1983-84), Alpha Zeta, Gamma Sigma Delta. Republican. Lutheran. Club: Ruritan (Grinnell, Iowa) (pres. 1979). Lodge: Rotary (bd. dir. 1982-88, v.p. 1985-86, pres. 1986-87). Avocations: golf, jogging, traveling, singing. Home: 604 Oak Park Dr Webster City IA 50595 Office: First State Bank 505 2d Ave Webster City IA 50595

SKAGGS, L. SAM, retail company executive; b. 1922; married. With Am. Stores Co., Salt Lake City, 1945—, chmn. bd., chief exec. officer, from 1966, formerly pres., now chmn. bd., also bd. dirs.; chmn. Sav-On Drugs Inc. (now Sav-on Osco), Anaheim, Calif., bd. dirs. Served with USAAF, 1942-45. Office: Am Stores Co PO Box 27447 709 E South Temple Salt Lake City UT 84127 •

SKALAGARD, HANS MARTIN, artist; b. Skuo, Faroe Islands, Feb. 7, 1924; s. Ole Johannes and Hanna Elisa (Fredriksen) S.; came to U.S., 1942, naturalized, 1955; pupil Anton Otto Fisher, 1947; m. Mignon Diana Haack Haegland, Mar. 31, 1955; 1 dau., Karen Solveig Sikes. Joined U.S. Mcht. Marine, 1942, advanced through grades to chief mate, 1945, ret., 1965; owner, operator Skalagard Sq., Rigger Art Gallery, Carmel, 1966—; librarian Mayo Hays O'Donnel Library, Monterey, Calif., 1971-73; painter U.S. Naval Heritage series, 1973—; exhibited in numerous one-man shows including Palace Legion of Honor, San Francisco, 1960, J.F. Howland, 1963-65, Fairmont Hotel, San Francisco, 1963, Galerie de Tours, 1969, 72-73, Pebble Beach Gallery, 1968, Laguna Beach (Calif.) Gallery, 1969, Arden Gallery, Atlanta, 1970, Gilbert Gallery, San Francisco; group shows: Am. Artists, Eugene, Oreg., Robert Louis Stevenson Exhibit, Carmel Valley Gallery, Biarritz and Paris, France, David Findley Galleries, N.Y.C. and Faroe Island, Europe, numerous others; represented in permanent collections; Naval Post Grad. Sch. and Library, Allen Knight Maritime Mus., Salvation Army Bldg., Monterey, Calif., Robert Louis Stevenson Sch., Pebble Beach, Anenberg ARt Galleries, Chestlibrook Ltd.,; lectr. Bd. dirs. Allen Knight Maritime Mus., 1973—, mem. adv. and acquisition coms., 1973-77. Recipient Silver medal Tommaso Campanella Internat. Acad. Arts, Letters and Scis., Rome, 1970, Gold medal, 1972; Gold medal and hon. life membership Academia Italia dell Arti e del Honoro, 1980; Gold medal for artistic merit Academia d'Italia. Mem. Navy League (dir. Monterey), Internat. Platform Assn., Sons of Norway (cultural dir. 1974-75, 76-77). Subject of cover and article Palette Talk, 1980, Compass mag., 1980. Home: 25197 Canyon Dr Carmel CA 93923 Office: PO Box 6611 Carmel CA 93921 Also: Dolores at 5th St Carmel CA 93921

SKÅNLAND, HERMOD, banker; b. Tromsö, Norway, June 15, 1925; s. Peder and Margit (Maurstad) S.; m. Jorid Henden, Oct. 14, 1972; 1 child, Mari Anne. MA in Econ., U. Oslo, 1951. Asst. Bur. Stats., Oslo, 1949-52; cons. to dir. gen. Ministry Fin., Oslo, 1952-71; dep. gov. Bank of Norway, Oslo, 1971-85, gov., 1985—; bd. dirs. Nordic Investment Bank, chmn., 1976-78, 86-88. Author: Norwegian Credit Market Since 1900, 1967, Dilemma of Incomes Policy, 1981, Central Banks and Political Authorities in Some Industrial Countries, 1984. Active various royal coms., delegations and bds.; chmn. Working Party. Rockefeller fellow Am. U., 1955; decorated Comdr. St. Olav (Norwegian) Order, 1987, Comdr. with star Finnish Lion and Icelandic Falcon Order. Home: Solvegen 1 B, 1177 Oslo 11 Norway Office: Norges Bank, Bankplassen 2, 0107 Oslo 1 Norway

SKARD, HALVDAN, cultural organization director; b. Oslo, Dec. 1, 1939; s. Sigmund and Aase Gruda (Koht) S.; m. Arnlaug Leira; 1 child, Halvard Leira. Student, U. Oslo, 1972. Cons. Studentsamskipnaden i Oslo, 1972-74; asst. dir. Rogaland Distriktshögskole, Stavanger, Norway, 1974-75; sec. of state Ministry of Edn., Oslo, 1976-81; sec. gen. Nordic Cultural Secretariat, Copenhagen, 1982-83; dir. Cultural Council of Norway, Oslo, 1983—; sec., chmn., mem. various govtl. commns. in Norway, 1965—; elected for polit. positions in govt., 1968—. Mem. Norwegian Union Local Authorities (exec. com. 1988—). Social Democrat. Lutheran. Office: Norsk Kulturraad Grev Wedels, plass PO Box 101 Sentrum, N-0102 Oslo Norway

SKARDA, RICHARD JOSEPH, clinical social worker; b. Santa Monica, Calif., Jan. 2, 1952; s. Robert Ralph and Cathryn Marie (Tourek) S. AA,

Los Angeles Valley Coll., Van Nuys, Calif., 1976; BA, U. Calif., Berkeley, 1978; MSW, UCLA, 1980. Lic. clin. social worker, Calif. Children's services worker Los Angeles County Dept. Children's Services, Panorama City, Calif., 1980-82; police service rep. Los Angeles Police Dept., 1982; psychiatric social worker Penny Lane, Sepulveda, Calif., 1983; children's services worker Ventura (Calif.) County Pub. Social Services Agy., 1983-85; head social work dept. Naval Med. Clinic, Port Hueneme, Calif., 1985—; part-time pvt. practice in clin. social work, Oxnard, Calif., 1987—. Served with USN, 1970-74. Mem. Nat. Assn. Social Workers, Acad. Cert. Social Workers, Calif. Soc. Clin. Social Work, U. Calif. Alumni Assn. Democrat. Roman Catholic. Office: Naval Med Clinic Port Hueneme CA 93043

SKARDAL, DOROTHY BURTON, American civilization educator; b. Omaha, July 24, 1922; d. William Mathew and Jennie (Nuquist) B.; m. Olav G. Skardal, June 12, 1953; children: Ellen Tone, Randi Anne. BA, Middlebury Coll., 1944; MA, Radcliffe Coll., 1945; PhD, Harvard U., 1963; LLD (hon.), Middlebury Coll., 1984. Instr. English, Iowa State U., Ames, 1946, Lawrence Coll., Appleton, Wis., 1946-48; instr. Am. lit. U. Oslo, 1965-71, lectr. Am. civilization, 1971-73, sr. lectr., 1973—; workshop chair European Assn. Am. Studies, 1982, 84. Author: The Divided Heart, 1974; editor: Essays on Norwegian-Am. Literature and History, 1986; numerous articles on Scandinavian-Am. lit. Bd. dirs. U.S. Ednl. Found. in Norway, Oslo, 1972—, The League of Norsemen, Oslo, 1977—. Decorated Knight's Cross First Class, Order St. Olav, Oslo, 1983; Fulbright fellow U. Oslo, 1950-51, Am. Council Learned Socs. fellow, 1952-53, research fellow Norwegian Research Council for Humanities, Oslo, 1964. Mem. Nordic Assn. Am. Studies, Norwegian-Am. Hist. Assn., Danish-Am. Heritage Soc., Assn. Am. Historians, Swedish-Am. Hist. Assn. Club: Am. Women's (Oslo). Home: Sorkedalsvn 229, 0315 Oslo 3, Norway Office: U Oslo, Box 1002, Blindern, 0315 Oslo Norway

SKAUGEN, MORITS, JR., investment company executive; b. Oslo, Dec. 17, 1955; s. Morits and Irmelin (Moren) S. Student Oslo Comml. Coll., 1970-74; B.S., Seattle U., 1978. pres. Carsten Corp., Seattle, 1977-78; dir. J. Lauritzen Group, Copenhagen, 1979-82; ptnr., mng. dir. Iko Maritime A/S, London, Oslo, 1982-84; chief exec. officer Norhav A/S, Oslo, 1984-85; ptnr., mng. dir. A/S Poseidon Holding, Oslo, 1985—. Served with Norwegian Navy, 1974-75. Office: A/S Poseidon, Vika Atrium, Munkedamsv 45, Oslo 1 Norway

SKEEN, DAVID RAY, computer systems administrator; b. Bucklin, Kans., July 12, 1942; s. Claude E. and Velma A. (Birney) S.; B.A. in Math., Emporia State U., 1964; M.S., Am. U., 1972, cert. in Computer Systems, 1973; grad. Fed. Exec. Inst., 1983, Naval War Coll., 1984; m. Carol J. Stimpert, Aug. 23, 1964; children—Jeffrey Kent, Timothy Sean, Kimberly Dawn. Cert. office automation profl. Computer systems analyst to comdr.-in-chief U.S. Naval Forces-Europe, London, 1967-70; computer systems analyst Naval Command Systems Support Activity, Washington, 1970-73; dir. data processing Office Naval Research, U.S. Navy Dept., Arlington, Va., 1973-78, dir. mgmt. info. systems Naval Civilian Personnel Command, Washington, 1978-80; dep. dir. total force automated systems Dept. Naval Mil. Personnel Command, Washington, 1980-85; dir. total force info. resource and systems mgmt. div. Chief Naval Ops., 1985—; lectr. Inst. Sci. and Public Affairs, 1973-76; cons. Electronic Data Processing Career Devel. Programs, 1975—; detailed to Pres.'s Reorgn. Project for Automated Data Processing, 1978, Pres.'s Fed. Automated Data Processing Users Group, Washington, 1978-80; assoc. prof. Sch. Engring. and Applied Sci., George Washington U. Served with USN, 1964-67, with Res., 1967—. Recipient Outstanding Performance award Interagy. Com. Data Processing, 1976. Mem. Sr. Exec. Assn., Am. Mgmt. Assn., Assn. Computing Machinery, Data Processing Mgmt. Assn., Naval Res. Assn. Contbr. articles to profl. jours. Home: 707 Forest Park Rd Great Falls VA 22066 Office: Dept Navy Washington DC 20370

SKEGGS, BRUCE ALBERT EDWARD, publishing company executive, former Australian politician; b. Sydney, Australia, Oct. 11, 1932; s. Albert Edward and Ethel Emily (Chown) S.; m. Evelyn Alison Gronn, Sept. 8, 1958; children: Philip, Julie, Robert, Margaret. Student pub. schs., Nailsworth, Australia. Journalist, The Argus, Melbourne, 1950-57, editor TV Week, 1957-60; chmn., mng. dir. Cabon Publ. Co. Pty. Ltd., Melbourne, 1960—; pub., mng. editor Australian Trotting Register, 1960—; ofcl. commentator Trotting Control Bd., Victoria, 1966-82; councillor City of Heidelberg, 1985—, chmn. parks and recreation; M.P. for Ivanhoe, 1973-82, temp. chmn. coms., 1979-82, mem. Victorian statute law rev. com., 1976-82, Parliamentary library com., 1976-79. Author: Golden Jubilee History, St. Georg'e, East Ivanhoe, 1979. State exec. Victoria Liberal Party Australia, 1961-73; hon. sec. Brit. Commonwealth Day Movement, 1972—; pres. Heidelberg Br. Liberal Party, 1982—; mem., vice chmn. Middle Yarra Adv. Council, 1974-82, 87—. Bd. mgmt. Austin Hosp., Melbourne, 1969-83, Royal Freemasons Homes, 1980-81, 84-88; alt. mem. Agnlican Synod, 1978-84; mem. mgmt. com. chaplaincy dept. Diocese of Melbourne, 1980—; pres. Grand Lodge Bd. Benevolence, 1982-84, dir. pub. relations United Grand Lodge of Victoria, 1984—; pres. The Freedom Coalition, 1984—; pres. adv. council Chinese Cultural Ctr.; mem. Heidelberg Heritage Com.; life bd. govs. Royal Children's Hosp., Austin Hosp. Recipient Queen's Jubilee medal; decorated Knight Order of St. John of Jerusalem, 1986. Mem. Australian Harness Racing Council (hon. pub. relations dir. 1973—), Inter-Dominion Harness Racing Council (hon. pub. relations dir. 1973—), Internat. Trotting Assn. (dir. publicity and promotions 1972—), Royal Soc. St. George (mem. com., 1988) , Heritage Assn. (pres. 1984—), Australian Journalists Assn. Anglican. Clubs: Royal Auto of Victoria, Cranbourne Harness Racing (com. 1979—, v.p. 1985—), East Ivanhoe Bowl, Parliamentary Bowl. Lodge: Masons. Office: 107 The Boulevard Ivanhoe, 3079 Victoria Australia

SKELTON, BRIAN GEOFFREY, marketing professional; b. London, June 21, 1955; s. Geoffrey Bernard and Daphne (Starkey) S.; m. Angelina Louise Dixon, Feb. 9, 1978; 1 child, Anna Louise. Degree, North Staffordshire Poly., Eng., 1976. Analyst Hawker Siddeley, London, 1976-77; programmer, tech. support mgr. Unichem Ltd., London, 1977-83; cons. Menorex Telex, Middlesex, Eng., 1983-84, product mgr., 1985-86, mktg. mgr., 1986—. Mem. Brit. Computer Soc., Inst. Data Processing Mgmt. Home: 14 Laurel Rd, West Wimbledon, London SW20 0PR, England Office: Menorex Telex, 96/104 Church St, Staines, Middlesex TW18 4XU, England

SKELTON, DOROTHY GENEVA SIMMONS (MRS. JOHN WILLIAM SKELTON), educator; b. Woodland, Calif.; d. Jack Elijah and Helen Anna (Siebe) Simmons; B.A., U. Calif., 1940, M.A., 1943; m. John William Skelton, July 16, 1941. Sr. research analyst War Dept., Gen. Staff, M.I. Div. G-2, Pentagon, Washington, 1944-45; vol. researcher, monuments, fine arts and archives sect. Restitution Br., Office Mil. Govt. for Hesse, Wiesbaden, German, 1947-48; vol. art tchr. German children in Bad Nauheim, Germany, 1947-48; art educator, lectr. Dayton (Ohio) Art Inst., 1955; art educator Lincoln Sch., Dayton, 1956-60; instr. art and art edn. U. Va. Sch. Continuing Edn., Charlottesville, 1962-75; researcher genealogy, exhibited in group shows, Calif., Colo., Ohio, Washington and Va.; represented in permanent collections Madison Hall, Charlottesville, Madison (Va.) Center. Mem. Nat. League Am. Pen Women, AAUW, Am. Assn. Museums, Coll. Art Assn. Am., Inst. for Study of Art in Edn., Dayton Soc. Painters and Sculptors, Nat. Soc. Arts and Letters (life), Va. Mus. Fine Arts, Cal. Alumni Assn., Air Force Officers Wives Club. Republican. Methodist. Clubs: Army Navy Country, Lake of the Woods (Va.) Golf and Country. Chief collaborator: John Skelton of Georgia, 1969; author: The Squire Simmons Family, 1746-1986, 1986. Address: Lotos Lakes Brightwood VA 22715

SKELTON, ROBERT BEATTIE, language educator; b. Auburn, Mich., Apr. 23, 1913; s. Glen Beattie and Irene (Richardson) S.; m. Mary Carmack, June 2, 1940; children—Susan, Robert Thomas, Rebecca and Melissa (twins). Student, Bay City (Mich.) Jr. Coll., 1934-35; A.B., Eastern Mich. U., 1937; M.A. (univ. scholar 1937-38), U. Mich., 1938, Ph.D. (Horace H. Rackham spl. fellow 1949-50, Am. Council Learned Socs. grantee Linguistics Inst. 1950), 1950; postgrad. (fellow), U. Brazil, 1942-43; postgrad. (Chilean Govt. fellow), U. Chile, 1943; postgrad., U. Salamanca, U. Paris, 1972, U. Perugia, 1975. Mem. faculty Auburn (Ala.) U., 1939-76, prof., 1954-76, research prof. comparative linguistics, 1967-76, head dept. fgn. langs., 1954-67; vis. scholar Linguistics Inst., 1967. Contbr. articles, monographs to profl. jours. Served from ensign to lt. USNR, 1943-46. Mem. Nat. Geog. Soc., Modern Lang. Assn., Am. Assn. Tchrs. French, Am. Assn. Tchrs. German, Am. Assn. Tchrs. Spanish and Portuguese, Linguistic Soc. Am., Inst. Internat. Edn. (asso.), Nat. Assn. Standard Med. Vocabulary, Am. Mus. Natural History (asso.), Acad. Tamil Culture (asso.). Home: 426 Scott St Auburn AL 36830

SKEWES-COX, BENNET, accountant, educator; b. Valparaiso, Chile, Dec. 12, 1918; came to U.S., 1919, naturalized, 1943; s. Vernon and Edith Page (Smith) S-C.; B.A., U. Calif., Berkeley, 1940; M.A., Georgetown U., 1947; B.B.A., Golden Gate Coll., 1953; m. Mary Osborne Craig, Aug. 31, 1946; children—Anita Page McCann, Pamela Skewes-Cox Anderson, Amy Osborne Skewes-Cox (Mrs. Robert Twiss). Asst. to press officer Am. Embassy, Santiago, Chile, 1941-43; state exec. dir. United World Federalists of Calif., 1948-50; pvt. practice acctg., San Francisco, 1953—; asst. prof. internat. relations San Francisco State U., 1960-62; grad. researcher Stanford (Calif.) U., 1962-63, Georgetown U., Washington, 1963-65; pres. Acad. World Studies, San Francisco, 1969—; sec. Alpha Delta Phi Bldg. Co., San Francisco, 1957—; lectr. in field. Mem. Democratic state central com. Calif., 1958-60, fgn. policy chmn. Calif. Dem. Council, 1959-61, treas. Marin County Dem. Central Com., 1956-62; founder, 1st. chmn. Calif. Council for UN Univ., 1976—; compiler World Knowledge Bank; bd. dirs. Research on Abolition of War; treas. Marin Citizens for Energy Planning. Served as lt. (j.g.), USNR, 1943-46. Mem. Assn. for World Edn. (internat. council 1975—), Am. Soc. Internat. Law, Am. Polit. Sci. Assn., San Francisco Com. Fgn. Relations, Am. Acctg. Assn., Calif. State Univ. Profs., AAUP, Nat. Soc. Public Accts., Fedn. Am. Scientists, UN Assn., Internat. Polit. Sci. Assn. World Federalists Assn. (nat. bd. dirs.). Clubs: University, Commonwealth of Calif., Lagunitas Country. Author: The Manifold Meanings of Peace, 1964; The United Nations from League to Government, 1965; Peace, Truce or War, 1967. Home: Monte Alegre PO Box 1145 Ross CA 94957 Office: Acad World Studies 2820 Van Ness San Francisco CA 94109

SKIBNIEWSKA, HALINA, architect; b. Warsaw, Poland, Jan. 10, 1921; d. Waclaw and Ewelina (Kuczowska) Erentz; m. Zygmunt Skibniewski, 1951. Educated Warsaw Tech. U. With Bur. Rebuilding of the Capital, Warsaw, 1945-47; asst., Warsaw Tech. U., 1945-54, lectr., 1954-62, acting prof., 1962-71, asst. prof., 1971-75, prof. extraordinary, 1975—; chief architect Design Office, 1953—; dep. to Seym, 1965—, vice-marshal of Seym, 1971-85; prin. works include schs., housing estates and Nat. Theatre, Warsaw. Chmn. central bd. Soc. for Polish-French Friendship, 1972—; dep. chmn. Council for Family Affairs, Council of Ministers, 1978—; mem. Consultative Council to Chmn. Council of State, 1986—. Publications include: Dziecko w mieszkaniu i osiedlu, 1969; Wyniki badan w zakresie budownictwa w Polsce dla ludzi z ciezkim uszkodzeniem narzadow ruchu, 1968; Rodzina a mieszkanie, 1974; co-author: Tereny otwarte w miejskim 'srodowisku mieszkalnym, 1979. Recipient State Prize 1st Class, 1972, 76, Order of Banner of Labour 2d Class, 1974, Honor prize Polish Architects Assn., 1978, Medal of 30th Anniversary of People's Poland, 1974, Lenin prize, 1979, Comdr. and Knight's Cross, Order of Polonia Restituta, Grand Officier Legion d'honneur, 1972. Mem. Assn. Architects of Polish Republic, Assn. Polish Urban Planners, Centro Internazionale di studio e documentazione dell' abitare, Academie d'Architecture France (corr.). Address: Ul Frascati 14m 4, 00-483 Warsaw Poland *

SKIDMORE, DONALD EARL, retired manufacturing company executive; b. Tacoma, May 12, 1920; s. Jake and Roxa J. (Young) S.; m. Ingeborg Johnsrud, Feb. 20, 1943; children—Donald E., Marilyn Kay, Sharon Ann. Student Racine Western Inst., 1937-41, Knapp Coll., 1946-48. Bookkeeper, acct. Ace Furnace & Steel Co., Tacoma, 1938-44, acct., 1946-50; ptnr., acct. Central Steel & Tank Co., Yakima, Wash., 1950-58, sec.-treas., dir. 1958-60, v.p., dir., 1966-67, 79-83, pres., dir., 1967-78. Mem. Yakima County Manpower Adv. Com., 1966-73; chmn. Citizens' Adv. Com. Vocat.-Tech. Edn.; bd. dirs. Yakima Sch. Dist. 7, 1965; Mem. council Evangel. Coll., Springfield, Mo., 1960-83, v.p., 1972-75; dir. Yakima Valley Youth for Christ, 1961-64, pres., lay council N.W. Coll. Assemblies of God, Kirkland, Wash., 1965-68, 71-74, bd. dirs., 1972-74, 76-84; internat. dir. Full Gospel Bus. Men's Fellowship Internat., 1974—, chmn. fin. com., 1980-81. Served with U.S. Army, 1944-46. Mem. Sheet Metal and Air Conditioning Contractors Nat. Assn. (local labor advisor 1959-66), Wash. Soc. C.P.A.s. Republican. Lodge: Lions (v.p. 1970-71). Home: 3402 Roosevelt Ave Yakima WA 98902-1559

SKIFF, RUSSELL ALTON, plastic company executive; b. Waterford, Pa., Feb. 26, 1927; s. Albert Alton and Leah Gladys (Allen) S.; B.S., U. Pitts., 1950; m. Dolores Theresa Molnar, June 25, 1950; children—Russell James, Sandra Lee, Eric Alan, Rebecca Lynn. Metall. chemist Jones & Laughlin Steel Co., Alliquippa, Pa., 1950-51; research and devel. chemist Gen. Electric Co., Erie, Pa., 1951-57; mgr. tech. sales and plant operation Hysol Corp. of Calif., El Monte, 1957-60; sr. research engr. autonetics div. N.Am. Aviation, Downey, Calif., 1960-62; pres. Delta Plastics Co., Inc. (now Delta D.P.C., Inc.), Tulare, Calif., 1962—. Served with USAAF, 1944-46. Mem. Constrn. Specifications Inst. Republican. Presbyterian. Club: Exchange (Calif.-Nevada dist. pres.-elect). Lodge: Lions (dir.). Contbr. articles to profl. jours. Home: 15170 Avenue 260 Visalia CA 93277 Office: Delta Plastics 983 E Levin Tulare CA 93274

SKILLMAN, ERNEST EDWARD, JR., real estate sales and management executive; b. New Orleans, Oct. 3, 1937; s. Ernest Edward and Helen Cecilia (Klein) S.; BA, La. State U., 1960, postgrad. in law, 1960-61; postgrad. Southeastern La. U., 1973. Engaged in real estate mgmt., Baton Rouge, 1964—, sales, 1969—. Sustaining mem. Republican Nat. Com., 1976—, life mem., 1980—, mem. congressional com., 1978—; mem. pres.'s club Democratic Nat. Com., 1979—; mem. Rep. Presdl. Task Force; mem. Jackson (La.) Assembly; Served with USN, 1961-64; Vietnam. Real estate broker, La. Mem. Aviation Mus. Assn. (charter life), Feliciana C. of C., Ams. Against Union Control, Res. Officers Assn. (life), Mil. Order World Wars (life), Am. Contract Bridge League (sr. master), U.S. Naval Inst., Navy League U.S., Am. Legion, Submarine Force Library and Mus. Assn. (life), Amvets (cmdr. 1985-87) (pres.) Foss-Landry Post #2 1985-87), Grad. Realtors Inst., Nat. Assn. Realtors, Baton Rouge Bd. Realtors, Sigma Chi (life). Roman Catholic. Clubs: Army and Navy, Rep. Senatorial (Washington), Camelot (Baton Rouge). Lodge: Kiwanis. Office: 3888 Brentwood Dr Baton Rouge LA 70809

SKINNER, ALASTAIR, accountant; b. Hamilton, Ont., Can., Apr. 4, 1936; s. Allistair and Isabelle (Drysdale) S.; m. Patricia Skinner; children: Lisa, Iain, James, Graeme. CA, Queens U., Kingston, Ont., Can., 1959; MBA, Harvard U., 1963. Cert. FCA, FCMA, CMC. Served to maj. Can. Army, 1954-71; nat. mng. ptnr. MacGillivray & Co. (name now Pannell Kerr MacGillivray), 1977-84; ptnr.-in-charge Toronto (Can.) office Spicer MacGillivray (name now Pannell Kerr MacGillivray), 1984-86; with Pannell Kerr MacGillivray, Toronto, 1986—. Co-author: profl. manuals. Fellow Inst. Chartered Accts. of Ont. (pres. 1983-84), Soc. Mgmt. Accts. of Can. (bd. dirs.); mem. Inst. Mgmt. Cons. of Ont., Can. Tax Found. (bd. govs.). Club: Albany (Toronto). Office: Pannell Kerr MacGillivray, Royal Bank Plaza, North Tower, Suite 1100, Toronto, ON Canada M5J 2P9

SKINNER, B. FRANKLIN, telecommunications company executive; b. Covington, Va., Nov. 4, 1931; s. B. Franklin and Charlotte Frances (Walton) S.; m. Ruth Ann Gee, Nov. 25, 1955; children: Ruth Anne, Christian Franklin, Lisa Page. B.A., U. Richmond, 1952, D.C.S. (hon.), 1985; L.L.D. (hon.), Jacksonville U., 1986; DHL (hon.), Interdenominational Theological Ctr., Atlanta, 1987. Div. traffic mgr. Chesapeake & Potomac Telephone Co., Richmond, Va., 1964-66, gen. comml. mgr., 1966-70, v.p. operating staff, 1970-73; v.p., gen. mgr. So. Bell Telephone & Telegraph Co., Charlotte, N.C., 1973-79; v.p. Fla. So. Bell Telephone & Telegraph Co., Miami, 1979-82; exec. v.p. mktg. and external affairs. co. hdqrs. So. Bell Telephone & Telegraph Co., Atlanta, 1982, pres., chief exec. officer, 1982—; dir. So. Bell, Atlanta, BellSouth Services, Birmingham, Citizens & So. Ga. Corp., Atlanta, Cen. Atlanta Progress. Trustee U. Richmond, Agnes Scott Coll., Atlanta; dir. High Mus. Art, Atlanta, Sci. and Tech. Mus.; bd. visitors Emory U., Atlanta; mem. United Negro Coll. Fund (nat. corp. campaign com.); chmn. nat. adv. bd. The Salvation Army. Served with U.S. Army, 1952-54. Recipient Top Mgmt. award Sales and Mktg. Execs., 1978, Reubin Askew Awareness award Greater Miami Urban League, 1980. Mem. Telephone Pioneers Am. (assn. pres. 1986-87), Atlanta C. of C. (bd. dirs.), Capital City Club, Commerce Club, Omicron Delta Kappa, Sigma Phi Epsilon, Pi Delta Epsilon. Baptist. Lodge: Rotary. Home: 675 Tuxedo Pl NW Atlanta GA 30342 Office: So Bell Tel & Tel Co 675 Peachtree St NE Room 4500 Atlanta GA 30375

SKINNER, DAVID BERNT, surgeon, educator; b. Joliet, Ill., Apr. 28, 1935; s. James Madden and Bertha Elinor (Tapper) S.; m. May Elinor Tischer, Aug. 25, 1956; children: Linda Elinor, Kristin Anne, Carise Berntine, Margaret Leigh. B.A. with high honors, U. Rochester, N.Y., 1958, Sc.D. (hon.), 1980; M.D. cum laude, Yale U., 1959. Diplomate: Am. Bd. Surgery (dir. 1974-80), Am. Bd. Thoracic Surgery. Intern, then resident in surgery Mass. Gen. Hosp., Boston, 1959-65; sr. registrar in thoracic surgery Frenchay Hosp., Bristol, Eng., 1963-64; teaching fellow Harvard U. Med. Sch., 1965; from asst. prof. surgery to prof. Johns Hopkins U. Med. Sch., also surgeon Johns Hopkins Hosp., 1968-72; Dallas B. Phemister prof. surgery, chmn. dept. U. Chgo. Hosps. and Clinics, 1972-87; prof. surgery Cornell U., 1987—; pres., chief exec. officer N.Y. Hosp., 1987—; dir. Omnis Surg. Inc., 1984-85; mem. President's Biomed. Research Panel, 1975-76; past cons. USPHS, Office Surgeon Gen. U.S. Navy. Co-author: Gastroesophageal Reflux and Hiatal Hernia, 1972; editor: Current Topics in Surg. Research, 1969-71, Jour. Surg. Research, 1972-83; co-editor: Surgical Treatment of Digestive Disease, 1985, Esophageal Disorders, 1985, Reconstructive Surgery of the Gastrointestinal Tract, 1985; mem. editorial bd.: Jour. Thoracic and Cardiovascular Surgery, Annals of Surgery, Surg. Gastroenterology; contbr. profl. jours., chpts. in books. Elder Fourth Presbyn. Ch., Chgo., 1976-87, clk. of session, 1978-82, 84-87; bd. visitors Cornell U. Med. Coll., 1980-87. Served to maj. M.C. USAF, 1966-68. John and Mary Markle scholar acad. medicine, 1969-74. Fellow ACS; mem. AMA, Internat. Surg. Group, Am., Western, So. surg. assns., Soc. Univ. Surgeons (pres. 1978-79), Am. Soc. Artificial Internal Organs (pres. 1977), Soc. Surg. Chmn. (pres. 1980-82), Am. Assn. Thoracic Surgery (council 1981-86), Soc. Vascular Surgery, Soc. Thoracic Surgery, Soc. Pelvic Surgeons, Soc. Surgery Alimentary Tract, Société Internationale de Chirurgie, Collegium Internationale Chirurgiae Digestivae, Am. Coll. Chest Physicians, Central Surg. Soc., Internat. Soc. Diseases Esophogus (v.p. 1983-87), Assn. Acad. Surgery, Halsted Soc., Soc. Clin. Surgery (pres. 1986—), Phi Beta Kappa, Alpha Omega Alpha. Clubs: Quadrangle (Chgo.); Cosmos (Washington). Home: 79 E 79th St New York NY 10021 Office: 525 E 68th St New York NY 10021

SKINNER, GORDON ROBERT BRUCE, internist, researcher; b. Glasgow, Scotland, Feb. 21, 1942; s. Robert Murray and Silva Dow (Wood) S.; m. Janet Rankin McLaren, Jan. 4, 1968; children—Fiona Elizabeth, Niall Fraser, David Iain. M.B.Ch.B., U. Glasgow, 1965; M.D., U. Birmingham, Eng., 1975. House officer Regional Hosp. Authorities, Glasgow, 1965-68; research fellow U. Birmingham, 1969-72, lectr., 1972-76, sr. lectr., 1976; cons. virologist Nat. Health Service, Eng., 1976—; dir. Vaccine Research Found. and Med. Research Internat., Herpes Vaccine Research Trust, Birmingham, Eng., 1982—. Patentee Skinner herpes vaccine, and alternate herpes vaccine from bovie mamm. virus, and virus treatment of cancer.Fellow Royal Coll. Ob-Gyn, Assn. Med. Microbiologists, Brit. Med. Assn. (treas. 1973-74). Home: 2 Paddock Dr, Dorridge West Midlands B93 8B2, England Office: Univ Birmingham, Vincent Dr, Birmingham West Midlands B15 2TJ, England

SKINNER-KLEE, JORGE, lawyer, diplomat; b. San Francisco, July 21, 1923; s. Alfredo and Dolores (Cantón Solórzano) S.-K.; m. Concha Arenales, Sept. 24, 1949; children: Cecilia Skinner-Klee Soler, Carolina Skinner-Klee Hempstead, Alfredo, Jorge. Licenciate in Jud. and Social Scis., U. San Carlos, Guatemala, 1951; D of Jud. and Social Scis. (hon.), Rafael Landívar Cath. U., Guatemala, 1980. Prof. sociology U. San Carlos, Guatemala, 1952-55; Minister of Fgn. Affairs Govt. Guatemala, Guatemala City, 1956-57; prof. sociology Rafael Landívar Cath. U., Guatemala, 1960-65, vice rector, 1969-79; councillor of state Govt. Guatemala, 1974-78, Congressman of the Republic, 1986—; dep. mem. Constituent Assembly Guatemala, 1955, 65, 78; mem. Permanent Tribunal for Arbitration, The Hague, The Netherlands, 1968—; amb. in charge of negotiations with G.B. on Belize question, 1959-76; del. several times to gen. assembly U.N.; bd. dirs. Banco Internat. Guatemala, Productos Duralita, Corrugadora Guatemala, others. Author: Indian Laws of Guatemala, 1954, Considerations on the Emergence of the Middle Class, 1965; contbr. articles to newspapers. Mem. Central Am. Jud. Commn. Orgn. of Centroam. Countries, 1955-57; seminar dir. Guatemalan Social Integration, 1955; planner Commn. for New Comml. Code, 1964-65. Named Grand Officier Legion of Honor, Govt. of France, 1954; recipient Grand Cross Order Quetzal, Guatemalan Govt., 1977; awarded numerous other internat. and nat. distinctions. Mem. Acad. Geography and History (pres. 1979-81). Mem. Nat. Ctr. Union Party. Clubs: Guatemalan Country, Caza Tiro y Pesca. Office: Skinner-Klee & Ruiz, 9-A Calle 3-72, Zona 1, Guatemala City Guatemala

SKIPPER, NATHAN RICHARD, JR., lawyer; b. Wilmington, N.C., May 29, 1934; s. Nathan Richard and Mary Dell (Sidbury) S.; m. Barbara Lynn Renton, Sept. 5, 1959 (div. June 1978); children: Nathan Richard III, Valerie Lynne; m. Karen Marie Haughton, Sept. 26, 1987. AB, Duke U., 1956, JD, 1962; AAS, Oakland Community Coll., 1980. Bar: N.Y. 1963, U.S. Dist. Ct. (so. dist.) N.Y. 1964, Mich. 1971, U.S. Dist. Ct. (ea. dist.) Mich. 1979. Assoc. Cravath, Swaine & Moore, N.Y.C., 1962-70; counsel financings Ford Motor Co., Dearborn, Mich., 1970-78; gen. counsel, sec. Volkswagen Am., Inc., Troy, Mich., 1978—. Served to capt. USAF, 1956-59, USAFR, 1962-75. Mem. ABA, Mich. Bar Assn., N.Y. State Bar Assn., Phi Delta Phi. Club: Grosse Pointe (Mich.) Yacht. Office: Volkswagen Am Inc 888 W Big Beaver Troy MI 48007-3951

SKJOLDAGER, HENRIK, bank executive; b. Denmark, Aug. 12, 1944; s. Emanuel and Kirsten (Søtofte) S.; m. Annelise Jensen; children: Annette, Mikael. Mng. dir. Kai Dige Bach AS, Herlev, Denmark, 1971-77, Snehvide Boligautomatik AS, 1977-84, The Bank of Copenhagen, 1984-88, Kai Dige Bach A/S, 1988—. Mem. Young Pres. Orgn. (chmn. 1987). Office: Kai Dige Bach A/S, Gl Klausdalsbrovej 480, DK-2730 Herlev Denmark

SKJORTEN, EINAR, civil engineer; b. Oslo, July 6, 1933; s. Einar and Ragnhild (Maseng) S.; m. Miriam Adrienne Donath, May 16, 1960; children—Ariel, Eldar. Sivilingenior, Tech. U. Norway, Trondheim, 1958; M.S., U. Ill., 1960. Cons. engr. Dr.Ing. A. Aas-Jakobsen, Oslo, 1960-61, Ing. E.N. Hylland, Oslo, 1961-64, Siv.ing. Apeland & Mjoset A.S., Oslo, 1964-74; ptnr., exec. Multiconsult A.S., Oslo, 1974—; v.p., dir. Norwegian Bldg. Research Sta., Oslo, 1970-76; dir. Norconsult A.S., Oslo, others; chmn. Com. for Computer Application in Norwegian Bldg. Industry, 1980—; dir. research program Norwegian Council Sci. and Indsl; mgr. dept. project mgmt. Multiconsult A.S., 1986—; project mgr. devel. programme for use of info. tech. Bldg. Industry of Norway, 1987—. Research, guest lectr. univ. Author: Bygningsstatikk for Ingeniorskolen, 1972, Datamaskinassistert tegning av Bygningskontruksjoner, 1983; co-author: Management and Information Technology, 1985; contbr. articles to profl. jours. Chmn. bd. dirs. Hosletoppen Skole, Baerum, Norway, 1976-79, local chpt Social Democratic party (Labor), Stabekk, Norway, 1979; mem. Baerum Steering Com. for Mcpl. Bldg., 1979—. Served to lt. Engrs., Norwegian Army, 1953-54. Fulbright grantee U. Ill., 1958-60. Mem. Norwegian Soc. Profl. Engrs. (chmn. sect. civil and structural engrs. 1966-67, mem. permanent com. for code of practice 1983—, chmn. exec. com. CAD/CAM conf. and exhbn. 1984, 85), Norwegian Assn. Cons. Engrs., Project Mgmt. Inst. of Pa., Norwegian Soc. for Project Mgmt., Norwegian Poly. Assn., Norwegian Petroleum Assn. Home: Rytterfaret 21, 1347 Hosle Norway Office: Multiconsult AS, Fornebuveien 1, 1324 Lysaker Norway

SKLAIR, LESLIE A., sociologist, educator; b. Glasgow, Scotland, June 22, 1940; s. Edward and Sadie (Goldman) S.; m. Freda Dyson, Dec. 17, 1969 (dec. 1981); 1 child, Jessica; m. Doro Marden, July 22, 1982; children: Aphra, Matilda. BA in Sociology, Philosophy, Leed (Eng.) U., 1964; MA in Sociology, MaMaster U., Hamilton, Ont., Can., 1965; PhD in Sociology, London Sch. Econs., 1969. Lectr. in sociology London Sch. Econs., 1970-81, sr. lectr., 1981—; cons. UN, N.Y.C., 1987. Author: Sociology of Progress, 1973, Organized Knowledge, 1974; numerous articles. Fellow Ctr. U.S.-Mex. Studies, U. Calif., San Diego, 1986-87. Mem. Brit. Sociol. Assn., Brit. Assn. China Scholars. Mem. Labour Party. Office: London Sch Econs, Houghton St, London WC2A 2AE, England

SKLAR, ALEXANDER, electric co. exec., educator; b. N.Y.C., May 18, 1915; s. David and Bessie (Wolf) S.; student Cooper Union, N.Y.C., 1932-35; M.B.A., Fla. Atlantic U., 1976; m. Hilda Rae Gevarter, Oct. 27, 1940; 1 dau., Carolyn Mae (Mrs. Louis M. Taff). Chief engr. Aerovox Corp., New Bedford, Mass., 1933-39; mgr. mfg., engring. Indsl. Condenser Corp., Chgo., 1939-44; owner Capacitron, Inc., 1944-48; exec. v.p. Jefferson Electric Co., Bellwood, Ill., 1948-65; v.p., gen. mgr. electro-mech. div. Essex Internat., Detroit, 1965-67; adviser, dir. various corp., 1968—; vis. prof. mgmt. Fla. Atlantic U., Boca Raton, 1971; lectr. profl. mgmt. U. Calif. at Los Angeles, Harvard Grad. Sch. Bus. Adminstrn., U. Ill. Mem. Acad. Internat. Bus., Soc. Automotive Engrs. Address: 4100 Galt Ocean Dr Fort Lauderdale FL 33308

SKLOVSKY, ROBERT JOEL, physician, educator; b. Bronx, N.Y., Nov. 19, 1952; s. Nathan and Esther (Steinberg) S.; m. Michelle Sklovsky-Welch, Dec. 21, 1985. BS, Bklyn Coll., 1975; MA, Columbia U., 1976; PharmD, U. of Pacific, 1977; D in Naturopathic Medicine, Nat. Coll. Naturopathic Medicine, 1983. Intern Tripler Army Med. Ctr., Honolulu, 1977; prof. pharmacology Nat. Coll. Naturopathic Medicine, Portland, Oreg., 1982-85; pvt. practice specializing in naturopathy Clackamas, Oreg., 1983—; cons. State Bd. Naturopathic Examiners, Oreg., Hawaii, Clackamas County Sherriff's Dept.; cons. Internat. Drug Info. Ctr., N.Y.C., 1983—; cons. Albert Roy Davis Scientific Research Lab, Orange Park, Fla. 1986. Recipient Bristol Labs. award, 1983. Mem. Am. Assn. Naturopathic Physicians, N.Y. Acad. Sci., AAAS. Office: 10808 SE Hwy 212 Clackamas OR 97015

SKOGEN, DUANE BLAIR, oil company executive; b. Hettinger, N.D., Sept. 4, 1932; m. Henry Joseph and Arlene Fern (Kelsey) S.; m. Arliss A. Berg, Dec. 27, 1952; children—Laurie Ann, Nancy Lynn, Connie Kay. B.S., S.D. Sch. Mines, 1956. Registered profl. engr., Mont., Tex. With Conoco Inc., Billings, Mont., 1962-71, mgr. ops. planning div., Houston, 1971-73, dir. U.S. mktg. and supply, 1973-74; dir. mfg. Douglas Oil Co., Los Angeles, 1974-77; refinery mgr. Conco Ltd., South Killingholme, U.K., 1977-81, mng. dir. refining, London, 1981—, also dir.; dir. A.P.T. (Immingham) Ltd., South Humberside, HOTT and COT(H), Benzene Mktg. Co., London; v.p., dir. Continental Oil Co. France, Stamford, Conn., 1982-86. Served as sgt. AUS, 1949-52; Korea. Mem. Am. Inst. Chem. Engring., Inst. Petroleum, Brit. Inst. Mgmt. (companion). Republican. Lutheran. Club: Wellington (London). Office: Conoco Ltd, Park House, 116 Park St, London W1Y 4NN, England

SKOK, WILLIAM HENRY, foreign service officer; b. Ogdensburg, N.J., Aug. 12, 1938; s. Joseph and Pauline (Beierle) S.; m. Dorothy Mary Pytlik, Aug. 10, 1963; children: William Raffaele, Pasquale Joseph. AB, Columbia U., 1961; postgrad. U. Md., 1969-70. Enlisted U.S. Navy, 1955, advanced through grades to lt. comdr.; ret. 1972; mgmt. intern Chase Manhattan Bank, N.Y.C., 1972-73; vice consul U.S. consulate, Turin, Italy, 1973-76; dep. prin. officer U.S. consulate gen., Curacao, Netherlands Antilles, 1976-77; comml. coordinator for Latin Am., State Dept., 1977-80; consul U.S. consulate gen., Naples, Italy, 1980-84; specialist internat. protection of intellectual property Office Bus. Practices, Dept. State, Washington, 1984—; head U.S. dels. to UNESCO WIPO meetings, also numerous other dels. dealing bilaterally with intellectual property and internat. trade issues. Decorated Joint Service Commendation medal Dept. Def. Mem. Am. Fgn. Service Assn. Republican. Methodist. Home: 6929 Woodstream Ln Seabrook MD 20706 Office: Office Bus Practices EB/BP Room 3531A Dept State Washington DC 20520

SKÖLDBERG, SVANTE, business association executive; b. Stockholm, July 6, 1931; s. Nils Karl and Sonja Elisabet (Heiron) S.; m. Solgerd Colliander, May 30, 1962; children—Ann, Henrik. M.B.A., Lund U., 1961. Mktg. cons. AB Mktg., Stockholm, 1961-64; product mgr. AB Findus, Bjuv, 1964-67; market and media dir. Svea Advt. Agy., Stockholm, 1967-68; mktg. dir. Kooperativa Förbundet, Stockholm, 1968-72; exec. v.p. Arvid Nordquist HAB, Stockholm, 1972-75, pres., 1975-78; pres. Nordium AB, Stockholm, 1978-80; pres. Swedish Advt. Assn., Stockholm, 1980—; dir. Tidningsstatistik AB, Solna, Beder Capital Fund, Stockholm, Reklamfilminformation, AB, Stockholm. Mem. Stockholm Mchts. Club, Swedish Mktg. Execs. Club. Lutheran. Home: Jagarstigen 61, 18146 Lidingö Sweden Office: Swedish Advertisers Assn, Holländargatan 20, 11185 Stockholm Sweden

SKOLER, LOUIS, architect, educator; b. Utica, N.Y., Apr. 5, 1920; s. Harry and Etta (Mitkoff) S.; m. Celia Rebecca Stern, Aug. 24, 1952; children: Elisa Anne, Harry Jay. BArch, Cornell U., 1951. Chief designer Sargent, Webster, Crenshaw & Folley, Syracuse, N.Y., 1951-60; design critic Cornell U., Ithaca, N.Y., 1956-57; pvt. practice architecture, Syracuse, 1956-69; mem. faculty Syracuse (N.Y.) U., 1959—, prof. architect 1965—, head of Masters in Architecture I, 1980-82, condr. internat. programs abroad, London, 1977, Scandanavia, 1985; ptnr. Architects Partnership, Syracuse, 1969-71; pres. Skoler & Lee Architects, P.C., Syracuse, 1971—; arbitrator Am. Arbitration Assn., 1980—; lectr. Nanjing Inst. Tech., People's Republic of China, 1986; designer internat. archtl. program Dept. Internat. Programs Abroad, Japan, summer 1988. Named 1st in Residential Design, Design-in-Steel, 1968-69; U.S. Travel grantee, 1981. Mem. AIA. Home: 213 Scottholm Terr Syracuse NY 13224 Office: Skoler & Lee Architects PC 1004 University Bldg Syracuse NY 13202

SKOLIMOWSKI, JERZY, film director; b. Warsaw, Poland, May 5, 1938; ed. Warsaw U., State Superior Film Sch., Lodz, Poland; m. Joanna Szczerbic. Scriptwriter for Innocent Sorcers (Wajda), Knife in the Water (Polanski), Poslizg (Lomnicki); dir., designer, editor, actor Rysopis, 1965; writer, dir., actor Walkover, 1965; writer, dir. Barrier, 1966; dir. Le Depart, 1967; writer, dir., actor Hands Up, 1967; dir. films include Adventurers of Gerard, 1969, The Deep End, 1971, King, Queen, Knave, 1972, Lady Frankenstein, 1976, The Shout, 1978, Moonlighting, 1982, Success Is the Best Revenge, 1984, The Lightship, 1985; appeared in films including Circle of Deceit, 1982, White Knights. Recipient Grand Prix, Internat. Film Festival, 1966, Silver Palm Cannes Film Festival, 1978. Author: Somewhere Close to Oneself, Somebody Got Drowned. Mem. Dirs. Guild Am.. Address: care Film Polski, ul Mazowiecka 6/8, 00-048 Warsaw Poland also: care Leading Artists Inc 445 N Bedford Dr Penthouse Beverly Hills CA 90212 *

SKOLNIK, MERRILL I., electrical engineer; b. Balt., Nov. 6, 1927; s. Samuel and Mary (Baker) S.; m. Judith Magid, June 4, 1950; children: Norma Jean, Martin Allen, Julia Anne, Ellen Charlotte. B.Engring., Johns Hopkins U., 1947, M.S. in Engring., 1949, D.Eng., 1951. Research scientist Johns Hopkins U., Balt., 1947-54; vis. prof. Johns Hopkins U., 1973-74; engring. specialist Sylvania Electric, Boston, 1954; staff mem. MIT Lincoln Lab., Lexington, Mass., 1954-59; research mgr. Electronic Communications, Timonium, Md., 1959-64, Inst. Def. Analyses, Arlington, Va., 1964-65; supr. radar div. Naval Research Lab., Washington, 1965—; mem. bd. visitors Engring. Sch. Duke U., Durham, N.C., 1977—. Author: Introduction to Radar Systems, 1962, 2d edit., 1980, Radar Handbook, 1970; editor: Radar Applications, 1988. Recipient Heinrich Hertz premium Instn. Electronic and Radio Engrs., London, 1964, Disting. Civilian Service award U.S. Navy, 1982; Meritorious Exec. award Sr. Exec. Service, 1986; Disting. Alumnus award Johns Hopkins U., 1979; named to Soc. of Scholars, Johns Hopkins U., 1975. Fellow IEEE (editor Proceedings 1986—, Harry Diamond award 1983, Centennial medal 1984); mem. Nat. Acad. Engring. Home: 8123 McDonogh Rd Baltimore MD 21208 Office: Naval Research Lab Washington DC 20375

SKOLOVSKY, ZADEL, concert pianist, educator; b. Vancouver, B.C., Can.; came to U.S., 1923, naturalized, 1929; s. Max and Kate (Jones) S.; m. Alice Maffett Glass, July 29, 1947 (div. 1953). Diploma, Curtis Inst. Music, 1937; studied piano with, Isabelle Vengerova and Leopold Godowsky; conducting with, Fritz Reiner and Pierre Monteux; violin with, Edwin Bachmann. prof. music Ind. U., 1976-87, prof. emeritus, 1987—; juror NYU Internat. Tchaikovsky Piano Competition, 1978, 3d Latin Am. Teresa Carreno Piano Competition, Caracas, Venezuela, 1978, U. Md. Internat. Piano Competition, 1981, Joanna Hodges Internat. Piano Competition, Palm Desert, Calif., 1983; tchr. master classes. Debut at Town Hall as winner of the Walter W. Naumburg award, 1939; appeared in recitals in Carnegie Hall, N.Y.C., 1939—, various states and Can., 1939—; soloist with N.Y. Philharmonic Symphony Orch.; soloist under condrs. Dimitri Mitropoulos, Charles Munch, Leonard Bernstein, Lorin Maazel, Erich Leinsdorf, Jan Kubelik, Paul Kletzki, Arthur Rodzinski, also Paul Paray; appeared as a soloist Lewishohn Stadium, N.Y. and, Robin Hood Dell, Phila., under condrs. Vladimir Golschmann, Pierre Monteux, Alexander Smallens; soloist with NBC Orch., Nat. Orch. Assn., Phila. Orch., Nat. Orch., Washington, San Francisco Symphony, Israel Philharmonic, Residentie Orch. at The Hague, L'Orchestre Nat. de Belgique, B.B.C. Scottish Orch., orchs. of Luxembourg, Lisbon, Portugal, Hilversum Radio, Holland, Paris, London, Ravinia, Chgo., N.Y.C.; also appeared on TV; first performance Second Piano Concerto by Prokofieff with N.Y. Philharmonic Orch. under Charles Munch, 1948; world premier Concerto No. 4 of Darius Milhaud with Boston Symphony, 1950; 1st extensive European tour, 1953; appeared with Residency Orch. of the Hague, 2d tour, appeared as soloist with Israel Philharmonic Orch. at opening concert World Festival Music, 1954, appeared in Mexico, 1965, European tour, Eng., Holland, Scandinavia, Belgium, 1965-66, 67, recital, Queen Elizabeth Hall, London, Eng., 1971, 73, recitals, B.C., 1975; concert tour of, S. Am., 1978, U.S., Can. and Europe, 1981-82, 1st concert tour of Far East, 1983, mus. films for TV., recorded for Columbia Masterworks Records, Philips Records; on concert tour, also condr. master classes, U.S., Europe, Israel, S.Am., Far East, 1986. Recipient prizes from Nat. Fedn. Music Clubs, 1943, Nat. Music League, 1940, Robin Hood Dell Young Am. Artists award 1943; recipient Walter W. Naumburg award, 1939. Democrat. Jewish. Club: Lotos (N.Y.C.).

SKONEY, SOPHIE ESSA, educational administrator; b. Detroit, Jan. 29, 1929; d. George Essa and Helena (Dihmes) Cokalay; Ph.B., U. Detroit, 1951; M.Ed., Wayne State U., 1960, Ed.D., 1975; postgrad. Ednl. Inst. Harvard Grad. Sch. Edn., 1986, 87; m. Daniel J. Skoney, Dec. 28, 1957; children—Joseph Anthony, James Francis, Carol Anne. Tchr. elem. sch. Detroit Bd. Edn., 1952-69, remedial reading specialist, 1969-70, curriculum coordinator, 1970-71, region 6 article 3 title I coordinator, 1971-83, area achievement specialist, 1984—; cons. in field. Mem. Wayne State U. Edn. Alumni Assn. (pres. bd. govs. 1979-80, newsletter editor 1975-77, 80—), Macomb Dental Aux. (pres. 1969-70), Mich. Dental Aux. (pres. 1980-81), Am.-Assn. Sch. Adminstrs., Wayne State U. Alumni Assn. (dir., v.p. 1985-86), Internat. Reading Assn., Mich. Reading Assn., Mich. Assn. State and Fed. Program Specialists, Profl. Women's Network (newsletter editor 1981-83, pres. 1985-87), Assn. for Supervision and Curriculum Devel., Delta Kappa Gamma, Beta Sigma Phi, Phi Delta Kappa. Roman Catholic. Home: 20813 Lakeland St Saint Clair Shores MI 48081 Office: Detroit Pub Schs 1121 E McNichols Detroit MI 48203

SKOOG, FOLKE KARL, emeritus botany educator; b. Fjärås, Sweden, July 15, 1908; came to U.S., 1925, naturalized, 1935; s. Karl Gustav and Sigrid (Person) S.; m. Birgit Anna Lisa Bergner, Jan. 31, 1947; 1 dau., Karin. B.S., Calif. Inst. Tech., 1932, Ph.D., 1936; Ph.D. (hon.), U. Lund, Sweden, 1956; D.Sc. (hon.), U. Ill., 1980. Teaching asst., research fellow biology Calif. Inst. Tech., 1934-36; NRC fellow U. Calif., Berkeley, 1936-37, summer 1938; instr., tutor biology Harvard U., 1937-41, research assoc., 1941; assoc., assoc. prof. biology Johns Hopkins U., 1941-44; chemist Q.M.C.; also tech. rep. U.S. Army ETO, 1944-46; asso. prof. botany U. Wis.-Madison, 1947-49, prof., from 1949, C. Leonard Huskins prof. botany, now emeritus.; Vis. physiologist Pineapple Research Inst., U. Hawaii, 1938-39; assoc. physiologist NIH, USPHS, 1943; vis. lectr. Washington U., 1946, U. Agr., Ultuna, Sweden, 1952; v.p. physiol. sect. Internat. Bot. Congress, Paris, 1954, Edinburgh, 1964, Leningrad, 1975. Editor: Plant Growth Substances, 1951, 80; Contbr. articles to profl. jours. Track and field mem. Swedish Olympic Team, 1932. Recipient certificate of merit Bot. Soc. Am., 1956. Mem. Nat. Acad. Scis. U.S., Bot. Soc. Am. (chmn. physiol. sect. 1954-55), Am. Soc. Plant Physiologists (v.p. 1952-53, pres. 1957-58, Stephen Hales award 1954, Reid Barnes life membership award 1970), Soc. Developmental Biology (pres. 1971), Am. Soc. Gen. Physiologists (v.p. 1956-57, pres. 1957-58), Internat. Plant Growth Substances Assn. (v.p. 1976-79, pres. 1979-82), Am. Soc. Biol. Chemists, Am. Acad. Arts and Scis., Deutsche Akademie der Naturforscher Leopoldina, Swedish Royal Acad. Scis. (fgn.). Home: 2248 Branson Rd Oregon WI 53575 Office: Dept Botany U Wis Madison WI 53706

SKOOG, WILLIAM ARTHUR, oncologist; b. Culver City, Calif., Apr. 10, 1925; s. John Lundeen and Allis Rose (Gatz) S.; A.A., UCLA, 1944; B.A. with gt. distinction, Stanford U., 1946, M.D., 1949; m. Ann Douglas, Sept. 17, 1949; children—Karen, William Arthur, James Douglas, Allison. Intern medicine Stanford Hosp., San Francisco, 1948-49, asst. resident medicine, 1949-50; asst. resident medicine N.Y. Hosp., N.Y.C., 1950-51; sr. resident medicine Wadsworth VA Hosp., Los Angeles, 1951, attending specialist internal medicine, 1962-68; practice medicine specializing in internal medicine, Los Altos, Calif., 1959-61; pvt. practice hematology and oncology Calif. Oncologic and Surg. Med. Group, Inc., Santa Monica, Calif., 1971-72; pvt. practice med. oncology, San Bernardino, Calif., 1972—; assoc. staff Palo Alto-Stanford (Calif.) Hosp. Center, 1959-61, U. Calif. Med. Center, San Francisco, 1959-61; asso. attending physician U. Calif. at Los Angeles Hosp. and Clinics, 1961-78; vis. physician internal medicine Harbor Gen. Hosp., Torrance, Calif., 1962-65, attending physician, 1965-71; cons. chemistry Clin. Lab., UCLA Hosp., 1963-68; affiliate cons. staff St. John's Hosp., Santa Monica, Calif., 1967-71, courtesy staff, 1971-72; courtesy attending med. staff Santa Monica Hosp., 1967-72; staff physician St. Bernardine (Calif.) Hosp., 1972—, San Bernardino Community Hosp., 1972—; chief sect. oncology San Bernardino County Hosp., 1972-76; cons. staff Redlands (Calif.) Community Hosp., 1972-83, courtesy staff, 1983—; asst. in medicine Cornell Med. Coll., 1950-51; jr. research physician UCLA Atomic Energy Project, 1954-55; instr. medicine, asst. research physician dept. medicine UCLA Med. Center, 1955-56, asst. prof. medicine, asst. research physician, 1956-59; clin. asso. hematology VA Center, Los Angeles, 1956-59; co-dir. metabolic research unit UCLA Center for Health Scis., 1955-59, 61-65; co-dir. Health Scis. Clin. Research Center, 1965-68, dir., 1968-72; clin. instr. medicine Stanford, 1959-61; asst. clin. prof. medicine, assoc. research physician U. Calif. Med. Center, San Francisco, 1959-61; lectr. medicine UCLA Sch. Medicine, 1961-62, assoc. prof. medicine, 1962-73, assoc. clin. prof. medicine, 1973—. Served with USNR, 1943-46, to lt. M.C., 1951-53. Fellow ACP; mem. Am., Calif. med. assns., So. Calif. Acad. Clin. Oncology, Western Soc. Clin. Research, Am. Fedn. Clin. Research, Los Angeles Acad. Medicine, San Bernardino County Med. Soc., Am. Soc. Clin. Oncology, Am. Soc. Internal Medicine, Calif. Soc. Internal Medicine, Inland Soc. Internal Medicine, Phi Beta Kappa, Alpha Omega Alpha, Sigma Xi, Alpha Kappa Kappa. Episcopalian (vestryman 1965-70). Club: Redlands Country. Contbr. articles to profl. jours. Home: 30831 Miradero Dr Redlands CA 92373 Office: 399 E Highland Ave Suite 201 San Bernardino CA 92404

SKOUSE, JOHN, shipping executive; b. Edinburgh, Scotland, Apr. 20, 1941; s. Mary Ellen Skouse; m. Jean Elizabeth McPherson; 1 child, Ewan John. BS in Bus. Adminstrn., Edinburgh U., 1963. Area mgr. Rowntree Mackitosh Confectionary, York, Eng., 1965-68; nat. mgr. Smiths Food Group, Lincoln, Eng., 1968-70; sales mgr. N.Am. Van Lines, Ft. Wayne, Ind., 1970-75; dir. mktg. Interconex, Inc., N.Y.C., 1977-83; v.p. shipping and forwarding Alfadhli & Aldarawish, Alkhobar, Saudi Arabia, 1983—; cons. Beirut, 1975-77. Mem. Inst. Freight Forwarders, Air Forwarders Assn., Brit. Businessmens Group Saudi Arabia, Country Gentlemens Assn. U.K., Royal Overseas League. Conservative. Roman Catholic. Home: 193 Colinton Rd, Edinburgh EH14, Scotland Office: Alfadhli & Aldarawish, PO Box 206, Alkhobar 31952, Saudi Arabia

SKOV, LISBETH ANDERSEN, publishing executive; b. Copenhagen, Apr. 21, 1949; d. Viggo and Gurli (Carlsen) Andersen; m. Soren Skov, July 7, 1984; children: Louise, Christel. MA, U. Aarhus, 1977. Editor Politiken Pub. Co., Copenhagen, 1977-80; editor Komma Pub. Co., Copenhagen, 1980-86, mng. editor, 1986-87, pub., 1987—. Mem. Den Danske Forlaegerforening (instr. 1987—, grantee 1982). Home: Langemarksvej 2, 2860 Soeborg Denmark Office: Komma Bookpublishers Ltd, Frederiksborgaade 26 POB 2163, 1016 Copenhagen Denmark

SKROWACZEWSKI, STANISLAW, conductor, composer; b. Lwow, Poland, Oct. 3, 1923; came to U.S., 1960; s. Pawel and Zofia (Karszniewicz) S.; m. Krystyna Jarosz, Sept. 6, 1956; children: Anna, Paul, Nicholas. Diploma faculty philosophy, U. Lwow, 1945; diploma faculties composition and conducting, Acad. Music Lwow, 1945, Conservatory at Krakow, Poland, 1946; L.H.D., Hamline U., 1963, Macalester Coll., 1972; L.H.D. hon. doctorate, U. Minn. Guest condr. in Europe, S.A., U.S., 1947—; Composer 1931—, pianist, 1928—, violinist, 1934—, condr., 1939—; permanent condr., music dir. Wroclaw (Poland) Philharmonic, 1946-47, Katowice (Poland) Nat. Philharmonic, 1949-54, Krakow Philharmonic, 1955-56, Warsaw Nat. Philharmonic Orch., 1957-59, Minnesota Orch., 1960-79; prin. condr., mus. adviser Halle Orch., Manchester, Eng., 1984—; musical advisor St. Paul Chamber Orchestra, 1986—. Composer: 4 symphonies Prelude and Fugue for Orchestra (conducted first performance Paris), 1948, Overture, 1947 (2d prize Szymanowski Concours, Warsaw 1947); Cantiques des Cantiques, 1951, String Quartet, 1953 (2d Prize Internat. Concours Composers, Belgium 1953); Suite Symphonique, 1954 (first prize, gold medal Composers Competition Moscow 1957), Music at Night, 1954, Ricercari Notturni, 1978 (3d prize Kennedy Center Friedheim Competition, Washington), Concerti for Clarinet and Orch., 1980, Violin Concerto, 1985, Concerto for Orch., 1985, Fanfare for Orch., 1987; also music for theatre, motion pictures, songs and piano sonatas, English horn concerto; rec. by Mercury, Columbia, RCA Victor, Vox, EMI, Angel. Recipient nat. prize for artistic activity Poland, 1953; First prize Santa Cecilia Internat. Concours for Condrs., Rome, 1956. Mem. Union Polish Composers, Internat. Soc. Modern Music, Nat. Assn. Am. Composers-Condrs., Am. Music Center. Office: Orch Hall 1111 Nicolett Mall Minneapolis MN 55403

SKUBISZEWSKI, PIOTR AUGUSTYN, art historian; b. Borzykowo, Poznan, Poland, Aug. 27, 1931; s. Ludwik and Aniela (Leitgeber) S.; m. Maria Krystyna Michalska, Nov. 16, 1959; 1 child, Marcin. MA, Poznan U., 1954, PhD, 1958. Lectr. Poznan U., 1953-64; researcher Inst. Art, Warsaw, Poland, 1964-67; prof. art history Warsaw U., 1967-81, vice dean faculty history, 1968-70, dir. Inst. Art History, 1970-81; prof. Poitiers (France) U., 1981—; vis. prof. Uppsala (Sweden) U., 1967, Kansas U., Lawrence, 1975. Author books on medieval art history, also articles and book revs. Mem. Assn. Polish Art Historians (sec. gen. 1965-68), Com. Art History of Polish Acad. Scis. (sec. gen. 1966-74, v.p. 1975-81), Poznan Learned Soc. Arts and Scis., Internat. Com. Art History. Roman Catholic. Home: 22 Ave Liberation, 86000 Potiers France Office: Poitiers U Dept Art History, 24 Rue de la Chaine, 86022 Poitiers France

SKULIMOWSKI, ANDRZEJ MACIEJ JACEK, educator; b. Wieliczka, Poland, July 3, 1958; s. Mieczyslaw Maciej and Halina (Kotulska) S. MSc in Electrical Engring., U. Mining & Metallurgy, Krakow, Poland, 1981, PhD, 1985; MSc in Math., Jagiellonian U., Krakow, 1982. Jr. asst. Inst. Automatic Control U. Mining and Metallurgy, Krakow, 1980-81, asst., 1981-82, sr. asst., 1982-85, asst. prof., 1985—; dir. research program Polish Acad. Scis., Warsaw, 1984—; reviewer Am. Math. Soc., Providence, 1986—; cons. Cos. in Poland, Switzerland and Fed. Republic Germany, 1980—. Author: Selected Problems of Multicriteria Optimization, 1988; contbr. articles to profl. jours. Mem. Polish Math. Soc., Am. Math. Soc. (reviewer 1986—), Polish Cybernetical Soc., German Soc. Math. Economy and Ops. Research. Roman Catholic. Home: Al Kijowska 10/84, 30-950 Crakow 23 Poland Office: U Mining & Metallurgy, Inst Automatic Control, PO Box 113, 30-950 Crakow Poland

SKULINA, THOMAS RAYMOND, lawyer; b. Cleve., Sept. 14, 1933; s. John J. and Mary B. (Vesely) S. A.B., John Carroll U., 1955; J.D., Case Western Res. U., 1959, LL.M., 1962. Bar: Ohio 1959, U.S. Supreme Ct. 1964, ICC 1965. Ptnr. Skulina & Stringer, Cleve., 1967-72, Riemer Oberdank & Skulina, Cleve., 1978-81, Skulina, Fillo, Walters & Negrelli, 1981-86, Skulina & McKeon, Cleve., 1986—; atty. Penn Cen. Transp. Co., Cleve., 1960-65, asst. gen. atty., 1965-78, trial counsel, 1965-76; with Consol. Rail Corp., 1976-78; dir. High Temperature Systems, Inc., Active Chem. Systems, Inc.; tchr. comml. law Practicing Law Inst., N.Y.C., 1970. Contbr. articles to legal jours. Income tax and fed. fund coordinator Warrensville Heights, Ohio, 1970-77; spl. counsel City of N. Olmstead, Ohio, 1971-75; pres. Civil Service Commn., Cleve., 1977-86, referee, 1986—, fact-finder SERB, Ohio, 1986—; spl. counsel Ohio Atty. Gen., 1983—. Served with U.S. Army, 1959. Mem. Am. Arbitration Assn. (labor panel 1988—), Nat. Assn. R.R. Trial Counsel, Internat. Assn. Law and Sci., ABA, Cleve. Bar Assn., Ohio Bar Assn. (bd. govs. litigation sect. 1986—), Fed. Bar Assn., Ohio Trial Lawyers Assn., Pub. Sector Labor Relations Assn. Democrat. Roman Catholic. Clubs: River Run Racquet, Lakewood Country. Home: 3162 W 165th St Cleveland OH 44111 Office: Skulina & McKeon 709 Ohio Savings Plaza 1801 E 9th St Cleveland OH 44113

SKUPIN, JANUSZ STANISLAW, biochemist, educator; b. Gniezno, Poland, Jan. 27, 1934; s. Jan and Pelagia (Kubasik) S.; M.Sc., U. Poznan, Poland, 1955, M.D., 1960, Dr. Scis., 1965; m. Aleksandra Mtynarczyk, Apr. 30, 1965; 1 son, Piotr. With Acad. Agr., Poznan, Poland, 1955—, dir. Inst. Food Sci., 1970-77, prof., 1973—, dir. dept. food biochemistry and analysis, 1970—; dir. Inst. Microbiology, Biochemistry and Food Analysis, 1983. Recipient numerous grants Rockefeller Found., U.S. Dept. Agr. Mem. Polish Biochem. Soc., Internat. Cereal Chemists Assn., Polish Acad. Scis. Author 2 books in field; contbr. articles to profl. jours. Home: 17 Michatowska, 60 645 Poznan Poland Office: 48 Mazowiecka, 606 23 Poznan Poland

SKUPINSKI, BOGDAN KAZIMIERZ, artist; b. Poland, July 16, 1942; came to U.S., 1971, naturalized, 1976; s. Kazimierz Stanislaw and Jrena Lucja (Kanar) S. B.A., Acad. Fine Arts, Krakow, Poland, 1969, M.A., 1971; cert., Ecole Nationale Superieure de Beaux Arts, Paris, 1971. Pres. the MacMurchy Co., N.Y.C. Graphic artist: painting Proclamation, 1968, Escape, 1968, Return, 1969, Good Journey, (permanent collection N.J. State Mus., 1971, The Stable, (permanent collection Library of Congress), 1971, Nouvel Ordre, 1970 (annual prize Ministry of Cultural Affairs of France), Gare du Nord, 1970 (award Commn. Fine Arts. Paris), anti-war themes, 1969-76; life and work of John F. Kennedy and Albert Michelson, 1969-76. Recipient Grand Prix Nat. Salon Young Artists, 1968; recipient People's Choice award 2d Nat. Graphic Rev., Karkow, 1969, ann. Bartoczek and Babrowski award Polish Ministry of Art and Culture, Warsaw, 1970, Cannon prize for graphics NAD, N.Y.C., 1971, 1st prize for prints and drawings Nat. Conn. Acad. Exhbn., Hartford, 1971, medal Internat. Exhbn. Graphic Art, Frechen, Germany, 1976; sci. fellow Acad. Fine Arts, Ecole Nationale Superieure de Beaux Arts, Kosciuszko Found. Fellow Pratt Inst.; mem. NAD. Democrat. Roman Catholic. Lodge: Masons. Home: PO Box 849 215 W 104th St Cathedral Sta New York NY 10025

SKWARCZYNSKI, MACIEJ LEON STEFAN, mathematician, educator, editor; b. Warsaw, Poland, Apr. 11, 1944; s. Stanislaw Tadeusz and Maria Elzbieta (Krynicka) S.; m. Irena Michalina Helena Anna Sawicka, Sept. 28, 1968. M.S., U. Warsaw, 1965; internat. student Stanford U., Palo Alto, Calif., 1966-68; Ph.D., U. Warsaw, 1969, Dr.Habil., 1979. Asst. U. Warsaw, 1965-67, sr. asst., 1968-69, asst. prof., 1969-79; research asst. Stanford U., 1967-68; assoc. prof. Radom Tech. U., Poland, 1980-84; assoc. prof. math. Agr. Acad., Warsaw, 1984—; dir. Inst. Math.-Physics, Radom Tech. U., 1980-82, Inst. Applied Math. and Stats., Warsaw, 1987; mng. dir. Math. Olympics, Warsaw, 1978; Leksykon Matematyczny edn. com. chmn. Wiedza Powszechna, Warsaw, 1975—; vis. prof. Bulgarian Acad. Sci., Sofia, 1980. Editor Prace Matematyczno-Fizyczne, 1982. Recipient medal State Council P.R.L. Za ofiarnosc i odwage, 1962. Mem. Polish Math. Soc., Am. Math. Soc., Polish Students Assn. (hon.). Roman Catholic. Avocation: sailing. Contbr. articles to profl. jours. Home: Smolenskiego 27a m 14, 01 698 Warsaw Poland Office: U Warsaw Dept Math, 009 01 Warsaw Poland

SLABE, JAMES F., financial executive; b. Johnstown, Pa., Nov. 29, 1940; s. Frank and Antoinette Marie (Draksler) S.; m. Elaine Werner, July 14, 1973. BA, Washington and Jefferson Coll., 1962; postgrad., U. Md., 1962-64. Div. controller Pfizer, Inc., N.Y.C., 1967-72; treas., controller Pharmacaps, Inc., Elizabeth, N.J., 1972-73; dir. profit planning McGraw-Hill, Inc., N.Y.C., 1973-78; v.p. fin. Parade Publs., Inc., N.Y.C., 1978-79; sr. v.p. fin. and adminstrn. Exec. Enterprises, Inc., N.Y.C., 1979—, also bd. dirs., 1980—; bd. dirs. The 21 Bldg. Corp., N.Y.C. Pub. Nat. Productivity Rev., Banks in Insurance Report, S Corporation Strategies and Benefits Law Journal. Treas. East Side Young Rep. Club, N.Y., 1968-70. Served as capt. U.S. Army, 1964-66. Mem. Fin. Execs. Inst., Assn. Am. Planners, Assn. Am. Controllers, Phi Beta Kappa. Roman Catholic. Home: 17 Mountainview Dr Mountainside NJ 07092 Office: Exec Enterprises Inc 22 W 21st St New York NY 10010

SLADDEN, RAYMOND, finance company executive; b. Malta, Aug. 24, 1955; s. Henry and Theresa (Formosa) S.; m. Diane Woods; 1 child, David. From asst. officer to sr. mgr. Airmalta Co. Ltd., 1978-85, gen. mgr.,

1986—. Mem. Chartered Inst. Bankers, Inst. Accts. Office: Airmalta Co Ltd, Head Office Finance Dept, Luqa Malta

SLADE, ADRIAN CARNEGIE, advertising writer, politician; b. London, May 25, 1936; s. George Penkivil and Mary Albinia (Carnegie) S.; m. Susan Elizabeth Forsyth, June 22, 1960; children: Nicola, Rupert. BA in Law, Cambridge U., 1959. Writer J. Walter Thompson Co., London, 1959-64; creative dir. S.H. Benson Ltd., London, 1964-71; mng. dir. Slade-Monico Bluff, London, 1971-75, Slade Bluff & Bigg, London, 1975-86, Slade Hamilton Fenech Ltd, London, 1986—. Pres. London Liberal Party, 1982-85; candidate Liberal Alliance, 1966, 74, 87; liberal mem. Gt. London Council, 1981-86; pres Liberal Com., 1987, Social and Liberal Dem., 1988. Home: 28 St Leonards Rd, London SW14 7LK, England Office: Slade Hamilton Fenech Ltd, 38 Clareville St, London SW147X, England

ŠLAPETA, IVAN, cinematographer; b. Olomouc, ČSSR, Czechoslovakia, Mar. 28, 1938; s. Lubomir and Ludmila (Sahankova) Š. Diploma in cinematography, Acad. Musical, Dramatic and Film Arts, Praha, Czechoslovakia, 1963. Cinematographer diplomate. Cameraman TV Ostrava, ČSSR, 1957; camera asst. Film Studio Barrandov, Praha, 1958-60, 2d cameraman, 1961-64, dir. photography, 1965—. Recipient Grand Prix (with Pavel Juracek), Oberhausen, 1966, Prix Italia (with Peter Weigel), Monte Carlo, 1969, Gold Globe (with Frantisek Vlacil), Karlovy Vary, 1978, Oscar nomination (with Maximilian Schell), Los Angeles, 1985. Mem. Assn. Film and TV Artists, Assn. Dramatic Artists. Roman Catholic. Clubs: Paleta Vlasti HC (Praha), Golf (Lisnice). Office: Film Studio Barrandov, Krizeneckeho 322, Prague 5, Czechoslovakia

SLATE, JOE HUTSON, psychologist, educator; b. Hertselle, Ala., Sept. 21, 1930; s. Murphy Edmund and Marie (Hutson) S.; m. Rachel Holladay, July 1, 1950; children: Marc Allan, John David, James Daryl. B.S., Athens Coll., 1960; M.A., U. Ala., 1965, Ph.D., 1970. Mem. faculty Athens (Ala.) State Coll., 1965—, prof. psychology, 1974—, chmn. behavioral scis., 1974—; pvt. practice psychology Athens, 1970—; v.p. Slate Security Systems, Hartselle, Ala. Author: Psychic Phenomena, 1988. Named hon. prof. Montevallo U., 1973. Mem. Am., Ala. psychol. assns., Inst. Parapsychol. Research (founder, pres.), Council for Nat. Register Health Service Providers in Psychology, NEA, Ala. Edn. Assn., Am. Soc. Clin. Hypnosis, Delta Tau Delta, Phi Delta Kappa, Kappa Delta Pi. Home: 1501 Hwy 31N Hartselle AL 35640 Office: Dept Psychology Athens State Coll Athens AL 35611

SLATER, DORIS ERNESTINE WILKE, business exec.; b. Oakes, N.D.; d. Arthur Waldemar and Anna Mary (Dill) Wilke; grad. high sch.; m. Lawrence Bert Slater, June 4, 1930 (dec., 1960). Sec. to circulation mgr. Mpls. Daily Star, 1928-30; promotion activities Lions Internat. in U.S., Can., Cuba, 1930-48; exec. sec. parade and spl. events com. Inaugural Com., 1948-49; exec. sec. Nat. Capital Sesquicentennial Commn., 1949-50, Capitol Hill Assos., Inc., 1951, Pres.'s Cup Regatta, 1951; adminstrv. asst. Nat. Assn. Food Chains, 1951-60; v.p., sec.-treas. John A. Logan Assos., Inc., Washington, 1960—; v.p., sec.-treas. Logan, Seaman, Slater, Inc., 1962—; mng. dir. Western Hemisphere, Internat. Assn. Chain Stores, 1964—. With pub. relations div. Boston Met. chpt. ARC, 1941-42; mem. Nat. Cherry Blossom Festival Com., 1949—; mem. Inaugural Ball Com., 1953, 57, 65. Methodist. Lion. Home and Office: 2500 Wisconsin Ave Washington DC 20007

SLATER, HELENE FORD SOUTHERN, public relations executive; b. Phila.; d. William Bette and Henrietta Harriet (Ford) Southern; B.A., New Sch. for Social Research, 1955, M.A., 1959; postgrad. Yeshiva U., Coll. City N.Y., Fordham U., Temple U., Howard U.; m. Chester E. Slater, June 22, 1955 (div. Dec. 1968). Reporter, columnist, feature writer various newspapers, 1940—; pres. Southern-Slater Enterprises, pub. relations, N.Y.C., 1955—; supr. Bur. Attendance, Bd. Edn. City N.Y., 1970-73. Pub. relations officer Shirley Chisholm Community Action Corp., 1972; pub. relations dir. UN Coll. Fund/Arthur Ashe Tennis Benefit, 1976-80; bd. dirs. New Harlem YWCA, 1980—; pub. relations dir. ann. careers conf. Pan-Hellenic Council, 1970-85. Recipient Outstanding Community Person award Radio Sta. WWRL, 1965; Achievement award Lambda Kappa Mu, 1971, Citation of Merit, 1973, Outstanding Soror of Yr., 1967, Distinguished Service Key, 1977; Achievement award Howard U., 1975, 80, Outstanding Person in the Community, Medgar Evers Community Radio (WNYE-FM), 1983; citation Barbados Bd. Tourism, 1983; Spl. Recognition award LKM Sorority 50th anniversary for pub. relations and editorial ability, 1987 . Mem. Nat. Assn. Media Women (charter mem., nat. pub. relations dir. 1973-80, Pres.'s award 1971, 79, Founder's cup 1974), Nat. Assn. Coll. Women, N.Y.C. Howard U. Alumni (pres. 1975-79), Coalition 100 Black Women, Nat. Assn. Negro Bus. and Profl. Women's Clubs. Editor: The Acorn, Lambda Kappa Mu Sorority Ann. House Organ, 1960-65, 77-81; The Media Woman, Nat. Assn. Media Women Ann. House Organ, 1966-67, 79. Home and Office: 360 W 22d St New York NY 10011

SLATER, S. DONALD, brokerge executive; b. N.Y.C., Apr. 8, 1927; s. Moses and Rose (Warshaw) S.; B.A. cum laude, Syracuse U., 1949; M.A., Columbia, 1951, postgrad., 1955; children—Donald, Julia. Investment cons. Standard & Poor's Corp., N.Y.C., 1951-53; lectr. econs. U. Conn., lectr. accounting and fin. Upsala Coll., 1954-55; investment banking and dir. research Shields & Co., N.Y.C., 1955-58; investment banking and research Blyth Eastman Dillon & Co., N.Y.C., 1958-61, E.F. Hutton & Co., N.Y.C., 1962-64; pres. Good Rds. Machinery Corp., pres. MainTek, Inc., Canton, Ohio, 1965-67; pres. Amadon Corp., Boston, 1964—; chmn. bd. Richardson Polymer Corp., Madison, Conn.; asst. prof. fin. Bentley Coll. Grad. Sch., Waltham, Mass. Bd. dirs. World Affairs Council, Boston. Served with US Navy; 1945-46. Mem. Tabard, Pi Sigma Rho, Pi Gamma Mu, Theta Beta Phi. Clubs: Columbia U. Alumni New Eng. (dir.); Badminton and Tennis (Boston). Author: The Strategy of Cash: A liquidity approach to maximizing the company's profits, 1974.

SLATTERY, ALICE, art educator; b. Chico, Calif., Mar. 15, 1945; d. Charles William and Ruth Elizabeth (Dakin) Mauldin. A.A. in Art, Coll. San Mateo (Calif.), 1965; B.A., Chico State Coll., 1967, M.A., 1968; MFA Syracuse U., 1984. Model, John Robert Powers Modeling Agy., Palo Alto, Calif., 1963-65; designer publs. office Chico State Coll., 1966-67; graphic artist Calif. State U., Chico, 1967-73; art instr. Live Oak (Calif.) High Sch., 1969; art instr. Sitka (Alaska) Community Coll., 1973-81; art instr. SARAC Fine Arts Camp, Sitka, 1974-75; art instr. Bur. Indian Affairs High Sch., Mt. Edgecumbe, Alaska, 1977; prof. art U. Alaska, Juneau, 1981—. Bd. dirs. Baranof Arts & Crafts Assn., chmn. ann. art show, 1976, v.p., exhibits chmn., 1977-81. Recipient numerous awards for artistry. Mem. Nat. Craft Council, Nat. League Am. Pen Women (v.p. 1980-81), Nat. Art Edn. Assn., Coll. Art Assn., Am. Crafts Council, AAUW, Graphic Communication Guild, Screen Printers Assn. Contbr. art exhibits to numerous art shows and museums. Office: Dept Fine Arts Univ Alaska 11120 Glacier Hwy Juneau AK 99801

SLATTERY, CHARLES WILBUR, biochemistry educator; b. La Junta, Colo., Nov. 18, 1937; s. Robert Ernest Slattery and Virgie Belle (Chamberlain) Tobin; m. Arline Sylvia Reile, June 15, 1958; children—Scott Charles, Coleen Kay. B.A., Union Coll., 1959; M.S., U. Nebr., 1961, Ph.D., 1965. Instr. chemistry Union Coll., Lincoln, Nebr., 1961-63; asst. prof., assoc. prof. chemistry Atlantic Union Coll., South Lancaster, Mass., 1963-68; research assoc. biophysics MIT, Cambridge, 1967-70; asst. prof., then prof. biochemistry Loma Linda U., Calif., 1970-80, prof. biochemistry-pediatrics, 1980—, chmn. dept., 1983—; vis. prof. U. So. Calif.-Los Angeles, 1978-79. Contbr. articles to profl. jours. NIH grantee, 1979-82, 86—, Am. Heart Assn. (Calif.), 1981-83, 83-84. Mem. Am. Chem. Soc., AAAS, Am. Dairy Sci. Assn., Am. Soc. Biol. Chemists, Am. Heart Assn. Thrombosis Council, Sigma Xi. Republican. Adventist. Office: Loma Linda Univ Sch of Medicine Dept of Biochemistry Loma Linda CA 92350

SLAUGHTER, FREEMAN CLUFF, dentist; b. Estes, Miss., Dec. 30, 1926; s. William Cluff and Vay (Fox) S.; student Wake Forest Coll., 1944; student Emory U., 1946-47, D.D.S., 1951; m. Genevieve Anne Parks, July 30, 1948; children—Mary Anne, Thomas Freeman, James Hugh. Practice gen. dentistry, Kannapolis, N.C., 1951—; mem. N.C. Bd. Dental Examiners, 1966-75, pres., 1968-69, sec.-treas., 1971-74; chief dental staff Cabarrus Meml. Hosp., Concord, N.C., 1965-66, 75; mem. N.C. Adv. Com. for Edn. Dental Aux. Personnel-N.C. State Bd. Edn., 1967-70; adviser dental asst. program Rowan Tech. Inst., 1974-76. Trustee N.C. Symphony Soc., 1962-68, pres. Kannapolis chpt., 1961; mem. Cabarrus County Bd. Health, 1977-83, chmn., 1981-83, acting health dir., 1981; vice chmn. Kannapolis Charter Commn., 1983-84; mem. City Council Kannapolis, 1984-85; Mayor protem, Kannapolis, 1984-85; active Boy Scouts Am., Eagle scout with silver palm. Served with USNR, 1944-46; ETO, MTO. Recipient Kannapolis Citizen of Yr. award, 1982; lic. real estate broker. Fellow Am. Coll. Dentists; mem. Am. Legion, Kannapolis Jr. C. of C. (v.p. 1952), Toastmasters Internat. (pres. Kannapolis 1963-64), ADA, Am. Assn. Dental Examiners (Dentist Citizen of Year 1975; v.p. 1977-79), So. Conf. Dental Deans and Examiners (v.p. 1969), N.C. Dental Soc. (resolution of commendation 1975), N.C. Dental Soc. Anesthesiology (pres. 1964), Southeastern Acad. Prosthodontics, So. Acad. Oral Surgery, Am. Soc. Dentistry for Children (pres. N.C. unit 1957), Internat. Assn. Dental Research, Cabarrus County Dental Soc. (pres. 1953-54, 63-64, 69), N.C. Assn. Professions (dir. 1976-80), Omicron Kappa Upsilon, Alpha Epsilon Upsilon. Clubs: Masons, Shriners, Kannapolis Music (pres. 1962-63), Rotary (dir. 1977-80). Office: Profl Bldg Kannapolis NC 28081

SLAUGHTER, JAMES LUTHER, III, graphic designer; b. Jenkins, Ky., Aug. 22, 1944; s. James Luther and Loretta (Winchester) S.; m. Susan Lee Brundige, Sept. 16, 1972. BS in Graphic Design, U. Cin., 1967. Graphic designer Shaw Studio Advt., Cin., 1967-69, E.F. MasDonald, Dayton, Ohio, 1969-70; ptnr., designer Slaughter & Slaughter, Inc., Cin., 1970—; cons. NIOSH, Cin., 1979; adj. faculty mem. No. Ky. U., Highland Heights, 1978-80. Contbr. articles to profl. jours. Mem. Concours Com. Arthritis Found., Cin., 1980-86; trustee Unity Ctr. Cin., 1986; bd. dirs. Appalachian Com. Devel. Assn., Cin., 1985-86, A Day In Eden Community Festival, Cin., 1986. Recipient Silver and Bronze medals The Advt. Club, Cin., 1980, Design Excellence award Internat. Typographic Composition Assn., 1980. Mem. Bus. and Profl. Advt. Assn. (workshop chmn. 1986), The Art Dirs. Club (Merit award 1970-85), Am. Inst. Graphic Arts, Nat. Model RR Assn.

SLAUGHTER, JANE MUNDY, author; b. Buchanan, Va., Oct. 2, 1905; d. Luther Thomas and Pearl Carnce (Karnes) Mundy; R.N., Jefferson Hosp., Roanoke, Va., 1926; m. Frank G. Slaughter, June 10, 1933; children—Frank G., Randolph M. Operating Room supr. Jefferson Hosp., 1923-24; pvt. duty nurse, 1924-33; freelance author, 1970—; author: Espy and the Catnappers, 1975; also 1st history of Fla. Med. Assn. Aux. Bd. dirs. Jacksonville (Fla.) YWCA, 1960-65. Mem. Fla. Hist. Soc., Jacksonville Hist. Soc., Fla. Fedn. Garden Clubs (life mem. Jacksonville), Fla. Med. Assn. Aux. (historian 1950). Democrat. Presbyterian. Club: Timuquana Country. Address: 5051 Yacht Club Rd Jacksonville FL 32210

SLAUGHTER, JOHN BROOKS, university administrator; b. Topeka, Mar. 16, 1934; s. Reuben Brooks and Dora (Reeves) S.; m. Ida Bernice Johnson, Aug. 31, 1956; children: John Brooks, Jacqueline Michelle. Student, Washburn U., 1951-53; B.S.E.E., Kans. State U., 1956; M.S. in Engring, UCLA, 1961; Ph.D. in Engring. Scis, U. Calif., San Diego, 1971; D.Engring. (hon.), Rensselaer Poly. Inst., 1981; D.Sc. (hon.), U. So. Calif., 1981, Tuskegee Inst., 1981, U. Md., College Park, 1982, U. Notre Dame, 1982; D.Sci. (hon.), U. Miami, 1983, U. Mass., 1983, Tex. So. U., 1984, U. Toledo, 1985, U. Ill., 1986, SUNY, 1986. Registered profl. engr., Wash. Electronics engr. Gen. Dynamics Convair, San Diego, 1956-60; with Naval Electronics Lab. Center, San Diego, 1960-75, div. head, 1965-71, dept. head, 1971-75; dir. applied physics lab. U. Wash., 1975-77; asst. dir. NSF, Washington, 1977-79; dir. NSF, 1980-82; acad. v.p., provost Wash. State U., 1979-80; chancellor U. Md., College Park, 1982-88; pres. Occidental Coll., Los Angeles, 1988—; bd. dirs., vice chmn. San Diego Transit Corp., 1968-75; mem. com. on minorities in engring. Nat. Research Council, 1976-79; mem. Commn. on Pre-Coll. Edn. in Math., Sci., and Tech. Nat. Sci. Bd., 1982-83; bd. dirs. Comml. Credit Corp., Balt. Gas and Electric, Monsato Co., Sovran Bank, Med. Mut. Liability Ins. Soc. Md., Martin Marietta. Editor: Jour. Computers and Elec. Engring, 1972—. Bd. dirs. San Diego Urban League, 1962-66, pres., 1964-66; mem. Pres.'s Com. on Nat. Medal Sci., 1979-80; trustee Rensselaer Poly. Inst., 1982; chmn. Pres.'s Com. Nat. Collegiate Athletic Assn. Naval Electronics Lab Center fellow, 1969-70; Recipient Engring. Alumnus award UCLA, 1978; Disting. Service award NSF, 1979; Recipient Disting. Service in Engring. award Kans. State U., 1981; recipient UCLA Engring. Disting. Alumnus of Year, 1978, U. Calif.-San Diego Disting. Alumnus of Year, 1982. Fellow IEEE (chmn. com. on minority affairs 1976-80), AAAS (dir. 1983—); mem. Nat. Acad. Engring., Nat. Collegiate Athletic Assn. (chmn. pres. commn.), Tau Beta Pi, Eta Kappa Nu, Alpha Phi Alpha. Office: Occidental Coll 1600 Campus Dr Los Angeles CA 90041 *

SLAUGHTER, LURLINE EDDY, artist; b. Heidelberg, Miss., June 19, 1919; d. Gilbert Emmings and Lurline Elizabeth (Heidelberg) Eddy; B.S., Miss. U. for Women, 1939; m. James Fant Slaughter, Jan. 27, 1946; children—Beverly Lowery, Anne Towles. Tchr. high sch., Silver City, Miss., 1939-41; clk. VA, Washington, 1941-42; one-woman shows Ahda Artzt Gallery, N.Y.C., 1967, Nat. Design Center, N.Y.C., 1967, 68, Delta State U., Cleveland, Miss., 1973, 84, Gulf States Gallery, Greenville, Miss., 1973, 76, 80, 84, Southeastern La. U., Hammond, 1977, Cheekwood Fine Arts Center, Nashville, 1978, Byars Gallery, Little Rock, 1984, San Pedro Theatre, San Antonio, 1981, Cottonlandia Mus., Greenwood, Miss., 1984 exhibited in group shows U. Fla., 1969, Brooks Art Mus., Memphis, 1970, Miss. State U., 1970, 85, Delta State U., 1971, 84; represented in permanent collection Miss. U. for Women, Miss. State U., Delta State U., Pine Bluff (Ark.) Art Ctr., Southeastern La. U., U. of South, Sewanee, Tenn., Eudora Welty Mepl. Library, Jackson, Miss.; represented in pvt. collections, Acapulco, Guadalajara, Mex., San Francisco, N.Y.C., so. states. Recipient Best in Show award Acapulco Ann., Hilton Hotel, 1979, Best in Show award Cottonlandia Mus., Greenwood, Miss., 1987. Tchr. Sunday Sch., Meth. Ch., 1953-67; pres. PTA; bd. dirs. Miss. Art Colony, 1965-85. Served as lt. (j.g.) USNR, 1942-45. Mem. Miss. Art Mus. and Mcpl. Gallery, Nat. Mus. for Women in the Arts (charter). Republican. Club: Humphreys Country. Address: Seldom Seen Plantation Silver City MS 39166

SLAWSKY, ZAKA ISRAEL, physicist, educator; b. Bklyn., Apr. 2, 1910; s. Simon and Mollie (Brimberg) S.; B.S., Rensselaer Poly. Inst., 1933; M.S., Calif. Inst. Tech., 1935; Ph.D., U. Mich., 1938; m. Dorothy Altman, Jan. 19, 1945; children—Albert Altman, Richard Charles. Faculty, Bklyn. Coll., 1939-40, Union Coll., Schenectady, 1940-41; staff Naval Ordnance Lab., White Oak, Md., 1941-75, chief physics research, 1960-75; faculty U. Md., College Park, 1946—, prof. physics, 1964—. Pres., Joint Bd. in Sci. Edn., Washington Area, 1969-70; pres. bd. trustees Georgetown Day Sch., 1956-63. Recipient Meritorious Civilian Service award USN, 1952, 58, Disting. Civilian Service medal, 1971. Fellow Am. Phys. Soc., Washington Acad. Sci.; mem. Fed. Prof. Assn. (pres. 1971), Washington Philos. Soc. Club: Cosmos (Washington). Contbr. articles on theory of high speed gas dynamics and molecular relaxation to profl. jours. Research on tech. of antimine warfare, torpedo hydrodynamics, guided and ballistic missiles, antisubmarine warfare. Patentee in field. Home: 4701 Willard Ave Apt 318 Chevy Chase MD 20815 Office: U Md Dept Physics College Park MD 20742

SLAYTER, JOHN HENRY, housing company executive, consultant, cattle farmer; Columbus, Ohio, Feb. 3, 1934; s. R. Games and M. Marie (Foor) S.; m. Marlene V. Patterson, Aug. 1, 1955 (div. Feb. 1971); children—Games Edwin, Mark Alan, John David, Julie Marie; m. Beverly Ann Billings, Aug. 28, 1971; children—Benjamin John, Megan Rebecca. B.S.M.E., Purdue U., 1956. Pres., owner Slayter Assocs., Inc., Elkhart, Ind., 1968-71; v.p. mfg. Multicon Corp., Columbus, 1971-73; v.p. div. mgr. Leadership Housing, Inc., Tokyo and Honolulu, 1973-75; pres. Glendale Corp., Oakville, Ont., Can., 1975-78; owner, operator Old Locust Farm, Inc., Newark, Ohio, 1978-82; v.p. research and engring. The Ryland Group, Inc., Columbia, Md., 1982-88, v.p., 1988—. Patentee in field. Dir. lay youth YMCA, Newark, Ohio, 1960-64; v.p., bd. dirs. Sheltered Workshop, Elkhart, 1965-71; founding mem. advanced bldg. tech. council Nat. Research Council of Nat. Acad. Scis.; mem. Republican County Exec. Com., Licking County, Ohio, 1980—. Served to 1st lt. U.S. Army, 1957-59. Mem. Nat. Cattlemens Assn., Nat. Inst. Building Scis., Design Council Industrialized Housing (founding), Nat. Assn. Homebuilders (chmn. bldg. systems council 1985, mem. exec com.). Lodges: Rotary (charter mem., dir.), Masons (32 degree). Avocation: beef cattle breeding. Home: 6052 Fairmount Rd SE Newark OH 43056

SLAYTON, RANSOM DUNN, consulting engineer; b. Salem, Nebr., Mar. 10, 1917; s. Laurel Wayland and Martha Ellen (Fisher) S.; B.S. with distinction, U. Nebr., 1938; postgrad. Ill. Inst. Tech., 1942, DePaul U., 1945-46; m. Margaret Marie Ang, Sept. 25, 1938; children—R. Duane, David L., Sharon J. Slayton Manz, Karla M. Slayton Fogel, Paul L. With Western Union Telegraph Co., Lincoln, Nebr., 1937-38, St. Paul, 1938-40, Omaha, 1940, Chgo., 1940-45; asst. prof. elec. engring. Chgo. Tech. Coll., 1945-46; with Teletype Corp., Chgo. and Skokie, Ill., 1946-82, lectr., China and Japan, 1978, 79, 80. Active vol. civic orgns., numerous ch. offices. Mem. IEEE (sr., life, numerous coms.), IEEE Communications Soc. (parliamentarian 1972-80, 82—, vice chmn. terminals com. 1980-82, chmn. 1983-84). Patentee in field. Home: 1530 Hawthorne Ln Glenview IL 60025

SLEDGE, ROBERT WATSON, history educator; b. Brownsville, Tex., Sept. 14, 1932; s. Robert Lee and Peggy (Watson) S.; m. Marjorie Stout, Aug. 14, 1956; children: Margaret Ann, Robert Lee II. BS, Southwestern U., 1953, BA, 1956; BD, So. Meth. U., 1960; MA, U. Tex.-Austin, 1964, PhD, 1972. Pastor Buda Methodist Ch., Tex., 1960-63; instr. history Nebr. Wesleyan U., Lincoln, 1963-64; prof. history McMurry Coll., Abilene, Tex., 1964—; vis. prof. Pan Am. U., Edinburg, Tex., 1974, 76; instr. pastors sch. So. Meth. U., Dallas, 1977-80, 84—. Author: Hands on the Ark (Jesse Lee prize 1972), 1975, The Methodist Excitement in Texas, 1984, God's Field, God's Building (Kate Warnick award 1986); editor: Pride of Our Western Praries, 1988; contbr. articles to profl. jours. Precinct chmn. Dem. Party, Taylor County, 1980-86 ; mem. gen. commn. archives and history United Meth. Ch. Served with U.S. Army, 1953-55. Mem. South Central Jurisdiction Com. Archives and History (chmn. 1984-88), Alpha Chi (nat. pres. 1983-87). Methodist. Avocations: tennis, hiking. Home: 8 Wynrush Circle Abilene TX 79606 Office: McMurry Coll Abilene TX 79697

SLEEMAN, BRIAN DAVID, mathematics educator; b. London, Aug. 4, 1939; s. Richard Kinsman and Gertrude Cecilia (Gamble) S.; m. Juliet Mary Shea, Sept. 7, 1963; children: Elizabeth Anne, Matthew Alexander, David James. BSc, Battersea Coll. Tech., London, 1963; PhD, U. London, 1966; DSc, Dundee (Scotland) U., 1975. Asst. lectr. math. U. Dundee, 1965-67, lectr., 1967-71, reader, 1971-78, prof., 1978—; vis. asst. prof. math. Courant Inst., N.Y., 1970-71; vis. prof. U. Tenn., Knoxville, 1976-77, Uppsala (Sweden) U., 1984. Author: Multiparameter Spectral Theory In Hilbert Space, 1978; co-author Differential Equations and Mathematical Biology, 1983; editor, assoc. editor math. jours. Fellow Royal Soc. Edinburgh, Inst. Math. and Its Applications; Am. Math. Soc., Edinburgh Math. Soc. Anglican. Office: U Dundee, Dundee DD1 4HN, Scotland

SLEIGHT, ARTHUR WILLIAM, chemist; b. Ballston Spa, N.Y., Apr. 1, 1939; s. Hollis Decker and Elizabeth (Smith) S.; A.B., Hamilton Coll., 1960; Ph.D., U. Conn., 1963; m. Betty F. Hilberg, Apr. 19, 1963; children—Jeffrey William, Jeannette Anne, Jason Arthur. Faculty, U. Stockholm, Sweden, 1963-64; with E.I. du Pont de Nemours & Co., Inc., Wilmington, Del., 1965—, research mgr. solid state/catalytic chemistry, 1981—; adj. prof. U. Del., 1978—. Recipient Phila. chpt. Am. Inst.. Chemists award, 1988. Mem. Am. Chem. Soc. (award Del. sect. 1978). Assoc. editor Materials Research Bull., 1977—; editorial bd. Inorganic Chemistry Rev., 1979—, Jour. Catalysis, 1986—, Applied Catalysis, 1987—, Solid State Scis., 1987—, Chemistry of Materials, 1988—, Materials Chemistry and Physics, 1988—, Jour. of Solid State Chemistry, 1988—; patentee in field; contbr. articles to profl. jous. Home: 111 Taylor Ln Kennett Square PA 19348 Office: DuPont Exptl Sta Wilmington DE 19898

SLEMMONS, ROBERT SHELDON, architect; b. Mitchell, Nebr., Mar. 12, 1922; s. M. Garvin and K. Fern (Borland) S.; B.A., U. Nebr., 1948; m. Dorothy Virginia Herrick, Dec. 16, 1945; children—David (dec.), Claire, Jennifer, Robert, Timothy. Draftsman, Davis & Wilson, architects, Lincoln, Nebr., 1947-48; chief designer, project architect Office of Kans. State Architect, Topeka, 1948-54; asso. John A. Brown, architect, Topeka, 1954-56; partner Brown & Slemmons, architect, Topeka, 1956-69; v.p. Brown-Slemmons-Kreuger, architects, Topeka, 1969-73; owner Robert S. Slemmons, A.I.A. & Assos., architects, Topeka, 1973—. Cons. Kans. State Office Bldg. Commn., 1956-57; lectr. in design U. Kans., 1961; bd. dirs. Kaw Valley State Bank & Trust Co., Topeka, 1978—. Bd. dirs. Topeka Civic Symphony Soc., 1950-60, Midstates Retirement Communities, Inc., 1986—; v.p. Ministries for Aging, Inc., Topeka, 1984—. Served with USNR, 1942-48. Mem. AIA (Topeka pres. 1955-56, Kans. dir. 1957-58, mem. com. on architecture for justice), Topeka Art Guild (pres. 1950), Kans. Council Chs. (dir. 1961-62), Greater Topeka C. of C., Downtown Topeka, Inc. Presbyn. (elder, chmn. trustees). Kiwanian (pres. 1966-67). Prin. archtl. works include: Kans. State Office Bldg., 1954, Topeka Presbyn. Manor, 1960-74, Meadowlark Hills Retirement Community, 1979, Shawnee County Adult Detention Facility, 1985. Office: 1515 1 Townsite Plaza Topeka KS 66603

SLESS, DAVID, communications researcher; b. Leeds, Yorkshire, Eng., Apr. 23, 1943. BA with honors, Leeds U., Eng., 1965; MSc, Durham U., Eng., 1975. Lectr. communication studies Sunderland Coll. Art, Eng., 1965 70; lectr. Sunderland Polytechnic, Eng., 1970-75; lectr. Flinders U. South Australia, 1975-78, sr. lectr., 1978-87; exec. dir. Communication Research Inst. Australia, Australia Capital Territory, 1987—. Author: Learning and Visual Communication, 1981, In Search of Semiotics, 1986. Grantee Austrian Research Grants Scheme, 1980-82, Australia Council, 1985. Mem. Australian Communication Assn. (pres. 1986-87). Office: Australian Nat Univ, Communication Research Inst, Liversidge St, Canberra 2601, Australia

SLETMO, GUNNAR KRISTOFFER, business educator, transportation consultant; b. Sandefjord, Norway, Jan. 3, 1937; s. Hans S. and Anna (Andersen) S.; children—Anne, Dag. Sivilokonom. Grad., Norwegian Sch. Econs. and Bus. Adminstrn., 1960; Ph.D., Columbia U., 1971. Lectr., Norwegian Sch. Econs. and Bus. Adminstrn., Bergen, Norway, 1960-69; assoc. prof. grad. sch. bus. Columbia U., N.Y.C., 1969-77; prof. U. Montreal, 1977—; chmn. Task Force on Deep-Sea Shipping, Ottawa, Ont., Can., 1984-85; dir. of Montreal-Tianjin mgmt. program, PRC, 1987—; cons. transp. various orgns., N.A., Europe. Author: Liner Conferences in the Container Age: U.S. Policy at Sea, 1981. Author books, articles, govt. reports. Mem. Am. Econ. Assn. Office: Ecole Hautes Etudes Commerciales, 5255 ave Decelles, Montreal, PQ Canada H3T 1V6

SLINN, RONALD JOHN ST. LEGER, forester, economist, educator; b. Sydney, Australia, Nov. 23, 1928; came to U.S., 1967; s. Herbert Frederick and Lillias Matilda (McLeod) S.; m. Edith Jean Watts, Jan. 19, 1952; children—Peter J. (dec.), Jennifer E., Barbara P., Ronald P. (dec.), Margaret A. B.Sc. in Forestry, Sydney U., 1950, diploma in forestry, 1950; M.S. in Forestry, Melbourne U., 1965; Ph.D. (fellow), Duke U., 1970. Officer in charge forest mgmt. research Australian Forest Research Inst., 1965-69; asso. prof. forest econs. Duke U., Durham, N.C., 1969-70; v.p. pulp, materials and tech. group Am. Paper Inst., N.Y.C., 1970—. Contbr. numerous articles on forest mgmt. and adminstrn. to profl. jours.; chmn., bd. visitors Duke U. Sch. Forestry and Environ. Scis.; mem. com. on indsl. energy conservation NRC; adv. mem. forest resources research com. Am. Forest Council Australian Commonwealth scholar, 1946-50. Fellow TAPPI; mem. Soc. Am. Foresters, Paper Industry Mgmt. Assn., Sigma Xi. Republican. Presbyterian. Club: Sky (N.Y.C.). Home: 17 Fieldston Rd Princeton NJ 08540 Office: Am Paper Inst 260 Madison Ave New York NY 10016

SLIWINSKI, MARIAN, physician, educator; b. Strzelce Wielkie, Poland, Feb. 2, 1932; s. Wladyslaw and Julia (Koprowska) S.; diploma physician Med. Acad., Lodz, Poland, 1955; m. Miroslawa Kaminska, June 7, 1956; 1 dau., Magdalena. Asst. Physiol. Inst. Med. Acad., Lodz, 1952-55, lectr. II Surg. Clinic and dir. Clin. Hosp., 1955-64, asst. prof., 1965; dir. edn. and research dept. Ministry of Health and Social Welfare, Govt. of Poland, 1964-70, vice-minister health and social welfare, 1970-72, minister health and social welfare, 1972-80; chief cardiosurgery Inst. Cardiology, Warsaw, 1980—; prof. medicine Med. Acad., Lodz, 1973—. Mem. Polish United Workers Party, Polish Cardiology Club. Office: Inst Cardiology, I Cardiosurgery Dept, Alpejska 42, Warsaw 4628, Poland

SLOAN, F(RANK) BLAINE, law educator; b. Geneva, Nebr., Jan. 3, 1920; s. Charles Porter and Lillian Josephine (Stiefer) S.; m. Patricia Sand, Sept. 2, 1944; children—DeAnne Sloan Riddle, Michael Blaine, Charles Porter. A.B.

with high distinction, U. Nebr., 1942, LL.B. cum laude, 1946; LL.M. in Internat. Law, Columbia U., 1947. Bar: Nebr. 1946, N.Y. 1947. Asst. to spl. counsel Intergovtl. Com. for Refugees, 1947; mem. Office Legal Affairs UN Secretariat, N.Y.C., 1948-78, gen. counsel Relief and Works Agy. Palestine Refugees, Beirut, 1958-60, dir. gen. legal div., 1966-78, rep. of Sec. Gen. to Commn. Internat. Trade Law, 1969-78, rep. to Legal Sub-com. on Outer Space, 1966-78; rep. UN delegation Vietnam conf., Paris, 1973; rep UN Conf. on Carriage of Goods by sea, Hamburg, 1978; prof. internat. law and orgn. Pace U., 1978-87, prof. emeritus, 1987—. Cons. UN Office of Legal Affairs, 1983-84, UN Water Resources Br., 1983; supervisory com., Pace Peace Ctr. Served with AC, U.S. Army, 1943-46. Decorated Air medal. Mem. Am. Soc. Internat. Law, Am. Acad. Polit. and Social Sci., Am. Arbitration Assn. (panel of arbitrators), Order of Coif, Phi Beta Kappa, Phi Alpha Delta (hon.). Republican. Roman Catholic. Contbr. articles to legal jours. Home: HCR-68 Box 72 Foxwind-Forbes Park Fort Garland CO 81133 Office: 78 N Broadway White Plains NY 10603

SLOAN, MARY JEAN, media specialist; b. Lakeland, Fla., Nov. 29, 1927; d. Marion Wilder and Elba (Jinks) Sloan. BS, Peabody Coll., Nashville, 1949; MLS, Atlanta U., 1978, S.L.S., 1980. Cert. library media specialist. Music dir. Pinecrest Sch., Tampa, Fla., 1949-50, Polk County Schs., Bartow, Fla., 1950-54; pvt. music tchr. Lakeland, 1954-58; tchr. Clayton County Schs., Jonesboro Ga., 1958-59; media specialist Eastualley Sch., Marietta, Ga., 1959—; coordinator conf. Ga. Library Media Dept., Jekyll Island, 1982-83, sec., Atlanta, 1982-83, com. chmn. ethnic conf., Atlanta, 1978, pres., 1984-85, state pres., 1985-86; program chmn. Ga. Media Orgns. Conf, Jekyll Island, 1988. Contbr. to bibliographies. Recipient Walter Bell award Ga. Assn. Instructional Tech., 1988. Mem. ALA (del. 1984, 85), NEA, Southeastern Library Assn., Am. Assn. Sch. Librarians, Soc. for Sch. Librarians, Internat., Ga. Assn. Educators (polit. action com. 1983), Beta Phi Mu, Phi Delta Kappa. Republican. Methodist. Home: 797 Yorkshire Rd NE Atlanta GA 30306 Office: Eastvalley Elem Sch 2570 Lower Roswell Rd Marietta GA 30067

SLOAN, MICHAEL LEE, author, computer science/physics teacher; b. Chgo., Jan. 24, 1944; s. Robert Earl Sloan and Cyril (Lewis) Glass; m. Claudia Ann Schultz, Sept. 27, 1969. B.S. in Physics, Roosevelt U., 1966, M.S., 1971. Tchr. physics Glenbard West High Sch., Glen Ellyn, Ill., 1966-79; computer cons. Midwest Visual, Chgo., 1979-82; sr. engr. Apple Computer, Rolling Meadows, Ill., 1982-85; asst. prof. Roosevelt U., 1971-73; tchr. computer sci./physics Ill. Math. and Sci. Acad., Aurora, 1987—; instr. Harper Coll., Palatine, Ill., 1984. Author: AppleWorks: The Program For the Rest of Us, 1985, Working with Works, 1987. Bd. dirs. Youth Symphony Orch., Chgo., 1977-78; trustee Body Politic Theatre, Chgo., 1981-82. Home: 411 W Park Ave Wheaton IL 60187

SLOAN, ROBERT FRANCIS, management consultant; b. Los Angeles, June 19, 1935; s. Lafayette F. and Frances (Walsh) S.; B.A. in Zoology, UCLA, 1957; Ph.D. in Oral Radiology, Osaka Dental U., 1977; m. Estela Alarid, June 8, 1961 (div. May 1982); m. Paula Sy., Apr. 22, 1987; children—Patrick, Cristina, Brett. Research asso. U. Calif. Med.-Dental Sch., Los Angeles, 1957-67; founding pres. Rocky Mountain Data Systems, 1967-70; founding exec. dir. Found. Orthodontic Research, 1968-70; exec. dir. InterAm. Orthodontic Seminar, 1964-70; mgmt. cons., Calif., 1978; chmn. bd. Radiol. Mgmt. Communications, Ltd., ITA Ltd., prof. Grad. Sch. of Business, U.S. Internat. U., San Diego, 1977-79; producer documentary and tech. films. Served to capt. M.S.C., U.S. Army, 1957-69. Recipient Bronze N.Y. Film Festival award, 1973, 79, Chris award, 1965, 73, Cine awards, 1964, 65, 74. Mem. ADA, Brit. Inst. Radiology, AMA, Found. Orthodontic Research (hon.), Socieda de Brasileira de Foniatria (hon. mem.). Editor: (book) Craniofacial Radiological Diagnosis and Management, 1988; developer Dental Telesis, 1988. Home: 10342 Wilkins Ave Los Angeles CA 90024

SLOAN, STEPHEN, real estate executive; b. N.Y.C., June 21, 1932; B.A., Washington and Lee U., 1954; m. Nannette Barkin, Feb. 24, 1957; children—Suzanne, Robert. Engaged in real estate, 1957—; ptnr. Milton Barkin Mgmt., 1959-71; pres. Lehman Realty Corp., Lehman Bros. Kuhn Loeb, Inc., N.Y.C., 1971-74; pres. World-Wide Realty Corp. subs. World-Wide Volkswagen, N.Y.C., 1974—; pres. Stephen Sloan Marine Corp., N.Y.C., 1979—; dir. Pacific Design Center, Los Angeles, Realty Found. N.Y., Aquirre Corp. Trustee, Horace Mann Sch., 1971—; chmn. Masters Angling Tournament, 1976—; trustee Am. Mus. for Fly Fishing, South St. Sea Port Mus., 19866; dir. Am. League Anglers Edn. and Research Found., vice-chmn. The Billfish Found. Mem. Internat. Game Fish Assn. (trustee; holder 19 world records), Citizens Com. for Urban Fishing (chmn.), Sloan Marine Assn. (chmn.), Internat. Oceanographic Assn., Am. League Anglers (dir.), Nat. Coalition for Marine Conservation, Fire Island Lighthouse Preservation Soc. (bd. dirs. 1984). Clubs: Explorers, Deep Sea, Chubb Cay, City Athletic, Balboa Angling, Japan Game Fish Assn., Big Game (France). Home: 510 Park Ave New York NY 10022 Office: 230 Park Ave New York NY 10169

SLOANE, BEVERLY LEBOV, writer, consultant; b. N.Y.C., May 26, 1936; d. Benjamin S. and Anne (Weinberg) LeBov; AB, Vassar Coll., 1958; MA, Claremont Grad. Sch., 1975, postgrad., 1975-76; grad. exec. program. Sch. Mgmt., UCLA, 1982; grad. exec. program UCLA Grad Sch. Mgmt., 1982; grad. intensive bioethics course Kennedy Inst. Ethics, Georgetown U., 1987; grad. advanced bioethics course Kennedy Inst. of Ethics, Georgetown U., 1988; m. Robert Malcolm Sloane, Sept. 27, 1959; 1 dau., Alison Lori. Circulation librarian Harvard Med. Library, Boston, 1958-59; social worker Conn. State Welfare, New Haven, 1960-61; tchr. English, Hebrew Day Sch., New Haven, 1961-64; instr. creative writing and English lit. Monmouth Coll., West Long Branch, N.J., 1967-69; freelance writer, Arcadia, Calif., 1970—. Mem. public relations bd. Monmouth County Mental Health Assn., 1968-69; adv. council tech. and profl. writing dept. English, Calif. State U., Long Beach, 1980-82; v.p. Council of Grad. Students, Claremont Grad. Sch., 1971-72, mem. Foothill Health Dist. (adv. council), County of Los Angeles, 1987—, task force edn. and cultural activities, City of Duarte, 1987-88, strategic planning task force com., task force edn. and cultural activities City of Duarte, 1987-88 (cert. of appreciation City of Duarte 1988, cert. of appreciation County of Los Angeles 1988) ; campaign com. for preeminence, Claremont Grad. Sch., 1986-87; trustee Ctr. for Improvement of Child Caring, 1981-83; mem. League Crippled Children, 1982—; bd. dirs. Los Angeles Commn. on Assaults Against Women, 1983-84; v.p. Temple Beth David, 1983-86; mem. community relations com. Jewish Fedn. Council Greater Los Angeles, 1985-87; bd. dirs. Los Angeles Commn. Assaults Against Women, 1983-84; del. Task Force on Minorities in Newspaper Bus., 1987— Coro Found. fellow, 1979. Fellow Am. Med. Writers Assn. (dir. 1980—, Pacific S.W. del. to nat. bd. 1980-87, chmn. various conv. coms., chmn. nat. book awards trade category 1982-83, chmn. Nat. Conv. Networking Luncheon 1983, 84, chmn. freelance and pub. relations coms. Nat. Midyr. Conf. 1983-84, workshop leader ann. conf. 1984, 85, 86, 87, nat. chmn. freelance sect. 1984-85, gen. chmn. 1985 Asilomar Western Regional Conf., gen. chmn. 1985, workshop leader 1985, program co-chmn. 1987, speaker 1988, program co-chmn. 1989), speaker 1985, 88, nat. exec. bd. dirs. 1985-86, nat. adminstr. sects. 1985-86, pres.-elect Pacific Southwest chpt. 1985-87, moderator gen. session nat. conf. 1987, chairperson general session nat. conf., 1986-87, chairperson Walter C. Alvarez Meml. Found. award 1986-87); mem. Women in Communications (dir. 1980—, v.p. community affairs 1981-82, N.E. area rep. 1980-81, chmn. awards banquet 1982, sem. leader ann. nat. profl. conf., 1985, program adv. com. Los Angeles chpt. 1987, chmn. Los Angeles chpt. 1st ann. Agnes Underwood Freedom of Info. Awards Banquet 1982, recognition award 1983, nominating com. 1982, 83, com. Women of the Press Awards luncheon 1988), Women in Communications (awards luncheon 1988), Am. Assn. for Higher Edn., AAUW (legis. chmn. Arcadia br. 1976-77, books and plays chmn. Arcadia br. 1973-74, creative writing chmn. 1969-70, 1st v.p. 1975-76, networking chmn. 1981-82, chmn. task force promoting individual liberties 1987-88, Woman of Achievement award 1986, cert. of appreciation 1987), Coll. English Assn., Am. Pub. Health Assn., Calif. Press Women (v.p. programs Los Angeles chpt. 1982-85, pres. 1985-87, state pres. 1987—), AAUP, Internat. Communication Assn., N.Y. Acad. Scis., Ind. Writers So. Calif., Hastings Inst., AAAS, Am. Med. Writers Assn. (pres.-elect Pacific S.W. chpt. 1985-87, pres. 1987—, nat. adminstr. sects. 1985-86, nat. exec. bd. dirs. 1985-86, chmn. nominating com. Pacific Southwest chpt., 1987—, workshop leader annual conf. 1984-87, steering com. Seminar on Med. Writing 1988, program planning com. for daylong program on med. writing, 1988), bd. dirs. Nat. Fedn. Press Women, Inc. 1987— (nat. co-chmn. task force recr minorities 1987—, delegate 1987—), chmn. state women of achievement com. 1986—), AAUW (chpt. Woman of Achievement award 1986, chmn. task force promoting individual liberties 1987-88, speaker 1987, recipient cert. of appreciation 1987), Soc. for Tech. Communication (workshop leader, 1985, 86), Kennedy Inst. Ethics, Soc. Health and Human Values, Assoc. Writing Programs. Clubs: Rotary of Duarte, Women's City (Pasadena), Vassar of So. Calif., Claremont Colls. Faculty House, Pasadena Athletic, Stock Exchange of Los Angeles, Town Hall of Calif. (vice chmn. community affairs sect. 1982—, speaker, 1986, instr. Exec. Breakfast Inst., 1985-86, mem. study sect. council, 1986—). Author: From Vassar to Kitchen, 1967; A Guide to Health Facilities: Personnel and Management, 2d rev. edit., 1977; mem. adv. bd. Calif. Health Rev., 1982-83. Home and Office: 1301 N Santa Anita Ave Arcadia CA 91006

SLOBODIEN, HOWARD DAVID, surgeon; b. Perth Amboy, N.J., July 25, 1923; s. Albert Leo and Anna Frances (Sontag) S.; B.S., Rutgers Coll., 1943; M.D., N.Y.U., 1947; m. Sally Doris Yerkes, May 9, 1950; children—David, Donald, Daniel, Douglas. Intern, Morrisania City Hosp., N.Y.C., 1947-48, resident, 1948-52; practice medicine specializing in surgery, Perth Amboy, 1955—; pres. John F. Kennedy Med. Center, Edison, N.J., 1967-70, dir. surgery, 1975-79; attending surgeon Gen. Hosp., Perth Amboy, dir. surgery, 1970-74; chief gen. surgery, past pres. med. staff Roosevelt Hosp., Edison; cons. surgery Meml. Hosp., South Amboy; clin. asst. prof. surgery Rutgers U. Med. Sch., 1971-84, mem. adv. council Office Consumer Health Edn., 1973-81; mem. adv. council Middlesex County Coll., 1968-78; v.p. Regional Health Facilities Planning Council, 1970-73. Editor N.J. Medicine, 1988—. Pack committeeman Cub Scouts, 1960-64; active steering com. Metuchen YMCA, 1962. Served with USNR, 1943-45, USAF, 1952-54. Diplomate Am. Bd. Surgery. Fellow ACS; mem. AMA, World, Pan-Am. med. assns., N.J. (trustee 1972-84, chmn. pub. relations council 1973-76, pres. 1982-83), Middlesex County (pres. 1970-71) med. socs., Pan-Pacific Surg. Assn., Am. Geriatric Soc., Royal Soc. Health, Am. Acad. Med. Adminstrs., Royal Soc. Medicine, N.J. Acad. Medicine (trustee 1974-78), Middlesex County Med. Assts. Assn. (county med. adviser 1973-80), N.J. Soc. Surgeons, Phi Beta Kappa. Clubs: Metuchen Country, Innisbrook. Home: 34 Linden Ave Metuchen NJ 08840 Office: 500 Lawrie St Perth Amboy NJ 08861

SLOCUM, DONALD WARREN, chemist. BS in Chemistry, BA in English, U. Rochester; PhD in Chemistry, NYU, 1963. Postdoctoral research assoc. Duke U., Durham, N.C., 1963-64; asst. prof. chemistry Carnegie Inst. Tech., Pitts., 1964-65; from asst. to assoc. prof. chemistry So. Ill. U., Carbondale, 1965-72; prof. So. Ill. U., 1972-81, adj. prof., 1981-84; program dir. Chem. Dynamics sect. Chemistry div. NSF, Washington, 1984-85; program leader div. ednl. programs Argonne (Ill.) Nat. Lab., 1985—; sr. scientist Gulf Research and Devel. Co., Pitts., 1980-82; vis. prof. U. Ill., 1970, U. Bristol, Eng., 1973, U. Cin., 1976; vis. fellow U. Bristol, 1972; vis. lectr. Carnegie-Mellon U. and U. Pitts., 1983-84; organized symposia on organometallic chemistry and catalysis; cons. in field. Contbr. more than 50 articles to profl. jours.; also papers, book chpts., and editorshops. Mem. AAAS, Am. Chem. Soc., Chem. Soc. Great Britain, Cen. States Univs. Inc. (bd. dirs. 1986—), Phi Lambda Upsilon, Sigma Xi. Office: Argonne Nat Lab 9700 S Cass Argonne IL 60439

SLOCUM, GEORGE SIGMAN, energy company executive; b. East Orange, N.J., Sept. 9, 1940. B.A., Cornell U., 1962, M.B.A., 1967. Mgmt. trainee Richardson-Merrell, Inc., 1962; v.p. Citibank N.A., 1967-78; v.p. fin. Transco Energy Co., Houston, 1978-80, sr. v.p., 1980-81, exec. v.p., chief fin. officer, dir., 1981-84, pres., chief operating officer, dir., 1984—; bd. dirs. Tex. Commerce Bank, Houston. Bd. dirs. Tex. Research League, Soc. for the Performing Arts, Houston; trustee Boy Scouts Am., Cornell U., U. Houston Found.; mem. alumni exec. council Cornell U. Grad. Sch. Mgmt. Served with U.S. Army, 1963-65. Mem. Am. Gas Assn. (exec. com., gas demand com., bd. fin. com.), Southeastern Gas Assn. (fin. com.). Home: 10776 Bridlewood Houston TX 77024 Office: Transco Energy Co 2800 Post Oak Blvd Box 1396 Houston TX 77251

SLOTTA, RAINER GÜNTER, archaeologist; b. Braunschweig, Niedersachsen, Fed. Republic Germany, May 1, 1946; s. Günter and Ursula (Riemschneider) S.; m. Elisabeth Kessler, Sept. 8, 1979; 1 child, Cornelius. PhD, U. Saarbrücken, Fed. Republic Germany, 1974. Conservator German Mining Mus., Bochum, Fed. Republic Germany, 1974-87, dir., 1987—. Author: Technische Denkmäler in der Bundesrepublik 5 vol., 1975-86, Einführung in die Industriearchäologie, 1982, Das Herder-Service, 1981, Das Carnall-Service, 1985. Recipient Gold medal Frontinus Soc., 1985. Office: German Mining-Mus, Am Bergbaumuseum 28, D-4630 Bochum Federal Republic of Germany

SLOWIK, RICHARD ANDREW, air force officer; b. Detroit, Sept. 9, 1939; s. Louis Stanley and Mary Jean (Zaucha) S.; m. Patricia Anne Lincoln; 1 stepchild, Amber Dawn. B.S., U.S. Air Force Acad., 1963; B.S. in Bus. Adminstrn., No. Mich. U., 1967; LL.B., LaSalle Extension U., 1969; M.B.A., Fla. Tech. U., 1972; M.S. in Adminstrn., Ga. Coll., 1979; M.A., Georgetown U., 1983; postgrad. cert., Va. Polytech. Inst. and State U., 1986. Commd. 1st lt. U.S. Air Force, 1963, advanced through grades to lt. col.; pilot Craig AFB, Ala., 1963-64, Sawyer AFB, Mich., 1964-68; forward air controller Pacific Air Forces, South Vietnam, 1968-69; pilot SAC, McCoy AFB, Fla., 1969-71; asst. prof. aerospace studies Va. Poly. Inst. and State U., Blacksburg, 1972-76; br. chief current ops. br. Robins AFB, Ga., 1976-80; asst. dep. chief ops. group Hdqrs. Air Force, Pentagon, Washington, 1980-82; Western Hemisphere and Pacific Area desk officer Nat. Mil. Command Center, Pentagon, Washington, 1982-83; mil. rep. Ops. Ctr., Dept. State, Washington, 1983-85; ops. officer 97th Bombardment Wing, Blytheville AFB, Ark., 1985—, chief base ops. and trg. div., 97th Combat Support Group, Blythville AFB, 1987-88, chief airfield mgmt. div. Eaker AFB, Ark., 1988—. Group ops. officer CAP, Marquette, Mich., 1967-68, Orlando, Fla., 1970-72, sr. programs officer, Blacksburg, 1972-76, Warner Robins, Ga., 1976-80, wing plans and programs officer, Washington, 1980—. Decorated Defense Meritorious Service Medal, 10 Air medals, 2 Air Force Meritorious Service medals, 2 Commendation medals, Cross of Gallantry with Palm, others; recipient Presdl. Medal of Merit, Presdl. Achievement award. Mem. Acad. of Mgmt., Air Force Assn., Am. Numis. Assn., Internat. Platform Assn., Mil. Order World Wars, Am. Def. Preparedness Assn., Am. Security Council, Order of Daedalians. Roman Catholic. Home: 1708 N Broadway Blytheville AR 72315 Office: Bombardment Wing Airfield Mgmt Eaker AFB AR 72317-5000

SLOWINSKI, JULIAN WALTER, clinical psychologist; b. Newark, Apr. 19, 1942; s. Julius W. and Nora H. (Majeski) S.; B.A., St. Benedict's Coll., Kans., 1965; M.S., Hahnemann Med. Coll., Phila., 1974; Psy.D., Rutgers U., 1977; m. Betty Jeannine Armbruster, Aug. 10, 1971; 1 child, Stefan Julien. Mem. Order of St. Benedict, 1960-68; chief psychologist Corinthian Guidance Ctr., Hahnemann Hosp., Phila., 1974-77; supr. child and family services Hall-Mercer Ctr., Pa. Hosp., Phila., 1977-80, dir. child and family outpatient services, 1980-85; clin. assoc. dept. psychiatry U. Pa. Sch. Medicine, 1978-85, clin. asst. prof., 1985—; clin. asst. prof. Hahnemann Med. Coll., 1974-85. Contbr. articles to profl. jours. and books. Lic. clin. psychologist, Pa.; diplomate marital and sex therapy Am. Bd. Family Psychology, Internat. Acad. Profl. Counseling and Psychotherapy. Fellow Phila. Soc. Clin. Psychologists; mem. Am. Psychol. Assn., Pa. Psychol. Assn., Am. Assn. Marriage and Family Therapy, Am. Assn. Sex Educators, Counselors and Therapists, (cert.) Acad. Psychologists in Marital Sex and Family Therapy, Soc. Sci. Study of Sex, Soc. Sex Therapy and Research. Home: 3924 Delancey Pl Philadelphia PA 19104 Office: Pa Hosp 700 Spruce St Suite 501 Philadelphia PA 19106

SLOWINSKI, ROMAN, educator, consultant; b. Poznan, Poland, Mar. 16, 1952; s. Lech and Melania (Michalska) S.; m. Teresa Maciejewska, May 31, 1975; children: Jan, Maria, Barbara. Bachelor's, K. Marcinkowski Meml. Coll., Poznan, 1969; MSc in Control Engring. with honors, Tech. U., Poznan, 1974, PhD in Ops. Research, 1977, Cert. in Ops. Research, 1981. Registered profl. engr., Poland. Asst. Tech. U. of Poznan, 1974-76, master asst., 1976-77, asst. prof., 1977-82, assoc. prof., 1982—; assoc. prof. U. Paris-Dauphine, 1986-87; visiting prof. U. Paris-Dauphine, 1981-82, Ecole Polytech. Fédérale de Lausanne, Switzerland, 1984; vice dir. Inst. Control Engring., T.U. Poznan, 1984-87; vice dean faculty of electrical engring. T.U. Poznan, 1987—; cons. Ctr. for Agrl. Research and Devel., Poznan, 1986—. Co-author: Operations Research for Computer Science, 1982 (Minister of Higher Edn. award 1983), Scheduling Under Resource Constraints, 1986; contbr. articles to profl. jours. Awarded the Hon. Distinction of Poznan City, 1980; hon. for Research Results Sci. Sec. of the Polish Acad.of Scis., 1981, tech. scis. dept. Polish Acad. of Sci., 1983. Mem. Am. Math. Soc., Assn. Francaise pour la Cybernétique, Economique et Technique, Polish Cybernetical Soc. (pres. Poznan chpt. 1986—), Polish Soc. for Computer Sci., Assn. Internat. de Cybernétique (hon.), Founds. of Control Engring. and Belgian Jour. of Operational Research (assoc. editor). Roman Catholic. Office: Politechnika Poznanska, Piotrowo 3a, PL 60 965 Poznan Poland

SLOWINSKI, WALLACE JOHN, health care company executive; b. Austin, Minn., Dec. 14, 1946; s. Wallace James and Manetta Lorain (Halverson) S.; A.A.S., Austin State Jr. Coll., 1967; B.A., Winona State U., 1978; M.B.A., Mankato State U., 1981; m. Sindy Kay Slowinski; children—Tawnya Dawn, Laura Lee. Meat cutter/union rep. George Hormel Co., Austin, 1967-76; pres. N. Am. Mgmt., Maple Grove, Minn., 1976—; personnel cons. United and Children's Hosps., St. Paul, 1978-80; v.p. adminstrn. Norstan Communications, Plymouth, Minn., 1980-82; personnel adminstr. East/West region Southwest Community Health Services, Albuquerque, 1982-84; asst. hosp. adminstr. Security Forces Hosp., Riyadh, Saudi Arabia, 1984-86; exec. v.p. Corporate Health Resources, Inc., Albuquerque, 1986-87; pres. John Slowinski Enterprises, Inc., Albuquerque, 1987—. Dir. edn. Ind. Sch. Dist. 492, Austin, Minn., 1974-76; del. Minn. State High Sch. Legis., Dist. 492, 1974-76; dept. chmn. AFL-CIO, Amalgamated Meat Cutters and Butcher Workmen local P-9, Austin, 1970-75. Mem. Am. Soc. Personnel Adminstrn. (accredited personnel mgr.), Nat. Assn. Office Products, Nat. Assn. Quick Printers. Republican. Roman Catholic. Clubs: Masons, Eagles. Home: 6234 Buenos Aires NW Albuquerque NM 87120 Office: Great Scott's Thrifty Printing 6601 4th St NW Albuquerque NM 87107

SLUSSER, EUGENE ALVIN, electronics manufacturing executive; b. Denver, Mar. 13, 1922; s. Jesse Alvin and Grace (Carter) S.; m. Anne L. Longley, Oct. 2, 1943; children: Robert, Jon, Carolyn. BS in Physics, U. Denver, 1947. Registered profl. engr., N.H. Staff mem. MIT Radiation Lab., Cambridge, 1942-45; project engr. Heiland Research Co., Denver, 1945-47; cons. Gen. Telephone System, N.Y.C., 1947-51; project engr. Airborne Inst. Lab., Mineola, N.Y., 1951-53; v.p. N.E. Electronics Corp., Concord, N.H., 1953-58; pres. Aerotronic Assocs., Inc., Contoocook, N.H., 1958-84, N.H. Automatic Equipment Corp., Concord, 1962—, E.A. Slusser & Assocs., Concord; bd. dirs. First Capital Bank. Patentee electronics field. Chmn. Hopkinton (N.H.) Water Bd., 1962-69, Hopkinton Planning Bd., 1971-77, Hopkinton Precinct Bd. Adjustment, 1977. Mem. Aircraft Owners and Pilots Assn. Lodge: Masons (32 degree). Home: RFD-3 Box 135 Hopkinton Village NH 03229 Office: 16 Centre St Concord NH 03301

SLUSSER, ROBERT WYMAN, aerospace company executive; b. Mineola, N.Y., May 10, 1938; s. John Leonard and Margaret McKenzie (Wyman) S.; B.S., MIT, 1960; M.B.A., Wharton Sch., U. Pa., 1962; m. Linda Killeas, Aug. 3, 1968; children—Jonathan, Adam, Robert, Mariah. Assoc. adminstr.'s staff NASA Hdqrs., Washington, 1962-65; with Northrop Corp., Hawthorne, Calif., 1965—, adminstr. mktg. and planning dept., space labs., 1965-68, mgr. bus. and fin. Warnecke Electron Tubes Co. div., Chgo., 1968-71, controller Cobra Program Aircraft div., Hawthorne, 1971-72, mgr. bus. adminstrn. YF-17 Program, 1972-75, mgr. adminstrn. F-18/Cobra programs, also mgr. F-18 design to cost program, 1975-78, mgr. adminstrn. F-18L program, 1978-79, mgr. engring. adminstrn., 1980-82, acting v.p. engring., 1982, mgr. data processing, 1983-84, v.p. info. resources, 1985—; mem., chief fin. officer, bd. dirs. So. Calif. Historical Found., 1987—; bd. dirs. PDES, Inc., 1988—. Grumman Aircraft Engring. scholar, 1956-60. Assoc. fellow AIAA. Home: 7270 Berry Hill Drive Rancho Palos Verdes CA 90274 Office: Northrop Aircraft Div One Northrop Ave Hawthorne CA 90250

SLYUNKOV, NIKOLAI NIKITOVICH, Soviet government official; b. Garadzets, Oblast Gomel, Belorussian, USSR, 1929. Grad., Belorussian Inst. Mechanization Agr., 1962. Mem. Communist Party Soviet Union, 1954—; with Minsk Tractor Plant, USSR, 1950-60; dir. Minsk Spare Parts Plant, 1960-65, Minsk Tractor Plant, 1965-72; mem. Cen. Com. Belorussian Communist Party, 1966-76; 1st sec. Minsk City Com. Belorussian Communist Party, 1972-74; dep. chair USSR GOSPLAN, 1974-83; 1st sec., mem. bur. Cen. Com. Belorussian Communist Party, 1983—. Office: Communist Party Soviet Union, Politburo, Moscow USSR *

SMALE, JOHN GRAY, diversified industry executive; b. Listowel, Ont., Can., Aug. 1, 1927; s. Peter John and Vera Gladys (Gray) S.; m. Phyllis Anne Weaver, Sept. 2, 1950; children: John Gray, Catherine Anne, Lisa Beth, Peter McKee. B.S., Miami U., Oxford, Ohio, 1949, LL.D. (hon.), 1979; LL.D. (hon.), Kenyon Coll., Gambier, Ohio, 1974; D.Sc. (hon.), DePauw U., 1983; D.C.L. (hon.), St. Augustine's Coll., 1985; LLD (hon.), Xavier U., 1986. With Vick Chem. Co., 1949-50, Bio-Research, Inc., N.Y.C., 1950-52; pres. Procter & Gamble Co., 1974-86, chief exec., 1981—, chmn. bd., 1986—, dir., 1972—; dir. Gen. Motors Corp.; mem. internat. council Morgan Guaranty Trust Co. Bd. dirs. United Negro Coll. Fund, United Way Am., Nat. Park Found.; mem. nat. adv. bd. Goodwill Industries Am., Inc.; emeritus trustee Kenyon Coll., Cin. Inst. Fine Arts. Served with USNR, 1945-46. Mem. Grocery Mfrs. Am. (bd. dirs.), Conf. Bd. (trustee), Bus. Council, Bus. Roundtable, Nat. Ctr. State Cts. (bus. and profl. friends com.), Internat. Life Scis. Inst. (CEO Council), Nutrition Found., Cin. Bus. Com. Clubs: Commercial, Commonwealth, Queen City, Cincinnati Country. Office: Procter & Gamble Co 1 Procter & Gamble Plaza Cincinnati OH 45202

SMALL, RICHARD DONALD, travel company executive; b. West Orange, N.J., May 24, 1929; s. Joseph George and Elizabeth (McGarry) S.; A.B. cum laude, U. Notre Dame, 1951; m. Arlene P. Small; children—Colleen P., Richard Donald, Joseph W., Mark G., Brian P. With Union-Camp Corp., N.Y.C., Chgo., 1952-62; pres. Alumni Holidays, Inc., 1962—, AHI Internat. Corp., Des Plaines, Ill., 1962—, All Horizons, Inc., 1982—; chmn. AHI, Inc., 1982—. Club: University (Chgo.). Home: PO Box 440 Glencoe IL 60022 also: 2202 Wailea Elua Wailea Maui HI 96753 Office: 1st Nat Bank Bldg 701 Lee St Des Plaines IL 60016

SMALL, RICHARD WILLIAM, biology educator; b. Taunton, Somerset, Eng., June 12, 1952; s. William John Mervyn and Grace Florence (White) S.; m. Alyson Florence Mary McGregor, Oct. 25, 1975; children: Jennifer, Lewis. BSc in zoology with honors, U. London, 1973; Diploma, Imperial Coll., London, 1976, PhD, 1977. Chartered biologist. Research assoc. Inst. Voor Dierkunde, Gent, Belgium, 1977; lectr. City of Liverpool Coll. Higher Edn., 1978-85; sr. lectr. biology Liverpool Poly., 1985—. Contbr. articles to profl. jours. Parish councillor, Scarisbrick Parish Council, Lancashire, 1983—. Mem. Inst. Biology, Soc. Nematologists, European Soc. Nematologists, Assn. Applied Biologists, Brit. Ecol. Soc. Mem. Green Party. Office: Liverpool Poly Byrom St, Liverpool L3 3AF, England

SMALL, WILFRED THOMAS, surgeon, educator; b. Boston, June 13, 1920; s. Fred Wentworth and Isabelle (Scott) S.; B.S., Bowdoin Coll., 1943; M.D., Tufts U., 1946; m. Muriel Yoe Gratton, Sept. 25, 1948; children—Wilfred Thomas, Richard Gratton, James Stewart, John Wentworth. Intern surg. service The Boston Children's Hosp., 1946-47, then research fellow; asso. in surgery Peter Bent Brigham Hosp., Harvard U., 1949-50; resident, chief resident in surgery New Eng. Med. Center, Tufts U., 1950-53; practice medicine specializing in surgery, Worcester, Mass., 1953—; asso. prof. surgery U. Mass., from 1973, now prof. surgery; mem. staff Meml. Hosp., 1953—, chief div. surgery, 1973-81; instr. Harvard U., 1949-50, Tufts U., 1952-60. Bd. dirs. Worcester Boys Club; mem. Worcester Art Museum, Worcester County Music Assn. Served to lt. (j.g.) USN, 1947-49. Diplomate Am. Bd. Surgery. Fellow ACS (pres. Mass. chpt. 1979); mem. New Eng. Surg. Soc., New Eng. Cancer Soc., Soc. Surgery Alimentary Tract, Mass., Pan Am. med. socs., AMA, Am. Trauma Soc., Worcester Econs. Club (past pres.), Worcester Council on Fgn. Relations. Episcopalian. Clubs: Tatnuck Country, Sakonnet Golf. Contbr. articles to profl. jours. Home: Warrens Point Rd Little Compton RI 02837 Office: 25 Oak Ave Worcester MA 01605

SMALL, WILLIAM ANDREW, mathematics educator; b. Cobleskill, N.Y., Oct. 16, 1914; s. James Arner and Lois (Patterson) S.; m. Bela Savkovich, Apr. 20, 1939; children: Lois (Mrs. Paul Gindling). James (dec.). B.S., U.S. Naval Acad., 1936; A.B., U. Rochester, 1950, M.A., 1952, Ph.D., 1958. Commd. ensign U.S. Navy, 1936, advanced through grades to lt. comdr., 1944; comdt. cadets, instr. DeVeaux Sch., Niagara Falls, N.Y., 1945-48; instr. U. Rochester, 1951-55; Alfred (N.Y.) U., 1955-56; asst. prof. math. Grinnell (Iowa) Coll., 1956-58, assoc. prof., chmn. dept., 1958-60; prof. math. Tenn. Tech. U., 1960-62, State Univ. Coll., Geneseo, N.Y., 1962-85; chmn. dept. math. State Univ. Coll., 1962-78; prof. emeritus, disting. service prof. SUNY, 1985—; Mem. exec. com. Arab People to Am. People Conv., Sharjah, United Arab Emirates, 1980; Fulbright-Hays lectr. math. Aleppo U., Syrian Arab Republic, 1964-65. Contbr. articles to profl. jours. Pres. Fedn. Am.-Arab Orgns., 1967—; Liberal Party candidate for N.Y. assemblyman, 1968. Mem. Math. Assn. Am., U.S. Naval Inst., Mil. Order World Wars, Ret. Officers Assn., Am.-Arab Antidiscrimination Com., Arab and Am. Peoples Assn., Phi Beta Kappa. Episcopalian. Club: Seneca Army Depot Officers. Lodge: Rotary. Home: 28 Court St Geneseo NY 14454

SMALLEY, ARTHUR LOUIS, JR., engineering and construction company executive; b. Houston, Jan. 25, 1921; s. Arthur I. and Ebby (Curry) S.; B.S. in Chem. Engring., U. Tex., Austin, 1942; m. Ruth Evelyn Britton, Mar. 18, 1946; children—Arthur Louis III, Tom Edward. Dir. engring. Celanese Chem. Co., Houston, 1964-72; mktg. exec. Fish Engring. Co., Houston, 1972-74; pres. Matthew Hall & Co., Inc., Houston, 1974—; dir. Scott-Ortech, Inc., Denver, Matthew Hall Internat. Ltd., London, Barnard and Burk Group, Inc., Baton Rouge, Northfield Nat. Bank, Houston. Life mem. Houston Livestock and Rodeo. Recipient Silver Beaver award Boy Scouts Am., 1963; registered profl. engr., Tex. Mem. Am. Inst. Chem. Engrs., Am. Petroleum Inst., Pres. Assn., Petroleum Club Houston. Republican. Episcopalian. Clubs: Rotary, Chemists of N.Y., Oriental (London); Houston. Internat. adv. bd. Ency. Chem. Processing and Design. Home: 438 Hunterwood Dr Houston TX 77024 Office: 1200 Milam St #3428 Houston TX 77002

SMALLEY, ROBERT MANNING, U.S. government official; b. Los Angeles, Nov. 14, 1925; s. William Denny and Helen (McConnell) S.; m. Lois Louisa Williamson, Nov. 28, 1948 (div.) m. Rosemary Sumner, Jan. 4, 1957; children—Leslie Estelle, David Christian. Student, UCLA, 1946-48. Radio news editor Mut. Radio Broadcasting System, Los Angeles, 1950-55; mgr. Agrl. Info. Inc., Sacramento, Calif., 1957-59; with Whitaker & Baxter, San Francisco, 1956-57, 59-61; sec. Mayor, San Francisco, 1961-63; asst. dir. pub. relations Republican Nat. Com., 1964; press sec. Republican vice presdl. candidate William E. Miller, 1964; dir. pub. relations Republican Nat. Com., 1965; v.p. Whitaker & Baxter, San Francisco, 1966-68; asst. pres sec. Republican vice presdl. candidate Spiro Agnew, 1968; spl. asst. Sec. Commerce, Washington, 1969-72; adminstrv. asst. U.S. Senator Robert P. Griffin, Washington, 1972-73; dir. corp. affairs Potomac Electric Power Co., Washington, 1973-75; U.S. rep. devel. assistance com. O.E.C.D., Paris, France, 1975-77; spl. asst. U.S. Senator Robert P. Griffin, Washington, 1977-78; asst. to campaign mgr. Reagan for Pres. Com., Washington, 1979; sr. advisor mgmt. communications IBM, 1979-82; dep. asst. sec. of state pub. affairs Dept. of State, Washington, 1982-87, U.S. ambassador to Kingdom of Lesotho, 1987—. Served with USN, 1944-46, PTO. Episcopalian. Home: American Embassy, Maseru 100, Lesotho Office: Dept of State 2201 C St NW Washington DC 20520

SMALLWOOD, GLENN WALTER, JR., utility company marketing representative; b. Jeffersonville, Ind., Oct. 12, 1956; s. Glenn Walter and Darlene Ruth (Zeller) S.; B.S. in Bus. Adminstrn., SE Mo. State U., 1978. Customer service advisor Union Electric Co., Mexico, Mo., 1979—; instr. Mexico Vo-Tech Sch., 1981; panelist on home design Mo. Extension Service, 1984. Coordinator local United Way, 1984; council mem. Great Rivers council Boy Scouts Am. Mem. Am. Mktg. Assn. (profl.), Nat. Eagle Scout Assn., Copper Dome Soc., Boy Scouts Am. Alumni Family, Mexico area C. of C., Semo U. Alumni Assn. Republican. Lodges: Optimist (cert. appreciation 1982, youth appreciation award 1974), Kiwanis (cert. appreciation 1984). Avocations: music; spectator sports; baseball; basketball; tennis. Office: Union Electric Co 321 W Promenade Mexico MO 65265

SMALLWOOD, ROBERT ALBIAN, JR., teacher; b. Phila., Oct. 3, 1946; s. Robert Albian and Mildred May (Miller) S.; BS, Rider Coll., 1969, MA, 1976; EdS, Rutgers U., 1986; m. Geraldine Ann Boozan, May 27, 1972; children: Amy Lynn, Daniel James. Cert. social studies tchr., secondary sch. prin., supr. curriculum and instrn., Pa.; cert. social studies and gen. bus. tchr., prin., supr., sch. bus. adminstr., asst. supt. bus., sch. adminstr. (supt.) N.J. Tchr. social studies Trenton Bd. Edn., 1973-76, tchr. bus. edn., 1975-76, sch. disciplinarian, 1976-84, acting asst. prin. Jr. High Sch. 2, 1980-83, tchr. U.S. history, 1983-87, chmn. social studies dept., 1984-85; tchr. U.S. history Trenton High Sch., 1987—; acting asst. prin. Carroll Robbins Elem. Sch., Jr. High Sch. #1, Jr. High Sch. #5, 1987—; mem. Dist.'s Affirmative Action Adv. Council; mem. Nat. Tchr. Corps Project, Trenton Area. Asst. ops. officer Trenton CD Unit, 1974-76, asst. disaster analysis officer, 1976, disaster analysis officer, 1976-79; trustee N.J. Council for Alcohol/Drug Edn., 1983—, mem. exec. com., 1985—, chmn. nominating com., 1985, 86, treas. 1987—; chmn. membership com. Hamilton Square Baptist Ch., 1981-82, chmn. Christian edn. com., 1982-85, supt. ch. sch., 1982-85, vice chmn. exec. bd., 1981-85, chmn., 1985—. Served with U.S. Army, 1969-72. Decorated Bronze Star medal, Army Commendation medal with oak leaf cluster, Joint Service Commendation medal. Mem. NEA, Nat. Council Social Studies, Vietnam Vets. Am., Am. Legion, Nat. Bus. Edn. Assn., Va. Geneal. Soc., Md. Geneal. Soc., Md. Hist. Soc., Geneal. Soc. Pa., Nat. Geneal. Soc., Phi Delta Kappa. Home: 2 Leese Ave Trenton NJ 08609

SMART, LARRY REGAN, telecommunications company executive; b. Sault Ste. Marie, Mich., Dec. 4, 1933; s. Lawrence Jonathan and Marguerite Mary (Cowell) S.; B.A., U. Mich., 1955, postgrad., 1956. Mgr., N.Y. Telephone Co., N.Y.C., 1960-64, dist. mgr., 1964-68, asst. treas., 1968-78, asst. v.p., asst. treas., 1978-83; asst. treas., dir. fin. NYNEX Corp., 1983—; treas., dir. Peter Rogers Assocs., Served to lt. USNR, 1957-60. Mem. Nat. Assn. Corp. Treas., Am. Soc. Fin. Profls., Money Mgrs., Bklyn. Heights Assn. Republican. Presbyterian. Club: William's. Home: 20 Pierrepont St Brooklyn Heights NY 11201 Office: 335 Madison Ave New York NY 10017

SMART, L(OUIS) EDWIN, employee and engineering services company executive; b. Columbus, Ohio, Nov. 17, 1923; s. Louis Edwin and Esther (Guthery) S.; m. Virginia Alice Knouff, Mar. 1, 1944 (div. 1958); children: Cynthia Stephanie, Douglas Edwin; m. 2d. Jeanie A. Milone, Aug. 29, 1964; 1 son, Dana Gregory. A.B. magna cum laude, Harvard U., 1947, J.D. magna cum laude, 1949. Bar: N.Y. State bar 1950. Assoc. firm Hughes, Hubbard & Ewing, N.Y.C., 1949-56; ptnr. firm Hughes, Hubbard, & Reed, N.Y.C., 1957-64; pres. Bendix Internat., dir. Bendix Corp. (and fgn. subs.), 1964-67; sr. v.p. external affairs Trans World Airlines, Inc., 1967-71, sr. v.p. corp. affairs, 1971-75, vice chmn., 1976, chmn. bd., chief exec. officer, 1977-78, chmn. bd., 1979-85; chmn. bd. and pres., chief exec. officer Transworld Corp. (now called TW Services Inc.), 1978-87, chmn. exec. com., dir.; chmn. bd. Hilton Internat. Co., 1978-86; chmn. exec. com., 1986—; bd. dirs. Canteen Corp., from 1973—, chmn. 1984—; chmn. exec. com., dir. Spartan Food Systems, Inc., 1979—; dir. Continental, N.Y. Stock Exchange, Sonat Inc.; trustee Com. Econ. Devel., 1977—, Conf. Bd., 1977—. Served to lt. USNR, 1943-46. Mem. ABA, N.Y. County Lawyers Assn., Phi Beta Kappa, Sigma Alpha Epsilon. Clubs: St. Croix Yacht, Economic, Presidents, Sky (N.Y.C.). Office: TW Services Inc 605 3d Ave New York NY 10158 *

SMART, MARY-LEIGH CALL (MRS. J. SCOTT SMART), farm operator, civic worker; b. Springfield, Ill., Feb. 27, 1917; d. S(amuel) Leigh and Mary (Bradish) Call; jr. coll. diploma Monticello Coll., 1934; student Oxford U., 1935; B.A., Wellesley Coll., 1937; M.A., Columbia U., 1939, postgrad., 1940-41; postgrad. N.Y. U., 1940-41; painting student with Bernard Karfiol, 1937-38; m. J. Scott Smart, Sept. 11, 1951 (dec. 1960). Dir. mgmt. Central Ill. Grain Farms, Logan County, 1939—; art collector, patron, publicist, 1954—; cons., 1970—; program dir., sec. bd. Barn Gallery Assocs., Inc., 1958-69, pres., 1969-70, 82-87, asst. treas., 1987—, hon. dir., 1970-78; curator Hamilton Easter Field Art Found. Collection, 1978-79, curator exhbns., 1979-86; owner Lowtrek Kennel, 1957-73, Cove Studio Art Gallery, 1961-68 (all Ogunquit, Maine). Mem. acquisition com. DeCordova Mus., Lincoln, Mass., 1966-78; mem. chancellor's council U. Tex., 1972—, U. N.H., 1978—; bd. dirs. Ogunquit C. of C., 1966, treas. 1966-67, hon. life mem., 1968—; bd. overseers Strawbery Banke, Inc., Portsmouth, N.H., 1972-75, 3d vice chmn., 1973, 2d vice chmn., 1974; bd. advisors Univ. Art Galleries, U. N.H., 1973—, v.p., bd. overseers, 1974-81, pres., 1981—; bd. dirs. Old York Hist. and Improvement Soc., York, Maine, 1979-81, v.p., 1981-82; mem. adv. com. Bowdoin Coll. Mus. Art Invitational Exhibit, 1975, '76 Maine Artists Invitational Exhbn., Maine State Mus., Maine Coast Artists, Rockport, 1975-78, All Maine Biennial '79, Bowdoin Coll. Mus. Art juried exhbn.; mem. jury for scholarship awards Maine Com. for the Skowhegan Sch. Painting and Sculpture, 1982-84; mem. nat. com. Wellesley Coll. Friends of Art, 1983—; adv. trustee Portland Mus. Art, 1983-85, fellow, 1985—; mem. mus. panel Maine State Commn. on Arts and Humanities, 1983-86; mem. adv. com. Maine Biennial, Colby Coll. Mus. Art, 1983; mem. council advisors Farnsworth Library and Art Mus., Rockland, Maine, 1986—. Served to lt. jg. WAVES, 1942-45. Mem. Am. Fedn. Arts, Am. Assn. Museums, Mus. Modern Art, Springfield Art Assn., Boston Mus. Fine Arts, Solomon R. Guggenheim Mus., Whitney Mus. Am. Art., Jr. League of Springfield, Inst. Contemporary Art Boston (corporator 1965-73). Republican. Episcopalian. Club: Western Maine Wellesley. Editor: Hamilton Easter Field Art Found. Collection Catalog, 1966; originator, dir. show, compiler of catalog Art: Ogunquit, 1967; Peggy Bacon-A Celebration, Barn Gallery, Ogunquit, 1979. Address: Rural Rt 2 Box 381 York ME 03909

SMEDRESMAN, INGEBORG FREUNDLICH, artist; b. Germany; came to U.S., 1937, naturalized, 1943; d. Paul and Erna Betty (Simon) Freundlich; B.S., U. Frankfurt, Germany, 1934; postgrad. in chemistry U. Zurich, Switzerland, 1934-37, art edn. Nat. Acad. Art Students League, Queens Coll; m. Sidney Smedresman, Aug. 10, 1937; children—Ingrid Braslow, Leonard C., Paulette Mehta, Suzanne van Oers. Art lectr. Forest Hills Jewish Center, 1966-68, Guggenheim Mus., 1973-76; art tchr. Queensboro Art Soc., 1969; art dir. Temple Beth El, Great Neck, L.I., 1969-75, YM-YWHA, Little Neck, 1975. One woman shows at Fine Arts Gallery, N.Y.C., 1970, Queens Coll., N.Y.C., summer 1975, 78, 81, 85, Harrison (N.Y.) Library, 1979, 80, Vleigh Place Library, 1984, Alley Pond Gallery, 1986, Alley Pond Eviron. Ctr., 1986; exhibited in group shows at ACA Gallery, 1959, Contemporary Art Gallery, 1965-66, Raymond Duncan Gallery, Paris, France, 1965-66, Ahda Arzt Gallery, N.Y.C., 1970, Ten Voorde Gallery, Amsterdam, 1973, Carrol Condit Gallery, White Plains N.Y., 1973, Westchester Art Soc., 1970-75; represented in permanent collections Godwin-Ternbach Mus. of Queens Coll., Pfizer Inc. Internat. Hdqrs., N.Y.C., City Hall, Moncton, N.B., Can., Israel Mus., Jerusalem; art instr. YM-YWHA, Flushing; lectr. Cooper-Hewitt Mus. Recipient art awards Paris Water Colors, 1965, 66, Suffolk County Artists, 1966, Queensboro Art Soc., 1975, 1st prize Westchester Art Soc., 1975. Mem. Art Students League N.Y. (life), Artists Equity Assn., Am. Chem. Soc. Home: 147-43 77th Rd Kew Garden Hills NY 11367

SMEETON, DONALD DEAN, clergyman, missionary, educator; b. Denver, May 3, 1946; s. Wilbur Rex and Anna (Sterk) S.; m. Dolores Marie Rosenkrans, June 1, 1967; children: Diane, David. BA, Cent. Bible Coll., Springfield, Mo., 1967; BS, Evang. Coll., Springfield, 1969; MA cum laude, Trinity Evang. Div. Sch., Deerfield, Ill., 1971; MA, Assemblies of God Theol. Sem., Springfield, 1977; PhD summa cum laude, Cath. U. Louvain, 1983. Ordained to ministry Assemblies of God Ch., 1971. Youth pastor N.W. Assembly of God, Mt. Prospect, Ill., 1969-71; adminstr. Teen Challenge, Brussels, 1971-72; tchr. Continental Bible Coll., Brussels, 1972-82; assoc. dean Internat. Corr. Inst., Brussels, 1982—. Author: Lollard Themes in the Reformation Theology of William Tyndale, 1986; contbr. numerous articles on history, theology and missions to profl. jours. Mem. Ecclesiastical History Soc., European Pentecostal Theol. Assn. (editor jour. 1982—, v.p. 1985-87). Office: Internat Corr Inst Chaussee de Waterloo 45, 1640 Rhode Saint Genese Belgium

SMEETS, PAUL MARIE, psychologist, educator; b. Heerlen, Limburg, Netherlands, May 20, 1940; s. Hubert Alphons and Maria Pauline (Severijns) S.; m. Anne-Marie Schrameyer, June 8, 1968; 1 child, Valerie. Doctorate in Psychology, U. Nijmegen, The Netherlands, 1963; Ed.D., Temple U., Phila., 1972. Psychologist, Huize Nieuwenoord, Baarn, Netherlands, 1965-68; research assoc. Woods Schs., Langhorne, Pa., 1968-71; psychologist Calif. Sch. for Deaf, Riverside, 1972-73; sr. lectr. dept. developmental psychology U. Leiden, The Netherlands, 1974—; research cons. Hamburg State Sch., Pa., 1969; lectr. U. Calif.-Riverside, 1973; research cons. Lega F. D'Oro, Osimo, Italy, 1982—. Contbr. articles to profl. jours., chpts. to books; editor, cons. editor, guest reviewer jours. Bur. Child Research Postdoctral fellow, 1971-72; recipient several research grants. Mem. Am. Assn. Mental Deficiency. Home: Rhijngeesterstraat Weg 82, 2343 BX Oegstgeest The Netherlands Office: U Leiden, Dept Devel Psychology, 2312 KM Leiden The Netherlands

SMEND, RUDOLF, theologian; b. Berlin, Oct. 17, 1932; s. Rudolf and Gisela (Hübner) S.; m. Dagmar Erlbruch, May 24, 1969. Student, U. Tübingen, Fed. Republic of Germany, 1951-52, Göttingen U., Fed. Republic of Germany, 1952-54, U. Basel, Switzerland, 1954-55; DTheol, 1958; DivD (hon.), Saint Andrews U., Scotland, 1979. Privat dozent U. Bonn, 1962-63; prof. theology Kirchliche Hochschule, Berlin, 1963-65, U. Münster, Fed. Republic of Germany, 1965-71, U. Göttingen, 1971—. Author: Die Entstehung des Alten Testaments, 1978, Die Mitte des Alten Testaments, 1986, Zur ältesten Geschichte Israels, 1987. Mem. Akademie der Wissenschaften, Soc. for Study of the Old Testament (hon.), Deutsche Forschungsgemeinschaft (v.p. 1986—). Home: 6 Thomas Dehler Weg, 3400 Göttingen Federal Republic of Germany Office: Theologicum, Platz der Göttinger Sieben 2, 3400 Göttingen Federal Republic of Germany

SMILEY, JOSEPH ELBERT, JR., evaluation engineer, librarian; b. Cin., Dec. 21, 1922; s. Joseph Elbert and Esther Marie (Lentz) S.; m. Leona Caroline Besenfelder, Aug. 23, 1953 (dec. Aug. 1986); 1 child, Mary Susan Smiley Liuzzi; m. Betty Concklin, May, 9, 1987. A.A., Edison Community Coll., 1978; B.A., U. S. Fla., 1981, M.A., 1983. Expediter VA, Miami, Fla., 1948-51, analyzer, 1953; evaluation engr. photographic equipment, CIA, Washington, 1953-75. Second v.p. pub. relations Country Club Estates Assn. Lehigh Acres, Inc., 1981-84, pres., 1984-86 ; coordinator, acting zone capt. Lehigh Acres Emergency Preparedness Com., 1983-84, chmn., 1984-86 . Served with U.S. Army, 1942-45, with USAF, 1951-52. Recipient commendation ribbon USAF, 1951; cert. of merit CIA, 1974, certs. of appreciation, 1975, 1981; letter of congratulations Gerald R. Ford, CIA, 1975. Mem. ALA, Fla. Library Assn., Internat. Platform Assn., Phi Theta Kappa, Kappa Delta Pi, Phi Kappa Phi, Beta Phi Mu. Republican. Roman Catholic. Club: KC. Home: 306 Dania St Lehigh Acres FL 33936

SMILIE, LARRY ALLEN, banker; b. Tokyo, July 30, 1953; s. Richard Clarence and Atsuko (Nagahashi) S.; Barbara Dean. A.A., Monterey Peninsula Coll., 1973; B.S., U. Calif.-Berkeley, 1976; M.B.A., San Francisco State U., 1978. Asst. v.p. Bank of Am., San Francisco, 1978-82, v.p., mgr., Los Angeles, 1984-88; v.p. lease sydications, asst. v.p. First Interstate Bank of Calif., San Francisco, 1982-84. Mem. Alpha Tau Omega. Clubs: Bachelors (San Francisco); Family. Home: 66 Partridge Dr San Rafael CA 94901 Office: Bank Amerilease 2 Embarcadero San Francisco CA 94111

SMILIE, MOLLIE KAY WILLIAMS, accountant, educator; b. Bradford, Pa., Aug. 11, 1949; d. Albert Franklin and Martha Rae (Moore) Williams; m. Christopher Stephen Arthur, Sept. 11, 1969 (div. Apr. 1976); 1 child, Erik Ian; m. Michael Steven Smilie, May 9, 1980. B.S., Colo. State U., 1979. C.P.A., Colo. Staff acct. Cady & Co., Fort Collins, Colo., 1979-80, Colo. State U., Fort Collins, 1980-81, asst. to controller, 1981-83, controller, 1983—; lectr. in field; mgmt. cons. Research Inst. of Colo., Fort Collins, 1985—; bd. dirs. Open Stage Inc., Ft. Collins. Dem. Precinct Chmn. Larimer County, Fort Collins, 1978; bd. dirs. Larimer County Boy Scouts Am., Fort Collins, 1979; bd. dirs. Colo. Com. on Acctg. Standards for Higher Edn., Denver, 1983—. Mem. Am. Inst. C.P.A.s, Colo. Soc. C.P.A.s, Nat. Assn. Coll. and Univ. Bus. Officers, Council on Govtl. Relations, Beta Alpha Psi. Republican. Unitarian. Avocations: acting; writing; horseback riding; skiing; travel. Home: 3509 N County Rd 23E LaPorte CO 80535 Office: Colo State U 202E Johnson Hall Fort Collins CO 80523

SMIT, HARM J., data communications and software consultant; b. Utrecht, Netherlands, Nov. 14, 1942; s. Peter A. and Margaretha (Bottema) S.; m. Monique Biehler, Feb. 18, 1966; children: Lars, Barbara. M.Sc., Tech. U. Delft (Netherlands), 1965. Systems programmer Philips Data Systems, Apeldoorn, Netherlands, 1965-71; computer systems researcher CII-Honeywell, Grenoble, France, 1971-74; project mgr. CIT-Alcatel, Velizy, France, 1974-77; project mgr. Thomson-Titn, Chilly Mazarin, France, 1977-82; tech. dir. B3I, Vauhallan, 1982—. Pres., Cultural Assn., Vauhallan, 1982—; mem. Environ. Def. Assn., Bievres, 1975—. Home: 31 rue de l'Eglise, Vauhallan, 91430 Essonne France Office: B3I 31 rue de l'Eglise, Vauhallan, 91430 Essonne France

SMITH, ALBERT CROMWELL, JR., investments consultant; b. Norfolk, Va., Dec. 6, 1925; s. Albert Cromwell and Georgie (Foreman) S.; B.S. in Civil Engring., Va. Mil. Inst., 1949; M.S. in Govtl. Adminstrn., George Washington U., 1965; M.B.A., Pepperdine U., 1975; m. Laura Thaxton, Oct. 25, 1952; children—Albert, Elizabeth, Laura. Enlisted USMC, 1944, commd. 2d lt., 1949, advanced through grades to col., 1970; comdr. inf. platoons, companies, landing force; variously assigned staffs U.K. Joint Forces, U.S. Sec. Navy, Brit. Staff Coll., Marine Staff Coll.; adviser, analyst amphibious systems; ret., 1974; pres. A. Cromwell-Smith, Ltd., Charlottesville, Va., 1973, head broker, cons. A. Cromwell Smith, Investments, La Jolla and Coronado, Calif., 1975—. Bd. dirs. Republicans of La Jolla, 1975-76; vestryman St. Martin's Episcopal Ch., 1971-73. Decorated Legion of Merit with oak leaf cluster, Bronze Star medal with oak leaf cluster, Air medal with 2 oak leaf clusters, Purple Heart. Mem. ASCE, Nat., Calif. assns. Realtors, San Diego, Coronado bds. Realtors, Stockbrokers Soc., So. Calif. Options Soc., SAR, Mil. Order Purple Heart. Club: Kona Kai. Author: The Individual Investor in Tomorrow's Stock Market, 1977; The Little Guy's Stock Market Survival Guide, 1979; Wake Up Detroit! The EVs Are Coming, 1982; The Little Guy's Tax Survival Guide, 1984; The Little Guy's Sailboat Success Guide, 1986, The Little Guy's Business Success Guide, 1988; contbr. articles to civilian and mil. publs. Office: 1001 B Ave Suite 319/320 PO Box 192 Coronado CA 92118

SMITH, ALEXANDER GOUDY, physics and astronomy educator; b. Clarksburg, W.Va., Aug. 12, 1919; s. Edgell Ohr and Helen (Reitz) S.; m. Mary Elizabeth Ellsworth, Apr. 19, 1942; children: Alexander G. III, Sally Jean. B.S., Mass. Inst. Tech., 1943; Ph.D., Duke U., 1949. Physicist Mass. Inst. Tech., Radiation Lab., Cambridge, 1943-46; research asst. Duke U., Durham, 1946-48; asst. prof. to prof. physics U. Fla., Gainesville, 1948-61; asst. dean grad. sch. U. Fla., 1961-69, acting dean grad. sch., 1971-73, chmn. dept. astronomy, 1962-71, prof. physics and astronomy, 1956—, Disting. prof., 1981—; dir. U. Fla. Radio Obs., 1956-85; cons. USN, USAF. Author: (with others) Microwave Magnetrons, 1958, (with T.D. Carr) Radio Exploration of the Planetary System, 1964 (also Swedish, Spanish and Polish edits), Radio Exploration of the Sun, 1966; (also numerous articles in field. Fellow Optical Soc. Am., Am. Phys. Soc., AAAS, Royal Micros. Soc.; mem. Am. Astron. Soc. (editor Photo-Bull. 1975—), Astron. Soc. Pacific, Internat. Astron. Union, Internat. Sci. Radio Union, Fla. Acad. Scis. (treas. 1957-62, pres. 1963-64, medal 1965), Assn. Univs. for Research in Astronomy (dir., cons.), S.E. Univs. Research Assn. (trustee 1981—), Soc. Photog. Scientists and Engrs., Sigma Xi (nat. lectr. 1968, past pres. Fla. chpt.), Phi Kappa Phi, Sigma Pi Sigma. Republican. Christian Scientist. Clubs: Athenaeum (past pres.), Woodside Racquet, Gainesville Golf and Country. Home: 1417 NW 17th St Gainesville FL 32605

SMITH, ALRICK LOCKHART, consulting reliability physicist; b. Nigel, South Africa, Sept. 16, 1947; came to Switzerland, 1980, naturalized, 1980; s. Allen Lockhart and Cora (Franken) S.; m. Dora Haenni, June 11, 1971; children—Craig Lockhart, Bryan Lockhart. B.Sc., U. St. Andrews, Scotland, 1972; B.Sc. with honors, U. Sussex, Eng., 1975, Dr.Phil.Nat., 1980, D.Sc. in Engring., Kensington U., 1983. Educator, research scientist Rhodesian Ministry of Edn., 1965-69, U. St. Andrews, 1969-72, U. Sussex, 1973-75, Oxford U., 1975; applied scientist/technologist LKB Produkter, Stockholm, 1975-76; South African Nat. Phys. Research Lab., Pretoria, 1976-78, South African Dept. Energy, Pretoria, 1978-79, South African Electricity Supply Commn., Johannesburg, 1979-80; cons. Motor Columbus Cons. Engrs., Baden, Switzerland, 1980-83; del. for Switzerland, Internat. Atomic Energy Agy. transp. risks oversight com.; chmn. 1st European Symposium on Materials Reliability, 1983; cons. Control Data Corp., Switzerland, Intakta Sarl, France, Frost and Sullivan Ltd., Eng., Mitsubishi Corp., Japan; lectr. in field. Editor: Reliability of Engineering Materials, 1984. Contbr. articles to profl. jours. Mem. Swiss Acad. Engring. Scis., Swiss Electrotech. Assn., Am. Phys. Soc., Am. Soc. Quality Control, IEEE Reliability Group, Scottish Univ. South Africa Assn., Russel Philos. Soc., U. St. Andrews Alumni Assn. (pres. So. African br. 1978-79), Soc. Reliability Engrs. Office: Postfach 1540, Baden 5401 Switzerland

SMITH, ANDREW PORTER, investment analyst; b. N.Y.C., Mar. 12, 1955; arrived in Eng., 1967; s. Thomas Franklin and Edyta (Klein) S.; m. Fiona Jane Pixley, Dec. 30, 1986. BA in Politics and Philosophy, Purdue U., 1976; MS, London Sch. Econs., 1977. Mng. dir. Capital Risk Ltd., London, 1982—, Global Analysis Systems Ltd., London, 1985-88; pres. Global Analysis Systems Inc., N.Y.C., 1986-88; mng. dir. London and Bishopgate Internat. Investment Mgmt. Plc., London, 1988—; sr. v.p. Paine Webber Internat. Trust, London, 1987-88; lectr. Keble Coll., Oxford, 1983-85; creator GAS100 Internat. Equity Index, London, 1986; cons. in field. Editor Jour. Internat. Studies, 1981-82, Atlantic Quar., 1983-84; contbr. articles to Wall St. Jour., Fin. Times. Mktg. cons. Internat. Child Care Soc., Bristol, Eng., 1987. Mem. Confedn. Brit. Industry, Royal Inst. Internat. Affairs, Strategic Planning Soc., Am. C. of C. Democrat. Office: London and Bishopgate, Internat Investment Mgmt PLC, 1 Temple Ave, London EC4Y 0HA, England

SMITH, ANTHONY WAYNE, lawyer, consultant; b. Pitts.; s. Anthony Woodward and Janey Mulhern (Coard) S.; m. Anya E. Freedel, June 20, 1930. B.A. with high honors, U. Pitts.; J.D., Yale U., 1934. Bar: N.Y. State 1935, U.S. Supreme Ct. 1940, D.C. 1947. Sec. to gov. Pa., 1932-33; with firm Donovan, Leisure, Newton & Lumbard, N.Y.C., 1934-37; pvt. practice law, Washington,, 1949—; asst. gen. counsel CIO, Washington,, 1937-56; asst. dir. state and city indsl. union councils CIO, 1941-55, exec. sec. housing com., 1937-39, 41-42, asst. sec. Latin Am. com., 1939-40; observer UN, 1954-56; atty. polit. edn. com. AFL-CIO., 1956-58; pres., gen. counsel Nat. Parks and Conservation Assn., 1958-80, spl. counsel, 1980—; comml. farmer, Franklin County, Pa., 1954—. Exec. committeeman Emergency Com. on Natural Resources, 1952-53, Citizens Com. on Natural Resources, 1953-78, C & O Canal Assn., 1954-71, Little Cove Assn., 1971—; del. various gen. sessions Internat. Union for Conservation of Nature, 1952—; pres. South Central Pa. Citizens Assn., 1962—; gen. counsel Citizens Permanent Conf. Potomac River Basin, 1968—; chmn. Environ. Coalition for N.Am., 1970—; co-chmn. Everglades Coalition, 1969—; observer to UN Conf. on Human Environ., Stockholm, Sweden, 1972, UN Environ. Programme, Geneva, Switzerland, 1973; mem. adv. com. to sec. state on UN Conf. on Human Environment, 1972; mem. adv. com. to sec. state UN Conf. Law of Sea, 1972-83; mem. U.S. Delegation, 1973-83; mem. adv. com. to Council on Environmental Quality on U.S.-USSR Sci. Exchange, 1974; mem. steering com. The Unfinished Agenda (Laurance S. Rockefeller Report on Environ.), 1976-77; bd. dirs. Council on Ocean Law, 1981—, Global Tomorrow Coalition, 1981—; mem. steering com. intensive timber harvest N.Y. State Andirondack Park Agy., 1980-82; spl. counsel Chesapeake Bay Found., 1980, Negative Population Growth, 1981—; mem. steering com. OSHA Environ. Network, indsl. union dept. AFL-CIO, 1980—chmn. cons. group on norms and incentives for population stabilization, 1982—; cons. Scholastic Mags., 1981—; spl. cons. Solarex Corp., 1982—; initiated legislation resulting in establishment of Atomic Energy Commn., 1945. Bd. editors Yale Law Jour. 1931-34; co-author Nat. Labor Relations Act, Fair Labor Standards Act; contbr. numerous articles to profl. jours. Served as 2d lt. AUS, 1926-30. Mem. Am. Farm Bur. Fedn., Pa., Franklin County farmers assns., Nat., Pa., Concord granges, Nat. Lawyers Club, Bar Assn. D.C., Assn. Bar City N.Y., Nat. Lawyers Club, Delta Tau Delta, Phi Mu Sigma, Delta Sigma Rho, Omicron Delta Kappa. Club: Yale (N.Y.C.). Home: 1330 New Hampshire Ave NW Washington DC 20036 also: Cove Mountain Farm 12462 Little Cove Rd Mercersburg PA 17236 Office: 1325 G St NW Suite 1003 Washington DC 20005

SMITH, ARTHUR LEE, lawyer; b. Davenport, Iowa, Dec. 19, 1941; s. Harry Arthur Smith (dec.) and Ethel (Hoffman) Duerre; m. Georgia Mills,

June 12, 1965 (dec. Jan. 1984); m. Jean Bowler, Aug. 4, 1984; children—Juliana, Christopher, Andrew. B.A., Augustana Coll., Rock Island, Ill., 1964; M.A., Am. U., 1968; J.D., Washington U., St. Louis, 1971. Bar: Mo. 1971, D.C. 1983. Telegraph editor Davenport Morning Democrat, 1962-64; ptnr. Peper Martin Jensen Maichel & Hetlage, St. Louis, 1971-82, Washington, 1983—; arbitrator Nat. Assn. Security Dealers, 1980—, Am. Arbitration Assn., 1980—. Served to lt. USN, 1964-68. Mem. ABA, D.C. Bar Assn., Mo. Bar Assn. (vice-chair ins. programs com. 1981-83, vice-chair antitrust com. 1983-86), Am. Judicature Soc., Securities Industry Assn. (legal and compliance div.), Am. Coll. Computer Lawyers, Fed. Bar Assn. Lodge: Order of Coif. Home: 1321 Darnall Dr McLean VA 22101 Office: Peper Martin et al 1730 Pennsylvania Ave NW Suite 400 Washington DC 20006

SMITH, BARBARA BARNARD, music educator; b. Ventura, Calif., June 10, 1920; d. Fred W. and Grace (Hobson) S. B.A., Pomona Coll., 1942; Mus.M., U. Rochester, 1943, performer's cert., 1944. Mem. faculty piano and theory Eastman Sch. Music, U. Rochester, 1943-49; mem. faculty U. Hawaii, Honolulu, 1949—; assoc. prof. music U. Hawaii, 1953-62, prof., 1962-82, prof. emeritus, 1982—; sr. fellow East-West Center 1973; lectr., recitals in Hawaiian and Asian music, U.S., Europe and Asia, 1956—; field researcher Asia, 1956, 60, 66, 71, 80, Micronesia, 1963, 70, 87, Solomon Islands, 1976. Author publs. on ethnomusicology. Mem. Internat. Soc. Music Edn., Internat., Am. musicol. socs., Soc. Ethnomusicology, Internat. Council for Traditional Music, Asia Soc., Am. Mus. Instrument Soc., Coll. Music Soc., Soc. for Asian Music, Music Educators Nat. Conf., Phi Beta Kappa, Mu Phi Epsilon. Home: 581 Kamoku St Apt 2004 Honolulu HI 96826

SMITH, BARBARA DAIL, nurse; b. Oklahoma City, July 15, 1949; d. James E. and Juanita E. (Butler) Berryhill; m. William Ben Smith, May 23, 1975; children: Rebecca Sue and James Ben. BS in Biology, Oklahoma City U., 1975, BS in Health Edn., 1984; RN diploma St. Anthony Hosp., 1979. Mgmt. nurse St. Anthony Hosp., Oklahoma City, 1979-83; cons. family help group cancer patients, 1981-83; nurse Oklahoma City Bd. Edn., 1983—. Author: (with others) Chemotherapy Cert. Program, 1981-82. Leader Camp Fire Orgn. Am., Oklahoma City, 1982-84; mem. Cen. Okla. Task Force Com. for children with spl. needs; mem. Oklahoma County Task Force Com. on Child Abuse; mem. spl. edn. task force com. Oklahoma City Pub. Schs., 1986-87; mem. gov.'s task force Child Abuse, 1985-86; mem. Okla. County Task Force on Children with Spl. Needs; mem. spl. edn. task force com. Oklahoma City Bd. Edn.; mem. exec. bd. Oklahoma City Fedn. of Tchrs. Local 2309 of the Am. Fedn. of Tchrs. Mem. Nat. Oncol. Nursing Soc., Okla. Oncol. Nursing Soc., Okla. City Sch. Nurses Soc. (pres. 1985-87), Oklahoma City Pub. Sch. Nurses (procedures com., sec. 1986-87), Sch. Nurse Orgn. Okla. (chair continuing edn./workshop com. 1985—, bd. dirs. 1985—), YWCA, Nat. Assn. Sch. Nurses, Beta Beta Beta. Democrat. Lodge: Fraternal Order of Police Ladies Aux.

SMITH, BARRY HAMILTON, foundation administrator, physician; b. Orange, N.J., Oct. 6, 1943; s. Kenneth Wright and Harriet (Barr) S.; m. Carley Eldredge, Dec. 13, 1969; children—Christopher, Sara. B.A., Harvard U., 1965; Ph.D., MIT, 1968; M.D., Cornell U., 1972. Intern, then resident N.Y. Hosp., N.Y.C., 1971-75; resident in neurosurgery Mass. Gen. Hosp., Boston, 1975-78; dir. Neurosci. Research Program MIT, Boston, 1975-78; dep. dir. Surg. Neurology Br. NIH, Bethesda, Md., 1978-83; sci. and med. dir. Dreyfus Med. Found., N.Y.C., 1983—; cons. Human Cell Biology Found., Princeton, N.J., 1982-87. Contbr. articles to profl. jours. Mem. exec. com. Nongovtl. Orgn./Dept. Pub. Info. UN. Served to comdr. USPHS, 1978-83. Recipient Commendation Medal award USPHS, 1982; EEO award, 1983. Mem. AMA, Soc. Neurosci., Am. Pain Soc. (audit com. 1983-85), Nat. Council Internat. Health, AAAS (UN DPI/NGO exec. com.), Phi Beta Kappa, Sigma Xi. Avocations: sailing; writing. Home: 40 E 94th St Apt 8A New York NY 10128 Office: Dreyfus Found 767 5th Ave New York NY 10153

SMITH, BETTY DENNY, county official, civic worker, fashion exec.; Centralia, Ill., Nov. 12, 1932; d. Otto and Ferne Elizabeth (Beier) Hasenfuss; student U. Ill., 1950-52, Los Angeles City Coll., 1953-57, UCLA, 1965, U. San Francisco, 1982-84; m. Peter S. Smith, Dec. 5, 1964; children—Carla Kip, Bruce Kimball. Free-lance fashion coordinator, Los Angeles and N.Y.C., 1953-58; instr. fashion Rita LeRoy Internat. Studios, 1959-60; mgr. Mo Nadler Fashions, Los Angeles, 1961-64; showroom dir. Jean of Calif. Fashions, Los Angeles, 1966—; staff writer Valley Citizen News, 1963; free-lance polit. book reviewer community newspapers, 1961-62. Bd. dirs. Pet Assistance Found., 1969-76; founder, pres., dir. Vol. Services to Animals of Los Angeles, 1972-76; mem. County Com. to Discuss Animals in Research, 1973-74; mem. blue ribbon com. on animal control Los Angeles County, 1973-74; dir. Los Angeles County Animal Care and Control, 1976-82, ind. legis. advocate for humane causes, 1969—; mem. State of Calif. Animal Health Technician Exam. Com., 1975—, chmn., 1979; chief fin. officer Coalition for Pet Population Control, 1987-88; dir. West Coast regional office Am. Humane Assn., 1988—; bd. dirs. Am. Soc. for Prevention of Cruelty to Animals, 1984—. Mem. exec. com. Rep. State Cen. Com., 1971-72; mem. Calif. Rep. Cen. Com., 1964-72; mem. Rep. Los Angeles County Cen. Com., 1964-70, mem. exec. com., 1966-70; chmn. 29th Congl. Central Com., 1969-70; sec. 28th Senatorial Central Com., 1967-68, 45th Assembly Dist. Central Com., 1965-66; mem. speakers bur. George Murphy for U.S. Senate, 1970; campaign mgr. Los Angeles County for Spencer Williams for Atty. Gen., 1966. Mem. Lawyers Wives San Gabriel Valley (dir. 1971-74, pres. 1972-73), Mannequins Assn. (dir. 1967-68), Internat. Platform Assn., Delta Gamma, Pi Phi Theta. Clubs: Los Angeles Athletic, Town Hall. Home: 1766 Bluffhill Dr Monterey Park CA 91754

SMITH, BRIAN CHRISTOPHER, psychiatric social worker, consultant, educator; b. Westgate-on-Sea, Eng., Nov. 7, 1937; s. Charles Frederick and Beatrice Clara (Penny) S.; m. Queenie Winifred Mastin, Aug. 22, 1964; children: Linda Anne, Alison Jane. Student, U. Edinburgh, 1962-66, U. St. Andrews, 1966-67. Cert. social worker, Eng. Prin. social worker Brit. Royal Army Med. Corps., 1979-80; sr. social worker, clinic coordinator Brighton (Eng.) Family Guidance Clinic, 1980-83; prin. social worker Ticehurst House Pvt. Hosp., Eng., 1983-86; cons. in social work Eng., 1986—; mem. council Electricity Consultative Com., Sussex, Eng., 1975—, Community Health Council, Eastbourne, Eng., 1978-79; mem. Mental Health Rev. Tribunal, Eng., 1975—. Contbr. articles to profl. jours. Active Framfield Conservative Assn., Sussex; councillor Framfield Council, Sussex, 1970; gov. Framfield Conservative Edn. Sch., Sussex, 1970; life gov., patron Royal Masonic Hosp., London, 1985. Fellow Royal Soc. Health, Royal Soc. Medicine. Anglican. Lodges: Masons (Old Ruymian, companion, mark master). Office: Brian C Smith & Co, PO Box 4, Uckfield TN22 5PZ, England

SMITH, BRIAN WILLIAM, lawyer, former government official; b. N.Y.C., Feb. 3, 1947; s. William Francis and Dorothy Edwina (Vogel) S.; m. Donna Jean Holverson, Apr. 24, 1976; children—Mark Holverson, Lauren Elizabeth. B.A., St. John's U., 1968, J.D., 1971; M.S., Columbia U., 1981. Bar: N.Y. 1972, D.C. 1975, U.S. Supreme Ct. 1976, U.S. Dist. Ct. N.Y. 1975, U.S. Dist. Ct. D.C. 1986. Atty., Am. Express Co., N.Y.C., 1970-73, CIT Fin. Corp., N.Y.C., 1973-74; assoc. counsel, mng. atty. Interbank Card Assn., N.Y.C., 1974-75, sr. v.p., corp. sec., gen. counsel, 1975-82; chief counsel to comptroller of currency, Washington, 1982-84; ptnr. Stroock & Stroock & Lavan, Washington, 1984—; mng. ptnr., 1986—. Served to capt., USAR, 1970-78. Mem. N.Y. State Bar Assn., ABA, D.C. Bar Assn., Assn. Bar City N.Y., Fed. Bar Assn. Clubs: N.Y. Athletic, City Washington. Home: 3646 Upton St NW Washington DC 20008 Office: Stroock & Stroock & Lavan 1150 17th St NW Suite 600 Washington DC 20036

SMITH, CARTER BLAKEMORE, broadcaster; b. San Francisco, Jan. 1, 1937; s. Donald V. and Charlotte M. (Nichols) S.; children: Carter Blakemore, Clayton M. AA, City Coll. San Francisco, 1958; BA, San Francisco State U., 1960; postgrad. N.Y. Inst. Finance, 1969-70; Assoc. in Fin. PLanning, Coll. for Fin. Planning, 1984. Announcer, Sta. KBLF, Red Bluff, Calif., 1954-56; personality Sta. KRE-KRE FM, Berkeley, Calif., 1958-63, Sta. KSFO, San Francisco, 1963-72, Sta. KNBR, San Francisco, 1972-83, Sta. KSFO, San Francisco, 1983-86, Sta. KFRC, San Francisco, 1986—; mem. faculty radio-TV dept. San Francisco State U., 1960-61. Mem. adv. bd. Little Jim Club Children's Hosp., 1968-71; bd. dirs. Marin County Humane Soc., 1968-73, San Francisco Zool. Soc., 1980—; trustee Family Service Agy. Marin, 1976-85; mem. alumni bd. Lowell High Sch. Recipient award San Francisco Press Club, 1965; named one of Outstanding Young Men in Am. U.S. Jaycees, 1972. Mem. Amateur Radio Relay League (life), Quarter Century Wireless Assn., Alpha Epsilon Rho. Office: Sta KFRC 500 Washington St San Francisco CA 94111

SMITH, CATHERINE MARY, educational administrator; b. Matewan, W.Va., Apr. 8, 1947; d. Benton B. and Rita Theresa (Morrison) S.; B.S. in Secondary Edn., W.Va. U., 1969, M.A. in Secondary English Edn., 1972; cert. in coop. vocat. edn. U. Md., 1979; cert. in edn. adminstr./supervision George Washington U., 1977. Tchr. English, Lackey High Sch., Charles County, Md., 1969-71; resident mgr. Univ. Trailer Ct., Morgantown, W.Va., 1971-72; tutor, counselor Potomac State Coll., W.Va. U., Keyser, 1972-73; chmn. dept. English, Gen. Smallwood Middle Sch., Charles County, 1973-75; chmn. dept. English, McDonough High Sch., Charles County, 1975-78, tchr. observer, 1978-79, asst. vice prin., tchr. coordinator coop. vocat. edn., 1979—; supervisory mgr. Dockside Sales, Inc., Alexandria, Va., 1972-75; partner real estate co., 1980—; grad. teaching asst. dept. curriculum and instrn. W.Va. U., 1973-74. Treas. bd. dirs. Charleston County Crime Solvers. Named Princess, Mountain State Forest Festival, 1968, Charles County Woman of Yr., 1984. Mem. Edn. Assn. Charles County, Md. Tchrs. Assn., Am. Vocat. Assn., Md. Vocat. Assn., AAUW, Soc. for Preservation Port Tobacco, Hist. Soc. of Charles County, Delta Kappa Gamma Soc. Internat. (pres.), Kappa Delta Pi. Democrat. Roman Catholic. Club: Bus. and Profl. Women's (1st v.p., chmn. various coms., Member of Month award 1981, 82). Home: 713 Prince Charles Dr La Plata MD 20646 Office: Route 2 Box 74-Q Pomfret MD 20675

SMITH, CHESTER LEO, lawyer; b. Kansas City, Mo., Jan. 23, 1922; s. Chester Leo and Alameda Mariposa (West) S.; m. Ann Smith; 1 dau., Blithe. BA, U. Chgo., 1942; JD, Harvard U., 1948. Bar: Ill. 1949, Calif. 1951. Asst. to v.p. Cuneo Press, Chgo., 1948-49; individual practice Los Angeles, 1951-87, ret., 1987. Author: Midway 4 June, 1942, 1962, (plays) My Empress Eva Darling, The Last Execution, Images of Che, Cross-Examination at Auschwitz; editor: (Wu Han): The Dismissal of Hai Jui, 1968; contbr. stories to, Collier's, Am. Legion mag. Served to 1st lt. Air Corps., USMCR, 1942-45. Decorated Air medal (3). Mem. Ill. Bar Assn., State Bar Calif., Beverly Hills Bar Assn. (chmn. internat. law com. 1971-76). Address: PO Box 49590 Los Angeles CA 90049

SMITH, CHRISTOPHER NORMAN, history and French language educator; b. Norwich, Norfolk, Eng., May 19, 1936; s. Reginald Edward and Monica Alice (Quinton) S.; m. Margaret Isabella Brown, Dec. 28, 1961; 1 child, Helen Frances Isabella. BA, Cambridge U., 1957, MA, 1960, PhD, 1969; diploma in edn., Oxford U., 1961. Asst. lectr. French U. Aberdeen, Scotland, 1966-68; lectr. Sch. Modern Langs. and European History, U. East Anglia, Norwich, 1968-74, sr. lectr., 1974—. Author: Alabaster, Bikinis and Calvados: an ABC of Toponymous Works, 1985, Jean Anouilh: Life, Work and Criticism, 1985 and editions of French Renaissance plays and emblem books; contbr. articles and revs. to profl. jours. Mem. Soc. for Seventeenth Century French Studies (treas., editor jour. 1978—). Anglican. Office: U East Anglia, Sch Modern Langs, Norwich NR4 7TJ, England

SMITH, CLYDE GAYLON, obstetrician/gynecologist; b. Caraway, Ark., Nov. 9, 1945; s. William Harry and Thelma Lee (Johnson) S.; m. Deanna Sue Holland, July 22, 1967; children—Craig, Keith. B.S., Harding U., 1967; M.D., U. Tenn., 1971. Diplomate Am. Bd. Ob-Gyn. Intern, Meth. Hosp., Memphis, 1972; resident in ob-gyn City of Memphis Hosp., 1973, Meth. Hosp., Memphis, 1974-75; practice medicine, specializing in obstetrics and gynecology, Memphis, 1976—; lectr. dept. nursing Meth. Hosp., 1976-82, Bapt. Meml. Hosp., 1983—; staff Bapt. East Hosp., Memphis, 1981—; clin. instr. dept. ob-gyn U. Tenn. Ctr. Health Scis., Memphis, 1977-88. Mem. devel. council Harding U., Searcy, Ark., 1975—, Harding Acad., Memphis, 1981—; adv. bd. Heartbeat, 1982, campaign div. chmn., 1981; sponsoring com., rev. editor Upreach, 1982—. Recipient AMA Physician Recognition award, 1976, 79, 82, 85, 88. Fellow ACS, Am. Coll. Obstetricians and Gynecologists (Recognition award 1976, 79, 82, 85, 88); mem. AMA, Tenn. Med. Soc., Memphis Shelby County Med. Soc., Soc. Obstetrical Anesthesia and Perinatology, Am. Fertility Soc., Am. Assn. Region Anesthesia, Am. Inst. of Ultrasound in Medicine, Nat. Perinatology Soc., So. Perinatal Soc., Memphis Obstetrical and Gynecol. Soc., Tenn. Obstetrical and Gynecol. Soc., Am. Assn. Gynecol. Laparoscopists. Mem. Ch. of Christ. Contbr. articles to profl. jours.; rev. editor Practical Gastroenterology, 1979—, Upreach, 1981-82. Home: 174 Grove Park Memphis TN 38117 Office: 6266 Poplar St Memphis TN 38119

SMITH, CLYN, JR., investment company executive, surgeon; b. Clovis, N.Mex., Dec. 7, 1919; s. Clyn and Rachel Virginia S.; m. Marilyn Decker, Nov. 13, 1943 (dec. 1962); children—Clyn, III, Sharon Jean, Brian Theodore; m. 2d, Pamela Dormody, Mar. 1, 1964; 1 dau., Mollie Kennard. A.B., Stanford U., 1940, M.D., 1944. Diplomate Am. Bd. Surgery. Intern, Alameda County Hosp., Oakland, Calif., 1943-44, resident, 1947-49; resident in surgery, Merritt Hosp., Oakland, 1946-47; practice medicine specializing in surgery, Monterey, Calif., 1949-84; staff Community Hosp. Monterey Peninsula, Carmel, Calif., Monterey Hosp.; cons. surgery U.S. Army Hosp., Ft. Ord, Calif., 1952-60; pres. Eastridge Corp., Clovis, 1958—, Univ. Heights Corp., Clovis, 1959—, Smith Investment Co., Monterey, 1964—, Fiesta Land, Inc., 1966-70; adv. dir. First Nat. Bank Monterey County, Monterey. Author profl. articles. Former bd. dirs. Monterey Bay area chpt. Nat. Multiple Sclerosis Soc., Monterey County br. Am. Cancer Soc., Arthur L. Swim Found. and Community Found. of Monterey County, Carmel Bach Festival, Econ. Devel. Corp. Monterey County; mem. Monterey County Republican Central Com., 1962-68. Served to capt. M.C., AUS, 1944-46. Fellow ACS; mem. Monterey County Med. Soc. (pres. 1956), AMA, Calif. Med. Assn., Am. Soc. Clin. Hypnosis, Monterey Bay Acad. Clin. Hypnosis (treas.-sec. 1968-70), Soc. Clin. and Exptl. Hypnosis, Monterey History and Art Assn., Navy League. Clubs: Old Capital, Rotary, Pacheco. Lodge: Masons. Office: Smith Investment Co 889 Pacific St Monterey CA 93940

SMITH, D. RICHARD, academic administrator; b. Lafayette, Ind., Dec. 27, 1930; s. Guy MacIlvane Smith and Hilda Emily Sattler; m. Virginia Lehker, Aug. 24, 1957; children: Richard Lehker, Steven Henry. BS, Purdue U., 1953, MS, 1957, PhD, 1960; postdoctoral study, Mich. State U., 1960-62, U. Mich., 1970, Harvard U., 1971, Cambridge U., 1971, Baruch Coll., 1972, CUNY, 1972, 74, 76; grad., Cuauhnahuac Instituto Colectivo de Lengua y Cultura, Cuernavaca, Morelos, Mexico, 1977. Dean, dir. Purdue U., Ft. Wayne, 1965-70; asst. to v.p. regional campus, dean continuing edn. Purdue U., West Lafayette, Ind., 1970-74, asst. to exec. v.p. and provost, prof. gen. studies, 1974-76, asst. dir. Internat. edn. and research, prof. gen. studies, 1976-79, assoc dir. internat. edn. and research and internat. programs in agr., prof. gen. studies, 1979—; con. accreditation examiner N.Cen. Commn. Higher Edn., Chgo. 1970—; bd. rep. Ind Consortium for Internat. Programs., 1976-87; accreditation chairperson The Am. Bd. Edn., Cumberland, Maine, 1980—; del. White House Conf. Libraries and Info. Services, Washington, 1979; liaison officer Midwest U. Consortium for Internat. Activities, 1976-77; dir. U.S. Presdl. Commn. World Hunger Symposium, 1981; supr. U.S. Peace Corps Counselling Office, 1986—; seminar speaker Chinese Acad. Sci, Beijing, 1981, Nanjing, People's Republic of China, 1981. Editor: An Inventory of Non-Traditional Instructional Activities, Patterns of Innovation. Bd. dirs. Ft. Wayne Fine Arts Assn., 1966-70, Ft. Wayne YMCA, 1968-70, Northeastern Ind. Mental Health Ctr., 1966-70, pres. Lafayette Symphony Found., 1985—. Served to cpl. U.S. Army, 1953-55. Purdue Research Found. fellow, 1958-60; vis. scholar Horace G. Racknam Sch. Grad. Studies, U. Mich., 1977. Mem. AAUP (assoc.), Assn. U.S. Univ. Dirs. of Internat. Agr. Programs., Patners of The Americas, Purdue Alumni Assn. (life). Lutheran. Clubs: Ft. Wayne Quest, Ft. Wayne Forthnightly. Home: 2851 Ashland West Lafayette IN 47906 Office: Purdue U AGAD Room 26C West Lafayette IN 47907

SMITH, DARRELL WAYNE, metallurgical engineering educator, consultant; b. Long Beach, Calif., July 31, 1937; s. Joseph Sidney and Bethel Irene (Monroe) S.; m. Marilyn Margaret Meese, Dec. 20, 1958; children: Mark Kevin, Barbara Dean, Paul Edwin. BS MetE, Mich. Technol. U., 1959; MS in Metallurgy, Case Western Res. U., 1965, PhD, 1969. Process metallurgist Babcock & Wilcox, Beaver Falls, Pa., 1959-62; project engr. Gen. Electric Co., Cleve., 1962-68, research metallurgist, 1968-70; prof. metall. engring. Mich. Technol. U., Houghton, 1970—; pres. SCS Assocs. Inc., Houghton, 1984—; bd. dirs. Peninsula Copper Industries, Hubbell, Mich., 1983—; metall. engring. cons. various corps. and nat. labs. Contbr. over 50 reports and papers in field. Mem. Am. Soc. Metals Internat., Am. Powder Metall. Inst. Republican. Home: Half Moon Beach Rt 2 Box 462 Chassell MI 49916 Office: Mich Technol U Dept Metall Engring Houghton MI 49931

SMITH, DAVID BURNELL, lawyer; b. Charleston, W.Va., Apr. 8, 1941; s. Ernest Dayton and Nellie Dale (Tyler) S.; m. Rita J. Hughes, Sept. 25, 1967. B.A., U. Charleston, 1967; J.D., U. Balt., 1972. Bar: Colo. 1972, Md. 1972, U.S. Supreme Ct. 1980, Ariz. 1983, U.S. Dist. Ct. Md. 1972, U.S. Dist. Ct. Colo. 1972, U.S. Ct. Appeals (4th cir.) 1972, U.S. Ct. Appeals (9th cir.) 1972, U.S. Ct. Appeals (10th cir.) 1983. Sales rep. Gulf Oil, Washington, 1967-72; sole practice, Littleton, Colo., 1972-83, Glendale, Ariz., 1983-86, Phoenix, 1986—; pro-tempore judge Wickenburg Mcpl. Ct., 1986—; presiding judge Peoria (Ariz.) Mcpl. Ct., 1987—. Vice pres. South Jefferson County Republicans, Lakewood, Colo., 1979, pres., 1980. Served with USCG, 1959-66. Mem. Nat. Assn. Criminal Lawyers, Am. Judicature Soc., ABA (vice-chmn. family law 1983), Colo. Bar Assn., Ariz. Bar Assn., Md. Bar Assn., Assn. Trial Lawyers Am., Colo. Trial Lawyers Assn., Ariz. Trial Lawyers Assn. Maricopa County Bar Assn. Lodges: Masons, Shriners, Elks. Home: 36418 N Wildflower PO Box 5145 Carefree AZ 85377-5145 Office: 4310 N 75th St Scottsdale AZ 85251

SMITH, DAVID ELVIN, physician; b. Bakersfield, Calif., Feb. 7, 1939; s. Elvin W. and Dorothy (McGinnis) S.; m. Millicent Buxton; children: Julia, Suzanne, Christopher Buxton, Christopher Buxton-Smith. Intern San Francisco Gen. Hosp., 1965; fellow pharmacology and toxicology U. Calif., San Francisco, 1965-67, assoc. clinical prof. occupational health and clinical toxicology, 1967—, dir. psychopharmacology study group, 1966-70; practice medicine specializing in toxicology and addictionology San Francisco, 1965—; physician Presbyn. Alcoholic Clinic, 1965-67, Contra Cost Alcoholic Clinic, 1965-67; dir. alcohol and drug abuse screening unit San Francisco Gen. Hosp., 2967-68; co-dir. Calif drug abuse info. project U. Calif Med. Ctr., 1967-72; founder, med. dir. Haight-Ashbury Free Med. Clinic, San Francisco, 1967—; research dir. Merritt Peralta Chem. Dependency Hosp., Oakland, Calif., 1984—; chmn. Nat. Drug Abuse Conf., 1977; mem. Calif. Gov's. Commn. on Narcotics and Drug Abuse, 1977—; nat. health adviser to former U.S. Pres. Jimmy Carter; dir. Benzodiazepine Research and Tng. Project, Substance Abuse and Sexual Concerns Project, PCP Research and Tng. Project; cons. numerous fed. drug abuse agys. Author: Love Needs Care, 1970, The New Social Drug: Cultural, Medical and Legal Perspectives on Marijuana, 1971, The Free Clinic: Community Approaches to Health Care and Drug Abuse, 1971, Treating the Cocaine Abuser, 1985, The Benzodiazepines: Current Standard Medical Practice, 1986, Physicians' Guide to Drug Abuse, 1987; co-author: It's So Good, Don't Even Try it Once: Heroin in Perspective, 1972, Uppers and Downers, 1973, Drugs in the Classroom, 1973, Barbiturate Use and Abuse, 1977, A Multicultural View of Drug Abuse, 1978, Amphetamine Use, Misuse and Abuse, 1979, PCP: Problems and Prevention, 1981, Sexological Aspects of Substance Use and Abuse, Treatment of the Cocaine Abuser, 1985, The Haight Ashbury Free Medical Clinic: Still Free After all these Years, Drug Free: Alternatives to Drug Abuse, 1987, Treatment of Opiate Dependence, Designer Drugs, 1988, others; also drug edn. films; founder, editor Jour. Psychedelic Drugs (now Jour. Psychoactive Drugs), 1967—; contbr. over 100 articles to profl. jours. Pres. Youth Projects, Inc.; founder, chmn. bd., pres. Nat. Free Clin. Council, 1968-72. Recipient Research award Borden Found., 1964, AMA Research award, 1966, Community Service award U. Calif. at San Francisco, 1974, Calif. State Drug Abuse Treatment award, 1984, Vernelle Fox Drug Abuse Treatment award, 1985. Mem. Am. Med. Soc. for Treatment of Alcoholism and Other Drug Dependencies, San Francisco Med. Soc., Am. Pub. Health Assn., Calif. Soc. Treatment of Alcohol and other Drug Dependencies (pres., bd. dirs.), Sigma Xi, Phi Beta Kappa. Unitarian. Home: 289 Frederick St San Francisco CA 94131 Office: 409 Clayton St San Francisco CA 94117

SMITH, DAVID SHIVERICK, ambassador, lawyer; b. Omaha, Jan. 25, 1918; s. Floyd Monroe and Anna (Shiverick) S.; m. June Noble, Dec. 8, 1945 (div. 1968); children:Noble, David Shiverick, Jeremy T., Bradford D.; m. Mary Edson, Feb. 14, 1972. Degre Superieur, Sorbonne, Paris, 1938; B.A., Dartmouth Coll., 1939; J.D., Columbia U., 1942. Bar: N.Y. 1942, Conn. 1950, D.C. 1954. Asso. Breed, Abbott & Morgan, N.Y.C., 1946-48; legal dept. ABC, N.Y.C., 1948-50; partner Chapman, Bryson, Walsh & O'Connell, N.Y.C. and Washington, 1950-54; spl. asst. to undersec. Dept. State, Washington, 1954; asst. sec. Air Force, 1954-59; dir. internat. fellows program Columbia U., 1959-75, coordinator internat. studies, 1960-75, asso. dean sch. internat. affairs, 1960-74; cons. AEC, 1959-60; partner Baker & McKenzie (and predecessor), N.Y.C. and Washington, until 1960-75, Martin & Smith (and predecessors), Washington, 1975-76, 77—; ambassador to Sweden 1976-77; dir. United Services Life Ins. Corp., Internat. Bank, United Interests Corp., IB Fin. Corp., USLICO Corp., Liberian Services, Inc.; mem. Council Fgn. Relations; dir. Fgn. Policy Assn.; mem. adv. council Sch. Advanced Internat. Studies, Johns Hopkins U., 1962—; pres., dir. Center for Inter-Am. Relations, N.Y.C, 1969-74. Adv. and contbg. editor: Jour. Internat. Affairs, 1960-74; editor: The Next Asia, 1969, Prospects for Latin America, 1970, Concerns in World Affairs, 1973, From War to Peace, 1974. Bd. dirs. Boys' Clubs Am., N.Y.C.; chmn. bd. advisers Nat. Trust Historic Preservation, 1963-70; bd. dirs., sec. Nat. Multiple Sclerosis Soc., 1965-70; alumni council Dartmouth Coll.; mem. adv. com. Nat. Cultural Center, Washington, 1959-62; chmn. bd. George Olmsted Found.; bd. dirs. Fedn. Protestant Welfare Agys., Inc. Served as lt. USNR, 1942-54; PTO; col. USAFR, 1955-75. Decorated Purple Heart. Mem. Am. Soc. Internat. Law, Internat., Am. fgn. law assns., ABA, N.Y. State Bar Assn., Conn. Bar Assn., Fed. Bar Assn. (v.p. for N.Y., N.J., Conn.), Pilgrims of U.S., France-Am. Soc., English-Speaking Union, Asia Soc., Hudson Inst., Washington Inst. Fgn. Affairs, Council Am. Ambassadors (dir., sec.), Phi Beta Kappa., Soc. Mayflower Descs., Soc. of Cin. Clubs: Brook (N.Y.C.); Metropolitan (Washington); Chevy Chase; Bathing Corp. of Southampton (Southampton, N.Y.), Meadow (Southampton, N.Y.). Home: 3029 Woodland Dr NW Washington DC 20008

SMITH, DONALD ALAN, advertising executive; b. Newark, Ohio, Dec. 4, 1934; s. Brooks and Ella (Jaeger) S.; B.F.A., U. Ga., 1956; children—Kirk Martin, Angela. Div. designer Dairypak, Athens, Ga., 1957—; pres. The Adsmith, Athens, 1960—; design cons. Athens Daily News, Athens Banner Herald, 1965-78, Athens Observer, 1979, Ga. Outdoor Advt., 1963-83, Athens Tempo mag., 1979; art dir. Athens mag., 1968-73. Exhibited artist including Rock and Roll '85, Flowers, Athens Portraits '86, Good Ole Boys and Good Ole Places, others. Served with U.S. Army, 1957-58. One man shows Rock, Roll n' Remember, 1985, Comediens, 1986, Flowers, 1986, Wildlife, 1986, Landscape, 1986, Portrait, 1986, Authors, 1987, Good Ole Boys, 1987, Georgia Landscape, 1987, Roots of Rock, 1987, 88. Recipient Design award Internat. Paper Co., 1970; 1st place awards Inst. Outdoor Advt., 1970; awards of excellence Deep South Advt. Show, 1971, 72; Gold Medal award Ga./Ala. Newspaper Advt. Execs. Assn., 1971; awards of excellence So. Creativity Show, 1972, 73, 79, merit awards, 1980, gold award, 1981, 3 merit awards, 1981; award Ga. Press Assn., 1975, Best of Show award, 1981; 1st place award So. Classified Advt. Mgrs., 1978; Outstanding Service award Ga. div. Am. Cancer Soc., 1980; Ga. Press award, 1981; 2d pl. Addy award, 1982; Archie awards, 1983, 84, 85, 86, 87, 88; Best of Print award Ga. Banking Assn., 1988; Am. Advt. Silver Medal award, 1983; citation Ga. Ho. of Reps., 1983, also others. Mem. Am. Advt. Fedn., Athens Ad Club (pres. 1983-84), Atlanta Advt. Club (Phoenix awards 1970, 74), Athens Area C. of C. (pub. relations chmn. 1965-70, Outstanding Service award 1965-66, ambassador of yr. 1983-84, community service award in arts 1986), Phi Beta Kappa, Phi Kappa Phi. Presbyterian. Home: 4 Tangelwood Ct Athens GA 30606

SMITH, DONALD EUGENE, aerospace engineer, consultant; b. Arcadia, Ohio, Sept. 18, 1934; s. Clyde Verlin and Evangeline (Smith) S.; m. Ieada Maggard, July 28, 1956; children—Margaret, Michael, Mark. B.S. in Phys. Sci., Ohio State U., 1959; M.S. in System Mgmt., George Washington U., 1973. Head dept., electronics engr. Columbus Tech. Inst., Ohio, 1964-66; sr. engr. tracking systems Bendix Field Engring. Corp., Columbia, Md., 1967-68, supr. tracking engr., 1968-71, mgr. engring., 1971-77, gen. mgr. network support, 1977-81, v.p. space ops., 1981-85, v.p. space transp. systems ops.,

1985-87, gen. mgr., 1987—. Served with U.S. Army, 1953-55. Mem. AIAA, U.S. Space Found., Nat. Space Club, Am. Astron. Soc. Current work: Reviewing management systems (including use of expert systems) to increase productivity in labor intensive areas of space tracking and data handling, managing efforts of operations personnel to return the U.S. Space Shuttle to flying status. Home: 15915 Laurelfield Houston TX 77059 Office: Bendix Space Transp Ops 600 Gemini Ave Houston TX 77058

SMITH, DONNA LILIAN, seminar executive; b. Phila., Oct. 8, 1944; d. Joseph Patrick and Mary Elizabeth (Veronica) Burke; student Calif. State U., Northridge, 1962-64; Assoc. degree, Fashion Inst. Calif., 1969. Cert. meeting profl. Fashion coordinator, 1963-68; dir. Fashion Mdsg. Inst., 1968-69; v.p. Fashion Inst. Design and Mdsg., 1969-78; pres., owner Seminars Internat., Los Angeles, 1979—; mem. adv. bd. Meeting West; producer fashion shows, cons. in field; mem. costume council Los Angeles County Mus. Art. Mem. Costume Soc. Am., Meeting Planners Internat., Los Angeles Conv. and Visitors Bur., U.S. C. of C. Fashion Group, Meeting Cons. Networks, Am. Soc. Travel Agts. (hon.). Roman Catholic. Office: 15910 Ventura Blvd Suite 1207 Encino CA 91436

SMITH, DRAYTON BEECHER, II, lawyer; b. Memphis, Apr. 15, 1949; s. Drayton Beecher and Margaret (Williams) S.; m. Ann Wallace Dewey, Aug. 25, 1973; children—Ann Margaret Wallace, Stephanie Dewey. B.A., Millsaps Coll., 1971; J.D., U. Tenn., 1974. Bar: Tenn. 1974, U.S. Tax Ct. 1975, U.S. Dist. Ct. (we. dist.) Tenn. 1979. Assoc. Montedonico, Heiskell & Davis, Memphis, 1974-77; sr. assoc. tax dept. Glankler, Brown, Gilliland & Chase, Memphis, 1977-82; sr. ptnr. tax dept. Beaty & Smith, Memphis, 1982—; gen. counsel Elvis Presley Enterprises, Inc., Memphis, 1980—; pres. D. Beecher Smith II, P.C., Memphis, 1982—; gen. counsel K-Sun Co., Memphis, 1984—. Pres. Episcopal Young Churchmen, Calvary Ch., Memphis, 1966-67, Youth Guidance Commn., Memphis, 1967; mem. estate planning council, Millsaps Coll., Jackson, Miss., 1986. Recipient cert. of appreciation, City of Memphis, 1982. Mem. ABA (taxation sect. 1974—), Tenn. Bar Assn. (com. on profl. responsibility), Memphis-Shelby County Bar Assn. (chmn. cts. com.), Kappa Sigma (alumnus adviser Rhodes Coll.; Man of Yr. award Alumni Assn. 1982, Outstanding 1st Yr. Vol. award 1983, cert. of appreciation 1983). Republican. Episcopalian. Club: University (Memphis). Home: 237 Windover Rd Memphis TN 38111 Office: Beaty & Smith 44 N 2d St Memphis TN 38103

SMITH, DWIGHT MORRELL, university chancellor, chemist; b. Hudson, N.Y., Oct. 10, 1931; s. Elliott Monroe and Edith Helen (Hall) S.; m. Alice Beverly Bond, Aug. 27, 1955; children—Karen Elizabeth, Susan Allison, Jonathan Aaron. B.A., Central Coll., Pella, Iowa, 1953; Ph.D., Pa. State U., 1957; ScD (hon.), Cen. Coll., 1986. Postdoctoral fellow, instr. Calif. Inst. Tech., 1957-59; sr. chemist Texaco Research Center, Beacon, N.Y., 1959-61; asst. prof. chemistry Wesleyan U., Middletown, Conn., 1961-66; asso. prof. Hope Coll., Holland, Mich., 1966-69; prof. Hope Coll., 1969-72; prof., chmn. dept. chemistry U. Denver, 1972-83, vice chancellor for acad. affairs, 1983-84, chancellor, 1984—. Editor Revs. on Petroleum Chemistry, 1975-78; contbr. articles to profl. jours. Chmn. Chs. United for Social Action, Holland, Mich., 1968-69; mem. Sch. Bd. Adv. Com., Holland, 1969-70; bd. commrs. Colo. Advanced Tech. Inst., 1984—; mem. adv. bd. United Way, Girl Scouts U.S., Freedoms Found. at Valley Forge, Inst. Internat. Edn., Jr. Achievement. DuPont fellow, 1956-57; NSF fellow Scripps Inst., 1971-72; recipient grants Research Corp., grants Petroleum Research Fund, grants NSF, grants Solar Energy Research Inst.; Mem. ch. bds. or consistories Reformed Ch. Am., N.Y., Conn., Mich. Mem. Am. Chem. Soc. (chmn. Colo. 1976, sec. Western Mich. 1970-71, Colo. sect. award 1986), AAAS, Catalysis Soc., Soc. Applied Spectroscopy, Sigma Xi. Clubs: Denver; University (N.Y.); Metropolitan. Home: 7 Sunset Ln Littleton CO 80121 Office: Office of Chancellor Univ Denver 2301 S Gaylord St Denver CO 80208

SMITH, EDWIN LEON, retired credit manager; b. Burlington, Iowa, Mar. 17, 1924; s. Paul Smith and Gertrude Eldora (Hollenback) Rhoades; m. Norma Geraldine McGaffee, July 14, 1943; 1 child, Bradley Warren. BSBA, U. Redlands, 1980. Credit mgr. Reynolds Metals, Los Angeles, 1956-63, Hoffman Electronics, El Monte, Calif., 1965-70, Thomson-C.S.F. Components Corp., Woodland Hills, Calif., 1973-86. Pres. Woodland Townehome Owners' Assn., 1975, 85-86; landscape chmn. Dove Creek Condominium Assn. Served with USNR, 1942-45, PTO. Fellow Nat. Inst. Credit; mem. Soc. Profl. Credit Mgrs., Woodland Hills C. of C. Republican. Presbyterian. Home: 6225 104 Shoup Ave Woodland Hills CA 91367

SMITH, ERIC PARKMAN, retired railroad executive; b. Cambridge, Mass., Mar. 23, 1910; s. B. Farnham and Helen T. (Blanchard) S.; A.B., Harvard U., 1932, M.B.A., 1934. Staff fed. coordinator transp., Washington, 1934; with traffic and operating depts. N.Y. New Haven & Hartford R.R., Boston and New Haven, Conn., 1934-53; with Maine Central R.R., Portland, 1953-82, sec. adv. bd. retirement trust plan, 1958-82, asst. treas., dir. cost analysis, 1970-82. Trustee parish donations 1st Parish in Concord, Unitarian-Universalist Ch., 1960—. Mem. New Eng. R.R. Club (pres. 1973-74), Louisa May Alcott Meml. Assn. (dir. 1984—, treas. 1987—), The Thoreau Soc. (dir. 1987—, treas. 1987—). Author: Verses on an Icelandic Vacation, 1965; contbr. The Meeting House on the Green, 1985. Home and Office: 35 Academy Ln Concord MA 01742-2431

SMITH, EVANGELINE CHRISMAN DAVEY (MRS. ALEXANDER MUNRO SMITH), civic worker; b. Kent, Ohio, May 30, 1911; d. Martin Luther and Berenice Murl (Chrisman) Davey; A.B. (Scholar), Wellesley Coll., 1933; postgrad. Akron U., 1933-34; m. Alexander Munro Smith, Oct. 5, 1935; children—Berenice Jessie Smith Hardy, Diantha Barret Smith Harris, Letitia Amy Smith Manley. Sec., Davey Tree Expert Co., Kent, 1934, dir., 1962-73, mem. dirs. adv. com., 1973-76; dir. Davey Investment Co., Kent, 1982-84; trustee Davey Investment Trust, 1984—. Trustee, Kent Free Library, 1957-77, pres., 1961-63; trustee Patton House, 1966-68, 79-81, historian, 1981—; mem. women's assn. Robinson Meml. Hosp., 1947—, mem. women's assn. governing bd., 1947-68; co-founder Kent council Girl Scouts U.S.A., sec., 1941-45; mem. Kent State U. Pres.'s Club, 1976—, Kent State U. Chestnut Soc., 1977—. Mem. Am. Legion Aux., D.A.R. (chpt. regent, 1966-68, registrar, 1973—), Daus. Am. Colonists (regent 1978-80, registrar 1980—), Colonial Dames XVII Century (chair nat. def.), Kappa Kappa Gamma, Phi Sigma Soc. Mem. United Church of Christ. Clubs: Akron Area Wellesley, Akron Woman's City. Home: 260 Whittier Ave Kent OH 44240

SMITH, G. E. KIDDER, architect, author; b. Birmingham, Ala., Oct. 1, 1913; s. F. Hopkinson and Annie (Kidder) S.; m. Dorothea Fales Wilder, Aug. 22, 1942; children: G.E. Kidder, Hopkinson Kidder. A.B., Princeton U., 1935, M.F.A., 1938; student, Ecole Americaine, Fontainbleau, France, 1935. Registered architect, N.Y., Ala., N.C. Architect Princeton Expdn. to, Antioch, Syria, 1938; designer, site planner, camoufleur with Caribbean Architect-Engr. on Army bases, Caribbean, 1940-42; own archtl. practice 1946—; lectr. numerous European archtl. socs., also many Am. univs. and museums; archtl. critic Yale U., 1948-49; vis. prof. MIT, 1955-56. Author: (with P.L. Goodwin) Brazil Builds, 1943, Switzerland Builds, 1950, Italy Builds, 1955, Sweden Builds, 1950, rev. edit., 1957, The New Architecture of Europe, 1961, The New Churches of Europe, 1963, A Pictorial History of Architecture in America, 1976, The Architecture of the United States, 3 vols, 1981; also contbr. articles to encys.; exhibits, Stockholm Builds, 1940, Brazil Builds, 1943; installed: Power in the Pacific, USN, 1945 (all at Museum Modern Art, N.Y.C); New Churches of Germany, Goethe House, N.Y.C., and Am. Fedn. Arts, 1957-58, Masterpieces of European Posters (donated), Va. State Mus., Richmond, 1958; Work of Alvar Aalto, Smithsonian Instn., 1965—, Am.'s Archtl. Heritage for, Smithsonian Instn., 1976, Smithsonian, 1976, photographs in collection, Mus. Modern Art, Met. Mus., N.Y.C. Served to lt. USNR, 1942-46. Recipient Butler prize Princeton, 1938; fellow Am. Scandinavian Found., 1939-40; Guggenheim Found. fellow, 1946-47; President's fellow Brown U., 1949-50; research Fulbright fellow Italy, 1950-51; research Fulbright fellow India, 1965-66; Samuel H. Kress grantee India, 1967; Brunner scholar, 1959-60; Graham Found. for Advanced Study in Arts-Nat. Endowment on Arts joint fellowship, 1967-69; Nat. Endowment Arts fellow, 1974-75; Ford Found. grantee, 1970-71, 75-76; decorated Order So. Cross Brazil; Premio ENIT gold medal Italy; recipient gold medal (archtl. photography) AIA, 1964; E.M. Conover award, 1965; subject of public TV spl., 1976. Fellow AIA, Internat. Inst. Arts and Letters (life; Switzerland); mem. Soc. Archtl. Historians, Assn. Collegiate Schs. of Architecture, Municipal Art Soc. N.Y.C., Coll. Art Assn. Episcopalian. Clubs: Century Assn. (N.Y.C.), Princeton (N.Y.C.), Badminton (N.Y.C.); Cooperstown Country. Address: 163 E 81st St New York NY 10028

SMITH, GEORGE SEVERN, lawyer; b. Van Wert, Ohio, Jan. 31, 1901; s. Harvey C. and Nella (Severn) S.; LL.B., Nat. U., 1928; m. Thelma Gertrude Horst, Jan. 12, 1935; 1 son, George Severn. Admitted to D.C. bar, 1931; chief license div. Fed. Radio Commn., 1929-32; asso. with Paul M. Segal, 1932-41; partner firm Segal, Smith & Hennessey, Washington, 1942-57. Smith, Hennessey & McDonald, Washington, 1958-62; legal adv. to commr. FCC, Washington, 1962-66, chief Broadcast Bur., 1967-71; del. Fed. Communications Bar Assn. to ho. of dels. Am. Bar Assn., 1958-59. Served as pvt. Med. Dept., U.S. Army, 1918-19. Mem. Am. Bar Assn., Fed. Communications Bar Assn. (Washington pres. 1957), Bar Assn. D.C. Republican. Methodist. Home: 5402 E Windsor Ave Apt 53 Phoenix AZ 85008

SMITH, GORDON PAUL, management consulting executive; b. Salem, Mass., Dec. 25, 1916; s. Gordon and May (Vaughan) S.; m. Ramona Chamberlain, Sept. 27, 1969; children: Randall B., Roderick F. B.S. in Econs, U. Mass., 1947; M.S. in Govt. Mgmt, U. Denver (Sloan fellow), 1948; postgrad. in polit. sci, NYU, 1948-50. Economist Tax Found., Inc., N.Y.C., 1948-50; with Booz, Allen & Hamilton, 1951-70; partner Booz, Allen & Hamilton, San Francisco, 1959-62, v.p., 1962-67, mng. pntr. Western U.S., 1967-69; partner Harrod, Williams and Smith (real estate devel.), San Francisco, 1962-69; state dir. fin. State of Calif., 1967-68; pres. Gordon Paul Smith & Co., Mgmt. Cons., 1968—; pres., chief exec. officer Golconda Corp., 1972-74, chmn. bd., 1974-85; pres. Cermetek Corp., 1978-80; bd. dirs., exec. com. First Calif. Co., 1970-72, Grenam Corp., 1976-85; bd. dirs. Madison Venture Capital Corp.; adviser task force def. procurement and contracting Hoover Commn., 1954-55; spl. asst. to pres. Republic Aviation Corp., 1954-55; cons., Hawaii, 1960-61, Alaska, 1963; cons. Wash. Hwy. Adminstrn., 1964, also 10 states and fed. agys., 1951-70, Am. Baseball League and Calif. Angels, 1960-62. Author articles on govt., econs. and edn. Mem. Calif. Select Com. on Master Plan for Edn., 1971-73; mem. alumni council U. Mass., 1950-54, bd. dirs. alumni assn., 1964-70; bd. dirs. Alumni Assn. Mt. Hermon Prep. Sch., 1963; bd. dirs. Palo Alto Stanford Med. Ctr., 1960-62, pres., chmn., 1962-66; chmn. West Coast Cancer Found., 1976-87 ; trustee, chmn. Monterey Inst. Internat. Studies, 1978—; trustee Northfield Mt. Hermon Sch., 1983—; mem. devel. council Community Hosp. of Monterey Peninsula, 1983—; bd. dirs. Friends of the Performing Arts, vice chmn., 1985—. Served to 1st lt., cav. AUS, 1943-46, ETO. Recipient spl. commendation Hoover Commn., 1955; Alumni of Year award U. Mass., 1963. Mem. Monterey History and Art Assn. (bd. dirs., vice chmn. 1985-87, chmn. 1987—), Calif. C. of C., Govtl. Research Assn., Am. Indsl. Devel. Council, San Francisco Mus. Art. Clubs: Carmel Valley (Calif.) Country; Monterey Peninsula Country. Home: 253 Del Mesa Carmel CA 93921

SMITH, HAMILTON OTHANEL, molecular biologist, educator; b. N.Y.C., Aug. 23, 1931; s. Bunnie Othanel and Tommie Harkey S.; m. Elizabeth Anne Bolton, May 25, 1957; children: Joel, Barry, Dirk, Bryan, Kirsten. Student, U. Ill., 1948-50; A.B. in Math, U. Calif., Berkeley, 1952; M.D., Johns Hopkins U., 1956. Intern Barnes Hosp., St. Louis, 1956-57; resident in medicine Henry Ford Hosp., Detroit, 1959-62; USPHS fellow dept. human genetics U. Mich., Ann Arbor, 1962-64; research asso. U. Mich., 1964-67; asst. prof. molecular biology and genetics Johns Hopkins U. Sch. Medicine, Balt., 1967-69; asso. prof. Johns Hopkins U. Sch. Medicine, 1969-73, prof., 1973—; asso. Institut für Molekularbiologie der U. Zurich, Switzerland, 1975-76. Contbr. articles to profl. jours. Served to lt. M.C. USNR, 1957-59. Recipient Nobel Prize in medicine, 1978; Guggenheim fellow, 1975-76. Mem. Am. Soc. Microbiology, AAAS, Am. Soc. Biol. Chemists, Nat. Acad. Sci. Office: Johns Hopkins U Sch Medicine Dept Microbiology 725 N Wolfe St Baltimore MD 21205

SMITH, HAROLD CHARLES, private pension fund executive; b. N.Y.C., Jan. 11, 1934; s. Harold Elmore and Hedwig Agnes (Gronke) S.; BA cum laude with honors, Ursinus Coll., 1955; MBA, NYU, 1958; M in Div., Union Theol. Sem., N.Y.C., 1958. Vice pres. YMCA Retirement Fund, Inc., N.Y.C., 1958-69, portfolio mgr., 1960—, assoc. sec., 1969-77, v.p., 1977-80, exec. v.p., 1980-82, pres. elect, 1982-83, pres., 1983—; assoc. prof. bus. and fin. L.I. U., 1969-71; trustee Bank Mart, Bridgeport, Conn.; bd. dirs. Mut. Ins. Co. Trustee YMCA Greater Bridgeport, 1975-79, Pension Funds United Ch. of Christ, 1968—, Springfield Coll. (Mass.), 1983—; bd. dirs. YMCA Greater N.Y., 1983—, Y Mut. Ins. Co., 1987—. Cert. fin. analyst. Mem. N.Y. Soc. Security Analysts, Am. Econs. Assn., Fin. Analysts Fedn. United Ch. of Christ. Clubs: Merchant's, Masons, Order Eastern Star. Author: Getting it All Together for Retirement, 1977. Home: 111 Ferry Ct S Stratford CT 06497 Office: 225 Broadway New York NY 10007

SMITH, HELEN CATHARINE, author; b. Chgo., June 7, 1903; d. J. A.; B.A., U. Calif. at Los Angeles, 1926; postgrad. U. Wis., 1954 56; M.So., Christian Coll., 1962, Ph.D., 1965, Psy.D., 1966; Ph.D. (hon.) Free U., hon. doctorate Gt. China Arts Coll., 1969, St. Olav's Acad., Sweden, 1969, Internat. Acad. Sovereign Order Alfred Gt., Eng., 1969; J.D., Ohio Christian Coll., 1969; Ph.D., U. Reno (Nigeria), 1975; m. H. C. Smith, June 7, 1932 (dec. 1972); children—Glen Dean, DeEtta Ellen (Mrs. Gerald L. Amdahl), George Dale. Tchr. 2d grade Maple Lawn Sch., Clinton, Wis.; legal sec., Janesville, Wis., Office of City Atty., Evansville, Wis., 1933—; v.p., dir. Blue Moon poetry mag., 1952-57. Recipient 1st pl. award for article Herdman Meml. Competition Brit. Press, 1957; John Francis Sims Meml. award for poetry, 1955; award of honor UN Day, Philippines, 1967; laurel wreath, gold medal Pres. Philippines, 1967; certificate recognition Nat. Poetry Day Com., 1972; Distinguished Service award Wis. Jaycees, 1975, certificate Am. Bicentennial Research Inst., 1975, Hall of Honor award U. Wis., 1988; named Hon. Poet Laureate (Am.-Visayan), 1967; Internat. Woman of 1975 with laureate honors by Imelda R. Marcos; inducted into Wis. Rock County Cultural Ctr. Hall of Honor, 1988. Fellow Intercontinental Biog. Assn.; mem. AAUW (awards poetry, short stories 1972), Wis. Regional Writers Assn. (sec. 1949-55, 61—, hon. life dir., leadership citation 1956, Jade Ring winner for short story 1957), Nat. League Am. Pen Women, Am. Poetry League, Wis. Fellowship Poets, Wis. Acad. Scis. Arts and Letters, Brit. Press Assn., United Poets Laureate Internat. (Karta award), Wis. Council for Writers (life, 2d pl. award for short story 1980), Centro Studie Scambi Internazionali Roma (medal of honor 1966-67, internat. exec. bd.), Wis. Edn. Assn., Wis. Regional Artists, State Hist. Soc. Wis., Accademia Internazionale Leonardo Da Vinci (Rome; Gold medallion 1972), Accademia Internazionale Di Pontzen, Am. Lit. Assn. (life), World Poetry Soc. (hon. life), UN Assn., Phi Beta Kappa (sustaining), Alpha Psi Omega, Sigma Iota XI. Author: Laughing Child, books I, II, III, 1945, 46, 47; Off the Record, 1949; From the Countryside, 1952; Stars in My Eyes, 1954; Wind-Falls, 1955; Chiaroscura, 1964; But Not Yet, 1973; You Can't Cry All the Time, 1975. Editor: Evansville Anthology of Verse, 1952, No. Spring, anthology, 1956; Chiaroscura, 1964; Helen's Sketch Book, 1978; contbr. articles, stories to numerous mags., newspapers, anthologies. Home: 455 S 1st St Apt 19 Evansville WI 53536

SMITH, HUESTON MERRIAM, engineer, consultant; b. Almeta, Tex., Dec. 19, 1912; s. Harry Merriam and Ruth Alice (Vansconcellos) S.; m. Edith Adele Fort, Dec. 12, 1970; 1 child, Joseph Hueston. BSEE, U. Mo., Rolla, 1938; profl. degree of electrical engring., U. Mo., 1982. Registered profl. engr. Mo., Tex., Kans., Ark. Asst. engr. Mo. Pub. Service Commn., Jefferson City, 1938-40; indsl. engr. Union Electric Co., St. Louis, 1947-50; chief engr. Fruin-Colnon Co., St. Louis, 1950-54; pres. Smith-Zurhelde & Assocs. Inc., St. Louis, 1954-65; sr. v.p. Thatcher & Patient Inc., St. Louis, 1965-69; prin. Hueston M. Smith & Assocs. Inc., St. Louis, 1969—. Mem. editorial adv. bd. Cons. Engr. mag., 1958-77, Bldg. Constrn. mag., 1960-74. City engr. Frontenac, Mo., 1957-59; chief of police City of Fontenac, 1952-54. Served to col. C.E. U.S. Army, 1940-46. Decorated Bronze Star. Mem. Cons. Engrs. Council U.S. (pres. 1960-61, bd. dirs. 1963-64), Cons. Engrs. Mo. (pres. 1965-67, bd. dirs. 1962-63), Mo. Soc. Profl. Engrs. (Outstanding Achievement award 1962), Soc. Am. Mil. Engrs., Res. Officers Assn. U.S., Ret. Officers Assn., Mil. Order of World Wars, Mo. Real Estate Assn., Nat. Rifle Assn., U. Mo.-Rolla Alumni Assn., Acad. Elec. Engrs. of U. Mo.-Rolla, Eta Kappa Nu. Club: Mo. Athletic. Lodge: Masons. Home: 711 E Monroe Ave Saint Louis MO 63122 Office: PO Box 9655 Saint Louis MO 63122

SMITH, JACK CARL, publisher; b. Cleve., Sept. 11, 1928; s. John Carl and Florence Agnes (O'Rourke) S.; m. Nannette June Boyd, Dec. 1, 1962; 1 dau., Colleen Wentworth. Student, Baldwin Wallace Coll., 1948-51, postgrad., 1958; B.A., Ohio U., 1954. Rep. Flying Tiger Line, Inc., Los Angeles, 1958-61; prin. Pub. Rep. bus., Cleve., 1961-64; pub. Penton Pub., Cleve., 1964—; dir. Central Cleve. Corp., Nat. Distbn. Terminals. Served with USAF, 1954-58. Mem. Am. Mgmt. Assn., Material Handling Inst., Am. Trucking Assn., Nat. Council Phys. Distbn. Mgmt., Family Motor Coach Assn., Recreation Vehicle Industry Assn., Am. Bus. Press, Mag. Pubs. Assn., Sci. Research Soc., Internat. Platform Assn., Sigma Xi, Sigma Chi. Club: Wings (N.Y.C.). Home: 457 Devonshire Ct Bay Village OH 44140 Office: Penton Pub Penton Plaza Cleveland OH 44114

SMITH, JAMES FINLEY, economist; b. Dallas, Nov. 4, 1938; s. Emerson Russell and Achsah Elizabeth (Foster) S.; m. Susan Schreiber, Aug. 18, 1962; children: Carter Emerson, Jamie, Curtis Noel, Marshall Edward. B.A., So. Meth. U., 1961, M.A., 1964, Ph.D., 1971. Math. analyst Sears, Roebuck & Co., Oak Brook, Ill., 1965-68; adminstrv. asst. to v.p. and treas. Sears, Roebuck & Co., Chgo., 1968-69, dir. econometric research, 1969-75; sr. economist Bd. Govs. FRS, Washington, 1975-77; dir. credit research Sears, Roebuck & Co., Chgo., 1977-80; chief economist Union Carbide Corp., Danbury, Conn., 1980-85; v.p. Wharton Econometric Forecasting Assocs., Phila., 1986; dir., chief economist Bur. Bus. Research U. Tex., Austin, 1987-88; prof. of fin. U. North Carolina, Chapel Hill, 1988—; pres. Nat. Bus. Econ. Issues Council, N.Y.C., 1981-83; cons. Pres.'s Council of Econ. Advisers, Washington, 1978-83; mem. econ. adv. bd. U.S. Dept. Commerce, 1977-80, 83—. Author: (with others) Economic Growth and Investment in Higher Education, 1987, The Chemical Industry in America, 1988, The New Texas Economy, 1988; contbr. articles to profl. jours. Served to lt. U.S. Army, 1961-62. NDEA fellow, 1962-65. Fellow Nat. Assn. Bus. Economists (v.p. 1988-89, dir. 1980-84, 1985-88); mem. Nat. Economists Club (bd. govs. 1984-87), Am. Econ. Assn., Economists Group Fed. Republic Germany, Soc. Bus. Economists (U.K.). Mem. United Ch. of Christ. Home: 3503 Pinnacle Dr Austin TX 78746 Office: PO Box 7459 Austin TX 78713

SMITH, JAMES GILBERT, electrical engineer; b. Benton, Ill., May 1, 1930; s. Jesse and Ruby Frances S.; m. Barbara Ann Smothers, July 29, 1955; 1 child, Julie. B.S. in Elec. Engring, U. Mo., Rolla, 1957, M.S., 1959, Ph.D., 1967. Instr., then asst. prof. U. Mo., Rolla, 1958-66; mem. faculty So. Ill. U., Carbondale, 1966—; prof. elec. engring. So. Ill. U., 1972—, chmn. dept. elec. scis. and systems engring., 1971-80. Served with AUS, 1951-53, Korea. Decorated Bronze Star. Mem. IEEE, Am. Soc. Engring. Edn., AAAS. Club: Rotary. Office: Coll Engring So Ill Univ Carbondale IL 62901

SMITH, JAMES HOWARD, accountant; b. Charleston, W.Va., Feb. 11, 1947; s. James Carlisle and Charlene Louise (Jones) S.; m. Kimberley Ann Johnson-Smith, Jan. 1, 1977; children: James Lloyd Woodward, Stephen Adam Carlisle. Student, Duke U., 1965-67, U. Tenn.-Nashville, summers 1970-72; BS, Belmont Coll., 1973; MBA, So. Ill. U., 1979. CPA, Tenn., D.C. Adminstr. Williams, Shields & Wildman, Attys., Nashville, 1973-75; tax law specialist IRS, Washington, 1975-77; supr. Ernst & Whinney, Washington, 1977-79; ptnr.-in-charge tax and fin. services Utility Group, Washington, 1979—. Speaker in field. Author: Federal Income Taxation of Rural Electric Cooperatives, 1982, Depreciation, Salvage, and Cost of Removal: A Critical Analysis, 1982. Treas. Waverly Hills Homeowners Assn., Arlington, Va., 1983, spokesman before county bd., 1983; treas. Animal Welfare League of Arlington (Va.), 1975-83, Animal Welfare Found. Arlington, 1983; v.p. Adam Walsh Child Resource Ctr. Greater Washington; bd. dirs. Missing Children of Greater Washington, 1985-88. Served with USN, 1967-70. Decorated Bronze Star medal with cluster, Purple Heart; recipient Spl. Achievement award U.S. Dept. Treasury, 1977. Fellow D.C. Inst. CPA's; mem. Am. Inst. CPA's, Tenn. Soc. CPA's, Nat. Assn. Accts. for Coops., Nat. Acctg. Assn., Duke U. Alumni Assn., So. Ill. U. Alumni Assn. Office: Ernst & Whinney Utility Group 1225 Connecticut Ave NW Washington DC 20036

SMITH, JEFFREY MICHAEL, lawyer; b. Mpls., July 9, 1947; s. Philip and Gertrude E. (Miller) S.; 1 son, Brandon Michael. BA summa cum laude, U. Minn., 1970; student U. Malaya, 1967-68; JD magna cum laude, U. Minn., 1973. Bar: Ga. 1973. Assoc. Powell, Goldstein, Frazier & Murphy, 1973-76; ptnr. Rogers & Hardin, 1976-79; ptnr. Bondurant, Stephenson & Smith, Atlanta, 1979-85, Arnall, Golden & Gregory, Atlanta, 1985—; vis. lectr. Duke U., 1976-77, 79-80; adj. prof. Emory U.; lectr. Vanderbilt U., 1977-82. Bd. visitors U. Minn. Law Sch., 1976-82. Mem. ABA (vice chmn. com. profl. officers and dirs. liability law 1979-83, chmn. 1983-84, vice chmn. com. profl. liability 1980-82, mem. standing com. lawyer's profl. liability 1981-85, chmn. 1985-87), State Bar of Ga. (chmn. profl. liability and ins. com. 1978—, trustee Inst. of Continuing Legal Edn. in Ga. 1979-80), Order of Coif, Phi Beta Kappa. Home: 145 15th St Unit 811 Atlanta GA 30361 Office: Arnall Golden & Gregory 55 Park Pl Atlanta GA 30335

SMITH, JEFFRY ALAN, public health administrator, physician, consultant; b. Los Angeles, Dec. 8, 1943; s. Stanley W. and Marjorie E. S.; m. Jo Anne Hague. BA in Philosophy, UCLA, 1967, MPH, 1972; BA in Biology, Calif. State U., Northridge, 1971; MD, UACJ, 1977. Diplomate Am. Bd. Family Practice. Resident in family practice NIH, Bethesda, Md., WAH, Takoma Park, Md., Walter Reed Army Hosp., Washington, Children's Hosp. Nat. Med. Ctr., Washington; dir. occupational medicine and environ. health Pacific Missile Test Ctr., Point Mugu, Calif., 1982-84; dist. health officer State Hawaii Dept. Health, Kauai, 1984-86; asst. dir. health County of Riverside (Calif.) Dept. Health, 1986-87; regional med. dir. Calif. Forensic Med. Group, Salines, Calif., 1987—. Fellow Am. Acad. Family Practice; mem. AMA, Am. Occupational Medicine Assn., Flying Physicians, Am. Pub. Health Assn. Home: 112 Seafoam Ave Monterey CA 93940 Office: PO Box 3274 Salinas CA 93912

SMITH, JEROME BURTON, entrepreneur; b. Chgo., May 4, 1930; s. Paul S. Smith and Della A. Smith Gross; B.S., Iowa State Coll., 1953; postgrad. Alexander Hamilton Bus. Inst., 1962; children—SaraLee Smith Broback, Bradley Lawrence. Pres., Arboreal Tree Service, Park Ridge, Ill., 1947-52; assoc. editor Am. Lumberman, Wood and Wood Products mags., Chgo., 1953-54; pub. relations rep. Weyerhaeuser Co., Tacoma, 1956-65; pres. Acad. Communicative Arts and Scis., Inc., Tacoma, 1962-69, Congress of Internat. Logging Championships, Inc., Tacoma, 1967-69; exec. v.p. Greenacres, Inc., Seattle, 1967-68; pres. Inversionismo S.A., Mexico City, 1973-78, Transworld Trade Tech., Inc., San Francisco, 1976—, High-Tech Homes, Inc., Los Altos, Calif., 1984—, Greenpages, Inc., Los Altos, 1985—; dir. Alpental Ski Inc., Snoqualmie, Wash., 1968-77; pres. Bahia Del Rincon, S.A. de C.V., Mexico City, 1967-78; mgr. Broadwalk Properties, Inc., Tacoma, 1968-77; owner Hyatt Hotel, Cabo San Lucas, Mex., 1973-78. Exec. mgr. United Citizens for Sound City Govt., Tacoma, 1958-64. Served to capt. USAF, 1955. Independent Republican. Presbyterian. Clubs: Tacoma Horse Polo, Mexico City Horse Polo; Woodbrook Hunt (dir.); Alpental Ski. Office: 177 Webster St Suite 248 Monterey CA 93940

SMITH, JODY BRANT, educator; b. Macon, Ga., May 7, 1943; s. Jody Bass and Gladys Irene (Patterson) S.; A.B., Mercer U., 1965; M.A., U. Miami, 1969, postgrad., 1970; m. Deborah Faye Everett, Aug. 20, 1971 (div. 1978); children—Heather Deborah, Jody Brant II; m. Germana D. Teixeira, Nov. 10, 1981. Asst. prof. philosophy and humanities Pensacola Jr. Coll., 1970-81, assoc. prof., 1981—; pres. Pyrrho Press, Inc., Gulf Breeze, Fla., 1974-77; pres. Image of Guadalupe Research Project, Inc., 1979-82; invited reader Indian Philos. Congress, New Delhi, 1975. Bd. dirs. Pensacola Right to Life, Inc., 1973-76, Fla. State Right to Life Com., Inc., 1974-75; provider written testimony U.S. Ho. of Reps. and U.S. Senate coms., 1975, 76, 83. Fla. Endowment for Humanities grantee, 1974; Nat. Endowment for Humanities summer fellowship, 1987. Fellow Am. Soc. Physical Research; mem. Cath. Philos. Assn., Physical Research Found., Beta Beta Beta. Coauthor: The Tilma—An Infrared Study, 1981; author: Guadalupan Studies, 1982; The Image of Guadalupe, 1983; The Guadalupe Madonna, 1983, rev. edit., 1985; contbr. articles to profl. jours. Home: 1503 E Lakeview Ave Pensacola FL 32503 Office: 1000 College Blvd Pensacola FL 32504

SMITH, JOHN KERWIN, lawyer; b. Oakland, Calif., Oct. 18, 1926; s. May Kerwin Smith; 1 dau., Cynthia. B.A., Stanford U.; LL.B., Hastings Coll. Law, San Francisco. Ptnr., Haley, Schenone, Birchfield & Smith, Hayward, Calif.; pres. Las Positas Land Co. Mem. Hayward Parks Commn., 1957, mem. city council, 1959-66, mayor, 1966-70; chmn. Alameda County Mayors Conf., 1968; chmn. revenue taxation com. League Calif. Cities, 1968; bd. dirs. Oakland-Alameda County Coliseum; pres. Hastings 1066 Found. Mem. ABA, Calif. Bar Assn., Alameda County Bar Assn., Am. Judicature Soc. Office: 1331 B St Hayward CA 94541

SMITH, JOHN WILLIAM, political scientist; b. Jamestown, N.D., Oct. 31, 1938; s. John William and Lena R. (Jordheim) S.; A.A., U. N.D., 1958; B.A., Northwestern U., 1960; M.A., U. Mich., 1963; m. Therese AL Hout, Nov. 22, 1980; children—Lena Jordan, Galen Dakota. Instr., U. Detroit, 1962-63, No. Mich. U., 1965-67; asst. prof. Indiana (Pa.) U., 1967-69; adj. prof. U. Detroit, 1970-82; vis. lectr. U. Mich., Dearborn, 1975—; instr. polit. sci. Henry Ford Community Coll., Dearborn, 1969—. Mem. Am. Polit. Sci. Assn., So. Polit. Sci. Assn., Western Polit. Sci. Assn., Assn. for Asian Studies, Mich. Conf. Polit. Sci. (pres. 1986-87). Contbr. chpts. to Riot in the Cities, 1970; City-Surburban Relations, 1979. Contbr. articles to profl. jours. Home: 21652 N Riverview Ct Birmingham MI 48010 Office: Henry Ford Community Coll Dearborn MI 48128

SMITH, JUSTINE TOWNSEND, recreational association executive; b. Evanston, Ill., June 28, 1936; d. William West and Justine Wilhelmina (Laituri) Townsend; m. Edward Charles Smith, Oct. 15, 1955 (div. 1983); 1 child, Leigh Ann. Student, Evanston Bus. Coll., 1954. Chief proofreader Melville series dept. English, 1965-70, asst. editor Library of Living Philosophers, Northwestern U., 1959-64; owner J.J. Creations, Buffalo Grove, Ill., 1972-79; ice skating profl. Northbrook Sports Complex, Ill., 1974, Watts Ice Rink, Glencoe, Ill., 1975; exec. dir. Ice Skating Inst. Am., Wilmette, Ill., 1981—; v.p. Women in Mgmt., Downers Grove, Ill., 1986. vice pres. Shelter Inc., Arlington Heights, Ill., 1980; active Jr. Achievement, Chgo., 1984. Mem. Am. Soc. Assn. Execs., Nat. Council Youth Sports Dirs. (pres.). Office: Ice Skating Inst Am 1000 Skokie Blvd Wilmette IL 60091

SMITH, KENNETH PATRICK, aeronautics company executive; b. Croydon, Surrey, Eng., June 7, 1940; s. Leslie Alan Williams and Patricia Smith; m. Hazel Howard-Dobbs, June 27, 1987; children: Mark Peter, Ian. Degree in mech. engring., RAF Halton, Buckinghamshire, Eng., 1960. Served with RAF, 1957-70; engring. officer RAF, Eng., 1957-70; engr. Fairey Aviation, Eng., 1970-73; sales mgr. Pall Corp., Portsmouth, Hants, Eng., 1973-76; comml. dir. A.P.M.E. Ltd. (subs. Pall Corp.), Portsmouth, Hants, Eng., 1976—; bus. cons., Chichester, West Sussex, 1980—. Fellow Inst. Dirs.; mem. Soc. Licensed Aeronautical Engrs. Mem. Conservative Party. Mem. Ch. of Eng. Club: Lions. Home: Compton House, Chestnut Walk, Tangmere, Chichester, West Sussex PO20 6HH, England

SMITH, KENNETH WYNDHAM, historian, educator, writer; b. Johannesburg, Republic South Africa, Sept. 11, 1939; s. George Alexander and Martha Alida (Standing) S.; m. Pamela Doris Maullin, July 14, 1962; children: Belinda, Hugh. BA, U. Witwatersrand, 1960; BA with honors, U. South Africa, 1963, MA, 1965; PhD, Rhodes U., 1975. Tchr. Hillview High Sch., Pretoria, Republic South Africa, 1961-63; personnel officer Ford Motor Co., Port Elizabeth, Republic South Africa, 1963-64; lectr. history U. North Sovenga, near Pietersburg, Republic South Africa, 1964-68; research fellow Inst. Social and Econ. Research Rhodes U., Grahamstown, Republic South Africa, 1969-71; lectr. U. South Africa, Pretoria, 1972—. Author: (history) The Campaigns Against the Bapedi of Sekhukune 1877-1879, 1967, From Frontier to Midlands: A History of the Graaff-Reinet District, 1786-1910, 1976; (novels under pseudonym Katherine Smith) Moonlight at Mopani, 1980; (under pseudonym Pamela Smith) The Search, 1981; (biography) Alfred Aylward: The Tireless Agitator, 1983; (novel) Tinde in the Mountains, 1986; (non-fiction) The Changing Past: Trends in South African Historical Writing, 1988; co-author: Africa North of the Limpopo, 1984. Home: 21 Pioneer Rd, Irene 1675, Republic of South Africa Office: U South Africa, Dept History, PO Box 392, Pretoria Republic of South Africa

SMITH, KENNITH LEO, artist, educator; b. Ralls, Tex., July 20, 1941; s. Leonard Henry and Christeene (Lowrance) S.; 1 dau., Stephanie. BS, Tex. Tech U., 1966, MS, 1971. Cert. tchr., Tex. One man shows: Lubbock Art Assn., 1979, Southwestern Med. Sch., 1982, Irving Art Assn., 1982, Artisans Gallery, Houston, 1982, Artisan's Studio, Dallas, 1983; group shows include: Am. Watercolor Soc., 1978, Lubbock Art Assn., 1978, Artist Workshop, Lubbock, 1979, Artisan's Studio, Dallas, 1980, 81, 82, 83, 84, 85, D'Art Dallas, 1983, 84, 85, Dallas Arts Dist., 1983; represented in permanent collections: Mus. of Tex. Tech U., Mus. of S.W., Sohio Oil Co., Furr's Inc., Tex. State Savs., Tex. Bank Dallas; head dept. art Mackenzie Jr. High Sch., Lubbock, 1966-70; head dept. art Dunbar-Struggs High Sch., Lubbock, 1970-80; owner Artisan's Studio, Dallas, 1980—; tchr. Brookhaven Coll., Dallas, 1981-82; drawing instr. Art Inst. Dallas, 1983—; curriculum developer State of Tex., 1975-80. Mem. Parks and Recreation Com., Lubbock, 1975-78. Recipient Best of Show award Tex. Tech. Mus., 1978; Merit award Tex. Fine Arts, 1983; Best of Show award Mus. Natural History Dallas, 1983, also Tex. Fine Arts Dallas region show, 1983; Grumbacher award, Bud Briggs award, Dick Blick-Northlight award Southwestern Watercolor Soc., 1985, High Winds medal Am. Watercolor Soc., 1986, La. Watercolor Internat. top award, 1986, Southwestern Watercolor Soc. top award and Grumbacher Gold Medal, 1986, Rocky Mountain Nat. Water Media, 1986—, others; named Knickerbocker Artist Am., Allied Artist Am. 73d annual, N.Y.C., 1st pl. artist and Craftsman of Dallas. Mem. Am. Watercolor Soc. (signature), West Tex. Watercolor Soc. (pres. 1978-79), Western Fedn. Watercolor Socs. (pres. 1979-80, merit award 1979), Tex. Watercolor Soc. (purchase award 1982), Southwestern Water Color Soc. (2d pl. SWS award, traveling exhibit), Western Fedn. Watercolor Socs. (Merit award 1987, 88), Am. Watercolor Soc. Methodist. Club: Tex. Fine Arts (dir. 1975-79). Author: Art Guide, 1977.

SMITH, LANI KAMIKI, musician, composer; b. Cin., June 9, 1934; s. Leonard Rice and Lillian Grace (Fittz) S.; m. Jama Dianne Dobberstein, Oct. 3, 1980. B.Mus., U. Cin., 1956, M.Mus., 1959. Served as organist and choir dir. for various chs., Ohio and Mich., 1954-81; music editor, composer, arranger Lorenz Pub. Co., Dayton, Ohio, 1967-82; freelance composer arranger 1000 works of sacred mus., numerous other pieces chamber ensemble, ballet, solo voice, orch., musicals, filmscores; part-time editor Lorenz Pub. Co., Calif., 1982—. Recipient Josef Bearns prize in composition, Columbia U., 1959. Grantee Rockefeller Found., 1967. Mem. Phi Mu Alpha, Pi Kappa Lambda. Home: 5460 White Oak Ave #E326 Encino CA 91316

SMITH, LAWRENCE G., bank executive; b. Washington, Mar. 20, 1938; s. George Joseph and Olive Ellen (Lawrence) S.; m. Myriam Bulhoes, Sept. 11, 1962 (div. 1977); children: Flavia, Erik; m. Marguerite Sinquefield Tarrant, Sept. 24, 1977. BA magna cum laude, Harvard U., 1959, MA, 1964, PhD, 1972. Sr. v.p. Citibank N.A., N.Y.C., 1964-84; various positions from exec. v.p. to pres., gen. mgr. Nat. Comml. Bank, N.Y.C., 1984—; bd. dirs. Langdon P. Cook, N.Y.C., Chgo. & Ill. Midland Rwy. Fulbright scholar, 1961. Office: Nat Comml Bank 245 Park Ave New York NY 10162

SMITH, MAGGIE, actress; b. Ilford, Eng., Dec. 28, 1934; d. Nathaniel and Margaret (Hutton) S.; m. Robert Stephens, 1967 (div. 1974); m. Beverley Cross, 1974. Ed., Oxford High Sch. Girls. dir. United British Artists, 1982—. Stage and film actress, 1952—; stage appearances include: New Face, N.Y.C., 1956, Share My Lettuce, 1957, The Stepmother, 1958, Rhinoceros, 1960, Strip The Willow, 1960, The Rehearsal, 1961, The Private Ear and The Public Eye, 1962, Mary, Mary, 1961; appearances at Old Vic, 1959-60, Nat. Theatre, London, 1963—; productions at Nat. Theatre include Private Lives, 1972, Othello, Hay Fever, Master Builder, Hedda Gabbler, Much Ado About Nothing, Miss Julie, Black Comedy, Stratford Festival, Ont., Can., 1976, 77, 78, 80, Antony and Cleopatra, Macbeth, Three Sisters, Richard III, Night and Day, London and N.Y.C., 1979-80; Virginia, London, 1981, Way of the World, Chichester Festival, London, 1984-85, Interpreters, London, 1985-86; films include: Othello, 1966, The Honey Pot, 1967, Oh What a Lovely War, 1968, Hot Millions, 1968, The Prime of Miss Jean Brodie, 1968 (Oscar award), Love and Pain and The Whole Damn Thing, 1971, Travels With My Aunt, 1972, Murder by Death, 1976, Death on the Nile, 1977, California Suite, 1978 (Oscar award), Quartet, 1978, Clash of the Titans, 1981, Evil under the Sun, 1981, The Missionary, 1982, A Private Function, 1984 (best actress award Brit. Acad. of Film & TV Arts, 1985), Lily in Love, 1985, A Room With a View, 1985, The Lonely Passion of Judith Hearne, 1987. Recipient Best Actress award Eve. Standard, 1962, 70, 82, 85; Best Film Actress award Soc. Filn and TV Arts U.K., 1968; Film Critics Guild, 1968; named Actress of Year, Variety Club, 1963, 72; Brit. Acad. Best Screen Actress, 1985; Taomina Gold award, 1985; decorated comdr. Brit. Empire. Office: care ICM Ltd, 388 Oxford St, London W1N 9HE, England also: care Fraser & Dunlop, 91 Regent St, London W1R 8RU, England *

SMITH, MARCIA JEAN, accountant, tax specialist, financial consultant; b. Kansas City, Mo., Oct. 19, 1947; d. Eugene Hubert and Marcella Juanita (Greene) S.; student U. Nebr., 1965-67; B.A. (Coll. Ednl. Opportunity grantee), Jersey City State Coll., 1971; M.B.A. in Taxation, Golden Gate U., 1976, postgrad., 1976-77; M.S. in Acctg., Pace U., 1982; Cert. of completion Cours Commerciaux de Geneve, 1985-86; Legal intern Port Authority N.Y., N.J., N.Y.C., 1972; legis. aide to Harrison A. Williams, U.S. Senator, Washington, 1973; tax accountant Bechtel Corp., San Francisco, 1974-77; sr. tax accountant Equitable Life Assurance Soc. U.S., N.Y.C., 1977; asst. sec. Equitable Life Holding Corp., N.Y.C., 1977-79, Equico Lessors, Inc., Mpls., 1978-79, Equitable Gen. Ins. Group, Ft. Worth, 1977-79, Heritage Life Assurance Co., Toronto, Ont., Can., 1978-79, Informatics, Inc., Los Angeles, 1978-79; sec. Equico Capital Corp., N.Y.C., 1977-79, Equico Personal Credit, Inc., Colorado Springs, Colo., 1978-79, Equico Securities, Inc., N.Y.C., 1977-79, Equitable Environ. Health, Inc., Woodbury, N.Y., 1977-79; tax sr. Arthur Andersen & Co., N.Y.C., 1979-82; pres. M.J. Smith Co., N.Y.C., 1983-85, prin. owner MJS Cons. Services Internat. Tax Cons., Boston, Mass., 1988—; cons. U.N., specialized agys., Geneva, 1985-87; tax cons.; real estate salesperson. Spl. advisor U.S. Congl. Adv. Bd.; human rights chmn. YWCA, Lincoln, Nebr., 1966-67. Recipient Certificate of Recognition, Central Mo. State Coll., 1965, Unicameral award State Neb., 1967, Mary McLeod Bethune award Jersey City State Coll., 1971. Mem. Am. Mgmt. Assn., Nat. Soc. Pub. Accts., Nat. Assn. Accts., Am. Acctg. Assn., Internat. Assn. Fin. Planners, Internat. Fin. Mgmt. Assn., NAA (Swiss Romande chpt.), Am. Women's Club of Geneva, Nat. Assn. Women Bus. Owners, Am. Assn. Individual Investors, AAUW, N.Y. Acad. Scis., AAAS, Nat. Hist. Soc., Nat. Assn. Tax Practitioners, Assn. Managerial Economists, Postal Commemorative Soc., Am. Mus. Natural History, Nat. Trust Historic Preservation, Internat. Tax Inst., Am. Econs. Assn., Internat. Platform Assn., U.S. Senatorial Club. Office: MJS Cons Services Internat Tax Cons 4 Copley Pl Suite 105 Boston MA 02116

SMITH, MARCUS WILFRID ALLISON, computer technology educator; b. Belfast, No. Ireland, Sept. 24, 1939; s. Marcus Edwin and Margaret Elizabeth Adams; m. Grace Ellen Jean Wilkinson, July 8, 1965; children: Susan Elisabeth, Kenneth Robert. BSc with honors, Queen's U. Belfast, 1961; PhD in Control Theory, Ulster Coll. No. Ireland Poly., 1978. Devel. engr. Short Bros. & Harland Ltd., Belfast, 1961-63; lectr. math. Coll. of Tech., Belfast, 1963-71; sr. lectr. analog computing Ulster Coll. Northern Ireland Poly., Jordanstown, No. Ireland, 1971-79, prin. lectr. computing, 1979-84; sr. lectr. computing U. Ulster, Jordanstown, No. Ireland, 1984-86, reader computing, 1986—; cons. in field. Contbr. numerous articles on determination of authorship, system identification and related applications of computer tech. to profl. and popular jours., 1978—. Fellow Inst. Math. and its Applications. Club: Johann Strauss Soc. of Gt. Britain. Office: Univ of Ulster at Jordanstown, Dept Info Systems, Newtown Abbey BT37 0QB, Northern Ireland

SMITH, MARK ALAN, personnel administrator; b. Lafayette, Ind., May 15, 1934; s. Mark Andrew and Sarah Fredissa (Palin) S.; children by previous marriage: Michelle Renee, Janene Marie. BA in Mus. Edn., BS in French, Ind. State U., 1957; MS in Adminstrn., George Washington U., 1976; postgrad., U. Pa. Wharton Sch., U. Denver Coll Law, U. Md. Coll. Law. Tech. writer Douglas Aircraft Co., Santa Monica, Calif., 1961-62; editor Copyright Law Office, Library Congress, Washington, 1963-64; asst. dir. personnel Holy Cross Hosp., Silver Spring, Md., 1964-65, dir. personnel adminstrn., 1965-80, dir. human resources adminstrn., 1080-82, asst. v.p., 1982—; instr. personnel mgmt. and labor relations Strayer Coll., Washington, 1970-73, bus. adminstrn. Cen. Mich. U. Grad. Sch., Washington extension, 1975-80; vis. lectr. George Washington U. Grad. Sch. Bus. Adminstrn., Washington, 1969, 70, 76; cons. to various hosps. in Md., Va. and Washington, 1967—. contbr. articles on orgn. devel. to profl. jours. Served with CIC, U.S. Army, 1957-60. Mem. Am. Hosp. Assn., Am. Soc. for Hosp. Personnel Dirs. (mem. labor relations com. 1970), Am. Soc. for Personnel Adminstrn. (accredited exec. in personnel, mem. pub. affairs com. 1975), Am. Mgmt. Assn., Washington Personnel Assn., Hosp. Council of Nat. Capital Area) Pres. Personnel dirs. div. 1969, 71), Md. Hosp. Personnel Adminstrn. Assn., Am. Soc. Law and Medicine, Phi Delta Kappa, Phi Mu Alpha Sinfonia, Blue Key. Home: 872 New Mark Esplanade Rockville MD 20850 Office: 1500 Forest Glen Rd Silver Spring MD 20910

SMITH, MICAH PEARCE, JR., advertising executive; b. Norman, Okla., Nov. 13, 1916; s. Micah Pearce and Julia Maud (Beeler) S.; m. Viola Sarajane Hatfield, June 1, 1946 (dec. Apr. 1986); children—Julia Annette, Carla Marie. Student U. Okla., 1936-41, corr. student, 1941-78. Dir. advt. Clinton Daily News (Okla.), 1946-53; dir. advt. Great Bend Daily Tribune (Kans.), 1953-55; ptnr., exec. v.p., gen. mgr. Indsl. Printing Inc., Oklahoma City, 1956-57; dir. advt. Daily Ardmoreite, Ardmore, Okla., 1958; dir. advt. Norman Transcript (Okla.), 1959-60; editor, pub. North Star, Oklahoma City, 1961; ptnr., exec. v.p. Gelders, Holderby & Smith, Inc., Oklahoma City, 1961-73; editor Chickasaw Times, Norman, 1970-78; fuels allocation officer State of Okla., 1973-80; chmn., pres., mgr. Media Mktg. Assocs., Inc., Oklahoma City, 1981—. Author syndicated newspapaer TV column; author, editor Genealogy of Smith, Pearce, Groom, Cecil et al. Sec. Ruling Council of Chickasaw Indian Tribe, Ada, Okla., 1971-79; coordinator gov. campaign State of Okla., 1969-70; deacon, trustee, elder Presbyn. Ch. Mem. Okla. Advt. Mgrs. Assn. (pres.), Am. Assn. Advt. Agy. Home and Office: 1525 Melrose Dr Norman OK 73069

SMITH, MICHAEL DENNIS, science business executive; b. Toronto, Can., Mar. 22, 1946; s. Leo and Jean S.; m. Lia Maria Vander Klugt, Dec. 22, 1973; children: Morgan Shane, Lindsay Jean, Philip Jacob George, Emily Anne. BS, U. Boston, 1968. Pres., chief exec. officer Northern Fortress Ltd., Toronto, 1982—; pres. Fortress Allatt Ltd., Toronto, 1983—, Fortress Sci. Ltd., Toronto, 1983—; bd. dirs. Eaton's Can. Ltd., Toronto, Can. Manoir Industries Ltd., Toronto, Tuckahoe Fin. Corp., Norwich Union Life Ins. Soc. Jewish. Club: Nat.

SMITH, MICHAEL PATRICK, producer, director; b. Canton, Ohio, Sept. 19, 1947; s. Melville Clement and Charlotte Julia (Dlugolecki) S.; B.A. in Communication Arts, Walsh Coll., 1969. Radio-TV-film producer-dir. Rodel Studios, Washington, 1973-75; producer-dir. radio-TV-motion pictures ARC, Washington, 1975-80; dir. audio-visual/broadcast media Fed. Emergency Mgmt. Agy., White House, Washington, 1980-87 ; dir. communications Designers & Planners, Inc., Washington, 1987—; minister music Bolling AFB, Washington, 1975-80; spl. asst. Res. Forces Policy Bd., 1983. Mem. U.S. Olympic Com.; mem. exec. council Washington Naval Recruiting Dist. Adv. Bd.; nat. pub. affairs chmn. Nat. Congl. Reception, 1980-83; pub. affairs officer U.S. Naval Acad.; lay lector Andrews AFB Chapel, 1980—. Served with USAF, 1969-73, lt. comdr. USNR, 1976—. Decorated Air Force Commendation medal, Navy Achievement medal. recipient Golden Eagle award CINE, 1971, 85; Public Relations award Council on Internat. Non-Theatrical Events, 1972; Disaster Relief Assistance award Johnstown Flood, 1977, Boston Blizzard, 1978, Hurricanes David, Frederick, 1979; Thomas Jefferson award, 1972, U.S. Safety Council award, 1976; cert. superior service/achievement Fed. Emergency Mgmt. Agy. Mem. Nat. Acad. TV Arts and Scis., Soc. Motion Picture and TV Engrs., Nat. Assn. Ednl. Broadcasters, Audio Engring. Soc., Assn. Naval Aviation, Navy League, Info. Film Producers Am., Washington Film Council (exec. bd.), Naval Res. Assn. (v.p. communications 1977—, pres. Kalmbach Ward Room, Washington chpt. 1980-83), Res. Officers Assn. (life, pres. D.C. chpt., pres. dept. Md. 1984, nat. pub. relations officer 1985-86, nat. jr. v.p. Navy, 1986-87, nat. historian 1987-88), nat. Navy exec. committeeman, 1988-90, Naval Order U.S., Naval Res. Assn. Am. Film Inst., Smithsonian Instn., U.S. Naval Inst., Bolling AFB Officers Assn., Am. Legion. Roman Catholic. Clubs: Army/Navy; Andrews AFB Officers; Toastmasters Internat., Ky Cols. Producer, dir., writer: Air Force Weekly, 1971-73; contbg. author Campus Navy Education and Training, 1976-77, Naval Air Res. NARTOPIX, Reservist, 1977—, The Officer mag., Crossroads, Naval Reservist News; editor, pub. Newsline, Naval Res. Assn. publ., 1977—, Now Hear This!, Res. Officers Assn. publ., 1986—. Composer: God Our Father, 1970. Home: 278 Southdale Ct Dunkirk MD 20754 Office: 2011 Crystal Dr Arlington VA 22202

SMITH, MIHAELA YVONNE, scientific research administrator; b. Bucharest, Romania, Feb. 29, 1948; d. Constantin Iancu Virginia (Botscu-Davidescu) Gref; m. Robert Eaton Smith, Apr. 26, 1976. Student in electronics/automation, Poly. Inst. Bucharest, 1967-69; Diploma in Econ. Cybernetics, Acad. Econ. Scis., Bucharest, 1975; Diploma in Social Scis., Transfer of Tech., U. Birmingham, Eng., 1978, PhD, 1982. Research asst. Internat. Ctr. for Forecasting Methodology, U. Bucharest, 1971-76, St. Anthony's Coll., Oxford U., 1977-80; research fellow, tech. policy unit U. Aston, Birmingham, 1979-84; officer sci. mgmt. and organizational program sci. adviser's office Commonwealth Sci. Council, London, 1984—. Contbr. articles to profl. jours. Mem. R&D Soc. (London), Strategic Planning Soc. (U.K.), Internat. Sci. Policy Found., World Future Soc., Internat. Impact Assessment Assn. Club: Royal Overseas (London). Home: 411, Gilbert House, Barbican, London EC2Y 8BD, England Office: Commonwealth Sci Council, Marlborough House, Pall Mall, London SW1Y 5HX, England

SMITH, NANCY LYNNE, journalist; b. San Antonio, July 31, 1947; d. Tillman Louis and Enid Maxine (Woolverton) Brown; m. Allan Roy Jones, Nov. 28, 1969 (div. 1975); 1 dau., Christina Elizabeth Woolverton Jones. B.A., So. Meth. U., 1968; postgrad. So. Meth. U., 1969-70, Vanderbilt U., 1964, Ecole Nouvelle de la Suisse Romande, Lausanne, Switzerland, 1962. Tchr. spl. edn. Hot Springs Sch. Dist. (Ark.), 1970-72; reporter, soc. editor Dallas Morning News, 1974-82; soc./celebrity columnist Dallas Times Herald, 1982—; stringer Washington Post, 1978; contbg. editor Ultra mag., Houston, 1981-82, Tex. Woman mag., Dallas, 1979-80, Profl. Woman mag., Dallas, 1979-80; mem. bd. advisors Ultra Mag., 1985—; appeared on TV series Jocelyn's Weekend, Sta. KDFI-TV, 1985. Bd. dirs. TACA arts support orgn., Dallas, 1980—, asst. chmn. custom auction, 1978-83; judge Miss Tex. USA Contest, 1984; mem. adv. bd. Cattle Baron's Ball Com., Dallas Symphony Debutante presentations; hon. mem. Dallas Opera Women's Bd., Northwood Inst. Women's Bd., Dallas Symphony League; mem. Friends of Winston Churchill Meml. and Library, Dallas Theatre Ctr. Women's Guild, Childrens' Med. Ctr. Auxiliary; mem. Community Council Greater Dallas Community Awareness Goals Com. Impact '88, 1985—. Mem. Soc. Profl. Journalists (v.p. communications 1978-79), Nat. Press Club, Dallas Press Club, DAR, Daus. of Republic of Tex. (registrar 1972), Dallas So. Memorial Assn., Dallas County Heritage Soc., Dallas Mus. Art League, Dallas Opera Guild. Club: Argyle (sec. 1983-84), The 500 (Dallas). Home: 5105 Mill Run Rd Dallas TX 75234 Office: Dallas Times Herald 1101 Pacific Ave Dallas TX 75202

SMITH, NEWMAN DONALD, financial executive; b. Chesterville, Ont., Can., Dec. 26, 1936; s. Clarke Harold and Ethelwyn Irene (Cross) S.; chartered acct., 1961; certified mgmt. acct.; 1966; chartered Inst. of Secretaries, 1967; m. Mary Elizabeth Murdoch, June 27, 1964; children—Clarke Murdoch, Brian Newman. With Coopers & Lybrand Inc., Ottawa, Ont., 1955-62; sec.-treas. Deloro Smelting & Refining Co. Ltd., Ottawa, 1963-69, M.J. O'Brien Ltd., Ottawa, 1963-69; exec. v.p., sec. Andres Wines Ltd. and subs., Winona, Ont., 1969—, also dir.; dir. Les Vins Andres du Quebec Ltee., Peller Wines of Calif., Watleys Ltd., Superior Wines Ltd., Andres Wines (B.C.) Ltd., Andres Wines (Alta.) Ltd., Andres Wines Atlantic Ltd. Fellow Chartered Inst. of Secs.; mem. Fin. Execs. Inst., Chartered Accts., Hamilton Mgmt. Accts., Chartered Inst. Secs. Clubs: Hamilton Golf and Country, Hamilton. Home: PO Box 7185, Ancaster, ON Canada L9G 3L4 Office: PO Box 550, Winona, ON Canada L0R 2L0

SMITH, NORMAN BRIAN, chemical company executive; b. Monton, Eng., Oct. 9, 1928; s. Vincent and Louise Smith; m. Phyllis Crossley, Apr. 2, 1955; children: David, Jane. BS, Manchester U., 1951, MS, 1952, PhD, 1954. With ICI, Harrogate, 1954-1985; textile devel. dir. ICI Fibres, Harrogate, 1969-72, dep. chmn., 1972-75, chmn., 1975-78; chmn. ICI Am. Inc., Wilmington, Del., 1981-83, Eng., 1983-85; chmn., pres. Imperial Chem. Industries Can., 1981-85; dep. chmn. Metal Box plc, Reading, Eng., 1985-86, chmn., 1986—, also bd. dir.; chmn. N.Am. Adv. Group, London, 1983-87; mem. Brit. Overseas Trade Bd., London, 1980-81, 83-87; bd. dirs. Lister & Co., London, Davy Corp., London; former bd. dirs. ICI Ltd., London, C-I-L Inc.;. Decorated Comdr. Brit. Empire Queen's Birthday Honours, London, 1980. Fellow Textile Inst.; mem. Brit. Textile Confedn. (pres. 1977-79). Mem. Ch. of Eng. Office: Metal Box plc, Queens House, Forbury Rd, Reading, Berkshire RG1 3JH, England

SMITH, NORMAN LEE, physician, medical educator; b. Logan, Utah, May 7, 1940; s. Norman P. and Alyce (Jorgensen) S.; m. Joan Carrigan, Jan. 31, 1969; children: Ann, Michael, Timothy, Emily, Melanie. BS, U. Utah, 1964, U. Calif., San Francisco, 1965, MD, 1968. Diplomate Am. Bd. Internal Medicine. Intern, then resident U. Utah Med. Ctr., Salt Lake City, 1968-74; chief med. resident U. Utah Affiliated Hosp., Salt Lake City, 1973-74; physician assoc. Meml. Med. Ctr., Salt Lake City, 1974—; assoc. clin. prof. U. Utah Sch. Medicine, Salt Lake City, 1975—; chmn. profl. edn. Am. Cancer Soc., Salt Lake City, 1976-77; vice chmn. dept. internal medicine LDS Hosp., Salt Lake City, 1982-84, chmn. gen. internal medicine task force, 1987—; dir., chmn. primary care project; med. dir. of Mind-Body Ctr., LDS Hosp., chmn. Utah State Unproven Health Practices Com., Salt Lake City, 1981-86; v.p. Collegium Aesculapium, Provo, Utah, 1984-86, pres., 1986-87. Contbr. articles to profl. jours. Chmn. Utah State Cost Containment, 1983; instr. Maturation Program, elementary schs., Salt Lake City, 1976-84; coach Little League Basketball, football, Salt Lake City, 1971-86. Served to maj. U.S. Army, 1970-72, Korea. Mem. AMA, ACP, Am. Soc. Internal Medicine, Acad. Psychosomatic Medicine, Phi Theta Kappa. Mormon. Lodge: Rotary. Office: Meml Med Ctr 2000 S 900 E Salt Lake City UT 84105

SMITH, PATRICK JOSEPH, writer; b. Cork, Ireland, Oct. 29, 1936; s. Patrick Joseph and Elizabeth (Cunne) S.; m. Berit Kaspar; children: Kathleen, Nicholas. BArch, U. Coll., Dublin, Ireland, 1960. Pvt. practice architecture London, 1960; pvt. practice architecture Stockholm, 1960-76, free-lance novelist, 1976-82; free-lance novelist Var, France, 1982—. Author: Having and Wanting, 1970, In London One Summer, 1972, En Liten Stad Pa Irland, 1976, Dying Light, 1979, There and Back, 1988. Swedish Union of Authors grantee, 1978, 80. Home: Villa Aves, 83460 Callian Var France

SMITH, PEGGY MARIE, government official; b. Balt., Nov. 21, 1940; d. John Weldon and Cecelia Agnes (Goddard) S. Student U. Md., 1978-79, Catonsville Community Coll., 1979-80. Various secretarial positions, until 1973; adminstrv. officer Health Care Financing Adminstrn., Balt., 1973-80; adminstrv. specialist Social Security Adminstrn., Balt., 1980-85, mgmt. analyst, 1985-87; social ins. claims examiner, 1987—. Vol. Mercy Hosp., Balt., 1960-62, Baltimore County Gen. Hosp., Balt., 1971; hotline counselor Lighthouse, Inc., Balt., 1975-77; tchr. Salem Lutheran Ch. Sch., Balt., 1962-67. Mem. Nat. Assn. Female Execs., Sierra Club, Cousteau Soc., Nat. Aquarium, Smithsonian Inst., Nat. Guild Hypnotists. Avocations: writing, mainly poetry; reading; psychology; parapsychology; gardening. Office: Social Security Adminstrn 6401 Security Blvd Baltimore MD 21235

SMITH, PETER WALKER, finance executive; b. Syracuse, N.Y., May 19, 1923; s. Stanley Sherwood and Elizabeth Wilkins (Young) S.; m. Lucile Elizabeth Edson, June 22, 1946; children: Andrew E., Laurie (Mrs. Samuel J. Falzone), Pamela C. (Mrs. Denison W. Schweppe, Jr.), Stanley E. B.Chem. Engring., Rensselaer Poly. Inst., 1947; M.B.A., Harvard U., 1948; LL.B., Cleve. Marshall Law Sch., 1955. Bar: Ohio 1955; Registered profl. engr., Ohio. Div. controller Raytheon Co., Lexington, Mass., 1958-66; v.p. finance, indsl. systems and equipment group Litton Industries Inc., Stamford, Conn., 1966-70; v.p. finance, treas. Copeland Corp., Sidney, Ohio, 1970-74; v.p. fin., treas., dir. Instrumentation Lab. Inc., Lexington, Mass., 1974-78; chief fin. officer, treas. Ionics, Inc., Watertown, Mass., 1978-80; v.p. fin., treas. Data Printer Corp., Malden, Mass., 1980-84, Orion Research Inc., Boston, 1984-87; pvt. practice cons. Concord, Mass., 1987—. Served to 1st. lt. AUS, 1943-46, 50-52. Mem. Fin. Execs. Inst., Acctg. Council, Machinery and Allied Products Inst., Am. Prodn. and Inventory Control Soc. (founder),

Rensselaer Soc. Engrs., Sigma Xi, Tau Beta Pi. Home and Office: 155 Monument St Concord MA 01742

SMITH, PHILIP CHADWICK FOSTER, maritime historian, editor; b. Salem, Mass., Feb. 17, 1939; s. Philip Horton and Elinor Colby (Mahoney) S.; children—Alexandra Chadwick, Hillary Webb; m. Gertrude Gouverneur Meredith Smith Stevenson, Dec. 21, 1983. B.A., Harvard U., 1961, postgrad. Grad. Sch. Design, 1961-63. Curatorial asst. Peabody Mus., Salem, Mass., 1963-66, curator maritime history, 1966-78, mng. editor The Am. Neptune, 1969-79, editor publs., 1978-79; curator Phila. Maritime Mus., 1979-84, editor/historian, 1979—; pres. Renfrew Group, Bath, Maine, 1982—; mem. U.S.-China 200 Bicentennial Com., 1984; project dir. Great Lakes Hist. Soc., Cleve., 1982-83; mem. adv. com. Eleutherian Mills-Hagley Found., Wilmington, Del., 1980-83; chmn. bd., pres. Corinthian Hist. Found., Phila., 1981-82; adj. prof. dept. Am. civilization U. Pa., 1981; bd. dirs. Council Am. Maritime Mus., 1977-79, chmn. publs. com., 1976-81, hon. fellow, 1985—; mem. Mus. Council Phila., 1980-84, Wenham Hist. Dist. Study Com. (Mass.), 1971-72, Soc. Nautical Research, Greenwich, Eng., 1969-79; curator maritime history Bostonian Soc., 1967-78. Author: A History of the Marine Society at Salem, 1766-1966, 1966; Portraits of the Marine Society at Salem in New-England, 1972; The Frigate Essex Papers: Building the Salem Frigate, 1798-1799, 1974; Captain Samuel Tucker, Continental Navy, 1976; The Artful Roux: Marine Painters of Marseille, 1978; The Privateers, 1979; The Empress of China (John Lyman Book award 1984, spl. citation for nonfiction Athenaeum of Phila. 1986), 1984; Philadelphia on the River, 1986; Hey Nellie Yoo-Hoo and Further Fugitive Pieces, 1986; editor: The Journals of Ashley Bowen of Marblehead, 1973; Mowee: An Informal History of the Hawaiian Island (C.E. Speakman, Jr.), 1978; Seafaring in Colonial Massachusetts, 1980; Sibley's Heir: A Volume in Memory of Clifford Kenyon Shipton, 1982; contbr. articles to hist. jours.; editorial adv. bd. American Neptune, A Quar. Jour., 1983—; editorial bd. Hist. Collections Essex Inst., 1975—, Samuel McIntire Papers, 1976—; editorial adv. com. Maine Maritime Mus., 1983—, corporator, 1984—; assoc. editor Colonial Soc. Mass., 1978-85. Bd. mgrs. Home for Aged Women, Salem, 1968-70; trustee Ropes Meml. Mansion, Salem, 1968-79; bd. dirs. Hist. Salem, Inc., 1966. Mem. U.S. Commn. Maritime History (founding), Colonial Soc. Mass. (corr.), Mass. Hist. Soc. (corr.), Internat. Congress Maritime Mus. (assoc.), Marine Soc. London (hon. gov. 1968—), N.Am. Soc. Oceanic History (founding; council 1976—, past chmn. publs. com.), Salem Marine Soc. (clk. 1963-79), Phila. Mus. Art. Republican. Clubs: Odd Volumes (Boston); Sunnybrook Golf (Plymouth Meeting, Pa.).

SMITH, PHILIP LAWTON, food company executive; b. LaGrange, Ga., Dec. 16, 1933; s. Hayden McKinley and Anne Mae (Slaughter) S.; m. Nancy Lou Fagan, Sept. 8, 1956; children: Kevin James, Stephen Eric, Scott Andrew. BBA with distinction, U. Mich., 1960, MBA with distinction, 1961. Account exec. Benton & Bowles, N.Y.C., 1961-65; v.p., account exec. Ted Bates, Inc., N.Y.C., 1965-66; product mgr. Gen. Foods Corp., White Plains, N.Y., 1966, product group mgr., 1966-69, mgr. advt. and merchandising Jell-O div., 1969-70, v.p. mktg. and devel., 1970-72, exec. v.p., 1972-73, mgr. strategic bus. unit, 1973-74, v.p., pres. pet foods div., 1974-77, v.p. U.S. grocery group, pres. Maxwell House div., 1977-79, exec. v.p. fin. and adminstrn., 1979-81, pres., chief operating officer, 1981-86, pres., chief exec. officer, 1987, chmn., 1987-88; chmn., chief exec. officer Pillsbury Co., Mpls., 1988—; vice chmn. Philip Morris Cos., N.Y.C., 1987—; trustee U.S. Trust Co. N.Y. Trustee Columbia Presbyn. Hosp. Office: Pillsbury Co 200 S 6th St Minneapolis MN 55402 *

SMITH, PHILLIP HARTLEY, steel company executive; b. Sydney, Australia, Jan. 26, 1927; came to U.S., 1950, naturalized, 1960; s. Norman Edward and Elizabeth (Williams) S.; m. Martha Frances Dittrich, June 4, 1955; children: Elizabeth, Thomas, Johanna, Alice, Margaret, Sarah. B.Engring. with 1st class honors in Mining and Metallurgy, U. Sydney, 1950; Metall. Engr., MIT, 1952; diploma indsl. relations, U. Chgo., 1958; LL.D., Grove City Coll., 1975. Successively trainee, metallurgist, foreman Indiana Harbor, Ind., Inland Steel Co., 1952-55; successively trainee, metallurgist, dir. purchasing and planning La Salle Steel Co., Hammond, Ind., 1956-64; with Copperweld Corp., Pitts., 1964-77; pres. Copperweld Corp., 1967-77, chmn., 1973-77; pres., chief exec. officer Bekaert Steel Wire Corp., Pitts., 1978-82; mng. ptnr. Hartley Smith & Ptnrs., 1982-84; chmn. Smith, Yuill & Co. Inc., 1984—; dir. Weirton Steel Corp., Scuul Ltd., Mitech Labs. Inc., Australian Essential Oils, Inc.; adj. prof. bus. Grove City Coll.; vis. dean sr. exec. program Dalien Inst. Tech., Peoples Republic of China. Editor: Mechanical Working of Steel, 1961; author: Essays in Management, A Guide to Young Managers on the Way Up. Trustee Grove City (Pa.) Coll., Berea (Ky.) Coll., 1978-85; chmn. Inroads Inc. Served as cadet officer Australian Mcht. Marine, 1942-43; Served as cadet officer Royal Australian Fleet Aux., 1943. Recipient Nat. Open Hearth Steelmaking award, 1955, Outstanding Chief Exec. Officer in Steel Industry award Fin. World, 1975; Nuffield scholar, 1949; Fulbright fellow, 1950. Mem. Sigma Xi. Presbyterian (elder, trustee). Clubs: University (Chgo.); Duquesne (Pitts.); Fox Chapel Golf, Rolling Rock (Ligonier, Pa.). Home: 102 Haverford Rd Pittsburgh PA 15238

SMITH, PHYLLIS MAE, health care consultant; educator; b. Couer d'Alene, Idaho, May 2, 1935; d. Elmer Lee Smith and Kathryn Alice (Newell) Wilson. Diploma, Lutheran Bible Inst., Seattle, 1956, Emanuel Hosp. Sch. Nursing, Portland, Oreg., 1959; student Coll. San Mateo, Calif., 1971. Staff nurse in surgery Emanuel Hosp., Portland, 1959-61, St. Vincent's Hosp., Portland, 1962-63; head nurse central service Sacred Heart Hosp., Eugene, Oreg., 1964-69; dir. central services Peninsula Hosp., Burlingame, Calif., 1969-74; pres. Phyllis Smith Assocs., Inc., Lewiston, Idaho, 1975-88; sr. tech. advisor, dir. ednl. programs, Parkside Material Mgmt. Services, Park Ridge, Ill., 1988—; lectr., cons. in field in over 8 countries. Contbr. to manuals, profl. jours. Mem. Internat. Assn. Hosp. Central Service Mgmt. (dir. edn. 1973-88, chmn. technician edn. and affairs com. 1978-88, John Perkins award, 1977, Chesire award 1977), Assn. for Advancement Med. Instrumentation, Nat. Assn. Female Execs. Episcopalian. Lodge: Eagles Aux. Avocations: fishing, walking, photography, chess, reading. Home and Office: 3730 11th St Lewiston ID 83501

SMITH, R. J., JR., oil company executive; b. Big Spring, Tex., Sept. 9, 1930; s. R. J. and Myrtle (O'Quinn) S.; m. Sarah Sue Holmes, Sept. 8, 1950 (div. 1962); children—Molly Smith Frank, Cassie Smith Bichler; m. 2d, Sandra Ann Schroeder, Jan. 21, 1971. Student, Abilene Christian U., 1948-50, So. Methodist U., 1951-52, Goethe U., Frankfurt, Germany, 1953-54; LL.D., Northwood Inst., 1983. Aero. engr. Chance-Vought Aircraft, Dallas, 1951-52; ind. oil operator, Dallas, 1960-62; ops. chief Leland Fikes, Dallas, 1963-66; owner, operator Texon Petroleum Corp (sold to Exxon USA 1983), Dallas, 1967-83; owner, pres. Cheyenne Petroleum Corp., Dallas, 1967—; owner, pres. Texan Petroleum Corp., Dallas, 1985—; dir. Sherry Lane Nat. Bank, Dallas. Bd. dirs. Effie and Wofford Cain Found., Dallas, 1979—, Lehndorff Minerals; chmn. bd. govs. Northwood Inst., Tex., trustee, West Baden, Ind., Midland, Mich. and Dallas, 1968—. Mem. Tex. Ind. Producers and Royalty Owners, Ind. Producers Assn. Am. Mid-Continent Producers Assn., N.Mex. Ind. Producers Assn. Republican. Clubs: Preston Trail Golf, Dallas Gun, Oak Cliff Country, University, Quadrant, Bent Tree Country (all Tex.); Del Mar Turf (Calif.). Office: Texan Petroleum Corp 2626 Cole Ave Suite 603 LB Dallas TX 75204

SMITH, RALPH CARLISLE, educational consultant; b. West New York, N.J., May 24, 1910; s. Alfred Thomas and Katharine (Haller) S.; m. Harriett V. Petersen, May 20, 1954. Chem.-Engr., Rensselaer Poly. Inst., 1931; J.D., George Washington U., 1939; M.A., U. N.M., 1955, Ph.D., 1962. Bar: D.C. 1940, U.S. Supreme Ct 1946; Registered profl. engr., N.Mex. Chemist E.I. duPont de Nemours & Co., Inc., 1931-35; engr. U.S. Patent Office, 1935-37, Colgate Palmolive Co., 1938-42; patent counsel Manhattan Project, Los Alamos, 1943-47; asst. dir. Los Alamos Sci. Lab., 1946-57; asst. to pres. nuclear electronic div. ACF Industries, 1957-60; mem. faculty N.Mex. Highlands U., 1961-78, prof. polit. sci., 1965-78, v.p., acad. dean, 1966-70, pres., 1970-72, counsel to pres., 1973-78; mem. law faculty U. N.M., 1950-57; cons. Teaching Machines, Albuquerque, 1961-65, Lytle Corp., Albuquerque, 1960-61, Columbia (Mo.) Coll., 1978—; County probate judge, Los Alamos, 1950-55, justice of peace, 1948-50, city magistrate, City of Las Vegas, 1977, Chmn. planning commn., Las Vegas, 1964-78. Co-author: The Effects of Atomic Weapons, 1950, History of Los Alamos Scientific Laboratory, 1961, 83; Co-editor: National Nuclear Energy Series, 1951. Editorial bd. Nat. Forum, 1984—. Republican candidate for Congress, 1956. Served to lt. col., C.E. AUS, 1942-47. Decorated Legion of Merit, Army Commendation medal. Fellow Am. Inst. Chemists; mem. Am. Phys. Soc., Am. Nuclear Soc., Am. Inst. Chem. Engrs., Am. Intellectual Property Law Assn., Order of Coif, Sigma Xi, Tau Beta Pi, Phi Kappa Phi. Home: 55 Terra Vista Ave San Francisco CA 94115

SMITH, RALPH EARL, virologist; b. Yuma, Colo., May 10, 1940; s. Robert C. and Esther C. (Schwarz) S.; m. Sheila L. Kondy, Aug. 29, 1961 (div. 1986); 1 child, Andrea Denise; m. Janet M. Keller, 1988. BS, Colo. State U., 1961; PhD, U. Colo., 1968. Postdoctoral fellow Duke U. Med. Ctr., Denver, 1968-70; asst. prof. Duke U. Med. Ctr., Durham, N.C., 1970-74, assoc. prof., 1974-80, prof. virology, 1980-82; prof., head dept. microbiology Colo. State U., Ft. Collins, 1983-88, prof., assoc. v.p. research microbiology, 1988—; cons. Bellco Glass Co., Vineland, N.J., 1976-80, Proctor & Gamble Co., Cin., 1985-86, Schering Plough Corp., Bloomfield, N.J., 1987—. Contbr. articles to profl. jours.; patentee in field. Asst. scoutmaster Boy Scouts Am., Durham, 1972-82, com. mem., Ft. Collins, 1986—; mem. adminstrv. bd. 1st United Meth. Ch., Ft. Collins. Eleanor Roosevelt fellow Internat. Union Against Cancer 1978-79. Mem. Am. Soc. Microbiology, N.Y. Acad. Scis., Am. Soc. Virology, Am. Assn. Immunologists, Am. Assn. Avian Pathologists, Gamma Sigma Delta. Democrat. Methodist. Home: 2406 Creekwood Dr Fort Collins CO 80525 Office: Colo State U VP Research Fort Collins CO 80523

SMITH, RANDOLPH LELAND, former army, officer, marketing executive; b. Mattoon, Ill., Nov. 3, 1939; s. Leland Prather and Hildred Ruth (Hall) S.; m. Joann Goodwin, Jan. 14, 1967; children—Karron Suzanne, Andrew Michael. B.S. in Aero. Engring., Calif. Poly. State U., 1962; M.B.A., N.Mex. State U., 1975. Commd. 2d lt., Ordnance Corps, U.S. Army, 1962, advanced through grades to lt. col., 1978; air def. officer, Fed. Republic Germany, 1962-64; comdr. 173d Ordnance Detachment, Ansbach, Fed. Republic Germany, 1964-65; chief quality assurance Pueblo Army Depot, 1966; comdr. B Co., 7th Support Bn., 199th Inf. Brigade, Vietnam, 1967-68; material officer 198th Maintenance Bn., Ft. Knox, Ky., 1968-69; spl. asst. to product mgr. Land Combat Support Systems, Redstone Arsenal, Ala., 1970-72; contract ops. officer 277th Supply and Service Bn., Danang, Vietnam, 1972-73; asst. prof. mil. sci. N.Mex. State U., Las Cruces, 1974-77; chief maintenance materiel sect., materiel support br. J-4, UN Command, U.S. Forces Korea, 8th Army, 1978-80; exec. officer U.S. Army Depot System Command, Chambersburg, Pa., 1980-81, dir. engring. and support systems, 1981-82; ret., 1982; mktg. mgr. Pueblo Diversified Industries, Colo., 1983-86, v.p. mktg., 1987—. Deacon Park Hill Baptist Ch., Pueblo, 1983-86; chmn. troop com. Boy Scouts Am., Pueblo. Decorated Bronze Star, Meritorious Service medal, Army Commendation medal. Mem. Am. Def. Preparedness Assn., Nat. Eagle Scout Assn., Beta Gamma Sigma. Address: 28390 Pongo Dr Pueblo CO 81006

SMITH, RAY WILLIAM, clergyman, counselor; b. Kirksville, Mo., Mar. 1, 1952; s. Norman George and Amber Lou (Fairley) S.; m. Kathryn Diane Marshall Siegrist, Dec. 28, 1974; children—Ashley Dianne Marshall, Travis William Sterling, Austin Andrew Bondurant. B.S., Central Mo. State U., 1974; M.Div., Austin Presbyn. Theol. Sem., 1978, D.Min., 1978;, Ed.D., Memphis State U., 1985. Lic. profl. counselor, Tex.; cert. counselor, Washington; ordained to ministry, Presbyn. Ch., 1978. Intern, First Presbyn. Ch. Galveston (Tex.), 1976-77; pastor Grace Presbyn. Ch., San Antonio, 1978-81, Shady Grove Presbyn. Ch., Memphis, 1981-85, 1st Presbyn. Ch., Spokane, 1986—; founder Christian Counseling Ctr. of Spokane; mem. ordination exam. com. Memphis Presbytery, 1981-82, Chinook Dist. Boy Scouts Am. Eagle Scout Bd. Rev. Com.; bd. dirs. San Antonio Urban Council, 1980, Family Service Memphis, Dismas House Memphis, mem. Hospice Com., San Antonio, 1981. Mem. Memphis Ministers Assn., Memphis Jaycees (dir.), Met. Inter-Faith Assn., Sales and Mktg. Execs. of Memphis (chaplain), Nat. Eagle Scout Assn., Presbyn. Musicians Assn., Am. Assn. Counseling and Devel., Christian Assn. Psychol. Studies, Assn. Mental Health Clergy, Presbyn. Inland Empire (com. on ministry), Conf. Contemporary Cosmology, Internat. Platform Speakers Assn., Delta Upsilon Internat., Kappa Delta Pi. Lodges: Toastmasters, Masons. Author book revs., articles, liturgical prayer collections; also How to Cope with Grief: A Series of Sermons, 1982; (manuscript and cassettes) Civil Religion in Texas, 1983. Home: West 835 Shoshone Spokane WA 99203 Office: South 318 Cedar St Spokane WA 41684

SMITH, REGINALD BRIAN FURNESS, anesthesiologist, educator; b. Warrington, Eng., Feb. 7, 1931; s. Reginald and Betty (Bell) S.; m. Margarete Groppe, July 18, 1963; children—Corinne, Malcolm. M.B., B.S., U. London, 1955; D.T.M. and H., Liverpool Sch. Tropical Medicine, 1959. Intern Poole Gen. Hosp., Dorset, Eng., 1955-56, Wilson Meml. Hosp., Johnson City, N.Y., 1962-63; resident in anesthesiology Med. Coll. Va., Richmond, 1963-64; resident in anesthesiology U. Pitts., 1964-65, clin. instr., 1965-66; asst. prof. 1969-71, assoc. clin. prof., 1971-74, prof., 1974-78, acting chmn. dept. anesthesiology, 1977-78; prof., chmn. dept. U. Tex. Health Sci. Center, San Antonio, 1978—; anesthesiologist in chief hosps. U. Tex. Health Sci. Center, 1978—; dir. anesthesiology Eye and Ear Hosp., Pitts., 1971-76; anesthesiologist in chief Presbyh. Univ. Hosp., Pitts., 1976-78. Contbg. editor: Internat. Ophthalmology Clinics, 1973, Internat. Anesthesiology Clinics, 1983; contbr. articles to profl. jours. Served to capt. Brit. Army, 1957-59. Fellow Am. Coll. Anesthesiologists, Am. Coll. Chest Physicians, A.C.P.; mem. Internat. Anesthesia Research Soc., Am. Soc. Anesthesiologists (pres. Western Pa. 1974-75), Tex. Soc. Anesthesiologists, San Antonio Soc. Anesthesiologists, AMA, Tex. Med. Assn., Bexar County Med. Soc. Republican. Episcopalian. Club: Oak Hills Country. Home: 213 Canada Verde San Antonio TX 78232 Office: 7703 Floyd Curl Dr San Antonio TX 78284

SMITH, RICHARD, artist; b. Letchworth, Herts., Eng., 1931; m. Betsy Scherman; children: Edward, Harry. Student, Luton Sch. Art, St. Albans Sch. Art, Royal Coll. Art. Tchr. St. Martin's Sch. Art, London, 1961-63; artist-in-residence U. Va., 1967, U. Calif. at Irvine, 1968, U. Calif. at Davis, 1976; one-man exhibitions include Kasmin Gallery, 1963, 67, Whitechapel Gallery, 1966; groups exhibitions include Pitts. Internat., 1961, New Shapes in Color, Amsterdam, Berne and Stuttgart, 1966-67, also Guggenheim Mus., Tate Gallery; represented in permanent collections Tate Gallery, Stuyvesant Found., Contemporary Art Soc., Ulster Mus., Walker Art Ctr. Served with RAF, 1950-52. Recipient Grand Prix, Sao Paulo Bienal, 1967; Scull prize 33d Bienniale de Venezia, 1966; Harkness travelling fellow, 1959-61. *

SMITH, RICHARD EMERSON (DICK), make-up artist; b. Larchmont, N.Y., June 26, 1922; s. Richard Roy and Coral (Brown) S.; m. Jocelyn De Rosa, Jan. 10, 1949; children: Douglas Todd, David. B.A., Yale U., 1944. Dir. make-up dept. NBC-TV, N.Y.C., 1945-59; freelance make-up artist and cons. 1959—. Television credits include Mark Twain, Tonight!, 1967 (Emmy award 1967); films include Requiem for a Heavyweight, 1962, The World of Henry Orient, 1963, Midnight Cowboy, 1968, Little Big Man, 1969, The Godfather, 1971, The Exorcist, 1973, The Godfather, Part II, 1974, The Sunshine Boys, 1975, Taxi Driver, 1975, Altered States, 1979, Scanners, 1980, Ghost Story, 1981, The Hunger, 1982, Amadeus, 1983 (Acad. award 1984), Starman, 1984, We're Back, Poltergeist III, 1987, Everybody's All-American, 1988. Office: 209 Murray Ave Larchmont NY 10538

SMITH, RICHARD JAY, orthodontist, educator; b. Bklyn., Aug. 10, 1948; s. Benjamin and Miriam (Cohen) S.; m. Linda Sharon Harris, Aug. 22, 1970; children: Jason Andrew, Owen Harris, Hilary Rachele. BA, Bklyn. Coll., CUNY, 1969; MS in Anatomy, Tufts U., 1973, DMD, 1973; PhD in Anthropology, Yale U., 1980. Asst. clin. prof. orthodontics U. Conn., Farmington, 1976-79; asst. prof. U. Md., Balt., 1979-81, assoc. prof., 1981-84; prof. orthodontics, biomed. sci., chmn. dept. orthodontics, adj. prof. anthropology Washington U., St. Louis, 1984—, assoc. dean, 1987—, cons. orthodontics Cleft Palate and Craniofacial Anomalies Team, 1984—; vis. assoc. prof. cell biology Sch. Medicine, Johns Hopkins U., Balt., 1980-84; orthodontic cons. St. Louis VA Med. Ctr., 1986—; staff Barnes Hosp., 1986—, St. Louis Children's Hosp., 1985—. Editor-in-chief Jour. Balt. Coll. Dental surgery, 1981-84. Contbr. numerous articles in orthodontics, anthropology, comparative biology to profl. jours. Am. Fund for Dental Health dental tchr. tng. fellow, 1977-78; NIH postdoctoral fellow, 1978-79. Fellow Internat. Coll. Dentists; mem. ADA, Alumni Assn. Student Clinicians (bd. govs. 1984—, Alan J. Davis award 1983), Am. Assn. Orthodontists, Am. Assn. Phys. Anthropologists, Internat. Assn. Dental Research. (pres. St. Louis sect. 1985—), Am. Assn. Dental Schs. Home: 816 S Bemiston Ave Clayton MO 63105 Office: Washington U Sch Dental Medicine 4559 Scott Ave Saint Louis MO 63110

SMITH, RICHARD WENDELL, lawyer; b. Lincoln, Nebr., May 29, 1912; s. Walter Charles and Mary Frances (Goodale) S.; m. Patricia Adelle Lahr, Apr. 8, 1947; children—Laurie Patricia, Barton Richard. A.B., Nebr. Wesleyan U., 1933; J.D., Harvard U., 1938. Bar: Nebr. 1938, U.S. Dist. Ct. Nebr. 1938, U.S. Ct. Claims 1949, U.S. Ct. Appeals (7th and 8th cirs.), U.S. Supreme Ct. 1955. Spl. agt. FBI, Dept. Justice, Washington, 1942-44; Ptnr. Woods, Aitken, Smith, Greer, Overcash & Spangler, Lincoln; apptd. by U.S. Dist Ct. as trustee in reorgn. of Am. Buslines, Inc., 1954-58; lectr. constrn. law Fed. Publs., Washington, 1974—. Contbr. articles to profl. jours. Bd. dirs., sec. Nebr. Wesleyan U., Lincoln, 1958-74; sec. Harvard Schs. and Scholarship Com., Lincoln, 1948—; treas. Nebr. Art Assn., Lincoln, 1984-86; bd. dirs. Lincoln Symphony Orch. Assn., Lincoln Community Theater, 1982-87. Served to lt. USNR, 1944-46. Mem. ABA (governing com. forum on constrn. industry 1983—), Nebr. Bar Assn. Republican. Lodge: Rotary (pres. 1981-82). Home: 916 Fall Creek Rd Lincoln NE 68510 Office: Woods Aitken Smith Greer et al 1500 American Charter Ctr Lincoln NE 68508

SMITH, ROBERT BURNS, magazine/newspaper executive; b. Columbus, Ohio, Feb. 24, 1929; s. Edwin Clyde and Blanche (Burns) S.; m. Marjorie Ann Otten. B.S., Ohio State U., 1949. Reporter, then asst. news editor Ohio State Jour., Columbus, 1948-59; with Columbus Dispatch, 1959—, mng. editor, 1968-80; editor-in-chief Ohio mag., 1980—, Living Single mag., 1980-86; v.p. Dispatch Features, Columbus, 1968—. Sec.-treas. James Faulkner Meml. Fund, Columbus, 1967—; trustee Ohio Hist. Soc., 1986—; mem. Ohio Privacy Bd., 1977-81. Served with USAF, 1951-55. Mem. Blue Pencil Ohio (v.p. 1969, pres. 1970), AP Ohio (v.p. 1974, pres. 1975), Mag. Pubs. Assn., Am. Soc. Mag. Editors, Regional Pubs. Assn. (dir. 1986—), Sigma Delta Chi, Delta Tau Delta. Presbyn. Clubs: Masons; York Temple Country (Worthington, Ohio). Home: 1456 Sandalwood Place Columbus OH 43229 Office: 40 S 3d St Columbus OH 43215

SMITH, ROBERT FRANK, microscopist, photomicrographer, educator; b. N.Y.C., Mar. 30, 1917; s. William and Barbara Elizabeth (Boesch) S.; m. Jacqueline Louise Brennan, June 20, 1936; children—Gail Smith Miller, Robert Frank (dec.), Wendy Smith Meehan, Gregory J. Student Columbia U., 1936-39; diploma Royal Microscopical Soc., Oxford, Eng., 1977. Registered biol. photographer in medicine and natural sci. Dir. microscopy and biol. photography Brookhaven Nat. Lab., Upton, N.Y., 1947-73; dir. biomed. communication, prof. microscopy, N.Y. State Coll. Vet. Medicine, Cornell U., Ithaca, N.Y., 1973-82, ret., 1982; prof. microscopy and photomicrography, Miner Inst. and SUNY, Plattsburgh, N.Y., 1983—; bd. dirs. for in-vitro cell biology and biotech plattsburgh U.; cons. C. Zeiss, Thornwood, N.Y., 1953-73, Nikon, Garden City, N.Y., 1975—, Smith Kline and French, Phila., 1955—, Am. Optical Co., Buffalo, 1980—; invited U.S. rep. in microscopy and photomicrography USSR, 1977; mem. Joint Task Force 7, organizer, dir. biol. photography Brookhaven Nat. Lab. med. survey of Marshallese people exposed to Hydrogen Bomb fallout, 1959-69; guest lectr. various univs. U.S. and Europe; Examined microscopically and photographed first moon rocks brought back by Apollo 11, 1969-70; author, condr. course in microscopy Med. Sch., U. Berne, Switzerland, 1970; author: Microscopy and Photomicrography, A Practical Guide, 1982; contbr. chpt. to book, articles to profl. jours. including Jour. Biol. Photographic Assn., Am. Lab., Visual Sonic Medicine, Natural History, Functional Photography, Am. Forests, Photographie und Forschung, African Violet Jour., AMA Archives of Ophthalmology; tech. editor Functional Photography, 1976—, contbr. bi-monthly column, 1976—. Served with USMC, 1944-45, PTO, Recipient cert. participation in USSR, USIA, 1977. Fellow Biol. Photographic Assn. (bd. govs. 1968-70, 4 Charles Foster Meml. Citations, 2 First awards, emeritus status), Royal Microscopial Soc.; mem. Rochester Acad. Sci. (hon.). Roman Catholic. Home: 11 Hunters Lane Ithaca NY 14850 Office: Functional Photography 101 Crossways Park W Woodbury NY 11797

SMITH, ROBERT MCDAVID, lawyer; b. Birmingham, Ala., Oct. 5, 1920; s. Maolin F. and Virginia (McDavid) S.; m. Eugenia Wimberly, Aug. 27, 1946; children—Eugenia Wimberly, Robert Patton, Felton Wimberly. B.A., U. N.C., 1942; LL.B., U. Ala., 1948; LL.M., Harvard U., 1949. Bar: Ala. 1949, U.S. Dist. Ct. (no. dist.) Ala. 1950, U.S. Ct. Appeals (5th cir.) 1952, U.S. Ct. Appeals (11th cir.) 1981, U.S. Supreme Ct. 1957. Assoc. Lange, Simpson, Robinson & Somerville, 1949-52, ptnr. 1952—; mem. Nat. Defendant Project, 1963-69. Mem. exec. com. Jefferson County (Ala.) Republican Party, 1965-68. Served to capt. AUS, 1942-46. Decorated Bronze Star. Fellow Am. Coll. Trial Lawyers; mem. ABA (chmn. sect. legal edn. and admission to bar), Am. Judicature Soc., Ala. Bar Assn. (chmn. com. legal edn.), Fed. Bar Assn. Republican. Methodist. Clubs: Kiwanis, Country, The Club, Downtown (Birmingham). Office: Lange Simpson Robinson & Somerville 1700 First Alabama Bank Bldg Birmingham AL 35203

SMITH, ROBERT SIDNEY, business executive; b. Charlotte, N.C., Feb. 26, 1945; s. Edward Mason and Virginia Irene Smith; m. Lynn Little. A.B. in Econs. and Bus. Adminstrn., Wofford Coll., Spartanburg, S.C., 1967. With mktg. dept. Humble Oil & Refining Co., 1971-72; v.p. Nat. Assn. Hosiery Mfrs., Charlotte, 1972-78, sr. v.p., 1978-82, pres., chief exec. officer, 1982—; ptnr., v.p. Green, Smith & Crockett Inc., 1978-82; mem. dist. Export Council; cons. in field. Chmn. research com. Mecklenburg County Republican Party, 1977-78; N.C. steering com. George Bush for Pres. 1988; sect. chmn. Charlotte United Way; pres. Charlotte Area Alumni Club Wofford Coll., 1977; chmn. bd. dirs. Leadership Charlotte Program, 1980-81; bd. dirs. Nat. Alumni Assn. Wofford Coll.; bd. dirs. U.S. Apparel Council, treas., 1982—; mem. industry sector adv. com. on textile for U.S. spl. trade rep. U.S. Dept. Commerce, also mem. mgmt. labor textile adv. com.; past mem. City Zoning Bd. Adjustment, Charlotte. Served to capt. USMC, 1967-70; Vietnam. Decorated Purple Heart; Vietnamese Cross Gallantry. Mem. Assns. Council of NAM (chmn. 1988-89), Nat. Assn. Mfrs. (bd. dirs.), Am. Soc. Assn. Execs. (key industry com.), Charlotte Textile Club. DAV, Sigma Alpha Epsilon (pres. Charlotte area alumni club 1980-81). Presbyterian. Home: 4733 Truscott Rd Charlotte NC 28226 Office: 477 S Sharon Amity Rd Charlotte NC 28211

SMITH, ROGER BONHAM, automotive manufacturing executive; b. Columbus, Ohio, July 12, 1925; s. Emmet Quimby and Bess (Obetz) S.; m. Barbara Ann Rasch, June 7, 1954; children: Roger Bonham, Jennifer Anne, Victoria Belle, Drew Johnston. Student, U. Mich., 1942-44, B.B.A., 1947, M.B.A., 1949. With Gen. Motors, Detroit, 1949—; treas. Gen. Motors, 1970-71, v.p. charge fin. staff, 1971-73; v.p., group exec. in charge of nonautomotive and def. group 1973-74, exec. v.p., 1974-80, vice chmn. fin. com., 1975-81, chmn., chief exec. officer, 1981—. Trustee Cranbrook Ednl. Community, Bloomfield Hills, Mich., Mich. Colls. Found., Detroit, Calif. Inst. Tech., Pasadena. Served with USNR, 1944-46. Mem. Bus. Council, Bus. Roundtable, Motor Vehicle Mfrs. Assn. (dir.). Clubs: Detroit, Detroit Athletic, Orchard Lake (Mich.) Country, Bloomfield Hills Country; Links (N.Y.C.). Home: Bloomfield Hills MI 48013 Office: Gen Motors Corp 3044 W Grand Blvd Detroit MI 48202

SMITH, RUSSELL WESLEY, management consultant, organizational development trainer; b. Penn Yan, N.Y., Jan. 23, 1947; s. Wesley Sanford and Gladys Klothe S.; m. Janice Larzelere, June 16, 1984; stepchildren—Gerald Allen, Christopher Michael. A.A.S., SUNY, 1973; B.S. cum laude, N.H. Coll., 1976. Project mgr. Robert Bell & Co., Balt., 1976-77; pres. Smith Klothe Assos., Warsaw, N.Y., 1983—; assoc. Resource Assos., Inc., Newmarket, N.H., 1979-84; assoc. Bus. Planning Group, Westport, Conn., 1985—; assoc. Cons. Capacities Group Inc., Cold Spring Harbor, N.Y., 1983—; assoc. Resource Mgmt. Group, Boston, 1984-85, Byrne Mgmt. Group, Inc., Medford, N.J., 1985—; cons. C. Todd, Inc., Haddenfield, N.J., 1978-79, Naus & Newlyn, Inc., Paoli, Pa., 1977-78. Served with Signal Corps, U.S. Army, 1966-68. Home and Office: Maple Winds 4768 Wilder Rd Warsaw NY 14569

SMITH, SAM DEVERE, industrial engineer; b. Rolla, Mo., Oct. 24, 1936; s. Levi P. and Eula G. (Christensen) S.; m. Norma Jean Leonard, Dec. 22, 1957; 1 child, Samra Dee. M of Engring., Mo. Sch. of Mines, 1960. Registered profl. engr., Kans. Designer Gen. Steel Ind., Granite City, Ill., 1961-68; design engr. Rockwell Mfg., Atchison, Kans., 1968-76; project engr. Rockwell Internat., Troy, Mich., 1976-79, Youngstown (Ohio) Steel Door, 1979-82; pvt. practice engr. transp. industry 1982—; pres. Smith Tranco Service Ltd., Richton Park, Ill., 1987—. Inventor intermodal transp. vehicle. Mem. ASME, Am. Soc. Quality Control (cert. reliability engr. 1981, quality engr. 1984), Assn. Am. R.Rs.(track train dynamics task force 1979-82). Home: 22418 Butterfield Dr Apt 107 Richton Park IL 60471

SMITH, SAMUEL CORNELIUS, aeronautical engineer, consultant; b. Haiti, West Indies; came to U.S., 1933, naturalized, 1933; s. Robert Thornley and Ann Elizabeth Smith; student M.I.T., 1949-52; B.S., Boston U., 1959; m. Brownielee McCullough, May 9, 1942; children—Claudia Ann, Adele Elaine, David Samuel. Mech. designer Colson Corp., Somerville, Mass., 1952-56, Harvard U., Cambridge, Mass., 1956-59; staff engr. Draper Lab., M.I.T., Cambridge, 1959-80, cons., 1980—. Recipient Apollo Achievement award NASA. Mem. AIAA, Armed Forces Communications and Electronics Assn., Inventors Assn. New Eng. Home: 210 Hartman Rd Newton Center MA 02159

SMITH, SCOTT ORMOND, lawyer; b. Altadena, Calif., Mar. 30, 1948; s. Donald Ormond and Jerry Ann (Shaw) S.; m. Antoinette Tribolet, Aug. 23, 1968 (div. 1983); children—Victoria, Jeffrey Ormond, Meagan Ashley; m. Barbara Lockert, May 8, 1985. B.S., U. So. Calif., 1971; J.D., Loyola U., Los Angeles, 1974. Bar: Calif. 1974, U.S. Dist. Ct. (so., no., cen. and ea. dists.) Calif. 1975, U.S. Ct. Appeals (9th cir.) 1975, U.S. Supreme Ct. 1984. Assoc. Foonberg & Frandzel, Beverly Hills, Calif., 1974-77; ptnr. Nelsen & Smith, Los Angeles, 1977-80; ptnr. Morganstern, Mann & Smith, Beverly Hills, 1980-83; sr. ptnr. Smith & Smith, Los Angeles, Calif., 1983—; lectr. Rutter Group, Calif., 1982—, Continuing Edn. of Bar, Calif., 1983—. Mem. ABA, Calif. State Bar, Los Angeles County Bar (treas. prejudgement remedies sect. 1984-85), Fin. Lawyers Conf. (bd. govs. 1982-86), Bankruptcy Study Group, Phi Alpha Delta, Beta Gamma Sigma. Republican. Presbyterian. Office: Smith & Smith 888 S Figueroa St 9th Floor Los Angeles CA 90017

SMITH, SELMA MOIDEL, lawyer, composer; b. Warren, Ohio, Apr. 3, 1919; d. Louis and Mary (Oyer) Moidel; student Los Angeles City Coll., 1936-37, U. Calif., 1937-39, U. So. Calif., 1939-41; J.D., Pacific Coast U., 1942; 1 son, Mark Lee. Bar: Calif. 1943, U.S. Dist. Ct. 1943, U.S. Supreme Ct. 1958. Gen. practice law; mem. firm Moidel, Moidel, Moidel & Smith. Field dir. civilian adv. com. WAC, 1943; mem. nat. bd. Med. Coll. Pa. (formerly Woman's Med. Coll. Pa.), 1953—, exec. bd., 1976-80, pres.-elect, 1980, pres., 1980-82. Decorated La Order del Merito Juan Pablo Duarte (Dominican Republic). Mem. ABA, Calif. Bar Assn. (servicemen's legal com.), Los Angeles Bar Assn. (psychopathic ct. com.), Los Angeles Lawyers Club (public defenders com.), Nat. Assn. Women Lawyers (chmn. com. unauthorized practice of law, social commn. UN, regional dir. western states, Hawaii 1949-57, mem. jud. adminstrn. com. 1960, nat. chmn. world peace through law com. 1966-67), League of Ams. (dir.), Inter-Am. Bar Assn., So. Calif. Women Lawyers Assn. (pres. 1947, 48, chmn. Law Day com. 1966, subject of oral hist. project, 1986), State Bar Conf. Com., Council Bar Assns. Los Angeles County (charter sec. 1950), Calif. Bus. Women's Council (dir. 1951), Los Angeles Bus. Women's Council (pres. 1952), Calif. Pres.'s Council (1st v.p.), Nat. Assn. Composers U.S.A. (dir. 1974-79, ann. luncheon chmn. 1975), Nat. Fedn. Music Clubs (nat. vice chmn. for Western region, 1973-78), Calif. Fedn. Music Clubs (state chmn. Am. Music 1971-75, state conv. chmn. 1972), Docents of Los Angeles Philharmonic (v.p. 1973-83, chmn. Latin Am. community relations 1972-75, press and public relations 1972-75, cons. coordinator 1973-75), Euterpe Opera Club (v.p. 1974-75, chmn. auditions 1972, chmn. awards 1973-75), ASCAP, Iota Tau Tau (dean Los Angeles, supreme treas.), Plato Soc. of UCLA, 1981—, discussion leader UCLA Constitution Bicentennial Project, 1985-87. Composer: Espressivo-Four Piano Pieces (orchestral premiere 1986). Home: 5272 Lindley Ave Encino CA 91316

SMITH, STEPHEN RALPH, business executive; b. Chgo., Sept. 26, 1945; s. Ralph E. and M. Imogene (Gard) S.; m. Patricia Moreno, Aug. 15, 1980; children: Paola Lucia, Carlo Alessandro/. BS, Case Inst. Tech., Cleve., 1967. With Airco Inc./Brit. Oxygen Co., N.Y.C., 1967-71; mgr. western hemisphere ops. Allied-Signal Corp., Morristown, N.J., 1971-75, dir. internat. devel., 1976-77, dir. internat. ops., 1977-79, dir. acquisitions, 1979-81; v.p., internat. gen. mgr. Drew Chem. Co., Boonton, N.J., 1981-82; mng. dir. Farmoplant S.P.A., Milan, 1982-85; pres., chief exec. officer Pochteca Corp., N.Y.C., 1982—, LPS Software Co., N.Y.C., 1986—; mng. dir. Winex Ltd., Guernsey, Eng., 1986-87; chmn. bd. dirs. Tianguis Ltd., London, Milan, 1985—; cons. Citicorp, N.Y.C., 1987—. Mem. European Venture Capital Assn., Swiss Venture Capital Assn.

SMITH, STEVEN SIDNEY, molecular biologist; b. Idaho Falls, Idaho, Feb. 11, 1946; s. Sidney Ervin and Hermie Phyllis (Robertson) S.; m. Nancy Louise Turner, Dec. 20, 1974. BS, U. Idaho, 1968; PhD, UCLA, 1974. Asst. research scientist Beckman Research Inst. City of Hope Nat. Med. Ctr., Duarte, Calif., 1982-84, staff Cancer Ctr., 1983—, asst. research scientist depts. Thoracic Surgery and Molecular Biology, 1985-87, assoc. research scientist molecular surgery dept., 1987—; cons. Molecular Biosystems Inc., San Diego, 1981-84. Contbr. articles to profl. jours. Grantee NIH, 1983—, Council for Tobacco Research, 1983—, March of Dimes, 1988—; Swiss Nat. Sci. Found. fellow Univ. Bern, 1968-73, Scripps Clinic and Research Found., La Jolla, Calif., 1978-82, NIH fellow, Scripps Clinic, 1979-81. Mem. AAAS, Pacific Slopes Biochem. Soc., N.Y. Acad. of Scies., Am. Soc. Cell Biology, Phi Beta Kappa. Republican. Office: City of Hope Nat Med Ctr 1500 E Duarte Rd Duarte CA 91010

SMITH, TAD RANDOLPH, lawyer; b. El Paso, July 20, 1928; s. Eugene Rufus and Dorothy (Derrick) S.; B.B.A., U. Tex., 1952, LL.B., 1951; m. JoAnn Wilson, Aug. 24, 1949; children—Laura, Derrick, Cameron Ann. Admitted to Tex. bar, 1951; assoc. firm Kemp, Smith, Duncan & Hammond, El Paso, 1951, partner, 1952—, mng. ptnr., 1975—; dir. El Paso Electric Co., M-Bank El Paso N.A., Property Trust Am.. Greater El Paso Devel. Corp., El Paso Indsl. Devel. Corp. Active United Way of El Paso; chmn. El Paso County Reps., 1958-61, Tex. Rep. State Exec. Com., 1961-62; alt. del. Rep. Nat. Conv., 1952, 62, del., 1964; trustee Robert E. and Evelyn McKee Found. 1970—; mem. devel. bd. U. Tex. El Paso, 1973-81, v.p., 1975, chmn. 1976; dinner treas. Nat. Jewish Hosp. and Research Ctr., 1977, chmn. 1978, presenter of honoree, 1985; bd. dirs. Southwestern Children's Home, El Paso, 1959-78, Nat. Conf. Christians and Jews, 1965-76, chmn. 1968-69, adv. dir. 1976—, Renaissance 400, El Paso, 1982—. Named Outstanding Young Man El Paso, El Paso Jaycees, 1961; recipient Humanitarian award El Paso chpt. NCCJ, 1983. Fellow Tex. Bar Found.; mem. ABA, Tex. Bar Assn., El Paso Bar Assn. (pres. 1971-72), El Paso C. of C. (dir. 1979-82), Sigma Chi. Republican. Methodist. Home: 1202 Thunderbird El Paso TX 79912 Office: Kemp Smith Duncan & Hammond 221 N Kansas 2000 MBank Plaza El Paso TX 79901

SMITH, TERRY GORDON, electronics production manager; b. Cin., Aug. 7, 1937; s. Clifford John and Vivan Aileen (Stone) S.; m. Sylvia Ann Gehl, Jan. 20, 1959 (dec. Dec. 1984); children: Donald Melvin, Terri Ann. Student, Arizona State U.; BA, U. Phoenix, MA in Mgmt., MBA. Mgr., owner Pharmacy, Phoenix, 1959-65; mgr. Super X Pharmacy, Scottsdale, Ariz., 1965-70; supr. Motorola, Inc., Phoenix, 1966-71, prodn. mgr., 1971—; mgmt. lectr. U. Phoenix, 1984—. Author: Metal Finishing Safety Manual, 1975. Mem. World Electroless Nickel Soc., Am. Mgmt. Assn., Am. Electroplaters Soc., Am. Soc. for Metal, Assn. for Mfg. Excellence. Republican.

SMITH, THOMAS BROUN, editor; b. Glasgow, Scotland, Dec. 3, 1915; s. John and Agnes (Brown/McFarlane) S.; m. Ann Dorothea Tindall, Feb. 3, 1940; 1 child, Carolyn Ann Ouchterlony. BA, MA, BCL, DCL, Oxford (Eng.) U., 1937-56; LLD, Edinburgh (Scotland) U., 1962; LLD (hon.), U. Cape Town, Republic of South Africa, 1959, U. Aberdeen, Scotland, 1969, U. Glasgow, Scotland, 1978. Bar: barrister at law Eng. 1938; adv. Scotland 1947; Queen's counsel 1956. Barrister London, 1938-39; adv. Edinburgh, 1947-49; prof. Scots law U. Aberdeen, 1949-58; prof. civil law U. Edinburgh, 1958-68, prof. Scots law, 1968-72; commr. Scottish Law Commn., Edinburgh, 1972-81; vis. prof. Tulane U. Law Sch., New Orleans, 1957-58, Harvard U. Law Sch., 1962-63, La. State U. Law Sch., 1973; Tagore prof. U. Calcutta, India, 1977. Author: Studies Critical and Comparative, 1963, Short Commentary on the Laws of Scotland, 1963, Property Problems in Sale, 1978, Basic Rights and their Enforcement, 1982, others; gen. editor: The Laws of Scotland: Stair Memorial Encyclopaedia; contbr. numerous articles to profl. jours. Lt. col. Territorial Army, Scotland, 1950-55. Served to lt. col. Brit. Army, 1939-46, ETO, MTO. Decorated knight bachelor Queen of Gt. Britain; named a hon. bencher Gray's Inn, 1987. Fellow Brit. Acad., Royal Soc. Edinburgh; mem. AAAS (fgn. hon. mem.), Law Soc. Scotland (hon.). Mem. Ch. of Scotland. Clubs: Naval and Mil. (London); New (Edinburgh). Home: 18 Royal Circus, Edinburgh EH3 6SS, Scotland Office: British Academy, 20-21 Cronwall Terr, London NW1 4QP, England

SMITH, THOMAS GREGORY, manufacturing company executive, wholesale distribution executive; b. Aurora, Ill., May 18, 1959; s. Dwight Emerson and Margaret Eloise (Garrett) S.; m. Lisa Jo Middleton, Jan. 27, 1979 (div. Mar. 1980); Stacey Lynn Marcum, Feb. 27, 1982; children: Michelle Lynn, Derek Mathew. Grad. high sch., West Aurora, Ill. Sales engr. Dwight Smith and Assocs., Aurora, 1980-81, v.p., gen. mgr., 1981-84, pres., gen. mgr., 1984—; pres., gen. mgr. Gregory Thomas, Inc., Aurora, 1981—; static cons. RCA Video Disk, Indpls., 1981-84. Mem. Nat. Electronics Distbr. Assn., Am. Fedn. Musicians, U.S. Ind. Telephone Assn., Elec. Overstress/Electrostatic Discharge Assn. (regional membership chmn. 1987-88), Am. Soc. Naval Engrs. Republican. Roman Catholic. Office: 834 N Highland Ave Aurora IL 60506

SMITH, THOMAS SHORE, lawyer; b. Rock Springs, Wyo., Dec. 7, 1924; s. Thomas and Anne E. (McTee) S.; m. Jacqueline Emily Krueger, May 25, 1952; children: Carolyn Jane, Karl Thomas, David Shore. BS in Bus. Adminstrn., U. Wyo., 1950, JD, 1959. Bar: U.S. Dist. Ct. Wyo. 1960, U.S. Ct. Appeals (10th cir.) 1960, U.S. Tax Ct. 1969, U.S. Supreme Ct. 1971. Ptnr. Smith, Stanfield & Scott, Laramie; atty. City of Laramie, Wyo., 1963-86; instr. mcpl. law U. Wyo., 1987. Dir. budget and fin. Govt. Am. Samoa, 1952-56; bd. dirs. Bur. Land Mgmt., Rawlins, Wyo., 1984—, Ivinson Hosp. Found., 1986—. Served 2d lt. USAF, 1944-46, ETO. Francis Warren scholar, 1958. Mem ABA, Wyo. Bar Assn. (pres. 1984-85), Albany County Bar Assn., Western States Bar Conf. (pres. 1985-86). Republican. Episcopalian. Lodges: Elks, Rotary. Office: Smith Stanfield & Scott 515 Ivinson PO Box 971 Laramie WY 82070

SMITH, VICTOR JOACHIM, artist; b. Grand Island, Nebr., Apr. 3, 1929; s. Victor Bordwell and Vesta Marie (Houf) S.; children—Melanie, Therese. B.A., Calif. State U., Long Beach, 1953, M.A., 1954. From instr. to assoc. prof. art Calif. State U., Long Beach, 1955-62; mem. faculty Calif. State U., Fullerton, 1962—; prof. art Calif. State U., 1968-81, prof. emeritus, 1981—, chmn. dept., 1976-77, vice chmn. dept., 1977-79. One-man exhbns. include, Comara Gallery, Los Angeles, 1960, 62, 66, 67, 69, Long Beach (Calif.) Mus. Art, 1959, Santa Barbara (Calif.) Mus. Art, 1962, Pasadena (Calif.) Art Mus., 1963, Los Angeles Mcpl. Art Gallery, 1968, Newport Harbor (Calif.) Art Mus., 1975, group exhbns. in, U.S., abroad; represented in numerous permanent collections. (Recipient over 70 awards for drawing and painting.). Home: Route 3 Box 778 Carbon Canyon CA 91710 Office: Art Dept Calif State U Fullerton CA 92634

SMITH, WALDO GREGORIUS, former government official; b. Bklyn., July 29, 1911; s. John Henry and Margaret (Gregorius) S.; m. Mildred Pearl Prescott, July 30, 1935; 1 dau., Carole Elizabeth Smith Levin. Student CCNY, N.Y., 1928-29; B.S. in Forestry, Cornell U., 1933. Forester, Forest Service, U.S. Dept. Agr., Atlanta, 1933-41, Ala. Div. Forestry, Brewton, 1941-42; engr., civil engring. technician Geol. Survey, U.S. Dept. Interior, 1942-71, cartographic technician, 1972-75; chmn. Public Transp. Council, 1975—; aide to indiv. legislator Colo. State Legis. Internship Program, 1987. Recipient 40 year Civil Service award pin and scroll; 42 Yr. Govt. Service award plaque. Registered profl. engr., Colo. Fellow Am. Congress Surveying and Mapping (life; sec.-treas. Colo. chpt. 1961, program chmn. 1962, reporter 1969, mem. nat. membership devel. com. 1973-74, rep. to Colo. Engring. Council 1976-77); mem. AAAS, Denver Fed. Center Profl. Engrs. Group (U.S. Geol. Survey rep. 1973-76, Engr. of Yr. award 1975), Nat. Soc. Profl. Engrs. (pre-coll. guidance com. 1986—), Profl. Engrs. Colo. (chpt. scholarship chmn. 1979—, advt. corr., service award 1983), Cornell U. Alumni Assn. (alumni secondary schs. com.), Common Cause, Colo. Engring. Council (chmn. library com. 1970—, spl. rep. Regional Transp. Dist., 1974-75; mem. sci. fair com. 1970-71; rep. ex officio Denver Pub. Library Found. Bd. Trustees 1975-80, Pres.' Outstanding Service award 1987), Fedn. Am. Scientists, Am. Soc. Engring. Edn., People for Am. Way. Contbr. proposals to science-for-citizens program and research applied to nat. needs program NSF. Contbr. articles to profl. jours. Home: 3821 W 25th Ave Denver CO 80211

SMITH, WALTER DELOS, accountant; b. Rensselaer, Ind., June 7, 1936; s. Walter Myron and Evelyn Geraldine (Murphy) S.; m. Yvonne Marie Dietz, Sept. 24, 1960; children—Michele, Michael, Kevin, Bryan, Denise, Derek. B.S. in Acctg., Walton Sch. Commerce, Chgo., 1960. C.P.A., Wis., Ill. Acct. Frazer & Torbet C.P.A.s, Chgo., 1960-66; asst. controller Rath-Packing Co., Waterloo, Iowa 1966-68; controller, treas. DeLeuw, Cather & Co., Chgo., 1968-72; corp. controller Mohawk Data Scis., Utica, N.Y., 1972-75; mgmt. cons. Walter D. Smith & Assocs., New Hartford, N.Y., 1975-76; v.p., gen. mgr. Flambeau-Plastics, Baraboo, Wis., 1976-83; prin. Walter D. Smith, C.P.A., Baraboo, 1983—; owner, pres. Fine Cabinet Shop, Inc., Baraboo, 1983—; mem. adv. panel U. Wis., Madison and Whitewater, 1981—; dir. Trachte Bldg. Systems, Sun Prairie, Wis. Pres. Downers Grove Drug Abuse Council, Ill., 1972; mem. Baraboo Area Opportunity Devel. Com., 1983—; bd. dirs. New Hartford Sch. Dist., 1974-76, Baraboo Sch. Dist., 1980-83. Served with AUS, 1955-56, Korea. Mem. Nat. Assn. Accts. (bd. dirs. 1966-67), Baraboo Toastmasters. Republican. Roman Catholic. Lodge: Kiwanis. Home: 809 Iroquois Circle Baraboo WI 53913 Office: Walter D Smith CPA 222 3d Ave Baraboo WI 53913

SMITH, WALTER JOSEPH, JR., lawyer, educator; b. N.Y.C., Feb. 23, 1936; s. Walter J. and Florence W. (Watson) S.; m. Felicitas U. Von Zeschau, Oct. 5, 1968; children—Caroline, Alexandria, Christopher. A.B., Hamilton Coll., 1958; LL.B., Columbia U., 1961. Bar: U.S. Ct. Mil. Appeals 1967, U.S. Dist. Ct. (D.C. dist.) 1967, U.S. Ct. Appeals (D.C. cir.) 1967, U.S. Supreme Ct. 1974, U.S. Ct. Claims 1975. Mem. Judge Advocate Gen.'s Office, U.S. Navy, Washington, 1966-68; trial atty., Washington, 1968-75; ptnr. Wilson, Elser, Moskowitz, Edelman & Dicker, Washington, 1975—; mng. ptnr., 1979—; adj. prof. law Antioch Sch. Law, 1981—. Pres. Dogwood Assn., 1982-83. Served to lt. USN, 1962-67. Recipient Pres.'s award Am. Soc. Pharmacy Law, 1984. Mem. ABA, Def. Research Inst., Counsellors, D.C. Bar Assn. Democrat. Roman Catholic. Clubs: Tuckahoe. Author: Insurance Protection in Product Liability. Office: Suite 880 600 Maryland Ave SW Washington DC 20024

SMITH, WALTER LEONARD, marine educator; b. N.Y.C., July 23, 1918; s. Leonard and Mary Elizabeth (Moog) S.; A.B., N.Y. U., 1945, M.S., 1947; m. Marjory Ellen Johnston, Dec. 27, 1967; children by previous marriage—Deborah, Colleen; 1 stepdau., Susan. Research fellow Warner Inst., N.Y.C., 1943; instr. St. Francis Coll., Bklyn., 1945-47, L.I. U., 1947-57; dir. pharm. sales and research Algin Corp., N.Y.C., 1957-61; asst. prof. Suffolk County Community Coll., Selden, N.Y., 1961-64, asso. prof., 1964-65, prof. head dept. life sci., 1965-68, prof. head dept. marine sci. and tech., 1969-77, prof. marine sci. and tech., 1977—; cons. Torigan Labs., 1954-58, Airborne Instruments, 1960, Shelter Island Oyster Co., 1961-66; dir. Goose Creek Ecol. Study, 1966-68. Co-chmn., Long Island Marine Resources Council, 1963; mem. PIADC Inst. Biological Safety Com. U.S Dept. Agr., 1988—, Plum Island Animal Disease Ctr., N.Y., 1988—, Marine Resources Council Bi-County Planning Bd., 1967—; bd. dirs., pres. Middle Atlantic Natural Sci. Council, Greenport, N.Y., 1972—; bd. dirs. L.I. chpt. N.Y. State Archeol. Assn., 1981—, pres., 1986—. Mem. World Mariculture Assn., Am. Inst. Bio. Scis., Nat. Shellfisheries Assn., N.Y. State Marine Edn. Assn. (exec. dir. 1977-81), Nat. Marine Edn. Assn., Inst. Biology of Gt. Britain. Club: Orient Yacht. Editor: Culture of Marine Invertebrate Animals, 1975. Home: PO Box 754 Orient NY 11957 Office: Suffolk County Community College Riverhead NY 11901

SMITH, WARREN ALLEN, recording studio corporate executive; b. Minburn, Iowa, Oct. 27, 1921; s. Harry Clark and Ruth Marion (Miles) S.; BA, U. No. Iowa, 1948; MA, Columbia U., 1949. Chmn. dept. Eng., Bentley Sch., N.Y.C., 1949-54, New Canaan (Conn.) High Sch., 1954-86; pres., chmn. bd. Variety Sound Corp., N.Y.C., 1961—; pres. Afro-Carib Records, 1971—, Talent Mgmt., 1982—, pres. AAA Recording Studio, 1985—; pres. Variety Rec. Studio, 1988—; instr. Columbia U., 1961-62. Pres., Taursa Fund, 1971-73. Book rev. editor The Humanist, 1953-58; editor (jour.) Taking Stock, 1967—; contbr. book revs. Library Jour.; syndicated columnist Manhattan Scene in W.I. newspapers. Served with AUS, 1940-44. Recipient Leavey award Freedoms Found. at Valley Forge, 1985. Mem. ASCAP, Mensa, Internat. Press Inst., Am. Unitarian Assn., Brit. Humanist Assn., Humanist Book Club (pres. 1957-62), Bertrand Russell Soc. (v.p. 1977-80, bd. dirs. 1977—), Mensa Investment Club (chmn. 1967, 73—). Signer Humanist Manifesto II, 1973. Avocation: teratology. Home: 1435 Bedford St Apt 10-A Stamford CT 06905 Office: Variety Rec Studios 130 W 42d St Room 551 New York NY 10036

SMITH, WESLEY CLAUDE, trucking company executive; b. Morland, Kans., Sept. 12, 1931; s. Harry Melroy and Bessie Lee (Dorton) S.; student Creighton U., Omaha, 1953-54; m. Marsha Kaye Perkins, July 29, 1971; children—Bradley C., Cynthia P., Daniel C., Brian C., Melissa K. Pres., chmn. bd. Magna Garfield Truck Line and Uintah Freightways, Salt Lake City, 1963—, Colt Trucking, Inc.; ptnr. Smith's Leasing, Salt Lake City. Bd. dirs. Transport Clearings Intermountain, 1969, chmn. bd., 1974-75, nat. chmn., 1975-76; bd. dirs. Rocky Mountain Tariff Bur., Western Hwy. Inst., Amicus-Latter Day Saints Hosp. Served with USAF, 1951-55. Mem. Am. Trucking Assn. (exec. com., v.p.), Utah Motor Transport Assn. (pres. 1973-75, dir., Service award), Regular Common Carrier Conf. (dir.), Salt Lake Internat. Round Table (pres. 1967), Salt Lake Transp. Club (v.p. 1965). Clubs: Salt Lake Rotary, Utah Elephant. Home: 4430 Viewcrest Dr Salt Lake City UT 84124 Office: 1030 S Redwood Rd Salt Lake City UT 84104

SMITH, WILBUR COWAN, lawyer; b. Aledo, Ill., July 16, 1914; s. Fred Harold and Anna Elizabeth (Cowan) S.; m. Teressa Phyllis Stout, Sept. 10, 1938; children—Roger Allen, Judith Ellen Smith Adams; m. Florence Ann Mackie, June 21, 1964; 1 dau., Donna Lee Pinkes; step-children—Diane Marie Linhart, Wayne Douglas Griffith, Nancy Ann LaFraugh. Student Colo. U., 1932-33, N.Mex. U., 1933; B.A., U. Iowa, 1937; J.D., Creighton U., 1954. Bar: Nebr. 1954, U.S. Dist. Ct. Nebr. 1954, U.S. Ct. Appeals (8th cir.) 1974. Salesman Gen. Foods Corp., 1939; civilian chemist U.S. Naval Ordnance, 1942-45; mgr. Omar Flour Mills, 1945-47; account exec. C.A. Swanson & Sons, 1948-49; dist. mgr. Brown-Forman Distillery, 1950-51; adminstrv. asst. to judge Douglas County, 1954-55; asst. city prosecutor Omaha, 1956; sole practice, Omaha, 1956-73; ptnr. Smith & Hansen, Omaha, 1973—. Pres., North High Sch. PTA, 1959-61, Belvedere Sch., 1954-56, Oak Valley, 1965-67; mem. bldg. com. YMCA, 1954-56; membership com. Boy Scouts Am., 1956-61; county del. Republican Party, 1962-82. Mem. ABA, Nebr. Bar Assn., Omaha Bar Assn., Am. Judicature Soc., Phi Alpha Delta. Methodist. Clubs: Odd Fellows, Masons, Shriners, United Comml. Travelers Protective Assn., Order Eastern Star. Office: Smith & Hansen 405 Farnam Bldg 1613 Farnam St Omaha NE 68102

SMITH, WILLIAM ARTHUR, artist; b. Toledo, Apr. 19, 1918; s. Bert Arthur and Catherine Jane (Doan) S.; m. Mary France Nixon, Sept. 30, 1939 (div. 1946); 1 son, Richard Keane; m. Ferol Yvonne Stratton, Oct. 10, 1949; children: Kim, Kathlin Alexandra. Student, Keane's Art Sch., Toledo, 1932-36, U. Toledo, 1936-37; M.A., U. Toledo, 1954. Newspaper work 1936-37; established studio N.Y.C., 1937; instr. Grand Central Art Sch., 1942-43; lectr. Acad. Fine Arts, Athens, 1954, U. Santa Tomas, Manila, 1955, Acad. Fine Arts, Warsaw, 1958; ofcl. del. Internat. Assn. Plastic Arts, Venice, 1954; mem. ofcl. del. to Russia under Cultural Exchange Agreement, 1958. Represented in, Met. Mus. N.Y.C., Library of Congress, Washington, one-man shows, Toledo Mus. Art, 1942, 52, Bucknell U., 1952, others, many fgn. cities during recent years; executed: mural Md. House, 1968; designed numerous U.S. postage stamps.; illustrator five books John Day Pub. Co. and others; author: Gerd Utescher; author, illustrator articles for various mags. Bd. dirs. Welcome House, v.p., 1966-73. Recipient Adolph and Clara Obrig prize for oil painting, 1953, Am. Artists Group prize for lithography Soc. Am. Graphic Artists, 1954, Knobloch prize, 1956, Winslow Homer Meml. prize, 1962, Am. Patriots' medal, 1974, Postal Commemorative Soc. prize, 1974; Dolphin fellow. Mem. Internat. Assn. Art (U.S. del. 1963, 66, 69, 73, exec. com. 1963-69, v.p. 1966-69, pres. 1973-76, hon. pres. 1976—, pres. U.S. nat. com. 1970-77, hon. pres. 1977—), NAD (sec. 1954-55, council 1953-56, 75-78, Watercolor award 1949, 51), Am. Watercolor Soc. (trustee 1949, pres. 1956-57, hon. pres. 1957—, Silver medal 1948, 52, 73, Stuart Watercolor prize 1954, Gold medal 1957, 65, Bronze medal 1972), Calif. Watercolor Soc., Audubon Artists, Phila. Watercolor Club, Nat. Soc. Mural Painters, Dutch Treat Club. Address: Bucks County Pineville PA 18946

SMITH, WILLIAM BASIL, manufacturing executive; b. Kansas City, Mo., Mar. 9, 1936; s. Theodore Winningham and Vera Ureth (Webb) S.; m. Nancy Lee Barker, June 22, 1957; children: Mark William Lee, Theodore Robert James. BSBA, U. Mo., 1958. cert. orthotist. Purchasing agt. Knit-Rite, Inc., Kansas City, 1959-67, distbn. mgr., 1967-68, exec. v.p., 1968-70, chmn. bd. dirs., 1970—, pres., 1973—; pres. Am. Bd. for Cert. in Orthotics and Prosthetics, Alexandria, Va., 1974-75. Mem. Am. Orthotic and Prosthetic Assn. (pres. 1985-86), Internat. Soc. Orthotists and Prosthetists. Home: 11000 Alhambra Leawood KS 66211 Office: Knit-Rite Inc PO Box 410208 Kansas City MO 64141-0208

SMITH, WILLIAM FRENCH, lawyer, former attorney general U.S.; b. Wilton, N.H., Aug. 26, 1917; s. William French and Margaret (Dawson) S.; m. Jean Webb, Nov. 6, 1964. A.B. summa cum laude, U. Calif., 1939; LL.B., Harvard U., 1942; hon. degrees, Pepperdine U., DePaul U., U. San Diego. Bar: Calif. 1942. Atty., sr. ptnr. Gibson, Dunn & Crutcher, Los Angeles, 1946-81, 85—; atty. gen. U.S., Washington, 1981-85; mem. Pres. Fgn. Intelligence Adv. Bd., Washington, 1985—; bd. dirs. Crocker Nat. Bank, San Francisco, 1971-81, Pullman, Inc., 1979-81, Pacific Mut. Life Ins. Co., 1970-81, RCA, 1985-86; now bd. dirs. Pacific Enterprises, Los Angeles, NBC Corp., N.Y.C., Am. Internat Group, N.Y.C., Pacific Telesis Group, Pacific Bell, San Francisco, Gen. Electric Co., N.Y.C., H.F. Ahmanson & Co., Los Angeles, Earle M. Jorgensen Co., Los Angeles, Fisher Sci. Group Inc., La Jolla, Calif., Weintraub Entertainment Group Inc., Los Angeles. Mem. U.S. Adv. Commn. on Internat. Ednl. and Cultural Affairs, 1971-78, Stanton Panel on Internat. Info., Edn. and Cultural Relations, 1974-75; U.S. del. The East-West Ctr. for Cultural and Tech. Interchange, Hawaii, 1975-77; mem. adv. council Sch. Govt., Harvard U., 1977—, mem. visiting com. Ctr. Internat. Affairs, Harvard U., 1986—; mem. adv. bd. Ctr. for Strategic and Internat. Studies, Georgetown U., Washington, 1978-82, 85—; mem. nat. bd. advisors Fedn. for Am. Immigration Reform (FAIR), 1985—; mem. nat. adv. com. Internat. Tennis Found. and Hall of Fame, Inc., 1985—, Nat. Legal Ctr. for the Pub. Interest, 1985—; mem. exec. com. The Calif. Roundtable, 1976-81, 85—, Calif. Community Found., 1980-81, 85—; bd. regents U. Calif., 1968—, chmn., 1970-72, 74-75, 76; bd. dirs. Legal Aid Found. Los Angeles, 1963-72; bd. dirs. Los Angeles World Affairs Council, 1970—, pres., 1975-78; dir. Am.-China Soc., 1987—; trustee Claremont McKenna Coll., 1967—, Ind. Colls. of So. Calif., 1969-74, Ctr. Theatre Group, Los Angeles Music Ctr., 1970-81, Henry E. Huntington Library and Art Gallery, 1971—, The Cate Sch., 1971-78, Northrop Inst. Tech., 1973-75; chmn. bd. trustees The Ronald Reagan Presdl. Library Found., 1985—; nat. trustee Nat. Symphony Orch., Washington, 1974—; mem. bd. fellows The Inst. Jud. Adminstrn., Inc., 1981—; chmn. Calif. Delegation to Rep. Nat. Conv., 1968, vice chmn., 1971, 76, 80, 88. Served to lt. USNR, 1942-46. Fellow Am. Bar Found.; mem. ABA (fellow sect. of litigation 1985—, standing com. law and nat. security 1985—), Los Angeles County Bar Assn., Am. Judicature Soc., Am. Law Inst., Calif. C. of C. (bd. dirs. 1963-80, pres. 1974-75), Order of Coif (hon.), Phi Beta Kappa, Pi Gamma Mu, Pi Sigma Alpha, Phi Delta Phi.

SMITH, WILLIAM HENRY PRESTON, free-lance writer; b. Pleasanton, Tex., Sept. 8, 1924; s. Sidney Newton and Willie Gertrude (Cloyd) S.; m. Frances Dixon, July 1, 1950; children: Juliet, Dixon, David. B.J., U. Tex., 1949. Reporter Dallas Morning News, 1949-52; advt. asst. Dallas Power & Light Co., 1952-55; dir. pub. relations Greater Boston C. of C., 1955-58; with New Eng. Telephone and Telegraph Co., Boston, 1958-86, asst. v.p.,

1966-75, corp. sec., 1975-83, dir. pub. relations, 1983-86; freelance writer Dover, Mass., 1986—. Bd. dirs., v.p. Mass. Soc. for Prevention Cruelty to Children; bd. dirs. Urban Dynamics Adv. Com.; mem. support policies com. United Way Mass. Served with paratroops U.S. Army, 1943-46. Decorated Purple Heart. Mem. Am. Soc. Corp. Secs., Friars, Sigma Delta Chi, Delta Kappa Epsilon. Republican. Clubs: Dedham Country and Polo, Down Town. Home and Office: 10 Turtle Ln Dover MA 02030

SMITH, WILLIAM MARTIN, financial executive; b. Chgo., Nov. 30, 1943; s. Sam and Helen Smith; BA, Mich. State U., 1965; JD, Chgo. Kent Coll. Law, 1973; m. Linda Carol Zimbalist, May 27, 1979; 1 child, Brian Alexander. Sr. v.p., dir. A.G. Becker, Inc., Chgo., 1972-77; bar: Ill. 1974; pres., chief operating officer Chgo. Bd. Options Exchange, 1977-79; pres., chief exec. officer N.Y. Futures Exchange, 1979-81, 1987—; gen. ptnr. Zimbalist Smith Ltd. Served to lt. (j.g.) USNR, 1966-69. Mem. Futures Industry Assn., Ill. Bar Assn. Club: Union League (Chgo.). Office: 125 Main St Suite 107 Westport CT 06880

SMITH, WILLIAM RAY, biophysicist, engineer; b. Lyman, Okla., June 26, 1925; s. Harry Wait and Daisy Belle (Hull) S. B.A., Bethany Nazarene Coll., 1948; M.A., Wichita State U., 1950; postgrad. U. Kans., 1950-51; Ph.D., UCLA, 1967. Engr., Beech Aircraft Corp., Wichita, Kans., 1951-53; sr. group engr. McDonnell Aircraft Corp., St. Louis, 1953-60; sr. engr. Lockheed Aircraft Corp., Burbank, Calif., 1961-63; sr. engr. scientist McDonnell Douglas Corp., Long Beach, Calif., 1966-71; mem. tech. staff Rockwell Internat., Los Angeles, 1973-86, CDI Corp.-West, Costa Mesa, Calif., 1986—; tchr. math. Glendale Coll., Calif., 1972; asst. prof. math. and physics Pasadena Coll. (now Point Loma Coll., San Diego), 1960-62, Mt. St. Mary's Coll., Los Angeles, 1972-73. Contbr. articles to sci. jours. Active Los Angeles World Affairs Council. Recipient citation McDonnell Douglas Corp., 1968; Tech. Utilization award Rockwell Internat., 1981; cert. of recognition NASA, 1982. Mem. N.Y. Acad. Scis., AAAS, AIAA, UCLA Chancelor's Assocs., Internat. Visitors Council Los Angeles, Town Hall Calif., Yosemite Natural History Assn., Sigma Xi, Pi Mu Epsilon. Republican. Presbyterian. Office: CDI Corp 3303 Harbor Blvd Costa Mesa CA 92626

SMITH, WILLIE TESREAU, JR., judge, lawyer; b. Sumter, S.C., Jan. 17, 1920; s. Willie T. and Mary (Moore) S. ; student Benedict Coll., 1937-40; A.B., Johnson C. Smith U., 1947; LL.B., S.C. State Coll., 1954, J.D., 1976; m. Anna Marie Clark, June 9, 1955; 1 son, Willie Tesreau, III. Admitted to S.C. bar, 1954; began gen. practice, Greenville, 1954; past exec. dir. Legal Services Agy. Greenville County, Inc.; state family ct. judge 13th Jud. Circuit S.C., 1977—. Mem. adv. bd. Greenville Tech. Edn. Center Adult Edn. Program and Para-Legal Program; past bd. dirs. Greenville Urban League; past trustee Greenville County Sch. Dist. Served with AUS, 1942-45, USAF, 1949-52. Mem. Am., Nat. (jud. council), S.C., Greenville County bar assns., Southeastern Lawyers Assn., Nat. Council Juvenile and Family Ct. Judges, Am. Legion, Greater Greenville C. of C. (past dir.), Phillis Wheatley Assn. (dir.), NAACP, Omega Psi Phi. Presbyterian (past chmn. bd. trustees Fairfield-McClelland Presbytery). Clubs: Masons, Shriners, Rotary. Home: 601 Jacob Rd Greenville SC 29605 Office: County Office Bldg S Main St PO Box 757 Greenville SC 29602

SMITH, WILLIS ALLEN, consultant, former food company executive; b. Balt., Oct. 26, 1919; s. Willis Alfred and Grace Lee (Roberts) S.; m. Joann Cobb, Aug. 29, 1970. Student, Johns Hopkins U., 1937-41, 46-48, Coll. William and Mary, Norfolk, Va., 1941-42. C.P.A., Md., Ohio, N.Y. Clk., Gas & Electric Co., Balt., 1936-41; acct. F. W. Lafrentz & Co., Balt., 1946-51; mgr. F.W. Lafrentz & Co., Salisbury, Md., 1952-53; partner F.W. Lafrentz & Co., Cleve., 1953-62, Main Lafrentz & Co., N.Y.C., 1963-74; comptroller CPC Internat. Inc., Englewood Cliffs, N.J., 1974-81, v.p., 1981-84; mem. bd. Internat. Acctg. Standards Com., 1979-82; lectr. Third Commodity Conf., Chgo., 1973, Internat. Acctg. Conf., N.Y.C., 1977, 10th Corp. Acctg. and Fin. Reporting Inst., Washington, 1979, Audit Mgmt. Conf., N.Y.C., 1982, Auditing and Acctg. Symposium, N.J., 1987. Contbr.: Accountants Handbook, 6th edit., 1981; articles to profl. jours. Pres. Vol. Bur. of Bergen County, Inc. Served with USNR, 1941-45, PTO. Mem. N.Y. State Soc. C.P.A.s (v.p. 1977-78, Outstanding Service award 1983), Fin. Execs. Inst., Nat. Assn. Accts., Am. Acctg. Assn., Am. Inst. C.P.A.s (v.p. 1982-83), Accts. Club (v.p.). Club: Ridgewood (N.J.) Country. Lodges: Masons, Shriners. Home: 815 Norgate Dr Ridgewood NJ 07450

SMITHERS, JOHN ABRAM, manufacturing executive; b. Middletown, N.Y., June 20, 1915; s. Francis Sydney and Eleanor (Boak) S.; m. Margaret McClure, Mar. 6, 1947 (div. May 1964); children: Margaret H., John Abram and Eleanor B. (twins), James P.; m. Jane Braitmayer Howell, June 13, 1964; stepchildren: Kathleen Howell, William D. Howell, Marian B. Howell. Customer and systems engr. IBM, 1935-47; ptnr. Red Hook Apple Industries, 1947-52; founder, treas. STAMP, Inc. (formerly Smithers Tools and Machine Products, Inc.), Rhinebeck, N.Y., 1948—, also bd. dirs.; founder, owner Sawkill Indsl. Park, Rhinebeck. Served to 2d lt. AUS, 1942-46. Mem. Council Industry Southeastern N.Y., Am. Def. Preparedness Assn., Am. Metal Stamping Assn. Clubs: Sippican, Beverly Yacht (Marion, Mass.). Home: Rd 2 Box 116 Red Hook NY 12571 Office: PO Box 391 Rhinebeck NY 12572-0391

SMITHSON, ALISON MARGARET, architect, writer; b. Sheffield, Eng., June 22, 1928; d. Ernest Gill and Alison Jessie (Malcolm) G.; m. Peter Denham Smithson, 1949; 3 children. Edn., Sunderland, South Shields, George Watson's Ladies Coll., Edinburgh and U. Durham. Asst., London County Council, 1949-50; pvt. practice architect with Peter Smithson, 1950—; prin. works include: Hunstanton Sch., Economist Bldg., London, Robin Hood Gardens, G.L.C. Housing in Tower Hamlets, Garden Bldg. St. Hilda's Coll., Oxford; exhbns.: Twenty-four Doors to Christmas, 1979; Christmas and Hogmanay, 1980-81; author: The Tram Rats; The Christmas Tree; Calendar of Christmas; Places Worth Inheriting; An Anthology of Christmas; An Anthology of Scottish Christmas and Hogmanay; Team 10 Primer; Euston Arch; AS in DS, An Eye on the Road, Upper Lawn, Solar Pavilion Folly; (novel) Young Girl; (with P. Smithson) Urban Structuring Studies; Ordinariness and Light; Without Rhetoric; The Heroic Period of Modern Architecture; The Shift: Monograph. Home: Cato Lodge, 24 Gilston Rd, London SW10 9SR, England

SMITHSON, PETER DENHAM, architect; b. Stockton-on-Tees, Eng., Sept. 18, 1923; s. William Blenkiron and Elizabeth (Denham) S.; m. Alison Margaret Gill, 1949; 3 children. Ed. Stockton-on-Tees Grammar Sch., U. Durham and Royal Acad. Schs., London. Asst. L.C.C., 1949-50; pvt. practice architect with Alison Smithson, 1950—; prin. works include: Hunstanton Sch., Economist Bldg., London, Robin Hood Gardens, G.L.C. Housing in Tower Hamlets, Garden Bldg. St. Hilda's Coll., Oxford, Amenity Bldg., U. Bath, Second Arts Bldg. 6 E, U. Bath; exhbns.: House of the Future, 1956, Milan Triennale, 1968; Venice Biennale, 1976; author: Urban Structuring Studies; Ordinariness and Light: Without Rhetoric; The Heroic Period of Modern Architecture; The Shift: Monograph; Bath Walks Within Walls; Oxford and Cambridge Walks. Address: Cato Lodge, 24 Gilston Rd, London SW10 9SR England

SMITHWICK, FRED, JR., hospital consultant; b. Washington, June 24, 1934; s. Fred and Genevieve (Davis) S.; A.A., Montgomery Coll., 1953; B.A., George Washington U., 1955, M.A., 1974. Asst. to pres. Dwoskin, Inc., Atlanta, 1956-63; dir. mktg. Moderncote, Inc., New Castle, Ind., 1963-70; v.p. Riverside Meth. Hosp., Columbus, Ohio, 1973-81, also sec. found.; pres. Physicians Profl. Mgmt. Corp., Columbus, 1981—; lectr. health care adminstrn. Ohio State U., George Washington U.; chmn. adv. com. Sch. Licensed Practical Nurses, Columbus Pub. Schs.; chmn. Health Resource Mgmt., Inc., Boca Raton, Fla. Fellow Royal Soc. Health (Gt. Britain), Am. Hosp. Assn.; mem. Am. Coll. Hosp. Adminstrs., Ohio Hosp. Assn., Delta Tau Delta. Methodist. Clubs: Porta Bella Yacht and Racquet (Boca Raton); Tower (Ft Lauderdale, Fla.). Lodge: Masons. Office: 4619 Kenny Rd Columbus OH 43220

SMITTER, RONALD WARREN, state judge; b. Pasadena, Calif., Nov. 14, 1951; s. Robert Claude and Kathryn Margaret (Brown) S.; m. Shannon Elaine Neilson, June 9, 1973; children: Sarah Kay, Robert William. B.A., U. Redlands, 1973; J.D., So. Meth. U., 1976. Bar: Tex. 1976, Calif., 1978, U.S. Dist. Ct. (so. dist.) Calif. 1978, U.S. Ct. Appeals (9th cir.) 1978. Assoc. Bonne, Jones & Bridges, Los Angeles, 1978-80, Morres, Polich & Purdy, Tustin, Calif., 1980-83; sole practice, Walnut, Calif., 1984—; judge pro tem Orange County Superior Ct., 1985—, workers compensation judge State of Calif.; mem. panel arbitrators, 1985—. Mem. ABA. Republican. Address: 1350 Front St Room 3047 San Diego CA 92101

SMOLDEREN, LUC HIPPOLYTE MARIE, Belgian diplomat; b. Anvers, Belgium, Feb. 7, 1924; m. Fiorella de Vinck de Winnezeele, Apr. 20, 1954; children: Violaine, Quentin, Ariane, Sybille. LLD, Catholic U., Louvain, Belgium, M in Philosophy and Letters. Atty. Brussels, 1950-53; with Ministry Fgn. Affairs, Brussels, 1953—; mem. del. to U N N.Y.C., 1956-58; mem. del. to NATO Paris, 1959-64; inspector of diplomatic posts Ministry Fgn. Affairs, Brussells, 1965-71; ambassador to Syria Damascus, 1972-76; permanent rep. to Atomic Agy. Vienna, 1976-80; ambassador to Morocco Rabat, 1981-85; ambassador to France Paris, 1986—. Contbr. articles to art and history jours. Named grand officier orders of Couronne de Belgique and Couronne de Chêne (Luxembourg); named commdr. orders of Léopold, Léopold II and Mérite Italien; named grand cordon Order Mérite Syrien. Mem. Soc. Royale de Numismatique de Belgique (v.p.), Acad. Royale d'Archéologie de Belgique. Office: Embassy of Belgium, 9 Rue de Tilsit, 75017 Paris France

SMOLKA, HORST, manufacturing executive; b. Hamburg, Ger., July 13, 1920; came to U.S., 1953, naturalized, 1962; s. Carl and Elisabeth (Schwendel) S.; Master's degree, Trade Coll. Hamburg, 1953; m. Anita Marianne Adermann, May 16, 1953; 1 son, Ronald Wilhelm. Tool maker apprentice Max Rentsch, Hamburg, Germany, 1937-40; tool maker machinist Hamburg Electric Works, 1949-53; machinist V & S Grinding, Chgo., 1953-54; model maker machinist Decker & Klingberg Co., Chgo., 1954-65, name changed Decker-Smolka Corp., 1965, pres., 1965—. Served with German Army, 1940-45. Prisoner of war, USSR, 1945-48. Home: 3031 N Nashville Ave Chicago IL 60634 Office: 5157-5165 W Homer St Chicago IL 60639

SMOLKA, THOMAS GORDON, manufacturing company executive; b. London, Feb. 27, 1936; s. Harry Peter and Lotty (Jaeckel) S.; m. Dalia Charlotte Semenowsky, Nov. 14, 1964; children—Alex Marc, Felix Albert, Ruth Merle. Exec. asst. to chmn. Gebauer & Lehrner, Vienna, Austria, 1958-59; exec. v.p. Tyrolia WMS, Vienna, 1959-70; dep. bus. mgr. AMF Tyrolia, Vienna, 1970-73; exec. v.p. Herz AG, Vienna, 1974-77; chmn., 1977—; non exec. dep. chmn. Inku AG, Vienna, 1984—, Matuschka, Austria, 1988— . Patentee ski bindings. Lay judge Labour Ct. Vienna, 1974-81. Recipient Olympic honorary medal Austrian Govt., 1964; named Kommerzialrat, Chancellor of Austria, 1976. Mem. Austrian Mech. Engring. Industries Assn. (bd. 1978—), Assn. Austrian Original Equipment Mfrs. (dir. 1982—), Austrian Sporting Goods Mfg. Assn. (dep. pres. 1964-73), Siegmund Freud Soc. (bd. 1980—). Jewish. Lodge: Masons. Home: 27 Norfolk Rd, London NW8 6AU, England Office: Herz Armaturen AG, 22 Richard Strauss Strasse, A 1232 Vienna Austria

SMOLLEN, LEONARD ELLIOTT, venture capitalist; b. N.Y.C., Jan. 1, 1930; s. Abner Charles and Madeleine (Ehrlich) S.; B.S., Carnegie Inst. Tech., 1951; M.S., Columbia U., 1952; M.E., Mass. Inst. Tech., 1962; m. Mindelle Deborah Hershberg, July 6, 1958; children: Rachel Anne, Jonathan Adam. Sr. engr. Sikorsky Aircraft, Bridgeport, Conn., 1953-57; engring. mgr. Allied Research Assos., Boston, 1957-61; tech. cons. Mitre Corp., Bedford, Mass., 1962-63; chief mech. engr. EG&G, Bedford, 1963-67, program mgr., 1967-69, dir. custom products and program mgmt., 1969-70; exec. v.p. Inst. for New Enterprise Devel., Belmont, Mass., 1971-77; exec. v.p. Venture Founders Corp., Waltham, Mass., 1976—; gen. ptnr. Venture Founders Capital, 1983—; bd. dirs. IVS Inc., Creare Inc., Telesis; lectr. Babson U.; research asso. Sloan Sch. Mgmt., MIT, 1970-71. Higgins fellow, 1952; Whitney fellow, 1960. Registered profl. engr., Conn., Mass. Mem. ASME. Club: Boston Yacht. Author: New Venture Creation: A Guide to Small Business Development, 1977; Source Guide for Borrowing Capital, 1977. Home: 10 Central St Winchester MA 01890 Office: 1 Cranberry Hill Lexington MA

SMOLUCHOWSKI, ROMAN, physicist, educator emeritus; b. Zakopane, Austria, Aug. 31, 1910; came to U.S., 1935, naturalized, 1946; s. Marian and Sophia (Baraniecka) S.; m. Louise Catherine Riggs, Feb. 3, 1951; children: Peter, Irene. MA, U. Warsaw, 1933; PhD, U. Groningen, Holland, 1935. Mem. Inst. Advanced Study, Princeton, 1935-36, instr., research asso. physics dept., 1939-41; prof. solid state scis., head solid state and materials program Princeton U., 1960-78; research assoc., head physics sect. Inst. Metals, Warsaw, 1936-39; research physicist Gen. Electric Research Labs., Schenectady, 1941-46; assoc. prof., staff Metals Research Lab., Carnegie Inst. Tech., 1946-50, prof. physics and metall. engring., 1950-56, prof. physics, 1956-60; prof. astronomy and physics U. Tex., Austin, 1978—; vis. prof. Internat. Sch. Solid State Physics, Mol, Belgium, 1963, Facultédes Sciences, Paris, 1965-66; lectr. Sch. Planetary Physics, Super-Besse, France, 1972; Fulbright prof. U. Sorbonne-Paris, 1955-56; lectr. Internat. Sch. Solid State Physics, Varenna, Italy, 1957, U. Liège, Belgium, 1956, Faculté des Scis., Paris, 1965-66; vis. prof. NRC of Brazil, 1958-59, Tech. U. Munich, 1974; mem. solid state panel Research and Devel. Bd., Dept. Def., 1949, sec. panel, 1950-61; mem. tech. adv. bd. Aircraft Nuclear Propulsion, 1950; chmn com. on magnetism Office Naval Research, 1952-56; chmn. com. on solids NRC, 1950-61, chmn. solid state scis. panel, 1961-67, chmn. div. phys. scis., 1969-75; mem. space sci. bd. Nat. Acad. Scis., 1969-75, mem. physics survey, 1963-66, 1969-72; adv. com. metallurgy Oak Ridge Nat. Lab., 1960-62, mem. com. on planetary and lunar exploration, 1980-84. Author: (with Mayer and Weyl) Phase Transformations in Nearly Perfect Crystals, 1952, (with others) Molecular Science and Molecular Engineering, 1959, The Solar System—Sun, Planets and Life, 1983; editor: (with N. Kurti) Monograph Series on Solid State, 1957, (with J. W. Wilkins and E. Burstein) Comments in Condensed Matter Physics, (with M. Glazer) Phase Transitions; (with others) Ices in the Solar System, The Galaxy and the Solar System; editor-in-chief: Crystal Lattice Defects and Amorphous Materials, Semiconductors and Insulators; asso. editor: Fundamentals of Cosmic Physics; Contbr. articles to profl. jours. Chmn. bd. trustees Simon's Rock Coll., 1971-72. Guggenheim Meml. fellow, 1974; fellow Churchill Coll. Cambridge U., Eng., 1974. Fellow Am. Phys. Soc. (chmn. div. solid state physics 1944-46), Am. Acad. Arts and Scis.; mem. AAAS, Internat. Astron. Union, Finnish Acad. Scis. and Letters, Am. Astron. Soc., Mex. Acad. Engring., Brazilian Acad. Scis., Sigma Xi, Alpha Sigma Mu, Pi Mu Epsilon. Home: 1401 Ethridge Ave Austin TX 78703 Office: U Tex Dept Physics and Astronomy Austin TX 78712

SMOOT, JOSEPH GRADY, academic administrator; b. Winter Haven, Fla., May 7, 1932; s. Robert Malcolm and Vera (Eaton) S.; m. Florence Rozell, May 30, 1955 (dec.); m. Irma Jean Kopitzke, June 4, 1959; 1 son, Andrew Christopher. B.A., So. Coll., 1955; M.A., U. Ky., 1958, Ph.D., 1964. Tchr., Ky. Secondary Schs., 1955-57; from instr. to asso. prof. history Columbia Union Coll., Takoma Park, Md., 1960-68, acad. dean, 1965-68; prof. history Andrews U., Berrien Springs, Mich., 1968-84, dean Sch. Grad. Studies, 1968-69, v.p. acad. adminstrn., 1969-76, pres., 1976-84; v.p. for devel. Pittsburg State U., Kans., 1984—; exec. dir. Pittsburg State Univ. Found., 1985—; commr. North Cen. Assn., 1987—, cons., evaluator, 1978—; cons. internat. edn; bd. trustees Loma Linda U., 1976-84, U. Ea. Africa, Baraton, Kenya, 1979-84, Hindsdale Hosp., Ill., 1973-84; chmn., bd. trustees Andrews Broadcasting Corp., 1976-84; bd. dirs. Internat. U. Thailand Found., 1987—. Contbr. articles to profl. jours. Bd. dirs. Pittsburg United Way, 1987— bd. advisors Pitts. Salvation Army. Recipient Disting. Pres. award Mich. Coll. Found., 1984. Fellow (assoc.) Inst. Early Am. History and Culture; mem. Am., So. hist. assns., Orgn. Am. Historians, soc. for Historians of Early Am. Republic, Phi Alpha Theta. Club: Crestwood Country. Lodge: Rotary (chmn. scholarship com. 1986) Home: 1809 Heritage Rd Pittsburg KS 66762 Office: Pittsburg State U Pittsburg KS 66762

SMREKAR, ERMINIO, architect; b. Trieste, Italy, Oct. 10, 1931; arrived in Australia, 1956; s. Carlo and Bruna (Tronconi) S.; m. Edda Caris, June 22, 1957; children: Patrizia, Barbara. Registered architect, Australia. Pvt. practice architecture Melbourne, 1965—. Named Cavaliere Ufficiale Italian Republic, 1973. Fellow Royal Australian Inst. Architects. Roman Catholic. Office: Smrekar Assocs, 35 Dryburgh St, West Melbourne Australia

SMUDHAVANICH, SUCHIN, banker; b. Yigor, Narathiwat, Thailand, Sept. 27, 1929; s. Sunthorn and Ubol (Pattaranond) S. BS, Thammasat U., Bangkok, 1952. CPA. Asst. v.p. Krung Thai Bank, Bangkok, 1970-86, v.p., 1986, sr. v.p., 1986—; chmn. Met. Investment & Trust Ltd., Bangkok, 1987—. Contbr. articles to profl. jours. Served to lt. Thai Army, 1956. Assoc. mem. Auditors and Accts. Assn. Thailand. Buddhist. Office: Krung Thai Bank Ltd, 35 Sukhumvit Rd, Bangkok 10110, Thailand

SMULAND, PHILIP LEE, clergyman, educator; b. Duluth, Minn., Oct. 22, 1951; s. Norman Hilmar and Mildred (Breedon) S.; m. Rhonda Ann Versher, Apr. 21, 1984. BA, U. Tex., Arlington, 1975; MA and MDiv, Westminster Theol. Sem., 1983. Ordained to ministry Presbyn. Ch., 1987. Tchr. 1st Presbyn. Ch., Manhattan Beach, Calif., 1984-85, intern pastor, 1985-87, assoc. pastor, 1987-88; pastor Covenant Presbyn. Ch., Harrisonburg, Va., 1988—; adj. prof. Nat. U., 1982—, Loyola-Marymount U., 1987—; asst. tchr. U. So. Calif.. 1984-86. Named one of Outstanding Young Men in Am., 1983. Mem. Phi Alpha Theta, Phi Delta Gamma. Republican. Home: 1411 Hillcrest Harrisonburg VA 22801 Office: Covenant Presbyn Ch 609 W Market PO Box 1477 Harrisonburg VA 22801

SMURFIT, MICHAEL W. J., manufacturing company executive; b. 1936. With Jefferson Smurfit Group PLC, Dublin, Ireland, 1961—, pres., from 1966, now chmn., chief exec. officer; pres. Jefferson Smurfit Corp., Alton, Ill., 1979-82, now chief exec. officer, chmn. bd., 1982—. Office: Jefferson Smurfit Corp 401 Alton St Alton IL 62002 *

SMUTNY, JOAN FRANKLIN (MRS. HERBERT PAUL SMUTNY), educator; b. Chgo.; d. Eugene and Mabel (Lind) Franklin; B.S. Northwestern U., M.A.; m. Herbert Paul Smutny; 1 dau., Cheryl Anne. Tchr., New Trier High Sch., Winnetka, Ill.; mem. faculty, founder, dir. Nat. High Sch. Inst., Northwestern U. Sch. Edn., Chgo.; mem. faculty, founder dir. high sch. workshop in critical thinking and edn., chmn. dept. communications Nat. Coll. Edn., Evanston, Ill., 1967—, exec. dir. high sch. workshops, 1970-75 , founder, dir. Woman Power Through Edn. Seminar, 1969-74 , dir. Right to Read seminar in critical reading, 1973-74 , seminar gifted high sch. students, 1973, dir. of Gifted Programs for 6, 7 and 8th graders pub. schs., Evanston, 1978-79, 1st-8th graders, Glenview (both Ill.) 1979—; dir. gifted programs Nat. Coll. of Edn., Evanston, 1980-82, dir. Center for Gifted, 1982—; dir. Bright and Talented and Project '86, North Shore Country Day Sch., Winnetka, Ill., 1982-86 ; dir. Job Creation Project, 1980-82; dir. new dimensions for women, 1973, dir. Thinking for Action in Career Edn. project, 1974-77 , dir. Individualized Career Edn. Program, 1976-79, dir. TACE, dir. Humanities Program for Verbally Precocious Youth, 1978-79; co-dir., instr. seminars in critical thinking Ill. Family Service, 1972-75 . Writer ednl. filmstrips in Lang. arts and Lit. Soc. for Visual Edn., 1960-74 ; mem. speakers bur. Council Fgn. Relations, 1968-69 ; mem. adv. com. edn. professions devel. act U.S. Office Edn., 1969—; mem. state team for gifted, IOE, Office of Gifted, Springfield, Ill., 1977; writer, cons. Radiant Ednl. Corp., 1969-71 ; cons. A.L.A., 1969-71 , cons., workshop leader and speaker in area of gifted edn., 1971—, coordinator of career edn. Nat. Coll. Edn., 1976-78 ; dir. Future Tchrs. Am. Seminar in Coll. and Career, 1970-72 ; cons. for research and devel. Ill. Dept. Vocat. Edn., 1973—; cons. in career edn. U.S. Office Edn., 1976—; evaluation cons. DAVTE, IOE, Springfield, Ill., 1977, mem. Leadership Tng. Inst. for Gifted, U.S. Office Edn., 1973-74; dir. workshops for high sch. students; dir. Gifted Young Writer's and Young Writer's conferences, 1978, 79; dir. Project '87, '88, '89 Nat. Coll. of Edn.; dir. Summer Wonders 1986-89; dir. Worlds of Wisdom and Wonder, 1978-89. Mem. Nat. Soc. Arts and Letters (nat. bd., 1st and 3d v.p. Evanston chpt., dir. 1983—), AAUP, Mortar Bd., Outstanding Educators of Am. 1974, Pi Lambda Theta, Phi Delta Kappa (chpt. v.p.). Editor, contbr. Maturity in Teaching, 1962. Writer ednl. filmstrips The Brother's Grimm, 1960, How the West Was Won, 1960, Mutiny on the Bounty, 1960, Dr. Zhivago, 1964, Space Odessey 2001, 1969, Christmas Around the World, 1973. Author of numerous books in field. Editor, Ill. Gifted Jour., 1982—. Contributing editor of numerous books in field. Contbr. articles to profl. jours. Reviewer of Programs for Gifted and Talented, U.S. Office of Edn., 1976-78. Home: 633 Forest Ave Wilmette IL 60091

SMYTH, CRAIG HUGH, fine arts educator; b. N.Y.C., July 28, 1915; s. George Hugh and Lucy Salome (Humeston) S.; m. Barbara Linforth, June 24, 1941; children: Alexandra, Edward Linforth (Ned). B.A., Princeton U., 1938, M.F.A., 1941, Ph.D., 1956; M.A. (hon.), Harvard U., 1975. Research asst. Nat. Gallery Art, Washington, 1941-42, officer-in-charge, dir. Central Art Collecting Point, Munich, Ger., 1945-46; lectr. Frick Collection, N.Y.C., 1946-50; asst. prof. Inst. Fine Arts, NYU, 1950-53, assoc. prof., 1953-57, prof., 1957-73, acting dir. Inst., acting head dept. fine arts Grad. Sch. Arts and Scis., 1951-53, dir. Inst., head dept. fine arts Grad. Sch., 1953-73; prof. fine arts Harvard U., 1973-85, prof. emeritus, 1985—; Kress prof. Ctr. for Advanced Study in Visual Arts Nat. Gallery Art, Washington, 1987-88; dir. Villa I Tatti, Harvard Center Italian Renaissance Studies, Florence, 1973-85; Art historian Am. Acad. in Rome, 1959-60; mem. U.S. Nat. Com. History Art, 1955-85; alt. U.S. mem. Comité Internat. d'Histoire de l'Art, 1970-83, U.S. mem., 1983-85; consultative chmn. adv. com. J. Paul Getty Ctr. History of Art and Humanities, 1982—; mem. architect selection com. J. Paul Getty Trust, 1983-84; mem. adv. com. Ctr. Advanced Study in Visual Arts, Nat. Gallery Art, Washington, 1983-85; mem. organizing com., keynote speaker 400th Anniversary of Uffizi Gallery, 1981-82; vis. scholar Inst. Advanced Study, Princeton, N.J., 1971, mem., 1978, visitor, 1983, 85-86; vis. scholar Bibliotheca Hertziana, Max Planck Soc., Rome, 1972, 73; mem. vis. com. dept. art and archaeology Princeton U., 1956-73, 85—; mem. Villa I Tatti Council, 1985—; mem. adv. com. Villa I Tatti, 1985—; trustee Hyde Collection, Glens Falls, N.Y., 1985-87, The Burlington mag., 1987—; mem. commn. Ednl. and Cultural Exchange between Italy and U.S., Rome, 1979-83. Author: Mannerism and Maniera, 1963, Bronzino as Draughtsman, 1971, Michelangelo Architetto (with H.M. Million), 1988; editorial adv. bd.: Master Drawings; contbr. articles on Michelangelo and St. Peter's (with H.M. Million) to profl. jours. Hon. trustee Met. Mus. Art, N.Y.C., 1968—. Served from ensign to lt. USNR, 1942-46. Decorated Legion of Honor France; sr. Fulbright research fellow, 1949-50. Fellow Am. Acad. Arts and Scis.; assoc. mem. Accademia Fiorentina della Arti del Disegno (academician); mem. Coll. Art Assn. Am. (dir. 1953-57, sec. 1956), Am. Philos. Soc., Phi Beta Kappa. Clubs: Harvard (N.Y.C.), Century Assn. (N.Y.C.). Address: PO Box 39 Cresskill NJ 07626

SMYTH, DAVID JOHN, economist; b. Twickenham, Eng., Apr. 19, 1936; came to U.S., 1967; s. John Richard and Ena Caryle (Stuart) S.; m. Jane Mair, July 19, 1969; children: Seamus John, Alexander David. B.Econs., U. Queensland, Australia, 1957, M.Econs., 1960; Ph.D., U. Birmingham, Eng., 1968. Lectr. econs. U. Queensland, 1957-60; univ. research scholar London Sch. Econs., 1960-63; lectr. econs., then sr. lectr. math. econs. U. Birmingham, 1963-67; prof. SUNY, Buffalo, 1967-70; prof. econs. Claremont (Calif.) Grad. Sch., 1971-76, chmn. dept., 1973-76; prof. econs. Wayne State U., Detroit, 1976-86, chmn. dept., 1976-85; LSU Found. Disting. prof. econs. La. State U., Baton Rouge, 1987—. Author: The Demand for Farm Machinery, 1970, Forecasting the United Kingdom Economy, 1973, Size, Growth, Profits and Executive Compensation in the Large Corporation, 1975; editor: Jour. Macroeconomics, 1977—; contbr. articles to profl. jours. Recipient award Bd. Govs. Wayne State U., 1980. Mem. Am. Econ. Assn., Econometric Soc., Royal Econ. Soc., So. Econ. Assn., Am. Fin. Assn., Econ. Soc. Australia and N.Z., Western Econ. Assn., Am. Agrl. Econ. Assn., AAUP (chpt. pres. 1975-76), Acad. of Scholars of Wayne State U. Home: 12812 Woodshire Pl Baton Rouge LA 70816 Office: La State U Dept Econs 2107 CEBA Baton Rouge LA 70803

SMYTH, NOEL FREDERICK, mathematics educator; b. Brisbane, Australia, May 16, 1958; s. Lyle Waldren and Gwen (McFadyen) S. BS with honors, Queensland (Australia) U., 1979; PhD, Calif. Inst. Tech., 1984. Lectr. in math. U. Wollongong, Australia, 1987—. Contbr. articles to math. jours. Grantee Australian Research Grants Com., 1988; research fellow Calif. Inst. Tech., 1984, U. Melbourne, Australia, 1984-86, U. New South Wales, Sydney, Australia, 1986-87. Mem. Soc. for Indsl. and Applied Math., Australian Math. Soc., Royal Scottish Country Dance Soc., Council for Scottish Gaelic. Presbyterian. Home: 43 The Crescent, Helensburgh 2508, Australia Office: U Wollongong, Northfield Ave, Wollongong 2500, Australia

SMYTHE-MACAULAY, DONALD CHARLES OGUNTOLA, oil company executive; b. Freetown, Sierra Leone, July 26, 1932; s. Christian Athanasius Everette and Agens Eloise (Smythe) Macaulay; m. Florence Amelia Reed, Dec. 24, 1962 (div. July 1984); children: Donald, David, Christopher, Dennis. BS, Lincoln U., 1960. Sales asst. BP West Africa, Ltd., Freetown, 1965-69, sr. sales asst., 1969-70, mktg. asst., 1970-73, sales mgr., 1973-77; mktg. mgr. BP Sierra Leone, Ltd., 1977-80, gen. mgr., 1980-85, mng. dir., 1985—; bd. dirs. S.L. Petroleum Refinery Co., Freetown, Whitex Industries Ltd., Freetown, S.L. Nat. Petroleum Co., Freetown. Commr. Sierra Leone Boy Scouts Assn., Freetown, 1975-87. Mem. Sierra Leone Inst. Mgmt., Internat. Meditation Soc. (nat. leader 1984—). Mem. All Peoples Congress. Methodist. Office: Sierra Leone Nat Petroleum, NP House Cotton Tree, Freetown Sierra Leone

SNAPP, ELIZABETH, librarian, educator; b. Lubbock, Tex., Mar. 31, 1937; d. William James and Louise (Lanham) Mitchell; BA magna cum laude, North Tex. State U., Denton, 1968, MLS, 1969, MA, 1977; m. Harry Franklin Snapp, June 1, 1956. Asst. to archivist Archive of New Orleans Jazz, Tulane U., 1960-63; catalog librarian Tex. Woman's U., Denton, 1969-71, head acquisitions dept., 1971-74, coordinator readers services, 1974-77, asst. to dean Grad. Sch., 1977-79, instr. library sci., 1977—, acting Univ. librarian, 1979-82, dir. libraries, 1982—, mem. adv. com. on library formula Coordinating Bd. Tex. Coll. and Univ. System, 1981—; del. OCLC Nat. Users Council, 1985-87, mem. by-laws com., 1985-86, com. on less-than-full-services networks, 1986-87; project dir. Nat. Endowment for Humanities consultancy grant on devel. core curriculum for women's studies, 1981-82; chmn. Blue Ribbon com. 1986 Gov.'s Commn. for Women to select 150 outstanding women in Tex. history; project dir. math./sci. anthology project Tex. Found. Women's Resources. Co-sponsor Irish Lecture Series, Denton, 1968, 70, 73, 78. Sec. Denton County Democratic Caucus, 1970. Recipient Ann. Pioneer award Tex. Women's U., 1986. Mem. ALA (standards com. 1983-85) Southwestern, Tex. (program com. 1978, Dist. VII chmn. 1985-86) library assns., Women's Collecting Group (chmn. ad hoc com. 1984—), AAUW (legis. br. chmn. 1973-74, br. v.p. 1975-76, br. pres. 1979-80, state historian 1986—), So. Conf. Brit. Studies, AAUP, Tex. Assn. Coll. Tchrs. (pres. Tex. Woman's U. chpt. 1976-77), Woman's Shakespeare Club (pres. 1967-69), Beta Phi Mu (pres. chpt. 1976-78; sec. nat. adv. assembly 1978-79, pres. 1979-80, nat. dir. 1981—), Alpha Chi, Alpha Lambda Sigma (pres. 1970-71), Pi Delta Phi. Methodist. Club: Soroptimist Internat. (Denton) (pres. 1986-88). Asst. editor Tex. Academe, 1973-76; contbg. author: Women in Special Collections, 1984, Special Collections, 1986; book reviewer Library Resources and Tech. Services, 1973—. Contbr. articles to profl. jours. Home: 1904 N Lake Trail Denton TX 76201 Office: TWU Sta PO Box 24093 Denton TX 76204

SNARE, CARL LAWRENCE, JR., business executive; b. Chgo., Oct. 25, 1936; s. Carl Lawrence and Lillian Marie (Luoma) S.; B.B.A., Northwestern U., 1968; postgrad. Roosevelt U.; postgrad. in econs. San Francisco State U., 1976-77. Cert. fin. planner. Asst. sec., controller Bache Halsey Stuart & Shields Inc. (now Prudential Bache), Chgo., 1968-73; controller Innisfree Corp. div. Hyatt Corp., Burlingame, Calif., 1973-76; cash mgr. Portland (Oreg.) Gen. Electric Co., 1976-79; chief fin. officer, controller Vistar Fin. Inc., Marina del Rey, Calif., 1979-82; v.p., treas. Carson Estate Co., Rancho Dominguez, Calif., 1988—; pres. Snare Properties Co., Rialto, Calif., 1984—, Snare Fin. Services Corp., Rialto, 1985—; registered investment advisor. C.P.A., real estate broker, cert. fin. planner, Calif. Mem. Am. Inst. C.P.A.s, Calif. Soc. C.P.A.s, Internat. Assn. Fin. Planners, Am. Inst. Fin. Planners. Founder Cash Mgmt. Assn., Portland, Oreg. Home: 1131 Wisteria Ave Rialto CA 92376 Office: 17925 S Santa Fe Ave Rancho Dominguez CA 90221

SNAVELY, WILLIAM PENNINGTON, economics educator; b. Charlottesville, Va., Jan. 25, 1920; s. Tipton Ray and Nell (Aldred) S.; m. Alice Watts Pritchett, June 4, 1942; children: Nell Lee, William Pennington, Elizabeth Tipton. Student, Hampden-Sydney Coll., 1936-37; B.A. with honors, U. Va., 1940, M.A., 1941, Ph.D., 1950; postgrad. (Bennett Wood Green fellow), Harvard, 1946-47. Mem. faculty U. Conn., 1947-73, prof. econs., 1961-73, chmn. dept., 1966-72, economist econ. edn. workshop, summers 1954, 55, 56; prof. econs. George Mason U., 1973-86, chmn. dept., 1973-81; acting dean CAS, summer 1981, 85-86, assoc. dean, 1982-85; prof. econs. Liberty U., 1986—; cons. Ford Found., Jordan Devel. Bd., Amman, 1961-62, 64-65, Lebanese Ministry Planning, Beirut, 1964-65, Saudi Arabian Central Planning Orgn., Riyadh, 1964-65, Am. U. Beirut, 1969-70, Bahrain Ministry Fin. and Nat. Economy, 1974, 75, 76, U.N., Jordan Nat. Planning Council, Amman, 1972; mem. Danforth Workshop, summer 1966; mem. adv. com. Willimantic Trust Co., Conn., 1968-73. Author: (with W.H. Carter) Intermediate Economic Analysis, 1961, Theory of Economic Systems, 1969, (with M.T. Sadik) Bahrain, Qatar and the United Arab Emirates, 1972; contbr. articles to jours.; articles Ency. Americana. Served to capt. AUS, 1942-46. Fellow Fund Advancement Edn. Harvard, 1951-52; faculty-bus. exchange fellow Chase Nat. Bank, N.Y.C., summer 1952; fellow Merrill Center Econs., summer 1957; Fulbright research fellow Rome, 1958-59. Mem. Am., So. econ. assns., Assn. Christian Economists, Assn. Comparative Econs., Va. Assn. Economists (pres. 1979-80), Phi Beta Kappa, Phi Kappa Phi. Home: 1551 Dairy Rd Charlottesville VA 22903

SNAVELY, WILLIAM PENNINGTON, JR., administrator mental retardation facility; b. Willimantic, Conn., Aug. 8, 1948; s. William Pennington and Alice Watts (Pritchett) S.; B.A., Muskingum Coll., 1970; M.S.W., U. Conn., 1973; m. Susan Lucy Badrick, May 11, 1974; 1 child, Mary Crystal. Dir. Tri County Geriatric Evaluation Service, Easton, Md., 1974-76; social work cons. House in the Pines, Easton, Md., 1975-77; dir. community services Holly Center, Salisbury, Md., 1976—. Mem. Gov.'s Com. to Promote Employment Handicapped, 1979-80, Md. Social Work Classification and Job Specification Task Force, 1979-80; mem. adv. bd. Eastern Shore Respite Care Program, 1980—; mem. profl. adv. bd. Epilepsy Assn. Md., 1984—; mem. Intensive Behavior Unit-Alt. Living Unit Adminstrv. Bd. Md. Eastern Shore, 1984—. Reciepent Elaine Pederson award, 1988. Mem. Internat. Platform Assn., Nat. Assn. Devel. Disabilities Mgrs. (dir. 1979-80, sec.-treas. 1980-82), Eastern Shore Devel. Disabilities consortium (founder, 1979), Nat. Assn. Social Workers (chmn. Eastern Shore unit Md. 1979-80, legis. coordinator and forensic screening coordinator 1986—, v.p. Md. chpt. 1980-82), Am. Assn. Mental Deficiency, Aircraft Owners and Pilots Assn., Locksmithing Inst. (cert.). Conglist. Mem. state adv. bd. United Cerebral Palsy Md., 1979-80. Home: Route 11 Box 344 Jeffrey St Salisbury MD 21801 Office: PO Box 2358 Snow Hill Rd Salisbury MD 21801

SNEED, MARIE ELEANOR WILKEY, retired educator; b. Dahlgren, Ill., June 12, 1915; d. Charles N. and Hazel (Miller) Wilkey; student U. Ill., 1933-35; B.S., Northwestern U., 1937; postgrad. Wayne State U., 1954-60, U. Mich., 1967; m. John Sneed, Jr., Sept. 18, 1937: children—Suzanne (Mrs. Geoffrey B. Newton), John Corwin. Tchr. English, drama, creative writing Berkley (Mich.) Sch. Dist., 1952-76. Mem. Mich. Statewide Tchr. Edn. Preparation, 1968-72, regional sec. 1969-70; mem. Pleasant Ridge Arts Council, 1982—, Pleasant Ridge Parks and Recreation Commn., 1982-88. Mem. NEA, Mich., Berkley (pres. 1961-62, 82-87) edn. assns., Oakland Tchr. Edn. Council (exec. bd. 1973-76), Student Tchr. Planning Com. Berkley (chmn. 1971-72), Phi Alpha Chi, Pi Lambda Theta, Alpha Delta Kappa, Alpha Omicron Pi. Club: Pleasant Ridge Woman's (pres. 1980-83). Home: 21 Norwich Rd Pleasant Ridge MI 48069

SNELL, GEORGE DAVIS, geneticist; b. Bradford, Mass., Dec. 19, 1903; s. Cullen Bryant and Katharine (Davis) S.; m. Rhoda Carson, July 28, 1937; children: Thomas Carleton, Roy Carson, Peter Garland. B.S., Dartmouth Coll., 1926; M.S., Harvard U., 1928, Sc.D., 1930; M.D. (hon.), Charles U., Prague, 1967; LL.D. (hon.), Colby Coll., 1982; Sc.D. (hon.), Dartmouth Coll., 1974, Gustavus Adolphus Coll., 1981, U. Maine, 1981, Bates Coll., 1982, Ohio State U., 1984. Instr. zoology Dartmouth Coll., 1929-30, Brown U., 1930-31; asst. prof. Washington U., St. Louis, 1933-34; research asso. Jackson Lab., 1935-56, sr. staff scientist, 1957—, emeritus, 1969—, sci. adminstr., 1949-50. Co-author: Histocompatibility, 1976; also sci. papers in field; editor: The Biology of the Laboratory Mouse, 1941. Recipient Bertner Found. award in field cancer research, 1962; Griffin award Animal Care Panel, 1962; career award Nat. Cancer Inst., 1964-68; Gregor Mendel medal Czechoslovak Acad. Scis., 1967; Internat. award Gairdner Found., 1976; Wolf Found. prize in medicine, 1978; award Nat. Inst. Arthritis and Infectious Disease-Nat. Cancer Inst., 1978; Nobel prize in medicine (with Dausset and Benacerraf), 1980; NRC fellow U. Tex., 1931-33; NIH health research grantee for study genetics and immunology of tissue transplantation, 1950-73 (allergy and immunology study sect. 1958-62); Guggenheim fellow, 1953-54. Mem. Nat. Acad. Scis., Transplantation Soc., Am. Acad. Arts and Sci., French Acad. Scis. (fgn. asso.), Am. Philos. Soc., Brit. Transplantation Soc. (hon.), Phi Beta Kappa. Home: 21 Atlantic Ave Bar Harbor ME 04609

SNIDER, JAMES RHODES, radiologist; b. Pawnee, Okla., May 16, 1931; s. John Henry and Gladys Opal (Rhodes) S.; B.S., U. Okla., 1953, M.D., 1956; m. Lynadell Vivion, Dec. 27, 1954; children—Jon, Jan. Intern, Edward Meyer Meml. Hosp., Buffalo, 1956-57; resident radiology U. Okla. Med. Center, 1959-62; radiologist Holt-Krock Clinic and Sparks Regional Med. Center, Ft. Smith, Ark., 1962—; cons. USPHS Hosp., Talihina, Okla., 1962—. Dir. Fairfield Community Land Co., Little Rock, 1968-88, Fairfield Communities, Inc., 1968-88. Mem. Ark. Bd. Pub. Welfare, 1969-71. Bd. dirs. U. Okla. Assn., 1967-70, U. Okla. Alumni Devel. Fund, 1970-74; bd. visitors U. Okla. Served to lt. comdr. USNR, 1957-62. Mem. Am. Coll. Radiology, Radiol. Soc. N.Am., Am. Roentgen Ray Soc., AMA, Phi Beta Kappa, Beta Theta Pi (trustee corp.), Alpha Epsilon Delta. Asso. editor Computerized Tomography, 1976—. Home: 5814 Cliff Dr Fort Smith AR 72903 Office: 1500 Dodson St Fort Smith AR 72901

SNIDERMAN, ALLAN DAVID, cardiologist, educator; b. Hamilton, Ont., Can., Oct. 17, 1941; s. Samuel and Mona (Carr) S.; m. Sarah Stobo Prichard; children: Sarah, Samuel, Robert, Jonathan, Andrew. MD, U. Toronto, 1965. Cert. cardiology specialist, Que. Intern Toronto Gen. Hosp., 1965-66; jr. asst. resident in medicine Royal Victoria Hosp., 1966-67, sr. asst. resident in medicine, 1967-68, resident in cardiorespiration, 1968-69, chief resident in medicine, 1969-70, fellow in cardiology, 1970-71, asst. physician div. cardiology, 1973-78, assoc. physician div. cardiology, 1978-80, sr. physician, 1981—, dir. div. cardiology, 1984—; asst. research biochemist div. metabolic diseases U. Calif., San Diego, 1971-73; asst. prof. exptl. medicine McGill U., 1973-76, assoc. prof. dept. medicine, 1976-80, Edwards prof. cardiology, 1978—, prof. medicine, 1981—. Fellow Royal Coll. Physicians and Surgeons Can. (cert. specialist in cardiology), Am. Coll. Cardiology, ACP; mem. Can. Cardiovascular Soc., Can. Soc. Clin. Investigation, Am. Soc. Clin. Investigation, Am. Fedn. Clin. Research, Alpha Omega Alpha. Office: Royal Victoria Hosp, Cardiology div, Montreal, PQ Canada H3A 1A1

SNOOK, JOHN MCCLURE, telephone company executive; b. Toledo, May 31, 1917; s. Ward H. and Grace (McClure) S.; m. Marjorie Younce (dec.); student Ohio State U., 1936-43. Instr. history, fine arts and scis. Ohio State U., Columbus; exec. v.p. Gulf Telephone Co., Foley, Ala., 1955-71, pres., 1971—. Chmn., Baldwin Sesquicentennial, 1969; mem. Baldwin County Bicentennial Commn.; pageant chmn., dir. Ft. Morgan Bicentennial Program, 1976; mem. hon. staff Gov. Ala., 1967—; past pres. Friends of Library Assn.; asso. sponsor Gulf Shores Mardi Gras Assn. Hon. a.d.c. lt. col. Ala.; hon. Ala. state trooper; recipient Citizen of Year award Gulf Shores, 1956-57. Mem. Ala.-Miss. Ind. Telephone Assn. (past pres.), Nat. Rifle Assn. (life), Am. Ordnance Assn., South Baldwin C. of C., Delaware County, Baldwin County (pres.) hist. assns., Defiance and Williams' Hist. Soc., Am. Mus. Nat. History Assn., Nat. Hist. Soc., Nat. Wildlife Fedn., Clan McLeod Soc., Smithsonian Assn., Am. Heritage Soc., Nat. Fedn. Blind, Ohio State Alumni Assn., Ala. Ind. Telephone Assn., Telephone Pioneers, Ind. Pioneers. Clubs: Lions (past pres.), Kiwanis (past pres.; asst. chmn. ann. Christmas Party and Parade). Office: Gulf Telephone Co Box 670 Foley AL 36535

SNOOK, JOHN RAMSEY, aircraft company executive; b. Hamilton, Ohio, July 21, 1938; s. John Clayson and Katharine (Ramsey) S.; m. Lydia Esther Rivera, June 21, 1969; 1 son, John Rivera. A.S.M.E., Idaho State U., 1965; B.S. Aero. Tech., Utah State U., 1968. Field rep. Pratt & Whitney Aircraft, Boeing 747 Flight Test, Seattle, 1969-70, Pan Am, Los Angeles, 1970-72, Douglas DC10-40 Flight Test, Yuma, Ariz., 1972, Douglas DC10 delivery, Long Beach, Calif., 1972-76; sr. field rep. Japan Air Lines, Tokyo, 1976-80, 83—, Pacific Southwest Airlines, San Diego, 1980-83. Served with USN 1956-62. Mem. VFW (quartermaster 1979-80, adjutant 1983-85, post comdr. 1986-87, dits. sr. vice comdr. 1987—). Home: 3-50 Osawa, 6 chome Mitakashi, Tokyo 181 Japan Office: Pratt & Whitney Aircraft, PO Box 36, Haneda Airport, Tokyo 144, Japan

SNOOK, QUINTON, constrn. co. exec.; b. Atlanta, July 15, 1925; s. John Wilson and Charlotte Louise (Clayson) S.; student U. Idaho, 1949-51; m. Lois Mullen, Jan. 19, 1947; children—Lois Ann Snook Matteson, Quinton A., Edward M., Clayson S., Charlotte T. Rancher, Lemhi Valley, Idaho, 1942—; owner, mgr. Snook Constrn., Salmon, Idaho, 1952—; owner Snook Trucking, 1967—, Lemhi Posts and Poles, 1980—. Mem. Lemhi County Commn., Dist. 2, 1980—. Mem. Am. Quarter Horse Assn., Farm Bur., Nat. Rifleman's Assn., Am. Hereford Assn., Idaho Cattlemen's Assn. Republican. Episcopalian. Club: Elks. Home: Route 1 Box 49 Salmon ID 83467

SNOOKS, GRAEME DONALD, economic historian; b. Perth, Australia, July 22, 1944; s. William Donald and Eleanor Violet (Williams) S.; m. Loma Rae Graham, Jan. 24, 1970; children: Adrian Graham, Roland William. BS in Econs., U. Western Australia, 1966, MS in Econs., 1968; PhD, Australian Nat. U., 1972. Tutor U. Western Australia, 1966-68; lectr. U. Queensland, Australia, 1971-72; lectr. Flinders U., Australia, 1972-74, sr. lectr., 1975-83, reader, 1984—; cons. visual arts bd. Australia Council, Sydney, 1974, S. Australian Premiers Dept., Adelaide, 1974-77, Arts Council Great Brit., London, 1978, British Pub. Record Office, London, 1984-86, BBC, London, 1986. Author: Depression and Recovery, 1974, Domesday Economy, 1986; editor:Australian Econ. History Rev., 1977—; contbr. articles to profl. jours. Australia Council grantee, 1974, Australian Research Council grantee, 1974-88. Mem. Econ. History Assn., Econ. History Soc., Econ. History Soc. Australia and New Zealand. Club: S. Australian Fly Fishing Assn. (Adelaide). Office: Flinders U, South Australia, Bedford Park Australia 5042

SNOWDEN, DIANA EMILY, utility company executive; b. N.Y.C., Oct. 29, 1947; d. Joseph Philip and Barbara Ellen (O'Mara) Loftus; m. Arthur Holburn Snowden II, June, 1, 1968 (div. Dec. 1982); children: Kirsten M., Arthur Neilan III. BA, Trinity Coll., 1968; MA, U. Alaska, 1983. Asst. v.p., treas. Westwood Mgmt. Corp., Bethesda, Md., 1970-73; dir. employee relations Anchorage Sch. Dist., 1973-79; v.p. indsl. relations Alascom and Tel Utilities, Inc., Anchorage, 1979-81; commr. Alaska Pub Utilities Commn., Anchorage, 1981-85; exec. dir. PNUCC, Portland, Oreg., 1985-86; v.p. human resources Pacific Power and Light, Portland, 1986—; cons. Alaska Gas Pipeline Adv. Bd., Anchorage, 1985—. Commr. Alaska State Human Rights Commn., Anchorage, 1976-81, chairperson; mem. Alaska Adv. Bd. U.S. Commn. on Civil Rights, 1979-81; bd. dirs. Anchorage Youth Adv. Bd., 1974-76, Bus Youth Exchange, 1986—, Goodwill Industries Oreg., Greater Bus. Group on Health, 1986—. Mem. Nat. Assn. Regulatory Utility Commrs., 1981-84. Republican. Roman Catholic. Home: 4405 SW Council Crest Dr Portland OR 97201 Office: Pacific Power and Light Co 920 SW 6th Ave Portland OR 97204

SNOWDON, LORD ANTHONY (ANTONY CHARLES ROBERT ARMSTRONG-JONES), photographer; b. London, Mar. 7, 1930; s. Ronald Owen Lloyd Armstrong-Jones and Anne, Countess of Rosse; m. Princess Margaret, 1960 (div. 1978); 2 children; m. Lucy Lindsay-Hogg, 1979; 1 dau. Ed., Eton Coll., Jesus Coll., Cambridge, Eng. Cons., Council Indsl. Design, 1962-87; editorial adviser Design mag.; artistic adviser The Sunday Times, Sunday Times Publications Ltd., London, 1962—; constable Caernarvan Castle, 1963—; mem. Civic Trust for Wales, Contemporary Art Soc. for Wales, Welsh Theatre Co.; v.p. Univ. Bristol Photographic Soc. Author: London, 1958; Assignments, 1972; Inchcape Review, 1977; Pride of the Shires, 1979; Personal View, 1979; Tasmania Essay, 1981; Sittings, 1982; co-author: (with S. Sitwell) Malta, 1958; (with John ussel and Bryan Robertson) Private View, 1965; (with Derek Hart) A View of Venice, 1972, Israel A First View, 1986, My Wales Like Lord Tony Pandy, 1987; TV documentaries: Don't Count the Candles (six awards), 1968; Love of a Kind, 1970; Born to be Small, 1971; Happy Being Happy, 1973; Mary Kingsley, 1975; Burke and Wills, 1975; Peter, Tina and Steve, 1977; photog. exhbns.: Photocall, London, 1958; photog. assignments: London, Cologne, Brussels, U.S., Can., Japan, Australia, Denmark, France, Holland. Mem. council Nat. Fund for Research for the Crippled Child; founder Snowdon award Scheme for Disabled Students, 1980; pres. (Eng.) Internat. Yr. of the Disabled; chair Snowdon Report on Integrating the Disabled, 1981; patron Nat. Youth Theatre, Metropolitan Union of YMCA's, British Water Ski Fedn., British Theatre Mus., Welsh Nat. Rowing Club, Circle of Guide Dog Owners, Snowdon Council; designed Snowdon Aviary, London Zoo, 1965, Chairmobile, 1972. Decorated 1st Earl, UK, 1961; recipient Cert. of Merit, Art Dirs. Club of N.Y., 1969, Soc. of Publication Designers, 1970, Wilson Hicks Cert. of Merit for Photocommunication, 1971; Soc. of Publication Designers' Award of Excellence, 1973; Design and Arts Dirs. award, 1978; Royal Photographic Soc. Hood award, 1979. Fellow Inst. British Photographers, Soc. Indsl. Artists and Designers, Royal Photographic Soc., Royal Soc. Arts, Manchester Coll. Art and Design; mem. Faculty Royal Designers for Industry, Council Royal Court Theatre, North Wales Soc. Architects (hon.), South Wales Inst. Architects (hon.). Home: 22 Launceston Pl, London W8 5RL, England

SNYDER, ALLEGRA FULLER, dance educator; b. Chgo., Aug. 28, 1927; d. R. Buckminster and Anne (Hewlett) Fuller; m. Robert Snyder, June 30, 1951 (div. Apr. 1975, remarried Sept. 1980); children: Alexandra, Jaime. BA in Dance, Bennington Coll., 1951; MA in Dance, UCLA, 1967. Asst. to curator, dance archives Mus. Modern Art, N.Y.C., 1945-47; dancer Ballet Soc. of N.Y.C. Ballet Co., 1945-47; mem. office and prodn. staff Internat. Film Found., N.Y.C., 1950-52; editor, dance films Film News mag., N.Y.C., 1966-72; lectr. dance and film adv., dept. dance UCLA, 1967-73, chmn. dept. dance, 1974-80, acting chair, spring 1985, prof. dance and dance ethnology, 1973—; vis. lectr. Calif. Inst. of Arts, Valencia, 1972; co-dir. dance and TV workshop Am. Dance Fest., Conn. Coll., New London, 1973; dir. NEH summer seminar for coll. tchrs. Asian Performing Arts, 1978, 81; coord. Ethnic Arts Intercoll. Interdisciplinary program, 1974-83, acting chmn., 1986; vis. prof. performance studies NYU, 1982-83; hon. vis. prof. U. Surrey, Guildford, Eng., 1983-84; bd. dirs. Buckminster Fuller Inst.; cons. Thyodia Found., Salt Lake City, 1973-74; mem. dance adv. panel Nat. Endowment Arts, 1968-72, Calif. Arts Commn., 1974; mem. adv. screening com. Council Internat. Exchange of Scholars, 1979-82; mem. various panels NEH, 1979-85; mem. adv. bd. Los Angeles Dance Alliance, 1978-84; cons. dance film series Am. Film Inst, 1974-75. Dir. film Baroque Dance 1625-1725, in 1977; co-dir. film Gods of Bali, 1952; dir. and wrote film Bayanihan, 1962 (named Best Folkloric Documentary at Bilboa Film Festival, winner Golden Eagle award); asst. dir. and asst. editor film The Bennington Story, 1952; created films Gestures of Sand, 1968, Reflections on Choreography, 1973, When the Fire Dances Between Two Poles, 1982; created film, video loop and text Celebration: A World of Art and Ritual, 1982-83; supr. post-prodn. film Erick Hawkins, 1964, in 1973. Also contbr. articles to profl. jours. and mags. Adv. com. Pacific Asia Mus., 1980-84, Festival of the Mask, Craft and Folk Art Mus., 1979-84; adv. panel Los Angeles Dance Currents II, Mus. Ctr. Dance Assn., 1974-75; bd. dirs. Council Grove Sch. III, Compton, Calif., 1976-81; apptd. mem. Adv. Dance Com., Pasadena (Calif.) Art Mus., 1970-71, Los Angeles Festival of Performing Arts com., Studio Watts, 1970; mem. Technology and Cultural Transformation com., UNESCO, 1977. Fulbright research fellow, 1983-84; grantee Nat. Endowment Arts, 1981, Nat. Endowment Humanities, 1977, 79, 81, UCLA, 1968, 77, 80, 82, 85. Mem. Am. Dance Therapy Assn., Congress on Research in Dance (bd. dirs. 1970-76, chairperson 1975-77, nat. conf. chair 1972), Council Dance Adminstrs., Am. Dance Guild (chairperson com. awards, 1972), Soc. for Ethnomusicology, Am. Anthropol. Assn., Am. Folklore Soc., Soc. Anthropology of Visual Communication, Soc. Anthropol. Study of Play, Soc. Humanistic Anthropology, Calif. Dance Educators Assn. (conf. chair 1972), Los Angeles Area Dance Alliance (adv. bd. 1978-84, selection com. Dance Kaleidoscope project 1979-81), Fulbright Alumni Assn. Home: 15313 Whitfield Ave Pacific Palisades CA 90272 Office: UCLA Dept Dance 124 Dance Bldg Los Angeles CA 90024

SNYDER, ARNOLD LEE, JR., retired air force officer, research director; b. Washington, Oct. 12, 1937; s. Arnold Lee and Frances May (Humbert) S.; B.C.E., George Washington U., 1960; M.S., U. Colo., 1966; Ph.D., U. Alaska, 1972; m. Patricia Dorine Ward, July 6, 1963; children—Heinrick Jason, Sonya Doreen, Ross Nansen. Commd. 2d lt. USAF, 1960, advanced through grades col., 1981, ret.; chief space environ. support system devel. sect. Air Force Global Weather Central, Offutt AFB, Nebr., 1972-76; chief ionospheric dynamics br. Geophysics Lab., Hanscom AFB, Mass., 1976-80; test dir. CONUS OTH-B radar system, Columbia Falls AFS, Maine, 1980-81; program dir. CONUS OTH-B radar System, Hanscom AFB, 1981-85; dir. Office of Tech. Support, 1985-87; tech. dir. U. Lowell Ctr. Atmospheric Research, 1987—; instr. Western New Eng. Coll., 1978-80; adj. prof. U. Lowell, 1987—. Recipient Legion Merit, Meritorious Service medal with one oak leaf cluster, Commendation medal USAF, research and devel. award, 1981; Def. Value Engring. award, 1984; Henry Harding scholar, 1955-56. Mem. Am. Geophys. Union, Am. Meteorol. Soc., Air Force Assn., Sigma Xi. Methodist. Contbr. articles to sci. jours. Home: 13 Gary Rd Chelmsford MA 01824 Office: U Lowell Ctr Atmospheric Research 450 Aiken St Lowell MA 01854

SNYDER, ARTHUR KRESS, lawyer, government official; b. Los Angeles, Nov. 10, 1932; s. Arthur and Ella Ruth (Keck) S.; m. Mary Frances Neely, Mar. 5, 1953; children—Neely Arthur, Miles John; m. 2d, Michele Maggie Noval, May 14, 1973; 1 dau., Erin-Marisol Michele; m. 3d, Delia Wu, Apr. 18, 1981. B.A., Pepperdine U., 1953; J.D., U. So. Calif., 1958; LL.D., Union U., 1980. Bar: Calif. 1960, U.S. Supreme Ct. 1982. Sole practice, Los Angeles, 1960-67; founder, pres. Arthur K. Snyder Law Corp., Los Angeles, 1981—; mem. City Council Los Angeles, 1967-85; pres. Marisol Corp., real estate and fgn. trade, 1978—; past instr. Los Angeles City Schs. Served to capt. USMC. Decorated La Tizona de El Cid Compeador (Spain), medal Legion of Honor (Mex.), Hwa Chao Zee You medal (Republic of China); numerous other commendations, medals, awards. Mem. Los Angeles County Bar Assn., Calif. Bar Assn., ABA, Internat. Bar Assn., Am. Trial Lawyers Assn., Am. Immigration Lawyers Assn., Am. Judicature Soc. Baptist. Club: Masons. Office: 355 S Grand Ave Suite 3788 Los Angeles CA 90071

SNYDER, CHARLES AUBREY, lawyer; b. Bastrop, La., June 19, 1941; s. David and Shirley Blossom (Haas) S.; m. Sharon Rae Veta, Aug. 29, 1963; children: David Veta, Shelby Haas, Claire Frances. B.B.A., Tulane U., 1963; J.D., La. State U., 1966. Bar: La. 1966. Assoc. firm. Milling, Benson, Woodward, Hillyer, Pierson & Miller, and predecessors, New Orleans, 1966-69, ptnr., 1969—; dir. Delta Petroleum Co., Petroleum Helicopters, Inc., Inc. Corp., La. Motel and Investment Corp. Trustee Kathlyn O'Brien Found., 1970, Touro Infirmary, bd. mgrs.; bd. dirs. New Orleans Speech and Hearing Ctr., pres., 1978-80; fellow La. Coll. Securities Counsel. Mem. ABA, La. Bar Assn. (chmn. sect. on corp. and bus. law 1982-83), New Orleans Bar Assn., La. Law Inst. (coms. on mineral code and revision of partnership law and community property law), Beta Gamma Sigma. Clubs: Metairie Country, Petroleum, Internat. House, Plimsoll. Home: 1659 Burbank Dr New Orleans LA 70122 Office: Milling Benson Woodward Hillyer Pierson & Miller 909 Poydras St Suite 2300 New Orleans LA 70112-1017

SNYDER, CLIFFORD CHARLES, plastic surgeon, educator; b. Fort Worth, Feb. 16, 1916; s. Charles L. and Olga (Agnas) S.; m. Mary Odessa Morris, Mar. 12, 1939; 1 child, Clifford Charles. B.S., U. Tenn., 1940, M.D., 1944. Diplomate Am. Bd. Surgery, Am. Bd. Plastic Surgery (examiner 1964-70, sr. examiner 1970-86). Intern U.S. Naval Hosp., Mare Island, Calif., 1944-45; resident in gen. surgery Jackson Meml. Hosp., U. Miami Sch. Medicine, Fla., 1946-49; resident in plastic surgery U. Tex. Med. Br., Galveston, 1949-52; instr. surgery U. Tex. Med. Br., 1952-53, asst. prof., 1953-54; asst. prof. surgery U. Miami Sch. Medicine, 1954-59, assoc. prof., 1959-67; chief plastic surgery Shriners Hosp. Crippled Children, Salt Lake City, 1967-88; chief surg. service VA Hosp., Salt Lake City, 1967-81; chief plastic surgery Variety Children's Hosp., Miami, 1956-66; pres. staff Variety Children's Hosp., 1960-66; attending Doctors Hosp., Coral Gables, Fla., 1955-66; hon. staff Doctors Hosp., 1966—; assoc. dean. U. Utah Sch. Medicine, Salt Lake City, endowed Clifford C. Snyder chair surgery, prof. emeritus dept. surgery; sr. plastic surgery cons. VA Hosp., Coral Gables, 1954-66, U.S. Air Force, Fla., 1956-66; mem. adv. bd. Crippled Children's Soc. Fla., 1956-66, Vocat. Rehab. Fla., 1960-66; mem. Fla. Gov.'s Com. Rehab., 1960-66; mem. specialists panel Ethicon, 1965—, chmn., 1970-75; mem. nat. surg. cons. com. VA, 1960-73, chief surgery com., 1974-78; faculty rep. Western Athletic Conf., 1976-80, bd. athletics, 1971-73, 75-81; mem. com. emergency services NRC, 1977. Mem. editorial bd. Jour. Plastic and Reconstructive Surgery, 1962-80, assoc. editor, 1957-63, editor internat. abstracts, 1963-69, co-editor, 1973-80, book rev. editor, 1973-80; assoc. editor Small Animal Clinician, 1965-80; spl. editor Vet. Medicine, 1965-80; contbr. over 155 articles to profl. jours. Served to lt. (s.g.) USNR, 1941-45. Recipient Best Prof. award U. Tex., 1953, U. Utah, 1974; Merit award Miami Dental Soc., 1959; Disting. Service award Fla. West Coast Dental Assn., 1960; Sci. Achievement award Fla. Med. Assn., 1961, 63; commendation VA Hosp., 1972; Ohio State U. Guest of Honor award, Ethicon Plastic Surgery citation, 1976; U. Tenn. Disting. Alumnus award, 1988. Fellow N.Y. Acad. Scis.; mem. Am. Assn. Plastic Surgeons (trustee 1964-76, v.p. 1973-74, pres. 1975-76), Am. Burn Assn., ACS (bd. govs. 1963-64, chpt. pres. 1964-66), Am. Coll. Vet. Surgeons (1st hon. mem., Mark Allam award), AMA, Am. Soc. Plastic and Reconstructive Surgeons (v.p. 1967-68, treas. Ednl. Found. 1962-67, trustee 1960-71), Am. Soc. Surgery of Hand, Am. Trauma Soc., Am. Assn. Hand Surgeons, Am. Animal Hosp. Assn. (hon.; Disting. Service award 1974), Am. Vet. Neurology Assn., Assn. VA Surgeons, Fla. Acad. Sci., Fla. Cleft Palate Assn. (pres. 1960-63), Fla. Med. Assn. (chmn. archives 1960-67), Fla. Soc. Plastic and Reconstructive Surgeons (pres. 1959-60), Fla. Med. Vet. Assn. (hon.), Internat. Congress Plastic Surgeons, Mexican-Am. Plastic Surgery Soc., Pan Am. Cancer Cytology Soc., Pan-Pacific Surg. Assn. (v.p. 1980-83), Plastic Surgery Research Council, Salt Lake Surg. Soc., Singleton Surg. Soc., Soc. Head and Neck Surgeons, Southeastern Plastic and Reconstructive Surgery Assn. (pres. 1962-63), So. Med. Assn. (sect. pres. 1964), So. Surg. Assn., Tex. Med. Assn., Am. Soc. Aesthetic Plastic Surgery, Utah Med. Soc. (del. 1977-81), Utah Hist. Soc. (pres. 1973), U. Utah Alumni Assn. (bd. dirs. 1975-80), Acad. Surg. Research, Plastic Surgery Soc. of the Americas (pres. 1986-87), Phi Kappa Phi, Alpha Delta Sigma, Alpha Epsilon Delta (Outstanding Achievement award 1971). Methodist. Office: U Utah Sch Medicine Dean's Office Salt Lake City UT 84132

SNYDER, FREDERICK EDWARD, legal educator; b. Kingston, N.Y., Apr. 3, 1944; s. John I. and Agatha (Flick) S. AB, Georgetown U., 1966, JD, 1974; MPhil, Yale U., 1969, PhD, 1970; LLM, Harvard U., 1977. Bar: Conn. 1974, N.Y. 1976, Mass. 1981. Law clk. to chief justice Conn. Supreme Ct., 1974; assoc. Baker & McKenzie, N.Y.C., 1975; assoc. Bingham Dana & Gould, Boston, 1976; fellow in law and humanities Harvard U. Law Sch., 1977, asst. dean, lectr. on law, dir. clin. programs, assoc. dir. East Asian legal studies, 1978-83, asst. dean for internat. and comparative legal studies, lectr. Latin Am. law, adminstr. grad. program, assoc. dir. East Asian legal Studies, 1983—; bd. dirs. Cambridge and Somerville Legal Services; pres. Cambridge Internat. Portfolio, Ltd. Named Fulbright Disting. Vis. Lectr., Universidad de Los Andes, Columbia, 1987. Mem. Ateneo Mexicano de Jurisprudencia (hon.), Inst. Politics and Constl. Law of U. La Plata (hon.), ABA, Critical Legal Studies Conf., Assn. Am. Law Schs. (pres. Sect. Grad. Studies). Democrat. Club: Harvard Faculty (bd. mgrs. 1980-83). Author: Law Politics and Revolution in Latin America: A Research Guide and Selected Bibliography, 1982; Latin American Society and Legal Culture, 1985; (with S. Sathirathai) Third World Attitudes Toward International Law, 1987. Office: Harvard U Law Sch Cambridge MA 02138

SNYDER, JED COBB, foreign affairs specialist, defense policy analyst; b. Phila., Mar. 24, 1955; s. David and Lynn Snyder; BA, Colby Coll., 1976; MA, U. Chgo., 1978, PhD candidate. Research asst. U. Chgo., 1979; asst. researcher Pan Heuristics div. R&D Assocs., Marina del Rey, Calif., 1979-80, assoc. researcher, asst. div. mgr., 1980-81, cons. 1982-83; cons. Sci. Applications, Inc., 1979-81, Rand Corp., Santa Monica, Calif., 1979-81, Los Alamos Nat. Lab., 1984; sr. spl. asst. to dir. Bur. of Politico-Mil. Affairs, Dept. State, Washington, 1981-82; research assoc. Internat. Security Studies Program, Woodrow Wilson Internat. Center for Scholars, Smithsonian Instn., Washington, 1982-84; founder, chmn. Washington strategy seminar, 1984, dep. dir., 1984-87; nat. security studies Hudson Inst., 1984-87; sr. research fellow Nat. Strategy Info. Ctr., 1988—; cons. Office of the Sec. Def., 1988; cons., 1984, Rand Corp., 1983—; John M. Olin fellow, 1987-88, Smith Richardson fellow, 1987-88; Herman Kahn fellow in nat. security studies, 1985-86, McArthur Sr. fellow, 1985-86; guest scholar Sch. Advanced Internat. Studies, Johns Hopkins U., Washington, 1982-83; guest scholar, professorial lectr., Washington, 1983-84; Inter-Univ. Seminar on Armed Forces and Soc. fellow, 1980; U. Chgo. fellow, 1979. Trustee Kents Hill (Maine) Sch. Mem. Internat. Inst. for Strategic Studies, Internat. Studies Assn., Council on European Studies, Mil. Ops. Research Soc., U.S. Naval Inst., Fgn. Policy Research Inst., AIAA, Am. Polit. Sci. Assn., Council on Fgn. Relations. Contbr. articles on U.S. fgn. policy and mil. def. to profl. publs. Home: 2201 L St NW Apt 602 Washington DC 20037 Office: Nat Strategy Info Ctr 1730 Rhode Island Ave NW Suite 601 Washington DC 20036

SNYDER, JOEL JAY, architect; b. Columbus, Ohio, Feb. 21, 1949; s. Joel Rice and Gloria (Mertz) S.; m. Christine Ann Wittmann, Mar. 13, 1982; children: Austin Wittmann, Philip Warren. BS, Ohio State U., 1972; postgrad. U. Ky., 1977, Harvard U., 1982. Registered architect, U.K., Ohio, N.Y., Pa., Ky., W.Va. Intern architect Eschliman & Assocs., Columbus, 1968-70, Acock, Trees & White, 1970, County Architects Office of Northamptonshire, Northampton, Eng., 1971, Ireland & Assocs., Columbus, 1972-73, Holroyd & Myers, 1973; architect Brubaker/Brandt, Inc., 1974-75, Feinknopf, Feinknopf, Macioce & Schappa, 1976; prin. Joel J. Snyder Assocs. Architecture and Planning, 1977—; pres. JS Assocs., 1982—; assocs. Sims Cons. Group, Lancaster, Ohio, 1983—; adj. prof. Ohio State U., Columbus, 1985—, bd. govs. Sch. Architecture Ohio State U., 1986—; mem. bd. advisors Ohio Bank and Savs. Co. Mem. AIA (chpt. pres. 1987—), Architects Soc. Ohio, Urban Land Inst., Am. Planning Assn., Constrn. Specifications Inst., Royal Inst. Brit. Architects, Inst. Urban Design., Ohio State U. Alumni Assn. (bd. govs.). Republican. Clubs: Columbus, Scioto Country. Avocations: travel; tennis; history. Home: 1892 Suffolk Rd Columbus OH 43221 Office: 744 S High St Columbus OH 43206

SNYDER, JOSEPH JOHN, author, lecturer, historian; b. Washington, Aug. 27, 1946; s. Joseph John and Amy Josephine (Hamilton) S.; m. Sally Hale Walker, July 4, 1973; children: Lauren Elizabeth, Brian Joseph Seth. BA in Anthropology, George Washington U., 1968; MA in Anthropology, U. N.Mex., 1973. With U.S. CSC, Washington, 1974-77; editor, writer U.S. Nat. Park Service, Harpers Ferry, W.Va., 1977-81; cons. editor Early Man mag., Evanston, Ill., 1978-83; cons. editor Sea Power Mag., 1987—; freelance writer, 1981—; lectr. Maya archaeology Norwegian-Caribbean Lines, Miami, Fla., 1982; cons. mus. design. Chmn. parks com. Neighborhood Planning Adv. Group, Croydon Park, Rockville, Md., 1980-81. Served with U.S. Army, 1970-71; Vietnam. Decorated Bronze Star. Mem. Soc. for History of Discoveries, Soc. Am. Archaeology, Council Md. Archaeology, Hakluyt Soc., Am. Com. to Advance Study of Petroglyphs and Pictographs (exec. sec. 1980—, editor Jour. Rock Art). Democrat. Contbg. editor Sea Power Mag., Arlington, Va., 1986—. Contbr. articles to popular mags. Home and Office: 2008 Ashley Dr Shepherdstown WV 25443-0158

SNYDER, LOIS DE ORSEY, public relations exec.; b. Whitinsville, Mass., Aug. 12, 1929; d. Francis X. and Germaine Gagnon De Orsey; A.B., Lenoir-Rhyne Coll., 1953; postgrad. Duke U., 1953-56; m. Harry M. Snyder, Jr. (dec. 1974); children: Stephen De Orsey, Melissa Anne. French tchr. Lenoir-Rhyne Coll., 1952-53; tchr. English, speech and drama Hickory (N.C.) High Sch., 1953-54; dir. public relations Hickory Furniture Mart, 1979-81; pvt. practice public relations, Hickory, 1981—. Pres., Hickory Dyslexia Found., Catawba County Arts Council, Hickory Landmarks Soc., ARC, Catawba County Mental Health Assn., N.C. Cerebral Palsy Assn.; lay reader St. Alban's Episc. Ch., Hickory. Recipient Outstanding Service award N.C. Assn. Cerebral Palsy, 1965. Mem. Catawba County Execs. Club, Internat. Platform Assn., Catawba County C. of C. (dir.), Lenoir-Rhyne Coll. Alumni Assn. (past pres., bd. dirs.), Alpha Psi Omega, Iota Epsilon Omega. Republican. Home: 1725 5th St Dr NW Hickory NC 28601-2388

SNYDER, LOUIS LEO, historian, emeritus educator; b. Annapolis, Md., July 4, 1907; s. Max and Mollie (Fainglos) S.; m. Ida Mae Brown, June 26, 1936. B.A., St. John's Coll., 1928; Ph.D., U. Frankfurt-am-Main, Germany, 1932. Jacob Schiff fellow polit. sci. Columbia U., N.Y.C., 1931-32; spl. corr. from Germany Paris edit. N.Y. Herald, 1928-31; mem. faculty CCNY, 1933-77, prof. history, 1953-77, prof. Ph.D. program, 1965-77, prof. history emeritus, 1977—; vis. lectr. Columbia U., N.Y.C., 1962; Fulbright vis. prof. U. Cologne, W. Germany, 1975; Rockefeller scholar Villa Serbelloni, Bellagio, Lake Como, Italy, 1979; cons. psychol. warfare br. War Dept., WWII; hon. dir. N.Y. Tchrs. Pension Assn., 1987. Author: Die persoenlichen und politischen Beziehungen Bismarcks zu Amerikanern, 1932, Race: A History of Modern Ethnic Theories, 1939, German Nationalism: The Tragedy of a People, 1952, The Meaning of Nationalism, 1954, The Age of Reason, 1955, The War: A Concise History, 1939-45, 1961, The Dynamics of Nationalism, 1964, The Making of Modern Man, 1967, The Blood and Iron Chancellor, 1967, The New Nationalism, 1968, Frederick the Great, 1970, Great Turning Points in History, 1971, The Dreyfus Affair, 1971, The Dreyfus Case: A Documentary History, 1973 (Anisfield-Wolf award), Varieties of Nationalism: A Comparative History, 1976, McGraw-Hill Ency. of the Third Reich, 1976; Roots of German Nationalism, 1978, Hitler's Third Reich: A Documentary History, 1982, Global Mini-Nationalisms: Autonomy or Independence, 1982, Louis L. Snyder's Historical Guide to World War II, 1982 (History Book Club selection), National Socialist Germany, 1984, Macro-Nationalisms: A History of the Pan-Movements, 1984, Diplomacy in Iron: The Life of Herbert von Bismarck, 1985, The Third Reich, 1933-45; A Bibliographical Guide to German National Socialism, 1987; co-author: (with R.B. Morris) A Treasury of Great Reporting, 1949; contbr. articles and revs. to profl. jours.; gen. editor: Anvil Van Nostrand-Krieger series of 130 original paperbacks in history and social scis.; assoc. editor: Intellect, 1974-77. Mem. adv. bd. Canadian Rev. Studies in Nationalism, 1973—, mem. council Am. Com. on History WWII, 1973—; bd. dirs. Copyright Clearance Ctr., 1977—. Served as 1st lt. USAAF, 1943-44. Recipient Alumni award of merit St. John's Coll., Annapolis, Md., 1969; recipient N.J. Writers Conf. citation, 1974, 75, 84, 86; fellow German-Am. Exchange, 1928-29; Ford Found. faculty fellow, 1952-53; Rockefeller Found. grantee, 1965-66; von Humboldt Found. grantee, 1972, 79; named to N.J. Literary Hall of Fame, 1987. Mem. Am. Hist. Assn., AAUP, Authors Guild (mem. nat. council 1973—); mem Assn. Former German-Am. Exchange Fellows; mem. Ret. Officers Assn., Conf. Group on German Politics, PEN, Phi Beta Kappa, Delta Omicron, Delta Tau Kappa. Home: 21 Dogwood Ln Princeton NJ 08540

SNYDER, RALPH HOWARD, automotive service executive; b. Manly, Iowa, July 16, 1923; s. Ralph Harnden and Gertrude Francis (Wendt) S.; student Iowa State U., 1941-43, 46; Brigham Young U., 1943-44; m. Opal Dorothy Peterson, Jan. 19, 1947; children—Donald Carleton, Douglas Eugene, Steven Leroy (dec.). Shop foreman Olds-Cadillac Agy., Estherville, Iowa, 1946-50; exptl. engr. Boeing Aircraft Co., Wichita, Kans., 1950-53; founder Snyder's Garage, Wichita, 1953—. Cons. with instrs. of local auto vocat. classes in various high schs. Active Boy Scouts Am., 1959-68. Chmn. Democratic precinct com., 1969-71. Served with USAAF, 1943-46. Mem. Automotive Service Assn., Soc. Automotive Engrs., Kans. Automotive Repair Assn. (pres.). Presbyterian (trustee 1971-74). Club: Bella Vista (Ark.) Country. Lodges: Masons, Shriners, Lions, Ea. Star, High Twelve. Home: Rt 5 Box 730 Augusta KS 67010 Office: 3419 E Harry St Wichita KS 67218

SNYDER, ROBERT MARTIN, consultant, retired government official; b. Lahmansville, W.Va., Sept. 6, 1912; s. Noah W. and Maggie M. (Varner) S.; m. Gail M. Hiser, Nov. 25, 1937; children—Rebecca J. (Mrs. Walbert Peters), Margaret A. (Mrs. John Bensenhaver), Shirley L. (Mrs. Jerry L. Williams), Robert Martin. B.S. in Agr, W.Va. U., 1937. Engaged in farming 1929-84; agrl. extension agt. Nicholas County, W.Va., 1937-41; adminstrn. commodity loans crop ins. and program performance AAA, Morgantown, W.Va., 1941-42; adminstrn. grain and oilseed program E central region AAA, U.S. Dept. Agr., 1942-47; asst. coordinator CCC, U.S. Dept. Agr., 1947-50, coordinator dairy, poultry, fruit and vegetable programs, 1950-52; chief agriculturist U.S. mission to Karachi, Pakistan FOA, 1952-54; counselor Am.embassy and dir. U.S. mission to Afghanistan, Kabul, Nairobi, Kenya, Uganda, Tanganyika and Zanzibar; councelor ICA, 1955-59; rep. ICA to, Brit. East Africa, 1959-60; food and agr. officer West African countries of Ivory Coast, Upper Volta, Niger, Dahomey, 1961-62; acting dir. U.S. AID Mission, Ivory Coast, 1962-63; attache U.S. Embassy, food and agrl. officer, Ivory Coast, 1963; agr. adviser, area office rep. AID mission to, Rhodesia and Nyasaland, 1964; attache, AID affairs officer Malawi, Africa, 1964-68; cons. World Bank, IBRD, 1967; detail officer fgn. direct investments Dept. Commerce, 1968; AID affairs officers Washington, 1968-69; food and agr. officer U.S. AID, Amman, Jordan, 1969-70; planning adviser Ministry Natural Resources, Nigeria, 1970-72; cons. 1972—; Mem. del. Gen. Mem. Agreements Tariffs and Trade Conf., Torquay, Eng., 1951; mem. Mus. Commn., Library Commn. Served to lt. USNR, 1944-46, PTO. Recipient nat. 4-H alumni award Nat. 4-H Congress, Chgo., 1982, Disting. Alumnus award W.Va. Coll. Agriculture and Forestry, 1987. Mem. Fgn. Service Assn., Am. Legion, W.Va. U. Alumni Assn., Am. Acad. Polit. and Social Sci., Soc. Internat. Devel., Internat. Platform Assn., U.S. Nat. Trust for Historic Preservation, Nature Conservancy, Commn. on Aging, Alpha Zeta. Clubs: Masons, Kiwanis, Explorers. Home: Noah Snyder Farm Route 1 Box 32 Lahmansville WV 26731

SNYDER, RONALD WARREN, marketing research and development company executive coffee roasting company executive; b. Phila., Feb. 6, 1947; s. Ronald Clark and Bertha Elizabeth S.; A.A.S., Gloucester County Coll., Sewell, N.J., 1972, B.S.B.A., Loyola U., Paris Extension, 1974, M.B.A., 1983. Owner, operator Eagle Advt., Inc., Springfield, Mo., 1973-74; profl. adventurer, 1974-78; chmn. bd., chief exec. officer Overseas Research & Devel. Inc., Springfield, 1979—; pres. and founder "Hey Mon" Coffee Ltd., 1985— ; Mo. coordinator Vietnam Vets. in Bus., 1979-82; mem. U.S. Senatorial Bus. Adv. Bd.; mem. nat. adv. bd. NSC. Served with USAR, 1966-69; Vietnam. Decorated Purple Heart, Combat Inf. badge. Mem. Am. Mgmt. Assn., Solar Lobby, Am. Assn. Small Research Cos., Internat. Shooters Devel. Fund, Nat. Rifle Assn. (life), Assn. M.B.A. Execs., Internat. Soc. Financiers, Springfield Area C. of C. Republican. Lutheran. Editor Vanguard mag., 1971-72. Home: 294-A Coffee Ln Everton MO 65646 Office: PO Box 267 Jewell Sta Springfield MO 65801

SNYDER, SUSAN LELAND, international trade executive; b. Washington, Nov. 10, 1945; d. Arthur Leland and Jane Peters. B.A., Mt. Holyoke Coll., 1967; postgrad. SUNY-Buffalo, 1967-70. Staff adviser Institut Francais de Gestion, Paris, 1971-73; mktg. strategist Compteurs Schlumberger, Paris, 1973-76; export dir. Schlumberger Instruments & Systemes, Velizy-Villacoublay, France, 1976-78; founder, pres. Pathfinder Corp. for Internat. Trade, Washington, 1978—; chmn. internat. mem. task force; mem. internat. com. Greater Washington Bd. of Trade, 1980—. Sec.-treas. French-Am. Com. for the Statue of Liberty, 1981-84; trustee, exec. dir. Com. for the Statue of Liberty Mus., 1985—; dir. Tilden Gardens, 1988—. Mem. Washington Flute Soc. Club: City Tavern (Washington). Office: Pathfinder Corp Internat Trade 1629 K St NW Washington DC 20006

SNYDER, THOMAS JOHN, osteopath; b. Monticello, Iowa, June 19, 1950; s. John Arvid and Laura Emma (Dirks) S.; m. LuAnne Carole Horner, June 17, 1972; children—Rachael, Mark, Andrea. B.A., Coe Coll., 1975; D.O., U. Osteo. Medicine, 1978. Cert. in internal medicine. Intern, Davenport Osteo. Hosp., Iowa, 1978-79; resident in internal medicine Normandy Hosp., St. Louis, 1979-82; asst. prof. U. Osteo. Medicine, Des Moines, 1982-83; staff physician Davenport Med. Ctr., Iowa, 1983—; staff physician Mercy Hosp., Davenport, 1984—, St. Lukes Hosp, Davenport, 1984—, Illini Hosp., Silvis, Ill., 1984—. Contbr. articles to profl. jours. Bd. dirs. Am. Cancer Soc., Scott County, 1984. Served with USMC, 1968-71. Mead Johnson fellow, 1982. Mem. Am. Heart Assn., Am. Lung Assn., Am. Diabetes Assn., Iowa Osteo. Med. Assn., Scott County Osteo. Assn. Mem. Reformed Ch. Am. Lodge: Rotary. Avocations: running, decoy collecting. Office: 3801 Marquette Suite 202 Davenport IA 52806

SNYDER, WARREN WILSON, management company executive, management consultant; b. Louisville, Aug. 8, 1945; s. Woodrow Wilson and Glenna Marie (Minor) S.; m. Donna Marie Farnham, July 17, 1971. B.Indsl. Design, Syracuse U., 1968; M.B.A., Old Dominion U., 1980. Graphics supr. planning and program devel. Norfolk (Va.) Redevel. Housing Authority, 1973-75; program mgr. Cerberonics, Inc., Alexandria, Va., 1975-78; v.p. ops. Atlantic DALFI, Inc., Norfolk, Va., 1978—, dir., San Diego, 1979—. Served to capt. USAF, 1968-73. Mem. Indsl. Design Soc. Am., Nat. Contract Mgrs. Assn., Alpha Xi Alpha. Home: 1364 Marshall Ln Virginia Beach VA 23455 Office: DALFI Inc 2125 Smith Ave Suite 202 Chesapeake VA 23320

SNYDER, WILLARD BREIDENTHAL, lawyer; b. Kansas City, Kans., Dec. 18, 1940; s. N.E. and Ruth (Breidenthal) S.; m. Lieselotte Dieringer, Nov. 10, 1970 (dec. Nov. 1975); m. Christa Wittman, June 1, 1978; children: Kim Green, Jackie Green, Rolf. BA, U. Kans., 1962, JD, 1965; postgrad., Hague Acad. Internat. Law, The Netherlands, 1965-66, U. Dijon, France, 1966; grad., Command and Gen. Staff Coll., Ft. Leavenworth, Kans., 1977. Sole practice Kansas City, Kans., 1970-80, 85—; trust officer, corp. trust officer Security Nat. Bank., Kansas City, 1980-83, corp. sec., 1983-85; pres. Real Estate Corp. Inc., 1984—; bd. dirs. Providence St. Margaret Health Ctr., Kansas City, Kans.; adv. bd. dirs. United Mo. Bankshares, Kansas City; West German consul for Kans., Western Mo., 1972—. Mem. Platte Woods (Mo.) City Council, 1983-84. Served with U.S. Army, 1967-70; served to lt. col. Kans. Army N.G. ARCOM, 1970, Bundesverdienst Kreuz (silver), 1987. Mem. Mo. Bar Assn., Kansas City Bar Assn., Kansas City Hosp. Attys., Kansas City Bd. Trade, Mil. Order of World Wars (chpt. comdr. 1983-84, regional comdr. 1987—). Office: care Security Bank Kansas City PO Box 1297 Kansas City KS 66117

SO, VICTOR ANG, gastroenterologist, internist, consultant; b. Amoy, Republic of China, Sept. 12, 1912; arrived in Philippines, 1923; s. Pit Huy and Pue (Ang) S.; m. Siok Gee Tan, Dec. 26, 1940; children: Isaac, Pacifico, Mary, Felisa, Linda, Juanito. A in Liberal Arts, Amoy U., 1933; AA, U. Philippines, Manila, 1936; MD, U. Santo Tomas, Manila, 1941. Diplomate Am. Bd. Gastroenterology. Intern U. Santo Tomas, 1940-41; pres. The Filipino Chinese Med. Soc., Manila, 1958-60, dir., 1960-74, adviser, 1974-83; bd. dirs. Beer Hausen Med. Specialty Scholarship Found., Manila, 1983—; treas. 4th Asian Pacific Congress Gastroenterology, Manila, 1972-73; panel discussor internat. symposium on hepatitis Gastroenterological Soc. of Republic of China, Manila, 1975; guest speaker Iloilo (Philippines) Med. Soc., 1975; co-founder Met. Gen. Hosp., Manila, 1968, bd. dirs. editor, researcher sci. work Jour. Philippine Fedn. Pvt. Med. Practitioners, 1969-73. Mem. The Filipino Chinese Med. Soc. (pres. 1958-60, bd. dirs. 1960-74, Appreciation award 1961, 74), Philippine Soc. Gastroenterology (bd. dirs. 1965-73). Office: Met Gen Hosp, 1357 G Masangkay St, Binondo, Manila Philippines

SOANES, DAVID LEE, architect, landscape architect, planner; b. Buffalo, July 18, 1950; s. Justus Arnold Thomas and Dorothy Ellen (Bonney) S.; B.Arch., U. Miami, 1973; M.L.A. (Univ. fellow), Cornell U., 1976; 1 dau., Summer Leigh; m. Susan Dobbs, July 4, 1985; stepchild: Kimberley Brown. Draftsman, Warshaw Assos., Miami, Fla., 1972, Drexler Assos., Miami, 1972-73; apprentice architect Wright Architect, Miami, 1973-74; apprentice architect, site planner Fred Thomas Assos., Ithaca, N.Y., 1974-76; cons. designer, Ithaca, 1976-77; architect/land planner PRC Toups, San Diego, 1977-80; pres., prin. architect, David Lee Soanes, Ltd., San Diego, 1980—; teaching asst. landscape architecture Cornell U., 1975-76. Registered architect, landscape architect, Calif. Mem. AIA, Am. Soc. Landscape Architects, Constrn. Specifications Inst., Nat. Trust Hist. Preservation, Tau Beta Pi. Baptist. Author: LaGrange Town Center, 1976; Bowdoin Park Study, 1976; designs include: master plan for Jamsil Center, Seoul, 1978, for Rancho San Diego, 1978, for Ram's Hill Country Club, 1979, for MX weapons system community for SAC, 1980, master plan Batam Centre, Indonesia, 1984. Home: 4737 Ocana Pl San Diego CA 92124

SOARES, EUSEBIO LOPES, anesthesiologist; b. Lisbon, Portugal, Oct. 20, 1918; s. Jose Lopes and Rosaria (Sousa) S.; M.D., U. Lisbon, 1942; m. Edviges Velasques Monteiro, Aug. 7, 1951; 1 dau., Maria Helena. Tng. in anesthesia, U.K., 1947-48; asst. prof. U. Lisbon Faculty Medicine, 1949-50; dir. dept. anesthesia Hosp. do Ultramar, Lisbon, 1952-56; sr. anesthesiologist Lisbon Civil Hosp., 1956-69; dir. dept. anesthesia Hosp. St. Ant. Capuchos, Lisbon, 1969—, also clin. dir.; vis. prof. Ibero-Latin-Am. Center Anesthesiology, Central U. Venezuela, 1969. Served as officer M.C., Portuguese Army, 1945-46. Fellow Royal Coll. Surgeons Eng., Royal Soc. Medicine; mem. World Fedn. Socs. Anesthesiologists (v.p. 1964), European Acad. Anesthesiology, Portuguese Soc. Anesthesiology (founder 1955, pres. 1955-57, 59-60), also socs. anesthesiology in Brazil, Argentina, Spain (hon.), Gt. Britain and Ireland, Belgium, U.S. Contbr. articles to profl. jours. Home: 15-6 deg-D., D Estefania, 1 100 Lisbon Portugal Office: Hosp St Ant Capuchos, Dept Anesthesia, 1 100 Lisbon Portugal

SOARES, MARIO ALBERTO NOBRE LOPES, president of Portugal, political party official; b. Lisbon, Dec. 7, 1924; s. Joã o Lopes and Elisa Nobre S.; m. Maria Barroso, 1949; 2 children; B.A. in History and Philosophy, U. Lisbon, 1951; J.D., Sorbonne, Paris, 1957. Founder, Movement for Democratic Unity (MUD), Lisbon, 1946, leader MUD Juvenil, mem. MUD Central Com., 1945-48, sec. presdl. candidature of Gen. Norton da Mattos, 1949; mem. exec. Social Dem. Action, 1952-60; mem. campaign com. for Humberto Delgado in presdl. elections, 1958; candidate as dep. for dem. opposition, Lisbon, 1965, 69; exiled to Sao Tome, 1968; in exile, Paris, 1970-74; tchr. U. Paris, 1970-74; asso. U. Rennes, 1970-74; co-founder, sec.-gen. Portuguese Socialist Party, 1973-86; minister fgn. affairs Portugal, 1974-75, 77-78; in charge of negotiations leading to independence of Guinea-Bissau, Mozambique, Angola 1974; minister without portfolio, 1975; dep. Constituent Assembly, 1975, Legis. Assembly, 1976; participant all major Socialist internat. summits, 1973—; v.p. Socialist Internat., from 1976; prime minister Portugal, 1976-78, 1983-85, pres. Portugal, 1986—; corr. various newspapers. Recipient Human Rights prize. Author hist. and polit. books. Office: Partido Socialista, Rua da Emenda 46, 1200 Lisbon Portugal *

SOARES DE MELLO, ADELINO JOSE RODRIGUES, mechanical engineer; b. Horta, Azores, Portugal, Oct. 3, 1931; s. Alfredo Luis and Hilda da Conceiç ã o (Rodrigues) S. de M.; Eng.Mec., Lisbon U., 1955; postgrad. Manchester (Eng.) Coll. Tech., 1956-57; m. Maria Odete Correia Baptista, Dec. 7, 1955; children—Joã o Carlos, Luis Miguel, Pedro Gonç alo. Mgr. mech. engrs. div. Profabril-Centro de Projectos, Sarl, Lisbon, 1958-68; dir. Tecnofabril-Industrias Mecanicas, Sarl, Lisbon, 1966-75; dir. Termec-Equipamentos Termicos de Coimbra, Lda, Portugal, 1968-71; mng. dir. Babcock & Wilcox Portuguesa, Sarl-Lisbon-Oporto, 1971-73; chmn. bd. dirs. Sorefame-Sociedades Reunidas de Fabricaç õ es Metalicas, Sarl, Amadora, Portugal, 1973-74; tech. rep. Brit. Ropeways Engrng. Co., Ltd., Sevenoaks, Eng., Rio de Janeiro, 1975-78; dir. Smec-Ind. Metalo Mecanicas, Ltda., Botucatu S.P., Brazil, 1975-78, Costa Pinto J.A., Ltda., Botucatu S.P., 1975-78, Sociedade Indul. de Concentrados, Sarl-Azinhaga, Portugal, 1978-81, Mot Sistemas de Movimentaç ao e Transporte, Lda, Lisbon, 1978-81, Metalurgica Duarte Ferreira, Sarl-Tramagal, Portugal, RUF, Lda, Lisboa, Portugal; indsl. cons. Com. Electromech. Industry, Ministry of Industry, 1980-84. Met. Vickers Elec. Co. Ltd. grantee, 1955-58. Mem. Associaç ao Portuguesa dos Industriais de Tomate (hon. sec. 1980-82), Ordem dos Engenheiros. Roman Catholic. Clubs: Automovel de Portugal, Met. Vickers Overseas. Columnist econ. affairs newspapers, 1982-84; contbr. articles to profl. publs. Home: Rua Maria Veleda, Quinta da Luz Torre 2-10, 1500 Lisbon Portugal Office: Avenida 5 de Outubro122 4, 1000 Lisbon Portugal

SOBCZYK, KAZIMIERZ, mathematics and mechanics educator; b. Radwanow, Poland, Mar. 17, 1939; s. Walenty and Marianna (Przepiora) S.; m. Elzbieta Anna Ferensztajn, Sept. 11, 1966; children—Joanna, Pawel, Jacek, Marcin. MS, U. Warsaw, 1960; PhD, Polish Acad. Scis., 1966, D Habilitowany, 1974. Research asst. Inst. Fundamental Technol. Research, Warsaw, 1961-65, adj., 1966-74, docent, 1977-82, prof. applied math., 1983—; research fellow NYU, N.Y.C. and MIT, Cambridge, 1970-71; Talbot-Crosbie fellow Glasgow U., 1975-76; vis. prof. Tech. U. Denmark, 1985. Author: Outline of Probability Theory, 1970; Methods of Statistical Dynamics, 1973; Stochastic Wave Propagation, 1985; Stochastic Differential Equations for Applications, 1985. Contbr. articles to profl. jours. Mem. Internat. Soc. Interaction of Mechanics and Maths., Am. Math. Soc., Polish Soc. Applied and Theoretical Mechanics. Roman Catholic. Avocation: gardening. Home: ul Anieli Krzywon 2 m 89, 01-391 Warsaw Poland Office: Inst Fundamental Technol Research, ul Swietokrzyska 21, 00-049 Warsaw Poland

SOBEL, HOWARD BERNARD, osteopathic physician; b. N.Y.C., May 15, 1929; s. Martin and Ella (Sternberg) S.; m. Ann Louise Silverbush, June 16, 1957 (dec. May 1978); children—Nancy Sobel Schumer, Janet Sobel Medow, Robert; m. Irene S. Miller, June 8, 1980; stepchildren—Avner Saferstein, Daniel Saferstein, Naomi Saferstein. A.B., Syracuse U., 1951; D.O., Kansas City Coll. Osteopathy and Surgery, 1955. Intern Zieger Osteo. Hosp., Detroit, 1955-56; gen. practice osteo. medicine Redford Twp., Mich., 1956-74, Livonia, Mich., 1974—; chief of staff Botsford Gen. Hosp., Farmington,

Mich., 1978; mem. faculty Mich. State U. Coll. Osteo. Medicine, 1969—, clin. assoc. prof. family practice, 1973—; mem. exec. and med. adv. coms. United Health Orgn. Mich.; mem. Venereal Disease Action Com., Mich.; apptd. to asst. impaired osteo. physicians Mich., 1983. Mem. Am. Osteo. Assn. (ho. of dels. 1981—), Mich. Assn. Osteo. Physicians and Surgeons (ho. of dels.), Am. Coll. Osteo. Rheumatologists, Coll. Am. Osteo. Gen. Practitioners, Osteo. Gen. Practice Mich., Wayne County Osteo. Assn. (pres.). Jewish. Home: 6222 Northfield St West Bloomfield MI 48322 Office: 28275 Five Mile Rd Livonia MI 48154

SOBH, ABDUL-NASSER, sales executive; b. Beirut, Mar. 14, 1961; s. Akram-Bahjat Sobh and Afaf-Rashed Rabaa; m. Joumama-Mohanna, Oct. 21, 1983. BS in Bus. Adminstrn., Beirut U., 1983, MBA in Mktg., 1984. Salesman Gen. Electric Co., Beirut, 1981-82; supr. salesman White-Westinghouse Electric Co., Beirut, 1983-84, Biter Metal Fabrication, Saudi Arabia, 1984-86; sales mgr. Abou Dawood Est. P&G, Saudi Arabia, 1986—; project cons. Arab Cons. Team, Saudi Arabia, 1985-86. Vol. Red Cross, Beirut, 1981-87, Lebanese Civil Def. Dept., Beirut, 1982. Recipient Mktg. Sparten award Lebanese Chem. Co., 1985. Mem. Lebanese Mgmt. Assn. Clubs: Bus. United, Chess Lebanese (Beirut). Lodge: Lions (Gold Lion 1986). Home: Kournish Maghaa Jihad Bldg, 511616 Beirut Lebanon Office: Abou Dawood Est, PO Box 252, Dammam 31411, Saudi Arabia

SOBINGSOBING, PEDRO JUANILLO, electrical engineer, educator; b. Albuera, Leyte, Philippines, Dec. 12, 1930; came to Saudi Arabia, 1975; s. Adriano Yuzon and Leoncia (Juanillo) S.; m. Socorro Rosillo Elatico, Nov. 10, 1956; children—Vicente Alex, Noel, Aleli, Santiago, Mildred, AlmaBella. AEE, Feati U., Philippines, 1964, BSEE, 1974; MSEE, U. Petroleum & Minerals, Saudi Arabia, 1978; tng. in X-Ray Spectroscopy, Eng., Fed. Republic Germany, 1985—. Communication specialist Page Communication Engrs., Vietnam, 1966-72; instr. electronics Philippines Technicum, 1972-74; maintenance supr. Page Communication Engrs., Iran, 1974-76; field supr. AVCO Tech. Dienste, Dhahran, Saudi Arabia, 1976-78; electronics engr. U. Petroleum and Minerals, Saudi Arabia, 1978—; cons. mgr. M.R. Abouhaimed Est., Saudi Arabia, 1978-82. Served with Philippines Armed Forces, 1954-64. Decorated Cert. of Merit, Cert. of 2d Honor. Mem. IEEE. Roman Catholic. Avocation: tennis. Home: Silahis St, Sta Ana, Manila The Philippines Office: Univ Petroleum & Minerals, UPM 373, Dhahran 31261, Saudi Arabia

SOBOL, BRUCE J., internist; b. N.Y.C., June 10, 1923; s. Ira J. and Ida S. (Gelula) S.; B.A., Swarthmore Coll., 1947; M.D., N.Y.U., 1950; m. Barbara Sue Gordon, Apr. 30, 1951; children—Peter Gordon, Scott David. Intern, Bellevue Hosp., N.Y.C., 1950-51, resident, 1951-52, N.Y. Heart Assn. fellow, 1953-55; resident VA Hosp., Boston, 1952-53; practice medicine specializing in internal medicine, White Plains, N.Y., 1955-59; dir. pulmonary lab. Westchester County (N.Y.) Med. Center, Valhalla, 1959-78; dir. med. research Boehringer Ingelheim, Ltd., Ridgefield, Conn., 1978-83; research prof. medicine N.Y. Med. Coll. Bd. dirs. Westchester Community Services Council, 1977-79; pres. Westchester Heart Assn., 1976-79. Served with inf. AUS, World War II; ETO. Diplomate Am. Bd. Internal Medicine. Fellow ACP, Am. Coll. Allergy, Am. Coll. Chest Physicians, N.Y. Acad. Scis.; mem. Am. Physiol. Soc., Am. Heart Assn., N.Y. Trudea Soc., Am. Thoracic Soc., Am. Fedn. Clin. Research. Contbr. numerous articles to profl. publs. Office: 275 Ridgebury Rd Ridgefield CT 06877

SOBOUTI, YOUSEF, astrophysicist, educator; b. Zanjan, Iran, Aug. 23, 1932; s. Ahmad and Omm-e-Kolsum (Sobouti) S.; m. Effat Barati, July 7, 1956; children: Farhad, SUsan, Farzin. BS, Tehran U., 1953; MA in Physics, U. Toronto, Ont., Can., 1960; PhD in Astronomy and Astrophysics, U. Chto., 1963. Tchr. high sch. Tabriz, Iran, 1953-56; lectr. math. U. Newcastle-on-Tyne, Eng., 1963-64; assoc. prof. physics Shiraz U., Iran, 1964-74, prof., 1970—; vis. assoc. prof. astronomy U. Pa., Phila., 1968-69; vis. sr. researcher U. Amsterdam, 1975-76; founder, dir. Biruni Obs., 1975—; vis. scholar U. Chgo., 1985-86; mem. internat. adv. com. 2d Marcel Grossman Meeting. Mem. editorial bd. Iran Jour. Sci. and Tech., 1984—; contbr. articles to prolf. jours. Recipient medal for excellence in research Iranian Ministry of Sci., 1978. Mem. Nat. Astron. Soc. Iran (v.p. 1974-78), Phys. Soc. Iran (bd. dirs. 1985—), Am. Astron. Soc., Internat. Astron. Union. Home: Gasr-e-Dasht Ave, 69 Street, Shiraz Iran Office: Dept Physics Shiraz U, Shiraz Iran

ŠOCHMAN, JAN, cardiologist, researcher; b. Prague, Czechoslovakia, June 6, 1956; s. Jan Šochman and Ludmila (Hantáková) Šochmanová. MD, Charles U., Prague, 1981. Intern Kolin Hosp., 1981-83; cardiologist Inst. Clin. and Exptl. Medicine, Prague, 1983—. Inventor catheterization techniques, 1986. Mem. Czech Cardiologic Soc. (com. mem. sect. invasive cardioangiology).

SOCKALINGAM, MUTHU, publishing company administrator; b. Gopeng, Selangor, Malaysia, May 20, 1935; s. Muthu Pillay and Alamel Ammal Seerangam; m. Edith Krishnan, Dec. 9, 1960; children: Shalini, Anita. BA with honors, U. Malaya, Singapore, 1959, diploma in edn., 1960; MLS, Rutgers U., 1965. Tchr. Sekolah Tuanku Abdul Rahman, Ipoh, Perak, Malaysia, 1960-63; lectr. Malayan Tchrs. Coll., Kuala Lumpur, Selangor, Malaysia, 1965-67; head textbook bur. Ministry of Edn., Kuala Lumpur, 1967-73; gen. mgr. Oxford U. Press, S.E. Asia, 1973-83; mng. dir. Penerbit Fajar Bakti Sdn Bhd, Malaysia, 1983—. Mem. council U. Malaya, 1978-90, Malaysian Exam. Council Kuala Lumpur, 1983-89. Mem. Malaysian Book Pubs. Assn. (v.p. 1977—). Office: Penerbit Fajar Bakti Sdn Bhd, 3 Jalan 13/3, 46200 Pataling Jaya Selangor, Malaysia

SOCOL, SHELDON ELEAZER, university official; b. N.Y.C., July 10, 1936; s. Irving and Helen (Tuchman) S.; B.A., Yeshiva U., 1958; J.D., N.Y.U., 1963; m. Genia Ruth Prager, Dec. 26, 1959; children—Jeffrey, Steven, Sharon. Asst. bursar Yeshiva U., N.Y.C., 1958-60, assoc. bursar, 1960-62, dir. student finances, 1962-70, sec., 1970—, chief fiscal officer, 1971-72, v.p. bus. affairs, 1972—. Mem. N.Y. State Adv. Council on Financial Assistance to Coll. Students, 1969-76; asst. dir. Tng. Inst. for Financial Aid Officers, Hunter Coll., City U. N.Y., 1970-71; presdl. adv. commn. Temple U., 1986; mem. N.Y.C. Regional Plan for Higher Edn. Regents Adv. Task Force, 1971-72. Pres., Minyon Park Estates, Inc. Mem. Nat. Assn. Coll. and Univ. Attys., NEA, N.Y. State, Met. N.Y.C. financial aid adminstrs. assns., Eastern Assn. Student Financial Aid Officers, Am. Mgmt. Assn., Am. Assn. for Higher Edn., Nat. Assn. Coll. and Univ. Bus. Officers, Middle States Assn. Colls. (mem. evaluation team commn. higher edn.), Carnegie Mellon U., Pa. Home: 136-18 71st Rd Kew Gardens Hills NY 11367 Office: Yeshiva University 500 W 185th St New York NY 10033

SODAWALLA, ANITA B., nurse, training and development consultant; b. Quezon City, Philippines, Dec. 5, 1942; came to U.S., 1972; d. Jose Canete Bustamante and Esperanza Manzano Carino; m. Badruddin Hussain Sodawalla, Dec. 26, 1975; 1 child, Ibrahim Badruddin. Diploma in Nursing, U. Philippines, 1968, MS in Nursing, 1971; BS in Nursing, Philippine Women's U., 1970; postgrad. Wayne State U., 1977-80. Charge nurse neonatal and pediatric ICU, Henry Ford Hosp., Detroit, 1972-73; instr., coordinator critical care Grace Hosp., Detroit, 1973-76; sr. instr. Harper Hosp. div. Harper-Grace Hosps., 1976-79, asst. dir. nursing Grace Hosp. div., 1980; pres., exec. dir. Critical Care Unltd., Inc., Southfield, Mich., 1979-84; dir. nursing services and continuing edn. Critical Care Profl. Services, 1980-84; pres., exec. dir. Profl. Success Systems, Inc., 1982-85, dir. human resources tng. and devel., 1986—; program coordinator, cons. Critical Care Edn. Ctr., 1984—; instr. Am. Heart Assn. Mich., Detroit, 1974—, bd. dirs. Macomb County Chpt., 1981-84; mem. First Presbyn. Ch. Detroit. Mem. Am. Assn. Critical Care Nurses, Nat. Assn. Female Execs., Nat. Assn. Nurse Cons. and Entrepreneurs. (founder, pres.), Philippine Nurses Assn. Mich. (life, pres., cons. 1975-78). Avocations: swimming, singing, reading.

SÖDERBAUM, OLOF PETER WILHELM, economist, researcher; b. Porjus, Sweden, May 23, 1937; s. Carl Emil and Kerstin Marianne (Lundgren) S.; m. Ingrid Elisabet Klint, Nov. 20, 1968 (dec. 1974); 1 child, Jakob; m. Eva Margareta Backman, June 9, 1978; children—Simon, Vilhelm, Hanna. B.A., Uppsala U. (Sweden), 1962, M.A., 1964, Ph.D. in Bus. Adminstrn., 1973. Asst. econs. Uppsala U., 1961-63; sec. Royal Acad. Engring. Scis., Stockholm, 1963-64; asst. prof. bus. adminstrn. Uppsala U., 1966-74; prof. econs. and environ. mgmt. Swedish Univ. Agrl. Scis., Uppsala, 1974—; internat. corr. Jour. Econ. Issues, Calif., 1983—. Author: Positional Analysis for Decision Making, 1973, Public Policy, Economics, Environment, 1978; also articles, book chpts. Expert Swedish Govt. com. prevention of cancer, Stockholm, 1979-84; bd. dirs. Environ. Ctr., Uppsala, 1974—, Environ. and Future, Uppsala, 1976—. Rotary Internat. fellow U. Lovain, Belgium, 1964-65. Mem. Assn. Evolutionary Econs., Assn. Social Econs., Internat. Assn. Agrl. Economists, European Assn. Agrl. Economists, Nordic Assn. Human Ecology. Avocations: sports; jogging. Home: Sömnadsvägen 31, S-752 Uppsala 57 Sweden Office: Swedish Univ Agrl Scis, Dept Econs, Box 7013, S-750 Uppsala 07 Sweden

SODERBERG, LENNART GOSTA, architect, consultant; b. Sundsvall, Sweden, May 21, 1923; s. Gosta Andrew and Gota Katarina (Petterson) S.; m. Margaretha Gunborg Anderson, July 7, 1951; children: Maria Katarina, Olla Kristina. Student, State Secondary Sch., 1943; BArch, Chalmers Tech. Coll., 1951. Registered architect, Sweden. Architect Brink, Orebro, Sweden, 1951-65, co-owner, 1965-72, prin., 1972-80; prin. Soderberg Arketektkowtor, 1980—. Prin. works include Orebro Gen. Hosp., Falu, Skoude, also numerous dist. hosps. Active Orebro Tech. Mus., 1983—. Mem. Sveriges Arketekters Rikstorbund. Lodge: Rotary. Home: Rantmastargat 64, Orebro Sweden S 70227

SÖDERKVIST, JAN MATS OLOF, engineer, consultant; b. Grängesberg, Sweden, Jan. 8, 1960; s. Erik Axel Olof and Kerstin Margareta (Oskarsdotter) s.; m. Kerstin Rosina Granlund, May 25, 1985. MSc in Engring., Royal Inst. Tech., Stockholm, 1983; Lic. in Engring., Royal Inst. Tech., 1984. Owner, cons. engring. HB Entema, Stockholm, 1985-87, Colibri AB, Stockholm, 1987—. Honor scholar Royal Inst. Tech., 1984; grantee Rotary Internat., Tucson, Ariz., 1982-83. Mem. Math. Assn. Am. Home: Torgnyvägen 48, 183422 Täby Sweden

SÖDERMAN, JACKIE (JEAN LUDVIG), filmmaker; b. Gotheburg, Sweden, May 27, 1927; d. John and Fanny Söderman; m. Eivor Johansson, Mar. 14, 1951; children: Dan Jackie, John Mikael. Ballet dancer The Gothenburg (Sweden) Opera, 1947-53, dancer, choreographer, 1953-55, dir., choreographer, 1955-64, gen. mgr., artistic dir., 1980-84; dir. The Royal Dramatic Theatre, Stockholm, 1964-67; producer, dir. Swedish TV, Gothenburg, 1967-80, head drama, music, 1984-88, producer, dir., 1988—. Office: Swedish TV, S-405 13 Gothenburg Sweden

SÖDERPALM, EWA ANNIKA, linguist, educator; b. Skara, Västergötland, Sweden, Mar. 12, 1939; d. Erik O. and Zoli C.J. (Collin) S.; divorced 1978; children: Annika, Agneta. BS in Speech Pathology and Therapy, U. Lund, Sweden, 1972, PhD in Phonetics, 1979. Lectr. Phonetics U. Lund, 1965-71; lectr. Speech Pathology Malmö U., Sweden, 1973-80; lectr., dir. Speech Pathology and Tng. Gothenburg U., Sweden, 1981—. Author: Röst-tal-och Språkrubbn, 1976, 2d edit. 1986. Mem. Internat. Assn. Logopedics Phoniatrics (bd. dirs.). Office: U Gothenburg, Dept Speech Pathology, Gröna str 11, S-413 Gothenburg 45 Sweden

SÖDERSTRÖM, HANS TSON, economist; b. Stockholm, Feb. 25, 1945; s. Torkel A.R. and Elisabet (Zielfelt) S.; Ekon dr. (Ph.D.), Stockholm Sch. Econs., 1974; m. Gunilla Seth, June 5, 1971; children—Christofer, Ebba, Marie. Sr. fellow Inst. Internat. Econ. Studies, U. Stockholm, 1971-84; assoc. dir., 1979-84; exec. dir. SNS Ctr. for Bus. and Policy Studies, Stockholm, 1985—; vis. fellow public and internat. affairs Princeton U., 1975; vis. scholar Stanford U., 1976; vis. research prof., bd. govs. Fed. Res. System, 1976; expert Govt. Commns. on Exchange Control and Wage Earners Funds, 1979-81; mem. SNS Econ. Policy Group 1980-81, chmn., 1984—; bd. dirs. SEB-Invest AB, 1980-85, Montagu Fondkomm, 1986-88. Ford Found. research fellow, 1975-76; recipient David Davidson prize in econs., 1971. Mem. Swedish Econ. Assn., Stockholm Stock Exchange, 1987, Swedish Shareholders Assn., 1984, Am. Econ. Assn., Liberal Econ. Club (chmn. 1984-85). Editor: Ekonomiste Debati, 1977-78, mem. editorial bd. 1979—, S-E Banken Quarterly Rev., 1983—; Author: Microdynamics of Production, 1974, Sweden-the Road to Stability, 1985, Getting Sweden Back to Work, 1986; contbr. articles to sci. jours. Home: Larsbergsvagen 27, S 181 Lidingo 38 Sweden Office: SNS, Sköldungagatan 2, S-114 Stockholm 27 Sweden

SODHY, LAKHMIR SINGH, health consultant; b. Kuala Lumpur, Selangor, Malaysia, Sept. 30, 1919; s. Sant Singh and Durga Devi Sodhy; m. Padma Watti, Apr. 18, 1942; children: Renuka, Himansu, Devika, Anil, Bina. MBBChir, U. Malaya, Singapore, 1952; Diploma in Pub. Health, U. London, 1957; Diploma in Indsl. Health, Royal Coll. Physicians and Surgeons, London, 1958. Med. officer Gen. Hosp., Kuala Lumpur, 1952-53; med. and health officer West Coast Penang, 1952-55; med. officer of health City of Kuala Lumpur, 1955-58, dir. health, 1958-72; sec. gen. Intergovtl. Com. on Population and Family Planning S.E. Asia, Kuala Lumpur, 1972-81; cons. World Bank, Washington, 1972-73, Evaluation of Health and Population, Kuala Lumpur, 1981—. V.p. Internat. Planned Parenthood Fedn., London, 1963-69. Recipient Gold medal Nat. Tuberculosis Assn., 1963, Ahli Mangku Negara award King of Malaysia, 1964, Kesetria Mangku Negara award King of Malaysia, 1966. Mem. Malaysian Med. Assn., Soc. Occupational Medicine, Coll. Gen. Practitioners. Lodge: Rotary (dist. gov. 1969-70). Home: 2B Crescent Ct, Brickfield, Kuala Lumpur 50470, Malaysia Office: 18A Crescent Ct, Brickfield, Kuala Lumpur Selangor 50470, Malaysia

SODNOM, DUMAAGIYN, Mongolian government official; b. 1933. Ed., Sch. of Fin. and Econs., Ulan Bator, Higher Sch. Fin. and Econs., U.S.S.R. With Ministry of Fin., Mongolia, 1950-54, dir. dept. in ministry, 1958-63, minister of fin., 1963-69, mem. Central Com., Mongolian People's Revolutionary Party, 1966—, first dep. chmn. State Planning Commn., rank of minister, 1969-72, chmn. State Planning Commn., 1972-84, dep. chmn. Council of Ministers, 1974-84, chmn., 1984—; mem. People's Great Hural (Assembly), 1966—. Address: Council of Ministers, Govt Palace, Ulan Bator Mongolia *

SODRE, ROBERTO COSTA DE ABREU, government official; b. June 21, 1918; m. Maria do Carma Melao; 2 daughters. LLB, Sao Paulo U., Brazil, 1942. Elected state rep. Nat. Dem. Union, 1950, 54, 58, chmn. Sao Paulo chpt., 1963; pres. Sao Paulo Legislature, 1960-62; joined Nat. Renewal Alliance, 1966; gov. State of Sao Paulo, 1966-71; sole practice law 1971-77, mem. adv. body to assist state govt., 1979; pres. Eletropaulo, 1982; minister fgn. affairs 1986—; former nat. com. mem. and sec.-gen. Nat. Dem. Union; mem. nat. com. Social Dem. Party, 1979. Pres. Nat. Coffee Council, 1981-82. Office: Ministry of Fgn Affairs, Brasilia Brazil *

SOEDERSTROM, ELISABETH ANNA, opera singer; b. Stockholm, May 7, 1927; d. Emanuel Albert and Anna (Palasova) S.; student Opera Sch., Stockholm, also pupil of Andrejewa Skilondz; m. Sverker Olow, Mar. 29, 1950; children—Malcolm, Peter, Jens. Appearances include Stockholm Opera, 1950, Salzburg Festival, 1955, Glyndebourne Opera, 1957, 59, 61, 63, 64, Met. Opera, 1959, 60, 62, 63, 83, 86-87; sang three leading roles in Rosencavalier within one year, 1959; toured USSR, 1966; others roles include Fiordiligi in Cosi Fan Tutte, Susanna and Countess in Figaro, Countess in Capriccio; radio, TV and concert appearances in U.S. and Europe; author: I Min Tonart, 1978, Sjung ut, Elisabeth!, 1986. Decorated Order of Vasa (Sweden); Stelle Della Solidarieta Dell'Italia; King Olav's reward (Norway); comdr. Most Disting. Order Brit. Empire; comdr. des Arts et des Lettres; named Singer of the Court (Sweden); recipient prize for best acting Royal Swedish Acad., 1965, Literis et Artibus award, 1969. Mem. Royal Acad. Music Gt. Britain (hon.). Address: Royal Opera House, Stockholm Sweden also: care Columbia Artists Mgmt 165 W 57th St New York NY 10019

SOEDJATMOKO, social scientist, university rector, retired; b. Sawahlunto, Sumatra, Jan. 10, 1922; s. K.R.T. Saleh Mangundiningrat and Isna Dikin; m. R. Adjeng Ratmini Subranti Gandasubrata, 1957. Dep. head fgn. press dept. Ministry of Info., 1945, chief editor Het Inzicht, 1946; dep. chief editor Siasat mag., 1947; del., later alt. perm. rep. to UN, 1947-51; mem. Indonesian Constituent Assembly, 1956-59; asso. editor Pedoman (daily), 1952-60; dir. P.T. Pembangunan, pub. co., 1953-61; vice chmn. del. to 21st UN Gen. Assembly, 1966; personal advisor to minister of fgn. affairs, 1967-77; ambassador to U.S., 1968-71; spl. advisor on social and cultural affairs to chmn. Nat. Devel. Planning Agy., 1971-80; rector UN U., Tokyo, 1980—; mem. Ind. Commn. on Disarmament and Security Issues, 1981; mem. Ind. Commn. on Internat. Humanitarian Issues, 1982. Recipient Magsasay award for internat. understanding, 1978. Co-editor: An Introduction to Indonesian Historiography, 1965; The Re-emergence of Southeast Asia: An Indonesian Perspective, Southeast Asia in World Politics, 1969; Development and Freedom, 1980; The Primacy of Freedom in Development, 1985; contbr. articles to periodicals and revs. Office: UN Univ Toho Seimei Bldg, 29th Floor Shibuya 2-chome, Shibuya-ku, Tokyo 150, Japan

SOEHARTO (SUHARTO), president of Indonesia; b. Kemusu, Jogjakarta, Indonesia June 8, 1921; ed. mil. schs. and Indonesian Army Staff and Command Coll.; m. Siti Hartinah, 1947; 6 children. Commd. officer Japanese-sponsored Indonesian Army, 1943, advanced through grades to full gen., 1966; from company to regt. comdr. Jogjakarta, Indonesia, 1946-53, regimental comdr. Central Java, 1953, div. comdr., 1956-59; dep. chief Army staff/comdr. Strategic Reserved Army Command, 1960-65, chief, 1965-68, supreme comdr., minister army, 1966, army chief of staff, 1966-67; dep. prime minister for def. and security, 1966; chmn. presidium of Cabinet, 1966-67; in charge def. and security, minister army, 1966; acting pres. Indonesia, chmn. presidium of cabinet in charge def. and security, 1967-68; pres. Indonesia, 1968—. Office: Office of Pres, Istana Merdeka, Jakarta Indonesia *

SOFFAIR, KEDDY JOSEPH, travel related services company executive; b. Baghdad, Iraq, Nov. 11, 1927; naturalized Brit. citizen; s. Joseph and Helloi Soffair; m. Bertine Dangoor, Oct. 14, 1948; children: Golda, Bernard, Elizabeth. BA in Econs., Am. U., Beirut, 1952. Dep. mgr. Am. Express Co., Tel Aviv, 1952-56; asst. mgr. Am. Express Co., London, 1956-63, sales mgr., 1963-70, tours devel. mgr., 1970-75; group sales mgr. Am. Express Co., U.K. and Ireland, 1975-80, dir. sales and mktg., 1980-86; dir. promotions Am. Express Co., U.K., 1986—; mem. Internat. Council Mus., 1980-83. Recipient U.K. incentive award Incentive and Exhbn. Assn., London, 1984. Fellow Inst. Travel Agts., European Travel Orgn. (council 1980—), Nat. Assn. Exhibitors (vice chmn. London 1965-80). Mem. Conservative Party, Jewish. Clubs: Annabel's, Les Ambassadors, Skal (London). Home: 44 Windermere Ave, London N3 3RA, England Office: Am Express Europe Ltd, Portland House StagP1, London SW1E 5BZ, England

SOGANDARES-BERNAL, FRANKLIN, biology educator, researcher, consultant; b. Ancon, C.A., Panama, May 12, 1931; came to U.S., 1951; s. Anastasio and Blanca Helena Bernal-Almillategui; m. Lucy Ann McAlister, 1960 (div. 1982); children—Franklin McAlister, Maria Helena, John Francis Marion. B.S., Tulane U., 1954; M.S., U. Nebr., Lincoln, 1955, Ph.D., 1958. Instr., asst. prof., prof. Tulane U., New Orleans, 1959-71, coordinator sci. planning, 1965-68; prof., chmn. zoology U. Mont., Missoula, 1971-72, prof. microbiology, 1972-74; prof. biology So. Meth. U., Dallas, 1974—, chmn. biology, 1974-76; cons. in pathology Baylor U. Med. Center, Dallas, 1974—, med. staff affiliate, 1978—, dir. Ctr. for Infectious Disease Research, Baylor Research Found., 1985—; research affiliate Nebr. State Mus., Lincoln, 1972—; pvt. practice cons. immunologist, Dallas, 1978—; cons. engr. Sputtertex Corp., Dallas, 1985; sci. adv. bd. EPA, Washington, 1980-82. Contbr. articles to profl. jours. Mem. Am. Soc. Parasitologists (council 1970-73, editorial bd 1964-67, H.B. Ward medal 1969), Am. Assn. Pathologists, Soc. Wildlife Diseases, Conf. Biol. Editors, N.Y. Acad. Scis., Am. Soc. Zoologists, Nat. Rifle Assn. (life). Democrat. Home: 10622 Royal Chapel Dr Dallas TX 75229 Office: So Meth Univ Dept Biology Dallas TX 75275

SOGANICH, JOHN, editor, financial columnist; b. Davidov, Slovakia, Aug. 3, 1928; came to Can., 1938; s. John and Susan (Nedzbala) S. Diploma in Journalism with honors, Ryerson Poly. Inst., Toronto, 1952. Editorial asst. No. Miner, Toronto, Ont., 1952-60; asst. editor The Fin. Post, Toronto, 1960-77, sr. editor, investments, 1977—; assoc. editor, Investor's Digest of Can., 1987—. Contbr. on investment matters for Mktg. mag., Canadian Mining Correspondent (former), Fin. Times, London. Mem. Can. Inst. Mining and Tech. Roman Catholic. Clubs: Engrs., Can. Address: 30 Rowanwood, Toronto, ON Canada M4W 1Y7

SOH, ERIC YOU KENG, corporate professional; b. Singapore, Feb. 9, 1954; s. Soh Tong Leong and Nyeo Swak Chew; m. Teo Mui Kwee, Aug. 29, 1987. Customer service rep. Singapore Airport Terminal Services, 1976-77; br. mgr. J.J. Travel/Transport Ltd., Brunei, 1978-79; buyer Bouygnes Offshore(s) Ptc. Ltd., Singapore, 1979-81; mgr. procurement dept. Sinarco Ptc. Ltd., Singapore, 1982-84; dir. Horig Equipment Services Ptc. Ltd., Singapore, 1987—, also bd. dirs.; rep. mgmt. services P.T. Salcon Sakti, Indonesia, 1982, 88—. Home: BLK 124, #09-219 Paya Lebar Way, Singapore 1438, Singapore Office: Hoirig Equipment Services Ptc Ltd, F05-08 GSM Bldg, Singapore 0718, Singapore

SOHN, LOUIS BRUNO, lawyer, educator; b. Lwów, Poland, Mar. 1, 1914; came to U.S., 1939, naturalized, 1943; s. Joseph and Fryderyka (Hescheles) S.; m. Elizabeth Mayo. LL.M., Diplomatic Sc.M., John Casimir U., 1935; LL.M., Harvard U., 1940, S.J.D., 1958. Asst. to Judge M. O. Hudson, 1941-48; research fellow Harvard Law Sch., 1946-47, lectr. law, 1947-51, asst. prof. law, 1951-53, John Harvey Gregory lectr. in world orgn., 1951-81, prof. law, 1953-61, Bemis prof. internat. law, 1961-81; Woodruff prof. internat. law U. Ga., 1981—; cons. U.S. ACDA, 1960-70, Office Internat. Security Affairs, Dept. Def., 1963-70; asst. to del. Permanent Ct. Internat. Justice, San Francisco Conf. UN, 1945; exec. sec. legal subcom. on atomic energy Carnegie Endowment for Internat. Peace, 1946; asst. reporter on progressive devel. internat. law Am. and Canadian bar assns., 1947-48; cons. UN secretariat, 1948, 69, legal officer, 1950-51; counselor internat. law Dept. State, 1970-71; U.S. del. to UN Law of Sea Conf., 1974-82; U.S. del. head Athens Conf. on Settlement Internat. Disputes, 1984. Author: Cases on World Law, 1950, Cases on United Nations Law, 1956, 2d edit., 1967, (with G. Clark) World Peace Through World Law, 1958, 3d edit., 1966, Basic Documents of African Regional Organizations, 4 vols, 1971-72, (with T. Buergenthal) International Protection of Human Rights, 1973, (with K. Gustafson) The Law of the Sea, 1984, International Organization and Integration: student edit. 1986; also articles on legal subjects; editor devel. internat. law: Am. Bar Assn. Jour, 1947-50; editorial bd.: Am. Jour. Internat. Law, 1958—. Recipient World Peace Hero award World Federalists of Can., 1974; Grenville Clark award, 1984; William A. Owens award for creative research in social and behavioral scis. U. Ga., 1985. Mem. Am. Soc. Internat. Law (exec. council 1954-57, v.p. 1965-66, hon. v.p. 1980-88,pres. 1988—), World Parliament Assn. (legal adviser 1954-64), Internat. Law Assn. (v.p. Am. br.), Am. Law Inst., ABA (hon., vice chmn. internat. law and practice sect. 1983—), Fedn. Am. Scientists (vice chmn. 1963, mem. council 1964-65, 68-69), Commn. Study Orgn. Peace (chmn. 1968—). Home: 540 S Milledge Ave Athens GA 30605 Office: U Ga Sch Law Athens GA 30602

SOKOL, ROBERT JAMES, obstetrician, gynecologist, educator; b. Rochester, N.Y., Nov. 18, 1941; s. Eli and Mildred (Levine) S.; m. Roberta Sue Kahn, July 26, 1964; children: Melissa Anne, Eric Russell, Andrew Ian. B.A. with highest distinction in Philosophy, U. Rochester, 1963, M.D. with honors, 1966. Diplomate Am. Bd. Ob-Gyn (assoc. examiner 1984-86), Sub-Bd. Maternal-Fetal Medicine. Intern Barnes Hosp., Washington U., St. Louis, 1966-67, resident in ob-gyn, 1967-70, asst. in ob-gyn, 1966-70, research asst., 1967-68, instr. clin. ob-gyn, 1970; Buswell fellow in maternal fetal medicine Strong Meml. Hosp.-U. Rochester, 1972-73; fellow in maternal-fetal medicine Cleve. Met. Gen. Hosp.-Case Western Res. U., Cleve., 1974-75, assoc. obstetrician and gynecologist, 1973-83, asst. prof. ob-gyn, 1973-77; asst. program dir. Perinatal Clin. Research Ctr., 1973-78, co-program dir., 1978-82, program dir., 1982-83, acting dir. obstetrics, 1974-75, co-dir., 1977-83, assoc. prof., 1977-81, prof., 1981-83, assoc. dir. dept. ob-gyn., 1981-83; prof. ob-gyn Wayne State U., Detroit, 1983—, chmn. dept. ob-gyn, 1983—; mem. grad. faculty dept. physiology Wayne State U., 1984—; chief ob-gyn Hutzel Hosp. 1983—; pres. Fund for Med. Research and Edn. Wayne State U., Detroit, 1988—; dir. C.S. Mott Ctr. for Human Growth and Devel., 1983—; past pres. med. staff Cuyahoga County Hosps.; mem. profl. adv. bd. Educated Childbirth Inc., 1976-80; sr. Ob cons. Symposia Medicus; cons. Nat. Inst. Child Health and Human Devel., Nat. Inst. Alcohol Abuse and Alcoholism, Ctr. for Disease Control, NIH, Health Resources and Services Adminstrn., Nat. Clearinghouse for Alcohol Info., Am. Psychol. Assn.; mem. alcohol psychosocial research rev. com. Nat. Inst. Alcohol Abuse and Alcoholism, 1982-86; mem. ob/gyn adv. panel U.S.

Pharmacopeial Conv., 1985—. Contbr. articles to med. jours., chpts. to books; reviewer med. jours.; mem. editorial bd. Jour. Perinatal Medicine; editor-in-chief Interactions: Programs in Clin. Decision-Making; researcher computer applications in perinatal medicine, alcohol-related birth defects, perinatal risk and neurobehavioral devel. Mem. Pres.'s leadership council U. Rochester, 1976-80; mem. exec. com. bd. trustees Oakland Health Edn. Program, 1987—; mem. voluntary alumni admissions com. U. Rochester, 1986—. Served to maj. M.C. USAF, 1970-72. Mem. AMA, Am. Coll. Obstetricians and Gynecologists (chmn. steering com. drug and alcohol abuse contract 1986-87), Soc. Gynecologic Investigation, Perinatal Research Soc., Assn. Profs. Gyn-Ob, Royal Soc. Medicine, Mich. Med. Soc., Wayne County Med. Soc., Central Assn. Obstetricians-Gynecologists, Research Soc. Alcholism, Soc. Perinatal Obstetricians (v.p., pres. elect 1987-88, pres. 1988—), Behavioral Teratology Soc., Am. Pub. Health Assn., Am. Med. Soc. on Alcoholism and Other Drug Dependencies, Internat. Soc. Computers in Obstetrics, Neonatology, Gynecology (v.p. 1987—), Internat. Platform Assn., Detroit Physiol. Soc. (hon.), Phi Beta Kappa, Sigma Xi, Alpha Omega Alpha. Republican. Jewish. Home: 5200 Rector Ct Bloomfield Hills MI 48013 Office: Dept Ob-Gyn Hutzel Hosp 4707 Saint Antoine Blvd Detroit MI 48201

SOKOLOV, SERGEY LEONIDOVICH, former Soviet minister of defense; b. Yevtpatoriya, Sebastopol, July 1, 1911. Grad. Mil. Acad. for Armoured and Mechanized Troops, 1947, Gen. Staff Mil. Acad., 1951. Food packer; then joined Army, 1932, with Tank Corps, Far East, 1934, then Europe; appointed Chief of Staff 32d Army, Karelia, 1941, chief comdr. (rank of col.), 1944, regimental comdr., then chief of staff of div., comdr. of div.; chief-of-staff, then first dep. comdr. Moscow Mil. Dist., 1960-64, Leningrad Mil. Dist., 1964, comdr. (rank of col-gen.), 1965-67; 1st dep. minister of def. (rank of gen.), 1967-84, minister of def. (rank of marshal), 1984-87; mem. CPSU, 1937—, candidate mem. Cen. Com., 1965-67, mem., 1968-87; mem. Politburo, 1985-87; dep. mem. Supreme Soviet, 1966—. Decorated 2 Orders of Red Banner, 2 Orders of Red Star and Order of Lenin. Address: Ministry of Defense, The Kremlin, Moscow USSR *

SOKOMANU, GEORGE ATI, president Republic of Vanuatu. Former dep. chief minister and minister of interior, New Hebrides; pres., Republic of Vanuatu, Port Vila, 1980—. Office: Office of Pres, Port Vila Vanuatu *

SOL, HENK GERARD, educator; b. Borger, Drenthe, Netherlands, Aug. 11, 1951; m. Jacqueline Jeannette Kuneman, June 7, 1975; children: Remco, Jeanine, Guido. MS in Ops. Research, Groninger U., Netherlands, 1974; PhD, Graniger U., Netherlands, 1982. Asst. prof. Groninger U., Netherlands, 1974-83; prof. Delft U. Tech., Netherlands, 1983—; cons. in field. Author: Simulations in Information Systems Development, 1982, Processes and Tools for Decision Support, 1982, Prototyping: A Modern Design Approach, 1986, DSS: A Decade in Perspective, 1986; mem. editorial bd.: Decision Support Systems Journal, 1985—, Journal Information and Management, 1986—. Mem. The Inst. for Mgmt. Sci., Soc. for Computer Simulation, Assn. for Computing Machinery. Home: Van HoudringeLaan 18, 2341-BK Oegstgeest The Netherlands Office: Delft U Tech, PO Box 356, 2600-AJ Delft The Netherlands

SOLAL, JEAN-LOUIS, shopping center industry executive; b. Algiers, Algeria, Apr. 29, 1928; s. Maurice and Suzanne (Stora) S.; B.A., George Washington U., 1950, M.A. in Internat. Law, 1951; m. Nicole Bussiere, Dec. 16, 1964; children—Marie-Christine and Alexandra (twins). Dir., Ets. Daveniere, Paris, 1951-53, Cie Finacie re d'Entreprise Industrielle Française, Paris, 1953-56; exec. attaché Cie Algerienne de Meunerie, Paris, 1956-62; founder, mng. dir. Ste. Française des Drugstores, Le Chesnay, France, 1962-72; pres. Consortium Parisien de l'Habitation, Le Chesnay, 1966-76; pres. Société des Centres Commerciaux, Paris, 1962—, Sociedad de Centros Comerciales España, Société de Centres Commerciales Belgique, French Shopping Ctr. Corp. Served with French Air Force, 1951-52. Decorated chevalier Ordre de la Couronne (Belgium), chevalier de la Legion d'Honneur (France). Mem. Internat. Council Shopping Centers (chmn. European com.). Clubs: Polo, Racing. Contbr. articles to profl. jours. Home: 91 Ave Henri-Martin, 75016 Paris France Office: 20 place Vendome, 75001 Paris France

SOLANA, FERNANDO, financier, educator; b. Mexico City, Feb. 8, 1931; s. Fernando and Concepcion (Morales) S. Grad. in polit. sci. Nat. U. Mex., 1964. Dir. Mañana weekly mag., 1957-66; prof. polit. sci., pub. adminstrn. and fin. Nat. U. Mex., 1962-77, vice chancellor, 1966-70; fin. dir. Conasupo, 1970-76; pres. bd., 1976-77; minister of commerce, 1976-77, of edn., 1977-82; pres., chief exec. officer Banco Nacional de Méx., 1982—; pres. bd. dirs. Inst. Mexicano Comercio Exterior, Banco Nat. Comercio Exterior, 1976-77; mem. com. public adminstrn. Secretariat Presidency, 1964-70; cons. to govt. and industry. Chmn. bd. El Colegio de Mex., Inst. Nacional de Antropología e Historia, 1977-82. Mem. Mexican Nat. Inst. Pub. Adminstrn., Found. Javier Barros Sierra, Consejo Consultivo Inst. Estudios Politicos, Econs. y Sociales del Partido Revolucionario Instl., Am. Polit. Sci. Assn., Am. Soc. Public Adminstrn., Asociación Mexicana de Bancos (pres. 1987—). Author, editor: History of Public Education in Mexico, 1981, Tan Lejos Como Llegue la Educación, 1982, Theory of Public Administration, 1984; others; essays, articles in field. Office: Banamex, 44 Isabel la Catolica, 06089 Mexico City Mexico

SOLANO, CARL ANTHONY, lawyer; b. Pittston, Pa., Mar. 26, 1951; s. Nick D. and Catherine A. (Occhiato) S. BS magna cum laude, U. Scranton, 1973; JD cum laude, Vilanova U., 1976. Bar: Pa. 1976, U.S. Dist. Ct. (ea. dist.) Pa. 1978, U.S. Ct. Appeals (3rd cir.) 1980, U.S. Ct. Appeals (5th cir.) 1981, U.S. Supreme Ct. 1982, U.S. Ct. Appeals (9th cir.) 1986. Law clerk Hon. Alfred L. Luongo U.S. Dist. Ct., Ea. Dist. Pa., Phila., 1976-78; assoc. Schnader, Harrison, Segal & Lewis, Phila., 1978-84, ptnr., 1985—. Mem. ABA, Pa. Bar Assn. (statutory law com. 1980—), Phila. Bar Assn., St. Thomas More Soc., Justinian Soc., Order of Coif, Pi Gamma Mu. Roman Catholic. Home: 619 Heritage Manor Ardmore PA 19003 Office: Schnader Harrison Segal & Lewis 1600 Market St Suite 3600 Philadelphia PA 19103

SOLARI, ROBERTO JORGE, manufacturing company executive; b. Ramos Mejía, Buenos Aires, Argentina, Dec. 23, 1941; s. Jorge Roberto and Velia (Dimanche) S.; m. Delia Susana Costa; children: Jorge Roberto, Christian Alejandro. B in Acctg., U. Buenos Aires, 1962, M in Bus. Adminstrn., 1965, M in Sociology, 1966, D in Adminstrn., 1972. CPA, Buenos Aires. Comptroller Ford Motor Co., Buenos Aires, 1966-72; comptroller Massey Ferguson Argentina, Buenos Aires, 1972, dir. fin., 1972-75, v.p., 1976-78, pres., gen. mgr., 1978—; chmn. bd. dirs. Cambridge Trade Co., Electra Holding, Knighthood Investments. Office: Massey Ferguson Argentina, Balacre 340, 1064 Buenos Aires Argentina

SOLER, DONA KATHERINE, civic worker; b. Grand Rapids, Mich., Mar. 7, 1921; d. Melbourne and Katherine Anne (Herbst) Welch; 1 child, Suzette Maria. Student pvt. and pub. schs., Grand Rapids, Mich. Artist-instr., metaphys. councilor, researcher, editor, pub. Psychic Exchange, 1979—. Author: What God Hath Put Together, 1979, Our Heritage From the Angels, 1981, Expose the Dirty Devil, 1984, Contemporary Poets of America (anthology), 1984, For Love of Henry, 1985, Greyball, 1986, House of Evil Secrets, 1986. Founder, 1st pres. South Coast Art Assn., San Clement, Calif., 1963-65, Orange Coast Cath. Christian Singles, 1970-73, Psychic Exchange, Orange County, 1979; founder, chief Lake Riverside Estates Communicators, Riverside, 1974-79. Mem. Rep. Nat. Com., Nat. Tax Limitation and Balanced Budget Com., Calif. Tax Reduction Movement, Halt Legal Reform, Internat. Platform Assn., Animal Assistance League of Orange County, Animal Protection Inst. Am., Greenpeace, People for the Ethical Treatment of Animals, Internat. Fund for Animal Welfare, World Wildlife Fund-U.S., Humane Soc. U.S., Am. Soc. Prevention Cruelty Toward Animals, In Def. of Animals, others.

SOLER, FRANCISCO ANGEL, ambassador, banker; b. San Salvador, El Salvador, Nov. 23, 1945; s. Angel Soler-Serra and Graciela (Leitzelar) de Soler-Serra; m. Evelyne Marie Carifalis, Jan. 26, 1975; children—Antonio, Lorenzo, Natalia, Cecilia. B.A. cum laude in Econs., Harvard U., 1967, M.B.A., 1970. Official asst. Citibank N.A., N.Y., San Salvador, 1967-68; sr. v.p. U.B.C. Inc., London, 1970-74; pres. H.B.S. Fin. Corp., London, 1974—; ambassador of El Salvador to European Econ. Community, Brussels, 1980—; dir. First Palm Beach Internat. Bank, Coral Gables, Fla., 1982-85, U.S. Can Co., Oakbrook, Ill., 1983—, chmn. Internat. Bancorp of Miami (Fla.) Inc., 1985—; hon. chmn. The Internat. Bank Miami, NA, Fla., 1985—. Roman Catholic. Avocations: golf; skiing. Office: Embassy of El Salvador, 3 Blvd St Michel, 1040 Brussels Belgium

SOLERI, PAOLO, architect, urban planner; b. Turin, Italy, June 21, 1919; came to U.S., 1955; m. Corolyn Woods, 1949 (dec. 1982); children: Kristine, Daniela. D.Arch., Turin Poly., 1946; hon. doctorates, Dickinson Coll., Moore Coll. Art, Ariz. State U. Fellowship with Frank Lloyd Wright, Taliesin West, Ariz., 1947-49; pvt. practice Turin and So., Italy, 1950-55; founder Cosanti Found., Scottsdale, Ariz. Major works include Earth House, Scottsdale, Ariz., 1956, Mesa City project, 1958-61, Outdoor Theatre, Inst. Am. Indian Arts, Santa Fe, 1966, Arcosanti (community for 5,000 people), nr. Cordes Junction, Ariz., 1970—, Minds for History Inst., 1986, Via Deliziosa, 1987; exhbns., Mus. Modern Art, N.Y.C., 1961, Brandeis U., Waltham, Mass., 1964, Corcoran Gallery, Washington, 1970, Space for Peace, 1985, also on tour, Xerox Center, Rochester, N.Y., 1976; collection Howe Architecture Library, Ariz. State U., Tempe; author 7 books. Recipient Craftsmanship medal AIA, 1963; Gold medal World Biennale of Architecture; Sofia, Bulgaria; Graham Found. fellow, 1962; Guggenheim Found. grantee, 1964-67. Address: Cosanti Found 6433 Doubletree Rd Scottsdale AZ 85253

SOLEY, ROBERT LAWRENCE, plastic surgeon; b. N.Y.C., Feb. 26, 1935; s. Max and Saide (Leader) S.; m. Judy Wasserman, June 16, 1963; children: John, Jill. BS, Yale U., 1956; MD, NYU, 1959. Diplomate Am. Bd. Surgery, Am. Bd. Plastic Surgery. Intern Bellevue Hosp., N.Y.C., 1959-60; resident in gen. surgery Mt. Sinai Hosp., N.Y.C., 1960-65; resident in plastic surgery Hosp. of U. Pa., Phila., 1967-69; practice medicine specializing in plastic surgery, White Plains, N.Y., 1969—; mem. staff, mem. med. bd. White Plains Hosp., 1985-88, chief sect. plastic surgery, 1988—; mem. staff Westchester County Med. Ctr., St. Agnes Hosp.; clin. asst. prof. plastic surgery N.Y. Med. Coll., Valhalla, 1972—. Contbr. articles to med. jours. Served to capt. M.C., USAF, 1965-67. USPHS grantee, 1968-69. Fellow ACS; mem. Am. Soc. Plastic and Reconstructive Surgery, Am. Soc. Aesthetic Surgery, N.Y. State Med. Soc., Westchester County Med. Soc. (chmn. sect. of plastic surgery 1981-84), Cleft Palate Assn., Am. Burn Assn. Lodge: Rotary (bd. dirs. White Plains chpt. 1982-85). Home: 30 Griffen Ave Scarsdale NY 10583 Office: 170 Maple Ave White Plains NY 10601

SOLIDUM, JAMES, fin. and ins. counselor; b. Honolulu, Mar. 12, 1925; s. Narciso and Sergia (Yabo) S.; student U. Hawaii, 1949-50; B.A., U. Oreg., 1953; m. Vickie Mayo, Aug. 14, 1954; children—Arlin James, Nathan Francis, Tobi John, Kamomi Teresa. Promotional salesman Tongg Pub. Co., 1953-54; editor Fil-Am. Tribune, 1954-55; master planning technician Fed. Civil Service, 1955-57; publs. editor Hawaii Sugar Planters Assn., 1957; field agt. Grand Pacific Life Ins. Co., 1957-59, home office asst., 1959-60, supr., 1960-62, asst. v.p., 1962-64; propr. J. Solidum & Assos., Honolulu, 1964—; pres. Fin. Devel. Inst., 1967—; v.p. Grand Pacific Life Ins. Co., 1983—; mem. Hawaii Econ. Devel. Corp., 1982—. Mem. adv. com. Honolulu dist. SBA, 1971-77, Philippine Consulate in Hawaii, 1959. Pres., Keolu Elementary P.T.A., 1960-62; mem. satisfaction com. Hawaii Visitors Bur., 1963-66; chmn. budget and rev. panel IV, Aloha United Fund, 1966-72, bd. dirs., 1971-77, 82—, chmn. bd., 1984; mem. mgmt. services com., 1977, mem. central com., 1977—, chmn. budget and allocations com., 1982-84, ; chmn. Kamehameha Dist. finance com. Aloha council Boy Scouts Am., 1966; vice chmn. Businessmen's Cancer Crusade, 1965; chmn. Operation Bayanihan, Hawaii Immigration Task Force, 1970; participant Oahu Housing Workshop, State of Hawaii, Hawaii chpt. HUD, 1970; mem. task force on housing and transp. Alternative Econ. Futures for Hawaii, 1973; chmn. Bicentennial Filipiniana, 1976; chmn. SBA Bicentennial Com., 1976; campaign chmn. State Rep. Rudolph Pacarro, 1964-68; mem. exec. com. Campaign for Reelection U.S. Senator Hiram L. Fong, 1970, Gov. William Quinn for U.S. Senate, 1976; Republican candidate for Hawaii Ho. of Reps., 1972; mem. Rep. Citizens Task Force on Housing, 1973; trustee St. Louis Alumni Found., 1970—, Kuakini Med. Ctr., 1984-86, trustee Palama Settlement, 1975-82, v.p., 1976, treas., 1980-82; bd. mgrs. Windward YMCA, 1964-67; bd. advisers St. Louis High Sch., 1963-64; bd. govs. Goodwill Industries; bd. dirs. Children's Center, Inc., 1975-77, bd. dirs. Hawaii Multi-Cultural Center, 1977—, treas., 1979; fin. chmn. St. Stephen's Parish Council, 1974—; bd. dirs. St. Louis Fine Arts Ctr., Hawaii Multi-Cultural Arts Ctr., 1977-81 . Served with AUS, 1945-47. C.L.U. Recipient Man of Year award Filipino C. of C., 1965; cert. of merit Aloha United Fund, 1971; Wisdom mag. honor award, 1974; Outstanding Alumnus honor medal St. Louis High Sch., 1976. Mem. C. of C. Hawaii (past v.p., dir.), Filipino C. of C. (past pres., com. chmn.), Am. Soc. C.L.U.'s, Honolulu Assn. Life Underwriters (past com. chmn., dir.), Hawaii Estate Planning Council, Hawaii Plantation Indsl. Editors Assn. (sec.-treas. 1957), St. Louis Alumni Assn. (pres. 1976, dir. 1964—), Phi Kappa Sigma. Republican. Roman Catholic. Home: 2622 Waolani Ave Honolulu HI 96817 Office: 1110 University Ave Honolulu HI 96826

SOLIMAN, JOHN ISKANDAR, engineering educator; b. Alexandria, Egypt, Sept. 24, 1926; s. Iskandar and Ines (Abdallah) s.; m. Gabrielle Zammit, July 17, 1953 (div. 1981); children—Andre, Monette. B.Sc., Alexandria U., 1948, M.Sc., 1950; Ph.D., U. London, 1955. Lectr. Alexandria U., Egypt, 1948-61; sr. sci. officer Brit. Iron and Steel Research Assn., London, 1961-62; lectr. Queen Mary Coll. U. London, 1962—; dir. Allied Automation Ltd., Croydon, Eng., chmn. internat. coms., Europe; organizer Internat. confs., Europe; prof. U. Rome, 1981—; vis. prof. univs. U.S.A., Europe; cons. multinat. corps.: United Techs., Allen Group, others. Contbr. articles to profl. jours. Egyptian Govt. scholar, 1951-55; Brit. Govt. and Industry grantee, 1962—. Mem. Inst. Mech. Engrs. Eng., Soc. Automotive Engrs. U.S., Soc. Mfg. Engrs. Club: Annabel's. Home and Office: Allied Automation Ltd, 42 Lloyd Park Ave, Croydon, Surrey CRO 5SB, England

SOLIN, JEAN, physician; b. Paris, Dec. 23, 1936; s. Marcel and Pauline (Ghips) S.; m. Anaik Benichon, Feb. 11, 1967; children: Boris, Gael. MD, U. Paris, 1964. Pneumonology Hosp. Tenon; Dermatology St. Covis Hosp.; practicing medicine Herold Hosp.; pediatrics Trousseau Hosp.; psychiatric Salpetriere; practicing medicine Ancien Externe des Hôpitaux de Paris; practice medicine specializing in pediatrics, sports medicine Lesigny, France. Contbr. articles to profl. jours. Served with French Navy, 1964-65. Mem. Syndicat Medecins Seine Marne (gen. sec. 1975), Action for Formation Found. (pres. 1985), Ordre Medecins Seine Marne (tituiary mem.), French Soc. Sport Medicine. Home: 94 Ave du Grand Morin, 77150 Lesigny France Office: Groupe Med Corot, 77330 Lesigny France

SOLKOFF, JEROME IRA, lawyer, consultant, lecturer; b. Rochester, N.Y., Feb. 15, 1939; s. Samuel and Dorothy (Krovetz) S.; m. Doreen Hurwitz, Aug. 11, 1963; children: Scott Michael, Anne Lynn. BS, Sch. Indsl. and Labor Relations, Cornell U., 1961; JD, U. Buffalo, 1964. Bar: N.Y. 1965, Fla. 1974, U.S. Dist. Ct. (we. dist.) N.Y. 1965. Assoc. Nusbaum, Tarricone, Weltman, Bilgore & Silver, Rochester, N.Y., 1964-66, Mousaw, Vigdor, Reeves, Heilbronner & Kroll, Rochester, 1966-70; sr. mcpl. atty. Urban Renewal Agy., Rochester, 1970-73; sole practice, Rochester, 1970-73; chief legal counsel Arlen Realty Mgmt., Inc., Miami, Fla., 1973-75; assoc. Britton, Cohen, Kaufman, Benson & Schantz, Miami, 1975-76; chief legal counsel First Mortgage Investors, Miami Beach, Fla., 1976-79; ptnr. Cassel & Cassel, P.A., Miami, 1979-82; sole practice, Deerfield Beach, Fla., 1982—; lectr. on fgn. investment practices in U.S., Eng., 1981-88, Montreal, Que., Can., 1981. Author: Fundamentals of Foreign Investing in American Real Estate and Businesses, 1981, Checklist of N.Y. Mortgage Foreclosure Procedures, 1970, History of Municipal Employee Unions, 1964. Bd. dirs. Jewish Community Ctrs. of South Broward, Fla., 1979—. Mem. ABA (sects. real property, trust and probate law), Fla. Bar Assn. (sects. real property, trust and probate law).

SOLLIER, CLAUDE, physician; b. Grand Bassam, Cote d'Tuoire, Apr. 17, 1928; d. Sollier Michel and Lecoq (Marguerite) S.; m. Poli de Gentili Françoise , June 26, 1952; children: Veronique, Jerome. MD, Faculté de Medecine de Paris, 1960. Externe Hopitaux, Paris, 1952-55; interne Hon. St. Lazare, Paris, 1956-58; chef Maternité, Figeac, 1962, Médecine, Figeac, 1972—. Mem. Amnesty Internat. Socialist. Roman Catholic. Home: 41 Allées Victor Hugo, 46100 Figeac France Office: Cabinet Méd, 13 Bis Rue du Canal, 46100 Figeac France

SOLOMENTSEV, MIKHAIL SERGEYEVICH, Soviet government official; b. Nov. 7, 1913. Grad. Leningrad Poly. Inst., 1940. Engr., Workshop foreman, chief engr., factory dir., Lipetsk and Chelyabinsk regions, 1940-54; sec., later 2d sec. Chal-yabinsk Regional Com. of Communist Party Soviet Union, 1954-57; chmn. Chelyabinsk Nat. Econ. Council, 1957-59; 1st sec. Karaganda Regional Com. Communist Party of Kazakhstan, 1959-62, 2d sec. Central Com., 1962-64; 1st sec. Rostov Dist. Com. of CPSU, 1964-66; sec. CPSU Central Com., 1966-67, head dept. heavy industry, 1967-71; chmn. Council of Ministers of R.S.F.S.R., 1971-83, mem. 1983—; chmn. CP Control Com., 1983—; chmn. Central Auditing Com., 1984-86; mem. Central Com. of CPSU, 1961—; cand. mem. Politburo, from 1971, now member ; dep. to U.S.S.R. Supreme Soviet, 1958—. Decorated Order of Lenin (6), Sixty Years of Armed Forces of USSR medal, others. Address: RSFSR Council of Ministers, 3 Delegataskaya ulitsa, Moscow USSR *

SOLOMON, ANTHONY MORTON, banker; b. Arlington, N.J., Dec. 27, 1919; s. Jacob and Edna (Yudin) S.; m. Constance Beverly Kaufman, Aug. 9, 1950; children: Adam, Tracy. BA in Econs., U. Chgo., 1941; MA in Econs. and Pub. Adminstrn., Harvard U., 1948, PhD, 1950. Jr. economist OPA, 1941-42; mem. Am. fin. mission to Iran 1942-46; securities analyst Bache & Co., N.Y.C., 1950-51; pub. First Nat. Indsl. Directory Mex., 1951-53; pres. Rosa Blanca Food Products Corp., Mex., 1953-61; dep. asst. sec. state for Latin Am., dep. asst. adminstr. for Latin Am., AID, 1963-65; asst. sec. state econ. affairs 1965-69; pres. Internat. Investment Corp. for Yugoslavia, London, 1969-72; adv. to chmn. ways and means com. Ho. of Reps., 1972-73; undersec. monetary affairs Treasury Dept., 1977-80; pres., chief exec. Fed. Res. Bank N.Y., 1980-85; now chmn. S.G. Warburg (U.S.A) Inc. (subs.), New York; lectr. Harvard Bus. Sch., 1961-63; chmn. AID mission to Bolivia, 1963; spl. cons. to Pres. Kennedy, chmn. mission U.S. Trust Ter., Pacific Ocean, 1963; mem. faculty Harvard U., 1961-63; cons. in field, pvt. investor, sculptor; founder criminal justice found. in Washington. dir. Syntex Corp., Palo Alto, Calif., S.G. Warburg Group (plc), subs.; advisor to mgmt. bd. Banca Commerciale Italiana; advisor Nomura Research Inst.; chmn. exec. com. Inst. for Internat. Econs.; mem. adv. bd. Blackstone Capital Fund; chmn. U.K. Equity Fund, Inc. Chmn. bd. Bellevue Hosp. Assn., P.S.1 Mus., Clocktower Mus.; mem. bd. Overseers Internat. Ctr. for Econ. Growth. Office: SG Warburg USA Inc Equitable Tower 787 7th Ave New York NY 10019

SOLOMON, DONALD WILLIAM, mathematics educator; b. Detroit, Feb. 6, 1944; s. Sidney C. and Bertha C. (Chaiken) S.; B.S. with distinction, Wayne State U., 1961, B.Medicine, 1961, M.S., 1963, Ph.D., 1966, M.D., 1968. Instr. math. Wayne State U., Detroit, 1966; asst. prof. math. U. Wis., Milw., 1966-68, asso. prof. math., 1970-74, asso. chmn. dept. math., 1975-78, chmn. div. natural scis., 1976-78, prof. math. scis., 1974—. NSF fellow, 1962, 63, 64-65; U. Wis. Grad. Sch. research grantee, 1967-68, 73-74; NSF research grantee, 1968-73. Mem. Am. Math. Soc., Math. Assn. Am., N.Y. Acad. Scis. Home: 924 E Juneau St Milwaukee WI 53202 Office: Dept Math Scis Univ of Wis Milwaukee WI 53201

SOLÒMON, JEAN-PIERRE See WYNNE, CAREY HOWARD, JR.

SOLOMON, JONATHAN, telecommunications executive; b. London, Mar. 3, 1939; s. Samuel and Moselle S.; m. Hester McFarland; June 10, 1966; 1 child, Gabriel. MA, U. Cambridge, Eng., 1963. Asst. prin. Board of Trade, London, 1963-67; prin. London Bd. of Trade, 1967-72, H.M. Treasury, London, 1973-80; asst. sec. Dept. Prices and Consumer Protection, London, 1980-85; undersec. Dept. Trade and Industry, London, 1980-85; dir. corp. strategy Cable & Wireless PLC, London, 1987—; supr. Sidney Sussex Coll., Cambridge, 1960-72, extra mural dept., U. London, 1963-72. Contbr. articles to tech. jours. Leader U.K. Delegation to Internat. Telecommunications Union Plenipotentiary Conf., Nairobi, Kenya, 1982. Mem. English Speaking Union. Jewish. Office: Cable & Wireless PLC, Theobalds Rd, London WC1, England

SOLOMON, JULIUS OSCAR LEE, pharmacist, hypnotherapist; b. N.Y.C., Aug. 14, 1917; s. John and Jeannette (Krieger) S.; student Bklyn. Coll., 1935-36, CCNY, 1936-37; BS in Pharmacy, U. So. Calif., 1949; postgrad. Long Beach State U., 1971-72; Southwestern Colls., 1979, 81-82; PhD, Calif. Inst. Hypnotherapy, 1988; m. Sylvia Smith, June 26, 1941 (div. Jan. 1975); children: Marc Irwin, Evan Scott, Jeri Lee; m. 2d, Ana Maria C. MacFarland, Apr. 5, 1975; children: George, Anamaria, Gabriella, Arthur. Cert. hypnotherapist; cert. hypnoanaesthesia therapist. Dye maker Fred Fear & Co., Bklyn., 1935; apprentice interior decorator Dorothy Draper, 1936; various jobs, N.Y. State Police, 1940-45; research asst. Union Oil Co., 1945; lighting cons. Joe Rosenberg & Co., 1946-49; owner Banner Drug, Lomita, 1949-53, Redondo Beach, Calif., 1953-72, El Prado Pharmacy, Redondo Beach, 1961-65; pres. Banner Drug, Inc., Redondo Beach, 1953-72, Thrifty Drugs, 1972-74, also Guild Drug, Longs Drug, Drug King, 1976-83; pres. Socoma, Inc. doing bus. as Two Hearts Help Clinic, 1983—. Charter commr., founder Redondo Beach Youth Baseball Council; sponsor Little League Baseball, basketball, football, bowling; pres. Redondo Beach Boys Club; v.p. South Bay Children's Health Center, 1974, Redondo Beach Coordinating Council, 1975; founder Redondo Beach Community Theater, 1975; active maj. gift drive YMCA, 1975; mem. SCAG Com. on Criminal Justice, 1974, League of Calif. Environ. Quality Com., 1975; pres. South Bay Democratic Club; mem. Dem. State Central Com., Los Angeles County Dem. Central Com.; del. Dem. Nat. Conv., 1972; chmn. Redondo Beach Recreation and Parks Commn.; mem. San Diego County Parks Adv. Commn., 1982; mem. San Diego Juvenile Justice Commn., 1986—; mem. San Diego County Adv. Com. Adult Detention, 1987—; mem. human resource devel. com., pub. improvement com. Nat. League of Cities; v.p. Redondo Beach Coordinating Council; councilman, Redondo Beach, 1961-69, 73-77; treas. 46th Assembly Dist. Council; candidate 46 Assembly dist. 1966; nat. chmn. Pharmacists for Humphrey, 1968, 72; pres. bd. dirs. So. Bay Exceptional Childrens Soc., Chapel Theatre; bd. dirs. So. div. League Calif. Cities, U.S.-Mexico Sister Cities Assn., Boy's Club Found. of San Diego County, Autumn Hills Condominium Assn. (pres.), Calif. Employee Pharmacists Assn., Our House, Chula Vista, Calif., 1984—; mem. South Bay Inter-City Hwy. Com., Redondo Beach Round Table, 1973-77; mem. State of Calif. Commn. of Californias (U.S.-Mexico), 1975-78; mem. Chula Vista Safety Commn., 1978, chmn., 1980-81; chmn. San Diego County Juvenile Camp Contract Com., 1982—; mem. San Diego County Juvenile Delinquency Prevention Commn., 1983—; spl. participant Calif. Crime and Violence Workshop; mem. Montgomery Planning Commn., 1983-86. Served with USCGR, 1942-45. Recipient Pop Warner Youth award, 1960, 1962, award of merit Calif. Pharm. Assn., 1962, award Am. Assn. Blood Banks, 1982. Diplomate Am. Bd. Diplomates Pharmacy Internat. Fellow Am. Coll. Pharmacists (pres.); mem. South Bay Pharm. Assn. (pres.), South Bay Councilmans Assn. (founder, pres.), Palos Verdes Peninsula Navy League (charter), Am. Legion, U. So. Calif. Alumni Assn. (life), Assn. Former N.Y. State Troopers (life), AFTRA, Am. Pharm. Assn., Nat. Assn. Retail Druggists, Calif. Pharmacists Assn., Hon. Dep. Sheriff's Assn., San Ysidro C. of C. (bd. dirs. 1985—), Fraternal Order of Police, San Diego County Fish and Game Assn., Rho Pi Phi (pres. alumni). Club: Trojan (life). Lodges: Elks (life), Masons (32 deg.; life), Lions (charter mem. North Redondo). Established Lee Solomon award for varsity athlete with highest scholastic average at 10 South Bay High Schs.

SOLOMON, MARK RAYMOND, law educator, lawyer; b. Pitts., Aug. 23, 1945; s. Louis Isadore and Fern Rhea (Josselson) S. BA, Ohio State U., 1967; MEd, Cleve. State U., 1971; JD with honors, George Washington U., 1973; LLM in Taxation, Georgetown U., 1976. Bar: Ohio, Mich. Tax law specialist corp. tax br. Nat. Office of IRS, 1973-75; assoc. Butzel, Long, Gust, Klein & Van Zile, Detroit, 1976-78; dir., v.p. Shatzman & Solomon, P.C., Southfield, Mich., 1978-81; prof., chmn. tax and bus. law dept., dir. MS in Taxation Program, Walsh Coll., Troy, Mich., 1981—; of counsel in tax matters Meyer, Kirk, Snyder and Safford, Bloomfield Hills, Mich., 1981—; adj. prof. law U. Detroit, 1977-81. Editor: Cases and Materials on Consolidated Tax Returns, 1978. Mem. ABA, Mich. Bar Assn., Phi Eta Sigma. Lodge: Kiwanis (bd. dirs). Avocation: bridge (life master). Home: 2109 Golfview Dr Apt 102 Troy MI 48084 Office: Meyer Kirk Snider and Safford 100 W Long Lake Rd Suite 100 Bloomfield Hills MI 48013

SOLOMON, MAXIMILIAN, merchant banker; b. Cleve., Oct. 19, 1946; s. Harry and Betty (Gerhardt) S.; m. Phyllis Gordon, Aug. 18, 1974 (dec.

1979). BA, Ohio State U., 1969; postgrad. Stanford U., 1979. Dir. instl. adv. services Friedberg Merc. Group, Toronto, Ont., Can., 1978—; mng. dir. The First Toronto Merc. Corp., 1979—, The First Merc. Corp., Toronto, 1984—, The First Merc. Corp. of N.Y., N.Y.C., 1984-85 , The First Merc. Currency Corp., Toronto, 1987—, The First Merc. Global Corp., Toronto, 1987—; gen. ptnr. The First Merc. Partnership., Toronto, 1984—, The First Merc. Convertible Debenture Partnership., Toronto, 1986—, The First Merc. Global Partnership., Toronto, 1987—, The First Merc. Double Gold Plus Partnership I, Toronto, 1987—, The First Merc. Double Gold Plus Partnership I, Toronto, 1987—, The First Merc. Double Gold Plus Partnership II, Toronto, 1987—, The First Merc. Internat. Partnership, Toronto, 1988—, The First Merc. Am. Partnership, Toronto, 1988—; pres., chief exec. officer, dir. The First Merc. Currency Fund, Inc., Toronto, 1985—; pres., chmn. bd. govs. The Toronto Options and Futures Soc., 1984-85; dir. The First Gulf Currency Corp., Toronto. Co-author study on Argus Corp. for Royal Commn. on Corp. Concentration, 1975-77. Mem. Toronto Soc. Fin. Analysts, Fin. Analyst Fedn., Nat. Futures Assn., Futures Industry Assn., The Toronto Futures Exchange. Jewish. Home: 212 Strathallan Wood, Toronto, ON Canada M5N 1T4 Office: The First Mercantile Currency, Fund Inc, 347 Bay St, Toronto, ON Canada M5H 2R7

SOLOMON, PAUL ALAN, environmental and analytical chemist; b. Boston, Dec. 14, 1956; s. Maurice and Ethel (Goodman) S.; m. Jocelyn Ileen Kritzer, June 9, 1985. BS in Chemistry with honors, U. Md., 1978; PhD in Chemistry, U. Ariz., 1984. Teaching asst. U. Ariz., Tucson, 1978-79, research asst., 1979-83, research assoc., 1983-84; research scientist Calif. Inst. Tech., Pasadena, 1984-88; chemist, air quality specialist technol. and ecol. services Pacific Gas and Electric, San Ramon, Calif., 1988—; cons. Tex. A&M U., Environ. Monitoring Services Inc., Newbury Park, Calif., Calif. Air Resources Bd., El Monte, Calif., 1986-87. Contbr. articles to profl. jours. Biochemistry scholar NSF, 1973; recipient John C. Ingang award U. Md., 1978. Mem. AAAS, Am. Inst. Chemists, Am. Chem. Soc. (Coryell award in Basic and Applied Nuclear Chemistry 1978), No. Calif. Ion Chromatography Users Group (award 1978), Air Pollution Control Assn., Alpha Chi Sigma, Phi Eta Sigma. Democrat. Jewish. Home: 4486 Sweet Shrub Ct Concord CA 94521 Office: Pacific Gas & Electric 3400 Crow Canyon San Ramon CA 94521

SOLOMON, RICHARD BENJAMIN, architectural and engineering company executive; b. S.I., N.Y., Sept. 3, 1942; s. Irving and Lillian Ray (Sheld) S.; B.A., U. Miami, 1968; m. Barbara Hoberman, Nov. 7, 1965; children—Martin Bradley, Daniel Louis. Specification writer T Trip Russell Assos., Miami, Fla., 1962-70; v.p., prin. Greenleaf/Telesca, Planners, Engrs., Architects, Inc., 1970-83; v.p., prin. APEC Cons., Inc., Architects, Planners, Engrs., Cost Cons., 1983—; instr. Miami Dade Community Coll., 1973; guest lectr. Fla. Internat. U., 1976—. Pres., Kendale Homeowners Assn., 1974. Served with USNR, 1963-65. Recipient various prizes Nat. Specifications Competition, 1970-74. Fellow Constrn. Specifications Inst. (nat. dir. 1977-79, v.p. 1983-84, pres. 1985-86, pres. Greater Miami chpt. 1972-73, Ben John Small Meml. award 1975, J. Norman Hunter Meml. award 1980). Home: 10000 SW 102d Ave Rd Miami FL 33176

SOLOMON, YONTY, pianist, educator; b. Cape Town, South Africa, May 6, 1938; came to Eng., 1961; s. David and Chase (Rudick) S.; B.Music, U. Cape Town, 1959; pvt. studies with Dame Myra Hess, London, 1960-61, Guido Agosti, Rome, 1965, Charles Rosen, Calif., 1973; RCM (hon.), Royal Coll. Music, London. Profl. concert pianist, 1962—; prof. piano Royal Coll. Music, London, 1978—; vis. artist in residence U. Nottingham (Eng.), 1979—; adjudicator Royal Overseas League Music Competitions, Commonwealth Music Competitions, 1973—; master-classes Prussia Cove Internat. Chamber Music, Cornwall, Eng., 1982. Author: Bach 48 Preludes and Fugues-Analysis and Commentaries, 1974; Schumann Symposium, 1975; Awareness in Piano Performance, 1984. Recipient numerous awards for excellence in music including Commonwealth Music award, 1962; Beethoven Prize, Harriet Cohen Internat. Music awards, 1967. Jewish. Office: Royal Coll Music, Prince Consort Rd, London SW7 England *

SOLOW, ROBERT MERTON, economist, educator; b. Bklyn., Aug. 23, 1924; s. Milton Henry and Hannah Gertrude (Sarney) S.; m. Barbara Lewis, Aug. 19, 1945; children: John Lewis, Andrew Robert, Katherine. BA, Harvard U., 1947, MA, 1949, PhD, 1951; LLD, U. Chgo., 1967, Brown U., 1972, U. Warwick, 1976, Tulane U., 1983; DLitt, Williams Coll., 1974, Lehigh U., 1977, Wesleyan U., 1982; DSc (hon.), U. Paris, 1975, U. Geneva, 1982; D of Social Sci., Yale U., 1986; DSc, Bryant Coll., 1988. Mem. faculty MIT, 1949—, prof. econs., 1958—, Inst. prof., 1973—; sr. economist Council Econ. Advisers, 1961-62, cons., 1962-68; cons. RAND Corp., 1952-64; Marshall lectr., fellow commoner Peterhouse, U. Cambridge, Eng., 1963-64; Eastman vis. prof. Oxford U., 1968-69; overseas fellow Churchill Coll., Cambridge; sr. fellow Soc. Fellows Harvard U., 1975—; dir. Boston Fed. Res. Bank, 1975-80, chmn., 1979-80; mem. Pres.'s Commn. on Income Maintenance, 1968-70, Pres.'s Com. on Tech., Automation and Econ. Progress, 1964-65. Author: Linear Programming and Economic Analysis, 1958, Capital Theory and the Rate of Return, 1963, The Sources of Unemployment in the United States, 1964, Growth Theory, 1970, Price Expectations and the Behavior of the Price Level, 1970. Bd. dirs., mem. exec. com. Nat. Bur. Econ. Research; trustee Inst. for Advanced Study, Princeton U., 1972-78. Served with AUS, 1942-45. Fellow Ctr. Advanced Study Behavioral Scis., 1957-58, trustee, 1982—; recipient David A. Wells prize Harvard U., 1951, Seidman award in Polit. Economy, 1983, Nobel prize in Econs., 1987. Fellow Am. Acad. Arts and Scis., Brit Acad. (corr.); mem. AAAS (v.p. 1970), Am. Philos. Soc., Nat. Acad. Scis. (council 1977-80), Acad. dei Lincei, Am. Econ. Soc. (exec. com. 1964-66, John Bates Clark medal 1961, v.p. 1968, pres. 1979), Econometric Soc. (pres. 1964, mem. exec. com.). Home: 528 Lewis Wharf Boston MA 02110 Office: MIT Dept Econs Cambridge MA 02139

SOLTANOFF, JACK, nutritionist, chiropractor; b. Newark, Apr. 24, 1905; s. Louis and Rose (Yomteff) S.; m. Esther Katcher, Sept. 29, 1959; children: Howard, Ruth C. Soltanoff Jacobs, Hillory Soltanoff Seaton. N.M.D. Mecca Coll. Chiropractic Medicine, 1928, U.S. Sch. Naturopathy and Allied Scis., 1951; D.Chiropractic, Chiropractic Inst. N.Y., 1956; postgrad. Atlantic States Chiropractic Inst., 1962-63, Nat. Coll. Chiropractic, 1964-65; PhD, diplomate in nutrition Fla. Natural Health Coll., 1982. Gen. practice chiropractic medicine, cons. in nutrition, N.Y.C., 1956-75, West Hurley, N.Y. and Boynton Beach, Fla., 1975—; lectr., cons. in field. Author: Natural Healing; pub. Warner Books; contbr. articles to profl. jours. Syndicated newspaper columnist. Fellow Internat. Coll. Naturopathic Physicians; mem. Am. Chiropractic Assn., Internat. Chiropractic Assn., Brit. Chiropractic Assn., N.Y. Acad. Scis., Am. Council on Diagnosis and Internal Disorders, Council on Nutrition, Ethcal Culture Soc. Unitarian. Instrumental in instituting chiropractic care in union contracts for mems. of Teamsters Union. Home: Route 28A PO Box 447 West Hurley NY 12491 also: 255 Venture Out Cudjoe Key FL 33480 Office: Route 28 and Van Dale Rd West Hurley NY 12491

SOLTÉSZ, ISTVÁN JÃNOS, editor-in-chief; b. Nyíregyháza, Szabolcs-Szatmár, Hungary, Feb. 28, 1926; s. István Soltész and Mária Gönczi; m. Ilona Bakó; children: István, Lászlo, Katalin. Editor in chief Magyar Nemzet, Budapest, Hungary. Author: A belpolitikai újaágírás, 1976, El kell menni katonának, 1982, Szoros porancsolat eljött, 1985. Mem. Secretariat Nat. Council Patriotic People's Front. Recipient Ferenc Rózsa award, 1974, Silver Rank Order of Work, Presdl. Council, 1972, Gold Rank, 1976, Order for Socialist Hungary, 1986. Mem. Assn. Hungarian Journalists (chmn. ethics com.). Mem. Hungarian Socialist Workers party. Home: Trombitas 15, H-1026 Budapest Hungary Office: Magyar Nemzet, Lenin krt 9-11, H-1073 Budapest Hungary

SOLTI, SIR GEORG, conductor; b. Budapest, Hungary, Oct. 21, 1912; naturalized Brit. citizen, 1972; s. Mor Stern and Theres (Rosenbaum) S.; m. Hedi Oechsli, Oct. 29, 1946; m. Anne Valerie Pitts, Nov. 11, 1967; 2 daus. Ed., Budapest Music High Sch.; Mus.D. (hon.), Leeds U., 1971, Oxford U., 1972, DePaul U., Yale U., 1974, Harvard U., 1979, Furman U., 1983, Sussex U., 1983, London U., 1986, Rochester U., 1987, Bologna (Italy) U., 1988. Mus. asst., Budapest Opera House, 1930-39, pianist, Switzerland, 1939-45; gen. music dir., Munich (Germany) State Opera, 1946-52, Frankfurt (Germany) City Opera, 1952-60, mus. dir. Royal Opera House Covent Garden, London, 1961-71, Chgo. Symphony Orch., 1969—, Orchestre de Paris, 1972-75; prin. condr. and artistic dir. London Philharm., 1979-83, condr. emeritus, London Philharm., 1983—; pianist Concours Internat., Geneva, 1942; guest condr. various orchs. including N.Y. Philharm., Vienna Philharm., Berlin Philharm., London Symphony, New Philharmonia, Bayerischer Rundfunk, Norddeutscher Rundfunk, Salzburg, Edinburgh, Glyndebourne, Ravinia and Bayreuth Festivals, Vienna State, Met. Opera; condr. concert tours with Chgo. Symphony to Europe, 1971, 74, 78, 81, 85, Chgo. Symphony to Japan, 1977, 86; prin. guest condr. Paris Opera Bicentennial Tour, 1976, rec. artist for London Records. Decorated Great Cross of the German Republic, knight comdr.'s cross, 1986 with Badge and Star; knight comdr. Order Brit. Empire; comdr. Legion of Honor, France; named to Order of Flag, Hungarian People's Republic, 1987; recipient grand prix du Disque Mondiale, 1959, 62, 63, 64, 66, 70, 77, 82; Grammy awards (27); Silver medal of Paris, 1984; Medal of Merit City of Chicago, 1987. Hon. fellow Royal Coll. Music (London). Office: Chgo Symphony Orch 220 S Michigan Ave Chicago IL 60604

SOLTIS, ROBERT ALAN, lawyer, photojournalist; b. Gary, Ind., Jan. 30, 1955; s. George William and Frances Marie (Jakob) S. AB (scholar), Ind. U., 1977; JD, DePaul U., 1982. Bar: Ill. 1982, Ind. 1982, U.S. Dist. Ct. (no. dist.) Ill. 1982, U.S. Dist. Ct. (no. and so. dists.) Ind. 1982, U.S. Ct. Apls. (7th cir.) 1983, U.S. Dist. Ct. Trial (no. dist.) Ill. 1984, Ind. Indsl. Bd. 1982; lic. instrument-rated pilot. Photographer Herald Newspapers, Merrillville, Ind., 1971-72; dep. coroner Lake County, Ind., 1972-78, spl. dep. sheriff, 1972-78; dep. coroner, Monroe County, Ind., 1975-76; area dir. Mayors Office of Urban Conservation, Gary, 1977-80; title examiner Law Bull. Title Services, Chgo., 1980; field clm. rep. Employers Ins. of Wausau, River Forest, Ill., 1980-82; assoc. Perz & McGuire, P.C., Chgo., 1982-84, McKenna, Storer, Rowe, White & Farrug, Chgo., 1984—. Co-host twice weekly TV show: Cancer and You, Bloomington, Ind., 1975-76; contbr. articles in field of cancer; photographer Petersens Pro Football and Baseball. Dir. pub. info. Am. Cancer Soc., Gary, 1977-79, Monroe County unit, 1975-76; pres. Gary Young Dems., 1977-78; precinct committeeman Dem. Party, Gary, 1978-82; bd. dirs. N.W. Ind. Urban League; chmn. Com. to Retain State Rep. William Drozda, 1978-82; mem., sponser Beverly Art Ctr.; vol. atty. S. Chgo. Legal Clinic, 1984—. Recipient Outstanding Reporter award Lake County Mar. of Dimes, 1973, Disting. Service award Am. Cancer Soc. Ind. Div., 1975-76; named Outstanding Young Men of Am., 1984. Mem. Ill. Bar Assn., Chgo. Bar Assn., Ind. Bar Assn., Lawyer-Pilots Bar Assn., Aircraft Owners and Pilots Assn., Glen Park Jaycees (founder, charter pres. 1977), Nat. Press Photographers Assn., Am. Soc. Mag. Photographers, Ind. U. Alumni Assn. (life). Roman Catholic. Club: Slovak (Gary). Avocations: flying, photography. Office: McKenna Storer Rowe White & Farrug 200 N LaSalle St #3000 Chicago IL 60601 Office: Sportschrome 10 Brinkeroff Palisades Park NJ 07650 Office: Nawrocki Stock Photo 432 S Michigan Ave Suite 1632 Chicago IL 60604

SOLVAY, JACQUES ERNEST, chemical company executive; b. Ixelles, Brussels, Dec. 4, 1920; s. Ernest John and Marie Helene (Graux) S.; m. Marie-Claude Boulin, Feb. 9, 1949; children—Anne-Christine (Countesse Jean du Petit Thouars), Marie Noël (Mrs. Claude Thibaut de Maisieres), Carole, Jean-Marie. Elec. and mech. degree U. Brussels, 1947. With Solvay & Cie, Brussels, 1955—, dir., 1967-71, chmn. bd., 1971—; dir. Société Generale de Banque, Brussels; chmn. Soltex Polymer Corp., 1974—. Chmn., Inst. Edith Cavell-Marie Depage, from 1970. Decorated comdr. Order of Leopold; knight Order Brit. Empire; Legion of Honor (France). Mem. Inst. Internat. de Physiqie et de Chimie (pres.), Fedn. des Industries Chimiques de Belgique (pres.), Belge-Brit. Union (pres.). Office: Solvay & CIE Societe Anonyme, 33 rue de Prince Albert, B-1050 Brussels Belgium also: Soltex Polymer Corp 3333 Richmond Ave Houston TX 77089 *

SOLZBACHER, WILLIAM ALOYSIUS, linguist, world affairs lecturer, retired government official; b. Honnef, Germany, Feb. 1, 1907; came to U.S., 1941, naturalized, 1947; s. Carl and Josepha (Schmitz) S.; student U. Bonn, 1926-28; Ph.D., U. Cologne, 1931; m. Regina Reiff, July 27, 1931; children—Josephine, (Mrs. Patrick Evetts Kennon), Irene (Sister Irene of Maryknoll), Regina (Mrs. Richard Oliver Rouse), Eve (Mrs. Richard D. Cuthbert). Interpreter, organizer internat. confs., 1925-39; founder, editor La Juna Batalanto (internat. youth mag. in Esperanto), 1926-34; faculty mem. Am. Peoples Coll. in Europe, Oetz, Tyrol, 1932-37; lecture tours, Europe, 1925-40, U.S., 1933; exiled by Nazis, as freelance writer, journalist, lectr. in Luxembourg and Belgium, 1933-40; escaped from Nazi-occupied Belgium and France, 1940; asso. editor Cath. Intercontinental Press, N.Y.C., 1942-50, treas., 1947-48, v.p., 1948-49; asst. prof. history and polit. sci. Coll. Mt. St. Vincent, 1950-51; fgn. lang. editor, chief program schedule sect. Voice of Am., Dept. of State, 1951-53; edni. dir. study tours, ASSIST, 1953-54; chief Monitoring Staff, Voice of America, 1954-67, in charge programs in Esperanto, 1960—, policy officer for Europe and Latin America, 1967-77, World Conf. Sociology, Liège, 1953, Amsterdam, 1956, Stresa, 1959, Washington, 1962, Varna, Bulgaria, 1970, World Esperanto Congress, Zagreb, 1953, Copenhagen, 1956, Brussels, 1960, The Hague, 1964, Tokyo, 1965, Madrid, 1968, Helsinki, 1969, London, 1971, Portland, 1972, Belgrade, 1973, Copenhagen, 1975, Athens, 1976, Reykjavik, 1977, Varna, 1978, Antwerp, 1982. Mem. Am. Sociol. Assn., Esperanto Assn. N.A. (past pres.), Internat. Commn. Esperanto and Sociol. (chmn.), World Esperanto Acad., Speakers Research Com. UN, Acad. Political Sci., MLA, Linguistic Soc. Am., The Polynesian Soc. (Wellington, New Zealand), Internat. Platform Assn., Soc. Sci. Study Religion, Am. Hist. Assn., Am. Acad. Polit. and Social Sci., Am. Assn. Advancement of Slavic Studies. Author: Walther Rathenau als Sozialphilosoph, 1932; Devant Hitler et Mussolini, 1933; Pie Xi contre les Idoles, 1939; Rome en de Afgoden van Onzen Tijd, 1940; Esperanto: The World Interlanguage (with George Alan Connor and Doris T. Connor), 1948, 3d edit., 1966; Say It In Esperanto, 1958. Contbr. encys. Home: 86-660 Lualualei Homestead Rd Waianae HI 96792

SOLZHENITSYN, ALEXANDER, author; b. Kislovodsk, Russia, Dec. 11, 1918; m. Natalya Reshetovskaya (div.); children: Ermolai, Ignat, Stepan; m. Natalia Svetlova. Corr. student in philology, Moscow Inst. History, Philosophy and Lit., 1939-41; degree in math. and physics, U. Rostov, 1941; Litt.D., Harvard U., 1978. Author: novel One Day in the Life of Ivan Denisovich, 1963, For the Good of the Cause, 1964, The First Circle, 1968, Cancer Ward, 1968, Stories and Prose Poems, 1971, August 1914, 1972; The Gulag Archipelago, 1918-1956, Part I, 1974, Part II, 1975, Part III, 1978, The Oak and the Calf, 1980; Letter to the Soviet Leaders, 1974, From Under the Rubble, 1975, Warning to the West, 1976, Lenin in Zurich, 1976, The Nobel Lecture, 1973; narrative poem Prussian Nights, 1977; (Harvard U. commencement address), A World Split Apart, 1978, East and West, 1980k, The Mortal Danger: How Misconceptions About Russia Imperial America, 1980; plays The Love-Girl and the Innocent, 1970, Candle in the Wind, 1974, Three Plays, 1985, October 1916, 1985. Arty. officer Russian Army, World War II. Recipient Nobel prize for lit., 1970, Templeton prize, 1983. Mem. Am. Acad. Arts and Scis. Home: Cavendish VT 05142 Address: care Farrar Strauss & Giroux Inc 19 Union Sq W New York NY 10003 *

SOM, MIHIR KUMAR, financial executive; b. Calcutta, West Bengal, India, Jan. 21, 1943; emigrated to Switzerland, 1973; s. Nikhil Prokash and Protima Som; m. Rosmarie Sieber, Sept. 10, 1970; children—Sanjoy Marcel, Anjan Michel. B.Commerce, U. Calcutta, 1962. Audit mgr. Wright, Stevens & Lloyd, London, 1969-72, Coopers & Lybrand, Geneva, 1973; fin. administr. Lockheed Aircraft, Geneva, 1974-77; fin. mgr. CSFB/Triad/Lockheed, Geneva, 1978-79; fin. dir. Lockheed Corp., Geneva, 1980—, dir. gen., 1986—. Fellow Inst. Chartered Accts. Eng. and Wales; mem. Inst. Chartered Accts. in India. Hindu. Home: Chemin Le Grenier 8, 1291 Commugny Switzerland

SOMARE, MICHAEL THOMAS, parliamentary leader; b. Rabaul, Papua New Guinea, Apr. 19, 1936; s. Ludwig Sana Somare and Bertha Painari Somare; married; 5 children. Hon. degrees from: Leicum Philippines, 1976, Australian Nat. U., Canberra, South Pacific U., U. Fiji, U. Papua New Guinea. Tchr. high schs., Papua New Guinea; interpreter Legis. Council Papua New Guinea; asst. edn. officer Papua New Guinea; supervisory officer-tchr., Madang; broadcast officer Dept. Edn., 1965; founder Pangu Party, 1966; mem. Papua New Guinea Legis. Council, 1968—, parliament leader, Pangu Party, 1968, 85—, chief minister, 1972-75, prime minister, 1975-80, 82-85, minister for natural resources, 1976-77, acting minister for police, 1978-80, leader of the opposition, 1980-82. Named Privy Councillor, 1977; Companion of Honour, 1979 Author: (biography) Sana. Address: Pangu Pati, PO Box 623, Port Moresby Papua New Guinea *

SOMASUNDARAN, PONISSERIL, engineering and applied science educator, consultant, researcher; b. Pazhookara, Kerala, India, June 28, 1939; came to U.S., 1961; s. Kumara Moolayil and Lakshmikutty (Amma) Pillai; m. Usha N., May 25, 1966; 1 child, Tamara. BS, Kerala U., Trivandrum, India, 1958; BE, Indian Inst. Sci., Bangalore, 1961; MS, U. Calif.-Berkeley, 1962, PhD, 1964. Research engr. U. Calif.-Berkeley, 1964; research engr. Internat. Minerals & Chem. Corp., Skokie, Ill., 1965-67; research chemist R.J. Reynolds Industries, Inc., Winston-Salem, N.C., 1967-70; assoc. prof. Columbia U., N.Y.C., 1970-78; prof. mineral engring. Columbia U., 1978-83, La Von Duddleson Krumb prof., 1983—; chmn. Henkry Kromb Sch. Mines Columbia U., 1988—, dir. Langmuir Ctr. for Colloids and Interfaces, 1987—; cons. numerous agys., cos., including NIH, 1974, B.F. Goodrich, 1974, NSF, 1974, Alcan, 1981, UNESCO, 1982, Sohio, 1984-85, IBM, 1984; mem. panel NRC; chmn. numerous internat. symposia and NSF workshops; mem. adv. panel Bur. Mines Generic Ctrs., 1983—; keynote and plenary lectr. internat. meetings. Editor books, including: Fine Particles Processing, 1980 (Publ. Bd. award 1980); editor-in-chief Colloids and Surfaces, 1980—; Henry Krumb lectr. AIME, 1988; contbr. numerous articles to profl. publs. Patentee in field. Pres. Keralasamajam of Greater N.Y., N.Y.C., 1974-75; bd. dirs. Fedn. Indian Assocs., N.Y.C., 1974—, Vols. in Service to Edn. in India, Hartford, Conn., 1974—. Recipient Disting. Achievement in Engring. award, AINA, 1980, Antoine M. Gaudin award Soc. Mining Engrs.-AIME, 1983, Achievements in Applied Sci. award 2d World Malayalam Conf., 1985, Robert H. Richards award, AIME, 1986, Arthur F. Taggart award Soc. Mining Engrs.-AIME, 1987, honor award Assn. Ind. in Am., 1988, honor award AIA, 1988; named Mill Man of Distinction, Soc. Mining Engrs.-AIME, 1983. Fellow Instn. Mining and Metallurgy (U.K.); mem. Soc. Mining Engrs. (bd. dirs. 1982-85, disting. mem., various awards), Engring. Found. (vice chmn. conf. com. 1983-85, chmn. conf. com. 1985—, bd. exec. com. 1985—), Nat. Acad. Engring., Am. Chem. Soc., N.Y. Acad. Scis., Am. Inst. Chem. Engrs., Soc. Petroleum Engrs., Internat. Assn. Colloid and Surface Scientists, Sigma Xi. Office: Columbia U 911 SW Mudd Bldg New York NY 10027

SOMBATSIRI, KRIT, economist, consultant; b. Bangkok, Thailand, Oct. 7, 1928; s. Phya Mahaisawan and Khunying Luen S.; m. Oonjai Amatayakul, May 4, 1962; 1 child, Kulit. LL.B., Thammasart U., Bangkok, 1948; B.S., Butler U., 1955; M.B.A., U. Mich., 1957; cert. econ. devel. Econ. Devel. Inst., 1968; Ph.D. in Econs. (hon.), Ramkhamhaeng U., Bangkok, 1983. Planning officer fiscal policy Nat. Econ. Social Devel. Bd., Bangkok, 1957-62, planning officer industry and power, 1963-65, dir. project div., 1965-70, dep. sec. gen., 1971-75, sec. gen., 1976-81; adv. operation planning Prime Minister's Office, Bangkok, 1982—; chmn. REDECO Cons. Firm, Bangkok, 1981—, Sangkasi Thai Galvanized Products, Bangkok, 1984-86. Trustee King Mongkut Inst. Tech., Bangkok (cert. appreciation 1984). Mem. Nat. Energy Com., Nat. Primary Edn. Com., Adv. Group Dep. Prime Minister, Economists Assn. Thailand. Buddhist. Avocation: expert on Thai cultural miniature tree (Bonsai tree). Home: 1095/1 Nakorn Chaisri Rd, Bangkok Thailand 10300

SOMERVILLE, WILLIAM GLASSELL, JR., lawyer; b. Memphis, July 27, 1933; s. William Glassell and Hilda (Deeth) S.; m. Mary Hateley Quincey, June 13, 1959 (div. Oct., 1985); children: William Glassell, John Quincey, Mary Campbell, Sarah Guerrant. AB, Princeton U., 1955; LLB, U. Va., 1961. Bar: Ala. 1961, U.S. Ct. Appeals (5th cir.) 1963, U.S. Supreme Ct. 1964, U.S. Ct. Appeals (8th cir.) 1968, U.S. Ct. Appeals (11th cir.) 1981. Law clk. to chief judge U.S. Dist. Ct. (no. dist.) Ala., 1961-63; assoc. Lange, Simpson, Robinson & Somerville, Birmingham, Ala., 1963-66, ptnr., 1966—; mem. supreme ct. adv. com. on rules of Ala. appellate procedure, 1972-77; mem. standing com. on Ala. rules of appellate procedure, 1979-86. Served with CIC, U.S. Army, 1955-58. Mem. ABA, Ala. Bar Assn., Am. Judicature Soc. Episcopalian. Clubs: Ivy (Princeton), Birmingham Country. Lodge: Rotary. Office: FAB Bldg Suite 1700 Birmingham AL 35203

SOMERWIL, JOHANNES, publishing company executive; b. Amsterdam, Oct. 2, 1926; m. Shirley Kathlyn Ayrton, Mar. 14, 1959. B.S., U. Amsterdam, 1943. Pres., Meulenhoff & Co., Amsterdam, 1943-78; mng. dir. Wolters N.V., Deventer, Netherlands, 1978—. Mem. DISTRIPRESS (bd. 1960-72, pres. 1972-73), Royal Dutch Publishers Assn. (bd. 1979-83), Internat. Publishers Assn. (pres. 1984-88). Office: Kluwer Group, Postbus 22981, 1100 DL Amsterdam The Netherlands

ŠOMLO, PETER, internist, consultant; b. Šahy, Czechoslovakia, Apr. 24, 1948; s. Stefan and Priska (Vermes) Š.; m. Beata Drobna, Nov. 6, 1981; children: Zuzana, Peter. MD, Komensky U., Bratislava, Czechoslovakia, 1972. Intern Gen. Hosp., Sahy, 1972-80, sub-chief med. officer internal med., 1980-85, chief med. officer internal med., 1985—. Contbr. articles to profl. jours. Mem. Czechoslovak Soc. Internal Med., Czechoslovak Soc. Cardiology, Czechoslovak Soc. Endocrinology. Home: 936 01, Sahy Czechoslovakia Office: Gen Hosp, 93601, Sahy Czechoslovakia

SOMMER, EMIL OTTO, III, financial executive; b. Bronxville, N.Y., July 9, 1947; s. Emil Otto and Elizabeth Arabell S.; B.A., Lafayette Coll., 1969; M.B.A., Cornell U., 1971; postgrad. George Washington U., 1973-74; m. Sandra Ann Kirk, May 18, 1974; children—April Ann, Eric Michael. Staff acct. Price Waterhouse & Co., N.Y.C., 1971, sr. acct., 1976-79, mgr., 1979; controller Transamerica ICS, Inc., N.Y.C., 1980—, v.p., 1982—, v.p. fin. and adminstrn., 1985-87; dir. of fin., chief fin. officer Paul, Weiss, Rifkind, Wharton & Garrison, 1987—. Served as 1st lt. Signal Corps, U.S. Army, 1972-74. Decorated Army Commendation medal, Joint Service Commendation medal. C.P.A., N.Y. Mem. Am. Inst. C.P.A.s, N.Y. State Soc. C.P.A.s (tech. com. fin. and leasing cos.), Am. Mgmt. Assn. Presbyterian. Club: Windmill. Home: 39 Evergreen Row Armonk NY 10504 Office: 1285 Ave of the Americas New York NY 10019

SOMMER, HOWARD ELLSWORTH, textile executive; b. Kansas City, Mo., May 1, 1918; s. Frederick H. and Edna O. (Olsen) S.; m. Sarah Scott McElevey, June 20, 1942; children: Scott E., Paul F. B.A. magna cum laude, Dartmouth Coll., 1940; M.B.A., Harvard U., 1942. With Wolf & Co. (C.P.A.s), Chgo., 1946-76; chmn. mng. group Wolf & Co. (C.P.A.s), 1960-76; dir. Jockey Internat., Kenosha, Wis., 1959—; sr. v.p., chmn. audit com. Jockey Internat., 1979—. Author: Procedural Routine for a Business Audit, 1947; also articles. Counsellor, Chgo. chpt. Boy Scouts Am. Served from 2d lt. to lt. col. AUS, 1942-46. Decorated Bronze Star, Commendation ribbon with oak leaf cluster; Croix de Guerre with palms; Medaille de la Reconnaissance (France). Mem. ASME, Assn. Cons. Mgmt. Engrs. (cert. of Award 1956, v.p. 1970-72), Inst. Mgmt. Cons. (cert. mgmt. cons., past dir.), Phi Beta Kappa, Chi Phi. Episcopalian (vestryman, warden). Clubs: Univ. (Chgo.) (pres., dir. 1959-61), Harvard Bus. Sch. (Chgo.) (dir. 1958-59); Indian Hill (Winnetka), North Shore Cotillion (Winnetka); Dartmouth (Chgo.); Halter Wildlife, Inc. (Kenosha, Wis.); Masons (32 deg.), Shriners. Office: 2300 60 St Kenosha WI 53140

SOMMER, NOEL FREDERICK, postharvest pathologist; b. Scio, Oreg., Jan. 21, 1920; s. John Frederick and Anna Effie (Holt) S.; m. Connie Inez Truxillo, May 1, 1946; 1 son, Gary Frederick. B.S., Oreg. State U., 1941; M.S., U., Calif.-Davis, 1952, Ph.D., 1955. Plant pathologist USDA, Raleigh, N.C., 1955-56; pomologist U. Calif.-Davis, 1956-80, chmn. dept. pomology, 1975-81, postharvest pathologist, 1981—; cons. Hawaii Dept. Agr., 1970, TRC Corp., 1973, Alexander and Baldwin Corp., 1975-76, Banco de Mexico, 1980, Bakki Steamship Co., 1981, UN Devel. Program-India, 1982; participant AID Devel. Project-Egypt, 1977-81. Contbr. articles to profl. jours. Served to maj. F.A. AUS, 1941-46. Fellow Institut Nationale de la Recherche Agronomique French Ministry of Agr., 1968-69; recipient Bronze medal Chambre d'Agriculture du Vaucluse, France, 1978. Mem. Mycol. Soc. Am., Am. Soc. Microbiology, Am. Phytopath. Soc., Am. Soc. Hort. Sci. Subspecialties: Plant pathology; Postharvest pathology. Office: U Calif Dept Pomology Davis CA 95616

SOMMER, PETER R., diplomat; b. Washington, Mar. 17, 1938; Two children. BA, Washington U., 1962; postgrad., L'Institut d'Etudes Politiques, Paris, 1962-63. Research analyst Dept. of Def. U.S. Mission to the

North Atlantic Treaty Orgn. in Paris, 1965-67; staff asst. Senate Com. on Appropriations, 1967-70; def. planning analyst NATO, Brussels, 1970-75; asst. for African Affairs Def. Security Assistance Agy. Dept. of Def., 1975-78; pol. mil. attache Am. Embassy, London, 1978-82; dir. for European and Soviet Affairs Nat. Security Council, 1982-87; U.S. ambassador to Malta 1987—. Office: Dept of State US Ambassador to Malta Washington DC 20520 *

SOMMER, THEO, editor, publisher; b. Constance, Germany, June 10, 1930; s. Theo and Else Sommer; m. Elda Tsilenis, 1952; 4 sons; m. Heide Granz, 1976. Educated Schwä bish-Gmünd, Tübingen; U. Chgo., Harvard U. Local editor Schwäbisch-Gmünd, 1952-54; polit. editor Die Zeit, Hamburg, W.Ger., 1958, dep. editor-in-chief, 1968, editor-in-chief, joint pub., 1973—; head of planning staff Ministry Def., 1969-70; lectr. internat. relations U. Hamburg, 1967-70; contbg. editor Newsweek; commentator German TV, radio. Publications include Deutschland und Japan zwischen den Mä chten 1935-40; Vom Antikominternpakt zum Dreimächtepakt, 1962; Reise in ein fernes Land, 1964, Reise ins andere Deutschland, 1986; editor: Denken an Deutschland, 1966; Schweden-Report, 1974. Mem. Deutsche Gesellschaft für Auswärtige Politik, Council Internat. Inst. Strategic Studies, Trilateral Commn. (steering com.). Home: Zabelweg 17, 2000 Hamburg 17 Federal Republic of Germany Office: Die Zeit, Pressehaus, Speersort, 2000 Hamburg 1 Federal Republic of Germany *

SOMMERSTEIN, ALAN HERBERT, classical literature educator; b. Birmingham, Eng., Oct. 25, 1947; s. Theophil and Millie Rose (Ostrovsky) S.; m. Rebecca Sally Hardoon, Aug. 29, 1971; children: Louise, Keith, Celia. BA, Cambridge U., 1968, PhD, 1971. Research fellow King's Coll., Cambridge, Eng., 1970-74; lectr. classical lit. U. Nottingham, Eng., 1974-83, reader in classics, 1983-88, prof. of Greek, 1988—. Author: The Sound Pattern of Ancient Greek, 1973, Modern Phonology, 1977; editor, translator The Comedies of Aristophanes, 6 vols., 1980-87; contbr. articles to profl. jours. Mem. Soc. for Promotion of Hellenic Studies (council 1980-83, 88—), Classical Assn. Jewish. Office: U Nottingham Dept Classics, University Park, Nottingham NG7 2RD, England

SOMMERVILLE, DAVID ARNOTT, advertising executive; b. Hamilton, Lanarkshire, Scotland, July 12, 1926; s. Archiblad and Elizabeth (Arnott) S.; children: Colin, Brian, Linda, Allan (dec.). Ed., Hamilton Acad., 1940-44; postgrad., various tng. colls., 1948-50. Publs. supr. Euclid (div. Gen. Motors), Newhouse, Scotland, 1950-59; group advt. mgr. R&J Dick Group, Glasgow, Scotland, 1959-63; dir. group bd. Brunning Group, London, 1964-74; mng. dir. Arnott Sommerville Advt., Glasgow, 1974—; bd. dirs. Arnott Currie, Glasgow. Com. advisor Coll. of Printing, Glasgow; trustee Scottish Disability Found. Fellow Inst. Practitioners in Advt. (chmn. 1966-68), Inst. of Dirs. Home: 39 Sutherland Ave, Glasgow G41, Scotland Office: Arnott Sommerville Advt, 8 Elliot Pl, Glasgow G38 EP, Scotland

SOMOGY, MILIVOJ VON, electronics engineer; b. Zagreb, Yugoslavia, Aug. 1, 1928; s. Milivoj and Draga von S.; M. in Electronics, Tech. U. Zagreb, 1954; m. Maria Markovic, July 19, 1952; 1 child, Gigi. With Neuberger Munich, 1954-56, Amal. Wireless, Sydney, Australia, 1957-60; sr. semiconductor engr. EMI, Australia, 1960-65; applications mgr. Fairchild, Hong Kong, 1965-67; gen. mgr. Motorola Hong Kong, 1967-69, dir. strategic mktg. Motorola Semicondrs.-Europe, Geneva, 1967-77, mng. dir. Motorola Semicondrs., Munich, 1977-80; corp. v.p., dir. strategic planning SGS/ATES, Milano/Munich, 1981-85, corp. v.p., pres. SGS Asia-Pacific, 1985-87, corp. v.p., pres. Asia-Pacific SGS-Thomson Microelectronics, 1987—. Roman Catholic. Home: 42 Seitner St, 8023 Pullach-Munich Federal Republic of Germany Office: 28 Ang Mo Kio Ind, Park 2, Singapore 2056, Singapore

SOMOGYI, JOZSEF, sculptor, educator; b. Austria, June 9, 1916; s. Já nos and Borbá la (Dió sy) S.; m. Maria Miske, 1945; 2 daus. Educated Budapest (Hungary) Coll. Fine Arts, 1942. Tchr. visual arts, 1945-63; prof. Budapest Coll. Visual Arts, 1963-74, rector, leading prof. sculpture sect., 1974—. Exhibitions include: World Exhibition, Brussels, 1958 (Grand prize), Venice Biennial, 1971; sculptures include works for civic and cultural bldgs. in Hungary and Vienna, monuments and sepulchres. Former mem. bd. dirs. Nat. Council Patriotic People's Front, Nat. Assembly, Presdl. Council. Recipient Kossuth prize, 1954; Munkácsy prize, 1956; Eminent Artist title, 1970; Labour Order of Merit, Golden Degree, 1976. *

SONCHIK, SUSAN MARIE, analytical chemist; b. Maple Heights, Ohio, Mar. 10, 1954; d. Stephen Robert and Gloria Ann (Hach) S. BS in Chemistry magna cum laude, John Carroll U., 1975; MS in Analytical Chemistry, Case Western Res. U., 1978, PhD in Phys. Chemistry, 1980. Asst. chemist Horizons Research Inc., Beachwood, Ohio, 1974-75; chemist specialist Standard Oil of Ohio, Warrensville Heights, Ohio, 1975-79; organic chemistry br. mgr. Versar, Inc., Springfield, Va., 1980-83; mgr. gas chromatography program IBM Instruments Inc., Danbury, Conn., 1983-87, radiation safety officer, 1985-87; expert witness, cons. Martin, Craig, Chester & Sonnenschein, Chgo., 1981-83; adv. engr. in advanced lithography IBM Corp., Essex Junction, Vt., 1987—; mem. exec. com. Am. Standard for Testing and Materials E-19, Phila., 1985-89; speaker in field. Author: African Walking Safari, 1985; editorial adv. bd. Jour. Chromatographic Sci., 1977—, guest editor, 1987. Troop leader Lake Erie council Girl Scouts Am., 1972-80, Southeastern Conn. council, 1983-87; leader Explorer Post, Greater Cleve. council Boy Scouts Am., 1977-78; managerial adviser Jr. Achievement, Warrensville Heights, Ohio, 1977-78; sci. fair judge Electrochem. Soc., 1977, 80, 81; asst. leader Internat. Folk Dancers, Newtown, Conn., 1985-87. Recipient Overall Best Paper award Eastern Analytical Symposium, 1984, First Gas Chromatograph award IBM Instruments Inc., 1985, contbn. award (tech. paper) 10th Internat. Congress of Essential Oils, Flavors, Fragrances, Washington, 1986. Mem. Am. Chem. Soc., ASTM (E-19 exec. com. 1985-89, subcom. chmn. 1986-87), Internat. Union for Pure and Applied Chemistry, Danbury Conservation Commn. (religion tchr. 1981-82, 83-84, 87-88), Nat. Assn. Female Execs., Iota Sigma Pi (pres. Northeast Ohio, 1978-79). Roman Catholic. Club: Green Mountain Hiking; Wilderness Soc.; No. Vt. Canoe Cruisers; Civilian Corp of Brigade of Am. Revolution. Avocations: camping, racquetball, dancing, travel, mountain climbing. Home: 14 Forest Rd Essex Junction VT 05452-3818 Office: IBM Corp Gen Tech Div Dept G40 Bldg 966-2 Essex Junction VT 05452

SONDERMAN, ROBERT ALAN, carpet and cotton manufacturing company executive; b. Conn., Sept. 4, 1944; s. Gerhard Eric and Louise (Rankin) S.; B.A. in Polit. Economy, Williams Coll., 1966; M.B.A. in Internat. Bus., Columbia U., 1968; m. Linda Ann Curtis, Dec. 9, 1972; children—David Ian, Michael Eric. With Richardson-Merrell Inc., U.S., 1968-71, Guatemala, 1971-72, Panama, advt./promotion mgr., San Juan, P.R., market mgr., Santo Domingo, Dominican Republic, 1972-76; area mgr. for N., S. and C. Am., Liggett & Myers Internat. Corp., Quito, Ecuador, 1976-78; gen. mgr. Inca Group, Caracas, Venezuela, 1978—. Mem. Sales and Mktg. Execs., Venezuelan/Am. C. of C., Carpet Mfrs. Assn. Home: Res Union 164, 4th Ave & 2d Trans, Los Palos Grandes 284 6409, Venezuela Office: Apartado 70150, Caracas 1071-A, Venezuela also: Jet Cargo Internat M271 PO Box 020010 Miami FL 33102

SONDHEIM, STEPHEN JOSHUA, composer, lyricist; b. N.Y.C., Mar. 22, 1930; s. Herbert and Janet (Fox) S. B.A., Williams Coll., 1950. Composer incidental music Girls of Summer, 1956, Invitation to a March, 1961; lyrics West Side Story, 1957, Gypsy, 1959, Do I Hear A Waltz?, 1965, Twigs, 1971; music and lyrics A Funny Thing Happened on the Way to The Forum, 1962, Anyone Can Whistle, 1964, Evening Primrose, 1966, Company, 1970, Follies, 1971, A Little Night Music, 1973, The Frogs, 1974, Pacific Overtures, 1976, Sweeney Todd, The Demon Barber of Fleet Street, 1979, Merrily We Roll Along, 1981, Sunday in the Park with George, 1984 (Pulitzer prize 1985), Into the Woods, 1986 (Tony award 1988); additional lyrics Candide, 1973; anthologies Side by Side by Sondheim, 1976, Marry Me a Little, 1981; film scores Stavisky, 1974, Reds, 1981; co-author film The Last of Sheila, 1973. Recipient Poses Creative Arts medal Brandeis U., 1982; Grammy award, 1984, 86. Mem. AAAL. *

SONG, JIN UN, neurosurgery educator; b. Taegu, KyungBuk, Korea, Dec. 27, 1925; s. Won Jae Song and Cha Jo Kang; m. Chung Shil, June 1, 1963; children: Inchan, Insoo, Inyoung. Degree, Kyungbook Med. Sch., Taegu, 1949, PhD, 1968. Diplomate Am. Bd. Neurol. Surgery. Intern Kyungbook Med. Sch. Hosp., Taegu, 1949-50, Bergen Pines (N.J.) County Hosp., 1957-58; resident in gen. surgery Korea U. Hosp., Seoul, Republic of Korea, 1956-57, Lutheran Med. Ctr., Bklyn., 1958-59; resident in neurology Kings County Hosp., Bklyn., 1959-60; resident in neurosurgery N.Y. Univ. Hosp., N.Y.C., 1960-63; fellow in neurosurgery Bellevue Med. Ctr., N.Y.C., 1963-64; chief, dept. neurosurgery Taegu Presbyn. Hosp., 1964-68; prof., chmn. dept. neurosurgery Cath. Med. Sch., Seoul, 1968—. Contbr. more than 200 articles to profl. jours. Served with Korean Army Med. Corps., 1950-56. Mem. Internat. Congress Neurosurgery, Asian Australasian Congress Neurosurgery, Korean Neurosurgical Soc., Eurasian Acad. Neurol. Surgery. Office: Cath Med Sch, 505 Bampodong, Kangnam-ku 135 Seoul Republic of Korea

SONGER, FRANCES VIRGINIA, marketing and motivational consultant; b. Atlanta, Feb. 13, 1957; d. Francis Harold and Lois Irene (Stringer) S.; m. Christopher Lee Clinkenbeard, Sept. 1, 1979 (div. 1980). B.A. in Exptl. Psychology magna cum laude, Ga. State U., 1982. Mgr., stores asst. Pepperidge Farm, Atlanta, 1976-82; mgr. S&A Corp., Atlanta, 1982-83; food and beverage asst. mgr., dir. meetings and banquets, sales dir. dir. mktg. Guest Quarters, Atlanta/Charlotte, 1983-87; hypnotherapist Hypnosis Motivation Inst., Atlanta, 1984-86; handwriting analyst, Atlanta, 1985-86; mktg. and image cons., public speaker, Total Mind Cons., Charlotte, N.C., 1987—; v.p. P.K.G.'s-Charlotte, N.C., 1988—. Mem. Nat. Assn. Female Execs., Blue Key, Psi Chi, Phi Kappa Phi. Republican. Avocations: photography, racquetball, gardening. Home: 6120 Old Providence Ln Charlotte NC 28226 Office: Total Mind Cons PO Box 220184 Charlotte NC 28222-0184

SONG JIAN, government official; b. Rongcheng County, Shangdong, People's Republic of China, 1932. Student, Harbin Tech. U., 1951-53, Moscow Bauman Poly. Inst. and Moscow U., 1953-58; postgrad., Moscow, 1958-61. Mem. Chinese Communist Party, 1947—; with Spaceflight Research Inst., 1961—; dir. Research Inst. for Devel. New Rocket Type, 1962; dep. head Cybernetics Research Office, 1962; developer several rocket research projects until 1979; dir. Inst. Info. Processing and Control, 1981; vice-minister of space industry 1982-84; alt. mem. Cen. Com. Chinese Communist Party, 1982-85; minister State Sci. and Tech. Commn., 1984; dep. head State Leading Group for Electronics Industry, 1984; mem. 12th Cen. Com. Chinese Communist Party, 1985; state councillor 1986—. Author 4 books; contbr. 60 articles on population theory to profl. jours. Mem. Automation Soc. (pres. 1980—), Systems Engring. Soc. (v.p. 1984—), Population Sci. Soc. (v.p. 1984—). *

SONG PING, Chinese government official; b. 1917, Ju County, Shandong Province. Student Cent. Party Sch., Inst. Marxism-Leninism, Yan'an. Joined Chinese Communist Party, 1937; formerly asst. dept. studies Cen. Party Sch.; dir. dept. studies Inst. Marxism-Leninism; formerly sec. gen. editorial dept. Xinhua Daily, Chonqging; past polit. sec. to Zhou Enlai, Nanjing; dir. orgn. dept. Harbin Trade Union Council, 1947; vice minister labour, 1953; vice chmn. State Planning Commn., 1957-63; sec. Chinese Communist Party, Gansu Province, 1973, 1st sec., 1977-81; vice chmn. Gansu Revolutionary Com., 1973, chmn., 1977-79; 2d polit. commissar Lanzhou mil. region People's Liberation Army, and 1st polit. commissar Gansu mil. dist., 1977-81; mem. 11th Cen. Com. Chinese Communist Party, 1977, mem. Presidium, 12th Cen. Com., 1982; vice minister State Planning Commn., 1981-83, chmn., 1983—; state councilor, 1983-88; vice chmn. State Environ. Protection Com., 1984. Address: care State Council, Beijing People's Republic of China *

SONG RENQIONG, government official; b. Liuyang County, Hunan Province, People's Republic of China, 1904; m. Zhong Yuelin. Grad., Liuyang High Sch. Joined Chinese Communist Party, 1926; with polit. dept. 5th Red Rgt. Chinese Red Army, 1932, polit. commissar Red Army Cadre Corps, 1934-35, with 28th Army Group, 1936, polit. commissar 129th Div. 8th Route Army; with cavalry rgt. Chinese Red Army, Hebei Province, 1938; lectr. Cen. Acad. Chinese Communist Party, 1943, alt. mem. Cen. Com., 1945-56; chmn. Nanjing Mil. Control Commn., 1949; vice chmn. S.W. China Mil. and Polit. Council, 1952; mem. Nat. Def. Council, 1954; minister 2d Ministry of Machine Bldg., 1958; vice chmn. Chinese People's Polit. Consultative Conf., 1965; alt. mem. Politburo 8th Cen. Com., 1966; mem. Secretariat CCP 11th Cen. Com., 1980, Presidium 4th Session of the 5th NPC, 1981, Presidium 5th Session of the 5th NPC, 1982; vice chmn. adv. commn. Chinese Communist Party 12th Cen. Com., 1985. Office: Chinese Communist Party, Beijing People's Republic of China *

SONKO, ANDRE, Senegal governtment official; b. Ngazobil, Senegal, Feb. 4, 1944. Grad., U. Dakar, 1968; postgrad., UCLA, 1970. With Orgn. and Method Bur., Republic of Senegal, 1972, dir., 1973-78; sec. gen. Republic of Senegal, Dakar, 1978-83, minister civil service and employment, 1983-87, minister of interior, 1987—. Address: Ministry of Interior, Dakar Senegal *

SONNENREICH, MICHAEL ROY, lawyer; b. N.Y.C., May 5, 1938; s. Emanuel Hirsch and Fay (Rosenberg) S.; m. Linda Beth Swartz, Sept. 4, 1961; children: Peter Charles, Nina Manya. Cert., Nat. U. Madrid, 1959; A.B., U. Wis., 1960; J.D., Harvard U., 1963. Bar: D.C. 1965, Mass. 1975, U.S. Ct. Mil. Appeals 1965, U.S. Supreme Ct. bar 1968, U.S. Tax Ct. 1980. Atty. Dept. Justice, Washington, 1966-68; spl. asst. to U.S. Atty. for D.C., 1968-71; dep. gen. counsel Fed. Bur. Narcotics and Dangerous Drugs, Dept. Justice, Washington, 1968-71; exec. dir. Nat. Commn. on Marijuana and Drug Abuse, Washington, 1971-73; sr. partner firm Sonnenreich & Roccograndi, Washington, 1973—; pres., dir. Integra Fund. Co-author 2 books; contbr. articles to profl. jours. Pres. Nat. Coordinating Council on Drug Edn., 1973-74; bd. overseers New Eng. Conservatory Music, trustee N.C. State Mus. Art Found., Clark U., Washington Opera; mem. Commn. of Nat. Mus. African Art and Commn. of Sackler Gallery, Smithsonian Inst. Served with U.S. Army, 1963-65. Mem. ABA. Home: 4720 Linnean Ave NW Washington DC 20008 Office: 600 New Hampshire Ave NW Suite 720 Washington DC 20037

SONNENSCHEIN, DAN JACOB, writer, electronic publisher; b. Haifa, Israel, Dec. 8, 1949; came to Can., 1950; s. Curt and Bronia (Schwebel) S.; B.A. in Psychology, U. B.C., 1971; M.Sc. in Math., Simon Fraser U., Burnaby, B.C., Can., 1978. Computer tng. coordinator Microtel Pacific Research, Burnaby, 1981-85; instr. computer Kwantlen Coll., Surrey, B.C., 1985-86; sr. writer Software Services, Vancouver, B.C., 1986-87; mgr. documentation Vertigo Systems Inc., 1986-87; owner Deskside Pub., Vancouver, 1987—. Author: A Guide to vi, 1986. Contbr. articles to profl. jours. Norman McKenzie scholar U. B.C., 1967; Eric Hamber Scholar, 1967; recipient Proficiency award Math. Assn. Am., 1967; book prize B.C. Math. Congress, 1967. Mem. Soc. for Tech. Communication, Math. Assn. Am. Jewish. Avocations: reading; walking; golf; music. Home: 109-1855 Nelson St, Vancouver, BC Canada V6G 1M9 Office: Deskside Pub Co, 1190 Melville, Suite 318, Vancouver, BC Canada V6E 3W1

SONNEVI, SVEN GÖRAN MANNE, poet; b. Lund, Sweden, Oct. 3, 1939; s. Bror August Sven Göransson and Maj Elly Ingeborg (Johansson) S.; m. Kerstin Birgitta Kronkvist, Aug. 5, 1961. Phil. cand., U. Lund, 1963. Author 11 books of poetry in Swedish, including Det omöjliga (The Impossible), 1975, Dikter utan ordning (Poems With No Order), 1983 (translated into Dutch, English, French, Turkish, German, Icelandic, and Finnish). Recipient Froding stipend Nat. Student Referendum, 1975, Aniara prize Librarians Assn., 1975, Bellman prize Swedish Acad., 1979, Gerard Bonnier prize, 1982, De Nios pris (Prize of the Nine), 1988. Mem. Swedish Writers Union, PEN. Home: Tralargrand 49, S-17547 Jarfalla Sweden

SONNINO, CARLO BENVENUTO, electrical manufacturing company executive; b. Torino, Italy, May 12, 1904; came to U.S., 1952, naturalized, 1959; s. Moise and Amelia S.; m. Mathilde Girodat, Jan. 21, 1949; children—Patricia, Frederic, Bruno. Ph.D., U. Milano, Italy, 1927, LL.B., 1928. Dir. research Italian Aluminum Co., Milano, 1928-34; pres. Laesa Cons. Firm, Milano, 1934-43; tech. adviser Boxal, Fribourg, Switzerland, 1944-52, Thompson Brand, Rouen, France, 1972-76; materials engring. mgr. Emerson Electric Co., St. Louis, 1956-72; staff scientist Emerson Electric Co., 1973—; prof. metall. engring. Washington U., St. Louis, 1960-68, U. Mo., Rolla, 1968—; cons. Monsanto Chem. Co., Wagner Co., other maj. firms, U.S., Europe. Decorated knight comdr. Italian Republic. Fellow Am. Soc. Metals, ASTM (hon.), Alpha Sigma Mu. Home: 7206 Kingsbury Blvd Saint Louis MO 63130 Office: Emerson E and S Div Emerson Electric Co 8100 Florissant St Saint Louis MO 63136

SONO, FUKUJIRO, electronics executive; b. Aug. 27, 1912; married. Grad. high sch., Kobe, Japan. With Kanebo, Ltd., from 1932; with TDK Electronics Co. Ltd., Tokyo, 1947—, previously pres., now chmn. Decorated Medal of Honor with Blue Ribbon. Home: 10-19 Mama, 2-chome, Ichikawa Japan Office: TDK Corp, 13-1 Nihon Bashi, 1-chome Chuo-ku, Tokyo 103, Japan *

SON SANN, prime minister of Democratic Kampuchea; b. Phnom-Penh, People's Republic Kampuchea, 1911; m. Mema Machhwa, 1940; 7 children. Ed. Ecole des Hautes Etudes Commerciales de Paris. Dep. gov. Provinces of Battambang and Prey-Veng, 1935-39; head Yuvan Kampuchearath (youth movement); minister fin., 1946-47; v.p. Council of Ministers, 1949; minister fgn. affairs, 1950; M.P. for Phnom-Penh and pres. Cambodian Nat. Assembly, 1951-52; gov. Nat. Bank Cambodia, 1954-68; minister of state (fin. and nat. economy), 1961-62; v.p. in charge economy, fin. and planning, 1965-67, pres. Council of Ministers, 1967; 1st v.p. in charge of econs. and fin. affairs, 1968; leader Khmer Peole's Nat. Front; involved in help for Khmer refugees, 1979; involved in anti-Vietnamese guerrilla war, 1979—; prime minister Coalition Govt. of Democratic Kampuchea, 1982—. Deocrated comdr. du Sowathara (Merite economique), grand officier Legion d'honneur, comdr. du Monisaraphon, medaille d'or du Regne; grand officier du Million d'Elephants (Laos). Avocation: Buddhist books. Avocation: Buddhist books. Office: Mission of Dem Kampuchea to UN 747 Third Ave 8th Floor New York NY 10027 *

SON SEN, Kampuchea government official; b. 1930; attended univ. in France, 1975-82. Chief of gen. staff Khmer Rouge Armed Forces, 1971-79, v.p., 1985—; second dep. prime minister, minister of def., 1975-79; mem. coordinating com. for nat. def. of coalition govt., 1982—, high comdr. Nat. Army, 1985—. Office: care Permanent Mission of Dem Kampuchea to UN 747 Third Ave New York NY 10017

SOO, FOOK MUN, orthopedic surgeon; b. Tanah Rata, Pahang, Malaysia, Jan. 8, 1943; s. Thong Peng and Yuet Lan (Mah) S.; m. Mei Lian Ooi, Sept. 20, 1973; 1 child, Mei Ping; m. Sik Yoke Yip; 1 child, Yew Sun. MBBS, U. Poona, India, 1969. Intern Sassoon Gen. Hosps., Poona, 1968-69; house surgeon Gen. Hosp., Penang, Malaysia, 1969-70; med. officer Gen. Hosp., Ipoh, Malaysia, 1970; orthopedic trainee Singapore Gen. Hosp., 1970-73; surg. registrar Royal Masonic Hosp., London, 1974; lectr. U. Malaysia, Kuala Lumpur, 1975-79; mem. staff Univ. Hosp., Kuala Lumpur, 1975-79, Subang Jaya Med. Ctr., Kuala Lumpur, 1985—, Assunta Hosp., Petaling Jaya, 1979—, Sentosa Med. Ctr., 1985—, Pantai Med Ctr., 1987—; practice medicine specializing in orthopedics Kuala Lumpur, 1975—. Fellow Royal Coll. Surgeons; mem. Western Pacific Orthopedic Assn.; life mem. Malaysian Med. Assn., Royal Mil. Coll. Old Boys Assn., Indian Grads. Assn., Malaysian Orthopedic Assn. (treas. 1984-86, v.p. 1986-87, pres. 1987-88). Buddhist. Clubs: Saujana Golf, Raintree, Royal Lake, Kelab Rahman Putra. Office: 9A Lorong Medan, Tuanu Satu, Kuala Lumpur 50300, Malaysia

SOO, SHAO LEE, mechanical engineer, educator; b. Peking, China, Mar. 1, 1922; came to U.S., 1947, naturalized, 1962; s. Hsi Yi and Yun Chuan (Chin) S.; m. Hermia G. Dan, June 7, 1952; children—Shirley A. Soo Gorman, Lydia M., David D. B.S., Nat. Chiaotung U., 1945; M.S., Ga. Inst. Tech., 1948; Sc.D., Harvard U., 1951. Engr. China Nat. Aviation, Calcutta and Shanghai, 1945-47; lectr. Princeton (N.J.) U., 1951-54, asst. prof., 1954-57, assoc. prof. mech. engring., 1957-59; prof. mech. engring. U. Ill., Urbana, 1959—; dir. S. L. Soo Assocs., Ltd., Urbana, 1980—, Kumar Cons., Inc., Springfield, Ill., 1986—; cons. NASA, NIH, Dept. Energy, EPA, NATO; mem. sci. adv. bd. EPA, 1976-78; adv. energy transp. World Bank, 1979; dir. Internat. Powder Inst., 1976—; NATO AGARD lectr.; Fulbright-Hays disting. lectr., 1974—, lectr. Chinese Acad. Sci., 1980; guest lectr. China-Japan Conf. Fluidizied Beds, 1985. Author 5 books on thermodynamics, energy conversion and multiphase flow; mem. editorial bd.: Internat. Jour. Multiphase Flow, 1972—, Jour. Pipelines, 1980—, Internat. Jour. Sci. and Engring., 1983; contbr. numerous articles to profl. jours. Recipient Applied Mechanics Rev. award, 1972, Disting. Lecture award Internat. Pipeline Assn., 1981; Alcoa Found. award, 1985. Fellow ASME; mem. ASEE, Combustion Inst., Fine Particle Soc. (chmn. fluidized beds com.), Chinese Acad. Sci. (invited), Sigma Xi, Pi Tau Sigma (hon.), Phi Kappa Phi. Methodist. Home: 2020 Cureton Dr Urbana IL 61801 Office: 1206 W Green St Urbana IL 61801

SOO, SUN WAH EDRIC, equipment rental and management consulting company executive; b. Taiping, Malaysia, May 17, 1947; s. Kok Chooi Soo and Yoke Ying Foong; m. Anne Mary Chan On Chee, Apr. 20, 1971; children—Rowena Soo Tzse-May, Aaron Soo Jun Khit, Colin Soo Jun Hao. Higher Nat. Diploma in Motor Vehicle Engring., Loughborough Coll., Eng., 1967, grad. London Bus. Sch., 1982, Royal Chartered Transport Inst. Eng., 1980. Regional mgr. Wearne Brothers, Malaysia, 1978-80, franchise gen. mgr., 1980-82, gen. mgr. Malaysia, 1981-82; group chief exec. and mng. dir. Initial plc UK, Malaysia, 1983—; dir. Dynaklen Services, Malaysia, 1983—, Kontrekleen Malaysia, 1983—, Initial Services (M) Sendirian Berhad, 1983—, Initial Environ. Services Sdn. Bhd., 1987—, Initial Automatic Services Sdn. Bhd., Initial Holdings (S) Pte Ltd., 1987—. Mem. Red Crescent Emergency Com., Malaysia, 1978. Sloan fellow London Bus. Sch., 1982-83. Fellow Brit. Inst. Mgmt., Am. Inst. Mgmt. (presidents council), Inst. Mktg. U.K., Inst. Road Transport Engrs. U.K.; mem. Soc. Auto Engrs., Chartered Inst. Transport, Malaysian Japanese Soc., Malaysian Buddhist Soc., Inst. Rd. Transport Engrs. (chmn. 1985), Automobile Assn. Malaysia (mem. com.). Lodges: Masons, Lions (bd. dir. 1977-78), Rotary. Home: 47 Rd 20/10 Paramount Garden, Petaling Jaya, Selangor Malaysia Office: Initial plc UK Group Cos in Malaysia, 255 Jalan Mahkota, Taman Maluri, Cheras, 55100 Kuala Lumpur West Malaysia

SOOFI, JAVAID SAEED, transportation company executive; b. Lahore, Punjab, Pakistan, Dec. 25, 1946; s. Muhammad Saeed Soofi and Rehmat Bibi; m. Raheela Javaid, Nov. 17, 1978; children: Qurat-ul-Ain, Nausheen, Nidah. FSc, F.C. Coll., Lahore, 1964; BS in Botany and Chemistry, Islamia Coll., Civil Lines, Lahore, 1967; MA in Adminstrv. Sci., U. Punjab, New Campus, Lahore, 1970. Med. rep. M/S Roche Sci. Services, Karachi, Pakistan, 1972; area sales mgr. M/S Seven-Up Bottling Co. Ltd., Lahore, 1975; asst. mgr. WACO div. M/S TAQ Cargo, Lahore, 1977-78; indsl. engring. analyst Pakistan Internat. Airlines, Karachi, 1979-84, career devel. officer, 1984—. Muslim. Office: Pakistan Internat Airlines, Career Devel Officer Manpower, Planning Div Head Office Bldg, Karachi Airport, Sind PAKINTAIR, Pakistan

SOONG, JAMES CHU YUL, Republic of China government official; b. Hsiangtan, Hunan, China, Mar. 16, 1942; s. Ta and Tiao-jung (Hu) S.; m. Viola Chen, Dec. 26, 1966; children—Chen-yuan, Chen-mai. LL.B., Nat. Chengchi U., 1964; M.A., U. Calif.-Berkeley, 1967; M.S.L.S., Cath. U., Washington, 1971; Ph.D., Georgetown U., 1974. Personal sec. to premier Exec. Yuan, Taipei, 1974-77; assoc. prof. Nat. Taiwan U., Taipei, 1975-79; dep. dir.-gen. Govt. Info. Office, Taipei, 1977-79, dir. gen. and govt. spokesman, 1979-84; dir. gen. Dept. Cultural Affairs, Kuomintang, 1984-87; dep. sec.-gen., Cen. Com., 1987—; research fellow Instn. Internat. Relations, Taipei, 1974—; personal sec. to Pres., Presdl. Office, Taipei, 1978—; mem. Central Standing Com., Kuomintang, 1988—; mng. dir. China TV Co., 1984—, Taiwan TV Enterprise, 1984—. Author: A Manual for Academic Writers, 1977; Politics and Public Opinion in the United States, 1978 (Dr. Sun Yat-sen Acad. and Cultural award 1978); How To Write Academic Papers, 1979; Keep Free China Free, 1982. Chmn. Motion Picture Devel. Found. of Republic of China, 1979-84; chmn. Hua-hsia Investment Corp.; bd. dirs. Chinese Inst. Pub. Opinion, 1980—, Nat. Fund for Lit. and Arts, 1982—. Decorated Order of Brilliant Star, Order of Cape of Good Hope, Order of Diplomatic Service of Merit, Order of Cloud and Banner; Eisenhower exchange fellow, Phila., 1982. Mem. Delta Phi Epsilon, Pi Sigma Alpha. Office: 11 Chugnshan S Rd, Taipei 10040, Republic of China

SOONG, WEI-TSUEN, psychiatrist; b. Taoyuan, Republic China, Nov. 23, 1945; s. Lin Fan Soong and Gin May Lin; m. Ko Ping Liu, May 19, 1973; children: Ta Tsen, Chung Tsen. MB, Nat. Taiwan U., 1971. Resident Nat.

Taiwan U. Hosp., Taipei, Republic China, 1972-76, cons., 1976—; lectr. Nat. Taiwan U., 1977-82, assoc. prof. psychiatry, 1982—; resident U. B.C., Vancouver, Can., 1978-80. Author: Early Infantile Autism and its Educational Intervention, 1987, Common Problems in Child Rearing, 2 vol., 1987; contbr. chptrs. to 6 books and articles to profl. jours. Founder Found. for Autistic Children and Adults in Taiwan, 1987; cons. Dept. Health, Republic China, 1986—. Fellow Royal Coll. Physicians Surgeons of Can.; mem. Chinese Soc. Neurology and Psychiatry (bd. dirs.), Chinese Nat. Assn. Mental Hygiene (bd. dirs., gen. sec.), World Fedn. Mental Health, Internat. Soc. Adolescent Psychiatry, Alumni Assn. Nat. Taiwan U. (named Top Ten Best Alumni, 1986). Office: Nat Taiwan Univ Hosp, No 1 Chang-Te St, Taipei Republic of China

SOONG CHANG-CHIH, Taiwan government defense official; b. Liaoning Province, China, June 10, 1916; s. Te-hsiang and Su-ching (Wang) S.; m. Cheng-ying Fong, May 7, 1943; children—Dah-wei David, Dah-ren Andy, Dah-yeong Michael, Dah-meei May. Grad. Chinese Naval Acad., 1937, Royal Naval Coll., Greenwich, Eng., 1946, Nat. Def. Inst. Taiwan, 1962, Taiwan Armed Forces U., 1969; Ph.D. (hon.), Konkuk U., Republic Korea, 1982; LL.D., Southeastern U., 1985. Commd. officer various Chinese Navy combat ships; comdr. Rating Tng. Sch., 1949-52, comdr. Landing Ship Squadron, 1954-55, supt. Chinese Naval Acad., 1955-62, comdt. 1st Naval Dist., 1962-65, chief of staff Navy Hdqrs., 1965-67; dep. comdr.-in-chief Navy, 1967-70, comdr.-in-chief, Navy, 1970-76, chief of gen. staff Ministry of Nat. Def., Taipei, Taiwan, 1976-81, minister, 1981-86; ambassador to Panama, 1987—; chmn. Found. Def. Industry Devel. Mem. standing com. Kuomintang party, 1978—. Decorated Cloud and Banner medal, 1st class, 4th class; various fgn. medals. Mem. Sino-Brit. Culture and Econ. Assn. Club: Taipei Golf. Office: Embassy of Republic of China, PO Box 4285, Panamá City 5 Republic of Panama

SOPER, JOHN WAYNE, science administrator, educator; b. Amarillo, Tex., Oct. 20, 1944; s. George Hannibal and Mary Gerardine (Maffey) S.; m. Christine Alece Lowe, July 14, 1979; children: Esther Wilhelm, Danielle Wilhelm. BA, Phillips U., Enid, Okla., 1967; PhD, U. Ark., 1973. Diplomate in clin. toxicology, clin. chemistry Am. Bd. Clin. Chemistry; cert. lab. dir. Am. Bd. Bioanalysis. Postdoctoral fellow Johns Hopkins U., Balt., 1973-78; instr. Mt. Sinai Sch. Medicine, N.Y.C., 1978-79, U.S. Naval Acad., Annapolis, Md., 1979-80; clin. assoc. U. Md. Hosp., Balt., 1980-82; asst. toxicologist Md. Med. Examiner's Office, Balt., 1982-86; clin. asst. prof. U. Md.-Balt., 1984-86; sci. dir. Med. Arts Lab., Oklahoma City, 1986—. Contbr. articles to profl. jours. Fellow NIH, 1969-72, 75-77, Carnegie-Mellon Found., 1977. Fellow Nat. Acad. Clin. Biochemistry, Am. Inst. Chemists; mem. Am. Assn. Clin. Chemistry, Am. Chem. Soc., Soc. Forensic Toxicologists, Am. Acad. Forensic Scis., Southwestern Assn. Toxicologists, AAAS, N.Y. Acad. Scis., Johns Hopkins Med. and Surg. Assn., Blue Key Nat. Honor Soc., Sigma Xi. Republican. Mem. Ch. of God. Avocations: photography; scuba diving.

SOPER, ROBERT LEE, manufacturing company executive; b. Eldora, Iowa, Aug. 10, 1921; s. William Henry and Leola (Cox) S.; student Carleton Coll., 1939-41; grad. Army Command and Gen. Staff Sch.; B.A., U. Mich., 1946; M.B.A. with distinction, Harvard U., 1948; m. Nancy Kenealy, Aug. 12, 1972; children—William Lee, Margaret Deane, Julie Elizabeth. Asst. credit mgr., mgr. data processing, Black & Decker Mfg. Co., Towson, Md., 1948-49; with Calif. Pellet Mill Co., San Francisco, 1950—, treas., 1960-71, exec. v.p., 1971-74, pres., 1974-83, chmn., 1983—; dir. Mission Nat. Bank, El Morro Industries Calif. Pellet Mill Ltd., Zeig Sheet Metal, CPM/Europe V.B., CPM/Europe S.A., CPM/Pacific Ltd. Served with USAAF, 1942-45; CBI, Decorated Air medal, D.F.C. Mem. Calif. C. of C., Calif. Mfrs. Assn., San Francisco C. of C., Calif. Council Internat. Trade, World Affairs Council. Clubs: Bankers, Commonwealth of Calif., Presidio Golf (San Francisco). Home: 2264 Hyde St San Francisco CA 94109 Office: PO Box 6806 San Francisco CA 94101

SOPHUSSON, FRIDRIK KLEMENZ, government minister; b. Reykjavik, Iceland, Oct. 18, 1943; s. Sophus A. Gudmundsson and Áslaug María Fridriksdóttir; children: Stefán, Áslaug, Gabríela, Helga. Candidate juris, U. Iceland, 1972. Tchr. Hlíoaskóli Lower Secondary Sch., Reykjavik, 1963-67; mgr. Icelandic Mgmt. Assn., Reykjavik, 1972-78; mem. Icelandic Parliament, Reykjavik, 1978—; minister of industry Reykjavik, 1987—; mem. Radio Council for Icelandic Broadcasting Service, Reykjavik, 1975-78, Nat. Research Council, Reykjavik, 1979-83. Chmn. Exec. Com. State Hosp., Reykjavik, 1984-87; pres. Ind. Party Youth Fedn., Reykjavik, 1973-77; vice-chmn. Ind. Party, Reykjavik, 1981—, mem. cen. com., 1969-77, 81—. Mem. Assn. Icelandic Lawyers. Lutheran. Office: Ministry of Industry, Arnarhvoli, 150 Reykjavik Iceland

SOPPELSA, JACQUES R., university president, geopolitical educator; b. Libourne, France, June 10, 1943; s. Raymond and Marthe (Guyet) S.; children—Muriel, Anne, Jean-Frederic, Alexandre. Agrégation de geographie, U. Paris, 1965, Doctorat d'Etat, 1976; Diplomé Etudes Superieurs, Ecole des Sciences Politique, Paris, 1973; Ancien Elève (hon.), Ecole Normale Superieure, St. Cloud, France, 1961-65. Prof. U. Paris, 1976—, now pres. U. Paris I (Sorbonne); pres. Centre d'Etudes Nord Americaines, Paris, 1977—, Institut National Superieur d'Etudes de Défense, Paris, 1982—. Author: Les Etats-Unis, 1971; L'Economie des Etats-Unis (award 1976), 1976; Geographie des Armements (award 1981); Des tensions et des armes, 1984, Lexique de géopolitique, 1988. Pres. French Rugby Fedn. Served to capt. French Army, 1968-69. Decorated chevalier Ordre National du Merite, Palmes Académiques; Knight Order of Malta. Mem. Fondation Nationale Etudes de Défense. Roman Catholic. Club: Cercle Edouard Herriot.

SÖRBOM, PER GUNNAR, historian, researcher; b. Uppsala, Sweden, June 22, 1940; s. Gunnar A.T. and Yvonne E. (Molin) S.; m. Gunilla E. Green; children: Johan G., Erik G. PhD, Uppsala U., 1972. Assoc. prof. history of sci. and ideas Uppsala U., 1972—; research sec. Swedish Council for Planning and Coordination of Research, Stockholm, 1986—; prof. pro tem U. Linköping, 1982-86; pres. Arte et Scientia KonsultAB, Sala, 1984—. Author: Läsning för Folket, 1972, Tao och de Tiotusen Tingen, 1979, Learning the Superior Skills of the Barbarians, 1982; guest appearances Swedish Broadcasting Corp., 1974—; contbr. articles to newspapers. Club: Sala Golf (hon. sec. 1974-76). Lodge: Rotary (pres. 1984-85). Home: O Tuleg 26, S-733 Sala 33 Sweden

SØRENSEN, BØRGE, librarian; b. Århus, Denmark, Feb. 22, 1942; s. Aksel and Inger (Ankersen) S.; divorced; children: Peter, Søren, Pernille; m. Birgit Sørensen, 1975; children: Mikkel, Jeppe. Diploma, Danish Sch. Librarianship, Copenhagen, 1965. Asst. county librarian Det sØnderjydske landes-bibliotek, Aabenraa, Denmark, 1965-69; cons. State Inspection for Pub. Libraries, Copenhagen, 1969-75; sec. Librarians Assn., Copenhagen, 1975-82; dir. Danish Library Bur., Ballerup, Denmark, 1982-86; city librarian Copenhagen Pub. Libraries, 1986—. Home: Ostre alle 115, 3270 Gilleleje Denmark

SØRENSEN, GEORG, political science educator; b. Fredericia, Denmark, Oct. 26, 1948; s. Georg Emmanuel and Gudrun Johanne (Andersen) S; m. Lisbet Iversen, Nov. 19, 1977; children: Mathilde, Sebastian. MA in Polit. Sci., Aarhus (Denmark) U., 1976; PhD in Social Sci., Aalborg (Denmark) U., 1983. Asst. prof. social sci., Inst. History Aarhus U., 1977-79; asst. prof. Inst. Devel. and Planning Aalborg U., 1979-81, assoc. prof. Internat. Studies Program, 1984—; guest lectr. various Swedish, Norwegian, Danish instns. 1981—; cons. Internat. Ctr. for Pub. Enterprise, Ljubljana, Yugoslavia, 1982, 84; workshop dir. European Consortium for Polit. Research, Colchester, Eng., 1984; apptd. examiner Copenhagen U., Aarhus U., Roskilde U., 1984—. Author, editor various books; contbr. articles to profl. jours. Chmn. bd. Bakkegaarden Kindergarten, Aalborg, 1982-86; bd. dirs Danish Assn. for Devel. Research, 1982-85. Research fellow Aalborg. U., 1981-83. Mem. Aaloborg U. Press (bd. dirs.). Home: 8 Skovbakkevej, 9000 Aalborg Denmark Office: Aalborg U, Internat Studies Program, 2 Fibigerstraede, 9220 Aalborg Denmark

SORENSEN, ROBERT C., social psychologist; b. Lincoln, Nebr., Sept. 7, 1923; s. Christian Abraham and Annis Sarah (Chaikin) S.; m. Marjorie Joyce Mattson, Sept. 11, 1943; children—Robert C.A., Katherine M. Simpson, David W.M. Student U. Nebr., 1940-42, Northwestern U., 1942-43; A.B., U. Chgo., 1944, M.A., 1948, Ph.D., 1954. Field examiner Chgo. regional office NLRB, 1945-46; indsl. relations dir. Scott Radio Labs., Chgo., 1946-48; dir. prelegal div. John Marshall Law Sch., Chgo., 1947-48; asst. prof. law U. Nebr. Coll. Law, Lincoln, 1948-52; ops. analyst Ops. Research Office, Johns Hopkins U., Chevy Chase, Md., 1952-54; dir. audience analysis dept. Radio Free Europe, Munich, 1954-59; dir. research This Week Mag., N.Y.C., 1959-61; v.p., dir. research D'arcy Advt. Co., N.Y.C., 1961-65; exec. dir. Ctr. for Advanced Practice, McCann-Erickson Inc., N.Y.C., 1965-67; pub. Psychology Today Mag., N.Y.C., 1967-68; pres. Robert C. Sorensen & Assocs. Inc., N.Y.C., 1968-85, Sorensen Mktg./Mgmt. Corp., N.Y.C., 1979—; v.p., dir. mktg. Warner Communications Inc., N.Y.C., 1972-74; prof. mktg. Grad. and Undergrad. Sch. Bus. Adminstrn., Rider Coll., Lawrenceville, N.J., 1981—; cons., expert witness in intellectual property and Anti-trust. Author: Adolescent Sexuality in Contemporary America. 1973, (with Viggo Mortensen) Free Will and Determinism, 1987; assoc. editor: Zygon: Jour. of Religion and Sci.; contbr. articles to profl. jours. V.p., councilor Inst. on Religion in an Age of Sci.; chmn. Scandinavian Semimar, Inc.; bd. dirs. Foster Parents Plan Internat., Foster Parents Plan U.S., Scandinavian Seminar Coll. (Copenhagen). Recipient UN award for civilian work in Korea, 1953. Mem. Market Research Council, Am. Sociol. Assn., Am. Assn. for the Advancement Sci., Am. Polit. Sci. Assn., Am. Assn. Pub. Opinion Research, Am. Mktg. Assn., U.S. Trademark Assn. Democrat. Unitarian. Club: University. Address: 210 E 72d St New York NY 10021

SORGE, JAY WOOTTEN, lawyer; b. Detroit, July 27, 1917; s. Ervin H. and Harriet Louise (Wootten) S.; m. Mary Jane Peterson, June 19, 1943. Student Washington and Lee U., 1935-36; A.B., U. Mich., 1939, J.D., 1942. Bar: Mich. 1942. Assoc. Hill Lewis Adams Goodrich & Tait, Detroit, 1945-52, ptnr., 1952-85; of counsel, 1986—; lectr. corp. law Detroit Coll. Law and Wayne State U. Law Sch., 1945-55. Trustee Fund for Henry Ford Hosp.; pres. Friends of Grosse Pointe Pub. Library, 1955-56, others. Served with USCG, 1942-45. Mem. Detroit Bar Assn., Mich. Bar Assn., ABA, Order of the Coif. Republican. Episcopalian. Clubs: Detroit, Country of Detroit. Home: 88 Touraine Rd Grosse Pointe Farms MI 48236 Office: Suite 3200 100 Tower Renaissance Center Detroit MI 48243

SORKIN, CHARLES K., accountant; b. Basel, Switzerland, Sept. 22, 1907; s. Niklaus and Luise (Rinek) S.; m. Mathilde Burggraf, Jan. 16, 1934 (dec. Dec. 1982); 1 child, Charles Klaus. Student, U. Basel, U. Akron, Western Res. U. CPA. Various positions in banking, industry and commerce Switzerland and Germany, 1927-39; various positions Akron, Ohio, 1939-46; pvt. practice pub. acctg. Akron, 1946-62; mng. ptnr. Sorkin, Lawson & Parker, CPAs, 1962-70; cons. Sorkin. Lawson & Parker, CPAs, 1970-72. Treas. Greater Akron Musical Assn.; founding sponsor principal chair endowment, co-sponsor concertmaster chair Mathilde and Charles K. Sorkin Fund; vol. chess tchr. schs. and insts. Germany and U.S.; tournament dir. U.S. Chess Fedn.; bd. dirs. Note For Life; active fundraising United Fund, Red Cross, Hosps., Akron (Ohio) Symphony Orch.; founder West Akron Kiwanis Found; voluntary audits, United Fund Agys., Akron Art Inst. Mem. Am. Inst. CPAs, Ohio Soc,. CPAs. Methodist. Clubs: Fairlawn Country, Akron Chess (Founder, honarary pres.), Sharon Golf. Lodges: Masons, Shriners, Kiwanis (past pres., founder West Akron club). Home: 100 Brookmont RII #104 Akron OH 44313

SORKIN, DAVID JAN, researcher; b. Chgo., Sept. 22, 1953; arrived in Eng., 1986; s. Sidney and Shirley (Levy) S.; m. Shifra Faye Sharlin, Dec. 19, 1976; children: Phoebe, Gideon, Isaac. BA, U. Wis., 1975; MA, PhD, U. Calif., Berkeley, 1975-83. Asst. prof. Brown U., Providence, 1983-86; research fellow Oxford (Eng.) U., 1986—. Author: Transformation of German Jewry, 1987; contbr. articles to profl. jours. Mem. Am. Hist. Assn., Assn. for Jewish Studies, Leo Baeck Inst. (exec. bd. 1987—). Office: St Antony's Coll, Oxford OX2 6JF, England

SORKIN, GERALD B., management and marketing executive; b. Bklyn., June 20, 1932; s. Nathan and Dora (Butlin) S.; A.B., Dartmouth Coll., 1953; m. Eleanor Smith, Sept. 30, 1956; children—Andrea Joyce, Lynn Harriet, Jessica Lee. Art dir., prodn. mgr. Wesley H. Porter, Advt., Los Angeles, 1953-56; advt. mgr. Plastix Footwear Corp., Los Angeles, 1956-58; mgr. sales promotion, brand mgr. Hunt Foods & Industries, Inc., Fullerton, Calif., 1958-63; prin. G.B. Sorkin & Co., Los Angeles, 1963-64; pres. Sorkin/Hudson, Los Angeles, 1964-67, 69-72; v.p. West Coast, Adams/Dana/Silverstein, Los Angeles, 1967-69; v.p. David W. Evans, Advt., Inc., Los Angeles, 1972-73, pres., 1973-77; ind. mktg. cons., 1977-78; dir. advt. Shapell Industries, Inc., Beverly Hills, Calif., 1978-79; dir. sales and mktg. Arvida Southern, Miami, Fla., 1979-82; sr. v.p. Venture Devel. Corp., Miami, 1982-83; v.p. mktg. ITT Community Devel. Corp., Palm Coast, Fla., 1983—; v.p., dir. Rinkled Raisin, Inc., Los Angeles, Diamond Fork Land Cattle Co., Cedar City, Utah; dir. David W. Evans, Inc., Salt Lake City, 1973-77; cons., franchising mktg., regional, nat., internat. mktg., builder mktg. Trustee, Eddie Cantor Charitable Found., 1972-79; dr. personnel com. chmn. Mid-Fla. ARC, 1988, 89.ommr. Wilshire Blvd. Temple Camps, 1973-79. Mem. Assn. Nat. Advertisers, Am. Resort and Residential Devel. Assn., Urban Land Inst., B'nai B'rith (Service awards 1973, 74, 75, 76). Republican. Jewish. Clubs: Rotary (pres. Flagler/Palm Coast Sunrise 1988—). Author, co-author TV scripts and movies. Home: PO Box 351554 Palm Coast FL 32035

SORREL, WILLIAM EDWIN, psychiatrist, educator, psychoanalyst; b. N.Y.C., May 27, 1913; s. Simon and Lee (Lesenger) S.; m. Rita Marcus, July 1, 1950; children: Ellyn Gail, Joy Shelley, Beth Mara. B.S., N.Y. U., 1932; M.A., Columbia, 1934, M.D., 1939; Ph.D., N.Y. U., 1963. Diplomate Am. Bd. Med. Psychotherapists; qualified psychiatrist, also certified examiner N.Y. State Dept. Mental Hygiene. Intern Madison (Tenn.) Sanitarium and Hosp., 1939; resident physician Alexian Bros. Hosp., St. Louis, 1940; officer instrn. St. Louis U. Sch. Medicine, 1940-41; asst. psychiatrist Central State Hosp., Nashville, 1941; assoc. psychiatrist Eastern State Hosp., Knoxville, 1942-44; assoc. attending neuropsychiatrist, chief clin. psychiatry Jewish Meml. Hosp., N.Y.C., 1946-59; assoc. attending neuropsychiatrist, chief clin. child psychiatry Lebanon Hosp., Bronx, N.Y., 1947-65; psychiatrist-in-chief Psychiatry Clinic, Yeshiva U., 1950-66, asst. prof. psychiatry, 1952-54, assoc. prof., 1954-58, prof., 1959-62, psychiatrist-in-chief, assoc. dir. Psychol. Center,, 1957-67; prof. human behavior Touro U., 1974-88; attending psychiatrist St. Clare's Hosp., N.Y.C., 1983—; asst. prof. clin. psychiatry Albert Einstein Coll. Medicine, 1986—; psychiat. cons. SSS, 1951, N.Y. State Workmens Compensation Bd., 1951—, Bronx-Lebanon Med. Ctr., 1985—; vis. psychiatrist Fordham Hosp., N.Y.C., 1951; attending neuropsychiatrist, chief mental hygiene service Beth-David Hosp., 1950-60; assoc. attending neuropsychiatrist Grand Central Hosp., 1958-66, Morrisania Hosp., 1959-72; psychiatrist-in-chief Beth Abraham Hosp., 1954-60; psychiat. cons. L.I. U. Guidance Center, 1955-60, Daytop Village, 1970-71; assoc. psychiatrist Seton City Hosp., 1955; guest lectr. U. London, 1947; vis. prof. Jerusalem, Israel Acad. Med., 1960, Hebrew U., 1960; mem. psychiat. staff Gracie Sq. Hosp., 1960—; chief psychiatry Trafalgar Hosp., 1962-72; vis. prof. psychiatry Tokyo U. Sch. Medicine, 1964; adj. prof. N.Y. Inst. Tech., 1968; vis. lectr. in psychiatry N.Y. U., 1971-73; Am. del. Internat. Conf. Mental Health, London, 1948; mem. Am. Psychiat. Commn. to USSR, Poland and Finland, 1963, Empire State Med., Sci. and Ednl. Found. Author: booklets Neurosis in a Child, 1949, A Psychiatric Viewpoint on Child Adoption, 1954, Shock Therapy in Psychiatric Practice, 1957, The Genesis of Neurosis, 1958, The Prejudiced Personality, 1962, The Schizophrenic Process, 1962, The Prognosis of Electroshock Therapy Success, 1963, Psychodynamic Effects of Abortion, 1967, Violence Towards Self, 1971, Basic Concepts of Transference in Psychoanalysis, 1973, A Study in Suicide, 1972, Masochism, 1973, Emotional Factors Involved in Skeletal Deformities, 1977, Cults & Cult Suicide, 1979; contbr. articles on the psychoses. Vice pres. Golden Years Found.; N.Y.C. chmn. Com. Med. Standards in Psychiatry, 1952-54. Recipient Sir William Osler Internat. Honor Med. Soc. Gold Key; 3d prize oil paintings N.Y. State Med. Art Exhibit, 1954; N.Y. Univ. Founders Day award, 1963; Presdl. Achievement award, 1984; others. Fellow Am. Psychiat. Assn. (life, pres. Bronx dist. 1960-61, del. council 1961-63, Gold medal 1974), Am. Assn. Psychoanalytic Physicians (pres. 1971-72, gov. 1972-88); mem. Eastern Psychiat. Research Assn., N.Y. State Soc. Med. Research, Am. Med. Writers Assn., A.M.A., N.Y. State, N.Y. County med. socs., N.Y. Soc. for Clin. Psychiatry, Assn. for Advancement Psychotherapy, Bronx Soc. Neurology and Psychiatry (pres. 1960-61, Silver medal 1970), Pan Am. Med. Assn. (trustee, asst. treas., pres. sect. on suicidology), Am. Acad. Psychotherapy, Assn. Research Nervous and Mental Disease, A.A.U.P. Home: 23 Meadow Rd Scarsdale NY 10583 Office: 263 West End Ave New York NY 10023

SORRELL, FURMAN YATES, mechanical engineering educator; b. Wadesboro, N.C., July 14, 1938; s. Furman Yates and Julia Lee (Little) S.; 1 dau., Shannon Lea. B.S., N.C. State U., Raleigh, 1960; M.S., Calif. Inst. Tech., 1961, Ph.D., 1966. Research engr. Pratt & Whitney Aircraft Corp., West Palm Beach, Fla., 1961-62; asst. prof. U. Colo., Boulder, 1966-68; mem. faculty N.C. State U., Raleigh, 1968—; asso. prof. mech. engring. N.C. State U., 1970-76, prof., 1976—; with Perry Assos. (Cons. Engrs.), 1974-75; tech. dir. N.C. Alt. Energy Corp., 1981-82 (on leave); cons. NASA, Langley Research Center, Babcox & Wilcox, Fram Corp., IBM, U.S. Army Chem. Systems Labs.; chmn. marine waste disposal panel NOAA Conf. Ocean Pollution and Monitoring, 1979-80. Contbr. articles to profl. jours. Grantee NSF, NOAA, NASA. Mem. Am. Geophys. Union, Am. Acad. Mechanics, Am. Phys. Soc., N.Y. Acad. Scis., ASME. Home: 930 Ralph Dr Cary NC 27511 Office: Box 7910 NC State U Raleigh NC 27695

SORRELL, MARTIN STUART, marketing services executive; b. London, Feb. 14, 1945; s. Jack and Sally (Goldberg) S.; m. Sandra Carol Ann Finestone, Apr. 25, 1971; children: Mark Richard Antony, Robert Alexander, Jonathan Edward Hugh. B.A., Christ's Coll., Cambridge U., 1966, M.A., 1970; M.B.A., Harvard U., 1968. Assoc., Glendinning Assocs., Westport, Conn., 1968; dir., v.p. Mark McCormack Orgn. London, 1969-72; dir. Pruway Investments Ltd., London, 1973-74, dir. James Gulliver Assocs., London, 1975-77; group fin. dir. Saatchi & Saatchi Co. P.L.C., London, 1977-86; chief exec. WPP Group P.L.C., 1985—. Fellow Inst. Dirs. Conservative. Jewish. Clubs: Reform (London); Harvard (London and N.Y.C.). Office: WPP Group, 27 Farm St, London W1, England Other: Rasor Communications Inc 10 E 53rd St New York NY 10022

SORSA, KALEVI, minister of foreign affairs Finland; b. Keuruu, Finland, Dec. 21, 1930; s. Kaarlo O. and Elsa S. (Leinonen) S.; m. Elli Irene Laakari, July 23, 1953. Ed. Sch. Social Sci. (now U. Tampere). Chief editor Vihuri, 1954-56; lit. editor Tammi pub. house, 1956-59; program asst. specialist UNESCO, 1959-65; sec.-gen. Finnish UNESCO Com., 1965-69; dep. dir. Ministry Edn., Govt. Finland, 1967-69, mem. Parliament, 1970—, minister for fgn. affairs, 1972, 75-76, 87—, prime minister, 1972-75, 77-79, 82-83, 83-87; chmn. fgn. affairs com, 1970-72, 77, 79-82; chmn. bd. adminstrn. Finnair, 1981—. Sec.-gen. Social Democratic Party Finland, 1969-75, pres., from 1975; chmn. Socialist Internat. Study Group on Disarmament, 1978-80; v.p., chmn. Socialist Internat. Adv. Council, 1980. Decorated Grand Decoration of Honor (Austria), Grand Cross Order of Dannebrog (Denmark), Grand Star Order of Star of Friendship Between Peoples of German Dem. Republic; Grand Cross Order Icelandic Falcon; Order of Banner (Hungarian People's Republic); 2d class Grand Cross Order St. Michael and St. George; Grand Cross Order Merit (Fed. Republic Germany); comdr. Grand Cross Order of White Rose Finland; Grand Cross Order of Orange-Nassau (Netherlands), Grand Cross Order of Merit of Polish People's Republic, Grand Cross Order of St. Marinus, Grand Cross Order of Merit of Senegal, Grand Cross Royal Order of No. Star (Sweden). Office: Valtioneuvoston Kanslia, Aleksanterinkatu 3D, 00170 Helsinki Finland *

SOSKEL, NORMAN TERRY, physician; b. Norfolk, Va., Sept. 1, 1948; s. Fred and Ruth (Chapel) S.; cert. piano teaching St. Louis Inst. Music, 1966; B.A., U. Va., 1970, M.D., 1974; m. Judith Anne Barrie, Apr. 9, 1980; children—Daniel Aaron, Shira Anne. Intern., Hosp. of St. Raphael-Yale U., New Haven, 1974-75; resident in internal medicine Salem (Va.) VA Hosp.-U. Va., 1975-77; pulmonary fellow U. Utah, Salt Lake City, 1977-80, instr. medicine, 1980-82, asst. prof. medicine, 1982-84, adj. instr. pathology, 1980-83; asst. prof. medicine U. Tenn., Memphis, 1984—; cons. in field. Recipient Paderewski medal Nat. Guild Piano Tchrs., 1967; Am. Lung Assn. fellow; Utah Heart Assn. grantee; Pulmonary Acad. award Nat. Heart-Lung-Blood Inst., 1980-84; Career Devel. and Merit Awards, 1984-87. Mem. Am. Lung Assn., Am. Thoracic Soc., ACP, AAAS, Nat. Speleological Soc., Western Connective Tissue Soc., So. Connective Tissue Soc., N.Y. Acad. Sci., Sigma Chi. Contbr. articles to profl. jours.; research in field of pulmonary connective tissues with respect to lung injury and development. Office: VA Hosp 1300 Jefferson Ave Room BB123 Research 151 Memphis TN 38104 Other: U Tenn Coleman Bldg 956 Court Ave Room 314 Memphis TN 38163

SÖTÉR, ISTVÁN, novelist literary historian; b. Szeged, Hungary, June 1, 1913; s. István and Jolán (Hreblay) S.; m. Veronika Jasz, 1939. Ed. U. Budapest, 1935, Ecole Normale Supérieure, Paris, 1936; Dr. honoris causa, U. Sorbonne Nouvelle, 1973. Prof. U. Szeged, 1948-52; prof., rector U. Budapest, 1952-83, rector, 1955; dir. Inst. Literary Studies of Hungarian Acad. Scis., 1956-83; rector Lorant Eotvos Univ. Budapest, 1963-66. Author novels and short stories: Walking in the Clouds, 1939, The Robber of the Church, 1942, The Ghost, 1945, The Fall, 1947, The Broken Bridge, 1948, The Eden, 1961, The Lost Lamb, 1974, Bakator, 1976, Tiszta Emma, 1978; Half Circle, 1979; Rings, 1980; author numerous critical essays and hist. monographs. Recipient Kossuth prize, 1954; decorated officier Ordre des Arts et Lettres, banner Order of Hungarian People's Republic. France. Mem. Internat. Comparative Lit. Assn. (pres. 1970-73), Hungarian PEN Club (v.p.), Hungarian Acad. Scis. *

SOTER, NICHOLAS GREGORY, advertising agency executive; b. Great Falls, Mont., Apr. 26, 1947; s. Sam Nick and Bernice (Bennett) S.; m. Kathleen Lyman, Feb. 20, 1970; children: Nichole, Erin, Samuel Scott, Kara, Stephen Andrew, Riley Kyle. BS, Brigham Young U., 1971. With McLean Assocs., Provo, Utah, 1970-75; chmn. bd., chief exec. officer Soter Assocs. Inc., Salt Lake City, 1975—; founder, pres. RS Corp., 1986-88, Plum C Corp., 1988; instr. advt. Utah Tech. Coll., Provo, 1971-75, Brigham Young U., Provo, 1980-84;founder, pres. RS Corp., 1986-88. Publisher: Journal of Joseph, 1979, Journal of Brigham, 1980, LaVell Edwards, 1980, Amos Wright, 1981, Moments in Motherhood, 1981, What It Means to Know Christ, 1981, Mormon Fortune Builders, 1982, Utah History, 1982; contbr. articles to profl. jours. Active Utah Valley Pub. Communications Council for Ch. Jesus Christ of Latter-day Saints, 1982-87, bd. dirs., 1987; bd. dirs. Utah Pilots Assn., 1988—; mem. adv. council. Monte L. Bean Life Sci. Mus., 1987—; Rep. dist. chmn. Recipient N.Y. Art Dir.'s The One Show award, Salt Lake Art Dirs. Communications Assn. of Utah Valley award. Mem. Communications Assn. Utah Valley (past pres.), Provo C. of C. (bd. dirs.), Innisbrook Network of Advt. Agys. (pres. 1986-87). Home: 1728 S 290 E Orem UT 84058 Office: Soter Assocs Inc 350 S 400 E Suite 300 Salt Lake City UT 84111

SOTIRHOS, MICHAEL, U.S. ambassador to Jamaica; b. N.Y.C., Nov. 12, 1928; m. Estelle Manos; 2 children. B.B.A., CCNY, 1950. Ptnr. Ariston Sales Co., Ltd., 1948, founder, chmn., 1958—; chmn. bd. Ariston Interior Designers, Inc., 1973-85; U.S. ambassador to Jamaica 1985—. Former mem. Nat. Vol. Service Adv. Council; former chmn. Internat. Ops. Com., Peace Corps; mem. nat. adv. council SBA, 1976; former chmn. Nat. Republican Heritage Groups Council. Recipient Man of Yr. award Nat. Rep. Heritage Groups Council. Address: US Ambassador to Jamaica care US Dept State Washington DC 20520 *

SOTO, JESUS-RAFAEL, artist; b. Ciudad Bolivar, Venezuela, June 5, 1923; ed. Sch. Fine Arts, Caracas. Dir., Sch. Fine Arts, Maracaibo, Venezuela, 1947-50; artist, Paris, 1950—; one-man exhbns. include Caracas, 1949, 57, 61, Paris, 1956, 59, 62, 65, 67, 69, 70, 79, Brussels, 1957, Essen, Germany, 1961, Antwerp, Belgium, 1962, Stuttgart, 1964, N.Y.C., 1965, 66, 71, 74; retrospective exhbn. Signals, London, 1965; represented in permanent collections Tate Gallery, Caracas Mus. Fine Arts, Albright-Knox Art Gallery, Buffalo, Cali (Colombia) Inst. Fine Arts, Stedelijk Mus., Amsterdam, Mus. Contemporary Arts, Sã o Paulo, Brazil, Moderna Museet, Stockholm, Kaiser Found., Cordoba, Argentina, Palace Fine Arts, Brussells, others. Recipient 'numerous awards including Wolf prize, São Paulo, 1963, David Bright Found. prize, 1964. Works include sculpture for garden Sch. Architecture, Univ. City of Caracas, murals and sculpture for Venezuelan pavilion. Office: 10 rue Villehardouin, 75003 Paris France *

SOTOMORA-VON AHN, RICARDO FEDERICO, pediatrician, educator; b. Guatemala City, Guatemala, Oct. 22, 1947; s. Ricardo and Evelyn (Von Ahn) S.; M.D., San Carlos U., 1972; M.S. in Physiology, U. Minn., 1978; m. Victoria Monzon, Nov. 26, 1971; children—Marisol, Clarisa, Ricardo, III.

Rotating intern Gen. Hosp. Guatemala, 1971-72; pediatric intern U. Ark., 1972-73, resident, 1973-75; fellow in pediatric cardiology U. Minn., 1975-78; research assoc. in cardiovascular pathology United Hosps., St. Paul, 1976; fellow in neonatal-perinatal medicine St. Paul's Children's Hosp., 1977-78, U. Ark., 1981-82; instr. pediatrics U. Minn., 1978-79; pediatric cardiologist, unit cardiovascular surgery Roosevelt Hosp., Guatemala City, 1979-81; asst. prof. pediatrics (cardiology and neonatology), U. Ark., Little Rock, 1981-83; practice medicine specializing in pediatric cardiology-neonatology, 1983—. Diplomate Am. Bd. Pediatrics, Sub-Bd. Pediatric Cardiology, Neonatal-Perinatal Medicine. Fellow Am. Acad. Pediatrics, Am. Coll. Cardiology, Am. Coll. Chest Physicians; mem. AMA, Ark. Med. Soc., N.Y. Acad. Scis., Am. Heart Assn., Guatemala Coll. Physicians and Surgeons, Guatemala Cardiology Soc., Central Ark. Pediatric Soc., So. Soc. Pediatric Research, Guatemala Assn. Critical Care. Clubs: Pleasant Valley Country (Little Rock); American (Guatemala). Home: 38 River Ridge Circle Little Rock AR 72207 Office: Med Towers II, Suite 800 Little Rock AR 72205

SOTTILE, JOHN HOOKS, diversified business executive; b. Miami, Fla., Nov. 29, 1947; s. James and Ethel Brundage (Hooks) S.; m. Ann Grubbs, Dec. 19, 1982; children: Sara Elaine, Rachel Ethel, John Nicholas. BS, U. Miami, 1971. Exec. asst. Goldfield Corp. div. AMEX, Melbourne, Fla., 1971-76, asst. to pres., 1976-83, v.p., 1983, pres., chief exec. officer, 1983—; v.p., dir. Fla. Orange Growers, Inc., Melbourne, 1967-83, pres., 1983—; v.p., dir. Indian Orange Groves, Melbourne, 1967-69, pres., 1983—; v.p., dir. Citrus Growers Fla., Inc., Melbourne, 1967-83, pres., 1983—; v.p., dir., Lake Byrd Citrus Packing Co., Melbourne, 1967-83, pres., 1983—; dir. Valencia Ctr., Inc., Melbourne, 1974-84, v.p., 1984; pres., dir. NASA Corp., Melbourne, 1977-80; v.p., dir. No. Goldfield Investments Ltd., Inc., Melbourne, 1983, pres., 1983—; v.p., dir. Black Range Mining Corp., Melbourne, 1983, pres., 1983—; v.p., dir. U.S. Treasury Mining Co., Melbourne, 1983, pres., 1983—; v.p., dir. San Pedro Mining Corp., Melbourne, 1983, pres., 1983—; v.p., dir. Fla. Transport Corp., Melbourne, 1983, pres., 1983—; v.p., dir. Power Corp. Am., Titusville, Fla., 1983-86, SE Power Corp., Titusville, 1983—; v.p., dir. Contractors Leasing Corp., Titusville, 1983, pres., 1983—; v.p., dir. Goldfield Consol. Mines Co., Melbourne, 1983, pres., 1983—; v.p., dir. Detrital Valley Salt Co., Melbourne, 1983, pres., 1983—. Mem. Soc. Mining Engrs. Democrat. Roman Catholic. Home: 2324 Brookside Way Indialantic FL 32903 Office: Goldfield Corp 100 Rialto Pl Suite 500 Melbourne FL 32901

SOUDER, DENNIS E., association executive; b. London, Ont., Can., Nov. 20, 1945; s. Mervyn Edward and Marjorie Alma (Orser) S.; m. Maureen Vicki Roydes, July 3, 1970 (div. 1979). BA, McMaster U., 1968. Cert. assn. exec. Registered rep. Greenshields, Inc., Toronto, Can., 1968-72; dir. Can. activities Phot Mktg. Assn., Toronto, 1972-73; gen. mgr. Brampton (Ont.) Bd. of Trade, 1973-75; exec. v.p. Can. Assn. Movers, Toronto, 1975-77; exec. dir. Hort. Trades Assn., Mississuga, Ont., 1977-80, Can. Nursery Trades Assn., Mississauga, 1978-80, Ont. Assn. Optometrists, Toronto, 1981—; lectr. Can. Soc. Assn. Execs., 1982, 88. Editor: Mag. Model Aviation Canada, 1973-75. Mem. Inst. Assn. Execs. (bd. dirs. 1983-87, chpt. pres. 1984-85, mem. editorial rev. bd.), Internat. Assn. Optometric Execs. (v.p. 1987-88, pres. elect 1988-89), Lorne Scots Regimental Assn. (sec. 1987-88), McMaster U. Alumni Council, 1988-89. Home: 47 Saint Clair Ave W, Suite 801, Toronto, ON Canada M4V 1K6 Office: Ont Assn of Optometrists, 40 Saint Clair Ave W, Suite 212, Toronto, ON Canada M4V 1M2

SOULAGES, PIERRE, painter; b. Rodez, France, Dec. 24, 1919; s. Amans and Aglae (Corp) S.; baccalauriat Philosphie Etudes secondaires au Lycee de Rodez, 1938; m. Colette Llaurens, Oct. 24, 1942. Paintings exhibited Lydia Conti Gallery, Paris, 1948-49, Louis Carre Gallery, Paris-N.Y.C., 1950-53, Galerie de France, Paris, 1956, 60-63, 67-72, Kootz Gallery, N.Y., 1954-65, Knoedler Gallery, N.Y.C., 1968; designer for ballet, theater, 1949, 51, for Louis Jouvet, Athenee, Paris, 1951; paintings in permanent collections Mus. Modern Art, N.Y.C., Musée d'Art Moderne, Paris, Museo de Arte Moderna, Rio de Janeiro, Tate Gallery of London, S.R. Guggenheim Mus., N.Y.C., Phillips Gallery, Washington, Mus. of Hamburg, Köln, Germany, Torino, Italy, Zurich, Switzerland, others; expositions retrospective in museums in Hanover, Essen, Den Haag, Zurich, Copenhagen, Paris, Pitts., Buffalo, Montreal, Vienna, Dakar, Lisbda, Madrid, Mexico, Caracas, São Paulo, Rio de Janeiro; M.I.T., 1962, Fine Arts Mus. Houston, 1966, Musée de Quebec, 1968, Centre Georges Pompidou, Paris, 1979, Musée du Parc de la Boverie, Liège, Belgium, 1980, others. Recipient Prix biennale de Tokyo, 1957, Prix de la Biennale de gravure de Ljubljana, Yougoslavie, 1959, Prix Carnegie, 1963, Prix des Arts de Paris, 1975, Prix Rembrandt, 1976, Grand Prix des Arts de la Ville de Paris, 1976, others. *

SOULAK, JOSEPH HAROLD, publishing executive; b. Adams, Wis., Mar. 25, 1932; s. Harold Joseph and Mary I. (Turski) S.; A.B., Providence Coll., 1960; postgrad. Boston U., 1960, Roosevelt U., 1969; m. Leanora Galante, Sept. 1, 1956 (div. Oct. 1971); 1 dau., Deborah; m. Judith A. Sharpe, Oct. 1975. Sports editor Lakeland Pubs., Grayslake, Ill., 1960-62, news editor, 1962-64, mng. editor, 1964-65; news editor Pawtuxet Valley Times, West Warwick, R.I., 1964; mgr. pub. relations Bastian-Blessing Co., Chgo., 1966-68; publs. mgr. Ryerson Steel, Chgo., 1969; dir. news services Ency. Brit., Inc., Chgo., 1969-75; pub., editor South Milw. Voice-Jour., Cudahy Free-Press, The Bay Viewer, Suburbanite (all South Milw.), 1975—; owner Voice Jour. Printing Co., Inc., 1987—; editor PR/Chicago, 1969-75; sec. Wis. Spectacle of Music, Inc., 1977; columnist, writer Waukegan (Ill.) News Sun, 1969-75. Mem. Lake County Safety Commn., 1961-65; mgr. pub. relations for Ill. Senator, 1964-75. Served with USN, 1952-56; Korea. Mem. Nat. Newspaper Assn., Wis. Press Assn., S. Milw. Assn. Commerce (dir., pres. 1976-85); Chgo. Press Club. Club: Kiwanis (dir. 1983). Office: 723 Milwaukee Ave South Milwaukee WI 53179

SOUM, EVELYN GABRIELLE, advertising executive; b. Colmar, France, May 25, 1947; d. Léon Lucien Wahl and Anna Kateline (Györi) Kowarski; m. Pierre Soum, April 10, 1969 (div. 1973); 1 child: Ludovic. Student, U. Paris, 1965-66; degree, Inst. D'Etudes Politiques, Paris, 1967. Sec. Selection du Readers Digest, Paris, 1968-71, promotion mgr., 1972-73; promotion asst. Estée Lauder, Paris, 1971; advt. and promotions mgr. Yves Rocher, Paris, 1974-77, internat. mktg. mgr., 1978; dir. Wunderman Belgium, Bussels, Belgium, 1977-78; founder, chmn. Cascades, Paris, 1980-85; chmn. Audour, Soum, Scali, McCabe, Sloves, Paris, 1985—. Pres.-elect. jury, Internat. Advt. Film Festival, Cannes, 1986. Mem. Cosmetic Exec. Women.

SOUMOY, PHILIPPE, finance company executive; b. Morialme, Namur, Belgium, Nov. 19, 1943; s. Jules and Marguerite (Deprez) S.; m. Vrebos Claudine, May 13, 1967; Sylviane, Gontran. Comml. engr., U. Louvain, Belgium, 1965. Trainee IBM Belgium, Brussels, 1965; auditor Arthur Andersen Belgium, Brussels, 1967-72, mgr., 1972-79; internat. auditor Tractionel, Brussels, 1979-86; fin. mgr. Tractebel, Brussels, 1986—. Mem. Fin. Execs., Fin. Analysts, Inst. Accts., Alumni I.A.G. (v.p.). Home: Jan Van Rijswijcklaan 94, 2018 Antwerpen Belgium Office: Tractebel, Place du Trone 7, 1000 Brussels Belgium

SOUROUJON D'ALCALA, BEN S., manufacturing company executive; b. Antwerp, Belgium, Feb. 15, 1927; s. Joseph and Beatrice S.; B.Sc. in Chemistry, Univ. Coll. N. Wales, 1948; m. Nelly Muller Zimmerman, Oct. 27, 1960; children: Jose, Beatrice, Jacqueline, Philippe, Andre. Pres., Industrias Reunidas SA, Mexico City, 1955-87. Clubs: Bella Vista Golf and Tennis, Avandaro Golf. Editor: Revista Belga, 1970-79; tennis reporter Jour. Français du Mexique; corr. Agence Belga Brussels. Office: 765 Paseo de las Palmas, Mexico City Mexico

SOURROUILLE, JUAN VITAL, government official; b. Buenos Aires, Aug. 13, 1940; m. Susana Romero Escobar; children: Diego, Maria Noel, Maria Florencia. Grad. Facultad de Ciencias Econs., Nat. U. Buenos Aires, 1963. Advisor Econ. and Social Devel. Inst., 1966, prof. macroecons., 1979-83; dir. Inst. Nat. de Estadisticas y Censos, 1970; undersec. Economia y Trabajo de la Nacion, 1970-71; mem. Commn. Directiva del Inst. de Desarrollo Economico y Social, 1972-83; sec. of planning 1983-85, minister of economy, 1985—; advisor Fed. Council Investigation; vis. researcher Harvard U.; cons. Econ. Commn. for Latin Am., Latin Am. Inst. Econ. and Social Planning, World Bank. Contbr. articles to profl. jours. Mem. Internat. Assn. Research in Income and Wealth, Acad. Council of Ctr. of Studies of State and Soc. *

SOUTHALL, IVAN FRANCIS, author; b. Melbourne, Victoria, Australia, June 8, 1921; s. Francis Gordon and Rachel Elizabeth (Voutier) S.; m. Joy Blackburn, Sept. 8, 1945; children—Andrew John, Roberta Joy, Elizabeth Rose, Melissa Frances; m. Susan Helen Westerlund, Nov. 11, 1976. Ed. pub. schs.; Victoria. Freelance writer, 1947—. Author over 50 books in 22 langs., including: Ash Road, 1965 (Book of Yr. 1966), To the Wild Sky, 1967 (Book of Yr. 1968), Bread and Honey, 1970 (Book of Yr. 1971), Josh, 1971 (Carnegie medal 1971), Fly West, 1975 (Book of Yr. 1976), The Long Night Watch, 1983 (Nat. Children's Book award 1986). Found. pres. Knoxbrooke Day Tng. Centre for Intellectually Handicapped, Victoria, 1967-69. Served as flight lt. Royal Australian Air Force, 1942-47, Europe. Decorated D.F.C., RAF; mem. Order Australia. Methodist. Club: Naval and Military (Melbourne). Home: PO Box 25, Healesville, Victoria 3777, Australia

SOUTHARD, PAUL RAYMOND, financial executive; b. Albany, N.Y., May 15, 1948; s. Harold G. and Frances L. (Shaylor) S.; BS, Rochester Inst. Tech., 1970. CPA, N.Y. Staff acct., Haskins & Sells, CPA's, Rochester, N.Y., 1969-70; sr. acct. Maurice F. Sammons & Co., CPAs, Rochester, 1970-73; fin. mgr. Radionics, Inc., Webster, N.Y., 1973-82, controller, 1982-87, Kitchen Concepts. Co., Fairport, N.Y., 1987—. Mem. N.Y. State Soc. CPAs, Rochester C. of C. (mem. small bus. council), Indsl. Mgmt. Council Rochester. Lodge: Kiwanis. Home: 1096 Everwild View Webster NY 14580 Office: Kitchen Concepts 1350 Fairport Rd Fairport NY 14450

SOUTHERN, SAMUEL D., utilities, oil and gas company executive; b. Plymouth, Eng., Sept. 19, 1909; m. Alexandra C.; 1 child, Ronald D. D. Engrng. (hon.), Tech. U. Nova Scotia, 1983. Chmn. ATCO Ltd., Calgary, Alta., Can., 1961—; chmn. Sentgraf Enterprises Ltd. Active City of Calgary Fire Dept., 1933—. Served with RCAF. Home: Rural Rt 9, Calgary, AB Canada T2J 5G5 Office: ATCO Ltd, 1600 909 11th Ave SW, Calgary, AB Canada T2R 1N6

SOUTHWORTH, HERBERT RUTLEDGE, historian; b. Canton, Okla., Feb. 6, 1908; s. Walton Rutledge and Lulah May (Shoemaker) S.; m. Suzanne Maury, Oct. 1, 1948. AB, Tex. Tech. Coll., 1933, MA, 1934; D in History, Sorbonne U., 1975. With Library Congress, Washington, 1934-38; journalist, editor Spanish Info. Bur., N.Y.C., 1938-39; free-lance journalist N.Y.C., 1939-41; journalist, propaganda analyst Office War Info., N.Y.C., 1942-43; dir. D sect. Psychol. Warfare Br. Office War Info., Algiers, Algeria, 1943; dir. Spanish broadcasts Office War Info., Rabat, Morocco, 1943-45; dir. U.S. Info. Office, Casablanca, Morocco, 1945-46; founder, gen. mgr. Soc. Africana Radiodifusion, Tangier, Morocco, 1946-60; hist. researcher France, 1961—; prof. U. Vincennes, Paris, 1979; regents prof. U. Calif., San Diego, 1974. Author: El mito de la cruzada de Franco, 1963, Antifalange, 1967, Guernica! Guernica!, 1977; contbr. articles to profl. jours. Mem. Soc. Spanish and Portuguese Hist. Studies, Soc. de Estudios de la Guerra Civil y del Franquismo. Home: Le Petit Prieure rue de l'Eglise, St Benoît du Sault, 36170 Indre France

SOUVEROFF, VERNON WILLIAM, JR., corporate executive, investor; b. Los Angeles, Aug. 12, 1934; s. Vernon William Sr. and Aileen (Young) S.; m. Aileen Patricia Robinson; children—Gail Kathleen, Michael William. B.S. in E.E., Stanford U., 1957; postgrad., Ohio State U., 1958-59. With Litton Industries, Beverly Hills, Calif., 1960-75; with ITT Corp., N.Y.C., 1975-87, corp. v.p., 1983-84, sr. v.p., 1984-87; pres. ITT Gilfillan, 1979-83; group exec. ITT Def. Space Group, 1983-84; dir. ITT Telecom and Electronics N.Am., 1984-86; pres., chief exec. officer ITT Def. Tech. Corp., 1986-87; bus. advisor, investor, corp. bd. dirs. 1987—; bd. dirs. Gilcron Corp., Avcron Corp.; mem. U.S. Def. Policy Adv. Com. on Trade, Washington, 1984—. Contbr. articles to profl. jours. Served as officer USAF, 1957-60. Recipient Exec. Salute award Los Angeles C. of C., 1981; Ring of Quality ITT Corp., 1983. Mem. IEEE, Nat. Contracts Mgmt. Assn., Electronics Industries Assn., Am. Def. Preparedness Assn., Nat. Security Indsl. Assn. Presbyterian. Club: Rancho Mirage Racquet (Calif.). Home: 425 Cameron St Alexandria VA 22314

SOUX, LUIS BERTRAND, engineering company executive; b. Potosi, Bolivia, Feb. 23, 1935; arrived in Venezuela, 1959; s. Augusto and Elena (Sanjinés) S.; m. Nelly Simonovis, Feb. 27, 1965. BS in Engring., Calif. Inst. Tech., 1957; MS in Elec. Engring., U. So. Calif., 1959; Ingeniero, U. Cen., Caracas, Venezula, 1967. Registered engr. Colegio de Ingenieros de Venezuela. Head dept. CADAFE, Caracas, 1959-67; sr. advisor Electricidad de Caracas, 1967-69; founder Inelectra S.A., Caracas, 1969, dir., 1969-72, pres., 1972-82, sr. council, 1982—; founder, pres. Inversiones INE, S.A., Caracas, 1974-80; founder, dir. Inelectra Servicios S.A., Caracas, 1979—; founder, v.p. Inversiones Edilectra S.A., Caracas, 1979—; founder, dir. Cen. Profl. Santa Paula, Caracas, 1977-82. Contbr. numerous papers and articles in field to confs. and profl. jours., articles on music to newspapers. Founding mem. Chamber Music Assn., Caracas, 1977; benefactor Amigos Teatro Teresa Carreño, Caracas, 1982; mem., donor Mus. Colonial Art, Caracas, 1985; donor L.B. Soux scholarships for postgrad. study, Caracas, 1987. Mem. IEEE (sr.), Assn. Venezolana Ingenieria Eléctrica y Mecánica, Soc. Venezolana Ingenieria Consulta, Assn. Venezolana Ejecutivos. Club: Los Cortijos (Caracas). Lodge: Lions. Home: Apartado 65521 Santa Paula, 1066A Caracas Venezuela Office: Inelectra SA, Edificio Inelectra, Av Circunyalación, del Sol Urb Santa Paula, 1066 Caracas Venezuela

SOUZA, HUGO ELADIO, development banker; b. Montevideo, Uruguay, Mar. 5, 1942; s. Eladio Agustin and Dora Maria (Bordabehere) S.; D.B.A., U. Uruguay, 1969; M.B.A., Am. U., 1978; m. Nibia Tato Souza, Nov. 7, 1968; children—Fabian, Mauro. Acct., Uruguay, 1969-75; mem. faculty dept. corp. fin. U. Uruguay, 1968-75; fin. mgr. IBM, Uruguay, 1968-75; ops. officer in charge of Ecuador, Colombia, English Caribbean, Cen. Am., Chile and Peru loans Inter-Am. Devel. Bank, Washington, 1975—; fellow in internat. banking Harvard U. (lectr., articles on internat. banking); Mem. Inter-Am. Acctg. Assn. Roman Catholic. Home: 7510 Shadywood Rd Bethesda MD 20817 Office: 1300 New York Ave Washington DC 20577

SOVERN, MICHAEL IRA, university president; b. N.Y.C., Dec. 1, 1931; s. Julius and Lillian (Arnstein) S.; m. Lenore Goodman, Feb. 21, 1952 (div. Apr. 1963); children: Jeffrey Austin, Eilzabeth Ann, Douglas Todd; m. Eleanor Leen, Aug. 25, 1963 (div. Feb. 1974); 1 dau., Julie Danielle; m. Joan Wit, Mar. 9, 1974. A.B. summa cum laude, Columbia U., 1953, LL.B. (James Ordronaux prize), 1955, LL.D. (hon.), 1980; Ph.D. (hon.), Tel Aviv U., 1982. Bar: N.Y. 1956, U.S. Supreme Ct. 1976. Asst. prof., then assoc. prof. law U. Minn. Law Sch., 1955-58; mem. faculty Columbia Law Sch., 1957—, prof. law, 1960—, Chancellor Kent prof., 1977—, dean Law Sch., 1970-79; chmn. exec. com. faculty Columbia U., 1968-69, provost, exec. v.p., 1979-80, univ. pres., 1980—; research dir. Legal Restraints on Racial Discrimination in Employment, Twentieth Century Fund, 1962-66; spl. counsel N.Y. State Joint Legis. Com. Indsl. and Labor Conditions, 1962-63; spl. counsel to gov. N.J., 1974-77; cons. Time mag., 1965-80; dir. Chem. Bank, AT&T, GNY Ins. Group., Orion Pictures Corp.; mem. N.J. Bd. Mediation Panel of Arbitrators; mem. panel arbitrators Fed. Mediation and Conciliation Service; bd. dirs. Asian Cultural Council, Shubert Orgn., Shubert Found., NAACP Legal Def. Fund; chmn. N.Y.C. Charter Revision Commn., 1982-83; co-chmn. 2d Circuit Commn. on Reduction of Burdens and Costs in Civil Litigation, 1977-80; chmn. Commn. on Integrity in Govt., 1986. Author: Legal Restraints on Racial Discrimination in Employment, 1966, Law and Poverty, 1969. Mem. Pulitzer Prize bd., 1980—, chmn. pro tem, 1986-87. Fellow Am. Acad. Arts and Scis.; mem. Council Fgn. Relations, Assn. Bar City N.Y., ABA, Am. Arbitration Assn. (panel arbitrators), Am. Law Inst., Nat. Acad. Arbitrators. Office: Columbia Univ 202 Low Library New York NY 10027

SOVIK, RUTH JOHNSON, religious organization executive, educator; b. St. Paul, Dec. 21, 1928; d. A.I. and Alma (Peterson) J.; m. Arne Sovik, Dec. 31, 1949; children: Ann Tenwick (dec.), Nord Christian, Liv Rebecca, Nathan Arne. B.A., St. Olaf Coll., 1950; M.A., Montclair State U., 1970. Cert. secondary sch. tchr. Corr. tchr. N.D., Fargo, 1950; missionary Am. Luth. Ch., Taipei, Taiwan (Republic of China), 1952-55; tchr. Internat. Sch., Geneva, 1964-65; editorial asst. World Council of Churches, Geneva, 1965-67, exec., 1973-80; tchr. English high sch., East Orange, N.J., 1969-71; gen. sec. World YWCA, Geneva, 1980-85; dep. gen. sec. World Council of Chs., 1986—. Mng. editor Internat. Rev. of Mission jour., 1973-77; editor, author revs., articles, reports, publs. in religious field. Home: 3 chemin de la Flechere, 1255 Veyrier Geneva Switzerland Office: World Council Chs, 150 rte de Ferney, 1211 Geneva 20, Switzerland

SOWA, KAZIMIERZ ZBIGNIEW, sociologist; b. Cracow, Poland, Aug. 16, 1942; s. Antoni Józef and Zofia Maria (Kozdeba) S.; m. Elizbieta Katarzyna; children: Jadwiga Zofia, Jan Kazimierz. MA, Jagiellonian U., Cracow, 1965, PhD, 1971, postgrad., 1977. Asst. Silesian Inst., Katowice, Poland, 1965-68; researcher Inst. Housing Economy, Warsaw, 1968-69; dir. Coop. Research Inst., Cracow, 1969-83; prof. Tchrs. Tng. Coll., RzeszóW, Poland, 1983—, Cen. Sch. Planning and Stats., Warsaw, 1985—; cons. State Orgn. Housing, Baghdad, Iraq, 1976-79, Bur. Cracow Devel., 1984-85; advisor Solidarity Trade Union, Cracow, 1980-81. Author: Miasto-Srodowisko-Mieszkanie, 1987, Wstep Do Socjologicznej Teorii Zrzeszen, 1988; (with others), editor: Szkice z Historii Socjologii Polskiej, 1983; contbr. articles to profl. jours. Mem. Polish Sociol. Assn. (officer 1981-83), Cracow Soc. Indsl. Activity (co-founder). Roman Catholic. Home: L Svobody 5/38, 30-093 Crakow Poland Office: Tchrs Tng Coll, ul Turkienicza 24, 35-059 Rzeszów Poland

SOWAH, SAMUEL ADJEI, entomologist, researcher; b. Accra, Ghana, Jan. 22, 1943; s. Charles Annang and Comfort Marteki (Martei) S.; m. Charlotte Adjorkor Quarcoo, Nov. 6, 1971; children: Ernest Adjetey, Michael Ablorh, Okoe, Akueteh, Sueley Ago, Suorkor. BS, U. Ghana, Legon-Accra, 1971. Entomologist in charge med. field unit Ministry Health, Bolgatanga, Ghana, 1971-74; sector chief WHO Onchocerciasis Control Programme, Tamale, Ghana, 1974-75; scientist Ouagadougou, Burkina, 1976; sector chief Lama-Kara, Togo, 1976-79, Bamako, Mali, 1979-84; zone chief Lama-Kara, 1984—. Contbr. articles to periodicals. Fellow Royal Soc. Tropical Medicine and Hygiene; mem. Am. Mgmt. Assn. Methodist. Office: WHO, Onchocercose BP 36, Kara Togo

SOWDER, FRED ALLEN, foundation administrator, alphabet specialist; b. Cin., July 17, 1940; s. William Franklin and Lucille (Estes) S.; m. Sandra Ann Siegman, July 15, 1961 (div. Sept. 1963); 1 child, William. Founder World Union for a Universal Alphabet, Cin., 1981—. State dir. Soc. Separationists, Cin., 1967-70; bd. dirs. ACLU of Ohio, ACLU Found., 1984—. Democrat. Home: 4020 Rose Hill Ave Cincinnati OH 45229 Office: World Union Universal Alphabet PO Box 252 Cincinnati OH 45201-0252

SOWDER, KATHLEEN ADAMS, marketing executive; b. Person County, N.C., Feb. 9, 1951; d. George W. and Mary W. (Woody) A.; BS, Radford Coll., 1976; MBA, Va. Poly. Inst., 1978; m. Angelo R. LoMascolo, Apr. 11, 1980; 1 child, Mary Jennifer. Asst. product mgr. GTE Sylvania, Waltham, Mass., 1978-79, product mgr. video products, 1979-80; comml.mktg. mgr. Am. Dist. Telegraph, N.Y.C., 1980-87; v.p. mktg. ESL, Rockland, Mass., 1987—, also exec. mem. Mem. Am. Mktg. Assn., Am. Soc. Indsl. Security (chair standing com. on phys. security). Republican. Home: 6 Treetop Ln Dobbs Ferry NY 10522 Office: ESL 1022 Hingham St Rockland MA 02370

SOWELL, VIRGINIA MURRAY, educator; b. Presidio, Tex., Mar. 23, 1931; d. Marshall Bishop and Mary Alice (Daniel) Murray; BA, Sam Houston State U., 1951; MA, Trinity U., 1957; PhD, U. Tex., 1975; children—John Houston, III, Paul Orin. Tchr. San Antonio (Tex.) Ind. Sch. Dist., 1951-52, 1955-58; asst. prof. San Antonio Coll., 1969-75, assoc. prof., 1976—; assoc. prof. spl. edn. Tex. Tech. U., Lubbock, 1976-85, asst. v.p. acad. affairs, 1984—, prof. 1985. Bd. govs. Tex. Sch. for Blind, v.p., 1983-86, pres., 1986-89; adv. com. Iowa Braille and Sight Saving Sch.; dir. vols. Witte Mus.; mem. research adv. com. Tex. Tech. U., 1981-82, pres. faculty senate, 1982-83; bd. dirs. Developmental Edn., Birth through Two, 1977—, SW Lighthouse for the Blind, 1984—, v.p., 1987, chmn. bd., 1988; pres. elect Visually Handicapped, 1986-87, pres, 1987-88. HEW grantee, 1977—, bd. dirs. AER Internat.; recipient Sammie K. Rankin award Tex. Assn. for Edn. and Rehab. of Blind and Visually Handicapped. Mem. Council for Exceptional Children (bd. govs. 1982-85, pres. div. visually handicapped 1987-88), Tex. Council Exceptional Children (treas. 1981-85), Tex. Div. Children with Learning Disabilities, Internat. Reading Assn., Assn. for Edn. and Rehab. of Blind (pres. S. Central region 1984-86, bd. dirs. 1988—), Am. Ednl. Research Assn., Assn. Edn. of Visually Handicapped (pres. South Central region 1984-86), Tex. Assn. Coll. Tchrs., AAUP, Phi Delta Kappa, Delta Kappa Gamma, Zeta Tau Alpha. Republican. Episcopalian. Home: 4610 28th St Lubbock TX 79410 Office: Tex Tech U Office Acad Affairs Box 4609 Lubbock TX 79409

SOWELL, W. R. (BILL), aviation company executive; b. Chipley, Fla., Nov. 8, 1920; s. Claude Tee and Eunice (Richardson) S.; student Centenary Coll., 1940-42; grad. Norton Bus. Coll., Shreveport, La., 1942; m. Nadine Martin, Sept. 1942 (div. Feb. 1971); children—J. Donald, Doris Dianne Sowell Preston, Deborah K., Sheri Denise. Owner, pres. Panama Airways, Inc. (now Sowell Aviation Co. Inc.), Panama City, Fla., 1945-53; pilot instr., flying supr. So. Airways, Bainbridge, Ga., 1950-53; founder, prin. owner, chmn. bd. pilot, instr. Sowell Aviation Co., Inc., Panama City, 1954—; chmn. bd. Sowell Aircraft Service, Inc., Panama City, 1964—; founder, pres., owner Pensacola (Fla.) Aviation Inc., 1964-72; airplane and instrument pilot examiner FAA, 1946-79; mem. Panama City Airport Bd., 1959-61, chmn., 1959-61; mem. Fla. Gov.'s Aviation Com., 1972-85, chmn., 1977-79. Served with AC, AUS, 1940-45. Mem. Airplane Owners and Pilots Assn., Quiet Birdmen, Nat. Aviation Transp. Assn., Fla. Aviation Trades Assn. (pres. 1970-72, dir.) Bay County C. of C. (dir. 1956-66, chmn. aviation com. 1962-63). Baptist. Clubs: Rotary, Masons, Shriners, Elks. Home: 3037 W 30th Ct Panama City FL 32405 Office: Panama City Bay County Mcpl Airport Panama City FL 32405

SOWERS, JOHN PHILLIP, industry administrator, consultant; b. Los Angeles, Apr. 22, 1947; s. Norman Joseph and Cora Marie (Cirino) S.; m. Linda Joyce Boyer, Sept. 5, 1980; 1 stepchild, Alisa Joy Boyer. Student, U. Calif., Santa Cruz, 1965-67, U. Calif., Hong Kong, 1967-68; BA, UCLA, 1969; postgrad., U. B.C., 1969-71; cert., U. So. Calif., 1987. Indsl. security investigator U.S. Dept. of Def., Los Angeles, 1976-78; mgr. security and safety Raytheon Co., Santa Barbara, Calif., 1978-81; sr. safety adminstr. Santa Barbara Research Ctr. Hughes Aircraft Co., 1981—; mem. Hughes Aircraft Environ. Affairs Subcom., Culver City, Calif., 1985—; owner, cons. Enviro-Tech, Santa Barbara, 1985—. Mem. Am. Soc. Safety Engrs., Santa Barbara C. of C. (hazardous waste subcom. 1985—).

SOWERWINE, ELBERT ORLA, JR., chemical engineer; b. Tooele, Utah, Mar. 15, 1915; s. Elbert Orla and Margaret Alice (Evans) S.; B. Chemistry, Cornell U., 1937, Chem. Engr., 1938; m. Norma Borge; children—Sue-Ann Sowerwine Jacobson, Sandra Sowerwine Montgomery, Elbert Orla 3d, John Frederick, Avril Ruth Taylor, Albaro Francisco, Octavio Evans, Zaida Margaret. Analytical chemist Raritan Copper Works, Perth Amboy, N.J., summers 1936, 37; research chem. engr. Socony-Vacuum Oil Co., Paulsboro, N.J., 1938-43; prodn. supr. Merck & Co., Elkton, Va., 1943-45; asst. plant mgr. U.S. Indsl. Chems. Co., Newark, 1945-48; project engr. and research dir. Wigton-Abbott Corp., Newark, 1948-50, Cody, Wyo., 1950-55; cons. engring., planning, indsl. and community devel., resource evaluation and mgmt. Wapiti, Wyo., also C.Am., 1955—. Commr. N.J., Boy Scouts Am., 1938-43; mem. Wapiti and Park County (Wyo.) Sch. Bds., 1954-58; dir. Mont. State Planning Bd., 1959-61; exec. bd. Mo. Basin Research and Devel. Council, 1959-61. Fellow Am. Inst. Chemists; mem. Am. Inst. Chem. Engrs., Am. Planning Assn., Nicaraguan Assn. Engrs. and Architects. Libertarian. Mem. Christian Ch. Researcher desulfurization of petroleum products, process control, alternate energy projects; patentee in petroleum and chem. processes and equipment. Home: Broken H Ranch Wapiti WY 82450 Office: Sowerwine Cons Wapiti WY 82450

SOWLE, DONALD EDGAR, management consultant; b. Mt. Pleasant, Mich., May 27, 1915; s. Sidney Edgar and Mary Agnes (West) S.; m. Gretchen Elizabeth MacRae, July 4, 1942; children: Lisa Sowle Cahill, Mary Ann Sowle Messing. B.S., Central Mich. U., 1940; postgrad., Harvard U., 1942, M.I.T., 1942; M.B.A., U. Chgo., 1950. Sales rep. Armour & Co., Grand Rapids, Mich., 1940-41; commd. 2d lt. USAF, advanced through grades to col., 1958; asst. dir. Jet Propulsion Lab., Calif. Inst. Tech., Pasadena, 1965-68; group v.p. Gulf & Western Industries, Los Angeles, 1968-69; dir. studies Congl. Commn. on Govt. Procurement, Washington, 1970-73; pres., chmn. bd. dirs. Don Sowle Assocs., Inc., Arlington, Va., 1973-81; adminstr. Fed. Procurement Policy, Washington, 1981-85; mgmt.

cons. 1985—; dir. Procurement Round Table, 1985; mem. adv. bd. Fed. Contracts Report, Bur. Nat. Affairs, 1965; nat. regent. Inst. Cost Analysis, 1981 instr. Georgetown U., 1961-65; bd. regents Kogod Sch. Bus.; adj. prof. and mem. adv. council procurement mgmt. program Kogod Coll. Am. U., Washington. Mem. adv. council Sch. Bus. Marymount U., 1985. Recipient Dept. Def. Joint Service Commendation medal, 1963; Legion of Merit award Sec. Def., 1964, Public Service award Los Angeles County, 1969, award Central Mich. U., 1968. Fellow Nat. Contract Mgmt. Assn. (bd. advisers); mem. U.S. C. of C. (procurement council 1985), Beta Gamma Sigma. Republican. Roman Catholic. Clubs: Capitol Hill, Officers. Home: 6643 McLean Dr McLean VA 22101

SOYINKA, WOLE, writer; b. Abeokuta, Nigeria, July 13, 1934; s. Ayo and Eniola S.; student U. Ibadan, U. Leeds (Eng.); married; 4 children. Staff Royal Ct. Theater, London; research fellow in drama U. Ibadan, 1960-61; lectr. in English U. Ife, 1962-63, research prof. dramatic lit., 1972, now prof. comparative lit., head dept. dramatic arts; artistic dir. Orisun Theater, 1960; chmn. Internat. Theatre Orgn., UNESCO. Recipient Prisoner of Conscience prize Amnesty Internat.; Jock Campbell-New Statesman Lit. award, 1969; John Whiting Drama prize, 1966; Dakar Negro Arts Festival award, 1966; Nobel Prize in Literature, 1986. Rockefeller Found. grantee, 1960. Author: (plays) The Lion and the Jewel, 1959, The Swamp Dweller, 1959, The Strong Breed, 1962, The Road, 1964, Kingi's Harvest, 1965, Madmen and Specialists, 1961, Before the Blackout, 1971, Jero's Metamorphis, 1974, Death and the King's Horsemen, 1975, Opera Wonyosi, 1978; (novels) The Interpreters, 1964, The Forest of a Thousand Demons, Idanre and Other Poems, 1967; Season of Anomy, 1973; (non-fiction) The Man Died; (poetry) Poems of Black Africa, 1975, Orgun Abibman, 1977, A Shuttle in the Crypt, 1972. Mem. Am. Acad. Arts and Letters. Office: Univ of Ife, Ile-Ife Nigeria *

SOYRIS, DOMINIQUE, psychiatrist; b. Montpellier, Herault, France, Dec. 10, 1954. MD, U. Montpellier, 1979. Practice medicine Beziers, France, 1980-82; intern 1982-86, resident, 1986—. Roman Catholic. Home: 165 Ave Charles de Gaulle, 92200 Neuilly sur Seine France Office: Hopital Bichat, 46 Rue Henri Huchard, 75018 Paris France also: Hopital Victor DuPour, Rue du Colonnel Prudhom, 95107 Argenteuil France

SOYUGENC, RAHMI, manufacturing exec.; b. Pazarcik, Turkey, May 5, 1931; s. Ismail and Ayse S.; came to U.S., 1954, naturalized, 1965; B.S. in Indsl. Engring., U. Evansville, 1959; M.S. in Indsl. Engring., Ill. Inst. Tech., 1964; m. Marjori Zurstadt, Sept. 10, 1960; children—Altay Yakup, Perihan Ayla. Systems analyst Am. Nat. Bank & Trust Co., Chgo., 1960-63; chief of ops. Chgo. Bd. Health, 1963-70; pres. Evansville Metal Products Co. (Ind.), 1970—, Keller St. Corp., Evansville, 1973—, pres., Nat. Anodizing and Plating Co., 1985—. Founder, dir. The Chicago Mosque. Recipient Meritorious Service award Chgo. Heart Assn., 1963, 66. Mem. Inst. Indsl. Engrs., Ops. Research Soc. Am., Am. Soc. Quality Control (chpt. pres.), Tri-State Council for Sci. and Engring. (region pres.), Turkish Am. Cultural Alliance (charter). Moslem. Clubs: Petroleum, Evansville Country. Lodge: Rotary. Home: 119 LaDonna St Evansville IN 47711 Office: Keller St Corp 2100 N 6th Ave Evansville IN 47710

SOZA, DUSHAN TRAVICE COLUMBAN, data processing executive; b. Colombo, Sri Lanka, July 16, 1956; s. Dudley Columban and Hyacinth Regina (Fernando) S. BSc in Elec. Engring. with honors, U. Reading, Eng., 1980. Design engr. Xionics Ltd., London, 1980-82; chief engr. Datatech Ltd., Colombo, 1982-87; gen. mgr. sales Computerlin Data Systems, Colombo, 1987—; dir. Bus. Forms Ltd., Colombo. Mem. Gen. Engring. Enterprise (dir.). Lodge: Rotary (bd. dirs. 1986-89). Home: 69/7 Bodhiraja Mawatha, Welikade Rajagiriya Sri Lanka

SPADOTTO, BEVERLY THERESE, editor; b. Syracuse, N.Y., July 11, 1951; d. Ted and Beverly Jean (Loughlin) S.; BA in Journalism, George Washington U., 1973; MA, U. So. Calif., 1975. Dir. pub. relations D'Arcy-MacManus & Masius, advt., Los Angeles, 1976-78; editor Rangefinder mag., Santa Monica, Calif., 1978-81; communications editor CJGNA Healthplans of Calif., Glendale, Calif., 1982-85; dir. communications U.S. Adminstrs., Inc., 1985—; owner BTS Prodns., Los Angeles, 1988—. Mem. Western Publs. Assn., Publicity Club Los Angeles, Sigma Delta Chi. Democrat. Roman Catholic. Home: 410 S Hobart Blvd Los Angeles CA 90020

SPAEH, WINFRIED HEINRICH, banker; b. Essen, W. Germany, Dec. 23, 1930; came to U.S., 1972; s. Josef and Anna (Belker) S.; Abitur, Gymnasium Essen-Werden, 1951; postgrad. Columbia U., 1961-62; m. Waltraut Schab, Aug. 15, 1964; children: Andrea, Olivier. With Dresdner Bank, Essen and Düsseldorf, 1951-60; with internat. banking div. Morgan Guaranty Trust Co. of N.Y., N.Y.C., 1961-66, v.p. German offices, Frankfurt, 1969, gen. mgr., 1972; exec. mgr. Dresdner Bank AG, Frankfurt/Main., 1975, dep. of mng. dirs., 1979-82, sr. officer, N.Y.C., 1982—; dir. Dresdner (SE Asia) Ltd., Singapore, 1978-80, Aseambankers Malaysia Berhad, Kuala Lumpur, 1977-80, P.T. Asian and Euro-Am. Capital Corp. Ltd., Jakarta, 1977-80. Mem. Deutsch-Australische Gesellschaft, Steuben-Schurz Gesellschaft, Nat. Planning Assn. (exec. com.), Inst. German Studies (bd. dirs. 1983—), Bankers Assn. Fgn. Trade (internat. adv. council 1982—), German-Am. C. of C. (bd. dirs. 1985—). Clubs: Overseas Bankers (London); Munchener Herrenclub; Union Internat. (bd. dir. 1981—) (Frankfurt); Belle Haven (Greenwich, Conn.). Home: 18 Calhoun Dr Greenwich CT 06830 Office: Dresdner Bank AG 60 Broad St New York NY 10004 also: Juergen-Ponto-Platz 1, Frankfurt Fed Republic Germany

SPAHICH, EKREM (ECK), journalist, realtor; b. Tuzla, Bosnia, Yugoslavia, Jan. 15, 1945; came to U.S., 1960, naturalized, 1966; s. Mo and Devleta H. (Aliefendic) S.; B.A. in Journalism, West Tex. State U., 1969, postgrad., 1972-84; m. Helen Sue Reid, Apr. 20, 1973; children—Michael, Holly. Public info. officer Borger unit Tex. Army N.G., 1972-73; area corr. Amarillo (Tex.) Daily News and Globe-Times, Sta. KVII-TV, Amarillo, 1972-88; reporter Borger (Tex.) News-Herald, 1972-78, asst. editor, 1978-79, editor, 1979-83; corr. UPI wire service, Dallas, 1980—; bd. dirs. Borger Satellite Workshop Ctr. Publicity dir. Hutchinson County Hist. Commn., 1975—; mem. Hutchinson County Sch. Bd., 1975-78, City of Borger Sports Commn., 1979-80. Served with U.S. Army, 1969-71. Decorated Bronze Star; named outstanding com. chmn., Tex. Hist. Commn., 1978, Tex. Hist. Found., Kerrville, 1979. Mem. Nat. Assn. Realtors, Panhandle Press Assn. (dir. 1980-82), VFW, Am. Legion, Borger Soccer Assn. (founding pres., 1978), Croatian Philatelic and Numismatic Soc. (founder, exec. dir.), Sigma Delta Chi. Baptist. Lodge: Order DeMolay (adv. council Borger chpt. 1977-81; various awards). Researcher Croatian history, philately and numismatism. Home: 1512 Lancelot Borger TX 79007

SPAIN, JAMES WILLIAM, foreign service officer, educator; b. Chgo., July 22, 1926; s. Patrick Joseph and Mary Ellen (Forristal) S.; m. Edith Burke James, Feb. 21, 1951; children: Patrick, Sikandra, Stephen, William. M.A., U. Chgo., 1949; Ph.D., Columbia U., 1959. Cons. sec. army 1949-50; with U.S. Fgn. Service, 1951-53; researcher, lectr. Columbia, 1955-62; mem. policy planning council State Dept., 1963-64; dir. Office Research and Analysis for Near East and South Asia, 1964-66; country dir. for Pakistan and Afghanistan, 1966-69; charge d'affaires Am. embassy, Rawapindi, 1969; consul gen. Istanbul, Turkey, 1970-72; minister Am. embassy, Ankara, 1972-74; diplomat-in-residence, vis. prof. history and govt. Fla. State U., Tallahassee, 1974-75; ambassador to Tanzania Dar es Salaam, 1975-79; ambassador to Turkey Ankara, 1980-81; ambassador to Sri Lanka 1985—; fgn. affairs fellow Carnegie Endowment for Internat. Peace and Rand Corp., Washington, 1982-84; adj. prof. polit. sci. Am. U., Washington, 1965-67. Author: The Way of the Pathans, 1962, The Pathan Borderland, 1963, American Diplomacy in Turkey, 1984. Served with U.S. Army, 1946-47, PTO. Fellow Ford Found., 1953-55; recipient Presdl. Exec. award, 1983. Mem. Middle East Inst., Council Fgn. Relations, Am. Fgn. Service Assn., Royal Central Asian Soc. Club: Cosmos (Washington). Address: US Ambassador to Sri Lanka care US State Dept Washington DC 20520

SPAIN, NETTIE EDWARDS (MRS. FRANK E. SPAIN), civic worker; b. Alexandria, La., Oct. 9, 1918; d. John Henry and Sallie Tamson (Donald) Edwards; student Alexandria Bus. Coll., 1936-37, Birmingham-So. Coll., 1958-59, Nat. Tng. Inst., United Community Funds and Councils Am., 1965-66; m. Frank E. Spain, May 18, 1974. Reporter, Alexandria Daily Town Talk, 1942-45; staff writer Brimingham (Ala.) Post, 1945-49; pub. relations dir. Community Chest, Birmingham, 1949-53; dir. info. services Pa. United Fund, Phila., 1953-55; asst. exec. dir. Ala. Assn. Mental Health, Birmingham, 1956-57; pub. relations dir. United Appeal, Birmingham, 1958-68, asst. exec. dir., 1968-71; asst. to pres. for devel. U. Ala., Birmingham, 1971-74, acting dir., 1975. Mem. public relations com. Ala. Heart Assn., Birmingham, 1972-75; bd. dirs. Kate Duncan Smith DAR Sch., Grant, Ala., 1981-82; bd. dirs. Children's Aid Soc., 1971-77, 79, v.p., 1976-77; bd. dirs. Jefferson-Shelby Lung Assn., 1972-75, Vol. Bur. Greater Birmingham, 1973-77, Hale County chpt. ARC, Hale County Library; advisor fin. Hale County Library Bd., 1988; adv. com. Jr. League, 1974-75; exec. com. Historic Hale County Preservation Soc.; hon. mem. president's council U. Ala., Birmingham; bd. dirs. Norton Center Continuing Edn., Birmingham-So. Coll.; charter mem. bd. Birmingham Children's Theater. Recipient 1st Place awards Nat. Photos for Fedn., 1966-67; citation Pa. United Fund, 1955, citation for service Jefferson-Shelby Lung Assn., 1975, citation Ala. Heart Assn., 1974, Vol. Bur. Greater Birmingham, 1977; award of Merit, Ala. Hist. Commn., 1977, Disting. Serveice award, 1987; Rotary Found. Paul Harris fellow; Benjamin Franklin fellow Royal Soc. Arts, London, U.S.A.; Citation, Veritas Club, Great Am. Citizen of Greensboro, Ala., 1987. Mem. Nat. Public Relations Council of Health and Welfare Services (dir. 1967-69), Birmingham Women's Com. of 100, Public Relations Council Ala. (hon. life), Order of Crown in Am., Ala. Hist. Soc., Nat. Soc. Colonial Dames Am., Nat. Trust for Historic Preservation, Met. Opera Guild, Guy E. Snavely Soc. (Birmingham-So. Coll.), Colonial Dames Am., DAR, First Families of Va., Birmingham Astron. Soc. (hon.). Episcopalian. Clubs: Lakeview Country (Greensboro, Ala.); Mountain Brook Country, Relay House, The Club; Northriver Yacht (Tuscaloosa); Greensboro Study; Progress Study; Cauldron. Home: Medley Greensboro AL 36744

SPALDING, FRANKLIN MATTHEW, dentist; b. Peoria, Ill., Oct. 17, 1942; s. Franklin M. and Mary Rose (Conklin) S.; m. Sandra E. Woodward, July 3, 1971. Student, Marquette U., 1960-62, U. Ill., 1963; DDS, U. Ill., 1967. Gen. practice dentistry Peoria, 1969—. Served to commdr. USN, 1967-69. Mem. ADA, Ill. State Dental Assn., Chgo. Dental Assn., Peoria Dental Soc. Office: 2305 S Jefferson Peoria IL 61605

SPALDING, HENRY A., mining engineer; b. Ky., Mar. 20, 1899; s. J.D. and Alice (Estes) S.; studied under personal tutors; m. Gertrude Petrey, Feb. 8, 1923 (dec.); children—Jack P. (dec.), Richard D. Gen., widely diversified engring. practice; inventor metall. processes; pres. H.A. Spalding, Inc.; mgr., part owner Old Va. Land Co.; mem. adv. bd. Ky. Geol. Survey. Co. Recipient Outstanding Citizen award Hazard (Ky.) civic clubs, 1958. Registered profl. engr. Fellow ASCE; mem. Am. Inst. Mining, Metall. and Petroleum Engrs. (Legion of Honor), Ky. Soc. Profl. Engrs. (pres. 1949-50, hon.), Ky. Acad. Sci., Appalachian Geol. Soc., Ky. Hist. Soc. Club: Filson. Co-author: Engineers Vest Pocket Book; contbr. articles to profl. jours. Home: 608 Broadway Hazard KY 41701 Office: Baker Bldg Hazard Ky 41701 also: 603 Ring Bldg Washington DC 20009

SPALVINS, JANIS GUNARS, transportation executive; b. Riga, Lativa, May 26, 1936; arrived in Australia, 1949; s. Peter Spalvins and Hilda (Dritmanis) Blumentals; m. Cecily Westall Rymill, Dec. 16, 1961; children: John Rymill and Richard Rymill. Group sec., dir. Camelec Group of Cos., South Australia, 1955-73; asst. gen. mgr. The Adelaide Steamship Co. Ltd., South Australia, 1973-77, chief gen. mgr., dir., 1977-81, mng. dir., 1981; dir., chief exec. David Jones Ltd., Australia, 1980, 1988—; bd. dirs. Howard Smith Ltd., The Adelaide Steamship Co. Ltd. Group, David Jones Ltd. Group, D.J's Properties Ltd. Group, Epstein & Co. Ltd., John Martin Retailers Ltd., Macmahon Holdings Ltd., Metro Meat Ltd., Nat. Consol. Ltd. Group, Petersville Sleigh Ltd. Group, Tooth & Co. Ltd. Group, Markheath Securites PLC-UK. Fellow Australian Inst. Mgmt.; mem. Inst. Dirs., Bus. Council Australia. Home: 2 Brookside Rd, Springfield Sth 5062, Australia Office: Adelaide Steamship Co Ltd, 123 Greenhill Rd, Unley Sth 5061, Australia

SPANGLER, ARTHUR STEPHENSON, JR., mental health administrator; b. Boston, June 20, 1949; s. Arthur Stephenson and Barbara Louise (Fellows) S.; m. Deborah A. Kauders, Nov. 27, 1971; children—Heather Anita, Rebecca Haley. BS, Hobart Coll., 1971; MEd, Boston Coll., 1974; ScD, Boston U., 1985; bd. cert. counselor; lic. psychologist, Mass.; lic. clin. social worker. Mass. Counselor, Met. State Hosp., Waltham, Mass., 1971-73; rehab. counselor J.T. Berry Rehab. Center, North Reading, Mass., 1974-75; program coordinator Shore Collaborative, Medford, Mass., 1975-76; dir. instl. sch. programs So. Shore Collaborative, North Weymouth, Mass., 1976-79; dir. mental retardation program South Shore Mental Health Center, Quincy, Mass., 1979-85; coordinator Outpatient Clinic, Boston Pain Ctr., Spaulding Rehab. Hosp., Boston, 1985-86; v.p., dir. behavioral medicine services Delphi Ctr., Quincy, 1985—; dir. indsl. disability mgmt. services, psychologist chronic pain program Miriam Hosp., Providence, 1987-88. Vol. counselor Multi-Service Ctr., Newton, Mass., 1973-75; bd. dirs. Newton-Wellesley-Weston-Needham Community Mental Health and Mental Retardation Ctr., Newton, 1976-80, pres. 1979-80. Mem. Boston Symphony Assn. Vols. Recipient award Nat. Assn. Retarded Citizens, 1974. Mem. Am. Psychol. Assn. (assoc.), Nat. Rehab. Assn., Am. Assn. for Counseling and Devel., Council for Exceptional Children, Assn. for Persons with Severe Handicaps, Soc. Behavioral Medicine New Eng. Pain Assn. Episcopalian. Speaker profl. assn. confs.; contbr. articles to profl. jours. Home: 88 Church St Weston MA 02193 Office: 44 Billings Rd Quincy MA 02171

SPANGLER, DAISY KIRCHOFF, educational consultant; b. Lancaster, Pa., Jan. 27, 1913; d. Frank Augustus and Lida Flaharty (Forewood) Kirchoff; BS, Millersville State Coll., 1963; MEd, Pa. State U., 1966, EdD, 1972; PhD, Stanton U., 1974; m. Francis R. Cosgrove Spangler, June 3, 1939 (dec.); children: Stephen Russell, Michael Denis. Tchr. rural sch., Providence, Pa., 1933-35, Rapho Twp., Pa., 1935-42, Mastersonville, Pa., 1942-51; elem. sch. prin. Manheim Central, Pa., 1952-66; tchr., Manheim, Pa., 1967-68; assoc. prof. elem. edn. Millersville U., Pa., 1968-78, prof. emeritus, 1978—, advisor Kappa Delta Phi, 1968-88; ednl. cons., 1978—. Dist. chmn. ARC, 1965-66; mem. Hempfield PTA, 1966-67. Mem. Pa. Edn. Assn., Pa. Elem. Prins. Assn., Assn. Pa. State Coll. and Univ. Profs., Nat., Lancaster (pres. 1963-64) prins. assns., Pa. Assn. Ret. State Employees, Pa. Assn. State Retirees, Lancaster Area Ret. Pub. Sch. Employees Assn., Am. Ednl. Research Assn., Manheim Tchrs. Assn. (pres. 1964-65), Hempfield Profl. Women, Am. Assn. Ret. Persons (chpt. pres. 1983-85, 88-89), Pi Lambda Theta (nat. com. 1980—, advisor Millersville U. 1968—, named outstanding advisor 1988—), Delta Kappa Gamma (pres. 1976-78). Lutheran (pres. Luth. Women 1966-67, 79-81). Club: Order Eastern Star. Home and Office: Route 7 Box 510 Manheim PA 17545

SPANGLER, RONALD LEROY, television executive, aircraft distributor; b. York, Pa., Mar. 5, 1937; s. Ivan L. and Sevilla (Senft) S.; student U. Miami (Fla.), 1955-59; children—Kathleen, Ronald, Beth Anne. Radio announcer Sta. WSBA, York, 1955-57; TV producer-dir. Sta. WBAL-TV, Balt., 1959-65; pres., chmn. bd. LewRon Television, N.Y.C., 1965-74; pres., chmn. bd. Spanair Inc., distbr. Rockwell Comdr. aircraft, Forest Hill, Md.; owner Prancing Horse Farm. Mem. Video Tape Producers Assn. N.Y., Rolls Royce Owners Club, Ferrari Clubs Am. Avocations: racing Ferrari automobiles. Home: PO Box 47 Bel Air MD 21014-0047

SPANN, GEORGE WILLIAM, management consultant; b. Cuthbert, Ga., July 21, 1946; s. Glinn Linwood and Mary Grace (Hiller) S.; B.S. in Physics with honors, Ga. Inst. Tech., 1968, M.S., 1970, M.S. in Indsl. Mgmt., 1973; m. Laura Jeanne Nason, June 10, 1967; children: Tanya Lynne, Stephen William. Engr., Martin Marietta Corp., Orlando, Fla., 1968-70; research scientist Engring. Expt. Sta., Ga. Inst. Tech., 1970-75; v.p., dir. Metrics, Inc., mgmt. and engring. cons., Atlanta, 1973-78, pres., dir., 1978—; v.p., dir. Exec. Data Systems, Inc., 1981—; mem. Ga. Energy Policy Council, Ga. Metrication Council, NASA applications survey group for Landsat follow-on; mem. com. on practical applications of remote sensing from space Space Applications Bd. Nat. Research Council; market research cons. NOAA, NASA, pvt. cos. Regents scholar, 1964. Mem. Am. Soc. Photogrammetry, Urban and Regional Info. Systems Assn., Atlanta Jaycees, Tau Beta Pi, Phi Kappa Phi, Sigma Pi Sigma. Author papers, reports. Home: 3475 Clubland Dr Marietta GA 30067 Office: 1845 The Exchange Suite 140 Atlanta GA 30339

SPANN, KATHARINE DOYLE, marketing, communications executive; b. Holton, Kans.; d. Edward James and Josephine (Hurla) Doyle; B.S., Emporia State Coll.; m. Hugh J. Spann (div. Feb. 1952); 1 dau., Susan Katharine. V.p. Bozell & Jacobs Advt. (formerly L.C. Cole Co.), San Francisco, 1951-76; pres. Katharine Doyle Spann Assos., 1977—; propr. Kate's Vineyard, Napa Valley, Calif.; exec. producer TV shows Doctors News Conf., The Ben Alexander Show, Land of Jazz, 1956—; communications counsel to health professions, 1970—. Bd. dirs. Heritage Fund, Napa Valley Opera House. Named Advt. Woman of Year, 1962; recipient El Capitan award Peninsula chpt. Pub. Relations Soc. Am., 1962, 66, Am. Silver Anvil award, Pub. Relations Soc. Am., 1962, 66, Excellence award Publicity Club of Bay Area, 1966. Mem. Am. Soc. Enology, Napa Valley Women in Wine, Calif. Vintage Wine Soc. (wine com.), Conferie des Chevaliers du Tastevin (events com.), Delta Sigma Epsilon. Club: Metropolitan (San Francisco). Home: 1447 S Whitehall Ln Saint Helena CA 94574

SPANN, RONALD THOMAS, lawyer; b. Chgo., Aug. 27, 1949; s. Daniel Anthony and Lorraine Marie (Gervasio) S. Student Sophia U., Tokyo, 1969, St. Mary's Coll., Rome, 1970; AB, U. Notre Dame, 1971; postgrad. Fordham Law Sch., diploma internat. trade law U. Fla., Inst. State and Law, Warsaw, Poland, 1976, Trinity Coll., Cambridge U., 1976; JD, John Marshall Law Sch., Chgo., 1977. Bar: Ill. 1977, D.C. 1980, U.S. Dist. Ct. (no. dist.) Ill., U.S. Ct. Appeals (7th cir.), N.Y. 1984, Fla. 1984, U.S. Dist. Ct. (so. dist.) Fla., U.S. Supreme Ct., U.S. Ct. Appeals (11th cir.) Fla., 1985; lic. real estate and mortgage broker. Assoc. solicitor U.S. Dept. Labor; trial atty. EEOC; law clk. to chief judge U.S. Dist. Ct. (no. dist.) Ill.; lobbyist Trade Assn. Execs. Food Industry, Ill., D.C., Va., Baker & McKenzie, Chgo., 1972-74; ptnr. firm Newman & Spann, Chgo.; sr. ptnr. Spann & Assocs., P.A., Miami, Berk, Spann & Bernstein, Fort Lauderdale, Fla.; pres. mediation dir. U.S. Arbitration and Mediation Service of S.E., Am. Arbitration Assn.; prof. Internat. Cancer Inst.; Instr. Ednl. Seminars, Inc. Bd. dirs. Edgewater Community Council, Advs. for Human Rights, South Fla. Lanes, Inc.; corr. Amnesty Internat., U.S.A.; co-founder AID-Ctr. One, Lamda Legal Def. and Edn. Fund, Inc. Recipient Real Estate Rehabilitator award Chgo. City Council, 1981, Internat. Disting. Leadership award, Man of Achievement award Am. Biog. Inst. Mem. ABA (former chmn. internat. human rights com., draft Model "Whistleblower" and mcpl. civil rights codes), Chgo. Bar Assn., Fed. Bar Assn. (former bd. dirs. Chgo. chpt., chmn. internat. human rights com.), Assn. Trial Lawyers Am., Christian Legal Soc., Lawyers in Mensa, Fla. Bar Assn., Broward County Bar Assn., Soc. Profls. Dispute Resolution, Nat. Assn. Realtors, Assn. Mortgage Bankers (former chair alt. dispute resolution com.).

SPARBERG, MARSHALL STUART, gastroenterologist, educator; b. Chgo., IL, May 20, 1937; s. Max Shane and Mildred Rose (Haffron) S.; m. Eve Edna, Mar. 15, 1987. B.A., Northwestern U., 1957, M.D., 1960. Intern Evanston Hosp., Ill., 1960-61; resident in internal medicine Barnes Hosp., St. Louis, 1961-63; fellow U. Chgo., 1963-65; practice medicine specializing in gastroenterolgy Chgo., 1967—; asst. prof. medicine Northwestern U., 1967-72, assoc. prof., 1972-80, prof. clin. medicine, 1980—; instr. Washington U., St. Louis, 1961-63, U. Chgo., 1963-65. Author: Ileostomy Care, 1969, Primer of Clinical Diagnosis, 1972, Ulcerative Colitis, 1978, Inflammatory Bowel Disease, 1982; contbr. numerous articles to profl. jours. Pres. Fine Arts Music Found., 1974-76; bd. dirs. Lyric Opera Guild, 1974—, Chamber Music Chgo., 1978-84; founding mem. Chamber Music Soc. North Shore, Chgo., 1984—. Served with USAF, 1965-67. Named Outstanding Tchr. Northwestern U. Med. Sch., 1972. Mem. AMA, ACP, Am. Gastroent. Assn., Chgo. Med. Soc., Chgo. Soc. Internal Medicine, Chgo. Soc. Gastroenterology (pres.), Chgo. Soc. Gastrointestinal Endoscopy (pres.). Democrat. Jewish. Office: 233 E Erie St Chicago IL 60611

SPARK, MURIEL SARAH, writer; b. Edinburgh, Scotland; d. Bernard and Sarah Elizabeth Maud (Uezzell) Camberg; (marriage dissolved); 1 son. Student, James Gillespie's Sch. for Girls, Edinburgh. Gen. sec. Poetry Soc., also editor Poetry Rev., 1947-49. Author: critical and biographical Child of Light, a Reassessement of Mary Shelley, 1951, John Masefield, 1953, (With D. Stanford) Emily Bronte: Her Life and Work, 1953, Mary Shelley, 1987; poems The Fanfarlo and Other Verse, 1952; fiction The Comforters, 1957, Robinson, 1958, The Go-Away Bird, 1958, Memento Mori (adapted for stage 1964, 1959, The Ballad of Peckham Rye, 1960 (Italian prize for dramatic radio 1962), The Bachelors, 1960, Voices at Play, 1961, The Prime of Miss Jean Brodie, 1961 (adapted for stage 1966, for film 1969, for TV 1978), The Girls of Slender Means, 1963 (adapted for TV 1974), The Mandelbaum Gate, 1965 (James Tait Black Meml Prize 1965), The Public Image, 1968, The Driver's Seat, 1970 (adapted for film 1972), Not to Disturb, 1971, The Hothouse by the East River, 1973, The Abbess of Crewe, 1974 (adapted as film Nasty Habits 1976), The Takeover, 1976, Territorial Rights, 1979, Loitering with Intent, 1981, Collected Stories I, 1967, Collected Poems I, 1967, The Stories of Muriel Spark, 1985 (Best Fgn. Collection of Short Stories, French NAC, 1987), The Only Problem, 1985, A Far Cry from Kensington, 1988; play Doctors of Philosophy, 1963; children's book The Very Fine Clock, 1969; Editor: (with D. Stanford) Tribute to Wordsworth, 1950, Selected Poems of Emily Bronte, 1952, The Bronte Letters, 1954, (with D. Stanford) Letters of John Henry Newman, 1957, My Best Mary, Selected Letters of Mary Shelley, 1953. Decorated Order Brit. Empire. Hon. mem. AAAL. Address: care Harold Ober Assocs 40 E 49th St New York NY 10017

SPARKS, BILLY SCHLEY, lawyer; b. Marshall, Mo., Oct. 1, 1923; s. John and Clarinda (Schley) S.; A.B., Harvard, 1945, LL.B., 1949; student Mass. Inst. Tech., 1943-44; m. Dorothy O. Stone, May 14, 1946; children—Stephen Stone, Susan Lee Sparks Raben, John David. Admitted to Mo. bar, 1949; partner Langworthy, Matz & Linde, Kansas City, Mo., 1949-62, firm Linde, Thomson, Fairchild Langworthy, Kohn & Van Dyke, 1962—. Mem. Mission (Kans.) Planning Council, 1954-63; mem. Kans. Civil Service Commn., 1975—. Mem. dist. 110 Sch. Bd., 1964-69, pres., 1967-69; mem. Dist. 512 Sch. Bd., 1969-73, pres., 1971-72; del. Dem. Nat. Conv., 1964; candidate for representative 10th Dist., Kans., 1956, 3d district, 1962; treas. Johnson County (Kans.) Dem. Central com., 1958-64. Served to lt. USAAF, 1944-46. Mem. Kansas City C. of C. (legis. com. 1956-82), Am., Kansas City bar assns., Mo. Bar, Law Assn. Kansas City, Harvard Law Sch. Assn. Mo. (past dir.), Nat. Assn. Sch. Bds. (mem. legislative com. 1968-73), St. Andrews Soc. Mem. Christian Ch. (trustee). Clubs: Harvard (v.p. 1953-54), The Kansas City (Kansas City, Mo.); Milburn Golf and Country. Home: 8517 W 90th Terr Shawnee Mission KS 66212 Office: City Center Sq 12th & Baltimore Sts Kansas City MO 64105

SPARKS, MEREDITH PLEASANT (MRS. WILLIAM J. SPARKS), lawyer; b. Palestine, Ill.; d. John L. and Laura (Bicknell) Pleasant; A.B. with distinction, Ind. U., 1927, A.M., 1928; Ph.D., U. Ill., 1936; J.D., Rutgers U., 1958; m. William J. Sparks, Dec. 31, 1930 (dec.); children—Ruth Sparks Foster, Katherine Sparks Crowl, Charles, John. Tchr. chemistry Rochester (Ind.) High Sch., 1928-29; chemist DuPont Co., Niagara Falls, N.Y., 1929-34, Northam Warren Co., N.Y.C., 1939; chem. patent agt. Am. Cyanamid Co., Bound Brook N.J., 1941-46; bars: Fla. 1958, U.S. Ct. Appeals (fed. cir.), U.S. Dist. Ct. (so. dist.) Fla., U.S. Supreme Ct.; patent agt., 1946-58; patent atty., 1958—; pres. Sparks Innovators, Inc., 1979-84. Recipient Disting. Alumni award Ind. U., 1987. Mem. Assn. Ind. U. Chemists (pres. 1950-51), Internat., Am., Fla., Coral Gables Bar Assns., Am., N.J., South Fla. patent law assns., Internat. Patent and Trademark Assn., Am. Chem. Soc., Nat. Assn. Women Lawyers (pres. 1981-82), AAUW, U. Ill. Pres. Council (life, homecoming honoree 1984), Phi Beta Kappa, Sigma Xi, Kappa Delta. Club: Zonta, Riviera Country (Coral Gables). Contbr. articles to profl. jours. Patentee in field. Home: 5129 Granada Blvd Coral Gables FL 33146 Office: The Law Center 370 Minorca Ave Coral Gables FL 33134

SPARKS, (THEO) MERRILL, entertainer, translator, poet; b. Mount Etna, Iowa, Oct. 5, 1922; s. David G. and Ollie M. (Hickman) S.; student U. Besancon (France), 1945; BA, U. So. Calif., 1948; postgrad. U. Iowa, 1948-51, Columbia U., 1951-52. Entertainer as singer, pianist, Los Angeles, Midwest, Fla., N.Y., N.J. areas, 1953—. Served with AUS, 1942-46. Co-recipient P.E.N. transl. award, 1968, Cross of Merit with Vernon Duke for cantata Anima Eroica, Order of St. Brigida, Rome, 1966. Mem. Am. Fedn. Musicians, Authors Guild, The Songwriters Guild, Vista, The Nat. Icarian Heritage Soc, ASCAP, Icarian Players, Modern Poetry Assn., Iowa Friends of the Library, Iowa Geneal. Soc. Composer songs including Sleepy Village,

1942, A Heart of Gold, 1956, Anima Eroica, 1966, An Italian Voyage, 1976, O Come and Join the Angels, 1982, Ballad of Ollie and Bart, 1983, Elegy, 1987, Ave Maria, 1988. poems pub. in mags. including Western Rev., Choice, Coastlines, South & West, N.Y. Rev. Books; poems included in: Arts of Russia, Primer of Experimental Poetry, The Portable 20th Century Russian Reader; play (musical) Icaria, 1986; co-editor, co-translator (with Vladimir Markov) Modern Russian Poetry, 1967. Club: Rotary. Home: PO Box 8 Mount Etna IA 50855 Office: 4620 SE 4th St #104 Des Moines IA 50315

SPAUN, WILLIAM BECKER, lawyer, retired; b. Atchison, Kans., Aug. 22, 1913; s. Floyd and Bertha (Becker) S.; J.D., U. Mo., Kansas City, 1936; m. Sidney Clyde Collins, Sept. 13, 1930 (dec.); 1 dau., Theon Spaun Martin; m. 2d, Mary Louise Robinson, Aug. 5, 1948 (dec.); children—William Becker, Mary Lou Spaun Montgomery, Robert R., Sarah Jean Fletcher, Shirley Anne Schindler. Admitted to Mo. bar, 1937; U.S. Supreme Ct., 1960; practice law, Hannibal, Mo., 1937-86; charter mem. World Peace Through Law Center, participant Washington conf., 1965. Regional fund chmn. ARC, 1961, nat. staff mem., 1943-44, nat. vice chmn. fund campaigns, 1963-64, local chpt. chmn., 1977-82; govt. appeal agt. SSS, 1968-72, chmn., 1972—. Recipient award for meritorious personal service WW II from ARC. Fellow Am. Coll. Probate Counsel, Harry S. Truman Library Inst. (hon.); mem. Am., Tenth Jud. Circuit (pres. 1958-60) bar assns., Mo. Bar (chmn. Law Day 1961, asso. editor jour. 1942-43), Am. Judicature Soc., Scribes. Republican.

SPEAR, HARVEY MILTON, lawyer; b. Providence, May 24, 1922; s. Alfred and Esther (Marcus) S.; m. Ruth Abramson, June 27, 1965; children: Jessica Eve, Elizabeth Anne. A.B., Brown U., 1942; LL.B., Harvard, 1948; M.A., George Washington U., 1949, LL.M., 1952, S.J.D., 1955. Bar: Mass. 1948, D.C. 1948, N.Y. 1954, U.S. Supreme Ct. 1954; C.P.A., Md. Asst. U.S. atty. D.C. 1948; legal asst. to chmn., asst. to vice chmn. SEC, 1948-50; spl. asst. to atty. gen., tax div. Dept. Justice, 1951-54; pvt. practice law N.Y.C., Washington, London, 1956—; sr. ptnr. Spear & Hill, N.Y.C., 1958-72; counsel Spear & Hill, 1972-75, Davis & Cox, N.Y.C., 1978-82, Cadwalader, Wickersham & Taft, N.Y.C., 1982—. Contbr. articles to legal jours. Treas. N.Y. County Democratic Com., 1963—; mem. Met. Opera Assn., 1961—; founding trustee Harlem Prep. Sch., 1967; vice chmn. Am. council Internat. U., Rome, Italy, 1972—; sec.-treas., bd. dirs. London Philharmonic Soc. (USA), Inc., 1968—. Served to maj. USMCR, 1942-45. Mem. ABA, N.Y. State Bar Assn., Bar Assn. City N.Y., Am. Inst. C.P.A.s. Home: 765 Park Ave New York NY 10021 also: Hither Ln East Hampton NY 11937 Office: 100 Maiden Ln New York NY 10038

SPEAR, HILDA D., language professional; b. Pinner, Middlesex, Eng., Aug. 27, 1926; d. Joseph Charles and Blanche E. (Collins) King; m. Walter E. Spear, Dec. 14, 1952; children: Gillian F., Kathryn A. BA with honors, U. London, 1951, MA, 1953; PhD, U. Leicester, 1972. Cert. tchr., Eng., 1946. Tchr. English London County Council, 1946-48, Leicester City Council, Eng., 1953-54; tutor English Leicester U., 1954-56; lectr. English Purdue U., West Lafayette, Ind., 1956-57, City Colls. Edn., Leicester, 1957-60; lectr. edn. Leicester U., 1965-67, lectr. English, 1967-68; lectr. English Dundee U., Scotland, 1969-87, sr. lectr., 1987—. Author: Remembering, We Forget, 1979 (Scottish Arts Council, Brit. Acad. and Carnegie awards 1979); co-author: Forster in Egypt, 1987; editor: Poems and Letters of C. H. Sorley (Scottish Arts Council award 1978), 1978, English Poems of C. S. Calverley, 1974; contbr. articles and revs. to profl. jours. Judge English-Speaking Union Debates, Scotland, 1977—, Scotsman Inter-Varsity Debates, 1982, 88; mem. panel Scottish Arts Council, Edinburgh, 1980-86. Fellow Internat. Biog. Assn. (life); mem. English Assn., Assn. Univ. Tchrs. Avocations: reading, writing, traveling, walking, animals. Office: Dundee U, Dundee, Angus DD1 4HN, Scotland

SPEARMAN, PATSY CORDLE, real estate broker; b. Richmond, Va., Aug. 23, 1934; d. Lee Pierce and Kathleen Jeanette (Munn) Cordle; m. David Hagood Spearman, Dec. 18, 1954; children: Kathleen Elizabeth, David Hagood. AA, Coll. William and Mary, Richmond, 1952; student, U. Ga., 1953-54; grad., Realtors Inst., 1979. Copywriter Cabell Eanes Advt. Agy., Richmond, 1952; clk. athletic dept. U. Ga., Athens, 1954-55; real estate saleswoman C. Dan Joyner & Co., Inc. (now Merrill Lynch Realty), Greenville, S.C., 1978—. Past pres. Women of Ch.; Presbyn. ch. Sunday sch. tchr. and youth leader. Recipient numerous awards for obtaining eye bank donors Lions Club and S.C. Eye Bank. Mem. Nat. Assn. Realtors (cert. residential specialist), Real Estate Securities and Syndication Inst., S.C. Assn. Realtors, Greenville Bd. Realtors, Pickens County Bd. Realtors (chmn. community services com.), Women's Council of Realtors, Million Dollar Club (charter, Greenville and Pickens County), Am. Vet. M.A. Aux., S.C. Vet. Aux. (treas.), Nat. Wildlife Fedn. (life), World Wildlife Fedn., Audubon Soc., Cousteau Soc., Smithsonian Inst. Clubs: Better Homes (Easley), Commerce (Greenville). Home: 505 Asbury Circle Easley SC 29640 Office: PO Box 327 Easley SC 29641

SPEARS, MARY ELLEN, psychologist, educator; b. Decatur, Ala., July 14, 1922; d. Andrew D. and Minnie Lucille (Dodson) Wiley; m. William D. Spears, June 8, 1974; children—Rebecca, William Dodson, Robert Andrew. B.S., Eastern Ky. U., 1944; M.S., Miss. State U., 1960; Ed.D., Auburn U., 1971. Teaching asst. Auburn U., 1968-70, instr. founds. of edn., 1970-72; asso. prof. behavioral scis. Pensacola (Fla.) Jr. Coll., 1972-78, prof. psychology and behavioral scis., head dept. behavioral scis., 1978—, dean Sch. Scis. and Social Scis., 1985—. Editor: Readings for Psychology and Youth, 1973. Mem. Southeastern Psychol. Assn., Am. Psychol. Assn., Northwestern Fla. Psychol. Assn., AAUW (sec. Auburn U. br. 1968-72, chmn. ednl. founds. Pensacola br. 1974-76), Psi Chi, Phi Delta Kappa, Delta Kappa Gamma. Democrat. Baptist. Home: 4556 Sabine Dr Gulf Breeze FL 32561 Office: 1000 College Blvd Pensacola FL 32504

SPECK, GEORGE, gynecologist; b. Boston, Jan. 4, 1911; s. Morris and Betty (Dulman) S.; student Harvard U., 1928-29; B.S. (with distinction) U. Mich., 1937; M.D. (with distinction), George Washington U., 1941; m. Doris Jean Deford, (dec.); m. Sylvia Salomon, Dec. 30, 1962; children—Besty Ellen Schlesinger, Betsy Ellen Nuell, David George. Intern, Cooper Hosp., Camden, N.J., 1941-42; resident in ob-gyn Bellevue Hosp., N.Y.C., 1942-45; instr. ob-gyn N.Y. U. Sch. Medicine, N.Y.C., 1943-45; clin. instr. preventive medicine George Washington U. Sch. Medicine, Washington, 1946-47, asst. clin. prof. ob-gyn, 1967—; clin. instr. Howard U., Washington, 1950-51. Trustee, Blue Shield of D.C., 1971—; mem. Alexandria (Va.) Public Health Adv. Commn., 1975-77. Diplomate Am. Bd. Ob-Gyn. Recipient Merit award George Washington U. Med. Alumni Assn., 1968, Alumni Service award, 1966. Fellow Am. Coll. Obstetricians and Gynecologists (founding), Internat. Coll. Surgeons, Am. Fertility Soc., Internat. Fertility Assn.; mem. Phi Beta Kappa. Contbr. articles to profl. jours. Address: 4324C Evergreen Ln Annandale VA 22003-3211

SPECK, HILDA, social worker; b. Stalybridge, Cheshire, England, Mar. 2, 1916; came to U.S., 1923; d. John Robert and Rose Ethel (Tymns) Smith; m. Wilmott Hilton Speck, Sept. 4, 1937 (dec. Jan 1968); foster children: Barbara Ann Beranek Renfrow, Winifred June Beranak Aguilar. Grad. high sch., Flint, Mich. Lic. social worker, Mich. Dir. social services The Salvation Army, Flint, 1945—; mem. establishing com. 4C Child Care Agy. Assisted in establishing Safe House for Victims of Domestic Violence, Flint, 1976-80; mem. Churchwomen United Convalescent Home; appt. clothing distbn. administr., Flint Civil Def.; mem. Red Feather Million Dollar Disaster Fund com. United Way, 1953; administered Salvation Army Rehab. Program, 1953; mem. Day Care co,m., Genesee County; mem. origional planning com. Planned Parent Orgn. Recipient Hands of Mercy award The Salvation Army, 1967, Centennial Youth award The Salvation Army, 1965, 20 Year Service award Big Brothers of Genesee County; named Woman of Week local radio sta., 1987. Mem. Council of Social Agys., Genesee County Commn. on Aging (v.p. 1971—), GLS Counties Health Planning Council Bd., Genesee County Emergency Task Force. Lodge: Zonta. Home: 2015 Stoney Brook Ct Flint MI 48507

SPECTER, ARLEN, U.S. senator; b. Wichita, Kans., Feb. 12, 1930; s. Harry and Lillie (Shanin) S.; m. Joan L. Levy, June 14, 1953; children: Shanin, Stephen. Student, U. Okla., 1947-48; B.A., U. Pa., 1951; LL.B., Yale U., 1956. Asst. counsel Warren Commn., Washington, 1964; magisterial investigator Commn. of Pa., 1965; dist. atty. City of Phila., 1966-74; ptnr. Dechert Price & Rhoads, Phila., 1974-80; mem. U.S. Senate from Pa., 1980—; lectr. law Temple U., 1972-75, U. Pa., 1968-72. Contbr. articls to profl. jours. Served to 1st U.S. Army, 1951-53. Recipient Youth Services award B'nai B'rith, 1966; recipient Sons of Italy award, 1968, Community Humanitarian award Baptist Ch., 1969, Man of Yr. award Temple Beth Ami, 1971, N.E. Catholic Outstanding Achivement award, 1973. Mem. Phi Beta Kappa. Republican. Jewish. Office: US Senate 331 Senate Hart Bldg Washington DC 20510 *

SPECTER, MELVIN H., lawyer; b. East Chicago, Ind., July 12, 1903; s. Moses and Sadie (Rossuck) S.; A.B., U. Mich., 1925; J.D., U. Chgo., 1928; m. Nellie Rubenstein, Feb. 1, 1927; children—Lois, Michael Joseph. Admitted to Ind. bar, 1928; individual practice law, East Chicago, Ind. 1928—. Bd. dirs. ARC (chpt. chmn. 1940-46), Community Chest Assn., Salvation Army Adv. Bd., pres., 1930-35; bd. dirs. Vis. Nurse Assn., pres., 1943-44; bd. dirs. East Chgo. Boys Club, 1958-65; trustee East Chicago Pub. Library, 1956-80, pres., 1957-67; pres. Anselm Forum, 1957-58; chmn. Brotherhood Week NCCJ, East Chicago, 1958-61; exec. bd. Twin City council Boy Scouts Am.; city chmn. U. Chgo. Alumni Found. Fund, 1951-55. Awarded James Couzen Medal for Inter-collegiate debate, U. Mich., 1924; citation for distinguished pub. service, U. Chgo. Alumni Assn., 1958. Citizenship award Community Chest Assn., 1965. Mem. Am. Ind. (del.), East Chicago (pres. 1942-44) bar assns., Am. Judicature Soc., Comml. Law League Am., Community Concert Assn. (dir. 1950-55), Wig and Robe Frat., Phi Beta Kappa, Delta Sigma Rho. Elk (exalted ruler 1945), K.P., Kiwanian (dir. 1946, 49-51, 52-55, pres. 1961); mem. B'nai B'rith. Home: 4213 Baring Ave East Chicago IN 46312 Office: 804 W 145th St East Chicago IN 46312

SPECTER, RICHARD BRUCE, lawyer; b. Phila., Sept. 6, 1952; s. Jacob E. and Marilyn B. (Kron) S.; m. Jill Ossenfort, May 30, 1981; children: Lauren Elizabeth, Lindsey Anne. BA cum laude, Washington U., St. Louis, 1974; JD, George Washington U., 1977. Bar: Mo. 1977, U.S. Dist. Ct. (ea. and we. dists.) Mo. 1977, U.S. Ct. Appeals (8th cir.) 1977, Ill. 1978, Pa. 1978, U.S. Dist. Ct. (ea. dist.) Ill. 1979, U.S. Ct. Appeals (7th cir.) 1979, Calif. 1984, U.S. Dist. Ct. (cen. dist.) Calif. 1985, U.S. Ct. Appeals (9th cir.) 1986, U.S. Dist. Ct. (so. dist.) Calif. 1987. Assoc. Coburn, Croft, Shepherd, Herzog & Putzell, St. Louis, 1977-79; ptnr. Herzog, Kral, Burroughs & Specter, St. Louis, 1979-82; exec. v.p. Uniqey Internat., Santa Ana, Calif., 1982-84; sole practice Los Angeles and Irvine, Calif., 1984-87; ptnr. Corbett & Steelman, Irvine, 1987—; instr. Nat. Law Ctr. George Washington U. 1975. Mem. ABA, Ill. Bar Assn., Mo. Bar Assn., Pa. Bar Assn., Calif. Bar Assn. Jewish. Home: 37 Bull Run Irvine CA 92720 Office: 18200 Von Karman Ave Suite 200 Irvine CA 92715

SPECTOR, JOHANNA LICHTENBERG, ethnomusicologist, educator emeritus; b. Libau, Latvia; came to U.S., 1947, naturalized, 1954; d. Jacob C. and Anna (Meyer) Lichtenberg; m. Robert Spector, Nov. 20, 1939 (dec. Dec. 1941). D.H.S., Hebrew Union Coll., 1950; M.A., Columbia U., 1960. Research fellow Hebrew U., Jerusalem, 1951-53; faculty Jewish Theol. Sem. Am., 1954—, dir., founder dept. ethnomusicology, 1962-85, assoc. prof. musicology, 1966-70, Sem. prof., 1970-85, prof. emeritus, 1985—. Author: Ghetto-und Kzlieder, 1947, Samaritan Chant, 1965, Musical Tradition and Innovation in Central Asia, 1966, Bridal Songs from Sana Yemen, 1960; documentary film The Samaritans, 1971, Middle Eastern Music, 1973, About the Jews of India: Cochin, 1976 (Cine Golden Eagle 1979), The Shanwar Telis or Bene Israel of India, 1978 (Cine Golden Eagle 1979), About the Jews of Yemen, A Vanishing Culture, 1986 (Cine Golden Eagle 1986, Blue Ribbon, Am. Film Festival 1986); religious and folk recs. number over 10, 000; contbr. articles to encys., various jours.; editorial bd. Asian Music. Fellow Am. Anthrop. Assn.; mem. Am. Ethnol. Soc., Am. Musicol. Soc., Internat. Folk Music Council, World Assn. Jewish Studies, Yivo, Asian Mus. Soc. (v.p. 1964—, pres. 1974-78), African Mus. Soc., Soc. Ethnomusicology (sec.-treas N.Y.C. chapt. 1960-64), Soc. Preservation of Samaritan Culture (founder). Home: 400 W 119th St New York NY 10027

SPEECE, RICHARD EUGENE, civil engineer, educator; b. Marion, Ohio, Aug. 23, 1933; s. Irvin Ward S. and Desta May (Speece); m. Jean Margaret Edscorn, Nov. 15, 1969; children: Eric Jordan, Lincoln Dana. B.C.E., Fenn. Coll., 1956; M.E., Yale U., 1958; Ph.D., MIT, 1961. Assoc. prof. civil engring. U. Ill., Urbana, 1961-65; prof. N.Mex. State U., 1965-70, U. Tex., Austin, 1970-74; Betz chair prof. environ. engring. Drexel U., Phila., 1974-88; Centennial prof. Vanderbilt U., Nashville, 1988—; cons. to govt., industry. Contbr. articles to profl. jours.; patentee in field. Recipient hon. mention for best paper Trans. Am. Fisheries Soc., 1973. Mem. Assn. Environ. Engring. Profs. (Disting. Faculty award 1970, disting. lectr. 1978, trustee 1981-83 Engring. Sci. award), ASCE (J. James Cross medal 1983), Am. Soc. Microbiologists, Water Pollution Control Fedn. (Harrison Prescott Eddy medal 1966), Am. Water Works Assn. Office: Vanderbilt U. Nashville TN 37235

SPEER, WILLIAM THOMAS, JR., banker; b. Boston, Feb. 17, 1936; s. William Thomas and Marie Dorothy (DeWolfe) S.; m. Glenda Jane Farris, Nov. 15, 1972; children: Jason Farris, Tyson DeWolfe, Courtland Conley, William Thomas III. A.A., Marin Jr. Coll., Kentfield, Calif., 1955; B.A. in Bus., Calif. State U.-Fullerton, 1962; postgrad. U. Calif.-San Francisco, 1955-56. Bank examiner Fed. Res. Bank, 1962-67, 68-70; exec. v.p. First Nat. Bank, Cañon City, Colo., 1967-68; v.p., then sr. v.p. Bank of Idaho, Boise, 1970-74; sr. v.p. Bank of N.Mex., Albuquerque, 1975; prin. organizer, founder, pres., chief exec. officer Am. Bank of Commerce, Boise, 1975—, also dir.; developer Willowgrove Estates, Meridian, Idaho, Rivers Bend Condominiums, McCall, Idaho; guest lectr. Boise State U.; cons. in field. Contbr. articles to profl. jours. Bd. dirs. Idaho chpt. Am. Heart Assn., 1983, chmn. bd., 1985; bd. dirs. Boise Philharm., 1984; active Pub. TV Sta., 1981-83. Served with U.S. Army, 1957-61. Recipient gov.'s appreciation award Idaho-Oreg. Lions Club, 1982. Mem. Am. Bankers Assn., Idaho Bankers Assn. (exec. council), Western Ind. Bankers Assn., Idaho Ind. Bankers Assn. (pres. 1986), Robert Morris Assocs., Nat. Assn. Home Builders, U.S. Indsl. Council, Greater Boise C. of C., Nat. Fedn. Ind. Bus., Idaho Water Users Assn. Clubs: Boise State U., Ducks Unltd., Hillcrest Country, Centurion. Lodge: Elks. Home: 1820 Montclair Dr Boise ID 83702 Office: 6850 Fairview Ave Boise ID 83704

SPELFOGEL, EVAN J., lawyer; b. Boston, Jan. 28, 1936; s. Morris R. and Helen S. (Steinberg) S.; m. Beverly Kolenberg; children—Scott, Douglas, Karen. A.B., Harvard U., 1956; J.D., Columbia U., 1959. Bar: Mass. 1959, N.Y. 1964, U.S. Supreme Ct. 1969. Atty., Office of Solicitor, U.S. Dept. Labor, Washington and Boston, 1959-60; atty. NLRB, Boston and N.Y.C., 1960-64; assoc. Simpson, Thacher & Bartlett, N.Y.C., 1964-69, Dewey, Ballantine, Bushby, Palmer & Wood, N.Y.C., 1969-77; ptnr. Fellner, Rovins & Gallay, N.Y.C., 1977-80, Summit, Rovins & Feldesman, N.Y.C., 1981—; adj. prof. law Baruch Coll., CCNY. Mem. ABA (sect. on labor and employment law, exec. council 1978-86, co-editor sect. newsletter 1976—, mem. ho. dels. 1987—), Fed. Bar Assn. (council on labor law), N.Y. State Bar Assn. (chmn. labor and employment law sect. 1977-78, exec. council 1975—, ho. of dels. 1978-79, com. on profl. discipline 1987—), Assn. of Bar of City of N.Y. (labor com. 1968-71, 87—), Am. Arbitration Assn. (nat. panel labor arbitrators), Phi Alpha Delta. Club: Harvard Varsity. Bd. editors Developing Labor Law: The Board, The Courts and the National Labor Relations Act, also co-editor-in-chief Supplements; contbr. articles to profl. jours. Home: 17 Parkside Dr Great Neck NY 11021 Office: 445 Park Ave New York NY 10022

SPELLER, ROBERT ERNEST BLAKEFIELD, book publisher; b. Chgo., Jan. 19, 1908; s. John Ernest and Florence (Larson) S.; m. Maxine Elliott Watkins; children—Robert Ernest Blakefield, Jon Patterson. Student Columbia U., 1929. Mng. editor Fgn. Press Service, 1930-31; pres. Mohawk Press, 1931-32, Robert Speller Pub. Corp., 1934-52, Record Concerts Corp., 1940-53, Robert Speller & Sons, Pubs., Inc., 1955—, Norellyn Press, Inc., 1960-83, Transglobal News Service, Inc., 1960—; pub. Hough's Ency. Am. Woods, 1957—; chmn. bd., pres., chief exec. officer Nat. Resources Publs., Inc., 1968-84; pres., dir. Transglobal Resources Devel. Corp., 1983—; pub. East Europe Mag., 1970—; sec., dir. Encoder Research & Devel. Corp., 1971—, Pecos Internat., Inc., 1974-77; v.p., dir. Pecos Western Corp. of Del., 1973-83; pres., chmn. bd. VTL Corp., 1986-87; pres. Contender Corp., 1986-87; dir. Gen. Research Corp., Fashion Form Mfg. Corp. Mem. founding bd. USO; trustee Philippa Schuyler Meml. Found. Served with Signal Corps, AUS, 1944-45. Founder Gourmet Soc. Club: Columbia U. (N.Y.C.). Office: 115 E 9th St New York NY 10003

SPELLMAN, DOUGLAS TOBY, advertising executive; b. Bronx, N.Y., May 12, 1942; s. Sydney M. and Leah B. (Rosenberg) S.; BS, Fairleigh Dickinson U., 1964; m. Ronni I. Epstein, Jan. 16, 1966 (div. Mar. 1985); children: Laurel Nicole, Daren Scott; m. Michelle Ward, Dec. 31, 1986. Media buyer Doyle, Dane, Bernbach, Inc., N.Y.C., 1964-66, Needham, Harper & Steers, Inc., N.Y.C., 1966; media supr. Ogilvy & Mather, Inc., N.Y.C., 1967-69; media dir. Sinay Advt., Los Angeles, 1969-70; chief ops. officer S.H.H. Creative Mktg., Inc., Los Angeles, 1969—; assoc. media dir. Warren, Mullen, Dolobowsky, Inc., N.Y.C., 1970—; dir. West Coast ops. Ed Libov Assocs., Inc., Los Angeles, 1970-71; media supr. Carson/Roberts Advt. div. Ogilvy & Mather, Inc., Los Angeles, 1971-72; assoc. media dir. Ogilvy & Mather, Inc., Los Angeles, 1972-73; media dir. Vitt Media Internat., Inc., Los Angeles, 1973-74; v.p., dir. West Coast ops. Ind. Media Services, Inc., Los Angeles, 1974-75; owner Douglas T. Spellman, Inc., Los Angeles, 1975-77, pres., chmn. bd., 1977-82; pres., chief operating officer Douglas T. Spellman Co. div. Ad Mktg., Inc., Los Angeles, 1982-85; pres., chief exec. officer, chmn. bd. Spellbound Prodns. and Spellman Media divs. Spellbound Communications, Inc., Los Angeles, 1984-86; gen. ptnr. Faso & Spellman, Los Angeles, 1984-86; chief operating officer, pres. Yacht Mgmt. Internat., Ltd., Los Angeles, 1984-86; v.p. media Snyder, Longino Advt. div. Snyder Advt., Los Angeles, 1985-86; advt./media cons., Los Angeles, 1986—; guest lectr. sch. bus UCLA, 1975, U. So. Calif., 1976. Served with U.S. Army Res. N.G., 1964-69. Mem. Aircraft Owners and Pilots Assn., Nat. Rifle Assn., Phi Zeta Kappa, Phi Omega Epsilon. Jewish. Clubs: Rolls Royce Owners, Mercedes Benz Am., Aston Martin Owners. Office: PO Box 180 Beverly Hills CA 90213

SPELLMAN, JOHN DAVID, electrical engineer; b. Beaver Dam, Wis., July 27, 1935; s. John Joseph and Elsie Marguerite (Schultz) S.; B.S. in Elec. Engring., U. Wis., 1959; m. Kathleen Burns King, May 26, 1972; stepchildren—Kathleen Biegel, Karen Silva, Kimberly Lyon. Jr. engr., part time, Malleable Iron Range Co., Beaver Dam, 1952-59; mem. tech. staff Rockwell Internat., Anaheim, Calif., 1961-85, lead engr., 1969-78, 81-85; mgr. ground instrumentation ops. unit Rockwell Internat., Vandenberg AFB, 1985—; cons. Data Processing, Santa Maria, Calif., 1965. Served to 1st lt. Signal Corps, AUS, 1959-61. Recipient U.S. Army Accomodation award, 1961, USAF Outstanding Achievement award for Civilian Personnel. Mem. Assn. Computing Machinery, Air Force Assn., Res. Officers Assn. Clubs: Birnam Wood Golf (Montecito, Calif.); Santa Maria Country. Contbr. publs. on minutemen data systems, PCM Telemetry systems. Home: 642 Meadowbrook Santa Maria CA 93455 Office: PO Box 5181 Vandenberg AFB CA 93437

SPELMAN, GRACE SUSAN, bank official; b. N.Y.C., Oct. 14, 1948; d. Marco A. and Gloria (Alvino) Vale; BS, Pa. State U., 1970; MA, New Sch. for Social Research, 1974; cert. in mgmt. Adelphi U., 1979, MBA, 1980. Bus. office rep. N.Y. Telephone Co., Rockville Centre, 1971-74; social worker Children's Aid Soc., N.Y.C., 1974-75; EEO officer Edwin Gould Services, N.Y.C., 1976-79; v.p. fin. instns. Bankers Trust Co., N.Y.C., 1979—; instr. mgmt. Adelphi U. Grad. Sch. Bus. Adminstrn., 1981—; notary pub. State N.Y., 1978—. Mem. Human Resource Planning Soc., Assn. MBA Execs., Am. Compensation Assn., Wall St. Compensation and Benefits Assn., N.Y. Compensation Assn., Adelphi U. Businesswomen's Alumni Assn. (pres. 1980-82). Office: 1 Bankers Trust Plaza New York NY 10017

SPENCE, JOHN DANIEL, real estate broker; b. Lethbridge, Alberta, Can., May 18, 1915; came to U.S., 1915, naturalized, 1943; s. Benjamin Abner and Clara May (Fullerton) S.; m. Phyllis Saxton Johnson, Feb. 4, 1939; children: Susan Kathleen Spence-Glassberg, John Daniel. A.B., Grinnell (Iowa) Coll., 1938; LL.D. (hon.), Rockford Coll., 1979. With Container Corp. Am., 1938-54, v.p., 1949-54; exec. Lanzit Corrugated Box Co., Chgo., from 1954; v.p. Consol. Paper Co., 1963; dir. devel. Rockford Coll., 1964-65, v.p., 1965-77, acting pres., 1977-79, cons., 1979—; bus. and ednl. cons., 1980—. Pres. Woodcrest Assn., Rockford, 1974-78; mem. adv. com. Forest Preserve Dist., Winnebago County, 1974—; chmn. adv. council Severson Dells Forest Preserve, 1976—; bd. dirs. John Howard Assn., to 1974-76; trustee Keith Country Day Sch., 1971-81, Children's Home of Rockford, 1973-76, Lake Forest Acad., to 1975, Pecatonica Prairie Path, 1975-85, Rockford Art Assn., 1980-83, Ctr. for Sight and Hearing Impaired, 1986—; trustee Highview Retirement Home, 1983—, pres., 1986-88, mem. community adv. bd. WNIU-FM, No. Ill. U., 1984—. Recipient Karl L. Williams award Rockford Coll. Alumni Assn., 1980, Service Above Self award Rockford Rotary Club, 1980. Mem. Profl. Secs. Internat. (adv. com.), Rockford C. of C. (dir. 1966-71, v.p.). Club: University (Chgo.). Lodge: Lions. Home and Office: 6710 Woodcrest Pkwy Rockford IL 61109

SPENCE, NICOL, language educator; b. Harare, Zimbabwe, July 29, 1924; s. William and Marie Rose (Tockert) S.; m. Andrée Henriette Friedrich, July 11, 1959; children: Robert Paul, Anita Rosemary. BA in Modern Langs., U. Leeds, Eng., 1948; PhD in Romance Philology, U. London, 1955. Asst. lectr. Queen's U., Belfast, Ireland, 1951-54, lectr., 1955-61, reader, 1961-66; asst. lectr. U. Coll. North Staffordshire, Keele, Eng., 1954-55; reader U. London Bedford Coll., 1966-79, prof. French linguistics, 1979-84. Author: A Glossary of Jersey French, 1960, poéme dé 12e siucle, 1964, Essays in Linguistics, 1976, Le Francais Contemporain, 1976; contbr. numerous articles to profl. jours. Mem. Soc. of Romance Linguistics, Soc. French Studies. Anglican. Home: Le Cresson Grande Route de Rozel, Saint Martin Jersey, Channel Islands

SPENCER, BILLIE JANE, lawyer; b. Caro, Mich., Sept. 16, 1949; d. William Norman and Jane Isabel (Putnam) S. AB in Econs., U. Miami, Coral Gables, Fla., 1971, LLM in Tax, 1980; JD, U. Fla., Gainesville, 1973; course cert. St. Catherine's Coll., Oxford U., 1973; grad. with highest distinction, Naval War Coll., Washington, 1988. Bar: Fla., Calif. Assoc. Frates Floyd, et. al., Miami, Fla., 1973-74; commd. lt. (j.g.) USNR, 1974, advanced through grades to comdr., 1988; judge advocate USNR, Subic Bay, Pensacola, 1975-78; sole practice San Francisco, and Stuart, Fla., 1978-85; asst. staff judge advocate USNR, Lemoore, Calif., 1982-83; DOD liaison USNR, Washington, 1985-88; civilian atty. USN, Mechanicsburg, Pa., 1988—; instr. econs. Fla. Inst. Tech., Jensen Beach, 1984-85; litigation cons. Castle & Cooke, Inc., San Francisco, 1979-83; clk. Ehrlichmann Watergate Trial team, Washington, 1974; del. state conf. on small bus., 1982. Mem. U.S. Naval Inst., Res. Officers Assn., The Navy League, Am. Mgmt. Assn. Republican. Unitarian. Home: 1441 Hillcrest Ct #202 Camp Hill PA 17011

SPENCER, EDSON WHITE, computer systems company executive; b. Chgo., June 4, 1926; s. William M. and Gertrude (White) S. Student, Princeton, 1943, Northwestern U., U. Mich., 1944; B.A., Williams Coll., 1948; M.A., Oxford (Eng.) U., 1950. With Sears, Roebuck & Co., Chgo., 1951-54, Honeywell, Inc., Mpls., 1954—; Far East regional mgr. Honeywell, Inc., Tokyo, 1959-65; corp. v.p. internat. ops. Honeywell, Inc., Mpls., 1965-69, exec. v.p., 1969-74, pres., chief exec. officer, 1974-78, chief exec. officer, 1978-87, chmn. bd., 1978—. Mem. Phi Beta Kappa. Office: Honeywell Inc Honeywell Plaza Minneapolis MN 55408 *

SPENCER, HARRY CHADWICK, minister; b. Chgo., Apr. 10, 1905; s. John Carroll and Jessie Grace (Chadwick) S.; m. Mary Louise Wakefield, May 26, 1935; children: Mary Grace Spencer Lyman, Ralph Wakefield. B.A., Willamette U., 1925, D.D. (hon.), 1953; M.Div., Garrett Bibl. Inst., 1929; M.A., Harvard U., 1932. Ordained to ministry Meth. Ch., 1931; pastor Washington Heights Ch., Chgo., 1931-33, Portage Park Ch., Chgo., 1933-35; rec. sec. bd. missions Meth. Ch., 1935-40, asst. exec. sec., 1940-45, sec. dept. visual edn., 1945-52, exec. sec. radio and film commn., 1952-56, gen. sec. TV, radio and film commn., 1956-68, asso. gen. sec. program council div. TV, radio and film communication, 1968-72; asso. exec. sec. joint commn. on communications United Meth. Ch., 1972, ret., 1973; sec. mass media, world div. Bd. Missions and Ch. Extension, 1964-72; Mem. exec. com. Nat. Council Chs. Broadcasting and Film Commn., 1952-73, chmn., 1960-63; mem. exec. com. Nat. Council Chs., 1960-63, mem. gen. bd., 1967-72, v.p. Central div. communications, 1969-72; chmn. constituting assembly World Assn. for Christian Broadcasting, 1963; mem. constituting assembly World Assn. Christian Communication, 1968, dir. assembly, 1975;

mem. adminstrv. com. Ravemco, 1950-70, Intermedia, 1970-72; vis. prof. Garrett Evang. Theol. Sem., 1975; lectr. in field. Exec. producer: TV series Learning to Live; radio series Night Call; motion pictures John Wesley, etc.; Contbr. articles on films to ch. publs. Trustee Scarritt Coll., 1967-74, emeritus, 1974—; bd. dirs. Outlook Nashville, 1977-83, sec., 1980; bd. dirs. Nashville chpt. UN Assn., 1976-83. Recipient award excellence art communications Claremont Sch. Theology, 1973; inducted into United Meth. Communicators Hall of Fame, 1983. Mem. United Meth. Assn. Communicators, World Assn. Christian Communications. Clubs: Kiwanis (Woodmont); Harvard (Nashville). Home: PO Box 150063 Nashville TN 37215

SPENCER, JOHN, surgery educator; b. Bedford, Eng., July 17, 1933; s. Arthur George and Nellie (Housden) S.; m. Gwyneth Ann Griffiths, Dec. 5, 1958; children: Stephen Mark, Joanna Mary, Helen Clare, Timothy Paul, Anthony John. MB, BS, U. London, 1957, MS, 1976. House surgeon Harrow Hosp., London, 1957; house physician Charing Cross Hosp., London, 1958; med. officer Uganda Med. Service, 1958-61; surg. registrar Bath City Hosps., Eng., 1962-64; surg. registrar Hammersmith Hosp., London, 1964-66, sr. surg. registrar, 1966-69; sr. lectr. Royal Postgrad. Med. Sch., London, 1970-87, reader in surgery, 1987—. Research fellow UCLA, 1969-70. Fellow Royal Soc. Medicine, Assn. Surgeons U.K.; mem. Brit. Soc. Gastroenterology, Surg. Research Soc. Home: 99 Brunswick Rd, London W5 1AQ, England Office: Royal Postgrad Med Sch, Ducane Rd, London W12 OHS, England

SPENCER, MARY MILLER, civic worker; b. Comanche, Tex., May 25, 1924; d. Aaron Gaynor and Alma (Grissom) Miller; 1 child, Mara Lynn. BS, North Tex. State U., 1943. Cafeteria dir. Mercedes (Tex.) Pub. Schs., 1943-46; home economist coordinator All-Orange Dessert Contest, Fla. Citrus Commn., Lakeland, 1959-62, 64; tchr. purchasing sch. lunch dept. Fla. Dept. Edn., 1960. Clothing judge Polk County (Fla.) Youth Fair, 1951-68, Polk County Federated Women's Clubs, 1964-66; pres. Dixieland Elem. Sch. PTA, 1955-57, Polk County Council PTA's, 1958-60; chmn. public edn. com. Polk County unit Am. Cancer Soc., 1959-60, bd. dirs., 1962-70; charter mem., bd. dirs. Lakeland YMCA, 1962-72; sec. Greater Lakeland Community Nursing Council, 1965-72; trustee, vice chmn. Polk County Eye Clinic, Inc., 1962-64, pres., 1964-82; bd. dirs. Polk County Scholarship and Loan Fund, 1962-70; mem. exec. com. West Polk County (Fla.) Community Welfare Council, 1960-62, 65-68; mem. budget and audit com. Greater Lakeland United Fund, 1960-62, bd. dirs., 1967-70, residential chmn. fund drive, 1968; mem. adv. bd. Polk County Juvenile and Domestic Relations Ct., 1960-69; worker children's services div. family services Dept. Health and Rehab. Services, State of Fla., 1969-70, social worker, 1970-72, 74-82, social worker OFR unit, 1977-81, pub. assistance specialist IV, 1984-88. Mem. exec. com. Suncoast Health Council, 1968-71; mem. Polk County Home Econs. Adv. Com., 1965-71; sec. bd. dirs. Fla. West Coast Ednl. TV, 1960-81; bd. dirs. Lake Region United Way, Winter Haven, 1976-81; mem. Polk County Community Services Council, 1978—. Mem. Nat. Welfare Fraud Assn., Fla. Congress Parents and Tchrs. (hon. life; pres. dist. 7 1961-63, chmn. pub. relations 1962-66), AAUW (pres. Lakeland br. 1960-61), Polk County Mental Health Assn., Fla. Health and Welfare Council, Fla. Health and Social Service Council, North Tex. State U. Alumni Assn. Democrat. Methodist. Lodge: Order of Eastern Star. Home: 535 W Beacon Rd Lakeland FL 33803 Mailing Address: PO Box 2161 Lakeland FL 33806

SPENCER, W(ALTER) THOMAS, lawyer; b. Crawfordsville, Ind., Aug. 6, 1928; s. Walter White and Jean Anna (Springer) S.; m. Patricia Audrey Raia, Mar. 30, 1974; children—Thomas Alfred, Jamie Raia. Student Wabash Coll., Crawfordsville, 1946-47; A.B., U. Miami-Coral Gables, 1950, J.D., 1956. Bar: Fla. 1956, U.S. Dist. Ct. (so. dist.) Fla. 1957, U.S. Dist. Ct. (no. dist.) Fla. 1963, U.S. Ct. Appeals (11th cir.) 1981, U.S. Supreme Ct. 1984. Assoc., Dean, Adams & Fischer, Miami, 1957-63; ptnr. Spencer & Taylor (George), Miami, 1963-81, Spencer & Taylor (Arthur), Miami, 1981—; mem. Fla. Ho. Reps., 1963-66; mem. Fla. Senate, 1966-68. Served to lt. USNR, 1952-55. Mem. ABA, Dade County Bar Assn., Am. Judicature Soc., Def. Research Inst., Fla. Def. Lawyers Assn. Democrat. Methodist. Clubs: Riviera Country, Coral Gables Country (Coral Gables); Bath (Miami Beach, Fla.). Home: 4520 Santa Maria St Coral Gables FL 33146 Office: Spencer & Taylor 19 W Flagler St Suite 1107 Miami FL 33130

SPENCER, WILLIAM EDWIN, telephone company executive, engineer; b. Kansas City, Mo., Mar. 22, 1926; s. Erwin Blanc and Edith Marie (Peterson) S.; student U. Kansas City, 1942; A.S., Kansas City Jr. Coll., 1945; B.S. in E.E., U. Mo., 1948; postgrad. Iowa State U., 1969; m. Ferne Arlene Nieder, Nov. 14, 1952; children—Elizabeth Ann, Gary William, James Richard, Catherine Sue. With Southwestern Bell Telephone Co., Kansas City, Mo., 1948-50, Topeka, 1952-61, sr. engr., 1966-69, equipment maintenance engr., 1969-76, engring. ops. mgr., 1976-79, dist. mgr., 1979—; mem. tech. staff Bell Telephone Labs., N.Y.C., 1961-62, Holmdel, N.J., 1962-66; U.S. Senatorial Club, 1985—. Mem. Rep. Presdl. Task Force, 1984—. Served with AUS, 1950-52. Recipient best Kans. idea award Southwestern Bell Telephone Co., 1972, cert. of appreciation Kans. Miss Teen Pageant, 1984. Registered profl. engr., Kans. Mem. Kans. Engring. Soc., Nat. Soc. Profl. Engrs., IEEE, Topeka Engrs. Club (past pres.), Telephone Pioneers Assn. (pres.), Nat. Geog. Soc., Kans. Hist. Soc., Am. Assn. Ret. Persons, U. Mo.-Columbia Alumni Assn., Nat. Travel Club. Republican. Patentee in field. Home: 3201 MacVicar Ct Topeka KS 66611 Office: 220 E 6th St Topeka KS 66603

SPENCER, WILLIAM HURLBUT FORCE, writer; b. Newport, R.I., Aug. 13, 1929; s. Lorillard and Katherine Emmet (Force) S.; m. Louise Thatcher Jones, Feb. 2, 1956 (div. Mar. 1960); children: William Force, Elizabeth Driggs; m. Valerie Taylor, Dec. 23, 1961. BS, Yale U., 1951; MS, U. Bridgeport, 1963. Tchr. Math. Fairfield (Conn.) Sch. System, 1957-72; owner, operator Lion's Paw Yacht, Antigua, 1972-79; dir. water sports Long Bay Hotel, Antigua, 1979-80; writer, researcher Antigua, 1980—. Author: Guide to the Birds of Antigua, 1981, Market, Kitchen & Table, A Bilingual Dictionary of Food, 1985. Served to lt. USN, 1951-54. Republican. Episcopalian.

SPENDER, SIR STEPHEN (HAROLD) K., poet, educator; b. Feb. 28, 1909; s. Edward Harold and Violet Hilda (Schuster) S.; m. Agnes Marie Inez, 1936; m. Natasha Litvin, 1941; 2 children. Ed. Oxford U.; D.Litt. (hon.), Montpellier U., Cornell Coll., Loyola U. Co-editor Horizon mag., 1939-41, Encounter, 1953-67; Elliston chair of poetry U. Cin., 1953; Beckman prof. U. Calif., 1959; vis. lectr. Northwestern U., Evanston, Ill., 1963; cons. poetry in English, Library of Congress, Washington, 1965; Clark lectr. Cambridge U., 1966; Mellon lectr., Washington, 1968; Northcliffe lectr. U. London, 1969; pres. English Ctr., PEN Internat., 1975—. Author: 20 Poems; Poems, the Destructive Element, 1934; The Burning Cactus, 1936; Forward from Liberalism, 1937; Trial of a Judge (verse play), 1937; Poems for Spain, 1939; The Still Centre, 1939; Ruins and Visions, 1941; Life and the Poet, 1942; Citizens in War and After, 1945; Poems of Dedication, 1946; European Witness, 1946; The Edge of Being, 1949; essay in The God That Failed, 1949; World Within World (autobiography), 1951; Learning Laughter (travels in Israel), 1952; The Creative Element, 1953; Collected Poems, 1954; The Making of a Poem, 1955; Engaged in Writing (stories), 1958; Schiller's Mary Stuart (transl.), 1958 (staged at Old Vic 1961); The Struggle of the Modern, 1963; Selected Poems, 1965; The Year of the Young Rebels, 1969; The Generous Days (poems), 1971; editor: A Choice of Shelley's Verse, 1971; D.H. Lawrence: novelist, poet, prophet, 1973; Love-Hate Relations, 1974; T.S. Eliot, 1975; W.H. Auden: a tribute, 1975; The Thirties and After, 1978; (with David Hockney) China Diary, 1982; Oedipus Triology (transl.), 1983 (staged Oxford Playhouse 1983); Journals 1939-1982, 1985; Collected Poems 1930-1985, 1985; (novel) The Temple, 1988. Inst. Advanced Studies fellow Wesleyan U., 1967; Oxford U. hon. fellow, 1973; decorated Queen's Gold medal for Poetry, 1971. Mem. Am. Acad. Arts and Letters (hon.), Nat. Inst. Arts and Letters (hon.), Phi Beta Kappa (hon.). *

SPENGLER, BRUNO, ambassador of Federal Republic of Germany to Papua New Guinea; b. Munich, Ger., Aug. 3, 1927; s. Emil and Anna (Goebel) S.; m. Karin Maentel, Feb. 14, 1967; 1 child, Gundula. Vice-consul, Istanbul, Turkey, 1961-65, Izmir, 1965-67; 2d sec., Islamabad, Pakistan, 1967-70; stationed Fgn. Office, Bonn, 1970-76; 1st sec., Kinshasa, Zaire, 1977-80, counselor, Paris, 1980-84; ambassador to Papua, New Guinea, Port Moresby, 1984—. Office: Embassy of Fed Republic Germany, PO Box 73, Port Moresby Papua New Guinea

SPERBER, DANIEL, physicist; b. Vienna, Austria, May 8, 1930; came to U.S., 1955, naturalized, 1967; s. Emanuel and Nelly (Liberman) S.; m. Ora Yuval, Nov. 29, 1963; 1 son, Ron Emanuel. M.Sc., Hebrew U., 1954; Ph.D., Princeton U., 1960. Tng. and research asst. Israel Inst. Tech., Haifa, 1954-55, Princeton U., 1955-60; sr. scientist, research adviser Ill. Inst. Tech. Research Inst., Chgo., 1960-67; asso. prof. physics Ill. Inst. Tech. Research Inst., 1964-67, Rensselaer Poly Inst., Troy, N.Y., 1967-72; prof. Rensselaer Poly Inst., 1972—; Nordita prof. Niels Bohr Inst., Copenhagen, 1973-74, NATO research fellow, vis., profl., 1974-77; vis. prof. G.S.I., Darmstadt, Fed. Republic Germany, 1983; sr. Fulbright research scholar, Saha Inst. Nuclear Physics, Calcutta, India, 1987-88. Contbr. 100 sci. papers to profl. jours. Served to capt. Israeli Army, 1950-52. Fellow Am. Phys. Soc.; mem. Israel Phys. Soc., N.Y. Acad. Scis., Sigma Xi. Jewish. Home: 1 Taylor Ln Troy NY 12180 Office: Dept Physics Renssalaer Poly Inst Troy NY 12181

SPERBER, PHILIP, business consultant, writer; b. N.Y.C., Feb. 29, 1944; s. Sol and Sally (Dolsky) S.; m. Doreen Faye Strachman, Dec. 27, 1969; children: Shoshana, Ryan, Sara, Jason. BS, N.J. Inst. Tech., 1965; JD, U. Md., 1969. Bar: Md., D.C., U.S. Ct. Appeals, U.S. Supreme Ct. Sales mgr. N.J. Electronics Corp., Kenilworth, N.J., 1965-68; ptnr. Blair, Olcutt, Sperber & Evans, Washington, 1968-71; v.p. Cavitron Corp., N.Y.C., 1971-77; group exec. Internat. Telephone & Telegraph Corp., Nutley, N.J., 1977-79; pres. REFAC Internat., Ltd., N.Y.C., 1979—; pres. APRO Sci., Morristown, N.J., 1975—, PDS Industries, Convent Station, N.J., 1977—; chmn. The Negotiating Group, Morris Twp., N.J., 1975—; mng. ptnr. Bear Devel. Group, Livingston, N.J., 1985—. Author: Intellectual Property Management, 1974 (N.J. Writers Conf. Citation 1975), Negotiating in Day-to-Day Business, 1976, The Science of Business Negotiation, 1979 (N.J. Writers Conf. Citation 1980), Corporation Law Department Manual, 1980 (N.J. Writers Conf. Citation 1981), Failsafe Business Negotiating, 1983 (N.J. Writers Conf. Citation 1984), Closing the Deal, 1985 (N.J. Writers Conf. Citation 1986), The Attorney's Practice Guide to Negotiations, 1985, International Transactions, 1986, A Negotiator's Views on How to Avoid Nuclear War, 1986, several others; over 90 pub. papers. Dir. N.J. Jaycees, Hillside, 1965-66, Md. Lions Internat., White Oak, 1970-71; pres. Runnymede Hills Civic Assn., Whippany, N.J., 1971-72, Consumer Clearinghouse, Morristown, N.J., 1977-78, Normandy Heights Civic Assn., Morris Twp.,N.J., 1986—; chmn., bd. trustees N.J. Literary Hall of Fame, Newark, 1986—; chmn. bd. trustees N.J. Inventors Congress and Hall of Fame, Newark, 1987—. Named one of Outstanding Young Men of Am. U.S. Jaycees, Tulsa, 1966; recipient Citation for Contbns. Am. Mktg. Assn., Newark, N.J., 1975, commendation for contbns. Am. Law Inst., Chgo., 1976, Plaque for Outstanding Performance Am. Mgmt. Assns., N.Y.C., 1978, Speaker Showcase award Internat. Platform Assn., Washington, 1983, Medal of Merit Pres. of U.S., Washington, 1987; decorated knight (hon.), Knights of Malta, Order of St. John of Jersalem, 1986. Fellow N.J. Inst. Tech. (alumni assn. council chmn. 1986—, Outstanding Alumnus award 1981); mem. Health Industry Mfrs. Assn. (del. 1976-77), Licensing Execs. Soc. (trustee 1977-79), Ultrasonic Industry Assn. (v.p. 1975-77), Am. Soc. for Testing and Materials (sect. chmn. 1976-77), ABA (legis. com. chmn. 1975-80), Am. Biog. Inst. (bd. dirs. 1986—), N.J. State Bar Assn. (councilman 1977-80), Am. Arbitration Assn. (judge; Outstanding Service award 1977), Am. Acad. Negotiation and Diplomacy (pres. 1984-86), Am. Inst. Chem. Engrs. (mktg. div.), IEEE (sr.), Tau Beta Pi (Eminent Engr. award 1986). Republican. Jewish. Clubs: President's (Newark); Sales and Internat. Execs. (N.Y.C.). Home: 30 Normandy Heights Rd Convent Station NJ 07961 Office: REFAC Internat Ltd 100 E 42d St New York NY 10017

SPERLICH, HAROLD KEITH, automobile company executive; b. Detroit, Dec. 1, 1929; s. Harold Christ and Elva Margaret (Stoker) S.; m. Polly A. Berryman, May 22, 1976; children: Sue, Scott, Terry L.; stepchildren: Laurie, Brian, Scott, Colleen. B.S. in Mech. Engring, U. Mich., 1951, M.B.A., 1961. With Aluminum Co. Am., 1951-54; v.p. car ops. Ford Motor Co., Detroit, 1957-77; v.p. product planning and design Chrysler Motors Corp., Highland Park, Mich., 1977-78, group v.p. engring., product devel., 1978-81, pres. N.Am. ops., 1981-84, pres., 1984-88, also dir. Active Detroit Community Fund. Served with USNR, 1954-57. Presbyterian. Club: Orchard Lake (Mich.) Country. Home: 3333 W Shore Dr Orchard Lake MI 48033 Office: Chrysler Motors Corp 12000 Chrysler Dr Highland Park MI 48288 *

SPERO, STANLEY LEONARD, broadcasting executive; b. Cleve., Oct. 17, 1919; s. Morris B. and Hermine (Harve) S.; m. Frieda Kessler, June 30, 1946; children—Laurie, Lisa, Leslie. BS cum laude, U. So. Calif., 1942; postgrad., Cleve. Coll., 1943. Account exec. Sta. WHKK, Akron, Ohio, 1946-48, Sta. KFAC, Los Angeles, 1948-52; account exec. Sta. KMPC, Hollywood, 1952-53, v.p., gen. sales mgr., 1953-68, v.p., gen. mgr., 1968-78; v.p. Golden West Broadcasters, 1978—; dir. Major Market Radio, Los Angeles, 1969. Pres. permanent charities com. entertainment industry, 1972; Served with U.S. Maritime Service, 1942-43. Mem. So. Calif. Broadcasters Assn. (chmn. 1972), Am. Advt. Fedn. (gov. 1972), Advt. Assn. West, Hollywood C. of C. (dir. 1972—, chmn. bd. dirs. 1985-87). Club: Hollywood Advertising (dir. 1972, pres. 1960-61). Home: 5027 Hayvenhurst St Encino CA 91436 Office: Sta KMPC 5858 Sunset Blvd Hollywood CA 90028

SPERRY, LEN T., psychiatry and preventive medicine educator; b. Milw., Dec. 1, 1943; s. Leonard V. and Wanda R. (Sadowski) S.; m. Patricia L. Garcia, June 11, 1977; children: Tracy, Christen, L. Timothy, Steven, Jonathon. BA, St. Mary's Coll., Winona, Minn., 1966; PhD, Northwestern U., 1970; MD, Centro Estudios Tecnologicos Universidad, Dominican Republic, 1981. Diplomate Am. Bd. Profl. Psychology, Am. Bd. Psychiatry and Neurology. Asst. prof. Marquette U., Milw., 1971-74; assoc. prof. U. Wis., Milw., 1974-75, U.S. Internat. U., San Diego, 1976-78; resident in psychiatry and preventive medicine Med. Coll. Wis., Milw., 1982-85; fellow in behavioral medicine U. Wis. Med. Sch., Milw., 1984-85; assoc. clin. prof. psychiatry, preventive medicine Med. Coll. Wis., Milw., 1986—; cons. Northeastern Ill. U., Chgo., 1970-71, Am. Appraisal Assn., Milw., 1972-76, Calif. Sch. Profl. Psychology, San Diego, 1977-79. Author: Learning Performance and Individual Differences, 1972, Together Experience, 1978; (with others) Contact Counseling, 1974, You Can Make It Happen: Self-Actualization and Organization, 1977, Adlerian Counseling and Psychotherapy, 1987; contbr. articles to profl. jours. Cons. mayoral campaign, South Bend, Ind., 1971. Northwestern U. fellow, 1969, Med. Coll. Wis. grantee, 1981. Mem. Am. Psychol. Assn. (sci. affair com. 1975-76), N. Am. Soc. Adlerian Psychology, Am. Psychiat. Assn., Assn. Christian Therapists, Wis. Psychiat. Assn. for Counselor Edn. and Supervision (chmn. publs. com., 1974-77).

SPERRY, ROGER WOLCOTT, neurobiologist, educator; b. Hartford, Conn., Aug. 20, 1913; s. Francis B. and Florence (Kraemer) S.; m. Norma G. Deupree, Dec. 28, 1949; children: Glenn Tad, Janeth Hope. B.A., Oberlin Coll., 1935, M.A., 1937, D.Sc. (hon.), 1982; Ph.D., U. Chgo., 1941, D.Sc. (hon.), 1977; D.Sc. (hon.), Cambridge U., 1972, Kenyon Coll., 1979, Rockefeller U., 1980. Research fellow Harvard and Yerkes Labs., 1941-46; asst. prof. anatomy U. Chgo., 1946-52, sect. chief Nat. Inst. Neurol. Diseases of NIH, also asso. prof. psychology, 1952-53; Hixon prof. psychobiology Calif. Inst. Tech., 1954-84, Trustee prof. Emeritus, 1984—; research brain orgn. and neural mechanism. Contbr. articles to profl. jours., chpts. to books.; Editorial bd.: Behavioral Biology. Recipient Oberlin Coll. Alumni citation, 1954; Howard Crosby Warren medal Soc. Exptl. Psychologists, 1969; Calif. Scientist of Year award Calif. Mus. Sci. and Industry, 1972; award Passano Found., 1973; Albert Lasker Basic Med. Research award, 1979; co-recipient William Thomas Wakeman Research award Nat. Paraplegia Found., 1972, Claude Bernard sci. journalism award, 1975, Disting. research award Internat. Visual Literacy Assn., 1979; Wolf Found. prize in medicine, 1979; Nobel prize in physiology or medicine, 1981, Realia award Inst. for Advanced Philos. Research, 1986. Fellow AAAS, Am. Acad. Arts and Scis., Am. Psychol. Assn. (recipient Distinguished Sci. Contbn. award 1971); mem. Royal Acad. (fgn. mem.), Nat. Acad. Scis., Am. Physiol. Soc., Am. Assn. Anatomists, Internat. Brain Research Orgn., Soc. for Study of Devel. and Growth, Psychonomic Soc., Am. Soc. Naturalists, Am. Zool. Soc., Soc. Developmental Biology, Am. Philos. Soc. (Lashley prize 1976), Am. Neurol. Assn. (hon.), Soc. for Neurosci., Internat. Soc. Devel. Biologists, AAUP, Pontifical Acad. Scis., Inst. for Advanced Philos. Research (Realia award 1986), Sigma Xi. Office: Calif Inst of Tech 1201 E California St Pasadena CA 91125 *

SPETNAGEL, THEODORE JOHN, civil engineer; b. Chillicothe, Ohio, May 26, 1948; s. Theodore S. and Lucille E. (Stuckey) S.; B.S., Clemson U., 1970; M.S., Ga. Inst. Tech., 1972; m. Nancy Carolyn Cunningham, Aug. 22, 1970; children—Theodore Allen, Elizabeth Graham. Engr., Appalachian Consulting Engrs., Kingsport, Tenn., 1967-70; design engr. Atlantic Building Systems, Atlanta, 1971-76, chief design engr., 1976-78; civil engr. Hdqrs., Ft. McPherson, Atlanta, 1978-79; chief minor constrn. sect. Hdqrs. U.S. Army Forces Command, Atlanta, 1979-84; dep. engr. Hdqrs. 2d U.S. Army, Forest Park, Ga. Timpanist, Atlanta Community Orch., 1977-80; deacon N.Decatur Presbyn. Ch., 1973-76, chmn. property com., 1975-76; elder Trinity Presbyn. Ch., 1978—, mem. choir, 1978-80, chmn. vol. personnel services com., 1980-81; bd. dirs. Wildwood Civic Assn., 1980—. Named Atlanta Young Engr. of Yr., 1980, 84; Atlanta Engr. of Yr. in Industry, 1977; Ga. Engr. of year in Govt., 1982; registered profl. engr., Ga., Ky., N.C., S.C., Tenn., Va., W.Va. Mem. Nat. Soc. Profl. Engrs. (bd. govs. Profl. Engrs. in Govt. div. 1981), ASCE, Ga. Soc. Profl. Engrs. (vice chmn. Profl. Engrs. in Govt. div. 1979-80, chmn. 1980-82), Atlanta Soc. Profl. Engrs. (dir. 1976-77, 79-80, treas. 1977-78), Soc. Am. Mil. Engrs. (asst. sec. Atlanta post 1981, dir. 1982-83), Tau Beta Pi, Chi Epsilon. Presbyterian. Home: 855 Kipling Dr NW Atlanta GA 30318 Office: Attn: AFKD-EN Ft Gillem Hdqrs 2d US Army Forest Park GA 30050

SPIEGEL, HERBERT, psychiatrist, educator; b. McKeesport, Pa., June 29, 1914; s. Samuel and Lena (Mendlowitz) S.; m. Natalie Shainess, Apr. 24, 1944 (div. Apr. 1965); children: David, Ann. B.S., U. Md., 1936, M.D., 1939. Diplomate: Am. Bd. Psychiatry. Intern St. Francis Hosp., Pitts., 1939-40; resident in psychiatry St. Elizabeth's Hosp., Washington, 1940-42; practice medicine specializing in psychiatry N.Y.C., 1946—; attending psychiatrist Columbia-Presbyn. Hosp., N.Y.C., 1960—; faculty psychiatry Columbia U. Coll. Physicians and Surgeons, 1960-82, spl. lectr., 1982—; adj. prof. psychology John Jay Coll. Criminal Justice, CUNY, 1983—; mem. faculty Sch. Mil. Neuropsychiatry, Mason Gen. Hosp., Brentwood, N.Y., 1944-46. Author: (with A. Kardiner) War Stress and Neurotic Illness, 1947, (with D. Spiegel) Trance and Treatment: Clinical Uses of Hypnosis, 1978; subject of book: (by Donald S. Connery) The Inner Source: Exploring Hypnosis with Herbert Spiegel, M.D.; Mem. editorial bd.: Preventive Medicine, 1972; Contbr. articles to profl. jours. Mem. profl. advisory com. Am. Health Found.; mem. pub. edn. com., smoking and health com. N.Y.C. div. Am. Cancer Soc.; mem. adv. com. Nat. Aid to Visually Handicapped. Served with M.C. AUS, 1942-46. Decorated Purple Heart. Fellow Am. Psychiat. Assn., Am. Coll. Psychiatrists, Am. Soc. Clin. Hypnosis, Am. Acad. Psychoanalysis, Internat. Soc. Clin. and Exptl. Hypnosis, William A. White Psychoanalytic Soc., N.Y. Acad. Medicine, N.Y. Acad. Scis.; mem. Am. Orthopsychiat. Assn., Am. Psychosomatic Soc., AAAS, AMA, N.Y. County Med. Soc. Office: 19 E 88th St New York NY 10128

SPIEGEL, SIEGMUND, architect; b. Gera, Germany, Nov. 13, 1919; s. Jakob and Sara (Precker) S.; ed. Coll. City N.Y., 1939-40, Columbia, 1945-50; m. Ruth Josias, Apr. 13, 1945; children—Sandra Renee, Deborah Joan. Came to U.S., 1938, naturalized, 1941. Draftsman, Mayer & Whittlesey, architects, N.Y.C., 1941-47, office mgr., 1947-55; pvt. practice architecture, East Meadow, N.Y., 1956—. Served with AUS, 1941-45; ETO. Decorated Purple Heart, Bronze Star, Croix de Guerre with palme (Belgium); recipient grand prize for instnl. bldgs. (for Syosset Hosp.), L.I. Assn., 1963; grand prize Human Resources Sch., 1966; grand prize Stony Brook Profl. Bldg., 1966; Beautification award, Town Hempstead, N.Y., 1969; Archi award for Harbour Club Apts., L.I. Assn., 1970, for Birchwood Blue Ridge Condominiums, 1974. Fellow Acad. Marketing Sci., L.I.U., 1971. Registered architect, N.Y., N.J., Mass., Md., Va., Pa., Conn., Ga., Vt., Tenn., N.H., Fla.; lic. profl. planner, N.J. Mem. AIA, N.Y. State Assn. Architects, East Meadow C. of C. (pres. 1966). Club: Kiwanis. Author: The Spiegel Plan. Contbr. articles to Progressive Architecture. Prin. works include: Syosset (N.Y.) Hosp., 1962; Reliance Fed. Savs. and Loan Assn. Bank, Queens, N.Y., 1961; Louden Hall Psychiat. Hosp., 1963; Human Resources Sch., Albertson, N.Y., 1964; Nassau Center for Emotionally Disturbed Children, 1968; Harbor Club Apt., Babylon, N.Y., 1968; Reliance Fed. Bank, Albertson, 1967; North Isle Club and Apt. Community, Coram, N.Y., 1972; County Fed. Savs. & Loan Assn., Commack, N.Y., 1972; Birchwood Glen Apt. Community, Holtsville, N.Y., 1972; Bayside Fed. Savs. & Loan Bank Plaza, Patchogue, N.Y., 1973; L.E. Woodward Sch. for Emotionally Disturbed Children, Freeport, N.Y., 1974, Birchwood Sagamore Hills, Blue Ridge and Bretton Woods Condominium Communities, Coram, N.Y., 1975, Maple Arms Condos, Westbury, N.Y., 1982, Dept. Pub. Works, Freeport, N.Y., Nuclear Molecular Resonance Bldg., 1983. Home: 1508 Hayes Ct East Meadow NY 11554 Office: 266 East Meadow East Meadow NY 11554

SPIEGEL, STANLEY LAWRENCE, mathematics educator, researcher; b. N.Y.C., Oct. 27, 1935; s. Sidney Daniel and Gertrude (Milsky) S.; m. Diana Lees, Aug. 13, 1972; children: Stephanie Berit, David Solomon, Sarah Caren. BS, NYU, 1957; AM, Harvard U., 1959, PhD, 1966. Postdoctoral fellow dept. meteorology MIT, Cambridge, 1966-68; research assoc. dept. math. Northeastern U., Boston, 1969-72; sr. scientist, EG & G Environ. Cons., Waltham, Mass., 1978-79, cons., 1978-85; prof. math. U. Lowell, Mass., 1973—; cons. Tri-Con Assocs., Cambridge, 1980-85; textbook reviewer for various pubs., 1974—. Contbr. articles to profl. jours. Apptd. mem. Brookline Town Meeting, Mass., 1981—; mem. Brookline Redistricting Commn., 1985, Brookline Fin. Com., 1986—. Fellow Air Force Office Sci. Research, 1981-83, 85—, Gen. Electric Co., 1957. Mem. N.Y. Acad. Scis., Am. Geophys. Union, Am. Meteorol. Soc., Sigma Xi, Pi Mu Epsilon. Jewish. Home: 39 Stetson St Bookline MA 02146 Office: U Lowell Math Dept One University Ave Lowell MA 01854

SPIEGELBERG, FRANK DAVID, lawyer; b. Washington, Aug. 21, 1948; s. Joseph H. and Ruth (May) S.; m. Linda Rae Gordesky, June 28, 1970; children: Adam Jay, Kimberly Joy. BA, Kent State U., 1970; JD, Duke U., 1973. Bar: Md. 1973, Tex. 1977, Okla. 1978, U.S. Ct. Mil. Appeals 1974, U.S. Dist. Ct. (ea. dist.) Okla. 1978, U.S. Ct. Appeals (10th cir.) 1978, U.S. Dist. Ct. (we. dist.) Okla. 1985, U.S. Supreme Ct. 1985. Assoc. Dukes, Troese, Mann & Wilson, Landover, Md., 1973; litigation atty. Cities Service Co., Tulsa, 1978-82, sr. litigation atty., 1982; atty. Apache Corp., Tulsa, 1982-86; of counsel Boesche, McDermott & Eskridge, Tulsa, 1986-87, ptnr., 1988—. Pres. Burning Tree Homeowners Assn., Tulsa, 1981-85, bd. dirs. 1981-85, 87—; mem. redistricting com. Union Sch. Bd., Tulsa, 1984. Served as capt. USAF, 1974-77. Recipient Air Force Commendation medal, 1977, cert. of Appreciation for seminar, Okla. Assn. Def. Counsel, 1982. Mem. Okla. Bar Assn., Tex. Bar Assn., Tulsa County Bar (grievance com.), Tulsa County Bar Assn., Assn. Trial Lawyers Am., Kent State U. Alumni Assn., Duke U. Alumni Assn., Sigma Phi Epsilon Alumni Assn. Home: 9032 E 67th St Tulsa OK 74133 Office: Boesche McDermott & Eskridge 800 Oneok Plaza 100 W 5th St Tulsa OK 74103

SPIELMAN, DAVID VERNON, insurance, finance and publications consultant; b. Humboldt, Iowa, Dec. 23, 1929; s. Elmo Bruce and Leona Belle (Blake) S.; m. Barbara Helen New, Nov. 24, 1956; children: Daniel Bruce, Linda Barbara. BA, U. Tex., 1966. Publs. engr. IBM Mil. Products, Kingston, N.Y., 1957-58; engring. writer Convair Astronautics div. Gen Dynamics Corp., San Diego, 1958-59; tech. publs. mgr. Ling-Temco Vought, Inc., Garland, Tex., 1960-62; tech. writer Ken Cook Pubs.-Tex. Co., Richardson, Tex., 1963-64; asst. coordinator Kuwait program U. Tex., Austin, 1964-66; ednl. writer Tex. Edn. Agy., Austin, 1966-74; real estate broker Dave Spielman Research Assocs., Austin, 1974—, ins. broker, 1974—; cons. Nat. Ctr. Vocat. Edn., Columbus, Ohio, 1974-75, Tex. State Auditor, Austin, 1976-77, U.S. Dept. Labor, Washington, 1975-78; exec. dir. Tex. Labor Ctr., Inc., 1978—. Counselor Distributive Edn. Clubs Am. Student Conf. Tex., Brenham, 1972; competition judge Tex. Carpenter's Apprentices, 1973-74; chpt. pres. Tex. Pub. Employees Assn., Austin, 1969-70. Served to sgt. maj. U.S. Army, 1952-53, with USAR 1947-50; served to cpl. USNG, 1950-52. Recipient Outstanding Vocat. Edn. Contributor, Tex. House and Senate. Mem. Acctg. Computer Machinery Assn. (newsletter editor 1958-59), Soc. Tech Writers and Editors (chpt. pres. 1960-61), Soc. Tech. Writers and Pubs. (chpt. pres. 1961-62), Soc. Tech. Communications (membership chmn. 1983-84), Tex. State Tchrs. Assn., Delta Pi (local sec., treas.). Democrat. Presbyterian. Lodges: Masons. Home and Office: 3301 Perry Ln Austin TX 78731

SPIELMANN, ZVI HERMANN, film producer; b. Kalusz, Poland, June 5, 1925; s. Mordekhai Markus and Sophie Zofiah (Rosenmann) S.; m. Miriam Rosner, May 13, 1952; children: Vered, Noa, Jaakov, Shlomit Dvora. Grad. high sch., Tel Aviv. Producer 1000 Little Kisses, 1981, Thieves in the Night, 1987; supr. prodn. films A Woman Called Golda, 1982, Remembrance of Love, 1984, Not Quite Paradise, 1985, TV series Desert Fever, 1988. Served to capt. inf. Israeli Def. Forces, 1950-52. Home: 16 Nordau Str, Herzliya 46541, Israel Office: Israfilm Ltd, 61 Pinsker, Tel Aviv 63568, Israel

SPIERS, TOMAS HOSKINS, JR., architect; b. Paris, Jan. 26, 1929; s. Tomas Hoskins and Blanca Genevive (DePonthier) S. (parents Am. citizens); student Mohawk Coll., 1946-48; B.A., Hobart Coll., 1951; M.Arch., Yale U., 1960; m. Nancy M. Fenold, Aug. 10, 1952; children—Merrick David, Jordan Henry, Corey Albert. Archtl. designer Pederson & Tilney, New Haven, 1955-60; mng. dir. Pederson & Tilney Italia SpA, Milan, Italy, 1960-66; v.p. European ops. Pederson/Tilney/Spiers, Milan, 1963-66; v.p. S.E. Asia, Louis Berger, Inc., Bangkok, Thailand, 1966-68; v.p. architecture Benatec Assos., Harrisburg, Pa., 1968-75, v.p. design, 1975-78, sr. v.p., 1979-87; pres., 1987—, also dir.; lectr. archtl. restoration Pa. State U., 1975-80; cons. Pa. Hist. & Mus. Commn., Bur. Historic Sites; mem. Pa. State Hist. Preservation Bd., 1980-84, chmn. 1986-88. Bd. dirs. Urban League of Harrisburg, Inc., 1977-84. Served with USNR, 1951-55. Registered architect, Pa., N.J., N.Y., Mass., Md., Ohio, Conn., S.C., R.I., Ind., Va., W.Va., D.C., Fla., Ga., Vt. Mem. Am. Arbitration Assn. (arbitrator 1974—), Assn. Preservation Tech. (bd. dirs., editor bull. 1979-82, v.p. 1984-87, pres. 1988—), AIA (com. on hist. resources 1977-88, exec. com. 1980-82, chmn. 1983), ASCE, Soc. Am. Mil. Engrs. Works include: restoration Gen. Knox quarters, Valley Forge, Pa., Eagle Hotel, Waterford, Pa., The Highlands, Whitemarsh, Pa., Washington Monument, Balt. Home: 357 N 27th St Camp Hill PA 17011 Office: 101 Erford Rd Camp Hill PA 17011

SPIGLER, RENATO GIACOMO CARLO, mathematics educator, researcher, writer; b. Venice, Italy, Nov. 10, 1947; s. Bernardy and Zaira (Tosatto) S. Laurea, U. Padova, Italy, 1972; Diploma, U. Bologna, Italy, 1975. Contract U. Padova, 1974-78, asst. prof., 1978-85, assoc. prof., 1985—; research scientist U. Wis., Madison, 1979-80, NYU, 1980-82, 83-85. Author 2 math. books; contbr. sci. articles to newspapers and profl. jours. Ministry Edn. fellow U. Padova, 1972-74; Fulbright scholar, 1983-85. Home: Via Anfossi 7, 35129 Padova Italy Office: U Padova, Via Belzoni 7, 35131 Padova Italy

SPIJKER, FREDERIK VAN'T, sales executive, consultant; b. Zwijndrecht, The Netherlands, Feb. 9, 1935; s. Lambert Jan Van't and Jacoba Trijntje (Klein-Essink) S.; m. Dicky Ineke Rolloos, Nov. 26, 1960; children: Henriette, Hans, Jacqueline, Arent. Student, Inst. Bus. Sci., Bilthoven, The Netherlands. Dir. mktg. D.v.d Ploeg BV, Barendrecht, The Netherlands, 1973-81; sales mgr. internat. area Sierra Europe BV, Heerlen, The Netherlands, 1982—; mng. dir. Sierra France Sarl, Logne, France, 1986, Internat. Mktg. Services, Ridderkerk, The Netherlands, 1987—. Served to lt. col. transport corps Royal Dutch Army Reserve, 1955. Clubs: Round Table, Fourty Plus (Zwijndrecht, Holl). Home: Pruimendijk 26 a, 2988 XN Ridderkerk The Netherlands Office: Sierra Chem Europe BV, Strijkviertel 82 a, 3454 PP De Meern The Netherlands

SPILKIN, MICHAEL, manufacturing company executive; b. Johannesburg, Transvaal, South Africa, Sept. 28, 1928; s. Samuel and Charlotte (Cohen) S.; m. Pamela Barnett, Oct. 15, 1958 (dec.); children—Wendy, Gary Roy; m. Sharon Erasmus, Apr. 22, 1979; 1 child, Nicholas Seth. Student Witwatersrand U., Johannesburg, 1950. Mgr., dir. Modern Scale Co. Ltd., Johannesburg, 1964, Steam and Mining, Johannesburg, 1968; chmn. Modcorp Ltd., Johannesburg, 1967; dir. S.M.E. Earthing & Lighting, Johannesburg, Kawenga Properties, Johannesburg, Michaels Agys., Johannesburg, Julkas Investments, Johannesburg. Co-sponsor: Selous Scouts, 1982 (best seller 1983). Mem. Scale & Weighing Machine Assn. (treas.) Jewish. Clubs: Wanderers (capt. 1955); Riviera Aquatic (Vereeniging). Office: PO Box 10190, Johannesburg 2000, Republic of South Africa

SPILLANE, MAURICE, software company executive; b. Dublin, Apr. 3, 1949; s. Maurice and Claire (Wall) S.; m. Patricia Byrne, Jan. 7, 1972; children: Niamh, Una, Deirdre, Aoife. Grad. sec. sch., Dublin. Auditor Civil Service, Dublin, 1967-71; acct. RTE, Dublin, 1971-72; dep. chief acct. NCCM Ltd., Kitwe, Zambia, 1972-76; mgr. data processing Braun Ltd., Carlow, Ireland, 1976-80; chief exec. officer RTS Ltd., Dublin, 1980—; also bd. dirs. and bd. dirs. subs.; v.p. MSA Ltd., London. Contbr. articles to U.S. and Irish mags. Recipient Mktg. award Am. Express, 1985. Fellow Assn. Cert. Accts.; mem. Prodn. and Ivnentory Control Soc., Irish Computer Soc. Office: RTS Ltd, Ballast house, O'Connell Bridge, Dublin 2, Ireland

SPILLER, GENE ALAN, nutritionist, clinical human nutrition research consultant, writer, editor; b. Milan, Italy, Feb. 19, 1927; came to U.S., 1950, naturalized, 1962; s. Silvio and Beatrice (Galli) S. D.Chemistry, U. Milan, 1949; M.S., U. Calif. Berkeley, 1968, Ph.D. in Nutrition, 1972. Cons. nutrition research and edn., Los Angeles, 1952-65; research chemist U. Calif.-Berkeley, 1966-67, assoc. specialist physiology dept., 1968-72; prin. scientist, head nutritional physiology Syntex Research, Palo Alto, Calif., 1972-80; cons. clin. nutrition research, Los Altos, Calif., 1981—; lectr. Mills Coll., Oakland, Calif., 1971-81, Foothill Coll., Los Altos, 1974—. Editor: Fiber in Human Nutrition, 1976; Topics in Dietary Fiber, 1978; Medical Aspects of Dietary Fiber, 1980; Nutritional Pharmacology, 1981; The Methylxanthine Beverages and Foods, 1984; CRC Handbook of Dietary Fiber in Human Nutrition, 1986; reviewer papers Am. Jour. Clin. Nutrition, 1976-83. Mem. Am. Inst. Nutrition, Am. Soc. Clin. Nutrition, Brit. Nutrition Soc., Am. Assn. Cereal Chemists, Am. Diabetes Assn. Club: Alpine Hills. Research on human nutrition; prin. investigator in human nutrition studies; dietary fiber and carbohydrates effect on human health; role of lesser known food components in nutrition; non-human primates as models for human nutrition. Office: PO Box 123 Los Altos CA 94022

SPILLNER, BERND, linguist, romance philology and general linguistics educator; b. Braunschweig, Germany, Mar. 20, 1941. B.A., Gymnasium, 1961; State diploma, U. Bochum, 1967, Ph.D., 1970. Head dept. applied linguistics Inst. Linguistics U. Bonn, Fed. Republic Germany, 1972-74; prof. U. Duisburg, Fed. Republic Germany, 1974—, dean, vice dean, faculty of langs., 1979-81; chmn. Sci. Commn. Rhetoric and Stylistics Assn. Internationale de Linguistique Appliquée, 1976—; v.p. GAL. Germany Soc. Applied Linguistics, 1982-86, pres. 1986—; corr. mem. Research Centre Multilingualism, Brussels, 1985—. Author: Symmetrisches und asymmetrisches Prinzip in der Syntax Marcel Prousts, 1971; Linguistik und Literaturwissenschaft Stilforschung, Rhetorik, Textlinguistik, 1974, Spanish edit., 1979. Editor: Rhetorik und Stilistik, 1977; Norm und Varietät, 1977; Methoden der Stilanalyse, 1984. Contbr. articles to profl. jours. Mem. Société de Linguistique de Paris, Gesellschaft für Angewandte Linguistik (v.p. 1986—), MLA, Società di Linguistica Italiana, Internat. Assn. Applied Linguistics (exec. bd. 1987—). Office: U Duisburg FB 3, Lotharstr 65, D-4100 Duisburg Federal Republic of Germany

SPINGARN, CLIFFORD LEROY, internist, educator; b. Bklyn., May 8, 1912; s. Alexander and Eleanor (Trinz) S.; A.B., Columbia, 1933, M.D., 1937; m. Eleanor Harrison, June 9, 1937; children—John Harrison, Alexandra. Intern, Mt. Sinai Hosp., N.Y.C., 1937-40, asst. attending physician, 1946-63, asso. attending physician, 1963—, chief parasitology clinic, 1956—; attending physician Doctors Hosp., N.Y.C., 1968—, chmn. com. on continuing med. edn., 1976—(disting. service award, 1988); pvt. practice internal medicine, N.Y.C., 1946—; instr. pharmacology Columbia, 1940-42; asst. clin. prof. preventive medicine N.Y. U., 1956-68; assoc. clin. prof. medicine Mt. Sinai Sch. Medicine, 1966-83, lectr. in medicine, 1983—. Trustee Milton Helpern Library Legal Medicine, 1982—; bd. dirs. N.Y. Faculty Continuing Med. Edn., 1982-86. Served from lt. (j.g.) to lt. comdr. M.C., USNR, 1942-46; now lt. comdr. ret. res. Diplomate Am. Bd. Internal Medicine. Fellow N.Y. Acad. Medicine, A.C.P.; mem. N.Y. Soc. Tropical Medicine, Am. Soc. Tropical Medicine and Hygiene, Am. Soc. Parasitologists, AAAS, Am. Soc. Internal Medicine, Med. Soc. County N.Y. (chmn. grievance com. 1969-72, chmn. bd. censors 1978-80, pres. 1981, trustee 1982-87, Disting. Service award 1986), Soc. Internal Medicine County New York (pres. 1965-67), N.Y. State Soc. Internal Medicine, N.Y. Cardiological Soc. (dir. 1971-73), Phi Beta Kappa, Sigma Xi, Alpha Omega Alpha. Author numerous papers. Home: 201 E 79th St New York NY 10021 Office: 66 E 80th St New York NY 10021

SPINKS, NELDA HUGHES, educator; b. Ruston, La., Sept. 3, 1928; d. Willie B. and Elizabeth Hughes; m. Wyman Allison Spinks, June 12, 1948; 1 son, Hugh Allison. BA, La. Tech. U.; MEd, U. Southwestern La.; Ed.D., La. State U. Cert. tchr., La. Instr. Acadia Baptist Acad., Eunice, La., 1954-63, Lafayette Parish Sch. Bd., 1963-67; asst. prof. U. Southwestern La., Lafayette, 1967-73, 75-87, assoc. prof., 1987—. Author: A Study of the Educational Needs of Potential Office Managers, 1974, (with others) Organizational Communication: A Practical Approach, 1987; guest editorial panelist Baptist Message newspaper, 1988—; panel of editors The State Bapt. Newspaper; contbr. articles to mags. Dir. Elizabeth Hughes Meml. Library, Bethel Bapt. Ch., Lafayette, 1987—. Recipient Postsecondary award Nat. Fed. Ind. Bus. Principles and Econs., 1987, career achievement award Connections, 1987; nominee Outstand Prof. award Amoco Found., 1987. Chmn., bd. dirs. U. Southwestern La. Bapt. Student Union; mem. dean's faculty adv. council U. Southwestern La., 1988—. Mem. Am. Bus. Communication Assn., Assn. Bus. Communication, S.W. Assn. Adminstrv. Services, Am. Mgmt. Assn. Nat. Collegiate Assn. for Secs. (sponsor), La. Assn. Bus. Educators (v.p. 1987—, pres.-elect 1988—), Nat. Fedn. Ind. Bus. (Outstanding Contributor award 1987), Lafayette C. of C. (edn. com. 1977), Kappa Delta Pi, Omicron Delta Epsilon, Delta Pi Epsilon (historian, editor newsletter 1987-88), Phi Delta Kappa, Phi Kappa Phi. Avocations: needlework, sports, reading. Home: 218 Brentwood Blvd Lafayette LA 70503 Office: U Southwestern La PO Box 41503 Lafayette LA 70504

SPIRY, JEAN LOUIS, oral surgeon; b. Paris, Nov. 24, 1949; married July 7, 1980; 1 child, Christelle. DDS. Chief of unity orthodontics Hosp. St. Louis, Paris, 1976—. Patentee in field. Laureat Indsl. Found. Home: 76 rue de Crimée, 75019 Paris France

SPISANI, FRANCO, mathematician, researcher; b. Ferrara, Italy, May 21, 1934; s. Mario and Dolores (Gaudenzi) S.; m. Giovanna Zappoli, June 1, 1965; children: Massimo, Vivana, Francesca. PhD, U. Degli Studi Padova, Italy, 1959. Founder, pres. Cen. Superiore di Logica E Scienze Comparate, Bologne, Italy, 1969—; founder, editor Internat. Logic Rev., Bologne, 1970—; hon. prof. Nat. U., Toronto, Can., 1971; mem. editorial bd. jour. Theoria, San Sebastian, Spain, 1985, philos. pubs. series, Melbourne, Australia, 1978. Author: General Theory of Directed Numbers, 1983. Mem. Internat. Burckhardt Acad., Internat. Inst. Arts and Letters (assoc., internat. award 1970), N.Y. Acad. Scis. Office: Centro Superiore di Logica, Galleria del Leone 3, Bologna Italy 40125

SPITLER, LEE WILLIAM, banker; b. Racine, Wis., Feb. 14, 1919; s. Marion Albert and Agnes Elizabeth (Lowe) S.; m. Helen Deloris Krejci, Mar. 19, 1949; children—Susan D., Lee William, Anne M., James E. B.S., U. Md., 1956; M.B.A., George Washington U., 1962; postgrad. advanced mgmt. program, Harvard U., 1963; grad., U.S. Air Force War Coll., 1959, U.S. Air Force Command and Staff Coll., 1955. Commd. 2d lt. U.S. Air Force, 1943, advanced through grades to col., 1954; chief personnel stats. div. Hdqrs. U.S. Air Force, Washington, 1950-54; asst. dir. statis. services U.S. Air Force, 1958-63; asst. comptroller Hdqrs. U.S. European Command U.S. Air Force, Paris, 1955-58; asst. comptroller Hdqrs. Air Tng. Command U.S. Air Force, Randolph AFB, Tex., 1963-64; ret. U.S. Air Force, 1964; v.p. Computax Corp., El Segundo, Calif., 1965-69; exec. v.p. Irving Bank Corp., N.Y.C., 1969-84; sr. exec. v.p. Irving Trust Co., N.Y.C., 1969-84; ret. 1984; dir. Turkiye Tutunculer Bankasi AS, Izmir, Turkey. mem. nat. adv. bd. Am. Security Council. Decorated Legion of Merit. Mem. Internat. Assn. Fin. Planning, Am. Bankers Assn., Am. Mgmt. Assn., Soc. for Mgmt. Info. Systems, Ret. Officers Assn., Nat. Assn. Uniformed Services, Mil. Order World Wars, Am. Assn. Mil. Comptrollers, Am. Legion, Am. Assn. Ret. Personnel, Air War Coll. Alumni Assn., First Fighter Group Assn. Clubs: Harvard, West Point Officers. Home: 38 Lauren Ln S Bricktown NJ 08723

SPITZ, GIDEON, hotel executive; b. Zandvoort, North Holland, Netherlands, Sept. 12, 1925; s. Raphael Jesaja and Anna Hermina (Wegerif) S.; m. Caroline Euwe, 1962 (div. 1966); 1 dau., Ester Judith. Student U. Amsterdam, 3 yrs. Dept. head Rubber Research Inst., Delft, Netherlands, 1950-53; head pub. relations dept. KLM Royal Dutch Airlines, Amsterdam, 1953-60; pres. Shipside Corp., N.Y.C., 1960-64, Dutch Combined Tourist Bd., Hilversum, Netherlands, 1964-70; dep. chmn. Golden Tulip Hotels, Hilversum, N.Y., 1970—. Served to lt. Dutch Army, 1947-50. Bd. dirs.The Netherlands and N. Am., Holland Promotion Found., The Netherlands, various hotel cos. Home: 9 Haenwyck, Laren, 1251 LM North Holland The Netherlands Office: Golden Tulip Hotels Internat, 2 Stationsweg, 1211 Hilversum The Netherlands other: Golden Tulip World Wide Hotels B V Lexington Ave New York NY 10022

SPITZ, HUGO MAX, lawyer; b. Richmond, Va., Aug. 17, 1927, s. Jacob Gustav and Clara (Herzfeld) S.; m. Barbara Steinberg, June 22, 1952; children—Jack Gray, Jill Ann Levy, Sally. A.A., U. Fla., 1948, B.Laws, 1951, J.D., 1967. Bar: Fla. 1951, S.C., 1955, U.S. Dist. Ct. (so. dist.) Fla. 1951, U.S. Dist. Ct. (ea. dist.) S.C. 1956, U.S. Ct. Appeals (4th cir.) 1957. Asst. atty. gen. State of Fla., Tallahassee, 1951; assoc. Williams, Salomon & Katz, Miami, Fla., 1951-54, Steinberg & Levkoff, Charleston, S.C., 1954-57; sr. ptnr. Steinberg, Spitz, Goldberg, Pearlman Holmes & White, Charleston, 1957—; lectr. S.C. Trial Lawyers Assn., Columbia, 1958—, S.C. U. Sch. Law, Columbia, 1975, S.C. Bar Assn., 1955—. Assoc. mcpl. judge Charleston, 1972-74, mcpl. judge, 1974-76; commr. Charleston County Substance Abuse Commn., 1976-79; bd. govs. S.C. Patient's Compensation Fund, Columbia, 1978-89; adv. mem., atty. S.C. Legis. Council for Workers' Compensation; chmn. bd. dirs. Franklin C. Fetter Health Ctr., Charleston, 1977-78; mem. S.C. Appellate Def. Commn., 1985-86; founding sponsor Civil Justice Found., 1986—; bd. dirs. Charleston Jewish Fedn., 1986—. Pres., Synagogue Emanu-El, 1969-71. Served with USN, 1945-46. Fellow S.C. Bar Assn., U. S.C. Ednl. Found; mem. ABA, Civil Justice Found., S.C. Law Inst., S.C. Trial Lawyers Assn. (pres. 1985-86), S.C. Claimants' Attys. for Worker's Compensation (exec. com. 1986), S.C. Worker's Compensation Ednl. Assn. (bd. dirs. 1978—), S.C. Law Inst., Am. Judicature Soc., N.Y. State Trial Lawyers Assn., Pa. Trial Lawyers Assn., Assn. Trial Lawyers Am. (mem. pres. council 1986—), Nat. Rehab. Assn., Nat. Orgn. Social Security Claimants' Reps. S.C. Bar (chmn. trial and appellate sect. 1982-83; ho. of dels. 1984-85), So. Assn. Workmen's Compensation Adminstrs., Nat. Inst. for Trial Advocacy (com. chmn. 1985). Democrat. Clubs: Hebrew Benevolent Soc. (pres. 1974-75), Jewish Community Ctr. (v.p. 1972-74) (Charleston). Home: 337 Confederate Circle Charleston SC 29407 Office: Steinberg Spitz et al PO Box 9 Charleston SC 29402-0009

SPITZBERG, IRVING JOSEPH, JR., association executive, lawyer; b. Little Rock, Feb. 9, 1942; s. Irving Joseph and Marie Bettye (Seeman) S.; m. Roberta Frances Alprin, Aug. 21, 1966 (separated 1988); children—Edward Storm, David Adam. B.A., Columbia U., 1964; B.Phil., Oxford U., 1966; J.D., Yale U., 1969. Bar: Calif. 1969, D.C. 1985. Asst. prof. Pitzer Coll., Claremont, Calif., 1969-71; fellow Inst. Current World Affairs, N.Y.C., 1971-74; vis. lectr. Brown U., Providence, 1973; prof. SUNY, Buffalo, 1980; dean of coll. SUNY, 1974-78; gen. sec. AAUP, Washington, 1980-84; exec. dir. Council for Liberal Learning of Assn. Am. Colls., Washington, 1985—; pres. The Knowledge Co., Bethesda, Md., 1985—; ptnr. Spirer, Spitzberg and Thorndike, 1988—; coordinator Alvan Ikoku coll., Nigeria, 1979-80; cons. Bd. Adult Edn., Kenya, 1973-74, Philander Smith Coll., Little Rock, 1978-80. Author and editor: Exchange of Expertise, 1978, Universities and the New International Order, 1979, Universities and the International Exchange of Knowledge, 1980; author: Campus Programs on Leadership, 1986, Racial Politics in Little Rock, 1987. Founder Coalition for Ednl. Excellence, Western N.Y., 1978-80; founding mem. Alliance for Leadership devel., Washington, 1985; counsel GASP, Pomona, (Calif.), 1969-71; Democratic Committeeman, Erie County, (N.Y.), 1978-80; founding pres. Internat. Found for St. Catherine's Coll., Oxford, 1986—. Recipient 1st place award Westinghouse sci. Talent Search, 1960; Kellett scholar Trustees of Columbia U., 1964-66. Mem. AAAS, Internat. Soc. Ednl., Cultural, and Sci. Exchanges. Jewish. Clubs; Federal, Columbia, Yale (Washington). Office: 1818 R St NW Washington DC 20009

SPITZER, ALLAN THOMAS, data processing executive; b. Honolulu, Aug. 31, 1955; s. Arthur Hoerman and Blanche Helen (van Oort) S.; B.A., U. Portland, 1977. With Standard Shoe Store Ltd., Honolulu, 1971-77, v.p., sec., gen. mgr., 1977-87; prin., chief exec. officer Automated Office Solutions, Honolulu, 1987—. Mem. U.S. C. of C., Hawaii C. of C., Nat. Fedn. Ind. Bus., Hawaii Visitors Bur., Hawaii Employers Council. Republican. Roman Catholic. Clubs: Outrigger Canoe, Red Carpet. Home: 1422 Nanaloko Pl Kailua HI 96734 Office: Standard Shoe Store Ltd 2213 Ala Moana Ctr Honolulu HI 96814

SPITZER, PETER GEORGE, healthcare information systems executive; b. Oradea, Romania, July 16, 1956; came to U.S., 1969; m. Anne Taylor, 1985. BS in Bioelec. Engring., MIT, 1979, MS in Elec. Engring. and Computer Sci., 1980; MD cum laude, Harvard U., 1980; MBA, UCLA, 1986. Sr. systems analyst Nat. Cash Register Co., Los Angeles, 1977—; dir. pathology diagnosis registry Peter Brigham Hosps., Boston, 1978-80; research analyst Mass. Gen. Hosp., Boston, 1978-80; resident obstetrician, gynecologist UCLA Ctr. for Health Scis., Los Angeles, 1980-81; v.p. Am. Med. Internat., Info. Systems Group, Beverly Hills, Calif., 1981-87; chief info. officer Tex. Children's Hosp., Houston, 1988—; asst. research prof. pediatrics Baylor Coll. of Medicine, Houston, 1988—. Smith-Kline Found. fellow, 1978-80. Mem. IEEE, Am. Hosp. Assn., Am. Mgmt. Assn., Data Processing Mgmt. Assn., Am. Acad. Med. Dirs., Eta Kappa Nu, Sigma Xi. Office: Tex Children's Hosp 1020 Holcombe #420 Houston TX 77030

SPITZER, WALTER OSWALD, epidemiologist, educator; b. Asuncion, Paraguay, Feb. 19, 1937; children—Paul, Pamela, Carl, Brenda. M.D., U. Toronto, 1962; M.H.A., U. Mich., 1966; M.P.H., Yale U., 1970. Gen. dir. Internat. Christian Med. Soc., 1966-69; asst. prof. clin. epidemiology McMaster U., Hamilton, Ont., Can., 1969-73; assoc. prof. McMaster U., 1973-75; prof. epidemiology McGill U., Montreal, Que., Can., 1975—; prof. medicine McGill U., 1983—, Strathcona prof. and chmn. dept. epidemiology and biostats., 1984—; cons. PanAm. Health Orgn., Washington, 1975, 77, Aga Khan Found., Geneva, 1983-84, Can. Ministry of Transport, 1977—. Editor Jour. Clin. Epidemiology, 1981—; contbr. articles to biomed. jours. Named Nat. Health Scientist of Can., 1981. Fellow Am. Coll. Epidemiology; mem. Can. Oncology Soc. (bd. dirs. 1983-85, pres. 1987—), Inst. Medicine of Nat. Acad. Scis. (U.S.). Mem. Liberal party. Anglican. Office: McGill U Purvis Hall, 1020 Pine Ave W, Montreal, PQ Canada H3A 1A2

SPITZLI, DONALD HAWKES, JR., lawyer; b. Newark, Mar. 19, 1934; s. Donald Hawkes and Beatrice (Banister) S.; m. Jacqueline Anne Spitzli, Mar. 3, 1979; m. Rita Angell, June 17, 1956; children—Donald Hawkes III, Peter Gilbert, Lori Anne, Seth Armstrong. A.B., Dartmouth Coll., 1956; LL.B., U. Va. 1963. Bar: Va. 1963. Assoc. Willcox, Savage, Lawrence, Dickson & Spindle, Norfolk, Va., 1964-67; atty. Eastman Kodak Co., Rochester, 1967-68; assoc. Willcox, Savage, Lawrence, Dickson & Spindle, Norfolk, Va., 1968-70, ptnr., 1971-77; pres. Marine Hydraulics Internat., Inc., Chesapeake, Va., 1978-80; sole practice, Virginia Beach, Va., 1980—; gen. counsel Chieftain Motor Inn, Inc., Jadon Farms, Ltd., Ocean Breeze Condominium, Ltd. Served to comdr. USNR, 1956-70. Mem. ABA, Va. Bar Assn. Episcopalian. Club: Yale (N.Y.C.). Office: PO Box 6059 Virginia Beach VA 23456

SPIVACK, GORDON BERNARD, lawyer, lecturer; b. New Haven, June 15, 1929; s. Jacob and Sophie (Ocheretianski) S.; m. Dolores Olivia Traversano, Jan. 16, 1956; children—Michael David, Paul Stephen. B.S. with philosophic orations and honors and exceptional distinction, Yale U., 1950, LL.B. magna cum laude, 1955. Bar: Conn. 1955, U.S. Supreme Ct. 1962, N.Y. 1970. Trial atty. antitrust div. Dept. Justice, Washington, 1955-60; asst. chief field ops. antitrust div. Dept. Justice, 1961-64, chief field ops. antitrust div., 1964-65, dir. ops. antitrust div., 1965-67; assoc. prof. law Yale U., New Haven, 1967-70; vis. lectr. Yale U., 1970-78; ptnr. Lord, Day & Lord, N.Y.C., 1970-86, Coudert Bros., N.Y.C., 1986—; speaker on antitrust law; mem. Pres.'s Nat. Commn. for Rev. Antitrust Law and Procedures, Washington, 1978-79. Contbr. numerous articles on antitrust law to profl. jours. Served with U.S. Army, 1950-52. Recipient Sustained Superior Performance award Dept. Justice, 1955-60. Fellow Am. Coll. Trial Lawyers; mem. ABA, N.Y. State Bar Assn., Bar Assn. City N.Y. Jewish. Clubs: The Sky, Yale (N.Y.C.); Woodbridge Country (Conn.). Home: 118 Townsend Terr New Haven CT 06512 Office: Coudert Bros 200 Park Ave New York NY 10166

SPIVACK, HENRY ARCHER, life insurance company executive; b. Bklyn., Apr. 15, 1919; s. Jacob and Pauline (Schwartz) S.; m. Sadie Babe Meiseles, Jan. 1, 1941; children: Ian Jeffrey, Paula Janis. Student CCNY, 1936-42; BBA, Am. Coll., Bryn Mawr, Pa., 1965. CLU. Comptroller Daniel Jones, Inc., N.Y.C., 1947-59; field underwriter Union Cen. Life Ins. Co., N.Y.C., 1959-79, mgr. programming dept., 1966-69, assoc. mgr., 1977-79; pension dir. Bleichroeder, Bing & Co., N.Y.C., 1975-77, sr. v.p. new confidence agy., 1979—; pension dir., employee benefit plan cons., pres. Profl. Benefit Planners Inc. N.J.; instr. N.Y. State Ins. Dept., C.W. Post Coll., L.I. U., N.Y. Ctr. for Fin. Studies; coordinator Ins. Dept. Yeshiva U., N.Y.; ins. courses instr.; also lectr., moderator. Contbr. articles to publs. Served with USN, 1943-46. Mem. Life Underwriters Assn. N.Y. (chmn. blood bank), Am. Soc. CLU's (past chmn. N.Y. chpt. pension sect., chmn. profl. liaison com.), Am. Soc. Pension Actuaries, Pensioneers at C.W. Post Coll., C.W. Post Coll. Tax Inst. and Fin. Planning Inst., Practising Law Inst., Internat. Assn. Fin. Planners, Internat. Assn. Registered Fin. Planners (cert.), Internat. Platform Assn., Greater N.Y. Brokers Assn. Lodge: K.P. (life; past dep. grand chancellor N.Y. state). Office: 2 Park Ave 3d Floor New York NY 10016

SPLITTSTOESSER, WALTER EMIL, plant physiologist; b. Claremont, Minn., Aug. 27, 1937; s. Waldemar Theodore and Opal Mae (Young) S.; m. Shirley Anne O'Connor, July 2, 1960; children: Pamela, Sheryl, Riley. B.S. with distinction (univ. fellow), U. Minn., 1958; M.S., S.D. State U., 1960; Ph.D., Purdue U., 1963. Plant breeder U. Minn., 1956-58; weed scientist S.D. State U., 1958-60; plant physiologist Purdue U., 1960-63, Shell Oil Co., Modesto, Calif., 1963-64; biochemist U. Calif., Davis, 1964-65; mem. faculty U. Ill., Urbana, 1965—; prof. plant physiology U. Ill., 1974—, head vegetable crops div., 1972-82; vis. prof. Univ. Coll., Dublin, Ireland, 1987, Univ. Coll., London, 1972; biologist Parkland Coll., Champaign, Ill., 1974; vis. research asso. Rothamsted Exptl. Sta., Harpenden, Eng., 1980; disting. vis. prof. Nagoya U. (Japan), 1982. Author: Vegetable Growing Handbook, 1979, 2d edit., 1984; contbr. over 200 articles to sci. jours.; rev. editor: Analytical Biochemistry, 1969-78, NSF, 1978-79; numerous others. Recipient J.H. Gourley award Am. Fruit Grower-Am. Soc. Hort. Sci., 1974; NIH fellow, 1964-65. Fellow Japanese Soc. Promotion of Sci.; Mem. Weed Sci. Soc. Am., Am. Soc. Hort. Sci. (rev. editor jour. 1969—), Am. Soc. Plant Physiologists, Japanese Soc. Plant Physiologists, Scandinavian Soc. Plant Physiologists, Sigma Xi, Alpha Zeta, Gamma Sigma Delta, Delta Theta Sigma, Phi Kappa Phi. Home: 2006 Cureton Dr Urbana IL 61801 Office: Univ Ill 1103 W Dorner Dr Urbana IL 61801

SPOCK, BENJAMIN MCLANE, physician, educator; b. New Haven, May 2, 1903; s. Benjamin Ives and Mildred Louise (Stoughton) S.; m. Jane Davenport Cheney, June 25, 1927 (div. 1976); children: Michael, John Cheney; m. Mary Morgan Councille, Oct. 24, 1976. B.A., Yale U., 1925, student Med. Sch., 1925-27; M.D., Columbia U., 1929. Intern in medicine Presbyn. Hosp., N.Y.C., 1929-31; in pediatrics N.Y. Nursery and Child's Hosp., 1931-32; in psychiatry N.Y. Hosp., 1932-33; practice pediatrics N.Y.C., 1933-44, 46-47; instr. pediatrics Cornell Med. Coll., 1933-47; asst. attending pediatrician N.Y. Hosp., 1933-47; cons. in pediatric psychiatry N.Y. City Health Dept., 1942-47; cons. psychiatry Mayo Clinic and Rochester Child Health Project, Rochester, Minn.; asso. prof. psychiatry Mayo Found., U. Minn., 1947-51; prof. child devel. U. Pitts., 1951-55; Western Res. U., 1955-67. Author: Baby and Child Care, 1946, (with J. Reinhart and W. Miller) A Baby's First Year, 1954, (with M. Lowenberg) Feeding Your Baby and Child, 1955, Dr. Spock Talks with Mothers, 1961, Problems of Parents, 1962, (with M. Lerrigo) Caring for Your Disabled Child, 1965, (with Mitchell Zimmerman) Dr. Spock on Vietnam, 1968, Decent and Indecent, 1970, A Teenagers Guide to Life and Love, 1970, Raising Children in a Difficult Time, 1974, Spock on Parenting, 1988. Presdl. candidate Peoples Party, 1972, advocator Nat. Com. for a Sane Nuclear Policy (SANE), co-chmn., 1962 . Served to lt. comdr. M.C., USNR, 1944-46. Office: PO Box 1890 Saint Thomas VI 00803-1890

SPOLAN, HARMON SAMUEL, banker; b. Phila., Dec. 12, 1935; s. Jay and Edythe (Greenberg) S.; m. Betty Jane Evnitz, Mar. 30, 1958; children—Michael, Suzanne. A.B., Temple U., 1957, LL.B., 1959; postgrad. Oxford U., 1966. Bar: Pa. 1960. Ptnr. Ravetz & Shuchman, Phila., 1960-68, Blair & Co., N.Y.C., 1968-72; v.p. Butcher & Singer, Phila., 1972-74; pres. Capital First Corp., Phila., 1974-75, State Nat. Bank, Rockville, Md., 1975-78, Jefferson Bank, Phila., 1978—; pres., bd. dirs. State Bancshares, Inc., Phila.; bd. dirs. Jefferson Bank, Phila., Capital Mortgage Co., Phila., Bryn Mawr Resources, Phila., Capital Corp. Resources, Phila.; lectr. law U. Pa., Phila., 1964-68. Author: Federal Aids to Financing, 1970; contbr. articles to profl. jours. Chmn. bd. Huntingdon Hosp., Willow Grove, Pa., 1982—; bd. dirs. YMHA, Phila., 1978—, Buten Mus., Phila., 1983, Anti-Defamation League, 1982. Named Man of the Yr., Nat. Assn. Women Bus. Owners, 1978; Disting. Alumnus, Central High Sch., 1975. Mem. ABA, Phila. Bar Assn. Democrat. Jewish. Clubs: Locust, Oxford and Cambridge (London). Home: 2106 Locust St Philadelphia PA 19103 Office: Jefferson Bank 250 S 18th St Philadelphia PA 19103

SPOONER, RONALD LEE, research company executive, engineer; b. Detroit, Oct. 8, 1939; s. Clarence D. and Eleanor (White) S.; MS in Engring. (I.F.C. fellow 1962, Gannett fellow 1963), U. Mich., 1963, MS in Math., 1965, PhD in Engring., 1967; m. Linda Ethel Ellis, June 15, 1962; children: Lisa, Susan, Carrie. Research engr. Cooley Electronic Lab, Ann Arbor, Mich., 1964-68; asso. dir. Bolt Beranek & Newman Co., Washington, 1968-72; v.p., founder Planning Systems Inc., Washington, 1972—. Adj. prof. dept. elec. engring. Catholic U. Am., Washington, 1968—. Treas. Annandale (Va.) Coop. Nursery Sch., 1972; mem. For Love of Children, Washington, 1968—. U. Fla. grantee, 1964. Mem. IEEE, Acoustical Soc. Am., Washington Acad. Scis., U.S. Naval Inst., Sigma Xi, Eta Kappa Nu, Tau Beta Pi, Phi Kappa Phi, Alpha Tau Omega. Clubs: Fairfax Tennis (Va.), Cosmos. Editor: IEEE Jours.; contbr. to profl. jours. Home: 8310 Summerwood Dr McLean VA 22102 Office: 7925 W Park Dr McLean VA 22102

SPORKEN, CHRISTIAAN PAUL, ethicist; b. Nieuwenhagen, The Netherlands, Mar. 18, 1927; s. Johan Joseph and Maria Elisabeth (Kremers) S.; Th.D., U. Nijmegen, 1957; Th.D., U. Leuven, 1961. Prof. moral theology Bergeyk-Eindhoven, 1957-68; dir. mgr. Bekkers Centrum, U. Nijmegen, 1968-74; prof. med. ethics med. faculty Rijksuniversiteit Limburg, 1974—, chmn. ethical com. Univ. Hosp., 1978—. Roman Catholic. Author: Ethiek en Gezondheidszorg, 6th edit., 1985; De Laatste Levensfase, 5th edit., 1977; Die Sorge um den Kranken Menschen, 1978, 3d edit., 1986; Sexualitat im Leben Geistig Behinderter, 1980; Eltern und ihr geistig behindertes Kind, 2d edit., 1980; Ayudando a morir, 1978; Heb jij qanvaard, dat ik sterven moet Stervenden en hun helpers, 1st and 2d edit., 1981; Hasst du denn bejaht, dass ich sterben muss?Eine Handreichung für den Umgang mit Sterbenden, 1981; Begleiding en ethiek, 1984; Begleitung in schwierigen lebans situationen, 1985; Was alte Menschen brauchen, 1986. Home: 25 Champs Elyseesweg, 6213 AA Maastricht The Netherlands Office: 53 Tongersestraat, 6200 MD Maastricht The Netherlands

SPRAGG, HOWARD EUGENE, church official; b. Boston, Sept. 15, 1917; s. Lee Hanford and Lillian (Hunter) S.; m. Jane Nichols, June 23, 1942; children: Susan E., Peter Hunter, Paul Alexander, Martha Ann, Deborah Townsend. A.B. summa cum laude, Tufts Coll., 1938; B.D., Chgo. Theol. Sem., 1947, D.D., 1968; D.D., Yankton Coll., 1956, Ursinus Coll., 1973, Northland Coll., 1974; L.H.D., Rollins Coll. Ordained to ministry Congl. Christian Chs., 1942; pastor in Chgo., 1942-48; gen. dir. P.R. mission Congl. Christian Chs., 1948-52; sec. Bd. Home Missions Congl. and Christian Chs., 1952-54, gen. sec. for adminstrn., 1954-58, treas., 1959-69; also treas. ten affiliated corps, including United Ch. Found. Annuity Congl. Ministers, Retirement Fund Lay Workers; treas. United Ch. Bd. Homeland Ministries, 1959-69, exec. v.p., chief exec. officer, 1969-84; fin. v.p. treas. United Church Found.; former mem. governing bd. Nat. Council Chs. Trustee Dillard U., Am. Coll., Madura, India; dir. workplace health fund; v.p., trustee Amistad Research Ctr.; founding trustee New Coll., Sarasota, Fla.; propr., mem. Boston Athenaeum. Mem. Soc. Arts, Religion and Culture (v.p.), Phi Beta Kappa. Home: Wolf Hill Rd Deering NH 03244

SPRAGUE, NORMAN FREDERICK, JR., surgeon, educator; b. Los Angeles, June 12, 1914; s. Norman F. and Frances E. (Ludeman) S.; m. Caryll E. Mudd, Dec. 27, 1941 (dec. Apr. 1978); children: Caryll (Mrs. Mingst), Norman Frederick III, Cynthia Sprague Connolly, Elizabeth (Mrs. Day); m. Erlenne Estes, Dec. 31, 1981. A.B., U. Calif., 1933; M.D., Harvard U., 1937. Intern Bellevue Hosp., N.Y.C., 1937; house surgeon Bellevue Hosp., 1938-39; pvt. med. practice Los Angeles, 1946—; mem. hon. staff Hosp. of Good Samaritan, Los Angeles; mem. staff St. Vincent Med. Ctr., Los Angeles; asst. clin. prof. surgery UCLA, 1951—; dir. emeritus Western Fed. Savs. & Loan Assn.; chmn. bd. dirs. Western Pioneer Co., 1961-63, Pioneer Savs. & Loan Assn., 1959-63; dir. Arden-Mayfair, Inc., 1966-69; also chmn. exec. com.; dir., mem. exec. com. Cyprus Mines Corp., 1959-79; trustee Mesabi Trust, 1964-76. Chmn. exec. com., v.p. Harvard Sch., 1954-65; mem. Community Redevel. Agy. City of Los Angeles, 1966-69, vice chmn., 1967-69; mem. Calif. Regional Med. Programs Area IV Council, 1970-75; bd. dirs., v.p. Calif. Inst. Cancer Research, 1974-80, pres., 1980-82; bd. dirs. Cancer Assoc., 1975-80; trustee UCLA Found., Marlborough Sch., Mildred E. and Harvey S. Mudd Found., Hollywood Bowl Assn., 1962-66; hon. trustee Calif. Mus. Found.; mem. exec. com., trustee Youth Tennis Found., 1960-70; trustee, pres. mem. exec. com. S.W. Mus.; founding trustee, Harvey Mudd Coll.; chmn. bd. trustees Carylland Norman Sprague Found., 1957—, Harvard Sch.; mem. bd. visitors UCLA Med. Sch.; mem. adv. com. Univs. Space Research Assn., Div. Space Biomedicine, 1982—; nat. bd. dirs. Retonitis Pigmentosa Internat. Served to maj. M.C. AUS, 1941-46. Decorated Bronze Star.; Recipient Bishop's award of Merit Episcopal Diocese Los Angeles, 1966; Highest Merit award So. Calif. Pub. Health Assn., 1968. Mem. AMA, Calif. Med. Assn., Los Angeles County Med. Assn. (pres. jr. sect. 1953), SAR, Am. Cattlemen's Assn., Symposium Soc., Tennis Patrons Assn. (dir. 1960-70), Delta Kappa Epsilon. Clubs: Faculty, California, Harvard, Lincoln, Los Angeles Country, Regency (Los Angeles). Home: 550 S Mapleton Dr Los Angeles CA 90024 Office: 3600 Wilshire Blvd Los Angeles CA 90010

SPRAOS, JOHN, economics professor; b. Athens, Greece, Nov. 4, 1926; arrived in Eng., 1946.; s. Menelaus and Penelope (Voudouroglu) S.; m. Mary Constance Whitwill, Sept. 26, 1956; children: Paul, Helen. MA, U. Edinburgh, Scotland, 1950. Research scholar U. Manchester, Eng., 1950-53; research fellow U. Sheffield, Eng., 1953-57; lectr. econs. U. London, 1957-64, reader econs., 1964-65, prof. econs., 1965-82, prof. emeritus, 1982—; chmn. Council Econ. Advisers, Greece, 1985—; cons. UN Conf. Trade and Devel., Geneva, 1974-75; mem. com. indexation experts UN, 1975; editorial adviser Penguin Books, 1967-77. Author: The Decline of the Cinema, 1962, Inequalising Trade?, 1983; mem. editorial bd. Review of Econ. Studies, 1955-65; contbr. articles to profl. jours. Chmn. Greek Com. Against Dictatorship, London, 1967-74. Mem. Am. Econ. Assn., Royal Econ. Soc. Office: University Coll, Gower St, London WC1E 6BT, England

SPRAWSON, BARRIE GILBERT, management consultant; b. Sutton Coldfield, Warwickshire, Eng., Nov. 19, 1939; arrived in Can., 1957; s. Gilbert Harry and Lily A. (Arkenstall) S.; m. Gillian Anne Spencer, Jan. 25, 1958; children: Garry Clive, Jonathan David, Andrew Barrie, Julia Patricia, Tricia Laura Karen. Student in advanced mgmt., Harvard U., 1982. V.p. Johnson & Higgins Willis Faber Ltd., Toronto, Ont., Can., 1964-74; ptnr.-in-charge human resources Peat Marwick & Ptnrs., Toronto, 1974-84; mng. prin. Sibson & Co., Toronto, 1984—; pres. Jr. Bd. Trade, Toronto, 1971-72; v.p., 2d dir. Johnson & Higgins Equity Corp., Toronto, 1972-74; chmn. Met. Toronto Compensation Com., 1975—; bd. dirs. Toronto Bd. Trade, 1973-74, chmn. compensation com., mem. labor relations com., 1975—; mem. mayor's compensation com. City of Toronto, 1976—; lectr. advanced mgmt. and indsl. relations Queens U., Kingston, Ont., 1983-87; speaker in field of human resource mgmt. Contbr. articles to various publs. Senator Jr. Chamber Internat. Named Queens Scout, Boy Scouts Assn., 1955. Mem. Can. Inst. Employee Specialists (pres. 1985-87). Conservative. Anglican. Clubs: Oakville, Albany (Oakville, Ont.), Empire. Home: 1417 Lakeshore Rd E, Oakville, ON Canada L6J 1L9 Office: Sibson & Co, 40 Dundas St W, Toronto, ON Canada M5G 2C2

SPRAY, PAUL, surgeon; b. Wilkinsburg, Pa., Apr. 9, 1921; s. Lester E. and Phoebe Gertrude (Hull) S.; m. Mary Louise Conover, Nov. 28, 1943; children—David C., Thomas L., Mary Lynn (Mrs. Thomas Branham). B.S., U. Pitts., 1942; M.D., George Washington U., 1944; M.S., U. Minn., 1950. Diplomate Am. Bd. Orthopedic Surgery. Intern U.S. Marine Hosp., S.I., 1944-45; resident Mayo Found., Rochester, Minn., 1945-46, 48-50; practice medicine specializing in orthopedic surgery Oak Ridge, Tenn., 1950—; mem. staff Oak Ridge Hosp., East Tenn. Baptist Hosp., Park West Hosp., Knoxville, Harriman Hosp., Tenn., Bapt. Hosp. of Roane County; Oak Ridge Associated Univs; vol. vis. cons., CARE Medico, Jordan, 1959, Nigeria, 1962, 65, Algeria, 1963, Afghanistan, 1970, Bangladesh, 1975, 77, 79, Peru, 1980, U. Ghana, 1982; AMA voluntary physician, Vietnam, 1967, 72; vis. assoc. prof. U. Nairobi, 1973; mem. teaching team of Internat. Coll. Surgeons to Khartoum, vis. prof. orthopedic surgery U. Khartoum, 1976; hon. prof. San Luis Gonzaga U., Ica, Peru; AmDoc vol. cons., U. Biafra Teaching Hosp., 1969; vis. prof. Mayo Clinic, 1988; sec. orthopedics overseas div. CARE Medico, 1971-76, sec. medico adv. bd., 1974-76, vice chmn., 1976, chmn., 1977-79, v.p. CARE, Inc., 1977-79, pub. mem. care bd., 1980—; chmn. Orthopedics Overseas, Inc., 1982-86, treas., 1986—; mem. U.S. organizing com. 1st Internat. Acad. Symposium on Orthopedics, Tianjin, China, 1983; mem. CUPP Internat. Adv. Council, 1986—; bd. dirs. East Tenn. Health Plan, 1987—. Mem. editorial bd. Contemporary Orthopedics, 1984—. Vice pres. Anderson County Health Council, 1975, pres., 1976-77; pres. health commn. Council So. Mountains, 1958-65, sec. bd. dirs., 1965-66; Tenn. pres. UN Assn., 1966-67; vice chmn. bd. Camelot Care Ctr., Tenn., 1979-82, chmn., 1982-86; chmn. bd. dirs. Camelot Found., 1986-87; Served to capt. AUS, 1946-48. Recipient various humanitarian awards including Sertoma Service to Mankind award, 1967, Freedom citation Sertoma, 1978, Medico Disting. Service award, 1980, 1st ann. Vocat. Service award Oak Ridge Rotary Club, 1979. Fellow ACS, Internat. Coll. Surgeons (Tenn. regent 1976-80, bd. councillors 1980-84, hon. chmn. bd. trustees 1981-83, trustee 1983-84, v.p. U.S. sect. 1982-83, mem. Surg. teams com. 1983—); mem. Societe International Chirugie Orthopedique et de Tramuatologie, So. Orthopedic Assn., Western Pacific Orthopedic Assn., Orthopedic Letters Club, Am. Fracture Assn., Am. Acad. Orthopedic Surgeons (mem. com. on injuries 1980—), AMA (Humanitarian Service award 1967, 72), Tenn. Med. Assn. (com. on emergency med. services 1978—), Alumni and Friends of Medico (pres. 1975-77), Peru Acad. Surgery (corr.), Peruvian Soc. Orthopedic Surgery and Traumatology (corr.), N. Am. Spine Soc., Mid-Am. Orthopedic Assn. Quaker. Club: Lions (Humanitarian award 1968, Ambassador of Goodwill award 1979). Home: 507 Delaware Ave Oak Ridge TN 37830 Office: 145 E Vance Rd Oak Ridge TN 37830

SPRECHER-GOLDBERGER, SUZANNE, virology science researcher, general microbiology educator; b. Pau, France, Nov. 13, 1940; d. Martin and Mania (Baum) G.; m. Nathan Sprecher, Oct. 23, 1962; children—Eli, David, Aaron. M. Zool. Scis., U. Brussels, 1962. Asst. virological scientist Pasteur Inst., Brussels, 1962—; research scientist Blood Transfusion Lab., Rouen, France, 1966-67; prof. microbiology Edith Cavell Hosp., Brussels, 1972—. Contbr. articles to profl. jours. Active Maison de la Culture Juive, Brussels, 1983—. Fellow Union Internationale Contre le Cancer, Geneva, Switzerland, 1976; recipient prize in sci. competition Rick Wouters, Belgium, 1978. Mem. Societe Belge D'Immunologie. Jewish. Lodge: B'nai B'rith. Avocations: reading, philosophy, culture, art, music. Home: 44 Ave E Theys, B-1410 Waterloo Belgium Office: Institut Pasteur de Brabant, 642 Rue England, B-1180 Brussels Belgium

SPRENG, DANIEL THEODOR, educator, researcher; b. Berne, Switzerland, Nov. 16, 1940; s. Hanns and Charlotte (Bertschinger) S.; m. Mary Magdalene Courtney; children: Kira Ann, Connor Patrick. Diploma in Physics, Swiss Fed. Inst. Tech., Zurich, 1965; MS, U. Kans., 1966; PhD in Materials Sci., Northwestern U., 1970. Researcher Swiss Aluminum Ltd., Neuhausen, Switzerland, 1971-73, sr. scientist, 1973-75, dir. ecology, 1976-82; fellow Inst. Energy Analysis, Oak Ridge, Tenn., 1975-76; researcher, lectr. Swiss Fed. Inst. Tech., Zurich, 1982—; cons. in field. Author: Net Energy Analysis, 1988, Energy Requirement of the Information Soc., 1987; contbr. articles to periodicals, jours.; patentee in field. Home: Burgstrasse 22, 8193 Eglisau Switzerland Office: Swiss Fed Inst Tech, ETH Zentrum, 8092 Zurich Switzerland

SPRENGER, KLAUS, management consultant; b. Hilden, Fed. Republic Germany, Apr. 18, 1946; s. Erich Gustav and Marianne Emma S.; m. Christiane Warmuth, Jan. 12, 1967; 1 child, Thorsten. Tech. degree in chemistry Bayer AG, Leverkusen, Fed. Republic Germany, 1977. Lab. asst. Bayer AG, Leverkusen, 1971-72; prodn. mgr. Coop-Waschmittelwerk, Düsseldorf, Fed. Republic Germany, 1972-75; sales mgr. Siolax, Gmbh, Hanau, Fed. Republic Germany, 1975-80, mgr. div., 1980-85; mgmt. and sales trainer VA-Akademie für Führen und Verkaufen, Sulzbach, Fed. Republic Germany, 1985—; cons. Brauer-Bund, Nuremburg, Fed. Republic Germany. Mem. SEPAWA. Evangelisch. Club: Tennis. Office: VA-Akademie für Fuhren und, Verkaufen, Hauptstrasse 123, D-6231 Sulzbach Hesse, Federal Republic of Germany

SPRIDDELL, PETER HENRY, corporate executive; b. Aug. 18, 1928; s. Thomas Henry and Eva Florence Spriddell; m. Joyce Patricia Haycock, 1952; 3 children. Student, Plymouth Coll.; MA, Oxford U.; postgrad., Harvard U. With Marks and Spencer, 1951—, alt. dir., 1970-72, full dir., 1972—, personnel dir., 1972-75, bldg. store ops., 1975-87, dir. estates and physical distbn., 1987—; bd. dirs. NFC, British Rail Property Bd. Pres. Oxford St. Assn., 1987; mem. council Templeton Coll. Oxford, 1978—, Town and Country Planning Assn., 1978—; v.p. Devon Hist. Bldg. Trust, 1978; liverman Worshipful Co. Paviers, 1984. Mem. British Council Shopping Ctrs. (sr. v.p. 1988). Club: Moor Park Golf. Home: 37 Main Ave Moor Park Estate, Northwood England Office: Marks and Spencer PLC, 47-67 Baker St, London England

SPRING, BONNIE JOAN, psychology educator, researcher; b. Hackensack, N.J., Oct. 9, 1949; d. John Edwin and Sonja Joan (Litwinowich) S.; B.A., Bucknell U., 1971; M.A., Harvard U., 1975, Ph.D., 1977. Lic. psychologist, Mass., Tex. Research scientist Biometrics Research, N.Y.C., 1975-78; instr. psychology Harvard U., Cambridge, Mass., 1977, asst. prof., 1977-82, assoc. prof., 1982-84; prof. Tex. Tech U., Lubbock, 1984—, dir. clin. tng., 1986—; lectr. psychiatry Columbia Coll. Physicians and Surgeons, N.Y.C., 1979-86; vis. lectr. nutrition MIT, Cambridge, 1979-80; staff psychologist Mass. Mental Health, Boston, 1981-84; research assoc. prof. psychiatry U. Md. Med. Sch., Balt., 1984—. Author: Psuchology, 1988; editor: Attention in Schizophrenia, 1979, Psychopharmacology, 1986—; mem. edit. bd. Jour. of Social and Clin. Psychology, 1985—. Contbr. articles to profl. jours. Mem. Harvard U. Com. on Status of Women, Cambridge, 1979-81; panel mem. com. on nat. needs for behavioral research personnel Inst. of Medicine, Nat. Acad. Scis., Washington, 1984-86; panel mem. nat. plan for research on schizophrenia NIMH, 1987. Nutrition grantee Ctr. for Brain Scis., 1980-81, Ford Found., 1981-82; Cognition grantee Kali-Duphar Labs., 1982-86; Schizophrenia grantee NIMH, 1980-84. Fellow Am. Psychol. Assn.; mem. AAAS, Am. Psychopathol. Assn., Soc. for Biol. Psychiatry, Am. Coll. Neuropsychopharmacology, Sigma Xi. Avocations: swimming, international travel. Office: Dept Psychology Tex Tech U PO Box 4100 Lubbock TX 79409

SPRING, DICK (RICHARD MARTIN SPRING), Irish political party leader; b. Tralee, Ireland, Aug. 29, 1950; m. Kristi Hutcheson; children: Aaron, Laura, Adam. B.A., Trinity Coll., Dublin; B.L., Kings Inn, Dublin. Minister of State Dept. Justice, Republic of Ireland, 1981, dep. prime minister, 1982-87, minister for environment, 1982-83, minister for energy, 1983-87; mem. Council of State, 1982-87; leader Labour Party, 1982—. Active Tralee Urban Dist. Council, 1979, Kerry County Council, 1979; pres. EEC Energy Council, 1984; mem. New Ireland Forum, 1985; negotiator Anglo Irish Agreement, 1986. Roman Catholic. Avocation: Rugby. Home: Dunroamin Cloonanorig, Tralee Ireland Office: Office of Leader, Labour Party, Dublin Ireland

SPRINGER, HUGH WORRELL, government official; b. St. Michael, Barbados, June 22, 1913; s. Charles Wilkinson and Florence Nightingale (Barrow) S.; m. Dorothy Drinan Gittens; children: Richild Diana, Mark Wakefield, Harold Jason, Stephen O'Connor. Student Harrison Coll. (Barbados), 1923-32; BA, Hertford Coll., Oxford U., Eng., 1936, MA, 1944; Barrister at Law, Inner Temple, London, 1938; hon. DSc Social Scis., Laval U., 1958; LLD, U. Victoria (B.C.), 1972, U. W.I., 1973, City Univ. (London), 1978, U. Manchester (Eng.), 1979, U. N.B., 1980, York U. (Can.), 1980, U. Zimbabwe, 1981, U. Bristol (Eng.), 1982, U. Birmingham (Eng.), 1983; D. Litt., U. Warwick (Eng.), 1974, U. Ulster, 1974, Heriot Watt Univ., 1976, U. Hong Kong, 1977, St. Andrews U. (Scotland), 1977; D.C.L., U. Oxford, 1980, U. E. Anglia, 1980. Acting prof. classics Codrington Coll., Barbados, 1938; sole practice law, Barbados, 1938-47; mem. House of Assembly, Barbados, 1940-47, exec. com., 1944-47; gen. sec. Barbados Labour Party, 1940-47; organizer, 1st gen. sec. Barbados Workers' Union, 1940-47; registrar Univ. West Indies, 1947-63, dir. Inst. Edn., 1963-66; acting gov. and comdr.-in-chief Barbados, 1964; dir. Commonwealth Edn. Liaison Unit, London, 1966, Commonwealth asst. sec. gen., 1966-70; sec. gen. Assn. Commonwealth Univs., London, 1970-80; gov.-gen. Barbados, 1984—. Bd. dirs. Sugar Industry Agrl. Bank, Hosp. Bd., Edn. Bd., Governing Body Harrison Coll., Queen's Coll., 1938-47; trustee Anglican Ch., 1981-84; chmn. Disciplinary Com. Bar, 1982-84, Nat. Tng. Bd., 1982-84, Income Tax Appeal Bd., 1983-84, Nat. Devel. Found., 1983-84, Mapps Coll., 1983-84, Friends of Scouting, 1983-84, mem. com. of Mgmt. of Assn. Mentally Retarded Children; others vol. service in Jamaica, West Indies, U.K., Ghana, East Africa, South Pacific, UN, Holland. Barbados scholar Harrison Coll., 1931; Guggenheim fellow, 1961-62; Harvard Ctr. for Internat. affairs fellow, 1961-62; sr. vis. fellow All Souls Coll., Oxford, 1962-63, (hon., 1988); Silver medal Royal Soc. Arts, Eng., 1970; Hon. fellow Hertford Coll., 1974; hon. prof. edn. U. Mauritius, 1981; Knight Grand Cross Order St. Michael and St. George; Knight Grand Cross, Royal Victorian Order, 1985; Knight of St. Andrew in Order of Barbados; comdr. Order of Brit. Empire. Anglican. Clubs: Athenaeum, Royal Commonwealth. Address: Office of Gov Gen, Government House, Bridgetown Barbados

SPRINGER, NEIL ALLEN, manufacturing company executive; b. Fort Wayne, Ind, May 2, 1938; s. Roy V. and Lucille H. (Gerke) S.; m. Janet M. Grotrian, Sept. 3, 1960; children: Sheri Lynn, Kelly Jean, Mark Allen. BS, U. Ind, 1960; MBA, U. Dayton, 1966. Staff asst. acctg. Internat. Harvester Co. (now Navistar Internat. Corp.), Bridgeport, Conn., 1966-68; asst. comptroller Internat. Harvester Co. (now Navistar Internat. Corp.), Fort Wayne, Ind., 1968-70; staff asst. Internat. Harvester Co. (now Navistar Internat. Corp.), Chgo., 1970-75, asst. corp. comptroller, 1975-77, v.p. fin., 1977-79, v.p. gen. mgr. trucks, 1979-81, pres. truck group, 1981-84, pres., chief operating officer, 1984-87; chmn., pres., chief exec. officer Navistar Internat. Transp. Corp., Chgo., 1987—; bd. dirs. Century Life Ins. Co., Waverly, Iowa; vice chmn. Am. Trucking Assn. Found., 1985—. Bd. dirs. Lutheran Home & Services for Aged, Arlington Heights, Ill., 1980—. Mem. Ill. Soc. CPA's. Office: Navistar Internat Transp Corp 401 N Michigan Ave Chicago IL 60611 *

SPRINGER, TIMOTHY JON, ergonomic consulting company executive; b. Fort Wayne, Ind., Nov. 12, 1952; s. Daniel Christian and Mabel Ann (Fuhrman) S.; m. Joyce Eileen McAllister, Sept. 1, 1973; children—Laura Trese, Benjamin Jon. Student, U.S. Naval Acad., 1970; B.A., Augustana Coll., 1974; M.A., U. S.D., 1976, Ph.D., 1978. Research asst. Dept. Transp., Vermillion, S.D., 1974-77, S.D. Hwy. Patrol, Pierre, 1977-78; assoc. research adminstr. State Farm Ins., Bloomington, Ill., 1978-82; assoc. prof. psychology Ill. State U., Normal, 1979-80; pres. Springer Assocs., Inc., St. Charles, Ill., 1982—. Author: Improving Productivity in the Workplace: Reports from the Field, 1986; (with others) Designing for High Technology Production Environments, 1987; ergonomics editor: Internat. Facility Management Assn. newsletter; contbr. articles to profl. jours. Patentee ergonomic forearm rest. Bd. dirs. Bethlehem Presch., St. Charles; mem. ch. council, deacon Bethlehem Luth. Ch., St. Charles. Mem. Human Factors Soc. Office: Springer Assocs Inc 1405 W Main St PO Box 1159 Saint Charles IL 60174

SPRINGSTEIN, KARL-AUGUST HERMANN, international technical consultant; b. Kiel, Germany, Nov. 3, 1918; s. Karl and Irma (Servus) S.; m. Traute Kramer, Jan. 22, 1948; children—Margot, Helmut. Physicist, U. Berlin, 1943. Physicist, dept. chief Telefunken, Berlin, 1943-45; chief engr. various communication and electronics cos., Berlin, 1945-55; chief engr. Dr.-Ing. Rudolf Hell GumbH, Kiel, W.Ger., 1955-61; research dir., tech. advisor of bd. Axel Springer Verlag AG, Hamburg, W.Ger., 1961-74; internat. tech. cons. Hamburg, W.Ger., 1975—; lectr. various univs.; freelance journalist in printing tech., pub., communications. Mem. Inst. Printing (London), Fuhrungskrafte der Druckindustrie (dir.). Mem. Evangelical Ch. Author tech. manual, 3 edits.; co-author several tech. manuals on printing tech.; contbr. articles to tech. publs. Home and Office: 27 Suelldorfer Muehlenweg, D-2000 Hamburg 55 Federal Republic of Germany

SPRINKLE, ROBERT LEE, JR., podiatrist; b. Winston-Salem, N.C., July 13, 1932; s. Robert Lee and Elton Elizabeth Sprinkle; children—Robert III, Karen, Ralph, Richard, Roy, Randy, Drouin. Student Salem Coll., 1952; BS, Ohio Coll. Podiatry, 1956; DPM, Pa. Coll. Podiatry, 1970. Practice medicine specializing in podiatry, Winston-Salem, 1957—; chmn. N.C. Bd. Podiatry Examiners, 1968-74; clin. assoc. prof. Dr. William M. School Coll. Podiatric Medicine; researcher reconstructive surgery human foot and ankle. Chmn. Mayor's Com. on Hiring the Handicapped, 1963-64; commr. Old Hickory council Boy Scouts Am., 1970-71, v.p., 1973-74, Silver Beaver award, 1969; pres. St. Leo's Parochial Sch. PTA, 1969-70; dir. Half Way House, 1965-66; chmn. Bishop McGuiness PTA, 1976. Paul Harris fellow Rotary Internat., 1971-72; grantee Schering, Inc., 1972-74; recipient St. George medal, 1971. Mem. Am. Podiatry Assn., N.C. Podiatry Assn. (past pres.), Piedmont Podiatry Assn., Am. Pub. Health Assn., Internat. Analgesia Soc. Democrat. Roman Catholic. Clubs: Forsyth Country, Twin City, Ardmore Community. Lodge: Rotary (dist. gov. 1976-77). Home: 1930 Swaim Rd Winston-Salem NC 27127 Office: Profl Bldg PO Box 5442 2240 Cloverdale Ave Suite 216 Winston-Salem NC 27113

SPRINKLE, ROBERT MARSHALL, international educational exchange executive; b. Granite City, Ill., Dec. 12, 1936; s. Marshall Roseboro and Jean Pomeroy (Miller) S.; B.A., U. Colo., 1959; student N.Mex. State U., 1963-64, U. Mich., 1964-65; m. G(ladys) Sandra Fisher, Mar. 31, 1967; 1 dau., Lisa Jean McKee. Dir. pub. relations, editor, dir. Internat. Student Visitor Service, USNSA/Ednl. Travel, Inc., N.Y.C., 1960-63; grad. asst., counselor N.Mex. State U. Guidance Center, 1963-64; program adv., adminstrv. coordinator U. Mich. Internat. Center, 1964-67; exec. dir., sec.-treas., dir. Assn. Internat. Practical Tng., Columbia, Md., 1967—, mem. internat. IAESTE adv. com., 1978-81; v.p. Network for Internat. Exchange, 1983-85; bd. dirs. Open Door Student Exchange, 1987—, Internat. Exchange Assn., 1985—, Worldwise 2000, 1988—; vice chmn., 1987-88. Bd. dirs. Nat. Council for Community Services to Internat. Visitors, 1969-73; mem. U.S. Nat. Commn. for UNESCO, Washington, 1969-75, 79-81, mem. exec. com., 1970-75, membership com. 1974-75, nominating com., 1974-75. Served to capt. AUS, 1959-60. Mem. Am. Assn. Higher Edn., Am. Fgn. Service Assn., Am. Soc. Engring. Edn., Am. Soc. Public Adminstrn., Am. Soc. Tng. and Devel. (exec. com. internat. div. 1982-83), Assn. Sandwich Edn. and Tng. (U.K.), Assn. World Edn., Nat. Assn. Fgn. Student Affairs, Soc. Internat. Devel., Soc. Intercultural Edn., Tng. and Research, Empire State Ry. Mus. Inc., Railroadians of Am. Inc., South Street Seaport Mus. Inc. Republican. Baptist. Office: Park View Bldg Suite 320 10480 Little Patuxent Pkwy Columbia MD 21044-3502

SPROULL, ROBERT LAMB, university president, physicist; b. Lacon, Ill., Aug. 16, 1918; s. John Steele and Chloe Velma (Lamb) S.; m. Mary Louise Knickerbocker, June 27, 1942; children: Robert F., Nancy M. AB, Cornell U., 1940, PhD, 1943; LLD (hon.), Nazareth Coll., 1983. Research physicist RCA labs., 1943-46; faculty Cornell U., 1946-63, 65-68, prof. physics, 1956-63, dir. lab. atomic and solid state physics, 1959-60, dir. materials sci. center, 1960-63, v.p. for acad. affairs, 1965-68; dir. Advanced Research Projects Agy., Dept. Def., Washington, 1963-65; v.p., provost U. Rochester, N.Y., 1968-70; pres. U. Rochester, 1970-84, pres. emeritus, 1984—; Prin. physicist Oak Ridge Nat. Lab., 1952; physicist European Research Assos., Brussels, Belgium, 1958-59; lectr. NATO, 1958-59; dir. John Wiley & Sons, Charles River Labs., United Technols. Corp., Xerox Corp., Bausch & Lomb; mem. sci. adv. com. Gen. Motors Corp, 1971-80, chmn., 1973-80; Mem. Def. Sci. Bd., 1966-70; Chmn. Def. Sci.-Bd., 1968-70; Mem. Naval Research Adv.

Com., 1974-76; mem. Sloan Commn. Higher Edn., 1977-79. Author: Modern Physics, 1956; Editor: Jour. Applied Physics, 1954-57. Trustee Deep Springs Coll., 1967-75, 83-87, Cornell U., 1972-77. Ctr. for Advanced Study in Behavioral Scis. fellow, 1973. Fellow Am. Acad. Arts and Scis.; mem. Telluride Assn. (pres. 1945-47), Inst. of Def. Analysis (trustee 1984—). Home: 6 Green Ridge Pittsford NY 14534 Office: U Rochester Rochester NY 14627

SPUFFORD, HONOR MARGARET, historian; b. Hartford, Eng., Dec. 10, 1935; d. Leslie Marshall and Mary (Johnson) Clark; m. Peter Spufford, July 7, 1962; children: Francis Peter, Bridget Margaret. MA with distinction, Leicester U., 1963, PhD, 1970; LittD, Cambridge (Eng.) U., 1986. Research fellow Lucy Cavendish Coll. Cambridge U., 1969-72; fellow Newnhan Coll., 1981—; hon. lectr. U. Keele (Eng.), 1974-78, sr. research fellow, 1978-81. Author: Contrasting Communities, 1974, Small Books and Pleasant Histories, 1982, Great Reclothing of Rural England, 1984. Fellow Royal Hist. Soc. Anglican. Home: 30 Bateman St, Cambridge CB2 1NB, England Office: Cambridge U Faculty History, West Rd, Cambridge CB3 9EF, England

SPUNT, SHEPARD ARMIN, realty executive, management and financial consultant; b. Cambridge, Mass., Feb. 3, 1931; s. Harry and Naomi (Drooker) S.; B.S., U. Pa., 1952, M.B.A., 1956; m. Joan Murray Fooshee, Aug. 6, 1961 (dec. June 1969); children—Erica Frieda and Andrew Murray (twins). Owner, Colonial Realty Co., Brookline, Mass., 1953—, Cambridge, 1960—; sr. assoc. Gen. Solids Assocs., 1956—; chmn. bd. Gen. Solids Systems Corp., 1971-74; trustee Union Capital Trust, Boston; incorporator Liberty Bank & Trust Co., Boston. Chmn., Com. for Fair Urban Renewal Laws, Mass., 1965—; treas. Ten Men of Mass., 1980. Pres., New Eng. Council of Young Republicans, 1964-67, 69-71; vice chmn. Young Rep. Nat. Fedn., 1967-69, dir. region I, 1964-67, 69-71; mem. Brookline Republican Town Com., 1960—; del. Atlantic Conf. Young Polit. Leaders, Brussels, 1973; bd. dirs. Brookline Taxpayers Assn., 1964—, v.p., 1971-72, pres., 1972—. Registered profl. engr., Mass. Mem. Nat. Soc. Profl. Engrs., Rental Housing Assn., Greater Boston Real Estate Bd., Navy League, Boston Athenaeum, Copley Soc. Boston. Lodges: Masons, Shriners. Author: (with others) A Business Data Processing Service for Small Business Practitioners, 1956; A Business Data Processing Service for Medical Practitioners, 1956, rev. edit., 1959. Author, sponsor consumer protection and election law legislation Mass. Gen. Ct., 1969—. Patentee in field of automation, lasers, dielectric bonding. Home: 177 Reservoir Rd Chestnut Hill MA 02167 Office: 21 Elmer St Cambridge MA 02238-0172

SPURGEON, EDWARD VAN RENSSELAER, manufacturing company executive; b. Santa Barbara, Calif., May 21, 1931; s. Robert Henry and Elizabeth (Delafield) S.; B.A., Dartmouth Coll., 1953, M.S., 1954; m. Patricia Ankeny Trebien Flynn, June 19, 1954; children—Edward van Rensselaer, Elizabeth D. With Gen. Elec. Co., 1966—, mgr. mfg. ops. indsl. controls, Salem, Va., mgr. mfg. kitchen systems ops., Kissimmee, Fla., sr. corp. cons., Fairfield, Conn., 1966-80, program mgr. corp. engring. and mfg., Bridgeport, Conn., 1980—. Pres., Roanoke (Va.) Childrens Home Soc., 1968; v.p. Roanoke Council Community Services, 1972; bd. dirs. Darien (Conn.) Arts Council, 1979. Served to lt., USNR, 1954-57. Mem. Am. Mgmt. Assn., Assn. Mfg. Excellence (bd. dirs. 1986—). Republican. Episcopalian. Clubs: Wee Burn Country (bd. dirs.), Noroton Yacht. Home: 35 Raiders Ln Darien CT 06820 Office: 1285 Boston Ave Bridgeport CT 06602

SPYROU, GEORGE ANDREWRANKIN, marketing professional, barrister; b. Glasgow, Scotland, Apr. 14, 1949; naturalized, 1972; s. Andrew George and Anne (Rankin) S.; m. Amanda E. Anninos, Dec. 1, 1984; 1 child, Peter Andrew Rankin. BA, Harvard U., 1971; BA in Law, Cambridge (Eng.) U., 1973, LLB, 1974, MA in Law, 1986. Bar: Eng., Wales. Assoc. atty. Cadwalader, Wickersham & Taft, N.Y.C., 1974-75, Healy & Baillie, N.Y.C., 1975-76; legal adviser Olympic Maritime, Monte Carlo, Monaco, 1977-80, Airship Industries, London, 1980-82; head internat. mktg. Airship Industries, London, N.Y.C., 1981—; legal adviser various transp. cos., London, 1980-85. Architect, designer houses in U.S. and Greece. Fellow Inst. Sales and Mktg. Mgmt. Clubs: Harvard (N.Y.C.); Signet Society (Cambridge); Royal Automobile (London). Home: 419 W Lyon Farm Greenwich CT 06831 Office: Airship Industries Inc 650 Fifth Ave New York NY 10019

SQUAZZO, MILDRED KATHERINE (OETTING), corp. exec.; b. Bklyn., Dec. 22; d. William John and Marie M. (Fromm) Oetting; student L.I. U. Sec.-treas., Stanley Engring., Inc. and v.p. Stanley Chems., Inc., 1960-68; founder, pres. Chem-Dynamics Corp., Scotch Plains, N.J., 1964-68; gen. adminstr., purchasing dir., Richardson Chem. Co., Metuchen, N.J., 1968-69; owner Berkeley Employment Agy. and Berkeley Temp. Help Service, Berkeley Heights, N.J., 1969—, Berkeley Employment Agy., Morristown, N.J., 1982, Bridgewater, N.J., 1987—; pres. M.K.S. Bus. Group, Inc., Berkeley Heights, 1980—; mgmt. cons., personnel fin.; lectr. Served with Nurse Corps, U.S. Army, 1946-47. Mem. Nat. Bus. and Profl. Women's Club. Office: 312 Springfield Ave Berkeley Heights NJ 07922

SQUILLACE, ALEXANDER PAUL, investment advisor; b. Missoula, Mont., Feb. 25, 1945; s. Dominick Paul and Kathleen Marie S.; B.S. in Bus. Adminstrn., Ohio State U., 1967; m. Miriam Palmer Patterson, June 17, 1967; children—Sandra, Scott, Brian, Susan. Investment analyst Nationwide Ins. Cos., Columbus, Ohio, 1967-69; instl. bond rep. Hornblower & Weeks-Hemphill, Noyes, Columbus, 1969-71, mgr. fixed income securities, Indpls., 1971-74; v.p. United Nat. Bank-United Nat. Corp., Sioux Falls, S.D., 1974-79; pres. Investment Mgmt. Group, Sioux Falls, S.D., 1979—, Farmers State Bank, Stickney, S.D., 1979—, Bormann Ins. Agy., Stickney, 1979—, Fin. Services Group Inc., 1984—; chmn. S.D. Investment Council, Postal Bus. Group Inc., 1986—; dir. Western Warehouse, Inc.; instr. Am. Inst. Banking. Named hon. citizen of Indpls., 1974; chartered fin. analyst. Fellow Fin. Analysts Fedn.; mem. Am. Inst. Banking, S.D. Bankers Assn., S.D. Investment Soc., Twin Cities Soc. Security Analysts, Ohio State Alumni Assn. Home: 2009 E 52d St Sioux Falls SD 57103 Office: 401 S 2nd Ave Sioux Falls SD 57102

SQUIRE, CLIFFORD WILLIAM, diplomat; b. Great Yarmouth, Norfolk, Eng., Oct. 7, 1928; s. Clifford John and Eleanor Eliza (Harpley) S.; m. Marie-José Carlier, July 6, 1959 (dec. 1973); children: Catherine, Stephen, Anne-Louise; m. Sara Laetitia Hutchison, May 22, 1976; children: James, Emma. BA, U. Oxford, 1951; diploma, Coll. Europe, Brugges, Belgium, 1952; PhD, Sch. Oriental and African Studies, London, 1979. Asst. dist. officer Nigerian Adminstrv. Service, Nigeria, 1953-59; sec. of embassy Brit. Fgn. Service, Bucharest, UN N.Y.C., Bangkok, 1959-72; counsellor Fgn. Office, London, 1972-76, Brit. Embassy, Washington, 1976-79; ambassador to Senegal, Mauritania, Guinea Dakar, Guinea Bissau, Cape Verde, 1979-82; under sec. Fgn. Office, London, 1982-84; ambassador Brit. Embassy, Tel Aviv, 1984—. Served to 2d lt. Brit. Army, 1947-49. Mem. Ch. of Eng. Club: Travellers. Office: Cambridge U Devel Office, Keynes House 24A Trumpington St, Cambridge CB2 1QA, England

SQUIRE, RUSSEL NELSON, musician, emeritus educator; b. Cleve., Sept. 21, 1908. B.Mus. Edn., Oberlin Coll., 1929; A.M., Case Western Res. U., 1939; Ph.D., NYU, 1942; postgrad. U. So. Calif. Dir. Oberlin Summer Music Sch., Ohio, 1929; dir. instrumental music instrn. Chillicothe Pub. Schs., Ohio, 1929-37; faculty Pepperdine U., Malibu, Calif., 1937-56, prof. music, 1937-56, now prof. emeritus, also chmn. fine arts div., 1940-56; faculty Calif. State U.-Long Beach, 1956-72, prof. music, 1964-72, now prof. emeritus; vis. prof. Pacific Christian Coll., 1970-74; prof. philosophy Sch. Edn., Pepperdine U., 1972-78; profl. theater orch. pianist, 1926-28; founder/propr./dir. Ednl. Travel Service involving study residencies in Europe, the Near East, China, India, Australia, Africa, Service, Agoura, Calif., 1958-84. Author: Studies in Sight Singing, 1950; Introduction to Music Education, 1952; Church Music, 1962; Class Piano for Adult Beginners, 1964, 3d edit., 1984; also contbr. articles to profl. jours. Founder/pres. Council for Scholarship Aid to Fgn. Students, Inc.; mem. Los Angeles County Music Commn., 1948-60; bd. dirs. Opera Guild So. Calif., 1948-60; pres. Long Beach Symphony Assn., 1963-64 (bd. dirs 1961-64). Mem. Music Tchrs. Assn. Calif. (br. pres. 1948-51), AAUP (chpt. founding pres. 1948-49), Phi Mu Alpha Sinfonia (life). Club: Twenty (Los Angeles), Bohemians (Los Angeles). Lodge: Rotary (Los Angeles, Long Beach). Home: PO Box 8355 Palm Springs CA 92263

SQUIRES, RICHARD FELT, research scientist; b. Sparta, Mich., Jan. 15, 1933; s. Monas Nathan and Dorothy Lois (Felt) S.; m. Else Saederup, 1 dau., Iben. B.S., Mich. State U., 1958; postgrad. Calif. Inst. Tech., 1961. Research biochemist Pasadena Found. for Med. Research, 1961-62; chief biochemistry sect. research dept. A/S Ferrosan Soeborg, Denmark, 1963-78; neurochemistry group leader CNS Biology sect. Lederle Labs. div. Am. Cyanamid Co., Pearl River, N.Y., 1978-79; prin. research scientist The Nathan S. Kline Inst. for Psychiat. Research, Orangeburg, N.Y., 1979—. Contbr. articles to profl. jours.; patentee in field. Nat. Inst. Neurol. and Communication Disorders and Stroke grantee, 1981-84. Mem. AAAS, Collegium Internationale Neuro-Psychopharmacologicum, Internat. Soc. Psychoneuroendocrinology, Soc. Neurosci., Internat. Soc. Neurochemistry, European Neurosci. Assn., Am. Soc. Neurochemistry, Am. Soc. Biochemistry and Molecular Biology, Am. Soc. Pharmacology and Exptl. Therapeutics. Home: 10 Termakay Dr New City NY 10956 Office: The Nathan S Kline Inst for Psychiat Research Orangeburg NY 10962

SRIDHAR, MIRLE SANNE GOWDA, librarian; b. Mirle, Karnataka, India, Feb. 6, 1949; s. Sanne and Ramamma Gowda; m. Suvarna Sridhar, Mar. 16, 1978; children: M.S. Sahana, M.S. Sneha. BS, Yuvaraja's Coll., Mysore, India, 1969; MLS, Manasa Gangothri, Mysore, 1972; MS, Bangalore (India) U., 1976, MBA, 1981. Asst. librarian U. Mysore, 1972-73; sr. tech. asst. Nat. Aero. Lab., Bangalore, 1973-77; asst. librarian Indian Inst. Mgmt., Bangalore, 1977-78; librarian ISRO Satellite Ctr., Bangalore, 1978—. Mem. Karnataka Library Assn. (life), Indian Assn. Spl. Libraries and Info. Ctrs. (life). Home: 41 Jagadeesh Nagar, Bangalore Karnataka 560093, India Office: ISRO Satellite Ctr, Vimanapura Post, Bangalore 560017, India

SRIDHAR, MYNEPALLI KAMESWARA CHANDRA, environmental scientist, educator; b. Vellatur, India, Dec. 8, 1942; s. Mynepalli Apparao and Mynepalli Venkata Subbamma; m. Mynepalli Kanakadurga Prasanna Devi, May 30, 1972; children: Srilatha, Pallavi, Preethi. ScB, Andhra U., 1961, MSc, M.S.U., 1964; PhD, Indian Inst. Sci., 1977. Demonstrator Andhra U., Machilipatnam, India, 1961; sr. research asst. Indian Inst. Sci., Bangalore, India, 1970-75, sci. officer, 1976-77; lectr. environ. sci. U. Ibadan, Nigeria, 1977-80, sr. lectr., head environ. health, 1980-83, from assoc. prof. to prof., 1983—; mem. consultancy servuces Coll. Medicine, 1984—; vis. lectr. Am. U. Beirut, 1980; vis. prof. Swiss Fed. Inst. for Water Resources and Water Pollution Control, Dubendorf, 1986-87. Contbr. over 100 articles to profl. jours., chpts. to books. Sec. Telugu Cultural Assn., Bangalore, 1966-68, Indian Cultural Assn., Ibadan, 1978-80, 85-87; community educator and consultant environ. mgmt. Nigerian Dept. Preventive and Social Medicine, 1978-87. Fellow M.S.U., 1962-64; Indian Inst. Sci. research fellow, 1964-70, Danish Internat. Devel. Agy. Danida fellow, 1984. Fellow Royal Soc. Health; mem. Royal Soc. Chemistry (chartered chemist), Inst. Water Pollution Control. Hindu. Club: Sr. Staff (Ibadan) (sec.). Home: 301 2d Block Nagar, Bangalore 560 036, India Office: U Ibadan, Ibadan Nigeria

SRIFUENGFUNG, CHAINARIN, bank executive; b. Bangkok, Thailand, Feb. 2, 1944; s. Kiarti and Janie S.; m. Suintharie Srifuengfung, Feb. 16, 1975; 1 child, Arayanie. Cert., Assumption Coll., Cholburi, Thailand, 1955; BS, Rochester Inst. of Tech., 1967. Consumer sales rep. Esso Standard Thailand, Bangkok, 1967-69; asst. mgr. mktg. & devel. Thai Investment & Securities Co., Bangkok, 1969-71; exec. dir. Chase Manhattan Investment Co., Ltd., Bangkok, 1971-74; deputy mng. dir. Cathay Trust Co., Ltd., Bangkok, 1975-83, advisor, 1983—; chmn. Thai Metropole Ins. and Warehouse Co., Ltd., Bangkok, 1980—; dir. Pennvasia, Hong Kong, 1983—, Guangdong Float Glass Co., Ltd., Shekou, People's Repub. China, 1985—; exec. v.p. First Bangkok Bank Ltd., 1986—. Office: First Bangkok City Bank Ltd, Head Office, 20 Yukhon 2 Rd, Bangkok 10100, Thailand

SRINIVASAN, MANDAYAM PARAMEKANTHI, software services executive; b. Mysore City, India, July 1, 1940; s. Appalacharya Paramekanthi and Singamma Budugan; came to U.S., 1970; B.S., U. Mysore, 1959, B.E. in Mech. Engring., 1963; M.S. in Ops. Research, Poly. Inst. N.Y., 1974, M.S. in Computer Sci., 1983; m. Ranganayaki Srirangapatnam, June 18, 1967. Costing engr. Heavy Engring. Corp., Ranchi, Bihar, India, 1963-70; inventory analyst Ideal Corp., Bklyn., 1970-75; systems analyst Electronic Calculus, Inc., N.Y.C., 1975-76; cons. in software, project leader Computer Horizons Corp., N.Y.C., 1976-85; pres. Compmusic, Bellerose, N.Y., 1985—; tchr., cons. in-house tng. Founding mem. governing council Vishwa Hindu Parishad of U.S.A., 1973—, pres. N.Y. State chpt., 1977-86. Mem. Assn. for Computing Machinery, IEEE, Inst. Engrs. (India). Republican. Hindu. Office: Compmusic Inc 8229 251st St Bellerose NY 11426-2527

SRINIVASAN, SAMUEL, physiatrist; b. Pasumalai, India, July 17, 1936; s. Appasrinivasan and Ruby Jemima Vethanayagam; m. Victoria Sathianathan, June 8, 1960; children: Reuben, David. MBBS, U. Madras, 1960; FRCS, Royal Coll. Surgeons, 1968. Diplomate Am. Bd. Phys. Medicine and Rehab. Registrar orthopaedic surgery Royal Lancaster (Eng.) Infirmary, 1966-68; surgeon Kalyani Hosp., Madras, 1969-70; orthopaedic surgeon Queen Victoria Hosp., Morecambe, Eng., 1970-73; resident U. Mich. Med. Ctr., Ann Arbor, 1976-79; dir. rehab. R.I. Hosp., Providence, 1979-84; practice medicine specializing in rehab. medicine Saginaw, Mich., 1984—; asst. prof. Brown U., Providence, 1979-84; chmn. Bd. Physical Therapy, State of R.I., 1981-84. Fellow Am. Acad. Physical Medicine and Rehab.; mem. AMA, Am. Acad. Thermology, Am. Soc., Clin. Evoked Potentials, Am. Assn. Electrodiagnosis and Electromyography, N.Y. Acad. Scis., Internat. Platform Assn. Republican. Episcopalian. Clubs: Saginaw Country, Centurian. Home: 850 Kenton Dr Saginaw MI 48603 Office: 830 S Jefferson Saginaw MI 48601

SRINIVASAN, SUMANGALI KIDAMBI, mathematics educator, researcher; b. Kancheepuram, Tamil Nadu, India, Dec. 16, 1930; s. Govindachari Kidambi and Rukmani Sumangali. B.A. with honors, Madras U., 1953, M.A., 1953, M.Sc., 1955, Ph.D., 1957. Postdoctoral fellow U. Sydney, Australia, 1957-58; Nat. Inst. Scis. sr. fellow U. Madras, 1958-59; sr. lectr. Indian Inst. Tech., Madras, 1959-61, asst. prof., 1961-67, prof., 1967-74, sr. prof. math., 1974—; vis. prof. U. Waterloo, Can., 1973, SUNY, Buffalo, 1971, ICTP, Trieste, 1971, 83, Nat. U., Singapore, 1982-83, Tech. U., Munich, w. Germany, 1983. Author: Stochastic Theory and Cascade Processes, 1969; Stochastic Point Processes and Their Applications, 1974; Stochastic Point Processes, 1974, Point Process Models of Cavity Radiation and Detection, 1988; co-author: (with R. Vasudevan) Introduction to Random Differential Equations and Their Applications, 1971; (with K.M. Mehata) Stochastic Processes, 1988, Introduction to Probability and Random Processes, 1981; (with G. Sampath) Stochastic Models of Spike Trains of Single Neurons, 1977; (with R. Subramanian) Probabilistic Analysis of Redundant Systems, 1980. Editor Solid Mechanics Archives, 1976—, Annals of Statistical Math., 1987—. Fellow Indian Acad. Scis., Tamilnadu Acad. Scis. (founder); mem. Operational Research Soc. India (v.p. 1972-74, pres. 1975-76), Indian Math. Soc., Bernoul. Soc. Home: 34 Srinivasa Iyengar St, West Mambalam, Madras Tamil Nadu 600033, India Office: IIT Dept Math, Guindi, Madras India

SRIVASTAVA, JAYA NIDHI, educator; b. Lucknow, India, June 20, 1933; d. Mahabir Prasad and Madhuri (Devi); came to U.S., 1959, naturalized, 1966; M.Math. Stats., U. Lucknow, 1954; Statistician's Diploma Indian Statis. Inst., Calcutta, 1958; Ph.D., U. N.C., 1961. Agrl. statistician, India, 1954-59; research asso. U. N.C., 1961-63; asso. prof. U. Nebr., 1963-66; prof. math. stats. Colo. State U., Ft. Collins, 1966—, chmn. Disting. Vis. Lectrs. Program in Stats., U.S. and Can., 1973-75; vis. prof. many instns. Fellow Am. Statis. Assn., Inst. Math. Stats.; mem. Indian Soc. Agrl. (pres. 1977, Excellence in Research prize 1960), Internat., Indian statis. insts., Bernoulli Soc., Am. Platform Assn. Author: (with S.N. Roy and R. Gnanadesikan) Analysis and Design of Certain Quantitative Multiresponse Experiments, 1971; co-editor: Survey of Combinatorial Theory, 1973; editor: Survey of Statistical Design and Linear Models, 1975; A Survey of Combinatorics and Optimal Design, 1980; Essays in Probability and Stats.; mem. editorial bd. Communications in Statistics, 1972, 86, Jour. Multivariate Analysis, Jour. Combinatorics, Info. and Systems Sci., 1976-84, Jour. Info. and Optimisation Sci., 1984—; founder, editor-in-chief Jour. Statis. Planning and Inference, 1976-84, chmn. governing bd., 1982—; contbr. articles to profl. jours. Office: Colo State U Dept Stats Fort Collins CO 80523

SSEMOGERERE, PAUL, minister foreign affairs. Pres. gen. Dem. party, Kampala, Uganda; former leader Opposition in Nat. Assembly, Uganda; minister of internal affairs Uganda, 1986-87, 2d dep. prime minister, minister fgn. affairs, 1987—. Office: Ministry of Fgn Affairs, Kampala Uganda *

STAAB, HEINZ A., chemist; b. Darmstadt, Germany, Mar. 26, 1926; m. Ruth Mueller, Aug. 22, 1953; children: Doris, Volker. BSc, U. Marburg, Fed. Republic Germany, 1949; Diploma in Chemistry, U. Tuebingen, Fed. Republic Germany, 1951; PhD, U. Frankfurt, Fed. Republic Germany, 1953; MD, U. Heidelberg, Fed. Republic Germany, 1960; PhD (hon.), Weizmann Inst., Rehovot, Israel, 1983. Research assoc. Max Planck Inst., Heidelberg, 1953-59; sucessively asst. prof, assoc. prof., prof. chemistry U. Heidelberg, 1959—; dir. Inst. Organic Chemistry, U. Heidelberg, 1964-76, head dept. organic chemistry, 1976—; bd. dirs. Max Planck Inst.; pres. Max Planck Soc. Contbr. articles to profl. jours. Recipient Bundesverdienstkreuz, Govt. Fed. Republic Germany, 1987. Mem. German Chem. Soc. (pres. 1984, 85, Adolf V Baeyer medal, 1979), Gesellschaft Deutscher Naturforsher v Aerzte (pres. 1981, 82), Deutsche Forschungsgemeinschaft (senator 1976-82, 84—), Heidelberger Acad. Wissenschaften (Nat. Sci. Council, sec. 1970-77), Austrian Acad. Scis., Acad. Leopoldina (chmn. chem. com. 1974—). Lodge: Rotary. Home: Schloss-Wolfsbrunnenweg 43, 6900 Heidelberg Federal Republic of Germany Office: Max Planck Gesellschaft, Rezidenstrasse 1-A, 8000 Munich 2 Federal Republic of Germany

STABLER, DONALD BILLMAN, business executive; b. Williamsport, Pa., Dec. 23, 1908; s. George William and Etta Mae (Billman) S.; m. Dorothy Louise Witwer, Aug. 10, 1952; 1 dau., Beverly Anne. B.S., Lehigh U., 1930, M.S., 1932, LL.D., 1974; LL.D., Dickinson Law Sch., 1981. Owner Donald B. Stabler (Contractor), Harrisburg, Pa., 1940-55; chmn. bd., chief exec. officer Stabler Cos. Inc., Stabler Constrn. Co., Protection Services Inc., State Aggregates Inc. (Transit Co.), Stabler Devel. Co., Stabler Land Co., Harrisburg, Pa., Ea. Industries, Inc., Elco-Hausman Constrn. Corp., Elco Paving, Inc., Center Valley, Pa., Work Area Protection Corp., St. Charles, Ill.; chmn. bd., chief exec. officer State Aggregates Inc., DBS Transit Co., Stabler Land Co., Stabler Devel. Co., Eastern Industries, Inc., Elco-Hausman Constrn. Corp., Elco Paving, Inc., Work Area Protection Corp.; bd. dirs. Millers Mut. Ins. Co., Harrisburg., Road Info. Program, Washington, pres., 1970-74, chmn. bd., 1975-78, chmn. emeritus, 1979—. Bd. dirs. Harrisburg Polyclinic Med. Center, Miami Heart Inst.; trustee Lehigh U. Recipient Silver Hard hat award Constrn. Writers Assn., 1973, Humanitarian award Lions, 1973, Nat. Automobile Dealers award, 1978, Man & Boy award Boys' Club, 1984, Man of Yr. March of Dimes, 1984, Rebuilding Am. award, CIT, 1985; decorated Knight Comdr., Order St. John of Jerusalem Knights of Malta.; named hon. Ky. Col. Mem. Am. Rd. and Transp. Builders Assn. (dir., award 1974), Assn. Pa. Constructors (dir., adv. bd., pres. 1949-50), U.S. C. of C., Pa. C. of C., Harrisburg C. of C. (adm. 1960), Am. Soc. Hwy. Engrs. (Industry Man of Year 1975), Harrisburg Builders Exchange, Nat. Soc. Profl. Engrs., Pa. Soc. Profl. Engrs. (Engr. of Yr. Harrisburg chpt. 1981), Com. of 100 Miami Beach (dir.), Pa. Soc. N.Y., Lehigh U. Alumni Assn. (pres. 1965-66, L-in-Life award 1972), Nat. Asphalt Paving Assn., Pa. Asphalt Paving Assn., Navy League, Chi Epsilon, Pi Delta Epsilon. Presbyterian. Clubs: Masons, Shriners, Jesters, Elks, Rotary, Tall Cedars; Surf (Miami Beach) (pres. 1974-76, chmn. bd. of govs. 1976-78); Bal Harbour (Miami), Beach Colony (Miami), Coral Reef Yacht (Miami); Indian Creek Country (Miami Beach); Tuesday (Harrisburg), Harrisburg Country (Harrisburg); Union League (Phila.); Saucon Valley Country (Bethlehem, Pa.). Home: Stray Winds Farm 4001 McIntosh Rd Harrisburg PA 17112 also: 236 Bal Bay Dr Bal Harbour FL 33154 Office: 635 Lucknow Rd Harrisburg PA 17110

STACEY, PETER JOHN, mathematician, educator; b. Chelmsford, Eng., Mar. 20, 1949; arrived in Australia, 1973; s. John and Elizabeth Ann (Thorne) S.; m. Kaye Christine Vale, June 24, 1972; children: Carol Elizabeth, Andrew Michael, Mark Richard. MA, Cambridge U., 1970; MS, Oxford U., 1971, PhD, 1973. Sr. tutor Monash Univ., Victoria, Australia, 1973-74; lectr. math. LaTrobe U., Bundoora, Australia, 1975-82, sr. lectr., 1982—, chmn. dept. math., 1984-87. Contbr. articles to profl. jours. Mem. Am. Math. Soc., London Math. Soc., Australian Math. Soc. Office: LaTrobe U, Dept Math, Bundoora 3083, Australia

STACK, DANIEL, lawyer, financial consultant; b. Bklyn., July 29, 1928; s. Charles and Gertrude (Heller) S.; m. Jane Marcia Gordon, Apr. 18, 1953; children: Joan, Gordon. B.A. cum laude, Bklyn. Coll., 1949; LL.B., Columbia U., 1952, LL.M., Georgetown U., 1955. Bar: N.Y. 1956. Asst. counsel ABC-TV, N.Y.C., 1959-60; gen. counsel IFC Securities Corp., N.Y.C., 1961-63; sec. pension com. Consol. Foods Corp., Chgo., 1967-69; v.p. legal Seaway Multi Corp. Ltd., Toronto, Ont., Can., 1969-72; v.p. mergers and acquisitions Acklands Ltd., Toronto, 1972-74; sr. v.p., sec., counsel Greenwich Savs. Bank, N.Y.C., 1978-81; sole practice, N.Y.C., 1982-85; ptnr. Brennen and Stack, N.Y.C., 1986—; cons. venture capital, corp. fin., mining, and oil, N.Y.C., 1982—; pres. Bus. and Fin. Resources, Inc., 1982-84; officer and dir. various public cos.; lectr., guest speaker on mergers and acquisitions; gen. counsel Greater N.Y. Safety Council, 1980—. Mem. Congl. mil. service acads. nominations com. and Civil Service intern selection com., 1978—; info. officer U.S. Naval Acad., 1972—. Served to lt. j.g. USNR, 1952-55, capt. Res. ret. 1981. Decorated Joint Service Commendation medal, 1981. N.Y. State Regents scholar, 1945-49. Mem. N.Y. State Bar Assn., N.Y. County Lawyer's Assn., ABA. Republican. Home: 8 Linda Dr Suffern NY 10901

STACK, PAUL FRANCIS, lawyer; b. Chgo., July 21, 1946; s. Frank Louis and Dorothy Louise Stack; m. Nea Waterman, July 8, 1972; children—Nea Elizabeth, Sera Waterman. B.S., U. Ariz., 1968; J.D., Georgetown U., 1971. Bar: Ill. 1971, U.S. Ct. Claims 1975, U.S. Tax Ct. 1974, U.S. Ct. Customs and Patent Appeals 1977, U.S. Supreme Ct. 1975. Law clk., U.S. Dist. Ct., Chgo., 1971-72; asst. U.S. atty. No. Dist. Ill., Chgo., 1972-75; ptnr. Stack & Filpi, Chgo., 1976—. Bd. dirs. Riverside Pub. Library, 1977-83, Suburban Library System, Burr Ridge, Ill., 1979-82; mem. Mayor's ad hoc adv. com. on Cen. Library, Chgo., Ill., 1987—. Mem. ABA, Chgo. Bar Assn. Presbyterian. Club: Union League (Chgo.). Home: 238 N Delaplaine Rd Riverside IL 60546 Office: 140 S Dearborn St Suite 411 Chicago IL 60603

STACK, STEPHEN S., manufacturing company executive; b. DuPont, Pa., Apr. 25, 1934; s. Steve and Sophie (Baranowski) Stasenko. BSME, Case Western Res. U., 1956; postgrad. Syracuse U. Registered profl. engr., Ill. Mech. engr. Kaiser Aluminum, Erie, Pa., 1956-58; instr. Gannon U., Erie, 1958-60, Syracuse (N.Y.) U., 1960-61; engring. supr. A. O. Smith Corp., Erie and Los Angeles, 1961-66; gen. mgr. Am. Elec. Fusion, Chgo., 1966-67; mgr. new products Maremont Corp., Chgo., 1967-69; dir. market planning Gulf and Western Ind., Bellwood, Ill., 1969-71; mgmt. and fin. cons. Stack & Assos., Chgo., 1971-76; pres. Seamcraft, Inc., Chgo., 1976—; mem. Ill. Legis. Small Bus. Conf., 1980, Gov.'s Small Bus. Adv. Commn., 1984—, Ill. State House Conf. on Small Bus., 1984, 86; del. White House Conf. on Small Bus., 1986. Patentee in liquid control and metering fields. Active Sem. Townhouse Assn., Lincoln Park Conservation Assn., Sheffield Neighbors Assn. Recipient Am. Legion award, 1948, Case Western Res. U. Honor key, 1956, Eagle Scout award, 1949. Mem. Ill. Mfrs. Assn. (bd. dirs. 1986—), Small Mfrs. Action Council (vice chmn. 1986-87, chmn. 1988—), Mfrs. Polit. Action Com. (exec. com. 1987—), Am. Mgmt. Assn., Pres.' Assn., Blue Key, Beta Theta Pi, Theta Tau, Pi Delta Epsilon. Clubs: Chgo. Execs., East Bank, Singapore (Mich.) Yacht, Fullerton Tennis (pres. 1971-79, treas. 1979-83, bd. dirs. 1983-86), Mid-Town Tennis, Lake Shore Ski (v.p. 1982). Office: 932 W Dakin St Chicago IL 60613

STACKELBERG, OLAF PATRICK VON, mathematician; b. Munich, Germany, Aug. 2, 1932; came to U.S., 1946, naturalized, 1947; s. Curt Frhrr. and Ellen (Biddle) von Stackelberg; m. Cora Elizabeth Sleighter, Sept. 4, 1954; children: John Sleighter, Peter Olaf, Paul Emmet. B.S. in Math, M.I.T., 1955; M.S., U. Minn., 1960, PhD. in Math, 1963. Asst. prof. math. Duke U., Durham, N.C., 1963-68; asso. prof. Duke U., 1968-76; prof., chmn. dept. math. Kent (Ohio) State U., 1976—; vis. asso. prof. U. Ill., 1969-70, U. London, Eng., 1974, Wesleyan U., summers 1965-76. Mng. editor: Duke Math. Jour, 1971-74; contbr. articles U.S. and fgn. jours. Served with Chem. Corps AUS, 1956-58. Alexander von Humboldt research fellow U. Stuttgart, Germany, 1965-66; NSF research grantee. Mem. Am. Math. Soc., Math. Assn. Am., Inst. Math. Stats., AAAS, AAUP, Fedn. Am. Scientists,

Assn. Computer Machinery, London Math. Soc. Home: 5924 Horning Rd Kent OH 44240 Office: Dept of Math Scis Kent State University Kent OH 44242

STACK-STAIKIDIS, WILLIAM JOHN, university dean, civil engineer; b. Athens, Nov. 20, 1933; came to U.S., 1955, naturalized, 1960; s. John C. and Christine V. (Chrysaki) Staikidis; m. Patricia Brown, June 9, 1955; 1 child, Christine Lisa Stack. B.S. in Applied Math, U. Athens, 1953; B. Civil Engring. with honors, N.C. State U., Raleigh, 1957, M. Civil Engring., 1961; Ph.D. studies, U. Calif., Berkeley, 1963-64; Ph.D. in Engring. and Sci, N.Y. U., 1970. Registered profl. engr., N.Y., N.J. Structural engr. Madigan & Hyland, Long Island City, N.Y., 1957-59, Meir Assocs., Raleigh, 1959-61; head research dept. Doxiades Assos. (Urban Planners), Athens, 1961-63; project engr. United Research Inc., Burlingame, Calif., 1963-64; project mgr. Tippetts, Abbett, McCarthy & Stratton, N.Y.C., 1964-66; participant with Edwards & Kelcey (in design of portion of Washington subway system), 1974-76; instr. math. and physics U. Athens, 1953-55; adj. prof. civil engring. CCNY, 1965-66; assoc. prof., head structures div. civil engring. dept. Newark Coll. Engring. of N.J. Inst. Tech., 1966-78; prof., dean Sch. Engring. Pratt Inst., Bklyn., 1978-85; dean Newark Coll. Engring. of N.J. Inst. Tech., 1985—. Author: (with others) Professional Engineers Examination, 1975; contbr. (with others) articles profl. jours. Recipient Robert Van Housen award for excellence in teaching N.J. Inst. Tech., 1975-76, James M. Robbins award for excellence in civil engring. edn., 1974-75; NSF Faculty fellow, 1969; Ford Found. grantee, 1963. Mem. Assn. Engring. Colls. N.Y. State (chmn. met. sect.), Nat. Soc. Profl. Engrs., ASCE, Am. Soc. Engring. Edn., Am. Concrete Inst., Sigma Xi, Chi Epsilon, Phi Kappa Phi. Home: 175 E 74th St New York NY 10021 Office: 323 King Blvd Newark NJ 07102

STADNICK, CYRIL, obstetrician, gynecologist; b. Tientsin, Republic of China, Nov. 15, 1946; s. Wladimir and Eugenia Stadnick; m. Célia Maria Pedrosa, July 25, 1974 (div. Mar. 1986); children: Alexandre Pedrosa, Ricardo Pedrosa. Student, Alliance Française, 1971, Goethe Inst., 1972; MD, U. Rio de Janeiro, 1972. Diplomate in Ob-Gyn. 1st asst. Fernando Pedrosa Clinic, Rio de Janeiro, 1973—; mem. staff Miguel Couto Mcpl. Hosp., Rio de Janeiro, 1974—, Silvestre Adventist Hosp., Rio de Janeiro, 1973—, Vassouras U., Rio de Janeiro, 1972-73, Snata Casa da Misericordia, Rio de Janeiro, 1973-74, São Lucas, Rio de Janeiro, 1986—, Samaritano Hosp., Rio de Janeiro, 1973—, Sã Vicente Hosp., Rio de Janeiro, 1987—, São Marcelo Hosp., Rio de Janeiro, 1973—; cons. Plastic Surgery Clinic, Rio de Janeiro, 1986—; laparoscopy cons. São Lucas, Rio de Janeiro, 1986—; chief Miguel Couto Maternity, Rio de Janeiro, 1977—; organizer Internat. Congress on Endoscopy, Rio de Janeiro, 1987. Author: (film) Laparoscopy, 1975; contbr. papers and articles to profl. publs. Dir. Med. Study Hall, Hosp. Silvestre, 1975-78, Hosp. Miguel Couto, 1977-79, Hosp. São Lucas, 1986—. Fellow Mastology Soc.; mem. Ibero Am. Endoscopy (founder 1985), Obstetrics and Gynecol. Soc., Human Reproduction Soc. Clubs: Caiçaras, Flamengo Soccer (Rio de Janeiro). Home: Visconde de Albuquerque 1324, Apt 302, 22450 Rio de Janeiro Brazil Office: Med Clinic, Alaulfo de Paiva 135/409, 22440 Rio de Janeiro Brazil

STADTLER, WALTER EDWARD, diplomat; b. N.Y.C., Apr. 4, 1936; s. Walter Henry and Paula (Nagl) S.; m. Maida Maria MacDonald, Mar. 4, 1937; children: Fiona, Walter Jr., Catriona. Student, Sorbonne U., Paris, 1955-56; AB, Fordham U., 1957; postgrad., Columbia U., 1957-58. With Dept. State 1962—; vice consul Am. Consulate, Southampton, Eng., 1962-63; third sec. Am. Embassy, London, 1963-64; econ. officer, second sec. Am. Embassy, Bonn, Fed. Republic of Germany, 1966-69; personnel officer Dept. State, Washington, 1966-69; counselor Am. Embassy, Bonn, Fed. Republic of Germany, 1980-82; second sec. Am. Embassy, Pretoria, South Africa, 1969-72, dep. chief of mission, 1982-85; first sec. Am. Embassy, Addis Ababa, Ethiopia, 1972-75, Stockholm, 1975-78; European affairs advisor U.S. Mission U.N., N.Y.C., 1978; mem. Royal Coll. Def. Studies, London, 1979, Sr. Seminar, Washington, 1985-86; ambassador Am. Embassy, Cotonou, Benin, 1986—. Served to capt. U.S. Army, 1958-62. Mem. Am. Fgn. Service Assn. Roman Catholic. Home: Am Embassy, 8008 Blvd de France, Cotonou Peoples Republic of Benin

STAEHLE, CHARLES MICHAEL, marine/ocean engineer; b. Lovell, Wyo., Oct. 4, 1938; s. Eddie Leroy and Frances Lenora (Glenn) S.; m. Margaret Elizabeth Allen, Jan. 21, 1963 (div. July 1982); children—Cynthia Marie, Mark Allen; m. Ruth Joyner, Dec. 31, 1983. B.S. in Physics, U. Okla., 1963. Project engr. oceanic div. Westinghouse Corp., Annapolis, Md., 1970-77; tech. mgr. NOAA, Washington, 1977-82; mgr. spl. programs Perry Offshore, Inc., Riviera Beach, Fla., 1982-84; pres., chief exec. officer Ocean Tech. Assocs., Inc., North Palm Beach, Fla., 1984—. Pres. Chase Creek Civic Assn., Arnold, Md., 1975. Served with USN, 1958-70, with Res. 1970—. Mem. Soc. Naval Architects and Marine Engrs., Marine Tech. Soc. (underwater physics com. 1981—, marine mining and minerals com. 1983—), Deep Submersible Pilots Assn., Naval Res. Assn., Navy Submarine League. Republican. Episcopalian. Lodge: Masons. Home: 2480 Treasure Island Dr Palm Beach Gardens FL 33410 Office: Ocean Tech Assocs Inc 3845 Investment Ln #4 Riviera Beach FL 33404

STAERK, HERBERT ERNST, engineer; b. Frankfurt, Germany, Feb. 13, 1930; s. Ernst August and Elisabeth Katharina (Friedrich) S.; m. Erika Beatrix Schmierer, Dec. 23, 1952; children: Manfred (dec.), Wolfgang, Jurgen. Diploma in engring., Frankfurt Engrs. Sch., Fed. Republic of Germany, 1953. Mgr. product instruments Hartmann & Braun AG, Frankfurt, 1960—. Contbr. articles on temperature measuring to profl. jours. Mem. German Electrotechnicans Orgn., German Engrs. Orgn., Orgn. Leading Staff, Orgn. for Measuring and Control Engrs. (exec. com. 1981—), Orgn. for Info. Tech. Engrs. (exec. com. 1981—), Leading Staff Orgn. of German Electrotechnical Mfrs.for Measuring and Automation (exec. com. 1981—), German Orgn. for Microelectronics. Club: ADAC (Munich). Home: Goethering 4, D6072 Dreieich Federal Republic of Germany Office: Hartmant & Braun AG, Postfach 900507, D-6000 Frankfurt 90 Federal Republic of Germany

STAFFELBACH, ANDRE, interior designer; b. Chur, Switzerland, July 24, 1939; came to U.S., 1962; s. Jacob and Anna (Della-Bella) S.; m. Jewel Van Beber, May 24, 1969; children—Anna Lisa, Deon Andre. Apprentice in Interior Design, Chur, 1955-59; Profl. Degree in Interior Architecture, Kunstgewerbeschule, Zurich, Switzerland, 1960-61. Interior architect Sporri Interiors, Zurich, 1960-62; interior designer E.R. Cole, N.Y.C., 1962-63, Town House Interiors, Chgo., 1963-65, Weston's, Dallas, 1965-66; pres. Staffelbach Designs, Dallas, 1966—; cons. Nat. Endowment Arts, Washington, 1976. Served with Swiss Army, 1959-62. Recipient Giants 100 award Interior Design Mag., 1983—; fellow Inst. Bus. Designers, Chgo., 1977. Mem. Inst. Bus. Designers (nat. pres. 1975-77, Disting. Merit award 1987), Nat. Council Interior Design (council 1981-83, nat. pres. 1984), Am. Soc. Interior Designers. Republican. Avocations: running; snow skiing. Author: Commercial Interiors International, 1986; contbr. articles to Interior Design Mag., Interiors Mag., Contract Mag., 1986. Home: 3116 Southwestern St Dallas TX 75225 Office: 2525 Carlisle Dallas TX 75201

STAFFORD, GODFREY HARRY, physicist; b. Sheffield, Apr. 15, 1920; s. Henry and Sarah Stafford; m. Helen Goldthorp, 1950; 3 children. M.Sc., U. CapeTown, 1941; Ph.D., Cambridge U., 1950; M.A., Oxford U., 1971; Ph.D., Cambridge U., 1950; D.Sc. (hon.), U. Birmingham, 1980. Head biophysics subdiv. Council for Sci. and Indsl. Research, Pretoria, S. Africa, 1951-54, Cyclotron Group, AERE, 1954-57; head proton linear accelerator group Rutherford Lab., 1957; head high energy physics div., 1963, dep. dir., 1966, dir., 1969-79, dir. Atlas and Rutherford Lab., 1975-79, dir. gen., 1979-81; U.K. del. IUPAP Com. on Particles and Fields, 1975-8; v.p. Inst. Physics Meetings Com., 1976-79; chmn. sci. policy com. CERN, 1978-81; master St. Cross Coll., Oxford, 1979-88. Contbr. articles to profl. jours. Decorated comdr. Order Brit. Empire; Ebden scholar U. Cape Town. Fellow Royal Soc., Inst. Physics (Glazebrook prize and medal 1981, pres. 1986-88); mem. European Phys. Soc. (pres. 1984-86), others. Office: Univ Oxford, Saint Cross Coll, Oxford OX1 3LZ, England also: Ferry Cottage, North Hinksey Village, Oxford OX2 0NA, England

STAFFORD, JOHN ROGERS, pharmaceutical and household products company executive; b. Harrisburg, Pa., Oct. 24, 1937; s. Paul Henry and Gladys Lee (Sharp) S.; m. Inge Paul, Aug. 22, 1959; children—Carolyn, Jennifer, Christina, Charlotte. A.B., Dickinson Coll., 1959; LL.B. with distinction, George Washington U., 1962. Bar: D.C. 1962. Assoc. Steptoe & Johnson, 1962-66; gen. atty. Hoffman-LaRoche, Nutley, N.J., 1966-67; group atty. Hoffman-LaRoche, 1967-70; gen. counsel Am. Home Products Corp., N.Y.C., 1970-74; v.p. Am. Home Products Corp., 1972-77, sr. v.p., 1977-80, exec. v.p., 1980-81, pres., 1981—, chmn., pres., chief exec. officer, 1986—; dir. Mfrs. Hanover Corp., Met. Life Ins. Co.; bd. trustees The Presbyn. Hosp. in the city of N.Y. Mem. adv. bd. The Whole Theatre Co.; bd. dirs. Cen. Park Conservancy, Pharm. Mfgs. Assn.; bd. trustees U.S. Council for Internat. Bus., Presbyn. Hosp., N.Y.C. Recipient John Bell Larner 1st Scholar award George Washington U. Law Sch., 1962, Outstanding Achievement Alumnus award, 1981. Mem. Am. Bar Assn., D.C. Bar Assn., Nat. Assn. Mfrs. (bd. dirs.). Clubs: Sky (N.Y.C.); Essex Fells (N.J.) Country, Links (N.Y.C.). Office: Am Home Products Corp 685 3rd Ave New York NY 10017

STAFFORD, JOHN TOBIAS, mathematics educator; b. Oxford, Eng., June 2, 1951; s. Godfrey Harry and Helen Goldthorpe (Clark) S.; m. Carolyn Anne Dean, June 27, 1987. BA, Cambridge (Eng.) U., 1972, MA, 1976; PhD, Leeds (Eng.) U., 1976. Research fellow Brandeis U., Waltham, Mass., 1976-78, Cambridge U., 1978-81; lectr. Leeds U., 1982-85, reader, 1985-88, personal chair, 1988—. Contbr. articles to profl. jours. Mem. London Math. Soc. (mem. editorial bd. 1987, Jr. Whitehead prize 1980). Office: Leeds U, Math Sch, Leeds LS2 9JT, England

STAFFORD, ROBERT THEODORE, U.S. senator, lawyer; b. Rutland, Vt., Aug. 8, 1913; s. Bert L. and Mable R. (Stratton) S.; m. Helen C. Kelley, Oct. 15, 1938; children—Madelyn, Susan, Barbara, Dianne. B.S., Middlebury Coll., 1935, LL.D., 1960; postgrad., U. Mich., 1936; LL.B., Boston U., 1938, LL.D., 1959; LL.D., Norwich U., 1960, St. Michaels Coll., 1967, U. Vt., 1970. Bar: Vt. bar 1938. City prosecutor Rutland, 1939-42; state's atty. Rutland County, 1947-51; dep. atty. gen. Vt., 1953-54; atty. gen. 1954-56, lt. gov., 1957-58, gov., 1959-60; mem. 87th to 92d Congresses, Vt.-at-large; apptd. U.S. Senate, 1971, elected, 1972—, chmn. com. on environment and public works, 1981-87; ranking mem. 1987—, chmn. edn. subcom., 1981-87, ranking mem., 1987—; ptnr. Stafford, Abiatell & Stafford, 1938-46; sr. ptnr. Stafford & LaBrake, 1946-51. Served as lt. comdr. USNR, 1942-46, 51-52; capt. Res. Mem. V.F.W., Am. Legion. Club: Elk. Home: 3541 Devon Dr Falls Church VA 22042 also: 64 Litchfield Ave Rutland VT 05701 Office: 133 Hart Senate Office Bldg Washington DC 20510

STAGNER, ROBERT DEAN, lawyer; b. Simi, Calif., May 23, 1950; s. Cecil William and Mary Jane (Davis) S.; m. Barbara Ann Crosby, Dec. 27, 1974; children: Rebecca Lyn, Brenda Deann. BA in History and Polit. Sci., Pasadena Coll., 1972; JD, Western State U., Fullerton, Calif., 1977. Bar: Calif. 1977, U.S. Dist. Ct. (cen. dist.) Calif. 1979. Ptnr. Stagner & Gregg, Orange, Calif., 1978—; officer, cons. Richard Walker Inc., Anaheim, Calif., 1976—, sec. 1978-81, bd. dirs.; gen. counsel Greater Am. Produce, Anaheim, 1978-84, acting pres. 1984; pres. Orion Constrn., Tustin, Calif., 1980-82; counsel Whittier Police Officers Assn., 1982—; cons. ballistics Kraemer Industries, Anaheim, 1985—, Exodus One Mktg., Placentia, Calif., 1985—, A.W. Schnitger, Encinada, Mexico, 1985—. Trainer USN Sea Cadet Corps, El Toro, Calif., 1984—; adult edn. Nazarene Ch., Chino, Calif., 1982-85. Named one of Outstanding Young Men Am., 1981. Office: 648 N Tustin Suite A Orange CA 92667

STAHEL, WALTER RUDOLF, industrial analyst, business consultant; b. Zurich, Switzerland, June 5, 1946; s. Walter Max and Frieda (Abrecht) S.; m. Christiane Andrée Collaud, Feb. 9, 1970; 1 son, Dominique Halim. Diploma, Swiss Fed. Inst. Tech., 1970. Architect, Bicknell & Hamilton, London, 1967-68, 71-72, Aebli & Sochalski, Zurich, 1970-71; design architect Obrist & Ptnr., St. Moritz, Switzerland, 1972-73; project mgr. Battelle Inst., Geneva, 1973-79; personal asst. to chief exec. officer Phymec Luxembourg S.A., Geneva, 1980-82; ind. researcher, bus. cons., Geneva, 1983—; chmn. ECOM Corp. S.A., Geneva, 1981—; pres. Medogen S.A., Geneva, 1984—; founder, dir. Product Life Inst., Geneva, 1982—; sec. gen. European chpt. Internat. Sci. Policy Found., Geneva, 1986—; sec. European Group Local Employment Initiatives, Brussels, 1987—; deputy sec. gen. Genera Assn., Geneva, 1988—. Author: Jobs for Tomorrow, 1981; Unemployment-Occupation-Profession, 1980; contbr. articles to profl. jours.; advisor Change, internat. tech. newspaper, London, 1983—. Recipient 1st prize Deutsche Gesellschaft für Zukunftsfragen, West Berlin, 1978, 3d prize Mitchell Prize Competition, Houston, 1982. Mem. Assn. Former Students of Swiss Fed. Inst. Tech. Home: 7 chemin des Vignettes, Conches, CH-1231 Geneva Switzerland Office: Inst de la Duree, PO Box 832, CH-1211 Geneva 3 Switzerland

STAHL, JOEL SOL, plastic-chemical engr.; b. Youngstown, Ohio, June 10, 1918; s. John Charles and Anna (Nadler) S.; B.Chem. Engring., Ohio State U., 1939; postgrad. Alexander Hamilton Inst., 1946-48; m. Jane Elizabeth Anglin, June 23, 1950; 1 son, John Arthur. With Ashland Oil & Refining Co. (Ky.), 1939-50, mgr. spl. products, 1946-50; pres. Cool Ray Co., Youngstown, 1950-51, Stahl Industries, Inc., Youngstown, 1951—, Stahl Internat., Inc., Youngstown, 1969—, Stahl Bldg. Systems, Inc., Youngstown, 1973—. Active Boardman Civic Assn., Boy Scouts Am., bd. mem. Ohio State U. Found., Community Chest, ARC. Named Ky. col., 1967. Mem. Regional Export Expansion Council, Soc. Plastics Engr., Soc. Plastics Industry, Internat. Platform Assn., Ohio Soc. N.Y., Tau Kappa Epsilon, Phi Eta Sigma, Phi Lambda Upsilon. Republican. Christian Scientist. Clubs: Citrus, Masons, Shriners, Rotary, Toastmasters (pres. 1949); Berlin Yacht (North Benton, O.); Circumnavigators. N.Y. Acad. Sci., Patentee insulated core walls, plastic plumbing wall. housing in continous process. Contbr. articles to profl. jours. Home: 530 E Central Blvd #1504 Orlando FL 32801 Office: 600-20 Federal Plaza W Youngstown OH 44503

STÅHL, LARS G., publishing executive; b. Kalmar, Småland, Sweden, May 21, 1940; s. Sven W. and Vivan S. G. (Dunge) S.; m. Henryka A. Karnecka, Feb. 14, 1978; children: Per, Rikard, Patrik. BS, U. Stockholm, 1963. Tchr. math. physics Äppelviksskolan, Bromma, Sweden, 1963-67; editor mag. Bergvall Pub., Stockholm, 1967-68, asst. pub. mgr., 1968-72; v.p. Nat. Sci. Esselte Studium, Stockholm, 1973-78, pres., 1982-85; pres. Almquist & Wiksell, Stockholm, 1978-82, Verbum AB, Stockholm, 1985—; v.p. Föreningen Svenska Läromedels producenter, Stockholm, 1980—, Worlddidac, Bern, Switzerland, 1983—; bd. dirs. Bonus, Stockholm, 1982—. Lutheran. Lodges: Rotary, Odd Fellows. Office: Verbum AB, PO Box 15269, S-15269 Stockholm Sweden

STAHL, LOUIS EDMUND, retired food company executive; b. Boston, June 20, 1914; s. Harry G. and Esther S.; B.S., M.I.T., 1936; m. Dorothy Judith Tishler, Dec. 17, 1939; children—Lesley, Jeffrey. Tech. dir., pres. Stahl Finish Co., Peabody, Mass., 1936-65; pres. Stahl Finish div. Beatrice Foods, Inc., Wilmington, Mass., 1965-70, group mgr. chem. group, 1970-72, pres. Beatrice Chem. div., 1972-78, v.p. Beatrice Foods, Chgo., 1976-79; dir. Stahl Investment Corp., Shawmut Mchts. Bank, Salem, Mass. Mem. Corp. devel. com. M.I.T.; pres. Rehab. Center for Aged, Swampscott, 1968—. Mem. Am. Chem. Soc., Am. Leather Chemists Assn. Office: 160 Commonwealth Ave Boston MA 02116

STAHL, MARILYN BROWN, interior designer; b. Boston, Dec. 11, 1929; d. Benjamin M. and Nettie D. (Glazer) Brown; B.S. in Art Edn., Mass. Coll. Art, 1951; m. Alvan L. Stahl, July 1, 1951; children—Robert, Barry, Kim. Instr. painting, Newton, Mass.; free-lance fabric designer, 1960-63; owner gallery, Newton, 1963-66, M.B. Stahl Interiors, Chestnut Hill, Mass., 1966; founder, pres. Maab Inc., mfrs. French furniture, 1979; pres. Decorators' Clearing House, Newton Upper Falls, Mass. Mem. Nat. Home Fashions League, Am. Soc. Interior Designers Industry Found., Nat. Home Fashions League Industry. Found. Home: 15 Manet Circle Chestnut Hill MA 02167 Office: Decorators' Clearing House 1029 Chestnut St Newton Upper Falls MA 02164

STAHL, PETER WILLIAM, archaeologist, researcher; b. Val-D'Or, Quebec, Can., Dec. 12, 1953; s. Ernst Helmut and Hildegard Ingebourg (Maier) S.; m. Ann Merrill Brower, Sept. 2, 1978; 1 child, Christina Mary. BA, U. Toronto, Ont., Can., 1975; MA, U. Calgary, Alta., Can., 1978; PhD, U. Ill., 1984. Research fellow Lowie Mus. U. Calif., Berkeley, 1984-85; research assoc. Inst. Archaelogy, London, 1985-87, hon. research fellow, 1987-88; adj. prof. SUNY Binghamton, 1988—, cons. Programa Antropologia para el Ecuador, 1980—, Escuela Superior Politécnica del Litoral, Ecuador, 1980—. Contbr. articles to profl. jours. Recipient S.H. Janes Silver medal, 1975; fellow Social Scis. Humanities Research Council, 1979-86. Mem. Soc. Am. Archaeology, Soc. Latin Am. Studies, Phi Kappa Phi. Lutheran. Office: SUNY Dept Anthropology Binghamton NY 13901

STAHL, STEPHEN MICHAEL, research laboratory executive, professor, lecturer; b. Wauseon, Ohio, Sept. 14, 1951; s. Howard Melvin and Nancy Elaine (Grime) S.; m. Cynthia Davis, Mar. 23, 1973; children: Jennifer Mary and Victoria Meredith. BS, Northwestern U., Evanston, Ill., 1973; MD, Northwestern U., Chgo., 1974; PhD, U. Chgo., 1976. Diplomate Am. Bd. Psychiatry and Neurology. Intern then residen; asst. dir. Stanford (Calif.) U. Med. Ctr., 1981-85; instr. Stanford U. Med. Sch., 1981-82, acting asst. prof., 1982-83, asst. prof., 1983-85; exec. dir. clin. neurosci. Merck Sharp & Dohme Research Labs., Harlow, Essex, Eng., 1985—; hon. sr. lectr. Inst. Psychiatry and Maudsley Hosp., London, 1985—, Inst. Neurology, Nat. Hosp. at Queen Sq., London, 1987—; adj. assoc. prof. Sch. Medicine UCLA, 1985—; vis. clin. investigator Inst. Psychiatry and Maudsley Hosp., London, 1985-86. Contbr. articles in psychopharmacology, psychiatry and neurology to profl. jours. Recipient A.E. Bennett, G.D. Searle and G. Milton Shy awards in Basic Research, 1974-75. Mem. Am. Acad. Child Psychiatry, Am. Coll. Neuropsychopharmacology, Am. Psychiatric Assn., British Assoc. of Psychopharmacology, British Pharmacology Soc., Soc. Biol. Psychiatry. Office: Merck Sharp & Dohme, Research Labs, Terlings Park Estwick Rd, Harlow, Essex CM20 2QR, England

STAHL, WERNER H., engineering educator; b. Diedorf, Germany, Oct. 24, 1938; s. Hans and Helene (Kraus) S.; m. Gertraud A. Pfeffer, Nov. 12, 1962; children—Manuel, Mario. Abitur, Oberreal Schule, 1958; Diploma Engring., Tech. U., Munich, 1963, Dr. Engring., 1965. Research and devel. engr., salesman, then product mgr. Krauss-Maffei AG, Munich, W.Ger., 1965-79; prof. mech. process tech. U. Karlsruhe (W.Ger.), 1979—. Patentee in field. Recipient Max Buchner prize (Dechema) for research on solid-bowl centrifuges, Frankfurt, 1976. Mem. AIME. Home: Stalbuehlweg 8, 6740 Landau Federal Republic of Germany Office: Institut für Mechanische, Verfahrenstechnick und Mechanik, Richard-Willstaetter Allee, 7500 Karlsruhe Federal Republic of Germany

STAHLBRAND, KARL LENNART, transportation executive; b. Kristianstad, Skane, Sweden, Oct. 12, 1926; m. Karin Gudrun Marianne Strömberg, May 7, 1950; children: Ulf Lennart, Leif Ove. Degree in engring., Norrköping (Sweden) Tech. Inst., 1955. Cert. in airline mgmt. Gas turbine designer Swedish Turbine Factory, Finspang, 1955-56; project engr. Scandinavian Airline System, Stockholm, 1956-59, supt. workshop, 1959-64, project mgr., 1983—; mgr. workshop Linjeflyg, Stockholm, 1964-70, leader F28 project, 1971-73, mgr. engring., 1973-79, project mgr., 1979-83. Author: Jet Engine Vibration Analysis, 1961, Analysis of Swedish Air Transports, 1974. Mem. Swedish Soc. Aeros. and Astros. Club: Viksjo Golf (Stockholm). Home: Hjalmvagen 11, 17561 Jarfalla Sweden Office: Scandinavian Airlines System, Kvarnbacksvagen 30, 16188 Stockholm Sweden

STAHR, ELVIS J(ACOB), JR., lawyer, conservationist, educator; b. Hickman, Ky., Mar. 9, 1916; s. Elvis and Mary Anne (McDaniel) S.; m. Dorothy Howland Berkfield, June 28, 1946; children: Stephanie Ann, Stuart Edward Winston, Bradford Lanier. AB, U. Ky., 1936; BA (Rhodes scholar), U. Oxford, Eng., 1938; BCL, 1939, MA, 1943; diploma in Chinese Lang., Yale U., 1943; LL.D., W.Va. Wesleyan Coll., Waynesburg Coll., 1959, Concord Coll., 1960, U. Md., U. Pitts., 1961, La. State U., Tex. Christian U., U. Ky., 1962, U. Notre Dame, 1964, Ind. State U., 1966, Brown U., 1967, Northwestern U., U. Fla., 1968, U. Tampa, 1972, Ind. U., 1976; D.Environ. Sci., Rollins Coll., 1973; Dr.Mil. Sci., Northeastern U., 1962; D.Pub. Adminstrn., Bethany Coll., 1962; D.H.L., DePauw U., 1963, Rose Poly Inst., 1965, Transylvania U., 1973; Litt.D., U. Cin., 1966, U. Maine, 1976; Pd.D., Culver-Stockton Coll., 1966; D.Sc., Norwich U., 1968, Hanover Coll., 1975. Bar: N.Y. State 1940, Ky. 1948, D.C. 1983, U.S. Supreme Ct. 1950. Practiced as assoc. Mudge, Stern, Williams & Tucker, N.Y.C., 1939-41; sr. assoc. Mudge, Stern, Williams & Tucker, 1946-47; assoc. prof. law U. Ky., 1947-48, prof. law, 1948-56; dean U. Ky. (Coll. Law), 1948-56, provost, 1954-56; exec. dir. Pres. Eisenhower's Com. on Edn. Beyond High Sch., 1956-57; vice chancellor professions U. Pitts., 1957-58; pres. W.Va. U., Morgantown, 1958-61; spl. asst. Sec. Army, Washington, 1951-52, cons., 1953; Sec. of the Army Dept. Def., Washington, 1961-62; pres. Ind. U., 1962-68, Nat. Audubon Soc., N.Y.C., 1968-79; sr. counselor Nat. Audubon Soc., 1979-81, pres. emeritus, 1981—; ptnr. Chickering & Gregory P.C., San Francisco, 1982-85; of counsel Chickering & Gregory, San Francisco, 1986—; dir. Acacia Mut. Life Ins. Co., 1968-85; pres. Univ. Assos., Inc., 1981—; exec. v.p. Pub. Resource Found., 1982—; sr. assoc. Cassidy & Assocs., Inc., 1984—; chmn. Washington Conservation Roundtable, 1986-87; dir. Chase Manhattan Corp., 1976-79, Fed. Res. Bank Chgo., 1966-68, dep. chmn., 1967, 68; Mem. Constn. Rev. Commn. Ky., 1949-56, Ind., 1967-68; mem. U.S. del. UN Conf. on Human Environment, Stockholm, 1972, Joint U.S.-USSR Com. on Cooperation for Protection of Environment, 1973, Internat. Whaling Commn., London, 1975, 78; mem. U.S. Aviation Adv. Commn., 1970-73, Nat. Commn. for World Population Yr., 1974; nat. chmn. U.S.O., 1973-76; pub. mem. Nat. Petroleum Council, 1974-79; mem. Summit Conf. on Inflation, 1974. Author: (with others) Economics of Pollution, 1971. Mem. Nat. Commn. on Accrediting, 1963-68; trustee Transylvania U., 1969-76, mem. founders bd., 1978-80; pres. Midwestern Univs. Research Assn., 1963-66; incorporator Argonne Univs. Assn., 1965, trustee, 1965-67; trustee Univs. Research Assn., 1965, mem. council presidents, 1965-68, chmn., 1968; bd. dirs. Alliance To Save Energy, 1977—, Resolve, 1977-81, Council Fin. Aid to Edn., 1966-69; chmn. higher edn. adv. com. Edn. Commn. States, 1966-68; mem. bd. Govtl. Affairs Inst., 1968-72, Pub. Adminstrn. Service, 1970-72, Inst. Services to Edn., 1965-67; chmn. Commn. on Fed. Relations, Am. Council on Edn., 1966-68; mem. exec. com. Nat. Assn. State Univs. and Land Grant Colls., 1965-68; mem. at-large bd. dirs. Am. Cancer Soc., 1970-76; trustee Com. Econ. Devel., 1964-82, hon. trustee, 1982—; mem. exec. bd. Nat. Assn. Ednl. Broadcasters, 1969-72; adv. council Electric Power Research Inst., 1973-77, Gas Research Inst., 1977-83, Population Inst., 1981—, FAIR, 1982—; mem. Govtl. Affairs Com. of Ind. Sector, 1980—; bd. dirs. Regional Plan Assn. Greater N.Y., 1970-75; evaluation panel Nat. Bur. Standards, 1975-77; adv. council Nat. Energy Project, Am. Enterprise Inst. Pub. Policy Research, 1974-76; chmn. Coalition Concerned Charities, 1972-78; mem. exec. bd. Am. Com. for Internat. Conservation, 1978-80; bd. dirs. World Environment Ctr., 1978-85, Environ. and Energy Study Inst., 1983—, Nat. Parks and Conservation Assn., 1988—, Nat. Water Alliance, 1983-86. Served 2d lt. to lt. col., inf. AUS, North Africa and China, 1941-45. Decorated Spl. Breast Order of Yun Hui (2) Army Navy and Air Force medal 1st class (China); Bronze Star medal with oak leaf cluster (U.S.); Order of Grand Cross (Peru).; Recipient Algernon Sydney Sullivan medallion of N.Y. So. Soc., 1936; named One of Am.'s Ten Outstanding Young Men U.S. Jr. C. of C., 1948; Meritorious Civilian Service medal Dept. Army, 1953, Disting. Civilian Service medal Dept. Army, 1971; Disting. Service award U. Ky. Alumni Assn., 1961; Disting. Service award Res. Officers Assn. U.S., 1962, Kentuckian of Year award Ky. Press Assn., 1961 and WHAS (Louisville), 1968, Conservation Service award Dept. Interior, 1979, Conservation Achievement award Nat. Wildlife Fedn., 1978, Barbara Swain award Nat. Resources Council Am., Award of Honor Natural Resources Council of Am., 1988; Sesquicentennial medal U. Mich., 1967, Centennial medal U. Ky., 1965; named Ky. Col. and gen.; La. and Neb. adm., Ind. Sagamore. Mem. Assn. U.S. Army (life, pres. 1965-68, chmn. council trustees 1969-74), Ind. Soc. of Chgo. (hon. life), Jr. C. of C. Internat. (hon. life senator), Assn. Am. Rhodes Scholars, ABA, Fed. Bar Assn., Kentuckians (pres. N.Y.C. 1976-79, life trustee), S.R., SAR, Ky. Bar Assn., D.C. Bar Assn., Ind. Bar Assn. (hon.), Disciples of Christ Hist. Soc. (life mem.), Phi Beta Kappa, Order of Coif, Sigma Chi (Balfour Nat. award 1936, Significant Sig 1961, dir. found. bd. 1974—, Order of Constantine 1981), Omicron Delta Kappa (dir. found. 1984—, Laurel Crown Circle award), Phi Delta Phi, Tau Kappa Alpha (Dist. Alumni award 1966), Merton Soc. (Oxford, Eng.); hon. mem. Blue Key, Beta Gamma Sigma, Alpha Kappa Psi, Kappa Kappa Psi. Presbyterian. Clubs: Army-Navy (Washington), City Tavern (Washington), Field (Greenwich); Pilgrims of U.S, Boone and Crockett. Home: Martin Dale Greenwich CT 06830 Office: Chickering & Gregory PC 1815 H St NW #600 Washington DC 20006

STAICU, PAUL, conductor, hornist; b. Bucharest, Romania, June 7, 1937; s. Ioan and Maria (Frânculescu) S.; grad. as Hornist magna cum laude, Prague Acad. Music, 1961; grad. as Condr., Vienna Acad. Music, 1970; m. Irina Botez, July 6, 1963; 1 son, Paul Cristian. Solo hornist Bucharest Philharmonic Orch., 1961-68; tchr. Bayreuth Sch., 1970, 75, 78, Gourdon Sch., 1976; prof. chamber music Bucharest Music Acad., 1966-78, prof. horn, 1969—; chief condr. chamber orch. Bucharest Music Acad., 1966-78, chief condr. symphony orch., 1975-78; chief condr. chamber and symphony orch. Constanta-Rumania, 1978—; numerous performances, tour Europe and U.S.A.; mem. internat. competition juries, Prague, 1968, 74, 78, 82, Munich, 1973, 80; recs. Recipient Cultural medal I Grade, Rumania, 1968, Herbert von Karajan Found. medal (as part of Camerata Orch.), 1974. Mem. Internat. Horn Soc., Internat. Biographical Assn. Concerts, recs., TV and radio performances. Home: 103 Bd Republicii, 70311 Bucharest Romania Office: 97 Mircea cel Batrin, 8700 Constanta Romania

STAIGER, BRUNHILD, language professional, researcher; b. Altlandsberg, Germany, July 4, 1938; d. Bruno and Brigitte (Jahn) S.; m. Rainer Esterer, May 11, 1974. Grad., Hamburg U., Fed. Republic Germany, 1964, PhD in Sinology, 1968. Asst. editor Chinese dept. Hamburg U., 1968-73; researcher Inst. Asian Affairs, Hamburg, 1973—, dep. dir., 1975—. Author: Das Konfuzius-Bild im Kommunistischen China, 1969; editor: China, 1980; co-editor: China Handbuch, 1974; regular contbr. China Aktuell. Mem. German Assn. Asian Studies (chairwoman China council 1979—), European Assn. Chinese Studies. Lutheran. Office: Inst Asian Affairs, Rothenbaumchaussee 32, 2 Hamburg 13 Federal Republic of Germany

STAIGER, RALPH CONRAD, educator, former association executive; b. N.Y.C., Sept. 10, 1917; s. Max Frederick and Marie Anna (Scheffmacher) S.; m. Marian Carpenter, Dec. 23, 1945; children: Charles Carpenter, Joan Marie. B.A., Columbia U., 1939; M.A., Tchrs. Coll., 1942; Ed.D., Temple U., 1952. Reading cons. Utica (N.Y.) Schs., 1952-62; prof. psychology, dir. reading clinic U. So. Miss., Hattiesburg, 1952-62; exec. dir. Internat. Reading Assn., Newark, Del., 1962-84; pres. Reading Cons. Services, 1984—; adj. prof. edn. U. Del., Newark, 1962-84; mem. internat. book com., 1974—, nat. adv. bd. Library of Congress Center for The Book, 1977—, chmn., 1984—; mem. U.S. Nat. Comm. for UNESCO, 1981-86; pres. U.S. Bd. on Books for Young People, 1985-86. Author: New Directions in Reading, 1967, The Teaching of Reading, 1973, Roads to Reading, 1979, Planning and Organizing Reading Campaigns, 1983. Bd. mgrs. Western br. YMCA, 1967-73. Mem. Nat. Conf. Research English (pres.), Alliance for Advancement Edn. (pres.), Council Communication Socs. (pres. 1981-83), Internat. Reading Assn. (dir.), Nat. Reading Conf. (dir.). Club: U. Wash.

STAINLAY, PETER THOMAS, airlines executive; b. Murwillumbah, New South Wales, Australia, Feb. 13, 1950; s. Leo A. and Annie A. (Proudfoot) S.; m. Wendy Dawn Stainlay, May 31, 1974; children: Andrew, Kimberley. Diploma Tech., New South Wales Inst. Tech., Sydney, 1973; diploma, Advanced Mgmt. Program, Havard U. Trainee Qantas Airways Ltd., Sydney, 1968-70, planning analyst, 1970-74, product mgr., 1974-77; mgr. Qantas Airways Ltd., Indonesia, 1977-80; dir. mktg. Qantas Airways Ltd., 1980-84, dir. corporate planning, 1984-86, sr. v.p. mktg., 1986-87, dep. chief exec. comml., 1987—; mem. adv. panel Sch. Mktg., New South Wales Inst. Tech., Sydney, 1985—. Club: Elanora Country (Sydney). Office: Qantas Airways Ltd, PO Box 489, Sydney, New South Wales 2001, Australia

STALEY, DELBERT C., telecommunications executive; b. Hammond, Ind., Sept. 16, 1924; s. Eugene and Nellie (Downer) s.; m. Ingrid Andersen, Mar. 16, 1946; children—Crista Staley Ellis, Cynthia, Clifford, Corinn. Student, Rose Poly. Inst., Hammond, 1943-44; grad. advanced mgmt. program, Harvard U., 1962; D. Engring. (hon.), Rose Hulman Inst. Tech., 1981; LL.D., Skidmore Coll., 1983. With Ill. Bell Telephone, 1946-76, v.p. ops., 1972-76; pres. Ind. Bell, 1976-78; v.p. residence mktg. AT&T, 1978-79; pres. N.Y. Telephone, 1979-83, chmn. bd., chief exec. officer, 1983; chmn. bd., chief exec. officer NYNEX Corp., White Plains, N.Y., 1983—, also dir.; dir. Dean Foods, Franklin Park, Ill., Ball Corp., Muncie, Ind., Bank N.Y., N.Y.C. Mem. com. econ. devel. Bus. Roundtable, Conf. Bd., N.Y.C. Partnership Inc.; mem. nat. bd. of govs. ARC, chmn., Greater N.Y.C.; vice chmn. United Way N.Y.C.; mem. United Way of Tri State. Served with U.S. Army, 1943-46, ETO. Recipient Puerto Rican Legal Def. and Edn. Fund award, 1981, Cleveland Dodge award YMCA Greater N.Y., 1983, New Yorker for N.Y. award Citizens Com. for N.Y., 1984. Mem. IEEE, Ind. Acad. (hon.), Telephone Pioneers Am. (pres. 1983-84). Presbyterian. Clubs: Westchester Country, Sky, Blind Brook, Exmoor, Royal Poinciana. Home: 100 Polly Park Rd Rye NY 10580 Office: Nynex Corp 1113 Westchester Ave White Plains NY 10604 *

STALKER, KENNETH WALTER, consulting engineer; b. St. John, Kans., Oct. 3, 1918; s. Walter Richard and Bertha (Bissett) S.; B.A., U. Colo., 1941; LL.B., LaSalle U., 1952; m. Eva Leona Teagarden, Feb. 7, 1947. Mfg. engr. Gen. Electric Co., Lynn, Mass., 1950-52; mgr. mfg. engring. and process devel. Aircraft Engring. Group, Gen. Electric Co., Cin., 1952-59, chief cons. engr. process advanced tech., 1965-81; mgr. engring. Goodman Mfg. Co., Chgo., 1959-64; mem. critical material task force Metal Property Council, 1980-81; cons. engr. Pratt & Whitney Aircraft, Spl. Metals Corp.; editorial adv. bd. Nat. Acad. Sci.; lectr. U. Ark. Precinct committeeman Cook County (Ill.) Republican Party, 1962-64; trustee Presbyn. Ch. of Wyoming (Ohio), 1978-81. Recipient managerial award Gen. Electric Co., 1956, William L. Badger Meml. award, 1970, award for outstanding contbns. Pratt & Whitney Aircraft, 1982-88. Mem. ASME, Soc. Mfg. Engrs., Soc. Automotive Engrs. Clubs: Masons, Shriners. Contbr. articles to trade jours. Patentee in field. Home and Office: 500 N Sequoyan Dr Fayetteville AR 72701 Other: 222 US Hwy 1 Suite 214 Tequesta FL 33469

STALLARD, WAYNE MINOR, lawyer; b. Onaga, Kans., Aug. 23, 1927; s. Minor Regan and Lydia Faye (Randall) S.; B.S., Kans. State Tchrs. Coll., Emporia, 1949; J.D., Washburn U., 1952; m. Wanda Sue Bacon, Aug. 22, 1948; children—Deborah Sue, Carol Jean, Bruce Wayne (dec.). Admitted to Kans. bar, 1952 pvt. practice, Onaga, 1952—; atty. Community Hosp. Dist. No. 1, Pottawatomie, Jackson and Nemaha Counties, Kans., 1955—; Pottawatomie County atty., 1955-59; city atty. Onaga, 1953-79; atty Unified School Dist. 322, Pottawatomie County, Kans., 1966-83. Bd. dirs. North Central Kans. Guidance Ctr., Manhattan, 1974-78; lawyer 2d dist. jud. nominating commn., 1980—; atty. Rural Water Dist. No. 3, Pottawatomie County, Kans., 1974—; chmn. Pottawatomie County Econ. Devel. Com., 1986—. Fund dr. chmn. Pottawatomie County chpt. Nat. Found. for Infantile Paralysis, 1953-54. Served from pvt. to sgt., 8th Army, AUS, 1946 to 47. Mem. ABA, Pottawatomie County, Kans. bar assns., Onaga Businessmen's Assn., Am. Judicature Soc., City Attys. Assn. Kan. (dir. 1963-66), Phi Gamma Mu, Kappa Delta Pi, Delta Theta Phi, Sigma Tau Gamma. Mem. United Ch. of Christ. Mason (Shriner); mem. Order Eastern Star. Home: 720 High St Onaga KS 66521 Office: Stallard & Roe 307 Leonard Onaga KS 66521

STALLWORTH, CHARLES DEROTHEA, JR., psychologist; b. Riderwood, Ala., July 4, 1940; s. Charles D. and Annie (Horn) S. B.S., Tenn. State U., Nashville, 1963, M.S., 1966; postgrad, Calif. Sch. Profl. Psychology, 1977-79, U. Ky., 1980, U. South Ala., summer 1967, Tuskegee Inst., summer 1968, Auburn U., summer 1969, Harvard U., summer 1975; Ph.D. in Psychology, Internat. Coll., 1983. Psychiat. asst. Hubbard Hosp., Nashville, 1964-66; counselor, math tchr. North Central High Sch., Chatom, Ala., 1969-70; supr. adult edn. Washington County Bd. Edn., Chatom, 1968-70; dir. counseling ctr. Albany State Coll., Ga., 1970—; cons. Peace Corps, 1979-82. Bd. dirs. Dougherty County CODAC, Inc., Albany, 1973-77, Albany Area Council V.D. Control, 1975-77. Recipient grants HEW, 1970-77, U.S. Office Edn., 1972. Mem. Am. Psychol. Assn. (assoc.), Alpha Phi Alpha. Democrat. Baptist. Research on impact of affective domain on learning outcomes and on application of cognative therapies as a means of controlling negative effects. Home: 805 4th Ave Albany GA 31705 Office: Albany State Coll Ctr for Student Devel Albany GA 31705

STALLWORTH, TERRESA LOUISE, psychiatrist; b. Tuscaloosa, Ala.; d. William Wesley and Louise Clara Catherine (Goodrich) S.; student Va. Intermont Coll., 1954-55; B.Mus. (Elsa Strong piano scholar, 1955-58), U. Tenn., 1959, M.D., 1963. Intern, U. Tenn. Meml. Hosp. and Research Center, 1963-64; resident in neurology City of Memphis Hosp., 1964-65; resident in psychiatry U. Mo., St. Louis, 1966-68, chief resident, 1968; clin. dir., asst. supt., acting supt. Lakeshore Mental Health Inst., Knoxville, Tenn., 1969-74; dir. community programs and specialty units, San Antonio State Hosp., 1974—; asso. clin. prof. psychiatry U. Tex. Health Scis. Center, San Antonio, 1974—; chmn. profl. adv. bd. Bexar County Mental Health/Mental Retardation Center, 1979-81; mem. profl. adv. bd. Horizon House Day Care Center. Concert pianist, various concerts Trinity U., St. Mary's U., Incarnate Word Coll., 1975—, concert appearances with San Antonio Symphony, city grant-sponsored concerts San Antonio State Hosp. Winner first prize Memphis and Mid-South piano contest, 1958. Diplomate Am. Bd. Psychiatry and Neurology, Am. Bd. Adminstrv. Psychiatry. Fellow Am. Psychiat. Assn.; mem. Tex. Psychiat. Assn. (com. on women), Bexar County Psychiat. Soc., AMA, Tex. Med. Assn., Bexar County Med. Soc., Alpha Omega Alpha. Clubs: Tuesday Music, NOW, Sigma Kappa Alumnae. Premier performance own Piano Sonata, 1980; contbr. article to profl. med. jour. Office: San Antonio State Hosp New Braunfels Ave San Antonio TX 78222

STAMATIOU, CONSTANTINE JOHN, banker; b. Vopos Magnisia, Thessaly, Greece, Nov. 3, 1937; s. John Constantine and Diane Spiros (Boukouvalas) S.; m. Mary Andrew Eliadis; children: John, Andrew, Diane, Costas. Fin. and Comml. Studies, U. Athens, Greece, 1956-65. Officer, br. mgr. Nat. Bank Greece, 1969-75; br. mgr. 1st Nat. City Bank, 1975-88; fin. mgr. Ergobank S.A., Athens, 1975—. Served with Greece Fin. Control, 1959-60. Home: 34 Thiatiron St, Nea Smirni, 171 10 Athens Greece Office: Ergobank SA, 69-75 Thessalonikis St, Moschato, 183 46 Athens Greece

STAMATIS, CONSTANTINE S., architect; b. Athens, Greece, Sept. 4, 1926; s. Stamatios C. and Eugenia A. (Philippides) S.; m. Elisabeth L. Arvaniti, Dec. 26, 1959 (div. Dec. 1961); 1 child, Alexander; m. Helen C. Tsaoussoglou, Aug. 12, 1962; 1 child, Eugenia Eva. Diploma in Architecture, Nat. Tech. U. of Athens, 1951. Registered architect, Greece. Design architect Social Security Authority, Athens, 1951-55, Labour Housing Authority, Athens, 1955-58, Nat. Tourist Orgn., Athens, 1958-66; pvt. practice architecture, Athens, 1966-75; dep. mng. dir. C.D. Kapsambelis & Assocs., Athens, 1975-84; mng. dir. C.D. Kapsambelis, C.S. Stamatis, P.D. Moundrouvalis, C.N. Karanopoulos and Assocs., Athens, 1984—; tech. advisor Hellenic Orgn. Small Scale Industries and Handicraft, Athens, 1972-81. Mem. Can. Mediterranean Inst. at Athens, 1984—, French-Hellenic Assn., Athens, 1960—; bd. dirs. Old People's Welfare Soc., Athens, 1973-84. Recipient 1st prize Abu Dhabi Nat. Oil Co. Bldg., 1975, 76, Zakum Devel. Co. Bldg., 1977, Abu Dhabi Investment Authority Bldg., 1980. Fellow Greek Archtl. Soc.; mem. Tech. Chamber of Greece, Archtl. Assn., Greek Polit. Soc., Athens Coll. Alumni Assn., European Cultural Found. (mem. Hellenic com.). Club: Yachting Club of Greece. Home: 58 Souidias St, 115 21 Athens Greece Office: 6 Sekeri St, 106 74 Athens Greece

STAMBERGER, EDWIN HENRY, farmer, civic leader; b. Mendota, Ill., Feb. 16, 1916; s. Edwin Nicolaus and Emilie Anna Marie (Yost) S.; m. Mabel Edith Gordon, Oct. 6, 1937; 1 child, Larry Allan. Farmer seed corn, livestock, machinery devel. Mendota, 1939—; bd. dirs. Mendota Coop. & Supply Co., 1949-67, pres., 1958-67. Mem. Mendota Luth. Ch. council, 1958-64, chmn. 1964, treas. northwest conf., 1966-68, trustee Bible camp; mem. Mendota Watershed Com., 1966-73, 77—, rev. and comment com. subregion and region Ill. Cen. Comprehensive Health Planning Agy., 1974-76; asst. in devel. Mendota Hosp., Mendota Lake; chmn. bldg. com. Mendota Luth. Home, 1972-73; bd. dirs. LaSalle County Mental Health Bd., 1969-74, U. Ill. County Extension, 1963-67, chmn. 1966-67; bd. dirs. Soil and Water Dist., 1968-73, vice chmn., 1971-73. Recipient Future Farmers Am. award. Mem. Am. Soc. Agrl. Engrs., Soil Soc. Am., Ill. Count Watersheds (founder), Smithsonian Inst., Mental Health Assn., People to People Internat., Platform Assn., Mendota C. of C. (Honor award 1974). Club: Mendota Sportsman's. Lodge: Lions (Mendota chpt. bd. dirs. 1965-67, Honor award 1981). Home and Office: Sabine Farm 4425 E 250th Rd Mendota IL 61342

STAMER, WOLFGANG, advertising agency executive; b. Hamburg, Fed. Republic of Germany, Feb. 1, 1930. Advt. dir., authorized mgr. Die Zeit, Hamburg. Home: Heinrich-Traun St 11A, D-2000 Hamburg 63, Federal Republic of Germany Office: Die Zeit, PO Box 106820, D-2000 Hamburg Federal Republic of Germany

STAMLER, WILLIAM RAYMOND, mining machinery manufacturing executive; b. Beckley, W.Va., Nov. 11, 1934; s. William Raymond and Mary Buford (Hodges) S.; m. Ellen Charlotte Boyd, Sept. 30, 1961; 1 child, Rose Mary. BA in Econs., U. of South, 1956. Commd. 2d lt. U.S. Air Force, 1956, advanced through grades to lt. col., 1977; resigned, 1965; pres. W.R. Stamler Corp., Millersburg, Ky., 1965-80, chmn., chief exec. officer, 1980—; chmn. Peoples Deposit Bank, Paris, Ky., 1975-84; mem. Ky. Dist. Export Council, 1982—; adviser dept. mining engring. U. Ky., Lexington, 1983—; bd. dirs. Bourbon Bank, Paris, Ky. Bd. dirs. Bourbon County YMCA, 1975-78; jr. warden St. Peter's Episcopal Ch., 1978; co-chmn. Ky. Gov.'s Product Liability Com., Frankfort, 1977; chmn. bd. Congressman's Service Acad. Rev., 1975-84; trustee Associated Industries of Ky., bd. dirs. 1976-79, U. of the South, 1977-84; Millersburg Mil. Inst., 1970-84, chmn. 1978-79. Decorated Commendation medal with oak leaf cluster; U. Ky. fellow. Mem. Bourbon County C. of C. (pres. 1971), Ky. C. of C. (bd. dirs. 1981-84), Nat. Stone Assn. (bd. dirs.), Ky. Coal Assn. (bd. dirs.), Res. Officers assn., Am. Mining Congress (chmn. product liability com. 1981-84, vice chmn. mfrs. div. 1983-87, chmn. 1988—, bd. dirs.), Am. Inst. Mining Engrs., Young Pres. Orgn., Mining Club N.Y., Kappa Alpha. Republican. Episcopalian. Clubs: Lex Yacht (commodore 1983-84), Lafayette (Lexington, Ky.); Cin.; Stoner Creek Country; King Coal, Spindletop Hall. Lodge: Rotary (pres. 1970). Home: 2 Mount Airy Dr Paris KY 40361 Office: WR Stamler Corp Main and Stamler Sts Millersburg KY 40348

STAMM, ANDRE MICHEL, pharmacy educator, consultant; b. Thann, France, Feb. 24, 1946; s. Thiebaut Aime and Marguerite Jeanne (Fehlbaum) S.; m. Helene Bernhard, Oct. 2, 1971; children—Sophie, Frederic. Degree in Pharmacy, Faculty of Pharmacy, Strasbourg, France, 1969, Ph.D., 1971, 75. Asst., Faculty of Pharmacy, Strasbourg, 1970-71, head asst., 1971-74, assoc. prof., 1975-77, prof., 1977—; cons. Pharmacy Industry, France, 1978—; vice dean, Faculty of Pharmacy, Strasbourg, 1980-83. Contbr. articles to profl. jours. Served to capt. French Army, 1973-74. Fellow Sci. and Tech. Pharmacy, Internat. Assn. Pharm. Tech. Office: Faculty Pharmacy, PO Box 24, 67401 Illkirch France

STAMP, TERENCE HENRY, actor; b. London, July 22, 1938; s. Thomas and Ethel Esther (Perrott) S. Actor: (films) include Billy Budd (Oscar nomination, Golden Globe award), 1960; Term of Trial, 1962, The Collector (Cannes Best Actor award), 1964, Alfie, 1964, Modesty Blaise, 1966, Far From the Madding Crowd, 1966, Poor Cow, 1967, Blue, 1967, Tales of Mystery, 1967, Theorem, 1968, Tales of Mystery, 1968, The Mind of Mr. Soames, 1969, A Season in Hell, 1971, Hu-man, 1975, The Divine Creature, 1976, Striptease, 1977, Meetings With Remarkable Men, 1978, Superman, 1978, Superman II, 1979, Meetings With Remarkable Men, 1980, The Bloody Chamber, 1982, The Hit, 1984, Legal Eagles, 1986, Wall Street, 1987, The Sicilian, 1986; (plays include) Dracula, The Lady From the Sea. Clubs: Brook's (London); Manchester. Address: care Duncan Heath Assocs, 162 Wardour St, London W1 England Office: care Fraser & Dunlop Ltd, 91 Regent St, London WRR 8RU, England *

STAMPER, DONALD LEE, emergency room physician; b. Middletown, Ohio, July 22, 1938; s. Chester Arthur and Garnet (Williams) S.; m. Beverly Jean Sticklen, Dec. 19, 1964; children—Amy Elizabeth, Melissa Kathleen. A.B., Miami U., Oxford, Ohio, 1968; D.O., Kansas City (Mo.) Coll. Osteo. Medicine, 1972. Patrolman, Middletown Div. Police, 1960-68; intern Grandview Hosp., Dayton, Ohio, 1972; ptnr. Franklin Family Clinic (Ohio), 1973—; police surgeon, Middletown; mem. staff Grandview Hosp. Capt., Middletown Police Res., 1982. Served with USN, 1955-59. Named Boss of Yr., Dayton Dist. Acad., 1978, Outstanding Citizen, City of Middletown, 1981. Mem. Ohio Osteo. Assn., Dayton Dist. Acad. Osteo. Medicine, Internat. Assn. Chiefs of Police, Alpha Phi Omega, Sigma Sigma Phi, Psi Sigma Alpha. Republican. Baptist. Home: 6119 Brookshire Ln Franklin OH 45005 Office: Franklin Family Clinic 10 Stadia Dr Franklin OH 45005

STAN, PATRICIA, savings consultant, real estate executive; b. Chgo., Oct. 10, 1952; d. Paul and Olga (Zyluk) S.; m. Donald Ross Crabtree, Feb. 27, 1982 (div.). Student Monmouth Coll., 1964-66; B.F.A., Drake U., 1969; postgrad. U. Houston, 1974-76, Houston Coll., 1977-78. Cert. tchr., Tex.; cert. real estate broker, Tex. Tchr., Spring Branch Meml. Ind. Sch. Dist., Houston, 1976-78; cons. Sam Feldt Co., Houston, 1978-80; counselor Doyle Stuckey Homes, Houston, 1980-82; pres. Stan Internat., Houston, 1981—; counselor Am. Classic Homes, Houston, 1982-83; cons. Savs. of America, Houston, 1983—. Patron Houston Mus. Fine Arts. Mem. Mensa, Tex. Edn. Assn., Nat. Women's Council Realtors, Houston Bd. Realtors, Tex. Real Estate Commn., Archaeol. Soc. Houston, Sierra Club, Kappa Kappa Gamma.

STANALAND, WILLIAM WHIT, JR., accountant; b. Benson Junction, Fla., Mar. 15, 1930; s. William Whit and Goldie (Merritt) S.; BS in Bus. Adminstrn., U. Fla., 1957, postgrad., 1959; postgrad. Rollins Coll., 1964; m. Norma Lee Ober, June 24, 1961; children—Sherry D., William Whit III, Terence B., Dana Lee; m. 2d, Sandra L. Swann, Dec. 1, 1971. Jr. acct. Pepsi Cola Bottling Co., 1957-58; acct. Wells, Laney, Earlich & Baer, 1958-59, A.J. Mixner, CPA, 1961-63; controller Halco Products, Inc., 1959-61; CPA, Orlando, Fla., 1963—. Served with USMC, 1948-52. CPA, Fla. Mem. Am., Fla. Insts. CPA's, Assn. Builders and Contractors, Associated Gen. Contractors of Mid-Fla., Mortgage Bankers Assn., Brevard Marine Assn., Cen. Fla. Tax Roundtable, Greater South Brevard C. of C. Clubs: Toastmasters; Coast (Melbourne); Eau Gallie Yacht. Lodge: Kiwanis. Home: 441 N Harbor City Blvd Unit C-20 Melbourne FL 32935 Office: 1600 Sarno Rd Suite 21 Melbourne FL 32935

STANDEISKY, ÉVA, historian; b. Pécs, Baranya, Hungary, Feb. 27, 1948; d. István and Margit (Matavovszky) S.; married; 1 child, Katalin. Historian, Eötvös Loránd U., Budapest, Hungary, 1971, PhD (hon.), 1974. Researcher Institut Party History, Budapest, Hungary, 1971—; reader faculty of law Eötvös Loránd U., Budapest, 1985—. Author: Literary Policy of Hungarian Communist Party 1944-48, 1987. Active Tradeunion, Bonn, Fed. Republic of Germany, 1982. Grantee Friedrich Ebert Stiftung, 1982. Mem. Hungarian Assn. History. Home: Nyul u 14, H-1026 Budapest Hungary Office: Institut for Party History, Alkotmány u 2, H-1054 Budapest Hungary

STANDIFER, HUGH AVERY, information systems consultant; b. Johnson County, Tex., Dec. 19, 1932; s. Mynis William and Lucy Kate (Lomax) S.; student Sam Houston State U., 1950, 70-71, U. Tex., Arlington, 1958, Central Tex. Coll., 1971-72, St. Edwards U., 1973; B.S. in Criminal Justice, Am. Tech. U., 1974; m. Bonnie K. Ruschmyer Juergens, Apr. 14, 1979; children by previous marriage—Hugh Marcus, William Herman, Penny Teresa, Patti Christine. Computer programmer Gen. Foods Corp., 1958-64; ops. mgr. Nat. Western Life Ins. Co., Austin, Tex., 1964-67; asst. div. chief for data processing Tex. Dept. Public Safety, Austin, 1967-73; info. systems dir. City of Austin, 1974-84; computer cons., Austin, 1984—; ptnr. Justan Enterprises, Data Processing Consultation and Services; pres. Tex. D.P.S. Credit Union, 1972; mem. rev. bd. Public Technology, Inc., 1975-76; instr. Tex. A&M U., 1969-74; mem. textbook selection com. Austin Ind. Sch. Dist., 1975-76, Gov.'s Commn. on Standards and Goals for Tex., 1975-76. Served with AUS, 1955-58. Mem. Met. Info. Exchange (pres. 1980), Govt. Mgmt. Info. Scis., Urban and Regional Info. Systems Assn., Library and Info. Tech. Assn., ALA, Tex. Assn. Govtl. Data Processing Mgrs. (exec. com., chmn. edn. com., v.p. 1981, pres. 1982). Lutheran. Pioneer in use of convict labor for clerical/data preparation activities. Office: PO Box 33160 Austin TX 78764

STANFORD, MELVIN JOSEPH, university dean, management consultant; b. Logan, Utah, June 13, 1932; s. Joseph Sedley and Ida Pearl (Ivie) S.; m. Linda Barney, Sept. 2, 1960; children: Connie Stanford Tendick, Cheryl Stanford Bohn, Joseph, Theodore, Emily, Charlotte, Charles, Sarah. B.S. (First Security Found. scholar), Utah State U., 1957; M.B.A. (Donald Kirk David fellow), Harvard U., 1963; Ph.D., U. Ill., 1968. Asst. audit supr. Utah Tax Commn., 1958-61; acct. Haskins & Sells, C.P.A.s, Boston, 1961-62; acctg. staff analyst Arabian Am. Oil Co., Dhahran, Saudi Arabia, 1963-66; teaching and research asst. U. Ill., Urbana, 1966-68; mem. faculty Brigham Young U., Provo, Utah, 1968-82; dir. mgmt. devel. programs Brigham Young U., 1970-73, prof. bus. mgmt., 1974-82; dean Coll. Bus. Mankato (Minn.) State U., 1982—; vis. prof. mgmt. Boston U., Europe, 1975-76. Author: New Enterprise Management, 1975, 82, Management Policy, 1979, 83; also articles, mgmt. cases. Founder Midwestern Jour. Bus. and Econs., 1985. Served with USAF, 1951-55; also Res. Mem. N. Am. Case Research Assn. (v.p. for research 1985-86, pres. 1987-88), Acad. Mgmt., Strategic Mgmt. Soc., SAR (pres. Utah 1978-79, nat. trustee 1979-80, Meritorious Service medal 1981), Alpha Kappa Psi, Phi Kappa Phi. Mem. Ch. Jesus Christ Latter Day Saints. Lodge: Kiwanis. Home: 221 Crestwood Dr North Mankato MN 56001 Office: Mankato State U Coll Bus 120 MH Mankato MN 56001

STANFORD, ROBERT AUGUST, editor; b. Akron, Ohio, Mar. 16, 1927; s. George Frederick and Margaret Hannah (Ruthenberg) S. BA with honor, U. Akron, 1956; lic. et arts et lettres avec mention bien, U. Paris, 1958. Asst. to pres. Dover Pubs., N.Y.C., 1962-64; copy editor McKinsey & Co., N.Y.C., 1965-66; gen. mgr. Burt Franklin Pubs., N.Y.C., 1967-68; dep. dir., adv. bd. N.Y.C. Dept. Social Services, 1968-78; mng. editor, co-owner N.Y. Native Newspaper, 1981-82; editor-in-chief In Touch Pubs., North Hollywood, Calif., 1984—; field ops. asst. U.S. Census Bur., Manhattan, N.Y.C.; part-owner That New Mag., Inc., NYC. Vol. Congresswoman Bella S. Abzug, N.Y.C., 1970-76. Served with signal corp U.S. Army, 1950-52. Mem. Phi Sigma Alpha. Democrat. Mem. United Ch. Christ. Home: 6842 Fulton St #7 North Hollywood CA 91605 Office: In Touch Pubs Internat Inc 7216 Varna St North Hollywood CA 91605

STANGELAND, LUDVIG BERNHARD, mechanical engineer, company executive; b. Bklyn., July 2, 1923; s. Ludvig E and Trine Louen) S.; m. Berit Heskestad, Aug. 23, 1947; 1 child, Geir. BSc in Mech. Engring. summa cum laude, U. N.H., 1949, MSc in Mech. Engring, 1950. Design engr. gas turbines Westinghouse Electric Corp., Lester, Pa., 1950-54; project engr. Exxon Corp. (formerly Esso Standard Oil Co.), Aruba, Netherlands Antilles, 1954-59; mgr. process engring. Norske Exxon (formerly Esso), Tonsberg, Norway, 1959-65; mgr. Valloy Refinery, 1965-68; chief engr., gen. prodn. mgr. Norsk Hydro AS, Karmoy, Norway, 1968—; chmn. bd. Skude Verft Skudenes, Norway, 1980—, br. office Rogalandsbanken, Haugesund, Norway, 1981—; bd. dirs. Saga Hotellene, Haugesund, Karmoy Industri. vice chmn. Karmoy Naeringsrad, 1974-80, Haugesund Industriforening, 1979-81; chmn. Industriens Kontakt/Samarbeidsorgan, Haugesund, 1975-81, Rogaland Industriforening, Stavanger, Norway, 1977-80. Recipient Participation Medal Norwegian Underground, 1943-45. Mem. Norwegian Soc. Grad. Engrs., Tau Beta Pi, Pi Mu Epsilon, Sigma Pi Sigma, Phi Kappa Phi, Theta Chi. Mem. Conservative Party. Lutheran. Lodge: Masons. Home: Stenderveien 37 5500, Haugesund Norway Office: Hydro Aluminum, N-4265, Havik Karmoy Norway

STANGUENNEC, ANDRE YVONS GEORGES, philosopher, educator, researcher; b. Toulon, France, June 7, 1941; s. Francois and Yvonnne (Monfort) S.; m. Danielle Deumien, Oct. 21, 1973; children: Fanny, Thomas. Baccalaureat, Rennes U., 1960; agregation, U. Paris, 1965; MA, U. Nantes, 1971, PhD in Philosophy, 1981. Faculty Profs. High Sch., France and Antilles, 1965-69; maitre de conf. U. Nantes, 1969—; researcher history and philosophy of life scis., history and philosophy of metaphysics. Author: L'homme et ses normes, 1981, Hegel Critique de Kant, 1985, Post-Kantian Studies, 1987, Philosophical Dictionary, 1988, Ethics and Poetry in Mallarmé, 1988; contbg. author Revue Philosophique de la France, Revue de Synthese, Archives de philosophie. Home: 117 rue Jean Fraix, 44400 Reze, Loire Atlantique France Office: U Nantes, Faculte des Lettres, Chemin de la Sensiveqq, 44400 Nantes France

STANICH, ALEXANDER ANTHONY, human resources executive; b. Fiume, Italy, Nov. 25, 1938; came to U.S., 1946, naturalized, 1948; s. Philip and Mercedes (Michelich) S.; m. Irene Spellman, May 23, 1964; children: Alex C., Diana J., Robert J. BS, NYU, 1967. Casualty underwriter Gt. Am. Life Ins., N.Y.C., 1962-65; mgr. group life ins. ASARCO, N.Y.C., 1965-67; mgr. employee benefits worldwide E.R. Squibb Corp., Princeton, N.J., 1967-72; corp. dir. benefits and ins. worldwide Gulton Industries,

Princeton, 1972-74; mgr. compensation and benefits Gt. No. Nekoosa Corp., Stamford, Conn., 1974-77; dir. compensation and benefits worldwide pension plan mgr., fixed income investments Estee Lauder Inc., N.Y.C., 1977-84; pres. Resource Solutions, 1981-87; v.p. employee relations Equitable Fin. Services, N.Y.C., 1984-87; pres. ASA Assocs. Human Resources and Mgrs. Acquisitions Cons., 1987—; prin. ASA Assocs., 1987—; pres. telecommunicaitons mktg. U.S. Telecom Systems, Inc., 1986; mem. human resources adv. com. Coll. of Ins., Vols. Am.; seminar chmn. benefits Am. Mmgt. Assn., 1972-76; cons. in field; bd. dirs. Atlantis Investments Inc., Fla. Served with U.S. Army, 1958-60. Mem. Life Office Mgmt. Assn. (bd. dirs.). Home: 280 Mountain Rd Wilton CT 06897

STANISCI, THOMAS WILLIAM, lawyer; b. Bkln., Nov. 16, 1928; s. Vito and Angela Marie (Martino) S.; m. Catherine Ellen Cullen, June 4, 1955; children—Thomas, Marianne, Ellen, William, Peter. B.A., St. John's Coll. Men, 1949, J.D., 1953, postgrad., 1954. Bar: N.Y. 1953, U.S. Dist. Ct. (so. and ea. dists.) N.Y. 1956; diplomate Am. Bd. Profl. Liability Attys. Assoc. Diblas Marasco & Simone, White Plains, N.Y., 1954-60; mem. Simone Brant & Stanisci, White Plains, 1960-66; mem. Shayne Dachs Stanisci & Harwood, Mineola, N.Y., 1966-83; sr. mem. Shayne Dachs Stanisci & Corker, Mineola, 1983—; lectr. Practising Law Inst., 1975-79; instr., lectr. Am. Mgmt. Assn., 1976-77; guest instr. Adelphi U., Hofstra U., 1975-79; guest speaker, panelist network and local tv. Served with U.S. Army, 1950-52. Mem. Am. Arbitration Assn., Nassau Suffolk Trial Lawyers Assn. (dir., 1978—), Nassau County Bar Assn. (lectr. acad. law), Assn. Trial Lawyers Am., Contbr. articles in field. Office: 250 Old Country Rd Mineola NY 11501

STANISLAO, JOSEPH, engineer, educator; b. Manchester, Conn., Nov. 21, 1928; s. Eduardo and Rose (Zaccaro) S.; m. Bettie Chloe Carter, Sept. 6, 1960. B.S., Tex. Tech. U., 1957; M.S., Pa. State U., 1959; D.Engring. Sci., Columbia U., 1970. Registered profl. engr., Mass. Asst. engr. Naval Ordnance Research, University Park, Pa., 1958-59; asst. prof. N.C. State U., Raleigh, 1959-61; dir. research Darlington Fabrics Corp., Pawtucket, R.I., 1961-62; from asst. prof. to prof. U. R.I., Kingston, 1962-71; prof., chmn. dept. Cleve. State U., 1971-75; prof., dean N.D. State U., Fargo, 1975—, acting v.p. agrl. affairs, 1983—, asst. to pres., 1983—; dir. Engring. Computer Ctr. N.D. State U., 1984—; pres. XOX Corp., 1985—. Contbr. chpts. to books, articles to profl. jours. Served to sgt. USMC, 1948-51. Recipient Sigma Xi award, 1968; recipient N.D. State U. Order of the Iron Ring, 1972, USAF Recognition award, 1979, ROTC Appreciation award, 1982. Sr. mem. Am. Inst. Indsl. Engrs. (v.p. 1964-65); mem. ASME, Am. Soc. Engring Edn. (campus coordinator 1979-81), Phi Kappa Phi, Tau Beta Pi (advisor 1978-79). Roman Catholic. Lodges: Lions; Elks. Home: 3520 Longfellow Rd Fargo ND 58102 Office: North Dakota State U Coll of Engring and Architecture Fargo ND 58105

STANKOVIC, MILORAD DRAGUTIN, physician; b. Leskovac, Yugoslavia, 1928; s. Dragutin Dusan and Olivera Stojan (Stosic) S.; M.D., U. Belgrade, 1955, specialty in pneumophthisiology, 1960; Ph.D. (hon.), Marquis Gruseppe Scicluna Internat. Univ. Found., 1984; m. Ana Kovacevic, 1962; children—Natalija, Katarina. Surgeon, physician infectious diseases Gen. Hosp. Leskovac, 1953-55; mil. physician, Dubrovnik, Yugoslavia, 1955-56; pneumophthisiologist Central Scholar Polyclinic, Belgrade, 1956-61; dir. antituberculosis dispensary, Stara Pazova, Indjija and Pecinci, Yugoslavia, 1962-64; chief antituberculosis dispensary TB Hosp., Apatin, Yugoslavia, 1964-73; chief antituberculosis dispensary Hosp. Med. Centre, Paracin, Yugoslavia, 1973-77; chief anti-Tb dispensary, Paracin, 1978; mem. Commn. for Med. Sci., Republic of Serbia, Belgrade, 1978, profl. supr. Pneumophthisiological Corps, 1983. Recipient Bronze medal for peace Albert Einstein Internat. Acad. Found., 1986. Mem. Serbian Med. Soc. (pres., mem. ct. honor 1978-81), Balkan Med. Union. Author: The Real View and the Prior Problems in the Fight against Tuberculosis, 1972; founder, editor Cancer, 1973, Archives of Pomoravlje, 1977-81, Archives of History of Medicine, 1982; contbr. over 100 articles to med. jours. Office: Medicinski Centar, Paracin Srbija Yugoslavia

STANLEY, EDWARD ALEXANDER, forensic scientist, geologist, technical and academic administrator; b. N.Y.C., Apr. 7, 1929; s. Frank and Elizabeth (Wolf) S.; m. Elizabeth Ann Allison, June 7, 1958; children—Karen, Scott. B.S., Rutgers U., 1954; M.S., Pa. State U., 1956, Ph.D., 1960. Geologist, Amoco Petroleum Co., Tulsa, 1960-62; prof. U. Del., 1962-64, U. Ga., 1964-77; assoc. dean research, chmn. geology dept. Indiana U. Pa., 1977-81; supr. Phillips Petroleum Co., Bartlesville, Okla., 1981-86, dir., comdg. officer N.Y.C. Police Dept. Crime Lab., 1986—; cons. geology, Athens, Ga., 1963-77, Indiana, Pa., 1977-81. Contbr. articles to profl. jours. Served to sgt. USAF, 1947-50. Grantee NSF, 1965-68, Office Water Resources Research, 1965-68, Nat. Acad. Sci., 1968, 73; exchange prof. Soviet Union. Fellow AAAS, Geol. Soc. Am.; mem. Am. Assn. Petroleum Geologists, Paleontol. Soc., Am. Acad. of Forensic Sci., Sigma Xi. Presbyterian. Avocations: photography; music; firearms. Home: 2004 Haverford Rd Ardmore PA 19003 Office: Crime Lab NY City Police Dept 235 E 20 St Room 836 New York NY 10003

STANLEY, H(ARRY) EUGENE, physicist, educator; b. Norman, Okla., Mar. 28, 1941; s. Harry Eugene and Ruth S.; m. Idahlia Dessauer, June 2, 1967; children: Jannah, Michael, Rachel. B.A. in Physics (Nat. Merit scholar), Wesleyan U., 1962; postgrad. (Fulbright scholar), U. Cologne, W. Ger., 1962-63; Ph.D. in Physics, Harvard U., 1967. NSF predoctoral research fellow Harvard U., 1963-67; mem. staff Lincoln Lab., M.I.T., 1967-68, asst. prof. physics, 1969-71, assoc. prof., 1971-73; Miller research fellow U. Calif., Berkeley, 1968-69; Hermann von Helmholtz assoc. prof. health scis. and tech. Harvard U.-M.I.T. Program in Health Scis. and Tech., 1973-76; vis. prof. Osaka (Japan) U., 1975; univ. prof., prof. physics, prof. physiology Sch. Medicine, dir. Center for Polymer Studies, Boston U., 1976—; Joliot-Curie vis. prof. Ecole Supérieure de Physique et Chimie, Paris, 1979; vis. prof. Peking U., 1981, Seoul Nat. U., 1982; dir. NATO Advanced Study Inst., Cargese, Corsica, 1985, 88; dir. IUPAP Internat. Conf. on Thermodynamics and Statis. Mechanics, 1986; cons. Sandia Nat. Lab., 1983—, Dowell Schlumberger Co., 1982—, Elscint Co., 1983-85; nat. co-chmn. Com. of Concerned Scientists, 1974-76-76. Author: Introduction to Phase Transitions and Critical Phenomena, 1971, Random Fluctuations and Pattern Growth, 1988; editor: Biomedical Physics and Biomaterials Science, 1972, Cooperative Phenomena Near Phase Transitions, 1973; On Growth and Form: Fractal and Non-Fractal Patterns in Physics, 1985; Statistical Physics, 1986, Fractals and Multifractals in Sci., Engring. and Medicine, 1989, Physica A; mem. editorial bd.: Physica, 1973—, Nuclear Physics D, 1983—, Jour. Statis. Physics, 1983—. Recipient Choice award Am. Assn. Book Pubs., 1972; Macdonald award, 1986; John Simon Guggenheim Meml. fellow, 1979-80. Fellow Am. Phys. Soc. (chmn. New Eng. sect. 1982-83), Nat. Acad. Scis. (non-linear sci. panel). Home: 50 Metacomet Rd Newton-Waban MA 02168 Office: Center for Polymer Studies Boston U Boston MA 02215

STANLEY, JAMES GORDON, engineering marketing executive, writer; b. Birmingham, Ala., Feb. 13, 1925; s. Joseph Gordon and Amy I. (Crocker) S.; B.S., U. Ala., 1949; m. children—Cynthia Ruth, Pamela Anne, Gordon Bruce, James Alan, Joseph Christopher; m. 2d, Patricia Ann Peuvion, 1969. Instr., Miss. State U. Extension, Jackson, 1956; tech. rep. S.E., Price Brothers Co., Dayton, 1957-59; project mgr., dept. mgr. Brown Engring. Co., Kennedy Space Center, Fla. and Huntsville, Ala., 1959-64; dir. engring., reliability Bendix Launch Support Div., 1964-67; mgr. reliability, systems engr. Dow Chem. Co., Kennedy Space Center, 1967-71, mgr. engring. mktg. Houston, 1971-73, contract research mgr., Midland, Mich., 1973-80, sr. project mgr. Houston, 1980—, assigned as project bus. mgr. Dow/Dept. Energy geothermal project, Lafayette, La., 1981-83; free lance writer. Served to lt. (j.g.) USNR, 1943-66. Recipient Toulmin medal for best article Mil. Engr. Mag., 1980. Mem. Cocoa Beach C. of C., Phi Gamma Delta. Baptist. Club: Elks. Contbg. editor for energy Nat. Def. Mag. Home: 2947 Meadowgrass Ln Houston TX 77082 Office: Dow Chem USA 400 West Belt S Houston TX 77042

STANLEY, JUSTIN ARMSTRONG, lawyer; b. Leesburg, Ind., Jan. 2, 1911; s. Walter H. and Janet (Armstrong) S.; m. Helen Leigh Fletcher, Jan. 3, 1938; children: Janet Van Wie Hoffmann, Melinda Fletcher Douglas, Justin Armstrong, Harlan Fletcher. A.B., Dartmouth Coll., 1933, A.M. (hon.), 1952, LL.D. (hon.), 1983; LL.B., Columbia U., 1937; LL.D. (hon.), John Marshall Law Sch., 1976, Suffolk U., 1976, Vt. Law Sch., 1977, Norwich U., 1977, Ind. U., 1981, Oklahoma City U., 1981. Bar: Ill. 1937. Since practiced in Chgo.; assoc. Isham, Lincoln & Beale, 1937-48, partner, 1948-66; partner Mayer, Brown & Platt, 1967—; v.p. Dartmouth Coll., 1952-54; asst. prof. law Chgo.-Kent Coll. Law, 1938-43, prof., 1943-46; Dir. Charles H. Shaw Co., Ellsworth Fin. Corp.; Pub. mem. disputes sect. Nat. War Labor Bd., 1943-44. Trustee Presbyn.-St. Luke's Hosp., Wells Coll., 1960-69, Rockford Coll., 1962-70; trustee Ill. Childrens Home and Aid Soc., pres., 1963-64. Served as lt. USNR, 1944-46. Recipient medal for excellence Columbia U. Law Sch., 1984. Fellow Am. Bar Found., Am. Coll. Trial Lawyers; mem. ABA (chmn. pub. utility sect. 1970-71, ho. of dels. 1973—, pres. 1976-77, chmn. commn. on professionalism. 1985-86, ABA medal 1986), Fed. Energy Bar Assn., Chgo. Bar Assn. (pres. 1967-68), Ill. Bar Assn. (Disting. Service award 1986), Alumni Council Dartmouth (pres. 1952), Am. Law Inst., Am. Judicature Soc., Alpha Delta Phi. Episcopalian. Clubs: Chicago (Chgo.), University (Chgo.), Legal (Chgo.), Commercial (Chgo.), Commonwealth (Chgo.), Law (Chgo.); Wausaukee (Wis.); Cosmos (Washington); Univ. (N.Y.C.), Century Assn. (N.Y.C.); R & A (St. Andrews, Scotland). Office: Mayer Brown & Platt 190 S LaSalle St Chicago IL 60603

STANLEY, LUTICIOUS BRYAN, JR., mechanical and civil engineer; b. Atlanta, Aug. 26, 1947; s. Luticious Bryan and Frances Aileen (William) S. B.S., So. Tech. Inst., 1974, 82; MS, Ga. State U., 1986. Registered profl. engr., Ga. Field engr. Jordan, Jones & Goulding, Inc., Atlanta, 1974-79; project mgr., engr. Mayes, Sudderth & Etheredge, Inc., Atlanta, 1979-82; field service engr. Westinghouse Electric Corp., Chattanooga, 1982-85, asst. regional projects mgr., Atlanta, 1985—; prin. LBS Enterprises. Served with USAR, 1969-75. Phi Theta Pi scholar, 1968. Mem. ASME. Christian Scientist. Lodge: Cobb County Lions (Rookie of Year award 1981). Author articles in field. Home: PO Box 5386 WSB Gainesville GA 30501 Office: 1299 Northside Dr WW Atlanta GA 30318

STANLEY, MALCHAN CRAIG, school system administrator, psychologist; b. Boston, Nov. 19, 1948; s. Harry Eugene and Ruth (Shultz) S.; m. Janice Perney, June 30, 1984; 1 child, Jessica. BA in Psychology, Antioch Coll., Yellow Springs, Ohio, 1971; MEd, Boston State Coll., 1975, postgrad., Boston Coll., 1987. Counselor Fernald Sch., Waltham, Mass., 1970-71, psychologist, 1975; tchr. Boston Pub. Schs., 1972-74; sch. psychologist EdCo, Inc., Brookline, Mass., 1975-76; school psychologist Greater Lawrence Ednl. Collaborative, Andover, Mass., 1976-77, exec. dir., 1977—; sec. adv. commn. Mass. Dept. Edn., 1981-84; treas. Mass. Orgn. Ednl. Collaboratives, 1988—. Chmn. Greater Lawrence Interagy. Task Force, 1980-83; treas. Mass. Orgn. Ednl. Collaboratives, 1988—. Mem. Assn. Supervision and Curriculum Devel., Am. Assn. Sch. Adminstrs., Phi Delta Kappa. Unitarian. Home: Gates Rd RD 1 Middleton MA 01949 Office: 10 High St Andover MA 01810

STANLEY, MARGARET DURETA SEXTON, speech therapist; b. Wells County, Ind., Aug. 7, 1931; d. James Helmuth and Bertha Anna (Kizer) Roberts; m. Gale Sexton, Nov. 21, 1950; children: Cregg Alan, Donna Sue, Sheila Rene; m. 2d, Charles Stanley, Mar. 24, 1979. BS, Ball State U., 1952, MA, 1963. Speech and hearing clinician Hamilton (Ohio) City Schs., 1955-59, Kettering (Ohio) Pub. Schs., 1959-60; speech, lang. and hearing clinician Muncie (Inc.) Community Schs., 1960—; dir. Psi Iota Xi Summer Clinic, Decatur, Ind., 1964; clinician Ball State U., 1965-77; supr. clinician Tri-County Hearing Impaired Assn., 1978-81. Compiler, editor curriculum for speech, lang. and hearing clinicians of Muncie Community Schs. Mem. Am. Speech and Hearing Assn. (cert. clin. competency in speech pathology), Ind. Speech and Hearing Assn., Am. Fedn. Tchrs., Muncie Fedn. Tchrs., Ind. Edn. Assn., Ind. Council Suprs. Speech and Hearing (pres. 1982-84), Adminstrv. Women's, Speech and Hearing Area Educators Ind. (founder, 1st. pres. 1984-86), Delta Kappa Gamma. Republican. Methodist. Lodge: Women Moose. Home: 3201 E Oaklawn Dr Muncie IN 47303 Office: 3201 S Macedonia St Muncie IN 47302

STANNARD, JAMES NEWELL, radiation biologist and toxicologist educator; b. Owego, N.Y., Jan. 2, 1910; s. Jay Ellis and Miriam (Newell) S.; m. Grace L. Kingsley, Aug. 7, 1935; 1 child, Susan L. Stannard Stumpf. AB, Oberlin Coll., 1931; MA, Harvard U., 1934, PhD, 1935. Instr. physiology U. Rochester, N.Y., 1935-39, asst. prof. radiation biology and biophysics, 1947-49, assoc. prof. radiation biology and biophysics, 1949-59, prof., 1959-75, prof. pharmacology and toxicology, 1952-75, emeritus prof., 1975—; assoc. dir. Atomic Energy Project U. Rochester, 1959-69; assoc. dean for grad. studies U. Rochester, N.Y., 1959-75; adj. prof. community medicine and radiology U. Calif.-San Diego, La Jolla, 1977—; asst. prof. pharmacology Emory U., Atlanta, 1939-41; sr. pharmacologist to prin. physiologist NIH, Bethesda, Md., 1941-47; vis. prof. U. Calif. Med. Ctr., San Francisco, 1954; cons. Battelle Pacific NW Lab., others; mem. task group Internat. Commn. on Radiol. Protection; chmn., mem. sci. coms., life mem. Nat. Council on Radiation Protection and Measurements; mem. adv. bd. Hanford Environ. Health Found. Author: Radioactivity and Health-A History, 1987; author, editor: Handbook of Experimental Pharmacology, vol. 36, 1973; editor: Radioisotopes in the Aquatic Environment, 1976; contbr. sci. articles to profl. jours. Sec. bd. dirs. Oaks North Mgmt. Corp. Number 1, San Diego. Served to lt. USN, 1944-46. Recipient cert. of appreciation HEW, 1970, cert. appreciation AEC, 1975, cert. appreciation EPA, 1977. Mem. Am. Indsl. Hygiene Assn., AAAS, Am. Soc. Pharmacology and Exptl. Therapeutics, Am. Physiol. Soc., Radiation Research Soc., Health Physics Soc. (dir. 1965-71, pres. 1969-70, editor, mem. editorial bd. 1975-81, Disting. Achievement award 1977), Biophys. Soc., Soc. Gen. Physiologists, Phi Beta Kappa, Sigma Xi. Home: 17441 Plaza Animado Apt 132 San Diego CA 92128 Office: U Calif San Diego M-022 La Jolla CA 92093

STANOMIR, DUMITRU, electronics engineer; b. Bucharest, Romania, Sept. 12, 1930; s. Gheorghe and Cleopatra (Petrusanu) S.; m. Mihaela Harabor, Aug. 4, 1942; 1 child, Ioan. D of Engring., Poly. Inst. Bucharest, 1954, PhD, 1973. Asst. dept. electronics Poly. Inst. Bucharest, 1954-61, lectr., 1961-74, prof. elec. engring., 1974—; reviewer Zentralblatt fur Mathematik, Fed. Republic of Germany, 1978—, Math. Revs., 1980—. Author: (with others) Mathematical Methods in Signal Theory, 1980, Theory of Electromechanical Systems, 1982, Electroacoustical Systems, 1984; contbr. articles to profl. jours. Mem. Am. Math. Soc. Home: PO Box 53-133, Bucharest Romania Office: Poly Inst of Bucharest, Polizu 1, Bucharest Romania

STANSELL, RONALD BRUCE, investment banker; b. Hammond, Ind., Apr. 9, 1945; s. Herman Bruce and Helen Rose Stansell; B.A., Wittenberg U., 1967; M.A., Miami U., Oxford, Ohio, 1969; m. Kathie Van Atta, Oct. 2, 1976; children—Kelsey, Kymberlie. Investment officer First Nat. Bank, Chgo., 1969-73; mgr. investments Chrysler Corp., Detroit, 1973; asst. v.p. A.G. Becker, Chgo., 1973-76; v.p. Blyth Eastman Dillon, Chgo., 1976-79; v.p. Dean Witter Reynolds Inc., Chgo., 1979-82; v.p. First Boston Corp., 1982-88; sr. v.p. Prudential-Bache Securities, Chgo., 1988—. Mem. Mettawa (Ill.) Zoning Bd., 1978-80; trustee Village of Mettawa, 1980—. Served with USMCR, 1968-69. Named to Pres.'s Club, Blyth Eastman Dillon, 1977, 78, 79. Mem. Bond Club Chgo., Investment Analyst Soc., Fixed Income Group. Clubs: Exmoon Country, Bob O'Link Golf; John's Island Country; Grandfather Golf; LaSalle. Home: Rural Rt #1 PO Box 49 Old Sch Rd Mettawa IL 60048

STANTON, EDWARD JAMES, JR., aerospace company executive; b. Pitts., Sept. 10, 1951; s. Edward James and Joann (Weyels) S. B.A. in History, Gannon U., 1974; M.B.A. in Mgmt. and Internat. Bus., U. Notre Dame, 1976. Constrn. insp. engring. and constrn. div. U.S.-Turkey ops. dept. Koppers Co., Inc., Eregli, Turkey, 1975; econ. and resources planning advisor space div., space shuttle integration segment Rockwell Internat., Downey, Calif., 1979-81, mgr. bus. devel., space sta. program, shuttle integration and satellite systems div., 1981-84, tech. planning advisor space sta. systems div., 1984-87, space transp. systems div., 1988—. Advisor Erie Hist. Soc., 1973-74; mem. Republican Nat. Com., 1981—. Served to 1st lt. U.S. Army, 1976-79. Recipient U.S. and Can. Mil. Parachute awards, 1977, 78; Pres. award Rockwell Internat., 1983. Mem. AIAA, Nat. Mgmt. Assn., Assn. M.B.A. Execs., Planetary Soc., Ctr. for Archaeostronomy, Gannon U. Alumni Assn., U. Notre Dame Alumni Assn., Pi Gamma Mu. Roman Catholic. Home: 1234 Cedars Ct B-22 Charlottesville VA 22901 Office: 12214 Lakewood Blvd Downey CA 90241

STANTON, JEANNE FRANCES, retired lawyer; b. Vicksburg, Miss., Jan. 22, 1920; d. John Francis and Hazel (Mitchell) S.; student George Washington U., 1938-39; B.A., U. Cin., 1940; J.D., Salmon P. Chase Coll. Law, 1954. Admitted to Ohio bar, 1954; chief clk. Selective Service Bd., Cin., 1940-43; instr. USAAF Tech. Schs., Biloxi, Miss., 1943-44; with Procter & Gamble, Cin., 1945-84, legal asst., 1952-54, head advt. services sect. legal div., trade practices dept., 1954-73, mgr. advt. services, legal div., 1973-84, ret., 1984. Team capt. Community Chest Cin., 1953; mem. ann. meeting com. Archaeol. Inst. Am., 1983. Mem. AAAS, ABA (chmn. subcom. D of com. 307 copyright sect. 1987-88), Ohio Bar Assn. (chmn. uniform state laws com. 1968-70), Cin. Bar Assn. (sec. law day com. 1965-66, chmn. com. on preservation hist. documents 1968-71), Vicksburg and Warren County, Cin. hist. socs., Internat. Oceanographic Found., Otago Early Settlers Assn. (asso.), Intercontinental Biog. Assn., Cin. Lawyers (pres. 1983, exec. com. 1978—), Cin. Women Lawyers (treas. 1958-59, nominating com. 1976). Clubs: Terrace Park Country, Cin. Club; Cincinnati. Home: 2302 Easthill Ave Cincinnati OH 45208

STANTON, WALTER OLIVER, electronics company executive; b. Canton, Ohio, Sept. 29, 1914; s. Bela Hayden and Edna (Keckley) S.; Elec. Engring., Wayne State U.; m. Mary Ann Wilcox; children—Sharon (Mrs. Robert Russell), Diana (Mrs. Grant Thornbrough), Pamela Stanton (Mrs. John O'Donnell). Pres. Pickering & Co., Inc., 1948—, Stanton Magnetics, Inc., 1966—, Pickering Impex S.A., Switzerland, Stanton Impex S.A. Fellow Audio Engring. Soc. (pres. 1957); mem. Newcomen Soc., Inst. Dirs. (London), Chief Exec.'s Forum. Home: 115 Lakeshore Dr North Palm Beach FL 33408 Office: Sunnyside Blvd Plainview NY 11803

STANTON, WILLIAM JOHN, JR., marketing educator; b. Chgo., Dec. 15, 1919; s. William John and Winifred (McGann) S.; m. Imma Mair, Sept. 14, 1978; children by previous marriage: Kathleen Louise, William John III. B.S., Ill. Inst. Tech., 1940; M.B.A., Northwestern U., 1941, Ph.D., 1948. Mgmt. trainee Sears Roebuck & Co., 1940-41; instr. U. Ala., 1941-44; auditor Olan Mills Portrait Studios, Chattanooga, 1944-46; asst. prof., asso. prof. U. Wash., 1948-55; prof. U. Colo., Boulder, 1955—; head mktg. dept. U. Colo., 1955-71, acting dean, 1963-64; assoc. dean U. Colo. (Sch. Bus.), 1964-67; vis. prof. summers U. Utah, 1946, 1949, U. Calif., Berkeley, 1950, Los Angeles, 1957; mktg. cons. to various bus. firms and govt. agys., 1950—. Author: Economic Aspects of Recreation in Alaska, 1953, (with Richard H. Buskirk) Management of the Sales Force, 7th edit, 1987 (also Spanish transl.), (with others) Challenge of Business, 1975, (with C. Futrell) Fundamentals of Marketing, 8th edit, 1987 (also Spanish, Portuguese and Indonesian transls.); (with M.S. Sommers and J.G. Barnes) Can. edit. Fundamentals of Marketing, 4th edit., 1985 Australian edit. (with K. Miller and R. Layton), 1986, Italian edit. (with R. Varaldo); mem. editorial bd. Jour. Mktg, 1963-69. Mem. Am., So., Southwestern, Western mktg. assns., Beta Gamma Sigma. Roman Catholic. Home: 1445 Sierra Dr Boulder CO 80302 Office: U Colo Campus Box 419 Boulder CO 80309

STANTON, WILLIAM TAYLOR, manufacturing engineer; b. Detroit, Oct. 27, 1926; s. Luther Dill and Maggie Ethel (Smith) S.; m. Sue Carol Reed, Feb. 19, 1960 (div. Jan. 1983); children: Terry, Steven, William. Registered profl. engr., Calif. Contract engr. various locations, 1966—. Lodge: Eagles, Moose. Home: PO Box 1124 Connersville IN 47331

STANWYCK, BARBARA (RUBY STEVENS), actress; b. Bklyn., July 16, 1907; d. Byron and Catherine (McGee) Stevens; m. Frank Fay, Aug. 26, 1928 (div. 1935); m. Robert Taylor, May 14, 1939 (div. 1951); 1 son. Ed. pub. schs., Bklyn. Began as chorus girl; later scored success in Burlesque, prod. by Arthur Hopkins; motion picture appearances include Meet John Doe, 1941, The Great Man's Lady, The Gay Sisters, 1942, Double Indemnity, 1944, My Reputations, 1945, Christmas in Connecticut, Two Mrs. Carrolls, 1946, The Bride Wore Boots, Strange Love of Martha Ivars, 1947, Cry Wolf, The Other Love, B.F.'s Daughter, 1948, Sorry Wrong Number, File on Thelma Jordon, The Lady Gambles, The Lie, East-Side, West-Side, The Furies, 1949, To Please a Lady, 1950, The Man in the Cloak, 1951, Clash by Night, 1951, Jeopardy, 1952, Titanic, 1952, Executive Suite, Witness to Murder, Escape to Burma, 1955, Cattle Queen of Montana, There's Always Tomorrow, 1956, Maverick Queen, 1956, These Wilder Years, 1956, Crime of Passion, 1957, Trooper Hook, 1957, Walk on the Wild Side, 1962, Roustabout, 1964, The Night Walker, 1965; TV shows The Barbara Stanwyck Theater, NBC-TV, 1960-61, The Big Valley, ABC-TV, The Colbys, 1985-87; appeared in: TV movie The Letters, 1973; TV mini-series The Thorn Birds (Emmy award 1983); guest star numerous TV shows. Recipient Emmy award, 1960-61, 66, hon. Acad. award, 1982, Am. Film Inst. award, 1987. Office: care A Morgan Maree & Assoc Inc 6363 Wilshire Blvd Los Angeles CA 90048 *

STAPLES, LYLE NEWTON, lawyer; b. Radford, Va., Feb. 16, 1945; s. Lester Lyle and Velma Jean (King) S.; m. Christie Mercedes Carr, Feb. 1, 1971; children: Scott Andrew, John Randolph, Brian Matthew, Melissa Ann. BA, U. Md., 1967, JD, 1972; LLM in Taxation, Georgetown U., 1977. Bar: Md. 1973, U.S. Supreme Ct. 1978, U.S. Tax Ct. 1981, U.S. Dist. Ct. Md. 1981, U.S. Ct. Appeals (4th cir.) 1981. Tax law specialist IRS, Washington, 1972-77; assoc. Hessey & Hessey, Balt., 1978-82, Rosenstock, Burgee & Welty, Frederick, Md., 1982-84; sole practice, Hampstead, Md., 1984—; vis. asst. prof. Towson (Md.) State U., 1981-82. Active Carroll County (Md.) ARC, Hampstead Bus. Assn., Hampstead Elem. Sch. PTA, North Carroll Mid. Sch. PTO, Greenmount, Md., Balt. Council Fgn. Affairs, Inc. Served with U.S. Army, 1968-69, Vietnam. Mem. ABA, Md. Bar Assn. Democrat. Methodist. Home: 4304 Royal Ave Hampstead MD 21074 Office: 926 S Main St PO Box 205 Hampstead MD 21074

STAPLETON, THOMAS DAVID, physician; b. Auburn, N.Y., Dec. 10, 1912; s. John Edward and Anna (McDermott) S.; AB, Georgetown U., 1934, MD, 1938; m. Wilhelmina Eileen Meagher, Apr. 6, 1942; children: David, Sheila, Miriam, William. Intern Georgetown U. Hosp., Washington, 1938-40; practice gen. medicine, Auburn, N.Y., 1940-42; resident Bklyn. Eye and Ear Hosp., Bklyn., 1946-48; practice medicine specializing in ophthalmology Auburn, 1948-84; staff mem. Auburn Meml. Hosp., now hon. staff; staff mem. Mercy Hosp., Auburn, pres. staff, 1958. Bd. dirs. United Fund; bd. trustees Auburn Community Coll., 1958-75, vice chmn., 1965-75. Served from lt. (j.g.) to lt. comdr., USNR, 1942-46; med. officer 4th Marine Div., 1942-45; hon. mem. Marine Corps Cayuga Meml. Detachment. Decorated Bronze Star, Purple Heart, numerous others. Diplomate Nat. Bd. Med. Examiners. Mem. Pan-Am. Assn. Ophthalmology, N.Y. State Ophthal. Soc., Internat. Assn. Ocular Surgeons. Am. Acad. Ophthalmology, AMA, N.Y. State (Pres.'s Citizenship award 1985), Cayugo County med. socs., N.Y. Acad. Scis., Bklyn. Eye and Ear Hosp. Alumni Assn., Internat. Platform Assn., Central N.Y. Eye and Ear Assn., N.Y. Acad. Scis., N.Y. Pa. League (affiliated with Major Leagues, pres. Auburn community baseball orgn. 1959-62, chmn. bd. 1962—, v.p. 1962-80), Georgetown U. Alumni Assn. (bd. govs.), Auburn C. of C., Am. Legion, VFW. Roman Catholic. Clubs: Owasco Country. Lodges: KC, Elks (dir.). Home: 130 Walnut St Auburn NY 13021

STAPP, BRUCE MICHAEL, government vocational rehabilitation evaluator; b. Oklahoma City, Dec. 25, 1944; s. Carl Herbert and Willie Lee (Broome) S.; children: Jonathan Michael, Benjamin Matthew. BBA, Central State U. Okla., 1973, MEd, 1974; postgrad. U. Okla., 1975-78; PhD, Calif. Coast U., 1988. Diplomate Internat. Acad. Behavioral Medicine, Counseling and Psychotherapy; cert. rehab. and career counselor; cert. vocational evaluation specialist; lic. profl. counselor; Nat. Bd. Cert. Counselor; Black Belt, Tae Kwon Do and Hapkido. Sr. vocat. rehab. counselor Okla. Dept. Human Services, Oklahoma City, 1974-78, sr. vocat. rehab. evaluator, Norman, 1978-80, Oklahoma City, 1980—; profl. counselor pvt. practice, Norman, 1986-87. Scouting coordinator Boy Scouts Am., 1985-86; active Statue of Liberty Ellis Island Found. Served with USN, 1965-67, Vietnam. Life fellow Am. Biog. Inst Research Assn., life fellow Internat. Biog. Assn., Research Bd. Advisors, Am. Biog. Inst. Mem. Internat. Platform Assn., (charter) Commanders Club, Disabled Am. Vets., U.S. Parachute Assn., Okla. Assn. Counseling and Devel., Okla. Career Devel. Assn., Am. Assn. Counseling and Devel., Nat. Career Devel. Assn., Kappa Delta Pi. Life mem. Cen. State Univ. Alumni Assn. (charter), Alumni Assn. Calif. Coast Univ., Statue of Liberty Ellis Island Found., Amateur Athletic Union, Korea Hapkido Assn., World Tae Kwon Do Fedn. Democrat. Baptist. Avocations: Karate, flying, paraplane piloting, skydiving, scuba diving, snow skiing, water skiing. Nat. Open Karate Olympics champion. Home: 1623 Glen Bo Dr Norman OK 73071 Office: Dept Human and Rehab Services 5813 S Robinson St Oklahoma City OK 73109-8521

STARCKE, EDGAR NOLTE, JR., prosthodontist; b. Seguin, Tex., May 28, 1938; s. Edgar Nolte and Gladys Geraldine (Lynch) S.; m. Margie Schwartz, July 22, 1962; children—Barbara Claire, John Christopher. Student Tex. Luth. Coll., 1956-58, U. Tex., 1958-59; D.D.S., U. Tex. Dental Br., Houston, 1963; cert. prosthodontics VA Med. Ctr. and U. Ala. Sch. Dentistry, Birmingham, 1970. Diplomate Am. Bd. Prosthodontics. Gen. practice dentistry, Seguin, 1965-67; staff dentist VA Med. Ctr., Amarillo, Tex., 1967-68; resident in prosthodontics U. Ala. Sch. Dentistry, 1968-70, instr., 1969-70; staff prosthodontist VA Med. Ctr., Atlanta, 1970-72; staff prosthodontist VA Med. Ctr., Houston, 1972-80, dir. prosthodontics residency, 1972—, asst. chief dental services, 1979-80, chief dental service, 1980—; clin. instr. Emory U. Sch. Dentistry, Atlanta, 1970-72; clin. asst. prof. U. Tex. Dental Br., 1973-79, clin. assoc. prof., 1979—; adminstrv. head preventive dentistry support ctr. VA Med. Ctr., 1983—; mem. faculty VA Physicians and Dentists In-Residence Program, 1985—. Contbr. articles to profl. jours. Co-developer Oralube saliva substitute. Pres. Spring Shadows Elem. Sch. PTA, Houston, 1983-84; hon. Tex. life mem. Tex. PTA, 1984. Served as capt. U.S. Army, 1963-65. VA grantee, 1974. Fellow Am. Coll. Prosthodontists (pres. S.E. Tex. sect. 1988-89); mem. ADA, Fedn. Prosthodontic Orgns., Am. Prosthodontic Soc., Am. Assn. Hosp. Dentists, S.W. Prosthodontic Soc., Psi Omega. Presbyterian. Avocations: art; antiques. Office: Chief Dental Service VA Med Ctr 2002 Holcombe Blvd Houston TX 77211

STAREK, HANS OTTO, librarian, technician; b. Vienna, Austria, June 1, 1932; s. Karl and Agnes (Rack) S.; m. Stefanie Brunner, Aug. 6, 1955; children—Johanna Eva Maria, Peter Michael. Grad. in Engring., Technologisches Gewerbe Museum-Vienna, 1951. Detail constructor AEG-Union, Vienna, 1951-55; project engr. Elektrobau AG, Vienna, 1955-56; design engr. Czeija & Nissl, commn. agt. Standard Telefon, librarian ITT Austria GmbH, Vienna, 1956—. Chmn. Stamp Collectors Club ITT Austria, 1970—. Mem. Sr. Club Czeija and Nissl, Arbeiter-Briefmarkensammlerverein. Roman Catholic. Office: Alcatel Austria Ag Dept NAB, Scheydgasse 41, A-1211 Vienna Austria

STARING, GRAYDON SHAW, lawyer; b. Deansboro, N.Y., Apr. 9, 1923; s. William Luther and Eleanor Mary (Shaw) S.; m. Joyce Lydia Allum-Poon, Sept. 1, 1949; children: Diana Hilary Agnes, Christopher Paul Norman. Student, Colgate U., 1943-44; A.B., Hamilton Coll., 1947; J.D., U. Calif.-Berkeley, 1951. Bar: Calif. 1952, U.S. Supreme Ct. 1958. Atty. Office Gen. Counsel, Navy Dept., San Francisco, 1952-53; atty. admiralty and shipping sect. U.S. Dept. Justice, San Francisco, 1953-60; assoc. Lillick McHose & Charles, San Francisco, 1960-64, ptnr., 1965—; titulary mem. Internat. Maritime Com.; bd. dirs. Marine Exchange at San Francisco, 1984-88, pres. 1986-88; instr. pub. speaking Hamilton Coll., 1947-48. Assoc. editor: Am. Maritime Cases, 1966—; contbr. articles to legal jours. Mem. San Francisco Lawyers Com. for Urban Affairs, 1972—; bd. dirs. Legal Aid Soc., San Francisco, 1974—, v.p., 1975-80, pres., 1980-82. Served with USN, 1943-46, comdr. Res. ret. Fellow Am. Bar Found., Am. Coll. Trial Lawyers; mem. ABA (chmn. maritime ins. com. 1975-76, mem. standing com. on admiralty law 1976-82, 86—), Fed. Bar Assn. (pres. San Francisco chpt. 1968), Bar Assn. San Francisco (sec. 1972, treas. 1973), Calif. Acad. Appellate Lawyers, Maritime Law Assn. U.S. (exec. com. 1977-88, v.p. 1980-84, pres. 1984-86), Brit.-Am. C. of C. (bd. dirs. 1987—), World Trade Club San Francisco, Mayor's San Francisco Shanghai Friendship Com., Propeller Club of U.S. Republican. Episcopalian. Home: 195 San Anselmo Ave San Francisco CA 94127 Office: 2 Embarcadero Ctr Suite 2600 San Francisco CA 94111

STARK, ANTHONY JAMES, marketing professional; b. Stafford, Eng., Oct. 17, 1961; s. William Burns and Joyce (Morton) S.; m. Elizabeth Mary Bonney, Dec. 15, 1984; 1 child, Oliver James. Grad. in Indsl. Measurement and Control, Birmingham Tech. Coll., Eng., 1982. Instrument technician Universal Grinding Wheel Co., Stafford, 1977-84; tech. sales engr. Pegler and Louden, Wolverhampton, Eng., 1984-86; sales and mktg. mgr. Rodyne, Ltd., Horsham, West Sussex, Eng., 1986—. Home: 38 The Pippins, Moss Pit, Stafford ST17 9DN, England Office: Rodyne Pneumatic Actuators, Foundry Lane, Horsham, West Sussex RH13 5TL, England

STARK, FRANKLIN CULVER, lawyer; b. Unityville, S.D., Apr. 16, 1915; s. Fred H. and Catherine (Culver) S.; m. Alice C. Churchill, Sept. 16, 1941 (dec. May 1975); children: Margaret C., Wallace C., Judith C., Franklin Culver; m. Carlyn Kaiser Stark, July 18, 1976. J.D., Northwestern U., 1940; A.B., Dakota Wesleyan U., 1937, LL.D., 1959. Bar: Ill. 1940, U.S. Supreme Ct. 1945, U.S. Tax Ct. 1945, U.S. Ct. Appeals (10th cir.) 1945, Calif. 1946; cert. taxation law specialist, Calif. Assoc. firm Sidley, McPherson, Austin & Burgess, Chgo., 1940-41, Fitzgerald, Abbott & Beardsley, Oakland, Calif., 1946-47; sr. mem. firm Stark, Wells, Rahl, Field & Schwartz, Oakland, 1947—; lectr. comml. law U. Calif. Sch. Bus., 1946-66. Editor: Ill. Law Rev, 1939-40; Contbr. articles to legal publs. Staff Office Gen. Counsel, OPA, Washington, 1941-42; bd. dirs. Merritt Peralta Found., Claremont Sch. Theology, Dakota Wesleyan U., Fred Finch Youth Ctr., 1970-82, Calif.-Nev. United Meth. Found., 1974-80, Oakland Meth. Found., 1952-82; chmn. bd. trustees Calif.-Nev. Meth. Homes, 1966-73; pres. Oakland Council of Chs., 1954-56; charter mem. World Peace Through Law Ctr.; former nat. pres. Campaign for UN Reform; nat. pres. Ctr. for UN Reform Edn. Served with USNR, 1942-45. Named Alumnus of Year for notable achievement Dakota Wesleyan U., 1966. Mem. Am., Calif., Alameda County bar assns., Oakland C. of C., Am. Trial Lawyers Assn., Phi Kappa Phi, Pi Kappa Delta, Phi Alpha Delta, Order Coif. Methodist. Clubs: Lakeview (Oakland); Commonwealth (San Francisco). Lodges: Masons; Shriners. Home: 333 Wayne Ave Apt E Oakland CA 94606 Office: Stark Wells Rahl Field & Schwartz 1999 Harrison St Suite 1300 Oakland CA 94612 also: Peri Exec Centre Suite 900 2033 N Main St Walnut Creek CA 94596

STARK, JESSE DONALD, physician; b. N.Y.C., Dec. 3, 1899; s. Eugene J. and Helen (Goldberger) S.; A.B., Cornell U., 1921; M.D., Jefferson Med. Coll., 1925; studied in Berlin, Vienna, Munich, 1925, 1930; m. Florence C. Seligmann, 1933 (dec.); m. 2d, Sara Miller Suchoff, Dec. 20, 1968. On staff Polyclinic Hosp., N.Y.C., 1934-35, Met. Hosp., N.Y.C., 1935-39; cons. roentgenologist Ft. Jay, Governor's Island, N.Y., 1935-41; vis. roentgenologist Gouverneur Hosp., N.Y.C., 1939-41, chief roentgenologist, 1946-61; attending cons. roentgenologist VA Hosp., Bronx, N.Y., 1946-47; instr. radiology N.Y. U. Coll. Medicine, 1935-49, asst. clin. prof. radiology, 1953-64, attending radiologist Clinic, 1935-41; asso. attending radiologist Univ. Hosp., 1954-58; instr. radiology N.Y.U.-Bellevue Post Grad. Med. Sch., 1949, asst. clin. prof. radiology, 1950-53; exec. dir. x-ray dept. Bird S. Coler Hosp., 1961-64, roentgenologist, 1964-71; dir. x-ray dept. Prospect Hosp., Bronx, 1968-85; cons. Surgeon Gen. U.S. Army, 1947-48, West Point Sta. Hosp., 1947, First Army, 1947—, Army of Occupation, Germany and Austria, 1948; U.S. rep. UNESCO. Meeting on Isotopes, Paris, 1957. Served as 2d lt., inf., U.S. Army, World War I; lt. col. M.C., AUS, 1941-50; col. M.C. U.S. Army Res., 1950; chief of X-Ray service and instr. U.S. Mil. Acad., West Point, N.Y., 1941-46. Decorated chevalier Mil. Order of St. Stephen, comdr. Mil. Order of St. Salvadore, Gold medal, Order of Macedonia; medal for merite scientifique Inst. Humanities Republic of France, Order of Lafayette, chevalier Legion of Honor, Croix de Guerre (hon.) (France); surgeon gen. Order of Lafayette; Gold medal of Merit (Free Poland). Diplomate Am. Bd. Radiology. Fellow Am. Coll. Radiology, Royal Coll. Health (Eng.); mem. N.Y. Acad. Scis., 7th Regt. Assn., N.Y. Soc. Med. Jurisprudence, Inst. Humanities Republic France, Radiology Soc. N.Am., AAAS, Soc. Am. Wars. AAUP, N.Y. Roentgen Soc., AMA, Assn. Mil. Surgeons U.S., Mil. Order World Wars, Res. Officers Assn., N.Y. Physicians Art Assn., West Point Soc. N.Y. Clubs: Army Navy (Washington); Cornell, Old Guard (N.Y.C.). Home: 965 Fifth Ave New York NY 10021

STARK, MILTON DALE, sports organization executive; b. Fellows, Calif., Apr. 28, 1932; s. Ernest Esco and Ruth Hazel (Keeney) S.; m. Katherine Margaret Boyd, Dec. 17, 1955 (div. June 1978); children: Mark Boyd, Kimberly Kay, Matthew Scott, Martin Dean; m. Diana Lynn Mead, July 26, 1980; 1 child, Ryan. AA, Taft Coll., 1956; BA, Whittier Coll., 1958, MEd, 1963. Cert. ednl. adminstr., Calif. Sec. Western Softball Congress, Hollywood, Calif., 1962-70; commr. Internat. Softball Congress, Anaheim Hills, Calif., 1966-75, sec., 1975-83, exec. dir., 1983—; sports cons. Whittier (Calif.) News, 1959-70. Editor in chief Softball Illus. mag., 1966-69; contbr. articles to softball mags. Served with USAF, 1951-55. Named to Internat. Softball Congress Hall of Fame, 1981. Republican. Home and Office: Internat Softball Congress 6007 E Hillcrest Circle Anaheim Hills CA 92807

STARK, PATRICIA ANN, psychologist; b. Ames, Iowa; d. Keith C. and Mary L. (Johnston) Moore. B.S., So. Ill. U., Edwardsville, 1970, M.S., 1972; Ph.D., St. Louis U., 1976. Counselor to alcoholics Bapt. Rescue Mission, East St. Louis, 1969; researcher alcoholics Gateway Rehab. Center, East St. Louis, 1972; psychologist intern Henry-Stark Counties Spl. Edn. Dist. and Galesburg State Research Hosp., Ill., 1972-73; instr. Lewis and Clark Community Coll., Godfrey, Ill., 1973-76, asst. prof., 1976-84, assoc. prof., 1984—, coordinator child care services, 1974-84; mem. staff dept. psychiatry Meml. Hosp., St. Elizabeth's Hosp., 1979—; supr. various workshops in field, 1974—; dir. child and family services Collinsville Counseling Center, 1978-82; clin. dir., owner Empas-Complete Family Psychol. and Hypnosis Services, Collinsville, 1982—; cons. community agys., 1974—; mem. adv. bd. Madison County Council on Alcoholism and Drug Dependency, 1977-80. Mem. Am. Psychol. Assn., Ill. Psychol. Assn., Midwestern Psychol. Assn., Nat. Assn. Sch. Psychologists, Am. Soc. Clin. Hypnosis, Internat. Soc. Hypnosis. Office: 2802 Maryville Rd Collinsville IL 62234

STARK, RICHARD BOIES, surgeon; b. Conrad, Iowa, Mar. 31, 1915; s. Eugene and Hazel (Carson) S.; m. Judy Thornton, Oct. 31, 1967. A.B., Stanford U., 1936; postgrad., U. Heidelberg, 1936-37; M.D., Cornell U., 1941. Diplomate Am. Bd. Plastic Surgery. Intern Peter Bent Brigham Hosp., Boston, 1941-42; asst. resident surgery Childrens Hosp., Boston, 1947; plastic surgeon Northington Gen. Hosp., Ala., 1945-46, Percy Jones Gen. Hosp., Mich., 1946; postwar fellow anatomy and embryology Stanford U., 1946-47; asst. resident, resident surgery, plastic and gen. surgery VA Hosp., Bronx, N.Y., 1947-50, N.Y. Hosp., 1947-50; instr. surgery Cornell U., 1950-52, asst. prof., 1952-55, assoc. prof., 1955; asst. attending surgeon N.Y. Hosp., 1950-55; asst. prof. surgery Columbia U., 1955-58, assoc. prof., 1958-73, prof. clin. surgery, 1973—; assoc. attending surgeon St. Luke's Hosp., N.Y.C., 1955-58, attending surgeon, 1958—; cons. Walter Reed Med. Ctr., 1970-77. Author: Plastic Surgery, 1962; Cleft Palate, 1968; Plastic Surgery at the New York Hospital 100 Years Ago; Aesthetic Plastic Surgery, 1980, Total Facial Reconstruction, 1985, Plastic Surgery of the Head and Neck, 1986; contbr. 30 chpts. to books, 180 articles to profl. jours.; assoc. editor Plastic Reconstructive Surgery, 1969-74; editor Annals Plastic Surgery, 1977-82; 14 one-man art shows, 1946—. Chmn. Medico Adv. Bd., 1976-77; mem., v.p. CARE Bd.; v.p. Wellborn Found., N.Y.C. Served with AUS, 1943-46. Decorated Bronze Star (U.S.); Medal of Honor (2) (Vietnam); cavallero Order of San Carlos (Columbia). Fellow ACS; mem. Am. Assn. Plastic Surgeons, Am. Soc. Plastic and Reconstructive Surgery (pres. 1966, Spl. Achievement award), Found. Am. Soc. Plastic and Reconstructive Surgery (pres. 1961-65), Am. Surg. Assn., Soc. Univ. Surgeons, French Soc. Plastic Surgeons, Brasilian Soc. Plastic Surgeons, Colombian Soc. Plastic Surgeons, Argentina Soc. Plastic Surgeons, Brit. Assn. Plastic Surgery, Peruvian Acad. Surgeons, N.Y. Surg. Soc., N.Y. Acad. Medicine (pres. Friends Rare Book Room), N.Y. State Med. Soc. (pres., sec., med. history), Halsted Soc. (pres. 1973-74), James IV Assn. Surgeons, Am. Soc. Aesthetic Plastic Surgery (pres. 1974-75). Home: 35 E 75th St New York NY 10021

STARKEY, RUSSELL BRUCE, JR., utility executive; b. Lumberport, W.Va., July 20, 1942; s. Russell Bruce and Dorotha Mable (Field) S.; m. Joan McClellan, May 27, 1966; children: Christine, Pamela, Joanne. BS, Miami U., Oxford, Ohio, 1964; grad. student U. New Haven, 1972-73, N.C. State U., 1974-75, U.S. Navy Schs., 1964-66, 68. Sr. engr., nuclear generation sect. Carolina Power & Light Co., Raleigh, N.C., 1973-74, sr. engr. ops. quality assurance, 1974, prin. engr., 1974-75, quality assurance supr. Brunswick Steam Electric Plant, Southport, N.C., 1975-76, supt. tech. and adminstrn., 1976, supt. ops. and maintenance, 1976-77, plant mgr. H.B. Robinson Steam Electric Plant, Hartsville, S.C., 1977-83, mgr. environ. services, Raleigh, 1984-85, mgr. nuclear safety and environ. services dept., 1985—; exec. dir. nuclear prodn. Pub. Service Ind., Jeffersonville, 1983-84. Served with USN, 1964-73. Mem. Am. Nuclear Soc., N.C. State Emergency Response Commn. (commr.). Lodge: Rotary. Home: 1508 Hemphill Dr Raleigh NC 27609 Office: PO Box 1551 Raleigh NC 27602

STARKWEATHER, FREDERICK THOMAS, data processing executive; b. Sioux City, Iowa, Feb. 24, 1933; s. Fred Ervin and Gertrude Faye (Madden) S.; m. Margot Glassen, Nov. 19, 1959; children: Thomas Frederick, Jerry Russell, Michael Glassen. BA in Math. and Physics, U. Nebr., Omaha, 1955. Mathematician Flight Determination Lab., White Sands Missile Range, N.Mex., 1955-56; supervisory mathematician Analysis & Computation, White Sands Missile Range, N.Mex., 1956-81; chief Data Scis. Div. Nat. Range Ops., White Sands Missile Range, N.Mex., 1981—; Nat. council rep. Am. Def. Preparedness Assn., Washington, 1980—; pres. White Sands Pioneer Group, White Sands Missile Range, 1983-86; bd. dirs. Assn. U.S. Army, Washington. Author hist. and genealog. books; contbr. book reviews and articles to newspapers and mags. Chmn. El Paso (Tex.) City Planning Commn., 1980-84; bd. dirs. El Paso County Hist. Soc., 1983-87; mem. El Paso County Hist. Commn., 1983—. Served with USAR, 1955-63. Recipient Profl. Secs. Internat. Exec. of Yr. award, 1987; named Disting. Alumnus U. Nebr., Omaha, 1985, Mgr. of Yr. Fed. Mgrs. Assn., White Sands Missile Range, 1984; recipient Conquistador City of El Paso award, 1980; cited for Services to Mankind Sertoma, El Paso chpt., 1985, Meritorious Civilian Service award U.S. Army, 1986, Cert. Appreciation for Patriotic Service U.S. Army, 1988. Mem. Fed. Mgrs. Assn. (bd. dirs.), Freedom Found. at Valley Forge (pres. El Paso chpt., George Washington Hon. medal 1982), El Paso C. of C. (assoc. dir. 1984—, bd. dirs.), Tau Kappa Epsilon (Hall of Fame 1986). Club: Toastmasters (dist. gov. 1970-71). Lodge: Masons. Home: 8010 Tonto Pl El Paso TX 79904 Office: Nat Range Ops Chief Data Scis Div White Sands Missile Range NM 88002

STARNES, JAMES WRIGHT, lawyer; b. East St. Louis, Ill., Apr. 3, 1933; s. James Adron and Nell (Short) S.; m. Helen Woods Mitchell, Mar. 29, 1958 (div. 1978); children: James Wright, Mitchell A., William B. II; m. Kathleen Israel, Jan. 26, 1985. Student St. Louis U., 1951-53; LLB, Washington U., St. Louis, 1957. Bar: Mo. 1957, Ill. 1957. Assoc. Stinson, Mag & Fizzell, Kansas City, Mo., 1957-60, ptnr., 1960—; ptnr. Mid-Continent Properties Co., 1959—, Fairview Investment Co., Kansas City, 1971-76, Monticello Land Co., 1973—; sec. Packaging Products Corp., Mission, Kans., 1972—. Bd. dirs. Mo. Assn. Mental Health, 1968-69, Kansas City Assn. Mental Health, 1966-78, pres., 1969-70; bd. dirs. Heed, 1965-73, 78-82, pres., 1966-67, fin. chmn. 1967-68; bd. dirs. Kansas City Halfway House Found., exec. com., 1966-69, pres., 1966; bd. dirs. Joan Davis Sch. for Spl. Edn., 1972-88, v.p., 1972-73, 79-80, pres., 1979-82; bd. dirs. Sherwood Ctr. for Exceptional Child, 1977-79, v.p., 1978-79. Served with AUS, 1957. Mem. ABA, Mo. Bar Assn., Kansas City Bar Assn., Kansas City Lawyers Assn. Presbyterian (deacon). Mem. adv. bd. Washington U. Law Quar., 1957—. Home: 1246 Huntington Rd Kansas City MO 64113 Office: Stinson Mag & Fizzell 2100 Boatmen's Ctr Kansas City MO 64105

STARNES, WILLIAM HERBERT, JR., chemist, educator; b. Knoxville, Tenn., Dec. 2, 1934; s. William Herbert St. and Edna Margaret (Osborne) S.; m. Maria Sofia Molina, Mar. 4, 1986. B.S. with honors, Va. Poly Inst., 1955; Ph.D., Ga. Inst. Tech., 1960. Research chemist Esso Research & Engring. Co., Baytown, Tex., 1960-62, sr. research chemist, 1962-64, polymer additives sect. head, 1964-65, research specialist, 1965-67, research assoc., 1967-71; instr. and research assoc. dept. chemistry U. Tex., Austin, 1971-73; mem. tech. staff AT&T Bell Labs., Murray Hill, N.J., 1973-85; prof., head dept. chemistry and life scis. Poly. U., Bklyn., 1985—; assoc. dir. polymer durability ctr. Poly. U., 1987—; vis. scientist Tex. Acad. Scis., 1964-67; chmn. chemistry subpanel AAAS Project 2061, 1985-86, mem. panel phys. scis. and engring., 1985-86; bd. doctoral thesis examiners Indian Inst. Tech., New Delhi, 1988. Mem. adv. bd. and bd. reviewers Jour. Vinyl Tech., 1981-83. Contbr. articles to profl. jours., chpts. to books. Patentee in field. NSF fellow 1958-60; recipient Profl. Progress award Soc. Profl. Chemists and Engrs. 1968, Disting. Tech. Staff award AT&T Bell Labs. 1982. Fellow AAAS, Am. Inst. Chemists (life); mem. Am. Chem. Soc. (bd. dirs. southeastern Tex. sect. 1970, speakers bur. div. polymer chemistry 1976—), N.Y. Acad. Scis. (life), Sigma Xi (M.A. Ferst award Ga. Inst. Tech. chpt. 1960), Phi Kappa Phi, Phi Lambda Upsilon (pres. Va. Poly. Inst. chpt. 1954-55). Current work: Degradation, stabilization, flammability, microstructures, and polymerization mechanisms of synthetic polymers, especially poly (vinyl chloride); free radical chemistry; carbon-13 nuclear magnetic resonance and organic synthesis. Subspecialties: Organic chemistry; Polymer chemistry. Office: Poly U Dept Chemistry and Life Scis 333 Jay St Brooklyn NY 11201

STARR, BARBARA SCHAAP, psychologist; b. Newark, Jan. 13, 1935; d. Louis George and Elsie (Dimond) Barron; B.A., Cornell U., 1956; M.Ed., Rutgers U., 1967, Ed.D., 1975; m. Robert M. Starr, Oct. 28, 1972; children: Renée Beth Levin, Michelle Anne Schaap. Psychologist, Glen Ridge (N.J.) Pub. Schs., 1971-80, Morris-Union Spl. Edn. Consortium, Passaic Twp., N.J., 1980-81; pvt. practice psychology, Livingston, N.J., 1977—; cons. psychologist Edn. Resource Ctr., 1984-87; adj. prof. Montclair State Coll., Upper Montclair, N.J., 1982. N.J. del. White House Conf. on Families, 1980; mem. nat. exec. com. Am. Jewish Congress, 1986—, nat. governing council, 1979—, v.p. state bd. N.J. region, 1979-87, sec., 1986—, nat. v.p., 1988—; trustee United Jewish Fedn. MetroWest, also chmn. task force on individual services, 1983-86; active Temple Emanu El, Livingston; mem. NOW, LWV, ACLU, Nat. Council Jewish Women. Mem. Am. Psychol. Assn. (divs. 17, 35, 37, 42), N.J. Psychol. Assn. (exec. bd. 1983—, sec. 1987-88), N.J. Acad. Psychology (trustee 1983—), Soc. Psychologists in Pvt. Practice, Assn. for Advancement of Psychology, N.J. Assn. for Advancement of Psychology, N.J. Assn. Women Therapists, Phi Beta Kappa, Kappa Delta Pi, Pi Lambda Theta, Kappa Delta Epsilon. Contbr. articles to profl. publs.

STARR, RINGO (RICHARD STARKEY), musician, actor; b. Liverpool, Eng., July 7, 1940; s. Richard and Elsie (Gleave) Starkey; m. Maureen Cox, Feb. 11, 1965 (div. 1975); children: Zak, Jason, Lee; m. Barbara Bach, Apr. 27, 1981. Drummer, vocalist mus. group, The Beatles, 1962-69; musician with Rory Storme's Hurricanes, 1959-62; solo performer, 1970—; recs. include Ringo the 4th, Sentimental Journey, Beaucoups of Blues, Ringo, Goodnight Vienna; film appearances with the Beatles include A Hard Day's Night, 1964, Help!, 1965, Yellow Submarine, 1968, Let It Be, 1970, TV film Magical Mystery Tour, 1967; individual film appearances include Candy, 1968, The Magic Christian, 1969, 200 Motels, 1971, Blindman, 1971, That'll Be the Day, 1973, Born to Boogie, also dir., producer, 1974, Son of Dracula, also producer, 1975, Lisztomania, 1975, Ringo Stars, 1976, Caveman, 1981, The Cooler, 1982, Give My Regards to Broad Street, 1984; appeared in TV miniseries Princess Daisy, 1983; star TV series Shining Time Station, PBS, 1989—. Decorated Order Brit. Empire; recipient numerous Grammy awards with The Beatles; inducted with The Beatles into Rock and Roll Hall of Fame, 1988. Home: 3 Savile Row, London W1, England *

STARR, WARREN DAVID, accountant, lawyer; b. N.Y.C., June 18, 1939; s. Benjamin and Beatrice (Danson) S.; m. Janet Sheila Berger, Dec. 25, 1960; children—Mark, Wendy. B.S. in Acctg., Queens Coll., 1959; J.D., NYU, 1965. C.P.A., N.Y.; bar: N.Y. 1966. Acct., Herbert Strauss & Co., N.Y.C., 1960-62, David Sieger & Co., N.Y.C., 1962-64, Walter Leipzig, N.Y.C., 1964-67; sr. ptnr. Starr and Co. (formerly Leipzig & Starr, C.P.A.s), Great Neck, N.Y., 1967—; ptnr. Starr & Starr, attys., N.Y.C., 1971—; dir. Hudson Shipping Co., Inc., N.Y.C. Trustee Cow Bay Manpower, Port Washington, N.Y., 1977-78; fundraiser United Jewish Appeal, Sands Point, N.Y., 1981-83. NYU Law Sch. grantee, 1963-65. Mem. Am. Assn. Atty.-C.P.A.s, ABA, N.Y. State Bar Assn. (tax sect.), N.Y. State C.P.A. Soc., Queens Coll. Alumni Assn. (trustee 1984—). Democrat. Jewish. Avocations: rare book collector; travel; tennis. Office: Starr & Co 9 Park Pl Great Neck NY 11021 Office: 350 Park Ave New York NY 10022

STARRETT, LOYD MILFORD, lawyer; b. St. Louis, Aug. 13, 1933; s. Loyd George and Edna (Switzer) S.; m. Michelle Miller, June 21, 1953 (div. Oct. 1965); children: Lucinda, Sarah Jean, Loyd Benjamin, Patricia Mary; m. Elaine Virginia MacGray, Apr. 8, 1967; children: A. Thomas Bower, Jo Ellen Bower, Amy S. Bower, Charles D. AB magna cum laude, Harvard U., 1953, LLB magna cum laude, 1958. Bar: Mass. 1959, U.S. Ct. Appeals (1st. cir.) 1959, U.S. Dist. Ct. Mass. 1960, U.S. Supreme Ct. 1965, U.S. Ct. Appeals (5th cir.) 1973, U.S. Ct. Appeals (11th cir.) 1984. Law clk. to chief judge U.S. Ct. Appeals (1st cir.), Boston, 1958-59; assoc. Foley, Hoag & Eliot, Boston, 1959-62, ptnr., 1963-85; ptnr. Fordham & Starrett, Boston, 1985—; v.p., sec. Modern Health Care Services, North Miami Beach, Fla., 1971—; bd. dirs. A.W. Hastings & Co., Manchester, N.H., clk., sec. 1973—. moderator Town of Rockport, Mass., 1975—, chmn. bd. appeals, 1976—; treas., bd. dirs. North Bay Council Boy Scouts Am., Danvers, Mass., 1986—; bd. dirs. Adoniram Judson Bapt. Assn., Malden, Mass., 1974—, moderator, 1979-81; bd. dirs. Am. Bapt. Chs. Mass., Boston, 1978—, Bapt. Home Mass., Kingston, 1984—, Am. Bapt. Chs., USA, Valley Forge, Pa., 1987—. Served to 1st lt. USAF, 1953-55. Mem. ABA, Mass. Bar Assn., Boston Bar Assn., Am. Judicature Soc., Nat. Inst. Trial Advocacy Advs. Assn., Am. Acad. Hosp. Attys., Mass. Moderators Assn. (bd. dirs. 1981-85, 86—). Home: 23 Granite St Rockport MA 01966 Office: Fordham & Starrett 260 Franklin St Boston MA 02110

STATE, DAVID, surgeon, educator; b. London, Ont., Can., Nov. 12, 1914; s. Louis and Sara (Rosenberg) S.; m. Avis Gae Lorberbaum, Nov. 25, 1945; children—Norman, Claudia, Leslie, Rosanne, Mathew. B.A., U. Western Ont., 1936, M.D., 1939; M.S., U. Minn., 1943, Ph.D., 1945. Diplomate Am. Bd. Surgery. Instr. surgery U. Minn. Med. Sch., Mpls., 1946-47, asst. prof., 1947-50, assoc. prof., 1950-52; dir. surgery Cedars of Lebanon Hosp., Los Angeles, 1952-58; prof., chmn. dept. surgery Albert Einstein Coll. Medicine, N.Y.C., 1958-71; prof. surgery Harbor/UCLA Med. Ctr., Los Angeles, 1971—, chmn. dept., 1971-81. Contbr. numerous articles to med. jours. Am. Diabetic Assn. grantee, 1978-83; Nat. Surg. Adjuvant Project grantee, 1979—. Mem. Allen O. Whipple Surg. Soc., AAAS, Am. Assn. History of Medicine, Am. Assn. Thoracic and Cardiovascular Diseases, ACS, Am. Gastroent. Assn., Am. Heart Assn. (sci. council cardiovascular surgery), Am. Soc. Artificial Internal Organs, Am. Surg. Assn., Am. Trudeau Soc., Halsted Soc., Inernat. Soc. Surgery, Los Angeles Surg. Soc., Med. Research Assn. Calif., Pacific Coast Surg. Assn., Transplantation Soc., Soc. Exptl. Biology and Medicine, Soc. Surgery of Alimentary Tract, Soc. Univ. Surgeons, Sigma Xi. Democrat. Jewish. Home: 1 Reata Ln Rolling Hills CA 90274 Office: Harbor/UCLA Med Ctr Dept Surgery Box 25 1000 W Carson St Torrance CA 90509

STATHIS, NICHOLAS JOHN, lawyer; b. Calchi, Dodecanese Islands, Greece, Feb. 27, 1924 (father Am. citizen); s. John and Sylvia (Koutsonouris) S.; student Columbia U., 1942-43, 44-48, A.B., 1946, J.D., 1948. Admitted to N.Y. bar, 1949; asso. James Maxwell Fassett, N.Y.C., 1948-50; asst. counsel to spl. com. to investigate organized crime in interstate commerce U.S. Senate, Washington, 1951; trial atty. Fidelity & Casualty Co. N.Y., N.Y.C., 1952; law sec. to Harold R. Medina, judge U.S. Ct. Appeals 2d Circuit, N.Y.C., 1952-54; spl. dep. atty. gen. N.Y. State Election Frauds Bur., Dept. Law, 1956; asso. firm Watson Leavenworth Kelton & Taggart, N.Y.C., 1954-60, partner, N.Y.C., 1961-81; partner firm Hopgood Calimafde Kalil Blaustein & Judlowe, N.Y.C., 1981-84; ptnr. firm Botein Hays & Sklar, N.Y.C., 1984—; lectr. Practising Law Inst., 1968-69. Pres., exec. dir., bd. dirs. Found. Classic Theatre and Acad., 1973—; bd. dirs. Concert Artists Guild, 1974—, Pirandello Soc., 1976—, Bklyn. Philharm. Orch., 1986—. Served with AUS, 1943-44. Mem. Assn. Bar City N.Y., Am., N.Y. State bar assns., Am., N.Y. patent law assns. Democrat. Greek Orthodox. Contbr. articles to profl. jours. Home: 53 Duncan Ave Jersey City NJ 07304 Office: 200 Park Ave New York NY 10166

STATIUS VAN EPS, LODEWIJK WILHELM, nephrologist; b. Aruba, Netherlands Antilles, Nov. 13, 1926; s. Johan Marin and Edna (Arends) Statius van E.; student Peter Stuyvesant Coll., Willemstad, Netherlands Antilles, 1942-45; H.B.S.-B., U. Amsterdam, 1953, M.D., 1954, Ph.D. thesis, 1954; m. Marie Jeanne Renée Hofte, July 17, 1954; children: Randolph, Reinout, Roelant. Internist trainee dept. medicine St. Elisabeth Hosp., Curaçao, 1954-57, U. Amsterdam, 1957-60; specialist in internal medicine, 1960; researcher nephrology U. Amsterdam, 1960-62; head dept. medicine St. Elisabeth Hosp., Curaçao, Netherlands Antilles, 1962-76, founder and head dialysis unit, 1969-76; head dept. medicine Slotervaarthospital, affiliated with Univ. Amsterdam, 1976—; mem. physicians exam. bd. U. Amsterdam. Bd. dirs. Netherlands Found. Cultural Coop.; founder Queen Beatrix Found. Against Tb, Netherlands Antilles, 1955; adv. to bd. dirs. Saint Rose Hosp., St. Maarten, 1984— Decorated officer Order of Orange Nassau; recipient

Cola Debrot award, 1984. Hon. mem. Netherlands Antilles Medicine; mem. Netherlands Soc. Internal Medicine, Netherlands Soc. Nephrology (bd. dirs. 1984—), Internat. Soc. Nephrology, Am. Soc. Nephrology, European Dialysis Transplant Assn., Assn. Européenne de Medecine Interne d'Ensemble. Roman Catholic. Contbg. author: Diseases of the Kidney (Earley and Gottschalk editors), 1979, 4th edit. (Shrier an Gottschalk editors), 1987, Non-Invasive Diagnosis of Kidney Disease (Lubec editor), 1983; contbr. numerous articles to profl. jours.; editor: Encyclopedia of the Netherlands Antilles, 1970, 2d edit., 1985; book on med. history and geog. pathology Netherlands Antilles, 1973. Home: Nassaukade 147, 1052 EH Amsterdam The Netherlands Office: Slotervaarthospital, Louwesweg 6, 1066 EC Amsterdam The Netherlands

STAUB, EUGÊNIO EMILIO, electronics company executive; b. Rio de Janeiro, Oct. 7, 1941; s. Emile Herman and Marion (Seeley) S.; m. Maria Theresa Staub, June 29, 1963. BS, Fundacão Getulio Vargas, São Paulo, Brazil, 1964. With Staub S.A. Indóstria e Comercio, São Paulo, 1956-72; mng. dir. Staub S.A. Indóstria e Comécio, São Paulo, 1970-72; mng. dir. IGB-Industria Comercio Gradiente Brasileiras SA, São Paulo, 1972-79, pres., 1979—; bd. dirs. FIESP, São Paulo. Served as 2d lt. arty. Brazilian Army Res., 1962-64. Mem. Conselho Nacional de Informatica e Automação (rep. CNI/CNC), Brazil-U.S.A. Bus. Council, Inst. Latino Am. (bd. dirs. 1986—). Clubs: Jockey, Atletico Paulistano (São Paulo), Soc. Harmonia Tênis. Home: Rua Galia 326-Jd Everest, 05602 Sao Paulo Brazil Office: Inds Gradiente Brasileiras SA, Rua Henrique Monteiro, 90 Pinheiros, 05423 Sao Paulo Brazil

STAUBLIN, JUDITH ANN, financial executive; b. Anderson, Ind., Jan. 17, 1936; d. Leslie Fred and Esta Virginia (Ringo) Wiley; student Ball State U., 1954-55, 69-70, Savs. and Loan Inst., 1962-67, U. Ga., 1974, Wright State U., 1975; children—Juli Jackson, Scott Jackson. Teller, Anderson Fed. Savs. and Loan Assn., Anderson, 1962-64, data processing mgr., 1965-70, loan officer, 1970-72, v.p. systems, 1972-74, fin. systems mktg., 1974-76; fin. dist. mgr. data centers div. NCR Corp., Atlanta, 1977-81, nat. sales mgr. EFT services Data Center Div., Dayton, Ohio, 1982-83; fin. dist. mgr. EFT and data services So. Thrift, Atlanta, 1983—. Active United Way. Mem. Am. Savs. and Loan Inst., Fin. Mgrs. Soc., Ga. Exec. Women's Network, Am. Soc. Profl. and Exec. Women, Anderson C. of C. Home: 6115 Woodmont Blvd Norcross GA 30092 Office: 5 Executive Dr NE Atlanta GA 30329

STAUFER, ALFRED J(OSE), aircraft company executive; b. San Jose, Costa Rica, Feb. 7, 1940; s. Josef Soelkner and Maria Obermayer (Riederer) S.; came to U.S., 1958, naturalized, 1968; student U. Ala., 1959-62; B.S. in Engring., U. Beverly Hills, 1979; m. Vicki Ann Schrack, Apr. 15, 1976; children—J. Chris, Eric P. Staff Mooney-Aerostar Aircraft Co., Kerrville, Tex., 1962-70; service mgr. N.Am. Rockwell AeroComdr. div., Albany, Ga., 1971-72; project engr. Piper Aircraft Corp., Vero Beach, Fla., 1972-73, supr. engring. projects, 1973-74, sr. engr., Lockhaven, Pa., 1974, regional mgr. Western Europe-Latin Am. internat. sales, 1974-79, adminstr. internat. worldwide distbn. and sales, 1979-80, dir. internat. sales, 1981-82, dir. internat. prodn. programs, 1983-87, dir. internat. sales and prodn. programs, 1988— . Served with Tex. Air N.G., 1963-69. Mem. Indian River County C. of C., Soc. Automotive Engrs., Am. Inst. Aeros. and Astronautics, Am. Mgmt. Assn. Club: Rotary Internat. Home: PO Box 1837 Vero Beach FL 32961 Office: Piper Aircraft Corp PO Box 1328 Corp Hdqrs Vero Beach FL 32961

STAUR, MARTIN JOHN, architect; b. Bridgeport, Conn., July 25, 1933; s. John and Julia Anna (Tudos) Staurovsky. Registered architect, Calif., N.Y., Conn., Ariz. Apprentice architect Anderson & Petrofsky, architects, Bridgeport, 1952-62; project architect A.J. Palmieri Co., Bridgeport, 1974-75, Bennett-Resnick Ptnrship, Westport, Conn. and Boston, 1976-78, Valus & Carpenter, Westport, 1979-80; architect Vineyard Realty Corp., White Plains, N.Y., 1980-83; prin. Martin J. Staur, AIA, Westport, 1983—; cons. architect Gassner Assocs., Westport, 1985—. Mem. AIA, Conn. Soc. Architects, Nat. Council Archl. Registration Bds. Republican. Roman Catholic. Avocations: building models; computers; gardening; sailing. Address: 11 Drumlin Rd Westport CT 06880

STAVROPOULOS, D(IONYSOS) JOHN, banker; b. Vicksburg, Miss., Jan. 19, 1933; s. John Dionysos and Olga (Balodemos) S.; m. Alexandra Gatzoyanni, Jan. 10, 1976; children: John, Theodore, Mark, Olga, Katerina. B.S., Miss. State U., 1955; M.B.A., Northwestern U., 1956. Chartered fin. analyst. With trust dept. First Nat. Bank of Chgo., 1956-69, internat. banking dept., 1970-76, sr. v.p. real estate dept., 1976-78, exec. v.p. comml. banking dept., 1979-80, chmn. credit strategy com., 1981—, chief credit officer, 1986—; v.p., dir. research Bache & Co., N.Y.C., 1969-70; instr. finance Northwestern U., 1962-68; dir. Central Ill. Public Service Co. Served with U.S. Army, 1951-53. Mem. Am. Bankers Assn., Assn. Res. City Bankers, Council Fgn. Relations (Chgo. com.), Robert Morris Assocs., (nat. dir.). Greek Orthodox. Clubs: Westmoreland Country; Economic (Chgo.). Office: First Chgo Corp 1 First National Plaza Chicago IL 60670

STAVROU, PATROCLOS, undersecretary to President; b. Nicosia, Cyprus, Jan. 21, 1933; s. Stavros and Helen (Pelekanou) S.; m. Mary Rodiou; 1 child, Niki. Faculty of Philosophy, U. Athens, Greece, Faculty of Law. Pvt. sec. to archbishop Athens, 1957-59; dir. ethnarchy office of Cyprus, sec. to archbishop Nicosia, 1959-60, dir. office of the Pres. of Cyprus, 1960-63, undersec. to Pres. of Cyprus, 1963—; chmn. joint staff com., Nicosia, 1963—. Author: Palamas and Cyprus, 1968 (Prize of the Acad. of Athens 1969), Cyprus, the Sweet Land, 1971. Bd. dirs. Archbishop Makarios III Found., Nicosia, 1978—, A. G. Leventis Found, Nicosia, 1982—; chmn. Nikos Kazantzakis Mus., Varvari, Heracleion of Crete, Greece, 1983. Mem. Soc. Cypriot Students. Christian Orthodox. Home: 6, Kalamatas St, 140 Nicosia Cyprus Office: Presdl Palace, Nicosia Cyprus

STAYER, JAMES MENTZER, history educator; b. Lancaster, Pa., Mar. 15, 1935; came to Can., 1968; s. Raymond R. and Helen (Mentzer) S.; m. Marica L. Sweet, Jan. 6, 1958 (div. Sept. 1984); children—Elizabeth, William, James. B.A., Juniata Coll., 1957; M.A., U. Va., 1958; Ph.D., Cornell U., 1964. Instr., Ithaca Coll., 1959-61; asst. prof. Bridgewater Coll., Va., 1962-65, Bucknell U., Lewisburg, Pa., 1965-68; asst. prof., assoc. prof. Queens U., Kingston, Ont., 1968-78, prof. history, 1978—, chmn. dept., 1981-82, 85—. Author: Anabaptists and the Sword, 1972; editorial bd. Archive for Reformation History, 1976—; editorial com. Sixteenth Century Jour., 1983—; cons. editor: Mennonite Quarterly Rev., 1983—. Mem. 16th Century Studies Conf. (council 1977-80), Am. Soc. Reformation Research. New Democrat. Avocations: Bicycling. Home: 142 Country Club Dr, Kingston, ON Canada K7M 7B6 Office: Queens Univ, Dept History, Kingston, ON Canada K7L 3N6

STAYMAN, SAMUEL M., investment company executive; b. Worcester, Mass., May 28, 1909; s. Morris and Fannie R. (Mittel) S.; m. Marjorie Schmukler, May 1, 1941 (dec. 1961); 1 child, Susan Stayman Madorsky; m. Josephine L. Wacht, Sept. 21, 1962. A.B., Dartmouth Coll., 1930, M.B.A., 1931. Pres. Vt. Woolen Mills, 1939-51; pres. Stamina Mills, 1952-65, S.M.S.A. Corp., N.Y.C., 1955—; mng. ptnr. Strand & Co., N.Y.C., 1966-81. Author: Expert Bidding at Contract Bridge, 1951, The Complete Stayman System of Contract Bidding, 1957, Do You Play Stayman?, 1965; originator Stayman Conv. Method of Bidding. Trustee, Am. Contract Bridge League Charity Found., 1970—. Mem. Am. Contract Bridge League. Clubs: Cavendish, Harmonie, Dartmouth, Regency Whist (N.Y.C.). Address: 2500 S Ocean Blvd Palm Beach FL 33480

STEAD, CHRISTIAN KARLSON, writer, poet; b. Auckland, New Zealand, Oct. 17, 1932; s. James Walter Ambrose and Olive Ethel (Karlson) S.; m. Kathleen Elizabeth Roberts, Jan. 8, 1955; children: Oliver William, Charlotte Mary, Margaret Hermione. BA, Auckland U. Coll., 1954, MA, 1955; PhD, U. Bristol, Eng., 1961; LittD, U. Auckland, 1982. Sr. lectr. in Eng. U. Auckland, 1960-63, assoc. prof., 1964-67, prof. in Eng., 1968-86, prof. Emeritus, 1986—; vis. fellow Univ. Coll. London, 1977; mem. internat. adv. bd., Cumberland Poetry Review, Malahat Review, Jour. Lit. Criticism, Yeats Annual. Author: numerous books including Whether the Will is Free, 1964, Quesada, 1975, Paris, 1984, Smith's Dream, 1971, The Death of the Body, 1986, The New Poetic, 1964, Poems of a Decade, 1983; editor New Zealand Short Stories, 1966, Measure for Measure: a Casebook, 1971, others; contbr. countless articles to periodicals. Active New Zealand Lit. Fund (chmn. adv. com., 1972-75, writer's rep., 1982-85). Decorated C.B.E. for services to New Zealand Lit., 1985; recipient Katherine Mansfield award-short story, 1961, Jessie MacKay award-poetry, 1972, others; Katherine Mansfield-Menton fellow, Nuffield Travelling fellow. Mem. New Zealand P.E.N. (chmn.). Home: 37 Tohunga Crescent, 1 Auckland New Zealand Office: U Auckland Eng Dept, Private Bag, Auckland New Zealand

STEAD, JAMES JOSEPH, JR., securities company executive; b. Chgo., Sept. 13, 1930; s. James Joseph and Irene (Jennings) S.; B.S., DePaul U., 1957, M.B.A., 1959; m. Edith Pearson, Feb. 13, 1954; children—James, Diane, Robert, Caroline. Asst. sec. C. F. Childs & Co., Chgo., 1955-62; exec. v.p., sec. Koenig, Keating & Stead, Inc., Chgo., 1962-66; 2d v.p., mgr. midwest municipal bond dept. Hayden, Stone Inc., Chgo., 1966-69; sr. v.p., nat. sales mgr. Ill. Co. Inc., 1969-70; mgr. instl. sales dept. Reynolds and Co., Chgo., 1970-72; partner Edwards & Hanly, 1972-74; v.p., instnl. sales mgr. Paine, Webber, Jackson & Curtis, 1974-76; v.p., regional instl. sales mgr. Reynolds Securities, Inc., 1976-78; sr. v.p., regional mgr. Oppenheimer & Co., Inc., 1978-88; sr. v.p., regional mgr. Tucker Anthony, 1988—; instr. Mcpl. Bond Sch., Chgo., 1967—. Served with AUS, 1951-53. Mem. Security Traders Assn. Chgo., Nat. Security Traders Assn., Am. Mgmt. Assn., Municipal Finance Forum Washington. Clubs: Executives, Union League, Municipal Bond, Bond (Chgo.); Olympia Fields Country (Ill.); Wall Street (N.Y.C.). Home: 20721 Brookwood Dr Olympia Fields IL 60461 Office: One S Wacker Dr Chicago IL 60606

STEARLEY, MILDRED SUTCLIFFE VOLANDT, foundation executive; b. Ft. Myer, Va., Aug. 3, 1905; d. William Frederick and Mabel Emma (Sutcliffe) Volandt; student George Washington U., 1923-24, 25-28; m. Ralph F. Stearley, Sept. 19, 1931. Elementary tchr. Brent Sch., Baguio, Philippines, 1929-30; staff aide vol. services ARC, also acting chmn., Charlotte, N.C., 1943, staff asst., Washington, 1943-47, Gray Lady vol., Okinawa, 1950-53, Brazil, Ind., 1954; trustee Air Force Village Found., San Antonio, 1975-78, sec. bd., 1975-77; sustaining mem. Tex. Gov.'s Com.; mem. 300 com. Bexar County Republican Com.; mem. decoration com. St. Andrew's Episc. Ch., San Antonio. Recipient commendation ARC, Washington, 1943. Mem. Army Daus., Am. Legion Aux., Army-Navy Club Aux., P.E.O. (life), Am. Security Council (nat. adv. bd.), San Antonio Mus. Assn., Smithsonian Inst., Pi Beta Phi. Episcopalian. Clubs: Ladies Reading (hon. mem.) (Brazil, Ind.); Lackland Officers Wives, Bright Shawl (San Antonio). Home: 4917 Ravenswood Dr Apt 311 San Antonio TX 78227

STEARNS, STEWART WARREN, charitable association executive; b. Denver, Apr. 8, 1947; s. Vinton H. and Marjorie L. (Tedro) S.; BS, Ea. N.Mex. U., 1970; MA, No. Ill. U., 1973; postgrad. SUNY, Albany, 1974—; m. Marjorie L. Fuller, Jan. 25, 1969; children—Theresa Lyn, Gregory Robert. Mng. editor Studies in Linguistics, DeKalb, Ill., 1972-73; instr. No. Ill. U., DeKalb, 1972-73; cons. AID, Guatemala, 1973-74; instr. Skidmore Coll., Saratoga Springs, N.Y., 1975; OAS fellow, Guatemala, 1976-77; asst. dir. Chaves County Community Action Program, Roswell, N.Mex., 1977-78; exec. dir. United Way Chaves County, Roswell, 1978-83,, Levi Strauss Found., 1983-85; exec. dir. Community Trust of Met. Tarrant County, 1985—. NDEA fellow, Dallas, 1970-71. Mem. Nat. Soc. Fund Raising Execs.

STEBBINS, GREGORY KELLOGG, treasurer; b. Lafayette, Ind., Jan. 10, 1951; s. Albert Kellogg and Nancy Ruth (Osborn) S. BS in Data Processing, Calif. Poly., Pomona, 1974; MBA, U. So. Calif., 1976; EdD, Pepperdine U., 1985. Account exec. Automatic Data Processing, Long Beach, Calif., 1977-78; salesman Grubb & Ellis, Los Angeles, 1978-81; v.p. Grubb & Ellis, Beverly Hills, Calif., 1981-83; regional mgr. Hanes Co., Beverly Hills, 1983-85; treas. U. Santa Monica (name formerly Koh-E-Nor U.), Los Angeles, 1983—. Mem. Am. Mgmt. Assn., Assn. MBA Execs., Organizational Devel. Network, The Planning Forum. Home: 3141 Mandeville Canyon Rd Los Angeles CA 90049 Office: Koh-E-Nor Univ 2101 Wilshire Blvd Santa Monica CA 90403

STECKLER, LARRY, magazine publisher and editor; b. Bklyn., Nov. 3, 1933; s. Morris and Ida (Beekman) S.; m. Catherine Coccozza, June 6, 1959; children: Gail Denise, Glenn Eric, Kerri Lynn, Adria Lauren. Student, CCNY, 1951. Assoc. editor Radio-Electronics mag., N.Y.C., 1957-62; electronics editor Popular Mechanics mag., N.Y.C., 1962-65; assoc. editor Electronic Products mag., Garden City, N.Y., 1965-67; editor Radio-Electronics mag., 1967—; editorial dir. Merchandising 2-Way Radio mag., N.Y.C., 1975-77; v.p., dir. Gernsback Publs., N.Y.C., 1975-84, pres., dir., 1984—; pub., editor-in-chief Radio-Electrons mag., 1985—; pub., editorial dir. Spl. Projects mag., 1980-84, Radio-Electronics Ann., 1982-84; pub., editor in chief Hands-On Electronics, 1984—; pub., editor-in-chief Radio-Electronics Experimenters Handbook, 1986—, Computer Digest, 1985—; pres. Claggk, Inc., 1986—; pub., editor-in-chief Modern Short Stories, The Magic Course, Eating In/Dining Out on Long Island, Faxsimile Newsletter, 1987—, Popular Electronics, 1988—; mem. electronics adv. bd. Bd. Coop. Ednl. Services, Nassau County, N.Y., 1975-77; pres. Electronics Industry Hall of Fame, 1985—; bd. dirs. Pub. Hall of Fame, 1987—. Author books, handbooks; pub.; contbr. articles to profl. jours. Bd. dirs. Nassau County council Camp Fire Girls, 1971-72. Served with U.S. Army, 1953-56. Recipient Coop. award Nat. Alliance TV and Electronic Services Assns., 1974, 75; inducted into Electronics Industry Hall of Fame, 1985. Mem. Internat. Soc. Cert. Electronic Technicians (chmn. 1974-76, 79-81, pres. 1985—, Pres.'s award 1985), Nat. Electronics Sales and Service Dealers Assn. (rec. sec. N.Y. State 1976-78, Man of Yr. award 1975, 85), Am. Mgmt. Assn., IEEE, Radio Club Am., Internat. Underwater Explorers Soc., Am. Soc. Bus. Press Editors (sr.), Internat. Soc. Performing Magicians (exec. dir.), Soc. Profl. Journalists. Club: L.I. Press. Home: 158 Whitewood Dr Massapequa Park NY 11762 Office: Radio-Electronics Gernsback Pub Inc 500 Bicounty Blvd Farmingdale NY 11735

STEDEFORD, AVERIL, psychotherapist, consultant; b. Chingford, Essex, Eng., May 19, 1932; m. Brian Stedeford, 1955; children: Christine, Elizabeth. B of Medicine, B of Surgery, U. Coll. and Hosp., London, 1955; diploma in child health, diploma in obstetrics, U. Coll. and Hosp., 1958; diploma in psycholog. medicine, Warneford Hosp., Oxford, Eng., 1975. Sr. registrar dept. psychotherapy Warneford Hosp., Churchill Hosp. Sir Michael Sobell House, Oxford, 1977-86; cons. Churchill Hosp. Sir Michael Sobell House, Oxford, 1986-88. Author: Facing Death, 1984. Mem. Royal Coll. Psychiatrists. Home and Office: 71 Sandfield Rd, Oxford OX3 7RW, England

STEDRONSKY, FRANK, film, television executive; b. Oak Park, Ill., Mar. 29, 1935; s. Frank Joseph Stedronsky; m. Alice Frances Sarlin, June 15, 1957; children: Linda, Jon, Jill, Scott. Student, Lyons Township Jr. Coll., 1955; BA in Journalism, U. Iowa, 1957. Gen. ptnr. Motivation Enterprises, Palatine, Ill., 1978—, also bd. dirs.; pres. Motivation Media, Inc., Glenview, Ill., 1969—, also bd. dirs.; treas. Motivation Mktg., Inc., Glenview, 1979—, also bd. dirs.; pres. Photo Impressions, Inc., Glenview, 1980—, also bd. dirs.; chmn. Sound Impressions, Inc., Des Plaines, Ill., 1976—, also bd. dirs.; pres. Motivation Media Far East Co., Ltd., Tai Pei, Republic of China, 1986—, also bd. dirs.; pres. Teleslide, Inc., Glenview, 1986—, also bd. dirs.; bd. dirs. The Bank & Trust Co. of Arlington Heights, Ill. Writer, director, producer: (films) The Stencil, 1961 (Chris award Columbus Film Festival 1961), Modern Mimeographing, 1962 (1st Place award Nat. Visual Presentation Assn. 1962), The Master, 1963 (1st Place award Nat. Visual Presentation Assn. 1963), A Snow Job, 1970 (Bronze award Internat. Film Festival of N.Y. 1970). Pres. Va. Lake Homeowners Assn. Palatine, 1975-76; regional dir. Crusade of Mercy Niles, Ill., 1968; sustaining mem. Rep. Nat. Com. Washington, 1980-87; charter mem. Rep. Presdl. Task Force Washington, 1984-87; sponsor Nat. Rep. Congl. Com. Washington, 1985; bd. dirs. Clearbrook Center for Mentally Handicapped Rolling Meadows, Ill., 1987—. Mem. Chgo. Audio Visual Producers Assn. (pres. 1983-86, disting. service award, 1986), Audio Visual Mgrs. Assn. (pres. 1968-69, pres. award 1969), U. of Iowa Alumni Assn. (life), Internat. Assn. for Multi-Image, Chgo. Film Video Council. Roman Catholic. Club: U.S. Senatorial (Washington). Home: 867 Virginia Lake Ct Palatine IL 60067 Office: Motivation Media Inc 1245 Milwaukee Ave Glenview IL 60025

STEEL, DAVID (MARTIN SCOTT), politician; b. Scotland, 1938; s. David Steel; m. Judith Mary MacGregor, 1962; 4 children. Grad., George Watson's Coll.; MA, Edinburgh U., 1960. Pres. Edinburgh (Scotland) U. Liberals, 1959, mem. students' rep. council, 1960; asst. sec. Scottish Liberal Party, 1962-64; M.P. 1964-66; mem. Parliamentary Del. to U.N. Gen. Assembly, 1967; sponsor bill to reform law on abortion, 1966-67; pres. Anti-Apartheid Movement of Great Britain, 1966-69; chmn. Shelter, Scotland, 1969-73; TV interviewer BBC, Scotland, 1964-65; presenter weekly religious programme STV, 1966-67, Granada, 1969; mem. Acton Trust, 1970—, Brit. Council Chs., 1971-75; mem. Council Mgmt. Ctr. for Studies in Social Policy, 1971-76; mem. adv. council European Discussion Ctr., 1971-76; mem. Privy Council, 1977; chief whip Liberal Party, 1970-75, leader, 1976—; v.p. Liberal Internat., 1978—; M.P. form Tweeddale, Ettrick and Lauderdale 1983—. Author: Boost for the Borders, 1964, Out of Control, 1968, No Entry, 1969, The Liberal Way Forward, 1975, A New Political Agenda, 1976, Militant for the Reasonable Man, 1977, New Majority for a New Parliament, 1978, High Ground of Politics, 1979, A House Divided, 1980, Border Country, 1985; (TV presentations) Partners in One Nation: a new vision of Britain 2000, 1985, (with Judy Steel) Mary Stuarts's Scotland, 1987; contbr. The Times, The Guardian, The Scotsman and others newspapers. Clubs: Cherry Dane, Ettrick Bridge, Selkirkshire. Office: House of Commons, London SW1A 0AA, England *

STEEL, KEITH WILLIAM, financial company executive; b. Moonie Ponds, Victoria, Australia, May 31, 1917; s. Percy William and Victoria Elizabeth (Alves) S.; m. Rosalind Nellie Whitaker, Dec. 13, 1940; children: Heather, Hilary, Linda. Jr. clk. AMP Soc., 1934-52; various positions Victoria, New South Wales, Queensland, New Zealand, 1952-57; mgr. New South Wales AMP Soc., 1957-63, asst. gen. mgr., 1963-66, gen. mgr., bd. dirs., 1966-79; chmn. Morgan Grenfell Ltd., Sydney, New South Wales, Australia, 1979—; dep. chmn. Time-Life Internat. (Australia) Pty. Ltd., 1979-84; chmn. Time-Life Internat. (Australia) Pty. Ltd., Sydney, 1984-86, Rheem Australia Ltd., Sydney, 1982-85; bd. dirs. CSR Ltd., chmn., 1984—; mem. Morgan Grenfell Holdings Ltd. Internat. Adv. Council, 1981—. Served to capt. Australian Armed Forces, 1940-46. Club: Union (Sydney)(pres. 1980-83), Royal Sydney Yacht Squadron (Melbourne), Pine Valley Golf (N.J.). Home: 36 Cherry St, Warrawee New South Wales 2000, Australia Office: Morgan Grenfell Australia Ltd, 70 Phillip St, Sydney New South Wales 2000, Australia

STEELE, ANITA (MARGARET ANNE MARTIN), law librarian, legal educator; b. Haines City, Fla., Dec. 30, 1927; d. Emmett Edward and Esther Majulia (Phifer) Martin; m. Thomas Dinsmore Steele, June 10, 1947 (div. 1969); children—Linda Frances, Roger Dinsmore, Thomas Garrick, Carolyn Anne; m. James E. Beaver, Mar. 1980. B.A., Radcliffe Coll., 1948; J.D., U. Va., 1971; M.Law Librarianship, U. Wash., 1972. Asst. prof. law U. Puget Sound, Tacoma, 1972-74, assoc. prof. law, 1974-79, prof. law, 1979—, dir. law library, 1972—. Contbr. articles to profl. jours.; mem. editorial adv. bds. various law book pubs., 1980—. Treas., Congl. Campaign Orgn., Tacoma, 1978, 80; mem. adv. bd. Clover Park Vocat.-Tech. Sch., Tacoma, 1980-82. Mem. Am. Assn. Law Libraries, Internat. Assn. Law Libraries, Am. Soc. Info. Sci. Republican. Home: 1502 Fernside Dr S Tacoma WA 98465 Office: U Puget Sound Sch of Law 950 Broadway Tacoma WA 98402

STEELE, COLIN ROBERT, librarian, consultant; b. Hartlepool, Durham, Eng., Mar. 2, 1944; s. Robert W. and Mary (Carter) S.; m. Anna Elizabeth Creer, July 22, 1967; children: Christopher, Jonathan. BA with honors, Liverpool U., Eng., 1965, MA, 1971; cert. in librarianship, U. Coll. London, 1967. Asst. librarian Bodleian Library Oxford (Eng.) U., 1967-76; dep. librarian Australian Nat. U., Canberra, 1976-80, librarian, 1980—. Author: English Interpreters of the Iberian New World, 1975, Major Libraries of the World, 1976; editor: Independent Mexico, 1972, Steady State: Zero Growth Libraries, 1978. Mem. Magellan Soc., 1980—; chair Australian Nat. Word Festival, 1983-87. Brit. Acad. Am. fellow, 1974; recipient Knight Cross of Queen Isabela La Catolica awarded by King of Spain, 1984. Mem. Australian Adv. Com. Bibliog. Services (council 1982—), Bibliog. Soc. Australia (council 1978-83), Library Assn. Australia and Britain, Hakluyt Soc., Oxford Bibliog. Soc. Club: Commonwealth (Canberra). Lodge: Rotary. Home: 11 Elsey St Hawker, Canberra ACT 2614, Australia Office: Australian Nat Univ, GPO Box 4, Canberra ACT 2601, Australia

STEELE, ELLEN LIVELY, business development executive, publishing executive; b. Fayette County, W.Va., Jan. 22, 1936; d. Alfred French and Sarah Ellen (Pritchard) L.; student N.Mex. State U., 1962-74; m. Henry Gilmer Steele, July 20, 1981; children—Gregory Benjamin Pake, Seana Ellen Pake. Civilian adminstrv. officer Dept. Army, White Sands Missile Range, N.Mex., 1962-67; mgr. Kelly Services Inc., Las Cruces, N.Mex., 1967-85; pres. Lively Enterprises, Inc., Las Cruces, 1967-76; sec., treas. Adam II, Ltd., Las Cruces, 1973-77; pres. Symposium Internat. Inc., Las Cruces, 1977-78, Asset & Resource Mgmt. Corp., Organ, N.Mex., 1978-83; lit. agt., prin. Ellen Lively Steele & Assos., 1979—; mng. partner AVVA III, Las Cruces, 1981-82, Internat. Alliance Sports Ofcls., Las Cruces, 1982—; mng. ptnr. Steele Lehnert, 1986—; ptnr., exec. producer Triple L Prodns., 1986—; dir. mktg. Los Cruces Conv.and Visitors Bur., 1984-85; dir. Santa Rosa Resources Corp., Denver; exec. GASCO Internat. Inc., Las Cruces, 1981-82; mem. N.Mex. State Senate, 1985—, co-chmn. higher edn. reform com., 1985, 86, mem. interim coms., jud. com., edn. com., criminal justice com., Human Needs & Aids com.; mem. nat. conf. state legislatures; N.Mex. Federated Rep. Women, Am. Legis. Exchange Commn.; mem. task force El Paso Electric Co. Rate Moderation; mem. firearms preemtion statute rev. Served with USAF, 1954-57. Mem. Internat. Assn. Fin. Planners, Sales and Mktg. Execs. Internat., Am. Mgmt. Assn., DAR. Episcopalian. Clubs: Order Eastern Star; Picacho Hills Country (Co-chmn. bd. dirs. 1980-84) (Las Cruces). Home: PO Drawer 447 Organ NM 88052

STEELE, GEORGE PEABODY, marine transportation executive; b. San Francisco, July 27, 1924; s. James Mortimer and Erma (Garrett) S.; m. Elizabeth Yates Fahrion, July 11, 1944 (div. May 1988); children: Jane Yates Steele Mitchell, James Fahrion; m. Betty McDonnell, May 20, 1988. BS, U.S. Naval Acad., 1944. Commd. ensign USN, 1944, advanced through grades to vice adm., 1973; service aboard submarines in Pacific, World War II; comdr. U.S.S. Hardhead, 1955-56; comdr. nuclear powered U.S.S. Seadragon (made 1st NW passage under ice to North Pole), 1959-61; comdr. Polaris missile sub U.S.S. Daniel Boone, 1963-66; head politico-mil. policy div. Europe/NATO br. Office Chief Naval Ops., 1966-68; comdr. Naval Forces, Korea, chief Naval adv. group, Korean Navy, comdr. Naval Component UN Command, 1968-70; comdr. Anti-Submarine Warfare Group 4, 1970-72; dep. asst. chief of staff Supreme Allied Comdr., Europe, SHAPE, Belgium, 1972-73; comdr. U.S. 7th Fleet, 1973-75; ret., 1975; exec. v.p., chief ops. officer Interocean Mgmt. Corp., Phila., 1976—, pres., 1978-85, chmn., chief exec. officer, 1981—; chmn. bd. dirs. Fgn. Policy Research Inst. Author: Seadragon, Northwest Under the Ice, 1962, (with H. Gimpel) Nuclear Submarine Skippers and What They Do, 1962, Vengeance in the Depths, 1963; contbr. articles to profl. publs. and newspapers. Decorated D.S.M., Legion of Merit with 4 gold stars, Navy Cross (Peru), Order of Rising Sun (Japan), Cloud and Banner (Republic China), Order Nat. Security of Merit (Republic Korea). Mem. Am. Bur. Shipping (bd. mgrs.), Am. Inst. Merchant Shipping (chmn. bd. dirs. 1986-87), U.S. Naval Inst. Episcopalian. Clubs: Univ., N.Y. Yacht; Union League (Phila.); Army-Navy, Army-Navy Country (Washington). Home: 225 S 18th St Apt 816 Philadelphia PA 19103 Office: Interocean Mgmt Corp Three Pkwy Suite 1300 Philadelphia PA 19102

STEELE, HOWARD LOUCKS, government official; b. Pitts., Jan. 27, 1929; s. Howard Bennington and Ruby Alberta (Loucks) S.; BS, Washington and Lee U., 1950; M.S., Pa. State U., 1952; Ph.D., U. Ky., 1962; m. Sally E. Funk, June 6, 1952 (div. 1977); children: John F., David A., Patricia A.; m. 2d, Jane R. Cornelius, July 30, 1977; 1 dau., Jennifer L. Sales mgr. Greenville (Pa.) Dairy Co., 1952-56; owner H.L. Steele Bulk Milk Hauling, Greenville, Pa., 1955-60; asst. prof. Clemson (S.C.) U., 1956-57, asso. prof., 1957-64; asso. prof. Ohio State U., Columbus, 1964-71; with Office Internat. Cooperation and Devel. U.S. Dept. Agr., Washington, 1971—, project mgr. AID, Bolivia, 1977-80, Honduras, 1980-82, Sri Lanka, 1982-84, Bur. Latin Am. and Caribbean AID, Washington, 1984—; instr. U. Md., College Park, 1974-76; vis. prof. U. Sao Paulo, Piracicaba, Brazil, 1964-66; partner Kingwood Acres Farm, Rockwood, Pa., 1966—. Recipient Nat. Forensic Union award; named One of Outstanding Young Men in U.S., U.S. Jaycees,

1965; cert. of merit Dept. Agr., 1975. Mem. Am. Agrl. Econs. Assn., Internat. Assn. Agrl. Economists, Sons Am. Revolution, Gamma Sigma Delta, Sigma Nu. Lodges: Masons, Shriners. Author: Comercialização Agri cola; contbr. to Agriculture, Lincoln Library of Essential Information; contbr. articles to profl. jours. Home: 5204 Holden St Fairfax VA 22032 Office: OICD Dept Agrl McGregor Bldg 14th St and Independence Ave Room 221 Washington DC 20250

STEELE, JAMES EUGENE, educational adminstr.; b. South Norfolk, Va.; s. James Edward and Blanche Eugenia (Munden) S.; B.S. in Music Edn., William & Mary Coll., Norfolk, 1961; M.Ed. in Ednl. Adminstrn. and Supervision, Temple U., 1972; Ed.D. in Ednl. Adminstrn., Nova U., 1965. Piccoloist, Norfolk Symphony Orch., 1951-73; dir. choral music Hampton (Va.) City Schs., 1960-65, supr. music, 1965—. Dir. fine arts div. Hampton Assn. Arts Humanities, 1967—. Mem. NEA, Va., Hampton edn. assns., Va. Assn. Sch. Execs., Hampton Instructional Suprs. Assn., Tidewater Regional Suprs., Va. Assn. Sch. Curriculum Devel., Va. Music Suprs. Assn., Va. Music Educators Assn., Music Educators Nat. Conf., Va. Choral Dirs. Assn., Va. Band and Orch. Dirs. Assn., Va. String Tchrs. Assn. Guest flute soloist Music Tchrs. Assn. Great Britain, 1962. Certified as tchr. supr., Va. Home: 132 Fayton Ave Norfolk VA 23505 Office: 1300 Thomas St Hampton VA 23669

STEELE, JOHN ROY, real estate broker; b. Detroit, Feb. 16, 1945; s. Wallace Lee Roy and Kay F. (Fitzpatrick) S.; B.A., Alma Coll., 1967; M.B.A., Central Mich. U., 1968; m. Beverly Louise Rauh, June 3, 1972; children—Josh Oliver, Matt Edward, Anne Elizabeth. Owner/broker Century 21 Steele, Realtors, Jackson, Calif., 1981—; partner/broker Century 21, Lewis-Steele, Realtors, Inc., Jackson and Truckee, Calif., 1976-81; v.p. Century 21 Foothill-Sierra council, 1987-88; dir. Amador Title Co., 1978-83, pres., 1978-79; ptnr. Computer World, Jackson, 1983-85. Bd. dirs. Trinity Episcopal Ch., Sutter Creek, Calif., 1978-79, 80-83, jr. warden, 1979; trustee Citizens for Progress, 1981-82; chmn. Amador County chpt. Easter Seals Telethon, 1985-88. pres. Amador Swim Team, 1986-87, 87-88; coach Mother Lode Youth Soccer League, 1984, 86; coach state finals Odyssey (Olympics) of the Mind, 1986, 87, 88. Mem. Amador County Bd. Realtors (bd. dirs. 1974-82, profl. standards com. 1988, pres. 1978), Calif. Assn. Realtors (dir. 1978). Clubs: Friends of the Library, Toastmasters (charter mem. 1987). Office: PO Box 210 Jackson CA 95642

STEELE, LORETTA A., systems analyst; b. San Diego, Mar. 21, 1952; d. Manuel and Lillie B. (Lincoln) S. B.A. in Psychology, U. Calif.-San Diego, 1976; postgrad., UCLA, 1978-80. Researcher, co-author UCLA Ctr. for Afro-Am. Studies, Los Angeles, 1979-80; pub., editor Computer Ads from Compustats, Los Angeles, 1981-82; pres. Compustats, Los Angeles, 1981-87, Lincoln & Steele InfoSystems, Los Angeles, 1988—; specialist System Devel. Corp., Santa Monica, Calif., 1981, Los Angeles Unified Sch. Dist., 1982; mem. Nat. Software Rev. Bd., 1984; computer instr. Wilshire Ctr. Community Involvement Assn., Inc., Immanuel Presbyn. Ch., Los Angeles, 1984; microcomputer specialist Summer Olympics Project, ABC, Los Angeles, 1984. Mem. Am. Soc. Profl. Cons., Nat. Council Negro Women, Democrat. Baptist.

STEELE, MICHAEL, conductor; b. Port-of-Spain, Trinidad, May 28, 1951; came to u.S., 1969. B.Mus., Temple U., 1974, M.Mus., 1988. Condr., So. Light Orch., Trinidad, 1976-78, Collegium Musicum, Trinidad, 1979—, Opera Ebony, Phila., 1984, Internat. Bachakadamie, Stuttgart, W.Ger., 1984, Savaria Symphony Orch., Szombathely, Hungary, 1986, Hungarian Radio and TV Orch., Budapest, Hungary, 1986; mus. assoc. Temple Opera, Phila., 1983-85, asst. mus. dir., 1985—, Solingen City Orch., Fed. Republic Germany, 1988 ; adjudicator Pan Trinbago, Trinidad, 1977-83, Nat. Parang Assn., Trinidad, 1977-78; coordinator of music U. W.I., Trinidad, 1979, instr., 1975. Composer song cycles and choral music; arranger. Recipient Beryl McBurnie award B. McBurnie Found., 1983, Am. Biog. Inst. Commemorative Medal of Honor, 1987; Sonderpreis, 9th Internat. Youth & Music Festival, Vienna, 1980; Sylvan E. Bowles scholar, 1970-74. Mem. Music Educators Nat. Conf., Music Tchrs. Assn. Trindiad, Alpha Lambda Delta. Episcopalian. Avocations: gourmet cooking; dance; theatre; weights; walking. Home: 940E Washington Ln Philadelphia PA 19138 Other: 16 Sapphire Crescent, Diamond Vale, San Diego Martin, Trinidad West Indies

STEELMAN, ROBERT JOE, pediatric dentist, researcher; b. Richland, Wash., Apr. 11, 1949; s. Earl and Betty Catherine (Young) S.; m. Marie Carol Hobson, Dec. 20, 1980. A.A.S., Columbia Basin Coll., Pasco, Wash., 1969; B.A., U. Wash., 1972; A.M., Washington U., St. Louis, 1974. D.M.D., 1982. Ecology researcher Washington U., 1974-76, med. researcher, 1976-78; resident in oral and maxillofacial surgery Emory U., Atlanta, 1982-83; pediatric dentist U. Tex. Health Sci. Ctr., Dallas, 1983-87; pediatric dental fellow Baylor Coll. Dentistry, Dallas, 1987—. Contbr. articles to profl. jours. Served as dental officer USPHS, 1983-87. Mem. ADA, Am. Assn. Dental Research, Am. Acad. Oral Medicine, Am. Acad. Oral Pathology, Student Clinicians of ADA, Sigma Xi, Omicron Kappa Upsilon, Alpha Epsilon Delta. Home: 9922 Knoll Krest Dallas TX 75238 Office: Baylor Coll Dentistry Dept Pediatric Dentistry Dallas TX 75246

STEEN, CARL BERTIL, educator, physician; b. Stockholm, Apr. 15, 1938; s. T. Bertil and Karin E.M. (Lindskog) S.; m. Gunilla A.M. Hornstein, June 1, 1968; 1 child, Mattias. M.D., U. Goteborg, 1964, M.D., Ph.D., 1977. Asst. dept. anatomy U. Goteborg, Sweden, 1958-64, asst. prof., 1978-80; physician-in-chief Vasa Hosp., Goteborg, 1976-80, resident Sahlgren Hosp. and Vasa Hosp., Goteborg, 1964-69, asst. physician-in-chief, Vasa Hosp., 1976-80; prof. U. Umea, Sweden, 1980-81; prof. Lund U., Sweden, 1981-88; prof. U. Göteborg, Sweden, 1988—; cons. WHO, mem. sci. council Swedish Nat. Bd. of Health and Welfare, Swedish Nat. Food Adminstrn. Bd. Contbr. internat. and Swedish textbooks on geriatric medicine and nutrition, profl. jours. Mem. Am. Geriatric Soc., Nordic Soc. on Gerontology, Swedish Geriatric Assn. (chmn.), Swedish Soc. for Nutrition (bd. dirs. 1975-78), Swedish Soc. for Research on Aging (sci. sec. 1975-83), Swedish Coll. Physicians, Internat. Union of Nutritional Scis. (com. on nutrition and aging 1979—), Internat. Psychogeriatric Assn. (bd. dirs. 1983—), Sci. Council of Fedn. Internat. des Assn. de personnes agees. Home: Skarsgatan 60, 412 69 Göteborg 65 Sweden

STEEN, ETIENNE, gynecologist, obstetrician; b. Lille, Nord, France, July 28, 1939; s. Julien and Jacqueline S.; m. Nicole Schmandt, Apr. 9, 1965; children: Ludovici, Bruno, Véronique, Olivier. D Medicine, Faculte de Medicine, Lille, France, 1964. Diplomate Soc. Specialists Ob-gyn. Chief of service Gyneco-Obstetrique Centre Hosp., Denain, 1969; practice medicine specializing in ob-gyn Denain, France, 1969—; mem. sr. attending staff Hosp. de Lille. Served with French mil. cooperative service, Burkina-Faso, 1966-67. Roman Catholic. Home: 91 Rue Duquesnoy, 59220 Denain France Office: 23 Rue Lozore Bernard, 59220 Denain France

STEEN, JOHN THOMAS, JR., lawyer, savings and loan executive; b. San Antonio, Dec. 27, 1949; s. John Thomas and Nell (Donnell) S.; m. Ida Louise Clement, May 12, 1979; children—John Thomas, Ida Louise Larkin. A.B., Princeton U., 1971; J.D., U. Tex., 1974. Bar: Tex. 1974, U.S. Dist. Ct. (we. dist.) Tex. 1976. Assoc. firm Matthews & Branscomb, San Antonio, 1977-82; ptnr. firm Soules, Cliffe & Reed, San Antonio, 1982-83; sr. v.p., gen. counsel Commerce Savs. Assn., San Antonio, 1983—, also dir.; bd. dirs. North Frost Bank, San Antonio, 1982-84. Trustee San Antonio Acad., 1976-81, 87—; v.p. Bexar County Easter Seal Soc., San Antonio, 1976-77; trustee, vice chmn. San Antonio Community Coll. Dist., 1977-82; bd. dirs. Tex. Easter Seal Soc., Dallas, 1977-80, San Antonio Research and Planning Council, 1978-81, Community Guidance Ctr., 1983-84; vice-chmn. Leadership San Antonio, 1978-79; mem. Fiesta San Antonio Commn., 1982-83; Bexar County commr., San Antonio, 1982, Tex. Commn. on Economy and Efficiency in State Govt., 1985—; Coliseum Adv. Bd., 1985—; pres. San Antonio Performing Arts Assn., 1984-85; chmn. World Affairs Council San Antonio, 1984-86; trustee United Way San Antonio, 1985—; bd. dirs. Accord Med. Found., 1987—; mem. adv. bd. U. Tex., San Antonio, 1987—. Served to 1st lt. USAR, 1973-81. Fellow San Antonio Bar Found., Tex. Bar Found. (life); mem. Tex. Bar. Assn., Santa Gertrudis Breeders Internat., Tex. and Southwestern Cattle Raisers Assn., San Antonio Acad. Alumni Assn. (pres. 1976-77), Phi Delta Phi. Clubs: Ivy (Princeton, N.J.); San Antonio German (pres. 1982-83), Order of Alamo, Tex. Cavaliers, San Antonio Country, Argyle, Conopus, Princeton (San Antonio and South Tex.) (pres. 1980-81). Home: 207 Ridgemont Ave San Antonio TX 78209 Office: Commerce Savs Assn 111 Soledad St Suite 600 San Antonio TX 78205

STEEN, PETER, actor, playwright; b. Randers, Denmark, Jan. 22, 1936; s. Thorkild and Bodil Agnete (Holleufer) S.; student U. Copenhagen, 1955-56, Actors Sch., Royal Theatre, Copenhagen, 1960-63; children by previous marriage—Morten, Rasmus. Debut, Royal Theatre, 1963, appeared in numerous prin. roles, 1963-74; also prin. roles in pvt. theatre, TV, films; dir. Royal Theatre, pvt. theatres, TV; debut as playwright at Royal Theatre, 1970, with play Jo Mere vi er Sammen, also dir.; mem. jury Nat. Theatre Acad., 1986; mem. Danish Film Council, 1968-72. Served with inf. Danish Army, 1954-55. Grantee in field. Mem. Danish Actors Assn., Danish Playwrights Assn., Danish Stage Dirs. Assn., Danish Film Workers Assn., Assn. for Danish Theatre History. Author: (TV plays) Fra Fem Til Syv, 1970, En Aegtemand, 1973, (with Peter Ronild) The Troubadour 1974, Bertel, 1986. Home: 12 Holbergsgade, 1057 Copenhagen Denmark

STEENBERG, BÖRJE KARL, forester; b. Stockholm, Aug. 6, 1912; s. Karl and Maja (Ohrstrom) S.; B.Sc., U. Stockholm, 1936, M.Sc., 1938, Ph.D., 1944, D.Sc., 1945; D.Forestry Sci., Royal Inst. Forestry, Stockholm, 1969; m. Elisa Hald, Oct. 15, 1940; children—Kjell, Ann. Mem. faculty Royal Inst. Tech., Stockholm, 1937—, prof., 1949—, emeritus, 1979—, head dept. paper tech., 1949—; asst. dir. gen. FAO, Rome, 1968-74; research dir. Swedish Forest Products Research Lab., 1944-68; cons. in field, del. internat. meetings. Recipient German Mitscherlich medal, 1960, Swedish Ekman Gold medal, 1961, Gold medal TAPPI, 1970. Mem. Royal Swedish Acad. Engring. Scis., Finnish Acad. Tech. Scis., Internat. Acad. Wood Sci., Royal Swedish Acad. Agr., Italian Acad. Forestry, N.Y. Acad. Sci. Clubs: Rotary, Travellers. Author papers in field. Home: 19 Ynglingagatan, 113 47 Stockholm Sweden Office: 53 Kristinas Väg, 100 44 Stockholm Sweden

STEENSON, TEDDY JAY, educator; b. St. Paul, Neb., Oct. 14, 1943; s. Lawrence August and June Elizabeth (Myers) S. BA in Edn., Kearney (Neb.) State U., 1961, MS in Edn., 1965; postgrad., Los Angeles Community Coll. and Mich. State U., 1977; student, Oomoto Sch. Traditional Japanese Arts, Japan, 1982. Instr. bus. edn., math. Hildreth (Neb.) Pub. Schs., 1965-71; instr. bus. edn. AFCENT Internat. Sch. U.S. Dept. Def. Dependents Schs. Systems, Brunssum, The Netherlands, 1971-73, Karamursel High Sch. U.S. Dept. Def. Dependents Schs. Systems, Turkey, 1975-86, Kubasaki High Sch. U.S. Dept. Def. Dependents Schs. Systems, Okinawa, Japan, 1975—; tchr. Sogetsu Sch. Ikebana (traditional Japanese flower arranging), Sei Tei (Japanese flower name). Mem. Am. Educators' Assn. Okinawa (treas 1980-83), NEA, Nat. Bus. Edn. Assn., Neb. St. Bus. Edn. Assn. (pres. 1970-71), European Bus. Edn. Assn., Phi Delta Kappa Okinawa Chpt. (treas. 1985-88). Lutheran. Lodges: Hildreth Lions NE (sec. 1970-71), Elks. Office: Kubasaki High Sch Okinawa Japan FPO Seattle WA 98773

STEFANESCU, DORU, mathematician, educator; b. Iasi, Romania, Jan. 19, 1952. MS, U. Bucharest, Romania, 1975, DSc, 1976, PhD, 1985. Tchr. math. Ind. Lyceum 19, Bucharest, 1976-80; asst. prof. math. U. Bucharest, 1980—; mam. Nat. Romanian Com. for Math. Competitions, Bucharest, 1978—; reviewer Math. Revs., U. Mich., Ann Arbor, 1980—, Zentralblatt fur Mathematik, West Berlin, 1984—. Author: Mathematical Models in Physics, 1984, (with others) 5 books on math. problems, 1975, 81, 85-86; contbr. articles to profl. jours. Fellow Scuola Matematica Interuniversitaria Italy; mem. Soc. Stiinte Matematice din R. S. Romania, Am. Math. Soc., Balkan Math. Union, Gesellschaft fur Angewandt Mathematik und Mechanik. Club: Casa Universitariolor (Bucharest). Home: PO Box 39-95, Bucharest Romania Office: U Bucharest Faculty Physics, Dept Math PO Box 52-11, Bucharest Romania

STEFANO, GEORGE B., neurobiologist, researcher; b. N.Y.C., Sept. 11, 1945; s. George and Agnes (Hendrickson) S.; m. Judith Mary Stefano, Aug. 24, 1968; 1 child, Michelle Laura. Ph.D., Fordham U., 1973. Mem. faculty N.Y.C. Community Coll., 1972-79, Medgar Evers Coll., CUNY, 1979-82; prof. cell biology, chmn. dept. biol. sci. SUNY-Old Westbury, 1982-86, asst. v.p. research, 1985—, dir. Gerontology Ctr., 1986—; pres., dir. East Coast Neurosci. Found., Dix Hills, N.Y., 1977-82; research coordinator dept. anesthesiology St. Joseph Hosp. and Med. Ctr., Paterson, N.J., 1979-82. Cofounder, mem. editorial bd. Molecular and Cellular Neurobiology. Contbr. articles to sci. jours. Nat. Acad. Scis. grantee, 1978, 80; NIMH grantee, 1979-83; project dir. ADA MHA-MARC, 1983—. Mem. Soc. Neurosci., N.Y. Acad. Sci., Gerontol. Soc. Am., AAAS.

STEFÁNSSON, ALEXANDER, Icelandic government official; b. Ólafsvík, Iceland, Oct. 6, 1922; m. Björg Hólmfriour Finnbogadóttir; 6 children. Grad. Coop.'s Comml. Coll., 1943. Dir. Coop. Soc. Olafsvik (Iceland); office mgr. Olafsvikurhreppur, Olafsvik, 1962-66, comml. mgr., 1964-79; dep. mem. Althing, Reykjavic, Iceland, 1972-74, mem., 1978—, dep. speaker Lower House of Parliament, 1979—, minister of social affairs, 1983-87; chmn. Comml. Council, 1964—; mem. bd. Union Harbour Authorities, 1969—; dep. chmn. bd. Fisheries Bank of Iceland, 1976—; dir. Utver Ltd., Olafsvik. Mem. exec. bd. Internat. Yr. of Disabled Com. Mem. Assn. of Local Authorities in Iceland (chmn. 1969-76), Assn. Local Authorities in Western Iceland (chmn. 1969-76). Mem. Progressive Party. Office: Progressive Party, PO 5331, Nastun 21, Reykjavik Iceland *

STEFFENS, HEIKO N., educator; b. Oldenburg, Niedersachsen, Germany, Apr. 11, 1938. Buehnenreife, Max-Reinhardt-Schule, Berlin, 1962; Lehrer examen, Pädagogische Hochschule, Bonn, 1967; Doctor, Pädagogische Hochschule, Westfalen-Lippe, Muenster, 1974. Actor, Kammerspiele, Paderborn, W.Ger., 1962-64; tchr. Hauptschule, Bad Honnef, W.Ger., 1967-70; sci. asst. Pädagogische Hochschule, Bielefeld, W.Ger., 1972-75; prof. Pädagogische Hochschule, Berlin, 1975-80; prof. arbeitslehre/ economics Tech. U., Berlin, 1980—; cons. Sender Freies Berlin, 1975-81; author, actor, cons. Westdeutscher Rundfunk, Köln, 1971—. Author: Career Education, 1975; Consumer Education, 1980; Industrial Robots, 1981; New Information-Technologies, 1986, New Technologies, 1988. Bd. dirs. Verbraucherzentrale Berlin e.V., 1976—; adminstrv. bd. Stiftung Verbraucherinstitut, Berlin, 1987—; juror Internat. Consumer Film Competition, Berlin, 1975-87, Ernst-Schneider-Film-Preis, Köln, 1981-83. Grantee, Stiftung Volkswagenwerk, Hannover, 1970-72, Graduiertenförderung, 1972-73. Mem. Soc. for Advancement Games and Simulations, Bundesfachgruppe füzÖkonomische Bildung, Gesellschaft fur Arbeit, Technik, Wirtschaft. Roman Catholic. Office: Technische U Berlin, Franklinstr 28/29, D-1000 Berlin Federal Republic of Germany

STEGEMEIER, RICHARD JOSEPH, oil company executive; b. Alton, Ill., Apr. 1, 1928; s. George Henry and Rose Ann (Smola) S.; m. Marjorie Ann Spess, Feb. 9, 1952; children: Richard Michael, David Scott, Laura Ann, Martha Louise. BS in Petroleum Engring., U. Mo., Rolla, 1950, cert. petroleum engr. (hon.), 1981; MS in Petroleum Engring., Tex. A&M U., 1951. Registered profl. engr., Calif. Various nat. and internat. positions with Unocal Corp. (formerly Union Oil Co.), Los Angeles, 1951—, v.p. sci. and tech. div., 1978-80, sr. v.p. corp. devel., 1980-85, pres., chief operating officer, 1985—, also bd. dirs. Patentee in field. Pres. World Affairs Council of Orange County, 1980-81; chmn. Brea (Calif.) Blue Ribbon Com, 1979-80; mem. math sci.-engring. adv. council Calif. State U., Fullerton; mem. chem. adv. council Calif. State U., Long Beach; bd. dirs. YMCA, Los Angeles, Martin Luther Hosp. Med. Ctr. Fellow Tenn. Gas Transmissions Co., 1951; recipient Engring. Merit award Orange County Engring. Council, 1980, Outstanding Engr. Merit award, Inst. Advancement Engring., 1981. Mem. Am. Petroleum Inst., Soc. Petroleum Engrs (lectr. 1978). Republican. Roman Catholic. Club: California (Los Angeles). Office: Unocal Corp Unocal Ctr Los Angeles CA 90051 *

STEGGLES, IRVING, mathematics educator, consultant; b. Gillingham, Eng., Apr. 20, 1945; s. Reginald William George and Zilpher Kathleen (Straw) S. M.A., Oxford U., 1966, diploma in edn., 1967. Schoolmaster, Royal Shrewsbury Sch., 1967, Monkton Combe Sch., Bath, Avon, 1967—, housemaster, 1977—; dir. Academic Tutorials, Bristol, 1984—, Mathematics in Edn. and Industry Schs. Project (chmn. Gen. Cert. of Sec. Edn. com. 1986—). Assoc. fellow Inst. Math. and Its Applications; fellow Victoria Inst.; mem. Math. Assn. U.K. (com. 1984—, reviewer, editorial com.), History of Math. Soc., London Math. Soc., Math. Assn. Am., Am. Math. Soc., Inst. Dirs., Mind Assn. Conservative. Baptist. Club: Oxford & Cambridge (London). Avocations: classical music, piano, organ, gastronomy, gardening. Home: 116 Hobleythick Ln, Westcliff-on-Sea, Essex SS0 0RJ, England Office: Monkton Combe School, Bath, Avon BA2 7HG, England

STEGMAN, CHARLES ("CHUCK") ALEXANDER, marketing professional; b. Denver, Apr. 17, 1959; s. Harvey Eugene and Mary Martha (Newell) S. BSEE, U. Colo., 1981. Regional dir. Sigma Phi Epsilon, Richmond, Va., 1981-82, chpt. devel. dir., 1982-83; sales rep. Lanier/Harris, San Francisco, 1983, legal account rep., 1983-84; mktg. rep. Businessland, Oakland, Calif., 1984-86, sr. mktg. rep., 1986; mktg. mgr. of networks Businessland, San Jose, Calif., 1987—; systems engring. instr. Businessland of San Jose, Calif., 1986-87. Mem. exec. bd. Alice B. Toklas Dem. Club, San Francisco, 1985—; mem. Harvey Milk Dem. Club, San Francisco, 1985-87; co-chmn. Molinari for Mayor, 1987; active Dem. Party. Recipient numerous computer sales awards; named one of Outstanding Young Men of Am., 1985. Mem. Sigma Phi Epsilon. Roman Catholic. Clubs: Comstock, Commonwealth. Home: 647 Castro St San Francisco CA 94114 Office: Businessland 1001 Ridder Park Dr San Jose CA 95131

STEHKÄMPER, HUGO FRANZ HEINRICH, archivist; b. Gelsenkirchen, Fed. Republic Germany, Apr. 5, 1929; s. Hugo Heinrich and Anna Henriette (Schubert) S.; m. Karola Stehkämper, Jan. 11, 1929; children: Ulrich, Christoph. Phil D., U. Münster, Westfalia, Fed. Republic Germany, 1954; grad., Archive Tng. Inst., Marburg/Lahn, Fed. Republic Germany, 1959. Asst. archivist State Archives, Münster, 1959-61; archivist Hist. Archives of City, Cologne, 1961-69, archive dir., 1969-70, adminstr., archive dir., 1970—; hon. prof. U. Cologne, 1987—. Contbr. articles to prof. jours.; editor: Cologne, The Holy Empire and Europe, 1971, Adenauer, Lord Mayor of Cologne, 1976. Mem. Hist. Commn. Westphalia, 1970, Curatorial Soc. Inst. Comparative Mcpl.History Münster, 1971; advisor Siftung Bundeskanzler Adenauer Haus Rhöndorf, 1985. Knight of St. Gregory-Ordre, Pope John Paul II, Rome, 1982. Mem. Soc. Rhenish History (sec. 1965), Assn. German Archivists (deputy chmn. 1969-77), Union German Hist. Assns. Cologne (chmn. 1985), Hansean Hist. Assn. (chmn. treas. 1973, dep. chmn. 1983, bd. dirs. 1973). Lodge: Rotary. Home: Am Hang 12, D-5060 Bergisch Gladbach 1 Federal Republic of Germany Office: Hist Archives of the City, Severinstrabe 222-228, D-5000 Cologne Federal Republic of Germany

STEIGER, DALE ARLEN, publishing consultant; b. LaCrosse, Wis., May 14, 1928; s. Walter Elmer and Doris Adeline (Howe) S.; student U. Wis., LaCrosse, 1945-46, 48-49; BA, Chgo. Acad. Fine Arts, 1951; postgrad. in bus. adminstrn. Drake U., 1958-62, Iona Coll., 1968; m. Alyce Ann Dyrdahl, Oct. 8, 1949; children—Christine Ann, Marta Louise. Art dir. Trane Co., LaCrosse, 1955, Look mag., Des Moines, 1956, promotions mgr. Cowles Subscription div., 1957-67, exec. v.p. Cowles Communications subdiv., 1960-71; v.p. mktg., asso. pub. Curtis Publs. Co., N.Y.C., 1971-72; pres. Dale Steiger Assocs., N.Y.C., 1972—, Blue Ribbon Reading Service, Rye, N.Y., 1979—; pres., pub. Videofinder mag., 1981—, Pulling mag., 1981—; pres. SUBCO, 1986; chmn. Hair and Beauty Inc.; pub. Hair and Beauty News, 1988—; lectr. direct mail and mktg. Served with AUS, 1946-48. Recipient Industry Achievement award Fulfillment Mgmt. Assn., 1979; Lee C. Williams award for outstanding contbns. to periodical pub. field, 1982. Mem. Mag. Publs. Assn., Audit Bur. Circulations, Fulfillment Mgmt. Assn. (pres., chmn. bd.), Nat. Soc. Art Dirs., VFW, Am. Legion. Republican. Presbyterian (elder). Clubs: Cornell (N.Y.C.); Westchester Country. Author: (with others) The Handbook of Circulation Management, 1980. Office: 488 Madison Ave New York NY 10022

STEIGER, FREDERIC, artist; b. Solwutz, Austria, Oct. 21, 1905; s. Michael and Ida (Schaeffer) S.; m. Netty Meth, Aug. 5, 1922 (div.); m. Ruby Eleanor Fevens; children—Trudi Kearns, Linda. Student, Olmouc (Austria) U. One man exhbns. include, Carroll Galleries, Toronto, Roberts Art Gallery, Toronto, Ont., Can., 1950, Odeon Theatre Gallery, Toronto and Ottawa, 1947, Ho. of Assembly, St. John's, Nfld., Can., 1960, Arts Club, Montreal, Que., Can., 1957, L'Art Francaise Art Gallery, 1957, Montreal Arts and Letters Club, 1960, T. Eaton Art Gallery, Toronto, 1972, 79, O'Keefe Centre Gallery, 1974, Galerie Lyson, Toronto, 1980-81, Linchrist Gallery, 1985, Ont. Inst. Studies in Edn., 1986, Queen's U., 1986, Karney-Daniels Art Gallery, 1986, Brampton Art Gallery, 1987; exhibited in group shows at Vancouver Art Mus., 1939, Royal Can. Acad., Montreal and Toronto, 1941, 45, Montreal Mus. Art, 1941, Ont. Soc. Artists, Art Gallery Toronto, 1938-40, Cummerford Gallery, N.Y.C., 1962; represented in permanent collections, IBM, 40 portraits, Nfld. Parliament Bldg., Meml. U. Nfld., St. John's, Hallmark Collection Can. Art, Imperial Oil Ltd., Toronto, Met. Toronto Pub. Library, Wellesley Hosp., Toronto, Royal Ins. Co., Toronto, Etobicoke Hydro-U of Saskatchewan; also pvt. collections; portrait of King Peter of Yugoslavia, 1974, Hon. William G. Davis, Premier of Ont, 1976, Hon. John C. Crosbie, M.P., 1983; work included in "Many Faces, Many Spaces," Artists in Ont., 1987, Discovery by Ruby Steiger. Recipient Bronze medal IBM Corp. Unitarian. Home and Studio: 316 The Kingsway, Apt 201, Islington, ON Canada M9A 3V3

STEIGER, OTTO, author, novelist; b. Thun, Berne, Switzerland, Aug. 4, 1909; s. Robert Steiger and Maria Steiger Wasmer; m. Rosmary Salber, 1949; children: Martin, Marianne. Ed. U. Berne, Switzerland, U. Paris. Author numerous novels, including: Spurlos vorhanden, 1980, Porträt eines angesehenen Mannes, 1981, Die Unreifeprüfung, 1984, Der Doppelgänger, 1985, Das Jahr mit elf Monaten, 1986, Vagabundenschule, 1986, Orientierungslauf, 1988; also numerous short stories, TV and radio plays. Recipient numerous prizes, awards, including Swiss Children's Books prize, 1980, cert. honor. Internat. Bd. Books for Young People; award City of Zurich. Mem. Swiss Authors Assn., Swiss Pen Club, Pro Litteris.

STEIMLE, RAOUL HENRI, neurosurgeon; b. Mex. City, Nov. 7, 1922; s. Frédéric and Mathilde (Vorburger) S.; m. Maria Bravo-Aguiar, Mar. 20, 1954; children: Pierre Paul, Dominique, Eric, Michèle, Philippe, Geneviève. BA, U. Stràsbourg, 1940, MD, 1951. Externe Hôpitaux de Paris, 1946; interne Hôpitaux de Strasbourg, 1948; clin. chief and asst. in surgery U. Stràsbourg, 1953; staff mem. Am. Brit. Cowdray Hosp., Mex. City, 1957; instr. neurology U. Mex., 1959; prof. neuro-anatomy Faculty of State of Mex., 1959; chief neurosurgeon Spanish Hosp., Mex. city, 1960-66; neurosurgeon U. Hosp., Besancon, France, 1966; assoc. prof. U. Hosp., 1968; full prof. neurosurgery U. Besancon, 1972—; chief neurosurgeon U. Hosp., 1972—; v.p. Physicians Order Dept. of Doubs, France, 1987. Author: Introduction à la Neurochirurgie, 1980; contbr. articles to profl. jours. Mem. ACS, Coll. Int. Surgeons: French Speaking and French Soc. for Neurosurgery, Mexican Soc. Neurosurgery, Chilean Soc. Surgery, European Soc. Pediatric Neurosurgery, French-Mexican Med. Soc. (counsellor), French Soc. History of Medicine, French Surg. Acad. (assoc.). Home: 26 rue F Carco, Besancon France Office: Hôpital J Minjoz, Bd Fleming, 25000 Besancon France

STEIN, BARBARA LAMBERT, marriage and family therapist; b. Detroit, Feb. 10, 1945; d. Joseph J. and Sylvia (Siegel) Lambert; m. David Joel Stein, Jan. 1, 1967; children—Craig Andrew, Todd Alexander. Student psychology Mich. State U., 1962-64; B.A. in Sociology, Wayne State U., 1966, postgrad. in psychiat. social work, 1972-74; M.S. in Counseling Psychology, Nova U., 1980; student, Art Inst. Ft. Lauderdale, 1985. Vol. abuse and neglect dept. Wayne County Juvenile Ct., Detroit, 1964-65; vol. D.J. Healy Shelter for Children, 1965-67; med. social worker Hutzel Hosp., Detroit, 1967-68; developer neighborhood teen drug program City of West Bloomfield (Mich.), 1970-71; med. social worker Extended Care Facilities, Inc., Birmingham, Mich., 1972-73; vol. group and occupational therapist Henderson Psychiat. Clinic Day Treatment Ctr., Ft. Lauderdale, Fla., 1977-78; pvt. practice family and marital therapy, Deerfield Beach, Coral Springs, and Boca Raton, Fla., 1980-85. Mem. Boca Raton Museum of Art (exec. chmn. antique show, sale and gala dinner fundraiser, 1988, co-chair mktg. mem. com.), The Friends of Photography, San Francisco, Mothers Against Drunk Driving, Sch. Edn. Bd. Temple Beth El of Boca Raton, until 1985; founding mem. Levis Jewish Community Ctr., Boca Raton. Recipient cert. of Meritorious Achievement, Henderson Psychiat. Clinic Day Treatment Ctr. Mem. Am. Assn. Marriage and Family Therapy (assoc.), Am. Psychol. Assn. (assoc.), Wayne State U. Alumni Assn., Nova U. Alumni Assn., Photogroup Miami, Camera Club of Boca Raton, Friends of Photography of San Francisco, Nat. Trust Historic Preservation, Opera Soc. Ft. Lauderdale,

Zool. Soc. Fla., Orton Dyslexia Soc., Assn. Children and Adults with Learning Disabilities, South County Jewish Fedn. (bd. dirs. until 1986, chmn. community relations council 1984-85, chmn. speakers bur. 1985-86).

STEIN, ELEANOR BANKOFF, judge; b. N.Y.C., Jan. 24, 1923; d. Jacob and Sarah (Rashkin) Bankoff; m. Frank S. Stein, May 27, 1947; children—Robert B., Joan Jenkins, William M. Student, Barnard Coll., 1940-42; B.S. in Econs., Columbia U., 1944; LL.B., NYU, 1949; grad. Ind. Jud. Coll., 1986. Bar: N.Y. 1950, Ind. 1976, U.S. Supreme Ct. 1980. Atty. Hillis & Button, Kokomo, Ind., 1975-76, Paul Hillis, Kokomo, 1976-78, Bayliff, Harrigan, Kokomo, 1978-80; judge Howard County Ct., Kokomo, 1980—; co-juvenile referee Howard County Juvenile Ct., 1976-78. Mem. Republican Women's Assn. Kokomo, 1980—; bd. dirs. Howard County Legal Aid Soc., 1976-80; dir. Howard County Ct. Alcohol and Drug Services Program, 1982—; bd. advisors St. Joseph Hosp., Kokomo, 1979—; bd. dirs. Kokomo Human Relations Commn., 1967-70. Mem. law rev. bd. NYU Law Rev., 1947-48. Mem. Am. Judicature Soc., Ind. Jud. Assn., Nat. Assn. Women Judges, ABA, Ind. Bar Assn., Howard County Bar Assn. Jewish. Clubs: Kokomo Country, Altrusa. Home: 3204 Tally Ho Dr Kokomo IN 49602 Office: Howard County Ct Howard County Courthouse Kokomo IN 46901

STEIN, ELLEN GAIL, urban planner; b. N.Y.C., May 19, 1951; d. Manuel W. and Bella (Skutel) Stein; B.A., SUNY-Stony Brook, 1972; M.U.P., Hunter Coll., 1976. Sr. research assoc. Nassau Suffolk (N.Y.) Regional Med. Program, 1976-77; sr. planner N.Y.C. Dept. Correction, 1977-79; group leader criminal justice Mayor's Office Ops., N.Y.C., 1979-81, dep. asst. dir. citywide spl. projects, 1981, dir. citywide audit implementaion, 1981-84; adminstr. Bur. Supplies, N.Y.C. Bd. Edn., 1984—. Mem. Assn. Sch. Bus. Ofcls., Nat. Inst. Govt. Purchasing Agts., Am. Soc. for Pub. Adminstrn., Am. Planning Assn. Home: 67 Park Terr E New York NY 10034 Office: 44-36 Vernon Blvd Long Island City NY 11101

STEIN, FRITZ HENRY, art gallery director; b. N.Y.C., July 25, 1932; s. Harve Carl and Hope Louise (Jonas) S.; B.A., U. R.I., 1955; postgrad. N.Y. Sch. Interior Design, 1965; children—Andrea, Pamela, Kimberly; m. Candice C. Scholz; children—Kristin, Kelly. Art dir. G. Fox Co., Hartford, Conn., 1955-60; co-owner Constn. Galleries, West Hartford, Conn., Gloucester, Mass., 1960-63; interior designer Silberman's of Norwich (Conn.), 1963-71; owner, mgr. Stone Ledge Studio Art Galleries, Noank, Conn. Mem. Groton (Conn.) Republican Town Com., 1980—. Dir. Groton Pub. Library. Mem. Noank Hist. Soc., Mystic Art Assn. (past pres. and dir.), Slater Mus. Republican. Roman Catholic. Club: Rotary (Paul Harris fellow). Home and Office: 59 High St Noank CT 06340 Office: 59 High St Box 237 Noank CT 06340

STEIN, GEORGE HENRY, historian, educator, administrator; b. Vienna, Austria, May 18, 1934; came to U.S., 1939, naturalized, 1948; m. Dorothy Ann Lahm, Nov. 22, 1963; 1 child, Kenneth. B.A. with honors (N.Y. State Regents scholar), Bklyn. Coll., 1959; M.A. in History (Regents fellow), Columbia U., 1960, Ph.D. in History (Pres.'s fellow), 1964. Lectr. history City Coll., CUNY, 1962-63; instr. dept. history Columbia U., N.Y.C., 1963-65; asst. prof. Columbia U., 1965-66; assoc. prof. dept. history SUNY-Binghamton, 1966-70, prof., 1970—, disting. teaching prof., 1973—, vice chmn. grad. affairs, 1974-76, v.p. acad. affairs, 1976-87, provost, 1985-87; manuscript evaluator and cons. to numerous publishers, 1964—. Author: The Waffen SS: Hitler's Elite Guard at War, 1939-45, 1966, paperback edit., 1984 (transl. into German, 1967, French, 1967, Spanish, 1973, Portuguese, 1970); contbr. articles on modern European history to scholarly publs.; editor: Hitler, 1968; contbr. book revs. to hist. jours. Served with USAF, 1953-57. NEH fellow, 1970-71. Mem. Am. Hist. Assn. (mem. conf. group on central European history, conf. group for use of psychology in history), Acad. Polit. Sci., Assn. of Contemporary Historians, Am. Assn. Higher Edn., Nat. Assn. State Univs. and Land Grant Colls. (mem. council acad. affairs 1976-87), Am. Council Edn. (exec. com. nat. council chief acad. officers 1983-85), Comite Internat. d'Histoire de la Deuxieme Guerre Mondiale (mem. Am. com. on history of 2d World War). Office: Dept History SUNY Binghamton NY 13901

STEIN, HERMAN DAVID, social sciences educator; b. N.Y.C., Aug. 13, 1917; s. Charles and Emma (Rosenblum) S.; m. Charmion Kerr, Sept. 15, 1946; children: Karen Lou Gelender, Shoshi Stein Bennett, Naomi Elizabeth. B.S.S., CCNY, 1939; M.S., Columbia U., 1941, D. Social Welfare, 1958; L.H.D., Hebrew Union Coll.-Jewish Inst. Religion, Cin, 1969. Family case worker, dir. pub. relations Jewish Family Service, N.Y.C., 1941-45; mem. faculty Sch. Social Work, Columbia U., N.Y.C., 1945-47, 50-64, prof. social scis., 1958-64, dir. research ctr., 1959-62; dean Sch. Applied Social Scis., Case Western Res. U., Cleve., 1964-68; provost for social and behavorial scis. Case Western Res. U., Cleve., 1967-71, provost, 1969-72, v.p., 1970-72, prof., 1972—; univ. provost Sch. Applied Social Scis., Case Western Res. U., 1986-88; dir. Global Currents Lectures, 1983-87 ; vis. prof. Sch. Social Work, U. Hawaii, Honolulu, winter 1971-72; fellow center for Advanced Study in Behavior Scis., 1974-75, 78-79; Dep. dir. budget and research dir. welfare dept. Am. Joint Distbn. Com. (European Hdqrs.), Paris, 1947-50; sr. adviser to exec. dir. UNICEF, 1976-82; cons. UNICEF, UN Social Devel. Div., 1960-83; adv. com. NIMH, 1959-71; mem. Bd. Human Resources, Nat. Acad. Scis., 1972-74; lectr. Sch. Social Work, Smith Coll., 1950-63, Harvard U. Sch. Public Health, 1971—; cons. Tecmar Inc., 1981-86. Author: The Curriculum Study of the Columbia University School of Social Work, 1960; co-author: The Characteristics of American Jews, 1965; Editor: (with Richard A. Cloward) Social Perspectives on Behavior, 1958, Planning for the Needs of Children in Developing Countries, 1965, Social Theory and Social Invention, 1968, The Crisis in Welfare in Cleveland, 1969, Organization and the Human Services, 1981; mem. editorial bd.: Adminstr. in Social work, 1976—; contbr. to profl. jours. Chmn. Mayor's Commn. on Crisis in Welfare in Cleve., 1968. Recipient Disting. Service award Council on Social Work Edn., 1970; René Sand award Internat. Council on Social Welfare, 1984. Mem. Am. Sociol. Assn., Soc. for Applied Anthropology, Council Social Work Edn. (pres. 1966-69), Internat. Assn. Schs. Social Work (pres. 1968-76), Nat. Assn. Social Workers (chmn. commn. internat. social welfare 1964-66), Internat. Conf. Social Welfare (mem. exec. com. 1976-80, bd. dirs. council internat. programs 1965, 77—, internat. adv. bd. 1986—), Club of Rome (assoc.). Office: Case Western Res U Adelbert Hall Cleveland OH 44106

STEIN, KONRAD MARK, physics educator; b. Prairie View, Tex., Sept. 14, 1952; s. Andrew Mark and Ruth Katherine (Hall) S.; m. Julie Chang, Oct. 10, 1985. B.S., U. Calif.-San Diego, 1974; Ph.D., U. Calif.-Riverside, 1982; M.S., Calif. State U.-Los Angeles, 1978. Systems engr., Jet Propulsion Lab., Pasadena, Calif., 1974-77; instr. physics Riverside City Coll., Calif., 1978-80, Calif. State U., 1980-81; prof. physics Goldenwest Coll., Huntington Beach, Calif., 1983—; vis. prof. physics Qing Hua U., Beijing, People's Republica China, 1984-85. Mem. Am. Phys. Soc., N.Y. Acad. Scis. Home: 4821 Parkglen Ave Los Angeles CA 90043

STEIN, LAUZENT JEAN, airline company executive; b. Paris, Nov. 8, 1946; s. Marc and Arlette (Simon) S.; m. Jacqueline Ricard, Feb. 2, 1977; 1 child, Cyril. Grad., Ecole Superieure Commerce, Paris, 1970. Product mgr. for N. Europe, Air France and Paris Vasagatan, 1972-76, mktg. , sales mgr. for Japan, Korea and Tokyo, 1976-80, advt. and promotions gen. mgr. for Paris, 1980-85, gen. mgr. for Scandinavia, Finland, Iceland and Stockholm, 1985—; sr. mem. French Fgn. Trade Council, 1986—. Contbr. articles to profl. publs. Mem. French C. of C. in Sweden (gen. sec. 1987). Office: Air France Vasagatan, 50 111 Stockholm 20 Sweden

STEIN, PAUL DAVID, cardiologist; b. Cin., Apr. 13, 1934; s. Simon and Sadie (Friedman) S.; m. Janet Louise Tucker, Aug. 14, 1966; children—Simon, Douglas, Rebecca. B.S., U. Cin., 1955, M.D., 1959. Intern Jewish Hosp., Cin., 1959-60, med. resident, 1961-62; med. resident Gorgas Hosp., C.Z., 1960-61; fellow in cardiology U. Cin., 1962-63, Mt. Sinai Hosp., N.Y.C., 1963-64; research fellow in medicine Harvard Med. Sch., Boston, 1964-66; asst. dir. cardiac catheterization lab. Baylor U. Med. Ctr., Dallas, 1966-67; asst. prof. medicine Creighton U., Omaha, 1967-69; assoc. prof. medicine U. Okla., Oklahoma City, 1969-73; prof. research medicine U. Okla. Coll. Medicine, Oklahoma City, 1973-76; dir. cardiovascular research Henry Ford Hosp., Detroit, 1976—. Author: A Physical and Physiological Basis for the Interpretation of Cardiac Auscultation: Evaluations Based Primarily on Second Sound and Ejection Murmurs, 1981. Contbr. articles to profl. jours. Am. Heart Assn. Council on Clin. Cardiology fellow, 1971, Council on Circulation fellow, 1972. Fellow Am. Coll. Cardiology, Am. Coll. Chest Physicians; mem. Am. Physiol. Soc., Central Soc. Clin. Research, ASME. Office: Henry Ford Hosp 2799 W Grand Blvd Detroit MI 48202

STEIN, RONALD MAX, advertising executive, consultant; b. London, Nov. 24, 1927; s. Harry and Frances (Flexser) S.; m. Rosalie Landau, Sept. 21, 1958; children: Val, Viv. Student, St. Martins's Sch. Art, London, 1945-47. Jr., staff Leon Goodman Displays, London, 1944; asst. to art dir. Royds Advt. Agy., London, 1945-55; studio mgr. Stowe & Bowden Advt., London, 1955-59; prin. Ronald Stein Advt. Cons., London, 1959—; publicity cons. Guild of Glass Engravers, London, 1979—. Illustrator (book): The Diabetic Cook Book, 1956; designer: Eve Club Souvenir Brochure, 1959, Guild of Glass Engravers catalogue, St. Lawrence Jewry Exhibition catalogue, 1986. Served with RAF, 1946-48, Italy, Austria. Mem. Publicity Club of London, Advt. Assn. (investigator 1980-87), Audit Bur. Circulation, Creative Circle, Inst. Dirs. (assoc. mem.), Periodical Proprietors Assn. (with indsl. intelligence). Conservative. Jewish. Office: Ronald Stein Advt Cons, 11 Cleve Rd, West Hampstead, London NW6 3RH, England

STEIN, THEODORE ANTHONY, biochemist, educator; b. St. Louis, Aug. 30, 1938; s. Leonard A. and Mathilda M. (Ellwangen) S.; BS, St. Louis U., 1960; MS, So. Ill. U., 1970, PhD, CUNY, 1987; m. Jeanette Heidemann, Aug. 30, 1975. Research instr. surgery Washington U. Sch. Medicine, St. Louis, 1972-75; research supr. surgery L.I. Jewish-Hillside Med. Center, New Hyde Pk., N.Y., 1975-76, research coordinator surgery, 1977—; asst. prof. surgery SUNY, Stony Brook, 1978—; biostats. cons. NIH grantee, 1962; Am. Liver Found. grantee. Mem. N.Y. Acad. Scis., Am. Fedn. Clin. Research, AAAS, Am. Pub. Health Assn., Sigma Xi. Republican. Roman Catholic. Contbr. articles to profl. jours. Home: 10 Glamford Ave Port Washington NY 11050 Office: LI Jewish Hillside Med Center New Hyde Park NY 11042

STEINBACH, UDO, polictical science educator; b. Pethau, Saxonia, German Democratic Republic, May 30, 1943; s. Arthur and Eva Margarete E. (Hammerich) S.; m. Rita E. Prothmann, Feb. 27, 1971; children: Anna, Armin, Ursula. Ph.D., U. Freiburg, 1970. Head dept. Middle East Stiftung Wissenschaft und Politik, Ebenhausen, W.Ger., 1971-75; head Turkish dept. Deutsche Welle, Köln, W.Ger., 1975; dir. Deutsches Orient-Inst., Hamburg, W.Ger., 1976—; pres. Arbeitsgemeinschaft Vorderer Orient für Gegenwartsbezogene Forschung und Dokumentation, W.Ger., 1976—; cons. Stiftung Volkswagenwerk, W.Ger., 1976-80. Author: Dhat al-Himma, 1971 (Freiburg Sci. Soc. award 1975); Grundlagen und Bestimmungsfaktoren der Aussen- und Sicherheitspolitik Irans, 1975; Kranker Wächter am Bosporus, 1979; editor: (with Gustav Stein) The Contemporary Middle Eastern Scene; Basic Issues and Major Trends, 1979; Europäisch-Arabische Zusammenarbeit. Rahmenbedingungen, Probleme, Aussichten, 1979; (with Rolf Hofmeier and Mathias Schönborn) Politisches Lexikon Nahost, 1981; (with Karl Kaiser) Deutsch-arabische Beziehungen, 1981; (with Werner Ende) Der Islam in der Gegenwart, 1983; (with Rüdiger Robert) Der Nahe und Mittlere Ostar-Politik und Gesellschaft, Wirtschaft, Geschichte und Kulbur, 1987. Mem. Deutsche Gesellschaft für Auswartige Politik, Deutsche Morgenländische Gesellschaf, Südosteuropa-Gesellschaft, Deutsch-Iranische Gesellschaft (chmn. Hamburg 1983—). Club: Club of Rome (Hamburg). Lodge: Rotary. Home: Bernadottestr 26, 2000 Hamburg 50 Federal Republic of Germany Office: Deutsches Orient-Inst, Mittelweg 150, 2000 Hamburg 13 Federal Republic of Germany

STEINBACK, THOMAS R., food service corporate manager; b. Evansville, Ind., May 17, 1950; s. Edward Oscar and Thelma Jean (Ellison) S.; B.A., Ambassador Coll., Eng., 1972; postgrad. Miss. State U., 1974-75; M.B.A., Syracuse U., 1980; m. Sherry Lynn Amos, Mar. 12, 1982; children: Lindsay Anne, Laura Jean, Chelsea Lynn. Cert. office automation profl. Exec. trainee Ambascol Corp., Eng., 1970-72; assoc. office mgr. Ambassador Coll., Pasadena, Calif., 1972-77; fin. loan counselor Syracuse (N.Y.) U., 1978-79; employee relations intern Gen. Electric Co., Syracuse, 1979, mgr. employee and community relations AEPD, Utica, 1979-82, mgr. communication programs-salaried relations AEPD, Syracuse, 1982-84; mgr. Profl. Relations Chgo. Pneumatic Tool Co., Utica, N.Y., 1984-87; corp. dir. human resources CIS Corp., Syracuse, 1987; pres. TRS Consulting, New Hartford, N.Y., 1987-88; exec. v.p. Rich Plan Corp., New Hartford, 1988—; adj. instr. AMA, Utica Coll., Empire State Coll., SUNY. Trustee ARC, Utica, 1980-82; chmn./trustee GE Employees Federated Service Fund, Utica, 1979-82; allstar mgr. New Hartford Lions Little League, 1982; pres. New Hartford ASA Girls Softball, 1984-85. Recipient Grad. Alumni award Syracuse U., 1980. Mem. Ambassador Internat. Cultural Found., Am. Soc. Personnel Adminstrs., Am. Mgmt. Assn., Assn. Grad. Bus. Students, Assn. M.B.A. Execs. Office: 4981 Commercial Dr Porkville NY 13495

STEINBAUGH, ROBERT P., management and finance educator; b. Mineral City, Ohio, Aug. 25, 1927; s. Paul W. and Blanche (Lechner) S.; m. Carolyn Ann Gates, Nov. 24, 1967. B.S., Ohio State U., 1950, M.A., 1952, Ph.D., 1957. Instr. Miami U., Oxford, Ohio, 1953-55, Ohio State U., Columbus, 1955-57; asst. prof. mgmt. and fin. Ind. State U.-Terre Haute, 1957-60, assoc. prof., 1960-63, prof. bus. adminstrn., 1963—. Mem. Acad. Mgmt., Am. Mgmt. Assn., Ohio State Alumni Assn., Beta Gamma Sigma, Delta Sigma Pi, Delta Pi Epsilon, Phi Delta Kappa, Phi Kappa Phi. Republican. Episcopalian. Lodge: Rotary. Home: 25 Monroe Blvd Terre Haute IN 47803 Office: Dept Mgmt Ind State U Terre Haute IN 47809

STEINBERG, HOWARD E., lawyer, holding company executive; b. N.Y.C., Nov. 19, 1944; s. Herman and Anne Rudel (Sinnreich) S.; m. Judith Ann Schucart, Jan. 28, 1968; children: Henry Robert, Kathryn Jill. A.B., U. Pa., 1965; J.D., Georgetown U., 1969. Bar: N.Y. 1970, U.S. Dist. Ct. (so. and ea. dists.) N.Y. 1973, U.S. Ct. Appeals (2d cir.) 1976. Assoc. Dewey, Ballantine, Bushby, Palmer & Wood, N.Y.C., 1969-76, ptnr., 1977-83; sr. v.p., gen. counsel, corp. sec. Reliance Group Holdings Inc., N.Y.C., 1983—; corp. sec. Data Resources, Inc., Lexington, Mass., 1978-79; bd. dirs. Days Inn Corp., Telemundo Group, Inc. Editor case notes: Georgetown Law Jour., 1968-69. Served to capt. JAGC AUS, 1972-74. Mem. ABA, N.Y. Bar Assn., Assn. Bar of City N.Y. Jewish. Club: University. Office: Reliance Group Holdings Inc 55 E 52d St New York NY 10055

STEINBERG, JANET DEBERRY, optometrist, educator, researcher; b. Phila., July 28, 1940; d. Bill and Florence (Kurtz) DeBerry; 1 child, J. Douglas Milner. Student Rider Coll., 1975-77; BS, Pa. Coll. Optometry, 1978, OD, 1981. Cons. Ophthalmic Eye Assocs., Levittown, Pa., 1982—; dir. Hopewell Valley Eye Assocs., Hopewell, N.J., 1982—; chief Low Vision Ctr., Scheie Eye Inst. dept. ophthalmology U. Pa., Phila., 1984—, also clin. assoc., 1985—; assoc. Louis A. Karp M.D. dept. opthalmology Pa. Hosp., Phila., 1987—; assoc. Louis A. Karp MD Dept. of Ophthalmology, Pa. Hosp., Phila., 1987—; asst. adj. prof. Pa. Coll. Optometry, Phila., 1983-85, mem. adj. faculty, 1986—; mem. N.J. Low Vision Panel, 1981—; cons. healthcare industry, 1985—. Fellow Am. Acad. Optometry; mem. Am. Optometric Assn. (Optometric Recognition award 1983-88), N.J. Optometric Assn., Central N.J. Optometric Assn., Assn. Research in Vision and Ophthalmology, Beta Beta Beta. Avocations: sailing, snorkeling, scuba. Office: Hopewell Valley Eye Assocs 84 E Broad St Hopewell NJ 08525 also: Scheie Eye Inst Low Vision Ctr 51 N 39th St Philadelphia PA 19104 also: Pa Hosp 7th and Spruce Sts Suite 100 Philadelphia PA 19106

STEINBERG, JILL ENID, computer sales executive; b. Jersey City, Oct. 27, 1955; d. Edwin Jay and Renee Ruth (Kaufman) S. B.A., U. Miami (Fla.), 1979. Salesperson luggage Burdine's, Miami, Fla., 1979-80, asst. mgr. area, 1980-81, commn. sales advanced consumer electronics, 1981-83, asst. mgr. computer sales, 1983-87, mgr. Computerbanc booth, 1987—; participant Apple seminar, 1983. Named outstanding salesperson So. Region, Hartmann Luggage, 1980; mem. Burdine's B Club. Mem. AAUW (com.), Nat. Assn. Female Execs., Alpha Kappa Delta, Delta Phi Epsilon. Lodge: Hadassah (life). Home: 15725 SW 88th Ct Miami FL 33157 Office: Computerbanc at Burdine's 7303 N Kendall Dr Miami FL 33156

STEINBERG, WARREN LINNINGTON, school principal; b. N.Y.C., Jan. 20, 1924; s. John M. and Gertrude (Vogel) S.; student U. So. Calif., 1943-44, UCLA, 1942-43, 46-47, BA, 1949, MEd, 1951, EdD, 1962; m. Beatrice Ruth Blass, June 29, 1947; children: Leigh William, James Robert, Donald Kenneth. Tchr., counselor, coach Jordan High Sch., Watts, Los Angeles, 1951-57; tchr. athletic coordinator Hamilton High Sch., Los Angeles, 1957-62; boys' vice prin. Univ. High Sch., Los Angeles, 1962-67, Crenshaw Hig Sch., Los Angeles, 1967-68; cons. Ctr. for Planned Change, Los Angeles City Sch., 1968-69; instr. edn. UCLA, 1965-71; boys' vice prin. LeConte Jr. High Sch., Los Angeles, 1969-71, sch. prin., 1971-77; adminstrv. cons. integration, 1977-81; prin. Gage Jr. High Sch., 1982-83, Fairfax High Sch., 1983—. Pres. Athletic Coordinators Assn., Los Angeles City Schs., 1959-60; v.p. P-3 Enterprises, Inc., Port Washington, N.Y., 1967-77, Century City (Calif.) Enterprises, 1966—. Vice pres. B'nai B'rith Anti-Defamation League, 1968-70; mem. adv. com. Los Angeles City Commn. on Human Relations, 1966-71, 72—, commr., 1976—, also chmn. edn. com.; pres. Los Angeles City Human Relations Commn., 1978—; mem. del. assembly Community Relations Conf. of So. Calif., 1975—; mem. citizens adv. com. for student integration Los Angeles Unified Sch. Dist., 1976-79; chmn. So. Calif. Drug Abuse Edn. Month com., 1970. Bd. dirs. DAWN, an anti-narcotics youth group. Served with USMCR, 1943-46. Recipient Beverly Hills B'nai B'rith Presdl. award, 1965; commended Los Angeles City Council, 1988. Mem. West Los Angeles Coordinating Council (chmn. case conf., human relations), Beverly-Fairfax C. of C. (bd. dirs. 1986—). Lodges: Lions (dir. 1960-62), Kiwanis. Contbr. articles on race relations, youth behavior to profl. jours. and newspapers. Home: 2737 Dunleer Pl Los Angeles CA 90064 Office: Fairfax High Sch 450 N Grand Ave Los Angeles CA 90054

STEINBORN, LEONARD, pharmaceutical company executive; b. Chgo., Apr. 29, 1946; s. Ben and Pearl (Burrows) S.; m. Sharon Diane Feinglass, Dec. 24, 1977; 1 child, Melissa Ilene. BS, Elmhurst Coll., 1976. Quality engr. Baxter Travenol Labs., Morton Grove, Ill., 1969-73; quality assurance supr. Hollister Inc., Lincolnwood, Ill., 1973-77; quality assurance auditor Am. Critical Care, Mount Prospect, Ill., 1977-78; compliance mgr. Searle Labs., Skokie, Ill., 1978-82; quality assurance mgr. Abbott Labs., North Chicago, Ill., 1982-84; strategic projects leader Abbott Labs., North Chicago, 1984—; lectr. in field. Author: The Quality Assurance Manual for the Pharmaceutical and Medical Device Industries. Mem. Am. Soc. for Quality Control (cert. quality engr.).

STEINBORN, (ERNST) OTTO H., physicist, educator; b. Dresden, Germany, May 8, 1932; s. Heinrich and Gertrud (Thomas) S.; diploma Tech. U. Dresden, 1959; Dr. phil. nat., U. Frankfurt-Main, 1965; habilitation, Tech. U. Berlin, 1970; m. Gudrun Mnich, Sept. 14, 1968. Research asst. U. Frankfurt-Main, W.Ger., 1961-67; research asso. Iowa State U., Ames, 1967-69; instr. phys. chemistry Tech. U. Berlin, 1969-70, prof., 1970-71; prof. U. Regensburg (W.Ger.), 1971—. Lutheran. Author articles on theoretical and phys. chemistry, nuclear physics. Office: U Regensburg Chemistry Inst, Universitätsstrasse 31, D-8400 Regensburg Federal Republic of Germany

STEINER, ROBERT FRANK, biochemist; b. Manila, Philippines, Sept. 29, 1926; came to U.S., 1933; s. Frank and Clara Nell (Weems) S.; m. Ethel Mae Fisher, Nov. 3, 1956; children: Victoria, Laura. A.B., Princeton U., 1947; Ph.D., Harvard U., 1950. Chemist Naval Med. Research Inst., Bethesda, Md., 1950-70; chief lab. phys. biochemistry Naval Med. Research Inst., 1965-70; prof. chemistry U. Md., Balt., 1970—; chmn. dept. chemistry U. Md., 1974—, dir. grad. program in biochemistry, 1985; mem. biophysics study sect. NIH, 1976. Author: Life Chemistry, 1968, Excited States of Proteins and Nucleic Acids, 1971, The Chemistry of Living Systems, 1981, Excited States of Biopolymers, 1983; editor: Jour. Biophys. Chemistry, 1972—. Served with AUS, 1945-47. Recipient Superior Civilian Achievement award Dept. Def., 1966; NSF research grantee, 1971; NIH research grantee, 1973-88. Fellow Washington Acad. Sci.; mem. Am. Soc. Biol. Chemists. Club: Princeton (Washington). Home: 2609 Turf Valley Rd Ellicott City MD 21043 Office: 5401 Wilkens Ave Baltimore MD 21228

STEINER, TIMOTHY JOHN, medical researcher; b. Hawkhurst, Kent, Eng., Apr. 26, 1946; s. Raymond Eugene and Barbara Ruth (Ward) S.; m. Susan Elizabeth Nee George, 1967. BSc with honors, Chelsea Coll., London, 1969, PhD, 1975; MB, BS, Charing Cross Hosp. Med. Sch., London, 1976. Cert. gen. med. council, 1978. Demonstrator in physiology Chelsea Coll., London, 1969-73; house physician, surgeon Charing Cross Hosp., London, 1977, lectr. in exptl. neurology, 1980-86, hon. cons., 1986—; sr. lectr. in clin. physiology Charing Cross and Westminster Med. Sch., London, 1986—; research head The Princess Margaret Migraine Clin., 1987—. Contbr. articles to profl. jours. Trustee, corr. The Way Ahead, London, 1987—. Research scholar Med. Research Council Gt. Brit. Chelsea Coll., London, 1967-69, research grantee. Fellow Med. Soc. London (council), Am. Heart Assn. (stroke council); mem. Internat. Headache Soc. (clin. trials study group), Inst. Med. Ethics, Soc. Pharm. Medicine (sci. subcom.), Royal Soc. Medicine (angiology forum com.). Home: 95 Kingston Hill, Kingston Upon Thames England KT2 7PZ Office: Charing Cross & Westminster Med Sch, St Dunstan's Rd, London England W6 8RP

STEINFINK, MURRAY, retail executive; b. N.Y.C., July 17, 1940; s. Jack and Stella; B.S. in Chem. Engring., CCNY, 1963; M.S. in Polymeric Materials, Bklyn. Poly. Inst., 1969; m. Susan Rose Wachs, June 15, 1963; children—Jaime, Jeremy. Product devel. chemist DuPont Co., Wilmington, Del., 1963-66; group leader adhesives products div. PPG Industries, Bloomfield, N.J., 1966-69; tech. dir. New Eng. Laminates Inc., Stamford, Conn., 1969-70; v.p. Skeist Labs. Inc., Livingston, N.J., 1970-73; dir. mktg. Ciba-Geigy Corp., Ardsley, N.Y., 1973-76; v.p. M. Lowenstein and Sons, Inc., N.Y.C., 1976-82, also pres. Splty. Products div.; sr. v.p. Revlon, 1982-83; v.p. Conair, Edison, N.J., 1983-85; chmn., chief exec. officer Splty. Retail Services Inc., 1985—; adj. prof. chem. engring. dept. Poly. Inst. Bklyn. Mem. Comml. Devel. Assn., Soc. Plastics Engrs., Am. Chem. Soc., Am. Inst. Chem. Engrs. Jewish. Patentee in field. Home: 329 Strawtown Rd New City NY 10956 Office: 150 E 58th St Suite 3400 New York NY 10155

STEINHAUS, RICHARD ZEKE, lawyer, educator; b. N.Y.; B.S., N.Y. U., 1951; J.D., Bklyn. Law Sch., 1955; L.H.D., N.Y. Coll. Podiatric Medicine, 1975; m. Joan Goodman, June 24, 1951 (div. 1982); children—Peter Michael, Richard Zeke; m. 2d, Mary K. Kopley, Sept. 25, 1982. Acct., Marks & Marks, CPA's, N.Y.C., 1951-55; admitted to N.Y. bar 1956, D.C. bar, 1961; pvt. practice N.Y.C., 1956-76; mem. firm Blinder, Steinhaus & Hochhauser, N.Y.C., 1965-76, Washington, 1961-70; vis. lectr. Ithaca Coll., 1973-85; asst. prof. N.Y. Coll. Podiatric Medicine, 1983—. Pres., Camp Vacamas Assn., 1965-68; acting police judge, Dobbs Ferry, 1965-66. Served with USN, 1945-47. Mem. Am. (mem. tax sect.), Internat., N.Y. State, Albany Bar Assns., Warren County (N.Y.) Bar Assn., N.Y. Magistrates Assns., Bar Assn. City of N.Y., Normanside C. of C. Democrat. Jewish. Clubs: Fort Orange (Albany, N.Y.); Alpine Suisse (Zermatt). Office: 90 S Swan St Albany NY 12210

STEINHORN, IRWIN HARRY, lawyer, educator, corporate executive; b. Dallas, Aug. 13, 1940; s. Raymond and Libby L. (Miller) S.; m. Linda Kay Shoshone, Nov. 30, 1968; 1 child, Leslie Robin. BBA, U. Tex., 1961, LLB, 1964. Bar: Tex. 1964, U.S. Dist. Ct. (no. dist.) Tex. 1965, Okla. 1970, U.S. Dist. Ct. (we. dist.) Okla. 1972. Assoc. Oster & Kaufman, Dallas, 1964-67; ptnr. Parness, McQuire & Lewis, Dallas, 1967-70; sr. v.p., gen. counsel LSB Industries, Inc., Oklahoma City, 1970-87; v.p., gen. counsel USPCI, Inc., Oklahoma City, 1987—; adj. prof. law Oklahoma City U. Sch. Law, 1979—; lectr. in field. Mem. adv. com. Okla. Securities Commn., 1986—. Served to capt. USAR, 1964-70. Mem. ABA, Tex. Bar Assn., Okla. Bar Assn. (sec., treas. bus. assn. sect. 1986-87, chmn. elect 1987-88), Com. to Revise Okla. Bus. Corp. Act, Phi Alpha Delta. Republican. Jewish. Club: Oklahoma City Golf and Country. Lodge: Kiwanis. Home: 6205 Avalon Oklahoma City OK 73118 Office: USPCI 2000 Classen Ctr Suite 500 S Oklahoma City OK 73106

STEINKRAUSS, WHIPPLE E., public service executive; b. Toronto, Ont., Can., Sept. 14, 1943; s. William Carl and Florence Beatrice Christine (Little) S. BA in Econs. and Psychology, Queens U., Kingston, 1964; MBA, U. Toronto, 1985. Mgr. pub. participation Met. Toronto Transp. Plan Rev., 1972-75; coordinator, pub. liason Royal Commn. on Met. Toronto, 1975-77; policy coordinator multi-culturalism and citizenship Ont. Ministry of Culture and Recreation, Toronto, 1977-79; dir. citizenship devel. Ont. Ministry of Citizenship and Culture, Toronto, 1979-86; exec. dir. support services Ont. Ministry Consumer Comml. Relations, Toronto, 1986—. Co-author: (with others) Report of the Royal Commission on Metropolitan Toronto, 1977. Bd. govs. YMCA of Met. Toronto, 1979-86. Mem. UN Assn. Can. (bd. dirs. 1971-74), Couchichiny Inst. Pub. Affairs (pres. 1976-78), Inst. Pub. Adminstrn. Can., Toronto Regional Group (mem. exec. com. 1982-84). Presbyterian. Home: 21 Dale Ave #715, Toronto, ON Canada M4W 1K3 Office: Ministry of Consumer Comml, Relations Services div, 10 Wellesley St E 6th fl, Toronto, ON Canada M7A 2H8

STEINLE, JOHN GERARD, health orgn. exec.; b. Havre, Mont., Nov. 8, 1916; s. Francis X. and Ada L. (de Lorimier) S.; BS, St. Mary's Coll., 1936; MA, U. So. Calif., 1937; LLB, St. Louis City Coll. Law, 1941; MS, Syracuse U., 1947; m. Joan E. Sinnott, Aug. 14, 1945, (div. June 1972); children: Susan (Mrs. Raymond Bebko), Elizabeth (Mrs. Jesse McFarland), Gretchen (Mrs. Sanford Prater), Jacquelynn (Mrs. Nickolas Leisos), Abbe Anne (Mrs. Michael Finn), Robyn; m. Bianca Santisteban, July 15, 1972. Adminstr. St. Louis City Infirmary, 1939-42; chief hosp. adminstrn. sect. USPHS, Washington, 1947-51, hosp. program dir., N.Y.C., 1951-54; pres. John G. Steinle & Assocs., Garden City, N.Y., 1954-70, Health Orgns., Systems and Planning Corp., Garden City, 1970-75, John G. Steinle and Assocs., Inc., 1975—; gen. counsel Face Up Profl. Skin Care Ctrs., Inc., Newport Beach, Calif., 1985—. Lectr. hosp. adminstrn. Columbia, 1952-59. Trustees Adelphi U., Garden City, 1953-62; chmn. bd. Madison Park Hosp., Bklyn., 1955-61. Served with AUS, 1942-46. Decorated Silver Star, Purple Heart. Mem. Assn. Med. Colls., AIA, Acad. Hosp. Cons. (pres. 1964-66), Internat. Hosp. Assn. Club: Princeton (N.Y.C.). Author: (with Ivan Belknap) The Community and Its Hospitals, 1963; Hospital Cost Management, 1982. Editor: Health and Hosp. Encys., 1974; cons. editor Hosp. Topics Mag. Contbr. articles to profl. jours. Home: 257A 3d St Palisades Park NJ 07650 Office: 888 W 16th St Newport Beach CA 92663

STEINMANN, GERHARD GUSTAV, immunopathologist; b. Osnabrueck, Fed. Republic Germany, June 10, 1948; s. Gustav Heinrich and Else Luise (Meyer-Buenemann) S.; m. Claudia Gertrud Foelger, Dec. 22, 1975; children: Julia, Sonja. Aerztl. Prüfg., U. Hamburg, Fed. Republic Germany, 1975, Approbation, 1977; Dr. med., 1977, Diplom Psychologie, 1977; Habilitation, U. Kiel, 1985. Diplomate German Bd. Pathology. Intern, U. Krankenhaus Eppendorf Hamburg, 1976-77; resident dept. pathology Kiel, 1977-79, asst. dept. pathology, 1980-85; research fellow Meml. Sloan-Kettering Cancer Ctr., N.Y.C., 1979-80, research group leader Thomae GmbH, Biberach an der Riss, Fed. Republic Germany, 1985—. Contbr. articles to profl. jours., chpts. to books. Served with Bundeswehr, 1967-69. Recipient Louise-Eylmann-Stiftung award, 1985; Ev. Studienwerk Villigst scholar, 1972; Deutsche Forschungsgemeinschaft-Bonn scholar, 1979; DFG grantee; Erich-Krieg prize, 1981. Mem. Internat. Soc. Lymphology, Am. Soc. Clin. Oncology, Am. Assn. for Cancer Research, Internat. Soc. for Exptl. Hematology, German Soc. for Pathology, Eurage. Office: Dr Karl Thomae GmbH, Postfach 1755, D-7950 Biberach an der Riss Federal Republic of Germany

STEINMETZ, JEAN CLAUDE, chemical company executive; b. Luxemburg, Sept. 26, 1953; s. Joseph Nicolas and Marie (Lahr) S. BS in Civil Engring. with honors, U. Birmingham, 1978, M in Indsl. Mgmt., 1979. Tech. engr. Du Pont S.A., Luxembourg, 1980; sales engr. Du Pont S.A., Geneva, 1980-81; mktg. engr. Du Pont S.A., Dusseldorf, Fed. Republic Germany, 1984; mgr. European automitive strategy program Gen. Electric Plastics, Bergen Opzoom, 1984-85; mgr. mktg. France Gen. Electric Plastics, Europe, 1986-87; mgr. mktg. European div. Gen. Electric Plastics, France and Spain, 1987—. Mem. Round Table. Club: Liberty Country (Thiverval). Home: 35 B15 reu Ml Gallieni, 7800 Versailles France

STEINMETZ, RICHARD BIRD, JR., minerals company executive, lawyer; b. Orange, N.J., Mar. 27, 1929; s. Richard Bird and Charlotte (Quinby) S.; m. Merriam Holly Miller, June 9, 1956; children: Richard Blair, Jonathan Bird, Edward Quinby. BA, Yale U., 1950; JD, Harvard U., 1955. Bar: N.Y. 1955. Assoc. Chadbourne, Parke, Whiteside & Wolff, N.Y.C., 1955-59; with Anaconda Co., N.Y.C., 1959-79, v.p., gen. counsel, 1971-79; v.p. Colt Industries Inc., N.Y.C., 1979-82; v.p., gen. counsel Pittston Co., Greenwich, Conn., 1982-84; exec. v.p., dir. Case, Pomeroy and Co., N.Y.C., 1984—. Served to capt. USMC, 1950-52. Mem. ABA, N.Y.C. Bar Assn., Assn. Gen. Counsel. Republican. Episcopalian. Home: 78 Zaccheus Mead Ln Greenwich CT 06831 Office: Case Pomeroy & Co Inc 6 E 43d St New York NY 10017

STELLER, ARTHUR WAYNE, educational administrator; b. Columbus, Ohio, Apr. 12, 1947; s. Fredrick and Bonnie Jean (Clark) S.; B.S., Ohio U., 1969, M.A., 1970, Ph.D., 1973. Tchr., Athens (Ohio) City Schs., 1969-71; curriculum coordinator, tchr. Belpre (Ohio) City Schs., 1971-72; prin. elem. schs., head tchr. learning disabilities South-Western City Schs., Grove City, Ohio, 1972-76; dir. elem. edn. Beverly (Mass.) Pub. Schs., 1976-78; adj. prof. Lesley Coll., Cambridge, Mass., 1976-78; coordinator spl. projects and systemwide planning Montgomery County Pub. Schs., Rockville, Md., 1978-80; asst. supt. Shaker Heights (Ohio), 1980-83. supt. schs. Mercer County Pub. Schools., Princeton, W. Va., 1983-85; supt. schs. Oklahoma City Pub Schs., 1985—. Bd. govs. Kirkpatrick Ctr.; mem. Oklahoma City Com. for Econ. Devel., Oklahoma Alliance Against Drugs, Oklahoma Zool. Soc. Inc.; selected for Leadership Okla. City, 1986; bd. dirs. Leadership Oklahoma City, ARC; bd. dirs. Okla. Centennial Sports Inc.; mem. Oklahoma Acad. for State Goals, State Supt.'s Adv. Council; mem. clin. experiences adv. com. U. Okla. Coll. Edn.; trustee Arts Council Oklahoma City, Omniplex Sci. and Arts Mus., Oklahoma City Area Vocat.-Tech. Dist. 22 Found.; mem. Urban Ctr. Ednl. Adv. Bd.; chmn. bd. dirs. Langston U.; active United Way Greater Okla., Sch. Mgmt. Study Group, Okla. Reading Council, Okla. City PTA; bd. dirs. Oklahoma County chpt. ARC, Jr. Achievement Greater Oklahoma City Bd., Oklahoma State Fair Bd., Last Frontier Council Bd. Charles Kettering Found., IDEA fellow, 1976, 78, 80; Nat. Endowment Humanities fellow, Danforth Found., 1987-88; 1977. Mem. Am. Assn. Sch. Adminstrs., Nat. Assn. Elem. Sch. Prins., Nat. Assn. Edn. Young Children, Nat. Sch. Pub. Relations Assn., Assn. Supervision and Curriculum Devel. (bd. dirs.), Internat. Soc. Ednl. Planning, Nat. Soc. Study Edn., Nat. Planning Assn., Council Basic Edn., Am. Edn. Fin. Assn., Ohio Assn. Elem. Sch. Adminstrs., Buckeye Assn. Sch. Adminstrs., Ohio Assn. Supervision and Curriculum Devel., Okla. Assn. for Supervision and Curriculum Devel., Okla. Assn. Sch. Adminstrs., Okla. Coalition for Pub. Edn., Okla. Commn. for Ednl. Leadership, Urban Area Supts. (Oklahoma br.), Ohio U. Alumni Assn. (nat. dir. 1975-78, pres. Cen. Ohio chpt. 1975-76, pres. Mass. chpt. 1976-78, life mem. trustee's acad.), World Future Soc. (life), Greater Oklahoma City C. of C. (exec. bd. dirs.), South Oklahoma City C. of C. (bd. dirs.), Oklahoma Heritage Assn., Heritage Hills Assn. (bd. dirs.), Nat. Eagle Scout Assn., Aerospace Found. (hon. bd. dirs.), Tau Kappa Epsilon Alumni Assn. (regional officer Mass. 1976-78, named Alumni Nat. Hall of Fame 1986), Kappa Delta Pi (life), Phi Delta Kappa (life). Methodist. Lodge: Rotary. Contbr. articles to profl. jours.; author: Educational Planning for Educational Success; editor: Effective Instructional Management; cons. editor, editorial bd. Jour. for Curriculum and Supervision. Home: 900 North Klein St Oklahoma City OK 73106

STELLERS, THOMAS JOE, educational administrator; b. Dover, Ohio, May 22, 1940; s. Joseph A. and Jane Elizabeth (Stieber) S.; m. Carol Jean Crichton, Aug. 28, 1971. B.S. in Edn., Bowling Green State U., 1962; postgrad. U. Pitts., 1963-64, So. Ill. U., 1965; M.Ed., Kent State U., 1968, Ph.D., 1973. Cert. tchr., high sch. prin., supt., Ohio. Biology tchr., yearbook adviser Austintown-Fitch High Sch., Austintown, Ohio, 1962-71, 72-74; univ. fellow Kent (Ohio) State U., 1971-72; supr. middle schs., supr. sci., Mahoning County Schs., Youngstown, Ohio, 1974-76, dir. adminstrv. services and mgr. data processing, 1976—; instr. yearbook workshops Kent State U., 1968-71, Northwood Inst. and Delta Coll., Mich., 1971-72; chmn. beginning computer awareness Ohio Statewide Ednl. Computer Fair, 1982, 84; chmn. software adv. com. Ohio Dept. Edn., 1987—. Edn. chmn. Am. Cancer Soc., 1977, United Way, 1979, 80; cooordinator Mahoning County Health Promotion Program; elder Christian Ch.Recipient No. One award Ohio's Project Leadership, 1985, First Dir.'s award, 1988; named Scott Assoc. Ohio Air Force Assn., 1987. Mem. Ohio Ednl. Data Systems Assn. (pres. 1985, 88, Outstanding Mem. award 1986), Ohio Ednl. Computer Mgmt. Council (bd.), Ohio Com. for Ednl. Info. Systems, Nat. Sci. Tchrs. Assn. (task force for establishing clearinghouse for research evaluation instruments), Ohio Ednl. Assessment Program (panel mem.), Ohio Jr. Acad. Sci. (dist. council), Buckeye Assn. Sch. Adminstrs. (ins. com.), Phi Delta Kappa, Sigma Phi Epsilon. Home: 2405 Vollmer Dr Youngstown OH 44511-1951 Office: 2801 Market St Youngstown OH 44507-1693

STELTZLEN, JANELLE HICKS, lawyer; b. Atlanta, Sept. 18, 1937; d. William Duard and Mary Evelyn (Embrey) Hicks; divorced; children: Gerald William III, Christa Diane. BS, Okla. State U., 1958; MS, Kans. State U., 1961; JD, U. Tulsa, 1981. Bar: Okla. 1981, U.S. Dist. Ct. (no., ea. and we. dists.) Okla. 1981, U.S. Tax Ct. 1982, U.S. Ct. Claims 1982, U.S. Ct. Appeals (10th cir.) 1983, U.S. Ct. Appeals (Fed. cir.) 1984, U.S. Supreme Ct. 1986; lic. real estate broker. Sole practice Tulsa, 1981—; lectr. Coll. of DuPage, Glen Ellyn, Ill., 1976, Tulsa Jr. Coll., 1981—; dietitian, Tulsa. Bd. dirs. Youth for Christ, Christian Living Ctr. Tulsa: Christian counselor 1st United Meth. Ch., Tulsa, 1986—, lay pastor, 1987—. Mem. Okla. Bar Assn., Tulsa County Bar Assn., Vol. Lawyers Assn. (bd. dirs.), Am. Dietetic Assn., Delta Zeta. Republican. Methodist. Home: 6636 S Jamestown Place Tulsa OK 74136 Office: 1150 E 61st St Tulsa OK 74136

STELZER, IRWIN MARK, economist; b. N.Y.C., May 22, 1932; s. Abraham and Fanny (Dolgins) S.; B.A. cum laude, NYU, 1951, M.A., 1952; Ph.D., Cornell U., 1954; m. Marian Faris Simian, 1981. Fin. analyst Econometric Inst., 1952; teaching fellow Cornell U., 1953-54; instr. U. Conn., 1954-55; researcher Twentieth Century Fund, 1953-55, economist W.J. Levy, Inc., 1955-56; sr. cons., v.p. Boni, Watkins, Jason and Co., Inc., 1956-61; lectr. N.Y. U., 1955-56, CCNY, 1957-58; researcher Brookings Instn., 1956-57; pres. Nat. Econ. Research Assos., Inc., 1961-85; pres. I.M. Stelzer Assocs. Inc., 1986—; dir. Energy and Environ. Policy Ctr., Harvard U., 1987—; economic columnist The Sunday Times, 1986—; assoc. mem. Nuffield Coll. Oxford; chmn. com. on adequate power supply FPC. Mem. Cornell U. Council; adv. com. revision of rules of practice and procedure Fed. Energy Regulatory Commn.; adv. council Electric Power Research Inst.; mem. Mayor's Energy Policy Adv. Group for N.Y.C.; adv. panel Pres.'s Nat. Commn. for Rev. of Antitrust Laws and Procedures; mem. Gov.'s Adv. Panel on Telecommunications; bd. governing trustees Am. Ballet Theatre; bd. dirs. U.S. Nat. Com., World Energy Conf.; mem. Fin. Adv. Bd. Pitkin County (Colo). Mem. Am. Econ. Assn., Am. Statis. Assn., Nat. Assn. Bus. Economists, So. Econ. Assn., Japan Soc., Phi Beta Kappa Assos., Phi Beta Kappa. Author: Selected Antitrust Cases: Landmark Decisions. Contbr. articles in econ. field. Home: PO Box 1008 Aspen CO 81612 Office: 126 E 56th St New York NY 10022

STEMMER, JAY JOHN, safety engineer, consultant; b. Wilkes-Barre, Pa., Apr. 29, 1939. BSCE, N.J. Inst. Tech., 1962; MBA, Calif. State U., Long Beach, 1969. Registered profl. engr., Calif.; cert. safety profl.; cert. hazard control mgmt. Engr. Factory Mut., N.J., 1973-77; cons. McKay & Assoc., Calif., 1977-81, Index Research, Calif., 1981-83, Fireman's Fund, Calif., 1983-85, AIG Cons., Calif., 1985-87; sr. cons. Argonaut, Calif., 1987—; assoc. prof. Sierra Coll., Los Angeles, 1979-80. Author: Medical Manual of Industrial Toxicology, 1965, Latin America, A Study of Air Transport Development and Potential in the Decade Ahead, 1970. Served to lt. USAF, 1962-65. Mem. NSPE, CSPE, Am. Soc. Safety Engrs., Am. Risk and Ins. Assn., Bd. Motion Pictures and TV Engrs., Screen Actors Guild, Actors Equity, AFTRA. Home: 1517 E Garfield Ave #84 Glendale CA 91205

STEMMER, NATHAN, philosopher and psycholinguist; b. June 14, 1925; s. Salomon and Ana (Lustig) S.; m. Ester Frydman, 1951; children—Jacob, Yoel, Shlomo. M.Sc., Hebrew U., Jerusalem, 1967, Ph.D., 1973. Lectr. Tel Aviv U., Israel, 1967-69; lectr. Bar Ilan U., Ramat Gan, Israel, 1969-75, sr. lectr. dept. philosophy, 1976—; mem. reading com. Jour. Child Lang., Cambridge, Eng., 1974-78; mem. adv. bd. Cambridge Ctr. for Behavioral Studies, Mass., 1985-88. Author: An Empiricist Theory of Language Acquisition, 1973; The Roots of Knowledge, 1983. Contbr. chpts. to books, numerous articles to profl. publs. Mem. Philosophy of Sci. Assn., Am. Philos. Assn., Assn. Study Child Lang., Internat. Soc. Applied Psycholinguistics. Home: 9 Diskin St, Jerusalem Israel Office: Bar Ilan Univ, Dept Philosophy, Ramat Gan Israel

STEMMY, THOMAS JOSEPH, accountant, educator, writer; b. Shenandoah, Pa., July 29, 1938; s. Thomas W. and Jean C. (Shemansky) S.; B.S. in Econs., Villanova U., 1960; M.Mgmt. Sci., Nat. Grad. U., 1977; m. Linda B. Cook, June 9, 1962; 1 dau., Lynn M. Fed. tax auditor IRS, Washington, 1960-63, rep. in pub. relations programs, 1961-63; tax auditor D.C. Govt., Washington, 1963; accountant, tax adviser T.J. Stemmy & Co., College Park, Md., 1963-73, Stemmy, Tidler & Co., College Park, 1973—; instr. U. Md., College Park, 1973—, faculty coordinator U. Md.-Univ. Coll. Coop. Edn. Program, 1982—; instr. fed. taxation Prince George's Community Coll., 1974-76; dir. Lakewood Harbor Estates, Inc., Fredericksburg, Va. Campaign mgr. for Mayor of College Park, 1968; mem. Md. Crime Investigating Commn., 1976; treas. Prince Georges County Cleanup Com., 1967-72; pres. College Park Bd. of Trade, 1971; mem. Am. Security Council, 1971; mem. Estate Planning Council Prince George's County, 1975; mem. Md. Ednl. Found., 1975-76; tchr. Confraternity Christian Doctrine, St. Matthias Ch.; basketball coach Lanham (Md.) Boys' Club, 1980. Served with AUS, 1960-66. Recipient Key to the City award College Park, 1971; C.P.A., Md., D.C. Mem. Md. Soc. C.P.A.'s, Md. State Sheriffs Assn., Md. State Toboggan Team Assn. (chmn. 1975), Am. Legion, Gamma Phi. Republican. Roman Catholic. Clubs: Kiwanis, Elks. Home: 9532 Elvis Ln Seabrook MD 20801 Office: 7338 Baltimore Ave College Park MD 20740

STEMPEL, ERNEST EDWARD, insurance executive; b. N.Y.C., May 10, 1916; s. Frederick Christian and Leah Lillian S.; m. Phyllis Brooks; children: Diana Brooks, Calvin Pinkcomb, Neil Frederick, Robert Russell. A.B., Manhattan Coll., 1938; LL.B., Fordham U., 1946; LL.M., NYU, 1949, D.J.S., 1951; LL.D. (hon.), Manhattan Coll., 1986. Bar: N.Y. 1946. With Am. Internat. Underwriters Corp., N.Y.C., 1938-53; v.p., dir. Am. Internat. Co. Ltd., Hamilton, Bermuda, 1953-63; chmn. bd. Am. Internat. Co. Ltd., 1963—; chmn., dir. Am. Internat. Assurance Co. (Bermuda) Ltd., Am. Internat. Reins. Co. Ltd., Bermuda; pres., dir. Am. Internat. Comml. Co. Inc., Bermuda; Sr. adviser mem. exec. com., dir. Am. Internat. Group Inc.; dir. C.V. Starr & Co. Inc., N.Y.C.; pres., dir. Starr Internat. Co. Inc.; dir. Am. Life Ins. Co., Wilmington, Del., Am. Internat. Life Ins. Co., P.R., La Interamericana (S.A.), Mexico, Mt. Mansfield Co., Inc., Stowe, Vt., Seguros Venezuela (C.A.), Caracas; chmn., dir. Australian Am. Assurance Co., Ltd., Am. Internat. Assurance Co. Ltd., Hong Kong; chmn. bd., dir. Philippine Am. Ins. Cos., Manila; dir. Am. Internat. Underwriters (Latin Am.), Inc., Bermuda, Am. Internat. Underwriters Mediterranean, Inc., Bermuda; Del. Am. Life Ins. Co., Wilmington, Pacific Union Assurance Co., Calif., Underwriters Adjustment Co., Panama. Served to lt. (s.g.) USNR, 1942-46. Mem. Am. Bar Assn., N.Y. State Bar. Clubs: Marco Polo (N.Y.C.), Royal Bermuda Yacht (Bermuda), Mid-Ocean (Bermuda), Coral Beach (Bermuda), Riddell's Bay Golf and Country (Bermuda). Office: Am Internat Co Ltd, PO Box HM 152, Hamilton HM AX, Bermuda

STENDAHL, BRITA KRISTINA, writer; b. Stockholm, Jan. 10, 1925; d. Johan Viktor and Olga Kristina Ingeborg (Normann) Johnsson; m. Krister Stendahl, Sept. 7, 1946; children: Johan, Anna, Daniel. Teol. kand, U. Uppsala, 1949, Fil kand, 1954, Fil dr hc, 1981. Tchr. high sch. Uppsala, Sweden, 1949-54; lectr. Scandinavian program, extension courses and freshman seminars, Harvard U., Cambridge, Mass., 1956-72, Boston Coll., Newton, Mass., 1972-73; freelance writer 1973—; sec. Cultural Inst. Ch. of Sweden, 1984—. Author:Søren Kierkegaard: An Analysis of His Aestetic Works, 1976, Sabbatical Reflections, 1979, The Force of Tradition, 1984, Att se och betrakta, 1988; contbr. numerous articles and revs. to profl. publs.; translator. Bd. dirs. Swedish Council for Planning and Coordination Research, 1986—. Radcliffe Inst. fellow, 1961-63. Mem. Arstasallskapet for Fredika Bremer-Studier (chmn. 1985—), Assn. Concerned With Devel. in Third World (bd. dirs. 1985—). Mem. Democratic Party. Lutheran. Home: Artillerig 30, 11451 Stockholm Sweden

STENEHJEM, LELAND MANFORD, banker; b. Arnegard, N.D., May 25, 1918; s. Odin N. and Lillie (Moe) S.; m. Judith H. Johnson, July 21, 1944; children—Leland Manford, Stephen Leslie, Joan Marie. B.S., N.D. State U., 1941; grad., U. Wis. Grad. Sch. Banking, 1948. With First Internat. Bank, Watford City, N.D., 1943—; exec. v.p. First Internat. Bank, 1961-66, pres., 1966—; chmn. State Bank Burleigh County, Bismarck, N.D., 1973—, First Nat Bank of Fessenden, N.D., 1983—; Mem. N.D. Banking Bd., 1958-63; mem. N.D. adv. council Farmers Home Adminstrn., 1957-60; bd. dirs. N.D. State U. Found. Pres. Good Shepherd Home, 1963—; Bd. dirs. N.D. State U. Alumni Assn., Greater N.D. Assn. Served as 2d lt. USMCR, World War II. Mem. Am. Bankers Assn. (past mem. exec. council), N.D. Bankers Assn. (past pres.), Ind. Bankers Assn. Am. (past pres.), Watford City Assn., Commerce (pres.), Alpha Tau Omega. Lutheran. Lodges: Mason, Elk, Lion (pres. Watford City), Rotarian (pres.), Shriners. Home: 100 SW 4th St Watford City ND 58854 Office: 100 N Main St Watford City ND 58854

STENFLO, CARL LENNART, physicist; b. Eksjö, Sweden, Nov. 27, 1939; s. Karl Daniel and Signe Ella (Röden) S.; children: Anna, Örjan, Daniel; m. Karin Elmhed, Aug. 16, 1987. Ph.D., Uppsala U., 1968. Prof. plasma physics Umeå U., 1971—. Contbr. articles to sci. jours. Home: Öbackav 6F, 902 44 Umeå Sweden Office: Umeå Univ, Dept Plasma Physics, 901 87 Umeå Sweden

STENNIS, JOHN CORNELIUS, senator; b. Kemper County, Miss., Aug. 3, 1901; s. Hampton Howell and Cornelia (Adams) S.; m. Coy Hines, Dec. 24, 1929 (dec.); children: John Hampton, Margaret Jane (Mrs. Womble). B.S., Miss. State U., 1923; LL.B., U. Va., 1928; LL.D., Millsaps Coll., 1957, U. Wyo., 1962, Miss. Coll., 1969, Belhaven Coll., 1972, William Carey Coll., 1975, Livingston U., 1984. Bar: Miss. Practiced in DeKalb, Miss.; mem. Miss. Ho. of Reps., 1928-32; dist. pros. atty. 16th Jud. Dist., 1931-37; circuit judge 1937-47; mem. U.S. Senate from Miss., 1947—, mem. armed services com., chmn. appropriations com.; pres. pro tempore U.S. Senate, 1987—. Active in promotion farm youth tng. programs; state chmn. Miss. 4-H Adv. Council. Mem. ABA, Miss. Bar Assn., Phi Alpha Delta, Phi Beta Kappa, Alpha Chi Rho. Presbyn. (deacon). Clubs: Mason, Lion. Office: 205 Russell Senate Bldg Washington DC 20510

STENSTROM, KARL GUNNAR, international manufacturing executive; b. Goteborg, Sweden, Feb. 23, 1946; arrived in Switzerland, 1987; s. Carl G. and Annie Stenstrom; m. Christina Goransson; children: Natasha, Christian, Tanya. BA, Goteborg Comml. Coll., 1967. Dist. mgr. Facit Inc., Secaucus, N.J., 1968-69; nat. sales mgr. Facit SA, Sao Paulo, Brazil, 1969-72; gen. mgr. A.M. Corp., Sao Paulo, Brazil, 1972-75; pres. Suveca-Electrolux Venezuela, Caracas, 1975-81, Swedish Match Latin Am., Coral Gables, Fla., 1981-87; pres., chief exec. officer lighter div. Swedish Match Corp., Nyon, Switzerland, 1987—; vice chmn. Cricket SA, Lyon, France, Cia Chilena de Fosforos, Santiago, Chile; bd. dirs. Cricket de Mexico, Feudor, Paris., Wilkinsson Sword. Lutheran. Home: 7 Chemin des Frenes, CH-1295 Geneva Switzerland Office: Swedish Match Consumer Goods, 5 Chemin du Canal, CH-1260 Nyon Switzerland

STENSTROP, ERNEST, architect; b. Chgo., Mar. 29, 1927; s. Carl Peter and Emma Fredericka (Jensen) S.; m. Lois L. Lavelle, May 9, 1953; m. Margaret K. Ewald, Dec. 4, 1971; children—Linda Sue, Leslie Ann, Victoria Kay, Janet. B.A., U. Ill., 1951. Designer, Chgo. Park Dist., 1953-64; designer, project mgr. Lawrence Monberg Assoc., Archtl. Engring. Cons., Kenosha, Wis., 1964-65; project mgr. A.M. Kinney Assoc. Inc., archtl. engring. cons., Skokie, Ill., 1965-68; project mgr. real estate and constrn. div. IBM Corp., Chgo., 1968-77, project mgr. real estate and constrn. div. IBM Corp., Atlanta, 1977—; co-founder, pres. Apparel Care Ctr., Inc., 1984—. Served with U.S. Army, 1945-47. Mem. AIA, Nat. Corp. Architects Com. Lodge: Masons. Archtl. works: Farm in the Zoo, Lincoln Park, Chgo.; Garfield Park Conservatory, Chgo.; Ott Chem. Co. Complex, Muskegon, Mich.; Merrimac Park Fieldhouse, Chgo.; Space Planner for numerous IBM Bldgs., Madison, Wis., Des Moines, South Bend, Ind., Lexington, Ky., Little Rock, Ark., Memphis, Metairie, La., Raleigh, N.C., Tulsa, Okla. Lutheran. Home: 455 Hackberry Ln Roswell GA 30076

STEPANEK, JOSEPH EDWARD, industrial development consultant; b. Ellinwood, Kans., Oct. 29, 1917; s. Joseph August and Leona Mae (Wilson) S.; m. Antoinette Farnham, June 10, 1942; children: Joseph F., James B., Antoinette L., Debra L. BSChemE, U. Colo., 1939; DEng in Chem. Engring., Yale U., 1942. Registered profl. engr., Colo. Engr. Stearns-Roger Mfg., Denver, 1939-45; from asst. to assoc. prof. U. Colo., Boulder, 1945-47; from cons. to dir. UN, various countries, 1947-73; cons. internat. indsl devel., U.S.-China bus. relations Boulder, 1973—; bd. dirs. 12 corps., 1973—. Author 3 books on indsl. devel.; contbr. 50 articles to profl. jours. Exec. dir. Boulder Tomorrow, 1965-67. Recipient Yale Engring. award Yale Engring. Assn., 1957, Norlin award U. Colo. 1978, Annual award India League of Am., 1982. Mem. AAAS. Democrat. Unitarian. Club: Yale (N.Y.C.). Home: 1622 High St Boulder CO 80302

STEPHAN, BODO, manufacturing company executive; b. Berlin, Mar. 9, 1939; s. Hans-Werner and Ilse Charlotte (Kretschmann) S.; m. Ingrid-Maria Seeger, Apr. 1, 1942; children: Viola-Dorothee, Katharina-Marguerite. Doctor's degree, U. Cologne, Fed. Republic Germany, 1966. Admitted to Bar, Berlin. Asst. prof. U. Berlin and Cologne, 1963-69; head sales mgr. F. Meyer Steelworks, Dinslaken, Fed. Republic Germany, 1970-73; div. mgr. AEG-Telefunken, Springe/Hannover, Fed. Republic Germany, 1974-80; sr. mgr. internat. div. AEG Cables, Moenchengladbach, 1980-82; chief exec. internat. ops. Krone AG, Berlin, 1983-85, chief exec. corp. controlling, 1986-87; mng. dir., major stockholder Kluessendorf AG, Berlin, 1988—, also bd. dirs. Author: Rechtsschutzbeduerfuis, 1966; contbr. articles to profl. jours. Consul ad honorem of Ecuador to Berlin. Fellow Assn. of C. of C., Berlin Industrialists Club, German Soc. Internat. Affairs, German Electronical Assn., Controllers Assn. Lutheran. Clubs: Club des Affaires, Econ. Politics Discussion Circle. Lodge: Kiwanis. Home: Am Hirschsprung 67, D-1000 Berlin 33 Federal Republic of Germany Office: Kluessendorf AG, Zitadellenweg 20 D-F, D-1000 Berlin 20 Federal Republic of Germany

STEPHAN, DENNIS EUGENE, infosystems professional; b. Big Spring, Tex., July 8, 1949; s. Eugene Dyer Stephan and Alta Mae (Claxton) Bart; 1 child, Danita Carol. BS in Indsl. Engring., U. Tex., Arlington, 1975; MS in Systems Mgmt., U. So. Calif., 1984; postgrad., Kans. State U., 1987-88. Commd. U.S. Army, 1975, advanced through grades to capt.; adminstrv. officer U.S. Army, Ft. Riley, Kans., 1977; mgr. database U.S. Army, Ft. Riley, 1977-80; data processing mgr. U.S. Army, Bremen, Fed. Republic Germany, 1980-83; automation mgmt. officer U.S. Army, Ft. Riley, 1983-84, info. ctr. mgr., 1985-86, info. services mgr., 1987; resigned U.S. Army, 1987; plans mgr. Directorate Info. Mgmt., Ft. Jackson, S.C., 1987—; chmn. Info. Mgmt. Users Group, Kans., 1983-85, Info. Systems Control Bd., S.C., 1988—; microcomputer cons. Tex. and Kans., 1983-87; info. systems cons., 1984-87. Devel. ednl. software, 1987. Mem. Assn. Computing Machinery. Home: 3611 Ranch Rd Apt 24-2 Columbia SC 29206 Office: Directorate Info Mgmt ATZJ-IM-RM Fort Jackson SC 29207-6010

STEPHAN, JEAN-YVES, ophthalmologist; b. Nantes, France, Mar. 7, 1939; divorced; 3 children. Degree in Medicine, Faculty Medicine Nantes, 1971. Examining ophthalmologist St. Nazaire (France) Hosp., 1974; practice medicine specializing in ophthalmology Nantes. Office: St Nazaire Hosp, 18 Ave de la Republique, 44600 Saint-Nazaire France

STEPHAN, JOHN JASON, historian, educator; b. Chgo., Mar. 8, 1941; s. John Walter and Ruth (Walgreen) S.; m. Barbara Ann Brooks, June 22, 1963. B.A., Harvard U., 1963, M.A., 1964; Ph.D., U. London, 1969. Research assoc. Social Sci. Center, Waseda U., Tokyo, 1969-70; mem. faculty U. Hawaii, Honolulu, 1970—; prof. history U. Hawaii, 1977—, chmn. E. Asian studies program, 1973-74, dir. program on Soviet Union in Pacific-Asia region, 1986—; research prof. Japan Found.; fellow U. Hokkaido, 1976-77; vis. prof. Inst. of Far East, Moscow, 1982, Inst. Econ. Research, Khabarovsk, USSR, 1982-83, Stanford U., 1986, Kennan Inst. for Advanced Studies, 1987; adj. research assoc. East-West Ctr., 1988—; disting. lectr. Fletcher Sch. of Law & Diplomacy Tufts U., 1986—. Author: Sakhalin: A History, 1971, The Kuril Islands: Russo-Japanese Frontier in the Pacific, 1974, The Russian Fascists, 1978, Hawaii Under the Rising Sun, 1984; Soviet-American Horizons on the Pacific, 1986. Sr. assoc. mem. St. Antony's Coll., Oxford (Eng.) U., 1977; Bd. dirs. Library Internat. Relations, Chgo., 1976-87; Hawaii rep. U.S.-Japan Friendship Commn., 1980-83. Fulbright fellow, 1967-68; Asia Found. grantee, 1974. Mem. Am. Assn. Advancement Slavic Studies, AAUP, Assn. Asian Studies, Authors Guild, Internat. House of Japan. Address: 4334 Round Top Dr Honolulu HI 96822

STEPHANY, URSULA KLARA JOHANNA, linguist, educator; b. Aachen, Fed. Republic Germany, June 30, 1937; d. Johannes and Johanna (Lahaye) S. Degree, U. Cologne, Fed. Republic Germany, 1963, PhD, 1969; degree, Ministry of Edn., Fed. Republic Germany, 1965; lic., U. Paris, Sorbonne, 1967. Research asst. Research Ctr. for Lang. Scis., Bloomington, Ind., 1965-66; tchr. lang. Staatl. Studienkolleg U. Cologne, 1966-70, Staal. Ingenieurschule, Cologne, 1967-68; asst. U. Cologne Dept. Linguistics, 1968-70, prof., 1972—. Author: Adjektivische Attributkonstruktionen, 1970, Aspekt, Temput, und Modalität, 1985; contbr. articles to profl. jours. Grantee Heinrich-Hertz-Stiftung, Düsseldorf, 1965-66, Am. Council Learned Socs., Wasington, 1966, Deutsche Forschungsgemeinschaft, Bonn, Fed. Republic Germany, 1977-78. Mem. Linguistic Soc. Am., Societas Linguistica Europaea, Deutsche Gesellschaft für Sprachwissenschaft. Office: U Cologne, Inst Sprachwissenschaft, 5000 Cologne 41 Federal Republic of Germany

STEPHEN, JOHN ERLE, lawyer, consultant; b. Eagle Lake, Tex., Sept. 24, 1918; s. John Earnest and Vida Thrall (Klein) S.; m. Gloria Yzaguirre, May 16, 1942; children: Vida Leslie Stephen Renzi, John Lauro Kurt. JD, U. Tex., 1941; postgrad. in internat. law, U. Mex., Northwestern U., 1942; postgrad., U.S. Naval Acad. Postgrad. Sch., 1944; grad. in internat. law, U.S. Naval War Coll., 1945. Bar: Tex. 1946, U.S. Supreme Ct. 1955, D.C. 1956, Mich. 1981. Gen. mgr. Sta. KOPY, Houston, 1946; gen. atty., exec. asst. to pres. Tex. Star Corp., Houston, 1947-50; ptnr. Hofheinz & Stephen, Houston, 1950-57; v.p., gen. counsel TV Broadcasting Co., Tex. Radio Corp., Gulf Coast Network, Houston, 1953-57; spl. counsel, exec. asst. to mayor City of Houston, 1953-56; spl. counsel Houston C. of C., 1953-56; v.p., gen. counsel Air Transp. Assn. Am., Washington, 1958-71, Amway Corp., Ada, Mich., 1972-83; cons. Austin, Tex., 1983—; chief protocol City of Houston, 1953-56; advisor Consulates Gen. of Mex., San Antonio, Houston, New Orleans, Washington, 1956-66; advisor Aviation Industry Employees Investment Fund, 1960-68; vis. lectr. Harvard U. Grad. Sch. Bus., Washington Fgn. Law Soc., Pacific Agribus. Conf.; cons. in field; mem., advisor U.S. Diplomatic Dels. to Treaty Confs. and U.S. Orgns., 1964-72. Author, editor in field. Bd. dirs. Houston Mus. Fine Arts, 1953-57, Contemporary Arts Assn., 1953-57, Tex. Transp. Inst., 1964-72. Served to comdr. USNR, 1941-46; mem. staff Supreme Allied Command, NATO, 1952. Mem. ABA (past chmn., mem. council, sect. public utility law), Am. Law Inst., World Peace Through Law Ctr. (past chmn. internat. aviation law com.), Fed. Bar Assn., D.C. Bar, State Bar Tex., State Bar Mich., FCC Bar Assn., Assn. ICC Practitioners, Am. Judicature Soc.; hon. mem. fgn. law socs. Clubs: Internat., Explorers, Houston Polo, Lakeshore, Saddle and Cycle, Breakfast, Nat. Aviation, Execs., Ky. Cols. Home: 6904 Ligustrum Cove Austin TX 78750

STEPHEN, NINIAN MARTIN, governor-general Australia; b. Oxford, Eng., June 15, 1923; s. Frederick and Barbara (Cruickshank) S.; LL.B., U. Melbourne, 1949; m. Valery Mary Sinclair, June 4, 1949; children—Mary, Ann, Sarah, Jane, Elizabeth. Called to Victoria bar, 1952, created queen's counsel, 1966; judge Victorian Supreme Ct., 1970-72; justice High Ct. of Australia, 1972-82; privy councillor, 1979; gov.-gen. of Australia, 1982—; dep. chancellor U. Melbourne, 1980-82. Served with Australian Army, 1941-46. Decorated AK, GCMG, GCVO, KBE, KStJ. Address: Government House, Canberra Australia *

STEPHEN, RICHARD JOSEPH, oral and maxillofacial surgeon; b. Joliet, Ill., Jan. 2, 1945; s. Joseph E. and Marcella M. (Pearson) S.; m. Jacqueline H. Thom, Aug. 5, 1967; children: Anne, Susan, George. Student, Lewis U., Lockport, Ill., 1962-65; DDS, Loyola U., Chgo., 1969; Cert. in Oral and Maxillofacial Surgery, Loyola U., Maywood, Ill., 1972. Practice dentistry specializing in oral and maxillofacial surgery Mt. Vernon, Ill., 1972—; cons. Ill. Cancer Council, Chgo., 1979—; Centralia (Ill.) Correctional Facility, 1980—, Vandalia (Ill.) Correctional Facility, 1980—. Fellow Am. Coll. Stomatologic Surgeons, Am. Soc. Oral and Maxillofacial Surgeons, Am. Dental Soc. of Anesthesiology, Internat. Assn. Oral Surgery, Internat. Assn. Maxillofacial Surgery. Lodges: Lions, Elks. Home: Rt #5 Box 226 Mount Vernon IL 62864 Office: 2413 Broadway Box 582 Mount Vernon IL 62864

STEPHEN, ROBERT FORRESTER, aviation company executive; b. Glasgow, Scotland, Jan. 25, 1926; s. Henry Brown Torrie and Mary Forrester (Gillchrist) S.; m. Jill Amabel Tod, Sept. 20, 1972; children—Andrew Henry, Robert Michael. B.Sc., St. Andrews U., 1952. Dir., Bristol Aeroplane Co., Melbourne, Australia, 1954-60; founder, mng. dir. Forrester Stephen Pl, Melbourne, 1960-74; mng. dir. Roband Engring. Distbrs., Melbourne, 1974—; dir. Eaglemont St. Ronans P.L., Melbourne, Melbourne Mail Order Pty. Ltd. Served as test pilot RAF, 1944-48. Presbyterian. Clubs: Commonwealth (Canberra); Naval and Military (Melbourne). Avocation: painting. Home: 22 Canberra Rd, Toorak Victoria 3412, Australia Office: Roband Engring Distributors, 1 Yarra Bank Rd, South Melbourne 3205, Australia

STEPHEN, SAMUEL JEYARAJA, cardiothoracic surgeon; b. Udugama, Galle, Sri Lanka, June 17, 1929; s. Thambipillai Rasiah and Grace Thangaratnam (Samuel) S.; m. Benitta Eugene Ferdinand, Oct. 25, 1967; children: Marie Priyanthie, Raviraj Ferdinand. Grad., U. London, 1947, U. Ceylon, 1955. Resident Health Services Clinic, Colombo, 1955-60; surgeon Thoracic Unit, Jaffna, Sri Lanka, 1963-67, Ratnapura, Sri Lanka, 1968-70; surgeon Gen. Hosp., Colombo, Sri Lanka, 1971—; tchr., examiner in anatomy, surgery and chest diseases Postgrad. Med. Sch. U. Colombo, 1974—; Hunterian prof. Royal Coll. Surgeons, London, 1987. Author clin. research papers in field. Recipient Distng. Citizen award Pres. Sri Lanka, 1987. Fellow Am. Coll. Cardiologists, Royal Coll. Surgeons, Ceylon Coll. Physicians (hon.); mem. Sri Lanka Med. Assn. (pres. 1986), Sri Lanka Coll. Surgeons (pres. 1988—), Gastroent. Soc. (mem. council 1987). Methodist. Lodges: Lions (host), Bonnie Doon. Home: 26 Gunasekera Ln, Borella, Colombo 8 Sri Lanka Office: Gen Hosp, Regent St, Colombo 7 Sri Lanka

STEPHENS, CHARLES WILLIAM, aerospace consultant, electronic engineer; b. Liberal, Kans., July 26, 1930; s. Ernest Virgil and Thelma Dorleska (Keating) S.; m. Mary B. Hoofnagle, Aug. 31, 1952; children—Craig A., Cathy J., Kirk M. B.S.E.E., U. Kans., Lawrence, 1952; postgrad. engring. studies, Bell Telephone Labs., N.Y.C., 1953-54. Mem. tech. staff Bell Telephone Labs. Inc., Whippany, N.J., 1953-54; v.p., dep. gen. mgr. Electronics & Def. Sector, TRW Inc., Redondo Beach, Calif., 1957-86, aerospace consultant, 1986—; mem. adv. bd. dept. elec. and computer engring. U. Kans., 1980—, chmn. adv. bd. Sch. Engring., 1981—; mem. bd. counselors sch. engring., U. So. Calif.; chmn. telecommunications and computer applications bd. Nat. Research Council, 1988—. Bd. mgrs. Torrance-South Bay Area YMCA, Calif., 1982; mem. Rolling Hills Covenant Ch., Calif., 1984—. Served with U.S. Army, 1954-56; Army Ballistic Missile Agy. Mem. Nat. Acad. Engring., AIAA, IEEE, Electronic Industries Assn. (bd. govs. 1983-86, bd. dirs. gov. div. 1983-86), Am. Men and Women of Sci., Sigma Xi, Sigma Pi Sigma, Eta Kappa Nu, Tau Beta Pi, Sigma Tau. Home: 2707 W 233 St Torrance CA 90505

STEPHENS, EDWARD CARL, university dean, writer; b. Los Angeles, July 27, 1924; s. Carl Edward and Helen Mildred (Kerner) S.; children: Edward, Sarah, Matthew. A.B., Occidental Coll., 1947; M.S., Northwestern U., 1955. Advt. exec. Dancer-Fitzgerald-Sample Inc., N.Y.C., 1955-64; prof. Medill Sch. Journalism, Northwestern U., Evanston, Ill., 1964-76; prof., chmn. dept. advt. S.I. Newhouse Sch. Pub. Communications, Syracuse U., N.Y., 1976-80, dean, 1980—; cons. Foote, Cone & Belding Communications. Author: (novels) A Twist of Lemon, 1958, One More Summer, 1960, Blow Negative!, 1962, Roman Joy, 1965, A Turn in the Dark Wood, 1968, The Submariner, 1974. Mem. George Polk Awards Com. Served as destroyer officer USN, 1943-46, PTO; served as sumbmarine officer USN, 1950-53, Atlantic; served as capt. USNR, 1968. Decorated Purple Heart. Mem. Am. Acad. Advt. (pres. 1976-77), Assn. Edn. Journalism and Mass Communication, Authors League, Nat. Acad. TV Arts and Scis. Episcopalian. Office: Syracuse U SI Newhouse Sch Pub Communications Syracuse NY 13210

STEPHENS, KENNETH DEAN, JR., communications executive; b. Logan, Utah, Dec. 8, 1942; s. Kenneth Dean and Dorothy Clara (Hoffler) S.; student U. Utah, 1961-63, Union Grad. Sch., Cin., 1988—; m. Julia E. Acevedo, Oct. 11, 1980; children—Trina Ridvan, Nick Jalal. Staff engr. Sta. KLOR-TV, Provo, Utah and Sta. KLRJ-TV, Las Vegas, Nev., 1958-61; chief engr. Sta. KUER-FM, Salt Lake City, and Sta. KOET-TV, Ogden, Utah, 1961-63; dir. TV research U. Utah, 1964-67; pres. Electronic Research Corp., Salt Lake City, 1968-71; mgr. Tele-San Juan, Inc, owner Sta. WTSJ-TV, San Juan, P.R., Sta. WPSJ-TV, Ponce, P.R. and Sta. WMGZ-TV, Mayaguez, P.R., 1970-74; pres. Broadcast Devels. Internat., St. Just, P.R., 1974-81; v.p. R&D, Focus Communications, Inc., Nashville, 1981-87; pres. The Vanguard Corp., 1987—. Broadcast cons. Universal House of Justice, Baha'i World Ctr., Haifa, Israel; designer Baha'i radio Stas., S.Am., Africa, U.S.; cons. for UN Sci. activities Baha'i Internat. Community (New York); prof. devel. communication Amoz Gibson Ctr., P.R. Author Lic. 1st class radiotelephone operator FCC. Mem. Am. Wind Energy Assn., PV Info. and Edn. Assn., Internat. Baha'i Audio-Visual Ctr., Soc. Broadcast Engrs., Internat. Inst. Communications. Baha'i. Patentee video rec., color TV projection, radar glasses for blind, color TV system, TV transmission, TV encryption/decryption system, direct broadcast satellite antenna, gated impulse modulator; developed color TV system used by NASA manned spacecraft. Office: HCO2 Box 14765 Arecibo PR 00612

STEPHENS, LARRY RALPH, history educator, publisher; b. Council Bluffs, Iowa, Nov. 10, 1940; s. Ralph L. and Agnes Leona (Fitzsimmons) S.; m. Betty Jean Tally, Aug. 29, 1965; children—Tally Jill, Libby Gail, Tyler Lane. B.A. in Ministry, Nebr. Christian Coll., Norfolk, 1964, B.Theology, 1964; M.A. in History, Fort Hays Kans. State Coll., 1968. Instr. history Northeast Mo. State U., Kirksville, 1968-73, asst. prof., 1974—; pub. Lancaster Excelsior Newspapers, Mo., 1980—. Author: Long Branch Lake Historical Resources: A History, 1975. Bd. dirs. Mo. Com. Humanities, NEH, 1984—, sec. 1986-87. Mem. Am. Hist. Assn., Am. Assn. State and Local History, Campus Vols. of Kirksville. Democrat. Mem. Christian Ch. Lodges: Masons, Rotary. Avocations: acting, gardening, raising Bantam chickens. Home: Route 2 Box 304A Kirksville MO 63501 Office: NE Mo State U Social Sci Dept Kirksville MO 63501

STEPHENS, LOWNDES FREDERICK, journalism educator; b. Frankfort, Ky., Sept. 27, 1945; s. James Willis and Harriet Connally (Barton) S.; m. Sally Lanier Smith, June 15, 1968; children—Sally Randolph, John Brent. B.A. in Econs., U. Ky., 1967, M.A. in Communications, 1969; Ph.D., U. Wis., 1975. Publs. officer Ky. div. Devel. Info., Frankfort, 1968-69; research economist Spindletop Research, Inc., Lexington, Ky., 1969-72; content research writer Ky. Ednl. TV Found., Lexington, 1972; editor Lake Superior project Inst. Environ. Studies, U. Wis.-Madison, 1972-74; dir. Communications Research Ctr., asst. prof. U. N.D., 1974-76; assoc. prof., prof. Coll. Journalism U. S.C., Columbia, 1976—; cons. Dept. Def., Am. Newspaper Pubs. Assn., U.S. Office Edn., CPC Internat.; faculty cons. Army Command and Gen. Staff Coll., 1979—; mem. nat. adv. panel George Polk Awards. Nat. Adv. bd., Am. Vets. Com., 1979—. Served to lt. col. USAR, 1985—. Rockefeller Found. grantee U. Wis., 1972-74. Fellow Inter-U. Seminar Armed Forces and Soc.; mem. AAUP, Internat. Communication Assn., Assn. Edn. Journalism and Mass Communications (chmn. internat. communication div., 1978-79, head Mass Communication and Soc. div. 1986-87), Am. Sociol. Assn., Assn. Consumer Research, So. Assn. Pub. Opinion Research, Sigma Delta Chi, Omicron Delta Kappa, Omicron Delta Epsilon, Kappa Tau Alpha. Democrat. Methodist. Editorial bd. World Press Ency., Pub. Relations Quar., Newspaper Research Jour. Contbr. articles to profl. jours. Home: 443 Brookshire Dr Columbia SC 29210 Office: U SC Coll Journalism Columbia SC 29208

STEPHENS, NORVAL BLAIR, JR., marketing consultant; b. Chgo., Nov. 20, 1928; s. Norval Blair and Ethel Margaret (Lewis) S.; m. Diane Forst, Sept. 29, 1951; children: Jill E., John G., Sandra J. (dec.), Katherine B., James N. B.A., DePauw U., 1951; M.B.A., U. Chgo., 1959. Asst. to v.p. ops. Walgreen Drug Co., Chgo., 1953-56; with Needham, Harper Worldwide (formerly Needham, Harper & Steers), Chgo., 1956-86; v.p. Needham, Harper Worldwide (formerly Needham, Harper & Steers), 1964-70, sr. v.p., 1970-72, exec. v.p. internat., 1972-74; exec. v.p., mng. dir. Needham, Harper Worldwide (formerly Needham, Harper & Steers), N.Y.C., 1974-75; exec. v.p. Chgo. office Needham, Harper & Steers, 1975-82, exec. v.p. internat., 1982-86; also dir.; pres. Deltacom, N.Y.C., 1971-76; pres. Norval Stephens Co., 1987—. Mem. Pelham (N.Y.) Bd. Edn., 1972-75; bd. advisors Barrington Area Arts Council, 1985-86, bd. dirs. 1987; trustee Village of Arlington Heights, Ill., 1961-65; commr., chmn. Plan Commn. Arlington Heights, 1965-67; trustee Meml. Library, Arlington Heights, 1966-67, Arlington Heights United Fund, 1963-67; bd. dirs. Lake Forest (Ill.) Children's Home, 1966-67, N.W. Community Hosp. Found., Arlington Heights, 1976—, vice chmn., 1987—; bd. dirs. Harper Coll. Ednl. Found., Palatine, Ill., 1977-86, pres., 1980-86; bd. dirs. Barrington Area Devel. Council, 1978—; bd. visitors, dir. alumni bd. DePauw U., 1979-83, pres., 1981-83, trustee, 1983—; exec. dir., Internat. Fedn. Advt. Agys., 1988—. Served with USMCR, 1951-53. Named Young Man of Year Arlington Heights Jaycees, 1964, Rector award DePauw U., 1976. Mem. Internat. Advt. Assn. (v.p. Midwest chpt. 1986-87), Am. Mgmt Assn., Am. Mktg. Assn., Chgo. Advt. Club, U. Chgo. Alumni Assn., DePauw U. Alumni Assn. (pres. 1977-79), Phi Beta Kappa, Delta Tau Delta (dir. Edn. Found. 1987—). Club: Larchmont Yacht. Home: 107 Fox Hunt Trail Barrington IL 60010 Office: 999 Plaza Dr Suite 400 Schaumburg IL 60173

STEPHENS, SIDNEY DEE, chemical manufacturing company executive; b. St. Joseph, Mo., Apr. 26, 1945; s. Lindsay Caldwell and Edith Mae (Thompson) S.; m. Ellen Marie Boeh, June 15, 1968 (div. 1973); m. 2d, Elizabeth Ann Harris, Sept. 22, 1973; 1 child, Laura Nicole. B.S., Mo. Western State U., 1971; M.A., U. Houston, 1980. Assoc. urban planner Met. Planning Commn., St. Joseph, Mo., 1967-71; prodn. acctg. assoc. Quaker Oats Co., St. Joseph, 1971-72, office mgr., personnel rep., Rosemont, Ill., 1972-73, employee and community relations mgr., New Brunswick, N.J., 1973-75, Pasadena, Tex., 1975-80; site personnel mgr. ICI Americas, Inc., Pasadena, Tex., 1980—; pvt. practice mgmt. cons., Houston, 1981—. Contbr. articles to profl. jours. Served with USNR, 1963-65. Mem. Am. Soc. Personnel Adminstrs., Houston Personnel Assn. (community and govtl. affairs com. 1984-85, 85-86). Republican. Methodist. Home: 16446 Longvale Dr Houston TX 77059 Office: ICI Americas Inc 5757 Underwood Rd Pasadena TX 77507

STEPHENS, SIMON DAFYDD GLYN, physician; b. Caerfyrddin, Dyfed, Wales, July 2, 1942; s. Thomas Glyn and Doris Keturah (Harry) S.; m. Janig Bodiou, July 21, 1970; children: Morwena, Erwan, Rhiannon. BSc, Charing Cross Hosp. Med. Sch. U. London, 1962, MBBS, 1965; MPhil, U. London, 1973; diploma in History of Medicine, Soc. of Apothecaries, London, 1980. Mem. Royal Coll. Physicians. Sci. staff mem. Med. Research Council Applied Psychology Unit and Nat. Physical Lab., Cambridge, Teddington, Eng., 1967-71; clin. research fellow Inst. of Sound and Vibration, Southampton, Eng., 1971-76; audiological medicine cons. Royal Nat. Throat, Nose and Ear Hosp., London, 1976-85; physician in charge Welsh Hearing Inst. Univ. Hosp. of Wales, Cardiff, 1986—; advisor Dept. Health and Social Security, London, 1986—; mem. Specialist Adv. Com. on Audiological Medicine, London, 1982—. Editor: Disorders of Auditory Function 2, 1976, Disorders With Defective Hearing, 1985, Adult Audiology, 1987, Measurement in Hearing and Balance, 1988. Sec. Celtic League, London, 1967-70. Recipient T.S. Littler prize British Soc. of Audiology, 1972, George Davey Howells Meml. prize in Otolangygology U. London, 1987. Mem. Internat. Assn. Physicians Audiology (sec. 1980-84), Internat. Soc. Audiology (asst. sec. gen. 1978—), British Assn. Audiological Physicians (sec. 1977-83, vice chmn. 1986—). Mem. Plaid Cymru Party. Home: Pen Y Bryn, Llan Faes, Llanilltud Fawr, De Morgannwg CF6 9XR, Wales Office: Welsh Hearing Inst, U Hosp Wales, Cardiff CF4 4XN, Wales

STEPHENS-BASSI, KAREN ANITA, manufacturing executive; b. Pasadena, Tex., Apr. 4, 1945; d. Patrick Kitchener and Francena (Ryan) McPearson; m. Phillip Von Stephens, Dec. 28, 1968 (div. Apr. 1981); m. Marco Vinicio Bassi, Dec. 3, 1984. BS, West Tex. State U., 1969, MFA, 1970. Cert. comml. investment mem. Tchr. Houston Ind. Sch. Dist., 1969-73, North Harris County Jr. Coll., Spring, Tex., 1973-76; instr. Market of Tex. Inc., Houston, 1976-79; v.p. Tecnomatic, Inc., Houston, 1979-81, chmn. bd., 1981-85; v.p., sec. bd. dirs. Mfrs. Group, Inc., Houston, 1981—; pres. Kaki Inc., San Leon, Tex. 1987—. Bd. dirs. Cultural Art Council of Houston, 1978-83. Mem. Instrument Soc. Am. Home: 3217 Iola Houston TX 77017 Office: Kaki Inc 1562 Railroad St San Leon TX 77539

STEPHENSON, ARTHUR EMMET, JR., investment company executive, banker; b. Bastrop, La., Aug. 29, 1945; s. Arthur Emmet and Edith Louise (Mock) S.; m. Toni Lyn Edwards, June 17, 1967. B.S. in Fin. magna cum laude, La. State U., 1967; M.B.A. (Ralph Thomas Sayles fellow), Harvard U., 1969. Chartered fin. analyst. Adminstrv. aide to U.S. Sen. Russell Long of La., Washington, 1966; security analyst Fidelity Funds, Boston, 1968; chmn. bd., pres. Stephenson & Co., Denver, 1969—, Stephenson Mcht. Banking Inc.; sr. ptnr. Stephenson Ventures, Stephenson Properties; chmn. bd. Charter Bank & Trust, Gen. Communications, Inc.; chmn. bd. dirs., pres. Circle Corp., Globescope Corp.; underwriting mem. Lloyd's of London; bd. dirs. Danaher Corp., River Oaks Industries, Inc., Satellink Corp., Signal Oilfield Services, Tex. Gas Transport Inc.; adv. bd. Thomas H. Lee Co. Fund, Captial Resource Ptnrs., L.P. adv. bd. Journ Bus. Venturing; pub. Denver Bus. Mag., Denver Mag., Vail Mag., Devel. Sales Catalog, Colo. Book. Mem. assocs. council Templeton Coll. at Oxford U., Eng.; mem. nat. steering com. Norman Rockwell Mus., Stockbridge, Mass.; past mem. Colo. small bus. council; mem. adv. bd. NYU Ctr. for Entrepeneurial Studies; del. White House Conf. Small Bus. Mem. Harvard Bus. Sch. Assn. (internat. pres.), Young Pres.'s Orgn. (dir. Inland Empire chpt. 1987—, membership chmn.-sec.-treas. 1988), Colo. Investment Advisers Assn. (treas., dir. 1975-76), Fin. Analysts Fedn., Denver Soc. Security Analysts (bd. dirs. 1975-77), Colo. Press Assn., Colo. Harvard Bus. Sch. Club (pres. 1979, chmn. 1980), Nat. Venture Capital Assn., Omicron Delta Kappa, Phi Kappa Phi, Beta Gamma Sigma, Kappa Sigma, Delta Sigma Pi. Clubs: Denver Press, Petroleum of Denver, Met. Denver Exec. (pres. 1979-80, chmn. 1980-81); Thunderbird Country (Rancho Mirage, Calif.); Annabel's (London); Harvard of N.Y., Harvard Bus. Sch. (N.Y.C., So. Calif., Orange County). Office: Stephenson & Co 100 Garfield St Denver CO 80206

STEPHENSON, IRENE HAMLEN, biorhythm analyst, consultant, editor, teacher; b. Chgo., Oct. 7, 1923; d. Charles Martin and Carolyn Hilda (Hilgers) Hamlin; m. Edgar B. Stephenson, Sr., Aug. 16, 1941 (div. 1946); 1 child, Edgar B. Author biorhythm compatibilities column Nat. Singles Register, Norwalk, Calif., 1979-81; instr. biorhythm Learning Tree Open U., Canoga Park, Calif., 1982-83; instr. biorhythm character analysis 1980—; instr. biorhythm compatibility, 1982—; owner, pres. matchmaking service Pen Pals Using Biorhythm, Chatsworth, Calif., 1979—; editor newsletter The Truth, 1979-85, Mini Examiner, Chatsworth, 1985—; researcher biorhythm character and compatibility, 1974—, selecting a mate, 1985—. Author: Learn Biorhythm Character Analysis, 1980; Do-It-Yourself Biorhythm Compatibilities, 1982; contbr. numerous articles to mags; frequent guests clubs, radio, TV. Office: Irene Hamlen Stephenson PO Box 3893 Chatsworth CA 91313

STEPHENSON, JOSEPH ELMER, surgeon; b. Pikeville, Ky., Oct. 3, 1917; s. Elmer D'Ester and Emabel (Bennett) S.; A.B., U. Ky., 1939; M.D., U. Louisville, 1942; m. Juanita Jeanice (Polly) Floyd, Dec. 30, 1939; children—Joseph Floyd, John Wesley, James Gibbs Rich. Diplomate Am. Bd. Surgery. Intern Charity Hosp. La., New Orleans, 1942-43; practice medicine, Elkhorn City, Ky., 1946-51; resident div. grad. medicine Tulane U. Med. Sch., 1951-54, fellow in gen. surgery Ochsner Found. Hosp. and Clinic, 1951-54; sr. surg. resident Lallie Kemp Charity Hosp., Independence, La., 1954-55; practice medicine specializing in gen. surgery, Ashland, Ky., 1956-83. Served to capt. M.C., USAAF, 1943-46. Fellow ACS; mem. Ky. Med. Soc., AMA, Boyd County Med. Soc., Ochsner Surg. Soc., Ky. Hist. Soc. (life), Sigma Chi (life), Alpha Kappa Kappa, Alpha Omega Alpha. Author 2 books. Home: 2726 Cumberland Ave Ashland KY 41101

STEPHENSON, ROBERT LLOYD, archeologist; b. Portland, Oreg., Feb. 18, 1919; s. George A. and Myrtle L. (Smith) S.; m. Georgie E. Boydstun, Jan. 5, 1946 (dec. July 1983); m. Patricia E. Elliott, July 26, 1984. B.A., U. Oreg., 1940, M.A., 1942; Ph.D., U. Mich., 1956. Lab. dir. U. Tex., San Antonio, 1940-41; field dir. River Basin Surveys, Smithsonian Instn., Tex., 1946-52, Mo., 1952-63, U.S., 1963-66; coordinator Nev. Archeol. Survey, U. Nev., Reno, 1966-68; dir. Inst. Archeology and Anthropology, U. S.C., 1968-84, research prof. emeritus, 1984—; state archeologist, Columbia, S.C., 1968-84; cons. in archeology Colville Consol. Indian Tribes, Nespelem, Wash., 1980. Asst. editor Am. Antiquity, 1960-63; asso. editor Plains Anthropologist, 1960-62; editor Plains Anthropologist, 1963, Nev. Archeol. Survey Reporter, 1966-68, Inst. Archeology and Anthropology's Notebook, 1969-84. Contbr. articles to profl. jours. Bd. dirs. U. S.C. Mus., 1971-75; mem. S.C. Rev. Bd. for Nat. Hist. Preservation Act, 1969-84; ex-officio mem. Camden Hist. Commn., 1971-84; mem. S.C. Heritage Trust Adv. Bd., 1976-84; mem. archeol. adv. com. TVA, 1972—. Served with USMC, 1942-46. Fellow Am. Anthrop. Assn.; mem. Nat. Assn. State Archeologists (pres. 1980-82); Soc. Profl. Archeologists (dir. 1977-79, pres. 1985-86), Soc. Am. Archeology, AAAS, Oreg. Hist. Soc., archeol. socs. Oreg., Tex., Nev., Mo., S.C., Md., Fla., Tenn., Soc. Vertebrate Paleontology, S.C. Acad. Sci., Nebr. Hist. Soc., Nat. Trust for Historic Preservation, Southeastern Archeol. Conf., Soc. for Hist. Archeology, Conf. on Historic Sites Archeology, Council on Am. Military Past (nat. dir. 1979-82, v.p. 1980-82), Sigma Xi. Republican. Episcopalian. Clubs: Condon, Toastmasters (dist. lt. gov. 1967-68, 70-72), Explorers. Home: 5831 Satchel Ford Rd Columbia SC 29206 Office: Univ SC Inst Archeology & Anthropology Columbia SC 29208

STEPHENSON, THOMAS EDGAR, physicist; b. Dahlgren, Ill., Oct. 19, 1922; s. Simon Gilmore and Lilly May (Atchisson) S.; B.S. in Physics, So. Ill. U., 1945; M.S. in Physics, U. Tenn., 1950; m. Helen Julia Mizzoni, June 8, 1946; children—Thomas Paul, Joan Priscilla, Timothy James, Michael David. Assoc. scientist Republic Aviation Corp., Farmingdale, N.Y., 1957-65; assoc. physicist Brookhaven Nat. Lab., Upton, N.Y., 1965-70; project engr. S.M. Stoller Corp., N.Y.C., 1970-73; nuclear licensing engr. Vepco, Richmond, Va., 1973-76; sr. nuclear engr. Burns & Roe Inc., Oradell, N.J., 1976-80; sr. engr. Stone and Webster Engring. Corp., N.Y.C., 1980—; adj. assoc. prof. physics L.I.U., Greenvale, N.Y., 1968-70. Served with AUS, 1943-46. Mem. Am. Phys. Soc., Am. Nuclear Soc. Episcopalian. Contbr. articles on physics to profl. jours. Home: 16 Briarfield Ln Huntington NY 11743 Office: 1 Penn Plaza New York NY 10001

STEPHENSON, TONI EDWARDS, publisher, investment management executive; b. Bastrop, La., July 23, 1945; d. Sidney Crawford and Grace Erleene (Shipman) Little; BS, La. State U., 1967; enrolled owner/pres. mgmt. program Harvard Bus. Sch.; m. Arthur Emmet Stephenson, Jr., June 17, 1967; 1 dau., Tessa Lyn. Computer programmer Employers Group Ins., Boston, 1967-68; systems analyst Computer Tech., Inc., Cambridge, Mass., 1968-69; sr. v.p., founder E. Stephenson & Co., Inc., Denver, 1971—, Stephenson Mcht. Banking, 1980—; gen. ptnr. Viking Fund; ptnr. Stephenson Properties, Stephenson Ventures, Stephenson Mgmt. Co.; pres., dir. Gen. Communications, Inc., Globescope Corp.; underwriting mem. Lloyd's of London; founder, dir. Charter Bank & Trust. Co-pub. Denver Bus. Mag., 1978—, Denver Mag., 1982—, Vail Mag., 1980—, Development Sales Catalog, 1980—, Colorado Book, 1986—; former dir. The Children's Hosp. Past pres. Children's Hosp. Assn. Vols. Mem. DAR, Delta Gamma. Clubs: Annabel's of London, Thunderbird Country, Petroleum. Office: E Stephenson & Co Inc 100 Garfield St Denver CO 80206

STEPIEN, WIESLAW ZBIGNIEW, archaeologist; b. Lodz, Poland, Apr. 3, 1947; s. Tadeusz and Helena (Werner) S.; m. Aleksandra Kazmierczak, Dec. 18, 1971; 1 child, Jakub. MS in Archaeology, U. Lodz, 1971. Asst. Polish Acad. Sci., Lodz, 1971-72, Mus. Archaeology and Ethnography, Lodz, 1972-73, U. Lodz, 1973-75, Cen. Maritime Mus., Gdansk, Poland, 1975-76; curator Cen. for Studies and Document Monuments, Lodz, 1976—; mgr. underwater excavations, Puck, Gdansk, 1970-85, air archaeology, Poland, 1979-87. Contbr. articles to profl. jours. Mem. Assn. Archaeology and Numismatics. Club: Aero Hot Air Balloon (Lodz) (chmn. 1986—). Home: 8A Hufcowa No 28, 94-107 Lodz Poland

STERCK, FREDDY, sales executive; b. Halle, Brabant, Belgium, July 16, 1954; s. Roger and Elisa (Cosyns) S. Diploma in commerce, H.O.R.I.H.A.N., Aalst, Belgium, 1972; diploma in hotel and fin. mgmt., Ecole Hoteliere, Lausanne, Switzerland, 1976; cert. in commerce, Inst. Soivay, Brussels, 1982. Asst. to gen. mgr. Hotel Arcade Stephanie, Brussels, 1976-77; mgr. sales Belgavia-Restobel, Brussels, 1977-79; with sales dept. Restaura S.A., Brussels, 1979-82, dir. sales, 1982—; dir. food and beverage Glacier Nat. Park/Greyhound, Mont., 1982; pres., chmn. bd. dirs. Le Scarabée S.A., Brussels, 1985—; sales dir. Ressaura S.A. subs GreyHound Corp., Brussels. Roman Catholic. Home: Ave des Scarabees 22 Box 9, 1050

Brussels Belgium Office: Restaura SA, De Bokck 54th Ave, 1140 Brussels Belgium

STERLING, SIR JEFFREY (MAURICE), shipping company executive, government official; b. Dec. 27, 1934; s. Harry and Alice Sterling; m. Dorothy Ann Smith, 1985; 1 daughter,. Student, Guildhall Sch. Music. With Paul Schweder and Co. (Stock Exchange), 1957-63; fin. dir. Gen. Guarantee Corp., 1963-64; mng. dir. Gula Investments Ltd., 1964-69; chmn. Sterling Guarantee Trust plc, 1969-85, The Peninsular and Oriental Steam Navigation Co., 1983—; chmn. European Ferries Group plc, 1987—; bd. dirs. British Airways, European Ferries; chmn. orgn. com. World ORT Union, 1969-73, mem. exec., 1966—, tech. services, 1974, v.p. Brit. ORT, 1978—; spl. advisor Sec. of State for Trade and Industry, 1983—. Dep. chmn. and hon. treas. London Celebrations Com. Queen's Silver Jubilee, 1975-83; chmn. Young Vic Co., 1975-83; chmn. govs. Royal Ballet Sch., 1983—; gov. Royal Ballet, 1986—; vice-chmn. and chmn. of the exec., Motability, 1977—. Decorated Knight, 1985, CBE, 1977. Clubs: Garrick, Carlton, Hurlingham. Office: The Peninsular and Oriental, Steam Navigation Co, 79 Pall Mall, London SW1Y 5EJ, England also: 17 Brompton Sq, London SW3, England *

STERLING, KEIR BROOKS, historian, educator; b. N.Y.C., Jan. 30, 1934; s. Henry Somers and Louise Noel (de Wetter) S.; B.S., Columbia U., 1961, M.A., 1963, Profl. Diploma, 1965, Ph.D., 1973; m. Anne Cox Diller, Apr. 3, 1961; children—Duncan Diller, Warner Strong, Theodore Craig. Asst. to dean Sch. Gen. Studies, Columbia U., N.Y.C., 1959-65, research grantee, Eng., 1965-66; instr. in history Pace U., N.Y.C. and Pleasantville, N.Y., 1966-71, asst. prof., 1971-74, assoc. prof., 1974-77, adj. prof., 1977—; ordnance br. historian U.S. Army Ctr. and Sch., Aberdeen Proving Ground, Md., 1983—; lectr. in gen. counselling Bklyn. Coll., City U. N.Y., 1967-68; asst. academic dean, adj. asst. prof. history, coordinator Am. studies program, dir. summer session Marymount Coll., Tarrytown, N.Y., 1968-71; asst. dean Rockland Community Coll., SUNY, Suffern, 1971-73; vis. prof. Mercy Coll., Westchester Community Coll., King's Coll., Nyack Coll., U. Wis., 1971, 75, 78-80, 83, Harford Community Coll., 1987—; co-project dir. Am. Ornithologists Union Centennial Hist. Project, 1976—; cons. Arno Press, Inc., 1973-78, Council State Colls. of N.J., 1974-75, NSF, 1983—; mem. Columbia U. Seminar on History and Philosophy of Sci., 1976—. Mem. Bicentennial Com. Tarrytown, 1975-76; archivist, historian section mammalogy Internat. Union Biol. Scis., 1985—. Served with U.S. Army, 1954-56. Grantee Theodore Roosevelt Meml. Fund, Am. Mus. Natural History, 1967, Nat. Geog. Soc., 1977, NSF/Am. Soc. Mammalogists, 1978, NSF, 1981-82, IREX, 1982, mem. Archives and 75th Anniversary Coms. Mem. Am. Soc. Mammalogists, Am. Ornithologists Union (co-chmn. Centennial Hist. Com., mem. Archives Com., grantee, 1976, 77), Am. Hist. Assn., Orgn. Am. Historians, Am. Soc. Environ. History (sec., mem. governing bd.; editor newsletter), History of Sci. Soc., Soc. for History in the Fed. Govt., Oral History Soc., Forest History Soc., Council on Am.'s Mil. Past, Soc. for History of Natural History, Rhinebeck (N.Y.) Hist. Soc. (trustee, pres. 1980-82), Harford County Com. of Md. Hist. Trust, Harford County Hist. Dist. Commn. (v.p. 1987—), Phi Alpha Theta. Democrat. Episcopalian. Author: Last of the Naturalists: The Career of C. Hart Merriam, 1974, 77; The Centennial History of the American Ornithologists Union (with M. G. Ainley), 1988; Serving the Line with Excellence: The History of the U.S. Army Ordinance Corps as Expressed through the Lives of its Chiefs of Ordnance, 1812-1987; editor: Notes on the Animals of North America (B.S. Barton), 1974; editor, contbr.: Natural Sciences in America, 1974, 68 vols., 1974, Biologists and Their World, 1978, 77 vols.; gen. editor, contbr.: The International History of Mammalogy, 1987—; editor, contbr. to numerous works in history Am. natural scis. and Am. military history. Home: 324 Webster St Bel Air MD 21014 Office: US Army Ordnance Ctr & Sch 216 Simpson Hall Aberdeen Proving Ground MD 21005 also: American Museum Natural History Dept Ornithology Central Park W at 79th St New York NY 10024

STERLING, ROBERT LEE, JR., investment company executive; b. Cleve., June 12, 1933; s. Robert Lee and Kathryn (Durell) S.; student U. Edinburgh (Scotland), 1955; B.A., Brown U., 1956; M.B.A., Columbia U., 1962; m. Deborah Platt, May 10, 1984; children—Robert Livingston, William Lee, Cameron Platt. Corp. research analyst Morgan Guaranty Trust, N.Y.C., 1962-63; asst. comptroller Western Hemisphere CPC Internat., N.Y.C., 1963-66; v.p. White, Weld & Co., Inc., N.Y.C., 1966-78; v.p. Merrill Lynch Asset Mgmt., 1978-80; v.p. Wood, Struthers & Winthrop Mgmt. Corp., N.Y.C., 1980-83; sr. v.p. Shearson/Am. Express Asset Mgmt., 1983—. Trustee, Lenox Hill Hosp., N.Y.C.; bd. dirs. Inst. Sports Medicine and Athletic Trauma; mem. adv. bd. Mus. Modern Art, Oxford U. Served to lt. USNR, 1956-60. Mem. New Eng. Soc. (past pres., J.P. Morgan medal), Nat. Trust Scotland (Edinburgh), St. Andrews Soc., St. Nicholas Soc., Pilgrims, Soc. Cincinnati, Alpha Delta Phi, Alpha Kappa Psi. Clubs: Round Hill (Conn.); Downtown, Univ. (N.Y.C.); Edgartown (Mass.) Yacht. Home: 16 Pheasant Ln Greenwich CT 06830 Office: 2 World Trade Ctr 106th Fl New York NY 10048

STERLING, ROBERT RAYMOND, educator; b. Bugtussle, Okla., May 16, 1931; s. Roland Pomeroy and Lillian (Neuman) S.; B.S., U. Denver, 1956, M.B.A., 1958; Ph.D., U. Fla., 1964; children—Robert, Kimberly. Asst. prof. social sci. Harpur Coll., Binghamton, N.Y., 1963-66; Sci. Faculty fellow Yale U., 1966-67; asso. prof., then prof. bus. adminstrn. U. Kans., Lawrence, 1967-70, Arthur Young disting. prof., 1970-74; dir. research Am. Acctg. Assn., 1972-74; Jesse Jones Disting. prof. Rice U., Houston, 1974-80, dean Grad. Sch. Adminstrn., 1976-80; Winspear disting. prof. U. Alta. (Can.), 1980-81; sr. fellow Fin. Acctg. Standards Bd., 1981-83; Garff disting. prof. bus. U. Utah, Salt Lake City, 1983—. Bd. dirs. Nat. Bur. Econ. Research, United Way, Trust Corp. Internat. Recipient Gold medal Am. Inst. C.P.A.s, 1968, 74; Bicentennial Disting. Internat. lectr., Europe, 1976; Hoover Disting. Internat. lectr., Australia, 1979. Fellow Acctg. Researchers Internat. Assn. (pres. 1974-80), Am. (v.p. 1975-76), S.W. (pres.) acctg. assns., Accts. for Public Interest (dir.); mem. Nat. Assn. Accts. (dir.), Houston Philos. Soc. (dir.). Author: Theory of the Measurement of Enterprise Income, 1970; (with William F. Bentz) Accounting in Perspective, 1971; Asset Valuation and Income Determination 1971; Research Methodology In Accounting, 1972; Institutional Issues in Public Accounting, 1974; (with A.L. Thomas) Accounting for a Simplified Firm, 1979; Toward a Science of Accounting, 1980; An Essay on Recognition, 1985; editor: Accounting Classics Series; editorial bd., dept. editor Accounting Rev.; editorial bd. Abacus; pub., editor Scholars Book Co. Home: 4409 Viewcrest Dr Salt Lake City UT 84124 Office: U Utah Coll Bus Salt Lake City UT 84117

STERMER, DUGALD ROBERT, designer, illustrator, writer, consultant; b. Los Angeles, Dec. 17, 1936; s. Robert Newton and Mary (Blue) S.; m. Jeanie Kortum; children: Dugald, Megan, Chris, Colin. B.A., UCLA, 1960. Art dir., v.p. Ramparts mag., 1965-70; freelance designer, illustrator, writer, cons. San Francisco, 1970—; founder Pub. Interest Communications, San Francisco, 1974; pres. Frisco Pub Group Ltd. Cons. editor Communication Arts mag., Palo Alto, Calif., 1974—; designer Oceans mag., 1976-82; editor: The Environment, 1972, Vanishing Creatures, 1980; author: The Art of Revolution, 1970, Vanishing Creatures, 1980; designer 1984 Olympic medals; illustration exhbn. Calif. Acad. Scis., 1986. Bd. dirs. Delancey St. Found., 1976—. Recipient various medals, awards for design and illustration nat. and internat. design competitions. Mem. Soc. Publ. Designers, Am. Inst. Graphics Arts, San Francisco Soc. Communicating Arts. Office: 1844 Union St San Francisco CA 94123

STERMER, NANCY LOUISE, personnel executive; b. Canandaigua, N.Y., Dec. 19, 1952; d. Gordon Ernest and Elaine Louise (Jones) S. B.A., Mich. State U., 1975; M.A., U. Mich., 1979. Cert. tchr. continuing edn., Mich. Teaching asst. Mich. State U., East Lansing, 1974-75; tchr. adult edn. Flint Community Schs., Mich., 1976; tchr. elem. edn., jr. high sch. Waterford Sch. Dist., Pontiac, Mich., 1976-80; tng. specialist Fed.-Mogul Corp., Southfield, Mich., 1981-83, office systems analyst and tng. specialist, 1983-86, info. systems coordinator, 1986; lead systems designer, trainer Comerica, Inc., Detroit, 1986-87, sr. tng. project mgr., 1987-88, human resources officer, sr. tng. project mgr., 1988—. Bd. dirs. Mich. chpt. Am. Lupus Soc., 1985-87. Named Outstanding Sr., Class of '75, Mich. State U., 1975. Mem. Nat. Assn. Female Execs., Assn. for the Devel. of Computer-Based Instrn., Nat. Tng. & Computers Network, Am. Soc. for Tng. & Devel., Soc. for Applied Learning Tech., Detroit Area Trainers Assn., Office Automation Mgmt. Assn., NOW, U. Mich. Alumnae, Kappa Delta Pi. Office: Comerica Inc 211 W Fort St Detroit MI 48275-2455

STERN, DUKE NORDLINGER, lawyer, consultant; b. Chgo., Apr. 14, 1942. B.S. in Econs., U. Pa., 1963; postgrad. U. Va. Law Sch., 1964; J.D., Temple U., 1968; M.B.A., U. Mo., 1969; Ph.D., 1972. Admitted to Mo. bar, 1969, U.S. Supreme Ct., 1978. Cert. Assn. Exec. 1979, Systems Profl., 1984, Mgmt. Cons., 1985; dir. Center for Adminstrn. Legal Systems, Duquesne U., Pitts., 1974-75; exec. dir., gen. counsel W.Va. State Bar, Charleston, 1975-79; pres. Risk & Ins. Services Cons., Inc., St. Petersburg, Fla., 1979-80, Duke Nordlinger Stern & Assos., Inc., St. Petersburg, 1980—, Duke Nordlinger Stern and Assocs., Ltd., London, 1985—, Duke Nordlinger Stern and Assocs., Ltd., Barbados, 1986—. Pres., W.Va. Legal Services Plan, Inc., 1978-79. Mem. Am. Soc. Assn. Execs. (cert.), Am. Arbitration Assn., Nat. Assn. Corp. Dirs., Am. Judicature Soc., ABA, Standard Com. on Lawyers' Profl. Liability, Assn for Systems Mgmy., Inst. Mgmt Cons. Author: An Attorney's Guide to Malpractice Liability, 1977, Case in Labor Law, 1977, An Accountant's Guide to Malpractice Liability, 1979, Avoiding Accountant's Malpractice Claims, 1982, Avoiding Legal Malpractice Claims, 1982; A Practical Guide to Preventing Legal Malpractice, 1983. Address: Duke Nordlinger Stern & Assocs Inc 1336 54th Ave NE Saint Petersburg FL 33703

STERN, ERIC PETRU, chemist; b. Arad, Romania, Jan. 1, 1941; s. Oscar and Palma (Friedman) S.; m. Ligia Renée Munoz, March 3, 1973; 1 child, Erika Cindy. Student, Humboldt U., Berlin, German Dem. Republic; diploma, Bucharest (Romania) U., 1963; MBA, Concordia U., Montréal, Que., Can., 1984. Chemist ICECHIM Research Inst., Bucharest, 1962-69; plant supr. Industria Lechera, Cayambe, Ecuador, 1969-73; chemist BPCO Inc. (formerly Esso Bldg. Products), Lasalle, Que., 1974—; mem. fire test com. Underwriter Can., Toronto, Ont., Can., 1975-77, ASTM Philadelphia, 1979—; abstractor Chem. Abstracts, Columbus, Ohio, 1973—. Contbr. articles to profl. jours.; patentee in field. Mem. Soc. Plastic Engrs., Am. Chem. Soc. Home: 5386 W Broadway, Montreal, PQ Canada H4V 2A4

STERN, ISAAC, violinist; b. Kreminiecz, Russia, July 21, 1920; came to U.S., 1921; s. Solomon and Clara S.; m. Nora Kaye, Nov. 10, 1948; m. Vera Lindenblit, Aug. 17, 1951; children: Shira, Michael, David. Student, San Francisco Conservatory, 1930-37; numerous hon. degrees including, Dalhousie U., 1971, U. Hartford, 1971, Bucknell U., 1974, Yale U., 1975, Johns Hopkins U., 1979, U. Md., 1983. Recital debut San Francisco, 1934; orchestral debut San Francisco Symphony Orch. (Pierre Monteux condr.), 1936; N.Y. debut, 1937; Carnegie Hall recital debut, 1943; N.Y. Philharm. debut (Arthur Rodzinski condr.), 1944; participated Prades Festival with Pablo Casals, 1950-52; soloist for first orchestral and recital performances at Kennedy Ctr., Washington; first Am. to perform in USSR after World War II, 1956; mem. Istomin-Rose-Stern trio, 1962-83 (Beethoven cycle w/Istomin & Rose 1970-71); performed in China at invitation of Chinese govt., 1979; performed world premieres of violin works by Bernstein, Dutilleux, Hindemith, Maxwell Davies, Penderecki, Rochberg and Schuman; has played with major orchestras, given countless recitals and performed at important festivals in the U.S., Europe, Israel, Far East, Australia and S. Am. Over 100 records, cassettes and CD's for CBS Masterworks, named Artist Laureate 1984 CBS Masterworks; made soundtrack for motion pictures Humoresque (Warner Bros.) and Fiddler on the Roof (United Artists); starred in soundtrack Tonight We Sing (20th Century Fox) and Journey to Jerusalem with Leonard Bernstein; documentary film From Mao to Mozart-Isaac Stern in China (Academy award 1981, Cannes Film Festival Special Mention), Carnegie Hall: The Grand Reopening, 1987 (Emmy award). Chmn. bd. Am.-Israel Cultural Found.; chmn., founder Jerusalem Music Ctr.; originating mem. Nat. Endowment for the Arts. Recipient numerous Grammy awards; Comdr. Ordre de la Couronne, 1974; Officier Legion d'Honneur, 1979; J.F. Kennedy Ctr. Honors, 1984; Commander's Cross of the Order of the Dannebrog, Denmark, 1985; Musician of the Year-ABC/Musical Am., 1986; Fellow of Jerusalem, 1986; Wolf Prize, 1987; Grammy Lifetime Achievement Award, 1987; numerous local city awards. Address: care ICM Artists Ltd 40 W 57th St New York NY 10019

STERN, MARC IRWIN, manufacturing and engineering company executive; b. Vineland, N.J., Apr. 17, 1944; s. Albert B. and Sylvia (Goodman) S.; m. Eva Suzanne Kuhn, Aug. 14, 1966; children: Adam Bryan, Suzanne Rona. B.A. cum laude in Polit. Sci., Dickinson Coll., Carlisle, Pa., 1965; M.A., Columbia U., 1966, J.D. magna cum laude, 1969. Bar: N.Y. 1969, N.H. 1975. Law clk. U.S. Ct. Appeals 2d Circuit, 1969-70; asso. Debevoise, Plimpton, Lyons & Gates, 1970-74; v.p., gen. counsel Wheelabrator-Frye Inc., Hampton, N.H., 1974-80; sr. v.p. Wheelabrator-Frye Inc., 1980-83; sr. v.p. adminstrn. The Signal Cos., Inc., La Jolla, Calif., 1983-85, Allied-Signal Inc., Morristown, N.J., 1985-86; mng. dir., chief adminstrv. officer The Henley Group, Inc., N.Y.C. and La Jolla, 1986—; bd. dirs. Signal Captial Corp., Fisher Sci. Group, Inc. Trustee Salk Inst. for Biol. Studies, La Jolla, San Diego Mus. of Art; bd. dirs. Dennis Conner Sports Inc., San Diego. Mem. ABA, Assn. Bar City N.Y., N.H. Bar Assn. Home: 1535 El Camino Del Teatro La Jolla CA 92037 Office: The Henley Group Inc 11255 N Torrey Pines Rd La Jolla CA 92037 also: The Henley Group Inc 375 Park Ave New York NY 10152

STERN, MICHAEL, journalist; b. N.Y.C., Aug. 3, 1910; s. Barnet and Anna (Agulansky) S.; B.S., Syracuse U., 1932; m. Estelle Goldstein, Nov. 11, 1934; children: Michael, Margaret. Reporter, Syracuse Jour., 1929-32, N.Y. Jour., 1932-33, Middletown Times Herald (N.Y.); staff writer McFadden Publs., 1935-42; adviser John Harlan Amen investigation into alliance between crime and politics in Kings County, N.Y., 1939-42; U.S. war corr. Fawcett Publs., 1942-45, fgn. corr., 1945—; lectr. Syracuse U. Bd. advs. The Intrepid Mus., N.Y.C., The " 21 " Heart Fund, N.Y.C. Clubs: Overseas Press (U.S.); Aquasanta Golf, Olgiata Golf (Rome). Named Syracuse U. Man of the Yr., 1986. Author: The White Ticket, 1936; Flight from Terror (with Otto Strasser), 1941; Into the Jaws of Death, 1944; No Innocence Abroad, 1954; An American in Rome (autobiography), 1963; Farouk, 1966; contbr. mags. Editor, publisher La Scienza Illustrata, 1948-49. Asso. producer The Rover film; exec. producer Satyricon, The Heroes, Love the Italian Way, Run For Your Life; host-narrator The City, CBS. Home: via Zandonai 95, 00194 Rome Italy

STERN, MICHAEL LAWRENCE, psychologist; b. N.Y.C., July 3, 1948; s. Abraham Isaac and Etta (Silverberg) S.; BA, Calif. State U., Long Beach, 1970; PhD, U. Wash., 1977; m. Karen Beth Rivard, July 26, 1981; children: Joshua Ethan, Rachel Lynn. Diplomate Am. Bd. Med. Psychotherapists; cert. employee assistance profl., sex therapist. Instr. dept. psychology U. Wash., Seattle, 1975-77; research assoc. dept. psychiatry U. Tenn. Med. Sch., Memphis, 1977-78; clin. dir. drug abuse program Fed. Correction Inst., Danbury, Conn., 1978-85, chief psychologist, 1985-86; dir. outpatient recovery ctr. Briarcliff Manor, N.Y., 1986—; pvt. practice clin. psychology, Danbury, 1981—; cons. Addiction Recovery Corp, Westchester, 1987—; adj. faculty Fairfield U., 1981—. U. Tenn. postdoctoral fellow, 1977-78. Mem. Am. Psychol. Assn., Assn. Advancement Behavior Therapy, Am. Assn. Sex Educators, Counselors, and Therapists, Conn. Psychol. Assn. Cons. editor TSA News, 1977-78. Home: Saw Mill Ridge Rd Newtown CT 06470 Office: 57 North St Suite 309 Danbury CT 06810

STERNBERG, DONNA GAIL (WEINTRAUB), retail company executive; b. Little Rock, Dec. 16, 1943; d. Charles Simon and Sadie Frieda (Lulky) Weintraub; m. Hans Joachim Sternberg, Feb. 19, 1967; children: Erich, Julie Ellen, Deborah Ann, Marc Samuel. B.A. cum laude, U. Tex., 1966; postgrad. Columbia U., 1966. Buyer, mgr. Goudchaux's, Inc., Baton Rouge, 1967-76, mdse. mgr., 1976-81, v.p., mdse. mgr. fur dept. Gouchaux/Maison Blanche, 1981—, mdse. mgr. design dept., 1988—. Founder women's div. Jewish Fedn. Greater Baton Rouge, 1970; chmn. women's div. La. United Jewish Appeal, 1972-74; nat. bd. dirs. women's div. United Jewish Appeal, 1972-76; regent Nat. Fedn. Republican Women; mem. community adv. com. La. State U. Honors Div., Baton Rouge, 1981—; mem. Nat. Commn. on Presdl. Scholars, 1982-86; mem. exec. com. Am. Israel Pub. Affairs Com., 1982—; bd. dirs., sec. Louisianians for Am. Security Polit. Action Com., 1983—; La. State chmn. alumni schs. com. Princeton U., 1987—; chmn. alumni recruiting Columbia Coll., 1985-86 . Alice Stetton fellow, Columbia U. Sch. Internat. Affairs, 1966. Mem. Baton Rouge Phi Beta Kappa Community Assn. (founder 1979, pres. 1979-81); pres. Erich Sternberg Found., 1986-87, v.p. 1988—; mem. adv. council Ctr. Internat. Studies Princeton U., 1987—. Mem. Phi Beta Kappa, Alpha Lambda Delta. Lodge: B'nai B'rith Women (charter pres. and founder Baton Rouge chpt. 1970-72). Office: PO Drawer 91102 Baton Rouge LA 70821-9102

STERNBERG, DONNA UDIN, lawyer; b. Phila., May 3, 1951; d. Jack and Frances (Osner) Udin; m. Harvey J. Sternberg; 1 child, Zachary Samuel. Student Tel Aviv U., 1971; BA, Northwestern U., 1973; JD, Loyola U., Chgo., 1976. Bar: Ill. 1976, Pa. 1979. Profl. actress, dancer, model, 1961-76; dancer Boishoi Ballet Co., 1965, 66, 67, Leningrad Kirov Ballet Co., 1966; actress Broadway prodn., 1966; appeared stage plays, TV and film roles, 1961-77; model nat. fashion mags. and publs., 1961-77; assoc. firm Ronald H. Balson & Assocs., Chgo., 1976-79, Mesirov, Gelman, Jaffe, Cramer & Jamieson, Phila., 1979-81; mem. firm Blank, Rome, Comisky & McCauley, Phila., 1981—. Active young leadership council Fedn. Allied Jewish Appeal, 1982-84; mem. Israel Bonds New Leadership Cabinet, 1982-87. Mem. ABA, Pa. Bar Assn., Phila. Bar Assn., Chgo. Bar Assn. Jewish. Club: Locust (Phila.). Office: Blank Rome Comisky & McCauley 4 Penn Ctr Plaza Philadelphia PA 19103

STERNBERGER, DOLF, political scientist, educator, writer; b. Wiesbaden, Fed. Republic Germany, July 28, 1907; s. Georg Sternberger and Luise Schauss; m. Ilse Rothschild, 1931. Dr. h.c. (hon.), U. Paris Sorbonne; Dr. phil h.c. (hon.), U. Trier, 1981. Prof. emeritus polit. sci. Heidelberg U., Fed. Republic Germany. Author: Der verstandene Tod, eine Untersuchung zu Martin Heideggers Existential- Ontologie, 1934, Panorama oder Ansichten vom 19 Jahrhundert, 1938, 1955, 13 Politische Radioreden, 1947, Figuren der Fabel, 1950, Aus dem Wörterbuch des Unmenschen, 1955, 1968, Lebende Verfassung, Studien über Koalition und Opposition, 1956, Uber den Jugendstil und andere Essays, 1956, Indische Miniaturen, 1957, Begriff des Politischen, 1961, Grund und Abgrund der Macht, 1962, Ekel an der Freiheit?, 1964, Die grosse Wahlreform, 1964, Kriterien-Ein Lesebuch, 1965, Ich Wünschte, ein Bürger zu sein, 1967, Heinrich Heine und die Abschaffung der Süunde, 1972, Schriften I Ubér den Tod, 1977, Schriften II Drei Wurzeln der Politik, 1978, Schriften III Herrschaft und Vereinbarung, 1980, Schriften IV Staatsfreundschaft, 1980, Schriften V Panorama, Schriften VI Vexierbilder des menschen, 1981, Die Politik und der Friede, 1986. Decorated Great Cross of Order of Merit; recipient Johannes-Reuchlin prize, Bavarian Acad. of Fine Arts, other awards. Mem. German Assn. Polit. Sci. (past chair), German PEN Club (past pres.), German Acad. Lang. and Lit. (hon. pres.). Office: Park Rosenhohe 35, 6100 Darmstadt Federal Republic of Germany *

STERNE, LAWRENCE JON, economic consulting firm administrator; b. Cambridge, Mass., Sept. 28, 1949; s. Russell Justin and Dorothea (White) S.; m. Susan Mains, Apr. 17, 1976; children—Marjorie Mains, Caroline Adams. B.A., Harvard U., 1972. V.p. Reynolds Research Assocs., N.Y.C., 1976-77, ECOM Cons., Inc., N.Y.C., 1977-78, Chem. Bank, N.Y.C., 1978-83, v.p., 1981—; sec. treas., dir. equity research Economic Analysis Assocs., Inc., Stowe, Vt., 1980—; pres. Paper and Forest Products Industry Analysts Group, N.Y.C., 1982-83. Clk. Stowe Bd. Sch. Dirs., 1985-87. Mem. N.Y. Soc. Security Analysts, Fin. Analysts Fedn. Avocations: reading, sailing, swimming.

STERNHELL, MARCUS ALLEN, advertising executive; b. Bklyn., Mar. 1, 1945; s. Maurice Louis and Mary (Rubenstein) S.; m. Joanne L. Chrils, Oct. 14, 1979. BA, U. Denver, 1969, MA, 1974. Account exec. Saxe Mitchell, Inc., Woodbury, N.Y., 1974-79; sr. account exec. Marsteller, Inc., N.Y.C., 1979-80; v.p., mktg. dir. Petite Bazaar, Ltd., 1980-84; pres., chief exec. officer Mark Sternhell Advt., Roslyn, N.Y., 1984—. Producer Time Changes (off Broadway show), 1972. Recipient Effie award Am. Mktg. Assn., 1979. Mem. Boat Owners Assn. of U.S., Nat. Marine Mfrs. Assn.,Nat. Assn. Marine Products and Services, U.S. Power Squadron, Coast Guard Aux., Carver Yacht Owners Assn. (bd. dirs.). Jewish. Avocations: boating, tennis, skiing. Office: Mark Sternhell Advt 125 Mineola Ave Roslyn Heights NY 11577

STERRETT, SAMUEL BLACK, lawyer, former judge; b. Washington, Dec. 17, 1922; s. Henry Hatch Dent and Helen (Black) S.; m. Jeane McBride, Aug. 27, 1949; children: Samuel Black, Robin Dent, Douglas McBride. Student, St. Albans Sch., 1933-41; grad., U.S. Mcht. Marine Acad., 1945; B.A., Amherst Coll., 1947; LL.B., U. Va., 1950; LL.M. in Taxation, N.Y.U., 1959. Bar: D.C. 1951, Va. 1950. Atty. Alvord & Alvord, Washington, 1950-56; trial atty. Office Regional Counsel, Internal Revenue Service, N.Y.C., 1956-60; ptnr. Sullivan, Shea & Kenney, Washington, 1960-68; municipal cons. to office vice pres. U.S. 1965-68; judge U.S. Tax Ct., 1968-88, chief judge, 1985-88; mem. Myerson, Kuhn & Sterrett, Washington, 1988—. Bd. mgrs. Chevy Chase Village, 1970-74, chmn., 1972-74; 1st v.p. bd. trustees, mem. exec. com. Washington Hosp. Center, 1969-79, chmn. bd. trustees, 1979-84; chmn. bd. trustees Washington Healthcare Corp., 1982-87; chmn. bd. trustees Medlantic Healthcare Group, 1987—; mem. Washington Cathedral chpt., 1973-81; mem. governing bd. St. Albans Sch., 1977-81; trustee Louise Home, 1979—. Served with AUS, 1943; Served with U.S. Mcht. Marine, 1943-46. Mem. Am., Fed., Va., D.C. bar assns., Soc. of the Cincinnati, Beta Theta Pi. Episcopalian. Clubs: Chevy Chase (bd. govs. 1979-84, pres. 1984), Metropolitan, Lawyers, Alibi, Alfalfa, Church of N.Y. Office: Myerson Kuhn & Sterrett 1330 Connecticut Ave NW Washington DC 20036

STERU, LUCIEN, psychiatrist, chemical company executive; b. Aug. 22, 1953; s. Marius and Sylvia (Coniver) S.; m. Dominique G. Hassid, Dec. 15, 1952; 1 child, Edouard. MD, Faculté de Médecine Pitie Salpetriere, Paris, 1981; Degree in Pharmacology, Faculté de Médecine Pitie Salpetriere, 1982. Resident in psychiatry Faculté de Médecine Pitie Salpetriere, 1980-83, pharmacologist, 1978-83; pres. Inst. for Tech. Evaluation of Medicines, Paris, 1983—; cons. in field, 1982-84. Contbr. articles to sci. jours.; patentee in field. Served to lt. health br. of mil., Paris, 1980-81. Mem. Assn. Francaise de Psychiatrie Biologique, Brit. Pharm. Soc. Home: 201 rue d'Alesia, 75014 Paris France Office: Inst for Tech Evaluation, Medicines, 93 Ave de Fontainebleau, 94270 Le Kremlin-Bicetre France

STETSON, JOHN CHARLES, business executive; b. Chgo., Sept. 6, 1920; s. John Charles and Dorothy H. (Eckman) S.; m. Gayle McDowell, Jan. 1, 1946; children: Sherry, Robert, Susan. B.S., Mass. Inst. Tech., 1943; postgrad., Northwestern U. Bus. Sch., 1946-48. Partner Booz Allen & Hamilton, Chgo., 1951-63; pres. pub. div. Houston Post Co., Houston, 1963-70; pres. A.B. Dick Co., Chgo., 1970-77; also dir.; sec. of the Air Force, Washington, 1977-79; nat. chmn. com. for employer support of guard and res. Dept. Def., Washington, 1980-81; pres. J.C. Stetson, Inc., 1981—; dir. Kemper Corp., NIBCO, Inc., Lawter Internat., Inc., Madison-Kipp Corp., 1st Ill. Corp., Helene Curtis, Inc., Lumberman's Mut. Casualty Co., Magna Photo Inc., Chgo. Tube and Iron, In, Laser Tech., Inc. Trustee Chgo. Symphony Orch. Served with USN, 1945-46. Recipient Disting. Service award Dept. Def., Disting. Service award also USAF. Clubs: Chicago, Chgo. Yacht, Knollwood. Home: 1834 Knollwood Dr Lake Forest IL 60045 Office: 222 W Adams Chicago IL 60606

STEUBEN, NORTON LESLIE, lawyer, educator; b. Milw., Feb. 14, 1936; s. Benjamin and Ria (Beerman) S.; m. Judith Ann Dickens, June 21, 1958; children: Sara Ann, Marc Nelson. A.B., U. Mich., 1958, J.D. with distinction, 1961. Bar: N.Y. 1962, Colo. 1975. Assoc., then ptnr. Hodgson, Russ, Andrews, Woods & Goodyear, Buffalo, 1961-68; mem. faculty U. Colo. Law Sch., Boulder, 1968—, prof. law, 1974—; of counsel Ireland, Stapleton, Pryor & Pascoe, Denver, 1980—; lectr. Law Sch., SUNY, Buffalo, 1961-68; officer Buffalo-Niagara Indsl. Devel. Corp., 1963-68, Buffalo Opportunities Devel. Corp., 1966-68. Author: Cases and Materials on Real Estate Planning, 1974, 2d edit., 1980, (with others) Problems in the Taxation of Individuals, Partnerships and Corporations, 1978, (with others) Problems in the Fundamentals of Federal Income Taxation, 1985, (with others) Problems in the Federal Income Taxation of Partnerships and Corporations, 1985; co-editor: Bittker, Fundamentals of Federal Income Taxation, 1983; contbr. articles to profl. jours. Mem. Boulder Human Rights Commn., 1969-72, chmn., 1972-74; mem. Boulder Landlord-Tenant Com., 1973-74; trustee Boulder Open Space Bd., 1976-81, vice chmn., 1978-79, chmn., 1979-81; trustee Congregation Har Ha-Shem, Boulder, 1978-79, v.p., 1979-81, pres., 1982-84; mem. Boulder Housing Authority, 1982—, vice chmn., 1984-85, chmn., 1985—. Recipient S.I. Goldberg award Alpha Epsilon Pi, 1957, Disting. Service to

Community award Buffalo Area C. of C., 1966, John W. Reed award U. Colo. Law Sch., 1970; Teaching Recognition award U. Colo.-Boulder, 1972, Teaching Excellence award, 1982. Mem. ABA, N.Y. State Bar Assn., Colo. Bar Assn., Boulder County Bar Assn., AAUP, Scribes (officer, editor Scrivener 1975-76, dir. 1979-82), Barristers Soc., Order of Coif, Tau Epsilon Rho. Democrat. Home: 845 8th St Boulder CO 80302 Office: U Colo 418 Fleming Law Bldg Boulder CO 80309

STEVENS, CHESTER WAYNE, real estate executive; b. Milw., May 24, 1925; s. Daniel Augusta and Genevieve (Kingston) S.; m. Bernice Louise Limberg, Nov. 8, 1947; 1 child, Doreen Louise Scholtes. Student, Augustana Coll., 1944. Mgr. ops. Plankinton Bldg., Milw., 1962-72; v.p. 1st Wis. Devel. Corp., Milw., 1972-78; pres., chief exec. officer Stevens Carley Co., Milw., 1978-81, C.W. Stevens Co., Milw., 1981-85; v.p. Towne Realty Inc., Milw., 1985—; cons. Milw. Redevel., 1981-82, Milw. Ins., 1983. Served with USAAF, 1943-46. Mem. Bldg. Owners and Managers Assn. (pres. 1972-73, dir. exec. com. 1976-82), Inst. Real Estate Mgmt. (pres. 1982, Mgr. of Yr., 1981), Milw. Bd. Realtors. Democrat. Lutheran. Club: Lake Ripley Country. Home: N 4439 Friedel Cambridge WI 53253 Office: Towne Realty Inc 710 N Plankinton Ave Milwaukee WI 53203

STEVENS, CLARK VALENTINE, lawyer; b. Detroit, Nov. 28, 1933; s. Valentine W. and Florence Mary (Potrykus) S.; m. Kathleen Rose Tobosky, Sept. 1, 1956; children—Mark, Glenn. B.S. in Acctg., U. Detroit, 1958; J.D., Wayne State U., 1967. C.P.A., Mich.; bar: Mich. 1967. Auditor, City of Detroit, 1958-60, IRS, 1960-65; tax mgr. Ernst & Ernst, 1965-69; mem. firm Regan & Stevens, 1969—; sec., dir. Mich. Rivet Corp., Warren, 1974—; bd. dirs. Tuff Machine Co., Warren, Mich., J.P.Tool Ltd., Ont., Can., Hercules Machine Tool & Die; pres., bd. dirs. Nat. Fitting Co., Warren, 1985. Mem. Mich. Bar Assn., Mich. Assn. C.P.A.s. Republican. Roman Catholic. Club: Grosse Pointe Yacht. Home: 843 S Rosedale Ct Grosse Pointe Woods MI 48236 Office: Regan & Stevens 1808 Penobscot Bldg Detroit MI 48226

STEVENS, DONALD KING, aeronautical engineer, consultant; b. Danville, Ill., Oct. 27, 1920; s. Douglas Franklin and Ida Harriet (King) S.; B.S. with high honors in Ceramic Engring., U. Ill., 1942; M.S. in Aeros. and Guided Missiles, U. So. Calif., 1949; grad. U.S. Army Command and Gen. Staff Coll., 1957, U.S. Army War Coll., 1962; m. Adele Carman de Werff, July 11, 1942; children—Charles August, Anne Louise, Alice Jeanne Stevens Kay. Served with Ill. State Geol. Survey, 1938-40; ceramic engr. Harbison-Walker Refractories Co., Pitts., 1945-46; commd. 2d lt. U.S. Army, 1942, advanced through grades to col., 1963; with Arty. Sch., Fort Bliss, Tex., 1949-52; supr. unit tng. and Nike missile firings, N.Mex., 1953-56; mem. Weapons Systems Evaluation Group, Office Sec. of Def., Washington, 1957-61; comdr. Niagara-Buffalo (N.Y.) Def., 31st Arty. Brigade, Lockport, N.Y., 1963-65; chief Air Def. and Nuclear br. War Plans div. 1965-67, chief strategic forces div. Office Dep. Chief Staff for Mil. Ops., 1967-69; chief spl. weapons plans, J5, U.S. European Command, Ger., 1969-72, ret., 1972; guest lectr. U.S. Mil. Acad. 1958-59; cons. U.S. Army Concepts Analysis Agy., Bethesda, Md., 1973—; cons. on strategy Lulejian & Assocs., Inc., 1974-75; cons. nuclear policy and plans to Office Asst. Sec. of Def., 1975-80, 84—; cons. Sci. Applications, Inc., 1976-78; Asst. camp dir. Piankeshaw Area council Boy Scouts Am., 1937; mem. chancel choir, elder First Christian Ch., Falls Church, Va., 1957-61, 65-69, 72—; elder, trustee Presbyn. Ch., 1963-65. Decorated D.S.M. (Army), Legion of Merit, Bronze Star. Mem. Am. Ceramic Soc., Assn. U.S. Army, U. Ill. Alumni Assn., U. So. Calif. Alumni Assn., Sigma Xi, Sigma Tau, Tau Beta Pi, Phi Kappa Phi, Alpha Phi Omega. Clubs: Rotary, Niagara Falls Country; Ill. (Washington); Terrapin. Contbr. articles to engring. jours.; pioneer in tactics and deployment plans for Army surface-to-air missiles. Address: 5916 5th St N Arlington VA 22203

STEVENS, ELISABETH GOSS (MRS. ROBERT SCHLEUSSNER, JR.), writer, journalist; b. Rome, N.Y., Aug. 11, 1929; d. George May and Elisabeth (Stryker) Stevens; m. Robert Schleussner, Jr., Mar. 12, 1966 (dec. 1977); 1 child, Laura Stevens. B.A., Wellesley Coll., 1951; M.A. with high honors, Columbia U., 1956. Editorial assoc. Art News Mag., 1964-65; art critic and reporter Washington Post, Washington, 1965-66; free-lance art critic and reporter Balt., 1966—; contbg. art critic Wall Street Jour., N.Y.C., 1969-72; art critic Trenton Times, N.J., 1974-77; art and architecture critic Balt. Sun, 1978-87. Author: Elisabeth Stevens' Guide to Baltimore's Inner Harbor, 1981, Fire and Water: Six Short Stories, 1982, Children of Dust: Portraits and Preludes, 1985; contbr. articles, poetry and short stories to jours., nat. newspapers and popular mags. Recipient A.D. Emmart award for Journalism, 1980, citation for critical writing Balt.-Washington Newspaper Guild, 1980; art critics' fellow Nat. Endowment Arts, 1973-74; fellow MacDowell Colony, 1981, Va. Ctr. for Creative Arts, 1982, 83, 84, 85, Ragdale Found., 1984; Work in Progress grantee for poetry Md. State Arts Council, 1986; Creative Devel. grantee for short fiction collection Mayor's Com. on Art and Culture, Balt., 1986. Mem. Coll. Art Assn., Am. Internat. Assn. Art Critics, Md. Writers Council, Balt. Writers Alliance, Balt. Bibliophiles, MLA., Popular Culture Assn., Authors Guild, Am. Studies Assn., Soc. Archtl. Historians. Home: 6604 Walnutwood Circle Baltimore MD 21212

STEVENS, GREG PETER, marketing professional; b. Nottingham, Eng., Sept. 9, 1946; s. Sam and Mabel (Boden) S.; m. Pamela Duncan; children: Amanda, Tim, Daniel, Debbie. Bus. systems salesman Olivetti Ltd., London, 1967-72; nat. sales mgr. 3M (U.K.) Ltd., Berks, Eng., 1972-81; sales dir. Moulinex Ltd., Surrey, Eng., 1981-86; mktg. and sales dir. Greenbrook Furniture, Essex, Eng., 1986, Belling and Co. Ltd., Middlesex, Eng., 1986-88, Gaggenau Electric (UK) Ltd., London, 1988—. Mem. Inst. of Dirs., Inst. Sales and Mktg. Mgmt., British Inst. Mgmt. Mem. Ch. of Eng. Home: 10 Erskine Close, Pamber, Heath, Hants RG26 6EP, England Office: Gaggenau Electric (UK) Ltd, Unit 2 Summit Centre, Heathrow, London England

STEVENS, J. PAUL, entrepreneur; b. Detroit, July 1, 1942; s. Constantine Jerome Dziuk and Mary Magdalene Stepanski; m. Alice Eaton, Jan. 6, 1959 (div. Dec. 1962); 1 child, David Paul; m. Georgia Jammie Bryant, July 1, 1963; 1 child, J. Paul Jr. BA, U. Mich., Ann Arbor, 1963, Rider Coll., Lawrenceville, N.J., 1966, Mich. State U., East Lansing, 1967. Lic. real estate broker, Mich. Treas. Stepanski Holdings, Alpena, Mich., 1955-59, Eaton Holdings, Ottawa, Ont., Can., 1959-62, Bryant Holdings, Alanson, Mich., 1963-82; cons. I.P.C., N.Y.C., 1962—, J.P. Stevens & Co. Ltd., N.Y.C. and Lansing, Mich., 1955—, Pitcairn Holdings, Jenkinstown, Pa., 1955—. Author: The Secret of Federal Budget Balancing, 1982; How to Prepare for the Crash of 1992, 1984. Recipient Internat. Banking award World Internat. Bank, 1962; named Knight of the Fourth degree KC, 1980. Life mem. Mich. State Numismatic Soc. (bd. dirs. 1962). Club: Capitol City Coin (Lansing) (treas. 1955—). Lodge: KC. Home and Office: 315 W Allegan St PO Box 15 III Lansing MI 48901

STEVENS, PATRICIA CAROL, university administrator; b. St. Louis, Jan. 11, 1946; d. Carroll and Juanita Donohue; AB, Duke U., 1966; MA, U. Mo.-Kansas City, 1974, PhD, 1982; m. James H. Stevens, Jr., Aug. 27, 1966 (div. Mar. 1984); children: James H. III, Carol Janet. Tchr. math, secondary schs., Balt., St. Louis, Shawnee Mission, Kans., 1966-71; lectr. U. Mo., Kansas City, 1975-76, research asst. affirmative action, 1976-79, coordinator affirmative action, 1979-82, instl. research assoc., 1982-84, acting dir. affirmative action and acad. personnel, 1984; dir. institutional research Lakeland Community Coll., 1984-86; asst. dean acad. affairs, math., engring. and tech. Harrisburg Area Community Coll., 1986—. Bd. dirs., v.p. Am. Cancer Soc. Jackson County, 75-84; council leader Hemlock Girl Scout U.S.A. bd. dirs., 1986—, PTA, 1975-77. Recipient Outstanding Service and Achievement award U. Mo. Kansas City, 1976; Jack C. Coffey grantee, 1978. Mem. Nat. Council Tchrs. Math., Mat. Assn. Am., Women in Leadership Inst., Am. Assn. Women in Community and Jr. Colls. (Pa. state coordinator 1988), Soc. Mfg. Engrs. (chmn.-elect 1988), Assn. Supervision and Curriculum Devel., Women's Equity Project, Nat. Assn. Student Personnel Adminstrs., Women's Network, Assn. Inst. Research, Phi Delta Kappa, (pres.), Phi Kappa Phi, Pi Lambda Theta, Delta Gamma (v.p., del. nat. conv. 1988, Cream Rose Outstanding Service award 1970). Home: 925 Pennsylvania Ave Harrisburg PA 17112 Office: Harrisburg Area Community Coll MET Dept 3300 Cameron Street Rd Harrisburg PA 17110

STEVENS, THEODORE FULTON, U.S. senator; b. Indpls., Nov. 18, 1923; s. George A. and Gertrude (Chancellor) S.; m. Ann Mary Cherrington, Mar. 29, 1952 (dec. 1978); children—Susan B., Elizabeth H., Walter C., Theodore Fulton, Ben A.; m. Catherine Chandler, 1980; 1 dau.; Lily Irene. B.A., U. Calif. at Los Angeles, 1947; LL.B., Harvard U., 1950. Bar: Calif., Alaska, D.C., U.S. Supreme Ct. bars. Pvt. practice Washington, 1950-52, Fairbanks, Alaska, 1953; U.S. atty. Dist. Alaska, 1953-56; legis. counsel, asst. to sec., solicitor Dept. Interior, 1956-60; pvt. practice law Anchorage, 1961-68; mem. Alaska Ho. of Reps., 1965-68, majority leader, speaker pro tem, 1967-68; U.S. senator for Alaska 1968—, asst. Rep. leader, 1977-85. Served as 1st lt. USAAF, World War II. Mem. ABA, Alaska Bar Assn., Calif. Bar Assn., D.C. Bar Assn., Am. Legion, VFW. Lodges: Rotary, Pioneers of Alaska, Igloo #4. Home: PO Box 879 Anchorage AK Office: 522 Hart Senate Bldg Washington DC 20510

STEVENSON, ARTHUR LAWRENCE, municipal official; b. Montreal, Que., Can., Dec. 17, 1935; s. Arthur Stevenson and Muriel Rufriange; m. Norma Sihvonen, June 8, 1957; children: Cathy, Peter. B in Commerce, Sir George Williams U., Montreal, 1965; MBA, Queens U., Kingston., Ont., Can., 1967. Adminstrv. supr. Texaco Can. Ltd., Montreal, 1960-65, mgr. adminstrv. services, 1967-71, asst. v.p. mktg., 1971-75; exec. dir. mgmt. services City of Toronto, 1975—; cons. City of Sao Paulo, Brazil, 1986-87, City of Chongqing, Peoples Republic of China, 1985-87, feasibility study Toronto Urban Inst., 1986-87. Exec. mem. Suomi Koti Finland House, Toronto, 1986-87. Mem. Adminstrv. Mgmt. Soc. (exec. bd., cert.), Inst. Pub. Adminstr. (chmn. nat. com. edn., tng., and devel. 1987). Home: 18 Lower Village Gate, Apt 306, Toronto, ON Canada M5P 3L7 Office: City of Toronto, Queen St City Hall, Toronto, ON Canada

STEVENSON, EARL, JR., civil engineer; b. Royston, Ga., May 8, 1921; s. Earl and Compton Helen (Randall) S.; B.S. in Civil Engring., Ga. Inst. Tech., 1953; m. Sue Roberts, Apr. 25, 1956; children—Catherine Helen, David Earl. Engr., GSA, Atlanta, 1959-60; engr., pres. Miller, Stevenson & Steinichen, Inc., Atlanta, 1960—; sr. v.p. Stevenson & Palmer, Inc., Camilla, 1984—; dir. Identification & Security Products, Inc., Atlanta. Served with USAAF, 1944-45. Registered profl. engr., Ga., Ala., S.C., Miss. Mem. Ga. Soc. Profl. Engrs., Water Pollution Control Fedn. Methodist. Home: 3163 Laramie Dr Atlanta GA 30339 Office: 2430 Herodian Way Smyrna GA 30080

STEVENSON, JAMES RICHARD, radiologist; b. Ft. Dodge, Iowa, May 30, 1937; s. Lester Lawrence and Esther Irene (Johnson) S.; m. Sara Jean Hayman, Sept. 4, 1958; children: Bradford Allen, Tiffany Ann, Jill Renee, Trevor Ashley. BS, U. N.Mex., 1959; MD, U. Colo., 1963; JD, U. N.Mex. 1987. Diplomate Am. Bd. Radiology, Am. Bd. Nuclear Medicine; Bar: U.S. Dist. Ct. N. Mex. Intern U.S. Gen. Hosp., Tripler, Honolulu, 1963-64; resident in radiology U.S. Gen. Hosp., Brook and San Antonio, Tex., 1964-67; radiologist, ptnr. Van Atta Labs., Albuquerque, 1970—; adj. asst. prof. radiology U. N.Mex., 1970-71; pres. med. staff AT & SF Meml. Hosp., 1979-80, trustee, 1982-83. Served to lt. col. USAR, 1963-70, Vietnam. Decorated Bronze Star. Allergy fellow, 1960. Fellow Am. Coll. Radiology (councilor 1981—), Am. Coll. Legal Medicine; mem. AMA (Physicians' Recognition award 1969—), Am. Coll. Nuclear Medicine (charter), Am. Coll. Nuclear Physicians (charter), Soc. Nuclear Medicine (v.p. Rocky Mountain chpt. 1975-76), Am. Inst. Ultrasound in Medicine, N.Am. Radiol. Soc., N.Mex. Radiol. Soc. (pres. 1978-79), N.Mex. Med. Soc. (chmn. grievance com.), Albuquerque-Bernalillo County Med. Soc. (scholar 1959), Nat. Assn. Health Lawyers, ABA (antitrust sect. 1986—), N. Mex. State Bar, Albuquerque Bar Assn., Sigma Chi. Republican. Methodist. Club: Albuquerque Country. Lodges: Elks, Masons, Shriners. Home: 3333 Santa Clara Dr SE Albuquerque NM 87106 Office: Van Atta Labs 8307 Constitution Dr NE Albuquerque NM 87110

STEVENSON, JOCKE SHELBY, lawyer; b. N.Y.C., June 12, 1934; s. Lincoln L. and Shirley (Grodnick) S.; m. Barbara Winokar, Oct. 7, 1970; 1 son, Marshall Lincoln. B.A., Yale U., 1956, J.D., 1959. Bar: N.Y. 1960, U.S. Dist. Ct. (ea. and so. dists.) N.Y. 1976, U.S. Ct. Internat. Trade 1978, U.S. Supreme Ct. 1981. Assoc. Marshall, Bratter, Greene, Allison & Tucker, N.Y.C., 1960-66; house counsel Burnham & Co., N.Y.C., 1966-70; sole practice, N.Y.C., 1971-77; ptnr. Hershcopf, Sloame & Stevenson, N.Y.C., 1978-80, Hershcopf, Stevenson, Tannenbaum & Glassman, N.Y.C., 1980—; adj. asst. prof. bus. law and polit. sci. Marymount Manhattan Coll., 1978-87; arbitrator N.Y.C. Small Claims Ct., 1977—, N.Y.C. Civil Ct., 1981—. Trustee Park Ave. Synagogue, N.Y.C. Mem. Assn. Bar City N.Y., N.Y. State Bar Assn. (com. on trusts and estates), ABA (com. sole practitioners and small firms). Clubs: Yale, University Glee (treas. 1987—) (N.Y.C.). Home: 400 E 85th St New York NY 10028 Office: 230 Park Ave Suite 3330 New York NY 10169

STEVENSON, JOHN REESE, lawyer; b. Chgo., Oct. 24, 1921; s. John A. and Josephine R. S.; m. Patience Fullerton, Apr. 10, 1943 (dec. 1982); children: Elizabeth F., Sally H. Stevenson Fischer, John Reese, Patience Stevenson Scott; m. Ruth Carter Johnson, May 21, 1983. A.B. summa cum laude, Princeton U., 1942; LL.B., Columbia U., 1949, D.J.S., 1952. Bar: N.Y. 1949, U.S. Supreme Ct. 1964. With firm Sullivan & Cromwell, N.Y.C., 1950—; mem. Sullivan & Cromwell, 1956-69, 75-87, of counsel, 1973-75, chmn., sr. partner, 1979-87, counsel, 1987—; legal adv. with rank of asst. sec. U.S. Dept. State, 1969-72, chmn. Adv. Com. on Pub. Internat. law, 1986—; adviser U.S. del. Gen. Assembly UN, 1969-74; chmn. U.S. del. Internat. Conf. on Air Law, The Hague, 1970; mem. U.S. del. Internat. Conf. on Law of Treaties, Vienna, 1969; ambassador, spl. rep. of Pres. Law of the Sea Conf., 1973-75; U.S. mem. Permanent Ct. of Arbitration, The Hague, 1969-79, 84—; U.S. rep. Internat. Ct. Justice, Namibia (S.W. Africa) case, 1970; spl. counsel U.S. del. Delimitation of Maritime Boundary in Gulf of Maine (Can. vs. U.S.A.), 1984; mem. OAS Inter-Am. Commn. on Human Rigths, 1987—; vice chmn. adv. bd. Ctr. for Strategic and Internat. Studies, U.S. Council for Internat. Bus. Arbitration Com.; prin. Ctr. Excellence in Govt.; bd. dirs. Bank of N.Y., Bank of N.Y. Co., Inc., Americas Soc. Author: The Chilean Popular Front, 1952; Contbr. articles to legal jours. Trustee Andrew W. Mellon Found.; trustee U.S. council ICC; pres., trustee Nat. Gallery Art. Fellow Am. Bar Assn. (hon.); mem. Am. Soc. Internat. Law (pres. 1966-68), N.Y. State Bar Assn. (chmn. com. on internat. law 1963-65), Internat. Law Assn., Institut de Droit Internat. (v.p. 1987-88), Assn. Bar City N.Y. (chmn. com. on internat. law 1958-61), Am. Arbitration Assn. (dir., chmn. exec. com.; chmn. internat. sect. law com.), Council on Fgn. Relations, Am. Law Inst., Ctr. for Strategic and Internat. Studies (vice chmn. adv. bd.), U.S. Council for Internat. Bus. (vice chmn. arbitration com.), Ctr. for Excellence in Govt. (prin.). Clubs: Links (N.Y.C.); Met. (Washington); Chevy Chase. Home: 1819 Kalorama Sq NW Washington DC 20008 Office: 1775 Pennsylvania Ave NW Washington DC 20006

STEVENSON, RAY, former health care management company executive; b. Marion, Ohio, July 25, 1937; s. Ray and Hazel (Emmelhainz) S.; m. Patricia Parker, June 17, 1960 (div. 1979); children: Jeffrey Parker, Kirk Andrew; m. Ellyn Gareleck, Feb. 8, 1985. BS, Ohio State U., 1959, MBA, 1967. Asst. adminstr. Children's Hosp., Columbus, Ohio, 1963-67; adminstr. Martin Meml. Hosp., Mt. Vernon, Ohio, 1967-71; sr. v.p. Hosp. Affiliates, Nashville, 1971-77; exec. v.p. Charter Med. Corp., Macon, Ga., 1977-79, pres., 1979-85; pres. R.S. Operators Inc., Atlanta, 1985—, R.S. Investors Inc., Atlanta, 1985—; mem. adj. faculty Ohio State U., 1979—; chmn. bd. dirs. World Link Corp., Atlanta, Filmworks Corp., Atlanta. Past chmn., bd. dirs. numerous hosps. and health-related orgns. Mem. Am. Coll. Hosps., Fedn. Am. Hosps. (bd. dirs. 1979-81), Nat. Assn. Psychiat. Hosps. Republican. Home: 1880 South Ocean Blvd Manalapan FL 33462 Office: RS Operators Inc 6487 Peachtree Indsl Blvd Atlanta GA 30360

STEVENSON, ROBERT MURRELL, music educator; b. Melrose, N.Mex., July 3, 1916; s. Robert Emory and Ada (Ross) S. AB, U. Tex., El Paso, 1936; grad., Juilliard Grad. Sch. Music, 1938; MusM, Yale, 1939; PhD, U. Rochester, 1942; STB cum laude, Harvard U., 1943; LittB, Oxford (Eng.) U.; Th.M., Princeton. Instr. music U. Tex., 1941-43, 46; faculty Westminster Choir Coll., Princeton, N.Y., 1946-49; faculty research lectr. UCLA, 1981, mem. faculty to prof. music, 1949—; vis. asst. prof. Columbia, 1955-56; vis. prof. Ind. U., Bloomington, 1959-60, U. Chile, 1965-66; cons. UNESCO, 1977. Author: Music in Mexico, 1952, Patterns of Protestant Church Music, 1953, La musica en la catedral de Sevilla, 1954, 85, Music before the Classic Era, 1955, Shakespeare's Religious Frontier, 1958, The Music of Peru, 1959, Juan Bermudo, 1960, Spanish Music in the Age of Columbus, 1960, Spanish Cathedral Music in the Golden Age, 1961, La musica colonial en Colombia, 1964, Protestant Church Music in America, 1966, Music in Aztec and Inca Territory, 1968, Renaissance and Baroque Musical Sources in the Americas, 1970, Music in El Paso, 1970, Philosophies of American Music History, 1970, Written Sources For Indian Music Until 1882, 1973, Christmas Music from Baroque Mexico, 1974, Foundations of New World Opera, 1973, Seventeenth Century Villancicos, 1974, Latin American Colonial Music Anthology, 1975, Vilancicos Portugueses, 1976, Josquin in the Music of Spain and Portugal, 1977, American Musical Scholarship, Parker to Thayer, 1978, Liszt at Madrid and Lisbon, 1980, Wagner's Latin American Outreach, 1983, Spanish Musical Impact Beyond the Pyrenees, 1250-1500, 1985; contbg. editor: Handbook Latin Am. Studies, 1976—; editor: Inter-Am. Music Rev, 1978—; contbr. to: New Grove Dictionary of Music and Musicians, 9 other internat. encys. Served to capt. U.S. Army, 1943-46, 49. Decorated Army Commendation ribbon; fellow Ford Found., 1953-54; Gulbenkian Found., 1966, 81; Guggenheim, 1962; NEH, 1974; recipient Fulbright research awards, 1958-59, 64, 70-71, 88-89, Carnegie Found. teaching award, 1955-56, Gabriela Mistral award OAS, 1985; Heitor Lobos Jury award OAS, 1988, Gold medal Sociedad Espanola de Musicologia, 1985; Orgn. Am. States medal, 1986, Cert. Merit Mexican Consulate San Bernardino, Calif., 1987. Mem. Am. Musicological Soc. (hon. life, Pacific SW chpt.), Real Academia de Bellas Artes, Hispanic Soc. Am., Am. Liszt soc. (cons. editor), Heterofonia (cons. editor). Office: UCLA Dept Music 405 Hilgard Ave Los Angeles CA 90024

STEVENSON, THOMAS HERBERT, management consultant, writer; b. Covington, Ohio, Oct. 16, 1951; s. Robert Louis and Dolly Eileen (Minnich) S.; m. Pamela F. Blythe, Mar. 10, 1979. BA, Wright State U., 1977. Teaching asst., research asst. Wright State U., 1975-77; teaching asst. Bowling Green State U., 1978; loan officer Western Ohio Nat. B Bank & Trust Co., 1979-80, asst. v.p. adminstrs., 1981-82, v.p. mgmt. services div., 1983-85; v.p., bank mgmt. cons. Young & Assocs., Inc., 1985-86, exec. v.p., 1987—; legis. impact analyst Community Bankers Ohio, 1985—; mem. exec. com. Owl Electronic Banking Network, 1981-85; mem. adv. bd. Upper Valley Joint Vocat. Sch. for Fin. Instns., 1981-85. Contbr. articles to profl. jours. Served to cpl. USMC, 1972-73. Recipient George Washington medal of Honor Freedom's Found., 1974. Mem. Am. Inst. Banking (adv. bd. 1982-85), Community Bankers Assn. Ohio, World Future Soc. Republican. Mem. Ch. of Brethren. Club: Eagles. Home: 9020 W U S Hwy 36 Covington OH 45318 Office: 121 E Main St Kent OH 44240

STEVER, HORTON GUYFORD, aerospace engineer, consultant; b. Corning, N.Y., Oct. 24, 1916; s. Ralph Raymond and Alma (Matt) S.; m. Louise Risley Floyd, June 29, 1946; children: Horton Guyford, Sarah, Margarette, Roy. A.B., Colgate U., 1938, Sc.D. (hon.), 1958; Ph.D., Calif. Inst. Tech., 1941; LL.D., Lafayette Coll., U. Pitts., 1966, Lehigh U., 1967, Allegheny Coll., 1968, Ill. Inst. Tech., 1975; D.Sc., Northwestern U., 1966, Waynesburg Coll., 1967, U. Mo., 1975, Clark U., 1976, Bates Coll., 1977; D.H., Seton Hill Coll., 1968; D.Engring., Washington and Jefferson Coll., 1969, Widener Coll., Poly. Inst. Bklyn., 1972, Villanova U., 1973, U. Notre Dame, 1974; D.P.S., George Washington U., 1981. Mem. staff radiation lab. MIT, Cambridge, 1941-42; asst. prof. MIT, 1946-51, asso. prof. aero. engring., 1951-56, prof. aero. engring., 1956-65, head depts. mech. engring., naval architecture, marine engring., 1961-65, asso. dean engring., 1956-59, exec. officer guided missiles program, 1946-48; chief scientist USAF, 1955-56; pres. Carnegie-Mellon U., Pitts., 1965-72; dir. NSF, Washington, 1972-76; sci. adviser, chmn. Fed. Council Sci. and Tech., 1973-76; dir. Office Sci. and Tech. Policy, sci. and tech. adviser to Pres., 1976-77; sci. cons., corp. dir. 1977—; dir. TRW, Schering-Plough; mem. secretariat guided missiles com. Joint Chiefs of Staff, 1945; sci. liaison officer London Mission, OSRD, 1942-45; mem. guided missiles tech. evaluation group Research and Devel. Bd., 1946-48; mem. sci. adv. bd. to chief of staff USAF, 1947-69, chmn., 1962-69; mem. steering com. tech. adv panel on aeros. Dept. Def., 1956-62; chmn. spl. com. space tech. NASA, chmn. research adv. com. missile and spacecraft aerodynamics, 1959-65; mem. Nat. Sci. Bd., 1970-72, mem. ex-officio, chmn. exec. com., 1972-75; mem. Def. Sci. Bd.; mem. adv. panel U.S. Ho. Reps. Com. Sci. and Astronautics; mem. Pres.'s Commn. on Patent System, 1965-67; chmn. U.S.-USSR Joint Commn. Sci. and Tech. Cooperation, 1973-77, Fed. Council Arts and Humanities, 1972-76; Pres.'s com. Nat. Sci. medal, 1973-77. Author: Flight, 1965; Contbr. articles to profl. publs. Past trustee Colgate U., Shady Side Acad., Sarah Mellon Scaife Found., Buckingham Sch.; trustee Univ. Research Assn., 1977—, pres., 1982-85; trustee Woods Hole Oceanographic Inst., 1980—, Univ. Corp. for Atmospheric Research, 1980-83; bd. dirs. Saudi Arabia Nat. Center for Sci. and Tech. bd., 1978-81; bd. govs. govs. U.S.-Israel Binat. Sci. Found., 1972-76. Recipient Pres.'s certificate of Merit, 1948, Exceptional Civilian Service award USAF, 1956, Scott Gold medal Am. Ordnance Assn., 1960, Disting. Pub. Service medal Dept. Def., 1969; comdr. Order of Merit Poland. Fellow AIAA (hon.; pres. 1960-62), Royal Aero. Assn., Am. Acad. Arts and Scis., Royal Soc. Arts, AAAS, Am. Phys. Soc.; mem. Nat. Acad. Engring. (chmn. aero. and space engring. bd. 1967-69, fgn. sec. 1984-88), Nat. Acad. Scis. (chmn. assembly engring. 1979-83), Nat. Conf. Bd. (sr. exec. council), Univs. Research Assn., 1982-84, Phi Beta Kappa, Sigma Xi, Sigma Gamma Tau, Tau Beta Pi. Episcopalian. Clubs: Cosmos (Washington); Bohemian (San Francisco); Century Association (N.Y.C.). Home: 1528 33d St NW Washington DC 20007 Office: Nat Acad Engring 2100 Constitution Ave NW Washington DC 20418

STEWARD, LINDA SUSAN, accountant; b. Columbus, Ohio, Oct. 26, 1956; d. James B. and Josephine (Johnson) S. BA in Econs. Lake Forest Coll., 1978; BS in Acctg. and Fin., Franklin U., 1979. econ. devel. profl. Acct. Nationwide Ins. Co., Columbus, 1976-79; acct. Kinnear Mfg. Co., Columbus, 1979-80; investment analyst dept. devel. State of Ohio, Columbus, 1980—; v.p. SRA & Assocs., 1986; pres. Number Crunchers Acctg. & Tax Service, 1986. Bd. dirs. Nat. Devel. Council, 1987. Mem. Am. Mgmt. Assn., Am. Soc. Exec. and Profl. Women, Nat. Assn. Accts., Assn. Bus. and Profl. Women in Constrn., Ohio Soc. C.P.A.s, Am. Mktg. Assn., Am. Women's Soc. C.P.A.s, Tech. Alliance Central Ohio, Columbus C. of C., Columbus Leadership Forum, Lake Forest Alumni Assn., Franklin U. Alumni Assn. Researcher in field. Office: 65 E State St Suite 200 Columbus OH 43215

STEWARD, PATRICIA ANN RUPERT, real estate consultant; b. Panama City, Panama, Apr. 20, 1945 (parents Am. citizens); d. Paul S. and Ernestina M. (Ward) Rupert; grad. Sch. of Mortgage Banking, Grad. Sch. of Mgmt., Northwestern U., 1979; m. Robert M. Levine, Oct. 28, 1978; children by previous marriage—Donald F. Steward, Christine Marie Steward. Vice pres. Asso. Mortgage & Investment Co., Phoenix, 1969-71; v.p., br. mgr. Sun Country Funding Corp., Phoenix, 1971-72, Freese Mortgage Co., Phoenix, 1972-74, Utah Mortgage Loan Corp., Phoenix, 1974-81; pres. Elles Corp., 1982—; condr. numerous seminars on mortgage fin. State chmn. Ariz. Leukemia Dr., 1977-78, mem. exec. com., 1979-80; troop leader Cactus Pine council Girl Scouts U.S.A., 1979-80; bd. dirs. Nat. Mental Health Assn., 1986-87, Ariz. Mental Health Assn., pres., 1986-87, bd. dirs., treas. Maricopa Mental Health Assn., 1984-85, v.p., 1985-86, pres., 1986-87; apptd. by state supreme ct. to Ariz. Foster Care Rev. Bd., 1984—, chairperson Bd. 8, 1986-87. Recipient cert. of appreciation Multiple Listing Service, Phoenix Bd. Realtors, 1975, Multiple Listing Service, Glendale Bd. Realtors, 1977. Lic. mortgage broker, Ariz. Mem. Ariz. Mortgage Bankers Assn. (dir. 1981-82, chmn. edn. com. 1981-82, founder continuing edn. seminar series 1981), Young Mortgage Bankers Assn. (chmn. exec. com. 1980-81), Cen. Ariz. Homebuilders Assn. Republican. Author: A Realtors Guide to Mortgage Lending, 1972. Office: Elles Corp 320 E McDowell Rd Suite 100 Phoenix AZ 85004

STEWART, ALBERT, JR., physician; b. Fayetteville, N.C., Sept. 23, 1920; s. Albert and Winnie Davis (Bruton) S.; student U. S.C., 1936-37; A.B., U. N.C., 1941; M.D., Washington U., 1944; m. Mary Inglesby DuBose, Oct. 5, 1951; children—Albert III, David DuBose, Paul Finley, Charles Inglesby, James Bruton. Intern, Barnes Hosp., St. Louis, 1944-45; fellow in medicine Washington U., St. Louis, 1946-47; ships surgeon Grace Line, N.Y.C., 1947; resident physician Meml. Hosp., Charlotte, N.C., 1948; fellow in gastroenterology Lahey Clinic, Boston, 1949; practice medicine specializing in internal medicine, Fayetteville, 1950—; physician VA Hosp., Fayetteville, 1950-51, cons., 1955-70; attending physician Cape Fear Valley Hosp., chief of staff, 1959; attending physician Highsmith Hosp., chief staff, 1965; clin.

assoc. prof. medicine U. N.C. Sch. Medicine, 1968-87; dir. East Coast Fed. Savs. and Loan Assn. Trustee, Highsmith-Rainey Meml. Hosp., 1983-86, N.C. Cancer Inst., 1978-86. Served as lt. (j.g.) USNR, 1945-46, to lt. M.C., 1952-54. Diplomate Am. Bd. Internal Medicine. Fellow A.C.P. (councillor N.C. chpt. 1982-85); mem. AMA, N.C. Med. Soc. (1st v.p. 1978-79), Cumberland County Med. Soc. (pres. 1952), Am. Soc. Internal Medicine, N.C. Soc. Internal Medicine (pres. 1981-82), Fayetteville Area C. of C. (dir. 1974-77), St. Andrew's Soc. of N.C. (dir. 1982—), Cape Fear Assembly (pres. 1970-73). Republican. Episcopalian. Club: Kiwanis (dir. 1980-81). Home: 1507 Morganton Rd Fayetteville NC 28305 Office: 114 Broadfoot Ave Fayetteville NC 28305

STEWART, ARLENE JEAN GOLDEN, designer, stylist; b. Chgo., Nov. 26, 1943; d. Alexander Emerald and Nettie (Rosen) Golden; B.F.A. (Ill. state scholar), Sch. of Art Inst. Chgo., 1966; postgrad. Ox Bow Summer Sch. Painting, Saugatuck, Mich., 1966; m. Randall Edward Stewart, Nov. 6, 1970; 1 child, Alexis Anne. Designer, stylist Formica Corp., Cin., 1966-68; with Armstrong World Industries, Lancaster, Pa., 1968—, interior furnishings analyst, 1974-76, internat. staff project stylist, 1976-78, sr. stylist Corlon flooring, 1979-80, sr. exptl. project stylist, 1980—; exhibited textiles Art Inst. Chgo., 1966, Ox-Bow Gallery, Saugatuck, Mich., 1966. Home: 114 E Vine St Lancaster PA 17602 Office: Armstrong Tech Ctr 2500 Columbia Ave Lancaster PA 17604

STEWART, CLARA WOODARD, advertising executive; b. Mineola, N.Y., May 1, 1952; d. Samuel Woodard and Irene (Colm) S.; BA in Broadcasting and Psychology, Mich. State U., 1974; MA in Journalism and Communications, U. Fla., 1975. Sales rep. Sta. WSBR, Boca Raton, 1976-77; media dir. Fred Wagenvoord Assoc., Inc., Boca Raton, Fla., 1977-81; v.p., sr. account exec., media dir. Birkenes & Foreman Advt., Boca Raton, 1981—, v.p. sr. account exec., media dir. Bd. dirs. Boca Raton Community Theater, 1977-78, publicity chmn., 1977-78; bd. dirs. United Way Greater Boca Raton, 1979—; pres. Friends of Boca Raton Public Library, 1981-83; mem. adv. bd. Boca Raton Symphony Orch., 1983-85; mem. Young Pres.'s Council Norton Gallery; treas. Friends of Caldwell Playhouse, 1984—. Mem. B/PAA (treas. Southeast Fla. chpt. 1984-87, bd. dirs. 1988—), Women in Communications, Advt. Fedn. Greater Ft. Lauderdale (bd. dirs. 1986—, sec. 1987-88, treas. 1988—), Am. Mktg. Assn. (sr. v.p. spl. programs, Gold Coast chpt., 1987-88) Mensa (SE regional public relations asst. 1978-80, treas. Palm Beach County 1981-83), Palm Beach County Hist. Soc. (newsletter editor 1980-82), Palm Beach County Geneal. Soc., Am. Film Inst., Nat. Trust Historic Preservation, BMW Car Club of Am., DAR, Phi Kappa Phi. Home: 6443 Parkview Dr Boca Raton FL 33433 Office: 2900 N Military Trail Suite 200 Boca Raton FL 33431

STEWART, DAVID HARRY, management consulting firm executive; b. Detroit, Oct. 16, 1939; s. Versile Harry and Alice Louise (Jackson) S.; m. Donna O.T. Lee, Jan. 5, 1980; 1 son, Eric Edward. B.A. in Philosophy, Calif. State U.-Long Beach, 1962. Computer programmer Aeronutronics, Newport Beach, Calif., 1959-63, Iowa State U., Ames, 1963-65; computer scientist Sch. Medicine U. So. Calif., Los Angeles, 1965-69; dept. head Rand Corp., Santa Monica, Calif., 1969-80; pvt. practice cons., Alexandria, Va., 1980-82; v.p. Viar and Co., Inc., Alexandria, 1982—; vis. fellow U. Copenhagen, Denmark, 1971. Bd. dirs. Los Angeles Regional Family Planning, 1976-77; mem. fiscal adv. com. Santa Monica Sch. Bd., 1980. Fellow Inst. for Advancement of Engring. (life), Phi Sigma Tau (life); mem. Assn. Computing Machinery, IEEE Computer Soc. (chpt. pres. 1978-80). Democrat. Club: Palos Verdes Yacht. Home: 7202 Rebecca Dr Alexandria VA 22307

STEWART, DAVID HYND, company executive, cattle breeder; b. Manzini, Swaziland, Aug. 14, 1928; s. Joseph Marcus and Jessie (Bennett) S.; m. Edulinda Marquerette Alves, Jan. 1, 1956; children—Sandra, Marina. Mng. dir. Stewart Investments Ltd., Siteki, Swaziland, 1973—. Senator Parliament of Swaziland, 1968; chmn. Bd. Swaziland Rwy., 1974; chmn. Sch. For Deaf, 1983; trustee Good Shepherd Hosp. Recipient King's medal His Majesty The King of Swaziland, 1970. Club: Manzini Lions (v.p. 1982-83). Lodge: Swaziland (asst. dir. ceremonies, jr. warden, 1987-88). Avocation: amateur photography. Home: Ngwenya Rd, Siteki Swaziland Office: Stewart Investments Ltd, Jacaranda Ave, Siteki Swaziland Office: PO Box 35, Siteki Swaziland

STEWART, DONALD BRUCE, actor, singer; b. S.I., N.Y., Nov. 14, 1935; s. George James and Florence Marian (Bonham) S.; m. Susan Clark Tremble, Nov. 5, 1973; children: Heather Michelle, Genevra Leigh. Student, Hastings Coll., 1953-55, Fla. State U. extension. Tester radio equipment Cessna Aircraft Co. Singer, Radio City Music Hall, 1960—; Broadway appearances in Camelot, 1961-62, The Fantasticks, 1962, Student Gypsy, 1963, Anyone Can Whistle, 1965; off Broadway roles in Jo, 1964, Babes in the Woods, 1965; starred in The Music Man, Sheets Theater, 1979; also numerous stock and night club appearances; starred as Michael Bauer in The Guiding Light, CBS-TV, 1968-85; star movies Lost, Carnival Magic, American Ninja; appeared in: numerous concerts with major symphony orchs. including N.C. and Ft. Lauderdale; appeared at, Kennedy Ctr. Host telethons for Cerebral Palsy, Easter Seals, March of Dimes; also benefit performances Am. Cancer Soc., Fight for Signt, United Jewish Appeal. Served as comdr., SAC USAF, 1956-61; Served as comdr. USNR, 1968-81; ret. comdr. Recipient Disting. Alumnus award Hasting Coll., 1984. Mem. Screen Actors Guild, Actors Equity, AFTRA. Office: care MSI Mgmt 250 W 57th St New York NY 10019

STEWART, DONALD FERGUSSON, development technologies educator; b. Bairnsdale, Australia, Feb. 12, 1938; s. John Fergusson and Gwenneth Alberta (Rees) S.; m. Laurel Jeanne Cock, Dec. 10, 1960; children: Mark, Rohan, Bryce. BS, U. Melbourne, Australia, 1958, MS, 1960, PhD, 1965. Chartered chemist, Australia. Sr. demonstrator in inorganic chemistry U. Melbourne, 1961-65, sr. research fellow in devel. technologies, 1985—; postdoctoral teaching fellow U. B.C., Vancouver, Can., 1965-66; research assoc. Princeton (N.J.) U., 1966; Leverhulme vis. fellow Leicester (Eng.) U., 1966-67; sr. research officer ICI Australia Ltd., Melbourne, 1967-73, sect. head, 1973-77; prof., head chem. tech. sect. Papua New Guinea U. Tech., 1977-84. Patentee; contbr. sci. papers to profl. publs. Mem. Australian Inst. Mining and Metallurgy (chmn. Papua New Guinea br. 1979-84), Royal Australian Chem. Inst., Papua New Guinea Inst. Chemistry (found. treas. 1984). Baptist. Office: Univ Melbourne, Parkville, Victoria 3052, Australia

STEWART, ERNEST WILLIAM, market research executive; b. Kansas City, Kans., Oct. 16, 1950; s. Ernest William Davey and Elizabeth Jeannette (Forbes) S.; m. Deborah Gayle Hofling, Dec. 8, 1979; children: Catherine Soteldo, Ernest William III. Student S.W. Mo. State U., 1968-71; B.S. in Communications, Lindenwood Coll., 1972; M.A. in Bus. Adminstrn. and Mktg., Webster U., 1982. Youth news editor St. Louis County Star, Overland, Mo., 1965-67; corr. St. Louis Post-Dispatch, 1971-72; writer/news editor Sta.-KMOX, St. Louis, 1972-73; reporter, then news editor St. Charles (Mo.) Jour., 1973-76; editorial dir. Ednl. Media Inc., St. Charles, 1976; dir. mem. relations St. Louis Tchrs. Credit Union, 1976-79; pub. relations rep. Mercantile Bancorp., St. Louis, 1979-82; dir. mktg. research Nat. Decorating Products Assn., St. Louis, 1982-86, dir market research and bus. devel., 1986—; tchr. seminars, condr. workshops in journalism, mktg.; cons. advt. agys. Recipient cert. excellence for best news story Suburban Newspapers Am., 1975, cert. appreciation Vocat. Indsl. Clubs Am., 1974, Pioneer award Mo. Credit Union League, 1978; named hon. Ky. col. Mem. Am. Mktg. Assn., Direct Mktg. Club St. Louis, Webster U. Alumni Assn. (long-range planning commn. 1982-86, bd. dirs. 1983—, pres. 1988—). Episcopalian. Author: (SBA Publ.) Starting a Retail Decorating Products Business. Contbr. numerous articles to decorating-products industry trade publs. Home: 323 E Jefferson Ave Kirkwood MO 63122 Office: Nat Decorating Products Assn 1050 N Lindbergh Blvd Saint Louis MO 63132

STEWART, EUGENE LAWRENCE, lawyer, trade association executive; b. Kansas City, Mo., Feb. 9, 1920; s. Edmund Dale and Mary Elizabeth (Raef) S.; m. Jeanne Ellen Powers, Oct. 19, 1945; children—Timothy, Terence, Brian. B.S., S.S., Georgetown U., 1947, J.D., 1951. Bar: D.C. 1951, U.S. Tax Ct. 1953, U.S. Ct. of Customs and Patent Appeals 1951-82, U.S. Ct. Appeals Fed. Circuit 1982, U.S. Ct. Appeals (3d cir.) 1985, U.S. Ct. Appeals (9th cir.) 1987, U.S. Ct. Appeals (11th cir.) 1988, U.S. Ct. Appeals (D.C. cir.) 1951, U.S. Ct. Internat. Trade 1958, U.S. Supreme Ct. 1967. Assoc. Steptoe & Johnson, Washington, 1951-56, ptnr., 1956-58; ptnr. Hume & Stewart, Washington, 1958-64; sole practice Law Offices of Eugene L. Stewart, Washington, 1964-69, 1978-83; ptnr. Lincoln & Stewart, Washington, 1969-73, Stewart & Ikenson, Washington, 1974-78, Stewart and Stewart, Washington, 1983—; adj. prof. law Georgetown U. Law Ctr., Washington, 1955-58; exec. sec. Trade Relations Council of U.S., Washington, 1962—. Contbr. articles to profl. publs. Pres., Sursum Corda, Inc. (low-income housing project), Washington, 1964-78. Served to lt. col. USAF, 1941-52; PTO. Recipient John Carroll award Georgetown U., 1966. Mem. ABA, D.C. Bar, Customs and Internat. Trade Bar Assn., Georgetown U. Alumni Assn. Inc. (pres. 1964-66). Republican. Roman Catholic. Office: Stewart and Stewart 1001 Connecticut Ave NW Washington DC 20036

STEWART, GEORGE TAYLOR, insurance executive; b. N.Y.C., Dec. 29, 1924; s. Fargo Calvin and Berthe Adelle (Pelleton) S.; m. Bonnie Elizabeth Myers, Sept. 14, 1946; children: Diane Barbara Stewart Carrington, Susan Gail Stewart Dupuis. A.B., Wesleyan U., Conn., 1947. Analyst Geyer & Co., Inc., 1948-54, Shelby Cullom Davis & Co., 1954-56; v.p. Blyth & Co., Inc., N.Y.C., 1956-65; chmn., chief exec. officer 1st Colony Life Ins. Co., Lynchburg, Va., 1965—; dir. Media Gen., Crestar Fin. Corp., Am. Mayflower Life Ins. Co. N.Y., Ethyl Corp. Author: Investing in American Business, 1964. Pres. The Corp. for Jefferson's Poplar Forest; chmn. bd. trustees Lynchburg Coll., 1977—, Salvation Army; trustee Va. Found. for Indep. Colls. Served as ensign USN, 1943-46, PTO. Recipient Lynchburg Bi-Centennial award, 1976, Lynchburg Pro Opera Civica award, 1982, award Navy League, 1981, Outstanding Businessman award Lynchburg Coll. Bus. Sch., 1982. Mem. Lynchburg C. of C. (pres.), N.Y. Soc. Security Analysts. Republican. Presbyterian (elder). Clubs: Metropolitan (N.Y.C.), Drug and Chemical (N.Y.C.); California (Los Angeles); Boonsboro Country (Lynchburg) (bd. dirs.), Piedmont, Waterfront. Office: First Colony Life Ins Co PO Box 1280 Lynchburg VA 24505

STEWART, IAN NICHOLAS, mathematics educator; b. Folkestone, Kent, Eng., Sept. 24, 1945; s. Arthur Reginald and Marjorie Kathleen (Diwell) S.; m. Avril Bernice Montgomery, July 4, 1970; James Andrew, Christopher Michael. BA, Cambridge U., Eng., 1966, MA, 1969; PhD, Warwick U., Coventry, Eng., 1970. Lectr. Warwick U., 1969-84, reader, 1984—; Humboldt fellow U. Tübingen, Fed. Republic Germany, 1974-75; vis. fellow U. Auckland, N.Z., 1976; assoc. prof. U. Conn., Storrs, 1977-78; prof. So. Ill. U., Carbondale, 1978, U. Houston, 1983-84. Author: Galois Theory, 1973, Concepts of Modern Mathematics, 1975, Catastrophe Theory and Its Applications, 1978, The Problems of Mathematics, 1987; editor: Longman-Pitman, London, 1975—, Mathematical Intelligencer, N.Y.C., 1980—, Dynamics and Stability of Systems, Oxford, Eng., 1986—, Nonlinearity, London, 1987—. Mem. Am. Math. Soc., London Math. Soc., Cambridge Philos. Soc., Sci. Fiction Writers Am., Save British Sci. Home: 8 Whitefield Close, Coventry CV4 8GY, England Office: U Warwick Math Inst, Gibbet Hill Rd, Coventry CV4 7AL, England

STEWART, ISAAC MITTON, lawyer, former chemical company executive, rancher; b. Salt Lake City, Dec. 30, 1904; s. Charles Biekley and Katherine (Romney) S.; m. June Woodruff, Dec. 16, 1927; children: Isaac Mitton, Charles Owen, June, Helen (Mrs. Richard B. Bennett), Wilford. Student, UCLA, 1923-24; J.D. with honors, George Washington U., 1928. Bar: Utah 1931, D.C. 1933. Adminstrv. asst. to Hon. Reed Smoot, U.S. senator from Utah, 1928-32; spl. asst. U.S. Senate Com. Finance, 1926-32; practiced law Washington, 1933-36; v.p. Union Carbide Corp., 1949-67, cons., 1967-81; dir., officer various corps.; dir. Consol. Freightways, Inc., 1958-83, cons., 1983-84; Owner Stewart Ranch, Kamas, Utah. Pres. Salt Lake (Mormon) Tabernacle Choir, 1962-75; Mem. adv. com. Senate Interstate and Fgn. Commerce Com. in a study fgn. trade; chmn. bus. and industry com. Nat. Citizens Commn. on Internat. Cooperation. Recipient George Washington U. Alumni Achievement award in law and pub. service, 1965. Mem. Am. Pioneer Trails Assn., Inc. (mem. adv. council), Am. Mothers Com., Inc. (adv. board), Phi Alpha Delta. Mormon. Home: Midway UT 84049 also: 77-048 Iroquois Dr Indian Wells CA 92210 also: Stewart Ranch RFD Kamas UT 84036 Office: Midway UT 84049

STEWART, JAMES, insurance broker; b. Germany, Nov. 25, 1912; s. Cecil Parker and Reine Marie Melanie (Tracy) S.; m. Martha, May 18, 1970; children: Tracy, James Cecil, Reine Elizabeth, Barry, China. Student, Harvard U., 1931. Salesman Electrolux Co., Los Angeles, Qui Soit Perfume, N.Y.C.; runner, stock clk. statis. dept. Bancamerica Blair Corp., N.Y.C., 1932-33; with classified advt. dept. New York Times; longshoreman Houston, Los Angeles, San Francisco, 1934; with publicity dept., cruise dir. French Line, N.Y.C., 1934-36; asst. marine mgr., br. mgr., br. supt., supt. ins. Am. Asiatic Underwriters, Shanghai, 1936-37, Hanoi and Saigon, 1938-39; sec., dir., supt. ins. Cie Franco-Americaine D'Assurances, 1936-39; embassy corr. for Paris-Soir, 1939; v.p. Frank B. Hall & Co., Inc., N.Y.C., 1939-42; ptnr., v.p., sec., chmn. and chief exec. officer, chmn. exec. com. Frank B. Hall & Co., Inc., 1945-78, also bd. dirs., 1945-84; bd. dirs. Frank B. Hall & Co. N.Y., Inc., 1970—; bd. dirs. Am. Mcht. Marine S/S Corp., Am. Homestead, Inc. Served with AUS, 1942; to lt. (s.g.) USNR, 1942-45. Decorated Shanghai medal, Asiatic Pacific medal. Mem. Assn. Average Adjusters of U.S., Am. Shipping Soc. Republican. Clubs: Racquet and Tennis, The Brook, India House (N.Y.C.); Deepdale Golf (Manhasset, L.I.); Everglades, Bath and Tennis (Palm Beach, Fla.); Sunningdale (Eng.) Golf; Travellers (Paris); Lyford Cay (Bahamas); Oslo (Norway) Golf; Southampton, Bathing Cup of Southampton, Nat. Golf Links of Am. (L.I.); Portland (London). Home: 42 W 58th St New York NY 10019 Office: Wall St Plaza New York NY 10005

STEWART, JAMES KEVIN, government official; b. Berkeley, Calif., Nov. 28, 1942; s. Berthold and Myrle (Minson) S.; m. Marise Rene Duff, Oct. 26, 1985; children: Daphne Brooks, Andrew MacLaren, James Kevin Spencer. B.S., U. Oreg., 1964; M.P.A., Calif. State U.-Hayward, 1977; grad. cert., U. Va., 1978; grad., FBI Nat. Acad., 1978. Chief of detectives Oakland Police Dept., 1976-81; instr. San Jose (Calif.) State U., 1978-81; spl. asst. atty. gen. Dept. Justice, Washington, 1981-82; dir. Nat. Inst. Justice, Washington, 1982—; guest lectr. U. Calif., Berkeley, Harvard U.; U.S. del. Council of Europe, Strasborg, France, 1984, U.N. Conf. on Crime Offenders, Milan, Italy, 1984. Bd. dirs. Alameda County Bd. Mental Health, 1979; chmn. conf. on reform of powers and rights respecting the investigation of criminal offenses and the apprehension of criminal offenders sponsored by the Soc. for the Reform of Criminal Law, Sydney, Australia, 1988—. Named Police Officer of Yr., Kiwanis Club of Oakland, 1976; recipient O.W. Wilson award for outstanding contbns. to law enforcement, 1986, Ennis J. Olgiati award Nat. Assn. Pre-Trial Services Agys., 1987, Predl. citation AIA, 1987, Nat. Criminal Justice Service award Nat. Criminal Justice Assn., 1988, Outstanding Nat. Contbn. to Policing Spl. award Police Exec. Research Forum, 1988; White House fellow, 1981-82. Mem. Internat. Assn. Chiefs of Police (dir. 1981-82), Police Mgmt. Assn. (founder, pres. 1979-81), White House Fellows Alumni, Nat. Acad. Assoc., Calif. Homicide Investigation Assn., Nat. Inst. Corrections (bd. dirs.), Crime Stoppers Internat. (bd. dirs.), Am. Judicature Soc., Calif. Peace Officers Assn. Delta Upsilon. Republican. Episcopalian. Club: University (Washington). Home: 6427 Lakeview St Falls Church VA 22041 Office: Dept of Justice Nat Inst Justice 633 Indiana Ave NW Washington DC 20531

STEWART, JAMES MAITLAND, actor; b. Indiana, Pa., May 20, 1908; s. Alexander Maitland and Elizabeth Ruth (Jackson) S.; m. Gloria McLean, Aug. 9, 1949; children: Michael, Ronald (dec.), Judy and Kelly (twins). B.S., Princeton U., 1932. Appeared in N.Y.C. in: Goodbye Again, 1932, Yellow Jack, Divided by Three and Page Miss Glory, 1934; motion pictures include Mr. Smith Goes to Washington, 1939, The Philadelphia Story, 1940, It's a Wonderful Life, 1946, Harvey U, 1950, Rear Window, 1954, Far Country, 1955 Man from Laramie, 1955, Strategic Air Command, 1955, A Man Who Knew too Much, 1956, Night Passage, 1957 Spirit of St. Louis, 1957, Vertigo, 1958, Bell, Book and Candle, 1959, It's a Wonderful World, 1959, Anatomy of Murder, 1959, The FBI, 1959, The Mountain Road, 1960, Two Rode Together, 1961 Mr. Hobbs Takes a Vacation, 1962, How the West Was Won, 1962, Take Her, She's Mine, 1963, Cheyenne Autumn, 1964, The Rare Breed, 1966, Flight of the Phoenix, 1966 Firecreek, 1968, Bandolero, 1968, Cheyenne Social Club, 1970, Fool's Parade, 1971, That's Entertainment, 1974, The Shootist, 1976, Airport '77, 1977, The Big Sleep, 1978, The Magic of Lassie, 1978; Right of Way, 1983; TV show The Jimmy Stewart Show, 1971-72, Hawkins Murder, 1973-74 (Recipient N.Y. Critics award for best male performance of 1939 in Mr. Smith Goes to Washington, Acad. award for performance in Philadelphia Story 1940, Berlin Film award 1962, Life Achievement award Am. Film Inst. 1980). Served to lt. col. Air Corps, World War II; brig. gen. USAF Res., 1959. Decorated D.F.C. with oak leaf cluster, Air medal, Croix de Guerre with palm; recipient Kennedy Ctr. medal for lifetime achievement, 1983, Spl. Career Oscar, 1984, Acad. Award, 1985, Presdl. medal of Freedom, 1985, Lifetime Achievement award Monterey Film Festival, 1988. Presbyterian. Office: ICM 8849 Beverly Blvd Los Angeles CA 90048 *

STEWART, JAMES WILLIAM, electrical engineer; b. Clarksville, Tex., July 23, 1926; s. Virgil Alfred and Effie Marie (Green) S.; m. Betty Gean Sutton, Apr. 24, 1945; children: James E., William W., Charles S. BSEE, Tex. Tech. U., 1950; MBA, Harvard U., 1956; cert. U.S. Army Command & Gen. Staff Coll., 1967. Mgr. bus. planning Ryan Aero. Co., San Diego, 1960-63; mgr. ops., spl. projects E-Systems, Inc., Dallas, 1963—; pres. Stewart-Sutton Enterprises, Inc. Sustaining mem. Republican Nat. Com. Served with USN, 1944-46, to maj. U.S. Army, 1950-60. Decorated Bronze Star. Mem. Res. Officers Assn., Second Inf. Div. Assn. (pres.), Tex. Tech. Elec. Engring. Assn., Nat. Property Mgmt. Assn., Assn. Old Crows, French Regiment de Corée (hon.), Tau Beta Pi, Phi Eta Sigma, Eta Kappa Nu, Alpha Chi. Republican. Presbyterian. Clubs: Forest Hollow (past pres.), Engrs., Harvard, Harvard Bus. (all Dallas). Address: 9040 Westbriar Dr Dallas TX 75228

STEWART, JEFFREY BAYRD, lawyer; b. Chgo., Feb. 6, 1952; s. Bruce A. and Harriet B. Stewart. A.B. magna cum laude (Rufus Choate scholar), Dartmouth Coll., 1974; J.D., Emory U., 1978. Bar: Ga. 1978. Ptnr., Arnall Golden & Gregory, Atlanta, 1978—. Mem. editorial bd. Emory Law Jour., 1977-78. Mem. ABA, State Bar Ga. Home: 724 Summit N Dr Atlanta GA 30324 Office: Arnall Golden & Gregory 1040 Crown Pointe Pkwy Suite 800 Atlanta GA 30338

STEWART, JOHN ANTENEN, physician; b. Hamilton, Ohio, Sept. 1, 1920; s. James E.B. and Rose Carol (Antenen) S.; m. Marian Louise Vail, June 23, 1945; children: John Vail, Robert Vail, Barbara Vail Stewart Keating. BS, U. Cin., 1942, MD, 1945. Diplomate Am. Bd. Ob-Gyn. Intern Harper Hosp., Detroit, 1945-46; at VA Hosp., 1946-48; resident Chgo. Maternity Ctr., 1948-49, Chgo. Lying-In Hosp., 1949, Ravenswood Hosp., Chgo., 1949-51; practice medicine specializing in ob-gyn Hamilton, Ohio, 1951—. Mem. Hist. Hamilton. Served to capt. M.C., U.S. Army, 1942-48. Fellow: Am. Coll. Ob-Gyn.; mem. Ohio State Med. Soc., Butler County Med. Soc., Hamilton Acad. Medicine, AMA, Royal Soc. Medicine, Am. Inst. Ultrasound Medicine, Am. Assn. Laparoscopists and Colposcopists, Am. Soc. for Colposcopy and Cervical Pathology, Royal Soc. Medicine, Am. Instn. Nuclear Magnetic Resonance, Am. Guild Organists, Ohio Genealogy Soc., Butler County Hist. Soc. Republican. Presbyterian. Home: 701 Oakwood Dr Hamilton OH 45013 Office: 240 Park Ave Hamilton OH 45013

STEWART, MARY CATHERINE, psychologist; b. Sault Ste. Marie, Mich.; d. Alexander Pringle and Marguerite Louise (Mc Carron) S.; A.B., U. Miami, 1941, M.S., 1960; m. Charles William Marker, Nov. 14, 1942 (div.); 1 son, Kevin Charles Stewart Marker. Human engring. analyst Boeing Co., Seattle, 1960-69; cons., Seattle, 1969-71, MITRE Corp., McLean, Va., 1971-74; research contract mgr. U.S. Dept. Transp., Washington, 1974-76; supervisory auditor psychologist GAO, Washington, 1976-78; established human factors group Idaho Nat. Engring. Lab. EG&G Idaho, Inc., Idaho Falls, 1978, mgr., 1978-82; profl. staff TRW Def. Systems Group, Norton AFB, Calif., 1982—. Mem. Human Factors Soc. (founder, 1st pres. Idaho chpt.). Office: TRW Def Systems Group Norton AFB CA 92409

STEWART, MICHAEL OSBORNE, university administrator; b. Sacramento, Aug. 25, 1938; s. Morris Albion and Marjorie Cathryn (McFarlin) S.; m. Lucille Arnette Cooper, June 11, 1961; children—Heather, Blaine. B.A., U. Calif.-Berkeley, 1960, M.A., 1961; Ph.D. Kans. State U., 1972. Asst. dean of students San Jose State U., Calif., 1965-66; assoc. dean of students Fort Hays State U., Kans., 1966-71, asst. v.p. acad. affairs, dir. instl. research, 1971-74; v.p. adminstrn. Peru State Coll., Nebr., 1974-79, U. S.D., Vermillion, 1979-82; v.p. bus. affairs, treas. Lawrence U., Appleton, Wis., 1982—; v.p., sec., treas. Lawrence Corp. Wis., 1983—; dir. Sch., Coll., Univ. Underwriters Ltd., 1987—. Mem. editorial bd. College and University Business Administration, 4th edit., 1981-82. Contbr. articles to profl. jours. Bd. dirs., chmn. Youth Care Inc., Hays, 1969-74. Served to capt. U.S. Army, 1961-65, col. Res., 1966. Alumni scholar U. Calif.-Berkeley, 1956-57; NDEA fellow, 1967-68. Mem. Kans. Assn. Student Personnel Adminstrn. (pres. 1970-71), Am. Assn. Univ. Adminstrns. (bd. dirs. 1979-82, chmn. audit budget com. 1982-84), Nat. Assn. Coll. Bus. Officers (small coll. and minority insts. com. 1985—, chmn. 1986—, task force on bus. competition 1987—), Central Assn. Coll. Bus. Officers (exec. com., idea exchange, publs., host coms. and programs 1974—), Appleton Taxpayers Assn. (bd. dirs. 1986), Theta Chi (nat. chaplain, sec. 1972-80). Democrat. Episcopalian. Lodge: Kiwanis (bd. dirs. Auburn club 1974, Appleton club 1984—, pres. 1988—). Avocations: collecting stamps, boating. Office: Lawrence Univ 115 S Drew St PO Box 599 Appleton WI 54912

STEWART, NORMAN LAWRENCE, college president; b. East St. Louis, Ill., June 20, 1942; s. Alfred and Helen (Grenard) S.; m. Nancy Lee Rosenthal, Aug. 28, 1966; children: Ian Andrew, Colin August, Brian Alfred. James scholar, U. Ill., 1960-61; B.A. with honors, diploma theology (asst. 1963-64), Wheaton (Ill.) Coll., 1963; honors scholarship, Near East Sch. Archaeology, Jerusalm, 1962; cert., Goethe Inst., W. Ger., 1964; fellow, U. Freiburg, W. Ger., 1964-65; honors fellow, Princeton Theol. Sem., 1966-67; M.A. (U.S. Steel Found. fellow), St. Louis U., 1971, Ph.D., 1972; Fulbright fellow, U. Bonn, W. Ger., 1971-72; LLD, Kobe U., Japan, 1987. Asst. dir. Dothan Archaeol. Expdn., Jenin, Israel, 1964; resident dir. Near East Sch. Archaeology, 1965-66; research asso. polit. archives W. German Fgn. Ministry, Bonn, 1971-72; mem. faculty Maryville Coll., St. Louis, 1972-77; asso. prof. history, asso. acad. dean Maryville Coll., 1975-77; acad. dean. Coll. Mt. St. Joseph, Cin., 1977-79; pres. Rockford (Ill.) Coll., 1979-87, Regent's Coll., London, 1984-87; mng. dir. Brakeley, John Price Jones, London, 1987—; co-founder Lincoln Acad., N.Y.C., 1966; bd. dirs. Rockford Devel. Corp., 1979-87. Author: Dothan Archaeological Expedition Tomb No. 1, 1964, German Relations with the Arab East, 1937-41, 1972. Trustee Kobe Coll., 1979—; trustee Lincoln Acad., Ill., 1979-87; bd. dirs. New Am. Theatre, Rockford, 1980-86, Swedish-Am. Hosp., 1980-87, Keith Country Day Sch., 1982-87; div. chmn. Rockford United Way, 1981; precinct committeeman, St. Clair County, Ill., 1972-73; adv. bd. St. Louis Metro Police Acad., 1976-77; bd. dirs. Vis. Nurses Assn., Cin., 1978-79. Mem. Am. Assn. Pres. Ind. Colls. and Univs., Internat. Assn. Univ. Pres., Council Ind. Colls., Archaeol. Inst. Am., Am. Hist. Assn., Phi Beta Kappa, Alpha Sigma Nu. Presbyterian. Home: 11 Talbot Rd, London N6 4QS, England

STEWART, PAUL ARTHUR, pharmaceutical company executive; b. Greensburg, Ind., Sept. 28, 1955; s. John Arthur and Alberta Jeannette (Densford) S.; m. Susan Rhodes, Dec. 20, 1975. B.S., Purdue U., 1976; MBA, Harvard Bus. Sch., 1987. Grad. asst. Purdue U., West Lafayette, Ind, 1977; asst. treas. Stewart Seeds, Inc., Greensburg, Ind., 1977-82, sec., treas., 1982-84; cons. The Boston Cons. Group, Inc., Chgo., 1986; founder, owner PASCO Group, mgmt. and computer cons., aircraft leasing, 1979-87; mgr. bus. planning-agrichems. Eli Lilly & Co., Indpls., 1987—. Mem. Greensburg-Decatur County Bd. of Airport Commrs., 1980-85, pres., 1980, 81, 83; mem. Decatur County Data Processing Bd., 1982-85. Mem. Ind. Seed Trade Assn. (dir. 1982-85, v.p. 1983-84, pres. 1984-85, chmn. legis. com. 1982-83), Am. Seed Trade Assn. (legis. com. 1983-85), Alpha Gamma Rho. Republican. Presbyterian. Office: Eli Lilly & Co Lilly Corp Ctr Indianapolis IN 46285

STEWART, PETER PAULS, distribution, real estate executive, religious and educational foundation administrator; b. Kansas City, Mo., May 26, 1920; s. Harry Ewing and Myrtle Marie (Pauls) S.; m. Elizabeth May Exall, July 18, 1942; children: Elizabeth Stewart Wally, Peter Bruce, Alan Gordon, Margaret Catherine, David Exall. BA in Econs. cum laude, Harvard U., 1942. Asst. mgr. Stoneleigh Hotel, Dallas, 1942; asst. gen. mgr. Tractores Universales, Mexico City, 1948; mgr. Auto Productos, Mexico City, 1949; asst. sales mgr. The Stewart Co., Dallas, 1950-54, pres., 1956—; ptnr. Auto

Convoy Co., Dallas, 1950-83; pres., founding dir. Thanks-Giving Sq. Found., Ctr. for World Thanksgiving, Nat. Thanksgiving Commn. City plan commr., 1958-60; past mem. bd. dirs. Dallas Mus. Fine Arts, Dallas Arboretum, Hockaday Sch., Dallas; pres. Dallas Assembly, 1970-71. Served to capt. AUS, 1943-46. Decorated Bronze Star. Recipient Linz award, 1970. Mem. Chief Execs. Orgn., Young Pres.' Orgn. Republican. Episcopalian. Clubs: Brook Hollow Golf, Tower (Dallas). Author: With United Hearts, 1975, The First Thanksgiving of the U.S., 1977, The World Gives Thanks, 1982, The First Step, 1987.

STEWART, W. RODERICK, manufacturing company executive; b. Norwood, Ohio, Mar. 22, 1916; s. Raymond Forrest and Estelle Marie (Keller) S.; m. Dolores Faye Doll., Apr. 15, 1944; 1 dau., Sharon Marie. BBA, U. Cin., 1939. Owner, dir. Music by Roderick Orch., 1934-49; v.p. Cin. Lithographing Co., 1949-63; owner, pres. Concrete Surfacing Machinery Co., Cin., 1963-71, Bossert Machine Co., Cin., 1963-71, R & C Tool & Mfg., Amelia, Ohio, 1970-71, Bourbon Copper & Brass, Cin., 1968-71; pres. Stewart Industries, Inc., Cin., 1971-80, chmn. bd., chief exec. officer, 1980-87; pres. Printing Machinery Co., Cin., 1976-86; chmn bd. dirs. Stewart Safety Systems, Inc., 1981—. Chmn., dir. Greater Cin. & Ky. chpt. Nat. Hemophilia Found., 1976-80; del. White House Conf. Small Bus., 1980; trustee Ohio Presbyn. Retirement Services. Served with USNR, 1942-45. Named Wyo. Citizen of Yr., 1987. Mem. Cin. C. of C. (Small Businessman of Yr. 1980), Lambda Chi Alpha. Presbyterian. Clubs: Maketewah Country, Northport Point Golf, Cin. (Man of Yr. 1979), Officers of World Wars. Lodges: Rotary, Masons, Shriners, Royal Jesters. Home and Office: 220 Linden Dr Wyoming OH 45215

STEWART-CLARKE, JOHN ERNEST, security company executive; b. Great Yarmouth, Norfolk, Eng., Dec. 30, 1928. Ed. Coll. Arts, Great Yarmouth, Coll. of Arts, Kidderminster, Ministry of Def., London, U. Bristol; M.A. in Human Resource Devel. Mgr., Gould Ltd., Norwich, Eng., 1945-49; prodn. exec. J. Corbett & Sons Ltd., Stourport, Eng., 1949-61; sales exec. Atkinsons Ltd., Bristol, 1961-70; cons. Securicor, London, 1970-80; dir. Security Tng. Ltd., Cheltenham, 1980-84; project exec., dir. Wirebird, Gloucester, Eng., 1984—; lectr. in aviation security, 1978—, Mid Glos Tech. Coll., Stroud, Eng., 1987—; broadcaster bus. affairs, 1985—; dir. M.V.C., Gloucester, Stewart-Clarke Assocs., Gloucester, Alert Security Confs. Ltd., 1980-84, Marnat Mktg. Ltd., 1980-83; cons. P & M Office Equipment, Gloucester, 1984—. Contbr. articles to profl. jours. Chmn. Crime Prevention Panel, Gloucester, 1979, Police and Community Com., Gloucester, 1982; vice chmn. Gloucester Conservative Assn., 1987—. Named Tng. Officer Grade A with honors, Rd. Transport Tng. Bd., London, 1978. Fellow Inst. Dirs., Inst. Indsl. Mgrs., Brit. Inst. Mgmt.; mem. Acad. Security Educators and Trainers (charter). Mem. Ch. of England. Clubs: Constitution (Bristol, Eng.); Conservative (Gloucester). Avocations: music; philately; ballroom dancing; writing. Home: The Willows, Crickley Hill Witcombe, Gloucestershire GL3 4UQ, England

STEYER, ROY HENRY, lawyer; b. Bklyn., July 1, 1918; s. Herman and Augusta (Simon) S.; m. Margaret Fahr, Feb. 21, 1953; children: Hume R., James P., Thomas F. A.B. with honors in Govt. and Gen. Studies, Cornell U., 1938; LL.B. cum laude, Yale U., 1941. Bar: N.Y. 1941, various fed. cts. from 1947, U.S. Supreme Ct. 1955. Assoc. firm Sullivan & Cromwell, N.Y.C., 1941-42, 46-52, ptnr., 1953—. Trustee N.Y.C. Sch. Vol. Program, 1974-78. Served to lt. USNR, 1943-46. Mem. Am. Coll. Trial Lawyers, ABA (chmn. com. on antitrust problems in internat. trade antitrust sect. 1959-62), N.Y. State Bar Assn., Assn. Bar City N.Y. (chmn. com. on trade regulation 1962-64), N.Y. County Lawyers Assn. (bd. dirs. 1972-78), Am. Judicature Soc., Am. Soc. Internat. Law, N.Y. Law Inst., Order of Coif, Phi Beta Kappa, Phi Kappa Phi. Clubs: Century Assn. (N.Y.C.), India House (N.Y.C.), Yale (N.Y.C.). Home: 112 E 74th St New York NY 10021 Office: Sullivan & Cromwell 125 Broad St New York NY 10004

STICH, OTTO, Swiss government official; b. Dornach, Canton Solothurn, Jan. 10, 1927; m. Trudi Stampfli. Grad., U. Basel, 1947, Dr. Econs., 1955. County magistrate of Dornach, 1957-65; head personnel office COOP Switzerland, 1971—, dep. dir., 1981—; nat. councillor, 1963-83, fed. councillor, 1983-84; head fed. dept. fin., Switzerland, 1984—, pres., 1988—. Social Democrat. Office: Chief Dept Finance, Bern Switzerland *

STICHWEH, RUDOLF, sociologist; b. Lemgo, Westphalia, Federal Republic of Germany, Aug. 26, 1951; s. Rudolf and Hella (Kullmann) S. Diploma, U. Bielefeld, 1977, PhD, 1983. Research assoc. Fritz Thyssen Stiftung, Cologne, Fed. Republic Germany, 1984-86, Max-Planck-Gesellschaft, Cologne, Fed. Republic Germany, 1985—, Maison des Scis. de l'Homme, Paris, 1987. Author: Zur Entstehung des Modernen Systems Wissenschaftlicher Disziplinen, 1984; (with others) Differenzierung and Verselbstaendigung, 1988; editor: Theorie als Passion, 1987; contbr. articles to profl. jours. Home: Mozartstrasse 2, D-5000 Cologne Federal Republic of Germany Office: Max-Planck-Inst, Lothringer Strasse 78, D-5000 Cologne Federal Republic of Germany

STICK, THOMAS HOWARD FITCHETT, architect; b. Balt., Feb. 28, 1938; s. Gordon M.F. and Anne Howard (Fitchett) S.; m. Rosalie Wade Reynolds, June 5, 1959 (div. Apr. 1982); children—H. Edward M., Alexander W., David F.; m. 2d Joyce C. Yeargin, July 25, 1982; stepchildren—Richard F. Carr Jr., Leah W. Carr, V. Maria Carr, John N. Carr. B.A. in Psychology, Yale U., 1960; postgrad. Md. Inst., 1962, U. Pa. Grad. Sch. Architecture, 1964. Registered architect, Pa., Md., Del., N.J., Va., Maine, N.Y., D.C., Mass., N.H., N.C., Vt.; cert. recommendation Nat. Council Archtl. Registration Bds. Architect, Vincent G. Kling & Ptnrs., Phila., 1964-74, B.J. Hoffman & Assocs., Berwyn, Pa., 1974; ptnr. Grim & Stick, Ardmore, Pa., 1975-77; prin. Stick Assocs., Gladwyne, Pa., 1977-80; corp. architect Gino's Inc., King of Prussia, Pa., 1980-81; mgr. constrn. adminstrn. Ballinger Co., Phila., 1981-83; sr. constrn. claims cons. MDC Systems Corp., Phila., 1984-85; chief architect Day & Zimmermann Inc., Phila., 1985—, discipline mgr. 1987—; v.p. F-S Found., 1986—, also bd. dirs. Photographer in one-man show Eastern Camera Gallery, 1972. Mem. AIA, Pa. Soc. Architects, Bldg. Ofcls. and Code Adminstrs. Internat., Constrn. Specifications Inst., Nat. Fire Protection Assn., Soc. War of 1812 (sec. 1977-82), Soc. of Cincinnati, Soc. Colonial Wars, SR, Descs. of Lords of the Md. Manors, Mil. Order of Loyal Legion of U.S., Huguenot Soc., Am. Clan Gregor Soc., St. Andrew's Soc. of Balt., St. George's Soc. of Balt., Zeta Psi. Republican. Episcopalian. Clubs: Merion Cricket (Haverford, Pa.); Yale, Peale (Phila.). Lodge: Sovereign Mil. Order of Temple of Jerusalem (comdr.), Sovereign Order of St. John of Jerusalem (Knight of Justice). Home: 1501 Monticello Dr Gladwyne PA 19035 Office: Day & Zimmermann Inc 1818 Market St Philadelphia PA 19103

STICKEL, EBERHARD ULRICH, mathematician; b. Stuttgart, Fed. Republic Germany, Aug. 24, 1958; s. Gerhard Franz Paul and Siglinde Klara (Foerstner) S.; m. Anne Stickel, Jan. 5, 1961. MS, Syracuse U., 1983; diploma in math., U. Ulm, Fed. Republic Germany, 1984; PhD, U. Ulm, 1985. Asst. prof. Ulm U., 1984-86; vis. prof. U. Western Ont., Can., 1986; cons. Arthur Andersen & Co., Stuttgart, 1986-87, WSGV, Stuttgart, 1987—. Contbr. articles to profl. jours. Mem. Am. Math. Soc., Deutsche Math. Vereinigung. Home: Hallschlag 149, 7000 Stuttgart 50 Federal Republic of Germany Office: WSGV, Lautenschlager Strasse, Stuttgart, Baden-Wuerttemberg Federal Republic of Germany

STICKLER, ALFONS CARDINAL, cardinal Roman Catholic Church; b. Neunkirchen, Vienna, Austria, Aug. 23, 1910. ordained 1937. Consecrated bishop Titular See Volsinium, 1983; then archbisho, proclaimed cardinal, 1985; chief Vatican librarian and archivist; deacon S. Giorgio of Velabro. Address: Citta del Vaticano, Rome Italy *

STICKLER, MITCHELL GENE, computer systems engineer; b. Fairmont, W.Va., Sept. 19, 1934; s. Elmer Daniel and Ruby Lee (Ball) S.; B.S. in Elec. Engring., W.Va. U., 1960; M.S. in Elec. Engring., U. Pitts., 1962; postgrad. Lehigh U., 1962-64; m. Janet Elaine Mankins, Aug. 6, 1960; children—Mitchell, Matthew, Mark, Patrick, Jason. Engr., Westinghouse Electric Corp., Youngwood, Pa., 1960-62; mem. tech. staff Bell Telephone Labs., Allentown, Pa., 1962-64, supr., 1964-68; v.p., dir. Virtual Computer Services, Union, N.J., 1968-70; systems cons. Pentamation Enterprises, Inc., Bethlehem, Pa., 1970-85, v.p. quality, 1985—. Served with USAF, 1954-57. Registered profl. engr., Pa. Mem. IEEE (computer group 1960—), Nat. Soc., Profl. Engrs. Home: Route 2 Box 31AA Schnecksville PA 18078

STICKNEY, ROBERT ROY, fisheries educator; b. Mpls., July 2, 1941; s. Roy E. and Helen Doris (Nelson) S.; m. LuVerne C. Whiteley, Dec. 29, 1961; children: Robert Roy, Marolan Margaret. BS, U. Nebr., 1967; MA, U. Mo., 1968; PhD, Fla. State U., 1971. Cert. fisheries scientist. Research assoc. Skidaway Inst. Oceanography, Savannah, Ga., 1971-73, asst. prof., 1973-75; asst. prof. Texas A&M U., College Station, 1975-78, assoc. prof., 1978-83, prof., 1983-84; prof. zoology, dir. Fisheries Research Lab., So. Ill. U., Carbondale, 1984-85; dir. Sch. of Fisheries U. Wash., Seattle, 1985—; chmn. S-168 com. So. Regional Coop. Research Project, 1981-84; bd. dirs. Western Region Aquaculture Consortium, 1987-88. Author: Principles of Warmwater Aquaculture, 1979, Estuarine Ecology of the Southeastern United States and Gulf of Mexico, 1984; editor Culture of Non-Salmonid Freshwater Fisheries, 1986, Reviews in Aquatic Sciences; contbr. articles to profl. jours. Served with USAF, 1959-63. Mem. Am. Fisheries Soc. (pres. fish culture sect. 1983-84, Tex. Aquaculturist of Yr. 1979), Am. Inst. Fish Research Biologists (past Tex. div. dir.), Am. Inst. Nutrition, World Aquaculture Soc. (bd. dirs.), Am. Soc. Limnology and Oceanography. Home: 17507 NE 133 Redmond WA 98052 Office: U Wash Sch Fisheries WH-10 Seattle WA 98052

STIEGLER, KARL DRAGO, mathematician; b. Zagreb, Yugoslavia, Oct. 24, 1919; s. Stephan and Catharina S.; m. Hildegard Sarco, Sept. 23, 1951; 1 child, Cornelia. MS in Math. and Theoretical Physics, U. Zagreb, 1946; PhD in Theoretical Physics, Tech. U., Munich, 1963. Prof. math. Engring Coll., Zagreb, 1946-50; research mathematician, constructor optical instruments Ghetaldus Co., Zagreb, 1950-56, chief dept. ophthalmol. optics, 1957-59; fellow faculty of math. Tech. U., Munich, 1964—; sci. cons. AFGA Camera Works, Munich, 1960—, Tech. U., Munich, 1964—; lectr. in field; active profl. internat. congs. Contbr. articles to profl. jours.; researcher in relativity, quantum physics, cosmology, theory of group representations, history and philosophy of math. scis. UNESCO research fellow Inst. Henri Poincaré, Sorbonne, U. Paris, 1954-55; hon. fellow Research Inst. History of Sci. and Tech., Deutsches Mus., Munich, 1964. Fellow Royal Astron. Soc. (London), Nat. Acad. Scis. (India), N.Y. Acad. Scis.; mem. Soc. Astronomica Italiana, Soc. Math. de France, Internat. Union Mathematicians, Deutsche Gesellschaft für Angewandte Optik. Office: Postfach 750 839, Munich 75 Federal Republic of Germany

STIEHL, CHARLES WILLIAM, physician, surgeon; b. South Milwaukee, Wis., Apr. 23, 1924; s. Carl Ernst and Marjorie (Simon) S.; m. Sarah D. Harding, Dec. 20, 1945 (div. 1957); children—Patti Stiehl Philbin, Carl Harding, Sarah Ann; m. Edith Ann Mauer, Nov. 1967; 1 child, Edith Ann. B.S., Northwestern U., 1942, B.M., M.D., 1947. Intern Columbia Hosp., Milw., 1947-48; resident St. Mary's Hosp., Milw., 1948-49; physician and surgeon Algoma Clinic, Wis., 1950-66; chief surgery Algoma Meml. Hosp., 1964—; med. dir. Heil Co., Milw.; owner Von Stiel Wine, Inc., Algoma, 1961—; pres. S&M Real Estate Corp., Algoma, 1958—. Author emergency medicine computer dictation software program; originator Von Stiehl natural cherry wine, stabilization natural cherry wine, aging wrap. Mem. Sch. Bd., 1954-58. Served with USNR, 1942. Mem. Wis. Med. Soc., Kewaunee County Med. Soc. (past pres.), Wis. Coll. Emergency Physicians, Acad. Indsl. Medicine, Beta Theta Pi, Nu Sigma Nu. Lutheran. Home and Office: 2740 W Forest Home Ave Milwaukee WI 53215

STIFEL, FREDERICK BENTON, pastor, biochemist, nutritionist; b. St. Louis, Jan. 30, 1940; s. Carl Gottfried and Alma J. (Clark) S.; m. Gail Joane Stewart, Aug. 10, 1963; children: Tim, Faith, Seth, Elizabeth. BS, Iowa State U., 1962, PhD, 1967; MDiv., Melodyland Sch. Theol., Anaheim, Calif., 1979. Ordained to ministry Evang. Presbyn. Ch., 1981. Lab. supr., research chemist U.S. Army Med. Research and Nutrition Lab., Denver, 1968-74, Letterman Army Inst. Research, San Francisco, 1974-76; intern pastor Melodyland Christian Ctr., Anaheim, 1979-80; assoc. pastor Faith Presbyn. Ch., Aurora, Colo., 1980—; chmn. Care of Candidates Com., Presbytery of West, Denver, 1985—; bd. dirs. Christian Family Services, Aurora; v.p. Love, Inc. of Metro Denver; regional coordinator Nat. Assn. Single Adult Leaders. Contbr. clin. med. and nutritional articles to profl. jours. Del. Iowa State Rep. Conv., Des Moines, 1964, Colo. State Rep. Conv., Denver, 1984; mem. parent adv. council, IMPACT drug intervention team Rangeview High Sch., Aurora, 1985—; vice chmn. Young Life com. Marin County, Calif., 1974-76. Served to capt. U.S. Army Med. Service Corps, 1967-70. Recipient Sci. Achievement award U.S. Army Sci. Conf., West Point, N.Y., 1968, 70. Mem. Am. Inst. Nutrition, Am. Soc. Clin. Nutrition, N.Y. Acad. Scis., Am. Sci. Affiliation, Evang. Theol. Soc., Phi Eta Sigma, Phi Kappa Phi, Alpha Zeta, Gamma Sigma Delta, Kappa Sigma, Sigma Xi. Home: 3492 S Blackhawk Way Aurora CO 80014 Office: Faith Presbyn Ch 11373 E Alameda Ave Aurora CO 80012

STIGLER, GEORGE JOSEPH, economist, educator; b. Renton, Wash., Jan. 17, 1911; s. Joseph and Elizabeth (Hungler) S.; m. Margaret Mack, Dec. 26, 1936 (dec. Aug. 1970); children: Stephen, David, Joseph. B.B.A., U. Wash., 1931; M.B.A., Northwestern U., 1932; Ph.D., U. Chgo., 1938; Sc.D., Carnegie Mellon U., 1973, U. Rochester, 1974, Helsinki Sch. Econs., 1976, Northwestern U., 1979; LL.D., Brown U., 1980. Asst. prof. econs. Iowa State Coll., 1936-38; asst. prof. U. Minn., 1938-41, asso. prof., 1941-44, prof., 1944-46; prof. Brown U., 1946-47; prof. econs. Columbia, 1947-58; Walgreen prof. Am. instns. U. Chgo., 1958—, dir. Center Study Economy and the State, 1977—; lectr. London Sch. Econs., 1948; vice chmn., dir. Securities Investor Protection Corp., 1971-74; dir. Chgo. Bd. Trade, 1980-83; bd. dir. Lynde and Harry Bradley Found., 1986. Author: Production and Distribution Theories, 1940, The Theory of Price, 1946, Trends in Output and Employment, 1947, Five Lectures on Economic Problems, 1949, (with K. Boulding) Readings in Price Theory, 1952, Trends in Employment in the Service Industries, 1956, (with D. Blank) Supply and Demand for Scientific Personnel, 1957, The Intellectual and the Market Place, 1964, 84, Essays in the History of Economics, 1965, The Organization of Industry, 1968, (with J.K. Kindahl) The Behavior of Industrial Prices, 1970, The Citizen and the State, 1975, The Economist as Preacher, 1982, The Essence of Stigler, 1986, Memoirs of an Unregulated Economist, 1988; Editor: Jour. Polit. Economy, 1972—; Contbr. articles to profl. jours. Mem. atty. gen.'s. com. for study anti-trust laws, 1954-55; mem. Blue Ribbon Def. Panel.; Trustee Carleton Coll. Recipient Nobel prize in econs., 1982; Guggenheim fellow, 1955; fellow Center for Advanced Study in Behavioral Scis., 1957-58; recipient Nat. Medal of Science, 1987. Fellow Am. Acad. Arts and Scis., Am. Statis. Soc., Econometric Soc., Nat. Acad. Sci.; mem. Am. Econ. Assn. (pres. 1964), Royal Econ. Soc. Am. Philos. Soc., History of Econs. Soc. (pres. 1977), Mt. Pelerin Soc. (pres. 1977-78). Office: Univ of Chgo Dept of Economics 1101 E 58th St Chicago IL 60637

STIGLITZ, MARTIN RICHARD, electrical engineer; b. Vienna, Austria, Mar. 24, 1920; came to U.S., 1939, naturalized, 1942; s. Georg Adolph and Maria (Brun) S.; B.S., Northeastern U., 1957, M.S. in Electronics Engring., 1959; M.B.A. in Mgmt., Western New Eng. Coll., 1977; m. Lenna Schoenberg, Dec. 10, 1950. Mech. engr. S.A. Woods Machine Co., Boston, 1939-51; electronics engr., research scientist Air Force Cambridge Research Labs., Hanscom AFB, Bedford, Mass., 1945-75; research electronics scientist Rome Air Devel. Command electromagnetic scis. div. U.S. Air Force, Bedford, Mass., 1985-88; tech. editor Horizon House-Microwave, Inc., Norwood, Mass., 1975-85, 85-88; dir. Solar Energy Tech. Inc., Bedford. Served with 11th Airborne div. U.S. Army, 1942-45. Decorated Air medal. Mem. IEEE, N.Y. Acad. Scis., Sigma Xi. Patentee solid state devices, med. instruments; contbr. over 50 articles to sci. and profl. jours. Home: 30 Woodpark Circle Lexington MA 02173

STIGSON, BJÖRN ROLAND, finance company executive; b. Madesjö, Kalmar, Sweden, Aug. 9, 1946; s. Stig Viking Leopold and Anna-Lisa Ottilia (Jonsson) Johansson; m. Karin Anna-Britta Hakeby, Feb. 10, 1968; children: Anna, Sara, Peter. MBA, Swedish Mgmt. Inst., Gothenburg, Sweden, 1969; student, Harvard U., 1981. Fin. analyst Kockums Group, Malmö, Sweden, 1969-71; fin. mgr. Elektriska Svetsningsaktiebolaget Group, Gothenburg, 1971-76; v.p. materials adminstrn. ESAB Group, Gothenburg, 1976-78, v.p. adminstrn. and fin., 1978-80, ex. v.p., 1980-82; pres., chief exec. officer Fläkt AB, Stockholm, 1983—; bd. dirs. SIAB, Stockholm, The Gen. Export Assn. Sweden, Stockholm. Served as sgt. Swedish Army, 1965-66. Mem. The Royal Swedish Acad. Engring. Scis. Lutheran. Clubs: Bachelors' (Gothenburg); Wermdö Golf and Country. Office: Flakt AB, Box 81 001, Nacka, 104 81 Stockholm Sweden

STILLEBACHER, GERHARD FRANZ, powder metallurgy company executive; b. Innsbruck, Austria, Nov. 25, 1933; s. Franz Josef and Margarethe M. (Heine) S.; m. Anna Maria Augustin, Feb. 8, 1957; children: Margarethe, Barbara. Diploma in welding engring., Welding Engring. Inst., Frankfurt, Fed. Republic Germany, 1959; diploma in elec. engring., Engring. Inst., Innsbruck, 1960; assoc. alumni, Columbia U., 1975; MBA/DBA, Occidental U./Inst. für Betrlebswirtschaft, Innsbruck, St. Louis, 1978. Application engr. Marlo Coil Co., St. Louis, 1960-61; chief engr., sales mgr. Marlo Italiana SpA, Milan, 1962-67; gen. mgr. Bound Brook Italia SpA, Bruneck, Italy, 1967-77; mng. dir. Redland/Wierer SpA, Kiens, Italy, 1978-84; mng. dir., v.p. GKN Bound Brook Italia SpA, Bruneck, 1984—; v.p. GKN-Saini SpA, Milan, 1987; bd. dirs. Mahindra Sintered Products, Poona, India. Named Cavaliere al Merito della Repubblica, Pres. of Italian Republic, Rome, 1978. Mem. Assn. Italian Sinterizzatori (pres. 1988—), Assn. German Engrs. Lodge: Rotary. Home: Loeffler 5, 39031 Bruneck, Brunico Italy Office: GKN Bound Brook Italia SpA, PO Box 68, 39031 Bruneck, Brunico Italy

STILLMAN, ALFRED WILLIAM, JR., design/support engineer; b. Biloxi, Miss., Sept. 11, 1942; s. Alfred William and Marie Ann (Hengen) S.; AA, Am. River Coll., 1966; BSEE, Calif. Poly. State U., 1970, BS in Applied Math., 1970, MS in Applied Math., 1973; ME in Indsl. Engring., Tex. A. and M. U., 1976; postgrad. elec. engring. N.J. Inst. Tech., 1977; PhD in Mgmt., Calif. Coast U., 1984; children: Shannon Lynn, Laura Marie. Cert. profl. logistician, instr. Calif. Community Colls. Engring. intern U.S. Army Material Command, Texarkana, Tex., 1973-75, electronic systems staff maintenance engr., Ft. Monmouth, N.J., 1975-77, mil. tactical data system integrated logistics support mgr. Office of Project Mgr., ARTADS, Ft. Monmouth, 1977-78, tactical ADP ILS Mgr., ILS dir. CORADOM, Ft. Monmouth, 1978-79, engring. mgr. regional dist. office Office of Project Mgr., Firefinder, Hughes Aircraft Co., Fullerton, Calif., 1979-80; prof. systems acquisition mgmt. Dept. Def. Systems Mgmt. Coll., Ft. Belvoir, Va., 1980-82; integrated logistics support engring. specialist, advanced systems div. Northrop Corp., Pico Rivera, Calif., 1982-83; program mgmt. rep. space systems group Rockwell Internat., Downey, Calif., 1983-84; product assurance project engr. Space Sta. Systems div. Rockwell Internat., Downey, Calif., 1984-85; mgr. product support, 1985-86; sr. mgr. ILS, Amex Systems, Inc., Compton, Calif., 1986-88, dir. ILS Gould, Inc. NavCom Systems Div., El Monte, Calif., 1988—; pres. AWS Assocs. Calif., Inc., Huntington Beach, 1983—; corp. v.p., div. pres. HOPE Assocs., Inc., Huntington Beach, 1983—; Served with USAF, 1962-66. Mem. IEEE, Am. Mgmt. Assn., Am. Inst. Indsl. Engrs. (sr.) Soc. Logistics Engrs. (sr.), Am. Def. Preparedness Assn., Am. Security Council, Tau Beta Pi. Presbyterian. Club: Acacia. Home: 705 W 40th #1 San Pedro CA 90731 Office: 4323 Arden Dr El Monte CA 91731

STILLMAN, LARRY BARR, paper company executive, entrepeneur; b. Salt Lake City, Oct. 27, 1941; s. Tilden Barr and Lydia (Osguthorpe) S.; m. Mari Liane Wood, Nov. 20, 1968; children: Shaney, Tyler, Ashley, Allison, Cassidy, Blakely. BS, U. Utah, 1969. Pres., founder Apple Beer Corp., Salt Lake City, 1965—; group v.p. Dixon Paper Co., Denver, 1969—; pres. La Bathtique, Salt Lake City, 1971—; mng. gen. ptnr. Hexad Investment, Salt Lake City, 1980—; mem. adv. council Scott Paper Co., Phila., 1983—. Author: Women in Business, 1981. Mem. exec. com. Com. of 100, Salt Lake City. Recipient Silver Addy award Am. Advt. Fedn., 1984. Mem. Delta Sigma Pi (pres. 1968). Office: Dixon Paper Co 3700 W 1987 S Salt Lake City UT 84130

STILLWAGON, GARY BOULDIN, radiation oncologist; b. Memphis, Dec. 30, 1951; s. Jack Wright and Ida Jean (Bouldin) S.; m. Leta Fern Miller, Jan. 20, 1979. B.S. in Physics, Ga. Inst. Tech., 1974, M.S. in Nuclear Engring. 1975, Ph.D., 1978; M.D., U. Tenn., 1983. Cert. FLEX, 1983; diplomate Nat. Bd. Med. Examiners, 1984, Am. Bd. Radiology in Radiation Oncology. Med. physicist Meth. Hosp., Memphis, 1974; research asst. Ga. Inst. Tech., Atlanta, 1975-78; radiation safety officer, and physicist VA Med. Center, Memphis, 1978-80, cons. radiation safety, 1980-83; fellow in radiation oncology Johns Hopkins U. and Hosp., Balt., 1983-87, asst. prof. oncology and radiology Johns Hopkins U. Sch. Medicine, Balt., 1987— ; Am. Cancer Soc. clin. fellow, 1986-87 ; vis. researcher radiobiology lab. U. Utah, 1978; cons. in radiation safety to various area hosps. Contbr. articles to profl. jours. Active Boy Scouts Am., Bapt. Ch. Sunday Sch. Dept. Energy fellow, 1976-78. Mem. Health Physics Soc., Am. Assn. Physicists in Medicine, Am. Nuclear Soc., Am. Soc. Therapeutic Radiology and Oncology, Am. Coll. Radiology, AAAS, AMA, Am. Soc. Clin. Oncology, Sigma Xi. Republican. Home: 4 Briar Grove Parkton MD 21120 Office: 600 N Wolfe St Baltimore MD 21205

STILZ, GERHARD, English philology educator; b. Schnait, Fed. Republic Germany, Nov. 12, 1940; s. Wilhelm and Marie (Schiller) S.; m. Heidrun Jobst, 1967. Staatsexamen, U. Tubingen, 1965, DPhil, 1967, habilitation, 1977. Asst. prof. Seminar for English Philology, U. Tubingen, Fed. Republic Germany, 1967-68, AR and AOR, 1970-77, privatdozent, 1977-80, prof., 1980-86, univ. prof., 1986—; prof. Inst. for Lit. Sci., U. Stuttgart, Fed. Republic Germany, 1981-83; vis. prof. U. Bombay, 1968-70, English and modern lang. dept., Flagstaff, Ariz., 1986; cons. Frankfurt Book Fair, 1986. Author: Anglo-Indian Short Story, 1980; co-author: Naturalism in England, 1983.; editor: Drama in Commonwealth, 1981; editor series Grundlagen zur Lit. in English. Fellow German Acad. Exchange Service, 1968-70, German Research Found., 1973-75, 77, Australia Council, 1983, Fulbright Commn., 1986. Office: U Tuebingen, Wilhelmstrasse 50 74, Tuebingen Federal Republic of Germany

STIMMEL, BARRY, internist, educator, university dean; b. Bklyn., Oct. 8, 1939; s. Abraham and Mabel (Bovit) S.; m. Barbara Barovick, June 6, 1970; children: Alexander, Matthew. B.S., Bklyn. Coll., 1960; M.D., State U. N.Y., Bklyn., 1964. Diplomate: Nat. Bd. Med. Examiners, Am. Bd. Internal Medicine. Resident Mt. Sinai Hosp., N.Y.C., 1964-65, 67-69; asst. dean admissions and student affairs Mt. Sinai Sch. Medicine, City U. N.Y., 1970-71, assoc. dean, 1971—, asst. prof. medicine, 1972-75, assoc. prof., 1975-84, prof. medicine and med. edn., 1984—, assoc. dean acad. affairs, 1975-81, dean admissions, acad. affairs and student affairs, 1981—, assoc. attending physician, 1975-84, attending physician, 1984—, acting chmn. dept. med. edn., 1980—; mem. com. planning, priorities and evaluation N.Y. Met. Regional Med. Program, 1971-73; adv. com. Nat. Center Urban Problems, City U. N.Y., 1970-71; adv. com. methadone maintenance Office of Drug Abuse Services State of N.Y., 1976-79; sci. adv. bd. Nat. Council Drug Abuse, 1976—. Author: Heroin Dependency: Medical, Social and Economic Aspects, 1975, Cardiovascular Effects Mood Altering Drugs, 1979, Pain, Analgesia, Addiction, 1982, Ambulatory Care, 1983; Editor: Advances in Alcohol and Substance Abuse, 1980—, Consumer Reports Drugs of Abuse, 1989; assoc. editor: Am. Jour. Drug and Alcohol Abuse, 1974-85; Contbr. chpts. to books, articles profl. jours. Served with M.C. USNR, 1965-67. Mem. Am. Assn. Physicians Assts. (adv. bd. 1972-73), Am. Assn. Higher Edn., AAUP, Soc. Study of Addiction to Alcohol and Other Drugs, Assn. Med. Edn. and Research Substance Abuse, Inst. Study of Drug Addiction, Am., N.Y. heart assns., Am., N.Y. State socs. internal medicine, Soc. Internal Medicine County of N.Y. (dir.), AAUP, Am. Coll. Cardiology, Greater N.Y. Coalition on Drug Abuse, N.Y. Acad. Medicine, Nat. Council Alcoholism, Research Soc. on Alcoholism, Am. Ednl. Research Assn., Am. Fedn. Clin. Research. Office: 100th St and Fifth Ave New York NY 10029

STIMSON, MIRIAM MICHAEL, educational administrator; b. Chgo., Dec. 24, 1913; d. Frank Sharpe and Mary Frances (Holland) S.; B.S., Siena Heights Coll., 1936; M.S., Instn. Divi Thomae, Cin., 1939, Ph.D., 1948. Joined Adrian Dominican Sisters, Roman Catholic Ch., 1935; mem. faculty Siena Heights Coll., Adrian, Mich., 1939-68, chmn. chemistry dept., 1948-68, dir. grad. studies, 1978—; research assoc. Fla. State U., Tallahassee, 1969; prof. Keuka Coll., Keuka Park, N.Y., 1969-78; lectr. Canisius Coll., 1961; mem. screening panel NSF, 1963. Speaker Ch. Women United, Penn Yan, N.Y., v.p., 1973-74, pres., 1974-76; chmn. pub. events com. Keuka Coll. Campaign 1970, Penn Yan, 1970-72; mem. Lenawee County Profl. Devel. Policy Bd., 1976—, chmn., 1979-80; mem. Lenawee County Home Health

Care Adv. Bd., 1981—, chmn., 1982-86; exec. com., bd. dirs. Mich. Consortium of Substance Abuse Edn., 1984—, v.p. 1986-87, pres. 1987-88. Mem. Am. Chem. Soc., Nat. Assn. Women Deans, Mich. Assn. Women Deans, Am. Assn. Counseling and Devel., Mich. Assn. Counseling and Devel., Am. Assn. Counseling Edn. and Supervision,. Home: 1126 E Siena Heights Dr Adrian MI 49221 Office: 1247 E Siena Heights Dr Adrian MI 49221

STINE, GORDAN BERNARD, dentist, educator; b. Charleston, S.C., Feb. 10, 1924; s. Abe Jack and Helen (Pinosky) S.; m. Barbara Berlinsky, Jan. 20, 1951; children—Steven Mark, Robert Jay. B.S. in Chemistry, Coll. of Charleston, 1944; D.D.S., Emory U., 1950. Lic. dentist, Ga., S.C. Assoc. to Dr. William McDowell, Charleston, 1953-54; pvt. practice gen. dentistry, Charleston, 1954-87; spl. asst. to pres. Med. U., S.C., Charleston, 1983—, clin. assoc. prof. community dentistry, 1983—, dir. Dental Continuing Edn., 1985—, bd. visitors, 1982, 83, chmn., 1982, chmn. Cultural Projects Council, 1984—, Continuing Edn. Adv. Com., 1986—; dental coordinator Area Health Edn. Ctrs., 1987—; instr. Trident Tech. Coll., 1981; mem. State Coll. bd. trustees, 1987-88; mem. dental adv. com. Div. Dental Health S.C. State Bd. Health, 1967-68; mem. regional adv. group S.C. Regional Med. Program, 1974-75. Chmn. S.C. Dental Polit. Action Com., 1973-74, 76-84, bd. dirs., 1973-85; bd. dirs. Coastal Carolina Fair Assn., 1957-61, 63-65, pres., 1965, 66; bd. dirs. Charleston Symphony Assn., 1963-68, pres. 1965, mem. pres.' council 1983-84; bd. dirs. Charleston Civic Ballet, 1968, S.C. Art Alliance, 1973-74, Charleston Concert Assn., 1967-73, Charleston Rwy. Hist. Soc., 1967-68; bd. dirs. Coastal Carolina council Boy Scouts Am., 1972, 74, 75, 82, 83, 84, v.p. for programs 1985, 86, adv. com. 1972, 74, 75, 82, 83, 84, 85, chmn. Kiawah Dist. 1982, chmn. coms.; bd. mem. Coll. Prep. Sch., 1963-67, vice chmn. 1964-66; mem. Task Force for Martin Luther King, Jr. Legal Holiday, YMCA of Greater Charleston, 1974-75, Martin King County Wide Birthday Celebration, 1975; founder Charleston Mini Parks, 1969, bd. mem., 1969-71, chmn., 1969, 71; bd. mem. Charleston Pride, 1967-86, chmn., 1973-74, 74-75, 83-85; chmn. dental div. Trident United Way, 1962, 69, bd. mem. 1970-73, 74-76, 78-80, 81-85, community welfare planning council 1967, 68, pres. 1982, exec. com. 1977-79, 81-84, chmn. coms.; chmn. fund raising dental div. Cancer Soc., 1956, 61, 66, 70, 71; chmn. Charleston County Democratic Party, 1968-72; Charleston County councilman 1975-84, chmn. 1979-80; alderman Ward 13 City of Charleston 1971-75; active pub. service coms. including S.C. Assembly on Growth, 1981, Trident Devel. Council 1972, legis. com. S.C. Assn. Counties 1979, 81, 82, Charleston Waterfront Park Adv. Com. 1982-83, Charleston Neighborhood Housing Services Bd. 1984; state senatorial candidate, 1975; vice chmn. Berkeley-Charleston-Dorchester Council of Govts., 1983-84, sec. 1985-88, mem., chmn. coms.; exec. com. Charleston Mus. 1980, bd. mem. 1977-78, steering com. 1978-80; chmn. Charleston Bicentennial Com. 1972-75; bd. mem. Carolina Art Assn. 1978; fund drive chmn. Roper Hosp. 1973; bd. mem. Coastal Fed. Credit Union 1979-80, pres. 1976; exec. com. Greater Charleston Safety Council, 1976-85, v.p., 1986-88; bd. mem. Trident Area Found., 1977-80, adv. bd., 1981-82; mem. steering com. Charleston campaign United Negro Coll. Fund, 1972, 73; bd. mem. Robert Shaw Boys Ctr., 1975-77, Mil. Services Ctr., 1979-82, Trident 100, 1980-81; chmn. State Health Fair Adv. Bd. for Nat. Health Screening Council, 1984-85; mem. Pres.' Adv. Council Winthrop Coll., 1984-85; mem. extension adv. bd. Clemson U., 1985, 86, chmn. 1987-88, statewide community devel. adv. com., 1985; bd. mem. Hebrew Benevolent Soc., 1968-71, pres., 1970, 71; bd. trustees Congregation Beth Elohim, 1959-64, pres., 1967, 68, Brotherhood pres., 1960; pres. Jewish Welfare Bd., 1970-71, mem. coms.; mem. YMCA. Served with USMC, 1942, with USN, 1945-46, 51-53; served with USNR, 1953-72, with USN Ret. Res. 1971-84. Named Coll. of Charleston Alumnus of Yr., 1966, Community Leader Am., 1968-71; recipient Hettie Rickett Community Devel. award, 1979, award adv. dental bd. Carolina Continental Ins. Co., 1983-84, Gov.'s Order of Palmetto award, 1985. Fellow Royal Soc. Health; mem. ADA, Coastal Dist. Dental Soc. (pres. 1954), Charleston Dental Soc. (pres. 1957-58), Am. Pub. Health Assn., Israel Dental Assn., Pierre Fauchard Acad., S.C. Dental Assn. (pres. 1974-75), Alpha Omega (pres. 1949-50, Disting. Service award 1976-77), Southeastern Alpha Omega Group (pres. 1960-78, charter mem.), Charleston Trident C. of C. (pres. 1972, bd. mem. 1968-74, 80), Tau Epsilon Phi. Clubs: Exchange Club of Charleston (pres. 1962), S.C. State Exchange (bd. dirs. 1965-68). Avocation: Gardening. Home: 2 Beverly Rd Charleston SC 29407 Office: Med Univ SC 171 Ashley Ave Charleston SC 29425

STINGEL, DONALD EUGENE, consultant; b. Pitts., Jan. 31, 1920; s. Eugene E. and Ruth I. (Liddell) S.; m. Rita Marie Sweeney, June 14, 1942; children—Donald M., Scott M., Janice L. B.S., Carnegie-Mellon U., 1941. Metall. engr. Union Carbide Corp., Alloy, W.Va., 1941; metall. engr. to works mgr. Union Carbide Corp., N.Y.C., 1946-65; pres. Alloys and Carbide div. Airco, Inc., 1965-68, Pullman Swindell, Pitts., 1969-77; chmn. Rodeway Inns Internat. and Lodging Systems, Inc., 1982-83; dir. Export-Import Bank U.S., Washington, 1977-81, Wean-United, Pitts., 1981—. Trustee Carnegie-Mellon U. Served to maj., Ordnance Dept., AUS, 1941-46; to lt. col., Transp. Corps, U.S. Army, 1950. Mem. Am. Iron and Steel Inst., Am. Inst. Mining and Metall. Engrs., Pitts. C. of C. (vice chmn. 1975-77). Republican. Clubs: Duquesne (Pitts.); Rolling Rock (Pa.) (Ligonier); Congressional Country, Country of N.C. Home: Country Club of NC Box 786 Pinehurst NC 28374

STINSON, DEANE BRIAN, auditor; b. Ottawa, Ont., Can., Nov. 12, 1930; s. Earl Minto and Clara Edna (Acres) S.; chartered acct. Inst. Chartered Accts. Ont., 1954; m. Patricia Ann Paynter, Aug. 25, 1956; children—Steven Wayne, Brian Richard, Andrew Alan. With Arthur A. Crawley & Co., Ottawa, 1949-54; staff chartered acct. Thorne, Ernst & Whinney, Sault Ste. Marie, Ont., 1958-59, audit partner, 1960-79, partner, 1980-86, sr. exec. ptnr., 1987— ; mem. Ont. Regional Mgmt. Council, 1980-86, mng. ptnr. 1980-86; adv. bd. Guaranty Trust Co., 1975—; pres. and chief exec. officer Sault Investments Ltd., Betwin Investments, Inc., Tille Investments Ltd., Tolstar Mgmt. Co. Adv. indsl. devel. com. Sault Ste. Marie, 1978-83; pres. Agate Venture (No. and Ea.) Inc., Venture Capital Corp.; mem. cultural task force Sault Ste. Marie, 1977-79. Fellow Inst. Chartered Accts. Ont.; mem. Can. Inst. Chartered Accts. (pres. chpt. 1965), Can. Tax Found. Progressive Conservative. Anglican. Club: Rotary (pres. 1978). Home: 15 Atlas Ave, Sault Ste Marie, ON Canada P6A 4Z2 Office: PO Box 578, Sault Ste, Marie, ON Canada P6A 5M6

STINSON, MARY FLORENCE, nursing educator; b. Wheeling, W.Va., Feb. 11, 1931; d. Rolland Francis and Mary Angela (Voellinger) Kellogg; m. Charles Walter Stinson, Feb. 12, 1955; children—Kenneth Charles, Karen Marie, Kathryn Anne. B.S. in Nursing, Coll. Mt. St. Joseph, 1953, postgrad., 1983; M.Ed., Xavier U., Cin., 1967; postgrad. U. Cin., 1981. Staff nurse contagious disease ward Cin. Gen. Hosp., 1953-54, asst. head nurse med. and polio wards, 1955, acting head nurse, clin. instr., 1955-56; instr. St. Francis Hosp. Sch. Practical Nursing, Cin., 1956-57; instr. Good Samaritan Hosp. Sch. Nursing, Cin., 1957-65; instr. refresher courses for nurses Cin. Bd. Edn. and Ohio State Nurses Assn. Dist. 8, 1967-70; coordinator sch. health office Coll. Mt. St. Joseph (Ohio), 1969-72, instr. dept. nursing, 1974-79, asst. prof., 1979—. Charter mem. Adoptive Parents Assn. St. Joseph Infant and Maternity Home; active Women's Com. for Performing Arts Series, Coll. Mt. St. Joseph; mem. St. Antoninus Rosary Altar Rosary and Sch. Soc., St. Antoninus Athletic Club, com. chmn., 1969-70; bd. dirs. Coll. Mt. St. Joseph Alumnae Assn., 1982-84, sec., 1968-69, v.p., 1969-70, pres., 1970-71, chmn. revision of constn., 1976-77; homecoming chmn. Coll. Mt. St. Joseph, 1970, co-chmn., 1977; mem. Gamble Nippert YMCA. Mem. Am. Nurses Assn., Ohio Nurses Assn., Southwestern Ohio Nurses Assn., AAUP. Democrat. Roman Catholic. Club: River Squares (v.p. 1967). Home: 5549 Cleander Dr Cincinnati OH 45238 Office: Coll Mt St Joseph 5701 Delhi Mount Saint Joseph OH 45051

STINSON, WILLIAM W., transportation executive; b. Toronto, Ont., Can., Oct. 29, 1933; children: Janet, Margo, James. B.A., U. Toronto, 1954; diploma in bus. adminstrn., U. W. Ont., 1955. Various positions Can. Pacific Rail, Toronto, 1950-66, supt. Toronto div., 1966-69; asst. gen. mgr. ops. and maintenance Pacific Region Can. Pacific Rail, Vancouver, 1969-71; gen. mgr. ops. and maintenance Pacific Region Can. Pacific Ltd., Vancouver, 1971, gen. mgr. ops. and maintenance Eastern Region, 1972-74; asst. v.p. ops. and maintenance Can. Pacific Rail, Montreal, 1974-76; v.p. ops. and maintenance Can. Pacific Ltd., Montreal, 1976-79; exec. v.p. Can. Pacific Rail, Montreal, 1979-81; pres., dir. Can. Pacific Ltd., Montreal, 1981-85, pres., chief exec. officer, 1985—; bd. dirs. Can. Pacific (Bermuda) Ltd, Can. Pacific Enterprises Ltd., Can. Pacific Express and Transport Ltd., Gen. Motors of Can. Ltd., Can. Pacific Forest Products Ltd., Can. Maritime Ltd., Harris Bankcorp Inc., Harris Trust and Savs. Bank, Marathon Realty Co. Ltd., Pan Can. Petroleum Ltd., Sun Life Assurance Co. Can., AMCA Internat. Corp., AMCA Internat. Ltd., Soo Line Corp, ROBCO Inc. Clubs: Mount Royal. Office: Can Pacific Ltd, PO Box 6042 Sta A, Montreal, PQ Canada H3C 3E4

STIPHO, ABDUL SALAM, civil engineer, educator; b. Mosul, Iraq, May 24, 1945; came to Saudi Arabia, 1978; s. Ayoub Stipho and Hassina (Hannah) Girgis; m. Huda D. Kattan, Oct. 7, 1974; children: Sally, Sarah. B.Sc. in Civil Engring., Baghdad U., 1966; Ph.D., U. Wales, 1978. Project capt. Ministry of Irrigation, Baghdad, 1969-71, mgr., Hindyah Project, Iraq, 1971-74; research officer Univ. Coll., Cardiff, Wales, 1977-78; mgr. engring. Dallah/Avco Co., Riyadh, Saudi Arabia, 1978-79, engring. advisor, 1979-86; asst. prof. engring. King Saud U., Riyadh, 1979—; dir. Duja Group of Cos., Riyadh, 1978-86. Co-author: Development in Soil Mechanics and Foundation Engineering, 1985. Contbr. articles to profl. jours. Served to 1st lt. Iraq Army, 1966-68. Iraq Ministry of Edn. scholar, 1962; England Ministry of Environment grantee, 1976. Fellow Geol. Soc. London; mem. Iraqi Soc. Engrs., ASCE. Roman Catholic. Club: Riyadh Sports. Avocations: stamp collecting; court tennis. Home: 2 Pollicott Close, Saint Albans, Hershire England Office: King Saud U Coll Engring, PO Box 800, Riyadh 11421, Saudi Arabia

STIREWALT, JOHN NEWMAN, coal company executive; b. Springfield, Ill., July 14, 1931; s. Newman Claude and Genevieve (Henton) S.; m. Joan Marie McCarthy, Dec. 26, 1957; children: Genevieve, Janice, James, Christopher. AB, U. Miami, 1953; grad. execs. program Carnegie-Mellon U. Grad. Sch. Indsl. Adminstrn., 1978. Salesman Kaiser Aluminum, Indpls., 1957-63; dist. sales mgr. Consol. Coal, Detroit, 1963-67, Cleve., 1967-73, gen. sales mgr., Detroit, 1973-76, asst. v.p., 1976-79; v.p. mktg. Youghiogheny and Ohio Coal Co., St. Clairsville, Ohio, 1979-81; v.p. mktg. Crown Coal and Coke Co., Pitts., 1981-85, Arch Mineral, 1985—; exec. reservist U.S. Dept. Interior emergency solid fuels adminstrn., 1971. Council chmn. Cub Scouts, Highland, Mich., 1976; mem. Mich. Energy Task Force, 1966; pres. bd. trustees Wheeling Country Day Sch., 1980-84; bd. trustees Wheeling Symphony. Served in U.S. Army, 1954-56. Mem. Sigma Chi. Presbyterian. Club: Bellerive Country. Home: 1009 Arlington Oaks Terr Chesterfield MO 63017 Office: Arch Mineral Corp Saint Louis MO 63102

STIRITZ, WILLIAM P., food company executive; b. Jasper, Ark., July 1, 1934; s. Paul and Dorothy (Bradley) S.; m. Susan Ekberg, Dec. 4, 1972; children—Bradley, Charlotte, Rebecca, Nicholas. B.S., Northwestern U., 1959; M.A., St. Louis U., 1968. Mem. mktg. mgmt. staff Pillsbury Co., Mpls., 1959-62; account mgmt. staff Gardner Advt. Co., St. Louis, 1963—; with Ralston Purina Co., St. Louis, 1963—; pres., chief exec. officer, chmn. Ralston Purina Co., 1981—; bd. dirs. Angelian Corp., Ball Corp., Centerre Bank, May Dept. Stores, S.C. Johnson & Son. Bd. dirs. Washington U., St. Louis. Served with USN, 1954-57. Mem. Grocery Mfrs. Assn. (dir.). Office: Ralston Purina Co Checkerboard Sq Saint Louis MO 63164

STIRLING, JAMES, architect; b. Glasgow, Scotland, Apr. 22, 1926; s. Joseph and Louisa (Fraser) S.; m. Mary Shand, 1966; children—Ben, Kate, Sophie. Student Liverpool Art Sch., 1942, Liverpool U., 1945-50. With firm James Stirling and James Gowan, London, 1956-63; individual practice architecture, London, 1963-70; prin. James Stirling and Michael Wilford, London, 1971—; William and Charlotte Shepherd Davenport vis. prof. archtl. design Yale U., 1967—; vis. prof. Akademie der Kunste, Dusseldorf (Germany), 1976—. Served to lt. 6th Airborne Div. British Army, 1943-45. Recipient Brunner award U.S., 1976, Alvar Aalto medal Finland, 1978; Royal Gold medal, 1980, Pritzker Architecture prize, 1981, Thomas Jefferson medal, 1986. Fellow AIA (hon.); asso. Royal Inst. British Architects; mem. Akademie der Kunste Berlin (hon.). Works include: engring. bldg. Leicester U., 1959-63, New Town Housing Runcorn, 1967-77, Stuttgart extension Nat. Art Gallery, 1977, 84, Fogg Mus., 1979-84, an extension of the Tate Gallery, London, 1980—; exhbns. Mus. Modern Art, N.Y.C., 1969, Venice Bienale, 1976. Author: James Stirling Buildings and Projects, 1976. Office: 75 Gloucester Pl, London W1H 3PF, England *

STIVENDER, DONALD LEWIS, mechanical engineer; b. Chgo., May 8, 1932; s. Paul Macon and Grace (Larsen) S.; m. Margaret Ann Lourim, Apr. 14, 1956; children—Anne, Robert, Carole. B.S. in Engring, U.S. Coast Guard Acad., 1954; M.S., U. Mich., 1959. Registered profl. engr. Research and devel. Research Labs., Gen. Motors Corp., Warren, Mich., 1959—, sr. research engr., 1968—; owner Stivender Engring. Assos., 1980—; cons. public domain engring. disciplines. Contbr. articles tech. jours. on diesel, gas turbine and spark ignition engine combustion, emission, constrn. and control aspects. Served with USCG, 1950-58. Mem. Soc. Automotive Engrs. (Arch T. Colwell award 1968, 69, 79, governing bd. 1971-73), ASME, Combustion Inst., Sigma Xi. Home: 1730 Hamilton Dr Bloomfield Hills MI 48013 Office: GM Research Labs Project Trilby 12 Mile and Mound Roads Warren MI 48090

STIVER, WILLIAM EARL, retired government administrator; b. Madison, Ind., Mar. 30, 1921; s. John Virgil and Anna Lynne (Ryker) S.; student Hanover Coll., 1947-49; B.S., U. Calif. at Berkeley, 1951, M.B.A., 1952; m. Norma A. Cull, June 11, 1944; children—Vicki, Raymond, Gena, John. With Fed. Ser., Bur. Census, Commerce Dept., Suitland, Md., 1952-79, chief budget and finance div., 1963-73, dep. assoc. adminstr. Social and Econ. Stats. Adminstrn., 1973-75, spl. asst., assoc. dir. for adminstrn. and field ops. Bur. of Census, 1975-77, electronic data processing staff coordinator, 1977-78, ret., 1979. Served with AUS; 1942-43, 45-46. Recipient Silver medal Commerce Dept., 1969. Mem. Phi Beta Kappa, Beta Gamma Sigma. Home: 8104 Kerby Pkwy Ct Fort Washington MD 20744

STOCK, RODNEY CLIFFORD, musicologist, editor; b. Westcliff-On-Sea, Essex, Eng., Sept. 8, 1929; arrived in Switzerland, 1958; s. Clifford William Charles and Barbara Beatrice (McKeone) S.; m. Renée Jeanne Bathilde Hue, Aug. 26, 1954; children: Rodolphe, Marie-Astrid. Licence ès Lettres, Sorbonne U., Paris, 1952; postgrad., Ont. Inst. Studies in Edn., Toronto, 1974, U. Geneva, 1979-84. Tchr. Schs. and Colls., Paris, 1950-51, Lons-le-Saunier, Jura, 1951-52, Le Mans, Sarthe, 1952-53; tchr. London, 1954-58, Geneva, 1958-66; sr. editor Internat. Bur. Edn., UNESCO, Geneva, 1977—; mem. council Faculty of Psychology and Edn. Geneva U., 1980-84; council mem. Archive Institut Jean-Jacques Rousseau, Geneva, 1982—. Author: (with others) Le Bureau International d'Education au Service du Movement Educatif, 1979; contbr. articles on comparative edn., literary and mus. criticism to profl. jours. Mem. Geneva Symphony Orch. Mem. Comparative Edn. Soc. Europe, Swiss Soc. for Research in Edn. Home: 19 Rue des Vollandes, 1207 Geneva Switzerland

STOCKFELT, TORBJÖRN SVEN HEMING, psychologist, educator; b. Laxsjö, Jämtland, Sweden, Dec. 24, 1928; s. Per Algot and Britta Barbara (Svensson) S.; m. Gerd Viola Wistrom, Aug. 12, 1950; children: Ola Per Valter, Jerker Sven Heming. BA, Uppsala U., Sweden, 1957, MA, 1958, PhD, 1964, Docent (hon.), 1967. Elem. sch. tchr. Swedish communes, 1952-60; univ. lectr. Uppsala U., 1960-64; research chief The Swedish Mil. Psychol. Inst., Stockholm, 1964-66; lectr., research leader The High Sch. for Physical Edn., Stockholm, 1966-69; prof. edn. and ednl. psychology Stockholm U., 1969—, research leader, supr., 1980—; prof. human services N.H. Coll. and Springfield Coll., 1988—; cons. in field, 1977—; chmn. sci. council Inst. for Enterprise Pedagogics, Stockholm, 1987. Author over 35 books on edn., psychology, fine arts; author fiction; contbr. articles to profl. jours. Home and Office: Kompassgatan 7, 413 16 Göteborg Sweden

STOCKHAUSEN, KARLHEINZ, composer; b. Modrath nr. Cologne, Germany, Aug. 22, 1928; student Musikhochschule, Cologne, 1947-51; student acoustical scis., U. Bonn, 1954-56; pupil Werner Meyer-Eppler, Olivier Messiaen; m. Doris Andreae, 1951; children—Suja, Christel, Markus, Majella; m. 2d, Mary Bauermeister, 1967; children—Tuleka, Simon. Composer, condr. first public score for electronic music; dir. Electronic Studio, Cologne; condr., tchr., editor rev. of serial music; performance own works, U.S., Can., 1964; with Westdeutscher Rundfunk Electronic Music Studio, Cologne, 1953—; artistic dir., 1963—; tchr. U. Pa., 1964; prof. Musikhochschule, Cologne, 1971. Composer: Kreuzspiel for six players, 1951; Spiel for orch., 1952; Eleven Piano Pieces, 1952-56; Punkte for orch., 1952; Kontrapunkte for ten instruments, 1952-53; Zeitmasze, 1955-56; Gesang der Junglinge, 1956; Gruppen for 3 orchs., 1955-57; Zyklus, Refrain, Carre for 4 choirs and 4 orchs., 1959; Kontakte for electronic sounds, piano and percussion, 1959-60; Momente for 4 choirs, 13 instruments, solo-soprano, 1962—; also numerous works for clarinet; Originale, mus. theatre, 1961; Plus-Minor, 1963; Mixtur for orch. and electronic modulators, 1964; Microphonie I, 1964, Telemusik, 1966, Hymnen, 1967, Stimmung, 1968, Mantra, 1970, Trans, 1971, Inori, 1974, Invisible Choirs, 1979, numerous other compositions; over 70 recs. of works. Foremost exponent of electronic music. Office: Westdeutscher Rundfunk, Wallrafplatz 5, D-5000 Koln Federal Republic of Germany *

STOCKS, RUNDELL KINGSLEY, management, construction, education and general consultant; b. Kokstad, Natal, South Africa, Feb. 14, 1925; s. Gerald Restall and Edith Hannah (Duffy) S.; m. Janet Alma Parish, Mar. 23, 1949 (dec. 1964); 1 dau., Virginia Anne Stocks Garde. Grad. Kingswood Coll., Grahamstown, South Africa, 1942. Chmn., mng. dir. Stocks Constrn., Port Alfred, South Africa, 1946-57; tech. clk. Vecor Ltd., Vanderbijlpark, 1957-60; gen. mgr. F.A. Poole Group, Pretoria, South Africa, 1960-64; dir., gen. mgr. Stocks Group, Pretoria, 1964-75; Pretoria dir. Eastern Province Bldg. Soc., 1970-86; chmn. non. exec. Habitech Group, Pretoria, 1975-85; chmn. Gem Valley Estates (Pty) Ltd., 1969—; external examiner U. Pretoria, 1970—. Served with South African Navy, 1943-46. Fellow Brit. Inst. Mgmt.; mem. South African Inst. Mgmt., South African Inst. Personnel Mgmt., South African Inst. Bldg. (pres. 1977-78), South African Inst. Welding. Christian Scientist. Home: Gem Valley Farm, Outside Pretoria, Transvaal Republic of South Africa Office: 442 Clark St, Waterkloof, Pretoria, Transvaal 0181, Republic of South Africa

STOCKTON, ALEXANDER DANIEL ALAN (SECOND EARL OF OVENDEN), publisher; b. Oswestry, Eng., Oct. 10, 1943; s. Maurice Victor and Katherine Margaret Alice (Ormsby-Gore) M.; grad. Eton, 1959; student U. Paris, 1959-60, U. Strathclyde, Glasgow, 1961-63; m. Helene Birgitte Hamilton, Sept. 10, 1970; children—Daniel Maurice Alan, Rebecca Elizabeth, Louisa Alexandra. Reporter, Glasgow Herald, 1963-65, Daily Telegraph, London, 1965-67; fgn. corr. Daily Telegraph, Paris, 1967-68; chief European corr. Sunday Telegraph, 1968-70; asst. corr. BBC, 1967-70; documentary producer Orgn. Radiofusion TV Franç aise, Paris, 1969-70; dir. Macmillan & Co. Ltd., London, 1970-76, dep. chmn., 1976-79, chmn. Macmillan Publishers Ltd., 1980—; dir. All-News Radio Ltd., Counterpoint Prodns. Ltd., St. Martin's Press Inc., N.Y.C. Trustee, gov. English Speaking Union, 1979—, Book Trade Benevolent Soc., 1976—, Archbishop Tenison's Grammar Sch., 1978-87, Mcht. Taylor's Sch., 1980-83, Lindemann Fellowship Com., 1980. Founder, 1st editor Strathclyde Telegraph, 1961-63. Mem. Livery of Worshipful Co. Mcht. Taylors, Worshipful Co. Newspapermakers and Stationers, Inst. Dirs., Publishers Assn. Tory. Mem. Ch. of England. Clubs: Carlton, Bucks, Beefsteak, Whites, Scribes, 1900, United and Cecil, R.A.C., Royal Yachting Assn., Whites, Pratts, Grouchos, R.A.C. Home: Flat 4, 46 Tite St, London SW3 4JA, England Office: 4 Little Essex St, London WC2R 3LF, England

STOCKWELL, BENJAMIN EUGENE, lawyer; b. Oklahoma City, Aug. 28, 1931; s. Benjamin Paul and Anna (Cunningham) S.; m. Marjorie Ethel Ribble, Apr. 4, 1952; children: Margaret Lynn, David Alan. B.A., U. Okla., 1952, LL.B., 1956. Bar: Okla. 1956. Practice in Oklahoma City, 1956-60, Norman, Okla., 1961—; mem. firm Benedum & Stockwell, 1961-62; then Stockwell & Pence (now Stockwell Law Offices); asst. prof. law, legal adviser to pres.'s office U. Okla., 1960-61; spl. lectr. U. Okla. (Coll. Law), 1971-77. Chmn. Cleveland County Bd. Health, 1963-64; mem. Okla. State Bd. Examiners Cert. Shorthand Reporters, 1971-76, chmn., 1974-76; Bd. dirs. Cleveland County Cancer Soc. Served to 1st lt. AUS, 1952-54. Mem. Okla. Bar Assn. (exec. com. 1965-68, v.p. 1969, chmn. spl. com. implementation jud. reform amendments 1967-69), Cleveland County Bar Assn. (past pres.), Okla. Inst. Justice, Order of Coif, Order of DeMolay Legion Honor, Scabbard and Blade, Phi Delta Phi, Pi Kappa Alpha, Pi Gamma Mu. Episcopalian. Lodge: Masons. Home: 1201 Lee St Norman OK 73069 Office: 119 E Main St PO Box 519 Norman OK 73070

STOCKWELL, OLIVER PERKINS, lawyer; b. East Baton Rouge, La., Aug. 11, 1907; s. William Richard and Lillie Belle (Dawson) S.; m. Roseina Katherine Holcombe, June 24, 1936; 1 child, Angell Roseina (Mrs. William C. Wright). LL.B., La. State U., 1932, J.D., 1968. Bar: La. 1932. Since practiced in Lake Charles; partner firm Stockwell, Sievert, Viccellio, Clements & Shaddock (and predecessor firm), 1933—; Dir. Lakeside Nat. Bank of Lake Charles; past dir. Gulf States Utilities Co.; past mem. jud. council La. Supreme Ct.; past mem. La. Commn. on Law Enforcement and Adminstrn. Criminal Justice; referee bankruptcy U.S. Dist. Ct. (we. dist.) La., 1938-46. Contbr. to La. Law Rev. Pres. Lake Charles Centennial; bd. dirs., mem. exec. com. Council for a Better La., pres., 1972; past bd. dirs. Pub. Affairs Research Council La., past bd. dirs. La. State U. Found.; past bd. suprs. La. State U., chmn., 1977-78, chmn. emeritus; past chmn. legal services adv. com. La. Joint Legis. Commn. on Intergovtl. Relations.; chmn. Paul H. Hebert Law Ctr. Council La. State U.; mem. Task Force on Excessive Govtl. Regulations. Served to lt. USNR, 1943-45. Research fellow Southwestern Legal Found. Fellow Am. Bar Found., Am. Coll. Trial Lawyers, Am. Coll. Probate Counsel; mem. Inter-Am. Bar Assn., Am. Judicature Soc., Internat. Bar Assn., ABA (past state chmn. jr. bar sect., mem. spl. com. adoption jud. conduct code;, chmn. La. membership com., sr. lawyers div.), La. Bar Assn. (past pres.), S.W. La. Bar Assn. (pres. 1942), Mid-Continent Oil and Gas Assn. (exec. com.), Comml. Law League, Internat. Assn. Ins. Counsel, Fedn. Ins. Counsel, Am. Law Inst. (life mem.), La. Law Inst. (past pres., chmn. mineral code com. 1986; chmn. 1987), chmn. emeritus, 1988, Lake Charles C. of C. (past pres., Civic award 1978), State Assn. Young Men's Bus. Clubs (past pres. Lake Charles), La. State U. Law Sch. Alumni Assn. (past pres.), Order of Coif, Henri Capitant, Lambda Alpha, Omicron Delta Kappa. Clubs: Kiwanis, Pioneer, City, Lake Charles Country, Boston of New Orleans, L of La. State U. (past pres.). Home: 205 Shell Beach Dr Lake Charles LA 70601 Office: 1 Lakeside Plaza Lake Charles LA 70601

STODDARD, FORREST SHAFFER, aerospace engineer, educator; b. Eglin AFB, Fla., Nov. 4, 1944; s. Edward Forrest and Esther Grace (Shaffer) S.; S.B., M.I.T., 1966, S.M., 1968; Ph.D., U. Mass., 1979; m. Mary Anne Maher Matthews, June 16, 1979; children—Joshua Forrest, Nathan Edward. Partner, chief engr. U.S. Windpower Inc., Burlington, Mass., 1977-80 ; wind power engring. cons., Amherst, Mass., 1980—; cons. Wind Systems Test Center, U.S. Dept. Energy Solar Energy Research Inst., Commonwealth of Mass.; asst. prof. mech. engring. U. Mass., 1982—; founder, pres. Pioneer Wind Power, Inc., 1982-87; cons., prin. investigator U.S. Dept. Energy, 1985-86; adj. research prof. alternative energy inst. West Tex. State U., 1987—; research prof. West Tex. State U., 1986—. Served to capt. USAF, 1968-72. Co-author Wind Turbine Engineering Design, 1987. Mem. Am. Wind Energy Assn. (dir., sec.), Am. Helicopter Soc., AIAA, Am. Solar Energy Soc., Friends of Earth, Sigma Xi. Mem. United Ch. Christ. Acting editor Wind Tech. Jour., 1979-82. Home: 63 Butter Hill Rd Pelham MA 01002 Office: PO Box 311 Amherst MA 01004

STODDARD, PATRICIA ANN, medical technologist, chemistry educator; b. Albert Lea, Minn., Apr. 5, 1930; d. Armond William and Lois Roberta (Remo) Olson Armstrong; m. Charles Gilbert Stoddard, Jan. 7, 1966; m. William Anton Hoogendijk, July 16, 1949 (div. Dec. 1964); 1 son, Christopher John. A.Sc., Clackamas Community Coll., 1973; B.A., Linfield Coll., 1976. Med. technologist King County Blood Bank, Seattle, 1962-63; surg. research technician Bishop Eye Research, Seattle, 1964-65; gen. supr. Willamette Falls Hosp., Oregon City, Oreg., 1965-68; adj. asst. prof. U. Portland, Oreg., 1977-86; dir. Willamette Animal Lab., Corbett, Oreg., 1969—. Author: Veterinarian Medicine for Small Animal Clinician, 1976, 77; Advances in Carriers and Adjuant for Veterinary Biologics, 1986. Instr. ARC, Vancouver, Wash., 1979—; flotilla past comdr. Coast Guard Aux., Vancouver, 1983. Mem. Am. Med. Technologists (Nat. Achievement award 1972, 74), Am. Soc. Microbiologists, Am. Inst. Biol. Sci., Am. Chem. Soc. (exec. bd. Portland sect. 1982—). Republican. Episcopalian. Club: Dolphin Yacht (Camas, Wash.). Home: PO Box 828 Camas WA 98607 Office: Willamette Animal Lab 9108 NE Sandy Blvd Portland OR 97220

STODDARD, PATRICK CLARE, military systems consultant; b. Grand Rapids, Mich., June 13, 1941; s. Frank Eudaly and Mary Clarann (Burns) S.; m. Anneliese Barg, Sept. 18, 1963; children—Patrick Frank, Conni Maryann. Student Cleve. Inst. Electronics, 1967-68, U. Md., 1961-63. Enlisted U.S. Air Force, 1959; radar technician, 1959-67, resigned, 1967; asst. engr. Univac div. Sperry Rand, Minn., 1967-68, field engr., 1968; systems engr. Hydrospace Challenger Research Inc., Md., 1968-73; sr. engr. Control Data Corp., Arlington, Va., 1973-74, prin. engr. computer scis., 1974-78, mil. systems cons., 1978—. Contbr. numerous studies in support of mil. systems devel.; patentee electronic oil slick control. Recipient Bill Norris Shark club award Control Data Corp., 1978. Roman Catholic. Home: 55 Mohegan Rd Noank CT 06340 Office: Control Data Corp 60 Hickory Dr Waltham MA 02154

STODDARD, WILLIAM BERT, JR., economist; b. Carbondale, Pa., Oct. 6, 1926; s. William Bert and Emily (Trautwein) S.; student Lafayette Coll., 1944-45; B.S., N.Y. U., 1950, A.M., 1952; m. Carol Marie Swartz, Feb. 28, 1970; 1 dau., Emily Coleman. Asst. chief accountant, budget dir. Hendrick Mfg. Co., Carbondale, Pa., 1952-54, asst. dir. prodn., 1956-68, also dir.; credit corr. U.S. Gypsum Co., N.Y.C., 1954-56; investment counselor, Carbondale, 1968-73, Ridgefield, Conn., 1973—; dir. First Nat. Bank Carbondale, 1968-73; bd. dirs. Lackawanna County Mfrs. Assn., Scranton, Pa., 1960-73. Treas., trustee Aldrich Museum Contemporary Art, Ridgefield, 1976—; bd. dirs. Ridgefield Library and Hist. Assn., 1977-85, 87—; trustee Ridgefield Library Endowment Fund Trust, 1985—. Served with U.S. Army 1946-47. Mem. Nat. Assn. Accountants, Am. Def. Preparedness Assn., Phi Alpha Kappa, Phi Delta Theta. Republican. Methodist. Clubs: N.Y. U. (N.Y.C.); Waccabuc (N.Y.) Country. Home: 59 Bridle Tr Ridgefield CT 06877 Office: 23 Catoonah St Ridgefield CT 06877

STOECKER, ROBERT GEORGE, paper company executive, economist; b. Hamburg, Germany, Dec. 13, 1925; s. Waldemar R. and Marie (Boehr) S.; m. Anne Marie Ritter, Nov. 14, 1953; children—Ralph B., Klaus M. Diploma in Econs., U. Heidelberg, 1953. Mgmt. trainee Bauer & Black, Chgo., 1954-56; merchandising cons. Container Corp. Am., Chgo., 1956-57; mktg. mgr. Europa Carton Ag, Hamburg, Germany, 1957-74, mgmt. bd., 1974—; adv. bd. Deutsche Bank Ag, Hamburg, 1977—. Home: Josthoehe 112, D-2000 Hamburg 63 Federal Republic of Germany Office: Europa Carton Ag, Spitalerstrasse 11, D-2000 Hamburg 1 Federal Republic of Germany

STOETZNER, ERIC WOLDEMAR, newspaper executive; b. Leipzig, Germany, Mar. 11, 1901; came to U.S. 1938, naturalized, 1944; s. Woldemar and Emma (Wolf) S.; student U. Leipzig, 1922; Dr. Econ. Sci., Frankfurt am Main, 1925; m. Fridel Henning-Gronau, Dec. 20, 1927 (dec. Sept. 1967); 1 dau., Renee. Advt. dir., bus. mgr., mem. bd. Frankfurter Zeitung, Germany, 1930-38; bus. mgr. mag. of Schurz Found., Phila., 1939-43; internat. analyst of pub. N.Y. Times, 1944-45, dir. fgn. bus. promotion, 1945-50, dir. fgn. advt., 1950-70, internat. cons., 1970—. Bd. dirs. Stamford Forum World Affairs. Decorated Chevalier de l'ordre du Merite Commercial de la France; Officer's Cross, German Order of Merit, 1953; Grand Cross, German Order Merit, 1981, recipient hon. plaque City of Frankfurt, 1979, Disting. Internat. Recognition award Fellowship Former Overseas Residents, 1984; named Symbol of 1938 Frankfurter Allgemeine Zeitung in report, Four Dramatic Lives of a Frankfordian, 1983. Mem. Internat. Advt. Assn. (hon. life; v.p. 1956-59), Confrerie des Chevaliers du Tastevin. Quaker. Club: Rotary (named Mr. Internationalist N.Y. chpt.). Subject of book by Horst Fischer: Werbung, Menschen, Politik: Die Stoetzner Story, 1986. Home: 376 Westover Rd Stamford CT 06902

STOHLER, MICHAEL JOE, dentist; b. Anderson, Ind., Mar. 26, 1956; s. Herbert Warren and Mary Jo (Philbert) S.; m. Mary Anne Poinsette, May 16, 1981; children: James Lawrence, Maria Christine. Student, Lake-Sumter Community Coll., Leesburg, Fla., 1974-76; BS, Ball State U., 1978; DDS, Ind. U., 1982. Gen. practice dentistry Anderson, 1982—. Mem. ADA, Ind. Dental Assn., East Cen. Dental Assn., Madison County Dental Assn., Acad. Gen. Dentistry, Acad. Dentistry for Handicapped, Anderson Personal Computer User's Group, Psi Omega. Lodge: Rotary (sgt.-at-arms Anderson chpt. 1986—). Home: 5839 Hobbs Dr Anderson IN 46013 Office: 2012 E 53d St Anderson IN 46013

STOIANOVICH, MARCELLE SIMONE, artist; b. Paris; d. Charles Caffe and Eugenie Le Nieffe; children: Christian, Diana Revson II. Student, Coll. Applied Arts, Paris, 1942-46. Book jacket designer Doubleday Edits., N.Y.C., 1954; archeol. draftsperson Smithsonian Inst., Washington, 1962; window decorator Guerlain Perfumes, Paris, 1975; film creditor Am. Films Festival, Deauville, France, 1975; assoc. editor L'Officiel de la Mode, Paris, 1976-81; jeweler Henri Bendel's, N.Y.C., 1983; free-lance artist N.Y.C. and Paris, 1983—. Permanent exhibits Venable/Nelage Galleries, Washington, D.C.; Lithographs, Original Print Collectors Group, N.Y.C. Mem. Met. Mus. Home: 60 Rector St Metuchen NJ 08840 Studio: 9 Rue Campagne Premiere, 75014 Paris France

STOIKOS, NICOLAS PAUL, economist; b. Volos, Greece, Nov. 30, 1959; s. Paul Nicolas Stoikos and Catherine (Apostolos) Stamatis. Diploma in bus. adminstrn., Grad. Sch. Indsl. Studies, Thessaloníci, Greece, 1983. Sales inspector 3M Hellas Ltd., Volos, 1985; dir. Astir & Co., Volos, 1986—; acct. Gen. Cement Co., Volos, 1987. Served with Greek Navy, 1983-84. Mem. Ecol. Motion Volos, Econ. Chamber of Greece. Mem. Christian Orthodox. Home and Office: 78 Democracy Ave, 37300 Agria-Volos, Magnesia Greece

STOILOV, GEORGI VLADIMIROV, architect; b. Kondofrey, Bulgaria, Apr. 3, 1929; s. Vladimir and Sophia Georgiev S.; m. Kina Kirilova, Apr. 3, 1958; 1 child, Georgi Georgiev. Grad., Faculty Architecture, Moscow, 1954; grad. in Urbanism, U. Paris, 1965. Mayor City of Sofia, Bulgaria, 1971—, minister of architecture and town planning, 1973—; rector Internat. Acad. Architecture, Sofia, 1986—; founder, sec.-gen. Secretariat Balkan Architects Confs., 1966—; vis. prof. NYU. Founder, chmn. Architecture and Soc. mag., 1984. Dep. Nat. Assembly of Bulgaria, 1967. Bulgarian Archtl. Laureate. Mem. AIA, Internat. Union Architects (pres. Paris sect. 1985-88, Paris sect., Bulgarian Archtl. Laureate), Union of Architects USSR (h.on., pres. 1981-89). Office: Union Architects Bulgaria, 1 Evogli Georgiev St, 1504 Sofia Bulgaria

STOJANOVIĆ, MIODRAG VLADIMIR, philologist educator, researcher; b. M. Krčmare, Serbia, Yugoslavia, July 30, 1934; s. Vladimir Dragutin and Gvozdenija S.; m. Milesa Aleksič, m. July 13, 1969; children: Vladimir, Ivana. Grad., U. Yugoslavia, Belgrade, 1957, magisterium, 1962, DSc, 1965. Prof. Latin high schs., Belgrade, 1960-70; researcher, neohelenist Inst. Balkan Studies U. Yugoslavia, Belgrade, 1971—, prof. classical langs., 1968-69. Author: Dositej Obradovic and Antiquity, 1971; (monograph) Haiduks and Klephts in Folk Poetry, 1984. Mem. Assn. for Ancient Studies (pres. 1976-81), Union of Profs.-esperantists Yugoslavia (pres. 1962-78). Home: Omladinskih Brigada, 49/III-31, 11070 Belgrade, Serbia Yugoslavia Office: Inst for Balkan Studies, Knez Mihailova 35/IV, 11000 Belgrade, Serbia Yugoslavia

STOKE, GORDON ALEXANDER, entrepreneur; b. London, June 28, 1921; s. Stephen and Barbara (Jamieson) S.; m. Doreen Le Poidevin, Nov. 16, 1944; children: Christopher, Nigel, Jeremy. Grad. high sch., Essex, Eng. Served to lt. Royal Navy, 1939-49; gen. mgr. Thompson & Norris Mfrs., London, 1950-55; dir. Credit Ins. Assn., London, 1955-65; chief exec. Portland Group Factors, London, 1965-68; group mng. dir. Elec. and Indsl. Securities, London, 1969-70; founder, dir. Preformations Group, London, 1970-83; bd. dirs. Lewis Electric Group, Maidenhead, Eng., G.S. Managerial Services Ltd., Sarisbury, Eng., Tower Works Group, Sarisbury, Vasayr Works Extec Hybrids, Sarisbury, 1983—. Decorated DSC; named to Order Brit. Empire. Mem. Am. Mgmt. Assn., Inst. Export, Inst. Credit Mgmt. (vice chmn. 1967), Brit. Inst. Mgmt. Mem. Liberal Party. Presbyterian. Home and Office: Holly Hill Ln, Sarisbury Green, Southampton SO3 6AH, England

STOKELY, WILLIAM BURNETT, III, corporation executive; b. Los Angeles, Sept. 18, 1940; s. William Burnett and Tamara S.; m. Kay Haslett, July 25, 1962; children: William Burnett, Stacy Ivie, Shelley Kay, Clayton Frank. Pres. The Stokely Co., Stokely Affiliated Fin. Enterprises, Inc.; dir. Industries Portela, C. por A., and Casa Linda (C. por A.), Navarrete, D.R., ; bd. dirs. Merchants Nat. Bank, Indpls., Bank of E. Tenn.-Knoxville. Mem. and past chmn. U. Tenn. Devel. Council, Knoxville; bd. trustees Berry Coll., past chmn. bd. visitors. Mem. Young Pres.'s Orgn., Penrod Soc. Indpls. (past pres.), Children's Mus. Indpls., U.S. C. of C. (past dir.), Ind. C. of C. (past dir.), Newcomen Soc. N.Am., Kappa Sigma, Omicron Delta Kappa. Clubs: Econs. (Indpls.), Hundred (Indpls.), Univ. (Indpls.), Indpls. Athletic (Indpls.); Crooked Stick Golf (Carmel, Ind.), Cherokee Country (Knoxville), Club LeConte (Knoxville), Melrose (Daufuskie Island, S.C.). Office: 620 Campbell Station Rd Station West Suite Y Knoxville TN 37922

STOKER, MICHAEL GEORGE PARKE, medical scientist; b. Taunton, Eng., July 4, 1918; s. Stanley Parke and Dorothy (Nazer) S.; M.B., Cambridge U., 1942, M.A., 1946, M.D., 1947; m. Veronica Mary English, Sept. 5, 1942; children—Christopher, Jennifer, Paul, Robin, Sally. Fellow Clare Coll., Cambridge U., 1948-58, now hon. fellow; prof. virology Glasgow (Scotland) U. Med. Sch., 1958-68; dir. Imperial Cancer Research Fund Labs., 1968-79; fellow Clare Hall, Cambridge U., 1979-87, pres., 1980-87, emeritus fellow, 1987—; hon. fellow Sidney Sussex Coll.; v.p., fgn. sec. Royal Soc., 1977-81. Served with Brit. Army, 1943-47. Decorated knight bachelor, comdr. Order Brit. Empire. Fellow Royal Soc.; mem. European Molecular Biology Orgn., European Acad. Arts and Scis.; fgn. hon. mem. Am. Acad. Arts and Scis., Czech Acad. Scis. Author papers in field. Office: Dept Pathology, Univ Cambridge, Cambridge England other: care Royal Soc, 6 Carlton House Terr, London SW1Y 5AG England

STOKES, ADRIAN VICTOR, computing executive; b. London, June 25, 1945; s. Alfred Samuel and Edna (Kerrison) S. B.Sc. with 1st class honors, Univ. Coll. London, 1966, Ph.D., 1970. Chartered chemist, 1969-70; research programmer GEC Computers Ltd., Borehamwood, Herts., 1970-71; sr. research fellow Inst. Computer Sci., U. Coll. London, 1971-77; sr. lectr. The Hatfield Poly., Herts., 1977-81; dir. computing W. Lambeth Health Authority, London, 1981—; mng. dir. C.A.T. Ltd., London, 1981—. Author: Concise Encyclopaedia of Information Technology, 1985, others. Contbr. articles to profl. jours. Mem. Social Security Adv. Com., London, 1980—; mem. Minister of State for Transport's panel of advisers on disability, 1983-85; mem. Dept. Health and Social Security com. on restrictions against disabled people, 1979-81, Disabled Persons' Transport Adv. com. 1986—. Order of Brit. Empire; officer of the Most Excellent Order, 1983. Fellow Brit. Computer Soc., Inst. Dirs.; mem. Computer Soc., Inst. Elec. and Electronic Engrs. Assn. Computing Machinery, Royal Soc. Chemistry, Brit. Inst. Mgmt. Avocations: philately; computing. Home: 97 Millway, Mill Hill, London NW7 4JL, England

STOKES, CARL NICHOLAS, lawyer; b. Memphis, Jan. 26, 1907; s. John William and Edith Isabell (Burgess) S. 1 child, Vicki Stokes Koehn. LL.B., U. Memphis, 1934. Bar: Tenn. 1934. Assoc., Norvell & Monteverde, 1934-38; clk. City Ct., Memphis, 1938-42; clk. Criminal Cts., Shelby County, Tenn., 1946-50; judge City Ct. and 1st Traffic Ct., Memphis, 1950-52; assoc. Shea and Pierotti, Memphis, 1952-62; v.p., gen. counsel Allen & O'Hara, Inc., Memphis, 1962-72; of counsel McDonald, Kuhn, Smith, Gandy, Miller & Tait, Memphis, 1972-76, Stokes, Kimbrough, Grusin & Kizer, P.C., Memphis 1976-82, Stokes, May, Grusin, Surprise & Kizer, P.C., Memphis, 1982-84. Hon. dir. Mid South Fair Assn.; life mem. Salvation Army Adv. Bd., Memphis, chmn., 1973-75; trustee Shrine Sch. for Handicapped Children; life elder Lindenwood Christian Ch. Served to capt. AUS, 1942-46. Recipient T.E. Kirkpatrick Ann. award Kiwanis Club Memphis, 1978; James W. Bodley Americanism award Am. Legion, 1980. Mem. Tenn. Bar Assn. (Merit award for pub. service 1958), ABA, Memphis Bar Assn., Shelby County Bar Assn. Clubs: Economic, English Speaking Union. Lodges: Masons (33 degree), Shriners (Memphis). Home: 2237 Massey Rd Memphis TN 38119 Office: Johnson Grusin Kee & May 780 Ridge Lake Blvd Memphis TN 91934

STOKES, CHRISTOPHER MAYNARD, airlines executive; b. Adelaide, Australia, Dec. 22, 1943; s. Philip Herbert and Jean (Edwards) S.; m. Rosemary Eileen Atterton, Jan. 13, 1967; children: Lydia J., Allison M., Lucy K. Diploma in Export, South Australian Inst., Adelaide, 1973, diploma in Mktg., 1975. Coordinator ticket sales Qantas Airways, Adelaide, 1978-80, coordinator sales devel., 1980-82, mgr. cargo, 1982-87; rep. Ansett Internat. Air Freight, South Australia, No. Territory, 1987—; lectr. air freight Inst. Export, Adelaide, 1982—; cons. perishable air freight, Adelaide, 1982—. Served to lt. Australian Army. Fellow Inst. Export; mem. Civil Aviation Inst. Anglican. Club: Royal South Australian Yacht Squadron (Adelaide).

STOKES, GORDON STEWART, physician; b. Sydney, New South Wales, Australia, Sept. 21, 1935; s. Robert Keith and Jessie Constance (Anderson) S.; m. Toni Patricia Kain, Apr. 11, 1961; children—Joanne, Peter, Jennifer, Robert. M.B.B.S. with honors II, U. Sydney, 1960, M.D., 1964; Dipl. Theology, Australian Coll. Theology, 1983. Resident med. officer Sydney Hosp., 1960-61; research fellow U. New South Wales, Kensington, 1962-64, Westminster Med. Sch., London, 1964-65; vis. scientist Nat. Heart Inst., Bethesda, Md., 1965-66; fellow, specialist Sydney Hosp., 1967-82; sr. staff specialist Royal North Shore Hosp., St. Leonards, New South Wales, 1983—; Leverhulme vis. reader U. Hong Kong, 1971; chmn. Sydney Hosp. Health Screening, 1978-83; vis. physician Women's Hosp. Crown St., Sydney, 1981-83. Co-editor: Use of Angiotensin Inhibitors, 1976; Hormones and the Kidney, 1980. Chmn. NSW br. Christian Med. Fellowship of Australia. Burroughs Wellcome prize dept. pharmacology U. Sydney, 1957; Overseas fellow, Nat. Heart Found., 1964. Fellow Royal Australian Coll. Physicians; mem. High Blood Pressure Research Council Australia. Anglican. Home: 15 McIntosh St, Gordon, New South Wales 2072, Australia Office: Royal North Shore Hosp, Clin Pharm Dept, Saint Leonards, NSW 2065, Australia

STOLEE, MICHAEL JOSEPH, education educator, consultant; b. Mpls., Aug. 22, 1930; s. Gullik R. and Adeline J. (Thomason) S.; m. Marilyn Sandbo, June 7, 1952; children—Margaret Kay, Anne Marie. B.A., St. Olaf Coll., 1952; M.A., U. Minn., 1959, Ph.D., 1963. Assoc. dean edn. U. Miami, Coral Gables, Fla., 1970-75, prof., 1963-75; dean Sch. Edn., U. Wis.-Milw., 1975-84, prof., 1975—; acting assoc. headmaster U. Sch. Milw., 1985-86; cons. sch. desegregation HEW, U.S. Dept. Justice, White House, NAACP, NAACP Legal Def. Fund, ACLU, states and sch. dists., Boston, Miami, Fla., Chgo., Phila., San Francisco, Mpls., Dallas, St. Louis, Pitts., Los Angeles, 1965—. Named Disting. Alumnus, St. Olaf Coll., Northfield, Minn., 1972. Mem. Am. Assn. Colls. Tchr. Edn. (govt. relations com. 1980-83), Phi Delta Kappa (area coordinator 1984—, pres. Milw. chpt. 1984-85). Democrat. Lutheran. Avocations: gardening, philately, photography. Home: 7033 N Lombardy Rd Milwaukee WI 53217 Office: U Wis-Milw PO Box 413 Milwaukee WI 53201

STOLL, ERIC D., consulting engineer; b. N.Y.C., Nov. 15, 1938; s. Duane C. and Bessie (Mosley) S.; B.E.E. magna cum laude, CCNY, 1961; M.E.E., N.Y. U., 1963, Ph.D. with honors, 1966, M.B.A., 1974. Mem. tech. staff Bell Telephone Labs., Murray Hill and Holmdel, N.J., 1961-68; program mgr. Bendix Corp. Nav. and Control Div., Teterboro, N.J., 1968-73; mgr. spl. programs ADT Security Systems Corp., N.Y.C., 1973-79; dir. engring. advanced tech. systems div. Austin Co., Fair Lawn, N.J., 1979-82; pres. Modulation Scis., Inc., Bklyn., 1982-85; owner Cons. Engring. Assocs., Teaneck, N.J., 1985—. Lic. profl. engr., N.Y., N.J. recipient Sandor I. Oesterreicher award Elec. Engring. Excellence, 1961, Founders Day award for outstanding scholarship N.Y.U., 1967. Fellow The Radio Club Am., Inc. (treas. 1987—); mem. IEEE, NSPE, N.J. Soc. Profl. Engrs., Bergen County Soc. Profl. Engrs. (v.p. 1986-87), Assn. Fed. Communications Cons. Engrs. (admissions com. 1986—), Inst. Mgmt. Scis. (pres. Met. N.Y. chpt. 1978-79, v.p. programs 1977-78), Tau Beta Pi, Eta Kappa Nu. Contbr. articles to profl. jours.; patentee in field. Home: 117 Hillside Ave Teaneck NJ 07666

STOLL, PETER, obstetrician and gynecologist; b. Neu-Isenburg, Germany, Jan. 13, 1916; s. Peter and Elise (Luft) S.; Dr. med., 1942; Dr.med.habil., 1953; m. Margot Freundlieb, Apr. 21, 1946; children—Eva, Walter, Peter, Margret, Georg, Christian. Mem. dept. ob-gyn U. Goettingen Faculty Medicine, 1948-50; mem. faculty U. Heidelberg (W. Ger.) Med. Sch., 1950—, prof. ob-gyn, 1958—, chmn. dept. Mannheim Hosp., U. Heidelberg Med. Sch., 1965—. Recipient Goldblatt award, 1975. Fellow Internat. Acad. Cytology; mem. German Soc. Ob-Gyn, German Soc. Cytology, Ob-Gyn Soc. Italy (hon.), Ob-Gyn Soc. Chile (hon.), German Soc. Balneology (hon.), German Soc. Adolescent Gynecology (hon.), German Soc. Pediatrics (corr.). Author med. textbooks: Gynecology, Cytology/Vitalcytology; Oncology; Preventive Gynecology and Obstetrics; nat. editor Acta cytologica. Home: Collinistrasse 5 18/19, 6800 Manheim Federal Republic of Germany

STOLL, RICHARD EDMUND, manufacturing executive; b. Dayton, Ohio, Aug. 5, 1927; s. George Elmer and Mary Francis (Zimmerle) S.; m. Vera Mae Cohagen; children: Richard Edmund, Linda Ann, Donna Gail. Student in mech. engring., MIT, 1945-47; MetE, Ohio State U., 1950. Registered profl. engr. Ill., Tex. Various staff and operating positions U.S. Steel Corp., Pitts., Chgo., Houston, 1952-78; gen. mgr. metall. services U.S. Steel Corp., Pitts., 1978-84, dir. quality mgmt. program and tech., 1983-84; corp. chief metallurgist Wheeling-Pitts. Steel Corp., Wheeling, W.Va., 1985-86, v.p., gen. mgr. flat rolled steel, 1986-87, v.p., gen. mgr., interum chief ops. officer, 1987—; cons. McElrath & Assocs., Mpls., 1984; bd. dirs. Ohio Valley Industry and Bus. Devel. Corp., Wheeling. Contbr. articles to profl. jours.; patentee in field. Served with C.E., U.S. Army, 1950-52. Fellow Am. Soc. Metals (chmn. 1963); mem. Am. Iron and Steel Inst., Am. Inst. Mining and Metallurgy (Nat. Open Hearth award 1957, bd. dirs. 1961-68), Am. Inst. Steel Engrs., Am. Soc. Metals. Republican. Roman Catholic. Clubs: Wheeling Country, Ft. Henry, Duquesne. Home: 1490 Candlewood Dr Pittsburgh PA 15241 Office: Wheeling-Pitts Steel Corp 1134 Market St Wheeling WV 26003

STOLLA, DANIEL PAUL, gynecologist, obstetrician; b. Marseille, France, Feb. 17, 1944; s. André Stolla and Edmée De Brienne; m. Yvonne Isnard May 15, 1965 (div. 1986); children: Valerie, Audrey; m. Christiane Tondi, Dec. 20, 1986. MD in Gynecology, U. Marseille, 1973, sexology clinic attestation, 1976. Extern Hosps. Assistance Publique de Marseille, 1966-69, attaché de consultation, 1973—; gynecologist, obstetrician Cabinet de Gynecologie Obstetrique Marseille, 1971—; attaché d' enseignement Clinique Faculte de Marseille, 1981-83. Home: 25 Chemin des Chasseurs, Vallon des Peyrards, 13015 Marseilles France Office: Cabinet de Gynelogie, 16 Place de Strasbourg, 13003 Marseilles France

STOLLMANN, RAINER E.G., literature educator; b. Bochum, Fed. Republic Germany, May 28, 1947; s. Georg and Erni S.; m. Christina Nilges, Dec. 15, 1972; children: Till and Max. Degree, U. Bochum, Fed. Republic Germany, 1973; PhD, U. Bremen, Fed. Republic Germany, 1977. Research cooperator Research Inst. U. Bremen, Fed. Republic Germany, 1980-85; research cooperator Studiengang Kulturwissenschaft, Bremen, Fed. Republic Germany, 1986—; dir. Dickinson Coll. (Pa.) Bremen Program, 1986—. Author: Aesthetisierung der Politik, 1978; author 3 radio programs; contbr. numerous articles to profl. jours. Home: Uhlandstr 5, D-2800 Bremen Federal Republic of Germany Office: Univ Bremen, P Weiss Str, D-2800 Bremen 33 Federal Republic of Germany

STOLTE, DIETER, broadcasting executive; b. Cologne, Fed. Republic of Germany, Sept. 18, 1934. Head dept. sci. Saarländischer Rundfunk, Saarbrücken, Fed. Republic of Germany, 1961-62; personal advisor to dir. gen. Zweites Deutsches Fernsehen, Mainz, Fed. Republic of Germany, 1962-67, controller dept. program planning, 1967-73, dir. programming, 1973-76, dir. gen., 1982—; dir., dep. dir. gen. Südwestfunk, Baden-Baden, Fed. Republic of Germany, 1976-82; hon. prof. music and art U. Hamburg, Fed. Republic of Germany, 1980. Editor: Integritas. Geistige Wandlung und menschliche Wirklichkeit, 1966, Fernsehkritik im Streit der Meinungen von Produzenten, Konsumenten, Rezensenten, 1969, Fernsehen-Ein Medium sieht sich selbst, 1976, Zwischen Pflicht und Neigung, 1988. Recipient Cross of Order of Merit, Officer's Cross of Order of Merit, Bavarian Order of Merit; named Hon. Citizen, State of Tenn. Mem. Internat. Acad. Arts and Scis. (mem. council), Nat. Acad. TV Arts and Scis. (mem. council), German Press Agy. (mem. adminstrv. council), TransTel (chmn. adminstrv. council), European Broadcasting Union (mem. adminstrv. council). Office: Zweites Deutsches Fernsehen, Postfach 4040, 6500 Mainz Federal Republic of Germany

STOLTE, LARRY GENE, computer processing company executive; b. Cedar Rapids, Iowa, Sept. 17, 1945; s. Ed August and Emma Wilhelmena (Tank) S.; B.B.A. with highest distinction (FS Services scholar), U. Iowa, 1971; m. Rebecca Jane Tappmeyer, June 13, 1970; children—Scott Edward, Ryan Gene. Tax and auditing acct. McGladrey Pullen & Co., Cedar Rapids, 1971-73; sr. v.p. TLS Co., Cedar Rapids, 1973—, also dir. Served to sgt. USMC, 1964-67. C.P.A., Iowa, Ill., Mo., Minn., Mich., Wis.; cert. mgmt. acct. Mem. Nat. Assn. Computerized Tax Processors (pres.), Nat. Assn. Accts., Am. Inst. C.P.A.'s, Am. Mgmt. Assn. Republican. Methodist. Home: 2107 Linmar Dr NE Cedar Rapids IA 52402 Office: TLS Co 425 2d St Se PO Box 1686 Cedar Rapids IA 52406

STOLTENBERG, THORVALD, government official; b. Oslo, Norway, July 8, 1931; m. Karin Stoltenberg; 3 children. Student, Austria, U.S. and Finland, 1952-54; degree in law, 1957. Joined Fgn. Service, Norway, 1958; vice consul Norwegian Embassy, San Francisco, 1959-61; sec. Norwegian Embassy, Belgrade, 1964-65; exec. officer Fgn. Minister's Secretariat, 1965-70; acting counsellor Embassy, Lagos, Nigeria, 1970; internat. sec. Norwegian Fedn. Trade Unions, 1970-71, 72-73, 81-83; state sec. Fgn. Ministry, Norway, 1971-72, Ministry of Defense, Norway, 1973-74, Ministry of Commerce and Shipping, Norway, 1974-76, Ministry of Fgn. Affairs, Norway, 1976-79; minister of defense Norway, 1979-81; dep. mayor Oslo 1985-87; fgn. minister Norway, 1987—; chmn. Nordic Aid Devel. Group, 1968, Norwegian Cons. Council on EC Affairs, 1971-72, 76-79; vice chmn. Norwegian del. to UN, 1971-72, 76-79; chmn. UN North South com., 1978-79. Mem. Oslo city council, 1984—, Mcpl. Exec. Bd., Oslo, 1984—; mcpl. counsellor, Oslo, 1984—; mem. fin. and planning coms., Oslo. Address: Ministry Fgn Affairs, Oslo Norway *

STONE, ALLAN GRAYSON, licensing representative; b. Bklyn., Jan. 5, 1926; s. Frank and Bertha (Lenner) S.; student Hamilton Coll., 1941-45, Adelphi Coll., 1944-48; m. Barbara Betsy Shore, 1948; children—Michael Sanford, Peter Lyle, Robert Adam. Vice-pres. Kagran Corp., N.Y.C., 1948-55; pres. Stone Assocs., N.Y.C., 1955-60, Licensing Corp. Am., N.Y.C., 1960-70; chmn. Hamilton Projects, Inc., N.Y.C., 1971—; dir. Herald Tribune Radio Network, Inc., Gateway Industries Inc., Def. Electronic Industries, Inc. Served with USNR, 1942-47. Clubs: Friars (N.Y.C.); North Shore Country (Glen Head, N.Y.); Boca West Golf (Boca Raton, Fla.). Home: 13 Grenfell Dr Great Neck NY 11020 Office: 215 Lexington Ave New York NY 10020

STONE, BARTLETT HENRY, gynecologist, educator; b. St. Johnsbury, Vt., Oct. 26, 1916; s. Edward Enos and Gladys Bennett (Newell) Stone; m. Mable Catherine Larbey, Dec. 22, 1942; children—Bartlett Dimick, Pamela Stone Kennedy. B.S., U. Vt., Burlington, 1938; M.D., 1941. Diplomate Am. Bd. Med. Examiners, Am. Bd. Obstetrics-Gynecology. Intern Springfield Hosp. (Mass.); resident in surgery New Eng. Deaconess Hosp., Boston; resident in obstetrics Boston Lying-In Hosp., resident in gynecology Free Hosp. for Women, Brookline, Mass., also fellow in gynecol. pathology; instr ob-gyn Harvard U. Med. Sch. Boston, 1954-86, emeritus, 1986—; active staff Newton Wellesley Hosp., Newton Lower Falls, Mass., 1952-82, assoc. staff, 1982-84, emeritus, 1986; obstetrician, gynecologist Brigham and Woman's Hosp., Boston, 1953-86, emeritus, 1986—; clin. assoc. gynecol. surgery Mass. Gen. Hosp., Boston, 1954-86, cons. 1986—; active staff gynecology and surgery New Eng. Deaconess Hosp., 1964-86, hon. staff men. 1986—; cons. ob-gyn Norwood (Mass.) Hosp., 1953-60, Sturdy Meml. Hosp., Attleboro, Mass., 1953-60, Mass. Eye & Ear Infirmary, Boston, 1957-60; trustee Ryder Meml. Hosp., Humacao, P.R., 1964-70. Contbr. articles in field to publs. Deacon Wellesley Hills Congregational Ch., 1960-63. Served to maj. U.S. Army, 1941-46; ETO, N. Africa. Fellow Am. Coll. Ob-Gyn, ACS, Am. Soc. Colposcopy and Cervical Pathology; mem. AMA (physicians achievement awards 1980-84), Mass. Med. Soc., Gynecol. Laser Soc. (founding) Am. Assn. Gynecol. Laparoscopists, Obstet. Soc. Boston, Am. Soc. Study Sterility, Am. Soc. Study Breast Disease, Phi Delta Theta. Republican. Congregationalist. Clubs: Mill Reef (Antigua, W.I.); Harvard (Boston); Wellesley, Wellesley Coll. Lodges: Masons, Shriners.

STONE, CHARLES KEMPTHORNE, barrister; b. Wellington, N.Z., Feb. 20, 1925; s. Arthur Richard and Gladys Ethel (Kempthorne) S.; student Scots Coll., Wellington, 1939-41; LL.B., U. N.Z., 1951; m. Alison Perry, Dec. 21, 1949; Sr. ptnr. Rudd Watts & Stone, Barristers, Solicitors, and Notary Public, Wellington; chmn. Wiggins Teape N.Z., Ltd., Glaxo N.Z., Ltd. Served with N.Z. Army, 1944-46. Decorated Queen's Jubilee medal, 1977. Mem. Royal Soc. N.Z., Australasian Inst. Mining and Metallurgy, Elec. Supply Authorities Assn. N.Z. (standing counsel). Clubs: Wellington, Mana Cruising. Home: 31 Wadestown Rd, Wellington New Zealand Office: PO Box 2793, Wellington New Zealand

STONE, DONALD D., investment and sales executive; b. Chgo., June 25, 1924; s. Frank J. and Mary N. (Miller) Diamondstone; student U. Ill., 1942-43; B.S., DePaul U., 1949; m. Catherine Mauro, Dec. 20, 1970; 1 child, Jeffrey. Pres., Poster Bros., Inc., Chgo., 1950-71, Revere Leather Goods, Inc., Chgo., 1953-71; owner Don Stone Enterprises, Chgo., 1954—; v.p. Horton & Hubbard Mfg. Co., Inc. div. Brown Group, Nashua, N.H., 1969-71, Neevel Mfg. Co., Kansas City, Mo., 1969-71. Mem. adv. bd. San Diego Opera; founder Don Diego Meml. Scholarship Fund; mem. bd. overseers U. Calif., San Diego, chancellor's assoc.; mem. exec. bd. Chgo. Area council Boy Scouts of Am. Served with U.S. Army, 1943-46. Clubs: Bryn Mawr Country (Lincolnwood, Ill.) (dir.), Carlton, La Jolla Beach and Tennis, La Jolla Country, Del Mar Thoroughbred. Home: 8240 Caminito Maritimo La Jolla CA 92037

STONE, ERNEST LYNN, educator; b. New Haven, Nov. 25, 1907; s. Wilbur Clayton and Emma (Benedict) S.; B.F.A., Yale U., 1936; postgrad. Tchrs. Coll. Columbia U., 1940; m. Semmeh Hall Sanjiyan, Jan. 11, 1928 (dec. Feb. 1978); children—Mary Victoria (Mrs. Russell Edward Leary), Ernest Lynn, Judith Cushing (Mrs. Leon Vincent Grabar); m. 2d, Ruth Lathrop Frager, Apr. 21, 1979. Art tchr. Bassett Jr. High Sch., New Haven, 1931-38, Hillhouse High Sch., New Haven, 1938-40; supr. art edn. New Haven Pub. Schs., 1940-70; asst. prof. art So. Conn. State U., 1953-61. Conn. coordinator for art in opera N.Y. Met. Opera Guild, 1950-60. Recipient 1st medal award, mural painting Soc. Beaux Arts-Architects (N.Y.), 1927, 29. Mem. Nat. Ret. Tchrs. Assn., Conn. Arts Assn., Assn. Ret. Tchrs. Conn., Conn. Watercolor Soc., Conn. Soc. Founders and Patriots (gov. 1965-66). Clubs: New Haven Paint and Clay (pres. 1949-52), Civitan (pres. 1961-62, dir. 1962-68, 72-78), Yale, New Haven Congregational (pres. 1945-46). Home: 139 Beecher Rd Woodbridge CT 06525 also: 4720 NE 3d Terr Fort Lauderdale FL 33334

STONE, FRANZ THEODORE, retired fabricated metal products manufacturing executive; b. Columbus, Ohio, May 11, 1907; s. Julius Frederick and Edna (Andress) S.; m. Katherine Devereux Jones, Feb. 23, 1935; children: Franz Theodore, Thomas Devereux Mackay, Raymond Courtney, Catherine Devereux Diebold. AB magna cum laude, Harvard U., 1929; hon. degrees, Canisius Coll., 1975, Ohio State U., 1976. Chmn. bd. Columbus McKinnon Corp., Amherst, N.Y., 1935-86. Chmn. emeritus Arts Council in Buffalo and Erie County, 1973-86; pres. Buffalo Philharmonic Orch. Soc., 1959-61, also life dir.; chmn. emeritus Studio Arena Theatre, Buffalo, 1968-86; Nat. Conf. of Christian and Jews Brother Sisterhood citation, 1986; First Arts award ARts Council and Greater Buffalo C. of C. Recipient Gold Key award Buffalo YMCA, 1966, Red Jacket award Buffalo & Erie County Hist. Soc., 1976, Disting. Citizen award SUNY, Buffalo, 1985. Clubs: (Fla.) Gulfstream Bath & Tennis, Ocean Club of Fla., Boca Raton Country Club, (W.VA.) The Greenbrier (Bflo) Buffalo Country Club, Buffalo Club, Saturn Club. Home: 1171 N Ocean Blvd Apt 4-CS Gulf Stream FL 33483

STONE, GREGORY MICHAEL, law enforcement, public safety consultant; b. Hartford, Conn., July 31, 1959; s. George William Jr. and Patricia Gertrude (Fitton) S. BA in Polit. Sci., Loyola U., Chgo., 1982; MS in Elect. Engring., Pacific Western U., PhD in Elect. Engring.; postgrad., Columbia Pacific U. Dir. advanced projects Sachs/Freeman Assocs. Inc., Lake Bluff, Ill., 1980-88; dir. pub. safety, nat. security services RJO Enterprises, Inc., Lanham, Md., 1988—; bd. dirs. Telescis. Internat. Ltd., Mundelein, Ill., Consolidated News Service, Mundelein, RCT:SFA Joint Venture, Lake Bluff; prin. Stone Industries Inc., Mundelein, 1982—; dir. systems engring. Airfone Inc., Oak Brook, Ill., 1983-84. Contbr. articles in field to profl. jours. Mem. Lake County Rep. Fedn., Waukegan, Ill., 1985—. Fellow Radio Club Am.; mem. AAAS, IEEE (chmn. Chgo. sect. vehicular tech. soc. 1983—), John Birch Soc., Am. Def. Preparedness Assn. (chmn. ops. security working group), Am. Soc. for Indsl. Security, Armed Forces Communications and Electronics Assn., Scientist's Inst. for Pub. Info., U.S. Naval Inst., SAR, Mayflower Soc.; assoc. mem. Internat. Assn. Chiefs Police, Nat. Sheriffs Assn., Internat. Assn. Bomb Technicians and Investigators, Internat. Narcotic Enforcement Officers Assn., Inc. Home: Box 485 Mundelein IL 60060 Office: RJO Enterprises Inc 4550 Forbes Blvd Lanham MD 20706

STONE, HOWARD LAWRENCE, lawyer; b. Chgo., Sept. 16, 1941; s. Jerome Richard Stone and Ceale (Perlik) Stone Tandet; m. Susan L. Saltzman, June 2, 1963; children—Lauren, David. Student U. Ill.-Chgo., 1960-61, U. Ill., Champaign, 1961; B.S.B.A., Roosevelt U., 1963; J.D., DePaul U., 1972. Bar: Ill. 1972, U.S. Dist. Ct. (no. dist.) Ill. 1972, U.S. Tax Ct. 1972, U.S. Supreme Ct. 1982; C.P.A., Ill. Agt. IRS, Chgo., 1964-72; spl. asst. U.S. atty. and chief fin. auditor and investigator No. Dist. Ill., Dept. Justice, Chgo., 1972-76; sr. ptnr. Stone, McGuire & Benjamin, Chgo., 1976—; lectr. in taxation. Author: Defending the Federal Tax Case: What To Do When the IRS Steps In, 1978; Client Tax Fraud—A Practical Guide to Protecting Your Rights, 1984. Co-editor, co-author: Handling Criminal Tax Cases: A Lawyers Guide, 1982; co-author: Federal Civil Tax Law, 1982; co-author: Negotiating to Win, 1985. Campaigner lawyers div. Jewish United Fund, Chgo., 1982—; com. mem., bd. dirs. Israel Bonds, Chgo., 1982—, U. Chgo.; chmn. U. Ill. Found. Geriatric Research Fund, 1984; bd. dirs. Gastro Intestinal Research Found., Chgo., 1978—. Mem. Chgo. Bar Assn., Ill. State Bar Assn., Fed. Bar Assn., ABA, Decalogue Soc. Lawyers, Am. Inst. C.P.A.s, Ill. C.P.A. Found., Am. Assn. Atty.-C.P.A.s, Ill. C.P.A. Soc. (resident lectr. in tax fraud 1976-84, chmn. Investment Advisers Act task force 1983-84). Jewish. Lodges: B'nai B'rith, Shriners. Office: Stone McGuire & Benjamin 55 E Monroe Suite 3740 Chicago IL 60603

STONE, HUBERT DEAN, editor, journalist; b. Maryville, Tenn., Sept. 23, 1924; s. Archie Hubert and Annie (Cupp) S.; student Maryville Coll., 1942-43; B.A., U. Okla., 1949; m. Agnes Shirley, Sept. 12, 1953 (dec. Mar. 1973); 1 son, Neal Anson. Sunday editor Maryville-Alcoa Daily Times, 1949; mng. editor Maryville-Alcoa Times, 1949-78, editor, 1978—; v.p. Maryville-Alcoa Newspapers, Inc., 1960—; pres. Stonecraft, 1954—. Vice chmn. Tenn. Great Smokey Mountain Park Commn., mem. mayor's adv. com. City of Maryville; mem. air service adv. com. Knoxville Met. Airport Authority; bd. dirs. United Fund of Blount County, 1961-63, 74-76, vice chmn. campaign, 1971-72, chmn. campaign, 1973, v.p., 1974, pres., 1975; vice chmn. bd. dirs. Maryville Utilities Bd.; bd. dirs. Blount County Hist. Trust, Nat. Hillbilly Homecoming Assn., Friendsville Acad., 1968-73, Alkiwan Crafts, Inc., 1970-73, Middle E.Tenn. Regional Tourism Group; dir. Foothills Land Conservancy, Smokey Mountains Passion Play Assn.; mem. adv. com. Blount County Alternative Center for Learning; chmn. Blount County Long Range Planning for Sch. Facilities; mem. adv. bd. Harrison-Chilhowee Bapt. Acad, mem. Leadership Knoxville. Served from pvt. to staff sgt. AUS, 1943-45. Decorated Bronze Star; named Outstanding Sr. Man of Blount County, 1970, 77, Hon. Order Ky. Cols., Commonwealth of Ky. Mem. Profl. Photographers of Am., Internat. Post Card Distbrs. Assn., Great Smoky Mountains Natural History Assn., Ft. Loudoun Assn., Tenn. Jaycees (editor 1954-55, sec.-treas. 1955-56), Blount County Arts/ Crafts Guild, Jr. Chamber Internat. (senator) Maryville-Alcoa Jaycees (life mem., pres. 1953-54), Blount County (v.p. 1971, 76, pres. 1977), Townsend (dir. 1969-71, 83-85, pres. 1983) chambers commerce, Tenn. Associated Press News Execs. Assn. (v.p. 1973, pres. 1974), Asso. Press Mng. Editors Assn., Tenn. Profl. Photographers Assn., Am. Legion, V.F.W., Chilhowee Bapt. Assn. (chmn. history com.) U. Okla. Alumni Assn. (life mem., pres. East Tenn. chpt. 1954-55), Sigma Delta Chi (life, dir. E. Tenn. chpt.). Baptist (trustee, pres. bd. trustees, deacon, chmn. evangelism, finance, personnel coms.). Mason, Kiwanian (pres. Alcoa 1969-70); Club: Green Meadow Country. Contbr. articles to profl. publs. Avocation: photographer U.S. Nat. Parks. Home: 1510 Scenic Dr Maryville TN 37801 Office: 307 E Harper Ave Maryville TN 37801

STONE, J. W., superintendent schools; b. Fortescue, Mo., Nov. 6, 1927; s. Perry Allen and May (Murrah) S.; BS, N.W. Mo. State Coll., 1956; MA, U. Mo., Kansas City, 1957, also postgrad. Farmer, Fortescue, Mo., 1944—; instr. Craig (Mo.) R-III High Sch., 1957-59; supt. schs., Holt County, Oregon, Mo., 1959-61, Craig R-III Sch. Dist., 1961—; del. to Hungary, USSR, Internat. Edn. Soc., 1968; mem. Mo. Adv. Council on Vocat. Edn., 1983—. Dist. dir. ARC, 1954—, bd. dirs. Midland Empire region, 1979—; bd. dirs. Heart Assn., Crippled Children's, March of Dimes, TB Soc., 1954—; mem. Town Bd., Fotescue, Mo., 1962-78; mayor City of Fortescue, 1968-78; chmn. Holt County Citizens Council, 1979—; vice chmn. Wesley Found., NW Mo. State U., 1970—; mem. regional empire com. bd. Girl Scouts, 1973-75; mem. com. Mo. Council Pub. Higher Edn., 1973; regional dir. Mo. Vocat. Rehab., 1967—; chmn. bd. N.W. Mo. Community Services, 1980—. Mem. 6th Congl. Dist., 1960—, 6th Congl. Legis. Dist., 1960—, Mo. Rep. State Com., 1960—; chmn. Holt County Rep. Cen. Com., 1954—; state com. del. to inauguration Pres. Reagan, 1981, 1985, Pres. Nixon, 1969, 1973; mem. Balance of State Planning Council, State of Mo., 1981—. dir. OEO Corp.; sec.-treas. NW Mo. Econ. Opportunity Corp., Maryville, Mo., chmn. bd., 1969-79; v.p. Mo. Council Chs., 1948-50; dir. Camps and Conf. W. Mo. Conf. United Meth. Ch., 1965—, mem. bd. adminstrv. fin., 1972—; chmn. N.W. dist. United Meth. Ch. Missions and Ch. Extension, 1976—; smem. Selective Service Bd. Mo. Region I, 1982, Appeals Bd. Western half of Mo., 1983; U.S. del. World Meth. Council Meeting, Dublin, 1976, Honolulu, 1981; Maryville dist. trustee Meth. Ch., 1960—. World del. Meth. Conf., Oslo, Norway, 1961; del. United Meth. Ch. Mo. West Conf. to World Meth. Council Evangelism, Jerusalem, 1974; world del. representing U.S. on Christian Edn., Tokyo, 1958; U.S. del. Comparative and Internat. Edn. Soc., Round-the-World, 1970, S. Am., 1971; world del. Meth. Conf. Nairobi, Kenya and London, 1986; bd. dirs. council of ministries Ms. Area United Meth. Ch., 1988—. Served with AUS, 1950-52. Mem. NEA, Nat., Mo. State assns. sch. adminstrs., Mo. State, Holt County (past pres.) tchrs. assns., Pi Omega Pi, Kappa Delta Pi, Tau Kappa Epsilon. Methodist (dist. lay leader 1968-84). Clubs: Masons (32 deg., Shriner), Order Eastern Star. Home: Fortescue MO 64452 Office: Craig MO 64437

STONE, JOHN TIMOTHY, JR., author; b. Denver, July 13, 1933; s. John Timothy and Marie Elizabeth (Briggs) S.; m. Judith Bosworth Stone, June 22, 1955; children: John Timothy, George William. Student Amherst Coll., 1951-52, U. Mex., 1952; BA, U. Miami, 1955. Sales mgr. Atlas Tag, Chgo., 1955-57; br. mgr. Household Fin. Corp., Chgo., 1958-62; pres. Janeff Credit Corp., Madison, Wis., 1962-72; pres. Recreation Internat., Mpls., 1972-74; pres. Continental Royal Services, N.Y.C., 1973-74; dir. devel. The Heartlands Group/Tryon Mint, Toronto, Ont., Can., 1987-88; bd. dirs. Madison Credit Bur., Wis. Lenders' Exchange. Author: Mark, 1973, Going for Broke, 1976, The Minnesota Connection, 1978, Debby Boone So Far, 1980, (with John Dallas McPherson) He Calls Himself "An Ordinary Man", 1981, Satiacum, The Chief Who's Winning Back the West, 1981, The Great American Treasure Hunt, 1983-86, Runaways, 1983, (with Robert E. Gard) Where The Green Bird Flies, 1984. Served with CIC, U.S. Army, 1957-59. Mem. Sigma Alpha Epsilon. Republican. Presbyterian. Clubs: Minarani, African First Shotters. Home: 1009 Starlight Dr Madison WI 53711 Office: Pubs Adv Group PO Box 5562 Madison WI 55705

STONE, MARTIN HOPE, orthopedic surgeon; b. Glasgow, Scotland, Mar. 30, 1956; s. Frederick Hope and Zelda (Elston) S.; m. Pauline Anne Johnson, May 16, 1986. MB, ChB, Glasgow U., 1979; MPhil in Bioengring., Strathclyde (Scotland) U., 1987. Jr. house officer medicine Gartnaval Gen. Hosp., Glasgow, 1979-80; jr. house officer surgery Victoria Infirmany, Glasgow, 1980; sr. house officer trauma surgery Western Infirmary and So. Gen. Hosp., Glasgow, 1980-81; gen. surg. tng. rotation Bristol Royal Infirmary, Bristol Childrens' Hosp., Ham Green Hosp., Weston Gen. Hosp. and Winford Hosp., Eng., 1981-84; orthopaedic registrar Glasgow Royal Infirmary, 1984-87; orthopaedic sr. registrar Southampton Gen. Hosp., Eng., 1987—. Johnson and Johnson travelling fellow, 1987. Fellow Royal Coll. Surgeons; mem. Brit. Med. Assn., Brit. Orthopaedic Assn.

STONE, MARVIN JULES, physician, educator; b. Columbus, Ohio, Aug. 3, 1937; s. Roy J. and Lillian (Bedwinek) S.; m. Jill Feinstein, June 29, 1958; children: Nancy Lillian, Robert Howard. Student, Ohio State U., 1955-58; S.M. in Pathology, U. Chgo., 1962, M.D. with honors, 1963. Diplomate: Am. Bd. Internal Medicine, Am. Bd. Hematology, Am. Bd. Med. Oncology. Intern ward med. service Barnes Hosp., St. Louis, 1963-64; asst. resident Barnes Hosp., 1964-65; clin. asso. arthritis and rheumatism br. Nat. Inst. Arthritis and Metabolic Diseases, NIH, Bethesda, Md., 1965-68; resident in medicine, A.C.P. scholar Parkland Meml. Hosp., Dallas, 1968-69; fellow in hematology-oncology, dept. internal medicine U. Tex. Southwestern Med. Sch., Dallas, 1969-70; instr. dept. internal medicine U. Tex. Southwestern Med. Sch., 1970-71, asst. prof., 1971-73, asso. prof., 1974-76, clin. prof., 1976—, chmn. bioethics com., 1979-81; mem. faculty and steering com. immunology grad. program, Grad. Sch. Biomed. Scis., U. Tex. Health Sci. Ct., Dallas, 1975, adj. mem., 1976—; dir. Charles A. Sammons Cancer Center, chief oncology, dir. immunology, co-dir. div. hematology-oncology, attending physician Baylor U. Med. Center, Dallas, 1976—; adj. prof. biology So. Meth. U., Dallas, 1977—; v.p. med. staff Parkland Meml. Hosp., Dallas, 1982; cons. in internal medicine Dallas VA Hosp., Presbyn. Hosp., Dallas. Contbr. chpts. to books, articles to profl. jours. Chmn. com. patient-aid Greater Dallas/Ft. Worth chpt. Leukemia Soc. Am., 1971-76, chmn. med. adv. com., 1978-80, bd. dirs., 1971-80; med. v.p. Dallas unit Am. Cancer Soc., 1977-78, pres., 1978-80; adv. bd. Baylor U. Med. Center Found.; mem. med. adv. bd. Dallas chpt. Lupus Found. Am., 1982—. Served with USPHS, 1965-68. Named Outstanding Full Time Faculty Mem. Dept. Internal Medicine, Baylor U. Med. Center, 1978, 87. Fellow ACP; mem. AAAS, Am. Rheumatism Assn., Reticuloendothelial Soc., Am. Assn. Immunologists, Am. Fedn. Clin. Research, Am. Soc. Hematology, Internat. Soc. Hematology, Internat. Soc. Preventive Oncology, N.Y. Acad. Scis., Am. Assn. Cancer Edn., AMA, Council on Thrombosis, Am. Heart Assn. (established investigator 1970-75), Am. Soc. Clin. Oncology, Am. Assn. for Cancer Research, So. Soc. Clin. Investigation, Tex. Med. Assn., Dallas County Med. Soc., Clin. Immunology Soc., Phi Beta Kappa, Sigma Xi, Alpha Omega Alpha. Office: Baylor U Med Ctr Charles A Sammons Cancer Ctr 3500 Gaston Ave Dallas TX 75246

STONE, MINNIE STRANGE, retired automotive service company executive; b. Palatka, Fla., Mar. 10, 1919; d. James Arrious and Pansy (Thomas) Strange; student Massey Bus. Coll., 1938-39; m. Fred Albion Stone, Nov. 30, 1939; children—Fred Albion, James Thomas, Thomas Demere. Sec., bookkeeper Sears, Roebuck & Co., Jacksonville, Fla., 1939-41; financial sec. U.S. Army, Macon, Ga., 1941, Atlanta, 1942; sec., bookkeeper Raleigh Spring & Brake Service, Inc. (name changed to Stone Heavy Vehicle Specialist) (N.C.), 1953-84, sec.-treas. corp., 1960-84, now dir., sec. Pres., YWCA, Wake County, 1973-76, bd. dirs., 1966-76; bd. dirs. Urban Ministry Center, Raleigh, 1983—. Mem. N.C. Mus. of History Assocs., Raleigh Council Smaller Garden Clubs (pres. 1960-61), N.C. Art Soc., Vol. Wake County Mental Health Assn., Monthly Investors Club, Coley Forest Garden Club. Republican. Baptist. Home: 920 Runnymede Rd Raleigh NC 27607 Office: 2200 Hwy 70 E Garner NC 27529

STONE, PAULA LENORE, lawyer; b. N.Y.C., Nov. 1, 1942; d. Milton H. and Pauline (Smith) Stone; m. Richard J. Chodoff, July 29, 1969 (dec. 1983). AB in Biology, Muhlenberg Coll., 1961; student Lehigh U., 1960, Jefferson Med. Sch., 1961-63; JD, Temple U., 1981. Bar: Pa. 1982. Med. cons. to trial lawyers, Bala Cynwyd, Pa., 1963-85, N.Y., 1985—; sole practice, Bala Cynwyd, 1982-85, N.Y., 1985—; of counsel firm Turrey Kepler, Norristown, Pa., 1985—. Editor Psychopharmacology Abstracts, Cancer Chemotherapy Abstracts, 1961-64; author: (with R. J. Chodoff) Doctor for the Prosecution, 1983. Mem. Assn. Trial Lawyers Am., Coll. Physicians, Phila., ABA, N.Y. Acad. Scis. (adv. com.), Pa. Bar Assn., ACLU. Democrat. Jewish. Address: Suite 8B 870 United Nations Plaza New York NY 10017

STONE, RALPH KENNY, lawyer; b. Bainbridge, Ga., Aug. 7, 1952; s. Ralph Patrick and Joyce (Mitchell) S.; m. Julie Ann Waldren, Aug. 24, 1974; children—Laura Lee, Rebecca. B.B.A. magna cum laude, U. Ga., 1974, J.D. cum laude, 1977. Bar: Ga. 1977, U.S. Dist. Ct. (so. dist.) Ga. 1977, U.S. Supreme Ct. 1980, U.S. Ct. Appeals (11th cir.) 1981. Staff acct. Price Waterhouse & Co., Columbia, S.C., 1974; assoc. Calhoun & Donaldson, Savannah, Ga., 1977; ptnr. Franklin & Stone, Statesboro, Ga., 1977-88; ptnr. Edenfield, Stone & Cox, Statesboro, Ga., 1988—; instr. taxation Ga. So. Coll., Statesboro, 1979-80. Sect. chmn. United Way Bulloch County, 1982, div. chmn., 1983, vice chmn. campaign, 1984, v.p., 1985-86; charter pres. Leadership Bulloch, Inc., 1984; chmn. Bulloch County Democratic Com., 1984—, Bulloch 2000 Com. 1986—; alt. del. Dem. Nat. Conv., 1988; sec. Ga. Assn. Dem. County Chairs, 1985; dist. chmn. Boy Scouts Am., 1985; pres. Forward Bulloch Inc., 1986; participant Leadership Ga., 1986—. Mem. ABA, State Bar Ga., Bulloch County Bar Assn. (pres. 1982-83), Statesboro-Bulloch County C. of C. (participant Tomorrow's Leaders program 1978, bd. dirs. 1982-83, chmn. govtl. affairs com. 1982-83, v.p. 1984-85, pres. 1986, chmn. bd. dirs. 1987), Phi Kappa Phi, Beta Alpha Psi. Baptist. Club: Optimist (bd. dirs. Statesboro 1978-79, 83-84, pres. 1980-81, dist. lt. gov. 1981-82, dist. youth activities and community service chmn. 1983-84). Home: 100 Lakeside Ct Statesboro GA 30458 Office: Edenfield Stone & Cox PO Box 1186 Statesboro GA 30458

STONE, SIR (JOHN) RICHARD (NICHOLAS), economist; b. Aug. 30, 1913; m. Winifred Mary Jenkins, 1936 (div. 1940); m. Feodora Leontinoff, 1941 (dec. 1956); 1 child; m. Giovanna Croft-Murray, 1960. Ed. Westminster Sch. and Gonville and Caius Coll., Cambridge, Eng.; Sc.D., Dr. h.c., Oslo and Brussels U., 1965, Geneva U., 1971, Warwick U., 1975, Paris, 1977, Bristol U., 1978. With C.E. Heath and Co. (Lloyd's Brokers), 1936-39, Ministry of Econ. Warfare, 1939-40, offices of War Cabinet, Central Statis. Office, 1940-45; dir. dept. applied econs. Cambridge, 1945-55; Leake prof. fin. and acctg. Cambridge, 1955-80; fellow King's Coll., Cambridge, 1945—; hon. fellow Gonville and Caius Coll. Cambridge, 1976—. Author: The Role of Measurement in Economics, 1951; The Measurement of Consumers Expenditure and Behaviour in the United Kingdom, 1920-1938, vol. I. (with others), 1954, vol. II (with D.A. Rowe), 1966; Quantity and Price Indexes in National Accounts, 1956; (with Giovanna Croft-Murray) Social Accounting and Economic Models, 1959; Input-Output and Nat. Accounts, 1961; (with Giovanna Stone) National Income and Expenditure, 1961; A Programme for Growth (gen. editor series with others) 1962-74; Mathematics in the Social Sciences and Other Essays, 1966; Mathematical Models of the Economy and Other Essays, 1970; Demographic Accounting and Model Building, 1971; Aspects of Economic and Social Modelling, 1980. Contbr. articles to profl. jours. Recipient Nobel prize in Econs., 1984. Fellow Econometric Soc. (pres. 1955), Brit. Acad.; mem. Am. Acad. Arts and Scis. (hon. mem.), Am. Econ. Assn., Internat. Statis. Inst., Royal Econ. Soc. (pres. 1978-80), Acad. Naz. dei Lencei. Home: 13 Millington Rd, Cambridge England

STONE, TREVOR WILLIAM, medical educator, researcher; b. Mexborough, Yorkshire, Eng., Oct. 7, 1947; s. Thomas William and Alice (Reynolds) S.; m. Anne Corina, Apr. 3, 1971. B in Pharmacy, U. London, 1969, DSc, 1983; PhD, U. Aberdeen, Scotland, 1972. Lectr. U. Aberdeen, 1970-77; sr. lectr. U. London, 1977-82, reader, 1982-86, prof. neuroscience, 1986—; cons. Beechams, Eng., 1987. Author: Microiontophoresis, 1985; editor: Purines: Pharmacology, 1985. Fellow Royal Soc. Medicine; mem. British Pharmacological Soc., Physiol. Soc., Soc. Neuroscience, N.Y. Acad. Scis. Office: Univ London, St Georges Med Sch, London SW17 ORE, England

STONE, VICTOR J., b. Chgo., Mar. 11, 1921; s. Maurice Albert and Ida (Baskin) S.; m. Susan Abby Cane, July 14, 1951; children—Mary Jessica, Jennifer Abby, Andrew Hugh William. A.B., Oberlin Coll., 1942; J.D., Columbia U., 1948; LL.D. hon., Oberlin Coll., 1983. Bar: N.Y. 1949, Ill. 1950. Assoc. Columbia U., N.Y.C., 1948-49; assoc. Sonnenschein, Chgo., 1949-53; research assoc. U. Chgo., 1953-55; asst. prof. law U. Ill., Champaign, 1955-57, assoc. prof. law, 1957-59, prof. law, 1959—, assoc. v.p. acad. affairs, 1975-78; mem. jud. adv. council State Ill., 1959-61; mem. com. jury instructions Ill. Supreme Ct., 1963-79, reporter, 1973-79; mem. Ill. State Appellate Defender Commn., 1973-83, vice chmn., 1973-77, 79-83. Trustee Oberlin Coll., 1982—; trustee AAUP Found., 1983—. Served as lt. USNR, 1942-46. Ford Found. fellow, 1962-63. Mem. ABA, Ill. Bar Assn. (chmn. individual rights and responsibilities 1971-72, mem. council civil practice and procedure 1978-82), Chgo. Bar Assn., Am. Judicature Soc., AAUP (gen. counsel 1978-80, pres. 1982-84 , pres. Ill. conf. 1968-70, pres. Ill. chpt. 1964-65, mem. council 1982—), ACLU (bd. dirs. Ill. div. 1986—). Co-editor: Ill. Pattern Jury Instructions, 1965, 71, 77; Civil Liberties and Civil Rights, 1977. Office: Coll Law U Ill 504 E Pennsylvania St Champaign IL 61820

STONE, WILLIAM BRUHN, English educator; b. Milw., May 31, 1929; s. William Herbert and Martha Emily (Bruhn) S.; B.A. with gen. honors, U. Chgo., 1948, M.A., 1957; m. Jane Bergman, Mar. 13, 1953; children: David, Daniel, Joyce. Instr. English, U. Ky., Lexington, 1958-61, Wis. State U., LaCrosse, 1961-62; lectr. English, Ind. U. N.W., Gary, 1962-71, 80—; asst. dir. composition U. Ill., Chgo., 1976-80; editorial cons. various pubs. Active member Amnesty Internat. U.S.A. Served with AUS, 1952-54; Korea. Mem. AAUP, Assn. Tchrs. Advanced Composition (v.p. 1984-87), Conf. Coll. Composition and Communication, Midwest Modern Lang. Assn., MLA, Nat. Council Tchrs. of English, Rhetoric Soc. Am., Anthony Powell Soc. (sec.-treas. 1983—), U.S. Chess Fedn., ACLU. Editor. Anthony Powell Communications, 1977-79; editorial bd. Jour. Advanced Composition, 1979—, contbg. editor, 1984—. Contbr. articles, revs. and poetry to profl. jours., articles to ency. Home: 5704 S Kenwood Ave Chicago IL 60637 Office: Indiana University Northwest Gary IN 46408

STONE, WILLIAM ROSS, research and development company executive, physicist; b. San Diego, Aug. 26, 1947; s. William Jack and Winifred (Beckcom) S.; m. Susan Letita Lane, Aug. 8, 1970; 1 child, Ann Michele. A.B. in Earth Sci., U. Calif.-San Diego, 1967, M.S. in Applied Physics, 1973, Ph.D. in Applied Physics, 1978. Research asst. U. Calif.-San Diego, 1967-69; sr. physicist Gen. Atomic, La Jolla, 1969-72; sr. engr. engring. div. Gulf Gen. Atomic, La Jolla, Calif., 1972-73; sr. scientist Megatek Corp., San Diego, 1973-80; prin. physicist, inverse scattering group leader IRT Corp., San Diego, 1980-86, research advisor, 1986-87; pres. Stoneware, Ltd., La Jolla, Calif., 1976— ; dir., chmn. Samaritan Inst., San Diego, 1984—. Editor: Vol. New Methods for Optical, Quasioptical, Acoustic and Electromagnetic Synthesis, 1981. Contbr. articles to various publs. Recipient medal San Diego Soc. Tech. Writers and Pubs., 1962. Mem. NRC, Nat. Acad. Sci., Internat. Radio Sci. Union, Optical Soc. Am., Acoustical Soc. Am., Soc. Exploration Geophysics, AAUP, Nat. Acad. Scis., IEEE Antennas and Propagation Soc. (coordinator profl. activities 1980-83, editor procs. 1984—), Assn. Computing Machinery Soc. Indsl. and Applied Maths., Soc. Photooptical Instrumentation Engrs., Phi Eta Sigma. Home: 1446 Vista Claridad La Jolla CA 92037

STONEHOUSE, JAMES ADAM, lawyer; b. Alameda, Calif., Nov. 10, 1937; s. Maurice Adam and Edna Sigrid (Thuesen) S.; AB, U. Calif., Berkeley, 1961; JD, Hastings Coll. Law, U. Calif., San Francisco, 1965; m. Marilyn Jean Kotkas, Aug. 6, 1966; children—Julie Aileen, Stephen Adam. Bar: Calif. 1966. Assoc. Hall, Henry, Oliver & McReavy, San Francisco, 1966-71; ptnr. firm Whitney, Hanson & Stonehouse, Alameda, 1971-77; sole practice law, Alameda, 1977-79; ptnr. firm Stonehouse & Silva, Alameda, 1979—; judge adv. Alameda council Navy League, 1978—. Founding dir. Alameda Clara Barton Found., 1977-80; mem. Oakland (Calif.) Marathon-Exec. Com., 1979; mem. exec. bd. Alameda council Boy Scouts Am., 1979—, pres., 1986-88, Lord Baden-Powell Merit award, 1988; mem. Nat. council Boy Scouts Am., 1986—; trustee Golden Gate Scouting, 1986—; bd. dirs. Lincoln Child Ctr. Found., 1981—, pres., 1983-85. Named Boss of Yr. Alameda Jaycees, 1977; Coro Found. fellow in pub. affairs, 1961-62. Mem. ABA, State Bar Calif., Alameda County Bar (vice chmn. com. office econs., 1977-78). Republican. Roman Catholic. Club: Commonwealth. Lodges: Rotary (dir. club 1976-78), Elks (past exalted ruler, all state officer 1975-76, all dist. officer 1975-77, 78-79) (Alameda). Home: 2990 Northwood Dr Alameda CA 94501 Office: Stonehouse & Silva 512 Westline Dr Suite 300 Alameda CA 94501

STONER, EDMUND CURTIS, JR., consulting engineer; b. Riverside, Calif., Oct. 20, 1903; s. Edmund Curtis and Margaret (Copley) S.; student Lafayette Coll., 1921-22; BSEE, Yale U., 1926; m. Margaret Dorman Hamilton, June 23, 1926 (dec. 1958); 1 child, Margaret Hamilton Schofield; m. Mary J. Garcia, 1960. Chief engr. ITT, Peru, Cuba and Spain, 1933-41; asst. v.p. Fed. Telephone & Radio, 1945-48; cons. engr. to minister of communications Govt. of Turkey, Ankara, 1948-51; chief engr. Gen. Telephone & Electronics Corp., Muskegon, Mich., 1954-58, chief engr., Tampa, Fla.,

1958-65; engr. planning dir. Gen. Telephone Co. Fla., 1965-68; cons. engr., 1969—. Served to lt. col. USAAF, World War II (col. Res. ret.). Decorated Bronze Star; Mil. Order Brit. Empire. Mem. IEEE, Rochester, Muskegon, Tampa chambers commerce, Order of Daedalians, OX-5 Aviation Pioneers, Order of Quiet Birdmen, Phi Kappa Psi. Presbyn. Clubs: University (Tampa, Fla.); Yale (NYC). Home: 310 S Burlingame Ave Temple Terrace FL 33617

STONG, JOHN ELLIOTT, retail electronics company executive; b. Elkater, Iowa, Sept. 20, 1921; s. Elliott Sheldon and Nora Elizabeth (Daly) S.; ed. U. Colo., 1943; m. Olive Miriam Foley, Dec. 11, 1943; children—Mary Mandelson, Jon, Miriam, Salesman, Purucker Music, Medford, Oreg., 1946-48, dept. mgr., 1949-56, store mgr., 1957, partner, 1958-61, owner, 1962-64; pres. Purucker Music Houses, Medford, 1965-67, Music West, Inc., Eugene, Oreg., 1968-70, Magnavox Centers, Medford, 1971—, Exec. Assist., Consultants Internat., 1972—. Served with USAF, 1943-45. Decorated Air medal. Mem. Nat. Assn. Music Mchts. (dir. 1969-72), Scull Mchts. Research Group (dir., chmn.). Republican. Roman Catholic. Home: 2120 Woodlawn St Medford OR 97501 Office: Cons Internat 117 N Central St Medford OR 97501

STOOP, NORMA MCLAIN, editor, author, photographer; b. Panama, C.Z., July 20, 1910; b. Harry Edward and Gladys (Brandon) McLain; student Penn Hall Jr. Coll., Carnegie Inst. Tech., New Sch., N.Y. U.; m. William J. Stoop, Jr., Sept. 20, 1932. Contbg. editor Dance Mag., N.Y.C., 1969-71, asso. editor, 1971-79, sr. editor, 1979—; sr. editor After Dark, 1978-82, also feature writer; also photographer, theater, ballet and film critic; entertainment editor sr. edit. WNYC-AM, 1980-83; chief film critic Manhattan Arts, 1983—, mem. editors panel Antioch U. summer writers workshop, 1988 ; mem. nat. adv. bd. TV Arts Studio, Inc. Mem. Poetry Soc. Am., Acad. Am. Poets, Dance Masters Am., Dance Critics Assn., TV Acad. Arts and Scis., Sigma Delta Chi. Clubs: Overseas Press, Deadline. Contbr. poems to Tex. Quar., Chgo. Rev., N.Y. Times, Arts in Society, Quest, Atlantic Monthly, Christian Sci. Monitor, others, 1958—, essays to Book Week in N.Y. Herald Tribune; represented in Best Poems of 1973, Exhibit of Dance Photography, Harvard U., Tufts Coll., 1975; MacNeil Lehrer News, 1988. Recipient award Dance Tchrs. Club Boston, 1977. Office: 33 W 60th St New York NY 10023

STOPH, WILLI, government official German Democratic Republic; b. Berlin, July 9, 1914; married; 4 children. Apprentice, then mason, foreman bricklayer, tech. architec, joined Communist Youth League of Germany, trade union mem., 1928; mem. Communist Party Germany, 1931—; participant anti-fascist resistance 1933-45, engaged in establishment anti-fascist-dem. order, 1945—; mem. cen. com. Socialist Unity Party Germany, 1950—; mem. Politburo of cen. com., 1953—, People's Chamber, 1950—; mem. Council of State, 1963—, dep. chmn., 1964-73, chmn. (head of state), 1973-76, minister of interior, 1952-55, minister nat. def. with rank gen. of army, 1956-60; dep. chmn. Council Ministers, 1954-64, premier, 1964-73, 76—. Decorated Karl Marx Order, Patriotic Order Merit, Hero of Labor, Order Lenin. Office: Office of Prime Minister, Berlin German Democratic Republic

STOPPARD, TOM, playwright; b. Zlin, Czechoslovakia, July 3, 1937; s. Eugene and Martha (Stoppard) Straussler; m. Jose Ingle, 1965 (div.); m. Miriam Moore-Robinson, 1972; 4 children. Journalist Western Daily Press, Bristol, Eng., 1954-58, Bristol Evening World, 1958-60; free-lance reporter 1960-63. Playwright, writer, 1963—; author: plays The Gamblers, 1965, A Separate Peace, 1966, Rosencrantz and Guildenstern Are Dead, 1967, Albert's Bridge, 1967, The Real Inspector Hound, 1968, After Magritte, 1970, Dogg's Our Pet, 1971, Enter a Free Man, 1972, Jumpers, 1972, Travesties, 1974, Dirty Linen and New-Found-Land, 1976, Night and Day, 1979, On the Razzle, 1981, The Real Thing, 1982 (Tony award for Best Play 1984), Rough Crossing, 1984, (adaptation) Dalliance, 1986, Hapgood, 1988; screenplays, including The Romantic Englishwoman, 1975, The Human Factor, 1979, Squaring the Circle, 1983; radio and TV plays, including The Dissolution of Dominic Boot, 1964, Where Are They Now?, 1970, Artist Descending a Staircase, 1972, The Dog it was that Died, 1983, Squaring the Circle, 1984, Four Plays for Radio, 1984, Rough Crossing, 1985, (with others) Brazil, 1985, Dalliance and Undiscovered Country, 1986, Largo Desolato, 1987, Empire of the Sun, 1987; novels Introduction Z, 1964, Lord Malquist and Mr. Moon, 1966; short stories. (Recipient John Whiting award 1967, Evening Standard award 1967, 73, 75, Prix Italia 1968); (Tony award 1968, 76, N.Y. Drama Critics Circle award 1968, 76). Ford Found. grantee, 1964. Home: Iver Grove, Iver, Bucks England Office: care Peters Fraser Dunlop, The Chambers 5th Floor, Chelsea Harbor, London SW10 OXF, England *

STOPPER, GUGLIELMO CARLO, wine company executive; b. Bolzano, Italy, Aug. 26, 1933; s. Gugliemo Carlo and Rosa Maria (Tutzer) S.; m. Maria Eleonora Sansoni, Dec. 8, 1933; children—Andrea, Alessandra, Antonio. Rer. Polit. et Soc., U. Florence (Italy), 1956. With Bur. for Econ., Pirelli, Milan, Italy, 1957-59; with sales dept. Montecatini, Milan, 1959-60, Frankfort/Main, W.Ger., 1960-68; market research dir. Pantasote Italy, Malgesso/Varese, Italy, 1968-72, also sales mgr. Industria Ossidi Sinterizzati brs. Pantasote N.J. U.S.A.; wine broker Stoppervini Wine Agy., Lugano, Switzerland, 1972—. Contbr. articles on econs. and wine mktg. to profl. jours. Served with Italian Air Force, 1957-58. Recipient First prize Istituto Studi Politici Internazionali Milan Via Clerici, 1956. Home: Via Castausio 28, Lugano Switzerland Office: Stoppervini, Via della Posta 2, CH-6900 Lugano Switzerland

STÖPPLER, SIEGMAR, economist, educator; b. Fed. Republic Germany, June 7, 1939; m. Annelie Hermschulte Stöppler, 1977; children: Ingmar, Henning, Annika. Diploma in Math., U. Frankfurt, 1965, PhD in Econs., 1972. Asst. researcher U. Frankfurt, 1966-72, assoc. prof., 1973-79, full prof., 1980—. Author: Dynamic Theory of Production, 1975, Dynamic Economic Systems, 1979, Forecasting & Production Planning, 1984; editor: Information & Production, 1985. Recipient Wolfgang Ritter prize, Bremen, 1985. Mem. Inst. Mgmt. Scis., TIMS, DGOR, Vetein für Socialpolitik. Home: Bismarckstr 129, D-2800 Bremen Federal Republic of Germany Office: Univ Bremen, Bibliothekstr, D-2800 Bremen Federal Republic of Germany

STORARO, VITTORIO, cinematographer; b. Rome, June 24, 1940; s. Renato and Teodolinda (Laparelli) S.; m. Antonia Cafolla, Dec. 29, 1962; children: Francesca, Fabrizio, Giovanni. Student, Duca D'Aosta, Rome, 1951-56, Centro Italiano Addestramento Cinematografico, Rome, 1956-58; Degree in Cinematography, Centro Sperimentale di Cinematografia, Rome, 1958-60. Cinematographer Titanus, 1968, Paramount, 1970, 81, 87, United Artist, 1972, 76-77, 20th Century Fox, 1976, 78, Columbia, 1981, 84-86, Cronard Communications, 1982, Warner Bros., 1983, NBC, 1984-85. Cinematographer films including Youthful Youthful, 1968, The Conformist, 1970, Last Tango in Paris, 1972, Nineteen Hundred, 1976, Apocalypse Now, 1976-77, Luna, 1987, Reds, 1979-80, One From the Heart, 1981, Wagner, 1982, Lady Hawke, 1983, Peter the Great, 1984-85, Ishtar, 1985-86, The Last Emperor, 1986-87, Tucker, 1987, New York Stories, 1988. Recipient Best Cinematography award N.Y. Film Critics, 1971, Acad. award Best Cinematographer: Apocalypse Now, 1980, Reds, 1982, The Last Emperor, 1988. Mem. Acad. Motion Picture Arts and Scis., Italian Assn. of Cinematographers (pres.). Home: Via Divino Amore 2, 00040 Frattocchie Marino Italy

STORCH, MARCUS, industrial gases and food storage company executive; b. Stockholm, July 28, 1942; s. Gilel and Anna (Westerman) S.; m. Gunilla E.K. Berglund, Aug. 27, 1972; children—Elisabeth, Tobias. M.Eng., Royal Inst. Tech., Stockholm, 1967. Product mgr. AGA AB, Stockholm, 1967-72, div. pres., 1972-79, exec. v.p., 1979-81, pres., chief exec. officer, 1981—; bd. dirs. Inter Innovation AB, Stockholm, The Swedish Employers' Confedn., Stockholm; pres. Indsl. Gases Com., 1980-82. Mem. CPI (chmn. 1982-84). Office: AGA AB, 18181 Lidingo, Stockholm Sweden

STORCK, JOACHIM W(OLFGANG), archivist, researcher, educator; b. Karlsruhe, Germany, Dec. 29, 1922; s. Willy Friedrich and Maria Theresia (Nosbisch) S.; m. Mary F. Hartrodt, Mar. 27, 1954 (dec. Apr. 1984); children: Daniel, Miriam, Tobias; m. Evelyn Holzapfel Grill, May 6, 1986. Student, U. Gottingen, 1945-47, U. Zurich, 1948-49; CPE, Cambridge U., 1954; PhD, U. Freiburg i.Br., 1957. Asst. lectr. Albert Ludwigs U., Freiburg i.Br., Fed. Republic Germany, 1960-64; research fellow Deutsche Forschungsgemeinschaft, Bad Godesberg, Fed. Republic Germany, 1965-68; asst. lectr. Philipps U., Marburg, Fed. Republic Germany, 1970-71; lectr. U. Mannheim, Fed. Republic Germany, 1971—; archivist, research fellow Deutsches Literaturarchiv Marbach/N, Fed. Republic Germany, 1971—; head dept. Martin Heidegger Archives, Marbach/N, 1976—. Author: Als der Krieg zu Ende war, 1973, Rainer Maria Rilke, 1975, Max Kommerell, 1985; Günter Eich, 1988; co-author, editor: Rilke heute, 1975, Rainer Maria Rilke and Osterreich, 1986. Mem. Rilke Gesellschaft (v.p. 1973—), Deutsche Schillergesellschaft (com. 1985—), Foundation R.M. Rilke (com. 1986—), H.v.Hofmannsthal Gesellschaft, Goethe Gesellschaft, Stefan George Gesellschaft. Mem. Social Democratic Party. Roman Catholic. Home: Theodor Heuss Strasse 9, D-7142 Marbach/N Federal Republic of Germany Office: Deutsche Schillergesellschaft, Schillerhohe 8-10, D-7142 Marbach/N Federal Republic of Germany

STOREY, DAVID MALCOLM, writer, dramatist; b. Wakefield, Yorkshire, Eng., July 13, 1933; s. Frank Richmond and Lily (Cartwright) S.; ed. Queen Elizabeth Grammar Sch., Wakefield, Yorkshire, Slada Sch. Fine Art, London; m. Barbara Rudd Hamilton, 1956; four children. Fellow Univ. Coll., London, 1974. Author: (plays) The Restoration of Arnold Middleton (Evening Standard award) 1967, In Celebration (Los Angeles critics award), 1969, The Contractor (N.Y. Critics prize), 1969, Home (N.Y. Critics prize), 1970, The Changing Room (N.Y. Critics prize), 1971, Cromwell, 1973, The Farm, 1973, Life Class, 1974, Night, 1976, Mother's Day, 1976, Sisters, 1978, Dreams of Leaving, 1979, Early Days, 1980; (novels) This Sporting Life (Macmillan award), 1960, Flight into Camden (Rhys Meml. prize 1961, Manghan award 1963), 1960, Radcliffe, 1963, Pasmore, 1972 (Faber Meml. prize), A Temporary Life, 1973, Edward, 1973, Saville (Booker prize), 1976, Sisters, 1978, A Prodigal Child, 1982, Present Times, 1984. Home: 2 Lyndhurst Gardens, London NW3 England Office: care Jonathan Cape Ltd, 30 Bedford Sq, London WC1B 3EL, England *

STORJOHANN, DARLYS WILLIAM, mortgage company executive; b. O'Neill, Nebr., Mar. 20, 1959; s. William James and Helen (Dohnal) S. Grad., Hume Fin., Century 21 Career Sch., Federated Tax Service; PhD, Clayton Theol. Inst.; BSBA, UCLA, 1987. Co-owner, mgr. World Western Farms, O'Neill, 1969—; pres. Tradefair Internat., Inc., Denver, 1977-83; pres., chief exec. officer World Western Investment Devel. Corp., North Hollywood, Calif., 1978—; ptnr. Greater Los Angeles First Mortgage Co., North Hollywood, 1983—; owner "That's Class" Limousine Service, West Hollywood, Calif., 1984—; tandem cons. AAA Mortgage Co., Ischua, N.Y., 1983-84; v.p. Fin. Digest Pub., West Hollywood, 1983—; pres., chief exec. officer Fin. Services Ednl. TV Network, North Hollywood, 1983-85—; chmn. bd. dirs. Calif. Life Mag., West Hollywood, 1978—; co-host Am. Congress on Real Estate, Burbank, Calif., 1985-88; owner Mountain States Constrn. Co., Mountain States Mining, Ltd., Mountain States Investment Co., Greater Nev. 1st Mortgage Co., Storjohann Farms, Asset One Mgmt. Co., World Wide Realty Corp. Author: Make Money Work for You, 1982; editor mag. Calif. Life, 1978-85, Mktg. Ideas Showcase, 1984. Chief exec. officer Fan Clubs of Am., Celebrity Concept Promotions, Sliver Screen Prodns., Hollywood Promotions, Miss Calif. Fan Club, Cindy Landis Fan Club, Flip Wilson Fan Club, Landis Promotions, Locklear Promotions, Heather Locklear Fan Club, Scott Baio Fan Club. Mem. World Mail Mktg. Assn. (pres., chief exec. officer, 1983—), Aircraft Owners and Pilots Assn., Nat. Assn. Fin. Cons., Nat. Notary Pub. Assn., Nat. Specialty Merchandisers Assn. Club: Eagle (Providence). Home: 279 S Beverly Dr Beverly Hills CA 90212 Office: Greater Los Angeles First Mortgage Co 12115 Magnolia Blvd Suite 137 North Hollywood CA 91607-2693

STORK, JOHN JOSEPH, management consultant; b. Godalming, Eng., Dec. 25, 1935; s. Joseph W. and Kathleen (Waddington) S.; m. Delphine M. Bowie, Feb. 1, 1963; children—Adam, Matthew. B. Commerce with honors, U. Leeds, 1958. Buyer, S. Simpson Ltd., London, 1958-60; client service exec. Attwood Stats. Ltd., London, 1960-62; research dir. Masius, Wynne-Williams Ltd., London, 1962-68; dir. D'Arcy MacManus & Masius Internat., London, 1968-74; chmn. John Stork Internat. Group, London, Amsterdam, Brussels, Frankfurt, Geneva, Oslo, Paris, Stockholm, 1974—; dir. C.G. Bevan Assocs. Ltd., London, 1979—, Dryflow Ltd, London, 1982—; chmn. Eel Pie Marine Ltd., London, 1983—, Stork Stafford Internat. Ptnrs. Inc., N.Y.C., 1983—. Served with Royal Navy, 1953-55. Club: Royal Thames Yacht (London). Office: John Stork Internat Group, 10 Haymarket, London SW1Y 4BP, England

STORKE, WILLIAM FREDERICK, film producer; b. Rochester, N.Y., Aug. 12; s. Legrand F. Sommerfeldt and Patricia Louise Storke; B.A. in Econs., UCLA, 1948; children—Victoria Jane, Adam John, William MacKenzie; m. 2d, Georgette MacKenzie Edwards, Feb. 22, 1970. With NBC, 1948—, successivley comml. editor guest relations dept. comml. supr., network sales West Coast, participating program sales, N.Y., dir. participating program sales, dir. program adminstrn., v.p. program adminstrn., 1948-57, v.p. programs East Coast, 1967-68, v.p. spl. programs, 1968—; pres. Claridge Group, Ltd. div. Trident TV Ltd., London, 1979—; exec. producer Oliver Twist, 1982; exec. v.p. Entertainment Ptnrs., Inc., 1982; producer To Catch a King, 1983, A Christmas Carol, 1984, The Last Days of Patton, 1985, A Special Friendship, 1986, Ted Kennedy, Jr. Story, 1986; exec. producer TV series Buck James, 1987-88. Mem. theatre panel Nat. Endowment for Arts, 1976-78. Served with USNR, 1943-46. Club: University (N.Y.C.). Home: 1060 Fifth Ave New York NY 10128

STORMS, CLIFFORD BEEKMAN, lawyer; b. Mount Vernon, N.Y., July 18, 1932; s. Harold Beekman and Gene (Pertak) S.; m. Barbara H. Grave, 1955 (div. 1975); m. Valeria N. Parker, July 12, 1975; children: Catherine Storms Fischer, Clifford Beekman. B.A. magna cum laude, Amherst Coll., 1954; LL.B., Yale U., 1957. Bar: N.Y. 1957. Assoc. atty. firm Breed, Abbott & Morgan, N.Y.C., 1957-64; with CPC Internat., Inc., Englewood Cliffs, N.J., 1964—; v.p. legal affairs CPC Internat., Inc., 1973-75, v.p., gen. counsel, 1975—, also mem. exec. com., bd. dirs. Trustee, mem. exec. com., bd. dirs. Food and Drug Law Inst.; mem. adv. com. Parker Sch. Fgn. and Comparative Law, Columbia U.; bd. dirs. CPC Ednl. Found. Mem. ABA (com. on corp. law depts.), N.Y. State Bar Assn., Assn. Bar City N.Y. (sec., com. on corp. law depts. 1979-81), Assn. Gen. Counsel, Phi Beta Kappa, Theta Delta Chi, Phi Alpha Delta. Clubs: Indian Harbor Yacht, Econ. N.Y., Yale (N.Y.C.); Milbrook, Board Room, Economic of N.Y. Home: 11 Serenity Ln Cos Cob CT 06807 Office: CPC Internat Inc International Plaza Englewood Cliffs NJ 07632

STOTESBERY, WILLIAM DAVID, computer technology corporation executive; b. Pitts., Sept. 30, 1952; s. Thomas J. and Joan (Beegle) S.; m. Mary C. Dudley, Jan. 21, 1975. BA, Tex. Christian U., 1974; MA in Pub. Affairs, U. Tex., 1977. Sr. cons. Peat, Marwick & Mitchell, Austin, Tex., 1977-82; pvt. mgmt. cons., Austin, 1982-83; dir. govt., pub. affairs Microelectronics & Computer Tech. Corp., Austin, 1983-88; corp. v.p. Westmark Systems, Inc., Austin, 1988—; bd. dirs. MBank Arboretum. Contbr. articles to profl. jours. Mem. Austin Community Devel. Commn., 1978-80; exec. com. Leadership Austin, 1983-87, curriculum chmn., 1983-84, chmn., 1986-87; bd. dirs. Austin Women's Ctr., 1983-86, pres., 1985-86. Mem. Austin C. of C. (bd. dirs. 1986-87). Office: Westmark Systems Inc 301 Congress Suite 1200 Austin TX 78701

STOTT, RICHARD KEITH, newspaper editor; b. Oxford, Eng., Aug. 17, 1943; s. Fred Brooks and Bertha (Pickford) S.; m. Penelope Anne Scragg, Apr. 18, 1970; children: Emily, Hannah, Christopher. Student, Clifton Coll., Bristol, Eng. Reporter Bucks Herald, Aylesbury, Eng., 1963-65, Ferrari Press Agy. Inc., Kent, Eng., 1965-68, Daily Mirror newspaper, London, 1968-79; features editor Daily Mirror, London, 1979-81, asst. editor, 1981-84, editor Sunday People sect., 1984-85, editor, 1985—, also bd. dirs.; editor Daily Mirror, 1985. Named Reporter of Yr. Brit. Press League, 1977. Office: Daily Mirror, Holborn Circus, London England EC1 PDQ

STOUDER, JOHN ALBERT, petroleum engineer, well pressure control educator; b. Louisville, Dec. 5, 1933; came to Norway, 1972; s. Ralph Eugene and Elizabeth (Chenoweth) S.; m. Barbara Roethe, Feb. 26, 1959 (div. Mar. 1978); children—Christoph Ralph, Bettina Eve; m. 2d Alfhild Martha Johansen, Dec. 1, 1978; children—Hans Oscar, Martha Elizabeth. B.A. in Biology, U. Louisville, 1955; M. Petroleum Engring., U. Okla., 1963. Coordinator, Stouder Drilling Co., Evansville, Ind., 1957-61, v.p., 1963-68; Sedneth II mgr. Sedco, The Hague, Netherlands, 1968-72; ops. mgr. Odfjell Drilling & Cons., Stavanger, Norway, 1972-78; adviser Norwegion Petroleum Directorate, Stavanger, 1978; pvt. practice petroleum engring. cons., also well pressure control instr., Sola, Norway, 1978—. Served to 1st lt. USAF, 1955-57. Baker Oil Tools scholar, 1963. Mem. Assoc. Photographers Internat., Nat. Rifle Assn. Am., Ha Pistolklubb, Soc. Petroleum Engrs., Am. Assn. Oilwell Drilling Contractors, Internat. Assn. Drilling Contractors, Tau Kappa Epsilon. Republican. Methodist. Home: Utsolavegen 20, 4050 Sola Norway Office: IJAS, Utsolavegen 20, 4050 Sola Norway

STOUGE, BARON NIELS SANDBERGH, odontologist, genealogist, heraldist; b. Ribe, Denmark, July 3, 1907; s. Baron Frederick Christian Sandbergh and Ingebord (Laursen) S.; student Cathedral Coll., Ribe, Royal Danish Odontological Coll., 1928; Dr. Phil. (hon.), U. Athens; m. Baroness Oddny S. Björns de Kornsá, Dec. 1, 1928; children: Finn, Bendt, Svend, Ingrid S. Staufeldt. Pvt. clinic odontology, 1932-82. Mem. com. Danish Red Cross. Decorated knight comdr. Royal Italian Order Saints Maurizzio e Lazzaro, knight comdr. Italian Crown Order, Papal Cross of Lateran 1st class, Grand cross Just Heredit. St. Agatha, knight comdr. justice Order St. John Jerusalem, vice-prior Priory of North; also various medals and plaques. Mem. Danish Odontological Soc. (hon.), Danish Geneal. Soc., Société Royal Franco-Belge Les Bienfaiteurs et Sauveteurs, Danish Heraldic Soc. (co-founder; v.p. 1946-58), Soc. Aragon Nobility in Denmark (pres.), Conseill St. Siege d'Archiveque, Internat. Platform Assn. Roman Catholic. Club: Royal Danish A. Home: Rosenvaengets Hovedvej 26, DK 2100 Copenhagen Denmark

STOUGH, CHARLES DANIEL, lawyer; b. Mound Valley, Kans., Dec. 6, 1914; s. Charles Daniel and Narka Pauline (Ice) S.; m. Mary Juliet Shipman, Feb. 13, 1936; children—Vera Rubin, Sally Randall Stough Bartlett. A.A., Kemper Mil. Sch., 1934; A.B., U. Kans., 1936, LL.B., 1938, J.D., 1968. Bar: Kans. 1938, Ill. 1938. City atty. City of Lawrence, Kans., 1947-67, City of Eudora (Kans.), 1949-85; spl. counsel, Douglas County Kans., 1951-85; sole practice, Lawrence, 1939-82; with firm Stough & Heck, 1982—; prof. local govt. law U. Kans., 1969-70. Mem. U. Kans. Spencer Mus., 1986; mem. Kans. Ho. of Reps., 1947-55, majority leader, 1951-53, speaker of house, 1953-55. Trustee, U. Kans. Endowment Assn., Nat. Parks and Conservation Assn., Washington. Served to lt. j.g. USNR, 1943-46. Recipient Ellsworth award U. Kans., 1980; named one of Outstanding Kansans U. Kans., 1986; named to Gallary of Outstanding Kansans, 1986. Trustee Hertzler Research Found., Halstead, Kans., 1983—. Mem. ABA (chmn. Local Govt. Law Sect. 1964-67), Kans. Bar Assn. (chmn. world Peace Through Law Sect. 1970—), Nat. Inst. Mcpl. Law Officers (trustee 1964-65), City Attys. Assn. (exec. com.). Republican. Congregationalist. Clubs: Kiwanis, Masons (Lawrence); Republican Vets. of Kans. (state pres. 1959-60).

STOUP, ARTHUR HARRY, lawyer; b. Kansas City, Mo., Aug. 30, 1925; s. Isadore and Dorothy (Rankle) S.; m. Kathryn Jolliff, July 30, 1948; children—David C., Daniel P., Rebecca Ann, Deborah E. Student, Kansas City Jr. Coll., Mo. 1942-43; B.A., U. Mo., 1950; J.D., 1950. Bar: Mo. 1950, D.C. 1979. Practice law Kansas City, Mo., 1950—; mem. firm Stoup & Thompson; mem. Lawyer to Lawyer Consultation Panel-Litigation, 1976—; chmn. U.S. Merit Selection Com. for Western Dist. Mo., 1981. Chmn. com. to rev. continuing edn. U. Mo., 1978-79; trustee U. Mo.-Kansas City Law Found., 1972—, pres., 1979-82; trustee U. Kansas City, 1979—. Served with USNR, 1942-45. Recipient Alumni Achievement award U. Mo.-Kansas City Alumni Assn., 1975, U. Mo.-Kansas City Law Found. Service award, 1987. Fellow Internat. Soc. Barristers, Am. Bar Found. (life mem.); mem. Kansas City Met. Bar Assn. (pres. 1966-67), The Mo. Bar (bd. govs. 1967-76, v.p. 1972-73, pres. 1974-75), ABA (ho. dels. 1976-80), Lawyers Assn. Kansas City, Mo. Assn. Trial Attys. (sustaining), Am. Assn. Trial Lawyers (sustaining), So. Conf. Bar Pres.'s (life), Mobar Research Inc. (pres. 1978-86), Phi Alpha Delta Alumni (justice Kansas City area 1955-56). Lodges: Optimists (pres. Ward Pkwy. 1961-62, lt. gov. Mo. dist. internat. 1963-64), Sertoma, B'nai B'rith. Home: 9002 Western Hills Dr Kansas City MO 64114 Office: Home Savs Bldg Kansas City MO 64106

STOUT, DONALD EVERETT, real estate developer and appraiser; b. Dayton, Ohio, Mar. 16, 1926; s. Thorne Franklin and Lovella Marie (Sweeney) S.; B.S., Miami U., 1950; m. Gloria B. McCormick, Apr. 10, 1948; children—Holly Sue, Scott Kenneth. Mgr. comml.-indsl. div. G.P. Huffman Realty, Dayton, 1954-58; leasing agt., mgr. Park Plaza, Dayton, 1959-71; developer 1st transp. center for trucking in Ohio; pres. devel. cos. Sunderland Falls Estates, Wright Gate Indsl. Mall, Edglo Land Recycle, pres. Donald E. Stout, Inc. Served with U.S. Army 1944-45, USN 1945-46. Named Outstanding Real Estate Salesman in Dayton, Dayton Area Bd. Realtors, in Ohio, Ohio Bd. Realtors, 1961. Lic. real estate broker, Ohio, U.S. Virgin Islands. Mem. Dayton Area Bd. Realtors (founder; 1st pres. salesman div. 1959, dir. 1959-60), Nat. Assn. Real Estate Bds., Soc. Real Estate Appraisers (sr. real estate analyst, dir. chpt. 1959-60, pres. chpt. 1964), Am. Inst. Real Estate Appraisers, Nat. Assn. Rev. Appraisers (charter), Soc. Indsl. Office Realtors, Res. Officers Assn., C. of C., Phi Delta Theta, Environ. and Hist. Preservationist. Clubs: Masons (32 deg.), Shrine. Contbr. articles to profl. jours. Office: 1336 Woodman Dr Dayton OH 45432

STOUT, GREGORY STANSBURY, lawyer; b. Berkeley, Calif., July 27, 1915; s. Verne A. and Ella (Moore) S.; m. Virginia Cordes, Apr. 23, 1948; 1 son, Frederick Gregory. A.B., U. Calif., 1937, LL.B., 1940. Bar: Calif. 1940. Practice law San Francisco, 1946, 52—; asst. dist. atty., 1947-52; mem. Penal Code Revision Commn. Calif.; chmn. com. State Bar Calif. Contbr. articles to profl. jours. Served to master sgt. AUS, 1942-45. Fellow Am. Coll. Trial Lawyers, Am. Bar Found.; mem. ABA, Fed. Bar Assn., Am. Bd. Trial Advocates, Nat. Assn. Def. Lawyers in Criminal Cases (sec. 1958-59, pres. 1962-63). Democrat. Episcopalian. Club: Bohemian. Home: 2389 Washington St San Francisco CA 94115 Office: 220 Montgomery St Suite 1010 San Francisco CA 94104

STOVALL, JERRY C(OLEMAN), insurance company executive; b. Houston, July 31, 1936; s. Clifford Coleman and Maxine (Lands) S.; m. Elsie Hostetter, June 20, 1959; 1 child, Brent Allen. BBA, U. Houston, 1968. Home office administr. Am. Gen. Life, Houston, 1955-63, agt., agy. mgr., 1963-66, agy. mgr., regional dir. agys., regional v.p., 1969-74; sr. brokerage cons. Conn. Gen. Life, Houston, 1966-69; sr. v.p., dir. mktg. Capitol Life Ins. Co., Denver, 1974-78; v.p., dir. mktg. Integon Life Ins. Corp., Winston-Salem, N.C., 1978-81; pres. Life of Mid-Am. Ins. Co., Topeka, 1981-85; pres. Victory Life Ins. Co., Topeka, 1981-85, chmn., pres., chief exec. officer, 1981-87, pres. Integon Life Ins. Corp., Winston-Salem, N.C., 1987—; past mem. Nat. Adv. Bd. for Internat. Assn. for Fin. Planning; past mem. pub. relations polciy com. Am. Council of Life Ins. Past vice chmn. maj. gifts drive United Way, Winston-Salem; past mem. exec. bd. Jayhawk area council Boy Scouts Am.; past bd. dirs. Kans. Capital area chpt. ARC, United Way Topeka; past mem. council Projects with Industry Menninger Found. Served with U.S. Army, 1955-57. Mem. Nat. Assn. Life Underwriters, Am. Soc. CLU's (Gold Key Soc.), Kans. Life Assn. (sec. treas., past legis. com.), Internat. Assn. Fin. Planners (past mem. nat. adv. bd.), Gideons. International Baptist. Clubs: Bermuda Run Country, Topeka Country. Office: Integon Life Ins Corp 500 W 5th St Winston-Salem NC 27152

STOVER, CARL FREDERICK, foundation executive; b. Pasadena, Calif., Sept. 29, 1930; s. Carl Joseph and Margarete (Müller) S.; m. Catherine Swanson, Sept. 3, 1954; children: Matthew Joseph, Mary Margaret Stover Marker, Claire Ellen; m. Jacqueline Kast, Sept. 7, 1973. B.A. magna cum laude, Stanford U., 1951, M.A., 1954. Instr. polit. sci. Stanford U., 1953-55; fiscal mgmt. officer Office Sec. Dept. Agr., 1955-57; asso. dir. conf. program pub. affairs Brookings Instn., 1957-59, sr. staff mem. govtl. studies, 1960; fellow Center Study Democratic Instns., Santa Barbara, Calif., 1960-62; asst. to chmn. bd. editors Ency. Brit., 1960-62; sr. polit. scientist Stanford Research Inst., 1962-64; dir. pub. affairs fellowship program Stanford U., 1962-64; pres. Nat. Inst. Pub. Affairs, Washington, 1964-70, Nat. Com. U.S.-China Relations, 1971-72; pres., dir. Federalism Seventy-Six, 1972-74; dir. cultural resources devel. Nat. Endowment for Arts, 1974-78; pres. Cultural Resources, Inc., Washington, 1978-85; bd. dirs. H.E.A.R. Found., 1976-86, treas., 1976-80, pres., 1980-86; pres., bd. dirs. Ctr. for World Lit., 1987—; pvt. profl. cons., 1970—; scholar-in-residence Nat. Acad. Public Adminstrn., 1980-82; cons. to govt., 1953—. Author: The Government of Science, 1962,

The Technological Order, 1963; Founding editor: Jour. Law and Edn, 1971-73; pub. Delos mag., 1987—. Treas. Nat. Com. U.S.-China Relations, 1966-71, 82-87, bd. dirs., 1966-74, 79—; bd. dirs. Coordinating Council Lit. Mags., 1966-68; trustee Inst. of Nations, 1962-76, Nat. Inst. Pub. Affairs, 1967-71, Kinesis Ltd., 1972—; vol. Nat. Exec. Service Corps, 1984—. Fellow AAAS; mem. Am. Soc. Public Adminstrn., Am. Com. on U.S.-Soviet Relations, Fedn. Am. Scientists, Soc. Internat. Devel., Jordan Soc. (dir. 1982-84), Nat. Acad. Pub. Adminstrn. (hon.), Phi Beta Kappa Assocs. (hon., lectr. 1972-87), Phi Beta Kappa. Democrat. Presbyterian. Club: City Tavern (Washington). Home: 4109 Metzerott Rd College Park MD 20740

STOVER, PHIL SHERIDAN, JR., investment consultant; b. Tulsa, Jan. 23, 1926; s. Phil Sheridan and Noma (Smith) S. Student, Yale, 1943-44, Denison U., 1944-45; B.S., U. Pa., 1948. With Nat. Bank Tulsa, 1948-70, v.p., 1956-64, sr. v.p., 1964-65, sr. v.p., cashier, 1965-70; owner Phil Stover & Assos., Tulsa, 1970—; pres., treas. Tulsalite, Inc. (mag. pubs.), 1973-79; vice chmn., dir. Tulsa Oiler Baseball Club, 1975-82, Springfield (Ill.) Redbirds Baseball Club; pres. Macon (Ga.) Baseball Club, 1980; dir. Redbirds Baseball Club, Louisville, 1982-86 ; ptnr. A Hotel, The Frenchmen, New Orleans, 1982—. Chmn. Tulsa County chpt. Nat. Found., 1956-59, Tulsa Met. Water Authority, 1961-70; vice chmn. Tulsa Utility Bd., 1957-70; Treas. adv. bd. Salvation Army. Served with USNR, 1944-46. Named Okla. Jr. C. of C. Outstanding Young Man, 1954. Republican. Presbyn. Address: University Club Tower 1722 S Carson St Tulsa OK 74119

STOWE, DAVID METZ, clergyman; b. Council Bluffs, Iowa, Mar. 30, 1919; s. Ernest Lewellyn and Florence Mae (Metz) S.; m. Virginia Ware, Nov. 25, 1943; children—Nancy F. (Mrs. Thomas Inui), Elizabeth A. (Mrs. Charles Hambrick-Stowe), Priscilla B. (Mrs. Thomas Nelson), David W. B.A., U. Calif. at Los Angeles, 1940; B.D., Pacific Sch. Religion, 1943, Th.D., 1953, D.D. (hon.), 1966; postgrad., Inst. Chinese Studies, Yale, 1945-46. Ordained to ministry Congl. Ch., 1943; asso. minister Berkeley, Calif., 1943-45, 51-53; missionary, univ. prof. Peking, China, 1947-50; chaplain, chmn. dept. religion Carleton Coll., 1953-56; edn1. sec. Am. Bd. Commnrs. and United Ch. Bd. World Ministries, 1956-62; prof. theology Beirut, Lebanon, 1962-63; exec. sec. div. fgn. missions Nat. Council Chs., 1963-64, asso. gen. sec. overseas ministries, 1965-70; also gov. bd.; counselor United Bd. Christian Higher Edn. in Asia; exec. v.p. United Ch. Bd. for World Ministries, 1970-85; cons. mission and religion in China 1985—; Mem. Commn. on World Mission and Evangelism, 1965-75, Theol. Ed. Fund, 1970-76; del. assemblies World Council Churches, 1961, 68, 75; mem. exec. council World Conf. on Religion and Peace, 1985—. Author: The Churches' Mission in the World, 1963, When Faith Meets Faith, 1963, Ecumenicity and Evangelism, 1970; also articles in religious books and periodicals. Mem. Am. Soc. Missiology, Internat. Assn. Mission Studies, Nat. Soc. Values in Higher Edn., Phi Beta Kappa, Pi Gamma Mu, Blue Key. Home: 54 Magnolia Ave Tenafly NJ 07670

STRACK, WILLIAM RICHARD, insurance company executive; b. N.Y.C., Feb. 3, 1936; s. William and Unity (Lockie) S.; m. Sheila Scanlon, July 9, 1960; children: Deborah, William, Tracy, Robert, Nancy, Karen. BS, NYU. CLU. Ins. agt. AETNA, N.Y.C., 1961-72, mgr. prodn., 1972-81; sr. v.p. U.S. Life Ins. Co., N.Y.C., 1982-85; pres., chief exec. officer All Am. Life Ins. Co. subs. of U.S. Life, Chgo., 1985—, also bd. dirs.; pres., chief exec. officer U.S. Life Ins. Co., Pasadena, Calif., 1987—, also bd. dirs. Served to sgt. U.S. Army, 1954-57. Mem. Nat. Assn. Life Underwriters, N.Y.C. Life Underwriters, N.Y. Chpt. CLU's, Million Dollar Round Table. Republican. Roman Catholic. Home: 255 Board Walk Park Ridge IL 60068 Office: All Am Life Ins Co 8501 W Higgins Rd Chicago IL 60631

STRAETZ, ROBERT P., retired business executive; b. Hillside, N.J., 1921. Grad., U. Chgo.; student, Advanced Mgmt. Program at Harvard U. Research chemist Manhattan Project, until 1946; with Textron Inc., 1946—; successively v.p., exec. v.p., pres. Textron Inc. (Homelite div.), until 1974, corp. group v.p., 1974-78, pres., chief operating officer, 1978-79, chmn. bd., chief exec. officer, 1980-84, chmn. bd., 1985-86. Office: care Textron Inc 40 Westminster St Providence RI 02903

STRAHLER, VIOLET RUTH, educational consultant; b. Dayton, Ohio, Sept. 30, 1918; d. Ezra F. and Bertha (Daniels) S. A.B. magna cum laude, Wittenberg U., 1944; M.A., Miami U., Ohio, 1959; Ed.D., Ind. U., 1972; LH.D. (hon.), Wittenberg U., 1986. Cert. tchr., supt., Ohio. Tchr. Miamisburg Pub. Schs., Ohio, 1944-51; tchr., counselor Dayton Pub. Schs., 1952-66, supr. sci. and math. curriculum, 1967-72, acting asst. supt. curriculum, 1972-73, exec. dir. curriculum services, 1973-85; instr. U. Dayton, Miami U., 1959-74; edn1. cons.; supervisor student tchrs., U. Dayton, 1986—. Author and co-author numerous textbooks, lab. guides. Editor newsletter Ohio Jr. Acad. Sci., 1950-52. Contbr. articles to profl. jours. Mem. Dayton/Montgomery County Arson Task Force; trustee Dayton Mus. Natural History. Ford Found. fellow, 1952-53; staff chmn. parish relations com. S. Park United Meth. Ch. . Mem. NOW, Am. Assn. Sch. Adminstrs., Buckeye Assn. Sch. Adminstrs. (life), Assn. Supervision and Curriculum Devel., Am. Chem. Soc., Nat. Sci. Tchrs. Assn. (life), Ohio Acad. Sci., Phi Delta Kappa. Methodist. Home: 5340 Brendonwood Ln Dayton OH 45415 Office: U Dayton Dept Tchr Edn Chaminade Hall 300 College Park Dayton OH 45469-0001

STRAIN, EDWARD RICHARD, psychologist; b. Indpls., Apr. 12, 1925; s. Edward Richard and Ernestine (Kidd) S.; m. Marsha Ellen Beeler, 1972; children: Douglas MacDonald, Chadwick Edward, Sarah Abigail, Zachary Richard. BA, Butler U., 1948; PhD, Duke U., 1952. Clin. psychologist Ohio State Med. Ctr., Columbus, 1952-53, Ind. U. Med. Ctr., Indpls., 1953-56; pvt. practice cons. psychology Indpls., 1956—; lectr. dept. psychology Butler U., Indpls., 1958-68; pres. Marion County (Ind.) Mental Health Assn., 1967-69. Pres. 500 Festival Assn., Indpls., 1961—, Perry Twp. (Ind.) Rep. Club, 1968-69. Founder, bd. dirs. Downtown Sr. Citizens Ctr., Indpls., 1958-62. Served with USNR, 1943-46. Mem. Lambda Chi Alpha. Episcopalian. Lodges: Masons, Rotary. Clubs: Indpls. Athletic, Indpls. Press. Office: 120 Monument Circle Suite 323 Indianapolis IN 48204

STRAIN, JOHN WILLARD, aerospace engineer; b. Ottumwa, Iowa, Dec. 31, 1929; s. John Wells and Agnes Gertrude (Kearns) S.; m. Elizabeth LaVonne Moment, Dec. 27, 1952 (dec.); children—James Anthony, Mary Therese, Michael Douglas, Meagan Kathleen. Student Upper Iowa U., 1947-48; B.A., U. No. Iowa, 1952. Supr., aero. rocket power plant engr. White Sands Proving Ground, N.Mex., 1954-55; mgr. Santa Cruz test and Hunters Point, Missile Systems div. Lockheed Missiles & Space Co., Sunnyvale, Calif., 1960-63, mgr. Ea. Test Range support, 1966-73, chief test engr. Aquila RPV/STD Program, 1975-78, factory test mgr. Army RPV Program, 1979-82, qualification and test engring. div. mgr., chief test engr., 1982-84, mgmt. proposal assignment, 1984—; owner Indsl. Systems Co. Bd. dirs. San Jose Civic Light Opera, 1971-73; treas. Assn. Unmanned Vehicle Systems, 1982-84. Served with AUS, 1952-54. Recipient Alumni Service award U. No. Iowa, 1981. Assoc. fellow AIAA; mem. Nat. Mgmt. Assn., AAAS, Inst. Environ. Scis. (sr.). Republican. Roman Catholic. Assoc. editor Missile Away mag. Am. Rocket Soc., 1954-55. Office: 1111 Lockheed Way Box 504 Sunnyvale CA 94086

STRAKA, RONALD MORRIS, physicist; b. Reading, Pa., Apr. 22, 1935; s. Morris Richard and Irene (Gurtowski) S.; B.Engring. Sci., Johns Hopkins U., 1957, postgrad., 1957-58; children—Erika Jane, Sonya Ellen. Research asst. Carnegie Instn. Washington, summer 1955, Astrophysics Lab., Johns Hopkins U., Balt., 1957-58; research physicist Air Force Cambridge Research Labs., Bedford, Mass., 1958-77; phys. scientist Air Force Systems Command Hdrqs., Andrews AFB, Md., 1977-79; physicist Air Force Geophysics Lab., Bedford, 1979—; NATO fgn. sci. cons. U. Athens (Greece), 1964. Dir. photography Boston Center Adult Edn., 1969-77. NSF grantee, 1964; recipient Sci. Achievement award USAF, 1971, 84. Mem. N.Y. Acad. Scis., Internat. Sci. Radio Union, Rockport Art Assn., U.S. Senatorial Club, U.S. Figure Skating Assn., Sigma Xi. Photography exhbns: Carl Siembab Gallery, Boston, DeCordova Mus., Lincoln, Mass., Boston Mus. Fine Arts, Mpls. Art Inst. Contbr. articles to profl. jours. Home: 38A Granite St Rockport MA 01966 Office: AF Geophysics Lab Hanscom AFB MA 01731

STRANDHAGEN, ADOLF GUSTAV, marine engineering educator; b. Scranton, Pa., May 4, 1914; s. Daniel Peter and Theresa Ann (Lylick) S.; m. Lucile E. Perry, Aug. 22, 1941; children—Karen, Gretchen. B.S., U. Mich., 1939, M.S., 1939, Ph.D., 1942. Asst. prof., research physicist Nat. Def. Research Council, Carnegie Inst. Tech. and Princeton U., 1942-46; assoc. prof. engring. sci. U. Notre Dame, 1946-50, prof., 1950—, chmn. dept. engring. sci., 1950-68; cons. U.S. Navy Mine Def. Lab., 1961-67; temporary staff U.S. Navy David Taylor Model Basin, 1958-60. Recipient Outstanding Engr. award St. Joseph chpt. ASME, 1958. Mem. Soc. Naval Architects and Marine Engrs. (mem. panel H-10 ship maneuvering 1965-75), Soc. Engring. Sci., ASME. Assoc. editor Jour. Vehicle Dynamics, 1972-80, Bull. on Ship Maneuvering, 1975; contbr. research papers and reports on hydrodynamics, ship maneuvering, applied math., probability theory to profl. jours. Office: U Notre Dame Coll Engring Notre Dame IN 46556

STRANGE, DONALD ERNEST, health care company executive; b. Ann Arbor, Mich., Aug. 13, 1944; s. Carl Britton and Donna Ernestine (Tenney) S.; BA, Mich. State U., 1966, MBA, 1968; m. Lyn Marie Purdy, Aug. 3, 1968; children: Laurel Lyn, Chadwick Donald. Asst. dir. Holland (Mich.) City Hosp., 1968-72, assoc. dir., 1972-74; exec. dir. Bascom Palmer Eye Inst./Anne Bates Leach Eye Hosp., U. Miami (Fla.), 1974-77; v.p. strategic planning and research Hosp. Corp. Am., Nashville, 1977-80, group v.p., Boston, 1980-82, regional v.p., 1982-87; chmn., chief exec. officer HCA Healthcare Can. 1985-87; exec. v.p., pres. health care group Avon Products, Inc., 1987—; lectr. Duke U., 1980, Harvard U., 1982—; dir. Polyclonal Sera Labs. Mem. Investments Orange Nassau Adv. Bd., Boston Mus. Fine Arts Council. Mem. Internat. Hosp. Fedn., Am. Coll. Healthcare Execs., Fedn. Am. Hosps., Washington Bus. Group on Health. Republican. Episcopalian. Clubs: Harvard, Old Hickory Yacht, Capt. Harbor P.S. Author: Hospital Corporate Planning, 1981.

STRASSER, GABOR, management consultant; b. Budapest, Hungary, May 22, 1929; s. Rezso and Theresa (Seiler) S.; m. Linda Casselman Pemble, Aug. 16, 1958 (div. 1976); children—Claire Margaret, Andrew John; m. Joke Verhoeff, Feb. 2, 1978; children: Steven Verhoeff, Tessa Christina. B.C.E., City Coll. N.Y., 1954; M.S., U. Buffalo, 1959; P.M.D., Harvard, 1968. Research engr. Bell Aircraft Co., Buffalo, 1956-61; project leader Boeing Airplane Co., Seattle, 1961-62; dept. head Mitre Corp., Bedford, Mass., Washington, 1962-68; v.p. Urban Inst., Washington, 1968-69; tech. asst. to pres.'s sci. adviser White House, 1969-71, exec. sec. pres.'s sci. and tech. policy panel, 1970-71; dir. planning Battelle Meml. Inst., Columbus, Ohio, 1971-73; pres. Strasser Assos., Inc., Washington, 1973—. Author, editor: Science and Technology Policies-Yesterday, Today, Tomorrow, 1973; Contbr. articles to profl. jours. Served to 1st lt., C.E. USAR. Recipient 1st nat. award Gravity Research Found., 1952. Mem. Am. Inst. Aeros. and Astronautics, IEEE, AAAS (chmn. indsl. sci. sect. 1974), Sigma Xi. Clubs: Cosmos (Washington), Harvard (Washington). Office: Strasser Assocs Inc 7305 Brookstone Ct Potomac MD 20854

STRASSER, GERHARD FRIEDRICH, German language and comparative literature educator; b. Landshut, Germany, Sept. 13, 1940; came to U.S., 1967; s. Friedrich Ludwig and Josephine (Buchner) S. M.A., Bavarian Ministry of Edn., Munich, Germany, 1965, M.A.T., 1967; Ph.D. in Comparative Lit., Brown U., 1974. Studienreferendar Goethe-Gymnasium, Regensburg, W.Germany, 1965-66; asst. tchr. secondary sch., Gymnasium Cham, W.Germany, 1966-67; instr. German Trinity Coll., Hartford, Conn., 1967-68, instr. French, 1968-69; asst. prof. German and comparative lit. Northwestern U., Evanston, Ill., 1973-79; asst. prof. German and comparative lit. Pa. State U., University Park, 1979-86, assoc. prof., 1986—; library reference asst. Brown U., Providence, 1972-73; Author: Lingua Universalis, 1988. Editorial cons. Random House, N.Y.C., 1984—; co-editor Comparative Literature Studies, 1988; mem. editorial bd. Symbola et Emblemata, Leiden, The Netherlands; contbr. articles to profl. jours. Grantee Am. Philos. Soc, 1985, Thyssen Found., 1988, German Acad. Exchange Service, 1987; Volkswagen Found. fellow, 1977, 78, 81-82; Fulbright Found. lectr., 1967-68, scholar, 1960-61; named to faculty honor roll Northwestern U., 1976-77. Mem. German Soc. for History of Sci., MLA, Am. Comparative Lit. Assn., Am. Assn. for Tchrs. of German, Midwest MLA, Soc. d'Etude du XVIIe siè. Avocations: classical music; travel; cross-country skiing. Home: 428 E McCormic State College PA 16801 Office: Pa State U Dept German University Park PA 16801

STRASSER, JOEL A., public relations executive, engineer; b. N.Y.C., Aug. 8, 1938; s. Albert Gerson and Nellie (Singer) S.; B.S., CCNY, 1961; m. Isabel Gallant, Aug. 15, 1965; children—Alison Debra, Andria Jocelyn, Jon Fredric. News editor Electronic Design mag., N.Y.C., 1962; space electronics editor Electronics mag. McGraw-Hill, N.Y.C., 1963-65; account exec. Lescarboura Advt., Inc., Briarcliff Manor, N.Y., 1965-67; N.Y. bur. chief Aerospace Tech. mag., N.Y.C., 1967-68; syndicated sci. columnist N.Am. Newspaper Alliance, N.Y.C., 1974-80; sr. v.p., founding dir. indsl. and sci. communications services Hill and Knowlton, Inc., N.Y.C., 1968-83; exec. v.p. Thomas L. Richmond, Inc., N.Y.C., 1983-85; sr. v.p., mng. dir. Dorf & Stanton Tech. Communications, N.Y.C., 1985—; adj. asst. prof. NYU, 1988—, adj. instr. Marymount Coll., Tarrytown, N.Y., 1981—; course leader, guest lectr. Am. Mgmt. Assn., 1976—, Am. Med. Writers Assn., 1983—; speaker Internat. Conf. on Energy Use Mgmt., 1977, 79, 81. Vice-pres., Citizens of Ramapo, 1969-70. Recipient Silver Anvil award Public Relations Soc. Am., 1980. Mem. Pub. Relations Soc. Am. (accredited, N.Y. chpt. pres., founding nat. chmn. tech. sect. 1985—, Presdl. citations 1986, 87), IEEE (sr.), Am. Astronautical Soc., Chem. Communications Assn., Nat. Assn. Sci. Writers, Internat. Solar Energy Soc., Internat. Assn. Bus. Communicators, Am. Med. Writers Assn. (guest lectr. 1983—); assoc. fellow AIAA. Jewish (v.p. temple 1980-83). Transmitted 1st color photograph by communications satellite, 1963; conducted 1st press interview by communications satellite, 1963. Speaker at socs. and assns., program coordinator Internat. Conf. on Energy Use Mgmt., Tucson, Los Angeles and West Berlin. Regular columnist High-Tech Marketing, Mid Atlantic Tech., O'Dwyer's PR Services Report, The Counselor; contbr. numerous articles to profl. jours. Home: 119 Smith Hill Rd Suffern NY 10901 Office: PO Box 203 Tallman NY 10982 also: 111 Fifth Ave New York NY 10003

STRATAS, TERESA (ANASTASIA STRATAKI), opera singer; b. Toronto, Ont., Can., May 26, 1938. Student, of Irene Jessner, 1956-59; grad., Faculty Music, U. Toronto, 1959. Winner Met. Opera auditions, 1959; major roles in opera houses throughout world include: Mimi in: La Bohème; Tatiana in: Eugene Onegin; Susanna in: The Marriage of Figaro; Nedda in: Pagliacci; Marenka in: The Bartered Bride; Violetta in: La Traviata; title role in: Rusalka; Jennie in: Mahagonny; created: title role in completed version of Lulu (Alban Berg), Paris Grand Opera, 1979; rec. artist: film appearances Kaiser von Atlantis; Zefirelli's La Traviata, Salome, Lulu, Paganini, Zarewitsch, Eugene Oregin. Decorated Order of Can.; recipient 3 Grammy awards, Emmy award, Drama Desk award, 1986, 3 Grammy nominations, Tony nomination, 1986; named Performer of Yr., Can. Music Council, 1979. Office: care Met Opera Co Lincoln Ctr Plaza New York NY 10023 *

STRATFORD, BRIAN REGINALD, psychologist, educator; b. Dewsbury, Yorkshire, Eng., June 20, 1931; s. Arthur and Winifred (Horner) S.; m. Maureen Patricia Hewitt, Aug. 3, 1957; children—Mark Richard John, Philippa Julia (dec.). D.Ed. in Psychology, U. Leeds, Eng., 1961; D.Ed., U. London, 1965; Ph.D., U. Nottingham, 1974. Sr. lectr. St. Mary's Coll., U. London, 1961-66; prin. lectr., research dir. psychology dept. Trinity Coll., U. Leeds, 1966-80; head studies spl. edn. U. Nottingham, Eng., 1980—; advisor Hong Kong Down's Syndrome Assn., 1986; research cons. Hong Kong Council Social Services, 1986—, European Down's Syndrome Assn., 1987—; cons., mem. adv. bd. Latin Am. Down's Syndrome Assn., 1987—; chief cons. Malta Down's Syndrome Assn., 1987—; vis. prof. Queensland U., Australia, 1985, New Delhi U., India, 1985, Acad. Scis., Prague, Czechoslovakia, 1986; chmn. Hong Kong Assn. for Sci. Study Mental Handicap. Author: Current Approaches to Down's Syndrome, 1985; also articles. Research advisor, chmn. research council Down's Syndrome Assn. Gt. Britain, London and Wales, 1981; active Down's Syndrome Research Com., Chgo., 1982; hon. sec. Home Farm Trust for Mentally Handicapped, Nottingham, 1982—; adv. bd. Ravenswood Found. for Jewish Handicapped People, Berkshire, Eng., 1983—. Grantee Down's Children's Assn., 1980—, Mental Health Found., 1982. Recipient Papal Knighthood Order of St. Gregory the Great, 1985. Fellow Royal Soc. Medicine, Brit. Psychol. Soc., Assn. Child Psychology and Psychiatry, Eugenics Soc. Roman Catholic. Avocations: music; painting. Home: Nottingham U, Lenton Hall, Nottingham NG7 2RD, England Office: U Nottingham Sch Edn, Nottingham NG7 2RD, England

STRATTON, JOHN CARYL, real estate executive; b. Chgo., July 11, 1920; s. John Frederick Otto and Dorothy Marjorie (Young) S.; BS cum laude, Princeton, 1949; MBA, U. New Haven, 1980; m. Lucille Waterhouse Hall, Mar. 13, 1974; children by previous marriage: Caryl Stratton Killing, John Caryl II, Susan Hall Levy, Evelyn Hall Brenton, Kenneth Hall. Chief liaison engr., Avco Mfg. Co., Stratford, Conn., 1950-55; pres. Yankee Engring. Service, Roxbury Conn., 1955—; pres. Stratton Realty, Roxbury, Conn., 1965—; dir. Auto Swage Products Inc.; lectr. U. Conn., 1968-74, Western Conn. State U., 1975-80; spl. adviser U.S. Congl. Adv. Bd. Chmn. Zoning Commn. Newtown, 1971-77; mem. Republican Nat. Com., Rep. Presdl. Task Force. Served with USAF, 1942-46. Decorated D.F.C., Air medal with oak leaf cluster; recipient Presdl. Achievement award, 1981. Mem. AIAA, Internat. Real Estate Fedn., Nat. Real Estate Exchange, Internat. Platform Assn., Newtown Bd. Realtors (pres. 1974, dir. 1975-79), New Milford Bd. Realtors, Conn. Assn. Realtors (v.p. 1981), Nat. Assns. Realtors, Internat. Platform Assn., Realtors Nat. Mktg. Inst. (cert. real estate salesman, cert. real estate broker), Am. Assn. Individual Investors, Internat. Arabian Horse Assn., Arabian Horse Club Conn., Mensa. Sigma Xi. Republican. Congregationalist. Clubs: N.Y. Athletic, Princeton. Address: Squire Rd Roxbury CT 06783

STRATTON, WALTER LOVE, lawyer; b. Greenwich, Conn., Sept. 21, 1926; s. John McKee and June (Love) S.; children—John, Michael, Peter (dec.), Lucinda. Student, Williams Coll., 1943; A.B., Yale U., 1948; LL.B., Harvard U., 1951. Bar: N.Y. 1952. Assoc. Casey, Lane & Mittendorf, N.Y.C., 1951-53; assoc. Donovan, Leisure, Newton & Irvine, N.Y.C., 1956-63; partner Donovan, Leisure, Newton & Irvine, 1963-84, Gibson, Dunn & Crutcher, 1984—; asst. U.S. atty. So. Dist. N.Y., N.Y.C., 1953-56; lectr. Practising Law Inst. Served with USNR, 1945-46. Fellow Am. Coll. Trial Lawyers; mem. ABA, N.Y. Bar Assn. Clubs: Round Hill, Indian Harbor Yacht (Greenwich, Conn.); Colo. Arlberg (Winter Park). Home: 434 Round Hill Rd Greenwich CT 06831 Office: 200 Park Ave New York NY 10166

STRAUB, F. BRUNO, Hungary government official; b. Jan. 5, 1914; s. Ferenc Straub and Terez Kren; m. Erzsebet Lichtneckert, 1940 (dec. 1967); m. Gertrud Szabolcsi, 1972; 2 daughters. Pres. Nat. Council for Environment and Nature Protection, 1978; dir. Inst. Enzymology, 1979—; v.p. Internat. Council Sci. Unions, 1974-76, pres., 1976-78; pres. Presdl. Council Hungarian People's Republic, 1988—. Home: Abranyi Emil u 3, H-1026 Budapest II Hungary Office: Inst Enzymology, Biological Research Ctr, Hungarian Acad Scis, H-1113 Budapest Hungary *

STRAUB, GERHARD HERBERT, manufacturing company executive; b. Munich, Germany, Aug. 11, 1936; s. Hugo and Maria (Jehle) S.; m. Gisela Ganzlin, Oct. 31, 1963; children: Stefan, Oliver, Florian. Diplom-Kaufmann, Ludwig-Maximilian U., Munich, 1964. Comml. referee Mamnesmann AG, Hüttenwerk Huckingen, Fed. Republic Germany, 1964-66; substitute mgr. Süddeutsche Etna-Werk GmbH, Munich, 1966-73, gen. mgr., 1973—; mem. plenary meeting Industrie und Handelskammer, Munich, 1982—; pres. Walter Lehmann-Stiftung, Bonn, 1984—; chmn. Mittelstandsausschuss im Landesverband der Bayerischen Industrie, Munich, 1985—. Comml. judge Landgericht Munich I, 1979—. Mem. Bundesverband Heizung Klima Sanitär (exec. bd. 1980-84, pres. 1984—), Landesverband Heizungs-, Klima- und Sanitärtechnik Bayern, Munich (exec. bd. 1975-79, 2d chmn. 1979—, 1st chmn. 1985—). Lodge: Rotary. Avocations: painting; hockey. Office: Suddeutsche Etna-Werk GmbH, Einsteinstrasse 104, D-8000 Munich Federal Republic of Germany

STRAUS, JOSEPH, lawyer, educator; b. Trieste, Italy, Dec. 14, 1938; s. Joseph and Kristina (Kocijancic) S.; m. Hildegard Thekla Ott; children: Alexander, Isabella. Diploma in law, U. Ljubljana, Yugoslavia, 1962; JD, U. Munich, 1968. Assoc. Law Office H. Nath, Munich, 1964-77, Law Office M. Kestenberg, N.Y.C., 1964-77, Law Office Chaim Rosenberg, Tel Aviv, 1964-77; mem. research staff Max Planck Inst. for Fgn. and Internat. Patent, Copyright and Competition Law, Munich, 1977-80, head dept., head library, 1980—; prof. intellectual property law U. Ljubljana, Yugoslavia, 1986—; cons. in field. Author or co-author 4 books and numerous articles. Mem. Internat. Assn. for Protection Indsl. Property (mem. exec. com., co-chair biotech. com. 1982—), Internat. Assn. for Advancement Teaching and Research in Intellectual Property (treas. 1987—). Club: tennis (Grosshesselohe). Home: Franz Reber Weg 7, 8000 Munich 71 Federal Republic of Germany Office: Max Planck Inst, Siebertstrasse 3, 8000 Munich Federal Republic of Germany

STRAUSS, ANDRE, educator, researcher, consultant; b. Strasbourg, France, Apr. 13, 1924; s. Maurice and Lucie (Rosenberg) S. Cert. teaching ability, U. Paris, 1946, Agregation and Doctorate, 1965; cert. prof. Cambridge U., 1948. Type-setter, machinist, 1945; secondary tchr. Lycee Pasteur, Strasbourg, France, 1948-57; dir. engring. dept. Lycee Voltaire, Paris, 1957-72; prof., dept. head, dir. Research Ctr., U. Pierre and Marie Curie, Paris, 1972-83; prof. cinema staging Institut des Hautes Etudes Cinematographiques, Paris, 1965-72; examiner for Ph.D., Imperial Coll., London, 1982—; prof. Paris Bus. Sch., 1957—; examiner French Nat. Sch. Magistracy, Paris, 1960—; pres. Ctr. Applied Studies in Communication, 1972—; lectr. summer session Am. U., 1961, U. Mich., 1961, U. Pa.-Carlisle, 1968; cons. Oxford-Pergamon U.; advisor So. Meth. U., Dallas, Paris. Author: La Fortune de Stendhal en Angleterre, 1965; Communication-Aeronautic-20th Century-Anglo American World, 1967; editor: 20th Century Trends of Thought, 1985; Artificial Intelligence, 1986; books of English poetry; contbr. articles to publs. in France, U.S., U.K., Austria. Founder Stendhal prize, 1966. Served as liaison officer French Armed Forces, World War II. Decorated Legion d'Honneur, comdr. Palmes Academiques, various war medals; recipient Silver Medal, City of Paris, 1968. Fellow Royal Soc. Arts, Manufacture and Commerce; mem. French Modern Lang. Assn. (pres. Paris 1960-78), Automatic Treatment of Lang. (adminstr. 1972—), Societe des Gens de Lettres de France, Societe des Ingenieurs et Scientifiques de France, Am. Soc. Collegiate Journalists. Office: Adfac Pl, Jussieu 4, 75005 Paris France

STRAUSS, FRANZ JOSEF, government official; b. Munich, Germany, Sept. 6, 1915; s. Franz and Walburga (Schiessl) S.; m. Marianne Zwicknagl, June 4, 1957 (dec. 1984); children: Max-Josef, Franz-Georg, Monika. Ed. U. Munich. Dep. dist. adminstr. Dist. Schongau, 1945, dist. adminstr., 1946-48; mem. German Parliament, 1949-78, Fed. minister for spl. affairs, 1953-55, for atomic affairs, 1955-56, of defence, 1956-62, Fed. minister of finances, 1966-69; ministerpresident of Bavaria, 1978—; mem. Bavarian Parliament, 1978—. Author: Entwurf für Europa, 1966; Herausforderung und Antwort: Ein Programm für Europa, 1968; Zusammenfassung Bundestagsreden, 1969-75 ; Bundestagsreden und Zeitdokumente, 1974-79; Die Finanzverfassung, 1969; Finanzpolitik-Theorie und Wirklichkeit, 1969; Deutschland, Deine Zukunft, 1975; Signale-Beiträge zur deutschen Politik, 1978; Zur Lage, 1980; Gebote der Freiheit, 1980; Verantwortung vor der Geschichte: Beiträge zur deutschen und internationalen Politik, 1985; Auftrag für die Zukunft: Beiträge zur deutschen und internationalen Politik, 1987; contbr. articles to profl. jours. Charter mem. Christian Social Union, 1945, sec. gen., 1949, chmn., 1961—. Served to 2d lt. German Army, 1939-45. Recipient hon. doctorates U. Detroit, Tech. U. Cleve., Kalamazoo Coll., DePaul U., U. Dallas, U. Md., U. Munich.; hon. prof. U. Santiago, Chile, Ctr. Research and Communications, Manila. Roman Catholic. Office: Bayer Staatskanzlei, Prinzregentenstr 7, D-8000 München Federal Republic of Germany Other: Christlich-Soziale Union, Nymphenburger Strasse 64, D-8000 Munich 19 Federal Republic of Germany

STRAUSS, JEANNE H., technical translator; b. Hamburg, Ger., Mar. 5, 1928; came to U.S., 1948, naturalized, 1954; d. Frederic and Julie Strauss; BA, Roosevelt U., 1956; MA, Loyola U., Chgo., 1960; PhD cert. in Spanish and French, U. Wis.-Madison, 1968. Legal sec. Montgomery Ward, Chgo., 1957-60; instr. Creighton U., Omaha, 1961-63; teaching asst. U. Wis., Madison, 1964-65; asst. prof. U. Wis.-Stevens Point, 1965-69, Western Ill. U., Macomb, 1969-71, U. Wis.-Superior, 1973-75; tech. translator, interpreter Phillips Petroleum Co., Bartlesville, Okla., 1975-86. Mem. Republican Senatorial Com., 1979—. Mem. Am. Assn. Tchrs. French, Am. Assn. Tchrs. Spanish and Portuguese, MLA, Am. Transl. Assn., ASME (affiliate); Philbrook Art Museum. Club: Toastmasters. Home: PO Box 78 Bartlesville OK 74005

STRAUSS, MARTIN HARRY, restaurant executive; b. San Francisco, Dec. 13, 1948; arrived in Can., 1972; s. Sol and Clara (Erlichman) S.; m. Arla Nitikman, Feb. 14, 1976; children: Jonathan N., Jay Samuel N. BA in Econs., Claremont Men's Coll., 1970; MBA in Fin., Columbia U., 1972. Exec. asst. BACM Industries, Ltd., Winnipeg, Man., Can., 1972-76; corp. sec. Kins Mgmt., Ltd., Winnipeg, 1976-80; mng. dir. Stage West Dinner Theatre, Winnipeg, 1980-86; dir. ops. Salisbury House of Can., Winnipeg, 1986—. Active Job-Finding Club of Man. (bd. dirs. 1986—). Mem. Man. Restaurant and Food Services Assn. (bd. dirs., 1986—). Lodge: Rotary (bd. dirs. Winnipeg club, 1986—). Home: 956 Queenston Bay, Winnipeg, MB Canada R3N 0Y2 Office: Salisbury House of Can, 212-530 Century St, Winnipeg, MB Canada R3H 0Y4

STRAUSS, SIMON, physician, radiologist; b. Bulawayo, Rhodesia (now Zimbabwe), Feb. 21, 1947; arrived in Israel, 1971; s. Eliezer and Freda (Kerem) S.; m. Janine Ilana Schmahmann, Aug. 9, 1973; children: Orit, Liron. B in Medicine and B in Surgery, U. Rhodesia, Salisbury, 1971. Intern in medicine Chaim Sheba Med. Ctr., Tel Hashomer, Israel, 1972-73, resident in radiology, 1973-78, staff mem. for ultrasound, 1983-86; fellowship in ultrasound Beth Israel Med. Ctr., N.Y.C., 1981-83; chief div. ultrasound Assaf Harofeh Med. Ctr., Zerifin, Israel, 1986—. Contbr. articles to profl. jours. Served to capt. Israeli Army, 1979-81. Mem. Israel Radiol. Soc., Israel Ultrasound Soc., Am. Inst. Ultrasound in Medicine. Jewish. Home: 6 Hashaked St, Kfar Shmaryahu 46910, Israel

STRAUSS, THOMAS, art critic; b. Budapest, Hungary, Apr. 4, 1931; s. Eugen and Aranka Fulop (Galy) S.; m. 1962 (div. 1966); 1 son, Igor. C.Sc. Charles U., Prague, 1961, habitation, 1966. Asst. lectr. aesthetics and theory arts Comenius U. Bratislava (Czechoslovakia), 1954—, asst. prof., 1966—, dir. Inst. Aesthetics, 1966-70; asst. curator Slovak Nat. Gallery, Bratislava, 1973-78; vice dir. Wilhelm Lehmbruck Mus., Duisburg, Ger., 1980-82, East European Inst. Culture, Cologne, 1986—. Mem. Assn. Visual Artists Slovakia (presidium 1966-70), Internat. Assn. Art Critics, Internat. Assn. Edn. Through Arts. Author: Artistic Thinking, 1962; A. Jasusch and the Birth of the East Slovakian Avanguarde, 1965; Art Now, 1968; Op-Art, 1969; Neoplasticism, 1970; L. Kassak, The Hungarian Contribution to Constructivism, 1975; Allegro barbaro. B. Bartók and the Visual Arts, 1981; Bonjour, Monsieur Kolar, 1984; The Strange Russian Painters, 1986; co-editor Estetika jour., 1964-71. Home: Ebertplatz 7, 5 Köln Federal Republic of Germany

STRAUSZ-HUPE, ROBERT, ambassador, author; b. Vienna, Austria, Mar. 25, 1903; emigrated to U.S., 1923, naturalized, 1938; s. Rudolph and Doris (Hedwig) Strausz-H.; m. Eleanor deGraff Cuyler, Apr. 26, 1938 (dec. 1976); m. Mayrose Ferreira Nugara, Aug. 22, 1979. A.M., Ph.D., U. Pa., 1944. Investment banker 1927-37; assoc. editor Current History, 1939-41; assoc. prof. polit. sci. U. Pa., 1946-52, prof., 1952—; spl. lectr., 1940-46; dir. Fgn. Policy Research Inst., 1955-69; U.S. ambassador Ceylon, 1970-72, to Belgium, 1972-74, to Sweden, 1974-76, to NATO, 1976-77, to Turkey, 1981—. Author: The Russian-German Riddle, 1940, Axis-America, 1941, Geopolitics, 1942, The Balance of Tomorrow, 1945, International Relations, 1950, The Zone of Indifference, 1952, Power and Community, 1956, (with Kintner, Cottrell, Dougherty) Protracted Conflict, 1959, (with W. Kintner, Stefan Possony) A Forward Strategy for America, 1961, (with others) Building the Atlantic World, 1963, In My Time, 1967, Dilemmas Facing the Nation, 1979; editor: The Idea of Colonialism, 1958, Orbis, 1957-69. Lectr. Air War Coll., 1953. Served to lt. col. AUS. Fellow Royal Geog. Soc.; mem. Council Fgn. Relations, Atlantic Council U.S. Lutheran. Clubs: Merion Cricket (Haverford, Pa.); Brook (N.Y.C.); Metropolitan (Washington). Address: Am Embassy, 110 Ataturk, 06688 Ankara Turkey

STRAVATO, CLAUDIA DELAUGHTER, state official; b. Dallas, May 25, 1942; d. Arman Dale and Nina Marie (Bear) DeLaughter; student Tex. Womans U., 1959-60, U. Tex., Arlington, 1961-66, U. Mo., 1967-70; B.S., West Tex. State U., 1974, M.A., 1977; children by previous marriage—Michael Armand, Anna Teresa. Adminstrv. asst. to pres. AMA, Dallas, 1961-67; dir. Panhandle div. Arthritis Found., Amarillo, Tex., 1971-73; dep. comptroller Tex. Comptroller of Public Accts., Austin, 1975—. Pres. Amarillo Rep. Womens Club, 1974-75; chmn. High Plains Womens Polit. Caucus, 1974, 79; founder, co-chmn. Amarillo Rape Crisis Service, 1975; state polit. action chmn. Tex. Womens Polit. Caucus, 1977; ofcl. recorder, mem. exec. com. Tex. Commn. for the Observance of Internat. Womans Yr., 1977; bd. dirs. Amarillo LWV, 1973, Tex. Abortion Rights Action League, 1978—, Tex. Women's Advocacy Project, 1982-85; founder, 1st pres. Amarillo Women's Network, 1980-81. Named Citizen of Yr., Nat. Assn. Social Workers, 1986, Outstanding Woman in State Govt., Tex. Gov.'s Office, 1987. Mem. Tex. Press Women (dir. 1984-85), Exec. Women in Tex. Govt. (founder, pres. 1985, 88), NAACP, ACLU (state dir. 1982-86, pres. High Plains chpt. 1982—). Unitarian. Home: 210 S Avondale Amarillo TX 79106

STRAW, GARY ROBERT, resort management executive; b. Springfield, Vt., Mar. 19, 1951; s. Robert Archie and Muriel Gwendolyn (Mayette) S.; m. Diane Leslie Durnall, Mar. 17, 1979; children: Gary Robert II, Megan June. Student, Deerfield Acad., 1970; BS, U. Vt., 1974. Gen. mgr. Point Sebago Resort, Casco, Maine, 1974-80; gen. mgr Meramec Valley Resort, Cuba, Mo., 1980-81; gen. mgr., dir. sales and mktg. Lost Valley Lake Resort, Owensville, Mo., 1981-86; pres. Straw and Assocs., Inc., Wash., Mo., 1986—, Straw and Assocs. Ohio, Inc., Port Clinton, 1986—, Straw & Assocs. Pa., Inc., Straw & Assocs. Wis., Inc., S and A Mktg., 1986—; guest speaker Coast To Coast, Inc., Marco Isle, Fla., 1987, Washington, 1987, U. Vt., 1975-78; sales and mktg. mgmt. Jellystone Park, Milw., 1987—, Tievoli Hills Resort, 1987, Clarksville, Mo., 1987, Erie Island Resort and Marina, Port Clinton, Ohio, 1987—, Hunter's Station, Tionesta, Pa., 1988—; Bent Oaks Resort, Lake Ozark, Mo., 1988—, Boulder Valley Ranch, Farmington, Mo., 1988—; cons. Patten Corp. Mid-Atlantic, 1988—, Bennett Funding Group, Inc., 1988—. Bd. dirs. El Vallejo Owners Assn., Wash., 1986-88. Mem. Ohio Residential and Resort Devel. Assn., Am. Residential and Resort Devel. Assn. Republican. Episcopalian. Home: 4448D Marin Harbor Port Clinton OH 43452 Office: 4495 W Darr-Hopfinger Rd Port Clinton OH 43452

STRAW, JIMMIE FRANKLIN, cost reduction consultant, writer, publisher; b. Pryor, Okla., Apr. 23; s. Walter L. and Katarine (Feild) S.; student public schs., Douglass, Kans.; m. DeLores Ann Satterfield, Feb. 28; children—Rebecca, Micaela, Joseph, Phillip, Andrei. Pres., TSA Import/Export Co., 1963-65, Redy Electronics Mfg. Inc., 1964-65, Trans-Global Merc., 1967-70, Internat. Trade & Devel. Corp., 1972-73, Jim Diamond Wigs, 1968-70, Discount Wig Centers, 1970-76, Peek-A-Boo Wig Shops, 1970-76, Salesway Corp., 1975-76; editor, pub. Bus. Opportunities Digest, Dalton, Ga., 1976—, Offshore Banking News, 1983—; writer, editor, pub. Bus. Intelligence Network Confidential Memos, Dalton, 1972—; founder, exec. dir. Am. Bus. Club, Dalton, 1974—; chmn. Aalpha Royale Advt., Dalton, 1971—; founder, exec. dir. Heritage Exchange, Dalton, 1982—; chief exec. officer First Am. Banking Ltd., Saipan, 1982—. Served with U.S. Army, 1964-67. Mem. Nat. Writers Syndicate (mem. editorial bd. of rev.), Mensa, Panjandrums (founder, coordinator). Author: The Complete Book of Money Making Opportunities, 1979; Financing Sources (annually); Finders Fee Guide (annually); editor, pub. Communications, newsletter Panjandrums, 1977-82. Home and Office: 301 Plymouth Dr NE Dalton GA 30720

STRAWINSKY, THEODORE, artist; b. St. Petersburg, Russia, Mar. 24, 1907; naturalized Swiss citizen, 1956; s. Igor and Catherine (Nossenko) Stravinsky; ed. in Switzerland and France, Andre Lhote's Acad., Paris; m. Denise Guerzoni, June 29, 1936; 1 dau., Catherine Jellatchitch. Painter in different media, 1927—; exhibited in France, Switzerland, Eng., Italy, N.Y.C., retrospective exhibition of 200 works 1921-86 Musée des Beaux Arts, Neuchatel, Switzerland, 1988; works include paintings on walls, mosaics, tinted glass windows, wall embedded glass blocks, tapestries, Switzerland, France, Belgium, Holland, Italy; designer theater sets and costumes in France, Belgium, Italy; represented in permanent collections European mus. and pvt. collections. Recipient medal Scis., Arts, Lettres of French Acad.; decorated comdr. Papal Order S. Gregorii Magni. Mem. Swiss Painters, Sculptors and Architects Assn. Roman Catholic. Author: Le Message de Igor Strawinsky, 1948, 80; Catherine and Igor Stravinsky, a Family Album, 1972; subject of Maurice Zermatten's Théodore Strawinsky, 1984, Fondazione Arch. Enrico Monti's "Théodore Strawinsky-Pitture murali sul Lago d'Orta", 1988; also numerous articles and revs. Home: 4 Chemin de la Florence, CH-1208 Geneva Switzerland

STRAWSON, GALEN JOHN, philosopher, educator, critic; b. Oxford, Eng., Feb. 5, 1952; s. Peter Frederick and Ann (Martin) S.; m. José Said, July 20, 1974; children: Emilie Manuela, Thomas Gregoire. BA, Cambridge U., 1973, MA, 1977; PhB, Oxford U., 1977, PhD, 1983; postgrad., Ecole Normale Superieure, Paris, 1977-78. Lectr. philosophy Oxford U. Univ. Coll., 1979-80, Exeter Coll., 1980-83, St. Hugh's Coll., 1983-85, New Coll., 1985-86, St. Hilda's Coll., 1986-87; fellow and tutor in philosophy Jesus Coll. Oxford (Eng.) U., 1987—. Author: Freedom and Belief, 1986; asst. editor lit. supplement London Times, 1978-87; cons. editor 1987—; contbr. articles to profl. jours. and revs. to newspapers. Mem. Mind Assn. Office: Oxford U Jesus Coll, Oxford OX1 3DW, England

STRAWSON, PETER FREDERICK, philosophy educator; b. London, Nov. 23, 1919; s. Cyril Walter and Nellie Dora (Jewell) S.; m. Grace Hall Martin, Oct. 27, 1945; children: Julia Katharine, Galen John, Robert Neville, Virginia Ann. M.A., Oxford U., 1940. Lectr. Univ. Coll. N. Wales, Bangor, 1946-47; lectr. Univ. Coll., Oxford, 1947-48, fellow, 1948-68; prof. metaphysics Magdalen Coll., Oxford U., 1968-87, prof. emeritus, 1987—; lectr., vis. prof. in many countries, including U.S.A., Can., Argentina, Mex., India, Israel, Yugoslavia, France, Fed. Republic Germany, Belgium. Author: Introduction to Logical Theory, 1952; Individuals, 1959; The Bounds of Sense, 1966; Logico-Linguistic Papers, 1971; Freedom and Resentment, 1974; Subject and Predicate in Logic and Grammar, 1974; Scepticism and Naturalism: Some Varieties, 1985; Analyse et Métaphysique, 1985. Served as capt. Brit. Army, 1940-46, U.K., Italy, Austria. Created knight bachelor, 1977. Fellow Brit. Acad.; mem. Am. Acad. Arts and Scis. (fgn. hon.), Mind Assn., Aristotelian Soc. (pres. 1969-70). Club: Athenaeum (London). Avocations: walking, reading English and French literature, travelling. Home: 25 Farndon Rd, Oxford England Office: Magdalen Coll, High St, Oxford England also: British Acad, 20-21 Cornwall Terr, London NW1 4QP, England

STREAM, ARNOLD CRAGER, lawyer, novelist; b. N.Y.C., Feb. 8, 1918; s. Mervyn and Sophia (Hyams) S.; m. Barbara Bloom, Oct. 1, 1967; children by previous marriages: Jane, Abigail, Richard, Raymond. B.A., CCNY, 1936; LL.D., St. Lawrence U., 1940. Bar: N.Y. 1940, D.C. 1942. Asst. U.S. atty. N.Y. Dist., 1940-43; partner firm Amen, Weisman & Butler, N.Y.C., 1948-55; exec. v.p., gen. counsel C & C TV Corp., 1955-60, Hazel Bishop, Inc., 1955-60; trial lawyer 1960—; sr. partner firm Monasch, Chazen & Stream, N.Y.C., 1973-82; sr. ptnr. firm Blum, Gersen, Dollard & Stream, N.Y.C., 1982—; trial counsel Gulfstream Aerospace Corp., Twentieth Century-Fox Film Corp., 1975-87; counsel French Embassy, N.Y.C., 1965-72; spl. counsel to TV industry; vis. lectr. Touro Coll. Sch. Law. Author: (novels) The Third Bullet, Bitter with Treason (Felix and I); short stories, book revs., tax series, series on constl. law; Contbr. articles to profl. jours. Served to lt. col. AUS, 1943-46. Mem. Bar Assn. City N.Y. Home: 33 Deepdale Dr Great Neck Estates NY 11021 Office: 270 Madison Ave New York NY 10016

STREAM, JAY WILSON, consultant; b. Farlan, Iowa, Apr. 17, 1921; s. Adrian M. and Theo (Bennett) S.; m. Dorothy McCullough, May 20, 1960; children: Carol, James, Cindy, Linda. Student, Milw. State Tchrs. Coll., 1943. Casualty ins. underwriter R.A. Napier & Co., Chgo., 1939-41; with Wallace Supply Mfg. Co., Chgo., 1941-42; quality control specialist Am. Torpedo (Amertorp), Franklin Park, Ill., 1942-43; home office rep. John Hancock Life Ins. Co., Chgo., 1946-48; partner ready-mix concrete co. Chgo., 1949-52; owner, operating officer Jay W. Stream Assocs., Midwest Land Corp., Hydrostructures, others; founder Village of Carol Stream, Ill., 1952-64; founder, pres., chmn. bd. Hawthorne Bank of Wheaton, Ill., 1961-68; dir. Hawthorne Bank of Wheaton, 1961—; cons. San Luis Obispo, Calif., 1970—; founder, chmn. steering com. World Arabian Horse Assn., 1967-72, 1st pres., 1972—. Head career devel., Wayne Newton, 1971-80; exec. producer several films and TV prodns. Mem. U.S. Trade Relations-U.S. Dept. Agr. Policy Adv. Com. for Trade. Served to 2d lt. USAAC, 1942-45. Republican. Home: 300 Greengate Rd San Luis Obispo CA 93401 Office: 1026 Chorro St Suite 1 San Luis Obispo CA 93401

STREAN, BERNARD M., retired naval officer; b. Big Cabin, Okla., Dec. 16, 1910; s. Ralph Lester and Maude (Hopkins) S.; m. Janet Lockey, June 12, 1935; children: Bernard M., Richard Lockey, Judy (Mrs. William S. Graves). B.S., U.S. Naval Acad., 1933; grad., Armed Forces Staff Coll., 1949, Nat. War Coll., 1958. Commd. ensign U.S. Navy, 1933, advanced through grades to vice adm., 1965; designated naval aviator 1935; assigned U.S.S. Pennsylvania, 1933-35, Naval Air Sta., Pensacola, Fla., 1935-36, U.S.S. Saratoga, 1936-38; assigned San Diego Naval Sta., 1938-39, Hawaii, 1939-40; assigned Naval Air Sta., Jacksonville, Fla., 1940-42; comdg. officer VF-1 U.S.S. Yorktown, 1943-44, Air Group 98, 1944-45, Air Group 75, 1945-46; head tech. tng. program sect. Office Chief Naval Ops., 1950-51; comdg. officer Air Transp. Squadron 8, 1951-54, Naval Sch. Pre-Flight Sch., 1954-56, U.S.S. Kenneth Whiting, 1956-57, U.S.S. Randolph, 1958-59; chief staff, aide to comdr. Naval Air Force, U.S. Atlantic Fleet, 1959-60; comdr. Fleet Air Whidbey, 1960-61, Patrol Force 7th Fleet, also U.S. Talwan patrol force, 1961-62; asst. chief naval ops. for fleet ops. 1962-64; comdr. Carrier Div. 2, Atlantic Fleet, 1964-65, World's 1st all-nuclear naval task force, 1964; dep. asst. chief for personnel Bur. Naval Personnel, Dept. Navy, Washington, 1965-68; chief naval air tng. Naval Air Sta., Pensacola, Fla., 1968-71; ret. 1971; v.p. O.S.C. Franchise Devel. Corp., 1971-75; chmn. bd. Solaray Corp., 1975-80; v.p. Huet-Browning Corp., Washington. Bd. dirs. U.S. Olympic Com., 1965-68; trustee No. Va. Community Colls., 1978-82. Decorated Navy Cross, (2) D.F.C. with 2 gold stars, Air medal with 7 gold stars, Legion of Merit, D.S.M., numerous area and campaign ribbons; Distinguished Service medal Greece; medal of Pao-Ting Republic China). Mem. Mil. Order World Wars, Loyal Order Carabao, Early and Pioneer Naval Aviators Assn. (pres. 1977-79), Arlington County Tax Assn. (vice chmn. 1978—), Md. Aviation Hist. Soc. (founder, bd. dirs. 1978-82), U.S. Naval Acad. Alumni Assn. Clubs: Army Navy (Washington); N.Y. Yacht; Washington Golf and Country (Arlington), Los Angeles Country. Address: 1200 N Nash St #846 Arlington VA 22209

STREAN, BERNARD MAX, JR., nautical cartographer; b. Pensacola, Fla., Mar. 6, 1936; s. Bernard Max and Janet (Lockey) S.; A.B., Earlham Coll., 1959; M.S., So. Ill. U., 1965; m. Florence Jones, May 7, 1973. Cartographic survey aide U.S. Geol. Survey, Arlington, Va., 1959, oceanographer sediment lab., Washington, 1963-64, hydrographic surveys, 1964-67, oceanographer marine geology, 1967-77, cartographer Def. Mapping Agency-Hydrographic Center, 1977-78, oceanographer Hydrographic/Topographic Center, 1978-81, cartographer, 1981—. Mem. Am. Assn. Petroleum Geologists, Am. Geophys. Union, Geol. Soc. Am., Nat. Geog. Soc., Seismol. Soc. Am., Internat. Assn. Volcanology and Chemistry of Earth's Interior. Episcopalian. Home: 6111 Colonial Terr Camp Springs MD 20748 Office: Def Mapping Agy Hydrographic Topographic Ctr Washington DC 20390

STREATOR, EDWARD JAMES, former diplomat; b. N.Y.C., Dec. 12, 1930; s. Edward James and Ella (Stout) S.; m. Priscilla Craig Kenney, Feb. 16, 1957; children: Edward James, III, Elinor Craig, Abigail Merrill. A.B., Princeton U., 1952. Commd. fgn. service officer Dept. State, 1956; assigned ICA, 1956-58; 3d sec. embassy Addis Ababa, Ethiopia, 1958-60; 2d sec. embassy Lome Togo, 1960-62; intelligence research specialist Office Research and Analysis for Africe, Dept. State, Washington, 1962-63, staff asst. to sec. state, 1964-66, chief polit.-mil. affairs unit, 1966-67; dep. dir. U.S. Mission to NATO Office Polit.-Mil. Affairs, 1967-68, dep. dir. polit. affairs, 1968-69; dep. dir. Office NATO and Atlantic Polit.-Mil. Affairs, Dept. State, 1969-73; dir. office 1973-75, dep. U.S. permanent rep. to NATO, dep. chief U.S. Mission to NATO, 1975-77; minister, dep. chief of mission Am. embassy, London, 1975-84; ambassador, U.S. rep. OECD Paris, 1984-87. Mem. U.S. dels. to NATO and OECD Ministerial Meetings, 1964, 66, 69-75, 85-87; mem. 10th SEATO Council Ministers Meeting, 1965; 2d spl. Inter-Am. Conf., 1965, Conf. Security and Coop., in Europe, 1973; mem. Council Royal United Services Inst.; exec. com. The Pilgrims, Internat. Inst. Strategic Studies; gov. Ditchley Found.; dir. Am. Friends of Blerancourt Mus.; chmn. U.S. Appeal Com., Prince's Bus. Trust; adv. dir. Am. C. of C., U.K. Served to lt. (j.g.) USNR, 1952-56. Episcopalian. Clubs: Met. (Washington); Brooks's, Buck's, Beefsteak Garrick (London); Mill Reef (Antigua). Address: c/o 32 Phillimore Gardens, London W87QF, England

STREEP, MERYL (MARY LOUISE STREEP), actress; b. Madison, N.J., June 22, 1949; d. Harry Jr. and Mary W. Streep; m. Donald J. Gummer, 1978; children: Henry, Mary Willa, Grace Jane. BA, Vassar Coll., 1971; MFA, Yale U., 1975, DFA (hon.), 1983; DFA (hon.), Dartmouth Coll., 1981. Ind. actress stage, screen 1975—. Appeared with Green Mountain Guild, Woodstock, Vt.; Broadway debut in Trelawny of the Wells, Lincoln Center Beaumont Theater, 1975; N.Y.C. theatrical appearances include 27 Wagons Full of Cotton (Theatre World award), A Memory of Two Mondays, Henry V, Secret Service, The Taming of the Shrew, Measure for Measure, The Cherry Orchard, Happy End, Wonderland, Taken in Marriage, Alice in Concert (Obie award 1981); movie appearances include Julia, 1977, The Deer Hunter, 1978 (Best Supporting Actress award Nat. Soc. Film Critics), Manhattan, 1979, The Seduction of Joe Tynan, 1979, Kramer vs. Kramer, 1980 (N.Y. Film Critics' award, Los Angeles Film Critics' award, both for best actress, Golden Globe award, Acad. award for best supporting actress), The French Lieutenant's Woman, 1981 (Los Angeles Film Critics award for best actress, Brit. Acad. award, Golden Globe award 1981), Sophie's Choice, 1982 (Acad. award for best actress, Los Angeles Film Critics award for best actress, Golden Globe award 1982), Still of the Night, 1982, Silkwood, 1983, Falling in Love, 1984, Plenty, 1985, Out of Africa, 1985 (Los Angeles Film Critics award for best actress 1985), Heartburn, 1986, Ironweed, 1987, A Cry in the Dark, 1988; TV film The Deadliest Season, 1977; TV mini-series Holocaust, 1978 (Emmy award); TV dramatic spls. Secret Service, 1977, Uncommon Women and Others, 1978. Recipient Mademoiselle award, 1976, Woman of Yr. award B'nai Brith, 1979, Woman of Yr. award Hasty Pudding Soc., Harvard U., 1980, Best Supporting Actress award Nat. Bd. of Rev., 1979, Best Actress award Nat. Bd. of Rev., 1982, Star of Yr. award Nat. Assn. Theater Owners, 1983, People's Choice award, 1983, 85, 86, 87. Office: care Internat Creative Mgmt 40 W 57th St New York NY 10019

STREET, ROBERT, retired university official, physicist; b. Wakefield, Eng., Dec. 16, 1920; s. Joe and Edith Elizabeth (Jones) S.; m. Joan Marjorie Bere, June 26, 1943; children—Alison Mary, Nicholas Robert. M.Sc., U. London, 1944, Ph.D., 1948, D.Sc., 1966. With Ministry Supppy, London, 1941-45; lectr. in physics U. Nottingham (Eng.), 1945-54; sr. lectr. U. Sheffield (Eng.), 1954-60; Found. prof. Monash U. (Australia), 1960-74; dir. Research Sch. Phys. scis., Australian Nat. U., Canberra Act, 1974-78; vice-chancellor U. Western Australia, Perth, 1978-86. Research, publs. in field. Decorated officer Order of Australia. Fellow Australian Acad. Sci., Inst. Physics, Australian Inst. Physics, Royal Soc. Arts; mem. Inst. Elec. Engrs. Club: Weld (Perth). Home: 60 Temby Ave, Kalamunda, WA 6076, Australia Office: U Western Australia, Nedlands, Perth 6009, Australia

STREETER, WILLIAM JOSEPH, manufacturing executive; b. Buffalo, Nov. 14, 1938; s. William John and Aletta (Hausbeck) S.; m. Petronella H. A. F. Steenman, Nov. 23, 1973; children: William, Mark, Andres, Michael. BS, Rochester Inst. Tech., 1960; MBA, NYU, 1971. Product engr. GAF Corp., Binghamton, N.Y., 1960-65; mgr. tech. services Powers Chemco Inc., Glen Cove, N.Y., 1966-70, also bd. dirs.; pres. Chemco Europe N.V., Soest, The Netherlands, 1971—. Author: The Silver Mania, 1984. Served with U.S. Army, 1963. Mem. Assn. for Quality Control (sr.), Soc. Photographic Scientists and Engrs. (sr.), Tech. Assn. Graphic Arts, Soest Businessmans Orgn. (bd. dirs. 1984-87). Roman Catholic. Office: Chemco Europe NV, De Beaufortlaan 28, 3768 MJ Soest The Netherlands

STREIBL, MAX, political official; b. Oberammergau, Fed. Republic Germany, Jan. 6, 1932; s. Max and Irene (Oswald) S.; m. Irmingard Junghans, 1960; 3 children. Grad., U. Munich. With Bavarian State Chancellery, 1960-62; mem. Bavarian State Parliament 1962—, Bavarian Minister for Land Devel. and Environmental Issues, 1970-77, Minister for Fin., 1977—; gen. sec. CSU Fed. Republic Germany, 1967-71; chmn. bd. Bayernwerke AG, Messerschmitt-Bölkow-Blohm, Energieversorgung Ostbayern, Bayerische Wasserkraft, ZDF (German Channel Two), Bayerische Landesbank, Flughafen München, Rhein-Main-Donau, Industrieverwaltungsgesellschaft, Fernsehstudio (TV Centre Munich), Deutsche Genossenschaftsbank. Contbr. articles to profl. jours. and newspapers. Decorated Bayerischer Verdienstorden, Grosses Bundesverdienstrkreuz mit Stern und Schulterband, others. Office: Bayerisches Staatsministerium, der Finanzen, Odeonsplatz 5, 8000 Munich 22, Federal Republic of Germany •

STREICH, ARTHUR HAROLD, financial planner; b. Mpls., Apr. 22, 1925; s. Herman Henry and Rose (Anderson) S.; B.A. in Journalism, Macalester Coll., 1952; m. Arlene June Ostlund, Aug. 30, 1947; children—Jennifer Streich Hallam, Jack, Paula Jo. Partner, S&E Publs., St. Paul, 1952-55; asst. sec. Northwestern Lumbermans Assn., 1955-57; gen. mgr. Nat. Electronics Conf., 1957-59; public relations exec. Mullen & Assos., Inc., Mpls., 1959-60; investment adviser Dempsey Tegeler & Co., Inc., Mpls., 1960-63; regional sales mgr. Dreyfus Corp., 1963-68; regional v.p. Anchor Corp., Chgo., 1968-69; regional v.p. wholesale sales and mgmt. Dreyfus Sales Corp., Chgo., 1969-72; regional v.p. Crosby Corp., Chgo., 1972-73; regional sales mgr. John Nuveen & Co., Chgo., 1973-74; owner Fin. Planning Services Co., Wayzata, Minn., 1974—. Republican candidate for mayor St. Paul, 1952. Served with USN, 1942-46. Mem. Nat. Assn. Security Dealers (registered prin.), Nat. Speakers Assn. Republican. Mem. Evang. Free Ch. Club: Toastmasters (Disting. Toastmaster). Address: 14431 Wellington Rd Wayzata MN 55391

STREICHER, JAMES FRANKLIN, lawyer; b. Ashtabula, Ohio, Dec. 6, 1940; s. Carl Jacob and Helen Marie (Dugan) S.; m. Sandra JoAnn Jennings, May 22, 1940; children—Cheryl Ann, Gregory Scott, Kerry Marie. B.A., Ohio State U., 1962; J.D., Case Western Res. U., 1966. Bar: Ohio 1966, U.S. Dist. Ct. (no. dist.) Ohio 1966. Assoc., Calfee, Halter & Griswold, Cleve., 1966-71, ptnr., 1972—; mem. Div. Securities Adv. Bd., State of Ohio; lectr. Case Western Res. U., Cleve. State U., Ctr. for Venture Devel. Trustee Cottillion Soc., Hiram House Camp, Soc. Crippled Children. Mem. ABA, Ohio State Bar Assn., Greater Cleve. Bar Assn. (chmn. corp., banking and bus. law sect. 1980-84), Ohio State U. Alumni Assn., Case Western Res. U. Alumni Assn., Newcomen Soc., Beta Theta Pi, Phi Delta Phi. Republican. Roman Catholic. Clubs: Hermit, Mayfield Country (bd. dirs. 1985—), Tavern, Union. Lodge: Rotary (Cleve.). Home: 50 Windrush Moreland Hills OH 44022

STREISAND, BARBRA JOAN, singer, actress; b. Bklyn., Apr. 24, 1942; d. Emanuel and Diana (Rosen) S.; m. Elliott Gould, Mar. 1963 (div.); 1 son, Jason Emanuel. Student, Yeshiva of Bklyn. N.Y. theatre debut Another Evening with Harry Stoones, 1961; appeared in Broadway musical I Can Get It for You Wholesale, 1962, Funny Girl, 1964-65; rec. artist Columbia Records; motion pictures include Funny Girl, 1968, Hello Dolly, 1969, On a Clear Day You Can See Forever, 1970, The Owl and the Pussy Cat, 1970, What's Up Doc?, 1972, Up the Sandbox, 1972, The Way We Were, 1973, For Pete's Sake, 1974, Funny Lady, 1975, The Main Event, 1979, All Night Long, 1981, Nuts, 1987; star, producer film A Star is Born, 1976; producer, dir., star Yentl, 1983; TV spls. include My Name is Barbra, 1965 (5 Emmy awards), Color Me Barbra, 1966; Gold record albums include People, 1965, My Name is Barbra, 1965, Color Me Barbra, 1966, Stoney End, 1971, Barbra Joan Streisand, 1972, The Way We Were, 1974, A Star is Born, 1976, Superman, 1977, The Stars Salute Israel at 30, 1978, Wet, 1979, (with Barry Gibb) Guilty, 1980, Emotion, 1984, The Broadway Album, 1986. Recipient Emmy award, CBS-TV spl. (My Name Is Barbra), 1964, Acad. award as best actress (Funny Girl), 1968, Golden Globe award (Funny Girl), 1969, co-recipient Acad. award for best song (Evergreen), 1976, Georgie award AGVA 1977, Grammy awards for best female pop vocalist, 1963, 64, 65, 77, 86, for best song writer (with Paul Williams),1977, Tony award (spl.award), 1970. Office: Creative Artists Agy Care Fred Spector 1888 Century Pk E Suite 1400 Los Angeles CA 90067 •

STRELAN, JOHN GERHARD, clergyman, educator; b. Ungarie, New South Wales, Australia, Nov. 10, 1936; s. Peter Gerhard and Erica Clara (Appelt) S.; diploma in theology Concordia Sem., Adelaide, S. Australia, 1959; Th.D., Concordia Sem., St. Louis, 1973; m. Bronwyn Helene Burgess, Mar. 6, 1965; children—Peter Gerhard, John William, Kylie Louise, Luana Jane. Ordained to ministry Luth. Ch., 1960; pastor Wangaratta Victoria,

Australia, 1960-62; circuit missionary Menyamya, Papua New Guinea, 1962-65; found. faculty mem., dean of studies, lectr. in N.T., Martin Luther Sem., Lae, Papua New Guinea, 1966-84, registrar, 1980-81; lectr. various seminars and workshops on religious movements in primal societies; guest lectr. Augustana Hochschule, Neuendettelsau, Bavaria; lectr. Luther Sem., North Adelaide, Australia, 1986—; v.p. Luth. Ch. Australia, 1987—. Bd. govs. Lae Internat. High Sch., 1980-83, chmn., 1983. Mem. Australian Assn. for Study of Religion. Composer hymn: Lord God our Guardian and our Guide; author: Search for Salvation, 1977; Glory be to Thee O Lord, 1979; Ephesians: A Commentary, 1981; The Letters of John: A Commentary, 1984; editor Bible Commentary series, 1982-84. Home and Office: Luther Seminary, 104 Jeffcott St, North Adelaide 5006, Australia

STRELETZKY, KATHRYN DIANE, sales executive; b. Bklyn., July 13, 1957; d. Donald Charles and Eleanor Jean (Galassi) S. B.A. with highest honors, Pa. State U.; MBA Coll. William and Mary, 1987. Sales exec. Procter & Gamble, Milw., Balt., 1979-81, 3M, Phila., Atlanta, 1982—; bd. dirs. Collegian, Inc. Regional coordinator Pa. State U. Alumni Admissions Com., Washington and No. Va., 1984—; treas. Whisperwood Homes Assn., Reston, Va., 1985-87. Mem. Cooperating for Growth, Pa. State Alumni Assn. (adv. bd. 1985), Exec. MBA Alumni Soc. of William & Mary, Phi Beta Kappa, Phi Kappa Phi. Republican. Roman Catholic. Home: 11269 Silentwood Ln Reston VA 22091

STREMBITSKY, MICHAEL ALEXANDER, school administrator; b. Smoky Lake, Alta., Can., Mar. 5, 1935; s. Alec and Rose (Fedoretz) S.; m. Victoria Semeniuk, Aug. 12, 1954; children: Michael, William-John. BA, U. Alta., 1955, BEd, 1958; MA, Columbia U., 1968, MEd, 1972. With Edmonton (Alta.) pub. schs., now supt. of schs. Bd. dirs. Glenrose Hosp. Mem. Am. Assn. Sch. Adminstrs., Am. Mgmt. Assn., Am. Sch. Bus. Ofls., Assn. for Supr. and Curriculum Devel., Can. Assn. Sch. Adminstrs., Can. Coll. Tchrs., Can. Edn. Assn., Conf. Alba. Sch. Suptds. (exec.), Council Ednl. Facility Planners Internat., Edmonton C. of C., Edmonton-Harbin (China) Friendship Soc., Edmonton Edn. Soc., U. Alta. Faculty Edn. Alumni Assn., Large City Sch. Supts., Nat. Assn. Ednl. Negotiators, Nat. Assn. Elementary Sch. Prins., Nat. Ukranian Profl. Bus. Club, Phi Delta Kappa. Lodge: Rotary. Office: Edmonton Pub Schs, Ctr for Edn, 1 Kingsway, Edmonton, AB Canada T5H 4G9

STREMPEL, ULRICH, editor, political scientist; b. Kiel, Fed. Republic Germany, Dec. 8, 1953; s. Juergen and Erika Margarete Marie (Sander) S.; m. Lise AnnePerreault, Aug. 9, 1975 (div. Nov. 1979). B.A. (Honors), U. Alta., Edmonton, Can., 1975, Ph.D., 1982; M.A., Carleton U., Ottawa, Ont., Can., 1977. Lectr. polit. sci. U. Alta., 1979-80, 81-82; adminstrv. intern Commn. of European Communities, Brussels, 1977-78; research fellow German Soc. for Fgn. Affairs, Bonn, 1982-84; editor Press and Info. Office of German Govt., Bonn, 1984-86; sr. officer, Govt. spokesman's group, Press and Info. Office of German Govt., Bonn. Contbr. articles to jours. and books; translator articles and monographs on internat. politics. Mem. working group on European politics Christian Democratic Union, 1985—; v.p. Can. Wolf Defenders, Edmonton, 1980-81. Grad. scholar Carleton U., 1975-76; Dissertation fellow U. Alta., 1980-81. Mem. German Soc. for Canadian Studies, German-Can. Soc., Europa Union. Lutheran. Avocations: chess, tennis, fine automobiles. Home: Grossenbuschstrasse 18, D-5205 Saint Augustin 2 Federal Republic of Germany Office: Informationsamt Bundesregierung, Welckerstrasse 11, D-5300 Bonn Federal Republic of Germany

STRENSKI, ROBERT FRANCIS, lawyer; b. Chgo., Oct. 10, 1947; s. Bernard F. and Harriet L. (Prokopiak) S. BS, U. Ill., 1969; JD, Washington U., St. Louis, 1973; postgrad. U. Colo., 1975. Bar: Mo. 1973, Colo. 1974. Acct. Motorola, Inc., Chgo., 1970; acct. City and County of Denver, 1973-74, asst. city atty., 1974—. Precinct committeeman Denver Democratic Com., 1976-78, dist. fin. chmn., 1977-78; arbitrator Better Bus. Bur., Denver, 1977—; mediator Ctr. for Dispute Resolution, Denver, 1980. Mem. Colo. Bar Assn., Denver Bar Assn., Nat. Inst. Mcpl. Law Officers (ethics com. 1985-88), Am. Arbitration Assn. (arbitrator). Democrat. Roman Catholic. Home: 410 Pearl St Denver CO 80203 Office: Law Dept City & County Denver 353 City and County Bldg Denver CO 80202

STRESEN-REUTER, FREDERICK ARTHUR, II, communications executive; b. Oak Park, Ill., July 31, 1942; s. Alfred Procter and Carol Frances (von Pohek) S.-R.; cert. in German, Salzburg (Austria) Summer Sch., 1963; B.A., Lake Forest Coll., 1967. Mgr. advt. Stresen-Reuter Internat., Bensenville, Ill., 1965-70; mgr. animal products mktg. Internat. Minerals & Chem. Corp., Mundelein, Ill., 1971-79, dir. animal products mktg., 1979-87, dir. communications, 1987—; pres. Brit. Iron Ltd., Lake Forest, Ill., 1984-86; lectr. mktg. U. Ill., 1977, Am. Mgmt. Assn., 1978; cons. mktg. to numerous agrl. cos., 1973—. lectr. Trustee, governing mem. Library Internat. Relations, 1978, Chgo. Recipient cert. of excellence Chgo. 77 Vision Show, 1977; Silver Aggy award, 1977; spl. jury gold medal V.I., N.Y. Internat. film festival awards, 1977; CINE Golden Eagle, 1980; Bronze medal N.Y. Internat. Film Festival, 1981, Silver medal, 1982; Silver Screen award U.S. Indsl. Film Festival, 1981. Mem. Nat. Feed Ingredients Assn. (chmn. publicity and publs. 1976), Nat. Agrl. Mktg. Assn. (numerous awards), Am. Feed Mfrs. Assn. (citation 1976, public relations com., conv. com.), Nat. Agrl. Mktg. Assn., Mid-Am. Commodity Exchange, 1984-86, USCG Aux., U.S. Naval Inst., Am. Film Inst., Bugatti Owners Club. Episcopalian. Club: Sloane (London). Contbr. articles to profl. jours. Home: Tryon Grove Farm 8914 Tryon Grove Rd Ringwood IL 60072 Office: Pittman-Moore Inc 421 E Hawley St Mundelein IL 60060

STRICH, MICHEL HENRY, surgeon; b. Grenoble, France, July 12, 1937; s. Andre J. and Marie (De Pinos) S.; m. Christel Mougenot, Mar. 25, 1966; children—Gilles, Caroline, Eric, Odile. Dr. Medicine, U. Reims, 1971. Extern Paris Hosp., 1959; intern Reims Hosp., 1967, anatomy asst., 1968; chef de clinique U. Paris, 1971; asst. of Paris Hosp., 1971—; head dept. surgery Orsay's Hosp., 1978—. Contbr. articles to profl. jours. Recipient spl. prize Reims Hosp., 1967. Mem. Surgeons of Paris Orgn. (sec.-gen. 1971-75), Medicine Writers Soc. Roman Catholic. Avocation: tennis. Home: 27 Avenue de Paris, 94300 Vincennes France Office: Hopital d'Orsay, place du Gen Leclerc, 91400 Orsay France

STRICH-MOUGENOT, CHRISTEL MARIE YVONNE, obstetrician, oncologist; b. Angers, France, Oct. 23, 1939; d. Jean and Rosenonde (Bertin) Mougenot; m. Michel Strich, Mar. 25, 1966; children: Gilles, Caroline, Eric, Odile. MD, U. Rheims, France, 1971. Cert. in gynecology, obstetrics and onocology. Externe Hosp. U. Paris, 1961; intern Hosp. U. Reims, 1967, asst. anatomy, 1968; chef de clinique U. Paris, 1971; asst. Hosp. Paris, 1971, attache of oncologist, 1980. Contbr. articles to profl. jours. Mem. Soc. Francaise Ob-gyn., Soc. de Cancerologie Privée (mem. lecture com.). Roman Catholic. Home: 27 ave de Paris, 94300 Vincennes France Office: Hosp Salpetriere, Blvd d l'Hosp, Paris France

STRICKLAND, EUGENE LEE, ret. air force officer, business executive; b. Richland Springs, Tex., May 18, 1917; s. John Hester and Annie Laura (Brown) S.; asso. in sci. and civil engring., North Tex. Agrl. Coll., 1937; grad. Armed Forces Staff Coll., 1948, Air War Coll., 1951, Nat. War Coll., 1957; m. Marion Davis, Sept. 1, 1945; children—Eugene Lee, Donald W., Leslie Jo. Commd. 2d lt. USAAF, 1939, advanced through grades to brig. gen. USAF; various assignments, U.S. and China, 1939-47; ops. officer 20th Air Force, Okinawa, 1952-54; comdr. air def. wing McGuire AFB, N.J., 1954-56; with war plans div. USAF and Joint Chiefs Staff, 1957-60; comdr. 81st Tactical Fighter Wing, Eng., 1960-62; dep. comdr. 3d Air Force, London, 1962-63; chief Middle East, Africa, and South Asia region Office Sec. Def., 1963-65; dir. internat. staff Inter-Am. Def. Bd., 1965-67; vice comdr. 4th Air Force, Hamilton AFB, Calif., 1967-69; exec. v.p. HOMCARE (HCI) Internat., 1970—. Decorated Legion of Merit with oak leaf cluster, D.F.C. with oak leaf cluster, Air medal with oak leaf cluster, Air Force Commendation medal, Purple-Heart, numerous area and unit ribbons. Mem. Air Force Hist. Soc., Air Force Assn., 14th Air Force Assn. Methodist. Lion. Address: 4101 E San Miguel Phoenix AZ 85018

STRICKLAND, ROBERT LOUIS, building materials and allied products company executive; b. Florence, S.C., Mar. 3, 1931; s. Franz M. and Hazel (Eaddy) S.; m. Elizabeth Ann Miller, Feb. 2, 1952; children: Cynthia Anne, Robert Edson. AB, U. N.C., 1952; MBA with distinction, Harvard, 1957. With Lowe's Cos., Inc., North Wilkesboro, N.C., 1957—, sr. v.p., 1970-76, exec. v.p., 1976-78, chmn. bd., 1978—, mem. office pres., exec. com., 1970-78, also bd. dirs.; founder Sterling Advt., Ltd., 1966; v.p., mem. adminstrv. com. Lowe's Profit-Sharing Trust, 1961-87, chmn. ops. com., 1972-78; mem. mgmt. com. Lowe's ESOP plan, 1978; bd. dirs. Revelstoke Cos. Ltd., Calgary, Can., Summit Communications, Winston-Salem, N.C., 1987—; panelist investor relations field, 1972—; speaker, panelist employee stock ownership field, 1978—; speaker London Instnl. Investor Conf., 1980; speaker on investment relations, London, Edinburgh, Paris, Zurich, Frankfurt, Geneva, Vienna, Amsterdam, Brussels, 1980—. Author: Lowe's Cybernetwork, 1969, Lowe's Living Legend, 1970, Ten Years of Growth, 1971, The Growth Continues, 1972, 73, 74, Lowe's Scoreboard, 1978, also articles. Mem. N.C. Ho. Reps., 1962-64, Rep. Senatorial Inner Circle, 1980—; mem. exec. com. N.C. Rep. Com., 1963-73; trustee U. N.C. Chapel Hill, 1987—; dir. U.S. Council of Better Bus. Burs., 1981-85; bd. dirs., v.p. Nat. Home Improvement Council, 1972-76; bd. dirs. N.C. Sch. Arts Found., 1975-79, N.C. Bd. Natural and Econ. Resources, 1975-76; bd. dirs., mem. govt. affairs com. Home Ctr. Inst.; trustee, sec. bd. Wilkes Community Coll., 1964-73; chmn., pres. bd. dirs. Do-It-Yourself Research Inst., 1981—; pres. Hardware Home Improvement Council City of Hope Nat. Med. Ctr., Los Angeles, 1987—. Served with USN, 1952-55, lt. Res. 1955-62. Named Wilkes County N.C. Young Man of Yr., Wilkes Jr. C. of C., 1962; recipient Bronze Oscar of Industry award Fin. World, 1969-74, 76-79, Silver Oscar of Industry award, 1970, 72-74, 76-79, Gold Oscar of Industry award as best of all industry, 1972, 87, Excellence award in corp. reporting Fin. Analysts Fedn., 1970, 72, 74, 81-82, cert. of Distinction Brand Names Found., 1970, Retailer of Yr. award, 1971, 73, Disting. Mcht. award, 1972, Spirit of Life award City of Hope, 1983. Mem. Nat. Assn. Over-the-Counter Cos. (bd. advisers 1973-77), Newcomen Soc., Employee Stock Ownership Assn. (pres. 1983-85, chmn. 1985-87), Scabbard and Blade, Phi Beta Kappa, Pi Kappa Alpha. Clubs: Twin City, Forsyth Country (Winston-Salem, N.C.); Hound Ears (Blowing Rock, N.C.); Roaring Gap (N.C.); Elk River (Banner Elk, N.C.). Home: 226 N Stratford Rd Winston-Salem NC 27104 Office: Lowe's Cos Inc PO Box 1111 North Wilkesboro NC 28656

STRICKLAND, THOMAS JOSEPH, artist; b. Keyport, N.J., Dec. 27, 1932; s. Charles Edward and Clementine Maria (Grasso) S. Student, Newark Sch. Fine and Indsl. Arts, 1951-53, Am. Art Sch., 1956-59, Nat. Acad. Sch. Fine Arts with Robert Philipp, 1957-59. judge local and nat. art shows; television guest; instr. painting and pastels Grove House; lectr. Exhibited in one man shows at, Hollywood (Fla.) Art Mus., 1972-76, Elliott Mus., Stuart, Fla., 1974, others; exhibited in group shows at, Am. Artists Profl. League, N.Y.C., 1958, 61, Parke-Bernet Galleries, N.Y.C., 1959, 61, 64, Exposition Intercontinentale, Monaco, 1966-68, Salon Rouge du Casino Dieppe, 1967, 7e Grand Prix Internat. de Peinture de la Cote d'Azur, Cannes, 1971, Hollywood Art Mus., 1972-76, Art Guild of Boca Raton, 1973, Stagecoach Gallery, 1973, Am. Painters in Paris, 1975; represented in permanent collections, St. Vincent Coll., Elliott Mus., Martin County Hist. Soc., Hollywood Art Mus., Salem Coll., Winston-Salem, N.C., St. Hugh Catholic Ch., Fla.; (Recipient Digby Chandler prize Knickerbocker Artists 1965, Best in Show Blue Dome Art Fellowship 1972, 1st Place, Fine Arts League, La Junta, Colo. 1973, Blue Ribbon award Cape Coral Nat. Art Show 1973, 1st prize Hollywood Art Mus. 1973, Charles Hawthorne Meml. award Nat. Arts Club Exhbn. 1977, 1st prize Miami Palette Club 1978, others.); Contbr. articles to profl. jours. Served with AUS, 1953-55. Mem. Blue Dome Art Fellowship, Pastel Soc. Am., Nat. Soc. Lit. and Arts, Grove House, Miami Palette Club. Roman Catholic. Home: 2595 Taluga Dr Miami FL 33133

STRICKLIN, CARL SPENCER, manufacturing company executive; b. Baconton, Ga., Nov. 23, 1917; s. Daniel Spencer and Alberta (Clarkson) S.; B.S. in Bus. Adminstrn., certificate in fin., Boston U., 1950; m. Constance Allen, Aug. 26, 1949; 1 child, Sandra Lee. Clk. stock control Eastern Air Lines, Miami, Fla., 1947; auditor Ernst & Ernst, Boston, 1950-54; asst. bus. mgr. Mass. Bible Soc., Boston, 1954-64, bus. mgr., 1964-74, dir., 1974-77, editor Comment, semi-monthly publ., 1974-77; v.p. fin., controller Eastern Reprodn. Corp., Waltham, Mass., 1977-79; treas. Ivy Packet Co., Inc., Canton, Mass., 1980-84, pres., 1985-88, chief exec. officer, 1988—. Treas., trustee Daystar Found., Inc., non-profit retirement home, Needham, Mass. Served with Q.M.C., U.S. Army, 1942-46. Mem. Mass. Soc. C.P.A.'s., Mass. Assn. Pub. Accountants, Nat. Soc. C.P.A.'s, Aircraft Owners and Pilots Assn., Norwood Aviation Club, Young Man's Christian Union Camera Club (treas.). Republican. Lodges: Masons, Shriners, Rotary (treas. Needham). Home and Office: 1019 Webster St Needham MA 02192

STRIDSBERG, ALBERT BORDEN, advertising specialist, editor; b. Wyoming, Ohio, July 22, 1929; s. Carl Alexander Herbert and Edith Vivian (Farley) S. BA with honors, Yale U., 1950; Diploma D'Etudes France, U. of Poitiers, Tours, France, 1951; postgrad., Am. U. Beirut, Lebanon, 1953-54; diploma, Direct Mktg. Inst. Copywriter Howard Swink Advt., Inc., Marion, Ohio, 1955 58; acct. supr. McCann Erickson, Co., Brussels, 1956-60, J. Walter Thompson Co., Amsterdam, The Netherlands, 1960-63; asst. to internat. exec. v.p. J. Walter Thompson Co., N.Y.C., 1963-67, internat. cons. spl. projects, acquisitions and diversifications, 1969-73; cons., coordinator Internat. Markets Advt. Agy., Inc., N.Y., London, 1967-69; editor-in-chief Advt. World mag., N.Y.C., 1975-77; lectr. in mktg. NYU, N.Y.C., 1978-84; lectr. in advt. Marist Coll., Poughkeepsie, N.Y., 1984—; U.S. corr. Media Internat. Mag., London, 1984—; adj. assoc. prof. NYU, 1966-78; ind. cons., free lance writer on advt. and mktg. issues, N.Y.C., 1973—. Author: Effective Advertising Self-Regulation, 1974, Progress Toward Advertising Self-Regulation, 1976, Controversy Advertising, 1977, Advertising Self-Regulation, 1980; editor N.Y. features Media Internat. mag., 1988; actor with Tricolor Theatre, Washington, 1952-54, Arcadian Players, Beirut, 1953-54. Choir dir. Episcopal Chs., Beirut, Brussels. Served as cpl. U.S. Army, 1951-53. Fulbright fellow U.S. Dept. of State, U. Poitiers, 1950-51, Ford Found. fellow, Beirut, 1953-54. Mem. Internat. Advt. Assn. (cons., project coordinator 1974-80), Am. Mktg. Assn., Product Devel. and Mgmt. Assn., Advt. Research Found., Direct Mktg. Assn., Am. Acad. Advt. Democrat. Episcopalian. Clubs: Yale (N.Y.C.), Elizabethan (New Haven). Home and Office: Media Internat Mag 28 S Clover St Poughkeepsie NY 12601

STRIEM, KAARL JAVIER, retail executive; b. Panama, Mar. 1, 1961; s. Haiman Lewin and Luz Gladys (Montero) S.; m. Mirna Mercedes Diaz de Striem, Apr. 9, 1966; 1 child, Jan Kaarl. BS, Ga. Inst. Tech., 1978. V.p. Tropicana Group, Panama, 1980-84; pres., gen. mgr. Karlestri S.A., Panama, 1984—; pres. Craftouch, Inc., Miami, Fla., 1987—; cons., Grupo Tropicana, 1980. negotiator Bilateral Treaties, Panama-Cen. Am., 1980; sub. dir. Users Assn. Colon Free Zone, Panama-Cen. Am., 1985-87. Mem. Assn. Furniture Mfrs. (dir. 1980), Chilean Indsl. Exposition, Brazilian Export Assn. Home: 14317 SW 62d St Miami FL 33183 Office: Craftouch Inc 9206 NW 106th St Medley FL 33178

STRIGNANO, JOSEPH ROBERT, architect; b. N.Y.C., June 25, 1932; m. Penny Strignano; 1 child, Barbara. B.Arch., Pratt Inst., 1952, B.Indsl. Design, 1958. Staff designer Nemirow Corp, N.Y.C., 1955-57, Gampel-Stoll Inc., 1957-58; v.p. design State Pavillion, N.Y.C., 1958-59; pres. Longacre Furniture Corp., N.Y.C., 1959-69; pres. J.R. Strignano & Assocs. Inc., N.Y.C., 1970-84. Recently created new collection of home furnishings for Concinnity div. I.W. Industries, Melville, N.Y. Office: JR Strignano and Assocs 300 E 59th St New York NY 10022

STRIMBU, VICTOR, JR., lawyer; b. New Philadelphia, Ohio, Nov. 25, 1932; s. Victor and Veda (Stancu) S.; m. Kathryn May Schrote, Apr. 9, 1955; children—Victor Paul, Michael, Julie, Sue. B.A., Heidelberg Coll., 1954; postgrad. Western Res. U., 1956-57; LL.B., Columbia U., 1960. Bar: Ohio 1960, U.S. Supreme Ct. 1972. With Baker & Hostetler, Cleve., 1960—, ptnr., 1970—. Mem. Bay Village (Ohio) Bd. Edn., 1976-84, pres., 1977-81; mem. Cleve. State U. Indsl. Relations Adv. Com., 1979—, chmn., 1982; mem. Bay Village Planning Commn., 1967-69; life mem. Ohio PTA; mem. Greater Cleve. Growth Assn.; bd. of trustees New Cleve. Campaign, 1987—. Served as pfc AUS, 1955-56. Recipient Service award Cleve. State U., 1980. Mem. Ohio Bar Assn., ABA, Greater Cleve. Bar Assn., Ohio Newspaper Assn. (minority affairs com. 1987—). Republican. Presbyterian. Clubs: Order of Nisi Prius, Cleve. Athletic. Office: Baker & Hostetler 3200 Nat City Ctr Cleveland OH 44114

STRINGER, DONALD HALL, insurance company executive; b. Brookhaven, Miss., Aug. 13, 1938; s. Flavil Hall and Ella V. (Bowman) S.; B.A., Harding Coll., Searcy, Ark., 1967; m. Betty Lee Cox, Nov. 30, 1973; children—Caroline, Kip, Colleen, Clint. Vice pres. Shannon Supply Co., Clinton, Ark., 1961-65; sci. tchr. Bradford (Ark.) public schs., 1967-68; group rep. Conn. Gen. Life Ins. Co., Houston, 1969-74; regional group mgr. Home Life Ins. Co., New Orleans, 1974-79, Dallas, 1979-82; founder, prin. Stringer & Assocs., ins. brokerage agy., Dallas, 1982-87, prin. G.S. Cons. Mem. pres.'s devel. council Harding Coll., 1974—; mem. Congressman Livingston's ins. and pension adv. com., 1978. Served with U.S. Army, 1959-65. Named Mgr. of Year, Home Life Ins. Co., 1977. Mem. Peruvian Paso Horse Registry of N.Am., Life Underwriters Assn., Nat. Health Underwriters Assn., Am. Assn. Owners and Breeders of Peruvian Paso Horses, Palomino Horse Owners and Breeders Assn., Palomino Horse Assn., Mensa. Republican. Mem. Ch. of Christ. Home: Route 2 Box 1005 Sanger TX 76266 Office: 1807 N Elm A124 Denton TX 76201

STRINGER, WILLIAM JEREMY, university official; b. Oakland, Calif., Nov. 8, 1944; s. William Duane and Mildred May (Andrus) S.; BA in English, So. Meth. U., 1966; MA in English, U. Wis., 1968, PhD in Ednl. Adminstrn., 1973; m. Susan Lee Hildebrand; children: Shannon Lee, Kelly Erin, Courtney Elizabeth. Dir. men's housing Southwestern U., Georgetown, Tex., 1968-69; asst. dir. housing U. Wis., Madison, 1969-73; dir. residential life, asso. dean student life, adj. prof. Pacific Luth., Tacoma, 1973-78; dir. residential life U. So. Calif., 1978-79, asst. v.p., 1979-84, asst. prof. higher and post-secondary edn., 1980-84; v.p. student life Seattle U., 1984—. Bd. dirs. N.W. area Luth. Social Services of Wash. and Idaho. Danforth Found. grantee, 1976-77. Mem. Am. Assn. Higher Edn., Nat. Assn. Student Personnel Adminstrs. (bd. dirs. region V), Am. Personnel and Guidance Assn., Phi Eta Sigma, Sigma Tau Delta, Phi Alpha Theta. Lutheran. Author: How to Survive as a Single Student, 1972; The Role of the Assistant in Higher Education, 1973. Home: 4553 169th Ave SE Issaquah WA 98027 Office: Seattle U Seattle WA 98122

STRINGFELLOW, JOHN, coal company executive; b. Rotherham, Yorkshire, Eng., Mar. 6, 1951; s. James Thomas and Dorothy Emilly (Mosely) S.; m. Rita Marilyn Pepper, Mar. 15, 1969; children: Marianne, Julia, Neil, Jon. Grad. process, mktg. and distbn. program, Harvard U., 1985; ONC in Civil Engring., Chesterfield Tech. Coll., 1973. Cert. Civil Engr. Engr., surveyor No. Strip Mining Ltd., Sheffield, Eng., 1970-75, site mgr., 1975-79, ops. mgr., 1979-81, prodn. dir., 1985—; v.p., ops., dir. Minicorp Inc., Somerset, Pa., 1981-85. Home: 1 St Andrews Rise, Walton Hall, Chesterfield, Derbyshire S40 3NJ, England Office: Northern Strip Mining Ltd, Minicorp House Carlton Rd, Worksop Nottinghamshire S81 7QF, England

STRITTMATTER, FREDERIC HENRY, banker; b. Lausanne, Switzerland, Sept. 1, 1953; s. Auguste Christian and Elisabeth Marguerite (Huber) S.; m. Myriam Nina Riat; children: Diane, Lactitia, Albane. MBA, Ecole HEC, Lausanne, 1979. Salesman Burroughs Co., Lausanne, 1979-80; mgr. sales NCR Corp., Lausanne, 1980-81; regional mgr. Tex. Instruments Corp., Lausanne, 1981-85; mgr. European sales ATS Co., Lausanne, 1985; orgn. mgr. Compagnie Financiere Espirito Santo, Lausanne, 1985—. Contbr. articles to profl. jours. V.p. Liberal Party, 1978-82. Home: La Chesaudaz, 1606 Forel Vaud Switzerland

STROBL, BERND KARL, civil engineer; b. Graz, Austria, June 26, 1953; s. Karl Friedrich and Edeltraud (Gaulhofer) S.; m. Maria Martina Eder, Nov. 10, 1966. Diploma in Engring. Tech., Tech. U., Graz, 1979. Supr. Energy Supply Auth. Kelag, Klagenfurt, Austria, 1972-78; project mgr. Pacher Cons. Co., Munich, 1979-82, Salzburg, Austria, 1982-85; dir. Geotechnik and Tunnelbau Cons. Engrs., Vienna, Austria, 1985-88; ind. cons. Vienna, 1988—; research proj. mgr. Inst. Soil Mechanics, Rock Mechanics and Found. Engring., Tech. U., Graz, 1986—. Mem. Chamber Austrian Profl. Engrs., Internat. Soc. Geomechanics, Austrian Soc. Traffic and Rd. Research. Roman Catholic. Home: Ferrogasse 71, A-1180 Vienna Austria Office: Geotechnik & Tunnelbau, Cons Engrs, Goethegasse 3/DG, A-1010 Vienna Austria

STRODE, JOSEPH ARLIN, lawyer; b. DeWitt, Ark., Mar. 5, 1946; s. Thomas Joseph and Nora (Richardson) S.; m. Carolyn Taylor, Feb. 9, 1969; children—Tanya Briana, William Joseph. B.S.E.E. with honors, U. Ark., 1969; J.D., So. Meth. U., 1972. Bar: Ark. 1972. Design engr. Tex. Instruments Inc., Dallas, 1969-70, patent agt., 1970-72; assoc. Bridges, Young, Matthews, Holmes & Drake, Pine Bluff, Ark., 1972-74, ptnr., 1975—. Bd. dirs. United Way Jefferson County, Pine Bluff, 1975-77, campaign chmn., 1983, pres., 1986, exec. com., 1983-87; bd. dirs. Leadership Pine Bluff, 1983-85. Mem. ABA, Ark. Bar Assn., Jefferson County Bar Assn., Pine Bluff C. of C. (dir. 1981-84), Ark. Wildlife Fed. (dir. 1979-81), Jefferson County Wildlife Assn. (dir. 1973-80, pres. 1974-76), Order of Coif, Tau Beta Pi, Eta Kappa Nu. Club: Kiwanis (lt. gov. Mo.-Ark. div. 1983-84, chmn. lt. govs. 1983-84). Home: Route 9 Box 908 Pine Bluff AR 71603 Office: 315 E 8th St PO Box 7808 Pine Bluff AR 71611

STROESSNER, ALFREDO, president of Paraguay, retired army officer; b. 1912. Ed. Mil. Coll., Asuncion. Formerly army chief of staff; took over govtl. authority in Paraguay upon resignation in May 1954, of Frederico Chavez who had been pres. since 1949; assumed office of pres., Aug. 15, 1954, pres. for life, 1977—. Address: Casa Presidencial, Avenida Mariscal Lopez, Asuncion Paraguay *

STROH, OSCAR HENRY, agricultural engineer; b. Harrisburg, Pa., Jan. 11, 1908; s. Simon Henry and Alice (Feaser) S.; B.S., U. Fla., 1948; grad. Command and Gen. Staff Coll., 1944, Armed Forces Indsl. Coll., 1954; Ph.D. in History, Internat. Inst. Advanced Studies, 1979; m. Geraldine Bradshaw, Dec. 18, 1936; children—Jon Robert, Dana Evelyn. Ofcl. photographer U. Fla., 1938-40; civil engr. U.S. Govt., 1952-67, Commonwealth of Pa., 1967-73; cons. engr., Harrisburg, 1973—. Pa. forest fire warden, 1931-71. Bd. dirs. Central Dauphin Sch. System, 1953-65; bd. govs. Daniel Boone Nat. Found., Birdsboro, Pa., 1969-83, Fishing Creek Valley Community Assn., 1949—; v.p. Am. Coll. Heraldry. Served to lt. col. AUS, 1940-47, 50-52; Korea. Named grand Prior Order St. John of Jerusalem, Knights Hospitallers; Knight grand cross Order St. Eugene de Trebizonde; Knight Grand Cross Byzantine Order Holy Sepulchre. Registered profl. engr., Pa., Vt. Mem. Nat. Soc. Profl. Engrs., Constrn. Specifications Inst., Co. Mil. Historians, Assn. Former Intelligence Officers, Palatines to Am. (past pres. Pa. chpt.), Mil. Order Fgn. Wars, SAR (pres.), Mil. Order World Wars, U.S. Horse Cavalry Assn. (charter). Lodge: Masons (32 deg.). Club: Sojourners. Author: Thompson's Battalion, 1975; Paxton Rangers; Pennsylvania German Tombstone Inscriptions, Vols. I, II; Dauphin County Tombstone Inscriptions, Vols. I-III; Heraldry in the U.S. Army; Story of the Hospitaller Order of St. John of Jerusalem: The Last Combat Sword of the American Army; Bugle Calls and Pistol Shots. Contbr. biweekly hist. column Paxton Herald, 1973-78. Home and Office: 1531 Fishing Creek Valley Rd Harrisburg PA 17112

STROH, WILLIAM HENRY, III, biotechnology and chemical management executive, consultant; b. N.Y.C., Feb. 11, 1937; came to W.Ger., 1972; s. William H. and Maria (Eger) S. M.S. in Chemistry, NYU, 1962, M.B.A., 1972. Prodn. specialist Agfa-Gevaert, Teterboro, N.J., 1963-65; asst. v.p. Aceto Chem., N.Y.C., 1965-67; group leader DuPont, Conn., 1967-70; mgr. planning and analysis W. R. Grace Co., Heidelberg, W.Ger., 1972-85; pres., chief exec. officer Bio-Consult, Berlin-Frankfurt, W.Ger., 1985—. Recipient Gold medal City U. Alumni Assn., 1962. Mem. Phi Lambda Upsilon, Zeta Psi (pres. 1960-62). Clubs: Union Internat. (Frankfurt); Baskerville Soc. (N.Y.C.) (pres. 1962). Home and Office: Bruder-Grimm Str 32, D-6000 Frankfurt 60 Federal Republic of Germany

STROJNY, MARIANO, clergyman; b. Bnin, Poland, Nov. 20, 1906; s. Mieczyslaw and Wloczewski (Boleslawa) S.; student U. Krakow, 1927-31; D.C.L., Lateran U., Rome, 1935. Ordained priest Roman Catholic Ch., 1931, monsignor, 1949; parish priest, Katowice, Chorzow, Poland, 1935, 37-38; dir. Pontifical Missions Works, 1937-39; notary Diocesan Tribunal Katowice, 1938-39; advocate Sacred Roman Rota, Rome, 1939-43; judge 1st Instance Tribunal Vicariate Rome, 1943-54, Tribunal Appeal Vicariate Rome, 1954-77; rector Pontifical Polish Coll., Rome, 1945-48, Pontifical Polish Inst., 1949-58; consultor Sacred Congregation for Oriental Ch., 1947-

73; comm. and consultor Sacred Congregation for Sacraments, 1940—; consultor of commn. Preparatory for Eastern Ch. Vatican Council, 1961-62; advocate Sacred Congregation Holy Office, 1966-72; procurator Sacred Congregation Causes of Beatification and Canonization of Saints, 1954—; mem. Supreme Tribunal Signatura Apostolica, 1960-85, Commn. for Sacred Congregation Doctrine of the Faith, 1960—; canon Patriarchal Archbasilica St. John Lateran, 1963—. Apostolic Supernumerary Protonotary, 1963—; corr. mem. European Acad. Arts, Scis. and Humanities, Paris, 1987—. Editor: Pius XII: In Memoriam, 1984. Recipient Anno Mariano silver medal from Pope Pius XII, 1954, Silver cup for sculpture Internat. Prize Arte Pro Arte Rome, 1972; Prix du Musée National at 13th internat. Grand Prix competition, Monte Carlo, 1978; decorated Order Polonia Restituta, 1963, 66. Sculptor Chopin, Rome, Marie Sklodowska Curie, Rome. Address: Casella Post, 9019 Aurelio, Rome 00165 Italy

STROKE, GEORGE WILHELM, physicist, educator; b. Zagreb, Yugoslavia, July 29, 1924; came to U.S., 1952, naturalized, 1957; s. Elias and Edith Mechner (Silvers) S.; m. Masako Haraguchi, Feb. 5, 1973. B.Sc., U. Montpellier, France, 1942; Ing.Dipl., Inst. Optics, U. Paris, 1949; Dr. ès Sci. in Physics, Sorbonne U., Paris, 1960. Mem. research staff and def. research staff MIT, 1952-63, lectr. elec. engring., 1960-63; asst. research prof. physics Boston U., 1956-57; NATO research fellow U. Paris, 1959-60; prof. elec. engring., head electro-optical sci. labs. U. Mich., 1963-67; prof. elec. scis. and med. biophysics SUNY-Stony Brook, 1967-79; mem. corp. mgmt. staff Messerschmitt-Bolkow-Blohm GmbH, Munich, W. Ger., 1980-84, chief scientist space div., 1984-86, chief scientist, Corp. Hdqrs.-Devel., 1986—; vis. prof. Harvard U. Med. Sch., 1970-73, Tech. U. Munich, 1978—; adviser laser task force USAAF Systems Command, 1964; govt. sci. cons. U.S. and abroad, 1964—; cons. NASA Electronics Research Ctr., Cambridge, Mass., 1966—; mem. commn. I, Internat. Radio Sci. Union, Nat. Acad. Scis., 1965—; cons. Am. Cancer Soc., 1972—; mem. NSF blue ribbon task force on ultrasonic imaging, 1973-74; mem. U.S. Ho. of Reps. Select Com., photog. evidence panel on Pres. J. F. Kennedy's assasination, 1978-79. MBB Corp. mem. Max-Planck Soc., 1982—; bd. dirs. Max-Planck Soc. Inst. Quantum Optics, 1986—. Recipient Humboldt prize, 1978. Fellow Optical Soc. Am., Am. Phys. Soc., IEEE. Contbr. articles to profl. jours. Author: An Introduction to Coherent Optics and Holography, 1966. Address: Messereschmitt-Bolkow-Blohm, GmbH Corp Hdqrs, Postfach 801169, D-8000, Munich 80 Federal Republic of Germany

STROM, BJORN GUNNAR ELOF, lawyer, rental company executive; b. Atvidaberg, Ostergotland, Sweden, Apr. 25, 1934; s. Elof Josef Fridolf and Svea Teresia (Olsson) S.; m. Ragnhild Astrid Anne-Marie Salskog, Oct. 6, 1957; 1 child, Catharina. M of Law, U. Stockholm, 1959. Bar: Sweden. Asst. justice, Civic Ct. Stockholm, 1959-62; mgr. Swedish Employers' Confedn., Stockholm, 1962-73, v.p., 1973-87; mng. dir. Swedish Fedn. Rental Property Owners, Kungsgatan, 1987—. Author: Gruppliv, 1963, Produktivt Samarbete, 1967, Langtidsuppdrag i Utlandet, 1976, Korttidsuppdrag I Utlandet, 1977, Utlandstjanst, 1981. Conservative. Lutheran. Home: Ekbackevagen 2, S 18146 Lidingo Sweden Office: Swedish Fedn Property Owners, Kungsgatan 29 Box 1707, S-11187 Stockholm Sweden

STROM, STAFFAN EINAR GUNNAR, physicist; b. Göteborg, Sweden, Sept. 14, 1934. MEE, Chalmers Inst. Tech., Göteborg, 1959, licentiate tech., 1963, D in Tech., 1967. Research assoc. dept. Theoretical physics, Chalmers Inst. Tech., 1959-69, docent, 1970-82, sr. research scientist, 1982-84; prof. electromagnetic theory Sch. Elec. Engring. Royal Inst. Tech., Stockholm, 1984—; vice-chmn. Swedish Nat. Com. Ursi, 1987—; chmn. Commn. B Swedish Nat. Com. Ursi, 1987—. Contbr. numerous articles to profl. jours. Mem. Soc. Indsl. Applied Math., Internat. Assn. Math. Physicists. Office: Royal Inst Tech, S-10044 Stockholm Sweden

STROMBERG, BJORN ARTHUR, publisher; b. Linkoping, Sweden, Oct. 23, 1935; s. Jean Arthur and Birgitta Margareta (Soderblom) S.; m. Gunilla Dennert, Oct. 24, 1970 (div. May 1972); m. Eva Cecilia Fagerstedt, Mar. 21, 1975; children: Eva Charlotte, Bjorn Thomas. Student San Francisco State Coll., 1961, U. Calif.-Berkeley, 1963, Ctr. d'Etude Industrielle, Geneva, 1968. Sales rep. San Francisco Progress, 1961-63; account exec. Lintas AB, Stockholm, 1963-65; adminstrv. dir. Industria, Stockholm, 1965-68; promotion mgr. Readers Digest, Stockholm, 1968-71; mktg. mgr. Byggforlaget, Stockholm, 1971-79; pub. BasPress Pub., Stockholm, 1979—. Author: How to Select Tradepress, 1975, 82. Conservative. Clubs: USA (pres. 1968-71), Swedish Am. Soc. (master 1971-78). Office: Modern Adminstrn Baspress Forlags, AB Brunnsgatan 9, 172 25 Sundbyberg Sweden

STROMGAARD, PETER, geographer, educator; b. Copenhagen, July 9, 1951; s. Svend Boje Stenholt and Ruth (Christiansen) S.; m. Dorte Ehlers, Apr. 27, 1984; children: Christian Sofus, Sofie Kirstine. BS in Geography and Biology, U. Copenhagen, 1974, MS in Geography, 1977, PhD in Geography, 1983. Officer provincial land use planning Dept. Agr., Zambia, 1978-80; acting coordinator Integrated Rural Devel. Program, Zambia, 1979-80; research fellow Inst. Geography, U. Copenhagen, 1980-86, assoc. prof., 1987—, chmn. study bd., 1985-87; chmn. study bd. Ctr. for African Studies, 1986-87; researcher field work Danish Agy. for Devel. Aid, Zambia, 1981, 85, 87, cons. soil and water resource, 1986; cons. land use planning, smallholder devel. scheme study European Devel. Fund/Cowiconsult, Cons. Engrs. and Planners, Copenhagen, 1985. Co-author: Introduction to Ecological Geography, 1987. Mem. Geografforbundet (editor jour. 1985—), Royal Danish Geog. Soc., Zambia Geog. Assn., Assn. Tropical Biology (mem. editorial bd. Biotropica jour.). Home: Gothersgade 156A 2th, 1123 Copenhagen Denmark Office: U Copenhagen Inst Geography, Oster Voldgade 10, 1350 Copenhagen Denmark

STROMHOLM, STIG FREDRIK, lawyer, educator; b. Boden, Sweden, Sept. 16, 1931; s. Fredrik and Gerda (Janson) S.; m. Gunilla Margareta Forslund, Aug. 9, 1958; children: Christina, Fredrik, Katarina. BA, Uppsala (Sweden) U., 1952, LLB, 1957, LLD, 1966; diploma in comparative law, Cambridge (Eng.) U., 1958; LLD, U. Munich, 1964; LLD (hon.), Lyons (France) U., 1980. Jr. judge Stockholm Ct. Appeals, 1961-66; lectr. Uppsala U., 1966-69, prof. law, 1969—, dean faculty law, 1973-79, vice rector, 1978—. Author various legal works, also fiction and criticisms. Served to capt. Swedish Army, 1968. Decorated comdr., officer and knight various orders. Mem. Royal Swedish Acad. Letters, History and Antiquities (pres. 1985—), Royal Uppsala Acad. Arts and Scis. (pres. 1979—). Lutheran. Club: Sällskapet (Stockholm). Home: Norra Rudbecktg 5, 75236 Uppsala Sweden Office: Juridicum Box 512, Riddartorgft 5, 75120 Uppsala Sweden

STRØMME, SIGMUND ELLING, publisher; b. Vardo, Norway, Apr. 8, 1923; s. Sigvard and Helga (Myhre) S.; m. Inger-Johanne Karset, Aug. 11, 1948; children—Stein Arild, Kristin, Harald. M.A., Univ. Oslo, 1949. Freelance journalist, lectr., translator, 1946-49; editor Tiden Norsk Forlag, Oslo, 1950-55; chief editor Cappelen Forlag A/S, Oslo, 1955-72, mng. dir., 1973-87, chmn. bd. dirs., 1987—. Pub. works on lit., publ., cultural affairs. Mem. Bd. Nat. Theatre, 1980—; v.p. Norwegian Nat. Commn., UNESCO, 1984—. Mem. Norwegian Pubs. Assn. (chmn. 1981-84), Scandinavian Pubs. Council, Internat. Pubs. Assn. (exec. com.), Council Norwegian Lang., Internat. PEN (v.p. Norway 1972-80). Home: 19 Vestbrynet, Oslo 11 Norway Office: Cappelen Forlag A/S, Kirkegatan 15, N-0153 Oslo 1 Norway

STRØMNES, FRODE JENS, psychologist; b. Trondenes, Norway, Jan. 4, 1937; s. Martin Olav Konrad and Petra Johanne (Lønning) S.; mag. art., Oslo U., 1963; fil. tri., Turun Yliopisto, 1971; m. Bjørg Imsland, 1 child, Gro; m. 2d, Liisa Helena Sulkakoski, 1968; children: Synniva, Hogne Martinus, Ingunn Loviisa. Lectr., Aarhus U., 1970; docent Åbo Akademi, 1972-75, 87—, acting prof. psychology, 1974; prof. psychology U. Tromsø, 1975—; dosentti Turun Yliopisto, 1976—. Active preservation old neighborhoods Turku, also ecology. Recipient grant Suomen Kulttuurirahasto, 1974; research fellow Norwegian Research Council, 1963-68, 71-74. Mem. Nordisk Sommeruniversitet, Nord. psykol. forskarförbund. Author: Prolegomena to a Theory of Semiotics, 1969; Associations or Addresses: A Study in Serial Verbal Learning, 1971; A New Physics of Inner Worlds, 1976; contbr. to profl. jours.; research on verbal learning. Home: Isbjornvg 8, N-9020 Tromsdalen Norway also: Huvilla No 10, Ruissalo, SF-20100 Turku 10 Finland Office: Institutt for Samfunnsvitenskap, Universitetet i Tromsø, N-9001 Tromsø Norway

STRÖMSTEDT, BO EUGEN, editor; b. Vasa, Finland, May 4, 1929; s. Harald and Hildur (Helin) S.; m. Margareta Henriksson, Jan. 3, 1953; children: Niklas, Lotten. B.A., U. Lund, 1950. Lit. critic Expressen, Stockholm, 1952-60, editor of arts, 1961-76, editor-in-chief, 1977—; bd. dirs. Dagens Nyheter AB, Stockholm, 1977—. Author essays on lit. and journalism. Recipient Gt. Journalistprize Åhlen & Åkerlunds Förlag, 1976. Office: Expressen, 105 16 Stockholm Sweden

STRONE, MICHAEL JONATHAN, lawyer; b. N.Y.C., Feb. 26, 1953; s. Bernard William and Judith Semel (Sogg) S.; m. Andrea Nan Acker, Jan. 27, 1979; 1 child, Noah Gregory. B.A. cum laude, Colby Coll., 1974; J.D., Fordham Law Sch., 1978. Bar: N.J. 1978, N.Y. 1979, U.S. Ct. Appeals (2d and 3d cirs.) 1979, U.S. Dist. Ct. (so. and ea. dists.) N.Y. 1979, U.S. Dist. Ct. N.J. 1979. Assoc. Ratheim Hoffman et al, N.Y.C., 1978-80, Botein Hays et al, N.Y.C., 1980-84; v.p., assoc. gen. counsel Gen. Electric Investment Corp., 1984—; v.p., gen. counsel Gindoff Enterprises Inc., 1985—. Bd. dirs. N.Y. chpt. Juvenile Diabetes Found., N.Y.C., 1981—, vice chmn., 1981-88; mem. fin. com. Juvenile Diabetes Found. Internat., 1981-86; asst. prin. bassist Westchester Symphony Orch., Scarsdale, N.Y., 1982, pres., 1982-87, chmn. bd., 1982—; vice-chmn. ann. dinner NCCJ, 1987. Mem. ABA (ERISA and significant legis. coms. 1985—, chmn. subcom. on joint ventures 1988—). Republican. Jewish. Home: Genesee Trail Harrison NY 10528 Office: Gen Electric Investment Corp 292 Long Ridge Rd Stamford CT 06904

STRONG, BETHANY JUNE, novelist, publisher, editor; b. Oklahoma City, June 13, 1906; d. Nicholas Henry and Anna Augusta (Spuhler) McLaughlin; m. John Donovan Strong, Sept. 2, 1928; children: Patricia, Virginia. BS in History of Ideas, Johns Hopkins U., 1966. Novelist, freelance writer, pub., editor Parable Press, Amherst, Mass., 1978—; cons. in field. Author: The King's Generalissima, 1976, First Love, 1978, Murder in the Mirror, 1985; also articles. Mem. Nat. Writers Club, Nat. League Am. Pen Women (pres. Conn. Valley br.). Roman Catholic. Avocation: photography.

STRONG, DOUGLAS MICHAEL, science administrator; b. Newport, Wash., Sept. 4, 1941; s. George Leslie Strong and Dorothea Gwenyth (Rednour) Foulkes; m. Geraldine Anne O'Melveny, Jan. 30, 1965; children: Michael Phillip, David Richard, Patricia Anne. BS, Gonzaga U., 1963; cert. med. technician, Sacred Heart Sch. Med. Tech., Spokane, Wash., 1964; PhD, Med. Coll. Wis., 1973. Commd. ensign USN, 1965, advanced through grades to comdr., 1977, ret., 1985; v.p. diagnostic research and devel. Genetic Systems, Seattle, 1985-88; dir. NW Tissue Ctr, 1988—; cons. Alta. (Can.) Govt., Edmonton, 1978-82, Pa. Regional Tissue and Transplant Bank, Scranton, 1978—, Controlled Chems., Inc., Ann Arbor, Mich., 1985—, Armed Forces Radiobiology Research Inst., Bethesda, Md., 1982-85, Genetic Systems, Seattle, 1982-85, Biotope, Seattle, 1982-85, Cellular Immunotherapy, Tucson, 1982-85; prof. dept surgery uniformed services U. Health Sci., 1978-85, dept. orthopedics U. Wash. Sch. Medicine, 1988—. Contbr. articles to profl. jours.; mem. numerous jour. editorial bds.; trumpet and guitar player in ch. choirs and numerous musical groups. Coach soccer Wheaton Boy's Club, Montgomery United Soccer Club, Montgomer County, Md., 1976-84, Rockville United Soccer Club. Recipient commendations Nat. Jud. Coll., Nat. Inst. Justice, Nat. Conf. Spl. Ct. Judges, Nat. Orgn. for Victims Assistance, Montgomery County Police Tng. Acad., Walter Reed Army Med. Ctr. Mem. AAAS, Am. Assn. Tissue Banks (Insp. Acceditation Com., 1988—), Am. Assn. Immunology, Internat. Inst. Refrigeration (sec. council U.S. 1976—), Soc. Cryobiology (sec. 1975-76), Am. Soc. Hist. Immunogenetics (standards com. 1986), Clin. Immunol. Soc. Roman Catholic. Home: 18624 94th Ave W Edmonds WA 98102 Office: Puget Sound Blood Ctr 921 Terry Ave Seattle WA 98104

STRONG, EARL POE, educator; b. Loundonville, Ohio, June 19, 1910; s. Otto and Luellen (Bassett) S.; B.A., Rider Coll., 1930; B.S., Indiana U. Pa., 1934; M.A., Ohio State U., 1937; Ed.D., NYU, 1943; m. Mildred Julius, June 15, 1937; 1 dau., Lou Ellen. Dep. collector in control sect. U.S. Treasury Dept., Cleve., 1930-32; tchr., head comml. dept. Manasquan (N.J.) High Sch., 1934-37; instr. bus. Coll. Commerce, U. Iowa, 1937-40; teaching fellow bus. edn. Sch. Edn., NYU, 1939-40; head D.C. Dept. Bus. in Pub. Schs., 1940-41; sr. tng. cons. CSC, Washington, 1941-42, dir. exec. devel. programs, 1952; research agt. in bus. edn. Vocat. Edn. Div., U.S. Office Edn., Washington, 1942-45; dir. utilization dept. Remington Rand, Inc., N.Y.C., 1946-48, cons. mgmt. problems, 1946-52; prof. mgmt., dir. bus. mgmt. service Coll. Commerce and Bus. Adminstrn., U. Ill.-Urbana, 1948-52 (pioneer in orgn. mgmt. aids and adv. service as univ. ednl. program of direct aid businessmen); prof. mgmt., asst. dean, dir. exec. devel. Coll. Bus. Adminstrn., Pa. State U., 1954-70, prof. emeritus, 1970—; prof. mgmt., dir. bur. bus. and govt. services, dir. exec. devel. programs Temple U., 1971-72, prof. emeritus, 1972; co-founder, dir. Gibraltar Inst., Buffalo, 1974—, pres., dean faculty, 1976; acad. dean S. Hills Bus. Sch., State College, Pa., 1979—, dir., 1979-81, dir. emeritus, 1981—; lectr. pub. adminstrn., Am. U., 1952-53; instr. evening and summer sessions Sch. Edn., U. Md., 1940-41; instr. bus. edn. and research adv. in bus. edn. Tchrs. Coll., Columbia U., 1941; instr. grad. sch. Dept. Agr., Washington, 1941-43; lectr. mgmt. and exec. devel. Coll. Prodn. Tech., Ashford, Eng., 1956-63; dir., seminar lectr. C.R. Poensgen-Stiftung, C.R. Poensgen-Kreis, Dusseldorf, W.Ger., 1970, 71, 72; seminar lectr. Greek Mgmt. Assn., Athens, 1972, Turkish Mgmt. Assn., Istanbul, 1972, Centro Jalisciense de Productividad, Guadalajara, Mex., 1971, 72, 73. Served as comdr. USNR, 1943-46. Fellow Coll. Prodn. Tech.; mem. Am. Mgmt. Assn., AAUP, Soc. Personnel Adminstrn., Delta Sigma Pi, Kappa Delta Pi, Pi Omega Pi, Gamma Rho Tau, Phi Sigma Pi, Phi Delta Kappa. Republican. Presbyn. Mason (32 deg.). Author or co-author textbooks and manuals on bus. mgmt. (books translated into Japanese, Arabic, Spanish, and Dutch). Home: 1337 S Garner St State College PA 16801 Office: Pa State U Bus Adminstrn Bldg Room 307B University Park PA 16802

STRONG, GEORGE GORDON, JR., litigation and management consultant; b. Toledo, Apr. 19, 1947; s. George Gordon and Jean Boyd (McDougall) S.; m. Annsley Palmer Chapman, Nov. 30, 1974; children: George III, Courtney, Meredith, Alexis. BA, Yale U., 1969; MBA, Harvard U., 1971; JD, U. San Diego, 1974. Bar: Calif. 1974, U.S. Dist. Ct. (cen. dist.) Calif. 1974; CPA, Calif., Hawaii, cert. mgmt. cons., U.S. customs house broker. Controller Vitredent Corp., Beverly Hills, Calif., 1974-76; sr. mgr. Price Waterhouse, Los Angeles, 1976-82, ptnr., 1987—; exec. v.p., chief operating officer Internat. Customs Service, Long Beach, Calif., 1982-84; chief fin. officer Uniform Software Systems, Santa Monica, Calif., 1984-85; exec. v.p. and chief operating officer Cipherlink Corp., 1986; pres. Woodleigh Lane, Inc., Flintridge, Calif., 1985-87; ptnr. Price Waterhouse, 1987—. Active Verdugo Hills Hosp. Adv. Council, Glendale, Calif., 1985. Mem. ABA, Calif. State Bar Assn., Los Angeles County Bar Assn., Am. Inst. CPA's, Calif. Soc. CPA's, Inst. of Mgmt. Cons., Harvard Bus. Sch. Assn. So. Calif. (v.p. 1986-87, pres. 1988—). Republican. Presbyterian. Clubs: Jonathan (Los Angeles), Flint Canyon Tennis (Flintridge), Olympic (San Francisco), Annandale Golf (Pasadena), Coral Beach and Tennis (Bermuda). Home: 4251 Woodleigh Ln Flintridge CA 91011 Office: 1880 Century Park E West Los Angeles CA 90067

STRONG, ROY COLIN, writer, former museum director; b. London, Aug. 23, 1935; grad. Queen Mary Coll., U. London; Ph.D., Warburg Inst., London; m. Julia Trevelyan Oman, 1971. Asst. keeper, then dir., keeper, sec. Nat. Portrait Gallery, London, 1959-74; dir. Victoria and Albert Mus., London, 1974-87; lectr. in Eng. and U.S., also contbr. to radio and TV; Ferens prof. fine art U. Hull, 1972; Wells lectr. Pierpont Morgan Library, 1974; mem. arts adv. com. Brit. Council; mem. archtl. adv. panel Westminster Abbey; chmn. arts panel Arts Council Gt. Britain; arranger numerous mus. exhbns. Recipient Shakespeare prize, 1980; knighted, 1982. Fellow Soc. Antiquaries; mem. Royal Archaeol. Inst. Clubs: Garrick, Grillions, Beefsteak (London). Author books on life and art of Tudor, Stuart and Victorian England, including: A Celebration, 1984, Art and Power, Renaissance Festivals, 1450-1650, 1984; contbr. articles to profl. jours.; reviewer for newspapers, radio and TV. Office: 3cc Morpeth Terr, London SW1P 1EW, England

STRONG, WILLIAM LEE, former manufacturing company executive; b. Jacksonville, Fla., Sept. 17, 1919; s. William M. and Hedwig C. (Ulm) S.; m. Betty Jean Stream, Dec. 13, 1941; children—William Lee, Thomas B., Robin E. Strong Vandever. AB in Econs., Occidental Coll., 1942; MBA, Harvard U., 1947. Budget dir. Byron-Jackson div. Borg Warner Corp., Los Angeles, 1954-56, controller, 1956-57; budget dir. Consol. Freightways, Inc., Menlo Park, Calif., 1957-60, treas., chief fin. officer, 1960-62; v.p. fin., treas., dir. Packard-Bell Electronics Corp., Los Angeles, 1962-65; treas. Allis-Chalmers Mfg. Co., Milw., 1965-68; v.p., treas. Continental Can Co., Inc., (now Continental Group, Inc.), 1968-75; sr. v.p., chief fin. officer Firestone Tire & Rubber Co., Akron, Ohio, 1976-77, exec. v.p., dir., 1978-81; dir. Transatlantic Fund, U.S. Life Corp.; guest lectr. various grad. bus. schs., other groups. chmn. bd. advisors Sch. Acctg. U. So. Calif. Served to lt. comdr. USN, 1942-54; PTO. Mem. Treas. Club N.Y., Phi Gamma Delta. Clubs: Harvard Bus. Sch. (N.Y.C.), Tennis (Rancho San Clemente). Home: 4020 Calle Marlena San Clemente CA 92672

STROUD, RICHARD HAMILTON, scientist, consultant; b. Dedham, Mass., Apr. 24, 1918; s. Percy Valentine and Elizabeth Lillian (Kimpton) S.; m. Genevieve Cecelia DePol, Dec. 20, 1943; children: William DePol, Jennifer Celia. B.S., Bowdoin Coll., 1939; M.S., U. N.H., 1942; postgrad., Yale U., 1947-48, Boston U. Sch. Edn., 1948-49. Asst. aquatic biologist N.H. Fish and Game Dept., Concord, 1940-41; jr. aquatic biologist TVA, Norris, Tenn., 1942, asst. aquatic biologist, 1946-47; chief aquatic biologist Mass. Div. Fisheries and Game, Boston, 1948-53; asst. exec. v.p. Sport Fishing Inst., Washington, 1953-55; exec. v.p. Sport Fishing Inst., 1955-81; sr. scientist Aquatic Ecosystems Analysts, Fayetteville, Ark., 1983—; founder, trustee Sport Fishery Research Found., Washington, 1967-88; research adv. Sport Fishing Inst., 1988—; cons. aquatic resources, 1981—, cons. editor fish sci. publs., 1982—; Pentelow lectr. U. Liverpool, Eng., 1975. Editor (ann. series) Marine Recreational Fisheries Symposia, 1982—, National Leaders of American Conservation, 1985, World Angling Resources and Challenges, 1985, Fish Culture in Fisheries Management, 1986, Management of Atlantic Salmon, 1988; contbr. articles to various publs. Bd. dirs. Nat. Coalition Marine Conservation, 1977—; chmn. Natural Resources Council Am., 1969-71, hon. mem., 1981—. Served with U.S. Army, 1942-46. Decorated Croix de Guerre with cluster.; recipient Conservation Achievement award Nat. Wildlife Fedn., 1975, 81, SOAR award Boy Scouts Am., 1972; named to Nat. Fishing Hall of Fame, 1984. Fellow Am. Inst. Fishery Research Biologists (emeritus, Outstanding Achievement award 1981), Am. Fisheries Soc. (pres. 1979-80, hon. life mem.); mem. Internat. Fish and Wildlife Agys., Freshwater Biol. Assn. (U.K.), Fisheries Soc. Brit. Isles. Republican. Club: Country (Pinehurst, N.C.). Office: PO Box 1772 Pinehurst NC 28374

STROUD, ROBERT EDWARD, lawyer; b. Chester, S.C., July 24, 1934; s. Coy Franklin and Leila (Caldwell) S.; m. Katherine C. Stroud, Apr. 8, 1961; children—Robert Gordon, Margaret Lathan. AB, Washington and Lee U., 1956, LLB, 1958. Bar: Va. 1959. Assoc. McGuire, Woods, Battle and Boothe, Charlottesville, Va., 1959-64; ptnr. Woods, Battle & Boothe, Charlottesville, Va., 1964—; mem. exec. com. McGuire, Woods, Battle & Boothe, 1980—; lectr. math. Washington and Lee U., 1957-59; lectr. bus. tax Grad. Bus. Sch., U. Va., Charlottesville, 1969-87, lectr. corp. taxation U. Va. Law Sch., 1985—; lectr. to legal edn. insts., lectr. in corp. law Washington & Lee Law Sch., 1984. Co-author: Buying, Selling and Merging Businesses, 1975; editor in chief Washington and Lee Law Rev., 1959; editor: Advising Small Business Clients, Vol. 1, 1978, 82, 87, Vol. 2, 1980, 84; contbr. articles to profl. jours. Pres. Charlottesville Housing Found., 1968-73; mem. mgmt. council Montreat Conf. Ct., N.C., 1974-77; trustee Presbyn. Found., 1972-73, Union Theol. Sem., Va., 1983—; bd. dirs. Presbyn. Outlook Found., 1974—, pres., 1985—; mem. governing council Presbyn. Synod of the Virginias, 1973-78, moderator, 1977-78; bd. dirs., v.p. U. Va. Tax Found., 1985—. Served to capt. inf. U.S. Army, 1958. Mem. ABA, Va. State Bar, Va. Bar Assn., Nat. Tax Inst., Am. Judicature Soc., Washington and Lee Law Sch. Assn. (pres. 1979-80), Phi Eta Sigma, Omicron Delta Kappa, Phi Delta Phi. Clubs: Boar's Head Sports, Redland (Charlottesville); Downtown, Bull and Bear (Richmond, Va.). Home: 104 Woodstock Dr Charlottesville VA 22901 Office: McGuire Woods Battle & Boothe PO Box 1288 5th St and E Jefferson St Charlottesville VA 22901

STROUGAL, LUBOMIR, premier Czechoslovakia; b. Veseli nad Luznici, Oct. 19, 1924; LL.D., Charles U., Prague, 1949. Mem. Communist Party Czechoslovakia, 1945—, mem. cen. com., 1958—, sec. cen. com., 1965-68, sec., mem. presidium and secretariat cen. com., chmn. bur. for directing party work in Czech lands, 1968-70; sec. Communist Party Regional Com., Ceske Budejovice, 1957-59; minister agr. and forestry, 1959-61, minister of interior, 1961-65, dep. Fed. Assembly, 1960-69; dep. premier, chmn. Econ. Council, 1968; mem. presidium central com., 1970—; dep. fed. assembly People's Chamber, 1969—; premier Czechoslovak Socialist Republic, 1970—. Decorated Order of Merit for Constrn., Order of Victorious February, Order of the Republic; recipient Gold medal FAO, UN. Address: Office of Premier, Prague Czechoslovakia *

STRUBBE, JOHN LEWIS, retired food chain store executive; b. Cin., June 27, 1921; s. John August and Emma Katherine (Coleman) S.; m. Nancy Richards Baer, Sept. 16, 1950; children: William Burrows, Laura, John Charles, Mary. B.S. in Gen. Engring, U. Cin., 1947, J.D., 1948. Bar: Ohio 1948, U.S. Supreme Ct. 1960, U.S. Patent Office 1950. Assoc. Wood, Arey, Herron & Evans, Cin., 1948-50; with The Kroger Co., Cin., 1950-86, sec., 1959-65, gen. atty., 1956-62, v.p., 1961-77, group v.p., 1977-85, sr. v.p., 1985-86. Gen. chmn. United Appeal Greater Cin., 1967; mem. Food Industry Productivity Task Force, 1972; past pres. Dan Beard council Boy Scouts Am.; past pres. bd. trustees Community Chest and Council of Cin. Area; vice chmn., mem. distbn. com. Greater Cin. Found.; v.p. devel. Cin. Ballet Co.; past trustee Meth. Union; vice chmn. U. Cin. Found.; bd. advisors to dean U. Cin. Coll. Bus. Adminstrn.; past chmn. bd. The Christ Hosp.; chmn. bd. Elizabeth Gamble Deaconess Home Assn. Served with USMCR, 1943-46, 50-52. Recipient U. Cin. Distinguished Alumnus award, chmn. award for devel. new food tech. Supermarket Inst., 1976, Brotherhood citation NCCJ, 1982; named Great Living Cincinnatian, Greater Cin. C. of C., 1986. Mem. Cincinnatus Assn. (past pres., dir.), Uniform Grocery Products Code Council (past chmn., pres.), Delta Tau Delta. Methodist. Clubs: Queen City, Cincinnati Country (Cin.); Commonwealth. Home: 661 Chardonnay Ridge Cincinnati OH 45226 Office: 704 Mercantile Library Bldg 414 Walnut St Cincinnati OH 45202

STRUBE, WILLIAM CURTIS, educator; b. St. Louis, Sept. 9, 1940; s. William Henry and Irene Louise Strube; B.A. in Econs., Monmouth (Ill.) Coll., 1962; M.B.A., U. Ariz., 1965; Ph.D. in Bus. Adminstrn., U. Ark., 1972; m. Janet Grace Hoetker, June 18, 1966; children—Kim Janette, Randall William. Part-time instr. U. Ark., 1968-69; mem. faculty Drury Coll., Springfield, Mo., 1969-70, asst. dean coll., then dean students, 1973-75, prof., dir. Breech Sch. Bus. Adminstrn., 1975—; pres. One Hour Photo Service, Inc.; v.p. Mergers-Acquisitions, Inc., Springfield, 1979; chmn. bus. adminstrn. Burlington No.; cons. in field. Bd. dirs. Springfield Boys Club, mem. Springfield Transit Task Force Com., Child Health Task Force of Child Advocacy Council; mem. St. John's Regional Med. Ctr. Adv. Council. Mem. Acad. Mgmt., S.W. Fedn. Adminstrv. Disciplines, Assn. Pvt. Enterprise Edn., Ozark Econ. Assn., Midwest Bus. Adminstrn. Assn., Midwest Econs. Assn., Omicron Delta Kappa, Phi Eta Sigma, Theta Chi. Presbyterian. Author papers in field. Home: 3709 Sugar Hill Springfield MO 65804 Office: Drury Coll Breech Sch Springfield MO 65802

STRUELENS, MICHEL MAURICE JOSEPH GEORGES, political science educator, foreign affairs consultant; b. Brussels, Belgium, Mar. 10, 1928; came to U.S., 1960, naturalized, 1966; m. Godelieve de Wilde, Aug. 2, 1949; children: Alain, Patricia, Brigitte, Bernard, Jean Paul (dec.). B.A., Coll. St. Pierre, Brussels, 1944; M.A., Antwerp U., Belgium, 1949; Ph.D., Am. U., Washington, 1968. Insp. econ. affairs Congo Govt., Leopoldville, 1950-54; chief insp. econ. affairs Congo Govt., 1954-55, dep. commr. transp., 1955-57; dir. Info. and Public Relations Office for Congo, Brussels, 1957-58, Congo Tourism Pavillion, Internat. World's Fair, Brussels, 1958-59; dir. gen. Belgian Congo and Ruanda Urundi Tourist Office, Congo, 1959; chmn. African Commn. Internat. Union Ofcl. Travel Orgns., Geneva, 1959-60; ofcl. Katanga rep. in U.S., N.Y.C., 1960-63; dir. gen. Internat. Inst. for African Affairs in Can., 1963-64; spl. asst. to prime minister Democratic Republic Congo; fgn. affairs minister, adviser to Congo UN del., adviser Congo embassy Democratic Republic Congo, Washington, N.Y.C., 1964-66; dir. Eurafrica, Consultants on Fgn. Affairs, Washington, 1966—; prof. polit. sci., French, internat. bus. Am. U., 1968—; dir. Center Research and Documentation on European Community, 1971—, E.C. Inst. in Europe, 1978—, U. Antwerp Exchange Program, 1979-83; dir. EPSCI/ESSEC (France) Exchange Program, 1980-84, chmn. internat. bus. dept., 1980-84; dir. exchange program Bus. Sch. of Poly., U. Madrid, 1981-84; investment adviser, 1977—; adminstr. French Parish, Ctr. Studies on Internat. Relations, Econs. and Bus., La Rochelle, France, 1987—; exec. v.p. Eglise St. Louis Corp., French-Speaking Union, Washington, 1974-75. Author: (with Inforcongo) Congo Belge et Ruanda-Urundi, 1958; monograph Le Canada à l'Heure de l'Afrique, 1964; The United Nations in the Congo - or ONUC and International Politics, 1976. Recipient Internat. Union Ofcl. Travel Orgns. Poster award Brussels, 1958, Etoile de Service en Argent King of Belgium, 1956; chevalier de l'Ordre Royal du Lion, 1957; Faculty award for outstanding contbn. to acad. program devel. Coll. Bus. Adminstrn., Am. U., 1979; Faculty award for outstanding teaching, 1980, 82, 84; Faculty award for outstanding service to Am. U., 1981. Mem. Phi Sigma Alpha. Clubs: Cosmos (Washington); Bukavu Royal Sports (founder 1950, pres. 1951-54, hon. pres. 1957) (Congo). Lodge: Rotary. Home: 1374 Woodside Dr McLean VA 22102

STRUHL, THEODORE ROOSEVELT, surgeon; b. N.Y.C., Jan. 5, 1917; s. Samuel and Florence (Kossoy) S.; m. Ruth Brand, Oct. 19, 1941; children—Karsten, Wendy. B.A., NYU, 1936, M.S., 1938; M.D., N.Y. Med. Coll., 1942, M.S. in Surgery, 1947; grad. Julliard Conservatory of Music, 1933. Diplomate Am. Bd. Abdominal Surgery, Am. Bd. Surgery. Intern Queens Gen. Hosp., Jamaica, N.Y., 1942-43; resident VA Hosp. Newington, Conn., 1947-48, Cumberland Med. Ctr., Bklyn., 1948-51; practice medicine specializing in surgery, Miami, Fla., 1951—; mem. staff Mt. Sinai Med. Ctr., Miami Beach, Fla., Jackson Meml. Hosp., Cedars of Lebanon Health Care Ctr. Variety Children's Hosp., South Shore Hosp., Miami Beach, Victoria Hosp.; former instr. in anatomy L.I. Coll. Medicine, N.Y.; instr. in surgery, instr. in anatomy and surg. anatomy U. Miami; instr. in surg. anatomy and surgery Mt. Sinai Med. Ctr.; med. adviser ARC of Dade County, Fla.; chief med. examiner Miami Beach Boxing Commn.; chief med. adviser World Boxing Assn., U.S. Boxing Assn.; med. adviser World Martial Arts, Judo and Karate; mem. Am. Bd. Quality Assurance and Utilization Rev. Physicians; formerly instr. in diving medicine Underwater Demolition Team Sch., U.S. Navy, Key West, Fla.; lectr., instr. in scuba diving, diving medicine; lectr. on medicine and surgery, cancer, artificial respiration, anatomy, hypnosis, boxing, weight lifting, judo, skin and scuba diving, swimming, water skiing, small craft, wrestling, music. Active ARC, 1936—, now bd. dirs., chmn. safety services ARC of Dade County; instr./trainer in CPR, instr. in advanced cardiac life support Am. Heart Assn.; former mem. N.Y. div. Olympic Wrestling Com. Served to maj. M.C., U.S. Army, World War II; ETO. Contbr. articles to profl. and sports publs. Fellow ACS, Internat. Coll. Surgeons (vice-regent Fla.), Am. Coll. Angiology, Internat. Acad. Proctology; mem. AMA (Physicians Recognition award 1986), So. Med. Assn., Fla. Med. Assn., Dade County Med. Assn., Israeli Med. Assn., Fla. Assn. Gen. Surgeons (charter), Med. Hypnosis Assn. Dade County (past pres.), Am. Coll. Angiology, Pan Am. Med. Assn., Am. Soc. Abdominal Surgeons, Am. Soc. Contemporary Medicine and Surgery, Med. Aspects of Atomic Explosion, Assn. Mil. Surgeons U.S., Am. Coll. Sports Medicine, Commodore Longfellow Soc., Miami Beach Power Squadron (charter), Am. Canoe Assn., Am. White Water Assn., Underwater Med. Soc., Photog. Soc. Am., Contin Hon. Soc. of N.Y. Med. Coll., Phi Delta Epsilon (past pres. chpt.). Democrat. Jewish. Holder black belt in judo; black belt in karate, 2d degree. Home: 44 Star Island Miami Beach FL 33139 Office: 1444 Biscayne Blvd Suite 304 Miami FL 33132

STRUL, GENE M., telecommunications company executive, former TV news dir.; b. Bklyn., Mar. 25, 1927; s. Joseph and Sally (Chartoff) S.; student journalism U. Miami (Fla.), 1945-47; m. Shirley Dolly Silber, Aug. 7, 1949; children—Ricky, Gary, Eileen. News dir. Sta. WIOD AM-FM, Miami, 1947-56; assignment editor, producer Sta. WCKT-TV, Miami, 1956-57, news dir., 1957-79; dir. broadcast news Miami News, 1957; free-lance writer newspapers and mags.; cons. dept. communications U. Miami, 1979, acting dir. public relations, 1979-80; v.p. Hernstadt Broadcasting Corp., 1980-81; dir. corp. communications Burnup & Sims, 1981—. Communications dir. United Way of Dade County, 1981. Served with AUS, 1945. Recipient Peabody award, 1975; Preceptor award Broadcast Industry conf., San Francisco State U.; Abe Lincoln awards (2) So. Baptist Radio-TV Conf.; Nat. Headliners awards (5); led Sta. WCKT to more than 200 awards for news, including 3 Peabody awards, Emmy award, 2 Nat. Sigma Delta Chi awards. Mem. Nat. Acad. Television Arts and Scis. (past gov. Miami chpt.), Radio-TV News Dirs. Assn., Fla. AP Broadcasters (past pres.), Greater Miami C. of C., Nat. Broadcast Editorial Assn., Sigma Delta Chi. Home: 145 SW 49th Ave Miami FL 33134

STRULOWITZ, JACK JOEL, management professional; b. Memphis, Oct. 20, 1942, s. Isidore and Adele (Katz) S.; m. Rhoda Susan Feuerstein, June 14, 1970; children—Donn Michael, Beth Hava. B.A., Rider Coll., 1966; M.Ed., Rutgers U., 1968. Edn. supr. N.J. State Prison, Trenton, 1966-67; edn. specialist N.J. Labor and Industry, Trenton, 1968-74; tng. officer N.J. Civil Service, Trenton, 1974-77; exec. asst. N.J. Atty. Gen., Trenton, 1978-80; exec. analyst N.J. Div. Motor Vehicles, Trenton, 1980—; mgmt. cons. Kessel Kitchen, Inc., Lawrenceville, N.J., 1982-83, Bridgewater Holding Co., 1976—. Pres. Rider Coll. Alumni Assn., Lawrenceville, 1982-84; vice chmn. Zoning Bd. Adjustment, 1978-85, chmn. Fedn. Planning Officials, Central N.J. chpt., 1979-85, Treas. Am. Jewish com., 1978—. Honorary Resolution, Township Lawrence N.J., 1982; Hope Chest Award Nat. Multiple Sclerosis Soc. N.Y.C., 1980. Bd. dirs. Adrams Hebrew Acad., 1980—, Jewish Fedn. Del. Valley, 1981-86, Jewish Family Services Del. Valley, 1980—, Jewish Community Relations council, 1981—; exec. com. Lawrence Township Club, 1977—; Dem. Mcpl. chmn., 1985-87. Lodges: Knights of Malta (Knighted 1986), Albert Einstein, B'nai B'rith (pres. 1982-85). Home: 18 Hamilton Ct Lawrenceville NJ 08648 Office: NJ Div Motor Vehicles 25 S Montgomery St Trenton NJ 08666

STRUTT, MAXIMILIAAN JULIUS OTTO, electronics engineer; b. Soerakarta, Java, Oct. 2, 1903; s. Julius Otto and Hendrika (Heusser) S.; BS in Eng., U. Munich, 1924; MS in Eng., Tech. U., Delft, Netherlands, 1926, D. Techn.Sc., 1927; Dr.Eng. (hon.), U. Karlsruhe (Germany), 1950; m. Elfriede Schaefer, Oct. 18, 1932; 1 dau., Helga (Mrs. C. Villalaz). Teaching asst., patent engr. Tech. U. Delft, 1926-27; research fellow Philips Co., Eindhoven, Netherlands, 1927-46, electronics cons., 1946-48; prof., dir. dept. advanced elec. engring. Swiss Fed. Inst. Tech., Zurich, 1948-74; indsl. electronics cons., 1948—; vis. prof. U. Calif., Berkeley, 1961, 62, 63, 66-67. Mem. sr. sci. adv. com. NASA Project, 1963. Recipient C.F. Gauss medal, 1954. Fellow IEEE; hon. mem. German and Japanese socs. Author numerous books, including: Skineffect en Temperatuurverdeeling in Electrische Geleiders, 1927; Lame'sche-Mathieu'sche- und verwandte Funktionen in Physik und Technik, 1932; Moderne Mehrgitter-Elektronenrohren, Band I and II, 1937-39; Ultra and Extreme Short Wave Reception, 1947; Ferritas, 1950; Anleitung zur Vorlesung Hohere Elektrotechnik I and II, 1957; Fortschritte der Hochfrequenztechnik, 1960; Vorlesung uber Feldtheorie, 1964; Vorlesung uber Lichttechik, 1965; Vorlesung uber Festkorpertechnik, Transistoren, Elektronenrohren, 1965; Semiconductor Devices, Vol. 1 Semiconductors and Semiconductor Diodes, 1966; also numerous articles. Research and numerous patents, including over 70 U.S. patents, on loudspeaker systems and room acoustics, in multigrid electron tubes, UHF tubes, transistor and laser circuits, fast automatic spectrography. Home: 59 Kraehbuehl, 8044 Zurich Switzerland

STRUVE, WALTER, historian, educator; b. Somers Pt., N.J., May 6, 1935; s. Louis W. and Mary La Forge (Russell) S.; m. Cynthia Rivers, Feb. 21, 1959; children—Adam David, John Frederick. A.B., Lafayette Coll., Pa., 1955; postgrad. Kiel U., Germany, 1955-56; M.A., Yale U., 1957, Ph.D., 1963; postgrad. Free U., Berlin, 1960-61. Instr. history Princeton U., N.J., 1961-64; instr. to prof. history CCNY, 1964—; assoc. Univ. seminars Columbia U., N.Y.C., 1973—; Fulbright research prof. Goettingen U., 1978-79. Author: Elites Against Democracy, 1973; Die Republik Texas, Bremen und das Hildesheimische, 1983; contbr. articles to profl. jours. Fulbright grantee, Germany, 1955-56; German Acad. Exchange Service research grantee, 1960-61, 78; Fritz Thyssen Found. grantee, 1979-80. Mem. Am. Hist. Assn., German Studies Assn., Immigration History Soc., Study Group on Internat. Labor and Working Class History, Conf. Group on Central European History. Home: 2727 Palisade Ave Riverdale NY 10463 Office: CCNY Dept History New York NY 10031

STRYKER, STEVEN CHARLES, lawyer; b. Omaha, Oct. 26, 1944; s. James M. and Jean G. (Grannis) S.; m. Bryna Dee Litwin, Oct. 20, 1972; children: Ryan, Kevin, Gerrit, Courtney. BS, U. Iowa, 1967, JD with distinction, 1969; postgrad. Northwestern Grad. Sch. Bus., 1969-70; M in Taxation, DePaul U., 1971. Bar: Iowa 1969, Tex. 1986; CPA, Ill., Iowa. Sr. tax acct. Arthur Young & Co., Chgo., 1969-72; fed. tax mgr. Massey Ferguson, Des Moines, 1972-74; fed./state tax mgr FMC Corp., Chgo., 1974-78; gen. tax atty. Shell Oil Co., Houston, 1978-81, asst. gen. tax counsel, 1981-83, gen. mgr., 1983-86, v.p., gen. tax counsel, 1986—. Mem. ABA, Texas Bar Assn., Iowa Bar Assn., Am. Inst. CPA's, Ill. Soc. CPA's, Iowa Soc. CPA's., Tax Execs. Inst., Am. Petroleum Inst. Republican. Home: 10819 Everwood St Houston TX 77024 Office: Shell Oil Co 1 Shell Plaza Suite 4570 Houston TX 77001

STUART, ALICE MELISSA, lawyer; b. N.Y.C., Apr. 7, 1957; d. John Marberger and Marjorie Louise (Browne) S. BA, Ohio State U., 1977; JD, U. Chgo., 1980; LLM, NYU, 1982. Bar: N.Y. 1981, Ohio 1982, N.Y. 1982, U.S. Dist. Ct. (so. dist.) Ohio 1983, U.S. Dist. Ct. (so. and ea. dists.) N.Y. 1985. Assoc. Schwartz, Shapiro, Kelm & Warren, Columbus, Ohio, 1982-84, Paul, Weiss, Rifkind, Wharton & Garrison, N.Y.C., 1984-85, Kassel, Neuwirth & Geiger, N.Y.C., 1985-86, Phillips, Nizer, Benjamin, Krim & Ballon, N.Y.C., 1987—. Surrogate Speakers' Bur. Reagan-Bush Campaign, N.Y.C., 1984. Mem. ABA, N.Y. State Bar Assn., Winston Churchill Meml. Library Soc., Jr. League, Phi Beta Kappa, Phi Kappa Phi, Alpha Lambda Delta. Republican. Presbyterian. Club: Women's Nat. Rep. (N.Y.C.). Office: Philips Nizer Benjamin Krim & Ballon 40 W 57th St New York NY 10019

STUART, DAVID EDWARD, anthropologist, columnist; b. Calhoun County, Ala., Jan. 9, 1945; s. Edward George and Avis Elsie (Densmore) S.; B.A. (Wesleyan Merit scholar 1965-66), W.VA. Wesleyan Coll., 1967; M.A. in Anthropology, U. N.Mex., 1970, Ph.D., 1972, postdoctoral student, 1975-76; m. Cynthia K. Morgan, June 14, 1971. Research assoc. Andean Center, Quito, Ecuador, 1970; continuing edn. instr. anthropology U. N.Mex., 1971, research archeologist Office Contract Archeology, 1974, research coordinator, 1974-77, asst. prof. anthropology, 1975-77, assoc. prof. anthropology, 1984—, asst. v.p. acad. affairs, 1987—; asst. prof. Eckerd Coll., St. Petersburg, Fla., 1972-74; cons. archeologist right-of-way div. Pub. Service Co. N.Mex., Albuquerque, 1977-78; cons. anthropologist Bur. Indian Affairs, Albuquerque, 1978, Historic Preservation Bur. N.Mex., Santa Fe, 1978-81, Nat. Park Service, 1980, Albuquerque Mus., 1981; sr. research assoc. Human Systems Research, Inc., 1981-83, Quivira Research Center, Albuquerque, 1984-86; bd. dirs. Table Ind. Scholars, 1979-83, pres., bd. dirs. Rio Grande Heritage Found., Albuquerque and Las Cruces, 1985-87; advisor Human Systems Research, Inc., Tularosa, N.Mex., 1978-80, Albuquerque Commn. on Hist. Preservation, 1984-86. Grantee Eckerd Coll., 1973, Historic Preservation Bur., 1978-80. Essayist award N.Mex. Humanities Council, 1986. Mem. Am. Anthrop. Assn., Royal Anthrop. Inst. Gt. Britain, N.Mex. Archeol. Council, N.Mex. Press Assn., Albuquerque Archeol. Soc. (pres. 1986—), Descs. Signers Declaration Independence, Sigma Xi, Phi Kappa Phi. Presbyterian. Co-author: Archeological Survey: 4 Corners to Ambrosia, N.Mex., 1976, A Proposed Project Design for the Timber Management Archeological Surveys, 1978, Ethnoarcheological Investigations of Shepherding in the Pueblo of Laguna, 1983; Author: Prehistoric New Mexico, 1981, 2d edit., 1984, 3d edit., 1988, Glimpses of the Ancient Southwest, 1985, others; columnist New Mexico's Heritage, 1983-87, 1985, others. Editor: Archeological Reports, No. 1, 1975, No. 2, 1981. Address: U NMex Dept Anthropology Albuquerque NM 87131

STUART, GERARD WILLIAM, JR., corporate executive; b. Yuba City, Calif., July 28, 1939; s. Gerard William and Geneva Bernice (Stuke) S.; student Yuba Jr. Coll., 1957-59, Chico State Coll., 1959-60; A.B., U. Calif., Davis, 1962; M.L.S., U. Calif., Berkeley, 1963; m. Lenore Frances Loroña, 1981. Rare book librarian Cornell U., 1964-68; bibliographer of scholarly collections Huntington Library, San Marino, Calif., 1968-73, head acquisitions librarian, 1973-75; sec.-treas., dir. Ravenstree Corp., 1969-80, pres., chmn. bd., 1980—; pres., chmn. bd. William Penn Ltd., 1981—. Lilly fellow Ind. U., 1963-64. Mem. Bibliog. Soc. Am., Phi Beta Kappa, Alpha Gamma Sigma, Phi Kappa Phi. Clubs: Rolls-Royce Owners; Grolier (N.Y.C.); Zamorano (Los Angeles). Home: 500 E Country Club Dr Yuma AZ 85365 Office: 2424 W 5th St Yuma AZ 85364

STUART, JOHN M., lawyer, author; b. N.Y.C., Apr. 3, 1927; s. Winchester and Maude Ruth (Marberger) S.; m. Marjorie Louise Browne, Dec. 11, 1954; children: Jane, Alice, Richard. BA, Columbia U., 1948, JD, 1951. Bar: N.Y. 1951, U.S. Supreme Ct. 1955. Assoc., Reid & Priest, N.Y.C., 1951-64, ptnr., 1965—; asst. sec. Minn. Power & Light Co., 1951-64. Recipient Internat. Brotherhood Magicians award, 1958-60, 1st prize in sci. fiction Phila. Writers Conf., 1958. Mem. ABA, N.Y. County Bar Assn., Sr. Republican. Methodist. Author: A Re-examination of the Replacement Fund, 1968; Avoiding Costly Bond Problems, 1980; (with Louis H. Willenken) Utility Mortgages Should be Reexamined, 1984; (with Majorie L. Stuart) (play) Make Me Disappear, 1969; (novel) You Don't Have to Slay a Dragon, 1976. Contbr. articles to mags. Magician, W. German TV magic spl., 1965; appeared in Spy at the Magic Show benefit for Project Hope, Manhasset, N.Y., 1967. Home: 31 Westgate Blvd Plandome NY 11030 Office: 40 W 57th St New York NY 10019

STUART, JOHN T., III, bank executive; b. Dallas, Aug. 12, 1936; m. Barbara White; children: John Michael, Melissa Elizabeth. BBA, U. Tex., 1958; postgrad., Southwestern Grad. Sch. Banking, 1969; grad. advanced mgmt. prog., Harvard Bus. Sch., 1978. With RepublicBank Dallas, 1962—, vice chmn., 1980-86, pres., chief operating officer, 1986—. Trustee Children's Med. Ctr., Dallas; mem. exec. com.; mem. devel. bd. U. Tex., Arlington, chmn. bus. sch. adv. council, 1971-72; pres. Dallas Assn. Retarded Citizens, 1971-73; mem. adv. bd. Aubrey Costa Inst., 1973-79; dir. Dallas Assembly, 1976-77. Served with U.S. Army, 1959-61. Recipient Disting. Alumnus award Coll. Bus. Adminstrn., U. Tex., Austin, 1980. Mem. Mortgage Bankers Assn. Am. (bd. govs. 1975-78), Tex. Mortgage Bankers Assn. (bd. dirs. 1973-76), Tex. Bankers Assn. (chmn. real estate sect. 1975), Dallas Clearing House, Am. Bankers Assn., Urban Land Inst., Cen. Bus. Dist. Assn., U. Tex. at Austin Ex-Students Assn. (pres., mem. exec. council 1969-71). Clubs: Dallas, Dallas Country, City, Harvard, Royal Oaks Country (past pres.). Office: RepublicBank Dallas NA Pacific & Ervay Sts Dallas TX 75201

STUART, ROBERT DOUGLAS, JR., U.S. ambassador to Norway; b. Hubbard Woods, Ill., Apr. 26, 1916; s. Robert Douglas and Harriet (McClure) S.; m. Barbara McMath Edwards, May 21, 1938; children: Robert Douglas III, James McClure, Marian Stuart Pillsbury, Alexander Douglas. B.A., Princeton U., 1937; J.D., Yale U., 1946. Bar: Ill. 1946. With Quaker Oats Co., Chgo., 1947-84; chief exec. officer Quaker Oats Co., 1966-81, chmn. bd. dirs., 1981-84; ambassador to Norway, 1984—; bd. dirs. U.A.L., First Nat. Bank of Chgo., Deere & Co., Molson Co., Ltd. Mem. Rep. Nat. Com., 1964-72; chmn. Ill. Reagan Bush Fin. Com., 1984; bd. dirs. William Benton Found., Chgo., 1980-84, Chgo. Urban League, 1963-84; trustee Princeton U., 1972-82, now trustee emeritus; trustee emeritus Tax Found., 1978-84. Served to maj. U.S. Army, 1942-45, ETO. Mem. Bus. Council. Republican. Presbyterian. Clubs: Chgo., Commercial, Old Elm; Shore Acres (Lake Forest, Ill.); River, Brooke (N.Y.C.). Lodge: Rotary. Office: American Embassy Oslo, Norway APO New York NY 09085-5381 also: Am Embassy, Drammensveine 18, Oslo 2 Norway *

STUART, WILLIAM DAVID, electrical engineer; b. Boyleston, Ind., June 25, 1932; s. John Edward and Mabel Ann (Weaver) S.; m. Barbara Josephine Vandervort, Nov. 10, 1956; children—David Joseph, Karen Lynne. B.S. in E.E., Purdue U., 1955, M.S., 1957; postgrad. Ohio State U., 1959-75. Registered profl. engr., Ohio, Md. Engr., Farnsworth Electronics Co., Fort Wayne, Ind., 1955-57; research asso. Ohio State U., 1959-61; project leader Battelle Columbus Labs. (Ohio), 1961-75; group leader IIT Research Inst., Annapolis, Md., 1975—; adj. instr. Prince George's Community Coll., 1980-83. Author: Radar Cross Section Handbook, 1970. Commr. Girls Softball, 1973-75; mem. com. Boy Scouts Am., 1968-72; chmn. student adv. services sci. Columbus Tech. Council, 1972-75. Served to 1st lt. AUS, 1957-58. Purdue Alumni scholar, 1951-55; Merit scholar, 1950-55. Mem. IEEE (sr. mem.; chmn. Columbus, treas. Balt.), Electromagnetics Soc., Applied Computational Electromagnetics, Soc., Am. Geophys. Union, Assn. Old Crows, Sigma Xi, Eta Kappa Nu. Democrat. Mem. Ch. of Christ. Home: 109 Claiborne Rd Edgewater MD 21037 Office: 185 Admiral Cochrane Dr Annapolis MD 21401

STUART-HAMILTON, IAN ALEXANDER, psychologist, researcher; b. Barrow in Furness, Cumbria, Eng., Nov. 26, 1959; s. Charles Alfred and Ruth Riley (Stuart) Hamilton. MA, Oxford U., 1981; PhD, Manchester U., 1984. Research assoc. Age and Cognitive Performance Research Ctr. U. Manchester, Eng., 1985—. Contbr. articles to profl. jours. Mem. Exptl. Psychology Soc. Office: Manchester U, ACPRC St Peter's House, M13 9PL, Manchester M13 9PL, England

STUBBS, DANIEL GAIE, management consultant; b. Charleston, S.C., Nov. 13, 1940; s. Daniel Hamer and Esther Virginia (Garlow) S.; m. Sherrill Ann Sloan, July 8, 1984; children: Kimberly, Allison, Don; student U. Fla., 1959-60; B.A., W.Va. U., 1965; postgrad. Temple U., 1965-67. Tchr., Sch. Dist. of Phila., 1965-67; rep. Am. Fedn. Tchrs., Washington, 1967; exec. sec. Calif. State Coll. Council, Am. Fedn. Tchrs., AFL-CIO, Los Angeles, 1967-68; rep. Am. Fedn. Tchrs., AFL-CIO, Los Angeles, 1968-69, dir. orgn. Balt. Tchrs. Union, 1969-70; employee relations specialist Calif. Nurses Assn., Los Angeles, 1971-72; exec. dir. United Nurses Assn. Calif., Los Angeles, 1972-74; labor relations cons. Social Services Union, Service Employees Internat. Union, Local 535, AFL-CIO, Los Angeles, 1974-76; exec. dir. Met. Riverside UniServ Unit, Calif. Tchrs. Assn., 1976-79, exec. dir. San Bernardino/Colton Uniserv Unit, 1979-80; gen. services adminstr. Housing Authority, City of Los Angeles, 1980-82; cons. Blanning & Baker Assocs., Tujunga, Calif., 1983-84; asst. exec. dir. adminstrv. services Los Angeles Housing Authority, 1984-86; mgmt. con., Los Angeles, 1986—; lectr. in field. Served with U.S. Army, 1961-62. Recipient W.Va. U. Waitman Barbe Prize for creative writing, 1965. Mem. So. Calif. Indsl. Relations Research Assn., Orange County Indsl. Relations Research Assn., Indsl. Relations Research Assn., UCLA Inst. Indsl Relations Assn., Soc. of Profls. in Dispute Resolution. Presbyterian. Club: Town Hall of Calif. Home: 3200 Fairesta St #11 La Crescenta CA 91214

STUBERT, HARALD GUNNAR, film company executive; b. Malmo, Sweden, Jan. 4, 1948; s. Sven and Anna (Petersson) S.; m. Anette Engstrom, May 15, 1978. BA, U. Lund, Sweden, 1973. Tng. officer SAAB Scania, Sodertalje, Sweden, 1974-75; cons. Stats. Cons., Stockholm, 1976-81; sr. cons. Bohlin & Stromberg Mgmt., Stockholm, 1982-83; pres. Bohlin & Stromberg Search, Stockholm, 1984, Esselte Cinema Internat., Stockholm, 1985—. Author: Stockholm Restaurants, yearly; contbr. articles to profl. jours. Club: Sallskapet. Home: Radmansgatan 18, 114 25 Stockholm Sweden Office: Esselte Cinema Internat, Box 9006, S-102 71 Stockholm Sweden

STUCKI, GRANT ALFRED, dentist; b. Delta, Utah, Oct. 2, 1928; s. Herman Wilford and Anna Elizabeth (Nelson) S.; student Brigham Young U., 1946-47, U. Utah, 1950-51; D.D.S., Northwestern U., 1954; student U. Louisville, 1954-55; m. Sharon Turner, Dec. 19, 1952; children—Sharee A., Grant Turner, Candice J., Randall M., Turner G., Taylor C. Attending dentist Ventura Correctional Sch. for Girls, Ventura, Calif., 1954-55; pvt. practice dentistry, Chgo., 1957-69, Torrance, Calif., 1972—; cons. dentist Ettie Lee Homes for Youth, 1975-80; cons. dentist Internat. Monetary Funders, 1978; advisor ASAI Germanium Research Inst, Tokyo, 1987—; worldwide distbr. Rights for Organic Germanium given by Maruyoshi Co., Japan. Co-author: A Natural Cure for Cancer. Pres., Internat. Commerce Exchange, Success Market Unltd., Internat. Retirement Accounts, Coastal Leasing Services. Bd. dirs. Ettie Lee Homes for Youth; instr. on Constn., Freeman Inst., The Iternat. AIDS Research Hosp. and Found., 1988. Served with USAF, 1955-57. Mem. Am. Endodontic Soc., Acad. Gen. Dentistry, Profl. Speakers Assn., Internat. Found. Profl. Excellence, Food for Millions Found., Donovan Acad. Orthodontics, Denticare Corp., Internat. Platform Assn. Republican. Mem. Ch. Jesus Christ of Latter-day Saints. Club: Toastmasters Internat. Office: 3318 E Anaheim St Long Beach CA 90804

STUDIHRAD, MILAN EINER, manufacturing company executive; b. Tyn Nad Vltavou, Czechoslovakia, Aug. 27, 1923; came to Italy, 1950; s. Jan and Feodora (Schmidtova) S.; m. Mercedes Doncovio, Oct. 3, 1983; Engr., Tech. U. Prague, 1949. Mng. dir. Thermo-O-Spray Ltd., Milan, Italy, 1952—, Finishing Equipment Ltd., Milan, 1956-67, Socit S.R.L., Milan, 1962-67. Contbr. articles to profl. jours. Pres., Union Constructors Finishing Equipment, Milan, 1977—; v.p. UPA-Equine Sect., Como, Italy, 1980—; v.p. European Com. Surface Treatment, CETS, Paris, 1983; dir. Anima-Nat. Assn. Mech. Industries, Milan, 1977—. Mem. Nat. Assn. Thoroughbred Breeders (dir. 1982-83) Thoroughbred Breeders Assn. Gt. Britain. Club: Jockey. Home: Via Cimarosa 12/4, 20144 Milan Italy

STUDLEY, HELEN ORMSON, artist, poet, writer, designer; b. Elroy, Wis., Sept. 8, 1937; d. Clarence Ormson and Hilda (Johnson) O.; m. William Frank Studley, Aug. 1965 (div.); 1 son, William Harrison. Owner RJK Original Art, Sherman Oaks, Calif., 1979—; designer Aspen Series custom greeting cards and stationery notes, lithographs Love is All Colors, 1982; represented in numerous pub. and pvt. collections throughout U.S., Can., Norway, Sweden, Austria, Germany, Eng., France; author poetry Love is Care, Changes, 1988. Active Luth. Brotherhood, Emmanuel Luth. Ch. Honors include display of lithograph Snow Dreams, Snow Queens at 1980 Winter Olympics, Lake Placid, N.Y., lithograph Summer Dreams, Summer Queens at 1984 Summer Olympics, Los Angeles; named finalist in competition for John Simon Guggenheim fellowship. Mem. Soc. Illustrators, Am. Watercolor Soc., Internat. Soc. Artists, Internat. Platform Assn., Calif. Woman's Art Guild. Club: Sons of Norway. Office: RJK Original Art 5020 Hazeltine Ave Sherman Oaks CA 91423

STUEDEMANN, ROLF P.T., engineer; b. Hamburg, Federal Republic of Germany, Apr. 24, 1925; arrived in Chile, 1947; s. Hans D. and Vera S. (Siemensen) S.; m. Adriana von Moltke (div. 1965); 1 child, Peter H.W.W.; m. Renate F. Niemeyer (dec. 1984); 1 child, Thomas Chr. W. Student, Tech. Sch., Berlin, Hamburg, 1940-44; degree in Comml. Engring., Escuela de Negocios, Valparaiso, Chile, 1979; degree in Advanced Mgmt. (hon.), Harvard U., 1977. Service mgr., salesman Goldmann, Janssen and Cia, Ltd., Valparaiso, 1958-60, sales and import mgr., 1960-62; salesman Olympia, Ltd., Santiago, Chile, 1962-63, sales mgr., 1963-65, v.p. service and assembling, 1965-66, v.p. sales, 1965-67, pres., 1967-85; chmn. Stuedemann S.A., Santiago, 1986—; assoc. prof internat. commerce Escuela de Negocios, Valparaiso, 1960-61. Mem. German Chamber of Industry and Commerce (bd. dirs. 1971-72, 77-78), Am. C. of C. (outreach fin. and investment com. 1987—). Lutheran. Lodge: Rotary of Ñuñoa (Santiago) (pres. 1987-88). Clubs: Deportivo Manquehue (Santiago), de Golf Sport Francés (Santiago). Home: Cardenal Belarmino 1252, Santiago-Vitacura Chile Office: Stuedemann SA, Ave Holanda 254, Santiago-Providencia Chile

STUHL, OSKAR PAUL, organic chemist; b. Wilhelmshaven, Germany, Dec. 23, 1949; s. Johannes Alexander and Johanna Wilhelmine (Hoelling) S.; Dipl. Chem., U. Duesseldorf, 1976, Dr.rer.nat., 1978. Tutor, Institut fuer Organische Chemie, U. Duesseldorf, 1975-76, sci. assoc., 1976-79; mgr. product devel. Drugofa GmbH, Cologne, W.Ger., 1980; mgr. sci. relations R.J. Reynolds Tobacco GmbH, Cologne, 1981—; cons. in field. Mem. editorial bd. Beitraege zur Tabakforschung Internat. Mem. Duesseldorf Museums Verein, Verein der Freunde des Hetjens-Museums, Verein der Freunde und Foerderer der U. Duesseldorf, Verein der Freunde des Stadtmuseums Duesseldorf, Met. Mus. Art (N.Y.C.), Verein zur Foerderung Deutsch-Japanischer Beziehungen. Mem. Gesellschaft Deutscher Chemiker, Gesellschaft Deutscher Naturforscher und Aerzte, Max-Planck-Gesellschaft, Am. Chem. Soc. (med. chemistry div., various other divs.), Chem. Soc. Japan, Royal Soc. Chemistry, Am. Pharm. Assn. (Acad. Pharm. Research and Sci., Acad. Pharm. Practice and Mgmt.), AAAS, Am. Soc. Pharmacognosy, Fedn. Internat. Pharmaceutic, Christlich Demokratische Union, CDU-Wirtschaftsvereinigung. Roman Catholic. Clubs: Vereinigung AC Duesseldorf; SCC; PCL (London); KDStV Burgundia-Leipzig (Zu Duesseldorf) im CV. Contbr. articles to profl. jours. Home: Ander Thomaskirche 23, D 4000 Duesseldorf 30, Federal Republic of Germany Office: RJ Reynolds Tobacco GmbH, Maria-Ablass Platz 15, D 5000 Cologne 1, Federal Republic of Germany

STUKALIN, BORIS IVANOVICH, diplomat; b. Tambov, USSR, May 4, 1923; s. Ivan Lukjanovich and Alexandra (Semenovna) S.; m. Olga Jakovlevna, Aug., 1949; children: Marina, Vladimir. BS in History, Tchrs. Coll., Voronesh City, USSR, 1951. Editor region newspapaer Young Communar, Voronesh, 1952-56, Communa, Voronesh, 1956-60; fellow Dept. Cen. Com. Communist Party of the Soviet Union, Moscow, 1960-63, 82-85; chief Com. of Pub. Russian Socialist Fed. Soviet Republic, Moscow, 1963-65; dep. chief editor newspapaer Pravda, Moscow, 1965-70; chmn. Pub. and Printing Com. of USSR, Moscow, 1970-82; ambassador to Hungary Budapest, 1985—. Dep. Supreme Council of USSR, Moscow, 1971; mem. Cen. Com. CPSU, Moscow, 1976. Office: Embassy USSR, Bajza u 35, Budapest VI Hungary

STULA, MICHAEL JAMES, businessman; b. N.Y.C., July 9, 1914; s. Fred and Irene (Melnik) S.; B.S., Ia. State U., 1938; m. Pauline A. Wickson, July 5, 1941; 1 dau., Linnea W. Insp., United Aircraft Co., East Hartford, Conn., 1940-42, foreman, 1942-45; owner Stula Agy., Colchester, Conn., 1945—; mayor Colchester, Conn., 1953-61; commr. Conn. Bd. Fisheries and Game, Hartford, 1957—, also chmn. Trustee, Cragin Meml. Library, Bacon Acad. Mem. New Eng. Outdoor Writers Assn., Nat. Assn. Real Estate Bds. Roman Catholic. Lodges: Elks, Lions. Address: 53 S Main St Colchester CT 06415

STUMPF, LOWELL C(LINTON), artist-designer; b. Canton, Ill., Dec. 8, 1917; s. Oral Baxter and Marie (Dawson) S.; grad. Chgo. Acad. Fine Arts; student L'Ecole de Beaux Arts, Marseille, France, 1945; m. Jacqueline Jeanne Charlotte Andree Lucas, Sept. 5, 1945; children—Eric Clinton, Roderick Lowell. Staff artist Internat. Harvester Co., Chgo., 1939-42, Nugent-Graham Studios, Chgo., 1945-47; free lance artist, designer, Chgo., 1947—. Served with AUS, 1942-45; NATO USA, ETO. Contbr. sci. and tech. illustrations, maps to Compton's Pictured Ency., Rand McNally & Co., Macmillan Co., Scott, Foresman & Co., Ginn & Co. textbooks, World Book Year Book, Field Enterprises Sci. Yearbooks, Childcraft Ann. and Library, World Book Dictionary. Home and Office: 7N161 Medinah Rd PO Box 25 Medinah IL 60157

STUMPF, STEPHEN ALAN, management consultant; educator; b. Rochester, N.Y., Dec. 28, 1949; s. Richard W. and Jacqueline A. (Mahar) S.; B.S. in Chem. Engring., Rensselaer Poly. Inst., 1971; M.B.A., U. Rochester, 1973; M. Phil., N.Y.U., 1978, Ph.D. in Bus. Adminstrn., 1978; m. Maria Jose Arnone, May 27, 1972; 1 son. Instr. mgmt. Grad. Sch. Bus. Adminstrn., N.Y.U., N.Y.C., 1977-78, asst. prof. mgmt. and organizational behavior, 1978-80, assoc. prof. mgmt. and organizational behavior, 1980—; dir. Mgmt. Simulations Projects Ctr., 1983—; cons. to AT&T Co., 1978-82, Citibank, 1979—, Dow Jones & Co., 1981—; Met. Life, 1986—. Bd. dirs. NYU Bus. Forum. Served to 1st lt. USAF, 1972-75. Spencer Found. grantee, 1979-81; NSF grantee, 1980-81, Social Sci. Research Council grantee, 1981-82; Fulbright scholar, 1986. Mem. Acad. of Mgmt., Am. Psychol. Assn., Am. Inst. of Decision Scis., Beta Gamma Sigma, Tau Beta Pi, Pi Lambda Upsilon. Republican. Roman Catholic. Author: Managing Careers, 1982; Choosing a Career in Business, 1984; contbr. articles on mgmt. to profl. jours. Home: 100 Bleecker St Apt 15D New York NY 10012 Office: 40 W 4th St New York NY 10012

STUREN, CARL OLOF, association executive; b. Stockholm, Feb. 20, 1919; s. Petrus and Kerstin (Wallbom) S.; M.C.W., Royal Inst. Tech., 1945; m. Winquist Solveig, July 11, 1943; children: Carl Olof, Lars Olof. Asst. comdr. Bldg. Bd. Stockholm City, 1944-47; tech. officer Swedish Standards Inst., 1947-49, dep. dir., 1950-56, dir., 1957-68; sec. gen. Internat. Orgn. Standardization, Geneva, 1969-86, sec. gen. emeritus, 1987—; UN expert indsl. standardization, Turkey, 1953-56, officer in charge UN Office, Ankara, 1954. Mem. Town Council Danderyd, 1962-68, chmn., 1966-68. Recipient Royal Gold medal Sweden, 1972, Astin Polk Internat. Standards medal, U.S.A., 1980, DIN Ehren ring award, 1981, Germany, Georg Garel award, France, 1985, ISO Golden award, 1986. Fellow Standards Engrs. Soc. (U.S.A.)(hon. life), Swedish Tennis Assn., Turkish Standards Inst., Standards Assn. New Zealand. Home: 10 ave de Champel, 1206 Geneva Switzerland Office: 1 rue de Varembe, 1211 Geneva Switzerland

STURGES, GLORIA JUNE, learning disabilities educator; b. Ingallas, Kans., Nov. 10, 1937; d. Donald Nathan and Dorothy Ellen (Whaley) Kitch; m. W.G. Bray, Jan. 22, 1960 (div. Apr. 1978); children—Lori Lynn, William Don; m. Sidney James Sturges. B.S. in Edn., Southeastern State U., 1959; M.A. in Edn., Webster U., 1975; postgrad. U. Kans., 1978-84, cert. learning disabilities specialty, 1984. Cert. tchr. elem. edn., Colo., Mo., reading and learning disabilities specialist, Mo. Tchr., Jefferson County Schs., Denver, 1959-60, Briggsdale, Colo., 1960-63, Colo. Sch. for Deaf and Blind, Colorado Springs, 1963-66, Bertha Heid Sch., Thornton, Colo., 1966-70; reading specialist Center Sch. Dist., Kansas City, Mo., 1970-78, learning disabilities specialist, 1985—; bus. exec. Sturges Co., Independence, Mo., 1982—. Active ARC, 1984—, Nat. Polit. Action, Kansas City, Mo., 1970—. conference presenter Emporia State U. Recipient Excellence in Edn. award ARC, 1984-85; Outstanding Achievement award Colo. for Deaf and Blind, 1963. Mem. Nat. Assn. Females Execs., NEA, Kappa Delta Pi. Republican. Baptist. Avocations: gourmet cooking; tennis; swimming; antiques. Home: 16805 Cogan Rd Independence MO 64055 Office: Red Bridge Sch 418 E 106th Terr Kansas City MO 64131

STURGES, JOHN SIEBRAND, consultant; b. Greenwich, Conn., Feb. 12, 1939; s. Harry Wilton and Elizabeth Helen (Niewenhous) S.; A.B., Harvard U., 1960; M.B.A., U. So. Calif., 1965; cert. EDP, N.Y.U., 1972; cert. exec. program. Grad. Sch. Bus., U. Mich., 1982; accredited Sr. Profl. in Human Resources, Personnel Accreditation Inst. 1986; cert. Life Office Mgmt. Assn., 1967; m. Anastasia Daphne Bakalis, May 6, 1967; children—Christina Aurora, Elizabeth Athena. With Equitable Life Assurance Soc. U.S., N.Y.C., 1965-79, mgr. systems devel., 1965-70, mgr. adminstrv. services, 1970-71, dir. compensation, 1971-75, v.p., personnel and adminstrv. services, 1975-79; sr. v.p. personnel Nat. Bank of N.Am., N.Y.C., 1979-82; corp. sr. v.p. adminstrn. and human resources Corroon and Black Corp., N.Y.C., 1982-84; mng. dir. human resources Marine Midland Bank, N.Y.C., 1984-87; mng. dir. Siebrand-Wilton Assocs., N.Y.C., 1986-87, pres., 1987—; adj. prof. Middlesex County Coll., 1987—. Lay reader St. Peters Episcopal Ch., Freehold, N.J., 1972—, vestryman, 1973—; bd. dirs. Freehold Area Hosp. Wellness Center, 1979—. Served to lt. USNR, 1960-65. Mem. Commerce Assocs., Am. Soc. Personnel Adminstrn. (v.p. 1988—), Am. Compensation Assn., Human Resources Planning Soc., Adminstrv. Mgmt. Soc., Employment Mgmt. Assn., Beta Gamma Sigma (dir. N.Y. 1978—), Phi Kappa Phi. Republican. Clubs: India House, Harvard (N.Y.C., Princeton, N.J.). Office: Siebrand-Wilton Assocs Inc PO Box 2498 New York NY 10008-2498

STURGES, SIDNEY JAMES, pharmacist, educator, investment and development company executive; b. Kansas City, Mo., Sept. 29, 1936; s. Sidney Alexander and Lenore Caroline (Lemley) S.; m. Martha Grace Leonard, Nov. 29, 1957 (div. 1979); 1 child, Grace Caroline; m. Gloria June Kitch, Sept. 17, 1983. BS in Pharmacy, U. Mo., 1957, post grad., 1959; MBA in Pharmacy Adminstrn., U. Kans., 1980; PhD in Bus. Adminstrn., Pacific Western U., 1980; cert. in Gerentology, Avila Coll., 1986. Registered pharmacist, Mo., Kans.; registered nursing home adminstr., Mo.; cert. vocat. tchr., Mo. Pharmacist, mgr. Crown Drugs, Kansas City, Mo., 1957-60; pharmacist, owner Sav-On-Drugs and Pharmacy, Kansas City, 1960-62; ptnr. Sam's Bargain Town Drugs, Raytown, Mo., 1961-62; pharmacist, owner Sturges Drugs DBA Barnard Pharmacy, Independence, Mo., 1962—; pres., owner Sturges Med. Corp., Independence, Mo., 1967-1977, Sturgess Investment Corp., Independence, 1967-1978, Sturwood Investment Corp., Independence, 1968—, Sturges Agri-Bus. Co., Independence, 1977—, Sturges Devel. Co., 1984—; instr. pharmacology Penn Valley Community Coll., 1976-84; instr., lectr. various clubs and groups. Contbr. articles to profl. jours. Bd. dirs. Independence House, 1981-83; mem. Criminal Justice Adv. Commn., Independence, 1982—. Recipient Outstanding award Kans. City Alcohol and Drug Abuse Council, 1982. Mem. Mo. Sheriffs Assn., Mo. Pharm. Assn. (pharmacy dr. 1981), Mo. Found. Pharm. Care, U. Mo. Alumni Assn. Home: 16805 Cogan Rd Independence MO 64055 Office: Sturges Co 13701 E 35th St Independence MO 64055

STURLASON, LEIF VIGGO, technical executive; b. Copenhagen, Denmark, Aug. 9, 1923; s. Sigurd Viggo and Edith Johanne (Hansen) S.; Mech. Engr., U. Cophenhagen, 1958; m. Gurli Israelson, Sept. 11, 1954; children: Runa, Asger. Research engr. Zeuthen & Aagaard, 1958-60; sect. leader Danfoss-Copenhagen, 1961-63; design-mgr. Danfoss-Nordborg, 1964-74, mgr. research, 1974-78, mgr. tech. services, 1978—, mem. Teknologirådet, 1974-80, DANDOK, 1977-83; mem. exec. com. Korrosionscentralen, 1982-84, chmn. bd., 1984—. Censor, AUC, Denmark, 1976—. Mem. Ingeniør-Sammenslutningen. Editor: Stud.-Techn., 1957-65. Patentee in field. Home: 16 Johs, Edwalds VEJ, 6400 Sonderburg Denmark

STURM, DONALD L., construction executive; b. 1932; married;. BA, CCNY, 1954; LLB, U. Denver, 1958; LLM, NYU, 1959. Atty. IRS, 1959-62; with Peter Kiewit Sons Inc., Omaha, 1963—, v.p., 1969-82, sr. v.p., 1982-86, vice chmn., 1986—, also bd. dirs.; sr. v.p. Kiewit U.S. Co. subs. Peter Kiewit Sons Inc., Omaha, from 1982, also bd. dirs.; chmn. Kiewit Holdings Group Inc., Norwalk, Conn., 1986—. Office: Kiewit Holdings Group Inc 800 Connecticutt Ave Norwalk CT 06856

STURM, WILLIAM CHARLES, lawyer; b. Milw., Aug. 4, 1941; s. Charles William and Helen Ann (Niesen) S.; m. Kay F. Sturm, June 10, 1967; children—Patricia, Elizabeth, Katherine, William, Susan. B.S. in Bus. Adminstrn., Marquette U., 1963, J.D., 1966. Bar: Wis. 1966, U.S. Dist. Ct. (ea. dist.) Wis. 1966, U.S. Supreme Ct. 1980. Sole practice, Milw., 1966-78; ptnr. Rausch, Hamell, Ehrle & Sturm, S.C., Milw., 1978-81, Rausch, Hamell, Ehrle, Sturm & Blom, Milw., 1981-83, Rausch, Hamell, Ehrle & Sturm, 1983—; asst. prof. Marquette U., 1982—; lectr. in field. Mem. adv. bd. Pallotine Order, 1985—. Recipient Editors award Wis. Med. Credit Assn., 1980. Mem. ABA, Wis. Bar Assn., Comml. Law League Am. (exec. council midwestern dist. 1981-83, 86-88, chmn. state membership com. 1981—, nat. nominating council 1984-86, 1987—, sec. midwestern dist. 1988—), Nat. Speakers Assn., Am. Bus. Law Assn., Midwest Bus. Law Assn. (sec. 1988—), Wis. Profl. Speakers Assn., Healthcare Fin. Mgmt. Assn., Beta Alpha Psi (faculty v.p. Psi chpt. 1985-88), Midwest Bus. And Health Assn. (v.p. proceedings 1987-88, v.p. program 1988—). Clubs: Westmoor Country (Milw.); Kiwanis (pres. 1979, lt. gov. div. 5, 1980) (Wauwatosa, Wis.). Contbr. articles to profl. jours. Office: 7500 W State St Milwaukee WI 53213

STURZENEGGER, OTTO, chemical company executive; b. Zurich, Switzerland, Feb. 27, 1926; came to U.S., 1948; s. Otto and Julia (Oertle) S.; m. Gerd Wold, Oct. 19, 1957; children—Elsie, Thomas O. B.S., Fed. Inst. Tech., Zurich, 1948; M.S., Okla. State U., 1949, Ph.D., 1953; grad. advanced mgmt. program, Harvard U., 1969; LHD (hon.), Mercy Coll., Dobbs Ferry, N.Y., 1982. Asst. to pres. Geigy Chem. Corp., Ardsley, N.Y., 1960-63, pres. mfg.-engring. div., 1963-69, pres. agr. chem. div., 1969-70; pres., chief exec. officer CIBA-GEIGY Corp., Ardsley, N.Y., 1970-78, chmn., chief exec. officer, 1978-86, chmn., 1978—; dir. CIBA-GEIGY A.G., Basle, Switzerland, 1986—; dir. NCNB Corp., Charlotte, N.C., IBM World Trade Corp., Armonk, N.Y., CIBA-GEIGY A.B., Basel, Switzerland. Bd. dirs. United Way Tri-State, N.Y.C., 1974-75; bd. govs. Kennedy Ctr., Washington, 1981; mem. adv. council N.Y. Med. Coll.-Hosp. Found., Valhalla, 1983-86. Recipient Westchester Man of Yr. award Gannett Newspapers, 1982. Mem. Sigma Xi. Office: CIBA-GEIGY Corp 444 Saw Mill River Rd Ardsley NY 10502

STUTMAN, LEONARD JAY, research scientist, cardiologist; b. Boston, Apr. 8, 1928; s. Herbert Hyman and Nellie (Wiener) S.; BS, MIT, 1948; MA, Boston U., 1949; MD, U. Rochester, 1953; m. Jeanne Ann Soblen, Dec. 23, 1951; children—Peter, David, Marc, Robin. Intern, resident medicine Bellevue Hosp., 1953-57; chief, med. services br. WPAFB, Dayton, Ohio, 1957-59; spl. advanced research fellow NIH, Nat. Heart Inst. 1959-61; instr. in clin. medicine N.Y. U. Coll. Medicine, 1956-61, asst. prof. pathology, 1961-65; assoc. prof. clin. medicine N.Y. Med. Coll., 1980—; head coagulation research lab. St. Vincent's Hosp. and Med. Center, N.Y., 1965—; attending physician St. Vincent's Hosp.; sr. attending physician medicine, sr. cardiologist Nyack (N.Y.) Hosp.; med. dir. Presdl. Life Ins. Co., Nyack, Urbaine Life Reins. Co., Tarrytown, N.Y. Dir. cardiac epidemiology study Ford Found. Vera Inst.; med. dir. Urbaine Life Reinsurance Co., Tarrytown, N.Y.; mem. Internat. Com. on Thrombosis and Hemostasis; vis. mem. arteriosclerosis group Rockefeller U., 1976—. Served as capt. USAF, 1957-59. Fellow Am. Coll. Cardiology, AAAS, ACP, N.Y. Acad. Medicine; mem. Am. Soc. Hematology, AMA, N.Y. Med. Soc., N.Y. Acad. Sci., Sigma Xi. Contbr. articles to profl. jours. Home: 250 Town Line Rd West Nyack NY 10994 Office: 153 W 11th St New York NY 10011

STYLIANOU, PETROS SAVVA, politician, journalist, writer; b. Kythrea, Cypress, June 8, 1933; s. Savvas and Evanthia Stylianou; m. Voula Tzanetatou, 1960; 2 daughters. Student, U. Athens, Greece, U. Salonika. With Panhellenic Com. of the Cyprus Struggle; pres. Cypriot U. Students, 1953-54; co-founder Dauntless Leaders of the Cypriot Fighters Orgn.; then joined liberation movement of Cyprus 1955; leader Nat. Striking Group; imprisoned 1956-59; mem. cen. com. United Dem. Reconstruction Front, 1959; dep. sec.-gen. Cyprus Labour Confedn., 1959, sec.-gen., 1960-62; with Cyprus Dem. Labour Fedn., 1962, sec.-gen., 1962-73, hon. pres., 1974—; mem. House of Reps., 1960-70, 1982—, sec., 1960-62; dir. Mus. Nat. Struggle, 1979-80; dep. minister of interior Govt. of Cyprus, 1980-82, spl. advisor to pres. on cultural affairs, 1982-85; founder, mng. dir. Kypriakos Logos mag., 1969—, Anaperikon Vima, 1970—; founder, pres. Pancyprian Com. for the Enclaved Greek Population, 1974—, Polit. Com. for the Cyprus Struggle, 1976—; mem. adminstrv. bd. Hellenic Inst. for Research in Rehabilitation, 1976—. mng. editor Ergatiki Foni newspaper, 1960-62, Ergatikor Agonas DEOK newspaper, 1962-63, Allaghi, 1963; contbr. articles and poetry. Mem. Internat. Council on Archives, 1975—, adminstrv. bd. Hellenic Inst. Research in Rehabilitation, 1976—; co-ordination coms. of 28 vocational and sci. orgns. Mem. Pancyprian Orgn. for Rehabilitation of Spastics (founder), Pancyprian Orgn. for Rehabilitation from Kidney Disease (founder), Orgn. for Rehabilitation of the Disabled, Orgn. for Rehabilitation from Haemophilia (founder), Orgn. for Rehabilitation from Myopathy, Cyprus Hist. Mus. and Archives (pres.), Pancyprian Olive Produce Orgn. (founder 1967),. Home: Kimononos 10 Engomi, Nicosia Cyprus Office: Stasicratous 16, Nicosia Cyprus *

STYLIANOUDIS, ALEXANDER NICOLAS, shipping company executive; b. Alexandria, Egypt, Feb. 19, 1930; came to Monaco, 1973; s. Nicolas Stylianos and Helen (Marchesi) S.; m. Inger Uno Olofson, Sept. 8, 1961 (div. 1970); 1 child, Nicolas. Cert. for foreigners comml. dept. Lund U., Malmo, Sweden, 1967. Asst. to mgr. Esso, Standard Oil, Athens, 1959-62; mgr. Dean Van Lines, Athens, Beirut, 1963-66; export mgr. Dux Internat., Malmo, Stockholm, 1967-73; asst. mgr. Onassis Group, Monte Carlo, 1973-75; mgr. Chandris Group, Pireaus, Monte Carlo, 1975—. Club: Glyfada Golf (Athens). Office: Atlantic Maritime Service SA, 20 Blvd Pr Charlotte Bloc D, 98000 Monte Carlo Monaco

STYMNE, BENGT A., management educator; b. Gävle, Sweden, Apr. 2, 1939; s. Sten A. and Ruth M.S. (Lindskog) S.; m. Ingrid Margareta Claeson, Dec. 29, 1958; children: Joakim, Ellika. D in Econ. Scis., Stockholm Sch. of Econs., 1970. Researcher Econ. Research Inst., Stockholm, 1961-64; research asst. U. Mich., Ann Arbor, 1964-65; program dir. Scandinavian Inst. Adminstrv. Research, 1966-70; prof. mgmt. European Inst. Advanced Studies Mgmt., Brussels, 1973-74; vis. fellow Templeton Coll., Oxford, Eng., 1977-78; vis. prof. Ecole Polytechnique and others, Paris, 1985-87; head Inst. Mgmt. Innovation and tech. Author books and articles on organizational strategies, work organizations and industrial democracy. Office: Stockholm Sch Econs, Box 6501, 113 83 Stockholm Sweden

STYNES, BARBARA BILELLO, association administrator; b. N.Y.C., Apr. 24, 1951; d. Sylvester Francis and Jacqueline Marie (Giardelli) Bilello; m. Frank Joseph Stynes, Aug. 24, 1969; children: Christopher Francis, Jeremy Scott. BA, Rutgers U., 1976. Mktg. rep. McNeil Consumer Products Co., Fort Washington, Pa., 1979-82, Met Path Inc., Des Plaines, Ill., 1982-85; mktg. coordinator Life program Meml. Hosp. and YMCA, Chattanooga, 1986—; mem. Chattanooga Area Wellness Council, 1986—, Chattanooga Area Healthcare Coalition, 1986—; dir. mktg. and communications, YMCA, Chattanooga, 1986—; fiber sculptor, 1975-77; weaver, 1976-79. Vol. Am. Heart Assn., 1972—, Spl. Olympics, Chgo., 1982-84; speaker Tenn. Safety Belt coalition, 1986—; clinic leader Am. Lung Assn., Chattanooga, 1986-88; chairperson fundraising, trustee Pine Grove Coop. Sch., New Brunswick, N.J., 1977-78; bd. dirs. Signal Mountain Newcomers Assn., Tenn., 1985-86. Mem. Nat. Assn. Female Execs., Am. Bus. Womans Network Chattanooga (chair membership), Fiber Arts Guild. Roman Catholic. Avocations: ballet, piano, aerobics. Home: 914 Dunsinane Rd Signal Mountain TN 37377

STYRON, WILLIAM, writer; b. Newport News, Va., June 11, 1925; s. William Clark and Pauline Margaret (Abraham) S.; m. Rose Burgunder, May 4, 1953; children: Susanna Margaret, Paola Clark, Thomas, Claire Alexandra. Student, Christchurch Sch., Davidson Coll.; A.B., Duke U., 1947, Litt.D., 1968. Fellow Am. Acad. Arts and Letters at Am. Acad. in Rome, 1953; fellow Silliman Coll., Yale, 1964—; hon. cons. Library of Congress.; jury pres. Cannes Film Festival, 1983. Author: novels Lie Down in Darkness, 1951, The Long March, 1953, Set This House on Fire, 1960, The Confessions of Nat Turner, 1967 (Pulitzer prize 1968, Howells medal Am. Acad. Arts and Letters 1970), Sophie's Choice, 1979 (Am. Book award 1980), In the Clap Shack, play, 1972, This Quiet Dust, 1982; also articles, essays, revs.; Editor: Best Stories from the Paris Review, 1959; adv. editor: Paris Rev, 1953—; Editorial bd.: The Am. Scholar, 1970-76. Decorated Commandeur de l'Ordre des Arts et des Lettres (France), Commandeur Légion d'Honneur (France); recipient Duke U. Disting. Alumni award, 1984, Edward MacDowell medal, 1988, Conn. Arts award, 1984, Prix Mondial del Duca, 1985, Edward MacDowell medal for excellence in the arts, 1988. Mem. Am. Acad. Arts and Scis., Am. Acad. Arts and Letters, Signet Soc., Harvard, Am. Acad. Arts and Letters, Académie Goncourt, Phi Beta Kappa. Democrat.

SU, CHING-SHEN, nuclear engineer, educator; b. Kwangtung, Republic of China, Oct. 10, 1930; s. Henry C. and Ying-ju (Wan) S.; m. Kuei-chen Lee, July 28, 1963; children: Chen-tung, Wendy, Wen-hui. BS, Naval Coll. Tech., 1954; MS, Nat. Tsing Hua U., 1963; PhD, Rensselaer Poly. Inst., 1966. From assoc. prof. to prof. Nat. Tsing Hua U., Hsinchu, Taiwan, 1967-75—; sr. research assoc. NRC, Marshall Space Flight Ctr., Huntsville, Ala., 1973-74; guest prof. Max Planck Inst für Chemie, Mainz, Fed. Republic of Germany, 1974-75; dir. Precision Instrument Devel. Ctr., Nat. Sci. Council, Taiwan, 1976-86; dean Coll. Nuclear Sci. Nat. Tsing Hua U. Taiwan, 1988—. Author: Vacuum Technology, 1978, Vacuum Engineering, 1986; contbr. articles to profl. jours. Served with Chinese Navy, 1954-61. Mem. Optical Engring. Soc. Taiwan (founder), Vacuum Soc. Republic of China (pres.), Nuclear Energy Soc. Taiwan, Biomed. Engring. Soc. Taiwan, Sigma Xi, Phi Tou Phi. Kuomintang. Confucian. Home: 90 New East Compound, 101 Kuang Fu Rd Sec 2, Hsinchu 30043, Republic of China Office: Inst Nuclear Sci, Nat Tsing Hua U, Hsinchu 30043, Republic of China

SUAREZ, JULIO CARLOS, petroleum engineer; b. Lima, Peru, June 17, 1941; s. Julio Suarez and Maria Lorca; m. Catalina Portocarrero, Jan. 10, 1969; children: Beatriz, Julio. BS in Petrloeum Engring., Nat. Engring. U., Lima, 1967. Prodn. engr. Belco Petroleum, Talara, Peru, 1966-68, petroleum engr., 1969-74; chief petroleum engr. Belco Petroleum, Peru, 1975-80; drilling engr. Asamera Oil, Jakarta, Indonesia, 1981—; mgr. drilling Asamera Oil, Bogota, Columbia, 1986, 87, 88. Mem. Indonesian Petroleum Assn., Soc. Petroleum Engrs. Roman Catholic. Club: Hilton Executive (Jakarta). Office: Asamera Oil, PO Box JL GATOH Subroto, Manggala Jakarta Indonesia Also: Tranversal 19, No 122-63, Bogota Colombia

SUAREZ GONZALEZ, ADOLFO, Spanish politician and lawyer; b. Cebreros, Avila, Spain, Sept. 25, 1932; s. Hipolito Suarez Guerra and Herminia Gonzalez Prado; Baccalaureat, San Juan de la Cruz Coll.; Dr. of Law cum laude, U. Madrid, 1958; m. Amparo Illana Elortegui, July 15, 1961; children: Maria Amparo, Adolfo, Laura, Sonsoles, Javier. Pvt. sec. to Nat. Del. for the Spanish Provinces, 1958-61; chief of cabinet of Vice Sec. of Nat. Movement. 1961-64; program dir. Spain's TV network, 1965-68; civil gov. Province of Segovia, Spain, 1968-69; dir.-gen. of Spanish Broadcasting TV System, 1969-73; family rep. to Spanish Parliament from Province of Avila, 1967-77; pres. of Dem. Union of Spanish People, 1975; minister sec.-gen. of Nat. Movement, from 1975; prime minister of Spain and pres. Council of Ministries, 1976-81; leader Unión Centro Democrático, 1977-81, leader Centro Democrático y Social, pres., 1982—. Recipient numerous decorations Mem. Madrid Bar Assn., Inst. of Polit. Studies, Spanish Trial Law Inst. Address: Centro Democratico y Social, Calle Jorge Juan 30-5, 28001 Madrid Spain *

SUAREZ-MURIAS, MARGUERITE C., emeritus language and literature educator; b. Havana, Cuba, Mar. 23, 1921; came to U.S., 1935, naturalized, 1959; d. Eduardo R. and Marguerite (Vendel) S.-M. A.B., Bryn Mawr Coll., 1942; M.A., Columbia U., 1953, Ph.D., 1957. Lectr. in Spanish Columbia U., 1954-56; pub. relations officer med. div. Johns Hopkins U., 1957-58; asst. prof. Spanish and French Sweet Briar Coll., 1958-59, Hood Coll., 1960-61; lectr. Cath. U., 1960-63, asst. prof., summers 1960-62, asso. prof., summers 1964-66; asst. prof. dept. langs. and linguistics Am. U., 1961-63, asso. prof., 1963-66; prof. dept. classical and modern langs. Marquette U., Milw., 1966-68; prof. Spanish and Portuguese U. Wis., Milw., 1968-83; chmn. U. Wis., 1972-75; guest prof. U. South Africa, Pretoria, 1980. Author: La novela romántica en Hispanoamérica, 1963, Antología estilística de la prosa moderna española, 1968, Essays on Hispanic Literature/Ensayos de literatura hispana, 1982; also various articles to profl. jours.; editor: Gironella's Los cipreses creen en Dios, 1969. Roman Catholic. Home: 3904 Saint Paul St Baltimore MD 21218 Winter Home: 27 Lee Dr Ocean Walk Saint Augustine FL 32084

SUBA, ANTONIO RONQUILLO, surgeon; b. Philippines, Apr. 25, 1927; came to U.S., 1952, naturalized, 1961; s. Antonio Mesina and Valentina Cabais (Ronquillo) S.; m. Sylvia Marie Karl, June 16, 1956; children—Steven Antonio, Eric John, Laurinda Ann, Gregory Karl, Timothy Mark, Sylvia Kathleen. M.D., U. St. Thomas, Philippines, 1952. Diplomate: Am. Bd. Surgery. Intern St. Anthony's Hosp., St. Louis, 1952-53; resident St. Louis County Hosp., St. Louis, 1953-57; trainee Nat. Cancer Inst., Ellis Fischel State Cancer Hosp., Columbia, Mo., 1957-59; chief surg. services U.S. Army, Bremerhaven, Germany, 1959-61; practice medicine specializing in gen. and hand surgery St. Louis, 1961—; pres., prin. ARS (P.C.), 1971-84. Contbr. feature articles to Philippine publs., 1946-51, articles to med. jours. Fellow A.C.S.; mem. AMA, Pan-Pacific, Mo. surg. assns., St. Louis Surg. Soc., Am. Assn. Hand Surgery. Club: K.C. Home: 12085 Heatherdane St Saint Louis MO 63131 Office: 1050 Dodge Dr Saint Louis MO 63026

SUBAK-SHARPE, GERALD EMIL, electrical engineering educator; b. Vienna, Austria, June 15, 1925; came to U.S., 1959, naturalized, 1967; s. Robert and Nelly (Brull) S.; m. Genell Jackson, Nov. 23, 1963; children: David, Sarah and Hope (twins). B.Sc. with 1st class honors, Univ. Coll., London, 1951; Ph.D., U. London, 1965; Sc.D., Columbia U., 1969. Research engr. Brit. Telecommunications Research, Taplow, Eng., 1951-58; mem. tech. staff Bell Labs., Murray Hill, N.J., 1959-64, cons., 1977-78; assoc. prof. elec. engring. Manhattan Coll., Bronx, N.Y., 1966-68; prof. elec. engring. CCNY, N.Y.C., 1968—; v.p. G.S. Sharpe Communications Inc., 1981—. Author: (with A.B. Glaser) Integrated Circuit Engineering, 1978; contbr. articles on network and semicondr. theory to profl. jours. Served as lt. Royal Warwickshire Regt., 1944-47. Recipient Prof. of Yr. award Eta Kappa Nu/CCNY, 1985-86. Fellow Instn. Elec. Engrs. (London); mem. IEEE (sr.), N.Y. Acad. Scis., Nat. Trust for Historic Preservation. Home: 606 W 116th St Apt 71 New York NY 10027 also: Knollcroft New Concord NY 12060 Office: CCNY Convent Ave and 140th St New York NY 10031

SUBBA, TANKA BAHADUR, university lecturer, researcher; b. Kalimpong, West Bengal, India, May 9, 1957; s. Moti Hang and Goma (Wati) S.; m. Rip Roshina Gowloog, Feb. 16, 1987. BA in Polit. Sci. with honors, Kalimpong Coll., India, 1977; MA in Sociology, N. Bengal U., Siliguri, 1979; PhD, N. Bengal U., 1985. Jr. research fellow N. Bengal U., 1981-84; lectr. N. Bengal U. Ctr. for Himalayan Studies, 1985—; mem. inter-dept. adv. com. Ctr. for Human Studies, Siliguri, 1985—. Author: the Quiet Hills, 1985; contbr. articles to profl. jours. Christian Inst. for Study Religion and Soc. research grantee, 1980-81; U. Grants Commn. research grantee, 1981-84. Mem. Indian Sociol. Soc. (life), Indian Inst. Hill Economy (life). Hindu. Office: N Bengal U, Ctr Himalayan Studies, Siliguri 734430, India

SUBRAHMANYAN, TIRUKOILUR RAJAGOPALAIYER, electronics and telecommunications engineer, consultant; b. Sattur, Tamil Nadu, India, Aug. 14, 1927; s. Tirukoilur V. and Swarnambal Rajagopalan; m. Sundarambal, July 7, 1947; children—Meenalochani, Varalakshmi. B.Engring., Coll. of Engring., Guindy, 1949. Cert. telecommunication engr. Tech. asst. All India Radio, Delhi, 1949-50; high frequency specialist, sales engr. Voltas Ltd., Bombay and Delhi, 1951-60, divisional mgr., mktg. exec., Delhi, Calcutta, Bombay, 1960-72; chief engr., Bombay, 1972-87; cons. Tata Projects Ltd., Bombay, 1987—. Editor: A Learner's Sanskrit-Hindi-Tamil-English Dictionary, 1980; author articles. Fellow Inst. of Electronics and Telecommunication Engrs. India (disting. fellow; v.p., chmn. Bombay 1977-78), Inst. Standards Engrs. India (treas. 1973-75); mem. IEEE (sr., v.p. India sect. 1972-73), Calcutta Mgmt. Assn. Hindu. Avocations: Philately; numismatics; photography; reading. Home: Kshama Plot 499, 13th Rd, Chembur,, Bombay 400 071 Maharashtra, India Office: Tata Projects Ltd, 24 Homi Mody St, Bombay, Maharashtra 400001, India

SUBRAMANIAM, SUPPIAH, air transport company executive; b. Kuala Lumpur, Fed. Territory, Malaysia, Mar. 23, 1942; s. Subramaniam Veerasamy and Sellamah Gopal; m. Indra Devi, June 3, 1972; 1 child, Surina. Stores record clk. Glaxo Labs., Selangor, 1960-61; clk. Nat. Electricity Bd., Kuala Lumpur, 1961-69; exec. acctg. officer U. Hosp., Kuala Lumpur, 1969-71; asst. acct. Kelang Port Authority, Selangor, 1971-72, acct., 1972-73; tech. cost acct. Malaysian Airline System, Selangor, 1973-76, cost acctg. controller, 1976-78, asst. accounts mgr., 1978-81, fin. projects mgr., 1981-82, mgr. mgmt. info. services, 1982-83, accounts mgr., 1983—; hon. treas. MAS Staff Multipurpose Coop. Soc., Selangor, 1983-85, vice chmn., 1985—. Fellow Chartered Assn. Cert. Accts.; mem. Chartered Inst. Mgmt. Accts. (assoc.), Malaysian Assn. CPA's. Clubs: Pantai Youngsters (hon. sec. 1966-72), Football Assn. (Kuala Lumpur) (pres. 1985—). Home: 10 Jalan SS19/3A, Subang Jaya Selangor 47500, Malaysia Office: Malaysian Airline System, Ground Floor Adminstrn Bldg, Subang Selangor 47200, Malaysia

SUBRAMANIAN, BALA, scientist, cardiologist; b. Madras, India, Oct. 5, 1940; s. Venkateswaran Iyer and Subbulakshmi S.; m. Shyamala Rajagopalan, July 14, 1965; children: Radha, Rajiv. MBBS, All India Inst. Med. Scis., New Delhi, 1962. Diplomate India Bd. Cardiology, Eng. Bd. Cardiology. Intern, then resident Armed Forces Med. Coll., Poona, India; sr. registrar Northwick Park Hosp., Harrow, Eng., 1977-79, cons. cardiology, 1979-83; dir. research Brunel Inst. for Bioengring., Uxbridge, Eng., 1983—. Author: Calcium Antagonists in Chronic Stabe Angina, 1983. Served to lt. col. Indian Army Med. Corps., 1962-77. Fellow Am. Coll. Cardiology, Am. Heart Assn. Home: 133 Preston Hill, Kenton, Middlesex HA3 9XE, England Office: 52 Harley St, London WIN 1AD, England

SUBRAMANIAN, SUNDARAM, electronics engineer; b. Emaneswaram, Madras, India, July 9, 1934; came to U.S., 1968; s. Sundaram and Velammal (Subbiah) S.; m. Hemavathy Vadivelu, Feb. 18, 1968; children: Anand Kumar, Malathy. BE, Madras (India) U., 1959; PhD, Glasgow (Scotland) U., 1967; MBA, Roosevelt U., Chgo., 1977. Research engr. Zenith, Inc., Chgo., 1968-75; project engr. Motorola, Inc., Chgo., 1975-77; prof. Chapman Coll., Orange, Calif., 1977-78; cons. MCS, Orange, 1978-80; project engr. Endevco, San Juan Capistrano, Calif., 1980-84; project mgr. Unisys Corp., Rancho Santa Margarita, Calif., 1984—; bd. dirs. P.S.B. Inc., Torrance, Calif., 1984—. Patentee in field. Bd. dirs. Tamil Nadu Found. Inc., Balt. and Washington, 1976-79; pres. S. India Cultural Assn., Villa Park, Calif., 1977-78. Mem. IEEE, Inst. Environ. Sci. (sr.). Office: Unisys Corp 30200 Bandaras Ranco Santa Margarita CA 92688

SUCHAN, HANS GEORG, management consultant; b. Peiskretscham, Upper Silesia, Dec. 12, 1925; s. Hans and Therese (Nierichlo) S.; Dr. oec.; m. Margot Eva Maria Krantz, 1931; children—Gabriele, Sabine. Cons. asst., Dr. Richter, C.P.A., Frankfurt, 1953-54; exec. mgr. revision and orgn. Koch & Mann, wholesale food, Wuppertal, 1954-56; cons. O. Martin mgmt. cons., Cologne, 1957-58; founder Suchan Unternehmensberatung BDU, 1958—, also mng. dir. Founder, mng. dir. Suchan Logistic Systems Gmbtt, 1969, Suchan Logistic Systems Ltd., London, 1980; founder Suchan Logistic Systems, San Francisco, 1981; cooperation with M.A.N. (Maschinenfabrik Augsburg-Nuernberg), Munich, 1975, M.A.N. Transportberatung Dr. Suchan, Steyr-Daimler-Puch AG, Vienna, FBS Fuhr-Betriebsservice, 1975; software cooperation with Wang, data and word processing, 1980. Mem. Bund Deutscher Unternehmensberater. Contbr. profl. jours. Author manual Wie Spare Ich Transportkosten, 1974. Home: 17 Mozart Strasse, D-6940 Weinheim Federal Republic of Germany Office: 13 Theodor Heuss Strasse, D-6940 Weinham Federal Republic of Germany

SUCHENWIRTH, RICHARD MATHIAS AUGUST, neurologist; b. Vienna, Austria, Nov. 1, 1927; s. Richard and Elisabeth (Kutsch) S.; MD, U. Munich, 1950; m. Gertrud Meyer zu Hörste, July 12, 1955; children: Richard G.H., Gertrud E.I., Dietlinde E.M., Roland H.R.; m. 2d, Barbara Freiin von Fuerstenberg, July 24, 1978; children: Lioba H.M., Leonhard O.M.J. Asst., Neurol. Clinic, Munich, Freiburg, Kiel (W. Ger.), 1951-62; head physician Neurol. Clinic Luebeck, 1962-66, Erlangen, 1967-70; med. supt. Neurol. Clin. Teaching Hosp., Kassel, 1970-81; pvt. dozent U. Kiel, 1965; prof. U. Erlangen (W. Ger.), 1972—. Pres. sci. com. Bekaempfung der Muskelkrankheiten Freiburg, W. Ger., 1972-74. Mem. Deutsche Gesellschaft für Neurologie, also others. Roman Catholic. Club: Lions. Author: Abbau der graphischen Leistung, 1967; Taschenbuch der klinischen Neurologie, 1975; Neurologische Begutachtung, 1977; An der letzten Türe, 1979; Pocket Book of Clinical Neurology, 1979; Neurologische Untersuchung, 1982; Warum Krank?, 1982; Therapie Neurologischer Krankheiten, 1988. Home: 12 Seesstrasse, D8036 Herrsching 2 Federal Republic of Germany

SUD, ISH, mechanical engineer; b. Calcutta, India, Oct. 6, 1949; s. Inder Sain and Santosh Vati (Law) S.; B.Tech., Indian Inst. Tech., Kanpur, 1970; M.S., Duke U., 1971, Ph.D., 1975. Design engr. T.C. Cooke, P.E., Inc., Cons. Engrs., Durham, 1974-77, dir. sect. energy mgmt. and spl. projects, 1978; sr. project engr., systems analyst Duke U., Durham, 1976-84, assoc. prof., 1983-87; pres. SUD Assocs., Cons. Engrs., Durham, 1979—. Mem. India Assn. (pres. 1973-74), ASHRAE, NSPE, ASME. Hindu. Contbr. articles to profl. jours. Home: 3004 Montgomery St Durham NC 27705 Office: 1805 Chapel Hill Rd Durham NC 27707

SUDARSKY, JERRY M., industrialist; b. Russia, June 12, 1918; came to U.S., 1928, naturalized, 1934; s. Selig and Sara (Ars) S.; m. Mildred Axelrod, Aug. 31, 1947; children: Deborah, Donna. Student, U. Iowa, 1936-39; B.S., Poly. U. Bklyn., 1942; D.Sc. (hon.), Poly. Inst. N.Y., 1976. Founder, chief exec. officer Bioferm Corp., Wasco, Calif., 1946-66; cons. to Govt. of Israel, 1966-67; founder, chmn. Israel Chems., Ltd., Tel Aviv, Israel, 1967-70; chmn. I.C. Internat. Cons., Tel Aviv, 1971-73; vice chmn. Daylin, Inc., Los Angeles, 1974-77, also dir.; pres. JMS Assos., Los Angeles, 1977—; vice chmn. bd. Jacobs Engring., Pasadena, 1985—. Bd. govs. Hebrew U., Jerusalem, hon. treas., 1968—; trustee Polytechnic U. N.Y., 1976—. Served with USNR, 1943-46. Mem. AAAS, Am. Chem. Soc., Sigma Xi. Clubs: Brentwood Country (Los Angeles). Home: 2220 Ave of the Stars Los Angeles CA 90067

SUDBRINK, JANE MARIE, sales and marketing executive; b. Sandusky, Ohio, Jan. 14, 1942; niece of Arthur and Lydia Sudbrink. B.S., Bowling Green State U., 1964; student in cytogenetics Kinderspital-Zurich, Switzerland, 1965. Field rep. Random House and Alfred A. Knopf Inc., Mpls., 1969-72, Ann Arbor, Mich., 1973, regional mgr., Midwest and Can., 1974-79, Canadian rep., mgr., 1980-81; psychology and ednl. psychology adminstrv. editor Charles E. Merrill Pub. Co. div. Bell & Howell Corp., Columbus, Ohio, 1982-84; sales and mktg. mgr. trade products Wilson Learning Corp., Eden Prairie, Minn., 1984-85; fin. cons. Merrill Lynch Pierce Fenner & Smith, Edina, 1986—; sr. editor Gorsuch Scarisbrick Pubs., Scottsdale, Ariz., 1988—. Mem. Am. Ednl. Research Assn., Nat. Assn. Female Execs. Lutheran. Home and Office: 1010 N Plum Grove Rd Schaumburg IL 60173

SUDBURY, DAVID ALAN, automobile sales executive; b. Vancouver, B.C., Can., July 30, 1948; s. Alan William and Muriel Leary S.; m. Jo Anne Karen Malanchuk, May 19, 1973; children: Jennifer, Paul. BA, U. Toronto, 1982. Analyst Gulf Oil Can., Toronto, 1972-74; credit mgr. Can. Motorola, Toronto, 1974-75; mgr. treasury Witco Chem. Can. Ltd., Toronto, 1975-79; dir. personnel Royal Doulton, Toronto, 1979-82; sr. corp. mgr. Honda Can., Inc., Toronto, 1982-86; v.p., gen. mgr. Honda Can. Fin., Inc., Toronto, 1987—, also bd. dirs. Mem. Personnel Assn. of Ont. (pres. 1982), Scarborough (Ont.) C. of C. Home: 634 Aspen Rd, Pickering, ON Canada L1W 3T7 Office: Honda Canada Finance Inc, 305 Milner Ave, Suite 301, Scarborough, ON Canada M1B 3V4

SUDDARTH, ROSCOE SELDON, diplomat; b. Louisville, Aug. 5, 1935; s. George Seldon and Anna (Urfer) S.; m. Michele Regine Lebas, Mar. 15, 1963; children: Anne, Mark. BA, Yale U., 1956, Oxford (Eng.) U., 1958; MA, Oxford (Eng.) U., 1961; MS, MIT, 1972; cert. Arabic lang. and area specialist program, Fgn. Service Inst., Beirut, 1965. Fgn. service officer Am. Embassy, Mali, Lebanon, Yemen Arab Republic, Libya, 1961-69; dep. chief-of-mission Am. Embassy, Amman, Jordan, 1974-79; exec. asst. to undersec. of State for Polit. Affairs U.S. Dept. State, Washington, 1979-81; dep. chief-of-mission Am. Embassy, Riyadh, Saudi Arabia, 1982-85; dep. asst. Sec. of State for Near Ea. and South Asian Affairs U.S. Dept. State, Washington, 1985-87; U.S. ambassador to Jordan 1987—. Co-author: Tales of the Foreign Service, 1971. Scholar Keasbey Found., Oxford U., 1956-58. Mem. Phi Beta Kappa. Episcopalian. Office: Am Embassy Amman Jordan APO New York NY 09892-5000 *

SUDHARMONO, Indonesian government official; b. Gresik, East Java, Indonesia, Mar. 12, 1927. Ed., Mil. Law Acad., 1956, Mil. Law Inst., 1962, Army Staff and Command Coll. Mil. officer Indonesian Army, 1945-72; state sec., minister Indonesia, Jakarta, 1973-88, v.p., 1988—. Address: Office Vice Pres, Jakarta Indonesia *

SUDILOVSKY, OSCAR, pathologist, educator; b. Rosario, Argentina, Nov. 8, 1933; s. Malquiel and Esther (Busel) S. M.D., U. Littoral, Rosario, Argentina, 1959; Ph.D., Case Western Res. U., Cleve., 1972. Chief tissue culture lab. U. Littoral, 1959-62; hon. fellow McArdle Lab. Cancer Research, U. Wis., Madison, 1969-71; asst. prof. pathology, Case Western Res. U., 1970-76, assoc. prof. pathology, 1976-87, prof. pathology, environ. health scis., oncology, 1987—, dir. Tissue Culture Lab. and Hybridoma Facility, 1976—, also assoc. prof. environ. health scis., 1985-87; dir. autopsy service Univ. Hosps. of Cleve., 1970-76; mem. pathology B study Sect. NIH. Contbr. articles to profl. jours. Nat. Council Sci. and Tech. Research (Argentina) fellow, 1959; NIH spl. research fellow, 1967-71. Mem. Am. Assn. Cancer Research, Tissue Culture Assn., Am. Assn. Pathologists, AAAS. Research on hepatocarcinogenesis, hybridomas and monoclonal antibodies; somatic cell genetics. Office: 2085 Adelbert Rd Cleveland OH 44106

SUDLER, LOUIS COURTENAY, realtor, baritone; b. Chgo., Feb. 25, 1903; s. Carroll H. and Susan B. (Culbreth) S.; m. Mary L. Barnes, Feb. 2, 1929 (dec. Oct. 1979); 1 child, Louis Courtenay; m. Virginia Brown, Apr. 21, 1984. Grad., Hotchkiss Sch., 1921; B.A., Yale U., 1925; D.Music (hon.), Southwestern Coll., Winfield, Kans., 1963, Augustana Coll., Rock Island, Ill., 1964, DePaul U., 1972; L.H.D. (hon.), Lake Forest Coll., 1972; D.F.A. (hon.), Northwestern U., 1973; D.Musical Arts (hon.), U. Ill.-Chgo., 1983, Am. Conservatory Music, 1986. Founder Sudler & Co., real estate, Chgo., 1927; leading baritone Chgo. Civic Opera, 1945-47; chmn. emeritus, sr. advisor Sudler Marling, Chgo., 1985—; dir. Upper Avenue Bank, 1962-79. Founder, host of Artists' Showcase, NBC-TV, 1960-65, WGN-TV, 1966-74; internat. appearances, 1946—; guest soloist symphony orchs., concert and marching bands; soloist inauguration Pres. Eisenhower, 1956; sung Nat. Anthem for Pres.'s Reagan, Ford, Nixon, Johnson and Kennedy; appearances oratorio socs., radio and TV; world premieres: Mass (Puccini), Prayer of St. Francis (Arne Oldberg), Abram and Sari (Elinor Remick Warren). Exec. chmn. John Philip Sousa Found.; bd. dirs. Chgo. Symphony Orch., pres., 1966-71, chmn., 1971-76, chmn. emeritus, 1976—. Recipient Peabody award, 1968; Flag of Honor, Am. Legion, 1952; Disting. Service medal State of Ill.; Order of Lincoln; Cross of Honor, Internat. Confedn. Music Socs.; Alumnus award Mich. State U., 1985; Sanford medal Yale U., 1980; Disting. Service to Music award Kappa Kappa Psi, 1985; Cliff Dwellers medal; McGaw medal; named Chicagoan of Yr. in arts Chgo. Jr. Assn. of Commerce, 1964; John Harvard Citizen of Yr., 1971; Sr. Citizen of Yr. Chgo., 1978; Sr. Citizen Hall of Fame Chgo., 1984; Nat. Fedn. Music Clubs; Music Mgr. of Yr., Chgo. of Edn.; Mgr. of Yr., Am. Symphony Orch. League; Hon. mem. Chgo. Symphony Orch., 1977; Edwin Franko Goldman Meml. citation, 1986; Hon. Dir. U. Tex. Longhorn band, 1986; Friends of Lit. citation for Artists' Showcase, 1965; Disting. Service award Lake Forest Fine Arts Alliance, 1985; Service award Music Ctr. North Shore, 1986; donor Sudler Flag of Honor and Sudler Cup awards for Sousa Found.; Sudler Internat. Wind Band Composition Competition held biennially; Louis Sudler prize in Arts endowed at Yale U., Princeton U., Stanford U., Mich. State U., Purdue U., Columbia U., Dartmouth Coll., Oberlin Coll., Harvard U., Rice U., MIT, John Hopkins U., Duke U., U. Chgo., Emory U. Mem. Nat. Fedn. Music Clubs, Friends of Lit., Soc. Colonial Wars, Yale U. Alumni Assn. (Yale medal 1986), Mu Phi Epsilon (hon. bd. dirs. meml. found.). Clubs: Chicago, Cliff Dwellers, Saddle and Cycle, Tavern, Arts, Casino, Commercial (Chgo.); Reagan. Office: 875 N Michigan Ave Chicago IL 60611

SUDYATMIKO, PRASASTO, lawyer, university dean, consultant; b. Pati, Java, Indonesia, Dec. 12, 1937; s. Robertus and Triningsih S.; m. Linda Wisenda, Apr. 11, 1967; children: Caecille Indriati, Stephanus. LM, U. Indonesia, Jakarta, 1963. Bar: Indonesia. Ptnr. Gunanto, Prasasto & Co., Jakarta; dean Faculty of Law, Cath. U. Atma Jaya, Jakarta, 1985—; bd. dirs. Mgmt. Instn. Prasetya Mulya, Jakarta. Chmn. Instn. for Nat. Unity, Jakarta, 1963-69; bd. dirs. dept. intellectual, legal and polit. studies Golongan Karya, Jakarta, 1985. Mem. Internat. Bar Assn., Indonesian Bar Assn. (vice chmn. Jakarta 1982-85, chmn. dept. for law improvement cen. bd. 1985), Indonesian Lawyer's Assn. (bd. dirs. dept. publ. 1986—), Asia Pacific Lawyer's Assn., Asean Lawyer's Soc. Home: 39 Jl Makaliwe Raya, Jakarta 11450, Indonesia Office: Gunanto Prasasto & Co, 96 Jl Bangka Raya - Pela, Jakarta Indonesia

SUEDFELD, PETER, psychologist, educator; b. Budapest, Hungary, Aug. 30, 1935; emigrated to U.S., 1948, naturalized, 1952; s. Leslie John and Jolan (Eichenbaum) Field; m. Gabrielle Debra Guterman, June 11, 1961 (div. 1980); children: Michael Thomas, Joanne Ruth, David Lee. Student, U. Philippines, 1956-57; B.A., Queens Coll., 1960; M.A., Princeton U., 1962, Ph.D., 1963. Research assoc. Princeton U.; lectr. Trenton State Coll., 1963-64; vis. asst. prof. psychology U. Ill., 1964-65; asst. prof. psychology Univ. Coll. Rutgers U., 1965-67, assoc. prof., 1967-71, prof., 1971-72, chmn. dept., 1967-72; prof., psychology U. B.C., Vancouver, 1972—; head dept. U. B.C., 1972-84, dean faculty grad. studies, 1984—; cons. in field. Author: Restricted Environmental Stimulation: Research and Clinical Applications, 1980; editor: Attitude Change: The Competing Views, 1971, Personality Theory and Information Processing, 1971, The Behavioral Basis of Design, 1976, Jour. Applied Social Psychology, 1975-82; contbr. articles to profl. jours. Served with U.S. Army, 1955-58. NIMH grantee, 1970-72; Can. Council grantee, 1973—; Nat. Research Council Can. grantee, 1973—; NIH grantee, 1980-84. Fellow Royal Soc. Can., Can. Psychol. Assn., Am. Psychol. Assn., Acad. Behavioral Medicine Research, Soc. Behavioral Medicine, N.Y. Acad. Scis.; mem. AAAS, Psychonomic Soc., Soc. Exptl. Social Psychology, Phi Beta Kappa, Sigma Xi. Office: U BC, Faculty Grad Studies, Vancouver, BC Canada

SUEDHOFF, CARL JOHN, JR., lawyer; b. Ft. Wayne, Ind., Apr. 22, 1925; s. Carl John and Helen (Lau) S.; m. Carol Mulqueeney, Apr. 10, 1954; children—Thomas Lau, Robert Marshall, Mark Mulqueeney. B.S., U. Pa., 1948; J.D., U. Mich., 1951. Bar: Ind. 1951, U.S. Dist. Ct. (no. and so. dists.) Ind. 1951, U.S. Ct. Appeals (7th cir.) 1957, U.S. Tax Ct. 1981. Assoc. mem. firm Hunt & Mountz, Ft. Wayne, 1951-54; ptnr. Hunt, Suedhoff, Borrorr & Eilbacher and predecessors, Ft. Wayne, 1955—; officer, dir. Inland Chem. Corp., Ft. Wayne, 1952-81; pres., dir. Lau Bldg. Co., Ft. Wayne, 1951-78, S.H.S. Realty Corp., Toledo, 1960-78; officer, dir. Inland Chem. P.R., Inc., San Juan, 1972-81, Northeast Cogen, Inc., others. Mem. Allen County Council, 1972-76, pres., 1974-76; mem. Allen County Tax Adjustment Bd., 1973-74, N.E. Ind. Regional Coordinating Council, 1975-76; bd. dirs. Ft. Wayne YMCA, 1961-63. Served with AUS, 1943-45. Mem. VFW (comdr. 1958-59), ABA, Ind. Bar Assn., Allen County Bar Assn., Beta Gamma Sigma, Phi Delta Phi, Psi Upsilon. Republican. Lutheran. Clubs: Univ. Mich. (pres. 1965-66), Friars, Ft. Wayne Country, Mad Anthony's. Office: 900 Paine Webber Bldg Fort Wayne IN 46802

SUEMATSU, HIROYUKI, medical professor; b. Niihama, Japan, July 12, 1935; s. Kano and Asako S.; m. Ikuko Suematsu, Feb. 4, 1967; children: Junko, Yoko. MD, U. Tokyo, 1961, PhD in Med. Sci., 1968. Asst. med. dept. U. Tokyo, 1962-70; asst. dept. psychosomatic med. Kyushu U., Fukuoka, 1970-71; lectr. Kyushu U., 1971-76; lectr. dept. psychosomatic med. U. Tokyo, 1977-84, asst. prof. psychosomatic, 1984-85, prof. psychosomatic med., 1986—. Author: Psychosomatic Diseases, 1977; editor: Psychosomatic Medicine, 1979, Anorexia Nervosa, 1985. Mem. Internat. Coll. of Psychosomatic Med. Home: 5-7-17 Shimouma, Setagaya-ku, Tokyo 154, Japan Office: U Tokyo Dept Psychomatic Med, 3-28-6 Mejirodai Bunkyo-ku, Tokyo 112, Japan

SUEMATSU, TSUNEMASA, association executive; b. Tokyo, Apr. 20, 1914; s. Kaiichiro and Masui (Ohishi) S.; m. Aiko Saitoh, Nov. 5, 1947; children—Mariko Ohno, Masako. B.Laws, Tokyo Imperial U., 1939. Liaison officer Fgn. Office, Tokyo, 1945-49; advisor finance Fin. Com., Ho. of Reps., Tokyo, 1949-77; insp. Govtl. Corp., Tokyo, 1977-80; exec. Soc. for World Peace Found., Tokyo, 1964—, Catholic Action Comrade Soc., Tokyo, 1980—; dir. Kasai Archtl. Planning, Inc. Mem. Soc. for World Peace, Union for World Fedn. (exec. 1968). Roman Catholic. Club: Nihon. Address: 4-7-25 Kita-Shinagawa, Shinagawa-ku, Tokyo Japan

SUEN, LAI-CHERNG, computer engineer; b. Taipei, Taiwan, Apr. 20, 1948; s. Ping-Haung and Hsueh-Yeh (Huang) S.; M.S., U. Notre Dame, 1974, Ph.D., 1977; came to U.S., 1972; m. Cheing-Mei Wang, July 26, 1977; children: Robert, Nancy. Supr. tech. staff Bell Labs., Naperville, Ill., 1977—. Mem. IEEE, Sigma Xi. Author: An Introduction to Fourier Analysis 1972; Boolean Algebra and Its Applications, 1972; Electronic Computer, vols. I and II, 1973; contbr. articles to profl. jours. Recipient AT&T Disting. MTS award, 1984. Home: 210 Ketten Dr Naperville IL 60540 Office: Bell Labs 2000 N Naperville Rd Naperville IL 60566

SUENENS, LEO JOSEPH CARDINAL, former archbishop; b. Brussels, Belgium, July 16, 1904; s. Jean and Jeanne Janssens; student Coll. Ste. Marie, Brussels, 1915-21; Ph.D., Gregorian U., Rome, 1924, B.C.L., 1927, S.T.D., 1929. Ordained priest Roman Cath. Ch., 1927; aux. bishop, vicar-gen. Archdiocese of Malines, 1945-61; consecrated bishop, 1945; archbishop of Malines-Brussels, primate Belgium, 1961-79, ret., 1979; elevated to cardinal, 1962; moderator Vatican Council, 1962-65; chancellor Louvain U.; pres. Belgian Bishops Conf., 1966—; mem. Pontifical Commn. for Revision Code of Canon Law. Recipient Templeton Found. prize in religion, 1976. Author: Theology of the Legion of Mary, 1954, The Right View of Moral Rearmament, 1954, The Gospel to Every Creature, 1957, Mary, the Mother of God, 1959, The Nun in the World, 1962, Love and Control, 1962, Christian Life Day by Day, 1964, Co-responsability in the Church, 1968, (with Archbishop M. Ramsey) The Future of the Christian Church, 1970, A New Pentecost?, 1975, Ecumenism and Charismatic Renewal, 1978, (with D. H. Camara) Charismatic Renewal and Social Action, 1979, Renewal and the Powers of Darkness, 1982, others. Address: Blvd de Smet, de Nayer 570, 1020 Brussels Belgium *

SUGANO, SHIGERU, publishing executive; b. Fukushima Prefecture, Japan, Aug. 9, 1924; s. Kenkichi and Fumi S.; m. Setsuki Kimura, May 3, 1952; children: Izumi, Aya. Grad. in econs., Waseda U., 1949. With Nihon Keizai Shimbun, 1949-69, advt. mgr. Nagoya office, 1961-63, Western office, 1963-67, Tokyo head office, 1967-69; dir. advt. Nikkei McGraw-Hill Co., Tokyo, 1969-74, dir., 1974-80; pres. Nikkei-McGraw-Hill Subscription Sales Co., 1980-85; auditor Nikkei-McGraw-Hill Subscription Sales Co., 1986—. Liberal Democrat. Buddhist. Home: 2-38-9-504 Matsubara, Setagaya-ku, Tokyo 156, Japan Office: Nikkei-McGraw-Hill Subs Sales Co, 1-1 Ogawamachi, Kanda Chiyoda-ku, Chiyoda-ku, Tokyo 101, Japan

SUGDEN, RICHARD LEE, pastor; b. Compton, Calif., Apr. 13, 1959; s. L. Fred Sugden and Nancy Jane (Motherwell) Coulter; m. Rebecca Lynn Travis, June 1981; children: Richard Lee II, Ryan Leon. BA, Pensacola (Fla.) Christian Coll., 1981. Ordained pastor, 1985. Assoc. pastor Chippewa Lake Bapt. Ch., Medina, Ohio, 1981-84; dir., evangelist Victory Acres Christian Camp, Warren, Ohio, 1985; asst. pastor Bible Bapt. Temple, Campbell, Ohio, 1985—; del. pastors' sch. 1st Bapt. Ch., Hammond, Ind., 1982—. Mem. Christian Law Assn., Buckeye Ind. Bapt. Fellowship. Republican. Home: 3208 Powersway Youngstown OH 44502 Office: Bible Bapt Temple 230 Lettie Ave Campbell OH 44405

SUGDEN, ROBERT, economics educator; b. Leeds, Eng., Aug. 26, 1949; s. Frank Gerald and Kathleen (Buckley) S.; m. Christine Margaret Upton, Mar. 26, 1982; children: Joe Robert, Jane Sarah. BA, U. York, 1970; MSc, Univ. Coll., Cardiff, Wales, 1971. Lectr. in econs. U. York, Eng., 1971-78; reader in econs. U. Newcastle upon Tyne, 1978-85; prof. econs. U. East Anglia, Norwich, Eng., 1985—. Author: (with others) The Principles of Practical Cost-Benefit Analysis, 1978, The Political Economy of Public Choice, 1981, The Economics of Rights, Co operation and Welfare, 1986. Office: Sch Econs and Social Studies, Univ East Anglia, Norwich NR4 7TJ, England

SUGIHARA, AKIO, city planner, architect; b. Fukui, Japan, Mar. 1, 1948; s. Takeo and Hitoe (Takemoto) S.; m. Yoko Atago, Apr. 4, 1976; children, Megumi, Yukiko. BS in Urban Engring., Tokyo U., 1970. Registered architect, Japan. Planner, architect Archtl. Design div. Kajima Corp., Tokyo, 1970-71, 73-85; planner Yachiyo Engring. Co., Tokyo, 1971-73; researcher Leisure Devel. Ctr., Tokyo, 1980-81; sr. planner Real Estate Devel. div. Kajima Corp., Tokyo, 1985-87, chief planner, mgr., 1987—; cons. Kajima Leasing Co., Tokyo, 1984—. Author: (with others) Leisure Development in Local Area, 1981, Flow System in Large Market, 1982; creator software program Money, 1984. Del. Kamata Devel. Conf., Ohta-ku, Tokyo, 1987—. Mem. The City Planning Inst. Japan, World Conf. Transport Research Soc. (charter mem. 1987—), Archtl. Inst. Japan, Tokyo U. Alumni Assn. Buddhist. Clubs: Meishin Assn. (Fukui, Tokyo). Home: 7-22-915 Sengawa 2-chome, Chofu-shi, Tokyo 182, Japan Office: Real Estate Devel div Kajima Corp, Fujikage Bldg 1-5, Motoakasaka 1-chome Minato-ku, Tokyo 107, Japan

SUGIHARA, TERUO, biologist; b. Kearny, N.J., June 19, 1949; s. Kyuichi and Shinobuko (Yamaguchi) S.; A.B., in Biology, Lafayette Coll., 1971; Ph.D. in Ecology, Rutgers U., 1981. Research asst. Rutgers U., 1972-77; cons. Betz Converse Murdoch, Plymouth, Meeting, Pa., 1979; project leader Rutgers U., 1977-80; sr. environ. specialist N.J. Dept. Environ. Protection, Trenton, 1981-84; biologist U.S. Army C.E., Phila., 1984—. Author and editor tech. bulletin, 1979. Served to 1st lt. U.S. Army, 1972. Mem. Am. Soc. Limnology and Oceanography, Ecol. Soc. Am., Am. Inst. Biol. Sci., Estuarine Research Fedn., N.J. Acad. Sci. Presbyterian. Home: 245 Cattell Ave West Collingswood NJ 08107

SUGIHARTO, BERNANDA, business executive; b. Malang, East Java, Indonesia, Aug. 27, 1946; s. Budiman and Suciati (Anna) S.; m. Felicitas Edritta Felina, Mar. 24, 1973; children—Fiorello-Michael, Jeromio-Michael. Degree in mech. engring. Bandung Inst. Tech., West Java, 1972. Cert. mech. engr. Sales engr. Astra Internat. Co., Jakarta, Indonesia, 1972; partsanalyst Inter Astra, Singapore, 1972-73; parts supr. United Tractors, Jakarta, Indonesia, 1973-74; project engr. Multi-Forest Co., Jakarta, 1974-76, project mgr., 1976-78; gen. mgr. industry and projects Sumalindo Group, Jakarta, 1978-85; dir. Kalbe Group, Jakarta, 1986—. Office: Kalbe Group, Enseval Bldg, Letjen Suprapto, Jakarta DKI 10002, Indonesia

SUGIKI, SHIGEMI, physician; b. Wailuku, Hawaii, May 12, 1936; s. Sentaro and Kameno (Matoba) S.; A.B., Washington U., St. Louis, 1957, M.D., 1961; m. Bernice T. Murakami, Dec. 28, 1958; children—Kevin S., Boyd R. Intern St. Luke's Hosp., St. Louis, 1961-62, resident ophthalmology, 1962-65; chmn. dept. ophthalmology Straub Clinic, Honolulu, 1965-70; chmn. dept. ophthalmology Queen's Med. Center, Honolulu, 1970-73, 80-83, 88—; assoc. clin. prof. ophthalmology Sch. Medicine, U. Hawaii, 1973—. Served to maj. M.C., AUS, 1968-70. Decorated Hawaiian NG Commendation medal, 1968. Fellow ACS; mem. Am., Hawaii med. assns., Honolulu County Med. Soc., Am. Acad. Ophthalmology, Contact Lens Assn. Opthalmologists, Soc. Eye Surgeons, Pacific Coast Oto-Ophthal. Soc., Pan-Pacific Surg. Assn., Am. Soc. Cataract and Refractive Surgery, Internat. Assn. Ocular Surgeons, Am. Soc. Contemporary Ophthalmology, Washington U. Eye Alumni Assn., Hawaii Ophthal. Soc., Research To Prevent Blindness. Home: 2398 Aina Lani Pl Honolulu HI 96822 Office: 1380 Lusitana St Suite 714 Honolulu HI 96813

SUGIMOTO, TSUNEAKI, internist; b. Dairen, Manchuria, Feb. 7, 1932; s. Tsuneki and Fuiko (Mitsufuji) S.; m. Kazu Hirota, Sept. 29, 1963; children: Yuko, Junko, Nobuyuki. MD, U. Tokyo, 1956. Intern U. Tokyo, 1956, resident, fellow, 1957, prof., 1983—; fellow U. Miss., University, 1965, Duke U., Durham, N.C., 1966; instr. Kanazawa U., Japan, 1968-72, assoc. prof., 1972-77; prof. Toyama Med. and Pharm U., Japan, 1977-83. Author: Atlas of Cardiac Arrhythmias, 1971. Home: 5-29-10 Shimouma, Setagaya-ku, Tokyo 154, Japan Office: Tokyo U Hosp, 7-3-1 Hongo, Bunkyo-ku, Tokyo 113, Japan

SUGITA, SHOICHI, electronic communications engineer, consultant; b. Tokyo, Jan. 4, 1935; s. Eiichi and Chii Sugita; m. Reiko Shimakata, Apr. 16, 1965; children: Minako, Toshiyuki. BE in Sci. and Engring., Waseda U., Tokyo, 1958. Engr. switching div. Nippon Electric Corp., Tokyo, 1958-66, engring. chief switching div., 1966-70, engring. mgr. switching div., 1970-78, mgr. switching div., 1978-84; chief engr. switching div. Nippon Electronic Corp., Tokyo, 1984-86; engring. gen. mgr. Internat. Digital Communication Corp., Tokyo, 1986-88; chief engr. switching group Nippon Elec. Corp., Tokyo, 1988—. Author: International Switching System, 1975; patentee in field. Mem. Inst. Electronics, Info. and Communication Engrs. Home: No 7-1, 2-Chome Nozawa, Setagaya-ku Tokyo Japan Office: No 1131 Hinode, Abiko-city Chiba, Japan

SUGIURA, BINSUKE, banker; b. Nov. 13, 1911; m. Chieko Sugiura. Grad., Tokyo U., 1935. With Kangyo Bank Ltd., 1935-52, Japan Long-Term Credit and Banking Co., Ltd., Tokyo, 1952—; now chmn. Japan Long-Term Credit and Banking Co., Ltd.; bd. dirs. Nippon Shinpan Co. Ltd., Fuji Kyuko Co. Ltd. Decorated Medal of Honor with Blue Ribbon, 1974. Mem. Japan Fedn. Econ. Orgns., Japan Fedn. Employers' Assns. Home: 31-5 Kamimeguro, 3-chome Meguro-ku, Tokyo 153, Japan Office: Long-Term Credit Bank Japan Ltd, 2-4 Otemachi, 1-chome Chiyoda-ku, Tokyo 100, Japan *

SUGIURA, HIDEO, automobile manufacturing company executive; b. Tokyo, Dec. 1, 1926; s. Takeshi and Sada (Sato) S.; m. Kazuko Nishida; children—Tomoko Sugiura Hagita, Fumihiko. B.S. in Physics, Kyoto Univ. Advisor, Honda Motor Co., Ltd., Tokyo, 1985—. Recipient Blue Ribbon medal Govt. of Japan, 1984. Mem. Japan Automobile Mfrs. Assn., Inc. (vice. chmn. 1982-85). Club: Tokyo Golf. Home: 2-28-5 Horinouchi Suginami-ku, Tokyo 166, Japan Office: Honda Motor Co Ltd, 2-2 1-Chome, Minamiaoyama, Tokyo 107, Japan

SUGIYAMA, KYOICHI, architect; b. Yokohama, Kanagawa, Japan, Mar. 13, 1951; s. Mitsuzo and Shizuko (Nishizima) S.; m. Chigako Ishikawa, Oct. 6, 1979; children: Masato, Manami. B of Engring., Nihon U., Tokyo, 1973, M of Engring., 1975, D of Engring., 1979. Registered architect, Japan. Architect, dir. System Sci. Cons., Inc., Tokyo, 1979—; sr. architect Japan Internat. Cooperation Agy., Tokyo, 1984-85, Manila, 1985-86, Puerto Montt, Chile, 1986-88, La Paz, Bolivia, 1986-87. Robert Kennedy scholar Nihon U., 1975, 77, Furuta scholar, 1976. Mem. Architectural Inst. Japan, The City Planning Inst. Japan. Home: 2 2 2203 311, Takeyama Midori-ku, Yokohama, Kanagawa 226, Japan Office: System Sci Cons Inc, Silver Takadanobaba Bldg, 3-18-11 Takada, Toshima-ku, Tokyo 171, Japan

SUGIYAMA, MEIKO, statistician, educator; b. Sapporo, Hokkaido, Japan, Feb. 22, 1934; d. Yosimiti and Mitsu Hori; BS, Tsuda Coll., 1957; m. Akira Sugiyama, June 18, 1965. Researcher pub. opinion research div. Broadcasting Culture Research Inst., Japan Broadcasting Co., Tokyo, 1957-76, sr. researcher, 1976-87; tchr. Tsukuba U., 1980, Tokyo U., 1981-85, Tsuda Coll., 1985; vis. scholar Worcester Coll Oxford U., 1987; vis. prof. Queen's Coll. CUNY, 1987-88; prof. Tokyo Woman's Christian U., 1988—. Recipient Good Citizenship prize Tsuda Coll., 1957. Mem. Am. Statis. Assn., Internat. Inst. Communications, Internat. Group for Study of Women, Behaviormetric Soc. Japan, Japan Statis. Soc., Tokyo YWCA. Home: Homat-East 205, Ichiban-cho 20-10 Chiyoda-ku, Tokyo 102, Japan Office: Tokyo Woman's Christian U, 4-3-1 Mitaka-shi, Tokyo 181, Japan

SUGIYAMA, TOKU MARY, school administrator; b. Sacramento, Sept. 6, 1921; d. Sakae and Kuniko (Kosaka) Koda; m. Yone J. Sugiyama, Apr. 5, 1952; m. George Y. Morishita, Mar. 23, 1942; (dec. Mar. 1949); children—Maeona, Carolyn, George. Jr. cert. U. Calif.-Berkeley, 1941; B.A., Towson State U., 1980, M.A., 1984. Tchr., Poston Relocation Ctr., Ariz., 1941-44; purchasing agt. U.S. Dept. Def., Tokyo Ordnance Depot, 1952-56; instr. Ikebana Sogetsu Sch., Tokyo, 1956-67, exec. dir. Sogetsu USA, sch. Japanese flower arrangement, 1967—. Recipient Mohan Sho, Sogetsu Sch., 1960, Sofu Sho, 1967, Flower Arranger of yr. award Nat. Council State Garden Clubs, 1979. Mem. Md. Fedn. Garden Clubs, Ikebana Internat. (charter), Balt.-Kawasaki Sitster City Cultural Com. Home: 959 Ellendale Dr Towson MD 21204

SUGRUE, DENIS LAMBERT, genitourinary pysician; b. Dublin, Ireland, Mar. 11, 1927; moved to Eng., 1950; s. Timothy and Mary Elizabeth (Lambert) S.; m. Helen Patricia O'Connell, Sept. 5, 1962; children—Rosaleen, Grainne. Matriculation Cert., Blackrock Coll., Dublin, 1944; Kitchener Scholar, U. Coll., Dublin, 1945. Registrar ear, nose and throat Royal Free Hosp., London, 1953-54; sr. registrar plastic surgery Plastic & Jaw Unit, Basingstone, Eng., 1954-57; cons. plastic surgery The Children's Hosp., Dublin, 1957-67; adv. Ministry of Health, cons. plastic surgeon Govt. Hosp., Tripoli, Libya, 1968; registrar venereology St. Thomas Hosp., London, 1969-70; sr. registrar venereology Wessex Region Hosp., Southampton, Eng., 1970-72; cons. physician North & Mid Staffforshire, Eng., 1972—; sr. clin. lectr. U. Birmingham, Eng., 1982—. Author: Sexual Infections, 1985; also articles. Regional Research Com. grantee, 1982. Mem. Med. Soc. Study Venereal Diseases. Roman Catholic. Avocations: public speaking; traveling. Mem. Irish rowing team 1948 Olympic Games, London. Home: 2 Fieldway Dairyfields, Stoke-on-Trent ST4 8AQ, England Office: Dept Genitourinary Medicine, Central Out-patient Dept, Stoke-on-Trent ST4 7PA, England

SUH, BO YOUNG, physician, researcher; b. Pusan, Republic of Korea, Jan. 28, 1948; came to U.S., 1976; s. Jong D. and Doo S. (Lee) S.; m. Sook H. Suh; children: Angela, Daniel. BS, Pusan Nat. Premedical Sch., 1969; MD, Pusan Nat. Medical Sch., 1973. Physician Army, Republic of Korea, 1973-76; resident in ob-gyn Bklyn. Hosp., 1978-79, Mt. Sinai Hosp., Hartford, Conn., 1979-82; practice medicine specializing in ob-gyn Portsmouth, R.I., 1982-83; research fellow U. Calif., San Diego, 1983-85; asst. prof. ob-gyn U. Colo., Denver, 1986—. Contbr. articles to profl. jours. Served to capt. 8th div. Korean Army, 1973-76. Mem. Am. Coll. Ob-gyn. Office: U Colo Dept Ob-Gyn 4200 E 9th Ave Denver CO 80262

SUH, PAUL MANSOO, missionary, educator; b. Seoul, Korea, Feb. 15, 1939; s. Kwang-Ok and Sang-Ok, Seung) S.; m. Aug. 28, 1962. BA, Dongkook U., Republic of Korea, 1962; MDiv, Chongshin Theology Seminary, Republic of Korea, 1967; MA, Kongkook U., 1970; PhD, Immanuel U., 1986. Ordained to ministry Presbyn. Ch., 1970. Mgr. Presbyn. Theol. Rev., Seoul, 1966-69; instr. Seoul Theol. Sem., 1966-69, G.P.A. Theol. Sem., Seoul, 1967-69; editor Christian Times, Seoul, 1968-69; exec. sec. G.P.A. Ch. in Korea, Seoul, 1969-70; dir. Dong-Ak Linguistic and Lit. Soc., Seoul, 1970—; pastor G.P.A. Ch. in Korea, Seoul, 1970—; missionary The 55th G.P.A. Ch. in Korea, Taegu, 1970; dir. Korea Mission in Indonesia, Jakarta, 1971—, supr. Korean Ch. Sch., Jakarta, 1974—; chmn. Hallelujah Inter-Service Inc., Jakarta, 1985—; coordinator Christian U. Indonesia, Ambon, 1987—. Editor: (book) Introduction to Korean Language and Literature, 1967; author: Study of Songs of Songgang, 1970, Christian Education of Indonesia, 1987. Recipient Presdl. medal Republic of Korea, 1977. Office: Korea Mission in Indonesia, PO Box 2355 Jkt, Jakarta 10001, Indonesia

SUHARA, AKIRA, paper company executive; b. Mar. 11, 1911; m. Fumiko Suhara. Grad., Tokyo Mercantile Marine U., 1934. Various positions Oji Paper Co., Ltd., 1943-49; with Honshu Paper Co., Ltd., 1949—, pres., now chmn.; vice chmn. Nippon Seishiren. Mem. Japan Fedn. Econ. Orgns. (treas.), Japan Fedn. Employer's Assns. (treas.). Home: 8-20 Kakinokizaka, 3-chome Meguro-ku, Tokyo 152, Japan Office: Honshu Paper Co Ltd, 12-8 Ginza, 5-chome, Tokyo 104, Japan *

SUHARTO See SOEHARTO

SUHARTOYO, S., ambassador; b. Yogyakarta, Indonesia, Sept. 2, 1926; married; 6 children. Grad., Gajah Mada U., Yogyakarta, 1955. Asst. lectr. Faculty of Tech., Gajah Mada U., Yogyakarta, 1954-58; bd. mgmt. Inst. for Research & Exploration of Mining and Industry, NV Molenvliet, Jakarta, Indonesia, 1958-61; dir. bd. mgmt. mech. industry and elec. equipment, Dept. Basic Industry and Mining, 1961-65; pres. dir. bd. mgmt. mech. industry/elec. and transport equipment Dept. Basic Industry, 1965-66; dir. gen. basic industry Dept. Industry, 1966-75, dir. gen. metal and mech. industry, 1975-78, dir. gen. basic metal industry, 1978-81; head investment coordinating bd. Republic of Indonesia, 1981-85; ambassador to U.K. and Ireland London, 1986—. Decorated commandeur in de Leopoldorde, 1975; recipient star Satya Lencana Pembangunan, 1962, star 3d class Mahaputra Utama, 1974. Roman Catholic. Club: Highgate Golf (London). Office: Embassy of Indonesia, 38 Grosvenor Sq, London W1X 9AD, England

SUISALA, EMONI TESESE, electric company executive; b. Apia, Western Samoa, Mar. 16, 1948; d. Tesese and Avaganofoa (Puni) T.; m. Tuipoloa Suisala, Jan. 26, 1978. Personal sec. to chmn. bd. Polynesian Airlines Ltd., Apia, 1966-71; sr. stenographer Health Dept., Apia, 1971-72; personal sec. to regional rep. United Nations Devel. Program, Apia, 1972-74; personal sec. Electric Power Corp., Apia, 1974-79, adminstrn. mgr., 1979—; prin. Tesese Secretarial Sch., Apia, 1966—. Mem. Comml. Edn. Soc. Australia. Seventh-Day Adventist. Office: Electric Power Corp, PO Box 2011, Apia Western Samoa

SUITER, JOHN WILLIAM, industrial engineering consultant; b. Pasadena, Calif., Feb. 16, 1926; s. John Walter and Ethel May (Acton) S.; B.S. in Aero. Sci., Embry Riddle U., 1964; m. Joyce England, Dec. 3, 1952; children—Steven A., Carol A. Cons. indsl. engr., Boynton Beach, Fla., 1955—. Instr. U. S.C. Tech. Edn. Center, Charleston, 1967-69. Served as pilot USAF, 1944-46. Registered profl. engr., Fla. Mem. Am. Inst. Indsl. Engrs., Soc. Mfg. Engrs. (sr.), Computer and Automated Systems Assn., Methods-Time Measurement Assn. (assoc.), Soc. Quality Control. Home: PO Box 5262 Grove City FL 34224

SUITNER, OTMAR, conductor; b. Innsbruck, Austria, May 16, 1922; s. Karl and Maria (Rizzi) S.; grad. Hochschule Musik, Mozarteum, Salzburg, 1943; m. Marita Wilckens, Feb. 14, 1948. Condr., Tiroler Landestheater, Innsbruck, 1943-44; condr., pianist, 1945-52; mus. dir., Remscheid, W.Ger., 1952-57; gen. mus. dir. Pfalzorch., Ludwigshafen, 1957-60, Staatsoper, Dresden, E.Ger., 1960-64, Staatsoper, Berlin, E.Ger., 1964—; hon. condr. NHK Symphony Orch., Tokyo, 1973—; prof. Hochschule Musik, Vienna, 1977—; guest condr. in San Francisco, Japan, Europe, Teatro Colon, Buenos Aires, also festivals in Bayreuth, Prague and Vienna; rec. artist EMI, Teldee, Deutsche Grammophon, Eterna, Denon records. Decorated commendatore Gregorius Order. Roman Catholic. Office: Berlin-Nieder-schönhausen, Platanenstrasse 13, Berlin German Democratic Republic

SUJO, CLARA DIAMENT, art historian. Dir. and founder Estudio Actual, Caracas, Venezuela, 1968—, CDS Gallery, N.Y.C., 1981—. Office: CDS Gallery 13 E 75 St New York NY 10021

SUJONO, HADI, physician, educator; b. Pacitan, East Java, Indonesia, May 25, 1929; m. Hermina S. Hadi, Dec. 15, 1965; children: Prim, Kresno, Puji. MD in Gen. Med., Gajah Mada U., Yogyakarta, Indonesia, 1962; cert. in gastroenterology, Kobe U., Japan, 1971; PhD, Padjadjaran U., Indonesia, 1982. Intern Padjadjaran U., 1968, chmn. div. gastroenterology dept. internal med., 1972—; vice chmn. Dept. Internal Med. Padjadjaran U. Hasan Sadikin Hosp., 1972-82; chmn. bd. postgrad. program med. specialist Padjadraran U., 1974-82; lectr. med. Padjadraran U., 1969—, chmn. gastroenterology team Hasan Sadikin Hosp., 1976—. Author: Gastroenterology, 1st ed.. 1975, 2d ed., 1981, 3d ed., 1983, 4th ed., 1986, Ultrasonography of Liver Cancer, 1983, Ultranosonography of Abdomen, 1985; editorial bd. Indonesian Med. Jour., 1982—, Indonesian Forum Gastroentero-Hepatology, 1984—; chief editor team Gastrointestinal Edoscopy book, 1986; contbr. articles to profl. jours.; papers in field.. Mem. steering com. Teaching Hosp., Bandung, Indonesia, 1972-73, pub. health workshop Padjadjaran U., 1978; chmn. regular sci. med. meeting Padjadjaran U., 1973-78; bd. dirs. postgrad. fellow forum subspeciality in gastroentero-hepatology, 1984—; adv. bd. Indonesian Boy Scouts, Bandung.Served with Indonesian mil., 1945-51. Decorated 1st Merit Honour for Independence, 2d Merit Honour for Independence, Merit Honour for Heroes. Recipient Labour Loyalty award U. Padjadaran, 1985. Mem. Internat. Soc. Internal Medicine, Asian Pacific Assn. for the Study of the Liver, Internat. Assn. for the Study of the Liver, Asian Pacific Assn. Gastroenterology, Counsilor of Asian Fed. Soc. for Ultrasound in Med. & Biol., World Fed. Soc. for Ultrasound in Med. and Biol., Indonesian Doctor Assn., Indonesian Soc. Internal Med., Indonesian Assn. Digestive Endocopy, Indonesian Soc. Gastroenterology (chmn. Bandung br.), Indonesian Assn. for the Study the Liver (chmn. Bandung br.), Indonesian Assn. Med. Ultrasonic (v.p.), Nat. Acad. Clin. Biochemistry. Muslim. Home: Jl Tamansari 29, Bandung 40116, Indonesia Office: Padjadjaran U Sch Med, Dept Internal Med, Jl Pasirkaliki 190, Bandung Indonesia

SUK, JOSEF, violinist; b. Prague, Czechoslovakia, Aug. 8, 1929; s. Josef and Maria (Vlkova) S.; grad. Prague Conservatory Music; m. Marie Poiakova, Apr. 26, 1951. Concert violinist throughout world; mem. Suk Trio; soloist Czech Philharmonic Orch. Recipient Grand Prix du Disque, Paris, 1960, 66, 68, 74; Edison prize, Amsterdam, 1972; Vienna Flotenuhr, 1974; Czechoslovac State prize, 1964; Grand Prix du Disque, 1978; named Artist of Merit, 1970. Nat. Artist, 1977. Home: 5 Karlovo Namesti, 12000 Prague Czechoslovakia

SUKUN, KAMIL MEHMET, publisher; b. Istanbul, Turkey, July 18, 1948; s. Ismail Nacil and Fatma Ayten (Akar) S.; B.A. in Fgn. Trade, Ankara Acad. Econ. and Comml. Scis., 1974; m. Perran Oztunc, Feb. 13, 1981; 1 child, Mehmet. Free-lance photographer, 1971-74; Veb Ofset Ileri Matbaacilik A.S., Istanbul; photog. cons. Ilbas Pub. Co., Istanbul, 1974, art dir., editor-in-chief Adam mag., Istanbul, 1975; editor-in-chief, EV (decorating) mag., 1976-83, Vizon (fashions) mag., 1977-83; founder pres. Profesyonel Ltd., Istanbul, 1983—; publisher Who's Who in Turkey-Gunumuz Turkiy esinde Kim Kimdir, 1984—; 1975, photo exhibitions in Turkey, Yugoslavia, Belgium; producer Vizon Show Internat. (fashion show), Istanbul, 1979—, Sofia and Cairo, 1982; cons. to Istanbul C. of C., 1986. Served to lt. Turkish Navy, 1979-80. Recipient Diploma award 7th Internat. Biennial Exhbn. Photography, 1971; Turkish Naval Forces Supporting Found. award, 1984; Turkish Found. Against Cancer cert., 1984; UNICEF Nat. Com. award, 1984, 85; UNICEF Presdl. award, 1985; Turkish Ministry of Health award, 1985. Mem. Istanbul Journalists Assn., Royal Photog. Soc. Gt. Britain. Club: Lions. Editor: The Fifty Residences of Turkey, 1981; author Adam mag. cover photograph selected and pub. in Photographis, 1978 (Zurich). Home: 72/17 Zincirlikuyu Cad Ulus, 80600 Istanbul Turkey Office: Profesyonel Ltd, Süleyman Nazif, SK 14/4, Nisantasi, Istanbul Turkey

SUKUP, EUGENE GEORGE, manufacturing company executive; b. Venus, Nebr., May 11, 1929; s. Louis and Dorothy Amelia (Buerkley) S.; m. Mary Elizabeth Bielefeld, Feb. 24, 1952; children: Charles Eugene, Steven Eugene. Grad. high sch., 1946. Owner, mgr. farm Dougherty, Iowa, 1951—; pres. Sukup Mfg. Inc., Sheffield, Iowa, 1963—, Sukup Enterprises Inc., Sheffield, 1968—. Patentee in field. Com. mem. Franklin County 4-H, 1958-64, N. Iowa Area Dist. mem. Sheffield-Chapin Community Sch. Bd., 1967-79; mem. Franklin County extension council, 1962-65; bd. regents Waldorf Coll., Forest City, Iowa; bd. dirs. Sheffield Care Ctr., 1976—, pres. 1981-82. Recipient Outstanding Young Farmer award Jr. C. of C., 1962, 4-H Alumni award, 1964, Iowa Gov.'s Spl. award, 1982. Mem. Farm Bur., Iowa Mgrs. Assn. Republican. Lutheran (ch. council 1960-62, 70-72, pres. 1962-71). Club: Sheffield Community. Home: Beeds Lake Hampton IA 50441 Office: PO Box 220 North Rd Sheffield IA 50475

SULASMI, MARIA THERESIA, pharmaceutical imports and distribution consultant; b. Cirebon, Indonesia, Sept. 10, 1917; d. Wie Hoo The and Gin Nio Tan; m. Ignatius Josef Subari, Nov. 30, 1939; children: Hwa Ing Angela, Swan Ing Ursula, Kian Hong Peter Hamidy. Grad. in pharmacy, Jadarta DKI, 1935. Agt. Fransch Algemeen Pharmacie, Jakarta, 1936-44; pharmacist KPM Hosp., Jakarta, 1946-60; dir. T.P. Japhar Pharm. Labs., Jakarta, 1959-69, P.T. Indria, Jakarta, 1960-66; advisor P.T. Dos ni Roha, Jakarta, 1965-88, advisor, 1988—; commr. P.T. Corsa Industries, Ltd. Office: PT Dos ni Roha, Jl Gatot Subrato Kav 6-7, 12930 Jakarta Indonesia

SULEIMAN, ABU BAKAR, physician; b. Johore Baru, Malaysia, Feb. 4, 1944; parents Suleiman Abdul Rahman and Petom Abdul Majid; m. Sukanya Tangtatsawas Abu Bakar; children: Zufar Suleiman Abu Bakar, Halina Jael Abu Bakar. MBBS, Monash U., Melbourne, Australia, 1968; Degree in (medicine), Singapore Nat. U., 1974. Med. Officer in Charge District Hosp., Pontain, Johore, Malaysia, 1970-71; med. officer Gen. Hosp., Johore (Malaysia) Baru, 1971-74; cons. nephrologist Dept. Nephrology Gen. Hosp., Kuala Lumpur, Malaysia, 1974-87; dir. Med. Services Ministry Health, Malaysia, 1987—. contbr. articles to profl. jours. Fellow Royal Australian Coll. Physicians; mem. Malaysian Med. Assn. (pres. 1986-87), Acad. Med. Malaysia (vice master 1985-88), Malaysian Soc. Nephrology (pres. 1984-86), Internat. Soc. Nephrology, Asian Pacific Soc. Nephrology.

SULEK, ANTONI, sociology educator; b. Barlogi, Lublin, Poland, Sept. 27, 1945; s. Jozef and Boleslawa (Struska) S.; m. Rozalia Rogala, Feb. 7, 1974; 1 child, Emilia. MA in Sociology, U. Warsaw, Poland, 1968, PhD, 1974. Asst. Inst. Sociology U. Warsaw, Poland, 1968-74, asst. prof. sociology, 1974—, vice dir. inst., 1981-84; asst. prof. sociology Higher Pedagogical Sch., Rzeszow, Poland, 1985-87, Lublin (Poland) Cath. U., 1987—. Author: (in Polish) Experiment in Social Research, 1979, Logic of Sociological Analysis, 1979, Methods of Sociological Analysis, 1986, Polish Reality and Methods of Coping With It, 1987; contbr. numerous articles to profl. jours. Mem. Solidarity Union, 1980-82. Mem. Polish Sociol. Assn. (all Polish bd., treas. 1978-81, Ossowski award 1979). Home: Gwiazdzista 31 Apt 62, 01 814 Warsaw Poland Office: U Warsaw, Inst Sociology, Warsaw 64, Poland

SULIOTIS, ELENA, opera singer; b. Athens, Greece, May 28, 1943; d. Constantino and Gallia (Cavalengo) S. Studied with Mercedes Liopart. Debut, Cavalleria Rusticana, Teatro San Carlo, Naples, 1964, as Abigail in Nabucco at La Scala, 1966, as Helen of Troy in Mefistofele, Chgo., 1966, as Lady MacBeth at Convent Garden, 1969; repertoire includes: Manon Lescaut, LaGiaconda, MacBeth, Norma, Otello, Aida, Luisa Mi-ler, Il Trovatore, Tosca, Loreley, la Forza del Destino; numerous recs. for Decca. Address: Villa il Poderino, Via Incontri 38, Florence Italy

SULIS, WILLIAM HERBERT, psychiatrist; b. Hamilton, Ont., Can., Oct. 5, 1955; s. Harold Wilson and Doreen Joan (Lee) S.; m. Ruth Doris Houghton, Oct. 8, 1983; children: Kara Marie, Tegan Jennifer. B.Sc. with honors, Carleton U., Ottawa, Ont., 1976; M.D., U. Western Ont., London, 1980, M.A., 1984. Med. intern U. Western Ont., 1980-81, resident in psychiatry, 1981-84; staff psychiatrist Psychogeriatric Clinic Victoria Hosp., London, Ont., 1984—; clin. lectr. psychiatry, U. Western Ont., 1984—. Fellow Royal Coll. Physicians Can.; mem. N.Y. Acad. Scis., Am. Math. Soc., Can. Math. Soc., Am. Phys. Soc., Am. Inst. Physics, Philosophy of Sci. Assn., Ont. Med. Assn., Can. Med. Assn. Anglican. Avocations: soaring; camping; movies. Home: 1234 Hillcrest Ave, London, ON Canada N5Y 4N1 Office: Victoria Hosp, Psychogeriatric Clinic, London, ON Canada N5Y 1N9

SULKUNEN, PEKKA JUHANI, social science researcher; b. Jyväskylä, Finland, July 15, 1948; s. Eino Olavi and Hilkka Liisa (Mannström) S.; m. Irma Hilda Piirainen, May 16, 1972; children: Santeri, Johanna, Ida. PhD in Social Scis., Helsinki U., Finland. Asst. U. Helsinki, 1973-77; dir. Social Research Inst. Alcohol Studies, Helsinki, 1983-86, researcher, 1981—; asst. lectr. U. Helsinki, 1983—. Author: Introduction to Sociology, 1987, Keys to Sociology, 1987; co-author Alcohol Control Policies In Public Health Perspective, 1975, Alcohol, Society And The State, 1981, The Suburban Pub. 1985 (Otava Found. prize 1986). Office: Social Inst Alcohol Studies, Kalevank 12, 00100 Helsinki Finland

SULLIVAN, ARNOLD C., corporation executive; b. Milw., Nov. 20, 1935; m. Joan Grossman, June 13, 1959; children: Gloria, Donald, Susan. BA, U. S.C., 1957; MA, So. Methodist U., 1959. With Fingerhut Corp., Minnetonka, Minn., 1965-75, sr. v.p., 1973-75; sr. v.p. Am. Can Co., 1975-81, exec. v.p., 1981—; bd. dirs. Fingerhut Corp. Mem. NAM, Am. Packaging Inst., Mpls. C. of C. Home: Werik Apartments 2327 Park Ave Cincinnati OH 45206

SULLIVAN, BARRY F., banker; b. Bronx, N.Y., Dec. 21, 1930; s. John J. and Marion V. (Dwyer) S.; m. Audrey M. Villeneuve, Apr. 14, 1956; children: Barry, Gerald P., Mariellen M., Scott J., John C. Student, Georgetown U., 1949-52; B.A., Columbia U., 1955; M.B.A., U. Chgo., 1957. Exec. v.p. Chase Manhattan Bank, N.Y.C., 1957-80; chmn., chief exec. officer 1st Chgo.-1st Nat. Bank Chgo., Chgo., 1980—; dir. Am. Nat. Corp. Dir. Econ. Devel. Commn., Chgo.; mem. Chgo. Urban League, Chgo. Central Area Com.; trustee Art Inst. Chgo., U. Chgo. Served with U.S. Army, 1952-54; Korea. Mem. Assn. Res. City Bankers, Trilateral Commn. Roman Catholic. *

SULLIVAN, CLAIRE FERGUSON, marketing educator; b. Pittsburg, Tex., Sept. 28, 1937; d. Almon Lafayette and Mabel Clara (Williams) Potter; m. Richard Wayne Ferguson, Jan. 31, 1959 (div. Jan. 1980); 1 child, Mark Jeffrey Ferguson; m. David Edward Sullivan, Nov. 2, 1984. BBA, U. Tex., 1958, MBA, 1961; PhD, North Tex. State U., 1973. Instr. So. Meth. U., Dallas, 1965-70; asst. prof. U. Utah, Salt Lake City, 1972-74; assoc. prof. U. Ark., Little Rock, 1974-77, U. Tex., Arlington, 1977-80, Ill. State U., Normal, 1980-84; prof., chmn. mktg. Bentley Coll., Waltham, Mass., 1984—; cons. Gen. Telephone Co., Irving, Tex., 1983, McKnight Pub. Co., Bloomington, Ill., 1983, dental practitioner, Bloomington, 1982-83, Olympic Fed., Berwyn, Ill., 1982. Contbr. mktg. articles to profl. jours. Named Outstanding Prof., So. Meth. U., 1969-70; Direct Mktg. Inst. fellow, 1981; Ill. State U. research grantee, 1981-83. Mem. Am. Mktg. Assn. (faculty fellow 1984-85), So. Mktg. Assn., Southwestern Mktg. Assn., Sales and Mktg. Execs. Boston, Beta Gamma Sigma. Republican. Methodist. Home: 9 Potter Pond Lexington MA 02173 Office: Bentley Coll Dept Mktg Waltham MA 02254

SULLIVAN, DOROTHY RONA, state official; b. Boston, Jan. 7, 1941; d. Lewis Robert and Dorothy (Hopkins) S.; B.A., Boston U., 1963; M.Ed., State Coll. Boston, 1966; C.A.G.S., Boston U., 1972; postgrad. Northeastern U., 1970-71, Boston Coll., 1974-78. Research asst., lay med. editor Boston Lying-in Hosp., 1963-64; employment counselor Mass. Div. Employment Security, Boston, 1964-66, sr. employment counselor, 1966-67, prin. employment counselor, 1967-70, employment office mgr., 1970-75, supr., 1975-78, chief research dept., 1978—, dir. def. employment analysis, 1985-87. Supr. community counselor interns and rehab. adminstrn. interns Northeastern U. Grad. Sch. Edn., 1968-74; supr. public adminstrn. interns Suffolk U., 1976; supr. econ. interns Boston U., 1979, Regis Coll., 1984. Recorder Gov.'s Conf. on Rehab., 1970, mem. Gov.'s Commn. Employment of Handicapped, 1972-78, Pres.'s Com. Employment of Handicapped, 1975-78; exec. bd. Greater Boston council Camp Fire Girls; R.S.V.P. adv. bd. Boston Commn. Affairs of the Elderly, 1977-78; mem. adv. com. equal employment opportunity practices Dept. Personnel Adminstrn., 1984-85. Mem. Nat. Vocat. Guidance Assn., Nat. Rehab. Assn. (Mass. sec. 1971-72, exec. bd. 1972-74, v.p. 1974-75, pres. 1976-77), Am. Fedn. State, County and Mcpl. Employees (exec. bd. local 164 1972-73, 74-76), Am. Assn. Counseling and Devel., Am. Personnel and Guidance Assn. (nat. recorder conf. 1968), Am. Acad. Polit. and Social Sci., Rockport Art Assn. (patron), Smaller Bus. Assn. New Eng., Am. Bus. Women's Assn. (del. nat. conv. 1980, 83, pres. Boston chpt. 1982, Woman of Yr., Boston chpt. 1983), Am. Soc. Pub. Adminstrn. (life), N.Y. Acad. Scis., Boston Ctr. for Internat. Visitors. Author: Boston Employment Service Guide, 1969; Massachusetts Cities and Towns, 1978-82; editor Mass. Trends, 1978-82; contbr. articles to profl. jours. Home: 33 Morey Rd Roslindale MA 02131 Office: Employment Security Bldg Govt Ctr Boston MA 02114

SULLIVAN, EARL ISEMAN, government official; b. Paducah, Ky., June 28, 1923; s. Jesse Iseman and Birdie S.; B.A., Western Ky. U., 1964, postgrad., 1965. Instr., Spencerian Coll., Louisville, 1965-75; Army edn. counselor Pentagon, Washington, 1975-78; dir. Army edn. Mil. Dist. Washington-Hoffman/DARCOM, 1978—. Vol. info. specialist Smithsonian Instn., 1977-79; v.p. Met. Organ Soc. D.C., 1976; asst. dir. Little Col. Theater, Louisville, 1958-59. Served with U.S. Army, 1947-48. Recipient Meritorious Civilian Service award Dept. Army, 1978, Outstanding Performance award, 1978, 80, Exceptional Performance awards, 1981, 83, 84; also awards for poetry and non-fiction, 1970-75. Mem. Adult Edn. Assn., Assn. Supervision and Curriculum Devel., Assn. Continuing Higher Edn., Ky. Soc., Hon. Order Ky. Cols., Soc. of Pilgrims of St. Mary's. Methodist. Club: Arts (Louisville). Contbr. poetry to anthologies. Home: 4 W Howell Ave Alexandria VA 22301 Office: 200 Stovall St Room 1N41 Hoffman II Alexandria VA 22332

SULLIVAN, EDWARD CUYLER, retired brewing company executive; b. Balt., Aug. 15, 1906; s. Charles Francis and Emma (Burgess) S.; m. Eileen Flanigan, Apr. 20, 1936 (dec.); 1 son, Pierce Edward; m. Adriane St. John Kleban, Aug. 1980. BA, Cath. U. Am., 1927. Trainee, then buyer Hutzler Bros., Balt., 1927-33; v.p. O'Neill's Dept. Store, Balt., 1933-41; dir. controls and operations Allied Stores Corp., N.Y.C., 1941-43; exec. v.p. Joskes Dept. Store, San Antonio, 1943-56; pres. Sterling Lindner Dept. Store, Cleve., 1956-59, Wolff & Marx Dept. Store, San Antonio, 1959-65; pres., dir. Lone Star Brewing Co., San Antonio, 1965-78; dir. Merc. Bank & Trust, San Antonio; pres. Tex. Brewers Inst. Pres. Research and Planning Council, San Antonio, 1963-65, San Antonio Symphony Soc.; Bd. dirs. Nat. council U.S.O., S.W. Found. Research and Edn.; v.p., bd. dirs. Tex. Tourist Council; bd. dirs. San Antonio-Air Force Community Council, San Antonio Livestock Expn.; trustee Our Lady of the Lake Coll. Recipient Golden Deeds award San Antonio Exchange Club, 1978; Brotherhood award NCCJ. Clubs: Argyle, San Antonio Country; Corpus Christi Yacht (Tex.).

SULLIVAN, EDWARD JOSEPH, electrotype company executive; b. Concord, N.H., May 17, 1915; s. Edward J. and Ida (Packard) S.; student St. Anslem's Coll., 1935-36; m. Dorothea M. Ash, Sept. 30, 1944; children—James Ash, Maureen Packard. Treas., Merrimack Electrotyping Corp., 1950-55, pres., 1955—; treas. Sheraton Properties Corp., 1961—; exec. v.p. Blanchard Press Corp., 1968-69; pres. Tridel Housing Devels., 1970—, Ho-Tei Corp., St. Thomas, V.I.; dir. Concord Fed. Savs. Bank; pres. Allied Photo Engraving Corp., 1964. Mem. Concord Hosp. Corp., U.S. Commn. on Civil Rights; chmn. bldg. fund Carmelite Monastery, Concord, 1950, St. Peters Ch. for Bishop Brady High Sch. Bldg. Fund, 1961; citizens com. Concord Housing Authority; commr. Concord Urban Renewal Assn.; v.p., bd. dirs. Diocesan Bur. Housing, Inc., Manchester, N.H., 1975—; bd. dirs. Carpenter Center, Inc., Manchester, N.H., Concord chpt. ARC, Concord Hosp. Served with USNR, 1942-46. Mem. Internat. Assn. Electrotypers and Stereotypers Union, Internat. Assn. Electrotypers and Stereotypers, Inc., Am. Legion, Aircraft Owners and Pilots Assn., Audubon Soc. N.H., Printing Inst. Am., One Hundred Club N.H. Elk. Republican. Roman Catholic. Club: Serra (v.p.). Kiwanian, K.C. Home: 99 Manor Rd Concord NH 03303 Office: 99 Manor Rd Concord NH 03303

SULLIVAN, EUGENE JOHN JOSEPH, manufacturing company executive; b. N.Y.C., Nov. 28, 1920; s. Cornelius and Margaret (Smith) S.; m. Gloria Roesch, Aug. 25, 1943; children: Eugene John Joseph, Edward J., Robert C., Elizabeth Ann Hansler. B.S., St. John's U., 1942, D.Commerce, 1973; M.B.A., N.Y. U., 1948. With chem. div. Borden, Inc., N.Y.C., 1946—; beginning as salesman, successively asst. sales Borden, Inc., 1957-58, exec. v.p., 1958-64; pres. Borden Chem. Co. div. Borden, Inc.; v.p. Borden, Inc., 1964-67, exec. v.p., 1967-73, pres., chief operating officer, 1973-79, chmn., pres., chief exec. officer, 1979-86, chmn. exec. com., 1987—; formerly adj. prof., now prof. St. John's U., 1987—; bd. dirs. Borden Co., F.W. Woolworth Co., Bank of N.Y., Warner Lambert Co., Discount Corp. of N.Y.; trustee Atlantic Mut. Ins. Co., D.C.N.Y. Corp. Trustee, sec. St. John's U.; trustee N.Y. Med. Coll.; chmn. Commn. on Cath. Health Care. Served as lt. USNR, 1942-46; lt. Res. Mem. Council Fgn. Relations, Knights of Malta, Knights of Holy Sepulchre. Clubs: University, Plandome Country, Westhampton Country. Office: Borden Inc 277 Park Ave New York NY 10172

SULLIVAN, GEORGE ALLEN, statistical analyst; b. Bronxville, N.Y., Dec. 1, 1935; s. George Dewey and Edna (Corzine) S.; A.B., Grinnell Coll., 1957; A.M., U. Rochester, 1959; Ph.D., U. Nebr., 1964; M. Govt. Adminstrn., U. Pa., 1976; m. Virginia Ann Weir, Apr. 9, 1960; children—Bonnie Len, Timothy Frank. Vis. scientist physics Rensselaer Poly. Inst., Troy, N.Y., 1964-66; sr. physicist Clevite Research Lab., Cleve., 1966-69; asst. prof. elec. engring. Air Force Inst. Tech., Dayton, Ohio, 1969-70; vis. scientist physics Chalmers U. Tech., Gothenburg, Sweden, 1970-71; statis. analyst Pa. Bd. Probation and Parole, Harrisburg, 1971—; specialist design and validation of parole decision guidelines instruments. Curtiss-Wright grad. fellow, 1958 59; NSF grad. fellow, 1963-64 Mem. Am. Statis. Assn. (Harrisburg chpt.), Nat. Speleological Soc., Pa. Assn. for Probation, Parole and Corrections, Phi Beta Kappa, Sigma Xi. Contbr. articles to profl. jours. Home: 4204 Kota Ave Harrisburg PA 17120 Office: 3101 N Front St Box 1661 Harrisburg PA 17105-1661

SULLIVAN, GEORGE EDMUND, editorial and marketing company executive; b. N.Y.C., Feb. 3, 1932; s. Timothy Daniel and Helen Veronica (Danaher) S.; m. Carole Ann Hartz, Sept. 4; 1954; children—Patricia Lynn, George Edmund, Michael Frank. B.A., Iona Coll., 1957; M.Ed., Rutgers U., 1961; Ph.D., Walden U., 1980. Tchr. English Holmdel Twp. and Keyport (N.J.) Pub. Schs., 1957-62; field mgr. regional mktg. Harcourt, Brace & World, Inc., N.Y.C., 1962-69; v.p. sales Noble & Noble, Publishers, Inc., 1969-72, sr. v.p., chief exec. officer, 1972-78; pres. Sullivan Ednl. Assos., Inc., West Orange, N.J., 1978—; dir. ednl. div. Hammond, Inc.; ednl. pub. cons. Edumedia Ltd., Kitchener, Ont., Can.; 4-H leader, 1957-59. Author numerous books on English lang., writing and map reading skills. Served with USAF, 1950-52. Mem. Assn. Am. Publishers (ofcl. rep. 1972-82), Keyport Edn. Assn. (pres. 1960-62), Am. Mgmt. Assn. Home: 127 Old Short Hills Rd Apt 200 West Orange NJ 07052

SULLIVAN, HENRY WELLS, Spanish literature educator, researcher; b. Southgate, Middlesex, U.K., Dec. 8, 1942; came to U.S., 1966; s. Henry John and Marie-Antoinette (Duigenan) S.; m. Constance Hubbard Rose, June 12, 1970 (div. 1973); m. Mary Eloise Ragland, June 14, 1975; 1 daughter, Caroline Alexandra. B.A., Queen's Coll., Oxford U., 1966, M.A., 1968; Ph.D., Harvard U., 1970. Teaching fellow Harvard U., Cambridge, Mass., 1966-69; asst. prof. NYU, 1969-71, U. Ill.-Chgo., 1971-77, Northwestern U., Evanston, Ill., 1977-78; sr. fellow Humboldt Found., Bonn and Hamburg, Germany, 1978-80; prof. Spanish lit., dept. chmn. U. Ottawa, Ont., Can., 1980-84; prof. Spanish lit. U. Fla., Gainesville, 1984—; mem. appraisals com. Ont. Council on Grad. Studies, 1983—. Author: Juan Del Encina, 1976; Tirso De Molina & The Drama of the Counter-Reformation, 1976; Calderon in the German Lands, 1983. Fellow NEH, Amsterdam, Netherlands, 1976, Guggenheim Found., 1984-85. Mem. MLA of Am. (com. for Spanish), Asociacion Internacional de Hispanistas, Asociacion Canadiense de Hispanistas. Home: 2640 NW 27th Terr Gainesville FL 32605 Office: U Fla ASB 235 Gainesville FL 32611

SULLIVAN, JAMES ANDERSON, lawyer; b. Wabash, Ind., July 1, 1925; s. Lawrence James and Mildred (Anderson) S.; m. Marily June Allen, Oct. 4, 1947; children—Timothy J., Patrick F., Katherine M. Sullivan Luce, Thomas S., James Anderson. A.B. magna cum laude, Ind. U., 1952, J.D. magna cum laude, 1954. Bar: Calif. 1955, U.S. Dist. Ct. (so. dist.) Calif. 1955, U.S. Ct. Appeals (9th cir.) 1955, U.S. Supreme Ct. 1963. Assoc. Gibson, Dunn & Crutcher, Los Angeles, 1954-56; mem. corp. legal staff Hughes Aircraft Co., Culver City, Calif., 1956-58, div. counsel, El Segundo, Calif., 1958-63, aerospace group counsel, Culver City, 1963-65; of counsel Sweeney Cozy & Diederich, Torrance, Calif., 1965-72; ptnr. Buck, Sullivan, Govendo & Bavetta, Redondo Beach, Calif., 1973-75; sole practice, Redondo Beach, 1975-84, Torrance, 1984—; mem. panel arbitrators Am. Arbitration Assn., Fed. Mediation and Conciliation Service; bd. dirs. EDP Environments, Inc., Torrance, Calif., Palos Verdes Breakfast Club, Palos Verdes Estates, Calif. Bd. dirs. South Bay Children's Health Ctr. Assn., Torrance, Calif. Served with USNR, 1943-46, PTO, 1950-51, Korea. John H. Edwards fellow, 1953-54. Mem. South Bay Estate Planning Council (pres. 1967-68), Order of Coif, Phi Beta Kappa, Phi Eta Sigma, Phi Delta Phi. Republican. Roman Catholic. Clubs: South Bay Athletic (Redondo Beach); Kiwanis (pres. Redondo Beach club 1981-82, Riviera Village club. 1985-86), Palos Verdes Breakfast (bulletin editor 1982-86, bd. dirs. 1986—). Address: The Plaza 4600 Lamont St Box-4111 San Diego CA 92109

SULLIVAN, JAMES KIRK, forest products company executive; b. Greenwood, S.C., Aug. 25, 1935; s. Daniel Jones and Addie (Brown) S.; m. Elizabeth Miller, June 18, 1960; children: Hal N., Kim J. B.S. in Chemistry, Clemson U., 1957, M.S., 1964, Ph.D., 1966; postgrad, MIT, 1975. Prodn. supr. FMC Corp., South Charleston, W.Va., 1957-62; tech. supt. FMC Corp., Pocatello, Idaho, 1966-69; mktg. mgr. FMC Corp., N.Y.C., 1969-70; v.p. govtl. and environ. affairs Boise Cascade Corp., Idaho, 1971—; dir. Idaho Bank & Trust Co. Contbr. articles to profl. jours.; patentee in field. Mem. Coll. of Forest and Recreation Resources com. Clemson U., Idaho Found. for Pvt. Enterprise and Econ. Edn., Idaho Research Found., Inc., adv. com. Idaho Task Force on Higher Edn.; chmn. adv. bd. U. Idaho Coll. Engring., pub. affairs com. NAM; pres. Bishop Kelly Found.; chmn. centennial campaign U. Idaho; trustee Idaho Children's Emergency Fund, Bishop Kelly High Sch.; past chmn. Bronco Athletic Assn. Served to 1st lt. U.S. Army, 1958-59. Mem. Am. Inst. Chem. Engrs., Am. Chem. Soc., Am. Inst. Chem. Engrs., Am. Paper Inst. (govtl. affairs com.), Bus. Week Found. (chmn. Bus. Week 1980), Bus. Roundtable (environ. com.), Idaho Assn. Commerce and Industry (bd. dirs.), C. of C. of U.S. (pub. affairs com.). Republican. Home: 5206 Sorrento Circle Boise ID 83704 Office: Boise Cascade Corp One Jefferson Sq Boise ID 83728

SULLIVAN, MICHAEL EVAN, investment and management company executive; b. Phila., Dec. 30, 1940; s. Albert and Ruth (Liebert) S.; BS, N.Mex. State U., 1966, MA (Ednl. Research Tng. Program fellow), 1967; BS, U. Tex., 1969; MBA, U. Houston, 1974; MS, U. So. Calif., 1976, MPA, 1977, PhD in Adminstrn., 1983; BS in Acctg., U. La Verne, 1981. Sr. adminstrv. and tech. analyst Houston Lighting & Power Co., 1969-74; electronics engr. U.S. Govt., Point Mugu, Calif., 1974-77; mem. tech. staff Hughes Aircraft Co., El Segundo, Calif., 1977-78; staff program adminstr. Ventura div. Northrop Corp., Newbury Park, Calif., 1978-79; div. head engring. div. Navastrogru, Point Mugu, 1979-82; br. head, div. head spl. programs Pacific Missile Test Ctr., (Calif.), 1983—; head operational systems integration office and assignments CNO-Dir. Research, Devel., and Acquisition in the Pentagon, Washington; pres., chmn. bd. Diversified Mgmt. Systems, Inc., Camarillo, Calif., 1978—. Author: The Management of Research, Development, Test and Evaluation Organizations; Organizational Behavior Characteristics of Supervisors-Public versus Private Sectors, Organizational Behavior Characteristics of Supervisors, Public versus Private Sectors; Self-Actualization in RDT & E Organizations; Self-Actualization in a Health Care Agency; others. V.p., bd. dirs. Ventura County Master Chorale and Opera Assn; bd. dirs. Southern Calif. Assn. of Pub. Adminstrn. (also mem. fin. com., programs com., student aid com.). Served with U.S. Army, 1958-62. Ednl. Research Info. Clearing House fellow, 1965-67. Mem. Am. Math. Soc., Math. Assn. Am., Am. Statis. Assn., IEEE, IEEE Engring. Mgmt. Soc., Am. Soc. Pub. Adminstrn., So. Calif. Assn. Pub. Adminstrn. (bd. dirs., various coms.), Am. Personnel and Guidance Assn., Fed. Mgrs. Assn., Am. Assn. Individual Investors, Mcpl. Mgmt. Assts. So. Calif., Acad. Polit. Sci., Assn. M.B.A. Execs., Phi Kappa Phi, Pi Gamma Mu. Home: PO Box 273 Port Hueneme CA 93041 Office: PO Box 447 Camarillo CA 93010

SULLIVAN, MICHAEL J., governor of Wyoming, lawyer; b. Omaha, Sept. 23, 1939; s. Joseph Byrne and Margaret (Hamilton) S.; m. Jane Metzler, Sept. 2, 1961; children: Michelle, Patrick, Theresa. BS in Petroleum Engring., U. Wyo., 1961, JD, 1964. Assoc. Brown, Drew, Apostolos, Barton & Massey, Casper, Wyo., 1964-67; ptnr. Brown, Drew, Apostolos, Massey & Sullivan, Casper, 1967—; gov. State of Wyo., Casper, 1987—. Trustee St. Joseph's Children's Home, Torrington, Wyo., 1986-87; bd. dirs. Natrona County Meml. Hosp., Casper, 1976-86. Mem. ABA, Wyo. Bar Assn., Assn. Trial Lawyers Am., Wyo. Trial Lawyers Assn. Democrat. Roman Catholic. Lodge: Rotary (pres. Casper club). Home: 5001 Central Ave Cheyenne WY 82002 Office: Office Gov State Capitol Cheyenne WY 82002-0010

SULLIVAN, NEIL MAXWELL, oil and gas company executive; b. McKeesport, Pa., May 25, 1942; s. Thomas James and Jane Mason (Ginn) S.; m. Margaret Pedrick, Aug. 10, 1974; children: Margaret Blair, Mason Pedrick. BS, Dickinson Coll., 1970; postgrad., Tulane U., 1970-74. Exploration geologist Bass Enterprises, Midland, Tex., 1976-77; dist. geologist ATAPCO, Midland, 1977-78, Anadarko Prodn. Co., Midland, 1978-79, chief geologist, 1979-80, v.p. exploration, regional mgr., Houston, 1980-82; exploration ops. mgr. Valero Producing Co., San Antonio, 1982-85, v.p. exploration, New Orleans, 1985-87; pres. Bluebonnet Petroleum Co., New Orleans, 1987—; mem. Dept. Interior Outer Continental Shelf Com. adv. bd., 1985-87. Editor: Guadalupian Delaware Mountain Group of West Texas and Southeast New Mexico, 1979, Ancient Carbonate Reservoirs and Their Modern Analogs, 1977, Petroleum Exploration in Thrust Belts and Their Adjacent Forelands, 1976. Bd. dirs. Permian Basin Grad. Ctr., Midland, 1979; com. chmn. Mus. of S.W., Midland, 1978. Served with USAF, 1964-68. Mem. Geol. Soc. Am., Am. Assn. Petroleum Geologists (cert. petroleum geologist), New Orleans Geol. Soc. (chmn. continuing edn. com. 1987—), South Tex. Geol. Soc. (nominating com. chmn. 1985), Soc. Econ. Paleontologists and Mineralogists (pres. Permian Basin sect. 1979). Lodge: Elks. Home: 1738 Milan St New Orleans LA 70115

SULLIVAN, NEIL SAMUEL, physicist, researcher, educator; b. Wanganui, Wellington, N.Z., Jan. 18, 1942; came to U.S., 1983; s. Reynold Richard and Edna Mary (Alger) S.; m. Robyn Annette Dawson, Aug. 28, 1965; children—Raoul Samuel, Robert Alexander and David Charles (twins). B.Sc. with 1st class honors, U. Otago, N.Z., 1964, M.Sc. in Physics, 1965; Ph.D. in Physics, Harvard U., 1972. Postdoctoral research Centre d'Etudes Nucleaires, Saclay, France, 1972-74, research physicist, 1974-82; prof. physics U. Fla., Gainesville, 1982—. Contbr. numerous articles on quantum solids and nuclear magnetism to profl. jours., 1971—. Recipient prix Saintour, College de France, Paris, 1978, prix LaCaze, Academie des Sciences, Paris, 1982; Fulbright exchange grantee, 1965; Frank Knox Meml. fellow Harvard U., Cambridge, Mass., 1965-67. Mem. Inst. Physics, Societe Francaise de Physique, European Phys. Soc., Am. Phys. Soc., AAAS. Current work: Investigation of fundamental properties of solid hydrogen and solid helium at very low temperatures; studies of molecular motions using nuclear magnetic resonance; orientational disorder in molecular crystals. Subspecialties: Condensed matter physics; Low temperature physics. Home: 4244 NW 76 Terr Gainesville FL 32606

SULLIVAN, PATRICK JAMES, lawyer; b. Orange, Calif., Sept. 17, 1943; s. Leo Charles Sullivan and Virginia (Wohosky) Souza; m. Pamela Pressler, Aug. 17, 1974; children: Shannon, Erin. BA, U. So. Calif., 1965; JD, Loyola U., Los Angeles, 1974. Bar: Calif. 1974, U.S. Ct. Appeals (9th cir.) 1978, U.S. Supreme Ct. 1979, U.S. Ct. Appeals (3rd cir.) 1983, U.S. Tax Ct. 1986. Trial atty. U.S. Dept. Justice, Washington, 1974-75; ptnr. Sullivan, Jones & Archer, San Diego and San Francisco, 1975-82, Sullivan & Jones, San Diego, 1982-83, Hewitt, Sullivan & Marshall, San Diego, 1983-85, Sullivan, DuVall & Noya, San Diego, 1986—; arbitrator San Diego Superior Ct., 1979-83; lectr. U. Calif. Securities Regulations Inst., 1985; chmn. Am. Law Inst. Anti-trust Conf., 1988. Served to 1st lt. U.S. Army, 1966-69; Vietnam. Decorated Bronze Star. Mem. ABA (litigation and antitrust sects.), Nat. Inst. Trial Adv. (faculty 1986—). Republican. Roman Catholic. Lodge: Rotary (Newhall, Calif.). Home: 335 Whitewood Pl Encinitas CA 92024 Office: Sullivan DuVall & Noya Wells Fargo Bank Bldg 101 W Broadway Suite 1400 San Diego CA 92101

SULLIVAN, TIMOTHY PATRICK, real estate developer; b. Phoenix, June 8, 1958; s. Jeremiah Joseph and Nancy Mignon (Otwell) S. BS in Animal Sci., Colo. State U., 1980; MBA, Ariz. State U., 1985. Lic. realtor, Ariz. Trust securities cashier The Ariz. Bank, Phoenix, 1980; owner Pronghorn Hereford Ranch, Ignacio, Colo., 1981—; assoc. J.J. Sullivan Realty, Scottsdale, Ariz., 1981-83; mng. ptnr. HKS Joint Venture Partnership, Scottsdale, 1983—; founder, corp. sec. Sullivan Devel. Corp., Scottsdale, 1983—. Alumni ambassador Colo. State U., Fort Collins; bd. dirs. Vol. Friends of Channel 8, Tempe, Ariz.; chmn. goodwill connections KAET-TV; chmn. mem. com. Cen. Ariz. ARC, 1986—; grad. Valley Leadership, Phoenix, 1988. Mem. Am. Hereford Assn., Colo. Hereford Assn., Alpha Zeta. Roman Catholic. Home: Pronghorn Hereford Ranch Ignacio CO 81137 Office: 4234 Winfield Scott Plaza Scottsdale AZ 85251

SULLO, ROSE ANN, sculptor, artist; b. N.Y.C., Mar. 27, 1919; d. Saverio and Rosina (Palumbo) Pesce; student Leonardi DaVinci Cultural Center, N.Y., 1934-37, Poppenhusen Inst., N.Y., 1936-37, Delphic Studios, N.Y., 1937, Cooper Union Inst., N.Y., 1937-39; m. Joseph A. Sullo, Oct. 12, 1947; children—Susan Ann, Donna Rose, Peter Adam. Free-lance profl. sculptor and artist; one woman shows include: Halifax Hist. Soc., Daytona Beach, Fla., 1978, Ormond Meml. Art Gallery, Ormond Beach, Fla., 1979; group shows: Brockton (Mass.) Art Center, 1972, United Fedn. Doll Clubs, Detroit, 1970, Los Angeles, 1971, Omaha, 1972, Louisville, 1973, Miami, 1974, San Francisco, 1976, San Diego, 1977, Hartford, Conn., 1973, 77, Seattle, 1972, Denver, 1978, N.Y.C., 1979, Akron, Ohio, 1979, Washington-Balt., 1980, St. Louis, 1981, Bedford, N.H., 1982, Kansas City, Kans., 1982, Patchogue, N.Y., 1982, Harrisburg, Pa., 1983, Ormond Beach, Fla., 1983, Flushing (N.Y.) Council Women's Clubs, 1977, 78, Nat. League Am. Pen Women, 1974, 75, 76, 77, 78, Daytona Automobile Conf. (Fla.), 1983, Daytona Community Coll., 1983, Daytona Mus. Arts and Scis., 1983; represented in permanent collections: Wee Lassie Doll Mus., Homstead, Fla., Mus. City N.Y., Strong Mus., Pittsford, N.Y., Morristown (N.J.) Mus. Arts and Scis.; presented work to Pres. Nixon, 1972. Del., art chmn. Flushing Council Women's Clubs, 1975—. Recipient many awards for art works and sculpture; Internat. Women's Year award, 1975; award of distinction for sculptural portraiture Deland Mus. (Fla.), 1983. Mem. Nat. Inst. Am. Doll Artist, Inc. (award of excellence 1970), Nat. League Am. Pen Women, (spl. award 1974), Sculpture, United Fedn. Doll Clubs, Dollology Club Washington, Doll Collector's Guild N.Y., Flushing Art League, Internat. Doll Clubs, Dutchess Art Assn., Internat. Doll Acad. Home: 16 Briar Hill Rd and Rt 52 Hopewell Junction NY 12533

SULMAN, CHARLES, oncologist; b. Perigueux, France, Mar. 4, 1942; m. Claudie Evelyne Goldschmidt, July 23, 1963; children: Michael David, Sandra. House physician U. Hosp., Lille, France, 1966-71, resident in nuclear medicine, 1969-70, resident in radiology and radiotherapy, 1970-71; biophys. asst. dr. U. Lille, 1968-74, dir. clin. teaching, 1976—; nuclear medicine asst. Oncol. Hosp., Lille, 1971-76; head dept. nuclear medicine Oncol. Hosp., 1976—; tchr. nuclear medicine Nat. Inst. Nuclear Scis. and Techniques, Paris, 1976; expert in nuclear medicine and med. decision making to profl. publs. Pres. Regional Jewish Community, Lille, 1984—; bd. dirs. French Jewish Consistory, Paris, 1984—. Mem. French Radiology Soc., Medicale Medecine Nucleaire et Electroradiology France, Soc. Francaise Biophysique et de Medecine Nuclaire France, Soc. Nuclear Medicine U.S., European Soc. Nuclear Medicine, European Soc. Med. Decision Making. Office: Clinique de la Louviere, 69 Rue de la Louviere, 59000 Lille France

SULTAN, ABD-EL-RAHMAN AHMED, architect; b. Cairo, Egypt, Nov. 4, 1947; came to Japan, 1974; s. Ahmed Mustafa and Sekina Ismail (Abd-Al-Lah) S.; m. Yasuko Emmei, Jan. 16, 1981. Dr.Arch., U. Tokyo, 1980, M.Arch., 1977; B.Arch., Ain Shams U., Cairo, 1968. Student/architect/cons. architect Hassan Fathy, Architect, Cairo, 1966—; prin. A.A. Sultan, Architect & Assocs., Cairo, Copenhagen, Tokyo, 1968-80; instr. dept. architecture Ain Shams U., Cairo, 1969-70; designer Krohn & Hartvig Rasmussen, Copenhagen, 1970-71; research fellow U. Tokyo, 1980-82; prin. A.A.S. Assocs., Internat., Tokyo, 1981—, Cairo, 1984—, cons. architect Greater Cairo Planning Commn., 1968-69, Simon Spies, Copenhagen, 1971, Fredriksberg Hotel, Copenhagen, 1971; cons. architect, planner UN Univ., Tokyo, 1978—; dir. Egypt Japan Steel Works, Cairo, 1985—. Archtl. works include: Tokyo H.I. Offices-Residences, Fiji JRD Hotel-Office-Shopping Ctr., Egyptian Pavilion Japan '85 Tsukuba Expo, ICA Houses, The Tokyo Mosque, Alexandria Nat. Steel Housing, U.A.E. Embassy, Saudi Embassy, Egyptian Embassy, Riyadh Hotel, Minato Community Ctr., LL House, SFI Apt. Bldg., Algeria M'sila Integrated Solar Village, Tokyo Setagaya Neighborhood Unit, MCI Apt. Bldg., Nat. Theatre Cairo; others; contbr. articles to profl. jours. Japanese Govt. fellow, 1980-81, scholar, 1974-80. Fellow Soc. Egyptian Architects; mem. Far East Soc. Architects and Engrs., Archtl. Inst. Japan, Archtl. Sect. Egyptian Syndicate of Engrs. Islam. Clubs: Mensa Japan, Fukuoka UNESCO Assn. Home: Shirogane-Dai 2-8-12, Minato-ku, Tokyo 108 Japan Office: Takanawa Toei Bldg #503, Takanawa 4-11-35, Minato-ku, Tokyo 108, Japan

SULTAN IBN ABDULAZIZ, PRINCE, Saudi Arabian minister of defense and aviation; b. 1924; s. King Abdul-Aziz ibn Saud. Pres., Royal Guard, Riyadh, Saudi Arabia; former minister of agr., minister of communications; minister of def. and aviation, 1962—; also insp.-gen.; mem. Saudi dels. to Arab and Islamic Summit Confs., state visits and UN Gen. Assembly sessions; chmn. Supreme Com. for Adminstrv. Reform; v.p. Supreme Council Higher Edn. Office: Ministry of Def and Aviation, Riyadh Saudi Arabia *

SULZBERGER, CYRUS LEO, writer; b. N.Y.C., Oct. 27, 1912; m. Marina Tatiana Lada, Jan. 21, 1942 (dec. 1976); children—Marina Beatrice (Mrs. Adrian Berry), David Alexis. Grad., Harvard, 1934. Columnist N.Y. Times, until 1978. Author: Sit-Down with John L. Lewis, 1938, The Big Thaw, 1956, What's Wrong with U.S. Foreign Policy, 1958, My Brother Death, 1959, The Test-DeGaulle and Algeria, 1962, Unfinished Revolution, 1965, History of World War II (Am. Heritage History), 1966, A Long Row of Candles, 1969, The Last of the Giants, 1970, The Tooth Merchant, 1973, Unconquered Souls, 1973, An Age of Mediocrity, 1973, The Coldest War, 1974, Postscript with a Chinese Accent, 1974, Go Gentle into the Night, 1976, The Fall of Eagles, 1977, Seven Continents and Forty Years, 1977, The Tallest Liar, 1977, Marina, 1979, How I Committed Suicide, 1982, Such a Peace: The Roots and Ashes of Yalta, 1982, The World and Richard Nixon, 1987, Fathers and Children, 1987. Recipient Pulitzer Prize citation, 1951; award for best consistent reporting from abroad Overseas Press Club Am., 1951; citations for excellence, 1957, 70; award for best book on fgn. affairs, 1973. Club: Metropolitan (Washington). Home: 25 Blvd du Montparnasse, 75006 Paris France

SULZBY, JAMES FREDERICK, JR., real estate executive; b. Birmingham, Ala., Dec. 24, 1905; s. James Frederick and Annie (Dobbins) S.; m. Martha Belle Hilton, Nov. 9, 1935; children: James Frederick III, Martha Hilton (Mrs. Robert J.B. Clark). Student, Howard Coll., Birmingham, 1925-26; AB, Birmingham-So. Coll., 1928; grad., Am. Inst. Banking, 1934; LittD, Athens Coll.; LHD, Samford U. With trust dept. First Nat. Bank of Birmingham, 1929-43; partner Sulzby Realty Co., 1943—; dir. Ala. Fed. Savs. & Loan Assn.; bd. dirs. Birmingham Area Bd. Realtors, pres., 1953; pres. Norwood Gardens, Inc. (housing project). Author: Birmingham As It Was in Jackson County, 1944, Birmingham Sketches, 1945, Annals of the Southside Baptist Church, 1947, Historic Alabama Hotels and Resorts, 1960, Arthur W. Smith, A Birmingham Pioneer, 1855-1944, 1961, Toward a History of Samford University, 1986. Trustee Rushton Lectures, Birmingham Civic Symphony Assn., Oak Hill Meml. Assn.; bd. dirs. Birmingham Sunday Sch. Assn., Ala. Baptist Publ. (emeritus mem.); mem. Birmingham Planning Commn., chmn., 1948-61; mem. adv. com. Civil War Centennial Commn.; historian 75th anniversary celebration for Birmingham, 1946; mem. adv. bd. Nat. Hist. Records; treas., mem. exec. com. Southside Bapt. Ch.; pres. Ala. Bapt. Young Peoples Union, 1932-33; bd. govs. Civic Theatre Birmingham, 1946-48; bd. dirs. Ala. Hall of Fame; chmn. Jefferson County Nat. Found. Infantile Paralysis, 1951-52, Jefferson County Hist. Commn.; mem. Cahaba Hist. Commn. Recipient Lit. award A.L.A., 1962. Mem. Newcomen Soc. U.S. (mem. Ala. com.), Ala. Hist. Assn. (pres. 1947-49, sec. 1950—), Ala. Bapt. Hist. Soc. (pres. 1947-49), Birmingham-Jefferson Hist. Soc., Birmingham Hist. Soc. (sec. 1945-50, trustee 1950—), Avondale Civic Assn. (pres. 1946, Am. Planning and Civic Assn., dir.), Ala. Assn. Realtors (pres. 1952), Ala. Writers Conclave (pres. 1950), Nat. Assn. Real Estate Bds. (dir. 1952-56), Ala. Acad. Sci, pres. 1965, trustee), Phi Beta Kappa, Phi Alpha Theta, Omega Tau Rho, Delta Sigma Phi, Omicron Delta Kappa. Democrat. Baptist. Clubs: Filson, Mountain Brook; Univ. (Tuscaloosa, Ala.). Home: 3121 Carlisle Rd Birmingham AL 35213 Office: Frank Nelson Bldg Birmingham AL 35203

SUMA, KOZO, cardiac surgeon, educator; b. Okayama, Japan, Sept. 11, 1932; s. Harumi and Toshie Suma; m. Hiroko Fujimoto, May 20, 1961; children: Naoki, Takeshi, Sachiko. MD, U. Tokyo, 1958, PhD, 1963. Intern U. Tokyo Hosp., 1958-59, asst. in surgery, 1963-70; Fulbright scholar, clin. and research fellow Mass. Gen. Hosp., Boston, 1966-67; chief surgeon

Sakakibara Juzen Hosp., Okayama, 1971-72; assoc. prof. surg. sci. Tokyo Women's Med. Coll., 1972-73, prof., 1973—, also chief surgeon cardiovascular surgery; chmn. sci. exhbn. World Congress Cardiology, Tokyo, 1978. Fellow Am. Coll. Cardiology; mem. Internat. Cardiovascular Soc. (councilor), Internat. Soc. for Artificial Organs, Japanese Assn. Thoracic Surgery (councilor), N.Y. Acad. Sci. Pioneer cardiac pacemaker in Japan; introduced hydrodynamical concept in cardiac surgery; developer hollow fiber oxygenator, treatment of Kawasaki disease. Home: 1-11-14 Chiyogaoka, Asoku, Kawasaki Japan Office: Tokyo Women's Med Coll, 2-1-10 Nishiogu Arakawa-ku, Tokyo 116, Japan

SUMARNO, ISHAK, banker; b. Jakarta, Indonesia, May 13, 1943; s. Kang So Tan and It Nio Jo; m. Tjandra Grace Supratik, Apr. 24, 1975; children—Joyce, Allen. Dipl.-Ing., Stuttgart U., West Germany, 1970. Registered profl. engr., West Germany. Sub-mgr. Bank Buana Indonesia P.T., Jakarta, 1976-84, mgr., 1984—. Recipient Cert. Commendation award Bankers Trust Co., 1981, Meritorious Achievement award Bankers Trust Co., 1981, Cert. of Attendance award Bank of Am., 1982. Club: Hilton Exec. (Jakarta), Bankers (Indonesia). Avocations: reading; music. Office: Bank Buana Indonesia PT, Asemka 32-35, Jakarta 11110, Indonesia

SUMARSONO, physician; b. Malang, Jawa Timur, Indonesia, Apr. 19, 1923; parents: Sumarno and Sumarni Yetti; m. Choufiah Tuti, July 23, 1960; children: Harjanto, Lukiwati, Aritono, Henny Kusumawati. MD, Airlangga U., Surabaya, Indonesia, 1958. Dir. Govt. Hosp., Labuha, Maluku, Indonesia, 1958-63; dir., supr. radiology and surgery Christian Hosp., Mojowarno, Jawa Timur, 1963—. Mem. Indonesian Med. Assn. Home: Jalan K H Hasyim Ashari 51, Jombang, Jawa Timur 61419, Indonesia Office: R S Kristen Mojowarno, Jalan Merdeka, Jombang, Jawa Timur Indonesia

SUMIDA, GERALD AQUINAS, lawyer; b. Hilo, Hawaii, June 19, 1944; s. Sadamu and Kimiyo (Miyahara) S.; m. Sylvia Whitehead, June 23, 1970. AB summa cum laude, Princeton U., 1966, cert. in pub. and internat. affairs, 1966; JD, Yale U., 1969. Bar: Hawaii 1970, U.S. Dist. Ct. Hawaii 1970, U.S. Ct. Appeals (9th cir.) 1970, U.S. Supreme Ct. 1981. Research assoc. Ctr. Internat. Studies, Princeton U., 1969; assoc. Carlsmith, Wichman, Case, Mukai & Ichiki, Honolulu, 1970-76, ptnr., 1976—; mem. cameras in courtroom evaluation com. Hawaii Supreme Ct., 1984—. Mem. sci. and statis. com. Western Pacific Fishery Mgmt. Council, 1979—; mem. study group on law of armed conflict and the law of the sea Comdr. in Chief Pacific, U.S. Navy, 1979-82; pres. Pacific and Asian Affairs Council Hawaii, 1982—, bd. govs., 1976—, Paul S. Bachman award, 1978; chmn. internat. com. Hawaii chpt. ARC, 1983—, bd. dirs., 1983; vice chmn. Honolulu Com. on Fgn. Relations, 1983—; pres., dir., founding mem. Hawaii Ocean Law Assn., 1978—; mem. Hawaii Adv. Group for Law of Sea Inst., 1977—; pres. Hawaii Inst. Continuing Legal Edn., 1979-83, dir., 1976—; pres., founding mem. Hawaii Council Legal Edn. for Youth, 1980-83, dir., 1983—; chmn. Hawaii Commn. on Yr. 2000, 1976-79; mem. Honolulu Community Media Council, exec. com., 1976-84, legal counsel, 1979-83; bd. dirs. Hawaii Imin Centennial Corp., 1983—, Hawaii Pub. Radio, 1983-88. Legal Aid Soc. Hawaii, 1984; mem. Pacific Alliance Trade and Devel., 1984—; founding gov. Ctr. Internat. Comml. Dispute Resolution, 1987—; v.p., exec. chmn. rules and procedures, Pacific Rim Found., 1987—; exec. com. Pacific Islands Assn., 1988—. Recipient cert. of appreciation Gov. of Hawaii, 1979, resolutions of appreciation Hawaii Senate and Ho. of Reps., 1979; grantee Japan Found., 1979. Mem. ABA, Hawaii Bar Assn. (pres. young lawyers sect. 1974, v.p. 1984), Japan-Hawaii Lawyers Assn., Am. Soc. Internat. Law, Japan-Hawaii Lawyers Assn., Hawaii C. of C. (energy com. 1981-87, chmn. 1985-87), Am. Judicature Soc., AAAS, Asia Pacific Lawyers Assn., Phi Beta Kappa. Democrat. Clubs: Yale (N.Y.C.); Plaza (Honolulu); Colonial (Princeton). Author: (with others) Legal, Institutional and Financial Aspects of An Inter-Island Electrical Transmission Cable, 1984, Alternative Approaches to the Legal, Institutional and Financial Aspects of Developing an Inter-Island, Electrical Transmission Cable System, 1986; editor Hawaii Bar News, 1972-73; contbr. chpts. to books. Home: 1130 Wilder Ave #1401 Honolulu HI 96822 Office: Pacific Trade Ctr 190 S King St Suite 2200 Honolulu HI 96813 also: Carlsmith Wichman Case Mukai Ichiki 1001 Bishop St Pacific Tower Suite 2200 Honolulu HI 96813

SUMME, GREGORY LOUIS, management consultant; b. Ft. Mitchell, Ky., Nov. 25, 1956; s. James Augustine and Mary Elizabeth (McQueen) S.; m. Susan Louise Stevie, Aug. 1, 1981; children: Heather, Erin. BSEE, U. Ky., 1978; MS, U. Cin., 1980; MBA with distinction, U. Pa., 1983. Design engr. Mostek Corp., Dallas, 1980-81; mktg. specialist Gen. Electric Plastics Europe, The Netherlands, 1982; sr. engagement mgr. McKinsey & Co. Inc., Atlanta and Hong Kong, 1983—. Contbr. articles to profl. jours. Mem. Atlanta Jaycees, 1983-85; dir. Boy Scouts Am. Explorers Council, Atlanta, 1984-86. Alex Proudfoot fellow Wharton Sch., U. Pa., 1981-83. Mem. IEEE, Eta Kappa Nu. Roman Catholic. Home: 1137 Morningside Pl Atlanta GA 30306 Office: 133 Peachtree St #2300 Atlanta GA 30303

SUMMERLIN, GLENN WOOD, advertising executive; b. Dallas, Ga., Apr. 1, 1934; s. Glenn Wood and Flora (Barrett) S.; student Ga. Inst. Tech., 1951-52; BBA, Ga. State U., 1956, MBA, 1967; m. Anne Valley, Oct. 16, 1971; 1 son, Wade Hampton; children by previous marriage: Glenn Wood III, Edward Lee. Prodn. mgr. Fred Worrill Advt., Atlanta, 1956-65; v.p. sales Grizzard Advt., Atlanta, 1965-74, pres., 1974—. Vice chmn. Polaris dist. Boy Scouts Am., 1967. Vice chmn. Ga. State U. Found., 1974; chmn. distributive edn. adv. com. DeKalb Coll., 1974-76; bd. founders Geo. M. Sparks Scholarship Fund; bd. dirs. Atlanta Humane Soc., 1971—, treas., 1973, 81-82, 84-86; mem. steering com. Com. to Honor Hank Aaron, 1982; lay rep. animal care com. Emory U., 1984-85; mem. adv. bd. Families in Action, 1985-86, Soc. Nonprofit Orgns. Recipient C.S. Bolen award So. Council Indsl. Editors, 1967; named Outstanding Young Man in DeKalb County, DeKalb Jaycees, 1967, Alumnus of Year, Ga. State U., 1973; recipient Direct Mail Spokesman award Direct Mktg. Assn., 1973. Mem. Mail Advt. Service Assn. (pres. N.Ga. chpt. 1959-60), Ga. Assn. Bus. Communicators (pres. 1966-67), Am. Mktg. Assn. (pres. Atlanta chpt. 1973-74), Ga. State U. Alumni Assn. (pres. 1971-72, dir. 1966-78), Sales and Mktg. Execs. Atlanta (dir. 1969-71), Ga. Bus. and Industry Assn. (bd. govs. 1974-76), Assn. Mail Advt. Agys. (pres. 1975-77), Nat. Soc. Fund Raising Execs. (bd. dirs. Ga. chpt. 1984), Southeastern Arms Collectors Assn., Ga. Arms Collectors Assn. (dir. 1974-76, Pres.'s award 1973), Tenn. Gun Collectors Assn., Tex. Gun Collectors Assn., Assn. Am. Sword Collectors (charter), Mid-Am. Antique Arms Soc. (charter), Mensa, Co. of Mil. Historians, Confederate Hist. Assn. Belgium, Nat. Assn. Advancement Humane Edn., Soc. Animal Welfare Adminstrs., World Soc. Protection Animals, Am. Humane Assn., Omicron Delta Kappa. Home: 1133 Ragley Hall Rd NE Atlanta GA 30319 Office: 1144 Mailing Ave SE Atlanta GA 30315

SUMMERS, BRIAN JOHN, economist; b. Rockville Centre, N.Y., May 1, 1945; s. Alexander John and Molly (Wiseman) S.; B.S., Rensselaer Poly. Inst., 1967; M.A. (NASA fellow), SUNY at Stony Brook, 1972. With Found. for Econ. Edn., Irvington, N.Y., 1973—, sr. staff, 1977—. Recipient George Washington Honor medal Freedoms Found., 1981. Contbr. articles to profl. jours., periodicals, chpts. to books; sr. editor The Freeman. Home: 30 S Broadway Irvington NY 10533 Office: 30 S Broadway Irvington NY 10533

SUMMERS, GENE, singer, music publishing company executive; b. Dallas, Jan. 3, 1939; s. David Hugh and Lena Pearl (Moore) S.; m. Deanna Lane Trentham, July 22, 1961; children: David Wayne, Steven Len, Gregory Shawn. Student, Howard Payne U., 1957, Arlington State U., 1957-58, So. Meth. U., 1969-70. Singer Sta. WFAA, Dallas, 1956-57; founder nat. touring band Rebels, 1957-59; singer CBS-TV, 1957-58; performer U.S. tours 1958-64; co-owner, exec. pres. Silicon Music Pub. Corp., 1965—; founder, pres. Domino Records, Dallas, 1968—; performer internat. tours 1975—; jouined Lake County Records, Switzerland, 1975, Big Beat Records, Europe, 1980; performer 1st Scandinavian Rock and Roll Meeting, 1981, 1st Festival Internat and Internat. Rockabilly tour, 1981; joined French TV, 1981; performer Sweden Tour, 1983; joined BBR/RCA Records Europe Sunrock Music, Vargarda, Sweden, 1983. Performer numerous TV appearances including: Milt Grant, Bill Bennett, Larry Kane, LeGrande Echiquire, Warner-Amex, 1983; performer numerous records: (singles) Straight Skirts, 1958, School of Rock 'n' Roll, 1958, Nervous, 1958, Twixteen, 1959, Almost 12:00 O'Clock, 1962, Dance Dance Dance, 1962, Big Blue Diamonds, 1963, Alabama Shake, 1964, The Clown, 1966, Who Stole the Marker from the Grave of Bonnie Parker, 1968, Hot Pants, 1971, Goodbye Priscilla, 1977, (albums) Rock 'n' Roll, Vol. 2, 1973, The Southern Cat Rocks On, 1975, Ballad of Moon Dog Mayne, 1976, Mister Rock and Roll, 1977, Texas Rocka and Roll, 1980, Gene Summer in Nashville, 1981, Early Rocking Recordings, 1981, Rocka-AúBoogie Shake, 1981, Dance Dance Dance, 1982, The Big Beat Show, 1982, Gene Summers Live in Scandanivia; performer movies, Backlot, 1984, No Safe Haven, 1986. Recipient Pittman award, 1970, Ritz Performance award, 1971. Mem. Broadcast Music Inc., Am. Guild Variety Artists, Nat. Fedn. Musicians, West Tex. Music Assn., Am. Film. Inst. Lodge: Moose (hon.). Home: 222 Tulane St Garland TX 75043 Office: Sunrock Music, Box 139, 44700 Vargarda Sweden

SUMMERS, HUGH BLOOMER, JR., chemical engineer; b. Lake City, Fla., Aug. 5, 1921; s. Hugh Bloomer and Hazel A. (Flory) S.; B.Chem. Engring., U. Fla., 1943; m. Betty Jane Karstedt, Aug. 17, 1946; children—Hugh Bloomer, III, Carole Anne. Research chem. engr. Dept. Agr., Olustee, Fla., 1947-65; chem. engr. Union Camp Corp., Savannah, Ga., 1965-86. Served with USNR, 1943-46. Registered profl. engr., Ga. Am. Inst. Chem. Engrs., Am. Chem. Soc. Democrat. Methodist. Author reports; patentee in field. Home: 17 Biscayne Blvd Lake City FL 32055-6501

SUMMERS, JOSEPH FRANK, author, publisher; b. Newnan, Ga., June 26, 1914; s. John Dawson and Anne (Blalock) S.; B.A. in Math., U. Houston, 1942; profl. certificate meteorology, U. Calif. at Los Angeles, 1943, U. Chgo., 1943; postgrad., U. P.R., 1943-44; M.A. in Math., U. Tex. at Austin, 1947; postgrad. (fellow math.) Rice U., 1947-49; m. Evie Margaret Mott, July 8, 1939; children—John Randolph, Thomas Franklin, James Mott. With Texaco Inc., Houston, 1933-42, 49-79, mgr. data processing, 1957-67, asst. gen. mgr. computer services dept., 1967-79, automation cons., 1979-83; pres. Word Lab Inc., Houston, 1983—; instr. math. AAC, Ellington Field, Tex., 1941-42, U. Tex. at Austin, 1946-47. Pres. Houston Esperanto Assn., 1934-39. Served to capt. AAC, 1942-46. Mem. Assn. Computing Machinery (pres. 1956-58), Nat. Assn. Accountants (past dir.), Am. Petroleum Inst. (mem. data processing and computing com. 1955-59). Author: Mathematics for Bombadiers and Navigators, 1942; Wholly Holey Holy, An Adult American Spelling Book, 1984. Contbg. author: American Petroleum Institute Drilling and Production Practices. Home: 5517 Tilbury Dr Houston TX 77056 Office: PO Box 732 Bellaire TX 77401

SUMMERSELL, FRANCES SHARPLEY, club woman; b. Birmingham, Ala.; d. Arthur Croft and Thomas O. (Stone) Sharpley; student U. Montevallo, Peabody Coll., Nashville; m. Charles Grayson Summersell, Nov. 10, 1934. Partner, artist, writer Asso. Educators, 1959—. Mem. D.A.R., Magna Charta Dames, U. Women's Club (pres. 1957-58), U.D.C. (state historian 1956-58, pres. Robert Emmet Rodes chpt. Tuscaloosa 1953-55), Daus. Am. Colonists (organizing regent Tuscaloosa 1956-63), English Speaking Union, Marquis Biog. Library Soc. (adv. mem.). Vice-chmn. Ft. Morgan Hist. Commn., 1959-63. Mem. Tuscaloosa County Preservation Soc. (trustee 1965-78, service award 1975), W. Ala. Art Assn., Nat. Trust Historic Preservation, Birmingham-Jefferson Hist. Soc. Clubs: Country, University (Tuscaloosa). Co-author: Alabama History Filmstrips, 1961; Viewing Alabama History Filmstrips, 1961; Florida History Filmstrips, 1963; Texas History Filmstrips, 1965-66; Ohio History Filmstrips, 1967 (Merit award Am. Assn. State and Local History 1968); California History Filmstrips, 1968; Illinois History Filmstrips, 1970. Home: 1411 Caplewood Tuscaloosa AL 35401

SUMMERSON, JOHN NEWENHAM, architectural historian; b. Darlington, Eng., Nov. 25, 1904; s. Samuel and Dorothea (Newenham) S.; ed. Univ. Coll., London; D.Litt. (hon.), univs. Leicester, Hull, Oxford and Newcastle; D.Sc. (hon.), U. Edinburgh; m. Elizabeth Hepworth, 1938; 3 children. Served in architects' offices and tchr. Edinburgh Coll. Art, 1929-30; on staff Architect and Bldg. News, 1934-40; dep. dir. Nat. Bldgs. Record, 1940-45; curator Sir John Soane's Mus., 1945-84; mem. Royal Commn. Hist. Monuments, Hist. Bldgs. Council; chmn. Nat. Council Diplomas in Arts and Design, 1960-69; lectr. history of architecture Birkbeck Coll., 1961-70; Slade prof. fine art Oxford U., 1958-59; Ferens prof. fine art U. Hull, 1960-61, 70-71; Slade prof. fine art Cambridge U., 1966-67; Bampton lectr. Columbia U., 1967-68. Trustee, Nat. Portrait Gallery, 1966-73. Decorated Royal Gold medal for Architecture, 1976; comdr. Order Brit. Empire, Companion of Honour, 1987. Fellow Brit. Acad., Soc. Arts; mem. Am. Acad. Arts and Scis. (hon.). Author: John Nash, 1934, Georgian London, 1945, 6th rev. edit., 1988, Heavenly Mansions, 1949, Sir John Soane, 1952, Sir Christopher Wren, 1953, Architecture in Britain, 1530-1830, 1953, 7th rev. edit., 1983, The Classical Language of Architecture, 1964, Book of John Thorpe, 1966, Inigo Jones, 1966, Victorian Architecture, 1970, The Life and Work of John Nash, 1980, The Architecture of the 18th Century, 1986. Address: 1 Eton Villas, London NW3 England Office: British Acad, 20-21 Cornwall Terrace, London NW1 4QP, England

SUMNER, GEORGE WILSON, JR., investment banker; b. Honolulu, May 7, 1927; s. George Wilson and Eva (Focke) S.; B.S., U.S. Naval Acad., 1949; m. Bebe Moody, Aug. 29, 1952; children—Elizabeth Hyde, George Wilson, III. Dir. personnel AMFAC, Honolulu, 1962; account exec. Dean Witter, Honolulu, 1962-67; v.p. Blyth & Co., Honolulu, 1967-71; v.p. E. F. Hutton & Co., now Shearson Lehman Hutton, Honolulu, 1972—. Bd. dirs. Hawaii Visitors Bur., 1960-62; pres. Bishop Mus. Assn., Honolulu, 1969-70, Kaui Keolani Children's Hosp., Honolulu, 1973-76; trustee St. Andrews Priory Sch.; dir. at large, exec. com. Am. Cancer Soc., N.Y.C., 1977-82. Served with USN, 1945-52. Recipient Disting. Service award Am. Cancer Soc., 1974. Mem. Investment Soc. Hawaii (pres. 1971-72). Episcopalian. Clubs: Oahu Country, Waialae Country, Plaza, Honolulu. Home: 3805 Old Pali Rd Honolulu HI 96817 Office: Shearson Lehman Hutton 1001 Bishop St Suite #2500 Pauahi Tower Honolulu HI 96813

SUMNER, RAYMOND, educator; b. Manchester, Eng., Feb. 28, 1929; s. Frank and Alice Anne (Lomas) S.; m. Kathleen Wilson, Feb. 19, 1955; children: Margaret Louise, Christine Helen, Timothy Michael. MEd, U. Manchester, 1965, PhD, 1972. Tchr. Egerton Park Sch., Lancashire, Eng., 1950-53, Cen. Grammar Sch., Manchester, Eng., 1953-56; tech. instr. Tech. Inst., Sierra Leone, 1956-60; head dept. St. Gregory's Tech. High Sch., Manchester, 1960-66; sr. research assoc., dept. edn. U. Manchester, 1966-70; asst. regional dir. Open U. Northwest Eng., 1970-72; head external relations dept. Nat. Found. for Ednl. Research, Slough, Eng., 1972—; cons. NFER-Nelson Pub. Co., Windsor, Eng., 1981—, UNESCO, Swaziland, 1979; vis. lectr. Brit. Council, Bangladesh, 1976. Author: The Role of Testing in Schools, 1987; co-author: Assessment Procedures in Schools, 1985, Achievement in Secondary School, 1974; contbr. articles to profl. jours. Gov. Frimley Ch. of Eng. Sch., Surrey, 1985. Recipient Platt prize U. Manchester, 1963. Mem. Brit. Psychol Soc. (sec. to com. 1983-87), Brit. Ednl. Research Assn. Club: Frensham Pond Sailing. Office: Nat Found Ednl Research, The Mere, Upton Park, Slough SL1 2DQ, England

SUMNERS, WILLIAM GLENN, JR., lawyer; b. Pueblo, Colo., Feb. 23, 1928; s. William Glen Sr. and Ruth Priscilla (Carmody) S.; 1 child from previous marriage, William Glenn III; m. Virginia Christine Thomson, June 16, 1985. BA, MA, U. Colo., 1951; postgrad., Colo. Sch. of Mines, 1954; LLB, U. Denver, 1954. Bar: Colo. 1954, U.S. Dist. Ct. Colo. 1954, U.S. Supreme Ct. 1962, U.S. Ct. Appeals (10th cir.) 1963, U.S. Ct. Claims 1982. Sole practice Denver, 1954-75; ptnr. Sumners & Fowler, Denver, 1975-80, Sumners & Miller, Denver, 1980-85, Sumners & Epprich, Denver, 1985—. Contbr. articles to profl. jours. Judge Denver Mcpl. Ct., 1962. Served with U.S. Army, 1945-47, PTO. Mem. ABA (chmn. internat. ins. law com. 1980-81, ins., negligence and compensation sect., internat. energy law sect.), Rocky Mountain Mineral Law Found. (trustee 1960-63, 80-85), Mountain States Legal Found. (bd. of litigation 1977—), Colo. Mining Assn. (bd. dirs. 1962—, pres. 1977), Internat. Bar Assn., Internat. Assn. Ins. Counsel, Ind. Petroleum Assn. Mountain States (bd. dirs. 1975). Office: 600-17th St #2600 S Denver CO 80202

SUMPTER, JERRY LEE, lawyer; b. Detroit, Aug. 13, 1942; s. Joseph Edward Sumpter and Telcie (Crager) Church; m. Santina Marie Cervi, Feb. 14, 1970; children—J.L., Shaundra. B.S. in Edn., Ball State U., 1966; J.D., Detroit Coll. Law, 1970. Bar: Mich. 1970. Cert. Nat. Bd. Trial Advocacy. Sole practice, Cheboygan, Mich., 1970—; prosecuting atty. County of Cheboygan, 1972-74; instr. criminal justice Alpena Community Coll., Mich., 1970—; speaker in field. Author: Civil Trial Strategy and Technique Notebook (2 vols.), 1983, Personal Injury: Discovery and Trial, 1986. Contbr. articles to profl. jours. Mem. Assn. Trial Lawyers Am., Mich. Bar Assn., Mich. Trial Lawyers Assn., Belli Soc., Delta Theta Phi. Home: 10805 Moonlight Bay Rd Cheboygan MI 49721 Office: PO Box 286 Cheboygan MI 49721

SUMRANPUTI, PAIBOON, real estate developer; b. Samut Sakorn, Thailand, Jan. 2, 1942; s. Hong and Kimkui Sumranputi; m. Somchai Rakkaew, Apr. 6, 1967; children: Pracha-prin, Bordin-torn, Amornrit. BEd, Sri-Nakrin U., Bangkok, 1963; M in Pub. Adminstrn., Nat. Inst. Devel. Adminstrn., Bangkok, 1969; postgrad., Columbia U., 1981, Thammasat U., Bangkok, 1987. Mgr. service sta. Esso Standard, Bangkok, 1969-72; sales mgr. Sakol Real Estate, Bangkok, 1972-75, Siam Realty, Bangkok, 1975-78; mktg. exec. Nava Nakorn, Bangkok, 1978-80; mktg. mgr., mng. dir. Inter-Life, Bangkok, 1980-83; gen. mgr. Thailand Indsl. Real Estate Devel. Co., Bangkok, 1983—. Lodge: Rotary. Home: 106/69 Sukhapibal 1 Rd, Klongkoom, Bangkapi 10230, Thailand

SUMRELL, GENE, research chemist; b. Apache, Ariz., Oct. 7, 1919; s. Joe B. and Dixie (Hughes) S.; B.A., Eastern N.Mex. U., 1942; B.S., U. N.Mex., 1947, M.S., 1948; Ph.D., U. Calif. at Berkeley, 1951. Asst. prof. chemistry Eastern N.Mex. U., 1951-53; sr. research chemist J. T. Baker Chem. Co., Phillipsburg, N.J., 1953-58; sr. organic chemist Southwest Research Inst., San Antonio, 1958-59; project leader Food Machinery & Chem. Corp., Balt., 1959-61; research sect. leader El Paso Natural Gas Products Co. (Tex.), 1961-64; project leader So. utilization research and devel. div. U.S. Dept. Agr., New Orleans, 1964-67, investigations head, 1967-73, research leader Oil Seed and Food Lab., So. Regional Research Center, 1973-84, collaborator, 1984— . Served from pvt. to staff sgt. AUS, 1942-46. Mem. Am. Chem. Soc., A.A.A.S., N.Y. Acad. Scis., Am. Inst. Chemists, Am. Oil Chemists Soc., Am. Assn. Textile Chemists and Colorists, Research Soc. Am., Phi Kappa Phi, Sigma Xi. Home: PO Box 24037 New Orleans LA 70184 Office: 1100 Robert E Lee Blvd New Orleans LA 70179

SUMTER, THOMAS LEE, consultant, educator; b. Topeka, Kans., Sept. 1, 1942; s. Thomas Harden and Viola Mae (Harding) S.; children—Thomas Allen, Michael Patrick; m. Beth Anne Balder, Feb. 14, 1981; 1 stepchild, Keri Lynn Anilionis. Student, Olympic Coll., 1963-64, U. Wash., 1964-66. Supr. Tally Corp., Seattle, 1964-68; project engr. Honeywell, Seattle, 1968-72; mfg. mgr. Contact Telecomm, Seattle, 1972-74; cons. Olympic Assocs., Seattle, 1974-80; prin. T.L. Sumter & Assocs., Kingston, Wash., 1980—; instr. project mgmt. Edmonds Community Coll., Wash., 1979-80. Adv. council on State Govt. Quality Assurance & Productivity, 1975; mem. Consumer Product Safety Commn., Sea Systems Quality Control, 1976. Recipient Letter of Commendation, USS Conquest, 1984. Mem. Am. Soc. Quality Control (sect. chmn. 1974—), Soc. Am. Mil. Engrs., Project Mgmt. Inst. Democrat. Congregationalist. Club: Kingston Yacht. Lodge: Kiwanis. Home: 12101 NE Olive Dr Kingston WA 98346 Office: T L Sumter & Assocs PO Box 7302 Kingston WA 98346

SUN, ALBERT YUNG-KWANG, biochemistry and neurochemistry educator; b. Amoy, Fukien, Peoples Republic of China, Oct. 13, 1932; came to U.S., 1959, naturalized, 1972; s. Pehcheng and SuiHo Kuo Wu; m. Grace Yen-Chi Cheung Sun, May 9, 1964; 1 child, Aggie Yee-Chun. B.S. in Agrl. Chemistry, Nat. Taiwan U., Taipei, 1957; Ph.D. in Biochemistry, Oreg. State U., 1967. Postdoctoral research assoc. Case-Western Res. U., Cleve., 1967-68; sr. research scientist Cleve. Psychiat. Inst., 1968-74; project dir. Ohio Mental Health Research Ctr., Cleve., 1972-74, research prof. neurochemistry, assoc. prof. biochemistry U. Mo., Columbia, 1974—; mem. adv. panel NSF, Washington, 1984-85. Editor: Neural Membranes, 1983. Advisor, Chinese Christian Fellowship Group, Columbia, 1974—. Grantee Nat. Inst. Alcohol Abuse and Alcoholism, 1974-78, 82—, Nat. Inst. Neurol. Com. Disease and Stroke, 1975-79, Nat. Cancer Inst., 1979-83. Mem. Research Soc. Alcoholism, Am. Soc. Neurochemistry, Internat. Soc. Neurochemistry, Am. Soc. Neurosci., Am. Soc. Biol. Chemists, Am. Chem. Soc. Current work: Structure-functional relationship of neural membranes using biochemical and biophysical approaches, study on the effect of aging and alcohol on membrane systems in the brain. Subspecialties: Biochemistry (medicine); Neurochemistry. Home: 2908 Shoreside Dr Columbia MO 65203

SUN, ROBERT ZU JEI, inventor, manufacturing company executive; b. Shanghai, July 5, 1948; s. David C.H. and Evelyn (Lee) S.; m. Nan Jennifer Ronis, Sept. 20, 1986; 1 child, Matthew Nyland. B.S. in Elec. Engring., U. Pa., 1970. Sr. project engr. Drexelbrook Engring. Co., Horsham, Pa., 1970-78; pres., chmn. bd. Suntex Internat., Inc., Easton, 1981—. Pres. Greater Easton Tech. Enterprise Ctr., Inc., 1986-87, Coalition of Religious and Civic Orgs., Easton, 1979-81. Inventor Mhing card game; patentee (4), the Twenty Four Game. Recipient 2 Excellence awards for Mhing pkg. Nat. Paperbox and Pkg. Assn., 1984-85. Office: 118 N 3d St Easton PA 18042

SUN, SHUNHUA, mathematics educator; b. Hangzhou, Zhejiang, China, Aug. 14, 1937; m. Shaolin Sun, Nov. 28, 1968; 1 child, Linyen. Student, Jiaotong U., Xian, China, 1962; MA, Sichuan U., China, 1965. Asst. Sichuan U., Chengdu, China, 1966-79; assoc. prof. Sichuan U., Chengdu, 1980-85, prof. dept. math., 1985—; vis. prof. Purdue U.,West Lafayette, Ind., 1981-82. Editor Northeastern Math. Jour., 1985—, Jour. Math. Research and Exposition, 1987—, Applied Math.: A Jour. Chinese Univs., 1985—, Jour. Engring. Math., 1985. Recipient awards Govt. Sichuan Province, China, 1983-85. Mem. Math. Soc. China, Am. Math. Soc. Office: Sichuan U Dept Math, Chengdu, Sichuan Peoples Republic of China

SUNAMURA, TSUGUO, coastal geomorphologist, coastal engineer; b. Tokyo, Apr. 1, 1941; s. Teiji and Jun (Hidaka) S.; B.Sc. in Phys. Geology, Tokyo Kyoiku U., 1964; M.Sc. in Civil Engring., U. Tokyo, 1969, Ph.D. in Coastal Engring, 1972; m. Reiko Ogiwara, Jan. 17, 1971. Coastal engr. research sect. Nippon Tetrapod Co., Ltd., 1964-67; research engr., then research assoc. Coast Engring. Lab., U. Tokyo, 1969-78; assoc. prof. Inst. Geosci., U. Tsukuba, 1978-87; prof., 1987—; vis. prof. civil engring. U. Del., 1978-79; instr. Chuo U., 1970-78, Chiba U., 1975-76. Mem. Geol. Soc. Am., Japanese Geomorphological Union, Japanese Soc. Civil Engrs., Assn. Japanese Geographers. mem. editorial bds. profl. publns.; contbr. articles to profl. jours. Home: 2-137-101 Namiki, Tsukuba, Ibaraki 305, Japan Office: U Tsukaba Inst Geosci, Ibaraki 305, Japan

SUNATRIO, SUN, surgeon, educator; b. Semarang, Indonesia, Jan. 18, 1945; parents: Soedarmo and Ning (Harijati) Sosrohardjono; m. Ratu Anfusiah, Sept. 28, 1970; children: Triany, Yuanita, Yan Adrian. MD, U. Indonesia, Jakarta, 1970. Head thoracic cardivascular dept., head subdept. thoracic cardiovascular anaesthesia U. Indonesia sch. of medicine, Jakarta, 1974—; head anaesthesiology dept., coordinator research and devel. U. Indonesia Sch. of Medicine, Jakarta, 1982—; head anaesthesiology and ICU Sumber Waras Hosp., Jakarta, 1978—; head anaesthesiology dept. Med. Faculty U. Tarumanegara, Jakarta, 1987; head anaesthesiology dept.met. med. ctr. Tarumanegara U., Jakarta, 1982—; mem. Presdl. Med. Team, Jakarta, 1975-76, Vice Presdl. Med. Team, 1976, med. equipment dept. Health Republic of Indonesia, 1978—; mem. med. operational team for separating Siamese twins, 1980, 87, 88; lectr. in field. Author: The Society for Indonesian Voluntary Sterilization, 1968, The Indonesian Society for Critical Care Medicine, 1980, Gynecology Yayasan Bina Pustaka-Jakarta, 1981, Lecture in Anaesthesiology, 1985; pub. Blackwell Sci. Pubs. Mem. Indonesian Assn. of Med. Drs., Indonesian Soc. of Anaesthesiologist (treas.), Indonesian Soc. for Critical Care Medicine (scientific com.), Indonesian Soc. Surgeons, Western Pacific Assn. of Critical Care Medicine. Home: Jl Pekayon 32, Pejaten Barat, Jakarta 12550, Indonesia Office: Cipto Mangunkusumo Hosp, Jalan Diponegoro 71, Jakarta 10002, Indonesia

SUNDARAM, MANJERI ANANTARAMAN, chemical executive; b. Calicut, Kerala, India, Mar. 7, 1933; s. Anantaraman M. S. and Lakshmi; m. Shantha , May 27, 1960; children: Geeta, Bhavani. MA in Eng. Lit., Madras U., Tamilnadu, 1956. Accounts service Indian Railways, Madras, Tamilnadu, Calcutta and Guwahati, 1956-74; joint fin. dir. Govt. India Railway Bd., New Delhi, 1974-77; fin. dir. Bongaigaon Refineries and Petro-Chems. Ltd., New Delhi, 1977-81; v.p. fin. Zuari Agro Chems. Ltd., Zuarinagar, Goa, 1981—. Contbr. articles to profl. jours. Mem. Pandu

Coll. Governing Council, Guwahati, 1965-73, Bd. Mgmt. Studies Goa U., 1987. Fellow UN-Under UN Devel. Programme For Study in U.S. and Can., Indian Inst. Rail Transport. Lodge: Rotary (Vasco-Da-Gama, Goa) (pres. 1986). Home: B-2, Zuarinagar, Goa 403 726, India Office: Zuari Agro Chems Ltd, Zuarinagar, Goa 403 726, India

SUNDBACK, SUSAN ELISABET, sociologist; b. Vasa, Ostrobothnia, Finland, Sept. 6, 1948; d. Holger Rafael and Isabel Elsa Amanda (Rosenholm) S.; m. Lauri Antero Karvonen, Aug. 26, 1977; children: Malin, Sven. BA, Abo Acad., 1972, MA in Social Sci., 1974, Licentiate in Philosophy, 1978. Lectr. in Sociology and Comparative Religion Abo Acad., Finland, 1975—; asst. The Donner Inst. Research in Religious and Cultural History in Abo/Turku, Abo, 1975-80; researcher Abo Acad., 1981-84, asst. in Sociology dept., 1985—. Contbr. articles to profl. jours. Lutheran. Office: Abo Acad Dept Sociology, Gezeliusgatan 2A, 20500 Abo Finland

SUNDERLAND, BARBARA ANNE, international marketing company executive, fund raising executive; b. Providence, R.I., Mar. 7, 1948; d. Everett Swan and Marica Anne (Galgas) S. BA, Brown U., 1977; MPH, U. Tex., 1988; MPH, U. Tex. Sch. Pub. Health, 1987. Cert. fund raising exec. Owner, Barbara Enterprises, Inc., Providence, 1962-78; exec. dir. Houston Area Parkinsonism Soc., 1979-82; pres. Sunderland Assocs., Internat. Mktg., Houston, 1982—; v.p. Van Dyke Travel Agy., Houston, 1983-85; cons. dept. neurology U. Tex. Med. Sch., 1982. Bd. dirs. R.I. Better Bus. Bur., 1975-78. bd. dirs. Am. Epilepsy Found., Houston chpt., 1983—; mem. edn. com. Houston Area Health Care Coalition, 1983; mem. Patient Edn. and Exchange Group, Health Meeting Planners; coordinator Houston Citywide Ways to Really Stop Smoking sponsored by NBC-TV, 1985-86; mem. mayor's Task Force Against Smoking in Pub. Places, City of Houston, 1985-86; bd. dirs. Parkinsonism Support Groups Am., Washington, 1981—; founder, pres. Stroke Found. of Tex., 1984; coordinator Feminist Majority of Houston, 1987. Recipient Jewish Vets. Brotherhood award, 1965, John Philip Sousa Music award, 1966, award J. Arthur Trudeau Ctr. for Retarded, 1975, Cert. of Appreciation City of Houston, 1985, 86, Cert. Appreciation Mayor of Houston and Dir. Health and Human Resources, 1986; recognized as Outstanding Female Bus. Owner, Dept. Labor, 1976. Mem. Nat. Soc. Fund Raising Execs. (spl. event award Houston chpt. 1982, bd. dirs. S.W. chpt., 1980-83, sec. 1982), Internat. Assn. Bus. Communicators, Nat. Assn. Female Execs., Women's Profl. Assn. (bd. dirs. 1980—) Clubs: Brown U. (pres., newsletter editor) (Houston); Forum; Combined Sch. Alumni (bd. dirs. 1978—). Author: The Stillborn and Neo-Natal Death Handbook for Grieving Parents, Professional Medical Support, Family, and Friends, 1987. Home and Office: PO Box 56754 Houston TX 77256 Office: 4950 Woodway Suite 606 Houston TX 77056

SUNDERLAND, DAVID KENDALL, real estate developer; b. Detroit, Mar. 25, 1930; s. Maurice Briggs and Helen (Bell) S.; B.A., Dartmouth Coll., 1952; postgrad. U. Mich. Sch. Bus. Adminstrn., 1956-58, Gen. Motors Inst., 1955-56; m. Brooke Williams, Sept. 13, 1975; children—Mark, Caryn, Matthew, Tracy. Fin. analyst Chevrolet div. Gen. Motors Corp., Detroit, 1955-58; budget mgr. Raytheon Co., Andover/Bedford, Mass., 1958-61, div. controller, Oxnard, Calif., 1961-64; v.p. Janss Corp., Los Angeles, 1964-68; pres. Gates Land Co., Colorado Springs, Colo., 1968—. Bd. regents U. Colo., 1978-86, chmn., 1984-85; bd. dirs. St. Francis Hosp., Colorado Springs, 1973-78; pres. Colorado Springs World Affairs Council, 1984-86. Served in USN, 1952-55. Named Colorado Springs Builder of Yr., 1975, Colo. Housing Industry Man of Yr., 1986; recipient Colo. Builders Disting. Service award, 1977; bronze leadership award Nat. Jr. Achievement, 1986. Mem. Colorado Springs C. of C. (bd. dirs. 1974-77, 84-87, chmn. 1988), Nat. Assn. Home Builders, Colo. Homebuilders Assn. (pres. 1979), Urban Land Inst. Republican. Club: Country of Colo. Office: 155 W Lake Ave Colorado Springs CO 80906

SUNDERMAN, FREDERICK WILLIAM, physician, educator, author, musician; b. Altoona, Pa., Oct. 23, 1898; s. William August and Elizabeth Catherine (Lehr) S.; m. Clara Louise Baily, June 2, 1925 (dec. 1972); children—Louise (dec.), F. William, Joel B. (dec.); m. Martha-Lee Taggart, May 3, 1980. B.S., Gettysburg Coll., 1919, Sc.D. (hon.), 1952; M.D., U. Pa., 1923, M.S., 1927, Ph.D., 1929. Diplomate Am. Bd. Internal Medicine, Am. Bd. Pathology (v.p. 1944-50 life trustee 1950—), Nat. Bd. Med. Examiners. Intern, then resident Pa. Hosp., 1924-26, assoc. charge chemistry div., physician, then chief metabolic clinic A and physician, 1935-47; mem. faculty U. Pa. Sch. Medicine, Phila., 1925-47; assoc. prof. research medicine, also lectr. U. Pa. Sch. Medicine; acting head med. dept. Brookhaven Nat. Lab., Upton, N.Y., 1947-48; chief chem. div. William Pepper Lab. Clin. Medicine, U. Pa. Med. Sch., 1933-47; prof. clin. pathology, dir. Temple U. Lab. Clin. Medicine, 1947-48; med. dir. govt. explosives lab. Carnegie Inst. Tech. and Bur. Mines, 1943-46; head dept. clin. pathology Cleve. Clinic Found., 1948-49; dir. clin. research M.D. Anderson Hosp. Cancer Research, Houston, 1949-50; dir. clin. labs. Grady Meml. Hosp., Atlanta, 1949-51; prof. clin. medicine Emory U. Sch. Medicine, 1949-51; chief clin. pathology Communicable Disease Center, USPHS, 1950-51; med. adviser Rohm & Haas Co., 1947-71; med. cons. Redstone Arsenal, U.S. Army Ordnance Dept., Huntsville, Ala., 1947-49; cons. clin. pathology St. Joseph's Hosp., Tampa, Fla., 1965-66; attending physician Jefferson Hosp., Phila., 1951—, dir. div. metabolic research, clin. prof. medicine, 1951-67, clin. prof. medicine, 1951-74, hon. clin. prof. medicine, 1975—; dir. Inst. Clin. Sci., 1965—; prof. pathology Hahnemann U. Med. Coll., 1970—, co-chmn. dept. lab. medicine, 1970-75; med. adviser and cons. bus. and industry, 1947—; dir. internat. seminars on clin. chemistry and pathology, 1947—. Author, editor 36 books on clin. chemistry and pathology; author over 295 articles.; author: Our Maderia Heritage, 1979, Musical Notes of a Physician, 1982; editor-in-chief Annals of Clin. Lab. Sci., 1970—; mem. editorial bd. Am. Jour. Clin. Pathology, 1973-77, Am. Jour. Indsl. Medicine, 1979-85; cons. editor Am. Jour. Occupational Medicine, 1979-85. Trustee Gettysburg Coll., 1967-79, chmn., 1972-74, hon. life trustee, 1979—, Bermuda Biol. Sta. for Research, 1986; bd. dirs. Musical Fund Soc., 1938—, Dwight D. Eisenhower Soc., 1984—, German Soc. Pa., 1986—; violin soloist Chautauqua Summer Series, eastern U.S., 1919-20; guest soloist Concerto Soloists of Phila., 1979, 83, 84. Recipient Naval Ordnance Devel. award, 1946; certificate appreciation War Dept., 1947; medal of honor Armed Forces Inst. Pathology, 1964; named Disting. Alumnus, Gettysburg Coll., 1963, recipient Meritorious Service award, 1979; Honor award Latin Am. Assn. Clin. Biochemistry, 1976. Fellow ACP (life); mem. Am. Assn. History Medicine, Am. Diabetes Assn., AMA, Am. Soc. Clin. Investigation, Royal Soc. Health, AAUP, Endocrine Soc., Am. Assn. Biol. Chemistry, AAAS, Am. Chem. Soc., Internat. Union Pure and Applied Chemistry (nickel subcom. Commn. on Toxicology), Inst. Occupational Health (Finland), Outokumpu Oy (Finland), Am. Assn. Clin. Chemists (award for outstanding efforts in edn. and tng. 1981), Coll. Am. Pathologists (founding gov., Pathologist of Yr. award 1962, Pres.'s Honor award 1984, disting. service award 1988), Am. Soc. Clin. Pathology (pres. 1951, archives com. 1977—, Ward Burdick award 1975, Continuing Edn. Distinguished Service award 1976), Assn. Clin. Scientists (pres. 1957-59, dir. edn. 1959—, diploma honor 1960, ann. goblet award 1964, Gold-headed cane 1974), Coll. Physicians of Phila. (sec. 1946-48, Disting. Service award 1980), Am. Indsl. Hygiene Assn., Am. Occupational Medicine Assn., Med. Soc. Pa., Nat. Soc. Med. Research, Nat. Acad. Clin. Biochemistry, Pan Am. Med. Assn., Pa. Assn. Clin. Pathology, Philadelphia County Med. Soc., Soc. Toxicology, Brit. Assn. Clin. Biochemists (hon.), Soc. Pharm. and Environ. Pathologists (hon.), Internat. Union Pure and Applied Chemistry, Inst. Occupational Health Finland (nickel subcom. commn. toxicology), Phi Beta Kappa, Sigma Xi, Alpha Omega Alpha, Phi Sigma Kappa, Alpha Kappa Kappa. Lutheran. Club: Union League (Phila.). Home and Office: 1833 Delancey Pl Philadelphia PA 19103

SUNDJAJA, RIDWAN SUHAEDI, finance educator, consultant; b. Bandun, Indonesia, Jan. 11, 1951; s. Solaeman and Hanna (Tanudjaja) S.; m. Dewi Juniarti, Apr. 11, 1979; 1 child, Dharma Putra. MBA, St. Louis U., Baguio City, Philippines, 1976; Doctorate in Econs., U. Katolik Parahyangan, 1977. Asst. dir. Bandung Inst. Accountancy, 1978-79; vice dean acad. affairs, faculty econs. UNPAR, Bandung, 1983-84, head mgmt. dept., faculty econs., 1985—; state examiner fin. and mktg. studies West Java, Bandung, 1983—; bd. dirs. Ridwan Assocs. Mgmt. Cons., Bandung, Dwisaha Pradana Corp., Bandung. Chmn. Edn. Teamwork for Neighboring Families, Bandung, 1984—, gen. elections for Pres. Neighboring Families, Bandung, 1985. Recipient Loyalty award Parahyangan Cath. U. Found., 1988. Mem. Indonesia Economist Assn. Club: Dadali Sports Ctr. (adviser 1985—). Home: Jl Lapangan Kebonwaru #8, Bandung 40271, Indonesia Office: U Katolik Parahyangan, Jl Merdeka 30, Bandung Indonesia

SUNDNES, GUNNAR, director Royal Norwegian Society of Science and Letters, educator; b. Trondheim, Norway, Feb. 21, 1926; s. Ole Sigvard and Gudrun (Folstad) S.; m. Laila Baglo, July 5, 1952; children—Gunnar, Lars Orjan, Marianne. Cand., U. Oslo, 1954; Ph.D., U. Bergen, 1971. Scientist, Inst. Marine Resarch, Bergen, 1953-56, Zoophysiol. U. Oslo, 1956-58; sr. scientist Inst. Marine Research, Bergen, 1958-72; prof. U. Trondheim, 1972-80; mem. Am. Fisheries Soc., Marine Biol. Assn. U.K., Royal Norwegian Soc. Sci. and Letters (exec. dir.). Home: Veimesterstien 21, 7000 Trondheim Norway Office: DKNVS, The Museum, E Skakkes Gt 47B, Trondheim Norway

SUNDY, GEORGE JOSEPH, JR., refractories reliability engineer; b. Nanticoke, Pa., Apr. 22, 1936; s. George Joseph Sr. and Stella Mary (Bodurka) S.; m. Stella Pauline Miechur, May 21, 1966; children: Sharon Ann, George Joseph III. BS, Pa. State U., 1958. Research engr. Bethlehem (Pa.) Steel Corp., 1959-85; reliability engr. Flo-Con Systems, Inc., Champaign, Ill., 1985—. Patentee in field. Mem. Am. Ceramics Soc., Iron and Steel Soc. AIME, Keramos, Sigma Tau. Democrat. Roman Catholic. Home: 604 E South Mahomet Rd Mahomet IL 61853 Office: Flo-Con Systems Inc 1404 Newton Dr Champaign IL 61821

SUNESSON, SUNE LARS, sociologist, educator; b. Stockholm, July 6, 1944; s. Lambert and Birgit S. (Adamsson) S.; m. Tullia Nielsen, 1965; children: Janna, Ossian, Livia. PhD, Stockholm U., 1974. Research asst. Stockholm U., 1967-68, asst. lectr., then instr., lectr., 1968-80; sr. research lectr., sr. research officer City of Stockholm, 1978-82; sr. lectr., docent Lund (Sweden) U., 1980-84, prof., head research dept. Sch. Social Work, 1984—; sci. adviser Nat. Bd. Health and Social Service, 1985—. Author: Politik Och Organisation, 1974, Byråkdati och historia, 1981, När man inte lyckas, 1981, Andra allt!, 1985, (with Kjell Nilsson) Konflikt, kontroll, expertis, 1988; also articles. Bd. dirs. Fountain House Malmo, Sweden, 1985—. Mem. Swedish Sociol. Assn. (chmn. 1984-86). Home: Regementsg 72, S-21751 Malmo Sweden Office: Lund U Sch Social Work, PO Box 23, S-22100 Lund Sweden

SUNG, C.B., multi-industry co. exec.; b. Shanghai, China, Feb. 1, 1925; came to U.S., 1947; naturalized, 1954; s. Tsing-Ching and Hsu-Ying (Ma) S.; BS, Chiao-Tung U., China, 1945; MS, M.I.T., 1948; MBA, Harvard U., 1950; m. Beulah C.H. Kwok, June 4, 1953; children—Dean, Wingate. From engr. to dept. chief Nanking-Shanghai Ry. Systems Adminstrn., China, 1945-47; devel. engr. instrumentation Ruge-de Forest, Inc., 1950-52; engr. research labs. Bendix Corp., 1952-62, asst. gen. mgr., 1962-64, gen. mgr., dir., 1964-67, corporate v.p. engring. and research, Detroit, 1967-69, v.p., group exec. advanced tech. group, Southfield, Mich., 1969-72, v.p., group exec. advanced concepts group, 1972-74; pres., chief exec. officer CMA Inc., Cleve., 1974-78; chmn. bd. Airborne Mfg. Co., Elyria, Ohio, 1975-79; chief exec. officer Etec Corp., Hayward, Calif., 1977-79; pres., chief exec. officer Unison Pacific Corp., San Bruno, Calif.; chmn. bd. Cleve. Controls, Inc., 1978—, Unison Internat., 1982—, Optimum Control Corp., 1984—, Buckett Corp., 1987—; dir. Varo, Inc., Capital Investment of Hawaii, Communication Intelligence Corp.; cons. in field. Mem. vis. com. Engring. Coll. U. Mich., Carnegie-Mellon U., Oakland U., Am. Found. Traditional Chinese Medicine. Fellow Cleve. Mus. Art, Pacific Forum (bd. dirs.); mem. Soc. Automotive Engrs., Sigma Xi. Patentee in field. Office: 1200 Bayhill Dr Suite 300 San Bruno CA 94066

SUNUNU, JOHN H., governor of New Hampshire; b. Havana, Cuba, July 2, 1939; m. Nancy Hayes, 1958; children—Catherine, Elizabeth, Christina, John, Michael, James, Christopher, Peter. B.S., MIT, 1961, M.S., 1962, Ph.D., 1966. Founder, chief engr. Astro Dynamics, 1960-65; pres. J. H. S. Engring. Co. and Thermal Research Inc., Salem, N.H., 1965-82; assoc. prof. mech. engring. Tufts U., 1966-82; assoc. dean Coll. Engring., Tufts U., 1968-73; mem. N.H. Ho. of Reps., 1973-74, Gov.'s Energy Council, 1973-78; chmn. Gov.'s Com. on N.H. Future, 1977-78; mem. Gov.'s Adv. Com. on Sci. and Tech., 1977-78; gov. State of N.H., Concord, 1983—. Chmn. Coalition of Northeastern Govs., 1985-86; vice chmn. Alliance for Acid Rain Control. Mem. Nat. Govs.' Assn. (vice chmn. 1986-87, chmn. task force on tech., task force on acid rain, chmn. 1987-88), Rep. Govs.' Assn. (chmn. 1985-86), New England Gov.s' Assn. (chmn. 1984-85, vice chmn. adv. commn. on intergovtl. relations). Republican. Roman Catholic. Office: Office of Gov State House Concord NH 03301 *

SUOJANEN, WAYNE WILLIAM, lawyer; b. Salem, Oreg., July 5, 1950; s. Waino Wiljam and Doris Grace (Stinson) S.; m. Deborah Kindler, Mar. 22, 1970; children: Rachel, Noah, Sarah. BA, Northwestern U., Evanston, Ill., 1972; SM, MIT, 1974, PhD, 1977; JD, U. Pa., 1980. Bar: Pa. 1980, U.S. Dist. Ct. (ea. dist.) Pa. 1981, U.S. Ct. Appeals (3d cir.) 1981. Assoc. Pepper, Hamilton & Scheetz, Phila., 1980-84, Hoyle, Morris & Kerr, Phila., 1985—. Joseph Scanlon fellow, MIT, 1974-75. Mem. ABA, Pa. Bar Assn., Phila. Bar Assn., Indsl. Relations Research Assn. Democrat. Home: 970 Lafayette Rd Bryn Mawr PA 19010 Office: Hoyle Morris & Kerr One Liberty Pl Suite 4900 1650 Market St Philadelphia PA 19103

SUONENLAHTI, MIKKO-JUSSI, management consultant; b. Rovaniemi, Finland, June 22, 1959; s. Juha Veikko and Ulla Raakel (Perisalo) S. Cert. in internat. bus., U. Copenhagen, 1981; BBA, Portland State U., 1983; MBA, Helsinki (Finland) Sch. Bus., 1987. Sales rep. Nokia Info. Systems, Helsinki, 1983-84, product mgr., 1984-85, mgr. sales, 1986-87; cons. mgmt. McKinsey & Co., Copenhagen, 1987-88; stategic planning mgr. Unisys, Helsinki, Finland, 1988—. Served with Finnish Army, 1979-80. Mem. Finnish Bus. Grads. Assn. (chmn. computer com. Helsinki chpt. 1983-85, chmn. internat. bus. com. 1985-87). Home: Otsolahdentie 16 B 102, 02110 Espoo Finland

SUOVANIEMI, OSMO ANTERO, physician; b. Kihnio, Finland, Aug. 2, 1943; s. Viljo Salomon and Meeri Mathilda (Vesanen) S.; Licentiate medicine, Helsinki U., 1972; m. Oili Sinikka Hautamaki, Jan. 6, 1964; children—Vesa, Joel, Ville. Resident Helsinki U. Hosp., 1963-68, 70-73; asst. dept. med. chemistry Helsinki U., 1969-72; pres. Labsystems Oy and Finnpipette Ky, Helsinki, 1971-86 , Eflab Oy, Helsinki, 1978-87 ; bd. dirs. Gen. Group Finnish Industry, 1978-86; pres., chmn. Biohit Oy, Helsinki, 1987—. . Recipient prize Finnish Soc. Inventors, 1976. Mem. Lab. Equipment Producers (dir.), Com. Finnish Comml. Secs., Assn. Finnish Health Care Industries (chmn. bd.), Finnish Fgn. Trade Assn. (council). Lutheran. Contbr. articles to profl. jours. Home: Kulopolku 6,, Helsinki 57, Finland Office: 9 Pulttitie, Helsinki 81,, Finland

SUPARGO, ASIANTO, psychiatrist; b. Jambi, Indonesia, July 15, 1948; s. Kammah S.; m. Ratna Lilyana, May 25, 1979; children: Theresia Elita, Agustinus William. MD, U. Sriwijaya, Palembang, Indonesia, 1977; degree in psychiatry, U. Indonesia, Jakarta, 1984. Med. officer Health Ctr., Sungai Lokan, Indonesia, 1977-79; mem. med. staff Gen. Hosp., Jambi, 1979-80, State Mental Hosp., Jakarta, 1980-84; officer med. health referral sect. Directorate of Mental Health, Ministry of Health Indonesia, Jakarta, 1984-85; med. officer med. care sect. State Mental Hosp., Jambi, 1985—; cons./coordinator community mental health integration Centre for the adavancement of Psychiatry and Mental Health, Jakarta, 1984-85; lectr. U. of Jambi, Acad. of Nursing , Jambi, 1986—. Contbr. research to psychiatry jour., 1983—. Mem. Indonesian Med. Assn., Indonesian Psychiatry Assn., Biol. Psychiatry Assn. Jakarta. Office: Jambi State Mental Hosp, Kenali Besar Km 9 5, Jambi 36001, Indonesia

SUPEK, IVAN, physicist, writer; b. Zagreb, Yugoslavia, Apr. 8, 1915; s. Rudolf and Marya (Ships) S.; m. Zdenka Tagliaferro; children: Iris, Silva, Ivan. Student in theoretical physics and philosophy, Zurich (Switzerland), Paris, Cambridge (Eng.), 1934-39; D of Sci., Heisenberg's Seminar, Leipzig, Germany, 1940. Prof. theoretical physics and philosophy of sci. U. Zagreb, 1945-70, rector, 1968, 70; head Inst. Philosophy of Sci. and Peace Yugoslav Acad. Scis. and Arts, Zagreb, 1965—. Author: (textbook) Teorijskafizika i Struktura Materije, 1st edit., 1949, Philosophy of Science and Humanism, 1979, Theory of Knowledge, 1974; (prose) On Atomic Volcanos, 2 vols., 1959; (plays) On Atomic Island, 1962, Heretic, 1969, Poet and Ruler, 1980, Lottery of Imperator, others; (novels) Discovery in the Lost Time, 1987, Trigon (triology), Crown Witness, 1984, others. Writings bridge sci. and lit. through devel. of quantum theoretical interpretations and peace efforts. Active internat. peace confs., mem. exec. com. Pugwash Conf., chmn. Yugoslav Pugwash chpt., host preparatory conf. World without Bomb, drafter Dubrovnik-Phila. statement urging world unity, among 13 signatories including Linus Pauling, Bertrand Russell, Jean Rostand, Alfred Kastler, Lord Boyd-Orr to issue appeal for Citoyens du Monde; founder Inst. Ruder Boskovic, Yugoslavia's 1st sch. of modern atomic theory, 1950, Interuniv. Ctr., Dubrovnik; mem. Yugoslav Parliament, Belgrade, 1963-67. Partisan during WWII. Recipient Life Work award Croatian Parliament. Humanist. Home: Rubeticeva 10, 41000 Zagreb Yugoslavia Office: Inst Philosophy Sci and Peace, Yugoslav Acad Sci and Arts, A Kovacica 5, 41000 Zagreb Yugoslavia

SUPRAMANIAN, VISWANATHAN, pediatrician; b. Kandavarayawpatti, South India, May 24, 1944; arrived in Malaysia, 1954; parents: Supramanian Perinan and Ganthimathi Somasundram; m. Mallika; children: Ganthimathi, Subramanian, Vallammai. MBBS, Madurai Med. Coll., Malaysia, 1970. Med. officer Taiping Gen. Hosp., Malaysia, 1971-75; registrar Penang Gen. Hosp., Malaysia, 1975-77; sr. house officer Amersham Gen. Hosp., Eng., 1977-79; registrar High Wycom Gen. Hosp., Eng., 1979-80; pediatrician Viswa Clin., Taiping, Eng., 1981—. Chmn. Subramaniam Temple com., Taiping, 1986-87; hon. treas. Boys Scouts Assn., Taiping, 1984—; bd. vis. Old People's Welfare Home, Taiping, 1987—; com. mem. Juvenile Rehab., Taiping, 1987—. Mem. Malaysian Pediatric Assn. Lodge: Lions Club (dir., chmn. med. projects 1982-87; Lion of Yr. 1986-87). Home: 54 Off JLN HJ Mohd Zain, Taiping 34000, Malaysia Office: 132 Main Rd, Taiping 34000, Malaysia

SUQUIA GOICOECHEA, ANGEL CARDINAL, cardinal Roman Catholic Church; b. Zaldivia, San Sebastian, Spain, Oct. 2, 1916. ordained 1940. Consecrated bishop Almeria, Spain, 1966, Malaga, 1969; archbishop Santiago de Compostela, Spain, 1973, Madrid, 1983; proclaimed cardinal 1985. Address: Arzobispado, Bailen 8, 28013 Madrid Spain *

SURBECK, LEIGHTON HOMER, lawyer; b. Jasper, Minn., Oct. 8, 1902; s. James S. and Kathryn (Kilpatrick) S.; m. Margaret H. Packard, 1976. B.S., S.D. State Sch. Mines, 1924; J.D. magna cum laude, Yale, 1927; L.H.D., S.D. Sch. Mines and Tech., 1957; LL.D., Central Coll., 1973; D.Humanitarian Services, Northwestern Coll., Iowa, 1980; LL.D., Hope Coll., 1986. Bar: N.Y. 1929. Law sec. to Chief Justice Taft, 1927-28; asso. Hughes, Schurman & Dwight, N.Y.C., 1928-34; mem. firm Hughes, Schurman & Dwight, 1934-37; mem. firm Hughes, Hubbard & Reed, N.Y.C., 1937—, of counsel, 1981—. Author: Success on the Job, 1957, The Success Formula that Really Works, 1986. Trustee Pacific Sch. Religion, Berkeley, Calif., 1962-80, Golden Gate U., San Francisco, 1979—, Central Coll., Pella, Iowa, 1966-78, Collegiate Boy's Sch., N.Y.C., 1975-78; chmn. Yale Law Sch. Fund, 1971-75. Served as col. AUS, 1942-45; chief econ. br. M.I. 1944-45. Recipient Yale medal Yale Alumni, 1975, Distinguished Service award Yale Law Sch., 1976; Horatio Alger award, 1977. Mem. Am., N.Y. State, N.Y. County bar assns., Assn. Bar City N.Y., Order of Coif, Sigma Tau., Delta Theta Phi. Mem. Marble Collegiate Ch. (elder 1962-78). Clubs: Down Town Assn, Siwanoy Country; Masons, University (N.Y.C.); Menlo Country (Woodside, Calif.). Home: 88 Faxon Rd Atherton CA 94025 Office: 1 Wall St New York NY 10005

SURBER, DAVID FRANCIS, public affairs consultant, syndicated TV producer, journalist; b. Covington, Ky.; s. Elbert and Dorothy Kathryn (Mills) S.; BA in Physics, Thomas More Coll., 1960; LLD (h.c.), London Inst. Applied Research, 1973. Owner, The P.R. Co., pub. affairs counseling, Covington, 1960—. Spl. corr. Am. newspapers to Vatican II, Rome, Italy, 1965. Mem. Bd. Adjustment (Zoning Appeals), Covington, 1964-84, chmn., 1971-84; chmn. Covington Environ. Commn., 1971-72, Commn. Strip Mining, 1967-68; mem. pub. interest adv. com. Ohio River Valley Water Sanitation Commn., 1976-82; mem. water quality adv. com. Ohio-Ky.-Ind. Regional Council Govts., 1975-82; mem. environ. adv. council City of Cin., 1981-84. Mem. rehab. com. Community Chest Greater Cin., 1972-78, mem. agy. admissions com., 1972-78, mem. priorities com., 1972-78. Pres. bd. dirs. Cathedral Found., 1968—; bd. dirs. Nat. Inst. Urban Wildlife, 1987—; trustee Montessori Learning Center, 1973-75, Bklyn. Spanish Youth Choir; founding mem. Mayor's Task Force on the Environment, Cin., 1972-73; mem. Ky. Nature Preserves Commn., 1976-79. Recipient Community Service award Thomas More Coll., 1975. Mem. AFTRA, Tri-State Air Com. (chmn. 1973-74), Izaak Walton League (pres. Ky. 1973, dir. Ky.; nat. dir.), ACLU, Mousquetaires d'Armagnac. Producer: Make Peace with Nature, WKRC-TV, Cin., 1973—, Strip Mining Must Be Stopped, 1972; Energy: Where Will It Come From; How Much Will It Cost, 1975; Atomic Power for Ohio, 1976; A Conversation With The Vice President, 1976; The Bad Water, 1977, The Trans-Alaska Pipeline: A Closeup Report, 1977. Office: 9 E Southern Ave Covington KY 41015-1447

SUREAU, CLAUDE GUY, obstetrician, gynecologist, educator; b. Paris, Sept. 27, 1927; s. Maurice and Rita (Jullian) S.; m. Janine Murset, Oct. 6, 1956; children: François, Véronique, Agnès. MD, U. Paris, 1955. Resident Paris Hosp., 1951-55; chief resident Paris U., 1956-59; asst. attending physician, asst. prof. St. V. de Paul Hosp., 1959-61, prof., chmn. ob-gyn. dept., 1974-76; assoc. attending physician, assoc. prof. U. Clinic Baudelocque, 1967-74, prof., chmn., 1976—; dir. Unit 262 Pathophysiology of Reproduction INSERM, 1983—. Author: Le Danger de Naitre, 1978, Clinical Perinatology, 1980, Immunologie de la Reproduction, 1983, La Maitrise de la Contraction Utérine, 1987. Recipient Chevalier de la Légion d'Honneur, 1977. Fellow Royal Coll. Obstetricians and Gynecologists, Am. Coll. Obstetricians and Gynecologists (hon.); mem. Intern. Fedn. Gynecologists and Obstetricians (pres. 1982-85, ethical com. pres. 1985—), French-Speaking Fedn. Gynecologists and Obstetricians (pres. 1986-88), European Asn. Gynecologists and Obstetricians (pres.1988). Roman Catholic. Home: 3 rue Pierret, 92200 Neuilly France Office: Clinique Universitaire, Baudelocque, 123 Blvd de Port-Royal, 75014 Paris France

SURFACE, STEPHEN WALTER, water treatment chemist; b. Dayton, Ohio, Feb. 25, 1943; s. Lorin Wilfred and Virginia (Marsh) S.; m. Suzanne MacDonald, Aug. 29, 1964 (div.); 1 child, Jennifer Nalani; m. Sinfrosa Garay, Sept. 16, 1978; children: Maria Lourdes, Stephanie Alcantara. BS, Otterbein Coll., 1965; MA, U. So. Calif., 1970; postgrad., U. Hawaii, 1971. Tchr. Hawaii State Dept. Edn., Honolulu, 1970-71; staff chemist Del Monte Corp., Honolulu, 1971; head chemist USNPearl Harbor, Honolulu, 1971-76, staff chemist, 1976—. Contbr. articles to profl. jours. Recipient DuPont Teaching award, U. So. Calif., 1966. Fellow Internat. Biog. Assn., Am. Inst. Chemists; mem. Am. Chem. Soc., Am. Water Works Assn., N.Y. Acad. Scis., Sigma Zeta, Phi Lambda Upsilon. Democrat. Methodist. Home: 94-1139 Noheaiki St Waipahu HI 96797 Office: Naval Facilities Engring Command Pacific div Pearl Harbor HI 96860-7300

SURIAN, ELVIDIO, music educator; b. Lussingrande, Istria, Italy, Jan. 10, 1940; s. Santo and Dobrilla (Ballarin) S.; m. Eugenia Venturi, Nov. 6, 1971; 1 child, Laura. BS, CUNY, 1962, MA, 1964; postgrad., NYU, 1965-70. Instr. music SUNY, Stony Brook, 1970; lectr. Lehman Coll., CUNY, N.Y.C., 1970-72; music librarian G. Rossini Music Conservatory, Pesaro, Italy, 1973-76, prof. music history, 1976—, mem. adminstrn. bd., 1986—; coordinator Répertoire Internat. Sources Musicales Group, Italy, 1975-83. Author: A Checklist of Writings on 18th Century French and Italian Opera, 1970; editor: D. Cimarosa, Orazi e Curiazi, 1986, Storia della Musica in Venezia, 1987; contbr. articles to music jours. Mem. Internat. Musicological Soc., Am. Musicological Soc., Italian Soc. Musicology (mem. exec. council 1976-79, 82-85), Am. Inst. for Verdi Studies (mem. adv. council). Roman Catholic. Home: Via Gallucci 3, 61100 Pesaro Italy Office: G Rossini Conservatorio Musica, Piazza Olivieri, 61100 Pesaro Italy

SURRAYA, MALIKA, physician; b. Jammu, Kashmir, India, Feb. 8, 1947; d. Mirza Inayat Ullah Baig and Sharaf Sultana; divorced. B Medicine and Sci., Fatiue Jinnah Med. Coll., 1963. Obstetrician, gynecologist 1969-70; women's med. officer Mpl. Corp., Gujranwala, Pakistan, 1971—; speaker PMA seminar, 1986. Home: Circular Rd, Gujranwala Pakistan Office: Municipal Dispensary, Noor Baina 5, Gujranwala Pakistan

SURYOUTOMO, HERMAN, food company executive; b. Pati, Indonesia, July 7, 1946; came to U.S., 1970; s. Kiem Hoo Oei and Lies Nio Ong; m.

Lusia Amalia Karnoatmodjo, Mar. 1, 1976; children: David Christopher, Nina Amelia, Jason Andrew, Tanya Christina. BS equivalent, Bandung Inst. Tech., Indonesia, 1970; MS, Washington U., St. Louis, 1972, DSc, 1975; MBA, Pepperdine U., 1984. Registered profl. engr., N.C., Ala.; registered civil engr., Calif. Sr. engring. specialist Jack Gillum & Assocs., St. Louis, 1974-75; div. and project mgr. Cygna Corp., San Francisco, 1975-82; chmn., chief exec. officer Innova Corp., Fremont, Calif., 1982—; pres. Innova Corp. of N.C., Raleigh, 1983—; owner, broker Prima Realty, Fremont, 1986—; pres., chief exec. officer Prima Foods Corp., Fremont, 1985—. Author: Organizational Effectiveness, 1984; contbr. articles to profl. jours. V.p., bd. dirs. Companion of Alameda County, Hayward, Calif., 1985—; bd. dirs. YMCA, Young Life Calif.-Nev. Named Fulbright Hays scholar, Washington, 1970; recipient Highest Achievement scholarship Dale Carnegie Schs., Oakland, Calif., 1976. Mem. ASCE. Roman Catholic. Lodges: Rotary, Toastmasters (officer 1985—). Home: 44433 Park Meadow Dr Fremont CA 94539 Office: Innova Corp 5411 Randall Pl Fremont CA 94538

SUSLAK, HOWARD ROBINSON, investment banking executive; b. N.Y.C., Apr. 24, 1920; s. Sigmund and Estelle (Robinson) S.; m. Adele Barnett, June 19, 1949; children—Brian Edward, Neil Scott, Valerie Estelle, Pamela Simone. Grad., Juilliard Sch. Music, 1942; B.A. magna cum laude, NYU, 1942; M.B.A., Wharton Sch., U. Pa., 1943. Asst. to pres. E.R. Squibb & Sons, N.Y.C., 1945-46; v.p. Metacan Mfg. Co., Bklyn., 1946-47; with MacDonald & Co., N.Y.C., 1947—; mgr. MacDonald & Co., 1948; in charge offices MacDonald & Co., Chgo., Pitts., Boston, Detroit, 1949-54; gen. ptnr. MacDonald & Co., 1954—, v.p., 1956-58, exec. v.p., 1958-62, pres., 1962—; chmn., mng. dir. Indsl. Mgmt. Cons., Ltd., London, 1949—; dir. George Hopkinson, Ltd., Kaz Mfg. Co. Inc., Phi Beta Kappa Assocs. Mem. N.Y.C. Planning Commn., 1965-66; bd. dirs. Weizmann Inst. Sci., Opera Orch. N.Y., Sch. Weber Electronics. Served with U.S. Army, 1943-44. Mem. Am. Mgmt. Assn., Newcomen Soc. N.Am., Phi Beta Kappa Assocs. Clubs: Economics, Harmonie, Phi Beta Kappa Alumni (N.Y.C.); Royal Automobile (London); Royal Automobile Country (Epsom, Eng.); Windham Mountain Ski. Home: 303 E 57th St New York NY 10022 Office: Rockefeller Center 630 Fifth Ave Suite 2166 New York NY 10111

SUSLAVICH, FRANK JOHN, automotive executive; b. Hudson, Mass., May 27, 1916; s. Andrew and Eva (Stakelunas) S.; diploma in acctg. Bentley Coll., Boston, 1937; m. Hortense Pounds, Sept. 3, 1949; children—Frank John, James, Jane, Gary, Gail. Acct., United Fruit Co., 1937-42; gen. acct. Bendix Aviation Corp., 1942-44; with Gen. Motors Corp., 1944-57, Atlantic regional mgr. Oldsmobile div., 1946-57; v.p., So. area dir. Chrysler Corp., 1957-59, asst. dir. corp. slaes, 1959-60, asst. gen. mgr. Plymouth div., 1960-61, gen. mgr. Manhattan sales and service ops., N.Y.C., 1963-84; v.p. Studebaker Corp., South Bend, 1961-63. Roman Catholic. Club: N.Y. Athletic.

SUSMAN, MORTON LEE, lawyer; b. Detroit, Aug. 6, 1934; s. Harry and Alma (Koslow) S.; m. Nina Meyers, May 1, 1958; 1 son, Mark Lee. B.B.A., So. Meth. U., 1956, J.D., 1958. Bar: Tex. 1958, U.S. Dist. Ct. (so. dist.) Tex. 1961, U.S. Ct. Appeals (5th cir.) 1961, U.S. Supreme Ct. 1961, U.S. Ct. Appeals (11th cir.) 1981. Asst. U.S. atty., Houston, 1961-64, 1st asst. U.S. atty., 1965-66, U.S. atty., 1966-69; ptnr. Weil, Gotshal & Manges and predecessor firm Susman & Kessler, Houston, 1969—. Served to lt. USNR, 1958-61. Recipient Younger Fed. Lawyer award Fed. Bar Assn., 1968. Fellow Am. Coll. Trial Lawyers, Tex. Bar Found.; mem. ABA, Tex. Bar Assn., Houston Bar Assn. Democrat. Jewish. Club: Houston, Houstonian; Crescent (Dallas). Home: 338 Hunters Trail Houston TX 77024 Office: Weil Gotshal & Manges 1600 Republic Bank Ctr Houston TX 77002

SUSSER, BERNARD ARNOLD, political philosopher, educator; b. N.Y.C., Nov. 16, 1942; s. Levi L. and Sarah (Thau) S.; m. Susan Mae Braun, June 12, 1966; children: Yair M., Shellie L., Donna N. BA, Yeshiva U., 1964; PhD, Columbia U., 1972. arrived in Israel, 1969;. Lectr. Columbia U., N.Y.C., 1971-72; from lectr. to assoc. prof. Bar Ilan U., Ramat Gan, Israel, 1972—, Tel Aviv U., 1972—; asst. prof. Vanderbilt U., Nashville, 1976-77; vis. fellow Oxford (Eng.) U., 1980-81; vis. prof. U. Va., Charlottesville, 1983-84; mem. research group to draft constn. for Israel; organizer, researcher constl. reform groups, Israel, 1985-87. Author: Political Philosophy of Martin Buber, 1981, Grammar of Modern Ideology, 1987; editor: Jewish Public Life, 1981, Political Reform for Israel, 1987. Served with Israeli Army. German Academic Exchange Program grantee German Govt., 1981, Ford Found. grantee, 1982-83. Home: Keren Hayesod 4A, Kfar Saba 44235, Israel Office: Tel Aviv U, Dept Polit Studies, Tel Aviv Israel also: Bar Ilan U, Ramat Gan Israel

SUSSEX, JAMES NEIL, psychiatrist, educator; b. Northcote, Minn., Oct. 2, 1917; s. Rollo and Florence (Bartholomew) S.; m. Margaret Ann Garty, Apr. 25, 1943; children: Margaret Eileen, Mary Patricia, Barbara Lorraine, Teresa Virginia. A.B., U. Kans., 1939, M.D., 1942. Diplomate: Am. Bd. Psychiatry and Neurology (dir. for child psychiatry 1966-70, dir. 1975-83, pres. 1982). Commd. lt. (j.g.), M.C. U.S. Navy, 1943, advanced through grades to comdr., 1955; intern (Naval Hosp.), Chelsea, Mass., 1942-43; resident psychiatry (Naval Hosp.), Vallejo, Calif., 1946-49; fellow child psychiatry Phila. Guild Guidance Clinic, 1949-51; asst. chief neuropsychiatry Naval Hosp., Bethesda, Md., 1951-55; resigned 1955; mem. faculty Med. Coll. Ala., 1955-68, prof. psychiatry, chmn. dept., 1959-68; psychiatrist-in-chief U. Ala. Hosps. and Clinics, 1959-68; faculty U. Miami Sch. Medicine, Fla., 1968—; prof. psychiatry U. Miami Sch. Medicine, 1970—, chmn. dept., 1970-83, spl. asst. to v.p. for med. affairs for geriatric medicine program, 1983-86; mem. adv. bd. Nat. Psychiat. Residency Selection Plan, 1965—; mem. Med. Adv. Bd. Ednl. Film Prodn., 1966—; cons. Bur. Research, U.S. Office Edn., 1966-72; dir. Ala. planning for Mental Retardation, 1964—; mem. psychiatry tng. rev. com. NIMH; mem. exec. com. Am. Bd. Med. Spltys., 1980-83. Editor: Jour. Ala. Soc. Med. History, 1957-63; editorial bd.: Jour. Am. Acad. Child Psychiatry, 1966-70. Mem. Assn. Soc. Profs. Psychiatry (chmn. 1967), AMA (ho. dels. 1966), So. Med. Assn. (chmn. sect. neurology and psychiatry 1965-66), Am. Assn. Psychiat. Services for Children (council 1966—, pres. 1972-74), Council Med. Splty. Socs. (bd. dirs. 1985—, sec. 1986—, pres.-elect 1978-88), Phi Beta Kappa, Nu Sigma Nu. Home: 6950 SW 134th St Miami FL 33156

SUSSMAN, DEBORAH EVELYN, design company executive; b. N.Y.C., May 26, 1931; d. Irving and Ruth (Golomb) S.; m. Paul Prejza, June 28, 1972. Student Bard Coll., 1948-50, Inst. Design, Chgo., 1950-53, Black Mountain Coll., 1950, Hochschule fur Gestaltung Ulm (Fulbright grantee), W.Ger., 1957-58. Art dir. Office of Charles and Ray Eames, Venice, Calif., 1953-57, 61-67; graphic designer Galeries Lafayette, Paris, 1959-60; prin. Deborah Sussman and Co., Santa Monica, Calif., 1968—; founder, pres. Sussman-Prejza and Co., Inc., Santa Monica, 1980—; speaker, lectr. UCLA Sch. Architecture, Archtl. League N.Y.C., Smithsonian Inst., Stanford Conf. on Design, Am. Inst. Graphic Arts Nat. Conf. at MIT, Design Mgmt. Inst. Conf., Mass.; spl. guest Internat. Design Conf., Aspen, Colo., Fulbright lectr., India, 1976; speaker NEA Adv. Council, 1985, Internat. Council Shopping Ctrs., 1986, USIA Design in America seminar, Budapest, Hungary, 1988. Mem. editorial adv. bd. Arts and Architecture Mag., 1981-85, Calif. Mag., Architecture Calif. Recipient numerous awards AIA Nat. Inst. Honors, 1985, 88, Am. Inst. Graphic Arts, Calif. Council AIA, Communications Arts Soc., Los Angeles County Bd. Suprs., Vesta award Women's Bldg. Los Angeles. Mem. AIA (hon.), Am. Inst. Graphic Arts (bd. dirs. 1982-85, founder Los Angeles chpt., chmn., 1983-84, numerous awards), Los Angeles Art Dirs. Club (bd. dirs., numerous awards), Alliance Graphique Internat., Architects, Designers and Planners Social Responsibility, SEGD. Democrat. Jewish. Avocation: photography. Office: Sussman-Prejza & Co Inc 1651 18th St Santa Monica CA 90404

SUSSMAN, LEONARD RICHARD, foundation executive; b. N.Y.C., Nov. 26, 1920; s. Jacob and Carrie (Marks) S.; m. Frances Rukeyser, May 9, 1942 (div. 1958); m. Marianne Rita Gutmann, May 28, 1958; children: Lynne, David William, Mark Jacob. A.B., NYU, 1940; M.S. in Journalism, Columbia U., 1941. Copy editor N.Y. Morning Telegraph, also news editor radio sta. WQXR, 1941; cable editor San Juan (P.R.) World Jour., also corr. Business Week mag., 1941-42; editor fgn. broadcast intelligence service FCC, 1942; press sec. to gov. P.R., 1942-43; dir. info. in N.Y. for Govt. P.R., 1946-49; regional dir., then nat. exec. dir. Am. Council Judaism, 1949-66; pub. affairs cons. Nationwide Ins. Cos. (and indsl. subsidiaries), 1955-57; mem. editorial com. Council Liberal Chs., 1956-59; exec. dir. Freedom House, 1967-88, Willkie Meml., 1970-88; sr. scholar in internat. communications Freedom House, 1988—; organizer, dir. Freedom House/Books USA, 1968-85; editor Freedom at Issue (bimonthly), 1970-81; mem. U.S. Conf. World Communication Yr./83, 1982-83: organizer acad. confs.; participant Internat. Conf. on Press Freedom, Venice, Italy, 1976, 77, Cairo, 1978, Talloires, 1981, 83, San Jose, Costa Rica, Johannesburg and Santiago, Chile, 1987, others.; mem. panel competition in space Congressional Office of Tech. Assessment, 1982-83. Author: American Press-Under Siege?, 1973, Mass News Media and the Third World Challenge, 1977, Glossary for International Communications: Warning of a Bloodless Dialect, 1983, Spanish version, 1987; editor: Three Years at the East-West Divide, 1983, Today's American: How Free?, 1986; contbr. sects. to books, articles in profl. jours. and newspapers; project dir.: Big Story-How The American Press and Television Reported and Interpreted The Crisis of Tet-1968 in Vietnam and Washington, 1977; editor: textbook series, also quar. mag. Issues, 1953-66; editorial bd. Polit. Communication and Persuasion. Trustee Internat. Council on Future of Univ., 1973-84; bd. dirs. World Press Freedom Com., 1977—; chmn. Friends of Survey Mag. Charitable Trust, London, 1978—; mem. U.S. Nat. Commn. for UNESCO, 1979-85, vice chmn., 1983-85; mem. U.S. delegations to internat. conf. on space, African Aid, UNESCO. Decorated Legion of Merit. Mem. Internat. Press Inst., Internat. Inst. Communication, Sigma Delta Chi (Annual First Amendment award 1988). Club: Century (N.Y.C.). Home: 215 E 73d St New York NY 10021 Office: 48 E 21st St New York NY 10010

SUSSMAN, MARC MITCHELL, international business executive, management consultant; b. N.Y.C., Mar. 31, 1956; s. Max and Ruth (Lindner) S; m. Sharon Tracy, Apr. 9, 1988. B.A., George Washington U., 1978; M.P.A., NYU, 1980. Mem. nat. staff Carter/Mondale Campaign, Atlanta, 1976; intern The White House, Washington, 1977; internat. affairs analyst Chem. Bank, N.Y.C., 1980-82; pres., chief exec. officer Alpha Internat. Mgmt. Group, Ltd., N.Y.C., 1982—; dir. Mormac, N.Y.C. Fund raiser Mondale Presdl. Campaign, N.Y.C., 1981-84, Friends of Ed Koch, N.Y.C., 1981, Hubert H. Humphrey Cancer Research Ctr., Boston, 1984—, Hubert H. Humphrey Fund, 1986—, Humphrey Exploratory Com., 1987—, Humphrey for U.S. Sen., 1988. Mem. NYU Alumni Assn., Internat. Platform Assn. Jewish. Club: Nat. Tennis Assn. (N.Y.C.). Avocations: tennis, collecting tennis art. Office: Alpha Internat Mgmt Group Ltd 145 W 58th St New York NY 10019

SUSSMAN, RALPH MAURICE, physician; b. N.Y.C., Apr. 15, 1908; s. Jacob and Taube Etta (Gertler) S.; student Columbia U., 1924, 26-28; M.D., L.I. Coll. Medicine, 1932; m. Frances Irene Goldberg, Sept. 12, 1929; children—Elizabeth Anne Sussman Socolow, Victoria Amy; m. 2d, Gertrude Hoddes Sneider, July 14, 1974. Intern, Beth Israel Hosp., N.Y.C., 1932-33, resident, 1933-35; practice medicine specializing in cardiology, N.Y.C., 1941—; adj. physician Beth Israel Hosp., N.Y.C., 1941-47, asso. physician, 1947-60, attending, 1960-77; asso. clin. prof. dept. medicine (cardiology) Mt. Sinai Sch. Medicine, City U. N.Y., N.Y.C., 1972-77; mem. staff Drs. Hosp., also chmn. com. coronary care. Bd. govs. Downstate Med. Center, 1970—; mem. Arthur Ross Found., 1975—; physician Draft Bd., 1942-45. Dazian Found. recipient, 1949-50. Diplomate Am. Bd. Internal Medicine. Fellow R.C.P. (asso.), N.Y. Acad. Medicine, A.C.P. (life), Am. Coll. Cardiology, Clin. Council Cardiology of Am. Heart Assn.; mem. N.Y. Cardiologic Soc. (exec. bd. 1975—), Soc. Internal Medicine N.Y. County (sec. 1977-78), Am. Geriatric Soc., N.Y. Acad. Scis., AMA, Alumni Assn. Downstate Med. Center (pres. 1974). Editor Lichonian, 1932; contbr. articles to med. jours. Home: 15 E 91 St New York NY 10128 Office: 1148 Fifth Ave New York NY 10128

SUSSNA, EDWARD, economist, educator; b. Phila., Nov. 26, 1926; s. Louis and Manya (Prytzycka) S.; m. Sylvia Fishman, Mar. 8, 1953; children—Audrey Francine, Ellen Sondra. B.A., Bklyn. Coll., 1950; M.A., U. Ill., 1952, Ph.D., 1954. Instr. U. Ill., 1952-54; asst. prof. Lehigh U., 1956-57; prof. bus. adminstrn. and econs. U. Pitts., 1957—; dir. Center for Econ. Edn., Grad. Sch. Bus., 1978—, dir. div. exec. devel.; vis. Fulbright prof. U. Tehran, Iran, adviser, 1972-73; cons. Bur. of Budget, Dept. HEW, Dept. Transp., UN Indsl. Devel. Orgn., Bell Telephone Co., Alcoa, Westinghouse Corp., NSF, Pitts. Nat. Bank, Japanese Regional Bankers Assn., others; vis. prof. UCLA, 1970, Ecole Superieure des Scis. Economiques et Commerciales, Paris, 1976-77, U. East Asia, Hong Kong and Macau, winter 1986; vis. scholar Internat. Inst. Mgmt., Berlin, spring 1982. Contbr. articles to profl. jours. Served with U.S. Mcht. Marine, 1944-47; Served with AUS, 1954-56. Vis. prof. under Ford Found. fellowship Harvard, 1960-61; guest scholar under Ford Found. fellowship Brookings Instn., Washington, 1962-63. Mem. Am. Econ. Assn., Am. Fin. Assn., Evaluation Research Soc., Econometric Soc., Inst. Mgmt. Scis., Strategic Mgmt. Inst., Beta Gamma Sigma, Omicron Delta. Home: 1538 S Negley Ave Pittsburgh PA 15217

SUTCLIFFE, ERIC, lawyer; b. Calif., Jan. 10, 1909; s. Thomas and Annie (Beare) S.; m. Joan Basché, Aug. 7, 1937; children: Victoria, Marcia, Thomas; m. Marie C. Paige, Nov. 1, 1975. A.B., U. Calif. at Berkeley, 1929, LL.B., 1932. Bar: Calif. 1932. Mem. firm Orrick, Herrington & Sutcliffe, San Francisco, 1943-85. Trustee San Francisco Law Library; bd. dirs. Merritt Peralta Found. Fellow Am. Bar Found; mem. ABA (chmn state regulation securities com. 1960-65), San Francisco Bar Assn. (chmn. corp. law com., 1964-65), San Francisco C. of C. (past treas., dir.), State Bar Calif., Phi Gamma Delta, Phi Delta Phi, Order of Coif. Clubs: Pacific Union, Bohemian (San Francisco). Home: 260 King Ave Piedmont CA 94610 Office: 600 Montgomery St San Francisco CA 94111

SUTCLIFFE, JAMES HELME, music critic, composer; b. Soochow, China, Nov. 26, 1929; s. Geoffrey Helme and Martha Rose (Wilkinson) S. Studied music with, G. Logie-Smith, 1941-47; BSc in Piano, Juilliard Sch. Music, N.Y.C., 1953; MA in Theory, Eastman Sch. Music, Rochester, N.Y., 1958. Asst. prof. music, opera dir. Duquesne U., Pitts., 1957-61; critic, author Opera News mag., Musical Am. mag., N.Y.C. Opera mag., London Opera Toronto Can. mag., Internat. Heralf Tribune, Paris, Opërnwelt, Zürich, 1964—; critic, author Opernwelt, Zürich, 1964—; tchr. piano Opera Can., Toronto. Author: Berlin, Hamburg, Vienna opera houses, Salzburg Festivals; (book) Die Bühnenwerke Benjamin Brittens, 1988; composer: orchestral, choral, piano education; Intro. and Allegro/Strings, Sonnet/Clarinet, 1956, Pictures for Percussion, Andante and Chorale, Theater Suite, 1957 (Benjamin Prize/Eastman Sch. Music), Elegy (Wind Orch.), 1959, Sinfonietta, 1960, Acad. Festival March, 1968, A Christmas Journey, 1986, Fröhliche Weihnachten, 1988. Served with U.S. Army, 1953-55. Home and Office: Wilmersdorfer Str 94, D-1000 Berlin 12 Federal Republic of Germany

SUTHERLAND, BRUCE, composer, pianist; pupil Halsey Stevens, Ellis Kohs, Ethel Leginska, Amparo Iturbi; b. Daytona Beach, Fla.; s. Kenneth Francis and Norma (Williams) S.; Mus.B., U. So. Calif., 1957, Mus.M., 1959. Harpsichord soloist with Telemann Trio in concert tour, 1969-70; tchr. master class for pianists U. Tex., Austin, 1971; dir. Bach festivals Music Tchrs. Assn. Calif., 1972-73, dir. Artists of Tomorrow Music Festivals Music Tchrs. Assn. Calif., 1984—, competitions performed in numerous contemporary music festivals in U.S., 1957—; piano faculty Calif. State U. at Northridge, 1977—; adjudicator music competitions and auditions Nat. Guild Piano Tchrs., others; dir. Brentwood-Westwood Symphony ann. competition for young artists, 1981—; composer: Allegro Fanfara for Orch., world premiere conducted by José Iturbi with Bridgeport Symphony Orch., 1970; Saxophone Quartet, 1971; Quintet for Flute, Strings, Piano, 1972; Notturno for Flute and Guitar, 1973; also string trio, piano and vocal works. Recipient grand prize Internat. Competition Louis Moreau Gottschalk, 1970; Stairway of Stars award Music Arts Soc., Santa Monica, 1973; named one of Los Angeles' Finest Piano Tchrs., New West Mag., 1977. Mem. Nat. Assn. Am. Composers and Condrs., Music Tchrs. Nat. Assn., Music Tchrs. Assn., Calif. Assn. Profl. Music Tchrs., Pi Kappa Lambda.

SUTHERLAND, DONALD, actor; b. St. John, N.B., Can., July 17, 1935; m. Shirley Douglas; 1 child, Kiefer. Ed., U. Toronto. Actor: London Acad. Music and Dramatic Art, Perth Repertory Theatre, Scotland, also Nottingham, Chesterfield, Bronley, Shieffield, (plays) including The Spoon River Anthology, The Male Animal, The Tempest, August for People (London debut), On A Clear Day You Can See Canterbury, The Shewing Up a Blanco Posnet, (films) including The Castle of the Living Dead, Dr. Terror's House of Horrors, The Dirty Dozen, 1967, Oedipus the King, Joanna, The Split, Start the Revolution without Me, The Act of the Heart, MASH, 1970, Kelley's Heroes, 1970, Alex in Wonderland, 1970, Little Murders, 1971, Klute, 1971, Steelyard Blues, 1973, Alien Thunder, The Master, Lady Ice, 1973, Don't Look Now, 1974, SPYS, 1974, The Day of the Locust, 1975, Cassanova, The Eagle has Landed, 1977, Animal House, 1977, Invasion of the Body Snatchers, 1978, The Great Train Robbery, 1979, Murder by Decree, 1979, A Man, A Woman and a Bank, Ordinary People, 1980, Eye of the Needle, 1980, Nothing Personal, Gas, The Disapperance, Blood Relative, Threshold, 1983, Crackers, 1984, Revolution, 1985, The Wolf at the Door, 1987, (TV shows and movies) including Marching to the Sea, The Death of Bessie Smith, Hamlet at Elsinore, The Saint, The Avengers, Gideon's Way, The Champions, The Winter of Our Discontent. Office: care Creative Artists Agy Inc 1888 Century Park E Los Angeles CA 90067 also: 760 N LaCienega Blvd Los Angeles CA 90069 *

SUTHERLAND, JOAN, coloratura soprano; b. Sydney, Australia, Nov. 7, 1926; d. McDonald S.; m. Richard Bonynge, 1954; 1 son. Student, Royal Coll. Music, London, 1951. Appeared concert and oratorio performances, Australia; appeared in: opera Judith, Syndey Conservatory of Music; debut Covent Garden in Magic Flute, 1952; other operatic performances include Handel's Acis and Galatea; heroine roles operas by, Bellini and Donizetti; Italian debut in Handel's Alcina, Teatro la Fenice, Venice, 1960, Bellini's Puritani, Glyndebourne Festival, Sussex, Eng., 1960, Bellini's Beatrice di Tenda, La Scala, 1961, Rossini's Semiramide, La Scala, 1962, Meyerbeer's Les Huguenots, La Scala, 1962, N.Y. debut, Carnegie Hall, 1961; Opera debut Lucia, 1961; opened Sutherland-Williamson Opera Co. tour, Australia, 1965; appeared: Handel's Julius Caesar, Hamburg Co. tour, Australia, 1965, Hamburg Opera, 1969, Bellini's Norma, Met Opera, 1970, opened, Lyric Opera Chgo. with, Semiramide, 1971, San Francisco Opera with, Norma, 1972, San Francisco Opera with, Trovatore, 1975, Met. Opera with, I Puritani, 1976, Met. Opera with, Esclamode, 1976, Vancouver Opera with, Le Roi de Lahore, 1977; premiered new prodn., Met. Opera in, Tales of Hoffmann, 1973; 1st prodn. in Am. in 80 years Esclarmonde, Massenet, San Fancisco Opera, 1974. Recipient Mobil Quest award, 1951; recipient Grammy award for best classical vocal soloist, 1981; named fellow Royal Coll. Music, 1981; decorated comdr. and dame comdr. Order Brit. Empire, comdr. and dame comdr. Order Australia. Office: care Ingpen and Williams, 14 Kensington Ct, London W8 5DN, England *

SUTHERLAND, JOHN ELLIOTT, writer, producer, educator; b. Williston, N.D., Sept. 11, 1910; s. Ronald and Adelaide Mae (Elliott) S.; student U. N.D., 1929-30; B.A., UCLA, 1937; m. Lysiane Wagner, 1952; children: Ronald, Eric, Diane. Grad. dir. dramatics and debate UCLA, 1938; prodn. mgr., writer, dialogue dir. Walt Disney Prodns., 1939-40; free-lance screenplay writer, Hollywood, 1941; writer-producer-dir. U.S. Army Signal Corps, other govtl. agys., 1941-45; writer, producer animated cartoons United Artists, Metro Goldwyn Mayer, 1946-55, live-action entertainment films Eagle Lion Motion Pictures Distributor, 1955-56; pres. John Sutherland Prodns., Los Angeles, 1946—, also Sutherland Learning Assos.; producer entertainment programs for ABC and CBS TV, 1972-76; writer, producer health multimedia learning systems U.S. Office of Edn. Housing Edn. Welfare, 1969-73, Capt. Kangaroo program CBS-TV, 1972-73. Mem edn. group Nat. Arthritis Commn., 1975; bd. visitors Grad. Sch. Edn. UCLA, 1974. Creator Thumper character in film Bambi, Walt Disney Prodns., 1939-40. Recipient 250 awards for creative excellence in documentary and ednl. films from domestic and internat. film festivals, 1950—; Sesquicentennial award for creative contbns. ednl. films U. Mich., 1967. Co-author: (feature film) Flight Command, 1941; (hist. novel) The Valiant, 1955. Conceived and produced 1st multi-media learning systems in continuing med. edn. Div. Nursing, USPHS, 1969-70. Address: 8700 Reseda Blvd Suite 108 Northridge CA 91324

SUTHERLAND, LOWELL FRANCIS, lawyer; b. Lincoln, Nebr., Dec. 17, 1939; s. Lowell Williams and Doris Genevieve (Peterson) S.; A.B., San Diego State Coll., 1962; LL.B., Hastings Coll. Law, 1965; m. Sandra Gaylynne Stengel, June 12, 1965; children—Scott Thorpe, Mark James, Sandra Doris. With Cooper, White & Cooper, attys., San Francisco, 1963-66; admitted to Calif. bar, 1966; with Wien & Thorpe, attys., El Centro, 1966-67; ptnr. Wien, Thorpe & Sutherland, El Centro, 1967-74, Wien, Thorpe, Sutherland & Stamper, 1973-74, Sutherland, Stamper & Feingold, 1974-77, Sutherland & Gerber, 1977—; ptnr. Sutherland & Sutherland, Ivy Shoppe; instr. bus. law Imperial Valley Coll., 1967. Pres. El Centro Active 20-30 Club, 1968-69; finance chmn. Salvation Army, 1972. Pres. bd. dirs. Boys Club of El Centro, 1969-71; bd. dirs. Imperial Gen. Hosp., 1971. Mem. Am., Calif., Imperial County Bar Assns., Am., Calif. (Recognition of Experience awards), San Diego (named Outstanding Trial Lawyer April 1981, Oct. 1983, Trial Lawyer of Yr. 1982), Trial Lawyers Assns., Thurston Soc., Nat. Bd. Trial Advs. (diplomate), Am. Bd. Trial Advocates (assoc.), Theta Chi. Mem. editorial staff Hastings Law Jour., 1964-65. Home: 1853 Sunset Dr El Centro CA 92243 Office: 300 S Imperial Ave 7 El Centro CA 92243

SUTHERLAND, NORMAN STUART, psychology educator, writer; b. Surbiton, Eng., Mar. 26, 1927; s. Norman McLeod and Celia Dickson (Jackson) S.; separated; children: Gay, Julia Claire. BA in Literae Humaniores with honors, Oxford U., 1949, BA in Psychology, Philosophy and Physiology with honors, 1953, PhD in Exptl. Psychology, 1957. Lectr. Oxford (Eng.) U., 1957-64; prof. exptl. psychology Sussex U., Brighton, Eng., 1965—; vis. prof. MIT, Cambridge, 1962-63, 64-65. Author: Breakdown, 1976, rev. edit., 1987, Discovering the Human Mind, 1982, Men Change Too, 1987, others; contbr. numerous articles to profl. jours., newspapers, chpts. to books. Served with RAF, 1949-51. Fellow Magdalen Coll., Oxford U., 1949-53, Merton Coll., 1961-64; John Locke prize scholar Oxford U., 1953. Mem. Exptl. Psychology Soc. (pres. 1979-80), Internat. Brain Research Orgn. Office: U Sussex, Lab Exptl Psychology, Brighton BN1 9QG, England

SUTHERLAND, ROBERT DONALD, librarian; b. North Bay, Ont., Apr. 15, 1953; s. Norman Ronald and Geneva (Soucie) S.; m. Elizabeth Ann Dennis, Sept. 3, 1977. BA in Psychology, U. Western Ont., 1976, MLS, 1983; EdB, Nipissing U., North Bay, Ont., 1978; MS in Psychology, U. Strathclyde, 1979. Tchr., prin. No. Lights Sch. Div., Camsell Portage, Sask., 1978-80; ednl. psychologist No. Lights Sch. Div., Prince Albert, Sask., 1980-81; v.p., learning asst. Yukon Tchrs. Assn., Mayo, Y.T., 1983-87; coordinator resource ctr. Yukon Coll., Whitehorse, Y.T., 1987—; chmn. Mayo Library Bd., Y.T., 1983-87. Chief Mayo Vol. Fire Dept., 1985—. Mem. Can. Library Assn., Yukon Tchrs. Assn. Clubs: Mayo Photography (pres. 1984-86); Community Sch. Band (Mayo) (bd. dirs. 1984-86). Home: 10 Hyland Crescent, Whitehorse, YK Canada Y1A 4P7 Office: Yukon College, PO Box 2799, Whitehorse, YK Canada Y1A 3H9

SUTHERLUND, DAVID ARVID, lawyer; b. Stevens Point, Wis., July 20, 1929; s. Arvid E. and Georgia M. (Stickney) S. BA, U. Portland, 1952; JD, U. N.Mex., 1957; postgrad., U. Wis., 1957. Bar: D.C. 1957, U.S. Supreme Ct. 1961. Atty. ICC, Washington, 1957-58; counsel Am. Trucking Assn., Washington, 1958-62; assoc. and ptnr. Morgan, Lewis & Bockius, Washington and Phila., 1962-72; ptnr. Fulbright & Jaworski, Washington and Houston, 1975-83; spl. counsel LaRoe, Winn & Moerman, Washington, 1983—; ptnr. Zwerling, Mark, Sutherland, Ginsberg & Lieberman, N.Y., 1987—; bd. dirs., gen. counsel Nat. Film Service, 1962-75; mem. family div. panel Public Defender Service for D.C., 1972-76. Founder, chmn. bd. govs. Transp. Law Jour, 1969-74. Vice chmn. Nat. Capitol Area council Boy Scouts Am., 1975-78; bd. regents U. Portland, 1985—. Served as spl. agt. CIC U.S. Army, 1952-54. Mem. ABA, Fed. Bar Assn., D.C. Bar Assn., Transp. Lawyers Assn., Am. Arbitration Assn. (nat. panel arbitrators 1970—), Am. Judicature Soc., Smithson Soc. (Smithsonian Instn.). Clubs: Nat. Lawyers; International, Lakewood (Washington). Home: 2130 Bancroft Pl NW Washington DC 20008 Office: 888 16th ST NW Washington DC 20006

SUTIC, DRAGOLJUB DOBROSAV, plant virologist, educator; b. Gornja Mutnica-Paracin, Yugoslavia, Nov. 3, 1919; s. Dobrosav Jovan and Milja Zivko (Zivkovic) S.; Dipl. ing. Agr., U. Belgrade, 1949, Dipl. Biol., 1954, Ph.D. in Phytopathology, 1955; m. Marija Vuletic, Dec. 24, 1949; children—Miroslav, Branislava, Dragoslava. Mem. faculty U. Belgrade, 1949—, prof. plant pathology Faculty Agr., 1969—, head dept., 1970—; mem. Internat. Com. Coop. Fruit Tree Virus Research, 1973—. Recipient Hon.

Plaque, Faculty of Agr.; Medal of Republic with Silver Wreath. Mem. Phytopath. Soc. Yugoslavia (v.p. 1976), French Acad. Agr. Mem. Orthodox Ch. Author books, manuals, research publs. in field. Home: 5 Drziceva, 11000 Beograd Yugoslavia Office: 6 Nemanjina, 11081 Zemun Yugoslavia

SUTOJO, HERU, economist, educator; b. Krawang, West Java, Indonesia, July 13, 1932; s. Tjokrosoemarto and Komariah Mangundihardjo; m. Oemi Alfia, July 14, 1941; children: Muti Srihartati, Wati Endang Setyowati, Benny Raharjo. M of Bus. Econs., U. Indonesia, Jakarta, 1958; MS, U. Wis., 1962. Tchr. high sch. Taman Siswa, Jakarta, 1951-58; instr. econs. U. Indonesia, Jakarta, 1958-62, assoc. prof., sr. lectr. econs., 1962—, head dept. mgmt., 1981-83, vice dean Sch. Econs., 1983—, sr. cons. The Mgmt. Inst., 1969-87; chmn. bd. Jasa Raharja, Accident Ins. Co., Jakarta. Chief editor: Mgmt. Usahawan Indonesia, 1972-81, sr. editor, 1981—. Head dept. highter edn. Bur. Fin. and Logistics, Republic of Indonesia, 1962-67. Mem. Am. Mgmt. Assn., Am. Risk and Ins. Assn., Internat. Ins. Soc. (bd. govs. 1985-87), World Productivity Congress, Indonesia Economist Assn. Islam. Home: Rawasari Barat I No 2, Jakarta Indonesia

SUTTER, ELIZABETH HENBY (MRS. RICHARD A. SUTTER), civic leader, management company executive; b. St. Louis, May 15, 1912; d. William Hastings and Alvina (Steinbreder) Henby; A.B., Washington U., St. Louis, 1931; m. Richard A. Sutter, June 15, 1935; children—John Richard, Jane Elizabeth, Judith Ann (Mrs. William Hinrichs). Sec.-treas. Sutter Mgmt. Co., St. Louis, Sutter Clinic, St. Louis; v.p. Downtown Med. Bldg., Inc., St. Louis, until 1985. Chmn. com. on mental health AMA Aux., 1960-62, v.p., 1962-63, 64-64, pres. 1965-66, editor Direct Line newsletter, 1967-74; assoc. editor MD's Wife, 1973-80; mem. adv. bd. Deaconess Hosp. Sch. of Nursing, St. Louis; trustee John Burroughs Sch., 1958-61, v.p. 1959, devel. commn., 1960-61; mem. Historic Bldgs. Commn. St. Louis County, 1957—, chmn., 1973—; chmn. Com. for Preservation Children's Teeth; mem. planning bd. Health, Hosp. Health, Welfare Council Met. St. Louis, 1955-64; pres. Aux. Central States Soc. Indsl. Medicine and Surgery, 1960-61; pres. St. Louis County Med. Soc. Aux., 1948-49, Mo. Med. Soc. Aux., 1952-53; sec. St. Louis County Health and Hosp. Bd., 1956-61, chmn., 1961; bd. dirs. Am. Lung Assn. Eastern Mo., exec. com., 1956-85, v.p., 1960-61; pres. Tb and Health Soc. of St. Louis, 1962-65; adv. council vol. services Nat. Assn. Mental Health, 1962-64; bd. dirs. Am. Cancer Soc., St. Louis, exec. com., 1954-64; bd. dirs. Mental Health Assn. St. Louis, 1960-61; mem. Practical Nursing Edn. Council, chmn. exec. com., 1959-60; mem. AMA Council on Mental Health Planning for Nat. Conf. on Mental Health, 1961; mem. adv. com. on women in services Dept. Def., 1969-72, vice chmn., 1971; participant 24th ann. global strategy discussion U.S. Naval War Coll., 1972; bd. govs. Washington U. Alumni, 1970-71, 75—, vice chmn. 1979-80, chmn., 1980-81; trustee Washington U., 1979-81; pres. Washington U. Arts and Scis. Century Club, 1970-71; bd. dirs. St. Louis Conv. and Tourist Bur., 1975-83, sec., 1980-82; bd. dirs. Health Services Agy., 1975-82; mem. East West Gateway Coordinating Council Task Force on Historic Preservation, 1975-81, University City Historic Preservation Commn., 1977; bd. dirs. Whitney Beach III Assn., Longboat Key, Fla., 1984-87; del. Mo. Republican Conv., 1972, 76, 80, 84, del. Nat. Rep. Conv., 1984. Named 1 of 10 Women of Achievement in good citizen category St. Louis Globe-Democrat, 1961; Alumna of Yr., Gamma Phi Beta, St. Louis, 1966; recipient St. Louis County Med. Soc. award of merit, 1964; Disting. Alumni citation Washington U., 1968, Disting. Alumni Service citation, 1977; Life Style award Eastern Mo. chpt. Am. Lung Assn., 1982; Meritorious Service award Am. Park and Recreation Soc., 1985. Mem. Mo. Hist. Soc., St. Louis Symphony Soc., AMA Aux. (hon. life), Mo. Med. Aux. (hon. life), Met. St. Louis Med. Aux. (hon. life). Presbyterian. Endowed Richard A. and Betty H. Sutter Vis. Professorship in Occ. and Insdl. Medicine Washington U., St. Louis. Home: 7215 Greenway Dr Saint Louis MO 63130

SUTTER, HARVEY MACK, cons. engr.; b. Jennings, La., Oct. 5, 1906; s. Josiah Harvey and Effie Relief (Murray) S.; A.B., U. Wichita, 1932; m. Julia Genevieve Wright, Sept. 19, 1936; children—James Houston, Robert Mack, Julia Ann (Mrs. Richard D. Boyd), John Norman. Design and prodn. engr. Boeing Aircraft, Wichita, Kans., 1936-38; supr. arts, crafts and coop. activities Bur. Indian Affairs, U.S. Dept. of Interior, 1938-42, chief procurement br. Bur. of Reclamation, Washington, 1946-54, chief div. procurement and property mgmt., 1954-58; asst. to adminstr. Bonneville Power Adminstrn., 1958-61, asst. to chief engr., 1962-66; cons. engr., 1967—; analyst, chief prodn. service WPB, Denver, 1942-44; chief div. supply C.E., Denver, 1944-46. Mem. exec. bd. Portland area Boy Scouts Am. Recipient Silver Beaver award. Presbyterian. Mem. Nat., Western woodcarvers assns., Internat. Wood Collectors Soc. Club: Electric of Oreg. Author or co-author books and articles on woodcarving. Home: 3803 SE Carlton Portland OR 97202

SUTTLE, STEPHEN HUNGATE, lawyer; b. Uvalde, Tex., Mar. 17, 1940; s. Dorwin Wallace and Ann Elizabeth (Barrett) S.; m. Rosemary Williams Davison, Aug. 3, 1963; children—Michael Barrett, David Paull, John Stewart. B.A., Washington and Lee U., 1962; LL.B., U. Tex., 1965. Bar: Tex. 1965, U.S. Dist. Ct. (no. and we. dists.) Tex. 1965, U.S. Ct. Appeals (5th cir.) 1967, U.S. Supreme Ct. 1970. Law clk. to presiding justice U.S. Dist. Ct., No. Dist. Tex., Ft. Worth, 1965-67; ptnr. McMahon, Smart, Surovik, Suttle, Buhrmann & Cobb, Abilene, Tex., 1970—. Pres. Abilene Boys Clubs, Inc., 1975-76; bd. dirs. Abilene Community Theater, 1979-80, Abilene Fine Arts Mus., 1977-78. Fellow Am. Coll. Trial Lawyers, Tex. Bar Found.; mem. Abilene Young Lawyers Assn. (outstanding young lawyer 1976), Tex. Young Lawyers Assn. (chmn. bd. dirs. 1973-76), Am. Judicature Soc. (bd. dirs. 1981-84), Abilene Bar Assn. (pres.), Tex. Bar Assn. (mem. coms. various sects.), ABA (chmn. young lawyers sect., award of merit 1976). Democrat. Episcopalian. Club: Abilene Country. Home: 1405 Woodland Trail Abilene TX 79605 Office: McMahon Smart Surovik Suttle Buhrmann & Cobb PO Box 3679 Abilene TX 79604

SUTTLE, WILLIAM WAYNE, lawyer, association executive; b. Marion, N.C., Dec. 4, 1933; s. Edgar Wayne and Ruth (Kincaid) S.; student U. N.C., 1952-55, LL.B., 1958; m. Mary Kyle Denton; children—William Eugene, John Reginald. Admitted to N.C. bar, 1958; individual practice, also solicitor County Criminal Ct. Marion, N.C., 1958-65; with N.C. Nat. Bank, Greensboro, 1965-66; pres. U.S. Jr. C. of C., 1966-67, chmn. bd., 1967-68; spl. asst. to dir. OEO, 1967-68, dir. S.E. region, Atlanta, 1968-70; exec. cons. U.S. Research and Devel. Corp., N.Y.C., 1970-72; counsel, v.p. Am. Ins. Assn., Atlanta, 1972-79, Washington, 1979-82, sr. v.p., 1982—. Bd. dirs. Contact Inc. Mem. Theta Chi, Delta Theta Phi. Democrat. Home: 2530-E S Arlington Mill Rd Arlington VA 22206 Office: 1130 Connecticut Ave NW Washington DC 20036

SUTTLES, DONALD ROLAND, educator, business consultant; b. Coldsprings, Ky., Nov. 14, 1929; s. Noah Elseworth and Bertha Viola (Seward) S.; m. Phyllis JoAnn McMullen, Dec. 12, 1952; children—Daniel, Ruth, Jonathan, Donna, Joanna, Stephen. Student U. Md., 1949-50, U.S. Naval Acad., 1951-52; BBA, U. Cin., 1959; MBA, Xavier U., 1966; Ed.D., U. N.C.-Greensboro, 1977. CPA, N.C.; cert. mgmt. acct.; cert. internal auditor. With Procter & Gamble Co., Cin., 1952-73, supr., 1959-60, indsl. engr., 1960-63, cost engr., 1963-64, mgr. prodn. planning, 1965-68, asst. security coordinator, 1968-70, dept. mgr., 1970-73; dir. bus. affairs Piedmont Bible Coll., Winston-Salem, N.C., 1973-80; assoc. prof. bus. Winston-Salem State U., 1978-87; prof. acctg. Catawba Coll., Salisbury, N.C., 1987—; also bus. cons. Deacon, tchr. Bible sch. Salem Bapt. Ch. Served with USAF, 1948-51. Mem. Am. Inst. CPA's, N.C. Assn. CPA's, Inst. Mgmt. Acctg., Inst. Cert. Mgmt. Accts., Inst. Internal Auditors. Republican. Home: 1715 Brewer Rd Winston-Salem NC 27127 Office: Catawba Coll Ralph W Ketner Sch Bus Salisbury NC 28144-2488

SUTTLES, VIRGINIA GRANT, advertising executive; b. Urbana, Ill., June 13, 1931; d. William Henry and Lenora (Fitzsimmons) Grant; student pub. schs., Mahomet, Ill.; m. John Henry Suttles, Sept. 24, 1977; step-children—Linda Suttles, Peg Suttles La Croix, Pamela Suttles Diaz, Randall. Media estimator and Procter & Gamble budget control Tatham-Laird, Inc., Chgo., 1955-60; media planner, supr. Tracy-Locke Co., Inc., Dallas and Denver, 1961-68; media dir., account exec. Lorie-Lotito, Inc., 1968-72; v.p., media dir. Sam Lusky Assos., Inc., Denver, 1972-86; ind. media buyer, 1984—; mktg. asst. mktg. dept. Del E. Webb Communities, Inc., Sun City West, Ariz., 1985—; lectr. sr. journalism class U. Colo., Boulder, 1975-80; condr. class in media seminars Denver Advt. Fedn., 1974, 77; Colo. State U. panelist Broadcast Day, 1978, High Sch. Inst., 1979, 80, 81, 82, 83. Founder, Del E. Webb Meml. Hosp. Found. Mem. Denver Advt. Fedn. (dir. 1973-75, 80-82, exec. bd., v.p. ops. 1980-81, chmn. Alfie awards com. 1980-81, advt. profl. of yr. 1981-82), Denver Advt. Golf Assn. (v.p. 1976-77, pres. 1977-78), Colo. Broadcasters Assn., Sun City West Bowling Assn. (bd. dirs. 1987—), Sun City West Women's Social Club. Republican. Congregationalist. Club: Denver Broncos Quarterback. Home: 21022 Sunglow Dr Sun City West AZ 85375 Office: First of Denver Plaza Bldg 633 17th St Suite 1616 Denver CO 80202

SUTTON, DOROTHY LOUISE, educator; b. Cherry Tree, Pa., Nov. 18, 1929; d. Paul and Viola Trudell (Leamer) S.; B.S. in Bus. Edn., Ind. State Coll., 1952; M.Ed., Pa. State U., 1956; postgrad. U. Colo., 1958, Pa. State U., 1964-65, Temple U., 1968, U. Pitts., 1970-72; m. William R. Ferencz, Dec. 28, 1946; 1 dau., Lucinda Kay Rollin. Tchr., Clarion-Limestone Joint High Sch., Strattonville, Pa., 1952-54; faculty Allegheny Coll., Meadville, Pa., 1954-61, Mohawk Valley Community Coll., Utica, N.Y., 1961-64; prof. secretarial sci. Harrisburg (Pa.) Area Community Coll., 1964-87, pres. faculty orgn., 1985-87, ret., 1987. Sec. bd. dirs. ARC, Meadville, 1956-61; mem. Harrisburg Nursing and Health Services Com., 1977-82. Mem. Exec. Women internat. (v.p. 1979-81, pres. 1981), Assn. Info. Systems Personnel (treas. 1981-82), Delta Pi Epsilon. Republican. Roman Catholic. Club: Soroptimist (pres. 1979-81). Home: 4301 Beaufort Hunt Dr Harrisburg PA 17110 Office: 3300 Cameron St Rd Harrisburg PA 17110

SUTTON, FREDERICK ISLER, JR., realtor; b. Greensboro, N.C., Sept. 13, 1916; s. Fred I. and Annie (Fry) S.; m. Helen Sykes Morrison, Mar. 18, 1941; children: Fred Isler III, Frank Morrison. Grad. Culver (Ind.) Mil. Acad., 1934; AB, U. N.C., 1939, student Law Sch., 1939-41. Lic. in real estate; cert. property mgr. Propr. Fred I. Sutton, Jr., realtor, Kinston, N.C., 1946—; comml. pilot, 1949—. Chmn. Kinston Parking Authority, Kinston Water Resources; pres. Lenoir County United Fund, 1969-70; trustee, dean U. N.C. Realtors Inst.; trustee Florence Crittenton Services; v.p. N.C. Real Estate Edn. Found.; deacon Presbyn. Ch. Served to lt. comdr. USNR, 1941-46. Named Kinston Realtor of Yr., 1963. Mem. Kinston Bd. Realtors (pres.), N.C. Bd. Realtors (v.p. 1957), N.C. Assn. Realtors (regional v.p., chmn. ednl. com., dir. Realtors Ednl. Found.), N.C. Assn. Real Estate Bds. (bd. dirs., v.p. 1958-60, 61, 63), Newcomen Soc., Am. Power Boat Assn. (7 Liter Hydroplane Nat. Champion 1951, Region 4 Champion 1976, 78-80, 82, Nat. High Point Champion 1982, Eastern Div. Champion 1982), U.S. Power Squadron (navigator, Kinston comdg. officer, adminstrv. officer dist. 27 1987), Kinston C. of C. (v.p.), SR. Lodges: Kiwanis (pres. Kinston chpt., bd. dirs.), Masons (32 deg.), Shriners, Elks. Home: 1101 N Queen St Kinston NC 28501 Office: Sutton Bldg PO Drawer 3309 Kinston NC 28501

SUTTON, JOHN EWING, judge, lawyer, accountant; b. San Angelo, Tex., Oct. 7, 1950; s. John F. Jr. and Nancy (Ewing) S.; m. Jean Ann Schofield, July 2, 1977; 1 son, Joshua Ewing; 1 stepson, Michael Brandon Ducote. B.B.A., U. Tex., 1973, J.D., 1976. Bar: Tex. 1976, U.S. Tax Ct. 1977, U.S. Ct. Claims, 1977, U.S. Dist. Ct. (no. dist.) Tex. 1977, U.S. Ct. Appeals (5th cir.) 1978, U.S. Dist. Ct. (we. dist.) Tex. 1979, U.S. Supreme Ct. 1980; C.P.A., Tex. With Daugherty, Kuperman & Golden, Austin, 1975-76; tax specialist Peat, Marwick, Mitchell & Co., CPA's, Dallas, 1976-77; ptnr. Shannon, Porter, Johnson, Sutton, and Greendyke Attys. at Law, San Angelo, Tex., 1977-87; judge 119th Dist. Ct. of Tex., 1987—. Treas. Good Shepherd Episcopal Ch., San Angelo, 1979-81; co-chmn. profl. div. United Way, San Angelo, 1980-82. Mem. ABA, Tex. Bar Assn., Tom Green County Bar Assn. (sec. treas. young lawyers 1977-78), Am. Inst. C.P.A.s, Tex. Soc. C.P.A.s (dir. 1980-87, pres. San Angelo chpt. 1980-81, mem. state exec. com. 1981-82, 86-87, state sec. 1986-87, chmn. profl. ethics com. 1985-86, Young CPA of Yr. 1984-85), Concho Valley Estate Planning Council (v.p. 1979-80, also dir.). Office: Tom Green County Courthouse San Angelo TX 76903

SUTTON, JOHN F., JR., law educator, university dean, lawyer; b. Alpine, Tex., Jan. 26, 1918; s. John F. and Pauline Irene (Elam) S.; m. Nancy Ewing, June 1, 1940; children: Joan Sutton Parr, John Ewing. J.D., U. Tex., 1941. Bar: Tex. 1941, U.S. Dist. Ct. (we. dist.) Tex. 1947, U.S. Ct. Appeals (5th cir.) 1951, U.S. Supreme Ct. 1960. Assoc. Brooks, Napier, Brown & Matthews, San Antonio, 1941-42; spl. agt. FBI, Washington, 1942-45; assoc. Matthews, Nowlin, Macfarlane & Barrett, San Antonio, 1945-48; ptnr. Kerr, Gayer & Sutton, San Angelo, Tex., 1948-50, Sutton, Steib & Barr, San Angelo, 1951-57; prof. U. Tex.-Austin, 1957-65, William Stamps Farish prof., 1965-84, A.W. Walker centennial chair, 1984—, dean Sch. Law, 1979-84. Editor: (with McCormick and Wellborn) Materials on Evidence, 6th edit., 1987; contbr. articles to profl. jours. Served to 1st lt. JAGC USAR, 1948-54. Fellow Am Bar Found., Tex. Bar Found. (life); mem. ABA (commn. on ethics 1970-76), State Bar Tex. (com. on rules of profl. conduct, com. adminstrn. rules of evidence), Order of Coif, Phi Delta Phi. Presbyterian. Clubs: Metropolitan, North Austin Rotary (pres. 1969), Lost Creek Country. Home: 11215 Research Blvd Austin TX 78759 also: 3830 Sunset Dr San Angelo TX 76904 Office: U Tex Law Sch 727 E 26th St Austin TX 78705

SUTTON, LEONARD VON BIBRA, lawyer; b. Colorado Springs, Colo., Dec. 21, 1914; s. Benjamin Edmund and Anne (von Bibra) S.; B.A., Colo. Coll., 1937; fellow Nat. Inst. Pub. Affairs, 1937-38; J.D., U. Denver, 1941; grad. Inf. Officers Sch., Ft. Benning, Ga., 1942; LLD (hon.) Colo. Coll., 1987. Bar: Colo. 1941, U.S. Supreme Ct., U.S. Tax Ct., Ct. of Claims, Customs Ct., U.S. Army Ct. Mil. Rev. Practiced law, Colorado Springs, 1941-42, 46-56; justice Colo. Supreme Ct., 1956-68, chief justice, 1960, 66; chmn. Fgn. Claims Settlement Commn. U.S., 1968-69; pvt. practice law, Denver and Washington, 1969—. Chmn. Colo. Statute Revision Com., 1964-67; del. various nat. and internat. bar assn. confs.; lectr.; past vice chmn. com. internat. cts. World Peace Through Law Commn.; past chmn. Colo. World Peace through Law Com., World Habeas Corpus Com.; hon. mem. N.J. World Trade Com., 1976—; mem. Colo. Democratic Central Com., 1948-56, mem. exec. com., 1948-58, chmn. rules com., 1955-56; del. Dem. Nat. Conv., 1952. Hon. trustee Inst. Internat. Edn., N.Y.C.; regent Dana Coll., Blair, Nebr., 1976-78; chmn. bd. govs. U. Denver, 1985—. Served from pvt. to capt., AUS, World War II. Recipient Grand Order of Merit Fed. Republic Germany, 1987. Mem. Colo. (Jr. Bar past chmn.), Internat., Inter-Am. (council), Am. (past chmn. com. on internat. cts., former mem. council sect. internat. law), Denver, D.C. bar assns., Mexican Acad. Internat. Law, Buenos Aires Bar Assn. (U.S. mem.), Am. Arbitration Assn., Washington Fgn. Law Soc. (pres. 1970-71, now hon. mem.), Royal Danish Guards Assn. Calif., Consular Law Soc. N.Y. (hon.), Phi Delta Phi. Episcopalian. Clubs: Wyoming One Shot Antelope Past Shooter's (pres. 1985-86); Colo. Harvard Bus. Sch. (assoc.); Masons, Shriners; Garden of Gods, Kissing Camels (Colorado Springs); Cosmos (Washington). Author: Constitution of Mexico, 1973. Contbr. articles on law, jud. adminstrn. and internat. relations to jours. Home: 3131 E Alameda Ave Apt 1908 Denver CO 80209

SUTTON, PAUL J., lawyer; b. N.Y.C., June 16, 1939; s. Jack and Frances (Drexler) Schwartzberg; m. Edith Diane Bers Sutton, Sept. 18, 1976; children: Daniel Richard, Lily Anna Bers. Student Indsl.Mgmt., Columbia U., 1960; student Welding Metallurgy, UCLA, 1963; BME, NYU, 1962; JD, Bklyn. U., 1967. Cer. Welder, Calif. Patent atty. Nolte & Nolte, N.Y.C., 1965-67, Darby & Darby, N.Y.C., 1967-69; patent counsel Gulf & Western Industries, Inc., N.Y.C., 1969-71; ptnr. Miskin & Sutton, N.Y.C., 1971-74, Sutton & Magidoff, N.Y.C., 1974-82; sr. ptnr. Sutton, Magidoff & Amaral, N.Y.C., 1982—. Author: Commercial Law, 1971; patentee telephone multidialing systems. Arbitrator civil court, City Of N.Y., 1979-86; co-founder Hallen Ctr. Edn., Mamaroneck, N.Y., 1975; chief judge Am. Patent Law Assn., N.Y.C., 1981. Mem. ABA (ethics and profl. responsibilities com., patent, trademark and copyright sect.), N.Y. Bar Assn. (antitrust law, patent and trademarks sects.), D.C. Bar Assn., Am. Intellectual Property Law Assn., N.Y. Patent, Trademark and Copyright Assn., Am. Judges Assn., Assn. Trial Lawyers Assn., Licensing Execs. Soc. Club: East Hampton, Yacht. Home: 300 Central Park West New York NY 10024 Office: Sutton Magidoff & Amaral 420 Lexington Ave New York NY 10170

SUTTON, RICHARD, cardiologist; b. Newport, Eng., Sept. 1, 1940; s. Dick Brasnett and Greta Mary (Leadbeter) S.; m. Anna Gunilla Cassö, Nov. 28, 1964; 1 child, Edmund. MBBS, U. London, 1964, DSc (Med), 1988. Registrar in cardiology St. George's Hosp., London, 1967-68; fellow in cardiology U. N.C., Chapel Hill, 1968-69; registrar, then sr. registrar Nat. Heart Hosp., London, 1970-76; cons. cardiologist Westminster and St. Stephen's Hosp., London, 1976—; hon. cons. cardiologist Italian Hosp., 1977—, S.W. Thames Regional Health, 1979—, St. Luke's Hosp., 1980—. Author: Foundations of Cardiac Pacing, 1988; contbr. chpt. to book, articles to med. jours. Fellow Royal Coll. Physicians, Am. Coll. Cardiology (Gov.'s award 1979, 82); mem. Brit. Med. Assn., Brit. Pacing and Electrophysiology group (co-founder, past sec., council mem.), Med. Research Soc., Royal Soc. Medicine. Anglican. Office: 149 Harley St, London W1N 1HG, England

SUTTON, TONY WAYNE, interior designer; b. Peoria, Ill., Oct. 3, 1955; s. Jerry Dean Sutton and Mary (Guylene) Rhodes; m. Tracey Lynn Matlick, Apr. 11, 1981; children: Alex Rhodes, Blake Rhodes. B in Interior Design, U. Ill., 1978. Interior designer Cen. Design Studio, Springfield, Ill., 1978-79, Est Est, Inc., Scottsdale, Ariz., 1980-84; pres., owner Est Est, Inc., Scottsdale, 1984—. Co-chmn. Scottsdale Culinary Festival, 1981, chmn., 1982; mem. Sick Kids Need Involved People; seminar host Southwestern Interior Design Phoenix Home and Garden mag.; bd. dirs Ctr. Arts Assn.; mem. Phoenix Zoo. Recipient Mame award Cen. Ariz. Sales and Mktg. Council, 1981. Mem. Men's League Scottsdale Ctr. for Arts (v.p. 1983, pres. 1984), Scottsdale Arts Ctr. Assn., Am. Cancer Soc., Ariz. C. of C., Phoenix C. of C., Scottsdale C. of C. Home: 5210 E Marconi Scottsdale AZ 85254 Office: Est Est Inc 7050 Main St Scottsdale AZ 85251

SUY, ERIK, law educator; b. Ghent, Belgium, Aug. 15, 1933; m. Ute Stenzel, Oct. 14, 1962; 1 child, Alexandra. JD, Ghent U., 1956; grad. Inst. Internat. Studies, Geneva, 1957; D of Polit. Sci., Geneva U., 1962. Prof. internat. law Leuven U., Belgium, 1963—; legal counsel UN, N.Y.C., 1974-83; dir. gen. UN Office, Geneva, 1983-87; advisor Office Minister External Affairs, Belguim, 1967-74; chief of cabinet, minister of external relations Regional Govt. Flanders, Belgium, 1987—. Author numerous books and articles. Mem. Inst. Internat. Law, Am. Soc. Internat. Law, Belgium Soc. Internat. Law, French Soc. Internat. Law, German Soc. Internat. Law, Mex. Acad. Internat. Law, Permanent Ct. Arbitration. Avocations: music, hiking, biking. Office: Law Sch, Tiense Str 41, 3000 Louvain Belgium

SUYDAM, PETER R., clinical engineer, consultant; b. Jersey City, Apr. 1, 1945; s. Stedman Mills and Winifred M. (Murphy) S.; m. Patricia Cunniff, Feb. 2, 1970 (dec. 1976); m. Jaimy Slifka, Feb. 11, 1978; children—Rycken Stedman, Stephen Michael. Student in engring. Rensselaer Poly. Inst.; student in pre-medicine, psychology, U. Rochester; B.S. in Bio-Engring., U. Ill.-Chgo., 1975. Cert. clin. engr.; cert. health care safety profl. Dir. clin. engring. Rush-Presbyn.-St. Luke's Med. Ctr., Chgo., 1975-81; pres. Syzygy, Inc., Chgo., 1978-81; lead auditor quality assurance Callaway Nuclear Power Plant, Union Elec. Co., St. Louis, 1981-84; sr. cons. Ellerbe Assocs., Inc., Mpls., 1984-86; div. mgr. CH Health Technologies, Inc., St. Louis, 1986—; staff cons. Joint Commn. on Accreditation for Hosps., Chgo., 1978-81; mem. tech. com. Safe Use of Electricity in Patient Care Areas of Health Care Facilities; mem. Bd. Examiners for Clin. Engring. Cert., 1980-85; com. mem. Midwest Med. Group Standards, Chgo. Hosp. Council, 1976-81. Contbr. articles to profl. jours. Served with USN, 1967-73. Mem. Assn. Advancement Med. Instrumentation (elec. safety com. 1980—), AAAS, IEEE (chpt. chmn. group on engring. in medicine and biology), Instrument Soc. Am., Am. Hosp. Assn., Nat. Space Inst., Nat. Fire Protection Assn. (health care, elec. and engring. sects.), Am. Soc. Hosp. Engrs., Am. Soc. Quality Control. Current work: Biotechnology applications in medicine and industry; quality assurance-all fields. Subspecialties: Biomedical engineering; Clinical engineering. Office: 11133 Dunn Rd Saint Louis MO 63136

SUYEMATSU, TOSHIRO, lawyer; b. Oakland, Calif., Aug. 27, 1918; s. Ben T. and Masa (Omaru) S.; m. Marina Franceschi, Sept. 30, 1945 (dec. 1950); m. Ellen Crowley, Apr. 30, 1954. B.A., U. Wyo., 1948, J.D., 1950. Bar: Wyo. 1951. Practiced in Laramie, Wyo., 1951-54, Cheyenne, Wyo., from 1954; mem. firm Suyematsu and Crowley, 1954-59, Miller, Suyematsu, Crowley, Duncan & Borthwick (and predecessor), from 1959; ct. apptd. U.S. atty. Wyo., 1977, 81. Legal chmn. Boy's State, 1951-52, Girl's State, 1953; govt. appeal agt. U.S. Selective Service; justice of peace, Cheyenne, 1957-58; chmn. Wyo. State Cancer Fund, 1952-54; sponsor Jr. Achievement; county treas. Republican Party, 1952; bd. dirs. Legal Services Laramie County. Served with AUS, 1941-46. Decorated Silver Star, Bronze Star, Purple Heart with cluster, Presl. Unit citation with 3 clusters; recipient Outstanding Performance award Dept. Justice, 1970, Dept. Justice dirs.' award, 1976. Mem. Wyo. Bar Assn., Cheyenne Bar Assn. (v.p. 1964, pres. 1966-67), UN Soc., Smithsonian Inst. Soc., Newcomen Soc. Club: Rotary. Office: PO Box 287 Cheyenne WY 82001

SUZMAN, JANET, actress; b. South Africa; BA, U. Witwatersrand, 1959; hon. degree Open U., 1984; m. Trevor Nunn, Oct. 17, 1969 (dec. 1986); 1 son. Leading roles with Royal Shakespeare Co. include Katharina in The Shrew, Beatrice in Much Ado about Nothing, Cleopatra in Antony and Cleopatra; TV roles include Viola in Twelfth Night, Joan in St. Joan, Clayhanger series, Robin Hood, Mountbatten Last Viceroy of India series, The Singing Detective Series; West End plays include Three Sisters, Hedda Gabler, Hello and Goodbye, The Greeks, Vassa, Andromache; films include Nicholas and Alexandra, Joe Egg, Nyjinsky, The Priest of Love., The Draughtsman's Contract, E La Nave Va. Directed Othello, South Africa and Chanel 4 TV. Recipient Best Actress award Evening Standard, 1973, 76, Plays and Players, 1976. Office: care William Morris (UK) Ltd, 31-32 Soho Sq, London W1, England

SUZUKI, BARNABAS TATSUYA, import/export manufacturing company executive; b. Hokkaido, Japan, Jan. 29, 1938; s. Mamoru and Hideko (Miura) S.; m. Tamiko Niwa, May 28, 1967; children: Lena, Mina. BL, Sophia (Jochi) U., Tokyo, 1963. Mgr. internat. div. Sanken Electric Co. Ltd., Tokyo, 1963-75; pres. TRANSTEKNE Internat. Inc., Tokyo, 1975—; rep. in Japan Airpax Corp., Cheshire, Conn., 1975—; bd. dirs. Sanken-Airpax Co. Ltd., Tokyo, Diesel kiki-Airpax Inc., Tokyo. Mem. The Pipe Club of Japan (sec. gen. internat.), Com. Internat. des Pipe Clubs (v.p.), Holland. Home: 9-17-11 Chiyoga-oka, Asawo-ku, Kawasaki 215, Japan Office: TRANSTEKNE Internat Inc, 405 Palm House, 1-20-2 Honmachi Shibuya-ku, Tokyo 151, Japan

SUZUKI, CHUMEI HIROAKI, advertising executive; b. Yokohama, Japan, Apr. 21, 1937; s. Takenosuke and Shizu Suzuki; m. Teruko Nakamoto, May, 1968; children: Kyoko, Takumi, Tasuku. BA, U. Tokyo, 1960; postgrad., Columbia U., 1965-66. Copywriter Hakuhodo Inc., Tokyo, 1960-65, creative dir., 1966-72, mgr. edn. and tng., 1973-77, mgr. account devel., 1980—; creative dir. McCann Erickson Hakuhodo, Tokyo, 1977-80; mem. jury Internat. Advt. Film Festival, Venice, Italy, 1972, Cannes, France, 1973. Recipient numerous awards for creative works and advertisements. Mem. Tokyo Copywriters Club, Project Mgmt. Inst. Roman Catholic. Home: Green Heights B3-301, 5-2 Kajiwara, Kamakura 247, Japan Office: Hakuhodo Inc, 2-7-3 Marunouchi, Chiyoda-ku, Tokyo 100, Japan

SUZUKI, GENGO, banker; b. Mino-Kamo City, Japan, Feb. 11, 1904; s. Seijiro Suzuki and Sumi Kani; grad. Taihoku Coll. Commerce, 1925; M.A. in Econs., U. Wis., 1927; m. Hide Motoda, Dec. 29, 1929 (dec. May 1975); children—Tsutomu, Sunao; m. 2d, Toshi Toki, July 7, 1976. Instr., then prof. econs. Taihoku Coll. Commerce, Taihoku, Taiwan, 1930-45; prof. econs. Taiwan Nat. U., 1945-48; dep. fin. commr. Ministry Fin., Japan, 1949-51, fin. commr., 1951-57; E.E. and M.P., fin. minister Japanese Embassy, Washington, 1957-60; exec. dir. IMF and IBRD, 1960-66; spl. asst. to minister fgn. affairs, minister fin., 1960-66; auditor Bank of Japan, Tokyo, 1966-70; chmn. Associated Japanese Bank (Internat.) Ltd., London, 1970-79, bd. counselor, 1979-87. Adv. bd. Mekong Com. ECAFE, UN, 1968-75; chief fin. mission on Ryukyus Island, 1968-69; vice chmn. Japanese com. bus. and industry adv. com. OECD, Paris, 1974-75; mem. European Atlantic Group, London, 1971-85. Mem. Internat. C. of C. (mem. council 1974-85, mem. commn. on ethical practices 1976-78). Trustee, Internat. Christian U., Tokyo, 1968—; bd. govs., Atlantic Inst. for Internat. Affairs, Paris, 1972—; councilor The Atlantic Council of U.S., 1986—; mem. joint com. on remunerations of exec. dirs. and their alternatives IMF-IBRD, 1977; trustee Rikkyo Sch. in Eng. Trust, Rudgwick, Eng., 1972—; bd. dirs. Per Jacobsson Found., Washington, 1970—; trustee ICU Cambridge House (Eng.), 1981—. Episcopalian. Clubs: Chevy Chase (Washington); Takanodai Country (ChibaKen, Japan); Royal Automobile (London and Epsom.).

Home: 6301 Stevenson Ave Apt 717 Alexandria VA 22304 Home: 2-5-13 Nukui-Kitamachi, Koganei-Shi Tokyo 184, Japan

SUZUKI, ISAO, educational researcher; b. Iwate, Japan, Jan. 3, 1925; s. Shosichi and Yukiyo Suzuki; m. Fujiko Sato, Oct. 21, 1955; children: Susumu, Mariko. LLB, Tokyo U., 1953. With Ministry Edn., Sci. and Culture, Tokyo, 1953-83, head gen. affairs div., minister's secretariat, 1974-76, dep. dir.-gen. elem. and secondary edn. bur., 1976-77, dep. dir.-gen., minister's secretariat, 1977-80, dir.-gen., minister's secretariat, 1980-82, dir.-gen. elem. and secondary edn. bur., 1982-83; commr. Agy. Cultural Affairs, Tokyo, 1983-85; dir. gen. Nat. Inst. Ednl. Research, Tokyo, 1985—. Author: Gakko Keiei no tame no Horitsu Jyoshiki, 1975, Kyoiku Hoki no Riron to Jissai, 1976, (with others) Kyoiku Gyosei Ho, 1982. Mem. Japan Ednl. Adminstrn. Soc. Home: 1-5-44 Takanawa, Minato-ku, Tokyo 108, Japan Office: Nat Inst for Ednl Research, 6-5-22 Shimomeguro Meguroku, Tokyo Japan

SUZUKI, JON BYRON, periodontist, educator; b. San Antonio, July 22, 1947; s. George K. and Ruby (Kanaya) S. B.A. in Biology, Ill. Wesleyan U., 1968; Ph.D. magna cum laude in Microbiology, Ill. Inst. Tech., 1971; D.D.S. magna cum laude, Loyola U., 1978. Med. technologist Ill. Masonic Hosp. and Med. Ctr., Chgo., 1966-67; instr. lab. in histology and parasitology Ill. Wesleyan U., Bloomington, 1967-68; med. technologist Augustana Hosp., Chgo., 1968-69; research assoc., instr. microbiology Ill. Inst. Tech., Chgo., 1968-71; clin. research assoc. U. Chgo. Hosps., 1970-71; clin. microbiologist St. Luke's Hosp. Ctr., Columbia Coll., Physicians and Surgeons, N.Y.C., 1971-73; assoc. med. dir. Paramed. Tng. and Registry, Vancouver, B.C., Can., 1973-74; dir. clin. labs. Registry of Hawaii, 1973-74; chmn. clin. labs. edn. Kapiolani Community Coll., U. Hawaii, Honolulu, 1974; lectr. periodontics, oral pathology Loyola U. Med. Ctr., Maywood, Ill., 1974—; lectr. periodontics Northwestern U. Dental Sch., Chgo., 1982—; NIH research fellow depts. pathology and periodontics Ctr. for Research in Oral Biology, U. Wash.-Seattle, 1978-80; prof. dept. periodontics and microbiology U. Md. Coll. Dental Surgery, Balt., 1980—; assoc. prof. div. dentistry and oral and maxillofacial surgery The Johns Hopkins Med. Inst., Balt., 1982—; practice dentistry specializing in periodontics Balt., Md.; cons. Dentsply Internat., York, Pa., U.S. Army, Walter Reed Med. Ctr., Washington, USN, Nat. Naval Med. Command, Bethesda, The Nutra Sweet Co., Deerfield, Ill.; mem. Oral Biology/medicine study sect. NIH, Bethesda, 1985—; vis. scientist to Moscow State U., USSR, 1972, NASA, Houston; lectr. Internat. Congress Allergology, Tokyo, 1973; lab. dir. Hawaii Dept. Health. Author: Clinical Laboratory Methods for the Medical Assistant, 1974; mem. editorial bd. Am. Health Mag.; contbr. articles on research in microbiology, immunology and dentistry to sci. jours. Instr. water safety ARC, Honolulu, 1973—. Recipient Pres.'s medallion Loyola U., Chgo., 1977; named Alumnus of Yr., Wesleyan U., 1977. Fellow Acad. Dentistry Internat., Am Coll. Dentists, Am. Coll. Stomatognathic Surgeons; mem. Am. Acad. Periodontology (diplomate), Am. Inst. Biol. Scis., Internat. Soc. Biophysics, Internat. Soc. Endocrinologists, Ill. Acad. Sci. (chmn. microbiology session of 65th ann. meeting 1972), AAAS, ADA, Am. Internat. Assn. Dental Research (pres. Md. chpt.), Am. Acad. Microbiology (diplomate), AAUP, N.Y. Acad. Scis., Sigma XI, Omicron Kappa Upsilon (nat. pres.), Beta Beta Beta, Blue Key. Home: 1819 Thornton Ridge Rd Baltimore MD 21204 Office: Dept Periodontics/Microbiology U Md 666 W Baltimore St Baltimore MD 21201

SUZUKI, NORIYUKI, federal agency administrator; b. Kobe, Hyogo, Japan, June 27, 1923; s. Ginta and Kaoru (Hanaoka) S.; m. Fusae Miura, Sept. 10, 1945; children: Motoyuki, Keiko. LLB, Kwansei Gakuin U., 1946. Dir. Miura Trading Co. Ltd., Kobe, 1946-49; staff mem. Nihon Steamship Co. Ltd., Kobe, 1949-58; pres. Y. Miura Co. Ltd., Tokyo, 1958-64, R.J. Del Pan (Japan) K.K., Tokyo, 1964—. Home: 5-16-3 Okusawa, Setagaya-ku Tokyo Tokyo 158, Japan Office: R J Del Pan (Japan) KK, 1-6-3 Honcho Nihonbashi, Chuo-ku Tokyo 103, Japan

SUZUKI, SABUROSUKE, corporate executive; b. Aug. 24, 1922; married. Grad., Tohoku U., 1946. With Nomura Securities Co., Ltd., from 1949; chmn. Ajinomoto Co., Inc., Tokyo; pres. Hayama Marina, Inc.; vice chmn. Japan Foods Sanitary Assn.; bd. dirs. Daiichi Hotel K.K. Home: 1001 Motoakasaka, 1-chome Minato-ku, Tokyo 107, Japan Office: Ajinomoto Co Inc, 5-8 Kyobashi, 1-chome Chuo-ku, Tokyo Japan *

SUZUKI, TATEYUKI, scientist, engineering educator; b. Kawagoe, Saitama, Japan, Apr. 28, 1945; s. Sentaro and Michiyo (Akiyama) S.; m. Kumiko Takaichi, Aug. 23, 1982; children: Ayako, Tomoyuki. B.S. in Engring., U. Tokyo, 1968, M.S. in Engring., 1970, Dr.Eng., 1973. Research fellow dept. aeros. U. Tokyo, 1973-74; lectr. Toyo U., Kawagoe, Japan, 1974-76, lectr. U. Saitama, Urawa, Japan, 1974—; research assoc. NASA-Ames Research Center, Moffett Field, Calif., 1976-77; assoc. prof. dept. mechanics Saitama Inst. Tech., Okabe, Japan, 1978-85, prof. gas dynamics, 1985—; dean., 1988— Author: Characteristics of a Blast Wave over Dust Deposit, 1982; co-editor: Comb. Explosion of Pulverized Coal, 1983; contbr. articles to profl. jours. Recipient research prizes Japan Pvt. Sch. Promotion Found., 1981, 82, 83; recipient research prizes Japan Securities Found., 1982, 88. Mem. Japan Soc. Heat Fluid Engring. (dir. 1985—), Kanto Inst. Engring. Edn., AIAA, Japan Soc. Mech. Engring. Buddhist. Home: 15-12 Minami-Torimachi, Kawagoe 350, Japan Office: Saitama Inst Tech, 1690 Fusaiji, Okabe 369 02, Japan

SUZUKI, TOSHIO, publishing executive; b. Tokyo, May 26, 1926; children—Ichiro, Chiyoko. Student Hosei U., Tokyo, 1942-46. Prodn. mgr. Time-Life Internat., Tokyo, 1946-59; prodn. mgr. and Tokyo office mgr. Asia Mags. Ltd., Hong Kong, 1960-71; pres. Japan Communications Ltd., Tokyo, 1971—, Incom Co., Ltd., Tokyo, 1972—. Mem. Butler council Marymount Coll., Tarrytown, N.Y. Fellow Japan Internat. Advt. Assn.; mem. Japan Fgn. Correspondent Club (assoc.). Buddhist. Home: 1-6-23 301 Sengoku, Bunkyo-ku, Tokyo 112, Japan Office: Incom Co Ltd, 1-23-6 Sekiguchi Bunkyo-ku, Tokyo 112, Japan

SUZUKI, YOSHIO, engineering and construction company executive; b. Kanagawa, Japan, Oct. 3, 1910; s. Chuji and Masu Suzuki; LL.B., Imperial U. Tokyo, 1933; m. Shigeko Saneyoshi, Oct. 19, 1936; children—Akiko Miyajima, Noriko Harada. With Ministry Commerce and Industry, 1933-52, comml. counsellor Japanese embassy to U.K., 1952-54; dir. heavy industry bur. Ministry Internat. Trade and Industry, 1954-57; dir. Export-Import Bank Japan, 1957-61; rep. dir., pres. JGC Corp., Tokyo, 1966-80, rep. dir., chmn. bd., 1980-88, dir., mem. exec. com., 1988—; rep. dir. Nikki-Universal Co., Ltd., 1967-85; mem. adv. group energy Agy. Natural Resources and Energy, 1978-83; commr. indsl. structure council Ministry Internat. Trade and Industry, 1980—; mem. Japanese Nat. Com., World Petroleum Congress, 1967-88. Decorated officer Legion of Honor (France); 2d Order of Sacred Treasure (Japan), Commandeur De l'Ordre De Léopold (Belgium). Mem. Fedn. Econ. Orgns. (councillor, 1967-88), Japan Petroleum Inst. (trustee, 1968-88), Japan Atomic Indsl. Forum (mng. dir.), Engring. Advancement Assn. Japan (pres. 1981-85). Club: Tokyo Rotary. Office: JGC Corp, 2-1 Ohtemachi 2-chome, Chiyoda-ku, Tokyo 100 Japan

SUZUKI, YOSHIO, banker; b. Tokyo, Oct. 12, 1931; s. Ichihei and Misako Suzuki; m. Yukiko Suzuki, Jan. 11, 1959; children—Yumiko, Kenta, Morio, Yuzo. Bachelor, Tokyo U., 1955, D.Econs., 1976. With Bank of Japan, Tokyo, 1955—, mgr. Matsumoto br., 1977-79, dep. dir. Inst. for Monetary and Econ. Studies, 1982-84, dir. inst., 1984-88, exec. dir. Bank of Japan, 1988—; vis. lectr. Tokyo U., 1972-73, Shinshu U., Matsumoto, Japan, 1978-79; mem. Japanese Govt. Tax Research Com., 1984—, Exam. Com. of Security Analysts, 1981—. Author: Effects of Monetary Policy (Nikkei Cultural prize for econ. lit. 1967), 1966; Money and Banking in Contemporary Japan (Economist's prize Mainichi Newspaper Co., Tokyo 1975), 1974; Monetary Economics in Contemporary Japan, 1983; Financial Deregulation and Monetary Policy, 1985; Money, Finance, and Macroeconomic Performance in Japan, 1986, Japan's Economy and Finance in a Changing World, 1987, The Japanese Financial System, 1988. Mem. Mont Pelerin Soc. (bd. dirs.), Japan Assn. Econs. and Econometrics, Forum for Policy Innovation, Japan Spl. Libraries Assn. (nat. bd. dirs. 1984—, Kanto dist. bd. dirs. 1984—). Club: Mangijo Country (Kanto dist.). Lodge: Economist Village. Home: 2-5-8 Kamitakaido, Suginami-ku, Tokyo 168, Japan Office: Bank of Japan, 2-2-1 Hongoku-cho, Nihonbashi Chuo-ku, Tokyo 103, Japan

SUZUKI, ZENKO, former prime minister of Japan; b. Yamada, Honshu, Japan, Jan. 11, 1911; ed. Fishery Tng. Inst., Ministry of Agr. and Forestry; m. Sachi, 1939; children—Shun'ichi, Motoko, Kazue, Chikako. Mem. Japanese Ho. of Reps., from 1947; mem. Socialist Party, 1947-49; mem. Liberal Party, 1949-55; mem. Liberal Dem. Party, 1955—, chmn. exec. council, 1968-82, pres., 1982; minister posts and telecommunications, 1960; minister health and welfare, 1965-67, minister agr. and forestry, 1976-77; prime minister of Japan, 1980-82. Office: care Liberal Democratic Party, 7, 2-chome, Hirakawacho, Chi yoda-ku, Tokyo Japan *

SVANHOLM, JOHN WILHELM, mining executive, mineral deposits authority; b. Stockholm, Sweden, Jan. 26, 1908; s. John August and Anna (Johanson) S.; m. Linda Manzanillo, Sept. 6, 1952; children—Ann-Marie Svanholm Cahuzac, John Lennart. Student Chalmers Tech. Inst., 1925-27; Engring. Diploma, State Tech. Inst. Vasteros, Sweden, 1931; postgrad. Stockholm U., 1953-54, 58, 59. Geophysicist A.B. Elektrisk Malmletning, Stockholm, 1933-35; assignment engr. (Germany, Romania, Yugoslavia), cons. geologist, mine mgr. Atlantic Gulf Pacific Co., Marinduque Iron Mines, Manila, Philippines, 1937-40; designer Pacific Naval Airbases Contractors, Cavite, Philippines, 1941; asst. chief geologist and chief engr. Benguet Consolidated Mining Co., Balatoc and Benguet Gold Mines Baguio, Philippines, 1951-52; tech. advisor Mineral Resources Corp., Rangoon, Burma, 1954-58, UN, N.Y.C., 1959-78; v.p., gen. mgr. Natural Resources Devel. Ltd., Tegucigalpa, 1983—; tech. advisor Govt. Burma, Rangoon, 1954-58, Internat. Atomic Energy Agy., Vienna, 1959-60, UN.D.P., N.Y.C., 1965-66, U.S. AID, Washington, 1973, UN Spl. Fund, 1966-78; mining engring. cons. Govt. of Honduras, 1968-79; presented papers on gold and uranium in Honduras Geol. Congresses in Cen. Am., 1976. Contbr. articles to profl. jours. Mem. Geol. Soc. Stockholm, AIME, Soc. Exploration Geophysicists. Lutheran. Home: Edificio Hasbun, 501 La Leona, Tegucigalpa DC Honduras Office: Natural Resources Devel Ltd, (Derena), Apartado 884, Tegucigalpa DC Honduras

SVANVIK, JOAR BO, surgeon, scientist; b. Kungsbacka, Halland, Sweden, Mar. 8, 1942; s. Ake Natanael and Marta Kerstin (Andersson) S.; m. Christina Anna Maria Staaf, Nov. 23, 1968; children—Nicklas, Robin, Anna. M.D., U. Gothenburg, Sweden, 1973, Ph.D., 1973. Resident Sahlgrens Hosp., Gothenburg, 1973-78; fellow U. Calif.-San Francisco, 1978-79; assoc. prof. surgery U. Gothenburg, 1979—. Editor: The Treatment of Ureteral Colic and Biliary Pain, 1982. Contbr. articles to med. jours., chpts. to books. Recipient research award Scandinavian Gastroenterol. Assn., 1984; NIH Internat. research fellow, 1978. Mem. Swedish Coll. Surgeons, Swedish Med. Assn., Soc. Surgery of the Alimentary Tract. Avocation: yachting. Home: Langasliden 16, 412 70 Gothenburg Sweden Office: Sahlgrens Hosp Dept Surgery, 413 45 Gothenburg Sweden

SVEBAK, SVEN EGIL, psychology educator; b. Verdal, Middle Norway, Norway, Dec. 17, 1941; s. Hans Georg and Dagny (Strand) S.; m. Randi Myrseth, Apr. 2, 1971; children: Annette, Teresa. Grad. in Psychology, U. Oslo (Norway), 1970; D in Philosophy, U. Bergen, Norway, 1982. Lic. Psychologist. Instr. of psychology U. Oslo, 1967-68; research asst. U. Bergen, 1968-70, asst. prof., 1970-76, assoc. prof., 1976—; vis. prof. Queens U. of Belfast, No. Ireland, 1987; lectr. of Behavioral Medicine Physiotherapy Coll. of Bergen, 1977—; cons. in Archtl. Design CUBUS A/S, 1970—. Editor: Psychological Service Armed Forces, 1986; assoc. editor Internat. Jour. of Psychophysiology, 1983—; contbr. articles to profl. jours. Recipient numerous research grants, 1972—. Mem. Soc. for Psychophysiological Research, Psychophysiology Soc., Internat. Orgn. of Psychophysiology, Reversal Theory Soc., Internat. Soc. for the Study of Individual Differences. Office: Dept of Somatic Psychology, U Bergen, Arstadveien 21, N-5009 Bergen Norway

SVEDA, MICHAEL, scientist, management and research consultant; b. W. Ashford, Conn., Feb. 3, 1912; s. Michael and Dorothy (Druppa) S.; m. Martha Augusta Gaeth, Aug. 23, 1936; children—Sally Anne, Michael Max. B.S., U. Toledo, 1934; Ph.D. (Eli Lilly research fellow), U. Ill., 1939. Tchr. chemistry U. Toledo, 1932-35, U. Ill., 1935-37; research, sales and product mgmt. positions E.I. du Pont de Nemours & Co., Inc., 1939-54; mgmt. counsel Wilmington, Del., 1955-59; dir. acad. sci. projects NSF, 1960-61; corp. assoc. dir. research FMC Corp., 1962-64; mgmt. and research counsel to academia, industry and govt. 1965—; lectr. univs., 1961—, fed. govt., groups, 1965—; mem. adv. com. on creativity in scientists and engrs. Rensselaer Poly. Inst., 1965—. Numerous appearances on pub. and comml. TV and radio. Named Outstanding Alumnus U. Toledo, 1954. Mem. Am. Chem. Soc., AAAS, Sigma Xi, Phi Kappa Phi, Alpha Chi Sigma, Phi Lambda Upsilon. Home: West Ln Revonah Woods Stamford CT 06905 Office: PO Box 3086 Stamford CT 06905

SVEDBERG, BJORN MAGNUS IVAR, communications company executive; b. Stockholm, July 4, 1937; s. Inge and Anna-Lisa (Lundstrom) S.; m. Gunnel Richardsdotter Nilsson, June 21, 1960; children—Camilla, Nina, Oscar, Rickard. M.S., Royal Inst. Tech., Stockholm, 1962; postgrad. U. Lausanne (Switzerland), 1972. With Telefonaktiebolaget L.M. Ericsson, Stockholm, 1962—, dept. mgr., 1970-72, chief engr., 1972-76, sr. v.p. research and devel., 1976-77, pres., 1977—; chmn. bd. Ellemtel Devel. Co., Ericsson Info. Systems AB, Ericsson Corp. U.S.A.; dir. LM Ericsson Telephone Co., AB Rifa, Ericsson Radio Systems AB, LM Ericsson Pty. Ltd., Australia, Compania Argentina de Telefonos S.A., Compania Entrerriana de Telefonos S.A., Argentina, Ericsson do Brasil Comercio Industria, SETEMER, Italy, Ericsson Inc., U.S.A. Bd. dirs. Fedn. Swedish Industries. Mem. Royal Swedish Acad. Engring. Scis., Swedish Acad. Scis. (assembly rep.). Home: Klovervagen 5, 161 36 Bromma Sweden Office: L M Ericsson Telefonplan, 126 25 Shockholm Sweden

SVEINAR, SVERRE, management consultant; b. Engerdal, Norway, Dec. 16, 1934; s. Bjarne and Astrid (Grindal) S.; m. Randi Aak, Mar. 14, 1935; children: Dag Aak, Snorre. BSBA, U. Minn., 1961. Machine operator Bur. Stats. in Norway, Oslo, 1956-57; programmer Archer Daniels Midland Co., Mpls., 1957-62; corp. data exec. Joh Johannson, Oslo, 1963-87; pres. Sverre Sveinar Systems, Asker, Norway, 1987—. Editor Kontakt mag., 1979—. Scoutmaster Gilwell council Internat. Boy Scouts, Asker, 1967—. Served to cpl. Norwegian Air Force, 1954-56. Mem. Norwegian Data Assn. (bd. dirs. 1968-72, bd. mem. point of sales com. 1985—), Internat. Assn. European Article Numbering (mem. ad-hoc com. Oslo chpt. 1974-86), Nat. Retail Mcht. Assn., Norwegian Polyteknisk Forening. Conservative. Lutheran. Clubs: Kjekstad Golf (Røyken, Norway); Asker (Norway) Tennis. Lodge: Gildespeiderne. Home: Grevlingåsen 30, 1370 Asker Norway Office: Sverre Sveinar Systems, Boks 219 Solstadlia 35, 1364 Hvalstad, Asker Norway

SVENBRO, JESPER, historian, educator; b. Landskrona, Sweden, Mar. 10, 1944; arrived in France, 1974; s. Werner and Ulla (Holmkvist) S.; m. Yvonne R. Llavador, Apr. 28, 1973; children: Anna Rosario, Francois Carl. Student, Yale U., 1969-70, Ecole Pratique, 1974-77; PhD in Classics, U. Lund, Sweden, 1977. Assoc. research fellow Swedish Inst. Rome, 1973-77; assoc. research fellow Nat. Ctr. Sci. Research, Paris, 1977-78, asst. research fellow, 1982-86, research fellow, 1986—; asst. Coll. France, Paris, 1978-80, Ecole Pratique, Paris, 1980-82. Author: (poems) Sarimner, 1984, others; (essays) La parola e il marmo, 1984, Phrasikleia, 1988; translator: (poems) F. Ponge, Ur Tingens Synpunkt, 1977; contbr. articles to profl. jours. Recipient Poetry prize Swedish Acad., 1979, 85. Mem. Ctr. Comparative Research Ancient Socs. Office: CRCSA, 10 Rue Monsieur-le-Prince, 75006 Paris France

SVENDSEN, ARNLJOT STRØMME, economist, educator; b. Oslo, Norway, Dec. 5, 1921; s. Ole A. Strømme and Dagmar (Baerem) S.; m. Bertha Ingunn Nygaard; children: Bergljot, Dagmar Terese. Degree in econs., U. Oslo, 1946. With Bank of Norway, Oslo, 1947-48, dep. bd. dirs., 1963-71; asst. prof. econs. The Norway Sch. Econs. and Bus. Adminstrn., Bergen, 1948-56, assoc., 1956-66, prof. maritime econs., 1966—, dir. inst., 1958—; mem. Nat. Ct. of Arbitration, Oslo, 1966-74; chmn. Internat. Adv. Group on Maritime Stats., 1970—; chmn. bd. dirs. Den Norske Credit Bank, Bergen, 1971—, Trajan Shipping Co., Bergen, 1976—, Hadrian Shipping Co., Bergen, 1976—. Author: Sea Transport and Shipping Economics, 1958, Trade Follow the Airlines, 1973. Chmn. bd. dirs. Theatre of Bergen, 1960—; chmn. Conservative Party, Bergen, 1967-71; dep. Norwegian Parliament, Oslo, 1973-77. Recipient Colombian Gold medal Comune di Genova, Italy, 1980. Mem. Assn. for Cultural Econs. Lodge: Order of St. Olaf (Knight 1973). Home: Endregaardsveien 3A, N 5019 Bergen Norway Office: Norwegian Sch Econs and Bus Adminstrn, Helleveien 30, N 5035 Bergen Norway

SVENSEN, BJORN, communications executive; b. Oslo, Oct. 28, 1949; s. Knut K. and Liv (Werner-Hansen) S.; m. Liv Almestad, Aug. 25, 1977 (div. 1984). Diploma, Inst. Mktg., 1969, Norwegian Bus. Mgmt. U., Oslo, 1977. Cons. Norwegian Trade Fair Orgn., Oslo, 1970-73; pub. relations officer Elkem A/S, Oslo, 1973-76; v.p. corp. communications Narvesen A/S, Oslo, 1976-80, Bergen (Norway) Bank, 1980-86, Kosmos Group, Sandefjord, Norway, 1986—. Chmn. Rover council Norwegian Boy Scouts Assn., 1972-76, internat. commr., 1976-77; mem. camp com., del. XIV World Boy Scouts Jamboree, Lillehammer, 1975. Recipient White Lilly award Norwegian Boy Scouts Assn., 1975, White Lilly award Danish Scout Assn., 1976, White Lilly award Finnish Scout Assn., 1976. Mem. Internat. Pub. Relations Assn. (nat. coordinator, council mem.), Norwegian Pub. Relations Assn. (pres. 1984-86). Home: Fjelltun Fjaerholmvn 31, 3132 Husoysund Norway Office: Kosmos Group, Strandpromenaden 9, 3200 Sandefjord Norway

SVENSON, CHARLES OSCAR, investment banker; b. Worcester, Mass., June 28, 1939; s. Sven Oscar and Edahjane (Castner) S.; m. Sara Ellen Simpson, Nov. 15, 1968; children: Alicia Lindall, Tait Oscar. A.B., Hamilton Coll., 1961; LL.B., Harvard U., 1964; LL.M., Bklyn. Law Sch., 1965. Bar: N.Y. 1965, U.S. Dist. Ct. (so. dist.) N.Y. 1965, U.S. Ct. Appeals (2d. cir.) 1965. Atty. Dewey, Ballantine, Bushby, Palmer & Wood, N.Y.C., 1964-68; v.p. Goldman Sachs & Co., N.Y.C., 1968-75; sr. v.p. Donaldson, Lufkin & Jenrette, N.Y.C, 1975—. Trustee Kirkland Coll., Clinton, N.Y., 1976-78; trustee Hamilton Coll., Clinton, 1979-83. Mem. ABA, N.Y. State Bar Assn., Assn. of Bar of City of N.Y. Clubs: Tuxedo (Tuxedo Park, N.Y.); Harvard (N.Y.C.). Home: 1185 Park Ave New York NY 10128 Office: Donaldson Lufkin & Jenrette 140 Broadway New York NY 10005

SVENSSON, JEAN HARALD YNGVE, management consultant; b. Molndal, Sweden, Apr. 2, 1917; s. Sven Harald and Anna Kristina (Persson) S.; m. Feb. 3, 1940; children: Per-Goran Orwall, Hakan Jenestrand. Engr., Chalmers Sch., Gothenburg, Sweden, 1937. Mgr. indsl. engring. co. Stockholm, 1940-48; sec. Engring. Employers Assn., Stockholm, 1948-66; dir. Swedish Employers Confedn., Stockholm, 1966-82, ret., 1982; owner, mgr. Yngve Svensson Mgmt. Service, Stockholm, 1983—; chmn. European Fedn. Productivity Services, 1960-64; lectr. on small bus. mgmt. in developing countries and Europe, 1971—, also mem. missions with ILO, others. Home and Office: Ynglingagatan 19, 113 47 Stockholm Sweden

SVENSSON, TORGNY H(ANS), pharmacologist, educator; b. Gothenburg, Sweden, May 13, 1945; s. Harry and Gunhild I. (Andersson) S.; m. Louise H. Linden, July 25, 1970; children: Martin H., Jenny E., Michael J. B.Medicine, U. Gothenburg, 1966, M.D., Ph.D., 1972. Postdoctoral fellow Yale U., New Haven, 1973-74; asst. prof. pharmacology Dept. Pharmacology, U. Gothenburg (Sweden), 1975-78, assoc. prof., 1978-83, prof. pharmacology Karolinska Inst., Stockholm, 1983—; vis. scientist The Salk Inst., LaJolla, Calif., 1981-82; cons. Astra Ltd., Södertalje, 1981—; adv. editor Archives of Pharmacology, Heidelberg, 1980—. Contbr. articles to profl. jours.; editor: Biogenic Amines and Affective Disorder, 1979; Recent Advances in the Treatment of Depression, 1981. Recipient Konrad and Helfrid Johansson's award for Med. Research, 1968, 69, 70; James Hudson Brown fellow, 1973-74. Mem. Swedish Med. Assn., Scandinavian Soc. Psychopharmacology, Soc. for Neurosci., Swedish Pharmacol. Soc. Liberal. Home: Ringvagen 9, Lidingo, 181 33 Stockholm Sweden Office: Karolinska Inst Dept Pharmacology, Box 60 400, 101 01 Stockholm Sweden

SVERDRUP, CATO FREDRIK, architect; b. Oslo, May 25, 1935; s. Cato A. and Ulla Johanne (Mathiesen) S.; m. Gun Ingalill Roth, Mar. 3, 1963; children: Carl Fredrik, Ulla Annette. BS in Naval Architecture and Marine Engring., MIT, 1958. Naval architect Burmeister & Wain Skibsvaerft A/S, Copenhagen, 1960-70, tech. dir., 1971-80, pres., 1980—; bd. dirs. MAN-B&W Diesel A/S, Copenhagen, Rasmussen & Schiøtz, Copenhagen. Bd. dirs. Elsinore (Denmark) Tech. Sch., 1974-78. Mem. Am. Bur. Shipping (Scandinavian com.), Soc. Naval Architects. Home: Vilvordevej 90, 2920 Charlottenlund Denmark Office: Burmeister & Wain Skibsvaerft A/S, Refshaleoen PO Box 2122, 1015 Copenhagen Denmark

SVETLANOV, YEVGENIY FYODOROVICH, composer, conductor; b. Moscow, Sept. 6, 1928. Student, Gnesiny Music Edn. Inst., USSR, Moscow Conservatoire. Asst. conductor Moscow Radio, 1954; conductor Bolshoi Theatre, Moscow, 1955-63; chief conductor Bolshoi Theatre, 1963-65; prin. conductor USSR State Symphony Orchestra, 1965—; prin. guest conductor London Symphony Orchestra, 1979—. Compositions include Preludes, 1945-51, Cantata Home Fields, 1949, Symphony, Tone-Poems Festival, 1950, Concerto, 1951, Daugava, 1953, Siberian Fantasy, 1953, Rhapsody, 1954, five Sonatas, 1946-52, five Sonatinas, 1946-51, Symphony, 1957, Beautiful Kalina, 1975; conductor Rusalka, Pskovityanka, The Czar's Bride, Sadko, Snow-Maiden, Prince Igor, The Sorceress, Not Only Love, Boris Godunov, October, Storm Along the Path, Paganini, Swan Lake, Night Town, Pages of Life, Chopiniana. Decorated Order of Lenin, 1975; named People's Artist of R.S.F.S.R. of USSR, 1968; recipient Lenin prize, 1972, Grand Prix (France), 1975, State Glinka prize, 1975, State prize in Music, 1983, other awards. Office: USSR State Symphony Orch, 31 Ulitsa Gorkogo, Moscow USSR *

SVIRSKY, ZIN, electrical contractor company manager; b. Krivoy Rog, Ukraine, USSR, Aug. 25, 1935. Project mgr. Electromontage-1, Lvov, USSR, 1960-63, Moldelectromontage, Kishinev, USSR, 1968-76, Newberry Energy Ltd., Edmonton, Can., 1977-81; constrn. mgr. State Contractors Inc., Edmonton, 1982-84, div. mgr., 1984-87; div. mgr. Toronto, Can., 1987—; pres. ZS Engring. Ltd., Edmonton, 1980-84. Mem. Assn. Profl. Engrs. Ontario, Assn. Profl. Engrs. Alta., Project Mgmt. Inst. Home: 133 Stillwater Cr, Willowdale, ON Canada M2R 3S3 Office: State Contractors Inc, 74 Martin Ross Ave, Downsview, ON Canada M3J 2L4

SVOBODA, ANGELA MAE, educator; b. Central City, Iowa, Apr. 10, 1929; d. Frank Joseph and Ann Marie (Vrba) S. Student Coe Coll., 1953-55; B.S. in Commerce, U. Iowa, 1956; M.S. in Edn., U. Mich., 1961; postgrad. U. No. Iowa, U. Iowa, Coe Coll., Appalachian State U. Exec. sec. I.O.A. Foods, Cedar Rapids, Iowa, 1947-53; departmental asst. to head bus. edn. dept. Coe Coll., Cedar Rapids, 1954-55; bus. tchr. Burlington (Iowa) Sr. High Sch., 1956-59; bus. tchr., office edn. coordinator Washington Sr. High Sch., Cedar Rapids, 1959—; public speaker. Mem. Iowa Office Edn. Assn., Iowa Vocat. Edn. Assn., Am. Vocat. Assn., Iowa Bus. Edn. Assn., Cedar Rapids Edn. Assn., Iowa State Edn. Assn., NEA (life), U. Iowa Alumni Assn. (life), Cedar Rapids Edn. Assn. (sec.), Profl. Secs. Inc., Daus. of Isabella (past pres. Cedar Rapids, past state v.p.), Czech Heritage Found., Pi Omega Pi, Delta Pi Epsilon, Delta Kappa Gamma. Democrat. Roman Catholic. Club: Quota (1st v.p. Cedar Rapids 1976-77, sec.-treas. dist. 7, 1975-76). Home: 4280 Cottage Pkwy SE Cedar Rapids IA 52403 Office: 2205 Forest Dr SE Cedar Rapids IA 52403

SVOBODA, JOANNE DZITKO, artist, educator; b. Jersey City, Dec. 24, 1948; d. John Richard and Joanna Frances (Rygiel) Dzitko; student Parsons Sch. Design, 1966, Kean Coll., 1970; B.A., Jersey City State Coll., 1970, M.A., 1975; postgrad. Tchrs. Coll., Columbia U., 1972; m. Peter W. Svoboda, Sept. 3, 1972; children—Kimberly Anne, Lauren Anne. Art tchr. YMCA, Jersey City, 1966-70, Henry Snyder High Sch., Jersey City, 1970-80; propr., craftsman, instr. Mountain Designers and Craftsmen, Long Valley, N.J., 1977-80; partner, craftsman, instr. Four Seasons Crafts, Chester and Long Valley, 1978-85; designer, estimator, v.p. Estate Contracting Inc., Long Valley, 1978—; tng. specialist Johnson & Johnson Baby Products, Skillman, N.J., 1984—; instr. interior design Jersey City Bd. Continuing Edn., 1974. Trustee, Jersey City Mus. Assn., 1973-79, chmn. fine arts dept., 1972-79; mem. curriculum revision com. Jersey City Bd. Edn., 1976; judge Distributive Edn. Clubs N.J., 1976, 77, 78; mem. Washington Twp. Shade Tree Commn., 1979-81, chmn., 1981; mem. Washington Twp. Hist. Heritage Commn., 1981-85, Washington Twp. Friends of the Library; publicity chmn. Washington Twp. Hist. Soc., 1980-81; mem. choir Our Lady of the Mountain Cath. Ch. Grantee, N.J. State Dept. Edn., 1973; awards N.J. Fedn. Jr. Woman's Clubs: black and white photography, 1979, crafts, 1979, 1st place color photography, 1980, free form, 1981. Mem. Am. Soc. Interior

Designers (affiliate), Federated Art Assn. N.J., Art Educators N.J., N.J. Designer Craftsmen. Democrat. Exhibited Courtney Gallery, Jersey City State Coll., 1970, 74, Long Valley, 1979-80; active encouraging establishment of hist. zone Long Valley, landmarks, Jersey City and Washington Twp.; contbr. articles in field to various publs. Home and Office: 180 A Welsh Rd Lebanon NJ 08833

SVOBODA, JOSEF, stage designer; b. Prague, Czechoslovakia, May 10, 1920; s. Josef and Ruzena (Mojzisova) S.; m. Hrubesova Libuse, Apr. 30, 1948; 1 child; Hejnova Syobodova Sarka. Akad. Arch., Vsumprum, Prague, 1949; Doctorat (hon.), Acad. Arts, London, Ohio U., 1977. Stage designer Nat. Theatre, Prague, 1947, head designer, 1951—; prof. Acad. Applied Arts, 1968—; prof. architecture Vsumprum, Prague; mem. Union Czech Dramatic Artists, 1975—. Stage designer for numerous theatres, worldwide. Decorated chevalier Ord des Arts et des Lettres, 1976; recipient Internat. Theatre award Am. Theatre Assn., 1976. Office: Laterna Magika, Liliova 9, Prague 1 Czechoslovakia also: Nat Theatre, Anenski nam 2, Prague 1 Czechoslovakia *

SWAEBE, GEOFFREY, foreign service officer; b. London, Mar. 23, 1911; s. Daniel and Deborah Dora (Abhrams) S.; m. Mary Angeline Mossman, Jan. 1942; 1 child, Geoffrey Jr. Exec. Florsheim Shoe Co., Chgo., 1935-38; divisional merchandise mgr. Thalhimers, Richmond, Va., 1938-48; gen. merchandise mgr. Pizitz Dept. Store, Birmingham, Ala., 1948-50; v.p., gen. mgr./dir. Hecht Co., Balt., 1950-62; chmn. bd., pres. May Dept. Stores Calif., 1962-72; bus. and mgmt. cons. 1972-81; ambassador UN, Geneva, Switzerland, 1981-83, U.S. Embassy, Brussels, Belgium, 1983—. Bd. dirs. Community Redevel. Agy. Commn., Los Angeles, Better Bus. Bur. Los Angeles, Greater Los Angeles Plans, Inc., Hollywood Bowl Symphony Assn. Served to capt. AUS, 1942-45. Decorated Bronze Star, Order of Merit Italian Republic. Republican. Office: Dept of State US Ambassador to Belgium Washington DC 20520 *

SWAEBE, RICHARD, diamond and precious gem dealer, international trade consultant; b. N.Y.C., Dec. 4, 1938; s. Leslie and Rosa (Landau) S.; m. Lily Kalkstein, Sept. 25, 1963; children—Theodore Aaron, Daniella. Pres., chmn. bd. Diamond Sales Co., Miami, Fla., 1963-82, Richard Swaebe, Inc., Miami, 1971—; dir., pres. Visual Fuse Inc., 1984—; cons. JCK Diamond and Precious Gem Indices, Smithsonian Instn., Dept. Mineral Sci., U.S. Treasury Dept., U.S. Dept. Justice, U.S. Atty.'s Office. Mem. exec. bd., soc. fellows Fla. Region Anti-Defamation League. Served with AUS, 1956-59. Mem. Diamond Dealers Club, Diamond Trade Assn., Am. Gem Trade Assn., Jewelers Bd. Trade. Republican. Jewish. Clubs: Bankers, Palm Bay, Jockey. Author: Diaquote-Gemquote Price Index, 1980. Office: 2451 Brickell Ave Miami FL 33129

SWAIM, JOHN FRANKLIN, physician, health care executive; b. Bloomingdale, Ind., Dec. 24, 1935; s. Max DeBaun and Edna Marie (Whitely) S.; m. Joan Dooley, Sept. 19, 1957 (div. Apr. 1979); children: John Franklin, Parke Allen, Pamela Ann; m. Peggy Lou Sankey, May 30, 1979; one child, Anne-Marie. BS cum laude, Ind. StateU., 1959; MD, Ind. U., Indpls., 1963. Diplomate Am. Bd. Family Practice. Med. dir. Parke Clinic, Rockville, Ind., 1969—; pres. Parke Investments Inc., Rockville, 1972—, Vermillion Health Care Corp., Clinton, Ind., 1977—; bd. dirs. Parke State Bank, Rockville. Author: One Year and Eternity, 1978; also contbr. articles to profl. jours. Coroner, Parke County, Ind., 1972-82. Served to capt. USAF, 1963-67, Vietnam. Decorated Bronze Star. Mem. Am. Acad. Family Physicians, AMA, Ind. State Med. Assn. (dist. pres. 1986—), Midwest Fin. Assn. Republican. Club: Hoosier Assocs. (Indpls.). Lodges: Elks, Masons, Shriners. Home and Office: Parke Clinic 503 Anderson St Rockville IN 47872

SWAIMAN, KENNETH FRED, pediatric neurologist, educator; b. St. Paul, Nov. 19, 1931; s. Lester J. and Shirley (Ryan) S.; m. Phyllis Kammerman Sher, Oct. 1985; children: Lisa, Jerrold, Barbara, Dana. B.A. magna cum laude, U. Minn., 1952, B.S., 1953, M.D., 1955; postgrad., 1956-58; postgrad. (fellow pediatric neurology), Nat. Inst. Neurologic Deseases and Blindness, 1960-63. Diplomate: Am. Bd. Psychiatry and Neurology, Am. Bd. Pediatrics. Intern Mpls. Gen. Hosp., 1955-56; resident pediatrics U. Minn., 1956-58, neurology, 1960-63; asst. prof. pediatrics, neurology U. Minn. Med. Sch., Mpls., 1963-66; asso. prof. U. Minn. Med. Sch., 1966-69, prof., dir. pediatric neurology, 1969—, exec. officer, dept. neurology, 1977—, mem. internship adv. council exec. faculty, 1966-70; Cons. pediatric neurology Hennepin County Gen. Hosp., Mpls., St. Paul-Ramsey Hosp., St. Paul Children's Hosp., Mpls. Children's Hosp. Author: (with Francis S. Wright) Neuromuscular Diseases in Infancy and Childhood, 1969, Pediatric Neuromuscular Diseases, 1979, (with Stephen Ashwal) Pediatric Neurology Case Studies, 1978, 2d edit., 1984; Editor: (with John A. Anderson) Phenylketonuria and Allied Metabolic Diseases, 1966, (with Francis S. Wright) Practice Pediatric Neurology, 1975, 2d edit., 1982; mem. editorial bd.: Annals of Neurology, 1977-83, Neurology Update, 1977-82, Pediatric Update, 1977 , Brain and Devel. (Jour. Japanese Soc. Child Neurology), 1980—, Neuropediatrics (Stuttgart), 1982—; editor-in-chief: Pediatric Neurology, 1984—; Contbr. articles to sci. jours. Chmn. Minn. Gov.'s Bd. for Handicapped, Exceptional and Gifted Children, 1972-76; mem. human devel. study sect. NIH, 1976-79, guest worker, 1978-81. Served to capt. M.C. U.S. Army, 1958-60. Fellow Am. Acad. Pediatrics, Am. Acad. Neurology (rep. to nat. council Nat. Soc. Med. Research); mem. Soc. Pediatric Research, Central Soc. Clin. Research, Central Soc. Neurol. Research, Internat. Soc. Neurochemistry, Am. Neurol. Assn., Minn. Neurol. Soc., AAAS, Midwest Pediatric Soc., Am. Soc. Neurochemistry, Child Neurology Soc. (1st pres. 1972-73, Hower award 1981), Internat. Assn. Child Neurologists (exec. com. 1975-79), Profs. of Child Neurology (1st pres. 1978-80), Phi Beta Kappa, Sigma Xi. Home: 420 Delaware St SE Minneapolis MN 55455 Office: U Minn Med Sch Dept Pediatric Neurology Minneapolis MN 55455

SWAIN, PHILIP RAYMOND, publishing co. exec.; b. Meriden, Conn., Nov. 30, 1929; s. Raymond Francis and Angela Catherine (Maslow) S. A.B. cum laude, Harvard U., 1950; M.B.A., Boston U. Tchr. Latin, Greek, pvt. schs., Cambridge and Still River, Mass., 1950-55; editor Ravengate Press, Cambridge, 1955-65, pres., 1965—. Mem. bd. advisers St. Benedict Acad., Still River. Mem. Book Builders of Boston. Roman Catholic. Club: Harvard. Author (as Philip Douglas): Saint of Philadelphia, The Life of Bishop John Neumann, 1977. Home: 56 Carpenter Ave Meriden CT 06450 Office: PO Box 103 Cambridge MA 02138

SWALES, WILLIAM EDWARD, oil company executive; b. Parkersburg, W.Va., May 15, 1925; s. John Richard and Ellen (South) S.; m. Lydia Eugena Mills, Dec. 26, 1948; children: Joseph V., Susan Eugena, David Lee. BA in Geology, W.Va. U., 1949, MS in Geology, 1951; grad., advanced mgmt. program Stanford U., 1968; DSc (hon.), W.Va. U., 1986; LLD (hon.), Marietta Coll., 1986. With Marathon Oil Co. (subs. USX Corp.), Findlay, Ohio, 1954-70, 74-87, mgr. Western Hemisphere and Australia div., 1967-70, spl. asst. to sr. v.p. prodn., internat., 1974, v.p. prodn., internat., 1974-77, sr. v.p. prodn., internat., 1977-82, also bd. dirs., chmn. bd., 1983-84, sr. v.p. exploration and prodn., 1983-84, pres., 1985-87, pres. Marathon Petroleum Co., 1982-83; vice-chmn. energy USX Corp., Pittsburgh, 1987—; bd. dirs. Tex. Oil & Gas Corp, Pitts. Nat. Bank, Pitts Nat. Bank Fin. Corp.; exec. v.p. Oasis Oil Co. of Libya, Inc., Tripoli, 1970-72, pres., 1972-74; exec. dir. USX Corp. Served with USN, 1943-45. Mem. Am. Petroleum Inst. (bd. dirs.), Am. Assn. Petroleum Geologists, Soc. Petroleum Engrs., Am. Geol. Inst., Nat. Petroleum Council, 25 Yr. Club Petroleum Industry. Clubs: Findlay Country, JDM Country, Laurel Valley Golf, Rolling Rock. Office: USX Corp 600 Grant St Pittsburgh PA 15230 *

SWALM, THOMAS STERLING, retired military officer, aerospace consultant; b. San Diego, Sept. 28, 1931; s. Calvin D. and Margaret A. (Rynning) S.; m. Charlene La Vern Garner, June 26, 1954; children: Edward Steven, Lori Ann. BS, U. Oreg., 1954; MS in Pub. Adminstrn., George Washington U., 1964; grad., Air Command and Staff Coll., 1964, Nat. War Coll., 1974. Commd. USAF, 1954, advanced through grades to maj. gen., 1982; instr. fighter-interceptor weapons sch. USAF, Tyndall AFB, Fla., 1956; pilot 434th Fighter-Day Squadron USAF, George AFB, Calif., 1957-58; pilot 50th Tactical Fighter wing, 10th Tactical Fighter Squadron USAF, Toul-Rosieres AFB, France and Hahn AFB, Fed. Republic Germany, 1958-61; hdqrs. 12th USAF, Waco, Tex., 1961-64; instr. pilot, flight examiner 4453d Combat Crew Tng. Wing USAF, Davis-Monthan AFB, Ariz., 1965-66; flight comdr. 12th tactical fighter wing USAF, Cam Ranh Bay AFB, Republic Vietnam, 1966-67; comdr. air-to-air flight, instr. USAF, Nellis AFB, Nev., 1967-70; comdr., leader Thunderbirds USAF, 1970-73; chief fighter attack div. USAF, Kirtland AFB, N.Mex., 1974-75, dep. dir. test and evaluation, 1975-76; from vice comdr. to comdr. 8th tactical fighter wing USAF, Kunsan AFB, Republic of Korea, 1976-78; comdr. 3d tactical fighter wing USAF, Clark AFB, Philippines, 1978-79; comdr. 57th fighter weapons wing, comdr. fighter weapons sch. USAF, Nellis AFB, Nev., 1979-80; comdr. 833d air div. USAF, Holloman AFB, N.Mex., 1980-81; comdr. tactical air warfare ctr. USAF, Eglin AFB, Fla., 1981-86; ret. USAF, 1986; pres. T. Swalm and Assocs., Ft. Walton Beach, Fla., 1986—; v.p. Applications Group International, Inc., Atlanta, 1986—. Mem. editorial bd. Jour. Electronic Def., 1983-86; contbr. articles to profl. jours. Hon. chmn. Heart Assn., Las Vegas, Nev., 1972; exec. dir. Boy Scouts Am., Las Vegas and Alamagordo, N.Mex., 1970-81. Decorated D.S.M., Legion of Merit with two oak leaf clusters, DFC, Air medal with 14 oak leaf clusters, Vietnam Service medal with three service stars, Republic Vietnam Campaign medal; recipient R.V. Jones Trophy Electronic Security Command, 1984. Mem. Air Force Assn., exec. advisor (Jerome Waterman award 1985), Thuderbird Pilots Assn., Old Mission Beach Athletic Club (founder), Assn. Old Crows (editorial bd., R.V. Jones trophy 1984), Order of Daedalians (flight capt.), Sigma Nu. Republican. Presbyterian. Office: PO Box 1836 Eglin AFB FL 32542-1836

SWAMINATHAN, JAGDISH, painter; b. June 21, 1928; m. Bhavani, 1955; 2 children. Student Delhi Poly., also Acad. of Fine Arts, Warsaw. Freedom fighter, trade unionist, journalist, writer children's books; later mem. Delhi State-Com. of Congress Socialist Party and Edn. weekly orgn. Mazdoor Awaz; sr. art tchr. Cambridge Sch., New Delhi; founder-mem. Group 1890, avant-garde group of India artists. Exhibited one man shows New Delhi, 1962, 63, 64, 65, 66, Bombay, 1966; group shows Warsaw, 1961, Saigon, 1963, Tokyo Biennale 1965, Art Now in India, London, Newcastle and Brussels, 1965-66, Seven Indian Painters, London, 1967, represented in pub. and pvt. collections in India and abroad. Founder, editor monthly jour. Contra, 1966. Jawaharlal Nehru research fellow. Mem. Internat. Assn. Arts (nat. com. 1967), Delhi Slipi Chakra (exec. com. 1967—). Office: care Gallery Chemould, Jahangir Art Gallery, Mahatma Gandhi Rd, New Delhi 110005, India *

SWAMINATHAN, MONKOMBU SAMBASIVAN, agricultural researcher; b. Kumbakonam, Tamil Nadu, India, Aug. 7, 1925; d. M.K. and S. (Thangam) Sambasivan; m. Mina Bhoothalingam Swaminathan, 1955; children—Soumya, Madhura, Nitya. B.Sc., Tranvacore U., 1944; B.Sc. in Agr., Coimbatore Agrl. Coll., Madras U., 1947; Assoc., Indian Agrl. Research Inst., New Delhi, 1949; Ph.D., U. Cambridge, U.K., 1952; D.Sc. (hon.), The Sardar Pater U., Vallabh Vidyanagar, 1970, Haryana Agrl. U., Hissar, 1973, The Andhra Pradesh Agrl. U., Hyderabad, 1973, The Andhra U., Waltair, 1972, G.B. Pant U., Pantnagar, 1974, Jodhpur U., 1975, Marathwada Krishi Vidyapeeth, Parbhani, 1975, Kumaon U., Nainital, 1975, Burdwan U., 1976, Agra U., 1978, Kerala Agrl. U., Trichur, 1978, Sri Venkateswara U., Tirupati, 1979, U. Agrl. Scis., Bangalore, 1980, Banaras Hindu U., Varanasi, 1981, Tech. U. Berlin, 1981, Mahatma Phule Agrl. U., Rahuri, 1982, Chandrasekhara Azad Agrl. U., Kanpur, 1982, U. Wis., 1983, Delhi U., India, 1984, U. Philippines, Diliman, Quezon City, 1984, Asian Inst. Tech., Bangkok, Thailand, 1985, U. Mangalore, India, 1986, U. Hyderabad, India, 1987, Agrl. U., Wageningen, The Netherlands, 1988, Assam Agrl. U., India, 1988, Oreg. State U., 1988. Tchr., researcher, research adminstr. Central Rice Research Inst., Cuttack, Indian Agrl. Research Inst., New Delhi, 1954-72; dir. gen. Indian Council Agrl. Research and sec. to Govt. India, Dept. Agrl. Research and Edn., 1972-79; sec. to Govt. India Ministry Agr. and Irrigation, 1979-80; acting dep. chmn. Planning Commn., Govt. India, 1980; mem. Agr., Rural Devel., Sci. and Edn. Planning Commn., Govt. India, 1980-82; dir. gen. Internat. Rice Research Inst., Los Banos, Philippines, 1982— ; vice chmn. tech. adv. com. Consultative Group on Internat. Agrl. Research, 1971-77, Protein-Calorie Adv. Group UN, 1972-77; chmn. first quinquennial rev. Internat. Rice Research Inst., 1976; chmn. UN Adv. Com. on Sci. and Tech. for Devel., 1980-83; pres. Internat. Fedn. Agrl. Systems for Devel., 1976-83; chmn., bd. trustees Internat. Council Research in Agroforestry, U.K., 1977-82; ind. chmn. FAO Council, Rome, 1981-85; mem. sci. and tech. adv. com. tropical diseases research WHO, 1983-85; hon. v.p. World Wildlife Fund, Geneva, 1985—; pres. Internat. Union for Conservation of Nature and Natural Resources, Geneva, 1984—; gen. pres. Indian Sci. Congress, Waltair, 1976; pres. SV Internat. Congress Genetics, New Delhi, 1983; mem. Nat. Commn. on Agr., 1971-77. Recipient Shanti Swarup Bhatnagar award, 1961; Mendel Meml. award Czechoslovak Acad. Scis., 1965; Birbal Sahni medal Indian Bot. Soc., 1966; Padma Shri, Pres. India, 1967; Ramon Magsaysay award, 1971; Padma Bhushan, Pres. India, 1972; Silver Jubilee Commemoration medal Indian Nat. Sci. Acad., 1973; Barclay medal Asiatic Soc., 1978; K. L. Moudgill prize, 1978; Borlaug award, 1979; Meghnad Saha medal Indian Nat. Sci. Acad., 1981; Rathindranath Tagore Prize, Visva Bharati U., 1981; R.D. Misra medal Indian Environ. Soc., 1982, R.D. Bennett Commonwealth prize, 1984; award Assn. for Women in Devel., Washington, 1985, Bicentenary medal U. Ga., 1985; Gen. Foods World Food prize, 1987, Albert Einstein Sci. award, 1986, World Food prize, 1987, Golden Heart Presdl. award, 1987. Fellow Indian Nat. Sci. Acad., Indian Acad. Scis., Royal Soc. London, Third World Acad. Scis., Nat. Acad. Scis. India (hon.), Swedish Seed Assn. (hon.), Nat. Acad. Sci. Italy (hon., fgn.), Royal Soc. Arts, London; mem. Nat. Acad. Scis. U.S. (fgn. assoc. 1977), All-Union Acad. Agrl. Scis. USSR (fgn.), Royal Swedish Acad. Agr. and Forestry (fgn.), Nat. Acad. Arts and Scis. (fgn. hon.). Address: B-4/142 Safdarjang Enclave, New Delhi 110029, India

SWAN, GEORGE STEVEN, law educator; b. St. Louis, Feb. 9, 1948; s. Raymond A. and Lorene (Kennedy) S. BA, Ohio State U., 1970; JD, U. Notre Dame, 1974; LLM, U. Toronto, 1976, SJD, 1983. Bar: Ohio 1974. Asst. atty. gen. state of Ohio, Columbus, 1974-75; jud. clk. Supreme Ct. Ohio, Columbus, 1976-78; asst. prof. Del. Law Sch., Wilmington, 1980-83, assoc. prof., 1983-84; prof. law St. Thomas U. Law Sch., Miami, Fla., 1984-88; jud. clk. U.S. Ct. Appeals 7th Cir., Chgo., 1988—. Contbr. articles to law jours. Mem. ABA, Ohio Bar Assn., Am. Polit. Sci. Assn. Republican. Roman Catholic. Office: 310 Fed Bldg South Bend IN 46601

SWAN, HARRY DAVID, private investigator, engineer, personnel and criminal justice consultant; b. Rochester, N.Y., Feb. 25, 1926; s. Harry and Florence (Ellison) S.; m. Pauline E. Gunnison, May 20, 1950 (div.); children—David, Lynne. A.S. in Commerce, Henry Ford Community Coll., Dearborn, Mich., 1965; B.S. in Criminal Justice, Madonna Coll., Livonia, Mich., 1977; M.A. in Criminal Justice, U. Detroit, 1980. Lic. pvt. investigator, Ky. Design checker Chrysler Corp., Highland Park, Mich., 1953-64, Hydramatic div. Gen. Motors, Ypsilanti, Mich., 1980, AC Spark Plug div. Gen. Motors, Flint, Mich., 1981, Alliance-Renault-AMC, Detroit, 1982; design engr. Corvette-Chevrolet, Gen. Motors, Warren, Mich., 1983; design checker Ford Motor Co., Dearborn, 1984-87; engine design checker ECS/Roush Performance Engring., Livonia, 1987-88; program engr., plastic products div., Redford, Mich., 1988—; chief exec. officer Covert Intelligence Agy. and Covert Pvt. Police, Lexington, Ky., 1983—. Served with USAAF, 1944-45. Mem. Am. Soc. for Indsl. Security, Sports Car Club Am., Delorean Internat. Club, Internat. Narcotic Enforcement Officers Assn., Internat. Assn. Chiefs of Police. Democrat. Presbyterian. Designer automotive chassis innovations, 1953-88. Address: 420 Redding Rd Suite 208 Lexington KY 40502

SWAN, HARRY KELS, curator; b. Somerville, N.J., Nov. 14, 1928; s. Peter Kenney and Martha Anita (Kels) S.; B.S. in Edn., Rutgers U., 1952, M.Ed., 1954. Curator/historian Liberty Village Ltd., Flemington, N.J., 1972-76; curator Washington Crossing State Park, Titusville, N.J., 1976-83, sr. hist. preservation specialist, 1983—; historian Am. Legacy Assn., Clinton, N.J.; historian, v.p. Washington Camp Ground Assn., Bound Brook, N.J.; pres. Daniel Morgan Meml. Found., Clinton; apptd. mem. hon. bd. scholars Liberty Park FDT, Denver, 1988; cons. in field. Mem. Somerset County (N.J.) Cultural and Heritage Commn., 1983—, N.J. Constitution Bicentennial Commn., 1986—; mem. hon. bd. scholars Liberty Park Found., Denver, 1988. Recipient Humanitarian Achievement award Am. Legacy Assn., 1981; Heritage award Raritan Valley SAR, 1982. Mem. South Bound Brook Hist. Soc. (founding trustee), Kappa Delta Pi, Delta Xi, Phi Delta Kappa, Republican. Mem. Dutch Reformed Ch. Author: History of South Bound Brook, New Jersey, 1964; Raritan's Revolutionary Rebel: Frederick Frelinghuysen, 1967; also monograph. Office: Washington Crossing State Park Box 337-A RD 1 Titusville NJ 08560

SWAN, JOHN (WILLIAM DAVID), premier of Bermuda; b. July 3, 1935; s. John N. and Margaret E. Swan; m. Jacqueline A. D. Roberts, 1965; 3 children. B.A., W.Va. Wesleyan Coll. Salesman real estate Rego Ltd., 1960-62; founder, chmn., chief exec. John W. Swan Ltd., 1962—; mem. Parliament of Bermuda, 1972—, formerly minister for marine and air services, then minister for labor and immigration, 1977-78, minister for home affairs, 1978-82, premier of Bermuda, 1982—; formerly parliamentary sec. for fin.; chmn. Dept. Civil Aviation; mem. Lloyd's of London. Chmn. bd. dirs. Bermuda Hosps. Mem. United Bermuda Party, Chief Execs. Orgn. World Bus. Council. Club: Royal Bermuda Yacht. Lodge: Rotary. Address: Office of Premier, Hamilton Bermuda *

SWANI, NARINDER MOHAN, textile engineering educator, academic administrator; b. Peshawar, India, June 19, 1927; s. Bishan Das and Banaras Kaur S.; m. Jette Jurlander, June 8, 1957; children: Anita, Anil. BA in Physics and Math., Govt. Coll., Lahore, India, 1946; BSc in Textiles, Leeds (Eng.) U., 1951, PhD in Textile Engring., 1964. Lectr. Keighley Tech. Coll., Eng., 1952-54, Percival Whitley Coll., Halifex, Eng., 1954-57; prof., head textile tech. dept. Delhi Coll. Engring., 1959-64, Indian Inst. Tech., New Delhi, 1964-72; dean students undergrad. studies Indian Inst. Tech., 1967-72, dir., 1972-78, 83—, prof. textile tech. dept., 1978-83; chief tech. advisor UNESCO Staff Devel. Ctr., Baghdad, Iraq, 1980-82. Contbr. articles to profl. jours. Fellow Textile Assn. (hon.), Textile Inst. (chmn. Indian adv. com. 1971—, recipient service medal 1985), Indian Nat. Acad. engring., Instn. Engrs. India (chmn. textile engring. div. 1984—); mem. Indian Soc. Tech. Edn. (pres. 1977-80), Assn. Engring. Edn. South and Central Asia (v.p. 1978-80). Hindu. Office: Indian Inst Technology, Hauz Khas, New Delhi 110 016, India

SWANN, DONALD IBRAHIM, composer and performer, freelance; b. Sept. 30, 1923; s. Herbert William Swann (dec.) amd Naguime Sultan; m. Janet Mary Oxborrow, 1955 (div. 1983); 2 children. Student, Westminster Sch., Christ Church, Oxford; hons. degree modern lang., Westminster Sch. Contributed music to London revues, including Airs on a Shoestring, 1953-54, as joint leader writer with Michael Flanders; Wild Thyme, musical play with Philip Guard, 1955; in At the Drop of a Hat, 1957, appeared for first time (with Michael Flanders) as singer and accompanist of own songs (this show ran over 2 yrs. in London, was part of Edinburgh Festival, 1959; Broadway, 1959-60; Am. and Can. tour1960-61; tour of Great Britain and Ireland, 1962-63); At the Drop of Another Hat (with Michael Flanders), Haymarket, 1963-64, Globe, 1965; Australia and New Zealand tour, 1964; US tour, 1966-67. Arranged concerts of owwon settings: Set by Swann, An Evening in Crete: Soundings by Swann; Between the Bars: an autobiography in music; A Crack in Time, a concert in search of peace. Musician in Residence, Quaker Study Ctr., Pendle Hill, USA, 1983; has worked in songwriting and performing partnerships with Jeremy Taylor, Sydney Carter, Frank Topping, John Amis; solo entertainments in theatres and concert halls (Stand Clear for Wonders with peace exploration songs). Founded Albert House Press for spl. publs., 1974. Compositions and Publs. include: Lucy and the Hunter, musical play with Sydney Carter; satirical music to Third Programme series by Henry Reed, ghosting for Hilda Tablet; London Sketches with Sebastian Shaw, 1958; Festival Matinis, 1962; Perelandra, music drama with David Marsh based on the novel of C.S. Lewis, 1961-62; Settings of John Betjeman Poems, 1964; Sing Round the Year (Book of New Carols for Children), 1965; The Road Goes Ever On, book of songs with J.R.R. Tolkien,,1968, rev. edn., 1978; The Space Between the Bars: a book of reflections, 1968; Requiem for the Living, to words of C. Day Lewis, 1969; The rope of Love; around the earth in song, 1973; Swann's Way Out: a posthumous adventure, 1974; (with Albert Friedlander) The Five Scrolls, 1975; Omnibus Flanders and Swann Songbook, 1977; Round the Piano with Donald Swann, 1979; (with Alex Davison) The Yeast Factory, music drama, 1979; Alphabetaphon: 26 essays A-Z (illustrated by Natasha Etheridge); songs and operas with Arthur Scholey: The Song of Caedmon, 1971; Singalive, 1978; Wacky and his Fuddlejig (children's musical play), 1978; Candle Tree, 1980; Baboushka (a Christmas cantata), 1980; The Visitors (based on Tolstoy), 1984; Brendan A-hoy! (with Evelyn Kirkhart and Mary Morgan) Mamahuhu (musical play), 1986; Envy (with Richard Crane), 1986. Avocation: going to the launderette. Address: 13 Albert Rd, London SW11 4PX, England

SWANSON, CHARLES RICHARD, accountant, oil and gas consultant; b. Tulsa, July 19, 1953; s. Donald Charles and Helen Kathryn (Smith) S.; m. Karen Marcelle Pfister, June 10, 1978; children—Kimberly Marcelle, Laura Kathryn. BA, Tulane U., 1975, MBA, 1977. CPA, Tex.; cert. data processing. Staff auditor Ernst & Whinney, Houston, 1977-79; sr. auditor, 1979-81, oil and gas cons., 1981-84, sr. mgr. energy industry services, 1984-87; ptnr. Swanson Petroleum Enterprises, Houston, 1979—; bd. dirs. Stratamodel, Inc., Houston, Swanson Geol. Services, Houston, Cygnet Group, Inc., Houston. Contbr. articles to profl. jours. Mem. Rep. Nat. Com., 1982. Teagle Found. scholar, 1971-75. Mem. Tulane Assn. Bus. Alumni (pres. 1982), Am. Inst. CPA's, Tex. Soc. CPA's, Petroleum Accts. Soc., Tex. Ind. Producers and Royalty Owners Assn., Ind. Petroleum Assn. Am., Houston Jaycees, Mensa, Delta Tau Delta (pres. 1971-75). Lutheran. Club: Krewe of Bacchus. Home: 511 Commodore Way Houston TX 77079 Office: Ernst & Whinney 333 Clay St Suite 3100 Houston TX 77002

SWANSON, DAVID HEATH, agricultural company executive; b. Aurora, Ill., Nov. 3, 1942; s. Neil H. and Helen J. (McKendry) S.; divorced; children: Benjamin Heath, Matthew Banford. B.A., Harvard U., 1964; M.A., U. Chgo., 1969. Account exec. 1st Nat. Bank Chgo., 1967-69; dep. mgr. Brown Bros. Harriman & Co., N.Y.C., 1969-72; asst. treas. Borden, Inc., N.Y.C., 1972-75; v.p., treas. Continental Grain Co., N.Y.C., 1975-77, v.p. chief fin. officer, 1977-79, gen. mgr. European div., 1979-81, exec. v.p. and gen. mgr. World Grain div., 1981-83, corp. sr. v.p., chief fin. and adminstrv. officer, 1983-86, group pres., 1985-86; pres., chief exec. officer Cen. Soya, Ft. Wayne, Ind., 1986—; bd. advisers Banco Popular de P.R., 1973-75; adv. bd. U.S. Export-Import Bank, 1985-86; mem. Gov.'s Agrl. Bd. Ind. Bd. dirs. Ft. Wayne Philharm., Internat. Policy Council on Agr. and Trade; mem. adv. bd. Purdue U. Agr. Sch. Mem. Council Fgn. Relations, Ind. C. of C. (bd. dirs.), Ft. Wayne C. of C. (bd. dirs.), Ft. Wayne Hist. Soc. (bd. dirs.). Republican. Congregationalist. Clubs: Am. Alpine (bd. dirs.), Scottish Deerhound of Am.; New Canaan (Conn.) Field, Racquet and Tennis, Links (N.Y.C.); Ft. Wayne Country; Explorers (bd. dirs., v.p., sec.). Office: Cen Soya Co Inc 1300 Ft Wayne Nat Bank Bldg Fort Wayne IN 46802

SWANSON, DONALD CHARLES, geologist; b. Canon City, Colo., Sept. 22, 1926; s. Charles William and Josephine Anne (Kramer) S.; B.S. in Gen. Arts and Sci., Colo. State U., 1950; B.S. in Geology, Tulsa U., 1956; postgrad. U. Okla., 1965-67; m. Helen Kathyrn Smith, June 10, 1950; children—Charles Richard, Jeffrey Stuart. Tax engr. and geologist Carter Oil Co., Tulsa, 1951-61; explorationist Humble Oil Co., Tex. and Okla., 1961-67; research geologist Exxon Prodn. Research Co., Houston, 1967-79; cons. geologist Swanson Geol. Services, Stratamodel, Inc., Houston, 1986—. Fellow Geol. Soc. Am.; mem. Am. Assn. Petroleum Geologists (recipient A.I. Levorsen awards 1969, 79), AAAS, Explorers Club, Sigma Chi. Lutheran. Contbr. articles to profl. jours., spl. publs. and books. Home: 510 Sandy Pont Houston TX 77079 Office: 7500 San Felipe Suite 520 Houston TX 77063

SWANSON, GEORGE ALBERT, wildlife and aquatic biologist; b. St. Paul, Dec. 5, 1929; s. George Alexandra and Alice Standish (Chandler) S.; m. Marlyn Marie Jones, Aug. 6, 1952; children—Sandra Marie, Lorie Alice. A.A., U. Minn., 1956; B.S., U. Minn.-St. Paul, 1959. Cert. profl. wildlife biologist. Fishery research biologist North Central Reservoir Investigations, Yankton, S.D., 1962-66; aquatic research biologist No. Prairie Wildlife Research Ctr., Jamestown, N.D., 1966-82, wildlife research biologist, 1982—. Patentee automatic plankton sampling system. Contbr. articles to profl. jours., chpts. to books. Served to staff sgt. USAF, 1950-54. Recipient Incentive award U.S. Fish and Wildlife Service, 1965, Spl. Achievement award, 1976, 81. Mem. Wildlife Soc., Ecol. Soc., Am. Soc. Limnology and Oceanography, Am. Benthological Soc., Am. Fisheries Soc. Lutheran. Club: Jamestown Eagles. Home: 1727 4th Ave NE Jamestown ND 58401

SWANSON, JENNIE ELIZABETH, educator; b. Atlanta, Aug. 5, 1932; d. Chester Arthur and Cleo Annie (McEachern) Williams; B.S., Northwestern U., 1954; M.S., No. Ill. U., 1972, Ed.D., 1976; m. Richard Edward Swanson, Apr. 24, 1954; children—Laurel Dee, Jeffrey Richard, Scott Edward. Public sch. tchr., 1954-69; psycho-ednl. diagnostician, 1969-72; mem. faculty Loyola U., Chgo., 1976-82, asst. prof. ob-gyn and pediatrics, 1979-82, dir. pre-start project depts. ob-gyn and pediatrics Stritch Sch. Medicine, 1978-82; dir. spl. services Community Unit Sch. Dist. 220, 1982—; mem. Gov. Ill. Com. Preventive Services, 1979-80; chmn. B-3 subcom. First Chance Consortium, 1978-80; chmn. INTER-ACT, 1979-80; cons. in field. Grantee HEW, 1973-76, 78-82. Mem. Council Exceptional Children, Assn. Maternal and Child Health, Nat. Perinatal Assn., Nat. Assn. Edn. Young Child, Northwestern U. Alumni Assn., Delta Delta Delta, Delta Kappa Gamma (scholar 1974). Lutheran. Author: (with others) Partners in Child Development, 1978. Office: 310 E James St Barrington IL 60010

SWANSON, NORMA LEE, quality assurance administrator; b. Kokomo, Ind., May 10, 1934; adopted d. Roy and Lora E. (Ewer) Hupp; m. Ray A. Swanson, Nov. 1, 1952 (div. Nov. 1972); children—Michael, Patrick, Lisa, Kelly. Student, St. Mary-of-the-Woods Coll. Nursing staff hosps. in Ill., 1952, 54, med. records adminstr., Ill., Iowa, 1964-77; med. records adminstr. and instrs. hosps., Khamis Mushayt, Saudi Arabia, 1977-80; quality assurance coordinator VA, Murfreesboro, Tenn., 1980-83, hosps. in Tabuk, Saudi Arabia, 1983-84; health systems specialist VA Med. Ctr., Marion, Ind., 1984-86, quality assurance specialist VA dist. 21, St. Louis, 1986—; cons. in field; Mem. Civic Theater, Murfreesboro, Tenn., 1981-84. Author: Adventures of Lee Kelly, 1976; editor: VA newsletter, 1982-83 Contbr. articles to profl. jours. Mem. Internat. Platform Assn., Speakers Bur.-Quality Assurance Assn., Am. Med. Record Assn., Illowa Med. Record Assn. (pres. 1975-77), Iowa Med. Record Assn. (program chair 1975-76), Nat. Assn. Quality Assurance Profls., Nat. Assn. Female Execs., Internat. Platform Assn. Club: Disabled Am. Vets. Comdrs. Lodges: Altrusa. Office: VA Med Ctr Dist 21 Saint Louis MO 63125

SWANSON, PAUL JOHN, JR., finance educator; b. Crawfordsville, Ind., May 10, 1934; s. Paul John and Helen (Bath) S. Student DePauw U., 1952; B.S. in Accountancy, U. Ill., 1959, B.S. in Econ. and Fin., 1960, M.S. in Fin., 1962, Ph.D., 1966. Grad. teaching asst. U. Ill., Urbana, 1960-65, grad. research asst., 1964-65; asst. prof. finance U. Cin., 1965-67, assoc. prof., 1967—, prof.-in-charge dept. quantitative analysis, 1967-68; pres. Paul Swanson and Assocs., Inc., 1983—; cons. local bus. and govt. agencies; mem. Perfect North Slope Ski Patrol, Ind. Served with AUS, 1956-58. Mem. Nat. Def. Exec. Res., Inst. Mgmt. Scis. (past pres. Miami Valley chpt.), Ops. Research Soc. Am., Am., Midwest finance assns., Fin. Analysts Soc., Inst. Chartered Fin. Analysts, Am. Statis. Assn., Delta Chi, Delta Sigma Pi. Republican. Episcopalian (treas., chmn. TV ministry com. 1983—, vestry). Home: 3441 Telford St Cincinnati OH 45220

SWANSON, RAYNOLD A., retired electronics executive; b. Ellsworth, Wis., Feb. 7, 1920; s. August J. and Ida M. (Hansen) S.; m. Millicent J. Wicklund, Dec. 27, 1947; children: Vern, Larry, Doug. Mech. draftsman Collins Radio, Cedar Rapids, Iowa, 1947-50, mech. engr., 1950-67; sect. head Harris Corp., Quincy, Ill., 1967-70; v.p. mfg., co-founder Quintron Corp., Quincy, 1970-82, exec. v.p., 1982-85, also bd. dirs. Patentee mech. stop. Town clk. Riverside (Ill.) Township, 1980—; bd. dirs. Chaddock Sch., Quincy, 1976—; advisor bd. dirs. Salvation Army, Quincy, 1975—; participant in chartering First Covenant Ch., Cedar Rapids, 1948. Served with U.S. Army, 1942-45, ETO. Lodge: Kiwanis (pres. Quincy 1984-85). Home: 2335 N 12th St Quincy IL 62301

SWANSON, RICHARD DENNIS, lawyer; b. Detroit, June 17, 1946; s. Richard H. and Elizabeth (McDevitt) S.; m. Lynne Battjes, Sept. 16, 1967; children: Monica, Sarah. BA, Grand Valley State Coll., 1968; MBA, Western Mich. U., 1969; JD, John Marshall Law Sch., 1977. Bar: Ill. 1977, Tenn. 1982, N.C. 1985. Asst. gen. counsel ITT N. Electric, Johnson City, Tenn., 1979-83; assoc. gen. counsel ITT Telecom Products, Raleigh, N.C., 1983-86; gen. counsel ITT World Directories, Brussels, 1986—. Mem. ABA, Wake County Bar. Office: ITT World Directories, 480 Ave Louise, B-1050 Brussels Belgium

SWANSON, ROBERT MARTIN, medical center administrator; b. Bell, Calif., Oct. 14, 1940; s. Harold M. and Elsie Lorraine (Allison) S.; AB, Long Beach (Calif.) State Coll., 1963; MA, U. Iowa, 1965; PhD, UCLA, 1970; m. Katharine Vivian Martin, Feb. 16, 1980. Dir., Office of Mental Health Research, U. Iowa, Iowa City, 1966-70; research dir. Health Planning Council, St. Paul, 1970-73; exec. dir. Kansas City (Mo.) Health Plan, 1973-75; asst. dir. St. Louis U. Hosps., 1975-80; asst. v.p. and chief planning officer St. Louis U. Med. Ctr., 1981-87, assoc. v.p., 1988—; dir. Organizational Research & Devel. Corp., Kansas City; dir., sec., chmn. awards com. Group Health Found. of Greater St. Louis; dir., sec., alliance for community health; clin. prof. St. Louis U. Grad. Program in Health and Hosp. Adminstrn., 1980—; adj. prof. Webster Coll., St. Louis, 1975-82; spl. cons. to Kansas City (Mo.) Health Dept., 1974-75; tech. cons. Health Services Adminstrn., HEW, 1973-75; coordinator St. Louis Community-Univ. Conf., 1977-80; mem. health affairs task force Mo. Cath. Conf., 1977. Named Adm. in Nebr. Navy, 1971; State of Iowa grantee, 1969. Mem. Nat. Assn. Hosp. Devel. (cert.), Am. Mgmt. Assn., Soc. for Advancement Mgmt., N.Am. Soc. Corp. Planners, Internat. Platform Assn., Advt. Club Greater St. Louis, Zeta Beta Tau. Republican. Eastern Orthodox. Contbr. articles on health services to profl. jours. Office: 3556 Caroline St Saint Louis MO 63104

SWANSON, ROY ARTHUR, classicist, educator; b. St. Paul, Apr. 7, 1925; s. Roy Benjamin and Gertrude (Larson) S.; m. Vivian May Vitous, Mar. 30, 1946; children: Lynn Marie (Mrs. Gerald A. Snider), Robin Lillian, Robert Roy (dec.), Dyack Tyler, Dana Miriam. B.A., U. Minn., 1948, B.S., 1949, M.A., 1951; Ph.D., U. Ill., 1954. Prin. Maplewood Elementary Sch., St. Paul, 1949-51; instr. U. Ill., 1952-53, Ind. U., 1954-57; asst. prof. U. Minn., Mpls., 1957-61; assoc. prof. U. Minn., 1961-64, acting chmn. classics, 1963-64, prof. classics, chmn. comparative lit., 1964-65; prof. English Macalester Coll., St. Paul, 1965-67; co-ordinator humanities program 1966-67; prof. comparative lit. and classics U. Wis.-Milw., 1967-70, chmn. classics dept., 1967-70, 86—, chmn. comparative lit., 1970-73, 76-83, coordinator Scandinavian studies program, 1982—; Cons. St. Paul Tchrs. Sr. High Sch. English, 1964. Author: Odi et Amo: The Complete Poetry of Catullus, 1959, Heart of Reason: Introductory Essays in Modern-World Humanities, 1963, Pindar's Odes, 1974, Greek and Latin Word Elements, 1981, The Love Songs of the Carmina Burana, 1987; Editor: Minn. Rev, 1963-67, Classical Jour, 1968-73; Contbr. articles to profl. jours. Bd. dirs. Lutheran Studies, Inc. Served with AUS, 1944-46. Decorated Bronze Star; recipient Disting. Teaching award U. Minn., 1962, Disting. Teaching award U. Wis.-Milw., 1974. Mem. Am. Philol. Assn., Am. Comparative Lit. Assn., Modern Lang. Assn., Soc. for Advancement Scandinavian Study, Phi Beta Kappa (pres. chpt. 1975-76), Phi Kappa Phi. Home: 11618 N Bobolink Ln Mequon WI 53092 Office: U Wis-Milw Dept Comparative Lit PO Box 413 Milwaukee WI 53201

SWANTZ, MARJA LIISA, social anthropologist, educator; b. Kuopio, Finland, Feb. 22, 1926; d. Armo Aaron and Aili Loviisa (Tanninen) Aro; candidate of Philosophy, U. Helsinki, 1947; Licenciate of Philosophy, U. Turku, 1966; Licenciate of Theology, U. Uppsala (Sweden), 1970, D.Th., 1970; m. Lloyd F. William Swantz, Nov. 27, 1954; children: Aili Mari, Eva Liisa, Lea June. Student sec. Student Christian Fedn. of Finland, 1950-51; faculty Tchr. Tng. Sch. for Women, Moshi, Tanganyika, 1952-56; faculty, trainer in Swahili lang. Internat. Tng. Centre, Hothorpe, Eng., 1957-60; research asso. U. Dar es Salaam, 1966-70, sr. research fellow, 1972-75; docent U. Uppsala, 1971; lectr. U. Helsinki, 1975-81, docent, 1975—, asst. prof., 1971-72, 75-81, dir. Inst. of Devel. Studies, 1981—; sr. fellow UNU World Inst. Devel Econs. Research, Annankatu, Helsinki; acting prof. cultural anthropol. U. Helsinki, 1986; dir. internat. research project, Tanzania, 1975-79; cons. govt. leaders and ministries, Tanzania; cons. Ministry Fgn. Affairs, Finland, Denmark, Norway; researcher UNICEF, field researcher, Tanzania, 1965-70, 72-75; vis. prof. U. Wis., summers 1982, 83. Chmn. Finland-Tanzania Friendship Soc., 1976-83; mem. nat. commn. and social sci. com., UNESCO, 1978—, also chmn. devel. com., hon. chmn., 1986—; bd. dirs. Finnish Missionary Soc.; mem. women's commn. Ecumenical Council of Finland; mem. Commn. on Chs.' Participation in Devel., World Council Chs.; bd. dirs. Scandinavian Inst. African Studies, 1982—. Served with Anti Aircraft, Finland, 1944. Acad. Finland sr. research fellow, 1977, 79, 86; Nat. Luth. Council U.S.A., grantee, 1952, Scandinavian Inst. African Studies, Uppsala, grantee, 1968; Cultural Found. of Finland grantee, 1973-75; Elin Wagner fellow, Sweden, 1967. Mem. Internat. Union Anthropol. and Ethnol. Scis. (permanent council), European Assn. Devel. Research and Tng. Insts. (exec. com., convenor working group on basic needs), Participatory Research Network in Europe (coordination com.), Finnish Anthropol. Soc. (mem. exec.), Finnish Lit. Soc. Lutheran. Author: Ritual and Symbol in Transitional Zaramo Society, 1970; Women in Development: Creative Role Denied?, 1985; contbr. articles to profl. publs. in Scandinavia, Eng., Africa; research in field. Home: 7A4 Tunturik, 00100 Helsinki 10 Finland Office: Annankatu 42C, 16 Helsinki Finland

SWAPP, CHARLES HENRY CHIPPENDALE, mechanical engineer; b. Brown's Town, Jamaica, Mar. 9, 1955; s. Elgin Bruce and Eda May (Dwyer) S. BSME with honors, The W.I. U., 1977. Engr. Reynolds Jamaica Mines, Ltd., Lydford, 1974-75, 77-81; mech. engr. Chippendale Engring., Claremont, Jamaica, 1981—. Inventor conveyor belt cleaner. Coach, Ramble United Youth Club, Jamaica, 1984—. Mem. Ch. of God Internat. Home: Claremont Jamaica Office: Chippendale Engring, Box 29, Claremont Jamaica

SWARTOUT, JEAN ANN, travel agency executive; b. Catskill, N.Y., Feb. 28, 1945; d. Charles Richard and Vera Mildred (Bower) S. Cert. travel cons. Inst. Cert. Travel Agts. Clk., W.T. Grant Co., Albany, N.Y., 1962-63; mail clk. Mchts. Mut. Ins. Co., Albany, 1963-65; bookkeeper Mountain View Coachline, West Coxsackie, N.Y., 1965-73; mgr. Argus Travel, Inc., West Coxsackie, 1973-84; owner, mgr. Country Side Travel, West Coxsackie, 1984-86, ptnr. West Coxsackie, N.Y., 1986—. Mem. Women In Travel Services, Town and Country Bus. and Profl. Women's Club (2d v.p. Coxsackie 1985-87, 1st v.p. 1987—). Roman Catholic. Avocations: music, reading, theatre, travel. Home: Mansion Sq Apt E-4 Coxsackie NY 12051 Office: Country Side Travel Rt 9-W West Coxsackie NY 12192

SWARTWOUT, JOSEPH RODOLPH, physician; b. Pascagoula, Miss., June 17, 1925; s. Thomas Roswell and Marshall (Coleman) S. Student, Miss. Coll., 1943-44; MD, Tulane U., 1951. Intern Touro Infirmary, New Orleans, 1951-52; asst. in obstetrics and medicine Tulane U., 1952-53, instr., 1955-60; Nat. Found. fellow Harvard U., 1953-55; asst. medicine Peter Bent Brigham Hosp., Boston, 1953-55; assoc. in obstet. research Boston Lying-In-Hosp., 1953-55; asst. prof. U. Pitts., 1960-61; assoc. prof. Emory U., Atlanta, 1961-66; assoc. prof. ob-gyn U. Chgo., 1967-80; chief ob-gyn at Prime Health, also clin. assoc. prof. U. Kans. Sch. Medicine, 1978-80; prof. dept. ob-gyn Mercer U. Sch. Medicine, Macon, Ga., 1980—, assoc. dean., 1982—. Fellow Am. Coll. Obstetricians and Gynecologists, Am. Heart Assn. (council clin. cardiology), Am. Acad. Reproductive Medicine; mem. AMA, Bibb County Med. Soc., Population Assn. Am., AAAS, Med. Assn. Ga., Assn. Profs. Ob-gyn, Am. Pub. Health Assn., Network Community Oriented Ednl. Instns. for Health Scis. corr.). Home: 319 Alexandria St Macon GA 31210 Office: Mercer U Sch Medicine Macon GA 31207

SWARTZ, B(ENJAMIN) K(INSELL), JR., archaeologist, educator; b. Los Angeles, June 23, 1931; s. Benjamin Kinsell and Maxine Marietta (Pearce) S.; m. Cyrilla Casillas, Oct. 23, 1966; children—Benjamin Kinsell III, Frank Casillas. A.A. summa cum laude, Los Angeles City Coll., 1952; B.A., UCLA, 1954, M.A., 1958; Ph.D., U. Ariz., 1964. Curator Klamath County Mus., Oreg., 1959-61, research assoc., 1961-62; asst. prof. anthropology Ball State U., Muncie, Ind., 1964-68, assoc. prof., 1968-72, prof., 1972—; vis. sr. lectr. U. Ghana, 1970-71; exchange prof. U. Yaoundé, Cameroon, 1984-85; field researcher N.Am., West Africa; exec. bd., pres. Am. Com. to Advance Study of Petroglyphs and Pictographs; bd. dirs. Council Conservation Ind. Archaeology. Editor: Archaeological Reports; contbr. revs. and articles to profl. jours.; author books, monographs in field including: West African Culture Dynamics, 1980, Indiana's Prehistoric Past, 1981. Klamath County chmn. Oreg. Statehood Centennial, 1959. Served with USN, 1954-56. Fellow AAAS, Am. Anthrop. Assn., Royal Anthrop. Inst., Ind. Acad. Sci.; mem. Current Anthropology (assoc.), Soc. Am. Archaeology, Soc. African Archaeologists in Am., Prehistoric Soc., Internat. Com. Rock Art, Assn. Field Archaeology, Sigma Xi, Lambda Alpha (nat. council, exec. sec.). Home: 3600 Brook Dr Muncie IN 47304 Office: Ball State U Dept Anthropology Muncie IN 47306

SWARTZ, CHRISTIAN LEFEVRE, lawyer; b. Mechanicsburg, Pa., Aug. 14, 1915; s. Christian Ira and Anna Frances (LeFevre) S.; m. Jean Althan Vanderbilt, Nov. 30, 1946 (div. 1964); children—Christian Arthur, James Vanderbilt, B.S., U. Pa., 1937; LL.B., Temple U., 1946; LL.M., George Washington U., 1950. Bar: Pa. 1947, D.C. 1947, U.S. Dist. Ct. D.C. 1947, U.S. Supreme Ct. 1955, U.S. Ct. Claims 1959, U.S. Ct. Appeals (D.C. cir.) 1959, U.S. Ct. Customs and Patent Appeals 1963. Assoc. James W. Batchelor Law Office, Washington, 1947-50, Julia B. Hopkins Law Office, 1950-51; asst. counsel facilities br. Naval Air Systems Command, Office of Gen. Counsel, Dept. Navy, Washington, 1951-72; sole practice, Washington, 1972—. Exhibited woodcarving in numerous shows. Served to lt. USNR, 1941-46. Mem. Fed. Bar Assn., D.C. Bar Assn., Nat. Woodcarvers Assn., No. Va. Carvers Assn. Republican. Presbyterian. Clubs: Capitol Hill, Capital Yacht (Washington); Corinthian Yacht (Ridge, Md.).

SWARTZ, JAMES RICHARD, investment company executive; b. Pitts., Oct. 4, 1942; s. Frank Thomas and Mary Elizabeth (Roth) S.; m. Susan Lee Shallcross, June 18, 1966; children: James Scott, Karin Lynn, Kristin Lee. AB, Harvard, 1964; MS in Indsl. Adminstrn., Carnegie-Mellon U., 1966. Asst. to v.p. mfg. Campbell Soup Co., Camden, N.J., 1966-68; sr. asso. Cresap, McCormick & Paget, N.Y.C., 1968-72; asst. v.p. G.H. Walker, Laird Inc., N.Y.C., 1972-74; v.p. Citicorp Venture Capital Ltd., N.Y.C., 1974-78; gen. partner Adler & Co., N.Y.C., 1978-83; mng. ptnr. Accel Ptnrs., 1983—; chmn. Patterson & Swartz, Inc., Princeton and San Francisco, 1983—; dir.Ungermann-Bass, Inc., Elcam Inc., Fleming Ventures, Netlink, Phys. Acoustics Corp., Sports Medicine Systems, Inc., Teleos Inc., WaferScale Integration, Inc.; chmn. Perceptron, Inc., pres. N.Y. Venture Forum, 1977-78. Mem. Nat. Venture Capital Assn. (chmn. bd. dir.). Republican. Clubs: Harvard (N.Y.C. and Princeton); Bd. Room, Racquet and Tennis (N.Y.C.); Nassau (N.J.). Home: 15 Hibben Rd Princeton NJ 08540 Office: One Palmer Sq Princeton NJ 08542

SWARZ, JEFFREY ROBERT, securities analyst, neuroscientist; b. Newark, Nov. 9, 1949; s. Irvin Brad and Blanche S. (Marcus) S.; m. Kathy Helen Kafer, June 20, 1976. B.S. with honors, U. Calif.-Irvine, 1971; Ph.D. (NIMH trainee 1971-74, NIH fellow 1975-76), U. Rochester, 1976. Postdoctoral fellow in neurovirology Johns Hopkins U. Sch. Medicine, 1976-79; staff fellow Infectious Disease br. NIH, Bethesda, Md., 1979-80; dir. biotech. group Teknekron Research Inc., McLean, Va., 1980-81; pres. AgroBiotics, Inc., Balt., 1981-82, Urbana, Ill., 1981-82; sr. scientist Pall Corp., Glen Cove, N.Y., 1982-83, sr. mktg. mgr. biotech., 1983-85; dir. mktg. and sales, 1985-86; biotech./health care analyst Goldman Sachs & Co., 1986—; cons. U.S. Senate Subcom. on Sci., Tech. and Space, 1979-80. Author: (with others) Genetic Engineering: Issues and Trends, 1982; contbr. numerous articles to profl. jours. Recipient Undergrad. Research award Bank of Am., 1970-71, Nat. Research Service award, 1976-79. Mem. Neurosci. Soc., Am. Chem. Soc., Soc. Indsl. Microbiology. Democrat. Jewish.

SWARZTRAUBER, SAYRE ARCHIE, marine consultant; b. Zion, Ill., June 23, 1929; s. Archie Douglas and Eleanor Miriam (Sayrs) S.; B.S. cum laude, Maryville (Tenn.) Coll., 1951; M.A., Am. U., 1964, Ph.D., 1970; m. Beryl Constance Stewart, June 27, 1953; children: Sayre Archie, Beryl Ann, Heidi, Holly. Commd. ensign U.S. Navy, 1952, advanced through grades to rear adm., 1976; comdr. River Squadron 5, Vietnam, 1968-69, U.S.S. Decatur, guided missile destroyer, 1970-71, Navy Recruiting Area 4, 1974-76; dep. chief staff Supreme Command Atlantic (NATO), 1976-79; co-dir. U.S.-Spanish Combined Staff, Madrid, 1979-81; dir. Inter-Am. Def. Coll., Washington, 1981-83; ret., 1983; apptd. rear adm. U.S. Maritime Service, 1984; supt. Maine Maritime Acad., 1984-86; Presdl. appointment Sec. of Navy Adv. Com., 1986; nat. and internat. lectr. strategic naval and maritime matters, 1973—. Ruling elder Presbyn. Ch. U.S.A., 1965—. Decorated Def. Disting. Service medal, Legion of Merit; Cross of Gallantry (Vietnam); Gran Cruz de Mérito (Spain); recipient Alfred Thayer Mahan award Navy League, 1974. Mem. U.S. Strategic Inst., Gamewardens of Vietnam, Am. Legion, U.S. Naval Inst., VFW, Mil. Order World Wars, Mensa, Phi Kappa Phi, Pi Gamma Mu, Pi Sigma Alpha, Theta Alpha Phi. Author: The Three-Mile Limit of Territorial Seas, 1972; contbr. articles, essays and revs. to profl. jours. Home: PO Box 589 Osterville MA 02655 Office: Mass Maritime Mag Editor Box D Buzzards Bay MA 02532

SWAYZE, JOHN CAMERON, SR., news commentator; b. Wichita, Kans., Apr. 4, 1906; s. Jesse Ernest and Christine (Cameron) S.; m. Beulah Mae Estes, Oct. 29, 1932; children: John Cameron Jr., Suzanne Louise Patrick. Student, U. Kans., 1925-27, Dramatic Sch., N.Y.C., 1928-29. Mem. editorial staff Kansas City (Mo.) Jour. Post, 1930-40, feature editor, 1940; news commentator Stas. KMBC/WHB, 1930-40; mem. news staff Sta. KMBC, 1940-45; news and spl. events dir. Western network NBC, Hollywood, Calif., 1946-47; radio and television news commentator NBC, N.Y.C., 1947-56; host Sightseeing with the Swayzes, N.Y.C., 1950—; TV comml. spokesman numerous sponsors, N.Y.C., 1956-81; reporter ABC, N.Y.C., 1956—. Author: Art of Living, 1979. Recipient Commentator award Alfred J. DuPont Found., 1950. Presbyterian. Clubs: Woodway Gun (Darien); Lambs (N.Y.C.); Nat. Press (Washington); Greenwich (Conn.) Country. Lodge: Order of DeMolay (Legion of Honor award 1938).

SWEARER, HOWARD ROBERT, university president; b. Hutchinson, Kans., Mar. 13, 1932; s. Edward Mays and Elloise (Keeney) S.; m. Janet Lois Baker, June 19, 1954; children: Nicholas Baker, Howard Randolph, Richard William. A.B., Princeton U., 1954; M.A., Harvard U., 1956, Ph.D., 1960. Prof. polit. sci. UCLA, 1960-67; program officer-in-charge office European and internat. affairs Ford Found., N.Y.C., 1967-70; pres. Carleton Coll., Northfield, Minn., 1970-77, Brown U., Providence, 1977-88; bd. dirs. Textron Inc., Bolt, Beranek & Newman, Wang Labs, Inc. Bd. dirs. Council on Library Resources, R.I. Pub. Expenditure Council, pres. 1986-88; trustee Brookings Instn.; exec. commr. Assn. of Am. U.; pres. R.I. Expenditure Council, 1986-88. Served to 1st lt. AUS, 1958-59. Mem. Council Fgn. Relations, Assn. Am. Univs. (exec. com.). Home: 55 Power St Providence RI 02906 Office: Brown U Providence RI 02912

SWEARINGEN, JOHN ELDRED, business executive; b. Columbia, S.C., Sept. 7, 1918; s. John Eldred and Mary (Hough) S.; m. Bonnie L. Bolding, May 18, 1969; children by previous marriage: Marcia L. Swearingen Pfleeger, Sarah K. Swearingen Origer, Linda S. Swearingen Arnold. B.S., U. S.C., 1938, LL.D. (hon.), 1965; M.S., Carnegie-Mellon U., 1939, D.Eng. (hon.), 1981; hon. degrees from other colls. and univs. Chem. engr. research dept. Standard Oil Co. (Ind.), Whiting, Ind., 1939-47; various positions Amoco Prodn. Co., Tulsa, 1947-51; gen. mgr. prodn. Standard Oil Co. (Ind.), Chgo., 1951; dir. Standard Oil Co. (Ind.), 1952, v.p. prodn., 1954, exec. v.p., 1956, pres., 1958, chief exec. officer, 1960-83, chmn. bd., 1965-83 (ret.); chmn., chief exec. officer Continental Ill. Corp., Chgo., 1984-87, chmn. exec. com., 1987, ret., 1987; dir. Lockheed Corp., Continental Ill. Corp., Continental Ill. Bank, Sara Lee Corp., AON Corp.; chmn. Nat. Petroleum Council, 1974-76, Am. Petroleum Inst., 1978-79. Mem. adv. bd. Hoover Instn. on War, Revolution and Peace, 1967—; trustee Carnegie Mellon U., 1960—, DePauw U., 1966-81, Chgo. Orchestral Assn., 1973-79; bd. dirs. McGraw Wildlife Found., 1964-75; bd. dirs. Automotive Safety Found., 1959-69, chmn., 1962-64; bd. dirs. Hwy Users Fedn. for Safety and Mobility, 1969-75, Northwestern Meml. Hosp., 1965—. Recipient decorations from govts. of Iran, Italy, Egypt, Phillipines; recipient Washington award Western Soc. Engrs., 1981, Gold medal for disting. achievement Am. Petroleum Inst., 1983; Laureate, Nat. Bus. Hall of Fame, Jr. Achievement, 1984. Fellow Am. Inst. Chem. Engrs.; mem. Am. Inst. Mining, Metall. and Petroleum Engrs. (Charles F. Rand Meml. gold medal 1980), Am. Chem. Soc., Nat. Acad. Engring., Phi Beta Kappa, Sigma Xi, Omicron Delta Kappa, Tau Beta Pi. Clubs: Mid-Am., Chgo., Racquet (Chgo.); Links (N.Y.C.); Bohemian (San Francisco); Eldorado Country (Indian Wells, Calif.); Old Elm (Lake Forest, Ill.); Glen View (Golf, Ill.). Office: 200 E Randolph Dr Suite 6538 Chicago IL 60601

SWEATMAN, PHILLIP JAY, retail company executive, financial executive; b. Norfolk, Va., Sept. 23, 1955; s. Julius Caleb and Lucille (Nollet) S.; m. Lynne Denise Baltic, June 27, 1980; children: Phillip Charles Julius, Adrienne Nicole.. BSBA in Econs., U. Denver, 1978; MBA in Fin., U. Pitts., 1982. Chartered fin. analyst. Asst. officer Mellon Bank Corp., Pitts., 1979-81, planning officer, 1983-84; fin. planning analyst Copperweld Corp., Pitts., 1981-83; bus. planning analyst Computer Sci. Corp., El Segundo, Calif., 1984-85, mgr. strategy, analyst, 1985-86; controller, asst. sec. CSC Comtec Inc., Farmington Hills, Mich., 1986-87; controller Franks Nursery & Crafts Inc, Detroit, 1987—; founder, pres., chmn. PSL Computer Services Ltd., Pitts., 1983—. Recipient Univ. Honors Scholarship U. Denver, 1976-78. Mem. Fin. Analyst Soc. Detroit, Controllers Council, Nat. Assn. Accts. Republican. Roman Catholic. Lodge: Rotary. Home: 25612 Livingston Circle Farmington Hills MI 48018 Office: Franks Nursery and Crafts Inc 6501 E Nevada Detroit MI 48034

SWEENEY, ERMENGARDE COLLINS, horse breeder; b. Falfurrias, Tex., Nov. 3, 1922; d. John and Ophelia (Fant) Sweeney; m. William Wallace Walton, Jr., Nov. 8, 1940 (div. 1972); children—William Walton III, Ermengarde Walton, Julia Walton. Student, Tex. Sch. Fine Arts, 1939-40. Horse breeder, exhibitor, Corpus Christi and Helotes, Tex., 1956—; pres. Paws Gulf Coast Humane Soc., Corpus Christi, 1978-87; lectr. in field. Bd. dirs., dir. region 5 of Tex. Human Info. Network, 1978-81. Mem. Arabian Horse Club of Am. Republican. Club: Corpus Christi Town. Contbr. to Arabian Horse Jour. in Eng. Address: 3461 Floyd St Corpus Christi TX 78411

SWEENEY, ERNESTINE KAY, nurse; b. Savannah, Ga., Oct. 26, 1959; d. James William and Jane Catherine (Brewer) S.; m. John Earl Foshee, Feb. 12, 1983 (div. 1988). A.D. in Nursing Sci., Northwestern State U., Shreveport, La., 1982. R.N., dental asst. Barksdale AFB, Bossier City, La., 1978-79; nurse orthopedics and neurosurgery Bossier Med. Ctr., 1982-87, nurse cardiac med. unit, 1987—. State officer Internat. Order Rainbow for Girls, 1977-80; vol. La. State Spl. Olympics, Bossier City, 1977-78. Mem. Am. Assn. Critical Care Nurses, NOW. Democrat. Roman Catholic. Lodge: Order Eastern Star. Avocations: writing short stories, collecting records, pen and ink sketching. Home: 3314 Schuler Dr Bossier City LA 71111 Office: Bossier Med Ctr 2105 Airline Dr 100 South Bossier City LA 71111

SWEENEY, GEORGE BERNARD, JR., broadcast executive, travel agency executive; b. Cleve., May 9, 1933; s. George Bernard and Ethel E. (Wise) S.; BS in Bus. Adminstrn., John Carroll U., 1955; MBA., U. Pa., 1957; m. Molly Jane O'Neill, July 13, 1963; children: Brian, Kelly, Mark, Kevin, Kim. With Exxon Corp., 1956-78, chmn., pres. Esso Pakistan Fertilizer Co., Karachi, 1969-74, v.p. Exxon Corp. and Exxon Chem. U.S.A., Houston, 1974-78; dir., prin. Chagrin Valley Co. Ltd., Cleve., 1977-81; dir. Nevamar Corp., Odenton, Md., Evergreen Capital Corp., Austin, Tex., Mapleleaf Capital Corp., Houston; chmn. bd. A/L Sports, Inc., Denver, 1979-83, Resource Bank, Houston, 1985-87; pres., prin. Questers, Inc., Houston, 1979—; pres., prin. Stas. KMUV/KPHD, Conroe, Tex., 1984—, Sweeney Broadcasting Co., 1984—; pres., prin. Travel Network Sweeney Travel Quest Inc., 1987—. Bd. dirs., v.p. Houston Symphony, 1976—; Resource Bank, Houston; trustee John Carroll U., Cleve., 1977—, Strake Jesuit Coll. Prep., Houston, 1979-85; trustee, chmn. bd. Trinity Coll., Washington, 1974-80; exec. bd. Wharton Grad. Sch., U. Pa., 1980-85; trustee, bd. dirs., exec. com. U. St. Thomas, Houston, 1982—; bd. dirs. Tex. Hunter-Jumper Assn., 1981-87; dir., v.p. Houston Hunter Jumper Charity Horse Show, 1983-88; chmn. "Friends of St. Francis" Franciscan Mission Service, Silver Springs, Md., 1987—, also bd. dirs. Served to 1st lt. Transp. Corps, U.S. Army, 1958. Recipient in Pakistan U.S. State Dept. citation of appreciation, 1974, John Carroll U. Centennial medal, 1986. Clubs: Houston, Houstonian Club. Home: Rt 1 Box 12 Macedonia Rd Hockley TX 77447-9712

SWEENEY, JAMES PATRICK, management consultant; b. Chgo., Feb. 3, 1952; s. James Thomas and Rita Marie (Quill) S.; m. Mona L. Maryjowski, Sept. 17, 1983; children: Matthew Quill, Kaelin Tauber. AB, U. Notre Dame, 1974; MS with honors, DePaul U., 1981. Staff cons. Arthur Andersen & Co., Chgo., 1974-76, sr. cons., 1976-79, mgr., 1979-82, sr. mgr.,

1982-85; ptnr. Arthur Andersen & Co., London, 1985-86, ptnr.-in-charge European health care cons. practice, 1986—; mem. faculty Am. Coll. Healthcare Execs., Chgo., 1981—; lectr. DePaul U. Chgo., 1983; vis. lectr. Royal Coll. Physicians, London, 1987. Commr. Bd. Police and Fire Commrs., Chgo., 1979. Mem. Healthcare Fin. Mgmt. Assn., Healthcare Mgmt. and Info. Systems Soc. Club: American, Aquilla (London). Home: 17 Drayton Gardens, London SW10 9RY, England Office: Arthur Andersen & Co, 2 Arundel St, London WC2R 3LT, England

SWEET, ALLEN ALEXANDER, microelectronics consultant, educator; b. Providence, July 5, 1943; s. Norman Allen and Caroline Elizabeth (Gunn) S.; m. C. Frances MacIver, July 12, 1980; children—Kaatje, John, Martin, Melinda, Andy, Jill. B.S. in E.E., Worcester Poly. Inst., 1966; M.S. in Physics/E.E., Cornell U., 1968, Ph.D., 1970. Sr. research engr. Monsanto Co., St. Louis, 1970-71; group leader Microwave Assocs., Burlington, Mass., 1971-75; mem. tech. staff Varian Assocs., Palo Alto, Calif., 1975-77; sect. head Watkins Johnson Co., Palo Alto, 1977-79; microelectronics cons., Menlo Park, 1979—; course instr. Tech. Service Corp., Silver Spring, Md., 1981—. Contbr. articles to profl. jours. Mem. IEEE (IEEE-MTT Microwave prize, 1977). Democrat. Episcopalian.

SWEETING, JOHN PAUL, advertising executive; b. Surrey, Eng., Dec. 30, 1933; s. James Henry and Helena S.; m. Valarie Ann Sweeting; children: Paul, Ian, Andrew. Student, City London Coll., 1954-59, U. Va., 1969. Account exec. Samson Clark & Co., London, 1954-62; account exec., client service dir., exec. dir. Lintas Ltd., London, 1962-72; dir. mktg. services and planning SSC&B Lintas Internat., London, 1972-85, corp. devel. dir., regional dir. for India, Pakistan, Korea and Japan, 1985—. Served as pilot officer RAF, 1952-54. Mem. Inst. Practitioners in Advt., Internat. Advt. Assn., European Assn. Advt. Agys. (mem. council). Club: Royal Automobile (London). Home: 2 Birchwood Ln, Chaldon, Chaterham, Surrey CR3 5DQ, England Office: Lintas Worldwide One Dag Hammarskjold Plaza New York NY 10017

SWENEY, FREDRIC, artist, writer; b. Holidaysburg, Pa., June 5, 1912; s. Charles Frederick and Ida (Haworth) S.; m. Ruth-B.-Hogan, June 13, 1937; 1 son, William Lee. Student Cleve. Inst. Art, 1931-33. Artist Cleve. Press, 1933-41; supr. tech. pub. Leece-Neville Co., Cleve., 1941-47; wildlife calendar artist Brown & Bigelow, St. Paul, 1949-79; instr. in graphics, head of graphics Ringling Sch. Art and Design, Sarasota, Fla., 1950-76. Author, illustrator: Techniques of Drawing and Painting Wildlife, 1959; Drawing and Painting Birds, 1961; Painting the American Scene, 1964; The Art of Painting Animals, 1983; The Art of Painting Cityscapes and the Urban Environment, 1985. Contbr. illustrations to popular mags., 1943-76. Group shows include Wild Wings Ann.; represented in permanent collections various corps. Recipient Nat. Offset Lithograph 1960-61; Lithographic Competition and Exhibit award, 1961; Design for Printing on Plastics award 2d Ann. Printing Exhbn., Mpls., 1962. Democrat. Presbyterian. Lodge: Masons. Home and Studio: 22244 SE 42d Ln Issaquah WA 98027-7215

SWENSON, ERICK NOAK, data processing executive, retired naval officer; b. Rochester, N.Y., June 12, 1926; s. Noak and Hulda Josephina (Sjellberg) S.; m. Annette Miller, Nov. 22, 1959; 1 child, Erika Margaret. BEE, U. Rochester, 1950; postgrad. U. Pitts., 1950-51, USN Postgrad. Sch., 1960-62. Registered profl. electrical engr., Calif. Enlisted USN, 1944, commd. ensign, 1951, advanced through grades to capt., 1975; electronics div. officer USS Missouri, 1951-52; ships supt. U.S. Navy Yard, San Francisco, 1952-53; quality control engr. Naval Ordnance div. Eastman Kodak Co., Rochester, N.Y., 1953-57; asst. Naval Tactical Data System project officer Dept. Navy, Washington , 1957-60, buships tech. rep. St. Paul, 1962-65, naval tactical data system project officer, Washington, 1965-75, ret., 1975; sr. scientist Hughes Aircraft Co., Fullerton, Calif., 1975-76, project mgr., 1976—; served as mil. adv. to NATO Indsl. Adv. Group on Naval Command and Control; coordinated naval command and control matters for U.S. and Allied Navies and involved in fgn. mil. sales; co-designer Naval Tactical Data System used world-wide for combat warships; instigated update of combat weapons system USN destroyers (KIDD class); pres. Physical Evaluation Bd., U.S. Navy, Washington, 1969-75; Pres. 1st Luth. Ch., Fullerton, Calif., 1981-83; mem. Mil. Service Academy Rev. Bd., 39th Congl. Dist., Fullerton, 1982—. Decorated Meritorious Service Medal; recipient Value Engr. award Hughes Aircraft Co., 1980, Naval Bd. Crest, Australian Dept. Def., 1975; N.Y. State Regents scholar 1946-50. Mem. IEEE, Am. Soc. Naval Engrs. (chmn. Long Beach/ Greater Los Angeles sect. 1987-88), USN League, Am. Def. Preparedness Assn., Nat. Railway Hist. Soc., USS Missouri Assn., Am. Battleship Assn., Fleet Res. Assn., U.S. Naval Inst., Australian Naval Inst. Home: 2073 Smokewood Ave Fullerton CA 92631 Office: Hughes Aircraft Co 1901 W Malvern Fullerton CA 92634

SWENSON, HAROLD FRANCIS, crisis management consultant; b. N.Y.C., Apr. 28, 1915; s. Charles Henry and Ethel Marie (Igoe) S.; A.B., Manhattan Coll., 1938; student Fordham U. Law Sch., 1938-41; m. Mildred Chandler, Dec. 31, 1943; 1 dau., Sally. Mem. law firm Root, Clark, Buckner & Ballantine, N.Y.C., 1938-41; spl. agt. FBI, 1941-47; indsl. relations exec. Gulf Oil, San Tome, Venezuela, 1947-52; employee relations and security exec. Sears, Roebuck & Co., Chgo., 1953-54; with State Dept., Washington, 1955-65, Def. Dept., Washington, 1965-68; pres., chief exec. officer, dir. Bishop's Service Inc., N.Y.C., 1969-73; v.p. surveys, mktg. and fgn. ops. Intertel Inc., Washington, 1974-78; with law dept., security exec. Chesebrough-Pond's Inc., Greenwich, Conn., 1978-86, crisis mgmt. cons. exec., 1986—. Polit. attache U.S. Embassy, Buenos Aires, Argentina, 1956-62. Served with USMCR, 1944-46. Mem. Soc. Former FBI Agts., Internat. Assn. Chiefs of Police, Am. Soc. Indsl. Security, Capital Marines, Mil. Order Carabao, U.S. Naval Inst., Mil. Order Fgn. Wars, Marine Corps. Hist. Soc., Bad Ems Golf Alumni, Air Crew Assn. of London, Epsilon Sigma Pi, Beta Sigma. Clubs: Chantilly Golf and Country (Centerville, Va.); Army-Navy (Washington); Pathfinders (London); American (Buenos Aires). Home: 4545 Forest Wood Trail Sarasota FL 34241 also: 3873 Tusico Pl Fairfax VA 22030

SWETCHARNIK, WILLIAM NORTON, visual artist, instructor, consultant; b. Phila., Oct. 18, 1951; s. Charles Jacob and Emily Wharton (Neil) S.; m. Sara Morris, Aug. 2, 1981. Student, R.I. Sch. Design, U. Calif. San Diego, Md. Inst. Art, Towson State U., Schuler Sch. Fine Arts, Art Students League, N.Y.C. Instr. Swetcharnik Studio, Mt. Airy, Md., 1980—; workshop instr. Md. Coll. Art and Design, Silver Spring; instr. Smithsonian Instn., Washington, 1986—; fellow, resident Yaddo, Saratoga Springs, N.Y., 1987. Works exhibited in group shows at CatepetL Gallery, Frederick, Md., 1977-81, Nat. Arts Club, N.Y.C., 1980-84, Washington County Mus. Art, Hagerstown, Md., 1981, Lever House Gallery, N.Y.C., 1982, Cork Gallery of Lincoln Ctr., N.Y.C., 1982, City Hall Courtyard Gallery, Balt., 1983, Md. Artists Exhbn. (first and third place awards), Balt., 1983, Md. State Legislature Bldg., Annapolis, 1976-83, Salmagundi Club (Dumond Meml. award 1981), N.Y.C., 1981-83, Harbor Gallery, 1982-83, Cold Spring Harbor, N.Y., 1982-83, Butler Inst. Am. Art, Youngstown, Ohio, 1982-83, Nat. Cathedral, Washington, 1984, N.J. Inst. Tech., 1984, Weinberg Ctr. Arts, Frederick, 1984, The Hermitage Mus., Norfolk, Va., 1984, Four Arts Soc., Palm Beach, Fla., 1984, Springville (Utah) Mus. Art., 1985. Fellow Millay Colony for the Arts, Austerlitz, N.Y., 1983, Cintas Found., N.Y.C., 1985-86; grantee Stacey Found., Quemado, N.Mex., 1983, Fulbright scholar to Spain, 1987-88; recipient Juror's and Dir.'s award Springville (Utah) Mus. Art, 1987. Mem. Pastel Soc. Am. Home and Studio: 7044 Woodville Mount Airy MD 21771

SWETLIK, WILLIAM PHILIP, orthodontist; b. Manitowoc, Wis., Jan. 31, 1950; s. Leonard Alvin and Lillian Julia (Knipp) S.; m. Cheryl Jean Klein, June 30, 1973; children: Alison Elizabeth, Lindsey Ann, Adam William Swetlik. Student, Luther Coll., Decorah, Iowa, 1968-70; DDS, Marquette U., 1974; MS in Dentistry, St. Louis U., 1977. Diplomate Am. Bd. Orthodontics. Resident in gen. dentistry USPHS, Norfolk, Va., 1974-75; practice dentistry specializing in orthodontics Green Bay, Wis., 1977—; instr. oral pathology NE Wis. Tech. Coll., Green Bay, 1979-86. Author: (with others) Orthodontic Headgear, 1977. Served as lt. USPHS, 1974-75. Fellow Coll. Diplomates Am. Bd. Orthodontics; mem. ADA, Am. Assn. Orthodontists, Wis. Dental Assn. (Continuing Edn. award 1986), Wis. Soc. Orthodontists, Orthodontic Edn. and Research Found., Brown Door Kewaunee Dental Soc. (program chmn. 1985-86, sec., treas. 1986-87, v.p. 1987-88, pres. 1988—), St. Louis U. Orthodontic Alumni Assn. (pres. 1988—), Acad. Gen. Dentistry, Violet Club of Am. Roman Catholic. Home: 3211 Tuckaway Ct Green Bay WI 54301-2611 Office: 2654 S Oneida St Green Bay WI 54304-5392

SWETMAN, GLENN ROBERT, educator, poet; b. Biloxi, Miss., May 20, 1936; s. Glenn Lyle and June (Read) S.; B.S., U. So. Miss., 1957, M.A., 1959; Ph.D., Tulane U., 1966; m. Margarita Ortiz, Feb. 8, 1964 (div. 1979); children—Margarita June, Glenn Lyle Maximilian, Glenda Louise. Instr., U. So. Miss., 1957-58, asst. prof., 1964-66; instr. Ark. State U., 1958-59, McNeese U., 1959-61; instr. English, Univ. Coll. Tulane U., 1961-64, spl. asst. dept. elec. engring., 1961-64; assoc. prof. La. Inst. Tech., 1966-67; prof., head dept. langs. Nicholls State Coll., Thibodaux, La., 1967-69, head dept. English, 1969-71, prof., 1971—. Partner, Breeland Pl., Biloxi, Miss., 1960—; stringer corr. Shreveport (La.) Times, 1966—; partner Ormuba, Inc., 1975—; cons. tech. writing Union Carbide Corp., Am. Fedn. Tchrs. State v.p. Nat. Com. to Resist Attacks on Tenure, 1974—. Subdiv. coordinator Republican party, Hattiesburg, Miss., 1964. Served with AUS, 1957. Recipient Poetry awards KQUE Haiku contest, 1964, Coll. Arts contest, Los Angeles, 1966, Black Ship Festival, Yoqosuka, Japan, 1967; Green World Brief Forms award Green World Poetry Editors, 1965. Mem. MLA, S. Central MLA, So. Literary Festival Assn. (v.p. 1975-76, 82-83, pres. 1984-85), Coll. Writers Soc. La. (pres. 1971-72, exec. dir. 1983—), IEEE, Am. Assn. Engring. Edn., La. Poetry Soc. (pres. 1971-74, 1986—), Internat. Boswellian Inst., Nat. Fedn. State Poetry Soc. (2d v.p., nat. membership chmn. 1972-74, pres. 1976-77), Nat. Soc. Scholars and Educators (bd. dirs. 1982—, sec. exec. bd. 1986—, sec. bd. dirs.), Am. Fedn. Tchrs. (chpt. pres. 1973-78), Nat. Fedn. State Poetry Socs. (1st v.p. 1975-76, exec. bd. 1972—), Phi Eta Sigma, Omicron Delta Kappa. Book reviewer Jackson (Miss.) State Times, 1961. Poems pub. in various publs. including Poet, Prairie Schooner, Trace, Ball State U. Forum, Film Quar., Poetry Australia, numerous others worldwide; (books of poems) Tunel de Amor, 1973; Deka #1, 1973; Deka #2, 1979; Shards, 1979; Concerning Carpenters, 1980; Son of Igor, 1980; A Range of Sonnets, 1981; Christmas, 1982; contbr. articles (147) to encys.; cons. editor (poetry) Paon Press, 1974—, Scott-Foresman, 1975; editorial bd. Scholar and Educator, 1980—. Home: 203 Four Point Dr Raceland LA 70394

SWETNAM, JAMES HUBBARD, priest, educator; b. St. Louis, Mar. 18, 1928; s. Henry Hubbard and Helen Mary (Luth) S. PhB, St. Louis U., 1953; BTh, St. Mary's (Kans.) Coll., 1960; B of Sacred Scripture, Pontifical Biblical Inst., Rome, 1962; PhD, U. Oxford, Eng., 1981. Ordained priest Roman Cath. Ch., 1958. Editor Pontifical Biblical Inst., Rome, 1962-75, 78—, instr., 1963-75, 78-84, prof., 1984—, vice rector, 1984—, dean biblical faculty, 1986—. Author: Jesus and Isaac, 1981; contbr. articles to profl. jours. Mem. Soc. Jesus, Cath. Biblical Assn. Am., Soc. New Testament Studies. Home and Office: Pontifical Biblical Inst, Via della Pilotta 25, 00187 Rome Italy

SWETT, FRANCISCO XAVIER, economist, government counselor; b. Guayaquil, Guayas, Ecuador, Oct. 26, 1946; s. Luis Alberto and Piedad (Morales) S.; m. Natalia Crespo, June 6, 1969; children: Natasha, Frances. Econs. Deg., Universidad Catolica, Quito, Ecuador, 1979; M.Pub. Affairs, Princeton U., 1974; B.A. with high honors, Wesleyan U., 1971. Pres., Nat. Planning Bd., Quito, 1978-79; econs. counsellor Central Bank of Ecuador, Guayaquil, 1980; pres., gen. mgr. Corporacion Estudios Economicos, Guayaquil, 1980-84; minister Ministry of Fin. and Pub. Credit, Quito, 1984-86; counselor to Pres. Republic of Ecuador, Quito, 1987—; cons. in field. Author: El Modelo de Desorrollo Agricole, 1983, La Deuda Externa del Ecuador, 1980, Financiameinto y Costo de la Educacion Ecuatoriana, 1978. Clubs: Princeton, Club de la Union.

SWETT, STEPHEN FREDERICK, JR., educator; b. Englewood, N.J., Sept. 14, 1935; s. Stephen Frederick and Frances (Gulotta) S.; B.A., Montclair State Coll., 1959, M.A., 1965; Ed.D. in Ednl. Adminstrn., Rutgers U., 1976; m. Annette Palazzolo, Nov. 18, 1961; children—Susan, Kimberly Ann, Stephen Laurence. Tchr., Long Branch (N.J.) High Sch., 1961-62, Roselle Park (N.J.) High Sch., 1962-73; research asst. Rutgers U., New Brunswick, N.J., 1973-74; instructional supr. Elmwood Park (N.J.) Schs., 1974-76, Morris Hills Regional Schs., Denville, N.J., 1976-77; asst. prin. Lawrence High Sch., Lawrenceville, N.J., 1977-79; prin. Stafford Intermediate Sch., Manahawkin, N.J., 1979—; participant NSF Inst. in physics, chemistry and math. Seton Hall U., 1964, Newark Coll. Engring., 1965, Stevens Inst. Tech., summers 1966-68. Served with AUS, 1959-61. Mem. Roselle Park Edn. Assn. (pres. 1971-73). Nat. Soc. Study Edn., Am. Assn. Physics Tchrs., Am. Inst. Physics, Am., N.J. assns. sch. adminstrs., Nat. Assn. Elementary and Middle Sch. Adminstrs., N.J. Assn. Elementary and Middle Sch. Adminstrs., Nat. Assn. Secondary Sch. Prins., Phi Delta Kappa (sec. Rutgers chpt. 1977-80, v.p. 1980-82, pres. 1983-84). Research on sch. fin. Home: 12 Louis St Old Bridge NJ 08857 Office: Stafford Intermediate Sch McKinley Ave Manahawkin NJ 08050

SWIDERSKI, JAN, actor, director; b. Chmielinec, Poland, Jan. 14, 1916. Ed. State Inst. Theatrical Arts, Warsaw. With theater Polski, Poznan, 1938-39, theater Miejski, Lublin, 1945, theater Wojska Polskiego, Lodz, 1946-49, theater Polski, Warsaw, 1949-55, theater Dramatyczny, Warsaw, 1955-67, theater Ateneum, Warsaw, 1967-81; prof. State Higher Theatrical Sch., Warsaw. Recipient Polish State prize 1st class, 1964, 76; Order of Banner of Labour 1st class, 1964; Artistic prize City of Warsaw, 1970; Minister of Culture and Arts prize 1st class, 1973; commdr. Cross with Star Order of Polonia Restituta, 1976; Festival of Polish TV Films and Spectacles prize, Olsztyn, 1978. Mem. Assn. Polish Theatre and Film Actors (mem. central bd. 1970—). •

SWIETELSKY, HELLMUTH FERDINAND, contractor; b. Traiskirchen, Baden, Austria, Mar. 23, 1905; s. Ferdinant Joseph and Maximiliane (Krenner) S.; m. Etelka Swietelsky Gordg, Sept. 10, 1942 (div.); children—Veronica Hovaguimiam, Ernest; m. 2d, Anita Sprangers, Mar. 26, 1965; children—Monique, Eva. Grad. Engr., Tech. U. Vienna (Austria), 1928, Senator honoris causa, 1980. Registered profl. engr. Vice mgr. Stuag Constrn., Vienna, 1928-36; mgr. Swietelsky Constrn., Linz, Vienna, Graz, Salesburg, Innsbruck, Spittal and Munich. Named Man of Yr., Internat. Road Fedn., Washington, 1965; decorated Goldenes Ehrenzeichen (Austria), 1967, Grosses, 1974, Silbernes, 1987. Home: Laudoneasse 7, 1080 Vienna Austria Office: Swietelsky Baugesellschaft, Tuchlauben 11, 1010 Vienna Austria

SWIFT, AUBREY EARL, lawyer, petroleum engineer; b. Tulsa, Sept. 21, 1933; s. Virgil and Edith (Jackson) S.; m. Modell Paulding, Oct. 5, 1951 (div.); children—Terry Earl, Vannessa Suzanne; m. Glenda Kay Arnce, Apr. 8, 1978 (div.); 1 son, Nickolas Gorman. B.S. in Petroleum Engring., U. Okla., 1955; J.D., S. Tex. Coll. Law, 1968. Bar: Tex. 1968, U.S. Supreme Ct. 1977. Petroleum engr. Humble Oil Co. div. Exxon, Houston, 1955-62; v.p. Mich.-Wis. Pipe Line, Houston, 1962-79, Am. Natural Gas Prodn., Houston, 1962-79; pres., chmn., chief exec. officer Swift Energy Co., Houston, 1979—; cons. Northwest Ala. Gas Dist., Hamilton, 1979—. Served to 1st lt. U.S. Army, 1956-57. Mem. Tex. Soc. Profl. Engrs., Soc. Petroleum Engrs. AIME, Order of Lytae, Tau Beta Pi. Presbyterian.

SWIFT, D(AVID) WILLIAM, optical physicist; b. London, June 22, 1936; s. William Houghton and Elizabeth Annetta (Smith) S.; m. Elisabeth Charlotte Fuchs, June 15, 1962. BSc in Physics with honors, U. Manchester, Eng., 1957; PhD, U. Cambridge, Eng., 1961. Research scientist N.V. Philips Gloeilampenfabrieken, Eindhoven, The Netherlands, 1960-64; project engr. European Space Tech. Ctr., Noordwijk, The Netherlands, 1964-67; sr. project engr. Pilkington P.E. Ltd., St. Asaph, Wales, 1967-68, dep. chief physicist, 1969-78, chief physicist, mgr. advanced tech., 1978-87, cons., 1987—; part-time tutor The Open Univ., U.K., 1971-84; vis. prof. Queen's U., Belfast, Northern Ireland, 1982. Cons. editor Engring. Optics; contbr. to tech. papers; patentee in field. Fellow Inst. Physics (chair optical group 1983-86, mem. industry com. 1983-87); mem. European Phys. Soc., Inst. Navigation. Office: Pilkington PE Ltd, Glascoed Rd, Saint Asaph, Clwyd LL17 0LL, Wales

SWIFT, JONATHAN, educator, tenor; b. Glasgow, Scotland, Apr. 26, 1932; came to U.S., 1948, naturalized, 1954; s. John Francis and Catherine Little (McGowan) S.; M.A., Wayne State U., 1957; postgrad. (Fulbright scholar), Ecole Normale Superieure de St. Cloud, Paris, 1954-55; cert. Conservatoire Nat. de Musique (France), 1955; postgrad. U. Mich., 1959, Cambridge U., 1981; Ph.D., Mich. State U., 1983. On-camera tchr. French, Sta. WTVS, Detroit, 1955-56, Am. lit., 1960-62; instr. French, Wayne State U., Detroit, 1955-60; tchr. English, French and social studies Detroit Public Schs., 1957-64; tchr. English and history Glasgow Corp. Schs., 1967; tchr. English and French, Livonia (Mich.) Public Schs., 1967; chmn. English dept. Stevenson High Sch., Livonia, 1970-78, dir. Sch. Global Edn., 1978—; sr. lectr. Mich. State U.; cons. to U.S. Dept. Edn., 1979, NEA pub. dept., 1979, Mich. State Dept. Edn., 1978, Gale Research Co., 1981, Globe Book Co., 1985; test writer Am. Coll. Testing Program, 1975-76; Internat. Reading Assn. lectr., Philippines, 1980, Hong Kong, 1984; lectr., curriculum cons. Debut in opera as Alfredo in La Traviata, 1961; leading tenor with Detroit Piccolo Opera Co., 1961-86, Detroit Grand Opera Assn., 1965, Mich. Opera Co., 1961-64; concert soloist with major symphonies in U.S., Can., Europe, Australia, 1961-81; appeared as tenor soloist in various radio and TV programs, 1961-81; rec. artist with Scotia and Andis (U.K.). Recipient French Govt. medal, 1954; tribute Mich. State Legislature, 1984, NEA Applegate-Dorros award, 1987, MEA Siddall Internat. award, 1987. Mem. NEA, Internat. Reading Assn., Nat. Council Tchrs. English (chmn. secondary sect. 1980-82), Assn. Tchr. Educators, Am. Assn. for Advancement of the Humanities, Mich. Council for Social Studies, Assn. Supervision and Curriculum Devel., Myasthenia Gravis Assn. (pres. 1968-69), Alliance Française, U.S./China Peoples Friendship Assn., Assn. of World Edn., Cousteau Soc., World Future Soc., Econ. Club of Detroit, Soc. Friends of St. George, Descs. of Knights of Garter. Roman Catholic. Contbr. articles and poems to profl. and lit. jours. Office: 33500 W Six Mile Rd Livonia MI 48152

SWIGGETT, HAL, writer, photographer; b. Moline, Kans., July 22, 1921; s. Otho Benjamin and Mildred (Spray) S.; ed. high sch.; m. Wilma Caroline Turner, Mar. 1, 1942; children—Gerald, Vernon. Staff photographer San Antonio Express-News, 1946-67, head dept., 1955-67; freelance writer/photographer San Antonio, 1947—, full-time, 1967—; ordained minister So. Baptist Ch. Served with USAAC, World War II. Recipient 10th ann. Outstanding Am. Handgunner award, 1982. Mem. Wildlife Unltd. (pres. chpt. 1955-58), Outdoor writers Assn. Am. (dir. 1969-72), Tex. Outdoor Writers Assn. (pres. 1967-68), Ducks Unltd., Nat. (life), Tex. (life) rifle assns., Internat. Handgun Metallic Silhouette Assn. (life), Game Conservation International. Republican. Contbg. author books game hunting, gun-oriented paperbacks; author: Hal Swiggett on North American Deer, 1980; editor spl. projects Harris Publs., Guns/Hunting, Tex. Fish & Game, guns/hunting sect. Christian Outdoorsman; contbg. editor Gun Digest, North Am. Hunter. Home: 539 Roslyn St San Antonio TX 78204

SWIHART, FRED JACOB, lawyer; b. Park Rapids, Minn., Aug. 19, 1919; s. Fred and Elizabeth Pauline (Judnitsch) S.; m. Edna Lillian Jensen, Sept. 30, 1950; 1 child; Frederick Jay. BA, U. Nebr., 1949, JD, 1954; M in Russian Lang., Middlebury Coll., 1950; grad., U.S. Army Command and Staff Coll., 1965. Bar: Nebr. 1954, U.S. Dist. Ct. Nebr. 1954, U.S. Ct. Appeals (8th cir.) 1977, U.S. Supreme Ct. 1972. Claims atty. Chgo. & Eastern Ill. R.R., 1954-56; atty. Assn. Amer. R.R.s, Chgo., 1956-60; assoc. Wagener & Marx, Lincoln, Nebr., 1960-61; prosecutor City of Lincoln, 1961-68; sole practice Lincoln, 1968—. Editor Law for the Aviator, 1969-71. Served to lt. col. U.S. Army, 1943-46, ETO, Korea, ret. col., USAR, 1979. Mem. ABA, Nebr. Bar Assn. Fed. Bar Assn., Assn. Trial Lawyers Am., Am. Judicature Soc., Aircraft Owners and Pilots Assn (legis. rep.), Nebr. Criminal Def. Attys. Assn., Nat. Assn. Legion of Honor, Internat. Footprint Assn., Am. Legion. Republican. Presbyterian. Lodges: Masons (knight comdr. of ct. of honor 1983), Shriners (potentate 1983). Home: 1610 Susan Circle Lincoln NE 68506 Office: 4435 O St Suite 130 Lincoln NE 68510

SWIMMER, JEROME, chemical company executive; b. Chgo., Nov. 11, 1915; s. Emanuel and Ida Stern S.; m. Shirley Swimmer, May 5, 1950; children: Glenn I., Mark L. BS, U. Ill., 1939; MS, Georgetown U., 1946. Registered profl. engr. in chem., Ill. Chemist chemical warfare div. U.S. Amry, 1941-44; chemist Manhattan dist. Atomic Energy Dept., 1945; owner, research dir. Nat. Biochemical Co., Chgo., 1946-79; pres., research dir. Geoliquids, Inc., Chgo., 1979—. Patentee in field. Mem. AAAS, Am. Chem Soc. Office: Geoliquids Inc 3127 W Lake St Chicago IL 60612

SWINBURNE, RICHARD GRANVILLE, philosopher, educator; b. Smethwick, Eng., Dec. 26, 1934; s. William H. and Gladys E. (Parker) S. BA with honors, Oxford (Eng.) U., 1957, BPhil, 1959, diploma in theology with distinction, 1960. Lectr., then sr. lectr. philosophy U. Hull, Eng., 1963-72; prof. philosophy U. Keele, Eng., 1972-84; Nolloth prof. philosophy Christian religion Oxford U., 1985—; Wilde lectr. natural and comparative religion Oriel Coll., Oxford U., 1975-78; vis. assoc. prof. philosophy U. Md., College Park, 1969-70; Forwood lectr. history and philosophy religion U. Liverpool, Eng., 1977; Marrett Meml. lectr. Exeter Coll., Oxford U., 1980; spl. lectr. theology U. London, 1981; Gifford lectr. U. Aberdeen, Eng., 1982-84; Edward Cadbury lectr. U. Birmingham, Eng., 1987; vis. prof. philosophy Syracuse (N.Y.) U., spring 1987. Author: Space and Time, 1968, rev. edit., 1981, The Concept of Miracle, 1971, An Introduction to Confirmation Theory, 1973, The Coherence of Theism, 1977, The Existence of God, 1979, German edit., 1987, Faith and Reason, 1981, The Evolution of the Soul, 1986, (with Sydney Shoemaker) Personal Identity, 1984, Japanese edit., 1987; editor: The Justification of Induction, 1974, Spanish edit., 1976, Space, Time and Casuality, 1983, Miracles, 1988; contbr. articles to profl. jours. Fereday fellow St. John's Coll., Oxford U., 1958-61, Leverhulme research fellow in history and philosophy sci. U. Leeds, Eng., 1961-63; disting. vis. scholar U. Adelaide, Australia, 1982. Home and Office: Oxford U Oriel Coll, Oxford 0X1 4EW, England

SWING, GAEL DUANE, college president; b. LaPorte County, Ind., Mar. 13, 1932; s. William Edward and Ruth Dorothy (Jessup) S.; m. Sandra Sue Scott, Apr. 13, 1957; children: Scott, Kristie, Janet. AB, Franklin (Ind.) Coll., 1954; MS, Ind. U., 1963; LLD, U. Indpls., 1984. Sales rep. Burroughs Corp., Indpls., 1954; successively dir. placement and admission counselor, dir. admissions, bus. mgr., v.p. devel. Franklin Coll., 1954-69; dir. spl. program services Office Devel., Washington U., St. Louis, 1969-73; exec. v.p. North Central Coll., Naperville, Ill., 1973-75; pres. North Central Coll., 1975—; mem. Ill. Bd. Higher Edn. Non-Pub. Adv. Com.; dir. Comml. Resources Inc.; mem. univ. senate United Methodist Ch. Recipient Alumni citation Franklin Coll., 1975. Mem. Fedn. Ind. Ill. Colls. and Univs. (exec. com.), Coll. Conf. Ill. and Wis. (chmn.), Nat. Assn. Schs., Colls. and Univs. of United Meth. Ch. (chmn. com. on ch. relations), Assoc. Colls. Ill. (bd. dirs.), Ednl. and Instl. Ins. Adminstrs. (chmn.), West Suburban Regional Acad. Consortium (bd. dirs.). Methodist. Clubs: Naperville Country; Union League (Chgo.). Office: North Central Coll Naperville IL 60566

SWINNEN, STEPHAN PATRICK, movement science and motor control researcher; b. Heusden, Limburg, Belgium, May 24, 1957; s. Petrus Gerard Swinnen and Alphonsine Dams; m. Lidy Nassen, Aug. 16, 1979; children: Ruben, Evelyne. Licenciate, Katholieke U. Leuven, Belgium, 1979, doctorate, 1986. Staff asst. Katholieke U. Leuven, 1979-83, 85-87, staff researcher, 1987—; staff research assoc. UCLA, 1983-85. Assoc. editor: Perceptual and Motor Skills jour., 1987; contbr. articles to profl. jours. Mem. N.Am. Soc. for Psychology of Sport and Phys. Activity, Am. Assn. for Health, Phys. Edn. Recreation and Dance. Home: P Beckersstraat 102, 3550 Heusden, Limburg Belgium Office: Katholieke U Leuven, Tervuurse Vest 101, 3030 Heverlee Belgium

SWINNERTON-DYER, (HENRY) PETER (FRANCIS), mathematician; b. Ponteland, Aug. 2, 1927; s. Leonard Schroeder and Barbara Winifred (Brackenbury) S-D.; M.A., Trinity Coll. Cambridge U., 1951; Sc.D. (hon.), Bath U., 1981. Research fellow Trinity Coll. Cambridge U., 1950-54, fellow, 1955-73, dean, 1963-73, prof. math., 1971—, vice chancellor, 1979-81, master St. Catharine's Coll., 1973-83, chmn. univ. grants com., 1983—, hon. fellow, 1981; vis. prof. Harvard U., 1971. Contbr. to math. jours. Commonwealth Fund fellow, U. Chgo., 1954-55. Mem. Royal Soc. (v.p. 1977-78), London Math. Soc. Home: Dower House Thriplow, Cambridgeshire England Office: Univ Grants Com, 14 Park Crescent, London W1N 4DH, England •

SWINTON, WILLIAM ELGIN, emeritus zoology educator; b. Kirkcaldy, Scotland, Sept. 30, 1900; s. William Wilson and Rachel Hunter (Cargill)

S. B.Sc., U. Glasgow, Scotland, 1922, Ph.D., 1931, D.Sc., 1971; LL.D., U. Toronto, 1975; Litt.D., U. Western Ont., 1977; D.Sc., Queen's U. Ont., 1982. Sci. staff Brit. Mus. Natural History, London, 1924-61; head life scis. Royal Ont. Mus., Toronto, 1961-63; dir. Royal Ont. Mus., 1963-66; prof. zoology U. Toronto, from 1966, now prof. emeritus; sr. fellow Massey Coll., Toronto. Author numerous books.; Contbr. articles to sci. jours. Served with Royal Navy, 1939. Fellow Royal Soc. Edinburgh, Royal Soc. Can., Royal Coll. Physicians and Surgeons, Acad. Medicine (Toronto); mem. Ont. Med. Assn., AAAS, N.Y. Acad. Scis., Am. Assn. Mus., Am. Mus. Natural History, Can. Mil. Inst., Am. Inst. Biol. Scis. Conservative. Presbyterian. Clubs: Athenaeum (London); Royal Can. Yacht, Arts and Letters (past pres.). Office: Massey Coll, 4 Devonshire Pl, Toronto, ON Canada M5S 2E1

SWISHER, ROGER CLAIRMAN, oil and gas drilling company executive; b. Glenrock, Wyo., Aug. 24, 1939; arrived in Norway, 1983; s. Dallas Roger and Lola Cleo (Allsup) S.; m. Ruth Elaine St. John, Dec. 16, 1958 (div.); children: Les, Sandy, Tareca, Brenda. Student, Tex. A&M U., 1964-65, U. Okla., 1975, 78, Rogaland Regional Coll., Norway, 1977. Driller Kerr-McGee Oil Ltd., Washington, 1962-63, Nevada Test Site, 1963-64; rig mgr. Kerr-McGee Oil Ltd., Mendoza, Argentina, 1964-65, Moran Bros. Inc., Calif., Wyo., Utah, 1965-72; supt. Moran Bros. Internat., Norway, 1972-79; operating mgr. Moran Bros. Inc., Tex., 1979-81; pres. Spur Resources, Tex., 1981-83; operating mgr. Morco A/S, Sola, Norway, 1983—; pres., chief exec. officer, chmn. R. H. Resources, Sola and Houston, 1985—; bd. dirs. Rogaland Oil and Gas, Houston. Co-inventor Advanced Hydraulic Drilling Rig, patented. Mem. Soc. Petroleum Engrs. Republican. Lodge: Eagle (sec. 1972-75). Office: R H Resources, PO Box 50, 4052 Royneberg Norway

SWITZER, JON REX, architect; b. Shelbyville, Ill., Aug. 22, 1937; s. John Woodrow and Ida Marie (Vadalabene) S.; m. Judith Ann Heinlein, July 7, 1962; 1 child, Jeffrey Eric. Student, U. Ill., 1955-58; BS, Millikin U., 1972; MA, Sangamon State U., 1981. Registered architect, Ill., Mo., Ohio, Colo. Architect Warren & Van Praag, Inc., Decatur, Ill., 1970-72; prin. Decatur, 1972-81, Bloomington, Ill., 1981-83; architect Hilfinger, Asbury, Cufaude, Abels, Bloomington, 1983-84; ptnr. Riddle/Switzer, Ltd., Bloomington, 1984-86; withbldg., design and constrn. div. State Farm Ins. Cos., Bloomington, 1986—. Served with U.S. Army, 1958-61. Mem. AIA (pres. Bloomington chpt. 1983, pres. Decatur chpt. 1976, v.p. Ill. chpt. 1986-87, sec. Ill. chpt. 1985, treas. Ill. chpt. 1984), Am. Econ. Assn., Nat. Trust Hist. Preservation, Decatur C. of C. (Merit Citation 1974, Merit award 1979). Republican. Presbyterian. Lodge: Masons (32d degree). Home: #9 Mary Ellen Way Bloomington IL 61701 Office: State Farm Ins Cos Bldg Design and Constrn Div One State Farm Plaza Bloomington IL 61701

SWITZER, ROBERT JOSEPH, lawyer; b. N.Y.C., Aug. 18, 1950; s. Sidney and Claire Devera (Bier) S. AB, UCLA, 1972; postgrad. U. Notre Dame, London, 1973; JD, Southwestern U., 1975. Bar: Calif., 1976, U.S. Dist. Ct. (cen. dist.) Calif. 1976, U.S. Sup. Ct. 1983. Legis. counsel Office of Chief Legislative Counsel Los Angeles City Council, 1977-79; assoc. editor Casenotes Publishing Co., Inc., Los Angeles, 1979—; congl. page U.S. Ho. of Reps., 1965. Commr., vice-chmn. City of West Hollywood Commn. on Rent Stabilization, 1987-88. Recipient Calif. State Senate Rules Com. Resolution in Honor of work as chmn. of UCLA Govt. Internship Program, 1971. Mem. Calif. Bar Assn. (standing com. on human rights 1985-88, conf. dels. 1985-86, conf. bar leaders 1984-85), Los Angeles County Bar Assn. (conf. bar leaders 1984-86, del. to State Bar Conf. Dels. 1987, 88), Lawyers for Human Rights (gov. 1981—, pres. 1984-85), Mcpl. Elections Com. Los Angeles (chmn. com. legislation). Home: 851 N Kings Rd #309 West Hollywood CA 90069

SWOLFS, MARC, engineering company executive; b. Ekeren, Belgium, Nov. 2, 1948; s. Maurice Swolfs and Elisabeth Mellen. Degree in mech. engring., U. Leuven, Belgium, 1971; MBA, U. Ghent, Belgium, 1972. Maintenance engr. UCO NV, Amougies, Belgium, 1974-75; project engr. UCO ENGRING NV, Ghent, 1975-78, 1978-79, dir.-mgr., 1979-80, mng. dir., 1980—; mem. mgmt. com. UCO NV, Ghent, 1984; mnging. dir. UCO CV, Ghent, 1987-88; dep. gen. mgr. UCO CV, 1988—. Recipient Export Oscar, Ministry Fgn. Trade, 1986. Mem. The Textile Inst. (Belgian sect. 1987—). Club: Internat. Flanders. Office: UCO NV, Bellevue 1, 9218 Ghent Belgium

SWOPE, CHARLES EVANS, banker, lawyer; b. West Chester, Pa., June 16, 1930; s. Charles S. and Edna (McAllister) S.; B.S., Bucknell U., 1953; J.D., Washington and Lee U., U. Va., 1959; attended Naval War Coll., Judge Adv. Gen. Sch., 1957, Indsl. Coll. Armed Forces, 1966, Command and Staff Coll., 1969; m. Stephanie Swope; 1 son, Charles E. Asso. firm Gawthrop & Greenwood, Attys., West Chester, Pa., 1959; pres., sr. trust officer 1st Nat. Bank, West Chester, 1965—, also dir.; pres. Eachus Dairy Co.; pres., dir. West Chester Corp.; dir. Denney-Reyburn Co., Madison Co., Penjerdel, Penn Mut. Fire Ins. Co., 1st Nat. Bank West Chester, Automobile Assn. Chester County; lectr. corp. law. Pres., West Chester Civic Assn., 1964; co-chmn. Chester County Heart Assn. Drive, West Chester Community Center Bldg. Drive, 175th Anniversary West Chester; mem. Nat. Football Found. and Hall of Fame; dir. Chester County council Boy Scouts Am., 1961-72; bd. dirs. Chester County Service, Swope Found. Trust; bd. dirs., v.p. West Chester U. Found.; pres. West Chester Found.; mem. Marine Corps. Scholarship Found.; chmn. Bus. and Indsl. Council of Chester County, pres., 1981; chmn. Easter Seal Soc. Chester County; mem. Com. to Restore Tun Tavern; trustee, West Chester U., 1962-72, pres. bd. trustees, 1966-72; trustee Chester County Devel. Fund, Charles S. Swope Scholarship Fund, Hatfield Home; YMCA trustee Chester County Hosp. Corp. Served to maj. USMC, 1952-55, col. Res. Decorated Legion of Merit, Nat. Def. medal, Navy Commendation medal, Meritorious Service medal; recipient Coll. Football Centennial award, 1970; Congressional Medal of Merit, 1981; Disting. Eagle Scout award Boy Scouts Am., 1983. Mem. Pa. Bankers Assn. (chmn. Legis. com. 1965, 70), U.S. Naval Inst., Assn. Univ. Trustees Pa., Am. Soc. Internat. Law, Chester County Bar Found. (v.p.), Greater West Chester C. of C. (pres. 1963), Marine Corps League Chester County (vice comdr. 1960-72), Freedoms Found., Am. Legion (life mem.), Chester County Hist. Soc., Marine Corps Res. Officer Assn. (nat. pres. 1982-83, vice chmn. bd. dirs.), Marine Corps Assn., Marine Corps League, Pa. C. of C., Navy League U.S., Washington and Lee Law Sch. Assn., Bucknell, West Chester U. alumni assns., Pa. Economy League, Brandywine Valley Assn., Maxwell Football Club, Phi Alpha Delta, Phi Kappa Psi. Republican. Methodist (ofcl. bd.). Clubs: West Chester (Pa.) Golf and Country; Union League (Phila.) Italian Social; Sky Top; Great Oaks Yacht and Country, Masons, Rotary (pres. West Chester, Pa., 1968-69, Paul Harris fellow), Elks. Home: 200 W Ashbridge West Chester PA 19380 Office: First Nat Bank 9 N High St West Chester PA 19380

SWOPE, GEORGE WENDELL, clergyman, educator; b. Norfolk, Va., Feb. 2, 1916; s. Dr. George W. and Nellie (Guthrie) S.; student Drexel U., 1940-41, U. Pa., 1941-42, Marshall U., 1960-63; AB, Eastern Coll., 1945; ThB, Eastern Bapt. Theol. Sem., 1945, DD, 1958, M. in Divinity, 1972; STB, Temple U., 1946; m. Winifred A. Devlin, June 26, 1940; children: George Wendell, Gregory Willard, Winifred Ruth. Ordained to ministry Bapt. Ch., 1945; pastor, Essington, Pa., 1940-43, Camden, N.J., 1943-46; dir. evangelism, Christian edn. Am. Bapt. Conv., 1946-54; pastor East Orange, N.J., 1954-58, Kenova, W.Va., 1958-63, Port Chester, N.Y., 1963-70; registrar Westchester Community Coll., 1970-74, asst. dir. guidance services, 1975-84; founder, owner Maplecroft Realty Ltd., 1988—. Pres. Nat. Alumni Assn., Ea. Bapt. Theol. Sem., 1956-58; pres. N.J. Bapt. Ministers Council, 1955-57, East Orange Protestant Council, 1955-56; mem. pastor's adv. com. Am. Bapt. Publs., 1957-62; vice chmn. press relation com. Am. Bapt. Conv., 1958-62, chmn. nominations com., 1962; chmn. commn. on Christian unity W.Va. Council Chs., 1958-60; pres. Port Chester Council Chs., 1969-70; mem. dept. evangelism Fed. Council of Chs., Nat. Council Chs. Chaplain East Orange His. Soc., 1957-58, mem. moderator council ordination Met. N.Y. Bapt. City Soc., also v.p.; chmn. ministers div. Planned Parenthood Assn. So. Westchester County; mem. Port Chester Anti-Poverty Commn.; chmn. mayor's commn. on community improvement Port Chester; chmn. Nat. Com. Engaged in Freeing Minds, 1976-79; exec. dir. Am. Family Found., 1979-81; minister-at-large Am. Bapt. Ch., 1985—; chmn. Diaconate in Bradford, Bradford Bicentennial Meml. Day Program; hospice vol., 1986—. Mem. SAR, Sunapee Region Bd. Realtors, Nat. Assn. Realtors. Lodges: Masons (past master), Rotary (past pres.), Westchester Country, Squires. Home: High St RFD 1 Box 49 Bradford NH 03221

SWYGERT, H. PATRICK, law educator, university vice-president; b. Phila., Mar. 17, 1943; s. LeRoy and Gustina (Rodgers) Huzzy; m. Sonja Branson, Aug. 22, 1969; children: Haywood Patrick, Michael Branson. AB in History, Howard U., 1965, JD cum laude, 1968. Bar: D.C. 1968, Pa. 1970, N.Y. 1970. Law clk. to presiding justice U.S. Ct. Appeals (3rd cir.), Phila., 1968-69; assoc. Debevoise, Plimpton, Lyons & Gates, N.Y.C., 1969-70; adminstrv. asst. to Congressman Charles B. Rangel, N.Y., 1971-72; spl. asst. dist. atty., Phila., 1973; from asst. prof. to prof. law Temple U., 1972—, v.p. adminstrn., 1982—. Bd. dirs. New Community Devel. Corp., HUD, 1980-82; gov.'s rep. Southeastern Pa. Transp. Authority, 1987—, also bd. dirs. Vice-chmn. Phila. Pub. Service Com., 1974-77, Sta. WHYY-TV, 1987; mem. exec. com. Pub. Law Ctr. Phila., 1980-88. Mem. ABA. Office: Temple U Broad & Montgomery Ave Conwell Hall 4th Floor Philadelphia PA 19122

SYCIP-WALE, FE LEE, physician; b. Cebu City, Philippines, July 19, 1935; d. Daniel Zarate Sycip and Tim Wa Lee; m. Sebellon M. Wale; children: Levi Japheth D. Wale, Mercedes Leah S. Wale. BS, U. Philippines, 1955; MD, Far Ea. U., Manila, 1961; diploma, London Sch. Hygiene and Tropical Medicine, 1973. Rotating resident Sillimal U. Med. Ctr., Dumaguete City, Philippines, 1961-63; cons. pediatrics Silliman U. Med. Ctr., Dumaguete City, Philippines, 1967-72, head extension service program rural communities, 1972—; intern Pittsfield (Mass.) Affiliated Hosps., 1963-64; resident pediatrics Children's Mercy Hosp., Kansas City, Mo., 1964-66; gen. practice resident Sweddish Covenant Hosp., Chgo., 1966. Mem. Philippine Pediatric Soc., Maternal and Child Health Assn. Philippines, Negros Oriental Med. Soc. Ldoges: Rotary, Gideon's Aux. Home: Oracion subdiv Banilad, Dumaguete, Negros Oriental Philippines Office: Silliman U Med Ctr, Extension Program, Dumaguete, Negros Oriental Philippines

SYED, ALI TAJ, manufacturing engineer; b. Karachi, Pakistan, Aug. 15, 1952; came to U.S., 1974, naturalized, 1979; s. Syed Jafar and Takreem Ali; m. Wajiha Zaidi, Apr. 20, 1986; 1 child, Mehdi Ali. B.S. in Mech. Engring., Engring. U. Lahore (Pakistan), 1973; M.S. in Indsl. Engring., Ill. Inst. Tech., 1975. Assoc. cons. Dr. M.Z. Hassan, Chgo., 1974-75; indsl. engr. Johnson Products Co., Inc., Chgo., 1975-76; indsl. engr. Rego Co., Marmon Group, Chgo., 1976-80, sr. mfg. engr., 1981-82; sr. mfg. engr. Abbott Labs., 1982—; cons. GRI Corp., Chgo., 1974-75, Computer Peripherals, Inc., Rochester, Mich., 1975-76, Charlotte Charles, Inc., Chgo., 1977-78; Fibrecraft Materials Corp., Niles, Ill. Mem. Am. Inst. Indsl. Engrs. Club: Bears Cricket (Chgo.). Home: 5445 N Sheridan Rd Chicago IL 60640 Office: Bldg AP4A Abbott Park North Chicago IL 60064

SYED, ASGHAR ALI, eye surgeon; b. Lahore, Punjab, Pakistan, Aug. 21, 1930; s. Ramzan Ali and Bibi (Khurshid) S.; m. Naeem Un Nisa; children: Abbas Ali, Jawad Ali. MBBS, King Edward Med. Coll., 1954; DOMS, Royal Infirmary Hosp., 1960. Physician Royal Infirmary Hosp., London, 1960; eye surgeon Ali Hosp., Lahore, Pakistan, 1962—; from asst. prof. to prof. ophthalmology Fatima Jinnah Med. Coll., Lahore, 1962-68, Sir Ganga Ram Hosp., Lahore, 1962-68. Contbr. articles to profl. jours. Home: 185 D Model Town, Lahore Pakistan Office: Ali Hosp, 21 Temple Rd, Lahore Pakistan

SYED, IBRAHIM BIJLI, medical physicist, educator; b. Bellary, India, Mar. 16, 1939; came to U.S., 1969, naturalized, 1975; s. Ahmed Bijli and Mumtaz Begum (Maniyar) S.; m. Sajida Shariff, Nov. 29, 1964; children—Mubin, Zafrin. B.S. with honors, Veerasaiva Coll., Bellary, U. Mysore, 1960; M.S. with honors and distinction, Central Coll., Bangalore, U. Mysore, 1962; diploma Radiol. Physics and Hosp. Physics, U. Bombay, 1964; D.Sc., Johns Hopkins U., 1972; Ph.D. (hon.), Marquis Giuseppe Scicluna Internat. U., Malta, 1985. Cert. hazard control officer, internat. health care safety profl.; Diplomate: Am. Bd. Radiology, Am. Bd. Health Physics. Lectr. physics Veerasaiva Coll., Bellary, U. Mysore, 1962-63; med. physicist, radiation safety officer Victoria Hosp., India, 1964-67, Bowring and Lady Curz on Hosp. and Post-grad Med. Research Inst., Bangalore, India, 1964-67; cons. med. physicist, radiation safety officer ministry of Health, Govt. of Karnataka, India, 1964-67, Bangalore Nursing Home, India, 1964-67; med. physicist, radiation safety officer. Halifax (N.S., Can.) Infirmary, 1967-69; dir. med. physics, radiation safety officer Baystate Med. Ctr, Springfield, Mass., 1973-79, assoc. prof. Springfield Tech. Community Coll., also adj. prof. radiology Holyoke Community Coll. (Mass.), 1973-79; asst. clin. prof. nuclear medicine U. Conn. Sch. Medicine, Farmington, 1975-79; cons. med. physicist Mercy Hosp., Springfield, also Wing Meml. Hosp., Palmer, Mass., 1973-79; med. physicist, radiation safety officer VA Med. Ctr., Louisville, 1979—, exec. officer radiation safety com., 1979—; prof. medicine (med. physics and nuclear cardiology) and nuclear medicine, U. Louisville Sch. Medicine, 1979—, dir. nuclear med. scis., 1980—; guest examiner Am. Bd. Radiology; mem. panel of examiners Am. Bd. Health Physics; Ph.D. thesis examiner U. Delhi, Internat. Inst. for Advanced Study, Clayton, Mo., 1985—; Internat. Atomic Energy Agy. tech. expert in nuclear medicine on mission to People's Republic of Bagladesh, 1986; founder, pres. Islamic Research Found. for Advancement of Knowledge, Louisville, 1988—. Pres. Springfield Islamic Center, 1973-79, India Assn., Louisville, 1980-81; v.p. Islamic Cultural Assn., Louisville, 1979-80, trustee, 1980—, vice chmn. bd. trustees, 1980-84, chmn. bd. trustees, 1984-86; vice chmn., bd. trustees Islamic Cultural Assn. of Louisville, Inc., 1987—; ordained minister for Islamic marriages, 1983—; legal advisor Islamic Cultural Assn. Louisville, 1986-87. Author: Radiation Safety for Allied Health Professionals; contbg. editor Journal of Islamic Food and Nutrition Council of America, 1986—; editor: Science and Technology for The Developing World, 1988; mem. editorial bd.: Jour. Islamic Med. Assn., 1981—; contbr. over 100 articles to sci. jours.; manuscript reviewer for Sci. and Med. Jours., 1973—. Trustee India Community Found. Louisville, 1980—, chmn. bd., 1984—; bd. dirs. Child Guidance Clinic, Springfield, 1973-79, Heritage Corp., Louisville, 1981—, others; active Am. Cancer Soc., Heart Fund. Recipient Disting. Community Service award India Community Found., 1982; WHO fellow, Govt. India scholar Bhabha Atomic Research Center, Bombay, 1963-64; USPHS fellow Johns Hopkins U., 1969-72. Fellow Inst. Physics (U.K.), Am. Inst. Chemists, Royal Soc. Health, Am. Coll. Radiology; mem. Am. Coll. Nuclear Medicine, Health Physics Soc., Am. Assn. Physicists in Medicine, Soc. Nuclear Medicine, Nat. Assn. Ams. of Asian Indian Descent (chmn. state pub. relations com. 1982—), Assn. Muslim Scientists and Engr. N. Am. (program chm. annual conf. 1987), AAUP, Soc. Nuclear Medicine India (life), Assn. Med. Physicists India (life), N.Y. Acad. Scis., Ky. Med. Assn., Jefferson County Med. Soc. (assoc.), Sigma Xi. Islamic. Home: 7102 Shefford Ln Louisville KY 40242 Office: 800 Zorn Ave Louisville KY 40202

SYED PUTRA IBNI AL-MARHUM SYED HASSAN JAMALULLAIL, Raja of Perlis; b. Aru, Malaysia, Nov. 25, 1920; student law, Kuala Lumpur; D.Letters (hon.), U. Malaya, 1963; m. Tengku Budriah binti Al-Marhum Tengku Ismail, 1941; 1 son. Made heir presumptive to throne of Perlis, 1938; served in Magistrate's Ct., then Land Office, then Courts, Kuala Lumpur, 1940-41; engaged in pvt. bus., 1941-45; ascended to throne, 1945; installed as Raja of Perlis, 1949; elected Timbalan Yang Dipertuan Agung by Conf. Rulers, 1960, Yang Dipertuan Agung, 1960. Decorated Darjah Itama Seri Mahkota Negara, 1958, D.K.M., 1965; 1st class Most Esteemed Family Order (Brunei), 1958; Sri Panglima Darjah Kinabalu, 1971. Office: care Press Attache Malaysian Embassy 2401 Massachusetts Ave NW Washington DC 20008 *

SYME, DANIEL BAILEY, clergyman, institution executive; b. Sharon, Pa., Feb. 6, 1946; s. Monte Robert and Sonia (Hendin) S.; m. Deborah Shayne, Mar. 28, 1977; 1 son, Joshua B.A., U. Mich., Ann Arbor, 1967; B.H.L., M.A.H.L., Hebrew Union Coll.-Jewish Inst. Religion, Cin., 1972; M.Ed., Columbia U., 1977, Ed.D., 1980. Ordained rabbi, 1972. Rabbi, Stamford Fellowship for Jewish Learning, Stamford, Conn., 1973-77; asst. dir. Nat. Fedn. Temple Youth, 1972-73; asst. nat. dir. edn. Union of Am. Hebrew Congregations, N.Y.C., 1973-77, dir., 1977—; asst. dir. Commn. Jewish Edn. for Reform Movement, N.Y.C., 1973-77, dir., 1977—; dir. Union Am. Hebrew Congregations TV Inst., N.Y.C., 1982-83, exec. asst. to pres., 1983-85, v.p., 1985—; chmn. Coalition for Alternatives in Jewish Edn., N.Y.C., 1978-80; mem. Nat. Assn. Temple Educators, 1972-84, Commn. on Teaching of Israel and Zionism, World Zionist Orgn., 1980-84; dir. at large Jewish Nat. Fund; dir. at large internat. bd. Meml. Found. for Jewish Culture. Contbr. articles to religious publs.; co-author: The Jewish Home, vols. 1-11, 1972-86, Finding God, My Body Is Something Special, Prayer Is Reaching, I'm Growing, I Learn about God, Books Are Treasures; author: The Jewish Home; exec. producer TV programs A Conversation with Menachem Begin, 1981, Choosing Judaism, 1981, To See the World through Jewish Eyes, 1983, A Conversation with Yitzchak Navon, 1983, You Can Go Home Again—Jewish Youth and Cults, 1984. Mem. Rabbinic Adv. Council, United Jewish Appeal, Nat. Religious Edn. Assn. (exec. bd.), Nat. Council for Jewish Edn. (exec. bd.). Office: Union Am Hebrew Congregations 838 Fifth Ave New York NY 10021

SYMMERS, WILLIAM GARTH, international maritime lawyer; b. Bronxville, N.Y., Nov. 30, 1910; s. James Keith and Agnes Louise (Shuey) S.; m. Marina Baruch, Apr. 25, 1936; children: Benjamin Keith, Ann St. Clair (Mrs. Edward L. Reed); m. Anne H. Ellis, Mar. 20, 1946; children: Barbara (Mrs. Thomas M. Bancroft, Jr.), Susan Friedman, Deborah. Grad., Lawrenceville (N.J.) Sch., 1929; AB, U. Va., 1933, JD, 1935. Bar: N.Y. 1937, U.S. Supreme Ct. 1940, D.C. 1953. Assoc. Bigham, Englar, Jones & Houston, N.Y.C., 1935-37; mem. Dow and Symmers, N.Y.C., 1940-56; ptnr. Symmers, Fish & Warner, N.Y.C., 1956—; admiralty counsel U.S. Maritime Commn., 1937-40; spl. counsel to naval affairs com. U.S. Ho. of Reps.; active investigation loss of SS Normandie, 1942; U.S. del., v.p. Antwerp Conf., Comité Maritime Internat., 1947; also del. Maritime Law Assn. U.S. to succeeding confs., Amsterdam, 1949, Brighton, 1952, Madrid, 1955, N.Y.C., 1966, Tokyo, 1968, Rio de Janeiro, 1977, Montreal, 1981; titular mem. Comité Maritime Internat., 1955—; mem. adv. com. on admiralty rules U.S. Supreme Ct., 1960-72. Contbr. articles to maritime publs. Mem. ABA, N.Y. State Bar Assn., Bar Assn. City N.Y. (chmn. admiralty com. 1953-56), Am. Soc. Internat. Law, Maritime Law Assn. (chmn. com. revision U.S. Supreme Ct. admiralty rules 1952-56, mem. exec. com. 1958-61, 1st v.p. 1964-66), Internat. Maritime Arbitration Orgn. (U.S. rep. 1978-81), Assn. Average Adjustors U.S.and U.K., St. Andrew's Soc. N.Y., English-Speaking Union U.S., Phi Delta Theta, Phi Delta Phi. Clubs: Down Town Assn., N.Y. Yacht (N.Y.C.); Indian Harbor Yacht; Field (Greenwich); Hillsboro (Pompano Beach, Fla.). Home: 444 E 52d St New York NY 10022 Office: 11 E 50th St New York NY 10022

SYMONDS, JOHNNIE PIRKLE, retired psycholgist; b. Wynnewood, Okla., Apr. 5, 1900; d. John Thomas and Lillie Belle (Driver) Pirkle; m. Percival Mallon Symonds, Dec. 25, 1922. BA, U. Tex., 1920, MA, 1921; postgrad. Columbia U., 1921-22, 26-27, 28-29, 30-31, NYU, 1975. Research asst. dept. psychology U. Tex., Austin, 1919-21; research assoc. Inst. Ednl. Research Tchrs. Coll. Columbia U., N.Y.C., 1921-22; psychologist Family Service Soc., Yonkers, N.Y., 1937-46; ret., 1960. Editor: Jour. Cons. Psychology, 1937-46; contbr. articles to profl. jours. Mem. Columbia Com. for Community Service, 1972—; active English in Action Program, English Speaking Union, Riverside Ch., N.Y.C., 1974-75, honored 91st anniversary mem., 1981. Mem. Am. Psychol. Assn., N.Y. State Psychol. Assn., Am. Assn. Applied Psychology, AAAS, Ednl. Press Assn., World Fedn. Mental Health, AAUW, Pi Lambda Theta, Kappa Delta Pi. Club: Appalachian Mountain (hon. award 50th anniversary mem. 1980). Home: 106 Morningside Dr Apt 71 New York NY 10027

SYNEK, M., physics educator, researcher; b. Prague, Czechoslovakia, Sept. 18, 1930; came to U.S., 1958, naturalized 1963; s. Frantisek and Anna (Kokrment) S.; m. Rosemarie Wahl, June 12, 1965; children—Mary Rose, Thomas Robert. Indsl. chemist Tech. Sch., Prague, 1946-50; cert. in liberal arts, Prague, 1951; M.S. in Physics with distinction, Charles U., Prague, 1956; Ph.D. in Physics, U. Chgo., 1963. Analytical chemist Indsl. Medicine Inst., Prague, 1950-51; research physicist Acad. of Scis., Prague, 1956-58; from asst. to assoc. prof. De Paul U., Chgo., 1962-67; prof. Tex. Christian U., Ft. Worth, 1967-71; lectr., researcher U. Tex.-Austin, 1971-75; tenured faculty U. Tex.-San Antonio, 1975—; sci. advisor Tex. Edn. Agy., Austin, 1971-73, U. Tex., 1971-73; advisor Student Physics Soc.. Researcher in laser-crystal energy efficiency, laser fusion, space lasers, approximate estimate of the extra-terrestial intelligence probability. Contbr. articles to sci. jours. Campaigner United Way, San Antonio, 1975—. Research grantee Robert A. Welch Found., 1968-71, 1976-83. Fellow AAAS, Am. Phys. Soc., Tex. Acad. Sci., Am. Inst. Chemists; mem. AAUP, Am. Assn. Physics Tchrs., Internat. Platform Assn., Disabled Am. Vets., Commdrs. Club, Am. Chem. Soc., Czechoslovak Nat. Council (dist. sec. Chgo. 1961-63), Sigma Xi (life), Sigma Pi Sigma. Roman Catholic. Home: 5300 NW Loop 410 San Antonio TX 78229

SYNGE, RICHARD LAURENCE MILLINGTON, biochemist; b. Liverpool, Eng., Oct. 28, 1914; s. Laurence M. and Katharine (Swan) S.; Ph.D.; ed. Winchester Coll., Trinity Coll., Cambridge (Eng.) U.; D.Sc. (hon.), U. East Anglia, 1977, U. Aberdeen, 1986; Ph.D. (hon.), U. Uppsala, 1980; m. Ann Stephen, 1943; 3 sons, 4 daus. Biochemist, Wool Industries Research Assn., Leeds, Eng., 1941-43; staff biochemist Lister Inst. Preventive Medicine, London, 1943-48; head dept. protein chemistry Rowett Research Inst., Aberdeen, Scotland, 1948-67; biochemist Food Research Inst., Norwich, Eng., 1967-76; hon. prof. Sch. Biol. Scis., U. East Anglia, 1968-84; vis. biochemist Ruakura Animal Research Sta., Hamilton, N.Z., 1958-59. Recipient (with A.J.P. Martin) Nobel prize for chemistry, 1952; John Price Wetherill medal Franklin Inst., 1959; named hon. fellow Trinity Coll., Cambridge U., 1972. Fellow Royal Soc. Chemistry, Royal Soc.; hon. mem. Royal Irish Acad., Royal Soc. N.Z., Am. Soc. Biol. Chemists. Mem. editorial bd. Biochem. Jour., 1949-55. Home: 19 Meadow Rise Rd, Norwich NR2 3QE, England

SY-QUENEL, CLAUDE-GERMAINE, otolaryngologist; b. Alger, Algeria, Mar. 14, 1944; d. Jean and Therese (Barboteu) Q.; m. Jacques Sy, Dec. 28, 1970; children: alexander, Dorothee, Camille. MD, Med. Faculty, Lille. Intern Dunkerque Hosp., France, 1970; resident C.H.R. Lille; practice medicine specializing in otolaryngology Dunkerque, France, 1979—; mem. staff Dunkerque Hosp., France, 1981—. Office: Liberal Practice, 19 rue des Soeurs Blanches, 59140 Dunkerque France

SYREN, KURT INGEMAR, business consultant; b. Gothenburg, Sweden, Nov. 5, 1931; s. Stig Gunnar Wilhelm and Debora Junia Cecilia (Tack) S.; M.B.A., Handelshögskolan, Gothenburg, 1962; D.B.A., U. Gothenburg, 1969; m. Anita Linnea Johansson, June 21, 1957; children: Mikael, Martin. With AB Bahco, Enkoping, Gothenburg, Norrkoping, 1954-58; engr., cost analyst Koppartrans Oljeaktiebolag, Gothenburg, 1959; instr. bus. adminstrn. U. Gothenburg, 1962-67, lectr. econs. and bus. adminstrn., 1970—; bus. cons., 1962—. Served with Swedish Army, 1952-53. Mem. Svenska Civilekonomforeningen, Gothenburg Press Assn. Mem. Swedish Ch. Club: Odd Fellows. Home: 28 Lingonvägen, 435 00 Molnlycke Sweden Office: Kurt Syrén, AB 29 Andra Langgatan, 402 31 Gothenburg Sweden

SYVERSEN, HARALD SYVER, corporate professional; b. Frogn, Norway, Feb. 1, 1938; s. Christian F. and Ellen (Lindblad) S.; m. Solveig Støa, Jan. 28, 1967; children: Jon Hrald, Wibecke. Student, Bautz & Hauge Comml., Tønsberg, Norway, 1955, NHH, Fredrikstad, Norway. Clk. A/S Greaker Cellulosefahr, Oslo, 1955-58; sales asst. A/S Greaker (Norway) Cellulosefabr, 1959-60, dept. mgr., 1960-66, asst. sales mgr., 1967-77; comml. mgr. A/S Greaker Industrier, 1977—; bd. dirs. Solberg Industrier, Fredrikstad, 1978—. Served with Norwegian navy, 1958-59. Lodge: Rotary. Home: Lyngstien 7, 1720 Greaker Norway Office: A/S Greaker Industrier, 1720 Greaker Norway

SZABADI, JUDITH, art historian, educator; b. Pápa, Hungary, Nov. 24, 1940; d. Bela and Vilma (Bartha) S. MA, U. Budapest, 1964, PhD in Art History, 1981. Editor Corvina Press, Budapest, 1964—; sr. lectr. Acad. of Art, Budapest, 1984—. Author: Endre Bálint, 1969, L. Gulacsy, 1969, J. Rippl-Ronay, 1978, Art Nouveau in Hungary, 1979, A magyar szecesszió müvészete, 1979, Jugendstil in Ungarn, 1982; contbr. articles to profl. jours. Research grantee Hungarian Acad. Scis.-Soros Found., 1986, 88. Mem. Hungarian Art Soc., Hungarian Art Found. Office: Corvina Press, Vörösmarty Ter 1, 1051 Budapest Hungary

SZABO, ISTVAN, film director; b. Budapest, Hungary, Feb. 18, 1938; s. Istvan and Maria (Vita) S.; m. Vera Gyurey, Dec. 29, 1961. Dir., Budapest Acad. Theatre and Film Arts, 1961. Began career as mem. Balazs B. Studio, Budapest; leading mem. Hungarian Film Studios, Budapest, 1961—, dep.

head Objektiv studio, 1980—; prof. Hungarian Film Sch., Budapest, from 1970; prof., docent Deutsche Film Fernsehakademie, Berlin, from 1982. Dir. short films: Concert, 1961, Variations Upon a Theme, 1961, Te (You), 1963, (Grand prix de Tours) Budapest, amiert szeretem (Budapest, Why I Love It), (series segment) Alom a hazrol (Dream About the House), 1971, (documentary) Kegyelet (Piety), 1967, Varosterkep (City Map) (Grand prix of Oberhausen 1977); TV plays: Osbemutato (Premier), 1974, Katzenspiel (Cat Play), 1982; full-length films: Almodozasok kora (The Age of Day-Dreaming), 1964, Apa (Father) (Grand prix of Moscow 1966), 1966, Tuzolto utca 25 (25 Fireman's Street) (Grand prix of Locarno 1974), 1973, Budapesti mesék (Budapest Tales), 1976, Bizalom (Confidence) (Silver Bear of Berlin 1980, Acad. award nomination 1981), 1979, Der Grüne Vogel (The Green Bird), 1979, Mephisto (Acad. award for best fgn. lang. film 1982, David di Donatello prize 1982, prize of Italian Critics, prize of Critics U.K. 1982), 1981, Redl ezredes (Col. Redl), (Brit. Acad. award 1986, Acad. award nomination 1986), 1985. Recipient Bela Balá zs prize, 1967, Kossuth prize, 1975; named Hon. Citizen City of New Orleans. Mem. Acad. Motion Picture Arts and Scis., Assn. Hungarian Film Dirs. and Artists. Office: Mafilm, 174 Lumumba, 1149 Budapest Hungary

SZABO, MAGDA (MRS. TIBOR SZOBOTKA), author; b. Debrecen, Hungary, Oct. 5, 1917; d. Alexis and Lenke (Jablonczay) Szabo; D. Phil. in Latin Philology, Debrecen U., 1940; m. Tibor Szobotka, June 5, 1948. Author numerous novels, short stories, dramas, others, trans. into 26 langs.; novels include Fresko, 1958; The Fawn, 1959; Island-Blue, 1959; Night of the Pig-Killing, 1960; Pilate, 1963; The Danaid, 1964; Genesis I, 22, 1967; Kathlin-Street, 1969; Lala the Fairy, 1965; Old Well, 1970; Old Fashioned Story, 1977; The Battle, 1982. Recipient Jozsef Attila prize, 1959, 72; Kossuth prize, 1978. Home: Julia utca 3, H-1026 Budapest II Hungary

SZABO, SANDOR, pathologist; b. Ada, Yugoslavia, Feb. 9, 1944; s. Gyorgy and Ilona (Komlos) S.; came to U.S., 1973, naturalized, 1981; M.D., U. Belgrade (Yugoslavia), 1968; M.Sc., U. Montreal (Que., Can.), 1971, Ph.D. (Med. Research Council Can. fellow), 1973; M.P.H., Harvard Sch. Pub. Health; m. Ildiko Mecs, Feb. 19, 1972; children—Peter, David. Intern, U. Belgrade Med. Sch. and Med. Center, Senta, Yugoslavia, 1968-69; vis. scientist Inst. Exptl. Medicine and Surgery, U. Montreal, 1969-70; resident in pathology Peter Bent Brigham Hosp. and Harvard U. Med. Sch., Boston, 1973-77, research fellow, 1975-77; asst. prof. pathology Harvard U., 1977-81, asso. prof., 1981—; cons. Recipient Physician's Recognition award AMA, 1976; Milton Fund award Harvard U., 1978; NIH grantee, 1978—. Mem. Am. Assn. Pathologists, Royal Coll. Pathologists, Am. Soc. Pharmacology and Exptl. Therapeutics, Soc. Exptl. Biology and Medicine, Am. Gastroenterol. Assn., Endocrine Soc., Internat. Acad. Pathology, N.Y. Acad. Scis. Roman Catholic. Contbr. articles to profl. pubs. Home: 46 Clearwater Rd Brookline MA 02167 Office: 75 Francis St Boston MA 02115

SZABO, ZOLTAN, research and continuing medical education organization administrator and educator; b. Szeged, Hungary, Oct. 5, 1943; came to U.S., 1967; s. Imre and Maria (Szikora) S.; m. Wanda Toy, Dec. 5, 1976; children: Eva, Maria. Student, U. Med. Sch., Szeged, 1962-65; PhD, Columbia Pacific U., 1983. Tech. dir. microsurgery lab. R.K. Davies Med. Ctr., San Francisco, 1972-80; dir. Microsurg. Research Inst., San Francisco, 1980—; research assoc. oral and maxillofacial surgery U. of the Pacific, San Francisco, 1980-83, adj. asst. prof., 1983—. Author: Microsurgery Techniques, vol. 1 1974, vol. 2 1984 (1st Place award for excellence in med. writing, 1982); contbr. chpt. books, articles to profl. jours. Served with U.S. Army, 1969-71, Vietnam. Recipient 1st prize sci. exhibit Am. Soc. Plastic and Reconstructive Surgeons, 1977, Cert. of Merit, AMA, 1978, Commendation, Accreditation Council for Continuing Med. Edn., 1984. Fellow Internat. Coll. Surgeons; mem. Hungarian Gynecol. Soc. (hon.), Medico-Dental Study Guild of Calif., Internat. Microsurg. Soc., Am. Fertility Soc., Am. Soc. Reconstructive Microsurgery (assoc.), Soc. for Study of Impotence. Office: Microsurg Research Inst 153 States St San Francisco CA 94114

SZABOLCSI, MIKLOS, Hungarian literary historian, educator; b. Budapest, Hungary, Mar. 3, 1921; s. Lajos and Elizabet (Meszaros) S.; m. Hedwig Margulesz, 1948; 1 child, Janos. Ph.D., Budapest U. of Scis., 1943. Tchr., Secondary Sch., Budapest, 1945-49; head dept. Ministry of Religious and Ednl. Affairs, Budapest, 1949-50; tchr. Secondary Sch., Budapest, 1950-53; dep. editor Literary mag. Csillag, Budapest, 1953-56; researcher, head Literary Inst., Budapest, 1956-81; dep. dir. Acad. Scis., Budapest, 1956-81; prof. Kossuth Lajos U., Debrecen, Hungary, 1964-70, Eotvos Lorand U., Budapest, 1979—; dir. gen. Hungarian Nat. Inst. Edn., Budapest, 1981—; vis. prof. Sorbonne, Paris, 1965-66. Author: Life and Work of Attila Jozsef, 1963, 77, 83; Methods of Poetry Analysis, 1968, 69; Sign and Cry, Problems of Avantgard and Neo-Avantgard, 1967, 82; The Clown as Self-Portrait of the Artist, 1971; co-editor: A Short Story of Hungarian Literature 1955-75; History of Hungarian Literature, Modern Period, 1975-76, Maia Curreats of XXth Century World Literature, 1987. Recipient state prizes for excellence in lit. Mem. Internat. Fedn. Modern Lang. and Lit. (pres. 1981-84), Assn., Internationale de Critiques Litteraires (v.p. 1971—), Societe Européene de Culture. Address: Orszagos Pedagogiai Intezet, Gorkij Fasor 17/21, Budapest VII Hungary

SZAJKOWSKI, BOGDAN, political scientist, educator, broadcaster; b. Wyrzysk, Poland, June 22, 1943; arrived in Eng., 1967; s. Pawel and Benedytka Henrieta (Trojanowska) S.; m. Martha Evelyn Dearlove, Oct. 6, 1973; children: Vara, Sophie, Nadia. Student, U. Warsaw, 1967; diploma Social Sci., U. Birmingham, 1969; MA in Econs., U. Manchester, 1980; PhD, U. Wales, 1987. Research scholar King's Coll., Cambridge, Eng., 1969-73; lectr. Australian Nat. U., Canberra, 1973-75, Univ. Coll., Dublin, Ireland, 1975-76; lectr. in comparative social instns. Univ. Coll., Cardiff, Wales, 1976—; cons. Ind. TV News, London, 1980—, BBC, London, 1986—, HTV, Wales, 1984—; mem. Council European Consortium Polit. Research, 1982. Author: The Establishment of Marxist Regimes, 1982, Next to God...Poland, 1983; editor-in-chief Communist Affairs, 1982-85; editor 3 vol. book Marxist Regimes: World Survey, 1981, 40 vol. series Marxist Regimes: Politics, Economics and Society, 1984—; editor Documents in Communist Affairs, 1977, 79, 81, 85. Mem. AAASS, NASES, European Bishop's Conf. Home: 11 Millbrook Rd, Dinas Powis CF6 4BZ, Wales Office: Univ Coll, Cardiff CF1 1XL, Wales

SZAJNA, JOZEF, set designer, theatre director; b. Rzeszow, Poland, Mar. 13, 1922; s. Julian and Karolina S.; Diploma graphics Acad. Fine Arts, Cracow, Poland, 1952, diploma Stage Designing, 1953; m. Bozena Sieroslawska, July 19, 1953; 1 child, Lukasz. Mem. faculty Acad. Fine Arts, Cracow, 1954-65; prof. scene-designing Acad. Fine Arts, Warsaw, Poland, 1972—; mgr., supr., dir., stage designer Nowa Huta (Poland) Theatre, 1955-66; stage dir. Teatr Stary, Cracow, 1966-70; mgr., theatre dir., designer Studio Teatr Galeria, Warsaw; scenography: Princess of Turandot, 1956, Akropolis, 1962, Macbeth, 1970; dir. plays: The Empty Field, 1965, The Bath House, 1968; author's performances: Faust, 1971, Witkacy, 1972, Replika, 1973, Gulgutiera, 1973, Dante, 1974, Cervantes, 1976, Majakowski, 1978, The Death on the Pear-Tree, 1978, Dante Alive, 1981, Dante Contemporary, 1985, Replika VII, 1986. Decorated knight and comdr. Cross of Order of Polonia Restituta; recipient Polish Reviewers award, 1957; Nowa Huta Artistic award, 1959; Minister of Culture and Arts (Poland) award, 1962, 71, 79; city of Cracow award, 1971; Gold medal Accademia Italia delle Arti e del Lavoro, 1981, Order Banner of Labour 1st Class, 1985, Medal Meritorious for Nat. Culture, 1986. Held prisoner concentration camps, Oswiehcim and Buchenwald. Mem. Internat. Assn. Soc. Européene de Culture, Art-AIAP (UNESCO) (hon. counsellor 1979). Numerous one-man and group exhbns., including Venice XXXV Biennial, 1970, Prague Quadrennial (gold medal), 1971, Warsaw (1st prize and gold medal), 1972, Moscow (Silver medal), 1974, São Paulo Biennial, 1979, Berlin, 1980, 1988, Moscow, 1987; Gold Centaur award Accademia Italia delle Arti del Lavoro, 1981, Oscar d'Julia '85 Accademia Italia, Artistic award Warsaw, 1986; prin. works include European Art Banner Italian Accademia d'Europa, Statue of Victory, Centro Studi E Richerche Delle Nazioni in Salsmaggiore, 1984, numerous others. Address: 14m8 Spasowskiego, 00-389 Warsaw Poland

SZAL, MARCEL MICHAEL, radiological physicist, biologist; b. McKees Rocks, Pa., Nov. 21, 1954; s. Valerian F. and Florence (Drost) S.; m. Kathleen Ann Koczur, June 20, 1981. M.S., U. Pitts., 1981. Radiol. physicist Mid-East Center for Radiol. Physics, Allegheny Gen. Hosp., Pitts., 1980-84, chief clin. physicist radiation therapy, 1984-86; clin. physicist Westmoreland Hosp., Greensburg, Pa., 1986-88; clin. physicist Triangle Radiation Oncology, Washington, Pa., 1988—. Mem. Nuclear Medicine Soc., Health Physics Soc., Am. Assn. Physicists in Medicine, Penn-Ohio Am. Assn. Physicists in Medicine (sec. 1986-87, pres. elect 1987-88). Home: 238 Helen St McKees Rocks PA 15136 Office: Washington Hosp Radiation Oncology Washington PA 15301

SZAL, RICHARD JOSEPH, research economist; b. Chgo., Feb. 19, 1946; s. Joseph Francis and Irene (Lewinski) S.; B.S., U. Ill.-Chgo., 1968; M.B.A., U. Hawaii, 1970; Ph.D., Duke U., 1973; 1 son, Mark David. Lectr. econs. N.C. State U., Raleigh, 1970-71; lectr. econs. Duke U., Durham, N.C., 1971-72, population studies fellow, 1970-72; research fellow in fgn. policy studies Brookings Instn., Washington, 1972-73, research asso., 1973-75; sr. economist ILO, Geneva, Switzerland, 1975—; cons. World Bank, Asian Devel. Bank. Mem. Am. Econs. Assn., Soc. Internat. Devel. Author: Poverty and Basic Needs: Evidence from Guyana and the Philippines, 1979; Considerations in the Design of Employment Generating Activities for Refugees; Food, Nutrition and Employment; contbr. articles to profl. publs. Home: 21 chemin de la Vigne Noire, CH-1290 Versoix Switzerland Office: Case Postale 500, CH-1211 Geneva Switzerland

SZAMOSI, ALFRED, radiologist; b. Budapest, Hungary, Nov. 1, 1928; s. Ludvig and Rosalina (Hartmann) S.; m. Karin I. Eklind, Dec. 29, 1959; children: Johan D.P., T. Gabriel. MD, Semmelweiss U., Budapest, 1954; D Med. Sci., Karolinska Inst., Stockholm, 1978. Intern and resident Karolinska Hosp., Stockholm, 1961-68, mem. staff, 1968—, vice head dept. thoracic radiology, 1970-84, head dept., 1984—; assoc. prof. radiology Karolinska Inst., 1978—; clin. lectr., 1984—. Fellow Swedish Soc. Thoracic Radiology (pres. 1986-88); mem. Swedish Med. Soc., Cardiovascular and Interventional Radiol. Soc. Europe.

SZATHMÁRY, LOUIS ISTVÁN, II, restaurateur; b. Rakospalota, Hungary, June 2, 1919; came to U.S., 1951, naturalized, 1963; s. Louis Istvan and Irene (Strauss) S.; m. Sadako Tanino, May 9, 1960; 1 dau., Magda. Ph.D., U. Budapest, 1944. Chef New Eng. Province Jesuits, Manresa Island, Conn., 1952-55; exec. chef Mut. Broadcasting System, N.Y.C., 1955-58; plant supt. Reddi Fox, Inc., Darien, Conn., 1958-59; exec. chef Armour & Co., Chgo., 1959-64; chef, owner Bakery Restaurant, Chgo., 1962—; owner Louis Szathmary Assos.; pres. Lou D'Or, Inc.; adj. prof. U. Nev., Las Vegas.; food columnist Inside Lincoln Park, Chgo. Sun Times. Author: The Bakery Restaurant Cookbook; author-editor: Cookery Americana, 16 vols. Mem. AFTRA, Chgo. Acad. Scis. (trustee emeritus), Nat. Restaurant Assn., Soc. Profl. Mgmt. Cons., Council on Hotel, Restaurant and Instl. Edn., Screen Actors Guild, Acad. Chefs U.S.A., Nat. Space Soc. (bd. govs.). Clubs: Grolier (N.Y.C.); Caxton, Cliff Dwellers, Chgo. Press. Office: 2218 N Lincoln Ave Chicago IL 60614

SZATMÁRI, MARIANNE, physician, consultant; b. Budapest, Hungary, Apr. 27, 1931; d. Tibor and Magda (Altai) S.; m. Béla Takács, Mar. 3, 1956 (dec. 1977). M.D., Semmelweis U., Budapest, 1955. Internist, Tetenyi u Korhaz, Budapest, 1955-58; gen. practice medicine, Budapest, 1958-79; gen. practice chief cons., Budapest, 1979-85; head dept. primary health care and rehab. Ministry of Health, 1985—. Author: Special Problems of General Practice, 1978; author numerous articles in field. Recipient award for extraordinary work Ministry of Health, Hungary, 1979. Mem. Societas Internationalis Medicinae Generalis (v.p. 1973—, internat. Hippokrates medal 1985, Heim medal 1985), Hungarian Sci. Soc. Gen. Practitioners (vice sec. gen. 1967—, Medicus Anonymus award 1977), Brit. Royal Coll. Gen. Practitioners, European Workshop on Research in Gen. Practice. Home: Balzac utca 48/b, 1136 Budapest Hungary Office: Magyar Altalanos Orvosok, Tudomanyos Egyesulete, Visegradi utca 47/c, Budapest Hungary

SZCZEPANSKI, JAN, sociologist; b. Poland, Sept. 14, 1913; s. Pawel and Ewa (Cholewa) S.; m. Eleonora Poczobut, 1937; 1 son, 1 dau. Educated U. Poznan; Dr. Honoris causa, Brno U., 1969, Lodz U., 1973, Warsaw U., 1979, Sorbonne, 1980. Asst., Poznan U., 1935-39; asst. Lodz U., 1945-52, extraordinary prof., 1952-63, prof., 1963—; chief sociol. dept. Inst. Philosophy and Sociology, Polish Acad. Scis., 1957-58, dep. dir., 1961, dir., 1968-75. Author: Structure of Intelligentsia in Poland, 1960; History of Sociology, 1961; Sociological Problems of Higher Education, 1963; editor numerous sociol. publs. Vice-chmn. all-Poland com. Nat. Unity Front, 1971-84; dep. to Sejm, 1957-60, 72-81, chmn. socio-econ. council, 1982-84; chmn. chief council of sci., higher edn. and tech. Ministry of Sci., Higher Edn. and Tech., 1973-82; chmn. sci. council Intercollegiate Inst. Research on Higher Edn., 1973—; mem. Council of State. Forced labor in Germany during Nazi occupation of Poland, 1939-44. Decorated comdr. Cross with Star of Order Polonia Restituta, 1969, Order of the Builders of People's Poland, 1974, hon. comdr. Order of Brit. Empire, 1978; recipient State prize 1st class, 1974. Mem. Assn. Internat. de Sociologie (bd. dirs.), Nat. Acad. Edn., Finnish Acad. Sci. and Lit., Am. Acad. Exact Scis. and Humanities (hon. mem. 1972), Am. Acad. Arts and Scis., Polish Acad. Scis. (v.p. 1972-80), Internat. Sociol. Assn. (pres. 1966-70).

SZCZESNY, RONALD WILLIAM, lawyer; b. Detroit, Nov. 26, 1940; s. Raymond Joseph and Sophie (Welc) S.; m. Rosemary Edna West, Sept. 30, 1961 (div. 1973); children—Timothy, Laurie, Kristen; m. Susan Joy Feragne, May 25, 1985. B.A. in Chemistry, Wayne State U., 1963, J.D., 1972. Bar: Mich. 1975, U.S. Dist. Ct. (ea. dist.) Mich. 1975, U.S. Tax Ct. 1975, U.S. Supreme Ct. 1983, U.S. Ct. Appeals 1985. Research chemist Wyandotte Chems., Mich., 1961-64; exptl. chemist Cadillac Motor Car Co., Detroit, 1964-66, gen. supr. material lab., 1966-69; materials engr., 1969-72, staff analysis engr. Gen. Motors Co., Warren, Mich., 1972-77; assoc. firm Zeff and Zeff & Materna, Detroit, 1977—. Mem. ABA, Assn. Trial Lawyers Am., Mich. Trial Lawyers Assn., Detroit Bar Assn., N.Y. Trial Lawyers Assn., Soc. Automotive Engrs., Advocates Bar Assn., Tex. Trial Lawyers Assn., Internat. Assn. Arson Investigators. Republican. Roman Catholic. Club: President's (U. Mich., Ann Arbor). Home: 27333 Spring Arbor Dr Southfield MI 48076 Office: Zeff and Zeff & Materna 607 Shelby St Detroit MI 48226

SZÉKELY, GÁBOR JÓZSEF, mathematician, educator; b. Budapest, Hungary, Feb. 4, 1947; s. Jeno and Gabriella (Steinherz) S.; married; children: Sylvia Agnes, Thomas David. PhD, Eötvös U., Budapest, 1971. Mgr. programs Budapest Semesters in Maths., 1985—; assoc. prof. math. dept. probability theory Eötvös U., Budapest, 1987—; vis. prof. Bowling Green State U., Ohio, 1988. Author: Paradoxes in Probability Theory and Statistics, 1986, Multivariate Statistical Analysis, 1986, Algebraic Probability Theory, 1988. Recipient of Rollo Davidson Math. prize Cambridge U., Eng., 1988. Home: Weslényi 66, 1077 Budapest Hungary Office: Eotvos U, Muzeum Krt 6-8, 1088 Budapest Hungary

SZEKER, GYULA, Hungarian government official; b. Szombathely, Hungary, Sept. 24, 1925; s. Janos and Karolina (Ferenczi) S.; m. Eva Apro; children—Laszlo, Gyula Jr. Degree Chem. Engring., Eotvos Lorand Univ., Budapest, 1949; Acad. D. Chem. Scis., Hungarian Acad. Scis., 1971. Chief engr. Hungarian Aluminum Industry, 1954-56, dep. of minister for Heavy Industries, 1956-63, minister's 1st dep., 1963-71, minister of state, 1971-75; dep. prime minister Council of Ministers, Budapest, 1975-80; chmn. State Office Tech. Devel., Budapest, 1980-84; pres. Hungarian Office for Standardization, 1984—; chmn. com. Nat. Atomic Energy Agy., Budapest, 1980-84 . Author: Position and Progress of the Hungarian Chemical Industry, 1965; Chemicalization in the National Economy, 1971; Chemical Accomplishments in the Development of Hungarian Industry, 1972; The Importance of Aluminum in Technical Development, 1975; Hungarian Aluminum Industry and the Socialist Economic Integration, 1975; The Aluminum Program, 1979; Hungarian Economy-World Economy, 1978; Development of Industry-Technical Development, 1982; Technical Progress and Competitiveness, 1984; Hungarian Development of Industry and Technology in the Years of 80's, 1984; Chemicalization and Hungarian Chemical Industry, 1985; contbr. articles to profl. jours. Office: Hungarian Office for Standardization, PO Box 24, Budapest H-1450 Hungary

SZETO, ANDREW YEUN-JONG, biomedical engineer; b. Canton, China, Jan. 8, 1949; s. Daniel Ming and Lien Chu S.; came to U.S., 1957, naturalized, 1967; m. Vivian Lim Ong, Sept. 1, 1979; children: Jonathan Mark, David Andrew. BS, UCLA, 1971, PhD, 1977; MS, U. Calif., Berkeley, 1973, M. in Engring., 1974. Elec. engr. Hughes Aircraft Co., Canoga Park, Calif., summers 1969-72; grad. research asst. biotech. lab. UCLA, 1975-77, postdoctoral scholar, summer 1977, vis. scholar, summer 1978; asst. prof. La. Tech. U., Ruston, 1977-80, assoc. prof. biomed. engring., 1980-82; dir. research and devel. La Jolla Tech., Inc., San Diego, 1982-83; assoc. prof. dept. elec. and computer engring. San Diego State U., 1983-86; prof. dept. elec. and computer engring , 1987; tech. cons. Transcutaneous Nerve Stimulators, La Jolla Tech., Inc., 1983-86; workshop organizer, 1978—. Recipient Ralph Crump award UCLA, 1977, Meritorius Profl. Performance and Promise award San Diego State U., 1986; Dept. Edn. grantee, 1978-82, 84-87, 87-90; NSF grantee, 1979-81. Mem. IEEE, Engrs. in Medicine and Biology Soc., Human Factors Soc., Biomed. Engring. Soc., Internat. Soc. Prosthetics and Orthotics, Am. Soc. Engring. Edn., Internat. Assn. Study of Pain, Sigma Xi (Researcher of Yr. 1981), Tau Beta Pi. Baptist. Contbr. articles to profl. jours. Home: 10445 Summerwood Ct San Diego CA 92131 Office: San Diego State U San Diego CA 92182

SZILAGYI, MIKE (MIKLOS) NICHOLAS, electrical and computer engineering educator; b. Budapest, Hungary, Feb. 4, 1936; came to U.S., 1981; s. Karoly and Ilona (Abraham) S.; m. Larissa Dorner, Feb. 23, 1957 (div. July 1970); 1 child, Gabor; m. Julia Levai, May 31, 1975; 1 child, Zoltan Charles. MS in Engring., Physics with honors, Tech. U. Leningrad, USSR, 1960; PhD, Electrotech. U. Leningrad, 1965; D Tech., Tech. U. Budapest, 1965; DSc with exceptional distinction, Hungarian Acad. Scis., 1979. Research asst. phys. electronics Tech. U. Leningrad, 1958-60; research assoc., Inst. Tech. Physics Hungarian Acad. Scis., 1960-66; head electron optics lab. Tech. U. Budapest, 1966-71; prof., head dept. phys. scis. K. Kando Coll. of Elec. Engring., Budapest, 1971-79, pres., 1971-74; cons. Deutsches Elektronen-Synchrotron DESY, Hamburg, Federal Republic of Germany, 1980-81; vis. sr. research assoc., applied and engring. physics Cornell U., 1981-82; prof. elec. and computer engring. U. Ariz., 1982—; sci. adv. Nat. Inst. Neurosurgery, Budapest, 1966-70; vis. prof. Enrico Fermi Inst., U. Chgo., Lawrence Berkeley Lab., U. Calif., Stanford Linear Accelerator Ctr., Stanford U., 1976-77, Inst. Physics, U. Aarhus, Denmark, 1979-81, 88, Delft U. Tech., The Netherlands, 1988—, U. Heidelberg, Fed. Republic of Germany, Max Planck Inst. Nuclear Physics, Heidelberg, 1984. Author nine books, including Introduction to the Theory of Space-Charge Optics, 1974, Fachlexikon Physik, 1979, Electron and Ion Optics, 1988; contbr. over 75 articles to profl. jours., also contbr. to internat. confs. UN Indsl. Devel. Orgn. fellow, 1976. Mem. IEEE (sr.), Am. Phys. Soc., Internat. Soc. Hybrid Microelectronics, European Soc. Stereotactic and Functional Neurosurgery, L. Eotvos Phys. Soc. (Brody prize 1964), J. Neumann Soc. for Computer Sci., Danish Phys. Soc., Danish Engring. Soc. Office: U Ariz Dept Elec and Computer Engring Tucson AZ 85721

SZIRMAI, ENDRE ANREAS FRANZ, physician, writer; b. Budapest, Hungary, Aug. 21, 1922; s. Károly Péter and Erzsébet R. (Schwartz) S.; Dr.med., MD, Med. U. Szeged, Hungary, 1947; PhD, Kobe U., Tokyo, 1961; Dr. med. lic., Innenministerium, Stuttgart, Germany, 1962; numerous hon. degrees from France, Hungary, Germany, Netherlands, Spain, U.S., Chile, Japan, Brazil, Ceylon, Mex., India, Italy, Can., Poland, Australia, USSR, New Zealand, Iraq, others. m. Ilona Mikes, Feb. 13, 1945; m. 2d, Marta , Feb. 8, 1951; 1 dau., Andrea. Physician specializing in clin. pathology, nuclear and gen. hematology, ob-gyn, oncology, myology, angiology, nuclear medicine; prof., hon. prof., 1954—; chmn. dept. nuclear hematology Inst. Nuclear Energy and asso. univs., London, 1960, Stuttgart, 1966—; prof. U. O.M., Des Moines, Iowa, 1965-88, U. Louisville, 1975—, U. San Diego, 1985—; founder Szirmai Archives. Proposed for Nobel Prize, 1969. Fellow Inst. Nuclear Energy and Coll. Angiology of N.Y., Royal Soc. Medicine, Royal Coll. Chemists; mem. Internat. Nomenclature Com. (pres.), German Acad. Sci., Hungarian Acad. Scis., N.Y. Acad. Scis., Mex. Acad. Gerontology (hon.), also numerous med., nuclear, and lit. assns. Author books, poetry and novels transl. into 35 langs., numerous abstracts in 49 langs., publs. on med. atomic energy, linguistic arts; editorial bd. several jours.; research biochem. methods, drugs; developer myotonometer, angiomyograph, myograph, utero-embryo cardiotonograph, electrocoagulometer; developer theories in medicine, philosophy, music and art; established Rutherford golden medal, Szirmai medal. Address: 11 Adolf-Kroener Strasse 11, D-7000 Stuttgart 1 Federal Republic of Germany

SZMUCH, OSCAR, language educator; b. USSR, July 2, 1943; came to U.S., 1966; s. Isaac and Genya (Fogel) S.; m. Eileen Robbins, Mar. 9, 1980; children—Genya, Orley Robbins, Mia Jayne. Exec. dir., owner Lang. Resources Internat., Sherman Oaks, Calif., 1975—; producer TV show R. Buckminster Fuller. Mem. adv. bd. Calif. State U.-Los Angeles; regional bd. dirs. Anti-Defamation League. Served with Israeli Def. Forces, 1963-66. Mem. Encino C. of C. (dir.). Home: 12212 Eagle Ridge Way Northridge CA 91326

SZOKOLAY, STEVEN VAJK, architectural educator; b. Budapest, Hungary, Nov. 22, 1927; emigrated to Australia, 1957; s. Bela Istvan and Marta (Tompa) S.; m. Edith Ditroi, Sept., 1955 (div.); children—Tash, Barsh; m. 2d Katalin Edelenyi, July 10, 1974. Grad. in Architecture, U. New South Wales, 1961; M.Arch., U. Liverpool, 1968; Ph.D., U. Queensland, 1978. Architect, Sydney and London, 1961-65; lectr. U. Liverpool, Liverpool and Nairobi, 1965-68; sr. lectr. Poly. of Central London, 1968-74; reader U. Queensland, Brisbane, 1974—, head dept. architecture, 1985—; dir. Solar Energy Devels., Brisbane, 1976—; cons. UNESCO, UNIDO, Turkey and Jordan, 1980, 83; mem. Planning Environ. Com. of Brisbane 1982—. Fellow Royal Australian Inst. of Architects; mem. Govt. Nat. Energy Research Council, Australian and New Zealand Archtl. Sci. Assn. (pres. 1980-81, chmn. com. heads of Australian schs. of architecture 1987—). Author: Environmental Science Handbook, 1980; World Solar Architecture, 1980, 6 others. Home: 50 Halimah St, Chapel Hill, Brisbane, Queensland 4069, Australia

SZORADI, CHARLES, architect; b. Matyasfold, Hungary, Nov. 2, 1923; came to U.S. 1957, naturalized, 1962; s. Nandor Stift and Margit (Tittl) S.; children: Charles Attila, Stephen Hill. Grad., Architecture Sch., Budapest Joseph Nador Inst. Tech., 1950. Registered architect, D.C., Md., Va., Pa. Architect, planner Hungarian Central Planning Office, 1950-56; architect Chatelain, Gauger & Nolan, Washington, 1957-60, Keyes, Lethbridge & Condon, Washington, 1962-68; architect, planner Doxiadis Assocs., Washington, 1968-71; chief architect Daniel, Mann, Johnson & Mendenhall, 1972; prin. Charles Szoradi, AIA, Architect and Planner, Washington, 1973—. Author: (with others) Washington On Foot, Encyclopedia of Architecture Graphic Standards. Nat. Endowment for Arts grantee, 1974-75. Commr. DC Woodley Park, 1980-83. Served with Hungarian Army, 1944. Grantee Nat. Endowment for the Arts, 1974-75. Mem. AIA (juror D.C. chpt. 1979, 84, Nat. Council Archtl. Registration Bds., graphic standards Ency. of Architecture, Hist. Preservation award 1981), Am. Planning Assn. Mem. Nat. Council Archtl. Registration Bds. Home and Office: 2822 28th St NW Washington DC 20008

SZTOMPKA, PIOTR, sociology educator; b. Warsaw, Poland, Mar. 2, 1944; s. Henryk and Helena (Zakrzewska) S.; m. Maria Lachowicz, Jan. 9, 1972 (div. 1975). MA in Law, Jagiellonian U., Krakow, Poland, 1966, MA in Sociology, 1967, PhD in Sociology, 1970. Postdoctoral fellow U. Calif., Berkeley, 1972-73; docent in habilitation Jagiellonian U., 1974-80, prof., 1980—, dean faculty philosophy and history, 1975-78, dir. Inst. Sociology, 1978—; vis. prof. Columbia U., N.Y.C., 1975-79, Johns Hopkins U. Ctr., Bologna, Italy, 1981-82, U. Mich., Ann Arbor, 1984-85, UCLA, 1987; chmn. sociol. commn. Polish Acad. Sci., Krakow, 1978-82, v.p. com. on sociology, Warsaw, 1984—. Author: System and Function, 1974, Sociological Dilemmas, 1979 (Polish Ministry award 1980), Masters of Polish Sociology, 1985, R.K. Merton: An Intellectual Profile, 1986, others. Active Polish United Workers Party, Krakow, 1971-81. Fulbright fellow, 1972; spl. vis. fellowship Am. Council Learned Socs., 1984. Mem. Polish Sociol. Assn. (sec. 1974-77), Internat. Sociol. Assn., European Council for Latin Am. Studies, Am. Sociol. Assn. Roman Catholic. Home: Jaracza 8/7, 31-143 PL Crakow Poland Office: Jagiellonian U Inst Sociology, Grodzka 52, 31-044 PL Crakow Poland

SZTRIK, JÁNOS, mathematics educator, researcher; b. Békéscsaba, Békés, Hungary, Sept. 20, 1953; s. Endre and Erzsébet (Juhász) S.; m. Rita Rigó, Dec. 18, 1982; 1 son, Attila. PhD, U. Debrecen, Hungary, 1981. Asst. U.

Debrecen, 1978-80, jr. researcher, 1980-85, researcher, 1985—, cons. dept. psychology, 1985—; adj. faculty U. Econs., Budapest, 1980—; cons. Tech. U. Budapest, 1987—. Contbr. articles to profl. jours. Recipient Pro Universitate award U. Debrecen, 1978. Mem. Bolyai Math. Soc., Neumann Computer Soc. Mem. Hungarian Socialist Workers' party. Roman Catholic. Home: Darabos 12, 5/27 Debrecen Hungary 4026 Office: U Debrecen, 4010 Debrecen Hungary

SZUBINSKA, BARBARA MARIA ANNA, artist; b. Skrzynno, Radom, Poland, Dec. 7, 1934; d. Czeslaw and Janina (Trybulska) S.; m. Bogdan Rutkowski, June 25, 1963. BA, Acad. Fine Arts, Warsaw, Poland, 1958. One-woman shows include Gallery L'Angle Aigu, Brussels, 1971-72, Gallery Libelt, Marburg, Fed. Republic Germany, 1972, Gallery Ingeleiv, Bergen, Norway, 1978, 81, Le Ctr. Artistique, Versoix, 1980, Galeries du Chateau, Avenches, Galerie du Bourg, Fribourg, Switzerland, 1985, Hergeroder Gallery, Bielefeld, 1986, Gallery BWA, Modern Art Gallery, Warsaw, Poland, 1963, 66, 72, 76, Gallery Wahl, Warsaw, 1987; exhibited in group shows in France, U.S., Can., Japan, Fed. Republic Germany, Italy, Eng., Sweden, Denmark, Finland, 1967—;. Home: PO Box 82, 00979 Warsaw 34 Poland

SZUHAY, JOSEPH ALEXANDER, human resources educator; b. Cambridge, Ohio, Feb. 28, 1925; s. David and Barbara (Orosz) S.; m. Joy Naomi Youppi, Nov. 21, 1946; children: Paige Melanie (dec.), Noel Joy (dec.) Brooke Jana. BS in Phys. Edn., U. Iowa, 1953, Cert. in Phys. Therapy, 1954, MS in Anatomy, 1956, PhD in Ednl. Psychology and Rehab. Counseling, 1961. Recreation therapist Iowa Hosp. for Severely Handicapped Children, Iowa City, 1952-53; instr. U. Iowa Sch. Phys. Therapy, Iowa City, 1954-61; phys. therapist Steindler Orthopedic Clinic-Mercy Hosp., Iowa City, 1959-61; dir. vocat. guidance adult day care program Southeastern Mental Health Ctr., Sioux Falls (S.D.) Coll., 1961-64, lectr. psychology, 1962-64; dir. rehab. counseling program U. Scranton Pa., 1964-74, prof., chmn. dept. human resources, 1974—; vocat. cons. Office Hearings and Appeals-Social Security Adminstrn.; vocat. cons. HEW (now HHS), 1962—, mem. policy adv. com. social and rehab. services, 1971-75; commr. Rehab. Services Adminstrn., 1975-76; ednl. cons. Pa. Bur. Visually Handicapped, 1968-69; cons. clin. and counseling psychology VA Hosps., 1971—; spl. projects cons. Teledyne Econ. Devel. Co., 1973—; mem. vis. cons. Regional Research Inst.-U. Wis., 1973—, cons. adv. council on rehab. counseling, 1974-76; rehab. counseling cons. U. Vt., 1976, U. R.I., 1977, Coppin State Coll., 1979-81, Lincoln U., 1981—, U. Md.-Eastern Shore, 1982—; mem. manpower task force Gov.'s Comprehensive Vocat. Rehab. Commn., 1967-68; mem. Gov.'s Regional Commn. on Health Care Bill, 1974. Co-author: (with Barry Newhill) Field Investigation and Evaluation of Learning Disabilities (6 vols.), 1981; editor: The History of the National Council on Rehabilitation Education, 1980; book reviewer: Psychiatry and Social Sci. Rev., Bestsellers; contbr. articles to profl. jours. Bd. dirs. Alcoholism and Drug Abuse Council, Northeastern Pa., 1965-71, pres., 1967-69, chmn. edn. com., 1966, 69, 70; bd. dirs. United Neighborhood Services, Lackawanna County, 1965-70, pres., 1968-69; bd. dirs. U. Scranton rep. Allied Services for Handicapped, 1967-78, Lackawanna County chpt. Nat. Found., 1969-72; bd. dirs., pres. Treatment and Rehab. Ctr., Northeastern Pa., 1970-75; bd. dirs. United Rehab. Services, Wilkes-Barre, 1985—, Operation Outcome, Scranton, 1985—, Scranton and Lackawanna County unit Vis. Nurses Assn., 1972-74, Scranton Mental Health and Mental Retardation Assn., 1971-78; adv. com. Regional Continuing Edn. Programs, 1978-82, Easter Seal Treatment Ctr., Scranton, 1979—. Mem. Am. Assn. for Counseling and Devel. (chmn. ethics com. 1965-70), Am. Psychol. Assn., Nat. Rehab. Assn., Nat. Council Rehab. Edn. (dir. region II 1969-71, dir. region III 1971-72, 77-83, chmn. legis. com. region III 1972-83), Nat. Council Rehab. Edn. (pres. 1974-75), Pa. Personnel and Guidance Assn., Pa. Rehab. Assn. (dir.), Northeastern Pa. Psychol. Assn., Phi Delta Kappa (treas. U. Scranton chpt. 1970-80). Home: 66 Woodland Way Clarks Summit PA 18411 Office: U Scranton Monroe and Linden Sts Scranton PA 18510

SZULC, TAD, journalist, commentator; b. Warsaw, Poland, July 25, 1926; came to U.S., 1947, naturalized, 1954; s. Seweryn and Janina (Baruch) S.; m. Marianne Carr, July 8, 1948; children: Nicole, Anthony. Student, U. Brazil, 1943-45; LHD (hon.), Am. Coll. Switzerland, 1987. Reporter AP, Rio de Janeiro, 1945-46; corr. at UN for UPI, 1949-53; mem. staff N.Y. Times, after 1953; corr. N.Y. Times, Latin Am., 1955-61; with Washington bur. N.Y. Times, 1961-65, 69-72, assigned to Spain and Portugal, 1965-68, assigned to Eastern Europe, 1968-69; commentator fgn. policy 1972—. Author: Twilight of the Tyrants, 1959, The Cuban Invasion, 1962, The Winds of Revolution, 1963, Dominican Diary, 1965, Latin America, 1966, Bombs of Palomares, 1967, United States and the Caribbean, 1971, Czechoslovakia since World War II, 1971, Portrait of Spain, 1972, Compulsive Spy: The Strange Career of E. Howard Hunt, 1974, The Energy Crisis, 1974, Innocents at Home, 1974, The Illusion of Peace, 1978, Diplomatic Immunity, 1981, Fidel Castro-A Critical Portrait, 1986. Decorated Cross of Chevalier of Legion d'Honneur France; recipient Maria Moors Cabot gold medal Columbia U., Medal of Honor, World Bus. Council, 1987, award for best book on fgn. affairs Overseas Press Club, 1979, 86. Clubs: Cosmos (Washington), Federal City (Washington); Overseas Press (award for best mag. interpretation fgn. affairs 1976; citations 1966, 74, 75, 77, 78) (N.Y.C.). Address: 4515 29th St NW Washington DC 20008

SZWALBENEST, BENEDYKT JAN, lawyer; b. Poland, June 13, 1955; s. Sidney and Janina (Bleishtif) S.; m. Shelley Joy Leibel, Nov. 8, 1981. BBA, Temple U., 1978, JD, 1981. Law clk. Fed. Deposit Ins. Corp., Washington, 1980; law clk. to presiding justice U.S. Dist. Ct. (ea. dist.) Pa., Phila., 1980-81; staff atty., regulatory specialist Fidelcor, Inc. and Fidelity Bank, Phila., 1981-86; spl. asst. to head of compliance and examinations dept. Fed. Res. Bank of N.Y., N.Y.C., 1986—. Author: Federal Bank Regulation, 1980. Mem. Commonwealth of Pa. Post-secondary Edn. Planning Commn., Harrisburg, 1977-79; trustee Pop Warners Little Scholars, Phila., 1981—. Mem. ABA (nat. sec., treas. law student div. 1980-81, Silver Key award 1980, Gold Key award 1981), Am. Judicature Soc., Am. Bankers Assn. (cert. compliance specialist, lectr. 1984—), Temple U. Sch. Bus. Alumni Assn. (sec. 1982-84, v.p. 1984-86, pres. 1986—, bd. dirs. gen. alumni assn. 1986—), Tau Epsilon Rho, Omicron Delta Epsilon. Home: 1107 Bryn Mawr Ave Bala Cynwyd PA 19004 Office: Fed Res Bank of NY 33 Liberty St New York NY 10045

SZYROCKI, JAN TADEUSZ, conductor; b. Laziska, Katowice, Poland, Dec. 29, 1931; s. Alojzy and Adelajda (Swietek) S.; m. Jolanta Baranowicz, June 27, 1959; children: Renata Szyrocka-Harquevaux, Anita. MS in Engring., Tech. U., Szczecin, Poland, 1956; diploma in piano class, State High Sch. Music, Szczecin, Poland, 1958; student in conducting, Royal Sch. Music, The Hague, The Netherlands, 1968-69, Vienna Music Coll., 1974-75; diploma in conducting, Acad. Music, Poznan, Poland, 1976. Founder, artistic dir., condr. Tech. U. Choir, Szczecin, 1952—, Boys Choir Nightingales, Szczecin, 1960-74, Vocal Ensemble Berzeretki, Szczecin, 1962-71, Collegium Maiorum, Szczecin, 1973-76, 82—; council mem., artistic dir. Internat. Choral Festival Miedzyzdroje, 1965—. Composer choral arrangements, theatrical music; records include 4 Polish albums, 1 French album and 3 German cassettes. Recipient 1st prize All Polish Competition for Student Choirs, 1957, 60-61, 63, 67, 69, 73-74, 87, Golden Cross Merit, 1962, 1st prize Netherlands competition, 1969, Knight's Cross Order of Rebirth Poland, 1972, 1st prize in Czechoslovak competition, 1977, 86, 1st prize Spanish competition, 1980, Officer's Cross Order of Rebirth Poland, 1980, Grade 1 State award Ministry Culture and Art, 1981, 85, 1st prize Brazilian competition, 1984, Grade 1 State award Ministry Sci. and Higher Edn., 1986, Wlodzimierz Pietrzak artistic award, 1986, Comdr.'s Cross Order of Rebirth Poland, 1988; named Szczecin Citizen of Yr., 1973. Mem. Polish Assn. Choirs and Orchs. (pres. Szczecin br. 1965—, Honorary Golden Badge with Laurel Crown 1983), Polish Musicians Assn., Henryk Wieniawski Music Assn. Roman Catholic. Home: Al Wyzwolenia 11/5, 70-552 Szczecin Poland Office: Szczecin Tech U Choir, Ul Wyspianskiego 1, 70-497 Szczecin Poland

TABACMAN, JORGE OSCAR, data processing executive, consultant; b. Mendoza, Argentina, Sept. 30, 1948; came to Australia, 1978; s. David and Elisa (Beckerman) T.; m. Graciela Alicia Schulman, Jan. 21, 1974; 1 child, Ana. High Bachelor in Exact Scis. Sci. Computer Operation Research, Ctr. High Studies in Exact Scis., Buenos Aires, 1975. Sr. cons. Computer Scis., Sydney, Australia, 1978-80, Idaps, Sydney, 1980-81, Honeywell, Sydney, 1981-82, TV Network 10; mgr. data processing Westfield Ltd., Sydney, 1982—; part-time lectr. Sydney Tech. Coll., 1984. Mem. Australian Computer Soc., Assn. Computer Machinery, Inst. Systems Analyst, EDP Auditors Assn. Jewish. Office: Westfield Ltd, 100 William St, 2011 Sydney Australia

TABAI, IEREMIA, president of Kiribati; b. Nonouti, Kiribati, 1950; student St. Andrew's Coll., Christchurch, New Zealand; grad. Victoria U., Wellington, New Zealand; married; 2 children. With Treasury Dept., Gilbert Islands (now Kiribati); elected to Ho. of Assembly, 1974, 78, leader of opposition, 1975-78, chief minister, 1978, also minister of local govt.; worked to secure independence of country; pres., minister fgn. affairs Republic of Kiribati, 1979—. Office: Office of Pres, Bairiki Republic of Kiribati *

TABAKOV, EMIL, orchestra conductor; b. Rousse, Bulgaria, Aug. 21, 1947; s. Russi Dimitrov and Biserka Mincheva (Vandeva) T.; m. Burjana Nikolaeva; 1 child, Julian. Student, Bulgarian State Conservatoire, Sofia, 1974. Conductor Rousse Philharm. Orch., 1976-79; conductor-chief Sofia Soloists Chamber Orch., 1979; chief conductor Sofia Philharm. Orch., 1985. Composer Symphony 1981, 83, 87, concert for Double Bass, Concerto for Percusion and others. Award Nikolai Malko Competition award for conductors, Kopenhagen, 1977. Office: Sofia Philharm, Sofia Bulgaria

TABALUJAN, HANS GERARD, automotive company executive; b. Jakarta, Indonesia, July 27, 1952; s. Carlo Hein and Stien Hilda (Kemboean) T.; m. Linda Adhihusada, Mar. 3, 1953; children: Norman Joseph, Yvette Leah. B in Econs., Monash U., Melbourne, Australia, 1973; MBA, Case Western Reserve U., 1975. Asst. to pres. Sumber Selatan Trading Co., Indonesia, 1976-80; pres. PT Century Batteries Indonesia, 1980—, PT Danmotors Vespa Indonesia, 1986—; bd. dirs. PT Danapaints Indonesia, PT Sumber Segar, PT Zindo Utama. Office: PT Zindo Utama, Jalan Letjen Suprato 400, Jakarta 10510, Indonesia

TABATA, YUKIO, engineering researcher; b. Maizuru, Kyoto, Japan, Sept. 29, 1948; s. Denji and Kimie (Yamazoe) T.; m. Masayo Tsuneyama, Oct. 10, 1974; children: Kayoko, Kentaro. BS, Shizuoka U., Japan, 1971; MS, Kanazawa U., Japan, 1974. With devel. dept. Ricoh Co., Ltd., Tokyo, 1974-79; with research ctr. Ricoh Reprographic Tech., Numazu, Shizuoka, Japan, 1979-86; assoc. research and devel engr. Ricoh Imaging Tech., Numazu, 1986—. Patentee electrical processes; inventor printing process. Co-founder Shizuoka U. Equestrian Club, 1970; mem. Good Will Guide, Tokyo, 1986—. Mem. Physical Soc. Japan, Inst. Image Electronics Engrs. Japan, Alumni Assn. Shizuoka U. Equestrian Club (chmn. 1975-83). Home: 49-8 Kamo, Mishima, Shizuoka 411, Japan Office: Ricoh Imaging Tech Research Ctr, 146-1 Nishisawada, Numazu, Shizuoka 410, Japan

TABATONI, PIERRE, economics educator, consultant, French government official; b. Cannes, France Feb. 9, 1923; s. Joseph and Rose (Altavelle) T.; m. Jacqueline Ferrat, 1949; 2 sons. Educated Lycée de Cannes, Faculties of Letters and Law, Aix-en-Provence, London Sch. Econs., Harvard U. Assoc. prof. econs. U. Algiers and Aix-en-Provence, 1950-54; prof. Aix-Marseilles U., dir. Inst. Bus. Adminstrn., 1950-54; prof. U. Paris from 1961, pres. U. Paris IX, 1968; counsellor for higher edn. Ministry of Edn., 1969-73; dir. cultural affairs French Embassy, Washington, 1973-75; Minister of Univs., Dir. for Internat. Univ. Relations, Ministry Univs., 1975-79; rector of Acad., 1980—; chancellor of Paris Univs.; v.p. European Inst. Mgmt. Research; assoc., cons. Sema Metra-SF. Author: Etudes sur l'incidence des impôts, 1950; (with others) Economics of Financial Institutions, 1963, Policy and Structures in Management Systems, 1975, Business and Financial Innovation, 1987. Decorated Chevalier Legion d'honneur; comdr. Palmes academiques; Ordre Nat. (Ivory Coast); Ordre Mérite (Fed. Republic of Germany); Ordre de Léopold (Belgium).

TABBA, MOHAMMAD MYASSAR, civil engineer; b. Damascus, Syria, Jan. 25, 1946; s. Baha-Eddin and Hayat (Arafe) T.; m. Noha Dakkak, July 24, 1973; children—Omar, Rima. B.Sc. in Engring., Damascus U., 1968; M.Engring., McGill U., 1972, Ph.D., 1979. Registered profl. engr., Que. Structural engr. M.Backler & Assocs., Montreal, Que., Can., 1972-73; project engr. Alcan Aluminum, Montreal, 1973-75; geotech. project engr. Lavalin, Montreal, 1978-81; geotech. specialist Hydro-Que., Montreal, 1981-83; chief engr. Al-Issa Cons. Engrs., Riyadh, Saudi Arabia, 1983-85; dir. projects SHARACO, Riyadh, 1985—; aux. prof. dept. civil engring. McGill U., 1981-83. Contbr. articles to profl. jours. Nat. Research Council Can. grantee, 1970-72, 75-78. Mem. ASCE, Am. Concrete Inst., ASTM, Que. Order Engrs. Office: SHARACO, PO Box 5500, Riyadh 11422, Saudi Arabia

TABBAA, RASHED, cardiologist; b. Damascus, Syria, Jan. 1, 1949; s. Mohammad Sami and Wejdan (Hashem) El-T.; m. Susan El-Bitar, July 9, 1974; children—Bishr, Hadi. M.B. CH.B., Alexandria U., 1972. Diplomate Am. Bd. Internal Medicine, Am. Bd. Cardiovascular Disease. Intern/Resident Huron Road, Cleveland, 1973-76; resident, Cleveland Clinic Cleveland, 1976-78; assoc. staff, dept. medicine Community Hosp., Indpls., 1978-79; dir. coronary care unit King Faisal Specialist Hosp., Riyadh, Saudi Arabia, 1978-81; acting dir. noninvasive cardiac lab. VA Med. Center, Houston, 1982—; active staff dept. medicine Methodist Hosp., Houston, 1982—; clin. asst. prof. Baylor Coll. Medicine, Houston, 1982—. Fellow Am. Coll. Cardiology; mem. Tex. Med. Assn., Soc. for Cardiac Angiography, Harris County Med. Sco., Am. Heart Assn. Office: 6560 Fannin #1530 Houston TX 77030

TABBIA, ALBERTO, film critic, journalist; b. Pilar, Argentina, Jan. 24, 1929; s. Angel and Sara (Ponce de León) T. MA in Lit., U. Nat. Buenos Aires, 1952. Corr. Internat. Film Guide, London, 1973—; freelance journalist Buenos Aires, 1974—; film critic La Opinión, Buenos Aires, 1974—, Tiempo argentino, Buenos Aires, 1981-86, La Nación, 1981—, Clarín, Buenos Aires, 1985—; mem. jury Goethe Inst., Buenos Aires, 1979, Berlin Film Festival, 1987. Co-editor: (film series) Flashback, 1958-65. Mem. Fédéation Internationale de la Presse Cinematographique. Office: La Nación, 557 Bouchard, 1106 Buenos Aires Argentina

TABENDEH, MAHMOUD, physician; b. Shiraz, Iran, July 23, 1945; s. Abolghasem Tabendeh and Robab Amani; m. Fatome Talle, Aug. 23, 1965; children: Babak, Ramak, Barmak. MD, Shiraz U., 1971. Diplomate Bd. Cardiologists, 1978. Enlisted med. corps Iranian Army, 1967, advanced through ranks to col., 1981; dir. cardiology dept. Shiraz Hosp., 1981—; cons. Shiraz Med. Sch., 1983—. Mem. Iran Med. Soc., N.Y. Acad. Sci. Office: Beheshti Shiraz Hosp, Zand Ave, Shiraz 71867, Iran

TABESH, YAHYA, mathematician; b. Tehran, Iran, Apr. 14, 1950; s. Mohammad Tabesh and Maryam Zand; m. Mojgan, Sept. 30, 1981; 1 child, Sina. BS, Sharif U. of Tech., Tehran, 1973; MS, Syracuse U., 1976. Lectr. math. Isfahan (Iran) U. of Tech., 1976-86, vice chancellor, 1980-81; lectr. math. Sharif U. of Tech., Tehran, 1986—; chmn. dept. math. Isfahan U. of Tech., 1981-83; chief research lab. Sharif U. of Tech., 1986—. Editor jour. Farhang-o-Andishe, 1981-82; assoc. editor jour. Nashre Riazi, 1986—; translator: First Book of Euclidis Elementa, 1981, Topology: A First Course, 1986. Fellow Atomic Energy Orgn.; mem. Iranian Math. Soc. (exec. com. 1981-83).

TABET, CHAFIC ELIAS, construction company executive; b. Bcharri, Lebanon, July 3, 1955; s. Elias Dimitri and Helene Said (Daher) T. PhD, N.D. de Jamhour, Beirut, 1974; LLM, St. Joseph U., Beirut, 1978; diploma de juriste conseil d'Entreprise, diploma d'Etudes superieures specialisees, Jean Moulin U., Lyon, France, 1978-79. Mktg. officer K. Assouad Est., Beirut, 1977-78; lawyer P. Ghannam Law Office, Beirut, 1979-81; bus. law educator Belgium Ctr. for Comml. Specialized Studies, Beirut, 1979-81; legal adv. Archirodon Overseas Co. Ltd., Jeddah, Saudi Arabia, 1981-82; v.p., legal adminstrv. and internat. affairs Saudi Arabian Trading and Constrn. Co., Riyadh, 1982—. Mem. Beirut Bar Assn., Andjce Lyon. Office: Saudi Arabian Trading & Const Co, PO Box 346, 11411 Riyadh Saudi Arabia

TABIS, BRUNO WALTER, JR., lawyer; b. Chgo., May 23, 1946; s. Bruno Walter and Anne Helen (Dziak) T.; m. Martha Ann Sorgatz, Jan. 25, 1969; 1 child, Elizabeth Katherine. B.S., U. Ill.-Urbana, 1973; J.D. with distinction, Ill. Inst. Tech.-Kent Coll. Law, 1973. Bar: Ill. 1973, U.S. Dist. Ct. (no. dist.) Ill. 1973. Atty. EPA, Chgo., 1973-75; sole practice, Chgo., 1975-77; ptnr. Anderson, McDonnell, Miller & Tabis, Chgo., 1977—; instr. Ill. Inst. Tech.-Kent Coll. Law, Chgo., 1980-81. Editor-in-chief: CBA-Communicator, 1983-86; editor CBA Record, 1986—; contbr. articles to profl. jours. Mem. ch. counsel St. Paul Luth. Ch., Wheaton, Ill., 1982—, v.p., 1984-86; commr. Lawyers Trust Fund Implementation Commn., Chgo., 1983-85; bd. dirs. Legal Clinic for Disabled, 1985—. Mem. Chgo. Bar Assn. (chmn. young lawyers sect. 1982-83, bd. mgrs. 1984-86), Ill. State Bar Assn. (real estate law sec. council 1987) ABA (chmn. directory com. young lawyers div. 1982-83), Legal Assistance Found. Chgo. (chmn. pvt. atty. involvement com. 1984—), Lawyers for Creative Arts (dir. 1979—, sec. 1980-81). Home: 1223 Howard Circle Wheaton IL 60187 Office: Anderson McDonnell Miller & Tabis 200 S Wacker Dr Suite 420 Chicago IL 60606

TABISZ, GEORGE CONRAD, physics educator; b. N.Y.C., Aug. 28, 1939; arrived in Canada, 1950; s. Edward Frank and Margaret Patricia (Hanratty) T.; m. Ellen Margaret Clark, Oct. 29, 1966; children: Marie-Isabelle, Edward. B of Applied Sci., U. Toronto, Can., 1961, MA, 1963, PhD, 1968. Postdoctoral fellow Centre Nat. de la Recherche Scientifique, Paris, 1968-70; asst. prof. physics U. Manitoba, Winnipeg, Can., 1970-75, assoc. prof., 1975-80, prof. physics, 1980—; vis. prof. theoretical chemistry U. Cambridge, Eng., 1976-77; vis. scientist Nat. research Council Can., Ottawa, Ont., 1983-84; mem. physics grant selection com. Nat. Sci. Engring. Research Council, Ottawa, 1985-88, chmn., 1987-88. NATO grantee, Brussels, 1975-84. Mem. Can. Assn. Physicists, Optical Soc. Am. Roman Catholic. Office: U Manitoba, Dept Physics, Winnipeg, MB Canada

TABISZEWSKI, EDWARD K(AZIMIERZ), consulting company executive; b. Warsaw, Poland, Jan. 19, 1927; s. Edward Michal and Kazimiera Maria (Zwierzynska) T.; m. Anna Maria Garbien, Aug. 26, 1948 (div. 1957); children—Maciej Andrzej, Jolanta Maria; m. Vreni Elisabeth Joerg, May 3, 1961; children—Mark George, Michael Andrew. M.A., Higher Sch. Commerce, Poland, 1949, M.B.A., Central Sch. Planning and Stats., Warsaw, 1952; M.Sc., Higher Sch. Econs., Cracow, Poland, 1956; postgrad. MIT, 1959-60. Dir. bus. devel. EAME, ITT (WD), Brussels, 1969-70, gen. mgr. Germany, Essen, Fed. Republic Germany, 1970-72; corp. dir. East-West devel. Borg Warner Corp., Brussels, 1973-82; v.p. European ops. Telephone Broadcasting Systems PLC, London, 1983; pres., chief exec. officer Bus. Devel. Cons. S.A., Montana, Switzerland, 1984—. Served to maj. Polish Underground Armed Forces (A.K.), 1942-45. Roman Catholic. Home: Residence du Rhone, CH-3962 Crans-Montant Switzerland Office: Bus Devel Cons SA, Residence du Rhone, CH-3962 Crans-Montanta Switzerland

TABNER, MARY FRANCES, educator; b. Rochester, N.Y., Dec. 11, 1918; d. William Herman and Mary Frances (Willenbacher) Arndt; m. James Gordon Tabner, June 27, 1942; 1 child, Barbara Jean. BA, SUNY, Albany, 1940, MA, 1959; postgrad., U. Rochester, Albany, 1944, 45, Northwestern U. (John Hay fellow), Albany, 1963-64, U. Manchester (Eng.), Albany, 1971-72. Tchr. history pub. schs. Mattituck, N.Y., 1940-43, Gorham, N.Y., 1943-46; tchr. pub. schs. Waterford, N.Y., 1949-55; tchr. social studies Shaker High Sch., Latham, N.Y., 1959-83, now also dir. Russian studies seminar, 1959-83, ret., 1983; tchr. ch. history Our Lady of Assumption Ch., Latham. Author bibliographies on Russian history, Am. studies. N.Y. State Regents independent study grantee, 1966. Mem. Nat. Council Social Studies, N.Y. State United Tchrs., Assn. Advancement Slavic Studies, SUNY, Albany Alumni Assn., History and Art Council Albany, Am., N.Y., Capital Dist. councils for social studies, Shaker Heritage Soc. (trustee, guide, tchr.), English Speaking Union, Am. Assn. Ret. Persons. Republican. Roman Catholic. Home: 557 Columbia St Cohoes NY 12047

TABONE, VINCENT, diplomat; b. Gojo, Malta, Mar. 30, 1913; s. Nicolo and Elisa (Galleja) T.; m. Maria Wirth, Nov. 21, 1941; children: Marilise, Colin, Helen, Vincent, Monica, Patricia, Anna. MD, St. Aloysius U., London; DOMS, Oxford (Eng.) U.; DMJ, U. Malta. Army med. officer Addention Hosp.; clin. officer Royal Lye Hosp., London; cons. Lup Hosp., Victoria Hosp., King George V Hosp., WHO; fgn. minister Malta. Sec. gen. Nationalist Party, Malta, 1962-74, dep. leader, 1974-77. Fellow Royal Coll. Surgeons. Home: 33 Carmel St, Saint Julians Malta

TABRISKY, JOSEPH, radiologist; b. Boston, June 23, 1931; s. Henry and Gertrude Tabrisky; B.A. cum laude, Harvard U., 1952; M.D. cum laude, Tufts U., 1956; m. Phyllis Eleanor Page, Apr. 23, 1955; children—Joseph Page, Elizabeth Ann, William Page. Flexible intern U. Ill. Hosp., 1956-57; resident in radiology Fitzsimons Army Hosp., 1958-60; instr. radiology Tufts U. Med. Sch., 1964-65; cons. radiologist Swedish Med. Center, Denver, 1966-68; chief radiologist Kaiser Found. Hosp., Harbor City, Calif., 1968-72; mem. faculty UCLA Med. Sch., 1972—, prof. radiol. scis., 1975—, vice chmn. dept., 1976—, exec. policy com. radiol. scis.; chmn. radiology dept. Harbor-UCLA Med. Center, 1975—, pres. faculty soc., 1979-80, exec. dir. MR/CT Imaging Ctr., bd. dirs. Research Ednl. Inst., Harbor Collegium/UCLA Found.; chief exec. officer Vascular Biometrics Inc.; steering com. Harvard U., 1952; cons. Los Angeles County Dept. Pub. Health; chmn. Los Angeles County Radiol. Standards Com., 1979. Mem. Harvard-Radcliffe Schs. Com.; bd. dirs., treas., Harbor-UCLA Med. Found.; chmn. UCLA Council for Ednl. Devel. Served to maj. M.C., U.S. Army, 1957-63. Diplomate Am. Bd. Radiology. Fellow Am. Coll. Radiology, Univ. Radcom Assn. (chief exec. officer 1987—); mem. Radiol. Soc. N. Am., Calif. Med. Assn., Calif. Radiol. Soc., Los Angeles Med. Assn., Los Angeles Radiol. Soc., Alpha Omega Alpha. Contbr. articles to med. jours. Office: 1000 W Carson St Torrance CA 90509

TABUCHI, MAMORU, general trading company executive; b. Osaka, Japan, Feb. 24, 1924; came to U.S., 1982; s. Iwao and Yoshiko (Nakamura) T.; m. Seiko Onodera, Mar. 7, 1958; children: Hiroko Toyoda, Keiko, Kumiko. B.A., Tokyo U. of Commerce, 1948; A.M.P., Harvard Bus. Sch., Boston, 1974. Sr. exec., mng. dir. Mitsui & Co., Ltd., Tokyo, 1981-85, pres., chief exec. officer, 1982-87, Mitsui & Co., USA, Inc., N.Y.C., exec. v.p., Mitsui & Co., Ltd., Tokyo, 1987—; mem. internat. adv. council Avon Corp., N.Y.C., 1986. Club: Sleepy Hollow Country. Avocation: golf. Home: Tokyo Japan

TACKER, EDGAR CARROLL, electrical engineering educator; b. Savannah, Tenn., Sept. 26, 1935; s. William Henry and Lue Marjorie (Wagner) T.; m. Florence Evelyn Maine, Jan. 20, 1956; children: Donna Carol, Karen Gail, Lara Ruth, David Franklin William. B.S. in Elec. Engring. with distinction, U. Okla., 1960; M.S.E.E., NYU, 1962; Ph.D. (Ford Found. fellow), U. Fla., 1964. Systems engr. Bell Telephone Labs., N.Y.C., 1960-62; asst. prof. elec. engring. U. Ark., Fayetteville, 1964-67; dir. Analog/Hybrid Computer Lab., 1964-67; assoc. prof. depts. systems sci. and elec. engring., computer Sci. Mich. State U., East Lansing, 1967-69; dir. Hybrid Simulation and Control Lab., 1967-69; assoc. prof. depts. elec. engring., chem. engring. and engring. sci., also dir. Coll. Engring. Hybrid Simulation Lab., La. State U., Baton Rouge, 1969-74; prof. systems and elec. engring. U. Houston, 1974-80, dir. systems engring. program, 1974-77; prof. elec. engring. U. Tulsa, 1980-88, chmn. dept., 1980-83; research prof. dept. elec. engring. and computer sci. U. Nev., Reno, 1988—; vis. asso. prof. U. Wis., Madison, 1973-74; systems engring. cons., 1970—. Asso. editor: Large-Scale Systems Jour; contbr. articles to profl. jours. Communications Devel. Tng. Program fellow Bell Telephone Lab., 1960-62; NASA Am. Soc. Engring. Edn. fellow, 1965; grantee Air Force Office Sci. Research , 1973-74, 80-81, 86, NSF, 1975-80, Office Naval Research, 1981-82, Naval Underwater Systems Ctr., 1982. Mem. IEEE, Am. Assn. Artificial Intelligence, Assn. for Computing Machinery.

TADIC, MARKO, mathematician, educator; b. Kolo, Duvno, Yugoslavia, Nov. 16, 1953; s. Pero and Kaja (Curkovic) T.; m. Ana Stanek, Aug. 11, 1979; children—Katarina, Marija, Petra. B.S., U. Zagreb, 1976, M.S., 1979, Ph.D., 1980. Asst., U. Zagreb, Yugoslavia, 1976-79, sci. asst., 1979-83, asst. prof., 1983-84, 85-86; research math. Max-Planck Inst. fur Math., Bonn, 1984-85, assoc. prof. 1986-87, prof. 1987—, head algebra and founds. of math. sect., 1983-84, 86—. Contbr. articles to profl. jours. Mem. Am. Math. Soc., Societe Mathematique de France, Assn. Math., Physics and Astronomers of Croatia. Home: Trzna 16A, Zagreb 41040, Yugoslavia Office: U Zagreb Dept Math, Marulicev Trg 19, Zagreb Yugoslavia

TADLIP, MARILOU PALICTE, librarian; b. Asturias, Cebu, Philippines, May 16, 1946; d. Leonardo Francisco C. and Luz Sacristan (Buenaventura)

Palicte; B.S.E., U. San Carlos, 1967; M.L.S., U. Hawaii, 1971; postgrad. U. San Carlos; cert. basic mgmt. Asian Inst. Mgmt., 1979; m. Olegario Tadlip, Jan. 14, 1968; children—Marie Louise Janet, Alexis Jude, Oleg Emmanuelle, Caesar John. Chmn. dept. library sci. U. San Carlos, Cebu City, Philippines, 1979, faculty, 1967—, acting dir. libraries, 1976-77, dir. libraries, 1977—; chmn. com. on libraries Philippine Assn. Accrediting of Schs., Colls. and Univs. Survey teams, 1976—; cons. Acad. Libraries Book Acquisition Systems, Inc. Mem. Bd. Trustees Cebu City, 1977—. Center for Cultural and Tech. Interchange between E. and W. grantee, Honolulu, 1970-71; Hawaii Library Assn. travel grantee, 1970-71; E & W Cultural Center grantee, 1970-71. Mem. Philippine Library Assn., Philippine Assn. Tchrs. of Library Sci., Philippine Accrediting Assn. Schs., Colls. and Univs., Cebu Librarians Assn., ALA, Cath. Library Assn., U. Hawaii Alumni Assn., Hui Dui Alumni Assn. Contbr. articles to profl. jours.; co-editor: A Union List of Filipiniana Holdings of the Member Institutions of ALBASA, Inc. The Sciences: Pure and Applied, 1978. Home: Saint Jude Acres,, Bulacao Pardo,, Cebu 6401, Philippines Office: The Library Univ of San Carlos, Cebu City 6401,, Philippines

TAFT, MARCUS, experimental psychologist, educator; b. Perth, Australia, Dec. 7, 1952; s. Ronald and Ellen Martha (Braumann) T.; m. Monica Louise Minz, Apr. 8, 1976 (div. Apr. 1987). BSc with honors, Monash U., Victoria, Australia, 1973, PhD, 1976. Research assoc. MIT, Cambridge, 1976-77; sr. tutor Monash U., 1978-80; lectr. U. New South Wales (Australia), 1981-86, sr. lectr., 1986—. Editorial bd. Internat. Jour. Cognitive Sci., 1987—; contbr. articles to profl. jours. Mem. Australian Psychol. Soc. (sec. div. sci. affairs 1983-85, 4th Year prize 1973). Office: U New South Wales, PO Box 1, Kensington, New South Wales 2033, Australia

TAFT, PERRY HAZARD, lawyer; b. Los Angeles, Jan. 23, 1915; s. Milton and Sarah T.; m. Callie S. Taft, Aug. 15, 1968; children by previous marriage—Stephen D., Sally L., Sheila R. Student U. Calif.-Berkeley, 1932-35; A.B., UCLA, 1936; LL.B., George Washington U., 1940. Bar: Calif. 1940. Spl. atty. Antitrust div. U.S. Dept. Justice, Los Angeles, 1941-42; dep. atty. gen. State of Calif., San Francisco, 1943-44; regional rep. Council State Govts., San Francisco, 1944-45; regional dir. govt. affairs Trans World Airlines, Los Angeles, 1945-47; Pacific coast mgr. Am. Ins. Assn., San Francisco, 1948-66; gen. counsel Assn. Calif. Ins. Cos., Sacramento, 1967-73; asst. city atty. City of Stockton, Calif., 1973-79; pres. Perry H. Taft, P.C., Stockton, 1979-85; dir. Compair, Inc., Burlingame, Calif. ; arbitrator Surplus Line Assn. Calif., 1965—. Contbr. articles to profl. jours. Bd. dirs. Stockton East Water Dist., 1979-83, pres., 1981-83; mem. San Joaquin County Water Adv. Com., 1982-85. Mem. State Bar of Calif., Psi Upsilon. Democrat. Clubs: Elkhorn Country, Yosemite. Home: 8615 Stonewood Dr Stockton CA 95209 Office: PO Box 7453 Stockton CA 95207

TAFURI, SPENCER ANDREW, treasurer, insurance executive, municipal administrator, treasurer; b. N.Y.C., Aug. 2, 1952; s. Joseph Thomas and Barbara (Sarvi) T.; m. Wynne Kovall, Oct. 22, 1977; children: Joseph, Melanie, Scott. BA in History, Rutgers U., 1975; MEd, Paterson Coll., 1977; MBA in Fin., Rutgers U., 1978, MBA in Acctg., 1980. Council pres. Borough of Emerson, N.J., 1982-85; adminstr.. treas. Borough of Little Ferry, N.J., 1982-86; treas. Borough of Riverdale, N.J., 1986—; chief fiscal officer Bergen County Mcpl. Joint Ins. Fund, Park Ridge, N.J., 1985—; adminstr. Twp. Saddle Brook, 1987—; chmn. Bergen County Treas. Group, Pascack Valley, N.J., 1984; chief exec. officer Meadows Assocs., Middletown, Conn., 1985—. Trustee Bergen County Community Action Program, 1983-84, Hackensack-Meadowlands Mcpl. Com., Lyndhurst, N.J., 1984; aide Sen. Cardinale, Cresskill, N.J., 1983-85. Recipient Meritorious Service award Borough of Emerson, 1985. Fellow Assn. Govt. Accts.; mem. Mcpl. Fin. Officers Assn., Tax Collectors and Treas. Assn. N.J., N.J. Mcpl. Mgrs. Assn., Bergen County Mcpl. Mgrs. Assn. Republican. Roman Catholic. Club: Emerson Rep. Lodge: Rotary (pres. Little Ferry/South Hackensack chpt. 1984-86, Outstanding Service award 1984). Home: 16 Sycamore Ave Emerson NJ 07630 Office: 91 Newark-Pompton Turnpike Riverdale NJ 07457

TAGG, FREDERICK GEORGE, manufacturing company executive, electrical engineer; b. London, Dec. 2, 1936; s. Frederick Arthur and Ivy Frances (Clarke) T.; m. Joyce Georgina Groom (dec. Aug., 1983), children: David John, Paul Andrew. Diploma in engring., Watford Tech. Coll., Eng., 1962. chartered engr., Eng. Engring. apprentice Rotax Ltd., Hemel Hempstead, Eng., 1954-58; design engr. Lucas Aerospace Ltd., Hemel Hempstead, 1958-67; project mgr. Hawker Siddeley Dynamic Ltd., Hatfield, Eng., 1967-68; product mktg. mgr. Walmore Electronics Ltd., London, 1968-77; mktg. mgr. internat. Burroughs O.E.M. Corp., Rickmansworth, Eng., 1977-83; dir. internat. ops. Plasma Graphics Corp., Warren, N.J., 1984-86; mng. dir. Craft Data Ltd., Chesham, Eng., 1985—; major of bd. Scan Craft Data A.S., Solna, Sweden, 1985—; bd. dirs. Craft Data Inc., Mission Viejo, Calif., Data Sign Ltd., Chesham. Contbr. articles to profl. jours. Mem. Inst. Electrical Engring., Inst. Electronics and Radio Engrs. Conservative. Mem. Ch. of Eng. Club: Sportsman (London). Office: Craft Data Ltd, 92 Broad St, Chesham Bucks England HP5 3ED

TAGGART, DAVID PAUL, cardiac surgeon, lecturer; b. Glasgow, Scotland, Jan. 7, 1987; s. Hugh Francis and Agnes (Graham) T. BM in CHB, Glasgow U., 1981. Intern, then resident Royal Infirmary, U. Glasgow, 1981-82, lectr. cardiac surgery, 1982—; dir. computing services. Reviewer: Brit. Med. Jour.; contbr. articles to sci. and med. jours. Scottish Hosps. Endowment research grantee, 1987. Fellow Royal Coll. Surgeons. Home: 10 Woodlands Gate, Glasgow G36 HX, Scotland Office: U Glasgow Royal Infirmary, Alexandra Parade, Glasgow G32 2ER, Scotland

TAGGART, LESLIE DAVIDSON, lawyer; b. Glasgow, Scotland, Aug. 28, 1910; came to U.S. (from Can.), 1920, naturalized, 1934; s. Frederick James and Petrina W. (Paterson) T.; m. Mary Mason Kerr, Sept. 27, 1940; children: Georgia M. Taggart Brackett, William K., Patricia A. Taggart Shepherd, Douglas G. A.B., Columbia U., 1931, LL.B., 1934. Bar: N.Y. 1934. Practiced in N.Y.C; former sr. partner Watson Leavenworth Kelton & Taggart; dir. Magnetic Analysis Corp., Mt. Vernon, N.Y.; lectr. Practising Law Inst. Past sec., bd. mgrs. St. Andrews Soc. N.Y. State. Mem. N.Y. Patent Law Assn., Am. Patent Law Assn. (past dir.), U.S. Trademark Assn. (past dir.), ABA, Am. Coll. Trial Lawyers, Phi Beta Kappa, Phi Sigma Kappa. Congregationalist. Clubs: Univ. (N.Y.C.); Patterson (Fairfield, Conn.). Home: 2 Melwood Ln Westport CT 06880

TAGGART, ROBERT BURDETT, communications company executive; b. Paterson, N.J., Apr. 6, 1943; s. Robert Burdett and Marjorie Stewart (Wiley) T.; m. Donna Fay Bledsoe, Feb. 14, 1973; children—David Robert. B.S., Northwestern U., 1967, M.S., 1968; Engr., Stanford U., 1970. Engr., mgr. Hewlett-Packard, Palo Alto, Calif., 1970-78; mgr. mech. engring. Comprint, Inc., Mountain View, Calif., 1978-80; engr. Apple Computer, Cupertino, Calif., 1980-82; founder, chief exec. officer, Chaparral Communications, Inc., San Jose, Calif., 1980—. Contbr. articles to profl. publs.; patentee in field. Mem. Soc. for Pvt. and Comml. Earth Stas. (pioneer). Republican. Presbyterian. Home: 348 Ramona Rd Portola Valley CA 94025

TAGLIAFERRI, LEE GENE, investment banker; b. Mahanoy City, Pa., Aug. 14, 1931; s. Charles and Adele (Cirilli) T.; B.S., U. Pa., 1957; M.B.A., U. Chgo., 1958; m. Maryellen Stanton, Apr. 29, 1962; children—Mark, John, Maryann. Div. comptroller Campbell Soup Co., Camden, N.J., 1958-60; securities analyst Merrill, Lynch, Pierce, Fenner & Smith, Inc., N.Y.C., 1960-62; asst. v.p. U.S. Trust Co. of N.Y., 1962-71; v.p. corporate finance div. Laidlaw & Co., Inc., N.Y.C., 1972-73; pres. Everest Corp., N.Y.C., 1973—; dir. Fairfield Communities Inc., UEC, Inc., LRA, Inc., Industrialized Bldg. Systems, Inc. Past pres. West Windsor Community Assn. Trustee Schuyler Hall, Columbia, Madison Sq. Boys Club. Served with AUS, 1953-55. K.C. Clubs: University of Pa., Princeton (N.Y.C.). Home: 77 Lillie St Princeton Junction NJ 08550 Office: 1 Penn Plaza New York NY 10001

TAGUBA, EDUARDO TUMALIUAN, physician; b. Tuguegarao, Cagayan, Philippines, Oct. 6, 1950; s. Julian Mallonga and Telesfora (Tumaliuan) T.; m. Darnette Zingapan, May 7, 1951; children: Trician Jan, Sheena Jan, John Edward, Marcelle Jan. MD, U. Santo Tomas, Manila, 1978. Diplomate Philippine Pediatric Soc. Intern Cagayan Provincial Hosp., Tuguegarao, 1978-80, mem. staff, 1987—; resident Lunsod NG Kabataan Hosp., Quezon City, Philippines, 1981-1984. Author: (with others) Dengue H-fever H-I Titer Determination, 1986 (Mead Johnson Co. research 2d prize). Mem. Philippine Med. Assn., Cagayan Med. Soc. Home: 15 Reyno St, Tuguegarao Cagayan Philippines Office: 92 Gonzaga St, Tuguegarao Cagayan Philippines

TAGUCHI, YOSHITAKA, architect; b. Urawa, Japan, Feb. 12, 1933; s. Washio and Masa Taguchi; m. Yukiko Misuda, Apr. 21, 1968; children: Naeko, Morihiko. B in Engring., Tokyo Inst. Tech., 1955. Dir. design div. Ministry Post and Telecommunication, Tokyo, 1979-84, dir. gen. bldg. dept., 1984-87; prin. Taguchi Yoshitaka Architect Office, Tokyo, 1987—; adviser The Saitama Bank, Japan, 1987—. Prin. works include Fukuoka Cen. Post Office, Nagoya Sorting Office, Sapparo Cen. Post Office, Miyazaki Cen. Post Office. Mem. Japan Inst. Architecture. Home: Tamagawa 3-3-12-203, Setagayaku, Tokyo 158, Japan Office: Ginza 1-24-2, Tokyo 104, Japan

TAHARA, HISASHI, paper company executive; b. Apr. 19, 1917; m. Yasuko Tahara. Grad., Keio U., 1941. Exec. dir. Honsyu Paper Mfg. Kabushiki Kaisha, from 1976; then v.p., now pres. Honshu Paper Mfg. Kabushiki Kaisha. Home: 1-1 Shiroganedai, Minato-ku, Tokyo Japan Office: Honshu Paper Co Ltd, 12-8 Ginza, 5-chome, Tokyo Japan *

TAHER, FOUAD, consulting company executive; b. Cairo, Oct. 26, 1923; m. Enaya Ahmad Hassan, 1949. BS, Cairo U., 1945; PhD, Stanford U., 1951. Lectr. Cairo U., 1951-59, assoc. prof., 1959-61; dir. gen. Ministry of Pub. Works, Cairo, 1961-64; inspector gen. Electricity Authority, Cairo, 1964-71; v.p. Rural Electrification, Cairo, 1971-77; counsellor Electricity Corp., Saudi Arabia, 1977-82; chmn. Elec. Power Systems Engring. Co., Cairo, 1982—; cons. Indsl. Devel. Ctr., League of Arab States, Cairo, 1974-76. Contbr. articles to profl. jours. Recipient Decoration of the Republic, Govt. Egypt, 1971. Fellow IEEE. Lodge: Rotary (pres. 1987-88). Home: 22 Ibn Zanki St Zamalek, Zamalek, Cairo Arab Republic of Egypt Office: Electric Power Systems Co, PO Box 125, Abbasseyah, Cairo Arab Republic of Egypt

TAHIR, MUSHTAQ AHMED, government official; b. Sialkot, Punjab, Pakistan, June 1, 1934; arrived in Saudi Arabia, 1977; s. Mian Mohammad and Bibi (Aisha) Ismail; m. Iqbal Begum, Mar. 23, 1953 (dec. Dec. 1971); children: Ikhlaq, Waqar, Shamas, Quamar, Tameez, Misbah-Ul-Haque. BA, Punjab U., 1964, MA in Adminstrv. Sci., 1967. Various ministerial posts Pub. Works Dept., Sialkot, 1952-57; divisional acct. Water and Power Devel. Authority, Lahore, Pakistan, 1958-69; asst. acct. Water and Power Devel. Authority, Sarghoda, Pakistan, 1973-76; programming officer Pres.'s Secretariat, Islamabad, Pakistan, 1970; accounts officer Evacue Trust Property Bd., Lahore, 1971-72; expert in indsl. follow-up Royal Commn., Saudi Arabia, 1977-78, expert in mgmt., 1978-79, expert in fin., 1980—; cons. Mid. East Trading Corp., Gujranwala, Pakistan, 1957-63. Author: Islam & Public Administration, 1966, Personnel Administration: Electricity: WAPDA, 1967, Financial Administration: Electricity: WAPDA, 1968. Mem. Geog. Soc. Muslim. Club: Recreation (Yanbu). Home: 7/309 Rangpura, Sialkot City Pakistan Office: Royal Commn Ho Fin, PO Box 30167, Yanbu Al-Sinaiyah Saudi Arabia

TAI, JOSEF, composer; b. Posen, German, Poland, Sept. 18, 1910; came to Palestine, 1934; Studies with Tiessen and Trapp, Berlin. Prof. piano and composition Jerusalem Acad. Music, 1937-53; dir. Electronic Music Ctr., Israel, 1959—; head dept. musicology Hebrew U., Jerusalem, 1965-71; pres. Israel sect., Internat. Music Council. Composer: (choreographic poem) Exodus, 1947; (symphonic cantata) A Mother Rejoices, 1949; (string orch.) Visions, 1950; Viola Concerto, 1954, 58, also five operas, four short operas, six piano concertos, 2 symphonies, four concertos string and wind instruments, others. Recipient Israel State prize, 1971. Mem. Acad. Arts West Berlin (ordinaire), Acad. Arts and Letters U.S. (hon.). Address: Hebrew Univ, Dept Musicology, Jerusalem Israel

TAI, SELWYN C., podiatric surgeon, consultant; b. Hong Kong, Oct. 31, 1950; s. En Shui and Jean T.; m. Helen Lim, June 2, 1979; 1 son, Gabriel. B.S.E., U. Pa., 1974; D.P.M., Ohio Coll., Podiatric Medicine, 1980. Dir., Community Foot and Ankle Clinic, Renton, Wash., 1981-85, Federal Way, Wash., 1984—; chief exec. officer Comfac, Seattle, Wash., 1981—. Mem. Internat. Coll. Podiatric Laser Surgery, Am. Podiatric Med. Assn., Am. Inst. Foot Medicine, Wash. State Podiatric Med. Assn., Internat. Coll. Podiatric Laser Surgery, IEEE, Federal Way C. of C. Home: PO Box 7178 Federal Way WA 98003 Office: Comfac 720 S 320th St Federal Way WA 98003

TAI, TSZE CHENG, aerodynamicist, researcher; b. Shaoxing, Chekiang, China, Apr. 29, 1933; came to U.S., 1963, naturalized, 1972; m. Shih Lin Sun, Aug. 27, 1965; children—Kuangheng, Kuangkai, Kuangshin. Diploma, Air Tech. Inst., Republic of China, 1957; MS, Clemson U., 1965; PhD, Va. Poly. Inst., 1968. Aircraft insp. Taoyuan Airbase, Taoyuan, Taiwan, 1958-63; research asst. Clemson U., 1963-65; grad. asst. Va. Poly. Inst., 1965-67, instr., 1967-68; research scientist David Taylor Research Ctr., Bethesda, Md., 1968—; chmn. panel U.S. Navy Aeroballistics Com., Washington, 1978-81; lectr. von Karman Inst. Fluid Dynamics, Belgium, 1980. Prin. Potomac (Md.) Chinese Sch., 1981-82; scientific officer fluid mechanics Office Naval Research, 1985-86. Recipient Eugene Brooks award Naval Ship Research and Devel. Center, 1979. Assoc. fellow AIAA; mem. Sigma Xi (chmn. awards com. 1979-80). Home: 10705 Tara Rd Potomac MD 20854 Office: David Taylor Research Ctr Code 166 3 Bethesda MD 20084

TAILLIBERT, RENE ROGER, architect; b. Chatres sur Cher, France, Jan. 21, 1926; s. Gaston and Melina (Benoit) T.; grad. Ecole Nationale Superieure des Beaux Arts, Paris, 1955; m. Beatrice Pfister, May 5, 1965; 1 child, Sophie Maria-Emma. Architecte en chef des Batiments Civils et Palais Nationaux, 1965—; architect Ministry Edn., Ministry Sports; curator Grand Palais, Paris, 1977-82, Palais de Chaillot, 1982—; cons. architect govts. Luxembourg, Tunisia, Jordan, Can., Ivory Coast. Served with French mil. forces, 1952-53. Decorated chevalier Legion d'Honneur, comdr. Ordre du Mérite National, Palmes academiques, Arts et Lettres, Officer Legion d'Honneur, 1972; recipient grand prix Nat. Architecture, 1976, Gt. Golden medal Soc. Arts and Industries, 1977; named Hon. Citizen City of New Orleans, 1987. Fellow Royal Soc. Arts (London); mem. Académie des Beaux-Arts, French Acad. Architecture (silver medal 1971), Cercle d'Architecture France. Roman Catholic. Club: Racing of France. Works include: Stadium Parc des Princes, Paris, 1972; stadium, Lille, 1976, Montreal, 1976; stadium for Olympic games, swimming pool Palais des Sports; U. Gabes, Tunisia, 1979; sport center, Chamonix, 1974; Olympic Sports Center, Luxembourg; sports center, Yamoussoukro, Ivory Coast; golf complex, Abidjan, Ivory Coast; Nat. Inst. Sport and Phys. Edn., Paris; Jordan Nat. Geog. Center, Amman; Piscine de Deauville, 1966; Faculté de pharmacie de Toulouse, 1979; Laboratoires pharmaceutiques à Castres, 1970; Complexe sportif et éducatif à Castres, 1977; editor: Construire l'Avenir, 1977. Office: 163 Ave de la Pompe, 75116 Paris France

TAIMUTY, SAMUEL ISAAC, physicist; b. West Newton, Pa., Dec. 20, 1917; s. Elias and Samia (Hawatt) T.; B.S., Carnegie Mellon U., 1940; Ph.D., U. So. Calif., 1951; m. Betty Jo Travis, Sept. 12, 1953 (dec.); children—Matthew, Martha; m. 2d, Rosalie Richards, Apr. 3, 1976. Physicist, U.S. Naval Shipyard, Phila. and Long Beach, Calif., 1942-46; research asst. U. So. Calif., 1947-51; sr. physicist U.S. Naval Radiol. Def. Lab., 1950-52, SRI Internat., Menlo Park, Calif., 1952-72; sr. staff engr. Lockheed Missiles & Space Co., Sunnyvale, Calif., 1972—; cons. physicist, 1971—. Mem. Am. Phys. Soc., Sigma Xi. Episcopalian. Mason. Contbr. articles to sci. publs. Patentee in field. Home: 3346 Kenneth Dr Palo Alto CA 94303 Office: Lockheed Missiles and Space Co PO Box 3504 Sunnyvale CA 94088

TAIPALE, KAARIN HANNA IRENE, architect; b. Helsinki, July 22; d. Pentti and Saara Elisabeth (Pesonen) T. MArch, Eidgenossisches Technische Hochschule, Zurich, Switzerland, 1972; MS in Hist. Prevention, Columbia U., 1983. Project architect Kalle Vartola Architects, Helsinki, 1974-81, Robert A. M. Stern Architects, N.Y.C., 1983-84; owner, prin. Kaarin Taipale Architects, Helsinki, 1985—; chmn. Seminar on Architecture and Urban Planning in Finland, Helsinki, 1986. Editor Finland Builds exhbn. catalog, 1986; editor-in-chief Arkkitehti, Finnish Archtl. Rev., 1988—; contbr. articles to profl. jours., newspapers. Fulbright scholar, N.Y.C., 1981. Mem. Finnish Assn. Architects, Internat. Council on Monuments and Sites. Lutheran.

TAIRA, FRANCES SNOW, nurse educator; b. Glasgow, Scotland, Feb. 27, 1935; came to U.S., 1959, naturalized, 1964; d. Thomas and Isabel (McDonald) Snow; m. Albert Taira, June 20, 1962; children—Albert, Deborah, Paul. B.S.N., U. Ill., 1974, M.S.N., 1976; Ed.D., No. Ill. U., 1980. Staff nurse various hosps., 1959-73; instr. nursing Triton Coll., 1976-81; asst. prof. nursing Loyola U., Chgo., 1981—. Mem. Am. Nurses Assn., Ill. Nurses Assn., U. Ill. Nursing Alumni Assn., Sigma Theta Tau, Phi Delta Kappa. Roman Catholic. Author: Aging: A Guide for the Family, 1983, Home Nursing: Basic Rehabilitation Care of Adults, 1986; contbr. articles to profl. jours. Home: 404 Atwater Ave Elmhurst IL 60126 Office: Loyola U Lake Shore Campus 6525 N Sheridan Rd Chicago IL 60626

TAISHOFF, LAWRENCE BRUCE, publishing company executive; b. Washington, Aug. 30, 1933; s. Sol Joseph and Betty (Tash) T.; A.B., Duke U., 1955; m. Pamela Sherwood, Apr. 4, 1986; children by previous marriage—Robert Paul, Randall Lawrence, Jonathan Bradford. Asst. dir. Sta. WTOP-TV, Washington, 1955-56; with Broadcasting Publs., Inc., Washington, 1958—, pres., pub., 1971—, chmn., 1982, also dir.; v.p. Jolar Corp., Washington, 1952-72, dir., 1958-72; gen. partner Jolar Assocs., Washington, 1972—; chmn. bd., pres. Graphictype, Inc., 1976-86, also dir.; chmn., pres. Solar Corp., 1982-86; chmn. Broadcasting-Taishoff Found., 1982—; trustee, mem. exec. com. Washington Journalism Ctr., 1982—; bd. dirs. Nat. Press Found., 1982—; mem. journalism and communications exec. com. Capital Campaign for Arts and Sci., Duke U., 1984—; mem. White House Press Corps, 1983—; mem. Met. Washington Bd. Trade, 1970—. Co-author radio and TV segment Britanica Book of the Year, 1983—. Team capt. pubs. div. United Givers Fund drive, 1965; mem. admissions adv. com. Duke Alumni Assn., 1968-70; mem. U.S. Senate and Ho. of Reps. Periodical Press Gallery, 1958—; trustee Broadcast Pioneers Ednl. Fund Inc., 1985; judge VFW Voice of Democracy contest, 1978—; mem. bd. judges Peabody awards, 1985—; mem. Am. U. Sch. Communications Disting. Adv. Commn., 1985—; mem. Founders Soc. Duke U., 1985—, The Mus. of Broadcasting Roundtable, 1988— . Served with AUS, 1956-58. Mem. Advt. Club Washington, Internat. Radio and TV Soc., Broadcast Pioneers (life, bd. dirs., exec. com. Broadcast Pioneers Library), White House Corrs. Assn., Mus. Broadcasting Roundtable, IEEE (sr.), Sigma Delta Chi, Zeta Beta Tau. Jewish. Clubs: Nat. Press, University (Washington); Woodmont Country (Rockville, Md.). Office: 1705 DeSales St NW Washington DC 20036

TAIT, JOHN REID, lawyer; b. Toledo, Ohio, Apr. 7, 1946; s. Paul Reid and Lucy Richardson (Rudderow) T.; m. Christina Ruth Bjornstad, Mar. 12, 1972; children—Gretchen, Mary. B.A., Columbia Coll., 1968; J.D., Vanderbilt U., 1974. Bar: Idaho 1974, U.S. Dist. Ct. Idaho 1974. Assoc. Keeton & Tait, Lewiston, Idaho, 1974-76, ptnr. Keeton & Tait, 1976-86, Keeton, Tait & Petrie, 1986—. Chmn. bd. No. Rockies Action Group, Helena, Mont., 1985-86, bd. dirs. 1981-88, Lewiston Hist. Preservation Commn., Idaho, 1975—, chmn., 1988—; bd. dirs. Idaho Legal Aid Services, Boise, 1975—, Idaho Housing Agy., Boise, 1984—. Served with U.S. Army, 1968-71. Mem. ABA, Assn. Trial Lawyers Am., Idaho Trial Lawyers Assn., Clearwater Bar Assn. (sec. 1974-76, pres. 1984-86). Democrat. Office: Keeton Tait & Petrie 312 Miller St PO Box E Lewiston ID 83501

TAITZ, MARSHALL MICHAEL, podiatrist; b. Pitts., Mar. 18, 1944; s. Irvin S. and Elizabeth Marie (Schucha) T.; BS, St. Joseph's U., 1966; DPM, Pa. Coll. Podiatric Medicine, 1979; m. Cathy Ettinger, Nov. 26, 1969; children—Cori, Joanna. Resident, Hosp. of Phila. Coll. Osteo. Medicine, 1979-80; staff St. Anne's Hosp., Fall River, Mass., 1980—, Charlton Meml. Hosp.; cons. podiatrist, dir. Southeastern Mass. Rehab. and Performance Ctr., 1980—; pvt. practice podiatry, Fall River, Mass., 1980—. Bd. dirs. Greater Fall River Diabetes Assn., 1980—, pres., 1986—, YMCA, Fall River. Served with USN, 1968-72. Mem. Am. Podiatry Assn., Mass. Podiatric Soc. Home: 58 Narragansett Ave Somerset MA 02726 Office: 673 Robeson St Fall River MA 02720

TAJIMA, TATSUYA, orthopedic and hand surgeon, educator; b. Sakaimachi, Japan, June 3, 1923; s. Heinai and Taka (Nagashima) T.; m. Masa Chono, Nov. 23, 1950; children—Naoya, Toru. M.D., Niigata Med. Coll., 1947; Ph.D., Postgrad. Sch. Niigata U., 1954. Resident in orthopedics, Albany Med. Coll., 1952-54; lectr. orthopedics Niigata U., 1954-58, assoc. prof., 1958-70, prof., chief orthopedics dept., 1970—, dir. Niigata U. Hosp., 1955-59; hon. dir. Niigata Hand Surgery Found., 1985—. Contbr. articles to profl. jours. Recipient Cultural Promotion award Niigata Nippo Co. newspaper, 1976. Mem. Japanese Orthopedic Assn. (pres. 1986-87), Internat. Soc. Orthopedic Surgery and Traumatology, Japanese Soc. Surgery of the Hand, Am. Soc. Surgery of the Hand (hon.), Am. Assn. Surgery of Trauma (hon.), Caribbean Soc. Surgery of Hand (hon.), German Speaking Soc. Hand Surgery (corr.), Brit. Soc. Hand Surgery, Internat. Fedn. Socs. Surgery of the Hand (pres. 1976-77, chmn. 3d Congress 1986). Corr. editor Jour. Hand Surgery, 1976—. Home: Aoyama-Shimmachi 19-2, Niigata 950 21, Japan Office: Niigata Hand Surgery Found, Shinko Cho 1 18, Niigata 950, Japan

TAKACS, MICHAEL JOSEPH, educator; b. N.Y.C., July 28, 1940; s. Michael and Elizabeth Agnes (Scharschmidt) T. AB in Sociology, Fordham U., 1964; MA in Sociology, St. John's U., 1968. Tchr. Bklyn. Prep. Sch., 1964-67, Turtle Hook Sch., Uniondale, N.Y., 1968-73, 74—, Nairobi U., 1971, Colegio San Ignacio, Rio Piedras, P.R. 1973-74; vis. scholar Robert Black Coll., Hong Kong U., 1975, Ramkamhang U., Bangkok, 1975. Vol. community outreach program Our Holy Redeemer Ch., Freeport, N.Y., L.I. Assn. for AIDS Care; adv. Nat. Jr. Honor Soc. Mem. Nat. Council for Social Studies, L.I. Council for Social Studies, N.Y. State Council for Social Studies. Roman Catholic. Home: 425 Newbridge Rd East Meadow NY 11554 Office: Turtle Hook Sch Jerusalem Ave Uniondale NY 11553

TAKADA, FUJIO, jewelry store owner; b. Osaka, Japan, Dec. 20, 1955; s. Fujikazu Takada and Misako Kusunoki; m. Ryoko Shimaoka, June 3, 1986; 1 child, Yuka. LLB, Kwansei Gakoin U., Nishinomiya, 1978; diploma in gemology, Gemological Inst. Am., Santa Monica, Calif., 1979. Pres., owner Takada Jewelry & Co., Ltd., Nishinariku, Japan. Gemological Inst. Great Britain fellow, 1980. Mem. Internat. Colored Stone Assn., Chibjo. Club: Ono Grand Country. Office: Takada Jewelry & Co Ltd, 1-11-22 Tamade Nishi, Nishinariku, Osaka 557, Japan

TAKAGI, NAOKO, credit card company executive; b. Tokyo, Sept. 2, 1955; s. Osamu and Kimiko (Mimura) T. BA, Waseda U., Tokyo, 1978. Mgr. planning div. Diamond Credit Co., Ltd., Tokyo, 1983-87, mgr. project div., 1987—; producer Morikawa Design Office, Tokyo, 1984—; advisor It's Inc., Tokyo, 1986—, I.T. Planning Corp., Tokyo, 1986—. Home: 5-12-11 Shimomeguro, Meguro-ku, Tokyo 153, Japan Office: Diamond Credit Co Ltd, 1-3-2 Dogenzaka, Shibuya-ku, Tokyo 150, Japan

TAKAHASHI, KAZUO, architect; b. Maebashi-shi, Gunma-ken, Japan, June 28, 1951; s. Tyuuzi and Kikuno Takahashi; m. Fumiko Takahashi; 1 child, Saito. BArch, Ashikaga Inst. Tech., Japan, 1974. Architect Ssekeikobo-K, Tokyo, 1976-78. Prin. works include Dohgi-House, 1981, K-House, 1982, Tomioka-Residence, 1985, Makiura-Residence, 1986. Home: 267 Rock-Machi, Maebashi-shi, Gunma-ken Japan Office: Kazu, 3-5-1-211 Kinuta, Setagaya-ku, Tokyo 157, Japan

TAKAHASHI, MICHIO, architect; b. Osaka, Dec. 27, 1925; s. Taneo and Asa Takahashi; m. Hideko Takahashi; children: Hiroko, Hiroshi, Yashushi. BArch, Tech. Coll. Miyakojima, Osaka, 1947. Chief product design Takenaka Komuten Co., Osaka, 1947-86, chief pub. relations sect., 1964-71; dir. engring. design Miki Design Office, Moriguchi, Japan, 1986—. Vice chmn. Com. Protection Against Fire and Take Refuge, Osaka, 1981-86; mem. Conf. Study and Communication on Archtl, Lows and Regulations, Japan, 1985—. Mem. Osaka Architects Office Soc. (bd. dirs. 1986). Home: I-51 Ryuouzan Hazu, Takarazuka 669-12, Japan Office: Miki Design Office, 2-10 Yagumonaka-machi, Moriguchi, Osaka Japan

TAKAHASHI, SHIOHIKO, architect; b. Niigata, Japan, Mar. 27, 1936; s. Katsue and Yoneko (Imai) T.; m. Fukiko Takahashi, Dec. 2, 1963; children: Jun, Ken, Mariko. B, Waseda U., Tokyo, 1959; MArch, Harvard U., 1965.

Registered architect. Mem. design staff Takenaka Komuten Co., Ltd., Tokyo, 1959-68, The Architects' Collaborative, Inc., Cambridge, Mass., 1965, Sert, Jackson & Assocs., Cambridge, 1966; exec. Urban and Archtl. Design, Inc., Tokyo, 1969-74; pres. S. Takahashi Architect & Assocs., Inc., Tokyo, 1975—; prof. Kanagawa U., Yokohama, Japan, 1973-86, Musashino Art U., Kodaira, Japan, 1986—. Author: Shopping Promenade, 1984, Planning of Shopping Malls, 1985; editor: Pedestrian Space, 1987; translator: Urban Structure, 1974. Pres. Shoyo Jr. High Sch. PTA, Fujisawa City, Japan, 1981, Shonan High Sch. PTA, Fujisawa City, 1987; leader Japan Toilet Soc., Tokyo, 1985—. Recipient Yokohama Townscape award Bashamichi Mall, 1985, Kaiko Plaza, 1985, Tokyo Archtl. award Archtl. Office Assn., Tokyo, 1986. Fellow Japan Inst. Architects, Archtl. Inst. Japan, Tokyo Soc. Architects and Bldg. Engrs. Home: 2-9-7 Matsugaoka, Kugenuma, 251 Fujisawa, Kanagawa Japan Office: S Takahashi Architect & Assocs Inc, 1-13-16 Shiba, Minato-Ku, Tokyo 105, Japan

TAKAHASHI, WATARU, environmental consultant; b. Ewa, Hawaii, Aug. 20, 1925; s. Zenjiro and Matsuno (Kodama) T.; m. Nobuko Toyama, Sept. 17, 1955; 1 child, Ann Eiko. BA in Chemistry, U. Hawaii, 1957; MA in Chemistry, Ind. U., 1959. Organic chemist U.S. Argl. Research Service, Peoria, Ill., 1961-62; indsl. hygiene chemist Dept. Health, Honolulu, 1962-65; marine chemist U. Hawaii, Honolulu, 1965-70, field epidemiologist, 1971-82; cons. Aiea, Hawaii, 1982—. Contbr. articles to profl. jours. Served with U.S. Army, 1950-52, PTO. Mem. AAAS, Am. Chem. Soc., Phi Beta Kappa. Home and Office: 98-1996 Hoala St Aiea HI 96701

TAKAHASHI, YASUSHI, automotive company executive; b. Tokyo, Aug. 25, 1956; s. Takeshi and Hiroko (Sugimoto) T. BS, Keio U., 1979, MS, 1981. Engr. Honda Research and Devel. Co. Ltd., Wako, Japan, 1983—; supr. Honda Research Am., Denver, 1983-84. Home: Nakayoshi-so 1-1 1-10-26 Nakacho, Asaka Saitama 341, Japan Office: Honda Research and Devel Co Ltd, 1-4-1 Chuo Wako, Saitama 351, Japan

TAKAHASHI, YOSHIKAZV, interior designer; b. Maebashi, Gumma-ken, Japan, Feb. 21, 1945; s. Chōji and Shige (Matsumoto) T.; m. Satoko Kobayashi, Jan. 25, 1970; 1 child, Norikazu. BA, Musashino Art U., Tokyo, 1967. Chief designer Kanko-Kikaku Sekkei-sha Architecture and Interior Design, Tokyo, 1967-78; head interior design Ishii Sekkei, Maebashi, Gumma-ken, Japan, 1978—; bd. dirs. Gumma Ednl. and Cultural Ctr., Maebashi, 1988—. Mem. Maebashi C. of C. (design cons. 1985—). Home: 1-6-5 Annaka, 379-01 Annaka-shi Japan Office: Ishii Sekkei Co Ltd, 2-7-12 Ootemachi, Maebashi-shi 371, Japan

TAKAHASHI, YOSHINDO, transport company executive; b. Tokyo, Apr. 21, 1931; s. Yoshio and Antonina Nikolaiuna (Razmowa) T.; m. Noriko Masago, Oct. 7, 1955; children—Hiroshi, Kaoru, Yukie. B.S., Aoyama Gakuin U., Tokyo, 1955. Mgr., Hino Motors Ltd., Tokyo, 1961-77; mgr. overseas ops. Hino Motors Ltd.; mng. dir. Hino Motors Hellas S.A., Athens, Greece, 1963-68, comptroller Thai Hino Motor Sales Ltd., Bangkok, Thailand, 1970-71; mng. dir. Okamoto Freighters Ltd., Tokyo, 1977—, Okamoto Internat. Ltd., Tokyo, 1977-85, Zen-Okamoto Enterprise Pte., Ltd., Singapore, 1983-85. Home: No 15-4-816, Higashi-nogawa 3-chome, Komae-Shi, Tokyo 201, Japan Office: Okamoto Freighters Ltd, #8-7 Hakozaki-cho, Nihonbashi Chuo-Ku, Tokyo 103, Japan

TAKAMINE, MASASHI MATTHEW, television company executive; b. Nagoya, Aichi, Japan, Apr. 24, 1935; s. Noboru and Shu Takamine; m. Kinuyo Mizutani, May 3, 1964; children: Fusako, Kyōko. B in Social Sci., Cath. U. Nagoya, 1959. Program dir. radio sta. Chubu Nippon Broadcasting Co., Nagoya, 1959-61, sales mgr. radio div., 1961-65, coordinator TV div., 1965-85, mgr. research mgmt., 1985-87, gen. mgr. programming and news ctr., 1987—. Active com. safe driving Japan Automobile Assn., 1976—; bd. dirs. fundraising Cath. U. Nagoya, 1987—. Recipient Gov's. award Aichi, 1950. Home: Tsuruha-cho, 3-8-2 Showa-Ku, Nagoya, Aichi 466, Japan Office: Chubu Nippon Broadcasting Co, 1-2-8 Shinsakae, Naka-ku, Nagoya, Aichi 460, Japan

TAKAMOTO, TOSHIHIKO, medical educator; b. Naze, Japan, Aug. 7, 1948; s. Takeshi and Tsuru T.; m. Kiyomi Hori, Mar. 21, 1974; children: Ken, Kaoru. MD, Kagoshima U., 1967-74; PhD, Tokyo Med. and Dental U., 1985. Diplomate Japan Bd. Gen. Medicine. Lectr. Tokyo Med. and Dental U., 1980—, asst. prof. cardiology, 1985—. Home: 3-14-9-1 Tsurumaki, Tama-Shi Tokyo 206, Japan Office: Tokyo Med & Dental U, 1-5-45 Yushima, Tokyo 113, Japan

TAKANO, KATSUO, mathamatics educator; b. Ibaraki, Japan, Sept. 3, 1944; s. Masutaro and Masa Takano; m. Suzuki Takano, 1974; children: Osamu, Tomoyo, Tatsuo. MS, Tokyo U. Edn., 1970. Asst. prof. Ibaraki (Japan) U., 1974-84, prof., 1984—. Office: Ibaraki U, 2-1-1 Bunkyo, 310 Mito Ibaraki, Japan

TAKANO, TORU, health club executive; b. Odawara, Japan, Apr. 17, 1957; s. Tadashi and Yuriko T. BS in Phys. Edn., Tsukuba U., 1982, MS in Phys. Edn., 1985. Planning mgr. People Co. Ltd., Tokyo; head instr. Croquet Assn., Japan. Co-author: Croquet No Susume, 1984. Recipient 1st prize Japan Open Croquet Singles Game, 1984, 86, 2d prize 1985, 3rd prize 1987. Mem. Japanese Soc. Leisure and Recreation Studies. Office: People Co Ltd, 8-5-30 Akasaka, Minato-ku, Tokyo 107, Japan

TAKASE, FUMIKO, educator; b. Nishinomiya, Hyogo, Japan, Mar. 23, 1927; d. Hisashi and Yukiko T. B.A., Berea Coll.-Ky. 1964; M.A., Mt. Holyoke Coll., 1966; postgrad. Tulane U., 1972-75. Instr. English, Mukogawa Girls High Sch., Nishinomiya, Japan, 1949-50, Yamate Girls High Sch., Kobe, 1950-52; asst. to dean women Kobe Coll., Nishinomiya, Japan, 1957-61, instr. English, 1966-70, asst. prof. English, 1970-77, prof. English, 1977—, chmn. dept. English, 1981-85, dir. Ctr. Women's Studies, 1985—; trustee Alumnae Assn., 1967-72, councillor, 1969-72; examiner English proficiency The Examining Com. of English Proficiency of Japan, 1971-72. Contbr. articles to profl. jours. Mem. Japan U. Women's Assn., MLA, Japan English Literary Soc., Japan Emily Dickinson Soc., Renaissance Soc. Am. (16th Century Studies). Home: 2-2-7 Kotoen, Nishinomiya, Hyogo 662, Japan Office: Kobe Coll, 4-1 Okadayama, Nishinomiya, Hyogo Japan

TAKASHI, OYABU, mathematician, physicist, physician; b. Kyoto, Japan, Aug. 9, 1949; s. Junichi and Fumiko Oyabu. Grad., Kyoto U., 1972; MD, Osaka (Japan) Med. Coll., 1979. Intern in phisiological dept. Oe shinryo-ku, Kyoto, Japan; practicing medicine specializing in internat. medicine Hodonomizu Hosp., Takatsuki, Japan; practicing medicine specializing in psychiatry Osaka. Mem. Am. Mathematical Soc., Société Mathématique de France, Mathematical Soc. of Japan, Biophys. Soc. of Japan, Soc. for Mathematical Biology. Home: Oe Kutsukake cho, 5-41 Nishikyo-ku, Nishikyo-ku, Kyoto Japan

TAKAZAWA, REIJI, architect; b. Hiroshima, Japan, June 22, 1942; s. Goro and Sachiko T.; m. Teruyo Takazawa; children: Kanji, Ryo, Satoshi. BS, Tokyo U., 1966. Registered architect, Japan. Sr. architect Kajima Corp., Tokyo, 1966-86; mng. dir. Avant Assocs., Inc., Tokyo, 1986—. Office: Avant Assocs Inc, 2-10-2 Nagatacho, Chiyopaku 100, Japan

TAKEDA, HARUO, insurance company executive; b. May 28, 1922; married. Grad., Tokyo U., 1947. With Tokyo Fire and Marine Insurance Co., 1947—, exec. dir., then pres. Home: 9-5 Nishikaigan, 1-chome Tsujido, Fujisawa Japan Office: Tokyo Fire and Marine Ins Co, 2-1 Marunouchi, 1-chome Chiyoda-ku, Tokyo Japan *

TAKEDA, KENNETH KINGO, orthodontist; b. Riverside, Calif., Dec. 24, 1929; s. Orisaburo and Umeko (Ando) T.; m. Mary Yamaguchi, Jan. 28, 1951; children—Matthew Curtis, Kristin Haruko. AA, Riverside Coll. (Calif.), 1949; BSCE, U. Calif.-Berkeley, 1951; DDS, U.Calif., San Francisco, 1965. Engring. draftsman U.S. Bur. Reclamation, Boulder City, Nev., 1949, jr. engr., Marble Canyon, Ariz., 1950; stress analyst Boeing Airplane Co., Seattle, 1951-53; structures engr. Douglas Aircraft Co., Long Beach, Calif., 1953-60; research engr. The Boeing Co., Seattle, 1961, 62, 63; practice dentistry specializing in orthodontics, Stockton, Calif., 1965—. Pres. chpt. Japanese Am. Citizens League, Lodi, Calif., 1984. Recipient Gabbs prize in dentistry U. Calif., 1965. Mem. U. Calif. Dental Alumni Assn., U. Calif. Orthodontic Alumni Assn., Calif. State Soc. Orthodontists, Pacific Coast Soc. Orthodontists, Am. Assn. Orthodontists, Am. Dental Assn., Calif. Dental Assn. (rep. ho. dels. 1972-73), San Joaquin Dental Soc. (pres. 1972-73), Omicron Kappa Upsilon, Delta Sigma Delta. Lutheran. Club: Kiwanis (Disting. Pres. 1977-78). Home: 626 Birchwood Dr Lodi CA 95240 Office: 532 W Harding Way Suite B Stockton CA 95204

TAKEDA, SHOZO, publishing executive; b. Tokyo, Aug. 30, 1914; d. Michitaro and Kimiko (Kayama) Kameda; m. Chieko Takeda, May 21, 1941; children—Mieko, Yumiko, Shoichiro. B.Engring., Kyoto U. (Japan), 1940. Pres., Yakugyo Jiho Co., Ltd., Tokyo, 1946—. Served with Japanese Navy, 1940-45. Buddhism. Home: 3-17-3, Minami-Yukigaya, Ota-Ku, Tokyo 145, Japan Office: Yakugyo Jiho Co Ltd, 2-36 Jimbocho, Chiyoda-ku, Tokyo 101, Japan

TAKEI, FUMIKO, English educator; b. Dallas, June 9, 1929; d. Seizo and Chiyo Kimura; m. Akira Takei, Apr. 29, 1954; children: Minoru, Koh. BA, Kobe Coll., Nishinomiya, Japan, 1953. Cert. Sogetsu flower arrangement instr. Tchr. Hamashobo Culture Sch., Yokohama, Kanagawa Perfecture, Japan, 1984—. Vol. (through Japan Bus. Assn. and So. Los Angeles Vol. Works) Gardena (Calif.) Retirement Ctr., 1980, Mothers Activity for the Asian Students from Abroad div. of Tokyo YWCA; Tokyo del. Internat. Student Assn., 1957. Home: 18-7 Isogodai, Isogo-ku, Yokohama Kanagawa, Japan 235

TAKEMAE, EIJI, political science educator; b. Suzaka, Japan, Aug. 4, 1930; s. Kikutaro and Tokuno (Kubo) T.; m. Atsuko Sugiyama, Mar. 26, 1961; 1 child, Kenichi. BA, Tokyo U. Edn., 1955; MA, Tokyo Met. U., 1963, PhD, 1971; cert., U. Hawaii, 1966. Lectr. Tokyo Met. U., 1969-74; lectr. Inst. Social Sci. Tokyo U., 1972-74; lectr. Hitotsubashi U., Tokyo, 1979, Chuo U., Tokyo, 1968—; prof. polit. sci. Tokyo Keizai U., 1974—; Fulbright vis. prof. U. Md., 1977-78. Author: Study of the U.S. Labor Policy for Japan, 1970, Untold History of the Allied Occupation of Japan, 1977, The Occupation and the Japanese Postwar History, 1980, Postwar Labor Reform, 1982, Witness to the History of the Occupation of Japan, 1983, GHQ, 1983; translator DDT Revolution (by C.M. Sams), 1986; collaborator: Democratizing Japan-The Allied Occupation, 1987. Recipient Disting. Book prize Japan Inst. Labor and Yomiuri Shimbun-sha, 1983. Mem. Japan Assn. Labor Law, Japan Polit. Sci. Assn., Japan Assn. Study of History of Occupation (pres. 1972-83). Buddhist. Home: 1129-52 Kisomachi, Machida-shi, Tokyo 194, Japan Office: Tokyo Keizai U, 1-7 Minamicho Kokubunji, Tokyo 185, Japan

TAKENAKA, SHIGEO, mathematics educator; b. Kobe, Hyogo, Japan, June 1, 1947; s. Kazue and Toshiko (Takenaka) T.; m. Emiko Sato, Mar. 21, 1972; children: Yoichi, Mitsuru. BS, Kyoto U., Japan, 1970, MS, 1972; DSc, Nagoya U., Japan, 1977. Research assoc. Nagoya U., 1972-77, lectr. math., 1977—. Yukawa Found. grantee Osaka U., 1977. Mem. Math. Soc. Japan, Am. Math. Soc., Inst. Math Stats. Office: Nagoya U, Dept Math Faculty Sci, Furo-cho Chikusa-ku, Nagoya 464, Japan

TAKESHITA, NOBORU, prime minister of Japan; b. Shimane Prefecture, Japan, Feb. 26, 1924; m. Naoko Endo, 1946; 3 daus. Grad. Sch. Commerce, Waseda U., 1947. Tchr. English, social studies, local secondary sch., Shimane Prefecture, 1947-51; mem. Shimane Prefectural Assembly, 1951-57; mem. Ho. of Reps., Diet, Tokyo, 1958—, parliamentary vice minister Ministry of Internat. Trade and Industry, 1963-64, dep. chief cabinet sec., 1964-66, chief cabinet sec., 1971-72, 74, minister of constrn., 1976, chmn. budget com. Ho. of Reps., 1978-79, minister of fin., 1979-80, 82-86, prime minister, 1987—; sec. gen. Liberal Dem. Party, 1986-87, pres., 1987—. Author: Waga michi o yuki (Seeking after the Path), 1979; Riso o mezashite (Pursuing an Ideal), 1981; Magokoro no seiji (Honest Politics), 1983. Holds rank of 5th dan, judo. Office: care Liberal Democratic Party, 1-11-23, Nagata-cho, Chiyoda-ku, Tokyo 100 Japan *

TAKESHITA, TORU, computer research scientist; b. Nishinomiya, Hyogo, Japan, Dec. 16, 1931; s. Hajime and Chiho (Kubota) T.; m. Yumiko Taniguchi, Oct. 20, 1962; children: Chikako, Jun. BA in Sci., U. Kyoto, Japan, 1957; PhD in Computer Sci., U. Beverly Hills, 1983. WitH Software Tech. IBM Japan Ltd., Tokyo, 1957—, mgr. Tokyo Research Lab., 1988—. Author 15 books related to computer programming; contbr. numerous articles to profl. jours. Mem. IEEE, Info. Processing Soc. Japan, Japan Soc. Software Sci. and Tech., Japan Soc. Artificial Intelligence. Home: 3 11 1 410 Soshigaya, Setagaya-ku, Tokyo 157, Japan Office: IBM Corp Tokyo Research Lab, 5 19 Samban-cho, Tokyo 102, Japan

TAKEUCHI, HIROYUKI, urologist, medical educator, researcher; b. Mitaka-Shi, Tokyo, Jan. 18, 1932; s. Rokuro and Harue Takeuchi; m. Reiko Fujil, Apr. 29, 1961; children—Tomoko, Motoshi. B.Engring., Shizuoka U. Hamamatsu, Japan, 1955; B.Medicine, Tokyo Med. and Dental U., 1959, M.D., 1964. Intern Enshu Med. Ctr., Hamamatsu, Japan, 1959-60; resident Tokyo Med. and Dental U. Hosp., 1960-64; asst. Tokyo Med. and Dental U., 1964-73, assoc. prof. dept. urology, 1973-84; vice dir. Shakai-Hoken Mishima Hosp., 1984-86, dir. 1986—. Fellow Japanese Soc. Urology, Japanese Soc. Fertility and Sterility, Japanese Soc. Traumatic Medicine; mem. Internat. Soc. Urology. Home: 10-2, Nakahara 4-Chome, Mitaka-Shi, Tokyo 181, Japan Office: Shakai-Hoken Mishima Hosp, 20-9 Minami-Honmachi Mishima-shi, Shizuoka Prefecture, Tokyo 411, Japan

TAKEYAMA, MINORU, architect, educator; b. Sapporo, Hokkaido, Japan, Mar. 15, 1934; s. Saiichiro and Misao (Saito) T.; m. Helle Klint, Dec. 5, 1964 (div.); 1 child, Indigo Klint; m. Rumi Okada, Dec. 21, 1972; children: Ken, Aki. BArch, Waseda U., 1956, MArch, 1958; MArch, Harvard U., 1960. Registered architect, Japan. Designer Sert, Gourley and Jackson, Cambridge, Mass., 1960-61; architect Jørn Utzon Architects, Denmark, 1961-62, Henning Larsen Architects, Copenhagen, 1962-63; lectr. Royal Acad. Fine Arts, Copenhagen, 1963-64; assoc. prof. Musashino Art U., Tokyo, 1965-70, prof., 1970—; pres. Minoru Takeyama and United Actions, Tokyo, 1965—. Author: Street Semiology, 1980, Language of Architecture, 1983; architect Musashino Art Univ. Bldg. no. 10, 1981, Sapporo Hosp., 1983, Renaissance Kyoto, 1985, Egyptian Embassy, Tokyo, 1986. Wheelwright fellow Harvard U., 1971; recipient Spl. award Union Internat. Architects, 1980, Bulgarian Assn. Architects, 1981. Mem. Japan Inst. Architects, Archtl. Inst. Japan (bd. dirs.), Japanese Soc. for Sci. Design. Home: 7-1-21-302 Minami-Aoyama, Minato-ku, Tokyo 107, Japan Office: Minoru Takeyama and United Action, 5-1-10-501 Minami-Aoyama, Minato-ku Tokyo 107, Japan

TAKINO, MASUICHI, physician; b. Santo-cho, Asago-gun Hyogo Prefecture, Japan, Apr. 14, 1905; s. Kichitaro and Yukiko (Toda) T.; grad. Nat. U. Japan, 1929; M.D., Kyoto U., 1934; m. Yoshiko Aoyagi, Nov. 17, 1930; 4 children. Lectr. internal medicine Kyoto (Japan) U., 1939-41; dir. dept. pathology Osaka Prefectural Sengokuso Hosp. of Pulmonary Tb, 1941-45; dir. Dainippon Zoki Inst. for Med. Research, 1947-61, Nippon Zoki Inst. for Constitutional Diseases, 1962-80; adviser Nippon Inst. Constl. Diseases, Osaka, Japan, 1985—; adv. Nippon Zoki Pharm. Co. Ltd., 1968-80; practice medicine specializing in allergy and autonomic nervous system, Osaka. Fellow Am. Coll. Chest Physicians (emeritus); mem. Japan Soc. Allergy (hon. mem., award 1970), Japan Soc. Internal Medicine (counselor), Japan Soc. Endocrinology (counselor), Japan Soc. Neurovegetative Research, counselor), Japan Soc. Angiocardiology (counselor) Japan Soc. Constn. (counselor), Internat. Soc. Biometeorology, Japan Christian Med. Assn.. Author: A New Direction in Asthma Treatment, 1952; (with Yoshitada Takino) Allergy and Asthma, 1956; (with Y. Takino and Kunikazu Sugahara) Pathogenesis and Therapy of Bronchial Asthma with Special Reference to Organ Vagotonia, 1976; Allergy and Autonomic Nervous System, 1979. Home: 1-3-7 Chiyogaoka, Nara 631, Japan Office: Shinmido Bldg, 5-19 Minami-Kyuhoji-Cho, Osaka 540, Japan

TAKINO, TATSURO, medical educator; b. Hyogo, Asago, Japan, Sept. 9, 1927; s. Toyoichi and Chie Takino; married; 3 children. M.D., Kyoto Prefectural U. Medicine, 1952, Ph.D. of M.D., 1957. Resident, Kyoto Prefectural U. Medicine (Japan), 1953-56, asst., 1956-57, instr., 1957-70, asst. prof., 1970-71, assoc. prof., 1971-79, prof. medicine, 1979—, also chmn. dept. internal medicine. Editor: Clinical Gastroenterology, 1983; Chronic Hepatitis, 1980; Liver Cirrhosis, 1979; Drug Induced Hepatic Injury, 1980. Bd. dirs. Emergency Assn., Kyoto, 1983; insp. Japan Alcohol Med. Assn., 1983. Nat. Edn. Dept. Tokyo grantee, 1981; Nat. Govt. Pub. Health grantee, 1977. Mem. Internat. Assn. Study of Liver, Japanese Assn. for Study of Liver, Internat. Hematol. Assn., Japan Internal Med. Assn. (councillor). Jodo Bud. Home: 17 Kusaki-cho, Tokiwa Ukyo-ku, Kyoto 616, Japan Office: 3d Dept Internal Medicine, Kyoto Prefectual U Medicine, Kawaramachi Hirokoji Kamigyo-ku, Kyoto 602, Japan

TAKKABUTR, CHEN, printing ink company executive; b. Pong, Phayao, Thailand, Sept. 5, 1940; s. Hong Tok Sae Liam and Chiew Tee Sae Liam; m. Urai Srichai, Nov. 30, 1975 (div. July 1981); children—Anat, Payak, Puttachart. Jr. degree in Bus. Adminstrn., Ramkhamhaeng U., Bangkok, 1978; sch. cert. New Method Coll., Hong Kong; Mathayom 8, Santiraj Bamrung, Bangkok, 1952-58. Reservationist, World Travel Service, Bangkok, Thailand, 1962-63, Alitalia Airlines, Bangkok, 1963-65, Pan Am. Airlines, Bangkok, 1965-67; salesman Berli Jucker Cl., Bangkok, 1968-70; dir. Toyo Ink Co., Bangkok, 1971-81; mng. dir. Krung Thai Ink Ltd., Bangkok, 1982—; dir. T.K.B. Trading Ltd., Bangkok; mem. printing ink quality control Printing Ink Standardization, 1982. Mem. Bangchan Indsl. Club: (chmn. 1980-81.) Democrat. Buddhist. Office: Krung Thai Ink Ltd, 88/8 Moo 2, Timland, Ngarmwongwarn 11000, Thailand

TAKLA, LARS ARNE, oil company executive; b. Odda, Hordaland, Norway, July 10, 1944; s. Hans and Anna (Kvammen) R.; m. Anne Grete Andersen, Nov.7, 1946; children: Erik, Espen, Lars Christian. MSc in Chem., Norwegian Inst. Tech., 1968. Chartered engr. Norway. Asst. research Inst. Tech. Elec. Chem., Trondheim, Norway, 1968-69; engr. lab. Norwegian Navy Lab. for Oil & Explosives, Bergen, 1969-70; engr. research and devel. Waardal Chem. Plant, Bergen, 1970-71; supr. research and devel. Norzink AS, Odda, Norway, 1971-74; supt. plant Norzink AS, Odda, 1974-77; sr. corrosion engr. Phillips Petroleum Co. Norway, Stavanger, 1977-80, chief offshore engr., 1980-81, mgr. govt. affairs, 1981-83, mgr. joint venture and planning, 1983-85, mgr. prodn. and pipeline ops., 1985, mgr. offshore ops., 1985-87, in charge of the facing ops. of 6 ekofisk platrforms, 1987—; bd. dirs. Sparventura AS, Sandnes. Bd. dirs. Odda Athletic Soc., 1973-77; chmn. bd. Tech. Soc. Hardanger, Odda, 1974-76. Served with Norwegian Navy, 1969-70. Mem. Norwegian Soc. Chartered Engrs. (profl. bd. mem. 1982-84), Soc. Petroleum Engrs. Conservative. Lutheran. Home: Agatv 13, 4300 Sandnes Rogaland Norway

TAL, JACOB, electronics executive; b. Tiberias, Israel, Nov. 29, 1940; s. Refael and Seniora Tboul; m. Rachel Alkony, Oct. 22, 1962 (div. 1978); 1 child, Tomer. BS, Technion, Haifa, Israel, 1966; MS, U. Minn., 1968, PhD, 1970. Research fellow U. Minn., Mpls., 1970-71; elec. engring. prof. U. Utah, Salt Lake City, 1971-78; research engr. Hewlett Packard, Palo Alto, Calif., 1978-81; founder, owner Motion Control Seminar, Mountain View, Calif., 1981—; founder, pres. Galil Motion Control, Palo Alto, 1983—; cons. Control Data, Mpls., 1970-75, Electro Craft, Mpls., 1970-78, Ford Motor Corp., Detroit, 1976-78, Burroughs Corp., Westlake, Calif., 1981-82. Author: Motion Control by Microprocessors, 1984, (with others) Incremental Motion Control, 1978; contbr. articles to profl. jours. Mem. IEEE, Electronic Motion Control Assn. Home: 49 Showers Dr #G-442 Mountain View CA 94040 Office: Galil Motion Control 1054 Elwell Ct Palo Alto CA 94040

TALAPATRA, KESHAB ANANDA, food technologist, consultant; b. Comilla, Bangladesh, Nov. 3, 1939; came to U.S., 1969, naturalized, 1980; s. Mukunda Lal and Kiran Bala (Roy) T.; m. Gitashri Bhattacharjee, Feb. 28, 1969; children—Sunit, Sudip. B.S. with honors, Calcutta U., India, 1958, M.S. in Tech., 1961, Ph.D., 1968; Ph.D., Pa. State U., 1974; M.B.A., Pepperdine U., 1981. Chem. prof. Bangabasi Coll., Calcutta, 1961-69; postdoctoral fellow Rutgers U., New Brunswick, N.J., 1969-71; grad. research asst. Pa. State U., University Park, 1971-73; food scientist Hunt-Wesson Foods, Inc., Fullerton, Calif., 1973-77; food technologist Star-Kist Foods, Inc., Terminal Island, Calif., 1977-80, sr. food technologist, 1980—; cons. food tech. various schs. and industries, 1974—. Patentee in field. Exec. mem. Bengali Assn. So. Calif., Pasedena, 1984. Research grantee Univ. Grants Commn., 1963-65. Mem. Am. Chem. Soc., Inst. Food Technologists, Am. Oil Chemists' Soc. Home: 809 Roxbury Dr Fullerton CA 92633 Office: Star-Kist Foods Inc 582 Tuna St Terminal Island CA 90731

TALARD, JEAN-PIERRE, sales executive; b. Paris, Feb. 25, 1942; m. Bernaux Danielle, July 21, 1966; 1 child, Agnes. Grad., Ecole Spéciale de Préparation aux Affaires, Paris, 1964; diploma in Acctg., Ecole Nouvelle d'Orgn. Econ. et Sociale, Paris, 1964; grad. in Mktg., Inst. Nat. Mktg., Paris, 1976. Clk. BRED Bank, Bezons, France, 1962-64, CSF Compagnie Générale de Télégraphie sans Fil, Paris, 1965-66; export salesman Reboul-SMT Packaging, Creteil, France, 1966-69, export area mgr., 1969-71, export product mgr., 1971-79, sales dir., 1979-87; sales dir. Avery Internat. France, 1987—. Treas. Conseiller du Commerce Extérieur de la France, Paris, 1975—. Roman Catholic. Home: 15 Rue Raynouard, F75016 Paris France Office: Avery Internat France SA, Rue Blaise-Pascal, 91380 Chilly-Mazarin France

TALASTERÄ, TAPIO ALTTI MATTI, freight company executive; b. Pori, Finland, June 23, 1938; m. Irma Anneli, Dec. 19, 1965; children: Johanna, Janne. Forwarder O.W. Hacklin Oy, Pori, 1956-61, dept. mgr., 1961-65; regional mgr. John Nurminen Oy, Pori, 1965-70; sales mgr. John Nurminen Oy, Helsinki, Finland, 1970-78; mem. mgmt. group John Nurminen Oy, 1972—; gen. mgr. internat. bus. John Nurminen Oy, Helsinki, Finland, 1978-85, dir. freight forwarding div., 1985—. Mem. Scandinavian Forwarding Assn. (bd. dirs. 1986), Finlands Forwarding Assn.(v.p. 1985), Internat. Fedn. Freight Forwarders Assns. (exec. com. 1986), Finnish Freight Forwarding Assn. (pres. 1988—). Home: Vanhan-Mankkaantie 20, 02180 Espoo Finland Office: John Nurminen Oy, Pasilankatu 2, 00240 Helsinki Finland

TALBERT, JAMES LEWIS, pediatric surgeon; b. Cassville, Mo., Sept. 26, 1931; s. William David and Frances (Lewis) T.; m. Alice Quintavell, July 25, 1958; children: William David, Alison Whitney. B.A., Vanderbilt U., 1953, M.D., 1956. Diplomate: Am. Bd. Surgery, Am. Bd. Thoracic Surgery. Intern, then resident in surgery Johns Hopkins Hosp., 1956-64, resident in pediatric surgery, 1964-65, Harvey Cushing fellow, 1958-59; instr. surgery, Garrett scholar pediatric surgery Johns Hopkins U. Med. Sch., 1965-66, asst. prof., 1966-67; mem. faculty U. Fla. Med. Sch., Gainesville, 1967—; prof. pediatric surgery, chmn. div., chief children's surgery U. Fla. Med. Sch., 1970—; mem. affiliated faculty VA Hosp., Gainesville; med. dir. Fla. Regional Med. Program for Diagnosis and Treatment Cancer in Children, 1970-73, N. Refferal Center Children's Med. Service Program Fla., 1970-80; chmn. Alachua County Emergency Med. Services Adv. Council, 1973-75; chmn. emergency med. services com. N. Central Fla. Health Planning Council, 1972-73; mem. Fla. Emergency Med. Services Adv. Council, 1973-75, 76-79. Author 105 articles in field; contbr. 16 chpts. to books. Served with USPHS, 1960-62. Recipient Founders medal, Roche award Vanderbilt U. Med. Sch., 1956. Fellow ACS (chmn. Fla. trauma com. 1969-77, gov.-at-large 1979-85, sec. bd. govs. 1982-85), Am. Acad. Pediatrics (exec. com. sect. oncology and hematology 1978-85), Am. Pediatric Surg. Assn. (founding mem.); mem. Am. Pediatric Surg. Assn. (chmn. trauma com. 1976-79), Pediatric Oncology Group (chmn. group retreat 1980), Am. Fedn. Clin. Research, Assn. Acad. Surgery, Soc. U. Surgeons, AMA, Univ. Assn., Emergency Med. Services, Soc. Pediatric Research, Am. Coll. Emergency Physicians, Am. Trauma Soc., Pediatric Surg. Biology Club, Am. Surg. Assn., Halsted Soc., Am. Assn. Surgery Trauma, Am. Burn Assn., Am. Pediatric Soc., Brit. Assn. Pediatric Surgeons, Soc. Internat. Chirurgie, So. Soc. Pediatric Research, So. Surg. Assn., Fla. Med. Assn., Fla. Heart Assn. (chmn. cardio-pulmonary resuscitation com. 1972-76), Fla. Assn. Pediatric Surgeons (pres. 1976-78), Fla. Assn. Pediatric Tumor Programs (pres. 1973—), Alachua County Med. Soc. (chmn. emergency med. services adv. com. 1973-75), Phi Beta Kappa, Alpha Omega Alpha, Phi Eta Sigma. Office: Box J-286 J Hillis Miller Health Ctr Gainesville FL 32610

TALBERT, RICHARD CLARK, management professional; b. Oak Park, Ill., Oct. 27, 1950; s. Austin Gertner and Kathryn Mary (Pokragac) T.; m. Patricia Parker, Mar. 16, 1974; children: Jeffrey, Kristin. Student, U. Ill., 1968-71. Cert. water specialist. Mgr. Rock Rd. Trailer, St. Louis, 1971-74; nat. dir. Narconon, Los Angeles, 1974-79; dealer Sunland Industries, Phoenix, 1981-85; pres., gen. ptnr. Northland Purewater div. Northland

Environ. Inc., Burbank, Calif., 1980—; pres. Northland Technologies Inc., Burbank, 1987—. Co-author, editor booklet Narconon. Active Citizens' Commn. on Human Rights, 1973—, Narconon Get Am. Off Drugs, Los Angeles, 1983—, Campaign Crusade for Religious Freedom, Hollywood, 1985—, Way to Happiness Found., 1985—. Mem. Calif. Solar Energy Industries Assn., Los Angeles Solar Energy Industries Assn., Orange County Solar Energy Industries Assn., Nat. Fedn. Ind. Bus., World Inst. of Scientology Enterprises, Water Quality Assn., Calif. C. of C., Burbank C. of C. Republican. Mem. Ch. Scientology. Office: Northland Environemtnal Inc 1115 Chestnut Burbank CA 91506

TALBOT, MATTHEW J., oil company executive; b. Sept. 4, 1937; s. Matthew J. and Margaret A. (Green) T.; m. Maureen Donlan, June 3, 1958; children: Maureen A., Matthew J., Kathleen M. BBA in Acctg., Iona Coll., 1963. Acct. S.D. Leidesdorf (now Ernst & Whinney), N.Y.C., 1961-67; sr. analyst Gen. Foods Corp., White Plains, N.Y., 1967-68; asst. to comptroller Tosco Corp., Los Angeles, 1968-70, comptroller, 1970-83, v.p., 1972-76, sr. v.p., 1976-78, exec. v.p., 1978-83; pres. Tosco Corp., Santa Monica, Calif., 1983—. Treas., bd. dirs. Ctr. Theatre Group, Los Angeles; trustee Craft and Folk Art Mus., Los Angeles. Mem. Am. Inst. CPA's, Fin. Execs. Inst. Roman Catholic. Office: Tosco Corp 2401 Colorado Santa Monica CA 90406

TALBOT, PHILLIPS, Asian affairs specialist; b. Pitts., June 7, 1915; s. Kenneth Hammet and Gertrude (Phillips) T.; m. Mildred Aleen Fisher, Aug. 18, 1943; children: Susan Talbot Jacox, Nancy, Bruce Kenneth. B.A., B.S. in Journalism, U. Ill., 1936; student, London Sch. Oriental Studies, 1938-39, Aligarh Muslim U., India, 1939-40; Ph.D., U. Chgo., 1954; LL.D. (hon.), Mills Coll., 1963. Reporter, Chgo. Daily News, 1936-38; corr. Chgo. Daily News, India and Pakistan, 1946-48, 49-50; asso. Inst. Current World Affairs, Eng. and India, 1938-41; part-time Inst. Current World Affairs, 1946-51; instr. U. Chgo., 1948-50, 1951; instr. U. Hawaii, 1953; exec. dir. Am. Univs. Field Staff, 1951-61; asst. sec. Near Eastern and S. Asian affairs Dept. State, 1961-65; U.S. ambassador to Greece 1965-69; pres. Asia Soc., N.Y.C., 1970-81; emeritus Asia Soc., 1981—; Phi Beta Kappa vis. scholar, 1973-74. Author: (with S.L. Poplai) India and America, 1958, India in the 1980s, 1983; editor: South Asia in the World Today, 1950. Trustee Inst. Current World Affairs, South-North News Service, East Asian History of Sci., Inc., China Inst. in Am., U.S.-Japan Found., United Bd. for Christian Higher Edn. in Asia. Served as 2d lt. cav. O.R.C., 1936; as 1st lt. 33d div. Ill. N.G., 1937-38; from lt. (j.g.) to lt. comdr. USNR, 1941-46. Mem. Assn. Asian Studies, Council Fgn. Relations, Pilgrims of U.S., Royal Soc. Asian Affairs. Presbyterian (elder). Clubs: Century Assn. (N.Y.C.); Cosmos (Washington). Address: 200 E 66th St New York NY 10021

TALBOTT, LINDA HOOD, educator, foundation executive, communications executive; b. Kansas City, Mo., Dec. 29, 1941; d. Henry H. and Helen E. (Hamrick) Hood; B.A. with highest distinction, U. Mo., 1962, M.A. (grad. fellow), 1964, Ph.D., 1973; postgrad. (postdoctoral fellow) Harvard U. Inst. Ednl. Mgmt., 1974; m. Thomas H. Talbott, Mar. 5, 1965. Prof. English, Met. Jr. Coll., Kansas City, Mo., 1963-67; prof. English, Queensborough Community Coll., Bayside, N.Y., 1967-68; prof. English, editor Nassau Rev., Nassau Community Coll., Garden City, N.Y., 1968-69; prof. English, adminstr. Lesley Coll., Cambridge, Mass., 1969; founding editor Tempo mag. and devel. officer U. Mo., Kansas City, 1969-76, dir. spl. projects Office of Chancellor, 1976—, adj. prof. edn., 1975—; pres. Talbott & Assocs., Kansas City, 1975—; exec. dir. Clearinghouse for Midcontinent Founds., Kansas City, 1975-85, pres., 1985—; dir. Kansas City Power and Light Co., 1983; lectr., cons. in field; mem. gov.'s adv. task force on literacy State of Mo., 1987—. Bd. dirs. exec. com. United Community Services/Heart of Am. United Way, 1974-82; mem. exec. com. The Central Exchange, 1978-85; bd. dirs. The Central Exchange Programming Corp., 1984—, Women's Employment Network, Kansas City, 1985—; mem. exec. com. Dimensions Unltd., Kansas City, 1973-77; commr. Kansas City Commn. on Status of Women, 1978-82; adminstrv. dir. Mid-Am. Assembly on Future of Performing Arts, 1979; chmn. Internat. Women's Yr. in Mid-Am. Symposium, 1975; del. Nat. Women's Conf., Houston, 1977; bd. advisors Ctr. for Mgmt. Assistance, Kansas City, 1979—; bd. advs. Kansas City Arts council, 1980-85, Long Term Care Project for Elderly Nat. Demonstration, Mid-Am. Regional Council, 1981-86, Women's Resource Service, U. Mo., Kansas City, 1971-85; hon. dir. Rockhurst Coll., 1977—; hon. trustee Truman Med. Ctr. Found., 1980—; bd. dirs. Greater Kansas City Mental Health Found., 1980-85, Starlight Theatre Assn., 1980—; bd. advisors Greater Kansas City Community Found., 1980-85; cons. R.A. Long Found., 1982—; mem. Community Care Funding Partners Council, 1982—; trustee Bus. and Profl. Women's Found., 1988—; mem. soc. fellows Nelson-Atkins Mus. Art, 1988—. Named Kansas City Tomorrow Leader, 1978; Chi Omega Pub. Service award, 1962; Outstanding Young Woman of Mo., 1967; Woman of the Yr. award, VFW, 1972; Outstanding Achievement award, U. Mo., Kansas City Sch. Edn., 1973; publ. awards, Nat. and Regional Council for Advancement and Support of Edn., 1971, 72, 73; Regional Citizen of Yr. award Mid Am. Regional Council, 1982; Am. Inst. for Public Service award, 1982; Outstanding Career Achiever in Greater Kansas City, Mo. Gen. Assembly citation, 1985; Harvard U. fellow, 1974, others. Mem. Am. Assn. Higher Edn. (coordinator 1973-75), AAUW, Council for Advancement and Support of Edn., Council on Founds., Women and Founds./Corp. Philanthropy, Soroptimist Internat., Mortar Bd., Phi Kappa Phi, Phi Theta Kappa, Phi Delta Kappa, Pi Lambda Theta, Delta Kappa Gamma, Chi Omega. Presbyterian. Clubs: Univ. Women's, Woodside Racquet, Kansas City, Mission Hills Country, Central Exchange. Author: The Community College in Community Service, 1973; Grantmaking in Greater Kansas City: The Philanthropic Impact of Foundations, 1976-80; editor, pub.: The Directory of Greater Kansas City Foundations, 1986, 88; editor: The Foundation Exchange, 1976—; A History of the University of Kansas City: Prologue to a Public University, 1976; A Brief History of Philanthropy in Kansas City, 1980; The Case for the Community Foundation, 1981; Perspectives on Trusteeship for the 80s, 1981; contbr. articles to profl. jours. Office: PO Box 22680 Kansas City MO 64113-0680

TALBOTT, THOMAS HOWARD, manufacturing company executive; b. Kansas City, Mo., Mar. 4, 1940; s. William B. and June K. (Boyce) T.; BA in Econs., U. Mo., Kansas City, 1963, MBA (fellow), 1965; m. Linda E. Hood, Mar. 5, 1965. With Mobil Oil Corp., 1965-73, staff analyst, N.Y., 1967-68, asst. to div. controller, Boston, 1968-69, div. supr. systems and indsl. engring., 1969, div. mgr. planning, systems and controls, Kansas City, Mo., 1969-73; project mgr. bus. planning and devel. C.J. Patterson Co., Kansas City, Mo., 1973-74, dir. fine food ops., 1974-75, asst. to pres., 1975-76, v.p. adminstrn., 1976-81, pres., 1981—, also dir. Hon. fellow Harry S. Truman Library Inst., 1976; active United Fund, 1969, Friends of Art, Univ. Assos., Philharmonic Assos.; adviser Jr. Achievement, 1973. Victor Wilson Scholar, 1958-62. Mem. U. Mo. Kansas City Alumni Assn. (Outstanding Alumni Achievement in Bus. award 1985), Omicron Delta Kappa, Phi Kappa Phi, Tau Kappa Epsilon. Presbyterian. Clubs: Univ., Woodside Racquet, Mission Hills Country. Home: 411 W 60th Terr Kansas City MO 64113 Office: 3947 Broadway Kansas City MO 64111

TALEB IBRAHIMI, AHMED, minister of foreign affairs of Algeria, physician; b. Setif, Algeria, Jan. 5, 1932; s. Sheikh Bachir Imrahimi and Halima Choukatly; m. Souad Houri, Mar. 4, 1966; children: Bachir, Saadeddine. Ed. Faculty Medicine, Algiers, Algeria, 1949-54; M.D., Faculty of Medicine, U. Paris, 1956. Dir. Jeune Musulman, 1952-54; with Union Genérále des Etudiants Musulmans Algériens, 1955-56, French Fedn. of FLN, 1956-57; imprisoned in France, 1957-62, in Algeria, 1964-65; physician Hospital Mustapha, Algiers, 1962-64; minister of nat. edn. Govt. Algeria, 1965-70, minister of info. and culture, 1970-77, minister and adviser to Pres., from 1977, now minister fgn. affairs; mem. exec. bd. UNESCO, 1968-74; mem. Polit. Bur. of FLN Party, 1979—. Author: Contribution à l'histoire de la médecine arabe au Maghreb, 1963; Lettres de Prison, 1966; De la Décolonisation à la Révolution Culturelle, 1973. Office: Ministry of Fgn Affairs, Algiers Algeria *

TALESE, NAN AHEARN, publishing company executive; b. N.Y.C., Dec. 19, 1933; d. Thomas James and Suzanne Sherman (Russell) Ahearn; m. Gay Talese, June 10, 1959; children: Pamela Frances, Catherine Gay. B.A., Manhattanville Coll. of Sacred Heart, 1955. Fgn. exchange student 1st Nat. City Bank, London and Paris, 1956; editorial asst. Am. Eugenics Soc., N.Y.C., 1957-58, Vogue mag., N.Y.C., 1958-59; copy editor Random House Pub., N.Y.C., 1959-64; assoc. editor Random House Pub., 1964-67, sr. editor, 1967-73; sr. editor Simon & Schuster Pubs., N.Y.C., 1974-81; v.p. Simon & Schuster Pubs., 1979-81; exec. editor, v.p. Houghton Mifflin Co., N.Y.C., 1981-83, v.p., editor-in-chief, 1984-86, v.p., pub., editor-in-chief, 1986-88; sr. v.p., pub., editorial dir. Doubleday & Co., N.Y.C., 1988—. Home: 109 E 61st St New York NY 10021 Office: Doubleday & Co 666 Fifth Ave New York NY 10103

TALFAH, ADNAN KHAYRALLAH, government official; b. Baghdad, Iraq, 1940; s. Khayrallah Talfah. BS in Mil. Scis., Mil. Coll., Iraq, 1961; MS in Mil. Scis., Staff Coll., Iraq, 1970; BS in Law and Politics, Mostansyriah U., Iraq, 1976, BS in English, 1980. Minister of state Republic of Iraq, 1977—, minister of def., 1977—, dep. comdr.-in-chief Armed Forces, 1979—, mem. Revolutionary Command Council. Mem. regional leadership Ba'ath Socialist Arab party, Iraq, 1977. Decorated Gen. Service medal, Palestine War medal, 1st Class Air Force medal; recipient Bravery medal Republic of Iraq, 1975, 1st class Rafidain medal Mil. style for distinct leadership during Iraq-Iran war Republic of Iraq, 1987, 7 Bravery medals for distinct leadership during Iraq-Iran war, 1987, 1st class Rafidain medal Civil style, 1st class Qadissiaht Saddam medal, 2 Bravery medals, 1988. Office: Ministry of Def, Baghdad Iraq

TALHOUARNE, YVES JEAN-MARIE, physician; b. Tercis, Landes, France, July 2, 1953; s. Raymond Jean and Jacqueline T. MD, Bordeaux U., France, 1980. Intern Hosp. Pau, France, 1978-79, Hosp. Dax, France, 1980-82; gen. practice medicine Dax, 1983—, practice medicine specializing in forensics, 1983—; med. expert Ct. Appeal, Pau, 1983, Social Security, Dax, 1983, ins. cos., 1983. Mem. Compagnie des Experts Cour D'Appel, Syndicat Nat. Medecins Stations Thermales. Roman Catholic. Home: 27 Rue La Lanac, 40180 Dax France Office: 46 Rue des Carmes, 40100 Dax France

TALLEY, WILLIAM GILES, JR., container manufacturing company executive; b. Adel, Ga., Sept. 25, 1939; s. William Giles and Mary (McGlamry) T.; B.S. in Bus. Adminstrn., U. S.C., 1961; m. Jacqueline Vickery, Apr. 14, 1962; children—William Giles, John Lindsey, Bronwyn Ashley. Mgmt. trainee Talley Veneer & Crate Co., Inc., Adel, 1961-62, plant mgr., salesman, Waynesboro, Ga., 1965-67; with Talley's Box Co., Leesburg, Fla., 1962-69, plant mgr., partner, 1967-69; gen. mgr. Growers Container Corp. Inc., Leesburg, 1969—; pres. Talley Acres, 1979—, pres. Talley Wood Products, Inc., 1985—; dir. Sunfirst Nat. Bank Lake County, Sun Bank N.A., Orlando, Fla. Bd. dirs. Leesburg Hosp. Assn. Served with USAAF, 1961. Mem. Leesburg C. of C. (dir.), Fla. Forestry Assn. (dir. 1977—), Sigma Alpha Epsilon. Democrat. Methodist. Clubs: Elks, Kiwanis. Home: Lake Griffin Leesburg FL 32748 Office: PO Box 817 Leesburg FL 32748

TALLEY-MORRIS, NEVA BENNETT, lawyer; b. Judsonia, Ark., Aug. 12, 1909; d. John W. and Erma (Rhew) Bennett; m. Cecil C. Talley, Jan. 1, 1946 (dec. Oct. 1948); m. Joseph H. Morris, Mar. 22, 1952 (dec. Dec. 1974). BA magna cum laude, Ouachita Coll., 1930; MEd, U. Tex., 1938, postgrad., 1939-41, PhD in Law, 1984; PhD in Law, World U., 1984. Bar: Ark. bar 1947, U.S. Supreme Ct. bar 1950. Tchr. high sch., prin. White County, Ark., 1930-42; student asst. U. Tex., summers 1937-41; ordnance insp. war service appointment U.S. Army Service Forces, 1942-45; law office apprentice, pvt. tutor North Little Rock, Ark., 1945-47; practiced in Little Rock, 1947—; del., mem. program coordinating com. World Peace through Law Conf., Manila, 1977, mem. pre-biennial goals and planning com., Madrid, 1978; program participant World Peace through Law Conf., Jerusalem conf., 1979, Brazil, 1981, Cairo, 1983; mem. com. on Client Security Fund, Ark. Supreme Ct., 1978-82, chmn. client security com., 1980-82; mem. Ark. Lawyers Com. for Appellate Cts., 1978; chmn. com. for Ark. lawyer writing awards Ark. Bar Assn. Found., 1981-86; program speaker 12th Biennial Conf. World Peace through Law, Berlin, 1985, Law of the World Conf., Seoul, 1987; co-chmn. Seminar on Family Law, Tokyo, 1987; invited del. IBC-Am. Biographical Inst. Internt. Congress, Singapore, 1988. Author: Family Law Practice and Procedure Handbook, 1973, Appellate Civil Practice and Procedure, 1975; contbr. articles to profl. publs. Chmn. Ark. Council on Children and Youth, 1952-54; participant People to People Program, citizen ambassador to Peoples Republic China, Beijing, 1985; program panelist, speaker Family Law Alternates, Seoul Conf., 1987; co-chmn. Tokyo, Japan Seminar on Family Law, 1987; invited del. as fellow IBC/ABI Internat. 15th Congress Joint Session for Biog. Insts., Singapore, 1988; program participant speaker Human Rights and World Peace Through Law. Named hon. mayor-pres. City of Baton Rouge, 1985. Fellow Ark. Bar Found. (bd. fellows), Internat. Biog. Assn., Am. Acad. Matrimonial Lawyers (gov. 1974-79), Phi Alpha Delta (hon.); mem. Nat. Assn. Women Lawyers (life, council del., pres. 1956-57, pres. NAWL Found. 1958, Achievement award 1962, hon. chmn. family law com. 1970-71), Ark. Assn. Women Lawyers (Outstanding Achievement award 1971, program chmn. 1977), Little Rock Assn. Women Lawyers, pres. 1950-51), North Little Rock Bus. and Profl. Women's Club (pres. 1951-52), AAUW (life), Am. Bar Assn. (mem. family law council 1958—, chmn. family law sect. 1969-70, ho. of dels., com. on late reports 1972-73, com. on hearings 1973-74, standing com. on memberships 1974-80, cert. of merit ann. conv. 1979, 80, judge Schwab legal essay contest 1980, sr. div. com. on alternates for dispute resolution 1986—), Ark. Bar Assn. (Distinguished Service to Legal Profession award 1970, chmn. family law reform com. 1960-61, ho. of dels. 1957-58, 74-78, Outstanding Lawyer-Citizen award 1978), Pulaski County Bar Assn. (chmn. com. on continuing legal edn. and programs 1978), World Assn. Lawyers (founding), Am. Judicature Soc. (cert. of appreciation 1979), Nat. Conf. Lawyers and Social Workers (exec. bd. 1962-66, 70-74), Smithsonian Assocs., U.S. Supreme Ct. Hist. Soc., Scribes-Legal Writers Assn., Phi Alpha Delta (1st woman hon.). Office: 1013 W Markham St Little Rock AR 72201

TALLMAN, JOHANNA ELEONORE, former library administrator; b. Luebeck, Germany, Aug. 18, 1914; came to U.S., 1923, naturalized, 1930; d. Friedrich Franz and Johanna Cornelia (Voget) Allerding; m. Lloyd Anthony Tallman, May 8, 1954. A.A., Los Angeles Jr. Coll., 1934; A.B., U. Calif. at Berkeley, 1936; cert. in Librarianship, 1937. Asst. librarian San Marino (Calif.) Pub. Library, 1937-38; various positions Los Angeles County Pub. Library, 1938-40, tech. reference librarian, 1940-42; asst. librarian Pacific Aero. Library, Hollywood, Calif., 1942-43; head librarian Pacific Aero. Library, 1943-44; librarian Engring. and Math. Scis. Library, U. Calif., Los Angeles, 1945-73; coordinator phys. scis. libraries U. Calif., Los Angeles, 1962-73; faculty Sch. Library Service, 1961-73; dir. libraries Calif. Inst. Tech., Pasadena, 1973-82; Dir. re-cataloging project U.S. Naval Ordnance Test Sta. Library., China Lake, Calif., 1951; cons. to indsl., research, ednl. instns., 1950-73; mem. trade adv. com. for library assts. Los Angeles Trade Tech. Coll., 1958-73. Author: Check Out a Librarian, 1985. Contbr. articles to profl. jours. Fulbright lectr. Brazil, 1966-67. Mem. ALA (chmn. engring. sch. libraries sect. 1949-50), Calif. Library Assn. (chmn. coll., univ. and research libraries sect. So. dist. 1954), Spl. Libraries Assn. (pres. So. Calif. chpt. 1965-66, chmn. sci.-tech. div. 1969-70), Librarians Assn. U. Calif. (pres. 1971). Club: Zonta. Home: 4731 Daleridge Rd La Canada CA 91011

TALLMAN, RUTH MARCHAK, aviation executive; b. Scranton, Pa., July 18, 1929; d. Michael and Mary (Hosko) Marchak; student Seton Hall Coll., 1948; m. Frank Gifford Tallman, III, Feb. 18, 1968. Fashion model Blue Book Modeling, Hollywood, Calif., 1944-48; sec. to controller, personnel mgr. Sta. KTLA-TV, Hollywood, 1955-63; owner Tallmantz Aviation Inc. Frank Tallman's Movieland of the Air Aircraft Mus., John Wayne Airport, Santa Ana, 1968—. Mem. Soc. Exptl. Test Pilots, Newport Harbor Art Mus., Ladies Aux. Whirly Girls, Nat. Aeronautic Assn., Aero Club so. Calif., 552 Club, Bob Hope Cultural Ctr. Palm Desert, Orange County Performing Arts Ctr., Eisenhower Luncheon. Roman Catholic. Clubs: Balboa Bay, Indian Wells Racquet, Mesa Verde Country, Rancho Las Palmas Country, Rancho Mirage. Home: 19713 Vista Caudal Newport Beach CA 92660 Office: 19711 Airport Way S John Wayne Airport Santa Ana CA 92707

TALMI, YOAV, conductor, composer; b. Kibbutz Merhavia, Israel, Apr. 28, 1943; diploma Rubin Acad. Music, Tel Aviv; postgrad. diploma Juilliard Sch. Music; m. Erella Gottesmann; 2 children. Assoc. condr. Louisville Orch., 1968-70; co-condr. Israel Chamber Orch., 1970-72; artistic dir., condr. Gelders Symphony Orch., Arnhem, 1974-80; prin. guest condr. Munich Philharm. Orch., 1979-80; artistic dir., condr. Israel Chamber Orch., 1984—; guest condr. Berlin Philharm., Munich Philharm., London Philharm., Philharmonia, Concertgebouw, Rotterdam Philharm., Israel Philharm., Tokyo Symphony, Detroit Symphony, Dallas Symphony, Rochester Philharm., Indpls. Symphony, others. Composer: Dreams for choir a capella, Music for Flute and Strings; Overture on Mexican Themes (recorded), 3 Monologues for Flute Solo (pub.); recs. include: Bruckner 9th Symphony, Tchaikowsky/Schoenberg, Bloch/Barber/Grieg/Puccini; (with Erella Talmi) works for flute and piano. Recipient Boskovitch prize for composition, Israel, 1965; Koussevitzky Meml. Conducting prize, Tanglewood, 1969; award Ruppert Found. Condr. competition, London, 1973. Home: 10 Yehuda St, Kfar Saba 44365 Israel Address: Shaw Concerts Inc 1900 Broadway New York NY 10023

TALTY, LORRAINE CAGUIOA, accountant; b. Makati, Manila, Philippines, July 3, 1957; came to U.S., 1973, naturalized, 1983; d. Leon Perez and Asuncion (Rodriguez) Caguioa; m. Kevin Michael Talty, Jan. 23, 1982. BBA in Acctg. magna cum laude, Chaminade U., Honolulu, 1979. Office mgr., comptroller Caro of Honolulu, 1976-82; acct. David Schenkein, CPA, Latham, N.Y., 1984-86; sales rep. Caromat Corp., Torrance, Calif., 1985-86; owner Kevlor Internat., mfrs. rep. agy., Fairport, N.Y., 1985—; acct. Cortland L. Brovitz & Co., CPA's, Rochester, N.Y., 1986-87; pvt. practice acctg., Fairport, 1986—. Newsletter editor Country Knolls West Civic Assn., Clifton Park, 1984-85, civic com. rep., 1985-86. Home: 34 Cambridge Ct Fairport NY 14450

TALVELA, MARTTI OLAVI, bass, opera and concert singer; b. Hiitola, Finland, Feb. 4, 1935; s. Toivo and Nelly T.; m. Anna Kaariainen, 1957; 3 children. Tchr. Lahti Music High Sch., 1958; with Royal Opera House, Stockholm, 1961-62; artistic dir. Savonlinna Opera Festival, Finland, 1972—. Performances, Deutsche Opera, Berlin, Staatsoper, Hamburg, Germany, Vienna, Austria, Munich, Germany, Royal Opera, Covent Garden, Met. Opera, N.Y.C.; debut, Met. Opera, N.Y.C., 1968; performances, La Scala, Milan, Italy, Rome, San Francisco, Tokyo, Bayreuth, Salzburg, 1962—, numerous recs., TV appearances. Recipient Finnish State prize, 1973. Office: Herbert H Breslin Inc 119 W 57th St New York NY 10019

TALYZIN, NIKOLAI VLADIMIROVICH, Soviet government official; b. Jan. 28, 1929, Moscow. Ed. Moscow Electrotechnical Inst. of Communications, grad. 1955. Electrician and technician-constructor 1944; engr., chief constructor, sr. scientist and dep. dir. Sci. Research Inst., 1955-65; dep. minister for Communications, 1965-75, minister, 1975-80; a vice-chmn. Council of Ministers, 1980-85, non-voting mem. of the Politboro, 1985—, head planning comm. Gosplan, 1985—, now chmn. Bur. for Social Devel. Mem. Central Com. of CPSU; dep. to Supreme Soviet of USSR (10th session); chmn. Central Bd. USSR-Finland Soc.; dr. and prof. tech. scis.; Laureate of State. Address: Bur for Social Devel, Office of Chmn, Moscow USSR *

TAM, BIT-SHUN, mathematician; b. Hong Kong, Feb. 21, 1951; s. Shiu-Chim Tam and Lin-Fung Hu. B.A. in Math., U. Hong Kong, 1973, Ph.D. in Math., 1977. Teaching asst. U. Hong Kong, 1973-78; postdoctoral fellow U. Waterloo, Can., 1978-79; instr. Auburn U., Ala., 1979-81; assoc. prof. Tamkang U., Taiwan, Republic of China, 1981-84, prof., 1984—. Editor Tamkang Jour. Math., 1982—. Contbr. research papers to profl. jours. Travel grantee Internat. Math. Union, 1983; research grantee Nat. Sci. Council Republic China, 1981—; hon. fellow U. Wis., Madison, 1987-88. Mem. Am. Math. Soc., Math. Assn. Am., Math. Soc. Republic China. Avocations: chess; reading; swimming; jogging; table tennis. Office: Dept of Math, Tamkang U, Taipei 25137 Republic of China

TAM, PAUL KWONG HANG, pediatric surgeon; b. Hong Kong, May 27, 1952; s. Shou Wa and Shui Chun (Tang) T.; m. Amy Yan Mi Chum, Dec. 26, 1981; 1 child: Greta Chun Huen. B Medicine and Sci., U. Hong Kong, 1976; M Surgery, U. Liverpool, England, 1984. Med. officer dept. surgery U. Hong Kong Queen Mary Hosp., 1977-83; research fellow dept. pediatric surgery Alder Hey Children's Hosp., Liverpool, 1983-84; lectr. dept. surgery U. Hong Kong, 1984-86; sr. lectr. dept. child health U. Liverpool, 1987—; hon. cons. Royal Liverpool Children's Hosp., Alder Hey, 1987—. Author book chpts. and contbr. articles to profl. pubs. Mem. British Assn. Paediatric Surgeons, British Paediatric Assn., Societe Internationale Chirugie, Assn. Surgeons of South Asia, Hong Kong Surg. Soc., Kong Kong Pediatric Soc. Roman Catholic. Club: Liverpool Paediatric. Office: Royal Liverpool Childrens Hosp, Alder Hey Eaton Rd, Liverpool L12 2AP, England

TAM, TSUN YAM, computer educator; b. Canton, China, May 16, 1949; came to U.S., 1955; s. Yan Soon and Man-Hok (Mok) T.; m. Patricia McDaniel Yacabacci, Dec. 11, 1983. B.S., NYU, 1974, M.A., 1978; student Cooper Union, 1968-71. Stuyvesant High Sch., N.Y.C., 1974-76; adj. asst. prof. NYU, 1974-76, asst. research scientist 1978-79, advisor, faculty, 1980-85; dir. info. systems Studley, Inc., N.Y.C., 1985—, instr. Inst. Audio Research, 1980-82; ptnr. chief engr. Ecompcon Ltd., Closter, N.J., 1983—; cons. Saab-Sania of Am., Orange, Conn., 1983-85; assoc. cons. engr. JBM Assocs., 1984—; cons. Regional Coll. Consortium, P.R., 1982; mem. com. N.Y. State Dept. Edn., 1976-79. Contbr. articles to profl. jours.; author: On the Upgrade 80-Micro; co-author: How To Work with Plastics and Equipment, 1974. Mem. Closter Nature Reserve (N.J.), 1983—. Hebrew Tech. Inst. scholar, 1972-74. Mem. IEEE, Assn. Computing Machinery, N.Y. Acad. Scis., Mensa, Leica Hist. Soc., AAAS, Phi Delta Kappa, Phi Kappa Lambda, Epsilon Pi Tau. Republican. Home: PO Box 655 Closter NJ 07624 Office: Studley Inc 300 Park Ave New York NY 10022

TAM, WILLIAM YU-KAY, psychiatrist; b. Hong Kong, Feb. 3, 1949; m. Mona Man-Wah Tsoi; children: Carol, Julian. MBBS, U. Hong Kong, 1972; PhD, U. London, 1983. Intern Queen Mary Hosp., Hong Kong, 1972-73, resident dept. psychiatry, 1973-77; resident Inst. Psychiatry, London, 1977-79; lectr. in psychiatry U. Hong Kong, 1975-81, sr. lectr. psychiatry, 1981—; research asst. U. London Inst. Psychiatry, 1977-79, sr. registrar, 1982-83; vis. asst. prof. U. Toronto, Ont., Can., 1986-87. Mem. Royal Coll. Psychiatrists, Soc. Psycho-physiol. Research, Neurosci. Soc., Hong Kong Pharmacology Soc. (founding mem.), Hong Kong Psychiat. Assn. (pres. 1986-88). Office: Queen Mary Hosp Dept Psychiatry, Hong Kong Hong Kong

TAMAMURA, TOSHIO, electronics company executive; b. Fukui, Japan, Jan. 29, 1948. Student, U. Electro-Communication, Tokyo, 1971. Mgr. research and devel. sect. Yokogawa Hewlett Packard, Tokyo, 1971—. Author: Know-how of Operational Amplifier, 1983; inventor Analog Integrated Circuits Tester, 1986. Office: Hewlett Packard Yokogawa, 9-1 Takakura cho, Hachioji Tokyo 192, Japan

TAMARIZ, JOSE LENIN, manufacturing company executive; b. Quito, Ecuador, Aug. 20, 1944; s. José Alfonso and Dolores Lucrecia (Crespo) T.; divorced; children: Jose Felix, Maria Eugenia, Alegria Maria. BS in Indsl. Engring., La. State U., 1971. Gen. mgr. COBALSA (Compañia Indsl. de Balsa Soc. Anónima), Guayaquil, Ecuador, 1984—; bd. dirs. Banco de Guayaquil. V.p. Assn. Football del Guayas, 1986-88. Mem. Inst. Indsl. Engrs. (sr.), Federación Ecuatoriana de Exportadores (pres. 1982-86, v.p. 1987—), Ops. Research Soc. Am., Inst. Mgmt. Scis. Roman Catholic. Clubs: Salinas Yacht, Barcelona Sporting (pres. 1978-82), Guayaquil Country. Home: PO Box 4348, Guayaquil Ecuador Office: COBALSA, PO Box 10473, Guayaquil Ecuador

TAMBAKOULIS, DIMITRIOS, construction company executive; b. Tsaritsani, Larisa, Greece, June 24, 1930; s. Anastasios and Theodora (Moukidou) T.; m. Flavia-Maria Fedi, Dec. 27, 1962; children: Theodora, Helen. Dott. in Civil Engring., U. Pisa, Italy, 1960. Area mgr. Fondedile S.P.A., Naples, Italy, 1960-61, Officine Reggiane S.P.A., R. Emilia, Italy, 1960-64; mgr. Ministry Pub. Works, Salonica, Greece, 1964-70; owner, pres. Themeliodomi SA, Salonica, 1970—, chmn. bd.; chmn. Geognosi SA, Asfalmak SA, Etena SA. Served to lt. Greek Army, 1957-59. Decorated cavaliere and cavaliere ufficiale della Repubblica Italy. Fellow Italian Comml. Chamber Salonica; mem. Union Hellenic Contractors, Tech. Chamber Greece. Mem. Christian Orthodox Ch. Office: Themeliodomi SA, 21 N Typa St, 546 46 Salonica Greece

TAMBOVTSEV, YURI A., professor, researcher; b. Leningrad, USSR, Dec. 4, 1948; s. Alexey I. and Tamara Y. (Below) T.; m. Shipolina. BA, Cuban State U., 1970; PhD, Leningrad State U. Asst. Novosibirsk State U., USSR, 1970; prof. Novosibirsk State U., 1977, sr. tchr., 1977-87, sr. research fellow, 1987—. Author: Consonantal Coefficient in Different Language Families, 1987. Mem. Finns-Ugric Soc., Ural-Altaic Soc., Phonetic Soc. of Japan. Office: Novosibirsk U, PO Box 124 Novosibirsk-90, 630090 Siberia USSR

TAMBURINE, JEAN HELEN, sculptor, painter, illustrator; b. Meriden, Conn., Feb. 20, 1930; m. Eugene E. Bertolli. Student, Art Students League, N.Y.C., 1948-50; student of Jon Corbino, John Groth, Carlo Ciampaglia, Elisabeth Gordon Chandler. Exhibited group shows Rockport (Mass.) Art Assn., North Shore Arts Assn., Gloucester, Mass., George Walter Vincent Mus., Springfield, Mass., Hudson Valley (N.Y.) Art Assn., Pearl S. Buck Found., Phila., Am. Artists Profl. League, N.Y., Acad. Artists Assn., Springfield, Pen and Brush, N.Y.; heritage bronze commd. by Wallingford (Conn.) Pub. Library, 1986; represented in permanent collections Conn. State Library, Middletown, Nashville Pub. Library, Strong Sch., Hartford, Conn., L'Heure Joyeux, Paris; also pvt. collections; author: Almost Big Enough, 1963, I Think I Will Go to the Hospital, 1965, How Now, Brown Cow, 1967. Recipient Assoc. Members prize Acad. Artists, Founders prize Pen and Brush, 1981, 1st prize for sculpture Arts and Crafts Assn. of Meriden, Conn.; named to Meriden Hall of Fame. Mem. Rockport Art Assn. (Martha Moore Meml. award 1983), North Shore Arts Assn., Acad. Artists Assn., Salmagundi Club, Am. Artists Profl. League, Am. Medallic Sculpture Assn., FIDEM, Authors Guild. Home and Office: The Bertolli Studio 73 Reynolds Dr Meriden CT 06450 also: PO Box 740 Rockport MA 01966

TAMINIAU, CAREL LODEWYK, article group manager; b. Elst, Netherland, June 6, 1943; s. Jan and Maria (Witte) T.; m. Evelyn De Mots, July 16, 1969; children: Jan Evert, Albert Carel. D in Econ. Sci., U. Amsterdam, 1969. Mktg. researcher Philips Internat., Eindhoven, Netherlands, 1969-70, Oestereichische Philips Industries, Vienna, Austria, 1970-71; cons. Svenska Philips AB, Stockholm, 1971-72, S.A. Philips Corp., Johannesburg, Republic South Africa, 1973-78; mgr. estimation and planning dept. Philips DAP div., Groningen, Netherlands, 1978-85, mgr. floor care, 1978-85, article group mgr., 1985—. Chmn. Roman Cath. Parish Com. Eelde/Paterswolde, Netherlands, 1977-84; chmn. parents com. Roman Cath. secondary Sch. St. Maarten, Haren, Netherlands, 1984-87; mem. town council City of Eelde. Christian Democrat. Home: Chopinweg 5, 9761JK Eelde Drente The Netherlands Office: Philips Internat DAP div, Europaweg 8, 9700AE Groningen The Netherlands

TAMIR, PINCHAS, science educator; b. Tel Aviv, Israel, June 6, 1928; s. Nahum Sternberg and Esther (Horowitz) Landau; m. Ruth Shomroni, Oct. 6, 1949; children: Hagit Azmon, Yuval Tamir. MS, Hebrew U., 1951; PhD, Cornell U., 1968. Tchr. Agrl. Secondary Sch., Pardeshana, Israel, 1956-66; research asst. Cornell U., Ithaca, N.Y., 1967-68; lectr. Hebrew U., Jerusalem, 1969-74, sr. lectr., 1974-78, assoc. prof., 1978-82, prof., 1982—; dirs. biology project Israel High Sch., 1968—; vis. prof. various univs. and research insts., 1974—. Editor, author Curriculum Implementation in Sci., 1979, Preserve and Inserve Edn., 1983, The Role of Curriculum Evaluations, 1984, others. Served to capt. Israeli Army, 1945-49. Mem. Am. Ednl. Research Assn., Nat. Assn. of Research in Sci. Teaching (jour. bd.), Assn. for Edn. of Sci. Tchrs., Assn. for Edn. of Tchrs. in Europe, Internat. Orgn. for Sci. and Technology Edn. Home: 22 Hagdood Haivri, Jerusalem 92345, Israel Office: Hebrew U, Sch of Edn, Jerusalem 91904, Israel

TAMMANY, ALBERT SQUIRE, III, savings and bank executive; b. Paget, Bermuda, Aug. 21, 1946; s. Albert Squire Jr. and Marion Genevieve (Galloway) T.; m. Teresa Reznor, Sept. 8, 1973. BA Stanford U., 1968; MBA, U. Pa., 1973. Budget and planning officer Tuskegee Inst., Ala., 1973-74; budget analyst controllers dept. Chase Manhattan Bank, N.Y.C., 1974-75; v.p., div. controller Wells Fargo Bank, San Francisco, 1975-78, v.p., retail group controller, 1978-79; v.p., controller Imperial Bank, Los Angeles, 1979-81, sr. v.p. fin., 1981-83; exec. v.p., First Network Savs. Bank, Los Angeles, 1983-87, pres., 1987—, also bd. dirs.; cons. Inst. for Services to Edn., Inc., 1973-74. Woodrow Wilson fellow U. Pa. Served with USMC, 1968-71. Wharton Pub. Policy fellow, 1972. Mem. Am. Bankers Assn. (trust ops. com.). Episcopalian. Clubs: Wharton, Stanford. Office: First Network Savs Bank 10100 Santa Monica Blvd Suite 500 Los Angeles CA 90067

TAMURA, HAJIME, Japanese government official; b. 1924. Grad., Keio U., Japan. Mem. Ho. of Reps., Japan, 1955—, former chmn. constrn. and fin. coms.; assoc. Noboru Takeshita; minister of labour, Japan, 1972-74, minister of transport, 1976-77, minister of internat. trade and industry, 1986—. Former chmn. pub. relations com. Liberal Democratic Party, Japan. Office: Ministry of Internat, Trade & Industry, 1-3-1 Kasumigaseki, Chiyoda-ku Tokyo Japan Office: Hitachi Metals Am 2400 Westchester Ave Purchase NY 10577

TAN, ENG MENG, biomedical scientist; b. Seremban, Malaysia, Aug. 26, 1926; came to U.S., 1950; s. Ming Kee and Chooi Eng (Ang) T.; m. Liselotte Filippi, June 30, 1962; children—Philip, Peter. B.A., Johns Hopkins U., 1952, M.D., 1956. Asst. prof. Washington U. Sch. Medicine, St. Louis, 1965-67; assoc. mem. Scripps Clinic and Research Found., LaJolla, Calif., 1967-70, mem., 1970-77, dir. Autoimmune Disease Ctr., 1982—; prof. U. Colo. Sch. Medicine, Denver, 1977-82; chmn. allergy and immunology research com. NIH, Bethesda, Md., 1980-84; mem. nat. arthritis adv. bd. HHS, Washington, 1981-85. Contbr. chpts. to books, articles to profl. jours. Named to Nat. Lupus Hall Fame, 1984; recepient U.S. Sr. Scientist award Humboldt Found., W. Ger., 1986. Mem. Arthritis Found. (pres. San Diego chpt. 1974-75), Am. Rheumatism Assn. (chmn. lupus com. 1980-82, pres. 1984-85), United Scleroderma Found. (ann. award 1982), Assn. Am. Physicians, Am. Soc. Clin. Investigation, Western Assn. Physicians (v.p. 1980-81), Am. Assn. Immunologists, Argentina Rheumatism Assn. (hon.), Australian Rheumatism Assn. (hon.). Research on characterization of autoantibodies in autoimmune diseases, systemic lupus erythematosus, scleroderma, sjogren's syndrome, myositis and mixed connective tissue disease; relationship of autoantibodies to pathogenesis; patentee in field. Home: 8303 Sugarman Dr La Jolla CA 92037 Office: Scripps Clinic and Research Found 10666 N Torrey Pines Rd La Jolla CA 92037

TAN, HUNG PHENG, banker, mathematician; b. Swatow, People's Republic of China, June 5, 1946; came to Singapore, 1955, naturalized, 1965; s. Keng Teck and Tai Miang (Aw) T.; m. Bee Oon Sim, June 24, 1979. B.Sc., Nanyang U., Singapore, 1968; M.A., SUNY-Buffalo, 1971, Ph.D., 1973. Systems analyst, programmer Govt. of Singapore, 1973-78; sr. systems analyst, dep. mgr. Banking Computer Services Pvt. Ltd., Singapore, 1978-81; data processing mgr., asst. gen. mgr. Bank of China, Singapore, 1981—. Reviewer math. revs. Contbr. articles to profl. jours. Chmn. residents' com. Prime Ministers Office, Singapore Govt. Serving as asst. supt. police Singapore Vol. Police Force, 1973—. Fulbright scholar, 1968-73. Mem. Data Processing Mgrs. Assn. Singapore (mem. council 1985—), Singapore Computer Soc., Assn. for Computing Machinery, Am. Math. Soc., Nat. U. Singapore Soc., Automobile Assn. Singapore. Office: Bank of China, 4 Battery Rd, Singapore 0104, Singapore

TAN, JOHN K., chemical company executive, educator; b. Fukien, China, Sept. 23, 1934; s. E. Ching Lam and Goct Sia (Kua) T.; m. Lily Go Tan, Mar. 4, 1967; children—Carolyn G., Edward John G., Herbert Joseph G., Steven Julian G. B.S. in Chem. Engring., Mapua Inst. Tech., Manila, 1960; M.Engring., Yale U., 1964; postgrad. Stevens Inst. Tech., Hoboken, N.J., 1964-68. Chem. engr. Globe Paper Mills, Inc., Malabon, Rizal, Philippines, 1960-61; supr. Internat. Chem. Industries Inc., Guiguinto, Bulacan, Philippines, 1961-62; grad. research asst. dept. chem. engring. Yale U., New Haven, 1962-64; sr. research chem. engr. Research Ctr., research and devel. div. Lever Bros. Co., Unilever Ltd., U.S.A., Edgewater, H.J., 1964-65; prin. research chem. engr., 1965-68; tech. mgr., tech. asst. to pres. Internat. Chem. Industries Inc., Guiguinto, Bulacan, Philippines, 1968-70; tech. cons. Econ. Devel. Found., Inc., Makati, Rizal, Philippines, 1968-70; asst. gen. mgr., tech. dir. Philippines Fermentation Indsl. Corp., Guiguinto, Bulacan, Philippines, 1970-73; prof. dept. dept. chemistry and chem. engring. Grad. Sch. Chem. Engring., Mapua Inst. Tech., Intramuros, Manila, Philippines, 1968-79; pres., gen. mgr., No. Chem. Sales Corp., Manila, Tex-Chem Mktg. Corp., Manila, 1972—; pres., chmn. bd. Bay Tank Yard, Inc., Manila, 1972—; exec. v.p. Lakeview Garments, Inc., Taguig, Metro-Manila, 1976-86; v.p., gen. mgr. Premier Steam Laundry Inc., Taguig, Metro-Manila, 1978-85; exec. v.p., gen. mgr. Multi-Land Devel. Corp., Manila, 1972—; advisor Nat. Bd. Advisors, internat. div. Am. Biog. Inst., Raleigh, N.C. Pres., Philippine Assn. Chem. Suppliers, Inc., Makati, Metro-Manila, 1983—. Trustee Philippine Cultural High Sch.; pres. Mapoa Inst. Tech. Chemistry and Chem. Engring. Alumni Assn.; trustee Prof. Lauro A. Limuaco Meml. Found. Conn. State Water Resources Commn. fellow Yale U., 1962-64; United Aircraft scholar Yale U., 1963-64; Univ. scholar Mapua Inst. Tech., Manila, 1955-60, Silver medalist in chem. engring., 1960; Internat. Biog. Assn. fellow, Cambridge, Eng., 1983—; named Outstanding Alumnus, Mapua Inst. Tech. Mem. Am. Inst. Chem. Engrs., Am. Chem. Soc., Yale Sci. and Engring. Assn., Sigma Xi, Eta Sigma Mu. Club: Yale of the Philippines. Home: 1973 Kasoy St, Dasmarinas Village, Makati, Metro-Manila Philippines Office: No Chem Sales Corp, 950 Soler St, Binondo, Manila Philippines

TAN, KENG HUAT, pharmacist; b. Klang, Selangor, Malaysia, Dec. 13, 1945; parents: Sam Hoe Tan and Rose Cheah Kim Lian. B of Pharmacy, U. Singapore, 1971. House pharmacist Ministry of Health, Kuala Lumpur, Malaysia, 1971-72; exec. pharmacist Hoechst Sdn. Bhd., Penang, Malaysia, 1972; mfg. pharmacist Barkath Pharma Sdn. Bhd., Shah Alam, Selangor, 1973; mgr. Grace Pharm. Pte. Ltd., Kuala Lumpur, 1974-79; mgr. pharm. wholesale div. Fima Supermarkets Bhd., Kuala Lumpur, 1979-80; mgr. Premier Pharms. Sdn. Bhd., Kuala Lumpur, 1980-84; prin. Tan Pharm. Co., Petaling Jaya, Malaysia, 1984—. Sec. Gerakan, Malaysia, Ampang br. 1974-75, dep. chmn. 1975-77, div. chmn. Selayang 1977-78; com. mem. Malaysian Chinese Assn., Petaling Jaya br. 1979-81, sec. sect. 4, Petaling 1981-82, chmn. 1982-86. Mem. Malaysian Pharm. Soc. Buddhist. Home: 34 Jalan SS 22/29, Damansara Jaya, Petaling Jaya Selangor 47400, Malaysia

TAN, KIAT W., garden director, botanist; b. Singapore, Feb. 13, 1943; came to U.S., 1961; s. Chee Tong and Siew Hong (Ong) T. B.A., Williams Coll., 1965; M.Sc., Mich. State U., 1967; Ph.D., U. Miami, 1974. Instr. biology Palm Beach Jr. Coll., Lake Worth, Fla., 1971-73; research asst. Marie Selby Bot. Gardens, Sarasota, Fla., 1973-76, asst. dir., 1976-83, dir. Orchid Identification Ctr., 1975-83, dir. Mus. Botany, 1980-83; asst. commr. Parks and Recreation Dept., Singapore, 1983-87, dir. Singapore Botanic Gardens, 1988—; com. mem. species survival orchids Internat. Union for Conservation of Nature, 1983-84; chmn. hort. activity Singapore Sci. Council, 1983; sec. Asean Orchid Congress, Singapore, 1984, Nature Reserves Bd., Singapore, 1983-88. Sec., Ministry Nat. Devel. Recreation Club Bldg. Fund, Singapore, 1983; hon. auditor Singapore Inst. Biology, 1983. Mem. Am. Orchid Soc. (hon. life, mem. conservation com. 1986—), Am. Hibiscus Soc. (hon. life), Singapore Gardening Soc. (life), Malayan Nature Soc. (life), Internat. Assn. Plant Taxonomy, Sigma Xi. Editor: 11th World Orchid Conf. Procs., Orchid Soc. S.E. Asia, Malayan Orchid Rev., Singapore Bot. Gardens Bull.; contbr. articles to profl. jours.

TAN, KIM LEONG, pediatrician, neonatologist, medical educator; b. Malaysia, Oct. 30, 1936; s. Chim Ean Tan and Siew Bo Yeoh; married, June 15, 1963; children: Min-Li, Min-Ching, Wei-Liang. MBBS, U. Singapore, 1962; DCH, U. London, 1967. Fellow Royal Coll. Physicians, 1977, Fellow Royal Australasian Coll. Physicians, 1978. Med. officer Ministry of Health, Singapore, 1963-68; lectr. U. Singapore, 1968-71, sr. lectr., 1971-75, assoc. prof., 1976-79; prof. Nat. U. Singapore, 1980—; hon. sci. advisor Internat. Ctr. Childhood Studies, U.K., 1982—; mem. Nat. Sci. Com. on Hepatitis and Related Disorders, Singapore, 1985—; chmn. Expert Com. on Immunization Program, Singapore, 1988—. Co-editor Procs. of 1st Asia Oceana Congress of Perinatology, 1979; mem. editorial bd. Jour. of AMA, 1984; designer phototherapy. Mem. panel of doctors Kim Seng Community Ctr. Night Clinic, Singapore, 1981—; mem. exec. com. Children's Aid Soc., Singapore, 1983—. Mem. Singapore Pediatric Soc. (chmn. research fund 1975—, Haridas Meml. lectr. 1972-77), Ob-gyn. Soc. Singapore (Benjamin Henry Sheares lectr. 1976), Brit. Med. Assn., Singapore Med. Assn., Acad. of Medicine. Home: 259 6th Ave, Dynasty Garden Ct 1, Singapore 1027, Singapore Office: Nat U Singapore Dept Pediatrics, Neonatal Unit, Singapore 0511, Singapore

TAN, KING TWOK, cardiothoracic surgeon; b. Singapore, Mar. 12, 1939; s. Teck-Lan Tan and Lan-Fang Han; m. Bih-Ju Tsai, Oct. 24, 1971; children: Ying Chien, Ying Ying. MD, Nat. Chiba U., Japan, 1967; postgrad., Japan Heart Inst., Tokyo Women's Med. Coll., 1968-74. Med. officer dept. cardiovascular and thoracic surgery Tan Tock Seng Hosp., Ministry of Health, Singapore, 1974-77, registrar, 1977-78, sr. registrar, 1978-80, cons. cardiothoracic surgeon, 1980-81; practice medicine specializing in cardiovascular and thoracic surgery Mt. Elizabeth Hosp., Singapore, 1981—; vis. cons. cardiothoracic surgeon Nat. U. Hosp., Singapore; lectr. People's Assn., Nat. Heart Assn. Fellow Am. Coll. Cardiology (assoc.). Club: Chinese Swimming; Pinetree & Country. Home: 24 Parkstone Rd, Singapore 1543, Singapore Office: 09-03 Mt Elizabeth Med Centre, Singapore 0922, Singapore

TAN, MANUEL A., physician. Home: Narciso St 1, Surigao City The Philippines

TAN, THOMAS NYANG KIANG, company executive; b. Beaufort, Malaysia, July 15, 1947; s. Siak Kui and Sau Kwan (Lam) T.; m. Swee Wah Yong, Jan. 2, 1974; children: Cissy, Shirley, Benno. Higher sch. cert. Sabah Coll., 1966. Sales supr. Rothmas of Pall Mall (Malaysia) Bhd., Sandakan, Sabah, 1967-70; br. mgr. Harper Gilfillan (Malaysia) Bhd., Sandakan, 1971-72; sales mgr. Motor and Leasing Sdn. Bhd., Sandakan, 1973-78, area mgr., 1979-81, gen. mgr., 1982-86; bd. dirs. Sabah Ports Authority, 1986—; dir. Higrowth Holdings Sdn. Bhd., 1987—; chmn. TNY Holding Sdn. Bhd., Kota Kinabaln, Sabah, 1981—; chief exec. Petrolubes, 1987—. Mem. com. Teochew Assn., Sandakan, 1982-83, sec., 1985, treas., 1986-87, mem. com., 1988—. Recipient Merit award Outward Bound Sch., Lumut, Malaysia, 1970. Mem. Jaycees. Club: Sandakan Golf. Office: Petrolubes Sdn Bld, WDT No 1 Pej Pos Batu 1 1/2, Sandakan, Sabah 90300, Malaysia

TAN, WILLINGTON KOK KONG CHUA, electrical wire manufacturing company executive; b. Manila, Nov. 25, 1948; s. Tong and Marciana (Chua) T.; B.S. in Elec. Engring., Mapua Inst. Tech., Manila, 1972; M.B.A., Ateneo de Manila U.; m. Judy Chua Ong, Oct. 12, 1975; children—Jon Wilbur, Janis Willa, Jed Warrick. Service supr. Citation Appliances & Electronics, Manila, 1970-74, asst. mgr., 1974-75; plant supr. Elta Industries, Inc., Manila, 1974; product design engr. Columbia Wire & Cable, Quezon City, Philippines, 1975-76, head dept. engring. and maintenance, 1976-79, asst. v.p. for engring./mfg., 1979-81, asst. v.p., 1981—; pres. Boom Mktg. Corp. Recipient cert. of appreciation Gen. Hdqrs. and Hdqrs. Service Group, Armed Forces Philippines, 1980. Mem. IEEE, Inst. Integrated Elec. Engrs. Philippines (chmn. plant tour com. and cert. of appreciation 5th Nat. Conv. 1980, nat. sec. 1986, vice chmn. ways and means com. nat. conv. 1983, 85, vice chmn. search for outstanding elec. engring educators 1983, Philippine sect. 1983), Philippine Motor Assn., Philippine Assn. Mech. and Elec. Engrs. Clubs: Rotary (treas. club and chmn. club world community service 1979-80, dir. club and chmn. club attendance com. 1980-81, Meritorious award 1980), Quezon City Sports (Quezon City). Research in devel. of Philippine manufactured 600 volt to 15,000 volt crosslink polyethylene power cable, 1978. Office: 75 Howmart Rd, Bo Kangkong, Quezon City Philippines

TAN, YOK KOON, real estate executive; b. Singapore, July 18, 1948; s. Kiam Toen and Giok Oh (Ng) T.; m. Chui Leng Chan, Mar. 26, 1979; children—York Siong, Suan Wi, Hoe Himm. LL.B. with hons., King's Coll. London, 1971; M.B.A., Columbia U., N.Y.C., 1974. Barrister-at-Law, Gray's Inn, Eng., Advocate & Solicitor, Supreme Court of Singapore. Exec. dir. Afro Asia Shipping Co. Pte. Ltd., Singapore, 1975—; dir. New Town Devel. Pte. Ltd., Singapore, 1980—; chmn., dir. Presidio Constrn. Pte. Ltd., Singapore, 1981—; dir. Ssangyong Cement Ltd., Singapore, 1974—. Clubs: British, Keppel. Avocations: swimming; tennis; new field and new experience. Office: Afro Asia Shipping Co Ltd, 63 Robinson Rd, Level 2 Afro Asia Bldg, Singapore 0106, Singapore

TANAKA, AIICHIRO, engineering seismologist; b. Kumamoto, Japan, Apr. 14, 1946; s. Noriyuki and Yuuko T.; m. Mieko Tanaka, July 31, 1950; children—Hideki, Michiyo, Toshiki. B.Engring., Kumamoto U., 1969, M.Engring., 1971. Research assoc. Kumamoto U., Japan, 1971—, lectr., 1985—; dir. Earthquake Engring. Promotion Soc., Kumamoto, 1985—. Mem. Archtl. Inst. Japan, Seismological Soc. Japan, Soc. Natural Disaster Sci., Internat. Assn. Earthquake Engring., Internat. Assn. Seismology and Physics of Earth's Interior, Jour. Physics Earth, Seismological Soc. Am., Earthquake Engring. Research Inst., European Earthquake Engring., numerous others. Office: Kumamoto Inst Tech, 4-22-1 Ikeda, Kumamoto 860, Japan

TANAKA, FUMIO, paper company executive; b. July 29, 1910; m. Fusako Tanaka. Grad., Kyushu U., 1935. With Oji Paper Co., Ltd., 1935—, previously pres., now chmn.; pres. Iida-cho Kamiryutsu Center Kabushiki Kaisha. Decorated Medal of Honor with Blue Ribbon. Mem. Japan Fedn. Employers' Assn. (vice chmn.), Japan Fedn. Econ. Orgns. (trustee). Home: 46-4 Utsukushigaoka, 3-chome Midori-ku, Yokohama 227, Japan Office: Oji Paper Co Ltd, 7-5 Ginza, 4-chome Chiyoda-ku, Tokyo 104, Japan *

TANAKA, HIROSHI, trading company executive; b. Kyoto, Japan, July 29, 1939; s. Okosu and Mie (Yamauchi) T.; m. Miyoko Tanaka, Oct. 4, 1964; children: Rie, Norimichi. B. Econs., Keio U., Tokyo, 1962. Sales mgr. Yaskawa & Co., Ltd., Tokyo, 1984-87, mgr., 1987—. Author: Basic language, 1981, C Language, 1986, Machine Language, 1987, Application Software, 1987. Home: E-210-876-2 Kita-Akitsu, Tokorozawa Saitama 359, Japan

TANAKA, HISAO, economist, educator; b. Tokyo, Feb. 11, 1924; s. Hanjiro and Hana (Tsuchiya) T.; B.C., Tokyo Comml. Coll., 1948; m. Reiko Ishiko, Feb. 18, 1953; children—Juichi, Mikihisa, Satoko. With Bank of Japan, Tokyo, 1948-80, asso. advisor econ. research dept., 1966, sr. research officer Inst. Developing Economies, 1974-80; prof. econs. Kyoto Sangyo U., Kyoto, Japan, 1980—; researcher Japanese Ministry Fgn. Affairs, 1961-62; vis. prof. Nagoya U. of Commerce, 1977-78. Mem. Am. Econ. Assn., Japan Soc. Internat. Econs., Japan and Yugoslavia Assn. (dir. 1980—); v.p. Acad. for Hong Kong and Taiwan in Japan, 1988—. Buddhist. Author: Finance and Banking in Eastern Europe, 1978; Oil Money and Asian Dollar in International Money Market, 1978; World Economy and Monetary Problems, 1980; Interest Rates in the World, 1983; Finance and Banking Systems in Socialist Countries, 1986. Home: 4-18-6 Minaminagasaki, Toshima-ku, Tokyo 171, Japan Office: 36 Motoyama Kamikamo, Kita-ku, Kyoto 603, Japan

TANAKA, JUNJI, educational administrator; b. Osaka, Japan, Nov. 22, 1929; s. Waichiro and Hide T.; B.A. in Econs., Kinki U., Japan, 1956; cert. in Librarianship, Doshisha U.; m. Chieko, Mar. 5, 1957; children—Keiji, Eiko. Local employee USIA, 1957; sr. advisor Am. Center, Osaka, Japan, 1970; exec. dir. Japan Inst. for Internat. Study, Osaka, 1973—; ednl. counseling services internat. student and personnel exchange programs. Recipient Meritorious Honor award USIA, 1968. Mem. Nat. Assn. Fgn. Student Advisors, Osaka C. of C. and Industry, Japan-Am. Soc. Buddhist. Lodge: Rotary. Home: 17-20, 4 chome, Kumano-cho, Toyonaka City, Osaka 650, Japan Office: Sanei Bldg, 3-20-9 Toyosaki, Oyodo-ku, Osaka 531, Japan

TANAKA, KATSUSHIGE, metal processing company executive; b. Kumamoto, Japan, June 27, 1930; s. Kanji and Nobuko T.; m. Emiko Tanaka, May 19, 1961; children: Keiko, Katsuyoshi. BS in Econs., Keio U., Tokyo, 1954; PMD, Harvard U., 1960. Mgr. fuel sect. Nippon Steel Corp., Tokyo, 1970-78, gen. mgr. fuel and ferrous materials dept., 1979-85, dir., 1985—. Home: 1-10-12 Denenchotu Ohta-ku, Tokyo 145, Japan Office: Nippon Steel Corp, Ote-machi Chiyoda-ku, Tokyo 100, Japan

TANAKA, KAZUMASA, data processing executive; b. Kawamoto, Shimane, Japan, Feb. 18, 1954; s. Masaki and Tatsuko (Tohma) T.; m. Sachie Okada, May 3, 1981. B of Agr., U. Tokyo, 1979. Sales rep. Info. Network Services, Tokyo, 1979—. Home: 2 24 62 4 1201, Tamagawa Ohta-ku, Tokyo 146, Japan Office: IBM Japan Ltd Dist Info Network, Services 6-3 Ohsaki 1-Chome, Shinagawa-ku, Tokyo 141, Japan

TANAKA, LEILA CHIYAKO, lawyer; b. Honolulu, Mar. 11, 1954; d. Masami and Bernice Kiyoko (Nakamura) T. BA in Japanese Lang., Am. Studies with distinction, U. Hawaii, Manoa, 1977; JD, U. Santa Clara, 1980. Bar: Hawaii 1980, U.S. Dist. Ct. Hawaii 1980. Sole practice 1980-81; law clk. state cir. ct. judge (2d cir.), Wailuku, Maui, Hawaii, 1981-82; spl. dep. atty. gen. Dept. of Atty. Gen., Hawaii, 1983, dep. atty. gen., 1983-88; housing unit supr. Hawaii Housing Authority, 1987-88, eviction hearings trial examiner, 1986-88; liability claims mgr. Hawaii Dept. Transp., 1988—; br. chief Hawaii Housing Authority, 1987—, housing unit supr., eviction hearings trial examiner, Hawaii Housing Authority, 1986—. Mem. ABA, Assn. Trial Lawyers Am., Pacific Rim Found., Orgn. Women Leaders, Phi Kappa Phi. Democrat. Buddhist. Office: State of Hawaii Dept Transp 869 Punchbowl St Honolulu HI 96813

TANAKA, MANABU, mechanical engineer; b. Shimouma-cho, Setagaya-ku, Japan, Oct. 23, 1947; s. Shouichi and Hideko (Amamiya) T.; m. Chizuko Hiki, May 2, 1980; 1 child, Tomoko. DEng., Tokyo Met. U., 1976. Researcher Tokyo Met. U., 1976-78; research assoc. Akita U., Japan, 1978-79, assoc. prof., 1979—. Grantee Ministry of Edn., Tokyo, 1980, 82; Housai Hyuuga grantee Iron and Steel Inst., Tokyo, 1985; grantee Shimazu Found., Kyoto, 1986. Mem. Japan Inst. Metals (Silver medal 1979). Home: 9-33 Tegatakyuuka-machi, Akita 010, Japan Office: Akita Univ, 1-1 Tegata-gakuen-cho, Akita 010, Japan

TANAKA, NORIHITO, manufacturing executive; b. Tokyo, Jan. 9, 1937; s. Minoru and Chiyo (Yoshizawa) T.; m. Eiko Osone, Jan. 17, 1967; children: Emi, Atsumi. Grad. from econ. faculty, Keio U., Tokyo, 1959. With Nihon Bed Mfg. Co. Ltd., Tokyo, 1959-70, mng. dir., 1970—; mng. dir. Nihon Tekko Co. Ltd., Tokyo, 1970—, pres., 1988—; mng. dir. Nihon Bed Sales Co. Ltd., Tokyo, 1970-87, v.p., 1987—. Home: 1-22-22 Minami Kugahara, Ota-Ku, Tokyo 146, Japan Office: Nihon Bed Mfg Co Ltd, 5-6-3 Ikegami, Ota-ku, Tokyo 146, Japan

TANAKA, STANLEY KATSUKI, optometrist, consultant; b. Honolulu, Sept. 19, 1932; s. Tomikichi and Hatsue T.; m. Esther K. Kokubun, Oct. 31, 1959; children—Glen A., Fay M. Student U. Hawaii, 1950-52; B.S., U. Okla., 1952; O.D. magna cum laude (Jackson award), Ill. Coll. Optometry, 1956. Enlisted U.S. Army, 1957, advanced through grades to col. Res., 1981; optometrist Hawaii Permanente Med. Group, Honolulu, 1968—; cons. opthalmic firms. Named Hawaii Optometrist of Yr., 1984. Mem. Am. Optometric Assn., Hawaii Optometric Assn., Armed Forces Optometric Soc., Contact Lens Soc., Am. Optometric Found., Optometric Extension Program, Beta Sigma Kappa. Democrat. Club: Toastmasters. Home: 2645 Oahu Ave Honolulu HI 96822 Office: 1010 Pensacola St Honolulu HI 96814

TANAKA, TETSUYA, manufacturing executive; b. Tottori-si, Tottori-ken, Japan, Dec. 7, 1919; s. Iwazo and Fumi Tanaka; m. Wakana Yamamoto, Oct. 15, 1944; children: Hitoomi, Yashiomi, Chiaki, Satoshi. BA in Econs., U. Kyoto, Japan, 1949; postgrad., U. Ill., 1955-56. Personnel mgr. Hitachi Chem. Co., Ltd., Tokyo, 1969-73, mgr. acctg., fin., 1973-74, dir., 1974-77, legitimative auditor, 1977-78; exec. dir. Hitachi Condenser Co., Ltd., Tokyo, 1978-83, legitimative auditor, 1983-87, advisor, 1987—. Served to 1st lt. Japanese Navy. Home: 964-7 Kashima Kashiwa-si, Chiba-ken 277, Japan Office: 1-31-1 Nishi Gatanda, Shinagawa-ku, Tokyo 141, Japan

TANAKA, WILLIAM HIROSHI, government official, retired; b. N.Y.C., Sept. 30, 1925; s. Fred Hisao and Mutsu (Kawasumi) T.; married; 1 child, Marina. MBA, Keio U., Tokyo, 1948. With woolen export dept. Takashimaya-IIDA Co., Ltd., Tokyo, 1948-55; with synthetic textile export dept. Marubeni-IIDA Co., Ltd., Tokyo and others, 1955-58; dir. Marubeni-IIDA GmbH., Hamburg and Düsseldorf, Fed. Republic Germany, 1958-67; chief rep. Marubeni Liaison Office, Vienna, Austria, 1967-69; head export industries UN Indsl. Devel. Orgn., Vienna, 1970-75, head tech. devel. and transfer br., 1976-85, internat. cons., 1986—; spl. sr. advisor Ministry of Trade and Industries, Male, Maldives, 1986-87, Ministry of Water Resources and Power, Beijing, People's Republic of China, 1986-87. Mem. Licensing Execs. Soc. Lodge: Lions (chmn. com. environment, anti-drugs and alcohol 1986-87, rep. to UN 1987) (Vienna). Home: Chimanistrasse 32, A-1190 Vienna Austria

TANARRO, FERNANDO MANUEL, financial consultant; b. La Coruña, Galicia, Spain, Feb. 11, 1933; s. Augusto Tanarro and Adela Nemiña. Degree in Econs., Cen. U., Barcelona, Spain, 1958; M in Taxation with honors, Inst. Católico de Adminstrn. e Industria, Madrid, 1964. Prof. U. Deusto, Bilbao-Vizcaya, Spain, 1969-71; ptnr. Price Waterhouse & Co., Barcelona-Catalunya, 1977—, Casals & Co., Barcelona-Catalunya, 1978—. Author: Investing in Spain, 1986; editor Exlusivas Económicas mag., 1987. Fellow Assn. Internal Accts., Assn. Authorized Pub. Accts., Inst. Taxation, Inst. Censores Cuentas; mem. Asociacion Española de Contabilidad y Adminstrn. de Empresas. Home: Casanova 59-61, 08011 Barcelona Spain Office: Price Waterhouse, Avenida de Roma 2 & 4, 08014 Barcelona Spain

TANASIE, PETRE, diplomat; b. Slatioara, Romania, Oct. 9, 1927; s. Savu G. and Gheorghita I. Tanasie; m. Silvia Iliescu; children: Mihaela, Adrian. Degree in Econs., Acad. Econ. Studies, Bucharest, 1951; D of Econs., Acad. Econ. Studies, 1962. Asst. prof. Acad. Econ. Studies, Bucharest, 1951-63, prof., 1967-69, 77-87; counsellor Romanian Embassy, Prague, 1963-67; dir. Ministry Fgn. Affairs, Bucharest, 1967-69, head, 1977-87; Romanian ambassador to Sri Lanka, India, and Nepal New Delhi, 1969-77; Permanent Ambassador from Romania UN, N.Y.C., 1987—. Author: Political Economy, 1958, International Cooperation in the Industrial Field, 1973, (with others) Encyclopedic Dictionary, 2 vols., 1964, Treaty of Economy, 2 vols., 1987. Recipient several medals, decorated several orders State Council of Romania. Office: Permanent Mission of Romania to the UN UN Bldg 573-77 Third Ave New York NY 10016

TANCHEV, PETER ZHELEV, 1st deputy chairman State Council of The People's Republic of Bulgaria; b. Gledka, Haskovo Dist., Bulgaria, July 12, 1920. Sec. standing com. Bulgarian Agrarian Union, 1949-51, mem. adminstrv. bd. and standing com., 1951, sec., 1957-75; minister of justice, 1962-66, dep. premier, 1966-71, 1st dep. premier, 1966-71, 1st dep. premier, 1971-74; 1st dep. chmn. State Council, 1974—. Address: State Council, Office First Dep Chairman, Sofia Bulgaria *

TANG, YUNG CHIEN (TOM), chemical company executive; b. Shanghai, China, May 4, 1919; came to U.S., 1945; s. Pei Tong and C.Y. (Wu) T.; m. Jane Yao Tang, Aug. 9, 1944. B.S. in Chem. Engring., Nat. Chekiang U., 1940, M.S., 1944; M.S. in Chem. Engring., U. Pitts., 1948; Ph.D., Columbia U., 1952. Div. mgr. Standard Packaging, Bklyn., 1964-66, group tech. dir., Clifton, N.J., 1966-67; pres., owner Tekni-Plex, Inc., Bklyn., 1967—. Patentee in field. Mem. Chinese Inst. Engrs. (pres. 1960-61, exec. mem. 1961-75). Home: 7855 Blvd East North Bergen NJ 07047 Office: Tekni-Plex Inc 68 35th St Brooklyn NY 11232

TANGE, KENZO, architectural educator; b. Osaka, Japan, Sept. 4, 1913; s. Tatsuyo and Tei Tange; m. Takako; 1 child, Noritaka Paul. Student, U. Tokyo, 1935-38, postgrad., 1942-45, PhD, 1959; DFA (hon.), SUNY, Buffalo, 1962; DEng (hon.), Technische Hochschule Stuttgart, Federal Republic of Germany, 1962; PhD in Architecture (hon.), Politecnico di Milana, Italy, 1964; PhD (hon.), U. Hong Kong, 1970, U. Sheffield, England, 1970, Harvard U., 1971, U. Buenos Aires, Argentina, 1978. Prof. U. Tokyo, 1946-74, prof. emeritus, 1974—; vis. prof. MIT, 1959-60, Harvard U., 1972; hon. prof. U. Nacional Rederico Villarreal, Peru, 1977, U. Buenos Aires, 1978. Author: Tradition and Creation in Japanese Architecture, 1960, A Plan for Tokyo 1960, 1961, Ise, 1962, Japan in the Future, 1966, Man and Architecture, 1970, Architecture and City, 1970; contbr. articles to profl. jours. Mem. adv. com. Gov. Tokyo, 1979-85, City Planning Inst. Japan. Recipient of prizes from Bldg. Soc. Japan, 1960, 65-66, 69-70, 79, 80, diploma Merit Internat. Olympic Com., 1964, Royal Gold medal Royal Inst. British Architects, 1965, Order Yugoslav Star on Necklace Yugooslavia, 1968, Order San Gregorio Magno from Apostolic Nunziature Vatican City, 1970, Order of Culture, 1988, Japan, Thomas Jefferson Meml. Architecture, 1970, Pritfzker Architecture prize, 1987 and numerous other awards. Mem. AIA (hon. fellow), Dem Ausserordentilichen Mitglid der Abteilyng Baukunst der Akademie der Kunst, Federal Republic of Germany, Am. Acad. Arts and Letters (hon.), Club Rome, Royal Acad. Arts and Letters, Belgium, Assn. Etranger a l'Inst. de France Acad. des Beaux-Arts, Archtl. Inst. Japan (hon. fellow), Japan Architects Assn. (pres. 1986—), Vatican Pantheon Acad. Arts and Letters, Correspondant Etrange de l'Acad. d'Architecture. Home: 1702, 2-3-34 Mita, Minato-ku, Tokyo 108, Japan Office: 7-2-21 Akasaka, Minato-ku, Tokyo Japan

TANGEN, HENRIK, investment company executive; b. Trondheim, Norway, Mar. 15, 1956; s. Egil and Marit (Sørlein) T.; m. Bodil Segtnan, Jan. 7, 1978; children: Christopher, Joachim. MS, Norwegian Inst. Tech., Trondheim, 1979; MBA, U. Denver, 1984. Project leader Ing. F. Selmer A/S, Oslo, 1981-83, chief real estate dept., 1984-85; v.p. Selmer Sande A/S, Oslo, 1985-86; pres., mng. dir. Consensus A/S, Trondheim, 1986—. Bd. dirs. Trondheim Fin. Forum, 1986—. Norges Teknisk-Naturviteskapelige Forskningsrad grantee, Oslo, 1983. Home: Nordsletveien 307, 7038 Trondheim Norway Office: Consensus A/S, 0 Tryggvasons Gt 48, 7000 Trondheim Norway

TANIGUCHI, TOKUSO, surgeon; b. Eleele, Kauai, Hawaii, June 26, 1915; s. Tokuichi and Sana (Omaye) T.; B.A., U. Hawaii, 1941; M.D., Tulane U., 1946; 1 son, Jan Tokuichi. Intern Knoxville (Tenn.) Gen. Hosp., 1946-47; resident in surgery St. Joseph Hosp., also Marquette Med. Sch., Milw., 1947-52; practice medicine, specializing in surgery, Hilo, Hawaii, 1955—; chief surgery Hilo Hosp.; teaching fellow Marquette Med. Sch., 1947-49; v.p., dir. Hawaii Hardware Co., Ltd. Served to capt. M.C., AUS, 1952-55. Diplomate Am. Bd. Surgery. Fellow Internat., Am. colls. surgeons; mem. Am., Hawaii med. assns., Hawaii County Med. Soc., Pan-Pacific Surg. Assn., Phi Kappa Phi. Contbr. articles in field to profl. jours. Patentee automated catheter. Home: 277 Kaiulani St Hilo HI 96720

TANII, AKIO, manufacturing executive; b. Apr. 20, 1928. Grad., Kobe Coll., 1948. With Matsushita Electric Indsl. Co., 1956—, now pres., also bd. dirs. Home: 7-18-4 Tsushima Fukui, 1-chome, Okayama 700, Japan Office: Matsushita Electric Indsl Co, 1006 Oaza Kadoma, Kadoma City Japan 571 *

TANKOOS, SANDRA MAXINE, court reporting executive; b. Bklyn., Nov. 12, 1936; d. Samuel J. and Ethel (Seltzer) Rich; m. Kenneth Robert Tankoos, Mar. 17, 1957; children: Robert Ian, Gary Russell, Jenine Sheryl. AA, Stenotype Inst., 1957; BA, Queens Coll., 1969; MA, C.W. Post Coll., 1973. Cert. stenotype reporter, 1959. Ct. reporter free lance, N.Y.C., 1957-70; tchr. Spanish, various high schs., L.I., 1970-76; pres. Tankoos Reporting, N.Y.C., 1976—, Ar-Ti Recording, Mineola, N.Y., 1977—. Contbr. articles to profl. jours. V.p., bd. dirs. Temple Sinai, Roslyn Hts., N.Y., 1979—, Liberal Jewish Day Sch., W. Hempstead, 1984—, LWV, Roslyn, 1969-75, NOW, Nassau County, 1975-77. Mem. Nat. Assn. Shorthand Reporters, Principal's Assn. Club: Numismatic (pres. 1973-78). Avocations: writing, piano. Home: 77 Shepherd Ln Roslyn Heights NY 11577 Office: Ar-Ti Recording Inc 223 Jericho Turnpike Mineola NY 11501 also: Tankoos Reporting Co 150 Nassau St New York NY 10038

TANKUS, HARRY, engineer, manufacturing company executive; b. Bialystok, Poland, Aug. 23, 1921; came to U.S., 1929, naturalized, 1929; s. Isador and Sima (Siegel) T.; m. Lila Beverly Lee, Sept. 9, 1947; children: Rolana, Ilyce. Diploma in engring., Armour Tech., 1942; student, U. Ill., 1946-47; grad. mgmt. course, U. Chgo., 1966. Inspection dept. head Buick div. Gen. Motors Co., Melrose Park, Ill., 1942-44; specification engr. Crane Packing Co., Chgo., 1946-53; chief engr. Crane Packing Co., 1953-62; asst. v.p. engring. Crane Packing Co., Morton Grove, 1962-64; asst. v.p. seals sales and engring., cons., mgr. seal div. Crane Packing Co., 1964-71, v.p. product sales, 1971-76, pres., 1976-82; chmn. John Crane-Houdaille, Inc., 1982-86; also dir. Crane Packing Co.; Bd. dirs. Inst. for Indsl. Innovation through Tribology, 1980—, Ill. Right to Work Com., Jr. Engring. Technol. Soc. in Ill., 1981-83, Ednl. Found.; bd. dirs. Oakton Community Coll. Ednl. Found., 1977—, pres., 1979-82. Contbr. articles to profl. jours. Bd. dirs Ill. Inst. Tech. Alumni, 1980—; v.p. university liaison Ill. Inst. Tech., 1986-87; mem. alumni bd. dirs. Alumni Council of 100, 1980-82; mem. adv. bd. Niles Twp. Sheltered Workshop; chmn. Nat. Conf. Fluid Power; chmn. indsl. div. Crusade of Mercy-United Way of Skokie Valley, 1980; mem. presdl. council Luth. Social Services of Ill.; trustee Rush North Shore Med. Ctr., 1981—; bd. dirs. United Way of Skokie Valley, 1981, gen. campaign chmn., 1981, v.p., 1982, pres., 1983, Chgo. United Way Crusade of Mercy, 1985—, Chgo. Lighthouse for the Blind, 1987—; bd. dirs. United Way Suburban Chgo., 1983. Served with U.S. Army, 1944-46. Decorated Purple Heart; recipient P.M. Ku award Am. Soc. Lubrication Engrs. Mem. Soc. Automotive Engrs. (chmn. seal program aerospace conf. 1965), ASME, Am. Soc. Metals, Western Soc. Engrs. (cert. of recognition), Am. Soc. Lubrication Engrs. (pres. 1975-76, P.M.KU award 1986), Am. Soc. Tool and Mfg. Engrs., Nat. Conf. on Fluid Power (gov. 1967, chmn. 1970), Am. Soc. Testing and Materials (chmn. subcom. on carbongraphite 1965). Clubs: Mason, Shriner, Moose, Rotary Internat. Office: 6400 Oakton St Morton Grove IL 60053

TANNENBAUM, HERBERT WALTER, lawyer; b. N.Y.C., May 13, 1935; s. Hyman Jack and Regina (Izan) T.; m. Muriel Golde, June 25, 1961; children—Ross, Eric, Brett. A.B., Amherst Coll., 1957; J.D., Georgetown U., 1967. Bar: Va. 1961, Fla. 1961. Sr. ptnr. Young, Stern & Tannenbaum, P.A., North Miami Beach, Fla., 1962—; chmn. bd. Turnberry Savs. and Loan Assn., North Miami Beach. Served with USAR, 1960, to lt., USCGR, 1961-68. Mem. North Dade Bar Assn. (pres. 1966-68), ABA. Democrat. Jewish. Address: 4800 Cleveland St Hollywood FL 33021

TANNENBERG, DIETER E. A., manufacturing and distributing company executive; b. Chevy Chase, Md., Nov. 24, 1932; s. E.A. Wilhelm and Margarete Elizabeth (Mundhenk) T.; m. Ruth Hansen, Feb. 6, 1956; 1 child, Diana Tannenberg Collingsworth. BSME, Northwestern U., 1959. Registered profl. engr., N.Y., Conn., Ohio, Ill., Ind., Wis., N.J. Supervising engr. Flexonics div. Calumet & Hecla, Inc., Chgo., 1959-61, chief engr., 1961-63, program mgr. advanced space systems, 1963-65, dir. mfg. services, 1965-67; dir. mfg. engring. SCM Corp., Cortland, N.Y., 1967-69; tech. dir. internat. Singer Co., N.Y.C., 1969-71; v.p. ops. internat. div. Addressograph-Multigraph Corp., Cleve., 1971-74; mng. dir. Addressograph Multigraph GmbH, Frankfurt/Main, W. Ger., 1974-78; v.p., gen. mgr. Europe, Middle East, Africa AM Internat. Inc., Chgo., 1978-79; pres. AM Bruning div., 1979-82, AM Multigraphics Div., Mt. Prospect, Ill., 1982-86; corp. v.p. AM Internat., Inc., 1981-83, corp. sr. v.p., 1983-86; chmn. bd. dirs., pres., chief exec. officer Sargent-Welch Sci. Co., Skokie, Ill., 1986—; chmn. Am. Internat. GmbH, Frankfurt, 1977-86; bd. dirs. Artra Group, Inc., Mathias Bauerle GmbH, St. Georgen, Fed. Republic Germany. Contbr. chpts. to handbooks, articles to tech., trade mags.; patentee in machinery field. Served with M.I., U.S. Army, 1953-56. Named Man of Yr. Quick Print Mag., 1985. Mem. Assn. Reprodn. Materials Mfrs. (bd. dirs. 1979-82, v.p. 1980-82), Nat. Assn. Quick Printers (bd. dirs. 1982-84), Nat. Printing Equipment and Supplies Mfg. Assn. (bd. dirs. 1983-86, chmn. govt. affairs com. 1985-86), Computer and Bus. Equipment Mfg. Assn. (bd. dirs. 1983-86), Soc. Am. Value Engrs. (hon. v.p. 1985—), Value Found. (trustee 1985—), Chgo. Council Fgn. Relations, ASME, Nat. Soc. Profl. Engrs., Pi Tau Sigma. Club: Economic (Chgo.). Office: Sargent-Welch Sci Co 7400 N Linder Ave Skokie IL 60077

TANNER, ALAIN, film maker; b. Geneva, Dec. 6, 1929. Films: Les Apprentis, 1964, Une Ville a Chandigarh, 1966, Charles, Dead or Alive, 1969, La Salamandre, 1971, La Retour d'Afrique, 1973, The Middle of the World, 1974, Jonah who will be 25 in the Year 2000, 1975, Messidor, 1979, Light Years Away, 1981, In the White City, 1983, No Man's Land, 1985, A Flame in my Heart, 1987. Office: Swiss Film Center, Munstergasse 18, 8001 Zurich Switzerland *

TANNER, DANIEL, educator; b. N.Y.C., Sept. 22, 1926; s. Jack and Lillian (Jupiter) T.; m. Laurel Nan Jacobson, July 11, 1948. B.S. with honors, Mich. State U., 1949, M.S., 1952; Ph.D. (Univ. Scholar), Ohio State U., 1955. Asst. prof. edn. San Francisco State Coll., 1955-60; asso. prof. edn., coordinator Midwest program on airborne TV instrn. Purdue U., 1960-62; asso. prof. edn., asso. dir. internat. program for edn. leaders Northwestern U., 1962-64; asso. prof. research div. tchr. edn. City U. N.Y., 1964-66; prof. edn., dir. Center for Urban Edn., U. Wis.-Milw. Sch. Edn., 1966-67; prof. edn., dir. grad. programs in curriculum theory and devel. Grad. Sch. Edn., Rutgers U., New Brunswick, N.J., 1967—; chmn. dept. curriculum and instrn. Grad. Sch. Edn., Rutgers U., 1969-71, faculty research fellow, 1974-75; vis. lectr. U. Kansas City, summer 1956, Tchrs. Coll. Columbia, summer 1966; vis. prof. Emory U., summer 1968, SUNY, Binghamton, winter 1968; vis. scholar U. London Inst. Edn., 1974-75; Mem. rev. bd. coll. work-study program U.S. Office Edn., 1965; cons. U. Tex. Med. Center, 1961-62, Chgo. Sch. Survey, 1964-65, Center Urban Edn., N.Y.C., 1964-65, West Chicago (Ill.) Sch. Survey, 1963-64, Nat. Ednl. TV Center, N.Y.C., 1963, Campbell County (Va.) Sch. Survey, 1970, Memphis Schs., 1977-78, ASCD Commn. on Gen. Edn., 1980-81, West Orange, N.J., Curriculum Study, 1984, ASCD Commn. on Secondary Sch. Practices, 1985, ASCD Ednl. Policy Task Force, 1985. Author: Schools for Youth: Change and Challenge in Secondary Education, 1965, Secondary Curriculum: Theory and Development, 1971, Secondary Education: Perspectives and Prospects, 1972, Using Behavioral Objectives in the Classroom, 1972, Curriculum Development: Theory into Practice, 2d edit., 1980, Supervision in Education, 1987; contbg. author: Curriculum Issues, 87th Yearbook NSSE, 1988, Ency. of Ednl. Research, 5th edit., 1982, Readings in Educational Psychology, 1963, Yearbook of the Association for Student Teaching, 1962, The Great Debate, Our Schools in Crisis, 1959, Educational Issues in a Changing Society, 1964, Programs, Teachers and Machines, 1964, Views on American Schooling, 1964, The Training of America's Teachers, 1975, Curriculum and Instruction, 1981; co-author: Teen Talk: Curriculum Materials in Communications, 1971; contbg. editor: Ednl. Leadership, 1969-74; mem. editorial bd.: Tex. Tech. Jour. Edn., Teaching Edn.; editorial cons.: Ency. of Ednl. Research, 5th edit., Jour. Ednl. Psychology; contbr. Atlantic Monthly, Bull. of Atomic Scientists and other nat. mags., ednl. jours. Trustee Delaware Valley Coll., Doylestown, Pa., 1981—. Fellow AAAS, John Dewey Soc. (bd. dirs. 1985-88); mem. Am. Ednl. Research Assn., N.Y. Acad. Sci., AAUP, Am. Polit. Sci. Assn., Am. Ednl. Studies Assn., Nat. Soc. Study Edn., Nat. Assn. Secondary Sch. Prins. (adv. council 1985—), Phi Kappa Phi, Phi Delta Kappa (Service award 1957). Home: Highwood Rd Somerset NJ 08873 Office: Grad Sch Edn Rutgers U New Brunswick NJ 08903

TANNER, HAROLD, investment banker; b. N.Y.C., May 7, 1932; s. Irving and Pauline (Steinlauf) T.; m. Estelle Newman, July 6, 1957; children: David, James, Karen. B.S., Cornell U., 1952; M.B.A., Harvard U., 1956. Vice pres., dir. Blyth & Co. Inc., N.Y.C., 1956-69; exec. v.p. New Court Securities Corp., N.Y.C., 1969-76, Blyth Eastman Dillon & Co., Inc., N.Y.C., 1977-80; partner Salomon Bros. Inc., 1980-81, mng. dir., 1981-87; pres. Tanner & Co., Inc., N.Y.C., 1987—; Co-founder Vol. Urban Cons. Group. Trustee Cornell U.; bd. dirs. Harvard Bus. Sch. Assocs. Served to lt. (j.g.) USNR, 1952-54. Clubs: Century, Harmonie. Home: 18 Kensington Rd Scarsdale NY 10583 Office: 101 E 52d St New York NY 10022

TANNER, LAUREL NAN, education educator; b. Detroit, Feb. 16, 1929; d. Howard Nicholas and Celia (Solvich) Jacobson; m. Daniel Tanner, July 11, 1948. BS in Social Sci, Mich. State U., 1949, MA in Edn., 1953; EdD, Columbia U., 1967. Pub. sch. tchr. 1950-64; instr. tchr. edn. Hunter Coll., 1964-66, asst. prof., 1967-69; supr. Milw. Pub. Schs., 1966-67; mem. faculty Temple U., Phila., 1969—; prof. edn. Temple U., 1974—; vis. professorial scholar U. London Inst. Edn., 1974-75; vis. scholar Stanford U., 1984-85, U. Chgo., 1988—; curriculum cons., 1969—; disting. vis. prof. San Francisco State U., 1987. Author: Classroom Discipline for Effective Teaching and Learning, 1978, La Disciplina en la enseñanza y el Aprendizaje, 1980; co-author: Classroom Teaching and Learning, 1971, Curriculum Development: Theory into Practice, 1975, 2d edit., 1980, Supervision in Education: Problems and Practices, 1987; editor Nat. Soc. Study Edn. Critical Issues in Curriculum, 87th yearbook, part 1, 1988. Faculty research fellow Temple U., 1970, 80, 81; recipient John Dewey Research award, 1981-82. Mem. Soc. Study Curriculum History (founder, 1st pres. 1978-79), Assn. Supervision and Curriculum Devel. (dir. 1982-84), Am. Ednl. Research Assn., Profs. Curriculum Assn. (Factotum 1983-84), Am. Ednl. Studies Assn., John Dewey Soc., Alumni Council Tchrs. Coll. Columbia U. Home: Highwood Rd Somerset NJ 08873 Office: Temple U Coll Edn Philadelphia PA 19122

TANNER, MARTIN STANLEY, lawyer; b. Salt Lake City, Mar. 27, 1955; s. George Stanley and Nona (Watson) T.; m. Patti Madsen, June 16, 1979; 1 child, David. BA, U. Utah, 1981; JD, Brigham Young U., 1984. Bar: Utah 1984, Ariz. 1986, Calif. 1987, U.S. Ct. Appeals (9th and D.C. cir.) 1986, U.S. Tax Ct. 1986, U.S. Ct. Appeals (10th cir.) 1987, U.S. Supreme Ct. 1987. Assoc. R. Dale Potter P.C., Salt Lake City, 1984-86, Snell & Wilmer, Phoenix, 1986-88; ptnr. Parsons, Behle and Latimer, Salt Lake City, 1988—; vol. atty. Utah Legal Services, Salt Lake City, 1984-86. Articles editor Utah Bar Jour., 1982-84; contbr. articles to profl. jours. Missionary Ch. Jesus Christ Latter-day Sts., Japan, 1974-76; explorer post leader Boy Scouts Am. Mem. ABA, Utah Bar Assn., Ariz. Bar Assn., Calif. Bar Assn., Phi Delta Phi. Republican. Mormon. Home: 3942 Pine Tree Dr Salt Lake City UT 84124 Office: Parsons Behle and Latimer 185 S State St Suite 700 Salt Lake City UT 84147-0898

TANNER, MAURI UUNO ENSIO, aerodynamic engineer; b. Närpiö, Finland, June 9, 1930; s. Uuno Oskar and Kerttu (Wahlroos) T.; m. Virpi Elina Pukonen, Nov. 30, 1952; children: Pekka, Leena. Diploma in engring., Tech. U., Helsinki, Finland, 1958; D in Engring., Tech. U., Brunswick, Fed. Rep. Germany, 1967. Chief research rock drill dept. Tampella Engring. Works, Tampere, Finland, 1958-61; aerodynamicist Deutsche Forschungs und Versuchsanstalt für Luft-und Raumfahrt, Göttingen, Fed. Republic Germany, 1961—. Contbr. articles to profl. jours. Mem. Deutsche Gesellschaft für Luft-und Raumfahrt, Suomen Teknillinen Seura. Home: Richard-Courant-Weg 13, 3400 Gottingen Federal Republic of Germany Office: Inst Theoretical Fluid Mech, DFVLR, Bunsenstrasse 10, 3400 Gottingen Federal Republic of Germany

TANNY, GERALD BRIAN, polymer chemist; b. Montreal, Que., Can., Dec. 26, 1945; s. Albert Morris and Jean (Levine) T.; m. Linda Barbera Salzedo, June 9, 1968; children—Micha, Shimon, Eitan. B.Sc. in Chemistry with honors, McGill U., Montreal, 1964, Ph.D. in Polymer Chemistry, 1970. Research assoc. Weizmann Inst. Sci., Rehovot, Israel, 1971-74, sr. scientist, 1974-78; assoc. research dir. Gelman Scis. Inc., Ann Arbor, Mich., 1978-86; v.p. advanced tech., 1986—; mng. dir. Membrane Filtration Tech. Inc. (name changed to Gelman Scis. Tech. 1984), Rehovot, 1980—; cons. in field. Contbr. articles to profl. jours. Grantee in field; Nat. Research Council Can. fellow, 1970-71. Mem. Am. Chem. Soc., Israel Plastics Assn. Jewish. Office: Gelman Sics Tech, Kiryat Weizmann, Rehovot Israel

TANOUS, HELENE MARY, physician; b. Zanesville, Ohio, Oct. 22, 1939; d. Joseph Carrington and Rose Marie (Mokarzel) Tanous; B.A., Marymount Coll., 1961; M.D., U. Tex., 1967. Intern, County Hosp., Los Angeles, 1967-68; resident in radiology U. So. Calif. Hosp., Los Angeles, 1969-71; practice medicine specializing in radiology, Los Angeles, 1972-73; instr. radiology U. So. Calif. Med. Sch., Los Angeles, 1971-72; asst. prof. diagnostic radiology Baylor Med. Sch., Houston, 1973-75; dir. med. student elective in diagnostic radiology Ben Taub Hosp., Houston, 1973-75; pvt. practice diagnostic radiology, Largo, Fla., 1975—; asst. prof. diagnostic radiology U. South Fla. Med. Sch., 1980—; dir. med. student edn. in Diagnostic Radiology. Pres., founder Children's Advocates, Inc.; bd. dirs. Fla. Endowment for Humanities, 1979-83. Diplomate Am. Bd. Radiology. Mem. AMA, So. Med. Assn., Fla. Med. Assn., Internat. Platform Assn., L'Alliance Francaise of Tampa (bd. dirs. 1984—, pres. 1985-87), Fedn. Alliances Francaises U.S.A. (bd. dirs. 1987—). Office: U South Fla Med Sch Dept Radiology 12901 N 30th St Box 17 Tampa FL 33612

TANOUS, PETER JOSEPH, banker; b. N.Y.C., May 21, 1938; s. Joseph Carrington and Rose Marie (Mokarzel) T.; B.A. in Econs., Georgetown U., 1960; m. Barbara Ann MacConnell, Aug. 18, 1962; children—Christopher, Helene, William. With Smith, Barney & Co., Inc. (now Smith Barney, Harris Upham & Co., Inc.), N.Y.C., 1963-78, 2d v.p., mgr. Paris office, 1967, v.p., 1968-78, resident European sales mgr., Paris, 1969-71, internat. sales mgr., N.Y.C., 1971-78, 1st v.p., 1975-78; chmn. bd. Petra Capital Corp., N.Y.C., 1978-81, now dir.; exec. v.p., Bank Audi (USA), N.Y.C., 1984—, dir. Bank Audi, Calif.; del. U.S.-Saudi Arabian Joint Econ. Commn. Bus. Dialogue; trustee Browning Sch., N.Y.C. Mem. internat. bd. advisers Ctr. Social Policy in Middle East, Brandeis U.; mem. adv. bd. Nat. Council U.S.-Arab Relations; bd. dirs. Kahlil Gibran Centennial Found.; trustee The Fleming Sch., N.Y.C. Served to 1st lt. AUS, 1961-63. Mem. Am. Geographical Soc. (councillor), Arab Bankers Assn. N.Am. (dir.), Georgetown U. Alumni Assn. (gov. 1968-71), Georgetown Club France (pres. 1968-71). Roman Catholic. Clubs: Met. (N.Y.C.); Automobile de France (Paris). Co-author: The Petrodollar Takeover, 1975; The Wheat Killing, 1979; author: The Earhart Mission, 1979. Home: 136 E 64th St New York NY 10021 Office: 600 Fifth Ave New York NY 10020

TAN SRI DATO' TEH, HONG PIOW, banker; b. Singapore, Mar. 14, 1930; s. Chong Ngee Teh; m. Puan Sri Datin Tay Sock Noy, Feb. 8, 1956; children: Teh Li Ming, Teh Li Hua, Teh Lee Pang, Teh Li Shian. BS, Pacific Western U., 1981, MBA, 1982, LLD (hon.), 1984; PhD in Fin., Clayton U., 1985. With Overseas-Chinese Banking Corp., Ltd., Singapore, 1950-59; sub-mgr. Malayan Banking Berhad, 1960, mgr. Kuala Lumpur br., 1962-64, area mgr. State of Selangor br., Apr. to Aug., 1964, gen. mgr. State of Selangor br., 1964-66; dir., exec. chmn. Pub. Bank Berhad, Kuala Lumpur, 1966-86, pres., chief exec. officer, 1986—; dir., exec. chmn. Pub. Fin. Berhad, Kuala Lumpur, 1966-86, exec. chmn., 1986—; chmn. Pub. Leasing and Factoring Sdn Berhad, Malaysia, London & Pacific Ins. Co. Berhad , Malaysia/Singapore, Tong Meng Industries Ltd., Singapore, Pub. Securities Ltd., Singapore; chmn., mng. dir. PB Trustee Services Berhad, Malaysia, Pub. Internat. Investment Ltd., Hong Kong; also industrialist, chmn., mng. dir. numerous cos. inc. in Malaysia, Singapore, Hong Kong, U.S.A., U.K., Can., Australia, New Hebrides. Recipient hon. titles: Dato Kurnia Sentosa, Pahang, 1966, Justice of Peace, 1967, Datuk - Darjah Sultan Ahmad Shah Pahang, 1978, Datuk - Sri Indera Mahkota Pahang , 1983 all from His Royal Highness the Sultan of Pahang; Dato Paduka Mahkota Johore, 1973, Dato Sri Paduka Mahkota Johore (The Most Honorable Order of the Crown of Johore), 1974, Dato Sri Setia Sultan Ismail Johore, 1978 all from His Royal Highness the Sultan of Johore, and Tan Sri - Panglima Setia Mahkota from His Majesty, the Yang DiPertuan Agong, 1983. Fellow Assn. Bus. Execs. U.K., Brit. Inst. Mgmt., Inst. Bank-Bank Malaysia, Inst. Adminstv. Accts. U.K., Inst. Adminstv. Mgmt. U.K. (hon. pres. Singapore br.), Inst. Bankers London, Inst. Bus. Adminstrn. Australia, Malaysian Inst. Dirs., Inst. Commerce U.K., Inst. Credit Mgmt. Ltd. U.K., Inst. Dirs. U.K., Inst. Indsl. Mgrs. U.K.; mem. Malaysia Soc. of Inst. Adminstrv. Accts., Malaysian Econ. Assn. (assoc.), Malaysian Inst. Mgmt., Teo Chew Assn. (Termerloh dist. hon. pres.) Pahang Darul Makmur, Eng Yong Tay Si Assn. Johore (hon. pres.), Teo Yeonh Huai Kuan Singapore (hon. adminstr.), Selangor Teo Chew Pooi Ip Assn. (dir.). Office: Public Bank Berhad, 6 Jalan Sultan Sulaiman, 50000 Kuala Lumpur Malaysia

TANTUM, CHARLES ALAN, state official; b. Trenton, N.J., Apr. 3, 1946; s. Charles Anderson and Eleanor Doris (Bozarth) T.; m. Jacquelyn Sue Buchko; children—Chryssa Sue, Cara Lyn. B.A., Western Md. Coll., 1968; A.A., Burlington County Coll., 1979; M.B.A., Monmouth Coll., 1981; cert. pub. mgr. Rutgers U., 1985. Field rep. N.J. Wage Bur., Trenton, 1971-75; investigator pvt. employment agencies N.J. Consumer Affairs, Trenton, 1975-81, supr., 1981, chief pvt. employment agencies, 1981—. Asst., Girl Scouts Am., 1983-84; leader Boy Scouts Am., 1962-64, recipient Order Arrow; soccer coach Pemberton Area Athletic League, 1985—. Served to capt. AUS, 1968-71, maj. USAR, 1971—. Episcopalian. Home: 313 Wissahickon Trail Browns Mills NJ 08015 Office: NJ Div Consumer Affairs Pvt Employment Agy 1100 Raymond Blvd Room 516 Newark NJ 07102

TANZER, CHARLES, emeritus teacher educator, writer; b. N.Y.C., Dec. 4, 1912; s. Benjamin and Anna (Schachter) T.; m. Beatrice Ball, June 28, 1957. B.S. in Biology with honors, L.I. U., Bklyn., 1933, L.H.D. (hon.), 1980; M.S. in Bacteriology, NYU, 1936, Ph.D., 1941; postgrad. U. Vt., 1944-46. Registered med. technologist. Asst. in bacteriology NYU Med. Sch., N.Y.C., 1934-38; tchr. sci. N.Y.C. pub. high schs., 1938-56; prin. N.Y.C. jr. high schs., 1957-65; prof. edn., coordinator sci. Hunter Coll., N.Y.C., 1965-73, prof. emeritus, 1973—; asst. prof. lab tech. Columbia U., 1944-51; adj. prof. biology L.I. U., 1951-63. Author: Biology and Human Progress, 1953, revised, 1986; Structure and Function in Living Things, 1966. Contbr. articles to profl. jours. Chmn. health com. Puerto Rican Study, P.R. and N.Y.C., 1955-56; chmn. pub. edn. Am. Cancer Soc., N.Y.C., 1963-72; chmn. Biology Testing com., Coll. Entrance Exam. Bd., 1951-56. Served to maj. U.S. Army, 1943-46, ETO. Named Disting. Alumnus of Yr., L. I. U., 1971; recipient Meritorious Service award, Sword of Hope Am. Cancer Soc., 1973. Mem. Nat. Assn. Biology Tchrs., N.Y. Biology Tchrs. Assn. (pres. 1955-57, 1st Honor award 1979), Sigma Xi. Democrat. Jewish. Avocations: photography; nature study. Home: 600 W 218th St New York NY 10034

TANZER, JED SAMUEL, lawyer, financial consultant; b. Arverne, N.Y., Nov. 16, 1947; s. David and Mildred (Bondy) T.; B.S. with honors in Social Sci., SUNY, Oneonta, 1970; J.D. cum laude, Syracuse U., 1978, M.B.A., 1978; m. Sally Jane Ketcham, July 10, 1971. Tchr., union grievance chmn. Central Sch. Dist., Windsor, N.Y., 1970-75; research asst. Sch. Mgmt., Syracuse (N.Y.) U., 1977-78; admitted to N.Y. State bar, 1979, Fed. Dist. Ct. bar, 1979, U.S. Tax Ct. bar, 1979; sr. atty. Ayco/Am. Express Corp., Albany, N.Y., 1978-82, assoc. regional mgr., 1982-85, v.p., regional mgr., 1986—; fin. cons., 1978—. Permanent teaching cert. N.Y. State. Mem. Am. Bar Assn. (com. state and local taxation 1981-82), N.Y. State Bar Assn., Justinian Law Soc., Beta Gamma Sigma, Kappa Delta Pi. Home: 1113 Autumn Chase Ct Marietta GA 30064 Office: 2839 Paces Ferry Rd Suite 1250 Atlanta GA 30339

TANZER, MARVIN LAWRENCE, biologist, educator; b. N.Y.C., Jan. 26, 1935; s. Joseph and Loretta Rose (Freundlich) T.; m. Betsy Chernoff, Dec. 19, 1954; children—Laura Sue, Andrew Ethan, Matthew Owen, Jennifer Elizabeth, S.B., M.I.T., 1955; M.D., N.Y.U., 1959. Lic. physician, Conn. Intern, asst. resident med. service Johns Hopkins Hosp., Balt., 1959-61; clin. and research fellow in medicine Mass. Gen. Hosp., Harvard Med. Sch., Boston, 1961-62; chief gen. physiology br. Fitzsimons Gen. Hosp., Denver, 1962-64; research fellow in medicine Mass. Gen. Hosp., 1964-65, asst. biologist, 1965-68; research assoc. in medicine Harvard Med. Sch., 1964-67, assoc. in medicine, 1967-68; investigator Marine Biol. Lab., Woods Hole, Mass., 1966-70, corp. mem., 1968—; tutor in biochem. scis. Harvard Coll., 1967-68; asst. prof. dept. biochemistry U. Conn., Sch. Medicine, Farmington, 1968-71, assoc. prof., 1971-75, prof., 1975—, dir. orthopaedic research lab., prof. dept. orthpaedic surgery, 1978—, prof., head dept. BioStructure and Function Sch. Dental Medicine, 1986—; vis. prof. U. Liege (Belgium), 1974-75; cons. and lectr. in field. Contbr. articles to profl. jours., chpts. to books; participant numerous profl. confs. Served to capt. USAR, 1962-64. Recipient numerous awards, grants and fellowships in medicine. Mem. Am. Soc. Bone and Mineral Research (adv. bd. 1978), Orthopaedic Research Soc., Am. Soc. Cell Biology, Tissue Culture Assn., Am. Heart Assn., Am. Soc. Biol. Chemists, AAAS, Am. Chem. Soc. (div. biol. chemistry), Nat. Bd. Med. Examiners (Diplomate), N.Y. Acad. Scis., Societe Belge de Biochimie, Belgian Connective Tissue Club, Sigma Xi, Alpha Omega Alpha. Office: U Conn Health Ctr Farmington Ave Farmington CT 06032

TAPIA, FERNANDO ANDRES, medical educator; b. Lima, Peru, Feb. 4, 1928; s. Ricardo and Ricardina (Mendieta) T.; m. Jacqueline Kay Graham, Sept. 5, 1959; children: Andres, Elisabeth Ann, Maria Luz, Nora Jean. BS, San Marcos U., Lima, 1954, MD, 1955. Fellow in internal medicine Cleve. Clinic, 1955-56, resident in cardiovascular disease, 1956-59; in-charge cardiologist Edgewater Hosp., Chgo., 1959-61; research assoc. High Altitude Inst. Cayetano Heredia U., Lima, 1961-67; prof. medicine and cardiology High Altitude Inst. Cayetano Heredia U., 1971—, coordinator postgrad. program in cardiology, 1977—; chief cardiology div. Cayetano Heredia Gen. Hosp., Lima, 1968—; staff San Borja Clinic, Lima, 1970—; pres. med. staff San Borja Clinic, 1981-82; exec. dir.. Miraflores Med. Inst., 1980-82; founder, pres. Coop. Service for Physicians and Allied Professions, 1966-75. Contbr. articles to profl. jours. USPHS fellow, 1956-58, grantee, 1961-67. Fellow Am. Coll. Cardiology; mem. Peruvian-N.Am. Med. Assn. (pres. 1964-66), Peruvian Soc. Cardiology (pres. 1979-81), Peruvian Congress Cardiology (pres. 1981), Peruvian Coll. Medicine (pres Region 3 1976-77, vice-dean 1984-85, dean 1986-87), Peruvian Soc. Angiology, Peruvian Soc. Internal Medicine, Am. Fedn. Clin. Research, Am. Heart Assn., Inter-Am. Soc. Hypertension. Roman Catholic. Office: San Borja Clinic, 333 Avenida Guardia Civil, Lima Peru

TAPLIN, OLIVER PAUL, classicist, educator; b. Kent, Eng., Aug. 2, 1943; s. Walter and Susan T.; m. Kim Stampfer, June 1964; children: Phoebe, Nat. BA, MA, Corpus Christi Coll., Oxford, 1968; PhD, Magdalen Coll. Oxford U., Eng., 1972. Jr. fellow Ctr. for Hellenic Studies, Washington, 1970-71; lectr. Bristol U., Eng., 1972-73; tutorial fellow, classics lectr. Magdalen Coll. Oxford U., 1973—; vis. prof. Dartmouth Coll., N.H., 1981, UCLA, 1987; cons. Nat. Theatre, London, 1981, Transatlantic Films, London, 1987-89. Author: Stagecraft of Aeschylus, 1977, Greek Tragedy in Action, 1978; founding editor Omnibus jour., 1981—; contbr. articles to profl. jours. Office: Magdalen Coll, Oxford OX1 4AU, England

TAPP, JOHN CECIL, physician, educator, futures trader; b. Horse Cave, Ky., Dec. 1, 1940; s. Ernest and Lottie Belle (Gill) T.; student David Lipscomb Coll., 1958-59, Western Ky. U., 1959-61; postgrad. Sch. Pharmacy, U. Ky., 1962; M.D., U. Louisville, 1966; divorced; children—John Randolph, Gregory Patrick. Diplomate Am. Bd. Family Practice, Nat. Bd. Med. Examiners, Am. Bd. Circulation Therapy. Intern, U. Louisville, 1966-67, resident in internal medicine, 1969-70; practice medicine, Bowling Green, Ky., 1971—; mem. staff Greenview Hosp., Bowling Green Warren County Med. Center; assoc. clin. prof. vol. faculty Coll. Allied Health Professions, U. Ky.; clin. instr. vol. faculty Travecca-Nazarene Coll., Nashville; mem. med. adv. bd. Bowling Green Jr. Coll.; dir. Prima Care Home Health Agy.; ptnr., pres. Animal House Pet Shop Inc.; ptnr., sec.-treas. Pearson Constrn. Co., Ltd.; ptnr. Tapp-Miller Internat. Travel Service for Profls. Served as maj. USPHS, 1967-69. Named to Hon. Order Ky. Cols. Fellow Am. Acad. Family Physicians; mem. Am. Acad. Bariatric Physicians, Am. Coll. for Advancement of Medicine, Ky. Acad. Family Physicians, Bowling Green. Med. Soc., Bowling Green-Warren County C. of C., Alpha Omega Alpha, Alpha Kappa Kappa, Kappa Psi. Office: 414 Old Morgantown Rd Bowling Green KY 40201

TAPPAN, DAVID S., JR., engineering, construction, natural resources management company executive; b. Hainan, People's Republic of China, May 27, 1922; m. Jeanne Boone. B.A., Swarthmore Coll., 1943; M.B.A., Stanford U., 1948. With sales and engring. dept. U.S. Steel Corp., 1948-52; adminstrv. asst. to v.p. of sales Fluor Corp., 1952-59, v.p. domestic sales, 1959-62, v.p. domestic and internat. sales, 1962-68, also. bd. dirs., sr. v.p., 1968-71; pres. Fluor Corp., Irvine, Calif., 1987-88; chmn., chief exec. officer, dir. Fluor Corp., Irvine, 1988—; pres. Fluor Engrs. & Constructors Inc. (now named Fluor Daniel Inc.), 1971-76, vice chmn. bd., 1976-82, pres., chief operating officer, 1982-84, chmn., chief exec. officer, from 1984; bd. dirs. Genentech Inc., Allianz Ins. Co., The Nat. Council for U.S.-China Trade Inc., Los Angeles-Guangzhou Sister City Assn., Nat. Energy Found.; bd. overseas exec. council on fgn. diplomats and adv. com. Export-Import Bank of U.S. Bd. dirs. Nat. Bus. Com. for Arts; chmn. Orange County Orgn.; councillor U. So. Calif. Sch. Bus. and Adminstrn., Stanford U. Grad. Sch. Bus. Served to lt. (j.g.) USNR, 1943-46. Mem. Am. Petroleum Inst., Los Angeles C. of C. (vice chmn., bd. dirs.). Office: Fluor Corp 3333 Michelson Dr Irvine CA 92730 *

TAPPAN, SANDRA HAZEN, private mental health counselor, dance school executive; b. Burlington, Vt., Sept. 25, 1940; d. Joseph and Elaine (Hazen) Rogow; B.A., Trinity Coll., 1979; M.S., U. Vt., 1983; m. Walter Howe Tappan II, Dec. 27, 1958; children—Suzanne E., Heidi L. Nat. cert. counselor Nat. Bd. Cert. Counselors, cert. Nat. Acad. Cert. Clin. Mental Health Counselors. Tchr. pre-sch., Enosburg Falls, Vt., 1967; owner, choreographer, tchr. Sandra Tappan Profl. Sch. Dance, St. Albans, Vt., 1968—; counselor CRASH, 1977-79, Planned Parenthood of Vt., 1979-80; tchr. Community Coll. Vt., 1982-84; cons. staff Northwestern Med. Ctr. Hosp., 1985—. Mem. Franklin County Planning Commn., 1974-76; exec. bd. United Way, 1984-85. Mem. Am. Assn. for Counseling and Devel, Am. Psychol. Assn. (assoc.), Republican. Home: 22 Rugg St Saint Albans VT 05478

TAPSELL, PETER, New Zealand government official, orthopedic surgeon; b. Rotorua, N.Z., Jan. 21, 1930; married; 4 children. M.B., Ch.B., Otago U., 1954. House surgeon Waikato Hosp., Hamilton, N.Z.; demonstrator in anatomy Sch. Medicine, Dunedin, N.Z.; resident surg. officer Dunedin Pub. Hosp., to 1958; trainee Royal Infirmary, Edinburgh, Scotland, 1958-59; resident surgeon Woolwich Hosp., London; resident in orthopedics Orthopedic Hosp., Oswestry, Eng., to 1961; orthopedic surgeon Rotorua and Queen Elizabeth hosps., from 1961; practice orthopedic surgery, N.Z., 1961—; former dep. mayor Rotorua City; M.P. for Eastern Maori, 1981—, minister of internal affairs, 1984-1987, minister civil def., until 1987, now minister forestry, lands, police, recreation and sport. Former chair N.Z. Maori Arts and Crafts Inst.; former mem. Phys. Environ. Conf., Tourist Devel. Council, Maori Adv. Council Health; former dep. chair Council Recreation and Sport; mem. council U. Waikato and Waikato Tchrs. Tng. Coll.; chair Ngati Whakaue Tribal Lands Inc. Ngarimu U. scholar; Fgn. Leader grantee, U.S., 1966; decorated mem. Order Brit. Empire, Queen's Jubilee medal. Fellow Royal Coll. Surgeons (Edinburgh), Royal Coll. Surgeons (Eng.). Avocations: hunting; fishing; skiing. Office: Ministry of Forestry, Wellington New Zealand *

TARANTA, ANGELO (VISCA), physician, educator; b. Rome, 1927; came to U.S., 1952, naturalized, 1956; MD, U. Rome, 1949. Diplomate Am. Bd. Internal Medicine, also sub-bd. Rheumatology. Intern, dept. internal medicine and pediatrics Univ. Hosp., Rome, 1949-50, resident, 1950-52; resident in medicine St. Mary's Hosp., Rochester, N.Y., 1952-53; resident in cardiology Irvington (N.Y.) House, 1953-54, research assoc., 1955-59, research dir., 1959-62; assoc. dir. Irvington House Inst., N.Y.C., 1965-71; research fellow in microbiology NYU Sch. Medicine, 1955-56, instr. in microbiology, 1955-58, adj. asst. prof. microbiology, 1958-60, asst. prof. medicine, 1960-65, assoc. prof., 1965-75, on leave of absence, 1975-79; dir. medicine Cabrini Health Care Ctr., N.Y.C., 1973—; prof. medicine, chief rheumatology and immunology div. N.Y. Med. Coll., 1979-85, chief div. humanities and ethics, 1985—; co-chmn. study group on heart disease in the young Inter-Soc. Commn. on Heart Disease Resources, 1972-78; bd. dirs. Am. Heart Assn., 1975-77; chmn. Council on Cardiovascular Disease in the Young, 1975-77; cons. in field. Author: (with M. Markowitz) Rheumatic Fever; editor (with E. Kaplan) Infectious Endocarditis; contbr. numerous articles to profl. publs. and textbooks. Fulbright travel award, 1952. Mem. Soc. Clin. Investigation, Am. Assn. Immunologists, N.Y. Acad. Medicine (chmn. sect. medicine 1980-87), Italian Rheumatology Assn. (hon.), Argentine Rheumatology Soc. (hon.). Office: Cabrini Med Ctr 227 E 19th St New York NY 10003

TARANTINO, LOUIS GERALD, lawyer, business consultant; b. Bridgeport, Conn., Sept. 7, 1934; s. Louis Gerald and Mary Louise (Boyle) T. BA, U. Pa., 1955, LLB, 1958. Bar: Conn. 1958, N.Y. 1960. Assoc. Beekman & Bogue, 1959-76, ptnr., 1968-76; chmn. Berkeley Mgmt. Assocs., Inc., Pitts., 1984—, also bd. dirs.; treas., dir. PERQ Systems Corp., Pitts.; bd. dirs. Beaver Valley Power Co., Beaver Falls, Pa., Advent Systems Ltd., Eng., Library Bur., Inc., Karpen Systems, Inc., KSI Bldg. Products, Knapp Investment Corp.; pres., bd. dirs. Polymar Roofs Inc., The Speechware Corp. Mem. Bar Assn. City N.Y., N.Y. Bar Assn., Conn. Bar Assn., SAR, Hugeunot Soc. Pa., St. Anthony Hall. Club: Knickerbocker, Broad St., St. Anthony (N.Y.C.); Duquesne (Pitts.). Home: 201 Grant St Sewickley PA 15143 Office: 1500 Liberty Ave Pittsburgh PA 15222

TARANTO, SERGIO ALBERTO, management consultant; b. Genoa, Italy, June 25, 1924; s. Carlo and Lea (Montagna) T.; m. Annamaria Ogliari, Feb. 18, 1952. B of Engring., U. Genoa, 1948. Mgr. sales Montedison, Milan, Italy, 1949-54; gen. mgr. Tudor Battery, Milan, 1954-71; mng. dir. Fiat Battery Bus., Milan, 1972-81; pres. Compagnia Generale Accumulatori, Milan, 1979-83; mgr. Fiat Components Bus., Torin, Italy, 1981-83; pres. Link Mgmt. Co., Milan, 1983—; tchr. Bus. Sch., Luiss U., Rome, 1984-86. Contbr. articles to profl. jours. Mem. Italian Assn. Battery Mfrs. (pres. 1974-83), Battery Council Internat. (bd. dirs. 1979-83), European Assn. Battery Mfrs. (v.p. 1978-83). Home: Via Vallazze 63, 20131 Milan Italy Office: Link Mgmt Cons, Via S Michele Del Carso 4, Milan Italy

TARASZKIEWICZ, WALDEMAR, physician; b. Wilno, Poland, July 6, 1936; came to U.S., 1979; s. Michal Taraszkiewicz and Nina (Lutomska) Dylla; m. Teresa Barbara Szwarc, Oct. 15, 1966. MD, Med. Acad., Gdansk, Poland, 1961, internal medicine specialty, 1967, internal medicine specialty II, 1972; family practice specialty, Am. Bd. Family Practice, 1985. Family physician Out Patient Clinic, Sopot, Poland, 1962-64; resident doctor U. Hosp., Gdansk, 1965-71; allergist Clinic of Allergy, Gdansk, 1965-75; physician Cardiology Dept., Gdansk, 1971-75, Hôpital Civil, Telagh, Algeria, 1975-79; surg. asst. Hinsdale (Ill.) Hosp., 1979-82; resident physician St. Mary of Nazareth Hosp., Chgo., 1982-85, emergency room physician, 1984-85; family practice medicine Brookfield, Ill., 1985-88, Westmont, Ill., 1988—; sr. asst. dept. cardiology Univ. Hosp., Gdansk, 1971-75; mem. adminstrv. com., pres. med. staff Hôpital Civil, Telagh, 1976-79. Contbr. articles to profl. jours. Recipient Bronze medal Polski Zwiazek Wedkarski, 1970, cert. 3d place, 1971. Fellow Am. Acad. Family Practice; mem. AMA (continuing edn. award), Ill. Med. Soc., Chgo. Med. Soc. (practice mgmt. com.), World Med. Assn., Am. Acad. Allergy and Immunology, Am. Coll. Allergy and Immunology, Polish Med. Alliance, N.Y. Acad. Scis. Office: 333 W 63d St Westmont IL 60559

TARAZ, AFSHIN, accountant; b. Tehran, Iran, Dec. 26, 1948; arrived in Eng., 1960; s. Manouchehr and Parvin (Derakhshan) T.; 1 child, Sarah. BA, U. Sussex, 1972; MSc, London Sch. Econs., 1973. Chartered acct., Eng. Acct. Peat Marwick Mitchell & Co., London, 1973-78, Arthur Andersen & Co., London, 1978-87, Ketlon (U.K.) Ltd., 1987—. Mem. Brit. Computer Soc. Conservative. Bahai. Home: 47 Dean Court Rd, Rottingdean Brighton, East Sussex BN2 7DL, England

TARG, WILLIAM, editor, writer; b. Chgo., Mar. 4, 1907; s. Max and Esther (Solomon) Torgownik; m. Anne Jesselson, May 1, 1933 (dec. Feb. 1965); 1 son, Russell; m. Roslyn Siegel, July 30, 1965. Student pub. schs. Editor-in-chief, v.p. World Pub. Co., 1942-64; editor-in-chief G.P. Putnam's Sons, N.Y.C., 1965-78; sr. editor G.P. Putnam's Sons, 1974—; also v.p.; pres. Targ Editions. Author: Indecent Pleasures, 1975, Secret Lives, 1982, Abacus Now, 1984; author, editor: Modern English First Editions, 1932, Lafcadio Hearn, 1936, 10,000 Rare Books and Their Prices, 1936, Adventures in Good Reading, 1940, Rare American Books, 1941, Poems of a Chinese Student, 1941, The American West, 1946, Carrousel For Bibliophiles, 1947, The Making of the Bruce Rogers Bible, 1949, A Reader for Writers, 1951, Bouillabaisse For Bibliophiles, 1955, Bibliophile in the Nursery, 1957; editor: Bookman's Progress (L.C. Powell), 1968, The Delacruze Stratagem. Clubs: Grolier, Rowfant. Home: 101 W 12th St New York NY 10011

TARGETTI, FERDINANDO, economics educator; b. Como, Italy, July 1, 1945; s. Lodovico and Anita (Cattania) T.; m. Boguslawa Kinda, Nov. 15, 1982. Laurea, U. Bocconi, Milan, Italy, 1970; cert. Cambridge U., 1975. Mem. faculty U. Bocconi, Milan, 1970—, U. Pavia, Italy, 1973; mem. faculty U. Trento, Italy, 1973—, assoc. prof. polit. economy, 1983—, prof. econ. policy, 1987—; vice-chmn. bd. Credito Lombardo Milano, 1979—; dir. Banca Agricola Milanese. Author: (in Italian) Value and Accumulation, 1978, Theory and Policy of Nicholas Kalbor, 1988; also numerous articles. Served to lt. Italian Air Force, 1968-69. Office: Via Vigevano 32, I-20144 Milan Italy

TARIGO, ENRIQUE E., vice president of Uruguay, lawyer, educator; b. Sept. 15, 1927; m. Susana Morador; children—Enrique, Miguel Angel, Alejandro, Gabriela, Juan Felipe. Grad., Faculty of Law and Social Scis., U. Montevideo, 1953. Mem., adminstrv. bd. U. de la Republica, until 1961; pres. dept. counseling services, 1962-64, mem. faculty of law, until 1978; journalist and polit. commentator after 1974; gen. mgr. daily newspaper El Dia, until 1978; columnist jour. Noticias, 1978-80; founder, writer, weekly jour. Opinar, 1980-85; v.p. Uruguay, 1985—. Author: El Juicio En Rebeldia, El Proceso Sucesorio, Estudios Sobre El Sodigo De Organizacion De Los Tribunales, Cinco Estudios Sobre La Prueba Testimonial, Curso De Derecho Procesal, numerous others. Mem. Coll. Lawyers Uruguay (bd. dirs.). Office: Office of the Vice Pres, Montevideo Uruguay *

TARIN, SHAUKAT FAYAZ, bank executive; b. Multan, Pakistan, Oct. 1, 1953; arrived in United Arab Emirates, 1985.; s. Jamshaid Ahmed and Mumtaz Tarin; m. Razalia Hussain, Feb. 22, 1980; children: Salman, Sara, Erum. MBA, U. Punjab (Pakistan), 1975. Sr. head country ops. support Citibank N.Am., Dubai, United Arab Emirates, 1985-87; gen. mgr. Citibank N.Am., Dubai, 1987—; mng. dir. Citicorp Gulf Fin., Ltd., 1987—. Mem. Am. Bus. Council of Dubai. Lodge: Rotaract (v.p. 1978-79). Home and Office: Citibank N Am, PO Box 749, Dubai United Arab Emirates

TARKOFF, MICHAEL HARRIS, lawyer; b. Phila., Oct. 3, 1946. B.A., U. Miami, 1968, J.D., 1971. Bar: Fla. 1973, U.S. Supreme Ct. 1976, N.Y. 1983, U.S. Tax Ct. 1984. Asst. pub. defender Miami Pub. Defender's Office, Fla., 1973-77; guest lectr. U. Miami Sch. Law, 1977; ptnr. Flynn, Rubio & Tarkoff, Miami, 1977-83; ptnr. Flynn and Tarkoff, Miami, 1983—; mem. substantial asst. in trafficking cases com. criminal law sect. Fla. Bar. Mem. Dade County Democratic Exec. Com., 1970-72, Tiger Bay; pres. Young Dems. of Dade County, Fla., 1971, trustee, 1973-75; legal counsel Dade County Dem. Com., 1978. Sponsor, South Fla. council Boy Scouts Am. Mem. ABA, Fla. Bar Assn. (narcotics practice, legis. com. criminal law sect.), Nat. Assn. Criminal Def. Lawyers (membership com., NORML legal com.), Fla. Criminal Def. Lawyers Assn. Office: 1414 Coral Way Miami FL 33145

TARM, FELIX, internist, medical researcher; b. Tallinn, Estonia, May 22, 1939; came to U.S., 1950, naturalized, 1960; s. Feliks and Eugenia (Semyonov) T.; m. Kay A. Mallicoat, Sept. 2, 1962; children: Susan A., Michael V., Viktor F. M.D., U. Iowa, 1965. Diplomate Am. Bd. Internal Medicine. Intern Med. Coll. Va., Richmond, 1966; fellow Mayo Clinic, Rochester, Minn., 1970-73, assoc. cons., 1973; physician, researcher, cons. Internal Medicine Specialists PA, Hutchinson, Kans., 1973—; lectr. Hutchinson Hosp. Corp., 1973—. Mem. editorial bd. jour. Postgrad. Medicine, 1979. Contbr. articles to profl. jours. Served to maj. U.S. Army, 1967-70. Recipient Outstanding Achievement in Internal Medicine award Mayo Found., 1973; FDA grantee; Mem. Mayo Clinic Assn., AMA (Physician's Recognition award, 1986), Am. Soc. Internal Medicine. Libertarian. Avocations: writing poetry; racquetball. Home: 43 Linksland Hutchinson KS 67502 Office: Internal Medicine Specialists PA 2020 N Waldron Hutchinson KS 67502

TARNOFF, JEROME, lawyer; b. Bklyn., June 22, 1931; s. Meyer and Anne (Soshnick) T.; children: Marcy Jane, Margery Lynne. AB, Syracuse U., 1952; JD, Columbia U., 1957. Bar: N.Y. 1957, Pa. 1983, U.S. Dist. Ct. (so. and ea. dists.) N.Y. 1960, U.S. Ct. Appeals (2d cir.) 1961. Ptnr., Sheldon and Tarnoff, N.Y.C., 1957-78, Feldesman, D'Atri, Tarnoff & Lubitz, N.Y.C., 1978, Baskin and Sears, P.C., N.Y.C., 1979-84, Baskin & Steingut P.C., 1984-85, Berger & Steingut, 1986—. Contbr. article to legal jour. Chmn. policy com. N.Y. Democratic Party, 1975-78, vice chmn. N.Y. County, 1978—, mem. nat. com., 1980—; mem. Community Planning Bd. #8, 1966-75; trustee Grand St. Settlement, Assoc. Y's of N.Y. Served with U.S. Army, 1952-54. Recipient Disting. Service award NAACP, 1975, cert. Achievement El Diario-La Prensa, 1977. Mem. ABA, Pa. State Bar, N.Y. State Bar Assn., Assn. Bar City N.Y., N.Y. County Lawyers, Am. Arbitration Assn. (nat. panel arbitrators), Phi Alpha Delta. Jewish. Clubs: Hollywood Golf (Deal, N.J.), Audubon. Lodge: Masons. Home: 1735 York Ave New York NY 10128 Office: 600 Madison Ave New York NY 10022

TARPLEY, JAMES DOUGLAS, journalism educator, magazine editor; b. Los Angeles, May 2, 1946; s. Clement Henry and Grace Lorraine (Everson) T.; m. Patricia Jean McIntosh, June 18, 1966; children: Tamara Jean, James David, Jonathan Eric. BS in Edn., SW Mo. U., 1968, MA in English, 1972; MA in Mass Communications, Cen. Mo. U., 1976; PhD in Journalism, So. Ill. U., 1983. Cert. tchr., Mo. Tchr. Eldon (Mo.) Pub. Schs., 1968-75; prof. journalism Evangel Coll., Springfield, Mo., 1976-87, Christian Broadcasting Network U., Virgina Beach, 1987—; guest lectr. Cen. Mo. U., SW Mo. U., So. Ill. U., U. Ohio summer journalism workshops, 1976—. Youth page editor Eldon Advertiser, 1972-76, mng. editor High Adventure, 1983-87, Criminal Justice Management, 1978-81, editor Ranger News, 1979-81, design and layout editor Vision Magazine, 1984-87; free-lance writer, contbr. biographical entries to profl. publ.; free-lance photographer; graphic artist, copywriter Disco-Fair advt. dept., 1964-68. Exec. com. Eldon PTA, 1971-74; youth dir. Eldon Assembly of God, 1968-75; Sunday sch. supt. Cen. Assembly of God, Springfield, Mo., 1978-82; mem. Sch. Effectiveness Evaluation Team Springfield Pub. Schs., 1985-86, 86-87. Recipient Mo. Journalism Tchr. Yr. award, 1976, Cert. of Merit Columbia U., 1984, Gold Medal of Merit Columbia U. Scholastic Press Assn., 1984; named Outstanding Grad., Dept. Mass Communication Cen. Mo. U. 1976; fellow U. Pa. and Freedom Found. project on press freedom, 1984, Nat. Newspaper Fund Fellow Dow Jones and U. Mo., 1975. Mem. Coll. Media Advisers (bd. dirs., chmn. various coms., pres. citation 1981, 84, 85), Soc. Coll. Journalists (exec. dir. 1983—, pres. citation 1981, 85), Assn. Edn. in Journalism and Mass Communication, Nat. Conf. Editorial Writers (com. scholarly research 1985—), Soc. Newspaper Design (edn. com. 1986-88), Broadcast Edn. Assn. (intern. com. 1984), Assn. Journalism Historians, Inst. Cert. Photographers, Mo. Tchrs. Assn., Evang. Press Assn., Pi Delta Kappa. Republican. Lodge: Kiwanis.

TARR, CHARLES EDWIN, physicist, educator; b. Johnstown, Pa., Jan. 14, 1940; s. Charles Larned and Mary Katherine (Wright) T.; m. Bex Suzanne Harrell, Sept. 4, 1964 (div. Feb. 1977); m. Gudrun Kiefer, Nov. 18, 1977. B.S. in Physics (Morehead scholar 1957-61), U. N.C., Chapel Hill, 1961, Ph.D., 1966. Research assoc. U. N.C., Chapel Hill, 1966, U. Pitts., 1966-68; mem. faculty U. Maine, Orono, 1968—; assoc. prof. physics U. Maine, 1973-78, prof., 1978—, chmn. dept., 1977-79, assoc. dean Coll. Arts and Scis., 1979-81, acting dean Grad. Sch., 1981-87, acting v.p. research, 1984-87, dean Grad. Sch., 1987—; gast docent U. Groningen, Netherlands, 1975-76; cons. in field. Contbr. articles to profl. jours. NASA grantee, 1970-72; NSF grantee, 1972—. Mem. Am. Phys. Soc., Assn. Computing Machinery, IEEE, Sigma Xi. Quaker. Home: 519 College Ave Orono ME 04473 Office: Univ Maine Grad Sch Orono ME 04469

TARR, KENNETH JAY, investment company executive; b. N.Y.C., Mar. 1, 1945; s. Julius and Alice (Tamres) T.; 1 child, Alexandra Jennifer. BA, U. Pa., 1967; MBA, Columbia U., 1971. With Chem. Bank, N.Y.C., 1971-73; asst. v.p. Standard and Poors/Inter Capital, N.Y.C., 1972-74; founder, mgr. S&P/Market Insights, N.Y.C., 1974-75; v.p. Kuhn Loeb and Co., N.Y.C., 1975-77; asst. v.p. Bessemer Trust Co., N.Y.C., 1977-80, v.p., 1980-82, sr. v.p., 1982—, dir. research, 1984. Mem. N.Y. Soc. Security Analysts. Clubs: N.Y. Yacht, Princeton (N.Y.C.). Office: Bessemer Trust Co 630 Fifth Ave New York NY 10111

TARRANT, JOHN EDWARD, lawyer; b. Dyersburg, Tenn., Nov. 25, 1898; s. John Morgan and Penelope A. (Fumbanks) T.; m. Mary Park Kaye, May 26, 1928; children: Mary Kaye Tarrant Durham, Eleanor Tarrant Newman, Penelope Tarrant Morton. B.S., U. Va., 1921; LL.B., Harvard U., 1923. Bar: Ky. 1923. Assoc. firm Simpson, Thacher & Bartlett, N.Y.C., 1922, Bruce, Bullitt & Gordon, Louisville, 1923-26; partner firm Bruce & Bullitt, 1926-40, Ogden, Tarrant, Galphin & Street, 1940-48, Bullitt, Dawson & Tarrant, 1948-70, Tarrant, Combs & Bullitt (and predecessor), 1970-80; ptnr. Wyatt, Tarrant & Combs, 1980-85, of counsel, 1985—; gen. counsel Fed. Land Bank, Fed. Intermediate Credit Bank, Louisville, 1930; spl. judge Ky. Ct. Appeals, 1948; chmn. bd. dirs. Louisville Investment Co., 1958-86; dir. Churchill Downs Inc., 1969-85, dir. emeritus, 1985—; dir. Citizens Fidelity Bank & Trust Co., 1957-69, adviser, 1969-71. Mem. Louisville Bridge Commn., 1954-57; mem. personnel bd. Ky. State Police, 1957-60; bd. dirs. Louisville Central Area Assn., 1966-68, NKC, Inc. (formerly Norton-Children's Hosps., Inc.), 1969-82; trustee YWCA, 1939-63, U. Louisville, 1966-70, Norton Meml. Infirmary, 1939-69. Served O.T.C., 1918, Camp Fortress Monroe, Va. Fellow Am. Bar Found. (life); mem. N.C. Soc. Cin., Ky. Soc. Colonial Wars, SAR, Am., Ky., Louisville bar assns., Am. Law Inst. (life), Jud. Conf. Sixth Circuit U.S. (life), Am. Judicature Soc. (life), Phi Beta Kappa, Kappa Sigma. Republican. Episcopalian. Clubs: Pendennis, Filson, Louisville Country, Jefferson (Louisville); Metropolitan (Washington). Home: Beech Grove 3740 Upper River Rd Louisville KY 40207 Office: 2600 Citizens Plaza Louisville KY 40202

TARRANTS, WILLIAM EUGENE, government official; b. Liberty, Mo., Dec. 9, 1927; s. Joseph Eugene and Mildred Jane (Wright) T.; m. Mary Jo Edman, Jan. 19, 1952 (div. 1981); children: James Timothy, Jennifer Lynn. B.Indsl. Engring., Ohio State U., 1951; M.S. in Indsl. Engring, 1959; Ph.D., N.Y. U., 1963. Registered profl. engr., Calif., Ohio, N.Mex. Instr. indsl. engring. Ohio State U., Columbus, 1958-59; asst. prof., research asso. N.Y. U., 1959-64; chief accident research div. Bur. Labor Stats., Dept. Labor, Washington, 1964-67; dir. manpower devel. div. Nat. Hwy. Traffic Safety Adminstrn., Dept. Transp., 1967-80; chief scientist Office of Program and Demonstration Evaluation, 1980-84; program analyst Office of Occupant Protection, 1984-87, program analyst evaluation staff, 1987—; also chmn. sci. and tech. info. advisory bd.; instr. Johns Hopkins U., 1984—; mem. planning and adminstrn. transp. safety Transp. Research Bd., Nat. Acad. Scis.; Cons. safety program eval. Indsl. Commn. Ohio, 1959. Contbr.: chpt.

to Selected Readings in Safety, 1973, Readings in Industrial Accident Prevention, 1980; Author: chpt. to A Selected Bibliography of Reference Materials in Safety Engineering and Related Fields, 1967, Dictionary of Terms Used in the Safety Profession, 1971, Measurement of Safety Performance, 1980, Handbook of Occupational Safety and Health, 1987, also manuals and articles in field; mem. editorial bd.: Jour. Safety Research, Accident Analysis and Prevention, An Internat. Jour.; editor-in-chief: Traffic Safety Evaluation Research Rev. Served to capt. USAF, 1951-57. Recipient Founder's Day award N.Y. U., 1963; 1st place Nat. Tech. Paper awards, 1961, 63, 67; cert. for outstanding performance Nat. Hwy. Traffic Safety Adminstrn., 1973, 86. Fellow Am. Soc. Safety Engrs. (dir., v.p. research and tech. devel., pres. 1977-78, chmn. acad. accreditation council 1978—, mem. fellow rev. bd. 1980—); mem. Am. Soc. Safety Research (trustee), Am. Inst. Indsl. Engrs., Human Factors Soc., System Safety Soc., Evaluation Research Soc., Vets. of Safety, Am. Nat. Standards Inst. (standards com.), Soc. for Risk Analysis, AAAS, Nat. Safety Council (chmn. research projects com. 1973-78, mem. exec. com. indsl. conf. 1977-78), Alpha Pi Mu, Kappa Delta Pi. Mem. Evangelical Covent Ch. (trustee, ch. chmn. 1976-80, 84-88). Home: 12134 Long Ridge Ln Bowie MD 20715 Office: 400 7th St SW Washington DC 20590

TARSON, HERBERT HARVEY, university administrator; b. N.Y.C., Aug. 28, 1910; s. Harry and Elizabeth (Miller) T.; m. Lynne Barnett, June 27, 1941; 1 son, Stephen. Grad., Army Command Gen. Staff Coll., 1942, Armed Forces Staff Coll., 1951, Adavnced Mgmt. Sch. Sr. Air Force Comdrs., George Washington U., 1954; B.A., U. Calif., Los Angeles, 1949; Ph.D., U.S. Internat. U., 1972. Entered U.S. Army as pvt., 1933, advanced through grades to maj., 1942; transfered to U.S. Air Force, 1947, advanced through grades to lt. col., 1949; adj. exec. officer Ft. Snelling, Minn., 1940-42; asst. adj. gen. 91st Inf. Div., 1942-43; chief of personnel, advance sec. Comd. Zone, ETO, 1944-45; dir. personnel services 8th Air Force, 1946-47; dep. dir. dept. info. and edn. Armed Forces Info. Sch., 1949-51; dir. personnel services Japan Air Def. Force, 1951-53, Continental Air Command, 1953-62; dir. adminstrv. services, spl. asst. to Comdr. 6th Air Force Res. Region, 1962-64; ret. 1964; asst. to chancellor L.I. U., Brookville, 1964-69; dean admissions Tex. State Tech. Inst., San Diego Indsl. Center, 1970-72; v.p. acad. affairs Nat. U., San Diego, 1972-75; sr. v.p. Nat. U., 1975—. Decorated Bronze Star medal with oak leaf cluster, Air Force Commendation medal with 2 oak leaf clusters. Fellow Bio-Med Research Inst.; mem. Doctoral Soc. U.S. Internat. U., Am. Soc. Tng., Devel., World Affairs Council, Air Force Assn., Navy League U.S., Pres.'s Assos. of Nat. U. (presidential life). Home: 4611 Denwood Rd La Mesa CA 92041 Office: Nat U 4141 Camino del Rio S San Diego CA 92108

TARTT, BLAKE, lawyer; b. Houston, Mar. 16, 1929; s. Herbert Blake and Bernice (Schwalm) T.; m. Barbara Jean Moore, Jan. 30, 1960; children: Blake III, Courtnay M. B.B.A., So. Methodist U., 1949, J.D. cum laude, 1959. Bar: Tex. 1959. Assoc. Fulbright & Jaworski, Houston, 1959-70; ptnr. Fulbright & Jaworski, 1970—; dir. Hycel, Inc., 1972-78. Served to 1st. lt. USAF, 1951-55, Korea. Decorated Air medal. Fellow Am. Bar Found. (chmn. fellows 1987), Tex. Bar Found. (chmn. bd. 1974-75, chmn. fellows 1978-79), Am. Coll. Trial Lawyers, Am. Bd. Trial Advocates (advocate); mem. ABA (ho. dels. 1976-82), Fed. Bar Assn., Internat. Assn. Ins. Counsel, Am. Judicature Soc. (bd. dirs. 1984—), So. Conf. Bar Pres. (pres. 1984), State Bar Tex. (dir. 1972-75, exec. com. 1975-76, pres. 1983-84), Houston Bar Assn., Am. Law Inst., Delta Theta Phi, Alpha Tau Omega. Episcopalian. Clubs: Coronado, Forest, Houston, Houstonian. Home: 3690 Inwood Dr Houston TX 77019 Office: Fulbright & Jaworski 1301 McKinney St Houston TX 77010

TARVER, MAE-GOODWIN, consulting company executive; b. Selma, Ala., Aug. 9, 1916; d. Hartwell Hill and R. Louise (Wilkins) T.; B.S. in Chemistry, U. Ala., 1939, M.S., 1940. Project supr. container shelflife Continental Can Co., Inc., Chgo., 1941-48, project engr. stats., 1948-54, quality control cons., research statistician, 1954-77; pres., prin. cons. Quest Assocs., Park Forest, Ill., 1978—; adj. assoc. prof. biology dept. Ill. Inst. Tech., Chgo., 1957-81. Bd. dirs. Ash Street Coop., Park Forest, Ill., 1976-85. Fellow Am. Soc. Quality Control (Joe Lisy award 1961, Edward J. Oakley award 1975, E.L. Grant award 1983); mem. Inst. Food Technologists, Soc. Women Engrs., Am. Statis. Assn., Park Forest C. of C. (pres. 1986), Sigma Xi. Home: 130 26th St Park Forest IL 60466

TASH, DUANE GEORGE, computer company administrator, computer systems consultant; b. Wilmington, Del., Feb. 2, 1944; s. Clarence Andrew and Margaret Louise (Forman) T. BS, U. Md., 1972; postgrad. East Coast Aero Tech. Sch., Lincoln, Mass., 1973, GTE Sylvania, Waltham, Mass., 1974. Research asst. U. Md., College Park, 1964-69; exhibit specialist Rogay, Inc., Rockville, Md., 1969-70; psychiat. intern Washington San. and Hosp., Takoma Park, Md., 1970-72; dir. Louis Joseph Auction Gallery, Inc., Boston, 1972-78; field service rep. Gen. Dynamics, Waltham, Mass., 1974-75; dist. service mgr. Gen. Dyanmics, Waltham, 1975-76; dir. Louis Joseph Auction Gallery, Inc., Boston, 1976; sr. customer service engr. Raytheon Data Systems, Norwood, Mass., 1976-80; product mgr. field engring. Data Gen. Corp., Westboro, Mass., 1980-86, mgr. field engring. systems maintainability engring. dept., 1986, mgr. Compatible Products Engring. Group, 1987-88; engring. specialist, cons. Seinie Tech., 1988—. Recipient Outstanding Aviation Performance award FAA, New Eng. region, Norwood, Mass., 1973. Home: 289 S Main St Hopedale MA 01747 Office: Data Gen Corp 50 Maple St Milford MA 01757

TASHIRO, HIDEO, dean dental educator, oral and maxillofacial surgeon; b. Mito, Japan, Apr. 15, 1930; s. Kiyotomo and Tomi (Kukita) T.; m. Kazuko Yamaoka, May 17, 1958; children—Eiko, Ikuko, Hideaki. B. Medicine, Kyushu U. (Japan), 1955; D. Med. Sci. (hon.), Kyushu U., 1962. Intern Kyushu U., Fukuoka, Japan, 1955-56, asst., 1956-61, assoc. prof., 1961-74, prof. oral surgery, 1974—, councillor, 1979-83, dean Univ. Dental Faculty, 1985—; dir. Univ. Dental Hosp., Fukuoka, 1979-81. Mem. Japanese Cleft Palate Assn. (councillor 1976—), Japan Soc. Head and Neck Tumors (councillor 1977—), Japanese Stomatological Soc. (councillor 1979-86d, Internat. Assn. Dental Research, European Assn. Maxillo-facial Surgery. Buddhist. Home: Higashiku Kasumigaoka 4-9-27, Fukuoka 813, Japan Office: Kyushu U, Higashiku Maidashi 3-1-1, Fukuoka 812, Japan

TASLEEM, RAFIQ AHMED, marketing executive; b. Multan, Punjab, Pakistan, Aug. 9, 1951; s. Manzoor Ahmed and Ghulam (Jannat) Khokhar; m. Rehanan Parveen, Mar. 15, 1984; 2 children. BS, Govt. Coll., Multan, 1971. Med. rep. Nordex Internat. Corp., Lahore, Pakistan, 1972-75; mgr. territory Abbott Labs Ltd., Karachi, Pakistan, 1975-77; med. sales officer Hoechst Ltd., Karachi, 1977-78; sales exec. Am. Life Ins. Co., Jeddah, Saudi Arabia, 1979-81; sales exec. Saudi Tech. Services and Trading, Riyadh, 1981-83, asst. br. mgr., 1983-85, br. mgr., 1985—; mgr. mktg. and sales Nat. Clay Bricks Industries, Riyadh, 1986, transport cons., 1986. Office: Saudi Tech Services and Trading, PO Box 20445, Riyadh 11455, Saudi Arabia

TASSÉ, YVON ROMA, engineer; b. St. Gabriel de Brandon, Que., Can., Oct. 1, 1910; s. Victor L. and Amilda (Laurendeau) T.; m. Pauline Boyer, Nov. 11, 1935; children: Suzanne, Michel, Ghislaine, Lucille, Denise, Yves, Jacques. BA cum laude, Coll. Ste.-Marie, Montreal, Que., 1930; BS in Applied Civil Engring. with great distinction, Ecole Polytech., Montreal, Que., 1935. Apparatus engr. Can. and Gen. Electric Co. Ltd., Montreal, 1937, Quebec, 1938-48; founder, ptnr. Tasse, Sarault & Assocs., Elec. and Mech. Cons. Engrs., Quebec, 1948-57; v.p., treas. Gen. Diesel Inc., Quebec, 1952-58; mng. dir. Indsl. and Trade Bur. of Met., Quebec, 1957-58; mem. Ho. Commons, 1958-62; appted. Parliametary sec. to Minister of Pub. Works 1959, ind. generalist, 1962—; bd. dirs. Fertek Inc., Montreal, Logistec Corp., Montreal. Successively dir., 2d v.p., 1st v.p., and pres. Que. Bd. Trade, 1950-54; chmn. bd. dirs. Hôpital de l'Enfant-Jesus, 1974-86; corp. warden Corp. of the Seven Wardens Inc., Soc. des Sept. gardiens inc., Can., 1985—; mem. Nat. Adv. Council on Aging, Can., 1986—. Mem. Assn. Profl. Engrs. Ont., Assn. Cons. Engrs. Can., Am. Inst. Elec. Engrs., Am. Inst. Heating and Air Conditioning, Inst. Mgmt. Consultants Que., Can. C. of C. Commerce (chmn., bd. dirs. 1954-57), Que. Holistic Med. Assn. (allied), Royal 22d Regt. Officers' Mess (hon.), Can. Corps. Commrs. (gov.). Conservative. Roman Catholic. Clubs: Cercle de la Garrison (Quebec). Office: 2052 Du-Bois Joli, Sillery, PQ Canada G1T 1E1

TASSIN, BERNARD LEON, radiologist; b. Garches, France, Nov. 9, 1942; s. Jacques and Christiane (Barberon) T.; m. Catherine Guerineau, Feb. 13, 1971; children: Amelie, Clementine, Gregoire. MD, Faculte Medecine, Paris, 1969, specialist, 1971. Diplomate French Med. Bd. Practice medicine specializing in radiology Rochefort, France, 1975—. Served with French mil. Mem. French Radiology Soc., Radiol. Soc. N.Am. Roman Catholic. Home: Rue de Vieux Pont, 17250 Pont L'Abbe d'Arnoult France Office: Cabinet de Radiologie, 51 Rue Toufaire, 17300 Rochefort France

TASSINARI, SILVIO JOHN, nuclear chemist; b. N.Y.C., June 2, 1922; s. Ceasar and Adrean (Bacchiani) T.; B.S., St. Michael's Coll., 1943, M.S., 1947; Ph.D., Internat. U., Kansas City, Mo., 1949; m. Lorraine I. Murtha, Oct. 18, 1952; children—Patricia Jeanne, Barbara Lynne. Nuclear chemist Brookhaven Nat. Lab., Upton, N.Y., 1951-71, radiation safety officer and health physicist, 1952; nuclear chemist, tech. dir. nuclear medicine VA Hosp., Bklyn., 1971-72; nuclear chemist Sch. Nuclear Med. Tech., VA Hosp., Northport, N.Y., 1972-84; pres., dir. L.I. Labs., Inc.; cons. nuclear medicine, radiation protection, hazardous material mgmt., computers, office automation. Mem. Congl. Adv. Bd. Health, Energy and Edn. Vice pres. Smithtown Central Sch. Dist. Bd. Edn., 1954-67. Served with USN, 1942-45, USNR, 1946-70, as group comdr., 1966-70 (commendation Sec. Navy). Fellow Am Inst Chemists, Am. Soc. Radiologic Technologists; mem. Soc. Nuclear Medicine, Health Physics Soc., N.Y. Acad. Scis., Am. Men and Women in Sci., Am. Inst. Chemists, U.S. Naval Inst., Sigma Xi. Republican. Roman Catholic. Home: 47 Moriches Rd Nissequogue Saint James NY 11780 Office: LI Labs Inc PO Box A Saint James NY 11780

TASSY, ALAIN, ophthalmologist; b. Marseilles, France, Jan. 20, 1941; s. Aime and Francine (Febrier) T.; m. Regine Chabanon-Pouget, Feb. 26, 1972; children: Sylvain, Estelle, Armelle. MD, U. Marseilles, 1966, D.E.A. in Neurophysiology, 1967. Resident U. Hosp., Marseilles, 1962-66, asst., 1966-74; clin. chief Med. U., Marseilles, 1966-74, head dept. ophthalmology, 1978—. Author: Local Ocular Drugs, 1973, 79, 86; contbr. articles to profl. jours. Mem. Trade Union Toulon Hosp. Physicians (treas. 1986—). Mem. Front Nat. Party. Roman Catholic. Office: Hosp Font-Pre, Ave Colonel Picot, 83100 Toulon France

TATAR, MARTIN LOUIS, advertising and public relations executive; b. Chgo., July 20, 1915; s. Max Goodman and Jennie (Kahn) T.; student Cornell U., 1933-35, Sarbonne U., 1945; m. Shirley Clubman, Feb. 7, 1943; children—Howard, Jerome. Profl. baseball player minor and maj. leagues, 1937-39; enlisted in U.S. Army, 1941, commd. 2d lt., 1942, advanced through grades to lt. col., 1968, ret., 1968; tng. officer, 1946-56; tng. officer and bn. comdr., Chgo., 1957-60; bn. and brigade comdr., Chgo., 1960-68; civilian dir. Army schs. U.S. Army, Ft. Sam Houston, Tex., 1968-71, info. officer, 1972-73, dep. chief advt. and info. Midwest recruiting, Skokie, Ill., 1973—; also Jewish lay leader, for U.S. Army; public speaker. Vol., Sr. Adult Activities, Chgo., 1968—; profl. sports ofcl., 1955—; active Holocaust Found., SCORE, Exec. Services Corps, Sos, Build, Better Bus. Bur. Decorated Purple Heart, Bronze Star medal; recipient 4 Chaplains Medal of Honor; Legion of Valour (Israel). Mem. Ret. Officers Assn., State Sports Ofcls., Am. Assn. Ethiopian Jews, North Shore Homeowners Assn., Lyric Opera Guild, Phi Epsilon Pi. Democrat. Jewish. Clubs: Chgo. Press, Zionist Orgn., Masons. Contbr. articles to profl. jours. Home: 4851 Davis St Skokie IL 60077

TATE, FRAN M., small business owner; b. Auburn, Wash., Oct. 5, 1929; dau. Frank Joseph and Theresa Mary (Bingesar) Pfulg; m. Rory Tate, Sept. 30, 1970 (div.); children—Michael C., Joseph M.; m. 2d, Juan Ramon Ramirez, Sept. 6, 1981 (div. May 1986). Student U. Wash. Gen. mgr., Sorensen Heating Co., Auburn, 1952-70; cons. Success Motivation Inst., Bellevue, Wash., 1970-72; field engr., draftsman, J. Dalton and Assocs., Point Barrow, Alaska, 1973-75; pres., owner Inupiat Water Delivery Co., Barrow, Alaska, 1977—; pres., owner Elephant Pot Sewage Haulers, Barrow, 1977—; pres., owner, operator Pepe's North of the Border Restaurant, Barrow, 1978—, pres., owner Tate Enterprises, Inc.; Burger Barn, Barrow, 1984—; disc jockey, Sta. KBRW, Barrow. Mem. Barrow Zoning commn. Recipient Boss of Yr. award Credit Women Internat., 1969; Outstanding Service award Barrow PTA; Alaska's Outstanding Women State Comm. for Status of Women, 1984. Mem. Barrow C. of C. (bd. dirs.), Blues Alley Music Soc., Nat. Geog. Soc., Smithsonian Instn., Jazz Heritage Found., Arctic Slope Scholarship Found., Nat. Assn. Female Execs. Roman Catholic. Club: Las Vegas Jazz.

TATE, JEFFREY, conductor; b. Salisbury, Wiltshire, Eng., Apr. 28, 1943; s. Cyril Henry T. and Ivy (Evans) Naylor. M.A., M.B., Chir., Cambridge U., Eng. Coach, asst. Royal Opera Covent Garden, London, 1970-77; coach, condr. Cologne Opera, W.Ger., 1977-79; condr. Gothenburg Opera, Sweden, 1978-80, Met. Opera, N.Y.C., 1980—; prin. condr. English Chamber Orchestra, 1985—; prin. guest condr. Geneva Opera, 1983. Recipient West-End-Theatre London, 1982. Office: care Royal Opera House, Covent Garden, London WC2E 7QA, England *

TATLIOGLU, GURAN MUSA, trading company executive; b. Susurluk, Turkey, Oct. 12, 1938; s. Mustafa Hilmi and Nuzhet (Bilik) T.; B.A., Istanbul U., 1960; postgrad NYU, 1961; M.B.A., U. of Pa., 1964; m. Lynne Virginia Hughes, Feb. 9, 1974; children: Julide Hikmet, Yasemin Ayse, Timur Guran. Mgmt. cons. Rohm and Haas Co., Phila., 1964, 67-69, distribution coordinator internat. div., 1969-71, mktg. coordinator for Turkey, Istanbul, 1971-76, resident mgr., Istanbul, 1976-82; vice chmn., dir. Akril Chem. Mfg. and Trading Co., Istanbul, 1983—; mng. dir. Julyas Overseas Ltd., Cambridge, Eng., Julyas Internat. Ltd., N.Y.C., Julyas Dis Ticaret A.S., Istanbul. Served with Turkish Army, 1965. Fellow Inst. Dirs.; mem. Cambridge and London Chambers of Commerce and Industry. Office: Julyas House, Carlby Rd Greatford, Stamford Lincs PE9 4PR, England

TATLYEV, SULEYMAN BAYRAM OGLY, Soviet government official. Head Main Adminstrn. for Chem. Industry, Azerbaidzhan Soviet Socialist Republic, 1966-70; candidate mem. Cen. Com. Azerbaidzhan Communist Party, 1971-76, mem., 1976—, mem. bur., 1978—; 1st dep. chair Council Ministers, Azerbaidzhan Soviet Socialist Republic, from 1978; now dep. chmn. Presidium USSR Supreme Soviet, Moscow. Address: USSR Supreme Soviet, Office Dep Chmn Presidium, Moscow USSR *

TATTERSALL, BRUCE, art historian; b. Rosyth, Fife, Scotland, Aug. 26, 1948; s. Robert and Olive Ada (Goble) T.; m. Elaine Williamson, May 25, 1974. MA, Edinburgh U., Scotland, 1970; DLitt, Edinburgh U., 1981; diploma in Museum and Art Gallery studies, Manchester U., Eng., 1972. Curator Wedgwood, Stoke-On-Trent, 1972-76; lectr. history of art North Staffordshire Polytechnic, Stoke-On-Trent, 1976-79; head of history of art Southampton Inst. Higher Edn., 1979—; external examiner Southampton U., Eng., 1980-85; vis. lectr. Gonville & Caius Coll., Cambridge, Eng., 1976. Author: Stubbs and Wedgwood, 1974; John Flaxman, 1979; contbt. articles to profl. jours. Anglican Home: Flat 29, Branksome Cour, Poole, Dorset England Office: Southampton Inst, East Park Terr, Southampton, Hampshire England

TATTERSALL, WILLIAM JAMES, industrial association executive, lawyer; b. Wilkes-Barre, Pa., May 11, 1932; s. James and Harriett (Moreau) T.; m. Joan M. Burns, Aug. 12, 1957; children—William J., James T., Christine M. B.A. in English, Moravian Coll., 1960; J.D., DePaul U., 1967. Bar: Ill. 1967. With Bethlehem Steel Corp., 1956-85, labor atty. indsl. relations dept., Bethlehem, Pa., 1967-73, mgr. state govt. affairs, 1973-79; asst. to mgr. Bethlehem Mines Corp., 1970-73; rep., negotiator 1974 Nat. Bituminous Coal Wage Agreement; dep. sec. gen. Internat. Iron and Steel Inst., Brussels, 1979—; Pres. Am. Club of Brussels, 1984-85, 85-86; counselor Boy Scouts Am., Brussels, 1984-85; lectr. Internat. Sch. Brussels, 1979-86; Mem. ABA, Ill. Bar Assn. Am. Iron and Steel Inst., The Metals Soc., Mid-Atlantic Legal Found., Pa. Soc., Institut Royal Des Relations Internats., Antique Automobile Club of Am. Club: Saucon Valley Country (Bethlehem). Lodge: Rotary. Office: Rue Colonel Bourg 120, B-1140 Brussels Belgium

TATUM, ALLYN CARR, lawyer, state official; b. Portia, Ark., Jan. 27, 1942; s. Algin Carr and Nina Ruth (Turney) T.; B.S. in Bus. Adminstrn., U. Ark., 1967, J.D., 1970; m. Lois Ann Galloway, Apr. 30, 1977; children—Lislie Rochelle, Juliet Kee. Admitted to Ark. bar, 1970; assoc. Highsmith, Harkey & Walmsley, Batesville, 1970-72; partner Highsmith, Tatum, Highsmith, Gregg & Hart, 1972-77; regional atty. Ark. Dept. Social Services, 1973-77; chmn. Ark. Workers Compensation Commn., 1977—; vis. prof. Ark. Coll., 1971-74; trust dept. advisor Citizens Bank, 1971-75; legal cons. White River Planning and Devel. Dist., 1972-77. Area Wide Comprehensive Health Planning Council, 1974-75; dir. Independence Fed. Bank, Independence Corp.; dir. Profl. Counseling Assocs. Inc., 1982-84, pres., 1985-86, also dir.; dir. Pro-Max, Inc.; mem. Atty. Gen.'s Task Force on Missing Children, 1985-87. Pres., East Side PTA, 1974-75; mem. pres. adv. council Ark. Coll., 1974-75; mem. adv. bd. Gateway Vo-Tech Sch., 1977-78; mem. Batesville (Ark.) Planning Commn., 1971-73, Community Sch. Bd., 1972-77; bd. dirs. Ark. Health Systems Found., 1974-75; bd. dirs. Delta-Hills Health Systems Agy., 1976-80, mem. exec. com., 1977; bd. dirs., exec. com. Ark. Health Coordinating Council, 1976-77; bd. dirs. North Central Ark. Mental Health Center, 1972-81, pres., 1974-80; chmn. exec. com. Region VI SW Assn. Mental Health Centers, 1977-80; bd. dirs. Batesville Community Theater, 1972; bd. dirs. Nat. Community Mental Health Inst., 1976-82, exec. com., 1977-78; bd. dirs. Nat. Council Community Mental Health Centers, 1975-82, pres., 1981-82; chmn. Ark. Gov.'s Task Force on Ark. Mental Health, 1986—; mem. adminstrv. bd., pastor parish com. First United Meth. Ch., Jacksonville, Ark. Recipient So. Senator award So. Bapt. Coll., 1974. Mem. So. Assn. Workers Compensation Adminstrs. (exec. com. 1971—, v.p. 1977, pres. 1978-79), ABA, Ark. (chmn. com. on mental disability 1985—), Independence County (pres. 1971-72) bar assns., Ark. Trial Lawyers Assn., Nat. Health Lawyers Assn., Internat. Assn. Indsl. Bds. and Commns. (nominating com. 1978-79, exec. com. 1985—), Assn. Rehab., Bus. and Industry (bd. dirs. 1985—), Scot Booster Club, Ark. Mental Health Assn., Batesville C. of C., Pi Kappa Alpha, Delta Theta Phi. Clubs: Kiwanis, Batesville Country (pres. 1974-75, dir. 1975-76). Home: 2708 Northeastern Ave Jacksonville AR 72076 Office: Ark Workmen's Compensation Commn Office of Chmn Justice Bldg Little Rock AR 72201

TATYREK, ALFRED FRANK, chemical engineer; b. Hillside, N.J., Jan. 23, 1930; s. Frank Peter and Frances (Luxa) T.; BS, Seton Hall U., 1954; postgrad. Rutgers U., 1956-57. Research chemist Bakelite div. Union Carbide, Bloomfield, N.J., 1953-58, U.S. Radium Corp., Morristown, N.J., 1959-62; analytical chemist insp. U.S. Army Chem. Procurement Dist., N.Y., 1962-64; research chemist U.S. Army Picatinny Arsenal, Dover, N.J., 1964-73; chem. engr. U.S. Army Armament Research & Devel. Ctr. Dover, 1973—. First aid instr. ARC, Essex County, N.J., 1969-82; chief first aid Maplewood (N.J.) CD 1971—; patrol dir. Nat. Ski Patrol, Phoenicia, N.Y., 1978-84, sr. patroller So. N.Y. region, 1979—. Mem. Magician's Round Table, Sigma Xi (pres. Picatinny chpt. 1974-75, 79-80, 85-86). Roman Catholic. Clubs: Alpine of Can., Appalachian Mountain, Sierra. Patentee chemiluminescent compounds and processes, crank case oil vacuum purification system for internal combustion engines; contbr. articles on mountaineering expdns. and adventures in the great mountain ranges of N.Am. and S.Am. and Africa to mags.; climbed Mt. Blanc, highest mountain peak in Europe; climbed to a summit of 19,730 on Mt. Kilimanjaro, highest mountain peak in Africa, 1972, also participant numerous mountain expdns. in U.S. and Can., including 3 first ascents in No. Cascades of Wash. (the SE Ridge of Mt. Goode, Aug. 1963, Peak 7732 via the NE Snow Chute, Aug. 1964, the E Ridge of Bear Mt., Aug. 1964); advanced scuba diving cert. Nat. Assn. of Underwater Instrs. Home: 27 Orchard Rd Maplewood NJ 07040 Office: US Army Armament Research Devel and Engring Ctr Dover NJ 07801

TAUB, RONALD H., merchandising executive; b. N.Y.C., July 16, 1929; s. Edward A. and Rose (Stoller) T.; m. Ethel Betty Flecker, June 1, 1952; children: Liba, Marcia, Zisl. BS in Bus. Edn., NYU, 1950; MS in Human Relations, Nat. Coll. Edn., 1982; LHD, Spertus Coll., Chgo., 1982. Chmn. Creative Displays, Inc., Chgo., 1957—. Inventor numerous display devices. Trustee Moriah Congregation, Deerfield, Ill., 1986—. Mem. Merchandising Execs. Club, Promotion Mktg. Assn. Am., Point of Purchase Advt. Assn. (guest speaker 1960—), Chgo. Advt. Club. Jewish. Clubs: Carlton, Internat. (Chgo.); Birchwood (Highland Park, Ill.). Home: 1154 Sheridan Rd Highland Park IL 60035

TAUBE, HENRY, chemistry educator; b. Sask., Can., Nov. 30, 1915; came to U.S., 1937, naturalized, 1942; s. Samuel and Albertina (Tiledetski) T.; m. Mary Alice Wesche, Nov. 27, 1952; children: Linda, Marianna, Heinrich, Karl. B.S., U. Sask., 1935, M.S., 1937, LL.D., 1973; Ph.D., U. Calif., 1940; Ph.D. (hon.), Hebrew U. of Jerusalem, 1979; D.Sc. (hon.), U. Chgo., 1983, Poly. Inst., N.Y., 1984, SUNY, 1985, U. Guelph, 1987; D.Sc. honoris causa, Seton Hall U., 1988. Instr. U. Calif., 1940-41; instr., asst. prof. Cornell U., 1941-46; faculty U. Chgo., 1946-62, prof., 1952-62, chmn. dept. chemistry, 1955-59; prof. chemistry Stanford U., 1962—, Marguerite Blake Wilbur prof., 1976, chmn. dept., 1971-74; Baker lectr. Cornell U., 1965. Recipient Harrison Howe award, 1961; Chandler medal Columbia U., 1964; F.P. Dwyer medal U. N.S.W., Australia, 1973; Nat. medal of Sci., 1976, 77; Allied Chem. award for Excellence in Grad. Teaching and Innovative Sci., 1979; Nobel Prize in Chemistry, 1983; Bailar medal U. Ill., 1983; Robert A. Welch Found. Award in chemistry, 1983; Disting. Achievement award Internat. Precious Metals Inst., 1986; Guggenheim fellow, 1949, 55. Mem. Am. Acad. Arts and Scis., Nat. Acad. Scis. (award in chem. scis. 1983), Am. Chem. Soc. (Kirkwood award New Haven sect. 1965, award for nuclear application in chemistry 1955, Nichols medal N.Y. sect. 1971, Willard Gibbs medal Chgo. sect. 1971, Disting. Service in Advancement Inorganic Chemistry award 1967, T.W. Richards medal NE sect. 1980, Monsanto Co. award in inorganic chemistry 1981, Linus Pauling award Puget Sound sect. 1981, Priestley medal 1985, Oesper award Cin. sect. 1986), Royal Physiographical Soc. of Lund (fgn. mem.), Nat. Acad. Scis., Am. Philos. Soc., Finnish Acad. Sci. and Letters, Royal Danish Acad. Scis. and Letters, Coll. Chemists of Catalonia and Beleares (hon.), Can. Soc. Chemistry (hon.), Hungarian Acad. Scis. (hon. mem.), Phi Beta Kappa, Sigma Xi, Phi Lambda Upsilon (hon.). Office: Stanford Univ Dept of Chemistry Stanford CA 94305

TAUBENFELD, HARRY SAMUEL, lawyer; b. Bklyn., June 27, 1929; s. Marcus Isaac and Anna (Engelhard) T.; m. Florence Spatz, June 17, 1956; children—Anne Gail Weisbrod, Stephen Marshall. B.A., Bklyn. Coll., 1951; J.D., Columbia U., 1954. Bar: N.Y. 1955, U.S. Supreme Ct. 1965, U.S. Dist. Ct. (so. and ea. dists.) N.Y. 1976. Assoc., Benjamin H. Schor, Bklyn., 1955-58; ptnr. Zuckerbrod & Taubenfeld, Cedarhurst, N.Y. and N.Y.C., 1958—; village atty. Village of Cedarhurst, 1977—; legis. chmn. counsel to Nassau County Village Ofcls., 1979-86; mem. legis. com. N.Y. State Conf. Mayors, 1979-87; arbitrator small claims ct. Civil Ct. City N.Y., 1970—; arbitrator Small Claims Dist. Ct. Nassau County, 1980—, Assessment Rev. Bd. Supreme Ct. Nassau County, 1981—; mem. Constitutional Bicentennial Com., 1987. Assoc. chmn. Am. Zionist Fedn., 1985-87; pres. Herut Zionists Am., 1977-79; v.p. Hartman YMHA, 1983-87; del. World Zionist Congress, 1977, 82, 87, mem. gen. Zionist council, 1977-83; bd. govs. Jewish Agy., World Zionist Orgn.; exec. Am. sect. bd. dirs. United Israel Appeal; trustee United Jewish Appeal; hon. vice chmn., bd. dirs. Jewish Nat. Fund, United Israel Appeal, Ams. for a Safe Israel. Served with USAR, 1948-56. Recipient Centennial award Jabotinsky Found., 1981; Betar Youth award World Betar 1982; award Internat. League for Repatriation of Russian Jews; Youth Towns of Israel Leadership award Israel Bonds Leadership; cert. of appreciation City N.Y. Mem. ABA, Nassau County Bar Assn. (mcpl. com. 1987, real property com. 1987), Internat. Assn. Jewish Lawyers and Jurists. Club: B'nai B'rith. Home: 288 Leroy Ave Cedarhurst NY 11516 Office: PO Box 488 575 Chestnut St Cedarhurst NY 11516

TAUCHI, HISASHI, pathologist, gerontologist; b. Gifu, Japan, Oct. 13, 1913; s. Shinichi and Shin (Miwa) T.; M.D., Nagoya Med. Coll., 1937, Ph.D., Dr.Med.Scis., 1944; m. Shinako Tanaka, Oct. 13, 1942; 1 child, Makoto. Asst. prof. pathology Nagoya U., 1943-44, prof., 1958-77, dean Faculty Medicine, 1974-76, prof. emeritus, 1977—; prof. Nagoya Women's Med. Coll., 1944-50, Nagoya City U., 1950-58; pres. Aichi Med. U., Nagakute, 1977-82, 85—, prof. pathology, 1977-83, prof., dir. Inst. Med. Sci. of Aging, 1983—; v.p. bd. dirs. Aichi Ika Daigaku, 1982—. Recipient Chunichi prize, 1970, Baelz prize, 1973; Japan Med. Assn. Med. prize, 1983. Mem. Japanese Pathol. Soc. (hon.; pres. 1974), Japan Geriatrics Soc. (hon.; pres. 1976-77), Japan Lung Cancer Soc. (hon.; pres. 1966-67), Japan Gerontol. Soc. (bd. dirs. 1981—, pres. 1987—), Japan Soc. for Biomed. Gerontology (chmn. gen. meeting 1981, bd. dirs. 1981—), Am. Gerontol. Soc., Japanese Cancer Assn. (councillor). Author: The Morphology of Aging, 1980, 87,

Aging of the Cells, 1981. Mem. editorial bd. Mechanisms of Aging and Devel., 1972-82. Contbr. papers in field. Home: 2-9 Yukimi-cho showa-ku, Nagoya 466, Japan Office: Aichi Med Univ, Yazako Nagakute, Aichi-ken 480-11, Japan

TAUFA'AHAU, HIS MAJESTY TUPOU, IV, King of Tonga; b. July 4, 1918; eldest son Viliami Tungi and Queen Salote Tupou III; ed. Newington Coll., Sydney U.; B.A., LL.B., 1942; m. Princess Mata'ahn, 1947; children: Tupouto'a, Pilolevu, 'Alaivahamama'o, 'Aho'citu. Minister of edn., 1943, minister of health, 1944-49, premier of Tonga, Fgn. Affairs, minister of Agr., 1949-65; king of Tonga, 1965—. Revised Tongan Alphabet, 1949, established teacher's tng. coll., 1944, high sch., 1947, broadcasting sta., 1961, govt. newspaper, 1964. First Chancellor U. South Pacific, 1970-73. Decorated knight Order Brit. Empire, Verdienstkreuz, Fed. Republic of Germany, 1979. Address: The Palace, Nuku'alofa Tonga

TAULANANDA, AJVA, agribusiness and industry executive; b. Trad, Thailand, Aug. 15, 1937; s. Chalao and Sroi T.; m. Yupadee Santirojprapai, Aug. 10, 1970; children: Isra, Achira. BA in Indsl. Engring., Chulalongkorn U., Bangkok, 1959; MS in Indsl. Engring., Iowa State U., 1969; PhD in Indsl. and Systems Engring., Ill. Inst. Tech., 1972. Chief tng. Thailand Mgmt. Devel. and Productivity Ctr., Ministry Industry, Bangkok, 1963-73; exec. dir. Thailand Mgmt. Assn., Bangkok, 1973-78; group v.p. Charoen Pokphand Group Cos., Bangkok, 1978—; chmn. agrl. com. Bd. Trade Thailand, Bangkok, 1987—; dep. minister Ministry Industry, Thailand, 1980. Fulbright scholar, 1967-69. Mem. Am. Soc. Agrl. Cons., Engring. Inst. Thailand (adviser 1986—), Assn. Thai Industry, Thailand Mgmt. Assn., C. of C. and Industry (chmn. working group on food, agr. and forestry), Thai C. of C. Buddhist. Clubs: Royal Bangkok Sports, Polo. Office: Charoen Pokphand Group Cos, 61 Kasemraj Rd Klongtoey, Bangkok 10110, Thailand

TAULI, ANDREW AMBUCAY, physician; b. Besao, Mountain Province, Philippines, Sept. 23, 1945; s. Alejandro Roman and Cirena (Ambucay) T.; m. Annabella Sebastian Tan, Dec. 16, 1976. BS, U. Philippines, 1967, Doctor of Medicine, 1972; DTM&H, Mahidol U., Bangkok, 1981. Intern Philippine Gen. Hosp., Manila, 1971-72; instr., resident physician Univ. Philippines Comprehensive Community Health Program, Laguna, 1972-74, chief resident, 1973-74; staff physician St. Theodore's Hosp., Sagada, Philippines, 1974, hosp. dir., 1975—; chmn. Mountain Province Med. Care Council, 1984-86. Commr. Cordillera Regional Consultative Commn., 1988—. Mem. Mountain Province Med. Soc., Phi Kappa Phi, Phi Kappa Mu. Episcopalian. Office: St Theodore's Hosp, Sagada Mountain Province, 2619, Philippines

TAVEIRA, TOMAS CARDOSO, architect, educator; b. Lisbon, Portugal, Nov. 22, 1938; s. Casimiro and Maria (do Patrocinio) T.; Archtl. degree Lisbon Sch. Fine Arts, 1966, Ph.D., 1974; postgrad. MIT; m. Amarilis de Jesus Cristina, Mar. 27, 1965; children—Silvia, Ricardo. Individual practice architecture, Lisbon, 1963—; faculty Lisbon Sch. Fine Arts, 1970—; owner, operator firm Tomas Taveira-Projects, Urban and Regional Studies, 1972—; prof. Lisbon Sch. Architecture, 1974—; dir. projects and bldgs; TV adviser. Chmn. Commn. Ministry Public Works Housing and Planning for New Urban Law, 1976-78; mem. Govtl. Commn. New Urban and Archtl. Studies, 1976. Served with armed forces, 1961-63. Mem. Internat. Fedn. Housing and Planning, Portuguese Author Soc., Internat. Union Architects, Am. Inst. Planners, Internat. Assn. Art Critics, Nat. Acad. Fine Arts, Portuguese Union Architects, Internat. Urban Planners Assn. Mem. Socialist party. Roman Catholic. Clubs: Tennis Internat., Sport Lisboa e Benfica, Literary. Author: The Discourse of the City, 1974; Martim Moniz Study of Urban Renewal, 1982; contbr. articles to newspapers, jours.; archtl. exhbns. Lisbon, Ports, Madrid, Berlin, Buenos Aires, Los Angeles. Home: Rua D João V n 21-6, 1200 Lisbon Portugal Office: 1st Fl 2 Ave de Republica, 1000 Lisbon Portugal

TAVEIRA, VASCO MANUEL DA COSTA, food company executive; b. Oporto, Portugal, Mar. 26, 1932; s. Manuel Vicente and Guilhermina Emilia (Cathou) T.; m. Elisabeth Lucie Morand, Nov. 16, 1968; children: Joana, Diana. Licence in Econs., Oporto U., 1961. Chartered acct. Clk. Espirito Santo Bank, Oporto, 1961; tchr. comml. sch., Abrantes, Portugal, 1961-62, comml. inst., Oporto, 1962-63; auditor internat. Nestle, Vevey, Switzerland, 1963-68; head acct. control Nestle Japan, Kobe, 1969-74; asst. head fin. and control div. Nestle Portugal, Lisbon, 1974-76, head fin. and control div., 1976—, also bd. dirs. Home: Lote 4-Corriola, 2775 Carcavelos Portugal Office: Nestle, Apartado 1807, 1018 Lisbon Portugal

TAVEL, CHARLES HUBERT GERARD, consultant; b. Basle, Switzerland, Nov. 13, 1918; s. Pierre-Georges-Robert and Genevieve (de Muralt) T.; m. Jacqueline Madeleine Hoch, June 15, 1957; children—Olivier, Alec. Chem. engr., Fed. Sch. Tech., Zurich, 1943, Ph.D., 1946, D.H.L. (hon.), 1984. Head prodn. dept. Firmenich & Co., Geneva, 1946-48; free lance journalist, Jour. de Geneve, 1948-50; dep. gen. dir. Battelle Meml. Inst., Geneva, 1953-66; sci. counselor Swiss Embassies, Washington and Ottawa, Ont., Can., 1967-70; head corporate planning Lonza AG, Basle, 1970-71; cons. in strategy, Geneva, 1973—; dir. Groupement Electronique, Lausanne, 1974—, Granit SA, Lausanne, 1973-83, CEPEC, Lausanne, 1964-67; chmn. OECD Working Group on Indsl. Innovation, Paris, 1971-76; mem. Standortgruppe, related to Swiss Ministry of Fgn. Affairs, 1976—. Author: The Third Industrial Age, 1975, 2d edit., 1980; Le Contact Patron Personnel, 1951; contbr. articles to profl. jours. Mem. central com. Parti Liberal, Geneva, 1951-55; co-founder, treas. Mus. Sci. History, Geneva, 1953. Served to capt., Swiss Army, 1940-73. Mem. Geneva Jr. C. of C. (founder, senator 1955), Swiss C. of C. (commn. sci. and research 1971-73), Classe Industrie and Commerce Soc. des Arts (pres. 1973-74). Home: la Chemin de Surville, CH1213 Petit-Lancy Geneva Switzerland Office: 29 Chemin de la Vendée, CH 1213 Petit Lancy Switzerland

TAVELLA, MICHAEL JOHN, electrical engineer, patent agent; b. Queens, N.Y., Sept. 13, 1952; s. Anthony T. and Berenice (Perrine) T.; m. Ki Sun Yi, Mar. 9, 1978; children: Min Jung, Anne Marie. BEE, Pratt Inst., 1975. Registered agt. U.S. Patent Office, 1979. Trainee engr. Am. Electric Power Co., N.Y.C., 1971-74; engr. Alaska Village Electric Co., Anchorage, 1976-82; utility engr. Alaska Pub. Utility Commn., Anchorage, 1982—; patent agt., Anchorage, 1980—. Patentee. Chmn. bd. Campbell Community Sch. Assn., 1987—; sec. Council Assns. Anchorage Community Schs., 1986-87. Roman Catholic. Home: 6900 Rovena St Anchorage AK 99502 Office: 420 L St Suite 100 Anchorage AK 99501

TAVERNIER, BERTRAND RENÉ MAURICE, film director, writer, producer; b. Lyon, France, Apr. 25, 1941; s. Rene and Genevieve (Dumond) T.; m. Claudine O'Hagan, Feb. 16, 1965; children: Nils, Tiffany. Lettres et Philosophie, Lycee Henri IV, Fénelon, Paris. Film asst., then critic, press agt., writer and film historian, 1960-73, film dir., 1973—. Dir. films including le Baiser de Judas, une Charge explosive, la Chance et l'Amour, l'Horloger de Saint-Paul (Prix Louis Delluc 1973), le Juge et l'Assassin (Cesar award 1976), Coup de torchon, 1981, la Mort en direct (Fgn. Press award 1979), Une semaine de vacances, 1980, Dimanche a la Campagne, The Clockmaker (Prix Louis Delluc), Que la Fete Commence, (Cesar awards), Des Enfants Gates, 1977, Round Midnight, 1986, La Passion Béatrice, 1987; joint screenplay la Trace, 1983. Home: 66 Blvd Malesherbe, Paris 75008 France *

TAY, JANNIE CHAN SIEW LEE, managing director; b. Ipoh, Malaysia, May 7, 1945; arrived in Singapore, 1971; d. Chee Keong and Loh Swee Lan; m. Henry Tay Yun Chwan, Mar. 15, 1969; children: Audrey Tay May Li, Michael Tay Wee Jin, Sabrina Tay May Yi. BSc in Physiology, Monash U., Melbourne, Australia, 1964, MSc in Pharmacology, 1970. Tutor Nat. U. Singapore, 1971-73; mgr. Lee Chay (Colombo Ct.), Singapore, 1974-79; mng. dir. Orchard Watch Co Pte Ltd., Singapore, 1975-79, The Hour Glass Pte Ltd., Singapore, 1979—. Chmn. Bal Masque Charity Ball for Community Chest of Singapore, 1984-88; patron Yuhua Community Service Com., Singapore, 1986; bd. dirs., sponsor Singapore First Film Festival, 1987 and dir. 1987—; chmn. sub-com. sch. mgmt. Canossian Sch. Hearing Impaired, 1985-88. Mem. Singapore Retail Mchts. Assn. (council 1986, sec.), Women Mgrs. Bus. Orgns. Singapore (chmn. 1987-88), Nat. Productivity Bd. (subcom. productivity in commerce sector 1985). Home: 40C Nassim Rd, Singapore 1025, Singapore Office: The Hour Glass Pte Ltd, 268 Orchard Rd, #18-01 Yen-San Bldg, Singapore 0923, Singapore

TAY, JEAN S., physician; b. Manila, Philippines, Sept. 1, 1957; d. Liong Kian and Victoria (So) T.; m. Stephen L. Uyboco, June 8, 1985. BS summa cum laude, U. Philippines, 1977, MD, 1981. Diplomate Philippine Bd. Medicine. Intern Brokenshire Meml. Hosp., Davao City, Philippines, 1981-82; rural health physician Dept. of Health, Davao City, 1982; pediatric intern. Med. Coll. Wis., Milw., 1983-84, Milw. Children's Hosp., 1984-86; neonatal clin. fellow U. Manitoba, Winnipeg, Can., 1986-87; neonatal research fellow U. Manitoba, Winnipeg, 1987—. Contbr. articles to profl. jours. Post doctoral fellow scholar Manitoba Health Research Council, 1987—. Fellow Royal Coll. Physicians and Surgeons Can., Am. Acad. Pediatrics; mem. Manitoba Med. Assn. Home: 402 115 Niakwa Rd, Winnipeg, MB Canada R2M 5A8

TAYA, MAAOUYA OULD SID AHMED, president of Islamic Republic of Mauritania; b. 1943. Minister of def. Mauritania, 1978-79, 81—, minister in charge of Permanent Sec., mil. com. for nat. recovery, 1979-81, army chief of staff, 1980-81, prime minister, 1981-84, pres., 1984—; chmn. mil. com. for Nat. Salvation, 1984—. Office: Office of Pres, Nouakchott Mauritania *

TAYLOR, ALAN FREDERICK, pharmaceutical research corporation executive, physician, researcher; b. Spalding, Lincolnshire, Eng., Nov. 2, 1929; came to U.S., 1975, naturalized 1984; s. Jonathan Frederick and Irene Maud (Major) T.; m. Ann Joaquina Temple-Raston, July 9, 1955; children—Sarah Louise, Katherine Ann, Joanna Clare, Deborah Jane. M.B., Ch.B. with honors in Medicine, St. Andrews U., 1955; D.C.H., Royal Coll. Physicians, Eng., 1957. Resident, Dundee Royal Infirmary and Royal Postgrad. Med. Sch., Hammersmith Hosp., 1955-57; resident in pediatrics and medicine Kingston Hosp., 1958-61; med. devel. dir. Organon Labs., London, 1961-71, mng. dir., 1971-73; mng. dir. Organon Internat., Oss, Holland, 1973-75; v.p. corp. devel. Organon Inc., West Orange, N.J., 1975-81; pres. Elan Pharm., Gainesville, Ga., 1981-84; corp. pres. Elan Corp., Athlone, Ireland, and Gainesville, Ga., 1984-85; ptnr. Devel. Southeast, Inc., 1985—; dir. Chateau Elan, Mulberry, Ga., 1982-85 ; mem. adv. bd. Seed Tech., Atlanta, 1984-86; pres. CytRx Corp., 1986—; mem. adv. bd. Integrated Healthcare Investments, Inc., 1987. Author: Alan Raston, various newspaper columns, med. and research articles in Brit. med. jours. Program chmn. Lanier Orch., Gainesville, 1983-86. Served as lt. Brit. Army, 1947-49, U.K., East Africa. Fellow Royal Soc. Medicine, Royal Hort. Soc.; mem. N.Y. Acad. Sci., Soc. for Study of Fertility, Shock Soc. Anglican. Clubs: Chattahoochee (Gainesville), Rotary. Home: 2421 Island Dr Gainesville GA 30501 Office: SIS PO Box 73 Duluth Atlanta GA 30136

TAYLOR, ALAN JOHN PERCIVALE, historian; b. Birkdale, Lancshire, Eng., Mar. 25, 1906; s. Percy Lees and Constance (Sumner) T.; 6 children; m. Eva Haraszti, 1976. Student Bootham Sch., York, Eng., Oriel Coll., Oxford U. (Eng.). Lectr. in modern history U. Manchester; lectr. in internat. history Oxford U., 1953-63, tutor modern history Magdalen Coll., 1938-63, fellow, 1938-76; Benjamin Meaker vis prof history Bristol U., 1976-78. Author: The Italian Problem in European Diplomacy, 1947-49, 1934; Germany's First Bid for Colonies 1884-85, 1938; The Habsburg Monarchy 1815-18, 1941, 2d edit., 1948; The Course of German History, 1945; From Napoleon to Stalin, 1950; Rumours of Wars, 1952; The Struggle for Mastery in Europe, 1848-1918, 1954; Bismarck, 1955; Englishmen and Others, 1956; The Trouble Makers: Dissent over Foreign Policy, 1792-1939, 1957; The Russian Revolution of 1917 (TV lecture script), 1958; The Origins of the Second World War, 1961; The First World War: an Illustrated History, 1963; Politics in Wartime and Other Essays, 1964; English History, 1914-1945, 1965; From Sarajevo to Potsdam, 1966; Europe: Grandeur and Decline, 1967; War by Timetable, 1969; Beaverbrook, 1972; The Second World War: an illustrated history, 1975; Essays in English History, 1976; The Last of Old Europe, 1976; The War Lords, 1977; The Russian War, 1978; How Wars Begin, 1979; Revolutions and Revolutionaries, 1980; Politicians, Socialism and Historians, 1980; A Personal History (autobiography), 1983, How War Ends, An Old Man's, Diary, 1984; editor: Lloyd George; twelve essays, 1971; Lloyd George, a Diary, 1971; Off the Record; political interviews 1933-43, 1973; My Darling Pussy: the letters of Lloyd George and Frances Stevenson, 1975. Address: 32 Twisden Rd, London NW5 1DN England

TAYLOR, ALLAN RICHARD, banker; b. Prince Albert, Sask., Can., Sept. 14, 1932; s. Norman and Anna Lydia (Norbeck) T.; m. Shirley Irene Ruston, Oct. 5, 1957; children: Rodney Allan, Leslie Ann. LLD (hon), U. Regina, Sask., 1987, Concordia U., Montreal, Can., 1988. With Royal Bank of Can., Toronto, Ont., Can., 1949—, mgr. main br., 1971-74; dep. gen. mgr. internat. div. Royal Bank of Can., Montreal, 1974-77, sr. v.p. internat. div., 1977-78, exec. v.p., 1978-83; pres., chief operating officer, dir. Royal Bank of Can., Toronto, 1983-86, now chmn., chief exec. officer, dir.; dir. Orion Royal Bank Ltd., London, TransCan. Pipelines Ltd., Toronto, Can. Pacific Ltd., Gen. Motors Can. Ltd., Oshawa, Ont., Internat. Monetary Conf., Washington. Mem. adv. com. Sch. Bus. Adminstrn., U. Western Ont., London; bd. dirs. Corp.-Higher Edn. Forum. Anglican. Clubs: Granite, Mississauga Golf & Country, National, Toronto, York (Toronto); Forest & Stream, Mount Royal, Royal Montreal Golf, St. James's (Montreal); Overseas Bankers' (London). Office: The Royal Bank of Can, Royal Bank Plaza, Toronto, ON Canada M5J 2J5

TAYLOR, ARTHUR ROBERT, academic administrator, business executive; b. Elizabeth, N.J., July 6, 1935; s. Arthur Earl and Marion Hilda (Scott) T. B.A. magna cum laude, Brown U., 1957, M.A. in Am. Econ. History, 1961; H.H.D., Bucknell U., 1975; L.H.D., Rensselaer Poly. Inst., 1975, Simmons Coll., 1975; LL.D., Mt. Scenario Coll., 1975. Asst. dir. admissions Brown U., Providence, 1957-61; with First Boston Corp., N.Y.C., 1961-70, asst. v.p., 1964-66, v.p., 1966-70, also dir.; v.p. fin. Internat. Paper Co., N.Y.C., 1970-71, exec. v.p., dir., 1971-72; pres. CBS Inc., N.Y.C., 1972-76; also dir. CBS Inc.; chmn. Arthur Taylor & Co., Inc., 1977—; dean faculty of bus. Fordham U., 1985—; dir. First Boston, Inc., Palm Beach County Utilities Corp., The Forum, Am. Patriots Inc., Pitney Bowes, Eastern Airlines, La. Land & Exploration Co.; Vols. in Tech. Assistance, Washington. Mem. steering com. Am. Friends of Bilderberg; trustee Brown U., Joffrey Ballet. Mem. Council Fgn. Relations, Trilateral Commn., Japan Soc., Phi Beta Kappa. Congregationalist. Clubs: Brook, Century (N.Y.C.); Met. (Washington); California (Los Angeles). Office: Fordham U Lincoln Ctr Campus 113 W 60th St New York NY 10023

TAYLOR, AUBREY ELMO, physiologist, educator; b. El Paso, Tex., June 4, 1933; s. Virgil T. and Mildred (Maher) T.; m. Mary Jane Davis, Apr. 4, 1953; children: Audrey Jane Hildebrand, Lenda Sue Brown, Mary Ann Smith. BA in Math. and Psychology, Tex. Christian U., 1960; PhD in Physiology, U. Miss., 1964; Postdoctoral fellow biophysics lab. Harvard U. Med. Sch., Boston, 1965-67; from asst. prof. to prof. dept. physiology U. Miss. Coll. Medicine, Jackson, 1967-77; prof., chmn. dept. physiology U. South Ala. Coll. Medicine, Mobile, 1977—; mem. pulmonary score com. Nat. Heart, Lung and Blood Inst., 1976; chmn. NIH Com., Manpower Com., 1986, RAP, 1983 . Author 4 books. Contbr. chpts. to books, articles to profl. jours. Assoc. editor Jour. Applied Physiology, 1984—; mem. editorial bd. Circulation Research, Am. Jour. Physiology, Microvascular Research, Microcirculatory and Lymphatic Research; editor Critical Care Medicine, 1987—. Served with U.S. Army, 1953-55. NIH grantee, 1967—; Lederle Faculty award, 1967-70; recipient Merit award, 1988—, Lucian award McGill U., 1988—. Fellow Am. Heart Assn. (circulation and cardiopulmonary council 1987—, chmn. So. regional rev. com. 1977-81, chmn. Energy Info. Adminstrn., CIA Review Com. 1986—, research com. 1987—); mem. Am. Physiol. Soc. (council 1984-87, chmn. membership com. 1985-87, pres. 1988—, Wiggers award 1987), Assoc. of Internat. Assn. of Bookkeepers, Microcirculatory Soc. (council 1977-81, pres. 1981-83, Landis award 1985), AAAS, Lymphology Soc. (recipient First Cecil Drinker award, 1988), N. Am. Soc. Lymphology, N.Y. Acad. Scis., Biophys. Soc., Sigma Xi. Democrat. Presbyterian. Current work: Cardio-pulmonary physiology; fluid balance, edema, microcirculation and capillary exchange of solute and water. Subspecialties: Physiology (medicine); Pul monary medicine, Royal Soc. of Medicine, Fedn. of Am. Socs. for Exptl. Biology (bd. mem. 1982—), NAS (mem. com. for Internat. Union of Psychol. Sci.). Home: 11 Audubon Pl Mobile AL 36606

TAYLOR, BERNARD FRANKLIN, laboratory administrator, microbiologist; b. Charles Town, W.Va., Mar. 21, 1930; s. Beverly Douglas and Harriet Elizabeth (Dotson) T.; m. Sylvia Adora Spriggs, Jan. 28, 1957; children—Bernard Franklin, Michael Lensen. Student Bluefield State Coll., 1951; B.S. in Biology cum laude, Storer Coll., 1952; M.S. in Microbiology and Pub. Health, Mich. State U., 1959, Rider Coll., 1961, Trenton Jr. Coll., 1964-65, Trenton State Coll., 1967; Ph.D. in Microbiology, Rutgers U., 1972; M.A. in Adminstrn. Rider Coll., 1980; cert. Inst. Med. Research, Camden, N.J. 1974, 79, 81. Bacteriologist Bur. Virology, Dept. Health, State of Mich., Lansing, 1954-56, virologist, 1956-59; instr. sci., coach football Elizabeth City (N.C.) State Tchrs. Coll., 1959-60; virologist div. labs. Dept. Health State of N.J., 1960-61, sr. virologist, 1961-62, prin. virologist, 1962-67, chief virologist, 1967-79, dir. pub. health lab. service div. pub. health and environ. labs., 1979—; med. technologist Helene Fuld Hosp., Trenton, 1961-64; co-adj. dept. biology Trenton State Coll., 1972—; co-adj. Mercer County Community Coll., 1981. Contbr. articles to profl. jours. Mem. juvenile cof. com. County of Mercer (N.J.); chmn. United Way campaign N.J. Dept. Health, 1973; asst. scoutmaster troop 31 Boy Scouts Am., Charles Town, 1949; govt. appointments include Nat. Def. Execution Reservist, Resource Mgmt. Officer, Office Def. Resources Fed. Emergency Mgmt. Agy. Recipient Ella P. Stewart Biology award, 1952. Mem. Am. Soc. Microbiologists, Am. Acad. Microbiologists (cert.), Am. Assn. for Lab. Animal Sci., Found. Infectious Disease, Assn. State and Territorial Pub. Health Lab. Dirs., Am. Soc. Pub. Adminstrs., Am. Pub. Health Assn., Nat. Assn. Biology Tchrs., N.Y. Acad. Scis., Sigma Xi, Beta Kappa Chi, Alpha Phi Alpha. Democrat. Lodge: Masons. Home: 438 Walnut Ave Trenton NJ 08609 Office: New Jersey State Dept Health CN 360 Trenton NJ 08625

TAYLOR, CARL LARSEN, lawyer; b. Honolulu, Apr. 9, 1937; s. William Henry and Dorothy (Gray) T.; m. Linda Ann Farrell, Aug. 3, 1963. AB, Harvard U., 1958, LLB, 1961. Bar: U.S. Ct. Appeals (D.C. cir.) 1965, U.S. Supreme Ct. 1969, U.S. Ct. Appeals (9th cir.) 1975, U.S. Ct. Appeals (2d cir., 4th cir.) 1977, U.S. Ct. Appeals (3d cir.) 1981, U.S. Ct. Appeals (7th cir.) 1982, U.S. Ct. Appeals (5th cir.) 1986, U.S. Ct. Appeals (10th cir.) 1987. Assoc. Hogan & Hartson, Washington, 1966-69, ptnr., 1978-80; gen. counsel Retail Clerks Internat. Assn., Washington, 1969-76; assoc. gen. counsel NLRB, Washington, 1976-78; ptnr. Kirkland & Ellis, Washington, 1980-87, Johnson & Swanson, Washington, 1987—. Served to lt. (j.g.) USN, 1961-65. Mem. Barristers. Club: Belle Haven (Alexandria, Va.). Office: Johnson & Swanson 555 13th St NW Suite 660 W Washington DC 20004

TAYLOR, CLAUDE I., airlines executive; b. Salisbury, N.B., Can., May 20, 1925; s. Martin Luther and Essie (Troope) T.; m. Frances Bernice Watters, Nov. 4, 1947; children: Karen, Peter. Student, Robinson Bus. Coll., 1942; R.I.A., McGill U. Extension, 1953; D.C.L. (hon.), U. N.B.; LL.D. (hon.), McMaster U. With Air Can., 1949—, gen. mgr. comml. planning, 1962-64, gen. mgr. marketing services, 1964-70, v.p. strategic devel., 1970-71, v.p. govt. and industry affairs, 1971-73, v.p. pub. affairs, 1973-76, pres., chief exec. officer, 1976-84, chmn. bd., 1984—; chmn. exec. com. and council Gov. Gen.'s Can. Study Conf., 1987; chmn. bd. Internat. Aviation Mgmt. Tng. Inst.; dir. GPA Group LTD. Hon. dir. Aviation Hall of Fame, Can. Nat. Exhbn. Assn.; past pres. Boy Scouts Can.; life gov. Douglas Hosp. Corp.; gov. Montreal Gen. Hosp. Decorated comdr. Order St. John, officer Order Can.; recipient Gordon R. McGregor Meml. Trophy Royal Can. Air Force Assn., 1980, Excellence in Communications Leadership award Internat. Assn. Bus. Communicators, Merit award B'nai Brith Can., McGill Mgmt. Achievement award, Human Relations award Can. Council Christians and Jews, Gold Medal award Adminstrv. Mgmt. Soc., Tony Jannus award, 1988. Fellow Soc. Mgmt. Accts. Can., Inst. Transport; mem. Internat. Air Transport Assn. (mem. exec. com., pres. 1979), Profl. Corp. Indsl. Accts. Que., Order of Can. (officer). Baptist. Clubs: Mt. Stephen (Montreal), Mt. Royal (Montreal), Forest and Stream (Montreal); Rideau (Ottawa). Office: Place Air Can. care Nicole Geoffrion, 500 René Levesque West, Montreal, PQ Canada H2Z 1X5 also: Air Canada Inc, 500 Dorchester 01700-2600, Montreal, PQ Canada H2Z 1X5

TAYLOR, CLYDE DONALD, foreign service officer; b. Armenia, Colombia, Sept. 30, 1937; came to U.S., 1940; s. Clyde Willis and Ruth Jean (Marstaller) T.; m. Virginia Lue Lundberg, Aug. 21, 1959; children: Mark, Courtney. B.A. in Polit. Sci., Wheaton Coll., 1959; M. Intenat. Service, Am. U., 1961; cert. econ. studies, Fgn. Service Inst. Dept. State, Washington, 1971; cert. nat. security, strategy and planning, Nat. War Coll., Washington, 1980. Commd. fgn. service office Dept. State, 1961; vice consul U.S. Embassy, Panama, 1964-66; econ.-comml. officer U.S. Embassy, Canberra, Australia, 1966-68; internat. economist Dept. State, Washington, 1968-71; chief econ.-comml. sect. U.S. Embassy, San Salvador, 1972-75; econ. devl. and fin. officer U.S. Embassy, Tehran, Iran, 1975-79; dep. asst. sec. internat. narcotic matters Dept. State, Washington, 1980; ambassador to Paraguay 1985—; U.S. Embassy Rep. Social Devel. Ctr., Tehran, 1975-78. Chmn. bd. dirs. Community Ch., San Salvador, 1973-74, 77-78; treas. Iran Am. Soc., Tehran, 1977-78. Recipient Meritorius award Bur. Econ. Affairs-Dept. State, 1970; recipient Meritorious award U.S. Embassy, Tehran, 1977, Presdl. Meritorious award, 1985. Mem. Am. Fgn. Service Assn. Presbyterian. Office: US Ambassador to Paraguay care US Dept of State Washington DC 20520 also: US Embassy 1776 Mariscal Lopez Ave Asuncion Paraguay APO Miami FL

TAYLOR, D(ARL) CODER, architect; b. Ft. Wayne, Ind., July 18, 1913; s. Frank A. and Edith (Zook) T.; m. Audrey Helen Larkin, June 5, 1944; children: Barbara Helen Taylor Reddy, Thomas Coder, Julie Marie Taylor Hitchins; m. Harriett Pribble Sinding, July 27, 1985. B.Arch., Carnegie Inst. Tech., 1935; spl. student, U. Wash., 1933. Draftsman Chgo., 1935; partner Zook & Taylor, architects, Chgo., 1939-42, Holsman, Holsman, Klekamp & Taylor, architects, Chgo., 1948-52, Yost & Taylor, architects and engrs., Kenilworth, Ill., 1952-60; chmn. Coder Taylor Assos., Inc., architects-engrs.-planners, Kenilworth, 1960-78; chmn. bd. Coder Taylor Assos., Inc., 1978-81, spl. cons., 1981—; cons. in field, 1935—. Contbr. articles to profl. jours.; prin. works include, Municipal Bldg., St. Charles, Ill., 1940, Prize Home No. 1, 1946 (Chgo. Tribune prize home competition), Sherman Garden Apts. 1951 (Chgo. chpt. AIA honor award), Kincheloe AFB, Mich., 1962 (Best Family Housing Project No. Area), Chanute AFB, Ill., 1959 (Best Family Housing Project Central Area), U.S. Naval Tng. Center, Great Lakes, Ill., 1964 (Merit award FHA), Swimming Pool House, Northfield, Ill., 1967 (Chgo. chpt. AIA-Chgo. Assn. Commerce and Industry distinguished bldg. award), 510 Green Bay Rd. Bldg, Kenilworth, Ill. (AIA-Chgo. Assn. Commerce and Industry award 1967), Roberts Residence, Lake Forest, Ill., 1968 (AIA-Chgo. Assn. Commerce and Industry dist. bldg. award), Glenview Pub. Library, 1970 (Chgo. chpt. AIA-Chgo. Assn. Commerce and Industry distinguished bldg. award), Kroch's & Brentano's stores, Chgo., 1961-77, Des Plaines Pub. Library, 1974 (Des Plaines C. of C. outstanding achievement award), Wilmette (Ill.) Park Dist. Recreation Center, 1974, Wilmette Village Adminstrn. Bldg. 1975, Glenview Central Fire Sta, 1976 (Glenview Appearance Commn. Outstanding Bldg. and Landscape award), Internat. Hdqrs Alpha Phi Frat., Evanston, Ill., 1975, Barrington Area Pub. Library, 1977; represented in spl. exhbns. and permanent collections, Art Inst. Chgo., Chgo. Hist. Soc., Wilmette Hist. Soc., Evanston Hist. Soc., Graham Found. Mem. Glenview (Ill.) Planning Commn., 1962-65; chmn. Glenview Appearance Commn., 1968-72, Picasso Day Com., Chgo., 1967; mem. fine arts com. Ill. Sesquicentennial Commn., 1967-68; exec. com., treas. Fedn. Open Lakefront, 1966-68; mem. tech. studies adv. com. Nat. Acad. Sci.-NRC, 1962—; mem. tech. panel, adv. com. HUD, Nat. Acad. Scis., Nat. Acad. Engring., 1969; nat. panel arbitrators Am. Arbitration Assn., 1952—. Served to lt. comdr. C.E. USNR, 1942-45. Recipient merit award for archtl. accomplishments Carnegie-Mellon U. Alumni Assn., 1982. Fellow AIA (dir. Chgo. chpt. 1965-66, pres. 1967, v.p. Ill. council 1968); mem. Ill. Assn. Professions (dir. 1968), Mich. Soc. Architects, Nat. Assn. Redevel. Ofcls., Tau Sigma Delta (pres. 1934- 35), Sigma Phi Epsilon (pres. 1934-35), Scarab (1934-35). Methodist. Club: North Shore Country (Glenview, Ill.). Home and Office: 727 Redwood Ln Glenview IL 60025

TAYLOR, DELLA MAE, nurse; b. Johnson City, Tenn., Apr. 15, 1932; d. Lee Roy and Honolulu Cornelius (Holly) Brewer; R.N., Meml. Hosp., Johnson City, 1953; student E. Tenn. State U.; diploma newspaper writing Newspaper Inst. Am., 1968; B.S., Steed Coll., 1978; postgrad. Emmanuel Sch. Religion, 1986—; m. John R. Taylor, Jr., Feb. 12, 1955 (dec. Oct., 1986); children: Aliesa Benea, Celeste Taylor. R.N., Tenn. Pediatric polio head nurse Meml. Hosp., Johnson City, 1953-54; staff nurse VA, Mountain Home, Tenn., 1954-55, 1961-64, part-time pvt. duty. 1964-78; staff nurse Meml. Hosp., Clarksville, Tenn., 1955-56; pediatric nurse U.S. Army Hosp.,

Augsburg, Germany, 1957-61; RN for life ins. exams, Jonesboro, Tenn., 1978—; instr. nursing, 1986—; owner Mama Bear's Fudge. Pres., Pageants III, Jonesboro, 1980-82; coordinator Pageants III Nationwide Youth Scholarship Pageant Corp., 1980-82. Chmn. precinct, 15th Dist. Democratic Com., 1977-78; mothers' chmn. Washington County March of Dimes; youth coordinator Washington County Heart Assn.; chmn. Dr. Charles Underwood Scholarship Fund, 1984. Recipient 2d prize for party time sausage pie Litton. Mem. Nurses Christian Fellowship, E. Tenn. State U Alumni Assn., Steed Coll. Alumni Assn., Nat. Assn. Female Execs., Unicoi C. of C., U.S. Pageants Assns., Bus. and Profl. Women's Club. Washington County Farm Bur. Democrat. Baptist. Home: Rt 8 Box 37 Taylor Dr Jonesboro TN 37659

TAYLOR, DOROTHY HARRIS, real estate broker; b. Richmond, Va., Nov. 3, 1931; d. Edgar Alan and Sadie (Wheeler) Harris; m. Gethsemane Jess Taylor (dec. Nov. 1964); children: Marlene J., Eric M., Andre E. Student, L.I. U., 1959, John J. Criminal Coll., 1974, Queen's Coll., 1983, 87, 88—, St. John's U., 1984, 86. Lic. real estate broker. Toll collector Port of N.Y. Authority, N.Y.C., 1967-80, tolls dispatcher, 1967; sales exec. Flushing Tribune, 1979; real estate salesperson Parkfield Realty, Queens Village, N.Y., 1982-83, Arro of Queens, 1983-84; real estate broker Arro of Queens, Queens Village, 1984-85, residential appraiser, N.Y.C., 1986—. Mem. Queens Council on Arts, 1987-88, Nat. Arbor Day Found., North Shore Animal Shelter League; mem. com. for disabled children Queens Coll.; charter mem. Nat. Mus. Women in Arts. Mem. Nat. Assn. Female Execs. (network dir. 1983-84), Am. Assn. Ret. Persons, Nat. Assn. of Unknown Players for Film, TV, and Print Modeling Arts, Inc. (charter), United Christian Evangelistic Assn. Democrat. Clubs: Dorcas Soc. (Bklyn.) (pres. 1957-58), Queens Coll. Women's. Lodges: Order Eastern Star, Heroines of Jericho, Lady of Knights. Avocations: gardening, crocheting, reading, contesting, interior decorating.

TAYLOR, EDWARD STEWART, physician, educator; b. Hecla, S.D., Aug. 20, 1911; s. Robert Stewart and Sylvia Frances (Dewey) T.; m. Ruth Fatherson, June 15, 1940; children: Edward Stewart, Elizabeth Dewey Taylor Bryant, Catherine Wells Taylor Lynn. B.A., U. Iowa, 1933, M.D., 1936. Diplomate Am. Bd. Ob-Gyn (dir. 1962-69). Intern, Hurley Hosp., Flint, Mich., 1936-37; splty. tng. ob-gyn L.I. Coll. Hosp., 1937-41; prof. ob-gyn, chmn. dept. Sch. Medicine, U. Colo., 1947-76, clin. prof., 1976-81, prof., chmn. emeritus, 1981—; cons. ob-gyn Fitzsimons Gen. Hosp.; attending obstetrician and gynecologist St. Joseph's Hosp., Rose Hosp. Med. Center, both Denver; nat. cons. ob-gyn to surg. gen. USAF, 1958-62. Author: Manual of Gynecology, 1952, Essentials of Gynecology, 4th edit.; editor: Beck's Obstetrical Practice, 10th edit.; editor-in-chief for obstetrics: Obstetrical and Gynecol. Survey. Trustee Denver Symphony Orch., 1979-85. Served to lt. col. AUS, 1942-45; surgeon 107th Evacuation Hosp., ETO. Fellow ACS, Am. Coll. Obstetricians and Gynecologists (Disting. Service award 1984); mem. AMA, Am. Gynecol. Soc. (v.p. 1974-75), Am. Assn. Obstetricians and Gynecologists (pres. 1970-71), Central Assn. Obstetricians and Gynecologists, S.W. Obstetrical and Gynecol. Soc., Am. Gynecol. and Obstetrical Soc., Assn. Profs. Ob-Gyn (pres. 1974-75), Western Surg. Soc., Finnish Gynecol. Soc. (hon.), Alpha Omega Alpha. Congregationalist. Club: Univ. (Denver). Home: 80 S Dexter St Denver CO 80222 Office: 4545 E 9th Ave Denver CO 80220

TAYLOR, ELIZABETH, actress; b. London, Feb. 27, 1932; d. Francis and Sara (Sothern) T. Student, Byron House, Hawthorne Sch., Metro-Goldwyn-Mayer Sch. Motion pictures include Lassie Come Home, 1942, There's One Born Every Minute, 1942, The White Cliffs of Dover, 1943, Jane Eyre, 1943, National Velvet, 1944, Life With Father, 1946, Courage of Lassie, 1946, Cynthia, 1947, A Date With Judy, 1948, Julia Misbehaves, 1948, Little Women, 1948, Conspirator, 1949, The Big Hangover, 1949, Father of the Bride, 1950, Father's Little Dividend, 1950, A Place in the Sun, 1950, Love is Better Than Ever, 1951, Ivanhoe, 1951, Elephant Walk, 1954, Rhapsody, 1954, Beau Brummel, 1954, The Last Time I Saw Paris, 1955, Giant, 1956, Raintree County, 1957, Cat on a Hot Tin Roof, 1958, Suddenly Last Summer, 1959, Holiday in Spain, 1960, Butterfield 8, 1960 (Acad. award best actress), Cleopatra, 1962, The V.I.P.'s, 1963, The Sandpiper, 1965, Who's Afraid of Virginia Woolf (Acad. award 1966), Taming of the Shrew, 1967, The Comedians, 1967, Reflections in a Golden Eye, 1967, Dr. Faustus, 1968, Boom!, 1968, Secret Ceremony, 1968, The Only Game in Town, 1969, X, Y and Zee, 1972, Under Milk Wood, 1971, Hammersmith is Out, 1972, Night Watch, 1973, Ash Wednesday, 1974, The Driver's Seat, 1975, The Blue Bird, 1976, A Little Night Music, 1977, Victory at Entebbe, 1977, The Mirror Crack'd, 1980, Return Engagement (TV), 1979, Between Friends, 1983, Malice in Wonderland (TV film), 1985, North and South (TV miniseries), 1985, The Young Toscanini, 1988; Broadway debut in The Little Foxes, 1981; narrator film documentary Genocide, 1981; appeared in play Private Lives, 1983; Hotel (TV series), There Must Be a Pony (TV film), Poker Alice (TV prodn.); author: (with Richard Burton) World Enough and Time; poetry reading, 1964, Elizabeth Taylor, 1965, Elizabeth Taylor Takes Off-On Weight Gain, Weight Loss, Self Esteem and Self Image, 1988. Active philanthropic, relief, charitable causes internationally; initiated Ben Gurion U.-Elizabeth Taylor Fund for Children of the Negev, 1982; nat. chmn. Am. Found. AIDS Research, 1985—, internat. fund, 1985—. Named Comdr. Arts and Letters (France), 1985; awarded Legion of Honor (France), 1987; recipient Aristotle S. Onassis Found. award, 1988. Office: Chen Sam & Assocs Inc 315 E 72d St New York NY 10021

TAYLOR, ELIZABETH JANE, investment consultant, real estate company executive; b. Tiffin, Ohio, Oct. 27, 1941; d. Albert Joseph Lucas and Mary Jane Siebenaller-Swander; m. Gaylen Lloyd Taylor, July 11, 1977. Student, Heidelberg Coll., 1961, Austin Community Coll., Tex., 1983-84. Cons., Hypnosis Conn., Ohio and Tex., 1967—; dir. regional mktg. Sibrow, Inc., Ottawa, Can., 1981-83; realtor assoc. Alliance Sales, Austin, 1985-88; assoc. Broadway Comml. Investments, 1988—; prin., Taylor & Assocs., Internat. Mktg. & Bus. Devel., Hong Kong, U.S., 1980—; tchr. mktg. and bus. develop., 1980—. Author: profl. column Austin Women Mag., 1984-86; (poetry) Letters from Home, 1986. Vice pres. Am. Congress on Real Estate, 1982-83; arbitrator Better Bus. Bur., 1984—; mem. speakers bur. Austin Woman's Ctr., 1985—; v.p. Austin World Affairs Council, 1984—; mem. adv. panel Austin Woman Mag., 1984-86. Nominated to Tex. Womens Hall of Fame, 1984. Mem. Nat. Assn. Female Execs. (network dir. 1980—). Avocations: writing, behavior research. Home: 3406 Danville Dr Cedar Park TX 78613

TAYLOR, ELLEN BORDEN BROADHURST, civic worker; b. Goldsboro, N.C., Jan. 18, 1913; d. Jack Johnson and Mabel Moran (Borden) Broadhurst; student Converse Coll., 1930-32; m. Marvin Edward Taylor, June 13, 1936; children—Marvin Edward, Jack Borden, William Lambert. Bd. govs. Elizabethan Garden, Manteo, N.C., 1964-74; mem. Gov. Robert Scott's Adv. Com. on Beautification, N.C., 1971-73; mem. ACE nat. action com. for environ. Nat. Council State Garden Clubs, 1973-75; bd. dirs. Keep N.C. Beautiful, 1973-85; mem. steering com., charter mem. bd. dirs. Keep Johnston County (N.C.) Beautiful, 1977-88; life judge roses Am. Rose Soc.; chmn. local com. that published jointly with N.C. Dept. Cultural Resources: An Inventory of Historic Architecture, Smithfield, N.C., 1977; co-chmn. local com. to survey and publish jointly with N.C. Div. Archives and History: Historical Resources of Johnston County, 1980-86. Mem. Nat. Council State Garden Clubs (life; master judge flower shows), Johnston County Hist. Soc. (charter), Johnston County Arts Council (bldg. com. 1960-65, trustee 1960-88, chmn. 1969-70, steering com., Spl. award for projects of Pub. Library Johnston County & Smithfield 1987), N.C. Geneal. Soc. (charter), Johnston County Geneal. Soc. (charter), Hist. Preservation Soc. N.C. (life), N.C. Art Soc. (life). Democrat. Episcopalian. Clubs: Smithfield (N.C.) Garden (charter; pres. 1969-71), Smithfield Woman's (v.p. 1976), DAR (organizing vice-regent chpt. 1976), Gen. Soc. Mayflower Descs. (life), Descs. of Richard Warren, Nat. Soc. New Eng. Women (charter mem. Carolina Capital chpt.), Colonial Dames Am. (life), Magna Charta Dames, Nat. Soc. Daus. of Founders and Patriots Am. Home: 616 Hancock St Smithfield NC 27577

TAYLOR, FANNIE TURNBULL, educator; b. Kansas City, Mo., Sept. 11, 1913; d. Henry King and Fannie Elizabeth (Sills) Turnbull; m. Robert Taylor, Dec. 2, 1938 (div. 1974); children: Kathleen Muir Taylor Isaacs, Anne Kingston Taylor Wadsack. BA, U. Wis., 1938; LHD (hon.), Buena Vista Coll., Storm Lake, Iowa, 1975. Mem. faculty U. Wis., Madison, 1941—, prof. social edn., 1949—, emeritus, 1979—, dir. Wis. Union Theatre, 1946-66, coordinator univ. systems arts council, 1967-70, assoc. dir. Ctr. Arts Adminstrn., 1970-72, coordinator Consortium Arts Ctr., 1976-84; cons. in field. Author: (handbook) The Arts as a New Frontier, also articles. Program dir. music Nat. Endowment Arts, 1966-67, program info. dir., 1972-76; bd. dirs. Wis. Arts Council, 1964-72, Wis. Found. Arts, 1976—, Madison Civic Music Assn., 1976-84, Madison Children's Mus., 1983-86; council chair Elvehjem Mus. Art, 1976—; mem. grant rev. com. Madison Civic Ctr., 1981-86, Madison Civic Ctr. Found., 1985—; bd. dirs. Wis. chpt. Nature Conservancy, 1963-84, chmn., 1976-77; bd. dirs. Shorewood Hills Found., 1976—, pres., 1976-81. Recipient Oak Leaf award Nature Conservancy, 1981. Fellow Wis. Acad. Scis., Arts and Letters; mem. Assn. Coll., Univ. and Community Arts Adminstrs. (exec. dir. 1970-72, Fannie Taylor award 1972), Am. Assn. Dance Cos. (bd. dirs. 1967-72), Nat. Assn. Regional Ballet (bd. dirs. 1975-77), Nat. Guild Community Schs. Arts (bd. dirs. 1977-80), Women in Communications (Writers' Cup 1980), U. Wis. Alumni Assn. (Disting. Service award 1979). Clubs: Madison Civics (pres. 1969-70), Madison, Univ. (pres. 1982-85), Blackhawk. Home: 1213 Sweet Briar Rd Madison WI 53705 Office: U Wis 5525 Humanities Madison WI 53706

TAYLOR, GARY LEE, marketing executive; b. Akron, Ohio, Mar. 28, 1953; s. Robert Eugene and Betty Jayne (Mayles) T.; m. Karen Sue Bates, Oct. 7, 1978; children: Lindsay Rose, Craig Scott. BBA in Mktg., U. Akron, 1975, MBA in Mktg., 1977. Media coordinator Rex Humbard Found., Akron, 1977-79, gen. mgr. advt., 1979-80, dir. mktg., 1980-82; pres., chief exec. officer InfoCision Mgmt. Corp., Akron, 1982—. Editor newsletter Telephone Fundraising News, 1986; contbr. articles to Religious Broadcasting mag., Fundrasing Mgmt. mag. Speaker, lectr. Nat. Religious Broadcasters Conv., 1982-87; chmn. bd. Profl. Transp. Services, Inc., 1988—. Republican. Methodist. Office: InfoCision Mgmt Corp 1755 Merriman Rd Akron OH 44313

TAYLOR, GEORGE, botanist; b. Feb. 15, 1904; s. George William and Jane (Sloan) T.; B.Sc. with 1st class honors in Botany, Edinburgh (Scotland) U., 1926, also D.Sc., Vans Dunlop scholar; LL.D. (hon.), Dundee, 1972; Dr.Phil. (hon.), Gothenburg, 1958; m. Alice Helen Pendrich, 1929 (dec. 1977); 2 children; m. 2d, Norah English (dec. 1967); m. 3d, Beryl, Lady Colwyn (dec. 1987). Mem. bot. expdn. to South Africa, Rhodesia, 1927-28; joint leader Brit. Mus. expdn. to Ruwenzori and mountains of East Africa, 1934-35; expdn. to S.E. Tibet and Bhutan, 1938; prin. in Air Ministry, 1940-45; dep. keeper botany Brit. Mus., 1945-50, keeper botany, 1950-56; dir. Royal Bot. Gardens, Kew, Eng., 1956-71; vis. prof. Reading (Eng.) U., 1969—; dir. Stanley Smith Hort. Trust, 1970—; Percy Sladen trustee, 1951-81; mem. council Nat. Trust, 1961-72, also chmn. gradens com.; mem. council RGS, 1957-61, v.p., 1964; mem. Ministry Transport Adv. Com. on Landscaping Treatment of Trunk Rds., 1956-81, chmn., 1969-81; hon. bot. adv. Commonwealth War Graves Commn., 1956-77. VMH, 1956; Fellow Royal Soc., RSE, LS, Royal Hort. Soc. (hon; mem. council 1951-73, v.p. and prof. botany 1974—, Veitch Gold medal 1963); mem. Linnean Soc. (bot. sec. 1950-56, v.p. 1956), Brit. Assn. Advancement Sci. (gen. sec. 1951-58), Bot. Soc. Brit. Isles (pres. 1955), Internat. Union Biol. Sci. (pres. div. botany 1964-69), Internat. Assn. Plant Taxonomy (pres. 1969-72), Royal Soc. Sci. (Uppsala, Sweden), Royal Bot. Soc. Netherlands (corr.), Bot. Soc. South Africa (hon.), Am. Orchid Soc. (hon.), Worshipful Co. Gardeners (hon. freeman), Royal Caledonian Hort. Soc. (Scottish hort. medal 1986). Clubs: Athenaeum; New (Edinburgh, Scotland). Author: An Account of the Genus Meconopsis, 1934, reprinted, 1985; contbr. articles on flowering plants to various periodicals. Office: care Royal Soc, 6 Carlton House Terr, London SW1 England

TAYLOR, GRAHAM DANIEL STEWART, lawyer; b. Wellington, New Zealand, Oct. 6, 1945; s. John James and Margaret Lillias (Beard) T.; m. Rosaleen Mary O'Flynn, Jan. 20, 1968; children—Eleanor, Charlotte, Rebecca, Richard. LL.B., Victoria U., New Zealand, 1967, LL.M. with honors, 1969; Ph.D., Cambridge U., 1972. Bar: High Ct., New Zealand, 1968, Supreme Ct., Victoria, 1978. Jr. lectr. Victoria U., Wellington, 1968-69; supr. numerous univ. colls., Cambridge, 1969-72; lectr. Monash U., Melbourne, 1972-74, sr. lectr., 1975-77; dir. research adminstrv. rev., council, Canberra, 1977-80; solicitor Brookfield Prendergast & Co., Auckland, 1981-82; legal counsel Office of Ombudsman, Wellington, 1982-87; barrister, 1987—. Author: Introduction to Australian Legal Process, 1975. Contbr. chpts. to books and articles to profl. jours. Contbr. papers to profl. confs. Mem. exec. com. Counterstroke New Zealand, 1982-83, pres., 1983-87. Named humanitarian trust student Cambridge U., 1969-71; New Zealand U. Grants Com. postgrad. scholar, 1970-72. Mem. New Zealand Law Soc., Internat. Assn. Procedural Law. Home and Office: 30 Clifton Terr, Wellington 6030, New Zealand 6001

TAYLOR, HENRY MILTON, Bahamas government official; b. Nov. 4, 1903; s. Joseph and Evelyn T.; m. Eula Mae Sisco; 3 stepchildren, 4 daughters from a previous marriage. Mem. Bahamas House of Assembly, from 1949; various political positions 1949-81; dep. gen. gov. The Bahamas, 1981-82, 84, gen. gov., 1988—. Author: My Political Memoirs, 1986. Address: PO Box N10846, Nassau The Bahamas also: Lucaya at Brentwood, 221 NE 44th St, Miami USA *

TAYLOR, JAMES WALTER, marketing professor; b. St. Cloud, Minn., Feb. 15, 1933; s. James T. and Nina C. Taylor; m. Joanne Syktte, Feb. 3, 1956; children: Theodore James, Samuel Bennett, Christopher John. BBA, U. Minn., 1957; MBA, NYU, 1960; D in Bus. Adminstrn., U. So. Calif., 1975. Mgr. research div. Atlantic Refining, Phila., 1960-65; dir. new product devel. Hunt-Wesson Foods, Fullerton, Calif., 1965-72; prof. Calif. State U., Fullerton, 1972—; cons. Knudsen, Inc., Los Angeles, 1975-82, Chiat Day Advt., Los Angeles, 1982-85, Moray Industries, Devonport, New Zealand, 1985—. Author: Profitable New Product Strategies, 1984, How To Create A Winning Business Plan, 1980, Competitive Marketing Strategies, 1986, The 101 Best Performing Companies In America, 1986. Served with USN, 1952-53. Fulbright scholar Ministry of Industry, Lisbon, Portugal, 1986-87. Mem. North Am. Soc. Corp. Planners, Am. Mktg. Assn., Strategic Mgmt. Assn., Assn. for Consumer Research, Acad. Mktg. Sci. Home: 3190 Mountain View Dr Laguna Beach CA 92651 Office: Calif State U Dept of Marketing Fullerton CA 92634

TAYLOR, JERRY FRANCIS, lawyer; b. Memphis, Oct. 2, 1934; s. Rex Brewster and Naomi (Robertson) T.; m. Jo(dy) Evelyn Katz, Mar. 5, 1971; 1 child, Deborah Pagan. BS, Memphis State U., 1956; JD, U. Tenn., 1963. Bar: U.S. Dist. Ct. Tenn. (we., mid. and ea. dists.) 1965, U.S. Dist. Ct. Miss. (mid. dist.) 1963, U.S. Ct. Appeals (6th cir.) 1970. Assoc. Krivcher & Cox, Memphis, 1963-65; sr. ptnr. Holt, Batchelor, Taylor & Spicer, 1965-80, Wilkes, McCullough & Taylor, Memphis, 1980—. Pres. Second Chance Inc. Fundraiser United Way Memphis, 1982; bd. dirs. Jeff Steinberg Ministries, 1983—, Outreach to Youth, Inc., 1983—. Served to capt. USAF, 1957-60. Law Sch. scholar Memphis-Shelby County Bar Assn., 1961. Mem. ABA, Tenn. Bar Assn., Memphis-Shelby County Bar Assn., Assn. Trial Lawyers Am. (state committeeman 1968), Tenn. Trial Lawyers Assn. (bd. govs. 1984—), Am. Bd. Trial Advocates (sec. Tenn. chpt. 1985-86, pres.-elect Tenn. chpt. 1987—), Lawyers Involved for Tenn. (trustee). Lodges: Masons, Shriners. Home: 1830 Kimbrough St Germantown TN 38138 Office: Wilkes McCullough & Taylor 1140 Sterick Bldg Memphis TN 38103

TAYLOR, JOANNA WANDA, philatelist, show promoter; b. Jersey City, May 17, 1942; d. Jan and Victoria Pelagia (Malecki) Sliski; m. Phillip Gray Vincent, Dec. 22, 1961 (div. May 1969), 1 child, Laurie Yvonne; m. Scott Harry Taylor, Jan. 5, 1970, 1 child, Joanna Victoria. BS in Microbiology, U. Md., 1966. Sanitarian Prince Georges County Dept. Health, Cheverly, Md., 1968-72; co-founder Scojo Stamps, Ridgely, Md., 1972—; co-founder, promoter S & S Enterprises, Balt., 1974—; auction agt. Scott H. Taylor, Ridgely, 1979—. Recipient Merchandising Excellence award at Nat., '81 Show, Ameripex '86 (Internat. Stamp Show), Bootholder. Mem. Am. Stamp Dealers Assn. (life), Am. Philatelic Soc. (life, expert com.), Scandinavian Collectors Club, Republican. Club: Tidewater Stamp (sec. 1985) (Easton, Md.). Avocations: gardening; crafts. Office: Scojo Stamps PO Box 423 Ridgely MD 21660

TAYLOR, JOB, III, lawyer; b. N.Y.C., Feb. 18, 1942; s. Job II and Anne Harrison (Flinchbaugh) T.; m. Mary C. August, Oct. 24, 1964 (div. Oct. 1978); children: Whitney August, Job IV; m. Sally Lawson, May 31, 1980. BA, Washington & Jefferson Coll., 1964; JD, Coll. William and Mary, 1971. Bar: N.Y. 1972, U.S. Dist. Ct. (ea. and no. dists.) N.Y. 1973, U.S. Ct. Appeals (2d cir.) 1973, U.S. Ct. Claims 1974, U.S. Tax Ct. 1974, U.S. Supreme Ct. 1975, U.S. Ct. Appeals (9th cir.) 1976, U.S. Ct. Mil. Appeals 1977, U.S. Ct. Appeals (D.C. and 10th cirs.) 1977, D.C. 1981, U.S. Ct. Internat. Trade 1981, U.S. Ct. Appeals (fed. cir.) 1982, U.S. Dist. Ct. (no. dist.) Calif. 1983, U.S. Ct. Appeals (6th cir.) 1987. Ptnr. Olwine, Connelly, Chase, O'Donnell & Weyher, N.Y.C., 1971-85, Latham & Watkins, N.Y.C., 1985—. Served to lt. USN, 1964-68. Mem. ABA, Assn. of Bar of City of N.Y. Republican. Episcopalian. Clubs: Racquet and Tennis (N.Y.C.); The Wee Burn Country (Darien, Conn.). Office: Latham & Watkins 885 3d Ave New York NY 10022-4802

TAYLOR, JOHN MCKOWEN, lawyer; b. Baton Rouge, Jan. 20, 1924; s. Benjamin Brown and May (McKowen) T.; 1 son, John McKowen. B.A., La. State U., 1948, J.D., 1950. Bar: La. 1950, U.S. Supreme Ct. 1960. Asso., Taylor, Porter, Brooks, Fuller & Phillips, Baton Rouge, 1951-55, Huckaby, Seale, Kelton & Hayes, Baton Rouge, 1955-58; ptnr. Kelton & Taylor, Baton Rouge, 1958-61; sole practice, Baton Rouge, 1961—. Served with AUS, 1943-46; to maj. USAR, 1946—; ATO, ETO, PTO. Mem. ABA, La. State Bar Assn., Baton Rouge Bar Assn., AAAS, Mil. Order of World Wars, Am. Radio Relay League, Sigma Chi. Republican. Presbyterian. Clubs: Baton Rouge Country, City of Baton Rouge, Baton Rouge Amateur Radio, Camelot. Home and Office: 2150 Kleinert Ave Baton Rouge LA 70806

TAYLOR, JOHN RUSSELL, art critic, editor; b. Dover, Kent, Eng., June 19, 1935; s. Arthur Russell and Kathleen Mary (Picker) T. B.A., Cambridge U., 1956, M.A., 1959; postgrad. Courtauld Inst. Art, London, 1956-58. Subeditor Times Ednl. Supplement, London, 1959-60; editorial asst. Times Literary Supplement, London, 1960-61; film critic The Times, London, 1962-73, art critic, 1978—; prof. cinema div. U. So. Calif., Los Angeles, 1972-78; editor Films and Filming, London, 1983—. Author: The Angry Theatre, 1962; Cinema Eye, Cinema Ear, 1964; The Art Nouveau Book in Britain, 1966; The Rise and Fall of the Wellmade Play, 1967; The Art Dealers, 1968; The Hollywood Musical, 1971; The Second Wave, 1971; Directors and Directions, 1975; Hitch, 1978, Strangers in Paradise, 1983, Alec Guinness, 1984, Orson Welles, 1986, others. Office: The Times, 200 Gray's Inn Rd, London WC1X 8E2, England

TAYLOR, JOHN WILLIAM RANSOM, editor; b. Ely, Cambridgeshire, Eng., June 8, 1922; s. Victor Charles and Florence Hilda (Ransom) T.; m. Doris Alice Haddrick, Sept. 7, 1946; children: Susan Hilda Haddrick, Michael John Haddrick. Design engr. Hawker Aircraft Ltd., Kingston upon Thames, Eng., 1941-47; editorial publicity officer Fairey Aviation Group, London, 1947-55; air corr. Meccano Mag., Liverpool, Eng., 1943-72; editor Air BP, London, 1956-72; editor-in-chief, compiler Jane's All the World's Aircraft, London, 1959—. Joint editor Guinness Book of Air Facts and Feats, London, 1974-84, History of Aviation Partwork, New English Library, London, 1972-73; contbg. editor Air Force Mag., Washington, 1971—, Jane's Defence Weekly, London, 1984-87; author 232 books, including Spitfire, 1946; (with D. Mondey) Spies in the Sky, 1972; (with K. Munson) History of Aviation, 1973, 2d edit., 1978; History of Aerial Warfare, 1974, (with R.A. Mason) Aircraft, Strategy and Operations of the Soviet Air Force, 1986, CFS-The Birthplace of Airpower, 1987. Contbr. articles in field to profl. jours. Dist. commr. Boy Scouts Assn., Surbiton, Surrey, Eng., 1964-69; warden Christ Ch., Surbiton Hill, 1976-80; pres. Chiltern Aviation Soc., Ruislip, Middlesex, Eng., 1979—. Recipient C. P. Robertson Meml. Trophy, Air Pub. Relations Assn., Ministry of Defence, London, 1959; Cert. of Honor, Commn. of Bibliography, History and Arts, Aero Club de France, Paris, 1971; Freeman, Liveryman, Freedom of the City of London, Guild of Air Pilots and Air Navigators, London, 1983; Order of Merit, World Aerospace Edn. Orgn., 1981. Fellow Royal Aero. Soc., Royal Hist. Soc., AIAA (assoc.), Académie Nationale de l'Air et de l'Espace. Mem. Ch. of England. Clubs: Royal Aero, RAF (hon. life) (London). Home and Office: 36 Alexandra Dr, Surbiton Surrey KT5 9AF, England

TAYLOR, KENDRICK JAY, microbiologist; b. Manhattan, Mont., Mar. 17, 1914; s. William Henry and Rose (Carney) T.; B.S., Mont. State U., 1938; postgrad. (fellow) U. Wash., 1938-41, U. Calif. at Berkeley, 1952, Drama Studio of London, 1985; m. Hazel Marguerite Griffith, July 28, 1945; children: Stanley, Paul, Richard. Research microbiologist Cutter Labs., Berkeley, Calif., 1945-74; microbiologist Berkeley Biologicals, 1975-86. Committeeman Mount Diablo council Boy Scouts Am., 1955, dist. vice-chmn., 1960-61, dist. chmn., 1962-65, cubmaster, 1957, scoutmaster, 1966; active Contact Ministries, 1977-80; bd. dirs. Santa Clara Community Players, 1980-84; vol. instr. English as a Second Lang., 1979-80; vol. ARC Blood Ctr., VA Hosp., San Jose. Served with AUS, 1941-46, lt. col. Res., ret. Recipient Scout's Wood badge Boy Scouts Am., 1962. Mem. Am. Soc. Microbiology (chmn. local com. 1953, v.p. No. Calif. br. 1963 65, pres. 1965-67), Sons and Daus. Mont. Pioneers. Presbyterian (trustee 1951-53, elder 1954—). Home: 550 S 13th St San Jose CA 95112

TAYLOR, LANCE JEROME, economics educator; b. Montpelier, Idaho, May 25, 1940; s. Walter Jerome and Ruth (Robinson) T.; m. Yvonne S.M. Johnsson, May 31, 1963; children: Ian Lance, Signe Marguerite. B.S. with honors, Calif. Inst. Tech., 1962; Ph.D., Harvard U., 1968. Instr. econs. Harvard U., Cambridge, Mass., 1967-68; asst. prof., assoc. prof. Harvard U., 1970-74; research assoc. MIT, Cambridge, 1968-70; prof. econs. MIT, 1974—; vis. prof. U. Brasilia, 1974, Pontifical Cath. U. Rio de Janeiro, 1981, U. Delhi, 1987-88; Marshall lectr. Cambridge U., 1986-87; cons. World Bank, UN, various fgn. govts. Author: Macro Models for Developing Countries, 1979, Models of Growth and Distribution for Brazil, 1980, Structuralist Macroeconomics, 1983. Fulbright fellow, 1962-63. Mem. Am. Econ. Assn., Royal Econ. Soc. Home: 95 Avon Hill St Cambridge MA 02140 Office: MIT Room E52-251C Cambridge MA 02139

TAYLOR, LINDA JEAN THORTON, information systems executive; b. Cambridge, Mass., Apr. 16, 1942; d. Ferdinand and Hazel Irene (Towne) Karamanoukian; m. John Robert Thornton, Jan. 21, 1961; 1 child, John Robert; m. 2d, F. Jason Gaskell, Nov. 30, 1978. AA in Bus. Adminstrn., West Los Angeles Coll., 1976; BS, West Coast U., 1978, MS in Bus. and Info. Scis., 1980. Cert. quality analyst. Asst. to chief indsl. engr. Pitts. Plate Glass Co., Boston, 1960-64; corp. sec., gen. mgr. Seaboard Planning Corp., Boston, 1967-67, Los Angeles, 1969-72; prin. Tay-Kara Mgmt., Los Angeles, 1972-73; chief systems adminstrn. Comp-La, Los Angeles, 1973-74; mgr. systems analysis Trans Tech Inc., Los Angeles, 1974-77; mgr. software engring. and tech. audit depts. System Devel. Corp., Los Angeles, 1977-81; v.p. Gaskell and Taylor Engring., Inc., Los Angeles, 1981-86; pres. Taylor and Zeno Systems, Inc., 1986—; mem. faculty, sr. lectr. West Coast U., Los Angeles, 1980—; vis. lectr. sr. seminar Calif. Poly. U., Pomona, 1978, 87; leader ednl. exchange del to People's Republic China; del. to 10th World Computing Congress, Internat. Fedn. Info. Processing, Dublin, Ireland, 1986; keynote speaker Hong Kong Computer Soc., Hong Kong Assn. for Advancement Sci. and Tech., 1987, NEC Inc. Software Engring. Lab., Tokyo, 1987. Appeared in 8 episodes of The New Literacy: An Introduction to Computers, Pub. Broadcasting System; mem. editorial bd.: Data Processing Quality jour. Chmn. bus. and profl. women's com. Calif. Rep. Cen. Com., 1974; mem. White House Com. on Workers Compensation, 1976; mem. fiscal adv. com. Santa Monica Unified Sch. Bd. Edn., 1979-81. Recipient Pub. Service award West Los Angeles C. of C., 1974. Mem. Assn. Women in Computing (pres. 1980-84, v.p. Los Angeles chpt. 1979-80), Nat. Computer Conf. (vice chmn., program com. 1980, mem. adv. com. 1983), Data Processing Mgmt. Assn. (v.p. South Bay chpt. 1979-80, bd. dirs. Los Angeles chpt. 1984, chmn. program com., media relations com. 1984 internat. conf., Individual Performance awards), IEEE (software engring. terminology task force 1980), Assn. Systems Mgmt. (sec. local chpt. 1974-75), EDP Auditors Assn., Assn. for Computing Machinery, Women in Mgmt., Nat. Assn. Women Bus. Owners, Ind. Computer Cons. Assn., Inst. for Cert. of Computer Profls. (bd. dirs.). Office: Taylor & Zeno Systems Inc 2040 Ave of the Stars Los Angeles CA 90067

TAYLOR, LISA SUTER, museum director; b. N.Y.C., Jan. 8, 1933; d. Theo and Martina (Weincerl) von Bergen-Maier; m. Bertrand L. Taylor III, Oct.

30, 1968; children: Lauren, Lindsay. Student, Corcoran Sch. Art, 1958-65, Georgetown U., 1958-62, Johns Hopkins U., 1956-58; D.F.A. (hon.), Parsons Sch. Design, 1977, Cooper Union, 1984. Adminstrv. asst. President's Fine Arts Com., 1958-62; membership dir. Corcoran Gallery Art, 1962-66; program dir. Smithsonian Instn., 1966-69; dir. Cooper-Hewitt Mus. Decorative Arts and Design, Smithsonian Instn., 1969-87, dir. emeritus, 1987—; Mem. adv. bd. Art Deco Soc., Fashion Inst. Tech., N.Y., Living Stage, Washington, Moore Coll. Art; mem. vis. com. Bank St. Coll.; cons. U. Cin. Grad. Sch. Art and Architecture; mem. Mayor's Adv. Council on Design. Co-dir. (film) A Living Museum, 1968; editor: Urban Open Spaces, 1979, Cities, 1981; The Phenomenon of Change, 1984, Housing: Symbol, Structure, Site, 1988. Recipient Thomas Jefferson award, 1976; Bronze plaque Johns Hopkins YMCA, 1958; medal of honor Am. Legion, 1951; Bronze Apple award Am. Soc. Indsl. Designers, 1977; named Trailblazer of Yr. Nat. Home Fashion League, 1981, Mcpl. Art Soc. award 1987, Joseph Henry medal, 1987, Dame of Honour Order of St. John of Jerusalem. Mem. Am., N.Y. State, N.Y.C. museum assns., Art Mus. Dirs. Assn., Mcpl. Arts Soc., Central Parks Conservancy, Am. Craftsmans Council, Archtl. League, Ceramics Circle, Needle and Bobbin Club, Smithsonian Instn. (Exceptional Service award 1969, Gold medal 1972, hon., Women's Council award 1979), Am. Soc. Interior Designers (hon.), AIA (hon.). Home: Seven Gates Farm Vineyard Haven MA 02568 Office: Cooper-Hewitt Mus 2 E 91st St New York NY 10128-9990

TAYLOR, ORVILLE WALTERS, historian; b. El Dorado, Ark., Sept. 20, 1917; s. William Oscar and Minnie Belle (White) T.; m. Evelyn Adelle Bonham, Dec. 5, 1942; children: Michael, Priscilla Taylor Norvell, Melissa, Penelope Taylor Pullen. AB, Ouachita Bapt. U., 1947; MA, U. Ky., 1948; grad. with honors Air Univ., 1952; PhD, Duke U., 1956. Instr. history Little Rock Jr. Coll., 1950-55; prof. history Bapt. Coll., Iwo, Nigeria, 1955-62, U. N.C., Asheville, 1963-65; prof., chmn. dept. Wesleyan Coll., Macon, Ga., 1965-69, Ga. Coll., Milledgeville, 1969-84, emeritus, 1984—; exec. sec., state historian Ark. History Commn., 1959; cons. Ministry of Edn., Nigeria, 1956-62; cons. NEH, 1972-79. Justice of peace, Pulaski County, Ark., 1952-55; chief fed. electoral officer Iwo Dist., Nigeria, 1957; vis./adj. prof. U. Ark., Duke U., E. Tex. State U., Coll. William and Mary, U. Ga., Ind. State U.; bd. dirs. Ark. Ednl. TV Assn., 1953-55; mem. nat. adv. com. Civil War Centennial Commn., 1959; Am. del. XIV Internat. Congress of the Hist. Scis., 1975. Served to capt. U.S. Army, 1941-46; lt. col. USAF (ret.), 1977—. Author: Negro Slavery in Arkansas, 1958, (with others) A History of Baptists in Arkansas, 1979, Religion in the Southern States, 1983, Persistence of the Spirit, 1986; contbr. articles and revs. to profl. jours. and encys. Am. Philos. Soc. grantee, 1968-69, NEH, grantee, 1969, 72, Shell Found. grantee, 1966, 67, 68. Mem. AAUP, Royal African Soc. (life), Am., So., Ark. (life, sec.-treas. 1954-55, Shader Meml. prize 1958) hist. assns., Fla. Hist. Soc., Ga. Assn. Historians (pres. 1973-74), Ga. Polit. Sci. Assn. (pres. 1970-71, Disting. Service award 1978), Assn. for Study Afro-Am. Life and History, Nat. Assn. for Ethnic Studies, Phi Beta Kappa, Phi Kappa Phi. Democrat. Baptist. Home: 800 Lantana Ave PO Box 3757 Clearwater Beach FL 34630

TAYLOR, PAUL, choreographer; b. Allegheny County, Pa., July 29, 1930; s. Paul B. and Elizabeth (Rust) T. Student, Syracuse U., 1949-52, Juilliard Sch. Music, 1952-53; hon. doctoral degrees include, Duke U., 1983, Conn. Coll., 1983, Syracuse U., Juilliard, SUNY at Purchase. Performed (with Paul Taylor Dance Co.) in over 300 U.S. cities and 34 overseas tours.; participated numerous arts festivals in 36 nations; PBS TV appearances include Dance in America, Live From the American Dance Festival, Two Landmark Dances, Three Modern Classics, The Taylor Company: Recent Dances; choreographer Aureole, 1962, Private Domain, 1969, Esplanade, 1975, Cloven Kingdom, 1976, Airs, 1978, Le Sacre du Printemps (the Rehearsal), 1980, Arden Court, 1981, Mercuric Tidings, 1982, Sunset, 1983, Roses, 1985, Last Look, 1985, Musical Offering, 1986; author: (autobiography) Private Domain, 1987 (Most Disting. Biography Nat. Book Critics Circle 1987). Recipient Internat. Circle of Criticism for Artistic Research and Cultural Exchange award Festival Nations, Paris, 1962; named Dancer of Year London's Dance and Dancers, 1965; decorated officier des Arts et Lettres France; prize for best fgn. attraction by Critics of Chile, 1966; Guggenheim fellow, 1961, 66, 83, MacArthur Found. fellow, 1985; recipient Capezio Dance award, 1967, Creative Arts award gold medal Brandeis U., 1978, Dance Mag. award, 1980, Samuel H. Scripps Am. Dance Festival award, 1983; Arts award state of N.Y., 1987. Office: Paul Taylor Dance Co 552 Broadway New York NY 10012 *

TAYLOR, PETER VAN VOORHEES, advertising and public relations consultant; b. Montclair, N.J., Aug. 25, 1934; s. John Coard and Mildred (McLaughlin) T.; BA in English, Duke U., 1956; m. Janet Kristine Kirkebo, Nov. 4, 1978; 1 son, John Coard III. Announcer, Sta. WQAM, Miami, 1956; announcer, program dir. Sta. KHVH, Honolulu, 1959-61; promotion mgr. Sta. KPEN, San Francisco, 1962; with Kaiser Broadcasting, 1962-74, Gen. Electric Broadcasting Co., 1974-78; program/ops. mgr. Sta. KFOG, San Francisco, 1962-66; mgr. Sta. WXHR AM/FM, Cambridge, Mass., 1966-67; gen. mgr. Sta. WJIB, Boston, 1967-70; mgr. FM div. Kaiser Broadcasting, 1969-72; v.p., gen. mgr. Sta. KFOG, San Francisco, 1970-78; pres. Taylor Communications, 1978—, No. Calif. Broadcasters Assn., 1975-77, Broadcast Skills Bank, 1975-76. Trustee, WDBS, Inc., Duke U., 1974-80; bd. dirs. San Francisco Better Bus. Bur., 1976-78. Served to lt. USCGR, 1957-63. Mem. Nat., Internat. radio clubs, Calif. Hist. Soc., Mus. Assn., Calif. Broadcasters Assn., San Francisco Symphony, Bay Area Publicity Club, San Francisco Advt. Club, Pub. Relations Soc. Am., Worldwide TV/FM Dx Assn. Clubs: Advt. Tennis Assn. (pres. 1975-77), San Francisco Tennis, Marina Tennis, Circle de L'Union, Olympic, Bacchus, The Family. Lodge: Rotary (bd. dirs. 1988—, dist. pub. relations chmn. 1986—). Home: 2614 Jackson St San Francisco CA 94115-1123 Office: 490 Post St Penthouse San Francisco CA 94102-1308

TAYLOR, RICK JOSEPH, tax executive; b. Escanaba, Mich., Feb. 24, 1956; s. Harold J. and Helen T. BS in Acctg., U. Wis., Green Bay, 1979; M in Taxation, U. Wis., Milw., 1985. CPA, Wis. Fin. acct. Shopko Stores, Green Bay, 1979-81; audit sr. Grant Thornton, Appleton, Wis., 1981-83; teaching asst. U. Wis., Milw., 1983-85; tax sr. Peat Marwick Main & Co., Milw., 1985-86, tax mgr., 1986-87; sr. tax mgr. Nat. Tax Office Peat Marwick Main & Co., Washington, 1988—. Author: (with others) CPA's Guide to Financial and Estate Planning After the Tax Reform Act of 1986, 1985 (Wis. Uniform Marital Property Act award), Trust and Estate Provisions, 1987, Income and Value Shifting; (newspaper column) Smart Money, 1986—, Income and Value Shifting, 1988; editor: (with others) Multistate Tax Almanac, 1986, 87; mem. editorial bd. Jour. of State Taxation, 1983—. Recipient Meldman Case Weine award Meldman Case Weine, 1985; taxation scholar U. Wis. Milw., 1983-84. Mem. Am. Inst. CPA's (Elijah Watts Sells award 1982), Wis. Inst. CPA's (mem. fin. planning com.),U. Wis.-Milw. Tax Assn. Roman Catholic. Home: 1123A Stuart St Arlington VA 22201 Office: Peat Marwick Main & Co 2001 M St NW Washington DC 20036

TAYLOR, ROBERT HENRY, political science educator; b. Greenville, Ohio, Mar. 15, 1943; arrived in Eng., 1980; s. Robert Earl and Mabelle Lucille (Warren) T.; m. Joan Margaret Lutton, June 27, 1967; children: Emily Sara, Edwin Daniel. BA, Ohio U., 1965; MA, Antioch Coll., 1967; PhD, Cornell U., 1974. Instr. Wilberforce (Ohio) U., 1967-69; lectr. U. Sydney, Australia, 1974-79; sr. lectr. in politics, dept. head Sch. Oriental and African Studies, London, 1980—. Author: Marxism and Resistence in Burma, 1984, The State in Burma, 1987, (with others) In Search of Southeast Asia, 1987; co-editor: Context, Meaning and Power in Southeast Asia, 1986. Mem. Assn. Southeast Asian Studies (chmn. 1986-88), Asian Studies Assn. Home: 78 Valley Rd, Welwyn Garden City, Herts AL8 7DP, England Office: Sch Oriental & African Studies, Malet St, London WC1E 7HP, England

TAYLOR, ROBERT JAMES, bank executive, accountant; b. Clayton, Mo., Mar. 16, 1943; s. James and Vernita (Dollar) T.; m. Janet Jeorgina Johnson, Nov. 14, 1975; children: Robert, Christopher, Bradley. BS, Washington U., St. Louis, Mo., 1966; M in Commerce, St. Louis U., 1969. CPA, Mo. Audit supr. Coopers & Lybrand, St. Louis, 1967-76; asst. controller Nat. Liberty Corp., Valley Forge, Pa., 1977-78; asst. v.p. Fed. Res. Bank of St. Louis, 1978—. Loan exec. United Way of Greater St. Louis, 1980; bd. dirs. Coll. Sch. of Webster Groves, Mo., 1982-85, treas. 1982-1985; mem. St. Louis County Welfare Adv. Bd., 1972-75, Friends St. Louis Art Mus., Mo. Bot. Garden, St. Louis Zoo Friends Assn., Rep. Pres. Task Force; mem. budget allocation com. United Way Child Care; bd. curators Lincoln U. Served with USCG, 1967-72. Mem. Am. Inst. CPA's, Nat. Assn. Black Accts. (pres. St. Louis chpt. 1976), Am. Inst. Banking (bd. dirs. St. Louis chpt. 1981-82), Nat. Arbor Day Found. Republican. Roman Catholic. Club: Washington Univ. Home: 15660 Sugar Ridge Ct Chesterfield MO 63017

TAYLOR, ROBERT LEE, information systems account executive, educator; b. Adrian, Mich., Jan. 9, 1944; s. Jack Raleigh and Virginia Dixon (Oakes) T.; m. Janice Grace George, Dec. 9, 1961; children—Robin, Lynne, David. A.A., Siena Heights Coll., 1974, B.A., 1976. With computer operation Gen. Parts div. Ford Motor Co., Rawsonville, Mich., 1965-66, prodn. monitoring supr., Saline Plant, Mich., 1966-75, methods and systems analyst, Ypsilanti Plant, Mich., 1975-77, data processing supr. Milan Plant, Mich., 1977-82, sr. systems analyst, Plastics, Paint and Vinyl div., Wixom, Mich., 1982-85; systems engr. Electronic Data Systems, Warren, Mich., 1985-86, systems engr. mgr. Romulus (Mich.) Parts Distbn. Ctr. Plant, 1986-87, customer service mgr., Toledo, 1987—; instr. data processing Siena Heights Coll., Adrian, 1985-86. Commr. Tecumseh Planning Commn., Mich., 1976-80, vice-chmn., 1981-82; trustee Tecumseh Bd. Edn., 1981-82, sec., 1983-84, chmn. citizens adv. com., 1983, chmn. computer adv. com., 1984, chmn. policy com., 1983-84; chmn. Tecumseh Area Laymen's Assn., 1983; mem. exec. com. Lenawee County Republican party, 1982—, precinct del., 1982—, chmn. computer com., 1984-86; state del. State of Mich., 1983-85, 87; founding advisor Evang. Free Ch. Adrian-Tecumseh, 1984-85, elder, 1986—, Sunday Sch. supt., 1984-87, chmn. Christian edn., 1986—, chmn. planning-bldg. com., 1987—; asst. Sunday Sch. supt. Berean Baptist Ch., Adrian, 1980-83; tchr. mentally impaired, 1977-83; deacon, Sunday Sch. supt., Grace Bible Ch., Tecumseh, 1973-76; chmn. bd. deacons First Bapt. Ch., Tecumseh, 1970-71, youth advisor, 1968-71, Layman of Yr., 1970; vice chmn. Tecumseh Area Crusade for Christ, 1973, facilities chmn. Lenawee County Crusade for Christ, 1986; chmn. Life Action Crusade, 1987. Served with USAF, 1961-65. Mem. Computer and Automated Systems Assn. (sr.) Mfg. Automation Protocol, Internat. Customer Services Assn., Soc. Mfg. Engrs. Republican. Avocations: golf, genealogy. Home: 603 Outer Dr Tecumseh MI 49286 Office: Electronic Data Systems PO Box 910 Toledo OH 43661

TAYLOR, ROBERT LEWIS, author, journalist; b. So. Ill., Sept. 24, 1912; s. Roscoe Aaron and Mabel (Bowyer) T.; m. Judith Martin, Feb. 3, 1945; children: Martin Lewis, Elizabeth Ann Taylor Peek. Student, Southern Ill. U., 1929; A.B., U. Ill., 1930-33. Corr. Am. Boy mag., 1935; reporter St. Louis Post Dispatch, 1936-39. Profile writer: New Yorker mag, 1939-63; Author: Adrift in a Boneyard, 1947, Doctor, Lawyer, Merchant, Chief; collection of mag. articles and stories, 1948, W. C. Fields: His Follies and Fortunes, 1949 (Signet classic edits. 1968; musical W.C. based on book 1971), The Running Pianist, 1950, Professor Fodorski, 1950 (musical All American based on book 1961), Winston Churchill: An Informal Study of Greatness, 1952, The Bright Sands, 1954, Center Ring, The People of the Circus, 1956, The Travels of Jaimie McPheeters, 1958 (TV series based on book, 1960; Signet classic edits. 1969), A Journey to Matecumbe, 1961 (film Treasure of Matecumbe 1976), Two Roads to Guadalupe, 1964, Vessel of Wrath: The Life and Times of Carry Nation, 1966, A Roaring in the Wind, 1978, Niagara, 1980; Tiare Tahiti, 1987; contbr. to: Reader's Digest, New Yorker, Sat. Evening Post, Life, Colliers, contbr., Esquire, Redbook. Served as lt. comdr. USNR, 1942-46. Recipient Pulitzer prize for The Travels of Jaimie McPheeters, 1959; recipient hon. mention award gen. reporting div. Sigma Delta Chi Desing. Service awards, 1939. Mem. Authors Guild, Delta Tau Delta. Clubs: Down East Yacht (Boothbay Harbor, Maine); Monte Carlo (Chapala, Mexico); Nautico (Ajijic, Mex.); Oceans Racquet (Daytona Beach, Fla.); Explorers.

TAYLOR, ROBERT LOVE, arbitrator, retired judge, consultant; b. Trenton, Tenn., Mar. 30, 1914; s. Hillsman and Katherine (Taylor) T.; m. Jerry C., Sept. 30, 1943 (dec. July 1972); children—Robert Love, Martha Taylor Smith; m. Virginia W., Feb. 14, 1974. LL.B., So. Law Coll.; J.D. (hon.), Memphis State U., 1967. Bar: Tenn. 1944, U.S. Supreme Ct. 1958, U.S. Ct. Appeals (6th cir.) 1952, U.S. Ct. Appeals (5th cir.) 1957, U.S. Tax Ct. 1977, Tex. 1979. Commr. ins. and banking State of Tenn., Nashville, 1951-52; chancellor Tenn. Chancery Ct., Memphis, 1960-68; judge Tenn. Ct. Appeals, Jackson, 1968-76; spl. atty. State of Tenn., Memphis, 1948-50, State of Miss., Memphis, 1950-51; pres. Realty Services Co., Boerne Title Co., Bandera Title Co.; cons. in field; bd. dirs. Bank of Leon Springs, San Antonio, Tex. Author report Black Market Sales of Infants in Tennesse, 1950. Mem. United Congl. Adv. Bd.; del. Democratic Nat. Conv., Chgo., 1957; chmn. Shelby County Dem. Exec. Com., Memphis, 1949-53; state comdr. Air Res. Assn., Nashville, 1946-47, judge adv., Washington, 1947-48. Recipient Cert. of Merit, Am. Legion, 1949; hon. life mem. DAV, Tenn. Hist. Commn., 1966. Mem. Tenn. Jud. Council, Tenn. Bar Assn. (chmn. labor sect. 1965), Regular Panel of Arbitrators, Fed. Mediation and Consiliation Service, Regular Regional Panel of Labor Arbitrators, U.S. Postal Service and Am. Postal Workers Union, AFL-CIO and Nat. Assn. Letter Carriers. Methodist. Club: Fair Oaks Country (Boerne, Tex.). Lodges: Rotary, Masons, K.T., Shriners. Home: 102 S Frey Boerne TX 78006 Office: Affiliated Profl Services Inc 216 E Blanco Boerne TX 78006

TAYLOR, RUSSEL REID, manufacturing company executive, educator; b. Gananoque, Ont., Can., Sept. 9, 1917; s. Howard William and Clara Helen (Reid) T.; B.Commerce, U. Toronto, 1938; D.B.A., Western Colo. U., 1978; divorced; children—Deborah Reid Souki, Cynthia Rowan Kane; m. Deborah Cohen, Nov. 22, 1986. Came to U.S., 1938, naturalized, 1951. Pres., Annis Furs, Inc., Detroit, 1955-61; chmn. Russel Taylor, Inc. div. Consol. Foods Corp., N.Y.C., 1961-78; dir. Minnetonka, Inc., Chaska, Minn., 1975—; adj. asst. prof. Fairleigh Dickinson U. Sch. Bus., 1971-78; asso. prof. Coll. New Rochelle (N.Y.), 1978-87, dir. H.W. Taylor Inst. Enterpreneurial Studies, 1987—; trustee Am. Liquid Trust, Boston, Keystone Money Trust, Boston, Keystone Bond Trust, Boston, Keystone Stock Trust, Boston, others. Author: Exceptional Entrepreneurial Women,1988. Dir. Gintel Fund, Gintel Erisa Fund, Gintel Capital Appreciation Fund, Greenwich. Bd. dirs. Jr. Achievement, Greenwich, Conn., 1974—. Served to lt. comdr. Royal Canadian Navy, 1943-46. Mem. Am. Arbitration Assn., (panel 1956—), Delta Upsilon. Clubs: Union League (N.Y.C.); Tequesta Country (Fla.); Greenwich Country. Home: 630 Steamboat Rd Greenwich CT 06830 Office: 512 7th Ave New York NY 10018

TAYLOR, SCOTT MAXFIELD, department store executive; b. Evanston, Ill., Aug. 13, 1953; s. Brett Maxfield and Gretchen Pauline (Porter) T., Jr. BA, Coe Coll., 1975; M in Mgmt., Northwestern U., 1977; MSC, New Sem., 1985. Sales mgr. Daytons, Mpls., 1977-78, asst. buyer, 1978-79; store mgr. Brett's Dept. Store, Mankato, Minn., 1979-80, buyer jr. dept., 1981-83, v.p., 1981-87, div. mdse. mgr., 1984-85, gen. mdse. mgr., 1985—, pres., 1988—, also bd. dirs. Bd. dirs. Blue Earth County Hist. Soc., Mankato, 1984-87; bd. dirs. Mankato Area Conv. and Visitors Bur., 1985—, chmn., 1987—; Presbyn. deacon, 1986—, moderator 1987—. George F. Baker scholar, 1975. Mem. Omicron Delta Epsilon. Lodge: Kiwanis (bd. dirs. 1984—). Avocation: curling. Home: Box 3642 Mankato MN 56002 Office: Bretts Dept Stores Box 609 Mankato MN 56002

TAYLOR, SHAHANE RICHARDSON, JR., ophthalmologist; b. Greensboro, N.C., Sept. 5, 1928; s. Shahane Richardson and Mary Hoke (Hooker) T.; A.B., U. N.C., 1955, M.D., 1959; m. Betty Jane Teague, Aug. 2, 1952; children—Shahane R. III, Anne Teague, Mary Hooker. Intern, N.C. Meml. Hosp., Chapel Hill, 1959-60; resident in ophthalmology U. N.C.-McPherson Meml. Hosp., 1960-63; practice medicine specializing in ophthal. surgery, Greensboro, N.C., 1963—; chief ophthalmology Wesley Long Hosp.; attending staff Moses Cone; staff Humana Hosp. (all Greensboro); cons. in ophthalmology N.C. State Employees Health Plan, Prudential Medicare, Title 19 program, Pilot Life Ins. Co.; vis. instr. opthal. surgery U. N.C., Chapel Hill, 1964-73; pres. North Central Peer Rev. Found. Mem. N.C. State Health Care Council, 1981. Served to capt., M.I., U.S. Army, 1951-54. Diplomate Am. Bd. Ophthalmology. Mem. AMA, So. Med. Assn., N.C. Med. Soc. (exec. council 1979-85), Med. Assn. U. N.C. (pres. 1981), Guilford County Med. Soc. (pres. 1977), Med. Rev. N.C. (bd. dirs. 1986—), Am. Acad. Ophthalmology and Otolaryngology, N.Y. Acad. Scis., Pan Am. Ophthal. Soc., So. Eye Surgeons, Mensa, Quarter Century Wireless Assn., Intertel. Episcopalian. Clubs: Greensboro Whist, Greensboro Country, Greensboro City (dir.). Home: 2207 Carlisle Rd Greensboro NC 27408 Office: 348 N Elm St Greensboro NC 27401

TAYLOR, SIDNEY, automotive executive, engineer; b. Manchester, Eng., Aug. 7, 1934; s. Robert Edward and Ethel (Sweatman) T.; m. Margaret Gwendoline Evans, July 23, 1955; children: Gillian Margaret, Christine Lynne, Robert Pearson. Various positions including chmn. automotive group, dir. TI Group PLC, London, from 1985, pres., mng. dir. automotive group and bundy. Mem. Inst. Mech. Engrs. (cert.), Inst. Prodn. Engrs. (cert.), Brit. Inst. Mgmt. Club: Royal Automobile (London). Office: TI Group PLC, 50 Curzon St Mayfair, London W1Y 7PN, England

TAYLOR, STEPHEN COLIN, biotechnologist; b. London, Sept. 16, 1953; s. John Telford and Joan Doris (Searles) T.; m. Lesley Ann Birkinshaw, May 6, 1955; children: Hannah Emily Louise, Ruth Elizabeth Ann. BSc, U. Kent, Canterbury, Eng., 1975; PhD, U. Warwick, Coventry, Eng., 1978. Sr. scientist ICI Corp. Lab., Runcorn, Eng., 1978-85; research and tech. mgr. ICI Bioproducts, Billingham, Eng., 1985—; hon. lectr. Durham U., Eng., 1985—. Patentee in field; contbr. articles to profl. jours. Mem. Soc. for Gen. Microbiology. Mem. Ch. of Eng. Club: Royal Soc. for Scottish Country Dancing (Richmond) (sec. 1986—). Office: ICI Bioproducts, PO Box 1, Billingham England TS23 1LB

TAYLOR, THEOPHILUS MILLS, clergyman, educator, church administrator; b. Cedarville, Ohio, June 22, 1909; s. Mills J. and Martha Slater (Dill) T.; m. Lois Dean McLaughlin, Mar. 12, 1936; children: Martha Renwick, Theophilus Mills III, Jessica Anne, Caroline Kerr. Student, Muskingum Coll., 1927-30, D.D. (hon.), 1944; B.Arch., U. Pa., 1935; M.Div., Pitts.-Xenia Theol. Sem., 1941; postgrad., U. Chgo., 1946; Ph.D. in Religion, Yale, 1956. Tchr. gen. sci., indsl. arts Woodstock Sch., India, 1935-38; ordained to ministry U.P. Ch., 1941; asst. pastor First Presbyn. Ch., Crafton, Pa., 1940-41; pastor U.P. Ch., Barnet Center, Vt., 1941-43; John McNaugher prof. N.T. lit. and exegesis Pitts.-Xenia Theol. Sem., 1943-59, dean dept. grad. studies, 1946-59; prof. Pitts. Theol. Sem., 1960-62; sec. gen. council Gen. Assembly U.P. Ch. U.S.A., 1962-72; also chmn. Ch. Exec. Devel. Bd., 1968-74; pres. Religion in Am. Life, 1970-73, mem. corp., trustee, 1974-79, emeritus trustee, 1980—; Asst. dir. archeol. excavations, Beitin, Jordan, 1957, 60; U.P. rep. Am. com. World Council Chs., 1946-48, del. constituting assembly, 1948; rep. to Conf. U.S.A. Mem. Chs., 1948-61; del. 16th Gen. Council of Alliance Ref. Chs., Geneva, 1948, 18th Gen. Council, Sao Paolo, 1959, 3d World Conf. on Faith and Order, Lund, Sweden, 1952, 4th conf., Montreal, 1963; del. 2d assembly World Council Chs., Evanston, Ill., 1954, adviser 3d assembly, New Delhi, 1961; mem. com. religion and pub. edn. Pa. Council Christian Edn., 1950-54; sec. joint drafting com. Conf. Ch. Union of Presbyn. U.S.A. and U.P. Chs., 1955-57; moderator gen. assembly U.P. Ch. U.S.A., 1958-59, chmn. commn. ecumenical mission and relations, 1959-62; mem. working com. Commn. Faith and Order, World Council Chs., 1952-71, mem. Commn., 1952-75, chmn. theol. commn. Holy Eucharist, faith and order, 1965-71; mem. exec. com., gen. bd., chmn. gen. constituent membership com. Nat. Council Chs., U.S.A., 1960-72; sec. Am. Council for Boys' Indsl. Home and Tech. Sch., Gujranwala, India, 1944-62. Author: Uncleanness and Purification in Paul, 1956, Survey of Theological Education (Africa, Middle-East and Asia), 1962; Assoc. editor: The United Presbyn, 1947-56; editorial council: Theology Today, Princeton, N.J., 1951-73; Contbr. editorials, articles, book revs. to religious jours.; chpts. to Stewardship in Contemporary Life, 1965, Assignment: Overseas, 1966, For Me to Live, 1972. Bd. dirs. Center for Interfaith Research on Religious Architecture; mem. corp. Nyack (N.Y.) Hosp., 1965-72; trustee Muskingum Coll., 1965-78, emeritus trustee, 1979—. Mem. Archaeol. Inst. Am., Soc. Bibl. Lit. and Exegesis, Guild for Religious Architecture, Presbyn. Hist. Soc. (pres. 1964-71), Studiorum Novi Testamenti Societas, Internat. Assn. for a Union of Democracies (mem. council 1972—, pres. 1973-85), Am. Oriental Soc. Home: Old Tabor House PO Box 7 Topsham VT 05076-0007

TAYLOR, THOMAS HUDSON, JR., import company executive; b. Somerville, Mass., June 8, 1920; s. Thomas Hudson and Virginia Gwendolyn (Wilson) T.; B.S. in Econs., Wharton Sch. Fin. and Commerce, U. Pa., 1947; m. Mary Jane Potter, Dec. 1, 1943; children—Thomas Hudson, III, James R., Jane, John E., Virginia. Acctg. exec. Collins & Aikman Corp., Phila., 1947-55, divisional controller automotive div., Albemarle, N.C., 1956-59, asst. dir. purchases, 1960-64; exec. v.p. Carolina Floral Imports, Inc., Gastonia, N.C., 1965-67, pres., treas., 1968—. County commr. Stanly County, Albemarle, N.C., 1962-66. Served to capt. USAAF, 1941-45. Decorated Air medal. Mem. Beta Theta Pi. Republican. Methodist. Clubs: Princeton, Gastonia City. Home: 4537 Forest Cove Rd Belmont NC 28012-8701 Office: Box 2201 Gastonia NC 28053

TAYLOR, WALTER WILLARD, archaeologist, educator; b. Chgo., Oct. 17, 1913; d. Walter Willard and Marjorie (Wells) T.; m. Lyda Averill Paz, Sept. 6, 1937 (dec. 1960); children: Peter Wells, Ann Averill Taylor Cover, Gordon McAuliffe; m. Nancy Thompson Bergh (div. 1970); m. Mary Henderson Swank (div. 1983). AB, Yale U., 1935; PhD, Harvard U., 1943. Archaeologist U.S., Mexico, Spain, 1935—; vis. lectr. Ariz. State Coll., Harvard U., U. Tex., U. Wash., Friends Internat. Seminars, Prisoner of War Camps in Germany, Escuela Nat. de Antropología e Historia, Mexico, U. Merida, Mexico, Mexico City Coll., So. Ill. U., Am. Anthrop. Assn.; fieldwork in Ga., Ariz., N. Mex., Spain, Coahuila, Sonora, Zacatecas, Mexico. Author: A Study of Archeology, 1983, Contributions to the Archaeology of Coahuila, Mexico, 1988. Served to capt. USMC, 1943-45, MTO, ETO. Rockefeller fellow, Guggenheim fellow; Kaplan research award Sigma Xi. Home: Calle Rosales #63, Alamos, 85760 Sonora Mexico

TAYLOR, WILLIAM, university administrator; b. Crayford, Kent, Eng., May 31, 1930; s. Herbert and Maud Ethel (Peyto) T.; m. Rita Hague, 1954; children—Anne Catherine, Rosemary Caroline, Richard William James. B.Sc. in Econs., London Sch. Econs., 1952; PGCE., Westminster Coll., London, 1953; Diploma in Edn., U. London, 1954, Ph.D., 1960; D.Sc. (hon.), Aston U., 1977; D.Litt. (hon.), Leeds U., 1979; D.Civil Law (hon.), U. Kent-Canterbury, 1981; hon. D., Open U., 1983, Loughboro U., 1984. Tchr., dep. prin. Kent County Council, 1953-59; sr. lectr., prin. lectr. various colls. Edn., 1959-64; lectr. U. Oxford, 1964-66; prof. U. Bristol, 1966-73; dir. U. London Inst. Edn., 1973-83; prin. U. London, 1983-85; vice chancellor U. Hull, 1985—; research adviser Dept. Edn. and Sci., Eng. and Wales, 1968-73; chmn. Nat. Found. for Ednl. Research, 1984—, Council Accreditation Tchr. Edn., 1984—; cons. in edn. Author: The Secondary Modern School, 1963; Society and the Education of Teachers, 1969; Heading for Change, 1972; Policy and Planning in Post Secondary Education, 1972; Research and Reform in Teacher Education, 1978, Universities Under Scrutiny, 1987; editor: Research Perspectives in Education, 1973; Educational Administration and the Social Sciences, 1969; Metaphors of Education, 1984. Chmn., U.K. nat. commn. UNESCO Ednl. Adv. Com., 1975-83; chmn. ednl. adv. council Ind. Broadcasting Authority, 1975-83; pres. English New Edn. Fellowship, 1981-86; pres. Council for Edn. in World Citizenship, 1980—. Decorated Comdr. Order of Brit. Empire, 1983. Fellow Coll. Preceptors, Commonwealth Council Ednl. Adminstrn., West Australian Inst. Ednl. Adminstrn.; mem. Worshipful Soc. Apothecaries London (liveryman). Home and Office: U Hull, Vice Chancellor, Hull England

TAYLOR, WILLIAM BARRETT, III, international marketing executive, lawyer; b. Winston-Salem, N.C., July 7, 1919; s. William Barrett, II, and Frances Dinsdale (Swann) T.; A.B., U. Tenn., 1941; J.D., U. Fla., 1950; postgrad. Oxford U., 1943, George Washington U., 1948, U. Denver, 1957, U. Md., 1958; m. Gwendoline Madge Abbott, May 1, 1945; children—Sally Hill (Mrs. Christopher Brunton), William Barrett IV, Richard A., Michael A. Admitted to Fla. bar, 1950, U.S. Supreme Ct. bar, 1953; commd. 2d lt. U.S. Air Force, 1941, advanced through grades to col., 1954; with 8th AF, 1942-45; with Office of Legislative Liaison, Office Sec. of Air Force, 1950-54; asst. chief of staff, chief of staff USAF Acad., 1955-58; with Joint U.S. Mil. Group, Spain, 1958-62; with Office of Asst. Sec. of Def., 1962-64; ret., 1964; internat. liaison McDonnell Douglas Corp., Washington, 1964-75; dir. internat. devel. Lykes Youngstown Corp., 1975-77; pres. Wm. B. Taylor Assocs., 1978—; commr. South Pacific Commn., Noumea, New Caledonia, 1969, sr. commr., 1970-74, with rank of dep. asst. sec. of state; v.p. Taylor Bros., Inc., Winston-Salem, 1947-50. Mem. Trans Atlantic council Boy Scouts Am., 1960-62; nat. chmn., bd. dirs. Nat. Alliance Sr. Citizens, coordinator Vols. for Nixon-Agnew, 1968; nat. co-chmn. Sr. Citizens for Nixon-Agnew, 1972; coordinator Sr. Citizens for Ford-Dole, 1976, Sr. Citizens for Reagan-Bush, 1980; chmn. srs. div. Reagan-Bush, 1984; nat. mem. Rep. Nat. Com. Mem. Am., Inter-Am., Fla. bar assns., Air Force Assn., Navy League,

Am. Def. Preparedness Assn., Armor Assn., Middle East Inst., Iran Am. Soc., Friends of Free China. Republican. Author: Pictorial History 14th Combat Bomb Wing, 1946. Home: 3209 N Columbus St Arlington VA 22207 Office: Suite 404 2201 Wilson Blvd Arlington VA 22201

TAYLOR, WILLIAM HALSTEAD, chemical pathologist; b. Wardle, Lancashire, Eng., Apr. 26, 1924; s. Thomas Halstead and Alice May (Hallett) T.; m. June Helen Thorniley, Sept. 7, 1950; children: Susan, John, Philippa, Rowena. BA, U. Oxford, Eng., 1946, BM, BCh, 1948, DM, 1957. House physician Postgrad. Med. Sch., London, 1948-49, Radcliffe Infirmary, Oxford, 1949; lectr., then sr. lectr. in clin. biochemistr U. Oxford, 1949-59, fellow, tutor St. Peter's Coll., 1957-59; head dept. chem. pathology Royal Liverpool (Eng.) Hosp., 1959—; dir. studies chem. pathology U. Liverpool, 1962-74; dir. Mersey Regional Metabolic Unit, 1965—. Author: Fluid Therapy and Disorders of Elctrolyte Balance, 1965; mem. editorial bd.: Clin. Sci. Jour., 1962-67; contbr. articles to profl. jours. U. Oxford Christopher Welch scholar, 1946. Fellow Royal Coll. Physicians; mem. Med. Research Soc., Assn. Clin. Biochemists, Assn. Clin. Pathologists. Club: 41 (Liverpool), Rotary. Home: 16 Salisbury Rd, Liverpool L19 0PJ, England Office: Royal Liverpool Hosp Duncan Bldg, Dept Chem Pathology, Liverpool L7 8XW, England

TAZEWELL, CALVERT WALKE (PSEUDONYM WILLIAM STONE DAWSON), retired air force officer, author, historian; b. Wilmington, Del., Apr. 13, 1917; s. Calvert W. and Sophie (Goode) T.; student Air Corps Tech. Sch., 1940, Air Tactical Sch., 1948, Sophia U., Tokyo, 1951, Air Command and Staff Sch., USAF Air. U., 1952, Ind. U., 1956; m. Beverly Mae LaCour, Jan. 14, 1943 (div. Apr. 1959); children—Lyn Diane, Patricia Marie, Beverly Ann; m. 2d, Belle Gordon, July 7, 1959 (div.); 1 son, William Bradford; m. 3d, Theresa Hoey, Feb. 20, 1976; adopted children—Valera Marie, Sabrina Maria; 7 stepchildren. Pvt., Va. NG, 1934-35; radio technician, San Antonio, 1936-37; pvt., USAC, 1937, m/sgt. weather observer and forecaster, 1941; commd. 2d lt. USAAF (by direct appointment while overseas), 1942, advanced through grades to lt. col. Airways and Air Communications Service; comml. multi-engine pilot; communications specialist on USAF meteorol. flight, flew over North Pole, 1947; during World War II developed and supervised for USAAF pioneer worldwide weather communications system, which principles and techniques accepted by World Meteorol. Orgn. and Internat. Civil Aviation Orgn.; apptd. officer Regular Army, 1947; transferred to USAF, 1948; comdr. 1951st AAGS Squadron, Nagoya, Japan, 1950-51; dep. dir. plans and requirements Hdqrs. 1808th AACS Wing, Tokyo, 1951-52; comdr. 1300th Student Squadron, Great Falls, Mont., 1953-54, 818th AC & W Squadron, Randolph, Tex., 1955-56, Kangnung Air Base, Korea, 1957, Takaoyama Air. Sta., Japan, 1958; dir. communications-electronics 314th Air div. Osan, Korea, 1956-57. Duluth Air Def. Sector, 1958-59; ret., 1959; civil def. coordinator Dade County, Fla., 1961; organizer chmn. Met. Dade County Public Library Adv. Bd., 1963-64; instr. N.Y. U., 1962-63, Old Dominion U., 1964-65; microcomputer mktg. systems specialist, 1977-82. Trustee, Assn. Preservation Va. Antiquities, 1967-69; bd. dirs. Boush-Tazewell-Waller House, Norfolk, 1982-83. Recipient awards Writers Digest, 1974, 75, Nat. Writers Club, 1976. Decorated Bronze Star. Mem. Norfolk Hist. Soc. (life mem., 1st pres., founder 1965), Va. History Fedn. (1st pres., founder 1967), Am. Radio Relay League. Amateur radio sta. operator, 1934—; amateur nutritionist, computerist. Contbr. articles on nutrition, electronics and history to periodicals in U.S., Gt. Britain. Address: PO Box 9917 Virginia Beach VA 23450

TEAGUE, BRUCE WILLIAMS, chiropractor; b. Dayton, Ohio, Sept. 6, 1947; s. Bige Barnett and Lena (Williams) T.; m. Germaine Lee Mullican, Oct. 15, 1977; children—Deanna, Katrina, Bret., Travis, Krystal. B.B.A., Eastern Ky. U., 1970; D.Chiropractic, Palmer Coll. Chiropractic, 1977. Chiropractor, pres., dir. Teague Chiropractic Ctr., Anchorage, 1980—. Mem. Am. Chiropractic Assn. (mem. council nutrition, council on sports injuries and phys. fitness), Internat. Chiropractic Assn., Alaska Chiropractic Soc., Palmer Coll. Alumni Assn. Lodges: Moose, Rotary. Office: Teague Chiropractic Ctr Huffman Plaza Suite 212 12350 Industry Way Anchorage AK 99515

TEAGUE, LAVETTE COX, JR., architectural educator; b. Birmingham, Ala., Oct. 8, 1934; s. Lavette Cox and Caroline Green (Stokes) T.; student Auburn U., 1951-54; B.Arch., MIT, 1957, M.S.C.E., 1965, Ph.D., 1968; M.Div. with distinction, Ch. Div. Sch. Pacific, 1979; cert. systems profl., 1985—. Archtl. designer Carroll C. Harmon, Birmingham, 1957, Fred Renneker, Jr., Birmingham, 1958-59; architect Rust Engring. Co., Birmingham, 1959-62, Synergetics, Inc., Raleigh, N.C., 1962-64, Rust Engring. Co., Birmingham, 1964-68; research asst., inst., research assoc. MIT, Cambridge, 1966-68; dir. computer services Skidmore, Owings & Merrill, San Francisco, Chgo., 1968-74; postdoctoral fellow UCLA, 1972; adj. assoc. prof. architecture and civil engring. Carnegie-Mellon U., Pitts., 1973-74; archtl. systems cons., Chgo., 1974-75, Berkeley, Calif., 1975-80, Pasadena, Calif., 1980-82, Altadena, Calif., 1982—; lectr. info. systems Calif. State Poly. U., Pomona, 1980-81, prof., 1981—; Fulbright lectr., Uruguay, 1983. Co-author: Structured Analysis Methods for Computer Information Systems, 1985. Recipient Tucker-Voss award M.I.T., 1967; Fulbright scholar, 1985. Mem. AIA (Arnold W. Brunner scholar 1966), Assn. Computing Machinery, Sigma Xi, Phi Eta Sigma, Scarab, Scabbard and Blade, Tau Beta Pi, Chi Epsilon. Episcopalian. Home: 1696 N Altadena Dr Altadena CA 91001 Office: 3801 W Temple Ave Pomona CA 91768

TEAGUE, PEYTON CLARK, chemist, educator; b. Montgomery, Ala., June 26, 1915; s. Robert S. and Sara McGehee (Clark) T.; m. Patricia Cussons Lamb, June 12, 1937; 1 dau., Norah Teague Grimball. Student, Huntingdon Coll., 1932-34; B.S., Auburn U., 1936; M.S., Pa. State U., 1937; Ph.D., U. Tex., 1942. Research chemist Am. Agrl. Chem. Co., Newark, 1937-39; instr. dept. chemistry Auburn U., Ala., 1941-42, asst. prof., 1943-45; research chemist U.S. Naval Research Lab, 1942-45; asst. prof. U. Ga., Athens, 1945-48, U. Ky., Lexington, 1948-50; assoc. prof. dept. chemistry U. S.C., Columbia, 1950-56, prof., 1956-82, disting. prof. emeritus, 1982—, assoc. dean grad. sch., 1966-68, chmn. grad. council, 1980-81, dept. dir. grad. studies, 1971-82; sec. grad. admission com. U. S.C., 1982—; vis. prof. Univ. Coll., Dublin, Ireland, 1963-64, 77; dir. Teague Hardware Co., Montgomery, Ala., 1955-74. Contbr. articles to sci. jours. Vestryman Trinity Episcopal Cathedral, 1968-71, lay reader, 1963—; bd. dirs. S.C. chpt. Arthritis Found., 1983-86; bd. dirs. Columbia Town Theatre, 1984-87. Recipient Outstanding Tchr. award U. S.C., 1976. Mem. Am. Chem. Soc. (chmn. S.C. sect. 1958-59), Phytochem. Soc. N.Am. (pres. 1969-70), S.C. Acad. Sci., Blue Key, Sigma Xi (pres. U. S.C. chpt. 1962-63), Phi Kappa Phi, Phi Lambda Upsilon, Phi Delta Theta. Club: Forest Lake Country. Lodge: Kiwanis. Home: 1550 Adger Rd Columbia SC 29205 Office: U SC Dept Chemistry Columbia SC 29208

TEAL, GORDON KIDD, physical scientist; b. Dallas, Jan. 10, 1907; s. Olin Allison and Azelia Clyde (Kidd) T.; m. Lyda Louise Smith, Mar. 7, 1931; children: Robert Carroll, Donald Fraser, Stephen O'Banion Teal. A.B. in Math. and Chemistry with spl. honors, Baylor U., 1927, LL.D., 1969; Sc.M. (Marston scholar), Brown U., 1928, Ph.D. (Univ. fellow, Metcalf fellow), 1931, Sc.D., 1969. Mem. research staff Bell Telephone Labs., N.Y.C., Murray Hill, N.J., 1930-53; research assoc. Columbia U., 1932-35; asst. v.p., dir. materials and components research Tex. Instruments, Dallas, 1952-55; asst. v.p., dir. research, dir. Central Research Labs. Tex. Instruments, 1955-61, asst. v.p. research and engring., 1961-62; asst. v.p., internat. tech. dir. Tex. Instruments, London, Paris and Rome, 1962-65; asst. v.p. in charge tech. devel., equipment group Tex. Instruments, 1967-68, v.p., chief scientist corp. devel., 1968-72; cons. to industry and govt. 1972—; 1st dir. Inst. Materials Research, Nat. Bur. Standards, Washington, 1964-67; cons. Dept. Def., 1956-64, 70-72, NASA, 1970-72, Nat. Bur. Standards, 1972-73, Tex. Instruments, Inc., 1972-77; chmn. exec. tech. devel. bd. Poly. Inst. Bklyn., 1963-72; mem. materials adv. bd. Nat. Acad. Scis.-NRC, 1960-64; mem. Nat. Acad. Scis. panels to Ceylon and India, workshops on indsl. research in Ceylon and India, 1970; mem. ad hoc com. on materials and processes for electron devices Nat. Acad. Scis.-NAE-NRC, 1970-72; mem. Nat. Acad. Sci.-Nat. Acad. Engring.-NRC adv. panel Inst. Applied Tech., Nat. Bur. Standards, 1969-75; chmn. Nat. Acad. Scis.-NRC adv. panel to Nat. Bur. Standards electronics technology div., 1972-75; chmn. panel for study research facilities and sci. opportunities in use of low and medium energy neutrons Nat. Acad. Scis.-NRC adv. panel electronics technology div., 1977-78; mem. Nat. Acad. Scis. panel to, Republic of China, Am. Workshop on Indsl. Innovation and Product Devel. in Taiwan, 1975. Contbr.: Transistor Technology, 1952, 58, Mikroelektronik, 1965, Washington Colloquium on Science and Society, 1967; chmn., co-editor: Technology Forecast for 1980, 1971; contbr. Bicentennial issue IEEE Transactions on Electron Devices, 1976; editorial adv. bd.: Internat. Jour. Solid State Electronics, 1960-68; contbr. chpts. to books, articles to profl. jours. Mem. pres.'s council Calif. Inst. Tech., 1969-71; trustee Brown U., 1969-74, trustee emeritus, 1974—; trustee Baylor U., Baylor U. Med. Center, Dallas, 1970-79; mem. vis. com. elec. engring. dept. U. Tex., Austin, 1969-73; mem. U. Tex. at Austin Sch. Arts and Scis. Found. Adv. Council, 1972-78; adv. council Coll. Natural Scis. Found., 1978—, Coll. Edn. Found., 1977—; hon. life mem. Coll. Natural Scis., 1985. Recipient Disting. Alumni award Baylor U., 1965; Inventor of Yr. award Patent, Trademark and Copyright Research Inst., George Washington U., 1966; Am. Acad. Achievement award, 1967; medal of Honor IEEE, 1968; Creative Invention award Am. Chem. Soc., 1970, also Doherty award Dallas-Ft. Worth chpt., 1974; 50th Anniversary Grad. Sch. citation Brown U., 1978; Omicron Delta Kappa outstanding alumnus award Baylor U., 1978; 25th anniversary first comml. silicon transistor citation by Tex. Instruments Inc., 1980; Semmy award Semicondr. Equipment and Materials Inst., 1984. Fellow IEEE (past dir., editorial bd., awards bd., Centennial medal 1984), Am. Inst. Chemists (50th ann. meeting honor scroll, fellows lectr. 1973), AAAS (v.p., chmn. indsl. sci. sect. 1969-70, mem. council 1968-71, mem. com. council affairs 1969-71, chmn. com. on industry, tech. and soc. 1972-74), Tex. Acad. Sci. (pres., hon. life fellow 1960), Washington Acad. Sci., Instn. Elec. Engrs. U.K. (chartered elec. engr.); mem. Nat. Acad. Engring. (aeros. and space bd. 1970-73), Council Sci. Socs. Dallas-Ft. Worth (dir., past chmn. bd., chmn. exec. com.), Am. Phys. Soc., Am. Chem. Soc., Electrochem. Soc., Dirs. Indsl. Research, Indsl. Research Inst., Sigma Xi, Sigma Pi Sigma (hon.), Kappa Epsilon Alpha. Clubs: Athenaeum (London); Cosmos (Washington). Address: 5222 Park Ln Dallas TX 75220

TEANNAKI, TEATAO, government official. V.p. Govt. of Kiribati, Bairiki, 1986—. Office: Office of Vice Pres, Bairiki Kiribati *

TEASLEY, EDGAR WILLIAM, association executive, realtor; b. Toccoa, Ga., Oct. 7, 1912; s. Edgar Carl and Pearle (Brown) T.; m. Margaret Pitney, Sept. 15, 1939; children: Stewart P., Russell W. AB in Econs., George Washington U., 1936. Exec. W.R. Grace & Co., N.Y.C., 1936-41; gen. mgr., owner Sta. WTNT, Augusta, Ga., 1947-49; self-employed land developer, home builder, realtor, Greenville, S.C., 1950-63; exec. v.p. Home Builders Assn., Greenville, 1963-85; pres. Am. Claims Service Corp.; exec. dir. Home Builders Ins. Trust, Home Builders Self Insurers Fund, Home Builders Pension Fund; founder, dir. Builder Lender Conf.; mem. Nat. Assn. Home Builders Monetary Task Forces, U.S. and internat., 1979-82. Editor, pub. Home Building Newsletter, 1961-86. Served with USNR, 1941-46. Recipient 8 awards as exec. v.p. Home Builders Assn. Greenville; named to Order of Palmetto. Mem. Am. Soc. Assn. Execs. (cert. assn. exec.), Internat. Platform Assn., Nat. Assn. Home Builders (life dir.), Am. Claim Service Corp. (pres.). Presbyterian (elder). Home: 8 Sunset Dr Greenville SC 29605 Office: 15 Wellington Ave Greenville SC 29609

TEATHER, DAVID CHARLES BARTON, educational administrator; b. Lytham St. Annes, Lancashire, Eng., Apr. 25, 1943; s. Bernard and Kathleen Mary (Barton) T.; m. Elizabeth Kenworthy, May 27, 1967; children: Ceri Jane, Ian Kenworthy. BS with honors, U. London, 1964, PhD, 1971. Lectr. U. London, 1967-70, U. Liverpool, Eng., 1970-73; sr. lectr. U. Otago, New Zealand, 1973-78, dir. Higher Edn. Devel. Ctr., 1978-83; vis. fellow U. New Eng., Armidale, Australia, 1984; dep. prin. Armidale Coll. Advanced Edn., Australia, 1984—; pres. New Zealand Coll. Edn., 1980-83. Editor: Staff Development in Higher Education, 1979, Towards the Community University, 1982, New Zealand Jour. Adult Learning, 1983-84; mem. editorial bd. Brit. Jour. Ednl. Tech., Jour. Distance Edn., Higher Edn. Abstracts, Jour. Ednl. TV; contbr. articles to profl. jours. Fellow Australian Inst. Mgmt., New Zealand Inst. Mgmt. Home: 164 Galloway St, Armidale NSW 2350, Australia Office: Armidale Coll Advanced Edn, Mossman St, Armidale NSW 2350, Australia

TEBBIT, NORMAN BERESFORD, former British secretary of state for trade and industry; b. Enfield, Eng., Mar. 29, 1931; s. Leonard and Edith Tebbit; m. Margaret Elizabeth Daines, 1956; 3 children. Ed. State Primary Schs., Edmonton County Grammar Sch. Comml. pilot, holder various posts Brit. Air Line Pilots' Assn., 1953-70; M.P. for Epping, 1970-74, for Chingford, 1974—; parliamentary pvt. sec. Dept. Employment, 1972-73; under-sec. of state Dept. of Trade, 1979-81; minister of state Dept. Industry, 1981; sec. of state for employment, 1981-83; sec. of state for trade and industry, from 1983; chmn. Conservative Party, until 1987. Served as pilot RAF, 1949-51. Office: House of Commons, Westminster, London SW1 England *

TEBEKA, JACQUES JACOB, computers and systems specialist, software company executive; b. Tunis, Tunisia, Feb. 28, 1935; s. Victor and Marie (Allal) T.; M.S., Ecole Polytechnique, Paris, 1958; M.S., Ecole Nationale Superieure des Mines de Paris, 1960; m. Majvor Goransson, June 25, 1960; children—Anita, Karina, Sabine. EDP mgr. Esso France, Paris, 1962, ops. research cons. Esso Mathematics and Systems, Florham Park, N.J., 1968-70; gen. mgr. Sci. Mgmt. Internat., Paris, 1970-74; advisor computers and systems BSN-Gervais Danone, Paris, 1974-79; gen. mgr. Groupe Dataid, Paris, 1979—. Author report to prime minister on computer specialists tng., 1980. Home: 37 Ave Bosquet, 75007 Paris France Office: 48 Ave Raymond Poincare, 75116 Paris France

TEBET, DAVID WILLIAM, television executive; b. Phila., Dec. 27, 1920. Student, Temple U., 1941. Publicity staff legitimate theatre prodns. for John C. Wilson, Theatre Guild, others; pub. relations Max Leibman Prodns., 1950—; sr. v.p. NBC-TV, N.Y.C.; v.p. talent NBC, Inc., 1959-75, sr. v.p., 1975-79; cons. Marble Arch Prodns., Studio City, Calif., 1979—; exec. v.p. Johnny Carson Prodns.; Mem. TV-radio and film adv. bd. Stevens Coll., Columbia, Mo. Named Man of Year Conf. Personnel Mgrs. W. Club: Friars (bd. govs. chmn. spl. events com., chmn. ann. testimonial dinners). Office: Carson Prodns Group 10045 Riverside Dr Toluca Lake CA 91602

TEBOUL, ALBERT, nuclear power director; b. Oujda, Morocco, Sept. 28, 1936; s. Charles and Reine (Sayag) T.; m. Arlette Creps, Apr. 27, 1968. Supérieure, Ecole d'électricité et de mécanique industrielles, Paris, 1959; grad., INSEAD, Fontainebleau, France, 1984. Engr. Metafram-Pechiney, Paris, 1960; engr. sci. research Ecole Centrale, Paris, 1960-61; engr. Thomson/CSF, Dijon, France, 1961-62, Soc. de Fabrication d'Elements Catologues, Bollene, France, 1962-65; staff mgr. Soc. de Fabrication d'Elements Catalytiques, Bollene, France, 1970-80, gen. mgr., 1982-85; gen. mgr. Cle Industrielle de Combustible Atomique Fritté, Paris, 1965; pres. Bollene, 1982-86; project mgr. Chain Fabric & Cen Cadarache, France, 1968-70; pres. Sofretes. Mengin, Montargis, France, 1980-82; dir. Centre d'Etudes Nucleairs de la Vallé du Rhône, Com. l'Energie Atomique, Bagnols sur Cèze, France, 1985—; with pub. relations dept. dale Carnegie Assocs., Avignon, France, 1979; fin. mgr. CRC, Jouy. en Josas, France, 1983. Patentee in field. Conseiller mcpl. Mairie Lapalud, 1971, 77. Recipient decree Govt. of France, 1984, 86, decree Chambre de Commerce et de L'Industrie de Vaucluse, 1986, Chevalier de L'ordre Nat. Dumerite, 1987. Mem. Licensing Exec. Soc., Française de L'energie Nucléaire, Inginner Soc. Française. Lodge: Rotary (Bourg. St. Andéol-Viviers-Le Teil). Home: Rue Bourgades Hautes, 84840 Lapalud, Vaucluse France Office: Centre d'Etudes Nucleaires, la Vallee du Rhone BP 171, 30205 Bagnols-sur-Ceze France

TEDDLIE, CHARLES BENTON, education research consultant, social psychologist; b. Winnfield, La., July 30, 1949; s. Charles Ray and Blanche (Wilson) T.; m. Karen Antoinette Lafontaine, Dec. 1972 (div. 1974); m. Susan Elizabeth Kochan, June 19, 1982; children: Kate, Timothy. B.S. cum laude, La. State U., 1972; M.A. in Social Psychology, U.N.C.-Chapel Hill, 1977, Ph.D., 1979. Vis. asst. prof. La. State U., Baton Rouge, 1979, adj. asst. prof., 1980-85; asst. prof. U. New Orleans, 1985—; internal research cons. La. Dept. Edn., Baton Rouge, 1980-85; pres. La Data, Baton Rouge, 1980—, asst. supr. for research and devel. La. Dept. Edn., 1988—. Contbr. articles to profl. jours.; editorial cons. Personality and Social Psychology Bull, 1980, Population: Behavioral, Social and Environ. Issues, 1977-79, Representative Research in Social Psychology, 1973-79; editorial cons. Ednl. and Psychol. Research, 1985—. Mem. Democratic Socialist Organizing Com., 1980—. Recipient Paul C. Young award La. State U., 1971-72. Mem. Am. Ednl. Research Assn., Am. Psychol. Assn., AAAS, Assn. Instl. Research, SAS Users Group Internat., Phi Kappa Phi. Democrat. Research on forecasting ednl. enrollment and policy trends, sch. efficiency and effectiveness studies, racial differences in social perception, mgmt. info. systems, communications research, self disclosure. Home: 6604-B Bellaire Dr New Orleans LA 70124 Office: U New Orleans Dept Ednl Leadership and Founds New Orleans LA 70148

TEDIN, DELIA M., interior decorator; b. Buenos Aires, Nov. 17, 1942; d. Horacio V. and Delia (Iriarte Udaondo) T.; m. Horadio Mazza (div.); children: Horacio, Delia, Sofia; m. Mariano T. Noblia; 1 child, Tristan.. BA, U. Buenos Aires, 1975; studied with, Michael Ham, Jesus Maria, Sagrado Corazon. With decorating firms Una Casa Diferente, 1982-85, Casa en Barrio Norte, Buenos Aires, 1984, Diseno, 1983; prin. Delia Tedin Ideas, Buenos Aires, 1976, 85. Contbr. to numerous publs. Mem. Decorators Assn. Republic Argentina (bd. dirs.), Orgn. Ferias Multiples, Colaboration Grupos Danza y Teatro. Clubs: Tennis Argentina, Yate Argentina. Office: Delia Tedin Ideas, Arenales 2450 207, 1425 Buenos Aires Argentina

TEENSMA, BENJAMIN NICOLAAS, educator; b. Pematang Siantar, Indonesia, Mar. 7, 1932; arrived in Netherlands, 1946; s. Benjamin Teensma and Henriëtte Wilhelmina Zegers De Beyl; m. Johanna Maria Vink, Sept, 1980. B of Philosophy, State U., Utrecht, 1958; PhD, State U., Amsterdam, 1966. Prof. Portuguese State U., Utrecht, Netherlands, 1958-65, Groningen, Netherlands, 1965-79, Leiden, Netherlands, 1979—; Author: D. Francisco M. de Melo, 1966, Estrada Real, 1985; co-editor: Franco Mendes' Memórias, 1975; contbr. articles to profl. jours. Mem. Dept. Langs. and Cultures of Latin Am., Leiden. Home: Sint Jacobsgracht 2A, 2311 PW Leiden The Netherlands Office: State U, Faculty of Letters PB 9515, 2300 RA Leiden The Netherlands

TEERLINK, J(OSEPH) LELAND, real estate developer; b. Salt Lake City, July 16, 1935; s. Nicholas John and Mary Luella (Love) T.; student U. Utah, 1953-55; m. Leslie Dowdle, Nov. 5, 1975; children: Steven, David, Andrew, Suzanne, Benjamin. Sales rep. Eastman Kodak Co., Salt Lake City, 1960-69; founder Graphic Systems, Inc., Salt Lake City, 1969-82, pres., 1969-79, chmn. bd., 1979-82; founder Graphic Ink Co., Salt Lake City, 1973, pres., 1975-79, chmn. bd., 1979-82; founder G.S.I. Leasing Co., Salt Lake City, 1975, pres., 1975-82; chmn. bd. Graphic Systems Holding Co., Inc., Salt Lake City, 1978-82; dir. leasing and acquisitions Terra Industries, Inc., real estate developers, 1982-86, ptnr., 1986—. Bd. dirs. ARC, Salt Lake City, 1979-82; vice consulate of the Netherlands for Utah, 1977—; mem. active corps of execs., SBA, 1979-83. Named Small Businessman of the Yr. for Utah, SBA, 1978. Mem. Graphic Arts Equipment and Supply Dealers of Am. (dir. 1978-82), Printing Industry of Am., Nat. Assn. Indsl. and Office Parks (pres. Utah chpt., 1986-87), Nat. Fedn. Ind. Businessmen, Salt Lake City C. of C., Salt Lake Bd. Realtors (life), Million Dollar Club. Republican. Mormon. Clubs: University. Lodge: Rotary. Home: 2984 Thackeray Pl Salt Lake City UT 84108 Office: 6925 Union Park Ctr Midvale UT 84047

TEETS, JOHN WILLIAM, diversifed company executive; b. Elgin, Ill., Sept. 15, 1933; s. John William and Maudie T.; m. Nancy Kerchenfaut, June 25, 1965; children: Jerri, Valerie Sue, Heide Jane, Suzanne. Student, U. Ill. Pres., ptnr. Winter Garden Restaurant, Inc., Carpenterville, Ill., 1957-63; v.p. Greyhound Food Mgmt. Co.; pres. Post Houses, Inc., and Horne's Enterprises, Chgo., 1964-68; pres., chief operating officer John R. Thompson Co., Chgo., 1968-71; pres., chief operating officer Restaurant div., also corp. v.p Canteen Corp., Chgo., 1971-74; exec. v.p., chief operating officer Bonanza Internat. Co., Dallas, 1974-76; chmn., chief exec. officer Greyhound Food Mgmt., Inc., Phoenix, 1976; group v.p. food service Greyhound Corp., Phoenix, 1976-81, group v.p. services group, 1980-81, vice chmn., 1980-82, chmn., chief exec. officer, 1981—, now also pres. and dir.; chmn., pres. Armour & Co., from 1981; vice chmn. President's Conf. on Foodservice Industry; mem. adv. bd. Phoenix and Valley of Sun Conv. and Visitors Bur., 1979-82. Recipient Silver Plate award, Golden Plate award Internat. Foodservice Mfrs. Assn., 1980. Mem. Nat. Automatic Mdsg. Assn., Nat. Restaurant Assn., Nat. Inst. Foodservice Industry (trustee), Am. Mgmt. Assn., Christian Businessmen's Assn. (chmn. steering com. 1977), Nat. Speakers Assn. Club: Arizona. Office: The Greyhound Corp Greyhound Tower Sta 3103 Phoenix AZ 85077 *

TEFFT, MELVIN, radiotherapist; b. Boston, Dec. 15, 1932; s. Louis and Anna (Krivian) T. B.A., Harvard U., 1954; M.D., Boston U., 1958. Diplomate: Am. Bd. Radiology, Nat. Bd. Med. Examiners. Intern Boston City Hosp., 1958-59; resident in radiology Mass. Meml. Hosp., Boston, 1959-62; fellow in radiation therapy Mass. Gen. Hosp., Boston, 1962-64; assoc. radiotherapist Mass. Gen. Hosp., 1971-73; assoc. prof. radiation therapy Harvard U., 1972-73; attending radiotherapist, dir. med. edn. Meml. Sloan-Kettering, Inst., N.Y.C., 1973-75; prof. radiology Cornell U., 1973-75; radiotherapist R.I. Hosp., 1975—, chmn. dept., 1984—, prof. radiation medicine Brown U., Providence, 1975—; chmn. radiation therapy com. Children's Cancer Study Group, 1979—. Contbr. numerous articles to profl. jours. Recipient research grants. Fellow Am. Coll. Radiology; mem. Am. Acad. Pediatrics, AAAS, Am. Assn. Cancer Research, Am. Coll. Nuclear Medicine, AMA, Am. Radium Soc., Am. Roentgen Ray Soc., Am. Soc. Clin. Oncology, Am. Soc. Preventive Oncology, Am. Soc. Therapeutic Radiology, Children's Hosp. Alumni Radiol. Soc., Children's Hosp. Staff Assn., European Soc. Pediatric Radiology, Internat. Soc. Pediatric Radiology, Mass. Med. Soc., Mass. Radiol. Soc., Med. Soc. County N.Y., Med. Soc. State N.Y., New Eng. Cancer Soc., New Eng. Roentgen Ray Soc., New Eng. Soc. Radiation Oncology, N.Y. Acad. Scis., N.Y. Roentgen Soc., Providence Med. Assn., Radiol. Soc. N.Am., Royal Coll. Radiologists, Royal Soc. Medicine, Soc. Nuclear Medicine, Soc. Pediatric Radiologists, Soc. Surg. Oncology. Office: Rhode Island Hospital Dept of Radiation Therapy 593 Eddy Street Providence RI 02903

TEGNER, SVEN ROLAND YELVERTON, physician, consultant, researcher; b. Halmstad, Sweden, June 20, 1946; s. Sven Olof and Myra Jessie (Fex) T.; m. Monica Karlsson, Nov. 8, 1975; children—Andreas, Cecilia. B.A., U. Lund, 1972, M.D., 1974; Ph.D., U. Linkoping, 1985. Registrar doctor Surgical clinic, Lulea, Sweden, 1974-80, Boden, Sweden, 1980-81, Orthopaedic Clinic, Linkoping, 1982-84, asst. dr., 1984-85, cons. physician, Boden, 1985—. Author: Cruciate Ligament Injuries, 1985; contbr. articles to profl. jours. Team physician, Lulea Ice Hockey Team, 1974—, Sweden Nat. Hockey Team, 1985—, Norrkoping Soccer Club, 1982-85. Mem. Swedish Orthopaedic Soc., Swedish Surgical Soc., Swedish Sports Medicine Soc., Scandinavian Orthopaedic Soc., Am. Coll. Sports Medicine, Internat. Soc. for Prosthetics and Orthotics, European Soc. Knee and Arthroscopic Surgery. Home: Repslagargatan 3A, 95135 Luleá Sweden Office: Central Hosp, Dept Orthopaedic Surgery, 96185 Boden Sweden

TEGTMEYER, CHARLES JOHN, radiologist, educator; b. Hamilton, N.Y., July 25, 1939; s. Charles Edwin and Eusebia (Petgrave) T.; BA (N.Y. Regents scholar) with honors, Colgate U., 1961; MD (USPHS Research scholar), George Washington U., 1965; m. Virginia Peters, June 1, 1965. Extern in surgery French Hosp., N.Y.C., 1964; surg. intern George Washington U. Hosp., Washington, 1965-66, surg. resident, 1966-68, resident in radiology, 1968-71; fellow in cardiovascular radiology Peter Bent Brigham Hosp., Boston, 1971-72; practice medicine specializing in radiology, Charlottesville, Va., 1972—; asst. prof. of radiology U. Va. Med. Center, Charlottesville, 1972-75, asst. prof. anatomy, 1973-77, dir. radiology edn. for med. students, 1972-81, assoc. prof. radiology, 1975-78, prof., 1978—, assoc. prof. of anatomy , 1977-87—, prof. of anatomy and cell biology, 1987— , dir. of angiography dept. radiology, 1974-87, prof. and chief div. angiography, internat. radiology and spl. procedures, 1987—; mem. staff U. Va. Hosp. Served to maj. AUS, 1966-72. Diplomate Am. Bd. Radiology (examiner June 1979, 81, 84-86), Nat. Bd. Med. Examiners. Fellow Am. Coll. Angiology, Am. Coll. Radiology, Soc. Cardiovascular and Interventional Radiology (fellow, sec.-treas. 1983, pres. 1986, exec. com. 1980-81, 83-87 and numerous other coms.); mem. Radiol. Soc. N.Am., Med. Soc. Va., Am. Roentgen Ray Soc., Eastern Radiol. Soc., AMA, Albemarle County Med. Soc., Trout Unltd., Sigma Xi, Nu Sigma Nu, Sigma Chi. Editorial bd. Radiographics, 1982-87, Current Problems in Diagnostic Radiology, 1981—; adv. editorial bd. Radiology, 1985-86, Diagnostic Imaging, 1983—; reviewer Radiology,

Am. Jour. Radiology, CHEST, JAMA, Jour. Urology. Contbr. numerous articles on angiography and interventional radiology to med. jours.; inventor of lymph duct cannulator. Home: Bass Hollow 2040 Earlysville Rd Earlysville VA 22936 Office: U Va Med Ctr Dept Radiology Charlottesville VA 22908

TEI, TAKURI, accountant; b. Korea, Feb. 25, 1924; s. Gangen and Isun (Song) T.; came to U.S., 1952, naturalized, 1972; diploma Concordia Theol. Sem., 1959; B.D., Eden Theol. Sem., 1965; M.Ed., U. Mo., 1972; m. Maria M. Ottwaska, Dec. 1, 1969; 1 dau., Sun Kyung Lee. Partner, Madeleine Ottwaska & Assos., St. Louis, 1968—; pres. TMS Tei Enterprises Inc., Webster Groves, Mo., 1969—; instr. Forest Park Community Coll. Mem. Am. Coll. Enrolled Agts. (pres. 1976—), Am. Accounting Assn., Am. Taxation Assn., Assn. Asian Studies, NAACP. Republican. Lutheran. Home and office: 7529 Big Bend Blvd Webster Groves MO 63119

TEICHER, MARCIA HARRIET, personnel consultant company executive; b. Bklyn., Mar. 31, 1947; d. Max and Bettina (Koerner) Fleschner; m. Arthur Mace Teicher, Nov. 23, 1974; 1 child, Craig Morgan. B.A., Queens Coll.-City U. N.Y., 1967. Sr. v.p., owner Smith's 5th Ave Agy., Inc., N.Y.C., 1965—; lectr. in field. Mem. Orgn. for Rehab. and Tng., Scarsdale, N.Y. Recipient Cert. Service award Lions Club, 1983. Mem. Advertising Women of N.Y., Assn. Personnel Cons. of N.Y. (cert., bd. dirs. 1979-80), N.Y. Chpt. of Am. Mktg. Assn. (bd. dirs. 1973—, Cert. award 1982, Cert. award 1984, publs. dir. 1984-85), Nat. Assn. Personnel Cons. Club: Castaways Yacht (New Rochelle). Avocations: boating; reading. Office: Smith's Fifth Ave Agy Inc 17 E 45th St New York NY 10017

TEICHLER, ULRICH CHRISTIAN, higher education educator, researcher; b. Stettin, Germany, July 23, 1942; s. Johannes and Erika (Petersen) T.; m. Yoko Urata; children: Nils-Erik Schinichiro, Matthias Tim Yoshio. Diplom-Soziologe, Free U. Berlin, 1968; Dr.Phil., U. Bremen, 1975. Research fellow Max-Planck Inst. Ednl. Research, Berlin, 1968-78; guest researcher Nat. Inst. Ednl. Research, Tokyo, 1970-72; prof. for research on higher edn. and work Comprehensive U. Kassel, Hessen, Fed. Republic Germany, 1978—, v.p., 1980-82; dir. Ctr. for Research on Higher Edn. and Work, Kassel, 1978—; fellow Netherlands Inst. for Advanced Study, Wassenaar, 1985; vis. prof. Sch. Edn. and Social Policy Northwestern U., Evanston, Ill., 1986—. Author: Faktoren und Zielvorstellungen der Hochschulreform in der Bundesrepublik Deutschland, 1970, Bibliography on Japanese Education, 1974, Theologie und gesellschaftliche Praxis, 1974, Der Arbeitsmarkt für Akademiker in Japan, 1975, Geschichte und Struktur des Japanischen Hochschulwesens, 1975, Hochschulexpansion und Bedarf der Gesellschaft, 1976, Das Dilemma der modernen Bildungsgesellschaft, 1976, Probleme der Hochschulzulassung in den Vereinigten Staaten, 1978, Admission to Higher Education in the United States, 1978, Aspekte der Studienreform, 1979, Die neuen Beamtenhochschulen, 1980, Perspektiven der Hochschulentwicklung in Bremen, 1980, Higher Education and the Needs of Society, 1981, Der Arbeitsmarkt für Hochschulabsolventen, 1981, Gesamthochschule-Erfahrungen, Hemmnisse, Zielwandel, 1981, Bildung und Beschäftigung, 1981, Ausserschulische Tätigkeitsbereiche für Absolventen sprach und literaturwissenschaftlicher Studiengänge, 1981, Beispiel praxisorientierten Studiums, 1981, Implementation of Higher Education Reforms: The German Gesamthochschule, 1981, Higher Education and the Labour Market in the Federal Republic of Germany, 1982, Öffnung der Hochschulen-auch eine Politik für die achtziger Jahre?, 1983, Berufs und Qualifikationsforschung, 2 vols., 1984, Hochschulzertifikate und betriebliche Einstellungspraxis, 1984, Higher Education in the Federal Republic of Germany, 1986, Higher Education in the European Community: Recognition of Study Abroad in the European Community, 1986, Studium und Beruf, 1986, Hochschule-Studium-Berufsvorstellungen, 1987; editor: Praxisorientierung des Studiums, 1979, Hochschule und Beruf, 1979, Neue Aufgaben der Hochschulen, 1980, Praxisorientierung als institutionelles Problem der Hochschule, 1980, Hochschule und Beruf-Forschungsperspektiven, 1981, Gesamthochschule Kassel, 1981, Integrierte Hochschulmodelle, 1982, Hochschule und Beruf in Polen und in der Bundesrepublik Deutschland, 1983, Berufstätigkeit von Hochschulabsolventen, 1983, The Compleat University: Break from Tradition in Germany, Sweden and the U.S.A., 1983, Hochschule und gesellschaftliche Entwicklung in Polen und der Bundesrepublik Deutschland, 1984, Forschungsgestand Hochschule, 1984, Hochschulentwicklung in den 60er Jahren, 1986; contbr. articles to profl. jours. Mem. Higher Edn. Council State Bremen, 1981-85. Mem. German Assn. Asian Studies (research council 1973—), German Sociol. Assn. (chair com. ednl. sect. 1980-84), German Acad. Exchange Service (selection com. 1980—), Soc. for Research into Higher Edn. (v.p. edn. 1986). Home: Haroldstr 11, D-3500 Kassel, Hessen Federal Republic of Germany Office: Wissenschaftliches Zentrum für, Berufs-und Hochschulforschung, Gesamthochschule Kassel, Henschelstr 4, D-3500 Kassel, Hessen Federal Republic of Germany

TEIKARI, VEIKKO OLAVI, industrial psychology educator; b. Jyväskylä, Finland, July 21, 1943; s. Onni Edward and Tyyne Hilja (Putkonen) T.; m. Eira Marjaana Eräntie, Nov. 1, 1969; children: Taru, Mika. D in Social Scis., U. Jyväskylä, 1977. Asst. Inst. Psychology U. Jyväskylä, 1967-68; sr. asst. Lab Indsl. Psychology U. Tech., Espoo, Finland, 1969-73, lab. mgr., 1973-84, prof., 1985—; leader Dept. Prodn. Mgmt. Helsinki U. Tech., 1986—. Author: Vigilanssi-ilmiön mittaamisesta ja selitysmahdollisuuksista, 1977; contbr. articles to profl. jours. Served with Finnish mil., 1963-64. Mem. Psychol. Soc. Finland, Ergonomic Soc. Finland. Home: Särkiniementie 10 C 16, 00210 Helsinki Finland Office: U Tech, Otakaari 4A, 02150 Espoo Finland

TEILHET, HILDEGARDE TOLMAN, author; b. Tucson, Nov. 22, 1906; d. Cyrus Fisher and Hannah Marthe (van Steen) Tolman; BA, Stanford U., 1926, postgrad., 1926-27; postgrad. U. Heidelberg (Ger.), 1927-28; m. Darwin L. Teilhet, Oct. 28, 1927; children: Marta, Saral, Jehanne. Manuscript editor Center for Advanced Study of Behavioral Scis., Stanford, Calif., 1964-72. Mem. Pen and Brush, Authors Guild, Mystery Writers Am., Nat. Soc. Lit. and Arts, Internat. Bibl. Centre, IPA, World Affairs Council, Assos. of Stanford U. Libraries (dir. 1976—, chmn. 1979-81, chmn. pub. Imprint 1976-79, 81-87), Alpha Phi. Democrat. Episcopalian. Author: (with Darwin L. Teilhet) The Ticking Terror Murders, 1935, The Crimson Hair Murders, 1936, The Feather Cloak Murders, 1938, The Broken Face Murders, 1940; sole author: Hero by Proxy, 1941; The Double Agent, 1945, The Assassins, 1946, The Terrified Society, 1947, The Rim of Terror, 1950, A Private Undertaking, 1953, Undertaking, 1958. Address: 14141 Miranda Rd Los Altos Hills CA 94022

TEIXEIRA, ANTONIO DA SILVA, banker; b. Pinhel, Beira Alta. Portugal, Apr. 6, 1932; s. Adriano and Angelina (Da Silva) T.; m. Maria Adosinda Sampaio, June 17, 1962; children: Ana Paula, Maria João, Luis Adriano, Antonio Pedro. Mining Engr., Inst. Superior Tech., Lisbon; Sr. Exec. (hon.), IMEDE, Lausanne, Switzerland, 1982. Dep. mgr. Minas de Jalles Lda., Vila Pouca de Aguiar, Portugal, 1958-64; cons. engr. CEO-Portugal, Lda., Lisbon, 1964-65; 1st class asst. INII-Portugal, Lisbon, 1965-70; exec. Banco de Fomento Nacional, Lisbon, 1970-76, mem. bd., 1976-82, dir., 1983—; tech. asst. Associação Indsl. Portuguesa, Lisbon, 1965-76; asst. researcher OCDE Pilot Team Project, Lisbon, 1966-68; lectr. Portugal, Angola, Mozambique; 1966-76. Contbr. articles to profl. jours. Mem. Ordem dos Engenheiros, Internat. IMEDE Alumni Assn., Assn. de Antigos Alunos Inst. Superior Tech. (v.p., dir.). Roman Catholic. Office: Banco de Fomento Nacional, Ave Casal Ribeiro 59, 1000 Lisbon Portugal

TEJWANI, GOPI A., scientist, educator; b. India, Mar. 1, 1946; came to U.S., 1973, permanent U.S. resident; B.S., Nagpur U., 1966, M.S. in Biochemistry, 1968; Ph.D. in Biochemistry, All-India Inst. Med. Scis., New Delhi, 1973; m. Raman; 1 son, Samir. Research asst. Nagpur U., India, 1968-69, All-India Inst. Med. Scis., 1969-73; research assoc. dept. microbiology St. Louis U. Sch. Medicine, 1973-74; postdoctoral fellow Roche Inst. Molecular Biology, Nutley, N.J., 1974-76; clin. asst. prof. dept. pharmacology Coll. Medicine, Ohio State U., Columbus, 1976-78, asst. prof., 1978-88, assoc. prof., 1988—; vis. prof. U. São Paulo, Brazil, 1978, Moscow (USSR) State U., 1981; condr. seminars, workshops, symposia; speaker profl. confs. U.S., India, Chile, Brazil, USSR, Poland, Greece, W.Ger., Eng., France , Italy, Australia; cons. Ortho Pharm. Corp., Raritan, N.J., also VA. Grantee, Ohio State U., 1979, Distilled Spirits Council U.S., 1979-80, Central Ohio Heart Chpt., 1980-81, Bremer Found., 1980-81, United Cancer Council, 1981-82, NIH, 1981-83, Weight Watchers Found. Inc., 1981-83, 84-86, Nat. Livestock and Meat Bd., 1983-84, Am. Health Asst. Fedn., 1986-88, Ohio Dept. Aging, 1988—; recipient Marion T. Colwill award, Ohio State U., 1980, faculty recognition award, 1982. Mem. AAAS, Am. Assn. Clin. Chemistry, Soc. Neurosci.(pres. Cen. Ohio chpt. 1987-88), Am. Soc. Pharmacology and Exptl. Therapeutics, Am. Soc. Biochem. Molecular Biologists. Asst. editor Recent Advances in Clinical Therapeutics, Vol. 3, 1983; referee Archives of Biochemistry and Biophysics, Science, Life Sciences, Investigative Radiology, Annals of Internal Medicine, Procs. of Nat. Acad. Scis.; contbr. writings to profl. publs. Office: Ohio State U College of Medicine Dept Pharmacology Columbus OH 43210 Home: 1945 Charmingfare St Columbus OH 43228

TE KANAWA, KIRI, opera and concert singer; b. Gisborne, N.Z., Mar. 6, 1944; d. Thomas and Elanor Te Kanawa; m. Desmond Park, Aug. 30, 1967; children—Antonia Aroha, Thomas Desmond. Student, St. Mary's Coll., Auckland, N.Z., 1957-60, London Opera Centre, 1966-69; D.Mus. (hon.), Oxford U., 1983. Joined Royal Opera House, London, 1971; appeared in role of Countess in: Le Nozze di Figaro, 1973; U.S. debut in Santa Fe Festival, 1971; Met. Opera debut as Desdemona in: Otello, 1974; appears regularly with all major European and Am. opera houses, including Australian opera cos., Royal Opera House Covent Garden, Paris Opera, Houston Opera, Munich Opera, La Scalla, others; appeared in film Don Giovanni as Elvira, 1979; recordings include Blue Skies, 1986, Kiri Sings Gershwin, 1987; PBS appearance: Great Performances: West Side Story, 1985. Decorated comdr. Order Brit. Empire, 1973, Dame Comdr. Brit. Empire, 1983. Office: care Basil Horsfield, L'Estoril (B), Avenue Princess Grace 31, Monte Carlo Monaco also: care Artists Internat Mgmt, London England *

TEKELIOGLU, MERAL, physician, educator; b. Ermenek, Konya, Turkey, Dec. 23, 1936; d. Sefik and Zeynep Tekelioglu; grad. Ankara (Turkey) Med. Faculty, 1961, specialist degree in histology-embryology, 1964, Docent, 1969; full prof., Faculty Medicine Hacettepe U., Ankara, 1975; m. Ziya Uysal, July 1961 (div. 1984); 1 son, Kaya. Asst. in histology-embryology Faculty Medicine, Ankara U., 1961-64, chief asst., 1964-69, docent dept. histology-embryology, Hacethpe U., 1969-75, prof., dir. dept. histology-embrology, 1979-83, Anka Med. Faculty, 1983—; full prof. histology-embryology Faculty Medicine, Hacettepe U., 1975-79; cons. election microscopy. Mem. Turkish Electron Microscopy Soc., European Soc. Anatomy, Royal Micros. Soc., Cytochem. Soc. of Oxford, European Pineal Study Group, Turkish Soc. Natural Protection, Clair Hall Cambridge (Eng.) U. (assoc.). Moslem. Author: (with others) The Cell: Fine Structure and Function, 1972, 74, 78, 82; Medical Embryology, 1984; articles on human brain morphology of slow-growing viral infections, degenerative diseases of the human central nervous system, related topics. Office: Sihhiye, Dept Histology-Embryology, Faculty of Medicine, Morphology Bldg, Ankara Turkey

TEKINEL, HÜSEYIN, electrical company executive; b. Kocaeli, Turkey, Aug. 24, 1932; s. Mustafa and Zehra (Yatağan) T.; m. Gülnar Kirimcan, May 22, 1958; children: Emine Özbay, Kemal Tekinel. MS in Elec. Power Engring., Tech. U. Istanbul, 1955. Reponcible engr. Relays and Metering Sect., Adapazari, 1956-59, 60-62; chief engr. Relays and Test Dept., Ankara, 1964-67; dir. networks div. Etibank, Ankara, 1967-70; bd. mem., asst. gen. mgr. Tek-Turkish Electricity Authority, Ankara, 1970-77; gen. mgr. ESAS-Elektrik Sanayii ve Ticcaret A.S., Kartal-istanbul, 1977-88; instr. Engring. Academi, Ankara, 1968-77, Middle East Tech. U., Ankara, 1963-68. Author: Electrical Power Transmission, 1976, Electrical Power Plants, 1976. Served to lt. Turkish Army, 1959-60. Recipient award Turkish Electricity Authority, Ankara, 1972. Mem. IEEE, Turkish Elec. Engrs. Chamber,. Clubs: Kartal Rotary, Enka Sport (Istanbul). Office: ESAS PK, Kartal, Istanbul Turkey

TELEKI, MARGOT WHITESON, marketing communications executive; b. Cleve., May 24, 1935; d. Milton D. and Ilon (Sarkany) Whiteson; grad. New Eng. Conservatory Music, 1952; student Radcliffe Coll., 1950-51, Harvard Extension U., 1950-51, Hunter Coll., 1951-52. Media exec. J. Walter Thompson Co., N.Y.C., 1958-60; head broadcast buyer Reach McClinton & Co., Inc., N.Y.C., 1960-62, media research mgr., 1962; research dir. Sta. WNEW, N.Y.C., 1963-64; sr. research analyst Young & Rubicam, N.Y.C., 1964-65; media exec. N.W. Ayer & Son, Inc., Phila., 1965-68; sr. editor Media-Scope Mag., N.Y.C., 1968-70, also columnist, 1969—; pres. Teleki Assocs., Ltd., N.Y.C., 1970-82; pres. TAL Communications, Inc., Morristown, N.J., 1982—. Club: Yale (N.Y.C.). Contbr. feature articles to various mags. and publs. Office: PO Box 9179 Morristown NJ 07960

TELEPAS, GEORGE PETER, lawyer; b. Kingston, N.Y., Nov. 20, 1935; s. Peter G. and Grace T.; m. Regina Tisiker, Sept. 6, 1969 (div.). B.S., U. Fla., 1960; J.D., U. Miami, 1965. Bar: Fla., 1965. Assoc., Preddy, Haddad, Kutner, & Hardy, 1966-67; assoc. Williams & Jabara, 1967-68; sole practice, Miami, Fla., 1968—. Mem. citizens bd. U. Miami. Served with USMC, 1954-56. Mem. ABA, Fla. Bar Assn., Colo. Bar Assn., Dade County Bar Assn., Assn. Trial Lawyers Am., Fla. Trial Lawyers Assn., Dade County Trial Lawyers Assn., Delta Theta Phi, Sigma Nu. Home: 1 Grove Isle Dr Apt 910 Coconut Grove FL 33133 Office: 1933 SW 27 Ave Miami FL 33145

TELESETSKY, WALTER, govt. ofcl.; b. Boston, Jan. 22, 1938; s. Keril and Nellie (Krelka) T.; B.S. in Mech. Engring., Northeastern U., 1960; M.B.A., U. Chgo., 1961; m. Sharron-Dawn Lamp, July 15, 1961; children—Stephanie Ann, Anastasia Marie. Mem. tech. staff The Mitre Corp., Bedford, Mass., 1962-68; sr. mem. tech. staff Data Dynamics, Inc., Washington, 1969; phys. scientist NOAA, Rockville, Md., 1970-71, U.S. Gate Project coordinator, 1972-74, dir. U.S. Global Weather Experiment Project Office, 1974, dir. Program Integration Office, 1975-77, dir. Programs and Tech. Devel. Office, 1977-79, dir. Programs and Internat. Activities Office, 1979-81, dep. asso. dir. for tech. services, chief AFOS ops. div. Nat. Weather Service, Silver Spring, Md., 1981-86, dir., Office of Systems Ops., 1986—; liaison to Nat. Acad. Scis. coms. on atmospheric scis., geophysics studies and internat. environ. programs, 1975-81; U.S. coordinator U.S./Japan Coop. Program in Natural Resources, 1980—; chmn. U.S.-Japan Marine Resources and Engring. Coordination Com., 1980—; U.S. del. governing council UN Environ. Program and World Meteorol. Orgn. Recipient Silver medal Dept. Commerce, 1975. Mem. AAAS, Am. Geophys. Union, Am. Meteorol. Soc. Contbr. articles to profl. publs. Home: 16 Eton Overlook Rockville MD 20850 Office: 8060 13th St Silver Spring MD 20910

TELL, BERTIL NILS, transportation executive; b. Stockholm, Sept. 6, 1947; s. Nils W. and Greta (Svensson) T.; m. Karin M. Emilsson, Sept. 11, 1971; children: David, Helena. MBA, Stockholm Sch. Econs., 1976-78, PhD, 1976, Docent, 1979. Assoc. prof. bus. adminstrn. Stockholm Sch. Econs., 1976-78; fin. mgr. Scandinavian Airlines Systems, Stockholm, 1978-81, controller traffic div., 1981-86, treas., 1986—. Author: A Comparative Study of Some Multiple-Criteria Methods, 1976, Investeringskalk i Praktiken, 1978; editor: Ekonomisk Styrning Under Inflation, 1984; contbr. articles to profl. jours. Fellow Planning Execs. Inst.; mem. Svenska Civilekonom Foreningen. Office: Scandinavian Airlines Systems, Dept UT, 16187 Stockholm Sweden

TELLEFSEN, BRYNJULF, college dean; b. Oslo, Dec. 12, 1945; s. Anders and Solveig (Klingenberg) T.; B.A. in Econs., Manchester (Eng.) U., 1969; M.Phil., Columbia U., 1974, Ph.D., 1977; m. Marianne Rasch-Nielsen, Jan. 29, 1971; children: Christian, Agnethe. Asst. prof. SUNY, Plattsburgh, 1973-77; program dir. Stiftelsen Norges Markedshoyskole (Sch. Mktg.), Oslo, 1977-88, dean, 1979-87; ptnr., bus. cons. Integrator A/S, 1988—. Chmn. Region 35 of Oslo Hoyre, 1983—. John M. Chapman fellow, 1972-74; Emery Found. fellow, 1975-77; Oslo Handelsstands Forening grantee, 1971-73; recipient George Hay Brown prize Columbia U., 1970. Mem. Norwegian Mktg. Assn. (dir. 1978-81), Am. Mktg. Assn., Brit. Inst. Mgmt., Norwegian Mktg. Research Assn., Esomar Polyteknisk Forening (Norway). Office: Postboks 210 Ø kern, Oslo 5, Norway

TELLER, AARON JOSEPH, chemical engineer; b. Bklyn., June 30, 1921; s. David and Mollie (Tascher) T.; m. Sherry R. April, June 30, 1946; 1 son, Richard Eric. B. Chem. Engring., Cooper Union, 1943; M. Chem. Engring., Bklyn. Poly. Inst., 1949; Ph.D., Case Inst. Tech., 1951. Research engr. Manhattan Project, 1942-44; devel. engr. Publicker Comml. Alcohol Co., 1944-45; prodn. mgr. Martin Labs., 1945-47; chief devel. engr. City Chem. Corp., 1946-47; chmn. chem. engring. and chem. depts. Fenn Coll., 1947-56; research prof., chmn. chem. engring. U. Fla., 1956-60; tech. dir. Mass Transfer, Inc., 1960-62; tech. dir. Colonial Iron Works, Inc., 1960-62, cons. tech. dir., 1962-64; ind. indsl. cons. 1947—; dean Sch. Engring. and Sci., Cooper Union, 1962-70; pres. Teller Environmental Systems, Inc., 1970-86; cons. Research Cottrell, 1986—. Editor: Liquid-Gas Operations (Perry's Chem. Engring. Handbook), 4th edit, 1963; Contbr. articles to profl. jours. Mem. Nat. Adv. Council on Air Pollution. Recipient Bus. Week environ. award, 1972, Valeur award, 1978. Fellow Am. Inst. Chem. Engring.; mem. Nat. Engrs. Commn. on Air Resources (chmn. commn. on resource economy 1972—), Am. Inst. Chem. Engrs. (chmn. Cleve. and Peninsular Fla. sects. 1953, 58, chmn. pollution control program 1958-61, chmn. air com. 1963-66, 22d ann. inst. lectr. 1972). Home: 3140 S Ocean Blvd Palm Beach FL 33480 Office: PO Box 1500 Somerville NJ 08876

TELLIER, PAUL M., Canadian government official; b. Joliette, Que., Can., May 8, 1939; s. Maurice J. and Eva M. (Bouvier) T.; m. Andree Poirier, June 6, 1959; children: Claude, Marc. B.A., U. Ottawa, 1959, L.LL, 1962; M.A., U. Montreal, 1963; B.Litt., Oxford U., 1966. Bar: Que. bar 1963. Asst. prof. U. Montreal, 1966-67; exec. asst. minister energy 1967-68; with Privy Council Office, Ottawa, Ont., Can., 1968-70; dep. sec. to Cabinet, exec. council Govt. of Que., 1970-72; dir.-gen. urban policy Ministry of State for Urban Affairs, 1972-73; joined Public Service Commn., 1974-75, exec. dir., 1975-76; asst. dep. minister fisheries and environ. Govt. of Can., 1976-77; dep. sec. to cabinet Fed.-Provincial Relations Office, 1977-79; dep. minister Indian affairs and no. devel. 1979-82, dep. minister energy, mines and resources, 1982-85; chmn. governing bd. Internat. Energy Agy., 1985; clk. of Privy Council and sec. to Cabinet Govt. of Can., Ottawa, 1985—; dir. Petro Can., Atomic Energy of Can. Ltd. Mem. Que. Bar, Inst. Public Adminstrn. Roman Catholic. Office: Privy Council Office, Langevin Block Rm 332, Wellington St, Ottawa, ON Canada K1A 0A3 also: care Internat Energy Agy, 2 rue Andre Pascal, 75775 Paris Cedex 16 France

TEMAM, ROGER M., mathematician; b. Tunis, Tunisia, May 19, 1940; s. Ange M. and Elise (Ganem) T.; m. Claudette Cukorja, Aug. 21, 1962; children: David, Olivier, Emmanuel. Agregation Math., U. Paris, 1962, DSc, 1967. Asst. prof. math. U. Paris, 1960-67, prof., 1967—; prof. Ecole Polytechnique, Paris, 1968-85. Author: (with I. Ekeland) Convex Analysis and Variational Problems, 1974, Navier-Stokes Equations, 1977, Mathematical Problems in Plasticity, 1983, Infinite Dimensional Dynamical Systems in Mechanics and Physics, 1988, Integral Manifolds..., 1988; contbr. 120 articles to sci. jours.; editor, assoc. editor profl. jours. Mem. Am. Math. Soc., Soc. Indsl. and Applied Math., Soc. Math Applications of Industry (founding pres. 1983-87).

TEMIN, HOWARD MARTIN, scientist, educator; b. Phila., Dec. 10, 1934; s. Henry and Annette (Lehman) T.; m. Rayla Greenberg, May 27, 1962; children: Sarah Beth, Miriam Judith. BA, Swarthmore Coll., 1955, DSc (hon.), 1972; PhD, Calif. Inst. Tech., 1959; DSc (hon.), N.Y. Med. Coll., 1972, U. Pa., 1976, Hahnemann Med. Coll., 1976, Lawrence U., 1976, Temple U., 1979, Med. Coll. Wis., 1981, Colo. State U., 1987, PM Curie, Paris, 1988. Postdoctoral fellow Calif. Inst. Tech., 1959-60; asst. prof. oncology U. Wis., 1960-64, assoc. prof., 1964-69, prof., 1969—, Wis. Alumni Research Found. prof. cancer research, 1971-80, Am. Cancer Soc. prof. viral oncology and cell biology, 1974—, H.P. Rusch prof. cancer research, 1980—, Steenbock prof. biol. scis., 1982—; mem. research policy adv. com. U. Wis. Med. Sch., 1979-85; mem. Internat. Com. Virus Nomenclature Study Group for RNA Tumor Viruses, 1973-75, subcoms. HTLV and AIDS viruses, 1985; mem. virology study sect. NIH, 1971-74, mem. dir.'s adv. com., 1979-83; cons. working group on human gene therapy NIH/RAC, 1984—, mem. Nat. Cancer Adv. Bd., 1986—; mem. NAS/IOM Com. for a Nat. Strategy for AIDS, 1986, NAS/IOM AIDS activities oversight com., 1987—; mem. Nat. Cancer Inst. (spl. virus cancer program tumor virus detection segment working group), 1972-73; sponsor Fedn. Am. Scientists, 1976—; sci. adv. Stehlin Found., Houston, 1972—; mem. Waksman award com. Nat. Acad. Sci., 1976-81; mem. U.S. Steel award com., 1980-83, chmn., 1982. Assoc. editor: Jour. Cellular Physiology, 1966-77, Cancer Research, 1971-74; exec. editor Molecular Carcinogenesis, 1987; mem. editorial bd.: Jour. Virology, 1971—, Intervirology, 1972-75, Proc. Nat. Acad. Scis, 1975-80, Archives of Virology, 1975-77, Ann. Rev. Gen., 1983, Molecular Biology and Evolution, 1983—, Oncogene Research, 1987—, AIDS, 1988—. Co-recipient Warren Triennial prize Mass. Gen. Hosp., 1971, Gairdner Found. Internat. award, 1974, Nobel Prize in medicine, 1975; recipient Med. Soc. Wis. Spl. commendation, 1971; Papanicolaou Inst. PAP award, 1972; M.D. Anderson Hosp. and Tumor Inst. Bertner award, 1972; U.S. Steel Found. award in Molecular Biology, 1972; Theobald Smith Soc. Waksman award, 1972; Am. Chem. Soc. award in Enzyme Chemistry, 1973; Modern Medicine award for Distinguished Achievement, 1973; Harry Shay Meml. lectr. Fels Research Inst., 1973; Griffuel prize Assn. Devel. Recherche Cancer, Villejuif, 1972; New Horizons lectr. Radiol. Soc. N.Am., 1968; G.H.A. Clowes lectr. award Assn. Cancer Research, 1974; NIH Dyer lectr. award, 1974; Harvey lectr., 1974, Charlton lectr. Tufts U., 1976, Hoffman-LaRoche lectr. Rutgers U., 1979, Yoder hon. lectr. St. Joseph Hosp., Tacoma, 1983; Cetus lectr. U. Calif., Berkeley, 1984; DuPont lectr. Harvard Med. Sch., 1985; Japanese Found. for Promotion Cancer Research lectr., 1985, Herz Meml. lectr. Tel-Aviv U., 1985, Amoros. Meml. lectr. U. West Indies, 1986; Albert Lasker award in basic med. sci., 1974; Lucy Wortham James award Soc. Surg. Oncologists, 1976; Alumni Disting. Service award Calif. Inst. Tech., 1976; Gruber award Am. Acad. Dermatology, 1981; mem. Central High Sch. Hall of Fame Phila., 1976; Pub. Health Service Research Career Devel. awardee Nat. Cancer Inst., 1964-74, 1st Hilldale award in Biolog. Sci. U. Wis., 1986, Braund Disting. vis. prof. U. Tenn., 1987, Eisenstark lectr. U. Mo., 1987, 1st Wilmot vis. prof. U. Rochester, 1987. Fellow Am. Acad. Arts and Scis., Wis. Acad. Sci. Arts and Letters; mem. Nat. Acad. Scis., Am. Philos. Soc., Tissue Culture Assn. (hon.). Office: Univ of Wis McArdle Lab 450 N Randall St Madison WI 53706

TEMIRKANOV, YURI KHATUEVICH, orchestra conductor; b. Nalchik, USSR, Dec. 10, 1938; s. Khatu Sagidovich and Polina Petrovna T.; grad. Leningrad Conservatory, 1966; m. Irina Guseva; 1 son. Chief condr. Leningrad Philharm. Orch., 1967-76, Kirov Opera and Ballet Theatre Orch., 1976-88; prof. Leningrad Conservatory, 1979—; chief guest condr. London Royal Philharm. Orch.; artistic dir. Leningrad Symphony Orch., 1988; mus. dir. operas: Peter I (Petrov), 1975, War and Peace (Prokofiev), 1976, Dead Souls (Schedrin), 1978, Pushkin (Petrov), 1979, Queen of Spades (Tchaikovsky), 1979; mem. Artistic Council Presidium, Ministry of Culture USSR. Winner 1st prize USSR Contest for Condrs., 1967, USSR State prize, 1976; named People's Artist of Kabardino-Balkarian Autonomous Republic, People's Artist of RSFSR. Mem. All-Russian Theatrical Soc. (vice chmn. bd.). Office: Leningrad Symphony Orch, Ul Brodskogo 2, Leningrad USSR *

TEMKIN, ROBERT HARVEY, accountant; b. Boston, Oct. 21, 1943; s. Max and Lillian (Giller) T.; m. Ellen Phyllis Band, Sept. 25, 1966; children—Aron, Rachel, Joshua. BBA, U. Mass., 1964. CPA, Mass., N.Y., Conn. With Arthur Young & Co., CPA's, 1964-72, 73—, ptnr., 1976—, nat. dir. auditing standards, 1980-88; controller SCA Services, Inc., Boston, 1972-73; mem. peer rev. com. SEC Practice Sect., Am. Inst. CPA's, 1982-84, auditing standards bd., 1984-88; adj. assoc. prof. NYU, 1982. Chmn. ad hoc com. low/moderate housing Town of Natick, Mass., 1972-73, mem. by-law revision com., 1972-73; mem. young leadership United Jewish Appeal, 1976-80; bd. dirs. Jewish Home for Elderly of Fairfield County, 1979—, pres., 1985-87; trustee Congregation Beth El, Norwalk, Conn., 1979—, pres., 1983-85, chmn. bd., 1986-87; mem. Bd. Edn., Weston, Conn., 1983-87, United Synagogue Am., chmn. audit com., mem. budget and fin. com.; mem. planning com. United Way Mass. Bay, Bus Adv. Council, U. Mass., also v.p.; bd. dirs. Jr. Achievement Stamford Area, 1978-80, spl. adv. nat. conf., 1967; trustee Am. Shakespeare Theatre/Conn. Ctr. for Performing Arts, 1981-84; mem. nat. adv. council United Synagogue Am., 1983-87, budget and fin. com., 1986—, chmn. audit com., 1987—, internat. v.p., 1988—; pres. Conn. Valley Region, United Synagogue Am., 1987-88; chmn. budget and fin. com. Synagogue Council Mass. Recipient Acctg. Alumni award U. Mass., 1978, Alumnus Award Sch. Mgmt. U. Mass., 1986. Mem. Am. Inst. C.P.A.s (staff dir. Commn. on Auditors Responsibilities 1976-78, mem. task force on auditor's report 1978-81, auditing standards bd. 1984—), Mass. Soc. C.P.A.s (Silver medal 1964, mem. profl. ethics com.), N.Y. State Soc.

C.P.A.s, Conn. Soc. C.P.A.s., Greater Boston C. of C. (dir.). Clubs: Bd. Rm. (N.Y.C.); Rolling Hills Country. Home: 1611 Commonwealth Ave West Newton MA 02165 Office: Arthur Young & Co One Boston Pl Boston MA 02109

TEMPERLEY, HOWARD REED, historian, educator; b. Sunderland, Eng., Nov. 16, 1932; s. Fred and May (Holland) T.; m. Rachel Stephanie Hooper, Sept. 29, 1966; 1 child by previous marriage, Alison; children by present marriage, Rebecca, Nicholas. BA, Oxford U., 1956; MA, Yale U., 1957, PhD, 1961. Asst. lectr. U. Wales, 1960-61; lectr. U. Manchester, Eng., 1961-67; sr. lectr. history U. East Anglia, Eng., 1967-80, prof. Am. history, 1980—. Author: British Antislavery, 1972; co-author: Introduction to American Studies, 1981; editor: Gubbins's Journals, 1980; editor Jour. Am. Studies, 1977-86. Served to 2nd lt. English Army, 1951-53. Mem. Brit. Assn. of Am. Studies (chmn.). Home: Arlington House, Arlington Ln, Norwich NR2 2DB, England Office: U of East Anglia, Sch English and American Studies, Norwich NR4 7TJ, England

TEMPLE, DAVID JOHN, company executive; b. Oshawa, Ont., Can., May 23, 1945; s. Herbert Weafer and Jessie Winnifred (Cunliffe) T.; m. Lynne MAry Taylor, Nov. 29, 1969. BSc, U. Guelph, Ont., 1967. Gen. mgr. Canplas Industries Ltd., Barrie, Ont., 1978-80, v.p., 1980-84, pres., chief exec. officer, 1984—; bd. dirs. Forsco Industries, Barrie. Mem. Barrie and Dist. C. of C. (bd. dirs. 1985—). Club: National Gold (Woodbridge, Ont.). Office: Canplas Industries Ltd, Box 1800 31 Patterson Rd, Barrie, ON Canada L4M 4V3

TEMPLE, PAUL NATHANIEL, investor, entrepreneur; b. Cin., Mar. 19, 1923; s. Paul Nathaniel and Alice Marie (White) T.; A.B., Princeton U., 1944; J.D., Harvard U., 1948; m. Karen Borgstrom, Aug. 3, 1944 (dec. 1981); children—Pamela Temple Abell, Lise Temple Greenberg, Robin Temple Kline, Thomas D.; m. Diane Elizabeth Brown, Nov. 27, 1981; 1 child, Paulina Diane Marie Temple; stepchildren—James Brown, Thomas Brown. Admitted to Calif. bar, 1948, D.C. bar, 1950; assoc. firm Pillsbury, Madison and Sutro, San Francisco, Washington, 1948-51; atty., exec. Celanese Corp., N.Y.C., 1952-54; internat. concessions negotiator Standard Oil N.J., N.Y.C., 1954-60; pres. Esso Affiliates, Spain, 1961-65; exec. v.p. Gas Natural S.A., Barcelona, 1965-69; pres., co-founder Weeks Natural Resources, Ltd., Westport, Conn., Hamilton, Bermuda, 1970-76; exec. chmn. Energy Capital plc, London, 1982-87, dir., 1979-87; chmn. bd. Energy Capital Devel. Corp., Rosslyn, Va., 1982—; chmn. bd. Dayspring Mining Corp., 1986—; bd. dirs. Global Media/Broadcasting Ltd., 1985-87; dir. Parent Care Ltd., 1988—; also investor petroleum exploration; co-founder Inst. Noetic Scis., 1973, bd. dirs., 1973—; founder Temple award for Creative Altruism, Washington, 1987; hon. sponsor for Christianity, Global Forum of Spiritual and Parliamentary Leaders for Human Survival, Oxford, 1988; master of ceremonies US.-U.S.S.R. Citizens Summit, Alexandria, Va., 1988; dir. The Temple of Understanding, 1987—. Served to ensign USNR, 1944-45. Recipient Civil Merit decoration, Spain, 1969. Mem. Am. C. of C. (pres. Spain 1969), State Bar Calif., Bar Assn. D.C., Inst. Noetic Scis. (co-founder, chmn. 1982—, dir.). Episcopalian. Clubs: Lyford Cay (Bahamas); Puerta de Hierro Golf (Madrid, Spain). Assoc. producer film Born Again, 1977-78, Broadway play Dance a Little Closer, 1983. Home: 1401 N Oak St Arlington VA 22209 Office: Suite 1400-1300 N 17 St Rosslyn VA 22209

TEMPLE, ROBERT WINFIELD, chemical company executive; b. New Albany, Ind., Feb. 25, 1934; s. Edgar Winfield and Kathryn (Rady) T.; m. Katrina Voorhis, Jan. 4, 1954 (div. Oct. 1970); children—James V., Robert K., Jennifer Anne; m. Katharine Ann Stobbs, Apr. 29, 1977 (div. June 1985); children—Andrew, Philip; m. Angela J., Aug. 5, 1986. B.S. in Chem. Engring., B.S. in Indsl. Mgmt., MIT, 1955; postgrad., Chem. Engring. Sch. MIT, 1955, Sch. Bus. Adminstrn. NYU, 1955-58, Mgmt. Devel. Program, Columbia U., 1966. Dist. sales mgr. ACF Industries, 1955-59; sr. staff cons. Arthur D. Little, Inc., 1959-64; dir. planning and devel. Am. Cryogenics, Inc., Atlanta, 1964-69; v.p. Williams Bros. Co., Atlanta, 1969-70; pres. Lang Engring., Coral Gables, Fla., 1970-74; pres. Western Process Co., Geneva and Houston, 1974-88; mgr. agribus., British-Am. Tobacco Co. dir. World Congress on Super Conductivity, Global Econ. Action Inst. Conf. on African Devel. Sunday sch. tchr.; chmn. MIT Enterprise Forum; bd. dirs. Dads Club Swim Team. Fellow Am. Inst. Chemists and Chem. Engrs.; mem. Am. Chem. Soc., Am. Mgmt. Assn., (seminar spkr.), Assn. Cons. Chemists and Chem. Engrs., Chem. Mktg. Research Assn., Internat. Food Technologists, MIT Alumni Assn. (past regional pres.). Presbyterian. Clubs: Cherokee Town and Country (Atlanta); Univ. (Houston). Contbr. articles to profl. jours. Home: 14134 Bluebird Ln Houston TX 77079 Office: Western Process Co PO Box 19435 Houston TX 77224

TEMPLETON, JOHN MARKS, JR., pediatric surgeon; b. N.Y.C. Feb. 19, 1940; s. John Marks and Judith Dudley (Folk) T.; B.A., Yale Coll., 1962; M.D., Harvard U., 1968; m. Josephine J. Gargiulo, Aug. 2, 1970; children—Heather Erin, Jennifer Ann. Intern, Med. Coll. Va., Richmond, 1968-69, resident, 1969; assoc. prof. pediatric surgery U. Pa. and Children's Hosp. of Pa., 1986—, assoc. prof., 1986—; chmn. bd. Templeton Growth Fund, Templeton World Fund, Templeton Income Funds, Templeton Global Funds, St. Petersburg, Fla., 1978—; bd. dirs. Templeton Emerging Market Fund, Templeton, Galbraith & Hansberger. Chmn. health and safety, exec. bd. Phila. council Boy Scouts Am.; Eastern Coll., Nat. Recreation Found., Melmark Home; pres. Pa. div. Am. Trauma Soc. Served with M.C., USNR, 1975-77. Mem. ACS, Am. Pediatric Surg. Assn., AMA, Am. Assn. Pediatricians, Phila. Coll. Physicians. Republican. Evangelical. Club: Union League (Phila.), Merion Cricket (Haverford). Assoc. editor: Textbook of Pediatric Emergencies, 1983. Office: 4 King St West, Toronto, ON Canada M5W 1M3

TENA, JUAN, mathematics educator, researcher; b. Monterrubio, Badajoz, Spain, Apr. 14, 1945; s. Antonio and Josefa (Ayuso) T.; m. Francisca Blanco, Nov. 12, 1977; children—Beatriz, Gabriel. M.D., U. Madrid, 1967; Diplome D'etudes Aprofondies, U. Grenoble, France, 1969, Ph.D., 1973; Ph.D., U. Madrid, 1973. Research asst. Laboratoire de Mathematiques Pures, Grenoble, 1970-73; assoc. prof. dept. algebra U. Valladolid, Spain, 1973-79, prof., 1982—; prof. dept. algebra U. Madrid, 1979-81, U. Santander, Spain, 1981. Author: Finitely Rationnels Sousgroups of a Elliptic Curve, 1975, Local Algebra, 1985. Mem. editorial com. Univ. Pub. Service, Valladolid, 1983—. Contbr. articles to profl. jours. Grantee French Govt., 1970-72, J. March Found., 1972-73. Mem. Real Sociedad Matematica Espanola, Am. Math. Soc., Soc. Math. France. Avocations: literature; philately. Home: Huelgas 1 7 B, 47005 Valladolid Spain Office: Facultad de Ciencias U Valladolid, Prado de la Magdale, 47005 Valladolid Spain

TENAGLIA, JOHN FRANC, broadcasting executive; b. Clairton, Pa., Jan. 17, 1935; s. Fileno Albert and Gina (Zucconi) T.; m. Judith Ann Droder, June 30, 1962; children: Christine Mary, Lisa Ann. BBA, U. Pitts., 1958. Gen. mgr. local affiliate ABC, Pitts., 1959-69; exec. v.p. GCC Communications Inc., Boston, 1970-80; prin. owner, pres., chief exec. officer TK Communications Inc., Bala Cynwyd, Pa., 1980—; bd. dirs. WK Cable, Junction City, Kans. Served with U.S. Army, 1954-56. Mem. Nat. Assn. Broadcasters. Republican. Roman Catholic. Office: TK Communications Inc One Bala Plaza Bala-Cynwyd PA 19004

TENDERA, MICHAEL PIOTR, cardiologist; b. Siemianozice, Poland, June 29, 1948; s. Pawel and Helena (Galusek) T.; m. Ewa M. Malecka, Dec. 27, 1972; children: Zofia, Pawel. MD, Silesian Med. Sch., Poland, 1972. Intern Silesian Med. Sch., 1972-73, resident, 1973-75, clin. instr., 1975-79, asst. prof., 1979-85, assoc. prof. cardiology, 1985—; research fellow Vanderbilt U., Nashville, 1982-83; dir. Radionuclide Cardiac Lab., Zabrze, Poland, 1983—, vice dir. 2d dept. cardiology, 1987—. Contbr. articles to profl. jours. Recipient J.K. Wende award Polish Cardiol. Assn., 1985. Mem. Polish Cardiology Assn. (br. treas. 1983-87), Am. Heart Assn., N.Y. Acad. Sci., European Soc. Clin. Respiratory Physiology. Roman Catholic. Home: Ul Reymonta 22-4, Katowice 40-029, Poland Office: Silesian Med Sch, 2d Dept Cardiology, Curie-Sklodowskiej 10, Zabrze 41-800, Poland

TENDLER, PAUL MARC, lawyer; b. N.Y.C., Oct. 22, 1943; s. Leonard and Gladys (Steisel) T.; m. Elaine Lynn Isaacson, Mar. 28, 1971; children—Jamie Meredith, Seth Evan. B.A., Queens Coll., N.Y.C., 1965; M.S., So. Ill. U., Carbondale, 1966; J.D., Howard U., 1969; postgrad. U. Pitts., 1969-70. Bar: D.C. 1980. Press asst to Congressman Begich, Washington, 1971; legis. asst. to Congressman Halpern, Washington, 1972, Congressman Rinaldo, 1973; dir. legis. research Cost of Living Council, Washington, 1973-74; asst. dir. govt. affairs Am. Nurses Assn., Washington, 1974-75; pres. Paul Tendler Assocs., Washington, 1975—; mng. ptnr. Tendler & Biggins, 1982—; adj. prof. Georgetown U., 1980-83, asst. prof., 1975-80; dir. bus. program Trinity Coll., Washington, 1983—. Author: The Federal Government at Work, 1976; An LPNs Guide to the Federal Government, 1978, 84. Ford Found. scholar, 1967-69. Mem. D.C. Bar Assn., Am. Arbitration Assn., ABA, Assn. Trial Lawyers Am., Delta Sigma Rho, Tau Kappa Alpha. Democrat. Jewish. Home and Office: 1090 Vermont Ave NW Washington DC 20005

TENGBOM, ANDERS, architect; b. Stockholm, Nov. 10, 1911; s. Ivar J. and Hjordis (Nordin) T.; m. Margareta Brambeck, May 21, 1937; children—Jonas, Anna, Svante, Lisen. Architect, Royal Inst. Tech., Stockholm, 1934; postgrad. Cranbrook Acad., 1936, Royal Acad. Stockholm, 1941. Pvt. practice architecture, Stockholm, 1938—; acting prof. architecture Royal Inst. Tech., 1947-48; mem. bd. Swedish Hosp. Fedn., 1962-70. Prin. archtl. works include Swedish Embassy Moscow, hosps. in Sweden, Venezuela, Saudi Arabia. Fellow AIA; mem. Nat. Assn. Swedish Architects (pres. 1963-65), Swedish Assn. Cons. Architects (pres. 1972-75), Royal Inst. Brit. Architects (hon. corr. mem. 1963), Royal Acad. Fine Arts (pres. 1980-86). Home: Canton 2, 17011 Drottningholm Sweden Office: Kornhamnstorg 6, 11127 Stockholm Sweden

TEN HORN, SINEKE GESINA HARMANNA MARGARETHA MARIA, medical sociologist; b. Veendam, Netherlands, June 4, 1951; s. Jacob and Liny (Abeling) ten H. M in Med. Sociology, State U., Groningen, Netherlands, 1973, D in Social Scis., 1982. Researcher, sci. staff mem. dept. social psychiatry State U., Groningen, 1973-82, sr. researcher, 1986—; coordinator collaborating ctr. social psychiatry WHO, Groningen, 1982-86; vis. sci. Central Inst. Mental Health, Mannheim, Fed. Republic Germany, 1986; cons. European office WHO, Geneva, 1978—. Editor: Psychiatric Case Registers in Public Health: World Wide Inventory, 1960-85, 86; mem. editorial bd. Maandblad Geestelijke Volksgezondheid, 1983-87, Tijdschrift Sociale Gezondheidszorg, 1983—, Revista Assn. Psichiatria y Neurologica, Spain, 1987—; contbr. articles to profl. publs. Bd. dirs. Forensic Psychiat. State Hosp., Groningen, 1983—, Found. Nursing Homes-Homes for Elderly, Groningen, 1986—; chmn. Groningen Regional Inst. Mental Health, 1985—. Am. Field Service fellow, 1968-69, World Health Orgn. fellow, 1975; grantee Netherlands Ministry Welfare, Health and Culture, 1973—. Mem. European Med. Sociologists, Dutch Assn. Sci. Journalists. Club: Soroptimists. Home: Aart Van der Leeuwlaan 7, 9721TE Groningen The Netherlands Office: U Groningen Dept Social Psychiat, Oostersingel 59, 9713EZ Groningen The Netherlands

TENIOLA, ALHAJI LATEEF, publisher; b. Ilesha, Oyo, Nigeria, Dec. 7, 1934; parents: Ali and Morin Abebi (Olatunji) T.; m. Yalayo Ogunsanmi Teniola, Dec. 12, 1956; children: Taiwo, Taju, Fatai, Bashir, Fatima, Jemila, Halima, Hafsat, Muda. Reporter Daily Service, Lagos, Nigeria, 1955-59; news editor Daily Express, Lagos, 1959-64; dir. Daily Sketch, Ibadan, Nigeria, 1964-67, Nigerian Rev., London, 1968-70; pub. Tech. Rev., Lagos, 1970—, Islamic Rev., Lagos, 1970—; treas. Union of Journalists, Lagos, 1962-69; chmn. Tech. Mags., Lagos, 1979-85, Lagos Radio-TV, 1979-83. Author: (religious books) Hajjan Saidan, 1963, Haji Alobo, 1965. Social Democrat. Islam. Home: FE 26 Biladu St, Ilesha Nigeria Office: Teniola Universal Group, 3 Ola Ayinde St, Ikeja Nigeria

TENNEY, MARK WILLIAM, civil engineer; b. Chgo., Dec. 10, 1936; s. William and Frieda (Sanders) T.; B.S., Mass. Inst. Tech., 1958, M.S., 1959, Sc.D., 1965; m. Jane E. Morris, June 1, 1974; children? Scott, Barbara. Design engr. Greeley & Hansen, Engrs., Chgo., 1959-61; asso. prof. civil engring. U. Notre Dame, 1965-73; chief exec. officer TenEch Engring., Inc., South Bend, Ind., 1973—. Served with C.E., AUS, 1959-60; maj. gen. USAR. USPHS research fellow, 1961-64. Diplomate Am. Acad. Environ. Engrs. Fellow ASCE; mem. Nat. Soc. Profl. Engrs., Am. Cons. Engrs. Council, Water Pollution Control Fedn., Am. Water Works Assn., Sigma Xi, Chi Epsilon, Phi Delta Theta. Clubs: South Bend Country, Landings Yacht and Golf, Columbia, Summit, Pickwick. Contbr. articles to profl. jours. Home: 2110 Niles-Buchanan Rd Niles MI 49120 Office: 744 W Washington St South Bend IN 46601

TENNEY, WILLIAM FRANK, physician; b. Shreveport, La., June 5, 1946; s. William Bonds and Pat (Patton) T.; m. Elizabeth Carter Steadman, Oct. 4, 1973; children: Amy Karen, William Allen. BA, Vanderbilt U., 1968; MD, La. State U., New Orleans, 1972. Diplomate Am. Bd. Pediatrics, sub-Bd. Pediatric Nephrology. Intern Grady Meml. Hosp., Atlanta, 1972-73; resident in pediatrics Emory U. Affiliated Hosps., Atlanta, 1973-74, fellow in pediatric nephrology and inorganic metabolism, 1974-76; practice medicine specializing in pediatric nephrology St. Helens, Oreg., 1976-79, Shreveport, 1979-85, Seattle, 1985—; mem. staff Children's Orthopedic Hosp. and Med. Ctr., Seattle; chief dept. pediatrics Swedish Hosp. Med. Ctr., Seattle, 1987—; clin. asst. prof. pediatrics La. State U. Sch. Medicine, 1979-85, U. Wash. Sch. Medicine, Seattle, 1985—; chmn. Renal com. Schumpert Med. Ctr., Shreveport, 1982, co-chmn. 1979-81, mem. 1983-84, co-dir. Renal Dialysis Unit, 1979-84, mem. renal transplantation com., 1984; cons. pediatric nephrology Shriner's Hosp. Crippled Children, Shreveport, 1979-84, Shreveport Regional Dialysis Ctr., 1979-84, Bossier Dialysis Ctr., Bossier City, La., 1983-84, Natchitoches (La.) Dialysis Facility, 1984. Author: (with others) Pediatric Case Studies, 1985; contbr. articles to profl. jours. Mem. Union Concerned Scientists, Cambridge, Mass., 1986—, Internat. Physicians for Prevention of Nuclear War, Boston, 1986—. Fellow Am. Acad. Pediatrics; mem. Am. Soc. Pediatric Nephrology, North Pacific Pediatric Soc., AMA, Wash. State Med. Assn., Internat. Soc. Peritoneal Dialysis, Empirical Soc. Emory U., King County Med. Soc., AAAS, Northwest Renal Soc., Southwest Pediatric Nephrology (mem. study group 1981-84). Home: 1133 16th Ave E Seattle WA 98112 Office: 1221 Madison St Seattle WA 98104

TENNSTEDT, KLAUS, conductor; b. Merseburg, Germany, June 6, 1926. Formerly gen. music dir., Dresden Opera, and dir., State Orch. and Theatre in Schwerin, German Democratic Republic, gen. music dir. and resident condr., Buehnen der Landeshauptstadt Kiel, Fed. Republic Germany, N.Am. debut, Toronto (Ont., Can.) Symphony, U.S. debut, Boston Symphony, 1974, named prin. guest condr., Minn. Orch., 1978, has since conducted all major orchs. of world, including Cleve. Symphony, Phila. Orch., N.Y. Philharm., Chgo. Symphony, Berlin Philharm., Israel Philharm.; prin. guest condr., London Philharm. Orch., music dir., London Philharm. Orch., 1983-87; prin. guest condr. recs. with, EMI Records, including all Mahler symphonies with London Philharm., Schumann symphonies with Berlin Philharm. Office: Columbia Artists Mgmt 165 W 57 St New York NY 10019

TENOPYR, MARY LOUISE WELSH (MRS. JOSEPH TENOPYR), psychologist; b. Youngstown, Ohio, Oct. 18, 1929; d. Roy Henry and Olive (Donegan) Welsh; AB, Ohio U., 1951, MA, 1951; PhD, U. So. Calif., 1966; m. Joseph Tenopyr, Oct. 30, 1955. Psychometrist, Ohio U., Athens, 1951-52, also housemother Sigma Kappa; personnel technician to research psychologist USAF, 1953-55, Dayton, Ohio, 1952-53, Hempstead, N.Y.; indsl. research analyst to mgr. employee evaluation N.Am. Rockwell Corp., El Segundo, Calif., 1956-70; asso. prof. Calif. State Coll.-Los Angeles, 1966-70; assoc. research educationist UCLA, 1970-71; program dir. U.S. CSC, 1971-72; dir. selection and testing AT&T, N.Y.C., 1972—; lectr. U. So. Calif., Los Angeles, 1967-70; vice chmn. research com. Tech. Adv. Com. on Testing, Fair Employment Practice Commn. Calif., 1966-70; adviser on testing Office Fed. Contract Compliance, U.S. Dept. Labor, Washington, 1967-73. Pres., ASPA Found.; mem. Army Sci. Bd. Fellow Am. Psychol. Assn. (bd. profl. affairs, edn. and training bd., mem. council reps., pres. div. indsl. organizational psychology); mem. Eastern Psychol. Assn., Am. Soc. Personnel Adminstrn. (bd. dirs. 1984-87), Nat. Acad. Sci. (coms. on ability testing, math. and sci. edn., panel on secondary edn.), Soc. Indsl. and Organizational Psychology (Recipient Profl. Practices award 1984), Nat. Council Measurement in Edn., Psychomatic Soc., Met. N.Y. Assn. Applied Psychology, Am. Ednl. Research Assn., Sigma Xi, Sigma Kappa, Psi Chi, Alpha Lambda Delta, Kappa Phi. Editorial bd. Jour. Applied Psychology, 1972-87; contbr. chpts. to books and articles to profl. jours. Home: 557 Lyme Rock Rd Bridgewater NJ 08807 Office: One Speedwell Ave Morristown NJ 07960

TENORIO, PEDRO PANGELINAN, government official; b. Saipan, Mariana Islands, Apr. 18, 1934; m. Sophia Tenorio; 8 children. Student, Territorial Coll. of Guam (now U. Guam). Formerly sch. tchr., bus. exec; former mem. Congress of Micronesia, also Marianas Dist. Legis.; v.p. Senate, chmn. program com. 1978-80, pres. Senate, 1980-82; gov. No. Mariana Islands, 1982—. Republican. Roman Catholic. Office: Office of Gov No Mariana Islands Saipan CM 96950 *

TEO, JOHN, engineer; b. Singapore, Singapore, Nov. 21, 1949; s. Kian Hua Teo and Quee Neo Wee; m. Tan Hwee Joo, Sept. 21, 1979; children: Karen Xiuxian, Kenneth XueQian. B of Mech. Engring., U. Singapore, 1973. Mgr. dept. Diethelm Pte Ltd., Singapore, 1976-82; sales mgr. CIS Superior Supply Pte Ltd., Singapore, 1982-84; gen. mgr. Material Handling Engring. Pte Ltd., Jurong, Singapore, 1984—. Served to capt. Singapore Army Intelligence, 1973-76. Mem. Mktg. Inst. Singapore, Singapore Robotics Assn. (asst. sec. 1987). Club: Internat. Brotherhood Magicians (v.p. 1982—, territorial v.p. 1985—) (Singapore). Home: 10 M Braddell Hill #01-49, 2057 Singapore Singapore Office: Material Handling Engring Pte Ltd, 8 Gul St 3, 2262 Jurong Singapore

TEO, KIM-SEE, marketing professional; b. Batu Pahat, Johor, Malaysia, Sept. 3, 1948; s. Kah-Seng Teo and San-Eng Lim; m. Cheng- Kian, May 27, 1980. BS with honors, U. Malaysia, 1975; LLB, U. London, 1983; advanced diploma mktg., Inst. Mktg., Singapore, 1985. Process engr. Nat. Semiconductor, Singapore, 1975-78; sr. process engr. SGS-ATES Semiconductor, Singapore, 1978; prodn., quality engr. Hewlett-Packard, Singapore, 1978-81; regional sales mgr. Interconics Chgo., Singapore, 1981-84; area mgr. Bourns Asia Pacific, Singapore, 1984-87; v.p. Bourns Asia Pacific, Hong Kong, 1987—. Mem. IEEE, Inst. Mktg. Eng., Am. Mktg. Assn., Am. Soc. Internat. Law, Brit. Inst. Mgmt., Internat. Biog. Assn., Hong Kong Mgmt. Assn. Home: 37 Barker Rd, 4-B The Peak, Hong Kong Hong Kong Office: Bourns Asia Pacific Inc, 18 Whitfield Rd 1401 Citicorp Bldg, Hong Kong Hong Kong

TEPPER, NEAL GARY, family therapist; b. Bklyn., Mar. 12, 1951; s. Leon and Bernice Rhoda (Fisher) T.; m. Nadine C. Claymore, Oct. 24, 1977; children: Beth, Wayland, David, Neal Jr.; B.A., State U. N.Y., Potsdam, 1972; M.A., U. N.D., 1973, B.S. in Edn., 1985. Group therapist St. Mike's Hosp., Grand Forks, N.D., 1972-73; tchr. courses Center Teaching and Learning, U. N.D., 1973-75, grad. teaching asst. dept. counseling and guidance, 1974-77, intern counselor Counseling Center, 1975-77; practicum guidance counselor Red River High Sch., Grand Forks, 1973-74; mental health clinician IV, Meml. Mental Health and Retardation Center, Mandan, N.D., 1977-79; dir. Children and Family Services for Standing Rock Sioux Tribe, Ft. Yates, N.D., 1978-81; dir. counseling United Tribes Ednl. Tech. Center, 1981-83; counselor Bur. Indian Affairs, Dept. Interior, Fort Totten, N.D., 1983-85; family therapist Lutheran Soc. Services of Minn., Grand Forks, N.D., 1985—; pvt. practice Prairie Psychol. Assocs., 1986—; bd. dirs. Understanding the Child, Grand Forks, N.D., 1976—, Options Inc., East Grand Forks; supr. NW Counseling, Crookston, Minn.; counselor Cathedral Parish. Mem. Polk County Child Protection Team. Mem. Am. Personnel and Guidance Assn., North Cen. Assn. Counselor Educators Assn., Mental Health Assn., Assn. Edn. of Young Children, N.D. Conf. Social Welfare. Lodge: Lions. Home: 118 7th St S Crookston MN 56716 Office: PO Box 985 Grand Forks ND 58206

TEPPER, R(OBERT) BRUCE, JR., lawyer; b. Long Branch, N.J., Apr. 1, 1949; s. Robert Bruce and Elaine (Ogus) T.; m. Belinda Wilkins, Nov. 26, 1971; children—Laura Katherine, Jacob Wilkins. A.B. in History, Dartmouth Coll., 1971; J.D. cum laude, St. Louis U., 1976, M.A. in Urban Affairs, 1976. Bar: Mo. 1976, Calif. 1977, Ill. 1978, U.S. Ct. Appeals (7th cir.) 1978, (8th cir.) 1976, (9th cir.) 1978, U.S. Dist. Ct. (cen., no. and so. dists.) Calif. 1978. Asst. gen. counsel St. Louis Redevel. Authority; 1976-77; assoc. Goldstein & Price, St. Louis, 1977-78, Loo, Merideth & McMillan, Los Angeles, 1978-82; sole practice, Los Angeles, 1982-84; ptnr., litigation supr. Kane, Ballmer and Berkman, Los Angeles, 1984—; spl. counsel to Solano County, San Diego, Santa Barbara, Hermosa Beach, Anaheim, Bakersfield, Lynwood, Norwalk, Redondo Beach, Oceanside, Ontario, Pasadena, Moreno Valley, West Covina, Whittier, Glendale and Hawthorne, Calif.; judge pro tempore Los Angeles County Mcpl. Ct., 1983—; grader State Bar Calif., 1980 84. Assoc. editor St. Louis U. Law Jour., 1974-76. Contbr. articles to legal jours. Grad fellow St. Louis U., 1973-76. Mem. Los Angeles County Bar Assn., Assn. Bus. Trial Lawyers, ABA. Republican. Jewish. Clubs: So. Calif. Dartmouth (bd. dirs. 1980-83), Los Angeles Athletic (Los Angeles). Home: 10966 Wrightwood Ln Studio City CA 91604 Office: Kane Ballmer and Berkman 354 S Spring St Suite 420 Los Angeles CA 90013

TERAO, TOSHIO, physician, educator; b. Shimizu, Japan, Jan. 18, 1930; s. Eiji and Mitsuko (Katagiri) T.; m. Setsuko Nishigaki, Nov. 13, 1961; children—Toshiya, Yasuo, Yoshio. Diploma U. Tokyo, 1953, M.D., 1970. Intern, Tokyo U. Hosp., 1953-54; sr. scientist Nat. Inst. Radiol. Sci., Chiba, Japan, 1963-67; research assoc. Mayo Clinic, Rochester, Minn., 1970-72; asst. U. Tokyo, 1972-77, lectr. in medicine 1977-79; prof. medicine Teikyo U., 1980—; dir. Teikyo U. Med. Hosp., 1987—. Author, editor in field. Mem. Am. Acad. Neurology, Japanese Soc. Internal Medicine, Japanese Soc. Neurology, Japanese Soc. Neuropathology, Japanese Soc. EEG and Electromyography, Japanese Soc. Psychiatry and Neurology, Japanese Soc. Cerebrovascular Disease, Sigma Xi. Office: Teikyo U, 2-11-1 Kaga, Itabashiku, Tokyo 173, Japan

TERASAWA, FUJIO, cardiologist; b. Kyoto, Japan, Jan. 3, 1931; s. Ichiro and Isuzu (Matsuhashi) T.; m. Emiko Hasegawa, Mar. 23, 1961; 1 child, Yasuko. MD Tokyo U., 1960. Research fellow 3d dept. internal medicine Faculty of Medicine, Tokyo U., 1959-68; head cardiac unit Yokufukai Geriatric Hosp., Suginami, Tokyo, 1968-74; research fellow 3d dept. internal medicine Faculty of Medicine, Tokyo U., 1975-78; head internal medicine Inst. Chemotherapeutics, Chiba, Japan, 1978-82; head internal medicine Natogaya Hosp., 1983-86; vice dir.Gyoda-Chuo Hosp., Saitima, Japan, 1987—. Mem. Japan Geriatric Soc. (councilor 1969—), Japanese Circulation Soc., Japanese Soc. Hypertension, Japanese Soc. Clin. Pharmacology and Therapeutics. Liberal Democrat. Contbr. articles to profl. jours. Avocations: art appreciation, especially copper-cut prints. Office: Gyoda-Chuo Hosp, 2-17-17 Fujimi-cho, Gyoda, Saitama 361, Japan

TERASAWA, MASANORI, photographer; b. Ogaki, Gifu, Japan, Oct. 18, 1945; s. Shuichi and Hisae (Tsukahara) T.; m. Kyoko Matsushita, Mar. 2, 1968; 1 child, Sayo. Photographer ELMO Co., Ltd., Nagoya, Japan, 1964-75, Ito Pro Photo, Fukuoka, Japan, 1975-78, Archtl. Photo Terasawa, Fukuoka, 1978—. Contbr. Architecture Monthly mag. Kindai Kenchiku, 1981; photographer (calendar and postcards) Prefecture of Fukuoka, 1980, 81. Home and Studio: 489-10 Susenji, Nishiku, Fukuoka Japan 819-03

TERBELL, JOSEPH BODINE, retired steel company executive; b. Chgo., June 6, 1906; s. Joseph Bodine and Marie Gladys (Green) T.; m. Phoebe Logan, 1931 (div. 1935); m. Merna Pace, 1936 (div. 1952); m. Lilyann J. Place, Oct. 3, 1952 (div. 1969); children—Gladys, Susan, Joseph B. Jr., Lawrence R.; m. Mary Matthiessen, June 10, 1970. B.S., Yale U., 1928. Salesman, Am. Manganese Steel, 1928-40; v.p. Am. Brake Shoe Co., N.Y.C., 1940-58; pres. Joliette Steel Ltd., Montreal, Que., Can., 1946-58; dep. commr. N.Y. State Div. Housing and Urban Renewal, N.Y.C., 1959-64; chief castings br. Dept. Commerce, Washington, 1958-59. Charter mem. Republican. Presdl. Task Force, Washington, 1981—, mem. Rep. Nat. Com., 1983—; mem. U.S. Def. Com., Fairfax, Va., 1983—; sponsor GOPAC, Washington, 1974—. Mem. Delta Psi. Episcopalian. Club: Yale. Home: 500 Mine Hill Rd Fairfield CT 06430

TERESA, MOTHER (AGNES GONXHA BOJAXHIU), nun, missionary; b. Skopje, Yugoslavia, Aug. 27, 1910. D.D. (hon.), U. Cambridge, 1977; Dr. med. (hon.), Cath. U. of Sacred Heart, Rome, 1981, Cath. U. Louvain (Belgium), 1982. Joined Sisters of Loreto, Roman Catholic Ch., 1928; came to India; founder Missionaries of Charity, Calcutta, India, 1950; opened

Nirmal Hriday Home for Dying Destitutes, 1952; started leper colony, West Bengal, 1964; founder Missionary Bros. of Charity, 1963, Internat. Assn. Coworkers of Mother Teresa and Contemplative Sisters and Brothers, 1976. Recipient Pope John XXIII Peace prize, 1971, Templeton Found. prize, 1973, Nobel Peace prize, 1979, Bharat Ratna (Star of India), 1980, U.S. Presdl. medal of Freedom, 1985; named hon. citizen of Assisi 1982. Address: Missionaries of Charity, 54A Lower Circular Rd, Calcutta 700016, India *

TERFLOTH, KLAUS, ambassador; b. Dusseldorf, Fed. Republic of Germany, May 20, 1929. JD, U. Bonn, Fed. Republic of Germany, 1953. Chef de cabinet European Communities Commn., Brussels, 1970-73; German ambassador to Rangoon, Burma, 1973-75; spokesman German Fgn. Ministry, Bonn, 1975-77; German ambassador to Tunis, Tunisia, 1977-80, Islamabad, Pakistan, 1980-84, Helsinki, Finland, 1984—. Office: Embassy Fed Republic of Germany, Fredrikinkatu 61, Helsinki Finland

TERMINI, DEANNE LANOIX, research company executive; b. New Orleans, May 2, 1943; d. Albert Oliver and Freida (Fisher) Lanoix; m. Raymond Joseph Termini, Sept. 4, 1965; 1 dau., Andrea. BA, Tulane U., 1964; MA, U. Tex., Austin, 1968. Research analyst Belden Assocs., Dallas, 1968-70, research assoc., 1970-75, v.p., 1975-79, sr. v.p., 1979-87, exec. v.p., 1987—, dir., 1979—; discussion leader Am. Press Inst., Reston, Va., 1983—; mem. Dallas Zoo Mktg. Com., 1986—. Author research reports. Active Greenhill Parents Assn., 1979-85, rec. sec., 1982-83, mem. math. subcom. bd. trustees, 1983-84; speaker European confs., 1986-87. Mem. Women in Communications, Am. Mktg. Assn., Internat. Newspaper Advt. and Mktg. Execs., Internat. Newspaper Mktg. Assn., Nat. Assn. Women Bus. Owners, Tulane U. Alumni Assn. Home: 13641 Far Hills Ln Dallas TX 75240 Office: Belden Assocs 2900 Turtle Creek Plaza Dallas TX 75219

TERPENING, VIRGINIA ANN, artist; b. Lewistown, Mo., July 17, 1917; d. Floyd Raymond and Bertha Edda (Rodifer) Shoup; m. Charles W. Terpening, July 5, 1951; 1 child by previous marriage, V'Ann Baltzelle Dlatrick. Studies with William Woods, Fulton, Mo., 1936-37; student Washington U. Sch. Fine Arts, St. Louis, 1937-40. Exhibited in one-woman shows at Culver-Stockton Coll., Canton, Mo., 1956, Creative Gallery, N.Y.C., 1968, The Breakers, Palm Beach, Fla., 1976; others; exhibited in group shows Mo. Ann., City Art Mus., St. Louis, 1956, 65, Madison Gallery, N.Y.C., 1960; Ligoa Duncan Gallery, N.Y.C., 1964, 78, Two Flags Festival of Art, Douglas, Ariz., 1975, 78-79, Internat. Art Exhibit, El Centro, Calif., 1977, 78, Salon des Nations, Paris, 1985, UN World Conference of Women, Narobi, Kenya, 1985; lectr. on art; jurist for selection of art for exhibits Labelle (Mo.) Centennial, 1972; chmn. Centennial Art Show, Lewiston, 1971, Bicenntenial, 1976; dir. exhibit high sch. students for N.E. Mo. State U., 1974; supt. ann. art show Lewis County (Mo.) Fair; executed Mississippi RiverBoat, oil painting presented to Pres. Carter by Lewis County Dem. Com., Canton, 1979. Mem. Lewistown Bicentennial Hist. Soc. Recipient cert. of merit Latham Found., 1960-63, Mo. Women's Festival Art, 1974, Bertrand Russell Peace Found., 1973, Gold Medallion award Two Flags Festival Art, 1975, Safeco purchase award El Centro (Calif.) Internat. Art exhibit, 1977; 1st pl. award LaJunta (Colo.) Fine Arts League, 1981; diploma Universita Delle Arti, Parma, Italy, 1981; Purchase award Two Flags Art Festival, 1981; award Assn. Conservation and Mo. Dept. Conservation Art Exhbt., 1982; paintings selected for Competition '84 Guide by Nat. Art Appreciation Soc., 1984; 1st pl. award New Orlean Internat. Art Exhibit, 1984, with Am. Women Artists at United Nations Conf. on Women, Nairobi, Kenya, 1985, Two Flags Festival of Art, 1986; named artist laureate, Nepenthe Mondi Soc., 1984, cert. on Arts for the Parks Nat., 1987. Mem. Artist Equity Assn., Inc., Internat. Soc. Artists, Internat. Platform Assn., Nat. Mus. Women in Art (charter), Animal Protection Inst. Mem. Disciples of Christ Ch. Address: Lewistown MO 63452

TERRAINE, JOHN ALFRED, author; b. London, Jan. 15, 1921; s. Charles William and Evelyn (Holmes) T.; m. Joyce Elizabeth Waite, 1945; 1 child. Educated Stamford Sch., Keble Coll., Oxford. Various positions with BBC, 1943-53; writer television series: The Great War, 1964; The Life and Times of Lord Mountbatten, 1968; The Mighty Continent, 1974; author: Mons, 1960; Douglas Haig: The Educated Soldier, 1963; The Western Front, 1964; Impacts of War, 1914 and 1918, 1970; Trafalgar, 1976; The Road to Passchendaele, 1977; To Win a War: 1918 The Year of Victory, 1978; The Smoke and The Fire, 1980; White Heat: the New Warfare 1914-18, 1982 (Chesney Gold medal Royal United Services Inst. 1982); The First World War, 1914-18, 1983; The Royal Air Force in the European War, 1939-1945, 1985. Recipient Documentary award Screenwriters' Guild, 1964; Script award Soc. Film and TV Arts, 1969. *

TERRELL, A. JOHN, university telecommunications director; b. Pasadena, Calif., Dec. 27, 1927; s. Harry Evans and Elizabeth (Eaton) T.; m. Elizabeth Schalk, June 6, 1949; children—Patricia Elyse, Marilee Diane, John Scott. Student, Chaffey Coll., 1947-48; B.B.A., U. N. Mex., 1952. Communications cons. Mountain States Tel. & Tel., Albuquerque, 1951-56; mgr. office and communications services A.C.F. Industries, Inc., Albuquerque, 1956-62; mgr. communications and services Norton Simon Industries, Inc., Fullerton, Ca., 1962-68; v.p. gen. mgr. Wells Fargo Security Guard Service Div. Baker Industries, Fullerton, Ca., 1968-71; adminstrv. mgr., budget adminstr. Hyland div. Baxter-Trevenol Labs. Inc., Costa Mesa, CA, 1971-77; exec. v.p. Am. Tel. Mgmt. Inst Inc., Newport Beach, Calif., 1977-78; telecommunications dir. UCLA, 1978—. Contbr. articles to profl. jours. Republican. candidate for state rep., Albuquerque, 1960; precinct chmn. and mem. Bernalillo County Rep. Central Com., 1961-62; Rep. candidate for N. Mex. State Bd. Edn., 2nd Jud. Dist., 1962; colonial aide-de-camp Gov. N. Mex., Santa Fe, 1968. Served with U.S. Mcht. Marine, 1944-45, U.S. Army, 1946-47, USAR, 1947-50. Mem. Nat. Assn. Accts. (dir. 1967-77) (Most Valuable mem. 1974-75), Telecommunications Assn., Am. Legion, Am. Legion Yacht Club , VFW. Episcopalian. Lodges: Greater Irvine Lions (charter pres. 1975-76), Albuquerque Jaycees (v.p., treas. 1956-62). Home: 1725 Port Charles Pl Newport Beach CA 92660-5319 Office: UCLA 405 Hilgard Ave CSBI Los Angeles CA 90024-1363

TERRELL, J. ANTHONY, lawyer; b. N.Y.C., Sept. 20, 1943; s. Claude M. and Kathleen L. (Prevost) T.; m. Karen E. Terrell, Aug. 8, 1969; 1 dau., Elizabeth S. B.A., NYU, 1965, LL.M. in Taxation, 1975; J.D., Villanova U., 1968. Bar: N.Y. Ptnr. Frueauff, Farrell, Sullivan & Bryan, N.Y.C., 1970-74, Reid & Priest, N.Y.C., 1974—. Mem. ABA (sect. corp., banking and bus. law, sect. taxation, tax-exempt financing com., sect. pub. utility law, vice chmn. corp. finance com., taxation and acctg. com.), Nat. Assn. Bond Lawyers. Clubs: Down Town Assn. (N.Y.C.); Belle Haven (Greenwich, Conn.); Coral Beach and Tennis (Paget, Bermuda). Home: Indian Harbor Greenwich CT 06830 Office: Reid & Priest 40 W 57th St New York NY 10019

TERRIS, LILLIAN DICK, psychologist, association executive; b. Bloomfield, N.J., May 5, 1914; d. Alexander Blaikie and Herminia (Doscher) Dick; B.A., Barnard Coll., 1935; Ph.D., Columbia U., 1941; m. Louis Long, Apr. 22, 1935 (dec. Sept. 11, 1968), 1 son, Alexander Blaikie Long; m. Milton Terris, Feb. 6, 1971. Instr. psychology Sara Lawrence Coll., Bronxville, N.Y., 1937-40; jr. personnel tech. SSA, Washington, 1941; sr. personnel clk. OWI, N.Y.C., 1941-43; dir. profl. examination service Am. Public Health Assn., N.Y.C., 1943-70, pres., 1970-79, pres. emeritus, 1979—; assoc. editor Jour. Public Health Policy, 1979—; bd. dirs. Profl. Exam. Service, Vis. Nurse Assn., Chittenden County, Vt. Recipient Nat. Environ. Health Assn. award, 1976; Cert. of Service award Am. Bd. Preventive Medicine, 1979. diplomate Am. Bd. Examiners in Profl. Psychology. Fellow Am. Psychol. Assn.; mem. Am. Public Health Assn., N.Y. State Psychol. Assn., Am. Coll. Hosp. Adminstrs. (hon. fellow), Phi Beta Kappa, Sigma Xi. Contbr. articles in field to profl. jours. Home: 208 Meadowood Dr South Burlington VT 05403 Office: 475 Riverside Dr New York NY 10027

TERRY, JAMES ANDREW, III, clinical psychologist, administrator, consultant; b. Chgo., July 7, 1935; s. James Andrew and Gussie Ola (Jones) T. B.A. in History, Roosevelt U.; M.S., Ill. Tchrs. Coll., 1966; Ph.D. in Clin. Psychology, Northwestern U., 1978. Cert. high sch. history, supervision, adminstrn., Ill. History tchr. Chgo. Bd. Edn., 1957-63; dir. and supr. jobs project YMCA, Chgo., 1964-68; dir. services Ebony Mgmt. Assocs., Chgo., 1968-69; dir. Englewood Mental Health Clinic, 1969—; cons. to indsl. cos. and agys.; condr. seminars for Ministry Edn. and Culture, Freeport Bahamas. Fellow Northwestern U. Med. Sch.; Dep. commr. of health for The Bur. of Mental Health, Alcoholism, and Substance Abuse Chgo. Dept. of Health. Recipient Health Services award Young Execs. in Politics, 1983. Mem. Am. Psychol. Assn., Ill. Psychol. Assn., Chgo. Psychol. Assn., Musicians Union, Kappa Alpha Psi. Roman Catholic. Contbr. articles to profl. jours. Home: 1916 S Hamlin St Chicago IL 60623 Office: 641 W 63d St Chicago IL 60621

TERRY, LINDA JOYCE, information and management consultant; b. Denver, Aug. 4, 1942; d. Paul Joyce and Helen Elisabeth (Barker) Terry; student W.Va. Wesleyan U., 1960-62, George Washington U., 1966-68, BA in Mgmt., Goddard Coll., Planfield, Vt., 1988; 1 son, Michael Karl Hinke. Clerk-typist Peace Corps, Washington, 1962-65; mgmt. analyst Nat. Archives and Records Service, Washington, 1965-68; sr. systems analyst Marine Midland Services Corp., Buffalo, 1968-72, U. Va., Charlottesville, 1973-75; mgmt. cons. Cincom Systems, Inc., Fairfax, Va., 1975-78; ind. mgmt. cons., Washington, 1978-79; mgmt. cons. Nolan, Norton & Co., Lexington, Mass., 1979-81; data mgmt. cons. Digital Equipment Corp., Maynard, Mass., 1981-84; dir. tng. and documentation Bachman Info. Systems, Inc., Lexington, 1984—, prin. cons. 1985; prin. cons. QED Infor. Scis., Inc. Wellesley, Ma., 1984; ind. mgmt. cons., 1985— . Co-chmn. Acton (Mass.) computer adv. com., 1982—; pres. Foggy Bottom Civic Assn., Washington, 1967-68. Mem. Orgn. Devel. Network. Office: 11 Percy Rd Lexington MA 01723

TERRY, NORMAN HARRY, production engineer; b. London, May 31, 1924; s. Thomas Harry and Annie May (Ebbage) T.; m. Miriam Antoinette Swan, Sept. 8, 1951; children: Paul, Stephen, Simon. Registered profl. engr., Eng. Apprentice Electroflo Instruments, London, 1940-45, supt., 1944-53; prodn. engr. E.M.I. Electronics, Hayes, Eng., 1953-58; project engr. Rank-Pullin Industries, London, 1958-60; sr. prodn. engr. Thorn Emi, Feltham, Middlesex, Eng., 1960—. Inventor circuit board pin, machine control system. Mem. Inst. Engrs. and Technicians. Avocations: model making; interior decoration. Home: 46 Barnfield Rd, London, Middlesex W5 1QT, England Office: Thorn E M I, Victoria Rd, Fetham, Middlesex TW13 7DZ, England

TERRY, SIR PETER (DAVID GEORGE), governor and commander-in-chief, Gibraltar; b. England, Oct. 18, 1926; s. James George and Laura Chilton Powell T.; me. Betty Martha Louisa Thomspson, 1946; 2 sons (1 dec.), 1 dau. Student, Chatham House Sch., Ramsgate, England. Joined RAF, 1945; commd. RAF Regt., 1946, pilot, 1953; instr. Staff Coll., 1962; comdg. officer, No. 51 Squadron RAF, 1966-68; comdg. officer RAF, El Adem, 1968-70; dir. air staff briefing Ministry of Def. RAF, 1970-71, dir. forward policy, 1971-74; asst. chief of staff (Policy and Plans) SHAPE, 1975-77; vice chief of air staff RAF, 1977-79; comdr.-in-chief and comdr. 2d Allied Tactical Air Force RAF, Germany, 1979-81; dep. comdr.-in-chief Allied Forces Cen. Europe, 1981; dep. Supreme Allied Comdr. Europe, 1981-84; gov. and commander-in-chief Gibraltar, 1985—. Club: Royal Air Force. Address: The Convent BFPO 52, Gibraltar *

TERSMEDEN, GERARD AREND HERMAN BENJAMIN, composer; b. Stockholm, Sweden; s. Gustaf Erik Benjamin and Hermine Maria Katarina (Versteegh) T.; ed. Sweden; m. Marianne Peggy Siocrona Britt, June 9, 1947; children—Christer, Per Olof. Composer works including Rhapsodie des Etoiles, 1979, Fleur du Cap, 1980, Reverie, 1974, Solitaire, 1947, Negresco, 1948, Prelude, Magnolia, 1949, Romantisk Rapsodi, 1950, Tiara, 1974, Mini Conserto, 1973, Mediterranean Rhapsody: Rapsodie des Memises, 1977, Till Hermine, 1976; and many others. Mem. various profl. music orgns. Club: Lyford Cay (Nassau, Bahamas). Home: Villa la Provencale 1297, Founex VD Switzerland

TERSTIEGE, HEINZ, materials scientist, association administrator; b. Münster, Fed. Republic Germany, June 18, 1934; s. Heinrich and Käte (Kalisch) T.; m. Joyce Pimenta, Dec. 13, 1975; children: Sabine, Birgit, Kai, Jörg. Student, Cambridge (Eng.) U., 1960; diploma engring., Tech. U. Berlin, 1962, D. Engring., 1966. Head of lab. Fed. Inst. Material Sci., Berlin, 1964-70, head dept., 1970—; cons. Inst. Nat. Tech. Indsl., Buenos Aires, 1974, Inst. Standards and Indsl. Research, Tehran, Iran, 1975, U. Tehran, 1976. Adj. editor Die Farbe Jour. Mem. Commn. Internat. l'Eclairage (sec. 1979—), Assn. Internat. de la Couleur (v.p. 1982-85, pres. 1986—), Deutsche Farbwissenschaftliche Gesellschaft (pres. 1982—), Grupo Argentino del Color (hon.), Optical Soc. Am., Intersoc. Color Council. Home: Wiesbadener Str 58 c, D 1000 Berlin 33 Federal Republic of Germany Office: Bundesanstalt für Materialf, Unter den Eichen 87, D 1000 Berlin 45 Federal Republic of Germany

TERUYOSHI, ISHIBASHI, mechanical engineer; b. Tokyo, May 16, 1940; children: Ryotaro, Maretoo. B in ME, Tokyo Met. U., 1964. Mech. engr. Sanki Engring. Ltd., Tokyo, 1964-70; mgr. engring. Nippon Roche Ltd., Fukoroi, Japan, 1970-78, Seikensha Ltd., Tokyo, 1978-81; dir. systems div. Nihon Millipore Ltd., Tokyo, 1981—. Patentee in field. V.p. Ultra-Filtration Membrane Characterization Com. Home: Minami Iriso 1 048-76, Sayam City, Saitama 350-13, Japan Office: Nihon Millipore Ltd, Kita Shinagawa 1-3-12, Shinagawa-ku Tokyo 140, Japan

TERZIAN, KARNIG YERVANT, civil engineer; b. Khartoum, Sudan, July 4, 1928; came to U.S.; s. Yeznig and Marie T.; m. Helen S., Dec. 21, 1958. B.A., B.S. in C.E., Am. U. Beirut, 1949; M.S. in C.E., U. Pa., 1954. Assoc., L. T. Beck & Assocs., 1956-60; prin. Urban Engineers, Inc., Phila., 1960—, now sr. v.p., sec.-treas., cons. major transp. projects in Pa., N.Y., N.J., Nigeria, Zaire. Bd. dirs. Armenian Sisters Acad., 1970-74. Mem. ASCE, ASTM, Prestressed Concrete Inst. Armenian Apostolic. Office: 300 N 3d St Philadelphia PA 19106

TERZIC, BRANKO DUSAN, international consultant, state official, engineer; b. Diepholz, W. Ger., June 19, 1947; came to U.S., 1950; s. Dusan Branko and Olivera (Beljakovic) T.; m. Judith Ware Antonic, Oct. 7, 1978; children—Dusan-Alexander, Elizabeth Alexandra Olivera, Branko G. III. B.S. in Energy Engring., U. Wis.-Milw., 1972. With Am. Appraisal Milw., 1970-72, 73-36; engr. Wis. Electric Power Co., Milw., 1972-73; v.p. Assoc. Utility Services, Milw., 1976-79; ptnr. Terzic & Mayer, Milw., 1979-81; mem. Wis. Pub. Service Commn., Madison, 1981-86; chmn. Wis. State Racing Bd., 1988—; pub. dir. Nat. Regulatory Research Inst., 1988—; v.p. The A.U.S. Consulting Group. Chmn. Fifth Congl. Republican Orgn., 1975-77. Publisher C.A. Turner Utility Reports, 1987—. Decorated comdr. Cross of Merit, Sovereign Mil. Order of Malta, Knight Grand Officer of Crown (Yugoslavia) Knight S.O.M. Constantine and St. George, Knight Order of Saints Maurice and Lazarus. Mem. Nat. Assn. Regulatory Utility Commrs. (chmn. engring. com. 1982—). Serbian Orthodox. Club: Milwaukee Athletic. Office: AUS Consulting Group 606 E Wisconsin Ave Box 92757 Milwaukee WI 53202

TERZOPOULOS, JOHN E., electrical company executive; b. Athens, Apr. 3, 1928; m. Aikaterini Louka, June 26, 1960; children: Sarah, Emmanouella. Tech. eng., Tech. U., Athens, 1950. Constrn supr. Ministry of Pub. Works, Alexandroupolis, Greece, 1950-51; pub. contractor Ministry of Pub. Works, Greece, 1953-65; mng. dir. Electroimpex S.A., Athens, 1965—. Served to 2d lt. Greek Army, 1952-53. Mem. Greek C. of C. (Export award 1983). Mem. Christian Orthodox Ch. Lodge: Rotary. Home: 24 Vroutou St, 11141 Athens Greece Office: Electroimpex SA, PO Box 52019, 14410 Metamorfosi Greece

TESA, TANYA K(OVACH), law firm executive; b. N.Y.C., June 24, 1947; d. Stephen P. and Tessie R. Kovach. BA, Bernard M. Baruch Coll., 1974; postgrad. CUNY, 1976-79. Owner, Mint Condition, Inc. Antiques, N.Y.C., 1969-72; disbursing agt. U.S. Bankruptcy Ct., So. Dist. N.Y., 1976—; exec. asst. to sr. mng. partner Summit Rovins & Feldesman, N.Y.C., 1972-85, spl. projects mgr., 1980-88; dir. communications, dir. legal recruitment Summit Rovins & Feldesman, N.Y.C., 1986-88; dir. adminstrn. Proskaur Rose Goetz & Mendelsohn, N.Y.C., 1988—; guest lectr. The New Sch. Social Research, 1987; exec. asst. to nat. chmn. Union Coll. 64th and 65th Ann. Funds, 1976-77; exec. asst. to chmn. Union Coll. Terr. Council, Schenectady, 1977-78; exec. asst. to chmn. Cornell U. Law Sch. Met. Campaign for Funds, 1979-83; exec. asst. to chmn. bd. Freedoms Found., Valley Forge, Pa., 1983-85; mem. Defender of Freedoms program, 1983-85; exec. asst. to nat. assoc. and v.p., fundraiser Boys Clubs Am., 1980-85; exec. asst. to mem. bd. dirs. and fundraiser I Love A Clean New York, Inc., N.Y.C., 1981-83; exec. asst. to chmn. bd. trustees Union Coll. Schenectady, 1982-86. First v.p. Ocean Bay Park Assn., Inc., Fire Island, N.Y., 1980—; mem. bd. Fire Island Assn., Inc., 1981—; bd. dirs. Ocean Bay Park Water Corp., 1985-88. Mem. Nat. Assn. Law Firm Mktg. Adminstrs., Assn. of Law Firm Adminstrs. Home: 20 Park Ave New York NY 10016 also: 145 Woodland Lake Naomi PA 18350 also: 19 Champlain Ocean Bay Park Fire Island NY 11770 Office: 445 Park Ave New York NY 10022

TESCH, EMMANUEL CAMILLE GEORGES VICTOR, iron company executive; b. Hesperange, Luxembourg, Dec. 9, 1920; s. Georges and Marie-Laure (Weckbecker) T.; m. Therese Laval; 1 child, François. Student Technisce Hochschule, Aachen, Germany; Metall. Engr., ETH, Zurich, 1948. Engr., Manufacture de Tabacs Heintz van Landeqyck, Luxembourg, 1948-51; mng. dir. SOGECO, Luxembourg, 1951-68; audiot ARBED, Luxembourg, 1958-68, dir., 1968-69; dir. del. to chmn., 1969-72, chmn., 1972—; chmn. TradeARBED, 1972-79; chmn. adv. bd. ARBED Finanz Deutschland GmbH; dir. SIDMAR S.A., Compagnie Maritime Belge, EUROFER, FININCO, Techno ARBED Deutschland GmbH, Eschweiler Bergswerks-Verein AG, Saarbergwerke AG, Dresdner Bank AG, Companhia Siderurgica Belgo-Mineira, Le Foyer S.A., SGNECO, S.A., Banque Generale du Luxembourg S.A. Decorated medal of Resistance (France); grand officer Ordre de merite civil et militaire d'Adolphe de Nassau, grand officer Ordre de la Couronne de Chêne (Luxembourg); comdr. Ordre de la Couronne (Belgium); comdr. Ordre d' Orange-Nassau (Netherlands); cavaliere Gran Croce (Italy); Order Tudor Vladimirescu (Romania); hon. knight comdr. Order Brit. Empire; Grosses Goldenes Ehrenzeichen mit Stern (Austria); Das grosse Verdienstkreuz mit Stern (W. Ger.); Encomienda de Numero Orden del Merito Civil (Spain). Mem. C. of C. Luxembourg (pres. 1974), Groupement des Industries Sidé rurgiques Luxembourgeoises (pres. 1973). Home: La Cléchère, Kockelscheuer, L-1899 Luxembourg Luxembourg Office: ARBED SA, 19 Ave de la Liberté, L-2930 Luxembourg Luxembourg

TESIO, VITTORIO, automobile company executive; b. Rome, Aug. 1, 1940; s. Vincenzo and Adriana (Miniero) T.; m. Vanda Fiumani, July 16, 1967; children: Francesco, Lorenzo. Dr. degree in Polit. Sci., U. Rome, 1964. Personnel officer Olivetti, Ivrea, Italy, 1966-72, personnel dir. Far East region, 1972-75, personnel dir. Italian div., 1975-79; orgn. and personnel dir. Teksid (Fiat Group), Torino, Italy, 1979-83; mgmt. devel. dir. Fiat S.p.A., Torino, 1983—. Served to 1st lt. Italian Air Force, 1964-65. Mem. Conf. Bd. (internat. human resources mgmt. council 1986—). Home: Via Susa 17, 10138 Torino Italy

TESORIERE, JOSEPH JOHN, shipping company executive; b. Hull, Yorkshire, Eng., Aug. 4, 1937; s. Joseph John Anderson and Frances May (Wiendley) T.; m. Ngaire Ann Thompson; children: Joseph, Rebecca, Lucy, Jason. Student, Alleyn's Coll., London, 1946-53. Shipping clk. Wm. Cory Shipowners, London, 1953-58, Royal Mail Lines, London, 1958-59; asst. steward P&O Lines, 1960; export mgr. Bayer U.K., London, 1960-64, Brit. Printing Corp., Somerset, Eng., 1964-82; dir. World Wide Exports Ltd., Holcombe, Somerset, 1982—. Contbr. articles on exporting to various publs. Sec. Holcombe Ch., Somerset, 1970-87, vice chmn. parish council 1964-74. Fellow Inst. Exports.

TESORO, GEORGE ALFRED, lawyer; b. Rome, Feb. 6, 1904; s. Alfred and Anna (Russi) T.; m. Gilda De Mauro, Mar. 18, 1934; children: Alfred W., Alexandra L. Tesoro Miller. J.D., U. Rome, 1925, D. Polit. Sci., 1929, Ph.D. in Taxation, 1930. Bar: D.C. 1948, U.S. Supreme Ct. 1965. Corp. lawyer, Rome, 1927-38; instr., lectr. taxation U. Rome, 1930-35; assoc. prof. pub. fin. and taxation U. Bari (Italy), 1935-38; news editor Sta. WOV, N.Y.C., 1941-42; lectr. in econs. Lawrence Coll., 1942; vis. prof., lectr., adj. prof. econs. Am. U., 1942-55; cons. Bd. Econ. Warfare, 1943; econ. analyst, chief sect. Fgn. Econ. Adminstrn. and Office Fgn. Liquidation Commn., 1944-46; economist, dep. econ. adv. Div. Econ. Devel. and Office Western European Affairs, Dept. State, 1946-55; sr. econ. officer, counselor U.S. Mission, Geneva, 1956-65; counsel Cox, Langford & Brown, Washington, 1965-69, Coudert Bros., Washington, 1969-82, Dempsey and Bastianelli, Washington, 1982-83; ptnr. Bosco, Curry & Tesoro, 1984—, chmn. emeritus Am. U. of Rome, 1985—; dir. Ferrero U.S.A., Inc., Bencor Corp. Am., Inc., others. Decorated comdr. Merito della Repubblica, 1971. Author: La Psicologia della Testimonianza, 1929; Le Penalità delle Imposte Dirette, 1930; Principii di Diritto Tributario, 1938; founder, editor Italian Jour. Fiscal Law, 1937-38. Office: 20 W 72d St New York NY 10023

TESSENDORFF, HEINZ, city official; b. Berlin, Apr. 26, 1931; s. Franz and Charlotte (Fortong) T.; m. Gudrun Ingrid Altmann; children: Haiko, Ronald, Kolja. Dr Ing, Tech. U., Berlin, 1962. Sci. asst. Berlin Waterworks, 1961-66, head dept., 1968-70, exec., bd. dirs., 1971—; exec., bd. dirs. Berlin Wastewater Works, 1971—. Recipient medal City of Paris, 1980. Mem. German Assn. Gas and Water Supply (pres. 1984-85), Union European Water Supply Assns. (pres. 1983-85), Internat. Water Supply Assn. (hon.; v.p. 1986—), Am. Water Works Assn. (hon.). Lidge: Lions. Home: Ilsensteinweg 58, D-1000 Berlin 38 Federal Republic of Germany Office: Berliner Wasser-Betriebe, Hohenzollerndamn 45, D-1000 Berlin 31 Federal Republic of Germany

TETERYCZ, BARBARA ANN, entrepreneur, advertising executive; b. Chgo., Jan. 23, 1952; d. Sylvester and Anne (Deutsch) T.; m. Robert Nathan Estes, Oct. 13, 1984. BA, U. Ill., 1974; postgrad. Parkland Coll., 1975-76, U. Ill., 1976-77. Teller, First Fed. of Champaign, Ill., 1974-75; cashier Kroger Co., Champaign, 1975-77; merchandise rep. RustCraft Greeting Cards, Champaign, 1977-78; sales rep. Hockenberg-Rubin, Champaign, 1978, John Morrell & Co., Champaign, 1978-80; account exec. Sta. WICD TV, Champaign, 1981-86; owner Left-Handed Compliments, Champaign; creator 1987, 88 left-handed calendar. Contbg. editor mag. Champaign County Bus. Reports, 1986. Vol. Am. Cancer Soc., 1985, U. Ill. Alumni Assn., 1985-88, Coms. to Elect and Re-elect Beth Beauchamp to City Council, Champaign, 1984, 87. Ill. State scholar, 1970-74. Mem. Ad Club of Champaign (finalist several copywriting contests), Internat. Platform Assn., Entrepreneurs Roundtable (founding), Women's Bus. Council, Urbana C. of C., Champaign C. of C. (pub. relations com., pres.'s club), Nat. Assn. Female Execs., Alpha Omega. Roman Catholic. Avocations: reading, writing, bicycling, bodybuilding. Home: 1615 Harbor Point Dr PO Box 873 Champaign IL 61820

TETLOW, WILLIAM LLOYD, computer executive; b. Phila., July 2, 1938; s. William Lloyd and Mary Eleanor (Ferris) T.; m. Amber Jane Riederer, June 13, 1964; children: Jennifer Kay, Rebecca Dawn, Derek William. Student, Cornell U., 1956-60; B in Gen. Edn., U. Omaha, 1961; MA, Cornell U., 1965, PhD, 1973. Dir. instl. research Cornell U., Ithaca, N.Y., 1965-70; dir. planning U. B.C., Vancouver, Can., 1970-82; div. dir. NCHEMS Mgmt. Products, Boulder, Colo., 1982-85; pres., dir. Vantage Info. Products, Inc., Boulder, 1985-87; pres., propr. Vantage Computer Services, Boulder, 1986—; cons. various univs. U.S., Can. and Australia, 1970—. Editor/author: Using Microcomputers for Planning and Decision Support, 1984; contbr. numerous articles to profl. jours. Council mem. Mt. Calvary Luth. Ch., Boulder, 1984-85. Served to 1st lt. AUS, 1961-63. Mem. Assn. Inst. Research (sec. 1973-75, v.p. 1980-81, pres. 1981-82). Republican. Lodges: Concordia, Tsawwassen. Home: 3650 Smuggler Way Boulder CO 80303 Office: Vantage Computer Services 1050 Walnut St Suite 212 Boulder CO 80302

TETZNER, RUTH (HALLARD), author; b. Flensburg, West Germany, Nov. 25, 1917; d. Werner and Agnes M. (Hach) Wodick; student Comml. High Sch., to 1936; m. Rudolf Tetzner, Mar. 17, 1948; 1 son, Ernst Otto. Free lance art and couture work, 1945-48; sec., mcht. clk. Fa. Hochtief AG, Stadt Essen, 1969-78; dozentin VH, high schs. and other instns. Founder, dir. Health Center, Essen, 1963-67. Recipient awards Verband Deutscher Schriftsteller, 1959-76, Freier Deutscher Autorenverband, 1974, Gedok-Bonn-Lübeck, 1973. Liberal Democrat. Author: (poems) Signale, 1974; (stories) Kreuzungen, 1978; Greta, 1967, 5th edit., 1981, Schlangenbeschwörer-Ind. Impressionen, Erzn. 1985, Ein Trip ins Paradies, Anti-Drogenroman und Dokumentation, 1986, Lyrik, Prosa in div. Anthologien; Neuer Realismus (in D.), 1964, div. essays, also div. essays and novels, 1956-82 (diaries) Neue Wege ünd Strassen 1956-82, 1983, others.

Home: 45 Fehlingstrasse, 2400 Lübeck-Travemünde Federal Republic of Germany

TEUBNER, GUNTHER CURT MAX, lawyer, educator; b. Herrnhut, Fed. Republic Germany, Apr. 30, 1944; s. Walter and Renate (Schmidt) T.; m. Enrica Mazza; children: Jonas, Nicola, Daniel. Student, U. Goettingen, 1963, U. Tuebingen, 1967; Dr. jur., U. Tuebingen, 1970, assessor, 1971; MA in Sociology of Law, U. Calif., Berkeley, 1974. Wissenschaftlicher asst. U. Tuebingen, Fed. Republic Germany, 1970-77, habilitation, 1977; prof. law sch. U. Bremen, Fed. Republic Germany, 1977—; vis. prof. Law Sch., U. Calif., Berkeley, 1980, Law Sch., U. Mich., 1987, Law Sch. Stanford, 1988; prof. European Univ. Inst., Florence, Italy, 1981; head law dept., 1984. Author: Standards und Direktiven in Generalklauseln, 1971, Public Status of Private Associations, 1974, Gegenseitige Vertragsuntreue, 1975, Organisationsdemokratie und Verbandsverfassung, 1978, Recht als Autopoietishces System; editor: Corporate Goverance and Directors' Liability, 1985, Dilemmas of Law in the Welfare State, 1985, Contract and Organization, 1985, Juridification of Social Spheres, 1988, Autopoeitic Law, 1987; contbr. articles to profl. jours. Recipient Leon-Petrazycki Sci. Internat. prize, 1981. Mem. Zivilrechtslehrervereinigung, Vereinigung für Rechtssoziologie, Gesellschaft für Rechtsvergleichung, Gesellschaft für Soziologie, Internat. Sociol. Assn., Law and Society Assn. Office: European U Inst, I-50016 San Domenico Italy

TEUGELS, JOZEF LODEWYK, mathematics educator; b. Londerzeel, Brabant, Belgium, Feb. 20, 1939; s. Karel Achilles and Maria Adolphina (Pas) T.; m. Rita Rosa Bettens, May 19, 1964; 1 child, Lieve Griet. Candidate in physics, U. Leuven, Belgium, 1961, lic. math., 1963; MS, Purdue U., 1966, PhD, 1967. Grad. asst. Purdue U., West Lafayette, Ind., 1964-67; from asst. prof. to assoc. prof. math. Cath. U. Leuven, 1967-73, prof., 1973—. Author: Regular Variation, 1987; contbr. articles to profl. jours. Fellow Inst. Math. Stats.; mem. London Math. Soc., Belgian Math. Soc., Internat. Statis. Inst. Roman Catholic. Home: Oude Nethensebaan 29, B-3050 Sint-Joris Weert Belgium Office: Katholieke U Leuven, Celestynenlaan 200B, B-3030 Heverlee Belgium

TEUSCHER, ADRIAN HUGO, pharmaceutical executive, consultant; b. Zurich, Switzerland, Aug. 19, 1944. Diploma in sci., Eth Zurich, Insead/Stanford, 1981, Imede, 1982. Mktg. mgr. Merck Sharp & Dohme, Zurich, 1971-74; area dir. Syntex Pharms., Zurich, 1975-82; gen. mgr. Prof. Postgrad. Services, Zurich, 1983-84, Jouveinal Pharma. AG, Zurich, 1985—; ptnr. HRMC Teuscher & Ptnrs KG, Zurich, 1982—. Editor: Guide Rouge Suisse 86/87, 1986. Served as capt., Swiss Army. Mem. Lic. Exec. Soc. Club: N.Y. Athletic. Lodge: Lions. Home: 56 Stoeckenstr, CH-8903 Birmensdorf Switzerland Office: HRMC Teuscher & Ptnrs KG, Neptunstr 33, CH-8032 Zurich Switzerland

TEUSCHER, GERHART, German language and literature educator, administrator; b. Isny, Germany, Feb. 24, 1934; came to Can., 1965, naturalized, 1978; s. Ludwig and Wilma (Münzing) T.; m. Marilyn Joan Philp, June 13, 1964; children: Richard John, Jonathan Brant. Diploma Übersetzer, U. Mainz, Fed. Republic Germany, 1959; M.A. in German Lang. and Lit., U. Toronto, Ont., Can., 1969; Ph.D. in German Lang. and Lit., SUNY-Buffalo, 1975. Instr. German Wesleyan U., Conn., 1963-65; lectr. McMaster U., Hamilton, Ont., 1965-67, asst. prof. German lang. and lit., 1967-75, assoc. prof., 1975-84, prof., 1984—, chmn. dept., 1982-87; translator, interpreter, editor Can. and Brit. embassies, Bonn, 1960-62; editorial asst. Langenscheidt Pubs., Munich, Fed. Republic Germany, 1962-63; rev. cons. to various profl. publs., 1964—; lectr., panelist various nat. and internat. confs. Translator, editor: Deutsche Lyrik des Barock (German Baroque Poetry by R. M. Browning, 1971), 1980. Contbg. editor (lexicography): Langenscheidt's Encyclopedic Dictionary, 1974. Translator, editor: Voyage from Stade to Quebec, 1983. Contbr. articles to profl. jours. Fellow Can. Council, 1971-74, Volkswagen Found., 1978; Fulbright scholar, 1955-56. Mem. Can. Assn. Univ. Tchrs., Ont. Assn. Tchrs. of German (exec. com. 1980-83), Assn. Translators and Interpreters of Ont., Am. Translators Assn. (assoc.) Lutheran. Home: 109 Little John Rd, Dundas, ON Canada L9H 4H2 Office: Dept Modern Langs, McMaster U, Hamilton, ON Canada L8S 4M2

TE WINKEL, MATTHEUS JOHANNES, personnel company executive; b. Enschede, Overyssel, The Netherlands, Sept. 11, 1938; s. Dirk J. and Geuvertje Antonia (Yzerman) T.; m. Carolina Wynands, Sept. 13, 1969; children: S. Pandu, Dirk Y. M of Metallurgy, Delft Tech. Univ., The Netherlands, 1967, M of Mining Engring., 1968; BS in Econs., Amsterdam Mcpl. U., 1972; postgrad., SIOO, Rotterdam, The Netherlands, 1973. Head of ore research Billiton Internat. Metals, Arnhem, The Netherlands, 1966-68; mgmt. cons. Berenschot Assocs., Amsterdam and Utrecht, The Netherlands, 1968-73; mgr. Health Care Sector Berenschot Assocs., Utrecht, 1978-81; sr. mgmt. cons. BMB Inc., Tilburg, The Netherlands and Brussels, 1973-78; exec. dir. Ziekenhuis Amstelveen, The Netherlands, 1981-86, Job Creation, The Hague and Amsterdam, 1987—; pres. mining sect. Royal Inst. Engrs., Amsterdam, 1972-82. Author: (with others) North Sea Energy, 1981, (with others) X-Raying Organizations, 1982, (with others) Adoption in the Netherlands, 1982. Pres. Beraadsgroep Ontwikkelingssamenwerking, Aalsmeer, The Netherlands, 1981—, Found. Devel. Coop., Aalsmeer, 1982—; mem. Beroepschriften Commisie, Aalsmeer, 1983—. Recipient Landsteiner Pin Red Cross Assn., The Hague, 1982. Fellow Mynbouwkundige Vereniging; mem. Koninklyk Geol. Mynbouwkundig Gendootschaap, Orde van Organisatie-Adviseurs. Office: Job Creation, Korte Poten 7, 2511 EB The Hague The Netherlands

TEXTER, E(LMER) CLINTON, JR., physician, educator; b. Detroit, June 12, 1923; s. Elmer Clinton and Helen (Rotchford) T.; m. Jane Starke Curtis, Feb. 19, 1949; children: Phyllis Cardew, Patricia Ann, Catherine Jane. B.A., Mich. State U., 1943; M.D., Wayne State U., 1946; postgrad., U. Detroit, 1946-47, N.Y. U. Postgrad. Med. Sch., 1948-49, Northwestern U., 1959-60, Williams Coll., 1975. Diplomate Am. Bd. Internal Medicine and Gastroenterology. Intern Providence Hosp., Detroit, 1946-47; Heart Assn. research fellow in medicine Cornell U. Med. Coll., N.Y.C., 1949-50; asst. physician to outpatients N.Y. Hosp., N.Y.C., 1949-50; asst. resident medicine 3d div. NYU, Goldwater Meml. Hosp., N.Y.C., 1950-51; instr. medicine Duke U. Sch. Medicine, Durham, N.C.; asst. physician Duke U. Hosp., 1951-53; asso. medicine Northwestern U. Med. Sch., Chgo., 1953-56; asst. prof. medicine Northwestern U. Med. Sch., 1956-61, assoc. prof., 1961-68; prof. physiology adj. U. Tex. S.W. Med. Sch., Dallas, 1969-72; coordinator allied health programs Temple (Tex.) Jr. Coll., 1969-72; prof. medicine, physiology, biophysics Coll. Medicine U. Ark., 1972—, Jerome S. Levy prof. medicine (gastroenterology), 1985—, dir. div. gastroenterology, 1972-85; asst. dean Coll. Health Related Professions U. Ark., Little Rock, 1972-73; assoc. dean U. Ark., 1973-75; mem. active staff Univ. Hosp., Little Rock, 1972—; assoc. chief staff for edn. Univ. Hosp., 1972-75; chief gastroenterology VA Hosp., Little Rock, 1972-79; dir. tng. program in gastroenterology, 1954-65; attending physician Northwestern Meml. Hosp., VA Lakeside Hosp., Chgo., 1953-68; asso. med. dir. Profl. Life & Casualty Co., Chgo., 1965-68; mem. adv. bd. Skokie Valley Community Hosp., 1959-68; chmn. dept. clin. physiology and clin. research ctr., cons. gastroenterology, publs. sects. Scott and White Clinic (Temple Tex.), 1968-72; cons. gastroenterology U.S. Naval Hosp., Great Lakes, 1963-68; cons. William Beaumont Regional Army Med. Center, El Paso, Tex., 1968—; surgeon gen. U.S. Army, 1970—; cons. St. Vincent Infirmary, Little Rock, 1973—, Doctors Hosp., Little Rock, Bapt. Med. Center, Little Rock, 1981—; dir. Ark. Digestive Disease Center, 1975—; cons. Ark. regional med. program Ark. Health Systems Found., 1972-76, Council on Drugs, 1958—; mem. select com. on role of dietary fiber in diverticular disease and colon cancer Life Scis. Research Office FASEB, 1980; del. Sino-Am. Conf. on Drug Therapy, Beijing and Shanghai, 1980; vis. prof. U. Fla., 1956, 69, U. Tenn., 1958, Cath. U. Leuven, 1962, 64, 71, 81, U. Zurich, 1964, Karolinska Inst., 1964, U. Gothenburg, 1964, U. Copenhagen, 1964, U. Rome, 1965, 67, 69, U. Ala., 1971. Author: Peptic Ulcer - Diagnosis and Treatment, 1955, Physiology of the Gastrointestinal Tract, 1968, The Aging Gut, 1983; Contbr. articles to profl. jours. Active Ark. Art Center, Ark. Symphony Soc.; bd. dirs. Wayne State Fund, Detroit, 1975—. Served with USNR, 1947-49. Recipient Disting. Service awards Wayne State U., 1969, 74; Clarence F.G. Brown fellow Inst. Medicine, Chgo., 1953-56. Fellow A.C.P.; mem. AMA (com. on med. rating phys. impairment 1960-64), Am. Gastroent. Assn., Am. Fedn. Clin. Research (chmn. gastroenterology 1956, 63), Stead Scholarship Soc. of Duke U., Am. Med. Writers Assn. (pres. 1973-74), Am. Assn. Study Liver Disease, Am. Soc. Gastrointestinal Edoscopy, Am. Physiol. Soc., Am. Soc. Clin. Pharmacology and Therapeutics (dir. 1971-76), Am. Coll. Gastroenterology (gov. So. region A 1978-79, bd. govs.-Ark 1988—, nat. affairs com. 1988—), Gasteroenterology Research Group (co-founder 1955, chmn. 1959), Internat. Soc. Gastrointestinal Motility (co-founder 1969, chmn. 1969-61), So. Soc. Clin. Investigation, Central Soc. Clin. Research, William Beaumont Soc. Gastroenterologists, Sigma Xi, Theta Alpha Phi, Delta Chi, Nu Sigma Nu. Episcopalian (lay reader 1968—, chalicer 1979—). Clubs: Little Rock, Chancellor's (Little Rock); Literary (Chgo.); John Evans of Northwestern U; Anthony Wayne Soc. (Detroit); Country Club of Va. (Richmond). Home: 11519 Tahoe Ln Little Rock AR 72212 Office: U Ark 4301 W Markham St Little Rock AR 72205

TEYSSANDIER, MARIE-JOSÉ, physician; b. Tulle, Corrèze, France, Sept. 3, 1931; s. Edmond and Paule (Jouhaud) T.; m. Ghislaine Huguet, Oct. 7, 1972; 1 child, Marie-Tatiana. MD, U. Marseille, France, 1956; cert. rehabilitation specialty, U. Paris, 1970, cert. manual medicine specialty, 1971. Commd. French Army, served to col., 1983; physician paratrooper North Africa, 1957-62; physician Pacific Islands, 1963-66, Versailles-Paris, 1966-70; physician Inst. Nat. des Invalides, Paris, 1970-72; physician manual medicine Attaché des Hôpitaux, Nice, 1972—; instr. U. Marseille, Madrid, Brussels, Milan, Nice. Author 10 med. books. Conseiller mcpl. Ville de Lieuche, 1971—. Decorated War Cross, 1959; named Chevalier, Ordre des Palmes Académiques, 1971, Chevalier, Ordre Nat. du Mérite, 1981. Mem. Soc. des. Gens de Lettres de France, Soc. Francaise de Médecine (sociétaire 1985), Orthopédique et Manuelle (v.p. 1985—), Syndicat Nat. Des. Médecins Ostéothérapeutes (v.p. 1986-87). Roman Catholic. Office: 42 rue Verdi, 06000 Nice France

THACKARA, JAMES SHERMAN, writer; b. Los Angeles, Dec. 7, 1944; s. James Justin and Ellen Louise (Schmid) T.; m. Davina Laura Anne Millard, July 7, 1975; children: Leila Anne, Theresa Anne. BA, Harvard U., 1967. Film writer Bino Cicogna Rome, 1969-70, World Film Services, London, 1970-72, Costa Gavras, Paris, 1975-88. Author: America's Children, 1984, Ahab's Daughter, 1987. Activist Campaign Against Soviet Psychiat. Abuses for Polit. Purposes, 1975-79; organizer Nuclear Emergency Trust, 1986—; mem. com. 50 Dems. Abroad London, 1980-87; mem. European-Atlantic Group, 1986-87. Mem. Internat. PEN.

THACKERAY, MILTON HOWARD, accountant; b. Provo, Utah, June 13, 1944; s. Milton Grover and Farol (Hassell) T.; m. Sandra Anne West, Dec. 29, 1966; children: Steven, Anne, William, James, Thomas, Milton, Mark. BS in Acctg., U. Utah, 1968, MBA, 1969. CPA, Utah, Wyo., N.Mex. Missionary, Latter-day Saints Ch., West Germany, 1963-66; staff acct. Main Hurdman, Salt Lake City, 1969-71, sr. acct., 1971-74, mgr., 1974-77; European liason ptnr. KMG Main Hurdman, Brussels, Belgium, 1977-80, ptnr. in charge govt. services, Salt Lake City, 1980-87; ptnr. Peat Marwick Main & Co., Salt Lake City, 1987—; pres. faculty adv. bd. U. Utah, Salt Lake City, chmn. com. on faculty resources devel. chmn. com. on Grad. Sch. Acctg., 1983-84; adj. faculty mem. Westminster Coll., Salt Lake City, U. Utah, 1987. High counselor U. Utah 2d Stake, Ch. of Jesus Christ of Latter-day Saints, Salt Lake City, 1982-85. Mem. Am. Acctg. Assn., Am. Inst. CPA's, Assn. Govt. Accts., Utah Assn. CPAs (v.p., chmn. forums and speakers subcom. state legis. com. 1984—, dir., pres. elect 1988), Beta Gamma Sigma, Beta Alpha Psi. (outstanding alumnus award 1986-87). Republican. Office: Peat Marwick Main & Co 60 E South Temple Suite 900 Salt Lake City UT 84177

THAHA, MUMTAZ, rural planner; b. Ranchi, Bihar, India, Aug. 11, 1947; d. Akbar and Nasima Akhtar; m. Abdul Lateef Thaha, Aug. 24, 1972; children: Shifan, Sheeba, Sheema, Shees. BA in Geography, Womens Coll., 1965; MA in Geography, Ranchi U., 1967, PhD in Regional Planning, 1973. Dep. dir. Nat. Inst. Rural Devel., Hyderabad, Andhra Pradesn, India, 1977—; course dir. various programs, 1977—; dir. various research projects, 1977—; guest faculty various tng. insts., 1977—. Author: Rural Settlement Env., 1987. Mem. Soc. for Internat. Devel. Home: E2 NIRD Campus R'Nagar, Hyderabad 500 030, India Office: Nat Inst of Rural Devel, Rajendranagar, Hyderabad 500 030, India

THAI, NGUYEN HOANG, economist, researcher; b. Saigon, Socialist Republic of Vietnam, Oct. 29, 1955; arrived in Canada, 1973; parents: Nguyen Van Sac and Phung Thi Trong. BA, Sherbrooke U., Que., Can., 1977; MA, Que. U., Montreal, 1988. Computer technician Lavalin, Inc., Montreal, Que., 1979-81; planning asst. Transp. Council, Montreal, 1981-82, asst. dir., 1982-83; researcher Que. U., 1985—. Mem. Assn. Economistes Quebecois. Home: 3415 Avon, Saint Hubert, PQ Canada J3Y-5A7 also: 7164 Nancy, Montreal, PQ Canada H3R 2L7

THAIN, DONALD HAMMOND, business administration educator; b. Toronto, May 6, 1928; s. William Edwards and Lucy May (Marsden) T.; m. Helen M. Steeves, Aug. 1952; children: Peter, Carol, John. MBA, Harvard U., 1953, D Bus. Adminstrn., 1955. Account exec. Spitzer, Mills and Bates, Toronto, 1948-51; research assoc. instr. Bus. Sch. Harvard U., Cambridge, Mass., 1951-57; prof. bus. adminstrn. U. Western Ont. (Can.), London, 1957—; bd. dirs. Denison Mines Ltd., Goodyear Can. Inc., Lawson Mardon Group Ltd., Silcop Ltd.; Magna internat. prof. bus. adminstrn., 1987. Author, co-author books on mgmt., 1956—; contbr. numerous articles to profl. jours. Recipient P.S. Ross award for best article in Bus. Quar., 1970, 77. Club: London Hunt and Country (golf capt. 1982). Home: 80 Sherwood Ave, London, ON Canada N6A 2E2 Office: U Western Ont, London, ON Canada N6A 3K7

THALL, RICHARD VINCENT, school administrator; b. San Francisco, Sept. 12, 1940; s. Albert Vincent and Alice Stella (O'Brien) T.; m. Ellyn Marie Wisherop, June 15, 1963; children: Kristen Ellyn, Richard Vincent Jr. AA, City Coll. San Francisco, 1961; BA, San Francisco State Coll., 1964; MA, San Francisco State U., 1971. Cert. elem. tchr., Calif.; cert. secondary tchr., Calif.; cert. community coll. tchr., Calif. Tchr. biology San Francisco Unified Sch. Dist., 1965-66; tchr. biology Mt. Diablo Unified Sch. Dist., Concord, Calif., 1966-79, program coordinator, 1979—; ranger/naturalist State of Calif., Brannan Island, 1973-78; naturalist Adventure Internat., Oakland, Calif., 1979-81; lectr. Princess Cruise Lines, Los Angeles, 1982-84, Sea Goddess, 1986—, Sun Lines, 1987—; Am. biology tchr., 1976. Author: Ecological Sampling of the Sacramento-San Joaquin Delta, 1976; Water Environment Studies Program, 1986; co-author: Project MER Laboratory Manual, 1982. Mem. Contra Costa County (Calif.) Natural Resources Commn., 1975-78, vice-chmn., 1977-78; active Save Mt. Diablo, Concord, 1969-76, v.p., 1974-75; mem. citizens com. Assn. Bay Area Govt. Water Quality, 1979-82, vice-chmn., 1980-82; active John Marsh Home Restoration Com., Martinez, Calif., 1977-78; mem. edn. adv. com. Marine World/Africa USAd, Vallejo, Calif., 1988—; troop com. chmn. Boy Scouts Am., Concord, 1984-86, asst. scoutmaster, 1985-87. Recipient Recognition and Excellence cert. Assn. Calif. Sch. Adminstrs., 1984, Wood Badge award Boy Scouts Am., 1986; grantee State Calif., 1982, 84. Mem. AAAS, Nat. Assn. Biology Tchrs., Nat. Audubon Soc., Am. Mus. Natural Hist., Nat. Geog. Soc., Smithsonian Instn. (assoc.). Republican. Roman Catholic. Home: 1712 Lindenwood Dr Concord CA 94521 Office: Mt Diablo Unified Sch Dist 1936 Carlotta Dr Concord CA 94519

THAM, SEONG CHEE, educator; b. Kuala Lumpur, Malaysia, Oct. 18, 1932; s. Chan Hung and Ngan (Wan) T.; B.A. with honors, U. Malaya, 1965; Ph.D., U. Singapore, 1970; m. Siew Oi Lan, Mar. 28, 1958; children—Edwin Soong Meng, Leonard Soong Choon, Leslie Soong Yue. Tchr., Meth. Boys' Sch., Kuala Lumpur, 1955-66; lectr. Lang. Inst., 1966-69; lectr. U. Singapore, from 1969, now assoc. prof. dept. Malay studies; Commonwealth Acad. fellow U. London, 1974; vis. scholar, Cornell U., 1985, Cambridge U., 1986; mem. Singapore Nat. Library Bd.; columnist Daily News, Berita Harian; adviser UNESCO project Study Southeast Asian Cultures; trustee Biopolitics Internat. Orgn. Mem. Inst. Southeast Asian Studies (trustee), Singapore Assn. Advancement of Sci. (v.p.), UN Assn. Singapore (pres. 1976-86, Internat. Sociol. Assn. Author: Malays and Modernization, 1977; Language and Cognition, 1977; Social Science Research in Malaysia, 1981; Literature and Society in Southeast Asia, 1981; Religion and Modernization Study of Changing Rituals Among Singapore's Chinese, Malays and Indians, 1984. Home: 34 Maryland Dr, Singapore 1027 Singapore

THAMES, REDDEN JEFFERSON, business executive; b. Elba, Ala., Oct. 31, 1932; s. Aaron Preston and Ruth (Bass) T.; A.B., Stetson U., 1958; B.D., So. Bapt. Theol. Sem., 1962, M.Div., 1970; m. Joanne Ellen Reeves, Sept. 1, 1952; children—Ruth, Nancy, Joe, Jim. Ordained to ministry So. Bapt. Ch., 1952; pastor chs., Lake View, S.C., 1962-67, Loris, S.C., 1967-70; dir. Horry County Dept. Social Services, Conway, S.C., 1970-73; dist. dir. S.C. Dept. Social Services, Columbia, 1973-85; v.p. WeCare Distbrs., Inc., Charlotte; dir. Catawba Regional Planning Council, 1973-81; v.p. Interval Mktg. Cons., Inc., North Myrtle Beach, S.C., 1981-82; v.p. pub. relations We Care Distbrs., Inc., Charlotte, N.C., 1983—. Bd. dirs. Dillon County Rural Recreation Commn., 1964—, Central Midlands Regional Planning Council, 1973—, Coastal Plains Mental Health Commn., 1971-73, Coastal Plains Regional Home Health Council, 1971-73; chmn. S.C., Nat. Multiple Sclerosis Soc. Named Rural Minister of Yr., Progressive Farmer mag., 1965, Outstanding Alumnus, Stetson U., 1971; Nat. Multiple Sclerosis Hope Chest award, 1982. Mem. Am. Mgmt. Assn., Adminstrv. Mgmt. Soc., Child Welfare League Am., Am. Public Welfare Assn. (human resources adv. com. 1975-79), CDN. Direct Sellers Assn. (govt. relations com. 1988—), Charlotte C. of C., CDN Cosmetic Assn. Lodge: Masons. Author: Dynamic Supervision, 1977. Office: PO Box 222138 Charlotte NC 28222

THAMS, JOHAN-PETTER BRYNJULF, business executive; b. Oslo, Apr. 11, 1916; s. Ulf Sparre and Lulu Marie (Jensen) T.; m. Gudrun Lorey, Sept. 10, 1939; (div. Jan. 1953); 1 son, Ulf; m. Irina Ostrovsky, July 15, 1953; children—Robert, Johan Georg. B.C., Oslo U., 1973; postgrad. Tech. Hochschule, Berlin, 1937-39; M.S., Teknisk Hoiskole, Trondheim, Norway, 1941. Registered chem. engr. Mgr., Cromtryck AB, Sweden, 1941-45, pres., 1945-80; pres. Chrome Print Inc., N.J., 1949-53; chmn. Chromtrykk AS, Norway, 1950—, Kromipaino OY, Finland, 1955—, Chrome Print Ltd., Eng., 1970—, Cromtryck AB, Vallingby, Sweden, 1980—. Patentee in printing and lacquering. Mem. commn. Swedish Standardisation Com., 1960—, Internat. Elec. Com., 1960—; chmn. Swedish Standardisation Com. Printed Circuits, 1980—. Club: Norske Selskap (Oslo). Home: Gronviksvagen 69, Stockholm 216140, Sweden Office: Cromtryck AB, PO Box 85, Vallingby 16212, Sweden

THANAWALLA, KHURSHED MEHERWANJI, management consultant, textile executive; b. Bombay, Dec. 24, 1942; s. Meherwanji Cursetji and Jer Meherwanji (Jassawalla) T. B.Comm., U. Bombay, 1964. Dep. mng. dir. Kisumu Cotton Mills Ltd., Kenya, 1965-82; dir. Rotary Screens of Asia Ltd., Singapore, 1974-84, Auto Ancilliary Mfrs. Sdm. Bhd., Malaysia, 1977-84, Kicosales Ltd., Nairobi, Kenya, 1965-84, Technoconsult Ltd., Guernsey, Channel Islands, 1977-83, Aseantech A.G., Zug, Switzerland, 1978-84, Khatau Internat. Ltd., Bombay, 1980-82; commr. P.T. Tubantia Kudus Spg. Mills, Kudus, Indonesia, 1978-83, P.T. Sumatex Subur, Padang, Indonesia, 1979-84; v.p. Bimag Machines Pvt. Ltd., Bombay, 1984—. Mem. Fedn. Kenya Employers (mgmt. bd.), Kenya Assn. Mfrs. (exec. com.), Textile Mfrs. Assn. Kenya (exec. com.), Kenya Govt. Textile Tng. Com., Kenya Govt. Textile Standards Com., Textile Machinery Mfrs. Assn. Zorastrian. Home: 16 LD Ruparel Marg, Bombay 400 006, India

THANAWALLA, TAJ HAIDERALI, insurance broker; b. Nairobi, Kenya, Sept. 7, 1940; s. Haiderali Gulamhussein and Khatija (Kassam) T.; Associateship of Corp. of Co. Secs., Balham & Tooting Coll. Commerce, 1959; Assoc., Inst. of Commerce and Mgmt., 1960; m. Parviz Noorali Rajan, Dec. 5, 1970; 1 son, Aly. With United Mktg. Internat., Ltd., Nairobi, 1963, 73—, mng. dir., 1974—, also dir.; mng. dir. Ryce Motors, Ltd., Nairobi, 1972-73; dir. H.G. Thanwalla, Ltd., Cambrian Agys., Ltd. Recipient cert. Jubilee Ins. Co., Ltd., 1976, 77, 78, 79, 80. Fellow Inst. Dirs. (London); mem. East Africa Jr. C. of C. (charter); assoc. mem. Inst. Credit Mgmt., Inst. Commerce (London), Chartered Inst. of Co. Secs. and Adminstrs. Mem. Nat. Ruling party. Moslem. Clubs: Nairobi, Mt. Kenya Safari, Nairobi Safari, Lukes, Vet Lab Golf, Sigona Golf.

THANI, SHEIKH ABDUL AZIZ BIN KHALIFA AL See AL-THANI, SHEIKH ABDUL AZIZ BIN KHALIFA

THANI, SHEIKH HAMAD BIN KHALIFA AL See AL-THANI, SHEIKH HAMAD BIN KHALIFA

THANI, SHEIKH KHALID BIN HAMAD AL See AL-THANI, SHEIKH KHALID BIN HAMAD

THANI, SHEIKH KHALIFA BIN HAMAD AL See AL-THANI, SHEIKH KHALIFA BIN HAMAD

THANI, SHEIKH NASIR BIN KHALID AL See AL-THANI, SHEIKH NASIR BIN KHALID

THAN-TRONG, HIEN, physician; b. Hue, Vietnam, Jan. 1, 1934; arrived in France, 1950; s. Phuoc Than-Trong and Hoang (Thi) Ve; m. Catherine Arigoni, May 6, 1958 (div. 1975). MD, U. Paris, 1966. Intern in cardiology and pneumology Compiegne (France) Hosp., 1961; intern in surgery Meaux and Senlis (France) Hosp., 1962; intern, then attaché cons. ob-gyn. Nanterre (France) Hosp., 1963-86, dir. family planning ctr., 1967-86; attaché in gynecol. cancerology U. Paul-Brousse Hosp., Villejuif, France, 1981-83; practice medicine specializing in ob-gyn. Paris, 1968—; practice medicine specializing in gynecology-oncology 1981—; attaché cons., 1976. Buddhist. Office: 37 rue Rousselet, 75007 Paris France

THAR, FERDINAND AUGUST (BUD), trade company executive; b. Paw Paw, Mich., Oct. 26, 1940; s. James Ferdinand and Louise Olga (Schmidt) T.; m. Siri Ashelman, Jan. 28, 1967; Jonathan Justin, Christina Sheri, Amanda Hope. BA, Mich. State U., 1964; postgrad., Boston U., 1964-65, Am. U., 1968-72, U. Ga. Sch. Internat. Law, 1978. Exec. dir. Ctr. Internat. Transp., East Lansing, Mich., 1979-82; program officer Govtl. Affairs Inst., Washington, 1964-73; assoc. dir. Battle Creek (Mich.) Unltd., 1980-83; pres. Eagle Trade, Battle Creek, 1983—; exec. dir. Great Lakes World Trade Ctr., Detroit, 1986; instr. Ednl. Services Exchange with China, 1987-88; U.S. del. 1st World Agrl. Fair, New Delhi, 1959-60, Internat. Farm Youth Exchange, Israel, 1962; mem. White House Conf. Internat. Cooperation, Washington, 1972, White House Conf. Balanced Growth, Washington, 1978; mem. NRC, Washington, 1979—, transp. research bd. Intergovtl. Relations Com., 1985—; guest govts. of France, Fed. Republic of Germany, Jamaica, Yugoslavia; cons., guest lecturer on internat. trade Peoples Republic of China, 1987-88, and Brit. R.R.s, French Nat. R.R., 1979; author devel. proposal agribus. project, 1982; cons. Great Lakes Regional Commn., Ann Arbor, Mich., 1984-85, Japanese Electronics Assn., Washington and Japan, 1984-86. Author: Influence of International Travel on Vocational Choice, 1963, Rural Youth in Michigan, 1964. Leader youth vol. group, Costa Rica, 1963. Mem. Am. Assn. Polit. Sci., Nat. Govs. Assn. (staff dir. 1973-83), World Trade Ctrs. Assn., Internat. Farm Youth Exchange, Gideons Internat.

THARAKAN, MATHEW PARAYIL KOCHUPAPPU, economics, management educator; b. Thycattuserry, India, Sept. 12, 1935; arrived in Belgium, 1966; s. Kochupappu P.A. and Rosamma (Kallivayalil) T.; m. Anne M. Belpaire, July 27, 1970; children: Joseph, Thomas. B in Commerce, Madras U., 1956; MBA, Marquette U., 1961; Degree in Devel., Louvain (Belgium) U., 1967, D of Econs., 1972. Chief of research Antwerp (Belgium) U., 1972-74, asst. prof., 1974-80, dir. Ctr. Devel. Studies, 1977-83, assoc. prof., 1981-86, prof., 1986-87, prof. ordinarus, 1987—; vis. prof. Nat. Inst. Bank Mgmt., Bombay, 1975, Jayawardenepur U., Sri Lanka, 1982, U. Louvain, Belgium, 1984-85; vis. scholar Inst. Internat. Econ. Studies, U. Stockholm, 1979; prof. European Inst. Advanced Studies in Mgmt., Brussels, 1981—; cons. Belgian Ministry Devel. Cooperation, Brussels, 1975-83, UN Indsl. Devel. Orgn., Vienna, 1976, 77, 79, Commn. European Communities, Brussels, 1977-78, World Bank, Washington, 1978. Author: Multinational Companies and A New International Division of Labor, 1979, (with others) Ajustements Structurels et Industries de Jute, 1979; editor: Intra-Industry Trade: Empirical and Methodological Aspects, 1983, (with others) Imperfect Competition and International Trade, 1984, Intra-Indistry Trade, Evidence & Extensions, 1988, Competetiveness of European Industry, 1988; contbr.

articles to internat. publs. Awarded fellowship Inter-Univ. Coll. Doctoral Studies, Brussels, 1982, U. Louvain, 1969-71, Ctr. Nat. Sci. Research, Paris, 1977-78; grantee Prime Minister's Secretariat for Sci. Policy, Brussels, 1985-86, Fund Collective Fundamental Research, Brussels, 1987. Mem. European Assn. Devel. Research Inst. (gov. 1987), Univ. Found. Brussels. Roman Catholic. Home: 19A Osylei, 2510 Mortsel Belgium Office: Univ Antwerp, 13 Prinsstraat, 200 Antwerp Belgium

THATCHER, DICKINSON, lawyer; b. Huntington Beach, Calif., May 26, 1919; s. Charles Harold and Gladys Belle (Dickinson) T.; m. Dale Nadine Mortensen, Feb. 2, 1952; children: Kirk R., Jeffrey L. BS, UCLA, 1941; postgrad. NYU, 1943-44, U. Paris, 1945-46; JD, Stanford U., 1948; LLM in Taxation, U. So. Calif., 1962. Bar: Calif. 1948, U.S. Ct. Claims 1956, U.S. Tax Ct. 1954, U.S. Supreme Ct. 1954. Dep. city atty. City of Los Angeles, 1948-51; credit atty. Union Oil Co., Calif., Los Angeles, 1951-54; trial atty. tax div. Dept. Justice, Washington, 1954-56; asst. U.S. atty. Los Angeles, 1956-57; sole practice Van Nuys, Calif., 1957-59, 72-88, North Hollywood, Calif., 1959-72. Contbr. articles to legal jours. Served with AUS, 1942-46. Mem. ABA, State Bar Calif. (disciplinary bd. 1970-72, client security fund 1973-75), Los Angeles County Bar Assn. (chmn. council, affiliated bar pres. 1968-70, exec. com. probate and trust law sect. 1985-88), San Fernando Valley Bar Assn. (pres. 1966). Home: 211 Bristol Rd Ojai CA 93023

THATCHER, MARGARET HILDA, prime minister U.K.; b. Oct. 13, 1925; d. Alfred Roberts; m. Denis Thatcher, 1951; 1 son and 1 dau. (twins). M.A., B.Sc., Somerville Coll., Oxford (Eng.) U. Research chemist, 1947-51; called to Lincoln's Inn, 1953, hon. bencher, 1975; M.P., 1959—, jt. parliamentary sec. Ministry of Pensions and Nat. Ins., 1961-64; sec. of state for edn. and sci., 1970-74; leader Conservative Party, 1975—; leader Opposition, 1975-79; prime minister, 1st lord of Treasury, 1979—. Hon. fellow Royal Inst. Chemistry, 1979, Freedom of Royal Borough of Kensington and Chelsea, 1979, Falkland Islands, 1983. Mem. Worshiphul Co. of Glorers, 1983. Address: 10 Downing St, London SW1 England *

THATTE, DILEEP, chemical company executive; b. Hyderbad, Andhra Pradesh, India, Jan. 31, 1951; s. V.D. Thatte and Vimal Thatte; m. Naina Thatte; children: Nandita, Ashwin. MS in Chem. Engring., U. Rochester, 1976; MBA, York U., Toronto, Ont., 1980. Registered profl. engr., Ont. Sales engr. Croda Can., Ltd., Toronto, Ont., 1976-77; sales engr. Calgon Can., Inc., Brampton, Ont., 1977-79, nat. sales mgr., 1980-86, mng. dir., gen. mgr., 1986—. Mem. Nat. Assn. Corr. Engrs., Can. Pulp and Paper Assn., Am. Water Works Assn., Assn. Profl. Engrs. of Ont. Office: Calgon Canada Inc, 27 Finley Rd, Brampton, ON Canada L6T 1B2

THAXTON, EVERETTE FREDERICK, lawyer; b. Charleston, W.Va., Jan. 11, 1938; s. Wilbur and Mildred F. (Gerwig) T.; m. Karen Caldwell, Dec. 29, 1967; children: James, LeeAnn, Emily. BA, U. Charleston, 1967; JD, W.Va. U., 1970. Bar: W.Va. 1970, Va. 1981, U.S. Ct. Appeals (fourth cir.) 1983. Cartographer, hwy. design technician W.Va. Dept. of Hwy., Charleston, 1961-63; dir. tax mapping W.Va. Tax Dept., Charleston, 1963-65; ptnr. Thaxton & Daniels, Charleston, 1970—. Served with USAF, 1955-61. Mem. ABA (various coms.), W.Va. Bar Assn., Assn. Trial Lawyers Am., W.VA. Trial Lawyers Assn., Am. Arbitration Assn. (panel arbitrators), Pi Gamma Mu, Aircraft Owners and Pilots Assn. Home: 502 Hillsdale Dr Charleston WV 25302 Office: Thaxton & Daniels 1115 Virginia St E Charleston WV 25301

THE, MARC POO KIAN, real estate director; b. Amsterdam, N.Holland, The Netherlands, Oct. 6, 1963; s. I.L. and H.E.W. (Zonnernberg) T. Assoc. Bus., Internat. Coll. Bus. Adminstrn., Ziest, 1984, BBA, 1986; postgrad., Henley Mgmt. Coll., London, 1987. Founder, pres. Foundation Integrand, Utrecht, The Netherlands, 1985—; mng. dir. Foundation Integrand Netherland, The Netherlands, 1986-87; mng. dir., founder Real Estate B.V., S. Hertogenbosch, The Netherlands, 1987—. Home: Hooge Steenweg 23, 5211 JN S-Hertogenbosch The Netherlands Office: Integrand, Ameland 70, 3524 AL Utrecht The Netherlands

THEINER, ERIC CHARLES, psychologist; b. N.Y.C., Sept. 27, 1935; s. Carl and Theresa Maria (Hahn) T.; B.S., Manhattan Coll., 1957; M.A., Syracuse U., 1960; Ph.D., U. Houston, 1966; m. Margaret A. Guill, July 16, 1977 (dec.); children—Cynthia, Eric. Cons., Ed N Hay & Assocs., Phila., 1969-70; mgr. assessment services ITT World Hdqrs., N.Y.C., 1970-72; clin. psychologist VA Med. Center, Memphis, 1972—, U. Tenn. Med. Sch., Memphis, 1972—; pvt. practice, 1972—; mem. bd. examiners in psychology State of Tex.; mem. faculty Memphis State U., 1972—, U. Ark., 1974—. Served with USAF, 1960-69. Mem. Tenn. Psychol. Assn., Biofeedback Soc. Tenn., Am. Psychol. Assn., Biofeedback Soc. Am., Tex. Psychol. Assn., D.C. Psychol. Assn., Soc. Behavioral Medicine, Southwestern Psychol. Assn., Soc. Personality Assessment, Soc. Air Force Psychologists, Miss. Psychol. Assn., Sigma Xi. Fellow Pa. Psychol. Assn. Contbr. articles to profl. jours. Home: 61 Belleair Dr Memphis TN 38104 Office: 2670 Union Ave Extended Suite 706 Memphis TN 38112

THEIS, ROBERT JEAN PAUL, philosopher, educator; b. Luxembourg, Jan. 1, 1947; s. Jean-Adolphe Theis and Marie Kieffer; m. Annette Nicole Bisdorff, July 20, 1978; children: Véronique, François, Marie-Luce. Lic. in Philosophy, Pontifical Gregorian U., Rome, 1970; M in Philosophy, U. Paris Sorbonne, 1973, D in Philosophy, 1975; M in Theology, Inst. Cath., Paris, 1974. Prof. Lycée, Luxembourg, 1980—; guest lectr. U. Saarbrucken, Fed. Republic Germany, 1982—; collaborator Filosofia Oggi, Genova, Italy, Kant-Studien, Mainz, Fed. Rep. Germany. Author: Le Discours Dédoublé, 1978; contbr. articles to profl. jours. Mem. Agrégé de l'Institut Grand-Ducal (section des Scis. Morales et Politiques) Ecole Pratique des Hautes Etudes (élève titulaire Ve sect.), Internat. Assn. Advancement of Hegelian Studies, Kant-Gesellschaft. Roman Catholic. Home: Rue Christophe-Colomb, 48 1349 Luxembourg Luxembourg Office: U Saarlandes, Fachbereich 5 3, D-6600 Saarbrücken Federal Republic of Germany also: Lycée Hubert-Clement, 2 rue Général Patton, L-4277 Esch/Alzette Luxembourg

THEOBALD, EDWARD ROBERT, lawyer; b. Chgo., Feb. 10, 1947; s. Edward Robert Theobald Jr. and Marie (Turner) Logan; m. Bonnie J. Singer, July 18, 1970; children: Debra Marie, Kimberly Ann. BA, So. Ill. U., 1969; JD, Ill. Inst. Tech.-Chgo. Kent Coll. Law, 1974. Bar: Ill. 1974, U.S. Dist. Ct. (no. dist.) Ill. 1974. Asst. state's atty. Cook County, Chgo., 1974-77, 77-79, supr. felony trial div., 1980-81; assoc. firm Conklin, Leahy & Eisenberg, Chgo., 1977; ptnr. firm Boharic & Theobald, Chgo., 1981-83; sole practice, Chgo., 1983—; legal advisor Sheriff of Cook County, Ill., 1986—. Named Number One Trial Atty. in Felony Trial Div. of Office of Cook County State's Atty., Felony Trial Div. Suprs., 1979. Mem. Chgo. Bar Assn. (bd. mgrs. 1985-87, labor and employment law com. 1983—), ABA (chmn. com. on sentencing alternatives young lawyers sect. 1982-83), Ill. Bar Assn., Assn. Trial Lawyers Am. Roman Catholic. Home: 7104 Grand Ave Downers Grove IL 60516 Office: 135 S La Salle St Suite 1246 Chicago IL 60603

THEOCARAKIS, BASIL, entrepeneur; b. Piraeus, Greece, Oct. 18, 1930; s. Nicholas Theocarakis and Anna (Tsoumas) Kontogeorgiou; m. Marina Alexandri, Jan. 15, 1961; children—Anna-Maria, Despina. J.D., Athens U., 1955. Pres., mng. dir. Theocarakis Group of Cos., 1980—. Served as officer Greek Army. Mem. Chamber Fine Arts. Avocation: oil painting. Home: 6 Ath Diakou Str, 152 37 Filothei Athens Greece Office: 169 Leoforos Athinon, 10447 Athens Greece

THEOCHARIS, REGHINOS D., university professor, consultant, author; b. Larnaca, Cyprus, Feb. 10, 1929; s. Demetrios and Florentia Z. (Mylonas) T.; m. Madeleine Loumbou, June, 6, 1954; children: Charis, Eleni. BSc in Econs., Athens Sch. of Econs. and Bus., 1946; PhD, London Sch. of Econs., 1958. Secondary sch. tchr. Larnaca Pub. Sch., 1949-51; insp. secondary schs. Cyprus Edn. Dept., 1953-56; researcher Research Dept. Bank of Greece, 1958-59; provisional minister of fin. Cyprus, 1959-60, minister of fin., 1960-62; gov. Bank of Cyprus, 1962-75; dir. gen. Centre of Planning and Econ. Research, Greece, 1978-81; univ. prof. Athens Sch. of Econs., Greece, 1975—. Author: Early Developments in Mathematical Economics, 1960, 2d edit., 1983; various books in Greek; contbr. articles to profl. jours. Hon. fellow London Sch. Econs., 1971. Greek Orthodox. Home: 2 Raidestou St, Kessariani, 16122 Athens Greece Office: Athens Sch Econs & Bus, Patision 76, 10434 Athens Greece

THEODOLI-BRASCHI, GIOVANNI ANGELO, investment banker; b. Bologna, Italy, May 1, 1942; s. Pio Theodoli and Adriana Moscatelli; JD, U. Bologna, 1966; MBA, Cornell U., 1972; m. Maria Milstein, Nov. 26, 1977; 2 children. Mktg. officer Texaco SpA, Italy, 1967-70; investment banker First Boston Corp., N.Y.C. and London, 1972-75; v.p. Europe, Citicorp Internat. Bank Ltd., London, 1975-82; dir. gen. Citibank España, Madrid, 1983-85; exec. dir. Citicorp Investment Bank, London, 1986-87; dir. so. Europe County Natwest Ltd., London, 1987—. Roman Catholic. Clubs: Circolo della Caccia (Rome); Annabel's, Hurlingham (London); Puerta de Hierro (Madrid). Office: County Natwest Ltd, 12 Throgmorton Ave, London EC2, England

THEODORAKIS, MIKIS, composer; b. Chios, Greece, 1925; ed. secondary sch., high sch., Greece, Athens Conservatorie, Paris Conservatorie; student of Oliver Messaien, Paris, 1953; m. Myrto Theodorakis, 1953; 1 son, 1 dau., Joined resistance against German occupation of Greece, 1943; arrested and deported during civil war, 1947-52; moved to Paris, 1954; returned to Greece, 1963; leader Lambrakis youth movement; mem. Parliament, 1964; arrested for political activities, 1967, released and exiled, 1970; returned to Greece at end of dictatorship, 1974, M.P., 1981, 85-86; works include: Epitaphios (poem by Iannis Ritsos, set to bouzouki music), 1958-59, ballet music for Antigone and Les Amants de Teruel, Sinfonia (oratorio), Adagio (for orchestra), Passacaglia, 1944-50, Orpheus (ballet), Assi-Gonia (scherzosinfonico), First Symphony, Carnaval (ballet) Sonatina No. 1 (for violin and piano), 1950-54, Epitaphios, Suita No. 1, 2, 3 (concerto for pianoforte), Oedipus Tyrannos (ballet), Sonatina No. 2 Petite Suite (piano), Paris, 1954, settings for poems by Eluard, and of Epiphania (Seferis), 1955-60; Axion Esti (oratorio), 1964, Mauthausen, Songs of Strife, Canto General, 10 Arcades, others; music for numerous films including The Barefoot Battalion, Zorba the Greek, Z, The Trojan Women, State of Siege, 1973; music for the Nat. Theatre of Greece; song cycles include The Hostage, 1962, The Ballad of Mauthausen, 1965, Romancero Gitano, 1967, Sun and Time, 1967, Ballads, 1975; numerous songs, oratorios. Recipient Gold medal Moscow Shostakovitch Festival, 1957, Corbey prize U.S.A., 1957, Comsomol prize, Moscow, 1957, First prize Athens Popular Song Festival, 1961, Sibelius award, London, 1963, Socrate prize, 1974. Author: Journals of Resistance, 1972; Culture et dimensions politiques, 1973. Address: 111 rue Notre Dame des Champs, 75006 Paris France also: Epifanous 1, Akropolis, Athens Greece *

THEODORE, GEORGE T., private investigator; b. Elmhurst, Ill., July 7, 1940; s. Ted and Alice (Nicopoulos) T. Cert. genealogy, Elmhurst Coll., 1965; cert. electronics, Triton Coll., 1967, cert. locksmithing, 1969. Pres. Tracer's, Inc., Elmhurst, 1961—. Mem. Am. Security Council, Nat. Genealogy Soc. Home: 197 Addison St Elmhurst IL 60126 Office: Tracers Inc 122 N York Rd Elmhurst IL 60126

THEODORE, WILLIAM JAMES, educational administrator; b. Chgo., Feb. 6, 1947; s. George and Winnie (Stafford) T.; m. Dana Yeargin, Mar. 1, 1980 (div. Nov. 1981). A.B., U. Mich., 1969, A.M., 1972; Ed.S., Wichita State U., 1981. Tchr. Tecumseh High Sch., Mich., 1970-72, Orleans Parish, La., 1972-76; prin. Nickerson Sch. Dist., Kans., 1980-82; tchr. Jefferson Parish Schs., Gretna, La., 1976-80, 1982-83; asst. prin. Arch Blenk High Sch., Gretna, 1983-84; prin., supt., Hillcrest Rural Sch. Dist., Cuba, Kans., 1984—. Mem. Nat. Assn. Secondary Prins., Nat. Assn. Elem. Prins., Kans. Unified Sch. Adminstrs., Assn. Supervisors Curriculum Devel., Am. Assn. Sch. Adminstrs., Kans. Assn. Sch. Adminstrs., Kans. Assn. Ednl. Negotiators, Kans. Assn. Elem. Prins., Phi Kappa Phi. Avocation: sports. Home: PO Box 85 Agenda KS 66930 Office: Hillcrest Rural Schs PO Box 167 Cuba KS 66940

THEODORIDES, MICHEL, pediatrician; b. Bordeaux, France, Apr. 2, 1935; s. Nicolas and Irene (Cutusi) T.; m. Henriette Bardy, Jan. 25, 1970; 1 child, David. MD, U. Bordeaux; fellow, Med. Acad. Paris, 1966. Cert. in pediatrics. Intern Children's Hosp., Bordeaux, 1960-66, chief of clinic, 1966-68, asst., 1968; pediatrician I.M.P. Antonne, Perigueux, France, 1968-71, I.R.P. d'Ailhaud Castelet, Perigueux, 1971, Ctr. Medico-Psycho-Pedagogics, Perigueux, 1972; attache Hosp. Perigueux, 1973. Departmental pres. UNICEF, 1983. Mem. French Pediatricians Soc. Home: 24650 Chancelade France Office: 22 Ave G Pompidou, 2400 Pergueux France

THEODOROPOULOS, DIMITRIOS MILTIADIS, chemist, educator; b. Athens, Greece, Sept. 15, 1926; s. Miltiadis John and Georgia Theodor (Zervas) T.; m. Helen Nanou, Mar. 25, 1958; children: Georgia, Melpomeni. BS in Chemistry, U. Athens, 1950, PhD, 1953. Vis. investigator The Rockefeller U., N.Y.C., 1953-56; assoc. lab. organic chemist U. Athens, 1956-57, docent tech., 1959-61, 62-65; vis. scientist U. Gothenburg, Sweden, 1957-59; asst. prof. Yale U., New Haven, 1961-62; research collaborator Brookhaven Nat. Lab., N.Y.C., 1965-67; assoc. Mt. Sinai Hosp., N.Y.C., 1965-67; dir. lab. organic chemistry U. Patras, Greece, 1967—, univ. pres., 1967-71; vis. prof. dept. biophysics U. Ill. Med. Ctr., Chgo., 1975, 79, dept. biol. chemistry U. Mons, Belgium, 1981, dept. biomed. Uppsala U., 1988; participant Internat. Peptide Symposia, 1959—; mem. European Peptide com., chmn. 19th European Peptide Symposium, 1986. Contbr. numerous articles in organic chemistry to sci. jours. Served with Greek Navy, 1947-49. Research Found. Greek fellow, 1953-56. Mem. Am. Chem. Soc., Chem. Soc. London, Greek Chem. Union. Mem. Christian Orthodox Ch. Home: 8 Macedonon, 115 21 Athens Greece Office: 231 Korinthou, Patras Greece

THEOHARIDES, THEOHARIS CONSTANTIN, pharmacologist, physician, educator; b. Thessaloniki, Greece, Feb. 11, 1950; s. Constantin A. and Marika (Krava) T.; m. Efthalia I. Triarchou, July 10, 1981; 1 child, Niove. Diploma with honors, Anatolia Coll., 1968, BA in Biology and History of Sci. and Medicine, Yale U., 1972, MS in Immunology, 1975, MPhil. in Endocrinology, 1975, PhD in Pharmacology, 1978, MD, 1983. Asst. in research biology Yale U., 1968-71, asst. in research pharmacology, 1973-78, exec. sec. univ. senate, 1976-78, research assoc. faculty clin. immunology, 1978-83; asst. prof. biochemistry and pharmacology Tufts U., 1983-88, assoc. prof., 1988—; co-dir. med. pharmacology curriculum, 1983-85, dir. med. pharmacology, 1985—; clin. pharmocologist Commonwealth Mass. Drug Formulary Commn., 1985—; spl. instr. modern Greek, Yale U., 1974, 77; vis. faculty Aristotelian U. Sch. Medicine, Thessaloniki, 1979. Trustee Anatolia Coll. 1984-85. Author book on pharmacology; contbr. numerous articles to profl. jours. Bd. dirs., v.p. for relations with Greece, Krikos, 1978-79; sec. Assn. Greeks t Yale, 1974-79, pres., 1982-83. Recipient Theodore Cuyler award Yale U., 1972; George Papanicoalou Grad. award, 1977; Med. award Hellenic Med. Soc. N.Y., 1979, 83; M.C. Winternitz prize in pathology Yale U., 1980; Disting. Service award Tufts U. Alumni Assn., 1986, Spl. Faculty Recognition award Tufts U. Med. Sch., 1987, 88. Mem. Hellenic Biochem. and Biophys. Soc., AMA, AAUP, N.Y. Acad. Scis., Am. Inst. History Pharmacy, AAAS, Soc. Health and Human Values, Am. Assn. History Medicine, Am. Soc. Cell Biology, Soc. Neurosci., Am. Fedn. Clin. Research, Conn. Acad. Arts and Scis., Am. Soc. Pharmacology and Exptl. Therapeutics, Hellenic Soc. Cancer Research, Hellenic Soc. Med. Chemistry, Internat. Soc. Immunopharmacology, Am. Soc. Microbiology, Am. Assn. Immunologists, Internat. Soc. History of Medicine, Mass. Med. Soc., N.E. Hellenic Med. Soc. (sec. 1984-85, v.p. 1985-86, 86-87), Hellenic Sci. Assn. Boston (bd. dirs. 1985), Internat. Anatolia Alumni Assn. (sec. 1984-85). Alpha Omega Alpha, Sigma Xi. Research on mechanisms of release of secretory products; hormonal induction of ornithine decarboxylase and membrane functions of polyamines; pathophysiology of mast cells. Home: 14 Parkman St Apt 2 Brookline MA 02146 Office: Tufts U Sch Med Dept Pharmacology 136 Harrison Ave Boston MA 02111

THEOLOGITIS, JOHN MICHAEL, financial consultant; b. Athens, Greece, July 16, 1956; s. Michael John Theologitis and Xanthippe Charilaos Picheon. MSCE, Nat. Tech. U. Athens, 1979; PhD, U. London, 1982. Tech. cons. Polemarcha-Epidaurus, Ltd., Athens, 1982; sci. research assoc. Nat. Tech. U., Athens, 1982-83; asst. mgr. mil. sales Karayannis Cos., Athens, 1984; mgr. fin. sect. Gen. Motors Corp. Hellas, Athens, 1985; pres., chief exec. officer Campus Ltd., Athens, 1985—; adv. to chief exec. officer Interam. Group Cos., Athens, 1986-87; investment mgr. Internat. Investment Cons., Athens, 1987—; sci. cons. European Econ. Community Program, 1982-84. Author: Tourism, Behavioral Modeling, 1984, Transportation Planning, 1985, Planning and Social Trends, 1985. Served with Greek Navy, 1983-84. Mem. UK Instn. Civil Engrs., TRANET, World Future Soc., ASCE, U.S. Transp. Research Bd., Greek Mgmt. Assn., U. London Convocation Assn., Am.-Hellenic C. of C., Tech. Chamber Greece. Greek Orthodox. Club: IAPA. Home and Office: 58 Voukourestiou St, 10673 Athens Greece

THEOPHILUS, GEORGE, banker; b. Choiseul, St. Lucia, June 7, 1936; s. Bernadette Faucher; m. Jeanne Lusca Cox, Mar. 8, 1931; children—Wendy Adele Claire, Lorne Danquah Cox. B.Sc. in Econ., London U. (External), 1963; M.A., Carleton U., 1969. Cons., Orgn. for Cooperation in Overseas Devel., Winnipeg, Man., Can., 1973—; mng. dir., chmn. St. Lucia Devel. Bank, 1981; dir. Nat. Comml. Bank, Castries, St. Lucia, 1981—. Chmn. Library Bd. Nat. Library, Castries, 1984—. Can. Internat. Devel. Agy. Commonwealth scholar, 1967-69. Fellow Internat. Bankers Assn. (hon.).

THEUT, C(LARENCE) PETER, maritime lawyer; b. Center Line, Mich., July 24, 1938; s. Clarence William and Anna Marie (Martens) T.; m. Judith Fern Trombley, Aug. 4, 1962; children: Elizabeth Anne, Kristin Claire, Peter Christopher, Sarah Nicole. BA, U. Mich., 1960, LLB, 1963. Bar: Calif. 1964, Mich. 1964, U.S. Dist. Ct. (no. dist.) Ohio 1968, U.S. Dist. Ct. (ea. dist.) Mich. 1968. Assoc. Overton, Lyman & Prince, Los Angeles, 1963-67; ptnr. Foster, Meadows and Ballard, Detroit, 1968-72; ptnr. Theut & Schellig, Mt. Clemens, Mich., 1972-80; ptnr. Hill, Lewis, Adams, Goodrich & Tait, Mt. Clemens, 1980-88, Butzel, Long, Gust, Klein & Van Zile, Detroit, 1988—; gen. counsel Nat. Marine Bankers Assn., Mich. Marine Dealers Assn. Mem. Calif. State Bar Assn., Mich. State Bar Assn., Macomb County Bar Assn., Maritime Law Assn., Nat. Marine Bankers Assn., Mich. Boating Industry Assn., ABA. Republican. Club: North Star Sail. Lodge: Kiwanis. Home: 38554 Hidden Ln Mount Clemens MI 48043 Office: Butzel Long Gust Klein & Van Zile 1650 1st Nat Bldg Detroit MI 48226

THEVATHASAN, IVOR GUNASEELAM, physician; b. Singapore, Aug. 18, 1940; s. Arthur W.S. and Gnana (Cooke) T.; m. Maureen Lim; 1 child, Alexander Walter. MB, BS, Calcutta U., 1967. Cert. in medicine. Physician Gunam Clinic, Singapore. Chmn., bd. vis. Children's Home, Singapore, 1987; bd. dirs. Singapore YMCA, 1986-89; bd. govs., bd. dirs. Oldham Hall Anglo-Chinese Sch.; mem. Malaysia-Singapore Vintage Car Register. Mem. Singapore Med. Assn., Coll. Gen. Practitioners. Club: Singapore Vintage Car. Lodge: Rotary (v.p., bd. dirs. 1985-86, past pres. Singapore Main club). Office: Gunam Clinic, 16 Cecil St, Singapore 02-02, Singapore

THEVENET, RENE, film expert and cons.; b. Lyons-Oullins, Rhone, France, May 5, 1926; s. Louis-Joannes and Marie (Deporte) T.; student U. Lyon, 1944-45, B.Philosophy, 1944; student law and lit. U. Paris, 1946-48; children: Jean-Louis, Francoise, Marie-Alice, Laurent, Eugenie. Founder, organizer Eaux Vives, Lyons, 1944-45; journalist for Enfin Film, Les Etoiles, L'Ecran Francais, Cinevie, Aux Ecoutes, Cinedigest and pub. relations officer and press officer, 1947-52; gen. sec., prodn. dir., adminstrv. dir. Co. P.A.C., 1950-55; pres. Contact Orgn., 1950-62; pres., mng. dir. Orgn. Cinematographique francaise, 1962-71; pres., mng. dir. Société Anonyme TV Cinema, 1972-75; mng. dir., pub. quar., Film Exchange, 1977-87; legal expert; producer or co-producer numerous films; author: Industrie et Commerce du Film en France, 1979. Decorated Knight of the Legion d'Honneur, Officer de l'Ordre des Arts et Lettres, Officer de l'Ordre du Mérit; dep. mayor Cannes, 1983. Mem. French Producers Motion Picture Assn. (exec. pres.), Ind. Film Producers Internat. Assn. (exec. pres.), Internat. Found. for Film and Audiovisual Communication (exec. pres.). Club: Rotary. Club de Cannes. Home and Office: 50 Ave Marceau, Paris 8 France also: Villa Dormus Solis, 1 bis Ave Roi Albert, 06400 Cannes France

THEVENON, DOMINIQUE, maxillo facial surgeon; b. Bourg-la-Reine, France, June 7, 1947; d. Felix and Claudine (Cotte) T.; children: Jean-Luc, Marie Odile. BS, Lyceum, France, 1965; MD, FAculty Medicine, Clermont, France, 1974. Resident Hosp. of Le Puy, France, 1972-74, Hosp. of Clermont Ferrand, France, 1975-79; clin. chief surgeon Faculty of Medicine, Clermont Ferrand, 1979-81; asst. Hosp. of Clermont Ferrand, 1979-81; surgeon Clin. Bon Secours, Le Puy, 1983—; practice medicine specializing in maxillo-facial surgery Le Puy, 1983—. Contbr. articles to profl. jours. Mem. French Soc. Stomatology and Maxillo-Facial Surgery, Coll. of Stomatologist Drs. and Maxillo-Facial Surgeons of France. Office: 37 Bis Place Du Breuil, 43000 Le Puy France

THIAGARAJAN, KUMARASWAMI, professional association administrator; b. Madras, India, Jan. 30, 1950; parents: Kumaraswami Thiruvannamalai and Kanthimathi (Kumaraswami) Munuswami; m. Vaidehi Thiagarajan, Apr. 12, 1984; 1 child, T.V. Susmita. BSc, Voorhees Coll.; DLitt, World U., 1983; PhD, Harmony Coll. Applied Sci., 1984; D Humanities (hon.), Collegium Sancti Spiritus, 1984; D Laws, Bodkin Bible Inst., 1984. Exec. sec. United Writers' Assn., Madras, 1975—; dep. gov. Am. Biog. Inst., N.C., 1988; dep. dir.-gen. Internat. Biog. Ctr., Cambridge, Eng., 1988. Author: Gandhiji's Teachings, 1978. Recipient Presdl. award Govt. of India, New Delhi, 1969, NIF Internat. awards NIF Weekly, New Delhi, 1975-80, Naraindoss Meml. award Current Events, India. Fellow Brit. Inst. Mgmt., World Lit. Council, Internat. Soc. Naturopathy, Am. Biog. Inst., United Writers Assn. India. Home and Office: United Writers Assn, 8 Warren Rd RR Flat 17-E, Mylapore, Madras 600 004, India

THIANDOUM, HYACINTHE CARDINAL, archbishop of Dakar; b. Poponguine, Senegal, Feb. 2, 1921; s. François Fari and Anne Ndiémé (Sene) T.; student Sem. Dakar, 1936-49; B.A. in Dogmatics and Social Scis., U. Propaganda, Gregorian U., Rome, 1955. Ordained priest Roman Catholic Ch., 1949; parish vicar, dir. works, Dakar, 1955-60; curate-dean cathedral, gen. vicar Dakar, 1960-62; archbishop of Dakar, 1962—; elevated to Sacred Coll. Cardinals, 1976; mem. Congregation of the Doctrine of the Faith, Rome, 5 yrs.; pres.-del. Synod of Bishops, 1977; pres. Conf. Bishops of Senegal and Mauritania, Symposium of Bishops Conf. Africa and Madagascar; mem. permanent com. Conf. Francophone West African Bishops; mem. Bishops Commn. Mass Media, Papal Commn. Social Communications Media, Congregation Religious and Secular Insts.; mem. council Gen. Secretariat of Roman Synod Bishops. Decorated grand cross Nat. Order Lion, 1976; comdr. Ordre National Français de la Légion d'Honneur, 1980; hon. chaplain Monastic Grand Cross Sovereign Order Malta, 1972. Office: de l'Archevêché, BP 1908, Dakar Senegal *

THIBAUT, MONIQUE, mycologist, allergologist, research director; b. Nogent, Seine, France; d. Raymond Thibaut and Marie Madeleine Labriet. MD, U. Paris, 1963, diploma in Biology, 1972, PhD, Faculty of Sci., 1970. Research asst. Nat. Ctr. for Sci. Research, Paris, 1963-67, research dep., 1967-77, master of research, 1977-84, dir. research, 1984—; vis. prof. Federal U., Rio de Janeiro, 1972; head med. mycology research sect. U. Paris VI, 1970—; cons. U. Pierre and Marie Curie, Paris, 1975—. Author: Mycotic Allergy Diseases, 1963 (recipient prize 1963); co-author monographs: Clinical Medical Mycology, 1975, Allergy, 1986; contbr. articles to sci. and med. jours. Recipient Silver medal Faculty of Medicine, U. Paris, 1964, Catherine Hadot prize Nat. Acad. Medicine, Paris, 1966, Laveran prize Sci. Acad., Paris, 1973. Mem. French Soc. Allergology and Clin. Immunology (Dexo prize 1965), French Soc. Parasitology, French Soc. Med. Mycology, Am. Soc. Microbiology, Mycol. Soc. Am. Office: Nat Ctr Sci Research, Parasitology Lab, 15 rue de l'Ecole de Medicine, 75006 Paris France

THIÉBAUD, JEAN-MARIE, physician; b. Pontarlier, France, Nov. 21, 1944; s. Marie-Louise T.; m. Geneviève Guilloz, July 11, 1969; children: Jean-Noel, Francois-Xavier, Josserand. MD with very high honors, Besançon (France) U., 1974, DEUG of Laws, 1980. Author: Histoire de L'eglise de Chaux Les Chatillon, 1979, Officiers Seigneuriaux et Anciennes Familles de Franche Comté, 1981-84, Petit Dictionnaire des Termes du Blason, 1982, Répertoire Héraldique de Franche=Comté, 1987, Le Château de Joux, 1987. Dep. mayor of Pontarlier, France, 1983—; pres. Joux Castle, France, 1983; nat. dep. Chambres des Professions Libérales, 1987. Recipient medal French Red Cross, 1981. Mem. Assn. des Professions de Sante de Pontarlier (pres. 1982), Chambre des Professions Libérales du Doubs (v.p.

1985—), Acad. de Besançon et de Franche-Comté, Bur. Nat. des Chambres des Professions Libérales, Union Syndicale des Médecins du Doubs (v.p. 1982), Conseil Francais D'Héraldique (pres. 1984—). Home and Office: 30 rue de la République, 25300 Pontarlier France

THIEBAUTH, BRUCE EDWARD, advertising executive; b. Bronxville, N.Y., Oct. 30, 1947; s. Bruce and Margaret Evelyn (Wiederhold) T.; m. Sherry Ann Proplesch, Aug. 31, 1968; 1 child, Bruce Revere. Student, Colby Coll., Waterville, Maine, 1965-66, Pace Coll., 1971; BA in Bus. Adminstrn. and Sociology magna cum laude, Bellevue Coll., 1972. Mgr. credit Gen. Electric Credit Corp., Croton Falls, N.Y., 1971; mgr. ops. Bridal Publs., Inc., Omaha, 1972-73; regional mgr. Bridal Fair, Inc., Omaha, 1973-74, sales mgr., 1974-76, chmn. bd., pres., 1976—; bd. dirs. Multi-Media Group, Inc., Fair Communications, Inc. Pub., bd. dirs. Bridal Fair mag. Served with USAF, 1966-70, Vietnam. Recipient Nat. Def. Service medal, Somers (N.Y.) League Citizenship and Pub. Service award, 1965. Mem. Nat. Small Bus. Assn., Nat. Assn. Broadcasters, Airline Passengers Assn., Bellevue Coll. Alumni Assn. Republican. Congregationalist. Office: 9315 Binney St Omaha NE 68134

THIELER, PETER, mathematics educator; b. Koenigsberg, East Prussia, Federal Republic of Germany, Aug. 22, 1943; arrived in Federal Republic of Germany, 1958; s. Erich Ernst and Ella Else (Wasgindt) T.; m. Johanna Gertrud Mevissen, Feb. 12, 1972; children: Robin Anselm, Anita Monika. Diploma in Math., U. Bonn, Federal Republic of Germany, 1971, PhD, 1974. With inst. for applied math. U. Bonn, 1971-75, akademischer rat, 1975-77; prof. math. Fachhochschule Darmstadt, Federal Republic of Germany, 1978-86; prof. Fachhochschule Flensburg, Federal Republic of Germany, 1987—; acting dir. Inst. Applied Math., Flensburg, 1987—. Served to lt. German Army, 1964-66. Recipient Scheffler Price award Scheffler-Bund, Solingen, Federal Republic of Germany, 1964. Mem. Deutsche Mathematiker Vereinigung, Gesellschaft für Angew. Math. und Mechanik, Soc. Mathématique Française, Soc. Indsl. and Applied Math., Am. Math. Soc. Home: Norderfelder Strasse 6, 2395 HUSBY, near Flensburg Federal Republic of Germany Office: Fachhochschule Flensburg, Kanzleistrasse 91-93, D-2390, Flensburg Federal Republic of Germany

THIERRY, FOUQUET-KISSEL, opera adminstrator; b. Paris, May 3, 1951; s. Jean and Eliane (Poussin) F. Student Lycee Louis-Le-Grand, Paris, 1966-71, Ecole Polytechnique, 1971-74. Adjoint de direction Opera de Paris, 1974-77, adminstr. du ballet, Paris, 1977-80, 83-85, charge de mission, 1980-83, dir. opera comique, 1988-87; dir. programs Paris Opera, 1987—; cons. Region Provence/Cote & Azur, Marseille, 1983-84; cons. Opera Bastille, 1983-85. Served with French Navy, 1973-74. Roman Catholic. Home: 62 Rue Taitbout, 75009 Paris France Office: Opera de Paris, 8 rue Scribe, 75009 Paris France

THIES, AUSTIN COLE, retired utility company executive; b. Charlotte, N.C., July 18, 1921; s. Oscar Julius and Blanche (Austin) T.; m. Marilyn Joy Walker, June 26, 1945; children: Austin Cole, Robert Melvin, Marilyn Leone. BS in Mech. Engring, Ga. Inst. Tech., 1943. With Duke Power Co., Charlotte, 1946—; mgr. steam prodn. Duke Power Co., 1963-65, asst. v.p., 1965-67, v.p. prodn. and operation, 1967-71, sr. v.p., 1971-82, exec. v.p., 1982-86, also dir.; past chmn. prodn. com., engring. and operating div. Southeastern Electric Exchange; chmn. tech. advisory com. Carolinas Va. Nuclear Power Assos.; chmn. N.C. Air Control Advisory Council. Mem. nat. adv. bd. Ga. Inst. Tech.; pres. Arts and Scis. Council; chmn. bd. dirs. Mercy Hosp.; trustee Alexander Childrens Center; bd. visitors Boy's Town.; 1st v.p. Sci. Museums of Charlotte; bd. dirs. Sci. Mus. Served with USNR, 1943-46. Decorated Purple Heart. Mem. Edison Electric Inst. (past chmn. engring. and operating div. exec. com.), IEEE, Charlotte C. of C., ASME (past chmn. Piedmont Carolina sect.), Am. Nuclear Soc., Air Pollution Control Assn., N.C. Soc. Engrs. (past pres., Engr. of Yr. 1985), Charlotte Engrs. Club (Disting. Service award 1984), Nat. Rifle Assn. (life), Kappa Sigma. Presbyterian (elder). Clubs: Rotary (past pres., dir. N. Charlotte), Cowans Ford Country (bd. dirs.), Quail Hollow Country (bd. dirs.), Charlotte City (bd. dirs.), Charlotte Ga. Inst. Tech. (past pres.), Charlotte Rifle and Pistol (past pres.). Home: 2429 Red Fox Trail Charlotte NC 28211 Office: 422 S Church St Charlotte NC 28242

THIGPEN, JAMES TATE, physician, oncology educator; b. Columbia, Miss., June 6, 1944; m. Louisa Berdie Kessler, June 14, 1969; children—Monroe Tate, James Howard, Samuel Calvin, Richard Allen, David Albert. B.S., U. Miss., 1964, M.D., 1969. Intern Strong Meml. Hosp., U. Rochester, N.Y., 1969-70; resident U. Miss. Sch. Medicine, 1970-71, fellow div. hematology/oncology dept. medicine, 1971-73, prof., dir. div. med. oncology dept. internal medicine, 1973—, also asst. prof. ob-gyn.; nat. med. del. from Miss. to Am. Cancer Soc., 1983-85, mem. nat. pub. issues com., 1983-85. Nat. bd. govs. ARC, 1981—. Fellow ACP; mem. AMA, Miss. Med. Assn., Central Med. Soc., Jackson Acad. Medicine, Miss. Acad. Scis., S.W. Oncology Group, Gynecologic Oncology Group, Am. Fedn. Clin. Research, Am. Assn. Cancer Edn., Am. Soc. Clin. Oncology, Am. Assn. Cancer Research, Am. Soc. Hematology, Soc. Gynecologic Oncologists, Am. Radium Soc. Baptist (deacon 1978—, Sunday sch. tchr. 1979-85). Club: Optimist (OI v.p. 1983-84). Home: 1135 Briarwood Dr Jackson MS 39211 Office: 2500 N State St Jackson MS 39216

THIJSSEN, JOHAN MARIA, biophysics researcher; b. Waalwijk, The Netherlands, May 12, 1939; s. Johan A. and Helena (Van Beijnen) T.; m. Louise M.C. Maas, Aug. 1, 1963; children: Norbert, Wouter, Maarten. MEngring. Sci., Tech. U., Delft, Netherlands, 1964; PhD, Cath. U., Nijmegen, Netherlands, 1969. Cert. med./clin. physicist. Jr. scientist dept. med. physics U. Nijmegen, 1963-64, sr. scientist Inst. Opthalmology, 1964-68, head biophysics lab., 1968—; cons. St. Radboud Hosp., Nijmegen, 1970—, Oldelft Inc., Delft, 1982—; project leader European Communities Concerted Action Program on Ultrasonic Tissue Characterization, Brussels and Nijmegen, 1982—; chmn. Nat. Com. on Safety Med. Ultrasound, 1983-86, Nat. Com. on Med. Tech. Assessment, 1987—; chmn. working party on med. imaging Nat. Sci. Found., 1985—. Editor: ultrasonic Tissue Characterization, 7 vols., 1980-87; chief editor: News in Physiol. Sci., 1988—; mem. editorial bd. Ultrasonic Imaging, 1986; contbr. over 100 articles on psychophysics, electrophysiology of visual system, echography and ultrasonic tissue characterization to sci. jours. Served to lt. 1st class Dutch Service Corps, 1959-61. Research grantee Nat. Sci. Found., 1970, 76, Health Orgn. TNO, 1975, 78, tech. Sci. Found., 1982, 85, 87, 88, Nat. Cancer Found., 1982, 85. Mem. Internat. Soc. for Ultrasound in Ophthalmology (sec. 1983—), European and World Fedns. for Ultrasound in Medicine (nat. del. 1979—), Internat. Orgn. for Med. Physics (nat. del. 1982—), Netherlands Soc. for Ultrasound in Medicine and Biology (past pres. 1978-83). Mem. Christian Dem. Party. Office: Catholic Univ, PO Box 9101, 6500 HB Nijmegen The Netherlands

THILLMANN, JOHN HORST, government official, urban planner; b. Amberg, Germany, July 15, 1946; came to U.S., 1952; s. Otto and Tina (Dietmyer) T.; m. Judy Ann Skurski, Jan. 25, 1969; 1 dau., Christiana. AB in Geography, U. Miami, 1969; MA in Bus. Mgmt., Central Mich. U., 1979; M in Urban Adminstrn. in Urban and Environ. Affairs, Va. Poly. Inst. and State U., 1978. City planner City of Rochester (N.Y.), 1970-72; assoc./sr. planner County of Fairfax (Va.), 1972-74, chief environ. planning, 1975-79; program/policy analyst Office of Policy Planning Evaluation, U.S. and EPA, Washington, 1979-82, chief program planning, 1983-85, dir. Washington ops. Office of Air and Radiation, 1985—; lectr. No. Va. Community Coll., Manassas, 1977, George Mason U., Fairfax, Va., 1979-80. Chmn. Fairfax County Environ. Quality Council, 1979-82; mem. Centreville dist. Fairfax County Planning Commn., 1982—; mem. Fairfax County Erosion Sediment Control Bd., 1982-84; mem. Fairfax County Goals for the Yr. 2000 Commn. N.Y. State Regents scholar, 1965; recipient spl. achievement award EPA, 1980, 84, silver medal, 1983, Bronze medal, 1985, 88. Mem. Am. Planning Assn., Gamma Theta Upsilon.

THINLEY, JIGMI YOSER, diplomat; b. Bumthang, Byakar, Bhutan, Sept. 9, 1995; s. Dorji Dasho and Karma (Lhatshor) T.; m. Rinsey Dem, Sept. 19, 1978; children: Leksang Pem Dechhey, Pem Sedo, Palden Tobgye. MPA, Pa. State U., 1975; grad. in Manpower Planning and Mgmt., Manchester (Eng.) U., 1982. Adminstrv. officer Ministry of Home Affairs, Thimphu, Bhutan, 1974-76; acting dir. Dept. Manpower, Thimphu, 1976-77, officer of spl. duty, 1977-79, dep. sec., 1979-82; sec. Royal Civil Service Commn., Thimphu, 1982-85; dir. Dept. Edn., Thimphu, 1985-87; permanent rep. Bhutan Mission to UN, N.Y.C., 1987—; mem. Nat. Edn. Policy, Thimpu, 1976-87; mem. bd. mgrs. Penden Cement Authority, Thimphu, Dungsem Cement Authority, Thimphu. Mem. Nat. Lang. Devel. Com., Bhutan, 1979—, Bd. Mgmt. Bhutan Particle Bd., Thimphu; chmn. Nat. Transport Service, Thimphu. Named Dasho by His Majesty the King of Bhutan. Mem. Internat. Assn. Permanent Reps. to UN, Nat. Soc. Wildlife. Address: Bhutan Mission to UN Two UN Plaza 27th Floor New York NY 10017

THIRANI, SUSHIL KUMAR, corporate executive; b. Calcutta, India, Oct. 20, 1930; s. Shri Krishnalal and Savitri Devi (Birla) T.; m. Sushila Rathi, Feb. 1950; children: Shashi, Suhasini, Anand. Chmn., mng. dir. Kores Ltd., Bombay, 1966—; bd. dirs. Kores Services Ltd., Kores Statinery and Equipment Ltd., Hong Kong, Koron Bus. Systems Ltd., Deeko India Ltd., Shashi Fin. Ltd., Futura Packaging Ltd., India, Pefco Industries Ltd. Mem. United Services. Hindu. Clubs: Bombay Presidency Golf, Bombay Gymkhana Ltd. Home: Westfield Estate B, Desai Rd, Bombay 40026, India Office: Kores Ltd, Off Dr E Moses Rd, Worli, Bombay 400018, India

THIRY, PAUL, architect; b. Nome, Alaska, Sept. 11, 1904; s. Hippolyte A. and Louise Marie (Schwaebele) T.; m. Mary Thomas, Oct. 26, 1940; children—Paul Albert, Pierre. Diploma, Ecole des Beaux Arts, Fontainebleau, France, 1927; A.B., U. Wash., 1928; D.F.A. (hon.), St. Martins Coll., 1970; D.Arts (hon.), Lewis & Clark Coll., 1979. Pvt. practice architecture 1929—; mem. Thiry & Shay, 1935-39; co-architect war work U.S. Navy Advance Base Depot, Tacoma, Fed. Pub. Housing Adminstrn. projects; community centers and appurtenances Port Orchard, Wash., 1940-44; practice in Salt Lake City, Alaska, Seattle, 1945—; pres. Thiry Architects, Inc., 1971—; architect in residence Am. Acad. in Rome, 1969. Author: (with Richard Bennett and Henry Kamphoefner) Churches and Temples, 1953, (with Mary Thiry) Eskimo Artifacts Designed for Use, 1978; Contbr. articles to profl. jours.; Projects exhibited and illustrated in books and periodicals.; Prin. works include Am. Embassy residence, Santiago, Chile (awarded Diploma Clegio de Arquitectos de Chile 1965); comprehensive plan Seattle Center (awarded A.I.A. citation for excellence in community architecture 1966); Seattle Coliseum (A.I.S.I. awards for design and engring. 1965), (A.I.S.C. award of excellence 1965), Washington State Library (AIA-ALA award 1964), U.S. 4th Inf. (Ivy) Div. Monument, Utah Beach, France, 1969 (hon. citizen Sainte Marie du Mont), Am. Battle Monuments Commn. Meml., Utah Beach, 1984; cons.: comprehensive plan Libby Dam-Lake Koocanusa Project, Mont.; cons. Chief Joseph Dam Powerhouse, Wash.; architect for Visitors Center (C.E. distinguished design award 1970, Chief of Engrs. cert. of appreciation 1974); cons.: New Melones Dam/Reservoir Project, Calif., 1972, Reregulating dam and powerhouse, Libby, Mont., 1977—; others.; works include coll. bldgs., chs., museums, and, govt. projects; also designer fabrics; carpets, furniture. Commnr. City of Seattle Planning Commn., 1952-61, chmn., 1953-54; rep. on exec. bd. Puget Sound Regional Planning Council, 1954-57; chmn. Central Bus. Dist. Study, 1957-60; mem. exec. com. Wash. State Hosp. Adv. Council, 1953-57; architect in charge Century 21 Expn., Seattle, 1957-62; mem. Dept. Interior Historic Am. Bldg. Survey Bd., 1956-61, vice chmn., 1958-61; mem. Joint Com. Nat. Capital, 1961, exec. bd., 1962-72; mem. President's Council Redevel. Pennsylvania Av., Washington, 1962-65; cons. FHA, 1963-67; cons. architect Nat. Capitol, 1964—; mem. Nat. Capital Planning Commn., 1963-75, vice chmn., 1972-75; mem. arts and archtl. com. J. F. Kennedy Meml. Library, 1964; mem. Postmaster Gen.'s Council Research and Engring., 1968-70; mem. Peace Corps Adv. Council, 1982-84. Decorated officier d'Academie with palms France; recipient Paul Bunyan award Seattle C. of C., 1949, Outstanding Architect-Engr. award Am. Mil. Engrs., 1977; named Distinguished Citizen in the Arts Seattle, 1962, Constrn. Man of Year, 1963; Academician N.A.D.; named to Coll. of Architecture Hall of Honor U. Wash., 1987. Fellow A.I.A. (pres. Wash. chpt. 1951-53, preservation officer 1952-62, chancellor coll. fellows 1962-64, chmn. com. nat. capital 1960-64, chmn. com. hon. fellowships 1962-64, Seattle chpt. medal 1984); mem. Nat. Sculpture Soc. (hon., Herbert Adams Meml. medal 1974, Henry Hering medal 1976), Am. Inst. Planners (exec. bd. Pacific N.W. chpt. 1949-52, hon. life), Am. Planning Assn. (hon. life, N.W. chpt. citation 1983), Soc. Archtl. Historians (life mem., dir. 1967-70), Nat. Trust Historic Preservation, Am. Inst. Interior Designers (hon.), Liturgical Conf. (life), Seattle Art Mus. (life), Seattle Hist. Soc. (hon. life), Oreg. Cavemen (hon.), Delta Upsilon, Tau Sigma Delta, Scarab (hon.). Clubs: Cosmos (Washington); Century (N.Y.C.); Architectural League N.Y. Home: 1017 E Blaine St Seattle WA 98102 Office: 800 Columbia St Seattle WA 98104

THISTLEWOOD, DAVID JOHN, art historian, design educator; b. Leeds, Eng., June 28, 1944; s. Harold and Ada (Grant) T.; m. Roslyn Mary Greene, July 27, 1968; children: Lucinda, Roslyn, Jevon. NDD, Leeds Coll. Art, 1964; MS, U. Newcastle, Eng., 1974; PhD, U. Liverpool, Eng., 1978. Lectr. design Leeds Poly., 1966-74; lectr., coordinating master design Sch. Architecture U. Liverpool, 1974—. Author: A Continuing Process, 1981, Herbert Read: Formlessness and Form, 1984; editor Jour. Art and Design Edn., 1986—. Trustee Nat. Art Edn. Archive, 1985—. Fellow Royal Soc. Arts; mem. Nat. Soc. for Edn. in Art and Design, Assn. Art Historians, Brit. Soc. Aesthetics. Office: U Liverpool, PO Box 147, Liverpool L69 3BX, England

THIVEGANON, VIMOL, finance company executive; b. Bangkok, June 1, 1948. Diploma in acctg., Bangkok Inst. Accts., 1965; cert. in bookkeeping, Faculty Secs., Guildford, Eng.; cert. in gen. edn., Panaphan Coll., Bangkok, 1963; cert. in English lang., U.S. Def. Lang. Inst., 1972; cert. in exec. skills, Alexander Hamilton Inst., 1980. Mem. staff Post Office U.S. Army, Korat Air Base, Thailand, 1966; asst. Civilian Personnel Office, Korat Air Base, 1966-67; acct. Fiscal Control Office, Korat Air Base, 1967-74; mgr. snack bar Ramasun Station USO, Udonthani, Thailand, 1974-75; mgr. internal auditing Chiangmai (Thailand) Trust Co. Ltd., 1976-85, mng. dir., 1986—. Home: 111/11 Faham Rd, Muang Chiengmai 50000, Thailand Office: Chiengmai Trust Co Ltd, 60-62 Chareonmuang Rd, Muang 50000, Thailand

THOANG, HO SI, chemistry researcher; b. Dongha, Quangtri, Vietnam, Apr. 10, 1938; parents Ho Cong On and Ngo Thi Khec; m. Tran Cam Nhung, Feb. 1, 1968; children: Ho Cam Hoai, Ho Hieu Giang. Degree in (chemistry), Hanoi U., Vietnam, 1959, Moscow State U., 1962; PhD, Moscow State U., 1967, DSc, 1974. Asst. Chemistry Dept. Hanoi U., Vietnam, 1962-64; research assoc. Chemistry Dept. Moscow State U., 1968-74; chief Lab. Catalysis, Ho Chi Minh City, Vietnam, 1975—; v.p. Vietnam Nat. Sci. Ctr., 1977—; dir. Inst. Chemistry VN NSC, Ho Chi Minh City, 1978—; pres. Ho Chi Minh City VN NSC, 1982—. Author: Activity and Physico-Chemical Properties of High Silica Zeolites, 1976,; contbr. articles to profl. jours.; editor: Jour. Chemistry, 1978—. Communist. Home: 140c Nam ky khoi nghia str, Ho Chi Minh City Quan I Vietnam Office: Inst Chemistry, 1 Mac Dinh Chi str, Ho Chi Minh City Quan I Vietnam

THOCAVEN, PIERRE JEAN, physician, psycho-sex therapist; b. La Chapelle-Auzac, France, Aug. 5, 1941; s. Jean-Gilbert and Irene (Tujague) T.; m. Danielle Boucher, Aug. 3, 1963; children: Catherine, Gilles. MD, U. Bordeaux, France, 1970; student, Bordeaux II U., 1986—, Juge Wise Ct., 1987—. Resident Mutualist Clinic, Pessac, France, 1974; resident physician Ruffec, France, 1969-70; resident surgeon functions for army Hosp. Robert Pique, Boreaux, 1968-69; cons. family planning 1973, AFNOR expert (in connection with ISO) for contraceptive products, 1975; gen. practice medicine Le Bouscat, France. Mcpl. councillor City of Le Bouscat, 1977-82, City of Bordeaux, France, 1987. Roman Catholic. Office: 49 rue Theophile Gautier, 33110 Le Bouscat France

THOM, CLARK WILSON, accountant; b. Glasgow, Scotland, May 22, 1937; emigrated to Swaziland, 1976; s. James and Annie Henderson (Murray) T.; m. Elizabeth Joan Gray Ferguson, Feb. 26, 1966; children—Anna Margaret Cochrane, Nina Mackenzie Clark. Ed. Jordan Hill Coll. Sch. Chartered acct., Scotland. Orgn. and methods officer Rhodesia and Nyasaland Tobacco Co., Harare, Zimbabwe, 1962-65; group acct., sec. CFC Furniture Co. Ltd., Lagos, Nigeria, 1966; fin. dir. BAT Zambia Ltd., Lusaka, 1968-71, Central Cigarette Mfg. Ltd., Lusaka, 1971-76; fin. controller Econ. Devel. for Equatorial and So. Africa, Mbabane, Swaziland, 1976-81; resident ptnr. firm Fisher, Hoffman, Stride, Spicer & Oppenheim, Mbabane, 1981—; dir. Nat. Indsl. Devel. Corp. Swaziland, 1984-85, Small Enterprise Devel. Co. Ltd., Mbabane, 1984-86. Chmn. bd. dirs. occupational bd. govs. Internat. Sch. Lusaka, 1973-76, chmn. 1976; bd. govs. Waterford Kamhlaba United World Coll., Mbabane, 1983—; chmn. bd. govs. Occupational Health Services Ltd., Manzini, Swaziland, 1984—. Mem. Inst. Chartered Accts. Scotland, Inst. Chartered Accts. South Africa, Swaziland Inst. Accts. (founder, tax coordinator 1985—, chmn. council 1986-87), Royal Commonwealth Soc. London. Presbyterian. Club: Mbabane Sports. Lodge: Rotary. Home: 6 North St, Mbabane Swaziland Office: Fisher Hoffman Stride & Co, PO Box 1478, Mbabane Swaziland

THOM, RONALD JAMES, architect; b. Penticton, B.C., Can., May 15, 1923. Educated Vancouver Sch. Art; LL.D. (hon.) Trent U., 1971; D.Eng. (hon.) Nova Scotia Tech. Coll., 1973. Began career as concert pianist; taught Vancouver Sch. Art and U. B.C. Sch. Architecture; ptnr. Thompson, Berwick, Pratt, Vancouver, B.C., 1958; prin. R.J. Thom Architects, Toronto, 1963—; lectr. numerous Can. univs. Contbr. articles to arts jours. Fellow Royal Archtl. Inst. Can.; mem. Royal Can. Acad. Arts, Ont. Assn. Architects, Archtl. Inst. B.C. Home: 95 Meadowcliffe Dr, Scarborough, ON Canada *

THOMA, ELMAR HERBERT, mathematician; b. Baden-Baden, Fed. Republic Germany, Sept. 10, 1926; s. Hubert Ambros and Friederike K. (Meyer) T.; m. Helga Christine Hagemann; children: Markus, Sebastian. PhD, U. Erlangen, Fed. Republic Germany, 1952. Asst. U. Munich, 1954-57, reader, 1957-59; vis. prof. U. Wash., Seattle, 1959-61; assoc. prof. U. Heidelberg, Fed. Republic Germany, 1961-64; full prof. U. Münster, Fed. Republic Germany, 1964-70, Tech. U. München, 1970—; dean Faculty Math. and Nat. Sci., U. Münster, 1968-69; dean Gen. Faculty of Nat. Scis., Tech. U. München, 1973-75. Co-editor Math. Annalen, 1974—. Mem. Deutsche Math. Vereinigung, Am. Math. Soc. Home: Lustheimstrasse 2, D-8000 Munich 60 Bavaria Federal Republic of Germany Office: Tech U Munchen, Math Inst, Arcisstrasse 21, D-8000 Munchen 2 Federal Republic of Germany

THOMA, KURT MICHAEL, designer, builder, photographer; b. Boston, Aug. 9, 1946; s. Kurt Richard and Janet (Holdsworth) T.; divorced; children by previous marriage—Heather Anne, Heidi. Student U. N.H., 1968. Clk., supr., asst. div. EDP coordinator, EDP coordinator, mut. funds div. 1st Nat. Bank Boston, 1968-69; v.p. cen. N.H. bldg. corp. Barry Dashner, Inc., 1969-72; field rep. Acorn Structures, Inc., 1972-75; v.p., treas. Design Structures Group, Inc., 1975-76; pres. Witthom Assocs., Inc., 1976-79; v.p. Confetti, Inc., 1978—; pres., treas., propr. Dessin Batir, Inc., Newport, R.I., 1979—. Served with U.S. Army N.G., 1966-72. Mem. Internat. and Am. Solar Energy Socs., Internat. Platform Assn. Republican. Christian Scientist. Avocations: writing, star class sailing, tennis, skiing, furniture design. Office: Dessin Batir Inc 12 Clarke St Newport RI 02840

THOMAN, MARK EDWARD, physician; b. Chgo., Feb. 15, 1936; s. John Charles and Tasula Mark (Petrakis) T.; A.A., Graceland Coll., 1956; B.A., U. Mo., 1958, M.D., 1962; m. Theresa Thompson, 1984; children—Marlisa Rae, Susan Kay, Edward Kim, Nancy Lynn, Janet Lea, David Mark. Intern, U. Mo. at Columbia, 1962-63; resident in pediatrics Blank Meml. Children's Hosp., Des Moines, 1963-65, chief resident, 1964-65, lt. comdr. USPHS, Washington, 1965-66, comdr. USNR, 1988—, cons. in toxicology, 1966-67; chief dept. pediatrics Shiprock (N.Mex.) Navajo Indian Hosp., dir. N.D. Poison Info. Center, also practice medicine, specializing in pediatrics Quain & Ramstad Clinic, Bismarck, N.D., 1967-69; dir. Iowa Poison Info. Center, Des Moines, 1969—; pvt. practice pediatrics, Des Moines, 1969—; sr. aviation med. examiner, accident investigator FAA, 1976—; faculty Iowa State U., U. Iowa, U. Osteo. Sci. and Health; dir. Cystic Fibrosis Clinic, 1973-82; dir. Mid-Iowa Drug Abuse Program, 1972-76; mem. med. adv. bd. La Leche Leauge Internat., 1965—; pres. Medic-Air Ltd., 1976—. Bd. dirs. Polk County Pub. Health Nurses Assn., 1969-77, Des Moines Speech and Hearing Center, 1974-79. Served with USMCR, 1954-58. Recipient N.D. Gov.'s award of merit, 1969; Cystic Fibrosis Research Found. award, 1975, Am. Psychiat. Assn. Thesis award, Diplomate Am. Bd. Pediatrics, Am. Bd. Med. Toxicology (examiner). 1962. Mem. AMA (del. 1970—), Polk County Med. Soc., Iowa State Med. Assn., Aerospace Med. Assn., Civil Aviation Med. Assn., Am. Public Health Assn., 1986—, Soc. Adolescent Medicine, Inst. Clin. Toxicology, Internat. Soc. Pediatrics, Am. Acad. Pediatrics, Cystic Fibrosis Club, Am. Acad. Clin. Toxicology (trustee 1969—, pres. 1982-84), Am. Assn. Poison Control Centers, Nat. Rifle Assn. (life), U.S. Naval Inst. Republican. Mem. Reorganized Latter-Day Saints Ch. Clubs: Flying Physicians, Aircraft Owners and Pilots Assn., Nat. Pilots Assn. (Safe Pilot award), Hyperion Field and Country. Editor-in-chief AACTION. Home: 6896 NW Trailridge Dr Johnston IA 50131 Office: 1426 Woodland Ave Des Moines IA 50309

THOMAS, ALAN, candy company executive; b. Evansburg, Pa., Jan. 1, 1923; s. William Roberts and Letta (Garrett) T.; student Rutgers U., 1941-42, 46-47; B.S., Pa. State U., 1949; M.S., U. Minn., 1950, Ph.D., 1954; m. Marguerite Atria, July 1, 1972; children—Garrett Lee, Michael Alan, Randall Stephen, Brett Eliot. Instr., Temple U., Phila., 1950-51, U. Minn., St. Paul, 1951-54; research asst. Bowman Dairy Co., Chgo., 1954-56; research project mgr. M&M Candies div. Mars, Inc., Hackettstown, N.J., 1956-60, product devel. mgr., 1961-64, chocolate research dir. 1964; v.p. research and devel. Mars Candies, Chgo., 1964-67; v.p. research and devel. M&M/Mars Div., Hackettstown, 1967-77, v.p. sci. affairs, 1977-78; gen. mgr. Ethel M, Las Vegas, 1978-83, cons., 1985; sr. cons. Knechtel Research Scis., Inc., Skokie, Ill., 1984; v.p. tech. Ferrara Pan Candy Co., Forest Park, Ill., 1986—. Chmn. industry council of industry liaison panel Food and Nutrition Bd., Nat. Acad. Scis./NRC, 1972-73; adv. U.S. del. Codex Alimentarius Com. on Cocoa and Chocolate Products, 1967-78. Served to 1st lt. inf. AUS, 1942-46. Recipient research award Nat. Confectioners Assn. U.S., 1971. Mem. AAAS, Grocery Mfrs. Am. (chmn. tech. com. 1975-76), Chocolate Mfrs. Assn. (chmn. FDA liaison com. 1975-77), Inst. Food Technologists, Am. Assn. Candy Technologists, Gamma Sigma Delta, Phi Kappa Phi. Home: 1625 Westwood Dr Las Vegas NV 89102 Office: Ferrara Pan Candy Co 7301 W Harrison St Forest Park IL 60130

THOMAS, CHARLES BENEDICT, mathematics educator; b. Maidstone, Kent, Eng., Aug. 17, 1938; s. Charles and Harriet Elizabeth (Watkinson) T.; m. Maria Jolanta Schmeidel, Sept. 17, 1966; children: C. Constantine, Gregory, Hanna. BA, Cambridge (Eng.) U., 1961, PhD, 1967. Research assoc. Cornell U., Ithaca, N.Y., 1965-67; lectr. U. Hull, Eng., 1967-69, Univ. Coll., London, 1969-79; univ. lectr., fellow Robinson Coll. Cambridge U., 1979—; vis. prof. Swiss Fed. Inst. Tech., Zürich, Switzerland, 1980—. Author: Elliptic Structures on 3-Manifolds, 1986, Characteristic Classes, 1987; contbr. articles to profl. jours. Served with RAF, 1956-58. Mem. London Math. Soc. (editor 1976-79), Am. Math. Soc., Max Planck Inst. for Math. (vis. 1980, 86, 88). Roman Catholic. Office: Dept Pure Math and Math Stats, 16 Mill Ln, Cambridge CB2 15B, England

THOMAS, CHARLES CARROLL, investment management executive; b. N.Y.C., Feb. 15, 1930; s. Charles Carroll and Miriam (Smith) T.; grad. Deerfield Acad., 1947; B.A., Yale U., 1951; m. Carolyn Rose Hirchert, June 16, 1951; children—Charles Carroll, Anne Hatheway, Megan Lloyd. Div. retail programs mgr. Mobil Oil Corp., Boston, 1953-63; exec. v.p. Lionel D. Edie & Co., N.Y.C., 1963-72; exec. v.p. Bank New Eng., Boston, 1972-76; v.p., dir. mktg. Loomis, Sayles & Co., Boston, 1976-85; pres. Concord Mgmt. Co., 1985—; co-pub. Cons. Compendium Inc., 1985—. Trustee, Deerfield Acad., 1975-78; trustee Babson Coll., 1976-82, 83—; trustee Cambridge Sch. of Weston (Mass.), 1976-82, New Eng. Home for Little Wanderers, 1983-86. Served with USAF, 1951-53. Mem. Assn. of Investment Mgmt. Sales Execs. (pres. 1980-81, dir. 1980-84), Air Force Assn. Republican. Congregationalist. Clubs: Yale of N.Y.C., Harvard of Boston, Concord Country. Home: 170 Barnes Hill Rd Concord MA 01742 Office: 33 Bedford St Concord MA 01742

THOMAS, DAVID ANSELL, retired university dean; b. Holliday, Tex., July 5, 1917; s. John Calvin Mitchell and Alice (Willet) T.; m. Mary Elizabeth Smith, May 18, 1946; 1 dau., Ann Elizabeth. B.A., Tex. Tech. Coll., 1937; M.B.A., Tex. Christian U., 1948; Ph.D., U. Mich., 1956. C.P.A., Tex. Accountant Texaco, Inc., 1937-42; asso. prof. Tex. Christian U., 1946-49; lectr. U. Mich., 1949-53; prof. accounting Cornell U., Ithaca, N.Y., 1953-84; asso. dean Cornell U. (Grad. Sch. Bus. and Pub. Adminstrn.), 1962-79, acting dean, 1979-81, dean, 1981-84. Author: Accelerated Amortization of Defense Facilities, 1958, Accounting for Home Builders, 1952; Contbr. numerous articles to publs.; Editor: Fed. Accountant, 1956-58. Pres. Exec. Investors, Inc.; exec. dir. Charles E. Merrill Family Found., 1954-57, Robert A. Magowan Found., 1957-60; adminstr. Charles E. Merrill Trust, 1957-81, Ithaca Growth Fund.; Bd. dirs. Ithaca Opera Assn., Cornell Student Agys. Served to capt. USAAF, 1942-46, PTO. Mem. Tex. Soc. C.P.A.'s, Nat. Assn. Accountants, Am. Accounting Assn., Phi Beta Kappa, Beta Alpha Psi. Clubs: Cornell of N.Y, University, Statler (pres., dir.). Home: 150 N Sunset Dr Ithaca NY 14850 Office: Samuel Curtis Johnson Grad Sch Mgmt Cornell U Ithaca NY 14853

THOMAS, DOUGLAS RONALD, advertising executive; b. London, Feb. 15, 1925; s. Harry Leonard and Constance Maude Thomas; married; children: Susan, David, Sally. Various positions Rank Orgns., 1956; mng. dir. Rank Advt. Films Ltd., London; Council mem. Advt. Assn., Advt. Standards Bd. of Fin.; pres. Cinema Advt. Assn., bd. dirs. Screen Advt. World Assn., London. Served to sgt. RAF, 1943-47. Fellow Inst. Chartered Secs. and Adminstrs., British Inst. of Mgmt., Inst. of Dirs. Mem. Ch. of England. Club: Arts (London). Office: Rank Advt Films Ltd, 127 Wardour St, London W1V 4AD, England

THOMAS, ERIC JAMES, chemistry educator; b. Stockport, Cheshire, Eng., Jan. 8, 1946; s. Eric and Margaret (Black) T.; m. Stella Margaret Grundy; children: Rebecca Clare, Richard James, Katharine Helen. BA, Cambridge U., 1968, MA, 1971, PhD, 1972. Lectr. chemistry King's Coll. U. London, 1973-79, Oxford (Eng.) U., 1979-88; prof. organic chemistry U. Manchester, Eng., 1988—; Fellow of the Exeter Coll. Oxford (Eng.) U., 1979-88. Contbr. research reports to profl. jours. Recipient Pfizer award, 1986; Higginbottom fellow in affiliation with the Royal Soc. of Chemistry, 1982. Office: U Manchester, Dept Chemistry, Manchester England M13 9RL

THOMAS, ETHEL COLVIN NICHOLS (MRS. LEWIS VICTOR THOMAS), educator; b. Cranston, R.I., Mar. 31, 1913; d. Charles Russell and Mabel Maria (Colvin) Nichols; Ph.B., Pembroke Coll. in Brown U., 1934; M.A., Brown U., 1938; Ed.D., Rutgers U., 1979; m. Lewis Victor Thomas, July 26, 1945 (dec. Oct. 1965); 1 child, Glenn Nichols. Tchr. English, Cranston High Sch., 1934-39; social dir. and adviser to freshmen, Fox Hall, Boston U., 1939-40; instr. to asst. prof. English Am. Coll. for Girls, Istanbul, Turkey, 1940-44; dean freshman, dir. admission Women's Coll. of Middlebury, Vt., 1944-45; tchr. English, Robert Coll., Istanbul, 1945-46; instr. English, Rider Coll., Trenton, N.J., 1950-51; tchr. English, Princeton (N.J.) High Sch., 1951-61, counselor, 1960-62, 72-83, coll. counselor, 1962-72, sr. peer counselor, 1986—. Mem. NEA, AAUW, Nat. Assn. Women Deans Adminstrs. and Counselors, Am. Assn. Counseling and Devel., Bus. and Profl. Women's Club (named Woman of Yr., Princeton chpt. 1977), Met. Mus. Art, Phi Delta Kappa, Kappa Delta Pi. Presbyn. Clubs: Brown University (N.Y.C.); Nassau.

THOMAS, FAIRWELL, biochemist, researcher; b. Kerala, India, Apr. 8, 1941; came to U.S., 1969; s. Thomas Puthiyathu and Ammukutty (Alexios) T.; m. Philsamma Vetticad, Apr. 17, 1971; children—Beena Fairwell, Neena Fairwell. B.S., St. Berchman's Coll., Kerala, 1960; M.S., U. Saugor, Rewa, India, 1963; Ph.D., Nat. Chem. Lab., U. Poona, 1967. Instr. Loyola Coll., Madras, India, 1960-61; lectr. Christian Med. Coll., Vellore, India, 1963; research fellow Nat. Chem. Lab., Poona, 1964-69; research assoc. U. Ga., Athens, 1969-72, Yale Med. Sch., New Haven, 1970; research chemist NIH, Bethesda, 1972—. Mem. Am. Soc. Mass Spectrometry, Assn. Scientists of Indian Origin in Am. Republican. Roman Catholic. Home: 5812 Kingswood Rd Bethesda MD 20814

THOMAS, GARNETT JETT, accountant; b. Farmington, Ky., July 27, 1920; s. Pinkney Madison and Ethel (Drinkard) T.; m. Nell Penton, May 23, 1981; stepchildren: Vernon Bice, Michael Bice, Gena Bice. BS, Lambuth Coll., 1947; student, U. Notre Dame, 1943-44; MS, Miss. State U., 1949. Clk., acct. Ill. Cen. R.R., Paducah, Ky., 1941-42; mgr. Coll. Bookstore, Lambuth Coll., Jackson, Tenn., 1946-47; acct. Miss. Agrl. and Forestry Expt. Sta., Mississippi State, 1948-60, chief acct., 1960-75, adminstrv. officer and chief acct., 1975-85; mem. adv. bd. Nat. Bank of Commerce of Miss., 1974—; pres. Starkville (Miss.) PBR Corp., 1977-84; fin. adminstr. seed tech. research internat. programs, Brazil, India, Guatemala, Columbia, Thailand, Kenya, 1958-85; bd. dirs. Govt. Employees Credit Union, 1967-86, pres., 1969-73. Contbr. articles to profl. publs. Served with USN, 1942-46. Decorated Bronze Star with oak leaf cluster. Mem. Nat. Assn. Accts., Assn. Govt. Accts., Am. Assn. Accts., Acad. Acctg. Historians, So. Assn. Agrl. Scientists. Republican. Methodist. Lodge: Rotary (pres. 1959-60, dist. gov. dist. 682, 1977-78, adv. com. to pres. 1979-80, dist. chmn. Poloplus). Home: 114 Grand Ridge Dr Starkville MS 39259

THOMAS, GEORGE JOSEPH, JR., life science educator, research scientist; b. New Bedford, Mass., Dec. 24, 1941; m. Martha Ann Sheehan, July 2, 1966; children: Elizabeth Ann, George Joseph, Jeanine Marie. B.A., Boston Coll., 1963; Ph.D., MIT, 1967. Research fellow King's Coll., London, 1967-68; asst. prof. Southeastern Mass. U., North Dartmouth, 1968-71, assoc. prof., 1971-74, prof. chemistry, 1974-87; dept. head, prof. cell biology and biophysics, U. Mo., Kansas City, 1987—. vis. scientist dept. biology Osaka (Japan) U., 1975-76, MIT, Cambridge, 1982-83; chmn. biophys. chemistry study sect. NIH, Bethesda, Md., 1979-83. Editorial bd.: Biophys. Jour, 1982-88; contbr. articles to sci. publs. Mem. Sch. Com. Westport, Mass., 1978-84, chmn., 1982-83; trustee Westport Free Public Library, 1975-78. Recipient Coblentz award Coblentz Soc., 1976. Mem. AAAS, Biophys. Soc., Am. Chem. Soc. Current Work: Structure and assembly of viruses and nucleoproteins; vibrational spectroscopy of nucleic acids and proteins. Subspecialties: Biophysical chemistry; Laser spectroscopy.

THOMAS, GEORGE WILLARD (BILL), micrographics quality control company executive, consultant; b. York, Pa., Jan. 26, 1927; s. George Washington and Ruth Jeanette (Lukens) T.; m. Juanita Anne Vinson, Feb. 6, 1948; children—Lynn Anne Thomas Nelson, George Willard Jr. Student York Jr. Coll. (Pa.), 1946-47; A.B., Gettysburg Coll. (Pa.), 1949; postgrad. U. Del.-Newark, 1949-51. Physicist, U.S. Navy, Panama City, Fla., 1951-56, Corona, Calif., 1956-71; owner, mgr. MicroFilming Services, Corona, 1971-79; pres. Neoteric Arts, Inc., Corona and Burnsville, Minn., 1972—; pres. MicroD Internat., Corona and Burnsville, 1973—; dir., v.p. Biotronic Devel Corp., Lakeville, Minn., 1987—. Contbr. articles in field. Commr. Inland Empire council Boy Scouts Am., Corona. Served with U.S. Navy, 1945-46. Recipient Disting. Merit award Boy Scouts Am., 1974; Merit award So. Calif. Micrographics Assn., 1980. Mem. Assn. Info. and Image Mgmt., Internat. Info. Mgmt. Congress, Can. Info. and Image Mgmt. Soc., Internat. Records Mgmt. Council, Am. Nat. Standards Inst., Records Mgmt. Assn. Republican. Office: Neoteric Arts Inc 15000 County Rd 5 Burnsville MN 55337

THOMAS, HANS MICHAEL, scientist; b. Zweibrücken, Germany, Nov. 29, 1920; s. Jakob and Kätchen (Ingold) T. B.Econ. Sci., U. Freiburg, 1948, Dr.rer.pol., 1950. Sec. Bundesverband Deutscher Volks-und Betriebswirte, Bonn, 1951-55; sci. collaborator Deutsche Forschungsgemeinschaft, Bad Godesberg, 1955-57; syndic Ludwig Scheer & Co. KG, Wuerzburg, 1957-62; comml. dir. Bastei Verlag and Gustav Luebbe Verlag, Bergisch Gladbach, 1962-64, Herlan & Co. Maschinenfabrik, Karlsruhe, 1964-66; ind. scientist, Ettlingen, Federal Republic Germany, 1966—. Contbr. articles to profl. jours. Mem. Internat. Conf. for Sociology of Religion, Centre interuniversitaire de Codicologie, Gesellschaft für Geistesgeschichte, others. Roman Catholic. Address: Brahmsstrasse 9, D-7505 Ettlingen Federal Republic of Germany

THOMAS, HENRI, author, poet; b. France, Dec. 7, 1912; s. Joseph and Mathilde Thomas; m. Jacqueline Le Beguec, 1957; 1 dau. Educated Strasbourg U. Teacher, until 1939; program asst. French sect. BBC, 1947-58; lectr. in French, Brandeis U., Mass., 1956-60; in charge German dept. Gallimard's Pub. House, Paris, 1960—. Author novels: Le seau à charbon, 1940, Le précepteur, 1942, La vie ensemble, 1943, Les déserteurs, 1951, La nuit de Londres, 1956, La dernière année, 1960, John Perkins (Prix Médicis 1960), Le promontoire (Prix Femina 1961), Le Parjure, 1964, La Relique, 1969, Le Croc des Chiffonniers, 1985, Une Saisin Volée, 1986; criticism: La chasse aux trésors, 1961, Tristan Le Déposséde, 1971; short stories: La Cible (Pirx St. Beuve 1956), Histoires de Pierrot et Quelques Autres, 1960, Les tours de Notre Dame (Prix des Sept); essyas: Le Porte-A-Faux, 1949, Sous le Lien de Temps, 1963, Le Migrateur, 1983; poetry includes: Póesies complètes, 1970, A Quoi tu penses, 1980, Joueur surpris, 1982;translator works by Goethe, Stifter, Iünger, Shakespeare, Pushkin. Recipient Prix Valéry Larbaud, 1970; decorated chevalier Legion d'honneur. Office: Editions Gallimard, 5 rue Sebastien-Bottin, 75007 Paris France

THOMAS, HUGH SWYNNERTON (LORD THOMAS), historian; b. Windsor, Eng., Oct. 10, 1931; s. Hugh Whitelegge and Margery Augusta (Swynnerton) T.; m. Vanessa Mary Jebb, May 5, 1984; children—Inigo, Isambard, Isabella. Prof. history U. Reading, London (Eng.), 1966-76, chmn. Centre Policy Studies, 1979—; life peer, 1981—. Author: The Spanish Civil War, 1961; Cuba of the Pursuit of Freedom, 1971; An Unfinished History of the World, 1979; Havannah, 1984, Armed Truce, 1986. Recipient Somerset Maugham prize, 1962; Nat. Arts Council Book award, 1980. Mem. Conservative Party. Mem. Ch. of England. Office: House of Lords, London SW1, England also: 29 Ladbroke Grove, London W11, England *

THOMAS, JEAN-CLAUDE, chemical engineer; b. Paris, June 10, 1931; s. Germain and Marguerite (Hutereau) T.; m. Alice Botevy, June 11, 1957; children: François, Philippe, Elisabeth. Degree in chem. engring., Ecole Nat. Superieure de Chimie, Paris, 1955; MA, U. Sorbonne, Paris, 1955. Chem. engr. Saint-Gobain Co., France, 1957-60; lab. mgr. Pechiney-Saint-Gobain Co., Lyon, France, 1960-69; plastic products devel. mgr. Rhone-Poulenc, Paris, 1970-80, auditor, 1980-81; cons. Communications Econs. et Sociales, Paris, 1981—. Inventor plastics. Roman Catholic. Home: 34 Avenue du Roule, 92200 Neuilly France Office: Communications Economiques, et Sociales, 10 Avenue de Messine, 75008 Paris France

THOMAS, JEREMY JOHN RHYS, sociologist, educator; b. Builth, Wales, Aug. 23, 1948; s. Norman Leslie Thomas and Beryl Audrey Gibson Wright; m. Barbara Mary Henshall, July 19, 1975 (div. 1980); children: Alexander, Oliver; m. Monika Helga Prützel, Oct. 6, 1980; children: Max, Anna. BA, U. Essex, Eng., 1970; MA, U. Sussex, Eng., 1974. Lectr. sociology Bristol (Eng.) Polytech., 1975-84, prin. lectr., 1984—; lectr. U. Essex, 1970-71; U. Sussex, 1974-75; research cons. Warner Bros., Burbank, Calif., 1987. Contbr. articles to profl. jours. Mem. Brit. Sociol. Assn. Anglican. Office: Bristol Polytech, Col Harbour Ln, Bristol BS16 1QY, England

THOMAS, JESS, tenor; b. Hot Springs, S.D., Aug. 4, 1927; s. Charles A. and H. and Ellen (Yocam) T.; m. Violeta Maria de Los Angeles Rios Andino Figueroa, 1974; children—Victor Justin, Lisa, Jess David. A.B., U. Nebr., 1949; M.A., Stanford, 1953; student, Otto Schulmann, San Francisco, 1953-57. Guidance counselor pub. schs. Hermiston, Oreg., 1949-52, Alameda, Cal., 1953-56. Winner San Francisco Opera audition, 1957; profl. debut, Baden State Theatre, Karlsruhe, Germany, 1958, appeared in, Stuttgart, Germany, 1959-64, Bavarian State Opera, Munich, 1959—, Munich Festival, 1960—, Bayreuth Festival, 1961—, Berlin Philharmonic, 1962, Met. Opera Co., 1962—, Venice, Italy Wagner Festival, 1963, Deutsche Oper, Berlin, 1961-64, Frankfurt Opera, 1963, Salzburg Summer Festival, 1964—, Vienna State Opera, 1964—, La Scala Opera, 1965, Opening Night New Met. Opera, 1966, Osaka Japan Festival, 1967, Convent Garden Opera, 1969—, Salzburg Easter Festival, 1969—, Paris Grand Opera, 1967—, San Francisco Opera, 1965—; sang Tristan in, Covent Garden, Met. Opera, Vienna State Opera, 1971—, Palacio de Bellas Artes, Mexico City, 1971—, Casals Festival, 1976—, Teatro Colon Opera, Buenos Aires, 1976—, Bolshoi Theatre, Moscow, 1971, appeared in, Wagner: The Film, 1983, rec. artist for, Angel Records, Deutsche Grammophon, Phillips, RCA, Columbia, N.Y. Philharmonic debut, 1967, Boston Symphony debut, 1967; pub. memoirs Kein Schwert Mir Der Vater, 1986. Named Kammersänger Bavarian State Govt., 1963; recipient San Francisco Opera medallion, 1972; named Kammersänger Austrian Govt., 1976; inducted into Acad. Vocal Arts Hall of Fame, Phila., 1986. Mem. Beta Theta Pi, Phi Delta Kappa. Home: PO Box 662 Tiburon CA 94920 Office: care Colbert Artists Mgmt 111 W 57th St New York NY 10019

THOMAS, JOHN MEURIG, chemist, scientist; b. Llanelli, Wales, Dec. 15, 1932; s. David John and Edyth Thomas; m. Margaret Edwards, 1959; 2 daughters. MA, U. Coll. of Swansea; PhD, Queen Mary Coll.; LLD (hon.), U. Wales, 1984; DLitt (hon.), CNAA, 1987. Sci. officer UKAEA, 1957-58, asst. lectr., 1958-59, lectr., 1959-65, reader, 1965-69; prof., head dept. of chemistry UCW, Aberystwyth, 1969-78; prof., head dept. physical chemistry, fellow King's Coll. U. Cambridge, 1978-86; dir., resident prof. Davy Faraday Research Lab. Royal Inst. Great Britain, 1986—; vis. prof. Tech. U. Eindhoven, The Netherlands, 1962, Pa. State U., 1963, 67, Tech. U. Karlsruhe, Fed. Republic Germany, 1966, Weizmann Inst., Israel, 1969, U. Florence, Italy, 1972, Am. U. in Cairo, 1973, IBM Research Ctr., San José, 1977, QMC, 1986—, Imperial Coll., London, 1986—, Acad. Sinica, Beijing, Inst. Ceramic Sci., Shanghai, 1986—; Winegard vis. prof. Guelph U., 1982, BBC Welsh Radio Annual lectr., 1978; Gerhardt Schmidt Meml. lectr., Weizmann Inst., 1979; Disting. vis. lectr., London U., 1980, Royal Soc.-Brit. Assn. lectr., 1980, Baker lectr., Cornell U., 1982-83, dist. lectr. in Chem., U. Western Ont., 1983, Sloan vis. prof., Harvard U., 1983, Disting. vis. lectr., Tex. A&M U., 1984, Salters lectr., Royal Instn., 1985, 86, Disting. vis. lectr. U. Notre Dame, Ind., 1986, Schuit lectr., Inst. Catalysis, U. Del., 1986, Battista lectr., Clarkson U., 1987, Hund-Klemm lectr., Max Planck Ctr., Stuttgart, 1987, Kenneth Pitzer lectr., U. Calif., Berkeley, 1988; Hon. bencher, Gray's Inn, 1987; mem. Radioactive Waste Mgmt. Com., 1978-80; mem. chem. com., SRC, 1976-78; mem. main com. SERC, 1986—; mem. adv. com. Davy-Faraday Labs, Royal Instn., 1978-80; sci. adv. com. Sci. Alexandria, 1979—; bd. govs., Weizmann Inst., 1982—; chmn. Chemrawn, IUPAC, 1987—; trustee BM, 1987—. Author: (with W.J. Thomas) Introduction to the Principles of Heterogeneous Catalysis, 1967; Pan edrychwyf ar y nefoedd, 1978, Heterogeneous Catalysis: theory and practice, 1988; contbr. articles in field. Office: The Royal Instn, 21 Albemarle St, London W1X 4BS, England *

THOMAS, JOSEPH PAUL, retail executive; b. Montego Bay, Jamaica, Jan. 9, 1950; s. Stanley Arthur and Theresa (Donegan) T.; m. Sharon Lyn Lyons, July 29, 1972; children: Justin Neil, Linley Kay, Sharon Lee. BS in Econs., U. West Indies, Kingston, Jamaica, 1970. Asst. to pres. Indsl. Chem. Co., Spanish Town, Jamaica, 1970-72; sales mgr. Tanner Ltd., Kingston, 1972-74; gen. mgr. Gator Ltd., Kingston, 1974-80, mgr. dir., 1980—; bd. dirs. Precision Arts Ltd., Kingston, 1975—, Wisynco Group Cos., Spanish Town, 1981—. Contbr. articles to profl. pubs. Mem. Jamaica Mfg. Assn. (pres. 1985-88), Pvt. Sector Orgn. Jamaica (bd. dirs.). Roman Catholic. Club: PWD Gun. Home: PO Box 874, Kingston 8, Kingston Jamaica Office: Gator Ltd, PO Box 69, Spanish Town, Saint Catherine Jamaica

THOMAS, KEVIN RICHARD, sales professional; b. Winchester, Eng., Sept. 24, 1955; s. Harry Arther and Nancy Mary (Caple) T.; m. Christina Nelson, Aug. 14, 1984. BS in Math. with honors, Southampton (Eng.) U., 1977. Tchr. Hall Mead Sch., London, 1977-80; engr. Marconi & Camberley, London, 1980-81; sales mgr. Sintrom Electronics Co., Reading, Eng., 1981-86, Advance Bryans Instruments Co., London, 1986—. Home: Mount Lodge, Hook Hill Ln, Woking, Surrey GU22 0QB, England Home: Advance Bryans Instruments, 14-16 Wates Way, Mitcham, Surrey England

THOMAS, LEO, pension, insurance and executive compensation consultant; b. Los Angeles, July 5, 1947; s. Leonard and Rose (Morris) T.; m. Bernice Roberts, Aug. 19, 1969; 1 child, Tod. BA, Occidental Coll., Los Angeles, 1968. With pub. relations com. Dem. Party, Los Angeles, 1968-69; ins. agt. Prudential Co., Los Angeles, 1969-77; fin. estate mgr. Hansch Fin. Group, Los Angeles, 1970—; pres. Thomas Fin. and Ins. Services, Inc., Los Angeles, 1980—; cons. Fin. Adv. Clinic, Los Angeles, 1982-84, Fin. Digest, Los Angeles, 1983-88, Life Ins. Leaders Round Table, Los Angeles, 1984-86. Contbr. articles to profl. jours. Mem. Nat. Tax Limitation Com., Washington, 1982-85, So. Poverty Law Council, Atlanta, 1982-88; charter mem. Statue of Liberty-Ellis Island Found., 1984-88; past pres. Young Dems., 1967. Named Agt. of Yr., Los Angeles Life Underwriters, 1983, 84, 85. Mem. Internat. Assn. Fin. Planners, Am. Soc. CLU's, Internat. Forum, Top of the Table. Jewish. Lodge: Kiwanis (bd. dirs. Los Angeles chpt. 1983-85). Office: Thomas Fin and Ins Service Inc 5900 Wilshire 17 Los Angeles CA 90036

THOMAS, LEONA MARLENE, medical records educator; b. Rock Springs, Wyo., Jan. 15, 1933; d. Leonard H. and Opal (Wright) Francis; m. Craig L. Thomas, Feb. 22, 1955; (div. Sept. 1978); children—Peter, Paul, Patrick, Alexis. B.A., Govs. State U., 1982, MHS, 1986; cert. med. records adminstrn. U. Colo., 1954. Dir. med. records dept. Meml. Hosp. Sweetwater County, Rock Springs, 1954-57; staff assoc. Am. Med. Records Assn., Chgo., 1972-77, asst. editor, 1979-81; asst. prof. Chgo. State U., 1984—; statistician Westlake Hosp., Melrose Park, Ill., 1982-84. Co. pres. Ill. Dist. 60 PTA, Westmont, Ill., 1972. Mem. Am. Med. Records Assn., Ill. Med. Records Assn., Chgo. and Vicinity Med. Records Assn. Democrat. Methodist. Home: 6340 F Americana Dr Apt 1101 Clarendon Hills IL 60514 Office: Chgo State U Coll Allied Health 95th at King Dr Chicago IL 60608

THOMAS, LEWIS, physician, educator, former medical administrator; b. Flushing, N.Y., Nov. 25, 1913; s. Joseph S. and Grace Emma (Peck) T.; m. Beryl Dawson, Jan. 1, 1941; children: Abigail, Judith, Eliza. BS, Princeton U., 1933, ScD (hon.), 1976; MD, Harvard U., 1937, ScD (hon.), 1986; MA, Yale U., 1969; ScD (hon.), U. Rochester, 1974, U. of Toledo, 1976, Columbia U., 1978, Meml. U. Nfld., 1978, U. N.C., 1979, Worcester Found., 1979, Williams Coll., 1982, Conn. Coll., 1983, U. Wales, 1983, U. Ariz., 1985, L.I. U., 1987; LLD (hon.), Johns Hopkins U., 1976, Trinity Coll., 1980; LHD (hon.), Duke U., 1976, Reed Coll., 1978; LittD (hon.), Dickinson Coll., 1980, Ursinus Coll., 1981, SUNY-Stony Brook, 1983; DMus. (hon.), New Eng. Conservatory Music, 1982; DHL (hon.), NYU Sch. Medicine, 1983; LittD (hon.), Drew U., 1983; PhD, Weizmann Inst., 1984. Intern Boston City Hosp., 1937-39, Neurol. Inst., N.Y.C., 1939-41; Tilney Meml. fellow Thorndike Lab., Boston City Hosp., 1941-42; vis. investigator Rockefeller Inst., 1942-46; asst. prof. pediatrics Med. Sch. Johns Hopkins U., Balt., 1946-48; asso. prof. medicine Med. Sch. Tulane U., New Orleans, 1948-50; prof. medicine Med. Sch. Tulane U., 1950; prof. pediatrics and medicine, dir. pediatric research labs. Heart Hosp., U. Minn., Mpls., 1950-54; prof., chmn. dept. pathology NYU Sch. Medicine, 1954-58, prof., chmn. dept. medicine, 1958-66, dean, 1966-69; prof., chmn. dept. pathology Yale U., New Haven, 1969-72, dean, Sch. Medicine, 1972-73; prof. medicine, pathology Med. Sch. Cornell U., N.Y.C., 1973—, prof. biology Sloan Kettering Inst. div., 1973—; adj. prof. Rockefeller U., N.Y.C., 1975—; pres., chief exec. officer Meml. Sloan-Kettering Cancer Ctr., N.Y.C., 1973-80, chancellor, 1980-83; pres. emeritus Meml. Sloan-Kettering Cancer Center, N.Y.C., 1984—; prof. SUNY-Stony Brook Health Scis. Ctr., 1984—; scholar-in-residence Cornell U. Med. Coll., 1988—; dir. 3d and 4th med. divs. Bellevue Hosp., 1958-66, pres. med. bd., 1963-66; cons. Manhattan VA Hosp., 1954-69; cons. to Surgeon Gen. Dept. Army, Surgeon Gen. USPHS; mem. pathology study sect. NIH, 1955-59, nat. adv. health council, 1960-64, nat. adv. child health and human devel. council, 1964-68; mem. commn. on streptococcal disease Armed Forces Epidemiol. Bd., 1950-62; mem. Pres.'s Sci. Adv. Com., 1967-70, Inst. Medicine, 1971, Nat. Acad. Scis., 1972—, mem. council and governing bd., 1979—; chmn. overview cluster subcom. Pres.'s Biomed. Research Panel, 1975-76; mem. Tech. Assessment Adv. Council, 1980—; bd. dirs., trustee Squibb Corp. Mem. N.Y.C. Bd. Health, 1956-69; mem. bd. sci. cons. Sloan-Kettering Inst. Cancer Research, 1966-72; mem. Sloan-Kettering Inst., 1973-83; bd. dirs. Josiah Macy Jr. Found., 1975-84; bd. sci. advisors Mass. Gen. Hosp., 1970-73, Scripps Clinic and Research Found., 1969-78; bd. dirs., research council Pub. Health Research Inst. of City N.Y., 1964-69; bd. overseers Harvard Coll., 1976-82; mem. sci. adv. com. Sidney Farber Cancer Inst., 1978—; mem. council Grad. Sch. Bus. and Pub. Adminstrn., Cornell U., 1978-82; mem. awards assembly Gen. Motors Cancer Research Found., 1978-83; asso. fellow Ezra Stiles Coll. Yale U. Author: Lives of a Cell, 1974, Medusa and the Snail, 1979, The Youngest Science, 1983, Late Night Thoughts on Listening to Mahler's Ninth Symphony, 1983; mem. editorial bd. Daedalus, Cellular Immunology, Am. Jour. Pathology. Trustee N.Y.C.-Rand Inst., 1967-71, The Rockefeller U., 1975—, Draper Lab., 1975-81, John Simon Guggenheim Meml. Found., 1975-85, Mt. Sinai Sch. Medicine, 1979-85, Ednl. Broadcasting Co., 1977-83, Menninger Found., 1980—; bd. dirs. Lounsbery Found., 1982—; chmn. bd. Monell Chem. Senses Ctr., 1982—; bd. advisors Kennedy Inst. Ethics, Georgetown U., 1982—; trustee Nat. Hospice, 1978—; mem. bd. overseers U. Pa. Sch. Nursing, 1983—; adv. council Program in History of Sci. Princeton U., 1982—; bd. dirs. Am. Friends Cambridge U., 1984—; mem. adv. com. Aaron Diamond Found., 1985—; dth Fund Book Program, 1982—. Served to lt. comdr. M.C. USNR, 1941-46. Recipient Disting. Achievement award Modern Medicine, 1975; Nat. Book award for Arts and Letters, 1975; Honor award Am. Med. Writers Assn., 1978; Med. Edn. award AMA, 1979; Bard award in medicine and sci. Bard Coll., 1979; Am. Book award, 1981; St. Davids Soc. award, 1980; Recipient Woodrow Wilson award Princeton U., 1980, award Cosmos Club, Washington, 1982; Richard Hopper Day award Phila. Acad. Natural Scis., 1985; Lewis Thomas award for communications ACP, 1986; Milton Helpern Meml. award, 1986; Ency. Brit. award, 1986; Alfred P. Sloan Jr. Meml. award, 1987; William B. Coley award Cancer Research Inst., 1987, Gold-Headed Cane award Am. Assn. Pathologists, 1988.. Fellow Am. Acad. Arts and Scis., Am. Rheumatism Assn.; mem. Nat. Acad. Scis., Am. Acad. and Inst. Arts and Letters, Am. Philos. Assn., Am. Soc. Exptl. Pathology, Practitioners Soc., Am. Acad. Microbiology, Peripatetic Clin. Soc., Am. Soc. Clin. Investigation, Am. Assn. Immunologists, Soc. Am. Bacteriologists, Assn. Am. Physicians (Kober medal 1983), Am. Pediatric Soc., N.Y. Acad. Scis. (pres.-elect 1988), Harvey Soc. (councillor), Scientists' Inst. for Pub. Info (chmn. bd. 1982— award for excellence in sci. communication), AAUP, Soc. Exptl. Biology and Medicine, Am. Soc. Clin. Oncology, Friends of History of Sci. Soc. (council 1982—), Council on Fgn. Relations, Interurban Clin. Club, Phi Beta Kappa, Alpha Omega Alpha. Club: Century Assn. Office: Cornell Univ Med Coll 1300 York Ave New York NY 10021

THOMAS, LEWIS EDWARD, laboratory executive, retired petroleum company executive; b. Lima, Ohio, May 18, 1913; s. Lewis Edward and Ilma Kathryn (Siebert) T.; B.S., Ohio No. U., 1935; M.S., Purdue U., 1973; m. Elinda Patricia Grafton, Dec. 21, 1939; children—Linda Thomas Collins, Stephanie Thomas Pawuk, Kathryn Thomas Ramsey, Deborah G. Asst. prof. chemistry Va. Mil. Inst., 1940-45; devel. engr. Sun Oil Co., Toledo, 1945-49, lab. supr., 1950-69, div. supr., 1969-73, lab. mgr., 1973-78; mgr. Toledo Symphony, 1978-79; mktg. staff Jones & Henry Labs., Toledo, 1979—; dir. First Fed. Savs. & Loan Assn.; vis. scientist to area high schs. Ohio Acad. Sci., 1960-67. Lay reader Episcopal Ch., 1962; pres., treas. Harvard Elem. Sch. PTA, 1953-54; mem. Mayor's Indsl. Devel. Com., Toledo, 1963-66; mem. Gov.'s Com. Statewide Health Planning Council, 1976—; mem. Lucas County Central Com., precinct committeeman Republican Party, 1958—; trustee Toledo Public Library, 1966-70, pres., 1969-70; trustee Toledo Lucas County Public Library, 1970—, v.p., 1971-72, pres., 1972-75, 85—; trustee U. Toledo, 1967—, vice chmn. bd., 1971-75; mem. adv. bd. St. Charles Hosp.; mem. Assn. Governing Bds. Univs. and Colls., 1969—; trustee Toledo Symphony Orch., 1981—; mem. governing bd. Northwest Ohio Council Girl Scouts U.S., 1981—; chmn. Northwest Ohio Easter Seals, 1983. Named Chem. Engr. of Year, Toledo Area, 1961, 63, 76; registered profl. engr., Ohio. Mem. Nat., Ohio (chmn. state conv. 1975), Toledo (trustee 1974—) socs. profl. engrs., Am. Inst. Chem. Engrs., Am. Chem. Soc. (pres. Toledo sect. 1960), Nat. Mgmt. Assn. (trustee Toledo chpt. 1962-70, nat. dir. 1968-70), Tech. Soc. Toledo (pres. 1968-69), Explorers Club, Sigma Xi, Pi Kappa Alpha, Tau Beta Pi, Nu Theta Kappa. Club: Toastmasters. Home: 4148 Deepwood Ln Toledo OH 43614 Office: PO Box 920 Toledo OH 43693

THOMAS, LINDSEY KAY, JR., research biologist, educator, consultant; b. Salt Lake City, Apr. 16, 1931; s. Lindsey Kay and Naomi Lurie (Biesinger) T.; m. Nancy Ruth Van Dyke, Aug. 24, 1956; children—Elizabeth Nan Thomas Cardinale, David Lindsey, Wayne Hal, Dorothy Ann. B.S., Utah State Agrl. Coll., 1953; M.S., Brigham Young U., 1958; Ph.D., Duke U., 1974. Park naturalist Nat. Capital Parks, Nat. Park Service, Washington, 1957-62, research park naturalist Region 6, Washington, 1962-63, research park naturalist Nat. Capital Region, Washington, 1963-66, research biologist S.E. Temperate Forest Park Areas, Washington, 1966, Durham, N.C., 1966-67, Great Falls, Md., 1967-71, research biologist Nat. Capital Parks, Great Falls, 1971-74, research biologist Nat. Capital Region, Triangle, Va., 1974—; instr. Dept. Agr. Grad. Sch., 1964-66; ecol. cons. Fairfax Count (Va.) Fedn. Citizens Assns., 1970-71; guest lectr. U. D.C., 1976. Asst. scoutmaster and scoutmaster, merit badges counselor Boy Scouts Am., 1958—, Scouters Tng. award, 1961. Recipient incentive awards Nat. Park Service, 1962; research grantee Washington Biologists Field Club, 1977, 82. Mem. AAAS, Bot. Soc. Washington, Ecol. Soc. Am., George Wright Soc., Nature Conservancy, Soc. Early Hist. Archaeology, Washington Biologists Field Club, Sigma Xi. Mormon. Contbr. articles profl. jours. Home: 13854 Delaney Rd Woodbridge VA 22193 Office: PO Box 209 Prince William Forest Park Triangle VA 22172 also: Nat Capital Region Nat Park Service Div Natural Sci Service 1100 Ohio Dr SW Washington DC 20242

THOMAS, MICHAEL TILSON, symphony conductor; b. Los Angeles, 1944; s. Ted and Roberta T. Studies with, Ingolf Dahl, U. So. Calif., others; student conducting, Berkshire Music Festival, Tanglewood, Mass.; student conducting (Koussevitsky prize 1968); LL.D., Hamilton Coll.; L.H.D. (hon.), D'Youville Coll., 1976. Asst. condr. Boston Symphony Orch., 1969, assoc. condr., 1970-72, prin. guest condr., 1972-74; also Berkshire Music Festival, summer 1970, 74; music dir., condr. Buffalo Philharmonic Orch., 1971-79; music dir., prin. condr. Great Woods Ctr. for Performing Arts, 1985; prin. condr. London Symphony Orch. Condr., dir., N.Y. Philharmonic Young People's Concerts, CBS-TV, 1971-77; vis. condr. numerous orchs., U.S., Europe, Japan; chief condr. Ojai Festival, 1967, dir., 1972-77; opera debut, Cin., 1975; condr.: Am. premiere Lulu (Alban Berg), Santa Fe Opera, summer 1979; prin. guest condr., Los Angeles Philharm., 1981-85, Am. premiere Desert Music (Steve Reich), 1984; prin. condr. Gershwin festival London Symphony Orch., Barbcan Ctr., 1987; recording artist CBS Masterworks, 1973—. Named Musician of Year, Musical Am. 1970; recipient Grammy award for Carmina Burana with Cleve. Orch., 1976, for Gershwin Alive with Los Angeles Philharm., 1983. Office: care Harold Holt Ltd, 31 Sinclair Rd, London W14 0NS, England also: Ronald Wilford Columbia Artists 165 W 67th St New York NY 10019 *

THOMAS, MILTON CARTER, II, lawyer; b. Union Point, Ga., Nov. 29, 1946; s. Milton Carter and Sarah Louise (Hillman) T.; m. Linda Susan Foglia, May 20, 1969 (div. 1976); 1 child, Erika Ree; m. Judy Webb, Aug. 29, 1986; 1 child, Sarah Stasia. BA, U. Conn., 1969, JD, 1972. Bar: Conn. 1977, Pa. 1974, U.S. Dist. Ct. Conn. 1976, U.S. Dist. Ct. (ea. and so. dists.) N.Y. 1980. Pvt. placement atty. Phoenix Mut. Life Ins. Co., Hartford, Conn., 1972-74; def. contracts adminstr. Dept. Def., Hartford, 1974-76; sole practice, Stamford, Conn., 1976—. Vice-pres., bd. dirs. Southfield Community Orgn., Stamford, 1982—; bd. dirs. Stamford Boys and Girls Club, 1986—, Community Housing Resource Bd., Stamford, 1986—. Served to capt. U.S. Army, 1969-74. Mem. ABA, Conn. Bar Assn. (com. juvenile justice), Darien/Stamford Bar Assn. Republican. Office: 49 Woodside St Stamford CT 06902

THOMAS, NATHANIEL CHARLES, clergyman; b. Jonesboro, Ark., June 24, 1929; s. Willie James and Linnie (Elias) T.; B.A., Miss. Indsl. Coll., Holly Springs, 1951; B.D., Lincoln U., 1954, M.Div., 1974; student Lancaster (Pa.) Theol. Sem., 1952-53; D.Div., Tex. Coll., Tyler, 1981; m. Juanita Fanny Jefferson, May 20, 1961 (dec. 1970); children—Gina Charlise, Nathaniel Charles, Keith Antony; m. 2d, Mary Elizabeth Partee, June 8, 1971. Ordained to ministry Christian Meth. Episcopal Ch., 1954; dir. Christian edn. 8th dist. Christian Meth. Episc. Ch., 1954-58; pastor in Waterford, Miss., 1949-51, Wrightville, Ark., 1955-57, Hot Springs, Ark., 1957-60, Little Rock, 1960-62, Mt. Pisgah Christian Meth. Episc. Ch., Memphis, 1966-67, Greenwood Christian Meth. Episc. Ch., Memphis, 1980-81; dir. Christian edn., adminstrv. asst. to Bishop B. Julian Smith, Christian Meth. Episc. Ch., Memphis, 1954-74, presiding elder South Memphis dist., 1971-74, sec. gen. conf. of ch., 1970-82, gen. sec. gen. bd. personnel services, 1978—, also mem. gen. connectional bd., program adminstr. ministerial salary supplement program, 1974—, asst. to sec. gen. Gen. Bd. Pensions, gen. sec. personnel services Gen. Bd., 1974-78; plan mgr. CME Ch. Group Fire & Casualty Ins. Plan, 1978—; sec. Ministerial Assn. Little Rock, 1960-62; v.p. youth work sect., div. Christian edn. Nat. Council Chs., del. World Council Chs. Conf., Upsalla Sweden, 1968. Dir. Haygood-Neal Garden Apts., Inc., Eldorado, Ark., 1969—, Smith-Keys Village Apts., Inc., Texarkana, Ark., 1968—, East Gate Village Apts., Inc., Union City, Tenn., 1971—; trustee Collins Chapel Health Care Center, Memphis, 1974—, Tex. Coll., 1981—; bd. dirs. Family Service Memphis, 1972-73; chmn. bd. dirs. Memphis Opportunities Indsl. Ctr., 1976-78. Mem. NAACP, Urban League, Community on Move for Equality, Memphis Interdenomminational Ministers Alliance, Memphis Ministers Assn., Tenn. Assn. Chs., Ark. Council Chs., Ark. Council Human Relations, Tenn. Council Human Relations, Family Service Memphis, A.B. Hill PTA. Author: Christian Youth Fellow Guide, 8th Episcopal District, 1959; Living Up to My Obligations of the Christian Methodist Episcopal Church, 1956; Steps Toward Developing an Effective Program of Christian Education, 1972; co-author: Worship in the Local Church, 1966; co-author, editor: Coming to Grips with the Teaching Work of the Church, 1966. Co-editor: Developing Black Families, 1975; compiling editor: Dedicated . . . Committed-Autobiography of Bishop B. Julian Smith, 1978—. Home: PO Box 9 Memphis TN 38101 Office: PO Box 74 Memphis TN 38101

THOMAS, P. JOSEPH, chemical company executive; b. Palai, India; s. Mathai Joseph and Mariam T.; m. Prem Lata, June 8, 1965; 1 child, Sonya. M.Sc., Kerala U., India, 1960; postgrad. St. Louis U., 1961-63; Ph.D., U. Miami, Fla., 1965. Research fellow Sch. Medicine, Harvard U., Boston, 1965-67; research assoc. Southwest Found., San Antonio, Tex., 1967-68; div. mgr. Hindustan Lever Ltd., Bombay, India, 1969-80; chief exec. Kay Labs. Pvt Ltd., Bombay, 1980—; prof. U. Bombay, 1980—; adviser Nat. Organic Chem. Industries Ltd., Bombay, 1985; dir. Epic Pvt Ltd., Bombay. Patentee plant growth stimulant weedicides. Mem. Am. Chem. Soc., Soc. Biol. Chemists, Dairy Sci. Assn., Assn. Food Sci. and Tech. Avocations: music; wine making. Home: 29 Silver Sands Juhu Tara, 400040 Bombay India

THOMAS, PAUL GREGORY, marine biologist, environmental consultant; b. Newcastle, NSW, Australia, July 15, 1958; s. Alan Raymond and Shirley (Mitchell) T.; m. Janine Anne Steadman, Nov. 4, 1959; children: Michael James, Sam Steadman. BS in Marine Biology, Zoology, James Cook U., Townsville, Australia, 1981; BS with hons., Tasmanian U., Hobart, Australia, 1983. Exptl. officer Roche Research Inst. Marine Pharmacology, Sydney, NSW, Australia, 1977-79, Australian Mus., Sydney, 1980-81; state coordinator BP Australia, Melbourne, Victoria, Australia, 1982-83; tutor marine sci. U. Tasmania, Hobart, 1983-84; marine scientist Australian Antarctic Div., Hobart, 1984—; cons. Ea. Marine Resources Ltd., Sydney, 1986-87; mgr. Barrier Reef Fisheries, Mackay, Queensland, Australia, 1987—. Author Uptake, Localisation and Deporation of Zinc in the Barnacle, 1983 (Ralston Trust award 1984); contbr. sci. articles and papers to profl. jours. Environ. cons. NW Bay Progress Assn., Hobart, 1986. Mem: Australian Marine Scientists Assn., Profl. Officers Assn. (state rep. 1987—), Australian Mariculture Assn., World Aquaculture Soc. Mem. Ch. of Eng. Office: Australian Antarctic Div, 8 Telina Dr, Beaconsfiled Mackay, 4740 Queensland Australia

THOMAS, REGINALD, foreign affairs diplomat.; b. Wels, Austria, Feb. 28, 1928; s. Leopold and Irma (Von Smekal) T.; m. Ingrid Renate Leitner, Nov. 26, 1960; children—Elisabeth, Alexander, Georg, Michael. J.D., U. Vienna (Austria), 1950. With Austrian Fgn. Service, 1951—; legation, Berne, 1952-56; dept. legal adviser on internat. law, Fgn. Ministry, Vienna, 1956-59; 1st sec. embassy, Tokyo, 1959-62; head office sec. gen. Fgn. Affairs, Vienna, 1962-68; ambassador to Pakistan, 1968-71, also Union of Burma, Japan, and Republic of Korea, 1971-75; head personnel div. Fgn. Ministry, Vienna, 1975-76, head dept. adminstrn., 1976-82, dep. sec. gen., 1978-82; ambassador to U.K., 1982-87. Decorated grand cross Japanese Order Rising Sun, Korean Order of Diplomatic Service, Jordanian Independence Order, Venezuelan Order of F. de Miranda; Hilal-i-Quaid-i-Azam (Pakistan). Mem. Austrian Assn. Fgn. Policy and Internat. Relations. Home: Schwarzenbergstrasse 8, 1010 Vienna Austria Office: Fed Ministry for Fgn Affairs, Ballhausplatz 2, A-1014 Vienna Austria

THOMAS, RICHARD L., banker; b. Marion, Ohio, Jan. 11, 1931; s. Marvin C. and Irene (Harruff) T.; m. Helen Moore, June 17, 1953; children: Richard L., David Paul, Laura Sue. B.A., Kenyon Coll., 1953; postgrad. (Fulbright scholar), U. Copenhagen, Denmark, 1954; M.B.A. (George F. Baker scholar), Harvard U., 1958. With First Nat. Bank Chgo., 1958—, asst. v.p., 1962-63, v.p., 1963-65; v.p., gen. mgr. First Nat. Bank Chgo. (London (Eng.) br.), 1965-66, v.p. term loan div., 1968, vice-chmn. bd., 1973-75, pres., dir., 1975—; sr. v.p., gen. mgr. First Chgo. Corp., 1969-72, exec. v.p., 1972-73; vice chmn. bd. 1973-74, pres., 1974—, also dir.; dir. CNA Fin. Corp., Sara Lee Corp., Chgo. Bd. Options Exchange. Trustee, past chmn. bd. trustees Kenyon Coll.; vice chmn. Rush-Presbyn.-St. Luke's Med. Ctr.; trustee Northwestern U.; chmn. bd., Orchestral Assn. Served with AUS, 1954-56. Mem. Chgo. Council Fgn. Relations (dir.), Phi Beta Kappa, Beta Theta Pi. Clubs: Sunningdale Golf (London); Economic (past pres.), Commercial, Chicago, Casino, Mid-America (Chgo.); Indian Hill (Winnetka, Ill.); Old Elm (Ft. Sheridan, Ill.). Office: 1st Chgo Corp 1 1st Nat Plaza Chicago IL 60670

THOMAS, ROBERT ALLEN, lawyer, consultant; b. Balt., Feb. 11, 1951; s. Robert Willis and Mildred Mary (Dooms-Hargis) T. BA, Allegheny Coll., 1973; MEd, Howard U., 1974; JD, New Eng. U., 1977; MBA, MPA, Boston U., 1988. Bar. Pa. 1977. Mem. staff U.S. Congress, 1973-75; legis. analyst taxation com. Mass. Ho. of Reps., 1975-77; sole practice, Meadville, Pa., 1977—; counsel Samuel T. Pees & Assocs., 1980—; dir. Amex Internat. Ltd., 1981—. Author: Ni Sekai Aida, 1986, Child of the American Raj, 1987, The Enemy Within, A Revisionist View of American Personnel Practices, 1988; contbr. articles to profl. publs. Bd. dirs. Martin Luther King, Jr. Scholarship Fund, 1982—; bd. dirs. Northwestern Legal Services Corp., 1980—, treas., 1982—, chmn. budget, personnel and fin. com., 1982—. Recipient Harry S. Truman Found. award, 1975. Mem. ABA, Pa. Bar Assn., Crawford County Bar Assn., NEA, Pa. State Edn. Assn., ACLU, NACCP. Democrat. Anglican. Address: 310-312 Chestnut St Meadville PA 16335

THOMAS, ROBERT RAY, management consultant; b. Columbus, Ohio, Dec. 14, 1926; s. Robert Ray and Esther Susan (Wolfe) T.; B.S. in TV Engring., Am. Inst. of Tech., 1950; m. Ann Lee Estes, Nov. 24, 1973; children—Sandra Ann, Robert Ray; 1 dau. by previous marriage, Margo Lynne. Electronic engr. Oakton Engring. Co., Evanston, Ill., 1949-50, Stewart Warner Corp., Chgo., 1950-51, Gen. Transformer Co., Homewood, Ill., 1951-53; electronic sales engr. Electronic Components Inc., Chgo., 1953-54; gen. mgr. West Coast, Miller Calson Services, Los Angeles, 1954-55; sales engr. R. Edward Steem Co., Chgo., 1955-59; dist. sales mgr. Motorola Semiconductor div. Motorola, Inc., Chgo. and Dallas, 1959-61; pres., chmn. bd. Enterprises Ltd. Co., Inc., Dallas, 1961—, pres. subs. Robert R. Thomas Co., 1961—, Rep. Mgmt. & Mktg. Counselors, 1969—; pres. Press Insulator Co., 1978—; co-founder CH&T Transformers Inc., 1983—; owner, pres. Westwood Creations, Inc., 1986—. Served with USAAF, 1945-46. Named Boss of Year, Big D chpt. Am. Bus. Womens Assn., 1965, Super Salesman by Purchasing Mag., Oct. 1975. Mem. Mfrs. Electronic Reps. Assn. (dir. S.W. chpt. 1964-69, pres. S.W. chpt. 1968-69), Sales and Mktg. Execs. of Dallas pres. (1977-78), S.W. Found. for Free Enterprise in Dallas (pres. 1976-77). Baptist. Lodge: Masons (Shriner). Office: 4134 Billy Mitchell Dr Dallas TX 75244

THOMAS, ROGER PARRY, interior designer, art consultant; b. Salt Lake City, Nov. 4, 1951; s. E. Parry and Peggy Chatterton T.; m. Marilyn Harris Hite, Nov. 21, 1976 (div. Apr. 1979); m. H. Andrea Wahn, Nov. 20, 1982. Student Interlochen Arts Acad., 1969; B.F.A., Tufts U., 1973. Pres. Miller-Thomas, Inc., Las Vegas, 1973-76; v.p. Yates-Silverman, Inc., Las Vegas, 1976-81; v.p. design Atlandia Design a Golden Nugget Co., Las Vegas, 1981—; curator Valley Bank Nev. Fine Art Collection. Bd. dirs. Nev. Dance Theatre; mem. McCarren Arts Adv. Bd., dir. Nev. Inst. Contemporary Art. Republican. Mem. Ch. of Jesus Christ of Latter-day Saints. Clubs: Sports Club, Country (Las Vegas). Office: Atlandia Design 3380 Arville St Las Vegas NV 89102

THOMAS, SUNDAY ASUQUO, chemistry educator; b. Abak, Akwa Ibom State, Nigeria, Feb. 18, 1951; s. Asuquo and Marit Thomas; m. Yetunde Temitope, Oct. 27, 1979; children: Aniekan, Iniobong, Uduak. BS in Chemistry with 1st class honors, Ahmadu Bello U., Zaria, Nigeria, 1975; PhD in X-ray Crystallography, Sussex U., Brighton, Eng., 1979. Sci. tutor Ind. High Sch., Ikot Ekpene, Nigeria, 1971-72; chemistry tutor Coll. Tech., Ilorin, Nigeria, 1975-76; grad. asst. Ahmadu Bello U., Zaria, 1976-77, asst. lectr., 1977-79, lectr., 1979-84, sr. lectr., 1984—; cons. Daje Tech. Co. Ltd., Kano, Nigeria, 1984; cons. in practical chemistry Nat. Edn. and Tech. Cen., Kaduna, Nigeria, 1986-87; chief examiner in chemistry Interim Joint Matriculation Bd., Zaria, 1986-87; moderator in chemistry Nat. Cert. in Edn., Zaria, 1983-87. Contbr. articles to profl. jours. Nat. pres. Nigeria Christian Grad. Fellowship, 1983-85; projects judge 6th Nat. Young Scientists competition, Kaduna, 1986; sec. Joint Chapel Council at Ahmadu Bello U., 1984-87. Recipient award for research and tng. Italian Govt. and 3d World Acad. Scis., U. Bologna, Italy, 1987-88. Mem. Am. Crystallographic Assn., Nigerian Assn. Math. Physics, Chem. Soc. Nigeria, Sci. Tchrs. Assn. Nigeria (vice chmn. Kaduna state br. 1982-83). Office: Ahmadu Bello U, Dept of Chemistry, Zaria Kaduna State Nigeria also: U Bologna care Prof Ripamonti, Dept Chemistry Via Selmi 2, 40126 Bologna Italy

THOMAS, WILLIAM ANDREW, computer and marketing consultant; b. Detroit, Sept. 9, 1962; s. Eugene Victor and Mary Elizabeth (Williams) T. Student, Shaw Coll., Detroit, 1976-78, Wayne State U., 1979-83, Ea. Mich. U., 1986—. Fin. planner Fin. Services Am., Bloomfield Hills, Mich., 1976-80; mktg. dir. Attainment Enterprises, Inc., Detroit, 1980-82, v.p., pub. relations, 1982-86, pres., chief exec. officer, 1986—; cons. Mich. Dept. Edn., Detroit, 1985—; cons. and mktg. researcher United Federated Exporting Co., Detroit, 1980-82; cons. Small Bus. Retailers Assn., Detroit, 1981-82, Boys Club of Detroit; lectr. in U.S., Can., Brazil, Africa, Asia. Asst. football coach Cass Tech. High Sch., Detroit, 1986—, head vollyball coach, 1986—; bd. dirs. Jr. Achievement, Detroit, 1979-80. Mem. Am. Mktg. Assn., Engring. Soc. Detroit, Entrepreneur Assn. Am., Internat. Financiers Am., Jaycees, Kappa Alpha Psi, Delta Sigma Pi. Clubs: Booster (Detroit) (pres.). Lodge: Masons. Office: Attainment Enterprises Inc 2727 2d Ave Suite 231 Detroit MI 48201

THOMASON, HARRY JACK LEE, JR., mechanical engineer; b. Washington, Apr. 12, 1953; s. Harry Emitte and Hattie Cornelia (Davis) T.; m. Ema Jean Bulaon, Dec. 15, 1974. AA, Prince Georges Community Coll., 1973; BS, U. Md., 1975. Cons. Thomason Solar Homes Inc., Ft. Washington, Md., 1975-79, v.p. engring., 1979-84; mech. engr. Naval Surface Weapons Ctr., Dahlgren, Va., 1984-86, White Oak, Md., 1986-87; energy conservation engr. Walter Reed Army Med. Ctr., Washington, 1987—; instr. solar house heating and cooling George Washington U., Washington, 1974-75. Contbr. articles to profl. jours. Patentee in field of solar energy. Recipient 1st place environ. award Isaac Walton League, 1971, spl. awards Washington Soc. Engrs., 1971, IEEE, 1971. Mem. ASME, Washinghton Soc. Engrs. Office: Walter Reed Army Med Ctr HSHL-EH Bldg 1 Washington DC 20307

THOMASON, ROBERT EARL, b. Pomona, Calif., July 28, 1932; s. Harl Louis and Carroll Edith (Smith) T.; m. Diane Louise Young, Aug. 23, 1952 (div. 1975); children—Elizabeth, Michelle, Robert, John, Mark; m. Vickie Ann Isbell, Mar. 28, 1975 (div. 1988); children—Victoria, Jason. B.Sc. in Agr., Calif. Poly. U., 1954. Tech. rep. Wilbur-Ellis Co., 1954-59; ranch mgr. DiGiorgio Corp., 1959-65; gen. mgr. Talwiwi Ranches, Litchfield Park, Ariz., 1965-69; dir. ops. Occidental-Libya Kufra Agrl. Project, 1969-72; agribus. rep. Occidental Petroleum Co., Saudi Arabia and Nigeria, 1972-82; mgr. environ. safety and adminstrn. services and leasehold devel. Occidental Oil Shale Inc., Grand Junction, Colo., 1974-81, v.p. environ. affairs, 1981-82; v.p. regulatory affairs Cathedral Bluffs Shale Oil Co., Grand Junction, 1982-86; safety and environment cons. Occidental de Colombia, 1986-88; mgr. environment and safety-Internat. Occidental Petroleum Corp., 1988—; v.p. Colo. Water Congress, Denver, 1983, pres., 1984. Mem. Am. Soc. Agrl. Engrs., Am. Soc. Agronomy. Republican. Office: care Oxy-USA Room 1725 PO Box 300 Tulsa OK 74102

THOMASSON, RAYMOND FRANKLIN, industrial chemist; b. Ansted, W.Va., Nov. 17, 1914; s. Charles L. and Mary Margaret (Holley) T. A.B., W.Va. U., 1940, B.S., 1940. Jr. chemist Wright Aero. Corp., Lockland, Ohio, 1940-41; chemist U.S. Rubber Co., Indpls., 1945-47; sr. health surveyor Monsanto Chem. Co., Miamisburg, Ohio, 1947-53; chemist C.& N.W. Ry., Chgo., 1953-57; sr. chemist Santa Fe R.R., from 1957; pvt. practice as cons. chemist, Cin., 1947-50, Dayton, Ohio, 1950-53; sr. health surveyor Chgo. Bd. Edn., 1971-81 . Mem. Naval Undersea Warfare Mus. Found. Served with AUS, 1942-45. Recipient Silver Beaver award Boy Scouts Am., 1986. Fellow Am. Inst. Chemists; mem. AAAS, Am. Chem. Soc., W.Va., Ind., Chgo. acads. sci., Franklin Inst., Am. Ordnance Assn., ASTM, Am. Accounting Assn., Art Inst. Chgo., NEA, Entomol. Soc., Washington, ALA, DAV, Am. Legion (life), The Nat. Assn. United Meth. Scouters (life), The Soc. John Wesley Fellows, Assn. Shrine Oriental Bands, De Molay Alumni Assn., others. Methodist. Lodges: Masons; Moose; Odd Fellows. Research in field. Home: 211 Wyoming St Charleston WV 25302

THOMKE, ERNST THEODOR, watch movement company executive; b. Biel, Berne, Switzerland, Apr. 21, 1939; s. Heinrich Ernst and Julia Johanna (Vetter) T.; m. Maria Katharina Pieren, Aug. 7, 1965; children—Sibylle Regula, Sabine Elisabeth, Niklaus Manuel. Student in chemistry and medicine U. Lausanne, U. Berne. Successively sales mgr. Swiss subs. Beecham AG, Berne, mktg. mgr., mktg. dir., mgr. European div.; pres. ETA SA Fabriques d'Ebauches, Grenchen, Solothurn, Switzerland, 1978-82, Ebauches SA, Grenchen, 1983-85, chief exec. officer, 1985—; exec. v.p. SMH Swiss Corp. for Microelectronics and Watchmaking Industries Ltd., 1985—. Office: ETA SA Fabriques d'Ebauches, Schildruststrasse 17, 2540 Grenchen, Solothurn Switzerland

THOMPSON, ALAN ERIC, economics educator; b. Sept. 16, 1924; s. Eric Joseph and Florence Thompson; m. Mary Heather Long, 1960; 4 children. M.A., U. Edinburgh, 1949, M.A. with 1st class honors, 1951, Ph.D., 1953. Asst. in polit. econ. U. Edinburgh, 1952-53, lectr. econs., 1953-59, 64-71; prof. econs. of govt. Heriot-Watt U., Edinburgh, 1972—; adviser to Scottish TV, 1966-76; Scottish gov. BBC, 1976-79; vis. prof. Grad. Sch. Bus., Stanford U. (Calif.), 1966, 68; chmn. adv. bd. econs. edn. Esmee Fairbairn Research Project, 1970-76; chmn. Kaiser Tech. and Devel. Trust, 1987—. Author: (with others) Development of Economic Doctrine, 1980; contbr. articles to profl. jours. M.P. Labour party, Dunfermline, 1959-64; mem. Scottish Com. Pub. Schs. Commn., 1969-70; mem. Joint Mil. Edn. Com. Edinburgh and Heriot-Watt Univs., 1975—, local govt. boundary commn. for Scotland, 1975-82; chmn. Northern Offshore Resources Study, 1974—; chmn. bd. govs. Newbattle Abbey Coll., 1980-82; bd. govs. Leigh Nautical Coll., 1981—; trustee Bell's Nautical Trust, 1981—. Served with Brit. Army, World War II. Carnegie Research scholar, 1951-52. Mem. Assn. Nazi War Camp Survivors (v.p. 1960—), Edinburgh Amenity and Transport Assn. (pres. 1970-75). Clubs: New, Edinburgh Univ. Staff (Edinburgh); Loch Earr Sailing. Office: Dept Econs Heriot Watt Univ, 31-35 Grassmarket, Edinburgh EH9 1SN, Scotland

THOMPSON, ARNOLD WILBUR, airport architect; b. Chgo., Oct. 26, 1926; s. Oscar and Emma S. (Terkelsen) T.; student U. Wis., 1944, U. Ky., 1945; B.S. in Architecture, U. Ill., 1950; m. Marian Harding, Dec. 30, 1950; children—Keith Arnold, Bruce Windsor, Douglas Scott. Project planner U.S. Public Housing Adminstrn., Chgo., 1950-52; cons. Bldg. and Furnishings Service YMCA, Chgo., 1952-55; regional architect Am. Airlines, Chgo., 1955-60, chief architect, 1960-64; pres. Arnold Thompson Assocs., Inc., N.Y.C., 1964-72; v.p. Lester B. Knight & Assocs., Inc., Riverside, Conn., 1972-77; pres. Arnold W. Thompson, P.C., Airport Facilities Cons., Hawthorne, N.Y., 1978-82; chmn. chief exec. officer Thompson Cons. Internat., Hawthorne, Reston, Va., Los Angeles, Washington, London, Miami, Fla., Chgo., 1982-85; chmn. Thompson Cons. Internat., Briarcliff Manor, N.Y., Dallas, Los Angeles, London, 1985—; chmn. bd. Potomac Assocs. Inc., Reston. Mem. New Castle Bd. Zoning Appeals, 1977-79; chmn. Chappaqua (N.Y.) Bd. Continuing Edn., 1980-86; bd. dirs. Bethel Nursing Home Corp., 1974-78. Served with U.S. Army, 1944-46. Registered profl. architect, N.Y., Conn., Fla., Ill., Ind., Ky., Mass., N.C., Pa., Va., Tex., also Nat. Council Archtl. Bds. Mem. AIA, ASCE, Am. Inst. Planners, Airport Cons. Council, Scarab. Congregationalist. Clubs: Wings (N.Y.C.); Whippoorwill (Armonk, N.Y.); Birchwood (Chappaqua). Office: Thompson Consultants Internat 575 N State Rd Briarcliff Manor NY 10510 also Office: 11733 Bowman Green Reston VA 22092 also Office: 452 NE 39th St Miami FL 33137 also Office: 8429 S Sepulveda Blvd Los Angeles CA 90065

THOMPSON, BRADBURY (JAMES), graphic designer; b. Topeka, Mar. 25, 1911; s. James Kay and Eunice (Bradbury) T.; m. Della Deen Dodge, Aug. 28, 1939; children—Leslie Dodge Keller, Mark Bradbury, David Dodge, Elizabeth Thompson Riley. A.B., Washburn U., 1934, D.F.A. (hon.), 1965; D.F.A. (hon.), R.I. Sch. Design, 1983. Dir. art Capper Publs., Inc., 1934-38, Rogers-Kellogg-Stillson, 1938-42; assoc. chief art sect. OWI State Dept., 1942-45. Art dir., Mademoiselle mag., 1945-59, Living for Young Homemakers, 1947-49; editor-designer, Westvaco Inspirations, 1938-62, 88; design dir., Art News mag., Art News Ann., 1945-72; design cons., Westvaco Corp., 1951-88, Famous Artists Schs., 1959-71, Pitney-Bowes, 1959-84, McGraw-Hill mags., 1960-77, Time-Life Books (Library of Art, 1965, Library of America, 1966, Foods of the World, 1966, The Swing Era, 1970), Field Enterprises Ednl. Corp., 1965-78, Harvard Bus. Rev., 1965-67, Cornell U., 1965-73; exhibited one man shows: AIGA Gallery, N.Y.C., 1959, 75, Washburn U., 1964, Cornell U., 1969, Rochester Inst. Tech., 1983, Internat. Typeface Corp., 1988; exhibited group shows: Alliance Graphique Internationale, Europe, 1955-67, Harvard, 1965, Yale, 1976, 87, Mus. Modern Art, N.Y.C. Faculty, Yale Sch. Art and Architecture, 1956-88. Author: Modern Painting and Typography, 1947, The Monalphabet, 1945, Alphabet 26, 1950; Designer for: books including Painting Toward Architecture, 1948, Photo-Graphic, 1949, Abstract Painting, 1951, Annual of Advt. Art, 1943, 54, Graphic Arts Prodn. Yearbook, 1948, 50, The Fiction Factory, 1955, Westvaco Am. Classics, 1958-83, The First 300 Years, 1967, Homage to the Book, 1968, The Quality of Life, 1968, The American Revolution: Three Views, 1975, the Washburn College Bible, 1979, Oxford edit., 1980; The Art of Graphic Design (Yale) 1988; Designer 985 U.S. Postage Stamps, 1958-88. Mem. Citizens Stamp Adv. Com., 1969—, 1st Fed. Design Assembly, 1973; bd. advisers Parsons Sch. Design, 1949-55; bd. govs. Phila. Mus. Coll. Art, 1956-59; bd. dirs. Perrot Meml. Library, 1966—, Am. Arbitration Assn., 1976-78; trustee Washburn U., 1972—. Recipient awards AIGA, 1948—; Gold T-Square Nat. Soc. Art Dirs., 1950; medals Art Dirs. Club, 1945, 47, 51 (2), 81 Soc. Publ. Designers, 1986, Type Dirs. Club medal, 1986; Distinguished Kansan award, 1983, Frederic Goudy award, Rochester Inst. Tech., 1983, Power of Print award Dimny, 1980; named to Art Dirs. Hall of Fame, 1977, N.Y. Printers Wall of Fame, 1983; Gold medal Sao Paulo Bienal, 1965; Silver medal, 1963;. Mem. Art Dirs. Club N.Y. (v.p., dir.), Am. Inst. Graphic Arts (dir., Gold medal 1975), Alliance Graphique Internationale, Soc. Illustrators, Alpha Delta, Delta Phi Delta. Congregationalist. Clubs: Dutch Treat, Riverside Yacht. Home: 25 Jones Park Riverside CT 06878

THOMPSON, BRUCE ALLAN, oil company executive, consultant; b. Alliance, Ohio, Apr. 24, 1938; s. George Otho and Gwendoline E. (Copeland) T.; m. Geraldine Ann Manley, June 15, 1963; children—Heather, Bruce, Jayson, Winston. B.S., Kent State U., 1960; M.S., Miami U., Oxford, Ohio, 1963. Cert. profl. geologist. Asst. dist. geologist Texaco Inc., Casper, Wyo., Billings, Mont., 1963-68; regional geologist Inexco Oil Co., Denver, Houston, 1968-79; exploration mgr. United Natural Resource, Denver, 1979-82; owner, mgr. Skull Creek Oil Co., Denver, 1982—; dir. Knee Hill Energy Co., Denver; cons. Viersen and Cochran, Denver, 1987—. Author: Stratigraphy of the Dunkard Basin, 1963; exploration guide Hydrocarbon Potential in Wyoming, 1974. Alt. del. Republican Party, Sedalia, Colo., 1984; active Ducks Unlimited, Castle Rock, Colo., 1983-84. Mem. Am. Assn. Petroleum Geologists, Am. Radio Relay League, Wyo. Geol. Assn. Houston Geol. Soc., Rocky Mountain Assn. Petroleum Geologists, Casper Petroleum Club, Denver Petroleum Club, Sigma Gamma Epsilon (Geol. Merit award 1962). Episcopalian. Clubs: Diehl Lake Country (Ohio) (fin. com. 1984—); Brown Palace (Colo.). Office: Skull Creek Oil 1615 California St Suite 615 Denver CO 80202

THOMPSON, DAVID ALFRED, industrial engineer; b. Chgo., Sept. 9, 1929; s. Clifford James and Christobel Eliza (Sawin) T.; children: Nancy, Brooke, Lynda, Diane, Kristy. B.M.E., U. Va., 1951; B.S. in Indsl. Engring, U. Fla., 1955, M.S. in Engring, 1956; Ph.D., Stanford U., 1961. Registered profl. engr., Calif. Research asst. U. Fla. Engring. and Industries Exptl. Sta., Gainesville, 1955-56; instr. indsl. engring. Stanford U., 1956-58, acting asst. prof., 1958-61, asst. prof., 1961-64, asso. prof., 1964-72, prof., 1972—, prof., asso. chmn. dept. indsl. engring., 1972—; prin. investigator NASA Ames Research Center, Moffatt Field, Calif., 1974—; cons. Dept. of State, Fed. EEO Commn.; maj. U.S. and fgn. cos.; cons. emergency communications center design Santa Clara County Criminal Justice Bd., 1975, Bay Area

Rapid Transit Control Center, 1977; clin. faculty med. sch. U. Calif., San Francisco; mem. com. for office computers Calif. OSHA. Dir., editor: documentary film Rapid Answers for Rapid Transit, Dept. Transp., 1974; contbr. articles profl. jours; editorial adv. bd.: Computers and Graphics, 1970—; reviewer: Indsl. Engring. and IEEE Transactions, 1972—. Served to lt. USNR, 1951-54. HEW grantee, 1967-70. Mem. Am. Inst. Indsl. Engrs., Human Factors Soc., IEEE, Am. Robotics Soc., Soc. Info. Display. Home: 101 Peter Coutts Circle Stanford CA 94305 Office: Stanford U Dept Indsl Engring Stanford CA 94305

THOMPSON, DAVID F., lawyer; b. Chgo., Oct. 19, 1942; s. Charles F. and Helen (Enright) T.; m. Monica McAleer, Dec. 15, 1973; children—Megan, Kristin. B.S., Loyola U., Chgo., 1965, M.S. in Indsl. Relations, 1966; J.D., Northwestern U., 1969. Bar: Ill. 1970, U.S. Dist. Ct. (no. dist.) Ill. 1970. Assoc., McDermott, Will & Emery, Chgo., 1969-72; asst. v.p. First Nat. Bank of Chgo., 1972-77; ptnr. Daleiden, Thompson & Tremaine, Ltd. and predecessors, Chgo., 1977—. Mem. ABA, Ill. State Bar Assn. Home: 1529 E Course Dr Riverwoods IL 60015 Office: Daleiden Thompson & Tremaine Ltd 20 N Wacker Dr Chicago IL 60606

THOMPSON, DEAN ALLAN, cattleman; b. Peru, Ind., Jan. 29, 1934; s. Paul Franklin and Pauline St. Clair (Thrush) T. Student Purdue U., 1952-54. Mgr. Thompson Farms, breeders registered Hereford cattle, Peru, 1956-69; owner Thompson Farms, Wartrace, Tenn. and Peru, 1970-87, Dean Thompson Prodns., Wartrace, Wartrace Records; chmn. bd. Instant Copy and Printing, Inc., Monterrey, Calif., 1976-86, Trenton Energy Inc., 1977-83, Bloomfield, Ind.; v.p., dir. 5B Cattle Co., Twin Bridges, Mont., 1986-87; ptnr., Brann-Thompson Ltd.; internat. beef cattle judge; dir. Maine Manna, Gorham. Bd. dirs. Thrush-Thompson Found. (formerly H.A. Thrush Found.), Peru; trustee Middle Tenn. State U. Found., 1981-83, 85—, chmn. fin. com., 1982-83, 85-87, exec. com., 1983-87, sec. 1988; precinct committeeman, chmn. Miami County (Ind.) Young Republican Com., 1962-67; treas. 5th Dist. Young Reps., 1965-66; elected elder Presbyterian Ch., 1986-88. Served with U.S. Army, 1955-56. Mem. Nat. Western (dir.), Ind. (dir. 1958-68, pres. 1960) polled Hereford assns., Ind. Cattleman's Assn. (founding dir.), Ind. Livestock Breeders Assn., Am. Hereford Assn. (v.p. pres.'s council 1981, pres. 1982), Tenn. Hereford Assn. (dir. 1977-81, v.p. 1979, pres. 1980-81). Clubs: Toastmasters (pres., area gov.); Columbia (Indpls.). Home and Office: 900 19th Ave S Nashville TN 37212

THOMPSON, DENNIS PETERS, plastic surgeon; b. Chgo., Mar. 18, 1937; s. David John and Ruth Dorothy (Peters) T.; m. Virginia Louise Williams, June 17, 1961; children: Laura Faye, Victoria Ruth, Elizabeth Jan. BS, U. Ill., 1957, BS in Medicine, 1959, MS in Physiology, MD, 1961. Diplomate Am. Bd. Surgery, Am. Bd. Plastic Surgery. Intern Presbyn.-St. Lukes Hosp., Chgo., 1961-62; resident in gen. surgery Mayo Clinic, Rochester, Minn., 1964-66, fellow in gen. surgery, 1964-66; resident in gen. surgery Harbor Gen. Hosp., Los Angeles, 1968-70; resident in plastic surgery UCLA, 1971-73, clin. instr. plastic surgery, 1975-82, asst. clin. prof. surgery, 1982—; practice medicine specializing in plastic and reconstructive surgery, Los Angeles, 1974-78, Santa Monica, Calif., 1978—; chmn. plastic surgery sect. St. John's Hosp., 1986—; mem. staff Santa Monica Hosp., UCLA Ctr. Health Scis., Brotman Med. Ctr.; chmn. dept. surgery Beverly Glen Hosp., 1978-79; pres. Coop. of Am. Physicians Credit Union, 1978-80, bd. dirs., 1980—, chmn. promotion com., 1983—, treas., 1985—. Contbr. articles to med. jours. Moderator Congl. Ch. of Northridge (Calif.), 1975-76, chmn. bd. trustees, 1973-74, 80-82. Am. Tobacco Inst. research grantee, 1959-60. Fellow ACS; mem. AMA (Physicians Recognition award 1971, 74, 77, 81, 84, 87), Calif. Med. Assn., Los Angeles County Med. Assn. (chmn. bylaws com. 1979-80, chmn. ethics com. 1980-81, sec.-treas. dist. 5 1982-83, program chmn. 1983-84, pres. 1985-86), Pan-Pacific Med. Assn., Am. Soc. Plastic Surgeons, Calif. Soc. Plastic Surgeons (chmn. bylaws com. 1982-83, chmn. liability com. 1983-85), Los Angeles Soc. Plastic Surgeons (sec. 1980-82, pres. 1982-88), Am.Soc. Plastic and Reconstructive Surgeons (pres. Los Angeles chpt. 1982-88), Lipoplasty Soc. N.Am., UCLA Plastic Surgery Soc. (treas. 1983-84), Am. Soc. Aesthetic Plastic Surgery, Western Los Angeles Regional C. of C. (bd. dirs. 1981-84, 86-88, chmn. legis. action com. 1978-80), Santa Monica C. of C., Phi Beta Kappa, Alpha Omega Alpha, Nu Sigma Nu, Phi Kappa Phi. Republican. Office: 2001 Santa Monica Blvd Santa Monica CA 90404

THOMPSON, DENNIS ROY, information management executive; b. Chgo., Apr. 11, 1939; s. Roy Gustav and Charlotte Rose (Schultz) T.; m. Donna Tello; children: Jesse, Kimbrelle. BSEE with honors, U. Ill., 1964; MS in Bus. Adminstrn., UCLA, 1967. Ops. research cons. Dart Industries, Los Angeles, 1969-70; pres. Seahill, Inc., Los Angeles, 1971-72; dir. credit analysis Comml. Credit Co., Balt., 1973-77; pres. Epicom, Inc., San Diego, 1978—; pub. RFP Publs., 1983—; lectr. data processing and computer sci. San Diego Community Coll. Patentee matchbook. Founder and past chmn. UNIX/C SIG, San Diego; sec., Annapolis (Md.) Libertarians, 1975; 1988 Libertarian Candidate for Calif. 44th Congl. Dist. Served with U.S. Army, 1959-61. Mem., Assn. Computing Machinery, IEEE, Data Processing Mgmt. Assn., Mensa. Club: Toastmasters (Able Toastmaster 1987). Office: RFP Publs 3647 Fairmount Ave San Diego CA 92105

THOMPSON, ELAINE VERA, political science educator; b. Sydney, Australia, Oct. 20, 1944; m. Bob Thompson, 1969; 2 children. B of Econs. with honors, U. Sydney, 1967, PhD, 1973. Tutor dept. govt. U. Sydney, 1967-72; lectr. Sch. Polit. Sci., U. New South Wales, Sydney, 1973-81, sr. lectr., 1981—; internat. visitor USIS, Dept. State, 1978; vis. prof. Pa. State U., State College, 1980, Am. U., Washington, 1980. Co-author: Changing the System, 1984; co-editor: Change the Rules, 1977, Australian Quar., 1985—; contbr. chpts. to books. Pres. Friends of A.B.C. Australian Am. Ednl. Found. Fulbright scholar, 1980, sr. Fulbright scholar, 1986. Mem. Australian Inst. Polit. Sci. (bd. dirs. 1978—), Australasian Polit. Studies Assn. (v.p. 1981-82, pres. 1982-83), Royal Australian Inst. Pub. Adminstrn. Office: U New South Wales, Sch Polit Sci, PO Box 1, 2044 Kensington Australia

THOMPSON, GEORGE LEE, manufacturing company executive; b. Denver, June 12, 1933; s. George H. and Frances M. (Murphy) T.; m. Jean G. Meier, Aug. 25, 1957; children: Shannon, Tracy, Bradley. B.S. in Bus, U. Colo., 1957; postgrad. in advanced mgmt, N.Y. U., 1969. With GTE Sylvania, Denvers, Mass., 1957-65, nat. sales mgr., 1965-67, mktg. mgr., 1967-68; v.p. sales entertainment products Batavia, N.Y., 1968-73; dir. mktg. Stamford, Conn., 1973-74; v.p. mktg. Servomation Corp., N.Y.C., 1974-76; exec. v.p. Servomation Corp., 1976-78, Singer Co., Edison, N.J., 1978-81; pres. Singer Co., 1981-83; pres. consumer products SCM Corp., N.Y.C., 1983-86; pres., chief exec. officer Smith-Corona Corp., New Canaan, Conn., 1986—; bd. dirs. Smith Corona Ltd., U.K., Singapore, Can. Mem. St. John Assn. (dir., pres.), Atrium Villa Assn. (dir., treas.), Chi Psi. Episcopalian. Clubs: New Canaan Field, Woodway Country, Seabright Lawn Tennis, Landmark, Seabrook Ocean. Home: 10 St John Pl New Canaan CT 06840 Office: Smith Corona Corp 65 Locust Ave New Canaan CT 06840

THOMPSON, GILBERT RICHARD, physician; b. Poona, India, Nov. 20, 1932; s. Richard Louis and Violet Mary (Harrison) T.; m. Sheila Jacqueline Deurvorst, June 14, 1958; children—Anna, Mark, Philip, Jennifer. M.B., B.S., St. Thomas Hosp. Med. Sch., 1956; M.D., U. London, 1963. Med. Research Council travelling fellow Mass. Gen. Hosp., Boston, 1966-67; hon. cons. physician Hammersmith Hosp., London, 1967—; hon. sr. lectr. Royal Postgrad. Med. Sch., 1967—; asst. prof. Baylor U. Coll. Medicine, Houston, 1972-73; vis. prof. McGill U., Montreal, Que., Can., 1981-82. Contbr. numerous sci. articles to profl. jours. Served to capt. M.C., Brit. Army, 1957-63. Recipient Lucian award Mc-Gill U.-Royal Victoria Hosp., 1982. Fellow Royal Coll. Physicians, Am. Heart Assn. (council on arteriosclerosis); mem. European Atherosclerosis Soc., Brit. Atherosclerosis Discussion Group, Royal Soc. Medicine (chmn. com. forum on lipids 1984-87). Roman Catholic. Avocations: fly-fishing; squash; skiing. Home: 3 Queen Anne's Gardens, London W4 1TU, England Office: Med Research Council, Lipoprotein Team, Hammersmith Hosp, London W12 OHS, England

THOMPSON, GRAHAM, building material executive; b. Harrow, England, Oct. 25, 1938; s. Leslie Arnold and Alice Elizabeth (Rhodes) T.; m. Gillian Margaret Rose, June 16, 1962; 1 child, Mark Andrew. BSc in Mech. Engring. with hons., U. Leeds, England, 1961. Chartered mech. engr. Devel. mgr. Butterley Brick Co. Ltd., Derby, Eng., 1963-66; prodn. mgr. Westbrick Ltd., Exeter, Eng., 1966-69; mng. dir. Westbrick Ltd., Exeter, 1969-75, chmn., 1975-77; mng. dir. Beazer Bldg. Materials, Exeter, 1983-84; chief exec. Tarmac Bricks and Tiles, Exeter, 1987—, Westbrick Ltd., Exeter, Eng., 1984—; mng. dir. Hawkins Tiles Ltd., Cannock, Eng., 1987—, Severn Valley Brick Co. Ltd., Avonmouth, 1988—. Fellow Inst. Energy, Inst. Ceramics; mem. Inst. Mech. Engrs., Brick Devel. Assn. (chmn. 1982-84, 86—), Nat. Fedn. Clay Industries (pres. 1987—). Mem. Social Democratic Party. Office: Westbrick Ltd, Pinhoe, Exeter EX4 8JT, England

THOMPSON, HERBERT ERNEST, tool and die co. exec.; b. Jamaica, N.Y., Sept. 8, 1923; s. Walter and Louise (Joly) T.; student Stevens Inst. Tech., 1949-51; m. Patricia Elaine Osborn, Aug. 2, 1968; children—Robert Steven, Debra Lynn. Foreman, Conner Tool Co., 1961-62, Eason & Waller Grinding Corp., 1962-63; owner Endco Machined Products, 1966-67, Thompson Enterprises, 1974—; pres. Method Machined Products, Phoenix, 1967; pres., owner Quality Tool, Inc., 1967—. Served to capt. USAAF, 1942-46. Decorated D.F.C., Air medal with cluster. Home: 14009 N 42d Ave Phoenix AZ 85023 Office: 4223 W Clarendon Ave Phoenix AZ 85019

THOMPSON, JAMES ROBERT, governor of Illinois; b. Chgo., May 8, 1936; s. James Robert and Agnes Josephine (Swanson) T.; m. Jayne Carr, 1976; 1 dau., Samantha Jayne. Student, U. Ill., Chgo., 1953-55, Washington U., St. Louis, 1955-56; J.D., Northwestern U., 1959. Bar: Ill. 1959, U.S. Supreme Ct. 1964. Asst. state's atty. Cook County, Ill., 1959-64; assoc. prof. law Northwestern U. Law Sch., 1964-69; asst. atty. gen. State Ill., 1969-70; chief criminal div. 1969, chief dept. law enforcement and pub. protection, 1969-70; 1st asst. U.S. atty. No. Dist. Ill., 1970-71, U.S. atty., 1971-75; counsel firm Winston & Strawn, Chgo., 1975-77; gov. Ill., 1977—; mem. joint com. to revise Ill. criminal code, mem. drafting subcom. Chgo.-Ill. bar assns., 1959-63, chmn. joint com. to draft indigent def. legis., 1966-68; mem. com. to draft handbooks for petit jurors in civil and criminal cases and for grand jurors Jud. Conf. Ill., 1959; mem. com. to draft uniform instrn. in criminal cases Ill. Supreme Ct.; co-dir. criminal law course for Chgo. Police and Indsl. Security Personnel, 1962-64; mem. Chgo. Mayor's Com. to Draft Legis. to Combat Organized Crime, 1964-67; adviser Pres.'s Commn. Law Enforcement and Adminstrn. Justice, 1966; mem. Pres.'s Task Force on Crime, 1967; lectr. Northwestern U. Law Sch., U. Calif.-Davis, Mich. State U., Nat., Ill., Ohio, N.D., Va., N.J., Ala., Md. and Ga. prosecutors' assns.; former bd. dirs. Chgo. Crime Commn.; v.p. Americans for Effective Law Enforcement, 1967-69. Co-author: Cases and Comments on Criminal Justice, 2 vols, 1968, 74, Criminal Law and Its Adminstration, 1970, 74; asst. editor-in-chief: Jour. Criminal Law, Criminology and Police Sci, 1965-69; bd. editors: Criminal Law Bull. Mem. ABA, Ill. Bar Assn. (past chmn. criminal law sect.). Republican. Office: Office of Gov 207 State House Springfield IL 62706 *

THOMPSON, JERE WILLIAM, retail food and dairy company executive; b. Dallas, Jan. 18, 1932; s. Joe C. and Margaret (Philp) T.; m. Peggy Dunlap, June 5, 1954; children: Michael, Jere W., Patrick, Deborah, Kimberly, Christopher, David. Grad. high sch., 1950; B.B.A., U. Tex., 1954. With Southland Corp., Dallas, 1954—; v.p. stores Southland Corp. (merged with Thompson Co. 1988), Dallas, 1962-73, exec. v.p., 1973-74, pres., 1974—, dir., 1962—, chief exec. officer, 1986—; bd. dirs. MCorp, Texstyrene Corp. Bd. dirs. St. Paul Hosp. Found. Served to lt. (j.g.) USNR, 1954-56. Office: Southland Corp 2828 N Haskell Ave Dallas TX 75221 *

THOMPSON, JOHN ALEXANDER, historian, educator; b. Coulsdon, Surrey, Eng., Oct. 23, 1938; s. Harold Charles and Viviane (Dragonetti) T.; m. Dorothy Joan Walbank, July 21, 1982. BA, Cambridge U., 1962, PhD, 1969. Asst. lectr. history Univ. Coll., London, 1966-68, lectr., 1968-71; asst. lectr. history Cambridge (Eng.) U., 1971-73, lectr., 1973—. Author: Reformers and War, 1987; contbr. articles to hist. jours. Served with RAF, 1957-59. Fellow Royal Hist. Soc.; mem. Orgn. Am. Historians, Soc. for Historians Am. Fgn. Relations, Brit. Assn. for Am. Studies. Home: 66 Grantchester Meadows, Cambridge CB3 9JL, England Office: St Catherine's Coll, Cambridge CB2 1RL, England

THOMPSON, JOHN OSBORNE, communication studies educator; b. Toronto, Feb. 21, 1947; arrived in Eng, 1970; s. Victor Arthur and Jean Alberta May (Ross) T.; m. Ann Harris, May 1, 1972. BA, U. Alberta, Edmonton, 1968, MA, 1972. Lectr. dept. communication studies U. Liverpool, Eng., 1972-84, lectr. in charge, 1984—. Author: Echo and Montana, 1980; (with Ann Thompson) Shakespeare, Meaning and Metaphor, 1987; editor: Monte Python: Complete and Utter Theory of the Grotesque, 1982. Chmn., film and video panel Merseyside Arts, Liverpool, 1984—. Mem. Semiotic Soc. Am., Internat. Assn. Semiotic Studies, Poetics and Linguistics Assn., British Film Inst. Office: U Liverpool Dept Communications, Liverpool L69 3BK, England

THOMPSON, JOHN P., retail food executive; b. Dallas, Nov. 2, 1925; s. Joe E. and Margaret (Philip) T.; m. Mary Carol Thomson, June 5, 1948; children: Mary Margaret, Henry Douglas, John P. B.B.A., U. Tex., 1948. With Southland Corp. (merged with Thompson Co. 1988), Dallas, 1948—, pres., 1961-69, chief exec. officer, 1969-86, chmn., 1969—, also bd. dirs. Office: Southland Corp 2828 N Haskell Ave Dallas TX 75221 *

THOMPSON, JOHN THEODORE, communications consultant; b. Decorah, Iowa, Mar. 5, 1917; s. Theodore Elmer and Bertha (Rod) T.; m. Dorothea Mae Green, Oct. 3, 1942; children—Jennifer Lynn, Melinda McLean; m. Jessie S. Bennett, Feb. 14, 1987. A.B., U. Mich., 1939. With Gen. Electric Co., 1939-58; mgr. distbn. sales electronics div. Gen. Electric Co., Schenectady, 1948-58; v.p. Raytheon Co., 1958-62; v.p. IT&T, 1962-67, sr. v.p., 1967-69; pres., chmn. bd., chief exec. officer Advance Ross Corp., 1969-70; v.p. Gen Telephone & Electronics Internat. Co., 1970-72; now vice chmn. Aarque Cos.; dir. Emery Air Freight Corp. Served to lt. (s.g.) USNR, 1943-46. Mem. Delta Upsilon. Clubs: Canadian (N.Y.C.); Greenwich Country, Indian Harbor Yacht. Home: 263 Overlook Dr Greenwich CT 06830

THOMPSON, K(ENNETH) REED, electrical engineer; b. Alma, Ga., Feb. 20, 1931; s. Howard and Larue (Head) T.; BEE, Ga. Inst. Tech., 1953, MSEE, 1954; m. Margaret Louise Drody, Mar. 22, 1952; children: Larry Stephen, Fred Lamar. With Ga. Power Co., Atlanta, 1950-52; with Gen. Electric Co., 1954—, systems engr., 1958-61, sr. systems engr., 1961-66, engring. unit mgr., 1966-71, GE Drive Systems Dept. engring. subsect. mgr., 1971-78, mgr. metal industry engring., Salem, Va., 1978-82, mgr. automated systems engring., 1982-84, mgr. advanced systems engring., 1985-87, project mgr., 1988—; adj. faculty Ga. Inst. Tech., 1953-54, U. Va. Extension, Roanoke, 1955-58; dir. Trendy Enterprises Inc.; bd. dirs. Order of the Engr., Va. Link, chmn., 1988—. Recipient Gen. Electric Cordiner award, 1963; registered profl. engr., Va. Mem. IEEE (sr. mem., region 3 chmn. 1982-83, dir. 1982-83, Centennial award 1984 Outstanding Service award 1986), Nat. Soc. Profl. Engrs., Va. Soc. Profl. Engrs. (dir. 1985-88, pres. Roanoke chpt. 1986-87, v.p. 1988—, Outstanding Service award 1987), Assn. Iron and Steel Engrs., Roanoke Valley Astron. Soc. (v.p. 1985-88), Va. Assn. Astron. Soc. (gen. chmn. 1986—), Tau Beta Pi, Eta Kappa Nu, Phi Kappa Tau. Club: Briaereans. Patentee in field (7 U.S., 7 fgn.). Office: Gen Electric Corp 1501 Roanoke Blvd Rm 151 Salem VA 24153

THOMPSON, LARRY ANGELO, lawyer, producer, personal manager; b. Clarksdale, Miss., Aug. 1, 1944; s. Angelo and Anne (Tuminello) T.; m. Pamela Edwards, Dec. 15, 1974 (div.). BBA, U. Miss., 1966, JD, 1968. Bar: Miss. 1968, Calif. 1970. In-house counsel Capitol Records, Hollywood, Calif., 1969-71; sr. ptnr. in entertainment law Thompson, Shankman and Bond, Beverly Hills, Calif., 1971-77; pres. Larry A. Thompson Orgn., Inc., 1977—; co-owner New World Pictures, 1983-85; lectr. entertainment bus. UCLA, U. So. Calif., Southwestern U. Law Sch. Co-chmn. Rep. Nat. Entertainment Com.; apptd. by Gov. of Calif. to Calif. Entertainment Commn. Recipient Show Bus. Atty. of Yr. award Capitol Records, 1971. Mem. Inauguration of Thompson Ctr. for Fine Arts in Clarksdale, Miss., 1986. Served with JAGC, U.S. Army, 1966-72. Mem. ABA, Miss. Bar Assn., Calif. Bar Assn., Inter-Am. Bar Assn., Hon. Order Ky. Colonels, Am. Film Inst., Nat. Acad. Recording Arts and Scis. Republican. Roman Catholic. Author: How to Make a Record Deal & Have Your Songs Recorded, 1975, Prime Time Crime, 1982; producer: Jim Nabors TV Show, 1977 (Emmy nominee), (series) Mickey Spillane's Mike Hammer, 1981, Bring 'Em Back Alive, 1982, Mickey Spillane's Murder Me, Murder You, 1982, (TV movies) The Other Lover, 1985, Convicted, 1986, Intimate Encounters, 1986, The Woman He Loved, 1988, (motion picture) Crimes of Passion, 1984, Quiet Cool, 1987, My Demon Lover, 1987. Home: 9451 Hidden Valley Pl Beverly Hills CA 90210 Office: 1440 S Sepulveda Blvd Suite 118 Los Angeles CA 90025

THOMPSON, LEE BENNETT, lawyer; b. Miami, Indian Ter., Mar. 2, 1902; s. P.C. and Margerie Constance (Jackson) T.; m. Elaine Bizzell, Nov. 27, 1928; children: Lee Bennett, Ralph Gordon, Carolyn Elaine (Mrs. Don T. Zachritz). B.A., U. Okla., 1925, LL.B., 1927. Bar: Okla. 1927. Since practiced in Oklahoma City; spl. justice Okla. Supreme Ct., 1967-68; past sec., gen. counsel, dir. Mustang Fuel Corp. Past sec. Masonic Charity Found. Okla.; past chmn. Okla. County chpt. ARC, past chmn. resolutions com. nat. conv.; founding mem. Dean's Council, U. Okla. Coll. Law; past dir. Oklahoma City Symphony Orch., Oklahoma City Community Fund. Served to col. AUS, 1940-46. Decorated Legion. of Merit; recipient Distinguished Service citation U. Okla., 1971; Rotary Found. Paul Harris fellow. Fellow Am. Bar Found. (past Okla. chmn.), Okla. Bar Found., Am. Coll. Trial Lawyers (past Okla. chmn.); mem. Oklahoma City C. of C. (past bd. dirs.), Oklahoma City Jr. C. of C. (past pres.), U.S. Jr. C. of C. (past dir., v.p.), ABA (del. 1972, past mem. com. law and nat. security, past mem. spl. com. on fed. ct. procedure), Okla. Bar Assn. (past mem. ho. dels., pres. 1972, Pres.'s award, profl. responsibility commn.), Oklahoma County Bar Assn. (past pres., Jour. Record award), Okla. Bar Found. (trustee 1971-76, 81-84), U. Okla. Alumni Assn. (past mem. exec. com.), U. Okla. Meml. Student Union (past pres., Greek Alumnus of Yr. award 1982), Oklahoma City Zool. Soc. (past bd. dirs.), Am. Judicature Soc., Mil. Order World Wars, Mil. Order Carabao, Am. Legion, Phi Beta Kappa (Phi Beta Kappa of Yr. 1982), Beta Theta Pi (past v.p., trustee). Democrat. Mem. First Christian Ch. (past deacon, life elder). Clubs: Mason (Shriner, Jester, 33 deg.), Rotary (past pres.), University, Men's Dinner (past mem. exec. com.), Oklahoma City Golf and Country, Beacon. Home: 539 NW 38th St Oklahoma City OK 73118 Office: 2120 First Nat Bldg Oklahoma City OK 73102

THOMPSON, LINDA RUTH, psychiatrist; b. Bristol, Va., May 17, 1941; d. Eugene Cassidy and Kitty Ruth (Corum) T.; A.B., King Coll., 1962; M.D., U. Va., 1966; children—Ethan Eugene, Daniel Richard. Diplomate Am. Bd. Psychiatry and Neurology. Intern, State U. of Iowa Hosp., Iowa City, 1966-67; resident in psychiatry U. Va. Hosp., Charlottesville, 1967-71; practice medicine specializing in psychiatry, Bristol, Va. Mem. Am. Psychiat. Assn., Tenn. Psychiat. Assn., Am. Psychoanalytic Assn., Washington Psychoanalytic Soc. Office: 1909 Euclid Ave Bristol VA 24201

THOMPSON, LOHREN MATTHEW, oil company executive; b. Sutherland, Nebr., Jan. 21, 1926; s. John M. and Anna (Ecklund) T.; children—Terence M., Sheila M., Clark M. Ed., U. Denver. Spl. rep. Standard Oil Co., Omaha, 1948-56; v.p. mktg. Frontier REF. co., 1967-68; mgr. mktg. U.S. region Husky Oil Co., Denver, 1968-72; v.p. Westar Stas., Inc., Denver, 1967-70; pres., chmn. bd. Colo. Petroleum, Denver, 1971—. Served with USAAF, 1944-46. Mem. Colo. Petroleum Council, Am. Petroleum Inst., Am. Legion. Democrat. Lutheran. Clubs: Denver Petroleum, Denver Oilman's Lodge: Lions. Home: 2410 Spruce Ave Estes Park CO 80517 Office: Colo Petroleum 4080 Globeville Rd Denver CO 80216

THOMPSON, LOUIS MILTON, agronomy educator; b. Throckmorton, Tex., May 15, 1914; s. Aubrey Lafayette and Lola Terry (Frazier) T.; m. Margaret Stromberg, July 10, 1937 (dec. Nov. 1972); children—Louis Milton, Margaret Ann, Glenda Ray, Carolyn Terry, Jerome Lafayette. B.S., Tex. A. and M. Coll., 1935; M.S., Iowa State U., 1947, Ph.D., 1950. Soil surveyor Tex., 1935-36, 39-40; instr. Tex. A. and M. Coll., 1936-39, 40-42; asst. prof. soils Iowa State U., Ames, 1947-50; prof. soils, head farm operation curriculum Iowa State U., 1950-58, assoc. dean agr. charge resident instrn., 1958-83, emeritus prof. agronomy, 1983—, assoc. dean emeritus, 1984—. Author: Soils and Soil Fertility, rev. edit, 1957, co-author rev. edit., 1978, Russian edit., 1983; Contbr. articles on weather-crop yield models and climate change to profl. jours. Served with AUS, 1942-46; col. Res. (ret.). Recipient Henry A. Wallace award disting. service to agr., 1982. Fellow AAAS, Am. Soc. Agronomy, Soil Sci. Soc. Am., Soil and Water Conservation Soc. (Pres.'s citation); mem. Am. Meteorol. Soc., Sigma Xi, Alpha Zeta (Tall Corn award 1957), Gamma Sigma Delta (nat. pres. 1956-58), Phi Kappa Phi (chpt. pres. 1961), Farm House (hon.). Presbyn. (elder). Club: Rotarian (past local pres.). Home: 414 Lynn Ave Ames IA 50010

THOMPSON, MALCOLM FRANCIS, electrical engineer; b. Charleston, S.C., Sept. 2, 1921; s. Allen R. and Lydia (Brunson) T.; BS, Ga. Inst. Tech., 1943, MS, 1947; postgrad. Mass. Inst. Tech., 1947-49; m. Ada Rose O'Quinn, Jan. 20, 1943; children: Rose Mary, Nancy Belle, Susan Elizabeth, Frances Josephine. Instr. dept. elec. engring. Mass. Inst. Tech., 1947-49; research engr. Autonetics Co., Anaheim, Calif., 1949-70; tech. dir. SRC div. Moxon, Inc., Irvine, Calif., 1970-73; engring. mgr., mgr. computers and armament controls. Northrop Aircraft Div., Hawthorne, Calif., 1973-87; ind. cons., 1987—. Served to capt. AUS, 1943-46. Mem. IEEE, Nat. Geog. Soc., Nat. Rifle Assn., Am. Ordnance Assn., Eta Kappa Nu. Patentee in field. Home and Office: 1602 Indus St Santa Ana CA 92707

THOMPSON, MARY JEAN, interior designer, lecturer; b. Salem, Oreg., Aug. 6, 1935; d. Lester Wayne and Bernis Laverne (Nelson) Schrunk; m. Newton L. Thompson, July 5, 1962 (div.); children—Craig L., Brooks D., K. Inga, Heidi A. B.A. cum laude in Music, Lewis and Clark Coll., 1957; B.A. cum laude in Interior Design, U. Utah, 1969. Designer, Clark Leaming Co., Salt Lake City, 1967-69; pres. Thompson Design Assocs., Inc., Reno, 1970—; pres. Faile Thompson Wardrobe Systems, 1987—. Bd. dirs. Community Concerts, 1975-76, Washoe Landmark Preservation, 1976-82, Sierra Nev. Mus. of Art, 1980—; co-chmn. Nev. Gov.'s Conf. for Women, 1988-89. Recipient McGraw Edison Lighting Excellence award, 1978; AIA honor award, 1981. Mem. Am. Soc. Interior Designers (cert. 1970, Merit award ASID/Wilsonart design competition 1983), Nat. Assn. Mirror Mfrs. (design award 1987), AIA (affiliate mem., dir. No. Nev. chpt. 1981-82). Interiors include: Western Nev. Community Coll., 1976, Reno Internat. Airport, 1981, Sparks Family Hosp., 1982, Westlake Community Hosp., 1984, Panorama Community Hosp., 1984, Harrah's Tahoe, 1983-84, Wellington (Fla.) Regional Med. Ctr., 1986, Inland Valley (Calif.) Med. Ctr., 1986, Roseville (Calif.) Community Hosp., 1986. Interiors featured in Designers West Mag., Dec. 1983, Interior Design Mag., Dec. 1983, Contract Mag., Feb. 1984, 88, Restaurant & Hotel Design, 1987.

THOMPSON, NANCY ETHELYN, association executive; b. Greene County, Ark., June 10, 1925; d. James Samuel and Nancy Theresa (Jackson) T. B in Philosophy, U. Chgo., 1949; postgrad. in journalism Northwestern U., 1950. Asst. to counsel to Pres. White House, Washington, 1964-65; sec., asst. treas. Internat. Econ. Policy Assn., 1967-84, v.p., sec., treas., 1984—; sec. Internat. Econ. Studies Inst., Washington, 1974-88. Mem. Literacy Council of No. Va., 1976—, pres., 1983-84, bd. dirs., 1981-85; del. Action in Community Through Service, Prince William County, Va., 1982-84, bd. dirs., 1986—; chmn. Winter Harmony Fest., Prince William County, 1984-85. Mem. Am. Soc. Assn. Execs., Nat. Assn. Execs., Nonprofit Fin. Mgrs. Roundtable, Women in Econs. Roundtable, Asia Soc. Republican. Episcopalian. Clubs: Montclair Country (Dumfries, Va.), Nat. Press. Home: 15604 Northgate Dr Dumfries VA 22026 Office: Internat Econ Policy Assn PO Box 27160 Washington DC 20005

THOMPSON, PAUL JAN DAVID, computer company executive; b. London, Dec. 30, 1957; s. John Matthew and Maria Johanna (Munk) T.; m. Sarah Maria Meier, Apr. 21, 1961. BSME, Imperial Coll. Sci. & Tech., London, 1979; MS in Indsl. Adminstrn., Carnegie-Mellon U., 1983. Devel. engr. Brown-Boveri & Co., Baden, Switzerland, 1979-81; maj. account sales rep. Hewlett-Packard Co., Geneva, 1983—. Imperial Coll. scholar, 1977. Mem. City and Guilds of London Inst. (assoc.). Home: 10 ave du Delay, CH-1110 Morges Switzerland Office: Hewlett-Packard SA, 7 rue du Bois-du-Lan, CH-1217 Geneva Switzerland

THOMPSON, PETER COLIN MICHAEL, manufacturing and trading company executive; b. Dundee, Scotland, Aug. 27, 1943; s. William Falase and Elspeth Baxter (Henderson) T. B.A., Sophia U., Tokyo, 1972. With Ben Line Steamers Ltd., U.K., Singapore, Hong Kong, Japan, 1962-78; gen. mgr.

Ben Line Steamers Ltd., Japan, 1972-78; dir. Sale Tilney (Japan) Ltd., Tokyo, 1979-82, pres., 1980-82; pres. ACI Japan Ltd., Tokyo, 1982—; dir. English Agy. (Japan) Ltd. Hong Kong and Japan, Acorns Internat. Inc., Japan, Auberges K.K., Japan; pres. Plastitherm K.K., Tokyo, 1980-84, Acorns Pacific Party, Ltd., Australia; pres. Overseas Affiliates KK, 1984—; chmn. Printos Packaging KK, 1984-86. Fellow Soc. Antiquaries Scotland. Clubs: East India, Caledonian (London); Tokyo, Press (Tokyo). Office: ACI Japan Ltd Yurakucho Bldg, 1-10-1, Yurakucho, Chiyoda-Ku Tokyo 100, Japan

THOMPSON, PETER LINDSAY, cardiologist, educator; b. Perth, Australia, Dec. 26, 1941; s. Reginald and Veronica (Donoghue) T.; m. Andrea Jane Stimson, Aug. 15, 1969; children: James, Alexandrea, Angus. BS, MB, U. Western Australia, Perth, 1965. Diplomate Am. Bd. Internal Medicine. Intern Royal Perth Hosp., 1965-67; asst. in medicine Peter Bent Brigham Hosp., Boston, 1970-72; cardiologist Sir Charles Gairdner Hosp., Perth, 1972—; practice medicine specializing in cardiology Perth, 1973—; clin. lectr. medicine U. Western Australia, 1976—; med. registrar Walter and Eliza Hall Inst., Melbourne, Australia, 1968; cardiology registrar Royal Melbourne Hosp., 1969. Author: Prognosis of Heart Attack, 1987; contbr. articles to med. jours. Fellow Royal Australasian Coll. Physicians, ACP, Am. Coll. Cardiology; mem. Nat. Heart Found. (bd. dirs. 1986—, chmn. heart attack com. 1987—), Australian Med. Assn. (pres. Western Australian br. 1986-87), Cardiac Soc. Australia and New Zealand (council 1986—). Roman Catholic. Club: Royal Freshwater Bay Yacht. Home: 10 Hobbs Ave Dalkeith, Perth 6009, Australia Office: 30 Kings Park Rd, West Perth 6005, Australia

THOMPSON, PHEBE KIRSTEN, physician; b. Glace Bay, N.S., Can., Sept. 5, 1897; d. Peter and Catherine (McKeigan) Christianson; M.D., C.M. Dalhousie U., Halifax, N.S., 1923; m. Willard Owen Thompson, M.D., June 21, 1923 (dec. Mar. 1954); children—Willard Owen, Frederic, Nancy, Donald. Came to U.S., 1923, naturalized, 1937. Intern Children's Hosp., Halifax, N.S., 1922-23; asst. biochemistry, dept. applied physiology Harvard Sch. Pub. Health, 1924-26; asst. and research fellow in medicine, thyroid clinic, Mass. Gen. Hosp., Boston, 1926-29; asst. in metabolism dept. (endocrinology) Rush Med. Coll. of U. Chgo. and The Central Free Dispensary Chgo., 1930-46; assoc. with husband in practice medicine, Chgo., 1947-54; mng. editor Jour. Clin. Endocrinology and Metabolism, 1954-61, cons. editor, 1961-65; editor Jour. Am. Geriatrics Soc., 1954-82; cons. editor Endocrinology, 1961-65; free-lance editor and writer. Recipient Thewlis award Am. Geriatrics Soc., 1966; cert. of appreciation Am. Thyroid Assn., 1966. Fellow Am. Med. Writers' Assn. (adv. com. 1955-60, v.p. Chgo. 1962), Am. Geriatrics Soc., Gerontological Soc. Am.; mem. Endocrine Soc., AAAS, Am. Genetic Assn., Am. Pub. Health Assn., Ill. Pub. Health Assn., Ill. Acad. Scis., Art Inst. Chgo. (life), Chgo. Hist. Soc. (life). Clubs: Univ.; Harvard; Canadian (corr. sec. 1968-73; mem. bd. 1973-76). Address: 4250 N Marine Dr #613 Chicago IL 60613

THOMPSON, RALPH NEWELL, former chemical corporation executive; b. Boston, Mar. 4, 1918; s. Ralph and Lillian May (Davenport) T.; m. Virginia Kenniston, Jan. 31, 1942; children: Pamela, Nicholas, Diana. B.S., MIT, 1940. Research engr. Middlesex Products Co., Cambridge, Mass., 1940-42; tech. dir. Falulah Paper Co., Fitchburg, Mass., 1945-48; staff engr. to v.p., div. gen. mgr. Calgon Corp., Pitts., 1948-70; v.p. mktg., corp. devel. Pa. Indsl. Chem. Corp., Clairton, 1970-74; gen. mgr. chem. div. Thiokol Corp., Trenton, N.J., 1974-76; group v.p.-chem. Thiokol Corp., Newtown, Pa., 1976-82; marine artist, specializing in lighthouses and historic sailing vessels 1982—; dir. Mulford Co. Inc., Mass., 1956-82, Thiokol Can. Ltd., 1975-82, Thiokol Chems., Ltd., Eng., 1976-82, Toray Thiokol Co. Ltd., Japan, 1976-82, Nisso-Ventron K.K., Japan, 1977-82, S.W. Chem. Services Inc., Tex., 1978-82, S.W. Plastics Europe (S.A.), Belgium, 1978-82, Dynachem. Corp., Calif., 1979-82, Carstab Corp., Ohio, 1980-82. Mem. Mt. Lebanon (Pa.) Civic League, 1950-74. Served with USNR, 1942-45. Recipient Goodreau Meml. Fund medal in chemistry, 1936. Fellow Am. Inst. Chemists; mem. TAPPI (contributor monograph series 1950-65), N.Y. Acad. Scis., Soc. Chem. Industry, Nat. Maritime Soc., Am. Soc. Marine Artists, Mil. Order World Wars, Pa. Soc., Soc. Descs. Colonial Clergy. Republican. Presbyterian.

THOMPSON, ROBERT ALLAN, aerospace engineer; b. Cleve., June 10, 1937; s. Roy Henry and Viola Alverta (Nehls) T.; B.S.E.E., Case Western Reserve U., 1958; postgrad. Cleve. State U., 1959, John Marshall Law Sch., 1970; Ph.D., Union Experimenting Colls. and Univs., 1979; m. Louise Alberta Saari, Nov. 27, 1970. Research engr. Sohio Satellite Tracking Sta., Standard Oil Research Lab., Cleve., 1958-63, acting dir., 1964-65; tchr. Cleve. Bd. Edn., 1958-65; dir. Warrensville Heights Planetarium and Space Sci. Program, 1964-65; tchr. spl. programs faculty Case Inst. Tech., 1965; dir. planning phase sci. div. Cleve. Supplementary Edn. Center, 1965-66; dir. James A. Lovell Regional Space Center, Milw., 1967-73; engring. and edn. cons., Chgo., 1973-78, Mystic, Conn., 1978—; pres., chmn. bd. Spatialworld Corp., 1982—, lectr. U. Wis., Milw., 1968-71; chmn. secondary math curriculum com. Cleve. Public Schs., 1963-64; mem. Wis. Aerospace Edn. Com., 1968-71; sec. Friends of Space Center, 1968-75. Recipient Leadership award Kiwanis Key Club, 1961; Goodwin Watson Inst. doctoral fellow, 1978-79. Registered profl. engr., Ohio, Wis., Conn., R.I. Fellow Brit. Interplanetary Assn.; mem. IEEE (sr. mem., exec. com., chmn. membership com. Cleve. sect. 1965-66), AAAS, AIAA (chmn. Wis. sect. 1969-70, sr. mem. Conn. sect. council mem. 1984-85, disting. lectr. 1987—), Cleve. Engring. Soc., Cleve. Astron. Soc. (mem. exec. com. 1966-67), Case Alumni Assn., Union Experimenting Colls. and Univs. Alumni Assn. Author: The New Egoshell-An Individualized Space Age Reality, 1980; co-author (with wife): Egoshell-Planetary Individualism Balanced Within Planetary Interdependence!, 1987; contbr. articles to encys. and profl. jours. Home: 401 Factory Sq Mystic CT 06355 Office: 301 Factory Square Mystic CT 06355

THOMPSON, TERENCE WILLIAM, lawyer; b. Moberly, Mo., July 3, 1952; s. Donald Gene and Carolyn (Stringer) T.; m. Caryn Elizabeth Hildebrand, Aug. 30, 1975; children: Cory Elizabeth, Christopher William. BA in Govt. with honors and high distinction, U. Ariz., 1974; JD, Harvard U., 1977. Bar: Ariz. 1977, U.S. Dist. Ct. Ariz. 1977, U.S. Tax Ct. 1979. Mem. Brown & Bain P.A., Phoenix, 1977—; legis. aide Rep. Richard Burgess, Ariz. Ho. of Reps., 1974; mem. bus. adv. bd. Citibank Ariz. (formerly Great Western Bank & Trust, Phoenix), 1985-86. Contbr. articles to profl. jours. Mem. Phoenix Mayor's Youth Adv. Bd. 1968-70, Phoenix Internat. Active 20-30 Club, 1978-81, sec. 1978-80, Valley Leadership, Phoenix, 1983-84, citizens task force future financing needs City of Phoenix, 1985-86; deacon Shepherd of Hills Congl. Ch. Phoenix, 1984-85; pres. Maricopa County Young Dems., 1982-83, Ariz. Young Dems., 1983-84, sec. 1981-82, v.p. 1982-83; exec. dir. Young Dems. Am., 1985, mem. exec. com. 1983-85; sec. Ariz. Dem. Com., 1984-87; bd. dirs. City Phoenix Mcpl. Ctr. Corp., 1987—, sec., 1987—. Mem. ABA, Ariz. Bar Assn. (securities council/law sect. 1988—, vice chmn. internat. law sect. 1978), Maricopa County Bar Assn., Nat. Assn. Bond Lawyers, Am. Acad. Hosp. Attys., Blue Key, Phi Beta Kappa, Phi Kappa Phi, Phi Eta Sigma. Home: 202 W Lawrence Rd Phoenix AZ 85013 Office: Brown & Bain PA PO Box 400 Phoenix AZ 85001

THOMPSON, THOMAS RONALD, industrial corporation executive; b. Gilman, Iowa, May 31, 1927; s. Thomas R. and Sarah Elizabeth (Westerfield) T.; B.A., U. Iowa, 1950; m. Evelyn M. Muckler, June 8, 1945; children—Thomas, Craig, Jann, Jill, Lori. With Lennox Industries Inc., Marshalltown, Iowa, 1950—, cost acct., 1950-52, asst. office mgr., 1952-53, office mgr., 1964-64, div. controller, 1964-76, v.p., gen. mgr. Midwest Div., 1976—; dir. Fidelity Brenton Bank, Marshalltown. Pres. Marshalltown Indsl. Bur., 1977-80; dir. Iowa Valley Community Coll., 1966-71, pres., 1969-71; vice chmn. United Way Drive, 1976, chmn., 1982, bd. dirs. United Way, 1974-81; bd. dirs. Marshalltown Area Community Hosp.; pres., bd. dirs., 1986-87; mem. nat. leadership com. Wartburg Coll.; chmn. Iowa Coll. Found., Marshalltown; endorsement chmn. Quakerdale Ptnrs. in Caring. Served with U.S. Army, 1945-46. Mem. Nat. Mgmt. Assn. (exec. adv. com. 1979—, silver knight award for mgmt., 1971), Iowa Mfrs. Assn. Republican. Congregationalist. Club: Rotary (dir. Marshalltown). Home: 1406 S 12th St Marshalltown IA 50158 Office: 200 S 12th Ave Marshalltown IA 50158

THOMPSON, TOMMY GEORGE, governor of Wisconsin; b. Elroy, Wis., Nov. 19, 1941; s. Allan and Julie (Dutton) T.; m. Sue Ann Mashak, 1969; children: Kellie Sue, Tommi, Jason. BS in Polit. Sci. and History, U. Wis., 1963, JD, 1966. Polit. intern U.S. Rep. Thomson, 1963; legis. messenger Wis. State Senate, 1964-66; sole practice Elroy and Mauston, Wis., 1966-87; mem. Dist. 87 Wis. State Assembly, 1966-87, asst. minority leader, 1972-81, floor leader, 1981-87; self-employed real estate broker Mauston, 1970—; gov. State of Wis., 1987—; alt. del. Rep. Nat. Conv., 1976. Served with USAR. Recipient med. award for Legis., Wis. Acad. Gen. Practice. Mem. ABA, Wis. Bar Assn., Phi Delta Phi. Roman Catholic. Office: Office of the Gov Room 115 E State Capitol PO Box 7863 Madison WI 53707-7863 *

THOMPSON, VIVIAN OPAL, nurse; b. Lebanon, Va., Nov. 30, 1925; d. Luther Smith and Cora Belle (Baugh) Thompson; R.N., Knoxville (Tenn.) Gen. Hosp., 1947. Supr. obstetrical dept. Knoxville Gen. Hosp., 1947-48; gen. duty nurse Clinch Valley Clinic Hosp., Richlands, Va., 1948-52, supr., 1957-61, 68-78, 78—; indsl. nurse, Morocco, Africa, 1952-56; charge nurse Bluefield Sanitarium, W.Va., 1961-65, Rochingham Meml. Hosp., Harrisonburg, Va., 1965-68. Democrat. Presbyterian. Home: 205 Pennsylvania Ave Richlands VA 24641

THOMPSON, WAYNE WRAY, historian; b. Wichita, Jan. 30, 1945; s. Clarence William and Elaine Maxine (Wray) T.; BA, Union Coll., Schenectady, 1967; student U. St. Andrews, Scotland, 1965-66; PhD, U. Calif., San Diego, 1975; m. Lillian Evelyn Hurlburt, June 28, 1969. Historian, USAF, 1975—. Served with AUS, 1971-72. Mem. Am. Hist. Assn., Orgn. Am. Historians, AF Hist. Found., Am. Mil. Inst., Air Force Assn., Soc. Historians Am. Fgn. Relations, U.S. Commn. on Mil. History, Inter-Univ. Seminar on Armed Forces and Soc., Assn. Asian Studies, Asia Soc., Phi Beta Kappa. Contbr. to Congress Investigates (Arthur M. Schlesinger, Jr. and Roger Bruns, editor), 1975. Editor Air Leadership, 1986. Home: 9203 St Marks Pl Fairfax VA 22031 Office: USAF Air Force History Hdqrs Bolling AFB DC 20332

THOMPSON, WESLEY DUNCAN, grain merchant; b. Blenheim, Ont., Can., Oct. 18, 1926; s. Wesley Gairdner and Anna Corneil (McCallum) T.; m. Patricia Florence Coatsworth, June 6, 1957; children—Wesley, Jennifer, Frank. B.A., U. Western Ont., London, Can., 1950. Pres. W.G. Thompson & Sons Ltd, Blenheim, Can., 1950—; v.p. Hyland Farms Ltd., Ridgetown, Ont.; bd. dirs. Standard Trust Co., Toronto. Office: W G Thompson & Sons Ltd, 122 George St, Blenheim, ON Canada N0P 1A0

THOMPSON, WILLIAM ALBERT, JR., consulting engineering company executive; b. Bluefield, W.Va., June 9, 1930; s. William Albert and Mary (Draper) T.; B.S. in Civil Engring., Va. Mil. Inst., 1952; m. Betty Presley Atkins, Aug. 1, 1952; children—William Albert III, James Carroll, Robert Ryland. Founder, prin. Thompson & Litton, Inc., Wise, Va., 1956—, pres., 1956-81, chmn., 1981—; mem. adv. bd. Dominion Bank, St. Paul, Va., 1974-83, chmn., 1982-83, mem. adv. bd. Dominion Banks Wise County, 1985—. Chmn. adv. bd., instr. Sch. of Mine Mgmt. Clinch Valley Coll., Wise, 1982-85; chmn. bd. trustees Eads Pension Trust, St. Louis, 1974-87; bd. dirs. Va. YMCA; elder Presbyn. Ch.; bd. dirs. Va. Resources Authority. Served to 1st lt. USAF, 1952-55. Registered profl. engr., Va., Fla., Ky., W.Va.; registered land surveyor, Ky. Recipient Chancellor's Cert Disting. Service Ch. Valley Coll. U. Va., 1985. Fellow ASCE. Engrs.; mem. NSPE, Cons. Engrs. Council Va. (past pres., Disting. Service award), Am. Cons. Engrs. Council (past dir.), Soc. Am. Mil. Engrs., Reserve Officers' Assn. U.S., Va. Soc. Profl. Engrs., Kappa Alpha Order. Home: 128 Orchard Ln Wise VA 24293 Office: PO Box 1307 Wise VA 24293

THOMPSON, WINSTON, ambassador extraordinary and plenipotentiary; b. Naisisili, Nacula, Fiji, July 8, 1940; s. Allan and Libera (Vunisa) T.; m. Queenie Pauline Reymond, Dec. 31, 1964; children: Lisa Ann, David Allan, Robert Leke. Diploma, Faculty of Agriculture, UWI, Trinidad, 1961; Associateship, Faculty of Agriculture, Uwi, Trinidad, 1962; Diploma in Agrl. Extension, U. Queensland, Australia, 1967. Sr. agriculture officer Ministry of Agriculture and Fisheries, Fiji, 1968-69, chief agriculture officer, 1969-71, dep. dir. agriculture, 1971-72, dir. agriculture, 1972-73, permanent sec., 1973-78; permanent sec. Ministry of Fin., Fiji, 1978-83; sec. Pub. Service Commn., Fiji, 1983-85; ambassador to the UN Fiji Mission to the UN, N.Y.C., 1985—; chmn. Fiji Pine Commn., 1976-85, Fiji Nat. Provident Fund, 1983-85. Club: United (Suva, Fiji). Office: Permanent Mission of Fiji to UN One United Nations Plaza 26th Floor New York NY 10017

THOMS, PAUL EDWARD, educational administrator, music education consultant; b. Louisville, Apr. 16, 1936; s. Samuel Carl and Augusta Susan (Muth) T.; m. Marion Carol Cox, Aug. 16, 1958; children—Monica Diane Hicks, Melinda Carol Unklesbay. Student, Ky. Wesleyan Coll., 1954-56, MusB, U. Ky., 1958; MusM, Miami U., Oxford, Ohio, 1965; postgrad. Ind. U., Millikin U., Calif. State Coll., Baldwin-Wallace Conservatory, Ohio State U. Rural music supr., Brown County, Ohio, 1958-60; dist. music coordinator, choral dir. Fairfield (Ohio) City Schs., 1960-82, dir. curriculum and pub. relations, 1982—; pres. north cen. div. Music Educators Nat. Conf. Contbr. articles to profl. jours.; choral condr.: (musicals) Guys and Dolls, Bye Bye Birdie, South Pacific, You're a Good Man, Charlie Brown, Hello, Dolly, Oliver, Godspell, The Sound of Music, others, (choral masterworks) Handel's Messiah, Haydn's Creations, Schubert's Mass in G, the Mozart Coronation Mass, Mozart's Requiem, the Mozart Lord Nelson Mass, others. Pres. Torch Internat.; bd. dirs. Hist. Hamilton, Ohio; trustee Rossville Hist. Preservation Assn. Recipient Ohio Senate Resolution, mayoral proclamation and Bd. Edn. resolution establishing Paul Thoms Day; named One of Ten Most Outstanding Sch. Music Dirs. in U.S. and Can., Sch. Musician mag. Mem. Nat. Assn. Jazz Educators, Am. Choral Dirs. Assn. (life), Fedn. Internat. Des Choeurs D'Enfants, Internat. Soc. for Music Edn., Nat. Thespian Soc. (hon., life), Ohio Music Edn. Assn. (past pres.), Tri-M (pres., bd. dirs.). Avocations: arts, antiques, historical restoration and preservation. Home: 128 S D St Hamilton OH 45013 Office: Fairfield City Schs 5050 Dixie Hwy Fairfield OH 45014

THOMSEN, THOMAS RICHARD, communications company executive; b. Avoca, Iowa, July 29, 1935; s. Howard August and Edna Mary (Walker) T.; m. Raylene Alice Tomes, Sept. 1, 1956; children: Jeffrey, Cathy. BSME, U. Nebr., 1958; MS, MIT, 1973. Engr. Western Electric Co., Omaha, 1957-64; mgr. Western Electric Co., Columbus, Ohio, 1964-72; v.p. Bell Sales West Western Electric Co., Morristown, N.J., 1979-80; asst. v.p. ops. staff AT&T, Basking Ridge, N.J., 1980-82; exec. v.p. Western Electric Corp., N.Y.C., 1982—; pres. AT&T Tech. Systems, Berkeley Heights, N.J., 1982—; bd. dirs. AT&T Credit Corp., Sandia Corp., Albuquerque. Trustee Rensselaer Poly. Inst. Mem. Telephone Pioneers Am. (former pres.), Pi Tau Sigma, Sigma Tau. Republican. Presbyterian. Club: Windows on the World. Home: 4 Powderhorn Dr Kinnelon NJ 07405 Office: AT&T Techs Inc One Oak Way Berkeley Heights NJ 07922

THOMSON, ALEXANDER BENNETT, JR., certified financial planner, tax and management consultant; b. Wyandotte, Mich., Sept. 1, 1954; s. Alexander Bennett and Norma Lee (Fields) T.; m. Rita Elizondo, May 8, 1982; 1 child, Luis Joaquin Elizondo. Student Eastern Mich. U., 1972-74, Kalamazoo Coll. 1975-77; M.A., Antioch Sch. Law, 1983; Cert. fin. planner. Pres. Thomson & Assocs., Ltd., Washington, 1977—; budget dir. The White House Conf. on Small Bus., 1979; asst. treas. Kennedy for Pres. Com. 1980, nat. scheduler, Geraldine A. Ferraro, 1984. Mem. Inst. Certified Fin. Planners, Internat. Assn. Fin. Planners, ABA, Am. Mgmt. Assn., Nat. Assn. Life Underwriters, Nat. Assn. Tax Practitioners, Nat. Assn. Security Dealers. Democrat.

THOMSON, DAVID TIMOTHY, retired principal; b. Seattle, Jan. 20, 1925; s. William Orville and Jessie (Cox) T.; m. Maria Hideko Okatsu; children: Timothy M., Kenneth J., Miguel M., Susan M. Student, Amherst Coll., 1943-44, Harvard U., 1944-48; MA, Pontificial U., Salamanca, Spain, 1965, U. Madrid, 1966. Diplomate Colegio Oficial de Licenciados y Doctorados de Ciencias y Letras. Dir. Eikaiwa Juku, Kyoto, Japan, 1954-62; prin. Colegio San Fernando, Salamanca, 1966-77, Colegio Antonio Machado, Salamanca, 1977-87. Author, editor: Spoken English, 4 vols., 1957-62. Served with USAAF, 1943-46, CBI. Mem. NEA, Assn. Nat. Espondylitis Anquilosante (bd. dirs. 1986—). Roman Catholic. Club: Salamanca Ateneo Salamantino. Home: Santa Marta de Tormes, Apartado 309, 37080 Salamanca Spain Office: Colegio Antonio Machado, C/San Pablo 21 Apartado 309, 37080 Salamanca Spain

THOMSON, GEORGE RONALD, lawyer, educator; b. Wadsworth, Ohio, Aug. 25, 1959; s. John Alan and Elizabeth (Galbraith) T. BA, Miami U., Oxford, Ohio, 1982, MA, 1983; JD, Ohio State U., 1986. Bar: Ill. 1986. Teaching fellow Miami U., 1982-83; dir. speech activities Ohio State U., Columbus, 1983-86; assoc. Peterson, Ross, Schloerb & Seidel, Chgo., 1986-87, Lord, Bissell & Brook, Chgo., 1987—; adj. prof. dept. communication Loyola U., Depaul U., Chgo, 1988—. Mem. Chgo. Inst. Art. Recipient Spl. Commendation Ohio Ho. of Reps., 1984, 85. Mem. ABA (tort and ins. sect. 1986—), Ill. State Bar Assn., Chgo. Bar Assn., Speech Communication Assn. Am., Amnesty Internat. (adminstr. 1978-82, 86—), Internat. Platform Assn., Am. Film Inst., Mortar Bd., Phi Beta Kappa, Phi Kappa Phi, Omicron Delta Kappa, Delta Sigma Ro, Tau Kappa Alpha, Phi Alpha Delta. Democrat. Presbyterian. Home: 2835 Pinegrove Unit 25 Chicago IL 60657 Office: Lord Bissell & Brook 115 S LaSalle St Chicago IL 60603

THOMSON, GERALD EDMUND, physician, educator; b. N.Y.C., 1932; s. Lloyd and Sybil (Gilbourne) T.; m. Carolyn Webber; children: Gregory, Karen. M.D., Howard U., 1959. Diplomate Am. Bd. Internal Medicine (bd. govs. 1985—). Intern SUNY-Kings County Hosp. Center, Bklyn., 1959-60; resident in medicine SUNY-Kings County Hosp. Center, 1960-62, chief resident, 1962-63, N.Y. Heart Assn. fellow in nephrology, 1964-65, asst. vis. physician, 1963-70, clin. dir. dialysis unit, 1965-67; practice medicine specializing in internal medicine N.Y.C., 1963—; attending physician SUNY Med. Bklyn. Hosp., 1966-70; instr. in medicine SUNY, Bklyn., 1963-68; clin. asst. prof. medicine SUNY, 1968-70; asso. chief med. services Coney Island Hosp., Bklyn., 1967-70; attending physician Presbyn. Hosp., 1970—; dir. nephrology Harlem Hosp. Center, N.Y.C., 1970-71; dir. med. services Harlem Hosp. Center, 1971-85, pres. med. bd., 1976-78; assoc. prof. medicine Columbia Coll. Physicians and Surgeons, 1970-72, prof., 1972—, Samuel Lambert prof. medicine, 1980—; exec. v.p. for profl. affairs Columbia-Presbyn Med. Ctr., 1985—; Mem. Health Research Council City N.Y., 1972-75; mem. med. adv. bd. N.Y. Kidney Found., 1971—; mem. Health Research Council, State N.Y., 1975-81; mem. hypertension info. and edn. adv. com. NIH, 1973-74, N.Y. State Adv. Com. on Hypertension, 1977-80; com. on non-pharm. treatment of hypertension Inst. of Medicine, Nat. Acad. Scis., 1980; mem. med. adv. bd. Nat. Assn. Patients on Hemodialysis and Transplantation, 1973-83; mem. adv. bd. Sch. Biomed. Edn., CUNY, 1979-83; mem. com. on mild hypertension Nat. Heart and Lung Inst., 1976, mem. clin. trials rev. com., 1980-85, mem. rev. panel, 1979; bd. dirs. N.Y. Heart Assn., 1973-81, chmn. com. high blood pressure, 1976-81; chmn. com. hypertension N.Y. Met. Regional Med. Program, 1974-76; mem. adv. com. Heart and Hypertension Inst. of N.Y. State, 1984; mem. N.Y. Gov.'s Health Adv. Council, 1981—, pub. Health Council, N.Y., 1983—, Joint Nat. Com. High Blood Pressure NIH, 1983-84, mem. rev. panel hypertension detection and follow-up program, 1980; mem. policy monitoring bd. study cardiovascular risk factors in young Nat. Heart, Lung and Blood Inst., 1984—; mem. panel on receiving and withholding med. treatment ACLU, 1984—; mem. Grad. Med. Edn. Commn., State of N.Y., 1984-86, mem. Commn. on End-State Renal Disease, 1985. Mem. adv. bd.: Jour. Urban Health, 1974—. Chmn. ad hoc com. on access to nursing homes Pub. Health Council State of N.Y. Recipient Nat. Med. award Nat. Kidney Found, N.Y., 1984, Outstanding Alumnus aeard Howard U., 1987, Dean's award Coll. Physicians and Surgeons Columbia U., 1986. Fellow ACP (Gov.'s council downstate region 1982—, chmn. com. health pub. policy 1982—, health care professoins com. 1987—), N.Y. Acad. Medicine (mem. com. medicine in soc. 1974-76); mem. AAAS, N.Y. Soc. Nephrology (pres. 1973-74), Am. Fedn. Clin. Research, Soc. Urban Physicians (pres. 1972-73), Am. Soc. Artificial Internal Organs, Assn. Program Dirs. in Internal Medicine, Pub. Health Assn. N.Y.C. (dir. 1983—), Physicians for Social Responsibility of N.Y. (dir. 1983—), Greater N.Y. Hosp. Assn. (quality assurance com. 1987), Alpha Omega Alpha. Home: 118 Whitman Dr Brooklyn NY 11234 Office: Harlem Hosp Center 506 Lenox Ave New York NY 10037

THOMSON, GRACE MARIE, nurse, minister; b. Pecos, Tex., Mar. 30, 1932; d. William McKinley and Elzora (Wilson) Olliff; m. Radford Chaplin, Nov. 3, 1952; children—Deborah C. Thomson Meshirer, William Earnest. Assoc. Applied Sci., Odessa Coll., 1965; extension student U. Pa. Sch. Nursing, U. Calif.-Irvine, Golden West Coll. RN, Calif., Okla., Ariz., Md., Tex. Dir. nursing Grays Nursing Home, Odessa, Tex., 1965; supr. nursing Med. Hill, Oakland, Calif.; charge nurse pediatrics Med. Ctr., Odessa; dir. nursing Elmwood Extended Care, Berkeley, Calif.; surg. nurse Childrens Hosp., Berkeley; med-surg. charge nurse Merritt Hosp., Oakland, Calif.; adminstr. Grace and Assocs.; active Watchtower and Bible Tract Soc.; evangelist for Jehovah's Witnesses, 1954—.

THOMSON, HARRY PLEASANT, JR., lawyer; b. Kansas City, Mo., May 9, 1917; s. Harry Pleasant and Alice F. (DeWolff) T.; m. Martha Jean Martin, May 3, 1941 (dec. 1981); children: Jane Anne (Mrs. Edward G. McCarthy), Carol Lee Thomson, Lisa Clair, (Mrs. John Porter). A.B., U. Mo., 1937, J.D., 1939. Bar: Mo. bar 1939, also U.S. Supreme Ct. bar 1959. Practiced in Kansas City; now of counsel Shughart, Thomson & Kilroy (P.C.); lectr. Mo. Continuing Legal Edn. Programs, 1961-78; Mem. Mo. Supreme Ct. Com. on Jury Instrns., 1962-81, chmn., 1977-81; mem. Commn. on Retirement, Removal & Discipline of Judges, 1972-81, chmn., 1980-81. Author: (with others) Missouri Approved Jury Instructions, 1964, 69, 73, 76, 78, 80; Mem. bd. editors: Mo. Law Rev, 1938-39; editorial adv. bd. Antitrust Law & Econs. Rev.; contbr. articles to profl. jours. Trustee U. Mo. Law Sch. Found., 1975-87, pres., 1979-81. Served to lt. USNR, 1942-46. Recipient certificate of appreciation for disting. service Mo. Bar, 1964; Spurgeon Smithson award Mo. Bar Found., 1979; Charles E. Whittaker award Kansas City Lawyers Assn., 1984; Litigator Emeritus award Kansas City Met. Bar Assn., 1985. Fellow Am. Coll. Trial Lawyers (regent 1967-68), Am. Bar Found.; mem. Lawyers Assn. Kansas City (past pres.), Kansas City Claims Assn. (past pres.), Internat. Assn. Ins. Counsel, Mo. Bar Assn. (bd. govs. 1967-71, exec. com. 1970-71), ABA, Am. Judicature Soc., Internat. Soc. Barristers, Order DeMolay Legion of Honor, Phi Beta Kappa, Order of Coif, Psi Chi, Sigma Chi, Delta Theta Phi. Clubs: University (pres. 1977), Carriage, Kansas City. Lodge: Rotary. Home: 1216 W 69th St Kansas City MO 64113 Office: 12 Wyandotte Plaza 120 W 12th St Kansas City MO 64105

THOMSON, JAMES AUSTIN, lawyer; b. Port Chester, N.Y., July 22, 1949; came to Australia, 1951; s. Ian Douglas and Maureen Winifred (Cazalet) T.; m. Lynne Dianne Anning, Dec. 22, 1973. LLB with honors, U. Western Australia, Perth, 1971, BA, 1974; LLM, Harvard U., 1975, SJD, 1981. Bar: Supreme Ct. Western Australia 1972, Victoria 1983, High Ct. Australia 1977, N.Y. 1987. Sr. atty. Crown Law Dept., Perth, 1973—; vis. prof. law U. Western Australia, 1977—; commr. Western Australia Law Reform Commn., Perth, 1982—; legal advisor Australian Constl. Conv., Melbourne, 1976-85; mem. standing com. State and Atty. Gens. of Perth, 1976—; Australian Del. UN Law of the Sea Conf., N.Y.C., 1979. Contbr. articles to profl. jours. Fulbright scholar, 1974, 86-87, Columbia U. scholar, 1986-87. Mem. Supreme Ct. Hist. Soc., Am. Soc. Legal History, Royal Australian Hist. Soc. Home: 44 Perina Way, City Beach 6015, Australia Office: Crown Law Dept, 109 Saint Georges Terr, Perth 6000, Australia

THOMSON, RICHARD MURRAY, banker; b. Winnipeg, Can., Aug. 14, 1933; s. H.W. and Mary T. BASC in Engring., U. Toronto, 1955; M.B.A., Harvard U., 1957; fellow course banking, Queen's U., 1958. With Toronto Dominion Bank, 1957—, asst. to pres. head office, 1963-68, chief gen. mgr., 1968-71, v.p., chief gen. mgr., dir., 1971-72, pres., 1972-77, chmn., chief exec. officer, 1978—, also bd. dirs., also dir.; Pres., chief exec. officer C.G.C. Inc., 1977-78; dir. Eaton's of Can., S.C. Johnson & Son Ltd., Union Carbide Can. Ltd., Cadillac Fairview Corp., Prudential Ins. Co. Am., Inc. Ltd., Internat. Thomson Orgn. Ltd., Inco Ltd. Vice chmn. bd. trustees Hosp. for Sick Children. Office: Toronto Dominion Bank, Toronto Dominion Ctr Box 1, 55 King St W, Toronto, ON Canada M5K 1A2

THOMSON, VIRGINIA WINBOURN, history educator, author; b. Oakland, Calif., Aug. 6, 1930; d. Harry Linn and Jennie Cook (Vineyard) T. A.A., San Mateo Coll., 1948; B.A., San Jose State Coll., 1951; M.A., U. Calif.-Berkeley, 1952. Cert. secondary tchr., Calif. Social sci. tchr. Capuchino High Sch., San Bruno, Calif., 1952-54, Watsonville High Sch., Calif., 1954-87; saleswoman and storyteller Home Interiors, San Mateo, 1963-64. Author: The Lion Desk, 1965; Short Talks Around The Lord's Table, 1985. Recipient Silver Pitcher award Home Interiors, 1964. Mem. Nat. Geog. Soc. (life),

AAUW (life), Nat. Writers Club Christian Writers Guild, Calif. Alumni Assn. (life), Phi Alpha Theta. Republican.

THONEY, ROGER NEIL, electrical engineer; b. Cin., Mar. 29, 1954; s. Albert Phillip and Margaret Ann (Erb) T.; BSEE, U. Ky., 1976, MBA, 1981, postgrad.; MSEE, Ohio State U., 1977, MS in Econs., U. Ky., 1988. Elec. engr. Procter & Gamble Co., Cin., 1977-80; engr. Cin. Gas and Electric Co., 1981-83, acting planning dir. nuclear engring. dept. W.H. Zimmer Nuclear Power Sta., 1983-84; sr. assoc. engr. IBM Corp., Lexington, Ky., 1984—. Ohio Elec. Utilities Inst. fellow, 1976; Eagles Nat. scholar U. Ky. Coll. Bus. and Econs., 1981. Recipient Outstanding Sr. Elec. Engring. award U. Ky. Dept. Elec. Engring., 1976, Jr. Elec. Engring. award, 1975. Mem. IEEE, Am. Mktg. Assn. Home: 85 Bon Jan Ln Highland Heights KY 41076

THONYA, LUCIUS MABASHA, government agency official; b. Songea, Ruvuma, Tanzania, Sept. 15, 1928; s. Daniel Msalapasi and Petra (Ukiva) T.; children from previous marriage: Athanas, Petra, Cuthbert, Imakulata, Lucia, Dora; married; children: Neema, Baraka, Furaha, Tumaini, Lekandali. Cert., Peramiho Cen. Sch., Tanzania, 1945, Peramiho Tchrs. Coll., 1947, U. London, 1965-66; postgrad., Poly. U., Toronto, Ont., Can., 1973-74. Tchr. lower primary sch. Gumbiro (Tanzania) Songes Dist., 1948-52; tchr., agrl. sch. dir. Middle Sch., Mpitimbi, Tanzania, 1953-54; headmaster, agrl.-in-charge sch. farm Peramiho Middle Sch., 1956-60, tutor, head Kishwahili dept., 1961-65, vice prin., 1966-68; head Kiswahili dept. Grade A Tchrs. Coll., Mpwapwa, 1969; officer-in-charge Ministry Edn., Dar Es Salaam, 1969- 73, dir. Printpak/Mtuu printing unit, 1973, coordination officer, 1974-83; ret. 1983; apptd. mgr. OUP Ministry Edn., Dar Es Salaam, 1985—; tchr. Benedictine Fathers, Songea, 1948-68; edn. officer Govt. Tanzania, Dar Es Salaam, 1969. Editor Tanzania Tchrs Jour., 1961, Tanzania Edn. Jour., 1969.; contbr. articles to profl. jours. Chmn. Tanzania Catholic Tchrs. Assn., Peramiho Diocese, 1957-60, Div. Local Council, Njelu, Tanzania, 1959-61, com. District Council, Songea, 1959-61. UNICEF Fellow Copp Clark & Hunter Rose Pubs., Toronto, 1973-74. Mem. Tanzania Authors Union, Pubs. Assn. Mem. Chama Cha Mapinduci Party. Home: Malimoja, PO Box 6668, Kibaha Tanzania Office: Oxford Univ Press, Maktaba Rd, PO Box 5299, Dar es Salaam Tanzania

THORBURN, JAMES ALEXANDER, humanities educator; b. Martins Ferry, Ohio, Aug. 24, 1923; s. Charles David and Mary Edna (Ruble) T.; m. Lois McElroy, July 3, 1954; children: Alexander Maurice, Melissa Rachel; m. 2d, June Yingling O'Leary, Apr. 18, 1981. BA, Ohio State U., 1949, MA, 1951; postgrad., U. Mo., 1954-55; PhD, La. State U., 1977. Head English dept. high sch., Sheridan, Mich., 1951-52; instr. English, U. Mo., Columbia, 1952-55, Monmouth (Ill.) Coll., 1955-56, U. Tex., El Paso, 1956-60, U. Mo., St. Louis, 1960-61, La. State U., Baton Rouge, 1961-70; assoc. prof. Southeastern La. U., Hammond, 1970—; testing and cert. examiner English Lang. Inst., U. Mich., 1969—; participant Southeastern Conf. on Linguistics. Contbg. author: Exercises in English, 1955, also poetry, short stories; book rev. editor: Experiment, 1958-87; editor: Innisfree. Served with F.A., AUS, 1943-46. Mem. MLA, Linguistic Assn. S.W., Avalon World Arts Acad., Linguistic Soc. Am., Am. Dialect Soc., Nat. Council Tchrs. English, Conf. on Coll. Composition and Communication, Internat. Poetry Soc., Internat. Acad. Poets, Sigma Delta Pi, Phi Kappa Phi, Phi Mu Alpha Sinfonia. Republican. Presbyterian. Home: 602 Susan Dr Hammond LA 70403 Office: Southeastern La U Dept English Hammond LA 70402

THORBURN, MARIGOLD JULIA, pathologist, educator; b. Sutton Coldfield, Eng., Feb. 9, 1935; arrived in Jamaica, 1960; d. David Alexander and Barbara (Chamberlain) Parsons; m. Ernest Carroll Thorburn, Mar. 4, 1961; children: Rachel Isabel, Barbara Juliet, Diana Ruth. MB ChB, U. Birmingham, Eng., 1957; MD, U. Birmingham, 1970. Intern United Birmingham Hosps., 1957-59; resident in pediatrics Children's Hosp., Cin., 1959; resident in pathology U. W.I., Kingston, Jamaica, 1962-64, research fellow dept. pathology, 1964-71, from lectr. to sr. lectr. dept. social and preventive medicine, 1972-75, assoc. lectr. depts. pathology, child health and social preventive medicine, 1975—; dir. Caribbean Inst. on Mental Retardation, Kingston, 1975-85, Early Stimulation Project, Kingston, 1975-84, 3D Projects, Spanish Town, Jamaica, 1985—; cons. UNICEF, UNESCO, Rehab. Internat., ILO, Pan Am. Health Orgn., 1977—. Author: Manual on Childhood disability, 1987; contbr. articles to med. jours., chpts. to books. Bd. dirs. Ptnrs. of Ams., Jamaica-West N.Y., 1973-87. Fellow Royal Coll. Pathology; mem. Med. Assn. Jamaica. Club: Liguanea (Kingston). Lodge: Soroptimist (Woman of Yr. Kingston club 1981). Home: 6 Courtney Dr, Kingston 10, Jamaica Office: 3D Projects, 14 Monk St, Spanish Town Jamaica

THORDARSON, MAGNUS THRANDUR, management consultant; b. Reykjavik, Iceland, May 2, 1952; s. Thorbur Baldur and Anna Christiane (Larusdottir) S.; m. Helga Thorvardardottir, June 13, 1975; children: Ragnhildur, Illugi, Petur Gautur. student Comml. Coll. Iceland, 1972, B.S. John F. Kennedy U., 1987. Mng. dir. Sig. Agustsson Ltd., Stykkisholmur, Iceland, 1976-83; v.p., gen. mgr. Royal Iceland Corp., Berkeley, Calif., 1983-87; owner M.Thordarson Cons., Claremont, Calif., 1987— ; vice chmn. Union of Scallop Producers, Reykjavik, 1980-83. Chmn. Ednl. Council Stykkisholmur, 1979. Lutheran. Address: 999 College Ave Claremont CA 91711

THORÉN, NILS OLOF, sales professional; b. Bo, Sweden, July 10, 1948; arrived in Saudi ARabia, 1983; s. Johan Olof and Lilly T.; m. Annukka, Aug., 18, 1949; children: Nicholas, Johanna, Christofer, Alexander. BS, Örebro (Sewden) Tech. Coll., 1968. Designer Abetong AB, Växjö, Sweden, 1970-74; structural engr. Asplunds Bygg AB, Örebro, 1974-77, Närkes Spännbetong AB, Örebro, 1977-80, Skanska, Kalmar, Sweden, 1980-83; design mgr. Alrashid-Abetong Co. Ltd., Riyadh, Saudi Arabia, 1983-87, sales and estimates mgr., 1987—. Served as officer Swedish Infantry, 1968-69. Home: Lunavagen 24, S-39351 Kalmar Sweden Office: Alrashid-Abetong Co Ltd, PO Box 6058, Riyadh 11442, Saudi Arabia

THORENS, JUSTIN, lawyer; b. Geneva, Sept. 15, 1931; s. Paul Louis and Germaine (Falquet) T.; m. Colette Françoise Vecchio, Mar. 28, 1963; children: Aline, Xavier. Lic. en droit, U. Genève, 1956, docteur en droit, 1963; postgrad., Freie U., Berlin, 1975, U. London, 1978. Cert. to practice law, Geneva, 1958. Atty. Geneva, 1956—; mem. law faculty U. Genève, 1967—, assoc. prof., 1970-73, prof., 1973—, dean law faculty, 1974-77, rector of univ., 1977-83; legal adviser, sec. gen. Geneva Chamber of Agriculture, 1961-72; alt. pres. Jurisdictional Ct., Geneva, 1971-78; mem. council UN Univ., Tokyo, 1986—, chmn. 1988—. Contbr. articels to profl. jours. Mem. Swiss Univs. Conf., (v.p. 1979-83), Conf. Swiss Rectors (v.p. 1981-83), Standing Conf. Rectors, Pres. and Vice Chancellors of European Univs. (council mem. 1982-84), Assn. Univs. Partiellement ou Entièrement de Langue Française (bd. dirs. 1978-81, vice chmn. 1980-83, 84-87, hon. vice chmn. 1987), European Ctr. for Higher Edn. (mem. adv. com. 1981, chmn. 1986—), Internat. Assn Univs. (bd. govs. 1980, bd. dirs. 1983, pres. 1985—). Home: 18 Chemin du Nant d'Aisy, 1246 Corsier Switzerland Office: Internat Assn Univs, 1 rue Miollis, 75732 Paris Cedex 15, France also: 7 rue de la Fontaine, 1206 Geneva Switzerland

THORGEIRSSON, GUDMUNDUR, physician, cardiologist; b. Djupavik, Stranadasysla, Iceland, Mar. 14, 1946; s. Thorgeir Gestsson and Asa Gundmundsdottir; m. Bryn dis Sigurjonsdottir, July 20, 1968; children: Thorgeir, Sigurjon Arni, Hjalti, Bogi, Asa Bryndis. MD, U. Iceland, 1973; PhD, Case Western Res. U., 1978. Diplomate Am. Bd. Internal Medicine, Am. Bd. Cardiovascular Disease. Intern., resident path. medicine U. Hosps., Cleve., 1974-80, teaching fellow, 1980-82; cardiologist Landspitalinn U. Hosp., Reykjavik, Iceland, 1982—; asst. prof. U. Iceland, 1985—; cons. Heart Prevention Clinic, Reykjavik, 1982—; bd. dirs. Icelandic Heart Assn., Reykjavik. Editor Icelandic Med. Jour., 1983—; contbr. articles to profl. jours. Icelandic Sci. Fund grantee, 1983-88. Fellow Am. Coll. Cardiology (assoc.), Soc. Scientarum Islandica; mem. Icelandic Med. Assn., Icelandic Cardiological Soc. (pres. 1985-87), ACP. Home: Klapparas 4, Reykjavik Iceland Office: Landspitalinn U Hosp, Reykjavik Iceland

THORHALLSSON, JON THOR, information technology educator, data processing executive; b. Reykjavik, Iceland, June 21, 1939; s. Thorhallur Arni Benediktsson and Sigridur Jonsdottir; m. Hrefna Beckmann, Jan. 31, 1964. Vordiplom, U. Giessen, Fed. Republic Germany, 1962, hauptdiplom, 1965, D Rer. Nat., 1967. Research assoc. U. Alta., Edmonton, Can., 1967-68, U. B.C., Vancouver, Can., 1968-69; instr. Red Deer Coll., Can., 1969-74; dir. computer service U. Iceland, Reykjavik, 1974-77, assoc. prof., head dept. info. tech., 1981—; dir. State and Municipal Data Processing Ctr., Reykjavik, 1977—; cons. Iceland Research Council, 1982—; chmn. Micromedia; bd. dirs. Univ. Computing Services U. Iceland. Contbr. articles to profl. jours. Mem. Icelandic Soc. Info. Process (pres. 1978-83), Icelandic Math. Assn., Icelandic Mgmt. Assn. (computer adv. com. 1982—), Icelandic Assn. Profl. Engr., Data Processing Mgmt. Assn. Home: Akurgerdi 31, Reykjavik Iceland Office: State and Municipal DP Ctr, Haaleitisbraut 9, Reykjavik Iceland

THORNBURG, FREDERICK FLETCHER, diversified businesses executive, lawyer; b. South Bend, Ind., Feb. 10, 1940; s. James F. and Margaret R. (Major) T.; children from previous marriage: James Brian, Charles Kevin, Christian Sean, Christopher Herndon; m. Patricia J. Malloy, Dec. 4, 1981. AB, DePauw U., 1963; postgrad., U. Notre Dame, 1965; JD magna cum laude, Ind. U., 1968. Bar: Ind. 1968, U.S. Tax Ct. 1970, U.S. Ct. Appeals (7th cir.) 1970, U.S. Supreme Ct. 1971. Tchr., coach U.S. Peace Corps, Colombia, 1963-65; law clk. to chief judge U.S. Ct. Appeals (7th cir.), 1968-69; assoc. Thornburg, McGill, Deahl, Harman, Carey & Murray, South Bend, 1969-75, ptnr., 1975-80; v.p. systems and services group Wackenhut Internat. Inc., Coral Gables, Fla., 1981-82, sr. v.p. adminstrn., 1982-86, pres., 1982-83, exec. v.p. 1986—; pres. Wackenhut Support Services, Inc., Wackenhut Services, Inc.; adj. prof. bus. law St. Mary's Coll., 1975-78; vice chmn., pvt. sec. adv. council Fla. Sec. of State; bd. dirs. The Wackenhut Corp. Assoc. editor in chief: Ind. Law Jour., 1967-68; contbr. articles to legal jours. Bd. dirs. YMCA, Channel 34, Symphony Orch. Assn. Fulbright scholar, Halleck scholar. Mem. ABA, Ind. Bar Assn., Dade County Corp. Counsel Assn., Order of Coif, Greater Miami C. of C. (bd. trustees), Phi Delta Phi, Alpha Delta Sigma. Clubs: Doral Country, Biltmore, Miami, Calusa Country. Lodge: Rotary. Office: Wackenhut Corp 1500 San Remo Ave Coral Gables FL 33146

THORNBURGH, DICK, U.S. attorney general, former governor of Pennsylvania; b. Pitts., July 16, 1932; s. Charles Garland and Alice (Sanborn) T.; m. Virginia Walton Judson, Oct. 12, 1963; children: John, David, Peter, William. B.Engring., Yale, 1954; LL.B. with high honors, U. Pitts., 1957; hon. degrees from 20 colls. and univs. Bar: Pa. 1958, U.S. Supreme Ct. 1965. Atty. firm Kirkpatrick & Lockhart, Pitts., 1959-69, 77-79, 87—; U.S. atty. for Western Pa. Pitts., 1969-75; asst. atty. gen. criminal div. U.S. Dept. Justice, Washington, 1975-77; gov. State of Pa., Harrisburg, 1979-87; now dir. Inst. Politics John F. Kennedy Sch. Govt., Harvard U.; U.S. atty. gen. dept. of justice, Washington, 1988—; del. Pa. Constl. Conv., 1967-68; bd. dirs. Rite Aid Corp., ARCO Chem. Co., Merrill Lynch & Co. Inc. Contbr. articles to profl. jours. Bd. dirs. Urban League Pitts., 1967-72, World Affairs Council Pitts. Fellow Am. Bar Found.; mem. Am. Judicature Soc. Republican. Home: Gateway Towers Apt 12 B Fort Duquesne Blvd Pittsburgh PA 15222 Office: US Dept of Justice Office of the Atty Gen 10th and Constitution Ave Washington DC 20530

THORNBURY, WILLIAM MITCHELL, lawyer, law educator; b. Kansas City, Mo., Feb. 11, 1944; s. Paul Cobb and Marguerite Madellaine (Schulz) T.; m. Joy Frances Barrett, Feb. 2, 1973; children: Barrett Mitchell, Adele Frances. B.A., UCLA, 1964; J.D., U. So. Calif., 1967, postgrad. 1967-69. Bar: Calif. 1968, U.S. Dist. Ct. (cen. dist.) Calif. 1968, U.S. Dist. Ct. (no. dist.) Calif. 1973, U.S. Dist. Ct. (so. dist.) Calif. 1980, U.S. Dist. Ct. (ea. dist.) Calif. 1980, U.S. Ct. Appeals (9th cir.) 1973, U.S. Ct. Claims 1980, U.S. Ct. Internat. Trade, 1981, U.S. Ct. Customs and Patent Appeals 1980, U.S. Ct. Mil. Appeals 1980, U.S. Supreme Ct. 1973, U.S. Ct. Appeals (Fed. cir.) 1984. Dep. pub. defender Los Angeles County Pub. Defender, 1969—, dep.-in-charge traffic ct., 1982-84, supervising atty. Juvenile Services div., 1984, dep. in charge, Inglewood, Calif., 1984-85; legal asst. prof. Calif. State U.-Los Angeles, 1983—; mem. adv. com. on alcohol determination State Dept. Health, 1984—; appointed to apprenticeship council by Gov. Deukmejian State of Calif., 1986—, chmn. equal opportunity com. 1987—; chmn., vice chmn. Santa Monica Fair Election Practices Commn., Calif., 1981-85; advisor on drunk driving Calif. Pub. Defenders Assn., 1984—; alt. mem. Los Angeles County Commn. on Drunk Driving, 1983-84; mem. steering com. Santa Monica Coalition, nominations com., 1984—; bd. dirs. Westside Legal Services, 1984-86, v.p., 1986-87; pres. Westside Legal Services, 1987-88. Columnist Calif. Defender; editor Drunk Driving Manual, 1984; contbr. article to Forum. Exec. bd. dirs. Santa Monica Young Rep., 1967-72, pres. 1972-73, treas. 1973-75, bd. dirs. 1968-72; delegate, precinct chmn., registration chmn. Los Angeles County Young Rep., 1968-70; chmn. legal com. Los Angeles County Rep. Cen. Com., 1977-81, 83-85; chmn. jud. evaluation com., 1978-80; pres. Santa Monica Rep. Club 1986—, bd. dirs., 1966—; bd. dirs. West Los Angeles Republican Club, 1986—; mem. Beverly Hills Rep. Club, Rep. State Cen. com., 1983-85, assoc. mem., 1980-83, 86—, Non-Partisan Candidate Evaluating Council, Inc. (bd. dirs. 1980-86, v.p. 1986—); mem. Pasadena Rep. Club, 1984—; bd. dirs. Santa Monicans Against Crime, 1979—; chmn. 44th Assembly Dist. Rep. Central Com. 1974-87; chmn. Western part of Los Angeles County for George Murphy for U.S. Senate, 1970, John T. LaFollette for Congress, 1970; campaign chmn. Donna A. Little for City Council, 1984; adv. Pat Geffner for City Council, 1979, 81; campaign mgr. Experienced Coll. Team, 1983. Recipient Outstanding Chmn. award Los Angeles County Rep. Party, 1974, sec.-treas. 1968-75, chmn. legal com. 1977-82, 83-85; named Outstanding Service to Rep. Party Legal Counsel, 1978; recipient award Am. Assn. UN, 1961. Mem. Los Angeles County Bar Assn. (vice chmn. indigent and criminal def. com., jud. qualification com. 1986-88, criminal justice com. 1986—, criminal law and law enforcement com., 1986-87), Santa Monica Bar Assn. (trustee 1976-77, 79—, chmn. legis. and publicity com., chmn. jud. evaluation com. 1982-84, pres.-elect 1984, pres. 1985-86, del. to state bar conv. 1974-86, liaison to Los Angeles County Bar Assn. 1986—), Los Angeles County Pub. Defenders Assn. (advisor, bd. dirs. 1980-88), ABA, Calif. Pub. Defenders Assn. (advisor), Santa Monica Hist. Soc., San Fernando Valley Criminal Bar Assn. (membership chmn. 1986—, bd. trustees 1986—, treas. 1987-88, pres.-elect 1988, chmn. judicial evaluations com. 1988), Assn. Trial Lawyers Am., Supreme Ct. Hist. Soc., Nat. Legal Aid and Defenders Assn., Nat. Assn. Criminal Def. Attys., Acad. Criminal Justice Scis., U. So. Calif. Law Alumni Assn., UCLA Alumni Assn., N.Y. Acad. Scis., Am. Assn. Polit. Sci., Criminal Law sect. of State Bar of Calif., Am. Soc. Criminology (life), Western Region Criminal Law Educators, Santa Monica C. of C. (inebriate task force 1980), Calif. Hist. Soc., Santa Monica Coll. Patron's Assn., Nat. Assn. Criminal Def. Counsel, Navy League (life, bd. dirs. 1979—, legis. chmn. 1982,), Nat. Rifle Assn. (life), Calif. Rifle and Pistol Assn. (life).

THORNE, JOHN THOMAS, indsl. instrument control system engr. and designer; b. Port Arthur, Tex., Apr. 17, 1926; s. Ernest Eugene and Mary (Wooldridge) T.; student Tex. Coll. Mines, 1944-45, LeTourneau Tech., 1949-50, Lamar Coll., 1952-53, Lee Coll., 1964-65; U. Houston, 1967-68, 78-79; m. Patricia McBride, Feb. 12, 1949; children—John Thomas, Ernest E., Alida Diane, Jerry Allen. Instrument technician Texas City Refining Inc. (Tex.), 1953-63; instrument and electronics instr. Lee Coll., 1963-66; instrument supr. Tech. Maintenance, Inc., Pasadena, Tex., 1963-67; ind. cons., Houston area, 1967-68; ind. cons. Diamond-Shamrock, Tenneco, U.S. Indsl. Chems., Olin Corp., 1967-68; instrument tech. dept. head San Jacinto Coll., 1966-68; regional systems mgr. Robertshaw Controls Co., Houston and Anaheim, Calif., 1968-70; ind. cons. Olin Corp., Pasadena Ind. Sch. Dist., 1970-72; mgr. tng. sales Tex-A-Mation Engring., La Porte, Tex., 1971-72; ind. cons. Forney Engring., Dallas also J.E. Sirrine Co., Houston, 1972; instrument designer Stubbs, Overbeck & Assos., Houston, assigned to Celanese Chm. Co., Bishop, Tex., 1972; instrument design supr. S.I.P., Inc., Houston, assigned to Shell Chem. Co., Houston, 1972-74; sr. instrument engr., design supr. Tellepsen Petro-Chem. Constrn. Co., Houston, 1974-79; prin. Thorne Cons. Service, Houston, 1979—. Mem. Tex. Senate Com. for Tech. and Vocational Edn., 1971-75; Tex. rep. for instrumentation HEW Conf., Los Alamos, 1967. Served with AUS, 1946, 50-53; with USAAF, 1946-49. Registered profl. engr. Mem. Instrument Soc. Am. (edn. dir. Houston sect. 1972-74), Am. Soc. Engring. Technicians, Internat. Platform Assn., Nat. Soc. Profl. Engrs. Club: Masons. Home: 16922 Blackhawk St Friendswood TX 77546 Office: PO Box 37 Friendswood TX 77546

THORNEYCROFT, BARON (GEORGE EDWARD) PETER, barrister, former politician; b. July 26, 1909; s. George Edward Mervyn and Dorothy Hope T.; m. Sheila Wells Page, 1938 (div. 1949); 1 son; m. 2d, Carla Roberti, 1949; 1 dau. Student Eton, Royal Mil. Acad., Woolwich. Commd. Royal Arty., 1930, resigned commn., 1933; called to bar, Inner Temple, 1935; practised Birmingham (Oxford Circuit), Stafford, 1938-45, Monmouth, 1945-66; parliamentary sec. Ministry of War Transport, 1945; pres. Bd. Trade, 1951-57; chancellor of Exchequer, 1957-58, resigned; minister of Aviation, 1960-62; minister Def., 1962-64; sec. of State for Def., 1964; chmn. SITPRO, 1968-75; chmn. Conservative Party, 1975-81; chmn. Trusthouse Forte Ltd., 1969-81, pres., 1982—; chmn. BOTB, 1972-74, Pye of Cambridge Ltd., 1967-69, Brit. Res. Ins. Co. Ltd., 1980—, Gil, Carvajal & Ptnrs. Ltd., 1981—, Cinzano U.K. Ltd., 1982-85; chmn. Pirello Gen. Cable Works Ltd., Pirelli Ltd.; dir. Securicor, Riunione Adratica de Sicurta, 1981—. Exhbns. of paintings, Trafford Gallery, 1961, 70. Mem. Royal Soc. Brit. Artists. *

THORNTON, CHARLES VICTOR, metals executive; b. Salt Lake City, Feb. 8, 1915; s. Charles Victor and Winnie May (Fitts) T.; m. Margaret Louise Wiggins, Apr. 17, 1937; children: Charles Victor III, Carolyn Louise (Mrs. John J. Moorhouse), David Frank. B.S. in Civil Engring., U. Utah, 1935; H.H.D., Ind. Inst. Tech., 1972. Engr., Truscon Steel Co., Youngstown, Ohio, 1935-37; dist. engr. Truscon Steel Co., Washington, 1937-40; chief engr. So. Iron Works, Inc., Alexandria, Va., 1940-45; pres. Thornton Industries, Inc., Ft. Worth, 1945-75; chmn. bd. Thornton Industries, Inc., 1975—; chmn. bd. Western Steel Co., Corpus Christi, Tex., 1971-84. Pres. Tarrant County Water Bd., 1984-86; past pres., chmn. bd. trustees emeritus Shriners Hosp. for Crippled Children.; adv. bd. dirs. Center for Transp. Recipient Good Neighbor of Yr. award Internat. Good Neighbor Council. Mem. ASCE (life), Ft. Worth C. of C. (pres. 1960), Am. Assn. Pvt. R.R. Car Owners (pres. 1982-83), Tau Beta Pi. Clubs: Shady Oaks Country, Fort Worth, Century II (bd. govs.), Exchange of Ft. Worth (past pres.). Lodges: Masons (33 degree s.r.), Shriners (past imperial potentate) Kiwanis (past pres., nat. adv. council 1986—, Merit of Honor award), Elks. Office: Suite 919 Ridglea Bank Bldg Fort Worth TX 76116

THORNTON, EDMUND B., business consultant exec.; b. Chgo., Mar. 9, 1930; s. George A. and Suzanne W. Thornton; B.A., Yale U., 1954; children from previous marriage: Thomas and Jonathan (twins), Susan and Amanda (twins); m. Susan Thorton; 1 child, Taylor. With No. Trust Co., Chgo., 1957-59; asst. sec., asst. treas. Ottawa Silica Co. (Ill.), 1959-61, v.p. corporate devel., 1961-62, pres., chief exec. officer, 1962-75, chmn. bd., chief exec. officer, 1975-83, chmn. bd., 1983-86; dir., v.p. Ottawa Nat. Bank. Del. Republican Nat. Conv., 1964-84, precinct committeeman, 1978—; chmn. LaSalle County Rep. Central Com., 1980—; pres. Ottawa Silica Co. Found. Served to lt. USMCR, 1954-56. Recipient Conservation Service award U.S. Dept. Interior, 1973. Mem. Ill. Mfrs.' Assn. (dir. 1969-75, chmn. 1975), NAM, Ill. State C. of C. (dir. 1972-78), U.S. C. of C., Nat. Indsl. Sand Assn. (dir. 1968-73), Explorers Club. Republican. Congregationalist. Clubs: Capitol Hill (Washington); Chicago, Racquet, U. Chgo. Lodge: Elks. Author various articles on historic preservation, history and mil. subjects. Home: PO Box 1 Ottawa IL 61350 Office: PO Box 949 Ottawa IL 61350

THORNTON, JENNIFER, documentation consultant; b. Leicester, Eng., July 24, 1946; d. John and Gwendolyn (Wilkinson) Harrison; m. Eric Kitchener Thornton, Apr. 7, 1969; 1 child, Samuel John. B.A. with honours in English Lang. and Medieval Lit., U. Durham, Eng., 1968; M.A. in Gen. Linguistics, U. Manchester, Eng., 1975. Tech. author Internat. Computers Ltd., Reading, Eng., 1968-72; editorial asst. Pergamon Press, London, 1972-73; sr. author Ferranti Computer Systems, Ltd., Manchester, 1978-79, prin. author, 1979-83, chief author, 1983-86, divisional documentation consultant, 1986—; lectr. gen. linguistics Manchester Poly., 1981; prin. U.K. expert in system documentation Internat. Standards Orgn., 1985—. Mem. tech. communications examination com. City and Guilds of London Inst., 1983—. Sub-editor Omega, 1972; contbr. articles to newspaper. Gov. St. James' Ch. of Eng. Primary Sch., Manchester, 1985—; mem. parochial ch. council, 1986—. Sci. Research Council grantee, 1976-78. Fellow Inst. Sci. and Tech. Communicators (council 1983—, bd. mgmt. 1985—, chmn. tech. and publs. com. 1985-86); mem. Inst. Elec. Engrs. (computing standards consultative com. 1985—, rep. to software devel. and system documentation com. British Standards Inst.), Soc. for Study of Artificial Intelligence and Simulation of Behaviour. Mem. Ch. of England. Home: 30 Willow Park Willow Bank, Manchester M14 6XT, England Office: Ferranti Computer Systems Ltd, Simonsway, Wythenshawe, Manchester M22 5LA, England

THORNTON, ROBERT KELSEY, English language educator; b. Huddersfield, Yorkshire, Eng., Aug. 12, 1938; s. Harold and Mildred Rought (Brooks) T.; m. Sarah Griffiths, Aug. 3, 1963 (div. 1975); children: Jason, Ben; m. Eileen Valerie Davison, July 4, 1976; children: Amy, Tom. BA, U. Manchester, Eng., 1960, MA, 1961, PhD, 1971. Lectr. Univ., Newcastle, Eng., 1965-75, sr. lectr., 1975-84, prof., 1984—. Author: G.M. Hopkins The Poems, 1975, The Decadent Dilemma, 1984; editor: The Midsummer Cushion, 1978, Ivor Gurney War Letters, 1985, Ivor Gurney Severn & Somme and War's Embers, 1987. Chmn. John Clare Soc., 1986—. Avocation: painting. Home: The Tannery, Dipton Mill Rd, Hexham NE46 1RT, England Office: The University, Sch English, Newcastle NE1 7RU, England

THORNTON, SPENCER P., ophthalmologist, educator; b. West Palm Beach, Fla., Sept. 16, 1929; s. Ray Spencer and Mae (Phillips) T.; m. Annie Glenn Cooper, Oct. 6, 1956; children: Steven Pitts, David Spencer, Ray Cooper, Beth Ellen. BS, Wake Forest Coll., 1951, MD, 1954. Diplomate: Am. Bd. Ophthalmology. Intern Ga. Bapt. Hosp., Atlanta, 1954-55; resident gen. surgery U. Ala. Med. Center, 1955-56; resident ophthalmology Vanderbilt U. Sch. Medicine, 1960-63, clin. instr. eye surgery, 1963-66; practice medicine specializing in ophthalmic surgery Nashville, 1960—; dir. cataract and corneal service Bapt. Hosp. Outpatient Surgery Ctr., Nashville, 1983—; mem. staff Mid State Bapt., chief ophthalmology service 1972-87; mem. staff Vanderbilt Hosp., Parkview Hosp.; guest prof. & vis. lectr. various univs., Sweden, 1987, Eng., 1986-87, Can., 1986, 87, South Africa, 1987, Switzerland, 1985, 87; instr. Moscow Inst. Eye Microsurgery, 1981, vis. lectr., 1982; instr. ophthalmic surgery Am. Acad. Ophthalmology Ann. Courses; vis. lectr. U. Vienna, 1982, 83, U. Munich, 1982, U. Zurich, 1982, 83, 84, U. Toronto, 1986; pres., chmn. bd. Spencer Thornton Profl. Assn., 1972—; Internat. lectr. lens implant symposiums, Eng., 1984-86, Spain, 1985, Australia, 1986; named to Am. Soc. Cataract and Refractive Surgery Cataract Leaders Council, 1987, internat. adv. com. European Implantlens Council, 1987. King Features syndicated newspaper columnist, 1959-60, feature writer, NBC radio and TV, 1958-60; author and co-author textbooks on cataract and refractive surgery; mem. editorial bd. Jour. Refractive Surgery, Jour. Am. Soc. Cataract and Refractive Surgery, Ocular Surgery News; contbr. articles to profl. jours. Pres. Eye Found. Tenn., 1974—; mem. alumni council Bowman Gray Sch. Medicine. Served to capt. M.C., AUS, 1956-58. Named among Outstanding Young Men of Yr., U.S. Jaycees, 1965. Fellow Internat. Coll. Surgeons, Royal Soc. Health (London), Am. Acad. Ophthalmology, ACS; mem. Nashville Acad. Ophthalmology (pres. 1974-75), Am. Intra-Ocular Implant Soc. (founding mem., del. to AMA 1980), Am. Soc. Cataract and Refractive Surgery (sci. adv. bd.), Keratorefractive Soc., Internat. Soc. Refractive Keratoplasty (sci. adv. bd.), AMA (Physician's Recognition award), Am. Med. Soc. Vienna (life), Tenn. Soc. Medicine, Nashville Acad. Medicine, Nat. Geog. Soc. (life), public relations chmn. 1979—), Phi Rho Sigma, Delta Kappa Alpha. Baptist. Home: 5070 Villa Crest Dr Nashville TN 37220 Office: 2010 Church St Nashville TN 37203

THORNTON, SUE BONNER, former librarian; b. nr. Fairfield, Tex.; d. John Carder and Mary (Bonner) T. A.B., U. Okla., 1920, A.B. in L.S, 1938, Mus.B. in Piano, 1921; M.A., Columbia U., 1932; postgrad., U. Hawaii, summer 1936. Music supr. Okla. pub. schs., 1921-25; head music dept. Northeastern State Coll., Tahlequah, Okla., 1925-32; librarian Northeastern State Coll., 1932-64. Author: The Bonner Family History. Mem. Central Area, Freestone County, B-RI museums; chmn. bd. trustees Freestone County (Tex.) Mus. Mem. NEA, ALA, Daus. Am. Colonists, Colonial Dames of 17th Century, Tahlequah C. of C., League Women Voters, United Ch. Women Tahlequah (chmn. 1960), D.A.R. (chmn. good citizens com. for Okla. 1958-60), Magna Charta Dames, Ams. Royal Descent, Plantagenet Soc., Soc. Descs. Knights Garter, Nat. Soc. U.S. Daus. 1812, Huguenot Soc. S.C., P.E.O., Order Washington Daus. Colonial Wars, Colonial Order of Crown, Tex. and Southwestern Cattle Raisers Assn., Pan Am. Round Table, Alpha Gamma Delta. Democrat. Presbyn. Clubs: History (Fairfield, Tex.);

Harvey Woman's (Palestine, Tex.); Soroptimist, Freestone County Country. Home: Route 1 Box 880 Fairfield TX 75840

THORPE, CALVIN E., lawyer, legal educator; b. Springville, Utah, May 22, 1938; s. Ronald Eaton and Lillian (Thorn) T.; m. Patricia Warren, Feb. 2, 1961; children—Amber, Jill, Marc, Linda, Michael. B.S. in Physics, Brigham Young U., 1962; M.S. in Engring., U. Pa., 1963; J.D., Seton Hall U., 1969. Bar: N.J. 1969, Tex. 1971, Utah, 1974, U.S. Dist. Ct. Utah 1974, U.S. Ct. Customs and Patent Appeals 1975, U.S. Ct. Appeals (10th cir.) 1980. Assoc. Law Offices Giles C. Clegg, Dallas, 1971-73; ptnr. Thorpe, North & Western, Sandy, Utah, 1973—; adj. assoc. prof. U. Utah, Salt Lake City, 1975—; lectr. Brigham Young U., Provo, 1983—; dir. I.E. Sensors, Inc., Salt Lake City. Chmn., mem. Sandy City Planning Commn., 1975-84; mem. Sandy City Bd. Adjustment, 1980-81; chmn. Sandy Econ. Devel. Council, 1984. Editor-in-chief, Utah Bar Journal, 1987—. Mem. Am. Planning Assn. (Utah chpt., Citizen Planner award 1985), Utah C. of C. (Total Citizen award 1986), Sandy Area C. of C. (chmn. 1985), Am. intellectual Property Law Assn., Sigma Pi Sigma. Mormon. Office: Thorpe North & Western 9662 S State St Sandy UT 84070

THORPY, FRANK THOMAS, airline executive; b. Invercargill, New Zealand, Aug. 23, 1919; s. Patrick Terence and Mary (White) T.; m. Pamela Patricia Kelliher, Sept. 10, 1964; children: Peter Frank, Michael John. Student, London Sch. Econs., 1939. Part-time dir. F.T. Thorpy Ltd., Auckland, New Zealand, 1946—; hon. consul Brazil New Zealand, 1967—; pub. relations cons. Varig Brazilian Airlines, Auckland, 1970-74, mktg. and sales mgr., 1974—; vice chmn. Bur. Importers and Exporters, 1960-69. Author: Wine in New Zealand, 1971, Complete Book of New Zealand and Australian Wines, 1973, New Zealand Wine Guide, 1976, Wine in Zealand, 1983, New Zealand Wine Diary, 1987; contbr. numerous articles to U.K., U.S., Australian, and New Zealand publs. Chmn. visual arts Auckland Festival Arts, 1960-69. Decorated knight Brazilian Order So. Cross, Cavaleiro da Ordem de Rio Branco, 1987, Greek War medal, 1940-41, Cruzeiro do Sol, 1973. Mem. Internat. Wine and Food Soc. (founder, past pres. Auckland), Royal New Zealand Yacht Squadron, Canterbury C. of C. Roman Catholic. Home: 135 Tamaki Dr, Mission Bay, Auckland New Zealand Office: Consul of Brasil, PO Box 4356, 8 Commerce St, Auckland New Zealand

THORSEN, JAMES HUGH, aviation director, airport manager; b. Evanston, Ill., Feb. 5, 1943; s. Chester A. and Mary Jane (Currie) T.; BA, Ripon Coll., 1965; m. Nancy Dain, May 30, 1980. Asst. dean of admissions Ripon (Wis.) Coll., 1965-69; adminstrv. asst. Greater Rockford (Ill.) Airport Authority, 1969-70; airport mgr. Bowman Field, Louisville, 1970-71; asst. dir. St. Louis Met. Airport Authority, 1971-80; dir. aviation, airport mgr. City of Idaho Falls (Idaho), 1980—. Bd. dirs. Crime Stoppers, 1987—. Named hon. citizen State of Ill. Legislature, 1976, Ky. Col.; FAA cert. comml. pilot, flight instr. airplanes and instruments. Mem. Am. Assn. Airport Execs. (accredited airport exec.), Internat. NW Aviation Council, Greater Idaho Falls C. of C. (bd. dir. 1986—), Mensa, Sigma Alpha Epsilon. Home: 1270 First St Idaho Falls ID 83401 Office: Mcpl Airport Idaho Falls ID 83401

THORSEN, NANCY DAIN, real estate broker; b. Edwardsville, Ill., June 23, 1944; d. Clifford Earl and Suzanne Eleanor (Kribs) Dain; m. David Massie, 1968 (div. 1975); 1 dau., Suzanne Dain Massie; m. James Hugh Thorsen, May 30, 1980. B.Sc. in Mktg., So. Ill. U., 1968, M.Sc. in Bus. Edn., 1975; grad. Realtor Inst., Idaho, 1983. Cert. resdl. and investment specialist. Personnel officer J.H. Little & Co. Ltd., London, 1969-72; instr. in bus. edn. Spl. Sch. Dist. St. Louis, 1974-77; mgr. mktg./ops. Isis Foods, Inc., St. Louis, 1978-80; asst. mgr. store Stix, Baer & Fuller, St. Louis, 1980; assoc. broker Century 21 Sayer Realty, Inc., Idaho Falls, Idaho, 1981—. Bd. dirs. Idaho Vol., Boise, 1981-84, Idaho Falls Symphony, 1982; pres. Friends of Idaho Falls Library, 1981-83; chmn. Idaho Falls Mayor's Com. for Vol. Coordination, 1981-84. Recipient Idaho Gov.'s award, 1982, cert. appreciation City of Idaho Falls/Mayor Campbell, 1982, 87, Century 21 Gold Assoc. award, 1987; named to Two Million Dollar Club, Three Million Dollar Club, 1987 ; named Top Investment Sales Person for Eastern Idaho, 1985, No. 1 Century 21 Agt. in Idaho, 1986, 87. Mem. Idaho Falls Bd. Realtors (chmn. orientation 1982-83, chmn. edn. 1983), So. Ill. U. Alumni Assn. Clubs: Newcomers, Civitan (Idaho Falls) (Civitan of Yr. 1986, 87). Office: Century 21 Sayer Realty Inc 403 First St PO Box 1606 Idaho Falls ID 83403

THORSHOV, ROY NORMAN, architect; b. Hudson, Wis., Mar. 13, 1905; s. Olaf and Helen (Hansen) T.; m. Sylvia Serum, Aug. 22, 1931; children: Sonja Louise, Jon Roland (dec.). B.Arch., U. Minn., 1928; diploma, Fontainbleau Sch. Fine Arts, 1929. Registered architect, Minn. Mem. Thorshov & Cerny, Inc. (architects), Mpls., 1927-60; pres. Thorshov & Cerny, Inc. (architects), 1935-60; mem. Thorsen & Thorshov Assos., Inc., 1960-87, v.p., treas.; mem. Minn. State Bd. Registration for Architects, Engrs. and Land Surveyors, 1966-72, sec.-treas., 1967-72, chmn. Mpls. Heritage Preservation Commn., 1972-76, sec., 1976. Architect: St. Francis Cabrini Ch, Mpls. (1st prize 1951), Richfield (Minn.) Central Elementary Sch. (honorable mention 1951), Clearwater County Meml. Hosp, Bagley, Minn. (top award AIA 1951), 1st Unitarian Soc Ch, Mpls. (2d prize Religious Arts Guild), Trinity Luth. Ch, La Crosse, Wis. (honor awards Progressive Architecture 1952, Minn. State Assn. Architecture awards for Elk River Steam Generating Plant, A.S. Aloe Bldg. St. Louis Park Med. Center 1952, honor awards for Am. Hardware Mut. Bldg., Mpls., 1st Christian Ch., Mpls. 1957, honor awards AIA for Fairmount Fed. Savs. and Loan Assn. (Minn.), St. Mary's Greek Orthodox Ch., Mpls. 1958, Dunwiddie Elementary Sch., Port Washington, Wis. 1959, Lyndale Homes, Mpls., Pearson Candy Co., St. Paul, Grandview Jr. High Sch., Mound, Minn. 1960, 1st honor award for Elliot-Twins Apts., U.S. Pub. Housing Authority 1964, 1st honor award AIA for Ebenezer Tower housing for elderly 1972). Pres. Kenwood Isles Condominium, 1987; bd. dirs. Sons of Norway Found.; bd. dirs. Pillsbury Waite Neighborhood Services, 1949-84, Hennepin County Bicentennial Commn., 1973-76. Decorated Knight's Cross 1st Class Royal Order St. Olav, comdr. Royal Order St. Olav, Norway). Fellow AIA (past sec., pres. Mpls. chpt.); mem. Am. Philatelic Soc., Minn. Soc. Architects (pres. 1964), Constrn. Specifications Inst., Inc. (dir. Minn. chpt. 1958-59), Minn. Hist. Soc., Walker Art Center, Torske-Klubben (pres. 1946-84), Hennepin County Hist. Soc. (dir., life mem., pres. 1971-82), Norwegian-Am. C. of C. (dir. upper Midwest chpt.), Norwegian-Am. Hist. Soc. (pres. 1979-81, dir.), Norwegian-Am. Mus. (dir., v.p. 1971), Nordmanns Forbundet (v.p. 1968, pres. 1971-75, dir. internat. bd. 1973—), Tau Sigma Delta, Tau Beta Pi. Clubs: Athletic (dir. 1958-60), Six O'Clock (pres. 1964), Ten Men's, Shriners. Home: 1425 W 28th St Minneapolis MN 55408

THORSON, MILTON ZENAS, paint and varnish company executive; b. Thorsby, Ala., Oct. 26, 1902; s. Theodore T. and Emma (Hokanson) T.; student Am. Inst. Banking, extension courses U. So. Calif.; Degree in Bus. (hon.); m. 3d, Helen Lob, Aug. 31, 1978. Chief teller Tenn. Valley Bank, Decatur, Ala., 1919-28; teller Security First Nat. Bank, Los Angeles, 1928-29; with Red Spot Paint & Varnish Co., Inc., Evansville, Ind., 1929-60, chmn. exec. bd., dir., 1961-79; chmn. exec. bd. Owensboro Paint & Glass Co. (Ky.); ; former mem. Regional Export Expansion Council, U.S. Dept. Commerce. Mem. Audubon Soc., Nat. Paint and Coatings Assn. (hon.), Soc. Plastic Engrs. (Plastic Industry Pioneer). Republican. Club: President's of U. Evansville (life). Contbr. tech. articles profl. jours. Home: Box 418 Evansville IN 47703 also: 527 Harbor Dr Key Biscayne FL 33149 Office: 110 Main St Evansville IN 47701

THORSTEINSSON, ÁRNI KRISTINN, sales executive; b. Reykjavik, Iceland, Mar. 5, 1922; s. Thorsteinn Gísli Árnason and Ásta Jónsdóttir; m. Sigridur Anna, Feb. 9, 1950; children: Anna, Ásta, Thorsteinn, Sveinn, Erna Thórunn, Ingibjörg Hólmfrídur. Rep. Hid islenska steinoliuhlutafelag, Reykjavik, 1941-46; div. chief, mgr. supply, import and purchasing dept. Oliufelagid h.f., Reykjavik, 1947—. Lodge: Lions, St. John's. Home: 10 Granaskjol, 107 Reykjavik Iceland Office: Oliufelagid HF, 18 Sudurlandsbraut, 108 Reykjavik Iceland

THORSTEINSSON, DAVID SCHEVING, food manufacturing company executive; b. Isafjordur, Iceland, Jan. 4, 1930; s. Magnus Scheving and Laura (Havstein) T.; m. Stefania Borg, May 21, 1966; children—Magnus, Gudrun, Stefania; m. Soffia Mathiesen, Apr. 18, 1953 (dec. Jan. 1964); children—Laura, Hrund, Jon. Cand. phil., U. Reykjavik, 1950. Prodn. mgr. S.L.A. Ltd., Reykjavik, 1951-57; mgr. SLA & Ljomi, Reykjavik, 1957-63; gen. mgr. Smjorliki, Sol Ltd., 1963-74, chief exec., 1974—; chmn., Indsl. Bank Ltd., Hydrol Ltd; vice-chmn. Tech. Devels. Ltd., dir. Gen. Ins. Ltd., Reykjavik; res. mem. bd. dirs. Nat. Bank Iceland, 1972-84, Central Bank, 1984—. Chmn., Red Cross Iceland, 1966-68, mem. Central Com. Liberal Party Iceland, 1979—; consul gen. Ireland, 1977—. Decorated knight Order Falcon. Mem. Fedn. Icelandic Industries (chmn. 1968-82), Fed. Icelandic Employers (vice chmn. 1984-85), European Free Trade Assn. Geneva (cons. com.), Joint Contact Group. Lutheran. Club: Rotary. Avocations: music; history; fishing. Home: 7 Mavanes, Gardabaer, Reykjavik Iceland Office: Sol Ltd, 14-21 Thuerholt, 105 Reykjavik Iceland

THOSTRUP, NILS, newspaper executive; b. Copenhagen, Denmark, July 20, 1936; m. Grete Lorentsen, 1960. Journalist Svendborg (Denmark) Avis, 1953-55, Fyens Stiftstidende, Odense, Denmark, 1956-58; copy editor Aalborg (Denmark) Amtstidende, 1959-65; mng. editor Jyllands-Posten, Viby J., Denmark, 1966-84, editor-in-chief, 1985—. Author: The Chinese Way, 1985, Reforms in China, 1987. Office: Jyllands-Posten, Groendalsvej, 8260 Viby J Denmark

THOTA, HAMSA A. P., microbiologist; b. India, July 14, 1948; came to U.S., 1972; s. Venkata Subbarao Naidu and Venkata (Subbamma) T.; B.S., Andhra U., 1968; M.S., U. Mysore, 1970; Ph.D., U. Ga., 1976; m. Sindhu Shah, June 26, 1976; children—Devi, Darshan. Shift-in-Charge, Modern Bakeries (Pvt) Ltd., India, 1970-71; grad. teaching asst. U. Ga., 1973-76; mgr. microbiology, head food analysis Rich-Seapak Corp., St. Simons Island, Ga., 1976—. Recipient Outstanding Research award Am. Oil Chemist's Soc., 1975. Cert. specialist in food, dairy and sanitation microbiology Nat. Registry Microbiologists of Am. Acad. Microbiology. Mem. Am. Soc. Microbiology, Inst. Food Technologists, Electron Microscopy Soc. Am., N.Y. Acad. Scis., Sigma Xi. Club: St. Simons Island Rotary (pres., dir., dist. gov.'s group rep.). Home: 121 Dunbarton Dr Saint Simons Island GA 31522 Office: Box 667 Saint Simons Island GA 31522

THOTTAPPILLY, GEORGE, virologist; b. Karoor, Kerala, India, Apr. 22, 1941; arrived in Nigeria, 1978; s. Kunjuvareed and Kunjalichy (Valiaveetil) T.; m. Aleyamma Kurien Melpurathu, Apr. 15, 1972; 1 child, Lisa. BS in Agr., Kerala U., 1962; MS in Agr., U. Goettingen, Fed. Republic Germany, 1964; PhD in Agr. with distincton, U. Giessen, Fed. Republic Germany, 1968. Sci. co-worker U. Giessen, 1968-69; postdoctoral research assoc. Mich. State U., East Lansing, 1970-71, research scientist, 1973-78; postdoctoral fellow Can. Nat. Research Council, Ottawa, Ont., 1971-73; virologist Internat. Inst. Tropical Agr., Ibadan, Nigeria, 1978—. Contbr. articles to profl. jours. Predoctoral fellow KAAD Found., 1965-66, Volkswagen Found., 1965-66. Fellow Indian Phytopathol. Soc., Nat. Acad. Sci.; mem. Am. Soc. for Virology, Am. Phytopathol. Soc., Soc. for Gen. Microbiology, Indian Virological Soc., Indian Botanical Soc., Inst. Biology, Internat. Working Group on Legume Viruses, N.Y. Acad. Scis., Nigerian Soc. Plant Protection, Root Crops Soc., Sigma Xi. Roman Catholic. Home and Office: Internat Inst Tropical Agr, PMB 5320, Ibadan Nigeria

THRALL, DONALD STUART, painter; b. Detroit, Mar. 29, 1918; s. Ernest Lawrence and Gertrude Marie (Aikenhead) T. B.A., Mich. State U., 1940; M.A., Columbia U. Tchrs. Coll., 1946; summer student, Skowhegan (Maine) Sch. Painting and Sculpture, 1947, Black Mountain (N.C.) Coll., 1948. Instr. painting and design Cass Tech. Sch., Detroit, 1949-55; ednl. coordinator Guggenheim Mus., N.Y.C., 1961-73; Bd. dirs. Mich. Watercolor Soc., 1950-55, Detroit Met. Art Assn., 1948-54; exhibiting mem. Detroit Inst. Arts, 1947-53. One-man exhbn., Contemporary Arts Gallery, N.Y.C., 1961, group exhbns. include, Met. Mus. Art, 1950, Detroit Inst. Arts, 1947-55 (award 1950, 53, 55), Mich. Artists invited survey show, 1951, Butler Inst. Am. Art, Youngstown, Ohio, 1950-52 (1st prize 1951), Whitney Mus., N.Y.C., 1953, Bklyn. Mus., 1961, others, group exhbns. include, Wildenstein Galleries, N.Y.C., 1952 (Hallmark Art prize), Downtown Gallery, N.Y.C., 1950-53, Detroit Artists Market, 1948-54, Scarab Gallery, Detroit, 1948-53 (award 1948, 51, 53, 54), Mich. Watercolor Soc., 1949-55 (award 1950, 52, 53, 55), Mich. State Fair, 1952 (1st prize 1952), Detroit Art Instr. Exhbn., 1946-53 (1st award 1946, 48, 50, 51, 53), 16th Serigraph Internat., N.Y.C., 1955, others; represented in permanent collections, Detroit Inst. Arts, Butler Inst. Am. Art, U. Mich. Mus. Art, Mus. Wayne State U., Cranbrook Acad. Art Mus., Bloomfield Hills, Mich., numerous pvt. collections, U.S. and abroad. Served with AUS, 1941-45. Guggenheim fellow, 1955. Mem. Mich. Acad. Sci., Arts and Letters, Beta Alpha Sigma (pres. 1940). Address: 945 West End Ave New York NY 10025

THRASHER, JAMES PARKER, writer; b. Waltham, Mass., Jan. 15, 1932; s. Linus James and Doris Melissa (Parker) T.; B.S. in Indsl. Adminstrn., Yale U., 1953; children: Deborah Anne, Linda Carol, Anne Elizabeth. With U.S. Steel Corp., Cleve., 1953-60; sales cons. Booz, Allen & Hamilton Internat., London, 1960 65; mgmt. cons. McKinsey & Co., Inc., London, 1965-67; v.p. for Europe, Integrated Container Service, Inc., London, 1967-69, pres., chief exec. officer, N.Y.C., 1970-75; v.p., dir. Interway Corp., N.Y.C., 1969-75, pres., chief exec. officer, dir., 1975-79, Transam. Interway, Inc. subs. Transam. Corp., San Francisco, 1979-81. Author: A Crisis of Values, 1985. Clubs: Yale. Home: 365 Lynn Cove Rd Asheville NC 28804

THRIFT, NIGEL JOHN, geographer, educator; b. Bath, Eng., Oct. 12, 1949; s. Leonard John and Joyce Mary (Wakeley) T.; m. Lynda Jean Sharples, May 1979; children: Victoria Caroline, Jessica Abigail. BA with honors, U. Wales, 1971; PhD, U. Bristol, 1979. Research officer U. Cambridge, Eng., 1976-78; research fellow U. Leeds, 1978-79; sr. research fellow Australian Nat. U., Canberra, 1980-84; reader U. Wales, Lampeter, 1984-87; reader dept. geography U. Bristol, 1987—; dir. Centre for Study of Britain and World Economy, 1984—. Author: Times, Spaces and Places, 1980, The Price of War, 1986; editorial bd. Soc. and Space, 1983; co-editor: Environment and Planning, 1979—. Fellow Royal Geog. Soc.; mem. Inst. Brit. Geographers (council). Office: Univ Bristol, University Rd, Bristol BS8 1SS, England

THRING, MEREDITH WOOLDRIDGE, chemical engineer, educator; b. Melbourne, Victoria, Australia, Dec. 17, 1915; came to Eng., 1919; s. Walter Hugh and Dorothy (Wooldridge) T.; m. Alice Margaret Hooley, Dec. 14, 1940; children—Susan Margaret Thring Kalaugher, John Meredith, Robert Hugh. B.A., Cambridge U., 1937, M.A., 1941, Sc.D., 1964; Dr. (hon.), Open U., 1982. Head combustion lab. Brit. Coal Utilisation Research Assn., London, 1937-46; head physics dept. Brit. Iron and Steel Research Assn., London, 1946-53; prof., head fuel tech. and dept. chem. engring. Sheffield U., 1953-64; prof., head dept. mech. engring. Queen Mary Coll., London U., 1964-81, prof. emeritus, 1981—; gen. supt. Internat. Flame Research Found., Ijmuiden, Holland, 1949-76; mng. dir. Fuel Combustion Ltd., Eng., 1984—, Thring Advanced Devels. Ltd., Eng., 1966—. Author: The Science of Flames and Furnaces, 1952, 62; Man, Machines and Tomorrow, 1972; How To Invent, 1977; The Engineer's Conscience, 1980; Robots and Telechirs, 1983. Recipient Robert Hadfield medal Iron and Steel Inst., 1949; Fellow Inst. Mech. Engring., (founder fellow); Inst. Energy (sr. fellow); pres. 1962-63, Inst. Physics, Instn. Elec. Engrs., Inst. Chem. Engrs. Mem. Ch. of England. Club: Athenaeum (London). Avocations: farming; wood carving. Home and Office: Bell Farm Brundish, Suffolk 1P13 8BL, England

THUEME, WILLIAM HAROLD, educator; b. St. Clair, Mich., Sept. 4, 1945; s. Harold Arthur and Delphine Betty (Buhl) T.; m. Nora Kathleen Koning, May 8, 1971; children—Benjamin William, Rebecca Kathleen, Jeffrey William, Sarah Kathleen. Student Port Huron Jr. Coll., 1963-64; B.A., Mich. State U., 1967, M.A., 1969; postgrad. Oakland U., 1971, U. Mich., 1971, San Francisco State U., 1975, U. Hawaii, 1975. Cert. tchr., Mich. Tchr. pub. schs., Charlotte, Mich., 1967-69, Ann Arbor, Mich., 1969—; fgn. travel coordinator Ambassadors Abroad Program, Amsterdam, Netherlands, 1968—; regional driver coordinator for Southeastern Mich., Avis Rent-a-Car, 1983—. Participant Skyhook II Project; elections coordinator Eaton County (Mich.) Republican Party, 1968, mem. nat. com., 1968—; mem. troop com. Council Boy Scouts Am., Ypsilanti; cub scout summer camp instr. Wolverne Council, 1987; coach of the angels Ypsilanti Am. Little League, 1988; active Mich. United Conservation Clubs, Big Brothers Am., Charlotte, Mich., Human Rights Watch, Nat. Security Caucus U.S., 1988—, Heritage Found., 1988—, Project Save OUr Schs., 1988—; elders quorum instr., exec. sec. Ch. of Jesus Christ of Latter-day Saints, 1976-81, adult spl. interest coordinator, 1982—, Sunday Sch. sec. Ann Arbor stake, 1983—; mem. Mich. Mormon Concert Choir, 1977—, Ypsilanti Mormon Choir. Recipient Spl. Recognition award Reagan Presdl. Campaign, 1981, Am. Security Council 30th Anniversary Spl. Recognition Cert. Mem. NEA, Mich. Edn. Assn., Internat. Reading Assn., Mich. Sheriffs Assn. (assoc.), Police Marksmanship Assn., Washtenaw Reading Council, Southeastern Mich. Reading Assn., Mich. Reading Assn., Mich. Assn. for Supervision and Curriculum Devel., Ann Arbor Edn. Assn., Am. Security Council, Am. Defense Inst., Found. for Christian Living, Nat. Geog. Soc., Am. Film Inst., Nat. Rifle Assn., Tri-County Sportsman League, Sigma Alpha Eta. Club: Washtenaw Sportsmen's (Ypsilanti). Lodge: Optimist (v.p. and dir. 1975-78) (Ann Arbor). Office: 25900 Greenfield Suite 418 Oak Park MI 48237

THULIN, INGRID, actress, director; b. Solleftea, Sweden, Jan. 27, 1929; d. Adam and Nana T.; m. Harry Schein, Sept. 15, 1956. Grad., Royal Dramatic Theatre Sch., Stockholm, 1951. Actress in numerous modern and classical plays Royal Dramatic Theatre, Stockholm, mcpl. theatres Malmo and Stockholm until 1962; actress Broadway, Italian stage, U.S. TV; films include: When Love Comes to the Village, 1950; Wild Strawberries, 1957; So Close to Life, 1958; The Face, 1958; The Judge, 1960; The Four Horsemen of the Apocalypse, 1961; Winter Light, 1962; The Silence, 1963; La Guerre est Finie, 1968; The Damned, 1970; Cries and Whispers, 1973; A Handful of Love, 1974; La Cage, 1975; Cassandra Crossing, 1976; Agnes Will Die, 1977; One and One, 1978; Broken Skies, 1982; The Rehearsal, 1983; Il Corsario, 1983; writer, dir. Swedish feature film Broken Skyes, 1983; dir. (short film) Devotion. Recipient numerous awards for acting excellence in theatre and films; named Best New Dir., Chgo. Film Festival, 1983. Address: Kevingestrand 7B, 18231 Danderyd Sweden

THULIN, LARS UNO, banker; b. Uddevalla, Sweden, Mar. 25, 1939; came to Norway, 1939; s. Haakon Erling and Signe Ingeborg (Thulin) Hansen; m. Anne Skard, Oct. 7, 1977. M.Sc., Norwegian Inst. Tech., 1965, Dr.Ing., 1970. Lectr., scientist U. Trondheim, 1965-70, dep. dean univ. planning unit, 1970-74; mng. dir. Norwegian Agy. Devel. Aid, Trondheim, 1974-75; undersec. Ministry Research and Edn., Oslo, 1975-76; undersec. Ministry Industry and Energy Oslo, 1976-77; exec. v.p. Den Norske Creditbank, Oslo, 1977—, mng. dir. den Norske Creditbank Plc., London, 1987—; chmn. bd. Ctr. for Indsl. Research, Oslo. Decorated Gt. Cross of Merit (Fed. Republic of Germany). Fellow Inst Petroleum U.K. Office: Den Norske Creditbank, Kirkegt 21, 1 Oslo Norway

THUMS, CHARLES WILLIAM, designer, consultant; b. Manitowoc, Wis., Sept. 5, 1945; s. Earl Oscar and Helen Margaret (Rusch) T. B. in Arch., Ariz. State U., 1972. Ptnr., Grafic, Tempe, Ariz., 1967-70; founder, prin. I-Squared Environ. Cons., Tempe, Ariz., 1970-78; designer and cons. design morphology, procedural programming and algorithms, 1978—. Author: (with Jonathan Craig Thums) Tempe's Grand Hotel, 1973, The Rossen House, 1975; (with Daniel Peter Aiello) Shelter and Culture, 1976; contbg. author: Tombstone Planning Guide, 5 vols., 1974. Office: PO Box 3126 Tempe AZ 85281

THUN, NILS, retired English educator; b. Uppsala, Sweden, Nov. 3, 1914; s. Arvid Frisendahl and Anna Elisabet Thun; m. Greta Dagny Wellenstam, May 2,1959. Fil mag, Uppsala U., 1939, Fil doktor, 1963. Schoolmaster secondary schs. 1942-62; docent Uppsala U., 1963-71; prof. English U. Umea (Sweden), 1971-79. Author: Reduplicative Words in English, 1963; contbr. articles on word formation and word history to profl. jours. Mem. Swedish Assn. U. Tchrs. (2d dep. chmn. 1967-69). Home: Tegnérgatan 38 A S-752 27, (018) 13 69 99 Uppsala Sweden

THUNE-HOLM, ANTON KRISTIAN, management consultant; b. Oslo, May 14, 1939; s. Erling and Ingeborg (Heltzen) Thune-Holm; m. Beda Thune-Holm, Aug. 3, 1963; children—Erling, Kirsti. B.Sc., Oslo Engring. Sch., 1963; M.B.A., N. European Mgmt. Inst., 1973. Sales engr. SAAS, Oslo, 1963-70, logistics mgr., 1970-72; mgmt. cons. Hartmark-Iras, Oslo, 1973-78; mktg. mgr. A-K Maskiner, Oslo, 1978-79; mng. dir. Oslo Consulting Group a/s, 1979—; chmn., pub. dir. Jour. Purchasing, 1980—; bd. dirs., chmn. 8 cos., 1988. Author: Control Valves, 1971; Purchasing, 1982; inventor aircraft starting system, 1972, magnetic signs, 1971. Chmn., Local Conservative Party, Oslo, 1973-77. Served with Norwegian Army, 1959-61. Mem. Brit. Inst. Mgmt., Am. Mktg. Assn. Home: Asdalsveien 42, 1166 Oslo 11, Norway

THURBER, DONALD MACDONALD DICKINSON, public relations counsel; b. Detroit, Feb. 3, 1918; s. Donald MacDonald Dickinson and Fayetta Cecelia (Crowley) T.; m. Margaret Worcester Dudley, June 6, 1964. A.B. magna cum laude, Harvard U., 1940. Pvt. tutor Detroit, 1937-39; house mgr. Cape Playhouse, Dennis, Mass., 1940; exec. sec. youth div. Democratic Nat. Com., 1940; membership sec. Harvard Club, N.Y.C., 1940; project supr. Detroit Council for Youth Service, 1941-43; rep. for Mich., Nat. Found. Infantile Paralysis, 1943-46; sec., adminstr. Wayne County (Mich.) chpt. 1946-50; exec. dir. Gov. Mich. Study Commn. on Deviated Criminal Sex Offenders, 1950-51; exec. sec. Mayor Detroit Com. Rehab. Narcotic Addicts, 1951-53; sec., asst. treas. Mich. Rotary Press, Inc., Detroit, 1953-54; pres. Mich. Rotary Press, Inc., 1954-58; exec. v.p. Pub. Relations Counselors, Inc., Detroit, 1958-61; pres. Pub. Relations Counselors, Inc., 1961—; bd. dirs. Evans Biocontrol, Inc., Broomfield, Colo. Mem. Mich. Crippled Children Commn., 1954-58, vice chmn., 1956-58; planning dir. Episcopal Diocese of Mich., 1958-62, mem. exec. council, 1963-66; cons. to Sec. Interior, 1962-68; mem. Nat. Park Trust Fund Bd., 1963-67; bd. regents U. Mich., 1958-63; mem. Mich. Bd. Edn., 1965-67; mem. bd. overseers com. to visit Harvard Coll., 1964-70; mem. Mich. Citizens Com. for Higher Edn. Planning, 1967-69; chmn. Wayne County Community Coll., 1968-72, trustee, 1968-74; mem. Adv. Com. on Higher Edn. Planning in Southeastern Mich., 1970-72; advisor Nat. Trust Hist. Preservation, 1972-78; bd. dirs. Nat. Park Found., 1974-80; mem. adv. council to Sec. Commerce, 1976-77; v.p. Detroit Grand Opera Assn.; mem. adv. com. Detroit Urban League, Community Music Sch., Detroit; trustee Clan Donald Lands Trust, Isle of Skye, Scotland, 1979—, St. Gregory's Abbey Found., Three Rivers, Mich.; mem. Mich. Hist. Commn., 1984-87; bd. dirs. Blue Cross-Blue Shield of Mich., 1986—, chmn. bd. exec. com., 1988—. Mem. Orch. Hall Assocs. Detroit, Detroit Hist. Soc., Mich. Hist. Soc., Friends of Detroit and Grosse Pointe Pub. Libraries, Mich. Natural Areas Council, Mich. Nature Assn., Clan Donald-U.S.A. (Gt. Lakes commr. emeritus, Mich. commr.), Soc. Colonial Wars, Soc. War of 1812, State Soc. of the Cincinnati of Pa., Mil. Order Loyal Legion U.S., Order Founders and Patriots Am., Colonial Order of Acorn, St. Nicholas Soc., Ancient and Honorable Artillery Commn. Democrat. Episcopalian. Clubs: University (Detroit), Prismatic (Detroit); Harvard (Eastern Mich., N.Y.C., Boston). Office: Pub Relations Counselors Inc 10 Rathbone Pl Grosse Pointe MI 48230

THURMOND, STROM, U.S. senator; b. Edgefield, S.C., Dec. 5, 1902; s. John William and Eleanor Gertrude (Strom) T.; m. Jean Crouch, Nov. 7, 1947 (dec. Jan. 1960); m. Nancy Moore, Dec. 22, 1968; children: Nancy Moore, J. Strom, Jr., Juliana Gertrude, Paul Reynolds. B.S., Clemson Coll., 1923; 14 hon. degrees. Bar: S.C. 1930. Tchr. S.C. schs., 1923-29; city atty., county atty., supt. edn. Edgefield County, 1929-33; state senator 1933-38, circuit judge, 1938-46, gov. of S.C., 1947-51; chmn. So. Govs. Conf., 1950; practiced in Alken, S.C., 1951-55; U.S. senator from S.C. 1955—; Del. Nat. Democratic Conv., 1932, 36, 48, 52, 56, 60; chmn. S.C. dels.; mem. Dem. Nat. Com., 1948; States Rights candidate for Pres. U.S., 1948; del. Nat. Republican Conv., 1968, 72, 76. Bd. dirs. Ga.-Carolina council Boy Scouts Am. Served with AUS; attached to 82d Airborne Div. for invasion 1942-46, Europe; maj. gen. Res. Decorated Legion of Merit with oak leaf cluster, Bronze Star with V, Purple Heart, Croix de Guerre France; Cross of Order of Crown Belgium; others; recipient Congl. Medal Honor, Soc. Nat. Patriots award, 1974. Mem. S.C. (past v.p.), ABA, Clemson Coll. Alumni Assn. (past pres.), also numerous def., vets., civic, fraternal and farm orgns. Baptist. Office: 218 Russell Senate Bldg Washington DC 20510 *

THURN UND TAXIS, PRINCE JOHANNES, business executive; b. Hofling, Germany, June 5, 1926; s. Prince Karl August and Princess Maria Anna (de Braganca) Thurn und Taxis; grad. High school Regensburg, 1946; pvt. banking studies, 1958; m. Mariae Gloria Gräfin und Herrin von Schönburg, Gräfin und Herrin zu Glauchau und Waldenburg, May 31, 1980;

children: Maria Theresia, Albert Erbprinz, Elisabeth. Pres. bd. dirs. banking, brewery, agr. and forestry cos. Head Thurn und Taxis Central Adminstrn. Decorated Order Malta, Rautenkrone. Verdienstorden der Bundesrepublik Deutschland. Mem. 1001 World Wildlife Fund, Wirtschaftsakademie Regensburg. Home and office: Castle 84, Regensburg, Bavaria Federal Republic of Germany

THWAITES, MICHAEL JONATHAN, diplomat; b. Sydney, New South Wales, Australia, May 10, 1944; s. Peter Nelson and Lavinia May (Pask) T.; m. Rosemary Eve Borthwick, July 5, 1969; children: Rayner Bartholomew, Hilary Christiane. B of Law with honors, U. Melbourne, Australia, 1967; MA, Oxford (Eng.) U., 1970; graduate, Nat. Defense Coll., Can., Kingston, 1988. Barrister, solicitor Supreme Ct. Victoria, Australia. From 3d to 2d sec. Australian Embassy, Manila, 1971-73; 1st sec. Australian Embassy, Washington, 1975-78; counsellor and dep. head of mission Australian Embassy, Moscow, 1981-84; dir. Can. and U.S. sect. Dept. Fgn. Affairs, Canberra, Australia, 1985-87; dep. high commr. for Australia, Ottawa, 1988—. Anglican. Club: Nat. Press (Canberra).

THYGESEN, THYGE PETER, architect; b. Fredericia, Denmark, Apr. 5, 1927; s. Jens Peter Carl and Anna Marna (Jensen) T.; m. Hanne Winther; children: Steen, Michael. Grad. in Architectur, Royal Acad. Fine Arts, Denmark, 1956. Registered architect, Denmark, Saudi Arabia. Architect Kai Borgen Co., Odense, Denmark, 1951-57, Kay Bogck-Hanson Co., Copenhagen, 1957-58, Erik Eriksen Co., Odense, 1958-60; chief architect Coop. Soc. Firm, Copenhagen, 1960-62; pvt. practice cons. architect Aarhus, Denmark, 1962-69; architect Malawi Govt., 1969-71; supr. architect Sch. Architecture, Aarhus, 1972-73; project coordinator Hordaland County Council, Bergen, Norway, 1973-77; chief architect Birch & Krogboe Overseas Corp., Saudi Arabia, 1977-80; project mgr. Idea Ctr., Jeddah, Saudi Arabia, 1981-84; chief architect Saudi Arabian-Bahrain Causeway Border Stas., 1984-86; project coordinator Copenhagen Internat. Airport extension program, 1986—. Contbr. articles to profl. jours. Served with Royal Danish Navy, 1950-51. Mem. Assn. Acad. Architects in Denmark, Fedn. Danish Architects. Home: G1 Kongevej 99 II tv, 1850 Frederiksberg Copenhagen Denmark Office: Skaarup & Jsepersen Cons, Architects & Planners AS, Landemaerket 9, 1119 Copenhagen K Denmark

THYVELIKAKATH, GEORGE XAVIER, chemistry educator; b. Cochin, India, Apr. 29, 1943; came to U.S., 1967; s. Anne Joseph (Chakiamury) T.; married; children—Mary, George, Manakil. B.Sc. in Chemistry, Kerala U., Cochin, India, 1965; M.S. in Chemistry, U. Southwestern La., 1971; Ph.D. in Chemistry, Okla. State U., 1975. Postdoctoral fellow U. Ark., Fayetteville, 1975-76, vis. asst. prof. chemistry, 1976-77; asst. prof. chemistry Oral Roberts U., Tulsa, 1977-80, assoc. prof., 1980-83, prof., 1983—; vis. prof. Northeastern Okla. State U., Tahlequah, 1978; cons. Metal Cleaning Corp., Tulsa, 1980-81; chem. lab. tech. staff Tulsa Jr. Coll., 1983—, adv. com. mem., 1983—. Author: Basic Organic Chemistry Laboratory Procedures, 1980; Cancer: Its Causes and Chemistry of Selected Anticancer Drugs, 1984. Contbr. articles to profl. jours. Convenor, Indian Nat. Congress Party Election Com., A Palluruthy, India, 1965; bd. dirs. Royal Oaks Condominium Homeowners Assn., Tulsa, 1980-82. Fellow Dow Research Corp., 1974, Gulf, 1975; recipient Outstanding Faculty award U. Ark., 1976-77, Oral Roberts U., 1979-80, Cert. Meritorious Service Okla. Sci. Tchrs. Assn., 1978; 1st recipient Performance award Oral Roberts U., 1984-85. Mem. Am. Chem. Soc. (sec. Tulsa sect. 1979-80, chmn. Tulsa sect. 1983), Okla. Acad. Sci. (chmn. sci. edn. sect. 1978—), Soc. Magentic Resonance Imaging, Sigma Xi, Phi Lambda Epsilon, Alpha Epsilon Delta. Roman Catholic. Club: Diana Arts (Kumbalanghy, Cochin) (pres. 1964-65). Current work: Cancer chemotherapy, mechanistic and systematic approach to drug design, complexation studies of medically important compounds, NMR studies for the detection of cancer, heart disease, etc.; NMR imaging of oil, water, and gas in rock samples, organic water and air pollutants, pesticides and herbicides; philosophy of education, professional ethics and human nature. Subspecialties: Organic chemistry; Nuclear magnetic resonance. Home: 6611 S Zunis Ave Tulsa OK 74136

TIAN, FENG, mathematics educator; b. Taizhou, People's Republic China, Apr. 30, 1940; s. Junjiu and Jinwen (Shen) T.; m. Shuying Li, May 1, 1969; children: Xu, Hui. B, Shandong U., Jinan, People's Republic China, 1961. Jr. mem. Inst. Math. Acad. Sinica, Beijing, 1961-78, asst. prof., 1978-80; asst. prof. Inst. Systems Sci, Acad. Sinica, Beijing, 1980-81, assoc. prof., 1981—; part-time prof. People's U. China, Beijing, 1979—, Huazhong Normal U., Wuhan, People's Republic China, 1983—, Nanjing (People's Republic China) Normal U., 1986—. Reviewer Math. Rev., Ann Arbor, Mich., 1981—, Zentralblatt fur Math., 1982—; vice editor in chief Math. in Practice and Theory Jour., 1983—; author: Optimization Method, 1979, Theory of Graph and Network Flow, 1986. Mem. Graph Theory Soc. China (trustee 1979-85, sec.-gen. 1985—), Chinese Math. Soc., Systems Engring. Soc. China, Am. Math. Soc. Home: Baofusi Bldg 919 104, Beijing 100086, People's Republic of China Office: Inst Systems Sci, Acad Sinica, Beijing 100080, People's Republic of China

TIAN JIYUN, government official of People's Republic of China; b. Feicheng County, Shandong, People's Republic of China, 1929. Sect. chief Dept. of Fin., Guizhou Province, 1954, dir. of gen. office, 1957; dep. dir. fin. monetary div. Office Fin. Monetary Div. and Office Fin. Econ. Affairs of Southwest China Bur. of Cen. Com., 1965; fin. and trade cadre Revolutionary Com., Sichuan Province, 1970; dir. fin. com. Sichuan Province People's Govt., 1975; joined Communist Party, 1945; mem. 12th Cen. Com. Chinese Communist Party, 1982—; dep. sec.-gen. State Council, Beijing, People's Republic of China, 1981-83, vice premier, 1983—, sec. gen., 1983-85; mem. Politburo, Secretariat of 12th Cen. Com., 1985—. Address: Office of Vice Premier, care State Council, Beijing People's Republic of China *

TIBBALDS, FRANCIS ERIC, architect; b. Brighton, Eng., Oct. 16, 1941; s. William Eric and Elsie Agnes (Wood) T.; m. Janet Grace McDonald, Sept. 6, 1969; children: Adam Dominic, Benedict Malcolm. Diploma in Architecture with distinction, The Poly. Sch. Architecture, London, 1966; M of Philosophy in Arts, Town Planning, U. Coll. London, 1969. Sr. architect planner Llewelyn-Davies, Weeks, Forestier-Walker & Bor, London, 1969-70; prin. architect planner Westminster City Council, London, 1970-72; dep. chief planning officer London Borough Lambeth, 1972-74; joint project dir. Group Five (Nigeria), Ilorin, Nigeria, London, 1974-75; dir. planning Llewelyn-Davies, Weeks, London, Saudi Arabia, Oman, Iran, 1975-78; prin. Tibbalds Colbourne Partnership, London, Cardiff, 1978—; external examiner Oxford (Eng.) Poly., Poly. Cen. London and Poly. South Bank; vis. lectr. various colls. Founding editor Urban Design Quarterly, 1978-84, Freeman of City of London; contbr. articles to profl. jours. Founder, chmn. Urban Design Group, London, 1978-86; chmn. PTRC: design and devel. com., 1983-85. Fellow Royal Soc. Arts, Faculty of Bldg., Royal Town Planning Inst. (pres. 1988); mem. Royal Inst. British Architects, London U. Town Planning Soc. (pres. 1968), Co. of Chartered Architects. Social Democrat. Office: 39 Charing Cross Rd, London WC2H OAW, England

TIBBITTS, KENT D., educator; b. Rexburg, Idaho, Sept. 21, 1937; s. Don Woodrow and Nora (Grant) T.; B.S. in Music Edn., U. Utah, 1964, M.S. in Ednl. Adminstrn., 1969; ednl. specialist Brigham Young U., 1978; m. Cecelia Ann Marcroft, Aug. 15, 1963; children—ViAnn, Don, Ernest, Ruth. Band dir. San Juan High Sch., Blanding, Utah, 1964-69; work and tng. specialist Utah Dept. Employment Security Blanding, 1969-70; Navajo Curriculum Center dir. San Juan Sch. Dist., Blanding, 1970-76, Navajo bilingual Title I dir., 1976-79, Title I media dir., 1979-81, dist. media and tech. dir., 1981-85; county drug and alcohol prevention coordinator, 1983-85; sch. dist. bus. adminstr. 1985—; bilingual/bicultural cons.; instr. coll. music, media. Chmn., San Juan County (Utah) Travel Council, 1970-74; bd. dirs. Utah Dept. Parks and Recreation, 1975—; treas. Kigalia Fine Arts Council, Blanding, 1976-82, 1985; mem. Blanding City Council, 1976; chmn. San Juan County Democratic Party, 1981-84. Served with U.S. Army, 1961-62. Recipient Creative Uses of Ednl. Tech. regional award AVID Corp., 1975, 1 of 10 Top Media Projects award Stanford U., 1974. Mem. Assn. Supervision and Curriculum Devel., Assn. Sch. Bus. Officials. Democrat. Mormon. Club: Lions (pres. club 1976-77) (Blanding). Author booklets, instructional kits on Navajo culture, lang.; producer films, filmstrips on Navajo lang. and cultures. Home: 574 W 100 S Blanding UT 84511 Office: 28 W 200 N Blanding UT 84511

TIBBITTS, SAMUEL JOHN, hospital administrator; b. Chgo., Oct. 7, 1924; s. Samuel and Marion (Swanson) T.; m. Audrey Slottelid, Aug. 28, 1949; children: Scott, Brett. B.S., UCLA, 1949; M.S., U. Calif.-Berkeley, 1950. Adminstrv. resident Calif. Hosp., Los Angeles, 1950-51; adminstrv. asst. Calif. Hosp., 1951-52, asst. supt., 1954-59, admistr., 1959-66; chmn. mgmt. com., asst. sec. Luth. Hosp. Soc. So. Calif., 1962-66, pres., 1966—; chmn. Pacificare Health Systems, 1979—; chmn. bd. Health Network Am., 1982—, Am. Healthcare Systems, 1983—; asst. supt. Santa Monica (Calif.) Hosp., 1952-54; pres. Commn. for Adminstrv. Services in Hosps., 1963, 64, 67, Calif. Health Data Corp., 1968-71; mem. Calif. Health Planning Council and Steering Com., 1968—, Los Angeles City Adv. Med. Council, 1971, 73, Pres.'s Com. Health Services Industry, Adv. Health Council, Calif., 1973; mem. adv. panel Pres.'s Cost of Living Council, Price Commn. and Pay Bd., Phase II; mem. Calif. Hosp. Commn., 1974—; mem. adv. bd. programs health service adminstrn. U. So. Calif. Bd. dirs. Calif. Hosp. Med. Center, Martin Luther Hosp., Henry Mayo Newhall Meml. Hosp.; trustee, exec. com. Blue Cross So. Calif., 1966-75. Served with M.C., U.S. Army, 1946-47. Recipient Service to Humanity award Luth. Mut. Life Ins. Co., Outstanding Achievement award Hosp. Council So. Calif., 1972, ACHE Gold Medal award, 1987, CAHHS Award of Merit, 1987; Lester Breslow Disting. lectr., 1983; named asso. officer most Venerable Order of St. John, 1972. Fellow Am. Coll. Hosp. Adminstrs.; mem. Am. Hosp. Assn. (chmn. council research and planning 1964-67, trustee 1968-70, chmn. bd. trustees 1978, Meritorious Service citation 1973, Trustees' award 1979), San Diego Hosp. Assn. (dir.), Calif. Hosp. Assn. (pres. 1968-69, trustee 1966-70, Ritz E. Heerman award 1960, Award of Merit, 1987), Hosp. Council So. Calif. (pres. 1961-62), U. Minn. Alumni Assn. Hosp. and Health Care Adminstrn. (hon.), Delta Omega. Home: 1224 Adair St San Marino CA 91108 Office: 1423 S Grand Ave Los Angeles CA 90015

TICHENOR, CHARLES BECKHAM, II, food-beverage executive; b. Indpls., s. Norman Beckham and Esther (Bremer) T.; B.S., Duke U., 1945; postgrad. Harvard U., 1947; m. Janet Salt; children—Charles Beckham III, Peter S., Suzanne P., Melissa N. Vice pres. Sealtest, Inc. (Kraft); pres., chmn., dir. Champale, Inc., Trenton, N.J.; dir. Doughtie's Foods, Inc., Balt., Motor Coils Mfg., Pitts., Dinamic Embellages Rombach, France, F.B. Johnston Printing Columbia, S.C., So. Tex. Oil Drilling & Exploration Co., San Antonio, N.Y.P Packaging Corp., Elizabeth, N.J., Yoo Hoo Chocolate Beverage Co., Carlstadt, N.J. Trustee Rider U., Lawrenceville, N.J.; U.S.Air Force War Coll., 1980; disting. chief exec. in residence, prof. Miss. State U. Served to lt. (j.g.) USNR, 1945-46; PTO, CBI. Mem. Duke Alumni Assn. (past pres.), U.S. Brewers Assn. (dir.), Am. Mgmt. Assn. Clubs: Nat. Assn. Corp. Dirs., Rotary Internat; Biltmore (Chgo.) Union League, Merion Cricket (Phila.); Cosmos (Washington), Aronimink (Newtown Square, Pa.). Mem. Davis Cup Tennis Team, 1941-42; twice U.S. table tennis champion, 1939-40. Office: PO Box MG Mississippi State MS 39762

TICKNER, ELLEN MINDY, lawyer; b. Phila., May 30, 1951; d. Arnold Charles and Priscilla Frances (Wertlieb) Klomparens. B.S., Northwestern U., 1973; postgrad. U. Miami, Coral Gables, Fla., 1973-74; J.D., DePaul U., 1976. Bar: Ill. 1977, Mich. 1977, U.S. Dist. Ct. (ea. dist.) Mich. 1979, U.S. Ct. Appeals (6th cir.) 1986. Legal research and writing instr. U. Detroit Sch. Law, 1976-77; staff atty. Juvenile Defender Office, Detroit, 1977-79; litigation atty. U. Mich. Inst. Gerontology, Ann Arbor, 1980; clin. instr. law U. Mich. Law Sch., Ann Arbor, 1980-82, clin. asst. prof. law, 1982-83; assoc. Raymond, Rupp, Wienberg, Stone & Zuckerman, P.C., Troy, Mich., 1984-87, assoc. Miller, Canfield, Paddock & Stone, Detroit, 1987—. Bd. dirs. Family Law Project, Ann Arbor, 1980-83, Mich. chpt. Nat. Com. for Prevention of Child Abuse, Lansing, 1980-82. Contbr. articles to legal jours. Mem. Women Lawyers Assn. of Mich. (bd. dirs. 1981-82), 13th Nat. Conf. Women and the Law (steering com. 1981-82), Assn. Trial Lawyers Am., Fed. Bar Assn., Mich. Trial Lawyers Assn., ABA (litigation sect.), Oakland County Bar Assn. (vice chmn. continuing legal edn. com. 1986-88, chair 1988), State Bar Mich., Detroit Bar Assn. Office: Miller Canfield Paddock & Stone 2500 Comerica Bldg Detroit MI 48226

TICOALU, JAMES, publisher; b. Manado, North Celebes, Indonesia, Oct. 21, 1942; s. Joseph and Caroline T.; B.S., Adventist Union Coll. Bandung, 1961; m. Nursanty Tampubolon, June 26, 1963; children—Nurlely, Welly, Kelly, Melky, Danny. Chmn., Indonesian Artists Found., 1967; dir. Bebas newspapers, 1969-71; dir. Internat. Book Service Inc., Jakarta, Indonesia, 1971—; chmn. Indonesia Library Found., 1971—, Ghakti Irian Jaya Found., 1980; pres., dir. Abaki Intermatra Ltd., 1975 . Mem. Indonesia Trade Chamber Commerce. Adventist. Club: Badminton. Home: 12 Jalan Museum, Jakarta Indonesia Office: Jalan Museum 12 POB 4012, Jakarta 10001, Indonesia

TIEDEMANN, ALBERT WILLIAM, JR., chemist; b. Balt., Nov. 7, 1924; s. Albert William and Catherine (Madigan) T.; B.S., Loyola Coll., Balt., 1947; M.S., N.Y. U., 1949; Ph.D., Georgetown U., 1958; m. Mary Therese Sellmayer, Apr. 6, 1953; children—Marie Therese, Donna Elise, Albert William III, David Lawrence. Teaching fellow N.Y. U., 1947-50; instr. chemistry Mt. St. Agnes Coll., 1950-55; chief chemist Emerson Drug div. Warner Lambert Pharm. Co., Balt., 1955-60; analytical supr. Hercules Powder Co., Allegany Ballistics Lab., Cumberland, Md., 1960-68; tech. service supt. Hercules Inc., Radford, Va., 1968-72; dir. Va. Div. Consol. Labs., Richmond, 1972-78; vice-chmn. Va. Toxic Substances Adv. Council, 1978—; dep. dir. for labs. Va. Dept. Gen. Services, 1978—Mem. sci. adv. com. Longwood Coll., 1983—. Served to lt. (j.g.) USNR, 1943-46; capt. Res., 1946—. Fellow Am. Inst. Chemists; mem. Am. Mgmt. Assn., Soc. Advancement Mgmt., chpt. v.p. 1983-84, chpt. pres. 1984-85), Am. Soc. Quality Control (chmn. Richmond sect. 1975-76, councilor biomed. div. 1978-80), U.S. Naval Inst., Naval Res. Assn. (dist. pres. 1954-57; nat. v.p. 1962-63, 65-69; nat. chmn. Navy Sabbath Program 1969-75; Nat. Meritorious Service award 1971, Twice a Citizen award 1978), Central Atlantic States Assn. Food and Drug Ofcls. (exec. bd. 1977-84, v.p. 1981-82, pres. 1982-83), Nat. Assn. Food and Drug Ofcls. (chmn. sci. and tech. com. 1981-85, sec.-treas. 1985-87), Assn. Ofcl. Analytical Chemists (editorial bd. 1986—, bd. dirs. 1987—), Analytical Lab. Mgrs. Assn. Home: 10511 Cherokee Rd Richmond VA 23235 Office: Consol Labs 1 N 14th St Richmond VA 23219

TIEDEMANN, EDWARD ERIC, nuclear engineer, researcher; b. Belleville, Ill., Feb. 9, 1954; s. Charles Edwin and Delores Ruth (Davidson) T.; m. Mary Ann Edwards, Apr. 24, 1977; children: Brent Edward, Kevin Andrew. B.S.M.E., U. of Ill., 1976. Registered prof. engr., Ill. Construction engr. Ill. Power Co., Havana, 1976-78, project mgmt. engr., Clinton, 1978-85, mem. tech. staff Clinton Nuclear Station, 1986-87, tech. adv. ops., 1987— . Donor, U. of Ill. Grants-In-Aid, Urbana, 1984—. James scholar U. Ill., 1972. Mem. ASME, Ill. Soc. Profl. Engrs. Republican. Office: Ill Power Co Clinton Nuclear Power Station Clinton IL 61727

TIEGEN, ELAINE MALIN, accounting company executive; b. Elizabeth, N.J., May 22, 1944; d. Bernard Edwin and Estelle (Radin) Malin; m. Robert A. Tiegen, Feb. 2, 1973 (div. Nov. 1975); 1 child, Heike-Ann M. BS in Acctg., Fairleigh Dickinson U., Madison, N.J., 1966. CPA, Fla. Staff auditor Peat, Marwick, Mitchell and Co., Miami, 1968-69; sr. staff auditor J.H. Cohn and Co., CPA's, Newark, N.J., 1969-71; with Clarence Rainess and Co., CPA's, N.Y.C., 1971-73; spl. asst. to sr. ptnr. Wiener, Stern and Hantman, CPA's, Miami, 1973-74; sr. specialist Laventhol & Horwath, Coral Gables, Fla., 1974-78, supr. dept. total acctg. services, 1978-79, mgr., 1979, head dept., 1980-83; prin. Elaine Malin Tiegen CPA, PA, Miami, 1983—; v.p. So. Fla. Interprofl. Council, 1984-85, pres., 1985-86; mem. small bus. rep. of adv. council Fed. Res. Bank of Atlanta, 1986—, chmn. 1988—. Mem. Am. Women's Soc. CPA's, Am. Soc. Women Accts (chpt. pres. 1975-76; Fla. Acct. of Yr. award 1976), Am. Inst. CPA's (small bus. council 1984-87, small bus. taxation com. 1987—), Fla. Inst. CPA's (recipient Disting. Service award Dade County chpt. 1980, 81, 82, gov. 1983-85, pres. chpt. 1984-85), Am. Arbitration Assn., Mensa. Office: 5401 Collins Ave #149 Miami Beach FL 33140

TIELU, FATU, utility company executive; b. Saleaaumua, Aleipata, Western Samoa, Dec. 23, 1959; s. Tiavatia and Sera Tielu; m. Rieko Yoneyama, July 4, 1981; children: Nada Fetuao, Yona Sebastian. B of Commerce in Accountancy, U. Auckland, New Zealand, 1982. CPA, Western Samoa. Chief acct. Dept. Edn. Apia, Western Samoa, 1982; asst. devel. officer Dept. Econ. Devel., Apea, 1982; fin. controller Dept. Econ. Devel., 1983-88, deputy gen. mgr. finance, 1988—; lectr. Nat. U. Samoa, 1988—. Treas. Apia Protestant Ch., 1983—. Mem. Western Samoa Soc. Acct. Office: Elec Power Corp, Beach Rd PO Box 2011, Apia Western Samoa

TIENARI, PEKKA JOHANNES, psychiatrist, educator; b. Pernio, Finland, May 27, 1931; s. Matti and Aino (Maatta) T.; m. Helena Rauhala, Apr. 29, 1954; children: Jukka Pekka, Janne Pekka. Lic. Medicine, U. Helsinki, Finland, 1957; MD, U. Helsinki, 1964. Resident Halikon Piirisairaala, 1953-55, Hesperia Hosp., 1955-59; resident U. Helsinki dept. psychiatry, 1959-61, asst. chief, 1961-65; prof., chmn. dept. psychiatry U. Oulu, Finland, 1965—; dean med. faculty U. Oulu, 1971-75; cons. psychiatrist Inst. Occupational Health, Helsinki, 1958-65, Out-Patient Clinic for Alcoholics, Helsinki, 1958-60, Clinic Marriage Guidance, Helsinki, 1958-59; lectr. psychiatry Social Coll., Helsinki, 1958-60; vis. prof. U. Rochester, N.Y., 1982. Author (with K.A. Achte and Y.O. Alanen) Textbook of Psychiatry, 1971; contbr. articles to profl. jours. NIH postdoctoral fellow NIMH, Bethesda, Md., 1967-68; WHO fellow, Eng., 1969. Mem. Finnish Psychiat. Assn. (pres. 1970-76), Scandinavian Assn. Psychiatrists (pres. 1978-82). Lodge: Rotary. Home: Rantakatu 13 B 3, 90100 Oulu Finland Office: Univ Cen Hosp, 90210 Oulu Finland

TIERNEY, ROBERT, artist, textile and graphic designer; b. Plymouth, Eng., Aug. 9, 1936; s. Cyril Fortescue and Hilda T.; student Plymouth Coll. Art, 1954-56; diploma in Art, Central Sch., London, 1956, postgrad., 1956-58; student Atelier Clay, Paris, 1959-60. Painter in watercolors, oil, design colors; textile/graphic designer cos. in U.K., Paris, Zurich, Vienna, also Denmark, Finland, Italy, Australia, Can., U.S., Japan, 1958—. Exhbn. debuts, London and Paris, 1958, N.Y.C. and Toronto, 1959; exhibited Can., 1979, Vienna, 1964—; works exhibited cities in U.S., Europe, Far East, 1982, 83, 84, 85, 86; touring exhbns., Japan, 1977-81, U.S., 1982, Kindly Acid, 1987, 88, 5 other works accepted by Victoria and Albert Mus., U.K., 1986 . Designer Tickenham Rugby Centenary scarf, U.K., 1971, scarf Mus. Fine Arts, Boston, 1979; work exhibited annually London Design Centre, Manchester, Paris, 1959—; paintings represented in permanent and pvt. collections; design works in pub. and govt. bldgs., pvt. residences, also archives Design Centre U.K., Victoria and Albert Mus., Boston Mus. Fine Arts; designed Royal Bouquet silk screen scarf to commemorate wedding of Prince of Wales, 1981. Registered Council Indsl. Design. Home: care 4 Lonsdale Villa, Plymouth PL4 7AS, England Office: care Council Industrial Design, The Design Ctr Haymarket, London SW1, England

TIERNO, PHILIP MARIO, JR., microbiologist, educator; b. Bklyn., June 5, 1943; s. Philip M. and Phyllis (Tringone) T.; BS, Bklyn. Coll. Pharmacy and R.L. Conolly Coll., L.I. U., 1965; MS, NYU, 1974, PhD, 1976; m. Josephine Martinez, Apr. 2, 1967; children: Alexandra Lorraine, Meredith Anne. Microbiologist, Luth. Med. Ctr., Bklyn., 1965-66; chief research microbiologist hemodialysis unit VA Hosp., Bronx, N.Y., 1966-70; chief microbiology div. NYU Med. Ctr. Goldwater Meml. Hosp., F.D. Roosevelt Island, N.Y., 1970-81; assoc. and cons. microbiologist Maimonides Med. Ctr., Bklyn., 1970-79; dir. microbiology dept. Univ. Hosp., NYU Med. Ctr., 1981—; adj. asst. prof. CUNY, 1974-76, Bloomfield (N.J.) Coll., 1975-82; assoc. prof. microbiology NYU Med. Sch., 1981—; cons. Office Atty. Gen. N.Y. State, NIH, and Dept. Health City of New York, 1981—. Pres., Flushing Taxpayers Assn., 1973-77; bd. dirs. Comprehensive Health Planning Agy. City N.Y., 1974-75, Norwood Bd. Adjustment, N.J., 1978-83, 86—, Norwood Bd. Edn., 1983-86; chmn. Norwood Environ. Commn., 1986—; co-founder, bd. dirs. Found. Sci. Research in Pub. Interest, S.I., N.Y., 1985—. Mem. AAAS, N.Y. Acad. Scis., Am. Acad. Microbiology, Am. Pub. Health Assn., Am. Soc. Microbiology, Phi Sigma, Alpha Epsilon Delta. Club: Optimists (v.p. Norwood 1978—). Lodge: Knights of Malta. Contbr. articles to profl. jours. Home: 30 Carter St Norwood NJ 07648

TIETKE, WILHELM, gastroenterologist; b. Niengraben, Germany, Oct. 15, 1938; came to U.S., 1969, naturalized, 1979; s. Wilhelm and Frieda (Schmeding) T.; M.D., U. Goettingen (W.Ger.), 1968; m. Imme Schmidt, Oct. 15, 1965; children—Cornelia, Isabel. Intern, Edward W. Sparrow Hosp., Lansing, Mich., 1970; resident in internal medicine Henry Ford Hosp., Detroit, 1971-73; fellow in gastroenterology, 1973-75; practice medicine specializing in gastroenterology, Huntsville, Ala., 1975—; mem. vol. faculty, cons. U. Ala., Huntsville, 1976; clin. assoc. prof. internal medicine, 1979—; pres. Gastroenterology Assocs. P.A., Huntsville, 1979—. Diplomate Am. Bd. Internal Medicine, Am. Bd. Gastroenterology. Fellow Coll. Gastroenterology; mem. AMA, Ala. Med. Soc., Am. Coll. Physicians, Am. Soc. Gastrointestinal Endoscopy. Lutheran. Lodge: Rotary. Home: 2707 Westminster Way Huntsville AL 35801 Office: 520 Madison St Suite A Huntsville AL 35801

TIGGES, JOHN THOMAS, writer, musician; b. Dubuque, Iowa, May 16, 1932; s. John George and Madonna Josephine (Heiberger) T.; m. Kathryn Elizabeth Johnson, Apr. 22, 1954; children: Juliana, John, Timothy, Teresa, Jay. Student Loras Coll., 1950-52, 57, U. Dubuque, 1960. Clk. John Deere Tractor Works, Dubuque, Iowa, 1957-61; agt. Penn Mut. Life Ins. Co., Dubuque, 1961-74; bus. mgr., bd. dirs. Dubuque Symphony Orch., 1960-68, 71-74; v.p., sec. Olson Toy and Hobby Inc., 1964-66; pres. JKT Inc., 1978-82; research specialist Electronic Media Services (Scripp-Howard); violinist. Author: (novels) The Legend of Jean Marie Cardinal, 1976, Garden of the Incubus, 1982, Unto the Altar, 1985, Kiss Not the Child, 1985, Evil Dreams, 1985, The Immortal, 1986, Hands of Lucifer, 1987, As Evil Does, 1987, Pack, 1987, Venom, 1988, Vessel, 1988, Slime, 1988, Come The Wraith, 1988, Salton Feast, 1988; (plays) No More-No Less, 1979, We Who Are About to Die, 1979; radio plays: Valley of Deceit, 1978, Rockville Horror, 1979, The Timid, 1982; TV drama: An Evening with George Wallace Jones, 1982; biographies: George Wallace Jones, 1983, John Plumbe Jr., 1983; co-author history book: The Milwaukee Road Narrow Gauge: The Bellevue, Cascade & Western, Iowa's Slim Princess, 1985; co-author: They came from Dubuque, 1983; co-author, editor: A Cup and a Half of Coffee, 1977; editorial asst. Julian Jour.; interviewer, spl. reporter Editorial Assocs., 1982-84; columnist Memory Lane; syndicated columnist Tough Trivia Tidbits; tchr. creative writing Northeast Iowa Tech. Inst.; co-founder Dubuque Symphony Orch., 1960; founder Julien Strings, 1972, Dubuque Sch. of Novel, 1978, Northeast Iowa Writers Workshop, 1981; co-host Big Broadcast Radio Program, WDBQ Radio, 1979-82; co-founder Sinipee Writers Workshop, 1985. Founder, bus. mgr. Dubuque Pops Orch., 1957. Recipient Nat. Quality award, 1966-70, Carnegie-Stout Library World of Lit. honors award, 1981. Fellow World Lit. Acad.; mem. Nat. Writers Club (profl.), Iowa Authors, Am. Fedn. Musicians, Internat. Platform Assn., Toy Train Collectors Club. Roman Catholic.Club: Dubuque Rails Model Railroad (co-founder 1987). Office: PO Box 902 Dubuque IA 10011

TIGLI, HUSEYIN, diversified manufacturing company executive; b. Egridir, Isparta, Turkey, Oct. 20, 1953; parents: Mehmet and Rahime (Cakiciaslan) T. BS, Columbia U., 1975, MS, 1978; MBA, Harvard U., 1981. Engr. Stauffer Chem. Co., Dobbs Ferry, N.Y., 1975-79; product mgr. Raychem Corp., Menlo Park, Calif., 1981-82; product mgr. Europe Raychem Corp., Pontoise, France, 1982-83, ops. mgr. Europe, 1983-85; gen. mgr. Europe Raychem, Pontoise, France, 1985—. Club: Harvard of France. Office: Raychem S A, BP 738, 95004 Cergy-Pontoise France

TIGNER, BROOKS K., journalist; b. Conroe, Tex., July 8, 1953; s. Charles Spencer and Margaret Ann (Knotts) T.; m. Genevieve Van Cauwenberge, June 28, 1986; 1 child, Ronan Guillaume. BA, Tex. A&M U., 1975; M.Internat. Mgmt., Am. Grad. Sch. Internat. Mgmt., Glendale, Ariz., 1980; MS, Columbia U. Grad. Sch. Journalism, 1984. Vol. Peace Corps, Liberia, 1975-77; gen. mgr. U.S. Import Assn., Monrovia, Liberia, 1977-79; asst. fin. officer Tolstoy Found., N.Y.C., 1980-83; econ. affairs journalist McGraw-Hill World News, Brussels, 1985—; cons., writer Mgmt. Ctr. Europe, Brussels, 1985—. Contbr. articles to publs. including: Businessweek, Internat. Mgmt., Securities Internat., Mgmt. Rev.

TIGRID, PAVEL, editor-in-chief; b. Prague, Czechoslovakia, Oct. 27, 1917; came to U.S., 1952; s. František and Erna (Singer) Schönfeld; m. Ivana Myška, Feb. 15, 1947; children: Deborah, Catherine, Gregory. Student, Charles U., Prague, 1936-39. Editor/announcer BBC, London, 1939-45; editor-in-chief Obzory (weekly newspaper), Prague, 1945-48; program dir. Radio Free Europe, Munich, Fed. Republic of Germany, 1950-52; editor-in-chief Svědectví-Temoignace, Paris, 1960—; lit. adviser Walker & Co., N.Y.C., 1960-68. Author: Printemps de Prague, 1968, Why Dubcek Fell, 1970, English, French, Czech., Spanish, Italian, Japanese edits., Why Dubcek Fell, 1970, Bitter Revolution, 78, French, Czech edits., Workers' Revolutions in Socialist Countries, 1984, others. Mem. Human Rights Help and Action Com., Paris, 1974. Office: Svedectvi-Temoignace, 30 rue Croix-des-Petits Champs, 75001 Paris France

TILAK, JANDHYALA BALA GANGADHARA, economist, educator; b. Tadepalligudem, India, May 15, 1952; s. Jandhyala Venkateswara Sastry and Subbalakshmi; m. Punyavati Dandibhotla; children: Kunj Vihari, Viswanath. BA, Andhra (India) U., 1972, MA in Econs., 1974; PhD, Delhi Sch. Econs., Delhi, India, 1980. Lectr. econs. U. Delhi, 1976-81; vis. fellow in econs. edn. Indian Inst. Edn., Pune, 1981-82; fellow Nat. Inst. Ednl. Planning and Adminstrn., New Delhi, 1982-87; cons. World Bank, Washington, 1987—. Author 2 books; contbr. numerous articles to profl. jours. Mem. Soc. for Study Regional Disparities (sec.), Inst. Econ. Growth Soc., Indian Assn. for Ednl. Planning and Adminstrn., Comparative Edn. Soc. India. Office: World Bank 1818 H St NW Washington DC 20433

TILBURY, ROGER GRAYDON, lawyer; b. Guthrie, Okla., July 30, 1925; s. Graydon and Minnie (Lee) T.; m. Margaret Dear, June 24, 1952; 1 dau., Elizabeth Ann. B.S., U. So. Calif., 1945; J.D., U. Kans., 1949; LL.M., Columbia, 1950; postgrad., Oxford (Eng.) U., 1949. Bar: Mo. bar 1950, Oreg. bar 1953. Practiced in Kansas City, Mo., 1950-53, Portland, Oreg., 1953—; asso. firm Rogers, Field, Gentry, Kansas City, Mo., 1950-53, Stern, Reiter & Day, Portland, 1953-56; partner firm Roth & Tilbury, 1956-58, Tilbury & Kane, 1970-72, Haessler, Tilbury & Platten, 1978-81; individual practice law Portland, 1981—; circuit judge pro tem., Oreg., 1972—, arbitrator and fact finder, 1973—; tree farmer; sec. Barrington Properties; mem. nat. panel arbitrators U.S. Mediation and Conciliation Service; atty. Animal Defender League, 1969-73; dir. Consol. Cargos, Inc. Dep. election commr. Kansas City, Mo., 1952-53; bd. dirs. Multnomah Bar Found. Served to lt. (j.g.) USNR, 1943-45. Battenfeld scholar, 1943. Mem. Oreg. State Bar, Soc. Barristers, Am. Arbitration Assn., Save the Redwoods League, East African Wildlife League, Nat. Wildlife Found., Am. Trial Lawyers Assn., Delta Tau Delta, Phi Delta Phi. Home: 9310 NW Cornell Rd Portland OR 97229 Office: 1123 SW Yamhill Portland OR 97205

TILBY, MICHAEL JOHN, language professional, educator; b. Harrow-on-the-Hill, Eng., Apr. 16, 1949; s. Edward James and Winifred Joan (Trist) T.; m. Susan Elizabeth Wharton. BA, Corpus Christi Coll., Cambridge, 1971, MA, 1975, PhD, 1976; postgrad., Ecole Normale Supérieure, Paris, 1973-74. Tutorial asst. U. Hull, Eng., 1975-76; lectr. comparative lit. U. East Anglia, 1976-77; fellow, lectr. French Selwyn Coll. U. Cambridge, 1977—, dir. studies in modern lang., 1980—, praelector, 1979-83, librarian, 1983-86, tutor, 1987—, tutor for admissions, 1987—; editor Selwyn Coll. Calendar, 1980-88. Author: A. Gide: Les Faux- Monnayeurs; editor: Nouvelles Choisies de P. Mérimée, P. Lainé, La Dentellière; contbr. articles to profl. jours. French Govt. scholar, 1973-74. Mem. Modern Humanities Research Assn., Soc. for French Studies (publicity officer, mem. exec. com. 1984—). Ch. of Eng. Home: 8 Norman Ct, Hemingford Grey, Huntingdon Cambridgeshire PE18 9BQ, England Office: U Cambridge, Selwyn Coll, Cambridge CB3 9DQ, England

TILL, JAAP W., communication network consultant; b. The Hague, The Netherlands, Nov. 15, 1944; s. Gerhard A. and Hermanna E. (VanHaersolte) V.; m. Jossine A. VanderPol, Apr. 18, 1969; children: Bettina, Olivier, Frederique. MS in Electronics, Delfi U. Tech., The Netherlands, 1972. Research scientist Akzo Corporate Research Labs., Arnhem, The Netherlands, 1973-79; datacommunications specialist Akzo Systems Consultancy, The Netherlands, 1979-84; prin. econs. James Martin Assocs., Amsterdam, The Netherlands, 1984—; orgn. advisor Sioo Sch. Mgmt. Sci., Utrecht, 1983; info. advisor Minister of Agriculture, The Hague, 1986; lectr. in field. inventor tillegraf, plector. Served to 2nd lt. The Netherlands Loyisties, 1967-68. Mem. Royal Engring. Soc. The Netherlands. Club: The Netherlands Computer User (bd. advisor). Home: Domineesberg Bergweg 16, Rhenen 3911 VB The Netherlands Office: James Martin Assocs, 873 De Boelelaan, 1082 RW Amsterdam The Netherlands

TILLER, CARL WILLIAM, retired church official; b. Battle Lake, Minn., Sept. 25, 1915; s. Carl J(ohn) and Edith (Wells) T.; m. Olive M. Foerster, June 21, 1940; children: Robert W., Jeanne L. (Mrs. John E. Peterson). B.A., Concordia Coll., Moorhead, Minn., 1935, LL.D., 1966; M.A. in Pub. Adminstrn, U. Minn., 1940. Budget sec., examiner Minn., 1936-41; exec. asst. to dir. Mcpl. Fin. Officers Assn., 1941-42; with U.S. Office of Mgmt. and Budget, 1942-72, spl. adviser budgetary devel., 1967-72; adj. prof. Am. U., 1952-70; assoc. sec. Baptist World Alliance, Washington, 1972-78; dir. Interchurch Center, N.Y.C., 1978-80; pres. and exec. dir. Interchurch Center, 1980-86; mem. gen. bd. Nat. Council Chs., 1963-75, treas., 1970-75; mem. gen. council Am. Baptist Conv., 1946-53, 54-60, 63-68, pres., 1966-67; Western treas. Bapt. World Alliance, 1956-72, rep. to UN, 1981—, sec. N.Am. Bapt. Fellowship, 1972-78, pres. D.C. Bapt. Conv., 1969-70; v.p. CARE Inc., 1972-78; mem. gen. bd. Am. Bapt. Chs. U.S.A., 1982-85, mem. com. on Christian unity, 1982-85, mem. bd. ednl. ministries, 1982-85; interim dir. Am. Baptist-Samuel Colgate Hist. Library, 1987-88. Contbr. articles to profl. jours. Active Am. Cancer Soc.; bd. dirs. Luther Rice Coll., 1971-77, chmn., 1973-76; bd. dirs. Japan Internat. Christian U. Found., treas., 1982-85; bd. dirs. Interreligious Service Bd. for Conscientious Objectors, 1983—, treas., 1988—. Mem. Am. Polit. Sci. Assn., Am. Soc. Pub. Adminstrn., Am. Acctg. Assn., Am. Bapt. Hist. Soc. (pres. 1982-85). Home: 528 Cumberland Ave Teaneck NJ 07666

TILLER, MARTHA RUSSELL, public relations executive, consultant; b. Temple, Tex., Jan. 20, 1940; d. John Lafayette and Cleo (Davidson) Russell; m. David Clyde Tiller, Nov. 26, 1966; 1 child, John Russell. BFA cum laude, U. Tex., 1961; student Nat. U. Mex., 1962, Piaget Inst. of Tex. Christian U., 1970. With radio-TV prodns. dept. U. Tex. and Sta. KTBC-TV, Austin, 1959-61; asst. to producer CBS TV, N.Y.C., 1961-64; with Goodson Todman Prodns., N.Y.C., 1964-66; dir. publs. Tex. Fine Arts Commn., Austin, 1967-69; press and social sec. to Mrs. Lyndon B. Johnson, Austin, 1973-76, also spl. asst. to Pres. Lyndon B. Johnson, Office of the Former Pres., Austin, 1972; dir. pub. info. S.W. Ednl. Devel. Lab., Austin, 1976, media specialist, 1969-72, writer, 1967; dir. pub. affairs Glenn, Bozell & Jacobs, Inc., Dallas, 1977-78; dir. pub. affairs U.S. Dept. HEW Region XII, 1978-79; dir. pub. relations Plaza of Ams. Hotel, Dallas, 1979-82; chmn., chief exec. officer Martha Tiller & Co. Pub. Relations Counselors, Dallas, 1982—. Creator, producer award-winning video Basic Steps to Fire Safety, 1981. Mem. cultural activities task force Goals for Dallas; mem. Sta. KLRN-TV Channel 9, Austin, Austin Symphony Orch. Soc., Town Lake Beautification Com. of Austin, Laguna Gloria Art Mus. and Guild, Austin; vice chmn. 8 Arts Ball, TACA Assn., 1981-82, bd. dirs., 1987—; nat. gifts chmn. Worldwide USO Gala, 1985; vice chmn. James K. Wilson Luncheon, 1982; bd. dirs. Dallas Symphony Orch. League, 1986—, Grand Heritage Ball Commn., 1986, Dallas Opera Women, 1984, Girls Club of Dallas, 1987—; mem. March of Dimes Women's Aux., Friends of LBJ Library (life), women's com. Dallas Civic Opera; bd. govs. Dallas Ballet, 1987—. Recipient Golden Key Pub. Relations award Am. Hotel/Motel Assn., 1982; named Nation's Top Broadcasting Coed, Am. Women Radio and TV, 1959. Mem. Pub. Relations Soc. Am., Tex. Pub. Relations Assn. (Best of Tex. award 1981), Women in Communications, Austin Natural Sci. Assn., Mortar Bd., Alpha Epsilon Rho. Clubs: Plaza Athletic, Park Cities, Bent Tree Country. Office: 2811 McKinney Suite 354 Dallas TX 75204-2547

TILLERY, BILL W., physics educator; b. Muskogee, Okla., Sept. 15, 1938; s. William Earnest and Bessie C. (Smith) Freeman; m. Patricia Weeks Northrop, Aug. 1, 1981; 1 child, Elizabeth Fielding; children by previous marriage: Tonya Lynn, Lisa Gail. B.S., Northeastern U., 1960; M.A., U. No. Colo., 1965, Ed.D., 1967. Tchr. Guthrie Pub. Schs., Okla., 1960-62; tchr. Jefferson County schs., Colo., 1962-64; teaching asst. U. No. Colo., 1965-67; asst. prof. Fla. State U., 1967-69; assoc. prof. U. Wyo., 1969-73, dir. sci. and math. teaching ctr., 1969-73; assoc. prof. dept. physics Ariz. State U., Tempe, 1973-75, prof., 1976—; cons. in field. Author: (with Ploutz) Basic Physical Science, 1964; (with Sund and Trowbridge) Elementary Science Activities, 1967, Elementary Biological Science, 1970, Elementary Physical Science, 1970, Elementary Earth Science, 1970, Investigate and Discover, 1975; Space, Time, Energy and Matter: Activity Books, 1976; (with Bartholomew) Heath Earth Science, 1984; (with Bartholomew and Gary) Heath Earth Science Activities, 1984, 2d edit. 1987, Heath Earth Science Teacher Resource Book, 1987, Heath Earth Science Laboratory Activity, 1987; editor Ariz. Sci. Tchrs. Jour., 1975—, Ariz. Energy Edn., 1978—. Fellow AAAS; mem. Nat. Sci. Tchrs. Assn., Ariz. Sci. Tchrs. Assn., Assn. Edn. of Tchrs. in Sci., Nat. Assn. Research in Sci. Teaching. Republican. Episcopalian. Home: 8986 S Forest Ave Tempe AZ 85284 Office: Dept Physics Ariz State U Tempe AZ 85287

TILLETT, GRACE MONTANA, ophthalmologist, real estate developer; b. Malone, N.Y., Dec. 5, 1924; d. Everett Reed and Althea Adela (Manson) Montana; m. Charles W. Tillett, Aug. 9, 1952; children—Charles, James, Avery. B.A., Syracuse U., 1946, M.D., 1949. Diplomate Am. Bd. Radiology, Am. Bd. Ophthalmology. Intern, Balt. City Hosps., 1949-50, resident, 1950-51; resident Johns Hopkins Hosp., Balt., 1951-53; practice medicine specializing in ophthalmology, Charlotte, N.C., 1957—; v.p. Prof. Optical Service, Charlotte, 1959—; pres. 2200 E. Seventh St. Real Estate Corp., Charlotte, 1965—; mem. staff Presbyn., Mercy, Charlotte Meml. hosps. Bd. dirs. Heart Assn. Charlotte, 1971-73, Dance Charlotte, 1978-79. Mem. Bus. and Profl. Women's Assn., Am. Acad. Ophthalmology, Am. Acad. Radiology, AMA, N.C. Med. Soc., Mecklenburg County Med. Soc., Charlotte Ophthalmol. Soc. Republican. Club: Charlotte Country. Office: 2130 Sharon Ln Charlotte NC 28211

TILLINGHAST, META IONE, civic worker; b. Newark, Nov. 14; d. Ralph Vincent and Florence Virginia (MacDonald) Muldoon; student Leland Powers Sch. of Spoken Word, Boston; m. Frederick William Tillinghast; children—Anne (Mrs. Robert Riley), Patricia (Mrs. Charles McLaughlin). Bd. dirs. Balt. chpt. ARC, 1955-58, chmn. Queen Anne's chpt. 1964-66, nat. bd. govs., 1966-69, Md. state fund chmn., 1969-71, Delmarva div. chmn. mems., funds, 1971-73, vols., 1971-74, coordinator community relations Eastern area, 1975-76; chmn. vols. nat. field office (now Eastern field office) ARC, Alexandria, Va., 1976-83, regional chmn. Eastern ops., 1983-86, chmn. vols. Del. chpt., 1986-88, chmn. vols. Nat. Historic Resources, 1986—, mem. nat. hist. resource com.; dir. ch. plays; chmn. United Fund Baltimore County (Md.) Women's div., 1950. Named vol. of year Md., ARC, 1965; recipient award Gen. Fedn. Women's Clubs, 1952. Mem. Md. No. Dist. Fedn. Women's Clubs (pres. 1953-55). Clubs: Women's Glyndon (pres. 1949-51), Talbot County Women's (pres. 1962-64), Women's Ten Hills (pres. 1940-42). Home: Nesbit Rd Rt 3 Box 24 Queenstown MD 21658

TIMAR, MATYAS, banker; b. Mohács, Hungary, July 10, 1923; s. Imre and Stefania (Fischoff) T.; m. Eva Vago, 1947; children: Julia, Zsofia. PhD of Jurisprudence, Eotvos Lorand U. Scis., Budapest, 1963; Dr. of Econ. Scis., Marx Karoly U. Econs., Budapest, 1969. Gen. mgr. Ministry for Fin., Hungary, 1949-55, dep. minister of fin., 1955-62, minister, 1962-67, dep. prime minister, 1967-75, chmn. econ. com. of govt., 1967-73, sec. of state, pres. Nat. Bank of Hungary, Budapest, 1975—. Author: Public Finance and Economic Management, 1964; In Reflections on the Economic Development of Hungary, 1967-73, 76; Equilibrium and Finance, 1983. Mem Hungarian Socialist Workers Party, 1943—; mem. cen. com. Hungarian Socialist Workers Party, 1966-85. Decorated Order of the People's Republic Residential Council Hungarian Peoples Republic, 1950, Golden Degree of Order of Labour, 1953, Order for Socialist Country, 1967, Order of Liberation, 1970. Address: Nat Bank of Hungary, Szabadsag Ter 8-9, H1850 Budapest Hungary

TIMBERLIN, BEVERLY JEAN, industrial supply company executive, business executive; b. Alvarado, Ind., Feb. 10, 1935; d. Lyle Spangler and Helen Juanita (Mason) Leas; m. David John Timberlin, Dec. 19, 1954; children: Michelle Renea, David Douglas. Student, Ball State U., 1953-54; AA, Jackson Community Coll., 1968; BA in Edn., Mich. State U., 1970, postgrad., 1970-73. Tchr. spl. edn. Jackson County Pub. Schs., Mich., 1970-73, Wichita Falls Pub. Schs., Tex., 1973-81; owner Sun Valley Distbrs., Phoenix, 1981—; corp. sec.-treas. Cupp's Indsl. Supply, Inc., Phoenix, 1981—; sec.-treas. ENSCO, Phoenix. Republican. Methodist. Avocations: swimming, gardening, golf, skiing. Home: 13431 N 68th Dr Peoria AZ 85345 Office: Cupp's Indsl Supply Inc 3418 W Flower St Phoenix AZ 85017 also: ENSCO 17816 N 25th Ave Phoenix AZ 85023

TIMBLIN, STANLEY WALTER, manufacturing executive; b. Butler, Pa., Feb. 16, 1937; s. William Cecil and Beulah (Rankin) T.; m. Mary Evelyn Cabe, June 7, 1959; children: Stephen Douglas, Jeffrey William, Dianne Elizabeth. BSEE, N.C. State U., 1960; M in Engring. Adminstrn., George Washington U., 1967. Registered profl. engr., Md. Quality control engr. Westinghouse Electric, Balt., 1960-64, test engring. supr., 1965-68, mgr. product reliability, 1968-70; corp. quality staff Westinghouse Electric, Pitts., 1970-71, engring. mgr. consumer services, 1971-73; pres., owner Tim-Tech Controls, Greensboro, N.C., 1973—. Contbr. numerous articles on quality control, 1965-71; patentee bldg. automation controls, refrigeration and security controls. Mem. IEEE, ASHRAE, Assn. Energy Engrs. Republican. Presbyterian. Club: Greensboro Engrs. Home: 4 Forest Hill Ct Greensboro NC 27410 Office: Tim Tech Controls Co 1109 S Chapman St Greensboro NC 27403

TIMBLO, MODU CAMOTIM, mining company executive; b. Assolna, Goa, India, Jan. 15, 1922; s. Ganesh Kamat and Jaiwanti (Ganesh) T.; m. Sushiladevi Tarcar, Feb. 29, 1948; children: Auduth, Dilip, Prashant. Owner, operator textile, semi-precious stones and pearls store, later expanded into gen. mdse. and import-export trade; with Sociedade de Fomento Industrial Private Ltd., Margao, Goa, India, now chmn., mng. dir.; dir. various Goa-based cos. Treas., Goa Pradesh Congress Com.; mem. All India Congress Com. Recipient Recognition of Outstanding Services Pres. Singh of India. Mem. Goa C. of C. and Industry, Goa Mining Assn., Goa Mineral Ore Exporters Assn. (pres.), Indian Mchts. Chamber, India Internat. Ctr. Club: Cricket of India Ltd. (Bombay). Office: Soc de Fomento Indsl Pvt Ltd, PO Box 31, Margao Goa 403601, India

TIMBUNGCO, EDUARDO REVOLTAR, broadcast executive; b. Lopez, Quezon, Philippines, Jan. 28, 1941; s. Cenon Looc and Balbina Lorete (Revoltar) T.; m. Anita Martin Montealegre, Sept. 4, 1971; children: Percival, Kenneth, Millicent. Cert., Feati U., Manila, 1964. Artist Rustan Mfg. Corp., Paranaque, Metro Manila, Philippines, 1964-66; sr. video technician ABS-CBN Broadcasting Corp., Quezon City, Philippines, 1968-72; spl. events technician Philippines Prodn. Ctr., Inc., Makati, Metro Manila, 1972-74; video technician Nat. Media Prodn. Ctr., Manila, 1974-77; TV program specialist Bendix-Siyanco, Taif, Saudi Arabia, 1977-80; TV producer, dir. Siyanco-SOCP, Taif, 1980-86; systems supr. RTV Malacañang, Manila, 1986—. Phase rep. Gatchalian Homeowners Assn., Las Pinas, Metro Manila, 1976-77; youth advisor Phase Eight-A Concerned Homeowners, 1986-87, pres., 1988—. Club: RTVM Band (Manila). Office: RTV Malacanang, Malacanang Palace, Manila Philippines

TIMERMAN, JACOBO, writer; b. Bar, Podal, USSR, Jan. 6, 1923; arrived in Argentina, 1928; s. Natan and Eva (Berman) T.; m. Risha Mindlin, May 20, 1950; children: Daniel, Hector, Javier. LHD (hon.), Brandeis U., 1981, Queens Coll., 1982. Translator Agence France Presse, Buenos Aires, 1953-56; writer La Razon, Buenos Aires, 1957-59, Clarin, Buenos Aires, 1959-60, El Mundo, Buenos Aires, 1960-62; editor, pub. Primera Plana, Buenos Aires, 1962-64, Confirmado, Buenos Aires, 1965-66, La Opinion, Buenos Aires, 1971-77; writer Buenos Aires, 1977—. Author: Prisoner Without a Name, 1981 (Los Angeles Times award 1981), The Longest War, 1982, Chile, Death in the South, 1987. Recipient David Ben Gurion award United Jewish Appeal, 1979, Golden Pen of Freedom award Internat. Fedn. Pubs., 1980, Conscience in Media award Am. Soc. Journalists and Authors, 1981. Jewish. Home and Office: Libertad 1584, Buenos Aires 1016, Argentina

TIMIO, MARIO, physician; b. Foligno, Perugia, Italy, Feb. 17, 1938; s. Felice and Anna (Gubbini) T.; m. Simonetta Gentili, June 17, 1949; children: Anna, Francesca, Carlo, Elisabetta. MD, Perugis Sch. Med., Italy, 1962. Diplomate in cardiology, internal medicine, work medicine. Asst. Med. Clinic U., Rome, 1962-66; asst. Inst. Med. Pathology U., Perugia, Italy, 1967-77; house physician Italian Hosp., London, 1968; researcher St. Mary's Hosp., London, 1968-69; head Dept. Internal Medicine, Foligno, Italy, 1978-87; dir. Hypertensive Ctr., Foligno, 1979—; tchr. U., Siena, Italy, 1986-87. Author: Myocardial Infarction, 1974, Stress and Cardiopathy, 1980; Editor: Heart in Renal Disease, 1987, jour. Medicina nei Secoli, 1985, Hypertension: Men, Facts, Theories, 1988. Mem. Internat. Soc. Hypertension, European Soc. Cardiology, Internat. Soc. Nephrology, Italian Soc. Cardiology, Italian Soc. History Medicine, Umbrian Soc. Journalist. Democrat. Roman Catholic. Clubs: Tennis (Perugia), Acad. Sci. and Art (Foligno). Home: Via XX Settembre N 22, 06100 Perugia Italy

TIMM, OLE, printing company executive; b. Copenhagen, Sept. 29, 1947; s. Jørgen and Ulla Timm; m. Hanne Andersen, May 18, 1969 (div. Oct. 1981); children: Tine, Jasper; m. Bibi Andersen, Oct. 19, 1985; 1 child, Philip. BS in Econs., Sch. Bus. and Adminstrn., Copenhagen, 1970, MS in Econs., 1972; postgrad., Harvard U., 1984. CPA, Denmark. Acct. Coopers & Lybrand, Copenhagen, 1972-76; internal cons. Gutenberghus Group, Copenhagen, 1976-77; asst. dir. London Editions, 1977; controller Gutenberghus Bladene A/S, Copenhagen, 1977-80, dep. dir., 1980-85; v.p., gen. mgr. Egmont H. Petersen A/S, Copenhagen, 1985—; bd. dirs., chmn. Dansk Metalvarefabrik A/S, Roskilde, Denmark, 1978—, Entertainment Denmark A/S, Copenhagen, 1986—. Home: Langebakken 12, 2960 Rungsted Kyst Denmark Office: Egmont H Petersen A/S, Herstedvang 12, 2620 Albertslund Denmark

TIMMANN, KLAUS-PETER, communications equipment company executive; b. Koenigsberg, Germany, July 14, 1940; s. Manfred and Annemarie (Lippold) T.; Abitur, Leibniz Coll., Hannover, W. Ger., 1959; interim degree Tech. U. Hannover, 1962; M.Sc. in E.E., U. Saarbruecken (W. Ger.), 1964; m. Marion E. Bartels, June 4, 1964; children—Jean Till, Mara. Elec. engr. aero. engring. and avionics dept. Collins Radio Co., Cedar Rapids, Iowa, 1971-72; mktg. mgr. Europe Motorola Co., Wiesbaden, W. Ger., 1972—; founder, mng. dir. TST Tele Security Timmann, Poecking, W. Ger., 1981—; dir. Timmann GmbH & Co., Tele Security Vertriebs KG, Tutzing, TSI Telesecurity Internat., Singapore. Clubs: Am. Cryptogram Assn., German Amateur Radio. Patentee in field. Home and Office: 3 Heinrichknotestrasse, D-8134 Poecking Federal Republic of Germany Office: Hauptstrasse 82, D-8132 Tutzing Federal Republic of Germany

TIMMERMAN, GEORGE BELL, JR., judge; b. Anderson, S.C., Aug. 11, 1912; s. George Bell and Mary Vandiver (Sullivan) T.; m. Helen Miller DuPre, Feb. 16, 1936. Student, The Citadel, 1930-34, LL.D. (hon.), 1950; LL.B., U. S.C., 1937, J.D., 1970. Bar: S.C. 1937. Practicing atty. Lexington, S.C., 1937-41, 46-55, 59-67; asst. chief trial atty. S.C. Pub. Service Authority, Charleston, 1941; judge 11th Jud. Circuit S.C., 1967-84, spl. circuit judge, 1984—; lt. gov. State of S.C., 1947-55, gov., 1955-59; pres. S.C. Democratic Conv., 1948, Lexington County Dem. Conv., 1950; S.C. Dem. committeeman, 1952-53; chmn. S.C. del. Dem. Nat. Conv., 1956; Dem. presdl. elector, 1964. Deacon Bapt. Ch. Served with USNR, 1942-46, PTO. Mem. ABA, S.C. Bar Assn., Am. Judicature Soc., Lexington C. of C., Am. Legion, Assn. Citadel Men (life), Citadel Inn of Ct. (bencher 1984—), Wig and Robe, Phi Delta Phi, Pi Kappa Phi, Blue Key.; mem. Woodmen of the World. Lodge: Lions. Home: PO Box 6 Batesburg SC 29006 Office: Main St Lexington SC 29072

TIMMERMANS, GILBERT LAMBERT, telecommunications company executive; b. Nerem, Limburg, Belgium, June 26, 1945; s. Joseph Julien and Maria Anna (Nijs) T.; m. Frieda Johanna Jackson, July 11, 1970; children: Peter, Yves. Student in indsl. engring., Rijksmijnbouwschool, Hasselt, Belgium, 1967; B in Econs., Post Univ. Centrum Diepenbeek, Belgium, 1974, MBA, 1978. Foundry prodn. mgr. Fabrique Nat. d'armes de guerre, Herstal, Belgium, 1969-71; foundry prodn. mgr. NOVA div. I.T.T., Tongeren, Belgium, 1971-75, engring. mgr., 1975-84, ops. mgr., 1984—. Bd. dirs. K.B.V.B. (Belgian football assn.). Served as sgt. arty Belgian Army, 1968. Home: Ginstraat 43, 3700, Tongeren, Limburg Belgium Office: NOVA div ITT, Overhaamlaan 44, Tongeren,, 3700 Limburg Belgium

TIMMINS, EDWARD PATRICK, lawyer; b. Denver, June 8, 1955; s. M. Edward and Elizabeth Jean (Imhoff) T.; m. Mary Joanne Deziel, Dec. 27, 1985; 1 child, Edward Patrick Jr. BA with honors, Harvard U., 1977; JD magna cum laude, U. Mich., 1980. Bar: Colo. 1981, U.S. Ct. Appeals (D.C. and 9th cirs.) 1982, U.S. Dist. Ct. Colo. 1984, U.S. Ct. Appeals (10th cir.) 1984. Law clk. to cir. justice U.S. Ct. Appeals (7th cir.), Chgo., 1980-81; trial atty. U.S. Dept. Justice, Washington, 1981-84; asst. U.S. atty. Denver, 1984—; dir., mem. Otten, Johnson, Robinson, Neff & Ragonetti P.C., Denver, 1985—. Sr. editor U. Mich. Law Rev., 1979-80. Harvard Nat. scholar, 1976. Mem. ABA, Colo. Bar Assn., Denver Bar Assn., Order of Coif, Internat. Platform Assn., Friends of Harvard Rowing. Office: Otten Johnson Robinson Neff & Ragonetti 950 17th St Suite 1600 Denver CO 80202

TIMMINS, JAMES DONALD, investment banker; b. Hamilton, Ont., Can., Oct. 3, 1955; came to U.S., 1979; s. Donald G. and Myrna L. (Seymour) T. B.A., U. Toronto, 1977; J.D., Queen's U., 1979; M.B.A., Stanford U., 1981. Investment banker Wood Gundy, Toronto, 1980, Salomon Bros., San Francisco, 1981-84; mng. dir. and chief exec. officer McKewon & Timmins, San Diego, 1984-87; ptnr. Hambrecht & Quist, San Francisco, 1987—. Home: 402 Stephen Rd San Mateo CA 94403 Office: Hambrecht & Quist 235 Montgomery St San Francisco CA 94104

TIMMONS, GERALD DEAN, pediatric neurologist; b. Rensselaer, Ind., June 1, 1931; s. Homer Timmons and Tamma Mildred (Spall) Rodgers; m. Lynne Rita Matrisciano, May 29, 1982; 1 child, Deanna Lynne; children from previous marriage: Jane Christina Timmons Mitchell, Ann Elizabeth, Mary Catherine. AB, Ind. U., 1953, MD, 1956. Diplomate Am. Bd. Psychiatry and Neurology. Intern Lima (Ohio) Meml. Hosp., 1956-57; resident Ind. U. Hosp., Indpls., 1957-59, 61-62; instr. neurology dept. Ind. U., Indpls., 1962-64; practice medicine specializing in psychiatry and neurology Indpls., 1962-64; practice medicine specializing in pediatric neurology Akron, Ohio, 1964—; chief pediatric neurology Children's Hosp. Med. Ctr., Akron, 1964—; chmn. neurology subcouncil Coll. Medicine Northeastern Ohio Univs., Rootstown, 1978—. Contbr. articles to profl. and scholarly jours. Served to capt. USAF, 1959-61. Mem. Summit County Med. Soc., Ohio Med. Soc., AMA, Am. Acad. Pediatrics, Am. Acad. Neurology (practice com. 1980—), Child Neurology Soc. (chmn. honors and awards com. 1978—), Am. Soc. Internal Medicine, Am. Electroencephalographic Soc. Republican. Methodist. Club: Cascade. Lodge: Rotary. Office: Akron Pediatric Neurology 300 Locust St Suite 370 Akron OH 44302

TIMMONS, GORDON DAVID, economics educator; b. Elbert, Tex., May 21, 1919; s. Walter James and Ella Mae (McCarson) T.; m. Jean Betty Kulhanek, Feb. 11, 1947; children: Kathy, Linda, Scott, Jim, Tamara, Dallas, Timothy, Kelly, Susanna. Student, U. Tex., 1937-40, U. Mont., 1961-64; BS, Utah State U., 1955; MS, Mont. State U., 1958. Enlisted USAF, 1939, advanced through grades to col., ret., 1961; instr. Columbia Basin Coll., Pasco, Wash., 1966—; pres. Assn. Higher Edn., 1969-72. Decorated Legion of Merit, Croix de Guerre (France). Mem. Northwest Econ. Conf. Democrat. Home and Office: Star Rt Box 39-A Olney TX 76374

TIMMRECK, JOE EDWARD, data processor; b. Longview, Wash., Oct. 8, 1950; s. Carmin C. and Betty (Snyder) T.; m. Janet Clipp; 1 dau., Jennifer. A.A. in Computer Sci., Lower Columbia Coll., 1970; student Weber State Coll., 1971-74. Engr. technician Ultrasystems, Ogden, Utah, 1973-75; system programmer St. Benedict's Hosp., Ogden, 1975-77; system analyst Jackson County (Oreg.), 1978-79; data processing mgr. Medford (Oreg.) Sch. Dist. 549C, 1979-83; writer, bus. cons. The Key Found., Point Roberts, Wash., 1987—. Founder, pres. Human Potentials Unltd., Medford, 1981-87; pub. The Obelisk, Medford, 1982-87. Mem. Am. Mgmt. Assn., Oreg. Assn. Ednl. Data Systems. Home and Office: 1905 Province Rd Point Roberts WA 98281

TIMOL, MAMOOJEE ESSOP, geriatrician; b. Rose-Hill, Mauritius, Sept. 10, 1937; arrived in France, 1960; s. Ismael Essop and Badat (Hafez) T.; m. Christiane Laurent; children: Karim, Kayvan, Tarik-Ludovic. Sch. Cert. of Cambridge, Islamic Coll., Port-Louis, Mauritius, 1956; Higher Sch. Cert. of Cambridge, Royal Coll. Sch., Port-Louis, 1958; student, Norwood Tech. Coll., London, 1959; MD, Faculte de Medecine Universite de Montpellier, France, 1969; Diploma in Gerontology and Geriatric Medicine, Faculte de

Medecine Universite de Montpellier, 1978, Diploma in Hygiene Hospitaliere, 1979, Diplome de la Reparation Juridique des Dommages Corporels, 1981. Lectr. biology, chemistry Islamic Coll., 1960-61; med. asst. children's unit, internal medicine, peritoneal and other extra renal dialysis Centre Hosp. de Nimes, France, 1966-69; pvt. practice specializing in geriatrics Bagnols sur Ceze, France, 1969—; cons. Inst. Medico Pedagogique, Bagnols sur Ceze, 1978—. Mem. Gaullist Party. Muslim. Clubs: Bridge (Bagnols sur Ceze, Avignon), Rotary. Address: 23 Place Mallet, Bagnols Sur Ceze 30200, France

TIN, SAW, mathematics educator; b. Mandalay, Burma, Oct. 4, 1938; s. Ngwe Seint U and Thin Kyi Daw; m. Pinlon Daw Thida, Nov. 11, 1973; children: Saw Yee Mon, Saw Min Htet, Saw Htet Aung. BSc, Mandalay U., 1960; MSc, U. Newcastle, Eng., 1970, PhD, 1973. Tutor Magwe Coll., Burma, 1960-62, 63-64, Mandalay U., 1962-63, 64-67; asst. lectr. Workers' Coll., Rangoon, Burma, 1967-68; asst. lectr. Rangoon Inst. Tech., 1968-80, leader engring. math., 1978—; lectr. math. Rangoon U., 1980-86, assoc. prof., 1986-88, prof., 1988—; sec. math. sci. div. Burma Research Policy Making Com., 1976—; cons. to Burmese Govt., 1983—. Fulbright scholar 1982-83. Home: 130 Kokine Rd, Pinlon Lodge, Rangoon Burma Office: Rangoon U, Dept Math, Rangoon Burma

TINBERGEN, JAN, economist; b. The Hague, Netherlands, Apr. 12, 1903; s. Dirk Cornelis and Jeannette (Van Eek) T.; D. Physics, Leiden U., 1929; hon. degree D.Econs., Helsinki, Durham, Amsterdam, Freiburg, Lisbon, Brussels, Strasbourg, Grenoble, Oslo, Paris, Bilbao, Ghent, Kiel, Bordeaux, Turin, Cluj, Cambridge; m. Tine Johanna de Wit, July 19, 1929; children—Tine (Mrs. Adriaan M. Van Peski) (dec.), Elsje (Mrs. Maurits J. Barendrecht), Hanneke, Marianne. Statistician, Central Bur. Stats., The Hague, 1929-45, temporarily attached to League of Nations Secretariat, 1936-38; dir. govt. Central planning bur., Netherlands, 1945-55; prof. Netherlands Sch. Econs., Rotterdam, 1933-73; cons. UN, World Bank, Netherlands, Surinam, UAR, Turkey, Venezuela; research dir. 20th Century Fund, 1960-62. Recipient Erasmus prize, 1967; Nobel prize econs., 1969. Mem. Nat., Royal Dutch, Royal Flemish, Am., Brit., French acads. sci., Econometric Soc., Am. Econ. Assn., Royal Statis. Soc. Mem. Dutch Labor Party. Author: Economic Policy: Principles and Design, 1956; The Design of Development, 1958; Shaping the World Economy, 1962; Lessons from the Past, 1964; Development Planning, 1967; Income Distribution: Analysis and Policies, 1975; co-author: Labor Plan, 1935, Warfare and Welfare, 1987. Home and Office: Netherlands Sch of Econs, Haviklaan 31, 2566 XD The Hague The Netherlands

TINBERGEN, NIKOLAAS, zoologist; b. The Hague, The Netherlands, Apr. 15, 1907; s. Dirk Cornelis and Jeannette (Van Eek) T.; m. Elisabeth Amelie Rutten, Apr. 14, 1932; children: Jacob, Catharina (Mrs. August Loman), Dirk, Jannetje, Gerardina (Mrs. S. Carleston). PhD, Leiden (Netherlands) U., 1932. Faculty Leiden U., 1933-49, prof. exptl. zoology, 1947-49; faculty Oxford (Eng.) U., 1949—, reader animal behavior, 1962-66, prof., 1966-74. Author: The Study of Instinct, 1951, Social Behaviour in Animals, 1953, The Herring Gull's World, 1953, Curious Naturalists, 1956, Animal Behavior, 1965, Signal for Survival, 1970, The Animal in its World, 2 vols., 1974; (with E.A. Tinbergen) Autistic Children, New Hope for a Cure, 1983; also articles and films including Signals for Survival (Italia prize 1969, Blue Ribbon N.Y. Film Festival 1971). Recipient Joint Nobel prize for physiology or medicine, 1973, Swammerdan medal, 1973, other awards. Fellow Royal Soc., 1962; mem. Nat. Acad. Scis., Am. Philos. Soc., Am. Acad. Arts and Scis. (fgn.), Akademie van Wetenschappen, Am. Mus. Natural History, Max Planck Gesellschaft, others. Home: 88 Lonsdale Rd, Oxford OX2 7ER, England

TINDALL, ROBERT EMMETT, lawyer, educator; b. N.Y.C., Jan. 2, 1934; s. Robert E. and Alice (McGonigle) T.; B.S. in Marine Engring., SUNY, 1955; postgrad. Georgetown U. Law Sch., 1960-61; LL.B., U. Ariz., 1963; LL.M., N.Y.U., 1967; Ph.D., City U., London, 1975; children—Robert Emmett IV, Elizabeth Mary. Mgmt. trainee Gen. Electric Co., Schenectady, N.Y., Lynn, Mass., Glen Falls, N.Y., 1955-56, 58-60; law clk. firm Haight, Gardner, Poor and Havens, N.Y.C., 1961; admitted to Ariz. bar, 1963; prin., mem. firm Robert Emmett Tindall & Assocs., Tucson, 1963—; asso. prof. mgmt. U. Ariz., Tucson, 1969—; vis. prof. Grad. Sch. of Law, Soochow U., Republic of China, 1972, Nat. Chengchi U., Republic of China, 1972, Schiller Coll., London, 1973, Grad. Bus. Centre, London, 1974; dir. grad. profl. programs Coll. Bus. and Public Adminstrn., U. Ariz., Tucson, 1975-81; investment cons. Kingdom of Saudi Arabia, 1981—; dir. entrepreneurship program, assoc. dir. Karl Eller Ctr. for Study of Pvt. Market Economy, U. Ariz., Tucson, 1984—; lectr. USIA in Eng., India, Middle East, 1974; lectr. bus. orgn. and regulatory laws Southwestern Legal Found., Acad. Am. and Internat. Law, 1976-80. Actor community theatres of Schenectady, 1955-56, Harrisburgh, Pa., 1957-58, Tucson, 1961-71; appeared in films Rage, 1971, Showdown at OK Corral, 1971, Lost Horizon, 1972; appeared in TV programs Gunsmoke, 1972, Petrocelli, 1974. Served to lt. USN, 1956-58. Ford Found. fellow, 1965-67; Asia Found. grantee, 1972-73. Mem. Am. Bar Assn., State Bar of Ariz., Internat. Bar Assn., Am. Bus. Law Assn., Acad. Internat. Bus., Screen Actors Guild, Honourable Soc. of Middle Temple (London), Phi Delta Phi, Beta Gamma Sigma (pres. Alpha chpt. Ariz. 1979-80). Clubs: Royal Overseas League (London); Racquet (Tucson). Author: Multinational Enterprises, 1975; contbr. articles on legal aspects of domestic and internat. bus. to profl. jours. Home: PO Box 43153 Tucson AZ 85733 Office: Coll Bus and Public Adminstrn U Ariz Dept Mgmt and Policy Tucson AZ 85721

TINDEMANS, LEO, minister foreign affairs Belgium; b. Zwijndrecht, Apr. 16, 1922; m. Rosa Naesens, 1960; 4 children. Ed. State U. Ghent, Catholic U. Louvain; D.Litt. (hon.), City U. London. Mem. Belgian Chamber of Deps., 1961; mayor of Edegem, 1965-76; minister of community affairs Govt. Belgium, Brussels, 1968-71, minister of agr. and middle class affairs, 1972-73, dep. prime minister, minister for budget and instl. problems, 1973-74, prime minister, 1974-78, minister of fgn. affairs, 1981—; vis. prof. Faculty Social Scis., Cath. U. Louvain (Belgium). Contbr. numerous articles, papers on constl. and internat. problems to jours. Pres. European People's Party; v.p. European Union of Christian Democrats. Recipient Charlemagne prize, 1976, St. Liborius medaille fur Einheit und Frieden, 1977. Office: Ministry Fgn Relations, Brussels Belgium *

TINDLE, CHARLES DWIGHT WOOD, broadcasting company executive; b. Bryn Mawr, Pa., Jan. 13, 1950; s. Charles Wood and Nancy (Sapp) T. Student, Kenyon Coll., 1968-71. Pres. Dwight Karma Broadcasting, Mesa, Ariz., 1971-76, Natural Broadcasting System, Mesa, 1976-79; producer, fellow Am. Film Inst. Ctr. for Advanced Film Studies, 1979-80; pres. Network 30, Scottsdale, Ariz., 1985—; owner Sta. KDKB-AM-FM, Mesa, Sta. KSML-FM, Lake Tahoe, Calif., Sta. KNOT-AM-FM, Prescott, Ariz., Sta. KBWA, Williams, Ariz. Recipient Peabody award U. Ga., 1976. Republican. Episcopalian. Home: 4959 E Red Rock Dr Phoenix AZ 85018 Office: Network 30 Inc 4416 N Scottsdale Rd #605 Scottsdale AZ 85251

TING, HOON CHIN, dermatologist, educator; b. Sitiawan, Perak, Malaysia, June 23, 1947; parents: Gooi Ling Chen and Lang Ing Hoon. MBBS, U. Malaya, Kuala Lumpur, Malaysia, 1972; diploma in dermatology, U. London, 1978; diploma in venereology, Soc. Apothecaries, London, 1984. Intern Univ. Hosp., Kuala Lumpur, 1972-73, resident, 1973-76, mem. staff, 1972-76; lectr. dept. medicine U. Malaya, Kuala Lumpur, 1976-84, assoc. prof. dept. medicine, 1984—; cons. Univ. Hosp., Kuala Lumpur, 1984—. Contbr. articles to profl. jours. Mem. Royal Coll. Physicians, Dermatological Soc. Malaysia (v.p. 1984-87). Home: 30 Jalan Setia Jasa, Bukit Damansara, 50490 Kuala Lumpur Malaysia Office: Univ Hosp, Dept Medicine, 59100 Kuala Lumpur Malaysia

TING, LAWRENCE SHAN-LI, plastics company executive; b. Kiang-su, China, Jan. 25, 1939; s. Wee Non and Hsiu Chin (Hsia) T.; B.S., Chinese Mil. Acad., 1961; m. Sylvia Tsong-Ching Fei, May 29, 1966; children—Iris Kwang-I., Joyce Kwang-Yu, Albert Kwang-Chin, Arthur Kwang-Hung. Commd. 2d lt. Chinese Army, 1957, advanced through grades to maj., 1971; ret., 1971; v.p., gen. mgr. Haw-yi Chem. Indsl. Corp., 1971-73; v.p. China Gulf Plastics Corp., Taipei, Taiwan, 1973-76, exec. v.p., 1976-83, also dir.; pres. Taiwan Indsl. Fastener Corp., 1983—, Alexander Stenhouse (Taiwan), 1984—, chmn. 1987— , Alexander Stenhouse Ins. Agy. Ltd., 1984—; chmn. 1987; dir. Taiwan Vinyl Chloride Monomer Corp., Taiwan Plasticizer Corp., Chin Cheng Investment Corp. Vice chmn. Chinese Taipei Olympic Com., 1975-82. Decorated Order Chi-Hsueh; Order Hwa Hsia; Order Phys. Edn.; Republic of China Nat. Def. scholar, 1964-66; Paul Harris fellow, 1981. Mem. Chinese Inst. Engrs., Taiwan Area Plastics Assn. (chmn.). Club: Taipei Rotary. Patentee household appliances. Home: 30 Lane 68 Hsin-Sheng, N Rd Sect III, 10474 Taipei Republic of China Office: 3 Tun Hwa S Rd, 10589 Taipei Republic of China

TING, SAMUEL CHAO CHUNG, physicist, educator; b. Ann Arbor, Mich., Jan. 27, 1936; s. Kuan H. and Jeanne (Wong) T.; m. Kay Louise Kuhne, Nov. 23, 1960; children: Jeanne Min, Amy Min; m. Susan Carol Marks, Apr. 28, 1985; 1 child, Christopher M. BS in Engring, U. Mich., 1959, MS, 1960, PhD, 1962, ScD (hon.), 1978; ScD (hon.), Chinese U. Hong Kong, 1987. Ford Found. fellow CERN (European Orgn. Nuclear Research), Geneva, 1963; instr. physics Columbia U., 1964, asst. prof., 1965-67; group leader Deutsches Elektronen-Synchrotron, Hamburg, W.Ger., 1966; asso. prof. physics M.I.T., Cambridge, 1967-68; prof. M.I.T., 1969—, Thomas Dudley Cabot Inst. prof., 1977—; program cons. Div. Particles and Fields, Am. Phys. Soc., 1970, Beijing Normal Coll., 1987, Chinese U. Hong Kong, 1987, Jiatong U., Shanghai, Peoples Republic China, 1987; hon. prof. Beijing Normal Coll., China, 1987,Jiatong U., Shanghai, 1987. Assoc. editor: Nuclear Physics B, 1970; contbr. articles in field to profl. jours.; editorial bd.: Nuclear Instruments and Methods; advisor Jour. Modern Physics A. Recipient Nobel prize in Physics, 1976, De Gasperi prize in Sci., Italian Republic, 1988; Am. Acad. Sci. and Arts fellow, 1975; Ernest Orlando Lawrence award U.S. Govt., 1976; Eringen medal Soc. Engring. Sci., 1977. Mem. Nat. Acad. Sci., Pakistani Acad. Sci. (fgn. mem.), Academia Sinica (fgn. mem.). Office: MIT Dept Physics 51 Vassar St Cambridge MA 02139

TINGEY, CAROL, psychologist, educator; b. St. James, Mo., Sept. 24, 1933; d. Willis Alma and Lola (Madsen) Tingey; B.S. magna cum laude, U. Utah, 1970, M.Ed., 1971, Ph.D., 1976; children—Richard, Blaine, James, Neil, Trish. Tchr. public schs., Salt Lake City, 1970, spl. edn. tchr., 1971-72; clin. instr. spl. edn. U. Utah, Salt Lake City, 1972-74; dir. staff devel. Utah State Tng. Sch., American Fork, Utah, 1974-75; asst. prof. spl. edn. U. No. Iowa, Cedar Falls, 1975-77; asst. prof. spl. edn. Trinity Coll., Washington, 1977-78; asst. prof. spl. edn. of severely handicapped George Mason U., Fairfax, Va., 1978-79; assoc. prof. edn. and tng. physically and multi-handicapped Northwestern State U. of La., Natchitoches, 1979-81; assoc. prof. spl. edn. Ill. State U., Normal, also coordinator program for physically handicapped, 1981-83; assoc. prof. psychology Utah State U., Logan, 1983—; bd. dirs. Nat. Down Syndrome Congress; researcher, cons. in field. Fellow Am. Assn. on Mental Deficiency (sec. Utah chpt. 1975, ednl. chmn. region VIII 1976-77, treas. edn. div. 1979-80), mem. Assn. for Severely Handicapped, Council for Exceptional Children (pres. Utah chpt. 1974-75), Assn. for Retarded Citizens, Phi Delta Kappa, Phi Kappa Phi. Author: Home and School Partnerships in Exceptional Education; Handicapped Infants and Children: Handbook for Parents and Professionals; New Perspectives on Down Syndrome; Down Syndrome: A Resource Handbook; Early Intervention--Hands on Strategies; contbr. articles to profl. jours.; recorded albums: Self Help Skills, Adaptive Behavior; Socialization Skills; Adaptive Behavior; Daily Living Tasks, Housekeeping Skills, Vocational Awareness, Community Helpers; editorial adv. bd. Exceptional Parent mag. Home: 1565 Rose Orchard Circle Logan UT 84321 Office: Utah State U 174 Devel Ctr/ Handicapped Persons Logan UT 84322

TINGLER, LOYD, retail trade company executive; b. Daviess County, Mo., Aug. 27, 1920; s. Lawrence Henry and Leah Mae (Robinson) T.; m. Arlene Marie Preston, Aug. 8, 1948; children—Martha, Elizabeth, Charles, James. Grad. Chillicothe (Mo.) Bus. Coll., 1941; postgrad. Harvard U., 1947. Mgr., Webb's Furniture Store, St. Petersburg, Fla., 1949-62; propr., dir. Loyd Tingler Furniture Inc., Pinellas Park, Fla., 1962—; dir. S.E. Bank of Pinellas Park, 1976-79; Chmn. Pinellas Park Water Mgmt. Dist., 1976-88; trustee 5th Ave Bapt. Ch., St. Petersburg, 1980—; bd. dirs. Boys' Club of Pinellas Park, 1965-73, Pinellas Park Girls' Club, 1971-72, Child Guidance Clinic of Pinellas Park, 1973-75, Bay Vista Civic Assn., 1957-72. Served with USN, 1942-47. Mem. Fla. Furniture Dealers Assn. (dir. 1972—). Nat. Home Furnishing Assn., Contractors and Builders of Pinellas County (dir. 1980-82), Pinellas Park C. of C. (dir. 1972-75, transp. chmn. 1972-75 named Citizen of Year 1979). Republican. Baptist. Clubs: Optimists (dir. 1967-70, Friend of the Boy award 1971), Kiwanis (Layman's award 1975), Pres.'s Moose. Home: 3611 93d Ave N Pinellas Park FL 34666 Office: 8010 US Hwy 19 Pinellas Park FL 34665

TINGLEY, GEORGE ALEXANDER, airline company executive; b. Providence, June 20, 1928; s. Edgar Burton and Alice Irene (MacDonald) T.; A.B., Brown U., 1951; M.S., UCLA, 1961; Dr.sc.techn., Swiss Fed. Inst. Tech., 1980; m. Katharina Regina Schenker, Aug. 23, 1968; 1 dau., Vanessa Alexandra. Engr., N. Am. Aviation, 1954-55; sales engr. G. M. Giannini and Epsco, 1955-58; test engr. Douglas Aircraft Co., Santa Monica, Calif., 1959-62; European sales mgr. Munzig Internat., Inc., Zurich, Switzerland, 1962-65; div. mgr. ops. research, sci. programming Swissair, Zurich, 1969-84; cons., 1985—. Served to lt. (j.g.) USNR, 1951-53. Mem. Airline Group of Internat. Fedn. Operational Research Socs. (mem. governing council 1975-81, pres. 1985-88), IEEE, Ops. Research Soc. Switzerland. Home: 8 Uebrichstrasse, Ch 8309 Nuerensdorf Switzerland Office: Swissair, CT Balsberg, Zurich Airport, CH-8058 Zurich Switzerland

TINKER, JACK, physician; b. Chorley, Eng., Jan. 20, 1936; s. Lawrence Schofield and Jessie (Keenesmith) T.; m. Maureen Ann Crawford, July 26, 1961; children—Andrew, Alastair. B.Sc., U. Manchester, 1957, M.B.Ch.B., 1960. Postgrad. med. dean Brit. Postgrad. Med. Fedn., London; hon. cons. intensive care medicine Middlesex Hosp., London; sr. consulting med. officer Sun Life of Can., London, 1983—. Series editor The Bloomsbury Series; editor Intensive Care Medicine; editor in chief Brit. Jour. Hosp. Medicine; editor: Care of the Critically Ill Patient; contbr. articles to profl. jours. Mem. Intensive Care Soc. (chmn. 1982), Brit. Med. Assn. Avocation: Cricket. Home: 1 Rectory Rd, London SW13, England Office: Brit Postgrad Med Fedn, 33 Millman St, London WC1, England

TINNISWOOD, PETER MAURICE, business educator; b. Surrey, Eng., May 30, 1951; s. Maurice Owen and Anne Katherine (Matchett) T.; m. Catharina Elizabeth Oeschger, Aug. 9, 1975. BA, Magdalen Coll., Oxford, 1973, MA, 1979; cert. in edn., Oxford U., 1974; MBA, European Inst. Bus. Adminstrn., 1981. Tchr. politics and econs. Repton Sch., Eng., 1974-76; tchr. in mgmt. Marlborough Coll., Eng., 1976-80, head faculty bus. studies, 1984-86, housemaster, 1985—; sec. gen. Franco-Brit. C. of C. and Industry, Paris, 1981-84; sec. Cambridge Bus. Studies Project Trust, 1984—; chief examiner Bus. Studies A. Level, Cambridge, 1984—. Home: Cotton House, Bath Rd, Marlborough, Wiltshire SN8 1NN, England Office: Marlborough Coll, Marlborough, Wiltshire SN8 1PA, England

TINSLEY, THOMAS VINCENT, JR., accounting company executive; b. Wilkes-Barre, Pa., Oct. 16, 1940; s. Thomas Vincent and Mary Clare (Green) T.; B.S. in Acctg., U. Scranton, 1963; grad. in programming Electronic Computer Programming Inst., 1966; m. Katherine Alice Swan, Oct. 15, 1966; children—Sara Elisabeth, Tracy Swan. Jr. acct. Peat, Marwick, Mitchell & Co., Balt., 1963-64; accounts receivable mgr., import acctg. mgr. Aimcee Wholesale Corp., N.Y.C., 1964-65; sr. acct. Richards, Ganly, Fries & Preusch, N.Y.C., 1965-66, Morris J. Weinstein, Groothius & Co., N.Y.C., 1966-69; supr. Brach Lane Hariton & Hirshberg, N.Y.C., 1969-70; owner mgr. Thomas V. Tinsley, Jr., C.P.A., Wilkes Barre, Pa. and N.Y.C., 1970-78; sr. partner Tinsley & Co., C.P.A.s, Wilkes-Barre and N.Y.C., 1978-83; pres. Tinsley & Co. P.C., Wilkes-Barre, Pa. and N.Y.C., 1984—; notary public, Luzerne County, Pa.; mem. faculty bank Found. for Acctg. Edn. Mem. Fairview Twp. Planning Commn., Fairview Twp. Zoning and Hearing Bd., 1979—. Served with USMCR, 1960-66. C.P.A., N.Y., Pa., N.J. Mem. Am. Arbitration Assn., Am., Pa. insts. C.P.A.s, Acctg. Research Assn., N.J., N.Y. State socs. C.P.A.s, Nat. Rifle Assn., U. Scranton Nat. Alumni Soc. (bd. govs. 1979—), Luzerne County Law Enforcement Officers and Assocs. Democrat. Roman Catholic. Clubs: Valley Country, N.Y. Athletic, World Trade Center, Union League (N.Y.C.); Nuangola Rod and Gun; West Side Tennis. Lodge: K.C. Home: Box 366 White Birch Ln Glen Summit Mountaintop PA 18707 Office: 10 W Northampton St Suite 500 Wilkes-Barre PA 18707

TIPPETT, MICHAEL KEMP, composer; b. London, Eng. Jan. 2, 1905; s. Henry William and Isabel (Kemp) T.; ed. Royal Coll. Music; Dr. Music (hon.) Cambridge U., 1964, Oxford U., Dublin U., Wales U., Leeds U. Formerly mus. dir. chorus and orch. soc., Oxted, Eng., tchr. French, Hazelwood Sch., until 1931; tchr. adult edn. dept. London County Council, 1932. Royal Arsenal Coop. Soc. Edn.; mus. dir. Morley Coll., London, 1940-51; dir. Bath Festival, 1969-74. Composer numerous orchestral works, including 4 symphonies, 1945, 58, 72, 77, 3 string quartets, 1935, 42, 46, Fantasia for piano, orch., 1942, orch. suite, 1948, Little Music for string orch., 1952, Variations on Theme by Correlli for string orch., 1953, piano concerto, 1955, 3 piano sonatas, 1937, 62, 73, Symphony No. 4, 1977, String Quartet No. 4, 1978, Triple Concerto, 1979, Piano Sonata #4, 1984, Moving into Aquarius, 1985; works for organ, choral works including A Child of our Time, 1944, The vision of St. Augustine, 1966, Crown of the Year; The Mask of Time, 1983; (operas) The Midsummer Marriage, 1952, King Priam, 1958-61, The Knot Garden, 1970, The Ice Break, 1977, also songs; author: Music of the Angels, 1980. Created knight, 1966; decorated comdr. Order Brit. Empire, Order of Merit. Address: care Schott & Co, 48 Great Marlborough St, London W1Y 2BN, England *

TIPPIT, JOHN HARLOW, lawyer; b. Marietta, Okla., July 22, 1916; s. Alva Ney and Edna Pearl (Harlow) T.; m. Ann Morse, Feb. 27, 1943; children—David H., Ann Maurine. B.A., U. Okla., 1940, LL.B., 1940. Bar: Okla., 1940, Colo., 1945, U.S. Supreme Ct., 1960. States atty. Love County, Okla., 1940; sole practice Denver, 1945-77, Boulder, Colo., 1978-83; ptnr. Tippit, Haskell & Welborn, Tippit & Haskell and Tippit & Whittington P.C., Boulder, 1947-48; dir. Buckingham Nat. Bank; pres., mng. ptnr. natural resources cos.; lectr. Rocky Mountain Mineral Law Found.; lectr. various legal confs. Co-author: American Law of Mining; contbr. articles to profl. jours. Vice pres. Denver council Boy Scouts Am.; pres. Red Rocks Assn.; bd. dirs., sec. Acad. Ind. Scholars. Served to lt. col. USAAF, 1940-44. Mem. ABA (chmn. sect. natural resources), Okla. Bar Assn., Colo. Bar Assn. (chmn. mineral law sect.), Denver Bar Assn. (trustee). Republican. Episcopalian. Clubs: Mile High Denver Country (Denver); Boulder Country. Home: 525 Aurora St Boulder CO 80302 Office: 305 Park West Bldg 250 Arapahoe St Boulder CO 80302

TIPPLE, ALLAN GRAHAM, town planning researcher; b. Harrogate, Eng., Feb. 17, 1949; s. Arthur Dawson Tipple and Agnes Barclay (Lazenby) Scholey; m. Susan Patricia Thirlwall, Sept. 5, 1970; children: Matthew, Eleanor, David, Nicholas. BA in Town Planning, U. Sheffield, Eng., 1970, MA in Town Planning, 1972; PhD, U. Newcastle, 1984. Town planner Kitwe (Zambia) City Council, 1972-75; sr. asst. planner North Yorkshire County Council, Northallerton, Eng., 1975-78; lectr. U. Sci. and Tech., Kumasi, Ghana, 1978-82, U. Newcastle upon Tyne, Eng., 1982-83; research officer Ctr. for Arcthl. Research and Devel. Overseas, 1983—; planner Nat. Housing Authority, Lusaka, Zambia, 1972-73; cons. World Bank, Washington, 1985-88; lectr. Ghana, Nigeria, Egypt, India, Zambia. Contbr. numerous articles on urban issues in Africa to profl. jours. Lay preacher Meth. Ch. Mem. Royal Town Planning Inst., Full Gospel Businessmen's Fellowship Internat. Home: 9 Woodburn Sq, Whitley Bay NE26 3JE, England Office: U Newcastle upon Tyne, Sch Architecture Ctr for, Archtl Research and Devel, Overseas, Newcastle NE1 7RU, England

TIPTON, CLYDE RAYMOND, JR., communications and resources development consultant; b. Cin., Nov. 13, 1921; s. Clyde Raymond and Ida Marie (Molitor) T.; m. Marian Gertrude Beushausen, Aug. 6, 1942; children: Marian Page Ashley, Robert Bruce. BS, U. Ky., 1946, MS, 1947. Research engr. Battelle Meml. Inst., Columbus, Ohio, 1947-49, sr. tech. adviser, 1951-62, coordinator corporate communications, 1969-73, v.p. communications, 1973-75, asst. to pres., 1978-79, v.p., corp. dir. communications and pub. affairs, 1979-86, ret.; staff mem. Los Alamos Sci. Lab., 1949-51; dir. research Basic, Inc., Bettsville, Ohio, 1962-64; asst. dir. Battelle Pacific N.W. Labs., Richland, Wash., 1964-69; pres., trustee Battelle Commons Co. for Community Urban Redevel., Columbus, 1975-78; cons. bus. communications and devel. Columbus, 1986—; secretariat U.S. del. 2d Internat. Conf. on Peaceful Uses Atomic Energy, Geneva, 1958; cons. U.S. AEC in Atoms for Peace Program, Tokyo, 1959, New Delhi, 1959-60, Rio de Janeiro, Brazil, 1961. Author: How to Change the World, 1982; editor: Jour. Soc. for Nondestructive Testing, 1953-57, The Reactor Handbook, Reactor Materials, vol. 3, 1955, vol. 1, 1960, Learning to Live on a Small Planet, 1974; patentee in field. Bd. dirs., past pres. Pilot Dogs; bd. dirs. Central Ohio United Negro Coll. Fund, Columbus Assn. for Performing Arts, Central Ohio resource bd. CARE, Pilot Guide Dog Found., Jazz Arts Group; bd. dirs., past pres. Architects Soc. Ohio Found., Greater Columbus Arts Council; chmn. bd. Battelle Scholars Program Trust Fund; mem. governing bd. Battelle Youth Sci. Program. Served with USAAF, 1943. U. Ky. Haggin fellow, 1947; Otterbein Coll. Sr. fellow, 1978. Mem. Am. Soc. Metals, NSPE/Prof. Engrs. in Industry (sec.), Ohio Soc. Profl. Engrs. (bd. dirs., treas., Disting. Service award), Pub. Relations Soc. Am., Sigma Xi, Alpha Chi Sigma. Episcopalian. Club: Athletic (Seattle). Lodge: Lions. Home and Office: 6475 Strathaven Ct West Worthington OH 43085

TIPTON, GARY LEE, personal services company executive; b. Salem, Oreg., July 3, 1941; s. James Rains and Dorothy Velma (Dierks) T.; B.S., Oreg. Coll. Edn., 1964. Credit rep. Standard Oil Co. Calif., Portland, Oreg., 1964-67; credit mgr. Uniroyal Inc., Dallas, 1967-68; partner, mgr. bus. Tipton Barbers, Portland, 1968—. Mem. Rep. Nat. Com., 1980—, Sen. Howard Baker's Presdl. Steering Com., 1980; apptd. Deputy Dir. Gen., Internat. Biog. Ctr., Cambridge, England, 1987—; mem. U.S. Congl. adv. bd. Am. Security Council, 1984—. Recipient Key to Internat. Biog. Cen., Cambridge, U.K., 1983, World Culture prize Accademia Italia, 1984, Presdl. Achievement award, 1982, cert. disting. contbn. Sunset High Sch. Dad's Club, 1972, 73. Fellow Internat. Biog. Assn. (life, Key award 1983) (U.K.); mem. Sunset Mall Mchts. Assn. (co-founder, treas. 1974-79, pres. 1982-83), Internat. Platform Assn., Smithsonian Assocs., Council on Fgn. Relations (vice chmn. steering com. Portland 1983-84, chmn. Portland com. on fgn. relations 1984-86), UN Assn. (steering com. UN day 1985). Office: Tipton Barbers 1085 NW Murray Rd Portland OR 97229

TIRAS, HERBERT GERALD, engineering executive; b. Houston, Aug. 11, 1924; s. Samuel Louis and Rose (Seibel) T.; m. Aileen Wilkenfeld, Dec. 14, 1955; children—Sheryle, Leslie. Student, Tex. A. and M. U., 1941-42; attended, Houston U., 1942-65, student, Nat. Defence U., 1986. Registered profl. engr., Calif. Cert. mfg. engr. in gen. mfg.; robotics; mfg. mgmt; gen. mgmt. Engr., Reed Roller Bit, Houston, 1942-60; pres. Tex. Truss, Houston, 1960-77; chief exec. officer Omnico, Houston, 1977—; Nat. Defense exec. res. resources officer, Region VI Fed. Emergency Mgmt. Agy., 1982—. Served to 1st lt. CAP, 1954-61. Mem. Machine Vision Assn., Nat. Defense U. Found., Soc. Mfg. Engrs., Robot Inst. Am., Robotics Internat., Marine Tech. Soc., Coll. and Univ. Mfg. Ednl. Council (nat. dir.), Assn. of the Indsl. Coll. of the Armed Forces. Lodge: Masons, Shriners. Home: 9703 Runnymeade Houston TX 77096 Office: PO Box 2872 Houston TX 77001

TIRET, HORACE MEDLIN, accountant; b. Pacific Grove, Calif., Oct. 23, 1915; s. Auguste Hubert and Annie Blaine (Eliot) T.; student Am. Inst. Banking, 1933-35; B.A., San Francisco Inst. Accountancy, 1941; postgrad. Golden Gate U., 1948-49; m. Elsie Christine Bleuss, Nov. 5, 1938; children—Sharon Lee, Jeffrey, Steven, Daniel, Michael. Bond cashier, Investment dept., Wells Fargo Bank, San Francisco, 1933-41; owner Tiret & Assos. (formerly Horace M. Tiret & Assos.), San Francisco, 1946—, pres., 1976-77, partner, 1977-80; pres. Concise Contact Lens Co., San Leandro, Calif., 1949-78, v.p., sec., 1978—, also dir. Chmn. troop com. Boy Scouts Am., San Francisco, 1955-60. Served with AUS, 1945-46. C.P.A., Calif. Mem. Calif. C.P.A. Soc., Am. Inst. C.P.A.'s, Am. Fuchsia Soc., Soc. Calif. Pioneers, Nat. Fuchsia Soc. Presbyn. Patentee in fuchsia field. Home: 168 Lunado Ct San Francisco CA 94127 Office: 250 Executive Park Blvd Suite 4800 San Francisco CA 94134

TIRKANITS, NICHOLAS MIKLOS, oil company executive, mining executive, civil engineer; b. Kiralyhaza, Czechoslovakia, July 7, 1923; came to Can., 1952; s. Nicholas and Elisabeth (Nagy) T.; m. Clara Margarethe Bedo, 1951; children—Elisabeth C., Beatrix C., Nicholas J., Thomas A. Diploma

Engr., Swiss Fed. Inst. Tech., Zurich, 1951; grad. Advanced Mgmt., McGill U., 1976. Registered profl. engr., Ont., Que. Asst. prof. Swiss Fed. Inst. Tech., Zurich, 1949-51; engr., cons., Toronto, Ont., 1952-60; sr. engr. Can. Pacific Ltd., Montreal, Que., 1960-79; chmn. Chipman Mining & Energy Corp. Ltd., Calgary, Alta., 1980-86; pres., chief exec. officer New Campbell Island Mines Ltd., Calgary, 1984—; pres., dir. Lundberg-Tirkanits & Assocs. Ltd., Profl. Engrs., Toronto, Calgary, Can., Austria, 1971—. Mem. Am. Geog. Soc., ASCE, Engring. Inst. Can., Order Engrs. Que., Assn. Profl. Engrs. Ont. Avocations: hunting; fishing; sailing. Home: 612 Elbow Dr SW, Calgary, AB Canada T2S 2H7 Office: New Campbell Island Mines Ltd, 820 138 4th Ave SE, Calgary, AB Canada T2G 4Z6

TIRTAKURNIA, SURYADI, paper company executive; b. Kalimantan, Indonesia, Nov. 26, 1946; s. Nio Yam and Siu Nai (Phua) The; m. Djuwita Lili, Dec. 1, 1968; children—Mulyadi, Hartini. Student pub. schs., Singapore. Vice dir. C.V. Sahabat, Jakarta, Indonesia, 1964-69, dir., 1969-72; dir C.V. The Venus, Jakarta, 1972-76; mng. dir. The Univenus Co., Ltd., Jakarta, 1976—.

TISCH, LAURENCE ALAN, diversified corporation executive; b. N.Y.C., Mar. 15, 1923; s. Al and Sadye (Brenner) T.; m. Wilma Stein, Oct. 31, 1948; children: Andrew, Daniel, James, Thomas. B.Sc. cum laude, N.Y. U., 1942; M.A. in Indsl. Engring, U. Pa., 1943; student, Harvard Law Sch., 1946. Pres. Tisch Hotels, Inc., N.Y.C., 1946—; chmn. exec. com. Loews Theaters, Inc. (co. name changed to Loews Corp.), N.Y.C., 1959-65, chmn. bd., 1960—, pres., 1965-69, chief exec. officer, 1969—; chmn. CBS Inc., N.Y.C., 1986, chmn., chief exec. officer, 1986—; pres., dir. CBS Inc., New York; chmn. CNA Fin. Corp. (subs. Loews Corp.), Chgo.; chmn. bd. CNA; dir. Automatic Data Processing Corp., Columbia Broadcasting System. Trustee, chmn. bd. N.Y. U.; trustee Legal Aid Soc., Met. Mus. Art, N.Y. Pub. Library, Carnegie Corp.; trustee-at-large Fedn. Jewish Philanthropies N.Y. Home: Island Dr North Manursing Island Rye NY 10580 Office: Loews Corp 666 Fifth Ave New York NY 10103 *

TISDALE, DOUGLAS MICHAEL, lawyer; b. Detroit, May 3, 1949; s. Charles Walker and Violet Lucille (Battani) T.; m. Patricia Claire Brennan, Dec. 29, 1972; children—Douglas Michael, Jr., Sara Elizabeth, Margaret Patricia, Victoria Claire. B.A. in Psychology with honors, U. Mich., 1971, J.D., 1975. Bar: Colo. 1975, U.S. Dist. Ct. Colo. 1975, U.S. Ct. Appeals (10th cir.) 1976, U.S. Supreme Ct. 1979. Law clk. to chief judge U.S. Dist. Ct. Colo., Denver, 1975-76; assoc. Brownstein, Hyatt, Farber & Madden, Denver, 1976-81, ptnr., 1981-87, also bd. dirs.; bd. dirs. Employer Services Program, Inc., Denver, Warner Devels., Inc., Vail, Colo.; lectr. Law Seminars, Inc., 1984—, Continuing Legal Edn. in Colo., Inc., 1984—, Nat. Bus. Insts., 1985—, ABA Nat. Insts. 1988; Colo. Law-Related Edn. Coordinator, 1982-88. Mem. ABA (mem. litigation sect. trial evidence com. 1981—, vice chmn. real property sect. com. on creditors rights in real estate fin. 1984—, vice chmn. real property sect. com. on real property law and needs of public 1984-85, 87—, chmn. 1987—, chmn. real property sect. subcom. on foreclosures in bankruptcy 1982—), Colo. Bar Assn. (conv. com. 1979—), Denver Bar Assn. (jud. adminstrn. com. 1978—), Am. Judicature Soc., Assn. Trial Lawyers Am., Colo. Trial Lawyers Assn., Law Club of Denver (sec. 1984-85), Phi Alpha Delta, Phi Beta Kappa. Democrat. Roman Catholic. Home: 10986 West 77th Ave Arvada CO 80005 Office: Brownstein Hyatt Farber & Madden 410 17th St Denver CO 80202

TISDALE, THOMAS EDWARD, mechanical engineer; b. Chgo., Mar. 14, 1942; s. Eugene Ephriam Tisdale and Modena (Hess) Pulliam; m. Mary Ellen Szarowicz, July 25, 1959 (div. Apr. 1977); children—Elizabeth Marie, Julie Anne, Thomas Edward. B.S. in Mech. Engring., San Jose State U., 1963; postgrad. Ill. Inst. Tech., 1966, U. Chgo. Engr., Cook Research Co., Morton Grove, Ill., 1963-65, Dale & Assocs., Chgo., 1965-69; project engr. U.S. Army, Charlestown, Ind., 1969-74, Sundstrand Corp., Rockford, Ill., 1974-77; project mgr. FMC Corp., San Jose, Calif., 1977-79, Abbott Labs., North Chicago, Ill., 1979—; cons. Dept. Energy, Idaho Falls, Idaho, 1977-79. Contbr. articles on engring. to profl. jours. Chmn. No. Ill. Heart Assn., Rockford, 1976, 77; mem. Young Republicans of Ill., Oak Park, 1968, 69. Mem. Soc. Mfg. Engrs. (cert.), ASME, Am. Def. Preparedness Assn., Robotics Internat. (cert. robotics engr.). Roman Catholic. Lodges: Eagles, Masons. Home: 827 Chatham Elmhurst IL 60126 Office: Abbott Labs AP4A/04B North Chicago IL 60064

TISDELL, CLEMENT ALLAN, economics educator, researcher, consultant; b. Taree, New South Wales, Australia, Nov. 18, 1939; s. Clement Alfred and Alma Jean (Lewis) T.; m. Marie-Elisabeth Eckermann, Dec. 7, 1968; children: Ann-Marie Elizabeth, Christopher Clement. B.Com. in Econs., U. New South Wales, Sydney, 1961; PhD, Australian Nat. U., Canberra, 1964. Temporary lectr. econs. Australian Nat. U., Canberra, 1964; vis. fellow Princeton U., 1965; vis. scholar Stanford U., 1965; lectr. econs. Australian Nat. U., Canberra, 1966-67, sr. lectr., 1967, reader in econs., 1967-72, prof. econs. U. Newcastle, New South Wales, Australia, 1972—; mem. acad. bd. Nat. Inst. Econs. and Indsl. Research, Melbourne, Victoria, Australia, 1984—; guest investigator Woods Hole (Mass.) Oceanographic Inst., 1986; dean faculty econs. and commerce U. Newcastle, 1977-78, 85-86; bursar Univ. House, Australian Nat. U., Canberra, 1966-68. Author: Science and Technology Policy, 1981, Wild Pigs, 1982; joint author: Economics in Canadian Society, 1986, Weed Control Economics, 1987; also other books and numerous articles to profl. jours. Jr. v.p. Australian Labor Party, Gateshead Branch, New South Wales, 1987. Postdoctoral traveling scholarship Autralian Nat. U., Canberra, 1965; William Evans vis. prof. U. Otago, New Zealand, 1988. Fellow Acad. Social Sci. in Australia; mem. Econs. Soc. Australia, Australian Agrl. Econs. Soc., Australian Inst. Internat. Affairs, Internat. Soc. Agrl. Econs. Mem. Anglican Ch. Club: Staff House (U. Newcastle). Home: 9 Kerri Close, 2290 Charlestown, New South Wales Australia Office: U Newcastle, Rankin Dr, 2308 Newcastle NSW Australia

TISSERAND, MICHEL GILBERT HENRI, ergonomist, engineer, researcher; b. Hericourt, France, Oct. 31, 1939; s. Rene Felicien and Odette Marie-Antoinette (Cerf) T.; m. Francoise Dominique Lambrioux, June 3, 1967; children: Philippe, Alain. Phys. engr., Inst. Nat. Scis. Appliquees, Lyon, France, 1964; Upper Ergonomics Diploma, Conservatoire Nat. Arts et Metiers, Paris, 1969. Researcher Nat. Safety Inst., Paris, 1966-69; chief biomechanics lab. Nat. Research and Safety Inst., Nancy, France, 1970-78, head ergonomics service, 1978—; prof. CNAM-CUCES, Nancy, 1975—; chmn. internat. working group Internat. Standard Orgn., 1984—. Contbr. articles to profl. jours. Mem. Assn. Francaise Normalisation, Soc. Ergonomie Langue Francaise, Applied Vision Assn., Soc. Automotive Engrs. Roman Catholic. Home: 12 Rue des Cottages, 54600 Villers Les Nancy France Office: Nat Research and Safety Ctr, Research BP 27 Ave de Bourgogne, 54501 Vandoeuvre France

TITI, OSCAR, banking company executive; b. Forli, Italy, May 10, 1945; s. Quinto and Clara (Cappelli) T.; m. Franca Formelli; 1 child, Michele. Doctorate in Indsl. Chemistry, U. Bologna, 1969; MBA, Columbia U., 1975. Process engr. Gulg Oil, L and Montreal, Can., 1970-73; officer Morgan Guaranty Trust, N.Y.C. and Milan, Italy, 1975-77; v.p. Sige Merchant Bank Milan, 1977-79; mng. dir. Barclays Internat. Fin., Milan, 1979-82; chief fin. officer Enoxy Inc., Zurich, Switzerland, 1982-83; mng. dir. A. Lazender, Milan, 1983—. Gen. Electric scholar, N.Y.C., 1974, Fullbright scholar, 1974. Roman Catholic. Office: A Lazender SPA, Via Giuditta Sidoli, 11, 20129 Milan Italy

TITTENSOR, RUTH MARGARET, ecological, environmental consultant; b. Warley, Essex, Eng., July 16, 1945. MA in Natural Scis., Oxford U., Eng., 1966; MS in Ecology, Edinburgh U., Scotland, 1969. Dir. Countryside Mgmt. Consultancy, West Sussex, Eng., 1971—; council mem. Sussex Trust Nature Conservation, 1971-74, specialist British Ecol. Soc., 1980—; examiner Cambridge Univ. Exams. Syndicate, 1985—; rep. Chichester (Sussex) Harbour Conservancy, 1986—. Author: A Sideways Look at Nature Conservation in Britain, 1981, Nature Conservation for Busy Farmers, 1986; contbr. articles to profl. jours. Grantee Royal Soc., 1971-75, British Ecol. Soc., 1985; fellow Oxford Univ., 1965, 79; Nat. Farmers' Union scholarship, 1979. Fellow British Inst. Agrl. Cons. (council mem. 1982—), mem. Inst. Biology, Inst. Chartered Foresters. Home and Office: Countryside Mgmt Consultancy, Walberton Green House, The St, Walberton, West Sussex BN18 0QB, England

TITUS, LARRY REED, electronics manufacturing company executive; b. Warren, Ohio, May 15, 1943; s. Leland R. and Elma A. (Gotthardt) T.; m. Barbara J. Kinnison, Sept. 8, 1962; children—Mary Jane, Rebecca Lynn, Debra Sue. B.B.A., Loyola U., Chgo., 1980; M.B.A., U. Chgo., 1984. Mgr. mgmt. info. systems ITT-Grinnell, 1974-78, ITT, 1978-81; mgr. mgmt. info. systems fixed div. Motorola Inc., Schaumburg, Ill., 1981-84, dir. internat. mgmt. info. systems, 1984-87, dir. European Info. Systems, 1987—. Vice pres. Joint Vocat. Edn., Warren, 1974; pres. Warren Sch. System, 1976; bd. dirs. Homeowners Assn., Palatine, Ill., 1984. Mem. Assn. System Mgmt. (bd. dirs. 1972-76), Data Processing Mgmt. Assn. (v.p. 1968-74), Nat. Assn. Accts. Republican. Club: Loyola U. Alumni. Lodge: Moose. Avocations: sports; reading. Office: Motorola Inc, Hagenauer Str 42, D-6200 Wiesbaden Federal Republic of Germany

TITUS, PAMELA LOUISE, real estate broker; b. Ft. Wayne, Ind., Aug. 15, 1953; d. Gene W. Eby and Louise Miller. B.S. in Speech and Hearing, Purdue U., 1975, M.S. in Speech Pathology with highest distinction, 1976. Speech pathologist Speech Pathology Assocs., Houston, 1977-80; profl. recruiter Diversified Human Resources Group, Houston, 1980-81, Key Personnel Pty., Ltd., Sydney, Australia, 1981-82; computer sales rep. ComputerLand, Houston, 1982-84; broker Coldwell Banker Comml. Real Estate Services, 1985—. Mem. Tex. Assn. Realtors, Houston Bd. Realtors, Internat. Council Shopping Ctrs.; Club: Houston Realty Breakfast. Presbyterian. Home: 11711 Memorial Houston TX 77024 Office: Coldwell Bankers 2500 West Loop S Houston TX 77027

TIWANA, NAZAR HAYAT, librarian; b. Kalra, India, Nov. 27, 1927; came to U.S., 1965; s. Khizar Hayat and Sultan (Bibi) T.; m. Sita Sarware Sahgal, Jan. 24, 1951; children—Yasmine, Omar. B.A. in Econs., Pembroke Coll., Cambridge, Eng., 1947; M.A. in L.S., U. Chgo., 1971. Reference librarian Chgo. Pub. Library, 1973-75, adminstrv. asst., 1975-76; adult services librarian Rogers Park Library, Chgo., 1976-79; dir. America's Ethnic Heritage Program, Chgo., 1979-81; head dept. Hild Regional Library, Chgo., 1981-83; reference librarian Mt. Prospect (Ill.) Library, 1985—; spl. staff asst. White House Conf. on Libraries and Info. Services, Washington, 1979; del. Ill. White House Conf. Librarian and Info. Services, 1978; del. State Dept. Adv. Conf. on Exchange of Internat. Info., Washington, 1979. Author: (with Don Schabel) Integrated Rural Information Systems, 1976. Assoc. Newberry Library, Chgo., 1981—. Recipient Spl. Service award Friends of Chgo. Pub. Library, 1979. Mem. ALA, Internat. Fedn. Library Assns., Ill. Libraries Assn., Art Inst. Chgo., Field Mus., Beta Phi Mu. Club: Chgo. Library. Home: 2620 W Pratt Blvd Chicago IL 60645

TIWARI, NARAYAN DUTT, minister of commerce; b. Balyuti, Uttar Pradesh, India, Oct. 18, 1925; s. Poornanand Tiwari; m. Sushila Tiwari, 1954. MA, LLB, Allahabad U., India. Freedom fighter India, 1942-47; mem. state assembly Govt. of Uttar Pradesh, India, 1952-62, 69-74; minister planning, labor and panchayats Govt. of Uttar Pradesh, 1969, minister fin. and parliamentary affairs, 1970-76, minister heavy industries and cane devel., 1973-76, chief minister, 1976-77, 84-85; leader of opposition Uttar Pradesh Congress (I) Legis. Party, 1977-80; mem. Lok Sabha, 1980—; minister planning Govt. of India, 1980-82, ministry of industry, 1981-83, 85-86, minister steel and mines, 1982-83, minister external affairs, 1986-87, minister commerce and minister finance, 1987-88; opposition leader, chmn. pub. accounts com., 1957; mem. Uttar Pradesh Vidhan Sabha, 1969; dep. chmn. State Planning Commn. Govt. of Uttar Pradesh, 1969, 80-81; sec. Polit. Sufferers' Distress Relief Soc. Office: Ministry of Commerce, North Block, New Delhi 110001, India *

TIZARD, BARBARA, education and child development researcher; b. London, Apr. 16, 1926; d. Herbert and Elsie (Kirk) Parker; m. Jack Tizard, Dec. 20, 1947 (dec. Aug. 1979); children: Bill, John (dec.), Jenny, Martin (dec.), Lucy. BA with honors, Oxford (Eng.) U., 1948; PhD in Psychology, U. London, 1957. Ednl. psychologist Child Guidance Clinic, London Hosp., 1957-60; lectr. dept. exptl. neurology Inst. Psychiatry U. London, 1963-67, research officer dept. child devel. Inst. Edn., 1967-71, sr. research fellow, 1971-77, tchr. reading, 1978-80, prof. edn., 1980—; dir. Thomas Coram Research Unit Inst. Edn., 1984—; cons. WHO, 1984—. Author: Early Childhood Education, 1975, Adoption: A Second Chance, 1977, (with others) Involving Parents in Nursery and Infant Schools, 1981, Young Children Learning, 1984, Young Children at School in the Inner City, 1988; coeditor: The Biology of Play, 1977; mem. editorial bd.: Jour. Child Psychology and Psychiatry, 1979—; contbr. numerous articles to profl. jours. Fellow Brit. Psychol. Soc. Office: U London Thomas Coram Research, Unit 41 Brunswick Sq, London WC1N 1AZ, England

TIZARD, ROBERT JAMES, government cabinet minister; b. Auckland, N.Z., June 7, 1924; s. Henry James and Jessie May (Phillips) T; m. Catherine Anne McLean, May, 1951 (div. 1983); children: Anne, Linda, Judith, Nigel; m. Mary Christina Macey, Dec. 1983; 1 child, Joseph Henry. MA in History with honors, Auckland U., 1952. Lectr. Auckland U., 1947-53; tchr. Mt. Albert Grammar Sch., Auckland, 1954-57, Tamaki Coll., 1960-63; M.P. Tamaki, Auckland, 1957-60, various dists., Auckland, 1963—; minister health, state services N.Z., 1972-74, minister fin., dep. prime minister, 1974-75, minister energy, sci. and tech., 1984-87, minister def., sci. and tech., 1987—. Served as flying officer Royal N.Z. Air Force, 1943-47. Mem. Labour Party. Club: Remuela Golf. Office: Minister Defense, Wellington New Zealand

TJAKRASUDJATMA, SUGANA, ophthalmologist; b. Cirebon, West Java, Indonesia, July 14, 1926; s. Gemo Tjakrasudjatma and Siti Kata; m. Sri Mulyaningsih; children: Henky Hanggana, Yanti Sri Hanggarianti, Ruby Harmawan Rubino. Student, St. Louis U., 1964-65; MD, U. Indonesia, 1959; Eye Specialist, 1962. Resident Med. Faculty U. Indonesia, Jakarta, 1959-64; med. staff Eye Hosp., Cicendo, Bandung, Indonesia, 1963-73; dir. Eye Hosp., Cicendo, 1973-79; head ophthalmology dept. U. Pajajaran, Bandung, 1973-85; dir. Hasan Sadikin Gen. Hosp., Bandung, 1979-84, Directorate Pub. Teaching Hosp. Ministry Health, Jakarta, 1983—; prin. investigator Helen Keller Inst., Bandung, 1976-78; head Eye Care Services West Java, Bandung, 1973-80; chmn. Eye Bank West Java, 19806; advisor WHO, New Delhi, 1976, 85, Bali, 1987; mem. Nat. Bd. Examiners Ophthalmology, Jakarta, 1979—. Contbr. to Cararacta Lentis, 1980;, Extraocular Infection, 1982; mem. bd. editors Ophthalmology Indonesiana, 1978—. Mem. functional group Golongan Karya, 1982. Mem. Indonesian Med. Assn. West Java (charter), Indonesian Ophthal. Assn. (chmn. West Java br. 1979—). Lodge: Lions (Bandung). Home: Jalan Tampomas 1, Bandung, West Java 40262, Indonesia Office: U Padjadjaran Med Faculty, Jalan Pasirkaliki 190, Bandung, West Java Indonesia

TJEKNAVORIAN, LORIS-ZARE, composer and conductor; b. Oct. 13, 1937; s. Haikaz and Adrine T.; m. Linda Pierce, 1964 (div. 1979); 1 child. Vienna Acad. Music, Salzburg Mozarteum; studied with Carl Orff. Teaching fellow U. Mich.; composer-in-residence Concordia Coll., also Ministry of Culture and Fine Arts; prin. condr. Teheran Opera, 1972-79; artist with RCA, 1976—; composer-in-residence Am.-Armenian Internat. Coll., La Verne U. (Calif.), 1979—; prin. assoc. London Symphony Orch.; chair bd. trustees Inst. Armenian Music, London, 1976-80; trustee Shahbanou Farah Found., Teheran; numerous internat. tours as condr. works include: Requiem for the Massacred, 1975; Simorgh (ballet), 1978; Lake Van Suite, Erebouni for 12 strings, 1978; Credo Symphony Life of Christ (opera), 1976; Liturgical Mass Violin Concerto; ballet suites for orchestra and documentary film scores. Decorated Order of Homayoun. Address: care Thea Dispeker 59 E 54th St New York NY 10022 also: care Basil Douglas Ltd, 8 St George's Terrace, London NW1 8XJ, England *

TJOKRODIPOERO, SOEWARDO, ophthalmalogist; b. Surabaya, East Java, Indonesia, June 8, 1931; s. Tjokrodipoero and Soelastri R.A.; m. Koeraisin Dewi, Apr. 15, 1960; children: Novie, Linda Dewi, Agustantie, Juni Astuti. MD, Surabaya, 1961. Cert. Ophthamalogist, Indonesia. Resident Gen. Hosp., Jember, Indonesia, 1964, head ophthamology dept., 1964—, vice dir., 1971—. Mem. Indonesian Ophthamol. Assn. Home: jl PB Sudirman 70, Jember, 68118 East Java Indonesia Office: RSU Jember Gen Hosp, jl Supriyadi 9, 68118 Jember Indonesia

TLASS, MUSTAFA ABDUL-KADER, government official, military officer; b. Arrastan, Syrian Arab Republic, May 11, 1932; s. Abdulkader Muhammad and Fatma Ahmad (Bakeer) T.; m. Lamiaa Hasan Al-Jabiry, 1958; children: Nahed, Firas, Manaf, Saria. Student, Mil Coll., Homs, Syrian Arab Republic, 1954; PhD in Mil. Sci. (hon.), Acad. Voroshelov, Moscow, 1980. Tchr. Al-Qraiya Sch., Al-Swaida, Syrian Arab Republic, 1950-52; 2d lt. armour weaponry Mil. Acad., Homs and elsewhere, Syrian Arab Republic, 1954; advanced through grades to maj. gen. Gen. Staff, Damascus, 1968; chief Nat. Security Ct., Homs, Syrian Arab Republic, 1965; pres. emergency mil. ct. Ministry of Def., Damascus, Syrian Arab Republic, 1966; dep. comdr.-in-chief Ministry of Def., Damascus, 1970, head, 1972; head mil. party com., gen. staff Ministry Def., Damascus, 1977—, dep. minister, chief gen. staff, 1968; mem. polit. bur. Al-Baa'th Arab Socialist Party, Damascus, 1969; appointed dep. chief supreme council Syrian and Egyptian forces 1973 war, Cairo and Damascus, 1973; mem. People's Assembly Syrian Parliamant, 1971—; dep. prime minister defence affairs Syrian Cabinet, 1972—. Author of mil. and hist. writings and poetry. Pres. Com. Geographic Encyclopedia; mem. regional command Al-Baa'th Arab Socialist Party, Damascus, 1965. Recipient Solenzara Inst. prize, 1986, The Syrian, Moroccan and Palestinian Liberation Orgn. Orders of Merit, Badge Mil. Honour Class of Knight, Senegalese Order and Lebanese Cedar Order of Ranking Officer, Meml. medal of 20th Anniversary of Soviet Victory in World War II. Mem. United Syrian-Egyptian Polit. Leadership. Muslim. Club: Photography Damacus. Home: Al-Rawda 58, Damascus Syria Office: Ministry of Defence, Omayad Square, Damascus Syria

TO, SIMON CHI KEUNG, trading company executive; b. Hong Kong, Nov. 2, 1951; s. Kau and Yin Ching (Ng) T.; m. Susana O.P. Sheung, Aug. 19, 1971; children: Evelyn Y.M., Benjamin N.M. BS in Mech. Engring., Imperial Coll. Sci. and Tech., London, 1973; MBA, Stanford U., 1975. Specialist internat. mktg. Cummins Engine Co. Inc., U.S.A., 1975-76; spl. asst. to chmn. and chief exec. officer Cummins Engine Co. Inc., Hong Kong, 1976-77, mgr. East Asia region, 1978-80; mgr. bus. planning and devel. Asia/Pacific region Manila, 1977-78; div. mgr. capital projects Hutchison China Trade Holdings Ltd., Hong Kong, 1980-81, gen. mgr., dir., 1981-82, mng. dir., 1982—; bd. dirs. Davenham Investments Ltd., Hong Kong Explosives Co. Ltd., Hunan HK Investment Co. Ltd., H-V Investment and Devel. Co. Ltd., Offshore Devel. Co. Ltd., Tovex Far East Ltd. Author computer-aided design used in archtl. application, 1973 (Outstanding Project Work award 1973).

TOBAR-ZALDUMBIDE, CARLOS, diplomat; b. Quito, Pichincha, Ecuador, Dec. 29, 1912; s. Carlos Manuel Tobar-Borgoño and Rosarion Zaldumbide; m. Adela Eastman, July 1, 1939; children: Mireya Tobar Eastman, Santiago Tobar Eastman, Aela Tobar Eastman. BSc, Villa St. Jean, Fribourg, Switzerland, 1931; Diploma in Law, Sorbonne U., 1937. 1st sec. Embassy of Ecuador, Lima, Peru, 1943-44; del. U.N. Conf., San Francisco, 1945; undersec. Ministry for Fgn. Affairs, Quito, Ecuador, 1945-52; minister Ministry for Fgn. Affairs, Quito, 1956-60; ambassador to France Paris, 1963-65, UN, N.Y.C., 1986—; prof. Universidad Central, Quito-Ecuador, 1954. Contbr. articles to profl. jours. Decorated Gt. Cross Isabel la Catolica, Govt. of Spain, Gt. Cross of Merit, Fed. Republic of Germany, Gt. Cross San Lorenzo,Govt. of Ecuador; named Grand Official Legion D'Honneur, Govt. of France. Roman Catholic. Club: Quito Tennis Golf (Ecuador). Office: Permanent Mission of Ecuador to the UN 820 2nd Ave New York NY 10017

TOBER, LESTER VICTOR, shoe company executive; b. St. Louis, Dec. 29, 1916; s. Abraham E.M. and Anna (Saifer) T.; m. Sylvia Isenburg, Aug. 4, 1940; children—Neil Steven, Robert Boyd, Cristie Elizabeth. B.S., U. Wis., 1935; postgrad., Washington U., 1936, U. Mo., 1936-39. Sec. Tober-Saifer Shoe Mfg. Co., St. Louis, 1955-65; v.p. Tober-Saifer Shoe Mfg. Co., 1966-68, exec. v.p., 1969-71, pres., 1974—; pres., chief exec. officer Tober Industries, Inc., 1977—. Active St. Louis Ambassadors, United Fund.; Trustee A.E. Tober Charitable Trust. Served to lt. (j.g.) USNR, 1944-46. Mem. Washington U. Eliot Soc., Zeta Beta Tau. Republican. Jewish (pres. temple brotherhood 1957). Clubs: St. Louis, Mo. Athletic; Naples (Fla.) Bath and Tennis. Lodge: Elk. Home: 19 Maryhill Saint Louis MO 63124 Office: Tober Industries Inc 1520 Washington Ave Saint Louis MO 63103

TOBIAS, LESTER LEE, psychological consultant; b. Bklyn., Oct. 11, 1946; s. Nathan and Charlotte T.; AB, Grinnell Coll., 1967; AM, U. Ill., 1971, PhD, 1972; m. Andrea Furmanek, July 10, 1977; children: Lauren, Julia. Instr. dept. univ. extension U. Ill., Urbana, 1970-72, intern U. Ill. Psychol. and Counseling Center, 1970-71, clin. counselor, 1971-72; psychologist Jefferson County (Colo.) Mental Health Center, Denver, 1972-73, team leader, psychologist, 1973-74; cons. to Denver OEO, Colo. Dept. Social Services, 1973-74; instr. Denver Community Coll., 1973-74; cons. psychologist Nordli, Wilson Assocs., Westborough, Mass., 1974-81, ptnr., cons. psychologist, 1981—; pres. Psychol. Services Internat., Inc., Westborough, 1983—. Contbr. articles to profl. and bus. publs. Bd. dirs. Worcester Big Bros., 1976. Meuhlstein Found. scholar, 1964-67; USPHS trainee, 1967-68. Mem. Nat. Psychol. Cons. to Mgmt., Am. Psychol. Assn. Home: 6 John St Westborough MA 01581-2511 Office: 2000 W Park Dr PO Box 5000 Westborough MA 01581-5000

TOBIAS, PHILLIP VALLENTINE, anthropologist, anatomist, educator; b. Durban, Republic South Africa, Oct. 14, 1925; s. Joseph Tobias and Fanny (Rosendorff) Norden. B.Sc., U. Witwatersrand, Johannesburg, South Africa, 1946, B.Sc.Honors, 1947, M.B.B.Ch., 1950, Ph.D., 1953, D.Sc., 1967; D.Sc. (hon.), U. Natal, 1980, U. Western Ont., 1986, U. Alta., 1987, U. Cape Town, 1988, Cambridge U., 1988. Lectr. in anatomy U. Witwatersrand, Johannesburg, 1951-52, sr. lectr., 1953-58, prof., head dept., 1959—, hon. prof. palaeoanthropology Bernard Price Inst. Palaeontol. Research, 1977—, hon. prof. zoology, 1981—, dir. Paleoanthropology Research Unit, 1979—; dean Sch. Medicine, 1980-82. Author: The African in the Universities, 1951, Chromosomes, Sex-Cells and Evolution, 1956, The Meaning of Race, 1961, Man's Anatomy, 1963, 4th edit., 1988, Olduvai Gorge, Vol. 2, 1967, vols. 4A and 4B, 1988, The Brain in Hominid Evolution, 1971, The Bushmen, 1978 (Anisfield-Wolf award Cleveland Found.), Man the Tottering Biped, 1982, Evolution of Human Brain, Intellect and Spirit, 1981, Dart, Taung and the "Missing Link", 1984, Hominid Evolution: Past, Present and Future, 1985; contbr. over 700 articles to profl. jours. Pres. non-racial Nat. Union South African Students, 1948-51, Edn. League of South Africa, 1952-57; founding mem. Nat. Edn. Union of South Africa, 1980—; mem. council South African Inst. Race Relations, 1974-75. Recipient Internat. Balzan Found. Prize, Milan, 1987. Fellow AAAS (hon.), Royal Soc. South Africa (hon.); mem. Inst. for Study of Man in Africa (founding pres. 1961-68, 1984-85), Anatomy Soc. of South Africa(founding pres.), South African Anthropol. Soc. (pres.), Assn. Sci. Writers South Africa (pres.), U.S. Nat. Acad. Scis., Internat. U. Anthropol. and Ethnol. Scis. (hon. life), Am. Acad. Arts and Scis. (hon.), Am. Assn. Anatomists (hon.). Lodge: Rotary (Paul Harris fellow). Office: U Witwatersrand Med Sch, Dept Anatomy, 7 York Rd Parktown, Johannesburg 2193, Republic of South Africa

TOBIASCH, VIKTOR KARL FRANZ, physician, educator; b. Prague, Austria (now Czechoslovakia), Aug. 1, 1912; s. Viktor and Anna (Dallendorfer) T.; M.D., U. Prague, 1937; m. Anneliese Maas, Aug. 18, 1959; children: Edda, Christina. Intern, Univ. Clinic, Prague, 1937-38; practice medicine specializing in internal medicine, Prague, 1938-42, Frankfurt, 1950-55, Munster (Germany), 1955-64; lectr. dept. internal medicine U. Munster, 1957-64, prof., 1963-73; prof. U. Ulm (Germany), 1973—; med. dir. Krankenanstalten, Isny, Germany, 1963-78; head Forschungsinstitut für Präeventivmedizin, Isny, 1973—. mem. sci. bd. Social-und Arbeits-medizin, Ulm Acad., 1978—; lectr. Naturwiss.-Techn. Akademie, Isny, 1980—. Roman Catholic. Club: Rotary (pres. 1974-75). Author: Ubergewicht-was tun?, 1974; Die Vermeidung der Risikofaktoren, 1977; Die psycho-physische Erschöpfung, 1977; Stress, biologisches Erbe, Segen oder Fluch?, 1979; Rheuma, ein Lehrbuch, 1981; Die beginnende zerebrale Insuffizienz, 1981; Mediz. Monatsschrift, 1955—. Hippokrates, 1964—; co-author: Lehrbuch d. inneren Medizin, 2d edit., 1978; Medica-Buch der gesamten Medizin, 9th edit., 1983. Home: Panoramastrasse 7972, Isny-Neutrauchburg Federal Republic of Germany

TOBIAS-JONES, BRIAN, oil field technology company executive; b. Newport, South Wales, Mar. 12, 1938; s. Arthur Rowland and Elizabeth

May (Hayes) Tobias-J.; grad. Newport Tech. Coll.; B.B.A., Pacific Western U., 1983; m. Shirley Yvonne Swenson, Sept. 1963; 1 son, Heath Meirion. Field engring. mgr. AMF Overseas Corp., Kuwait, 1973-75, mgr. Mid East, 1975-76, mgr. Africa and Mid East, 1976-77, mgr. Europe, Africa and Mid East, 1977-79, mgr. Eastern Hemisphere, London, 1980-82; pres. Petro Industries, Inc., Dallas, 1983—, Tobias-Potter Investments Inc., London, Paris, Dallas, 1987—; ptnr., pres. Tex. Costal Petroleum Inc., Tex. Coastal Securities Inc. Bd. dirs. internat. affairs Olympian Investment Co., Inc.; tchr. Bd. dirs. Greenhills Found., Dallas. Served with Brit. Army, 1956-58. Fellow Inst. Sales Mgmt. Mem. Christian Ch. Home: 6611 Missy Dr Dallas TX 75252 Office: Tex Coastal Petroleum 4965 Preston Park Blvd #1 Plano TX 75075

TOBIN, CALVIN JAY, architect; b. Boston, Feb. 15, 1927; s. David and Bertha (Tanfield) T.; m. Joan Hope Fink, July 15, 1951; children—Michael Alan, Nancy Ann. B.Arch., U. Mich., 1949. Designer, draftsman Arlen & Lowenfish (architects), N.Y.C., 1949-51; with Samuel Arlen, N.Y.C., 1951-53, Skidmore, Owings & Merrill, N.Y.C., 1953; architect Loebl, Schlossman & Bennett (architects), Chgo., 1953-57, v.p., 1953-57; v.p. Loebl Schlossman & Hackl, 1957—; Chmn. Jewish United Fund Bldg. Trades Div., 1969; chmn. AIA and Chgo. Hosp. Council Com. of Hosp. Architecture, 1968-76. Archtl. works include Michael Reese Hosp. and Med. Center, 1954—, Prairie Shores Apt. Urban Redevel, 1957-62, Louis A. Weiss Meml. Hosp, Chgo., Chgo. State Hosp, Central Community Hosp, Chgo., Gottlieb Meml. Hosp, Melrose Park, Ill., West Suburban Hosp, Oak Park, Ill., Thorek Hosp and Med. Center, Chgo., Water Tower Pl., Chgo., Christ Hosp., Oak Lawn, Greater Balt. Med. Ctr., Shriners Hosp. for Crippled Children Chgo., also numerous apt., comml. and community bldgs. Chmn. Highland Park (Ill.) Appearance Rev. Commn., 1972-73; mem. Highland Park Plan Commn., 1973-79; mem. Highland Park City Council, 1974—, mayor pro-tem, 1979—; mem. Highland Park Environ. Control Commn., 1979-84, Highland Park Hist. Preservation Commn., 1982—; bd. dirs. Young Men's Jewish Council, 1953-67, pres., 1967; bd. dirs. Jewish Community Centers Chgo., 1973-78. Served with USNR, 1945-46. Fellow AIA (2d v.p. Chgo. chpt.), Pi Lambda Phi. Jewish. Clubs: Standard, Highland Park Country. Home: 814 Dean Ave Highland Park IL 60035 Office: Loebl Schlossman & Hackl 845 N Michigan Ave Chicago IL 60611

TOBIN, GERALD J., lawyer; b. Bklyn., Sept. 11, 1935; s. David and Dorothy (Gnatowsky) T.; m. Helene Pomerantz, June 24, 1956; children—Alyson Beth, Stacey Lynn, Adam Scott. B.A., U. Miami, 1959, J.D., 1962. Bar: Fla. 1962, N.Y. 1980, U.S. Supreme Ct. 1965, U.S. Ct. Appeals (5th cir.) 1964, U.S. Ct. Appeals (11th cir.) 1981. Sole practice, Miami, Fla., 1962—; Judge Mcpl. Ct., City of Miami, 1965-72; chief judge, 1970-72; chmn. bd. Nat. Corrections Constrn. Inc., Nat. Corrections Mgmt. Inc. Bd. dirs. P.R.I.D.E.-Fla Prison Industries, 1982—, Big Bros., Miami, Congregation Bet Breira. Home: 12005 SW 64th St Miami FL 33183

TOBIN, HAROLD WILLIAM, lawyer; b. San Francisco, Apr. 7, 1922; s. Robert Douglass and Rita Mary (Lannon) T.; m. Julie DeLaveaga, Aug. 3, 1946; m. Shirley Ellen Traynor, Jan. 5, 1965; children: Douglass Michael, Kathleen, Harold William, Jr., Suzanne, Neil McKinley. Student U. San Francisco, 1940-42, U.S. Air Corp Aviation Cadet Sch., 1942-43; JD, U. San Francisco, 1946. Bar: Calif. 1949, U.S. Dist. Ct. (no. dist.) Calif. 1949, U.S. Ct. Apls. 1949. U.S. atty. War Crimes Trials, Manila, Phillipines, 1946-48; assoc. Hone & Lobree; assoc. Benjamin L. McKinely, 1951-53; ptnr. Jacobsen & Tobin, 1953-57, Tobin and Ransom, 1957-67; sole practice San Francisco, 1970-71, Antioch, Calif., 1971—. Mem. San Francisco Rep. County Central Com., 1949-51, 70-71; pres., VIP San Francisco Archdiocesan Council Cath. Men, 1958-59. chmn. Antioch Police Commn., 1977-81; sec. Bay Area Rapid Transit Citizens. Served with USAAF, 1942-43. Mem. ABA, Contra Costa County Bar Assn., State Bar Calif. (pres. conf. barristers 1957-58), Bar Assn. San Francisco (past dir.), Assn. Trial Lawyers Am. Club: Barristers of San Francisco (past pres.). Catholic. Home: 2100 Reseda Way Antioch CA 94509 Office: 2830 Lone Tree Way Antioch CA 94509

TOBIN, JAMES, economics educator; b. Champaign, Ill., Mar. 5, 1918; s. Louis Michael and Margaret (Edgerton) T.; m. Elizabeth Fay Ringo, Sept. 14, 1946; children: Margaret Ringo, Louis Michael, Hugh Ringo, Roger Gill. AB summa cum laude, Harvard U., 1939, MA, 1940, PhD, 1947; LLD (hon.), Syracuse U., 1967, U. Ill., 1969, Dartmouth Coll., 1970, Swarthmore Coll., 1980, New Sch. Social Research, 1982, NYU, 1982, Bates Coll., 1982; LHD (hon.), Hofstra U., 1983; LLD (hon.), U. Hartford, 1984, Colgate U., 1984; D in Econs. (hon.), New U. Lisbon, 1980; LLD (hon.), U. New Haven, 1986; LHD (hon.), Hofstra U., 1983, Gustavus Adolphus Coll., 1986; D in Social Scis. honoris causa, U. Helsinki, 1986. Assoc. economist OPA, WPB, Washington, 1941-42; teaching fellow econs. Harvard U., Cambridge, Mass., 1946-47, with Soc. Fellows, 1947-50; assoc. prof. econs. Yale U., New Haven, 1950-55, prof. emeritus, 1955—, Sterling prof. econs., 1957—, prof. emeritus, 1988—; mem. Council Econ. Advisers, 1961-62, Nat. Acad. Scis. Author: National Economic Policy, 1966, Essays in Economics-Macroeconomics, vol. 1, 1972, The New Economics One Decade Older, 1974, Consumption and Econometrics, vol. 2, 1975, Asset Accumulation and Economic Activity, 1980, Theory and Policy, Vol. 3, 1982, Policies for Prosperity, 1987. Served to lt. USNR, 1942-46. Recipient Nobel prize in econs., 1981; Social Sci. Research Council faculty fellow, 1951-54. Fellow Am. Acad. Arts and Scis., Econometric Soc. (pres. 1958), Am. Statis. Assn., Brit. Acad. (corr.); mem. Am. Philos. Soc., Am. Econ. Assn. (John Bates Clark medal 1955, v.p. 1964, pres. 1971), Acad. Scis. Portugal (fgn. assoc.), Phi Beta Kappa. Home: 117 Alden Ave New Haven CT 06515 Office: Yale Univ Dept Economics PO Box 2125 New Haven CT 06520

TOBITA, SHIGEO, English educator; b. Tokyo, Dec. 22, 1927; s. Tokiwa and Tsurue (Yamada) T.; B.A., Aoyama Gakuin U., 1952; M.A., Waseda U., 1954, postgrad., 1957; m. Tomoko Mori, Sept. 30, 1957; children—Hiroko, Kyoko, Miyuki. Lectr., Aoyama Gakuin U., 1957-60, asst. prof., 1960; asst. prof. Otaru Coll. Commerce, 1963-69; prof. English, Chuo U., Tokyo, 1969—; research scholar Carleton Coll., 1976, U. N.C., Chapel Hill, 1978-79; lectr. Keio U., 1980—. Mem. MLA, Japan English Lit. Soc., Japan Am. Lit. Soc., Japanese Assn. Am. Studies, Japan Ukiyo-e Soc. Translator: Catch-22 (Joseph Heller), 1969; Travesty (John Hawkes), 1979; Good as Gold (Joseph Heller), 1981; Neighbors (Thomas Berger), 1982, An Artist of the Floating World (Kazuo Ishiguro), 1988, Tempory Shelter (Mary Gordon), 1988, (with Kazuo Ishiguro) An Artist of the Floating World, 1988; Co-editor: Shogakukan-Random House English-Japanese Dictionary, 1973-74; Spirit English-Japanese Dictionary, 1987. Home: 6-6 3-chome Kinuta, Setagaya-ku 157 Tokyo Japan Office: Chuo U, 742-1 Higashi-nkano, Hachiojishi Tokyo 192-03, Japan

TOCKMAN, GERALD, lawyer; b. St. Louis, Sept. 29, 1937. B.A., Washington U., St. Louis, 1958, J.D., 1960. Bar: Mo., Ill. 1960, D.C. 1971, Calif. 1984, U.S. Supreme Ct. 1976. Sole practice, St. Louis, 1960—. Mem. ABA, Mo. Bar Assn., Ill. Bar Assn., St. Louis Bar Assn., Assn. Trial Lawyers Am. Contbr. articles to profl. jours. Office: 319 N 4th St Suite 1001 Saint Louis MO 63102

TODARO, MICHAEL PAUL, economics educator, consultant; b. N.Y.C., May 14, 1942; s. George Joseph and Annette (Piccini) T.; m. Donna Renee Crickenberger, June 17, 1974; 1 dau., Lenora Jean. B.A., Haverford Coll., 1964; M.Phil., Yale U., 1966, Ph.D., 1967. Vis. lectr. Makerere U. Uganda, 1964-65; vis. sr. lectr. U. Nairobi, Kenya, 1968-70, 74-76; assoc. dir. Rockefeller Found., N.Y.C., 1968-76; vis. prof. U. Calif.-Santa Barbara, 1976-77; dpe. dir. Population Council, N.Y.C., 1977; prof. econs. NYU, 1977—; sr. assoc., cons. Population Council, 1978—; cons. Fund for Peace (Inst. for Study of World Politics), N.Y.C., 1979—. Author: Internal Migration in Developing Countries, 1976; Economics for a Developing World, 1982; Economic Development in the Third World, 1985; co-author: Economic Theory, 1969; mem. editorial bd. Population and Devel. Rev., 1976—. Fellow: Woodrow Wilson Found., 1966, NDEA, 1966; Compton Found. grantee, 1981-84. Mem. Council on Fgn. Relations, Am. Econs. Assn., Internat. Union for Sci. Study of Population, Population Assn. Am., Phi Beta Kappa. Roman Catholic. Home: 150 E 61st St New York NY 10021 Office: NYU Dept Econs 269 Mercer St New York NY 10003

TODD, ALEXANDER ROBERTUS (BARON TODD OF TRUMPINGTON), educator; b. Glasgow, Scotland, Oct. 2, 1907; s. Alexander and Jane (Lowrie) T.; m. Alison Sarah Dale, Jan. 30, 1937 (dec. 1987); children—Alexander Henry, Helen Todd Brown, Hilary Alison. B.Sc. (Carnegie Research scholar 1928-29), U. Glasgow, 1928; D.Sc., 1938; Dr.phil.nat., U. Frankfurt am Main, 1931; D.Phil., Oxford U.-Eng., 1933; M.A., U. Cambridge-Eng., 1944; LL.D. (hon.)., univs. Glasgow, Melbourne, Edinburg, Cal., Manchester, Hokkaido; Dr.rer.nat. (hon.), U. Kiel; D.Litt. (hon.), U. Sydney; D.Sc. (hon.), univs. London, Exeter, Warwick, Sheffield, Liverpool, Oxford, Leicester, Durham (Eng.), Wales, Madrid (Spain), Aligarh (India), Strasbourg (France), Harvard, Yale, Mich. (U.S.), Paris (France), Adelaide (Australia), Strathclyde (Scotland), Australian Nat. U., U. Cambridge, U. Philippines, Tufts U., Chinese U. Hong Kong, Hong Kong U. Mem. staff Lister Inst. Preventive Medicine, London, 1936-38; reader biochemistry U. London, 1937-38; prof., dir. chem. labs. U. Manchester-Eng., 1938-44; prof. organic chemistry U. Cambridge-Eng., 1944-71, also fellow Christ's Coll., 1944—, master, 1963-78, chancellor U. Strathclyde, 1963—; dir. Fisons Ltd., London, 1963-78. Nat. Research Devel. Corp., London, 1968-76; vis. prof. Calif. Inst. Tech., 1938, U. Chgo., 1948, U. Sydney, 1950, MIT, Cambridge, 1954, U. Calif., 1970, Tex. Christian U., 1980; chmn. adv. Council Sci. Policy, 1952-64, Royal Commn. Med. Edn., 1965-68. Chmn. Nuffield Found., London, 1936-80; chmn. govs. United Cambridge Hosps., 1969-74; chmn. trustees Croucher Found., Hong Kong, 1980-87, 88—. Created knight, 1954, baron (life peer), 1962; Order of Merit (U.K.); Order Rising Sun (Japan); recipient Nobel prize for chemistry, 1957; Pour le Merite (W. Germany), 1966; Lomonosov medal U.S.S.R. Acad. Sci., 1978; medals various chem. socs., sci. orgns., including Royal Copley medals Royal Soc., 1949; named master Salter's Co., 1961. Fellow Royal Soc. (pres. 1975-80), Australian Chem. Inst. (hon.), Manchester Coll. Tech. (hon.), Royal Soc. Edinburgh (hon.), Royal Coll. Physicians London (hon.), Royal Coll. Physicians, Sure, Glasgow; mem. French, German, Spanish, Belgian, Swiss, Japanese chem. socs. (all hon.), Australian, Austrian, Ghana, Polish acads. sci., Acad. Natural Philosophy Halle (Germany), Am. Philos. Soc., N.Y. Acad. Sci., Nat. Acad. Scis. (U.S.A.), AAAS (all fgn. mem.), Chem. Soc. (pres. 1960-62), Internat. Union Pure and Applied Chemistry (pres. 1963-65), Soc. Chem. Industry. Contbr. articles to profl. jours. Office: Christ's Coll, Cambridge CB2 3BU, England

TODD, JOHN ODELL, insurance company sales professional; b. Mpls., Nov. 12, 1902; s. Frank Chisholm and Mary Mable (Odell) T.; AB, Cornell U., 1924; CLU, Am. Coll., 1933; m. Katherine Sarah Cone, Feb. 21, 1925; children: John Odell, George Bennett. Spl. agt. Equitable Life Assurance Soc., Mpls., 1926-28; ins. broker, Mpls., 1928-31; spl. agt. Northwestern Mut. Life Ins. Co., Mpls., 1931-38, Evanston, Ill., 1938—; ptnr. H.S. Vail & Sons, Chgo., 1938-43, Vail and Todd, gen. agts. Northwestern Mut. Life Ins. Co., 1943-44; sole gen. agt., Chgo., 1944-51; pres. Todd Planning and Service Co., life ins. brokers, 1951—; founder, hon. chmn., prin. John O. Todd Orgn., Exec. Compensation Specialists and Cons., 1970—; faculty lectr. C.L.U. Insts., U. Conn., 1952-53, U. Wis., 1955-57, U. Calif., 1956, U. Hawaii, 1966; host interviewer ednl. Films Series of the Greats, 1973-74. Pres. Evanston (Ill.) 1st. Ward Non-Partisan Civic Assn., 1956-57; trustee Evanston Hist. Soc., 1973-76; bd. dirs. First Congl Ch., Evanston, 1987—. Recipient Golden Plate award Am. Acad. Achievement, 1969; Huebner Gold medal for contbn. to edn., 1978; named Ins. Field Man of Year, Ins. Field Pub. Co., 1965; Ill. Room in Hall of States dedicated to him by Am. Coll., 1981. Mem. Nat. Assn. Life Underwriters (John Newton Russell award 1969), Assn. Advanced Life Underwriters (pres. 1963-64), Am. Coll. Life Underwriters (trustee 1957-78), Chgo. Life Underwriters Assn. (dir. 1938-41, Disting. Service award 1984), Northwestern Mut. Spl. Agts. Assn. (pres. 1955-56), Life Agy. Mgrs. Assn. (dir. 1945-48), Northwestern Mut. Assn. Agts. (pres. 1957-58), Chgo. Life Trust Council, Million Dollar Round Table (pres. 1951, qualifier 52 consecutive yrs.), Psi Upsilon, Sphinx Head. Republican. Clubs: Evanston Univ.; Glen View. Author: Taxation, Inflation and Life Insurance, 1950; Ceiling Unlimited, 1965, 5th edit., 1984; contbg. author to text Huebner Foundation, 1951.

TODD, NORMA JEAN ROSS, retired government official; b. Butler, Pa., Oct. 3, 1920; d. William Bryson and Doris Mae (Ferguson) Ross; student spl. courses Pa. State U., 1944-46, Yale U., 1954-57; m. Alden Frank Miller, Jr., Apr. 16, 1940 (dec. Feb. 1975); 1 son, Alden Frank III; m. 2d, Jack R. Todd, Dec. 23, 1977. Exec. mgr. Donora (Pa.) C. of C., 1950-57, Donora Community Chest, 1950-57; office mgr. Donora Golden Jubilee, 1951; staff writer Herald-Am., Donora, 1957, city editor, 1957-70; asso. editor Daily Herald, Donora, 1970-73; service rep. Pitts. Teleservice Center, Social Security Adminstrn., HHS, 1977-83. Mem. Mayor's Adv. Council, Donora, 1965-69, Citizens' Adv. Council, Donora, 1965-69; mem. Donora Bd. Edn., 1954-60, pres., 1960; mem. Donora Borough Council, 1970-72; bd. dirs. Mon Valley chpt. ARC, 1964—, sec. bd., 1966—; bd. dirs. Washington County Tourism Agy., 1970—, sec., 1972—; bd. dirs. Washington County History and Landmarks Found. 1971-80, sec., 1975-80; bd. dirs. Mon Valley council Camp Fire Girls, 1965-79, Mon Valley Drug and Alcoholism Council, 1971-78; bd. dirs. United Way Mon Valley, 1973-82, chmn. pub. relations, 1973-74. Recipient Fine Arts Festival of Pa. Poetry first prize award Fedn. of Women's Clubs, 1987. Mem. Pa. Soc. Newspaper Editors, Pitts. Press Club, Donora C. of C. (pres. 1971-72), DAR (regent Monongahela Valley chpt. 1974-77), Washington County Poetry Soc. (pres. 1967-69), Washington County Fedn. Women's Clubs (rec. sec. 1964-66). Clubs: Order Eastern Star (worthy matron 1966-67), White Shrine of Jerusalem (high priestess 1973-74), Order of Amaranth (royal matron 1966, dist. dep., grand rep. W.Va. 1979-80), Donora Forecast (pres. 1962-63), Donora Unidon (pres. 1965-66, 56-57). Home: Overlook Terr Donora PA 15033 also: 1310 McKean Ave Donora PA 15033

TODD, OLIVIER RENÉ, writer, journalist; b. Paris, June 19, 1929; s. Julius Oblatt and Helen (Thompson) Todd; m. Anne Marie Nizan, July 13, 1948 (div. 1971); children: Emmanuel, Camille; m. France Huser, Dec. 24, 1982; children: Samuel, Aurélia. MA in Philosophy, Cambridge U., 1952; Lic. ès lettres, Sorbonne, Paris, 1954. Tchr. Lycée Internat. du Shape, Saint-Germain, France, 1956-62; univ. asst. Ecole normale de Saint Cloud (France), 1962-64; reporter Nouvel Observateur, Paris, 1964-69, asst. editor, 1970-77; columnist, mng. editor l'Express, Paris, 1977-81; guest columnist Newsweek Internat., 1970-76. Author: Une demi-campagne, 1957, La traversée de la Manche, 1960, Des trous dans le jardin, 1969, L'année du crabe, 1972, Les canards de Ca Mao, 1975, La marelle de Giscard, 1977, Portraits, 1979, Un fils rebelle, 1981, Un cannibale tès convenable, 1982, Une légère de bois, 1983, Jacques Brel, une vie, 1984, La balade du chômeur, 1985, Cruel Avril, the Story of the Fall of Saigon, 1987. Served with French Army. Home: 12 rue de Tournon, 75 006 Paris France

TODD, RICHARD ANDREW, actor, writer; b. Dublin, Ireland, June 11, 1919; s. Andrew William and Marvill (Agar-Daly) Palethorpe-Todd; m. Catherine Grant-Bogle (div. 1970); children: Peter, Fiona; m. Virginia Anne Mailer; children: Andrew, Seumas. Ed. privately, Shrewsbury, England. Author: (autobiographies) Caught in the Act, 1986, In Camera; began theatrical career London, 1937; founder, mem. Dundee (Scotland) Repertory, 1938-39, 1947-49; stage appearances include An Ideal Husband, London, 1965, Dear Octopus, 1967, Equus, Australia, 1975, Nightfall, Republic of South Africa, 1979, This Happy Breed, 1980, The Business of Murder, London, 1981-86; formed Triumph Theatre Co., 1970; TV appearances include Wuthering Heights, Doctor Who; films include The Hasty Heart, 1949, Stage Fright, 1950 (Hollywood Golden Globe), Lightning Strikes Twice, 1951, Rob Roy, 1954, The Dam Busters, 1955, A Man Called Peter, 1955, The Virgin Queen, 1955, Saint Joan, 1957, Chase a Crooked Shadow, 1957, Never Let Go, 1961, The Longest Day, 1962, Operation Crossbow, 1965, The Last of the Long-Haired Boys, 1968, Asylum, 1972. Recipient Brit. Nat. Film Award, Picturegoer Award, Daily Express-Tribunal Award. Club: Army and Navy (London). Address: Little Ponton House, near Grantham Lincolnshire, England also: Chinham Farm, Faringdon England

TODD, SHIRLEY ANN, educational counselor; b. Botetourt County, Va., May 23, 1935; d. William Leonard and Margaret Judy (Simmons) Brown; m. Thomas Byron Todd, July 7, 1962 (dec. July 1977). B.S. in Edn., Madison Coll., 1956; M.Ed., U. Va., 1971. Cert. tchr., Va. Elem. tchr. Fairfax County Sch. Bd., Fairfax, Va., 1956-66, 8th grade history tchr., 1966-71, guidance counselor James F. Cooper Intermediate Sch., McLean, Va., 1971-88, dir. guidance, 1988—; chmn. mktg. Lake Anne Joint Venture, Falls Church, Va., 1979-82, mng. ptnr., 1980-82. Del. Fairfax County Republican Conv., 1985. Fellow Fairfax Edn. Assn. (mem. profl. rights and responsibilities commn. 1970-72, bd. dirs. 1968-70), Va. Edn. Assn. (mem. state com. on local assns. and urban affairs 1969-70), NEA, No. Va. Counselors Assn. (hospitality and social chmn., exec. bd. 1982-83), Va. Counselors Assn. (exec. com. 1987), Va. Sch. Counselors Assn., Am. Assn. for Counseling and Devel. Baptist. Club: Chantilly Nat. Golf and Country (v.p. social 1981-82) (Centreville, Va.). Avocations: golf, tennis. Home: 6543 Bay Tree Ct Falls Church VA 22041 Office: James F Cooper Intermediate Sch 977 Balls Hill Rd McLean VA 22101

TODD, ZANE GREY, utility executive; b. Hanson, Ky., Feb. 3, 1924; s. Marshall Elvin and Kate (McCormick) T.; m. Marysnow Stone, Feb. 8, 1950 (dec. 1983); m. Frances Z. Anderson, Jan. 6, 1984. Student, Evansville Coll., 1947-49; BS summa cum laude, Purdue U., 1951, DEng (hon.), 1979; postgrad., U. Mich., 1965. Fingerprint classifier FBI, 1942-43; electric system planning engr. Indpls. Power & Light Co., 1951-56, spl. assignments supr., 1956-60, head elec. system planning, 1960-65, head substation design div., 1965-68, head distbn. engring. dept., 1968-70, asst. to v.p., 1970-72, v.p., 1972-74, exec. v.p., 1974-75, pres., 1975-81, chmn., 1976—, chief exec. officer, 1981—; chmn., pres. IPALCO Enterprises, Inc., Indpls., 1983—; chmn. bd., chief exec. officer Mid-Am. Capital Resources, Inc. subs. IPALCO Enterprises, Inc., Indpls., 1984—; gen. mgr. Mooresville Pub. Service Co., Inc., Ind., 1956-60; bd. dirs. Mchts. Nat. Bank, Mchts. Nat. Corp., Am. States Ins. Co., Environ. Quality Control, Inc.; chmn. 500 Festival Assocs., Inc., pres., 1987; dir. Indpls. Pvt. Industry Council. Contbr. articles to tech. jours. and mags. Mem. adv. bd. St. Vincent Hosp.; bd. dirs. Commn. for Downtown, YMCA Found., Crime Stoppers Cen. Ind., Corp. Community Council, Indpls. Ctr. for Advanced Research; mem. adv. council, trustee Christian Theol. Sem.; chmn. bd. trustees Ind. Cen. U. (now U. Indpls.); bd. govs. Associated Colls. of Ind.; chmn. U.S. savs. bond program State of Ind.; mem. Conf. Bd., Nat. and Greater Indpls. adv. bds. Salvation Army; mem. adv. bd. of Clowes Hall. Served as sgt. AUS, 1943-47. Named Disting. Engring. Alumnus, Purdue U., 1976, Knight of Malta, Order of St. John of Jerusalem, 1986. Fellow IEEE (past chmn. power system engring. com.); mem. ASME, NSPE, NAM (bd. dirs.), Am. Mgmt. Assn. (gen. mgmt. council), Power Engring. Soc., Ind. Electric Assn. (bd. dirs., past chmn.), Edison Electric Inst. (bd. dirs.), Ind. Fiscal Policy Inst. (bd. govs.), Ind. C. of C. (bd. dirs.), Indpls. C. of C. (bd. dirs.), Mooresville C. of C. (past pres.), Newcomen Soc. (chmn. Ind.), Eta Kappa Nu, Tau Beta Pi. Clubs: Columbia, Indpls. Athletic (past bd. dirs.), Meridian Hills Country (bd. dirs.), Skyline (bd. govs.). Lodges: Rotary, Lions (past pres.). Home: 7645 Randue Ct Indianapolis IN 46278 Office: Indpls Power & Light Co 25 Monument Circle Indianapolis IN 46206

TODMAN, TERENCE A., ambassador; b. St. Thomas, V.I., Mar. 13, 1926; s. Alphonso and Rachel (Callwood) T.; m. Doris T. Weston, July 26, 1952; children: Terence A., Patricia, Kathryn, Michael. BA, Poly. Inst., P.R., 1951; MPA, Syracuse U., 1953; postgrad., Am. U., 1953-54; hon. degree, Colgate U., 1981; LLD (hon.), Syracuse U., 1986; D in Pub. Service (hon.), Morgan State U., 1986; LLD (hon.), Boston U., 1987. Asst. personnel officer Govt. V.I., 1951; internat. relations officer State Dept., 1952-54; fgn. affairs officer 1955, U.S. nominee UN intern program, 1955; adviser U.S. delegation UN Gen. Assembly, 1956-57; U.S. rep. UN trusteeship council petitions com. and com. rural econ. devel. 1956-57; 2d sec., polit. officer Am. embassy Beirut, Lebanon, 1960-61, Tunis, 1961-63; counselor, dep. chief mission Am. embassy Lome, 1965-68; dir. Office E. African Affairs, State Dept., 1968-69; U.S. ambassador to Chad, 1969-72, Republic Guinea, 1972-74, Costa Rica, San Jose, 1975-77; asst. sec. state 1977-78; ambassador to Spain, 1978-83, Denmark, 1983—. Trustee Coll. of the Virgin Islands. Served to 1st lt. AUS, 1945-49. Recipient Superior Honor award State Dept., 1966, Medal of Honor Govt. of V.I., Grand Cross of the highest order of Isabela la Catolica (Spain), Presdl. Disting. Service award, 1985. Mem. Am. Fgn. Service Assn., Council on Fgn. Relations. Office: US Embassy Denmark APO New York NY 09170

TODOROV, DOBROMIR TODOROV, mathematics educator; b. Sofia, Bulgaria, Oct. 7, 1948; parents: Todor Todorov Stoyanov and Zora Ivanova (Georgieva) Todorova; m. Stoyka Hristova Yordanova, Mar. 3, 1974; 1 child, Todor. MA, U. Sofia, 1972, PhD, 1985. System programmer Inst. for Computing Technique, Sofia, 1972-77; asst. prof. Karl Marx Inst. Econs., Sofia, 1977—. Contbr. articles profl. jours. Mem. Union Bulgarian Mathematicians, Am. Math. Soc. Home: Dimitar Blagoev 50 A, 1606 Sofia Bulgaria Office: Karl Marx Inst Econs, Dept Mathematics, 1100 Sofia Bulgaria

TODOROV, RADOSVET, information scientist; b. Sofia, Bulgaria, Mar. 31, 1946; m. Mariana Todorova. M in Physics, Faculty Scis., Algiers, Algeria, 1970; PhD in Info. Sci., Humboldt U., 1979. Researcher Bulgarian Acad. Scis., Sofia, 1973-76, 79—. Author: Scientific Communication in Physics, 1986; contbr. articles to profl. jours.; mem. editorial adv. bd. internat. jour. Scientometrics, 1988—. Office: Bulgarian Acad Scis, 7 Noemvri 1, 1000 Sofia Bulgaria

TODOROV, STANKO, politician; b. Pernik region, Bulgaria, Dec. 10, 1920; m. Sonya Todorova, 1947; 2 sons. Active Resistance Movement, 1941-44; mem. Nat. Assembly; minister of agr. Govt. of Bulgaria, 1952-58; sec. cen. com. Bulgarian Communist Party, 1958-59, 66-71, full mem. politburo, 1961—; dep. prime minister 1959-66; permanent Bulgarian rep. to Council for Mut. Econ. Assistance, 1962-66; chair Council of Ministers, 1971-81, Nat. Assembly, 1981—. Decorated Order of the October Revolution, 1981. Office: Narodno Sobranie, Sofia Bulgaria *

TODOROV, TZVETAN, scientific researcher; b. Sofia, Bulgaria, Mar. 1, 1939; arrived in France, 1963; s. Todor Todorov Borov and Haritina (Peeva) Todorova; m. Martine Van Woerkens, June 18, 1971 (div. Sept. 1980); 1 child, Boris; m. Nancy L. Huston, May 16, 1981; 1 child, Lea. Grad., U. Sofia, 1961; Doctorat, U. Paris, 1966, Doctorat és lettres, 1970. Research asst. Ecole des Hautes Etudes en Scis. Sociales, Paris, 1964-67; vis. lectr. Yale U., New Haven, 1967-68; sci. researcher Ctr. Nat. de la Recherche Sci., Paris, 1968—; vis. prof. Columbia U., N.Y.C., 1974, 77, 80, 83, 86; bd. dirs. Ctr. de Recherches sur les Arts et le Langage, Paris. Author: The Fantastic, 1970, Theories of the Symbol, 1977, The Conquest of America, 1982, Literature and Its Theorists, 1984; editor Poetique, 1970-79. Office: Ctr Research Arts and Lang, 44 rue de la Tour, 75016 Paris France

TODOROVIC, RADMILO ANTONIJE, veterinarian, technical development executive; b. Zabojnica, Yugoslavia, Oct. 30, 1927; came to U.S., 1960; s. Antonije Ilija and Rajka (Otasevic) T. m. Lillian Djukic, June 9, 1960; children: Jovan, Ilija, Joan, Jane. DVM, U. Belgrade, Yugoslavia, 1953; MS, U. Wis., 1963; PhD, U. Ill., 1967. Diplomate Am. Coll. Vet. Medicine. Veterinarian Vetinary Hosp., Bare-Knic, Yugoslavia, 1953-55; asst. prof. U. Belgrade, 1955-60; veterinarian Am. Breeders, Madison, Wis., 1960-63; dir. Ctr. Tropical Agr., Cali, Colombia, 1968-78; assoc. prof. Tex. A&M U., College Station, 1968-80; mgr. research and devel. Internat. Minerals & Chem. Corp., Terre Haute, Ind., 1980—, research veterinarian, 1983—; research veterinarian Colombian Inst. Agr., Bogota, 1968-72; cons. U.S. Aid-Vet Dept., Lima, Peru, Micronesia, 1969-73; invited speaker World Vet. Congress, 1970, 75, Agrl. Seminar, China, 1984. Contbr. over 120 articles to profl. jours. and textbooks. Postdoctoral fellow N. Atlantic Treaty Pact. Mem. Am. Vet. Med. Assn., Ill. Soc. Med. Research, Conf. on Research Workers in Animal Diseases, Soc. Protozoologists, Assn. Univ. Profs., AAAS, Latin Am. Assn. Agrl. Scis., Colombian Vet. Med. Assn., N.Y. Acad. Sics., Soc. Tropical Vet. Medicine, Ind. State Vet. Med. Assn., Smithsonian Assocs., U.S. Animal Health Assn., Am. Assn. Indsl. Vets., Sigma Xi, Phi Sigma, Phi Zeta. Home: 1355 Winterberry Ct Terre Haute IN 47802 Office: Internat Minerals & Chem Corp PO Box 207 Terre Haute IN 47808

TODSEN, DANA ROGNAR, cancer center executive; b. St. Petersburg, Fla., Oct. 8, 1947; s. Birger Rognar and Elsie (Ewin) T.; m. Janis Hellman, June 13, 1970; children—Matthew Kristian, Jennifer Alana. B.A., U. South Fla., 1970, M.A., 1976. Assoc. dir. So. Health Found., Tampa, Fla., 1976-78; dir. U. Tampa, 1978-82; mng. dir. St. Anthony's Devel. Found., St. Petersburg, 1982-85; dir. devel. Moffitt Cancer Ctr., Tampa, 1985—; ptnr. McElroy, Todsen, Inc.; pres. Todsen & Assocs., Brandon, Fla., 1983—. adj. instr. Hillsborough Community Coll., 1978, U. S.Fla., 1980; cons. Exec. Service Corp. Tampa. Contbr. articles to profl. jours. Bd. dirs. Children's

Home Soc., 1983—, Leadership, Tampa Bay, 1987—, bd. dirs. 1987—; mem. Leadership Tampa, 1981—; cons. Big Bros. and Big Sisters Tampa, Met. Ministries, Tampa Community Health Ctr., Suicide and Crisis Ctr. Mem. Nat. Assn. Fund Raising Execs. (cert.), Nat. Assn. Hosp. Devel., Am. Coll. Healthcare Mktg., Sales & Mktg. Execs Internat., Mil. Affairs Council, Council for Advancement and Support Edn., Philanthropic Action Council, Greater Tampa C. of C., Tampa Tiger Bay, Alpha Tau Omega. Democrat. Methodist. Club: Tampa. Home: 3918 Applegate Circle Brandon FL 33511 Office: Moffitt Cancer Ctr PO Box 280179 Tampa FL 33682

TOET, ALEXANDER, electronics researcher; b. Apeldoorn, Netherlands, Oct. 12, 1955; s. Johannus and Jenny (Pasman) T. MSc in Physics and Meteorology, U. Utrecht, Netherlands, 1982; PhD in Physics, U. Utrecht, 1987. Image processing, vision researcher U. Utrecht, Netherlands, 1982-86, Philips Electronics Co., Eindhoven, Netherlands, 1986—, Inst. Sensory Physiology, Soesterberg, Netherlands, 1986—; cons. U. Hosp. Utrecht, 1982-86. Contbr. articles to profl. jours. Mem. IEEE, Internat. Assn. Pattern Recognition, Assn. Research in Vision and Ophthalmology. Home: Albert van Dalsumlaan 845, 358HT Utrecht The Netherlands Office: Univ Utrecht, Princetonplein 5, NL 3508 TA Utrecht The Netherlands

TOFIAS, ALLAN, accountant; b. Boston, Apr. 13, 1930; s. George I. and Anna (Seidel) T.; m. Arlene Shube, Aug. 30, 1981; children: Bradley Neil, Laura Jean Silver. B.A., Colgate U., 1951; M.B.A., Harvard U., 1956. C.P.A., Mass. Sr. acct. Peat, Marwick, Mitchell & Co., Boston, 1956-60; mng. ptnr. Tofias, Fleishman, Shapiro, & Co. P.C., Boston, 1960—. Mem. town meeting Town of Brookline (Mass.), 1970-77, mem. fin. adv. bd., 1975-81; mem. New Eng. Bapt. Health Care Corp., 1985—; bd. dirs. West Newton YMCA, 1986—, Boston Aid for Blind, 1988—. Served to lt. (j.g.) USNR, 1951-54. Mem. Am. Inst. C.P.A.s, Mass. Soc. C.P.A.s, Nat. C.P.A. Group (exec. com. 1983-88, vice chmn. 1985-88), N.Eng.-Israel C. of C. (mem. exec. com.). Clubs: Wightman Tennis (Weston, Mass.) (treas. 1974-76); Newton Squash and Tennis (Mass.) (bd. dirs. 1966—). Lodge: Moses Michael Hays. Home: 59 Monadnock Rd Wellesley MA 02181 Office: Tofias Fleishman Shapiro & Co PC 205 Broadway Cambridge MA 02139

TOFTNER, RICHARD ORVILLE, engineering executive; b. Warren, Minn., Mar. 5, 1935; s. Orville Gayhart and Cora Evelyn (Anderson) T.; BA, U. Minn., 1966; MBA, Xavier U., 1970; m. Jeanne Bredine, June 26, 1960; children: Douglas, Scott, Kristine, Kimberly, Brian. Sr. economist Federated Dept. Stores, Inc., Cin., 1967-68; dep. dir. EPA, Washington and Cin., 1968-73; mgmt. cons. environ. affairs, products and mktg., 1973-74; prin. PEDCo Environ., Cin., 1974-80; trustee PEDCo trusts, 1974-80; pres. ROTA Mgmt., Inc., Cin., 1980-82; gen. mgr. CECOS, 1982-85, cons., 1985—; v.p. Smith, Stevens & Young, 1985-88; real estate developer, 1980—; adj. prof. U. Cin.; chmn. bd. dirs. Toxitrol Internat., Inc., 1987—; lectr. Grad. fellowship rev. panel Office of Edn., 1978—; advisor, cabinet-level task force Office of Gov. of P.R., 1973; subcom. Nat. Safety Council, 1972; nominee commr. PUCO, Ohio; Cin. City mgr. Waste Task Force, 1987—. Served with AUS, 1954-57. Mem. Soc. Advancement Mgmt., Water Pollution Control Fedn., Engring. Soc. Cin., Cin. C. of C. Republican. Lutheran. Clubs: Columbia (Indpls.); Bankers (Cin.). Contbr. articles to mgmt. planning and environ. to periodicals, chpts. in books; developer Toxitrol. Home: 9175 Yellowwood Dr Cincinnati OH 45251 Office: 4700 Ashwood Dr Suite 100 Cincinnati OH 45241

TOFTNESS, CECIL GILLMAN, lawyer, consultant; b. Glasgow, Mont., Sept. 13, 1920; s. Anton Bernt and Nettie (Pedersen) T.; m. Chloe Catherine Vincent, Sept. 8, 1951. A.A., San Diego Jr. Coll., 1943; student Purdue U., Northwestern U.; B.S., UCLA, 1947; J.D., Southwestern U., 1953. Bar: Calif. 1954, U.S. Dist. Ct. (so. dist.) Calif. 1954, U.S. Supreme Ct. 1979. Sole practice, Palos Verdes Estates, Calif., 1954—; dir., pres., chmn. bd. Fisherman & Mchts. Bank, San Pedro, Calif., 1963-67; dir., v.p. Palos Verdes Estates Bd. Realtors, 1964-65. Chmn. Capital Campaign Fund, Richstone Charity, Hawthorne, Calif., 1983. Served to lt. (j.g.) USN, 1938-46, ETO, PTO. Named Man of Yr., Glasgow, 1984. Mem. South Bay Bar Assn., Southwestern Law Sch. Alumni Assn. (class rep. 1980—), Internat. Physicians for the Prevention of Nuclear War (del. 7th World Congress, 1987), Themis Soc.-Southwestern Law Sch., Schumacher Founder's Circle-Southwestern Law Sch. (charter). Democrat. Lutheran. Lodges: Kiwanis (sec.-treas. 1955-83, v.p., pres., bd. dirs.), Masons, K.T. Home: 2229 Via Acalones Palos Verdes Estates CA 90274 Office: 2516 Via Tejon Palos Verdes Estates CA 90274

TOGASAKI, SHINOBU, corporate executive; b. San Francisco, Aug. 17, 1932; s. Kikumatsu and Sugi (Hida) T.; m. Toshiko Kawaguchi, Nov. 24, 1959; children: John Shinobu, Ann Mariko. BS in Math., Duke U., 1954; postgrad., Stanford U., 1954-56. Math. programmer IBM, 1956—; sr. programmer IBM, Palo Alto, 1970-87; mgr. applications devel. Service Bur. Corp., Palo Alto, 1961-64, sr. analyst, 1964-68; systems architect devel. lab. Service Bur. Corp., San Jose, Calif., 1968-70; chief fin. officer Robin Hood Ranch, Inc., 1976—, mgr. architecture & strategy Hewlett Packard Corp., San Jose, 1987—; cons., mktg. support rep. Pres. Friends Outside Santa Clara County, 1983-84. Mem. Am. Mgmt. Assn., AAAS, Am. Statis. Assn., Assn. Computing Machinery, Inst. Mgmt. Sci., Palo Alto C. of C., Sigma Pi Sigma. Home: 2367 Booksin Ave San Jose CA 95125 Office: 555 Bailey Ave San Jose CA 95150

TOGONU-BICKERSTETH, FUNMI ADENIKE, psychology educator, gerontologist; b. Otan-Aiyegbaju, Oyo, Nigeria, Apr. 16, 1949; d. Gabriel Olatunji Faniran and Bola Oyedeji Adedewe; m. Gilbert Lanre Togonu-Bickersteth; 1 child, Olutoyin Bolaji. BS with honors, U. Ibadan, Nigeria, 1971; M in Social Sci., Bryn Mawr (Pa.) Coll., 1974, PhD, 1978. Lectr., social work coordinator Del. State Coll., 1976-79; lectr. psychology Univ. Ife, Ile-Ife, Nigeria, 1979—; cons. Div. Social Services, Wilmington, Del., 1978. Juvenile ct. panel mem. Oyo State Ministry Justice, Ile-Ife, 1984-86. Mem. Am. Gerontol. Assn., Internat. Sociol. Assn. Club: Zonta (Ile-Ife) (sec. service com.). Home: Rd 12, House 28, UNIFE, Ile-Ife, Oyo Nigeria Office: Univ Ife, Dept Psychology, Ile-Ife Nigeria

TOINET, MARIE-FRANCE, political scientist; b. Paris, Jan. 11, 1942; d. Paul-Marie and Manon (Adam) T. Diploma, Inst. Etudes Politiques, Paris, 1963; PhD, U. Paris, 1969; postgrad. Kennedy Sch. Govt., Harvard U., 1969-70. Researcher Nat. Found. Polit. Sci., Paris, 1963—, dir. research, 1987—, mem. bd., 1973-80, 86—; vis. asst. prof. U. Calif., Irvine, 1974; vis. assoc. prof. U. Iowa, Iowa City, 1978; dir. research U. Paris I, 1980-83; conf. master Inst. Polit. Studies, Paris, 1981-83; vis. prof. Yale U., New Haven, Conn., 1984, U. Mich., Ann Arbor, 1984. Author: Le Congres des Etats-Unis, 1972, Les Etats-Unis et leurs populations, 1980, La chasse aux sorcieres, 1984, Le systeme politique des Etats-Unis, 1987. Harkness fellow Commonwealth Fund, N.Y.C., 1968-70, Fulbright fellow, 1978, Eisenhower fellow, Phila., 1987. Mem. French Polit. Sci. Assn., Am. Polit. Sci. Assn. (Congl. fellow 1968-69). Home: 21 rue du Vieux Colombier, 75006 Paris France Office: Nat Found Polit Sci, 27 rue St Guillaume, 75007 Paris France

TOKITA, TSUTOMU, seed company executive; b. Kasukabe, Saitama, Japan, Mar. 30, 1935; s. Taisuke and Setsu T.; m. Setsuko Tokita, Oc.t 28, 1963; children: Iwao, Osamu, Yûko. M in Hort., Chiba Nat. U., 1957. Prodn. mgr. Tokita Seed Co., Ltd., Kasukabe, 1957-68, exec., 1968-71; pres. Tokita Seed Co., Ltd., Omiya, Saitama, Japan, 1971—. Editor: Seed Production Technology of Vegetables, 1968; breeder Senposai vegetable variety, 1986. Mem. Kasukabe-City Edn. Com., 1971. Recipient Golden Prize Commodity Devel., Japan Econ. Jour., 1987. Mem. Japan Seed Trade Assn. (dir. 1978). Home: 5912-3 Kasukabe, 344 Kasukabe Japan Office: Tokita Seed Co Ltd, 1-069 Nakagawa, 330 Omiya Japan

TOKORO, MASAAKI, architect; b. Kōbe, Japan, Apr. 4, 1929; s. Yasuji and Yae (Musashino) T.; m. Haruko Tatsuno; 1 child, Asao. B in Engring., Nihon U., Tokyo, 1957. Chief architect M. Warder Studio, Tokyo, 1955-56; architect designer Takenaka Komuten, Tokyo, 1956-58; pres. M. Tokoro Architect and Assocs., Tokyo, 1958—; guest lectr. Nihon U., 1971-85. Recipient Concours award Kanagawa Prefecture Govt., 1968. Fellow Tokyo Soc. Architects and Bldg. Engrs. (House Design Concours award 1983); mem. Japan Inst. Architects (chmn. bd. editors 1978), Japan Inst. Architect, Archtl. Inst. Architect. Mem. Tokyo Christian Reformed Ch. Club: Blue Red and Blue. Home: G-1303 Suncity, 3-27 Nakagai Itabashiku, Tokyo 174, Japan Office: Kugimannishi Bldg 410 3-14, Yotsuya Shinjukuku, Tokyo 160, Japan

TOLAND, JOHN WILLARD, historian, writer; b. La Crosse, Wis., June 29, 1912; s. Ralph and Helen Chandler (Snow) T.; m. Toshiko Matsumura, Mar. 12, 1960; 1 dau., Tamiko; children by previous marriage: Diana Toland Netzer, Marcia. B.A., Williams Coll., 1936; student, Yale Drama Sch., 1936-37; L.H.D., Williams Coll., 1968, U. Alaska, 1977, Western Conn. U., 1986. Mem. adv. council Nat. Archives. Author: Ships in the Sky, 1957, Battle: the Story of the Bulge, 1959, But Not in Shame, 1961 (Best Book Fgn. Affairs award Overseas Press Club), The Dillinger Days, 1963, The Flying Tigers, 1963, The Last 100 Days, 1966 (Best Book Fgn. Affairs citation Overseas Press Club), The Battle of the Bulge, 1966, The Rising Sun (Van Wyck Brooks award for non-fiction), 1970 (Best Book Fgn. Affairs award Overseas Press Club, Pulitzer prize for non-fiction), Adolf Hitler, 1976 (Best Book Fgn. Affairs award Overseas Press Club, Gold Medal Nat. Soc. Arts and Letters), Hitler, The Pictorial Documentary of His Life, 1978, No Man's Land, 1980 (Best Book Fgn. Affairs citation Overseas Press Club), Infamy, 1982; (novels) Gods of War, 1985, Occupation, 1987; also short stories. Served to capt. USAAF, 1942-46, 1947-49. Mem. Authors Guild, Accademia del Mediterraneo., Western Front Assn. (hon. v.p.). Home: 1 Long Ridge Rd Danbury CT 06810

TOLEDANO, MINDA BAGO-OD, physician; b. Esperanza, Philippines, Sept. 6, 1951; d. Santos and Florencia (Balane) Bago-od; m. Henry Madrid Toledano, May 5, 1979; children: Camille, Carlo Emmanuel. MD, Manila Cen. U. Resident Perpetual Help Hosp., Manila, 1974-76, vis. cons., 1985-86; sr. resident Jose Fabella Meml. Hosp., Manila, 1976-85, vis. cons., 1985-86; vis. cons. Las Pinas Drs. Hosp., De Ocampo Hosp., Hillside Gen. Hosp., Manila, 1985-86; cons. Ebin Sina Med. Ctr., Taif, 1986—. Mem. Manila Med. Soc., Muntinlupa Med. Soc. Home: 68 Kamagong Rd, Pilar Village, Metro Manila Las Pinas, Philippines

TOLEDANO, ROGER ROBERT, canal company executive; b. Panama City, Panama, July 20, 1940; s. Robert Solomon and Margot (de Lima) T.; m. Lucia Wegener, Sept. 26, 1963; children: Rogelio Antonio, Roberto Eduardo, Michelle Madelene. BSME, Bradley U., 1962. Mech. engr. Panama Canal Co., Panama City, 1962-67, mech. engr. supr., 1967-82; gen. engr. supr. Panama Canal Commn., Panama City, 1982—; dep. sec. Primer Banco de Ahorro, Panama City, 1980—; owner Wegtol, S.A. Cons., 1983—. V.p. SOS Orphanage Village, Panama City, 1987—, bd. dirs., 1986. Fellow ASHRAE, NSPE (canal area rep. 1982-86, mem. internat. affair com. 1987—), Sociedad Panamena de Arquitectos e Ingenieros. Club: Canal Radio (bd. dirs. 1986-87). Lodge: Rotary (pres. 1984-85). Home: PO Box 1021, Panama City Panama

TOLENTINO, PAULINO DEFANTE, agriculturalist; b. Iloilo City, Philippines, Apr. 7, 1926; d. Mariano Viscerra Tolentino and Estrella (Debuque) Defante; m. Leticia Enrile; children: Paulino Jr., Paz Estrella, Fatima Sarah. AA, Silliman U., Dumaguete City, Philippines, 1948; MD, U. Santo Tomas, Manila, 1953; M in Nat. Security Adminstrn., Nat. Def. Coll. Philippines, Ft. Bonifacio, Metro Manila, 1975. Mem. U.S. Armed Forces in Far East, Panay, Philippines, 1941-45; practice medicine specializing in thoracic vascular surgery Far Eastern U., Rizal Provincial Hosp., Metro Manila, 1960-70; v.p./treas. Radio Communications of Philippines, Inc., Metro Manila, 1961—; pres. Paulino D. Tolentino, Inc., Metro Manila, 1965—, Tolentino Tech. Inst., Inc., Metro Manila, 1972—, Ind. Sagay-Escalante Planters, Inc., Negros Occidental, Philippines, 1985—; trustee Sugar Industry Found., Inc., 1987—; bd. dirs. Sugar Philippines, Inc. Trustee Cen. Philippine U., Jaro, Iloilo, 1978—, chmn., 1978-80, 82-84; v.p. Vet. Fedn. Philippines, 1976-78. Served to lt. col. Philippine Constabulary, 1975—. Recipient Disting. Service award Cen. Philippine U., Disting. Alumnus award Silliman U., 1978, Most Outstanding Alumnus award U. Santo Tomas, 1984. Mem. Philippine Amateur Radio Assn. (life). Roman Catholic. Home: 312 Manga Ave, San Juan, Metro Manila Philippines Office: Radio Communication Philippines, New York St Cubao, Quezon City Philippines

TOLIN, BRUCE GEORGE, food products executive; b. Chgo., June 22, 1957; s. Stanley and Anita (Kasindorf) T.; m. Andrea Deborah Schornstein, Sept. 21, 1985; 1 child, Heather. BS in Food Sci., U. Ill., 1981; postgrad. mktg., Northwestern U. Food scientist, internat. mktg. Union Carbide Corp., Chgo., 1981-84; mktg. mgr. Intek Internat. Food Products, Inc., Barrington, Ill., 1984-86, v.p., 1987—; pres. Toltran Ltd., Barrington, Ill., 1985—. Patentee Human Language Computer Interpretor Program. Mem. Inst. Food Technologists (editor internat. newsletter, 1981—), Am. Translators Assn., Am. Liszt Soc. Republican. Home: 1485 Powder Horn Dr Algonquin IL 60102

TOLIN, DONALD LEE, lawyer, steel company executive; b. Casper, Wyo., Aug. 29, 1953; s. Sidney and Cecelia (Baer) T.; m. Vickie Lynn Davison, Sept. 4, 1977, children: Cecelia Anne, Sarah Dawn, Joshua Abraham, David Joseph. BS in Acctg. with honors, U. Wyo., 1975, JD, 1978. Bar: Wyo. 1978, U.S. Tax Ct. 1978, U.S. Ct. Appeals 1978; CPA, Wyo. Sole practice Casper, 1978—; v.p., treas., corp. counsel Casper Iron & Metal, Inc., 1972—, also bd. dirs. Chair Wyo. state adv. com. U.S. Commn. Civil Rights, 1986-88, 88—; active Am.-Israel Pub. Affairs Com.; organizaer, chmn. Wyo. Jewish Assn. Mem. ABA (chmn. div. com. 1978, council real property probate and trust div.), Wyo. State Bar, Wyo. Trial Lawyers Assn., Am. Inst. CPAs, Wyo. Soc. CPAs, Am. Assn. Attys./CPAs, Natrona County Bar Assn., Inst. Scrap Iron and Steel (sec.-treas. Rocky Mountain chpt. 1977-79, v.p., pres. 1981-83, nat. dir. 1981-83, environ. and legis. chmn.), Steel Service Ctr. Inst., Am. Welding Soc., ASTM, Casper Area C. of C. Lodges: Shriners, Masons. Home: 561 Walsh Dr Casper WY 82601 Office: Casper Iron & Metal Inc 3200 W 13th St Casper WY 82601

TOLKUNOV, LEV NIKOLAYEVICH, Soviet government offical, journalist; b. Bukreyevka, Kursk, USSR, Jan. 22, 1919. Ed., Gorky Inst. Literature, Moscow, Higher Party Sch. Communist Party Soviet Union. Sub-editor, mil. corr. Pravda, 1938-44; dep. exec. sec., head dept. for a lasting peace For a People's Democracy, 1947-51; dep. editor, then editor People's Democracies Pravda, 1951-57; employee of apparatus of Cen. Com. Communist Party Soviet Union, 1957-65, dep. chief dept. for liaison with Communist and worker's parties in other Communist countries, 1961-65; editor-in-chief Izvestia, 1965-75, 83-84; chmn. bd. Novosti Press Agy., 1976-83; mem. Communist Party Soviet Union, 1943—; candidate mem. Cen. Com. Communist Party Soviet Union, 1966-76, mem., 1976—; dep. to USSR Supreme Soviet, Moscow, 1966—, chair Soviet of the Union of, 1984—, chair Soviet Com. for European Security, 1984—. Decorated Order of Lenin (twice), Red Banner of Labour (three times), Red Star, Order of Oct. Revolution, Order of People's Friendship, Order of the Patriotic War, and other medals. Office: Soviet of the Union, Office Chmn, Moscow USSR *

TOLL, JOHN SAMPSON, university president, physics educator; b. Denver, Oct. 25, 1923; s. Oliver Wolcott and Merle d'Aubigne (Sampson) T.; m. Deborah Ann Taintor, Oct. 24, 1970; children: Dacia Merle Sampson, Caroline Taintor. B.S. with highest honors, Yale U., 1944; A.M., Princeton U., 1948, Ph.D., 1952; D. Sc., U. Md., 1973, U. Wroclaw, Poland, 1975; LL.D., Adelphi U., 1978. Mng. editor, acting chmn. Yale Sci. mag., 1943-44; with Princeton U., 1946-49, Proctor fellow, 1948-49; Friends of Elementary Particle Theory Research grantee for study in France, 1950; theoretical physicist Los Alamos Sci. Lab., 1950-51; staff mem., assoc. dir. Project Matterhorn Forrestal Research Center, Princeton, 1951-53; prof. chmn. physics and astronomy U. Md., 1953-65; pres., prof. physics SUNY, Stony Brook, 1965-78, U. Md., 1978—; 1st dir. State U. N.Y. Chancellor's Panel on Univ. Purposes, 1970; physics cons. to editorial staff Nat. Sci. Tchrs. Assn., 1957-61; U.S. del., head sci. secretariat Internat. Conf. on High Energy Physics, 1960; mem-at-large U.S. Nat. Com. for Internat. Union of Pure and Applied Physics, 1960-63; chmn. research adv. com. on electrophysics to NASA, 1961-65; mem. gov. Md. Sci. Resources Adv. bd., 1963-65; mem., also chmn. NSF adv. panel for physics, 1964-67; mem. N.Y. Gov.'s Adv. Com. Atomic Energy, 1966-68; mem. commn. plans and objectives higher edn. Am. Council Edn., 1966-69; mem. Hall of Records Commn., 1979; bd. dirs. Dairy Council, 1979—, Washington/Balt. Regional Assn., 1980—; mem., chmn. adv. council Princeton Plasma Physics Lab, 1979—; mem. Adv. Council of Pres.'s, Assn. of Governing Bds., 1980—, So. Regional Edn. Bd., 1980—; mem. exec. com. Nat. Assn. Univs. and Land Grant Colls., 1980—; mem. Greater Balt. Com., Inc., 1980—; bd. dirs. Def. Systems Mgmt. Coll., 1982—; AAU rep. on Assembly of Nat. Post Edn. Assn., 1982—; mem. univ. programs panel of energy research bd. Dept. Energy, 1982—; mem. Washington-Balt. Regional Assn., 1983-84, Ctr. for the Study of the Presidency, 1983-84; mem. SBHE Adv. Com., 1983—, Md. Gov.'sChesapeake Bay Council, 1985; mem. resource com. State Trade Policy Council Gov.'s High Tech RoundtableMd. Dept. Econ. Devel., 1986—; marine div. chmn. NASULGC, 1986; bd. dirs. Am. Council on Edn., 1986; bd. trustees Aspen Inst. for Humanities, 1987. Contbr. articles to sci. jours. Recipient Benjamin Barge prize in math. Yale U., 1943, George Beckwith medal for Proficiency in Astronomy, 1944, Outstanding citizen award City of Denver, 1958, Outstanding Tchr. award U. Md. Men's League, 1965, Nat. Golden Plate award Am. Acad. Achievement, 1968; named Washingtonian of Yr., 1985; John Simon Guggenheim Meml. Found. fellow Inst. Theoretical Physics U. Copenhagen; John Simon Guggenheim Meml. Found. fellow U. Lund, Sweden, 1958-59. Fellow Am. Phys. Soc.; mem. Am. Assn. Physics Tchrs., Fedn. Am. Scientists (chmn. 1961-62), Washington Acad. Scis., Philos. Soc. Washington, Assn. Higher Edn., Nat. Sci. Tchrs. Assn., Yale Engring. Assn., Phi Beta Kappa, Sigma Xi (sci. achievement award U. Md. chpt. 1965), Phi Kappa Phi, Sigma Pi Sigma, Omicron Delta Kappa (hon.). Club: Cosmos. Office: UoMd Office of Pres Adelphi MD 20783

TOLL, ROBERTA DARLENE (MRS. SHELDON S. TOLL), b. Detroit, May 14, 1944; d. David and Blanche (Fischer) Pollack; B.A., U. Mich., 1966; M.S.W., U. Pa., 1971; student Ctr. for Humanistic Studies, 1986; m. Aug. 11, 1968; children—Candice, John, Kevin. Dir. counselors Phila. Family Planning, Inc., 1971-72; psychologist Lafayette Clinic, Detroit, 1972-73; social worker Project Headline, Detroit, 1973-75; pvt. practice clin. psychology, Bloomfield Hills, Mich., 1975—; adj. prof. U. Detroit, Oakland Community Coll. Bd. dirs. Detroit chpt. Nat. Council on Alcoholism. Cert. social worker, Mich. Fellow Masters and Johnson Inst.; mem. Nat. Assn. Social Workers. Democrat. Club: Franklin Hills Country. Home and Office: 640 Lone Pine Hill Rd Bloomfield Hills MI 48013

TOLLE, DONALD JAMES, emeritus teacher educator; b. Roxbury, Kans., May 29, 1918; s. Edgar Earl and Sadie M. (Lott) T.; m. Mary Alice McNeill, July 24, 1945; children: Donald MacDavid, Louise Margaret, Theresa Love. A.B., Fla. So. Coll., 1940; M.A., U. Fla., 1947; Ed.D., Fla. State U., 1957. Tchr. Palmetto (Fla.) Jr.-Sr. High Sch., 1940-42, Winter Haven (Fla.) High Sch., 1946-47, Monticello (Fla.) Jr. High Sch., 1947-48; prin. Jefferson County High Sch., Monticello; also supervising prin. Monticello Pub. Schs. (W), 1949-51; instr. St. Petersburg (Fla.) Jr. Coll., 1951-55, dean of men, 1953-58, dean instrn., 1958-66; dean acad. studies Fla. Jr. Coll., Jacksonville, 1966-67; assoc. prof. higher edn., assoc. dir. community coll. coop. internship program So. Ill. U., Carbondale, 1967-71; prof. higher edn. So. Ill. U., 1971-84, prof. emeritus, 1984—; vis. prof. Appalachian State U., summer 1964; acting prof. U. South Fla., 1965-66. Co-author book; contbr. articles to profl. jours. Mem. Fla. Gov's Advisory Com. Law Enforcement Edn., 1964-66; mem. exec. com. Fla. Council for Edn. in Politics, 1958-66, Fla. Assn. Colls. and Univs., 1958-66, sec. treas., 1960-61; cons. to several jr. colls. Served with USAAF, 1942-45. Home: 907 Skyline Dr Carbondale IL 62901

TOLLEY, MICHAEL JOHN, university educator; b. Barnsley, Eng., Aug. 1, 1938; arrived in Australia, 1965; s. Charles John and Mary (Bainbridge, now Sunde) T.; m. Inga Juel Sunde, July 29, 1961; children—Ann Edith, Philip Michael. B.A. (hons.), London U., 1959, Ph.D., 1974. Lectr. Palmerston North U. Coll., N.Z., 1961-65; lectr. U. Adelaide (So. Australia), 1965-72, sr. lectr., 1972-82, reader, 1982—. Mem. Religious Soc. of Friends. Editor: William Blake's Designs for Edward Young's Night Thoughts, 1980; The Stellar Gauge, 1980; contbr. articles to profl. jours. Office: U Adelaide, Dept English, PO Box 498, 5001 Adelaide Australia

TOLMAS, HYMAN CYRIL, pediatrician; b. New Orleans, Feb. 1, 1922; s. Charles and Cecile (Bressler) T.; B.S., Tulane U., 1943; M.D., Tulane Med. Sch., 1945; m. Constance D. Cohen, July 9, 1950; children—Jean Ann, Alan Leon. Intern, Charity Hosp. La., New Orleans, 1945-46, resident pediatrics, 1946, 48-50; practice medicine specializing in pediatrics, New Orleans, 1950—; mem. med. adv. com. New Orleans Speech & Hearing Center, 1964—; chief, coordinator pediatrics Hotel Dieu Hosp., New Orleans, 1960-65; sr. vis. pediatrician Touro Infirmary, New Orleans, 1950—, dir. adolescent unit, 1978—; mem. staff Mercy, East Jefferson Gen., Lakeside Hosps., New Orleans; pres. med. staff Mercy Hosp., 1972, trustee, 1973—, v.p. bd., 1976-77, pres., 1977—; clin. prof. pediatrics Tulane Med. Sch., 1965—. Bd. dirs. ARC, 1953-54; coordinator med. center Tulane Alumni Fund. Served to lt. (j.g.) USNR, 1946-48. Recipient Med. award City of New Orleans, 1963, Orleans Parish Med. Soc., 1967. Fellow Am. Acad. Pediatrics (exec. com. adolescent sect. 1981-84, now program dir. adolescent sect., chmn. com. on adolescence, state chpt. 1978—, Outstanding Contbr. award in adolescent medicine 1985); mem. New Orleans Pediatric Soc. (pres. 1963-65), La. Pediatric Soc. (sec. 1968-70), Orleans Parish Med. Soc., AMA, La. Med. Soc., New Orleans Grad. Med. Assembly, Tulane Med. Alumni Assn. (dir. 1981-84), Am. Soc. Pub. Service (Thomas Jefferson award 1982). Club: Bacchus Carnival (New Orleans). Contbr. articles to nat. jours.; mem. editorial bd. Internat. Jour. Adolescent Medicine. Home: 466 Crystal St New Orleans LA 70124 Office: 2017 Metairie Rd Metairie LA 70005

TOLSMA, PIETER JARIG, automotive executive; b. Heer, Limburg, The Netherlands, Aug. 7, 1939; m. Anna Van Putten, Sept. 27, 1962; children: Eric, Marjolijn. ING degree in Mech. Engring., HTS, Den Haag, The Netherlands, 1960. Sales engr. Intechmij, Den Haag, 1963-71, sales mgr., 1971-75; gen. mgr. Landré-Intomech, Vianen, The Netherlands, 1975-79; dep. mng. dir. Econosto NV, Rotterdam, The Netherlands, 1979-88; mng. dir. Werkmetaal B.V., Vianen, The Netherlands, 1988—. Served to capt. Dutch Ordnance, 1960-63. Lodge: Lions (pres. Zoetermeer, The Netherlands club 1986-87). Home: 34 Tichelberg, 2716 LM Zoetermeer The Netherlands

TOLSTAYA, TATIANA NIKITICHNA, writer, editor; b. Leningrad, May 3, 1951; d. Nikita Alexsevich Tolstoy and Natalia Michailovna Lozinskaya; m. Andrej Valentinovich Lebedev, May 11, 1974; children: Artemij Andreevich, Alexej Andreevich. Grad. in Classical Philology, Leningrad U., 1974. Diplomate in philology. Editor Nauka Pub. House, Moscow, 1974-83. Author: The Golden Porch, 1987; contbr. articles to mags. and newspapers. Mem. PEN Internat. Russian Orthodox. Home: Bolshaya Polianka 37, Apt #2, 109180 Moscow USSR

TOM, LAWRENCE, computer graphics engineering executive; b. Los Angeles, Jan. 21, 1950; s. Tommy Toy and May (Fong) T. BS, Harvey Mudd Coll., 1972; JD Western State U., San Diego, 1978. Design engr. Rockwell Internat., Los Angeles, 1972-73; design engr. Rohr Industries, Inc., Chula Vista, Calif., 1973-76, sr. design engr., 1980, computer graphics engring. specialist, 1980-83; pvt. practice design engring. cons., Los Angeles, 1975-77; sr. engr. Rohr Marine, Inc., Chula Vista, 1977-79; chief exec. officer Computer Aided Tech. Services, San Diego, 1983-87; software cons. Small Systems Software, San Diego, 1984-85; computer graphics engring. specialist TOM & ROMAN, San Diego, 1986—; dir. western region Computervision Users Group, 1986-88, vice chmn. 1988—; cons. in field. George H. Mayr Found. scholar, 1971; Bate Found. Aero. Edn. scholar, 1970-72. Mem. Aircraft Owners and Pilots Assn. Office: 7770 Regents Rd Suite 113-190 San Diego CA 92122

TOM, PING, trading company executive, lawyer; b. Chgo., Apr. 15, 1935; s. Y. Chan and Lillian (Goo) T.; m. Valerie Ching Oct. 11, 1958; children—Darryl, Curtis. B.A. in Econs., Northwestern U., 1956, J.D., 1958. Bar: Ill. 1958. Vice pres. Chinese Noodle Mfg., Chgo., 1958-66; v.p. Chinese Trading Co., Chgo., 1966-72, pres., 1972—; pres. Lekel Pail Co., Chgo., 1980—, Mah Chena Corp., Chgo., 1980—, Griesbaum Meat Co., Chgo., 1981—; bd. dirs. Madison Fin. Co. holding corp. Madison Nat. Bank, Niles, Ill., 1st Nat. Bank, Wheeling, Ill.; prin. Chgo.-United; legal advisor Chinese Benevolent Assn., Chgo. Pres. Chinese Am. Civic Council, Chgo., 1973; trustee Hull House Assn., Chgo.; bd. dirs. South Side Planning Bd., Chgo.; bd. dirs. exec. com Chgo.'s Sister City Commn; mem. Chgo.'s World's Fair Corp., State of Ill. Devel. Fin. Authority; mem. bd. of advisors Mercy Hosp., Chinese Am. Service League; chmn. Chinatown Parking Corp.; pres. Chinese-Am. Devel. Corp.; mem. bldg. jury Chgo. Cen. Library Design. Mem. Chinatown C. of C. (pres. 1983). Club: Econ., Exec. (Chgo.);

Park Ridge Country. Home: 6945 Lexington Ln Niles IL 60648 Office: Chinese Trading Co 2263 Wentworth Ave Chicago IL 60616

TOMA, MAIAVA IULAI, Samoan diplomat; b. Apia, Western Samoa, July 5, 1940; m. June Carruthers, Jan. 15, 1982; 1 dau., Lillian Audrey. Ed., Soots Coll., Wellington, N.Z., Victoria U., Wellington. With Western Samoan Pub. Service Prime Ministers Dept., 1964—, sr. commr. S. Pacific Commn., 1973-74, sec. Govt. Western Samoa, 1975-77, 82—, permanent rep. to UN, 1977—; ambassador to U.S.A.; high commr., Ottawa, Can. Office: Mission of Western Samoa to UN 820 2d Ave Suite 800 New York NY 10017

TOMALIA, DONALD ANDREW, chemical company scientist; b. Owosso, Mich., Sept. 5, 1938; s. Andrew Vincent and Mary (Kondel) T.; children from previous marriage: Lynne Marie, Laurel Anne, Donald Andrew, Elizabeth Leigh; m. Janet E. Büchtenkirch, Aug. 2, 1986. B.A. in Chemistry, U. Mich., 1961; postgrad., Bucknell U., 1962; Ph.D. in Phys. Organic Chemistry, Mich. State U., 1968. Project leader Dow Chem. Co., Midland, Mich., 1966-68, group leader, 1968-71, research mgr., 1971-76, assoc. scientist, 1976-79, sr. assoc. scientist, 1979-84; research scientist Dow Chem. Co., Midland, 1984—; invited internat. lectr. Polymer Soc. Japan, Tokyo, 1978, 84, Kyoto U. and Internat. Com. Cationic Polymerization, Japan, 1980, others; adj. prof. chemistry U. S. Fla. Author: (with others) Functional Monomers, Vol. 2, 1974; contbr articles to profl. jours.; holder 74 patents in field. Recipient Indsl. Research award, 1978, 86; Disting. lectr. award Japan Soc. Polymer Sci., 1984. Mem. Am. Chem. Soc., AAAS, Sigma Xi. Home: Rt 6 463 W Chippewa River Rd Midland MI 48640 Office: Dow Chem Co 1710 Bldg Midland MI 48640

TOMAN, MIHAEL, research ecologist; b. Kamna Gorica, Slovenia, Yugoslavia, Mar. 13, 1953; s. Jozica Toman; m. Barbara Ravnik, Aug. 25, 1979; 1 child, Valentina. BS in Biotech., Edvard Kardelj U., Ljubljana, Yugoslavia, 1978, MS, 1982, PhD, 1987. Probationer Boris Kidric Inst. Chemistry, Ljubljana, 1978-80, research asst., 1980-85, researcher, 1985—; univ. asst. biotech. faculty Edvard Kardelj U., 1982-88; univ. tchr., 1988—. Author: Our Waters, 1987; contbr. articles to profl. jours. Recipient Presernova Nagrada U. Ljubljana, 1978, Krkina Nagrada Pharm. Industry, Novo Mesto, Yugoslavia, 1982; Award for Innovation Community of Ljubljana, 1986. Mem. Yugoslav Entomol. Soc. Roman Catholic. Home: Bratovseva Pl 8, 61000 Ljubljana Yugoslavia Office: Boris Kidric Inst Chemistry, Majdrihova 19, 61000 Ljubljana, Slovenia Yugoslavia

TOMAR, WILLIAM, lawyer; b. Camden, N.J., Oct. 10, 1916; s. Morris and Katie (Sadinsky) T.; m. Bette Brown, Nov. 28, 1942; children—Richard T., Dean Jonathon. LL.B. cum laude, Rutgers U., 1939. Bar: N.J. 1940, Fla. 1975, D.C. 1978, U.S. Sup. Ct. 1953. Sr. ptnr. Tomar, Seliger, Simonoff, Adourian & O'Brien, Haddonfield, N.J., 1958—;mem. faculty Ctr. Trial and Appellate Advocacy, Hastings Coll. Law, U. Calif., 1971-86, Nat. Coll. Advocacy, Harvard U. Law Sch., 1973-75. Mem. UN Speakers Bur., UNICEF, 1960—, mem. adv. bd. Salvation Army, 1967-84, N.J. Student Assistance Bd., 1987—, Inst. Med. Research, 1967—, Touro Law Sch., 1981; N.J. Capital Punishment Study Commn., 1972-73, bd. dirs. South Jersey Assn. Performing Arts, Boy Scouts of Am. Camden County Council, 1985—, Haddonfield Symphony Soc., 1985—; bd. trustees Cooper Hosp., Univ. Med. Ctr.; mem. planning com. World Peace Through Law Center, 1970—; trustee Cooper Med. Center, 1979—. Fellow Am. Coll. Trial Lawyers; mem. ABA (com. on nuclear energy 1966), Assn. Trial Lawyers Am. (assoc. editor jour. 1966—, gov. 1963-64, nat. parliamentarian 1964-70, nat. exec. com. 1964-70, chmn. seminars 1965 lectr. student advocacy program 1968—), World Assn. Lawyers (founding mem. 1974—), N.J. Bar Assn. (fee arbitration com. 1972-74, 75-77), Trial Lawyers of N.J. (cert. by Supreme Ct. of N.J. as civil trial atty., recipient trial bar award 1977), N.J. Worker's Compensation Assn. (trustee 1958-83), N.Y. Trial Lawyers Assn., Phila. Trial Lawyers Assn., Camden County Bar Found. (bd. trustees 1986—), Camden County Bar Assn. (com. on relations of bench and bar 1964—, com. on worker's compensation 1956—, adult edn. com. 1975—). Office: 41 S Haddon Ave Haddonfield NJ 08033

TOMÁS, CARLOS MARIA, public relations executive, priest; b. Reus, Tarragona, Spain, June 27, 1926; s. José T. and Gertrudis V. (Bravo) T. Lic. in Law, U. Barcelona, Spain, 1951; Lic. in Philosophy, Faculties Borja, Sant Cugat Vallés, Spain, 1960; Grad. in Econs. and Social Scis., Sociales et Economiques, Paris, 1967. Cert. laywer, pub. relations practicioner; ordained priest Roman Cath. Ch., 1964. Atty. Ministry Home Affairs, Madrid, 1953-56; dir. pub. relations Escuela Superior de Adminstrn. y Direccion de Empresas, Barcelona, 1966—. Co-author: Relaciones Públicas, 1978, Nuevo Manual de Relaciones Públicas, 1981; contbr. articles to profl. jours. Mem. Internat. Pub. Relations Assn. (past chmn. membership com.), European Confedn. of Pub. Relations (past pres. CEDET), Internat. Assn. Bus. Communicators, Spanish Pub. Relations Assn. (past v.p.), Barcelona Bar Assn. Office: ESADE, Ave Pedralbes 60, 08034 Barcelona Spain

TOMAS, JESUS BALICANTA, surgeon; b. Laoag City, Ilocos Norte, Phillipines, Dec. 22, 1950; d. Eugenio Garma and Justa (Balicanta) T. BS in Premedicine, U. Santo Tomas Coll. Sci., Manila, 1970; MD, Manila Cen. U. Coll. Medicine, 1976. Intern Armed Forces of Philippines V. Luna Meml. Med. Ctr., Quezon City, Philippines, 1976-77; physician St. Agnes Gen. Hosp., Quezon City, 1978-79; pre-licensure rural heath tng. Presdl. Secutrity Command Sta. Hosp., Manila, 1978; physician, surgeon East Ave Med. Ctr., Quezon City, 1979-83; med. specialist, surgeon Batac (Philippines) Gen. Hosp., 1984—. Recipient Pag-Ibig award Supreme Drug Abuse Council, Inc., Manila, 1985; named Outstanding Physician Profl. Community Leader Service, Inc., Manila, 1986. Mem. Philippine Med. Assn., Ilocos Norte Med. Assn. Lodge: Lions. Home: 17 Balintawak St, Laoag City Philippines Office: Batac Gen Hosp, National Hwy, Batac Philippines

TOMASEK, FRANTISEK CARDINAL, archbishop of Prague; b. Studenka, Czechslovakia, June 30, 1899; s. Frantisek and Zdenka (Vavreckova) T.; D.D., Faculty Theology, Olomouc, 1938. Ordained priest Roman Catholic Ch., 1922; tchr. religion, 1922-34; asst. Pedagogik-Catechetik, Theol. Faculty SS Cyril and Methodius, Olomouc, 1934-40; sch. insp. religion, 1940-46; lectr., then prof. pegadogics and catechetik Faculty of Theology, Olomouc, 1949-65; aux. bishop of Olomouc, 1965-77; apostolic adminstr. Archdiocese Prague, 1977—; archbishop of Prague, primate of bohemia, 1977; elevated to Sacred Coll. Cardinals, 1977. Author monographs, articles; editor: Letters on Education, 1934-47. *

TOMASEK, JAROSLAV, machinery, chemical and ordnance products company executive; b. Trebic, Czechoslovakia, Apr. 26, 1931; came to U.S., 1972, naturalized, 1978; s. Martin and Marie Tomasek; M.S.E.E., Tech. U. Prague, 1956; Ph.D., Czechoslovak Acad. Scis., 1965; m. Hana Krasna, Nov. 6, 1959. Sr. research engr. several research instns., Czechoslovakia, 1956-72; sr. design engr., chief engr., engring. mgr. Electro-Craft Corp., Hopkins, Minn., 1972-85, FMC Corp., Mpls., 1985—. Mem. IEEE (sr.), ASTM, U.S. Metric Assn. Co-author: (in Czech) Semiconductor Switching Devices, 1970; editor, co-author: DC Motors, Speed Controls, Servo Systems, 1973; contbr. numerous articles to tech. jours., also conf. papers; patentee electronic switching devices and circuits, fundamental expertise in high-performance switching servo amplifiers, brushless DC servo systems. Home: 10024 South Shore Dr Minneapolis MN 55441 Office: FMC Corp 1300 S 2d St Minneapolis MN 55459-0043

TÓMASSON, TÓMAS ÁRMANN, Icelandic ambassador to USSR; b. Reykjavik, Iceland, Jan. 1, 1929; s. Tómas and Gudrun (Thorgrímsdóttir) T.; children: Jón, Ingibörg, Tómas, Árni. BA, U. Ill., 1952; MA, Fletcher Sch. Law and Diplomacy, 1953; postgrad. Russian Inst., Columbia, 1953-54. Icelandic fgn. service officer, 1954; sec. of Embassy, Moscow, 1954-58; officer Ministry Fgn. Affairs, Reykjavik, 1958-60; 1st sec., counsellor of Embassy, Paris, 1960-66; dep. permanent rep. of Iceland to NATO and OECD, 1960-66; chief of div. Ministry Fgn. Affairs, 1966-69, chmn. def. com., dep. sec. gen., 1970-71; permanent rep. of Iceland on North Atlantic Council, ambassador to Belgium and EC, 1971-77; permanent rep. to UN, 1977-82; ambassador to France and permanent rep. to OECD and UNESCO, also accredited to Spain, Portugal, Cabo Verde, 1982-84; ambassador to Belgium and EC; Icelandic rep. to NATO, 1984-86; ambassador to the USSR, 1987—. accreditad to German Democratic Republic, Hungary, Romania, Bulgaria and Mongolia. Decorated Grand knight Order of Falcon, Iceland and Belgian, French, Luxembourg, Portuguese and Swedish orders. Mem. Cercle Royal Gaulois Artistique et Lttéraire. Home: care Utanrikisraduneytid, Reykjavik Iceland Office: Embassy of Iceland, Khlebny per 28, Moscow USSR

TOMASZEWSKI, JEREMIASZ JERZY, clinical biochemist, educator, laboratory diagnostic consultant; b. Lublin, Poland, Apr. 18, 1930; s. Wladyslaw and Genowefa (Jargiello) T.; m. Halina Elzbieta Wloch, Jan. 1, 1950; children—Tatiana, Tomasz. M.Chemistry, Slodowska-Curie U., Lublin, 1961; D. Natural Sci., U. Lublin, 1966; D. Med. Sci., Med. Acad., Lublin, 1973. Dep. dir. Central Clin. Lab., Lublin, 1961-66; head reserch ctr. Med. Acad., Lublin, 1967-79, head dept. clin. biochemistry environ. and toxicology, 1980—; mem. Nat. Specialist Bd. of Lab. Diagnostic, Warsaw, 1978—; v.p. Nat. Commn. for Lab. Equipment, Warsaw, 1979—. Contbr. numerous articles in field to profl. jours. Mem. Internat. Fedn. Clin. Chemistry, Polish Soc. Lab. Diagnostics (mem. exec. bd. 1972-79), Commn. in Clin. Pathol. Com. Polish Acad. Sci. Roman Catholic. Office: Dept Clin Biochemistry &, Environ Toxicology,, Jaczewskiego 8,, 20-950 Lublin Poland

TOMASZEWSKI, MACIEJ RYSZARD, law educator; b. Warsaw, Poland, Jan. 2, 1941; s. Antoni and Felicja Zofia (Gut) T.; m. Anna Elzanowski, June 27, 1964 (div. 1975); 1 child, Piotr; m. Walentyna Ambrozewski, Mar. 8, 1975; children: Katarzyna, Malgorzata. LLM, U. Warsaw, 1964, LLD, 1973. Adj. prof. law U. Warsaw, dir. postgrad. studies, 1975—; arbitrator Ct. Arbitration, Polish Chamber Fgn. Trade, Warsaw, 1985—. Co-author, editor: International Commercial Law, 1984; co-author: System of Common Economic Law of Comecon Countries, 1987; contbr. articles on pvt. internat. law to legal jours. Recipient Gold Cross Merit, Council State, 1985. Mem. Internat. Law Assn., Assn. Friends French Legal Culture, Inst. Internat. Bus. Law and Pzache, Internat. C. of C. (corr.). Home: UL Lesniewsla 2, 03 582 Warsaw Poland Office: U Warsaw, UL Krakowskie Przedmiescie 26/28, Warsaw Poland

TOMAZI, GEORGE DONALD, electrical engineer; b. St. Louis, Dec. 27, 1935; s. George and Sophia (Bogovich) T.; m. Lois Marie Partenheimer, Feb. 1, 1958; children: Keith, Kent. BSEE, U. Mo., Rolla, 1958, Profl. EE (hon.), 1970; MBA, St. Louis U., 1965, MSEE, 1971. Registered profl. engr., Mo., Ill., Wash., Ohio, Calif., Va. Project engr. Union Electric Co., 1958-66; dir. corp. planning Gen. Steel Industries, 1966-70; exec. v.p. St. Louis Research Council, 1970-74; exec. v.p. Hercules Constrn. Co., St. Louis, 1974-75; dir. design and constrn. div. Mallinckrodt, Inc., St. Louis, 1975—. Author: P-Science: The Role of Science in Society, 1972, The Link of Science and Religion, 1973. Active Nat. Kidney Found.; bd. dirs. U. Mo. Devel. Council, St. Louis Artists Coalition; elder Luth. Ch. Served with U.S. Army, 1959-61. Mem. NSPE, IEEE, Japan-Am. Soc., AAAS, Am. Inst. Chem. Engrs., Am. Def. Preparedness Assn., U. Mo. Alumni Assn. (bd. dirs. 1972-78), Sigma Pi. Club: Engrs. (pres. 1985-86), Mo. Athletic. Lodge: Rotary. Office: Mallinckrodt Inc 675 McDonnell Blvd Saint Louis MO 63134

TOMAZINIS, ANTHONY RUDOLF, city planning educator; b. Larissa, Greece, June 24, 1929; came to U.S., 1956, naturalized, 1966; s. Rodolfos A. and Christofily (Papamargaritou) T.; m. JoAnn R. Frank, June 24, 1962; children: Christina, Marina, Alexis. BCE, Assoc. Schs. Nat. Tech. U. Greece, 1952; M of City Planning, Ga. Inst. Tech., 1959; PhD in Planning, U. Pa., 1963. Mem. faculty U. Pa., Phila., 1962—, assoc. prof. city planning, 1966-77, prof. city and regional planning and civil engring., 1977—, chmn. transp. research group, inst. environ. studies, 1969-79, dir. Transp. Studies Center, 1969-79, chmn. univ.-wide program in transp. Transp. Studies Center, 1977—, chmn. faculty senate, 1984-87; chmn. grad. liberal studies program U. Pa., 1987—; pres. A.R. Tomazinis & Assocs., Inc.; cons. transp. and urban planning; transp. planning cons. Del. Valley Regional Commn., 1965-72, Doxiadis & Asso., Athens, Greece, 1961-64, OECD, Paris, 1970-74, Govt. Iran, 1976; mem. travel forecasting com. Transp. Reserach Bd.; Fulbright prof. city planning U. Paris, 1973-74; cons. Institut de Recherche des Transports, Paris, 1973-74. Served with Greek Armed Forces, 1953-54. Decorated medal of Meritorious Acts King of Greece, 1949. Mem. Am. Inst. Cert. Planners, Inst. Transp. Engrs. (assoc. editor Jour. Advanced Transp., Transp. Planning and Tech.), Am. Hellenic League (Phila. pres. 1967-71, 81-85, dir. 1971-80), AAAS, Regional Scis. Assn., Am. Soc. Planning Ofcls., Univ. City Arts League, Fedn. Am. Hellenic Socs. of Greater Phila. (pres. 1977-79). Club: Hellenic University. Home: 15 University Mews 45th and Spruce Sts Philadelphia PA 19104 Office: U Pa Translab 3400 Walnut St Philadelphia PA 19104

TOMBET, ANDRE, lawyer; b. Geneva, Mar. 2, 1927; s. Adolphe and Alice-Helene (Meyer) T.; LL.B., U. Geneva, 1950; postgrad. Sch. Law, London U., 1951; LL.M., Yale U., 1954; m. Dorothea von Bradsky, Sept. 7, 1957; children—Ariane, Alain. Admitted to Geneva bar, 1952; asso. firm White & Case, N.Y.C., 1954-56; individual practice law, Geneva, 1961—; legal adv. permanent dels. to UN, Geneva and fgn. cos.; dir. Swiss Deposit and Creditbank, 1984—; vice-chmn. bd. Hotel and Country Club Le Mirador, 1971—. Trustee Martin Bodmer Found., 1980—; pres. Igor Carl Faberge Found., 1983. Capt., mil. justice, 1968-80. Sterling fellow, 1953. Mem. Swiss Fedn. Lawyers, Geneva Law Soc., Internat. Bar Assn., Geneva Bar Assn. (mem. council 1984—), Internat. Assn. for Protection Indsl. Property, Swiss Soc. Bibliophiles, Internat. Assn. Bibliophiles (mem. council 1986), Soc. Geneva State Archives (mem. com. 1970—, v.p. 1983—). Clubs: Cercle De La Terrasse, Golf (com. 1983—), Am. Internat. (v.p. 1983-84, mem. exec. com. 1983—) (Geneva); Le Mirador Country (gov.); Yale (N.Y.C.). Home: 12 Chemin du Nant d'Argent, 1223 Cologny Switzerland Office: rue du Marche, 1211 Geneva 3, Switzerland

TOMBS, SIR FRANCIS (LEONARD), electric company executive; b. May 17, 1924; s. Joseph and Jane Tombs; m. Marjorie Evans, 1949; 3 daughters. BSc in Econs., Birmingham Coll. Tech.; LLD (hon.), Strathclyde U., 1976; DTech. (hon.), Loughborough U., 1979; DSc (hon.), Aston U., 1979, U. Lodz, Poland, 1980, U. Cranfield, 1985; DLitt. (hon.), U. Bradford, 1986. With GEC, 1939-45, Erith, 1957-65; with Birmingham Corp., 1946-47, Brit. Electricity Authority, Midlands; then with Cen. Electicity Authority, Merseyside and N. Wales, 1947-57; with C.A. Parsons, Erith, 1965-68, James Howden and Godfrey Ltd., 1968-69; successively dir. engring., dep. chmn., chmn. South of Scotland Electricity Bd., 1969-77; chmn. Electricity Council, 1977-80, Weir Group, 1981-83, Turner and Newall, 1982—; chmn. Rolls-Royce, 1985—; bd. dirs. N.M. Rothschild and Sons, Shell-U.K.; mem. Standing Commn. on Energy and the Environment , 1978—, SERC, 1982-85. Chmn. Engring. Council, 1985—, ACARD, 1985-87, ACOST, 1987—; mem. Nature Conservancy Council, 1978—. Decorated Knight, 1978. Mem. IEE (pres. 1981-82), Assn. Brit. Orchestras (chmn. 1982-86). Office: Honington Lodge, Honington, Shipston-upon-Stour, Warwickshire CV36 5AA, England *

TOMER, HERMAN DEEMAR, information systems management executive; b. New Kensington, Pa., May 3, 1949; s. Neil Charles and Artene Donna (Olivo) T.; m. Barbara Ann Corsi, Apr. 20, 1985; children: Lisa, Neil, Danielle, Sara, Lauren, Leslie. BS, Edinboro U., 1971. Mem. mktg. staff IBM, Pitts., 1977-81; dir. mgmt. info. systems Internat. Group of Allegheny Internat., London, 1981-82, Advanced Info. Programs, Pitts., 1983-86; staff v.p. info. services Allegheny Internat., Pitts., 1986-87; staff v.p. info. services Sonoco Products Co., Hartsville, S.C., 1987—. Mem. Pitts. World Affairs Council, 1977—. Served to lt. commdr. USN, 1971-77, Vietnam. Mem. Brit. Inst. Mgmt., Soc. for Info. Mgmt., Pitts. Info. Execs. Republican. Roman Catholic. Lodge: Rotary. Avocations: photography, travel, golf. Home: 200 Park Ave Hartsville SC 29550 Office: Sonoco Products Co 400 N 2d St Hartsville SC 29550

TOMICH, LILLIAN, lawyer; b. Los Angeles, Mar. 28, 1935; d. Peter S. and Yovanka P. (Ivanovic) T. AA, Pasadena City Coll., 1954; BA in Polit. Sci., UCLA, 1956, cert. secondary teaching, 1957, MA, 1958; JD, U. So. Calif., 1961. Bar: Calif. Sole practice, 1961-66; house counsel Mfrs. Bank, Los Angeles, 1966; ptnr. Hurley, Shaw & Tomich, San Marino, Calif., 1968-76, Driscoll & Tomich, San Marino, 1976—; dir. Continental Culture Specialists Inc., Glendale, Calif. Trustee, St. Sava Serbian Orthodox Ch., San Gabriel, Calif. Charles Fletcher Scott fellow, 1957; U. So. Calif. Law Sch. scholar, 1958. Mem. ABA, Calif. Bar Assn., Los Angeles County Bar Assn., Women Lawyers Assn., UCLA Alumni Assn., Town Hall and World Affairs Council, Order Mast and Dagger, Iota Tau Tau, Alpha Gamma Sigma. Office: 2297 Huntington Dr San Marino CA 91108

TOMIMOTO, MASASUKE, leasing executive; b. Tokushima, Japan, May 21, 1934; s. Zenichi and Yasuko (Morinaga) T.; m. Kazuko Okuma, Jan. 4, 1959; children: Kyoko, Noriko. B, Tokushima U., 1957. Cert. elec. engring. Sales engr. Ataka & Co., Tokyo, 1957-69; mgr. Showa Leasing Co., Tokyo, 1969-71, gen. mgr., 1971-76, v.p., 1979-84, dir., gen. mgr., 1984—; dir., gen. mgr. Itel Japan, Tokyo, 1976-79. Home: 4-37-10, Kinuta, Tokyo Setagaya-ku 157, Japan Office: Showa Leasing Co Ltd, 3-10-43, Minami-Aoyama, Tokyo Minato-ku 107, Japan

TOMIYASU, HIDEO, town planning consultant, architect; b. Nagasaki, Kyushu, Japan, Feb. 6, 1928; s. Junichi and Tome T.; m. Michiko Tanei, Mar. 8, 1958; children: Yoko, Shun, Ken. B in Engring., Tokyo U. Registered first class architect, Japan. With Ichiura Urban Devel. & Housing Cons., Tokyo, 1954-62, ptnr. Osaka br., 1962-81, pres., 1981—; with Project Planning Assn., Toronto, Ont., Can., 1962-63; vis. prof. Osaka U., 1971—, Tokyo U., 1986—. chief planner Senri New Town, 1963-68, Senboku New Town, 1964, Tama New Town (West), 1970—. Mem. Japan Archtl. Inst., Town Planning Cons. Assn. (bd. dirs.). Home: 3-2-5-708 Minamiosawa, Hachioji, Tokyo 192-03, Japan Office: Ichiura Urban Planning Cons, 5-1-10-201 Minami Adyama, Tokyo Minato-ku 107, Japan

TOMKINS, BRUCE ALLEN, chemist; b. Providence, Aug. 2, 1951; s. Chester and Leonora B. Tomkins. B.A., U. Conn., 1973; M.S., U. Ill., 1975, Ph.D., 1978. Staff chemist analytical chemistry div. Oak Ridge Nat. Lab., 1978—. Mem. Am. Chem. Soc., Am. Inst. Chemists, Phi Beta Kappa, Sigma Xi, Phi Kappa Phi. Contbr. articles to profl. jours. Home: 103 E Holston Ln Oak Ridge TN 37830 Office: Oak Ridge Nat Lab Bldg 2026 MS 043 Oak Ridge TN 37831-6043

TOMKO, JOZEF CARDINAL, cardinal Roman Catholic Church; b. Udavake, Kosice, Czechoslovakia, Mar. 11, 1924. ordained 1949. Consecrated bishop Titular See Doclea, 1979; proclaimed cardinal 1985; sec.-gen. Synod Bishops; Pro-Prefect Congregation for the Evangelization of Peoples. Address: Villa Betania, Via Urbano VIII 16, 00165 Rome Italy *

TOMLINSON, JOHN RACE GODFREY, education educator; b. Manchester, Eng., Apr. 24, 1932; s. John Angell and Beatrice Elizabeth Race (Godfrey) T.; m. Audrey Mavis Barrett, Mar. 27, 1954; children: John, Susan, Janet, Graham. BA, Manchster U., 1953, MA, 1955. Tchr. LEA, Stoke-on-Trent, Eng., 1958-60; adminstrv. officer LEA, Shropshire County, Eng., 1960-63; asst. edn. officer LEA, Lancashire County, Eng., 1963-67; dep. dir., then dir. edn. LEA, Cheshire County, 1967-85; dir. Inst. Edn. U. Warwick, Warwickshire, 1985—; chmn Schs. Curriculum Award com., Eng., 1982—, Manpower Services Commn., Eng., 1985—. Editor Grenville Papers, 1963-65; co-editor Changing Government of Education, 1986. Served to flight lt. RAF, 1955-58. Commdr. Order of British Empire. Fellow Brit. Inst. Mgmt., Coll. Preceptors, Royal Soc. Arts; mem. Royal No. Coll. Music. Clubs: Army and Navy, Royal Overseas (London). Office: Univ Warwick Inst Edn, Coventry CV4 7AL, England

TOMLINSON, ROBERT JOHN, energy industry legal executive; b. Detroit, May 4, 1936; s. Harry John and Helen Adele (Strauss) T.; m. Margaret Armstrong, June 9, 1962 (div. 1977); 1 child, Justin Hudspeth. BA in Econs., U. Mich., 1958; JD, Wayne State U., 1961. Bar: Mich. 1962, Wash. 1972. Internat. atty. Parke Davis & Co., Detroit, 1962-68; assoc. Heritier & Abbott, Detroit, 1969-70; atty. Mich. Consol. Gas Co., Detroit, 1970-72; sr. v.p. legal Wash. Energy Co. & Subs., Seattle, 1972—; bd. dirs. Mercer Ins. Co., Hamilton, Bermuda. Mem. ABA, Am. Soc. Corp. Secs. (pres. n.w. region 1978-79), Pacific Coast Gas Assn. (legal adv. com. 1977—, legal sect. chmn. 1977, 78, 80, 85), N.W. Gas Assn., Chi Phi. Clubs: Bellevue Athletic (Wash.); Seattle Athletic. Home: 6321 Seaview Ave NW Seattle WA 98107 Office: Washington Energy Co 815 Mercer St Seattle WA 98109

TOMLINSON, STEPHENSON ANTHONY, surgeon; b. Cayman Islands, W.I., Nov. 14, 1950; s. Anthony Daniel and Chrissie Bell (Martin) T.; m. Margaret Evans, Jan. 1, 1973 (div. 1976). B of Surgery, Univ. of the W.I., 1973. House med. officer Univ. W.I. Hosp., Kingston, Jamaica, 1973-74, emergency officer, 1974-75, anesthetist, 1975-76; gen. surgeon Queen Elizabeth Hosp., Bridgetown, Barbados, 1976-77, East Birmingham (Eng.) Hosp., 1977-78, Wordsley (Eng.) Hosp., 1978-79; med. officer Cayman Islands Hosp., Grand Cayman, 1979-83; pvt. practice medicine specializing in gen. surgery Grand Cayman, 1983—; advisor Grand Cayman Cancer Support Soc., 1985-87. Organizer Grand Cayman Parks Programme, 1987. Mem. Brit. Med. Assn., Cayman Island Med. and Dental Soc. (exec. officer 1980-81), Grand Cayman C. of C. (adv. officer health com. 1984-85). Home and Office: PO Box 273, Grand Cayman West Indies

TOMLINSON, WILLIAM HOLMES, management educator, retired army officer, b. Thornton, Ark., Apr. 12, 1922; s. Hugh Oscar and Lucy Gray (Holmes) T.; m. Dorothy Payne, June 10, 1947 (dec.); children: Jane Axtell, Lucy Gray, William Payne; m. Florence Mood Smith, May 1, 1969 (div.); m. Suzanne Scollard Gill, Mar. 16, 1977. BS, U.S. Mil. Acad., 1943; grad. Air Command Staff Coll., 1958; MBA, U. Ala., 1960; MS in Internat. Affairs, George Washington U., 1966; grad. U.S. Army War Coll., 1966; grad. Indsl. Coll. Armed Forces; PhD in Bus. Adminstrn., Am. U., 1974; postgrad. Advanced Mgmt. Program, Harvard U., 1968, 69. Commd. 2d lt. U.S. Army, 1943, advanced through grades to col., field arty., 1966; service in Philippines, Japan; aide de camp, comdg. gen. 8th Army, 1945-48; mem. Office of Undersec. Army, Pentagon, Washington, 1961-64; comdr. 2d Bn., 8th Arty. and 7th Div. Arty., S. Korea, 1964-65; faculty Indsl. Coll. Armed Forces, Ft. McNair, Washington, 1966-72, ret., 1973; faculty U. North Fla., Jacksonville, 1973—, assoc. prof. mgmt., 1976—; vis. prof. U. Glasgow, Scotland, fall 1987; mem. Nat. Def. Exec. Res., Fed. Emergency Mgmt. Agy., 1976—. Decorated Bronze Star, Legion of Merit, Philippine Liberation medal, Japanese Occupation medal; recipient Freedom Found. award, 1973, Sr. Profl. in Human Resources. Mem. Acad. Mgmt., NE Fla. for Nat., Am. Soc. Personnel Adminstrn., Indsl. Relations Research Assn., Acad. Internat. Bus., European Internat. Bus. Assn., Co. Mil. Historians, Nat. Eagle Scout Assn., Nat. Employee Services Assn. (pres. 1987), Co. Mil Historians, West Point Soc. N. Fla. (pres. 1976), Mil. Order Stars and Bars (Fl. state comdr.), Beta Gamma Sigma. Presbyterian (elder). Clubs: Army Navy, Army Navy Country, Fla. Yacht, Kappa Alpha Order. Lodges: Masons (32 deg.), Shriners, Rotary. Contbr. articles and case studies to profl. jours. and books. Home: 1890 Shadowlawn Jacksonville FL 32205 Office: U North Fla Dept Mgmt 4567 S St Johns Bluff Rd Jacksonville FL 32216

TOMOBUCHI, MITSUHIRO, trading company executive; b. Neyagawa, Osaka, Japan, Feb. 11, 1957; s. Banji and Misako T.; m. Takako Tomobuchi, May 10, 1986. BS in Metallurgy, Kyoto U., Japan, 1980. With machinery dept. Kawasho Corp., Tokyo, 1980-83, with electronic systems dept., 1983—. Home: 4-39-1-319 Narashinodai, Funabashi 274, Japan Office: Kawasho Corp, World Trade Ctr Bldg 30F, 4-1 Hamamatsu-cho, 2-chome, Tokyo Minato-ku 105, Japan

TOMPANE, MARY BETH, management consultant; b. Hollywood, Calif., Sept. 27, 1928; d. Richard Earl and Mary Elizabeth (McGregor) Goss; A.A., Phoenix Coll., 1948; postgrad. No. Ariz. U., Ariz. State U., 1946-55; M.Banking Mgmt., U. Calif., Riverside, 1973; m. Eugene F. Tompane, Nov. 4, 1950; children—Michael, Richard, Donald, John. Mgmt. analyst, 1955-69; dept. head Boswell Hosp., Sun City, Ariz., 1969-72; non profit orgn. cons., Phoenix, 1972—; travel agt., Phoenix and Tempe, Ariz., 1972-81; interim exec. dir. Girl Scouts U.S.A., from 1981; mem. nat. women's bd. Northwood Inst., 1980—. Pres. YWCA of Maricopa County, 1962-65, Phoenix Day Nursery, 1965-67, Anytown USA, 1967-69, Friends of Thunderbird, 1975-77, Family Service Phoenix, 1980; Horizona chmn. Bicentennial City of Phoenix, 1974-76; bd. dirs. Tempe United Way, 1981-86, Tempe Regional Valley of the Sun United Way, 1986—, Tempe Community Council, 1982-85. Named Woman of Year, Phoenix, 1965. Mem. Internat. Assn. Vol. Edn., Dirs. of Vols., Am. Assn. Assn. Execs. Republican. Episcopalian.

TOMPKINS, CURTIS JOHNSTON, college dean; b. Roanoke, Va., July 14, 1942; s. Joseph Buford and Rebecca (Johnston) T.; m. Mary Katherine

Hasle, Sept. 5, 1964; children: Robert, Joseph, Rebecca. B.S., Va. Poly. Inst., 1965, M.S., 1967; Ph.D., Ga. Inst. Tech., 1971. Indsl. engr. E.I. DuPont de Nemours, Richmond, Va., 1965-67; instr. Sch. Indsl. and Systems Engrng., Ga. Inst. Tech., Atlanta, 1968-71; assoc. prof. Colgate Darden Grad. Sch. Bus. Adminstrn., U. Va., Charlottesville, 1971-77; prof., chmn. dept. indsl. engrng. W.Va. U., Morgantown, 1977-80; dean Coll. Engrng., 1980—; mem. engrng. accreditation commn. Accreditation Bd. for Engrng. and Tech., 1981-86; chief fin. officer Inst. Ndsl. Engrs., 1987-88, pres., chmn. bd., 1988—; mem. exec. bd. Engrng. Deans Council, 1985—, vice chmn., 1987—; mem. Commn. on Engrng. Edn., Nat. Assn. State Univs. and Land Grant Colls., 1985—; cons. corps., govt. agys., ednl. instns.; lectr. various univs. Author: (with L.E. Grayson) Management of Public Sector and Nonprofit Organizations, 1983; contbr.: chpt. to Ency. of Profl. Mgmt, 1978, 83. Bd. dirs. Public Land Corp. of W.Va., 1980—; mem. faculty Nat. Acad. Voluntarism, United Way Am., 1976—; mem. Morgantown Water Commn., 1981-87, Morgantown Utility Bd., 1987—; mem. steering com. W.Va. Conf. on Environment, 1985—. Mem. Am. Soc. Engrng. Edn. (chmn. indsl. engrng. div. 1981-82, v.p. pub. affairs 1985-87, bd. dirs. 1985-87, v.p. 1986-87), Inst. Indsl. Engrs. (sr., v.p. publs. 1983-85, v.p. edn. and research 1985-87, trustee 1983—, pres.-elect 1987-88, pres. 1988-89), Am. Assn. Engrng. Socs. (bd. govs. 1987-90, exec. com. 1987—), Jr. Engrng. Tech. Soc. (bd. dirs. 1988—), Sigma Xi, Phi Kappa Phi, Tau Beta Pi, Alpha Pi Mu. Methodist. Home: 1453 Anderson Ave Morgantown WV 26505 Office: Coll Engrng WVa U Morgantown WV 26506

TOMPKINS, JOSEPH BUFORD, JR., lawyer; b. Roanoke, Va., Apr. 4, 1950; s. Joseph Buford and Rebecca Louise (Johnston) T.; m. Stewart Hamilton Gamage, Feb. 28, 1976; children—Edward Graves, Claiborne Forbes. B.A. in Politics summa cum laude, Washington and Lee U., 1971; M.P.P. in Pub. Policy, Harvard U., 1975, J.D., 1975. Bar: Va. 1975, U.S. Dist. Ct. D.C. 1982, U.S. Ct. Appeals (D.C. cir.) 1976, U.S. Ct. Appeals (5th cir.) 1977, U.S. Ct. Appeals (11th cir.) 1982, U.S. Ct. Appeals (3d cir.) 1983, U.S. Ct. Appeals (6th cir.) 1985, U.S. Supreme Ct. 1977. Assoc. Sidley & Austin, Washington, 1975-79, ptnr., 1982—; assoc. dir. Office of Policy and Mgmt. Analysis, criminal div. U.S. Dept Justice, Washington, 1979-81, dep. chief fraud sect. criminal div., 1981-82. Contbr. articles to legal publs. Mem., vice chmn. Va. Commn. Health Regulatory Bds., Richmond, Va., 1984-86, chmn., 1986—. Recipient Spl. Commendation, U.S. Dept. Justice, 1981. Mem. ABA (criminal justice sect., mem. white collar crime com., 1980—, chmn. task force on computer crime; 1982—), Va. Bar Assn., D.C. Bar Assn., Fed. Bar Assn., Phi Beta Kappa. Democrat. Methodist. Home: 6102 Woodmont Rd Alexandria VA 22307 Office: Sidley & Austin 1722 Eye St NW Washington DC 20006

TOMPKINS, RAYMOND EDGAR, lawyer; b. Oklahoma City, July 13, 1934; s. Charles Edgar and Eva Mae (Hodges) T.; m. Sue Anne Sharpe, June 10, 1963; children: Matthew Stephen, Christopher T., Katherine Anne. BS, Okla. State U., 1956; JD, U. Okla., 1963. Bar: Okla. 1963, U.S. Dist. Ct. (no. dist.) Okla. 1963, U.S. Dist. Ct. (we. dist.) Okla. 1964, U.S. Ct. Appeals (10th cir.) 1965, U.S. Supreme Ct. 1968, U.S. Dist. Ct. (ea. dist.) Okla. 1969, U.S. Ct. Appeals (9th cir.) 1981, U.S. Ct. Appeals (4th cir.) 1986. Ptnr. Hanson, Peterson & Tompkins, Oklahoma City, 1963-66, 68-80; adminstrv. asst. U.S. Congress, 1966-68; ptnr. Linn & Helms, Oklahoma City, 1980—. Chmn. bd. trustees Okla. Ann. Methodist Conf.; mem. Okla. State Rep. Exec. Com. Served to maj. USAR, 1956-71. Recipient award of Honor Oklahoma City Bi-Centennial Commn., 1976. Mem. ABA, Okla. County Bar Assn., Okla. Bar Assn. (Law Day award), Am. Judicature Soc., Blue Key. Club: Lions (Oklahoma City). Home: 329 NW 40th Oklahoma City OK 73118 Office: Bank of Okla Bldg Suite 1200 Oklahoma City OK 73102

TOMPKINS, ROBERT GEORGE, physician; b. Portland, Oreg., May 29, 1923; s. George Henry and Minnie (Davies) T.; m. Rosemarie Nowicki, June 6, 1948 (dec. 1960); children: Timothy Michael, Mary Eileen, George Henry, Robert George. B.S., U. Wash., 1943; M.B., Northwestern U., 1947; M.D., 1949; M.S., U. Minn., 1954. Diplomate Am. Bd. Internal Medicine. Intern King County Hosp., Seattle, 1948-49; resident King County Hosp., 1949-50; fellow, 1st asst. Mayo Found., Rochester, Minn., 1950-54; practice medicine specializing in cardiology and internal medicine Tulsa, 1954—; mem. staff St. Francis Hosp., chief staff, 1964, med. dir., 1968-86; clin. prof. medicine Tulsa Med. Coll. and U. Okla. Med. Coll.; v.p., med. dir. William K. Warren Med. Research Center; med. chmn. Guatemala Mission Hosp., Diocese Oklahoma City and Tulsa; coordinator planning program Okla. Regional Med. Program; mem. Tulsa Health and Hsp. Planning Council; bd. dirs. St. Francis Hosp., 1968-86. Contbr. articles to profl. jours; editor: Jour. Okla. State Med. Assn, 1974-86. Decorated knight Equestrian Order Holy Sepulchre of Jerusalem, Vatican); Knight Sovereign Mil. Order of Malta. Fellow A.C.P., Royal Coll. Medicine, Am. Coll. Cardiology; mem. AAAS, AMA, Am. Diabetic Assn., Am. Heart Assn., Tulsa County Heart Assn. (pres. 1959), Am. rheumatism Assn., Mayo Alumni Assn., Alpha Kappa Kappa. Club: K.C. Home: 6551 S Darlington Tulsa OK 74136 Office: 6161 Yale St S Tulsa OK 74136

TOMPSON, MARIAN LEONARD, association executive, b. Chgo., Dec. 5, 1929; d. Charles Clark and Marie Christine (Bernardini) Leonard; m. Clement R. Tompson, May 7, 1949 (dec. 1981); children: Melanie Tompson Kandler, Deborah Tompson Mikolajczak, Allison Tompson Fagerholm, Laurel Tompson Davies, Sheila Tompson Dorsey, Brian, Philip. Student public and parochial schs., Chgo. and Franklin Park, Ill. Co-founder La Leche League (Internat.), Franklin Park, Ill., 1956; pres. La Leche League (Internat.), 1956-80, dir., 1956—; exec. dir. Alternative Birth Crisis Coalition, 1981-85; cons. WHO; bd. dirs. North Am. Soc. Psychosomatic Ob-Gyn, Natural Birth and Natural Parenting, 1981-83; mem. adv. bd. Nat. Assn. Parents and Profls. for Safe Alternatives in Childbirth, Am. Acad. Husband-Coached Childbirth; mem. profl. adv. bd. Home Oriented Maternity Experience; guest lectr. Harvard U. Med. Sch., UCLA Sch. Public Health, U. Antioquia Med. Sch., Medellin, Columbia, U. Ill. Sch. Medicine, Chgo., U. W.I., Jamaica, U. N.C., Nat. Coll. of Chiropractic, Am. Coll. Nurse Midwives, U. Parma, Italy, Inst. Psychology, Rome, Rockford (Ill.) Sch. Medicine, Northwestern U. Sch. Medicine; mem. family com. Ill. Commn. on Status of Women, 1976-85; mem. perinatal adv. com. Ill. Dept. Pub. Health, 1980-83; mem. adv. bd. Internat. Nutrition Communication Service, 1980—; bd. cons. We Can, 1984—; exec. adv. bd. United Resources for Family Health and Support, 1985-86. Author: (with others) Safe Alternatives in Childbirth, 1976, 21st Century Obstetrics Now!, 1977, The Womanly Art of Breastfeeding, 3d edit, 1981, Five Standards for Safe Childbearing, 1981; author prefaces and forwards in 7 books; columnist: La Leche League News, 1958-80, People's Doctor Newsletter, 1977—; contbr. articles to profl. jours.; assoc. editor: Child and Family Quar., 1967— ; mem. med. adv. bd. East West Jour., 1980—. Recipient Gold medal of honor Centro de Rehabilitacao Nossa Senhora da Gloria, 1975. Office: 9616 Minneapolis Ave Franklin Park IL 60131

TOMS, KATHLEEN MOORE, nurse; b. San Francisco, Dec. 31, 1943; d. William Moore and Phyllis Josephine (Barry) Stewart; RN, AA, City Coll. San Francisco, 1963; BPS in Nursing Edn., Elizabethtown (Pa.) Coll., 1973; MS in Edn., Temple U., 1977; MS in Nursing, Gwynedd Mercy Coll. 1988; m. Benjamin Peskoff; children from previous marriage: Kathleen Marie Toms, Kelly Terese Toms. Med.-surg. nurse St. Joseph Hosp., Fairbanks, Alaska, 1963-65; emergency room nurse St. Joseph Hosp., Lancaster, Pa., 1965-69, blood, plasm and components nurse, 1969-71; pres. F.E. Barry Co., Lancaster, 1971—; dir. inservice edn. Lancaster Osteo. Hosp., 1971-75; coordinator practical nursing program Vocat. Tech. Sch., Coatesville, Pa., 1976-77; dir. nursing Pocopson Home, West Chester, Pa., 1978-80, Riverside Hosp., Wilmington, Del., 1980-83; assoc. Coatesville VA Hosp., 1983—; chief Nurse, 1984—; with VA Cen. Office; trainee assoc. chief Nursing Home Care Unit, Washington; mem. Pa. Gov.'s Council on Alcoholism and Drug Abuse, 1974-76; mem. Del. Health Council Med.-Surg. Task Force, 1981—; dir. Lancaster Community Health Center, 1973-76; lectr. in field. Served to maj. Nurse Corps, USAR, 1973—. Decorated Army Commendation medal; recipient Community Service award Citizens United for Better Public Relations, 1974; award Sertoma, Lancaster, 1974; Outstanding Citizen award Sta. WGAL-TV, 1975; U.S. Army Achievement award, 1983. Mem. Elizabethtown, Temple U. Alumni Assns., Pa. Nurses' Assn. (dir.), Sigma Theta Tau, Iota Kappa. Inventor auto-infuser for blood or blood components, 1971. Home: 400 Summit House 1450 West Chester Pike West Chester PA 19380 Office: Coatesville VA Med Ctr Black Horse Pike Coatesville PA 19320

TOMTER, PER, mathematician; b. Moss, Norway, June 16, 1939; s. Anders and Liv Anker (Hassel) T. Candidatus magisterii, U. Oslo, 1962, Candidatus Realium, 1965; Ph.D., U. Calif.-Berkeley, 1969. Asst. in maths. U. Oslo, 1962-66, prof., 1970-77, 80—; prof. U. Tromso, Norway, 1977-79; gastforscher Sonderforschungsbereich, U. Bonn, W.Ger., 1971-72; vis. prof. dept. math. U. Calif., Los Angeles, 1985, San Diego, 1986. Contbr. articles to profl. jours. Fulbright grantee, 1965. Mem. Norwegian Math. Soc., Am. Math. Soc. Lutheran. Avocations: judo; travel; history. Office: U Oslo Matematisk Inst, Blindern, 3 Oslo Norway

TOMUSCHAT, HANS CHRISTIAN ULRICH, lawyer, educator; b. Stettin, Fed. Republic of Germany, July 23, 1936; s. Ernst and Erica (Schoder) T.; m. Heide E. Mohr (div. 1986); children: Julia, Philipp. BA, U. Heidelberg, Fed. Republic Germany, 1959, JD, 1964, PhD, 1970. Prof., dir. inst. internat. law U. Bonn, Fed. Republic Germany, 1972; Author books in field constl. pub. internat. law; contbr. articles to profl. jours., 1964-87. Mem. U.N. Human Rights Com., N.Y.C., Geneva, 1977-86, U.N. Internat. Law Commn., Geneva, 1985-1991. Recipient prize Legatum Visserianum, Netherlands, 1964. Mem. Internat. Commn. Jurists, German Assn. Internat. Law (council), Assn. German Tchrs. Constl. Law (bd. dirs. 1986-87). Home: Kautexstrasse 43, D-5300 3 Bonn Federal Republic of Germany Office: Inst Völkerrecht, Adenauerallee 24-42, 1 Bonn Federal Republic of Germany

TONDA, RICHARD DALE, mechanical engineer; b. Oskaloosa, Iowa, Apr. 12, 1952; s. Richard William and Betty Lee (Trinkle) T.; m. Vicki Lynn Sterling, Aug. 5, 1972; children—Richard Aaron, Heather Richelle. B.M.E., Gen. Motors Inst., 1975; M.S. in Engrng. Mechanics, Mich. State U., 1976; Ph.D., Tex. A&M U., 1986. Registered profl. engr., Tex., Mich. Jr. engr. Oldsmobile div. Gen. Motors Corp., Lansing, Mich., 1974-75; research asst. Mich. State U., East Lansing, 1975-76; asst. prof. Coll. Engrng., Tex. A&M U., College Station, 1976-79; head, proving grounds Tex. Transp. Inst., Tex. A&M U. System, College Station, 1978-80; mgr. materials and structures lab. Tex. Transp. Inst., Tex. A&M U., College Station, 1983-84, mgr. automotive research program, 1980-87; assoc. prof. mech. engrng. GMI Engrng. & Mgmt. Inst.; dir. Engitech, Inc., College Station. Author: Graphics for Engineers III, 1978. Mem. Soc. Automotive Engrs., Tex. Soc. Profl. Engrs. (chpt. pres. 1983-84, Outstanding Young Engr. 1984), Soc. Automotive Engrs. (Ralph Teeter award for Outstanding Engrng. Educator 1987), ASME, Soc. Plastics Engr. Republican. Methodist. Lodge: Masons. Current work: Research in automotive emissions and fuel economy, vehicle handling and design; work in area of solid mechanics research into constitutive behavior of high-performance, fiber-reinforced composites, especially as they apply to determining and predicting fracture behavior of the composite. Subspecialties: Mechanical engineering; Composite materials.

TONEGAWA, SUSUMU, biology educator; b. Nagoya, Japan, Sept. 5, 1939; came to U.S., 1963; s. Tsutomu and Miyoko (Masuko) T.; m. Mayumi Yoshinari, Sept. 28, 1985; 1 child, Hidde Tonegawa. B.S., Kyoto U., Japan, 1963; Ph.D., U. Calif.-San Diego, 1968. Research asst. U. Calif.-San Diego, 1963-64, teaching asst., 1964-68; mem. Basel Inst. Immunology, Switzerland, 1971-81; prof. biology MIT, Cambridge, 1981—. Editorial bd. Jour. Molecular and Cellular Immunology. Decorated Order of Culture, Emperor of Japan; recipient Cloetta prize, 1978, Avery Landsteiner prize Gesselschaft für Immunologie, 1981, Louisa Gross Horwitz prize Columbia U., 1982, award Gairdner Found. Internat., Toronto, Can., 1983, Robert Koch Found. prize, Bonn. Rep. of West Germany, 1986, co-recipient Albert Lasker Med. Research award, 1987, Nobel prize in Physiology or Medicine, 1987; named Person with Cultural Merit Japanese Govt., 1983. Mem. NAS (fgn. assoc.), Am. Assn. Immunologists (hon.), Scandinavian Soc. Immunology (hon.). Office: MIT 77 Massachusetts Ave Cambridge MA 02139 *

TONEV, TOMA VASSILEV, mathematician, educator, researcher; b. Sofia, Bulgaria, Apr. 5, 1945; s. Vassil Jossifov and Zarina Kostova (Boyadzhieva) T.; m. Elena Todorova Lyubenova, Dec. 29, 1974; children—Daniela, Vassilena. Magister in Math., U. Sofia, 1969; Ph.D. in Math. and Physics, Moscow State U., 1973. Instr. U. Sofia, 1968-69, asst. prof., 1969-83, lectr., 1977—; research fellow Bulgarian Acad. Scis., Sofia, 1974-83, assoc. prof. math., 1983—; invited lectr. Banach Centre, Warsaw, Poland, 1978, 82, Internat. Centre Theoretical Physics, Trieste, Italy, 1988, Oberwolfach, Fed. Republic of Germany (FRG), 1985, 86, U. Md., 1986; vis. prof. Moscow State U., 1978, U. Ulm, FRG, 1985, Hokkaido U. Sapporo, Japan, 1987, U. Saarlandes, FRG, 1986; reviewer Math. Revs., Ann Arbor, Mich., 1975—, Zentralblatt fur Mathematik, Berlin, 1982—; sec. Internat. Confs. Complex Analysis, Varna, Bulgaria, 1981, 83, 85, 87. Editor: Complex Analysis, 1985, 86; Serdica-Bulgarian Math Pubs., 1987—; Pliska-Studia Math. Bulgaria, 1988. Recipient Young Researcher prize with hon. diploma Union Balkan Mathematicians, 1975. Fellow Union Scientists in Bulgaria; mem. Am. Math. Soc., Polish Math. Soc., Deutsche Math. Vereinigung, Union Bulgarian Mathematicians. Home: Chataldzha St 2-A, BG-1527 Sofia Bulgaria Office: Bulgarian Acad Scis Inst Math, PO Box 373, BG-1090 Sofia Bulgaria

TONG, JOHN YEH CHANG, oil executive; b. Shanghai, China, Aug. 1, 1931; s. Teh Foo and Lee Chuan (Chang) T.; m. Vivinne Ting, Oct. 5, 1956; children—Patricia, Peggy, Jackson, Jefferina, Jefferson, Pollyana. B.A., St. Vincent Coll., 1952; M.A., Columbia U., 1954. Ptnr., Granja Arco-Iris, Passo Fundo-RGS, 1957-63; dir. Tabacaria Londres, Rio de Janeiro, 1964-71, Granoleo S/A, Porto Alegre, Brazil, 1975—; cons. Socopa Corretora, Sao Paulo, 1972-75. Author: A Bolsa e a Bossa, 1971; A Bigamia Monetaria, 1980. Contbr. articles to profl. jours. Roman Catholic. Avocations: tennis; swimming. Home: Rua Bororo 315 Porto Alegre, Rio Grande do Sol Brazil Office: Granoleo S/A, Ave Cavalhada 4050, 90.000 Porto Alegre Rio Grande do Sol Brazil

TONG, PEARCE, film producer; b. Shanghai, China, Feb. 2, 1935; m. Wai-Ling. Student, English Coll., Hong Kong, 1949-55, Bus. Adminstrn. Inst., Hong Kong, 1956-59. Sales mgr. Nat. Cash Register Co., Hong Kong, 1960-62; owner Hong Kong Recording Co., 1963-69, Empire Records, Hong Kong, 1963-69; pres. Pearce Comml. Studios Ltd., Hong Kong, 1970-74; producer Leo Burnett Advt. Agy., Hong Kong, 1975-77; dir. Nancy Kwan Films Ltd., Hong Kong, 1978-80; producer Shaw Studio, Hong Kong, 1981-85; exec. producer Magnum Films Ltd., Hong Kong, 1986-87; producer owner Pearce Prodns., Hong Kong, 1988—. Home and Office: Pearce Prodns, C4-16F Great George Bldg, Causeway Bay A3135 Hong Kong

TONGREN, JOHN DAVID, computer security company executive, management consultant; b. Erie, Pa., Dec. 1, 1942; s. John Corbin and Alice Jeanette (Jones) T.; m. Nancy Cowie, Aug. 28, 1965 (div. Dec. 1972); 1 son, Jon Eric; m. Kathleen McKay, Feb. 14, 1981. B.A., DePauw U., 1964; M.B.A., U. Mich., 1965; postgrad. Calif. Coast U., Santa Ana, 1987—. Cert. info. systems auditor; cert. systems profl., cert. mgmt. acct. Cost study coordinator U. Louisville, 1971-72; sr. internal auditor Westinghouse Co., Columbus, Ohio, 1972-74, corp. audit mgr.-audit systems, Pitts., 1974-78; mgmt. cons. Alexander Grant & Co., Chgo., 1978-79, nat. dir. computer acctg. and auditing, 1979-81; pres. Tongren & Assocs., Muskegon, Mich., 1981—; dir. edn. EDP Auditors Found., Chgo., 1983-85. Vice-pres. Saddle Lake Property Owners Assn., Grand Junction, Mich., 1983. Mem. EDP Auditors Assn. (pres. Pitts. chpt. 1975-76, bd. dirs. Chgo. chpt. 1986-88), Inst. Internal Auditors, Inst. Cert. Mgmt. Accts., Info. Systems Security Assn., Meeting Planners Internat., Computer Security Inst.

TONKIN, HUMPHREY RICHARD, university president; b. Truro, Cornwall, Eng., Dec. 2, 1939; came to U.S., 1962; s. George Leslie and Lorna Winifred (Sandry) T.; m. Sandra Julie Winberg, Mar. 9, 1968 (div. 1981); m. Jane Spencer Edwards, Oct. 1, 1983; 1 child, Sebastian George Tonkin. B.A., St. John's Coll., Cambridge, Eng., 1962, M.A., 1966; A.M., Harvard U., 1966, Ph.D., 1966. Asst. prof. English U. Pa.-Phila., 1966-71, assoc. prof., 1971-80, prof., 1980-83, vice-provost undergrad. studies, 1971-75, coordinator internat. programs, 1977-83, master Stouffer Coll. House, 1980-83; pres. State Univ. Coll., Potsdam, N.Y., 1983—; vis. prof. English Columbia U., N.Y.C., 1980-81; dir. Ctr. Research and Documentation on World Lang. Problems, Rotterdam and N.Y.C., 1983—; mem. editorial bd. Spenser Studies, Duquesne Studies in Lang. and Lit., Spenser Ency.; mng. editor Language Problems and Language Planning. Author: bibliography Sir Walter Ralegh, 1971; Spenser's Courteous Pastoral, 1972; bibliography Esperanto and International Language Problems, 4th edit., 1977; (with Jane Edwards) The World in the Curriculum, 1981, The Faerie Queene, 1989; contbr. articles, studies, revs. to profl. jours. Pres. Pa. Council Internat. Edn., 1980-81; bd. dirs. World Affairs Council Phila., 1979-83, Partnership in Service-Learning, 1985—, Global Perspectives in Education, 1985—, Council Internat. Exchange of Scholars, 1985—. Recipient Lindback award for disting. teaching, 1970; Frank Knox fellow Harvard U., 1962-66; Guggenheim fellow, 1974. Fellow Acad. Esperanto; mem. Universal Esperanto Assn. (pres. 1974-80, 86—, rep. to UN 1974—), Spenser Soc. (pres. 1983-84, former dir.), Renaissance Soc. Am. (former dir.), Esperanto Studies Assn. Am. (pres. 1977—). Home: 69 Pierrepont Ave Potsdam NY 13676 Office: State Univ Coll Potsdam NY 13676

TONKIN, LEO SAMPSON, educational adminstrator; b. Suffern, N.Y., Apr. 2, 1937; s. Leo S. and Ann (Petrone) T. A.B., Johns Hopkins, 1959; postgrad., Sch. Advanced Internat. Studies, 1962-63; J.D., Harvard, 1962; Dr. Pedagogy, St. Thomas Aquinas Coll., 1973. Legis. asst. to U.S. Congressman; then Sen. Charles McC. Mathias, Jr., of Md., 1962-63; asso. counsel U.S. Ho. of Reps. Select Com. on Govt. Research, 1964; spl. cons. Ho. Spl. Subcom. on Edn., 1965-66; exec. dir. D.C. Commrs. Council on Higher Edn., 1965-66; pres. Leo S. Tonkin Assos., Inc., 1966—; founder, dir., chmn. bd. Washington Workshops Found., 1967—; Mem. White House Conf. on Edn., 1965, White House Conf. on Youth, 1971; spl. asst. to chmn. U.S. Ho. of Reps. Select Com. on Crime, 1972; mem. bd. plebe sponsors U.S. Naval Acad., 1977—; v.p. London Fedn. Boys' Clubs, 1980—; mem. adv. panel Nat. Commn. for Protection of Human Subjects of Biomed. and Behavioral Research, HEW, 1976-77. Contbr. articles to mags. Bd. dirs. Washington Choral Arts Soc., 1971-73, Nat. Coordinating Council on Drug Edn., 1973, Nat. Student Ednl. Fund, 1974—; chmn. Wall Street Seminar Found., 1978—; chmn. bd. trustees St. Thomas Aquinas Coll., 1966-73, continuing trustee, 1973-78, trustee, chmn. emeritus, 1978—; chmn. bd. trustees City of Phila. Govt. Honors Program; trustee Southeastern U., 1966-73; asso. bd. trustees Immaculata Coll., 1966-73; mem. advisory bd. Pub. Affairs and Govt. Degree Program, Mt. Vernon Coll., 1971-74; bd. dirs. YMCA, Washington, 1969-71. Recipient Americanism award, Valley Forge Freedoms Found, Americanism award, 1973. Mem. Johns Hopkins Alumni Assn. of Washington (pres. 1969-72). Clubs: Georgetown (Washington), City Tavern (Washington), Nat. Press (Washington), Capitol Hill (Washington), Capitol Yacht (Washington); Harvard (N.Y.C.). Home: Watergate South 700 New Hampshire Ave NW Washington DC 20037 Office: 3222 N St NW Washington DC 20007

TOO, C. C., retired Malaysian government official; b. Kuala Lumpur, Malaysia, Mar. 31, 1920; s. Too Choo Sun and Lum Yoke Yue. War Diploma in Sci., Raffles Coll., 1947; DSc (hon.), 1988. Sec. to Chinese Nationalist consul-consul gen. of Kuala Lumpur, 1946-50; research asst. to head Emergency Info. Service, dir. ops. staff, 1951-53; Chinese asst. to head psychol. warfare sect. Ministry Home Affairs, Kuala Lumpur, 1955-56, head, 1956-83; cons. in field; controller Kuala Lumpur div. Civil Def. Corps, 1956-61; participant internat. confs. and seminars. Named hon. mem. Order of Brit. Empire, hon. citizen New Orleans, 1962; decorated Malaysia Commemoration silver medal, 1964, Panglima Setia Mahkota with title Tan Sri, 1986; recipient Johan Mangu Negara award for psychol. warfare, 1957. Fellow Royal Soc. Arts (Gt. Britain); mem. Civil and Fgn. Service Assn. Malaysia, Inst. Pub. Relations, Royal Photog. Soc. Gt. Britain (assoc.), Nat. Rifle Assn., Photog. Soc. Am., Nat. Geog. Soc., Am. Mus. Natural History, Automobile Assn. Malaysia, The Planetary Soc. U.S.A., Cactus and Succulent Soc. Am., Aloe, Cactus and Succulent Soc. Zimbabwe, Selangor Shooting Assn. Malaysia, Malayan Nature Soc., Malayan Hist. Soc., Royal Asiatic Soc. Home: 20 Jalan Inai, 55100 Kuala Lumpur Malaysia

TOOHEY, MARIYA ANNE, state trade representative; b. Detroit, Mar. 31, 1956; d. James Lawrence and Evelyn Jean (Narancich) T. BA in German Lit., U. Mich., 1977; MA in Internat. Mgmt., Am. Grad. Sch. Internat. Mgmt., 1978. Trainee Kuehne & Nagel, Cologne and Hamburg, Fed. Republic Germany and Paris, 1979-80; sales/price analyst Ford Germany Parts and Service Ops., Cologne, 1980-84, merchandising specialist, 1984-85; mgr. trade coordination State of N.C. European Office, Dusseldorf, Fed. Republic Germany, 1985—. Mem. Thunderbird Alumni Assn. Europe, German-Am. C. of C. Republican. Roman Catholic. Office: State of NC European Office, Wasserstrasse 2, 4000 Dusseldorf Federal Republic of Germany

TOOKEY, ROBERT CLARENCE, consulting actuary; b. Santa Monica, Calif., Mar. 21, 1925; s. Clarence Hall and Minerva Maconachie (Anderson) T.; BS, Calif. Inst. Tech., 1945; MS, U. Mich., 1947; m. Marcia Louise Hickman, Sept. 15, 1956; children: John Hall, Jennifer Louise, Thomas Anderson. Actuarial clk. Occidental Life Ins. Co., Los Angeles, 1945-46; with Prudential Ins. Co. Am., Newark, 1947-49; assoc. actuary in group Pacific Mut. Life Ins. Co., Los Angeles, 1949-55; asst. v.p. in charge reins. sales and service for 17 western states Lincoln Nat. Life Ins. Co., Ft. Wayne, Ind., 1955-61; dir. actuarial services Peat, Marwick, Mitchell & Co., Chgo., 1961-63; mng. partner So. Calif. office Milliman & Robertson, cons. actuaries, Pasadena, 1963-76; pres. Robert Tookey Assos., Inc., 1977—. Committeeman troop 501 Boy Scouts Am., 1969-72. Served to lt. (j.g.) USNR, 1943-45, 51-52. Fellow Soc. Actuaries, Conf. Actuaries in Pub. Practice; mem. Am. Acad. Actuaries, Pacific States Actuarial Club, Pacific Ins. Conf. Clubs: San Gabriel Country; Rotary (Pasadena); Union League (Chgo.). Home: 1249 Descanso Dr La Canada CA 91011 Office: 1249 Descanso Dr La Canada CA 91011

TOOL, H. RAYMOND, b. Kansas City, Mo., Feb. 3, 1938; s. Herman R. and Lillian M. (Pruitt) T.; B.S., U. Kansas City, 1960; M.S., U. Mo., 1963; Ph.D., Heed U., 1979; m. Brenda L. Toot, Mar. 25, 1961; children—Harold R., Carol D. Sales mgr. Hach Chem. Co., 1965-74; exec. v.p., sec. Branchemco, Inc. Jacksonville, Fla., 1974-88; pres. Indsl. Materials Corp., Jacksonville, 1977—, Designs Unltd., 1977—; ptnr. Western Way Warehouse, 1976-88. Mem. Am. Chem. Soc., ASHRAE, Tech. Assn. Pulp and Paper Internat., Am. Mgmt. Assn., Nat. Assn. Corrosion Engrs., Am. Inst. Chemists, Fla. Soc. Environ. Analysts. Republican. Presbyterian. Clubs: Masons, Shriners. Home: 10864 Crosswicks Rd Jacksonville FL 32216 Office: 8286 Western Way Circle Jacksonville FL 32216

TOOLEY, JOHN, opera house executive; b. Rochester, Kent, Eng., June 1, 1924; s. H.R. and E.R. Tooley; grad. Magdalene Coll., Cambridge U.; m. Judith Morris, 1951 (marriage dissolved 1965); children: Sarah, Fiona, Rachel; m. 2d, Patricia Bagshawe, 1968; 1 son, Benjamin. Sec., Guildhall Sch. Music, 1952-55; asst. to gen. adminstr. Royal Opera House, Covent Garden, London, 1955-60, asst. gen. adminstr., 1960-70, gen. adminstr., 1970-80, gen. dir., 1980-88. Served with Rifle Brigade, 1943-47. Created knight, 1979; decorated commendatore Italian Republic. Club: Garrick (London). Home: Avon Farm House, Stratford-sub-Castle, Salisbury Wiltshire, England Office: Royal Opera House, Covent Garden, London WC2E 9DD England

TOOMEY, THOMAS MURRAY, lawyer; b. Washington, Dec. 9, 1923; s. Vincent L. and Catherine V. (McCann) T.; m. Grace Donohoe, June 22, 1948; children: Isabelle Marie Toomey Hessick, Helen Marie, Mary Louise, Thomas Murray. Student, Duke U., 1943-44, Catholic U. Am., 1942-43, 45-47; J.D., Catholic U. Am., 1949. Bar: D.C. 1949, Md. 1952. Sole practice Washington, 1949—; sec., dir. Allied Capital Corp. and subs., Washington and Ft. Lauderdale, Fla.; founder, organizer, dir. Pepsi-Cola Bottling Co. of Hartford-Springfield, Inc.; dir. Pepsi-Cola Bottling Co. of New Haven, Inc., Donohoe Cos. Inc., Washington, Nat. Capital Bank, Washington. Chmn. aviation and transp. coms. Met. Washington Bd. Trade, 1954-76, bd. dirs., 1962-77; chmn. dedication Dulles Internat. Airport, 1962; trustee Cath. U. Am.; founding trustee Heights Sch. Served to 1st lt. USMC, 1942-46, 50-52. Recipient Ann. Alumni Achievement award Cath. U., 1977. Mem. ABA, D.C., Md. bar assns., Bar Assn. D.C., Am. Judicature Soc., Comml. Law League Am., Nat. Assn. Small Bus. Investment Cos. (chmn. legal com. 1968-72), Friendly Sons St. Patrick (pres. 1983), Sovereign Mil. Order of Malta (Fed. Assn. U.S.A.). Clubs: Congressional Golf and Country, Kenwood Golf and Country; Univ. (Washington), Army and Navy (Washington); Tower (Ft. Lauderdale), Lago Mar Beach (Ft. Lauderdale); Rehoboth Beach (Del.); Country. Home: 6204 Garnett Dr Chevy Chase MD 20015 also: 2000 S Ocean Dr Apt 1410 Fort Lauderdale FL 33315 Office: 1625 Eye St NW Washington DC 20006

TOPENCHAROV, VLADIMIR VLADIMIROV, mathematics educator; b. Sofia, Bulgaria, July 15, 1933; s. Vladimir Evtimov and Ivanka lazarova (Doktorova) T.; m. Irina N. Balkandjieva, Feb. 5, 1955 (dec. 1984); 1 child, Vladimir. Degree in engring., Tech. U. Sofia, 1957, D Engring., 1963; D Natural Scis. in Math., Tech. U. Dresden, German Dem. Republic, 1983. Asst. prof. Tech. U. V.I. Lenin, Sofia, 1957-63, assoc. prof., 1964-69, prof. math., 1969—, chief dept. algebra, 1988—; expert UNESCO U. Alger, Algeria, 1963; vis. prof. U. Dijon, France, 1965-67; dir. Research Inst. Edn., Sofia, 1969-71; sr. advisor State Council Presidency of P.R. Bulgaria, 1972-82; dir. Ctr. Applied Math., Sofia, 1970-81. Author: Linear Algebra, 1982, Higher Education in Bulgaria, 1983, Teachers in Bulgaria, 1986, others. Mem. Nat. Commn. for UNESCO, Bulgaria, 1972—; cons. Internat. Inst. for Edn. Planning, UNESCO, Paris, 1983—. Recipient medal Cyrille and Mathode State Council, 1986, Merite Ednl. Worker award State Council, 1987, many others. Mem. Bulgarian Tchrs. Union, Union Bulgarian Mathematicians, Union Bulgarian Scientists, Bulgarian Sci. and Tech. Union, Am. Math. Soc. Home: Blvd Tolbuhin 73, 1000 Sofia Bulgaria Office: Tech Univ V Lenin, PO Box 384, 1000 Sofia Bulgaria

TOPLITZ, GEORGE NATHAN, lawyer; b. Winsted, Conn., June 13, 1936; s. Morris and Rose (Dolinsky) T.; m. Janet S. Strauss, July 30, 1961 (div.); children—Jill, Wendy, Anna; m. Kimilene A. Snead, Nov. 25, 1979. B.A., U. Conn., 1958; LL.B., Boston U., 1961. Bar: N.Y. 1964, U.S. Dist. Ct. (so. dist.) N.Y. 1968, U.S. Dist. Ct. (ea. dist.) N.Y. 1968, U.S. Ct. Appeals (2d cir.) 1986, U.S. Supreme Ct. 1987. Claims atty. Royal-Globe Ins. Co., surety dept., N.Y.C., 1963-65; surety atty. Transam. Inst. Co., N.Y.C., 1965-67; assoc. Max E. Greenberg, Cantor, Reiss, N.Y.C., 1967—, ptnr., 1974-88; ptnr. Max E. Greenberg, Cantor, Trager, Toplitz, 1988—; lectr. Am. Mgmt. Assn., 1974-76, Am. Assn. Cost Engrs., 1974-75, Sch. Continuing Edn. NYU, 1975; NW Ctr. Profl. Edn., 1988. Served with U.S. Army, 1961-63. Recipient Letter of Commendation for acting vol. spl. master Supreme Ct. N.Y., 1982, 84, 85, 86, 87, 88. Mem. N.Y. State Bar Assn., N.Y. County Lawyers Assn., ABA, Assn. Trial Lawyers Am., Internat. Platform Assn. Office: 100 Church St New York NY 10007

TOPOL, CHAIM, actor, producer, director; b. Tel Aviv, Israel, Sept. 9, 1935; s. Jacob and Rela (Goldman) T.; B.Sc.; m. Galia Finkelstein, 1956; 3 children. Founder Green Onion, satirical theatre, 1956, Mcpl. Theatre of Haifa (Israel), 1959; star London stage prodn. Fiddler on the Roof; actor, producer, dir. Genesis Project, filming the Bible, N.Y.C.; films include Cast a Giant Shadow, 1965, Sallah, 1966, Before Winter Comes, 1969, A Time for Loving, Fiddler on the Roof, 1971, The Public Eye, Flash Gordon, Follow Me, 1972, Galileo, 1974, For Your Eyes Only, 1980; (TV) The House on Garibaldi Street, 1979; TV miniseries include: The Winds of War, 1983, Queenie, 1987. Recipient Golden Globe award San Francisco Film Festival. Author: (autobiography) Topol by Topol, 1981. Address: 108 Dizengoff St, Tel Aviv Israel *

TOPOLSKI, JERZY, historian, educator; b. Poznan, Poland, Sept. 20, 1928; s. Wladyslaw Topolski and Halina (Pietrzynska) Topolska-Cychnerska; m. Zofia Kulejewska, Apr. 21, 1954 (div. 1958); m. 2d Maria Barbara Antczak, Sept. 9, 1961 (div. 1978); m. 3d Maria Danuta Labedzka, July 29, 1978. M.Polit. Economy, U. Poznan, 1950; Ph.D., U. Torun (Poland), 1951. Asst., U. Poznan, 1951; fellow Acad. Social Scis., Warsaw, 1951-54; prof. asst. Polish Acad. Scis., 1954-56, docent Polish Acad. Scis.-U. Poznan, 1956-61; prof. U. Poznan, 1961—, also vice dir. Inst. History, 1968-81, dir. inst., 1981—. Author: Birth of Capitalism in Europe, 1965, 2d edit., 1976; Methodology of History (State award 1969), 1968; Theory of Historical Knowledge, 1983; co-author, editor: History of Poland (State award 1978), 1976. Judge, State Tribunal, Warsaw, 1982; pres. Polish Com. of Hist. Scis., 1984—. Decorated Comdr.'s Cross Order Polonia Restituta (Poland). Mem. Polish United Workers Party. Office: U Poznan Inst History, Marchlewskiego 124/126, 61-874 Poznan Poland

TOPPING, GRAHAM, chemist; b. Wigan, Lancashire, Eng., Aug. 28, 1940; s. James and Dorothy (Astley) T.; m. Elizabeth Hornby Crawford, Oct. 2, 1965; children: Michael, Deborah. BSc in Chemistry, U. Liverpool, 1961, BSc in Oceanography, 1962, PhD in Oceanography, 1967. Scientist Royal Soc., London, 1963-64; lectr. U. Strathclyde, Glasgow, Scotland, 1966-70; scientist dept. agr. and fisheries Scotland Marine Lab., Aberdeen, 1970—; cons. Intergovtl. Oceanographic Commn., Paris, UN Environment Programme, Nairobi, Kenya; mem. adv. com. marine pollution Internat. Council Exploration of Seas, Copenhagen, Denmark, 1985—. Contbr. articles to profl. jours. Town Councillor Borough of Kintore, Scotland, 1967-69. Recipient John Murray Travelling Studentship, Royal Soc., 1963-64. Fellow Royal Soc. Chemistry; mem. Inst. Water and Environ. Mgmt. Mem. Ch. England. Home: 7 Allandale Gardens, Kintore, Aberdeenshire AB5 OUT, Scotland Office: Dept Agr & Fisheries for Scotland, Victoria Rd, Aberdeen Scotland

TOPRAC, A. ANTHONY, chemical company executive; b. Istanbul, Turkey, Feb. 12, 1920; s. Anthony A. and Despina (Tserkez) T.; B.S. in Chem. Engring., Robert Coll., 1942; M.S., U. Minn., 1947; Ph.D., Lehigh U., 1950; m. Dena Comninos, June 15, 1952; children—Dennis A., Anthony J., Paul K. Teaching and research asst. Lehigh U., 1947-50; asst. prof. civil engring. U. Tex., Austin, 1950-53, asso. prof., 1954-60, prof., 1961-73, dir. Structures Fatigue Research lab., 1963-73; mng. dir. Interchem-Hellas S.A., Athens, Greece, 1973—, also dir.; lectr. in field. Recipient Cert. award, James F. Lincoln Found., 1947; Lincoln Gold medal, Am. Welding Soc., 1954. Fellow Am. Soc. Civil Engrs. Greek Orthodox. Contbr. articles in field to profl. jours. Office: 196 Syngrou Ave, Kallithea, 17671 Athens Greece Home: 17 Mavromihali St, Philothei, Athens Greece

TOREN, ROBERT, photojournalist; b. Grand Rapids, Mich., Oct. 9, 1915; s. Clarence J. and Helen (Holcomb) T.; student Winona Sch. Profl. Photography, 1957, West Coast Sch. Photography, 1959-62; m. Miriam Jeanette Smith, July 17, 1940. Photographer, Harris and Ewing, Washington, 1938-39, Versluis Studios, Grand Rapids, Mich., 1939-43, prodn. mgr., 1940-43; owner, photographer Toren Galleries, San Francisco, 1946-70; photographer Combat Tribes of World, Rich Lee Orgn., 1978-84, Darien jungle expdn. Am. Motors, 1979; feature writer Auburn (Calif.) Jour., El Dorado Gazette, 1983-87. One man shows various univs.; prints in permanent collections: Photog. Hall of Fame, Coyote Point Mus., San Mateo County Hist. Mus.; photog. column San Mateo Times; lectr. Am. Pres. Lines, Coll. San Mateo, Peninsula Art Assn., Mendicino Art Center. Historian City of Foster City; vice chmn. Art Commn. Foster City. Trustee, West Coast Sch.; bd. dirs. Foster City Art League, Hillbarn Theatre, San Mateo County Arts Council; mem. art com. San Mateo County Fair, 1979-87 ; coordinator, dir. Georgetown (Calif.) Mountain Mus., 1982—. Served from pvt. to staff sgt. AUS, 1943-46. Mem. Calif. Writers (br. pres.), Profl. Photographers Am. Presbyn. Author: Peninsula Wilderness. Illustrator: The Tainted Tree, 1963. Editor: The Evolution of Portraiture, 1965; The Western Way of Portraiture, 1965, Conquest of the Darien, 1984. Home: 3140 Cascade Trail Cool CA 95614

TORFFIELD, MARVIN, artist; b. Bklyn., July 25, 1943; s. Barnett Philip and Rina (Shapiro) T. B.F.A., Pratt Inst., 1965; M.F.A., Yale U., 1970. Vis. fellow Advanced Ctr. Visual Studies, MIT, 1970; research fellow Harvard U., 1972. Exhibited group shows Jewish Mus. N.Y., 1969, Paula Cooper Gallery, 1977, Central Park, 1980, Leo Castelli Gallery, 1983, 35th IDCA, 1985, Sert Gallery, Harvard U., 1986. Patentee high fidelity-stereo sound system. Fellow Nat. Endowment for Arts, 1970, Guggenheim Found., 1975; Pollock-Krasner Found. grantee, 1986-87; MacDowell Colony residency, Peterborough, N.H., July-Sept., 1988. Office: PO Box 292 New York NY 10013-9998

TORFS, EDMOND LOUIS, insurance company executive, educator; b. Antwerp, Belgium, July 12, 1947; s. François and Mariette (Dries) T.; m. Adrienne Van Mechelen; children: Inke, Wim. Lic. in physics, Vrye U., Brussels, 1969; PhD in Physics, U. Antwerp, Belgium, 1976. Asst. prof. U. Antwerp, 1969-77; devel. mgr. Royale Belge Ins. Co., Brussels, 1977—; prof. Boston U., Brussels, 1984—, U. Brussels, 1987—. Office: Royale Belge Ins Co, Vorstlaan 25, B 1170 Brussels Belgium

TORGERSON, FERNANDO GORDON, university dean emeritus; b. Plaza, N.D., Mar. 5, 1918; s. Nels and Marie (Hafthorn) T.; m. Gertrude Irene Hall, Aug. 14, 1949 (dec. 1978); m. Louise (Steinmetz) Frazer, 1981. B.A., State Tchrs. Coll., Minot, N.D., 1939; M.S., Columbia U., 1949; Ph.D., U. Minn., 1956. Assoc. dir. spl. services Montefiore Hosp., N.Y.C., 1962-66; asst. prof. Columbia Sch. Pub. Health and Adminstrv. Medicine, 1962-66; dir. Calif. Office Health and Welfare Agy., 1966-67; dean Grad. Sch. Social Work, U. Tex. at Arlington, 1967-78, dean emeritus, 1978—; cons. in field; cons. to U.S. Army surgeon Gen., 1959-62. Author articles. Mem. social work professional advisory bd. Emory U.; mem. criminal justice policy, devel. com. N. Tex. Council Govts.; mem. Tex. Urban Devel. Commn., 1970—; mem. Chancellors Council U. Tex. System. Served with U.S. Army, 1941-62. Lodge: Rotary. Home: 555 Franklin Dr Arlington TX 76011

TORGERSON, LARRY KEITH, lawyer; b. Albert Lea, Minn., Aug. 25, 1935; s. Fritz G. and Lu (Hillman) T. BA, Drake U., 1958, MA, 1960, LLB, 1963, JD, 1968; MA, Iowa U., 1962; cert., The Hague (The Netherlands) Acad. Internat. Law, 1965, 69; LLM, U. Minn., 1969, Columbia U., 1971, U. Mo., 1976; PMD, Harvard U., 1973, EdM, 1974. Bar: Minn. 1964, Wis. 1970, Iowa 1970, U.S. Tax Ct. 1971, U.S. Supreme Ct. 1972, U.S. Dist. Ct. Minn. 1964, U.S. Dist. Ct. (no. dist.) Iowa 1971, U.S. Dist. Ct. (ea. dist.) Wis. 1981, U.S. Ct. Appeals (8th cir.) 1981. Asst. corp. counsel 1st Bank Stock Corp., Mpls., 1963-67; v.p., trust officer Nat. City Bank, Mpls., 1967-69; sr. mem. Torgerson Law Firm, Northwood, Iowa, 1969—; trustee, gen. counsel Torgerson Farms, Northwood, 1977—, Redbirch Farms, Kensett, Iowa, 1987—, Sunburst Farms, Grafton, Iowa, 1987—, Gold Dust Farms, Bolan, Iowa, 1988—; chmn., gen. counsel Internat. Investments, Mpls., 1983—, Transoceanic, Mpls., 1987—; pres., gen. counsel Torgerson Investments, Northwood, 1984—, Torgerson Properties, Northwood, 1987—. Mem. ABA, Am. Judicature Soc., Iowa Bar Assn., Minn. Bar Assn., Wis Bar Assn., Mensa, Psi Chi, Circle K, Phi Alpha Delta, Omicron Delta Kappa, Pi Kappa Delta, Alpha Tau Omega, Pi Delta Epsilon, Alpha Kappa Delta. Lutheran.

TORIOLA, ABEL LAMINA, physical education educator; b. Kaduna, Nigeria, Jan. 25, 1959; s. Michael Alabi and Helen Paulina (Okere) T.; m. Olutoyin Mobolaji Akinwale, June 13, 1987; 1 child, Temilolu. BS in Phys. Edn., U. Ife, Ile-Ife, Nigeria, 1980, MA in Phys. Edn., 1983, PhD in Phys. Edn., 1987. Coordinator pre-degree phys. edn. program U. Ife (name now Obafemi Awolowo U.), 1985-87; coach U. Ife, 1980-87; sec. Olympic Standard Swimming Pool Com. U. Ife, 1984-87; students' adviser academic matters U. Ife, 1985-87; cons. U. Benin, Nigeria, 1986-87. Mem. Nigerian Assn. Phys. Health Edn. and Recreation, Nigerian Assn. Sports Sci. and Medicine. Methodist. Club: U. Ife Staff. Office: Inst Phys Edn, Obafemi Awolowo U, Ile-Ife Oyo State, Nigeria

TORKI, MOSTAFA AHMAD, psychology educator; b. Meet Gazal, Garbia, Egypt, Mar. 2, 1940; s. Ahmad Abulmagd and Fatima Mohmmad T.; m. Nihad Salah-AlMarasi, July 21, 1951; children: Iman, Lamia, Ahmad, Hazem. BA, Cairo U., 1962, MA, 1968; PhD, Kuwait U., 1973. Research asst. Nat. Ctr. Social Criminological Researches, Cairo, 1963-68; demonstrator Kuwait U., 1968-73, asst. prof., 1973-80, assoc. prof., 1980—; cons. Ministry of Edn., Kuwait, Ctr. Community Service, Kuwait U. Hon. fellow U. Minn. 1983; grantee Kuwait U., 1985. Mem. Am. Psychological Assn., Internat. Assn. Cross Cultural Psychology, Internat. Council Psychologists. Clubs: Heliopolis (Arab Republic Egypt), Kuwait U. Home: Villa 15 Shuwaick, 13096 Kuwait Kuwait Office: Kuwait U Dept Psychology, PO Box 23558, 13096 Kuwait Kuwait

TORKILDSON, RAYMOND MAYNARD, lawyer; b. Lake City, S.D., Nov. 19, 1917; s. Gustav Adolph and Agnes (Opitz) T.; m. Sharman Elizabeth Vaughn, Sept. 8, 1956; children—Stephen, Thomas. S.B., U. S.D., 1946; J.D., Harvard U., 1948. Bar: Calif. 1949, Hawaii 1950. Assoc. James P. Blaisdell, Honolulu, 1949-52; ptnr. Moore, Torkildson & Rice and successors, Honolulu, 1955-64; exec. v.p. Hawaii Employers Council, Honolulu, 1964-67; ptnr. Torkildson, Katz, Jossem, Fonseca & Moore and predecessors, Honolulu, 1967-72, sr. ptnr., 1972—. Mem. mgmt. com. Armed Forces YMCA, Honolulu, 1971; treas. Hawaii Republican Com. 1977-83. Served with U.S. Army, 1941-46; lt. col. Res. ret. Mem. ABA, Hawaii Bar Assn. Roman Catholic. Clubs: Oahu Country, Pacific (Honolulu).

TORNAGHI, LUIZ CARLOS, finance company executive; b. Rio de Janeiro, Dec. 29, 1943; s. Newton and Anna Maria (Costa) T.; m. Maria, Apr. 18, 1966; children: Luiz, Anna, Isabel. Degree in engring., Pontificia U. Catholica, 1967; MBA, Harvard U., 1973. Mgr. prodn. planning and control Gillette do Brasil, Rio de Janeiro, 1967-71; mgr. mergers and acquisitions UNIBANCO, Rio de Janeiro, 1973-75; pres. Sena Internat. ltd., Rio de Janeiro, 1973-83; chmn. SGI-Holdings, N.Y.C., 1978-81; pres., chief exec. officer Acel Investments ltd., Rio de Janeiro, 1983—, Acel S.C.R., Rio de Janeiro, 1986—; chmn. bd. Amplus Informática, Rio de Janeiro, Coifa Pecúlio e Pensões, Rio de Janeiro, Ameise Com. Ind., Rio de Janeiro. Author: Trading Companies. Sub sec. planning Ministry Edn. and Culture, Brazil, 1979-80; exec. sec. Corredor Carajás, São Luis, Brazil, 1980-82. Recipient Comenda da Ordem do Timbira, Govt. Maranhão, Brazil, 1981. Mem. Clube de Engenharia, Instituto Brasileiro de Execs. Financeiros. Clubs: Jockey, Iatch. Home: Ave Rui Barbosa, 80, 22250 Rio de Janeiro Brazil Office: Acel Investimentos, Ave Rio Branco, 181, 20040 Rio de Janeiro Brazil

TORNBLOM, BJORN (GOTTFRID), aviation executive, aviation consultant; b. Kristinehamn, Varmland, Sweden, July 6, 1918; s. Berndt Gottfrid and Signe Valborg Johanna (Engblom) T.; m. Magnhild Emma Hakansson, Sept. 13, 1941; 1 child, Birger. M. Engring., Royal Inst. Tech., Stockholm, 1942. Aircraft project engr. Royal Swedish Air Force, Stockholm, 1942-43; chief engr. Scandinavian Airways Ltd., Norrtalje, Uppland, 1943-48; head aviation br. Tech. Inst. Stockholm, 1942-47; asst. chief engr. Swedish Airlines, Stockholm, 1948-49; mgr. prodn. Scandinavian Airlines System, Stockholm, 1949-54, chief engr., 1954-56, v.p. ops., 1956-60, v.p. engring. and maintenance, 1960-69, exec. v.p. tech. and ops., 1969-81; cons., sr. ptnr. Scandinavian Aviation Cons.-Scanavia, Stockholm, 1982—; dir. Linjeflyg, Stockholm, 1967-82, Crownair/Swedair, Stockholm, 1971-77, Scanair, Stockholm, 1975-80, Transair, Malmo, Skane, 1976-81, Scanavia A/S, Oslo, 1981—, Scanavia A.B., Stockholm, 1982—. Named Hon. Disting. Citizen, State Wash., 1971; recipient Tech. Mgmt. award Air Transport World, 1978; Thulin medal in Bronze, 1968, Gold, 1977. Mem. Royal Swedish Aero Club (Carl August Wicander medal in Silver 1985), Swedish Soc. Aeros. and Astronautics (chmn. 1955-57), Swedish Aviation Hist. Soc., Internat. Air Transport Assn. (chmn. tech. com. 1976), Assn. European Airlines. Home: Aniaravagen 15, S175 60 Jarfalla Sweden Office: Scanavia-Scandinavian, Aviation Cons, Drottningholmsvagen 31-33, S-112 42 Stockholm Sweden

TORNEDEN, ROGER L(EE), insurance executive; b. Lawrence, Kans., Feb. 2, 1944; s. William E. and Lelia M. (Kindred) T.; B.S. in Indsl. Mgmt., U. Kans., 1966, M.S. in Ops. Research, 1967; Ph.D. in Internat. Bus., N.Y. U. 1974; m. Lisa Meredith Ross, Dec. 18, 1982; children: Jennifer, Stephanie. Corp. planning analyst ARCO, N.Y.C., 1967-69; sr. fin. analyst J.C. Penney, N.Y.C., 1969-72, dir. ops. analysis Sarma-Penney, Brussels, 1972-74, Japan project dir., Kobe, 1974-77, dir. internat. devel., N.Y.C., 1977-81, dir. econ. affairs, N.Y.C., 1982-87; v.p. mktg. Am. Internat. Group, N.Y.C., 1988—; asst. prof. mktg. Baruch Coll., 1978-84; bd. dirs. Lenox Manor Owners, Inc.; internat. cons. disposal fgn. ops.; bd. dirs. Am. C. of C. in Japan, 1976-77; bd. dirs. YMCA of Greater N.Y., 1988—. Served with USNR, 1961-65. Recipient Outstanding Performance award Bd. Govs. Am. C. of C. in Japan, 1977; Commodity Trader of Yr. award Internat. Moneyline, 1984. Mem. Nat. Retail Mgmt. Assn. (internat. com.), Soc. Applied Econs., Japan Soc. Republican. Lutheran. Author: Foreign Disinvestments by U.S. Multinational Corporations, 1975; contbr. articles to profl. jours. Home: 176 E 77th New York NY 10021 Office: Am Internat Group 70 Pine St New York NY 10270

TORNELL, DAVID ROBERT, manufacturing company executive; b. Mexico City, Nov. 3, 1939; s. David R. Tornell and Guadalupe Romo; m. Cecilia Lopez Ortega, May 20, 1964; children: Cecilia, Lucy, Emily, Veronica, Bety, Rocio. CPA, Nat. U. Mex., Mexico City, 1961; MBA, Inst. Poly. Nat., Mexico City, 1973. Credit and collection mgr. H. J. Heinz Mex., Mexico City, 1964-66; asst. mng. dir. Mallory Battery Co., Mexico City, 1966-69; various fin. positions H. J. Heinz Mex., Mexico City, 1969-73; mng. dir. Timex Group, Mexico City, 1973-80; v.p. fin. Alfa Industries-Food Sector, Mexico City, 1980-81; mng. dir. Rassini Rheem, Mexico City, 1982-86, Fruehauf De Mex., Mexico City, 1986-87, SKF Mex., Mexico City, 1987—; cons. Secofin, Mexico City, 1984—. Mem. Mex. Inst. Fin. Execs., Mex. Inst. Pub. Accts., Nat. Assn. Accts. Home: Gabriel Mancera 1112, 03100 Mexico City Mexico

TÖRNQVIST, ULLA MARGARETHA, controller; b. Gothenburg, Sweden, July 31, 1949. BS in Econs., U. Gothenburg, 1971, D of Econs., 1976; postgrad., European Inst. for Advanced Studies in Mgmt., Brussels, 1973-75. Research asst., sr. lectr. U. Gothenburg, 1972-77, 79-82, dir. doctoral program, 1981-82, assoc. prof., docent, 1986; postgrad. fellow U. Wis., Milw., 1976-77; research scientist Research Inst. of Swedish Nat. Def., Stockholm, 1977-78, 78-79; research asst. Internat. Inst. for Applied Systems Analysis, Laxenburg, Austria, 1978, European Inst. Bus. Adminstrn., Fontainebleau, France, 1979; cons. Bohlins Revisionsbyrå AB, Stockholm, 1982-84; controller AB Volvo, Gothenburg, 1984—; v.p. Swedish Ops. Research Assn., Stockholm, 1977-79. Author: The Choice of Accounting Principle, 1986; contbr. articles to profl. jours. Swedish Inst. research scholar, Brussels, 1974. Mem. Swedish Assn. for Bus. Economists, Swedish Planning Execs. Inst., Rotary Fellows Alumni Assn. (Found. award Milw. chpt. 1976). Club: Swedish Mountaineering (Gothenburg) (pres. 1987—). Home: Kompassgatan 7, 413 16 Gothenburg Sweden Office: AB Volvo, 405 08 Gothenburg Sweden

TOROEAN, MANGIRING L., financial company executive; b. Parapat, Indonesia, Feb. 15, 1944; s. H. L. Toroean and M.A. Tobing; m. Rosita Sirait; children: Meriaty Alice Hasian, Peter Martin Helmut, Irving Marcos Christopher, Ivan Paima Rex Namora. Student, U. Indonesia/Agrl. Inst., Bogor, Indonesia, 1968; MBA, Grad. Sch. Mgmt-IPPM, Jakarta, Indonesia, 1985. Asst. lectr. U. of Indonesia/Agrl. Inst, Bogor, 1967-68; asst. cons. Mgmt. Found., Jakarta, 1970-71; fin., adminstrv. mgr. Jakarta, 1971-74, exec. devel. program, 1974, account, credit officer, 1975-77, head credit div., 1978-82, head mktg. policy, 1982-83, project mgr., 1983-84; head fin. services, banking Citicorp Global Payment Prod, Jakarta, 1984—. Author: Product Knowledge and Marketing Policy, 1983; editor: Conduct Brainstorming Customer Service Excellence Program, 1983. Mem. Alumni Assn. MBA-Indonesia (treas. 1986—). Club: Exec. (Jakarta). Lodge: Lions (Melvin Jones award 1985). Home: Jalan Permata Berlian, Blok Q No 19, Permata Hijau, Jakarta Indonesia Office: Citibank/Citicorp Global Payment Products, JL Jenderal Sudirman Kav 70A, Jakarta Indonesia

TORRANCE, ELLIS PAUL, educational psychologist, educator; b. Milledgeville, Ga., Oct. 8, 1915; s. Ellis Watson and Jimmie Pearl (Ennis) T.; m. Jessie Pansy Nigh, Nov. 25, 1959. B.A., Mercer U., 1940; M.A., U. Minn., 1944; Ph.D., U. Mich., 1951. Tchr. Midway Vocational High Sch., Milledgeville, 1936-37; tchr., counselor Ga. Mil. Coll., 1937-40, prin., 1941-44; counselor student counseling bur. U. Minn., 1945; counselor counseling bur. Kans. State Coll., 1946-48, dir., 1949-51; dir. survival research field unit Stead AFB, Nev., 1951-57; dir. Bur. Ednl. Research, 1958-64; prof. ednl. psychology U. Minn., 1958-66; chmn., prof. dept. ednl. psychology U. Ga., 1966-78, Alumni Found. disting. prof., 1974-85; Alumni Found. disting. prof. emeritus 1985—. Author: Torrance Tests of Creative Thinking, Thinking Creatively in Action and Movement, Style of Learning and Thinking, and Sounds and Images; contbr. articles to jours., mags., books. Trustee Creative Edn. Found.; founder Nat. Future Problem Solving Problem and Bowl, Nat. Scenario Writing Contest. Torrance Ctr. for Creative Studies, Torrance Creative Scholars, and Mentors Network established in his honor at U. Ga. Fellow Am. Psychol. Assn.; mem. Am. Ednl. Research Assn., Am. Soc. Group Psychotherapy and Psychodrama, Creative Education Leadership Council, Nat. Assn. Gifted Children, Phi Delta Kappa. Baptist. Home: 183 Cherokee Ave Athens GA 30606

TORRE, ANTHONY MANUEL, industrial services company executive; b. Lugo, Spain, Nov. 2, 1929; came to U.S., 1961, naturalized, 1968; s. Antonio and Matilde (Vila) T.; M.S. in Elec. Engring., Havana U., 1953; Automation and Instruments Engr., Delft U., 1956; m. Dulce M. Sanchez, Mar. 20, 1968; children—Nestor, Aldo. Asst. chief engr. Shell Oil Co., 1954-61; chief engr. Phillips Petroleum Corp., 1961-68; refinery maintenance mgr. Continental Oil Co., 1968-70; refinery engring. and maintenance mgr. Texaco Oil Co., Panama, 1970-73; gen. mgr. I.M.I.S.A., Barcelona, Spain, 1973—; pres. bd. dirs. Alamo Indsl. S.A., Barcelona, 1980—. Mem. Internat. Maintenance Inst., IEEE, Am. Welding Soc. Republican. Roman Catholic. Inventor radiation heater for synthetic fibers, electromech. speed changer. Home: 93-95 Pso Bonanova, 08017 Barcelona Spain Office: 54 Pablo Alcover, 08017 Barcelona Spain

TORRECILLAS, BLAS, mathematician; b. Almeria, Spain, Sept. 24, 1958; s. Pedro Torreciallas and Maria Jover; m. Amalia Fernandez, Sept. 8, 1984; 1 chiild, Pedro. Grad., U. Granada, Spain, 1980, PhD, 1983. Asst. prof. U. Granada, 1980-82, tchr., 1983-86; assoc. prof. U. Grenada, 1986—. Author: (monograph) Sheaf Over the Spectrum of Noncommunication Rins, 1980, Homological Aspect of Torsion Theory, 1983. Fellow Govt. of Spain, 1980; Fulbright Found. fellow, Gainesville, Fla., 1982-83. Home: Pintor Lopez Mezquita 2, 5th Floor, 18002 Granada Spain Office: U Granada, 18071 Granada Spain

TORRES, ANTHONY IGNATIUS, educator; b. Chgo., July 5, 1929; s. Anastasio and Bivina (Garcia) T.; B.S., No. Ill. U., 1954; M.Ed., DePaul U., 1956, Ed.S., 1958; Ed.D., Loyola U., Chgo., 1973. Tchr., Chgo. Public Schs., 1954-66; adminstr. Ill. Office of Edn., 1966-72; prin. Park Ridge (Ill.) Public Schs., 1972-76; dir. personnel Prairie State Coll., Chicago Heights, Ill., 1976-77; supt. schs., River Grove, Ill., 1977-79, Sauk Village, Ill., 1979-87; dir. adminstrv. services, Bellwood, Ill., 1987—. Bd. govs. United Republican Fund; mem. Ill. Ednl. Facilities Authority, 1979—; bd. dirs. United Way Suburban Cook County, 1981—; bilingual chmn. Nat. Adv. and Coordination Council, 1984—. Recipient Those Who Excel award Ill. State Bd. Edn., 1978. Mem. Am. Assn. Sch. Adminstrs., Ill. Assn. Sch. Adminstrs., Am. Assn. U. Adminstrs., Phi Delta Kappa (Service award Loyola U. chpt.). Club: Columbia Yacht (Chgo.). Contbr. articles in profl. jours., column on edn. to local newspapers. Home: 1700 N North Park Chicago IL 60614

TORRES, ERIKA VOGEL, college administrator; b. Fulda, Hessen, W. Ger., Mar. 22, 1939; came to U.S. 1962, naturalized, 1966; d. Hermann Josef and Ella Mathilde (Schneider) Vogel; m. Angelo Torres, Jr., Mar. 2, 1974; children—Karen Doris, Christopher Hans, Alexandra Eran. B.S., U. Bridgeport, 1973, M.S., 1975, Diploma 6th Year Profl., 1977; Ph.D., Columbia Pacific U., 1982. Instr., U.S. Army Edn. Ctr., W.Germany, 1966-71, mil. test proctor, 1969-71; exec. sec., adminstrv. asst. U. Bridgeport, Conn., 1972-76, admissions counselor, 1976-77, dir. grad. admissions, 1977-79; dean records and registrar Post Coll., Waterbury, Conn., 1979—, instr. German, 1983-84; tchr. German, Ind. German Lang. Schs. of Conn., Westport, 1983—; coll. registrar Norwalk Community Coll., 1979-88. Editor: Post College Catalog, 1980—, Admissions Viewbook, 1981-83. Mem. Am. Assn. Collegiate Registrars and Admissions Officers, Nat. Assn. Female Execs., Am. Personnel Guidance Assn., Am. Assn. Tchrs. German, Nat. Assn. Vets. Program Adminstrs. Avocations: reading, travel, theosophy. Home: 97 Wilson St Bridgeport CT 06605

TORRES, EUGENIO, electrical engineer; b. San Juan, P.R., May 14, 1950; s. Eugenio and Pura (Agosto) T.; A.E.E., U. P.R., 1971; E.E.T., Wentworth Inst. Tech., Boston, 1973; B.S. in Mfg., Western Mich. U., 1985; m. Elba; children—Eugenio F., Herbert, Elizabeth. Prodn. supr. Union Carbide, Inc., P.R.; automation specialist Honeywell, Inc., Rio Piedras, P.R.; account mgr. Mal del Caribe, Santurce, P.R.; applications engr. comml. mktg. Carrier Corp., Syracuse, N.Y.; engr. internat. group Rapistan div. Lear Seigler, Grand Rapids, Mich.; now tech. and sales support mgr. Ammeraal Conveyor Belting, Grand Rapids. Served with P.R. Air N.G., 1975-78, N.Y. Air NG, 1978-80; capt. Mich. Army NG, 1981—. Cert. mfg. engr. in robotics, engring. technician. Mem. IEEE, ASHRAE, Internat. Material Mgmt. Soc., Delta Phi Theta, Alpha Phi Omega. Roman Catholic. Clubs: Exchange, Nyang, Mich. Army N.G. Officers, Prang NCO. Home: 2050 Foxboro Ct NW Grand Rapids MI 49504 Office: PO Box 1245 Grand Rapids MI 49501-1245

TORRES, GUIDO ADOLFO, water treatment company executive; b. Esmeraldas, Ecuador, Aug. 29, 1938; s. Carlos M. and Nora I. (Andrade) T.; m. Lupe N. Duran, Aug. 29, 1964; children: Guido, Alex, Juan Jose. B of Chem. Engring, Cen. U. Ecuador, 1967. Chief of study group Indsl. Devel. Ctr. Ecuador, Quito, 1965-69, tech. asst. to exec. dir., 1969-70; researcher Frakes Water Treatment Plant, Luverne, Minn., 1970-71; researcher Andean Water Treatment Soc. Anonima, Quito, 1972-84, gen. mgr., 1984-85, pres., 1985—. Author: Industrial Water Treatment; contbr. articles on water treatment to jours.; developer water treatment chems., equipment. Fellow Chem. Engring Coll. Ecuador (pres. 1976); mem. Am. Inst. Chem. Engrs., Am. Water Works Assn., Quito Indsl. Chamber, Quito C. of C., Quito Small Industry Chamber. Club: Castillo Amaguana. Home: 261 Miravalle, Quito Pichincha, Ecuador Office: Andean Water Treatment Soc, Belgica 161 PO Box 3297, Quito Pichincha, Ecuador

TORRES, ISRAEL, oral and maxillofacial surgeon; b. El Paso, Tex., Sept. 5, 1934; s. Francisco Mendoza and Manuela (Gallardo) T.; m. Karen Marie Hensley, Aug. 22, 1970; children—Michael, George Stanley, Dianna. B.S., Tex. Western Coll., 1958; D.D.S., U. Tex.-Houston, 1963; postgrad. Health Sci. Ctr., Houston, 1963-66; diploma (hon.) XX Reunion de Provincia, Juarez, Chihuahua, Mexico, 1970, Ateneo Odontologica Mexicano, Valle de Bravo, Mexico, 1973, Colegio de Cirujanos Mexicanos, Juarez, 1975, 84. Cert. instr. Advanced Cardiac Life Support, 1986—; diplomate Am. Bd. Oral and Maxillofacial Surgery. Resident in oral surgery Methodist Hosp., Houston, 1963-64, Ben Taub Hosp., Houston, 1964-65, Hermann Hosp., Houston, 1965-66; practice dentistry specializing in oral and maxillofacial surgery, El Paso, 1966—; mem. staff Sun Towers Hosp., chief oral and maxillofacial surgery, 1975, 76, 77; instr. pathology El Paso Community Coll., 1975-76; lectr. in field. Contbr. articles to Jour. Oral/Maxillofacial Surgery. Bd. dirs. Am. Cancer Soc., El Paso, 1971-73, El Paso Cancer Treatment Ctr., 1971-74; bd. dirs. West Tex. Health Systems Agy., 1980-82, chmn., 1981-82; med. adv. com. W. Tex. Council of Regional Health. Recipient Bowie Exes award, El Paso, 1982, Mexican Consul Gen. Award of Appreciation, 1986, Mexican Social Security Service Award of Appreciation, 1986. Fellow Am. Coll. Oral and Maxillofacial Surgeons, Am. Assn. Oral and Maxillofacial Surgeons, Internat. Assn. Oral and Maxillofacial Surgeons, Southwest Soc. Oral and Maxillofacial Surgeons, Acad. Internat. Dental Studies, Pan Am. Med. Assn., EPSDT (dental adv. and rev. com. 1985-86), Tex. Soc. Oral and Maxillofacial Surgeons. mem. El Paso Dist. Dental Soc. (pres. 1979), U. Tex. Dental Br. alumni Assn. (life), Nat. Rifle Assn. (life), Tex. Rifle Assn. (life), Am. Found. for N.Am. Wild Sheep, Internat. Sheep Hunting Assn. Republican. Roman Catholic. Clubs: Anthony Rod and Gun, Grand Slam (life). Avocations: high mountain sheep hunting; outdoor activities. Home: 416 Lindbergh St El Paso TX 79932 Office: 1201 E Schuster Bldg 4-A El Paso TX 79902

TORRES, JORGE HORACIO, marketing executive; b. Parana, Entre Rios, Argentina, Oct. 13, 1945; s. Andres Cesar and Rosa (Dimenza) T.; m. Susana Graciela Wildner-Fox, Feb. 20, 1971; children—Susana G. Germana, Maria J. Luciana, Santiago Alexander A. B.S., G. Belgrand Mil. Acad., Santa Fe, 1962; Electronics Engr., Buenos Aires U., 1968; Licenciate in Bus. Administrn., El Salvador U., 1982. Registered profl. engr. Project mgr. SADE OBRELMEC, Buenos Aires, 1969-72; engring. mgr. ESIN Cons., Buenos Aires, 1972-73; tech. mgr. SADE, Caracas, Tegucigalpa, 1976-79, comml. mgr., Buenos Aires, 1979-85, mktg. gen. mgr. Sade Indsl. Group, Buenos Aires, 1985—. Undersec., Province Entre Rios, Argentina, 1973-74, state sec., Province Entre Rios, 1974-76. Served to lt. Argentinian Army, 1962—, res. Mem. Engring. Profl. Council, Entre Rios Engring. Profl. Coll., Argentina Engrs. Ctr., IEEE, Planetary Soc. Roman Catholic. Home: Juan Francisco Segui 3560-P2B, 1425 Buenos Aires Argentina Office: Sade Saccifim, Av San Martin 4970 Florida, 1602 Buenos Aires Argentina

TORRES, KENNETH LAWRENCE, pump manufacturing company executive; b. Bombay, India, June 7, 1944; s. Cecil Lawrence and Florence (Rogers) T.; m. Jean Rogers, July 27, 1968; children—Dawn Torres, Ashley. B.Sc. in Engring., Sheffield U., 1964. Mng. dir. Torres Engring. & Pumps Ltd., Sheffield, Eng., 1981—. Patentee pump design. Office: Torres Engring & Pumps Ltd, 28 Sanderson St, Sheffield S9 2TW, England

TORRES, LORETTA RUBY, automotive company executive; b. Hopkinsville, Ky., July 5, 1946; d. James Vincent and Joan Wilma (Wilson) Dennett Fiore; m. George Joseph Torres, June 1, 1963; children—Georginna Jo, Daniel Andrew, Tammara Lyn. Student, Whatcom Community Coll., U. N.Mex., U. Wis.; Cert. in Service Mgmt., Calif. Poly. U.-Gen. Motors, 1986. Cert. emergency med. technician, Wash. Mem. retail staff Ben's Dept. Store, 1973-74, mgr. supr. The Hawthornes', Pt. Roberts, Wash., 1975-76; mem. staff warranty claims Lee Galles Oldsmobile, Albuquerque, 1978-82, service advisor, 1982-85. Service, part dir. Baca Motors Inc., Belen, N.Mex., 1985—. Pres., PTA, Acoma Elem. Sch., Albuquerque, 1970-72; emergency med. technician Pt. Roberts Community Fire Dept., Wash., 1975-76; mem. Blaine Boosters Assn., Wash., 1976-77, mem. AIEC adv. council San Juan Community Coll. Republican. Roman Catholic. Avocations: reading; gardening; yoga; art; dancing. Office: Baca Motors Inc 101 Rio Communities Belen NM 87002

TORRES, MELBA BALDEO, internist; b. Mauban, Quezon, Philippines, Oct. 17, 1932; d. Amadeo Desembrana and Leona Asinas (Mayuga) Baldeo; m. Alfredo Castañeda Torres, Feb. 2, 1958; children: Melodia, Melinda, Melissa, Ildebrando. BA, Far Ea. U., Manila, 1952, MD, 1958; M of Pub. Health, U. Philippines, 1964. Resident physician pediatrics dept. Far Eastern Univ., Manila, 1958-59; physician E. Rodriguez Health Ctr., Mandaluyong, Philippines, 1959-60; med. officer Office of Provincial Health Officer, Manila, 1960-72, acting asst., 1972-76; sr. med. officer Ministry Health, Port Harcourt, Nigeria, 1976-80; prin. Sch. Health Tech., Port Harcourt, Rivers State, Nigeria, 1976-85; cons. Ministry Health, Port Harcourt, Nigeria, 1980-85; med. practitioner Torres Med. and Surg. Clinic, Manila, 1985—; med. officer counterpart of WHO Med. Officer for Rizal Health Devel. Project 4001, Pasig, Manila, 1970-76; mem. adaptation for basic health services scheme of standing orders for community health officer, suprs. and assts. com., 1980. Mem. Kababaihang Rizalista, Mandaluyong, Manila, 1974—, Sacred Heart Soc., Rivers State, Nigeria, 1980-85, Apostleship Prayer, Mandaluyong, 1987—; pres. Our Lady Perpetual Help Assn., Rivers State, 1976-85. Mem. Philippine Med. Assn., Philippine Assn. for Advancement Sci., Mandaluyong Med. Soc. (councilor 1972-74). Mem. Nationalist Party. Roman Catholic. Home: 842 Fabella, Manila, Mandaluyong 1501, Philippines Office: Torres Med and Surg Clinic, 19 T Bernardo, Manila, Mandaluyong 1501, Philippines

TORRESY, FRANK LOUIS, industrialist, financier; b. Genoa, Italy, May 2, 1921; came to U.S., 1955, naturalized, 1964; s. Alfredo and Elvira (Muzio) Torresi; LL.D. summa cum laude, U. Genoa, 1943, D.Econs.Scis., 1945; m. Joana Augusta de Almeida; children—Viviana, Alfredo, Frank Louis, Jr., Natalie. Admitted to bar, 1946; practice law, Genoa, 1946; founder, pres. Resinas Sinteticas Del Norte de Espana, Barcelona, Spain, 1949-51; dir. Societa Idro Elettrica Ligure, Genoa, 1951-54, Chem. & Indsl. Engring. Ltd., Zurich, Switzerland, 1955-57; founder, dir., pres. Internat. Devel. and Investment Co. Ltd., Nassau, Bahamas, 1958-69, also dir. related subs.; founder, pres. Celulose de Angola S.A., 1969-77; major shareholder, chmn. Empar Empreendimentos e Participacoes S.A., Rio de Janeiro, 1977—. Served to capt. Italian Army, 1941-45. Decorated War Merit Cross. Republican. Roman Catholic. Clubs: Lyford Cay (Nassau); Deepdale (N.Y.C.); Gavea (Rio de Janeiro); Puerta de Hierro (Madrid).

TORTELIER, PAUL, cellist, composer; b. Paris, Mar. 21, 1914; s. Joseph and Marguerite (Boura) T.; m. Madeleine Gaston (div. 1943); 1 child, Anne; m. Maud Monique Martin; children: Pascal, Maria Tortelier de la Pau, Pomone. Grad. with honors, Conservatoire Nat. de La Musique, Paris, 1935; D of Music (hon.), Leicester (Eng.) U., 1972, Oxford U., 1975; D.H.C. (hon.), Aston U., Birmingham, Eng., 1979. 1st cellist Opera Monte Carlo, 1935-37; cellist Boston Symphony Orch., 1937-40; prof. music Conservatoire Nat. Supèrieur de la Musique, Paris, 1956-69, Folkwang Hochschule Musik, Essen, Fed. Republic Germany, 1969-75, Conservatoire Nat. de Region, Nice, 1978-80; 1st cellist Soc. des Concerts du Conservatoire, Paris, 1946-47. Composer: Spirales, 1943, Suite for Solo Cello, 1946, Symphony Israelienne, 1956, The Great Flag (Hymn for the United Nations), 1959, Violin and Piano Concerto for performance with orch., 1965, Offrande, 1970, Alla Maud, 1973, Sonata Breve "Bucephale", 1983, Romance and Dance Variations, 1985, Sonata Breve "Mon Cirque", 1987. Supporter United World Colls., 1985—. Recipient Great Prize for Recording Bach Cello Solo Suites (2). Fellow Royal College of Music; mem. Royal Acad. Music (hon.), Soc. des Auteurs et Compositeurs. Lodge: Lions (comdr. Helsinki, Finland, 1983). Home: care M A de Valmalete, Bldg Gaveau 11 Ave Delcassé, 75635 Paris France Office: Mariedi Anders Artists Mgmt 535 El Camino Del Mar San Francisco CA 94121 also: care MA de Valmalete, Bldg Gaveau 11 avenue Delcasse, 75635 Paris France

TOSATO, ANGELO, biblical scholar; b. Venice, Italy, Dec. 29, 1938; s. Egidio and Cecilia (Valmarana) T. Lic. in Philisophy, Gregorian U., 1960, PhD in Theology, 1972; PhD in Scripture, Bibl. Inst., Rome, 1982. Prof. Lateran U., Rome, 1975, Gregorian U., Rome, 1984—, Bibl. Inst., Rome, 1985—; cons. Commn. for Relations with Jews, Vatican, 1981—. Author: Il Matrimonio Israel, 1982; contbr. papers on bibl. matters to numerous publs. Mem. Italian Bibl. Assn. (sec. 1987—). Roman Catholic. Home: Via della Scrofa 70, 00186 Rome, Lazio Italy

TOSUNLAR, AKIF ZAFER, small business owner, computer systems dealer; b. Istanbul, Turkey, Dec. 17, 1950; s. Huseyin Behcet and Melahat (Saygel) T.; m. Julia Claire Parker-Jones, July, 3, 1973; children: Lara Claire Filiz, Olivia Yeliz. Student, Bosphorus U., 1971-73, 74-75. Mgr. ops. Tourism Transport, Ltd., Istanbul, 1969-73; sr. cons. Anglo-World Travel, Ltd., Bournemouth, Eng., 1976-80; mng. dir. Euro Package Tours, Ltd., Bournemouth, 1980-87; owner Silversands Tours/Computers, Poole, Eng., 1987—. Mem. Tourism Soc. Muslim.

TOTH, BENEDICT JOHN, physician; b. Vasboldogasszony, Hungary, Nov. 28, 1910; came to U.S., 1937, naturalized, 1942; s. Benedek Joseph and Maria (Doka) T.; M.D., U. Budapest, 1936; m. June Eileen Riley, Feb. 16, 1946; children—John Thomas. Intern, Univ. Hosps., Budapest, 1935-36; resident New Rochelle (N.Y.) Hosp., 1937-42; instr. pathology U. Budapest, 1935-36; chief radiology dept. St. Francis Hosp., Olean, N.Y., 1941-56, Salamanca Dist. Hosp., 1941-56, Tri-county Meml. Hosp., Gowanda, N.Y., 1953-70, Gowanda State Hosp., 1955-70, Cuba (N.Y.) Meml. Hosp., 1942-71, Chaffee Meml. Hosp., Springville, N.Y., 1956-70, Port Allecany Hosp., 1948-68, Wellsville (N.Y.) Meml. Hosp., 1943-47; cons. radiologist Cuba Meml. Hosp., 1971-82; chmn. com. N.Y. State Hosp. and Schs., 1965-66. Diplomate Am. Bd. Radiology. Mem. Cattaraugus County Med. Soc. (pres. 1961), N.Y. Radiol. Soc., Am. Coll. Radiology, AMA, N.Y. Med. Soc., Buffalo Radiol. Soc., Pa. Radiol. Soc., Radiol. Soc. N.Am., Am. Cancer Soc., Nat. Gastroent. Soc. Republican. Presbyterian. Club: Coral Gables (Fla.) Country. Contbr. articles in field to profl. jours. Address: 5317 Orduna Dr Coral Gables FL 33146

TÓTH, FERENC LÁSZLÓ, economist; b. Szeged, Hungary, Sept. 20, 1953; S. Ferenc Istvan and Mària (Hasdell) T.; m. Éva Hizsnyik; 1 child, Dániel. MSC, Karl Marx U. Econs., Budapest, Hungary, 1978, PhD, 1982. Research scholar Inst. for Computer Scis., Budapest, 1978-83, Internat. Inst. for Applied Systems Analysis, Laxenburg, Austria, 1984—. Contbr. articles to profl. jours. Office: Internat Inst Applied Systems Analysis, Schlossplatz 1, A-2361 Laxenburg Austria

TOUBON, JACQUES, politician; b. Nice, France, June 29, 1941; s. Pierre-Constant and Yolande (Molinas) T.; m. Lise Weiler, 1982. Student, Inst. d'Etudes Politiques and Ecole Nat. d'Adminstrn., Lyons, France. Civil servant Govt. of France, 1965-76; chef de cabinet to Minister of Agr., 1972-74, Minister of Interior, 1974; tech. adviser Office of Prime Minister, 1974-76; dir. Fondation Claude Pompidou, 1970-77; asst. se.-gen. Rassemblement pour la République, 1977-81, sec.-gen., 1984—; dep. to Nat. Assembly, 1981—. Decorated Chevalier du Mérite Agricole. Home: 243 Blvd St Germain, 75007 Paris France Office: Assemblee Nationale, 73555 Paris France *

TOUCHARD, JACQUES JEAN HENRY, physician; b. Bordeaux, Gironde, France, Mar. 17, 1921; s. Georges Pierre and Ellen Louise (Labroue) T.; m. Alice Colette Theilacker, Jan. 11, 1945; children: Yves, Kathleen, Florence, Marie-Pierre, Frédéric. MD, U. Bordeaux, 1947, diploma in radiology, 1957. Asst. radiologist Bergonié Found., Bordeaux, 1957-67, chief dept., 1967—; cons. dept. otorhinolaryngology, Bordeaux Hosp.; mem. Corps Epidemiol. Reference Office. Hon. councilor Clairac, Lot et Garonne, 1955. Mem. Radiotherapie section de Soc. Française de Radiologie, European Soc. Therapeutic Radiology and Oncology. Home: rue Bertrand de Goth 152, 33800 Bordeaux, Gironde France Office: Found Bergonié, rue de Saint Genes 180, 33076 Bordeaux, Gironde France

TOUFFAIRE, PIERRE JULIEN, physician; b. Orange, Vaucluse, France, Aug. 22, 1933; s. Rene C. and Pierrette G. (Vaubourg) T.; m. Josette Leontine Lotti, Nov. 25, 1961; children—Michel, Jean. Bac., U. Toulon, 1951; Ancien Extern Hosp., Marseille, France, 1957; M.D., U. Marseille, 1963. Practice medicine, Saint-Maximin, France, 1961—. Roman Catholic. Home: Allée des Aubepines, Saint-Maximin France Office: 4500 Point Lookout Rd Orlando FL 32808

TOUGH, ALLEN M(AC NEILL), psychology educator, writer; b. Montreal, Que., Can, Jan. 6, 1936; s. David Lloyd and Margaret Phyllis (Allen) T.; m. Elaine Posluns, June 10, 1981; children: (by previous marriage) Susan Anne, Paul Allen. B.A., U. Toronto, 1958, M.A., 1962; Ph.D., U. Chgo., 1965. Tchr. Scarborough (Ont.) Bd. Edn., 1959-61; asst. prof. U. Toronto, Ont., 1964-66; asst. to full prof. adult learning and future studies Ont. Inst. Studies in Edn. and U. Toronto, 1966—; cons. editor Adult Edn. Jour., 1967-73; conf. chmn. Nat. Seminar Adult Edn. Research, Toronto, 1969; v.p. UNESCO Meeting, Paris, 1979; cons. Nat. Inst. Edn., 1978-79. Author: Learning Without a Teacher, 1967, Adult's Learning Projects, 2d edit, 1979, Expand Your Life, 1980, Intentional Changes, 1982, Fundamental Priorities, 1986; developed conceptual framework and original interview questions for studying self-planned learning. Kellogg fellow, 1962; Can. Council scholar, 1964; Ont. Inst. grantee, 1966-77. Mem. Am. Psychol. Assn., World Futures Studies Fedn., World Future Soc., Brit. Interplanetary Soc., Internat. Soc. for Study of Human Ideas on Ultimate Reality and Meaning, Soc. for Utopian Studies. Office: Ont Inst Studies in Edn, 252 Bloor St W, Toronto, ON Canada M5S 1V6

TOUQ, MUHYIEDDEEN SHABAN, university dean; b. Amman, Jordan, Apr. 15, 1944; s. Shaban Touq and Kairiah Moula; m. Hiba Nabulsi, June 15, 1977; children: Toleen, Yanal. BA, Jordan U., Amman, 1966; MA, Ball State U., 1969; PhD, Purdue U., 1972. Prof. psychology U. Wis., Eau Claire, 1972-73, United Arab Emirates Univ., Al-Ain, Arab Republic Egypt, 1973—; dean Coll. Edn. United Arab Emirates Univ., Al-Ain, United Arab Emirates, 1984—; dean Arab Community Coll., Amman, 1980-81; prof. psychology Jordan U., Amman, 1973—, head dept., 1976-78, advisor to pres., 1979-82, dean of students, 1982-84; cons. World Bank, Washington, 1977; exec. bur. UNESCO Inter-Youth Yr., Barcelona, Spain, 1985; bd. dirs. Internat. Council of Teaching, Washington, 1987—. Author: Educational Psychology, 1984, General Psychology, 1986; contbr. over 20 research articles to profl. jours. Originated 8 youth clubs and forums in Jordan, 1982-84; bd. dirs. SOS Villages, Amman, 1983-84, Edn. Council Amman, 1983, Ministry of Edn. Research Council, 1980-84, Moslem Girls Assn., 1980-84. Fulbright scholar Inst. Internat. Edn., 1968. Mem. Am. Ednl. Research Assn., Am. Psychol. Assn., Nat. Assn. on Gifted Edn. Home and Office: Box 13223, Amman Jordan

TOUR, ROBERT LOUIS, opthalmologist b. Sheffield, Ala., Dec. 30, 1918; s. R.S. and Marguerite (Meyer) T.; Chem.E., U. Cin., 1942, M.D., 1950. Intern, U. Chgo. Clinics, 1950-51; resident U. Calif. Med. Center-San Francisco, 1951-54; practice medicine, specializing in ophthalmology, San Francisco, 1954-76, Fairbanks, Alaska, 1976-79, Phoenix, 1979—; mem. staff John C. Lincoln Hosp., Humana Hosp., Boswell Meml. Hosp., Del Webb Meml. Hosp.; clin. prof. ophthalmology U. Calif.-San Francisco, 1974-76. Served to maj. AUS, 1942-45. Diplomate Am. Bd. Ophthalmology. Fellow ACS, Am. Acad. Ophthalmology; mem. Ariz. Ophthal. Soc., Phoenix Ophthal. Soc., Calif. Assn. Ophthalmology, Contact Lens Assn. Ophthalmologists, Pacific Coast Oto-Ophthal. Soc., Pan-Am. Assn. Ophthalmology, AMA, Ariz. Med. Assn., Maricopa County Med. Soc., Assn. Research in Vision and Ophthalmology, F.C. Cordes Eye Soc., Sigma Xi, Nu Sigma Nu, Alpha Tau Omega, Tau Beta Pi, Alpha Omega Alpha, Phi Lambda Upsilon, Omicron Delta Kappa, Kappa Kappa Psi. Clubs: Masons, K.T., Lions, Shriners. Home: 1016 E Lois Ln Phoenix AZ 85020 Office: 755 E McDowell Rd Phoenix AZ 85006

TOURE, ABDOURAHMANE, former minister of commerce of Senegal; b. Matam, Senegal, Sept. 3, 1943; s. Iba Toure and Goubal Dieng; m. Marie Toure; 5 children. Maitrise en Scis. econ., U. Caen, France; Brevete, Ecole Nat. d'Adminstrn., Senegal; M.B.A., Ecole des Hautes Etudes, Montreal, Que., Can. Various positions in Presidency of Republic of Senegal, minister of commerce, Dakar, until 1988. Decorated chevalier de l'Ordre du Lion. Mem. Parti Socialiste. Musulmane. Address: Ministere du Commerce, 23 rue Calmette, B P 4057 Dakar Senegal *

TOURE, MOHAMED ALI, professional society administrator; b. Dakar, Senegal, Feb. 20, 1949; s. Moustapha and Rouguietou (Diallo) T.; m. Mariame Tiam, Nov. 30, 1976; children: Rouguietou, Moustapha, Said Nour, Mohamed Fadel, Bineta. Maths. Baccalauract, Lycee Blaise Diagne, Dakar, 1967; Electricity-Mechanics Engr. diploma, Ecole Speciale de Mecanique et Electricité, Sudria, Paris, 1975. Dep. head of staff Senelec Power Authority, Dakar, Senegal, 1975-79, head of staff (research), 1979; gen. mgr. Sinaes, Dakar, 1980-86; mem. profl. staff Islamic Found. Sci., Tech. and Devel., 1986—. Recipient Internat. Africa award, 1980, 85. Muslim. Lodge: Rotary. Avocations: public relations; foreign language; civilizations; philology. Home: Bopp rue 1 No 103, Dakar Senegal Office: IFSTAD, PO Box 9833, Jeddah 21423, Saudi Arabia

TOURE, YEYA TIEMOKO, science educator; b. Gao, Mali, 1952; s. Tiemoko Hakirou and Aïssa (Aboulaye) T.; m. Hindou Keita, Sept. 16, 1976; children: Abdoulaye, Youssouf, Tiemoko. MS, Ecole Normale Superieure, Bamako, Mali, 1974; PhD, Ctr. Pedagogique Superieure, Bamako, 1979, U. Marseilles, France, 1985. Prof. Biology Girls Sch., Bamako, 1975-76; prof. Cellular Biology and Genetics, researcher Ecole de Medecine et Pharmacie, Bamako, 1979—; prof. Radical Entomolgy Inst. Supérieur de Formation et de Recherche Appliquée, Bamako, 1985—; dir. gen. Ctr. Nat. de la Recherche Sci. et Tech., Bamako, 1986—; mem. expert com. on biology and control of vector WHO, Geneva, 1985-89, temp. advisor on applied field research on malaria, 1987-89. Contbr. more than 30 articles to profl. jours. Research grantee WHO, 1981—, Internat. Atomic Energy Agy., 1984—. Fellow Royal Soc. Tropical Medicine and Hygiene, Italian Soc. Parasitology. Mem. Union Dem. du Peuple Malien. Muslim. Office: Ctr Nat de la Recherche, Sci et Tech, rue 408 Lajiabougou, BP 3052 Bamako Mali

TOUREK, STEVEN CHARLES, lawyer; b. Evanston, Ill., Apr. 28, 1948; s. Charles Frank and Gertrude Jean (Steiner) T., Jr.; m. Ann Elizabeth Elliott, Sept. 13, 1969; children—Peter S., Samuel C. B.A., Dartmouth Coll., 1970; M.A., Cambridge U., 1974, LL.B., 1975; postgrad. Yale U. Law Sch., 1970-71. Bar: Minn. 1976, Wis. 1981, U.S. Dist. Ct. Minn. 1976, U.S. Dist. Ct. (we. dist.) Wis. 1982, U.S. Ct. Appeals (8th cir.) 1981. Asst. dean Dartmouth Coll., Hanover, N.H., 1971-72; assoc. Oppenheimer, Wolff, Foster, Shepard & Donnelly, St. Paul, 1975-79; ptnr. Winthrop & Weinstine , St. Paul, 1979—. Dir Vol. Action Ctr., St. Paul, 1977-78; dir., treas. Bd. Edn. Ind. Sch. Dist. 197, West St. Paul, 1980-83; trustee, bd. dirs. Dodge Nature Ctr., West St. Paul, 1982—. Bd. dirs. Family Service Greater St. Paul, 1986-87, Found. for Excellence, 1987—. Reynolds fellow, 1973-74; Hattie M. Strong Found. fellow, 1972-73; Rufus Choate scholar, Dartmouth Coll., 1966-70. Mem. Minn. Bar Assn., Wis. Bar Assn., Minn. Trial Lawyers Assn., Assn. Trial Lawyers Am., ABA, Found. for Excellence in Edn. (bd. dirs. 1986—), Phi Beta Kappa. Lutheran. Clubs: Cambridge U. Boat (pres. 1974-75), Cambridge Blues Com. (chmn. 1974-75). Lodge: Rotary (bd. dirs. Midway chpt. 1985-86). Office: Winthrop & Weinstine 1800 Conwed Tower 444 Cedar St Saint Paul MN 55101

TOURETZ, LILLIAN CAROLE CONRAD, psychotherapist; b. N.Y.C., Oct. 17, 1923; d. Philip and Rose Helen Stetsky; B.A., Hunter Coll., 1944; M.S.W., N.Y.U., 1968; m. Martin Conrad, June 3, 1944; children—David, Donna; m. 2d, Arthur Touretz, May 28, 1977. Asst. mgr. N.Y.C. Housing Authority, 1946-49; pres. Profl. Workers AFL-CIO, 1947-49; lectr., cons. in field, 1952-78; psychotherapist Pelham (N.Y.) Family Service, 1968-77; pvt. practice psychotherapy, Hartsdale, N.Y., 1977—; field instr. Adelphi U., 1972-77. Chmn. United Jewish Appeal; v.p. regional bd. B'nai B'rith, chpt. pres. B'nai B'rith, 1981-84, pres. Council of Pres. Mem. Nat. Assn. Social Workers, Soc. Clin. Social Work Psychotherapists, Hunter Coll., N.Y.U. alumni assns. Democrat. Address: 55 Edgewood RD Hartsdale NY 10530

TOURNIER, JEAN-CLAUDE, controller; b. Paris, Dec. 1, 1933; s. Jacques and Marcelle (Gandy) T.; m. Marie-José Bagot, Mar. 19, 1956; children: Jacques, Véronique, Jean-Baptiste, Anne-Sophie, Pascale. Diploma, Inst. d'Etudes Politiques, Paris, 1954; lic., Faculté de Droit, Paris, 1955. Attaché de direction Air France, Paris, 1958-61; analyst Banque de Neuflize, Schlumberger, Paris, 1962; cadre, chef de service Spie Batignolles, Contrôle de Gestion, Paris, 1963—. Author: Gagner de l'argent à la Bourse, 1974, Savoir gérer l'entreprise face à l'inflation, 1977, Table des méthodes d'évaluation d'une entreprise, 1982, L' impôt sur la fortune, 1983, Gerer un mini-portefeuille en Bourse, 1986. Served with French Air Force, 1955-57. Mem. Soc. Forestiere du Chabet (adminstr. 1973-80), French Fin. Analysts Soc., Spie Epargne (pres. conseil de surveillance 1986, v.p., chmn.). Roman Catholic. Home: 149 Boulevard Malesherbes, 75017 Paris 17 France Office: Spie Batignolles, 1 rue de l' Entreprise, 95863 Cergy Pontoise Cedex France

TOURNIER, MICHEL, author; b. Paris, Dec. 19, 1924; s. Alphonse and Marie-Madeleine (Fournier) T. Ed. U. Paris, Sorbonne, U. Tubingen. In radio and TV prodn., 1949-54; press attaché, Europe, 1955-58; head lit. services Editions Plon, 1958-68; author: Vendredi ou les limbes du Pacifique, 1967; Le Roi des Aulnes, 1970; Les meteores, 1975; Le vent paraclet, 1977; Le coq de bruyere, 1978; Des clefs et des serrures, 1979; Gaspard, Melchior et Balthazar, 1980, La Goutte d'Or, 1986. Decorated officer Légion de'Honneur; recipient grand prix du Roma Acad. Française, 1967; prix Goncourt, 1970. Mem. Academie Goncourt.

TOURTELLOTTE, MILLS CHARLTON, mechanical and electrical engineer; b. Great Falls, Mont., Dec. 26, 1922; s. Nathaniel Mills and Frances Victoria (Charlton) T.; m. Dorothy Elsie Gray, Sept. 16, 1947; children—Jane Tourtellotte Collins, Kathryn Tourtellotte Bauman, Thomas. B.S., Ill. Inst. Tech., 1947, M.S., 1952. Registered profl. engr., Ill., Mich., Tex. Engr., Automatic Electric Co., Chgo., 1947-49, Inland Steel Co., East Chicago, Ind., 1952-56; sr. project engr. Gulf States Tube div. Quanex Corp., Rosenberg, Tex., 1956—; fallout shelter analyst Fed. Emergency Mgmt., Washington, 1970—. Contbr. papers to tech. lit. Patentee mech. and elec. devices. Election judge Ft. Bend County Republican Party, 1965; chmn. 4H Adult Leaders Assn., 1968; song leader, tenor in choir local Methodist Ch. Named Friend of 4H, Ft. Bend County Extension Service, 1968; named Eagle Scout, Order of the Arros, Boys Scouts Am., 1987 . Mem. Nat. Soc. Profl. Engrs., ASME, Tex. Soc. Profl. Engrs. (edn. chmn. 1969), Fluid Power Soc., Am. Soc. for Engring. Edn. (industry chmn. 1969), Assn. Iron and Steel Engrs. (life), VFW (life, quartermaster 1984). Office: Quanex Corp Gulf State Tube div PO Box 952 Rosenberg TX 77471

TOUVA, PAUL, Solomon Islands government official; b. July 11, 1946; married; 4 children. Student, St. Gregory Coll., Campbell Town, New South Wales, Australia, 1964-68. With Lands Dept., Solomon Islands, 1969—, adminstrv. officer valuer, 1976—; former minister natural resources, former dep. speaker Nat. Parliament, former minister fgn. affairs, now minister econ. planning Solomon Islands, Honiara. Roman Catholic. Address: Ministry Econ Planning, Honiara Solomon Islands *

TOUYZ, STEPHEN WILLIAM, clinical psychologist; b. Cape Town, Republic of South Africa, Aug. 29, 1950; s. Harry and Tilly (Woolfowitz) T.; m. Rennette Dawn Elk, Jan. 18, 1976; children—Justin Lawrence, Lauren Marissa. B.S., U. Cape Town, 1972, Ph.D., 1976; B.S. with honors, U. Witwatersrand, 1974. Sr. tutor U. Cape Town, 1974-75; sr. research asst. Groote Schuur Hosp., Cape Town, 1974-75, intern psychologist, 1976-78; staff psychologist Royal Prince Alfred Hosp., Sydney, Australia, 1978-80; clin. lectr. U. Sydney, 1979—; head clin. psychology unit Royal Prince

Alfred Hosp., Sydney, 1980—; cons. psychologist anorexia nervosa unit Northside Clinic, Sydney, 1979-84, Royal Prince Alfred Hosp., 1983—, Lynton Pvt. Hosp., 1984—; field supr. U. Sydney, 1979—. Author: Grune and Stratton, 1984. Research grantee Council for Sci. and Indsl. Research, 1973-76, Nat. Health and Med. Research Council Australia, 1983-87, Ramaciotti Found., 1983-84. Fellow Internat. Coll. Psychosomatic Medicine; mem. Australian Psychol. Soc., Australian Behaviour Modification Assn., Australian Soc., Psychiat. Research, Am. Psychol. Assn. (affiliate). Office: Dept of Psychiatry, Royal Prince Alfred Hosp, Camperdown NSW 2050, Australia

TOV, EMANUEL, theology educator; b. Amsterdam, The Netherlands, Sept. 15, 1941; s. Juda and Toos (Neeter) Toff; m. Lika Aa, Dec. 3, 1964; children: Ophirah, Ariel, Amitai. BA, Hebrew U., Jerusalem, 1964, MA, 1967, PhD, 1973. Prof. of bibl. studies Hebrew U., 1980—, chmn. bibl. dept., 1982-84; vis. prof. U. Pa., Phila., 1980-81, 1985-86; Grinfield lectr. on Septuagint Oxford (Eng.) U., 1982—; bd. dirs. Computer Assisted Tools Septuagint Studies, Jerusalem/Phila. Editor Hebrew U. Bible Project, 1981—. Jewish. Office: Hebrew U, Dept of Bible, Jerusalem Israel

TOVEY, MALCOLM JILLARD, accountant; b. Oldham, Lancashire, Eng., Mar. 7, 1948; s. Sydney and Lilian (Platt) T.; m. Pauline Eastwood, May 15, 1974 (div. Dec. 1982); 1 child, Suzanne Michelle. Cert., Inst. Chartered Accts. Eng. and Wales, 1973. Acct. James Hardman and Co., Oldham, 1965-80; dep. chief acct. Mecca Leisure, Ltd., London, 1980-83, fin. systems mgr., 1983-85; fin. dir. Travelscene, Ltd. div. Mecca Leisure Group PLC, London, 1985-87; fin. cons. Mecca Leisure Group, PLC, London, 1987, mgmt. info. services mgr., 1987—; fin. dir. Interwork Garments, Ltd., Atherton, Lancashire, 1978-80/. Mem. Ch. of Eng. Office: Mecca Leisure Ltd, 76 Southwark St, London SE1 OPP, England

TOVSTONOGOV, GEORGIY ALEKSANDROVICH, theatrical director, educator; b. Tbilsi, Georgia, Russia, Sept. 28, 1915; s. Aleksandr and Tamara (Papitashvili) T.; ed. Lunacharsky Inst. Theatrical Art; m., 2 sons. Actor and asst. dir. Jr. Theatre, Tbilisi, 1931; dir. Griboyedov Russian Drama Theatre, Tbilisi, 1938-46, Central Children's Theatre, Moscow, 1946-49, Leningrad Komsomol Theatre, 1950-56; chief dir. Leningrad State Drama Theatre, 1956—; chmn. directing Leningrad Inst. Theatre, Music and Cinema, 1962—; prodns. include: Kremlin Chimes, 1940, School for Scandal, 1942, Pompadours, 1954, Irkutsk Story, 1960, Woe from Wit, 1962, Virgin Soil Upturned, 1964, Three Sisters, 1964, The Idiot, 1966, Merchants, 1966, Khanuma, 1973. Recipient State prize, 1950, 52, 68; named People's Artist, 1957; decorated Order of Lenin (2), Order of Red Banner. Co-editor Theatre monthly; author: Notes on the Theatre, 1960; Talking about Directing, 1962; On Being a Director, 1965; My Thoughts at Large, 1972. Address: Leningrad State Acad, Bolshoi Drama Theatre, 65 Fontanka, Leningrad USSR *

TOVUA, JOSEPH PAUL, government official; b. Honiara, Solomon Islands, July 11, 1946; s. Joseph and Melania (Solony) T.; children: Isabella, Thomas, Paul, Melchior, Cassiano, Linus, Gloria, Pauline, Felicia, Paul Jr. Grad., Marist Bros. Coll., 1968. Valuer Solomon Island Govt., 1975-76, lands officer, 1975-76; mem. Nat. Parliament Solomon Island, 1976—; minister natural resources Solomon Island Govt., 1976-81, minister fgn. affairs, 1984—. Mem. United Party. Roman Catholic.

TOWBIN, A. ROBERT, investment banker; b. N.Y.C., May 26, 1935; s. Harold Clay and Minna (Berlin) T.; m. Irene K. Lyons, Sept. 15, 1957; children: Minna Joyce, Abraham Robert, Zachary Harold. B.A., Dartmouth Coll., 1957. With Asiel & Co., N.Y.C., 1958-59; with L.F. Rothschild, Unterberg, Towbin Holdings, Inc. (merged with C.E. Unterberg, Towbin Co. 1977), N.Y.C., 1959-86, vice chmn., 1961-86; mng. dir. Shearson Lehman Bros., Inc., N.Y., 1987—; dir. AVX Corp., Anthology Film Archives, Shearson Small Capitalization Fund. Hon. mem. N.Y. State Council Arts; bd. dirs. Grand St. Settlement, St. David's Sch., Marymount Sch. Mem. Securities Industry Assn., Bond Club N.Y. Clubs: Stock Exchange Luncheon, Harmonie (N.Y.C.); Nat. Golf Links Am.; N.Y. Yacht. Home: 1010 Fifth Ave New York NY 10028 Office: Shearman Lehman Bros Inc Am Express Tower World Fin Ctr New York NY 10285

TOWERS, BERNARD LEONARD, medical educator; b. Preston, Eng., Aug. 20, 1922; s. Thomas Francis and Isabella Ellen (Dobson) T.; m. Carole Ilene Lieberman; 1 child, Tiffany Sabrina; children by previous marriage: Helena Marianne, Celia Marguerite, Julie Carole. M.B., Ch.B., U. Liverpool, 1947; M.A., U. Cambridge, 1954. House surgeon Royal Infirmary, Liverpool, 1947; lectr. U. Bristol, 1949-50, U. Wales, 1950-54, Cambridge U., 1954-70; fellow Jesus Coll., 1957-70, steward, 1961-64, tutor, 1964-69; dir. med. studies 1964-70; prof. pediatrics UCLA, 1971-84, prof. anatomy, 1971—, prof. psychiatry, 1983—, convenor, moderator medicine and soc. forum, 1974—; co-dir. Program in Medicine, Law and Human Values, 1977-84; cons. Inst. Human Values in Medicine, 1971-84; adv. bd. Am. Teilhard Assn. for Future of Man, 1971—; v.p. Teilhard Centre for Future Man, London, 1974—. Author: Teilhard de Chardin, 1966, Naked Ape or Homo Sapiens?, 1969, Concerning Teilhard, 1969; also articles, chpts. on sci. and philosophy.; Editor anat. sect.: Brit. Abstracts Med. Scis, 1954-56, Teilhard Study Library, 1966-70; adv. bd.: Jour. Medicine and Philosophy, 1974-84. Served to capt. RAMC, 1947-49. NIH grantee, 1974-78; NEH grantee, 1977-83. Fellow Cambridge Philos. Soc., Royal Soc. Medicine; mem. Brit. Soc. History of Medicine, Soc. Health and Human Values (pres. 1977-78), Anat. Soc. Gt. Britain, Worshipful Soc. Apothecaries London, Am. Assn. for Study Mental Imagery, Western Assn. Physicians, Sociètè Europèenne de Culture Venise. Office: U Calif Ctr Health Scis Los Angeles CA 90024-1763

TOWERS, GARRY SUTHERLAND, tobacco company executive; b. Blantyre, Malawi, Jan. 9, 1948; s. Walter and May (Sutherland) T.; m. Eleanor Kathleen Bickford, Feb. 24, 1971; children—Sarah, Marc. Student Falcon Coll., Zimbabwe, 1963-66. Gen. mgr. tobacco estates, Malawi, 1970-77; mng. dir. Tobacco Devel. Co., Chipata, Zambia, 1978—; dir. Zambia & Overseas Tobacco Co., Lusaka. Presbyterian. Office: 21488 PO Box 510454, Chipata Zambia

TOWERY, CURTIS KENT, lawyer; b. Hugoton, Kans., Jan. 29, 1954; s. Clyde D. and Jo June (Curtis) T. BA, Trinity U., 1976; JD, U. Okla., 1979. Bar: Okla. 1980. Mem. Curtis & Blanton, Pauls Valley, Okla., 1980-81; lawyer land and legal dept. Trigg Drilling Co., Oklahoma City, 1981-82; adminstrv. law judge Okla. Corp. Commn., Oklahoma City, 1982-85; counsel Curtis & Blanton, Paul's Valley, Okla., 1985—; bd. dirs. First Nat. Bank of Pauls Valley, Okla., Clyde Towery Inc., Trinity Exploration Corp.; adminstrv. law judge Okla. Dept. Mines, 1985—. Assoc. Okla. Mus. Art, 1985—, Okla. Symphony Orch., 1987; v.p. Assoc. Bd. Ballet Okla., 1988—. Mem. ABA, Okla. Bar Assn., Am. Assn. Petroleum Landmen, Internat. Assn. Energy Economist, Okla. City Assn. Petroleum Landmen, Phi Alpha Delta, Sigma Nu. Democrat. Presbyterian. Clubs: Young Men's Dinner Club (Oklahoma City), Faculty House. Lodges: Rotary, Elks. Home: 9009 N May Ave Sutton Pl 179 Oklahoma City OK 73120 Office: Curtis & Blanton 123 W Paul Pauls Valley OK 73075

TOWEY, MARIE ELIZABETH, nursing administrator, educator; b. Salem, Mass., Jan. 13, 1934; d. Daniel and Mary Catherine (Buckley) Linehan; m. Carroll Francis Towey, Aug. 24, 1957; children—Mary Ellen Towey Roth, Michael Carroll, Kevin James. Diploma Burdett Coll., 1952; R.N., Salem Hosp. Sch. Nursing, 1955; postgrad. Boston Coll. Sch. Nursing, 1956-61; B.S., Salem State Coll., 1975, M.Ed. in Health Counseling and Guidance, 1978. R.N., Mass., Va., D.C. Md. Staff nurse Salem Hosp. and Mass. Gen. Hosp., 1955; nursing instr. Salem Hosp. (Mass.), 1955-59, med. nursing supr., 1960-61; staff nurse Twin Oaks Nursing Home, Danvers, Mass., 1961-71, Mt. Pleasant Hosp., Lynn, Mass., 1971; social worker, nurse NIMH Tng. Grant, Malden Ct. Clinic (Mass.), 1972-73; region IV coordinator North Shore Council on Alcoholism, Danvers, 1973-74; community mental health nurse Danvers-Salem Community Mental Health Resources Unit, Salem, 1974-78; nurse instr. Med. Aid Tng. Sch., Washington, 1978-79, Fairfax County Div. Continuing Edn. med. div., Woodson High Sch. (Va.), 1979-80; dir. nursing and health services ARC, Alexandria, 1980-81; dir. nursing services Med. Personnel Pool, Alexandria, 1981-82, adminstr., 1982-84; adminstr. ambulatory care ctr. Medic 24-Ltd., Baileys Crossroads, Va., 1984—; adminstr. Am. Med. Services, Springfield, Va., 1984-85; dir. nursing service Camelot Hall Nursing Facility, Arlington, Va., 1985-86, Clinton Convalescent Ctr., Md., 1986; sr. med. rev. specialist Intracorp, Falls Church, Va., 1986—; lectr. in field. Co-author planning grant in mental health and mental retardation, 1978. Sec. Mass Soc. of D.C.,1987-88; area chmn. Burke Centre Conservancy (Va.), 1981-88 ; mem. town meeting Danvers Town Govt., 1971-78; pres. Mass. Region IV Mental Health and Mental Retardation Adv. Council, 1977-78; sec., treas. Mass. Area Bd. Coalition, 1977-78; trustee Danvers State Hosp., 1977-82; community mental health resources devel. unit com. chmn. Danvers-Salem Area Mental Health Retardation Bd., 1973-78, pres., 1975-77; chmn. emergency med. services com. North Shore Council on Alcoholism, 1972-76; mem. adv. com. for adult edn. North Shore Region, 1974-75; mem. Danvers Task Force on Deinstitutionalization, 1975-76; bd. dirs. Archdiocesan Council Cath. Nurses, 1969-72. Recipient Merit and Appreciation certs. various agys., socs. and hosps. Mem. Am. Nurses Assn. (membership com. 1983—), Va. Nurses Assn. (hospitality com. 1983), Va. Assn. Home Health Agys. (chmn. region I legis., rep. 1984-86), D.C. Nurses Assn. (conf. com. 1982), Health Adminstrs. Assn. of Nat. Capitol Area, Salem Hosp. Alumnae Assn. (past treas. and chmn. program 1956-58, 60-64), Alexandria C. of C. Republican. Club: Danvers Garden (pres., chmn. civic beautification 1972-77). Home: 10639 Canterberry Rd Fairfax Station VA 22039 Office: Intracorp 5205 Leesburg Pike Falls Church VA 22041

TOWNE, CLAUDIA CIACCO, data processor; b. N.Y.C., Apr. 6, 1945; d. Francesco and Angelina (Gaultieri) Ciacco; B.A., Hunter Coll., N.Y.C., 1966; M.B.A., U. Conn., 1986; m. Gene Leonard Towne, Dec. 23, 1967. Graphics systems analyst Mergenthaler Linotype Co., N.Y.C., 1966-68; systems analyst Service Bur. Corp., Honolulu, 1968-71; systems and programming mgr. Automatic Data Processing, Inc., N.Y.C., 1971-79; info. systems mgr. Berol USA, Danbury, 1979-84; corp. dir. mgmt. info. systems IPCO Corp., White Plains, N.Y., 1985—. Bd. dirs. Greater Danbury Area Jr. Achievement, 1980-83. Mem. Data Processing Mgmt. Assn.

TOWNER, LAWRENCE WILLIAM, historian, librarian; b. St. Paul, Sept. 10, 1921; s. Earl Chadwick and Cornelia Josephine (Mallum) T.; m. Rachel E. Bauman, Nov. 28, 1943; children: Wendy Kay Towner Yanikoski, Kristin Anne Towner Moses, Lawrence Baumann (dec.), Elizabeth Gail, Peter Mallum, Michael Chadwick. BA, Cornell Coll., Mt. Vernon, Iowa, 1942, LHD; MA, Northwestern U., 1950, PhD, 1955; LHD; LittD (hon.), Lake Forest Coll.; LHD, U. Ill., Chgo., 1986. History master Chgo. Latin Sch., 1946-47; instr., then asst. prof. history MIT, Cambridge, 1950-55; asso. prof. history Coll. William and Mary, Williamsburg, Va., 1955-62; editor William and Mary Quar., Williamsburg, Va., 1956-62, mem. bd. editors, 1970-71; fellow Ctr. Study History of Liberty, Harvard U., Cambridge, Mass., 1961-62; librarian Newberry Library, Chgo., 1962—, pres., 1975-86, pres. emeritus, 1986—; vis. prof. English Northwestern U., 1968-70; professorial lectr. U. Chgo., 1968. Contbr. numerous articles to mags., profl. jours.; bd. editors: Am. mag., History and Life. Mem. council Eleutherian Mills, Hagley Found., Chgo., 1965-69, 77-78, Inst. Early Am. History, Williamsburg, Va., 1970-73, 79-82; trustee Grinnell (Iowa) Coll., 1966-72, Latin Sch. Chgo., 1970-72, Mus. Contemporary Art, 1972-75; bd. dirs. Ill. Humanities Council, 1974-78, chmn., 1976-78; mem. exec. com. Fedn. Pub. Programs in the Humanities, 1977-78; bd. govs. Henrotin Hosp., 1977-86. Served to lst lt. pilot USAAC, World War II. Decorated Chevalier of Arts and Letters Govt. of France, 1986. Mem. Am. Hist. Assn. (mem. council 1973-75), Orgn. Am. Historians, Bibliog. Soc. Am., Ind. Research Libraries Assn. (chmn. bd. 1976-78), Colonial Soc. Mass., Va. Hist. Soc., Mass. Hist. Soc., Modern Poetry Assn. (pres. 1967-69, trustee 1962-75), Am. Antiquarian Soc., Phi Beta Kappa. Clubs: Cosmos (Washington); Harvard (N.Y.C.); Caxton, Economic, Wayfarers (Chgo.) (pres. 1983-84). Home: 101 E Bellevue Pl Chicago IL 60611 Office: The Newberry Library 60 W Walton St Chicago IL 60610

TOWNES, CHARLES HARD, physics educator; b. Greenville, S.C., July 28, 1915; s. Henry Keith and Ellen Sumter (Hard) T.; m. Frances H. Brown, May 4, 1941; children: Linda Lewis, Ellen Screven, Carla Keith, Holly Robinson. B.A., B.S., Furman U., 1935; M.A., Duke U., 1937; Ph.D., Calif. Inst. Tech., 1939. Mem. tech. staff Bell Telephone Lab., 1939-47; assoc. prof. physics Columbia U., 1948-50, prof. physics, 1950-61; exec. dir. Columbia Radiation Lab., 1950-52, chmn. physics dept., 1952-55; provost and prof. physics MIT, 1961-66, Inst. prof., 1966-67; v.p., dir. research Inst. Def. Analyses, Washington, 1959-61; prof. physics U. Calif. at Berkeley, 1967-86, prof. physics emeritus, 1986—; Guggenheim fellow, 1955-56; Fulbright lectr. U. Paris, 1955-56, U. Tokyo, 1956; lectr., 1955, 60; dir. Enrico Fermi Internat. Sch. Physics, 1963; Richtmeyer lectr. Am. Phys. Soc., 1959; Scott lectr. U. Cambridge, 1963; Centennial lectr. U. Toronto, 1967; Lincoln lectr., 1972-73, Halley lectr., 1976; dir. Gen. Motors Corp.; mem. Pres.'s Sci. Adv. Com., 1966-69, vice chmn., 1967-69; chmn. sci. and tech. adv. com. for manned space flight NASA, 1964-69; mem. Pres.'s Com. on Sci. and Tech., 1976. Author: (with A.L. Schawlow) Microwave Spectroscopy, 1955; author, co-editor: Quantum Electronics, 1960, Quantum Electronics and Coherent Light, 1964; editorial bd.: (with A.L. Schawlow) Rev. Sci. Instrument, 1950-52, Phys. Rev, 1951-53; bd.: (with A.L. Schawlow) Phys., Rev, 1951-53, Jour. Molecular Spectroscopy, 1957-60, Procs. Nat. Acad. Scis, 1978—; contbr. articles to sci. pubIs. Trustee Calif. Inst. Tech., Carnegie Instn. of Washington, Pacific Sch. Religion; mem. corp. Woods Hole Oceanographic Instn. Recipient numerous hon. degrees and awards, including; Nobel prize for physics, 1964; Stuart Ballantine medal Franklin Inst., 1959, 62; Thomas Young medal and prize Inst. Physics and Phys. Soc., Eng., 1963; Disting. Public Service medal NASA, 1969; Wilhelm Exner award Austria, 1970; Niels Bohr Internat. Gold medal, 1979; Nat. Sci. medal, 1983, Berkeley citation U. Calif., 1986; named to Nat. Inventors Hall of Fame, 1976, Engring. and Sci. Hall of Fame, 1983. Fellow Am. Phys. Soc. (council 1959-62, 65-71, pres. 1967, Plyler prize 1977), Optical Soc. Am. (hon., Mees medal 1968), IEEE (medal of honor 1967), Calif. Acad. Scis.; mem. Am. Philos. Soc., Am. Astron. Soc., Am. Acad. Arts and Scis., Nat. Acad. Scis. (council 1969-72, 78-81, chmn. space sci. bd. 1970-73, Comstock award 1959), Société Française de Physique (council 1956-58), Royal Soc. (fgn.), Pontifical Acad. Scis., Max-Planck Inst. for Physics and Astrophysics (fgn. mem.). Office: Dept Physics U Calif at Berkeley Berkeley CA 94720

TOWNSEND, EARL CUNNINGHAM, JR., lawyer, author, composer; b. Indpls., Nov. 9, 1914; s. Earl Cunningham and Besse (Kuhn) T.; m. Emily Macnab, Apr. 3, 1947; children: Starr (Mrs. John R. Laughlin), Vicki M. (Mrs. Christopher Katterjohn), Julia E. (Mrs. Edward Goodrich Dunn, Jr.), Earl Cunningham III, Clyde G. Student (Rector scholar), De Pauw U., 1932-34; A.B., U. Mich., 1936, J.D., 1939. Bar: Ind. 1939, Mich. 1973, U.S. Supreme Ct. 1973, U.S. Ct. Appeals (4th, 6th, 7th cirs.), U.S. Dist. Ct. (no. and so. dists.) Ind., U.S. Dist. Ct. (ea. dist.) Va., U.S. Dist. Ct. (ea. dist.) Mich. Sr. partner firm Townsend & Townsend, Indpls., 1940-69; sr. partner Townsend, Hovde & Townsend, Indpls., 1969-84, Townsend, Yosha & Cline, Indpls., 1984-86, 1986—; individual practice Roscommon, Mich., 1973—; dep. prosecutor, Marion County, Ind., 1942-44; radio-TV announcer WIRE, WFBM, WFBM-TV, Indpls., 1940-49, 1st TV announcer Indpls. 500 mile race, 1949, 50; Big Ten basketball referee, 1940-47; lectr. trial tactics U. Notre Dame, Ind. U., U. Mich., 1968-79; chmn. faculty seminar on personal injury trials Ind. U. Sch. Law, U. Notre Dame Sch. Law, Valparaiso Sch. Law, 1981; Roscommon, Mich.; founder, v.p., treas. Am. Underwriters, Inc., Am. Interinsurance Exchange, 1965-70; mem. Com. to Revise Ind. Supreme Ct. Pattern Jury Instructions, 1975-83; lectr. Trial Lawyers 30 Yrs. Inst., 1986. Author: Birdstones of the North American Indian, 1959, also articles in legal and archeol. fields; composer: Moon of Halloween. Founder, life fellow Roscoe Pound Am. Trial Lawyers Found., Cambridge, Mass.; cofounder, dir. Meridian St. Found.; mem. fin. and bldg. coms., bd. dirs., later life trustee Indpls. Mus. Art; life trustee Ind. State Mus.; trus Judge Cale J. Holder Meml. Scholarship Fund, Ind. U. Law Sch.; trustee Cathedral High Sch., Indpls.; mem. Ind. U. Found.; mem. Dean's Council, Ind. U.; life dir. Indpls./Marion County Hist. Soc.; fellow Meth. Hosp. Found. Recipient Ind. Univ. Writers Conf. award, 1960; Hanson H. Anderson medal of honor Arsenal Tech. Schs., Indpls., 1971; named to Council Sagamores of Wabash, 1969, Hon. Ky. Col., 1986; Ind. Basketball Hall of Fame; hon. chief Black River-Swan Creek Saginaw-Chippewa Indian tribe, 1971. Fellow Ind. Coll. Trial Lawyers (pres. 1984—), Ind. Bar Found., Indpls. Bar. Found. (disting., charter), Internat. Acad. Trial Lawyers, Internat. Soc. Barristers; mem. Ind. Trial Lawyers Assn. (pres. 1963-64, life dir. 1981—), ABA (com. trial techniques 1964-76, com. aviation and space 1977—), Ind. State Bar Assn. (del. 1977-79), Indpls. Bar Assn., 34th Dist. (Mich.) Bar Assn., State Bar Mich., Assn. Am. Trial Lawyers (v.p. Ind. 1959-60, bd. govs. 7th jud. circuit 1966-68, assoc. editor Jour. 1964—), Am. Bd. Trial Advocates (diplomate, pres. Ind. chpt. 1982-85), Bar Assn. 7th Fed. Circuit, Roscommon County Bar Assn., Lawyers Assn. Indpls., Am. Judicature Soc., Am. Arbitration Assn. (panel), ASCAP, Ind. Archaeol. Soc. (founder, pres.), Indpls. C. of C., Ind. State C. of C., Genuine Indian Relic Soc. (co-founder, chmn. frauds com.), Ind. Hist. Soc., Trowel and Brush Soc. (hon.), U. Mich. Pres.'s Club, U. Mich. Victors Club (charter), Soc. Mayflower Descs. (gov. 1947-49), Key Biscayne C. of C., Delta Kappa Epsilon, Phi Kappa Phi. Republican. Methodist. Clubs: Mason (32 deg., Shriner), Players, U. Mich. (local pres. 1950), Columbia, Indpls. Athletic, Key Biscayne Yacht. Home: 5008 N Meridian St Indianapolis IN 46208

TOWNSEND, FRANK MARION, physician, educator; b. Stamford, Tex., Oct. 29, 1914; s. Frank M. and Beatrice (House) T.; m. Gerda Eberlein, 1940 (dec. div. 1944); 1 son, Frank M.; m. Ann Graf, Aug. 25, 1951; 1 son, Robert N. Student, San Antonio Coll., 1931-32, U. Tex., 1932-34; M.D., Tulane U., 1938. Diplomate: Am. Bd. Pathology. Intern Polyclinic Hosp., N.Y.C., 1939-40; commd. 1st lt. M.C., U.S. Army, 1940, advanced through grades to lt. col., 1946; resident instr. pathology Washington U., 1945-47; trans. to USAF, 1949, advanced through grades to col., 1956; instr. pathology Coll. Medicine, U. Nebr., 1947-48; asso. pathologist Scott and White Clinic, Temple, Tex., 1948-49; asso. prof. pathology Med. Br. U. Tex., Galveston, 1949-59; dir. labs. USAF Hosp., Lackland AFB, 1950-54; cons. pathology, chief cons. group Office Surgeon Gen. Hdqrs. USAF, Washington, 1954-55; cons. Office Surgeon Gen. Hdqrs. SAF, 1955-63; dep. dir. Armed Forces Inst. Pathology, Washington, 1955-59; dir. Armed Forces Inst. Pathology, 1959-63; vice comdr. aerospace med. div. Air Force Systems Command, 1963-65; ret. 1965; practice medicine specializing in pathology San Antonio, 1965—; dir. labs. San Antonio State Chest Hosp.; consulting pathologist Tex. Dept. Health hosps., 1965-72; clin. prof. pathology U. Tex. Med. Sch., San Antonio, 1969-72; prof., chmn. dept. pathology Health Sci. Ctr. U. Tex. Med. Sch., 1972-86, emeritus chmn., prof., 1986—; cons. U. Tex. Cancer Center-M.D. Anderson Hosp., 1966-80, NASA, 1967-75; mem. adv. bd. cancer WHO, 1958-75; mem. Armed Forces Epidemiology Bd., 1983—; bd. govs. Armed Forces Inst. Pathology, 1984—. Mem. editorial bd. Tex. Med. Jour., 1978-86; contbr. articles to med. jours. Mem. adv. council Civil War Centennial Commn., 1960-65; bd. dirs. Alamo Area Sci. Fair, 1967-73. Decorated D.S.M., Legion of Merit; recipient Founders medal Assn. Mil. Surgeons, 1961. Fellow ACP, Coll. Am. Pathologists (edn. advisor on accreditation, South Central states regional commr. lab. accreditation 1971-84), Am. Soc. Clin. Pathologists (Ward Burdick award 1983), Aerospace Med. Assn. (H.G. Moseley award 1962); mem. Tex. Med. Assn., AMA, Internat. Acad. Aviation and Space Medicine, AAAS, Tex. Soc. Pathologists, Am. Soc. Allied Health Professions, Am. Assn. Pathologists, Internat. Acad. Pathology, Acad. Clin. Lab. Physicians and Scientists, Soc. Med. Consultants to Armed Forces. Club: Torch. Home: Box 77 Harwood TX 78632 Office: U Tex Health Sci Ctr Dept Pathology 7703 Floyd Curl Dr San Antonio TX 78284

TOWNSEND, HAROLD GUYON, JR., publishing company executive; b. Chgo., Apr. 11, 1924; s. Harold Guyon and Anne Louise (Robb) T.: A.B., Cornell U., 1948; m. Margaret Jeanne Keller, July 28, 1951; children—Jessica, Julie, Harold Guyon III. Advt. salesman Chgo. Tribune, 1948-51; gen. mgr. Keller-Heartt Co., Clarendon Hills, Ill., 1951-62; pub. Santa Clara (Calif.) Jour., 1962-64; pres., pub. Dispatch-Tribune newspaper Townsend Communications, Inc., Kansas City, Mo., 1964—; dir. United Mo. City Bank. Chmn., Suburban Newspaper Research Commn., 1974—; dir. Certified Audit Bur. of Circulation, 1968-72. del. Rep. Nat. Conv., 1960; chmn. Mission Hills Rep. Com., 1966-77; bd. dirs. Kansas City Jr. Achievement, 1966-68, Kansas City council Girl Scouts U.S.A., 1969-71, Kansas City council Boy Scouts Am., 1974, Kansas City chpt. ARC, 1973-79, Kansas City Starlight Theater, Clay County (Mo.) Indsl. Commn.; treas., trustee Park Coll., Parkville, Mo., 1970-78. Mem. adv. com. North Kansas City Hosp.; bd. dirs. Taxpayers Research of Mo., 1978—, Nelson Gallery Friends of Art, 1980-85. Served with inf. AUS, World War II. Mem. Kansas City Advt. and Sales Club, Kansas City Press Club, Suburban Press Found. (pres. 1969-71), Suburban Newspapers Am. (pres. 1976-77), Kansas City Printing Industries Assn. (pres., dir.), Printing Industries of Am. (pres. non-heatset web sect. 1980-82), North Kansas City C. of C. (dir., pres. 1964-70), Univ. Assocs. (treas. 1977-80), Sigma Delta Chi, Pi Delta Epsilon, Phi Kappa Psi. Clubs: University (treas. 1977); Indian Hills Country; Hinsdale (Ill.) Golf; Mission Valley Country, Field (Sarasota, Fla.). Home: 829 W 54th Terr Kansas City MO 64112 Office: 7007 NE Parvin Rd Kansas City MO 64117

TOWNSEND, J. RUSSELL, JR., insurance executive; b. Cedar Rapids, Iowa, Nov. 21, 1910; s. J. Russell and Mabel (Ferguson) T.; B.S., Butler U., 1931; M.B.A., U. Pa., 1933; m. Virginia Holt, Aug. 1, 1938; 1 son, John Holt. CLU, registered health underwriter. Field asst. Equitable Life Ins. Co. Iowa, 1933-50, gen. agt., 1950-69, gen. agt. emeritus, 1969—; mng. asso. J. Russell Townsend & Assos., 1969—; assoc. prof. emeritus bus. adminstrn. Butler U., Indpls., 1982; cons. Ind. Dept. Ins., 1948-50; mem. Ind. Ho. of Reps., 1946-48, Ind. Senate, 1956-64; lectr., writer ins. field. Chmn. Indpls. Bicentennial Com., 1975-76; pres. Indpls. Jaycees, 1940. Served with USNR, 1942-46; lt. comdr. Res. ret. Recipient 25-year teaching award Am. Coll. C.L.U.s, 1960; Alumni Achievement award Butler U., 1979. Mem. Indpls. chpt. C.L.U.s (past pres.), Ind. Life Underwriters Assn. (past v.p.), Ret. Officers Assn. (past pres. Indpls. chpt.), Ind. Soc. Assn. Execs., Naval Res. Assn., Navy League U.S., Am. Soc. C.L.U.'s, AAUP, Am. Soc. Risk and Ins., Ind. Acad. Sci., Sales and Marketing Execs. Council, U.S. Naval Inst., Phi Delta Theta (past pres. Indpls. alumni club). Republican. Presbyterian. Clubs: Columbia, Meridian Hills Country, Indpls. Literary, Kiwanis (dir. Ind. Found., lt. gov. Ind. dist. internat. 1975-76), Indpls. Press, Ft. Harrison Officers, Masons, Sojourners (Indpls); Army and Navy (Washington); Crystal Downs Country (Frankfort, Mich.) (past pres.); U. Pa. Faculty. Contbr. articles to trade mags. Home: 8244 N Pennsylvania St Indianapolis IN 46240 Office: 906 Investors Trust Bldg 107 N Pennsylvania St Indianapolis IN 46204

TOWNSEND, LAWRENCE WILLARD, theoretical physicist, educator; b. Jacksonville, Fla., May 13, 1947; s. Willard Hyram and Marion Patricia (McCann) T.; m. Linda Susan Summerlin, June 5, 1969; children—Laura Suzanne, David Matthew, Jeremy Peter. B.S., U.S. Naval Acad., 1969; M.S., U.S. Naval Postgrad. Sch., 1970; Ph.D., U. Idaho, 1980. Research asst. prof. physics Old Dominion U., Norfolk, Va., 1980-81; research scientist Langley Research Ctr., NASA, Hampton, Va., 1981-87, sr. research scientist 1988— , prin. investigator NASA space radiation protection research program, 1982—; mem. adj. faculty Old Dominion U., Norfolk, Va., 1981—; mem. NASA Space Station radiation panel, 1985-87, NASA Life Scis. radiation panel, 1987—, U.S. Dept. Energy Medium Energy Nuclear Data Working Group, 1986—; mem. adv. com. HUGS at CEBAF, 1986— . Treas. Va. peninsula chpt. Full Gospel Businessmen's Fellowship Internat., 1983, pres., 1979, 85, 86, v.p. Palouse River chpt., 1978. Served to lt. comdr. USN, 1969-77. Whittenberger Found. fellow, 1979-80; NASA Spl. Achievement award, 1984. Mem. Am. Phys. Soc. Sigma Xi (award 1980-81). Contbr. articles to profl. jours. Office: NASA Langley Research Center Mail Stop 493 Hampton VA 23665

TOWNSEND, SUSAN ELAINE, social service institute administrator, hostage survival consultant; b. Phila., Sept. 5, 1946; d. William Harrison and Eleanor Irene (Fox) Rogers; m. John Holt Townsend, May 1, 1976. BS in Secondary Edn., West Chester State U., 1968; MBA, Nat. U., 1978; PhD in Human Behavior, La Jolla U., 1984. Biology tchr. Methacton Sch. Dist., Fairview Village, Pa., 1968-70; bus. mgr., analyst profl. La Jolla Research Corp., San Diego, 1977-79; pastoral asst. Christ Ctr. Bible Therapy, San Diego, 1980-82, also bd. dirs.; v.p., pub. relations World Outreach Ctr. of Faith, San Diego, 1981-82, also bd. dirs.; owner, pres., cons. Townsend Research Inst., San Diego, 1983—; teaching assoc. La Jolla U. Continuing Edn., 1985—. Author: Hostage Survival-Resisting the Dynamics of Captivity, 1983; contbr. articles to profl. jours. Religious vol. Met. Correctional Ctr., San Diego, 1983—, San Diego County Jail Ministries, 1978—. Served to comdr. USN, 1970-76, USNR, 1976—. Mem. Naval Res. Assn. (life), Res. Officers Assn. (Outstanding Jr. Officer of Yr. 1982), Navy League U.S. (life), West Chester U. Alumni Assn., Nat. U. Alumni Assn. (life), La Jolla U. Alumni Assn., Past Pres.'s Assn., Gen. Fedn. Women's Clubs (pres. Peninsula club 1983-85, pres. Parliamentary law club 1984-86, pres. 1985—),

Calif. Fedn. Women's Clubs (v.p.-at-large San Diego dist. 25 1982-84). Office: 1060 Alexandria Dr San Diego CA 92107

TOWNSHEND, JACK, geomagnetism and seismology scientist; b. Brandywine, Md., Apr. 24, 1927; m. Frieda Wybenga, Nov. 22, 1952; children—Donna Lynn, Donald Gilbert, Brenda Jean. Student George Washington U., 1950, U. Wis.-Madison, 1960-62. Mail carrier U.S. Post Office, Brandywine, Md., 1943-45; sci. aid Cheltenhan Obs., Md., 1946-49; geophysicist Coast and Geodetic Survey, Washington, 1949-55, tng. officer, Fredericksburg, Va., 1955-63; chief Coll. Obs., Fairbanks, Alaska, 1963—; lectr. in field. Contbr. articles to profl. jours. Vice pres. Alaska State Bd. Edn., Juneau, 1979-83; lay leader Methodist Alaska Missionary Conf., Anchorage, 1972-76. Served with U.S. Army, 1945-46. Recipient Silver medal Coast and Geodetic Survey, 1962, Disting. Service award, 1964; Superior Service to Pub. award Dept. Commerce, 1967. Fellow Explorers Club; mem. AAAS, Am. Geophys. Union, Nat. Assn. State Bds. Edn. (bd. dirs. 1981-82). Club: Farthest North Press (Fairbanks) (pres. 1970). Lodge: Kiwanis (lt. gov. Pacific Northwest dist. 1971-72, Layman's award 1969). Office: College Obs 800 Yukon Dr Fairbanks AK 99775-5160

TOYE, WENDY, theatrical producer, film director, actress, choerographer, dancer; b. May 1, 1917; d. Ernest W. and Jessie (Ramsay) Toye. First profl. appearance as Mustard-seed in A Midsummer Night's Dream, 1929; prin. dancer in Hiawatha, 1931, Marigold, Phoebe in Toad of Toad Hall; producer dances, Royalty, Christmas, 1931-32; danced in C.B. Cochran's The Miracle, Lyceum, 1932; masked dancer in Ballerina, Gaiety, 1933; mem. Ninette de Valois original Vic Wells Ballet, prin. dancer for Ninette de Valois in the Golden Toy, Coliseum, 1934; toured with Anton Dolin's ballet (choreographer for divertissments and short ballets), 1934-35; in Tulip Time, Alhambra, then Markova-Dolin Ballet as prin. dancer and choreographer, 1935; in Love and How to Cure it, Globe, 1937; arranged dances and ballets for many shows and films including most of George Black's prodns. for next 7 years, notable Black Velvet, also prin. dancer, 1939, Shakespearean season, Open Air Theatre, 1939; theatre prodns.: Big Ben, Bless the Bride, Tough at the Top, The Shepherd Show, Prince's; co-dir., choreographer Peter Pan, N.Y., And so To Bed; co-dir., choreographer Feu-d'Artifice, Paris, Night of Masquerade, Q, Second Threshold, Vaudeville; choreography for Three's Company in Joyce Grenfell Requests the Peasure, Fortune, Wild Thyme, Duke of York's Lady of the Wheel, Lyric, Hammersmith, Majority of One, Phoenix, Magic Lantern, Saville, As You Like It, Old Vic, Virtue in Danger, Mermaid and Strand, Robert and Elizabeth, Lyric, On the Level Saville, Midsummer Night's Dream, Shakespeare quartercentenary Latin Am. tour, 1964, Soldier's Tale, Edinburgh Festival, 1967, Boots and Strawberry Jam, Nottingham Playhouse, 1968, The Great Waltz, Drury Lane, 1970, Showboat, Adelphi, 1971, She Stoops to Conquer, Young Vic, 1972, Cowardy Custard, Mermaid, 1972, Stand and Deliver, Roundhouse, 1972, R loves J, 1973, The Confederacy, 1974, The Englishman Amused, Young Vic, 1974, Follow the Star, Chichester, 1974, Westminster Theatre, 1976, Made in Heaven, 1975, Make Me a World, 1976, Oh Mr. Porter, 1977, Dance for Gods, Conversations, 1979, Colette, Comdey, 1980, Gingerbread Man, Water Mi 11, 1981, This Thing Called Love, 1983; assoc. producer Singin in the Rain, 1983, Noel & Gertie, 1984, Celimare, 1984, Barnum, 1985, Mad Woman of Chaillot, 1985, Torvill & Dean Ice Show World Tour, 1985, Once Upon a Mattress, 1985, Kiss Me Kate, 1986, Unholy Trinity, 1986, Copenhagen, 1986, Miranda, 1987; opera prodns: Bluebeard's Castle, Sadler's Wells and Brussels, The Telephone, Sadler's Wells, Russalka, Sadler's Wells, Fledermaus, Coliseum and Sadler's Wells, Orpheus in the Underworld, Seraglio, Bath Festival, 1967, The Impresario, Don Pasquale, 1968, The Italian Girl in Agliers, 1968, La Cenerentola, Merry Widow, 1979, Orpheus in the Underworld, 1981, ENO North: The Mikado, 1982, Italian Girl in Algiers, ENO, 1982; films directed include: The Stranger Left no Card, The Teckman Mystery, Raising a Riot, The Twelfth Day of Christmas, Three Cases of Murder, All for Mary, True as a Turtle, We Jointed the Navy, The King's Breakfast, Cliff in Scotland, A Goodly Manor for a Song, Girls Wanted - Istanbul, Trial by Jury (TV); prodns. for tv include: Golden Gala, ATV, 1978, Follow the Star, BBC, 1979, Strangers in Town, 1981; appeared with and was choreographer for Camargo Soc.; guest artist with Sadler's Wells Ballet and Mme. Rambert's Ballet Club; went to Denmark as prin. dancer with Brit. Ballet, organized by Adeline Genee, 1932; trained with Euphen MacLaren, Karavina, Dolin, Morosoff, Legat, Rambert, Silver Jubilee medal, 1977. Address: care David Watson, Simpson Fox, 52 Shaftesbury Ave, London W1V 7DE, England *

TOYODA, EIJI, automobile manufacturing company executive; b. Kinjo, Nishikasugai, Aichi, Japan, Sept. 12, 1913; s. Heikichi and Nao T.; m. Kazuko Takahashi, Oct. 19, 1939; children: Kanshiro, Tetsuro, Shuhei, Sonoko. B.M.E., Tokyo U., 1936. Bd. dirs. Toyota Motor Corp., Aichi, Japan, 1945—, mng. dir., 1950-53, sr. mng. dir., 1953-60, exec. v.p., 1960-67, pres., 1967-82, chmn., 1982—; chmn. Towa Real Estate Co., Ltd.; exec. dir. Toyota Central Research and Devel. Lab., Inc.; dir. Aichi Steel Works, Ltd., Toyoda Machine Works Ltd., Toyoda Automatic Loom Works Ltd., Aisin Seiki Co. Ltd.; auditor Toyoda Tsusho Corp.; pres. Japan Automobile Mfrs. Assn., Inc., 1972-80; vice chmn. Keidanren, 1984—. Author: Toyota Fifty Years in Motion, 1988. Mem. Japan Automobile Mfrs. Assn. (supreme adv. 1980), Japan Motor Indsl. Fedn. (adv. 1980), Fedn. Econ. Orgns. (vice chmn. 1984). Office: Toyota Motor Corp, 1 Toyota-cho Toyota-shi, Aichi 471, Japan *

TOYODA, SHOICHIRO, automobile company executive; b. Nagoya, Japan, Feb. 27, 1925; s. Kiichiro and Hatako Toyoda; m. Hiroko Mitsui, Feb. 10, 1953; children: Atuko, Akio. B in Engring., Nagoya U., 1947; D in Engring., Tohoku U., 1955. Dir. Toyota Motor Co., Ltd., 1952-61, mng. dir., 1961-67, sr. mng. dir., 1967-72, exec. v.p., 1972-81; pres. Toyota Motor Sales Co., Ltd., 1981-82, Toyota Motor Corp., 1982—; bd. dirs. Nippondenso Co., Ltd., Toyota Motor Sales, U.S.A., Torrance, Calif., Nagoya Broadcasting Network; chmn. bd. dirs. Inst. Internat. Econ. Studies. Trustee Keizai-Doyukai, Tokyo, 1970—; exec. mem. Keidanren, Tokyo, 1984—; v.p. CHUBU Econ. Fedn., Nagoya, 1984—; consul gen. Honorario de Costa Rica, Nagoya, 1984—. Recipient Medal with Dark-Blue Ribbon Govt. of Japan, 1972, The Deming Prize, 1980, Medal with Blue Ribbon Govt. of Japan, 1984. Mem. Japan Authomobile Mfrs. Assn., Inc. (pres. 1986—), Japan Motor Indsl. Fedn., Inc. (pres. 1986—). Office: Toyota Motor Corp, 1 Toyota-Cho, Toyota Aichi 471, Japan

TOYOMURA, DENNIS TAKESHI, architect; b. Honolulu, July 6, 1926; s. Sansuke Fujimoto and Take (Sata) T.; m. Akiko Charlotte Nakamura, May 27, 1949; children—Wayne J., Gerald F., Amy J., Lyle D. BS in Archtl. Engring., Chgo. Tech. Coll., 1949; cert., U. Ill., Chgo., 1950, 53, 54; student, Ill. Inst. Tech., Chgo., 1953-54; cert., U. Hawaii-Dept. Def., Honolulu, 1966-67, 73. Lic. architect, Ill., Hawaii; lic. real estate broker, Ill. Designer, draftsman James M. Turner, Architect, Hammond, Ind., 1950-51, Wimberly and Cook, Honolulu, 1952, Gregg, Briggs & Foley, Architects, Chgo., 1952-54; architect Holabird, Root & Burgee, Architects, Chgo., 1954-55, Loebl, Schlossman & Bennett, Architects, Chgo., 1955-62; prin. Dennis T. Toyomura, AIA, Architect, Honolulu, 1963-83, Dennis T. Toyomura, FAIA, Architect, Honolulu, 1983—; fallout shelter analyst Dept. Def., 1967—; cert. analyst multi-distaster design, Dept. Def., 1973; cons. Honolulu Redevel. Agy., City and County of Honolulu, 1967-71; sec., dir. Maiko of Hawaii, Honolulu, 1972-74; mem. steering com. IX world conf. World Futures Studies Fedn., U. Hawaii, 1986; conf. organizer pub. forum 10th Hawaii Conf. in High Energy Physics, U. Hawaii, 1985; bd. dirs. Research Corp. U. Hawaii, State of Hawaii, Pacific Canal of Hawaii; mem. Hawaii State Found. on Culture and the Arts, 1982-86; mem. Gov.'s Com. on Hawaii Econ. Future, 1984; archtl. mem. Bd. Registration for Profl. Engrs., Architects, Land Surveyors and Landscape Architects, State of Hawaii, 1974-82, sec. 1980, vice chmn. 1981, chmn., 1982; mem. Nat. Council Engring. Examiners, 1975-82; mem. Nat. Council Archtl. Registration Bds., Western region del. 1975-82, nat. del. 1976-82; appointments include Research Corp., U. Hawaii, 1986-89. Ecclesiastical del. commr. state assembly, Synod of Ill., United Presbyn. Ch. U.S.A., 1958, alt. del. commr. nat. gen. assembly, 1958, del. commr. Los Angeles presbytery, 1965; bd. session 2d Presbyn. Ch., Chgo., 1956-62, trustee, 1958-62; trustee 1st Presbyn. Ch., Honolulu, 1964-66, 69-72, sec., 1965, bd. sessions, 1964-72, 74-79; founding assoc. Hawaii Loa Coll., Kaneohe, 1964; mem. adv. commn. drafting tech. Leeward Community Coll., U. Hawaii, 1965—; mem. Hawaii State Found. on Culture and the Arts, 1984-86; bd. dirs. Lyon Arboretum Assn., U. Hawaii, 1976-77, treas., 1976. Served with U.S. Army, 1945-46. Recipient cert. appreciation Leeward Community Coll./U. Hawaii, 1971—, Human Resources of U.S.A. award Am. Bicentennial Research Inst., 1973; Outstanding Citizen Recognition award Cons. Engrs. Council Hawaii, 1975; Cert. Appreciation, Gov. of Hawaii, 1982, 86, commendation, 1983; resolution and cert. commendation Hawaii Ho. of Reps. and Senate, 1983. Fellow AIA (Coll. Fellows 1983, bd. dirs. Hawaii Soc. 1973-74, treas. 1975, Pres.'s Mahalo award 1981); life mem. AAAS, Acad. Polit. Sci., Am. Acad. Polit. and Social Scis., N.Y. Acad. Scis., Chgo. Art Inst., Chgo. Natural History Mus., Honolulu Acad. Arts, Nat. Geog. Soc.; mem. Council Ednl. Facility Planners Internat. (bd. govs. N.W. region 1980-86), Bldg. Research Inst. (adv. bd. of Nat. Acad. Sci.), Ill. Assn. Professions, ASTM, Constrn. Specifications Inst., Constrn. Industry Legis. Orgn. (bd. dirs. 1973-81, 83—, treas. 1976-77), Japan-Am. Soc., Hawaii State C. of C. (bd. dirs. 1984-87), U. Hawaii Kokua O'Hui, O'Nahe Popo (bd. dirs. 1984—), Alpha Lambda Rho, Kappa Sigma Kappa. Clubs: Malolo Mariners (purser 1964, skipper 1965) (Honolulu); U. Hawaii Pres.', Hawaii Loa Coll. Pres.'. Home: 2602 Manoa Rd Honolulu HI 96822 Office: Dennis T Toyomura FAIA Architect 1370 Kapiolani Blvd Honolulu HI 96814

TOZAKI, SEIKI, import-export company executive; b. Mar. 18, 1910; m. Misao Tozaki. Grad., Tokyo Coll. Commerce, 1934. With C. Itoh & Co. Ltd., Tokyo, 1934—, pres., from 1970, now chmn.; also chmn. C. Itoh & Co. (Am.) Inc., N.Y.C. Recipient medal of Honor with Blue ribbon, 1972. Office: C Itoh & Co 335 Madison Ave New York NY 10017 *

TOZER, THEODORE WILLIAM, mortgage company executive; b. Bloomington, Ill., Feb. 3, 1957; s. William Thomas and Joan Marie (Heberlein) T.; m. F. Sandra Williams, Mar. 28, 1981. BS, Ind. U., 1978. CPA, Ill., Ohio.; cert. mgmt. acct. Staff acct. Borg-Warner, Chgo., 1978, Armco, Inc., Middletown, Ohio, 1979; mgr. investment ops. BancOhio Nat. Bank, Columbus, Ohio, 1979-85; controller BancOhio Mortgage Co., Columbus, Ohio, 1985-86, chief fin. officer, 1986—. Mem. Nat. Assn. Accts., Am. Inst. CPA's. Home: 3258 Palomar Ave Columbus OH 43229 Office: BancOhio Mortgage Co 51 N High St Columbus OH 43251

TRABUCCHI, GIUSEPPE, trading company executive; b. Padova, Italy, Nov. 9, 1945; s. Cherubino and Carla (Gola) T.; m. Jibek Rakhimdjanovna Baltabaeva, Nov. 30, 1971; children—Marco-Abai, Maria-Aijan. Maturita classica Liceo Alle Stimate, Verona, Italy, 1963; Laurea Ingegneria Elettrotecnica, Padova U., Italy, 1969; Specialisation Long distance Energy Transmission, Moscow Power Inst., 1971. Prodn. mgr. ITALSIDER S.p.A., Marghera, Italy, 1971-72; export mgr. SIRCE S.p.A., Milan, 1973-76; tech. and purchasing mgr. INTERMAN & S.E.D., Rome and Jeddah, Saudi Arabia, 1976-77; gen. mgr. SOGECRED S.A., Fribourg, Switzerland, 1978—. Home: R te d'Avry 7, 1753 Matran (FR) Switzerland Office: SOGECRED SA, 55 Blvd de Perolles, 1700 Fribourg Switzerland

TRACEY, JAY WALTER, JR., lawyer; b. Rocky Ford, Colo., June 13, 1925; s. Jay Walter and Margaret Louise (Bish) T.; m. Elizabeth Longfellow Henry, Nov. 1, 1952; children: Jay Walter, William H., Anne E., John B. BS, Yale U., 1949; LLB, Harvard U., 1952. Bar: Colo. 1952, U.S. Dist. Ct. Colo. 1952, U.S. Ct. Appeals (10th cir.) 1958. Assoc. Holland & Hart, Denver, 1952-57, ptnr., 1957-71, 72—; pres. Von Frellick Assocs., Inc., Denver, 1971-72; dir. Ctr. for Dispute Resolution, Denver, 1984-88. Councilman, City of Cherry Hills Village (Colo.), 1965-70, mayor pro tem, 1966-70, mem. Home Rule Charter Conv., 1966; trustee Denver Country Day Sch., 1967-70. Served with U.S. Army, 1943-46. Decorated Purple Heart. Mem. ABA, Colo. Bar Assn., Denver Bar Assn., Colo. Yale Assn. (pres. 1971-72), Assn. Yale Alumni (del. 1975-78), Harvard Law Sch. Assn. Colo. (pres. 1962-63), Harvard Law Sch. Assn. (v.p. 1963-64). Republican. Episcopalian. Clubs: University, Denver Country, Arapahoe Tennis, Mile High. Lodge: Rotary (Denver chpt. bd. dirs. 1980-82, 1st v.p. 1981-82). Office: Holland & Hart PO Box 8749 Denver CO 80201

TRACT, HAROLD M., lawyer; b. N.Y.C., May 18, 1926; s. Meyer and Mary (Nadler) Trachtenberg; m. Natalie A. Meyerowitz, Nov. 16, 1958; children—Marc M., Laurence T. B.A., U. Wis., 1948; J.D., Harvard U., 1951. Bar: Mass. 1951, N.Y. 1953. Assoc. Rein, Mound & Cotton, N.Y.C., 1952-62, ptnr., 1962-85; sr. ptnr. Kroll & Tract, 1985—; dir. The Mercantile and Gen. Reins. Co. Am., N.Y. Surety Co., Cherry Valley Coop. Ins. Co., Gerling Am. Ins. Co., Navigators Ins. Co., Navigators Group, Inc.,J.P. Woods (Bermuda) Ltd., Nasco N.Am. Inc., Toa-Re Ins. Co. Am., First United Am. LIfe Ins. Co., Preferred Life Ins. Co. of N.Y., Colonial Indemnity Ins. Co., Nordstern Ins. Co. Am., Ins. Fedn. N.Y. Inc.; bd. govs. Internat. Ins. Seminars Inc.; mem. arbitration panels Am. Arbitration Assn., N.Y. Ins. Exchange. Served with A.C., U.S. Army, 1944-46. Mem. ABA, City Bar Assn. N.Y., N.Y. County Lawyers, Nat. Assn. Ins. Commrs. (mem. adv. com. on reins., adv. com. on internat. insurer relations). Jewish. Clubs: Metropolitan, Harvard (N.Y.C.), Old Westbury Golf and Country. Editorial bd.: Ins. and Reins. Internat., Exec. Newsletter, Internat. Ins. Fin. Services newsletter. Home: 105 Fir Dr East Hills NY 11576 Office: 500 Fifth Ave New York NY 10110

TRACY, ALOISE See SHOENIGHT, PAULINE ALOISE SOUERS

TRACY, HONOR LILBUSH WINGFIELD, writer, journalist; b. Bury St. Edmunds, Suffolk, Eng., Oct. 19, 1913; d. Humphrey Tracy and Christabel May Clare Miller. Ed. Grove Sch., Highgate, London. Fgn. corr. The Observer, 1947-50; Dublin corr. Sunday Times, London, 1950; columnist Daily Telegraph, 1973—; author of numerous books including: (travel books) Kakemono: A Sketchbook of Postwar Japan, 1950; Mind You, I've Said Nothing! Forays in the Irish Republic, 1953; Silk Hats and No Breakfast, 1957; Spanish Leaves, 1964; Winter in Castille, 1973; The Heart of England, 1983; (fiction) The Deserters, 1954; The Straight and Narrow Path, 1956; The Prospects are Pleasing, 1958; A Number of Things, 1959; A Season of Mists, 1961; The First Day of Friday, 1963; Men at Work, 1966; The Beauty of the World (Am. title Settled in Chambers), 1967; The Butterflies of the Province, 1970; The Quiet End of Evening, 1972; In a Year of Grace, 1975; The Man From Next Door, 1977; The Ballad of Castle Reef, 1979; contbr. numerous articles to profl. jours. and popular mags. Home: 1 Mead House, Heahfield Ln, Chislehurst Kent, England Office: care Daily Telegraph, 135 Fleet St, London EC4 4BL, England *

TRAFICANTE, DANIEL DOMINICK, chemist; b. Hoboken, N.J., Nov. 20, 1933; s. Paul and Mary T.; m. Doris Marilyn Poley, Aug. 20, 1955 (div. 1983); children—Daniel D., Mark S., Christopher, Dawn; m. Margaret Mary Kelly, May 19, 1984. B.S., Syracuse U., 1955; Ph.D., MIT, 1962. Commd. 2d lt. U.S. Air Force, 1956, advanced through grades to capt. 1960, resigned, 1967; dir. undergrad. labs. MIT, Cambridge, 1968-70, dir. nuclear magnetic resonance lab., 1970-78; dir. nuclear magnetic resonance lab. Yale U., New Haven, 1978-81; dir. Nuclear Magnetic Resonance Inst., Cranford, N.J., 1981-83; dir. chem. instrumentation NSF, Washington, 1983-85; research fellow, dir. life scis. nuclear magnetic resonance consortium Monsanto Co., Chesterfield, Mo., 1985-86; dir. Nuclear Magnetic Resonance Concepts; dir. nuclear magnetic resonance research lab. and prof. chemistry and medicinal chemistry U. R.I., 1986—. Recipient Letter of Commendation award Syracuse U., 1987. Author: Chemistry, 1978. Contbr. articles to profl. jours. Mem. Am. Chem. Soc.

TRAGER, BERNARD H., lawyer; b. New Haven, July 18, 1906; s. Harry L. and Ida R. (Ruttenberg) T.; m. Mina R. Trager, Aug. 25, 1929 (dec. July 1987); children—Roberta Trager Cohen, Philip. LL.B., NYU, 1928. Bar: Conn. 1929. Sole practice, 1929-60; sr. ptnr. Trager & Trager, Bridgeport, Conn., 1960-80, pres. Trager & Trager, P.C., 1980—; trustee Peoples Savs. Bank of Bridgeport, 1964-78, trustee emeritus, 1978—. Mem. Gov.'s Commn. Gambling, 1965-71; chmn. Conn. Bd. Pardons, 1959-73; life trustee U. Bridgeport; pres. Hundred Club Conn., 1976-77; mem. Bridgeport Mayor's Commn. Human Rights, 1958-62; chmn. Nat. Community Relations Adv. Council, 1953-55; pres. Conn. Conf. Social Work, 1948-49; mem. Bridgeport Fin. Adv. Commn., 1966-75; bd. dirs. Council Jewish Fedns. and Welfare Funds, 1954-61; trustee Nat. Health and Welfare Retirement Assn., 1955-68, Bridgeport Area Found., 1967-81; bd. dirs. Bridgeport Hosp., 1970—, also mem. profl. com. Mem. Bridgeport Bar Assn. (pres. 1959-61), Conn. Bar Assn. (pres. 1964-65), ABA (ho. dels. 1965-66), Fairfield Bar Assn. Jewish. Club: Algonquin of Bridgeport (pres. 1979-80). Home: 25 Cartright St Apt 2G Bridgeport CT 06604 Office: Trager & Trager PC 1305 Post Rd Fairfield CT 06430

TRAHAIR, RICHARD C. S., psychologist, educator; b. Melbourne, Australia, Sept. 10, 1935; s. Bernard Alexander and Isobel Alzina (Stewart) T.; m. Susan Elisabeth Jeffrey, Feb. 22, 1960 (div. 1979); children: Catherine, Nicholas, Andrew, Elizabeth. BA with honors, U. Melbourne, 1962, PhD, 1966. Registered psychologist. Tutor, lectr. U. Melbourne, 1958-66; sr. lectr. La Trobe U., Melbourne, 1967—, dep./acting head Chisholm Coll., 1980-82. Author: The Humanist Temper, 1984; contbr. articles to profl. jours. and published monographs on the history of psychoanalysis. Mem. Australian Psychol. Soc., Australian Soc. Hypnosis. Club: Melbourne Cricket. Home: PO Box 2, Flinders 3929, Australia Office: La Trobe Univ, Kingsbury Dr, Bundoora 3083, Australia

TRAHAN, MARGARET FRITCHEY, co-owner wholesale food distributing company; b. Harrisburg, Pa., May 3, 1934; d. John Augustus and Dorotha Amy (Warren) Fritchey; m. Henry Voltaire Trahan, Jr., Sept. 29, 1956; children—Henry Voltaire III, Randall Scott. B.S. in Bus. Edn., Cedar Crest Coll., 1955; B.E. in Curriculum & Instrn., Fla. Atlantic U., 1971. Corr. course writer Acad. Health Scis., U.S. Army, San Antonio, 1976-77, team chief, individual analysis and design. br., 1977-80, dep. chief individual tng. analysis and design br., 1980-81; satellite TV program dir. U.S. Army Health Services Command, San Antonio, 1981-84; chief individual tng. in forces br. Acad. of Health Scis., U.S. Army, San Antonio, 1984-85; co-owner, operator Circle T Farms, San Antonio, 1985—. Vol. worker Army Community Services, 1966-67, ARC, 1966-74; pres. sr. state officer club, sr. 1st v.p. Tex. soc. Children of the Am. Revolution, 1979-81, sr. nat. v.p. south central region, 1978-80, sr. nat. historian, nat. conv. vice chmn., 1980-82, hon. sr. nat. v.p. nat. soc., 1982-85. Recipient Outstanding Performance award Acad. of Health Scis. and Sec. of Army, 1958, 79, 80; commendation cert. ARC, 1967, U.S. Army Community Services, 1974, Nat. Soc. Children Am. Revolution, 1980; Exceptional Performance award U.S. Army Health Services Command and Acad. of Health Scis., 1981, 83, 84; Comdr.'s award for civilian service Dept. Army, 1985; named one of Notable Women of Tex., 1983-84. Mem. AAUW, Fed. Ednl. Tech. Assn., Assn. Edn. and Communication Tech., Armed Forces Pub. Affairs Council, Nat. Assn. Female Execs., Am. Mgmt. Assn., Hilton Sea Island Tower Assn. (v.p., bd. govs. 1987—), DAR (rec. sec. Alamo chpt. 1975-76), Organizing Soc. (pres. Brownsville, Tex. 1988—). Republican. Lutheran. Club: U.S. Army Theater Support Communications Officers Wives (pres. 1968-69), Sr. Nat. Officers'. Lodge: Ladies of the Shrine. Avocations: tennis, seashells, swimming, knitting, latchhook. Home: PO Box 2576 South Padre TX 78597-2576 Office: Circle T Farms 9322 Oak Downs San Antonio TX 78230

TRAICOFF, ELLEN BRADEN, psychologist; b. Gary, Ind.; d. Charles Leonard and Blossom (Riggin) Braden. BS, Ind. U., 1971, MS, 1974; D of Psychology, Forest Inst. Profl. Psychology, 1987; grad., Family Inst. Chgo., 1978. Edn. and family therapist Cath. Family Services, 1974-78; child and family specialist Porter Starke Services, Valparaiso, Ind., 1978-79; dir. family violence programming Southlake Ctr. Mental Health, Merrillville, Ind., 1979-83, dir. forensic services, 1983-84; cons. Lake County (Ind.) Dept. of Pub. Welfare, 1984-86; psychologist Walbash Valley Hosp., Lafayette, Ind., 1987-88, Touchstone Group Clin. Psychiat. Affiliates, Chgo., 1988—. Contbr. articles to profl. jours. Del. White House Conf. on Families, 1980. Mem. Am. Assn. Marriage and Family Therapy (clin.), Family Inst. Chgo. Alumni Assn. Office: Touchstone Group Westmont Ill Mercy Hosp Chicago IL 60139

TRAIL, GEORGE ARTHUR, III, diplomat; b. Chambersburg, Pa., Oct. 16, 1936; s. George Arthur and Elizabeth Aurelia (Feldman) T.; m. Mary Jo Weaver, Sept. 1, 1961; children: Regina, Angela, George Arthur, Amy. A.B., Franklin and Marshall Coll., 1958; B.S., U. Houston, 1965. Commd. fgn. service officer Dept. State, 1965; consul. Am. Consulate, Kaduna, Nigeria, 1973-75; first sec. Am. Embassy, Bangkok, Thailand, 1976-78; dep. dir. West African Affairs Dept. State, Washington, 1978-80; consul. gen. Am. Consulate Gen., Johannesburg, South Africa, from 1980; U.S. ambassador to Malawi 1988—. Served to lt. USN, 1959-65. Recipient Meritorious Honor Dept. State, 1970. Mem. Fgn. Service Assn., Omicron Delta Epsilon, Phi Sigma Kappa. Office: Am Embassy, PO Box 30016, Lilongwe Malawi *

TRAIN, JOHN, investment counselor, author; b. N.Y.C., May 25, 1928; s. Arthur Cheney and Helen (Coster) T.; m. Maria Teresa Cini di Pianzano, 1961 (div. 1976); children: Helen, Nina, Lisa; m. Frances Cheston, July 23, 1977. BA, Harvard U., 1950, MA, 1951. Founder, mng. editor Paris Rev., 1952-54; staff Asst. Sec. Army, Washington, 1954-56; staff asst. de Vegh & Co., 1956-58; pres. Train, Smith Counsel (and predecessor firms), N.Y.C., 1958—, Chateau Malescasse, Lamarque-Margaux, Bordeaux, France, 1970-81; columnist Forbes mag., 1977-83, Harvard mag., 1983—; bd. dirs. PK English Trust Co., London, Pkbank, N.Y., Nat. Banking Corp. Author: Dance of the Money Bees, 1973, Remarkable Names, 1977, Even More Remarkable Names, 1979, Remarkable Occurrences, 1978, Remarkable Words, 1980, The Money Masters, 1980, Remarkable Relatives, 1981, Preserving Capital, 1983, Famous Financial Fiascos, 1984, John Train's Most Remarkable Names, 1985, The Midas Touch, 1987; contbr. articles to various mags. Chmn. Italian Emergency Relief Com., 1976-77; pres. Afganistan Relief Com.; 1986—; trustee Harvard Lampoon, Cambridge, Mass., 1974—; trustee, treas. World Monuments Fund. Served with U.S. Army, 1954-56. Decorated commendatore Ordine del Merito della Repubblica, commendatore Ordine Della Solidarieta (Italy); chevalier Ordre Franco-Outremerien (France). Clubs: Century, Racquet and Tennis; Metropolitan (Washington); Brooks's (London); Travellers (Paris); Order Colonial Lords of Manors, The Pilgrims. Office: Train Smith Counsel 345 Park Ave New York NY 10154

TRAISSAC, LOUIS, otorhinolaryngological cancer surgeon; b. Bordeaux, France, Mar. 17, 1936; s. Robert and Marie Marthe (Montau) R.; m. Renée Pouyanne; children: Benoit, Marie-Laure, Loïc, Emmanuelle, Quitterie. MD, U. Medicine, Bordeaux, 1963. Intern then resident Regional Hosp. Ctr., Bordeaux, 1960-64, 66-67; chief clinic Hosp. Ctr. and U. Bordeaux, 1967-71, prof., 1972—, chief of service, 1974—, research dir., 1973—. Inventor voice prosthesis, larynx tube. Mem. Otorhinolaryngology Soc. Bordeaux (sec. gen. 1970—), Found. G. Portmann (mem. internat. bur. 1972—), French Soc. Otorhinolaryngology, French Soc. Cancerologie, Italian Soc. Otorhinolaryngology (hon.). Roman Catholic. Clubs: Lions (Merignac); Ligue d'Aquitaine de Voile (Bordeaux). Home: Domaine de Camot, 33370 Tresses France Office: Service ORL Ctr des Specialites, 89 rue des Sablieres, 33077 Bordeaux Cedex France

TRAMIER, HENRY JEAN LOUIS, plastic surgeon; b. Avignon, Dec. 1, 1938; s. Elie and Gabrielle (Blayac) T.; m. Genevieve Molines, 1963 (div. 1970); 1 child, Sophie; m. Christiane Mouren, Jan. 10, 1970; children: Blaise, Vincent. Student, Sch. Fine Arts, Avignon; MD, U. Marseille, France, 1964. Intern Hosp. de Marseille, 1963, chief clinic orthopedic surgery and traumatology, 1970-72, cons. plastic and hand surgery, 1970-75, clinic tchr., 1980—; asst. surgeon Hosp. of Tunis, 1965-66; substitute surgeon Hosp. Brignoles, 1969; practice medicine specializing in plastic surgery Marseille; cons. plastic and hand surgery Hosp. of Aubagne, France, 1972—; staff plastic surgeon hand service Hotel Dieu, Marseille, 1973—. Contbr. numerous articles to med. jours.; exhibited paintings in group shows in France and U.S. Named laureate Nat. Acad. Medicine, 1973. Fellow Internat. Coll. Surgeons, T. Skoog Soc. ; mem. French Soc. Orthopedic Surgery and Traumatology, French Soc. Plastic and Reconstructive Surgery, Marseille Surg. Soc., French Soc. for Surgery of Hand (assoc.), French Coll. Plastic Reconstructive and Aesthetic Surgery, Societe Française des Chirurigiens Esthetique Plasticies, College des Praticiens de l'Hospitalisation Privée de Provence (founder, treas.), Association Mediterraneenne des Chirurgiens Esthetique Plasticiens (founder, treas.), Caisse de Retraite des Medecins de France. Roman Catholic. Home: 43 Rue St Jacque, Marseille 13006, France Office: Euroclinik S A, 43 Rue St Jacques, Marseille 13006, France

TRAMMELL, HOMER CONRAD, business consultant; b. Laurel, Miss., Oct. 10, 1937; s. Homer Lee and Evie Louisa (Breazeale) T.; m. Gail Elaine Lacy, Feb. 14, 1960. BBA, U. Miss., 1964; postgrad., Ind. U., 1968-71, Purdue U., 1968, Ind. State U., 1969. Jr. exec. Sears, Roebuck and Co., Vicksburg, Miss., 1964-67; asst. mgr. Western Auto Co., Jackson, Miss., 1967; tchr. Northwestern Sch. Dist., Kokomo, Ind., 1967-71; bus. cons.

Trammell Assocs., Kokomo, 1971—; co-owner TJ's Steak 'N Such restaurant; pres. TAM Group, Bus. Cons.; bd. dirs. Schoolhouse Smorgasboard., Inc. Pres. Promised Land, Inc., Kokomo, 1974—; v.p. bd. dirs. Kokomo Rescue Mission, 1982-84, pres. 1984—, Served with USAF, 1956-60. Mem. Soc. for the Advancement of Mgmt. (v.p. 1962-63, pres. 1963-64), Ind. Gospel Music. Assn. (founder, pres. 1976-78), Christian Motorcyclists Assn. (found Ind. chpt.). Mem. Ch. of God. Home: 13018 E 340 S Greentown IN 46936 Office: Trammell Assocs PO Box 388 Kokomo IN 46901

TRAMPEDACH, KURT GEORG, computer and communications company executive; b. Kassel, Hessen, Germany, Nov. 13, 1943; s. Konrad and Marie-Luise (Jonsson) T.; m. Siegrid Bader, Apr. 28, 1967; 1 child, Timothy. Abitur, Goetheschule, Kassel, 1964; Diplom, Universitat Karlsruhe, Fed. Republic Germany, 1970, Dr. rer. pol., 1973. Data processing planning mgr. Robert Bosch GmbH, Stuttgart, Fed. Republic Germany, 1973-79; dir. bus. planning Audi NSU AG, Ingolstadt, Fed. Republic Germany, 1979-81; dir. strategic planning and market research Siemens AG, Munich, Fed. Republic Germany, 1981-87 ; mng. dir. So. Europe No. Telecom Europe Ltd, London, England, 1987—; lectr. U. Tubingen, 1978-80. Contbr. articles to profl. jours. DAAD doctoral fellow MIT, 1971. Avocations: playing wind instruments; bicycle racing; tennis. Home: 4 Dukes Ln, Gerrards Cross, Bucks SL9 7JZ, England Office: No Telecom Europe Ltd, No Telecom House, St Cloud Way, Maidenhead Berkshire SL6 8XB, England

TRAN, CHI HUU, physician; b. Da Phuoc Hoi, Bentre, Republic Vietnam, Apr. 28, 1929; arrived in France, 1981; s. The Huu and Sau Thi (Truong) T.; m. Tuyet-Nga Bui; children: Tuyet Hong, Tuyet Hoa. Sci. degree, Faculty Sci., Toulouse, France, 1952; MD, Med. Sch. Saigon, Vietnam, 1958, Med. Sch. Paris, 1967. Diplomate French Bd. Pulmonary Disease. Med. doctor Hong Bang Hosp., Saigon, 1960-63; chmn. dept. chest disease Med. & Surg. Ctr. Villiers St. Denis, Charly, France, 1968-69; asst. prof. Med. Sch. Saigon, 1970-72, assoc. prof., 1973-75, vice dean, 1974-75; practice medicine Issy-Les-Moulineaux, France, 1966—; Vice chmn. Vietnam Anti-Tb Assn., Saigon, 1970-74, Vietnam Thoracic Diseases Assn., 1972-74; adviser Ministry Health Republic Vietnam, 1972-73. Served to lt. Med. Corps Republic Vietnam Army, 1957-60. Mem. French Pulmonary Diseases Assn. Home: 2 Rue Blanchard, 92220 Bagneux France Office: 72 Victor Cresson, 92130 Issy Les Moulineaux France

TRAN, MINH SON, physician; b. Cholon, South Vietnam, June 12, 1938; s. Hoi Van and Xuan-thi (Nguyen) T.; m. Pauline Anne Vanty Nguyen; children: Jacques Minh-Son Tran, Pierre Minh-Son. Cert. in phys. and biol., Faculty of Scis., Saigon, Vietnam, 1959; MD, Saigon U., 1967. Lt., MD 43d Regiment 18th Div. Army Republic South Vietnam, 1967-68; capt., surgeon Ban Me Thuot (South Vietnam) Mil. Hosp., 1968-69, Hosp. for Paralytic, Vung Tau, South Vietnam, 1969-70, Gen. Republic Hosp. Saigon, 1970-75; physician Paris U., 1978—. Prisoner-of-war Saigon, 1975-76; polit. refugee in Paris, 1978—. Mem. Sci. Assn. Acupuncturist Med. Drs. France. Roman Catholic. Home and Office: 3 Valentina Terechkova, 93270 Sevran France

TRAN, NANG TRI, electrical engineer, physicist; b. Binh Dinh, Vietnam, Jan. 2, 1948; came to U.S., 1979, naturalized, 1986; s. Cam Tran and Cuv Thi Nguyen; m. Thu-Huong Thi Tong, Oct. 14, 1982; children: Helen, Florence, Irene. B.S.E.E., Kyushu Inst. Tech., Kitakyushu, Japan, 1973, M.S.E.E., 1975; Ph.D., U. of Osaka Prefecture, Sakai, Japan, 1978. Research assoc. U. of Calif.-Irvine, 1979; engr., research scientist Sharp Electronics, Irvine, 1979-80; sr. research scientist Arco Solar Industries, Chatsworth, Calif., 1980-84; research specialist, task leader 3M Co., St. Paul, 1985—. Contbr. articles to profl. jours.; patentee in field. Scholarship fellow Vietnamese Govt., Japan, 1968-73, grad. scholarship fellow Rotary Internat., Japan, 1973-75, predoctoral fellow Japanese Govt., 1975-78. Mem. IEEE, Am. Vacuum Soc., Japan Soc. of Applied Physics, Japan Soc. of Physics.

TRÂN, QUANG HAI, ethnomusicologist; b. Linh Dong Xa, Vietnam, May 13, 1944; s. Van Khe and Thi Suong (Nguyen) T.; diploma Nat. Conservatory of Music, Saigon, Vietnam, 1961; diploma Cambridge (Eng.) U., 1965 diploma Centre d'Etudes de Musique Orientale, Institut de Musicologie, Paris, 1969; MusD (hon) Internat. U. Found., 1987; Ecole Pratique des Hautes Etudes; Cultural Doctorate World U., 1988; m. Bach Yen, June 17, 1978; 1 dau., Thi Minh Tam. Tchr., Centre Studies for Oriental Music, Paris, 1970-75; ethnomusicologist Musée de l'Homme, Paris, and Musée National des Arts et Traditions Populaires, Paris, 1975—; instr. U Nanterre, Paris X, 1987; composer: Nho miên thuong du (Nostalgia of the Highlands) (for 16-stringed zither), 1971, Xuân Vê (The Spring is coming back) (for 16-stringed zither), 1971, Ao thanh (Magic Sound), 1973, Ve Nguon (Return to the Sources) (in cooperation with Nguyen Van Tuong) (electroacoustical music), 1975, Shaman, 1982, Hat haigiong, 1982, Tiêng hat dàn môi Mông, 1982, Nui Ngu Sông Huong (for monochord), 1983, Nam Bac Môt Nhà (for 16-string zither), 1984, Voyage chamanique (for voice), 1986, Tro vê nguôn côi, 1988; also numerous songs; composer film music for: Long Vân Khanh Hôi, 1980; author, performer of numerous records on Vietnamese music. Recepient Grand prize for Vietnam/Tran Quang Hai and Bach Yen, Record Acad., 1983. Mem. Soc. Ethnomusicology, Asian Music Soc., Internat. Folk Music Council, Internat. Musicological Soc., Internat. Assn. Sound Archives, UNESCO Internat. Council Museums and Collections of Mus. Instruments, Soc. Musicology, Centre d'Etudes de Musique Orientale, Association française des Archives Sonores, Société des Auteurs des Compositeurs et des Editeurs de la Musique, Center for Sci. Research (research team), French Soc. Ethnomusicology (founding mem.), French Assn. Research in South East Asia (founding mem.), Assn. Française de Recherche sur l'Asie du Sud Est, Centre Internat. d'Etudes Vietnamiennes, Assn. Preserving and Developing Vietnamese Songs, Assn. Vietnamese Artists and Writers in Europe, Am. Biol. Inst. and Research Assn. (dep. gov. 1987—), Internat. Biol. Assn. (dep. dir. gen. 1987, dep. dir., 1987—)Recipient Médaille d'Or de la musique Académie Culturelle Asiatique, 1986. Contbr. numerous articles to music publs., revs. to numerous music mags.; recs. Home: 12 rue Gutenberg, F-94450 Limeil Brevannes France Office: Departement d'ethnomusicologie, Musee de l'Homme, 75116 Paris France

TRAORE, MOUSSA, president of Mali, army officer; b. Kayes, Sept. 25, 1936; ed. Cadets Coll., Kati, tng. coll., Fréjus, France. Lt. army, Mali, 1964, col. army, from 1971 brig gen. 1978, at Armed Forces Coll., Kati until 1968, led military coup. 1968; pres. Mali, 1968—; prime minister Mali, 1968-80; minister of def. and security, 1978—; minister of interior, 1978-79; pres. conf. of heads of state Union Douaniere Etats l'Afrique Noire, 1970. Pres. mil. com. Nat. Liberation, 1968—; sec.-gen. Nat. Council Union Démocratique du Peuple Malien, 1979-80 formerly member, Cen. Exec. Bureau. Served as non-commd. officer French Army. Address: Office of the Pres, Bamako Mali *

TRAPOLIN, FRANK WINTER, insurance executive; b. New Orleans, Jan. 29, 1913; s. John Baptiste and Florence Bertha (Winter) T.; B.S. in Econs., Loyola U. of South, New Orleans, 1935; m. Thelma Mae Mouledoux, Oct. 27, 1937; children—Timothy, Patricia Couret, Jane Oaksmith, Anne Britt. Agt., Godchaux & Mayer, New Orleans, 1935-42, 46-51; pres. Trapolin-Couret Ins. Agy., Inc., New Orleans, 1953—; mem. faculty Loyola U.; ins. cons. Former pres. Cath. Human Relations Commn. Greater New Orleans, Associated Cath. Charities New Orleans, Maryland Dr. Homeowners Assn., Loyola U. Alumni Assn.; former chmn. adv. bd. New Orleans Juvenile Cts., Ursuline Nuns New Orleans; former scoutmaster Boy Scouts Am.; former v.p. Community Relations Council Greater New Orleans, New Orleans Jr. C.of C., La. Interch. Conf.; former trustee United Fund Greater New Orleans Area; tng. officer 8th Coast Guard Dist. Aux.; former mem. adv. bd. Coll. Bus. Adminstrn., Loyola U., Mother-house of Sisters of Holy Family; former bd. dirs. St. John Berchman Orphanage, New Orleans Interfaith Conf., St. Elizabeth's Home for Girls, Cath. Book Store Found., Manresa Retreat House; adv. bd. New Orleans Track Club; founder, Serra Run for Vocations. Served with USN, 1942-46, 51-53, with Res. Recipient Merit cert. City of New Orleans, 1972; Order of St. Louis. Mem. La. Assn. Ins. Agts., Nat. Assn. Ins. Agts., New Orleans Ins. Exchange, Navy League, Mil. Order World Wars, Greater New Orleans Exec. Assn. (pres. 1985, named Exec. of the Year 1985), New Orleans Photog. Soc., Sierra Club, Blue Key. Democrat. Roman Catholic. Clubs: Sertoma (pres. New Orleans 1955-56), Serra (pres. New Orleans 1973-74), Internat. House, New Orleans Track, New Orleans Yacht, Pass Christian Yacht. Lodge: KC (4 deg.). Patentee gunnery, tng. and machinery devices for USN. Home: 119 Audubon Blvd New Orleans LA 70118-5538 Office: Trapolin-Couret Agy 837 Gravier St Suite 1212 New Orleans LA 70112-1514

TRAPP, LOUIS ANDRE, JR., lawyer; b. N.Y.C., July 21, 1930; s. Louis A. and Katherien (Schuster) T.; A.B., Rutgers U., 1951; LL.B., Columbia, 1956; m. Margaret P. Martines, Apr. 13, 1956; children—Amy Sayre, Louis A. III. Admitted to N.Y. bar, 1957; assoc. Reynolds, Richards, LaVenture, Hadley & Davis, N.Y.C., 1956-65, ptnr., 1966-87, Putney, Twombly, Hall & Hirson, 1988—; justice Village Plandome (N.Y.), 1967-76, trustee, 1976-86, dep. mayor, 1983-86. Chief Plandome Vol. Fire Dept., 1972-74; bd. dirs. N.Y. Young Republican Club, 1957-59; trustee Soc. of St. Johnland, 1971-76, v.p., 1975-76; bd. dirs., sec. Halcyon Found.; bd. dirs., v.p. St. Johnland Nursing Home, Inc., 1975-76; trustee Am. Mus. in Britain. Served to 1st lt. USAF, 1951-53. Mem. Assn. Bar City N.Y., Am. N.Y. State bar assns., N.Y. State Magistrates Assn., Phi Delta Phi. Republican. Episcopalian (vestry). Clubs: Downtown Assn. (N.Y.C.); Plandome Field and Marine (pres. 1969-70), St. Croix Country. Home: 35 Central Dr Plandome NY 11030 Office: Bar Bldg 36 West 44th St New York NY 10036

TRASK, FREDERICK KINGSBURY, JR., former banker; b. Short Hills, N.J., Oct. 8, 1907; s. Frederick K. and Katharine Stagg (Jacquelin) T.; m. Margaret Moulton Pope, June 14, 1930; children—Jacquelin Trask Duffek, Jane Trask Freund, Frederick K. III, Frances Pope Trask Wozencraft. A.B., Harvard U., 1930; postgrad. Am. Inst. Banking, 1931-32, NYU Bus. Extension Coll., 1932-33. With N.Y. Trust Co., N.Y.C., 1930-35; with Farmers Deposit Nat. Bank, Pitts., 1935-46, asst. cashier, 1940-43, asst. v.p., 1943-44, v.p., 1944-46; organized Payson & Trask, 1947, gen. partner, 1947-78; dir. N.Y. Met. Baseball Club, Inc., 1962-79; dir. Gt. No. Paper & Gt. No. Nekoosa Corp., 1949-83; dir. Gen. Reins. Corp., 1951-83; trustee U.S. Trust Co. N.Y., 1949-82; asst. dir. Contract Settlement, Washington, 1944-45. Pres., Soc. N.Y. Hosp., 1961-65, bd. govs., 1954—; councilman Borough of Sewickley, 1941-45; bd. dirs. Family Service Assn., Pitts., 1941-44, 46; mem. Helen Hay Whitney Found., 1947—, trustee, sec.-treas., 1947-78; trustee China Med. Bd. N.Y., 1956-76. Served as maj. Army Service Forces and Fin. Dept., AUS, 1942-43, lt. col., 1943-44. Republican. Episcopalian. Clubs: Old Capital (Monterey, Calif.), Harvard, Union (N.Y.C.); Sea Pines Golf, Bear Creek Golf (Hilton Head, S.C.); Burlington Country (Vt.). Home: 97 Del Mesa Carmel Carmel CA 93923

TRAURIG, LEONA, researcher, orthomolecular therapist; b. Chgo., Aug. 14, 1934; d. Daniel and Sonia (Lemson) Leviton; m. Walter Bernard Traurig, Nov. 6, 1955; children—Marcia, William, Donald. R.N., Jackson Meml. Hosp., Miami, Fla., 1955. Asst. charge nurse labor and delivery Jackson Meml. Hosp., 1955-56; dir. employee health services Larkin Gen. Hosp., Miami, 1972-73; med. examiner, Miami, 1973-82; pres. Miami Med. Assocs., 1982—; cons. Life Extension Found., Hollywood, Fla., 1982—; organizer-vol. Sch. Systems Clinics, Dade County, Fla., 1970-79; cons. Girl Scouts Am., 1968-74, Home for Aged, 1979—(both Miami). Contbr. articles to profl. jours. Vol. examiner Am. Cancer Soc., Miami, 1982—; vol. counselor health fairs Am. Heart Assn., Miami, 1980-83; vol. coordinator summer camp clinics clinics Girl Scouts U.S.A., Miami, 1971-73. Recipient Best All Round Nurse award Alumnae Assn. Jackson Meml. Hosp., 1955; Appreciation award Dade County (Fla.) Sch. Bd., 1979. Mem. Am. Heart Assn., Am. Nurses Assn., Nat. Bus.-Profl. Assn., Ctr. Chinese Medicine, Life Extension Found. Democrat. Jewish. Address: 13149 SW 91 Ct Miami FL 33176

TRAUTWEIN, JAMES WILLIAM, optoelectric component company executive; b. Washington, Mo., Aug. 24, 1935; s. Edwin Herman and Octavia (Raymond) T.; student S.E. Mo. U., 1953-55; B.S.E.E., Mo. U., Rolla, 1957; M.S. in Solid State Physics, Western Ky. U., 1967; 1 dau., Susan. Engring. trainee Gen. Electric Co., Owensboro, Ky., Tyler, Tex. and Syracuse, N.Y., 1957-58, research engr., Owensboro, Ky., 1958-60, design engr., 1960-63, engring. mgr., 1963-67; engring. supr. Monsanto, Decater, Ala., 1967; design engr. Tex. Instrument Inc., Dallas, 1967-69, engring. mgr., 1969-72, project mgr., 1972-74; mktg. mgr. TRW Optron, Carrollton, Tex., 1975-80; v.p. mktg. Optek, McKinney, Tex., 1980—; condr. tech. seminars. Boys' counselor Royal Ambassadors, Owensboro, Ky., 1960-66; counselor Jr. Achievement, Owensboro, 1964-67. Registered profl. engr., Mo., Ky. Mem. IEEE, Profl. Engrs. Soc. (v.p. Green River br. 1966), Mark Twain Soc. Republican. Lutheran. Author: Increasing Speeds of Response in Photocell, 1967; contbr. articles to profl. jours. Office: 345 Industrial Blvd McKinney TX 75069

TRAVELSTEAD, CHESTER COLEMAN, former educational administrator; b. Franklin, Ky., Sept. 25, 1911; s. Conley and Nelle (Gooch) T.; m. Marita Hawley, Aug. 1, 1936; children—Coleman, Jimmie. A.B., Western Ky. State Coll., Bowling Green, 1933; M.Music, Northwestern U., 1947; Ph.D., U. Ky., 1950; D.Hum., Morehead State U., 1975; Ph.D., John F. Kennedy U., Buenos Aires, 1975; L.H.D., U. N.Mex., 1980. Tchr., prin. rural and consol. schs. Mecklenberg County, Va., 1931-32, 33-35; tchr. gen. sci., math., music Picadome High Sch., Lexington, Ky., 1935-37; dir. music Henry Clay High Sch., Lexington, 1937-42; personnel supr. Lexington Signal Dept., Dept. War, 1942-43; supr. music Lexington pub. schs., 1945-47; rep. Investors Diversified Services, Inc., 1947-48; coordinator in-service tchr. edn. Ky. Dept. Edn., 1950-51; asst. prof. edn., asst. dean Coll. Edn., U. Ga., Athens, 1951-53; dean Sch. Edn., U. S.C., Columbia, 1953-56; dean Coll. Edn. U. N.Mex., Albuquerque, 1956-68; v.p. acad. affairs U. N.Mex., 1968-76, provost, 1976-77; Mem. Nat. Council Accreditation Tchr. Edn., 1960-66, chmn., 1963-65. Author books; contbr. articles in field to profl. jours. Pres. bd. dirs. N.Mex. Symphony Orch., 1977-78, 84-85. Served with USNR, 1943-45, PTO. Mem. NEA, Nat. Soc. Study Edn., Soc. Advancement Edn., AAUP, Phi Kappa Phi, Phi Delta Kappa., Kappa Delta Pi. Home: 320 Fontana Pl NE Albuquerque NM 87108

TRAVERS, W. LAWRENCE, health care executive; b. Syracuse, N.Y., Nov. 1, 1943; s. Walter Roy and Elizabeth Laurene (Hicks) T.; BS, Coll. of Emporia (Kans.), 1965; MSW, Syracuse U., 1972; postgrad. in Pub. Adminstrn., Nova U., Ft. Lauderdale, Fla., 1978-82; postgrad. in law Columbia Pacific U., 1982—. Cert. social worker, counselor, N.Y. Cons. alcoholism treatment Hutchings Psychiat. Ctr. of N.Y. State, Office of Mental Health, Syracuse, 1972-73, program dir. alcoholism rehab. unit, 1973-76, program dir. psychogeriatric day treatment/outpatient services, 1976-80, mental health outpatient service, 1980-86, program dir. mentally ill. chem. abuse sr. adv. panel, 1986—; pvt. practice, Marietta, N.Y.; bd. dirs. Franklin Med. Lab. Sch., Westbury, N.Y., 1980. Dem. party official, 1974-76. Recipient sci. achievement award Chem. Rubber Co., 1965. Fellow Am. Orthopsychiat. Assn.; mem. Acad. Cert. Social Workers (diplomate), Nat. Assn. Social Workers (clin. register), Am. Coll. Addiction Treatment Adminstrs. Presbyterian. Home: 2420 Patterson Rd Marietta NY 13110 Office: Hutchings Psychiat Ctr Box 27 Univ Sta Syracuse NY 13210

TRÁVNIK, IGOR, research, development specialist; b. Bratislava, Czechoslovakia, Oct. 1, 1942; s. Karol and Greta (Jankova) T.; m. Eliska Sevcikova, Oct. 26, 1966; children: Robert, Boris. Degree in Constrn. Engring., Slovak Tech. U., 1964; M of Econ. Scis., Bratislava Bus. Sch., 1975. Asst. Ustav Ekonomiky A Organzacie Stavebnictva, Bratislava, 1964-71, researcher, 1971-76, research group leader, 1976-82, dept. mgr., 1982-84, vice dir. research, development, 1984—; faculty constrn. Slovak Tech. U., 1980—; cons. Slovakian Ministry Bldg., 1982—. Author: (with others) Network Analysis, 1973. Mem. research and devel. adv. group Com. of Communist party, Bratislava, 1981—. Mem. Czechoslovak Assn. Sci. and Technique. Office: Inst Economy and Orgn, Ruzova Dol 27, 82469 Bratislava Czechoslovakia

TRAXLER, WILLIAM BYRD, lawyer; b. Greenville, S.C., July 10, 1912; s. David Byrd and Mary Willey (Gatling) T. Student The Citadel, 1929-30, U. Tex., 1930-32; J.D., George Washington U., 1940. Bar: D.C. 1940, S.C. 1940, U.S. Ct. Appeals (4th cir.) 1960. Ptnr. Hinson, Traxler and Hamer, Greenville, 1950-58, Rainey, Fant, Traxler and Horton, 1958-60; sole practice, Greenville, 1960—. Bd. dirs. Phyllis Wheatly Assn., 1954, Vis. Nurse Assn., Greenville, 1957-59, United Way, Greenville, 1976; vice-chmn. bd. health City of Greenville, 1960-70; life mem. The Citadel Endowment Fund. Served to capt. U.S. Army, 1942-46. Recipient Alumni Achievement award George Washington U., 1946. Mem. S.C. Bar Assn., Greenville County Bar Assn. (pres. 1976), Greenville C. of C. (chmn. of yr. 1967, chmn. taxation com.), George Washington Law Assn. (life), Law Sci. Acad., George Washington U. Law Assn. (life), Phi Alpha Delta, Beta Theta Pi. Club: Torch (pres. 1956). Author: Military Government in Germany, 1960; Political Third Parties, 1968; History of the Fourteenth Amendment, 1974; The Jury Numbers Game, 1976; Medieval Harmony, 1982. Club: Greenville Country (bd. govs. 1982-85). Home: 100 Trails End Greenville SC 29607 Office: PO Box 10031 Greenville SC 29603 also: 606 E North St Greenville SC 29603

TRAYNOR, J. MICHAEL, lawyer; b. Oakland, Calif., Oct. 25, 1934; s. Roger J. and Madeleine (Lackmann) T.; m. Shirley Williams, Feb. 11, 1956; children: Kathleen, Elizabeth, Thomas. B.A., U. Calif., Berkeley, 1955; J.D., Harvard U., 1960. Bar: Calif. 1961, U.S. Supreme Ct. 1966. Dep. atty. gen. State of Calif., San Francisco, 1961-63; spl. counsel Calif. Senate Com. on Local Govt., Sacramento, 1963; assoc. firm Cooley, Godward, Castro, Huddleson & Tatum, San Francisco, 1963-69, partner, 1969—; advisor 2d Restatement of Restitution, 1981-85, 3d Restatement of Unfair Competition, 1986—, 1988 revisions 2d Restatement of Conflict of Laws; mem. Joint Commn. on Fair Jud. Election Practices, 1976-79; lectr. Boalt Hall Sch. Law U. Calif.-Berkeley, 1982—; cons. Rand Corp., 1986—. Contbr. articles to legal jours. Trustee Head-Royce Sch., Oakland, 1974-83, chmn., 1980-82. Served to 1st lt. USMC, 1955-57. Fellow Am. Bar Found.; mem. Am. Law Inst. (council 1985—), Bar Assn. San Francisco (pres. 1973), Sierra Club Legal Def. Fund (treas. 1979—). Home: 3131 Eton Ave Berkeley CA 94705 Office: Cooley Godward Castro Huddleson Tatum One Maritime Plaza Alcoa Bldg Suite 2000 San Francisco CA 94111

TREACY, RICHARD PATRICK, I, construction executive; b. Dublin, Ireland, Nov. 25, 1942; s. Edward Allen Treacy and Mary Cummins; children: Richard Patrick II, Robert Edward, Juliette Mary. Mng. ptnr. Treacy & Thomas, Dublin, 1963—; cons. in field. Staff officer St. John Ambulance Brigade Ireland, 1956—. Faculty of Bldg. fellow, London, 1978. Mem. Irish Inst. Tng. and Devel., Nat. Assn. Master Painters and Decorators Ireland (pres. 1977, 87), Constrn. Industry Fedn. (v.p. 1987-88). Office: Lr Sandyford Rd, Dumdrum, Dublin 16, Ireland

TREAT, WILLIAM WARDWELL, banker, former judge; b. Boston, May 23, 1918. AB, U. Maine, 1940; MBA, Harvard U., 1947. Bar: Maine 1945, N.H. 1949, U.S. Supreme Ct. 1955. Judge N.H. Probate Ct., Exeter, 1958-83; pres., chmn. bd. Bank Meridian N.A. (formerly Hampton Nat. Bank), 1958-84, chmn., 1984—; chmn. Towle Mfg. Co.; bd. dirs. Exeter & Hampton Electric Co., Unitil Co., Colonial Group, Inc., Amoskeag Bank Shares, Inc.; faculty Nat. Coll. for State Judiciary, Reno, 1975—; chmn. N.H. Jud. Council, 1976-83; adv. bd. Nat. Ctr. for State Cts., 1973-80; pres. Nat. Coll. Probate Judges, 1968-77, pres. emeritus, 1977—; mem. Nat. Fiduciary Acctg. Standards Project, 1975—, Am. Assembly on Death, Taxes and Family Property, 1976—. Author: Treat on Probate, 3 vols, 1968, Local Justice in the Granite State, 1961; contbr. articles to profl. jours.; editor: Probate Court Manual, 1976, Focus on the Bank Director: The Job, 1977. Mem. Rep. Nat. Com., 1954-58, 60-64; mem. U.S. del. to 42d Gen. Assembly of UN; presdl. elector, sec. U.S. Electoral Coll., 1956, 60; del.-at-large Rep. Nat. Conv., 1960, program chmn., 1964; bd. dirs., v.p. Hundred Club of N.H.; trustee Franklin Pierce Coll., 1985—. Mem. Am. Law Inst., ABA, N.H. Bar Assn., Am. Bankers Assn. (exec. com. community bankers div. 1975-78, chmn. div. communications com. 1976, chmn. task force bank dirs. program 1976-77), N.H. Bankers Assn. (legis. com. 1975-77, fed. legis. com. 1977—), Am. Judicature Soc. (bd. dirs. 1971-77), New Eng. Law Inst. (adv. bd. 1969-76), Soc. Cin., Soc. Mayflower Descendants in State of N.H. Clubs: Harvard, Tavern, St. Botolph, Somerset (Boston); Royal Poinciana, Port Royal (Naples, Fla.); Bald Peak Colony (Melvin Village, N.H.). Home: PO Box 498 Hampton NH 03842 Office: 100 Winnacunnet Rd Hampton NH 03842

TREECE, JAMES LYLE, lawyer; b. Colorado Springs, Colo., Feb. 6, 1925; s. Lee Oren and Ruth Ida (Smith) T.; m. Ruth Julie Treece, Aug. 7, 1949 (div. 1984); children—James (dec.), Karen, Teryl Wait, Jamilyn Smyser, Carol Crowder. Student Colo. State U., 1943, Colo. U., 1943, U.S. Naval Acad., 1944-46; B.S., Mesa Coll., 1946; J.D., U. Colo., 1950; postgrad. U. N.C., 1976-77. Bar: Colo. 1952, U.S. Dist. Ct. Colo. 1952, U.S. Ct. Appeals (10th cir.) 1952, U.S. Supreme Ct. 1967. Assoc., Yegge, Hall, Treece & Evans and predecessors, 1951-59, ptnr., 1959-69; U.S. atty., Colo., 1969-77; pres. Treece, Bahr & Arckey, P.C. and predecessor firms, Littleton, Colo., 1977—; mcpl. judge, 1967-68; mem. faculty Nat. Trial Advocacy Inst., 1973-76, Law-Sci. Acad., 1964. Chmn. Colo. Dept. Pub. Welfare, 1963-68; chmn. Colo. Dept. Social Services, 1968-69; mem. Littleton Bd. Edn., 1977-81. Served with USNR, 1944-46. Recipient awards Colo. Assn. Sch. Bds., 1981, IRS, 1977, FBI, 1977, DEA, 1977, Fed. Exec. Bd., 1977. Mem. Fed. Bar Assn. (pres. Colo. 1975), Colo. Bar Assn. (bd. govs.), Denver Bar Assn. (v.p., trustee). Republican. Lutheran. Home: 7210 E Euclid Dr Englewood CO 80111 Office: 2596 W Alamo Ave Littleton CO 80120

TREGLOWN, JEREMY DICKINSON, editor; b. May 24, 1946; s. Geoffrey and Beryl T.; m. Rona Bower, 1970 (div. 1982); 3 children; m. Holly Eley (nee Vrquitart), 1984. MA, BLitt, Oxford (Eng.) U.; PhD, U. London. Lectr., Lincoln Coll., Oxford U., 1974-77, Univ. Coll. London, 1977-80; asst. editor The Times Literary Supplement, London, 1980-82, editor, 1982—. Vis. fellow All Souls Coll., 1986. Gen. editor Plays in Performance series, 1981-85; editor: The Letters of John Wilmot, Earl of Rochester, 1980; Spirit of Wit, 1982, The Lantern-Bearers and other Essays by Robert Louis Stevenson, 1988; contbr. to Plays and Players, The Guardian, Observer, Sunday Times; contbr. articles on poetry and drama to academic jours.

TREIKI, ALI A., Libyan ambassador to the United Nations; b. Misrata, Libya, 1938; m. Aisha Dihoum; children: Amal, Suzan, Mohamed, Amina. BA, U. Behghazi (Libya), 1960; PhD, Toulouse (France) U., 1967. Minister plenipotentiary Libyan Araba Jamahiriya, 1970; sec. of state Fgn. Affairs of Libya, 1971-77; fgn. sec. of Libya 1977-81; sec. of liaison Fgn. Affairs of Libya, 1981-82; ambassador and permanent rep. UN, 1982-84, 86—; sec. people's com. People's Bur. for Fgn. Liaison, 1984-86; v.p. gen. assembly UN, 1987; non-resident A.E. and P. Can.; chmn. Arab Group of the UN, N.Y., 1987; del. Nan-Aligned Movement, Orgn. Islamic Conf., Orgn. African Unity, League Arab States, Group of 77; bd. trustees UNITAR. Mem. Arab-Am. Anti-Discrimination Com., Washington, 1987—. Recipient 22 hon. medals various countries. Office: Mission Socialist People's Libyan Libyan Arab Jamahiriya to UN 309-315 East 48th St New York NY 10017

TREJO, JOSÉ DIAZ, accountant, stockbroker, consultant, insurance executive, financial planner; b. Carrizo Springs, Tex., Feb. 11, 1948; s. Elisandro Briones and Maria Trinidad (Diaz) T. AA, Coll. DuPage, 1969; BA in History, No. Ill. U., 1971. CPA, Ill; lic. ins. producer, Ill. Revenue acctg. and banking Spector Industries, Inc., Bensenville, Ill., 1977-81; revenue auditor State of Ill., Springfield, 1982-84; practice acctg. Trejo & Assocs., Itasca, Ill., 1985—; cons. in taxes, personal and corp. fin. planning, bus. valuation, audits, and other areas of field; gen. securities rep. HD Vest Investment Securities, direct participation programs rep. HDVIS. Mem. Am. Inst. CPA's (tax div. 1986-87, personal fin. planning div. 1986-87), Ill. CPA Soc. (review instr., faculty mem., personal fin. planning, banks, and continuing profl. edn. coms.), Hispanic Alliance Career Enhancement, Midwest Assn. Hispanic Accts. (chmn. pvt. practioners com.), Nat. Assn. Securities Dealers, Securities Investors Protection Corp. Roman Catholic. Home: 320 N Elm St Itasca IL 60143

TREJOS, DIEGO, architect; b. San Jose, Costa Rica, June 26, 1937; s. Jose Joaquin and Clara (Fonseca) T.; Architect, Universidad Nacional Autonoma de Mexico, 1960; m. Sylvia Cadaval, Dec. 5, 1959; children—Ana Lorena, Carlos Eduardo, Diana Sylvia. Architect, Escalante Van Patten, Costa Rica, 1960; architect, partner, Aica Sacmag, Costa Rica, Mex. and P.R., 1961-66; cabinet minister of the Presidency and Pub. Security, Govt. of Costa Rica, 1966-70; exec. pres. Co. T.R. Engrs. and Architects and its housing div., San Jose, 1970—; cons. Desarrollos Tecnicos S.A., 1983; mem. academic council architecture Autonomous U. C.Am., 1977; pres. jury, 1979. Mem. Architects and Engrs. Coll. Costa Rica (bd. dirs. 1965-66), Costa Rica Architects Assn. (bd. dirs. 1964-65), Am. Hereford Assn. Mem. Unidad Party. Roman Catholic. Clubs: Indoor, Hacienda Montelimar in the Peninsula of Nicoya, Guanacaste, Costa Rica. Major archtl. works include Del Monte Bldg., 1981, Sociedad Seguros de Vida, 1977, St. Claire Coll. Gymnasium, 1966,

Ashford Tower Apartment Bldg., P.R., 1964; author: Memoirs of the Minister of the Presidency to the Congress (Asamblea Legislativa) of Costa Rica, 1967, 68, 69, 70; Recreational centers, San Jose met. area. Home: Box 5573, San Jose Costa Rica Office: Box 5573, San Jose Costa Rica

TRELEAVEN, PHILLIPS ALBERT, publishing company executive; b. Oak Park, Ill., July 20, 1928; s. Harry William and Mary Elizabeth (Gregory) T. B.A., Duke U., 1950; A.M., Boston U., 1959; D.B.A. (hon.), Unity Coll., 1988. With G. K. Hall & Co., Boston, 1956-60, 61-67, 69-79; pres. G. K. Hall & Co., 1969-78, chmn. bd., 1970-78; underwriter mcpl. bonds Scharff & Jones, New Orleans, 1959-61; instr. in polit. economy Boston U., 1967-69; vis. lectr. econs. Unity Coll., 1979—; Owner Odyssey Hill Farms, Thorndike, Maine, 1971-75; pres., pub. Thorndike Press, 1977-87, chmn. bd. dirs., 1988—; pres. pubs. and communications group Sr. Service Corp., 1987—. Selectman, Thorndike, 1979-81; trustee Unity Coll., 1985—. Served with AUS, 1950-53. Mem. Phi Beta Kappa. Home: One Mile Rd Thorndike ME 04986 Office: PO Box 155 Thorndike ME 04986

TRELFORD, DONALD GILCHRIST, editor; b. Coventry, England, Nov. 9, 1937; s. Thomas Staplin and Doris (Gilchrist) T.; m. Janice Ingram (div. 1978); children—Sally, Timothy, Paul; m. Katherine Louise Mark, July 31, 1978; 1 dau., Laura Louise. M.A., Cambridge U., 1961. Reporter, sub-editor Coventry Standard, 1961, Sheffield Telegraph, 1961-63; editor Times of Malawi, 1963-66; corr. in Africa Observer, Times, BBC, 1963-66; dep. news editor Observer, London, 1966, asst. mng. editor, 1968, dep. editor, 1969-75, editor, 1976—, also dir.; mem. council Roehampton Inst. Higher Edn., 1976-80, Journalists for Europe; judge Brit. Press Awards, Olivier Theatre Awards. Editor: Siege, 1980, Sunday Best, 1981-83; author: County Champions, 1982; Snookered, 1986, (with Garry Kasparov) Child of Change, 1987. Patron, Milton Keynes Civic Forum. Served as pilot officer RAF, 1956-58. Named Newspaper editor of Yr., Granada TV, London, 1983; Internat. Editor of Yr., World Press Rev., 1984. Mem. Internat. Press Inst. (Brit. exec. com. 1976—). Anglican. Clubs: Garrick, MCC (London). Office: The Observer, 8 Saint Andrew's Hill, London EC4V 5JA, England

TRELL, ERIK YNGVAR, physician, scientist, educator; b. Trollhattan, Sweden, June 4, 1939; s. Yngvar and Karin (Trell) Gustavsson; m. Lena Margareta Alm; children: Karl Oskar, Kristina Elisabet. Intern, then resident in internal medicine Malmo (Sweden) Gen. Hosp. Lund U., 1962-73, assoc. prof. dept. preventive medicine, 1973-82, assoc. prof. dept. community and preventive medicine, 1982-87; assoc. prof. internal medicine Linköping (Sweden) U. Hosp., 1973; prof. family and preventive medicine dept. community health scis. Linköping (Sweden) U. Hosp., 1987—; adviser WHO, Internat. Agy. for Research on Cancer. Contbr. articles ot profl. jours.; patentee in field. Mem. Internat. Soc. for Study of Time, others. Office: Linköping U Dept Health Sci, Bangatan 5, Malmo Sweden

TRELOAR, MURRAY EDWARD, pathologist; b. Toronto, Can., Mar. 16, 1949; s. John Edward and Jean Gladys (Murray) T.; m. Margaret Anne Menagh, Aug. 11, 1973. BS, U. Toronto, 1972, MD, 1975. Pathologist Stratford (Ont.) Gen. Hosp., 1980-81, chief pathologist, 1981-84; chmn. lab. medicine Oshawa (Ont.) Gen. Hosp., 1984—; lab. dir. Oshawa Clinic, 1987—. Fellow Royal Coll. Physicians Surgeons Can. (Hematological Pathology com. 1985—), Am. Soc. Clin. Pathologists, Coll. Am. Pathologists (Delegate 1984—); mem. Ont. Med. Assn. (mem. council lab. medicine sect. 1986—, vice-chmn. 1988—),, Can. Med. Assn., Can. Assn. Pathologists, Alpha Omega Alpha. Home: 67 Glenmanor Dr, Oshawa, ON Canada L1J 5A3 Office: Oshawa Gen Hosp, 24 Alma St, Oshawa, ON Canada L1G 2B9

TREMAIN, ALAN, hotel executive; b. Kent, Eng., Aug. 18, 1935; came to U.S., 1966; s. Archibald and Elizabeth (Morris) T.; m. Anita P. DeVienne, July 31, 1961; children: Warren, Nathlie, Hugo, Philippe. Grad., Westminster Hotel Sch., 1952, Canterbury Sch. Econs., 1962; LL.B., La Salle Sch., Chgo., 1971. Chef de Pertie Grosvenor House, London, 1954-55; food and beverage mgr. Peninsula, Hong Kong, 1956-57; gen. mgr. Warners Hotel, also The Russley, Christchurch, New Zealand, 1958-64, Menzies, Sydney, Australia, 1964-65, Empress Hotel, Vancouver, B.C., Can., 1966-69; pres. Planned Food Facilities (Internat.) Ltd., Toronto, 1970-72; resident mgr. Sheraton Boston, 1972; mng. dir. Copley Plaza Hotel, Boston, 1972—; pres. Hotels of Distinction, Inc., Boston. Author: A Guide to the Fine Art of Living, 1963, A Meal for To-Night, 1965. Decorated officer Order Brit. Empire (U.K.); recipient Culinary Merit award from Cercle Epicurien Mondel, Paris, 1956. Fellow Hotel and Catering Inst. (U.K.), founding mem. Internat. Soc. Chefs de Cuisine (chmn. 1954). Clubs: Mason, Montreal Badminton and Squash, Brae Burn Country, Rolls Royce Owners. Address: Copley Plaza Copley Sq Boston MA 02116

TREMAYNE, ERIC FLORY, lawyer; b. Washington, Nov. 29, 1945; s. Bertram William and Frances (Lewis) T.; m. Barbara Ann Williams, Sept. 18, 1982. B.A., Westminster Coll., 1967; J.D., Washington U., St. Louis, 1973. Bar: Mo. 1973, U.S. Dist. Ct. (ea. and we. dists.) Mo., 1973. Assoc. Tremayne, Lay, Carr, Bauer and Nouss, Clayton, Mo., 1973-77, ptnr., 1978—; dir. Vortex Engring. Inc., St. Louis. St. Louis. Campaign aide Citizens for Kit Bond, St. Louis, 1972. Served to sp. 4 U.S. Army, 1968-70. Mem. St. Louis County Bar Assn. (Outstanding Young Lawyer, 1981, pres. 1983-84), Bar Assn. Met. St. Louis. Republican. Anglican. Clubs: St. Louis Beta Theta Pi (v.p. 1978—), Sports Car Club Am. (instr. 1979—). Home: 433 Eatherton Valley Rd Chesterfield MO 63017 Office: Tremayne Lay Carr Bauer & Nouss 120 S Central Suite 540 Clayton MO 63105

TREMBLAY, FRANCIS WILFRED, education consultant, educator; b. Lebanon, N.H., Mar. 10, 1925; s. Albert Napoleon and Mary Ann (Gagnon) T.; m. Eugenia Howson, July 21, 1952 (div. Feb. 1973); 1 child, Mary Irene; m. Micheline Francoise Poirier, Nov. 25, 1974; children—Sophie, Annie, Catherine, Paul Gauthier. B.A., U. N.H., 1949; B.E., Wash. State U., 1950, M.Ed., 1953; Ed.D., Brigham Young U., 1980. Cert. pub. sch. adminstr., Calif. Tchr. Mullan Pub. Schs., Idaho, 1950-51, Palouse Pub. Schs., Wash., 1951-53; prin. Warm Springs Elem. Sch., Calif., 1954-58; supt. Smith River Union Sch., Calif., 1958-62, Placer Hills Union Sch., Meadow Vista, Calif., 1962-68; cons. Calif. Dept. Edn., Sacramento, 1968-87; adj. prof. Chapman Coll., Orange, Calif., 1981—; mem. Nat. Com. on Migrant Student Record Transfer System, 1980. Pres. Del Norte County Tchrs. Assn., Calif., 1963, N. Coast Adminstrs. Assn., Calif., 1963; mem. Common Cause, Sacramento, 1984. Served with USN, 1943-46, PTO. Nat. Def. Inst. Scholar, 1965, 66, 67. Mem. Calif. Assn. Sch. Adminstrs., Calif. Assn. Compensatory Edn., Phi Delta Kappa. Democrat. Unitarian. Home: 6937 Ellsworth Circle Fair Oaks CA 95628 Office: Calif State Dept Edn Sacramento CA 95814

TREMPONT, JACQUES A., former ambassador, educator, b. St. Gilles, Belgium, Apr. 7, 1925; s. Alexis and Lucienne T.; student U. Oxford, 1949-50, U. Valladolid, 1948-50, Academie de Droit Internation de La Haye, 1947-50; Dr. Law, U. Louvain, 1951, Lic.Sc.Pol. and Diplomatiques, 1951, B.A. Phil., 1950, cand. philosophie et lettres, 1948; m. Nadine Masoin, June 23, 1953; children: Dominique-Jacques, Anne-Isabelle, Catherine. With Mil. Govt. in Germany, 1945-49; with NATO, Paris, 1952-54, World Bank, Washington, 1954-56, ICHEC, 1958-73, U. Pro Deo, Rome, 1973-76; internat. monetary adv., 1957—; mem. faculty Collegium Romanum Pro Deo, 1976—; AEP to UN, 1978-80; chmn. Molimex Engring. Decorated chevalier Order of Leopold (Belgium); knight Grand Cross, Order Vila Viçosa (Portugal); knight comdr. Order of Cedar (Lebanon), Nat. Order (Peru), Order Condor of Andes (Bolivia). Clubs: Cercle Royal Gaulois, Cercle des Nations, Club Val Duchesse (Brussels). Home: 15 Ave de la Folle Chanson, B-1050 Brussels Belgium

TRENNEPOHL, GARY LEE, finance educator; b. Detroit, Dec. 6, 1946; s. Leo Donald and Wilma Mae (Tiensvold) T.; m. Sandra K. Yeager, June 9, 1968; children: Paige E., Adrienne A. BS, U. Tulsa, 1968; MBA, Utah State U., 1971; PhD, Tex. Tech U., 1976. Asst. prof. aero. studies Tex. Tech U., Lubbock, 1972-74; asst. prof. fin. Ariz. State U., Tempe, 1977-80, assoc. prof., 1980-82; prof. U. Mo., Columbia, 1982-86, dir. Sch. Bus., 1984-86; prof. fin. Tex. A&M U., College Station, 1986—, head dept., 1986—. Author: An Introduction to Financial Management, 1984; assoc. editor Jour. Fin. Research, 1983—; contbr. articles to profl. jours. Served to capt. USAF, 1968-72. Decorated Commendation medal with oak leaf cluster, Vietnam Service medal. Mem. Fin. Mgmt. Assn. (bd. dirs. 1987-88, v.p. 1987-88), So. Fin. Assn., Southwestern Fin. Assn. (bd. dirs. 1983-84, pres. 1986), Midwest Fin. Assn. (bd. dirs. 1985—). Republican. Lutheran. Home: 2010 Pebblestone College Station TX 77840 Office: Tex A&M U Coll Bus College Station TX 77843

TRESMONTAN, OLYMPIA DAVIS, psychotherapist, marriage and family counselor; b. Boston, Nov. 27, 1925; d. Peter Konstantin and Mary (Hazimanolis) Davis; B.S., Simmons Coll., 1946; M.A., Wayne State U., 1960; Ph.D. (Schaefer Found. grantee), U. Calif., Berkeley, 1971; m. Dion Marc Tresmontan, Sept. 15, 1957 (dec. Mar. 1961); m. 2d, Robert Baker Stitt, Mar. 21, 1974. Child welfare worker San Francisco Dept. Social Service, 1964-66; sensitivity tng. NSF Sci. Curriculum Improvement Study, U. Calif., Berkeley, 1967-68; individual practice psychol. counseling, San Francisco, 1970—; dir. Studio Ten Services, San Francisco, Promise for Children, San Francisco, 1981-88; tchr. U. Calif. extension at San Francisco, 1971-72, Chapman Coll. Grad. Program in Counseling, Travis AFB, 1971-74; clin. cons. Childworth Learning Ctr., San Francisco, 1976-80; cons. project rape response Queen's Bench Found., San Francisco, 1977; adv. bd. Childrens' Multicultural Mus., San Francisco, 1988—. Active Friends San Francisco Pub. Library, Internat. Hospitality Com. Bay Area; bd. dirs. Childworth Learning Center, 1976-80. Mem. Am. Psychol. Assn., Am. Orthopsychiat. Assn., Am. Assn. Marriage Counselors, Calif. Assn. Marriage, Family and Child Therapists, Assn. for Study of Dreams. Club: Commonwealth. Author: (with J. Morris) The Evaluation of A Compensatory Education Program, 1967; (Karplus edit.) What is Curriculum Evaluation, Six Answers, 1968. Home: 2611 Lake St San Francisco CA 94121

TREURNICHT, ANDRIES PETRUS, political official; b. Piketberg, Republic of South Africa, Feb. 19, 1921; s. Andries Petrus and Hester Johanna (Albertyn) T.; m. Engela Helena Dreyer, Jan. 18, 1949; children: Elsa, Lise, Elana, Andriette. BA, U. Stellenbosch, Republic of South Africa, 1941; MA, U. Capetown, Republic of South Africa, 1951, PhD, 1957. Minister religion Dutch Reformed Ch., Republic of South Africa, 1946-60, editor die kerkbode, 1960-67, assessor, 1965-69; editor Hoofstad Perskor, Republic of South Africa, 1967-71; mem. parliament Nat. Party, Republic of South Africa, 1971—; dep. minister Republic of South Africa Govt., 1976-79, minister, 1979-82; leader Conservative Party, Republic of South Africa, 1982—, Ofcl. Opposition Party, Republic of South Africa, 1987—. Author 16 books; contbr. articles on culture, politics and religion to profl. jours. Decorated Republic of South Africa Govt. Office: Box 1842, 0001 Pretoria Republic of South Africa

TREVINO DÍAZ, JOSUÉ, electronics and communications engineer, religion educator; b. Monterrey, Mexico, Oct. 21, 1959; s. Josué Trevino and Hermila Esthela Díaz. Degree in Electronics and Communications Engring., U. Autonoma de Nuevo Leon, Monterrey, 1984. Cert. engineer. Computer programmer Gamesa, Monterrey, Nuevo Leon, Mexico, 1981. Counsellor Internat. Fellowship of Evang. Students, 1984—. Baptist. Home: MM Lacas 320, Colonia Deportivo Obispado, 64010 Monterrey Nuevo Leon, Mexico

TREVOR, BRONSON, economist; b. N.Y.C., Nov. 12, 1910; s. John Bond and Caroline Murray (Wilmerding) T.: A.B., Columbia Coll., 1931; m. Eleanor Darlington Fisher, Nov. 8, 1946; children—Eleanor, Bronson, Caroline. Own bus., 1931—; dir., asst. sec. Northwestern Terminal R.R., 1952-58; chmn. bd. Texinia Corp., Former dir. chmn. fin. com. Gen. Hosp. of Saranac Lake mem. Council for Agrl. and Chemurgic Research, Am. Forestry Assn. Mem. Republican County Com. of N.Y. County, 1937-39; leader in primary election campaigns N.Y. County, 1937, 38, 39 to free local Rep. party orgn. from leftwing affiliations; mem. Nat. Rep. Club. Served with U.S. Army, 1942, World War II. Mem. N.Y. State C. of C., S.A.R., Soc. Colonial Wars. Clubs: Union, Knickerbocker, Racquet and Tennis, Piping Rock. Author: (pamphlet) The United States Gold Purchase Program, 1941; also numerous articles on econ. subjects. Home: Paul Smith's NY 12970 Office: POB 182 Oyster Bay NY 11771

TREVOR, WILLIAM (WILLIAM TREVOR COX), playwright; b. May 24, 1928; s. James William and Gertrude Cox; m. Jane Ryan, 1952; 2 children. Ed. St. Columba's Coll., Trinity Coll. Author TV plays, including: The Mark-2 Wife, O Fat White Woman, The Grass Widows, The General's Day, Love Affair, Secret Orchards; radio plays include: Beyond the Pale (Giles Cooper award 1980), Autumn Sunshine (Giles Cooper award 1982), The Penthouse Apartment; plays: Going Home, 1972, A Night with Mrs. da Tanka, 1972, Marriages, 1973, Scenes from an Album, 1981, The Old Boys, 1964 (Hawthornden prize), The Love Department, 1966, The Day We Got Drunk on Cake, 1967, The Ballroom of Romance, 1972 (adapted for BBC-TV 1982), Angels at the Ritz (RSL award), 1975, The Children of Dynmouth (Whitbread prize), 1976, Lovers of their Time, 1978, Other People's Worlds, 1980, Beyond the Pale, 1981, Fools of Fortune (Whitbread prize), 1983, A Writer's Ireland, 1984, News from Ireland, 1986, Nights At The Alexandra, 1987. Recipient Allied Irish Banks award for lit., 1976; decorated comdr. Order Brit. Empire, 1977. Mem. Irish Acad. Letters.

TREVOR-ROPER, H(UGH) R(EDWALD) (BARON DACRE OF GLANTON), historian, author, educator; b. Jan. 15, 1914; s. B.W. E. Trevor-Roper; m. Alexandra Howard-Johnston, 1954. Student Charterhouse, Christ Ch., Oxford, Eng., 1945-57. Research fellow Merton Coll., 1937-39; censor, 1947-52; Regius prof. modern history, fellow Oriel Coll. Oxford U., 1957-80; master of Peterhouse, Cambridge, Eng., 1980-87; dir. Times Newspapers Ltd., 1974-88. Author: Archbishop Laud, 1940; The Last Days of Hitler, 1947; The Gentry 1540-1640, 1953; Historical Essays, 1957; The Rise of Christian Europe, 1965; Religion, The Reformation and Social Change, 1967; The Philby Affair, 1968; The European Witch-Craze of the 16th and 17th Centuries, 1970; The Plunder of the Arts in the Seventeenth Century, 1970; Princes and Artists, 1976; A Hidden Life, 1976; Renaissance Essays 1985; Catholics, Anglicans and Puritans, 1987; editor: Hitler's Table Talk, 1953; (with J.A. W. Bennett) The Poems of Richard Corbett, 1955; Hitler's War Directives 1939-45, 1964; Essays in British History Presented to Sir Keith Feiling, 1964; The Age of Expansion, 1968. Address: The Old Rectory, Didcot Oxon England

TRIBBLE, DAGMAR HAGGSTROM (MRS. ELSTON J. TRIBBLE), artist; b. N.Y.C.; d. Olaf Albin and Ida (Sabini) Haggstrom; m. Elston J. Tribble, July 15, 1933; 1 child, Martha Watkins (Mrs. James Malcolm McKinnon). Student, Parsons Sch. Design, N.Y. and Paris, 1928, Art Students League, 1930-32, Farnsworth Sch. Painting, 1949-50. Tchr. fashion illustration Parsons Sch. Design, 1929-32; designer sportswear and beachwear Travelo Corp., N.Y.C., 1933-45; founder, pres. The Garden State Watercolor Soc., 1969—. One-woman shows at Beard Sch., Orange, N.J., Monmouth Coll., West Long Branch, The Present Day Club, Princeton, N.J., 1968, 71, 73-75, 77-78, 82, M.S. Kungsholm, 1971-74, M.S. Sagafjord, 1971, United Nat. Bank, Fenwood, N.J., 1972, others; exhibited in group shows at Cape Cod Art Assn., 1963, Knickerbocker Artists Ann. Exhbn., 1963, Westfield Art Assn. State Show, 1963-64, Hunterdon County Art Ctr. Ann., 1963-64, Catherine Lorillard Wolfe Art Show, 1964, Nat. Arts Club shows, Met. Mus. Art, Nat. Acad., N.Y.C., Am. Water Color Soc. anns., 1967—, Nat. Assn. Women Artists anns., 1967—, Nat. Assn. Women Artists Internat., Paris, 1969, Garden State Watercolor Soc. anns., 1970—, Am. Watercolor Soc. Ann. Traveling Exhbn., 1972, N.J. State Cultural Ctr., Trenton, 1977; represented in pvt. collections. Recipient Agnes B. Noyes award, 1962, Windsor Newton award, 1963, Captain's Barn award for Watercolor Westfield Art Assn. State Show, 1964, Steinback Co. award for watercolor Festival of Fine Art Exhbn., 1964, Am. Artist medal merit, Am. Watercolor Soc., 1965, Jane C. Stanley Meml. prize, Nat. Assn. Women Artists, 1966. Mem. Am. Watercolor Soc. (hon.), Garden State Watercolor Soc. (pres. 1970—; Squibb award 1973), Nat. Assn. Women Artists, Princeton Art Assn. (pres. 1968-69). Clubs: Nat. Arts (N.Y.C.), Salmagundi. Home: 12 Battle Rd Princeton NJ 08540

TRIBBLE, RICHARD WALTER, brokerage executive; b. San Diego, Oct. 19, 1948; s. Walter Perrin and Catherine Janet (Miller) T.; m. Joan Catherine Sliter, June 26, 1980. BS, U. Ala., Tuscaloosa, 1968; student, Gulf Coast Sch. Drilling Practices, U. Southwestern La., 1977. Stockbroker Shearson, Am. Express, Washington, 1971-76; ind. oil and gas investment sales, Falls Church, Va., 1976-77; pres. Monroe & Keusink, Inc., Falls Church and Columbus, Ohio, 1977-87; fin. cons. Merrill Lynch Pierce, Fenner & Smith, Inc., Phoenix, 1987—. Served to cpl. USMC, 1969-71. Republican. Methodist. Office: 40 N First Ave Phoenix AZ 85003

TRIBLE, PAUL SEWARD, JR., senator; b. Balt., Dec. 29, 1946; s. Paul Seward and Katherine (Schilpp) T.; m. Rosemary Dunaway; children: Mary Katherine, Paul Seward III. B.A., Hampden-Sydney Coll., 1968; J.D., Washington and Lee U., Lexington, Va., 1971. Bar: Va. 1971. Law clk. to U.S. dist. judge Albert V. Bryan, Jr., 1971-72; asst. U.S. atty. Eastern Dist. Va., 1972-74; commonwealth's atty. Essex County, Va., 1974-76; mem. 95th-97th congresses from 1st Dist. Va., U.S. Senate, 1982—. Mem.: Washington and Lee Law Rev. Mem. Va. Jaycees (named Outstanding Young Man of Va. 1978). Republican. Episcopalian. Clubs: Ruritans, Lions, Kiwanis. Home: Kilmarnock VA 22482 Office: US Senate Washington DC 20510

TRIBOUILLARD, DANIEL LOUIS, fashion executive; b. Paris, Jan. 8, 1935; s. Rene and Denise (Begon) T.; m. Nicole Marlhiou, Feb. 22, 1969; children: Nathalie, Virginie. Grad. high sch., France. Designer, gen. mgr. Leonard, Paris, 1958-86, pres., 1987—. Mem. Found. Du Futur, Paris, 1986. Recipient Merite Nat., France, 1984, Arts et Lettres, 1983. Club: Maxim's Bus. Office: Leonard, 19 Ave de L'Opera, 75001 Paris France

TRIGG, CHARLES WILDERMAN, writer; b. Balt., Feb. 7, 1898; s. Samuel Holland and Mary E. (Wilderman) T.; grad. Balt. Poly. Inst., 1914; B.S. in Chem. Engring., U. Pitts., 1917; M.A., U. So. Calif., 1931, M.S., 1934, postgrad., 1950-55; postgrad. U. Calif. at Los Angeles, 1936-38; m. Ida Faye Conner, Dec. 17, 1932 (dec. Aug. 1973); m. 2d, Avetta Hoffman Danford, Jan. 11, 1975. Fellow Mellon Inst. Indsl. Research, Pitts., 1916-20; chemist, prodn. mgr. King Coffee Products Corp., Detroit, 1920-23; sales promotion mgr. John E. King Coffee Co., Detroit, 1923-24; with E.R. Bohan Paint Co., Los Angeles, 1924-27; tchr. Los Angeles Pvt. High Sch., 1927-30; asso. prof. chemistry Cumnock Coll., Los Angeles, 1930-36, dean men, 1936-38; tchr. Eagle Rock High Sch., Los Angeles, 1938; coordinator Air Corps Inst., 1941-43; instr. East Los Angeles Jr. Coll., 1945-46; instr. Los Angeles City Coll., 1938-43, 46-49, coordinator, 1949-50, asst. dean, 1950-55, dean instruction, 1955-63, dean emeritus, prof. emeritus, 1963—; lectr. U. So. Calif., 1946, 59-60. Served to lt. comdr. USNR, 1943-45. Named Eagle Scout Boy Scouts Am., 1914. Mem. Math. Assn. Am. (sect. chmn. 1952-53; mem. nat. bd. govs. 1953-56), Nat. Council Tchrs. Math., Sch. Sci. and Math. Assn., Assn. Los Angeles Jr. Coll. Adminstrs. (pres. 1957-58), Sigma Xi, Alpha Chi Sigma, Phi Lambda Upsilon, Phi Delta Kappa, Pi Mu Epsilon, Alpha Mu Gamma. Author: Mathematical Quickies, 1967. Mem. editorial bd. Los Angeles Math. Newsletter, 1954, Jour. Recreational Math., 1971—. Mem. editorial staff Math. Mag., 1949-63. Contbr. numerous articles to profl. jours. Book reviewer, 1961—. Patentee in the field of instant coffee. Address: 2404 Loring St San Diego CA 92109

TRIGO, TOMÁS, film location manager, film liaison; b. La Paz, Bolivia, Oct. 9, 1956; came to U.S., 1957; s. Julio Trigo-Ramirez and Linda Trigo; m. Linda Kesner, Apr. 15, 1980; 1 child, Raquel. Student, Calif. Poly., 1978-79; BS in Geography, Calif. State U., Fullerton, 1980. Cert. Assn. Am. Geographers. Location scout for films Bridge to Cross, Lorimar Prodns., 1985, Lime Street, Columbia Pictures, 1985, George Washington-II, MGM-United Artists, 1986, Amerika, ABC TV, 1986, Broadcast News, 20th Century Fox, 1987, Suspect, Tri-Star Prodns., 1987; location mgr. films Gardens of Stone, Tri-Star Prodns., 1986, Stillwatch, Zev Braun Pictures, 1986, Hamburger Hill, Paramount Pictures, 1987, "Zits", Elliot Kastner Prodns., 1987, War and Remembrance, ABC TV, 1987. Recipient Representativo Honorario, Tarija, Boliva. Taoist. Home: PO Box 8274 Charlottesville VA 22906 Office: Trigo Assocs, Casilla 6308, La Paz Bolivia

TRIMBLE, GEORGE SIMPSON, industrial executive; b. Phila., Oct. 12, 1915; s. George Simpson and Edna Mae (Mytinger) T.; m. Janet Anna Bogue, Apr. 15, 1939; children: Robert Bogue, Frank George. S.B., Mass. Inst. Tech., 1936. With The Martin Co., Balt., 1937-67; successively draftsman, design engr., chief fluid dynamics, mgr. aerodynamics, mgr. advanced design, v.p. advanced design The Martin Co., 1937-55, v.p. engring., 1955-60, v.p. advanced programs, 1960-67; dir. Advanced Manned Missions Program, NASA, Washington, 1967; dep. dir. Johnson Spacecraft Center, Houston, 1967-69; pres., dir. Bunker Ramo Corp., Oak Brook, Ill., 1970-80; dir. Richardson Co., Des Plaines, Ill., 1978-82, Martin Marietta Corp., 1970-78; owner, pres. Carefree Engine Co. (Ariz.), 1981—; cons. Sci. Adv. Bd. Aero Vehicle Panel, 1959-61, Office Dir. Def., Research and Engring. Trustee Devereux Found., 1968—, chmn. bd. trustees, 1976-79. Fellow AIAA; mem. Tau Beta Pi. Home: PO Box 1355 Carefree AZ 85377 Office: Carefree Engine Co Carefree AZ

TRIMBLE, THOMAS JAMES, utility company executive; b. Carters Creek, Tenn., Sept. 3, 1931; s. John Elijah and Mittie (Rountree) T.; m. Glenna Kay Jones, Sept. 3, 1957; children: James Jefferson, Julie Kay. BA, David Lipscomb Coll., 1953; JD, Vanderbilt U., 1956; LLM, NYU, 1959. Bar: Tenn. 1956, Ariz. 1961, U.S. Dist. Ct. Ariz. 1961, U.S. Dist. Ct. D.C. 1963, U.S. Ct. Appeals (10th cir.) 1971, U.S. Supreme Ct. 1972, U.S. Ct. Appeals (9th cir.) 1975. From assoc. to ptnr. Jennings, Strouss & Salmon, Phoenix, 1960-87; sr. v.p., gen. counsel S.W. Gas Corp., Las Vegas, Nev., 1987—. Mem. editorial bd. Vanderbilt U. Law Rev., 1954-56 Mem Pepperdine U. Bd. Regents, Malibu, Calif., 1981—, sec., mem. exec. com., 1982—; mem. bd. visitors Pepperdine Sch. Law, Malibu; pres. Big Sisters Ariz., Phoenix, 1975, bd. dirs., 1970-76; chmn. Sunnydale Children's Home, Phoenix, 1966-69, bd. dirs., 1965-75; pres. Clearwater Hills Improvement Assn., Phoenix, 1977-79, bd. dirs., 1975-80; trustee Nev. Sch. of Arts, 1988—. Served to 1st lt. JAGC, USAF, 1957-60. Fellow Ariz. Bar Found. (founding); mem. ABA, Ariz. Bar Assn. (editorial bd. Jour. 1975-80), Am. Gas Assn. (legal sect. mng. com.), Pacific Coast Gas Assn. (legal adv. com. 1987—), Energy Ins. Mut. Ltd. (bd. dirs. 1988—), Order of Coif, Phi Delta Phi. Republican. Mem. Ch. Christ. Club: Spanish Trail Country (Las Vegas). Lodge: Kiwanis (pres. Phoenix 1972-73). Home: 5104 S Turnberry Ln Las Vegas NV 89113 Office: Southwest Gas Corp PO Box 98510 5241 Spring Mountain Rd Las Vegas NV 89102-8510

TRIMMEL, MICHAEL ANDREAS, environmental scientist educator, psychologist; b. Vienna, Austria, Apr. 26, 1952; s. Michael and Elfriede (Lischka) T.; m. Ursula Hochwimmer, May 20, 1985; 1 child, Karin. MS, Höhere Technische Lehranstalt, Vienna, 1971; PhD, U. Vienna, 1977. Registered profl. engr., Austria. Lab. technician, asst. U Vienna Psychol. Inst., 1974-80; asst. prof. U. Vienna Med. Faculty, 1980—; collaborator U. Vienna Neurosurgery Clinic, 1980-87, U. Vienna Inst. Psychology, 1980—; cons. to Fed. Republic of Germany Govt., Bonn, 1986—. Contbr. of sci. articles to profl. jours. Mem. Berufsveband Österr. Psychologen, Berufsveband of Lower Austria (chmn. 1981—), British Psychophysiology Soc., German Psychophysiology Soc., German Soc. Psychology, Soc. Psychophysiol. Research, N.Y. Acad. Scis. Roman Catholic. Home: Joseph-Dabschstr 5/16, A-2102 Bisamberg Austria Office: U Vienna, Inst Environ Hygiene, Dept Medical Psy, Kinderspitalg 15, A-1095 Vienna Austria

TRINDER, CHRISTOPHER GERARD, economics researcher; b. London, Mar. 31, 1950; s. Royce William Stoll and Josephine (Parisio) T.; m. Karen Jayne Giles, Oct. 27, 1979. MA in Econs. with honors, Cambridge (Eng.) U., 1972. Researcher, lectr. econs. U. Essex, Eng., 1973-75; research fellow U. York, Eng., 1975-79; researcher Nat. Inst. Econ. Social Research, London, 1980—; lectr. London Sch Econs., London, 1982-85; mem. edit. bd. Econ. and Social Research, London, 1986—. Author: Parents and Children: Incomes in Two Gererations, 1983. Mem. council and exec. com. Nat. Children's Bur., London, 1976-79. St. John's Coll. scholar Cambridge U., 1971-72, Wrenbury scholar, 1972-73. Club: Civil Service Recreation (London). Office: Nat Inst Econ and Social Research, 2 Dean Trench St, Smith Sq, London SWIP 3HE, England

TRINGALE, ANTHONY ROSARIO, insurance executive; b. Syracuse, N.Y., Apr. 20, 1942; s. Anthony and Susan Marie (Cerio) T.; B.S.F.S., Georgetown U., 1967; CLU, Am. Coll. Life Underwriters, 1973; m. Myranda Lou Atwell, Aug. 1, 1964; children—Anthony William, Michael Paul, Mark David, Amber Marie. Cert. mktg. exec. Office mgr. trainee N.Y. Life Ins. Co. No. Va., 1965-66, office mgr. Fairfax, 1966, field underwriter, 1966-68, asst. mgr., 1968-73, mgmt. asst., home office, N.Y.C., 1973, gen. mgr. Pitts. gen. office, 1973-76; gen. mgr. Acacia Mut. Life Ins. Co., Annandale, Va., 1976-83; fin. and ins. planner, mgmt. and mktg. cons., 1983-86; pres. Ins. Cons. Group (iCG), Annandale, 1986—; pres., Acacia Prodn. Clubs, 1984, 86; field rep. to mktg. com. Acacia Mut. Fed. Savs. Bank, 1983-86; bd. dirs. Acacia Fed. Savs. Bank; lectr. estate and fin. planning, bus. ins. and communications; mem. steering com. Entrepreneurship Forum, Washington, 1982—; nat. adv. bd. The Entrepreneurship Inst., Columbus, Ohio, 1985—. Trustee SME-I Accreditation Inst., Memphis State U.; chmn. mktg. edn. adv. bd. Commonwealth of Va., 1988—; chmn. Va. MEAB, 1988—; liason rep. Am. Soc. CLU's, Bryn Mawr, Pa.; founding vice chmn. Fairfax Orgn. Christians/Jews United in Service (FOCUS); arbitrator Fairfax County Dept. Consumer Affairs; lector, extraordinary minister Nat. Shrine of Immaculate Conception; past chmn. planned giving com. ARC; v.p. bd. dirs. Jeane Dixon's Children to Children Found.; chmn. VIP panel United Cerebral Palsy campaign, 1978-86, bd. dirs. 1985—, mem. exec. com. 1988—; vice chmn. bd. mktg. and distributive edn. Fairfax County Schs. (past chmn.), 1988—; vice chmn. adv. bd. ExCounty Vocation Inc. Mem. No. Va. Soc. CLUs (past pres.), Am. Soc. CLU's (liaison team rep.), No. Va. Assn. Life Underwriters (treas. 1972), Assn. Advanced Life Underwriting, Sales and Mktg. Execs. Met. Washington (pres. 1979-80, exec. com. 1982-84), Nat. Assn. Life Underwriters (nat. mgmt. award Gen. Agts. and Mgrs. Conf., 1976-83; exec. com. 1984-85, life, qualifying) No. Va. Estate Planning Council (exec. com. 1985—, 3d v.p. 1988), Internat. Platform Assn. (trustee, bd. govs.), No. Va. Gen. Agts. and Mgrs. Assn. (pres. 1980-81, dir. 1982-83), Greater Washington Assn. Health Underwriters, Fairfax County C. of C. (legis. com., small bus. com.), Annandale C. of C., Sales and Mktg. Execs. Internat. (area dir., internat. dir. 1982-84, regional v.p. 1984-85, sr. v.p. 1986-87, trustee), Nat. Italian Am. Found, Council of 1000. Roman Catholic (lector, instr.). Contbr. articles in field of personal and business fin. strategies to Md. Bus. Observer; local radio host for fin., bus. news, and community news programs. Home: 8805 Sandy Ridge Ct Fairfax VA 22031 Office: Ins Cons Group 7700 Little River Turnpike Suite 222 Annandale VA 22003

TRINH, HÔ TÔN, language educator; b. Hànôi, Socialist Republic of Vietnam, Sept. 28, 1920; s. Hô Vân and Tôn Thi (Tinh) Tuong; m. Nguyen Thi, 1945; children: Hoàng Hoa, My Duê, Duy Châu, Mac Tu. Activist Dept. for Arts Propaganda, Nghê Tinh, Socialist Republic of Vietnam, 1945-54; research fellow Ministry for Propaganda, Hànôi, 1954-59; sci. sec. Inst. for Lit., Hànôi, 1959-68, sub-dir., 1968-75, dir., 1985—; prof. Vietnamese State U., Hànôi, 1981. Author: The West: Literature and Man, 1969, 2d edit., 1971, Literature: Sources and Creation, 1973, Literary Dialogue, 1986. Mem. Budapest Sci. Acad. (hon.), Vietnamese Writers' Assn., Nat. Commn. for UNESCO (v.p. 1985—), Assn. Asian Social Sci. Research Councils (v.p. 1985-87). Office: Inst for Lit, 20 Lythaito, Hanoi Socialist Republic of Vietnam

TRINH VAN-CAN, JOSEPH-MARIE CARDINAL, archbishop of Hanoi (Vietnam); b. Trac But, Vietnam, Mar. 19, 1921. Ordained priest Roman Catholic Ch., 1949; held various offices in Hanoi archdiocese; ordained titular bishop of Ela (with personal title of archbishop) and coadjutor archbishop of Hanoi, 1978, elevated to Sacred Coll. Cardinals, 1979, Archbishop of Hanoi, 1978—; titular ch. St. Mary in Via. Mem. Congregation: Evangelization of Peoples. Office: Archveche, 40 Pho Nha Chung, Hanoi Vietnam *

TRINTIGNANT, JEAN-LOUIS, actor; b. Piolene, France, Dec. 11, 1930; s. Raoul and Claire Tourtin; m. Colette Dacheville, 1954 (div.); m. 2d Nadine Marquand; 3 children. Student Faculte de Droit, Aix en Provence. Theatre debut, 1951; film roles, 1955—; plays include: Macbeth, Jacques ou la Soumission (Ionesco), Hamlet, Bonheur, impaire et passe (Sagan); films include: Si Tous Les Gars du Monde, La Loi Des Rues, And God Created Woman, Club de Femmes, Les Liaisons Dangereuses, L'Ete Vilent, Austerlitz, La Millieme Fenetre, Plein Feux Sur L'Assasin, Coeur Battant, The Game of Truth, Horace, 1962, Les Sept Peches Capitaux, The Easy Life, 11 Successo, Nutty, Naughty Chateau, La Bonne Occase, Mata-Hari, Un Jour a Paris, Is Paris Burning, The Sleeping Car Murder, A Man and a Woman, Enigma, Safari Diamants, Trans-Europ Express, Mon Amour, My Night at Maud's, The Conformist, The Crook, Without Apparent Motive, The Outside Man, The French Conspiracy, The Sunday Woman, Under Fire, others. Address: care Artmedia, 10 avenue Georges V, 75008 Paris France *

TRIPATHI, RAMESH CHANDRA, ophthalmologist, researcher; b. Jamira, India, July 1, 1936; came to U.S., 1977, naturalized, 1983; s. Arjun and Gandhari Tripathi; m. Brenda Jennifer Lane, May 20, 1969; children: Anita, Paul. I.Sc., Lucknow Christian Coll., 1954; MD, Agra Med. Coll., 1959; M of Surgery in Ophthalmology, Lucknow U., 1963; PhD, U. London, 1970. Diplomate in Opthalmology Royal Coll. Surgeons and Physicians, Royal Coll. Pathologists. Ophthalmic resident Lucknow U. Med. Coll., Kanpur, 1959-63; fellow Univ. Eye Clinic, Ghent, Belgium, 1964; ophthalmic registrar Southwest Middlesex Hosp., U.K., 1965-67; fellow, registrar, chief clin. asst. Inst. Ophthalmology, Moorfields Eye Hosp., London, 1967-72; lectr. U. London, 1968-70, sr. lectr., 1970-77; cons. Moorfields Eye Hosp., London, 1972-77; prof. ophthalmology U. Chgo., 1977—, prof. The Coll., 1979—, sec. dept. ophthalmology, 1977—, attending ophthalmologist, attending ocular pathology and cons. pediatric tumor bd., 1978-80; mem. med. staff U. Chgo. Med. Ctr., 1977—, dir. Eye Pathology Labs., 1977—; cons. attending ophthalmologist Oak Forest Hosp., 1986—, dir. Ophthalmology Resident Program, chmn. Instnl. Rev. Bd., 1988—; cons. Nat. Eye Inst., 1981—, NIH; vis. prof. Yeshiva U., N.Y.C., 1973, U. Wurzberg, Fed. Republic Germany, 1974, U. Toronto, 1979, Jefferson U., Phila., 1979, Columbia U., N.Y.C., 1981, U. Oxford, Eng., 1984, 86, Nat. Autonomous U. Mex., Mexico City, 1981, Hôtel Dieux de Paris, 1975, various others; preceptor MS and PhD degree candidates in ophthalmology and visual sci., U. Chgo.; presenter over 200 sci. papers at nat. and internat. meetings, seminars and symposia. Exec. editor Exptl. Eye Research, 1987—; editorial bd. Ophthalmic Research, 1974—, Lens Research, 1983—, Ophthalmic Literature, 1974-76; exec. editor Cornea, 1981-86; assoc. editor Afro-Asian Jour. Ophthalmology, 1981—; contbr. over 300 articles to sci. publs., 25 chpts. to books. Chmn. Med. Council Assn. Indians in Am., Chgo., 1983, v.p., 1986—; bd. dirs. Indo-Am. Ophthal. Soc. World Eye Found.; mem. Chgo. Found. for Med. Care, 1977; pres. Vision Research Found., 1987—. Recipient Ophthalmology prize Royal Soc. Medicine, London, 1971, Royal Eye London prize Ophthal. Soc. London, 1976, State awards, 1987, 88, Outstanding Citizen award, 1984, Honor award Alcon Research Inst., 1987; Med. Research Council London grantee, 1972-75, Nat. Eye Inst. USPHS grantee, 1977—; named Litchfield lectr. U. Oxford, Eng., 1986. Fellow Royal Soc. Medicine London (council 1973-76), Royal Coll. Pathologists, Internat. Coll. Surgeons U.S. (vice regent 1984-86), Am. Acad. Ophthalmology (honor award 1984), Nat. Acad. Scis. (India); mem. AMA, Physiol. Soc. London, Fedn. Am. Socs. for Exptl. Biologists, Assn. Indians in Am. (v.p. 1986—, Honor award 1983), Nat. Fedn. Asian Indians (Honor award 1986), India Med. Assn. (bd. dirs. 1984-85, Disting. Physicians award 1987), Royal Microscopical Soc., Pan Am. Assn. Ophthalmology, Ophthalmological Soc. U.K., Oxford Ophthalmological Soc., Contact Lens Assn. Ophthalmologists, Internat. Acad. Pathologists, Am. Assn. Pathologists, Electron Microscopical Soc. Am., Am. Assn. University Profs., Internat. Soc. Eye Research, Soc. for Exptl. Biology and Medicine, Am. Glaucoma Soc. Club: Quadrangle. Home: 5545 S Harper Ave Chicago IL 60637 Office: U Chgo Eye Research Labs 939 E 57th St Chicago IL 60637

TRIPODI, MARY ANN, physical education educator; b. Massillon, Ohio, Feb. 3, 1944; d. Domenico A. and Margaret P. (Cicchinelli) T. B.S., Kent State U., 1966, M. Ed., 1970, postgrad., 1981—. Instr. phys. edn. Canton (Ohio) South High Sch., 1966-69; instr. health and phys. edn. Notre Dame Coll., Cleve., 1969-71; instr. health and phys. edn. U. Akron (Ohio), 1971-80, coordinator women's sports clubs, 1971-79, asst. prof. health and phys. edn., 1980—, asst. to dir. athletics, 1979-85, asst. athletic dir., 1985—, head coach women's volleyball, 1971-75, head coach women's basketball, 1971-81, dir. coaching workshops, 1981—; cons. Ohio Female Athletic Found., 1982-83. Mem. AAHPER and Dance, Nat. Assn. Phys. Edn. Coll. Women, Fin. Aid and Ethics and Eligibility (chmn. 1974-80), Midwest Assn. Phys. Edn. Coll. Women, Ohio Assn. Health, Phys. Edn., Recreation and Dance, Ohio College Assn. (chmn. elect curriculum div. women's phys. edn. sect. 1971, mem.-at-large 1972), Ohio Assn. Intercollegiate Sports for Women (N.E. dist. commr. 1974-77), Ohio Female Athletic Found. (trustee, v.p.), Cleve. Women's Phys. Edn. and Recreation Assn., Pi Lambda Theta, Delta Psi Kappa. Roman Catholic. Contbr. articles to profl. jours. Clubs: University, Touchdown, Varsity A Assn. (Akron, Ohio). Home: 1303 Cedarwood Dr Kent OH 44240 Office: Jar Annex U Akron Akron OH 44325

TRIPODI FALCO, JORGE ALBERTO, film director, producer; b. Capital Federal, Buenos Aires, Argentina, Feb. 26, 1948; arrived in Chile, 1976; s. Francisco Antonio and Delia Dora (Falco) T.; m. Silvia Bianchi, Aug. 17, 1969 (div. 1976); 1 child, Lucas; m. Gloria Aksman, Feb. 26, 1977 (div. 1986); 1 child, German Tripodi. Student, U. Buenos Aires, 1969-73, Tech. Nat., Buenos Aires, 1973-75; hon. degree, Mcpl. de Avellaneda, Buenos Aires, 1972. Asst. dir. films Buenos Aires, 1973-75; asst. dir. publicity films Cinemania, Buenos Aires, 1975, Buenos Aires and Santiago, Chile, 1976-79; asst. dir. publicity films Stuart-Carvaial Producciones, Buenos Aires and Santiago, 1979-81, Cinemania, Buenos Aires and Santiago, 1981-82, Novo Latino, Buenos Aires, 1982-85; films dir. publicity films Flehner Films, Buenos Aires, 1986; films dir., producer publicity films Jorge Tripodi Prodns., Santiago, 1982. Recipient numeous awards including Clio award, USA, 1982, Festival Iberoamericano de la Publicidad awards, 1981, Chileno del Spot Publicitario awards, 1982, 83, 84, 85, 86, 87, Festival del Cine Publicitario Artistico Argentino, 1982, 84, 85, 86, others. Mem. Soc. de Productores, Assn. de Productores. Roman Catholic. Office: Jorge Tripodi y Cia Ltd, Maria Luisa Santander, Suite 0363, Santiago Chile

TRIPP, JOHN WILLIAM, management consulting, managerial seminars and professional placement company executive; b. Seattle, Oct. 13, 1931; s. Harry A. and Grace D. (Hill) T.; m. Rosemary F. Aldridge, Sept. 12, 1952 (div. 1972); children—John William, Bradley J., Kelly, Kerry. B.S. in Chem. Engring. with honors, Wash. State U., 1954. Gen. mgr. subs. Union Oil Co. Calif., 1956-71; founder, prin. John W. Tripp & Assocs., Colorado Springs, Colo., 1971—. Author: (manuals) Essentials of Project Management, 1978; Essentials of Systems Management, 1978; Structured Documentation, 1984. Pres. Skyway Condominium Assn., Colorado Springs, 1979-82, Four O'Clock Condominium Assn., Breckenridge, Colo., 1981—. Mem. Mgmt. Adv. Services Roundtable, Assn. for Computing Machinery, Pvt. Employment Agy. Council (treas. 1982-83), Colorado Springs C. of C. Home: 911 Stewart Pl Colorado Springs CO 80910 Office: John W Tripp & Assocs 2940 E Fountain Blvd Colorado Springs CO 80910

TRIPP, MARIAN BARLOW LOOFE, public relations company executive; b. Lodge Pole, Nebr., July 26; d. Lewis Rockwell and Cora Dee (Davis) Barlow; B.S., Iowa State U., 1944; m. James Edward Tripp, Feb. 9, 1957; children: Brendan Michael, Kevin Mark. Writer, Dairy Record, St. Paul, 1944-45; head, product promotion div., public relations dept. Swift & Co., Chgo., 1945-55; mgmt. supr., v.p. public relations J. Walter Thompson Co., N.Y.C. and Chgo., 1956-74; v.p. consumer affairs, Chgo., 1974-75; pres. Marian Tripp Communications Inc., Chgo., 1976—. Mem. Public Relations Soc. Am., Am., Ill. home econs. assns., Chgo. Home Economists in Bus., Am. Inst. Wine and Food (exec. com., trustee Chgo. chpt.), Les Dames d'Escoffier, Chgo. Network. Episcopalian. Club: Fortnightly. Office: 70 E Walton Pl Chicago IL 60611

TRIPP, THOMAS NEAL, lawyer, political consultant; b. Evanston, Ill., June 19, 1942; s. Gerald Frederick and Kathryn Ann (Siebold) T.; m. Ellen Marie Larrimer, Apr. 16, 1966; children: David Larrimer, Bradford Douglas, Corinne Catherine. BA cum laude, Mich. State U., 1964; JD, George Washington U., 1967. Bar: Ohio 1967, U.S. Ct. Mil. Appeals 1968, U.S. Supreme Ct. 1968. Sole practice, Columbus, Ohio, 1969—; real estate developer, Columbus, 1969—; chmn. bd. Black Sheep Enterprises, Columbus, 1969—; polit. cons. Keene, Shirley & Assocs., Washington, 1986—; vice chmn. bd. Sun Valley-Elkhorn Assn., Idaho, 1983-85, chmn. 1986—; vice chmn. Sawtooth Sports, Ketchum, Idaho, 1983-85; legal counsel Wallace F. Ackley Co., Columbus, 1973—; polit. cons. Keene, Shirley & Assocs., Washington, 1986—; bd. dirs. KWRP Broadcasting Corp., 1986—; presiding judge Ohio Mock Trial Competition, 1986-87. Trustee Americans for Responsible Govt., Washington, GOPAC; mem. Bob Dole for Pres. Nat. Fin. Com., 1987-88; mem. Peace Corps Adv. Council, 1981-85; mem. U.S. Commn. on Trade Policy and Negotiations, 1985—; campaign mgr., fin. chmn. Charles Rockwell Saxbe, Ohio Ho. of Reps., 1974, 76, 78, 80; campaign mgr. George Bush for Pres., 1980, nat. dep. field dir., 1980; mem. alumni admissions council Mich. State U., 1984—; regional co-chmn. Reagan-Bush, 1984, mem. nat. fin. com., 1984; mem. Victory '84 fin. com.; mem. Victory '88 fin. com. Bush-Quayle; Rep. candidate 2d U.S. Congl. Dist., Idaho, 1988. Served to capt. U.S. Army, 1967-69. Fellow Pi Sigma Alpha; mem. Vietnam Vet. Am., Phi Delta Phi. Republican. Avocations: swimming, tennis, skiing, writing, political essays. Home: 5420 Clark Statie Rd Gahanna OH 43230-1956

TRIPPE, CHARLES WHITE, financial and development executive; b. N.Y.C., Jan. 30, 1935; s. Juan Terry and Elizabeth (Stettinius) T.; m. Pamela Reid; children: Charles Jr., James R., Elizabeth, Carie. BS in Engring., Yale U., 1957; MBA, Harvard U., 1959. V.p. fin. Intercontinental Hotels, N.Y.C., 1962-66; v.p., treas. Pan Am, N.Y.C., 1966-69, v.p. planning, 1969-71; v.p. corp. devel. Pan Am., N.Y.C., 1971-77; v.p. planning Bell & Howell, Chgo., 1978-85; ptnr. and founder Trippe & Co., Greenwich, Conn., 1985—; chmn., chief exec. officer AMPRO Corp.; chmn. Liberia Devel. Corp., The Liberia Co.; pres. Bermuda Properties, Ltd. Club: Links (N.Y.C.), Round Hill (Greenwich), Indian Hill (Winnetka, Ill.).

TRIPPODO, NICK CHARLES, physiologist, research laboratory head; b. Galveston, Tex., Sept. 27, 1945; s. Pete and Rena (Menotti) T.; B.S., Stephen F. Austin State U., 1968, M.S., 1969; Ph.D., U. Tex. Med. Br., 1974; m. Linda Sue Evers, Aug. 26, 1967; children—Joseph Brent, Julie Robin. Research asso. U. Miss. Sch. Medicine, Jackson, 1974-75, instr., 1975-76; staff mem. Alton Ochsner Med. Found., New Orleans, 1976-79, hypertension research coordinator, 1979-88; hypertension laboratory of vascular physiology head, 1988; peptide pharmacology sect. head Squibb Inst. for Med. Research, Princetown, N.J., 1988—; asst. prof. La. State U. Med. Sch., 1976-84, assoc. prof., 1984—, Tulane U. Med. Sch. Recipient research award Bay Area Heart Assn., 1973; USPHS research grantee, 1978—. Mem. Am. Physiol. Soc. (fellow cardiovascular sect.), Am. Heart Assn. (fellow 1975-76, research grantee 1977-78; investigator 1985-88), Am. Fedn. for Clin. Research, Internat. Soc. for Heart Research, Internat. Soc. Hypertension, Soc. Exptl. Biology and Medicine. Contbr. book chpts. and articles to profl. publs. Home: 5239 Trenton St Metairie LA 70006 Office: 1516 Jefferson Hwy Jefferson LA 70121

TRISCHLER, THOMAS JOSEPH, urban architect; b. Pitts., Sept. 27, 1952; s. Floyd David and Gloria Neldine (Fusting) T.; m. Jana Lee Abrams; 1 child, Brittany Taryn. Registered architect, Calif. B.S. in Architecture, U. So. Calif., 1974; MBA, degree in urban land economics, real estate fin., mktg., strategic analysis UCLA, 1986. Designer, Ben-Ami Shulman Registered Bldg. Designers, Los Angeles, 1972, George Barnes Architect, Northridge, Calif., 1973-74; assoc. urban planner, urban designer East Los Angeles Community Union Planning Dept., 1972-73; urban planner, urban designer Community Planning & Devel. Co., 1974-75, Irvine Co., 1975; project mgr. Danielian Moon, Ilg and Assocs., Newport Beach, Calif., 1975-77, Rolly Pulaski & Assocs., 1977-78; office mgr., project mgr. Brion Jeannette & Assocs., 1978; sr. design architect Albert C. Martin & Assocs., Los Angeles, 1978-80; project architect-dir., mgr. computer implementation WZMH Group, Inc., 1981—; prin. Trischler Assocs., Orange, 1983—, The TA/TAG Venture, Newport Beach, Calif., 1986—; co-founder Situs Devel., Orange, Calif., 1987—; active in reformation of archtl. licensing laws, 1977-80. Prin. works include Thousand Oaks Pub. Library, Calif. (design award), The Atrium Office Bldg., Irvine, Calif. (design award), Plaza Alicante Office Bldg., Garden Grove, Calif. (design award), Hyatt Regency Alicante, Garden Grove (design award). Com. coordinator East Los Angeles Community Union, 1972-73; mem. Ad Hoc Com. to Incorp. East Los Angeles, 1972-74; speaker career day programs Boy Scouts Am., 1978—. Calif. State scholar, 1970-74; recipient cert. of appreciation East Los Angeles Area C. of C., 1974. Mem. AIA (assoc. pres.), U. So. Calif. Alumni Assn., Assn. U. Related Research Parks, Urban Land Inst., Am. Planning Assn.; pres. Orange County chpt. 1979-80, assoc. dir. Calif. council 1980, mem. coms. 1979-80, numerous certs. and awards 1977—). Roman Catholic. Clubs: Back Bay Rugby Football. Office: 1745 W Katella Ave Suite E Orange CA 92667

TRIVEDI, BAL C., financial consultant; b. Mahuva, Gujarat, India, Mar. 23, 1943; s. Chhotalal J. and Bhanuben Trivedi; m. Urmila B., Jan. 19, 1969; 1 child, Shilpa B. BSc, St. Xavier's Coll., 1961; BSME, Bihar Inst. Tech., Sindri, India, 1965; MSME, U. Houston, 1976, MBA in Fin., 1978. Registered profl. engr., Tex.; registered securities prin. Engring. supr. Bechtel Power Corp., Houston, 1974-77, 79-84; sr. engr. Brown & Root Corp., Houston, 1977-79; fin. cons. Merrill Lynch, Houston, 1984-85, First Met. Fin. Services, Houston, 1985—; chmn. Mech. Engring. Soc., Binar Inst. Tech., 1965; pres. NDT Corp., Houston, 1981-83, Metropolis, Inc., Houston, 1984—. Mem. Nat. Productivity Council, Bombay, 1967-70. Mem. ASME, NSPE, Nat. Assn. Realtors, Nat. Assn. Securities Dealers. Hindu. Home: 3919 Mayfield Oaks Ln Houston TX 77088 Office: First Met Fin Services 6420 Hillcroft St Houston TX 77081

TRIVEDI, MANMOHAN MANUBHAI, computer engineer, computer engineering educator; b. Wardha, India, Oct. 4, 1953; s. Manubhai J. and Tanuben M. (Trivedi) T.; m. Nayana N. Mehta, Aug. 22, 1982. B.Engring. with honors, Birla Inst. Tech. and Sci., 1974; M in Engring., Utah State U., 1976, PhD, 1979. Jr. engr. Uranus Electronics, Surat, India, 1974; teaching and research asst. Space Dynamics Lab., Utah State U., Logan, 1975-79; assoc. prof. elec., computer engring. La. State U., Baton Rouge, 1979-86; assoc. prof. elec. and computer engring U. Tenn., Knoxville, 1986—; cons. to govt. agys. and industry, 1981—. Mem. La. State U. Faculty Senate, 1984-85; tech. cons. to govt., industry; Author, co-editor Advances in Image Analysis Applications, 1988; assoc. editor Internat. Jour. Approximate Reasoning, IEEE Transactions on Sytems and Cybernetics; guest editor Optical Engring. Jour.; moderator, chmn. Robotics Session in Compusat-88, Interdisciplinary Computing Satellite Symposium, 1988; contbr. articles to Robotics, Image Analysis, Computer Vision and Remote Sensing Jours. Grantee U.S. Army, U.S. Dept. Energy, U.S. Def. Mappaing Agy., TVA, Oak Ridge Nat. Lab., other govt. agys.; grad. research scholar Utah State U., 1976. Mem. IEEE (sr.), IEEE Systems, Man and Cybernetics Soc. (chmn. pattern recognition, image processing, computer vision tech. com. 1986—), Computer Soc. IEEE (chmn. robotics tech. com. 1987—, Intersoc. Cooperation Com.), Am. Soc. Photogrammetry and Remote Sensing, Am. Assn. Artificial Intelligence (co-chmn. conf., Orlando, Fla. 1987), Applications of Artificial Intelligence (conf. chmn. 1988—), Pattern Recognition Soc., Internat. Soc. Optical Engring., Sigma Xi, Phi Kappa Phi, Tau Beta Pi. Avocations: reading, hiking, travel, photography. Home: 3636 Taliluna Apt 203 Knoxville TN 37919 Office: U Tenn Ferris Hall Dept Elec and Computer Engring Knoxville TN 37996

TRLIN, ANDREW DRAGO, sociology educator; b. Auckland, New Zealand, Sept. 30, 1942; s. Mate and Rose (Vegar) T.; m. Annette Noble Beasley, Dec. 7, 1967; children: Matthew, Natasha, Alexander, Belinda, Miranda. BA with honors, Victoria U. of Wellington, New Zealand, 1965, MA with distinction, 1967; PhD, Massey U., Palmerston North, New Zealand, 1975. Asst. master Mt. Roskill Grammar Sch., Auckland, 1966; jr. lectr. geography Massey U., 1967-68, lectr., 1969-71, lectr. sociology, 1972-74, sr. lectr., 1975-84, reader, 1985—; vis. fellow dept. demography Australian Nat. Univ., Canberra, 1974-75, 82. Author: Now Respected Once Despised: Yugoslavs in New Zealand, 1979; editor: Social Welfare and New Zealand Society, 1977; co-editor: New Zealand and International Migration, 1986; contbr. articles to profl. jours. Mem. social planning sub-com. Palmerston North City Council, 1983-86. Recipient Plaketa award Matica Iseljenika Hrvatske, Zagreb, Yugoslavia, 1981; Med. Research Council of New Zealand grantee, 1978. Mem. Internat. Union Sci. Study Population, New Zealand Demographic Soc., New Zealand Geog. Soc. Roman Catholic. Office: Massey U Dept of Sociology, Private Bag, Palmerston North New Zealand

TROHAN, WALTER, newspaperman; b. Mt. Carmel, Pa., July 4, 1903; s. E. Henry and Bernice (Skindzier) T.; m. Carol Rowland, Mar. 17, 1929; children: Carol (Mrs. Wayne A. Glover), Walter, Nancy (Mrs. Robert W. Dollar). A.B., U. Notre Dame, 1926; D.Litt., Lincoln Coll., 1958. Reporter Daily Calumet, Chgo., 1922, Daily Calumet (City News Bur.), Chgo., 1927-29; with Chgo. Tribune, 1929-71, became asst. Washington corr., 1934; exec. dir. Chgo. Tribune (Washington bur.), 1947-49, chief, 1949-69, columnist, 1960-71; spl. assignments. South Am., 1936, 41, Europe, 1940, Summit Confs., 1955, 60, 61, Fgn. Ministers Confs., 1957, 59, Paris Peace talks, 1968, Turkey, Iran, Greece, 1971; news commentator W.G.N., M.B.S., 1951-69. Author: Political Animals, 1975; Editor: Jim Farley's Story; The Roosevelt Years, 1948; Contbr. to various mags. Emeritus trustee Lincoln Coll. Decorated comdr. Order of Isabel La Catholica Spain; granted Knighthood St. John of Jerusalem; recipient Captive Nations medal; named to Sigma Delta Chi Washington Hall of Fame, 1973. Mem. White House Corr. Assn. (pres. 1937-38), Overseas Writers, Chgo. Hist. Soc., J. Russel Young Sch. of Expression. Roman Catholic. Clubs: Gridiron (pres. 1967); Red Circle (Washington); Civil War Round Table (Chgo.), Baker Street Irregulars (Chgo.) (hon.); Bohemian (San Francisco). Address: 5711 Phelps Luck Dr Columbia MD 21045 also: Carrowmeer House, Newmarket-on-Fergus County Clare Ireland

TROISI, BARBARA DAVIES, reading specialist; b. Rahway, N.J., June 16, 1937; d. Thomas Edward and Ruth Marie (Ohlott) Davies; BS, N.Y.U., 1959, postgrad., 1981—; (dissertation in progress); MA, Fairleigh Dickinson U., 1979; m. Frank X. Troisi, Aug. 22, 1959; children: Pamela Ann, Morgan Andrew. Tchr. English, Cliffside Park (N.J.) Sr. High Sch., 1959-62; reading tchr. Pascack Valley Regional High Sch., Hillsdale, N.J., 1976-78, reading specialist, 1979—; cons. in field. NYU Alumni Scholar, 1955-59; Alcoa scholar, 1955-59; recipient Founders Day award NYU, 1959. Mem. N.J. Assn. Learning Cons., N.J. Reading Assn., Nat. Council Tchrs. English, Internat. Reading Assn., Assn. for Supervision & Curriculum Devel., Kappa Delta Epsilon. Republican. Roman Catholic. Clubs: Jr. Women's of Upper Saddle River, Women's of Upper Saddle River. Contbr. articles to profl. jours. Avocations: writing children's and short stories. Office: Pascack Valley Regional High Sch Piermont Rd Hillsdale NJ 07642

TROLLE, CLAUS, wine and spirits company executive; b. Gentofte, Denmark, Apr. 2, 1946; s. Niels and Hertha (Nielsen) T.; m. Marianne Wrem, Jan. 27, 1968; children: Louise, Casper, Peter. MBA, Copenhagen Sch. Econs. and Bus. Adminstrn., 1974. Product mgr. Quaker Oats Corp., Copenhagen, 1970-75; sales and mktg. dir. Danish Distilleries, Copenhagen, 1975-80; mktg. dir. Beauvais subs. The Volvo Group, Copenhagen, 1980-83; mktg. mgmt. cons. Rebild Mktg. Mgmt., Copenhagen, 1983-86; sales and mktg. dir. Better Brands subs. Danish Distilleries Group, Copenhagen, 1986—; cons. in mktg. and mgmt. Served with Royal Danish Guard, 1967-69. Home: Rorsovej 4, 2920 Charlottenlund Denmark

TROMBOLD, WALTER STEVENSON, supply company executive; b. Chanute, Kans., June 21, 1910; s. George John and Margaret (Stevenson) T.; m. Charlotte Elizabeth Kaufman, Dec. 28, 1941; children: Joan Kleitsch, Lynn Oliphant, Walter Steven, David George, Charles Phillip. BS in Bus., U. Kans., 1932; AA, Iola Jr. Coll., 1930; spl. degree, Balliol Coll., Oxford U., 1943. Asst. mgr. S.H. Kress & Co., 1932-38; counselor Penn Mut. Life Ins. Co., 1938-41; field mgr. Travelers Ins. Co., Kansas City, 1938-41; with Reid Supply Co., Wichita, Kans., Kansas City, Mo., Topeka, Kans. 1946-86, pres. Trombold Consultation Service, 1986—, also chmn. bd. dirs. Bd. dirs., officer YMCA, 1922—; merit badge councilor Boy Scouts Am.; bd. dirs. Camp Fire Girls; life mem. PTA, 1953—, pres., 1952; chmn. personnel adv. bd. City of Wichita (Kans.), 1956—; commr. Gen. Assembly Presbyn. Ch. USA, past deacon, elder, trustee; commr. Synods of Mid-Am., Presbytery of So. Kans.; assoc. chmn. Nat. Laymen's Bible Week, 1972-86. Served to lt. comdr. USN, 1941-45. Recipient various awards including Honor Man Wichita Swim Club, 1970, Disting. Service award to Youth YMCA, 1970, Service award to Swimmers Kansas City High Sch. Activities, 1975. Mem. Kans. U. Alumni Assn. (life), Kans. C. of C., Wichita C. of C., Sales and Mktg. Execs. (bd. dirs., v.p.), Textile Care and Allied Trades Assn., Alpha Tau Omega. Clubs: Old Timer (sec., treas. 1964-86, Honor Man of Yr. 1977), Wichita Racquet, Knife and Fork Internat. (bd. dirs., v.p.), Univ. (chmn. bd. dirs., v.p.). Lodges: Rotary, Masons (32 deg.). Republican. Home: 340 Hillsdale Wichita KS 67230

TROMPETA, JESUS IGLESIAS, lawyer, law educator; b. Banga, Aklan, Philippines, Dec. 24, 1928; s. Rafael and Andrea (Iglesias) T.; m. Bellaflor G. Villanueva, Aug. 12, 1978; 1 child, Andree V. AA, U. Philippines, Manila, 1950, BS in Edn., 1952, LLB, 1967; postdoctoral, Pepperdine U., 1975. Bar: Philippines 1967, N.Y. 1983, U.S. Dist. Ct. (no. and so. dists.) N.Y. 1983, U.S. Ct. Appeals (9th cir.) 1983. Instr. Manila City Schs., Philippines, 1952-62; supervising registar Philippines Dept. of Commerce, Manila, 1962-68; instr. law Philippine Coll. of Commerce, Manila, 1967-68; legal asst.

McGarry Law Offices, Los Angeles, 1972-74; instr. Los Angeles Unified Sch. Dist., 1974-84; sole practice Los Angeles, 1983—; legal asst. Kwan Law Offices, Los Angeles, 1968-74. Pres. Filipino Am. Polit. Orgn., Los Angeles, 1969-82. Recipient Plaque of Honor Sulu Unltd., 1977, Plaque of Appreciation City of Los Angeles, 1981. Mem. ABA, Assn. Trial Lawyers Am., State Bar Calif. (cert. completion performance skills tng. program, 1987), Integrated Bar of Philippines, Filipino Am. Educators Assn. (v.p. 1975-76), Filipino Am. Council of So. Calif. (exec. sec. 1970-72, pres. 1986—), Philippine Lawyers Assn. (treas. 1980—, Plaque of Honor 1980), U. Philippine Alumni Assn. (cert. of honor 1973, Plaque of Spl. Recognition 1980, Outstanding Alumnus award 1987), Asian Am. Edn. Commn. (commr. 1974-83, Cert. of Appreciation 1980, 82), United Filipino Am. Assembly of So. Calif. (bd. dirs. 1972-76). Club: Filipino (pres.). Office: 3580 Wilshire Blvd Suite 2080 Los Angeles CA 90010

TROMPF, GARRY WINSTON, history and religious studies educator; b. Sydney, New South Wales, Australia, Nov. 27, 1940; s. William Henry and Irene Catherine (Perryman) T.; m. Robyn Rowena Brewster; children: Sharon, Carolyn, Sasha, Leilani, Joshua. BA with honors, U. Melbourne, Australia, 1962; Diploma in Edn. with honors, U. Melbourne, 1963; MA, Monash U., Melbourne, 1965, Oxford U., London, 1969; PhD, Australian Nat. U., 1974. Teaching fellow Monash U., Melbourne, 1964-65; lectr. in history Oxford U., 1965-67, U. Western Australia, Perth, 1967-69; lectr. in religiousstudies U. Papua New Guinea, Port Moresby, 1972-75, sr. lectr. in religious studies, 1975-77, prof. history, 1983-85; sr. lectr. in religious studies U. Sydney, 1978-82, assoc. prof., head religious studies, 1986—; vis. prof. history U. Calif., Santa Cruz, 1974-75, 82, 88; vis. prof. religion and social scis. State U. Utrecht (The Netherlands), 1984; vis. prof. Jung Inst., Zurich, 1984. Author: Friedrich Max Muller, 1978, Idea of Historical Recurrence, 1979; editor: Prophets of Melanesia, 1977, The Gospel is not Western, 1987, (with C. Loeliger) New Religious Movements in Melanesia, 1985. Chmn. Human Rights Assn., Papua New Guinea, 1985. Brit. Free Passage scholar Brit. Council, 1965-67; Fulbright-Hays travelling scholar Australian-Am. Found., 1975; Charles Strong lectureship Charles Strong Trust, 1980. Mem. Australian Assn. Study of Religion. Home: 58 Boundary Rd, 2076 Waroonga, New South Wales Australia Office: U Sydney, Dept Religious Studies, 2006 Sydney, New South Wales Australia

TROTIN, GAÉTAN HONORE, ear and throat specialist; b. Montourtier, Mayenne, France, Dec. 7, 1947; s. Honore Eugene and Renee Pascale (Boismal) T. MD, U. Paris, 1977. Diplomate in ear and throat specialty. Ear and throat specialist Bichat Hosp., Paris, 1977-80, St. Louis Hosp., Paris, 1980—, Beaujon Hosp., Clichy, France, 1981—. Author: Le Sarcoidose Maladie Familiale, 1977. Mem. French Soc. Otolaryngology. Club: Stode Lavallois. Home: 5 Rue Parmentier, 92200 Neuilly France Office: 22 Allees Leon Gambetta, 92110 Clichy France

TROTMAN, DAVID JOHN ANGELO, mathematician; b. Plymouth, Devon, Eng., Sept. 27, 1951; came to France, 1975; s. John Andrew and Rosalie Belinda Wynlane (Lodge) T.; m. Marie-Helene Gabrielle Cuyer, Aug. 28, 1975; children: Laura, Lucy, Daniel. BA in Math., U. Cambridge, Eng., 1972, MA, 1977; MSc, U. Cambridge, 1973; PhD in Math., Warwick U., Eng., 1978; D'es. Sc., U. Paris XI, Orsay, France, 1980. Asst. prof. U. Paris-Sud, Orsay, 1975-80, 83—; prof. U. Angers (France), 1980-83; vis. assoc. prof. Cornell U., Ithaca, N.Y., 1986, U. Hawaii, Honolulu, 1987. Contbr. articles to profl. jours. Recipient Adams Essay prize St. John's Coll., Cambridge, 1971. Mem. Soc. Math. of France, London Math. Soc., Am. Math. Soc. Roman Catholic. Home: 50 Blvd Saint Marcel, 75005 Paris France Office: U Paris-Sud, Dept Math, Batiment 425, 91405 Orsay France

TROTT, DENNIS CHARLES, lawyer; b. Ft. Wayne, Ind., Oct. 31, 1946; s. Charles and Eileen (Collins) T.; m. Nancy J. Servis, Aug. 4, 1973; children: Eileen Susanne, Duncan Eric. AB, Ind. U., 1968; JD, U. Mich., 1973. Bar: N.Y. 1974, U.S. Dist. Ct. (so. dist.) N.Y. 1974, U.S. Ct. Appeals (2d cir.) 1974, U.S. Ct. Mil. Appeals 1985, U.S. Ct. Internat. Trade 1986, U.S. Tax Ct. 1986, U.S. Supreme Ct. 1986. Assoc. Haight, Gardner, N.Y.C., 1973-75, Breed, Abbott, N.Y.C., 1975-77; ptnr. Henderson & Koplik, N.Y.C., 1985—; pres., chief exec. officer Luke Enterprises, Inc., N.Y.C., 1988—. Bd. dirs. Neighborhood Housing Services of N.Y.C., 1985—. Served with U.S. Army, 1968-70. Mem. Assn. of Bar of City of N.Y., N.Y. County Lawyers Assn., Maritme Law Assn. Home: 304 Sherman St Brooklyn NY 11218 Office: Henderson & Koplik 950 3rd Ave New York NY 10022

TROUT, MARGIE MARIE MUELLER, civic worker; b. Wellston, Mo., Apr. 27, 1923; d. Albert Sylvester and Pearl Elizabeth (Jose) Mueller; student Webster Coll., 1944-45; cert. genealogist Bd. Cert. Genealogy; m. Maurice Elmore Trout, Aug. 24, 1943; children—Richard Willis, Babette Yvonne. Sec. offices Robertson Aircraft Corp., St. Louis, 1942; speed lathe and drill press operator Busch-Selzer Diesel Engine Co., St. Louis, 1942-43; Cub Scout den mother, Vienna, Austria, 1953-55, Mt. Pleasant, Mich., 1955, London, 1956-57; leader Nat. Capitol council Girl Scouts U.S.A., Bethesda, Md., 1963-65; co-chmn. Am. Booth YWCA and Red Cross Annual Bazaars, Bangkok, Thailand, 1970-72; worker ARC, Vientiane, Laos, 1959-60, Bangkok, 1970-72; activities co-chmn., exec. bd. mem. Women's Club Armed Forces Staff Coll., Norfolk, Va., 1975-77; mem. Am. Women's Clubs, Embassy Clubs, Internat. Women's Clubs Vienna, 1952-55, London, 1956-59, Vientiane, 1959-61, Bangkok, 1969-72, Munich, Germany, 1965-69, Norfolk, 1975-77. Crochet articles exhibited Exhibition of Works of Art by the Corps Diplomatique, London, Eng., 1958. Home: 6203 Hardy Dr McLean VA 22101

TROUT, MONROE EUGENE, pharmaceutical company executive; b. Harrisburg, Pa., Apr. 5, 1931; s. David Michael and Florence Margaret (Kashner) T.; m. Sandra Louise Lemke, June 11, 1960; children: Monroe Eugene, Timothy William. AB, U. Pa., 1953, MD, 1957; LLB, Dickinson Sch. of Law, 1964, JD, 1969. Intern Great Lakes (Ill.) Naval Hosp., 1957-58; resident in internal medicine Portsmouth (Va.) Naval Hosp., 1959-61; chief med. dept. Harrisburg State Hosp., 1961-64; dir. drug regulatory affairs Pfizer, Inc., N.Y.C., 1964-68; v.p., med. dir. Winthrop Labs., N.Y.C., 1968-70; med. dir. Sterling Drug, Inc., N.Y.C., 1970-74, v.p., dir. med. affairs, 1974-78, sr. v.p., 1978—; pres., chief exec. officer Am. Healthcare Systems, Inc., 1986—, chmn., 1987—, also bd. dirs.; dir. Magnetic Resonance Inc., Med. Magnetics, Inc., Friends of the Nat. Library of Medicine; adj. assoc. prof. Bklyn. Coll. Pharmacy; spl. lectr. legal medicine Dickinson Sch. Law; mem. Sterling Winthrop Research Bd., 1977-86; sec. Commn. on Med. Malpractice, HEW, 1971-73; cons. HEW, 1974; mem. Joint Commn. Prescription Drug Use, 1976-80; mem. profl. adv. bd. Comml. Credit Corp., 1976-78, Control Data Corp., 1978-82; mem. Council Sci. and Indsl. Research, 1976-78. Editorial bd.: Hosp. Formulary Mgmt, 1969-79, Forensic Science, 1971—, Jour. Legal Medicine, 1973-79, Reg. Tox. and Pharmac, 1981—, Medical Malpractice Prevention, 1985—; Contbr. articles to profl. jours. Exec. com. White House Mini Conf. on Aging, 1980; Republican dist. leader, New Canaan, Conn., 1966-68; mem. Town Council New Canaan, 1978-86 , vice chmn., 1985-86 ; bd. dirs. New Canaan Interchurch Service Com., 1965-69, Athletes Kidney Found., Circle in Sq. Theater Inc., 1984-86 ; trustee Dickinson Sch. of Law, Cleve. Clin., 1971-87, Albany Med. Coll., 1977-86, Morehouse Med. Sch., St. Vincent DePaul. Ctr. for the Homeless; vice chmn. Health Commn. for Food and Shelter, Inc.; mem. Nat. Health Advisory Bd. AAA, N.Y. State Commn. Substance Abuse, 1978-80; chmn. bd. ACLM Found., 1983-87. Served to lt. comdr. USNR, 1956-61. Recipient Alumni award of merit U. Pa., 1953; Named Tenn. Col. Fellow Am. Coll. Legal Medicine (v.p., pres., bd. govs.); mem. AMA (Physicians Recognition awards 1969, 72, 76, 82, 85), Med. Execs. (pres. 1975-76), Delta Tau Delta. Lutheran. Office: 1205 Prospect Suite 520 La Jolla CA 92037

TROUTMAN, BRUCE WEBER, health maintenance organization administrator; b. Dayton, Ohio, Mar. 15, 1947; s. H. Eugene and Margaret (Weber) T.; m. Kay Stevens, May 16, 1981; 1 child, Brian H. B.S., Ohio State U., 1969; D.O., Chgo. Coll Osteo. Medicine, 1973. Intern Zieger Botsford Hosp., Detroit, 1974; practice m,edicine Mich., 1974-86; med. dir. Health Plus Mich., Flint, 1986—; physician reviewer Profl. Rev. Orgn., Genesee, Lapeer, Shiawassee counties, Mich., 1976-86 ; med. dir. two health maintenance orgns., 1984-86; cons. health maintenance orgns. Mem. Am. Osteo. Assn., Mich. Assn. Osteo. Physicians and Surgeons, Lapeer Osteo. Soc., Nat. Bd. Osteo. Examiners,,Group Health Assn. Am. (med. dirs. div.), Lapeer C. of C. (bd. dirs. 1983-84). Republican. Lutheran. Lodge: Optimists (bd. dirs. 1981-85, 85—, v.p. 1983-84). Avocations: photography, cross country skiing, raising racoons, landscaping. Home: 2033 Gray Rd Lapeer MI 48446 Office: Health Plus 2050 S Linden Rd Flint MI 48507

TROUTMAN, CHARLES HENRY, III, lawyer; b. Wooster, Ohio, Mar. 25, 1944; s. Charles Henry and Lois Margaret (Dickason) T. B.A., Wheaton Coll., 1966; J.D., Am. U., 1969; M.Comparative Law, So. Meth. U., 1970. Bar: Ill. 1969, D.C. 1969, Guam 1973, U.S. Ct. Appeals (9th cir.) 1973, Trust Territory Pacific Islands, 1973, U.S. Supreme Ct. 1976, Commonwealth of No. Mariana Islands 1978. Asst. atty. gen., Guam, 1970-74; assoc. Cronin, Troutman & Assocs., Guam, 1974-75; atty. gen., Guam, 1975-77; counsel Dept. Edn., Guam, 1977-78; compiler of laws Govt. of Guam, Agana, 1978—, acting atty. gen., 1987. Mem. ABA, Fed. Bar Assn. (sec. local chpt.), Am. Soc. Internat. Law, Christian Legal Soc., Guam Bar Assn. Democrat. Presbyterian. Home: PO Box 455 Agana GU 96910 Office: 238 Archbishop FC Flores St PDN Bldg 7th Floor Agana GU 96910

TROUTWINE-BRAUN, CHARLOTTE TEMPERLEY, psychologist, educator, clergywoman; b. Newton, Mass., Nov. 27, 1906; d. Joseph and Libbie (Kempton) Temperley; BS, Simmons Coll., 1927; postgrad. Boston U., 1947-49; MA, Northeastern U., 1966; BES, Internat. Ch. Ageless Wisdom, 1981; m. Arklay S. Richards, Nov. 28, 1928 (div. 1942); children—Whitman Albin, Lincoln Kempton, Sylvia Caroline; m. 2d, Harry Troutwine, May 3, 1945 (div. 1954); m. 3d, Charles E. McCrum, 1961 (div. 1965); m. 4th, Lester Lewis Walsh, Feb. 16, 1968 (div. Feb. 1972); m. 5th, George Braun, Feb. 6, 1975 (dec. Oct. 1975). Pvt. sec. pres. Hygrade Sylvania Electric Corp. Salem, Mass., 1927-28; pvt. and dept. exec. sec. Dr. Stanley Cobb, Bullard prof. neuropathology Harvard U. Med. Sch., 1928-31; part-time work, various positions, 1931-51; exec. dir. Postgrad. Med. Inst., 1951-57; mgr. Postgrad. Information Services, Lederle Labs. div. Am. Cyanamid Co., Pearl River, N.Y., 1957-60; exec. sec. postgrad. med. edn., Hahnemann Med. Coll. and Hosp. also exec. dir. Mary Bailey Inst. Cardiovascular Research, 1961; counselor, tchr. psychology Holliston High Sch., 1965-66. Caseworker Friends of Framingham Reformatory; counselor Falmouth (Mass.) High Sch., 1966-74; psychotherapist Hallgarth Clinic, 1975—. Speaker for Am. Epilepsy League. Mem. Mass. Tchrs. Assn. (life), Spiritual Frontiers Assn. (life), N.E.A. (life), Nat. Ret. Tchrs. Assn. (life), Nat. Assn. Sch. Counselors (charter, life), Assn. Research Enlightenment, Soc. Mayflower Descs. (life), Simmons Coll. Alumnae Assn., AAUW, Med. Soc. Execs. Assn. (emeritus), Am. Soc. Psychical Research, States Med. Postgrad. Assn. (past sec.), Mass. Psychol. Assn., Am. Spiritual Healing Assn. (life, healing mem., mem. adv. bd.), Spiritual Frontiers Fellowship (life), World Fedn. Healers (healer mem.), Mass. Healers Assn. Author articles in med. and spiritual fields. Mem. Soc. of Friends. Home: 83 Falmouth Ct Bedford MA 01730

TROWBRIDGE, ALEXANDER BUEL, JR., trade association executive; b. Englewood, N.J., Dec. 12, 1929; s. Alexander Buel and Julie (Chamberlain) T.; m. Eleanor Hutzler, Apr. 18, 1981; children by previous marriage: Stephen C., Corrin S., Kimberly. Grad., Phillips Acad., Andover, Mass., 1947; AB cum laude, Princeton U., 1951; LLD (hon.), D'Youville Coll., 1967, Hofstra U., 1968, Hobart Coll. and William Smith Coll., 1975. With Calif. Tex. Oil Co., 1954-59; ops. mgr. Esso Standard Oil S.A. Ltd., Panama C.Z., 1959-61; div. mgr. Esso Standard Oil S.A. Ltd., El Salvador, 1961-63; pres., mgr. div. Esso Standard Oil Co., P.R., 1963-65; asst. sec. commerce for domestic and internat. bus. U.S., 1965-67; sec. of commerce 1967-68; pres., chief exec. officer Am. Mgmt. Assn., N.Y.C., 1968-70; pres. The Conf. Bd., Inc., N.Y.C., 1970-76; vice chmn. bd. Allied Chem Corp., 1976-80; bd. dirs. Nat. Assn. Mfrs., 1978—, pres., 1980—; bd dirs. New Eng. Mut. Life Ins. Co., PHH Group, Waste Mgmt., Inc., Rouse Co., Sun Resorts Ltd. N.V.; mem. internat. adv. com. Nikko Securities Internat. Co. Trustee Phillips Acad., Andover, Mass.; bd. dirs. Enterprise Found.; mem. Pres.'s Task Force on Pvt. Sector Initiatives, Pres.'s Commn. on Social Security, 1982; mem. Nat. Commn. on Exec. Legis. and Jud. Salaries, 1985. Served with USMCR, 1951-53; maj. Res. Decorated Bronze Star with combat V; recipient Arthur Flemming award, 1966, Pres.'s E cert. for export service, 1968. Mem. Council Fgn. Relations. Clubs: Metropolitan, Georgetown City (Washington); Links, University (N.Y.C.). Home: 1823 23d St NW Washington DC 20008 Office: Nat Assn Mfrs 1331 Pennsylvania Ave NW Suite 1500 Washington DC 20004

TROY, JOSEPH F., lawyer; b. Wilkes-Barre, Pa., Aug. 16, 1938; s. Sergei and Shirley Jean T.; m. Brigitta Ann Balos, June 9, 1962; children: Darcy Kendall, Austin Remy. B.A., Yale U., 1960; LL.B., Harvard U., 1963. Bar: Calif. 1964, D.C. 1979. Assoc. Hindin, McKittrick & Marsh, Beverly Hills, Calif., 1964-68; partner Hindin, McKittrick & Marsh, 1968-70; pres. Troy Casden Gould, Los Angeles, 1970—; lectr. Calif. Continuing Edn. of Bar, 1972-80; dir. World Trade Bank N.A., 1983—. Author: Let's Go: A Student Guide to Europe, 1962, Accountability of Corporate Management, 1979. Pres. Los Angeles Chamber Orch. Soc., 1968-75, chmn. bd., 1975-78, vice chmn., 1978-81; bd. dirs. Music Center Opera Assn., 1972—, exec. v.p., mem. exec. com., 1987—; hon. consul of Tunisia, Los Angeles, 1984-88. Reid Hall fellow U. Paris, 1958. Mem. ABA, Calif. State Bar, D.C. Bar, Los Angeles County Bar Assn. (chmn. bus. and corp. law sect. 1977-78), French Am. C. of C. of U.S. (exec. v.p. 1983-85), French Am. C. of C. of Los Angeles (pres. 1982-84). Clubs: Beach, Regency (Los Angeles); Yale (N.Y.C.) (bd. dirs. Los Angeles); California (Los Angeles); Center (Newport Beach); St. James's (London). Office: 1801 Century Park E Suite 1600 Los Angeles CA 90067

TROYAT TARASOFF, HENRI, writer; b. Nov. 1, 1911; s. Tarasoff Aslan and Abessolomoff (Lydie) T.; m. Marie a Marguerite Saintagne, Sept. 23, 1948; 2 children. Ed. Lycee Pasteur, and Law Faculty, U. Paris. Mem. Acad. Francaise 1959—; Legion d'honneur. Publs.: Faux-jour (Prix Populiste), 1935, L'araigne (Prix Goncourt), 1938, La neige en deuil (Grand prix litteraire de Monaco), 1952, Tant que la terredurera (three vols.), 1947-50, Les semailles et les moissons (five vols.), 1953-58, La lumiere des justes (five vols.), 1960-63, Les Eygletiere (three vols.), 1965-67, Les heritiers de l'avenir, 1968, Anne Predaille, 1973, Le Moscovite, 1974, La Derision, 1983, numerous others; (biographies) Dostoievsky, Pouchkine, Tolstoi, Gogol, Catherine la Grande, Pierre le Grand, Alexandre Ier, Ivan le Terrible, Tchekhov, Tourgueniev, Gorki, Flaubert. Office: Acad Francaise, 23 quai de Conti, 75006 Paris France

TROZZOLO, ANTHONY MARION, chemist; b. Chgo., Jan. 11, 1930; s. Pasquale and Francesca (Vercillo) T.; m. Doris C. Stoffregen, Oct. 8, 1955; children: Thomas, Susan (Mrs. Bruce Hecklinski), Patricia, Michael, Lisa, Laura. B.S., Ill. Inst. Tech., 1950; M.S., U. Chgo., 1957, Ph.D., 1960. Asst. chemist Chgo. Midway Labs., 1952-53; assoc. chemist Armour Research Found., Chgo., 1953-56; mem. tech. staff Bell Labs., Murray Hill, N.J., 1959-75; Charles L. Huisking prof. chemistry U. Notre Dame, 1975—; vis. prof. Columbia U., N.Y.C., 1971, U. Colo., 1981, Katholieke Universiteit Leuven, Belgium, 1983; vis. lectr. Academia Sinica, 1984, 85; AEC fellow, 1951, NSF fellow, 1957-59; Phillips lectr. U. Okla., 1971; P.C. Reilly lectr. U. Notre Dame, 1972; C.L. Brown lectr. Rutgers U., 1975; Sigma Xi lectr. Bowling Green U., 1976, Abbott Labs., 1978; M. Faraday lectr. No. Ill. U., 1976; F.O. Butler lectr. S.D. State U., 1978; Chevron lectr. U. Nev.-Reno, 1983; Hesburgh Alumni lectr. U. Notre Dame, South Bend, Ind., 1986, disting. lectr. sci., 1986. Assoc. editor: Jour. Am. Chem. Soc, 1975-76; editor: Chem. Reviews, 1977-84; editorial adv. bd. Accounts of Chem. Research, 1977-85; contbr. articles to profl. jours; patentee in field. Fellow N.Y. Acad. Scis. (Halpern award in Photochemistry 1980), AAAS, Am. Inst. Chemists; mem. Am. Chem. Soc. (Disting. Service award St. Joseph Valley sect. 1979, Coronado lectr. 1980), AAUP, Sigma Xi. Roman Catholic. Home: 1329 E Washington St South Bend IN 46617 Office: U Notre Dame Notre Dame IN 46556

TRPIS, MILAN, scientist, educator; b. Mojsova Lucka, Slovakia, Czechoslovakia, Dec. 20, 1930; came to U.S., 1971, naturalized, 1977; s. Gaspar and Anna (Sevcikova) T.; m. Ludmila Tonkovic, Dec. 15, 1956; children: Martin, Peter, Katarina. M.S., Comenius U., Bratislava, 1956; Ph.D., Charles U., Prague, 1960. Research asst. Slovak Acad. Sci., Bratislava, 1953-56; sci. asst. Slovak Acad. Sci., 1956-60, scientist, 1960-62, ind. scientist, 1962-69; ecologist-entomologist East Africa-Aedes research nit, WHO, Dar es Salaam, Tanzania, 1969-71; asst. faculty fellow dept. biology U. Notre Dame, 1971-73, asso. faculty fellow, 1973-74; asso. prof. med. entomology Johns Hopkins U. Sch. Hygiene and Pub. Health, 1974-78, prof., 1978—, dir. labs. med. entomology; research asso. U. Ill., Urbana, 1966-67, Can. Dept. Agr., Lethbridge, Alta., 1967-68; dir. Biol. Research Inst. Am., 1971-79; external dir. research Liberian Inst. Biomed. Research, 1981—; dir. AID project on transmission of river blindness in areas of Liberia and Sierra Leone; dir. WHO research grant; tech. adv. com. US AID Vector Biology and Control Project, 1986—; trainer doctoral students, Africa, Asia, Cen. Am., 1979—. Editor: Jour. Biologia, 1956-71, Jour. Entomol. Problems, 1960-72; zool. sect.: Jour. Biol. Works, 1960-71; Contbr. articles to profl. jours. Dir. WHO project on prophylactic drugs for river blindness, Liberia, 1985-87. Recipient Slovak Acad. Sci., 1st prize for research project. Mem. AAUP, Am. Inst. Biol. Sci., AAAS, Am. Mosquito Control Assn., Am. Soc. Parasitologists, Helminthol. Soc. Washington, Am. Soc. Tropical Medicine, Entomol. Soc. Am., Am. Genetic Assn., N.Y. Acad. Scis., Johns Hopkins U. Tropical Medicine Club, Smithsonian Assocs., Sigma Xi, Alpha chpt. Delta Omega. Home: 1504 Ivy Hill Rd Cockeysville MD 21030 Office: Johns Hopkins U 615 N Wolfe St Baltimore MD 21205

TRŘÍŠKA, JOSEF, medievalist, historian; b. Rychnov, Czechoslovakia, Sept. 10, 1922; s. Josef and Josefa (Königová) T.; m. Božena Müllerová, Dec. 22, 1956; 1 child, Alena. PhD, Charles U., Prague, Czechoslovakia, 1950. Grammar sch. tchr. Hradec Králové, Czechoslovakia, 1950-53; sci. researcher Acad. Scis., Prague, 1953-66, Charles U., Prague, 1966—. Author 10 books, 72 articles. Mem. Internat. Soc. for History of Rhetoric. Office: Charles University, Ovocny trh 5, Prague Czechoslovakia

TRTPATHI, KRISHAN K, microbiologist; b. Abohar, India, Nov. 5, 1952; s. Shankar Prasad and Mukta Devi T.; m. Geeta Rani, June 28, 1974; 1 child, Vandana. BSc with honors in Microbiology, Punjab U., 1973, MSc with honors in Microbiology, 1976, PhD in Microbiology, 1987. Jr. microbiologist Ranbaxy Labs. Ltd., New Delhi, 1976-77; chemist for research and devel. Unichem Labs. Ltd., Ghaziabad, India, 1977-78; devel. scientist asst. Indian Drugs & Pharms. Ltd., Gurgaon, India, 1978-81; dep. asst. dir. Central Research Inst., Kasauli, India, 1981—. Editor proceedings nat. seminars; contbr. research articles to profl. publs. WHO fellow, 1987. Mem. Semple's Club, Assn. Microbiologists India, Indian Soc. Microbiology. Hindu. Club: Officers (Kasauli). Home: St 1 Jain Nagar, Abohar Punjab 152 116, India Office: Central Research inst, Kasauli Solan 173 205 India

TRÜBESTEIN, GUSTAV KLAUS, physician, educator; b. Kassel, Ger., Sept. 30, 1939; s. Gustav and Ursula (Umland) T.; MD, U. Heidelberg, 1964; m. Renate May, Oct. 13, 1972; children: Eva, Michael. Internist, Univ. Clinic W.Berlin, 1964-66, Univ. Clinic Tuebingen, 1966-70, Univ. Clinic Bonn, 1970—; prof. U. Bonn Med. Faculty, 1977-80, prof., 1980—. Grantee Deutsche Forschungsgemeinschaft. Fellow Internat. Coll. Angiology; mem. German Soc. Angiology, German Soc. Internal Medicine, Internat. Soc. Thrombosis, Haemostasis, N.Y. Acad. Scis. Author 6 books, papers in field. Office: Weimarstrasse 38, D-5205 Sankt Augustin Federal Republic of Germany

TRUDEAU, PIERRE ELLIOTT, former Canadian prime minister, lawyer; b. Montreal, Que., Can., Oct. 18, 1919; s. Charles-Emile and Grace (Elliott) T.; m. Margaret Sinclair, Mar. 4, 1971 (div.); children: Justin Pierre, Alexandre Emmanuel, Michel Charles-Emile. B.A., Jean de Brebeuf Coll., Montreal, 1940; LL.L., U. Montreal, 1943; M.A., Harvard U., 1945; student, Ecole des Sciences Politiques, Paris, London Sch. Econs.; numerous hon. degrees. Bar: Called to Que. bar 1943, created Queen's counsel 1969. Practiced law in Montreal; jr. economist staff Privy Council, Ottawa, Ont., Can.; asso. prof. law, mem. Inst. Pub. Law U. Montreal, 1961-65; mem. Ho. of Commons, 1965—; parliamentary sec. to prime minister 1966-67; minister justice, atty. gen. Can., 1967-68; leader Liberal party 1968—; prime minister Can., 1968-79, 80-84; leader of opposition in parliment, 1979-80, mem. Privy Council,, 1979—; mem. law firm Heenan Blaikie and predecessor firms, 1984—; co-founder Cité Libre (monthly rev.); del. France-Can. Interparliamentary Assn., 1966, UN, 1966. Author: Federalism and the French Canadians, 1968, Réponses, 1967; co-author: Deux Innocents en Chine, 1961; editor: La Gréve del'Amiante, 1956; contbr. articles to profl. jours. Decorated Order of Companions of Honor (Gt. Britain). Mem. Canadian Bar Assn., Montreal Civil Liberties Union, Royal Soc. Can. Liberal. Roman Catholic. Office: Heenan Blaikie, 1001 de Maisonneuve, Montreal, PQ Canada H3A 3C8

TRUDEL, JOHN DAVIS, electronics company executive; b. Trenton, N.J., Aug. 1, 1942; s. LeRoy Renee and Elizabeth Etta (Reading) T. BEE cum laude, Ga. Inst. Tech., 1964; MEE, Kans. State U., 1966. Research and devel. project engr. Collins Radio Co., Richardson, Tex., 1966-67; sr. engr. Sanders Assocs., Inc., Nashua, N.H., 1967-68; sr. electronic system engr. LTV Electrosystems, Inc., Greenville, Tex., 1968-69; sr. engr. Collins Radio Co., Richardson, 1969-70; project engr. F & M Systems, Co., Dallas, 1970-71; pres. Sci. System Tech., Inc., Richardson, 1971-74; product mgr. portable oscilloscopes Tektronix, Inc., Beaverton, Oreg., 1974-82, mgr. application mktg. Lab. Instrument div., 1983-84, v.p. mktg. Cable Bus Systems Corp., Beaverton, 1982-83; mktg. mgr. Tektronix Labs., 1984-87; gen. mgr. spl products team, 1988—. Primary author of MAGIC, gen. purpose microwave computer-aided design program; contbr. articles to profl. jours. Mem. nat. adv. bd. Am. Security Council, 1974—. Recipient Scholastic award Lambda Chi Alpha, 1963-64; Western Electric scholar, State of N.J. scholar, McLendon scholar; NDEA Grad. fellow. Mem. IEEE, Assn. Old Crows, Am. Mktg. Assn., Nat. Avionics Soc., Automatic R.F. Techniques Group, Am. Electronics Assn., Aircraft Owners and Pilots Assn., Tau Beta Pi, Eta Kappa Nu. Roman Catholic. Office: Tektronix Labs MS 50-222 PO Box 500 Beaverton OR 97077

TRUEMAN, DEBORAH CHERYL, mathematician; b. Melbourne, Victoria, Australia, Feb. 2, 1955; d. Frederick Arthur and Beryl Victoria (Potter) T. B.A. (Double Honours), Monash U., Clayton, Victoria, 1978, Ph.D., 1981, A.Mus. A. (A.M.E.B), 1986. Tutor Monash U., 1981-83, sr. tutor, 1984-85; lectr. Swinburne Inst. Tech., Hawthorn, Australia, 1986—; reviewer Math. Revs., Ann Arbor, Mich., 1983—. Contbr. articles to profl. lit. Australian Commonwealth Univ. scholar Monash U., 1973, Commonwealth postgrad. research awardee, 1979-81. Mem. Australian Math. Soc., Am. Math. Soc., Inst. Math.Stats., Australian Stat. Soc. Mem. Ch. of England. Office: Hawthorn (Melbourne), Dept of Math Swinburne Inst, Tech PO Box 218, Hawthorn, Victoria 3122, Australia

TRUKAN, BOHDAN, TV and film dir., producer; Ph.D., Nat. Theater Acad., Warsaw, Poland. Actor, Teatr Polski, Teatr Kameralny, Warsaw, 1950-52; with Polish Broadcasting Corp., Warsaw, 1955-70, staff producer, dir. artistic programs, 1958-70, chief producer, opera and music theater, 1960-63, film dir., instr. profl. tng. for TV dirs., 1959-62; vis. artistic co-dir. Nat. Theater, Kielce/Radom, Poland, 1962-63; freelance theater dir.; vis. prof. U. Wis., U. Houston, U. Calif., Bklyn. Coll., Hunter Coll. N.Y.U.; dir. films; Teatre Klasyczny, Warsaw, Film Polski, Warsaw Film Studies, Brit. Broadcasting Corp., Opera Piccola, London, O.R.T.F.-Radiodiffusion TV Francaise, Paris, Compagnie du Cothurne, Centre Dramatique National de Lyon (France), Teatro Piccolo di Milano (Italy), Richard Milne Ltd., London; drama prodns. include: The Man with a Flower in His Mouth, School for Wives, La Mandragola, Widowers' Houses, Uncle Vanya, A Month in the Country, Smoke, Back to Lisbon, Pierre Grassou, Borderland, Shred of Evidence, Arms for America, Lady Windermere's Fan. Tango, The Maids; opera prodns. include: Bastien et Bastienne, Zelise et Valcour, The New Don Quixote, Casanova, Ushiko and Narikhira (world premiere), Cosi Fan Tutte, also ballet prodns.; TV producer, dir. musicals, concerts, recitals, variety programs; Judith E. Wilson lectr. on drama Cambridge U., 1981. Mem. Polish Theatre and Film Artists Assn. (dir. 1967-69, mem. drama dirs. group theatre), Writers Guild Poland, Internat. Writers Guild, Internat. Film and TV Producers Guild, Internat. Theatre Inst. (del. XIV World Congress 1971), Acad. TV Arts and Scis. (juror 29th Am. Film and TV Festival 1987). Address: 6410 Strickland Ave Brooklyn NY 11234

TRUMBLY, WILLIAM DALE, geologist; b. Osage County, Okla., Sept. 27, 1921; s. Oliver William and Mary Frances (Cornett) T.; m. Earlene Elizabeth Cox, Dec. 31, 1945; children—William D., Mary Adair Trumbly Leslie, Toya Trumbly Thomas, James E., Nancy I. BS in Mil. Sci. and Tactics, Okla. State U., 1943; BS in Geology, U. Okla., 1947. Geologist, Tex. Pacific Coal & Oil Co., Midland, 1947-51, Republic Natural Gas Co., Midland and

Oklahoma City, 1952-62; assoc. geologist Mobil Oil Corp., Oklahoma City, 1962-69; regional geologist Royal Resources Corp., Oklahoma City, 1969-70; chief geologist Vanderbilt Resources Corp., Oklahoma City, Dallas, 1970-73; pres., owner Trumbly Petroleum Cons., Inc., Dallas, 1973—. Served to 1st lt. AUS, 1943-45. Contbr. articles to profl. jours. Decorated Bronze Star, Purple Heart with Cluster. Mem. Soc. Ind. Profl. Earth Scientists, Am. Assn. Petroleum Geologists (ho. of dels. 1970-72, 77-80, ins. com. 1977-78), Oklahoma City Geol. Soc. (exec. com. 1965-69, pres. 1968-69), Dallas Geol. Soc. (pres. 1982-83). Roman Catholic. Club: Energy (charter) (Dallas).

TRUMPY, HERMANN JAKOB, hotel executive; b. Zurich, Switzerland, Jan. 5, 1936; s. Hermann and Olga (Auer) T.; m. Regula Elisabeth Thalmann, Aug. 31, 1937; children—Hermann Emil, Alfred Robert, Regula Anna Olga, Thomas Hermann Ernst. Student Comml. Bus. Sch. Clos Rousseau Cressier-Neuchatel Switzerland, 1952-53; With Hotel Trumpy, Zurich, 1959—, owner, mgr., 1972—; owner, mgr. Rehota AG, Zurich, 1965—. Mem. Swiss Soc. Hotelers, Swiss Soc. Restaurants, Tourist Soc., Zurich, Swiss Tourist Orgn., Conf. des. Chevaliers du Tastevin de Clos de Vougeot, Conf. des Chevaliers des Coteaux de Champagne. Club: Hittnau Golf. Home: Alte Landstrasse 112, Zollikon, 8702 Zurich Switzerland Office: Hotel Trumpy, Sihlquai 9, 8005 Zurich Switzerland

TRUONG CHINH (FORMERLY DANG XUAN KHU), former chairman State Council of Vietnam Socialist Republic; b. Nam Dinh, Vietnam, 1907. Sec., Revolutionary League of Vietnamese Youth until 1930, imprisoned by French, 1930-36, worked as journalist, 1936-39, imprisoned, escaped to Yenen, 1939, returned to Vietnam, 1941; sec.-gen. Community Party of Indo-China, later Lao Dong party, 1941-56; chmn. standing com. Nat. Assembly Dem. Republic Vietnam, 1960-76, Nat. Assembly Socialist Rep. Vietnam, 1976-81; pres. State Council, 1981-86; chmn. Nat. Def. Council; chmn. Com. for Drafting Constn. Socialist Republic Vietnam, 1975-76. Sec. gen. Communist Party Vietnam, 1986. Decorated Order of Lenin. Office: 1 Hoang Van Thu St, Hanoi Socialist Republic of Vietnam *

TRUSDELL, MARY LOUISE CANTRELL, retired state educational administrator; b. Chandler, Okla., Oct. 24, 1921; d. George Herbert and Lois Elizabeth (Bruce) Cantrell; m. Robert William Trusdell, Jan. 7, 1943; children—Timothy Lee, Laurence Michael. BA, Ga. So. Coll., 1965; MEd, U. Va., 1974. Dir. spl. learning disabilities program Savannah Country Day Sch., Ga., 1960-65; learning disabilities tchr. Richmond pub. schs., Va., 1966-73; dir. New Community Sch., Richmond, 1974-75; dir. Fed. Learning Disabilities Project, Dept HEW, Mid. Peninsula, Va., 1975-76; supr. programs for learning disabled Va. Dept. Edn., Richmond, 1976-86; bd. dirs. Learning Disabilities Council, Richmond, Very Spl. Arts, Va., 1986—; mem. adv. com. Learning Disabilities Research and Devel. Project, Woodrow Wilson Rehab. Ctr., Fisherville, Va., 1983. Bd. dirs. Savannah Assn. Retarded Children, 1957-60, Meml. Guidance Clinic, Richmond, 1966-69. Named Tchr. of Yr., Learning Disabilities Ctr., Richmond, 1972. Mem. Assn. for Children and Adults with Learning Disabilities, Orton Dyslexia Soc. (pres. capital area br. 1968-70, nat. bd. dirs. 1970-72, Va. br. 1986—). Presbyterian. Avocations: camping, travel, theater, reading.

TRUSSEL, HAROLD JUNIOR, school principal; b. Montpelier, Idaho, July 4, 1936; s. William and Wanda Matilda (Jaussi) T.; m. Vilate Gardner, Jan. 21, 1961; children—Reed William, Bryan Gardner, Allison. B.S., U. Utah, 1963, M.S., 1968, Ednl. Specialist, 1972; postgrad. U. Fla., 1977. Tchr., South High Sch., Salt Lake City, 1970-73; acting prin. SE Jr. High Sch., Salt Lake City, 1972-73; prin. Lincoln Jr. High Sch., Salt Lake City, 1974-75, Jordan Intermediate Sch., Salt Lake City, 1975-78, Bryant Intermediate Sch., Salt Lake City, 1978-84, West High Sch., Salt Lake City, 1984—; chmn. Utah State Middle Sch. Com., 1981-83, Utah Jr. High Adv. Com., 1984—; dir. Nat. Tchr. Corps, Salt Lake, 1976-78. Organizer, officer Freedom Clubs for Am., Salt Lake City, 1979—; coach Little League Baseball, Salt Lake City, 1968-70; mem. Town Council Meeting, Salt Lake City, 1976; mem., speaker Utah Pub. Productivity Fair, 1983; mem. Gov.'s Criminal and Juvenile Justice Commn., 1987—. Recipient Valley Forge Freedoms Found. medal, 1983; named Best High Sch. Prin. Utah, Utah Holiday Mag., 1985. Mem. Salt Lake Adminstrs. Exec. Council, Salt Lake Assn. Secondary Sch. Adminstrs. (chmn. adminstr. edn. com. 1981-82, chmn. profl. rights and responsibility com. 1979-80), Nat. Assn. Secondary Sch. Prins., Phi Delta Kappa. Lodge: Kiwanis (Bonneville, Internat.). Address: West High Sch 241 N 300 W Salt Lake City UT 84103

TRUSSELL, FREDRICK GEORGE, test engineer, reactor operator, consultant; b. Albuquerque, Mar. 5, 1950; s. Travis L. and Enid L. (Wells) T.; m. Kathryn D. Stringfellow, June 1, 1968 (div. Oct. 1968); m. Patricia Humphries, Oct. 23, 1974; children: Travis, Todd, Cody, Danny, Mike. B in Nuclear Engring., Columbia Pacific U., 1984. Reactor operator U.S. Navy, 1972-80; field technician Eberline Instrument Co., Albuquerque, 1980; reactor operator Sandia Nat. Labs., Albuquerque, 1981—, test engr., Pantex, Tex., 1986—. Author: ACRR Operators Manual, 1983, ACRR Experimenters Manual, 1984, Multiple Listing Software, 1984. Bernalillo County chmn. Am. Diabetes Assn. Bike Ride, 1984; foster parent, 1987—. Club: Optimists (charter, bd. dirs. 1981-83, 84-85, v.p. 1983-84). Office: 7256 Sandia Nat Labs PO Box 5800 Albuquerque NM 87185

TRUSSLER, SIMON, journal editor, lecturer; b. Tenterden, Kent, Eng., June 11, 1942; s. John and Joan (Ovenden) T.; m. Glenda Leeming, Aug. 23, 1966 (div. 1984); children: Nicholas, Anna; m. Laverne Anderson, Aug. 29, 1984; 1 child, Jonathan. BA, Univ. Coll., London, 1963, MA, 1966. Founding editor Prompt, 1962-64, Theatre Quarterly, 1967-81, New Theatre Quarterly, 1984—; editorial asst. Plays and Players, 1964-67; co-editor Encore, 1965; London theatre critic Tulane Drama Rev. (later Drama Rev.), 1965-70; theatre critic Tribune, London, 1966-72; radio critic The Listener, London, 1969; vis. lectr. London program Tufts U., 1973-81, U. Kent, 1984-86; lectr. City Univ., London, part-time 1980-82; vis. prof. drama dept. U. Calif., Santa Barbara, 1983; sr. lectr. drama Goldsmiths' Coll., U. London, 1986—; gen. editor Writer-File series, London, 1985—; editor Theatre Internat., Internat. Theatre Inst., Paris, 1981-83, Swan Theatre Plays series, 1986—. Author: (critical studies) John Osborne, 1969, The Plays of John Osborne, 1969, The Plays of Arnold Wesker, 1971, The Plays of John Whiting, 1972, The Plays of Harold Pinter, 1973, John Arden, 1973, Edward Bond, 1976, (theater documentation) (with Charles Marowitz), Theatre at Work, 1967, A Classification for the Performing Arts, 1974, Annual Bibliography of Theatre Studies, 1975-76, 77, David Edgar: A Theatre Checklist, 1979, Royal Shakespeare Company: An Annual Record, 1979-86, New Theatre Voices of the Seventies, 1981, Twentieth-Century Drama, 1982; editor: New English Dramatists 13, 1968, Burlesque Plays of the Eighteenth Century, 1969, 4 Elizabethan and Jacobean Plays for Methuen Student Edit. series, 1983-87, 8 for Swan Theatre Play series. 1986-87. Home: Great Robhurst, Woodchurch, Ashford Kent TN26 3TB, England Office: U London, Goldsmiths Coll, Drama Dept, New Cross, London SE14 6NW, England

TRUTTER, JOHN THOMAS, consulting company executive; b. Springfield, Ill., Apr. 18, 1920; s. Frank Louis and Frances (Mischler) T.; m. Edith English Woods II, June 17, 1950; children: Edith English II, Jonathan Woods. BA, U. Ill., 1942; postgrad., Northwestern U., 1947-50, U. Chgo., 1947-50; LHD (hon.), Lincoln Coll., 1986. Various positions Ill. Bell, Chgo., 1946-58, gen. traffic mgr., from asst. v.p. of pub. relations to gen. N. Suburban mgr., 1958-69, v.p. pub. relations, 1969-71, v.p. operator services, 1971-80, v.p. community affairs, 1980-85; pres. John T. Trutter Co., Inc., Chgo., 1985—; mem. personnel staff AT&T, N.Y.C., 1955-57; pres., chief exec. officer Chgo. Conv. and Visitors Bur., 1985-88; pres. Chgo. Tourism Council, 1988—; bd. dirs. State Nat. Bank, Evanston; mem. adv. bd. Alford and Assocs., Chgo., 1984—, Chgo. Apparel Industry Assn., 1987—. Co-author: Handling Barriers in Communication, 1957, The Governor Takes a Bride, 1977. Past pres. Hull House Assn.; chmn. United Cerebral Palsy Assn. Greater Chgo., v.p. nat. bd.; bd. dirs. Chgo. Crime Commn., Abraham Lincoln Assn., v.p. English Speaking Union, City Colls. Chgo. Found., Lyric Opera Chgo.; past chmn. Childrens Home and Aid Soc.; v.p. Orch. Ill., hon. vice chmn., bd. dirs.; bd. dirs. Upper Ill. Valley Assn.; treas. Chgo. United, 1970-85; mem. Ill. Econ. Devel. Commn., 1985, Commn. on Improvement Cook County Circuit Ct. System, 1985—, Civic Com. for Domestic Relations Ct. Div., 1986—; past presiding co-chmn. NCCJ; bd. dirs. Ill. Humane Soc. Found.; chancellor Lincoln Acad. Ill., 1985—; numerous others; bd. govs. Northwestern U. Library Council, 1984—; trustee Lincoln (Ill.) Coll., 1987—; mem. State Ill. Assembly Sch. Problems Council, 1985—, spl. commn. on adminstrn. of justice in Cook County, 1986—. Served to lt. col. U.S. Army. Decorated Legion of Merit; recipient Outstanding Leadership award Chgo. West Project, 1985, Laureate award Lincoln Acad. Ill., 1980, Outstanding Civic Leader award Am. Soc. Fundraisers, Humanitarian of Yr. award, New Directions award SSMC, 1987. Mem. Pub. Relations Soc. Am., Sangamon County Hist. Soc. (founder, past pres.), Ill. State Hist. Soc. (pres. 1985-87), U. Ill. Alumni Assn. (bd. dirs.), Alpha Sigma Phi, Phi Delta Phi. Clubs: Tavern, Economic, Mid-America, City (v.p.). Home and Office: 630 Clinton Pl Evanston IL 60201

TRYBUS, RAYMOND J., university dean, research administrator, clinical psychologist; b. Chgo., Jan. 9, 1944; s. Fred and Cecilia (Liszka) T.; m. Sandra A. Noone, Aug. 19, 1967; children—David, Nicole. B.S., St. Louis U., 1965, M.S., 1970, Ph.D., 1971. Lic. psychologist, Md., D.C. Clin. psychologist Jewish Vocat. Service, St. Louis, 1968-71; clin. psychologist Gallaudet U., Washington, 1971-72, research psychologist, 1972-74, dir. demographic studies, 1974-78, dean grad. studies and research, 1984-88; assoc. provost, prof. psychology Calif. Sch. of Profl. Psychology, 1988—. dean Gallaudet Research Inst., 1978-84; cons. Mental Health Ctr. for Deaf, Lanham, Md., 1982—, Congl. Research Service, 1982—, McGill U. Nat. Study Hearing Impairment in Can., 1984—. Contbg. author: The Future of Mental Health Services for the Deaf, 1978, Hearing-impaired Children and Youth with Devel. Disabilities, 1985; editor Jour. Am. Deafness and Rehab. Assn. Grantee NIMH, Spencer Found., Tex. Edn. Agy., W.K. Kellogg Found. Mem. Am. Assn. Univ. Adminstrs. (bd. dirs.), Assn. Internat. Assn. Study of Interdisciplinary Research, Am. Psychol. Assn., Soc. Research Adminstrs., AAAS, Roman Catholic. Home: 6342 Cibola Rd San Diego CA 92120 Office: 6212 Ferris Square San Diego CA 92121

TRYON, EDWARD POLK, physics educator; b. Terre Haute, Ind., Sept. 4, 1940; s. Philip Freeland and Elizabeth Marsh (Banker) T. A.B., Cornell U., 1962; Ph.D., U. Calif., Berkeley, 1967. Research asso. Columbia U., N.Y.C., 1967-68; asst. prof. Columbia U., 1968-71; asst. prof. physics Hunter Coll., CUNY, 1971-73, asso. prof., 1974-79, prof., 1979— (on leave 1977-78, 86); vis. mem. Inst. Advanced Study, Princeton, 1977-78. Contbr. articles to profl. jours. Cornell Nat. Scholar, 1958-62; Hon. Woodrow Wilson fellow, 1962-64; NSF fellow, 1962-64; CUNY scholar, 1982-83. Mem. Am. Phys. Soc., N.Y. Acad. Scis., Phi Beta Kappa, Sigma Xi (nat. lectr. 1982-84), Phi Kappa Phi. Office: Dept Physics Hunter Coll New York NY 10021

TRZASKO, JOSEPH ANTHONY, psychologist; b. Jamaica, N.Y., June 4, 1946; s. Joseph Anthony and Lottie Marion (Nadraus) T.; B.A. cum laude, U. N.H., 1967; M.A., U. Vt., 1969, Ph.D., 1972; m. Ann Elizabeth Kidd, June 26, 1971; 1 son, Joshua Damon. Cert. bahavioral therapy, 1976. Prof. dept. psychology Mercy Coll., Dobbs Ferry, N.Y., 1969—; postdoctoral internship Ridge State Home and Tng. Sch., Colo. Dept. Insts., 1980; staff psychologist St. Dominic's Intermediate Care Facility for Developmentally Disabled, Blauvelt, N.Y., 1980—; cons. psychologist Jewish Guild for Blind, N.Y.C., 1983—, Orange County A.H.R.C., Middletown, N.Y., 1985—; pvt. practice clin. psychology. NDEA fellow U. Vt., 1967-69; NSF faculty research participation grantee Ednl. Commn. States/Nat. Assessment Ednl. Progress, 1976. Mem. Am. Psychol. Assn., Internat. Council Psychologists, AAUP, Am. Ednl. Research Assn. Roman Catholic. Home and Office: 30 Lake Dr Somers NY 10589

TSAGAMILIS, HERCULES, physician; b. Salonica, Macedonia, Greece, Jan. 27, 1933; s. Spyros and Maria (Kallitsopoulos) T.; m. Lydia Tziros, Dec. 11, 1969; 1 child, Alexander. MD, U. Salonica Med. Sch., 1958. Intern Mil. Med. Sch., Salonica, 1958-60; sr. resident in ear, nose and throat surgery Gen. Hosp. Piraeus, Greece, 1960-63; chief ear, nose and throat surgery Naval Hosp., Salamina Isles Naval Base, Greece, 1964-68; med. officer submarines USN, San Francisco and San Diego, 1965; chief Naval Hosp. Piraeus, 1965-69; mem. staff Naval Hosp. Phila., 1970-71; fellow Pa. U., Phila., 1970-71; chief ear, nose, and throat dept. Naval Hosp. Athens, 1972-78, 80-85, commdr., dir. admissions office, 1986-87; mem. med. staff Gen. Staff Hellenic Navy, Athens, 1978-80; pres. Supreme Med. Com. Hellenic Navy, Athens, 1987—, Rear Admiral-Surgeon Gen., 1988—. Fellow Am. Acad. Facial Plastic-Reconstructive Surgery, Internat. Coll Surgeons; mem. Hellenic Otorinolaryngology Soc. Club: Ekali (Ekali Attiki). Home: 25 Ikarias St, 14565 Ekali-Athens Greece Office: 35 Vas Sofias Ave, 10675 Athens Greece

TSAI, GERALD, JR., financial services corporation executive, specialty retailing executive; b. Shanghai, China, Mar. 10, 1928; came to U.S., 1947, naturalized, 1954; s. Gerald and Ruth (Lea) T.; m. Marlyn Kathryn Fritz Chase, Mar. 24, 1969; children: Gerald Van, Veronica Lee, Christopher. B.A., M.A., Boston U., 1949. Security analyst Bache & Co., N.Y.C., 1951-52; with Fidelity Mgmt. & Research Co., Boston, 1952-65; v.p. Fidelity Mgmt. & Research Co., 1960-63, dir., 1961-65, exec. v.p., 1963-65; chmn. Tsai Mgmt. & Research Corp., N.Y.C., 1965-68; exec. v.p., dir. CNA Fin. Corp., N.Y.C., 1968-86; chmn. bd., chief exec. officer Associated Madison Cos., Inc., 1978-86; exec. v.p., dir. Am. Can Co., 1982-86, vice chmn., chief exec. officer, from 1986, pres., 1987; chmn., chief exec. officer, pres. Primerica Corp. formerly Am. Can Co., 1987—. Office: Associated Madison 200 Park Ave New York NY 10166 also: Primerica Corp American Ln Greenwich CT 06836 *

TSAI, PUO-FUON, architectural educator; b. Taipei, Taiwan, Republic of China, Feb. 1, 1928; s. Hsin-Tai and Lan-Ying (Yeh) T.; m. Ming-Yeh Tsai Wu; children: Tsai Chueh-Hung, Tsai Cheng-Chih, Tsai Su-Fang, Tsai Su-Fung. BS of Architecture and Engring., Nat. Cheng-Kung U., Republic of China, 1951. Licensed architect, Republic of China. Chief designer Haigo Shen and Assocs., Taipei, Taiwan, Republic of China, 1961-64; prof. Dept. Architecture Tan-Kung U., Taipei, 1967-68, Dept Architecture and Urban Design Chinese Culture U., Taipei, 1966—. Author: Architectural Working Drawing, 1975, The Architect as Developer, 1978, The Third Generation Architect and Concept, 1978, The Pedestrian System/Theory and Practice, 1985; contbr. articles to profl. jours. Mem. spl. project Shin-yi Taipei Urban Design Com. Recipient Perpetual Hounour award Nat. Arts Exhibition, Republic of China, 1976, Gold Cup award Nat. Assn. Architects, 1976, Outstanding School fellow Nat. Taipei Inst. Tech., 1981. Mem. Taipei Architects Assn. (pres. 1983-85), Constitution Nat. Union Architect Assn. (dir. managing 1980—), Architecture Inst. Republic of China (dir. managing 1983—), Archtl. Inst. Japan, Taipei Assn. Interior Designers. Club: Rotary Taipei NW. Home: 6F-5 N 288 Kuang-Fu S Rd, Taipei Republic of China 10554 Office: PF Tsai and Assocs, 5F NO 0 Sec 1 Chang-An E Rd, Taipei 10404 Republic of China

TSAKALOS, STRATOS VASILIOS, pharmaceutical company executive; b. Fities, Agriniou, Greece, Nov. 11, 1948; s. John and Angeliki (Agelouli) T.; married; children: John, Angelica. BS, U. Salonica, Greece, 1972; MS, U. London, 1975. Dir. fin. F. Hoffmal La Roche Co., Athens, Greece, 1978-80; asst. gen. mgr. Smith Kline and French Hellas S.A., Athens, 1980-83; gen. mgr. Smith Kline and French Labs S.A., Athens, 1983—; adj. lectr. Inst. Mktg., Athens, 1978-85. Home: 11A R Ferraiou St, 151 21 Peuki Attikis Greece

TSAKONAS, GEORGE, surgeon; b. Egira, Greece, Jan. 6, 1937; s. Dennis and Athina T.; m. Ernestine Van Vilsteren, Sept. 5, 1965; children—Michele, Dennis. M.D., Med. Sch. Munich U., 1962. Intern Cath. Med. Center, Jamaica, N.Y., 1962-63; resident Cath. Med. Center of Bklyn. and Queens, 1963-66, Luth. Med. Center, Bklyn., 1966-68; practice medicine specializing in surgery, Bklyn., 1968—; mem. staff Luth. Med. Center, Meth. Hosp., Kings County Med. Center; clin. instr. SUNY-Downstate Med. Center, Bklyn. Fellow A.C.S., Internat. Coll. Surgeons; mem. Royal Soc. Medicine, Bklyn. Surg. Soc., N.Y. State Med. Soc., Kings County Med. Soc. Club: Richmond County Country. Home: 91 E Loop Rd Staten Island NY 10304 Office: 820 Broadway Brooklyn NY 11206

TSANG, PETER KWOKYIU, mechanical engineer; b. Hong Kong, Nov. 14, 1950; s. So and Wing Fun (Leung) T.; m. Pik Ngan Tam. Cert. in mech. engring., marine engring. Marine engr. World-Wide Shipping Co. Ltd., Hong Kong, 1971-77, Golden Peak Mainline Co. Ltd., Hong Kong, 1977-78; engring. supt. Grinstead Shipping Co. Ltd., Hong Kong, 1978-80; engr., then mech. and maintenance engr. China Light & Power Co. Ltd., Hong Kong, 1980—. Mem. ASME, Inst. Mech. Engrs., Inst. Marine Engrs., Hong Kong Inst. Engrs. Home: 75 3d St Sect I Fairview Park, Yuen Long New Territories, Hong Kong Hong Kong Office: China Light & Power Co Ltd, 147 Argyle St, Kowloon Hong Kong

TSAO, EDMUND SIU-HU, surgeon, educator; b. Hong Kong, June 19, 1930; s. E-Kant and Mabel (Chan) T.; M.D., Ling-Nan U. Med. Coll., Canton, 1954; m. Florentine Annita Su-Di Leung, Nov. 12, 1957; 1 dau., Alice Meng-Shao. Surgical resident Pei-King No. 6 People's Hosp., 1954-60; attending surgeon Chung Shan Med. Coll., Canton, 1961-68, Hosp. Da-Wang State Farm, Si-Hui County, Quangdong Province, 1969-76; prof. surgery, dir. div. hepatobiliary surgery Sun Yat-sen U. Med. Scis., Canton, 1976—. Mem. Chinese Med. Assn. Author: Clinical Oncology, 1974; Current Diagnosis and Treatment, 1977. Home: 464 Dong Fong Zhong Rd 2/F, Canton People's Republic of China Office: 1st Affiliated Hosp, Sun Yat-sen U Med Scis, Chung Shan Er Rd, Canton People's Republic of China

TSE, CHRISTOPHER P., chemical company executive. BS, U. Hawaii, 1972; MBA, La Salle U., St. Louis, 1987. Med. technologist Smith-Kline Bio-Sci. Labs., Honolulu, 1968-73; clin. chemist Kopp Clin. Labs., Ottawa, Ont., 1973-80; dir. tech. services Dow Diagnostic div. Dow Chem. Co., Indpls., 1980-82; ops. mgr. Kopp Clin. Labs., Toronto, Ont., 1982—; dir. clin. chemistry Kopp Clin. Labs., Ottawa, Ont., 1982—. Mem. Can. Soc. Clin. Chemists (bd. dirs. Ottawa chpt. 1986-87), Am. Soc. Clin. Chemistry, Adminstrv. Mgmt. Soc., Clin. Ligand Assay Soc. Office: Kopp Clinical Labs, 1095 Carling Ave, Ottawa, ON Canada K1Y 4P6

TSE, JOHN WAI-KWONG, radiochemical comany executive; b. Hong Kong, July 8, 1951; arrived in Can., 1970; s. Henry H. and S.K. (Cheung) T.; m. Lettice Hung Lam; children: Jeanie, Jeshurun. BS in Pharmacy, U. Alta., Can., 1974, MS in Bionucleonics, 1977, PhD in Radiopharmacy, 1982. Teaching asst. U. Alta., 1975-82; pharmacist Sprague Drug, Edmonton, Alta., 1975-76; radiopharmacist Cross Cancer Inst., Edmonton, 1977-79; pres. Internat. Radiochem. Ctr. Can., Edmonton, 1979—; pres. World Trade Devel. Inc., Can., 1985—, Petro-Tracer Inc., Can., 1985—; adj. asst. prof. U. Alta., 1984—; bd. dirs. Alliance Press, Can. Chief editor Renewal monthly newspaper, 1986—. Pres. Can.-Asian Resources Inst., Alberta, 1984—; bd. dirs. Chinese Christian and Missionary Alliance Ch., Alberta, 1974—, Chinese Christian Mission, 1986—. Alta. Environ. Research Trust grantee, 1983-84; Alta. Heritage Fund scholar, 1981-82. Mem. Edmonton Council for Advanced Tech., Alberta Pharm. Assn., Can. Inst. Mining, Can. Inst. Mgmt. Office: Internat Radiochem Ctr Inc, 8444-45 St, Edmonton, AB Canada T6B 2N6

TSE, STEPHEN YUNG NIEN, insurance executive; b. Shanghai, China, Feb. 14, 1931; came to U.S., 1949; s. Koong Kai Tse and Teh-Ying Koo Tse; student Ripon Coll., 1951-52; BBA, U. Wis., Madison, 1955; m. Margaret Miray Lock, Sept. 7, 1957; children: Chida, Chiming, Chiyung, Chikai. V.p. investments Am. Internat. Assurance Co., Hong Kong, 1962-64, fin. v.p., 1964-70; v.p. fgn. investments Am. Internat. Group, Inc., N.Y.C., 1971-82, sr. v.p. Fgn. Investments, 1982—; pres., chief exec. officer AIG Assocs., 1986—; bd. dirs. Am. Life Ins. Co., Am. Internat. Assurance Co., Transatlantic Fund, Am. Internat. Underwriters, Ltd., Equitable Investment Co., Hong Kong Carpet Mfrs. Ltd., Worldwide Looms, Ltd., AIG Realty Inc., C.V. Starr & Co., Inc. Mem. Beta Theta Pi. Clubs: Sky, Club at the World Trade Ctr., India House, Hong Kong Country, Am. of Hong Kong, Royal Hong Kong Golf, Singapore Country. Office: Am Internat Group Inc 70 Pine St New York NY 10270

TSEKHMISTRO, IVAN ZAKHAROVITCH, educator, philosopher; b. Orel, USSR, July 7, 1937; s. Zakhar Kononovitch and Anastassija (Rakosiy) T.; m. Lyudmila Nikolayevna Nesterova; children: Roman, Irina. B of Engring, Kharkov State U., USSR, 1959, D of Philosophy, 1977. Engr. Sibgiprotrans, Novosibirsk, USSR, 1959-62; prof. Kharkov State U., 1980—. Author monographs Dialectics of Plurality and Wholicity: The Qyantum, Properties of the World as a Whole, 1972, Plurality and Wholicity Dialectics and Continuum, 1977, The Search of the Quantum Conception of the Physical Basis of Consciousness, 1981, The Conception of Wholicity, 1987. Communist. Office: Kharkov State U, 4 Dzerzhinsky Sq, 310077 Kharkov USSR

TSENG, HUNG-LU, health science facility administrator; b. Nautou, Taiwan, Republic of China, Nov. 30, 1927; s. Zu-Kuan and Yee-Sai (Lin) T.; m. Lee Chiun-Huai, Oct. 4, 1954; children: Ling-Yuan, Tsuan-Chien, Chih-Chien, Der-Chien. MB, Nat. Taiwan U., Taipei, 1951. Resident to chief resident Nat. Taiwan U. Hosp., Taipei, 1951-56; chief med. dept. Provincial Taichung (Republic of China) Hosp., 1958-62; prof. Chung-Kou Med. Coll., Taichung, 1959-62, Chung-San Med. Coll., Taichung, 1962-64; vis. dr. Nat. Taiwan U. Hosp., Taipei, 1961-62; pres. Shin-Sheng Hosp., Taichung, 1962—. Bd. dirs. Red Cross Soc. Taichung City, 1974—. Mem. Med. Assn. Taichung City, Taichung Life Line Assn. (bd. dirs.)ž, Chinese Soc. Immunology, Nat. Taiwan U. Alumni Assn. (bd. dirs.), Golf Assn. Taichung City (bd. dirs.), Chinese Life Line Assn. (bd. dirs.), Chinese Internal Medicine. Lodge: Rotary (dist. gov. 1988—). Home and Office: 100 Min-Chuan Rd, Taichung Republic of China

TSENG, WEN-PING, cardiologist; b. Chang-Hwa, Taiwan, Republic of China, Jan. 15, 1924; s. Chi-Chin and Chin-Kwei (Chang) T.; m. Tsui-Wei, Chou, Sept. 7, 1945; children—Hui-Jen, Yea-Fan, Ham-Min, Tzy-Mei. M.D., Nat. Taiwan U., Taipei, 1953; D.Med. Sci., Osaka Mcpl. Med. Ctr. (Japan), 1960. Resident Nat. Taiwan U. Hosp., Taipei, 1953-57, staff physician, 1958—, vice supt., 1978-83, instr. medicine Med. Coll., 1961-67, assoc. prof., 1967-75, prof., 1975—, prof., chmn. Sch. Rehab., 1980-86. Author: Blackfoot Disease, 1979. Fellow Am. Coll. Cardiology, Am. Coll. Chest Physicians, Internat. Coll. Angiology, Royal Soc. Medicine; mem. Am. Heart Assn., Internat. Soc. Cardiology, N.Y. Acad. Sci., Republic China Soc. Cardiology, Formosan Med. Assn., Chinese Med. Assn., Chinese Med. Info. and Service Assn. (chmn. 1981), Chinese Hypertension Assn. (chmn. 1986). Home: 2d Floor 2 Lane 71, An-Ho Rd, Taipei 106 Republic of China Office: Nat Taiwan U Hosp, Dept Medicine, 1 Chang-te St, Taipei Republic of China

TSERING, DAWA, Bhutan government official; b. Sept. 29, 1935; married; two sons, three daus.; B.A. with honours in econs. and polit. sci. U. Calcutta, 1956, LL.B., 1959. Dir. edn. Govt. of Bhutan, 1960-64, dep. sec. gen. devel. wing, 1964-65, sec. gen., 1965-69, minister planning and devel., 1969-72; with Dept. Fgn. Affairs, 1970-72, minister for fgn. affairs, 1972—; debator Calcutta U., 1958-59; sec. of cabinet; chmn. Nat. Urban Devel. Corp.; acting chmn. Chukha Hydel Project; pres. Bhutan Olympic Com.; chmn. Nat. Edn. Com., ESCAP; v.p. UN Gen. Assembly; gov. for Bhutan in World Bank, 1981—, Asian Devel. Bank, 1982—; chmn. Nat. Assembly, 1964—. Recipient Druk Thuksel medal, 1966, Coronation Gold medal, 1974, High Decoration awarded by Republic of Korea. Mem. Nat. Sports Assn. (pres.). Club: Royal Golf (v.p.). Office: Ministry of Fgn Affairs, Thimphu Bhutan

TSEU, LAWRENCE KUM WING, dentist; b. June 23, 1932; s. Joseph Yuk Woon and Lillian (Choy) T.; m. Evelyn Kojima, Dec. 24, 1953; children: Larilyn, Shauna, Janell, Lawrence Jr., Andrew. B.S., Brigham Young U., 1958; D.D.S., Northwestern U., 1962. Intern Queen's Hosp., Honolulu, 1963; gen. practice dentistry 1962—; instr. dental assts. Kapiolani Community Coll., Honolulu, 1968-69; treas. Hawaii Soc. Dentistry for Children, Honolulu, 1965-66; dental cons. Queen's Hosp., 1970-73; staff St. Francis Hosp., 1965—; chmn. State Hawaii Bd. Dental Examiners, 1982—. Served with USAF, 1951-55. Mem. ADA, Hawaii Dental Assn., Am. Assn. Dental Examiners, Coll. Physician's and Surgeons of U. Pacific, Acad. Gen. Dentistry, Honolulu County Dental Soc., U.S. Air Force Assn., C. of C. Hawaii, Tri Beta Biol. Honor Soc., Delta Sigma Delta. Clubs: Honolulu, Mercedes of Am. Office: 1441 Kapiolani Blvd Suite 708 Honolulu HI 96814

TSHIMBALANGA, KASONGO MUKKENDI, import-export company executive; b. Kasansa, Kasai Orient, Zaire, July 18, 1940; s. Kapongo and Kanjinga (Mbombo) Tambwe; m. Mamina Mona Mamina, Oct. 8, 1983; children: Kanjinga, Tshimanga, Kamwanya, Mukendi, Kabemba, Tambwe, Mabuku, Kalonji, Ngomba, Mbombo, Tshiabu. Grad. in Commerce, Institut Superieur Commerciale, Kinshasa, Zaire, 1971. Fin. dir. SODIMCA,

Kinshasa, 1965-87; adminstrv. dir. PAPEZA sarl, Kinshasa, 1972-87; assoc. mgr. SIECO sprl, Kinshasa, 1982—, 1987—. Decorated bronze, silver and gold medal Merite Civil, gold medal merite Sport (Kinshasa). Mem. Aneza C. of C., Comite Prof. Imprim. Aneza (pres. 1982-87, gold medal 1985), Fedn. Zaioise Football (pres. 1975-76). Lodge: Rotary. Address: BP 8342, Kinshasa Zaire

TSIRPANLIS, ZACHARIAS, humanities educator; b. Kos, Greece, June 13, 1938; s. Nicolas Tsirpanlis and Kalliopi Klutsi, m. Cathy Sivva, Oct. 23, 1978; children: Kalliopi, Evangelia. MA, U. Thessaloniki, Greece, 1961, PhD, 1968. Asst. prof. U. Thessaloniki, 1965-70, keeper hist. archives, 1970-72; assoc. prof. U. Ioannina, Greece, 1972-75, prof., 1975—. Author: Cardinal Bessarion's Bequest, 1967, The Macedonian Students in Rome, 1971, Documents from Vatican Archives, 1973, The Greek College in Rome, 1980, Register of the Venetian Candia, 1985. Mem. Soc. Macedonian Studies, Soc. Slavic Studies, Soc. Greek Historians, Cyprus Research Ctr., Inst. for Balkan Studies. Home: Mitropoleos 26, 546 24 Thessaloniki Greece Office: U Ioannina, Ioannina Greece

TSITLIK, JOSHUA E., biomedical engineer, educator; b. Zhitkovichi, Belorussia, USSR, Nov. 22, 1939; came to U.S., 1976; s. Anatoli and Dina (Kunda) T.; m. Victoria Plaks, Jan. 6, 1968; 1 child, Ann. M.S. in Elec. Engring., Leningrad Poly. Inst., USSR, 1964, Ph.D. in Elec. Engring., 1972; M.S. in Clin. Engring., Johns Hopkins Sch. Medicine, 1980. Various positions in engring. and metrology, USSR, 1964-76; research asst., assoc. Johns Hopkins U. Sch. Medicine, Balt., 1977-80, instr. biomed. engring. and medicine, 1980-84, asst. prof., 1984—. Translation editor Jour. of Engring. Cybernetics, 1982-84; cons. editor (jour.) Medical Electronics, 1988—; guest editor Annals of Biomed. Engring., 1987; author of abstracts, book chpt., articles. Patentee in field. Bd. dirs. Levindale Hebrew Geriatric Ctr. and Hosp., Balt. 1982-84. NIH grantee, 1984. Mem. IEEE (sr., chmn. Balt. chpt. Engring. in Medicine and Biology 1986-88), Biomed Engring Soc., Cardiovascular System Dynamics Soc. Democrat. Jewish. Lodge: B'nai B'rith. Home: 121 Northway Rd Reisterstown MD 21336

TS'O, PAUL ON-PONG, biophysical chemist, educator; b. July 17, 1929. B.S., Lingnan U., 1949; M.S., Mich. State U., 1951; Ph.D., Calif. Inst. Tech., 1955. Teaching asst. Calif. Inst. Tech., 1952-55, research fellow biology div., 1955-61, sr. research fellow, 1961-62; assoc. prof. biophys. chemistry dept. radiol. scis. Johns Hopkins U., Balt., 1962-67; prof. Johns Hopkins U., 1967-73; prof., dir. div. biophysics Johns Hopkins U. Sch. Hygiene and Pub. Health, 1973—, prof. dept. environ. health scis. div. environ. health biology, 1980—; cons. Nat. Cancer Inst., 1972-75; mem. study sect. A on biophysics and biophys. chemistry NIH, 1976-80; mem. Clearinghouse on Environ. Carcinogens, Nat. Cancer Inst., 1976-80; mem. European expert com. on biophysics UNESCO. Editor: Basic Principles in Nucleic Acid Chemistry, Vol. I and II, 1974, The Molecular Biology of the Mammalian Genetic Apparatus, Vol. I and II, 1977; co-editor: The Nucleohistones, 1964, Chemical Carcinogenesis, Part A and Part B, 1974, Polycyclic Hydrocarbons and Cancer: Environment, Chemistry and Metabolism; and Molecular and Cell Biology, Vol. 1 and 2, 1978, Vol. 3, 1981, Carcinogenesis: Fundamental Mechanisms and Environmental Effects, 1980, Interrelationship Among Aging, Cancer and Differentiation, 1985, Structure and Function of the Genetic Apparatus, 1986; mem. editorial bd. Molecular Pharmacology, 1964—, Biophys. Jour, 1969-72, Biochimica et Biophysica Acta, 1971-81, Cancer Rev, 1973—, Jour. Environ. Health Scis, 1976-81; asso. editor: Cancer Research, 1975-87; mem. editorial adv. bd.: Biochemistry, 1966-74, Biopolymers, 1979—; contbr. over 300 articles and revs. to profl. jours. Named Md. Chemist of Yr., 1981; named One of 1000 Most Cited Scientists, Citation Index, 1965-78. Fellow AAAS; mem. Biophys. Soc. (chmn. public sci. policy com. 1972-76, council mem. 1975-78, exec. bd. 1975), Am. Soc. Biol. Chemists, Am. Soc. Microbiology, Am. Soc. Cell Biology, Biology Alliance for Public Affairs (chmn. organizing com. 1973-76), Am. Assn. Cancer Research, Am. Chem. Soc., Academia Sinica, European Acad. Arts, Scis. and Humanities, Sigma Xi. Office: Johns Hopkins U Div Biophysics Sch Hygiene and Pub Health Baltimore MD 21205

TSOKHAS, KOSMAS, economics researcher, author; b. Melbourne, Victoria, Australia, Oct. 4, 1953; s. John and Malama (Karikios) T; m. Helen Margaret Lang. BA with honors, U. Melbourne, 1976, MA, 1979, PhD, 1982. Tutor U. Melbourne, 1976, sr. tutor, 1977, lectr., 1978; postdoctoral fellow Australian Nat. U., Canberra, 1983-85, research fellow, 1986—. Author: A Class Apart, 1984, Beyond Dependence, 1986. Home: 54 Ballarat St Fisher, Canberra 2611, Australia Office: Australian Nat U, PO Box 4, Canberra 2601, Australia

TSOTSOROS, STATHIS, economist, management executive; b. Nafpactos, Greece, Apr. 22, 1949; s. Nicolaos and Julia (Mandelos) T.; m. Helen Harissis, Feb. 24, 1974; children: Nicolaos, Dimitris. MS in Elec. Engring., Nat. Tech. U., Athens, 1972; BS in Econs., U. Athens, 1978; PhD in Econs., Pantios Sch. Polit. Scis., AThens, 1982. Registered profl. engr. Dist. engr. Pub. Power Corp., Arcadia, Greece, 1974-75, head tech. sector, 1975-76; dist. dir. Pub. Power Corp., Arcadia-Argolis, 1976-81; dir. by gov. Pub. Power Corp., Athens, 1983-84; cons. Ministry of Energy, Greece, 1981-83; v.p. and governing council in charge Econ. Affairs Fin. and Mining Trust, Athens, 1984-85; v.p. and mng. dir. Bus. Reconstrn. Orgn., Athens, 1984-86; v.p. exec. com., dir. gen. Orgn. for Planning and Environ. Protection of Athens, 1986—; cons. Hellenic Agy. for Local Govt. and Devel., Athens, 1987—; chmn. 5-yr. plan formulation com. Ministry of Energy and Natural Resources, Greece, 1982-87, chmn. 5-yr. plan formultation com. of Ministry of Nat. Economy, Attica Region, 1988—. Author: Economic and Social Mechanisms in the Highland Regions (1715-1828), Problematic (financially unstable) Industrial Enterprises and Public Law N. 1386/83; contbr. articles to profl. jours. Served as cpl. Army, Greece, 1972-73. Grantee Comml. Bank of Greece, 1984, Nat. Bank of Greece, 1987. Mem. Panhellenic Soc. Mech. and Elec. Engrs., Tech. Chamber of Greece, Econ. Chamber of Greece. Hellenic Socialist Party. Greek Orthodox. Home: 47 Ventouri St, 15562 Cholargos, Athens Greece Office: OPEPA, 30 Fokionos Negri, 11361 Athens Greece

TSU, JOHN B., university administrator; b. China, Dec. 1, 1924; s. Tsu Kwei and Tsu Cheng-shih; m. Susan Fu, Jan. 22, 1966. LL.B., Imperial U., Tokyo, Japan, 1943; M.A., Georgetown U., 1949; Ph.D., Fordham U., 1953. Prof. polit. sci., co-dir. Inst. Far Eastern Studies, Seton Hall U., 1958-60; prof. Inst. Far Eastern Studies, Seton Hall U. (Asian Studies), dir. inst., 1960-77; dir. Inst. Far Eastern Studies, Seton Hall U. (Carnegie Chinese and Japanese program), 1961-77, dir. internat. studies, 1974-77; dir. Nat. Def. Lang. Inst., 1963-65, Chinese Dictionary Project, 1965-66; prof. and dir. Multicultural Inst.; spl. asst. to pres. U. San Francisco, 1977-83; founder, dir. Asian-Pacific Inst., John F. Kennedy U., 1985—; also dir. John F. Kennedy U. in Japan, 1987—; vis. prof. East-West Ctr., U. Hawaii, 1966; pioneer in introducing Chinese and Japanese in Am. secondary schs.; mem. univ. seminar on China, Columbia U.; exec. sec. Sino-Am. Amity, 1953-55; cons. Ctr. for 20th Century Studies, U. Wis., 1969—; dir. Chinese/Japanese-English Bilingual Inst., U.S. Office Edn.-Seton Hall U., 1974-77; advisor Asian Am. Assembly, CCNY, 1977-83; vis. scholar Hoover Instn., Stanford U., 1983-85; commr. Edn. Commn. of the States, 1983—. Author: Sino-Soviet Relations, 1949-1952, 1953, The World of Asia, 1966; contbr. to: Funk & Wagnalls Ency; articles to profl. jours. Mem. Pres.'s Nat. Adv. Council on Edn. for Disadvantaged Children, 1971-73; mem. Nat. Adv. Council on Ethnic Heritage Studies, HEW 1975-80; trustee Dhara Realm U., 1977—; mem. Calif. Gov's Transition Adv. Com., 1982-83, Calif. Gov.'s Adv. Council, 1983—. Mem. Am. Assn. UN (chmn. ednl. com. Newark chpt. 1964-66, chpt. trustee), Chinese Lang. Tchrs. Assn. (chmn. 1967-69), Assn. Japanese Lang. Tchrs. (exec. com.), Am. Polit. Sci. Assn., Assn. Asian Studies, MLA, Am. Assn. Internat. Law, Am. Acad. Polit. and Social Sci. Home: 1366 Manzanita Dr Millbrae CA 94030 Office: John F Kennedy U 12 Altarinda Rd Orinda CA 94563

TSUCHIYA, SUMA, artist; b. Ueno, Mie, Japan, Feb. 12, 1924; d. Hinomatsu and Kachi Kawase; m. Kimio Tsuchiya, Jan. 25, 1950 (dec. Aug. 1984) 1 child, Kiyoharu. Degree in teaching, Mie U., Tsu, 1945. Pres. Suma Bright Art Inst., Osaka, Japan, 1968—; lectr. Osaka Arts Coll., Japan, 1982—. Author: The World of Brilliant Image Art, 1988; patentee in field. Recipient Japan Display Design prize Japan Display Design Assn., 1978, Gonstrn. Industry Lighting Design prize Daiko Denko, 1979, 17th Internat. Art Exhbn. award The Mainichi News Papers, 1988. Mem. Designers Assn., Artists, Architects and Industrialists Assn., Lighting Acad. Circles, Salon de Finale Assn. (Salon de Internat. Art Exhbn. prizes 1985, 86, 87, 88). Mem. Liberal Democratic Party. Buddhist. Home and Office: Suma Bright Art Inst, 2-10-14 Sugimoto, Sumiyoshi-ku, Osaka 558, Japan

TSUJI, TAKESHI, electronics company executive; b. Osaka, Osaka Prefecture, Japan, May 21, 1943; parents: Tasaburo Okada and Seiko Tsuji; m. Ieko Nishida, Apr. 13, 1965; children: Daisuke, Yoko, Kaori. Grad. in English Literature, Kansai Foreign Lang. U., Osaka, 1965. Cert. engr. Sales mgr. Signode Nippon Ltd., Kobe, Japan, 1975-80; mktg. mgr. Signode K.K., Kobe, 1980-85, dir., gen. mgr., 1985-87; pres., chief exec. officer KKEMS Inc., Osaka, 1988—; mng. dir. K.K. Eiko, Osaka, 1988—; pres. Indentification Tech. Inst., Kobe, 1986—. Mem. Automatic Identification Mfrs. Assn., Tech. Transfer Inst., Automotive Industry Action Group. Home: 8-3-8 Kasugadai Nishiku, 673-02 Kobe, Hyogo Japan Office: KKEMS, Elcoh Bldg 5F, 1-18-15 Esaka-Cho, Suita City 564, Japan

TSUJII, KAZUMASA, steel company executive; b. Hyogo, Japan, Oct. 15, 1927; s. Sakuna and Kikuno T.; m. Akemi Maeda, Jan. 26, 1953; children: Kazuhide, Michiko. BS in Mech. Engring., Kobe Tech. Coll., 1949. With Nakayama Steel Works, Ltd., Osaka, 1949-77; dir. Nakayama teel Works, Ltd., Osaka, 1977-83, mng. dir., 1983-87, sr. mng. dir., 1987—; bd. dirs. The Iron and Steel Inst. Japan, 1982-83. Patentee coil inventions. Served as officer Japanese Navy, 1943-45, Hiroshima. Mem. Kansai Econ. Fedn. Sodo Buddhist. Home: 3-27-6, Habikigaoka, Habikino, Osaka Japan 583 Office: Nakayama Steel Works Ltd, 1-66, 1-chome, Osaka Taisho-ku 551, Japan

TSUKAZAKI, SEIKI, licensing practitioner; b. Hiroshima, Japan, Jan. 4, 1911; s. Giichi and Fumi (Takatsuki) T.; m. Fusa Otaguro, Nov. 21, 1935; children: Yoko, Mikiko. BS, Rikkyo U., Japan, 1935. Clk. Furukawa Electric Industry and Towa Paint, Tokyo, 1935-38; chief dir. Shandon (People's Republic China) Fertilizer Import & Distbn. Control Assn., 1938-043; mng. dir. Mitami Aeronautical Devices Research Inst., Nagano Prefecture, 1944-45; rep. Licensing Service Ctr., Tokyo, 1957—; adadvisor Hihon Kogyo Shimbum, Tokyo, 1965-67; bd. dirs. Tokai Water Analysis & Control Office. Contbr. articles to profl. jours. Fellow Inst. Internat. Licensing Practitioners; mem. Japan Assn. Future Research. Episcopalian. Home: 1-3-5 Sakuragaoka Kugenuma, Kanagawa-ken 251, Fujisawa City Japan Office: Licensing Service Ctr 25-12, Toranomon 1-chome, Minato-ku, Tokyo 105, Japan

TSUKIO, YOSHIO, architectural educator; b. Nagoya, Aichi, Japan, Apr. 26, 1942; s. Kenzo and Miyoko Tsukio; m. Takako Tsukamoto, May 2, 1970 (div. Apr. 1987). BA, U. Tokyo, 1965; MS, 1967, PhD, 1978. Lic. architect. Pres. Urban Systems Inc., Tokyo, 1972-75; sr. researcher Leisure Devel. Ctr., Tokyo, 1975-76; assoc. prof. Nagoya U., Japan, 1976-88, prof., 1988—. Author: Realised Utopias, 1980, City as A System, 1981, Business Environments in the Age of Information, 1987, Restructuring of Construction Industry, 1988. Named Honorable Citizen, City of Balt., 1980. Mem. Archtl. Inst. of Japan, City Planning Inst. of Japan, Ops. Research Soc. of Japan, Japanese Soc. for Artificial Intelligence. Office: Nagoya Univ, Furo-Cho, Nagoya, Aichi Chikusa-ku 464, Japan

TSUKIOKA, MITSUKO (HSIU-JEN LIU), commercial firm executive; b. Taipai, Taiwan, Republic of China, Mar. 22, 1940; came to Japan, 1965.; s. Tien and Shao (Lin) Liu; m. Yasunori Matsumura, Sept. 24, 1959; children: Lie-Jun, Kan-Li, Lie-Shin, Chien-Chia. BBA, Lincoln U., San Francisco, 1984. With Japan Showa Kosan Co., Ltd., Tokyo, 1966-73, Sanshi Co., Ltd., Tokyo, 1973-80; pres. So An Co., Ltd., Taipei, Taiwan, 1979—, Sanwa Shoji Co., Ltd., Tokyo, 1980—; exec. Pres. Ent. Corp., 1975—, Ky. Fried Chicken, Taiwan, 1980—. Recipient 30th Anniversary medal and Letter of Appreciation, Magistrate of Nan-Tao Prefecture, Taiwan, 1981, Social Service Silver medal, Minister of Interior, Taiwan, 1982, Hua-Hsia medal, Pres. of Republic of China, 1987, others. Home: Sanwa Bldg 4th Floor, 4-21-4 Ryohgoku, Sumida-ku, Tokyo 130, Japan Office: Sanwa Shoji Co Ltd, 1-20-1 Shinkawa, Chuo-ku, Tokyo 104, Japan

TSUNASHIMA, KUNIO, executive recruiting consultant; b. Yokohama, Japan, Feb. 28, 1949; s. Tatsuo and Hisae T.; m. Shigeko, Aug. 27, 1975; children: Takako, Asako. BA, Keio U., Tokyo, 1971; MBA, U. Pa., 1974. Chief staff corp. planning dept. Nomura Securities Co., Ltd., Tokyo, 1971-78; mgmt. cons. McKinsey & Co., Ltd., Tokyo, 1978-86; mng. dir., Japan br. mgr. Russell Reynolds Assocs., Inc., Tokyo, 1986—. Author: (with others) Growth Strategy for the Mature Industry, 1980, Strategy for Corporate Revolution, 1986. Home: King Homes 61 6-5-36, Minami-Aoyama Minato-ku, Tokyo 107, Japan Office: Russell Reynolds Assocs Inc, Time & Life Bldg, 17th Floor, 3-6 Otemachi 2-chome Chiyoda-ku, Tokyo 100, Japan

TSUNEYOSHI, TADAO, bearings manufacturing executive; b. Kamakura, Kanagawa, Japan, Feb. 18, 1943; s. Tadayasu and Michiko (Sakami) T.; m. Toshiko Tachi, Nov. 12, 1965; children: Rika, Yuki. M of Engring., Tokyo Met. U., 1966, M of Mech. Engring., 1968. Researcher Tsugami Co., Nagaoka/Niigata, Japan, 1968-74; asst. to gen. mgr. Ataka Machine Tool Co., Tokyo, 1974-75; assoc. sales engr. Nihon Timken Kabushiki Kaisha, Tokyo, 1975-77; mgr. Nihon Timken Kabushiki Kaisha, Yokohama, Japan, 1977-85, gen. mgr., rep. dir., 1985—; v.p. Am. Auto Parts Assn. in Japan, 1986-88, pres. 1988—. Mem. Japan Soc. Precision Engring. Club: Izawa Tennis Garden (Fujisawa, Japan). Home: B-5-4 Shonan Lifetown, Fujisawa Kanagawa 252, Japan

TSUSHIMA, NOBUKO, internist, cardiologist; b. Yoichi, Japan, May 7, 1937; d. Masayoshi and Matsue (Saito) T. MD, Hokkaido (Japan) U., 1962, PhD, 1967. Intern Hiroo Tokyo Mcpl. Hosp., 1962-63; resident in internal medicine Hokkaido U., 1963-67; staff internal medicine Tonan Hosp., Sapporo, Japan, 1967-72, chief internal medicine, 1972-81; chmn. internal medicine Nat. Cardiovascular Ctr., Suita, Japan, 1982—; chief physician artificial organs dept. Cleve. Clinic, 1976-77. Inventor intravital video microscopic system, 1979. Mem. Cerebro-Vascular Disease Research Assn. (dir. 1979-80), Am. Soc. Microcirculation, European Soc. Microcirculation, Japanese Soc. Microcirculation, Japanese Soc. of Circulation-Internal Medicine-Angiology-Diabetes Mellites and Autonomic Nervous System Disorders. Lodge: Soroptimists (pres. 1979-80, program advisor 1980-82, Golden Gavel 1980). Home: 203 D-10, 3-chome Aoyamadai, Suita Japan 565 Office: Nat Cardiovascular Ctr, 5-7-1 Fujishirodai, Suita 565, Japan

TSUSHIMA, YUKO, novelist; b. Tokyo, Mar. 30, 1947; d. Shuji and Michiko T.; 2 children. B.A., Shirayuri Women's Coll., 1968. Author novels: Child of Fortune (women's lit. award 1978), 1978; Territory of Light (Noma award for new writers 1979), 1979; By the River of Fire, 1983; Silent Trader (Kawabata lit. award 1983), 1984. Mem. Japan Writer's Assn., Lit. Women's Assn. Office: care Japan PEN Club Room 265, 9-1-7 Akasaka Minato-Ku, Tokyo Japan

TSUTSUMI, YOSHIAKI, transportation executive. s. Yasujiro T.; married; 3 children. Owner Seibu Lions Football Team, 1979—; pres. Seibu Ry. Co. Ltd., Tokyo. Office: Seibu Railway Co Ltd, 16-15 Minami Ikebukuro 1-Chome, Toshima-ku, Tokyo 171, Japan *

TSUYOSHI, NAKAMURA, insulation engineer; b. Nagoya, Aichi, Japan, Feb. 12, 1926; s. Mitsushiro and Teruyo Nakamura; m. Toshiko Sato, May 6, 1956; 1 child, Akane. BS, Gakushuin U., Tokyo, 1955. Mem. staff Suzuka (Japan) plant Asahi-Dow Co., 1955-63; mem. research and devel. staff Asahi-Dow Co., Osaka, 1963-65, Tokyo, 1965-66, 71-74; mem. research and devel. lab. staff Asahi-Dow Co., Suzuka, 1966; mgr. Sapporo (Japan) plant Asahi-Dow Co., 1974-76; mem. research and devel. staff Asahi-Dow Co., Tokyo and Sapporo, 1976-82; mem. research and devel. lab. staff Asahi-Chem. Industry Co., Tokyo, Kawasaki, 1966-67, Takatsuki, 1967-71; mgr. Sapporo office Dow-Kakoh Co., 1982-85; mem. research and devel. staff Dow-Kakoh Co., Sapporo, 1982-86; pvt. practice in housing cons. Sapporo, 1986—. Patentee in field; contbr. articles to profl. jours. Pres. Hiroshima Tennis Assn.; mem. Sapporo Tennis Assn. Mem. Northern Regions Ctr. (study soc. 1983—), Study Soc. Window Cold Region House, Archtl. Inst. Japan, Hokkaido Housing Conf. Home and Office: 4-5-4 Hokushin-cho, Sapporo-gun, Hokkaido, Hiroshima-cho 061-11, Japan

TSVETKOV, EVGENY PETROVITCH, geophysicist, writer; b. Velikie-Luky, USSR; arrived in Israel, 1976; s. Peter Simeon and Praskovia Nikonov (Bystrov) T.; m. Fanya Moses Pismen, Aug. 1, 1947; children: Ekaterina, Peter. MSc in Physics, Moscow State U., 1965; PhD in Geophysics, Inst. Earth Physics, Moscow, 1971. Research scientist Inst. Earth Physics Acad. Scis., Moscow, 1965-70, sr. researcher, 1973-74; sr. engr. Inst. Hydroproject, Moscow, 1970-71; sci. editor Znanie-Sila (sci.-lit. mag.), Moscow, 1971-73; research scientist Weizmann Inst. Sci., Rehovot, Israel, 1976-78; vis. prof. geophysics Tel Aviv U., 1980, project chief Sch. Engring., 1982-86; sr. researcher Geophys. Engring. Ormat Turbine, Yavne, Israel, 1980-82; writer Australia, 1986—; chief project geophys. applied turbulence Inst. Chem. Hydrodynamics, CCNY, 1983-85. Author 2 novels and collected stories (in Russian); editor numerous books; contbr. sci. and popular articles to various publs. Mem. PEN. Home: 16 Carroll St, Hughes Canberra ACT 2605, Australia

TU, HO CHUNG, pediatrician-neonatologist; b. Viet-nam, Jan. 1, 1946; came to U.S., 1974; s. Ho Thuc Tu and Vo Thi Cang., m. Tran Hoang Lan; children—Ho Hoang Viet, Ho Viet Dung, Ho Dung Anh. M.D., Vietnam, 1971. Resident, Jamaica-Queen Gen. Hosp. (N.Y.), fellow in neonatology Jackson meml. Hosp./U. Miami (Fla.), 1979-81; dir. neonatology Mt. Sinai Med. Ctr., Miami, 1981—. Inventor exchange-transfusion machine. Vice chmn. Free Vietnamese League, Washington; chief exec. bd. Vietnamese-Am. Republican Heritage Council. Office: Pediatrics Dept Mount Sinai Med Ctr Miami FL 33140

TU, WEI-MING, historian, philosopher, writer; b. Kunming, Yunnan, China, Feb. 26, 1940; came to U.S., 1962, naturalized, 1976; s. Shou-tsin (Wellington) and Shu-li (Sonia Ou-yang) T.; m. Helen I-yu Hsiao, Aug. 24, 1963 (div.); 1 son, Eugene L.; m. Rosanne V. Hall, Mar. 17, 1982; children: A. Yalun, Mariana Mei-ling B. B.A., Tunghai U., 1961; M.A., Harvard U., 1963; Ph.D., 1968. Vis lectr. humanities Tunghai (Taiwan) U., 1966-67; vis. lectr. East Asian studies Princeton U., 1967-68, asst. prof., 1968-71; asst. prof. history U. Calif., Berkeley, 1971-73; assoc. prof. U. Calif., 1973-77, prof., 1977—; vis. prof. Chinese history and philosophy Harvard U., 1981-82, prof. Chinese history and philosophy, 1982—, chmn. com. on study of religion, 1984-87, chmn. dept. East Asian langs. and civilizations, 1988—; vis. prof. dept. philosophy Peking U., 1985; disting. vis. prof. depts. philosophy and history Taiwan U., 1988; mem. joint com. on Chinese studies Am. Council of Learned Socs.; adviser East Asian program Woodrow Wilson Ctr.; gov. Inst. East Asian Philosophy, 1983—; pres. Contemporary Mag., Republic of China, 1986—. Author: Neo-Confucian Thought in Action—Wang Yang-ming's Youth, 1976, Centrality and Commonality—An Essay on Chung-Yung, 1976, Humanity and Self-Cultivation—Essays in Confucian Thought, 1980, Confucian Ethics Today: The Singapore Challenge, 1984, Confucian Thought: Selfhood as Creative Transformation, 1985, The Way, Learning, and Politics: Perspective on the Confucian Intellectual, 1988; editorial bd.: Asian Thought and Soc., 1976—, Harvard Jour. Asiatic Studies, 1983, Philosophy East and West, 1984—; contbr. articles Philosophy East and West, Jour. Asian Studies, Daedalus, The Monist, Chinese lang. jours. and newspapers. Bd. dirs. Chinese Cultural Found., 1978—. Am. Council Learned Socs. fellow, 1968-69; research grantee Center East Asian Studies, Harvard U., 1968-69; research grantee Humanities Council Princeton U., 1970-71; research grantee U. Calif., 1973-74; sr. scholar Com. on Scholarly Communication with People's Republic of China Nat. Acad. Scis., 1980-81; Fulbright-Hays research scholar Peking U., 1985. Fellow Soc. for Study of Value in Higher Edn.; mem. Am. Soc. for the Study Religion, Am. Acad. Arts and Scis., Assn. Asian Studies (dir. 1971-75), Am. Hist. Assn., Soc. Asian and Comparative Philosophy, Am. Acad. Religion, Conf. Study of Polit. Thought, AAAS, Asia Soc. N.Y. (assoc. China Council). Office: Harvard U Dept East Asian Langs and Civilizations Cambridge MA 02138

TUBBS, EDWARD LANE, banker; b. Delmar, Iowa, Apr. 17, 1920; s. Clifton Marvin and Mary Ellen (Lane) T; m. Grace Barbara Dyer, Nov. 27, 1941; children: Steven, Alan, William. BS, Iowa State U., 1941. With Iowa State U. Agrl. Extension Service, Newton, 1942; farm owner and mgr., 1944—; instr. Vets. On-Farm, DeWitt (Iowa) Schs., 1957-58; v.p., dir. Jackson State Bank, Maquoketa, Iowa, 1959-66; chmn., pres., dir., trust officer Maquoketa State Bank, 1966—; pres., dir. Ohnward Bancshares, Inc.; chmn., dir. First Central State Bank, DeWitt; pres., dir. Mabsco Agrl. Services, Inc., 1982-87; supt. banking State of Iowa, 1987—; bd. dirs. Iowa Bankers Ins. Services, Iowa Bus. Growth Corp.; lectr. banking schs.; Exchange del. USSR, 1959-85; hon. dir. Walnut Hill Bank, Living History Farms, 1987—. Pres. Elwood (Iowa) Sch. Bd., 1956-62; treas. City of Maquoketa, 1975-81; mem. People to People; trustee Sharar Found., Clinton Coll., 1983-86; v.p., bd. dirs. Timber City Indsl. Devel. Corp.; treas. Maquoketa Community Services, 1967-80; trustee Iowa 4-H Found., 1987—, Hoover Presdl. Library Assn. Inc. Served with AUS, 1942-43. Recipient 4 H Club Alumni award, 1962, Century Farm award Iowa Dept. Agr., 1976; named Jaycee Boss of Year, 1970; Iowa Agrl. Extension Assn. award, 1982. Mem. Bank Adminstrn. Inst., Am. Bankers Assn. (dir., council 1984-86), Iowa Bankers Assn. (treas. 1978-79, pres. 1980-81), Iowa Transfer System (dir. 1978-81), Iowa Ind. Bankers, Am. Legion, Isaac Walton League, Iowa Cattlemen's Assn., Farm Bur., Iowa State U. Alumni Assn. (dir., Floyd Andre award for Disting. Service to Agriculture 1985), Maquoketa C. of C. (dir. 1966-69), Order of Knoll (Pres.'s Circle Iowa State U.), Internat. Platform Assn., Gamma Sigma Delta, Alpha Zeta. Republican. Mem. United Ch. of Christ. Lodge: Rotary (Paul Harris fellow). Author articles in field. Home: 820 Niles St Maquoketa IA 52060 Office: 203 N Main St Maquoketa IA 52060

TUBBS, JERRY RONALD, university administrator; b. Reed City, Mich., Dec. 12, 1932; s. Roy Walter and Mildred Josephine (Holmquist) T.; m. Lorraine Bertha Grein, Nov. 21, 1953; children: Deborah Michelle, Michael Roy. BS in Acctg., Ferris State Coll., 1961; postgrad., Inst. Ednl. Mgmt., Harvard U., 1973; MA in Ednl. Adminstrn., Cen. Mich. U., 1978. Bus. mgr. Ferris State Coll., Big Rapids, Mich., 1960-63; controller Louvers & Dampers, Inc., Somerset, Ky., 1963-64; internal auditor Cen. Mich. U., Mt. Pleasant, 1964-65, exec. asst. to v.p. bus. and fin., 1965-70, v.p. bus. and fin., 1970—, treas., trustee, 1980—; chmn. Higher Edn. Adminstrn. Referral Service, Washington, 1977-85. Bd. dirs. Isabella County United Way, 1966-74, United Way Mich., 1982-85; mem. supervisory com., bd. dirs. Isabella County (Mich.) Govtl. Employees Credit Union, 1965-70; mem. citizens adv. com. City Mt. Pleasant, 1966-68; treas., chmn. budget com., mem. exec. com. Isabella County Commn. Aging, 1975-79; vice chmn. Isabella County Econ. Devel. Corp., 1978-83; mem. Mid Mich. Devel. Corp., 1982-86; treas., trustee Christ The King Luth. Chapel, 1967-70; mem. bldg. com. Immanuel Luth.Ch., 1982-85; treas. Beal city Bus. Assn., 1982—; sec. Art Reach Mid Mich., 1981-85; bd. dirs. Cen. Mich. U. Devel. Fund, 1980—; Mt. Pleasant Area Vols. for Literacy, 1986-88; sec. 1987-88. Served with USN, 1951-54. Mem. Mich. Assn. Coll. and Univ. Bus. Officers, Nat. Assn. Coll. and Univ. Bus. Officers (bd. dirs. 1986—), Cen. Assn. Coll. and U. Bus. Officers (exec. com. 1983-86), U. Personnel Assn., Nat. Assn. Phys. Plant Adminstrs., VFW (life), Sigma Iota Epsilon. Club: President's (Mt. Pleasant). Home: 591 Fairway Dr Weidman MI 48893 Office: Cen Mich U 133 Warriner Hall Mount Pleasant MI 48859

TUBBY, ROGER WELLINGTON, government administrator, educator; b. Greenwich, Conn., Dec. 30, 1910; s. George Prentiss and Frances Reynolds (Kidder) T.; m. Anne Williams, Mar. 8, 1936; children: Suzanne (Mrs. L. Batra), Jean (Mrs. R. Sherwood), Peter, Brenda (Mrs. J. Chandler). Student, Choate Sch., 1923-29; A.B., Yale U., 1933; postgrad. law sch., London Sch. Econs., 1935-36. Reporter Bennington (Vt.) Banner, 1938-40, mng. editor, 1940-42; info. specialist Bd. Econ. Warfare, 1942-44; dir. info. Fgn. Econ. Adminstrn., 1944-45, asst. to adminstr., 1945; dir. info. Office Internat. Trade, Dept. Commerce, 1945-46; press officer Dept. State, 1945-49, exec. asst. press relations, 1950; asst. press sec. White House, 1950-52; acting press sec. to Pres. Oct.-Dec. 1952, press sec., Dec. 1952; personal asst. to Democratic presdl. candidate, 1956; co-pub. Adirondack Daily Enterprise, Saranac Lake, N.Y., 1953-70, Lake Placid News, 1957-70; faculty Paul Smith's (N.Y.) Coll., 1959-61, dir. devel., 1972-75; dep. commr. ops. and planning N.Y. State Dept. Parks and Recreation, 1975-77; asst. sec. for pub.

affairs Dept. State, 1961-62; ambassador U.S. rep. to European office UN, other internat. agys., Geneva, 1962-69; acting dean, dean acad. relations Fgn. Service Inst., Dept. State, 1969-72; adj. prof. Plattsburgh State U. Del., 1981-82; numerous internat. confs.; mem. Gov.'s Commn. Sports and Winter Olympics; gov.'s rep. to 1980 Winter Olympics; exec. dir. North Country Econ. Council; chmn. Olympic Accommodations Corp.; dir. Key Bank, Saranac Lake, N.Y., Champlain Valley Physicians' Hosp., Plattsburgh, N.Y., Biotechnology Corp., Lake Placid; News dir. Dem. Nat. Com., 1960; Dem. candidate for Congress from 30th N.Y. Dist., 1974. Trustee Trudeau Inst., Potsdam Coll. Found.; trustee emeritus Coll. of Atlantic, Bar Harbor, Maine; chmn. Fgn. Policy Council, Lake Placid; pres. Adirondack North Country Assn.; bd. dirs. Adirondack Conservancy; chmn. Com. on the Adirondacks; past pres., dir. Adirondack Park Assn.; mem. N.Y. State Com. on Acad.-Industry Relations; chmn. Gov.'s Tourism Adv. Council; mem. Gov.'s Task Force on Revitalized Area Devel.; chmn. adv. com. Adirondack North Country Assn. Recipient Disting. Service awards SUNY-Plattsburg, SUNY-Potsdam; Paul Harris fellow Rotary Internat. Mem. Acad. Polit. Sci., Com. on the Present Danger, Council Am. Ambassadors, Am. Fgn. Service Assn. Home: Trudeau Rd Saranac Lake NY 12983

TUBIANA, MAURICE RENÉ, oncologist; b. Constantine, Algeria, Mar. 25, 1920; s. S. and Fortunée (Nathan) T.; m. Monique Peindarie, June 3, 1953; 1 child, Catherine. MD, Paris U., 1945, MA in Physics and Math., 1946. Intern Paris U. Hosp., 1946-50; assoc. prof. biophysics Paris U., 1952-62, prof. radiotherapy, 1962—; chief lab. isotopes Inst. Gustave-Roussy, Villejuif, France, 1952-59, chief radiation dept., 1959-76, dep. dir. in charge sci. research, 1976-82, dir., 1982—; cons. WHO, Geneva, 1962—, IAEA, Vienna, Austria, 1962—. Author: Le Refus du Réel, 1977; contbr. over 300 articles to profl. jours. Served with French Army, 1940-44. Decorated Legion of Honor; recipient I.H. Gray medal, 1981, Breur medal, 1985. Mem. Internat. Soc. Radiation Oncology (pres. 1977-81), Internat. Soc. Radiology (pres. 1986—), French Acad. Sci., French Acad. Medicine. Home: 53 Bis, Quai des Grands Augustins, 75006 Paris France Office: Inst Gustave-Roussy, 39 Rue Camille Desmoulins, 94800 Paris France

TUCAPSKY, ANTONIN, composer, conductor, educator; b. Opatovice, Czechoslovakia, Mar. 27, 1928; s. Vaclav and Josefa (Sirkova) T.; student Janacek Acad. Music, Brno, 1950-51; student Masaryk U., Brno, 1947-51, Ph.D., 1969; m. Beryl Musgrave, Oct. 13, 1972. Prof. music, Tchrs. Tng. Coll., Novy Jicin, 1955-59; lectr. music pedagogical faculty Ostrava U., 1959-73; condr. Moravian Tchrs. Choir, Czechoslovakia, 1964-73; lectr. music theory and composition Trinity Coll. Music, London, 1975—; compositions include: In Honorem Vitae, Lauds (choral), 1977, The Time of Christmas, Before Trees Stir, (choral), 1978, The Sacrifice cantata, 1977, Missa Serena oratorio, 1979, Pocket Music-Wind Quintet, Four Dialogues clarinet and piano, 1979, Comoedia Cantata, 1982, Suite for Oboe and Piano, 1983, Sonata for Classical Guitar, 1984. Sonata per Violino Solo, 1985, Veni, Sancte Spiritus (choral), 1985, The Undertaker opera, 1987. Mem. Composers Guild Gt. Britain, Royal Soc. Musicians Gt. Britain, Czechoslovak Soc. Arts and Scis. Author: Janacek's Male Choruses, 1971; recording artist: Supraphon, 1969, Bediver Records Ltd., 1979. Home: 50 Birchen Grove, London NW9 85A, England

TUCHMAN, BARBARA WERTHEIM, historian, writer; b. N.Y.C., Jan. 30, 1912; d. Maurice and Alma (Morgenthau) Wertheim; m. Lester R. Tuchman, 1940; children: Lucy, Jessica, Alma. B.A., Radcliffe Coll., 1933; D.Litt., Yale U., Columbia U., Harvard U., Brown U., N.Y. U., Norte Dame U., Smith Coll., William and Mary Coll., Darmouth Coll. Research asst. Inst. Pacific Relations, N.Y.C., 1934, Tokyo, 1935; editorial asst. The Nation, N.Y.C., 1936, Spain, 1937; staff writer War in Spain, London, 1937-38; Am. corr. New Statesman and Nation, London, 1939; with Far East news desk, OWI, N.Y.C., 1944-45; Jefferson lectr., 1980. Author: The Lost British Policy, 1938, Bible and Sword, 1956, The Zimmerman Telegram, 1958, The Guns of August, 1962 (Pulitzer prize), The Proud Tower, 1966, Stilwell and the American Experience in China, 1971 (Pulitzer prize), Notes from China, 1972, A Distant Mirror, 1978, Practising History, 1981, The March of Folly, 1984, The First Salute, 1988; contbr. to Fgn. Affairs, N.Y. Times, others. Trustee Radcliffe Coll., 1960-72, N.Y. Public Library, 1980—. Decorated Order Leopold 1st class Belgium. Fellow Am. Acad. Arts and Letters (pres. 1978-80), Smithsonian Council, AAAL (Gold medal for history 1978); mem. Authors Guild (treas.), Authors League (council), Soc. Am. Historians (pres. 1971-73). Club: Cosmopolitan. Home: Cos Cob CT 06807 Office: care Russell & Volkening 50 W 29th St New York NY 10001

TUCHMAN, SIDNEY, drycleaning company executive, seminar leader; b. Indpls., July 28, 1924; s. Sam and Pearl (Friedman) T.; married; children: Mitchell, Ellen, Kathy. Student, Rose Poly. Inst., 1943-44. Ptnr. Tuchman Cleaners, 1947-60, pres., 1960—; co-founder Apparelmaster; dir. Johson Group Inc.; pres. and founder Tuchman Tng. Systems; cons., guest lecturer Ind. U. and Purdue U.; tng. cons. United Way; conducted workshops Deloitte Haskins & Sells, Holiday Inn, Hilton Hotels, Merchants Nat. Bank, Sta. WRTV (McGraw-Hill), Dial One franchising cos., Blue Cross and numerous others; keynote speaker Apparelmaster Conv., Atlanta, 1981, Australian and N.Z. Drycleaners Assn., 1981. Author: (audio cassettes and books) How to Attract and Hold Customers and Clients, Professional Selling Power; contbr. articles to profl. jours. V.p. Better Bus. Bur., Indpls., 1973, Jewish Welfare Fedn., Indpls., 1969; pres. Indpls. Hebrew Congregation, 1977-78; chmn. Block Forum Series, 1987—. Served with Signal Corps, U.S. Army, 1943-46. Recipient Spirit of Service award Nat. Inst. Dry Cleaners, 1966, 68, 69; Nat. award Am. Inst. Laundering, 1974, Spirit of Life award City of Hope Hosp., 1983. Mem. Indpls. Cleaners and Launderers (pres. 1973-74), Ind. Drycleaners and Launderers Assn. (pres. 1978-79), Internat. Rountable of Drycleaners (pres. 1979-80, Best Ann. Presentation award 1981), Inst. Ind. Launderers, Internat. Fabricare Inst., Am. Mgmt. Assn. Jewish. Clubs: Broadmoor Country, Kiwanis. Home and Office: 8145 Ridley Ct Indianapolis IN 46260

TUCK, JIM MARSHALL, author, editor; b. Geneva, July 24, 1925; s. Somerville Pinkney and Beatrice Mitchell (Beck) Fahnestock T.; m. Mary Chase Nicholson, Oct. 13, 1956 (div. 1960); children: Katherine Dorsey Marshall; m. Maria Cruz Ruiz, Mar. 14, 1984. BA in History, Princeton U., 1951. Regional editor Fodor's Modern Guides, N.Y.C., 1970-83; book critic Travelmex, Guadalajara, Mex., 1985—. Author: The Holy War in Los Altos, 1982, Pancho Villa and John Reed, 1984, Engine of Mischief: An Analytical Biography of Karl Radek, 1988; contbr. articles, book revs. and short stories to profl. jours. Mem. Ams. for Dem. Action, 1981—. Served with USMCR, 1943-46, 52-54. Recipient Francisco Zarco prize, Mexican Tourism Council, 1968, Diploma of Honor, Romanian Govt., Bucharest, 1980, Huesped Distinguido, State Jalisco, Mex., 1985. Mem. Travel Writers Orgn. (v.p. 1987-88), Soc. Southwestern Authors, ACLU, Am. Legion. Unitarian-Universalist. Club: Princeton (N.Y.C.). Home and Office: Apartado Postal 31-548, CP45050 Guadalajara, Jalisco Mexico

TUCK, MURRAY, accountant, insurance company executive; b. Bklyn., Nov. 12, 1920; s. Samuel and Rose (Green) T.; grad. with honors Pace Inst. Sch. Acctg., N.Y.C., 1945; student Pace Inst. Ins., 1949-50; m. Leah Samuels, Aug. 6, 1971; 1 child by previous marriage, Susan (Mrs. R. Greenbaum), stepchildren—Edward Schultz, Charlotte (Mrs. K. Hoek), Larry Schultz. Jr. Acct., Morris Traum & Co., C.P.A.s, Bklyn., 1938-39; jr. acct. Mathew Weiss & Co., C.P.A.s, Bklyn., 1939-40, supervising sr. acct., 1940-45; asst. dept. head internal audit dept. United Mchts. and Mfrs., Inc., N.Y.C., 1945-52; comptroller TransRadio Press Service, Inc., N.Y.C., 1952-57, Bus. Factors, Inc., N.Y.C., 1957-62; pvt. practice acctg., Farmingdale, N.Y., 1950—; prin. Murray Tuck, ins. broker, Farmingdale, 1950—; ins. cons. Assn. for Help of Retarded Children, Inc., Nassau, N.Y., 1965—, Suffolk, N.Y., 1967—; mem. C.W. Post Coll. Fin. Planning Inst., 1980. Pres., Farmingdale Sr. High Sch. PTA, 1963-65; chmn. Farmingdale Community Scholarship Fund, 1962-67; sec., v.p. Group for Childrens Welfare, Central Islip, N.Y., 1961-65; treas. Farmingdale Little League Assn., 1956—; treas. Farmingdale Youth Council, Inc., 1956—; founder and donor Farmingdale Community award, 1962-65, Farmingdale Fireman award, 1962-65; co-committeeman Farmingdale Salvation Army, 1960-61; mem. Farmingdale Adult Edn. Adv. Com., 1955-60; mem. Farmingdale Police Aux., 1960-70; air raid warden, Farmingdale, 1944-50; notary pub. N.Y., 1960; Republican committeeman, Farmingdale, 1966-76; bd. dirs. Advancement for Commerce and Industry, Inc., pres., 1971-73, bd. dirs., 1974-78. Recipient Farmingdale Classroom Tchrs. Honor award 1963, cert. of appreciation Farmingdale CAP, 1964, Disting. Service plaque Advancement for Commerce and Industry, 1972, 74, cert. of service Farmingdale Youth Council, 1964, cert. of merit N.Y. Gov. Rockefeller. 1961, Village of Farmingdale, 1981; Citizen of Yr. award Kiwanis-Lions-Rotary Club, 1981, Congress U.S. Proclamation, 1981, Oyster Bay citation, 1980, 81, numerous other awards for community service; accredited in accountancy and taxation Nat. Accreditation Council; enrolled to practice with U.S. Treasury Dept. Mem. Nat. Soc. Pub. Accts., Nat. Assn. Ins. Agts., Empire State Accts. Assn., C.W. Post Coll. Tax Practicioners Forum, Nat. Assn. Enrolled Agts. Jewish. Editor: ARC Lamplighter, 1965-69; contbr. numerous articles on ins. and taxes to various publs. Home and Office: 670 Conklin St Farmingdale NY 11735

TUCKER, CHARLES RAY, metalworking company executive, sales and service engineer; b. Somerset, Ky., Jan. 18, 1950; s. Arthur William and Mildred Gladys (Taylor) T.; m. Charlotte Ann Wood, July 26, 1969; children—Shawn Dell, Ryan Scott. Student, U. Cin., 1968-70; grad. engring. program Cin. Milacron, 1970. Registered mech. engr., Ky., Miss. Asst. engring. lab mgr. Tecumseh Products Co., Somerset, Ky., 1971-76, engring. lab mgr., Tupelo, Miss., 1977-82; tech. sales mgr. Cin. Milacron, Grand Prairie, Tex., 1982-84; sales rep. E.F. Houghton & Co., Valley Forge, Pa., 1984—; lectr. in field. Named So. Div. Performer of Year E.F. Houghton & Co., 1985. Mem. Somerset-Pulaski County Jaycees (bd. dirs. 1976). Democrat. Baptist. Avocations: golf; fishing; hunting; travel.

TUCKER, FLORENCE DENSLOW, writer, retired government official; b. Greenville, Miss., Nov. 12, 1925; d. Victor Amos and Martha Buchannan (Binkley) Denslow; m. Joseph Nathaniel Tucker Jr., Nov. 9, 1946 (dec.); children: Joseph Nathaniel III, Frederick Steven, James Denslow; m. Noel Francis Parrish, June 25, 1983 (dec. Apr. 1987). Diploma piano, Ward-Belmont Coll., Nashville, 1945; studied piano with Michael Field, N.Y.C., 1945-46; B of Music Edn., Delta State U., Cleveland, Miss., 1960; MS in Counseling, U. So. Miss., 1971; EdD, George Washington U., 1982. Tchr. music Gulfport (Miss.) pub. schs., 1959-63; recreation therapist VA Hosp., Gulfport, 1964-70; edn. counselor USAF, Miss. and Japan, 1971-74, edn. services officer, Republic of Korea, 1974-75, asst. dir. sr. tng. CAP nat. hdqrs., 1975-77; EEO officer D.C. Dept. Labor, 1977-80; bur. chief complaints processing and adjudication Office EEO, U.S. Geol. Survey, Reston, Va., 1980-82, mgr. human resources, Dept. Interior, 1982-84; internat. forum coordinator Pres.'s Com. on Employment of Handicapped, 1985; commr. Alexandria Commn. on Aging, Va., 1985—, chmn. edn. and cultural affairs com., sec., 1987—; vis. prof. Kunsan Tchrs. Coll., Kunsan Jr. Coll., 1974-75; apptd. mem. del. People-to-People Internat. Ambassador Program, Beijing, Peoples Republic China and Hong Kong, 1988; workshop leader, cons. and lectr. in field; bd. dirs. Wake Assocs., Ltd., Washington, 1980-84. Columnist on aging issues, Alexandria (Va.) Gazette-Packet, feature writer, 1988—; contbr. articles to profl. jours. Organizer, pres. Gulfport chpt. Parents-Without-Ptnrs., 1962-64; charter mem. Westminster Presbyn. Ch., Gulfport, 1961; mem. Nat. Council on Aging. Recipient Outstanding Vis. Prof. award Kunsan Tchrs. Coll., 1974, Kunsan Jr. Coll. award for promoting tchr. exchange program, also certs. of commendation. Mem. Women in Communication, Nat. Assn. Female Execs., Am. Soc. Profl. and Exec. Women, NATO Def. Coll. Anciens Assn. U.S., Va. Assn. on Aging, Phi Delta Kappa. Club: The Famous Tuskegee Pilots World War II. Home: Stonehurst 9302 Arlington Blvd Fairfax County VA 22031

TUCKER, GEORGE MCKINLEY, JR., construction company executive; b. Balt., Apr. 7, 1934; s. George McKinley and Carolyn Elizabeth (Simmons) T.; B.E., Johns Hopkins U., 1954; grad. Dale Carnegie course; m. Patricia Jane Smith, Aug. 6, 1955; children—Michael Spencer, Barrett Lee. With Whiting-Turner Contracting Co., Towson, Md., 1957—, div. mgr., 1969-73, v.p., 1973—. Mem. ch. vestry Trinity Episcopal Ch., Long Green, Md., 1971-76, 83—, coordinator youth confirmation program, 1972-84, sr. warden, 1973-76, 86—, jr. warden, 1983-86, head usher, 1978—; coach, mgr. Community Little League Baseball, Optimist Basketball and Football, Jacksonville, Md., 1968-75; active Balt. area council Boy Scouts Am., 1971-74. Served to 1st lt. C.E., U.S. Army, 1955-57. Mem. ASCE, Republican. Episcopalian. Home: 4207 Ravenhurst Cr Glen Arm MD 21057 Office: 300 E Joppa Rd Towson MD 21204

TUCKER, HOWARD MCKELDIN, investment banker, consultant; b. Washington, Apr. 1, 1930; s. Howard Newell and Bessie Draper (McKeldin) T.; B.A., U. Va., 1954; postgrad. NYU Grad. Sch. Bus. Adminstrn., 1956; m. Julia Spencer Merrell, Feb. 1, 1952; children—Deborah, Mark, Alexander, H. David; m. 2d, Megan Evans, Aug. 17, 1979. Investment research J.P. Morgan & Co., N.Y.C., 1954-59; pension investment dept. Morgan Guaranty Trust Co., N.Y.C., 1959-61; registered rep.-analyst Mackall & Coe, Washington, 1962-69; dir. internat. dept., analyst Legg Mason Wood Walker & Co., Washington, 1969-79; with Govt. Research Corp./Nat. Jour., 1979-82, Potomac Asset Mgmt., 1982—; cons. Washington Analysis Corp., 1985—, ; writer London Investment Jour.; dir. Monarch Enterprises, Inc., Uniflight, Inc.; Sci. Mgmt. Assocs., Inc., Jeffrey Bigelow Assocs.; mem. task force on balance-of-payments U.S. Dept. Treasury, 1967—; co-organizer U.S.-Ger. Parliamentary Exchange, 1980-82; observer OECD, 1980-82; spl. overseas visitor Australian Govt., 1982. Trustee Nat. Cathedrala Sch. for Girls, 1972-78; chmn. missionary devel. fund Episcopal Diocese of D.C., 1974; vestryman Christ Episcopal Ch., Georgetown, 1962-65; del. Va. Republican Conv., 1968; co-dir. Andover-Exeter Washington Intern Program, 1976-86; mem., trustee Washington Cathedral chpt., 1966-72; patron West Europe program Woodrow Wilson Ctr., 1985—. Served with USN, 1950-56. Chartered fin. analyst. Mem. Washington Soc. Investment Analysts, Fin. Analysts Fedn., Nat. Economists Club, Cogswell Soc. Clubs: Naval and Mil. (London), Nat. Press, A.K.C., B.O.M.C., Harvard Coop, Georgetown Visitation Tennis, Saints and Sinners. Author: Literature in Medicine. Contbr. articles to fin. jours.; book revs. to Washington Post. Home: 2038 18th St NW Washington DC 20009 Office: 5247 Wisconsin Ave NW Suite 5 Washington DC 20015

TUCKER, JOYCE ELAINE, lawyer, state human rights administrator; b. Chgo., Sept. 21, 1948; d. George M. and Vivian Louise T. B.S., U. Ill., 1970; J.D., John Marshall Law Sch., 1978. Bar: Ill. 1978. Substitute tchr. Chgo. Public Schs., 1970-71; mental health specialist Tinley Park (Ill.) Dept. Mental Health, 1970-74; coordinator Title VII Program, Ill. Dept. Mental Health, Chgo., 1974-76, chief mental health equal employment opportunity officer, 1976-79; acting dir. Ill. Dept. Equal Employment Opportunity, Chgo., 1979-80; dir. Ill. Dept. Human Rights, Chgo., 1980—. Mem. Nat. Bar Assn., Cook County Bar Assn. (Spl. Achievement award 1980), Am. Bar Assn., Chgo. Bar Assn. Mem. African Methodist Episcopal Ch. also: 619 Stratton Office Bldg Springfield IL

TUCKER, MARC STEPHEN, education policy analyst, author; b. Boston, Nov. 15, 1939; s. David Jones and Natalie (Croman) T.; m. Linda Beth Hepler, Sept 27, 1964 (div. 1973); children: Matthew, Joshua; foster child, Julie Beers. AB, Brown U., 1961; MSS, George Washington U., 1982. Lighting dir., camera Sta. WGBH-TV, Boston, 1962-64, asst. dir. edn. div., 1964-66; asst. to pres. Edn. Devel. Ctr., Newton, Mass., 1966-71; asst. dir. NWREL, Portland, Oreg., 1971-72; assoc. dir. Nat. Inst. Edn., Washington, 1972-81; dir. Project on Info. Tech. and Edn., Washington, 1981-84; exec. dir. Carnegie Forum on Edn. and the Econ., Washington, 1985-87; pres. Nat. Ctr. on Edn. and the Economy, Rochester, N.Y., 1988—; prof. edn. U. Rochester, 1988—; staff dir., prin. author Carnegie report-A Nation Prepared: Teachers forthe 21st Century, 1986. Chmn., pres. Brass Chamber Music Soc., Annapolis, Md., 1980-81; mem. bd. advisors Apple Edn. Found., 1984-85, bd. visitors Wake Forest U., 1987—, bd. visitors U. Pitts. Sch. of Edn., 1987—, bd. advisors Bank St. Coll. Edn. Ctr. for Children and Tech., 1987—. Democrat. Home: 429 Cobbs Hill Dr Rochester NY 14610 Office: Nat Ctr on Edn and the Economy Suite 500 39 State St Rochester NY 14614

TUCKER, PAUL WILLIAM, retired petroleum company executive; b. Liberty, Mo., Dec. 21, 1921; s. Nova William and Georgia May (Cuthbertson) T.; m. Beverly Caryl Livingston, June 2, 1943; children: Ann Caryl Tucker Worland, Linda Tucker Smith. B.S., William Jewell Coll., 1942, LL.D., 1968; M.S. in Chemistry, La. State U., 1944; Ph.D. in Chemistry, (George Breon fellow), U. Mo., 1948; postgrad., U. Ill., 1946. Registered profl engr., Okla. Chemist, spectroscopist Tenn. Eastman Corp., Oak Ridge, 1944-46; chemist Phillips Petroleum Co., Bartlesville, Okla., 1948-49; tech. rep. Phillips Petroleum Co., 1949-60, asst. dir. public affairs, 1960-62; mng. dir. U.K. Ltd., London, 1962-68; v.p. gas and gas liquids U.K. Ltd., Europe-Africa, London, 1969-73; v.p. gas and gas liquids public affairs and govt. relations U.K. Ltd., 1973-74; mgr. internat. gas and gas liquids Bartlesville, 1974-78; v.p. gas and gas liquids div., natural resources group 1978-80, v.p. gas and gas liquids group, 1980-85. Contbr. articles to profl. jours. Recipient Disting. Services award N.Mex. Petroleum Industries Com., 1956, Citation of Achievement William Jewell Coll., 1979. Fellow Inst. Petroleum U.K., Instn. Gas Engrs. U.K.; mem. Okla. Soc. Profl. Engrs., Nat. Soc. Profl. Engrs., Am. Chem. Soc., AAAS, Sigma Xi, Alpha Chi Sigma, Phi Lambda Upsilon. Republican. Baptist. Club: Hillcrest Country (Bartlesville).

TUCKER, ROBERT DENNARD, health care products executive; b. Tifton, Ga., July 18, 1933; s. Robert Buck and Ethel Margaret (Dennard) T.; m. Peggy Angelyn Smith, June 23, 1957; children: Robert Barron, Jennifer Lee. BBA, Ga. State U., 1958. With sales and sales mgmt. Johnson & Johnson Inc., New Brunswick, N.J., 1958-68; v.p., gen. mgr. ASR Med. Industries, N.Y.C., 1968-72, Howmedica Suture div. Pfizer Inc., N.Y.C., 1972-75; exec. v.p., chief operating officer R. P. Scherer Corp., Detroit, 1976-79; pres., chief operating officer Scherer Sci. Inc., Atlanta, 1980—, also bd. dirs; chmn., chief exec. officer Scherer Health Care Inc., Atlanta, 1980—, also bd. dirs.; bd. dirs. Nat. Travel Mgmt., Atlanta, Biofor Inc., Waverly, Pa. Pub: Tuckers of Devon, 1983; author, pub.: Descendants of William Tucker of Throwleigh, Devon. Chmn. bd. Health Industries Mfrs. Assn. polit. action com., Washington, 1983-85; trustee, past pres. Ga. Horse Found., Atlanta; trustee Brenau Coll., Gainesville, Ga., 1985—. Served with USN, 1951-54, Korea. Recipient Disting. Service award Brenau Coll., 1987. Mem. Nat. Assn. Mfrs., Health Industries Mfrs. Assn. (bd. dirs. 1979-86, disting. service recognition 1981, 86), Pharm. Mfrs. Assn., Thoroughbred Owners and Breeders Assn. Ky. and Ga. (Man of Yr. 1984). Republican. Methodist. Clubs: Cherokee (Atlanta); Big Canoe (Ga.). Home: 405 Townsend Pl Atlanta GA 30327 Office: Scherer Healthcare Inc 2859 Paces Ferry Rd Suite 590 Atlanta GA 30339

TUCKER, SHERIDAN GREGORY, child psychiatrist, clinical psychopharmacologist; b. Bossier City, La., Feb. 26, 1950; s. William Samuel and Marie Regina (Nevarez) T.; m. Jaylene D. Lambert, Dec. 30, 1977; children—Julia Elizabeth, Elliott Thomas, Oliver Michael. B.S., U. Mo.-Kansas City, 1972; M.D., U. Kans., 1975. Diplomate Am. Bd. Psychiatry and Neurology. Resident in psychiatry U. Kans., Kansas City, 1975-78. chief dept. psychiatry U.S. Army, Ft. Polk, La., 1978-80; fellow dept. psychiatry Kans. U. Med. Ctr., Kansas City, 1980-82, clin. asst. prof., 1984—; staff dir. div. adolescent services Kans. Inst., Olathe, 1985, staff cons., staff dir. Pre-Adolescent Services; child psychiatrist Psychiat. and Psychol. Cons., Prairie Village, Kans., 1985—. Contbr. articles to profl. jours. Served to maj. U.S. Army, 1978-80. Mem. Am. Acad. Child Psychiatry, Am. Acad. Clin. Psychiatrists, Am. Psychiat. Assn., N.Y. Acad. Scis., Assn. Child Psychology and Psychiatry. Republican. Episcopalian. Avocation: computing. Office: Psychiat and Psychol Cons 4121 W 83rd St Suite 150 Prairie Village KS 66208

TUCKER, STEPHEN GUYNN, data processing consultant; b. Atlanta, Aug. 14, 1946; s. Benton Aubry and Marion Lee (Haymore) T.; B.S. with honors in Bus. Edn., U. Ga., 1977; children—Adam, Amber, Carrie. Programmer, analyst Service Bur. Corp., Dallas, 1968-70; devel. programmer, analyst IBM, White Plains, N.Y., 1970-74, systems engr., Atlanta, 1974-77, systems engr., Jacksonville, Fla., 1977-80; mgr. systems programming Advanced Micro Devices Co., Sunnyvale, Calif., 1980-81; dir. data processing services Fla. Associated Services div. Am. Heritage Life Ins. Co., Jacksonville, 1981-82; owner Tucker Enterprises, data processing consulting firm, Jacksonville, 1982-85, Columbia, S.C., 1985—; systems engr. Nat. Advanced Systems, Columbia, S.C., 1985—. Served with USAF, 1969-70. Cert. in data processing Inst. Cert. Computer Profls., also cert. in computer programming (systems). Mem. Data Processing Mgmt. Assn., EDP Auditors Assn., Assn. Systems Mgmt. Home: PO Box 1467 Columbia SC 29202-1467

TUCKER, WANDA HALL, writer; b. Los Angeles, Feb. 6, 1921; d. Frank Walliston and Hazel Gladys (Smith) Hall; AA, Citrus Coll., 1939; m. Frank R. Tucker, Apr. 16, 1943; children—Frank Robert, Nancy Irene. Society editor Azusa (Calif.) Herald, 1939-42, editor, 1942-43; city editor San Marino (Calif.) Tribune, 1943-45; editor Canyon City (Calif.) News, 1953; reporter Pasadena (Calif.) Star-News, 1953-73, city editor, 1973-75, day mng. editor, 1975, mng. editor, 1975-81, sr. mng. editor, 1981-84, dir. internship program, 1976-79, mem. editorial bd., 1982-84; editor, assoc. pub. Foothill Inter-City Newspapers, 1984-86; communications cons., Palm Desert, Calif., 1986—. Mem. rent rev. commn. City of Palm Desert, Calif.; bd. dirs. Silver Spur Ranch Assn. Recipient writing award Calif. Newspaper Pubs. Assn., 1965; named Woman of Year, Pasadena Women's Civic League, 1974, Pasadena chpt. NAACP, 1977, Emer Bates Meml. award, 1981. Mem. Nat. Soc. Newspaper Columnists, Sigma Delta Chi. Clubs: Desert Press; Greater Los Angeles Press (writing awards 1971-72).

TUCKER, WILLIAM E., lawyer, consultant; b. Okla., Sept. 2, 1937; s. Owen and Dixie (Stiles) T.; m. Nancy L. Henkins, Nov. 25, 1956; children—Desiree, Gayle. B.S., S.D. Sch. Mines and Tech., 1956; J.D., Okla. U., 1962. Bar: Okla. 1962, Colo. 1962. With legal dept. J. M. Huber Corp. and Marathon Oil Co., Denver and Tulsa, 1962-65; asst. atty. gen. Colo., 1965-74; ptnr. Tucker & Brown, Denver, 1974-80, Denver and Washington, 1982—; White House counsel, 1980-81; chmn. drafting com. Am. Tort Reform Assn. 1986-87; mem. civil justice model legis. com. Am. Legis. Exchange Council, 1986; chief parliamentarian White House Conf. Small Bus., 1986; mem. internat. observing team to Phillipine elections, 1986; lectr. on civil justice reform; cons. on presdl. transition Korean Govt., 1988. Contbr. articles to profl. jours.; author: Transition Report on the Reagan Transition. State chmn., nat. gen. counsel Young Republicans; active polit. campaigns; officer, bd. dirs. Edison Found.; bd. dirs. Air Force Acad. Found. Inc.; co-chmn. Am. Tort Reform Assn. Legal Commn., 1987—. Served to 2d lt. C.E., U.S. Army, 1958. Methodist. Clubs: Denver Athletic, Racquet World (Denver); Delphi (Washington); Regency Sport and Health (McLean, Va.). Office: Western Fed Savs Bldg Suite 1330 718 17th St Denver CO 80202 Also: 1701 Pennsylvania Ave NW Suite 1000 Washington DC 20006

TUCKWELL, HENRY CLAVERING, mathematics educator; b. Adelaide, Australia, Mar. 17, 1943; s. Eric Clavering Tuckwell and Laura Margaret (Higgins) Richards. BSc, U. Adelaide, 1964, MSc, 1970; MS, U. Chgo., 1973, PhD, 1974. Lectr. U. B.C., Vancouver, Can., 1975-79; asst. prof. UCLA, 1979-80; lectr. Monash U., Melbourne, Australia, 1980-84, sr. lectr., 1985—; vis. assoc. prof. UCLA, 1982, U. B.C., 1983, U. Wash., Seattle, 1986; vis. prof. UCLA, 1987. Author: Introduction to Theoretical Neurobiology Vol. 1 and 2, 1988, Elementary Applications of Probability Theory, 1988, Stochastic Processes in the Neurosciences, 1988; chief editor: Jour. of Theoretical Neurobiology, 1980-87; contbr. 55 articles to profl. jours. Mem. Australian Statis. Soc., Am. Math. Soc., Am. Phys. Soc., Am. Psychol. Assn. (affiliate), Victorian Music Tchrs. Assn. (assoc.). Office: Monash U, Dept Math, Clayton Victoria 3168, Australia

TUCNY, PETR HENRY, architect, industrial aesthetics educator; b. Praha, Czechoslovakia, June 26, 1920; s. Henry and Jarmila (Fott) T.; m. Gita Tucna Mendikova, Feb. 28, 1976; children: Jan Henry, Petr Nicholas, Andrew. Architect, Ceske vysoke uceni technicke, Prague, 1946; M.F.A., Vysoka Skola Umelecko-Prumyslova, Prague, 1948; Ph.D., Carolus U., Prague, 1952, C.Sc. in Esthetics, 1956. Freelance architect, designer, Prague, 1943—; prof. Akademia Sztuk Pieknych, Warsaw, 1961, 62-63; prof. Hochschule Fur Ind. Formgestaltung, Halle/Saale, German Dem. Republic, 1963, 65-66; lectr. prof. Hochschule fur Gestaltung, Ulm, Federal Republic Germany, 1965-68; freelance designer Svaz Ceskych Vytvarnych Umelcu-Praha, Prague; prof. design, indsl. esthetics Hochschule für Bildende Kuenste, Hamburg, 1982—. Chief designer Laboratorni Pristoje, Prague, 1960-76, Belzer Werk, Wuppertal, Federal Republic Germany, 1965-80, Poggenpohl KG, Herford, Federal Republic Germany, 1970—, Stavostroj, Nove Mesto, Czechoslovakia, 1962—, ZTS-Martin, Czechoslovakia, 1976—.

Author: Teoreticke zaklady technicke estetiky, 1951; Princip obraznosti v architekture a v prum. vytvarnictvi, 1954; Fysiologicke zaklady esteticke reakce, 1952; expositions delivered USA, Japan, Finland, France, Italy, Bulgaria, Spain, Belgium, Ireland, Can., India, Vietnam, Hungary, Netherlands, Soviet Union, Sweden, Germany. Mem. Czechoslovak Indsl. Design Orgn. (sec.-gen. 1964-67), Czechoslovak Com. Indsl. Design (pres. 1966-70), Czechoslovak Soc. Tech. Esthetic (pres. 1962-70), Council Czechoslovak Indsl. Design, Czechoslovak Fedn. Fine Artists. Home: Jasna II/16, CS 14700, Prague 4 Czechoslovakia

TUDOR, JAMES CAMERON, diplomat; b. St. Michael, Barbados, Oct. 18, 1918; s. James Arthur and Irene Maguerite (Millar) T. MA, Keble Coll., Oxford, England, 1948. Master history Combermere Sch., Barbados, 1946-49, Queen's Coll., Guyana, 1949-52; master social studies Modern High Sch., Barbados, 1952-61; minister edn. Govt. of Barbados, 1961-67, minister fgn. affairs, 1967-72, 87—, ambassador to France, Holland, Germany, 1972-75, ambassador to UN, 1976; majority leader Senate of Barbados, 1986—. Named Knight Commanders St. Michael and St. George Her Majesty Queen Elizabeth II. Mem. Democratic Labour Party. Office: Ministry of Fgn Affairs, Bridgetown, Saint Michael Barbados

TUĞCU, NEJAT, tourism and hotel company executive, information systems expert; b. Antalya, Turkey, Mar. 27, 1945; s. Cavit Fikri and Ayse (Sapci) T.; m. Seyhan Kozanoğlu, May 26, 1976. BS in CE magna cum laude, Robert Coll., Istanbul, Turkey, 1967; MS in Structures, Cornell U., 1969, PhD in Structures and Theoretical and Applied Mechanics, 1970. Data processing and sr. systems analyst Geiger-Berger Cons., N.Y.C., 1970-72; dep. gen. mgr. computer ctr. Boğazici U., Istanbul, 1972-75, asst. prof. computer sci., 1975-80; dep. gen. mgr. Hisarbank, Istanbul, 1980-83; sr. comml. project mgr. Intes Constrn. and Contracting, Inc., Istanbul, 1983-86; exec. Seven Hills Internat. Tourism, Hotel and Trade, Inc., Istanbul, 1986—; ptnr., prin. Infotek Enformasyon Sistem A.S., Istanbul, 1980-87. Co-editor Master Plan for Istanbul and Marmara Ports, 1974. Fellow Cornell U., 1967-68. Islam. Lodge: Rotary (sec. Istanbul-Findikli chpt. 1982-83, v.p. 1983-84, pres. 1984-85. Home: Mirgün-Istinye Cad, 67 Park Apt Emirgan, Istanbul 80850, Turkey Office: Seven Hills Internat Tourism Hotel and Trade Inc, Gaziumurpasa Cad 38/6, Bimar Plaza Balmucu, Istanbul 80700, Turkey

TU'IPELEHAKE, PRINCE FATAFEHI, prime minister of Tonga; b. Nuku' alofa, b. Tonga, Jan. 7, 1922; s. Vilame Tungi and Salote Tupou III; ed. Newington Coll., Sydney, Australia; Catton Agr. Coll., Queensland, Australia; m. Princess Melenaite Tupou Moheofo; children: Mele Siuilikutapu Kalanivalu-Fotofili, Elisiva Fusipala Hahano Vahai, Sione Ngu Uluvalu Takeivulai Tukuaho, Lavinia Mataotaone Maafu, Ofeina'e he Langi Tuku' aho, Viliami Tupoumalohi Mailefihi Tuku' aho. Vis. agrl. officer, 1944-49; gov. Vava'u, 1949-55, Ha' apai, 1955; minister of lands, 1953; prime minister of Tonga, 1965—, also minister for agr.; chmn. Tonga Commodities Bd. Decorated comdr. Order Brit. Empire. Address: Office of Prime Minister, Nuku'alofa Tonga *

TUITA, SIOSAIA ALEAMOTU'A LAUFILITONGA, deputy prime minister and minister of lands, survey and natural resources of Tonga; b. Lapaha, Tongatapu, Aug. 29, 1920; s. Isileli Tupou and Luseane Halaevalu (Fotofili) T.; m. Fatafehi Vilai Tupou, Oct. 15, 1949; children: Siosaia Ma'ulupekotofa, Tu'ilokomana, Tupou 'Ahome'e Faupula, Tu'ihalafatai. Ed. Tupou Coll., Tonga, Wesley Coll., Auckland, N.Z. Oxford (Eng.) U., 1966. Court interpreter and registrar, Supreme Ct., 1945; asst. sec. Prime Minister's Office, 1954; registar of Supreme Ct., 1954, acting gov. of Vava'u, 1956, gov., 1957; hon. Minister of Lands and Survey & Natural Resources, 1965—, of Police, 1964-65; chmn. Niuafo'ou evacuation, 1965; assumed title of Tuita, 1972; named Condr. of the Brit. Empire by Her Majesty Queen Elizabeth !!, 1977, Baron Tuita of Utungake by His Majesty King Taufa'ahau Tupoy, IV, 1980; chmn. Royal Land Commn. and Nat. Standing Com. on energy; mem. His Majesty Privy Council, His Majesty Cabinet Ministers, Legislative Assembly. Served to lt. officer, Tonga Def. Service, N.Z. Army, 1942-43. Methodist. Club: Helepeku (Tonga). Mem. Tonga Rugby Football Union. Avocations: rugby and cricket. Address: Office of Deputy Prime Minister, PO Box 5, Nuku'alofa Tonga

TUKIAINEN, TURO KAARLO JALMARI, industrial executive; b. Helsinki, Finland, s. Lauri K.J. and Miria Annikki (Lydecken) T.; m. Anne Katrine Arnesen, July 1, 1961; children: Merit, Anne, Lauri. Master's of Law, Helsinki U., 1964; MBA, Inst. Europeen d'Adminstrn. des Affaires, Fountainebleu, France, 1967. Lawyer A. Ahlstrom Corp., Helsinki, 1967-70, A. Ahlstrom Corp. Karhula Works, Karhula, Finland, 1970-72; gen. mgr. A. Ahlstrom Corp. Karhula Works, 1972—; bd. dirs. A. Ahlstrom Corp., Helsinki, 1980—; bd. dirs. Kotka (Finland) Telephone Co., Instrumentarium. Bd. dirs. Port of Kotka. Served to capt. Finland Reserve, 1956-57. Decorated knight 1st. class Order Lion (Finland), Chevalier Ordre Nat. Merit (France), Silver medal Armed Forces (Finland); named Hon. Consul (France). Mem. French-Finland Chamber Commerce, Kymi County Chamber Commerce (chmn. 1974-82, chmn. industry subcom. 1982—), Inst. Europeen d'Adminstrn. des Affaires (nat. adv. bd.). Conservative. Lutheran. Clubs: Kotka (bd. dirs. 1972—), Pörssikluri. Home: Karhulantie 70, 48600 Karhula Finland

TULL, THERESA ANNE, foreign service officer; b. Runnemede, N.J., Oct. 2, 1936; d. John James and Anna Cecelia (Paull) T. B.A., U. Md., 1972; M.A., U. Mich., 1973; postgrad. Nat. War Coll., Washington, 1980. Fgn. service officer Dept. State, Washington, 1963—, dep. prin. officer, Brussels, Saigon, Danang, 1973-75; prin. officer Cebu, Philippines, 1977-79; dir. office human rights, 1980-83; charge d'affaires, Am. Embassy, Vientiane, Laos, from 1983; ambassador to Guyana, 1987—. Recipient Civilian Service award Dept. of State, 1970, Meritorious Honor award, 1977. Mem. Am. Fgn. Service Assn. Club: Cathedral Choral Soc. (Washington). Home: care Waldis 416 N Washington Ave Moorestown NJ 08057 Office: Am Embassy Box V APO San Francisco CA 96346 *

TULL, WILLIS CLAYTON, JR., librarian; b. Crisfield, Md., Feb. 22, 1931; s. Willis Clayton and Agnes Virginia (Milbourne) T.; student U. Balt., 1948, Johns Hopkins U., 1956; B.S., Towson (Md.) State Coll., 1957; M.L.S., Rutgers U., 1962; postgrad. Miami U., Oxford, Ohio, 1979. m. Taeko Itoi, Dec. 18, 1952. Tchr., Hereford Jr.-Sr. High Sch., Parkton, Md., 1957-59; aide Enoch Pratt Free Library, Balt., 1959-61, profl. asst., 1962-64; coordinator adult services Washington County Free Library, Hagerstown, Md., 1964-67; asst. area librarian Eastern Shore Area Library, Salisbury, Md., 1967; br. librarian Balt. County Pub. Library, Pikesville, Md., 1968-71, asst. area br. librarian, Essex, Md., 1971-72, sr. info. specialist, Catonsville, Md., 1972-87; on-line supr., Towson Md., 1988—. Mem. Republican Central Com. Baltimore County, 1971-72. Served with U.S. Army, 1949-52. Mem. Amnesty Internat., Internat. Rescue Com., U.S. Com. for Refugees, Accuracy in Media, Com. for a Free Afghanistan, Com. for the Free World, Inst. Religion and Democracy, Nat. Intelligence Study Ctr., Raoul Wallenberg Com. U.S., Freedom to Read Found., Freedom House, Friends Dem. Ctr. Cen. Am., World Future Soc., Md. Library Assn. (chmn. intellectual freedom com. 1969-70), Md. Assn. Adult Edn. (regional coordinator Western Md. 1965-67), Unitarian and Universalist Geneal. Soc. (founder, dir. 1971-87), Md. Geneal. Soc., Soc. War of 1812, SAR, Del. Geneal. Soc., Chesapeake Bay Found., Nature Conservancy, Tidewater Geneal. Soc., Va. Geneal. Soc., Md. Hist. Soc., St. George's Soc. Balt., Eastern Shore Soc. Balt. City, Asia Soc., Balt. Council on Fgn. Affairs, Star Spangled Banner Flag House Assn., Kappa Delta Pi. Clubs: University. Contbr. to profl. and geneal. jours. Home: 10605 Lakespring Way Hunt Valley MD 21030 Office: 320 York Rd Towson MD 21204

TULLIS, EDWARD LEWIS, retired bishop; b. Cin., Mar. 9, 1917; s. Ashar Spence and Priscilla (Daugherty) T.; m. Mary Jane Talley, Sept. 25, 1937; children—Frank Loyd, Jane Allen (Mrs. William Nelson Offutt IV). AB, Ky. Wesleyan Coll., 1939, LHD, 1975; BD, Louisville Presbyn. Theol. Sem., 1947; DD, Union Coll., Barbourville, Ky., 1954, Wofford Coll., 1976; LHD, Claflin Coll., 1976, Lambuth Coll., 1984. Ordained to ministry Methodist Ch., 1941; service in chs. Frenchburg, Ky., 1937-39, Lawrenceburg, Ky., 1939-44; asso. pastor 4th Ave. Meth. Ch., Louisville, 1944-47, Irvine, Ky., 1947-49; asso. sec. ch. extension sect. Bd. Missions, Meth. Ch., Louisville, 1949-52; pastor First Meth. Ch., Frankfort, Ky., 1952-61, Ashland, Ky., 1961-72; resident bishop United Meth. Ch., Columbia, S.C., 1972-80, Nashville area, 1980-84; ret. United Meth. Ch., 1984; instr. Bible Ky. Wesleyan Coll., 1947-48; instr. Louisville Presbyn. Theol. Sem., 1949-52; mem. Meth. Gen. Conf., 1956, 60, 64, 66, 68, 70, 72, Southeastern Jurisdictional Conf., 1952, 56, 60, 64, 68, 72, bd. mgrs. Bd. Missions, 1962-72, mem. bd. discipleship, 1972-80, v.p. Gen. Council on Fin. and Adminstrn., 1980-84; Chaplain Ky. Gen. Assembly, 1952-61; chmn. Frankfort Com. Human Rights, 1956-61, Mayor's Advisory Com. Human Relations, Ashland, 1968-72. Author: Shaping the Church from the Mind of Christ, 1984. Contbr. articles to religious jours. Sec., bd. dirs. Magee Christian Edn. Found.; trustee Emory U., 1973-80, Alaska Meth. U., 1965-70, Ky. Wesleyan Coll., Martin Coll., Lambuth Coll., McKendree Manor, Meth. Hosps., Memphis, Lake Junaluska Assembly, 1966—. Recipient Outstanding Citizen award Frankfort VFW, 1961, Mayor's award for outstanding service, Ashland, 1971. Club: Kiwanis. Home: 2 S Lakeshore Dr Lake Junaluska NC 28745

TULLOCH, GEORGE SHERLOCK, JR., electrical equipment distribution company executive; b. Bklyn., Aug. 18, 1932; s. George Sherlock and Dorothy (Gooch) T.; m. Edyth Benson Woodroofe, June 16, 1956; children: Michael, Daniel, Lindsay. B.A. in History, Amherst Coll., 1954; LL.B., U. Mich., 1959. Bar: N.Y. 1960, Mo. 1983. Assoc. Breed, Abbott & Morgan, N.Y.C., 1959-66; sec., asst. gen. counsel Westvaco Corp., N.Y.C., 1966-78; v.p., sec., gen. counsel, dir. Graybar Electric Co., N.Y.C., 1978—; dir. Blue Cross and Blue Shield Mo. Served to 1st lt. USMCR, 1954-56. Mem. ABA, Assn. Bar City N.Y., Met. St. Louis Bar Assn., Am. Soc. Corp. Secs. Home: 4954 Lindell Blvd Saint Louis MO 63108 Office: Graybar Electric Co Inc 34 N Meramec Ave PO Box 7231 Saint Louis MO 63177

TULLY, DANIEL P., investment company executive; b. 1932; married. BBA, St. Johns U., 1953. With Merrill Lynch, Pierce, Fenner & Smith, Inc., N.Y.C., 1955—, acct. clerk, 1955-59, acct. exec. trainee, 1959-63, asst. to mgr. Stamford, Conn. office, 1963-70, mgr., 1970-71, v.p., 1971-79, dir. individual sales, 1976-79, exec. v.p., 1979-82, pres. individual services group, 1982-84, pres. consumer mktg., from 1984, now chmn., pres., dir.; with Merrill Lynch & Co. (parent), N.Y.C., 1955—, former exec. v.p., now pres., chief operating officer, dir. Served U.S. Army, 1953-55. Office: Merrill Lynch & Co Inc One Liberty Plaza 165 Broadway New York NY 10080 *

TULLY, RONALD, librarian, information scientist; b. Edinburgh, Midlothian, Scotland, Aug. 4, 1960; s. James and Davinia Laing (Anderson) T.; m. Charisse Ann Bird, Sept. 25, 1982; children: Emma Siobhan, Craig Ewan. BA in Librarianship, Robert Gordons Inst. Tech., Aberdeen, Scotland, 1981. Library asst. Royal Soc. Edinburgh, Scotland, 1981; asst. librarian Royal Coll. Surgeons Edinburgh, 1981-83; medical/sci. librarian Christie Hosp. and Holt Radium Inst., Manchester, Eng., 1983-85; publs. and adminstrn. mgr. Merck, Sharp & Dohme Ltd., Hoddesdon, Eng., 1985—. Mem. Library Assn. (assoc.), Inst. Info. Scientists. Home: 69 Star St, Ware Hertfordshire SG1 27AQ, England Office: Merck Sharp & Dohme Ltd, Hertford Rd Hoddeson, Hertfordshire EN1 19BU, England

TUMAY, MEHMET TANER, geotechnical consultant, educator; b. Ankara, Turkey, Feb. 2, 1937; came to U.S., 1959; s. Bedrettin and Muhterem (Uybadin) T.; m. Karen Nuttycombe, June 15, 1962; children—Peri, Suna. B.S. in Civil Engring., Robert Coll. Sch. Engring. (Turkey), 1959; M.C.E., U. Va., 1961; postgrad. UCLA, 1963-64; Ph.D., Tech. U. Istanbul (Turkey), 1971; Fugro-Cesco postdoctoral research fellow U. Fla., Gainesville, 1975-76. Instr. civil engring. U. Va., Charlottesville, 1961-62; asst. prof. civil engring. U. Louisville, 1962-63; teaching fellow UCLA, 1963-64; asst. prof. civil engring. Robert Coll. Sch. Engring., Istanbul, 1966-71; asso. prof. dept. civil engring. Bogazici U., Istanbul, 1971-75; assoc. prof. then prof. civil engring., coordinator geotech. engring. La. State U., Baton Rouge, 1976—; maitre de conferences Ecole Nationale des Ponts et Chaussees, Paris, 1980—; geotech. cons. Sauti, Spa, Cons. Engrs., Italy, 1969-72, SOFRETU-RATP, Paris, 1972-73, D.E.A., Cons. Engrs., Istanbul, 1974-75, BOTEK, Ltd., Istanbul, 1975—, Senler-Campbell Assos., Louisville, 1979—, Fugro Gulf-Geogulf, Houston, 1980—; cons. UN Devel. Program, 1982-84, 87; cons. in field. Contbr. articles to profl. jours. AID scholar, 1975-76; qualified fallout shelter analyst and instr. Dept. Def.; lic. civil engr., La., Turkish Chamber of Civil Engring; NSF grantee, 1982—; French Ministry External Relations scholar, 1982. Fellow ASCE; mem. Am. Soc. Engring. Edn., ASTM, La. Engring. Soc., Turkish Soil Mechanics Group (charter), Turkish Chamber Civil Engrs., Internat. Soc. Soil Mechanics and Found. Engring., Sigma Xi, Chi Epsilon, Tau Beta Pi. Home: 1915 W Magna Carta Pl Baton Rouge LA 70815 Office: La State Univ Dept Civil Engring Baton Rouge LA 70803

TÜMER, HÜSEYIN VACIT, paint company executive; b. Ankara, Turkey, Mar. 9, 1930; s. Cemal and Zehra T.; m. A Gönül Gücü, Oct. 7, 1953; 1 child, Sedef. M in ChemE, U. Ankara, 1951, PhD in Indsl. Chem., 1957. Asst. gen. mgr. Turyag Oil and By-Products A.S., Izmir, Turkey, 1953-68; gen. mgr. Dyo Sadolin A.S., Izmir, 1968-74; exec. v.p. Yasar Holding A.S., Izmir, 1974-80; gen. mgr. Otomobilcilik Ve Ticaret A.S., Izmir, 1980-86; pres. dir. Pt. Danapaints Indonesia, Jakarta, 1986—; lectr. Ege U., Izmir, 1955-61. Patentee Improved Raney Nickel Catalyst; contbr. articles to profl. jours. Research fellow So. Regional Research Lab., 1961-62. Mem. Izmir C. of C. (vice-chmn. 1982-85). Moslem. Lodge: Rotary (Izmir). Office: Pt Danapaints Indonesia, JL Pemuda-Pulogadung, 13001 Jakarta Indonesia

TUNG, BETTY WONG, ski apparel company executive; b. Shanghai, China, Feb. 23, 1944; d. Foo Yuan and Joanna (Chen) Wong; came to U.S., 1962; m. Michael Hong-nien Tung, Dec. 23, 1967; children—Patricia J., Eric M. B.S. in Chemistry, U. Calif.-Berkeley, 1966; M.S. in Phys. Chemistry, U. So. Calif., 1967. Research engr. NCR Corp., El Segundo, Calif., 1967-73; engring. specialist Northrop Corp., Hawthorne, Calif., 1973-78; pres. Fera Internat. Corp., Torrance, Calif., 1978—; dir. F.Y. Garments Ltd., Singapore, Ski Industries Am., 1985—. Contbr. articles to profl. jours.; patentee electroless plating bath. Mem. Hong Kong Trade Devel. Assn. (exec.), Electrochem. Soc., Ski Industries Am. (bd. dirs.), Ski Fedn. Office: Fera Internat Corp 20603 Earl St Torrance CA 90503

TUNG, ROSALIE SUET-YING, educator; b. Shanghai, China, Dec. 2, 1948; came to U.S., 1975; d. Andrew Yan-Fu and Pauline Wai-Kam (Cheung) Lam; B.A. (Univ. scholar), York U., 1972; M.B.A., U. B.C., 1974, Ph.D. in Bus. Adminstrn. (Univ. fellow, Seagram Bus. fellow, H.R. MacMillan Family fellow), 1977; m. Byron Poon-Yan Tung, June 17, 1972; 1 dau., Michele Christine. Lectr., diploma div. U. B.C., 1975, lectr. exec. devel. program, 1975; prof. mgmt. Grad. Sch. Mgmt., U. Oreg., Eugene, 1977-80; vis. scholar U. Manchester (Eng.) Inst. Sci. and Tech., fall 1980; vis. prof. UCLA, spring 1981, Harvard U., 1988, prof. mgmt. Wharton Sch. Fin., U. Pa., Phila., 1981-86; disting. prof. bus. adminstrn., dir. internat. bus. ctr. U. Wis., Milw., 1986—. Mem. Acad. Internat. Bus. (treas.), Acad. Mgmt. (bd. govs.),Internat. Assn. Applied Psychology, Am. Arbitration Assn. (comml. panel arbitrators). Roman Catholic. Author 7 books; contbr. articles to profl. jours. Office: U Wis-Milw Sch Business PO Box 17441 Milwaukee WI 53217

TUNHAMMAR, GÖRAN MAGNUS, lawyer, lobbyist; b. Stockholm, Dec. 22, 1946; s. Elam and Margaretha (Mathiasson) T.; m. Johanna Katarina Areskoug, Oct. 6, 1978; children: Katarina, Gustaf. BSc, U. Lund, 1974, LL.M., 1975. Asst. judge Dist. Ct., Kristianstad, Sweden, 1975-77; mgr. employment policy Swedish Employers Confedn., Stockholm, 1977-80, mgr. and counsel personnel abroad, 1983-85, v.p. govt. and parliament relations, 1985—; assoc. law firm Almgren, Forkman and Liedholm, Malmö, Sweden, 1980-82; dep. mem. The Swedish Labour Ct., Stockholm, 1986—. Chmn. Nordic Soc., Stockholm div., 1986—. Mem. Internat. Law Assn., Swedish Econ. Soc., Bus. Mgmt. Soc. Lodge: Rotary. Office: Swedish Employers Confedn, Sodra Blasieholmshamnen 4A, S-10330 Stockholm Sweden

TUNKU ABDULLAH IBNI ALMARHUM TUANKU ABDUL RAHMAN, business consultant; b. Kuala Pilah, Malaysia, May 2, 1925; s. Tuanku Abdul Rahman and Che Engku Maimunah; Diploma in Public Adminstrn., Malay Coll., Kuala Kangsar, 1936-41; student U. Glasgow, 1948-51; m. Chesterina Sim Zecha, Apr. 21, 1973; children—Tunku Iskandar, Tunku Marinah, Tunku Kamil, Tunku Yaacob, Tunku Yahya, Tunku Halim, Tunku Soraya. Mem. Malaysian Civil Service, 1952-63; mem. Malaysian Parliament, 1964-74; chmn. Malayan Cement Bhd., Malaysia Borneo Fin. Bhd., Taisho Marine & Fire Ins. (M) Bhd., The Melewar Corp. Sdn. Bhd., MBf Holdings Bhd.; dir. various cos. Pres., Malaysian Assn. Youth Clubs, 1954-66, Malaysian Youth Council, 1966-72, Asian Youth Council, 1972-80. Islam. Clubs: The Lake, Selangor, Bankers. Office: 22d Floor, Plaza MBf Jalan Ampang, Kuala Lumpur 50450, Malaysia

TUNMER, WILLIAM ERNEST, JR., psycholinguist, educator, lecturer; b. San Antonio, June 23, 1947; arrived in Australia, 1980; s. William Ernest Tunmer Sr. and Bettye (Eaker) Lynn; m. Lucy Howard Hastings, Apr. 14, 1979; 1 child, Ross Phillip. BS, U. Tex., 1970, PhD in Psycholinguistics, 1979. Research asst. Dept. Psychology, U. Tex., Austin, 1972-73, research assoc., 1973-76, teaching asst., 1976-77, instr., 1978; sr. research assoc. div. bilingual and internat. edn. S.W. Ednl. Devel. Lab., Austin, 1978-80; research fellow in edn. and psychology U. Western Australia, Nedlands, 1980-81, lectr. dept. edn., 1982-86, sr. lectr., 1987-88; prof. Massey U., New Zealand, 1988—; vis. scholar Ctr. for Cognitive Sci., U. Tex., Austin, 1985, Sch. Edn., Stanford (Calif.) U., 1985. Cons. editor: Jour. Child Devel., 1984—, Jour. Ednl. Psychology, 1985—, Brit. Jour. Devel. Psychology, 1986; mem. editorial bd. Reading Research Quar., 1986—; contbr. articles to profl. publs. and chpts. to books. Research grantee Nat. Inst. Edn., 1979, Edn. Research and Devel. Com., Canberra, Australia, 1982, Devel. Assistance Com., U. Western Australia, 1984, Edn. Com. Spl. Grant Research, U. Western Australia, 1985-87, Australian Research Grants Scheme, Canberra, 1986-87. Mem. Internat. Reading Assn., Australian Assn. for Research in Edn., Am. Edn1. Research Assn., Am. Psychol. Assn., Phi Eta Sigma, Phi Epsilon Tau, Phi Kappa Phi. Home: 18 Ihaka, Palmerston North New Zealand Office: Massey U. Dept Edn, Palmerston North New Zealand

TUNON, JEAN CLAUDE, company executive; b. Paris, June 26, 1925; s. Gregorio Manuel and Jeanne (Stassart) T.; m. Maud Josephine Elias, Aug. 24, 1950; 1 child, Gregorio Juan. Diploma Humanities, Coll. St. Barthelemy, Liège, Belgium, 1943; Diploma Higher Comml. Studies, Institut Normal des Scis. Commerciales, 1949, Diploma Profl. Acct., 1950; postgrad. U. Liège, 1959-61; cert. Harvard U. Grad. Sch. Bus. Adminstrn., 1971, Advanced Mgmt. Program, 1975. Assoc. Spinoy, Forbras and Tunon Accts., Liege, Belgium, 1950-56; prof. acctg. and mktg. Institut Normal des Scis. Commerciales, Liege, 1950-61; pres. Internat. Ctr. Corr. Studies, Liege, Paris, Geneva, Monaco, 1950-71; prof. retailing and selling Higher Commercial Schs., Liège, 1954-56; pres., ednl. dir. Tunon Internat. Hospitality Sch., 1964—; pres. Monaco Congres et Tourisme, Monte-Carlo, 1964—; pres. Harry Winston-Monte-Carlo Jewels, 1971—; chmn. bd. Europe Voyages, Paris, 1982—, Tunon Formation and France Formation, Paris, 1983—, Tunon Temporim, Paris, 1984—, Am. Bus. Sch., Lyon, France, 1985—, ESdeSUP, Paris and Marseille, France, 1986, Univ. Hartford at Paris, 1986. Served with U.S. Army, 1944-47; res. capt. Belgian Air Force, 1948. Mem. Econ. Council State Monaco, 1973-79; mem. World Bus. Council, 1976—; mem. High Com. for Tourism of State Monaco, 1972—. Decorated Commandeur de l'Ordre d'Isabelle la Catholique d'Espagne, Chevalier de l'Ordre de la Couronne de Belgique, 1965, Chevalier de l'Ordre de Leopold de Belgique, 1968, Chevalier des Palmes Academiques; recipient Silver medal City of Paris, 1980, Vermeille medal City of Paris, 1985, Silver Medal, Tourism in Spain, 1981. Mem. Am. Legion (Silver Medal), Nat. Fedn. Pvt. Schs., Monaco Travel Agys. Assn. (founding pres.), French Assn. Travel Agts. (dir.), Am. Assn. Travel Agts., Universal Fedn. Travel Agts. Assn., Harvard Alumni Assn. South of France and Monaco (pres.). Clubs: Skal (Monaco) (v.p. 1975—); Harvard Bus. Sch. (France); Cercle Interallie (Paris); Jockey (Deauville); Monaco Ambassadors, Monte-Carlo Country; Yacht (Monaco); Automobile (Monaco). Lodge: Rotary (sec. gen. 1965—). Address: 3 rue L Aureglia, BP 75 Monte Carlo CEDEX 98002, Monaco

TUN TIN, government official for Burma. Prime minister Rangoon, Burma, 1988. Address: Office of Prime Minister, Rangoon Burma *

TUOHY, (JOHN FRANCIS) FRANK, writer, educator; b. Uckfield, Eng., May 2, 1925; s. Patrick Gerald and Dorothy (Annandale) T. BA, Cambridge (Eng.) U., 1946. Lectr. U. Turku, Finland, 1947-48; prof. English lang. and literature U. Sao Paulo, Brazil, 1950-56; contract prof. Jagiellonian U., Krakow, Poland, 1958-60; vis. prof. Waseda U., Tokyo, 1964-67; writer-in-residence Purdue U., Lafayette, Ind., 1970-71, 76, 80. Author: (novels) The Animal Game, 1957, The Warm Nights of January, 1960, The Ice Saints, 1964 (Geoffrey Faber Meml. prize and James Tait Black Meml. prize, 1964), Portugal, 1969; (stories) The Admiral and the Nuns, 1962 (Katherine Mansfield Prize, 1960, Soc. of Authors travelling scholarship, 1963), Fingers in the Door, 1970, Winter's Tales, 1971, Live Bait, 1979 (William Heinemann award, 1979); (biography) W.B. Yeats, 1976; (TV play) The Japanese Student, 1973; contbr. stories to Encounter. Recipient E.M. Forster Meml. award, 1971. Fellow Royal Soc. Lit.; mem. PEN, Soc. Authors. Home: care A D Peters and Co Ltd, 10 Buckingham St, London WC2N 6BU, England also: Lloyd's Bank Ltd, Uckfield, Sussex England *

TUOHY, WILLIAM, journalist; b. Chgo., Oct. 1, 1926; s. John Marshall and Lolita (Klaus) T.; m. Johanna Iselin, Nov. 24, 1964; 1 son, Cyril Iselin. B.S., Northwestern U., 1951. Copy boy, reporter, night city editor San Francisco Chronicle, 1952-59; assoc. editor, nat. polit. corr., fgn. corr. Newsweek mag., 1959-66; Vietnam corr. Los Angeles Times, 1966-68; Middle East corr. Los Angeles Times, Beirut, 1969-71; bur. chief Los Angeles Times, Rome, 1971-77, London, 1977-85, Bonn, Fed. Republic Germany, 1985—. Author: Dangerous Company, 1987. Served with USNR, 1944-46. Recipient Nat. Headliner award for Vietnam bur. coverage, 1965; Pulitzer prize internat. reporting (Vietnam), 1969; Overseas Press Club award for best internat. reporting (Middle East), 1970. Address: care Los Angeles Times Fgn Editor Los Angeles CA 90053

TUOMILEHTO, JAAKKO OLAVI, medical scientist; b. Ilmajoki, Finland, Dec. 24, 1946; s. Oiva Ilmari and Rauha Heleena (Rahnasto) T.; m. Kaija-Maria Pohtola, June 29, 1968 (div. Sept. 1982); children: Henri Pekka, Petteri Matti, Tuomas Jaakko; m. Eva Wolf; 1 child, Kristian Paul Wolf. MD, U. Turku, Finland, 1973, M of Polit. Sci., 1975; PhD, U. Kuopio, Finland, 1975. Research fellow U. Kuopio, 1972-77, prof. community medicine, 1977-78, 82-83, 86; sr. researcher dept. epidemiology Nat. Pub. Health Inst., Helsinki, Finland, 1978-80; chief internat. cardiovascular data ctr. WHO, 1984-86; dept. dir. Helsinki, Finland, 1987—; med. officer Regional Office for Western Pacific, WHO, Manila, 1980-82; med. officer Province of North Karelia, Joensuu, Finland, 1974; mem. Nat. Blood Pressure Com. of Finland, 1975-77, Med. Research Council of Acad. Finland, 1977-80; prin. investigator North Karelia Project, 1977—; cons. WHO, Geneva, 1983—. Author: The North Karelia Project, 1981; contbr. articles to sci. jours. and books. Lutheran. Home: Huttumyllyntie 17, 00920 Helsinki Finland Office: Nat Pub Health Inst, Mannerheimintie 166, 00280 Helsinki Finland

TUPASI, THELMA ESTELA, physician; b. Nueva Vizcaya, Philippines, Sept. 13, 1940; d. Vicente Tupasi and Eulalia Flojo; m. Claver P. Ramos; children: Rainerio George, Vicente Miguel, Ma. Regina, John Paul. MB cum laude, U. Philippines, Quezon City, 1961, MD with distinction, 1964. Assoc. prof. U. Philippines Coll. of Medicine, Philippine Gen. Hosp., Manila, 1972-83; chief lab. research div. dept. health Research Inst. Tropical Med., Manila, Philippines, 1981-84; dir. Research Inst. Tropical Med., Manila, 1984-86; pres. Tropical Disease Research Found., Makati, Philippines, 1984—; cons. infectious disease sect. Makati Med Ctr; mem. WHO Acute Respiratory Infection Tech. Adv. Group. Rockefeller Found. fellow, 1967-69; named an Outstanding Young Scientist, Nat. Acad. Sci. and Tech., 1980, an Outstanding Woman in Nation's Service, Lions Internat., 1983. Fellow Infectious Disease Soc. Am. (corr.). Office: Tropical Disease Research Found, Makati Med Ctr, 2 Amorsolo St, Makati Philippines

TUPOUTO'A, Crown Prince of Tonga, government official; b. Nuku'alofa, Tonga, May 4, 1948; s. Taufa'ahau Tupou IV and Halaevalu Mata'aho; ed. public schs., Tonga, N.Z., Switzerland; grad. Royal Mil. Acad., Sandhurst, Eng. Joined Ministry Fgn. Affairs Tonga, 1970, minister of fgn. affairs and def., 1979—. Commd. col.-in-chief Tonga Def. Services and Royal Guards, 1969. Address: Ministry Fgn Affairs, PO Box 821, Nuku'alofa Tonga

TURBERGUE, HENRI JEAN MARIE, physician; b. Rixheim, Alsace, France, Nov. 19, 1951; s. Charles Joseph and Marcelle Marie (Herz) T. MD, Medicine Faculty Strasbourg, France, 1976. Med. student Civil Hosp. Strasbourg, 1969-74; resident cardiology service Civil Hosp., Mulhouse, France, 1975-76; gen. practice medicine Taillecourt, France,

1978—; cons. in field. Author: Coronary Heart Disease Socio-Profl. Factors, 1976. First town councilor Taillecourt Town council, 1984—. Served as med. officer France Health Service Air Army, 1977-78. Mem. Assn. Med. Urgencies of Region of Montbeliard. Roman Catholic. Club: Audincourt Invest. Home and Office: 67 Rue Sous Bois, 25400 Taillecourt, Doubs France

TURBIAUX, MARCEL LUCIEN, psychologist; b. Paris, May 15, 1935; s. Marcel Emmanuel Joseph and Lucienne Louise (Gaillot) T. M.S. in Psychology, U. Sorbonne, Paris, 1954; diploma in Psychopathology, Inst. Psychology, Paris, 1955, diploma in social psychology, 1957; D.Psychology, U. Paris, 1964. Registered psychologist, Paris. Attache to personnel mgr. Regie Autonome des Transports Parisiens, Paris, 1957, tech. sec. hygiene and health com., 1958-74, head dept. security of work, 1975—; expert Internat. Labour Office, Geneva, 1973; lectr. Poly. Sch., Paris, 1976; cons. Secursol, Paris, 1972-80, 85. Co-author: Encyclopedie Pratique de Psychologie, 1979, Melanges de Mythologie Francaise, 1980. Contbr. articles to profl. publs. Recipient Mil. Merit award Ministry of Def., 1972, Nat. Merit award Ministry of Def., 1974. Mem. Security of Work Commn., Internat. Railways Union, French Nat. Acad. History. Club: Ergonomics. Avocations: history; theater; art. Home: 16 Quai de la Megisserie, 75001 Paris France Office: Regie Autonome Transports Parisiennes, 120 122 Rue du Mont-Cenis, 75018 Paris France

TURCAN, ROBERT ALAIN, Roman and Gallo-Roman archaeology educator, historian; b. Paris, June 22, 1929; s. Pierre Joseph Marie and Yvonne Georgette (Bayle) T.; m. Marie Jeanne Marguerite Deleani, Dec. 28, 1956; children: Isabelle, Pierre, Anne Marie. Student Lycée Louis le Grand, Paris, 1949-52; lic. agregation (hon.), Ecole Normale Supérieure, Paris, 1952-53, 54-55. With Ecole Française de Rome, 1955-57; asst. prof. Latin, U. Lyon, 1957-63, prof. Latin lit., 1963-74, prof. Roman and Gallo-Roman archaeology, 1974-87, U. Paris IV, 1987—. Roman: dir. antiquities Rhône-Alpes, Lyon, 1975-76; dir. research Ctr. d'Etudes Romaines et Gallo-Romaines, Lyon, 1975-84. Author: Sarcophages romains à représentations dionysiaques, (Reinach award 1967), 1966; Religions de l'Asie, 1972; Mithras Platonicus, 1975; Mithra et le mithriacisme (Saintour 1982), 1981; Firmicus Maternus, L'erreur des religions païennes, 1982; Numismatique romaine du culte métroaque, 1983; Héliogabale et le sacre du soleil, 1985; Vivre à la cour des Césars, 1987. Recipient Jeanbernat award Inst. de France, Acad. des Inscriptions et Belles Lettres, 1959. Corr. mem. Deutsches Archäologisches Inst. zu Berlin, Inst. de France. Roman Catholic. Home: 3 Residence du Tourillon, 69290 Craponne France Office: U Paris IV, Inst Art et Archeologie, 3 Rue Michelet, 75006 Paris France

TURGAY, ATILLA, physician, psychiatrist, researcher; b. Ankara, Turkey, June 16, 1946; came to Can., 1977; s. Mustafa and Beyhan Turgay; m. Cigdem Savran, June 10, 1972; children—Suna, Efe. M.D., Hacettepe U., 1970, specialist in psychiatry, 1974; degree magna cum laude in psychiatry, Ottawa U., 1979. Resident in psychiatry and child psychiatry U. Ottawa, 1977-79, chmn. div. child and adolescent psychiatry, dept. psychiatry, 1984—; dir. adolescent inpatient psychiatry McMaster U., chief dept. psychiatry Children's Hosp. of Eastern Ont., Ottawa, 1980—. Contbr. articles to profl. jours. Mem. Am. Psychiat. Assn., Can. Psychiat. Assn., Can. Acad. Child Psychiatry (chmn. com. edn. primary physicians). Home: 1935 Highridge Ave, Ottawa, ON Canada K1H 5H1 Office: Childrens Hosp Eastern Ont, 401 Smyth Rd, Ottawa, ON Canada K1H 8L1

TURIEL, MAURIZIO, cardiologist; b. Milan, Italy, Oct. 16, 1948; s. Isacco and Lina (Zagdoun) T.; student Pharmacology Inst., Milan, 1972-73; M.D., U. Milan, 1973. Italian govt. research grantee II Med. Clinic of U. Milan, 1974, specialist in pneumology, 1976, in cardiology, 1978, in hygiene and preventive medicine, 1985; research fellow I, Med. Pathology Inst., 1981; cons., chief cardiopulmonary sect. Analysis Lab. Center; research fellow Cardiovascular Research unit Royal Postgrad. Med. Sch., London, 1986—. Mem. Italian Soc. Cardiology, Societas Europaea Physiologial Clinical Respiratoriae. Jewish. Contbr. articles to profl. publs. U.S. Home: 19 Vetta D'Italia, 20144 Milan Italy

TURINA, SRECKO, analytic chemist; b. Rijeka, Yugoslavia, Jan. 17, 1931; s. Zvonimir and Vjekoslava (Ursicic) T.; grad. U. Zagreb, 1954, Sc.D., 1960; m. Nada Indjic, Feb. 13, 1960; children—Ariana, Dalibor. Head lab. material testing Prvomajska machine tools factory, Zagreb, Yugoslavia, 1958-65; head lab. chem. analysis Inst. Material Sci., U. Zagreb, 1965—; lectr. chromatography. Recipient Nikola Tesla award for tech. scis., Republic of Croatia, 1981. Mem. Croatian Chem. Soc., Statis. Soc. Croatia. Author: Thin Layer Chromatography. Home: 31 A V Bubnja, 41000 Zagreb Yugoslavia Office: 1 Salaja, 41000 Zagreb Yugoslavia

TURK, THOMAS NORMAN, mfg. co. exec.; b. New Castle, Pa., Dec. 9, 1938; s. Charles Julian and May Matilda (Cowperthwaite) T.; A.A., Golden West Coll., 1973; B.A., Calif. State U., 1976; M.B.A., Nat. U., 1982; m. Coleen Budd, Dec. 28, 1969; children—Thomas Jeffrey, Casey Thomas, Tiffany Ann. With Eaton-Leonard Corp., Carlsbad, Calif., 1976-87, materials mgr., 1978-87, Sierracin/Magnedyne Corp., Carlsbad, 1988—. Served with USMC, 1956-58. Cert. profl. in inventory mgmt. Mem. Am. Prodn. and Inventory Control Soc. (v.p. edn. 1981-82, pres. 1983-84, bd. dirs. 1984-86), Soc. Mfg. Engrs. (cert. mfg. engr.), Internat. Platform Assn., Computer Automated Systems Assn. Democrat. Home: 31710 Oak Glen Rd Valley Center CA 92082 Office: 2258 Rutherford Rd Carlsbad CA 92008

TURKAT, DAVID MARK, psychologist; b. Bklyn., Apr. 7, 1952; s. Michael M. and Phyllis R. (Schiff) T.; B.A. magna cum laude, Brandeis U., 1973; M.A., La. State U., 1974, Ph.D., 1978. Psychologist, Rockdale Mental Health Clinic, Conyers, Ga., 1977-78, Ga. Mental Health Inst., Atlanta, 1978; program evaluation specialist Div. Mental Health and Mental Retardation-Community Support Project, Atlanta, 1978-80; pvt. practice clin. and cons. psychology, Atlanta, 1979—; cons. U. Ga., 1980—, Miss. Dept. Mental Health, 1981—; mem. consumer com. Mental Health Assn. Met. Atlanta, 1978-80; commentator mental health radio series, 1981—; producer, host health news talk show on cable TV, Atlanta, 1981-83; host Soap Opera Psychology, Sta. WXIA-TV, Atlanta; host entertainment talk show on cable TV Mem. alumni council Brandeis U., 1978—, pres., 1986—; mem. prodn. com. Access Atlanta, 1980—. Recipient Caber award for best local cable talk show, 1982; PSA award Inst. for Mental Health Initiatives, 1984; Menninger Found. fellow, 1980—. Mem. Assn. for Media Psychology (chmn. prodn. and program com. 1982—, v.p. 1982-84), Am. Psychol. Assn., Gen. Semantics Inst., Southeastern Psychol. Assn., Ga. Psychol. Assn. (media award 1983), Mental Health Assn. Ga. Contbr. articles to profl. jours. Office: 3390 Peachtree Rd Suite 544 Atlanta GA 30326

TURLEY, J. WILLIAM, lawyer; b. Van Nuys, Calif., Jan. 11, 1948; s. Billy Brown and Kathryn Ann (Kuniak) T.; children: Timothy Jay, Damon Andrew. BA, U. Mo., 1970, JD, 1974. Bar: Mo. 1974, U.S. Dist. Ct. (we. dist.) Mo. 1974, U.S. Dist. Ct. (ea. dist.) Mo. 1974. Stockholder Wesner, Turley & Kempton, Inc., Sedalia, Mo., 1975-84; ptnr. Carnahan, Carnahan & Turley, Rolla, Mo., 1984-87, Robinson, Turley, Turley & White, 1987—; atty. City of Sedalia, 1976; pros. atty. Pettis County, Sedalia, 1976; Author: Trial Handbook for Missouri Lawyers, 1984; contbr. articles to profl. jours. Chmn. Sedalia Dem. Com., 1982. Mem. Mo. Bar Assn. (bd. govs. 1986—), Assn. Trial Lawyers Am. (bd. govs. 1985—), Mo. Assn. Trial Attys. (pres. 1985), Jaycees, Scribes. Democrat. Roman Catholic. Lodge: Moose. Home: PO Box A Newburg MO 65550 Office: Robinson Turley Turley & White PO Box 47 Rolla MO 65401

TURLEY, JAMES ANTHONY, JR., lawyer; b. N.Y.C., Aug. 2, 1918; s. James Anthony and Wilhelmine Agusta (Moje) T.; AB, Middlebury Coll., 1941; JD, Duke U., 1948; postgrad. in internat. law Georgetown U., 1955; m. Georgette Kouchakji-Sabbagh, June 27, 1953; children: Elizabeth Anne, Sue Anne Bedford, Mary Rose McDevitt, James Anthony III, Sean Anthony. Bar: N.Y. 1950, U.S. Supreme Ct. 1954, U.S. Ct. Mil. Appeals 1954, U.S. Ct. Claims 1955. Sole practice law, 1950-53; appellate govt. counsel Dept. Def., Washington, 1953-56; trust cons. trust dept. Hanover Bank (merged with Mfrs. Hanover Trust Co. 1960), N.Y.C., 1956-60, asst. v.p. Mfrs. Hanover Trust Co., 1959-76, v.p. trust devel. dept., 1977-81; gen. counsel Dept. Gen. Services, Div. Real Property, City of N.Y., 1981-82; ptnr. firm Van Nuys, Turley & Nelson, N.Y.C., 1982-83; solo practice, 1984—; speaker on estates; mem. faculty Practising Law Inst., Am. Mgmt. Assn. Mem. adv. bd. Muscoot Interpretative Farm, Somers, N.Y., 1975-80; chmn. Somers (N.Y.) Assessment Rev. Bd., 1976—. Trustee Somers Hist. Soc., 1980—; chmn. Landmarks Preservation Com., 1985-88. Served to maj. USMCR, 1941-46, 53-56. Mem. Westchester County Bar Assn. (chmn. sect. estates and trusts, mem. surrogate's ct. com.), Internat. Acad. Estate and Trust Law (academician, mem. exec. council 1982-86), Greater N.Y. Estate Planning Council (dir. 1962-66), Fed. Bar Council of N.Y., N.J. and Conn. (co-chmn. tax workshop), Consular Law Soc. (trustee 1984—, v.p. 1985—). Roman Catholic. Clubs: Princeton (N.Y.), Friendly Sons of St. Patrick of N.Y.C. and Westchester County, Ancient Order Hibernians, Somers Hist. Soc. (N.Y.) (trustee 1982—), Am. Irish Hist. Soc. Home: RD 4 Lalli Dr Katonah NY 10536 Office: 175 Main St White Plains NY 10601

TURLEY, ROBERT JOE, lawyer; b. Mt. Sterling, Ky., Dec. 6, 1926; s. R. Joe and Mavis Clare (Sternberg) T.; m. Mary Lynn Sanders, Dec. 17, 1948 (div.); children—Leighton Turley Isaacs, Lynn Turley McComas, R. Joe, Mavis Lee. Student Berea Coll., 1944-45, St. Mary's Coll. (Calif.), 1945-46; LL.B., U. Ky., 1949. Bar: Ky. 1949, U.S. Dist. Ct. (ea. dist.) Ky. 1950, U.S. Ct. Appeals (6th cir.) 1958, U.S. Supreme Ct. 1959. Ptnr. Mooney & Turley and successor firms, Lexington, Ky., 1949-84, Turley & Moore, Lexington, 1984—; chmn. Fed. Jud. Selection Commn. Ky., 1985—; gen counsel Shriners Hosps. for Crippled Children, 1976-77, trustee, 1981—. Served with USNR, 1944-46. Diplomate Nat. Bd. Trial Advocacy, 1980. Fellow Am. Coll. Trial Lawyers; mem. Ky. Bar Assn., ABA, Assn. Trial Lawyers Am. Republican. Baptist. Clubs: Lafayette, St. Ives Jour., Champions Golf. Lodges: Masons, Shriners. Contbr. articles to legal jours. Home: 111 Woodland Ave Lexington KY 40502 Office: Turley & Moore 134 N Limestone St Lexington KY 40507

TURNBULL, GEORGE HENRY, marketing executive; b. London, Oct. 17, 1926; s. Bartholomew and Pauline (Konrath) T.; m. Marion Anne Wing, Mar. 14, 1950; children: Deborah, Penelope, Robert. Student, King Henry VIII Sch., Coventry, England; BSc (hons.) Mechanical Engring., Birmingham U., England. P.A. to technical dir. Standard Motors Ltd., Coventry, Eng., 1950-51; liaison officer between Standard Motors and Rolls Royce, Eng., 1951-53; exec. with experimental dept. Standard Motors, 1954-55; mgr. works Petters Ltd., Staines, Eng., 1955-56; mgr. div. cars Standard Motors, Coventry, 1956-59; gen. mgr. Petters Ltd., Coventry, 1959-62; dir., gen mgr. Standard-Triumph Internat., Coventry, 1962—; dep. chmn. Standard-Triumph Internat., 1969; dir. British Leyland Motor Corp., Birmingham, Eng., 1967; dep. mng. dir. British Leyland Motor Corp., Birmingham, 1968-73, mng. dir., 1973; mng. dir. British Leyland Austin Morris, Birmingham, 1968-73; chmn. Truck and Bus Div. British Leyland, Birmingham, 1972-73; v.p., dir. Hyundai Motors, Seoul, Republic of Korea, 1974-77; cons. to chmn. Iran Nat. Motor Co., Tehran, 1977-78, dep. mng. dir., 1978-79; chmn. Talbot U.K., Birmingham, 1979-84; mng. dir. group Inchcape Plc., London, 1984-85, chief exec. group, 1985-86, chmn., chief exec., 1986—; bd. dirs. Bank in Liechtenstein Ltd., 1988—. Chmn. Korea-Europe Fund Ltd., 1987—; bd. dirs. Euro-Asia Cen., 1987—. Fellow Inst. Mech. Engrs., Inst. Prodn. Engrs.; mem. Soc. Motor Mfgs. and Traders (pres. 1982-84, dep. pres. 1984—), Indsl. Soc. (chmn. 1987), Birmingham C. of C. (mem. council 1972, v.p. 1973). Office: Inchcape Plc, 40 St Mary Axe, London EC3A 8EU, England

TURNBULL, JEFFREY JOHN, architectural educator; b. Melbourne, Australia, Nov. 21, 1937; s. Raymond Frederic and Agnes (Cunningham) T. BArch, U. Melbourne, 1960, diploma in Town, Regional Planning, 1962; MArch, U. Calif., Berkeley, 1962. Registered architect, Victoria, Australia. Lectr. architecture U. Melbourne, 1964-87, sr. lectr., 1988—. Contbr. articles to archtl. jours., chpt. to book. Mem. Royal Australian Inst. Architects (assoc.). Home: 649 Drummond St #9, Carlton North, Victoria 3054, Australia Office: U Melbourne, Parkville 3052, Australia

TURNER, ARTHUR CAMPBELL, political science educator, author; b. Glasgow, Scotland, May 19, 1918; naturalized, 1958; s. Malcolm and Robina Arthur (Miller) T.; m. Anne Gordzialkowska, Jan. 21, 1950; 1 child, Nadine (Mrs. M.J. O'Sullivan). M.A. with 1st class honors, U. Glasgow, 1941; B.A. with 1st class honors in Modern History, Queen's Coll., Oxford U., 1943, M.A., 1947, B.Litt., 1948, M.Litt., 1979; Ph.D., U. Calif., Berkeley, 1951. Lectr. history U. Glasgow, 1945-51; asst. prof. history U. Toronto, 1951-53; Commonwealth Fund fellow U. Calif., Berkeley, 1948-50, vis. prof., summers 1950, 66, 71, 78; assoc. prof. polit. sci. U. Calif., Riverside, 1953-58, prof., 1958—, chmn. div. social scis., 1953-61, dean grad. div., 1960-61, chmn. dept. polit. sci., 1961-66; prof. internat. relations, govt. Claremont Grad. Sch., part-time 1962-72; vis. prof. UCLA, 1967, Pomona Coll., 1977; Exec. com. Inst. World Affairs, 1960—, dir., 1965. Author: The Post-War House of Commons, 1942, Free Speech and Broadcasting, 1944, Mr. Buchan, Writer: A Life of the First Lord Tweedsmuir, 1949, Scottish Home Rule, 1952, Bulwark of the West: Implications and Problems of NATO, 1953, Towards European Integration, 1953, Pakistan: The Impossible Made Real, 1957, The Unique Partnership: Britain and the United States, 1971; co-author: Control of Foreign Relations, 1957, The Regionalization of Warfare, 1985; (with L. Freedman) Tension Areas in World Affairs, 1964, Power and Ideology in the Middle East, 1988; contbr.: Ency. Americana Annual, 1957—; mem. editorial com., U. Calif. Press, 1959-65, 80-83, chmn., U. Calif. Press, 1962-65. Recipient Cecil prize, 1939; Blackwell prize U. Aberdeen, 1943, 51; Rockefeller research grantee Cambridge, 1959-60; NSF travel grantee, 1964; Wilton Park fellow, 1966, 76; Santa Barbara Seminar on Arms Control fellow, 1983. Mem. Am. Soc. Internat. Law, Am., Canadian hist. assns., Am. Polit. Sci. Assn., Hist. Assn. (Eng.), Phi Beta Kappa. Republican. Home: 1992 Rincon Ave Riverside CA 92506

TURNER, CHRISTOPHER JOHN, diplomat; b. Aug. 17, 1933; s. Arthur Basil and Joan Meddows (Taylor) T.; m. Irene Philomena de Souza, 1961; 2 daughters. MA, U. Cambridge. Dist. officer Diplomatic Service, Tanganyika, Tanzania, 1958-61, dist. commr., 1961-62; magistrate, regional local cts. officer Diplomatic Service, 1962-64, sec. sch. adminstrn., 1964-69; dist. agt. Anglo-French Condominium of New Hebrides, 1970-73, devel. sec., 1973, fin. sec., 1975, chief sec., 1977-80; adminstrv. officer staff planning Hong Kong, 1980-82; gov. Turks and Caicos Islands 1982-87; gov. Montserrat West Indies, 1987—. Served with RAF, 1951-53. Decorated OBE, 1977; recipient Vanuatu Independance medal, 1981. Office: Government House, Plymouth, Montserrat West Indies also: 98 Christchurch Rd, Winchester SO23 9TE, England *

TURNER, EVAN HOPKINS, art museum director, educator; b. Orono, Me., Nov. 8, 1927; s. Albert Morton and Percie Trowbridge (Hopkins) T.; m. Brenda Winthrop Bowman, May 12, 1956; children: John, Jennifer. A.B. cum laude, Harvard U., 1949, M.A., 1950, Ph.D., 1954. Head docent service Fogg Mus., Cambridge, Mass., 1950-51; curator Robbins Art Collection of Prints, Arlington, Mass., 1951; teaching fellow fine arts Harvard U., 1951-52; lectr., research asst. Frick Collection, N.Y.C., 1953-56; gen. curator, asst. dir. Wadsworth Atheneum, Hartford, Conn., 1956-59; dir. Montreal Mus. Fine Arts, Que., Can., 1959-64, Phila. Mus. Art, 1964-77, Ackland Art Mus., 1978-83, Cleve. Mus. Art, 1983—; adj. prof. U. N.C., Chapel Hill, 1978—; adj. prof. art history U. Pa. Mem. Assn. Art Mus. Dirs., Coll. Art Assn. Am., Am. Mus. Assn., Am. Fedn. Arts. Clubs: Union (Cleve.); Franklin Inn (Phila.); Century Assn. Home: 3071 N Park Blvd Cleveland OH 44118 Office: The Cleve Mus of Art 11150 East Blvd Cleveland OH 44106

TURNER, FRED L., fast food franchiser executive; b. 1933; married. B.S., De Paul U., 1952. With McDonald's Corp., Oak Brook, Ill., 1956—, exec. v.p., 1967-68, pres., chief adminstrv. officer, 1968-77, chief exec. officer, 1977-87, chmn., 1977—, also dir.; bd. dirs. Baxter Internat. Inc. Served as 1st lt. U.S. Army, 1943-45. Office: McDonald's Corp 1 McDonald's Plaza Oak Brook IL 60521 *

TURNER, GEORGE PEARCE, investment company executive; b. Dallas, Aug. 22, 1915; s. Fred Horatio and Florence (Phillips) T.; m. June Lori Haney, Feb. 4, 1943 (div. 1976); children—Bruce Haney, Brian Phillips, Mark Richardson; m. Kathryn Blank Hauf, June 1976. Student, U. Tex., 1932-33, 35-36, 40-41, So. Methodist U., 1934; BA in Internat. Relations cum laude, U. So. Calif., 1962, MS in Internat. Pub. Adminstrn. summa cum laude, 1966; PhD in Econs./Internat. Relations, Columbia Pacific U., 1982, PhD. in Pub. Adminstrn./Internat. Relations, 1985. Archtl. designer Los Angeles, 1946-48; prin. Lieburg & Turner (cons. engrs.), Pasadena, Calif., 1947-48; pres. Radiant Heat Engring., Inc., Pasadena, 1948-53; exec. asst. to dir. fgn. subsidiaries S.Am. Fluor Corp. Ltd., Los Angeles, 1953-54; exec. staff Coast Fed. Savs. & Loan Assn., 1954-55, Holmes & Narver, Inc., Los Angeles, 1955-61; mgr. project devel. S.Am. ops. Southwestern Engring. Co., Los Angeles, 1962; pres. Haney Devel. Corp., 1964—, Fomento e Inversiones Quisqueyanos C. por A., Santo Domingo de Guzman, Dominican Republic, 1967—; gen. mgr. for Venezuelan ops. Hale Internat. Inc., Caracas, 1970-71; dir., mgr. Consortium Lomas de La Lagunita, Caracas, 1970, Consortium Desarrollos Urbanos, Valencia, Venezuela, 1970; pres. Haney Investment Corp. (HANCO), 1974—, Casa Fomiq, 1978—, Caribbean Vagabond Ltd., Grand Cayman Island, B.W.I., 1981—, Kay Pearce & Turner, Ltd., Newtown Square, Pa., 1981—; sec. Integrated Industries of Atlantic County (N.J.); gen. partner N.Y. Ave. Parking Assocs., Atlantic City, 1980—; cons. econ. devel., 1963—; adviser, provisional pres., Dominican Republic, 1965-66, constl. pres. of republic, 1966-68; projects programmer Nat. Planning Inst. Peru Tri-Partite Mission, 1963-65; ofcl. OAS adviser Nat. Office Tourism Dominican Republic, 1966-67, Nat. Office Cultural Patrimony, Liga Mcpl. Dominicana, 1967-68; cons., dir. projects, programming, tech. matters Mission Recovery and Rehab., Dominican Republic, 1965-67; dep. dir. Tech. Assistance Mission Dominican Republic, 1967-68; cons. assignments for program assistance Inter-Am. Tng. Ctr., Fed. U. Ceara, Brazil; OAS adviser on tech. assistance to Chile, Argentina, Uruguay, Peru, Brazil, 1962-68; cons. Wildwood Ocean Towers, N.J., 1969-70; cons. Capital Investment Devel. Corp., Downing Ctr., Downingtown, Pa., 1971-77; dir. for Project Monitor and owners agt., hosp. tower Hahnemann Med. U. and Hosp., Phila., 1975-78; pres. Urban Planning and Devel. Corp., Exton, Pa., 1978-79; cons., corp. sec., v.p. Constrn., Devel. and Properties Mgmt. Group, Integrated Industries Inc., Exton, 1978—; ltd. ptnr. Marsh Creek Assocs. Two, 1985—; appointed to faculty Columbia Pacific U., 1987. Author: An Analysis of the Economy of El Salvador, 1961, The Alliance for Progress: Concept Versus Structure, 1966, Some Observations on the Decade of the 1960's—U.S. vis-a-vis Latin America, 1982, Latin American Odyssey, 1985; Contbr. articles to profl. publs. Served with USAF, 1941-45. Decorated OAS Medal of Honor; citation for valiant service in Dominican Republic, 1965-66; ofcl. OAS Commendation for program contbns., Peru, Dominican Republicn, Brazil, Venezuela, 1969. Mem. Delta Phi Epsilon, Alpha Sigma Lambda. Home: 8 Fox Run Ln Newtown Square PA 19073 Office: Kay Pearce & Turner Ltd PO Box 419 Newtown Square PA 19073

TURNER, HENRY BROWN, business executive; b. N.Y.C., Sept. 3, 1936; s. Henry Brown III and Gertrude (Adams) T.; m. Sarah Jean Thomas, June 7, 1958 (div.); children: Laura Eleanor, Steven Bristow, Nancy Carolyn. A.B., Duke U., 1958; M.B.A., Harvard U., 1962. Controller Fin. Corp. of Ariz., Phoenix, 1962-64; treas., dir. corporate planning Star-Kist Foods, Terminal Island, Calif., 1964-67; dir., 1st v.p. Mitchum, Jones & Templeton, Los Angeles, 1967-73; asst. sec. Dept. Commerce, Washington, 1973-74; v.p. fin. N-Ren Corp., Cin., 1975-76; v.p. Oppenheimer & Co., N.Y.C., 1976-78; exec. v.p., mng. dir. corporate fin. Shearson Hayden Stone Inc., N.Y.C., 1978-79; sr. mng. dir. Ardshiel Inc., 1980-81, pres., 1981—; bd. dirs. Info. Techs., Inc., MacDonald & Co., Pembrook Mgmt. Co., Nat. Car Rental Systems, Inc., Golden State Vinters Inc. Sponsor Jr. Achievement, 1964-67. Served to lt. USNR, 1958-60. Coll. Men's Club scholar Westfield, N.J., 1954-55. Mem. Fed. Govt. Accountants Assn. (hon.), Duke Washington Club, Omicron Delta Kappa. Home: 1100 Park Ave Apt 8A New York NY 10028 Office: Ardshiel 230 Park Ave New York NY 10169

TURNER, JOHN NAPIER, member of Canadian parliament; b. Richmond, Eng., June 7, 1929; s. Leonard and Phyllis (Gregory) T.; m. Geills McCrae Kilgour, May 11, 1963; children: Elizabeth, Michael, David, Andrew. BA with honors in Polit. Sci., U. B.C., Can., 1949; BA, Oxford U., Eng., 1951, BCL, 1952; MA, Oxford U., 1957; postgrad., U. Paris, 1952-53; LLD (hon.), U. New Brunswick, 1968, York U., Toronto, 1969; D. of Civil Law (hon.), Mt. Allison U., N.B., 1980. Bar: Eng. 1953, Que. 1954, Ont. 1968, B.C. 1969, Y.T. 1969, N.W.T. 1969, Barbados 1969, Trinidad 1969. With Stikeman, Elliot, Tamaki, Mercier and Turner, Montreal, Que., McMillan Binch, Toronto, 1976-84; M.P. for St. Lawrence-St. George Montreal, 1962-68, Ottawa-Carleton, 1968-75; parliamentary sec. to Minister of Northern Affairs and Nat. Resources, 1963-65; minister without portfolio 1965-67; registrar-gen. Govt. of Can., 1967-68, minister of consumer and corp. affairs, 1968, solicitor-gen., 1968, minister of justice and atty.-gen. of Can., 1968-72, minister of fin., 1972-75, prime minister of Can., 1984; leader Liberal Party Can., 1984—; former parliamentary sec. to Minister of Northern Affairs and Natural Resources; created Queen's Counsel Parliament of Can., 1968; current positions include minister without portfolio, registrar gen., minister consumer and corp. affairs, solicitor gen., minister justice and atty. gen., minister fin. Author: Senate of Canada, 1961, Politics of Purpose, 1968. Can. Track Field Champion, 1950-51; mem. English Track and Field Team. Mem. Eng. Bar Assn., Grey's Inn London, Bar assns. of Ont., Que., B.C., Barbados, Trinidad. Liberal. Roman Catholic. Clubs: St. James, Mt. Royal, Montreal Racquet (Montreal); Cercle Universitaire d'Ottawa; Country (Aylmer, Que.); Queen's Badminton and Racquet; York (Toronto); The Vancouver. Home: 541 Acacia Ave, Ottawa, ON Canada K1M 0M5 Office: Liberal Party of Canada, 200 Laurier Ave W, Ottawa, ON Canada K1P 6M8 also: Office of Leader of Opposition, 409-S House of Commons, Ottawa, ON Canada K1A 0A6

TURNER, LOYD LEONARD, advertising executive, public relations executive; b. Claude, Tex., Nov. 5, 1917; s. James R. and Maude (Brown) T.; m. Lee Madeleine Barr, Apr. 13, 1944; children: Terry Lee, Loyd Lee. Student, Tex. Tech. U., 1935-36, Okla. Bapt. U., 1936-37; B.A., Baylor U., 1939, M.A., 1940; postgrad., U. Pa., 1940-42. Instr. dept. English U. Pa., Phila., 1940-42; pub. relations coordinator Consol. Vultee Aircraft Corp., San Diego, 1946-48; dir. pub. relations Consol. Vultee Aircraft Corp., Fort Worth, 1948-53; asst. to pres. Fort Worth div. Gen. Dynamics Corp., 1953-72; exec. asst. to pres. and chmn. bd. Tandy Corp., Fort Worth, 1972-76; v.p. Tandy Corp., 1976-85; sr. v.p. Witherspoon & Assocs., Inc., Fort Worth, 1986—, also bd. dirs.; mem. Gov.'s Com. on Public Sch. Edn., Tex., 1966-69; pres. Tex. Council Major Sch. Dists., 1968-69. Author: The ABC of Clear Writing, 1954. Bd. dirs. Tarrant County chpt. ARC, 1956-59; bd. dirs. Pub. Communication Found. for N.Tex., 1970-76, Tex. Com. Public Edn., 1961-69; bd. dirs. Fort Worth Child Study Ctr., 1974-81, 85-88, v.p., 1986-88; bd. dirs. Parenting Guidance Ctr., 1976-78, Longhorn council Boy Scouts Am., 1976—, One Broadway Plaza, 1978—; planning and research council United Way, Tarrant County, 1976-80; bd. dirs. Casa Manana Musicals, 1978—, pres., 1978-80; bd. dirs. Fort Worth Citizens Organized Against Crime, 1976—, vice chmn., 1978—; bd. dirs. Jr. Achievement Tarrant County, 1982-87, North Central chpt. March of Dimes, 1983-84; mem. Christian edn. coordinating bd. Bapt. Gen. Conv., Tex., 1976-80; trustee Fort Worth Pub. Library Bd., 1953-63, pres., 1958-63; trustee Fort Worth Bd. Edn., 1959-71, pres., 1965-71; trustee Baylor U., Waco, Tex., 1980—. Served with USAAF, 1942-46. Named Library Trustee of Yr. Tex. Library Assn., 1961; Paul Harris fellow Rotary Internat., 1983; recipient Silver Beaver award Boy Scouts Am., 1986. Mem. Pub. Relations Soc. Am. (pres. N.Tex. chpt. 1977), Pub. Rel. Soc. Am. (Paul M. Lund Pub. Service award 1980), Nat. Mgmt. Assn., Tex. Congress of Parents and Tchrs. (hon. life mem.), West Tex. C. of C. (bd. dirs. 1982-87, v.p. 1985-87, Leadership award 1966, 69), NEA (pres. Best Bd. of Large Sch. Systems in U.S. 1968), Tex. Assn. of Sch. Bds. (bd. dirs. 1966-71, Outstanding Service award 1971), Advt. Club of Fort Worth (pres. 1977-78), Air Force Assn. (Spl. citation 1962), Assn. for Higher Edn. of N. Tex. (vice chmn. 1979-82), Fort Worth C. of C. (bd. dirs. 1974-76, 78-81, 83-87, vice chmn. 1985-87), Arts Council of Fort Worth (dir. 1973-75, 80—), Tex. Assn. Bus. (bd. dirs. 1979-82, 83-87), Tex. Research League (bd. dirs. 1979-87), Baylor U. Devel. Council (pres. 1975-77), Baylor U. Alumni Assn. (bd. dirs. 1958-61), Fort Worth Safety Council (bd. dirs. 1980-83), Am. Advt. Fedn. (Silver Medal award 1981), Fort Worth Art Assn., Soc. Profl. Journalists-Sigma Delta Chi (pres. Fort Worth chpt. 1961-62). Baptist. Clubs: Admirals, Century II, Frog, Knife and Fork (pres. 1965-66), Colonial Country. Lodge: Rotary (pres. 1974-75; William B. Todd Service Above Self award 1987). Home: 3717 Echo Trail Fort Worth TX 76109 Office: Witherspoon & Assocs Inc 1000 W Weatherford Fort Worth TX 76102

TURNER, PHILIP WILSON, design engineer; b. Cambridge, Cambridgeshire, Eng., Aug. 16, 1921; s. Arthur Edgar and Minnie Rose (Williams) T.; B.Sc., London U., 1945; M.A., Cambridge U., 1946. Physicist, Spencer Moulton, Bradford-on-Avon, Eng., 1946-48, chief scientist, 1948-49; sr.

designer, dir. Moulton Devels., Bradford-on-Avon, 1949-59; design engr. Cambridge U., 1959-69; sr. design engr. engring. dept., 1969-84, cons., 1984—; cons. in field. Patentee in field. Fellow Plastics and Rubber Inst.; mem. Inst. Mech. Engrs., Inst. Physics, Soc. Application of Research, Inst. Inventors. Club: Everyman (Bath, Avon, Eng.). Avocations: philosophy; music; model making; musical instrument construction; tennis. Home: Cabbage Moore, Great Shelford, Cambridge CB2 5NB, England Office: Engring Dept Cambridge U, Trumpington St, Cambridge CB2 1PZ, England

TURNER, RALPH HERBERT, sociologist, educator; b. Effingham, Ill., Dec. 15, 1919; s. Herbert Turner and Hilda Pearl (Bohn) T.; m. Christine Elizabeth Hanks, Nov. 2, 1943; children: Lowell Ralph, Cheryl Christine. B.A., U So. Calif., 1941, M.A., 1942; postgrad., U. Wis., 1942-43; Ph.D., U. Chgo., 1948. Research assoc. Am. Council Race Relations, 1947-48; faculty UCLA, 1948—, prof. sociology and anthropology, 1959—, chmn. dept. sociology, 1963-68; chmn. Acad. Senate U. Calif. System, 1983-84; vis. summer prof. U. Wash., 1960, U. Hawaii, 1962; vis. scholar Australian Nat. U., 1972; vis. prof. U. Ga., 1975, Ben Gurion U., Israel, 1983; vis. fellow Nuffield Coll. Oxford U., 1980; disting. vis. prof. Am. U., Cairo, Egypt, 1983; adj. prof. China Acad. Social Scis., Beijing, People's Republic China, 1986; faculty research lectr. UCLA, 1986-87. Author: (with L. Killian) Collective Behavior, 1957, 2d edit., 1972, 3d edit., 1987, The Social Context of Ambition, 1964, Robert Park on Social Control and Collective Behavior, 1967, Family Interaction, 1970, Earthquake Prediction and Public Policy, 1975, (with J. Nigg, D. Paz, B. Young) Community Response to Earthquake Threat in Southern California., 1980, (with J. Nigg and D. Paz) Waiting for Disaster, 1986; editorial cons., 1959-62; editor: Sociometry, 1962-64; acting editor: Ann. Rev. of Sociology, 1977-78; assoc. editor, 1978-79, editor, 1980-86; adv. editor: Am. Jour. Sociology, 1954-56, Sociology and Social Research, 1961-74; editorial staff: Am. Sociol. Rev., 1955-56; assoc. editor: Social Problems, 1959-62, 67-69; cons. editor: Sociol. Inquiry, 1968-73, Western Sociol. Rev., 1975-79; editorial bd. Mass Emergencies, 1975-79, Internat. Jour. Critical Sociology, 1974—, Symbolic Interaction, 1977—. Mem. behavioral scis. study sect. NIH, 1961-66, chmn., 1963-64; dir.-at-large Social Sci. Research Council, 1965-66; chmn. panel on pub. policy implications of earthquake prediction Nat. Acad. Scis., 1974-75, also mem. earthquqke study delegation to Peoples Republic of China, 1976; Mem. com. social edn. and action Los Angeles Presbytery, 1954-56. Served to lt. (j.g.) USNR, 1943-46. Recipient Faculty prize Coll. Letters and Scis. UCLA, 1985; Faculty Research fellow Social Sci. Research Council., 1953-56; Sr. Fulbright scholar U.K., 1956-57; Guggenheim fellow, U.K., 1964-65. Mem. Am. Sociol. Assn. (council 1959-64, chmn. social psychology sect. 1960-61, pres. 1968-69, chmn. sect. theoretical sociology 1973-74, chmn. collective behavior and social movements sect. 1983-84, Cooley-Mead award 1987), Pacific Sociol. Assn. (pres. 1957), Internat. Sociol. Assn. (council 1974-82, v.p. 1978-82), Soc. Study Social Problems (exec. com. 1962-63), Am. Acad. Arts and Scis., Soc. for Study Symbolic Interaction (pres. 1982-83, Charles Horton Cooley award 1978), AAUP. Home: 1126 Chautauqua Blvd Pacific Palisades CA 90272 Office: UCLA 405 Hilgard Ave Los Angeles CA 90024

TURNER, RALPH WILSON, JR., broadcasting executive clergyman; b. Shreveport, La., Jan. 18, 1948; s. Ralph W. and Gladys Pearl (Ma Gouirk) T.; m. Sandra Elaine Aymond, May 23, 1970; children: Christopher Layne, Cory Wilson. BA cum laude in Speech Edn., La. Coll., 1970; MRE, New Orleans Bapt. Theol. Sem., 1973. Ordained to ministry Bapt. Ch., as deacon, 1972. Assoc. pastor and minister edn. 1st Bapt. Ch., Farmerville, La., 1968-71, 1st Bapt. Ch., Summit, Miss., 1971-73, 1st Bapt. Ch., Slidell, La., 1973-75, 1st Bapt. Ch., Port Arthur, Tex., 1975-76; minister edn. and bus. adminstr. 1st Bapt. Ch., Beaumont, Tex., 1976-79; assoc. dir. missions, teaching and tng. Greater New Orleans Bapt. Assn., 1979-81; dir. media services dept. La. Bapt. Conv., 1981—, also state dir. The ACTS Satellite Network, 1983—; state coordinator Bapt. Telecommunication Network, 1983—; guest faculty New Orleans Bapt. Theol. Sem., 1979-80, 84, 87; Sunday sch. dir. St. Tammany Bapt. Assn., Slidell, 1973-75; ch. tng. dir. Concord Bapt. Assn., Farmerville, 1970-71; mem. Commn. for Ch. and Youth Agy. Relationships (nat. pres. 1988-90, founding editor nat. newsletter Youthscope 1985—); Merit badge counselor, exec. bds. New Orleans Area, Three Rivers and Attakapas councils Boy Scouts Am., 1973—, relationships v.p., 1983—, Nat. Religious Relationships Com., 1988; dist. rep. Nat. Eagle Scout Assn., 1975-79, participant Nat. Boy Scout Teleconf., 1988; faculty mem. Bapt. Week at Philmont Scout Ranch, 1978, 80, 88, dir. Protestant Wk. Philmont Ranch, 1987, 88, Protestant Chaplain gen. Nat. Jamboree, 1985, mem. Nat. Protestant Com., 1980—; deacon Calvary Bapt. Ch., Alexandria, 1987, assoc. chmn., 1988, mem. Nat. Religious Relationships Com., 1988—; La. Baptist Message Guest Editorial Panel, 1988—. Recipient Alexandria (La.) Civitan Citizenship award, 1969, 70; Silver Beaver award Boy Scouts Am., 1982; Good Shepherd award Nat. Assn. Baptists for Scouting, 1980; Nat. God and Service recognition (Protestant), 1986; Bronze Pelican award Cath. Com. on Scouting, 1986, Nat. Promotion award ACTS Network, 1986, 87. Mem. Nat. Assn. of Ch. Bus. Adminstrs., La. Bapt. Religious Edn. Assn., Bapt. Public Relations Assn., Met. Assn. of Religious Edn. Dirs., So. Bapt. Religious Edn. Assn., Golden Triangle Religious Edn. Assn., Nat. Audio-Visual Assn., Tex. Bapt. Public Relations Assn., La. Cable TV Assn. (assoc.), Southwestern Bapt. Religious Edn. Assn., Nat. Assn. Local Ch. Communicators (charter), Assn. Bapt. for Scouting (nat. bd. 1978—), Internat. TV Assn., Assn. for Ednl. Communications and Tech., La. Assn. for Ednl. Communications and Tech., Internat. Platform Assn., Nat. Assn. Local Cable Programmers, Am. Assn. Media Specialists, Assn. State ACTS Dirs. (founder, chmn., 1st pres. 1986-88, 88-89), Young Men's Bus. League of Beaumont, Alpha Phi Omega (life mem.; chpt. founder). Republican. Lodges: Lions, Rotary (newsletter editor 1976, chorister 1976), . Author: Training Sunday School Workers, 1982; How To Use Audiovisuals; The Church Video Answerbook: A Nontechnical Guide for Ministers and Lay Persons, 1986; contbr. articles to religious, adminstrv. and scouting publs. Avocations: writing, computers, photography. Office: LBC Media Services 1250 MacArthur Dr PO Box 311 Alexandria LA 71309

TURNER, ROBERT FOSTER, lawyer, government official, educator, writer; b. Atlanta, Feb. 14, 1944; s. Edwin Witcher and Martha Frances (Williams) T.; m. Debra Lou Herwig, Apr. 13, 1979. A.B., Ind. U., Bloomington, 1968; postgrad., Stanford U., 1972-73; J.D., U. Va., 1981. Bar: Va. 1982, U.S. Supreme Ct. 1986. Research assoc., pub. affairs fellow Hoover Instn. on War, Revolution and Peace, Stanford U., 1971-74; spl. asst., legis. asst. U.S. Sen. Robert P. Griffin, 1974-79; assoc. dir. Ctr. Law and Nat. Security, U. Va., Charlottesville, 1981, 87—, sr. fellow, 1985-86; spl. asst. undersec. for policy Dept. Def., 1981-82; counsel Pres.'s Intelligence Oversight Bd., White House, 1982-84; prin. dep. asst. sec. for legis. and intergovtl. affairs Dept. State, 1984-85; pres. U.S. Inst. Peace, Washington, 1986-87; lectr. in law and in govt. and fgn. affairs U. Va., 1988—. Author: Myths of the Vietnam War: The Pentagon Papers Reconsidered, 1972, Vietnamese Communism: Its Origins and Development, 1975, The War Powers Resolution: Its Implementation in Theory and Practice, 1983, Congress, the Constitution and Foreign Affairs, 1988, Nicaragua v. United States: A Look at the Facts, 1987; (with John Norton Moore) The Legal Structure of Defense Organization, 1986, International Law and the Brezhnev Doctrine, 1987; contbr. articles to profl. jours. Pres. Endowment of U.S. Inst. of Peace, 1986-87; trustee Intercollegiate Studies Inst., 1986—. Served to capt. U.S. Army, 1968-71, Vietnam. Grantee Hoover Press, 1972, Earhart Found., 1980, Inst. Ednl. Affairs, 1980, Carthage Found., 1980. Mem. ABA (chmn. com. on exec.-congl. relations, sect. internat. law and practice 1983-86, adv. com. on law and nat. security 1984-86, standing com. on law and nat. security, 1986—), Bd. of Research Cons., Inst. Fgn. Policy Analysis, Mensa, Am. Soc. Internat. Law, Nat. Eagle Scout Assn. Home: 8222 La Faye Ct Alexandria VA 22306 Office: U Va Sch of Law Ctr for Law and Nat Security Charlottesville VA 22901

TURNER, ROSS JAMES, investment corporation executive; b. Winnipeg, Man., Can., May 1, 1930; s. James Valentine and Gretta H. (Ross) T.; children: Ralph, Rick, Tracy Lee. Student, U. Man. Extension, 1951, Banff Sch. Advanced Mgmt., 1956. Various sr. operating and mgmt. positions Genstar Corp., San Francisco, 1961-76, chmn., pres., chief exec. officer, 1976-86, also bd. dirs.; chmn. Genstar Investment Corp., San Francisco, 1986—; chmn., bd. dirs. Rio Algom Ltd., Gt. West Life Assurance Co., Fed. Industries Ltd.; bd. dirs. Oxford Properties Can. Ltd., Western Corp. Enterprises, Inc. Bd. dirs. YMCA, San Francisco; mem. Bay Area Internat. Forum. Fellow Soc. Mgmt. Accts. Can.; mem. San Francisco C. of C. (past pres., dir.). Clubs: Mt. Royal (Montreal); Toronto; Vancouver; Rancho Santa Fe Golf; Pacific Union, Peninsula Golf and Country (San Francisco). Office: Genstar Investment Corp 801 Montgomery San Francisco CA 94133

TURNER, WALTER FRANKLIN, electronics company executive; b. Chgo., Feb. 8, 1934; s. Walter Franklin and Mary (Campanale) T.; m. Jean Ann McDermott, Jan. 29, 1969; children: Paul E., Teresa E., Tracey L. BBA, Loyola U., Los Angeles, 1955. Mktg. rep. IBM, Los Angeles, 1959-69; regional mgr. Farrington Mfg. Co., Los Angeles, 1969-70; nat. acct. mgr. Telex Computer Products, Los Angeles, 1970-73; regional mgr. Value Computing, Los Angeles, 1973-82; pres. JCA Software, Inc., Irvine, Calif., 1982-87; v.p. mktg., sales Essential Software, Inc., Sherman Oaks, Calif., 1987—. Served to lt. USN, 1955-59. Office: JCA Software Inc 18201 Von Karman Ave Irvine CA 92715

TURNER, WELD WINSTON, industrial psychologist; b. St. Paul, July 25, 1931; s. Frank and Hazel Thirza (Weld) Prevratil; B.S. Commerce, Okla. State U., 1954; M.S., Purdue U., 1955, Ph.D., 1959; m. Helen Theo Kralicek, June 12, 1953 (div. 1969); children—Jean Ann, Alan Weld. Personnel evaluation asso. Gen. Motors Inst., Flint, 1955-60; supr. personnel research B.F. Goodrich Co., Akron, 1960-67; sr. manpower adv. Mobil Oil Corp., N.Y.C., 1967—; lectr. adult edn. div. U. Akron, part-time. Served with U.S. Army, 1951-52. Mem. Am. Psychol. Assn., Soc. Indsl. Organizational Psychology, Assembly for Sci. and Applied Psychology, Sigma Xi, Phi Kappa Phi, Pi Gamma Mu. Home: 601 Rosery Rd Apt 3905 Largo FL 34640

TURNER, WILLIAM BOB, management and financial consultant, educator, lecturer; b. Fresno, Calif., July 3, 1920; s. William Burton and Grace (Calhoun) T.; m. Phyllis Vivian Hain, Apr. 2, 1940; children—Jacqulyn Lee Turner Gruchala, Pamela Turner Kartiganer, Donna Turner Diaz. B.S., UCLA, 1948; M.S., Golden State U., 1952; B.A., Columbia Pacific U., 1980, Ph.D., 1984. Lic. nursing home adminstr., Calif. Mgr., contract adminstr. Sunstrand/Turbo, Pacoima, Calif., 1955-59; mgr. mgmt. control Marquardt Corp., Van Nuys, Calif., 1959-64; div. controller Purolator Products, Inc., Newbury Park, Calif., 1964-67; controller A. & W. Internat., Inc., Santa Monica, Calif., 1967-70; exec. v.p. Wyndon Corp., Century City, Calif., 1970-80, dir., 1972-80; pres. Del Rey Mgmt., Sherman Oaks, Calif., 1979—; v.p. Sandpebbles Corp., Canoga Park, Calif., 1976-82; prof. Golden State U., Los Angeles, 1985—; cons. in field, 1965—; asst. prof. Calif. State U.-Dominguez Hills, 1976-80, Golden State U., Los Angeles, 1952-56, adminstr. Quizmasters seminars, 1976—; exec. trustee Magnolia Investments, 1982; mem. Calif. Senate Select Com. on Small Bus., 1986—. Author: The Administrator, 1977; Study Manual for NHA Exam, 1980; A-I-T Study Manual for the California Exam, NHA, 1982, Cram for NAB Exam, 1987. Republican precinct worker, 1952-68. Served with U.S. Army, 1944-45. Fellow Am. Coll. Health Care Adminstrs. (Educator of Yr. 1985); mem. Nat. Assn. Accts. Populist. Lodges: De Molay (past comdr., dean, chevalier, Cross of Honor, Legion of Honor, past master councilor), Masons. Home: 13902 Huston St Sherman Oaks CA 91423 Office: Golden State U 1111 W 6th St Los Angeles CA 90017

TURNER, WILLIAM COCHRANE, international management consultant; b. Red Oak, Iowa, May 27, 1929; s. James Lyman and Josephine (Cochrane) T.; m. Cynthia Dunbar, July 16, 1955; children: Scott Christopher, Craig Dunbar, Douglas Gordon. BS, Northwestern U., 1952. Pres., bd. dirs. Western Mgmt. Cons., Inc., Phoenix, 1960-74, Western Mgmt. Cons. Europe, S.A., Brussels, 1968-74; U.S. ambassador, permanent rep. OECD, Paris, 1974-77, vice chmn. exec. com., 1976-77, U.S. rep. Energy Policy Commn., 1976-77; mem. U.S. dels. internat. meetings, 1974-77, western internat. trade group U.S. Dept. Commerce, 1972-74; chmn. Argyle Atlantic Corp., Phoenix, 1977—; chmn. European adv. council, 1981—, Asia Pacific adv. council AT&T Internat., 1981—; mem. European adv. council IBM World Trade Europe, Africa, Mid. East Corp., 1977-80; mem. Asia Pacific adv. council Am. Can Co., 1981-85, Gen. Electric of Brazil adv. council Gen. Electric Co., Coral Gables, Fla., 1979-81, Caterpillar of Brazil adv. council Caterpillar Tractor Co., Peoria, Ill., 1979-84, Caterpillar Asia Pacific Adv. Council, 1984—, adv. com. Trade Negotiations, 1982-84; bd. dirs. Goodyear Tire & Rubber Co., Akron, Ohio, Salomon Inc., N.Y.C., Atlantic Inst. Found., Inc., mem. internat. adv. council Avon Products, Inc., N.Y.C., 1985—; mem. Spencer Stuart adv. council Spencer Stuart and Assocs., N.Y.C., 1984—; chmn., mem. internat. adv. council Advanced Semiconductor Materials Internat. NV., Bilthoven, The Netherlands, 1985—; bd. dirs. The Atlantic Council of the U.S., Washington, 1977—; co-chmn. internat. adv. bd. Pacific & Asia Christian U., Kona, Hawaii, 1985—; bd. dirs. World Wildlife Fund/U.S., 1983—, The Conservation Found., 1985—; bd. govs. Joseph H. Lauder Inst. Mgmt. and Internat. Studies, U. Pa., 1983—; trustee Heard Mus., Phoenix, 1983-86; trustee Am. Grad. Sch. Internat. Mgmt., 1972—, chmn. bd. trustees, 1987—; bd. govs. Atlantic Inst. Internat. Affairs, Paris, 1977—; adv. bd. Ctr. Strategic and Internat. Studies, Georgetown U., 1977-81; mem. European Community-U.S. Businessmen's Council, 1978-79; bd. govs. Am. Hosp. of Paris, 1974-77; trustee Nat. Symphony Orch. Assn., Washington, 1973-83, Am. Sch., Paris, 1976-77, Orme Sch., Mayer, Ariz., 1970-74, Phoenix Country Day Sch., 1971-74; mem. nat. councils Salk Inst., 1978-82; mem. U.S. Adv. Com. Internat. Edn. and Cultural Affairs, 1969-74; nat. rev. bd. Ctr. Cultural and Tech. Interchange between East and West, 1970-74; mem. vestry Am. Cathedral, Paris, 1976-77; pres., bd. dirs. Phoenix Symphony Assn., 1969-70; chmn. Ariz. Joint Econ. Devel. Com., 1967-68; exec. com., bd. dirs. Ariz. Dept. Econ. Planning and Devel., 1968-70; chmn. bd. Ariz. Crippled Children's Services, 1964-65; treas. Ariz. Rep. Com., 1956-57; chmn. Ariz. Young Rep. League, 1955-56. Recipient East-West Ctr. Disting. Service award, 1977. Mem. U.S. Council Internat. Bus. (trustee, exec. com. 1977—), Council Fgn. Relations, Phoenix 40. Episcopalian. Clubs: Met., Links (N.Y.C.), Plaza (Phoenix), Paradise Valley (Ariz.) Country, Bucks (London). Office: 4350 E Camelback Rd Suite 240-B Phoenix AZ 85018

TURNER, WILLIAM IAN MACKENZIE, JR., paper company executive; b. Sharon, Pa., Jan. 17, 1929; s. William Ian MacKenzie and Marjorie (Merrick) T.; m. Ann McCreery, June 13, 1953; children: William Ian MacKenzie III, Julia McCreery, James Zachry, Carol Merrick. B.A. in Mech. Engring. with honors, U. Toronto, Ont., Can., 1951; M.B.A. with distinction, Harvard U., 1953; LLD (hon.), Mt. Allison U., 1984; DCL (hon.), Bishop's U., 1987. Pres., Power Corp. Can., Ltd., Montreal, 1966-70; dir., pres., chief exec. officer, dir. Consol.-Bathurst, Ltd., Montreal, 1970-82; chmn., chief exec. officer Consol.-Bathurst, Inc., 1982—; dir. Celanese Can. Ltd., Canadian Marconi, A. Johnson & Co. Inc., CB Pak Inc., Schroders P.L.C., Bombardier, Inc., Power Corp. Can, Provigo, Inc., Newmont Mining; chmn. adv. bd. Wells Fargo Internat. Chmn. bd. govs. Royal Victoria Hosp.; chmn. Brit. N.Am. Com.; bd. dirs., exec. com. Montreal Symphony Orch.; chancellor Bishop's U., 1987. Named to Order of Can., 1987. Clubs: Montreal Amateur Athletic Assn. (Montreal), Montreal Racket (Montreal), Mount Royal (Montreal), Saint James (Montreal), Hillside Tennis (Montreal); Nat. (Toronto), Toronto (Toronto), York (Toronto); Brook (N.Y.C.), Knickerbocker (N.Y.C.). Office: Consol-Bathurst Ltd, 800 Dorchester Blvd W, Montreal, PQ Canada H3B 1Y9

TUROFF, CAROLE RUTH, lawyer, newspaper columnist; b. Cleve., June 14, 1937; d. Sam and Edna (Siegel) Lecht; B.A., Am. Internat. Coll., 1961; J.D., Cleve. Marshall Law Sch., 1970; m. Jack N. Turoff, Aug. 19, 1961; children—Hyleri Beth, Raechel Dawn, Elana Kay, Avril Jo. Admitted to Ohio bar, 1970; individual practice law, Cleve., 1970—; spl. counsel to atty. gen. Ohio, 1971-84; real estate broker Cuyahoga Realty, Cleve., 1976—; columnist Cleve. Press, 1974-81; tchr. English, Richmond Heights (Ohio) High Sch., 1961-62; lectr. in field. Chairperson community March of Dimes; active various polit. campaigns; del. Am. Israeli Polit. Affairs com., Israel task force; worker with Ralph Nader in Consumer Fraud; mem. exec. com. Cleve. Congress; founder Women in Divorce; founder The Carole Turoff Legal Clinic, 1987; session chairperson Internat. Woman's Yr. UN, Mexico, 1975; TV reporter Nat. Women's Conf., Houston; mem. corporate and profl. women's cabinet State of Israel Bonds. Recipient trophy as keynote speaker Internat. Woman's Yr. program, NASA. Mem. Internat. Platform Assn., Am. Trial Lawyers, Ohio, Cleve. bar assns., Nat. Women Lawyers. Democrat. Jewish. Club: Nat. Bd. Am. Mizrachi Women. Home: 2569 Snowberry Ln Pepper Pike OH 44124 Office: 2289 Lee Rd Cleveland Heights OH 44118

TUROFF, JACK NEWTON, lawyer, business consultant; b. Cleve., Dec. 8, 1933; s. Herman and Jean Y. (Pearlman) T.; m. Carole R., Aug. 19, 1961; children—Hyleri, Raechel, Elana, Avril. B.S. in Bus. Adminstrn., Ohio State U., 1955, J.D., 1960. Bar: Ohio 1960, U.S. Dist. Ct. (no. dist.) Ohio 1961, U.S. Supreme Ct. 1969. Asst. atty. gen. State of Ohio, 1960-62; sole practice, Cleve., 1960-62; assoc. Dudnik, Komito, Nurenberg, Plevin, Dempsey & Jacobson Assn., Cleve., 1963-64; ptnr. Turoff & Turoff, Cleve., 1965-81, 82—; ptnr. Koplow, Pomerantz, Turoff & Turoff Co., L.P.A., Cleve., 1981-82; cons. and lectr. in field of bus. Bd. dirs., sec. Jewish Children Group Homes, 1962-78; mem. Democratic Exec. Com., 1963-79; state steering rep. Senator Henry Jackson Presdl. campaign, 1980; active Dem. county congl. campaigns; chmn. bd. Neighborhood Counseling Service, 1980—; bd. dirs. West Side Community Mental Health Ctr. 1982—. Served with USAF, 1956-59, USAFR, 1959-70. Recipient Service award Big Bros. Am., 1975, Outstanding Service award Neighborhood Counseling Service, 1983. Mem. Ohio State Bar Assn., Am. Trial Lawyers Assn., Greater Cleve. Bar Assn., Cuyahoga County Bar Assn., Ohio Harness Horsemen's Assn. (bd. dirs. 1983—). Lodge: KP. Home: 2569 Snowberry Ln Pepper Pike OH 44124 Office: Nat City Bank Bldg 629 Euclid Ave Suite 420 Cleveland OH 44114

TURPIN, GÉRARD CHRISTIAN, endocrinologist, educator, consultant; b. Nov. 11, 1939; s. Raymond Alexandre and Simone Henriette (Gaillochet) T.; m. Anne-Lise Colette Rambert, Nov. 24, 1964; children: Eric, Sylvie. MD, U. Paris, 1964. Extern Hosps. of Paris, 1960-64, intern, 1964-70; clin. specialist Hosps. and Acad. of Paris, 1970-80, prof. medicine, 1980—; dir. Ctr. for Study and Research for Endocrinological and Metabolic Disorders, 1984—. Author: Why, When, How to Treat Hyperlipoproteinemias, 1982, 87, Pediatric Hyperlipidemias, 1985; author numerous articles on endocrinology and metabolism. Served to lt. French Army, 1964-65. Mem. French Endocrine Soc. (treas. 1979-84), Med. Soc. of Paris Hosps. Office: Hopital le pitie-Salpetriere, 83 Boulevard de l'Hopital, 75013 Paris France

TURSSO, DENNIS JOSEPH, business executive; b. St. Paul, Apr. 13, 1939; s. Joseph Bias and Cecelia Beatrice (Solheid) T.; m. Sharon Ann Benike, June 6, 1964 (div. 1975); 1 child, Jason Bradford; m. 2d, Jacqueline Mary Hoffmann, Oct. 19, 1977; children—Shannon and Missey Michele (twins). Student U. Minn., 1959-61. Sales mgr. Sten-C-Labl Inc., St. Paul, 1958-65; salesman Dymo Industries, Berkeley, Calif., 1965-68; with Dawson Patterson, St. Paul, 1968—; pres., chief exec. officer Tursso Cos. holding co., St. Paul, 1980—; bd. dirs. Venture Capital Fund St. Paul Port Authority; bd. dirs. Summit Nat. Bank, St. Paul, Blackourn Co., Shamrock Inc., Omaha. Advisor SBA, St. Paul, 1981-83; bd. dirs. Childrens' Home Soc. St. Paul. Recipient Star Club sales awards Dymo Industries, 1966, 67. Mem. Nat. Fed. Ind. Bus., Soc. Packaging Engrs., St. Paul C. of C. (cert. of merit, Outstanding Businessman 1987). Clubs: St. Paul Athletic, St. Paul, University, Minnesota, Decathlon, Pool and Yacht, Town and Country. Address: Tursso Cos 223 Plato Blvd E Saint Paul MN 55107 Office: Tursso Co Plant 3540 Midway Blvd Fort Dodge IA 50501

TURTOLA, RISTO PEKKA, architect; b. Marttila, Finland, Jan. 6, 1934; s. Viljo Abel and Irma Silvia (Lindstrom) T.; Architect, Polytech. U. Helsinki, 1964; m. Anja Marita Roos, June 5, 1960. Designing architect Olli Kivinen, Helsinki, 1964-68; leading architect Kauria-Turtola, Helsinki, 1965—; teaching asst. Poly. U. Helsinki, 1971-72, specialized tchr., 1976. Served with Pioneers, 1961-62. Recipient 1st prize Kokkola, Koivuhaka City Planning Competition, 1964, Tampere, Pispala Nordic City Planning Competition, 1968; 3d prize Turku, Univ. and City Planning Competition, 1976. Mem. Assn. Finnish Architects. Home: 8 Pohjoisranta, 00170 Helsinki Finland Office: 2 Rauhankatu, Helsinki Finland

TUSJIMOTO, MASASHI, data processing executive; b. Hyogo, Japan, Sept. 5, 1951; m. Hiroka Tsujimoto, Feb. 8, 1980; 2 children. B. of Indsl. Engring., Kansai U., Osaka, Japan, 1974. Engr. Nihon Computer System, Osaka, 1974-77, Ashisuto, Tokyo, 1977-85; mng. dir. SAS Software K.K., Tokyo, 1985—. Home: Kounan-cho 5-2-21-404, Higashinadaku-kobe, Hyogo Japan

TUSTIN, RICHARD DON, psychologist; b. Masterton, New Zealand, Apr. 20, 1948; s. John Noel and Esme Therese (Jones) T.; m. Jocelyn Norma Watson, Jan. 9, 1971; children: Jeremy Dougal, Nicholas James. BA with hons., Victoria U., Wellington, New Zealand, 1970; MA, Victoria U., 1973; PhD, Auckland U., New Zealand, 1977. Psychologist Dept. Justice, Wellington, New Zealand, 1970-75; chief clin. psychologist Minda, Inc., Adelaide, Australia, 1977—; teaching fellow U. Auckland, 1976-77. Contbr. articles to profl. publs. Pres. Glenelg Resident Assn., Adelaide, 1984—. Fellow New Zealand Psychol. Soc.; mem. Australia Behavior Modification Assn. (state pres. 1985-87, nat. pres. 1987—). Office: Minda Inc, Ilfra Combe Ave, Adelaide 5048, Australia

TUTIN, DOROTHY, actress; b. London, Apr. 8, 1930; d. John and A.E. (Fryers) T.; m. Derek Waring, 1963; 2 children. Ed. Royal Acad. Dramatic Art, London. Appeared at Stratford Festival, 1958, 60, took part in Shakespeare Meml. Theatre tour of Russia, 1958, Shakespeare recital before Pope, Vatican, 1964; prin. roles: Rose, The Living Room; Katherine, Henry V; Sally Bowles, I am a Camera; St. Joan, The Lark; Catherine, The Gates of Summer; Hedwig, The Wild Duck; Viola, Twelth Night; Ophelia, Hamlet; Dolly, Once More, with Feeling; Portia, The Merchant of Venice; Cressida, Troilus and Cressida; Sister Jeanne, The Devils, 1961, 62; Juliet, Romeo and Juliet; Desdemona, Othello; Varya, The Cherry Orchard, 1961; Prioress, The Devils, Edinburgh, 1962; Polly Peachum, The Beggar's Opera, 1963; Queen Victoria, Portrait of a Queen, 1965, N.Y., 1968; Rosalind, As You Like It, 1967; Cleopatra, Antony and Cleopatra, 1977; Madam Ravanskaya, The Cherry Orchard; films include: The Beggar's Opera, The Importance of Being Earnest, A Tale of Two Cities, Cromwell, Savage Messiah, The Shooting Party; TV appearances include: Henry VIII Anne Boleyn, 1974, South Riding, 1976, The Double Dearler, 1980, The Eavesdropper, 1981, The Combination, 1981, Life After Death, 1981, La Ronde, 1982, King Lear, 1982, Landscape, 1982, The Father, 1986, A Kind of Alaska, Murder with Mirrors, The Demon Lover. Recipient Evening Standard award as best actress, 1960; Variety Club of G.B. award for best film actress, 1972; Soc. of West End Theatre award for actress of the year in a revival, 1976. Address: care Barr Burnett, 2-3 Golden Sq, London W1 England

TUTINS, ANTONS, electronics/audio engineer; b. Ludza, Latvia, May 2, 1933; s. Francis and Veronika (Seipulniks) Tutins; came to U.S., 1950, naturalized, 1963; student U. Minn., 1951-55; BS in Elec. Engring., Ill. Inst. Tech., 1970; MBA, U. Chgo., 1974; m. Raita Snebergs, July 8, 1961; 1 child, Robert. With Motorola Communications div., Chgo., 1964-73; applications engring. supr. Knowles Electronics, Inc., Franklin Park, Ill., 1973-77, product engring. mgr., 1977-81; engring. mgr. Perma Power Electronics Inc., Chgo., 1982—. Served with USN, 1955-57. Mem. IEEE, Acoustical Soc. Am., Chgo. Acoustical and Audio Group (pres. 1977-78), Audio Engring. Soc., Midwest Acoustics Conf. (exec. com., pres. 1980), Latvian Cath. Student Assn. Dzintars (pres. 1979-81), Am. Latvian Cath. Assn. (registered agt. 1978—, v.p. 1985), Motorola Engring. Club (pres. 1970-71). Roman Catholic. Home: 1338 Briar Ct Des Plaines IL 60018 Office: 5601 W Howard Ave Chicago IL 60648

TUTT, CHARLES LEAMING, JR., educator, mechanical engineer; b. Coronodo, Calif., Jan. 26, 1911; s. Charles Leaming and Eleanor (Armit) T.; m. Pauline Barbara Shaffer, Aug. 16, 1933 (dec. Aug. 1981); children: Charles Leaming IV, William Bullard; m. Mildred Dailey LeMieux, Aug. 7, 1982. B.S.E., Princeton U., 1933, M.E., 1934; D.Eng., Norwich U., 1967. Student engr. Buick Motor div. Gen. Motors Corp., Flint, Mich., 1934-36; engr. chassis unit sect. Buick Motor div. Gen. Motors Corp., 1936-38, spl. assignment engr., 1938-40; asst. prof. mech. engring. Princeton U., 1940-46; staff asst. ASME, N.Y.C., 1940-44; asso. editor Product Engring. mag. McGraw-Hill Pub. Co., N.Y.C., 1944-46; asst. to pres. Gen. Motors Inst., Flint, 1946-50; adminstrv. chmn. Gen. Motors Inst., 1950-60, dean engring., 1960-69, dean acad. affairs, 1969-74; pres. Sunnyrest Sanitarium, Colorado Springs, Colo., 1982—. Contbr. articles to profl. jours. Mem. adv. com. Sloan Mus., Flint, 1965-82; trustee Norwich U., Northfield, Vt., 1963-76; bd. dirs. Engring. Found., N.Y.C., 1963-75, chmn., 1967-73; v.p. Friends of Pike Peak Library Dist., 1985, pres., 1986-87; mem. adv. bd. Pikes Peak Community Coll., 1986—. Fellow ASME (life, v.p. 1964-66, pres. 1975-76); mem. Soc. Mfg. Engrs. (dir. 1972-78), Am. Soc. Engring. Edn., Soc.

Automotive Engrs., Colo. Soc. Profl. Engrs., Engrs. Council for Profl. Devel. (dir. 1975-80), Am. Soc. Metals, Soc. of Cin. in State of Va., Sigma Xi, Delta Tau Delta, Tau Beta Pi. Clubs: Flint City, University (Flint); Wigwam (Deckers, Colo.); Princeton (N.Y.C.); Cooking, Cheyenne Mountain Country (Colorado Springs); Broadmoor Golf. Home: 20 Loma Linda Dr Colorado Springs CO 80906

TUTTLE, TONI BRODAX, swimming pool company executive; b. Bklyn., July 19, 1952; d. Abraham Paul and Marilyn (Monte) Brodax; m. Roy Lee, May 21, 1978; 1 son, Sean Monte. student Lesley Coll., 1972; B.A. in Journalism, U. R.I., 1974. Reporter Mexico City Daily News, 1972; freelance photographer/writer N.Y. Yankees, Communications Group, Ft. Lauderdale, Fla., 1974-78; editorial asst. Boating Mag., N.Y.C., 1974-76; pub. relations cons. B. Altmans Dept. Store, N.Y.C., 1975-76; dir. pub. relations Windjammer Barefoot Cruises, Miami, Fla., 1976-78; account exec. Art Jacobson Advt., Miami, 1978-79; v.p. Tuttle's Pool Co., Inc., Miami, 1979—. Jewish. Home: 6740 SW 94th St Miami FL 33156

TUTU, DESMOND MPILO, South African ecclesiastic; b. Klerksdorp, Republic of South Africa, Oct. 7, 1931; m. Leah Nomalizo Shenxane; children: Trevor Thamsanqa, Theresa Thandeka, Naomi Nontombi, Mpho Andrea. Diploma in teaching, Pretoria (Republic of South Africa) Bantu Normal Coll., 1953, BA, U. South Africa, 1954; licentiate in theology, St. Peter's Theol. Coll., Republic of South Africa, 1960; postgrad, King's Coll., U. London; D.D. (hon.), Gen. Theol. Sem., N.Y., 1978, Aberdeen U., Scotland, 1984, Trinity Luth. Sem., 1985, Trinity Coll., Hartford, Conn., 1986, Chgo. Theol. Sem., 1986, U. West Indies, Trinidad and Tobago, 1986, Oberlin Coll., 1986, U. of the South, 1988, Emory U., 1988; D.C.L. (hon.), Kent (Eng.) U., 1978; LL.D. (hon.), Harvard U., 1979, Claremont Grad. Sch., 1984, Temple U., 1985, 86, Mt. Allison U., Sackville, N.B., Can., 1988, Northeastern U., 1988; Th.D. (hon.), Ruhr U., 1981; 81; S.T.D. (hon.), Columbia U., 1982, Dickinson Coll., 1984; L.H.D. (hon.), St. Paul's Coll., 1984, Howard U., 1984, Morehouse Coll., 1986, Cen. U., 1986, CUNY, 1986; H.H.D. (hon.), Wilberforce U., 1985; Ph.D. (hon.), U. Rio, Rio de Janiero, 1986. Ordained priest Anglican Ch., 1961. Schoolmaster, 1954-57; parish priest, 1960—; lectr. Fed. Theol. Sem., 1967-69; lectr. UBLS Roma, Lesotho, 1970-72; assoc. dir. theol. edn. fund World Council Chs., Bromley, Kent, 1972-75; dean of Johannesburg, Republic of South Africa, 1975-76; bishop of Lesotho, 1976-78, of Johannesburg, 1985-86; archbishop of Cape Town, Republic of South Africa, 1986—; sec.-gen. South African Council Chs., 1978-85; vis. prof. Anglican Studies, N.Y. Gen. Theol. Sem., 1984; pres. All Africa Conf. of Chs., 1987—; chancellor U. Western Cape, Republic of South Africa, 1988—. Author: Crying in the Wilderness, 1982, Hope and Suffering, 1983 (both collections of sermons and addresses). Vice chmn. Internat. Alert, 1986; mem. disbursements adv. com. Fund for Edn. in South Africa, N.Y.C., 1988; mem. com. of honor for meml. to Imre Nagy and companions Hungarian Human Rights League, 1988. Recipient Prix d'Athene Onassis Found., 1980, Family of Man gold medallion, 1983, Martin Luther King Jr. Humanitarian award Ann. Black Am. Hero and Heroines Day, 1984; Nobel prize for peace, 1984, Martin Luther King Jr. Peace award, 1986, Internat. Integrity award John-Roger Found., 1986, Pres. award Glassboro State Coll., 1986, World Pub. Forum award City of San Rafael, Calif., 1986, Order of So. Cross Govt. of Brazil, 1987, Order of Merit Govt. of Brazil, 1987, Pacem in Terris award Quad Cities, 1987, Albert Schweitzer Humanitarian award Emmanuel Coll., 1988; recipient Freedom of the City Florence, Italy, 1985, Methyr Tydfil, U.K., 1986, Durham, Eng., 1987, Hull, Eng., 1988; King's Coll. fellow, 1978. Mem. NAACP (life), World Council Global Co-operation. Address: Bishop's Court, Claremont, Cape Town 7700, Republic of South Africa also: South African Council Chs, 42 De Villiers St, PO Box 4921, Johannesburg Republic of South Africa

TUTUOLA, AMOS, author; b. 1920, Abeokuta, W. Nigeria; s. Charles and Esther Tutuola; m. Victoria Tutuola, 1947; 8 children. Educated Mission Schs. Worked on father's farm; trained as coopersmith; with Nigeran Broadcasting Corp., Ibadan, 1945—; vis. fellow U. Ife (Nigeria), 1979; assoc. internat. writing program U. Iowa, Iowa City, 1983. Author: The Palm-Wine Drinkard (2d prize Turin, Italy 1985), 1952; My Life in the Bush of Ghosts (2d prize Turin, Italy 1985), 1954; Simbi and the Satyr of the Jungle, 1955; The Brave African Huntress, 1958; The Feather Woman of the Jungle, 1962; Ajaiyi and His Inherited Poverty, 1967; The Witch Herbalist of the Remote Town, 1981; Wild Hunter in the Bush of the Ghosts, 1982. Served with RAF, World War II. Named hon. citizen City of New Orleans, 1983. Home: PO Box 2251, Ibadan Nigeria *

TUUL, JOHANNES, physics educator, researcher; b. Tarvastu, Viljandi, Estonia, May 23, 1922; came to U.S., 1956, naturalized, 1962; s. Johan and Emilie (Tulf) T.; m. Marjatta Murtoniemi, July 14, 1957 (div. Aug. 1971); children—Melinda, Melissa; m. Sonia Esmeralda Manosalva, Sept. 15, 1976; 1 son, Johannes. B.S., U. Stockholm, 1955, M.A., 1956; Sc.M., Brown U., 1957, Ph.D., 1960. Research physicist Am. Cyanamid Co., Stamford, Conn., 1960-62; sr. research physicist Bell & Howell Research Center, Pasadena, Calif., 1962-65; asst. prof., assoc. prof. Calif. State Poly. U., Pomona, 1965-68; vis. prof. Pahlavi U., Shiraz, Iran, 1968-70; chmn. phys. earth sci. Calif. State Poly. U., Pomona, 1971-75, prof. physics, 1975—; cons. Bell & Howell Research Center, Pasadena, Calif., 1965, Teledyne Co., Pasadena, 1968; guest researcher Naval Weapons Center, China Lake, Calif., 1967, 72; resident dir., Calif. State U. Internat. Programs in Sweden and Denmark, 1977-78. Author: Physics Made Easy, 1974; contbr. articles in field to profl. jours. Pres. Group Against Smoking Pollution, Pomona Valley, Calif., 1976; foster parent Foster Parents Plan, Inc., Warwick, R.I., 1964—; block capt. Neighborhood Watch, West Covina, Calif., 1982-84. Brown U. fellow, 1957-58; U. Namur (Belgium) research grantee, 1978; Centre Nat. de la Recherche Scientifique research grantee, France, 1979; recipient Humanitarian Fellowship award Save the Children Fedn., 1968. Mem. Am. Phys. Soc., AAAS (life), Am. Assn. Physics Tchrs., N.Y. Acad. Scis. Republican. Roman Catholic. Research in energy conservation and new energy technologies. Office: Calif State Polu U 3801 W Temple Ave Pomona CA 91768

TUUTTI, HEIKKI, educator; b. Lappeenranta, Finland, Jan. 19, 1946; s. Edvard and Ida Maria (Piispa) T.; Marja Katrina Kaippa, June 24, 1968; children: Antti, Saija. Degree in (dental surgery), U. Helsinki, Finland, 1971; MSc in Social Sci., U. Kuopio, Finland, 1985; PhD, U. Kuopio, 1986. Diploma of Finnish Bd. Pub. Health. Dental health officer Municipality of Ilomantsi, Finland, 1972-74; cons. Inst. for Mentally Retarded, Liperi, Finland, 1975-79; asst. prof. U. Kuopio, 1975-79; sr. lecturer U. Dar Es Salaam, Tanzania, 1979-82; project mgr. DSM Dental Sch., Kuopio, 1982-86; team leader devel. project DSM Dental Sch., Dar Es Salaam, 1986—; vice chmn. U. Kuopio, 1970; bd. adminstrs. U. Kuopio, 1976-79. Editor: Dev Coop Between University, 1984; Jour. J. Tanz Dental Assn., 1987. cons. Ministry Edn. Finland, 1978-79. Served to ensign Finnish Army, 1964-65. Mem. Internal Assn. for Dental Research, Internal Assn. Dentistry for Handicapped, Fedn. Dentaire Internal, Tanzanian Med. Assn. Lodges: Rotary, Lion. Home: Sammalniementie 1 D 1, 70700 Kuopio Finland Office: MMC Dental Sch Dev Project, Box 70043, Dar Es Salaam Tanzania

TVEIT, MARTIN TORVALD, scientific foundation administrator; b. Ålvik, Kvam, Norway, Sept. 8, 1923. Diploma, Imperial Coll. Sci. and Tech., London; MSc, U. Minn., 1954; PhD, U. London, 1954. Pres., chief exec. officer World Confedn. Productivity Sci., Oslo. Mem. World Acad. Art and Sci., Swedish Acad. Engring. Sci. Office: World Confedn Prod Sci, Akersgt 64, Oslo 1, Norway

TWEEDALE, MARTIN MIDDLETON, philosopher, educator; b. Trenton, N.J., Oct. 10, 1937; arrived in N.Z., 1971; s. Joseph Tweedale and Gertrude Elizabeth (Lippincott) T.; m. Dellene Marie Moreland, Feb. 1, 1964; children: Ian Middleton, Jennifer Yust. BA, Princeton U., 1959; PhD, UCLA, 1965. Asst. prof. U. Pitts., 1965-69, UCLA, 1969-71; sr. lectr. U. Aukland, N.Z., 1971-88; prof. medieval and ancient philosophy, philosophy of lang., metaphysics U. Alberta, Can., 1988—. Author: Abailard on Universals, 1976. Mem. Am. Philos. Assn., Medieval Acad. Am., Internat. Soc. Medieval Philosophy. Home: 11606 72nd Ave, Edmonton, AB Canada T6G 0C1 Office: Philosophy Dept, Univ Alberta, Edmonton, AB Canada T6G 2E5

TWELLS, JOHN LAWRENCE, manufacturing and distributing company executive; b. Flint, Mich., Feb., 1934; s. Robert and Margaret Shaw (MacKillop) T.; m. Mary Jane Jentzen, Nov. 1961; children: Linda, John Lawrence, Robert William. BBA, U. Toledo, 1957; postgrad., Marquette U., 1975; MBA, Columbia Pacific U., 1981, DBA, 1983. Lab., terr. mgr., nat. accounts rep. Motorcraft/Autolite div. Ford Motor Co., Dearborn, Mich., 1950-63; dist. mgr., regional sales mgr. MOPAR div. Chrysler Corp., Detroit, 1963-67; asst. gen. mgr. NAPA Genuine Parts Co., Atlanta, 1967-68; gen. mgr. John MacKillop and Co., Inc., Poland, Ohio, 1968—; parts mktg. mgr. Dresser Industries, Waukesha (Wis.) Engine div. 1973-76; mgr. replacement and OEM parts profit ctr. Baker Material Handling Corp., 1976-78; gen. sales mgr. Amweld Bldg. Products Inc., Garretsville, Ohio, 1978-82, asst. gen. mgr., 1982, gen. mgr., 1983-87; pres., chief exec. officer Mesker Door Co., St. Louis, 1987—; lectr. in field. Contbr. articles on microfiche, inventory control, personnel selection, motivation and evaluation to profl. jours. Deacon Immanuel Presbyn. Ch., Milw., 1974-76. Served with U.S. Army, 1957-59. Recipient Disting. Mktg. award Sales and Mktg. mag., 1980. Mem. Am. Prodn. and Inventory Control Soc., Constrn. Specifications Inst., Sales and Mktg. Execs. Internat., Am. Inst. Indsl. Engrs., Am. Def. Preparedness Assn., Am. Legion, VFW, Tau Kappa Epsilon. Republican. Lodge: Rotary. Home: 8996 Sherwood Dr NE Warren OH 44484 Office: PO Box 5214 Poland OH 44514

TWIDALE, C(HARLES) R(OWLAND), geomorphologist, educator; b. Lincolnshire, Eng., Apr. 5, 1930; s. George Wilfred and Gladys May (West) T.; ed. Wintringham Grammar Sch., Grimsby; B.Sc., U. Bristol, 1951, M.Sc., 1953, D.Sc., 1977; Ph.D., McGill U., 1957; m. Kathleen Mary Gargini, Apr. 21, 1956; children—Nicholas, Richard Jonathan, Amanda Elizabeth. Research officer, div. land research Commonwealth Sci. and Indsl. Research Orgn., Canberra, 1952-57; mem. faculty dept. geography, geology, U. Adelaide, 1958—; vis. prof. geology and geophysics U. Calif., Berkeley, 1971; vis. prof. geology U. Tex., Austin, 1979. Nuffield Commonwealth bursary, 1965; NSF sr. fgn. scientist fellow, 1965-66, also vis. prof. Rensselaer Poly. Inst., Troy, N.Y. Fellow Royal Soc. South Australia (pres., 1975-76), Geol. Soc. Am., Royal Geog. Soc.; mem. Geol. Soc. Australia, Royal Soc. South Australia (Verco medal 1977). Author: Geomorphology, 1968; Structural Landforms, 1971; Analysis of Landforms, 1976; Granite Landforms, 1982; contbr. articles to profl. jours. Home: 7 Brecon Rd, Aldgate, Aldgate South Australia, 5154, Australia Office: Univ Adelaide, Geology & Geophysics Dept, Adelaide South Australia, 5000, Australia

TYANO, SHMUEL, psychiatrist; b. Tel-Aviv, Apr. 6, 1939; s. Abraham and Nina (Mandil) T.; m. Ginette Fride, 1965; children: Galia, Lital. MD, U. Strasbourg, France, 1965; MSc, Tel-Aviv U., 1972. Supr. Psychotherapy Inst., Tel-Aviv, 1972; head div. child and adolescent Psychiat. Dep. Geha Psychiat. Hosp., Tel-Aviv, 1977—, also bd. dirs.; assoc. prof. psychiatry Tel-Aviv U., 1984—; chmn. child psychiat. sect. med. sch. Tel-Aviv U., 1984. Co-author: (with others) Psychiatry, 1987. Served to lt. col Israeli military, 1968. Mem. Israel Med. Assn. (chmn. Israel Med. Sci. Council), Israel Psychiat. Assn. (sec. 1975-78), Israel Child and Adolescent Psychiat. Assn. (pres. 1983-87), Internat. Soc. Adolescent Psychiatry (v.p. 1985), World Psychiatry Assn. of Child Psychiatry (reporter 1986). Jewish. Home: 29 Tagore St, 69203 Tel-Aviv Israel Office: Geha Psychiat Hosp, PO Box 72, Petah-Tikva Israel

TYLER, EWEN WILLIAM JOHN, mining executive, geologist; b. Sheffield, Eng., Aug. 24, 1928; came to Australia, 1940; s. William Harold and Ethel (Matthew) T.; m. Aldyth Dorothy Watts, March 3, 1951; children—Brett, Jane, Timothy. B.Sc. with honours, U. Western Australia, Perth, 1949. Geologist, Geita Gold Mining Co., Ltd. (Tanzania), 1949-59; dir. Tanganyika Holdings Ltd., London, 1959-69, Melbourne, Australia, 1969-75; dir. Tanaust Proprietary Ltd., Melbourne, 1975-78, Ashton Mining Ltd., Melbourne, 1978—. Fellow Geol. Soc. London, Geol. Soc. Australia; mem. Instn. Mining and Metallurgy, Australasian Inst. Mining and Metallurgy. Anglican. Clubs: Melbourne, Royal Automobile of Victoria (Melbourne). Office: Ashton Mining Ltd, 441 Saint Kilda Rd, Melbourne Victoria 3004, Australia

TYLER, HAROLD RUSSELL, JR., lawyer, former government official; b. Utica, N.Y., May 14, 1922; s. Harold Russell and Elizabeth (Glenn) T.; m. Barbara L. Eaton, Sept. 10, 1949; children: Bradley E., John R., Sheila B. Grad., Philips Exeter Acad., 1939; AB, Princeton U., 1943; LLB, Columbia U., 1949. Bar: N.Y. 1950. Pvt. practice N.Y.C., 1950-53, 55-60; mem. firm Gilbert & Segall, 1957-60, 61-62; asst. U.S. atty. 1953-55, asst. atty. gen. U.S. charge civil rights div., 1960-61; commr. N.Y.-N.J. Waterfront Commn., 1961-62; U.S. dist. judge So. Dist., N.Y., 1962-75; dep. atty. gen. U.S., 1975-77; mem. firm Patterson, Belknap, Webb & Tyler, N.Y.C., 1977—; adj. prof. law NYU Sch., 1966-75; vis. lectr. Inst. Criminology, Cambridge, 1968; vice chmn. Adminstrv. Conf. USA, 1975-77. Bd. dirs. Fed. Jud. Center, Washington, 1968-72; trustee Practising Law Inst., N.Y.C., William Nelson Cromwell Found., Law Center Found. Mem. ABA (standing com. on fed. judiciary). Home: Indian Hill Rd Bedford NY 10506

TYLER-SLAUGHTER, CECIL LORD, housing relocation specialist; b. Peoria, Ill., Oct. 15, 1958; s. William Albert and Verline Marie (Tyler) Scott. Student Ill. State U., 1974-78. Adminstrv. intern Ill. State U., Normal, 1974-76; child care coordinator Community Action Agency, Peoria, 1976-79; program coordinator Learning Tree Prep. Sch., Peoria, 1980-83; housing relocation specialist Salvation Army, Peoria, 1984—. Investigative reporting journalist Face to Face, 1982; interviewer radio news format, 1983. Cons. NAACP, Peoria, 1984; leader 4H Club, Peoria, 1980-83; election judge Peoria Democratic Party, 1984. Recipient 4H Silver Clover Leadership award, 1983, Save the Children Spl. Honor Mayor Office, Atlanta, 1981; White House fellow Presdl. Commn., 1983. Mem. George Washington Carver, ARC, Smithsonian Inst. Orthodox Jewish. Home: 1904 Grand View Peoria Heights IL 61614 Office: Cen Ill Eastern Iowa Salvation Army Hdqrs 413-415 Adams NE Peoria IL 61612

TYNELL, LARS VICTOR, national librarian of Sweden; b. Stockholm, Apr. 6, 1923; s. Knut and Lizzie (Moll) T.; m. Signe Baath, Dec. 21, 1946; children: Elsa, Maria. Fil.lic., Stockholm U., 1949. With Royal Library, Stockholm, 1946-66, 77-88, dept. head, 1960-66, nat. librarian, 1977-88, emeritus, 1988—; dir. Stockholm City Library, 1966-77; bd. dirs. Bibliotekstjanst AB, Lund, Sweden. House of Emigrants, Vaxjo, Sweden, 1978-88, Nordinfo, 1978-85, Delegation Sci. and Tech. Info., Stockholm, 1979-88. Contbr. articles on librarianship to profl. jours. Mem. Swedish Library Assn. (bd. dirs. 1974-78), Internat. Fedn. Library Assns. (chmn. nat. library sect. 1982-85). Office: Royal Library, Box 5039, S-10241 Stockholm Sweden

TYÖRINOJA, REIJO JUHANI, theology educator; b. Tampere, Finland, Aug. 26, 1948; s. Aarne Oskari and Toini Tellervo (Lehtinen) T.; m. Pirjo Helena Kurikka, Dec. 31, 1971; children: Anu, Samuli, Tuomas. D in Theology, U. Helsinki, Finland, 1984, docent in theol. ethics and philosophy of religion, 1986. Asst. U. Helsinki, 1983-85, asst. prof., 1986-87, chief asst., 1987—; Author: The Grammar of Faith, 1984; contbr. articles to profl. jours. Mem. Soc. Internat. pour L'Etude de la Philosophie Médiévale. Lutheran. Home: Myllykallionrinne 2 C 23, 00200 Helsinki 20 Finland Office: Univ Helsinki, Neitsytpolku 1b, SF-00140 Helsinki Finland

TYRAN, BENJAMIN, business consultant; b. Little Falls, N.Y., Apr. 21, 1921; s. Harry and Rose (Hryb) T.; B.S. in Edn., Rider Coll., 1944; M.B.A., N.Y. U., 1950; postgrad. Am. U., 1952, 53; m. Jeanne Marie Deckman, July 12, 1947; children—Garry K., Cynthia J., Craig K. Econ. analyst Standard Oil Co. Calif., N.Y.C., 1949-51; research economist Labor-Mgmt. Maritime Com., Washington, 1951-52; petroleum price economist MSA, Washington, 1952-54; gen. sales mgr. Am. Ind. Oil Co., 1954-60; founder, pres., dir. Ind. Petroleum Supply Co., San Francisco and N.Y.C., 1960-72; petroleum cons., Burlingame, Calif., 1973-77; chmn. dir. Isle of Man Petroleum, Ltd., U.K.; pres. dir. Natomas Internat. Corp., Natomas of Can., Ltd., Ind. Petroleum Supply—U.K., Ltd., London, Natomas of Arabia, Ltd., Ind. Petroleum Supply Eastern, Tokyo, 1965-72; sec.-treas., dir. Tarfa, Inc., Ashland, Oreg., 1976-79; v.p., dir. Natomas Co., San Francisco, 1963-72, Ind. Indonesian Am. Petroleum Co., 1966-72; chmn., pres., dir. Doorcraft, Inc., Harrisburg, Oreg., 1976—; exec. v.p. Clay-Jones Overseas Ltd., San Francisco, 1976-83; dir., chmn. exec. com. West Indies Oil Co., Antigua, W.I., 1965-72; dir., mem. exec. com. Natomas Co., San Francisco, 1963-72; dir. Sunshine TV, Inc., Medford, Oreg. Mem. San Francisco Com. Fgn. Relations; trustee So. Oreg. State Coll. Found., 1976—, pres., 1979-84; chmn. Ashland Econ. Devel. Commn., 1981—; pres. Council for Econ. Devel. in Oreg., 1983-84; bd. dirs. Oreg. Econ. Devel. Corp.; mem. Council for Advanced Sci./Engring. Edn. of Oreg.; mem. Oreg. Gov.'s Trade Mission to Middle East, 1984, to Far East, 1985; trustee Rogue Valley Manor, Medford, 1985—; mem. N.W. Indsl. Devel. Council; mem. Medford/Jackson County Econ. Devel. Council, 1984—, exec. com. Internat. Trade Inst. Portland (Oreg.) State U., 1987—. Recipient award for distinguished accomplishments in world bus. Tau Kappa Epsilon, 1972, Distinguished Alumnus award Rider Coll., Trenton, N.J., 1972; Pres.'s medal for outstanding service So. Oreg. State Coll., 1984; Outstanding Service award Council for Econ. Devel., 1983-84, Glenn Jackson Meml. Award for Econ. Devel. Medford C. of C., 1986. Mem. Am. Econ. Assn., Acad. Polit. Sci., World Affairs Council, Tau Kappa Epsilon. Club: Family (San Francisco). Home and Office: 1120 Prospect St Ashland OR 97520

TYRIE, ANNE VALERIE, geologist, educator; b. Edinburgh, Scotland, Oct. 10, 1954; arrived in Can., 1980; d. Thomas Palmer and Isobella Wilkie (Smillie) T.; m. Ian David Boud, Aug. 30, 1976 (div. Aug. 1985); m. Michael William Horsfall, Sept. 1, 1985. BS in Geology with honors, U. Manchester, Eng., 1977, MS in Planetology, 1979, PhD in Pattern Recognition, 1981. Chartered acct. trainee Arthur Andersen and Co., Manchester, 1977-80; research geologist W.G. Wahl Ltd., Toronto, Ont., Can., 1980; geologist Ont. Geol. Survey, Toronto, Can., 1980-81, geophysicist, 1981-82, rev. geologist, 1982-83; asst. prof. U. Toronto, 1983—; v.p. research Real/Data Corp., Toronto, 1987—; cons. Philip A. Lapp Ltd., Toronto, 1986—; mem. various coms. U. Toronto, 1983—. Co-editor Second International Proceedings on Recent Crustal Movements in Africa, 1987; contrb. numerous articles to profl. jours. Dir. Women in Sci. Engring. Can., 1984—; instr. Peel Summer Acad., 1985; mem. Speakers Bur., Mississauga, Ont., 1985—, Open Doors Govt. Program, Toronto, 1984—. Grantee Natural Scis. Engring. Research Council, 1984-87, U. Toronto, 1986-88, Digital Equipment Corp., 1987-88. Mem. Can. Aero. Space Inst., Can. Remote Sensing Soc., Can. Hydrographic Soc. (fin. mgr. jour. 1985—), Am. Soc. Phtogrammetry, Inst. Environ. Studies, Com. Advanced Remote Sensing Study Groups., Ont. Assn. Remote Sensing (pres. 1988). Club: Elmwood (Toronto). Office: U Toronto Survey Scis, Erindale Campus, Mississauga, ON Canada L5L 1C6

TYRL, PAUL, mathematics educator, researcher, consultant; b. Prague, Czechoslovakia, Dec. 24, 1951; came to U.S., 1970, naturalized, 1978; s. Vladimir Tyrl and Marta (Kocian) Kocian. G.E.D. diploma, WIN Learning, Ctr., 1972; B.A. with honors, Jersey City State Coll., 1977, M.A., 1980; postgrad., Rutgers U., 1980—. Cert. tchr secondary edn., higher edn., N.J. Quality controller Agfa-Perutz, Munich, W. Ger., 1969-70; technician AT&T, Kearny, N.J., 1970-73; acquisition librarian Jersey City State Coll., 1973-74, post office supr., 1974-76, math. lab. dir., 1976-79, instr. math., 1979-80; instr. math. Hudson County Community Coll. (N.J.), 1980-82, asst. prof., coordinator math., 1982-84; prof., chmn. math., curriculum dir., acad. coordinator Coll. New Rochelle (N.Y.), 1984—; researcher Rutgers U., New Brunswick, N.J., 1980—; cons. Jersey City Bd. Edn., N.J., 1982—. Contbr. articles to profl. jours. Mem. Nat. Council Tchrs. Math. (reviewer and referee), Am. Math. Assn., N.Y. Acad. Scis., Am. Ednl. Research Assn., Math. Assn. Am., Am. Math. Assn. Two-Yr. Colls., Am. Math. Soc., Am. Mus. Natural History, Smithsonian Instn. Roman Catholic. Office: New Rochelle Coll School of New Resources 125 Barclay St New York NY 10007

TYSK, LENNART INGEMAR, psychiatrist; b. Linkoping, Sweden, May 12, 1935. D in Med. Sci., U. Uppsala, Sweden, 1985. Sr. med. officer Psychiat. Clin. Gavle (Sweden) Hosp., 1979—. Contbr. articles to profl. jours. Office: Psychiat Clin, Gavle Hosp, S-801 Gavle 17 Sweden

TYSON, MIKE G., professional boxer; b. N.Y.C., June 30, 1966; s. John Kilpatrick and Lorna Tyson; m. Robin Givens, Feb. 7, 1988. Defeated Trevor Berbick to win WBC Heavyweight Title Nov. 1986, defeated James Smith to win WBA Heavyweight Title, Mar. 1987, defeated Tony Tucker to win IBF Heavyweight Title, Aug. 1987, defeated Michael Spinks to IBF Heavyweight Title, June 1988. Hon. sports chmn. Cystic Fibrosis Assn. N.Y., 1987—, Young Adult Inst., N.Y.C., 1987—. Office: care Reel Sports Inc 9 E 40th St New York NY 10016

TYSON, PAMELA ANN, state official; b. Teaneck, N.J., June 17, 1953; d. Theodore Randall and Barbetta (Plescia) T. BA cum laude, SUNY, Stony Brook, 1977; MSW, U. Conn., 1984. Cert. social worker, Mass. Dir. Stony Brook Women's Ctr., N.Y., 1974-75, Lab. Behavior Assessment, Stony Brook, 1975-78; social worker Mass. Soc. Prevention Cruelty Children, Holyoke, Mass., 1979-83; exec. dir. New Eng. Learning Ctr. Women in Transition, Greenfield, Mass., 1983-85; dir. Western Mass. Exec. Office Human Services, Springfield, 1985—, spl. asst. to sec., 1986—; bd. dirs., com. chmn. Hampshire Council Children, Northampton, Mass., 1980-82; founder Ann. Western Mass. Confs. on Human Services. Contbr. articles to profl. jours. Founder Franklin County Women's Issues Network; chmn. Springfield Homeless Coalition, Western Mass. Hispanic Adv. Commn.; mem. Mass. Rural Devel. Com., Franklin County Mental Health Task Force, Hampshire/Franklin County Sexual Abuse Task Force, Mass. Human Services Providers, Mayor's Task Force on Deinstitutionalization, Mayor's Task Force on Early Intervention, Springfield Homeless Human Rights Commn., Nat. Com. Prevention Child Abuse, Assn. Advancement Behavior Therapy Social Work Group for Study Behavioral Methods, Franklin County Charter Commn.; bd. dirs. Springfield Infant Mortality and Teenage Pregnancy Coalition. Democrat. Presbyterian. Lodge: Zonta. Avocations: movies, reading. Office: Western Mass Exec Office Human Services 436 Dwight St 3d Floor Springfield MA 01103

TYSON, ROY KNOX, lawyer, commercial and residential real estate broker; b. Houston, May 30, 1942; s. Alfred Knox and Katherine (Archer) T.; children—John Knox, Dorothy Katherine. A.B., Southwestern U., 1964; J.D., So. Meth. U., 1971. Bar: Tex. 1971, U.S. Dist. Ct. (no., so. and ea. dists.) Tex., U.S. Ct. Appeals (5th cir.), U.S. Tax Ct., U.S. Ct. Mil. Appeals, U.S. Supreme Ct. Assoc., Sorrell, Anderson & Sorrell, Corpus Christi, Tex., 1971-73, Touchstone, Bernays & Johnston, Dallas, 1973-76; atty. Southwestern Bell Telephone Co., Dallas, 1976-84; ptnr. Burleson, Pate & Gibson, 1984—; comml. and residential real estate broker. Served to lt. (j.g.), USNR, 1965-68. Recipient Law Enforcement Assistance award Dept. of Justice, 1970. Mem. ABA, Dallas County Bar Assn. Episcopalian. Home: 3400 Normandy Ave Dallas TX 75205 Office: Burleson Pate & Gibson 2414 N Akard St Dallas TX 75201

TYSZKIEWICZ, KRZYSZTOF JAN BENEDYVT, cinematographer; b. Warsaw, Poland, Oct. 21, 1942; arrived in Fed. Republic Germany, 1970; s. Krzysztof M. Stanislaw and Barbara (Rechowicz) T.; m. A. Nicola Tyszkiewicz, Mar. 23, 1979; children: Aleksandra Goya Beata, Wiktoria Kosma Nike. Student, Ecole du Louvre, Paris, 1964-65, Hornsey Coll. Art, London, 1965. Freelance still photographer Paris, 1966-68; chief cameraman Spark S.A., Geneva, 1968-69; freelance cinematographer, dir. Hamburg, 1970—. Recipient 1st prize for Tau Levica Labiryiut, Oberhausen, 1962, Bronze Lion for Polio, Cannes, 1971, Silver Lion for Patex, Cannes, 1985. Mem. Polish Cinematographer Assn. Roman Catholic. Home and Office: Rothenbaumchaussee 207, 2000 Hamburg 13 Federal Republic of Germany

TYTELL, PEARL LILY (MRS. MARTIN KENNETH TYTELL), examiner disputed documents; b. N.Y.C., Aug. 29, 1918; d. Harry and Yetta (Feigenbaum) Kessler; student St. John's U., 1941-43; B.S., N.Y. U., 1962, M.A., 1968; m. Martin Kenneth Tytell, May 23, 1943; children—Peter, Pamela. Examiner disputed documents, N.Y.C., 1950—; lectr. on handwriting, typewriter identification, detection forgery colls., univs., 1955—; lectr. N.Y. U., 1955-57; mem. faculty N.Y. Inst. Criminology, N.Y.C., 1958; cons. govtl. agys., law firms; expert witness in city, state, fed. cts., U.S. and Commonwealth P.R. Sec. Along The Hudson Home Owners Assn., 1960—. Mem. AAAS, Internat. Assn. Chiefs of Police (asso.), Eastern Bus. Tchrs. Assn. Club: N.Y. Univ. Co-author: The Confrontation of Anonymous Letter Writers. Home: 3031 Scenic Pl Riverdale NY 10463 Office: 116 Fulton St New York NY 10038

TYUSHKEVICH, STEPAN ANDREEVICH, educator; b. Mingitui, Kuitunskii, USSR, Dec. 25, 1917; s. Andrei Ivanovich and Ekaterina Grigorievna (Berdnikova) T.; m. Irena Gerontievna; children: Alexander, Stanislav. Diploma in Elec. Engring., V.I. Ulyanov (Lenin) Electrotech.

Inst., Leningrad, 1941; postgrad., Lenin Mil.-Polit. Acad., Leningrad, 1952. Engr. elec., designer Metal Plant, Leningrad, 1941; Komsomol party worker of regiment, commissar and dep. regiment commdr. for polit. work USSR Army, Leningrad, Volhovskii, Ukrania, 1941-45; dep. comdr. for polit. work, propagandist Mil. Units Soviet Army, 1945-55; adj. sr. tchr. philosophy Lenin Higher Polit. Acad., Moscow, 1955-68; head sci. bd., sr. sci. worker Inst. Mil. History USSR Ministry Defence, Moscow, 1968—; advanced through grades to Maj.-Gen. USSR Army, 1941-86, retired, 1968; lectr. Soc. of Knowledge, 1951—; participant World Sociol. Congresses, also del. Author: Necessity and Accidentity in War, 1962, Philosophy and Military Theory, 1975, The World-Wide-Historical Importance of Victory in the Great Patriotic War, 1970, 1975, War and Modern Times, 1968; collaborator and editor of numerous books and articles in field. Recipient Patriotic War Order I and II degrees, Order of the Red Star, For Service For Motherland Armed Forces III degree. Mem. Soviet Sociol. Assn., Internat. Research Com. (v.p. 1978—). Communist. Office: USSR Ministry Defence, Inst Military History, Universitetskii prospekt, 14, Moscow USSR

TZADUA, PAULOS CARDINAL, archbishop of Addis Ababa, Ethiopia; b. Addifinni, Ethiopia, Aug. 25, 1921; s. Tzadua and Tensaye (Hailu) Asgeda. Dr. Polit. Sci., Cath. U. Milan, 1957, Dr. Law, 1958. Ordained priest, 1944. Elected bishop, 1973; appointed archbishop of Addis Ababa, 1977; elevated to Sacred Coll. of Cardinals, 1985. Translator: The Fetha Nagast (The Law of the Kings). Contbr. articles to profl. jours. *

TZAFERIS, EFTHYMIOS, diplomat; b. Cairo, Mar. 28, 1927; s. Vassilios and Angelika (Vidouris) T.; m. Rica Pothitos, Mar. 11, 1978; children: Helen Stergiou-Tzaferis, Vassilios. LLB, U. Paris, 1957. Attache Greek Ministry of Fgn. Affairs, 1957-59, 3d sec., 1959-61; consul of Greece Greek Ministry of Fgn. Affairs, Treiste, Italy, 1961-63; 2d sec. Greek Ministry of Fgn. Affairs, 1963-64; consul of Greece Greek Ministry of Fgn. Affairs, Naples, 1964; with Greek Embassy Greek Ministry of Fgn. Affairs, Rome, 1964-65; 1st sec. Greek Ministry of Fgn. Affairs, 1965; with Greek Embassy Greek Ministry of Fgn. Affairs, Buenos Aires, 1965-66; with Greek Ministry of Fgn. Affairs, Athens, 1966-67; with Greek Embassy Greek Ministry of Fgn. Affairs, Budapest, Hungary, 1967-69; counsellor 2d class Greek Ministry of Fgn. Affairs, 1969-70; charge d'affaires en pied Greek Ministry of Fgn. Affairs, Lagos, Nigeria, 1970-72; counsellor 1st class Greek Ministry of Fgn. Affairs, 1972-73; with Greek Ministry of Fgn. Affairs, Athens, 1973-74; ambassador of Greece Greek Ministry of Fgn. Affairs, Khartoum, Sudan, 1974-77; with Greek Ministry of Fgn. Affairs, Athens, 1977-81; ambassador of Greece Greek Ministry of Fgn. Affairs, Rabat, Morocco, 1981-85, Australia, New Zealand, Fiji, Papua New Guinea, Tonga, We. Samoa, Vanuatu, 1985—. Greek Orthodox. Clubs: Nat. Press, Hellenic (Canberra, Australia). Home: 115 Empire Cir, Yarralumla, Canberra 2600, Australia Office: Embassy of Greece, 9 Turrana St, Yarralumla, Canberra 2600, Australia

TZALLAS, NIOVE, painter; b. Jannina, Greece, Jan. 26, 1938; d. George and Kaliroi (Papastergiou) Georgopoulos; m. Neocosmos Tzallas, Aug. 21, 1959. Student, Athens Sch. Beaux Arts, 1955-58, Atelier Andre Lhote, France, 1958-59, Cen. Sch. Arts and Crafts, Eng., 1959-61. One-woman shows: Paris, 1962, Rome, 1963, Gallery of Royal Soc. Painters, London, 1964, Gallery du Damier, Paris, 1968, Gallery de U. Paris, 1969, 72, Mus. de Havre, France, 1971, Galerie Vallombreuse, Biarritz, France, 1974, Gallery Mouffe, Paris, 1975, Gallery Bernheim-Jeune, Paris, 1982, BH Corner Gallery, London, 1985, 86, Everarts Galerie, Paris, 1988; exhibited in floating exhbns. aboard S.S. Pegassos, S.S. Semiramis, 1966, S.S. Olympia, 1967; exhibited in group shows: Salon des Independants, Grand Palais des Champs Elysées, 1973-87, Grand Prix Internat. de la Baie des Anges, Nice, France, Galerie Riviera, Nice, 1974, Galerie Blaise St. Maurice, Paris, 1974-77, Galerie l'Arthotèque, Monte Carlo, 1975, Salon Populiste, Paris, 1975, Maison de la Culture à Ville-neuve-la Garenne, 1976-77, Ctr. Culturel de Mussidan, Dordogne, France, 1977, The Breakers Gallery, Palm Beach, Fla., 1976-78, Ctr. European Delobbe à Olloy Sur Viroin, Belgium, 1978, Galerie la Roue, Paris, 1978-79, Salon de l'Art Libre, Paris, 1978-79, Festival d'Art Graphique d'Osaka, Japan, 1983-84, Mus. de Luxembourg, Paris, L'Union des Femmes Peintres et Sculpteurs, 1981, 82; represented in permanent collections: Mus. Modern Art, Haiffa, Israel, Bibliotheque Nat. de la France, Paris, Nat. Bank of Greece. Home: 15 Ekalis St, 145 61 Kifissia, Psyhiko, Attica Greece

TZELIOS, CHRISTOS GEORGE, accountant; b. Politsani, No. Epirus, Oct. 12, 1934; s. George Demetrios and Sevasti (Papachronis) T.; came to U.S., 1956, naturalized, 1962; student Athens U. Law Sch., 1954-56; B.B.A. in Pub. Accountancy, City Coll. N.Y., 1963; m. Vivi Rigas, Jan. 16, 1972; children—Aristotle, Alexander. Accountant, AMF Pinspotters, N.Y.C., 1958-60; tax accountant Royal McBee Corp. subs. Litton Industries, N.Y.C., 1961-65, Agrico Chem. subs. Continental Oil Co., N.Y.C., 1965, Colt Industries, N.Y.C., 1966-68; owner, operator Tzelios Bus. Service, bus. cons. and planning, Astoria, N.Y., 1968—; owner, pres. Hellenic Book Club, 1973—. A founder, mem. bd. dirs. Astoria Restoration Assn., 1977—; treas. Greek-Am. Democratic Com., 1976—. Mem. City Coll., Baruch Coll. alumni assns. Greek Orthodox. Club: Hellenic Univ. Office: 22-55 31st St Astoria NY 11105

TZINER, AHARON E., labor studies and business administration educator, researcher, lecturer, consultant; b. Bucharest, Romania, Aug. 4, 1950; came to Israel, 1955; s. Moshe and Hana-Mina (Rozenberg) T.; m. Shoshana Hager, Nov. 1, 1972; children—Shlomi, Ifat-Malca. B.A. in Psychology of Math., Bar-Ilan U., 1973, M.A. in Social, Indsl. and Orgnl. Psychology, 1975; Ph.D. in Labor Studies, Tel-Aviv U., 1981. Sr. research officer Israel Def. Forces Dept. Behavioral Scis., Ramat-Gan, Israel, 1975-79; cons., research project dir. Israeli Aircraft Industries, Lod, 1979-80; asst. prof. Shenkar Coll. Textile Tech. and Fashion, Ramat-Gan, 1982-83; asst. prof. Tel-Aviv U., Ramat-Aviv, 1981-84, assoc. prof., 1984—; reviewer Jour. Applied Psychology, 1984, 85. Author monographs; contbr. articles to profl. jours. Served to capt. Israeli Army, 1975-79. Recipient Spl. Rank Promotion award Israel Def. Forces, 1978; Disting. Doctoral Research award Tel-Aviv U., 1980; Mem. Israel Psychol. Assn. (expert div. social and vocat. psychology 1979), Am. Psychol. Assn., Internat. Assn. Applied Psychology, Acad. Mgmt. U.S.A. Club: Univ. Faculty. Avocations: social work; study Jewish culture scripts; music; theatre. Office: Tel-Aviv U, Dept Labor Studies, Tel-Aviv Israel

UBAY, ALBERTO QUILANTANG, former Philippine provincial governor; b. Merida, Leyte, Philippines, Sept. 14, 1908; s. Braulio Isidro and Maria (Quilantang) U.; m. Milagros Realiza, Dec. 20, 1938; children—Rebecca Ubay Camara, Franklin R. A.A., Silliman U., Dumaguete City, Philippines, 1931; LL.B., Philippine Law Sch., Manila, 1935. Bar: Philippines 1935. Sec. to Congressman Carlos Tan, Leyte, 1932-33; mem. Merida Mcpl. Council, 1937-41; asst. provincial fiscal officer, then acting provincial fiscal officer Zamboanga Province, Philippines, 1946-48; mem. Congress of Philippines from Zamboanga del Norte Province, 1954-69; judge Ct. of First Instance, Caloocan City, Philippines, 1970-78; gov. Provincial Govt. Zamgoanga del Norte, 1980-86; chmn. Provincial Bd., 1980-86, Provincial Peace and Order Council, Provincial Devel. Council, Provincial Agrl. Council, Provincial Agrl. Exec. Council, Provincial Sch. Bldg. Selection Com., Barangay Rds. Provincial Selection Com., Provincial Nutrition Council, Provincial Population Commn., Provincial Sch. Bd., 1980-86. Founder, author laws establishing Zamboanga del Norte Nat. Agrl. Coll., 1960, Katipunan Nat. Agrl. Sch., 1961, Sindangan Nat. Agrl. Sch., 1962, Zamboanga del Norte Sch. Arts and Trades, 1963, Siocon Nat. Vocat. Sch., 1962, Rizal Meml. Nat. Vocat. Sch., 1964, Dipolog Sch. Fisheries, 1964; chmn. United Way Philippines, Zamboanga del Norte, 1980-86, provincial chpt. ARC, 1980-86, Zamboanga del Norte council Girl Scouts, Zamboanga del Norte council Boy Scouts, 1980-86; provincial chmn. polit. party Kilusang Bagong Lipunan, 1984-86; mem. Ch. Mil. Liaison Group, Dipolog City, 1980-86. Recipient numerous awards and honors in appreciation of leadership and services as legislator, judge and gov., 1954-86. Mem. Integrated Bar of Philippines (chpt. pres. 1974). Roman Catholic. Avocations: gardening, flowering plants. Lodge: K.C. (grand knight 1940).

UBEROI, MAHINDER SINGH, aerospace engineering educator; b. Delhi, India, Mar. 13, 1924; came to U.S., 1945, naturalized, 1960; s. Kirpal Singh and Sulaksha (Kosher) U. B.S., Punjab U., Lahore, India, 1944; M.S., Calif. Inst. Tech., 1946; D.Eng., Johns Hopkins U., 1952. Registered profl. engr. Mem. faculty U. Mich., Ann Arbor, 1953-63, prof. aeros., 1959-63, vis. prof., 1963-64; prof. aerospace engring. U. Colo., Boulder, 1963—, chmn. dept. aerospace engring., 1963-75; fellow F. Joint Inst. for Lab. Astrophysics, Boulder, 1963-74; hon. research fellow Harvard U., 1975-76; invited prof. U. Que., Can., 1972-74. Council mem. Ednl. TV Channel 6, Inc., Denver, 1963-66. Guggenheim fellow Royal Inst. Tech., Stockholm, Sweden, 1958; exchange scientist U.S. Nat. Acad. Scis.; exchange scientist Soviet Acad. Scis., 1966. Mem. Am. Inst. Aeros. and Astronautics (mem. council Rocky Mountain sect. 1963-66), Am. Phys. Soc., Am. Soc. Engring. Edn., Air Force Assn., Tau Beta Pi. Home: 819 6th St Boulder CO 80302

UCHENDU, INNOCENT CHUKWUEMEKA, food products executive; b. Ikenanzizi, Nigeria, Apr. 24, 1939; s. Fred Ukaegbu and Agnes U.; m. Patience Ifeyinwa, June 24, 1967; 1 child, Ikechukwu Chigozie; m. Vera Ekwutosi, June 4, 1988. BSc in Polit. Sci. with honors, U. Ibadan, Nigeria, 1966. Tchr. Cath. Mission Umuahia, Ea. Nigeria, 1956-60; clk. Govt. Ea. Nigeria, Enugu, 1960-63, adminstrv. officer, 1960-63; mktg. trainee Lever Bros. Nigeria Ltd., Apapa, 1966; mgr. personnel Mobil Oil Nigeria Ltd., Lagos, 1974-77; mgr. manpower devel. Food Specialities Nigeria Ltd., Lagos, 1978—, exec. dir., 1980—; chmn. Golden Guinea Breweries Ltd., Umuahia Imo State, 1987—. Chief Agbara Community, Agbara Ogun State, 1986, Alike Community, Alike Obowo Imo State, 1987. Mem. Nigerian Inst. Mgmt., Inst. Personnel Mgmt. Club: Lagos Country. Lodge: Rotary. Office: Food Specialities Nigeria Ltd, 19/21 Indsl Ave Ilupeju, PMB 21164 Ikeja Lagos Nigeria

UCHIDA, MORIYA, manufacturing company executive; b. Kyoto, Japan, Jan. 27, 1929; d. Katsuya Uchida and Kiyoko Motoyama; m. Kuniko Morita Uchida, Apr. 28, 1959; children: Michiya, Sarah. MS, Tokyo Inst. Tech., 1953, DEng, 1961. With Teijin, Ltd., Iwakuni, Japan, 1953—; researcher Teijin Research Lab., Iwakuni, Japan, 1953-55; chief researcher Synthetic Fiber Lab., Iwakuni, Japan, 1955-61; mgr. Tech. Planning Sect., Tokyo, 1961-67, Basic Research Lab., Tokyo, 1967-71; dep. dir. Cen. Research Lab., Tokyo, 1971-73; gen. mgr. Patent and Licensing Dept., Tokyo, 1973-76, Research & Development Dept., Tokyo, 1976-77; dir. Product Devel. Inst., Tokyo, 1977-79, Teijin, Ltd., Tokyo, 1979—; lectr. Tokyo Inst. Tech., 1973—, Gunma U., 1981—, Tokyo Agrl. and Engring. U., 1986—; bd. dirs. Engring. Acad. of Japan, 1987—. Author: International Technological Strategy, 1985, The Advanced Composite Materials, 1986, Intellectual Capital, 1987, New Industrial Innovation, 1987. Spl. mem. Council for Sci. and Tech., 1987—, Council Aeros., Electronics and other Advanced Technologies, 1986-87; mem. Com. Long-Range Planning Indsl. Tech., 1977-81; com. mem. Sci. Council, 1985—. Mem. Japan Chem. Soc. (bd. dirs. 1973-76), Soc. Fiber Sci. and Tech. Japan (bd. dirs., editor 1981-83, v.p. 1982-84), Soc. Polymer Sci. Japan (v.p. 1984-88), Internat. Union of Pure and Applied Chemistry (mem. CHEMRAWN com. 1979-87), Sci. Council Japan. Clubs: Kojun-sha, Okura Health (Tokyo). Lodge: Internat. House. Office: Teijin Ltd, 2-1-1 Uchisaiwaicho, Tokyo 100, Japan

UDOKA, ARNOLD BENJAMIN, dancer, choreographer; b. Indot Abak, Akwa Ibom, Nigeria, Aug. 14, 1958; s. Benjamin Udo and Veronica (Ikwo). BA in Theatre Arts with honors, U. Calabar, 1982; MA in Dance Studies, Laban Ctr. for Movement and Dance, London, 1987. Prin. dancer, choreographer Calabar U. Theatre, Nigeria, 1976-82, student demonstrator dance, 1979-81, grad. asst. dance, 1984-85, choreographer, 1984—; dancer Adzido Pan-African DAnce Ensemble, London, 1986—; sessional tchr. Laban Ctr. for Movement and Dance, U. London, 1987—; dance tutor Commonwealth Inst., London, 1987—; dance educator, coordinator Jenako Arts, London, 1987—; chief choreographer Akwa Ibom State Dance Contingent, 1988; dance model Gala Books Ltd., London, 1987. Choreographer numerous dances including Ndem-Mmong, 1979, Teh Defilement, 1979, New Generation, 1980, We the Dead, 1981, Awake Awake and Alive, 1982, Song of the Sea, 1986, Abaikpa Idehhe Akang Iba, 1988 (Nigerian Festival Silver winner); author: (play) In Disruptions Like, That, 1983; author numerous poems. Dir. socials Nat. Youth Service Corps., Borno State, Nigeria, 1982-83. Recipient Scholar Cross River State Govt., 1979-82; named Commonwealth Acad. Staff Scholar, 1985—. Mem. Black Dance Devel. Trust Eng. Roman Catholic. Clubs: Palmwine Drinkers, Reggae (staff adviser 1984—). Home: 56 Ikot Okoro Rd, Abak Akwa Ibom Nigeria Office: Dept Theatre Arts, U Calabar, Cross River State Nigeria

UDOLPH, JÜRGEN, linguist; b. Berlin, Fed. Republic Germany, Feb. 6, 1943; s. Georg and Charlotte (Knappek) U.; m. Maria Woitalla, June 11, 1971; children: Susanne, Martin, Anja. MA, U. Göttingen, Fed. Republic Germany, 1971, PhD, 1978. Sci. asst. U. Göttingen, 1972-79; sci. employee Acad. Sci. at Mainz, Mainz and Göttingen, Fed. Republic Germany, 1979—. Author: Studies in Slavic River-Names, 1979, Investigations in Slavic and Indoeuropean Toponymics, 1975—. Henning-Kaufmann grantee, 1983. Mem. Internat. Commn. for Slavic Onomastics. Home: Steinbreite 9, D3405 Rosdorf Federal Republic of Germany Office: Dept Linguistics, Humboldtallee 13, 3400 Göttingen Federal Republic of Germany

UDRISTE, CONSTANTIN NICOLAE, mathematics educator; b. Turceni, Gorj, Romania, Jan. 22, 1940; s. Nicolae C. and Dumitra (Iordache) U.; m. Aneta Anghel, Aug. 21, 1965; children: Daniel Ion, Sorin Adrian. Diploma, U. Timisoara, Romania, 1963; D of Math., Babes-Bolyai U., Cluj-Napoca, 1971. High sch. math. tchr. Bucharest, Romania, 1963-64; asst. prof. Poly. Inst., Bucharest, 1964-70, lectr., 1970-76, prof., 1976—. Author: Problems and....., 1980, Minima and Maxima, 1980, Algebra, Geometry and Differential Equations, 1982; rev. U. Mich. Math. Revs., 1986—, Zentralblatt für Mathematik, Berlin, 1973—; editorial bd. Math. Gazette, Bucharest, 1978-86; contbr. over 70 articles to math. jours. Dep. Popular Council Nicolae Bălcescu, Bucharest, 1965-70. Recipient Dragomir Hurmuzescu prize Acad. of R.S.R., 1985. Mem. Soc. Math. Scis. Romania, Tensor Soc. Japan, Profs.' Council Transport Faculty, Am. Math. Soc. Office: Poly Inst, Splaiul Independentei 313, 77590 Bucharest Romania

UDWADIA, FIRDAUS ERACH, engineering educator, consultant; b. Bombay, Aug. 28, 1947; came to U.S., 1968.; s. Erach Rustam and Perin P. (Lentin) U.; m. Farida Gagrat, Jan. 6, 1977; children: Shanaira, Zubin. BS, Indian Inst. Tech., Bombay, 1968; MS, Calif. Inst. Tech., 1969, PhD, 1972; MBA, U. So. Calif., 1985. Mem. faculty Calif. Inst. Tech., Pasadena, 1972-74; asst. prof. engring. U. So. Calif., Los Angeles, 1974-77, assoc. prof., 1977-83, prof. mech. engring., civil engring. and bus. adminstrn., 1983-86; prof. engring. bus. adminstrn. U. So. Calif., 1986—; also bd. dirs. Structural Identification Computing Facility U. So. Calif.; cons. Jet Propulsion Lab., Pasadena, Calif., 1978—, Argonne Nat. Lab., Chgo., 1982-83, Air Force Rocket Lab., Edwards AFB, Calif., 1984—. Contbr. articles to profl. jours. Bd. dirs. Crisis Mgmt. Ctr., U. So. Calif. NSF grantee, 1976—. Mem. AIAA, ASCE, Am. Acad. Mechanics, Soc. Indsl. and Applied Math., Seismological Soc. Am., Sigma Xi (Earthquake Enging. Research Inst., 1971, 74, 84). Home: 2100 S Santa Anita Arcadia CA 91006 Office: U So Calif University Park 364 DRB Los Angeles CA 90089-1114

UEDA, NOBUO, insurance company executive, educator; b. Musashino, Tokyo, July 9, 1950; s. Kinjiro and Shizue (Kodama) U.; m. Yuko Umezawa, Nov. 23, 1981. B Commerce, grad. Journalism Inst., Keio U., Japan, 1974. Cert. real estate agt., Tokyo. Chief clk. Meiji Mut. Life Ins. Co. div. Mitubishi Group, Tokyo, 1974-78, mem. standing com., labor union, 1979-82, asst. mgr. credit mgmt. fin. sect., 1982-83, asst. mgr., buyer real estate investment sect., 1983-84, mgr. tenant leasing sect., 1985—. Contbr. articles to industry publs. Mem. Ofcl. Agts. Life Ins. Assn., Assn. Yukichi Fukuzawa, Ins. Inst. Keio U. (chief. sec.). Clubs: Tokyo Mita, Lundens Country. Home: 3-10-11 Kichijiyoji-Honchyo, Musashino City Tokyo 180, Japan Office: Meiji Mut Life Ins Co, 2-1-1 Marunouchi Chiyoda ku, Tokyo 100, Japan

UEDA, NOBUYA, architect, educator; b. Himeji, Hygo, Japan, July 26, 1940; s. Nobuo and Kunie (Hirose) U.; m. Tomoko Murakami. MArch, Kyoto U., Japan, 1965, U. Calif., Berkeley, 1967. Lic. 1st class architect, Japan. Chief architect Nikken Sekkei Ltd., Osaka, Japan, 1965—; jr. architect Skidmore, Owings and Merrill, San Francisco, 1967-68; asst. prof. Okla. State U., Stillwater, Okla., 1970-71; lectr. Akashi (Japan) Technol. Coll., 1984—; archtl. advisor World Bank, Seoul, South Korea and Washington, 1977-78, FAO UN, Bangkok and Rome, 1976-76. Author: Designing Wholesale Markets for Asian Cities, 1975. Fulbright grantee, 1966. Mem. Japan Inst. Architects (profl.), Archtl. Inst. Japan, Archtl. Assn. Japan. Home: 3-2-13 Sakasedai, 665 Takarazuka Japan Office: Nikken Sekkel Ltd, 5-21-1 Koraibashi, Higashi-ku, Osaka 541, Japan

UEHARA, MICHAEL ANTHONY, writer; b. Honolulu, Oct. 21, 1957; s. Kiyoshi Jerry and Chieko (Shimabukuro) U.; m. Mary Ann Cummins, May 26, 1979 (div. July 1983); m. Frances Jane Pirie, Oct. 11, 1984. BA, U. Wash., 1979. Copywriter Ketchum Advt. Japan, Tokyo, 1983—; editor-in-chief The Magazine, The Ray Kay Group, Tokyo, 1986—; creative cons. Thai Airways Internat., Tokyo, 1986—. Recipient 1st prize Asiaweek Mag. Short Story competition, 1986.

UEHLING, BARBARA STANER, educational administrator; b. Wichita, Kans., June 12, 1932; d. Roy W. and Mary Elizabeth (Hilt) Staner; m. Stanley Johnson; children: Jeffrey Steven, David Edward. B.A., U. Wichita, 1954; M.A., Northwestern U., 1956, Ph.D., 1958; hon. degree, Drury Coll., 1978; LL.D. (hon.), Ohio State U., 1979. Mem. psychology faculty Oglethorpe U., Atlanta, 1959-64, Emory U., Atlanta, 1966-69; adj. prof. U. R.I., Kingston, 1970-72; dean Roger Williams Coll., Bristol, R.I., 1972-74; dean arts scis. Ill. State U., Normal, 1974-76; provost U. Okla., Norman, 1976-78; chancellor U. Mo.-Columbia, 1978-86, U. Calif., Santa Barbara, 1987—; sr. vis. fellow Am. Council Edn., 1987; cons. higher edn. State of N.Y., 1973-74; cons. North Central Accreditation Assn., 1975-86; mem. nat. educator adv. com. to Comptroller Gen. U.S., 1978; mem. commn. on mil.-higher edn. relations Am. Council on Edn., 1978-86; bd. dirs. Merc Bancorp, Inc., 1979-86; Meredith Corp., 1980—. Author: Women in Academe: Steps to Greater Equality, 1978; contbr. articles to profl. jours. Bd. dirs., chmn. Nat. Ctr. Higher Edn. Mgmt. Systems; bd. dirs. Am. Council on Edn., 1979-83, treas., 1982-83; trustee Carnegie Found. for Advancement of Teaching, 1980-86; mem. adv. com. Nat. Ctr. for Food and Agrl. Policy; bd. dirs. Resources for the Future; mem. NCAA Select Com. on Athletics, 1983-84, NCAA Presdl. Commn.; pres. elect Western Coll. Assn.; mem. Nat. Council on Ednl. Research, 1980-82; mem. Bus.-Higher Edn. Forum, Am. Council on Edn. Social Sci. Research Council fellow, 1954-55; NSF fellow, 1956-57; NIMH postdoctoral research fellow, 1964-67; named one of 100 Young Leaders of Acad. Change Mag. and ACE, 1978; recipient Alumni Achievement award Wichita State U., 1978; Alumnae award Northwestern U., 1985. Mem. Am. Assn. Higher Edn. (dir. 1974-77, pres. 1977-78), Western Coll. Assn. (pres.-elect 1988), Internat. Com. for Study of Ednl. Exchange (chair 1988—), Sigma Xi. Office: U Calif Santa Barbara Office of Chancellor Cheadle Hall Santa Barbara CA 93106

UEMATSU, YOICHI, architect; b. Mino, Osaka, Japan, July 17, 1950; s. Masayuki and Jun (Nunoi) U.; m. Masumi Tanaka, June 13, 1987. BE, Waseda U., Tokyo, 1974. Registered architect, Tokyo. Architect Irie Miyake Architects and Engrs., Tokyo, 1974—. Home: 2-14-4-503 Gakuen-Nishi Machi, Kodaira, Tokyo 187, Japan Office: Irie Miyake Architects and Engrs, 2-8-10 Toranomon, Minato-Ku, Tokyo Japan

UEMURA, MASARU, petrochemical company executive, educator; b. Tokyo, July 13, 1930; s. Yoshio and Hideye (Shimada) U.; m. Keiko Tanishima, Dec. 25, 1957; children: Hiroko, Kayoko. Bachelor's, Tokyo Inst. Tech., 1953, Doctorate, 1984. Researcher lab. NihonDenshi Co., Tokyo, 1953-56, Bayer Japan Ltd., Tokyo, 1956-58; mgr. polymer lab. Tosoh Corp., ShinNanyo/Yamaguchi, Japan, 1958-72; head Tokyo Lab., 1972-77; prof. Mie Nat. U., Tsu, Japan, 1983—; dir., head lab. Shindaikyowa Petrochem. Co., Yokkaichi, Japan, 1977—; cons. engr. Nat. Authority Sci. and Tech., Tokyo, 1962; leader, del. Internat. Orgn. Standard, Ottawa, Budapest, 1976-79, del. Moscow, Baden-Baden, Montreau, Pernociuso, 1971-75; mem. UNESCO, Tokyo, 1977—. Patentee in field. Mem. TAPPI, Internat. Union Pure and Applied Chemistry, Chem. Soc. Japan, Soc. Polymer Sci. Japan, Japan Cons. Engrs. Assn. Home: 1-26-11 Hanegi Setagaya, Tokyo 156, Japan Office: Shin Daikyowa Petrochem Co, 1-3-1 Kasumi, Yokkaichi 510, Japan

UENO, JUN, architect; b. Tokyo, July 17, 1949; s. Takashi and Kazue (Oomori) U.; m. Yooko Hirakawa, Dec. 2, 1979; children: Ryoo, Natsumi. B in Engring., Chiba U., 1973, M in Engring., 1976. Architect Takeo Adachi Architect & Assoc., Tokyo, 1976-79; chief architect T. Mohri Architect & Assocs., Tokyo, 1980-83; sub-chief architect sect. Iino Fudosan Kaisha Ltd., Tokyo, 1983—; profl. mem. Survey Team of Rural Fisheries Devel. Project in Solomon Islands, Japanese Govt., 1982-83. Fellow Archtl. Inst. Japan. Club: Diamond Exec. (Tokyo). Office: Iino Fudosan Kaisha Ltd, 1-1 Uchisaiwai-cho 2 choome, Chiyoda-ku Tokyo 100, Japan

UENO, SHIGEKI, accountant; b. Kofu, Yamanashi, Japan, Mar. 3, 1949; s. Masao and Haruko (Ashizawa) U.; m. Mieko Yajima, Oct. 10, 1981; children: Toshiki, Emi. BCS, Chuo U., Tokyo, 1971; MBA, Aoyamagakuin U., Tokyo, 1979. CPA, Japan. With Yazaki, Kofu, 1973-75; mgr. Toda CPA's, Tokyo, 1975-79; officer Ueno CPA's, Kofu, 1979—. Mem. Japan Fedn. CPA Assn., TKC Nat. Fedn. Accts. Club: Internat. Resort Service. Home: 378 Horinouchi-machi, Kofu Yamanashi 400, Japan Office: Ueno CPA, 684-6 Kamiimai-machi, Kofu Yamanashi 400, Japan

UENO, TOMIKO F., forestry company executive; b. Mie, Japan, May 26, 1930; s. Fusataro and Masuye (Higashi) U.; m. Kohei Ueno, Nov. 20, 1953; children: Fusako, Takuro, Toyotsugu. AB, Tokyo Kaseigakuin U., 1952. Pres., chief exec. officer Ueno & Co. Ltd.(name changed to Ueno Corp.), Tokyo, 1975—; bd. dirs. Ueno Ringyo Ltd., Tokyo. Mem. Forestland Owners Assn. Japan. Office: Ueno Ringyo Ltd, 5-17 Fuyuki, 135 Koto-tu Tokyo Japan

UFFEN, ROBERT JAMES, geophysics educator, professional engineer; b. Toronto, Ont., Can., Sept. 21, 1923; s. James Frederick and Elsie May (Harris) U.; m. Mary Ruth Paterson, May 3, 1949; children—Joanne, Robert. B.A.Sc., U. Toronto, 1949, M.A., 1950; Ph.D., U. Western Ont., 1952, D.Sc. (hon.), 1970; D.Sc. (hon.), Queen's U., 1967, Royal Mil. Coll., 1978, McMaster U., 1983. Registered profl. engr., Ont. Prin. univ. coll U. Western Ont., London, 1961-65, dean Coll. Sci., 1965-66; chmn. def. research bd. Govt. of Can., Ottawa, Ont., 1967-69, chief sci. advisor to cabinet, 1969-71; dean applied sci Queen's U., Kingston, Ont., 1971-80, prof. geophysics, 1971—, coordinator summer program for sci. tchrs., 1986—; bd. dirs. Ctr. for Resource Studies; mem. NRC Can., 1963-66, Sci. Council Can., 1967-71; chmn. Can. Engring. Manpower Council, 1972-74; mem. Fisheries Research Bd. Can., 1975-78. Contbr. articles to profl. jours. Regent Colls. Applied Arts and Tech., Ont., 1966-75; vice chmn. Ont. Hydro, Toronto, 1975-79; commr. Royal Commn. on Asbestos, Ont., 1980-84, Truck Safety, Ont., 1981-83; chmn. Ont. Exploration Tech. Fund., 1980-83. Served to lt. Royal Can. Army, 1941-45. Decorated officer Order of Can.; recipient Centenial Medal, Can., 1967. Fellow AAAS, Royal Soc. Can., Geol. Soc. Am.; mem. Am. Geophys. Union, Assn. Profl. Engrs. Ont. (councillor 1975-79, Citizenship award 1985). Club: Rideau (Ottawa). Home: 1504 185 Ontario St, Kingston, ON Canada K7L 2Y7 Office: Queen's Univ, Miller Hall, Kingston, ON Canada K7L 3N6

UGAI, TOSHIYA, banker; b. Kobe, Hyogo Prefecture, Japan, Dec. 25, 1926; s. Keiji and Koshizu (Itoh) U.; m. Mariko Murata, Nov. 26, 1953; children: Yukari Suzuki, Hiroshi Ugai, Junji Murata. B in Econs., Kobe U. Econs. (Japan), 1950. Mem. staff Bank Tokyo Ltd., Osaka, N.Y.C., Nagoya, Tokyo, 1950-69; dep. gen. mgr., Singapore office, 1969-74, acting gen. mgr. systems and methods div., Tokyo, 1974-75, gen. mgr. Toa Rd. office, Kobe, 1975-78; gen. mgr. fgn. div. The Chiba Kogyo Bank Ltd., Tokyo, 1978-81, dir., gen. mgr. fgn. div., 1981-85, sr. counselor fgn. div., 1985-87, sr. counselor internat. div., 1987—. Served with Japanese Navy, 1945. Mem. Bankers Club. Buddhist. Clubs: Chotaro Country (Chiba Prefecture, Japan); Small Kindness Movement (Tokyo). Home: 486-61 Totsuka-cho, Totsuka-ku, Yokohama Kanagawa-ken 244, Japan Office: The Chiba Kogyo Bank Ltd, 11-2 1-chome Kyobashi Chuo-ku, Tokyo 104, Japan

UGRIN, BÉLA, photojournalist, film producer; b. Endröd, Hungary, July 19, 1928; came to U.S., 1962, naturalized, 1967; s. Gáspár and Regina (Gyuricza) U.; m. Emmanuella Caravageli, Feb. 12, 1964; 1 son, Gregory Alexander. Grad., Inst. Photojournalism, Munich, W. Ger., 1960; BA, U. Houston, 1977; MA, Tex. So. U., 1980. Freelance mag. photographer Munich, and N.Y.C., 1959-66; chief photographer Westport (Conn.) News,

1967-69; staff photographer Houston Post, 1969-77, chief photographer, 1978-84; lectr. in field. Ind. film producer, 1985—; assoc. dir. Houston ISD's Dept. Tech., 1986—; producer-dir., (cultural TV documentary) André Kertész: A Poet With the Camera, 1986, (ednl. video series) Take Command, 1986-87, (ednl. video series) Technology and Education Today, 1988; contbr. articles on video prodns., photography and travel to various publs. Mem. Soc. Profl. Journalists.

UHDE, GEORGE IRVIN, physician; b. Richmond, Ind., Mar. 20, 1912; s. Walter Richard and Anna Margaret (Hoopes) U.; m. Maurine Elizabeth Whitley, July 27, 1935; children—Saundra Uhde Seelig, Thomas Whitley, Michael, Janice. M.D., Duke U., 1936. Diplomate: Am. Bd. Otolaryngology. Intern Reading (Pa.) Hosp., 1936-37, resident in medicine, 1937-38; resident in otolaryngology Balt. Eye, Ear, Nose and Throat Hosp., 1938-40, U. Oreg. Med. Sch., Portland, 1945-47; practice medicine specializing in otolaryngology Louisville, 1948—; asst. prof. otolaryngology U. Louisville Med. Sch., 1945-62, prof. surgery (otolaryngology), head dept., 1963—, dir. otolaryngology services, 1963—; mem. staffs Meth., Norton's-Children's, Jewish, St. Joseph's, St. Anthony's, St. Mary and Elizabeth's hosps.; cons. Ky. Surg. Tb Hosp., Hazlewood, VA Hosp., Louisville, U. Louisville Speech and Hearing Center. Author 4 books.; Contbr. articles to profl. jours. Bd. dirs. Easter Seal Speech and Hearing Center. Served to lt. col. M.C. U.S. Army, 1940-45, ETO. Recipient Disting. Service award U. Louisville, 1972. Fellow A.C.S., Am. Acad. Ophthalmology and Otolaryngology, So. Med. Soc.; mem. N.Y. Acad. Scis., Am. Coll. Allergists, Am. Acad. Facial Plastic and Reconstructive Surgery, AAAS, Assn. U. Otolaryngologists, AAUP, Assn. Mil. Surgeons U.S., Am. Laryngol., Rhinol. and Otol. Soc., Am. Audiology Soc., Soc. Clin. Ecology, Am. Soc. Otolaryngology Allergy, Centurian Otol. Research Soc. (Ky. rep.), Am. Council Otolaryngology (Ky. rep. 1968—), Hoopes Quaker Found., SAR (life), Alpha Kappa Kappa. Democrat. Methodist. Clubs: Filson, Big Spring Country, Jefferson. Home: 708 Circle Hill Rd Louisville KY 40207 Office: Med Towers Louisville KY 40202

UHERIK, ANTON, psychophysiologist; b. Malé Dvorany, Czechoslovakia, Sept. 12, 1930; m. Irma Horváthová; 1 child, Adela Uherik Laktišová. PhD, Comenius Univ., Bratislava, Czechoslovakia, 1955. Head psychophysiology dept. Inst. Experimental Psychology-Slovak Acad. Scis., Bratislava, 1954—. Author: Electrical Activity of the Skin, 1965, The Psychophysiological Properties of Man, 1978, Man Is Just Man, 1988; contbr. numerous articles in field to profl. jours. Home: Švermova 11, 831 01 Bratislava Czechoslovakia Office: Slovak Acad Scis, Inst Experimental Psychology, Kocelova 15, 821 08 Bratislava Czechoslovakia

UHL, EDWARD GEORGE, retired manufacturing executive; b. Elizabeth, N.J., Mar. 24, 1918; s. Henry and Mary (Schiller) U.; m. Maurine B. Keleher, July 19, 1942; children: Carol Uhl Nordlinger, Kim, Scott, Cynthia Uhl McKitrick; m. Mary Stuart Brugh, Sept. 17, 1966. B.S., Lehigh U., 1940, D.Sc. (hon.), 1975. Engr. guided missiles Martin Co., 1946-51, chief project engr., 1951-53, v.p. engring., 1953-55, v.p. ops., 1955-56; v.p., gen. mgr. Orlando div. Martin Co., Fla., 1957-59; v.p. tech. adminstrn. Ryan Aero. Co., 1959-60, v.p., div. mgr., 1961; pres., chief exec. officer, dir. Fairchild Industries, 1961-76, chmn. bd., chief exec. officer, dir., 1976-86; dir. Md. Nat. Bank, Md. Nat. Corp., Vanguard Technologies Internat., Inc. Trustee Johns Hopkins U.; chmn. bd. trustees Lehigh U.; bd. nominations Aviation Hall Fame. Served from 2d lt. to lt. col. Ordnance Corps AUS, 1941-46. Recipient Hamilton Holt award Rollins Coll., 1965. Fellow AIAA; mem. Air Force Assn., Am. Def. Preparedness Assn. (John C. Jones award 1975), Soc. Automotive Engrs., Phi Beta Kappa, Tau Beta Pi. Clubs: Assembly (Hagerstown); Maryland (Balt.); Talbot Country (Easton); Sky (N.Y.C.).

UHL, PHILIP EDWARD, marine artist; b. Toledo, Aug. 19, 1949; s. Philip Edward and Betty Jean (Mayes) U. Student, Dayton Art Inst., 1967-68, Art Students League, 1974. Creative dir. Ctr. for Civic Initiative, Milw., 1969-71; art dir. Artco Advt. Agy., Honolulu, 1972-73; artist, photographer Assn. Honolulu Artists, 1974-77; pres. Uhl Enterprises div. Makai Photography, Honolulu, 1977—, Videoscapes div. Channel Sea TV, Honolulu, 1977—; cons. Pan Am. Airways, N.Y.C. and Honolulu, 1979-84, ITTC Travel Ctr., Honolulu, 1982-83, Royal Hawaiian Ocean Racing Club, Honolulu, 1985-86, Sail Am.-Am.'s Cup Challenge, Honolulu, 1985-86; bd. dirs. Sail Fest Hawaii. Co-producer video documentary White on Water, 1984 (Emmy 1984); producer Joy of Life, 1988 (recipient Golden Monitor award Internat. TV Assn.); pub., art dir. mags., promotional publs. Pan Am. Clipper Cup, 1980, 82, 84 and Kenwood Cup, 1986; photographer: (book) Nautical Quarterly, 1983 (Soc. Publ. Designers award 1984); contbr. numerous articles, photos to yachting publs. worlwide. vol. VISTA, 1969-71. Mem. Am. Soc. Mag. Photographers, U.S. Yacht Racing Union, Royal Hawaiian Ocean Racing Club (cons.), Royal Corinthian Yacht Club, Waikiki Yacht Club. Mem. Am. Film Inst., Internat. Platform Assn., Soc. Internat. Nautical Scribes, Honolulu Creative Group. Office: UHL Enterprises Century Ctr Suite 3-757 1750 Kalakaua Honolulu HI 96826

UHLMANN, WERNER SIGMUND, industry executive; b. Berlin, Germany, June 16, 1935; arrived in Sweden, 1939; s. Erich Leopold and Hildegard (Neumann) U.; m. Gertrud Birgitta Ohson, Nov. 2, 1962 (div. 1987); children: Robert, Helena, Henrik. MBA, Sch. Econ., Gothenburg, Sweden, 1965. Mgr. fin. dept. Asea A.B., Vasteras, Sweden, 1964-68, 73-75; fin. dir. Asea Electric Party, Ltd., Melbourne, Australia, 1968-73; asst. fin. dir. Industri AB Euroc, Malmo, Sweden, 1975-78, 1975-78, sr. v.p., corp. treas., 1978—; bd. dirs. Finans Scandic A.B., Stockholm; alternate dir. Allemans Fond 3; auditor Sparbanken Skane, Malmo, 1983—. Nat. treas. Ronservative Student-Forbundet, 1962-65, Stockholm Jr. C. of C. Internat., 1975. Conservative. Christian. Home: Polgatan 69, S-21611 Malmo Sweden Office: Industri AB Euroc, PO Box 30600, S-20062 Malmo Sweden

UHRMAN, CELIA, artist, poet; b. New London, Conn., May 14, 1927; d. David Aaron and Pauline (Schwartz) U. BA, Bklyn. Coll., 1948, MA, 1953; PhD, U. Danzig, 1977; postgrad. Tchrs. Coll., Columbia U., 1961, CUNY, 1966, Bklyn. Mus. Art Sch., 1956-57, PhD (hon.), LittD, 1973; cert. Koret Living Library U. of San Francisco, 1982. One-woman shows: Leffert Jr. High Sch., Bklyn., 1958, Flatbush C. of C., N.Y.C., 1963, Conn. C. of C., New London, 1962; exhibited in group shows: Smithsonian Instn., Washington, 1958, Springfield (Mass.) Mus. Fine Arts, 1959, Bklyn. Mus., 1959, Old Mystic (Conn.) Art Center, 1959, Carnegie Endowment Internat. Center, N.Y.C., 1959, Lyman Allyn Mus., New London, 1960, Palacio de La Virrelna, Barcelona, Spain, 1961, YMCA, Bklyn., 1962, UFT Art Exhibit, N.Y.C., 1963, Soc. of 4 Arts, Palm Beach, Fla., 1964, Perspective 68, Monte-Carlo, Monaco, 1968, George W. Wingate High sch., Bklyn., 1967, Premier Salon Internat., Charleroi, Belgium, 1968, Palme d'or Beaux Arts, Monte-Carlo, 1970, 72, Dibuix-Joan Miro Premi Internacional, Barcelona, 1970; N.Y. Art Festival, 1970, Internat. Platform Assn. Art Show, Washington, 1971, 73, Ovar Mus., Portugal, 1974, others; represented in permanent collections: Bklyn. Coll., Ch. of Evangel, Bklyn.; tchr. N.Y.C. Sch. System, 1948-82; ptnr. Uhrman Studio, 1973-83; hon. rep. U.S., Centro Studi E Scambi Internazionali, Rome, mem. Internat. Com., 1969. Hon. life mem. World Poetry Day Com., Inc. and Nat. Poetry Day Com., 1977. Recipient award Freedoms Found., George Washington medal of honor, 1964, Diplome d'Honneur Palme d'Or des Beaux Arts Exhbn., Monaco, 1969, 72, Diploma and Gold medal, Centro Studi E Scambi Internazionali, 1972; decorated Order of Gandhi Award of Honour, Knight Grand Cross, 1972; personal poetry certificate WEFG Stereo, 1970; Gold Laurel award Esposizione Internazionale D'Art Contemporain, Paris, 1974; named Poetry Translator Laureate World Acad. Lang. and Lit., 1972, Poet of Mankind Acad. Philosophy, 1972; cert. of appreciation Bd. Edn. of N.Y.C., 1982. Fellow World Lit. Academy Eng.; mem. Internat. Arts Guild (comdr. 1966—), World Poetry Soc. Intercontinental (rep. at large 1969—), Internat. Acad. Poets (founding fellow), N.Y. Artists Equity. Author: Poetic Ponderances, 1969, A Pause for Poetry, 1970, Poetic Love Fancies, 1970, A Pause for Poetry for Children, 1973, The Chimps Are Coming, 1975, Love Fancies, 1987. Home: 1655 Flatbush Ave Apt and Studio C106 Brooklyn NY 11210

UJAGER, ANWAR MASIH, ophthalmologist; b. Gojra, Chenderke, Pakistan, Sept. 3, 1937; s. Ujader and Taj; m. Catherine Sidiki, July 20, 1968; children: Tahreem, Huma, Aneeqa. MBBS, Nishter Med. Coll., Multan, Pakistan, 1963; Diploma Ophthalmology, Royal Coll. Surgeons, Dublin, Ireland, 1970, Royal Coll. Surgeons, London, 1971. Sr. house surgeon Gateshead and Dist. Hosp. Com., Eng., 1966-67, Mildmay Mission Hosp., London, 1968-69, Norfolk and Norwich (Eng.) Hosp., 1969-70, Sussex Eye Hosp., Brighton, Eng., 1970-71; med. officer Pennel Meml. Hosp., Bannu, Pakistan, 1963-65, Mission Hosp., Peshawar, Pakistan, 1965-66; head eye dept. Sussex Eye Hosp., Peshawar, Pakistan, 1971-74, med. dir., 1974—; hon. lectr. Khyber Med. Coll., Peshawar; cons. State Bank, Peshawar, 1974-87, Am. Consulate, Peshawar, 1974-87; pennel physician Am. Embassy, Islamabad, Pakistan, 1974-87. Contbr. articles to profl. jours. Pres. Anti Leprosy Assn., Peshawar; mem. Fed. Adv. Council, Govt. Pakistan, Islamabad, 1980-87, Fed. Leprosy Control Bd., 1983-87, Service and Devel. Com. Christian Conf. Asia, Singapore, 1982-86; exec. mem. mng. com. Red Crescent Soc. Recipient Gold medal Lahore Diocese Ch. Pakistan, 1982, Bolan award Bolan Cultural Soc., Quetta, 1984, Ophthalmology fellow Internat. Coll. Surgeons, Chgo., 1985, TAMGA-e-IMTIAZ award Pres. Pakistan, 1988. Fellow Pakistan Acad. Ophthalmology; mem. Ophthal. Soc. of the Pakistan (exec. mem.), Ophthal. Soc. U.K., Pakistan Red Crescent Soc. (Peshawar exec. com.). Home and Office: Mission Hosp, Peshawar Pakistan

UKPONG, JUSTIN SAMPSON, priest, educator, religious institute dean; b. Etinan, Cross River, Nigeria, Dec. 26, 1940; s. Sampson Akpan and Elizabeth Eshiet (Ekwere) U. BA in Philosophy, Bigard Sem., Enugu, Nigeria, 1963, BD, 1968; MA in Bibl. Theology, Pontifical Urban U., Rome, 1978, PhD in Bibl. Theology, 1980. Ordained priest Roman Cath. Ch., 1967; diploma in social administrn. and journalism. Asst. priest Cath. Cathedral, Calabar, Nigeria, 1968-69; adminstr. Cath. Cathedral, Calabar, 1974-76; lectr. U. Calabar, 1980-81; lectr./prof. Cath. Inst. West Africa, Port Harcourt, Nigeria, 1981—; acting rector 1985-86, faculty dean, 1986—. Author: African Theologies New, 1984, Sacrifice: African and Biblican, 1987, Introduction to African Theology, 1988; editor Bible and Life mag. 1984—, Incarnation Monograph Series, 1986—; contbr. articles to profl. jours. Misereor study fellow, Can., 1969; Missio research grantee, Nigeria, 1982. Fellow Cath. Bibl. Assn. Am.; mem. West African Assn. Theol. Insts. (sec. 1987—), Nigerian Assn. Bibl. Studies, Cath. Theol. Assn. Nigeria, Port Harcourt Music. Soc. Home: PO Box 270, Etinan Nigeria Office: Cath Inst West Africa, PO Box 499, Port Harcourt Nigeria

UKPONG, SAMUEL JAPHET, manufacturing firm director, college researcher; b. Nkpat Enin, Nigeria, Mar. 20, 1949; s. Japhet Job and Hannah Japhet Ukpong; grad. Regina Ceoli Coll., 1969; diploma Yaba Coll. Tech., 1972; B.A. in Bus. Adminstrn., B.A. in Philosophy, Columbia Pacific U., 1981, D.D. Clayton U., 1984; m. Ekaette S. Umoh, July 2, 1977; children—Enobong Samukpong, Onofiok Samukpong, Iniedidiong Samukpong. With Central Bank of Nigeria, Lagos, 1970-76; fgn. exchange officer U. Calabar, 1976-81; Nigerian regional mgr. C.P.S. Assos. A.G., Chur, Switzerland, 1978-84; vis. prof. Atma U. India, 1985-87; pres., chief exec. officer Ema Sam Agys. Ltd., Calabar, Nigeria, 1978-84 ; chmn. Sajju Internat. Ltd., 1982—; vice chmn. Seagas (Nigeria) Ltd., 1981—; exec. dirs. Esa Power Ltd. 1988—; pres. Sajju Inst. and Research Found., Calabar, 1987—. Chmn., Nkpat Enin Youth Assn., 1978-82; chmn. tech. com. Nkpat Enin Local Govt., 1981-82; patron sr. staff assn. Coll. Tech., Calabar, 1980-81; pres. Christian youth fellowship Qua Iboe Ch., Calabar, 1978-81. Mem. Nigeria Inst. Mgmt. (asso.), Am. Mgmt. Assn. Internat., Alexander Hamilton Inst. U.S.A. Clubs: Police, Sports (Calabar). Author: You Need Your Needs, 1979, Reason With Me, 1980, Why Only Jesus Christ, 1980, Downfall No End, 1981, Spiritual Unfoldment Program, 15 vols. Home: PO Box 1130, 52 Umo Orok St, Calabar Nigeria Office: 58 Ekpo Abasi St, PO Box 1130, Calabar Nigeria

UKROPINA, JAMES ROBERT, energy company executive, lawyer; b. Fresno, Calif., Sept. 10, 1937; s. Robert J. and Persida (Angelich) U.; m. Priscilla Lois Brandenburg, June 16, 1962; children—Michael Steven, David Robert, Mark Gregory. A.B., Stanford U., 1959, M.B.A., 1961; LL.B., U. So. Calif., 1965. Bar: Calif. 1966, D.C. 1980. Assoc. firm O'Melveny & Myers, Los Angeles, 1965-72; partner O'Melveny & Myers, 1972-80; exec. v.p., gen. counsel Santa Fe Internat. Corp., Alhambra, Calif., 1980-84, dir., 1981-86; exec. v.p., gen. counsel Pacific Enterprises, Los Angeles, 1984-86, pres., dir., 1986—; bd. dirs. Security Pacific Corp., Lockheed Corp.; lectr. in field. Editor-in-chief: So. Calif. Law Rev, 1964-65. Trustee Occidental Coll.; mem. adv. council Stanford Bus. Sch.; mem. Calif. Econ. Devel. Corp. Bd. Served with USAF, 1961-62. Mem. Am. Bar Assn., Calif. Bar Assn., Los Angeles County Bar Assn., Beta Theta Pi. Club: Calif. Office: Pacific Enterprises 801 S Grand Los Angeles CA 90017

ULAKOVICH, RONALD STEPHEN, real estate developer; b. Youngstown, Ohio, Nov. 17, 1942; s. Stephen G. and Anne (Petretich) U. B.S., Indsl. Engring. Coll., 1967; M.S., Method Engring., Ill. Inst. Tech., 1969. Methods engr. Supreme Products, Chgo., 1964-66; pres. Contract Chair, 1966-70; v.p. sales Amrep Corp., Rosemont, Ill., 1970-73; pres. Condo Assoc., Ltd., Arlington Heights, Ill., 1973—, Am. Resorts Internat. Ltd., 1983. Named Employee of Yr., 1965; recipient Nat. Home Builders Grand award, 1977, Million Dollar Circle award Chgo. Tribune, 1978, Cert. of Recognition award Congressional Com., 1982, Cert. of Merit award Pres. Reagan's Task Force, 1984; named to Ky. Col.State of Ky., 1982. Mem. Am. Assn. Investors, Apt. Owners Assn., Real Estate Soc. of Syndicators and Investors, Am. Resort and Resdl. Devel. Assn. Roman Catholic. Avocations: auto racing, golf. Home: 510 Van Buren St East Dundee IL 60118

ULANHU, former vice president People's Republic of China; b. Suiyan, 1904; m. Yun Liwen. Attended Mongolian-Tibetan Sch., Peking, 1922-24, Far Eastern U., Moscow. Joined Chinese Communist Party, 1925; head edn. dept. Nationalities Inst. under Anti-Japanese Mil. and Polit. Acad., Yenan, 1941; alt. mem. 7th Cen. Com. Communist Party, 1945; chmn. Inner Mongolia People's Govt., 1947-67; comdr. Polit. Commissar Inner Mongolia Mil. Region, People's Librarian Army, 1947-67; mem. Standing Com., Chinese People's Polit. Consultative Conf., 1949, exec. chmn. nat. com., 1978, vice pres., 1978-83; vice minister Nationalities Affairs Commn., 1949, minister, 1954; vice premier State Council, 1954-82; chmn. Nationalities Commn., 1954-67; 2d sec. North China Bur., Cen. Com. Chinese Communist Party, 1965; appointed col. gen., 1955; alt. mem. Politburo, 8th Cen. Com., Chinese Communist Party, 1956-67; criticized and ousted from office in Cultural Revolution, 1967; mem. 10th Cen. Com., Chinese Communist Party, 1973, mem. Cen. Com. and Politburo, 11th Cen. Com., 1977, mem. Cen. Com. and Politburo, 12th Cen. Com., 1982-85; vice chmn. standing com. 4th Nat. People's Congress, 1975-83, permanent chmn. presidium, 5th Nat. People's Congress, 1980, vice chmn. standing com. 7th Nat. People's Congress, 1988—; dir. United Front Work Dept., Chinese Communist Party, 1977-82; mem. Presidium, 12th Congress Chinese Communist Party, 1982; vice pres. People's Republic of China, 1983-88. Address: Nat People's Congress, Office Vice Chmn, Beijing Peoples Republic of China *

ULBRECHT, JAROMIR JOSEF, chemical engineer; b. Ostrava, Czechoslovakia, Dec. 16, 1928; s. Josef and Leopolda U.; m. Vera Krafneter, July 10, 1952; children: Jan Stanislav, Magdalena Vera. Ing., Czech Inst. Tech., Prague, 1952, Ph.D., 1958. Dept. head Research div. (Synthetic Rubber Co.), Zlin, Czechoslovakia, 1958-63; head lab. engring. rheology Czechoslovak Acad. Scis., Prague, 1963-68; prof. chem. engring. U. Salford, Eng., 1968-78; prof., chmn. dept. chem. engring. SUNY, Buffalo, 1978-83; chief div. chem. process metrology Nat. Bur. Standards, Washington, 1984—. Author: Non-Newtonian Liquids, 1967, Mixing of Liquids by Mechanical Agitation, 1985; editor: Chemical Engineering Communications, 1976; contbr. numerous articles to profl. jours. Recipient Outstanding Scholarship award Czech Acad. Scis., 1965, 67; Alexander von Humboldt fellow, 1967. Mem. Am. Inst. Chem. Engrs., Inst. Chem. Engrs. (London), Soc. Rheology, Brit. Soc. Rheology, N.Y. Acad. Scis. Office: Div Chem Process Metrology Bldg 221 Room B250 Washington DC 20234

ULBRICHT, ROBERT E., lawyer, savings and loan executive; b. Chgo., Dec. 1, 1930; s. Emil Albert and Vivian June (Knight) U.; m. Betty Anne Charleson, June 20, 1953; 1 dau., Christine Anne. A.B., U. Ill., 1952, M.A., 1953; J.D., U. Chgo., 1958. Bar: Ill. 1958, U.S. Dist. Ct. (no. dist.) Ill. 1959. Research atty. Am. Bar Found., Chgo., 1957-59; asst. trust counsel Continental Ill. Nat. Bank & Trust Co., Chgo., 1959-60; assoc. law firm Cummings and Wyman, Chgo., 1960-68; gen. atty., sec., sr. v.p. Bell Fed. Savs. & Loan Assn., Chgo., 1968—; instr. Aurora Coll., Coll. DuPage. Mem. nominating com. Dist. 41 Sch. Bd., 1970-71, vice chmn., 1971; chmn. dist. area fund raising Glen Ellyn council Girl Scouts Am., 1970. Bd. dirs. Glen Ellyn (Ill.) Pub. Library, 1979-85, pres., 1983-84. Served with AUS, 1953-55. Mem. Chgo. Bar Assn., Ill. Bar Assn., ABA. Clubs: Glen Oak Country, Glen Ellyn Tennis. Bd. editors Chgo. Bar Record, 1970-73; contbr. articles to legal jours. Office: 79 W Monroe St Chicago IL 60603

ULEHLA, IVAN, physics educator; b. Skalica, Czechoslovakia, Oct. 17, 1921; s. Miloslav and Anna Marie (Tilschova) U.; m. Ludmila Ulehlova, Oct. 31, 1942 (div. 1966); children: Ivan, Josef, Katerina; m. Libuse Pouchla, Sept. 9, 1966; 1 child, Premysl. RNDr, Charles U., 1949. Asst. Charles U., Prague, Czechoslovakia, 1949-51, Komensky U., Bratislava, Czechoslovakia, 1951-54; sr. researcher Inst. Nuclear Physics, Prague, Czechoslovakia, 1954-60; asst. prof. physics Tech. U., Prague, Czechoslovakia, 1960-63, prof., 1963-67; dir. Nuclear Ctr. Charles U., Czechoslovakia, 1975-85, prof. physics, 1967—; vice-dir. Joint Inst. Nuclear Research, Dubna, USSR, 1964-67; sci. sec. 1st Conf. on Atomic Energy, Geneva, 1955, spl. asst. 2d Conf., 1958. Author book on nuclear physics, 1962, books on physics and philosophy, 1962, 64, 82. Decorated Order of Labor (Czechoslovakia). Mem. European Phys. Soc., Czechoslovakian Acad. Scis. (corr.), Czechoslovakian Union Math. and Physics (pres. 1981-87). Home: Vavrenova 1169, 14200 Prague 4 Czechoslovakia Office: Charles Univ, Nuclear Ctr V, Holesovickach 2, 18000 Prague 8 Czechoslovakia

ULERICH, WILLIAM KEENER, publishing company executive; b. Latrobe, Pa., Apr. 18, 1910; s. William Wesley and Anna (Keener) U.; m. Edith O. Orton, May 26, 1934 (div. 1950); 1 dau., Constance K.; m. Alethea M. Jones, Aug. 23, 1950. A.B., Pa. State U., 1931; LL.D., Dickinson Sch. Law, 1977. Editor Daily Times, State College, Pa., 1931-45; asso. prof. journalism Pa. State U., 1934-45; pub. Clearfield (Pa.) Daily Progress, 1946; chmn. bd. dirs. Ind. Broadcasters, Inc., Indiana, Pa., 1949—, Clearfield Broadcasters, Inc.; dir. County Nat. Bank, Clearfield. Bd. dirs., past pres. Clearfield Meml. Hosp.; trustee Pa. State U., 1952-57, 64-85, v.p. bd. trustees, 1973-76, pres. bd. trustees, 1976-79, pres. emeritus, 1985. Served with AUS, World War II. Mem. Pa. Newspaper Pubs. Assn. (pres. 1952). Methodist. Home: 724 S 2d St Clearfield PA 16830 also: N-1003 Longboat Key Towers Longboat Key Club Rd Longboat Key FL 33548 Office: 206 Locust St Clearfield PA 16830

ULERY, DANA LYNN, statistical computing consultant; b. East St. Louis, Ill., Jan. 2, 1938; d. Harry H. Tanzer and Meriam (Corn) Mueller; m. Harris E. Ulery, Aug. 15, 1959 (div. Jan. 1979); children: Bradford T., Terrie L.; m. William H. Fellner, Feb. 29, 1980. BA in Math. and English Lit., Grinnell Coll., 1959; MS in Computer Sci., U. Del., 1972, PhD in Applied Sci., 1975. Research engr. NASA Jet Propulsion Lab., Pasadena, Calif., 1960-63; programmer Getty Oil Co., Delaware City, Del., 1963-64; postdoctoral research assoc. U. Del., Newark, 1975-76; sr. software engr. E.I. duPont de Nemours & Co., Wilmington, Del., 1977-82, cons. supr., 1982-87, statis. computing cons., 1987—; lectr. U. Del., Newark, 1970-77; vis. lectr. Inst. Stats. and Computer Sci., Cairo, Egypt, spring 1976; cons. Am. U., Cairo, spring 1976. Author: (with others) Concepts in Computer Science, 1976; creator software system Lineal, 1974; contbr. articles to profl. jours. Yonkers honor Scholar, 1956-59; Unidel research fellow, 1973-76; U. Del. research fellow, 1971-73. Mem. Assn. Computing Machinery, Am. Statis. Assn., IEEE Computer Soc., Am. Soc. Quality Control, AAAS, Chem. Industry Data Exchange, Fabric and Suppliers Linkage Council, Am. Nat. Standards Inst. X-12 Com., Sigma Xi. Home: 18 Squirrel Ln Newark DE 19711 Office: Applied Stats Group Engring Dept EI DuPont de Nemours & Co Wilmington DE 19898

ULIJN, JAN MARINUS, linguist, educator; b. Oss, The Netherlands, June 19, 1944; s. W.M.C. and H.F. (van den Oever) U.; m. P.H.W. van Dommelen, Dec. 19, 1968; children: Giel, Brigit, Rein. BA in French Lang. and Lit., Nijmegen U., The Netherlands, 1966, MA in Romance Linguistics, 1968, PhD in Social Scis., 1978; diploma in applied linguistics and scis., Besançon (France) U., 1967. Sr. lectr., assoc. prof. Eindhoven (The Netherlands) U. Tech., 1969—; vis. researcher lab. exptl. psychology Nijmegen U., 1977-78; vis. scholar sch. edn. dept. linguistics Stanford (Calif.) U., 1979-80; prof. psycholinguistics TESOL Summer Inst., Oreg., 1984; vis. scholar Shanghai (People's Republic of China) Jiaotong U., 1987; vice chmn. research ctr. tech. knowledge transfer and communication Eindhoven U. Tech., 1986, chmn. sect. applied linguistics, 1987, bd. dirs. post-graduate program tech. and linguistics, 1987. Editor: Reading for Professional Purposes (methods), 1985; co-editor: Reading for Professional Purposes (studies), 1984; contbr. articles to profl. jours.; mem. editorial bd. Jour. Research on Reading, 1978—, Reading in a Fgn. Lang., 1982—. Recipient Palmes Académiques French Govt., 1984. Fellow Soc. Tech. Communication; mem. Assn. Néerlandaise Linguistique Appliquée (founder, treas. 1972-73), Internat. Reading Assn. (Research award 1982), Linguistic Soc. Am., Studiekring voor Technische Informatie en Communicatie, Wetenschappelijk Redacteuren Kring, Dutch Assn. Lang. Tchrs. (chmn. French didactics commn. 1972-76). Roman Catholic. Home: Buizerdlaan 2, 5672 VS Nuenen The Netherlands Office: Eindhoven U Tech, Den Dolech 2, 5600 MB Eindhoven The Netherlands

ULLAH, FATTAH, physician; b. NW Frontier Province, Pakistan, Jan. 20, 1916; s. Subhan Ullah and Muslima; m. Nasseem Akhtar Fattahullah, Nov. 19, 1948; children: Nilofar, Nighat, Waqar, Kaukab, Shahab. MBBS, U. Bombay, 1945. Diplomate Pakistan Bd. Family Practice. Practice medicine specializing in Tb. Abbottabad, Pakistan, 1950-87. Hon. health officer Mcpl. Com. Abbottabad, 1963—. Served to capt. dr. Pakistan Army, 1945-50. Mem. Physicians Med. Assn. (pres. 1985-87), Islamic Med. Drs. Assn. (pres. 1986-87). Mem. Jamate-Islami party. Muslim. Home: 1996 Wioarullah Rd, Abbottabad Pakistan *Died, Nov. 27, 1987.*

ULLENDORFF, EDWARD, Orientalist; b. Jan. 25, 1920; s. Frederick and Cilli (Pulverman) U.; M.A., U. Jerusalem, 1941; D.Phil., Oxford U., 1951; M.A. (hon.), U. Manchester (Eng.), 1962; D.Litt. (hon.), St. Andrews U., Scotland, 1972; m. Dina Noack, Apr. 27, 1943. With Govt. Palestine, 1946-48; mem. faculty Oxford Inst. Colonial Studies, 1948-49; lectr., then reader Semitic langs. St. Andrews U., 1950-59; prof. Semitic langs. U. Manchester, 1959-64, prof. Ethiopian studies, 1964-82; prof. Semitic langs. U. London, 1979-82; cataloguer Ethiopian manuscripts Royal Library Windsor Castle, 1952; mem. adv. bd. Brit. Library, 1975-83; Schweich lectr. Brit. Acad., 1967. Recipient Imperial Ethiopian Gold medallion, 1960; Haile Selassie Internat. prize for Ethiopian Studies, 1972. Served with Armed Forces, 1941-46; Eritrea and Ethiopia. Fellow Brit. Acad. (v.p. 1980-82); mem. Anglo Ethiopian Soc. (chmn. 1965-68), Assn. Brit. Orientalists (chmn. 1963-64), Soc. O.T. Study (pres. 1971), Royal Asiatic Soc. (v.p. 1975-85). Author: The Definite Article in the Semitic Languages, 1941; Exploration and Study of Abyssinia, 1945; Catalogue of Ethiopian Manuscripts in the Bodleian Library, Oxford, 1951; The Semitic Languages of Ethiopia, 1955; The Ethiopians, 1959, 3d edit., 1973; (with Stephen Wright) Catalogue of Ethiopian MSS in Cambridge University Library, 1961; Comparative Semitics in Linguistica Semitica, 1961; (with S. Moscati and others) Introduction to Comparative Grammar of Semitic Languages, 1964; An Amharic Chrestomathy, 1965; The Challenge of Amharic, 1965; Ethiopia and the Bible, 1968; (with J. B. Pritchard and others) Solomon and Sheba, 1974; Studies in Semitic Languages and Civilizations, 1977; (with M. A. Knibb) Book of Enoch, 1978; The Bawdy Bible, 1979. Annotator/translator: Emperor Haile Selassie, My Life and Ethiopia's Progress, 1976; (with others) The Amharic Letters of Emperor Theodore of Ethiopia to Queen Victoria, 1979; (with C.F. Beckingham) The Hebrew Letters of Prester John, 1982; A Tigrinya Chrestomathy, 1985, Studia Aethiopica et Semitica, 1987, The Two Zions, 1988; joint editor Studies in Honor of G. R. Driver, 1962; Ethiopian Studies, 1964. Contbr. articles and revs. to scholarly jours. Chmn. editorial bd. Bull. Sch. Oriental and African Studies, 1968-78; editor Jour. Semitic Studies, 1961-64. Home: 4 Bladon Close, Oxford OX2 8AD, England

ULLMAN, MARIE, manufacturing company executive; b. Linlithgo, N.Y., Mar. 19, 1914; d. Max and Sarah (Jaffe) Michaelson; R.N., Bklyn. Hosp., 1935; m. Robert Ullman, Aug. 15, 1935. Pres., sec.-treas. Ullman Devices Corp., Ridgefield, Conn., 1938—; dir. State Nat. Bank Conn., Ridgefield. Mem. C. of C. Ridgefield, Bklyn. Hosp. Nurses Alumnae. Home: 43 Chestnut Hill Rd Wilton CT 06897 Office: PO Box 398 Ridgefield CT 06877

ULLMANN, ERNST, art historian, educator; b. Reichenberg, Czechoslovakia, Dec. 19, 1928; s. Ernst and Martha (Tallowitz) U.; m. Helga Wiese, Aug. 7, 1954; children: Christian, Bettina, Mathias, Reinhard. MA, U. Halle, German Dem. Republic, 1956, PhD, 1960; PhD Habilitation, Karl Marx U. Leipzig, German Dem. Republic, 1967, Dr. sc. phil., 1973. Aspirant U. Halle, 1956-60; chief asst. Karl Marx U. Leipzig, 1960-64, lectr., 1964-71, reader art hist., 1971—; dir. Inst. Art History U. Leipzig, 1964-68; dep. dir. Section for Art Scis. U. Leipzig, 1977-79. Author: Leonardo da Vinci, 1980, The World of Gothic Cathedrals, 1982, Raffael, 1983; co-editor: History of German Art 2 vols., 1981-83. Chmn. working group History Art Ministry Edn., 1982. Recipient Gustav Hertz prize U. Leipzig, 1984, Nat. prize German Dem. Republic, 1985, Vaterländischer Verdienstorden, 1982. Fellow Princeton U. Inst. for Advanced Studies; mem. Saxon Acad. Scis., Com. Internat. Histoire Art, Internat. Assn. Art Critics, Gesellschaft Denkmalpflege (chmn. 1982—),. Office: Karl Marx U, Karl Marx Platz 9, 7010 Leipzig German Democratic Republic

ULLMANN, LIV, actress; b. Tokyo, Japan, Dec. 16, 1938; d. Viggo and Janna (Lund) U.; m. Hans Stang, 1960 (div. 1965); 1 dau., Linn, by Ingmar Bergman; m. Donald Saunders, Sept. 7, 1985. Student pub. sch.; studies with dramatic coach, London, Eng.; 8 hon. doctoral degrees in arts and humanities. Starred in Diary of Anne Frank, repertory troup, Stavanger, Norway; became established actress of classic stage and film roles in Norway; appeared as Ingmar Bergman's leading lady in film Persona, 1966; many other films directed by Bergman; also films in U.S., Can., Mex., France, Italy, Germany, S.Am., Switzerland, England; starred as Nora in A Doll's House in N.Y. Shakespeare Festival prodn. Vivian Beaumont Theater, Lincoln Ctr., N.Y.C.; appeared on Broadway in Anna Christie, 1977, I Remember Mama, 1979, Ghosts, other stage appearances include Old Times, West End, London, 1985-86, Mother Courage, Nat. Theatre, Oslo, Norway; author: Changing, 1977, translated into over 20 langs (Book-of-Month Club), Choices, 1984, translated into over 20 langs. Ofcl. goodwill ambassador UNICEF, 1980—. Decorated officier of Arts and Letters, France, The Order of St. Olaf, King of Norway; recipient Dag Hammarskjold Hon. medal; named best actress by either N.Y. Film Critics or Nat. Soc. Film Critics U.S. for 6 yrs. in a row. Home: Drammensviens 91, Oslo Norway Office: care Robert Lantz 888 Seventh Ave New York NY 10106

ULLRICH, (NOEL) BRUCE, management consultant; b. New Plymouth, N.Z., June 23, 1938; s. August and Daisey Winifred (McKeekan) U.; m. Jeannette Axelsen, Dec. 8, 1962; children: Jane, Matthew, Michael. B of Commerce, U. Canterbury, Christchurch, N.Z., 1964. Clk. in accountancy Morris Patrick & Co. (now Peat Marwick Group), Christchurch, 1957-61, ptnr., 1962-73; bus. cons. Christchurch, 1974—; founder, dir. Merrimack Holdings Ltd. Vice-chmn. Xth Brit. Commonwealth Games Organizing Com., Christchurch, 1970-74; bd. govs. Christchurch Boys High Sch., 1972-82, chmn., 1974-75; mem. council U. Canterbury, 1970—; chmn. N.Z. Himalayan Expdn. Organizing Com., Christchurch, 1975; bd. dirs. N.Z. Olympic Com., Wellington, 1977—; gen. team mgr. N.Z. team XIth Commonwealth Games, Brisbane, Australia, 1982, XIIIth Commonwealth Games, Edinburgh, Scotland, 1986; chef de mission N.Z. Olympic team, Seoul, Republic of Korea, 1988. Fellow Inst. Dirs.; mem. N.Z. Soc. Accts. Club: U. Canterbury Assn. (founding chmn. 1962-67), Canterbury. Home: 19 Kotare St, Fendalton, Christchurch 4, New Zealand

ULLRING, SVEN BANG, civil engineer, business executive; b. Hammerfest, Norway, Dec. 16, 1935; s. Sven Rolf Knösen Hoff and Benedicte Elisabeth (Hvide Bang) U.; m. Bodil Margaretha Glimstedt; children: Petter Henrik, Pia Benedicte, Caroline Elisabeth. Degree, Ecole Poly., U. Lausanne, Switzerland, 1958; MS in Civil Enging., ETH, Swiss Fed. Inst. Tech., Zurich, 1960. Design engr. AB Skanska, Malmo, Sweden, 1962-63; project engr. Hydro-Electric Project, Ceylon, 1963-64; mgr. project, then mgr. contracts for Middle East, S.E. Asia, Africa, South Am. Ceylon Steel Mill, 1964-72, head internat. secretariat, 1972-77, chief engr., 1975, regional dir. for Middle East and North Africa, 1981-85; pres., chief exec. officer Det Norske Veritas, Hovik, Norway, 1985—; chmn. Norwegian Postal Bd.; bd. dirs. Norwegian Export Council, chmn. subs. Contbr. articles to profl. jours. Served with Royal Norwegian Engrs., 1961-62. Mem. Den Polytekniske Foreningen, Norwegian Inst. Civil Engrs. Home: Gustav Vigelandsvei 16, N-0274 Oslo Norway Office: Det Norske Veritas, Veritasveien 1 POB 300, N-1322 Hovik Norway

ULRICH, GERTRUDE ANNA, retired nurse; b. Steinauer, Nebr., Oct. 19, 1922; d. Fred, Jr. and Matilda (Rinne) U.; R.N., Lincoln (Nebr.) Gen. Hosp., 1960; postgrad. Wesleyan U., Lincoln, 1960-61, B.S. in Natural Scis., 1972; postgrad. U. Nebr., 1967-68, Omaha U., 1966. Instr. Lincoln (Nebr.) Gen. Hosp. Sch. Nursing, 1960-61, 66-67; staff nurse Lincoln Gen. Hosp., 1961-62, 68-71; missionary nurse to Turkey, United Ch. Bd. World Ministries, N.Y.C., 1963-64; camp nurse Girl Scouts U.S.A., Nebraska City, Nebr., summer 1964; staff nurse Homestead Nursing Home, 1964-66; nursing supr. Tabitha Home, Lincoln, 1972-80, med. record supr., 1975-80; evening nursing supr. Homestead Nursing Home, Lincoln, 1980-87. Lincoln Found. ednl. grantee, 1971; named Nurse of Week, Sta. KFOR, 1973, 76. Mem. Am. Nurses Assn. Mem. Reformed Ch. Am. Home: 410 S 41 Lincoln NE 68510

ULRICH, KLAUS HERMANN AUGUST OTTO, mathematician, researcher; b. Zorge, Harz, Fed. Republic Germany, Apr. 23, 1954; s. Hermann and Else (Thomas) U. Student, U. Hanover, Fed. Republic Germany, 1971-76, Dr. rer. nat., 1981. Asst. Inst. Math., U. Hannover, Fed. Republic Germany, 1976—; univ. asst. Inst. Math., Tech. U. Clausthal, Fed. Republic Germany, 1982-84; researcher Inst. Applied Math., U. Hannover, Fed. Republic Germany, 1985—. Author: Das Levi-Oka-Problem, 1981; contbr. articles to profl. jours. Mem. Deutsche Mathematiker-Vereinigung, Österreichische Mathematische Gesellschaft, Soc. Math. de France, Am. Math. Soc., Soc. Indsl. Applied Math., Sociedade Brasileira de Matemática Aplicada e Computacional. Home: Grethe-Jürgens Strasse 32, D-3000 Hannover 51 Federal Republic of Germany Office: Inst Applied Math U Hannover, Welfengarten 1, D-3000 Hannover 1 Federal Republic of Germany

ULRICH, PAUL GRAHAM, lawyer, author, editor; b. Spokane, Nov. 29, 1938; s. Donald Gunn and Kathryn (Vandercook) U.; m. Kathleen Nelson Smith, July 30, 1982; children—Kathleen Elizabeth, Marilee Rae, Michael Graham. B.A. with high honors, U. Mont., 1961; J.D., Stanford U., 1964. Bar: Calif. 1965, Ariz. 1966, U.S. Supreme Ct. 1969. Law clk. judge U.S. Ct. Appeals, 9th Circuit, San Francisco, 1964-65; assoc. firm Lewis and Roca, Phoenix, 1965-70; ptnr. Lewis and Roca, 1970-85; pres. Paul G. Ulrich PC, Phoenix, 1985—; owner Pathway Enterprises, 1985—; judge pro tem Ariz. Ct. Appeals Div. 1, Phoenix, 1986; instr. Thunderbird Grad. Sch. Internat. Mgmt., 1968-69, Ariz. State U., Coll. Law, 1970-73, 78, Scottsdale Community Coll., 1975-77, also continuing legal edn. seminars. Author: Applying Management and Motivation Concepts to Law Offices, 1985; editor, contbr.: Arizona Appellate Handbook, 1978—; Working with Legal Assistants, 1980, 81; Future Directions for Law Office Management, 1982; People in the Law Office, 1985-86; contbg. editor Law Office Economics and Management, 1984—; contbr. numerous articles to profl. jours. Mem. Ariz. Supreme Ct. Task Force on Ct. Orgn. and Adminstrn., 1988—; bd. visitors Stanford U. Law Sch., 1974-77. Served with U.S. Army, 1956. Recipient continuing legal edn. award State Bar Ariz., 1978, 86, Harrison Tweed Spl. Merit award Am. Law Inst./ABA, 1987. Mem. ABA (chmn. selection and utilization of staff personnel com., econs. of law sect. 1979-81, mem. standing com. legal assts. 1982-86, co-chmn. joint project on appellate handbooks 1983-85, co-chmn. fed. appellate handbook project 1985—, chmn. com. on liaison with non-lawyer orgns. Econs. of Law Practice sect. 1985-88), Ariz. Bar Assn. (chmn. econs. of law practice com. 1980-81, co-chmn. lower ct. improvement com. 1982-85, co-chmn. Ariz. Appellate handbook project 1976—), Maricopa County Bar Assn., Calif. Bar Assn., Am. Law Inst., Am. Judicature Soc. (Spl. Merit Citation 1987), Phi Kappa Phi, Phi Alpha Delta, Sigma Phi Epsilon. Republican. Presbyterian. Home: 107 E El Caminito Rd Phoenix AZ 85020 Office: 3030 N Central Ave Suite 1000 Phoenix AZ 85012

ULTAN, LLOYD, historian; b. Bronx, N.Y., Feb. 16, 1938; s. Louis and Sophie U.; B.A. cum laude, Hunter Coll., 1959; M.A., Columbia U., 1960. Asso., Edward Williams Coll., Fairleigh Dickinson U., Hackensack, N.J., 1964-74, asst. prof. history, 1974-75, asso. prof., 1975-83, prof., 1983—; cons. in field. Gen. sec. Bronx Civic League, 1964-67; v.p. bd. trustees Bronx County Hist. Soc., 1965-67, 77-84, curator, 1968-71, pres., 1971-76, historian, 1986—; founding mem., dir. Bronx Council on Arts, 1968-71; chmn. Bronx County Bicentennial Commn., 1973-76. Bronx Borough Pres.'s Bicentennial Adv. Com., 1974-76; program guidelines com. N.Y.C. Dept. Cultural Affairs, 1976-77; bd. dirs. Nat. Shrine Bill of Rights, Mt. Vernon, N.Y., 1983—; mem. N.Y.C. Com. on Cultural Concerns, 1982—; bd. sponsors Historic Preservation com. St. Ann's Ch. Morrisania, 1987—; bd. dirs. 91 Van Cortlandt Owners Corp., 1986— . N.Y. State Regents Coll. Teaching fellow, 1959; elected to Hunter Coll. Alumni Hall of Fame, 1974; Fairleigh Dickinson U. Fifteen Yr. awardee, 1979, Twenty Yr. awardee, 1984. Mem. Am. Hist. Assn., AAUP, N.Y. Hist. Soc., Phi Alpha Theta, Alpha Chi Alpha, Sigma Lambda. Editor, Bronx County Hist. Soc. Jour., 1964—, Bronx County Hist. Soc. Press, 1981—; author: The Beautiful Bronx, 1920-50, 1979; Legacy of the Revolution: The Valentine-Varian House, 1983; co-author: The Bronx in the Innocent Years, 1890-1925, 1985. Home and Office: 91 Van Cortlandt Ave W Bronx NY 10463

ULVEGÄRDE, DAG EVERT, advertising executive; b. Göteborg, Sweden, Nov. 12, 1941; s. Sven G. and Gerty A. (Karlsson) U.; m. Helene Brink, Nov. 10, 1971; children: Hanna, Sofia, Adam. MA in Bus. Advt., U. Gothenburg, Sweden, 1966. Asst. to fin. dir. SDS, Sundsvall, Sweden, 1967-69; devel. exec. RUI, Stockholm, 1969-71; fin. dir. Stendahl Annonsbyrå, Göteborg, 1971-80; mng. dir. Mktg. Gruppen, Göteborg, 1980—; chmn. Media Mktg. Ltd., London, 1986—, Media Mktg. Ltd., Oslo, 1987—, System media Mktg., Dusseldorf, Fed. Republic Germany, 1987—. Home: Kaprifolvagen Box 104, 430 41 Kullavik Sweden Office: Mktg Gruppen AB, Vasagatan 7 Box 3183, 400 10 Goteborg Sweden

ULVUND, STEIN ERIK, psychology researcher; b. Nesbyen, Norway, Aug. 11, 1952; s. Karl and Birgit Ulvund; m. Annie Ulvund, June 18, 1977; children: Camilla, Cathrine, Caroline. Degree in ednl. psychology, U. Oslo, 1977, PhD, 1986. Research fellow U. Oslo, 1976-77; researcher Norwegian Research Council, Oslo, 1978-80; research asst. U. Oslo, 1980-83, lectr., 1983-86, assoc. prof., 1986—. Editor Scandinavian Jour. of Ednl. Research, 1988—; author Cognitive Development in Infancy, 1988; contbr. articles to profl. jours. Office: Inst for Ednl Research, Box 1092 Blindern, Oslo Norway

UMBACH, CLAYTON AUGUST, JR., publisher; b. New Orleans, Aug. 30, 1930; s. Clayton August and Gladys (Meyer) U.; B.J., U. Mo., 1952; m. Patricia J. Young, Oct. 16, 1954; children—Clayton August, III, Ellen Kay, Alice Claire. With Gulf Pub. Co., Houston, 1956—, dir. book pub. div., 1962—, corp. v.p., 1979—; chief exec. officer, dir. Gulf Pub. Video subs. Gulf Pub. Co., Houston, 1982—; lectr. S.W. Writers Conf., Rice U., publishing program Tex. A&M U., U. Houston. Disaster info. dir. Harris County chpt. ARC, 1965-70. Served with inf. AUS, 1952-54, Korea. Mem. Harris County C. of C. (info. com. 1964-66), Am. Soc. Tng. and Devel., Internat. Assn. Bus. Communicators, Tex. Pubs. Assn. (dir. 1979—, pres. 1981—), Houston Area Booksellers Assn. (dir. 1973-85, 87—), Am. Film Inst., Smithsonian Inst., Phi Theta Kappa. Lutheran. Clubs: Houston Press, Plaza. Author: How to Prepare for Management Responsibilities, 1964. Home: 8006 Neff St Houston TX 77036 Office: Gulf Pub Co PO Box 2608 Houston TX 77252-2608

UMBRIACO, MICHEL PAUL, academic administrator; b. Montreal, Que., Can., May 7, 1949; s. Raphaël and Marielle (Bédard) U.; m. Lucie Lavoie, May 31, 1987. BA, Sem. de St. Jean, Que., 1970; BS, U. Montreal, 1972, MA, 1976; postgrad., U. Laval, Que., 1987—. Lectr. U. Montreal, 1971-73; v.p. Media-Que. Inc., Montreal, 1971-73; asst. gen. dir. Télé-univ., Quebec, 1973-79, dir. service communications, 1979-87; invited researcher Can. Work Place Automation Research Ctr., Laval, Que., 1987-89.; dir. Corp. pour l'Avancement des Nouvelles Applications des Langages Inc; v.p. Services Médiatiques Univs. du Que., 1982-87. Contbr. articles to profl. jours. Mem. Interprovincial Assn. for Telematics (v.p., pres. 1983-87), Groupe Que becois de Télématique et Médiatique (treas. 1984-87, chmn. 1986), Assn. des médias et de la technologie en éducation au Can. Club: Garrison (Que.). Office: Télé-université, 2635 Hochelaga (7th), Ste-Foy, Québec, PQ Canada GIV 4V9

UMBRICHT, VICTOR HERMANN, Swiss diplomat, association executive; b. Endingen, Switzerland, Oct. 25, 1915; s. Simon and Caroline (Meisel) U.; m. Elisabeth Fresard; children—Christopher, Monique, Madeleine. Student, U. Bern, U. Lausanne and U. Paris; Internat. Law, U. Berne, 1939; D. honoris causa, U. Basel, 1966, U. Zurich, 1987. Mem. Swiss Bar. Entered Swiss Diplomatic Service, 1941, assigned to embassies Ankara, London, Washington, 1941-53; dep. dir. ops. for Europe, Africa and Australia, World Bank, Washington, 1953-57; head ops. Swiss treasury, Berne, 1957-60; pres. Ciba Corp., N.Y.C., 1962-65; sr. fin. adviser, pres. Monetary Council UN Mission to Belgian Congo (now Zaire), 1960-61, chmn. FAO-Industry Coop. Program, 1966-70, mem. Mekong Adv. Bd., 1968-76, chief UN mission to Bangladesh, 1972-73, head UN mission to Pakistan, 1973-74, participant missions to Vietnam, mediator for East African Community, Kenya, Tanzania and Uganda, 1978-86; vice-chmn. Internat. Com. Red Cross, Geneva, 1970-86; chief of missions to Southeast Asia, India, Pakistan, Israel, Central America, 1971-77. Recipient Grotius medal, The Hague, 1984. Roman Catholic. Home: 25 Steinenring, CH4051 Basel Switzerland Office: Ciba-Geigy Ltd, Klybeckstrasse 141,, CH4002 Basel Switzerland

UMEDA, ZENJI, manufacturing company executive; b. Wakayama Prefecture, Japan, Sept. 13, 1913; s. Zemichi and Kei Umeda; grad. Kyoto Imperial U., 1939; m. Fusako Hirota; children—Yoshitsugu, Kayoko, Kazuyo, Yoshihiro. Chmn., Kawasaki Heavy Industries Ltd., Tokyo; vice chmn. Nikon Zosen Kogyokai. Decorated Blue Ribbon medal, Miti award, 1974. Mem. Shipbuilders Assn. Japan (pres. 1981). Office: Kawasaki Heavy Industries Ltd, 16-1 Nakamachidori, 2 chome, 1 Kuta-ku,, Kobe Japan *

UME-EZEOKE, PHILIP ORJI, hotel company executive, consultant; b. Amichi, Nigeria, Apr. 25, 1919; s. Michael Umeagugoesi Ezeoke and Martha Nganuba Ume-Ezeoke; m. Angela Enu Okolo, Nov. 26, 1949; children—Philip Chukwudi, Fidelia Omata, Obijiofor, Nwamaka, Uchechukwu, China; Arinze, C'Nonso. Diploma in edn., Higher Coll., Yaba, Lagos, Nigeria, 1944; diploma in adminstrn., U. Ibadan, 1955. Cert. pub. adminstr. A. Owner, dir. Washington Meml. Coll., Onitsha, Nigeria, 1947-51; adminstrv. sec. Local Govt. Council, Nnewi, Anambra, 1952-55; regional adminstrv. officer Nigerian Broadcasting Corp., Enugu, 1956-70, controller (tng.), Lagos, 1960-67; controller Broadcasting Corp. of Biafra, 1967-69; mng. dir. Ume-Ezeoke Enterprises Ltd., Enugu, 1970—; promoter, bd. dirs. Mulumba Assurance Co. Ltd., Lagos, 1978—. Author: Amichi, Before They Die, 1984; Knights of Saint Mulumba Nigeria. Zonal chmn. Nat. Party of Nigeria, Anambra State, 1978-83; nat. sec. Boy Scouts of Nigeria, Lagos, 1961-66; mem. bd. edn. Nnewi Local Govt., 1972-75; patron Igwebuike Social Club, Amichi, 1980, Akulue Uno Social Club, Amichi, 1981. Mem. Nigerian Inst. Mgmt. (assoc.). Roman Catholic. Home: 55 Annang St, Enugu Anambra State, Nigeria Office: Ume-Ezeoke Enterprises Ltd, 5 Awolowo St, Enugu Anambra Nigeria

UMEGAKI, HARUKI, insurance company executive, architect, city planner; b. Kawasaki, Kanagawa, Japan, Mar. 29, 1951; s. Yoichiro and Tatsuko (Iwaya) U. Student, Toya (Isaka) U.; BS in Engring., Yokohama Nat. U., Japan, 1973. Asst. Dai-ichi Mut. Life Ins. Co., Tokyo, 1973-78, mgr., 1978—. Recipient Bldg. Constructor Soc. prize for the Toshiba Bldg., 1985. Mem. Archtl. Inst. Japan. Home: 1-1-7 Moto-Akasaka Minato-ku, Tokyo 107, Japan Office: Dai-ichi Mut Life Ins Co, 1-13-1 Yuraku-cho Chiyoda-ku, Tokyo 100, Japan

UMEGAKI, YOICHIRO, radiologist, consultant; b. Komori, Japan, Mar. 3, 1922; s. Yasuji and Yoshie (Akashi) U.; m. Tatsuko Iwaya, Feb. 21, 1949 (div.); 3 children; m. Toyoko Isaka, Mar. 26, 1962. M.D., U. Tokyo, 1945, D. Med. Sci., 1953. Resident in radiology U. Tokyo, 1945-51, Tokyo Cancer Inst., 1951-54; asst. prof. radiology Chiba U. (Japan), 1955-58; prof. radiology Shinshu U., Natsumoto, Japan, 1958-62; chief radiology Nat. Cancer Ctr., Tokyo, 1962-71; head clin. research Nat. Inst. Radiol. Scis., Chiba, 1971-79, research cons., 1979—; head radiology Cancer Inst., Tokyo, 1979-81; mem. Sci. Council of Japan, 1985—. Author: Textbook of Radiology, 1956; Textbook of Radiotherapy, 1966; patentee Moving Field Radiotherapy, 1957; editor: Progress in computerized Tomography, 1979—, GANN, 1963-79, Japanese Jour. Cancer Clinics, 1962—, Nippon Acta Radiologica, 1970-76, Japanese Jour. Clin. Oncology, 1971-78. Dep. sec. congress XII Internat. Congress Radiology, Tokyo, 1969; pres. VII Internat. Conf. Use of Computers in Radiotherapy, 1980; pres. VII Joint Congress Med. Informatics. Japanese Med. Assn. grantee, 1976; Ministry of Health and Welfare grantee, 1965—; recipient project leader award Ministry Edn., 1979. Hon. fellow Am. Coll. Radiology; mem. Japanese Assn. Radiotherapy Systems (hon.), Japanese Soc. Med. Infos. (dir. 1982—), Japanese Cancer Soc. (councilor), Sci. Council Japan, Japanese Soc. Cancer Therapy (councilor), Japanese Soc. Med. Electronics (hon.). Club: Internat. of Radiotherapy (Eng., France). Home and Office: 1787 Okura, Machida 194-01, Tokyo Japan

UMEH, JOHN ANENECHUKWU, educator, estate surveyor; b. Nnobi, Nigeria, Oct. 3, 1934; s. Ogbuefi Michael Eze-Ifedi and Rebecca Oyeafor (Uzokwe) U.; m. Rich Enujioke Oti, May 25, 1968; children: Nnenna, Obiageli, Chukwueloka, Chiamaka, Nnaedozie, Ayikamba, Ezechukwukwadolu. B.Sc. in Estate Mgmt., U. London, 1962, M.Sc., 1970; MA, Pembroke Coll., Cambridge U., Eng., 1964. Tutor Prince Secondary Comml. Coll., Onitsha, Nigeria, 1953-54; tutor, then asst. prin. Etukokwu Secondary Comml. Coll., Onitsha, 1955-57; tech. asst. town planning sect. Architects Dept. London County Council, 1962 summer; mem. faculty U. Nigeria, 1962—, prof. estate mgmt., 1974—, head dept., 1973—; dean Faculty Environ. Studies, 1975-77, 81—; dep. vice-chancellor Enugu Campus U. Nigeria, 1983-86; cons. in field, 1971—; vis. prof. U. Aberdeen, 1981, Strathclyde U., Glasgow, Scotland, 1988; mem. Traditional Medicine Bd. for Anambra State Nigeria, 1987—; mem. convocation U. London, 1962—. Author: Compulsory Acquisition of Land and Compensation in in Nigeria, 1973, Feasibility and Viability Appraisal, 1977, Land Policies and Compulsory Acquisition of Private Lands for Public Purposes in Nigeria, 1978, Land Condemnation and Compensation in Nigeria Since 1970, 1982, Nkenu-The Yes-Bird, 1982, Okponku Abu, 1982, Ije Ngwele Aghu, 1982, Songs of the Harmattan, 1983; c0-editor: University of Nigeria 1960-85: An Experiment in Higher Education, 1986; editor-in-chief: Tropical Environ., 1973; contbr. articles to profl. jours. Fellow Royal Instn. Chartered Surveyors, Rating and Valuation Assn., Nigerian Instn. Estate Surveyors and Valuers (gov.); mem. Internat. Assn. Human Biologists, Internat. Ctr. Land Policy Studies, Estates Surveyors and Valuers Registrations Bd. Nigeria, Internat. Real Estate Fedn. (rep. standing com. 1973—), Internat. Real Estate Fedn. (v.p. profl. and ednl. exchanges com. 1984—, cert. merit 1986),. Home: House 2 U Nigeria, Enugu Nigeria Office: U Nigeria, Dept Estate Mgmt, Enugu Nigeria

UMMINGER, BRUCE LYNN, federal executive, scientist, educator; b. Dayton, Ohio, Apr. 10, 1941; s. Frederick William and Elnora Mae (Waltemathe) U.; m. Judith Lackey Bryant, Dec. 17, 1966; children—Alison Grace, April Lynn. B.S. magna cum laude with honors in biology, Yale U., 1963, M.S., 1966, M.Phil., 1968, Ph.D., 1969; postgrad., U. Calif., Berkeley, 1963-64; cert., U. Cin., 1975, Fed. Exec. Inst., 1984. Asst. prof. dept. biol. scis. U. Cin., 1969-73, assoc. prof. dept. biol. scis., 1973-75, acting head dept. biol. scis., 1973-75, prof. dept. biol. scis., 1975-81, dir. grad. affairs, 1978-79; program dir. regulatory biology program NSF, Washington, 1979-84, dep. dir. cellular bioscis. div., 1984—, acting div. dir., 1985-87; sr. advisor on health policy Office of Internat. Health Policy Dept. State, Washington, 1988—; exec. sec. Nat. Sci. Bd. Com. on Ctrs. and Individual Investigator Awards, 1986-88; mem. NSF rev. panel Research Improvement in Minority Instns., 1986, 87, U.S.-India Coop. Research Program, 1981-82, U.S.-India Exchange of Scholars Program, 1979-81; mem. sr. exec. panel exec. potential program Office Personnel Mgmt., 1988—; mem. space shuttle proposal rev. panel in life scis. NASA, 1978, research assocs. award com., 1985—; mem. adv. screening com. in life scis. Council for Internat. Exchange of Scholars, 1978-81; liaison rep. nat. heart, lung and blood adv. council NIH, 1979-87, interagy. research animal com., 1984, interagy. working group internat. aspects biotech., 1988; sci. adv. com. Arlington Pub. Schs., 1987—; adv. bd. Campbell Comml. Coll., Cin., 1977-79. Contbr. articles to profl. jours.; assoc. editor Jour. Exptl. Zoology, 1977-79; editorial adv. bd. Gen. and Comparative Endocrinology, 1982. Mem. world mission com. Ch. of the Redeemer, New Haven, 1967-68; mem. Sunday Sch. steering com., Sunday Sch. treas. Calvary Episcopal Ch., Cin., 1972-73, sr. acolyte, 1972-77, adult edn. com., 1975-76. Recipient George Rieveschl Jr. Research award U. Cin., 1973; Outstanding Performance award and Sustained Superior Performance, NSF, 1981, spl. achievement award, 1985, Sr. Exec. Service Performance award, 1986, 87; U. Cin. Grad. Sch. fellow, 1977—; NSF fellow, 1964; research grantee NSF, 1971-79. Fellow AAAS (council 1980-83; mem. program com. 1989 annual meeting 1988; chairperson-elect sect. G.-Biol. Scis. 1987-88, chairperson 1988-89; mem. steering group sect. com. G 1987-90), N.Y. Acad. Scis.; mem. Am. Soc. Zoologists (sec., mem. exec. com. 1979-81; chmn. nominating com. 1981; sec. div. of comparative physiology and biochemistry 1976-77; chmn. Congl. Sci. Fellow Program com. 1986-88), Am. Physiol. Soc. (program adv. com. 1978-81, program exec. com. 1983-86; mem. steering com., comparative physiology sect. 1978-81; sec. Am. Physiol. Soc.-Am. Soc. Zoologists Task Force on Comparative Physiology 1976-78), Am. Inst. Biol. Scis. (chmn. selection com. congl. sci. fellow in zool. scis 1987), Sr. Execs. Assn., Sigma Xi (Disting. Research award U. Cin. chpt. 1973, pres. U. Cin. chpt. 1977-79). Clubs: Mory's Assn. (New Haven), Yale (Washington). Lodges: Masons, K.T., Shriners, Order Eastern Star. Home: 4087-B S Four Mile Run Dr Arlington VA 22204 Office: NSF Div Cellular Bioscis 1800 G St NW Washington DC 20550

UNDERDAL, ARILD KARSTEN, political science educator; b. Bodø, Nordland, Norway, Aug. 13, 1946; s. Karstein and Amanda (Eliassen) U.; m. Else Børmer, Dec. 27, 1972; 1 child, Siri. MA, U. Oslo, 1972, PhD, 1982. Research asst. U. Oslo, 1973-77, assoc. prof. polit. sci., 1979-85, prof., 1988—; research fellow Fridtjof Nansen Inst., Oslo, 1977-79; prof. Norway Sch. Mgmt., 1986-87; chmn. dept. polit. sci. U. Oslo, 1981-82; chmn. bd. Norwegian Inst. Internat. Affairs, 1986-88. Author: The Politics of International Fisheries Management, 1980; (with others) Norsk Oljepolitikk og Fiskerinaeringens Interesser, 1983; editor Cooperation and Conflict, 1986-89. V.p. Norwegian Student Union, Oslo, 1969. Served with Norwegian Air Force, 1969-70. Mem. Internat. Studies Assn., Nordic Polit. Sci. Assn. (sec.). Home: Nyquistv 2A, N-1176 Oslo Norway Office: U Oslo, Blindern Campus, N-0317 Oslo Norway

UNDERHILL, JACOB BERRY, III, retired insurance company executive; b. N.Y.C., Oct. 25, 1926; s. Jacob Berry, Jr. and Dorothy Louise (Quinn) U.; m. Cynthia Jane Lovejoy, Sept. 9, 1950 (div. Sept. 1962); children: David Lovejoy, Kate Howell Underhill Kerwin, Benedict Quinn; m. Lois Beachy, Nov. 2, 1963 (div. July 1987); m. Betsy F. Ashton, Oct. 17, 1987. Grad., Phillips Exeter Acad., 1944; A.B., Princeton U., 1950. Editor Courier & Freeman, Potsdam, N.Y., 1950-53; reporter Democrat & Chronicle, Rochester, N.Y., 1953-56; chief editorial writer St. Petersburg (Fla.) Times, 1956-59; asso. editor McGraw Hill Publ. Co., N.Y.C., 1959-61, Newsweek, N.Y.C., 1961-63; asst. press sec. to Gov. N.Y., 1963-67; dep. supt., 1st dep. supt. State N.Y. Ins. Dept., 1967-72; v.p., sr. v.p., exec. v.p., dir., vice chmn. bd., pres. N.Y. Life Ins. Co., N.Y.C., 1972-86. Bd. dirs. Manhattan Eye, Ear and Throat Hosp., Better Bus. Bur. of Met. N.Y., Greater N.Y. Fund; trustee Nat. Trust for Historic Preservation. Served with USNR, 1944-46. Clubs: Players, Links (N.Y.C.); Noyac Golf and Country (Sag Harbor, N.Y.). Home: 410 E 57th St New York NY 10022

UNDERWEISER, IRWIN PHILIP, mining company executive, lawyer; b. N.Y.C., Jan. 3, 1929; s. Harry and Edith (Gladstein) U.; m. Beatrice J. Kortchmar, Aug. 17, 1959; children: Rosanne, Marian, Jeffrey. B.A., CCNY, 1950; LL.D., Fordham U., 1954; LL.M., NYU, 1961. Bar: N.Y. 1954. With firm Scribner & Miller, N.Y.C., 1951-54, 56-62; partner firm Feuerstein & Underweiser, 1962-73, Underweiser & Fuchs, 1973-77, Underweiser & Underweiser, 1977—; v.p., sec. Sunshine Mining Co., Kellogg, Idaho, 1965-70, chmn. bd., 1970-78, pres., 1971-74, 77, v.p., 1977-83; vice chmn., dir. Underwriters Bank and Trust Co., N.Y.C., 1969-73; dir. Anchor Post Products, Inc. Bd. dirs. Silver Inst. Inc.; gen. counsel, mem. bus. council Friends City Center Music and Drama, N.Y.C., 1966-67; pres. W. Quaker Ridge Assn., 1969-70; treas. Scarsdale Neighborhood Assn. Presidents, 1970-71. Served with AUS, 1954-56. Mem. Am., N.Y. State bar assns., Bar Assn. City N.Y., Phi Beta Kappa, Phi Alpha Theta. Home: 7 Rural Dr Scarsdale NY 10583 Office: 405 Park Ave New York NY 10022

UNDERWOOD, EDWIN HILL, lawyer; b. Bainbridge, Ga., Mar. 28, 1920; s. Edwin Hendon and Gladys (Legg) U.; m. Cynthia Ann Greiner, Feb. 1950 (div. 1967); children: Vance, Hill, Molly; m. Elizabeth Jane Morgan, Apr. 24, 1968; children: Michael, Samanthia, Dorothy, Edith. AB, U. Fla., 1941; JD, U. Miami, Coral Gables, 1948. Bar: Fla. 1948. Sole practice Key Biscayne and Miami, Fla., 1948—; bd. dirs. Key Biscayne Bank and Trust Co., Fla., Guaranty Life Ins., Jacksonville, Fla. Pres. Marine Council Greater Miami, Fla., 1966. Served to capt. U.S. Army, 1940-46, ETO. Mem. ABA (tort and ins. practice sect., antitrust law sect.), Fla. Bar, Dade County Bar Assn. (bd. dirs. 1956-59), Internat. Assn. Ins. Counsel, Dade County Def. Bar Assn., Fla. Def. Lawyers Assn., Law Sci. Acad. Am., Maritime Law Assn. U.S., Am. Judicature Soc. Democrat. Episcopalian. Clubs: Key Biscayne (Fla.) Yacht (commodore 1964), Key Biscayne Beach (pres. 1960); Miami; Palm Bay (Fla.); Capital City Country (Tallahasse, Fla.), Coral Reef Yacht, Fishers Island. Home: 605 Ocean Dr Key Biscayne FL 33149

UNDERWOOD, RALPH EDWARD, infosytems specialist; b. Houston, Sept. 26, 1947; s. Harry Anson and Ethel Jackson Underwood; m. Linda Sue Merkel, Apr. 10, 1976. BS in Biology, Baker U., 1969; JD, Washburn U., 1973; MS in Computer Sci., Kans. U., 1984. Bar: Kans, 1973. Free-lance stock and options trader Prairie Village, Kans., 1974-79; mem. staff BDM Corp., Leavenworth, Kans., 1982-84; sr. research and devel. engr. Ford Aerospace and Communications Corp., Colorado Springs, Colo., 1984-87, subcontract adminstr., 1987—. Patentee in field. Mem. ABA, IEEE, Armed Forces Communications and Electronics Assn., Kans. Bar Assn., Upsilon Pi Epsilon, Sigma Phi Epsilon (social chmn. 1968, asst. ho. mgr. 1968, sec./treas. sr. council 1969), Phi Alpha Delta. Office: Ford Aerospace & Communications Corp 10550 State Hwy 83 Colorado Springs CO 80921

UNDERWOOD, ROBERT RICHARD, hotel manager; b. Oct. 30, 1954; s. Wilhelm and Mona (LaFortune) U.; m. Barbara Maduray, Apr. 3, 1956. Cert. advance level, Seychelles Coll., 1972; diploma hotel and catering inst. mgmt., Middlesec Poly. at Hendon, London, 1976. Asst. mgr. London Steak Houses, London, 1973-76; with mktg. dept. Horwath & Horwath, London, 1973-76; trainee Coral Strand Hotel, Seychelles, 1976-77, food and beverage asst. mgr., 1977-79; temp. asst. mgr. Norfolk Hotel and Baccus Club, Nairobi, Kenya, 1977-79; food and beverage mgr. Lesotho Hotels Ltd., 1979-80, dep. mgr., 1980-81; food and beverage mgr. Coral Strand Hotel, Seychelles, 1981-83, gen. mgr., 1983—. Lectr., advisor Nat. Youth Service, hotel. schs. Mem. Hotel Catering and Instnl. Mgmt. Assn., Seychelles Hotels Assn. (sec. 1985-87, chmn. 1987—). Tourist Office Adv. Com. Lodges: Rotary (pres. 1985-86, treas. 1986-87), Seychelles. Home: Vista Do Mar Estate, Mahe Seychelles Office: Coral Strand Hotel, Beau Vallon, Box 400, Mahe Seychelles

UNDEUTSCH, UDO HEINZ-HERMANN, psychology educator; b. Weimar, Germany, Dec. 22, 1917; s. Paul and Maria (Niggemeyer) U.; m. Hanna Bierfreund, Jan. 9, 1946; children: Klaus, Ursula, Barbara, Elisabeth, Inge. M.A. in Psychology, Fr. Schiller U.-Jena, 1942, Dr.rer.nat., 1941. Asst. prof. Fr. Schiller U., Jena, 1941-45; assoc. prof. psychology U. Mainz, 1946-51; prof. psychology U. Cologne, 1951—. Author: Psychologische Untersuchungen am Unfallort, 1962; Die psychische Entwicklung der heutigen Jugend, 1966, Sicherheit im Betrieb, 2d edit. 1965; Psychologische Impulse für die Verkehrsicherheit, 1977. Editor: Forensische Psychologie, 1967. Pres. Com. Safety for the Child, 1972, Research Group the Human Factor in Traffic Safety, Koln, 1968. Recipient Bundesverdienstkreuz 1st class (Fed. Republic Germany); Golden Diesel Ring, Assn. Motor Journalists, 1984, officer Order of King Leopold II (Belgium). Mem. Deutsche Gesellschaft für Psychologie, Berufsverband Deutscher Psychologen. Roman Catholic. Home: Farnweg 1, D5020 Frechen Federal Republic of Germany

UNDY, ROGER, management educator, academic administrator; b. Nottingham, Eng., Nov. 2, 1938; s. Harold and Harriet (Holmes) U.; m. Kathleen Claire Stevenson, Sept. 19, 1959; children: Kim, Ruth. BA, Oxford (Eng.) U., 1972. Research assoc. Oxford U. Ctr. Mgmt. Studies, 1972-75, research fellow, 1975-77, fellow in indsl. relations, 1977-80, sr. tutor, 1980-83; fellow Templeton Coll. Templeton Coll. Oxford Ctr. Mgmt. Studies, 1983—, dir. Oxford Inst. Employee Relations, 1985—, dean, 1988; cons. Eng. and Europe, 1977—. Author: Change in Trade Unions, 1981, Ballots and TU Democracy, 1984; contbr. articles to profl. jours. Labour Party candidate Parliament, Bridgwater, Eng., 1974. Mem. Assn. Univ. Tchrs. Mem. United Reformed Ch. Home: 6 Feilden Grove, Headington, Oxford England Office: Oxford U Templeton Coll, Kennington, Oxford OX1 5NY, England

UNGER-HAMILTON, ROMANA JULIA, archaeologist, researcher; b. Berlin, May 30, 1946; d. Boris Wladimir Blacher and Gerty Herzog-Blacher; m. C. Unger-Hamilton, 1968 (div. 1973) children: Felix, Ferdinand; m. John Hope Mason, 1986. BA with 1st class hons., Inst. Archaeology, U. London, 1981, PhD, 1985. Researcher Inst. Archaeology, 1985—. author articles in field. Grantee Sci. and Engring. Research Council, Eng., 1985—. Mem. Palestine Exploration Fund. Office: Inst Archaeology, 31-4 Gordon Sq, London WC1, England

UNGRAD, HELMUT MARIA, electrical manufacturing company executive; b. Vienna, Austria, Nov. 29, 1929; came to Switzerland, 1957; s. Franz and Helene (Schmidberger) U.; m. Elisabeth Vollenweider, May 23, 1957; children: Christine, Franz, Isabelle, Eva. Diploma in Engring., Tech. U., Vienna, 1952, D in Tech., 1966. Project. engr. Brown Boveri, Vienna, 1952-57; devel. engr. Brown Boveri, Baden, Switzerland, 1957-60, head devel. dept., 1960-64, head dept. indsl. networks, 1964-66, gen. mgr. sales protection, relays, 1966-80, gen. mgr. mktg., power systems, 1981—, gen. mktg. corp. staff, 1985—. Co-author: Modern Protection, 1987; patentee in field; contbr. articles to profl. jours. Head music sch., Oberrohrdorf, 1977-87. Mem. IEEE, Com. Internat. Grand Resaux Elec. (convenor 1980—), Swiss Elec. Soc., Internat. Elec. Com. (convenor working group 1964-66). Roman Catholic. Clubs: Railway (Zurich); Nat. Geog. Soc. Home: Luxmattenstr 19, CH5452 Oberrohrdorf Switzerland Office: Brown Boveri, Haselstr 1, CH5401 Baden Switzerland

UNNO, KENZO, architect; b. Tokyo, Apr. 1, 1949; s. Shiro and Yoshi (Kubota) U.; m. Masako Takayama, Aug. 31, 1984; 1 child, Haruka. B of Engring., Sci. U. Tokyo, 1974. Various archtl. and constrn. positions Tokyo, 1974-80; owner Umi Kenchikuka Kobo, Toyko, 1980—. Contbr. articles to profl. jours. Recipient various design awards. Mem. Tokyo Soc. Architects and Bldg. Engrs. Home and Office: 11-19 Higashi-komatsugawa, 4-chome, Edogawa-ku Tokyo 132, Japan

UNO, SOUSUKE, government official; b. Moriyama, Shiga, Japan, Aug. 27, 1922; s. Chouji and Ito (Fujimoto) U.; m. Chiyo Hirose, Feb. 22, 1949; children: Yuriko, Noriko. Student, Kobe (Japan) U. of Commerce, 1943. Mem. Shiga Prefectural Assembly, 1951-58, Japanese Ho. of Reps., 1960—; parlimentary vice minister internat. trade and industry Govt. Japan, 1966-67; dir. gen. Def. Agy. Japanese Ministry of State, 1974, dir. gen. Sci. and Tech. Agy., 1976-77, dir. gen. Adminstrv. Mgmt. Agy., 1979-80, minister internat. trade and industry, 1983, minister fgn. affairs, 1987—. Author: Domoi Tokyo, 1948, Shoya Heibe Gokumonki, 1971, (collections of haiku) Obyo, 1963, Benikuma, 1978, others. Dir. div. fin. policy research council, Liberal Dem. Party, dep. chmn. research commn. on tax system, dep. sec. gen., 1973, chmn. diet affairs com., chmn. pub. relations com., acting sec. gen., 1982-83, 86-87, chmn. spl. com. for introduction pvt.-sector vitality into pub. works. Served with Japanese Imperial Army, 1943-45. Office: Ministry Fgn Affairs, 2-2-1 Kasumigaseki Chiyodaku, Tokyo 100, Japan

UPADHYAYA, SHAILENDRA KUMAR, government official; b. India, Sept. 13, 1929; s. Gopal Prasad and Uma Devi U.; m. Sharmistha Upadhyaya; m. Beena Sharma; 3 s., 1 dau. Grad., Benares Hindu U. Founding mem. Communist Party of Nepal, 1950, mem. cen. com. and polit. bureau, 1950-56; founder Progressive Communist Party of Nepal, 1958; asst. minister Forests, Food and Agriculture, 1962-64; mem. Nat. Panchayat, Nepal, 1963-71; minister in charge of Panchayat Nepal, 1965, minister fgn. affairs, 1986—, minister land reform, from 1986; vice-chair Nat. Planning Commn., Nepal, 1969; minister home and Panchayat Nepal, 1970-71, minister land reforms and info., 1970-71; perm. rep. UN, 1972-78; ambassador to Argentina, Chile, Peru and Brazil 1977-78; exec. chair Inst. 3d World Econ. Studies, Nepal 1982—. Decorated Prabal Gorkha Dakshin Bahu (Order Right Hand of Gurkha) first class. Home: 5/108 Jawala Khel, Lalitpur, Khathmandu Nepal Office: Ministry of Fgn Affairs, Kathmandu Nepal *

UPHOFF, JAMES KENT, education educator; b. Hebron, Nebr., Sept. 1, 1937; s. Ernest John and Alice Marie (Dutcher) U.; m. Harriet Lucille Martin, Aug. 6, 1962; 1 child, Nicholas James. B.A., Hastings Coll., 1959; M.Ed., U. Nebr., 1962, Ed.D., 1967. Tchr., Walnut Jr. High Sch., Grand Island, Nebr., 1959-65, dept. chmn., 1962-65; instr. dept. edn. U. Nebr., Lincoln, 1965-66; curriculum intern Bellevue (Nebr.) Pub. Schs., 1966-67; asst. prof. edn. Wright State U., Dayton, Ohio, 1967-70, assoc. prof., 1970-75, prof. edn., 1975—, co-dir. pub. edn. religion studies ctr., 1972-75, dean br. campuses, 1974-79, dir. lab. experiences, 1982—; vis. prof. U. Dayton, 1968-69. Author: (with others) Summer Children: Ready or Not For School, 1986; editor: Dialogues on Developmental Curriculum K and I, 1987. Phi Delta Kappa scholar, 1969. Mem. adv. com. pub. edn. fund Dayton Found., 1985—; mem. Luth. Ch. council, 1987—. Mem. NEA, Ohio Edn. Assn. (devel. commn.), Western Ohio Edn. Assn. (pres. 1974-75, exec. com. 1979-85), Assn. Supervision and Curriculum Devel. (dir. 1974-79), Ohio Assn. Supervision and Curriculum Devel. (v.p. 1972-73), Nat. Council Social Studies (religion com.), Ohio Council Social Studies (profl. concerns com.), Dayton Area Council Social Studies (pres. (1970-71, 85-87), LWV Greater Dayton (edn dir 1981-85), Ohio Council Chs. (edn. com. 1973-75), Phi Delta Kappa (chpt. pres. 1983-84), Kappa Delta Pi. Republican. Lodges: Rotary (editor; dir. 1974-79), Optimists (pres. 1983-85). Home: 150 Spirea Dr Dayton OH 45419 Office: Wright State U 320 Millett Edn Dayton OH 45435

UPPAL, TAJ BAHADUR, microbiologist, physician; b. Peshawar, Pakistan, Aug. 11, 1937; s. Karam and Sham (Kapoor) U.; m. Amal Tiwana, Mar. 18, 1948; childrn: Farooq Salman. BSc, Islamia Coll., Peshawar, 1955; MBBS, King Edward Med. Coll., Lahore, 1961; Diploma in Bacteriology, London Sch. Hygiene, London, 1965. Rotating intern St. Luke's Hosp., Newburgh, N.Y., 1962-63; med. resident St. Luke's Hosp., Newburgh, 1963-64; asst. prof. microbiology Khyber Med. Coll., Peshawar, 1965-77, prof. microbiology, 1977—; mem. Tech. Com., Pakistan Sci. Found. Islamabad, 1976; mem. expert com. Govt. Pakistan, 1980; mem. expert microbiology bd. of communicable and infectious diseases Pakistan Med. Research Council, 1981; mem. specialist com. pathology Coll. Physicians, Karachi, 1985. Author: Manual of Superficial Mycotic Infections, 1984; contbr. articles to profl. jours; reviewer Internat. Nomenclature of Infectios Disease, 1985. Mem. Assn. Clin. Pathology, Am. Soc. Microbiology. Home: 22 Chinar Rd University Town, Peshawar Pakistan Office: Khyber Med Coll, Peshawar Pakistan

UPSTON, JOHN EDWIN, diplomat; b. Maxwell AFB, Ala., Apr. 17, 1935; s. John E. and Claudia (Smith) U.; m. Cristina Paige Brookes, Jan. 1986; children: John Edwin, III, Michael Gignoux, Bennett Coit, Leland Craven. Student, Va. Mil. Inst., 1954-55; student in internat. relations, Harvard U., 1957; AB, Stanford, 1958. Founding adminstr. Mental Research Inst., Palo Alto, Calif., 1959-61; dir. Mental Research Inst., 1961—; bus. developer N.Y.C., San Francisco, 1961—; creator, producer Career Westinghouse Broadcasting Network TV series, 1961; mem. mgmt. planning policy implementation staff Dept. State, Washington, 1964-65; adv. Internat. Orgn. Affairs, 21st-22d UN Gen. Assembly; mem. permanent U.S. Mission to UN, N.Y.C., 1966-69; assoc. Burnham & Co., investment bankers, N.Y.C., 1969-70; exec. dir. Sec. of State's Com. Facilitate Internat. Travel, 1970—; spl. asst. undersec. State for mgmt. 1970-72; U.S. rep. regional meeting European Nat. Commn., Varna, Bulgaria and Bucharest, Rumania; U.S. adviser Gen. Conf. UNESCO, Paris, 1972, Nairobi, Kenya, 1976; gen. mgr. Mediphone, Inc., 1961; v.p., dir. Broadcast Devel. Corp., N.Y.C., 1962—; founder and pres. Caribbeana Council, Washington and Barbados, W.I., 1977-81; coordinator Caribbean Affairs, Bur. Inter-Am. Affairs, Dept. State, Washington, 1981-86; U.S. ambassador to Rwanda 1986—; mem. White House Task Force for P.R., 1981-86; presdl. del. to Independence of Antigua, 1981. Past dir. Tolstoy Found.; mem. Caribbean Conservation Assn., Barbados; mem. task force on U.S. immigration policy Council on Fgn. Relations; bd. dirs. Crossroads Africa, Inc.; hon. mem. Population Crises Com., Washington. Recipient Superior Honor award State Dept., 1973. Club: Knickerbocker (N.Y.C.). Home: Hidden Valley Farm Lovettsville VA 22080 Office: Dept State Washington DC 20520 Office: US Ambassador to Rwanda care US Dept of State Washington DC 20520

UPTHEGROVE, FRANKLIN JOHN, clergyman; b. Lima, Ohio, Dec. 18, 1921; s. George F. and Mary E. (Thomas) U.; BS in Edn., Ohio U., 1958; BD, Crozer Theol. Sem., 1961, M Div, 1972; postgrad. Conwell Sch. Theology, 1963-65, Hartford Sem., 1964; DD (hon.), Eastern Neb. Christian Coll., 1970; m. Margaret children—Sylvia M. Gable, Barbara J. Richardson, Rita J.; stepchildren—Robert H. Reid, Milton Reid, Joseph Reid. Ordained to ministry United Ch. of Christ, 1961; pastor Mt. Zion Baptist Ch., Athens, Ohio, 1954-58, 1st Bapt. Ch., Rutland, Ohio, 1954-58, St. Paul's Bapt. Ch., Utica, N.Y., 1966-82; ret., 1982; organizer Antioch United Ch. of Christ, Phila., 1961, pastor, 1961-66; substitute tchr. secondary edn., Phila., 1960-66, Utica, 1966—. Mem. youth com. North br. Phila. YMCA, 1964-66; spl. examiner personnel dept. Civil Service, Phila., 1965-66; mem. Selective Service System, N.Y.C., 1983—; chmn. housing com. Utica Community Action Commn., 1966—; chmn. bd. Utica Community Action, Inc.; mem. Mohawk Valley Regional Econ. Devel. Council, N.Y. State; pres., bd. dirs. Mid-Utica Neighborhood Preservation Corp., 1975—; exec. dir. Commn. Human Relations City of Utica; gen. counsel Mohawk Valley Community Coll; mem. Selective Service Bd., 1983—, Gov's. Econ. Devel. Commn. N.Y. State; pres. Black Ministerial Alliance, Utica-Rome, 1980-85, Mid-Utica Neighborhood Preservation Corp., 1979—. Bd. dirs. Cosmopolitan Center, Utica, Utica Found. Served with USNR, 1943-46. Recipient citation Chapel of Four Chaplains, 1965. Mem. N. Central Ministerium (Phila. pres. 1966), Inter-Ch. Child Care Soc. Phila. (bd. dirs.). Office: 219 Leah St Utica NY 13502

UPTON, GRAHAM JOHN GILBERT, statistics educator; b. Edinburgh, Scotland, Jan. 22, 1944; s. Albert John and Doreen Elizabeth (Hobbs) U.; m. Susan Amy Joy Fisher, July 29, 1967 (div. Sept. 1987); children: Robin, Christopher. BSc, U. Leicester, Eng., 1965; MSc, U. Birmingham, Eng., 1966, PhD, 1970. Lectr. math. stats. U. Newcastle, Newcastle-upon-Tyne, Eng., 1968-73; lectr. math. U. Essex, Colchester, Eng., 1973-88, sr. lectr., 1988—; vis. prof. U. Dokkyo, Saitama, Japan, 1986; chief examiner U. Cambridge (Eng.) Local Exam. Syndicate, 1984—; vis. expert Orgn. for Econ. Co-operation and Devel., Paris, 1985—. Author: Analysis of Cross-Tabulated Data, 1978, Spatial Data Analysis By Examplevol. 1, 1985, vol. 2, 1988. Recipient Leverhulme prize U. Leicester, 1965. Fellow Royal Statis. Soc.; mem. Biometric Soc. Office: U Essex, Wivenhoe Park, Colchester England

UPTON, HERBERT HAWKES, JR., printing company executive; b. Ann Arbor, Mich., Sept. 21, 1925; s. Herbert Hawkes and Ellen (Canfield) U.; m. Anne Lloyd Drake, Sept. 15, 1950; children—William Lloyd, Joseph Hawkes, Mary Stoddart. B.B.A., U. Mich., 1948. Vice pres., gen. mgr. Double A Products Co., Manchester, Mich., 1956-66; pres., prin. owner Malloy Lithographing, Inc., Ann Arbor, 1971—; dir. NBD Bank, Ann Arbor. Pres. Ann Arbor Amateur Hockey Assn., 1965. Served to ensign USN, 1944-46; PTO. Mem. Ann Arbor Area Graphic Arts Assn. (bd. dirs. 1983—), Ann Arbor C. of C. (bd. dirs. 1984—). Episcopalian. Club: Barton Hills Country.

URABÉ, SHIZUTARO, architect; b. Kurashiki, Japan, Mar. 31, 1909; s. Mankichi Urabé; m. Shigeko Urabé, Sept. 7, 1918; children: Taro, Shinro, Tetsuro. BE, Kyoto U., Japan, 1934. Mgr. B. & R. dept. Kurashiki Rayon, Osaka, Japan, 1949-62; pres. S. Urabe & Assoc. Architects, Osaka, 1962-81, chmn., 1981-85, corp. advisor, 1985-87; corp. advisor Urabesekkei, Osaka, 1987—; asst. chmn. DAS, Osaka, 1956-82, counselor, 1982—; part-time lectr. Osaka U., 1954-55, Kyoto U., 1962-66. Editor: Furusato no Sumai, 1962. Hon. mem. Archtl. Inst. Japan (prize 1965, grand prize 1986); mem. Japan Inst. Architects. Buddhist. Home: 1 7 8 Kotoen, Nishinomiya 662, Japan Office: Urabesekkei, 1 12 39, Umeda, Kita-ku, Osaka 530, Japan

URBACH, EPHRAIM ELIMELECH, historian, educator, president Israel Academy Sciences and Humanities; b. Wloclawek, Poland, May 25, 1912; s. Israel Joseph and Haya Esther (Spiegel) U.; student Jewish Theol. Sem., Breslau, Poland and U. Breslau, 1930; D. Litt., U. Rome, 1936; Ph.D. (hon.), Weizmann Inst. Sci., Rehovot, Israel, 1980, Ben-Gurion U. of Negev, 1984; D.H.L. (hon.), Jewish Theol. Sem. N.Y., 1982, Tel Aviv U., 1986; m. Hanna Pinczower, 1944. Ordained rabbi, 1934; chaplain Brit. Army, 1941-45; sr. lectr. Jewish Theol. Sem., Breslau, 1938; tchr. Rehavia Gymnasium, Jerusalem, 1938-41; dir. Ma'ale secondary sch., Jerusalem, 1945-50; supr. secondary schs. Israel Ministry Edn., Jerusalem, 1950-53; lectr. in Talmud and Midrash, Hebrew U., 1953-58, prof. Talmud and Midrash, 1958-80, prof. emeritus, 1980—; pres. Israel Acad. Scis. and Humanities, Jerusalem, 1980-86. Recipient prize for Jewish studies Govt. Israel, 1955; Kaplun prize Hebrew U., Jerusalem, 1969; Leib Jaffe prize Keren Hayesod, 1970; Ch. N. Bialik prize Tel-Aviv Municipality, 1982. Mem. Acad. Hebrew Lang., Am. Acad. Jewish Studies (corr.), World Union Jewish Studies (pres.). Author: The Tossaphists: Their History, Writings and Methods, 1955, 4th edit., 1980; The Sages: Their Concepts and Beliefs, 1979, paperback edit. 1987; The Halakha: The Sources and Development, 1984. Office: care Israel Acad Scis &, Humanities, PO Box 4040, Jerusalem 91040, Israel

URBAN, JAMES ARTHUR, lawyer; b. West Palm Beach, Fla., Feb. 18, 1927; s. Arthur Joseph and Elsie Elizabeth (Wespeaker) U.; m. Alice Burmah Steed, June 21, 1952; children: James Arthur, Katherine Elizabeth. A.B., Duke U., 1950; J.D. with high honors, U. Fla., 1953. Bar: Fla. 1953. Since practiced in Orland; mem. firm Carlton, Fields, Ward, Emmanuel, Smith, Cutler & Kent (P.A.); dir. Fla. Legal Services, Inc., 1975-76. Bd. visitors Coll. Law Fla. State U., Tallahassee, 1973-79, mem. council advisers, 1975-79; mem. pres.'s council U. Fla., Gainesville, 1976-77; charter mem. Indsl. Devel. Commn. Mid-Fla., 1977—. Served with U.S. Army, 1945-47. Recipient Outstanding Alumnus award U. Fla. Law Rev. Alumni Assn., 1975. Fellow Am. Coll. Probate Counsel, Am. Coll. Real Estate Lawyers, Am. Bar Found.; mem. Am. Bar Assn. (Ho. of Dels. 1976-80), Am. Law Inst., Fla. Bar (author, lectr. continuing legal edn. program 1968—, pres. 1974-75), Fla. Bar Found. (dir. 1975—, pres. 1977-79), Nat. Conf. Bar Founds. (dir. 1979—), Orlando C. of C. (dir. 1971-73), Phi Kappa Phi, Theta Chi. Episcopalian. Clubs: Rotary (Orlando), Citrus (Orlando), Univ., Country (Orlando). Home: 1614 Pepperidge Dr Orlando FL 32806 Office: Carlton Fields et al PO Box 1171 Orlando FL 32802 also: 1601 CNA Tower Orlando FL 32801

URBAN, MARTIN, museum director; b. Liebemühl, Germany, Dec. 16, 1913; s. Julius Urban; ed. U. Königsberg, U. Bonn, U. Kiel; prom. Dr. phil., 1950; prof., 1980; m. Ruth Henneberg, 1942; children: Agnes, Dagmar, Petra, Gabriele. Asst., custodian Schleswig-Holsteinisches Landesmus., Schleswig, Schloss Gottorf, 1950-62; dir. Found. Seebüll Ada and Emil Nolde, Neukirchen, W. Ger., 1963—. Author papers on art in Middle Ages, 20th century, especially German expressionism and Emil Nolde, Catalogue Raisonne of Nolde's oil paintings. Address: Nolde Stiftung Seebüll, 2268 Neukirchen Federal Republic of Germany

URBANCZYK, STANISLAW, linguist; b. Kwczala, Poland, July 27, 1909; s. Jan and Zofia (Glownia) U.; m. Alina Nitsch, June 20, 1936 (dec. July 1985); children: Stanislaw, Kazimierz, Anna. PhD, Jagellonian U., Krakow, Poland, 1939, habilitation, 1945; D honoris causa, Salzburg U. Prof. linguistics U. Torun, Poland, 1947—; prof. U. Poznan, Poland, 1948-56, U. Krakow, 1956-69; prof. Polish Acad. Scis., Krakow, 1953-79, pres. com. linguistics, 1987; cons. Inst. Polish Lang., Krakow, 1979—. Author: Zdania Rozpoczynane Wyrazem co w Jezyku Polskim, 1939, Biblia Królowej Zofii a Staroczeskie Przeklady Pisma sw, 1946, Religia Pog. Slowian, 1947, Szkice z Dziejów Jezyka Polskiego, 1968, Slowniki ich Rodzaje i Uzytecznosc, 1978, (with others) Encyklopedia Wiedzy o Jezyku Polskim, 1978, Prace z Dziejów Jezyka Polskiego, 1979, (with J. Reichman) Slownik gwar Polskich, 1979—, (with others) Gramatyka Historyczna Jezyka Polskiego, 4th edit., 1981, (with R. Olesch), Die Altpolnischen Orthographien des 16. Jahrhunderts, 1983, Zarys Dialektologii Polskiejch, 7th edit., 1984, (with others) Slownik Staropolski, 8 vols., Biblia Królowej, 1971; contbr. articles to profl. jours. Mem. Com. Polish Linguistics (pres. 1968-71), Soc. Friends of Polish Lang. (pres. 1984). Roman Catholic. Home: Rakowicka 10 B/10, 31 511 Crakow Poland Office: Inst Polish Lang, Straszewskiego 27, Crakow Poland

URBIK, JEROME ANTHONY, financial services executive; b. Chgo., Oct. 30, 1929; s. Anthony Frank and Sophie Elizabeth (Stripeikis) U.; married, 1956; children: Laura M., Michael A., Anthony J., Mary L., John T. BA in Philosophy, St. Mary's Coll., Techny, Ill., 1953; student, Am. Coll., 1970. CLU, chartered fin. cons. Field underwriter Mut. of N.Y., Chgo., 1955-59; merchandising specialist Mut. of N.Y., N.Y.C., 1959; pvt. practice brokerage cons. Northfield, Ill., 1960-64; chief exec. officer Hinsdale (Ill.) Assocs. Fin. Services Corp., 1964—; v.p. Interstate Coll. Personology, Sacramento, 1982—. Contbr. articles on industry to profl. mem. editorial bd. Leaders Mag., 1981—. Mem. adv. council congressman Henry Hyde, Nat. Rep. Com., Washington; mem. fin. com. Judy Koehler senate campaign, Hinsdale; mem. Small Bus. Devel. Ctr., Lewis U., Lockport, Ill. Named Small Bus. Acct. of Yr. for State of Ill. SBA, 1987. Mem. Am. Soc. CLU's (bd. dirs. 1970—), Gen. Agts. Mgrs. Conf. (pres. 1967-68), Nat. Assn. Life Underwriters, Chgo. Orchestral Assn., Chgo. Lyric Opera. Roman Catholic. Home: 474 E South St Elmhurst IL 60126 Office: Hinsdale Assocs Fin Service Corp 119 E Ogden Hinsdale IL 60521

URCIUOLI, J. ARTHUR, investment banker; b. Syracuse, N.Y., Nov. 13, 1937; s. Joseph R. and Nicoletta Anne (Phillips) U.; m. Margaret Jane Forelli, Aug. 13, 1966; children: Karen Sloan, Christian Joseph Arthur. B.S., St. Lawrence U., 1959; J.D., Georgetown U., 1966; grad. Advanced Mgmt. Program, Harvard Bus. Sch., 1982. Bar: N.Y. 1966. Atty. Brown, Wood, Fuller, Caldwell & Ivey, N.Y.C., 1966-69; internat. investment banker, dir. internat. fin. Merrill Lynch, N.Y.C., Paris, 1970-78; pres. Merrill Lunch Internat., 1978-82; chmn. Merrill Lynch Internat. Bank, London; dir. banking div. Merrill Lynch Capital Markets, 1980-84; sr. v.p. Merrill Lynch Bus. Fin. Services, Merrill Lynch Co., 1984—, also bd dirs. Contbr. articles to profl. jours. Trustee St. Lawrence U., 1976—; bd. dirs. United Way, Greenwich, Conn., 1978-81. Served to capt. USMC, 1959-63. Mem. Securities Industry Assn. (chmn. sales and mktg. com. 1987—). Republican. Congregationalist. Clubs: Harvard (N.Y.C.); N.Y. Yacht, Riverside (Conn.) Yacht; Rocky Point (Old Greenwich, Conn.). Office: Merrill Lynch Pierce Fenner & Smith Inc 717 5th Ave New York NY 10022

URE, ALAN WILLIS, construction company executive; b. Glasgow, Scotland, Mar. 30, 1926; s. Colin McGregor and Edith Hannah Eileen Willis (Swinburne) U.; m. Mary Christine Henry, Apr. 11, 1953; children: Fiona Mary, John William, Alison Joan. MA, Cambridge U., 1950. Trainee engr. Trollope & Colls, Ltd., London, 1950-52, engr., 1952-55, mgr., 1955-64, tech. dir., 1964-69, dir., 1969-82, mng. dir., 1982-85; dep. mng. dir. Trollope & Colls Holdings, Ltd., London, 1984—; mng. dir. Trollope & Colls Mgmt. Ltd., London, 1980-82; pres. Nat. Fedn. Bldg. Trades employers, 1981-82; pres. Constrn. Health and Safety Group, London, 1980-86; v.p. Fedn. Internationale Europeenne de la Construction, Paris, 1982-85; bd. dirs. Constrn. Industry Tng. Bd., 1982-85; chmn. Nat. Joint Council for the Bldg. Industry, 1988—. Contbr. articles to profl. jours. Mem. Royal Commn. on Civil Liability and Compensation for Personal Injury, London, 1974-78; mem. U.K. Govt. Adv. Com. on Asbestos, London, 1976-79. Served with Royal Navy, 1944-47. Decorated Comdr. Brit. Empire. Recipient Royal Naval Res. Officers Decoration. Mem. Ch. of Eng. Club: Naval (London). Home: 28 Hambleside Ct, Hamble Hants SO3 5QE, England

URIBE, JOEL JUAREZ, cardiologist; b. Acapulco, Mex., Dec. 10, 1948; s. Joel Juarez Guzman and Gloria Uribe Garcia; m. Lourdes Sanchez Diaz, Sept. 5, 1971; children—Joel Juarez, Jacob, Jessica. M.D., U. Mex., 1973. Diplomate Am. Bd. Internal Medicine, Am. Bd. Cardiovascular Diseases. Intern Regina (Sask., Can.) Gen. Hosp., 1971-72; resident in internal medicine U. Tex. Health Scis. Ctr., San Antonio, 1973-76; fellow in cardiology Emory U. Sch. Medicine, Atlanta, 1976-79; chief internal medicine dept. Acapulco Gen. Hosp., 1979-82; prof. medicine U. Mex. Med. Sch., 1980-88; cardiologist Scripps Meml. Hosp., Chula Vista, (Calif.) Community Hosp. Chula Vista, 1982—; Bay Hosp. Med. Ctr. Fellow Am. Coll. Chest Physicians, Am. Coll. Cardiology; mem. Soc. Mex. Cardiologia, Soc. Mex. Medicina Interna, AMA. Address: 754 Medical Center Ct Suite 203 Chula Vista CA 92010

URIBE VILLEGAS, OSCAR, sociologist; b. Toluca, Mex., Nov. 6, 1928; s. M. Rafael and Luz (Villegas) Uribe. BS, Nat. Prep. Sch., Mex., 1948; post-grad., Nat. Sch. Anthropology, Mex., 1949-52, Sch. Polit. and Social Scis., Mex., 1951-54, Coll. Mex., 1957-62. Researcher, coordinator Inst. Investigaciones Sociales Nat. U. Mex., Coyoacán, 1952-72; titular researcher Nat. U. Mex., 1972—, prof. sch. polit. and social scis., 1953-58; cons. Consejo Nat. Turismo, 1964—. Author: Técnicas Estadísticas para Investigadores Sociales, 1958, La Matemática la Estadística y las Ciencias Sociales, 1963, Curvas Sociográficas, 1969, Causación Social y Vida Internacional, 1958, El A.B.C. de la Correlación, 1962, 25 Conceptos de Uso sociológico, 1965, Sociolingüística Concreta, 1970, Los Elementos de la Estadística Social, 1971, Sociolingüística Doctrinaria, 1971, Situaciones de Multilingüismo en el Mundo, 1972, El Progreso, 1973, La Sociolingüística Actual, 1974, Las Disciplinas Sociolingüísticas, 1976, Imágenes del Hombre en la Rusia zarista y en la Unión Soviética, 1977, Issues in Sociolinguistics, 1977, Para una Sociología del Cercano Oriente, 1978, Koinoniología, 1979, En Pro de la Amistad Mexicano-Finesa, 1980, Progreso e Independencia, 1984, El Enfasis Sociológico en Socio-Lingüística, 1984, Una Iniciación a la Lingüística Otomiana,1985, La Identidad Nacional en el Caso de India, 1986, El Mexicano, Mentalidad Mexicana de Habla Castellana, 1987, De Rerum Humana Natura y la Universitas Mexicana, 1987, Ensayos Marginales, 1987; Aux. editor Revista Mexicana de Sociología, 1952-66; mem. editorial bd. Internat. Jour. Sociology Lang., Revista Interamericana de Sociología. Recipient Presea Presencia Estado Mex., 1984. Mem. Mex. Sociol. Assn., Internat. Sociol. Assn. (council 1966-70), Ctr. Research Bilingualism (corr.), Assn. Internat. Polit. Sci., Inst. Internat. Sociology, Soc. Linguistica Italiana, Soc. Lingua Portuguesa, Inst. Mex. Culture, Consejo Culture Estado Mex., Soc. Mex. Estudios Semioticos (pres.), Internat. Assn. Semiotic Studies. Home: 117 Palestina, 02080 Mexico City 16 Mexico Office: Inst Investigaciones Sociales, 2a Torre de Humanidades, 90 piso CU, 20 DF Coyoacan Mexico

URITESCU, DORIN VASILE, linguist, researcher; b. Fibis, Timis, Romania, Apr. 30, 1946; s. Aurel and Marioara (Pepa) U.; m. Gabriela Garofeanu, Oct. 9, 1971; children: Ramona Maria, Ioana Gabriela. Degree in philology, U. Timisoara, Romania, 1969, PhD in Philology, 1978. Researcher The Ctr. Sci. Research Romanian Acad., Timisoara, 1970-75; vis. prof. linguistics U. Chgo., 1982-84; researcher Ctr. Social Studies U. Timisoara, 1975-82, 1984—; dialectology researcher Ctr. Social Studies, U. Timisoara, 1985—. Author: Synchrony and Diachrony. Phonetics of the Dialects in Northern Banat, 1987, Formal and Natural in Phonological Evolution; (with others) Atlas Linguarum Europae, 1983, Treatise of Romanian Dialectology, 1984, The New Linguistic Atlas of Romania. Crisana, Supplement to the Dictionary of Selected Indo-European Synonyms; contbr. articles to profl. jours. Grantee Polish Acad. Sci., 1973, Fulbright scholar, 1982-84. Mem. Romanian Soc. Philol. Studies, Romanian Soc. Romance Linguistics, Romanian Nat. Com. Atlas Linguarum Europae, Linguistic Soc. Am. Home: Bd Cetătii 60, ScB Apt 10, 1900 Timisoara Timis Romania Office: U Timisoara, Bd V Parvan 4, 1900 Timisoara Timis Romania

URMER, DIANE HEDDA, management firm executive, financial officer; b. Bklyn., Dec. 15, 1934; d. Leo and Helen Sarah (Perlman) Leverant; m. Albert Heinz Urmer, Sept. 2, 1952; children: Michelle, Cynthia, Carl. Student U. Tex., 1951-52, Washington U., St. Louis, 1962-63; BA in Psychology, Calif. State U.-Northridge, 1969. Asst. auditor Tex. State Bank, Austin, 1952-55; v.p., controller Enki Corp., Sepulveda, Calif., 1966-70, also dir., 1987—; v.p., fin. Cambia Way Hosp., Walnut Creek, Calif., 1973-78; v.p., controller Enki Health & Research Systems, Inc., Reseda, Calif., 1978—, also dir. Contbr. articles to profl. jours. Pres. Northridge PTA, 1971; chmn. Northridge Citizens Adv. Council, 1972-73. Mem. Women in Mgmt. Club: Tex. Execs. Avocations: bowling, sailing, handcrafts, golf. Office: Enki Health and Research Systems Inc 6660 Reseda Blvd #203 Reseda CA 91335

UROKOHARA, TOMIO, automobile parts executive; b. Tokyo, Apr. 23, 1925; d. Shigekazu and Ito (Urokohara) Yokoyama; m. Kiyoko Yano, Nov. 23, 1952; children: Akihiko, Haruhiko. LLB, Tokyo U., 1949. With Tominaga & Co., Ltd., Tokyo, 1949-65; gen. mgr. sales Nichiryo, Ltd., Tokyo, 1965-67; gen. mgr. adminstrn. Tokai Cold Forming Co., Ltd., Nagoya, Japan, 1967-70; exec. v.p. Toakai TRW & Co. subs. TRW, Inc., Nagoya, 1970—. Served with Japanese Army. Buddhist. Home: 2-2-9-205 Daiko-Minami, Higashi-ku, Nagoya 461, Japan Office: Tokai TRW & Co Ltd, 1203 Ushiyama-cho, Kasugai 486, Japan

URQUHART, BRIAN EDWARD, former UN official; b. Bridport, Dorset, Eng., Feb. 28, 1919; s. Murray and Bertha (Rendall) U.; m. Sidney Damrosch Howard, Apr. 26, 1963; children—Rachel, Charles; children from previous marriage—Thomas, Katherine, Robert. Ed. Oxford U., Eng.; D.C.L., (hon.), 1986; LL.D., Yale U., 1981, Tufts U., 1985, CUNY, 1986, Grinnell U., 1986, SUNY-Binghamton, 1986; D. Univ., U. Essex, Eng., 1981; degree (hon.) U. Colo., 1987, U. Keele, Eng., 1987. Entered Brit. Army, 1939, advanced to maj., 1943; served in North Africa, Sicily, and Europe; demobilized 1945; ofcl. UN Secretariat, N.Y.C., 1945-86, under sec.-gen. for spl. polit. affairs, 1974-86; scholar-in-residence Ford Found., N.Y.C., 1986—. Decorated Order Brit. Empire, KCMG. Club: Century (N.Y.C.). Author: Hammarskjold, 1972, A Life in Peace and War, 1987; also articles and revs. Home: 131 E 66th St New York NY 10021 Office: Ford Found 320 E 43rd St New York NY 10017

URQUHART, JAMES BURWELL, III, research engineer, thermodynamicist, computer systems consultant; b. Pitts., Mar. 18, 1944; s. James Burwell Jr. and Eva Marie (Williams) U.; m. Eleanor Mack, July 29, 1967; children—Susan, Melanie, Katherine. BSME magna cum laude, Duke U., 1966; MSME, Ga. Inst. Tech., 1968. Registered profl. engr., Fla. Research engr. Boeing Co., Huntsville, Ala., 1968-72, Pratt & Whitney, West Palm Beach, Fla., 1972-79, 85, United Tech. Research Ctr., West Palm Beach, 1979-85, 86-88; chmn. bd. Computer Applications, Inc. Contbr. articles to profl. jours. Patentee in field. Recipient commendation NASA/Boeing Co., 1971. Mem. U.S. Golf Assn., Phi Beta Kappa, Sigma Xi, Tau Beta Pi, Pi Mu Epsilon, Pi Tau Sigma. Episcopalian. Office: UTOS Inc PO Box 10966 Palm Beach Gardens FL 33410

URQUHART, STEPHEN E., lawyer; b. Quincy, Mass., Mar. 2, 1949; s. Raymond Miles and M. Eileen (MacDonald) U.; m. Katherine Driscoll, Mar. 15, 1970; 1 child, Stephen M. AB, Boston Coll., 1976, JD, 1979. Bar: Mass. 1979, U.S. Dist. Ct. Mass. 1980. Legis. aide Mass. Ho. of Reps., Boston, 1976; counsel B.C. Legal Assistance Bur., Waltham, Mass., 1976-79; assoc. Law Offices of Robert J. Ladd (formerly Law Offices of Roland I. Wood), North Andover, Mass., 1980-88, Law Offices Nicholas Macaronis, Lowell, Mass., 1988—. Precinct capt. Edward M. Kennedy for Senator, Mass. 1979-80; campaign worker various Dem. candidates. Recipient cert. of merit United World Federalists, 1974. Mem. ABA, Mass. Bar Assn., Mass. Acad. Trial Attys., Am. Arbitration Assn., Internat. Platform Assn., Phi Beta Kappa. Methodist. Club: Clan Urquhart (Va.). Home: PO Box 610 Danville NH 03819 Office: 9 Central St Lowell MA 01852

URRUTIA-CÁRDENAS, HERNÁN, Spanish language educator, researcher; b. Valdivia, Chile, Mar. 10, 1940; s. Luis Urrutia-Ibánez and Blanca Cárdenas-Bravo; m. Orietta Cabrera-Concha, Nov. 16, 1942; children: Gabriel, Isabel. Lic. Philology, U. Complutense, Madrid, 1972, D in Hispanic Philology, 1974. Prof. Spanish grammar U. Austral, Valdivia, 1966-75; prof. Spanish philology U. Deusto, Bilbao, Spain, 1976—; prof. Spanish linguistics U. Basque Country, Bilbao, 1980—; dir. Inst. Philology, U. Austral, Valdivia, 1974-75; dir. dept. Hispanic linguistics U. Deusto, Bilbao, 1976—, vice dean faculty philosophy and letters, 1976-80, dir. phonetics lab., 1982—. Author: Lengua Y Discurso en la Creación Léxica, 1978; co-author: MAnual de Ortografia, 1976, Gram. Transfor. Del Español, 1982, Esquema de Morfosintaxis Hrca del Español, 1983, Las Sibilamtes em el Vizcaino, 1988; contbr. numerous articles to profl. jours. Grantee U. Austral, Valdivia, 1964, Govt. of Basque Country, Bilbao, 1982, Ministry of Edn. and Sci., Madrid, 1983. Mem. Spanish Soc. Linguistics (bd. dirs. 1982-84), Spanish Soc. Applied Linguistics. Roman Catholic. Club: Fadura (Vizcaya, Spain). Home: Avenida de Amaya, 26 2d A, 48940 Lejona Vizcaya, Spain

URRY, VERN WILLIAM, research psychologist; b. Salt Lake City, Sept. 20, 1931; s. Herbert William and Emma Irene (Swaner) U.; B.A., U. Utah, 1955; M.S., 1962; Ph.D., Purdue U., 1970; m. Billie Jeanne Nevius, Sept. 24, 1957; 1 dau., Gloria Jeanne. Research psychologist U.S. Army Enlisted Evaluation Center, Fort Benjamin Harrison, Ind., 1961-67; head systems and programming Measurement and Research Center, Purdue U., West Lafayette, Ind., 1967-70; asst. dir. Bur. Testing, U. Wash., Seattle, 1970-72; personnel research psychologist U.S. Office Personnel Mgmt., Washington, 1972-86; pvt. practice, 1986—. Served with U.S. Army, 1952-54. Recipient Cert. of Achievement, U.S. Army Enlisted Evaluation Center, 1967, others. Mem. AAAS, Am. Psychol. Assn., Psychometric Soc., Internat. Platform Assn., N.Y. Acad. Scis., Phi Kappa Phi. Contbr. articles to various publs. Home and Office: 806 Tepic Dr El Paso TX 79912-1720

URSI, CORRADO CARDINAL, archbishop of Naples; b. Andria, Italy, July 26, 1908; s. Riccardo and Apollonia (Sterlicchio) U.; ed. Seminario Regionale di Molfetta, Bari, Italy. Ordained priest Roman Catholic Ch., 1931; with Pontifical Regional Seminary of Molfetta, vice rector, later rector, 1931-51; mem. Congregation Cath. Edn.; bishop Nardó (Italy), 1951; archbishop of Acorensa, 1961; archbishop of Naples, 1966—; elevated to Sacred Coll. Cardinals, 1967. Address: Largo Donnaregina 23, 80134 Naples Italy *

URSIN, BJØRN, research geophysicist, petroleum geophysics educator; b. Danzig, Poland, Sept. 5, 1943; s. Rolf and Christel Dorothea (Bloeck) U.; m. Elin Haldogaard, May 11, 1973 (separated); children: Kristin, Jørgen, Marit; m. Else-Britt Pettersen, Sept. 30, 1967 (div. Oct. 1972); 1 child, Line. MSc CE, Norwegian Inst. Tech., Trondheim, 1970, PhD, 1976; MSc, U. Grenoble, France, 1971. Research asst. Norwegian Inst. Tech., Trondheim, 1969-73; scientist Computing Ctr., Univ. Trondheim, 1973-74; research mgr. Geophys. Co. of Norway, Høvik, 1975-79; group leader Petroleum Tech. Research Inst., Trondheim, 1979-84; research dir. Merlin Profilers, Trondheim, 1984; v.p. research and devel. Seismic Research and Devel., Trondheim, 1985—; adj. assoc. prof. petroleum geophysics Norwegian Inst. Tech., 1979-84, adj. prof., 1985—. Contbr. over 25 papers to internat. sci. jours.; editor: Geophys. Prospecting, 1986—. Recipient Norwegian Geophys. Award Norseis, Oslo, Norway, 1985. Mem. Royal Astron. Soc., European Assn. Exploration Geophysicists, European Geophys. Soc., Soc. Exploration Geophysicists (translations com. 1979—), IEEE (sr. mem.), Soc. Indsl. and Applied Math., Nordic Assn. Applied Geophysics, Norwegian Geophys. Soc., European Assn. Signal Processing, Norwegian Signal Processing Soc., Norwegian Assn. Automatic Control, Norwegian Soc. Chartered Engrs. Home: Fjordgata 7, N-7010 Trondheim Norway Office: Seismic Research and Devel, PO Box 1965 Moholtan, N-7002 Trondheim Norway

URSO, PAUL, immunologist; b. Sicily, Italy, Aug. 3, 1925; came to U.S., 1930, naturalized, 1936; s. Paolo and Melchiorra (Garufi) U.; B.S., St. Francis Coll., 1950; M.S., Marquette U., 1952; Ph.D., U. Tenn., 1961; children—Theresa M. Urso Schweizer, Peter J. Research assoc. Dept. Biology, Oak Ridge Nat. Lab., 1958-59; predoctoral fellow U. Tenn., Oak Ridge Inst., Nuclear Studies, 1959-61; asst. and assoc. prof. biology Seton Hall U., S. Orange, N.J., 1961-71; sr. scientist/immunologist Oak Ridge Assoc. U., Oak Ridge, 1971-81; asst. prof. microbiology/immunology Morehouse Sch. Medicine, Atlanta, 1981—; cons. ORNL, 1961-63, ORAU, 1963-70; mem. com. NIH, 1983—. Adv. grads., Seton Hall U. 1965-70; bd. dirs. Oak Ridge Community Playhouse, 1979-80, Cath. High, Knoxville, 1974-75; v.p. Parents without Partners, Oak Ridge, 1979; mem. St. Mary's Ch. choir, Oak Ridge, 1974-81, Sacred Heart Ch. Choir, Atlanta, 1982—; baseball coach Oak Ridge Boys Club, 1971-74, Our Lady of Sorrows, Tacoma Park, Md., 1953-55. Served with Signal Corps, U.S. Army, 1944-46; PTO. Marquette U. grad. asst., 1950-52; ORINS at U. Tenn. predoctoral fellow, 1959-61; NIH grantee, 1964-67, 83-87; Dept. Energy/EPA Co., grantee, 1978-81; grantee NIH/MBRS, 1983-87, 87—, AID, 1985-86, 87-88. Mem. Am. Assn. Immunologists, Reticuloendothelial Soc., Transplantation Soc., Internat. Soc. Exptl. Hematologists, Soc. Am. Zoologists, Internat. Soc. Developmental and Comparative Immunology, Radiation Research Soc., Sigma Xi (v.p. 1968-69, pres. 1969-70, Seton Hall U.). Roman Catholic. Clubs: Parents without Partners, Oak Ridge Community Playhouse, Swingin Singles Sq. Dance, Southside Theatre Guild (Fairburn, Ga.). Contbr. articles to profl. jours. Office: 720 Westview Dr SW Atlanta GA 30310

URSTADT, CHARLES DEANE, real estate and publishing executive; b. N.Y.C., June 13, 1959; s. Charles Jordan and Elinor McClure (Funk) U.; m. Lynn Caroline Jackson, May 19, 1984. BA cum laude, NYU, 1982. News reporter Sta. WNYC-TV, N.Y.C., 1979-80; adminstrv. asst. Mayor's Press Office, City of N.Y., 1980-81; asst. v.p. Pearce, Urstadt, Mayer & Greer, Inc., 1981-84, v.p., mem. exec. com., 1984-86, sr. v.p., sec., 1986—; pub., editor-in-chief N.Y. Constrn. News, 1984—. Chmn. Young Reps. of Bronxville, 1984-85; Village Rep. Campaign Com. of Bronxville, N.Y., 1984-85, Young People for O'Rourke Campaign, 1986; mem. adv. bd. Community Housing Improvement Program, Inc., 1987—; bd. dirs. 61 East 86th St. Owners Corp., 1987—, Forum 500 (N.Y. Rep. State Com.), 1987—, The Ensemble Studio Theater, 1988—, East Side Assn., 1988—. Mem. Bldg. Contractors Assn., Nat. Assn. Home Builders, Internat. Platform Assn., Fairfield County Home Builders Assn., L.I. Builders Inst., Rockland County Builders Assn., Assoc. Builders and Owners of Greater N.Y., Builders Inst., N.Y. Bldg. Congress (bd. dirs. 1988—), Urban Land Inst. Clubs: Nat. Realty, Links. Office: Pearce Urstadt Mayer & Greer Inc 90 Park Ave New York NY 10016

USERA, JOHN JOSEPH, dean, chemistry educator, researcher, consulting statistical analyst; b. Cleve., Mar. 18, 1941; s. Libertad Vivas and Beatrice (Ramirez) U.; m. Maria Bernadette Borszich, Sept. 6, 1969; children: Helen E., Karena M., Pamela Y. B.S., Black Hill State Coll., 1971, BS in Edn., 1972; M Natural Sci., U. S.D., 1978, MA, 1980; PhD, Kans. State U., 1984. Registered analytical chemist, Kans.; cert. secondary sch. chemistry tchr., S.D. Teaching asst. S.D. Sch. Mines, Rapid City, 1973-74; sci./math. instr. Shannon County Schs., Batesland, S.D., 1971-73; chemistry/physics instr. Bon Homme Sch. Dist., Tyndall, S.D., 1974-81; chemistry lectr. U. S.D., Springfield, 1979-80; lectr. in stats. Pitts. State U., 1986—, dean instructional services ans instl. research, 1987—; chemistry and stats. prof. Labette Community Coll., Parsons, Kans., 1981-87; dir. forensic lab. Labette Community Coll., 1982—. Author: Science Anxiety, 1984. Contbr. articles to profl. jours. Served to sgt. USMC, 1965-69, Viet Nam. Named S.D. Tchr. of Yr., S.D. Edn. Assn., 1980. Fellow Am. Inst. Chemists; mem. Am. Chem. Soc., Am. Chem. Soc. (analytical chemistry sect.), Two-Yr. Coll. Chemistry Conf., Assn. for Instl. Research, Am. Mgmt. Assn., Soc. for Coll. and Univ. Planning, Am. Assn. for Higher Edn., Nat. Sci. Tchrs. Assn., Kans. Edn. Assn., NEA, Maths. Assn. of Am., Kans. Sci. Tchr. Assn., Sigma Delta Nu, Pi Mu Epsilon. Roman Catholic. Lodge: K.C. Avocations: computers; reading; classical music. Home: 3102 Briggs Parsons KS 67357 Office: Labette Community Coll 200 S 14th St Parsons KS 67357

USHER, GEORGE GEOFFREY, chemical company executive; b. Toronto, Ont., Can., Oct. 25, 1958; s. Thomas Clemens and Pamela Margaret (Sale) U.; m. Shelagh Heather MacPherson, Sept. 22, 1984; 1 child, Samantha Margaret. BS in Agriculture, U. Guelph, Ont., 1982. Chem. technician Dextran Products Ltd., Toronto, 1982-84, prodn. mgr., 1984-85, v.p., 1985-86, pres., 1986—. Office: Dextran Products Ltd, 421 Comstock Rd, Scarborough, ON Canada M1L 2H5

USHER, SIR LEONARD GRAY, retired news association executive; b. Paeroa, New Zealand, May 29, 1907; s. Robert and Mary Elizabeth (Johnston) U.; m. Mary Gertrude Lockie, Nov. 30, 1940 (div. 1962); children: Lala Athene Frazer, Miles Gray; m. Jane Hammond Derne, July 11, 1962 (dec. 1984). Tchrs. certificate, Auckland Tng. Coll., 1926-27; B.A., Auckland U., 1934. Headmaster schs. Fiji, 1930-43; pub. relations officer Govt. of Fiji, 1943-56; exec. dir. Fiji Times & Herald, Suva, 1956-73; dir. Fiji Times & Herald, 1973-77; editor Fiji Times, 1958-73; organizing dir. Pacific Islands News Assn., 1974-85, councillor, life mem., 1985—; chmn. bd. Fiji Devel. Bank, 1978-82, Suva Stock Exchange, 1979—, Island Bottlers (Fiji) Ltd., 1980-86; dep. chmn. Nat. Bank Fiji, 1974-82, Fiji Times-Herald, 1975-77; dir. Fiji Air Ltd., Fiji Liquefied Gas Carriers Ltd., Connoisseur Products (Pacific) Ltd., John P. Young and Assocs. (Fiji) Ltd., Mt. Pleasant Ltd. Mem. Fiji Broadcasting Commn., 1954-56, Fiji Visitors Bur., 1953-56, Fiji Library Adv. Com.; pres. Fiji Bd. Fire Commrs., 1967-70, 75-76; councillor Suva, 1962-71, 75-77, mayor, 1967-70, 75-76; mem. council U. South Pacific, 1975-78; trustee Fiji Crippled Children Soc., 1965—, pres., 1971-74; sec. Fiji Press Council, 1986—. Served with inf. Fiji Army, 1942-45. Decorated comdr. and knight comdr. Order Brit. Empire. Mem. Royal Commonwealth Soc. (sec. Fiji). Methodist. Clubs: Mason (master Fiji 1949-50, 74-75), United Grand Lodge Eng. (past grand standard bearer 1985), Defence (trustee), Fiji Arts (trustee), United (trustee) (Suva); Royal Automobile (Sydney); Grammar (Auckland). Home: GPO Box 14432, Suva Fiji Office: 24 Des Voeux Rd, GPO Box 14432, Suva Fiji

USHIO, JIRO, manufacturing executive; b. Himeji, Hyogo Prif, Japan, Feb. 12, 1931; s. Kenji and Mitsuko U.; m Hitomi Haruko; children: Shiro, Sachiko. BA Polit. Sci., Tokyo U., 1953. Pres. Ushio Inc., Tokyo, 1964-78, chmn., chief exec. officer, 1978—; dir. Daini Den Den Co., Tokyo, 1984—; chmn. Internat. U. Japan, Niigata, 1987—. Author: Activity Principle for Youth, 1981. Mem. Tax Commn. Prime Minister's Office, Econ. Council, Indsl. Structure Council, U. Council. Mem. Inst. Social Engring. (pres. 1969—), Japan Assn. Corp. Execs. (vice chmn.), Matsushita Sch. Govn. and Mgmnt. (exec. trustee). Home: 1-50-30 Denenchohfu Ohota-ku, Tokyo 145, Japan Office: Ushio Inc, Asahi-Tokai Bldg 19F2-6-1, Ohtemachi Chiyodaku Tokyo 100, Japan

USHIODA, KENJIRO, manufacturing company executive; b. Tokyo, June 4, 1926; s. Takejiro and Tei U.; m. Emeko Muto; children: Yoichiro, Atsuko. With Myokenya, Tokyo, 1946-66; pres. Toyo Sash Co. Ltd., Tokyo, 1966—, Tostem Cera Co. Ltd., Tokyo, 1968—; pres. Toyo Exterior Co. Ltd., Tokyo, 1974-80, chmn., 1980—; pres. Viva Home Co. Ltd., Saitama, 1977-86, chmn., 1986—. Recipient Medal of Honor with Blue Ribbon Prime Minister of Japan, 1987. Mem. Japan Metal Sash Inst. (chmn. 1986), Japan Curtain Wall Mfrs. Assn. (chmn. 1986). Office: Toyo Sash Co Ltd, 3-8-9 Hosoda, Katsushika-ku, Tokyo 124, Japan

USMAN, RAZIEF, trading and plantation company owner; b. Jakarta, Indonesia, Oct. 13, 1957; s. Nur Usman and Cut Nursiah Raja Sabi. Economy degree, Gajah Mada U., Yogyakarta, Indonesia, 1986. Pres. dir. PT. Ubertraco, Jakarta, 1979—; exec. dir. PT. Purindo Ranandra & Coy, Jakarta, 1983—, PT. Trivicindo Internat., Jakarta, 1983—, PT. Inesia Sparta Industria, Jakarta, 1985—; pres. dir. PT. Sari Alam Sakti Manunggal, Jakarta, 1986—, PT. Irako Engring., Jakarta, 1986—, PT. Lanmorindo Abadi Sentosa, Jakarta, 1986—, PT. Ubertraco Mina Fishery, Jakarta, 1986—; mgr. fin. Human Welfare Found., Jakarta, 1986—; pres. dir. Pandu Buana Nusantara Sdn. Bhd., Malaysia, 1987—, Buhmann Inc., Austin, Tex., 1985—, PT. Ubertraco Cons., Jakarta, 1984—, PT. Gamindacon Inter Cons., Jakarta, 1983-86. Chmn. Gaperda, Aceh, Indonesia, 1987. Office: PT Sari Alam Sakti Manunggal & Group, 16A Jl Tebet Timur Raya, Jakarta Selatan 12820, Indonesia

USTINOV, NICOLAI H. G. See GEDDA, NICOLAI H. G.

USTINOV, PETER ALEXANDER, actor, director, writer; b. London, Eng., Apr. 16, 1921; s. Iona and Nadia (Benois) U.; m. Isolda Denham, 1940 (div.); 1 child, Tamara; m. Suzanne Cloutier, Feb. 15, 1954 (div. 1971); children: Pavla, Igor, Andrea; m. Helen du Lau d'Allemans, 1972. Student, Westminster Sch., London, Mr. Gibbs Prep. Sch., London, London Theatre Sch.; D.Mus. (hon.), Cleve. Inst. Music, 1967; LL.D. (hon.), U. Dundee, 1969, LaSalle Coll. of Phila., 1971; Litt.D. (hon.), U. Lancaster, 1972; Doctorate (hon.), U. Toronto, 1984. Stage appearances include The Wood Demon, 1938, The Bishop of Limpopoland, 1939, First Night, 1940, Swinging the Gate, 1940, Fishing For Shadows, 1940, Hermione Gingold Revue, 1940, Diversion No. 1 Revue, 1940, Diversion No. 2 Revue, 1941, Squaring The Circle, 1941, Frenzy, 1948, Love in Albania, 1949, The Love of Four Colonels, 1951-52 (N.Y. Critics award, Donaldson award), Romanoff and Juliet, 1956 (Evening Standard drama award), Photo Finish, 1962, The Unknown Soldier and His Wife, 1968, 73, Who's Who in Hell, 1974, King Lear, 1979, 80, Beethoven's Tenth, 1983-84; film appearances include One of Our Aircraft is Missing, 1941, The Way Ahead, 1944, Private Angelo, 1949, Odette, 1950, Quo Vadis, (Acad. award nomination for Best Supporting Actor), 1951, Hotel Sahara, 1951, Beau Brummel, 1953-54, The Egyptian, 1954, We're No Angels, 1955, Lola Montez, 1955, The Spies, 1955, An Angel Over Brooklyn, 1955, The Sundowners, 1960, Spartacus, 1960-61 (Acad. award for Best Supporting Actor), Romanoff and Juliet, 1961, Billy Budd, 1962, Topkapi, 1963, John Goldfarb, Please Come Home, 1964, Blackbeard's Ghost, 1967, The Comedians, 1967, Hot Millions, 1968, Viva Max, 1969, Hammersmith Is Out, 1971, Big Truck and Poor Clare, 1971, One of Our Dinosaurs is Missing, 1974, Logan's Run, 1975, Treasure of Matecumba, 1975, The Last Remake of Beau Geste, 1976, The Purple Taxi, 1977, Death on the Nile, 1977, The Thief of Baghdad, 1978, Ashanti, 1979, Charlie Chan and the Curse of the Dragon Queen, 1980, Evil Under the Sun, 1981, Memed, My Hawk, 1982, Appointment With Death, 1988; dir.: (plays) Squaring the Circle, 1941, Love in Albania, 1949, No Sign of the Dove, 1952, A Fiddle at the Wedding, 1952, Romanoff and Juliet, 1956, Photo Finish, 1962, 64, Half Way Up the Tree, 1967, The Unknown Soldier and His Wife, 1968, 69, 73, (operas) L'Heure Espagnole (Ravel), Covent Garden, 1962, Gianni Schicchi (Puccini), Covent Garden, 1962, Erwartung (Schoenberg), Covent Garden, 1962, The Magic Flute (Mozart), Hamburg Opera, 1968; dir., scenery and costume designer: operas Don Giovanni (Mozart), Edinburgh Festival, 1973; dir., producer, set and costume designer: operas Don Quichotte (Massenet), Paris Opera, 1973; dir., producer: operas The Brigands (Offenbach), The German Opera, Berlin, 1978, The Marriage (Moussorgsky), Piccola Scala, 1981, Marva, The Flood (Stravinsky), Piccola Scala, 1982, Katjakabanowa (Janacek), Hamburg Opera, 1985; appeared on radio, London (BBC), Germany, Belgium, Rome, Paris, N.Y.C., Hollywood; TV appearances include In All Directions (host, producer, co-star), BBC, History of Europe, BBC, Einstein's Universe, PBS and BBC, 1979, Barefoot in Athens (Emmy award), Storm in Summer (Emmy award), The American Revolution, CBS, (George Peabody award), Omnibus (Emmy award), The Well Tempered Bach (Emmy award nomination), PBS, 1984, 13 at Dinner, CBS, 1985, Deadman's Folly, CBS, 1985, Peter Ustinov's Russia, 1985, Appointment with Death, 1987, World Challenge, occassional political commeantaries, BBC; recordings include Mock Mozart, The Grand Prix of Gibraltar, Peter and the Wolf, Nutcracker Suite, The Soldier's Tale (Stravinsky) (with Jean Cocteau), Hary Janos (Kadaly), London Symphony Orch., The Little Prince (St. Exupery) (narration), The Old Man of Lochnager; author: (plays) House of Regrets, 1942, Blow Your Own Trumpet, 1943, The Banbury Nose, 1944, The Tragedy of Good Intentions, 1945, The Indifferent Shepherd, 1948, Frenzy, 1948, The Man In the Raincoat, 1949, The Moment of Truth, 1951, The Love of Four Colonels, 1951, High Balcony, 1952, No Sign of the Dove, 1954, Romanoff and Juliet, 1956, The Empty Chair, 1956, Photo Finish, 1962, The Life in My Hands, 1964, The Unknown Soldier and His Wife, 1967, Halfway Up the Tree, 1967, Who's Who in Hell, 1974, Overhead, 1981, Beethoven's Tenth, 1983, others, (films) The Way Ahead (with Eric Ambler), 1942-43, School for Secrets, 1946, Vice Versa, 1947, Private Angelo, 1949, Romanoff and Juliet, 1961, Billy Budd (with DeWitt Bodeen), 1962-63, The Lady L, (with Ira Wallach), 1964, We Were Only Human, 1967, Hot Millions (with Ira Wallach), 1968, Memed, My Hawk, 1982, Appointment with Death, 1988 (short stories) Add a Dash of Pity, 1960, Frontiers of the Sea, 1966, (novels) The Loser, 1961, Krumnagel, 1971, (autobiography) Dear Me, 1977, My Russia, 1983, Ustinov in Russia, 1987. Served in Brit. Army, 1942-46. Comdr. Order of the Brit. Empire, 1975; recipient Disting. Service award UNICEF, 1975, Prix de la Butte, 1978, award for Best Actor Variety Club of Great Britain, 1979; rector U. Dundee, 1968, 71-73; Commandeur Des Arts et Des Lettres, 1985; elected to Acad. Fine Arts, Paris, 1988. Office: care William Morris Agy UK Ltd, 31/32 Soho Sq, London W1V 5DG, England *

UTADA, KATSUHIRO, food company executive; b. Hiroshima, Japan, Aug. 26, 1925; s. Chikatsu and Hide U.; m. Minako; children—Akihiro, Rumiko. B. Laws, Tokyo U., 1947. Dir., Ajinomoto Co., Inc., Tokyo, 1971-73, mng. dir., 1973-75, exec. mng. dir., 1975-79, exec. v.p., 1979-81, pres., 1981—; dir. Ajinomoto Gen. Foods, Ajinomoto Danone, Knorr Foods; chmn. Unami Mfrs. Assn. of Japan. Club: Tokyo Lions. Office: Ajinomoto Co Inc, 1-5-8, Kyobashi, Chuo-ku, Tokyo 104 Japan *

UTAYBA, MANI IBN SAID AL- See OTAIBA, MANA SAID AL-

UTIGER, RONALD ERNEST, engineering executive; b. Wallasey, Cheshire, Eng., May 5, 1928; s. Ernest Frederick and Kathleen (Cram) U.; married; 2 children. MA, Oxford (Eng.) U., 1950. Economist Courtaulds

Co., Can. and Eng., 1950-61; comml. and econ. analyst Brit. Aluminum Co., Ltd., 1961-62, fin. controller, 1962-65, comml. dir., 1965-68, dep. mng. dir., 1968, mng. dir., 1968-79, chmn., 1979-82; interim chmn., chief exec. officer Brit. Nat. Oil Corp., 1979; mng. dir., dep. chmn. TI Group plc, London, 1981-84, chmn., mng. dir., 1984-86, chmn., 1986—, also bd. dirs.; mem. Confed. Brit. Industry Council; bd. dirs. Brit. Alcan Aluminum plc, Gerrards Cross, Eng., Ultramar plc, London. Bd. dirs. Brit. Library. Decorated comdr. Brit. Empire. Mem. Brit. Inst. Mgmt. Office: TI Group plc, 50 Curzon St, London W1Y 7PN, England

UTLEY, JON BASIL, real estate and franchise developer, journalist; b. Moscow, Mar. 10, 1934; came to U.S., 1939, naturalized, 1952; s. Arcadi and Freda (Utley) Berdichevsky; m. Ana Maria Hijar, 1978. BS, Georgetown U., 1956; student U. Munich, 1952, Alliance Française, Paris, 1956. Mgr., Am. Internat. Underwriters, Cali, Colombia, 1959-60; editor, pub. Bogotá Bull., 1960-61; v.p. Universal Investors Services, Nassau, 1962-67; real estate developer, Washington, 1968—; mng. gen. ptnr. Kimwill Oil Assocs., Warren, Pa., 1978—; vice-chmn. fin. com. Needle in a Haystack (franchisers) 1986—; fgn. corr. Jour. of Commerce, Internat. Reports, S.Am., 1969-74; columnist Times of the Ams., 1974—, assoc. editor, 1981—; columnist Washington Inquirer, 1981—, Washington Times, 1981-82; contbg. editor Conservative Digest, 1984—; editorial adv. bd. Internat. Reports, 1981—; lectr. Accuracy in Media (treas., bd. dirs. 1985—), Freedoms Found. Valley Forge, commentator Voice of Am., 1985—; contbr. articles to Washington Post, Harvard Bus. Rev., Nat. Rev., Human Events, Miami Herald, Lincoln Rev., others. Observer Guatemalan elections Georgetown U. Ctr. for Strategic Studies, 1985, mem. exec. adv. council Conservative Caucus, trustee Ctr. for Internat. Relations, adv. com. Solidarity Endowment. Mem. Apt. and Office Bldg. Assn., Council Inter-Am. Security (bd. dirs. 1988—). Republican. Clubs: Nat. Press, Army-Navy, Council Nat. Policy. Office: 1239 Ranleigh Rd McLean VA 22101

UTOMO, RUDY TJIPTO, engineering executive, consultant; b. Kendal, Cent. Java, Indonesia, Jan. 8, 1935; m. Jeanne Susanti, Sept. 17, 1964; children: Samuel, Daniel, Timothy, Michael. BCE, Bandung Inst. Tech., 1963. Pres., dir. P.T. Wijaya Kusuma Contractors, Jakarta, Semarang, 1967—; chmn. P.T. Emindo Engring., Jakarta, Surabaya, 1970—, P.T. Furindo Kencana (Furniture), Jakarta, 1970—; dir. P.T. John Holland Construction Industry, Jakarta, 1972-86; chmn. P.T. Elang Laut Trading Industry, Jakarta, Palembang, 1972—, P.T. Tripranoto Trading, Jakarta, 1973—; chief cons. P.T. Tripranoto Sri Cons., Jakarta, 1977—; cons. P.T. Intisar Primula (Computer), Jakarta, 1985—. Krida Bhakti award First Lady of Indonesia (Taman Mini Park 1975, Mus. Taman Mini 1980, Imax Theater Keong Emas 1984). Lodges: Lions, Blind Welfare. Office: P T Wijaya Kusuma Contractors, Jl Gondangdia Lama 32, Jakarta, Pusat 10350, Indonesia

UTTERSTROM, JOHN RAYMOND, missiles systems executive; b. Vancouver, B.C., Can., Oct. 8, 1922; s. John and Gertrude Wilhemina (Hanson) U.; m. Mary Agnes Deffries, Sept. 24, 1947; children—Vicki Ann, Thomas Raymond, Mary Susan, Kathy Jo. B.S.E.E., U. Wash., 1948. With Boeing Co., Seattle, 1948-83, successively analyst, successively group leader, dept. head, chief engr., dir. engring., program mgr., 1948-80, v.p. Missile Systems div., 1980-83; pres. Boeing Mgmt. Assn. Pres. bd. dirs. Wash. State Spl. Olympics. Served to lt., USAAF, 1942-45. Recipient Ann. Honors, Aviation Week, 1961. Fellow AIAA (assoc. dir. Outstanding Aerospace Engring. award 1980, Wright Meml. Lectureship 1985, Edward Wells award 1984); mem. Sigma Xi, Tau Beta Pi. Clubs: Overlake Golf and Country (Bellevue, Wash.); Seattle Yacht. Patentee AC modulation suppressor. Deceased Dec. 1986. Home: 9830 Shoreland Dr SE Bellevue WA 98004 Office: PO Box 3999 MS 84 30 Seattle WA 98124

UTZ, JOHN PHILIP, physician, medical educator; b. Rochester, Minn., June 9, 1922; s. Gilbert C. and Marion H. (Hoy) U.; m. Dorothy Mary Griffin, July 2, 1947; children: Margaret, Christopher, Charles, Jonathan, Stephen. Student, Notre Dame U., 1940-42; B.S., Northwestern U., 1943, M.D., 1946; M.S., Georgetown U., 1949. Diplomate: Am. Bd. Internal Medicine. Intern Mass. Meml. Hosp., 1946-47; researcher Lab. Infectious Diseases, 1947-49; chief infectious disease service Lab. Clin. Investigation, Nat. Inst. Allergy and Infectious Diseases, NIH, Bethesda, Md., 1952-65; prof. medicine, chmn. div. immunology and infectious disease Med. Coll. Va., Richmond, 1965-73; instr. Sch. Medicine, Georgetown U., Washington, 1952-56; asst. prof. medicine Sch. Medicine, Georgetown U., 1956-62, assoc. prof., 1962-65, dean Sch. Medicine, 1973-78, prof., 1973—; lectr. dept. preventive medicine Howard U., 1960-73; fellow Mayo Found., Rochester, Minn., 1949-52; vis. investigator Pasteur Inst., Paris, France, 1962-63, 82; cons. U.S. Dept. State, El Salvador, 1953, Costa Rica, 1954; cons. Hoffmann-La Roche Co., Nutley, N.J., 1965-78, Clin. Center, NIH, Bethesda, 1965-85, VA, 1965—; 32d ann. Howard Lilienthal Meml. lectr., 1982. Co-author: Medical Mycology, 1st, 2d, 3d edits; Bd. editors: Jour. Infectious Diseases, Antimicrobial Agents and Chemotherapy. Pres. Nat. Found. Infectious Diseases, 1972-75; trustee Am. Type Culture Collection, 1978-86, vice chmn., 1980-81, chmn., 1981-83; mem. sci. adv. bd. Leonard Wood Found., 1980-83. Served with AUS, 1943-45. Recipient Ruth Gray award, 1973; Disting. Alumni award Northwestern U., 1977; Armine T. Wilson lectr. Wilmington, 1982. Mem. Am. Fedn. Clin. Research, A.C.P., Am. Coll. Chest Physicians (gov. D.C. chpt. 1978-84), Am. Clin. and Climatol. Assn., Soc. Exptl. Biology and Medicine, Am. Thoracic Soc., Am. Assn. Immunologists, So. Soc. Clin. Investigation, Infectious Disease Soc. Am., Am. Soc. Microbiology, Am. Coll. Clin. Pharmacology and Chem. Therapy, Internat. Soc. Human and Animal Mycology, Soc. Clin. Investigation, Assn. Am. Physicians, Med. Mycol. Soc. Am. (council, pres. 1974-75), Academie Royale des Sciences D'Outre Mer (Belgium), Academie Nat. de Medecine (France), Alpha Omega Alpha. Office: Georgetown U Hosp Washington DC 20007

UY, NORMA LUGSANAY, pediatrician; b. Gingoog City, Philippines, Feb. 8, 1952; d. Tun Sy and Sotera (Kho) Lugsanay; m. Rolando A. Uy, Oct. 30, 1976; children: Melody Gaile, Ruth Lalaine, Earl Roland. MD, Cebu Inst. Med., Cebu City, Philippines, 1975. House physician Maria Reyna Hosp., Cagayan De Oro City, Philippines, 1977-82; resident physician pediatrics No. Mindanao Regional Tng. Hosp., Cagayan De Oro City, 1983-86, med. specialist, 1987—. Mem. Inner Wheel Club, West Cagayan De Oro, 1977—. Mem. Philippine Acad. Family Physicians, Philippine Med. Women Assn., Misamis Oriental Med. Soc. (asst. treas. 1987), Ham 10 Inc., Doctors Care. Home: 31 St Nazareth Subdivision, Cagayan De Oro City, Misamis Oriental Philippines Office: Northern Mindanao Regional Tng, Hosp, Cagayan De Oro City, Misamis Oriental Philippines

UZAWA, HIROFUMI, economics educator; b. Yonago, Tottori, Japan; July 21, 1928; s. Tokio and Toshiko (Uzawa) U.; m. Hiroko Aoyoshi, Dec. 1, 1958; children: Tohru, Satoru, Marie. BS in Math., U. Tokyo, 1951; PhD in Econs., Tohoku U., Sendai, Japan, 1963. Research assoc. Stanford U., Palo Alto, Calif., 1956-59, assoc. prof. econs. and stats., 1960-64; asst. prof. econs. and math. U. Calif.-Berkeley, 1959-60; prof. econs. U. Chgo., 1964-69; prof. U. Tokyo, 1969—, dean Faculty Econs., 1980-82. Author (in Japanese): Social Costs of the Automobile (Mainichi prize 1974), 1974; Reexamination of Modern Economics, 1977; Preference, Production, and Capital; Optimality, Equilibrium, and Growth; Transformation of Modern Economics; Towards a Theory of Public Economics; editor: Studies in Linear and Non-Linear Programming, 1958. Recipient Matsunago prize Matsunaga Meml. Found., 1969, Yoshino prize Chuo-Koron Sha, 1970; named A Person of Cultural Merit, Govt. Japan, 1983; fellow Advanced Ctr. for Behavioral Scis., Palo Alto, 1960-61. Fellow Econometric Soc. (pres. 1976), Royal Econ. Soc., Am. Econ. Assn. (fgn. hon.), Am. Acad. Arts and Scis. Office: U Tokyo, Hongo 7-3-1, Bunkyo-ku, Tokyo 113, Japan

VACCARO, RAUL EDUARDO, lawyer, business executive; b. Panama City, Republic of Panama, Nov. 3, 1932; s. Carlos Eduardo and Silvia Leonor (Torres) V.; m. Maria Esperanza Mora, Apr. 18, 1953; children—Raul Eduardo, Gina, Carlos, Leopoldo, Roberto, Esperanza. B.S. and L., LaSalle Coll., Panama City, 1951, Diploma in Commerce Sci., 1949; Iur. Dr., Panama U., Panama City, 1962. Asst. mgr. First Nat. City Bank, Panama City, 1954-63; exec. v.p. Overseas Mgmt., Panama City, 1963-79; sr. ptnr. Bufete Raul E. Vaccaro, Panama City, 1975—; pres. World Mgmt. Co., Panama City, 1979—; pres. Assn. Panamena Ejecutivos, Panama City, 1973-74, Bank of Investment, Panama City, 1974-87, Pan Am. Council Mgmt., Panama City, 1975-79; v.p. World Council Mgmt., The Hague, The Netherlands, 1975-79. Contbr. articles to the Great Transition. Exec. v.p. YMCA, Panama City. Decorated Commendatore (Italy). Mem. Interam. Bar Assn., Internat. Tax Planning Assn., Instituto de Derecho Bancario, Panama Bar Assn., Am. C. of C. (diploma 1984), Panama C. of C., Panama Council Pvt. Enterprise (hon.). Roman Catholic. Clubs: Union, Golf (Panama City). Lodge: Rotary. Avocations: history; classical music. Office: World Mgmt Co of Panama Inc, Fco Boyd Ave and 51st St, PO Box 1703, Panama City 1 Republic of Panama

VACHON, LOUIS-ALBERT CARDINAL, archbishop; b. St. Frederic, Que., Can., Feb. 4, 1912; s. Napoleon and Alexandrine (Gilbert) V. D.Ph., Laval U., 1947, hon. degree, 1982; D.Th., St. Thomas Aquinas U., Rome, 1949; hon. degrees, U. Montreal, McGill and Victoria, 1964, Guelph U., 1966, Moncton U., 1967, Bishop's, Queen's and Strasbourg U., 1968, U. Notre Dame, 1971, Carleton U., 1972, Laval U., 1982. Superior, Grand Seminaire Québec Quebec, 1955-59; superior gen. Le Séminaire de Qué., 1960-77; prof. philosophy Laval U., 1941-47, prof. theology, 1949-55, vice-rector, 1959-60, rector, 1960-72; protonotary apostolic 1963-77, aux. bishop of Que., 1977-81, archbishop of Que. and primate of Can., 1981—, apptd. Cardinal with title St. Paul of the Cross, 1985; Past pres. Corp. Laval U. Med. Centre; mem. Sacred Congregation for Clergy, Vatican, 1986—; adminstrv. bd. Nat. Order of Qué., 1985—, CAn. Conf. Cath. Bishops, 1981—. Author: Espérance et Présomption, 1958, Verité et Liberte, 1962, Unité de l'universite, 1962, Apostolat de l'universitaire catholique, 1963, Memorial, 1963, Communauté universitaire, 1963, Progres de l'universite et consentement populaire, 1964, Responsabilite collective des universitaires, 1964, Les humanites aujourd'hui, 1966, Excellence et loyauté des universitaires, 1969, Pastoral Letters, 1981—. Hon. pres. La Société des etudes grecques et latines du Québec; assoc. mem. bd. Quebec Symphony Orch.; bd. govs. Laval U. Found. Decorated officier de l'Ordre de la Fidelité française, companion Order of Can., du Conseil de langue française, Ordre nat. du Qué. Fellow Royal Soc. Can.; mem. Canadian Assn. French Lang. Educators (pres. 1970-72), Assn. Univs. and Colls. Can. (pres. 1965-66), Conf. Rectors and Prins. Que. Univs. (pres. 1965-68), Internat. Assn. Univs. (dep. mem. adminstrv. bd. 1965-70), Assn. des universites partiellement ou entierement de langue française (adminstrv. bd. 1961-69), Internat. Fedn. Cath. Univs. (adminstrv. bd. 1963-70), Ordre des francophones d'Amérique. Office: 1073 Blvd St-Cyrille ouest, Sillery, Quebec, PQ Canada G1S 4R5

VACHON, MICHEL, printing company executive; b. Montreal, Que., Can., July 25, 1947; s. Charles A. and Gilberte (Lemieux) V.; m. Suzanne Larose, Aug. 1, 1970; children: Annick, Luc. BA, Sem. St-Thérese, Can., 1969; BSc in Indsl. Engring., U. Montreal, 1973. Project engr. Eastern Coated Papers, Dorval, Que., 1973-78; prodn. mgr. Delpro Corp., Dorval, 1978-79; ops. mgr. Imprimerie Chartier, St. Hyacinthe, Que., 1979-86, gen. mgr., 1986—. Mem. Order Engrs. Que. Home: 128 Thomas Chapais, Boucherville, PQ Canada J4B 5E8

VACHON, REGINALD IRENEE, engineer; b. Norfolk, Va., Jan. 29, 1937; s. Rene Albert Vachon and Regina (Galvin) Radcliffe; student U.S. Naval Acad., 1954-55; B.M.E., Auburn U., 1958, M.S., 1960; Ph.D., Okla. State U., 1963; LL.B., Jones Law Sch., 1969; m. Mary Eleanor Grigg, Jan. 16, 1960; children—Reginald Irenee, Eleanor Marie. Engr., Hayes Internat., 1958; instr., research asst. Auburn U., 1958-60, research asso., 1961, asso., prof., 1963-78; research and devel. engr. E.I. DuPont, 1960; aerospace engr., technologist NASA Marshall Space Flight Center, summers, 1964, 65; pres. Vachon Nix & Assocs., 1977—, VNA Systems Inc., 1982—; chmn. bd. Optimal Systems Internat., Inc., 1969—; chief operating officer Thacker Constrn. Co., Thacker Orgn. Inc., 1981—; admitted to Ala. bar, 1971. Served with U.S. Army, 1960-61. Registered profl. engr., Ala., Ga., Miss., La., Wis., Tex. Fellow ASME; mem. Am. Inst. Aeros. and Astronautics, Nat. Soc. Profl. Engrs., Ala. Bar Assn., Am. Bar Assn. Roman Catholic. Club: Cosmos (Washington). Contbr. articles to profl. jours.; patentee in field. Home: 1414 Epping Forest Atlanta GA 30319 Office: PO Box 467069 Atlanta GA 30346

VADIM, ROGER PLEMIANNIKOV, film director; b. Paris, Jan. 26, 1928; s. Igor and Marie-Antoinette (Ardilouze) Plemiannikov; m. Brigitte Bardot, 1952 (div.); m. Annette Stroyberg, 1955 (div.); m. Jane Fonda, 1967 (div.); m. Catherine Schneider 1975 (div.); children—Christian, Vania, Nathalie, Vanessa. Screenwriter, asst. dir. Marc Allegret, Francoeur Studios, 1947-56; reporter Paris Match, 1952-54; driver Ferrari Motor Cars, France, Italy, Eng., Germany, 1953-60; ind. film dir., screenwriter, 1956—; films include: Et Dieu crea la Femme, 1956, Sait-on-Jamais, 1957, Les Bijoutiers du Clair de Lune, 1958, Les Liasons Dangereuses, 1959, Et Mourir de Plaisir, 1960, Le Repos de Guerrier, 1963, Le Vice et la Vertu, 1963, Chateau en Suede, 1964, La Ronde, 1964, La Curee, 1966, Barbarella, 1968, Metzengerstein (Spirits of the Dead), 1969, Pretty Maids All in A Row, Si Don Juan Etait une Femme, 1973, La Jeune Fille Assassinee, 1975, La Femme Fedete, 1976, Night Games, 1981, Suprise Party, 1983; dir. (TV) Beauty & the Beast; publications: Memoirs du diable, 1975, The Hungry Angel, 1983, Bardot Deneuve Fonda, 1986. *

VAGNEUR, KATHRYN OTTO, accountant, rancher, author; b. Aurora, Ill., Feb. 23, 1946; d. Harold William and Afton (Bryner) Otto; m. Gerald Ronald Terwilliger, Oct. 19, 1968 (div. 1974); 1 dau., Jocelyn Marie; m. Clyde O. Vagneur, Aug. 24, 1979. BS in Math., U. Utah, 1968; MS in Agribus. Mgmt., Ariz. State U., 1979. CPA, Colo. Computer systems designer U. Utah Libraries, Salt Lake City, 1966-68; research asst. in computer systems Carnegie-Mellon U., 1968-70; owner, mgr. Evening at Arthurs Restaurant, Aspen, Colo., 1973-76; self-employed tax cons. Phoenix, 1977-78; with Touche Ross & Co., Colorado Springs, Colo., 1978-82; ptnr., fin. mgr. V Bar Lazy V Ranch, Peyton, Colo., 1978—; ptnr. Vagneur & Firth, Colorado Springs, 1982—; pres. The Marlwood Corp., Colorado Springs; chmn. Excellence in Bus. Seminar Series, 1987-88. Chmn. bd. dirs. Pikes Peak Ctr.; del. Rep. State Conv., 1982, White House Small Bus. Conf., 1986; bd. dirs. Springs Into Action Econ. Devel. Strategy, 1987-88; mem. Gov.'s Econ. Devel. Action Council, 1987; 4-H leader. Mem. Am. Inst. CPAs, Nat. Soc. Accts. for Coops., Colo. Soc. CPAs, Nat. Assn. Accts., Jr. League, Am. Salers Assn., Nat. Cattlemen's Assn. (featured speaker 1986 Beef Profit Conf.), Nat. Fedn. Ind. Bus., Colorado Springs C. of C. (com. chmn.), Am. Quarter Horse Assn., Beta Alpha Psi, Alpha Zeta. Author: A Financial Analysis of Cooperative Livestock Marketing, 1978; contbr. articles to mags. Home: 14725 Jones Rd Peyton CO 80831 Office: Vagneur & Firth 830 N Tejon Suite 303 Colorado Springs CO 80903

VAGO, PIERRE, architect; b. Budapest, Hungary, Aug. 30, 1910; arrived in France, 1927; s. Joseph and Ghita (Lenart) Vago; m. Nicole Cormier, Dec. 1968; children: Jean-Pierre, Florence, Michel, Catherine. Ed. Ecole Spec. Architecture, Paris, 1928-32; hon. degrees several univs. Practice architecture, Paris, 1934-85; designed many buildings in several countries; participant many internat. competitions; prof. at several univs. Writer many publs. in various countries. Served as lt. French Navy, 1939-45. Decorated chevalier Légion d'Honneur, médaille de la Resistance, officer of Arts and Lettres (France); commandeur St. Gregoire le Grand (Vatican); many others. Mem. Internat. Union Architects (hon. pres.), AIA (hon.), Paris Acad. d'Architecture, Berlin Akad. der Künste, Internat. Acad. Architecture, and others. Roman Catholic. Office: 17 Quai Voltaire, 75007 Paris France

VAGRIS, JAN JANOVICH, Soviet government official; b. Latavia, USSR, 1930. Grad., Latvian State U. Mem. Communist Party Soviet Union, 1958—; dep. chair city exec. com. People's Deps. Elgava, USSR, 1958-67; 2d sec. city com. Latvian Communist Party, Elgave and Liepaja, USSR, 1958-67; 1st sec. Liepaja city com. Latvian Communist Party, 1967-73, mem. cen. com., 1971—, head dept. adminstrv. orgns. cen. com., 1973-78, 1st sec. Riga City com., 1978—; candidate mem. Bur. Cen. Com. Latvian Communist Party, 1978-81, mem., 1981—; now dep. chmn. Presidium USSR Supreme Soviet, Moscow. Address: USSR Supreme Soviet, Office Dep Chmn, Moscow USSR *

VAGUE, JEAN MARIE, physician; b. Draguignan, France, Nov. 25, 1911; s. Victor Francois and Marie (Voiron) V.; m. Denise MArie Jouve, Sept. 3, 1936; children: Philippe, Thierry, Irene (Mrs. Claude Juhan), Maurice. Baccalaureat, Cath. Coll., Aix en Provence, France, 1928; MD, Marseilles (France) U., 1935. Intern, Hotel Dieu Conception, Marseilles, 1930, resident, 1932-39; practice medicine specializing in endocrinology, Marseilles, 1943—; assoc. prof. Marseilles U., 1946-57, prof., clinic endocrinology, 1957—. Dir. Ctr. Alimentary Hygiene and Prophylaxis Nutrition Diseases Nat. Rys. Mediterranean region, 1958—; expert chronic degenerative diseases (diabetes) WHO, 1962—. Served to lt. French Army, 1939-40. Decorated Cross Legion Honor, Acad. Palms, knight pub. health, knight mil. merit, War Cross. Mem. Endocrine Soc. U.S., Am. Diabetes Assn., Royal Soc. Medicine (London), European Assn. for Study Diabetes, Spanish, Italian, French (past pres.) socs. endocrinology, French Acad. Medicine, Spanish Acad. Medicine, French lang. Diabetes Assn. (past pres.). Author: Human Sexual Differentiation, 1953, Notions of Endocrinology, 1965, others; research includes demonstration of diabetogenic and atherogenic power of obesity with topographic distbn. fat in upper part of body, evolution of android diabetogenic obesity from 1st stage of efficacious hyperinsulinism to less efficacious hyperinsulinism and hypoinsulinism-neuro-germinal degeneration, degenerative lesions of germinal epithelium and nervous system. Home: 411 Ave du Prado E-6, 13008 Marseilles France Office: Clinique Endocrinologique, Hopital U de la Timone, Blvd Jean-Moulin, 13385 Marseilles France

VAICAITIS, RIMAS, engineering educator; b. Sakiai, Lithuania, Apr. 30, 1941; came to U.S., 1960; s. Kostas and Marcele (Vaivada) V.; m. Jone Aukse Paplenas, June 19, 1965; children: Rima, Krista. BS, U. Ill., 1966, MS, 1967, PhD, 1970. Asst. professor civil engring. Columbia U., N.Y.C., 1970-75, assoc. prof., 1975-80, dir. inst. flight structures, 1977—, prof., 1980—; research engr. NASA, Hampton, Va., 1976-77; pres. Vibraccoustics Inc., West Nyack, N.Y., 1984—. Contbr. numerous articles to profl. jours. Named Disting. Alumnus U. Ill., 1984; fellow NASA, 1975-77, NSF wind engring. studies scholar, 1977-79. Mem. AIAA, ASCE, KASA Lithuanian Fed. Credit Union (pres. 1987, bd. dirs. 1981-86). Roman Catholic. Office: Columbia U Dept Civil Engring New York NY 10027

VAIL, IRIS JENNINGS, civic worker; b. N.Y.C., July 2, 1928; d. Lawrence K. and Beatrice (Black) Jennings; grad. Miss Porters Sch., Farmington, Conn.; m. Thomas V.H. Vail, Sept. 15, 1951; children—Siri J., Thomas V.H. Jr., Lawrence J.W. Exec. com. Garden Club Cleve., 1962—; mem. women's council Western Res. Hist. Soc., 1960—; mem. jr. council Cleve. Mus. Art, 1953—; chmn. Childrens Garden Fair, 1966-75, Public Square Dinner, 1975; bd. dirs. Garden Center Greater Cleve., 1963-77; trustee Cleve. Zool. Soc., 1971—; mem. Ohio Arts Council, 1974-76, pub. sq. com. Greater Cleve. Growth Assn.; mem. endangered species com. Cleve. 200 Soc. Recipient Amy Angell Collier Montague medal Garden Club Am., 1976, Ohio Gov.'s award, 1977. Episcopalian. Clubs: Chagrin Valley Hunt, Cypress Point, Kirtland Country, Union, Colony, Women's City of Cleve. (Margaret A. Ireland award). Home: Hunting Valley Chagrin Falls OH 44022

VAILLANCOURT, DONALD CHARLES, corporate communications executive; b. Newark, Dec. 30, 1943; s. Vincent J. and Margaret Kathleen (Pasch) V.; A.A., Thomas Edison Coll., 1975, B.A., 1976; M.A., William Paterson Coll. of N.J., 1982; J.D., Pace Sch. Law, 1985; m. Dianne Daugherty, Oct. 2, 1987. Reporter, Newark Star Ledger, 1962-64; night editor UPI, Newark, 1964-65; reporter, editor Newark News, 1965-71; asst. dir. public relations Grand Union Co., Wayne, N.J., 1971-75, dir. public relations, 1975-76, dir. corp. communications and consumer affairs, 1976-80, v.p. corp. communications and consumer affairs, 1980-85, corp. v.p., officer corp. communications and consumer affairs, 1985—. Bd. dirs. Better Bus. Bur. Bergen, Passaic and Rockland Counties; chmn. family council Essex County Geriatrics Center. Recipient Honor award Food Edn., Cornell U., 1975. Mem. Food Mktg. Inst. (govt. relations com.), N.Y. State Food Mchts. Assn. (legis. relations com.), N.J. Food Council (former chmn.), N.J. C. of C. (pub. relations com.). Episcopalian. Home: 467 Chestnut St Nutley NJ 07110 Office: 201 Willowbrook Blvd Wayne NJ 07470

VAILLARD, MIGUEL MEDINA, federal official; b. San Rafael, Veracruz, Mex., Feb. 24, 1943; s. Miguel Medina Ceballos and Beda (Vaillard Romero) Vaillard de Medina; m. Zoila Fernandez de Medina, Aug. 17, 1968; children: Miguel Medina Fernandez, Maria del Carmen Medina Fernandez. B in Mechanical Engring., U. Veracruz, 1965; MS in Nuclear Engring., U. Mex., Mexico City, 1968. Research assoc. U. Mex., Mexico City, 1968-71; research assoc. on loan Nuclear Research Ctr., Karlsruhe, Fed. Republic Germany, 1969-70; nuclear engr. Commn. Fed. de Electricidad, Mexico City, 1971-81, head dept. nuclear engring., 1981-83; asst. dir. energy application Nuclear Research Inst., Mexico City, 1984; dir. gen. Nat. Nuclear Safety Commn., Mexico City, 1984—. Contbr. articles to profl. jours. Mem. Am. Nuclear Soc. (pres. Latin Am. chpt. 1987-88). Roman Catholic. Home: Villa Guerrero 22, Vergel Coyoacan, 14340 Mexico City Mexico

VAINSTEIN, GUSTAVO ALFREDO, television executive; b. Buenos Aires, Dec. 9, 1949; arrived in France, 1976; s. Carlos and Dora (Wainer) V. M in Sociology, U. Buenos Aires, 1972; M in Communication, U. Paris, 1978. Dir. local TV programming La Pampa, Argentina, 1974-75; programmer Radio Nacional, Buenos Aires, 1975-76; instr. Inst. Nat. de L'Audiovisuel, Paris, 1977-83, mgr. mktg., 1983-87; mgr. mktg., dir. programs Region Cable, Lille and Nice, France, 1987—; cons. Instituto Interamericano De Ciencias Agricolas, Argentina, 1976, UNESCO, France, 1980. Writer (radio program) Conquest of Future, 1974. Home: 138 Blvd Auriol, 75013 Paris France Office: Region Cable, 43 Mal de Laitre Tassienr, 59350 Saint Andre France

VAISEY, DAVID GEORGE, librarian; b. Tetbury, Eng., Mar. 15, 1935; s. William Thomas and Minnie (Payne) V.; m. Maureen Anne Mansell, Aug. 7, 1965; children: Katharine, Elizabeth. BA, Oxford U., Eng., 1959, MA, 1962. Archivist Staffordshire County Council, Stafford, Eng., 1960-63; from asst. librarian to sr. asst. librarian Bodleian Library, Oxford, Eng., 1963-75, keeper of western manuscripts, 1975-86, Bodley's librarian, 1986—; dep. keeper Oxford U. Archives, 1966-75; vis. prof. dept. library studies UCLA, 1985; commr. Royal Commn. Hist. Manuscripts, 1987. Served to 2d lt. Brit. Army, 1954-56. Fellow Exeter Coll., Oxford, 1975; hon. research fellow, Univ. Coll., London, 1987. Fellow Royal Hist. Soc., Soc. Antiquaries. Office: The Bodleian Library, Oxford OX1 3BG, England

VAIVODS, JULIJANS CARDINAL, Latvian ecclesiastic; b. Vorkova, Latvia, Aug. 18, 1895. Ordained priest Roman Catholic Ch., 1918. Chaplain various schs., 1918-23; vicar gen., Liepaja, Latvia, from 1944; apostolic activity curtailed by polit. situation, in exile, 1958-60; vical gen., Riga, Latvia, 1962-64; attended Vatican II, 1964; consecrated titular bishop of Macriana Maior, apostolic adminstr. diocese of Riga and diocese of Liepaja, 1964; elevated to Sacred Coll. of Cardinals, 1983. Author catechetical books and theatrical works for youth. Address: Pils Iela 2, 226047 Riga Latvia USSR *

VAJDA, MIHÁLY, philosopher, educator; b. Budapest, Hungary, Feb. 10, 1935. Diploma, Eötvös L. U., Budapest, 1958; PhD, Acad. Scis., Budapest, 1967. Research fellow Acad. Scis., 1962-73; vis. prof. U. Bremen, Fed. Republic Germany, 1977-80; vis. fellow Columbia U., N.Y.C., 1985; vis. prof. New Sch. Social Research, N.Y.C., 1987; Ashley Fellow Trent U., Pterborough, Ont., Can., 1988. Author: Bracketed Science, 1968, On Phenomenology, 1969, On Fascism, 1976, State and Socialism, 1981. Ashley fellow Peterborough, Ont., 1988. Home: Duránci u 29, H-1116 Budapest Hungary

VAJRABHAYA, THAVORN, botanist, educator; b. Bangkok, Thailand, Apr. 2, 1934; s. Sahas and Choey (Tan) V.; B.S., Cornell U., 1955, Ph.D., 1960; m. Montakan Hanutsaha, Apr. 2, 1967; children—Vajrapat, Twitee. Mem. faculty Chulalongkorn U., Bangkok, 1960—, prof. botany, 1973—, vice rector planning and devel., 1978-85, dean Grad. Sch., 1986—. Recipient Orchid Tissue Culture award Royal Hort. Soc. Thailand, 1974; Honor award for devel. tissue culture techniques in orchids, Agrl. Sci. Soc. Thailand. Mem. Internat. Assn. Plant Tissue Culture (nat. corr.), Photog. Soc. Thailand, Sigma Xi, Phi Alpha Xi. Buddhist. Author articles in field. Home: 26 Sukhumvit Rd, Soi 59, Bangkok 10110 Thailand Office: Chulalongkorn U, Phya Thai Rd, Bangkok 10500, Thailand

VAKIL, HASSAN CHARHARSOUGH, general and thoracic surgeon; b. Shiraz, Iran, Apr. 4, 1934; came to U.S., 1958; s. Mohammed Mehdi and

Robab Vakil; m. Virgie M. Tshudy, Mar. 9, 1967; children—Jeffrey Jahan, Mark Mehdi. B.S., U. Tehran, 1954, M.D., 1958. Rotating intern Jersey City Med. Ctr., 1959; resident in gen. surgery Pa. Hosp. Phila., 1960-64; resident in thoracic surgery Allegheny Gen. Hosp., Pitts., 1964-66, Glen Dale Hosp., Md., 1964-66; sr. resident in thoracic surgery Emory U. Hosps., Atlanta, 1966-67; practice medicine specializing in gen. and thoracic surgery, Media, Pa., 1967—; mem. staff Riddle Meml. Hosp., chief div. surgery, 1981—; cons. in thoracic surgery Elwyn Inst. (Pa.), Fair Acres, Pa. Fellow ACS, Am. Coll. Chest Physicians; mem. AMA, Pa. Med. Soc., Delaware County Med. Soc., Am. Cancer Soc. (dir. Delaware County unit). Republican. Club: Springhaven (Wallingford, Pa.). Office: Riddle Meml Health Care Ctr Suite 105 PO Box 603 Media PA 19063

VAKIL, SADEGH MEISSAMI, electrical engineer, educator; b. Arak, Iran, Sept. 18, 1935; came to U.S., 1955; s. Hassan Meissami and Sedigheh (Ghaffari) V.; m. Simeen Mojtabai, Aug. 20, 1966 (div. 1972); 1 child, Maryam Maureen. BEE, U. Mo., 1958, MEE, 1959; MA in Physics, U. Calif., Berkeley, 1966, postgrad., 1962-69. Research assoc. Boeing Co., Seattle, 1960-63; sr. research engr. Lockheed Corp., Sunnyvale, Calif., 1963-69; assoc. prof. Arya-Mehr U. Technology, Teheran, Iran, 1969-82; lightning, nuclear protection specialist Collins div. Rockwell Internat., Cedar Rapids, Iowa, 1984—; cons. Rockwell Internat., Los Angeles, 1970; vis. prof. U. London, 1980-81; researcher Toulouse (France) Inst. Tech., 1981-82. Contbr. articles to profl. jours. Welfare rep., organizer Arya-Mehr U. Technology, 1971-79. Mem. IEEE, Eta Kappa Nu, Tau Beta Pi.

VALA, DAYASAGAR RAO, cardiologist; b. Mahboobnagar, India, July 14, 1943; s. Gopal Rao and Vimala Devi Vala; m. Nirmala Makunoor, Oct. 31, 1965; children: Madhavi, Deepti. B of Surgery, Osmania Med. Coll., 1964; D of Cardiology, Christian Med. Coll., Madras, India, 1975. Sr. med. house officer Northamptonshire (Eng.) Hosp., 1966, St. Stephen's Hosp., London, 1966-67, Wharfdale (Eng.) Gen. Hosp., 1967-68, Dartford Dist. Hosp., Kent, Eng., 1968-69; chief resident in internal medicine Berkshire Med. Ctr., Pittsfield, Mass., 1969-71; prof. cardiology Kakatiya Med. Coll., India, 1978-79; cons. cardiologist C.D. Deshumukh Cardiovascular Research Ctr., Hyderabad, India, 1980—. Contbr. articles to profl. jours. Fellow Royal Coll. Physicians Edinburgh, Royal Coll. Physicians and Surgeons Can.; mem. Cardiol. Soc. India (sec. Hyderabad chpt. 1983-86), N.Y. Acad. Scis., Share Med. Care. Home: House #12-13-374, St #18, Tarnaka, Hyderabad 500017, India Office: CD Deshmukh Research Ctr, Vidyanagar, Hyderabad India

VALANCE, MARSHA JEANNE, library director, story teller; b. Evanston, Ill., Aug. 2, 1946; d. Edward James Jr. and Jeanne Lois (Skinner) Leonard; m. William George Valance, Dec. 27, 1966 (div. 1976); 1 child, Marguerite Jeanne. Student Northwestern U., 1964-66; AB, UCLA, 1968; MLS, U. R.I., 1973. Children's librarian trainee N.Y. Pub. Library, N.Y.C., 1968-69; reference librarian Action Meml. Pub. Library (Mass.), 1969-70; mgr. The Footnote, Cedar Rapids, Iowa, 1976-78; assoc. editor William C. Brown, Dubuque, Iowa, 1978-79; library dir. Dubuque County Library, Dubuque, 1979-81; library dir. G.B. Dedrick Pub. Library, Geneseo, Ill., 1981-84; library dir. Grand Rapids (Minn.) Pub. Library, 1984—; workshop coordinator, participant, sect. chmn. profl. confs. Author: (with others) Mystery, Value and Awareness, 1979; Pluralism, Similarities and Contrast, 1979; contbr. articles to publs. Troop leader Mississippi Valley Council Girl Scouts U.S.A., Cedar Rapids, 1976-78; mem. liturgy com. St. Malachy's Roman Cath. Ch., Geneseo, 1983; com. judging clinic 4-H, Moline, Ill., 1984; trustee KAXE No. Community Radio, 1986—, ICTV, 1988-90; sec. Grand Rapids Community Services Council, 1986; coach Itasca County 4-H Horse Bowl Team, 1987; organizer Grand Rapids Storyfest, 1987; program chmn. Spotlight on Books Conf., 1989—. Iowa Humanities Bd. grantee, 1981, Minn. Library Found. grantee, 1985, 86, 87, Blandin Found. grantee, 1986, Arrowhead Regional Arts Council grantee, 1987. Mem. ALA, Minn. Library Assn., Iowa Libraries of Medium Size (sec. 1981), Northlands Storytelling Network (bd. dirs. 1988-90), Nat. Assn. Preservation and Perpetuation Storytelling, NCIC, Alliance Info. and Referral Services, DAR (constn. chmn. 1983-84), Am. Morgan Horse Assn., Mississippi Valley Morgan Horse Club, North Cen. Morgan Assn., Alpha Gamma Delta. Club: Geneseo Jr. Women's (internat. chmn. 1983-84). Home: 1405 7th Ave SE Grand Rapids MN 55744-4083 Office: 21 NE 5th St Grand Rapids MN 55744

VALAVANIS, MANOLIS, insurance company executive; b. Athens, Greece, Apr. 22, 1952; s. Aristidis and Vassiliki (Anagnostopoulou) V.; m. Effie Neri, Nov. 30, 1981; children: Aristidis, Vassilis. ScB magna cum laude, Brown U., 1975; masters degree, Yale U., 1975-76. Group actuarial asst. Travelers Ins. Co., Hartford, Conn., 1976-80; regional supr. Am. Life Ins. Co., Wilmington, Del., 1980-83; mng. dir. Continental Hellas Ins. Co., Athens, Greece, 1983—. Mem. Soc. Actuaries, Am. Acad. Actuaries. Home: 34 Geranon Str, 11364 Athens Greece Office: Continental Hellas Ins Co, 253 Syngrou Ave, 17122 Athens Greece

VALDES, MANUEL FERNANDO, lawyer; b. Santiago, Chile, Nov. 27, 1933; s. Manuel C. and Rosa (Wood) V.; m. Ximena Cox, Dec. 18, 1955; children: Manuel Francisco, Jose Ignacio, Ana Luisa, Maria Magdalena, Ximena Carolina. LLB, U. Chile, 1954. Founder 1st Farmers Coop., Santa Cruz, Chile, 1958-68; sole practice law Santa Cruz, 1962-70; ptnr. Guzman and Valdes, Santiago, 1987—; mem. Farmers Arbitration Ct., Santa Cruz, 1965-70; pres. 1st Confedn. Farmers Union, Santiago, 1967-73, Confedn. Prodn. and Commerce, 1975-81; intamer Chile chpt. Council Commerce and Prodn., 1978—, Pacific Basin Econ. counicl, 1979—; mem. Exports Corp., 1977-83; bd. dirs. Banco de Crédito e Inversiones, 1980—; chmn. bd. dirs. Industria Maquinaria Agricola Coloso Inc., Santiago, 1987—. Decorated Ordem Rio Branco, Brazil, 1980. Mem. Nat. Farmers Assn. (pres. 1983-87). Roman Catholic. Club: Union (Santiago). Home: Lota 2845 Providencia, Santiago 9, Chile Office: Agustinas 785, Suite 552, Santiage 1, Chile

VALDONIO, GIULIO CESARE, aircraft company executive; b. Milan, Italy, Dec. 3, 1937; s. Camillo and Francesca (Bedoni) V.; m. Bianca Bellini, Apr. 20, 1970; children: Francesca, Marco. DAero, Engring. Poly., Milan, 1960; MA in Aero Engring., U. Mich., 1962. Jr. structural engr. Aermacchi SPA, Varese, Italy, 1961, systems engr., 1963-65, chief systems engr., 1965-67, chief of preliminary design, 1967-77, dir. advanced studies, 1977-81, gen. mgr., 1981—; engr. instr. U. Mich., Ann Arbor, 1963. Fellow Royal Aero. Soc. Office: Aermacchi SPA, Via Sanvito, 80 21100 Varese Italy

VALEANI, BERNARD MARIE, real estate developer; b. Hanoi, French Indochina, Dec. 4, 1945; s. Charles Christian and Simone Greó de Boyrie V.; m. Claudia Bové, July 2, 1970; Celia, Charles-Edouard. DS in Law, Paris U., 1969; DS in Bus. Adminstrn., Dauphine U., Paris, 1970. Jr. exec. CGIB, Paris, 1970-72; mgr. Midland Bank, Paris, 1972-82; gen. mgr. Architecture Renovation Constrn., Paris, 1982—. Club: Maxim's Bus. Home: 32 Ave Charles Floquet, 75007 Paris France Office: ARC, 108 Rue de Richelieu, 75002 Paris France

VALENTINE, GEORGE DOUGLAS, ambassador; b. Calgary, Alta., Can., Feb. 5, 1932; s. John Cuthbert and Evelyn Mary (LaMarche) V.; married, July 27, 1963; children: Deborah, Christopher, Mark. BA, U. British Columbia, Vancouver, 1953. Vice consul Canadian Consulate, Dusseldorf, Fed. Republic Germany, 1963-67; comml. counselor Canadian Embassy, Bogota, Columbia, 1967-69, ambassador, 1980-83; consul Canadian Consulate, Rio de Janiero, 1969-73; dir. Fgn. Investment Rev. Agy., Ottawa, Can., 1972-75; comml. counselor Canadian Embassy, Tehran, Iran, 1975-78; consul gen. Canadian Consulate Gen., Dallas, 1978-80; ambassador to Columbia, 1980-83; dir. gen. Dept. External Affairs, Ottawa, 1983-85; ambassador Canadian Embassy, Riyadh, Saudi Arabia, 1985—. Office: Embassy of Canada, POB 94321, Riyadh 11693, Saudi Arabia

VALENTINE, HERMAN EDWARD, computer company executive; b. Norfolk, Va., June 26, 1937; s. Frank and Alice Mae (Heigh) V.; m. Dorothy Jones, Nov. 27, 1958; children: Herman Edward, Bryce Thomas. B.S. in Bus. Adminstrn., Norfolk State Coll., 1967; grad. student, Am. U., 1968, Coll. William and Mary. Asst. bus. mgr. Grad. Sch., Dept. Agr., 1967, exec. officer, 1967-68; bus. mgr. Norfolk State Coll., 1968; pres. Systems Mgmt. Am. Corp., Norfolk, 1969—, now also chmn.; star ambassador City of Norfolk, Va.; bd. dirs. Greater Norfolk Corp, Operation Smile; sponsor trustee U. of Va. Darden Sch. of Bus.; president's council, Old Dominion U.; adv. bd. Tidewater Vets. Meml. Project.; bd. dirs. Greater Norfolk Corp. Star ambassador City Norfolk; adv. council of the Va. Stage Co.; pres. council Am. Inst. Mgmt.; bd. dirs. 70001 Tng. & Employment Inst., Cooperating Hampton Rds. Orgn. for Minorities in Engring., Operation Smile; sponsor trustee U. Va. Darden Sch. Bus.; pres.'s council Old Dominion U.; adv. bd. Tidewater Vets. Meml. Project. Named Entrepreneur of Yr. Dept. of Commerce Minority Bus. Devel. Agy.; recipient Presdl. Citation, 1984, Cert. of Merit City of Chg., 1985, Presdl. Citation Nat. Assn. Equal Opportunity in Higher Edn., 1981, McDonald's Hampton Roads Black Achievement award United Negro Coll. Fund., 1986, Disting. Service award Va. State Conf. NAACP, 1985, Citizen of Yr. award William A. Hunton YMCA, 1986, Nat. Bus. Leadership award Tidewater Minority Purchasing Council, 1984, Meritorious Service award United Negro Coll. Fund., 1982, Outstanding Community Service award Va. State Conf. NAACP, 1984, Delicados, Inc. award, 1986, Supplier of Yr. award Nat. Minority Supplier Devel. Council, 1987, Va. Outstanding Businessperson of Yr. award Black Pres.'s Roundtable Assn., 1987, Colgate Whitehead Darden award, U. Va., 1987, cert. of recognition Lt. Gov. of the Commonwealth of Va., 1987. Mem. Am. Mgmt. Assn., Tidewater Regional Polit. Assn. (founder, chmn.), Navy League, Armed Forced Communication and Electronics Assn.

VALENTINE, JEFFREY, association executive; b. Phila., Sept. 28, 1940; s. Joshua Morton and Olga W. (Wilson) V.; 1 child, Karen. B.S., St. Louis U., 1964, postgrad., 1966-68. Programmer, systems analyst Honeywell Electronic Data Processing, Wellesley Hills, Mass., 1964-66; account exec. Semiconductor div. Tex. Instruments, New Eng., 1966-68; New Eng. sales exec., Mid-Atlantic regional mgr. Electronic Instrumentation Co., 1968-70; pres. Nat. Free Lance Photographers Assn., Doylestown, Pa., 1970—; pres., dir. Towne Print & Copy Ctrs. Inc.; exec. dir. Nat. Paralegal Assn., 1982—; pres. Paralegal Assocs., Inc., 1982—; pres., chief operating officer Doylestown Parking Corp., 1977-88; dir. Law Enforcement Supply. Co., Doylestown, Valtronics Supply Co., Towne Print & Copy Ctrs. Inc., Doylestown, Doylestown Stationery and Office Supply, Energy Mktg. Assocs. Inc., Doylestown; pres. Paralegal Pub. Corp., 1983; pub. Paralegal Jour.; pres. Valco Enterprises Inc., 1986—, Paralegal Employment Systems, Inc., 1988. Author: Photographers Bookkeeping System, 1973, rev., 1978, Photographers Pricing Guides, 1971, 1972, 74, 75, Available Markets Director's-4 Vols, 1973-77, National Model Sources Directory, Annual Paralegal Salary & Employment Survey, 1985, 86-88; also articles, bulletins, pamphlets. Exec. sec. Doylestown Bus. Assn., 1972-78, pres., 1979, 83, v.p., 1981. Mem. London Coll. Applied Scis., Nat. Fedn. Paralegal Assns., Photog. Industry Council, Nat. Assn. Legal Assts., Am. Soc Assn. Execs., Soc. Assn. Mgrs., Nat. Fedn. Ind. Business (mem. action council com.), Nat. Parking Assn., Nat. Office Products Assn., Graphic Arts Assn. Delaware Valley, Nat. Assn. Federally Licensed Firearms Dealers, Nat. Compostition Assn., Internat. Platform Assn. Office: 10 S Pine St PO Box 693 Doylestown PA 18901

VALENTINE, STEPHEN KENNETH, JR., lawyer, broadcasting commentator; b. Detroit, Apr. 27, 1940; s. Stephen K. and Bernice M. (Falger) V.; m. Frances M. Craig, Oct. 20, 1967; children—Joanna, Victoria, Veronica. B.S., U. Detroit, 1962, J.D. (gen. scholar), 1966. Bar: Mich. 1967, Fla. 1970, U.S. Dist. Ct. (ea. dist.) Mich. 1967, U.S. Ct. Appeals (6th cir.) 1969, U.S. Supreme Ct. 1971. Appraiser, adminstrv. asst. Detroit Bd. Assessors, 1962-66; assoc. Colombo, Vermuelen & Colombo, Detroit, 1966-68; mem. Stephen K. Valentine, Jr. and Assocs., P.C., West Bloomfield, Mich., 1968—; mem. ct. rule revision com. Mich. Supreme Ct., 1975-80; mediator Oakland County Circuit Ct., 1979—; claims referee Oakland County Probate Ct., 1979—; participant Legal Forum, Sta. WOMC; commentator Sta. WJR; U.S. govt. appeal agt., 1970-71; seminar lectr. Fed. Bar Assn., 1978-79. Mem. pres.'s adv. council U. Detroit, 1961-62. Mem. ABA (litigation sect. bus. torts com.). Mich. Bar Assn. (rep. assembly 1973-76, 76-79, chmn. dist. ct. com. 1969-77, vice chmn. trial ct. com. 1979-83), State Bar Mich. (civil procedures com. 1971-78, econs. com. 1972-74, profl. liability ins. com. 1978-81), Fla. Bar Assn., Detroit Bar Assn. (pub. adv. com. 1979—), Nat. Advocates Soc., Am. Trial Lawyers Assn., Mich. Trial Lawyers Assn., Comml. Law League Am., Am. Arbitration Assn. (panel arbitrators 1969—). Roman Catholic. Home: 5850 Middlebelt Rd West Bloomfield MI 48322 Office: Valentine & Assocs PC 5767 W Maple Rd Suite 100 West Bloomfield MI 48322

VALENTINO (VALENTINO GARAVANI), fashion designer; b. Milan, Italy, May 11, 1932. Student, Academia Dell'Arte, Paris. Worked with Designer Jean Desses; and Guy Laroche; owner, operator Valentino Piu, Milan and Rome, 1960—, Valentino Boutique Inc., N.Y.C., 1966—. Office: 24 via Gregoriana, Rome Italy also: 823 Madison Ave New York NY 10021 *

VALETTE, JEAN PAUL, author; b. Paris, Oct. 21, 1937; s. Jean and Monique (Lavie) V.; m. Rebecca M. Valette, Aug. 6, 1959; children—Jean-Michael, Nathalie, Pierre. Baccalaureate, U. Poitiers (France), 1954. Diplome, Hautes Etudes Commerciales de Paris, 1959; Ph.D., U. Colo., 1962. Acct., Arthur Andersen, 1964-66; research economist Charles River Assocs., 1966-69. Author: Lisons, 1968; The Role of Transportation in Regional Economic Development, 1971; France, A Cultural Review Grammar, 1973; C'est comme ca, 1978, 86; Spanish for Mastery, 1980, 84, 88; Con. Mucho Gusto, 1980, 1984, 88; French for Mastery, 1975, 81, 88; Contacts: langue et culture francaises, 1976, 1981; French Fluency, 1985; Rencontres, 1985; Situaciones, 1988. Mem. Am. Assn. Tchrs. French, Am. Assn. Tchrs. Spanish and Portuguese. Address: 16 Mt Alvernia Rd Chestnut Hill MA 02167

VALIATHAN, MARTHANDA VARMA SANKARAN, cardiac surgeon; b. Mavelikara, Kerala, India, May 24, 1934; s. Marthanda Varma and Janaki Amma Valiathan; M.B., B.S., Med. Coll. Trivandrum, 1956; M.Surgery, U. Liverpool (Eng.), 1960; m. Ashima Sethi, Nov. 15, 1964; children—Manna, Manish. Resident in gen. surgery Greenwich Dist. Hosp., London, 1958, United Liverpool Hosp., 1959, Jefferson Med. Coll. Hosp., Phila., 1961; sr. lectr. surgery Postgrad. Inst., Chandigarth, India, 1963; resident in cardiovascular surgery Johns Hopkins Hosp., 1965, George Washington U. Hosp., 1966, Georgetown U. Hosp., 1967; instr. surgery Georgetown U. Hosp., 1969; cons. cardiac surgery Safdarjung Hosp., New Delhi, 1972; prof. cardiac surgery, dir. Sree Chitra Tirunal Inst. Med. Scis. and Tech., Trivandrum, 1974—; examiner cardiothoracic surgery Univs. Madras, Bombay and Calcutta, India; mem. panel experts WHO. Recipient Sci. and Tech. prize Govt. of Kerala, India, 1980, Padma Sri Pres. of India, Om Prakash Bhasin Nat. award Govt. of India, Pres. India Birla Nat. award. Fellow Royal Coll. Surgeons Eng., Royal Coll. Surgeons Edinburgh, Royal Coll. Phys. and Surg. Can., Am. Coll. Cardiology, Indian Acad. Scis., Nat. Acad. Med. Scis.; mem. Assn. Cardiovascular Surgeons India, Cardiol. Soc. India, Inst. Med. Sci. (governing council), Soc. Thoracic Surgeons, Assn. Thoracic and Cardiovascular Surgeons (corr.). Hindu. Home: 6 Katakompally Housing Scheme, Pulayanar Kotta, Trivandrum 695011, India Office: Sree Chitra Tirunal, Inst Med Scis and Tech, Trivandrum 695 011, India

VALICANGIL, OMER, pharmaceutical company executive; b. Istanbul, Turkey, Aug. 9, 1952; s. Sitki and Melahat (Ozulu) V.; m. Alison Jane Standley, Aug. 11, 1984. BS in Chem. Engring., Bosphorus U., 1975; MS in Biochem. Engring., U. Wales, 1977. Research asst. U. Coll. Swansea, U.K., 1977-80; head chem. production CIBA-GEIGY Pharms., Istanbul, 1982-84, mktg. projects mgr., 1985; dep. mgr. CIBA-GEIGY Pharms., SE Asia, Basle, Switzerland, 1986-87; head quality control Hoffman-LayRoche, Istanbul, 1988—; cons. in loss prevention. Co-author: Occupational Health and Safety, 1987; contbr. articles to profl. jours. Sci. Research Council U.K. grantee, 1977, 79. Mem. Am. Inst. Chem. Engrs., Inst. Chem. Engrs. U.K. (chartered engr.). Moslem. Club: Levent Tennis. Lodge: Rotary. Home: Levazim Sb Sitesi A-1 Blok 46, 80600 Istanbul Turkey Office: Roche Mustahzarlari AS, PK 16 Levent, 80622 Istanbul Turkey

VALIMAHOMED, SALIM AKBARALI, investment banker; b. Uganda, Nov. 25, 1948; came to U.S., 1967; s. Akbarali V. and Roshankhanoo (Jamal-Merali) Vaiya; m. Maurisse Taylor Gray, Apr. 24, 1982; 1 child, Zahra. BSCE, U. R.I., 1971; MHA, Duke U., 1974; MS in Mgmt., Stanford U., 1978. Assoc. Booz Allen & Hamilton, N.Y.C., 1974-79; v.p., ptnr. Kidder, Peabody & Co., N.Y.C., 1980-86; pres. Longview Inc., N.Y.C., 1986—. Prin. investigator NIH report: Supply/Demand for Hemophilia Products in U.S., 1978. Chmn. Nat. Com. Aga Khan Found. U.S., Washington, 1984-87. Mem. Internat. Hosp. Fedn., Asia Soc., Inst. Stategic Planning. Club: Union League (N.Y.C.). Home: 2 Heywood Rd Pelham Manor NY 10803 Office: Longview Inc 157 E 57th St New York NY 10022

VALIN, REGINALD PIERRE, communications executive; b. London, Mar. 8, 1938; s. Pierre Louis and Molly Doreen (Butler) V.; m. Brigitte Karin Leister; 1 child, Claire. Student, Emanuel Sch., 1949-56. Dir. Charles Barker City, London, 1971-73, mng. dir., 1973-76, chief exec., 1976-79; chmn., chief exec. officer Valin Pollen Ltd., London, 1979-84, Valin Pollen Internat., London, 1984-87, The VPI Group, London, 1987—; bd. dirs. Bus. in the Community, London, 1985—; chmn. UPI N.Am., Inc. Mem. Ch. of Eng. Office: The VPI Group, 32 Grosvenor Gardens, London SW1, England

VALINET, STANLEY S., entrepreneur; b. Indpls., Nov. 13, 1916; s. Arthur R. and Mary (Burnstein) V.; children: Greg, Steve, Pam. BA, Ind. U., 1937, postgrad., 1937-39. Pres., chief exec. officer VD Corp., Indpls., Tru-Lite Research Labs, Indpls., NRC Corp., Indpls. Contbr. articles to profl. jours. Mem. Profl. Farmers Am. Club: Columbia Athletic. Office: NRC Corp Investments div PO Box 857 Carmel IN 46032

VALK, ROBERT EARL, corporate executive; b. Muskegon, Mich., Aug. 21, 1914; s. Allen and Lulu (Schuler) V.; m. Ann Parker, August 9, 1941 (div. July 1959); children: James A., Sara C.; m. Alice Melick, Dec. 29, 1960; children: Marie, Susan. B.S. in Mech. Engring, U. Mich., 1938. With Nat. Supply Co., 1938-55; plant mgr. Nat. Supply Co., Houston, 1945-48; works mgr. Nat. Supply Co., Toledo, Houston and Gainesville, Tex., 1949-55; asst. v.p. prodn. Electric Auto-Life Co., Toledo, 1956; v.p., group exec. gen. products Electric Auto-Life Co., 1956-60; gen. mgr. mfg. automotive div. Essex Internat., Inc., 1960-66, v.p. corp., gen. mgr. automotive div., 1966-74; pres. ITT Automotive Elec. Products Div., 1974-80; v.p. ITT N.Am. Automotive Ops. Worldwide, 1980-86; chmn. Asset Timing Corp., 1986—; dir. Woodstream Corp., Lititz, Pa., Digital Appliance Controls, Inc., Hoffman Estates, Ill.; trustee Henry Ford Health Care Corp., Detroit. Trustee Cottage Hosp., Grosse Pointe; chmn. adv. bd. St. Luke's Episcopal Ch. Home; bd. dirs. Inst. Advanced Pastoral Studies. Mem. Am. Soc. Naval Engrs., Soc. Automotive Engrs., Am. Ordnance Assn., Am. Mgmt. Assn., Air Force Assn., Am. Mfrs. Assn., Wire Assn., Nat. Elec. Mfrs. Assn., Engring. Soc. Detroit. Republican. Episcopalian. Clubs: Country (Detroit), Yondotega, Economics (Detroit); Grosse Pointe, Bay View Yacht; Little Harbor (Harbor Springs, Mich.). Home: 80 Renaud Rd Grosse Pointe Shores MI 48236 Office: 500 Stephenson Hwy Suite 405 Troy MI 48083

VALLBONA, RIMA-GRETEL ROTHE, Spanish educator, writer; b. San José, Costa Rica, Mar. 15, 1931; d. Ferdinand Hermann and Emilia (Strassburger) Rothe; BA/BS, Colegio Superior de Señoritas, San José, 1948; diploma U. Paris, 1953; diploma in Spanish Philology, U. Salamanca, Spain, 1954; MA, U. Costa Rica, 1962; D in Modern Langs., Middlebury Coll., 1981; m. Carlos Vallbona, Dec. 26, 1956; children: Rima-Nuri, Carlos-Fernando, María-Teresa, María-Luisa. Tchr., Liceo J.J. Vargas Calvo, Costa Rica, 1955-56; faculty U. St. Thomas, Houston, 1964—, prof. Spanish, 1978—, head dept. Spanish, 1966-71, chmn. dept. modern fgn. lang., 1978-80; vis. prof. U. Houston, 1975-76, Rice U., 1980-81, U. St. Thomas, Argentina, summer 1972, Rice U. program in Spain, summer 1974. Mem. scholarship com. Inst. Hispanic Culture, 1978-79, 88, chmn., 1979, bd. dirs., 1974-76, 88—, chmn. cultural activities, 1979, 80, 85, 88; bd. dirs. Houston Pub. Library, 1984-86. Recipient Aquileo J. Echeverria Novel prize, 1968; Agripina Montes del Valle Novel prize, 1978; Jorge Luis Borges Short Story prize, Argentina, 1977; lit. award SW Conf. Latin Am. Studies, 1982; Constantin Found. grantee for research U. St. Thomas, 1981; Ancora lit. award, Costa Rica, 1984. Mem. MLA, Am. Assn. Tchrs. Spanish and Portuguese, Houston Area Tchrs. of Fgn. Langs., S. Cen. MLA, SW conf. Orgn. Latin Am. Studies, Latin Am. Studies Assn., Inst. Internat. de Lit. Iberoam., Latin Am. Writers Assn. of Costa Rica, Inst. Hispanic Culture of Houston, Casa Argentina de Houston, Inst. Lit. y Cultural Hispanico, Phi Sigma Iota, Sigma Delta Pi (hon.). Roman Catholic. Club: Nat. Writers. Author: Noche en Vela, 1968, Yoland Oreamuno, 1972, La Obra en Prosa de Eunice Odio, 1981, Baraja de Soledades, Las Sombras que Perseguimos, 1983; (short stories) Polvo de Camino, 1971, La Salamandra Rosada, 1979, Mujeres y Agonias, 1982, Cosecha de Pecadores, 1988; mem. editorial bd. Letras Femeninas, U.S.; co-dir. Foro Literario, Uruguay, Alba de América; contbr. numerous articles and short stories to lit. mags. Home: 3002 Ann Arbor St Houston TX 77063 Office: 3812 Montrose Blvd Houston TX 77006

VALLÉE, PIERRE-GABRIEL, electronics executive; b. Saint-Etienne, Loire, France, Nov. 16, 1941; s. Raymond and Solange (Broch) V.; m. Feliciana (Garayar-Escudero); 1 child, Isabelle. MS in Engring., Ecole Nat. Supreme Arts et Metiers, Paris, 1964; MBA in Econs., U. Paris, 1966. Engr. Pont-A-Mousson, Nancy, France, 1968-72; gen. counsel Socea-Balency, Rueil-Malmaison, France, 1972-74; controller Thomson Visualisation Traitement, Paris, 1975-76; v.p. fin. and legal Co. Internat. Info., Paris, 1977-78; exec. officer Thomson-CSF, Paris, 1979-81; v.p. fin. and adminstrn. Thomson-CGR, Paris, 1983—; v.p. Gen. Electric CGR, Paris, 1988—; bd. dirs. Sopha Med., Paris, 1985—. Contbr. articles to profl. jours. Mem. Nat. Acctg. Assn. Home: 29, Rue de la Cote, 92500 Rueil-Malmaison France Office: Thomson-CGR, 33, Ave Du Maine-Tour MM, 75015 Paris France

VALLENILLA, ALFREDO ANTONIO, oil company executive; b. Caracas, Venezuela, Sept. 28, 1956; s. Alfredo and Carmen Cecilia (Fernandez) V.; m. Martha Rodriguez, Mar. 17, 1984; children: Vanessa, Viviana. Diploma in Engring., U. Católica, Caracas, 1979; MS, Stanford U., 1982. Cons. Cottin, Doth and Assocs., Caracas, 1982-84; mgr. ops. Paiven S.A., Caracas, 1984-86, gen. mgr., 1986—; bd. dirs. Blocker de Venezuela, Caracas; cons. Sercontec S.A., Caracas, 1985—; comml. adviser HydroPower Industries, Caracas, 1986—. Mem. Colegio de Ingenieros de Venezuela, Stanford U. Alumni Assn. Venezuela. Roman Catholic. Office: Paiven SA, Apartado 66297, Caracas 1061A, Venezuela

VALLERY, JANET ALANE, industrial hygienist; b. Lincoln, Nebr., Apr. 4, 1948; d. Gerald William and Lois Florence (Robertson) V.; B.S., U. Nebr., Lincoln, 1970; diploma Bryan Meml. Sch. Med. Tech., Lincoln, 1971. Med. technologist Lincoln Gen. Hosp., 1971-72; congressional sec., 1973; lab. scientist Nebr. Dept. Health, 1973-79; sr. safety indsl. hygienist Nebr. Dept. Labor, 1979-85; indsl. hygienist U.S. Dept. Labor OSHA, 1985—; cons. in field. Mem. Am. Conf. Govt. Indsl. Hygienists, Am. Soc. Clin. Pathologists (assoc.), Arabian Horse Assn. Nebr., Nebr. Dressage Assn., Am. Indsl. Hygiene Assn., Am. Legion Aux. Republican. Methodist. Home: 4900 S 30th St Lincoln NE 68516 Office: 6910 Pacific St Rm 100 Omaha NE 68106

VAMBERY, MARIE JOSEPHE, drug company executive, consultant; b. Oran, Algeria, Aug. 3, 1950; d. Jean and Santina (Linteris) Radenac; m. Robert George Vambery, Mar. 5, 1976. Lic. in English, U. Paris, 1969; M.B.A., Ecole de Haut Enseignement Commercial, Paris, 1971, Columbia U., 1973. Brand supr. Procter & Gamble Co., Paris, 1973-76; product mgr. L'Oreal Co., N.Y.C., 1976-77; sr. product mgr. Block Drug Co., Inc., Jersey City, 1979-81, dir. new products, 1981-87, product group mgr., 1987—; sr. product mgr. CPC Internat. Best Foods, Englewood Cliffs, N.J., 1979-81. Author: Marketing in the French Tire Industry, 1971. Fulbright Found. scholar, 1971; Johnson Wax Found. fellow, 1971, French Govt. Fgn. Office fellow, 1972. Mem. Am. Mgmt. Assn., Am. Mktg. Assn. Club: Essex County Country (West Orange, N.J.). Home: Wildwood Ave Llewelyn Park West Orange NJ 07052 Office: Block Drug Co Inc 257 Cornelison Ave Jersey City NJ 07302

VAN, GEORGE PAUL, healthcare company executive; b. Isle Maligne, Que., Can., Feb. 12, 1940; s. Raymond Murdoch and Germaine Marie (Brassard) V.; B.A., McGill U., 1961; D.H.A., U. Toronto, 1963; m. Janine Marie Irene Therese Yvette Boily, Sept. 15, 1962; children—John, Robert, Caroline. Sr. cons. Agnew Peckham and Assos., Toronto, Ont., Can., 1963-65; chief exec. officer, exec. dir. Misericordia Corp., Edmonton, Alta., Can., 1965-68; chief operating officer, exec. v.p. Texpack, Ltd., Brantford, Ont., 1968-70, also bd. dirs.; group v.p. Will Ross, Inc., Milw., 1970-73; exec. v.p. Nortek, Inc., Cranston, R.I., 1973-77, also bd. dirs.; pres., chief operating officer Hosp. Affiliates Internat. Inc. subs. INA Corp., Nashville, 1977-80, also bd. dirs.; chmn., pres., chief exec. officer Health Group Inc., Nashville, 1980-84; chmn., chief exec. officer Columbia Corp. (formerly Franklin Corp.), Nashville, 1984-88, hon. chmn., 1988—. Bd. dirs. Tulane U. Med. Ctr., 1977-80, Nashville Inst. for the Arts, 1987-88, Nashville Symphony, 1987-88; bd. overseers U. Pa. Sch. of Nursing, 1979-82, 84-88, assoc. trustee U. Pa., 1979-82, 84-88. Recipient several scholarships. Mem. Am. Coll. Healthcare Adminstrs., Am. Coll. Healthcare Execs., Am. Hosp. Assn. Clubs: Westside, Griffith Island, Cumberland, Nashville City. Contbr. articles to profl. jours. Home: 1608 Chickering Rd Nashville TN 37215

VAN AAL, JAN L., advertising executive; b. Alicante, Spain, Mar. 4, 1935; arrived in France, 1951; s. Henri E.M. and Maria del Carmen (Pomares) Van A.; m. Monique S. Besnard, Mar. 30, 1965; children: Catherine, Francois, Valerie, Stephanie. Degree in internat. affairs, Inst. D'Etudes Politiques, Paris, 1959; MS in Mgmt., Northwestern U., Evanston, Ill., 1984. Asst. account exec. Dorland, Paris, 1959-61; account exec. Darland, Paris, 1961-65; account supr. Dorland and Grey, Paris, 1965-69, supr. mgmt., mng. dir., 1969-73; pres., chief exec. officer Grey Paris, 1977—, Grey Communication France, Paris, 1985—. Author: Connivence, 1982, Au Clair de La Pub, 1986. Mem. Assn. Advt. Agys. (bd. dirs. 1978-84, v.p. 1980-84, pres. 1984-85), Fedn. Nationale Publicite (pres. 1984-85). Office: Grey Communication France, 23 Rue Linois, 75015 Paris France

VAN ALSTYNE, VANCE BROWNELL, arbitration management consultant; b. Rochester, N.Y., Feb. 3, 1924; s. Guy Brownell and Jessie Cary Van A.; B.A., U. Rochester, 1948; LL.B., Blackstone Coll. Law, 1964; m. Jane Kotary, Aug. 12, 1950; children—Cary B., Stacey E. Research asst. Gilbert Assos., Inc., N.Y.C., 1950-56; corp. sec., v.p., dir. R.C. Simpson & Staff, Inc., Newark and Ridgewood, N.J., 1956-74, pres., dir. R.C. Simpson, Inc., Ridgewood, 1975—. Served to 2d lt. USAF, 1943-45. Decorated Air medal. Mem. Am. Mgmt. Assn., Indsl. Relations Research Assn., Am. Arbitration Assn., Internat., Swiss-Icelandic Salmon Assns. Home: 175 Brush Hill Rd Kinnelon NJ 07405 Office: United Jersey Bank Bldg PO Box 567 Ridgewood NJ 07451

VAN ALSTYNE, W. SCOTT, JR., lawyer, educator; b. East Syracuse, N.Y., Sept. 21, 1922; s. Walter Scott and Cecil Edna (Folmsbee) Van A.; m. Margaret Reed Hudson, June 23, 1949 (div.); children: Gretchen Anne, Hunter Scott; m. Marion Graham Walker, May 3, 1980. B.A., U. Buffalo, 1948; M.A., U. Wis., 1950, LL.B., 1953, S.J.D., 1954. Bar: Wis. 1953. Assoc. Shea & Hoyt, Milw., 1954-56; asst. prof. law U. Nebr., 1956-58; individual practice law Madison, Wis., 1958-72; prof. law U. Fla., 1973—; lectr. law U. Wis., 1958-72; lectr. Cambridge-Warsaw Trade Program Cambridge U. (Eng.), 1976; vis. prof. law Cornell U., 1977, U. Leiden, Netherlands, 1988; spl. counsel Gov. of Wis., 1966-70; bd. dirs. non-resident div. State Bar Wis., 1981—, pres., 1988—; bd. govs. State Bar Wis., 1988—. Contbr. articles to profl. jours. Mem. Gov.'s Commn. on Edn., Wis., 1969-71. Served with AUS, 1942-45, 61-62; col. Res., ret. Decorated Legion of Merit. Mem. SR (N.Y.), Holland Soc. (N.Y.), Order of Coif, Phi Beta Kappa, Omicron Delta Kappa, Phi Delta Phi. Republican. Presbyterian. Clubs: Madison, Ft. Rensselaer. Office: Holland Law Center U Fla Gainesville FL 32611

VAN ANDEL, HENDRIK, consulting and engineering firm executive; b. Almkerk, Netherlands, Nov. 12, 1943; s. Abraham and Cornelia (Kamp) Van A.; m. Neeltje Jacoba Francina Millenaar; children—Abraham, Jacobus. B.Sc., Hogere Tuinbouw Sch., Utrecht, 1960-64; B.Sc. in Econs., M.O. Economie en Statistiek, Leiden, 1967; M.Sc. in Bus. Adminstrn., Erasmus U., Rotterdam, 1971. Cons., Food Industries Research & Engring., Wageningen, Netherlands, 1966-71, project mgr., 1971-76, mng. dir., 1976—; dir. Nethconsult, Rotterdam, 1982—. Contbr. articles on food handling and microcomputing to profl. jours.; Mem. Vereniging Afgestudeerden Erasmus Univ., CP/M Users Group (chmn. 1983), Royal Inst. Engrs., Orgn. Netherlands Cons. Engrs. Home: Trajanusplein 1, 4041 AK Kesteren The Netherlands Office: Food Industries Research and Engring, Nude 46, 6702 Wageningen The Netherlands

VAN ANTWERPEN, FRANKLIN STUART, federal judge; b. Passaic, N.J., Oct. 23, 1941; s. Franklin John and Dorothy (Hoedemaker) Van A.; m. Kathleen Veronica O'Brien, Sept. 12, 1970; children: Joy, Franklin W., Virginia. BS in Engring. Physics, U. Maine, 1964; JD, Temple U., 1967; postgrad., Nat. Jud. Coll., 1980. Bar: Pa. 1969, U.S. Dist. Ct. (ea. dist.) Pa. 1971, U.S. Ct. Appeals (3d cir.) 1971, U.S. Supreme Ct. 1972. Corp. counsel Hazeltine, Corp., N.Y.C., 1967-70; chief counsel Northampton County Legal Aid Soc., Easton, Pa., 1970-71; assoc. Hemstreet & Smith, Easton, 1971-73; ptnr. Hemstreet & Van Antwerpen, Easton, 1973-79; judge Ct. Common Pleas of Northampton County (Pa.), 1979-87, U.S. Dist. Ct. (ea. dist.) Pa., Phila., 1987—; adj. prof. Northampton County Area Community Coll., 1976-81; solicitor Palmer Twp., 1971-79; gen. counsel Fairview Savs. and Loan Assn., Easton, 1973-79; judge Ea. Dist. U.S. Dist. Ct. Recipient Booster award Bus. Indsl. and Profl. Assn., 1979; George Palmer award Palmer Twp., 1980, Man of Yr. award Atlantic Contractors Assn., 1981. Mem. ABA (com. on jud. edn.), Pa. Bar Assn., Northampton County Bar Assn., Am. Judicature Soc. Clubs: Pomfret (Easton); Union League (Phila.). Office: US Dist Ct 7614 US Courthouse Independence Mall W Philadelphia PA 19106

VANAT, LAURENT-RAYMOND, business consultant; b. Geneva, Oct. 5, 1961; s. Raymond and Marguerite (Haller) V.; m. Carole Ledune, June 22, 1985. Lic. es. Scis. Comml. et Indsl., U. Geneva, 1983. Mgr. area sales Kustner S.A., Geneva, 1983-86; bus. cons. Societe Fiduciaire Suisse, Geneva, 1987—. Bd. dirs. The European Missionary Assn. Internat., 1987—. Evangelical. Home: 37 Moillebeau, Geneva 1209, Switzerland Office: Societe Fiduciaire Suisse, Guissepe Motta 50, Geneva 1204, Switzerland

VAN AUKEN, ROBERT DANFORTH, educator; b. Chgo., Oct. 31, 1915; s. Howard Robert and Mable (Hanlon) Van A.; student Guilford Coll., 1933-35, Gen. Motors Inst. Tech., 1936-38, U. Pitts., 1953-54; BS, U. Dayton, 1958; MA, U. Okla., 1967; m. Ruth Bowen Cutler, Nov. 24, 1939; children: Robert Hanlon, Joseph Marshall, David Danforth, Howard Evans, Jonathan Lewis. Commd. aviation cadet U.S. Air Force, 1938; advanced through grades to lt. col., 1961; fighter pilot, squadron comdr., ops. officer, 1939-45; asst. air attaché, Paris, 1946-49; staff officer, Pentagon 1950-53; procurement-prodn. staff officer Wright-Patterson AFB, 1954-58, Tinker AFB, 1958-60, Holloman AFB, 1960-61, ret., 1961; personnel officer U. Okla., Norman, 1962-65, mem. faculty, 1965—, asst. prof. mgmt., 1979-83, prof. emeritus bus. adminstrn., 1983—, dir. student programs and career devel. Coll. Bus. Adminstrn., 1975-79; mgmt. cons., 1963—. Decorated Silver Star, Purple Heart. Mem. Oklahoma City Personnel Assn., Acad. Mgmt., Internat. Platform Assn., Ret. Officers Assn., Mil. Order of World Wars, Order of Deadalians, 5th Air Force Meml. Found., 49th Fighter Group Assn., 31st Fighter Officers Assn., Beta Gamma Sigma, Delta Sigma Pi. Republican. Clubs: Lions, Masons. Contbr. monographs in field. Home: 420 Highland Rd Midwest City OK 73110 Office: U Okla 307 W Brooks St Norman OK 73019

VAN BASTELAER, ALOIS, statistician; b. Merksem, Belgium, Apr. 6, 1950; arrived in The Netherlands, 1976.; married;. M in Sociology, U. Nymegen, The Netherlands, 1972, PhD in Social Scis., 1982. Researcher dept. sociol. methodology U. Utrecht, 1973; lectr. dept. sociology U. Oran, Algeria, 1973-75; researcher dept. cultural and religious psychology U. Nymegen, 1976-82; sr. statistician Cen. Bur. Stats., Heerlen, The Netherlands, 1982-85, sr. researcher, project mgr., 1985—. Author: Organizational Stress and the Personnel Officer, 1982; contbr. articles to profl. jours. Mem. Internat. Statis. Inst., Dutch Soc. Statisticians. Roman Catholic. Office: Cen Bur Stats, PO Box 4481, 6401 CZ Heerlen The Netherlands

VAN BENDEGEM, JEAN PAUL, mathematics educator; b. Gent, Belgium, Mar. 28, 1953; s. Egbert and Yvonne (Hutsebaut) Van B.;. Licenciaat wiskunde, Rijksuniversiteit, Gent, 1976, Licenciaat wijsbegeerte, 1979, PhD, 1983. Research asst. Nat. Sci. Found., Gent, 1979-84, sr. research asst., 1984-86, research assoc., 1986—; prof. Rijksuniversitair Centrum, Antwerp, Belgium, 1984—, Vrije Univ., Brussels, 1985—. Author: Finete, Empirical Mathematics, 1987; editor: Theory and Experiment, 1987; mem. editorial bd. Philosophica, Communication and Cognition, Wiskunde en Onderwijs, Logique et Analyse; contbr. articles to profl. jours. Mem. Humanistische Vereniging, 1984; served with Civil Service, 1979-81. Fulbright-Hays grantee Commn. for Ednl. Exchange, Ctr. for Philosophy of Sci., Pitts., 1985. Mem. Philosophy of Sci. Assn., Am. Math. Soc., Sherlock Holmes Soc. of London. Office: Rijksuniversiteit Gent, Rozier 44, B-9000 Gent Belgium

VAN BEVER, WILLEM FLORENT MARIA, pharmaceutical company executive; b. Aalst, East Flanders, Belgium, Sept. 30, 1943; s. Jules and Elza (Schouppe) Van B.; m. Micheline Jacops, Aug. 3, 1966; children—Filip, Sofie, Wim. B.Sc. in Pharmacy, U. Gent, Belgium, 1966; M.Sc. in Medicinal Chemistry, U. Mich., 1968, Ph.D. in Medicinal Chemistry, 1969. Asst. dir. research and devel. Janssen Pharmaceutica, Beerse, Belgium, 1975-77, v.p., 1977-82, v.p. internat., 1983—; sci. adviser Fedn. Belgian Chem. Industry, Brussels, 1980—, Fedn. Belgian Industries, Brussels, 1981—; mem. Nat. Adv. Bd. Sci. Affairs Belgium, Brussels, 1982—. Contbr. articles to profl. jours. Mem. Flemish Chem. Soc., Am. Chem. Soc., Belgian Pharm. Soc. Club: Fifty-One (Turnhout, Belgium) (chmn. 1980-81). Avocation: tennis. Home: Brandelweg 7, 8510 Kortijk-Marke Belgium Office: Janssen Pharmaceutica NV, Turnhoutseweg 31, 2340 Beers Belgium

VAN BILJON, WILLEM JOHANNES, geologist; b. Pretoria, South Africa, Feb. 16, 1929; s. Stephanus and Betty (Couzyn) Van B.; m. Sophie Susanna Coetzee, June 27, 1953; children—Stephanus, Willem (dec.), Erli, Lynette M.Sc., U. Pretoria, 1951; Ph.D., U. Witwatersrand, 1959. Lectr., U. Witwatersrand, Johannesburg, South Africa, 1951-62; prof. U. Orange Free State, Bloemfontein, 1963-67; prof. Rand Afrikaans U., Johannesburg, 1967-83; counsellor for sci. and tech. Council Sci. and Indsl. Research Pretoria, Bonn, W.Ger., 1984—; cons. in field. Contbr. articles to profl. jours.; editor: Some Sedimentary Basins of Southern Africa, 1978; The Limpopo Belt, 1983. Chmn. Parent tchrs. Orgn., Joahnnesburg, 1972. Recipient Havenga prize in geology South African, Akademie vir Wetenskap en Kuns, Pretoria, 1984. Mem. Geol. Soc. South Africa (pres. 1972-73, Honnours award 1983), Associated Sci. and Tech. Socs. South Africa (pres. 1982). Club: American (Bonn). Home: Ela Brändström Str 150, 5300 Bonn 3 Federal Republic of Germany Office: South African Embassy, Auf der Hostert 3, 5300 Bonn 2 Federal Republic of Germany

VAN BOVEN, GEERT JEAN RAOUL, engineer; b. Wetteren, East Flanders, Belgium; s. Etienne and Maria (Melkebeek) Van B.; m. Kath Lavaert, July 20, 1983. BEE, Cath. U. Louvain, France, 1981. Sales engr. Tecnomatix, Antwerp, Belgium, 1982-84; sales mgr. Sidel, Gent, Belgium, 1985-86; mktg. and sales mgr. Olivetti, Brussels, Belgium, 1986—; bd. dirs. mktg. co., Gent. Home: Bommelsrede 16, 9210 Heusden, East Flanders Belgium Office: Olivetti, De Beaulieulaan 2 Bus J, 1000 Brussels Belgium

VANCE, JAMES, manufacturing company executive; b. Cleve., May 20, 1930; m. Dolores Bernadette Doyle, July 6, 1957; 1 child, James J. B.A. cum laude, Baldwin Wallace Coll., 1955; J.D. magna cum laude, Cleve. Marshall Law Sch., 1960. Asst. treas., asst. to v.p. fin. and adminstrn., financial analyst Republic Steel Corp., 1956-68; treas. Addressograph & Multigraph Corp., Cleve., 1968-72; v.p. fin. Cin. Milacron Inc., 1972-77; vice chmn., dir. Dayton-Walther Corp., 1977-87; sr. v.p., gen. counsel, sr. bus. advisor Varity Corp., Toronto, 1987—; dir. Citation Cos., Amertool Corp., Gen. Automation, Min-Cer (S.A.), Mexico, Dwisa of Paris, Dayton-Est of Vesoul, Fiday of Asnieres, France; lectr. bus. law Baldwin Wallace Coll., 1961-63. Vice chmn. United Appeal, 1959; mem. Citizens League Cleve., 1960—; mem. fin. com. YMCA, 1961—; mem. Greater Cleve. Growth Center, 1963—; Vice chmn. fin. com. Cuyahoga Republican Party, 1968-69. Served with inf. AUS, 1951-52. Decorated Bronze Star. Mem. Cleve. Soc. Security Analysts, Am., Ohio bar assns., Fin. Execs. Inst., Am. Ordnance Assn., Nat. Machine Tool Builders Assn., Machinery and Allied Products Inst., Am. Mgmt. Assn., Cin. Indsl. Inst., Ohio C. of C., Alpha Tau Omega, Delta Theta Phi. Club: Cleve. Treasurers (dir.). Home: 6600 Wyman Ln Cincinnati OH 45243 Office: Varity Corp, 595 Bay St, Toronto, ON Canada M5G 2C3

VANCE-GILBERT, CAROLE AMY, insurance company executive; b. Hartford, Conn., Sept. 22, 1942; d. Lester George Harding and Violet Edla Peterson; m. Bruce Gilbert, Feb. 1988. Instr., Inst. Computer Mgmt. div. Litton Industries, 1967-69; mgr. computer ops., dir. ednl. seminars Computer Mgmt. Inst., Detroit, 1969-73; mgr. computer ops. Shatterproof Glass Corp., Detroit, 1973-75; with City Nat. Bank, Detroit, 1975-79, asst. v.p., 1979; sec., dir. research tech. Hartford (Conn.) Ins. Group, 1979-86; ptnr. Vance Communications Ltd., Glastonbury, Conn., 1986—. Mem. Assn. Systems Mgmt. Republican. Episcopalian. Home: 96A Lakeside Dr Lebanon CT 06249

VAN CLEAVE, WILLIAM ROBERT, international relations educator; b. Kansas City, Mo., Aug. 27, 1935; s. Earl Jr. and Georgiana (Offutt) Van C.; m. Nancy Miriam Hession, 1987; children: William Robert, II, Cynthia Kay. B.A. in Polit. Sci. summa cum laude, Calif. State U., Long Beach, 1962; M.A. in Govt. and Internat. Relations, Claremont (Calif.) Grad. Sch., 1964, Ph.D., 1966. Mem. faculty U. So. Calif., 1967-87, prof. internat. relations, 1974-87, dir. def. and strategic studies ctr., 1971-87; univ. prof., dir. Ctr. for Def. and Strategic Studies Southwest Mo. State U., 1987—; sr. fellow Hoover Instn., Stanford U., 1981—; chmn. Strategic Alternatives Team, 1977—; acting chmn. Pres.'s Gen. Adv. Com. on Arms Control, 1981-82; spl. asst. Office Sec. Def., mem. Strategic Arms Limitation Talks (SALT) delegation, 1969-71; mem. B team on Nat. Intelligence Estimates, 1976; mem. exec. panel, bd. dirs. Com. Present Danger, 1980—; dir. transition team Dept. Def., 1980-81; sr. nat. security advisor to Ronald Reagan, 1979-80; mem. nat. security affairs adv. council Republican Nat. Com., 1979—; resident cons. R & D Assocs., 1976—; research council Fgn. Policy Research Inst., Inst. Fgn. Policy Analysis; co-dir. Ann. Internat. Security Summer Seminar, Fed. Republic Germany; trustee Am. com. Internat. Inst. Strategic Studies, 1980—; vis. prof. U.S. Army Advanced Russian Inst., Garmisch, Fed. Republic Germany, 1978-79; cons. in field, mem. numerous govt. adv. coms. Co-author: Strategic Options for the Early Eighties: What Can Be Done?, 1979, Tactical Nuclear Weapons, 1978, Nuclear Weapons, Policies, and the Test Ban Issue, 1987; author: Fortress USSR, 1986; bd. editors: Orbis, Internat. Security Rev. Global Affairs. Co-chmn. Scholars for Reagan, 1984. Served with USMC, 1953-57. Recipient Freedom Found. award, 1976, Outstanding Contbn. award Air War Coll., 1979, award teaching excellence U. So. Calif., 1980, 86; named Outstanding Prof. U. So. Calif., 1977, Disting. Alumnus Claremont Colls., 1978; Woodrow Wilson fellow, 1962, NDEA fellow, 1963-65. Mem. Internat. Inst. Strategic Studies (U.S. com.). Home: Rt 3 Box 691 Rogersville MO 65742 Office: Ctr for Def and Strategic Studies Southwest Mo State U Springfield MO 65804-0095

VANCURA, STEPHEN JOSEPH, radiologist; b. Norton, Kans., June 26, 1951; s. Cyril William J. and Clara Mae (Ruthstrom) V.; B.A. magna cum laude, Kans. State U., 1972; M.D., Kans. U., 1976; m. Lydia Acker, Dec. 10, 1976. Intern in medicine Letterman Army Med. Center, San Francisco, 1976-77, resident in radiology, 1977-80; practice medicine specializing in radiology, 1980—; chief dept. radiology Darnall Army Hosp., Ft. Hood, Tex., 1980-82; pvt. practice diagnostic radiology, 1982—. Served to maj. M.C., U.S. Army, 1976-82 Recipient Ollie O. Mustala award in clin. pharmacology Kans. U. Med. Center, 1974; A. Morris Ginsberg award in phys. diagnosis Kans. U. Med. Center, 1975; Resident Tchr. of Yr. award Letterman Army Med. Center, 1979; Staff Tchr. of Yr. award Darnall Army Hosp., 1982. Trembly Meml. scholar, 1972. Diplomate Am. Bd. Radiology. Mem. Am. Coll. Radiology, Inter-Am. Coll. Radiology, Radiologic Soc. N. Am., AMA, Tex. Med. Assn., Am. Inst. Ultrasound in Medicine, Tex. Radiol. Soc., Central Tex. Physicians Assn., Sigma Xi, Alpha Chi Sigma, Alpha Omega Alpha. Club: Killeen Exchange. Home: 913 Nola Ruth St Harker Heights TX 76543 Office: Metroplex Hosp Dept Radiology 2201 S Clear Creek Rd Killeen TX 76541

VANDAELE, EMILE JOSEPH, business executive; b. St. Eloois Vijve, Belgium, May 10, 1929; s. Adiel Raymond and Zulma Maria (Devaere) V.; m. Christianna Vanacker, July 24, 1957; children: Bart, Marleen, Annemieke, Kristien, Filip, Mark, Peter, Katelyn. Degree in comml. scis. with honors, Hoger Handel Inst., Waregem, Belgium, 1948; degree in textiles, Prov. Inst., Kortrijk, Belgium, 1953. Co-owner, mng. dir. Bekaert Australia Party, Ltd., Blackburn Vic, Australia, 1956-61; co-owner, mng. dir. Aubedal Pty, Ltd., Blackburn Vic, Australia, 1958-61, Ter Molst Internat., TerMolst, Oostrozebeke, Belgium, 1962—, Euromonta, Oostrozebeke, Belgium, 1965—; fgn. trade advisor Ministry of Commerce, Brussels, 1987—; mng. dir. Ter Molst Internat. N.V., Belgium, Ter Molst N.V., Euromonta N.V., Belgium; pres. Erindale Weavers Ltd., Can.; bd. dirs. Turrella Textiles Pty Ltd., Australia, Nibeltex Industries Ltd., Nigeria. Home: Molstenstraat 40, 8780 Oostrozebeke Belgium Office: Molstenstraat 44, 8780 Oostrozebeke Belgium

VAN DAM, BERNARDUS, employee relations executive, management consultant; b. Groningen, Netherlands, Apr. 14, 1936; s. Christiaan Hendrik and Cornelia (Paans) Van D.; m. Janneke Van Soelen, May 20, 1966; children—Christiaan Hendrik Pieter, Johanna Elisabeth Cornelia. M.B.A., Century U., 1981, Ph.D., 1983; M.A., Webster U., 1984. Mgr. employee relations Dow Chem. Co., Terneuzen, Netherlands, 1964-74; dir. indsl. relations Nederhorst/Vicon, Gouda and Nieuw Vennep, Netherlands, 1974-78, Borg Warner Europe, Etten-Leur, Netherlands, 1978-83; internat. mgmt. cons., Hoeven, Netherlands, 1983—; lectr. mgmt. and social scis. Webster U., 1985—. Contbr. articles to profl. jours. Mem. supervisory bd. Enzico, Amsterdam, 1975—. Served with Royal Dutch Air Force, 1955-57. Mem. Christian Democratic Party. Mem. Christian Reformed Ch.

VAN DE BOVENKAMP, SUE ERPF, charitable organization executive; b. N.Y.C.; d. George Norton and Bettina Lions (Hearst) Mortimore; student Gardner Sch., Art Students League, Cooper Union; m. Armand Grover Erpf, 1965; children: Cornelia Aurelia, Armand Bartholomew; m. Gerrit Pieter Van de Bovenkamp, Aug. 11, 1973. Pres. Armand G. Erpf Fund, N.Y.C., 1971—; founder, hon. chmn. Erpf Catskill Cultural Ctr., 1972—. Bd. advisors, founder N.Y. Zool. Soc., 1971—, William Beebe fellow, 1983—; fellow in perpetuity Met. Mus. Art, 1977; life fellow Pierpont Morgan Library, 1974—; mem. council of friends Whitney Mus. Am. Art, 1971-77; mem. Whitney Circle, 1978—; bd. dirs. Catskill Ctr. for Conservation and Devel., 1983-86; mem. adv. council, dept. art history and archaeology Columbia U., 1972—, established univ. seminar on uses of oceans, 1977, mem. adv. council Translation Ctr., 1986; life conservator N.Y. Pub. Library, 1980; fellow Frick Collection; 1971—; mem. council Agribus. Council, Inc., 1979-87; founder, life mem. World Wildlife Fund, 1973—, bd. dirs., 1984—; mem. pres.'s council Columbia U., 1973-78. Life mem. Mus. City N.Y., 1972—, mem. pres.'s council, 1971—. Mem. N.Y. Acad. Scis., The Planetary Soc. Office: The Armand G Erpf Fund 640 Park Ave New York NY 10021

VAN DECKER, DENIS JOSEPH RENE, software/communication company executive; b. North York, Ont., Can., July 26, 1962; s. Marcel Jean-Marie and Donna Diane (Veinot) Van D. BS in Chem. Engring., U. Waterloo, Toronto, Ont., 1985. Internat. software rep. Netron, Inc., Downsview, Ont., 1985-86; voice info. systems practitioner PAN Info., Toronto, 1986—; tech. v.p. Phonetix Corp., Toronto, 1987—; bd. dirs., chief exec. officer Personalized Audio Visual News Info., Toronto; cons. Telemagix, Inc., Toronto, 1986—. Mem. Ont. Liberal Policy Com., 1986—. Mem. Univ. Waterloo Alumni Assn. (v.p., bd. dirs.). Roman Catholic. Club: Engrs. in Toronto. Home: 256 Jarvis, #4A, Toronto, ON Canada M5R-2C3 Office: Phonetix Corp, 1290 Bay St Suite 202, Toronto, ON Canada M5R 2C3

VAN DEMARK, ROBERT EUGENE, orthopedic surgeon; b. Alexandria, S.D., Nov. 14, 1913; s. Walter Eugene and Esther Ruth (Marble) Van D.; m. Bertie Thompson, Dec. 28, 1940; children: Ruth Elaine, Robert, Richard. B.S., U. S.D., 1936; A.B., Sioux Falls (S.D.) Coll., 1937; M.B., Northwestern U., 1938, M.D., 939; M.S. in Orthopedic Surgery, U. Minn., 1943. Diplomate: Am. Bd. Orthopedic Surgery. Intern Passavant Meml. Hosp., Chgo., 1938-39; fellow in orthopedic surgery Mayo Found., 1939-43; 1st asst. orthopedic surgery Mayo Clinic, 1942-43; orthopedic surgeon Sioux Falls, 1946—; attending orthopedic surgeon McKennan Hosp., pres. med. staff, 1954, 70; attending orthopedic surgeon Sioux Valley Hosp., pres. staff 1951-52; clin. prof. orthopedic surgery U. S.D., 1953—, adj. prof orthopedic anatomy, 1983—; med. dir. Crippled Children's Hosp. and Sch., 1952-84; chief hand surgery clinic VA Hosp., Sioux Falls.; dir. S.D. Blue Shield. Editor: S.D. Jour. Medicine; Contbr. articles to med. jours. Bd. dirs. S.D. Found. for Med. Care, 1976-83; hon. chmn. S.D. Lung Assn., 1982. Served from lt. to maj. U.S. Army, 1943-46. Recipient citation for outstanding service Pres.'s Commn. for Employment Physically Handicapped, 1960; Service to Mankind award Sertoma Internat., 1963; award for dedicated services to handicapped S.D. Easter Seal Soc., 1969; Robins award for outstanding community service, 1971; Humanitarian Service award United Cerebral Palsy, 1976; Alumni Achievement award U. S.D., 1977; Disting. Citizen award S.D. Press Assn., 1978; U. S.D. Med. Sch. Faculty Recognition award, 1980; outstanding contbns. to Handicapped Children award S.D. State Dept. Health, 1985; named Humanitarian of Yr. S.D. Human Services Forum, 1987. Fellow ACS (pres. S.D. chpt. 1952, 53); mem. Am. Assn. Med. Colls., Assn. Orthopaedic Chairmen, Am. Acad. Orthopedic Surgery, Clin. Orthopedic Soc., Am. Assn. Hand Surgery, Am. Coll. Sports Medicine, Mid-Am. Orthopedic Assn., Am. Acad. Cerebral Palsy, S.D. Med. Assn. (pres. 1974-75, Disting. Service award 1987), Sioux Falls Dist. Med. Soc., SAR, 500 1st Families Am., Sigma Xi, Alpha Omega Alpha, Phi Chi. Lutheran. Clubs: Optimist, Minnehaha Country. Home: 2803 Ridgeview Way Sioux Falls SD 57105 Office: 1301 S 9th Ave Sioux Falls SD 57105

VAN DEN BERG, JAN TEUNIS, mechanical engineer; b. Hague, Netherlands, May 6, 1941; came to Brazil, 1949, naturalized, 1977; s. Teunis and Helena Petronella (Ros) Van den B.; m. Marise Wollmann, Sept. 15, 1973; children—Jan Marcello, Luis Roberto. Mech. Engr., Fed. U. Parana, Curitiba, Brazil, 1964. Registered profl. engr., Brazil. Maintenance engr. City of Curitiba, Parana, 1965—, maintenance dir. dept. pub. works, 1984-85; maintenance dir. dept. materials, 1986-87, chief of fleet maintenance URBS-Curitiba City Bus Corp., 1987—; cons. Festugato Cummins, Curitiba, 1975-84, Lacombe Turbo, Curitiba, 1979—, Comando de Ingenieria, Paraguayan Army, Asuncion, 1981—; researcher in field. Mem. Parana Inst. Engring. Roman Catholic. Club: Graciosa Country (Curitiba). Avocations: reading; scale model armored vehicles. Home: Rua Joaquim Inacio Taborda, Ribas 744-Ap 502, Curitiba, Parana 80430 Brazil Office: URBS City of Curitiba, Bus Corp, Ave Pres Afonso Camargo, Est Rodoferroviaria, 80050 Curtiba Parana Brazil

VANDENBERGHE, RONALD GUSTAVE, accountant, real estate developer; b. Oakland, Calif., July 1, 1937; s. Anselm Henri and Margaret B. (Bygum) V.; B.A. with honors, San Jose State Coll., 1959; postgrad. U. Calif. at Berkeley Extension, 1959-60, Golden Gate Coll., 1961-63; CPA, Calif.; m. Patricia W. Dufour, Aug. 18, 1957; children: Camille, Mark, Matthew. Real estate investor, pres. VandenBerghe Fin. Corp., Pleasanton, Calif., 1964—. Instr. accounting U. Cal., Berkeley, 1963-70; CPA, Pleasanton, 1963—. Served with USAF. Mem. Calif. Soc. CPAs. Republican. Presbyterian. Mason (Shriner). Home: PO Box 803 Danville CA 94526 Office: 20 Happy Valley Rd Pleasanton CA 94566

VANDEN BOSSCHE, URBAIN, computer company executive, management and marketing consultant; b. Leopoldsburg, Belgium, July 20, 1930; s. Emil Theodoor Vanden Bossche and Marcelle Dehaut; m. Lily Franssen, Oct. 17, 1953; children: Philip, Veronique. Grad. in acctg. and econs., U. Ghent, Belgium, 1952. Mem. sales support dept. IBM, Ghent, 1952-56; dir. Securex, Ghent and Brussels, 1957-62; head. new data processing div. Siemens, Brussels, 1963-66; mng. dir. Univac, Brussels, 1967-69; gen. mgr. SGBA, 1970-72, Matra-Benelux, Brussels and Amsterdam, 1973-74; mng. dir. Nixdorf, Belgium, 1975-80; gen. mgr. Caci, Belgium, 1980-82; mng. dir. Telexcomputer Products, Belgium and Luxemburg, 1983-86; European mktg. dir. Tandy Corp., Brussels, 1986-87; sr. v.p. mktg. and sales Trident Tech. Holding, Brussels, 1988—; Mem. Fiscal Advisors, acctg. experts. Club: 51 Internat. (pres. Brussels 1981-82, vice gov. dist. 101, 1987—); American Common Market. Home: Ijsvogellaan 39, B-1850 Grimbergen Belgium Office: Trident Tech Holding, Ave F Roosevelt 30, 1150 Brussels Belgium

VAN DEN BROEK, GERARD JOHANNES, cultural anthropologist; b. Rijswijk, The Netherlands, July 18, 1953; s. Gerard and Josephine Elza H. (Jongsma) V. BA in Anthropology, U. Leiden, The Netherlands, 1977, MA in Anthropology, 1980; postgrad., Free Acad. Arts, 1980-81; D Social Scis., U. Leiden, The Netherlands, 1986. Prof. cultural anthropology/ethnocommunication Inst. Cultural and Social Studies, U. Leiden, 1984-86. Feature editor Mare, 1984-87; reviewer Semiotica, Word and Image, Current Anthropology, Bijdragen Koninklijk Inst. voor Taal, Land en Volkenkunde; contbr. articles on bot. classification, 18th century philosophy, hunting and fishing to profl. jours. Grantee Netherland Soc. Pure Sci. Research, The Hague, 1983, 84; Fulbright scholar, Netherland Am. Commn. Ednl. Exchange, Amsterdam, 1984. Mem. Semiotic Soc. Am., Internat. Commn. Ethnobotany, Netherlands Soc. Pacific Cultures. Home: Van Assendelftstraat 3g, Oegstgeest 2342 AR, The Netherlands Office: Inst Cultural and Social Studies, Stationsplein 12, Leiden 2300 RA, The Netherlands Office: Rabobank Nederland, PO Box 17100, 3500 HG Utrecht 3500 HG, The Netherlands

VAN DEN BROEK, LODEVICUS CHRISTIAAN, small business owner; b. The Netherlands, Nov. 24, 1944; s. Christiaan and Wilhelmina (Van Poppel) v.d. B.; m. Angela Koolen, Jan. 10, 1980. Grad., Soc. Acad., Breda, The Netherlands, 1971; Drs, Tilburg (The Netherlands) U., 1977. Head personnel dept. Galvanitas, Oosterhout, 1971-73; with personnel dept. Tilburg U., 1973-78; head personnel dept., cons. Camps, Obers & Co. Registered Accts., Eindhoven, The Netherlands, 1978-80; prin. v.d. Broek & Ptnrs., Breda, 1980—. Author: Type Organ En Type Sociaal Beleid, 1977, Funktioneringsgesprekken en beoordelen, 1983, 2d edit., 1985, 3d edit., 1986; contbr. articles to profl. jours. Served with Dutch mil., 1965-67. Mem. Nederlandse Vereniging voor Personeelbeleid, Nederlands Inst. voor Efficiency. Home: Schubertlaan 23, 4837 CP Breda The Netherlands Office: van den Broek & Ptnrs, Schubertlaan 23, 4837 CP Breda The Netherlands

VANDENBROEK, PAUL, otolaryngologist, educator; b. Paris, The Netherlands, Feb. 11, 1935; m. Joyce Dröge. MD, U. Utrecht, The Netherlands, 1961; PhD, U. Nymegen, The Netherlands, 1968. Resident in surgery Doctor's Hosp., N.Y.C.; resident in otolaryngology Radband Hosp., Nijmegen, The Netherlands, 1966-68; prof. otolaryngology, head and neck surgery Cath. U., Nijmegen, The Netherlands; chmn. dept. otolaryngology U. Nymegen. Contbr. articles to profl. jours. Bd. dirs. Dutch Cancer Assn. Hon. fellow U. Liverpool, U.K., 1970. Office: Cath U, Nijmegen The Netherlands

VANDENBROUCKE, LUC M., managing director; b. Kortrijk, Belgium, July 19, 1950; s. Joseph Vandenbroucke and Dina Vandaele; m. Martine Demeyere, Mar. 30, 1973; children: Tom, Bart, Koen, Pieter. Student, Katholieke Universiteit Leuven, Belgium, 1973, Internat. Trade Invest Inst., Antwerp, Belgium, 1979. Mgr. sales Barco Electronics, Kortrijk, 1975-77, product mgr., data displays, 1977-79, comml. dir., indsl. producer, 1979-81; mgr. sales, mktg. Barco Video Systems, Kortrijk, 1982-83; mgr. mktg., computer graphics products Barco Video and Communication, Kortrijk, 1983-85; dir. mkgt., sales Barco Industries and Creative Systems, Kortrijk, 1985-88, gen. mgr., dir., 1988—. Office: Barco-Industries Creative Systems, TH Sevenslaan 106, 8500 Kortrijk Belgium

VANDENBURGH, EDWARD CLINTON, III, lawyer; b. Chgo., Sept. 27, 1915; s. Edward Clinton and Charlotte (Knowles) V.; m. Mary M. Chandler, 1939; children—Edward C. IV, Lael, Jean, Anne; m. Beverly A. Hibbot, 1959; Children—Lynn, John D. B.S., Iowa State U., 1937; LL.B., Duke, 1940; M.P.L., John Marshall Law Sch., 1947. Bar: Iowa bar 1940, Ill. bar 1946. Since practiced patent law; adj. prof. John Marshall Law Sch., 1959-78. Author: Trademark Law and Procedure, 2d edit, 1968; Contbr.: Ency. Patent Practice and Invention Management, 1964. Served with Transp. Corps AUS, 1944-46. Recipient Jefferson medal for outstanding contbn. to field of patent, trademark and copyright law, 1978. Mem. Am. Patent Law Assn., ABA (editor 1963-69, sec. 1971-73, vice chmn. 1974, chmn. elect 1975, chmn. 1976, patent, trademark and copyright sect.), Ill. Bar Assn., Holland Soc. N.Y. Home: 6988 S Pleasant Hill Rd Elizabeth IL 61028

VANDENDRIESSCHE, PHILIPPE R.H., sound engineer; b. Nivelles, Belgium, Apr. 22, 1958; s. Michel and Renée (Andrieux) V.; m. Catherine Paulus, Apr. 18 1981; children: Antoine, Martin. Degree in (electronics), Inst. Reine Astrid, Mons, Belgium, 1977; Student, Inst. des Arts de Diffusion, Louvain-La-Neuve, Belgium, 1981. Technician Radio Diffusion TV Belgium, Brussels, 1981-82; sound engr. Numerous films, TV, and Commls., 1982—; tchr. Beaux Arts Acad., Charleroi, Belgium, 1983—, Inst. des Arts de Diffusion, Louvain-La-Neuve, Belgium, 1984-88. Sound engr. Info. Service of Def., Evere, Belgium, 1983. Mem. Audio Engring. Soc. Home and Office: Allee Des Bouvrevils 5, B1400 - Nivelles Belgium

VANDENHENDE, RENE ANDRÉ, pharmaceutical company executive; b. Kortrijk, Belgium, June 21, 1939; s. George Vandenhende and Henriette Vandenbogaerde; m. Jeanine Buysens, Sept. 2, 1965; children: Veerle, Koen, Karel, Kristof. DVM, U. Ghent, 1964. Mgr. tech. services Sanders, Brussels, 1965-70; mgr. animal health Belgium Upjohn, Puurs, Belgium, 1971-78; mgr. animal health Holland Upjohn, Puurs, 1974-78, area mgr. animal health Europe, 1978-86; area dir. animal health European ops. Brussels, 1986—; also bd. dirs. Home: Bosduifweg 15, 2850 Keerbergen Belgium Office: Upjohn, Rue de Geneve 10, 1140 Brussels Belgium

VAN DEN HEUVEL, ROBERT C., financial company executive; b. Eindhoven, Holland, June 23, 1945; s. Cornelis J. and Agnes (Vandersommen) V.; m. Marijke E.J. Crul, Oct. 8, 1969; 1 child, Alexandra. LLB, U. Utrecht, Netherlands, 1968. Treas. Douwe Egberts N.V., Utrecht, 1970-78; mng. dir. Wilma Internat., Antwerp, Curacao, 1978-82; mem. bd. mgmt. Fokker Royal Aircraft Factory, Amsterdam, 1982-87; mng. dir. Oranje-Nassau Groep B.V., Amsterdam.zo, Netherlands, 1987—; bd. dirs. Royal Schelde, Holland, Desmacon B.V., Holland, Commerzbank Nederland N.V., Holland, Hollinda B.V., The Hague. Served to capt. infantry, 1968-70. Clubs: Amstel (Amsterdam); De Pan Golf. Office: Oranje-Nassau Groep BV, PO Box 22885, 1100 DJ Amsterdam ZO The Netherlands

VAN DE PAVERD, PETRUS ALOYSIUS, financial economist; b. Amsterdam, Netherlands, Jan. 24, 1931; s. Johannes Theodorus and Maria Helena (Bohnenn) Van de P.; m. Elisabeth Maria van der Hoek, Sept. 6, 1956; children—Joseph L.M., Petrus J., Elzelina M.C., Christina A.M., Clemens J.P. B.A. Econs., U. Amsterdam, 1953, M.A., 1958; Charterd fin. analyst Chartered Fin. Inst. Va., 1967. Head research Nederl. Credietbank, Amsterdam, 1956-63; security analyst G.S. & Co., Value Line, Equity Interest, N.Y.C., 1963-70; investment adviser van Lanschot, 's-Hertogenbosch, 1970-76; investment mgr. pension fund Akzo, Arnhem, Netherlands, 1976-82; cons. econs., Arnhem, 1982—; dir. EFFAS, Paris, 1973—; gen. mgr. external contracts Bank Mees Hope, Amsterdam, 1987—. Speaker, chmn. nat. and internat. confs.; contbr. articles to profl. jours. Treas., relious orgns.; chmn. ednl. orgns.; advancement chmn. Boy Scouts Am., Ossining, N.Y., 1967-70. Mem. N.Y. Soc. Security Analysts, Dutch Soc. Security Analysts, Chartered Fin. Inst. Va., Dutch Soc. Avocations: history; painting; travel. Home: Laan van Klarenbeek 93, 6824 Arnhem The Netherlands

VANDEPLANQUE, XAVIER, physician; b. Tourcoing, Nord, France, Jan. 13, 1947; d. Gerard and Thérèse V.; m. Marie-Françoise Bécourt, July 7, 1969; children: Marie-Laure, Geraldine. MD, U. Lille (France), 1973. Pvt. practice in gen. medicine Bailleul-Sire-Berthoult, France, 1974—, pvt. practice in homeopathy, 1980—. Mem. Confederation Française des Soc. D'Homeopathie et de Biotherapies (founder, v.p. 1980—), Soc. Med. Artesienne de Perfectionnement Continu en Biotherapie (founder, pres. 1980—), As de Coeur (founder, pres. 1987), Assn. Med. Anthroposophique. Home and Office: 4 Rue de la Neuville, 62580 Bailleul-Sire-Berthoult France

VAN DER AVERT, MARCEL-ALENA-LEOPOLD, real estate executive; b. Antwerp, Belgium, Sept. 20, 1954; s. Leopold and Tharsilla (V.D. Cruys)) VanD.; m. Lydia-Elisabeth-Rieger; 1 child, Valerie. B in Polit. Sci., St. Ignatius U., Antwerp, 1976; B in Pedagogics, U. Antwerp, 1978, M in Econ. Sociology, 1978. Scientific researcher Antwerp Pub. Welfare Work, 1978-79; econs. tchr. High Sch. of Antwerp, 1980-81; exec. search cons. Constant and Ptnrs., Brussels, Belgium, 1981-82; comml. dir. Wooncentrum Real Estate, Antwerp, 1983-85; sr. exec. Group Onderlinge Dienst Voor Wöningbouw Real Estate, Antwerp, 1985—; mng. dir. Hermes Consulting Internat., Antwerp, 1986—. Mem. Union of Real Estate Brokers of Belgium (Pres. 1986—). Home: De Hulsten 135, 2153 Zoersel Belgium

VANDERBEEK, DUANE LLOYD, construction company executive; b. Adams, Nebr., July 17, 1942; s. B. Frank and Minnie J. (Hietbrink) V.; m. Carol E. Daum, June 11, 1965; children: Todd D., Tami C. Student Nat. Bus. Inst., Lincoln, Nebr., 1959-65. Loan service mgr. H. A. Wolf Co., Inc., Lincoln, 1959-65; exec. v.p. Duane Larson Constrn. Co., Lincoln, 1965—; pres. HBAL Credit Union, Lincoln, 1979; builder, developer, council chmn. Homebuilders Assn. Lincoln, 1975—. Cubmaster Boy Scouts Am., 1977; coach team 6 City Recreation Girls Softball, Lincoln, 1979; mem. fin. com. St. Marks United Meth. Ch., Lincoln, 1982. Served with USNG, 1964-70. Recipient Outstanding Service awards Homebuilders Assn. Lincoln, 1976, 80. Mem. Am. Legion. Republican. Clubs: Bowling Team, Softball Team (Lincoln). Lodge: Elks. Home: 1140 Cobblestone Dr Lincoln NE 68510 Office: Duane Larson Constrn Co 201 S 84th St Lincoln NE 68510

VAN DER ELST, GASTON, linguist; b. Antwerp, Belgium, Dec. 10, 1946; s. Joseph and Hortence (Van Mechelen) V.D. Elst; m. Reinhilde Nickel. Lic. Wijsbeg and Letter, U. Leuven, 1969, D Wijsbeg and Letter, 1979; D Philosophy Habil, U. Erlangen, 1980. Faculty mem. U. Marburg, Fed. Republic Germany, 1970-76; faculty mem. U. Erlangen (Fed. Republic Germany)-Nurnberg, 1976—, prof. German lang., 1983—, akademischer oberrat, 1986—. Author: Verbsemantik, 1982, Aspekte Zur Entstehung der NHD Schriftsprache, 1987. Office: U Erlangen, Nurnberg Bismarckstrasse 1, D8520 Erlangen Federal Republic of Germany

VANDEREYCKEN, WALTER, psychiatrist, sexologist; b. Tienen, Belgium, May 11, 1949; s. Lodewijk and Yvonne (Oversteyns) V.; m. Anne Vanautgaerden, July 30, 1974; 1 child, Sofie. M.D., U. Leuven, Belgium, 1974, M.A. in Sexology, 1979; Ph.D. in Medicine, U. Leiden, Netherlands, 1984. Cert. neuropsychiatrist. Clin. dir. dept. Behavior Therapy Univ. Psychiat. Ctr., Kortenberg, Belgium, 1979—; assoc. prof. U. Leuven, 1985—. Author: Anorexia Nervosa, 1984; Family Approach to Eating Disorders, 1988. Editor: Abnormal Eating Behavior, 1981, Management of Sexual Problems, 1983; editor-in-chief Dutch Jour. Sexology, 1980-86; co-editor-in-chief Dutch Jour. Psychiatry, 1985—. Mem. Internat. Coll. Psychosomatic Medicine, Soc. Psychotherapy Research (U.S.A.), Soc. Behavioral Medicine (U.S.A.). Home: Leuvenselaan 85, B-3300 Tienen Brabant Belgium Office: Univ Psychiatric Ctr, Leuvensesteenweg 517, B-3070 Kortenberg, Brabant Belgium

VANDERHADEN, GARY LEE, state official, municipal policy advisor; b. Watertown, N.Y., May 19, 1950; s. Robert Edward and Marilyn Celeste (MacDonald) V.; m. Maria-Cristina Tolentino, Aug. 20, 1977. BA with honors, Queen's U., Kingston, Ont., 1972, M in Pub. Adminstrn., 1974. Research asst. Queen's U., Kingston, 1974-76; planning and policy officer Govt. of Northwest Territories, Yellowknife, 1977-78, policy advisor, 1978-82, dir. policy, legis., 1982—. Author: Interest Groups in the Northern Territories, 1977. Pres. Yellowknife Direct Charge Coop. Ltd., 1980. Regents scholar State of N.Y., 1968; recipient award for excellence in Latin Studies Beaver Coll., 1968. Mem. Inst. Pub. Adminstrn. of Can., Can. Evaluation Soc. Presbyterian. Clubs: Yellowknife Ski; Yellowknife Chess. Home: 802 Fraser Tower, 5303-52 St, Yellowknife, NT Canada X1A 1V1 Office: Govt of Northwest Territories, Box 1320, Yellowknife, NT Canada X1A 2L9

VAN DER KLOOSTER, ADRIAN, holding company executive; b. Lekkerkerk, The Netherlands, Dec. 4, 1939; s. Dimmen and Maayke (de Jong) Van der K.; m. Lamberta Hendrika Van der Meijden, Mar. 23, 1946; children: Michiel Adriaan, Joost Reinout. Ing., HTS, 1961; Ir, Tech. U. Delft, 1968. Div. mng. dir. Pakhoed Holding B.V., Rotterdam, Netherlands, 1968-78; dir. corp. devel. Van Gelder Papier N.V., Amsterdam, Netherlands, 1978-80; mng. dir. NeSBIC B.V., The Hague, Netherlands, 1981-83, bd. dirs., 1983—; pres. Cats Holding B.V., 1983—; mng. dir. Fineca B.V., 1984—, Leeuwarder Papierwarenfabriek B.V., 1985—; pres. bd. Pie Med B.V., 1982—, Software Enterprises Europe B.V., Zeepfabriek De Klok B.V., Hollandia Offset Beheer B.V., 1983—; bd. dirs. Nedap N.V., Nyloplast B.V., Du-MED B.V. Mem. bd. Indsl. Innovation, Utrecht, Netherlands, 1982-84. Mem. Royal Inst. Engrs. Home: Straatweg 278, 3054 AP Rotterdam The Netherlands Office: Cats Holding BV, Straatweg 278, 3054 AP Rotterdam The Netherlands

VAN DER KROEF, JUSTUS MARIA, political science educator; b. Djakarta, Indonesia, Oct. 30, 1925; came to U.S., 1942, naturalized, 1952; s. Hendrikus Leonardus and Maria Wilhelmina (van Lokven) van der K.; m. Orell Joan Ellison, Mar. 25, 1955; children: Adrian Hendrick, Sri Orell. B.A., Millsaps Coll., 1944; M.A., U. N.C., 1947; Ph.D., Columbia U., 1953. Asst. prof. fgn. studies Mich. State U., 1948-55; Charles Dana prof., chmn. dept. polit. sci. U. Bridgeport, Conn., 1956—; vis. prof. Nanyang U., Singapore, U. Philippines, Quezon City, Vidyodaya U., Sri Lanka Colombo; dir. Am.-Asian Ednl. Exchange, 1969—; Chmn. editorial bd. Communications Research Services, Inc., Greenwich, Conn., 1971-80; mem. internat. adv. bd. Union Trust Bank, Stamford, Conn., 1974-88, adv. bd., 1988—; mem. nat. acad. adv. council Charles Edison Meml. Youth Fund; bd. dirs. WUBC-TV, Bridgeport, Conn., 1978-80. Author: Indonesia in the Modern World, 2 vols., 1954-56, Indonesian Social Evolution. Some Psychological Considerations, 1958, The Communist Party of Indonesia: Its History, Program and Tactics, 1965, Communism in Malaysia and Singapore, 1967, Indonesia Since Sukarno, 1971, The Lives of SEATO, 1976, Communism in Southeast Asia, 1980, Kampuchea: The Endless Tug of War, 1982, Since Aquino: The Philippine Tangle and the U.S., 1986; Editorial bd.: World Affairs, 1975—, Jour. Asian Affairs, 1975—, Asian Affairs, 1980—, Asian Profile, 1983—, Jour. of Govt. and Admn., 1985—, Jour. of Econ. and Internat. Relations, 1987—; mng. editor: Asian Thought and Society, 1986—; book rev. editor: Asian Thought and Soc, 1976-85. Mem. City Charter Revision Com. City of Bridgeport, 1983-86. Served with Royal Netherlands Marine Corps, 1944-45. Sr. fellow Research Inst. Communist Affairs, Columbia U., 1965-66; fellow U. Queensland, Brisbane, Australia, 1968-69; research fellow Inst. Strategic Studies, Islamabad, Pakistan, 1982—; research fellow Mellon Research Found., 1983; research fellow Internat. Ctr. Asian Studies, Hong Kong, 1983—. Mem. Univ. Profs. Acad. Order (nat. pres. 1970-71), Pi Gamma Mu, Phi Alpha Theta, Lambda Chi Alpha, Alpha Sigma Lambda Phi Sigma Iota. Home: 165 Linden Ave Bridgeport CT 06602

VANDERLAAN, RICHARD B., marketing company executive; b. Grand Rapids, Mich., Sept. 2, 1931; s. Sieger B. and Helen (Kerr) V.; cert. liberal arts Grand Rapids Jr. Coll., 1952; cert. mech. engring. U. Mich., 1955; cert. indsl. engring. Mich. State U., 1960; cert. Harvard Bus. Sch., 1970; m. Sally E. Conroy, Mar. 26, 1982; children—Sheryl Vanderlaan, Pamella Vanderlaan DeVos, Brenda Vanderlaan Thompson. Tool engr. Four Square Mfg. Co., Grand Rapids, 1950-60; sales engr. Ametek, Lansdale, Pa., 1960-63; br. mgr. J.N. Fauver Co., Grand Rapids, 1964-68; v.p. Fauver Co. subs. Sun Oil Co., Grand Rapids 1968-76, exec. v.p., 1976-80; pres. House of Printers, Inc., 1980-82, also dir.; pres. Richard Vanderlaan Assocs., 1982—. Named eagle scout Boy Scouts Am. Mem. Mfrs. Agts. Nat. Assn., Soc. Automotive Engrs. Republican. Clubs: Birmingham Country, Oakland Hills Country, Economic of Detroit, Detroit Athletic. Avocations: golf, tennis. Office: 22157 Metamora Dr Birmingham MI 48010

VAN DER LELY, CORNELIS, manufacturing company executive, inventor; b. Maasland, Holland, Mar. 2, 1920; arrived in Switzerland, 1959; s. K. and M. (van der Vlugt) van der L.; m. Maartje J. den Hollander, Sept. 18, 1954; children: Harold, Olaf, Ronald, Celesta, Alexander. Pres., founder Lely Cos., Australia, Can., U.S., Holland, Switzerland, Eng., France, Germany,, Austria, Italy, 1945—. Internat. patentee in farm machinery, hydraulics, prefabricated houses, torque converters, indsl. equipment. Recipient Seminatore d'oro, Salone della Macchina Agricola, Italy, 1972, Koning Willem I Plaquette, Holland, 1983, Officier in de Orde van Oranje Nassau, 1985. Office: Lely, Butzenweg 20, CH6300 Zug Switzerland

VAN DER MEER, SIMON, accelerator physicist; b. The Hague, Netherlands, Nov. 24, 1925; s. Pieter and Jetske (Groeneveld) van der M.; m. Catharina M. Koopman, Apr. 26, 1966; children—Esther, Mathijs. Engring. degree in physics, Poly. U., Delft, Netherlands, 1952; Dr. (hon.) U. Geneva, 1983, U. Amsterdam, Netherlands, 1984, U. Genoa, Italy, 1985. Research engr. Philips Physics Lab., Eihdhoven, Netherlands, 1952-55; sr. engr. CERN European Orgn. Nuclear Research, Geneva, 1956—. Co-recipient Nobel prize for physics, 1984. Mem. Royal Netherlands Acad. Scis. (corr.), (fgn. hon.) AAAS. Office: European Orgn Nuclear Research, 1211 Geneva 23 Switzerland

VAN DER MEULEN, JOSEPH PIERRE, neurologist, medical school dean; b. Boston, Aug. 22, 1929; s. Edward Lawrence and Sarah Jane (Robertson) VanDer M.; m. Ann Irene Yadeno, June 18, 1960; children—Elisabeth, Suzanne, Janet. A.B., Boston Coll., 1950; M.D., Boston U., 1954. Diplomate: Am. Bd. Psychiatry and Neurology. Intern Cornell Med. div. Bellevue Hosp., N.Y.C., 1954-55; resident Cornell Med. div. Bellevue Hosp., 1955-56; resident Harvard U., Boston City Hosp., 1958-60, instr., fellow, 1962-66; assoc. Case Western Res. U., Cleve., 1966-67; asst. prof. Case Western Res. U., 1967-69, assoc. prof. neurology and biomed. engring., 1969-71; prof. neurology U. So. Calif., Los Angeles, 1971—; also dir. dept. neurology Los Angeles County/U. So. Calif. Med. Center; chmn. dept. U. So. Calif., 1971-78, v.p. for health affairs, 1977—, dean Sch. Medicine, 1985-86; vis. prof. Autonomous U. Guadalajara, Mex., 1974; pres. Norris Cancer Hosp. and Research Inst., 1983—. Contbr. articles to profl. jours. Mem. med. adv. bd. Calif. chpt. Myasthenia Gravis Found., 1971-75, chmn., 1974-75, 77-78; med. adv. bd. Amyotrophic Lateral Sclerosis Found., Calif., 1973-75, chmn., 1974-75; mem. Com. to Combat Huntington's Disease, 1973—; trustee Calif. Hosp. Med. Ctr., Good Hope Med. Found., Eisenhower Med. Ctr., Doheny Eye Hosp., House Ear Inst., Los Angeles Hosp. Good Samaritan, Children's Hosp. of Los Angeles, St. Thomas Aquinas Coll.; bd. dirs. Assn. Acad. Health Ctrs., The Scott Newman Found; pres. Scott Newman Ctr. Served to lt. M.C. USNR, 1956-58. Nobel Inst. fellow Karolinska Inst., Stockholm, 1960-62; NIH grantee, 1968-71. Mem. Am. Neurol. Assn., Am. Acad. Neurology, Los Angeles Soc. Neurology and Psychiatry (pres. 1977-78), Mass., Ohio, Calif. med. socs., Los Angeles Acad. Medicine, Alpha Omega Alpha (councillor). Home: 39 Club View Ln Rolling Hills Estates CA 90274 Office: U So Calif 1985 Zonal Ave Los Angeles CA 90033

VAN DER MOTTEN, MICHEL LYDIE GILBERT, machinery executive; b. Gent, Belgium, Sept. 11, 1959; s. Oscar Maurice Van Der Motten and Stefanie Hybel. Diploma in Textile Tech., Higher Inst. for Textile and Rubber, Gent, 1976, diploma in Rubber and Plastic Tech., 1979. Prodn. mgr. Thouadec, Heusden, Belgium, 1979-80; engring. mgr. Socomer, Gent, 1980-81; product mgr. machinery div. Interensco, Antwerp, Belgium, 1981—. Home: Lange Groenstraat 2, 9720 Depinte Belgium

VANDER MYDE, PHILIP LOUIS, architect; b. Whiteside County, Ill., Apr. 4, 1931; s. Louis John and Ann Marie (Pals) Vander M.; student Central Coll., 1949-50; BA in Arch., U. Minn., 1958; m. Martha T. Grier, Mar. 15, 1969; children—Jane Gray, John Philip, Martha Maslin. Architect, Vosbeck-Ward & Assos., Alexandria, Va., 1962-64; asso. partner Vosbeck Vosbeck & Assos., Alexandria, 1966; ptnr. VVKR Partnership, Alexandria, 1967-70, mng. ptnr. Md. Office, University Park, 1970-80; prin. VVKR Inc., Alexandria, Va., 1980-83; mng. ptnr. for architecture Dewberry & Davis, Fairfax, Va., 1983-87; ptnr. Senseman/VanderMyde, Alexandria, 1987—. Mem. Alexandria Hosp. Corp., 1981—; bd. dirs. Southeast Fairfax Devel. Corp., 1988. Served to capt. USNR , 1959—. Recipient Honor award Bicentennial Design awards, AIA; 16 design awards, 1970-86; registered architect, Va., Md., D.C., N.C., Tenn., Pa., Mich., N.J., Ill., W.Va., Del., also Nat. Council Archtl. Registration Bds. Mem. AIA (pres. Potomac Valley chpt. 1977-78), Seminary Hill Assn., Vauxcleuse Citizens Assn. (pres.), Washington Bd. Trade, Minn. Alumni Assn., Sigma Alpha Epsilon (past pres.). Republican. Presbyterian. Clubs: Belle Haven Country, Potomac Soc., Holland Soc. N.Y. Lodge: Rotary (bd. dirs. 1987). Archtl. works include Prince Georges Gen. Hosp., 1977, U. Md. Law Library, 1978, Frederick County Courthouse, 1979, Md. Dept. Agr. Headquarters, 1980, Inglewood Office Complex, 1981, Wolf Trap Ctr. for Performing Arts, 1984, First Am. Bank of Va., 1987, Birchwood Office Complex, 1988, Columbia Ctr. II Hotel, 1988, Youngstar Space Acad., 1988. Home: 1100 N Howard St Alexandria VA 22304 Office: Senseman/VanderMyde 5845 Richmond Hwy Suite 800 Alexandria VA 22303

VAN DER PADT, ARIE, mechanical engineer; b. Mar. 14, 1932. Student, Delft Univ. Tech., The Netherlands, 1950-55. With Doorne's Bedrijfswagenfabriek, Eindhoven, The Netherlands, 1958—, also chmn. bd. mgmt. Office: Doorne's Bedrijfswagenfabriek, Geldropseweg 303, Nb 5645 TK Eindhoven The Netherlands

VANDERPLOEG, KENNETH PAUL, business executive; b. Grand Rapids, Mich., Oct. 26, 1941; s. Frederick and Eva Mae (Harvey) Vander P.; m. Sue Ann Tornga, Sept. 6, 1963; children—Laura E., Michele Ann. A.A.S., Grand Rapids Jr. Coll., 1962; B.B.A., Western Mich. U., 1964. Asst. controller Lawndale Industries, Aurora, Ill., 1969-72; asst. controller Cracker Jack, Chgo., 1972-74; controller IMS Internat., Ambler, Pa., 1974-76, Cummins Allison Corp., Glenview, Ill., 1976-78; chief exec. officer Quickprint, Downers Grove, Ill., 1978—. Served with U.S. Army, 1966-68. Methodist. Club: Rotary (Downers Grove) (bd. dirs. 1982-84, treas. 1985-86). Office: Quickprint 415 Ogden Ave Downers Grove IL 60515

VAN DER POEL, PIETER WILLEM, chemical researcher; b. Barendrecht, Zuid-Holland, The Netherlands, Aug. 20, 1931; s. Adrianus and Maaike (Nolen) van der P.; m. Adriana Oosterwijk, Feb. 9, 1961. Chem. Engr., Tech. U., 1957, D.Tech. Scis., 1958. Registered profl. chem. engr. Asst. to Prof. Waterman, Tech. U., Delft, The Netherlands, 1956-58; research chemist Centrale Suiker Mij., Amsterdam, 1958-66, head central lab., 1966-83; research dir. C.S.M. Suiker bv, 1983—; v.p. Commn. Internationale Technique Sucriere, Tienen, Belgium, 1983—, pres. subcom., 1982—; mem. adv. bd. Sugar Tech. Revs., Amsterdam, 1983—; mem. awarding com. Verein Deutscher Zuckertechn., 1988—; lectr. in field. Contbr. numerous articles to profl. jours. Patentee in field. Mem. Koninklijke Nederlandse Chemische Vereniging, Verein Deutscher Zuckertechniker, Am. Soc. Sugar Beet Technologists. Mem. Dutch Reformed Ch. Avocations: photography; botany; gardening. Home: Westerkim 7, Prinsenbeek, 4841 BP Noord-Brabant The Netherlands Office: Centraal Laboratorium CSM Suiker BV, Valveeken 6, NL-4815 HL Breda The Netherlands

VANDERPOOL, WARD MELVIN, management and marketing consultant; b. Oakland, Mo., Jan. 20, 1917; s. Oscar B. and Clara (McGuire) V.; m. Lee Kendall, July 7, 1935. MEE, Tulane U. V.p. charge sales Van Lang Brokerage, Los Angeles, 1934-38; mgr. agrl. div. Dayton Rubber Co., Chgo., 1939-48; pres., gen. mgr. Vee Mac Co., Rockford, Ill., 1948—; pres., dir. Zipout, Inc., Rockford, 1951—, Wife Save Products, Inc., 1959—; chmn. bd. Zipout Internat., Kenvan Inc., 1952—, Shevan Corp., 1951—, Atlas Internat. Corp.; pres. Global Enterprises Ltd., Global Assos. Ltd.; chmn. bd. dirs. Am. Atlas Corp., Merzat Industries Ltd.; trustee Ice Crafter Trust, 1949—; bd. dirs. Atlas Chem. Internat. Ltd., Shrimp Tool Internat. Ltd.; mem. Toronto Bd. Trade; chmn. bd. dirs. Am. Atlas Corp., Am. Packaging Corp. Mem. adv. bd. Nat. Security Council; mem. Rep. Nat. Com., Presdl. Task Force, Congrl. Adv. Com. Hon. mem. Internat. Swimming Hall of Fame. Mem. Nat. (dir. at large), Rock River (past pres.) sales execs., Sales and Mktg. Execs. Internat. (dir.), Am. Mgmt. Assn., Rockford Engring. Soc., Am. Tool Engrs., Internat. Acad. Aquatic Art (dir.), Am. Inst. Mgmt. (pres. council), Am. Ordnance Assn., Internat. Platform Assn., Heritage Found., Ill. C. of C. Clubs: Jesters, Elks, Rockford Swim, Forest Hills Country, Exec., Elmcrest Country, Pyramid, Dolphin, Marlin, Univ. Lodges: Masons, Shriners. Home: 374 Parkland Dr SE Cedar Rapids IA 52403 also: Richview Rd #308, Toronto, ON Canada M9A 5C1 Office: Box 242A Auburn St Rd Rockford IL 61103 also: 111 Richmond St W, Suite #318, Toronto, ON Canada M5H 1T1

VANDERROEST, ROBERT D., dentist; b. Kalamazoo, June 21, 1927; s. Richard and Emma (Stuut) VanderR.; m. Ruth A. Zwart, July 17, 1950; children—Lynn Carol, Karen Lee, Julie Diane, Steven Robert. D.D.S., U. Mich., 1954. Practice dentistry, Portage, Mich., 1954—; trustee Am. Nat. Bank, Portage, 1979-86; mem. dental hygiene adv. bd. Kalamazoo Valley Community Coll., 1978-86; bd. dirs. Mich. Acad. Dentistry for the Handicapped, 1980-83; lectr. Pres., Portage Pub. Schs. Bd. Edn., 1956-70, Kalamazoo Valley Intermediate Sch. System Bd., 1970—, Mich. Assn. Retarded Children, 1984-86. Served with C.E., U.S. Army, 1946-48. Recipient Community Service award Assn. Retarded Children, 1979; deacon Bethany Reformed Ch., 1961-64, elder, Southridge Reformed Ch., 1976-79. Mem. Kalamazoo Valley Dental Soc. (pres. 1962-63), ADA, Mich. Dental

Assn. (Dental Citizen of Yr. 1984). Lodges: Optimists (pres. 1960), Rotary (Portage). Avocations: hunting, stamp collecting, photography, sailing, power boating. Home: 7603 Primrose Ln Portage MI 49081 Office: 200 E Centre Ave Portage MI 49081

VAN DER STICHELEN ROGIER, JEAN, coal company executive; b. Roeselaere, Flanders, Belgium, Jan. 3, 1929; s. Louis Amedee and Marie Louise (Lenaerts) van der S.; m. Jane Vanden Perren, Dec. 10, 1952; children: Eric, Richard, Catherine, Axel. B in Civil Mining Engring., U. Louvain, Belgium, 1952; B in Econs., Inst. Hautes Etudes Commls., Brussels, 1970. Mining engr. N.V. Limburg-Maas Co., Eisden, Belgium, 1952-63; chief Bur. Courtoy, Brussels, 1963-64; dep. dir. mines N.V. Kempense Steekolenmijnen, Eisden, 1964-73; engr. comml. dept. N.V. Kempense Steekolenmijnen, Brussels, 1973-76, comml. dir., 1976—. Mem. Belgian Mining Engrs. (mng. dir. 1980—), Bourse Indsl. Belgique (pres. 1986—), Fedn. Charbonnière de Belgique (bd. dirs. 1982—). Home: 18 Allee de la Frenaie, B1300 Wavre Brabant Belgium Office: NV Kempense Steenkolenmijnen, 21 Ave des Arts, Bte 9, 1040 Brussels Belgium

VAN DER VELDE, BERT VICTOR, airline executive, consultant; b. Amsterdam, The Netherlands, Oct. 27, 1945; s. Leonard and Willy (Wolff) Van Der V. B.B.A., U. Atlanta, 1972. Salesman, De Groot & Co., Amsterdam, 1963-68; internat. sales mgr. The Winfo Corp., London, 1968-70, concern controller, 1972-77; controller, sales mgr. Balton-Linbal Group, Amsterdam, 1978-81; corp. planner Reiss & Co. Group, Amsterdam and Lagos, Nigeria, 1981-82; mng. dir., The Winfo Corp., Alphen aan den Ryn, Holland, 1982—; export cons. The Stolzer Corp., N.Y.C., 1969-70; fin. cons. Electronium BV Group, Ede, Holland, 1983-85; export cons. Johannus of Am. Inc., Vancouver, Wash., 1983-85, L.C.N. BV, Schiphol, Holland, 1982-84; sr. exec. MARTINAIR Holland N.V., Amsterdam, 1985—.Author: Travelogue, 1978; Afgekort, 1984. Served with Dutch Army, 1965-67. Recipient Children's Friend Soc. award, 1975. Mem. Nat. Geog. Soc., Internat. Chaplains Assn., Mensa Nederland. Home: Bezembinder 115, 2401 Alphen aan den Ryn The Netherlands Office: The Winfo Corp, PO Box 314, 2400 Alphen aan den Ryn The Netherlands

VAN DER WEE, HERMAN FRANS ANNA, economics educator; b. Lier, Antwerpen, Belgium, July 10, 1928; m. Verbreyt Monique, Feb. 27, 1954; children: Dominique, Barbara. PhB, U. Leuven, Belgium, 1949, LLD, 1950, MA in Political-Social Scis., 1951, D Hist. Sci., 1963. Research fellow Harvard U., Cambridge, Mass., 1968, Woodrow Wilson Internat. Ctr., Washington, 1975-76; vis. fellow Inst. Advanced Study, Princeton, N.J., 1981-82; vis. scholar Stanford (Calif.) U., 1982; vis. fellow All Souls Coll., Oxford, Eng., 1985; prof. Erasmus U., Rotterdam, The Netherlands, 1987; vis. prof. U. Paris IV, 1987-88; prof. U. Leuven, 1967—; dean Faculty Econ., Polit. Scis., Brussels, 1972-75; chmn. Dept. Econs. Univ. Leuven, 1972-74; dir. Leuven Univ. Press, 1972-82, Postgrad. Workshop Quantitative Econ. History, 1970—. Author: Growth of the Antwerp Market, 1963, The Economic Development of Europe, 1988, La Banque Nationale de Belgique, 1975, Prosperity and Upheaval, 1986, Rise and Decline of Urban Industries, 1988. Recipient De Stassart prize Royal Acad. Belgium, 1968, Quinquennial Solvay prize Nat. Found. Sci. Research Belgium, 1981, Fulbright-Hayes scholar, 1975, 1981. Fellow: British Acad.; mem. Royal Acad. Belgium, Royal Acad. Netherlands, Internat. Assn. Econ. History, (pres. 1986—). Office: Centrum voor Economische Studies, Van Evenstraat 2b, 3000 Leuven, Brabant Belgium

VAN DER WILDT, ALBERT, cinematographer; b. Amsterdam, The Netherlands, Sept. 27, 1942. Grad., Dutch Film Sch., Amsterdam, 1965. Cinematographer/dir. Y es Nuestra, 1983, Passage, 1985, (with Derek May) The Boulevard of Broken Dreams, 1987, Image of a Child, 1988. Served with Dutch Army, 1961-63. Recipient Prix d'Amsterdam, Hilverum Film Festival, 1986. Mem. Audiovisuele Beroeps Vereniging. Home and Office: JM Coenenstraat 25, 1071WD Amsterdam The Netherlands

VANDEVENTER, JANICE LEIGH, cartographer, flight instructor; b. Long Beach, Calif., Aug. 10, 1944; d. Owen Jerome and Laurence Elizabeth (Monninger) V.; B.A. in Geography, UCLA, 1966. Cartographer, Automobile Club So. Calif., Los Angeles, 1966-70, sr. cartographer, 1970-72, research coordinator, 1972-74, chief cartographer, supr. 1974—; flight instr. Falcon Air, Long Beach, 1975—. Recipient FAA Safety Pin, 1974. Active choir New Life Community Ch., Artesia, Calif. Mem. Am. Congress Surveying and Mapping, Nat. Computer Graphics Assn., Los Angeles Area C. of C., Aircraft Owners and Pilots Assn., Sweet Adelines, Goldenaires Quartet (lead singer, group named novice quartet champions 1982), UCLA Alumni Assn., Alpha Xi Delta. Home: 5141 E Burnett St Long Beach CA 90815 Office: Automobile Club So Calif 2601 S Figueroa St Los Angeles CA 90007

VANDEVER, WILLIAM DIRK, lawyer; b. Chgo., Aug. 1, 1949; s. Lester J. and Elizabeth J. V.; m. Kathi J. Zellmer, Aug. 26, 1983; children: Barton Dirk, Brooke Shelby. BS, U. Mo., Kansas City, 1971, JD with distinction, 1974. Bar: Mo. 1975, U.S. Dist. Ct. (we. dist.) Mo. 1975. Dir. Popham Law Firm, Kansas City, Mo., 1975—; lectr. med. malpractice various hosps. and colls., Kansas City, Mo., 1979—. Issue editor U. Mo.-Kansas City Law Rev., 1974. Mem. Mo. Assn. Trial Attys., Kansas City Met. Bar Assn. (treas., sec., pres. exec. com. 1986—, elected to 16th Jud. Commn., 1988—), Kansas City Bar Found. (treas. 1986—), Phi Delta Phi, Beta Theta Pi. Home: 11800 Central Kansas City MO 64114 Office: Popham Law Firm 1300 Commerce Trust Bldg Kansas City MO 64106

VAN DINE, VANCE, investment banker; b. San Francisco, July 2, 1925; s. Melvin Everett and Grace Winifred (Harris) Van D.; m. Isabel Erskine Brewster, Sept. 8, 1956; 1 dau., Rose M. (dec.). B.A., Yale U., 1949; LL.B., NYU, 1955. Assoc. Morgan Stanley & Co., N.Y.C., 1953-59, 61-63; ptnr. Morgan Stanley & Co., 1963-75; mng. dir. Morgan Stanley & Co. Inc., N.Y.C., 1970-83, adv. dir., 1983—; cons. Internat. Bank for Reconstn. and Devel., 1959-61. Author: The Role of the Investment Banker in International Transactions, 1970, The U.S. Market After Controls, 1974. Bd. dirs. Yale U. Alumni Fund, Rec. for Blind, Inc., N.Y.C.; trustee L.I. U., Cancer Research Inst., N.Y.C.; gov. dir. Fgn. Policy Assn. Served with USN, 1943-46. Recipient Yale Class of 1949 Disting. Service award, 1983. Republican. Episcopalian. Clubs: Union, Piping Rock, N.Y. Yacht, Seawanhaka Corinthian Yacht, Church, Yale of N.Y.C, Met. Opera. Home: 1165 Park Ave New York NY 10128 Office: Morgan Stanley & Co 1251 Ave of Americas New York NY 10020

VANDIVER, FRANK EVERSON, university president, author, educator; b. Austin, Tex., Dec. 9, 1925; s. Harry Shultz and Maude Folmsbee (Everson) V.; m. Carol Sue Smith, Apr. 19, 1952 (dec. 1979); children: Nita, Nancy, Frank Alexander; m. Renée Aubry, Mar. 21, 1980. Rockefeller fellow in humanities, U. Tex., 1946-47, Rockefeller fellow in Am. Studies, 1947-48, M.A., 1949; Ph.D., Tulane U., 1951; M.A. (by decree), Oxford (Eng.) U., 1963; H.H.D. (hon.), Austin Coll., 1977. Apptd. historian Army Service Forces Depot, Civil Service, San Antonio, 1945, Air U., 1951; prof. history La. State U., summers 1953-57; asst. prof. history Washington U., St. Louis, 1952-55; asst. prof. history Rice U., Houston, 1955-56, assoc. prof., 1956-58, prof., 1958-65, Harris Masterson Jr. prof. history, 1965-79, chmn. dept. history and polit. sci., 1962-63, dept. history, 1968-69, acting pres., 1969-70, provost, 1970-79, v.p., 1975-79; pres., chancellor N. Tex. State U., Denton and Tex. Coll. Osteo. Medicine, 1979-81; pres. Tex. A&M U., College Station, 1981-88; Harmsworth prof. Am. history Oxford U., 1963-64; vis. prof. history U. Ariz., summer 1961; master Margarett Root Brown Coll., Rice U., 1964-66; Harman lectr. Air Force Acad., 1963; Keese lectr. U. Chattanooga, 1967; Fortenbaugh lectr. Gettysburg Coll., 1974; Phi Beta Kappa assoc. lectr., 1970—; vis. prof. mil. history U.S. Mil. Acad., 1973-74; hon. pres. Occidental U., St. Louis, 1975-80; bd. dirs. GTE Southwest. Editor: The Civil War Diary of General Josiah Gorgas, 1947, Confederate Blockade Running Through Bermuda, 1861-65: Letters and Cargo Manifests, 1947, Proceedings of First Confederate Congress, 4th Session, 1953, Proceedings of Second Confederate Congress, 1959, A Collection of Louisiana Confederate Letters; new edit, J.E. Johnston's Narrative of Military Operations; new edit, J.A. Early's Civil War Memoirs, The Idea of the South, 1964; author: Ploughshares Into Swords: Josiah Gorgas and Confederate Ordnance, 1952, Rebel Brass: The Confederate Command System, 1956, Mighty Stonewall, 1957, Fields of Glory, (with W. H. Nelson), 1960, Jubal's Raid, 1960, Basic History of the Confederacy, 1962, Jefferson Davis and the Confederate State, 1964, Their Tattered Flags: The Epic of the Confederacy, 1970, The Southwest: South or West?, 1975, Black Jack: The Life and Times of John J. Pershing, 1977 (Nat. Book Award finalist 1978), (address) The Long Loom of Lincoln, 9th rev., 1986; also hist. articles.; mem. bd. editors: U.S. Grant Papers, 1973—. Confederate Inaugural Centennial speaker Va. Civil War Centennial, 1962; mem. adv. council Civil War Centennial Commn.; cons. NEH, 1966-72; mem. adv. council, office chief mil. history Dept. Army, 1969-74; exec. dir. Am. Revolution Bicentennial Commn. Tex., 1970-73; mem. selection com. Ft. Leavenworth Hall of Fame Assn. U.S. Army, 1971-72, 74-81, 83-84; bd. dirs. Inst. Civil War Studies, 1975-80; chmn. adv. council U.S. Mil. Hist. Research Collection, Carlisle Barracks, Pa., 1972-75; mem. Nat. Council for Humanities, 1972-78, vice-chmn., 1976-78; adv. com. U.S. Army Command and Gen. Staff Coll., 1984—; bd. sect. Navy Adv. Bd. Edn. and Tng., 1984-86; mem. U.S. Army Adv. Panel ROTC Affairs, 1984—; cons., mem. Army Sci. Bd., 1986-88; bd. dirs. Assn. Am. Colls., 1982, GTSW, 1987, The Conf. Bd., 1987; Mem. Internat. Edn. Commn., Am. Council Edn., 1982. Recipient research grants Am. Philos. Soc., 1953, 54, 60; Guggenheim fellow, 1955-56; Huntington Library research grant, 1961; laureate Lincoln Acad., Ill., 1973; Carr P. Collins prize Tex. Inst. Letters, 1958, Harry S. Truman award Kansas City Civil War Round Table, Jefferson Davis award Confederate Meml. Lit. Soc., 1970, Fletcher Pratt award N.Y. Civil War Round Table, 1970, First Outstanding Alumnus award Tulane U. Grad. Sch., 1974, Outstanding Civilian Service medal Dept. Army, 1974, Nevins-Freeman award Chgo. Civil War Round Table, 1982, T. Harry Williams Meml. award, 1985; named hon. mem. Sons of Republic of Tex., 1986. Fellow Tex. Hist. Assn.; mem. Am. Hist. Assn., So. Hist. Assn. (asso. editor jour. 1959-62, pres. 1975-76), Tex. Inst. Letters (past pres.), Jefferson Davis Assn. (pres., chmn. adv. bd. editors of papers), So. Am. Historians (councillor), Tex. Philos. Soc. (pres. 1978), Civil War Round Table (Houston), Orgn. Am. Historians, Sons of Republic of Tex. (hon.), Phi Beta Kappa, SAR of Tex. (hon.). Clubs: Cosmos, Army and Navy (Washington); Briarcrest Country (College Station); Austin, Headliners (Austin). Office: Tex A&M Univ Office of the President College Station TX 77843-1246

VAN DONKELAAR, PIETER, mechanical engineer, environmental consultant; b. Dordrecht, The Netherlands, Oct. 1, 1927; arrived in Belgium, 1986; s. Anthonie Adrianus and Geertje (Volker) van D.; m. Marjolene Suzanne Bergman, Sept. 27, 1955; children: Anthonie Rudolf, Louisette Marjolene, Carla Bianca, Nelleke Katinka, Ilse Anushka, Albine Mariken. ME, Technol. U., Delft, The Netherlands, 1954. Chief insp. Hispano Suiza, Breda, The Netherlands, 1954-56, asst. factory mgr., 1956-57; factory mgr. Becht & Dyserinck, Rucphen, The Netherlands, 1957-58; chief engr. Outboard Marine Belgium, Brugge, 1958-79, dir. environ. affairs, 1979-87; environ. cons. Greentech Research, Herbeumont, Belgium, 1987—; chmn. PL-14 Coordinating European Council, London, 1977—; lectr. Tech. Acad. Esslingen, Fed. Republic Germany, 1983—. Author: Modern Two-Stroke Lubrication, 1987; contbr. numerous articles on quality control, product liability, environ. affairs, electric cars, two-stroke lubricants, and econs. to profl. jours.; inventor electric car. Served with arty. Dutch Army, 1948-50. Decorated knight Order of Crown (Belgium); recipient European quality award European Orgn. Quality Control, 1979, ann. presdl. award, 1981. Mem. Internat. Wassersportgemeinschaft, Royal Inst. Engring., Am. Soc. for Quality Control (sr.), Belgische Vereniging van Automobiel Ingenieurs, Assn. pour Sauvegarde de Leman, Assn. Vehicules Electriques Routiers Europe, Internat. Profl. Assn. for Environ. Affairs, Soc. for Risk Analysis. Home: Velodreef 91, Essen, B2190 Antwerp Belgium Office: Greentech Research SPRL, Voie du Four 23, B6803 Herbeumont Luxembourg, Belgium

VAN DYKE, GENE, energy company executive; b. Normal, Ill., Nov. 5, 1926; s. Harold and Ruby (Gibson) Van D.; B.S. in Geol. Engring., U. Okla., 1950; m. Kerstin Rohr, Feb. 27, 1981; children—Karen, Scott, Janice, Mary Katherine. Geologist, Kerr-McGee, Oklahoma City, 1950; chief geologist S.D. Johnson Co., Wichita Falls, Tex., 1950-51; ind. geologist and oil operator, 1951-58; partner Van Dyke and Mejlaender, Houston, 1958-62; owner, pres. Van Dyke Oil Co. (name now Van Dyke Energy Co.), Houston, 1962—; also dir.; dir. Van Dyke Netherlands, Inc. Served with AC, U.S. Army, 1945. Mem. Am. Petroleum Inst., Ind. Petroleum Assn. Am., Am. Assn. Petroleum Geologists, Am. Assn. Petroleum Landmen, Tex. Mid-Continent Oil and Gas Assn. Republican. Methodist. Clubs: Houston, Houston Petroleum, Houston City. Compiler index of geol. articles in South La. Home: 3815 Olympia Houston TX 77019 Office: Van Dyke Energy Co One Greenway Plaza Houston TX 77046

VAN DYKE, JON MARKHAM, lawyer, educator; b. Washington, Apr. 29, 1943; s. Stuart Hope and Eleonora (Markham) Van D.; m. Sherry Phyllis Broder, Feb. 12, 1978; children—Jesse Bernard, Eric Gabriel, Michelle Tiare. B.A., Yale U., 1964; J.D., Harvard U., 1967. Bar: D.C. 1968, Calif. 1970, Hawaii, 1976. Asst. prof. law Cath. U., Washington, 1967-69; law clk. Calif. Supreme Ct., San Francisco, 1969-70; vis. fellow Ctr. for Study of Democratic Instns., Santa Barbara, 1970-71; assoc. prof. law Hastings Law Sch., U. Calif.-San Francisco, 1971-75, prof., 1975-76; prof. law Law Sch., U. Hawaii, Honolulu, 1976—, assoc. dean, 1980-82; project dir., law of the sea Sea Grant Coll. Program, 1979—; research assoc. Environment and Policy Inst., East-West Ctr., Honolulu, 1982-84, adj. research assoc. Resource Systems Inst., 1986—; mem. exec. bd. Law of the Sea Inst., Honolulu, 1982-88; dir. U. Hawaii Inst. for Peace, 1988—. Author: North Vietnam's Strategy for Survival, 1972; Jury Selection Procedures: Our Uncertain Commitment to Representative Panels, 1977; editor: Consensus and Confrontation: The United States and the Law of the Sea Convention, 1985; International Navigation: Rocks and Shoals Ahead?, 1988. Mem. Reapportionment Commn., Honolulu, 1981-82, ACLU Litigation Com., Honolulu, 1986-87, Hawaii Bicentennial Commn. of U.S. Constitution, 1987. Named Outstanding Prof. Hawaii Assn. of Plaintiffs Attys., 1984; recipient Presdl. Citation for Teaching Excellence, 1987. Mem. Am. Soc. Internat. Law, Hawaii State Bar Assn., Internat. Council Environ. Law, Amnesty Internat. USA Legal Adv. Council. Home: 4191 Round Top Dr Honolulu HI 76822 Office: U Hawaii Law Sch 2515 Dole St Honolulu HI 96822

VAN DYKE, JOSEPH GARY OWEN, computer consulting executive; b. N.Y.C., Dec. 21, 1939; s. Donald Wood and Gladys Ann (Tague) Van D.; m. Lynne Diane Lammers; June 25, 1966; children: Alison Baird, Jeremy Wood, Matthew Kerr. BA, Rutgers U., 1961; postgrad., R.I. Sch. of Design, 1962, Am. U., 1964-67. Computer programmer System Devel. Corp., Paramus, N.J., 1962-64; sect. head computer tech. div. System Devel. Corp., Falls Church, Va., 1964-67; project mgr. Informatics Inc., Bethesda, Md., 1967-70; dept. dir. Informatics Inc., Rockville, Md., 1970-74, v.p., gen. mgr., 1974-78; owner, pres. J G Van Dyke and Assoc., Inc., Bethesda, 1978—; chmn. bd., chief exec. officer The Outreach Group, Inc., 1987—. Bd. dirs. Westbrook Sch., Bethesda, 1981-82, St. Columba's Ch., Washington, 1980-84; founder Computer Edn. Workshop, Bethesda, 1981; coach MSI soccer, Bethesda, 1979—. Mem. Inst. Elec. Engring. Democrat. Episcopalian. Home: 5117 Dalecarlia Dr Bethesda MD 20816 Office: 6701 Rockledge Dr 250ᴮBethesda MD 20817

VANE, JOHN ROBERT, pharmacologist; b. Worcestershire, Eng., Mar. 29, 1927; s. Maurice and Frances Florence V.; B.Sc. in Chemistry, U. Birmingham, 1946; B.Sc. in Pharmacology, Oxford U., 1949, D.Phil., 1953, D.Sc., 1970; D.Med. (hon.), U. Cracow (Poland), 1977, Copernicus Acad. Medicine, Cracow; Doctor (hon.), Rene Descartes U., Paris, 1978; D.Sc. (hon.), CUNY, 1980, Aberdeen U., 1983, N.Y. Med. Coll., 1984, Birmingham U., 1984, U. Surrey, 1984, Camerino U., Italy, 1984; m. Elizabeth Daphne Page, Apr. 4, 1948; children—Nicola, Miranda. Fellow, Therapeutic Research Council, Oxford U., 1946-48; researcher worker Sheffield U., 1948-49, Nuffield Inst. Med. Research, Oxford U., 1949-51; Stothert research fellow Royal Soc., 1951-53; instr., then asst. prof. pharmacology Yale U. Med. Sch., 1953-55; mem. faculty Inst. Basic Med. Scis., Royal Coll. Surgeons Eng., 1955-73, prof. exptl. pharmacology, 1966-73; group research and devel. dir. Wellcome Found. Ltd., Beckenham, Kent, 1973-85; bd. dirs. William Harvey Research Inst., St. Bartholomew's Hosp. Med. Coll., London, 1986—. Decorated knight bachelor; recipient Baly medal Royal Coll. Physicians; Albert Lasker Basic Med. Research award; Peter Debye prize; Nuffield Gold medal; Ciba Geigy Drew award Drew U.; Feldberg Found. prize; Dale medal Soc. for Endocrinology, 1981; Nobel prize in medicine, 1982; Galen Medal Worshipful Soc. Apothecaries, 1983; Louis Pasteur Found. prize, Santa Monica, Calif., 1984. Fellow ACP (hon.), Inst. Biology, Royal Soc., Brit. Pharm. Soc.; mem. Polish Pharm. Soc. (hon.), Physiol. Soc., Royal Acad. Medicine Belgium, Royal Netherlands Acad. Arts and Scis., Polish Acad. Scis. (fgn.), Am. Acad. Arts and Scis. (fgn. hon.), Soc. Drug Research, Nat. Acad. Scis. (fgn. assoc.). Co-editor: Adrenergic Mechanisms, 1960; Prostaglandin Synthetase Inhibitors, 1974; Metabolic Functions of the Lung, Vol. 4, 1977; Handbook of Experimental Pharmacology, 1978; Prostacyclin, 1979; Interactions Between Platelets and Vessel Walls, 1981; contbr. numerous articles to profl. jours. Home: White Angles, 7 Beech Dell, Keston BR2 6EP Kent, England Office: William Harvey Research Inst, St Bartholomew's Hosp Med Coll, London EC1M 6BQ, England

VANE, SYLVIA BRAKKE, anthropologist, cultural resource management company executive; b. Fillmore County, Minn., Feb. 28, 1918; d. John T. and Hulda Christina (Marburger) Brakke; m. Arthur Bayard Vane, May 17, 1942; children—Ronald Arthur, Linda, Laura Vane Ames. A.A., Rochester Jr. Coll., 1937; B.S. with distinction, U. Minn., 1939; student Radcliffe Coll., 1944; M.A., Calif. State U.-Hayward, 1975. Med. technologist Dr. Frost and Hodapp, Willmar, Minn., 1939-41; head labs. Corvallis Gen. Hosp., Oreg., 1941-42; dir. lab. Cambridge Gen. Hosp., Mass., 1942-43, Peninsula Clinic, Redwood City, Calif., 1947-49; v.p. Cultural Systems Research, Inc., Menlo Park, Calif., 1978—; pres. Ballena Press, Menlo Park, 1981—; cons. cultural resource mgmt. So. Calif. Edison Co., Rosemead, 1978-81, San Diego Gas and Elec. Co., 1980-83, Pacific Gas and Elec. Co., San Francisco, 1982-83, Wender, Murase & White, Washington, 1983—, Yosemite Indians, Mariposa, Calif., 1982-84, San Luis Rey Band of Mission Indians, Escondido, Calif., 1986—, U.S. Ecology, Newport Beach, Calif., 1986—, Riverside County Flood Control and Water Conservation Dist., 1985—. Author: (with L.J. Bean), California Indians, Primary Resources, 1977, The Cahuilla and the Santa Rosa Mountains, 1981. Contbr. chpts. to several books. Bd. dirs. Sequoia Area council Girl Scouts U.S., 1954-61; bd. dirs., v.p., pres. LWV, S. San Mateo County, Calif., 1960-65, cons. San Francisco council Girl Scouts U.S., 1962-69. Fellow Soc. Applied Anthropology; mem. Southwestern Anthrop. Assn. (program chmn. 1976-78, newsletter editor 1976-79), Am. Anthropology Assn., Soc. for Am. Archaeology. Mem. United Ch. of Christ. Office: Ballena Press 823 Valparaiso Ave Menlo Park CA 94025

VAN EEKELEN, WILLEM FREDERIK, government official; b. Utrecht, The Netherlands, Feb. 5, 1931; m. Johanna Wentink; 2 children. Student, Utrecht U., Princeton U., 1950-52; degree in law, Utrecht U., 1954, Ph.D. cum laude, 1964. Mem. Netherlands Diplomatic Service, 1957-77, Lower House of Parliament, 1977-78, 81-82; state sec. defense The Netherlands, 1978-81, state sec. fgn. affairs, 1982-86; minister of def. 2d Lubbers govt., The Netherlands, 1986-88. Office: care Ministry of Def, Amsterdam The Netherlands *

VAN ELZAKKER, ANTON HENDRICK MARIE, biochemist; b. Bergen op Zoom, The Netherlands, June 25, 1935. PhD in Biochemistry, Tech. U., 1959. Prof. physics and biology European Coll., Luxemburg, 1965-69; headmaster Veurs Coll., Leidschendam, The Netherlands, 1969-74; product mgr. Astra Pharmaceutics, Den Haag, The Netherlands, 1974-80; asst. mgr. marketing Hassle A.B., Gothenburg, Sweden, 1980-81; dir. clin. research Warner-Lambert, Amsterdam, 1981—. Editor: (with others) (book) Beta-blockade and Anaesthesia, 1979. Mem. Dutch Soc. Cardiology, European Soc. Cardiology. Home: Starkenborglaan 3, Oegstgeest The Netherlands Office: Warner-Lambert, Postbus 3G4 Kruisweg 327B, 2130 AJ Hoofddorp The Netherlands

VAN ESSCHE, JOHN REMI, film company executive; b. Hoeilaart, Belgium, Aug. 26, 1927; s. Victor and Melanie Van E.; m. Georgette Vandooren; children—Hugo, Gert, An. Diploma in bus. U. Louvain (Belgium), 1949. Sales mgr. Fabelta S.A., Belgium, 1951-70;dir. UCB-div. Sidac Films, Gent, Belgium, 1970—, dir., 1984—; dir. conversion div. UCB Belgium; chmn. Conversion Cos. in Europe; vice chmn. Brit. Sidac, 1973; chmn. Med. Industries, U.S.; dir. Sidex Ltd., Gt. Brit. Club: Orde Prince (Belgium). Home: Jezus Eikse Steenweg 22A, 1990 Hoeilaart Belgium Office: UCB Film Sector, Ottergemse Steenweg 801, 9000 Gent Belgium

VAN GALEN LAST, HENDRIK, writer; b. Bandung, Java, Indonesia, Feb. 13, 1921; came to Holland, 1934; S. Gerrit Van Galen Last and Elmire Vroom; m. Marie Stevels, May 24, 1944 (dec. May 1979); children: Marc, Eefje, Dick. Cert. tchr. history. Literary critic Haags Dagblad, The Hague, Holland, 1947-48; cultural adivsor Sticusa, Amsterdam, Holland, 1948-56; researcher Found. Sci. Research, The Hague, 1958-62; tchr. history Lycée, Amsterdam, 1962-74; tchr. Sch. Tchrs. in History, The Hague, 1974-83; writer The Hague, 1945-69; columnist Nieuwe Rotterdamse Courant, 1968-71, NRC-Handelsblad, 1971—. Author: President Dramakutra, 1957, De Waanzin van Ajax, 1979, De spoken van W.F. Hermans, 1986; editor: Correspondence Ter Braak-Du Perron, 4 vols., 1962-68, Libertinage, Amsterdam, 1949-53; contbr. articles to profl. jours. Mem. Maatschappij Voor Ned. Letterkunde. Home: 407 Amerbos, Amsterdam 1025 ZH, Holland

VAN GELDER, SANDER, manufacturing executive; b. Amsterdam, Holland, Oct. 2, 1937; s. Leo and Henie (Weich) van G.; m. Ruth Heller, Mar. 20, 1962; children—Danny, Marc, Rachel. Engr., Tech. Hochschule Pforzheim (Ger.), 1958; degree econs. Inst. Soc. Wetensch., 1962. Mgr., Kon Byenkorf/Beheer, Amsterdam, 1958-60; mgr. Jewellery Chain, Eindhoven, 1960-62, pres., Jewel Diamond Group, Utrecht, 1962-74; pres. Internat. Trade Group, Zeist, 1974-78; pres. Group of Cos., Vale do Lobo, Portugal, 1978—; dir. Gen. Tourism, Lisbon, 1981-83. Patentee in field. Decorated Bronze Medallion, King of Greece, 1956; Design award Jewellery Designs, Fedn. Gold and Diamonds, 1970; Tourist award Spanish Tourist Orgn., 1982-84. Mem. Dutch Jewellery Orgn., Merito Turistico Portuges Govt., Portuges Red Cross (pres. 1972-78). Home: Rua da colina 454, 8100 Vale do Lobo, Algarve Portugal Office: Vale do Lobo Lda, 8100 Vale do Lobo, Algarve Portugal

VAN GILDER, DEREK ROBERT, lawyer, engineer; b. San Antonio, Feb. 26, 1950; s. Robert Ellis and Genevieve Delphine (Hutter) Van G.; m. Charlene Frances Madison, Jan. 21, 1984. Student, U.S. Mil. Acad., 1969-71; BS in Civil Engring., U. Tex., 1974, JD, 1981; MBA, U. Houston, 1976. Bar: Tex. 1981, U.S. Ct. Appeals (9th cir.) 1981, Calif. 1982, U.S. Dist. Ct. (cen. dist.) Calif. 1982, U.S. Dist. Ct. (ea. and so. dists.) Tex. 1982, U.S. Ct. Appeals (5th cir.) 1982, U.S. Dist. Ct. (we. dist.) Tex. 1983; registered profl. engr. Tex., La., N.M., Calif. Engr. various engring cos., Houston, Longview and Austin, Tex., 1974-81; assoc. Thelen, Marrin, Johnson & Bridges, Los Angeles, 1981-82, Bean & Manning, Houston, 1982-85; sole practice Houston, 1985-86; prin. Van Gilder & Assocs., Houston, 1986—; instr. Houston Community Coll., 1981—. Mem. ABA, Houston Bar Assn., Am. Arbitration Assn. (panel arbitrators), Houston Med.-Legal Soc., Nat. Soc. Profl. Engrs., Tex. Soc. Profl. Engrs. Republican. Roman Catholic. Club: Houston City. Office: 11 Greenway Plaza Suite 2222 Houston TX 77046

VAN GILS, GILBERT JAN, sales professional; b. Merksem, Belgium, May 16, 1938; s. Corneel and Adele (Hufkens) Van G.; m. Jacqueline Angeline Kreydt, Aug. 7, 1962; children: Pascale, Muriel. Grad. in mktg., Trade and Tech. Sch., Antwerp, 1958; postgrad., U. Antwerp, 1974-77. Service engr. Gevaert Photo Products, Antwerpen, 1961-63; photolab mgr. Unicolor Co., Brussels, 1963-66, LTPP Co., Valence, France, 1966-68; European field mgr. Pako Corp., Antwerpen, 1968-73; mng. dir. Pako Europe, Antwerpen, 1973-78; pres., chief exec. officer Ampaco/Amdipro Co., Antwerpen, 1979—. Served with Belgian mil., 1958-61. Roman Catholic. Home: Damhertenlaan 12, 2232 Schilde Antwerpen Belgium Office: NV Ampaco/NV Amdipro, Middelmolenlaan 110, 2100 Deurne Antwerpen Belgium

VAN GULICK, ARNOLD JOHANNES WILHELMUS, marketing executive; b. den Bosch, The Netherlands, July 10, 1942; s. Arnold A.C.M. and Henriëtte (Beekwilder) van G.; m. Martina Timmers, Oct. 14, 1944; children: Maritt, Christiane. H.B.S.b., St. Janslyceum, den Bosch, 1961. Sales exec. Bruynzeel, Zaandam, The Netherlands, 1964-68; merchandising mgr. EDAH, Helmond, The Netherlands, 1968-71; product mgr. Bensdorp, Bussum, The Netherlands, 1971-77; mktg. mgr. Melkunie, Woerden, The Netherlands, 1977-82; dir. sales and mktg. Johma, Losser, The Netherlands, 1982-84; gen. mktg. mgr. Coberco Group Cos., Zutphen, The Netherlands, 1984—. Served with Dutch Arty., 1962-64. Office: Coberco ba, Stationsplein 37, Zutphen 7200 AB, The Netherlands

VANHAEFTEN, CARL FREDERICK, former federal agency administrator; b. Santa Cruz, Calif., Jan. 12, 1923; s. Karel August Rudolf and Anna Bartholda (Faure) vanH.; m. Dorothy G. Wolthuis, Aug. 30, 1946 (div. July 1968); children: Karel A.R., Linda, Eileen; m. Roberta K. Taylor, Oct. 31, 1969. B.S., Royal Coll. Tropical Agr., The Netherlands, 1945. Investigator U.S. Mil. Intelligence Unit, The Hague, 1946-47; German youth activities officer U.S. Army, Augsburg, 1947-48; edn. adviser 2d Armored Cav. Regt., Augsburg, 1948-50; chief info. and edn. (2d Air Div.), Landsburg, Germany, 1950-51; fgn. student adviser Coll. Agr., U. Maine, 1952-53; agrl. tng. specialist U.S. mission to European Regional and Other Orgns., 1953-54; chief FOA agrl. tng. br. Europe and Latin Am., 1954-56; dep. and acting chief div. econ. assistance to Spain for food and agr. 1956-60; dir. program econ. assistance for food and agr. Cambodia, 1960-63, Morocco, 1964-65; asst. dir. U.S. AID mission to Vietnam, 1965-68, spl. asst. war on hunger, 1968-70; mid-career tng. Johns Hopkins, 1970-71; chief rural devel. div. Latin Am. Bur., AID, 1972-75; cons. internat. devel., 1975—. Served with Underground Resistance Movement, World War II, in Holland. Recipient U.S. Medal of Freedom, 1946; Vietnam Agrl. medal, 1968. Home: 2840 Linden Ln Falls Church VA 22042

VANHANDEL, RALPH ANTHONY, librarian; b. Appleton, Wis., Jan. 17, 1919; s. Frank Henry and Gertrude Mary (Schmidt) Van H.; m. Alice Catherine Hogan, Oct. 27, 1945; children: William Patrick, Karen Jean, Mary Jo. BA, U. Wis., 1946; AB, U. Mich., 1947. Head librarian Lawrence (Kans.) Free Pub. Library, 1947-51, Hibbing (Minn.) Pub. Library, 1951-54; library dir. Gary (Ind.) Pub. Library, 1954-74, Wells Meml. Pub. Library, Lafayette, Ind. (name now Tippecanoe County Pub. Library), 1974-84; mem. Ind. Library Cert. Bd., 1969-84, Ind. State Library and Hist. Bldg. Expansion Commn., 1973-81. Named Ind. Librarian of Year, 1971, Sagamore of Wabash, 1984. Mem. Anselm Forum (sec. 1964, v.p. 1965), ALA, Ind. Library Assn. (pres. 1963-64), Kans. Library Assn. (v.p. 1951). Clubs: KC, Rotary. Home: 3624 Winter St Lafayette IN 47905

VANHANEN, TATU, political science educator; b. Vuoksenranta, Finland, Apr. 17, 1929; s. Taavi and Anna (Jantunen) V.; m. Anni Tiihonen, July 15, 1951; children: Rauno Juhani, Matti Taneli, Tuomo Tahvo. Candidate, Sch. Social Scis., Finland, 1958, licentiate, 1963; D Social Scis., U. Tampere, Finland, 1968. Editor Kyntäjä Rural Youth Union, Helsinki, Finland, 1959-61; chief article service Agrarian Party/Ctr. Party, Helsinki, 1962-69; acting assoc. prof. U. Jyväskuylä, Finland, 1969-72; researcher Acad. Finland, Helsinki, 1972-74; assoc. prof. U. Tampere, Finland, 1974—. Author: Power and the Means of Power, 1979, The Emergence of Democracy: A Comparative Study of 119 States, 1850-1979, 1984. Grantee Acad. Finland, 1970—, Scandinavian Inst. Asian Studies, 1976, 80, 84; Fulbright scholar, 1973-74. Mem. Assn. for Politics and Life Scis., Internat. Polit. Sci. Assn., Finnish Polit. Sci. Assn. (pres. 1986—). Mem. Center Party. Lutheran. Home: Vanha Lahnuksentie, 02970 Espoo 97 Finland Office: U Tampere, PO Box 607, 33101 Tampere Finland

VAN HARE, GEORGE FREDERICK, JR., chemical engineer; b. Jersey City, N.J., Oct. 8, 1923; s. George Frederick and Anna Price (Kuckler) Van H.; B in Chem. Engring., Pratt Inst., 1948; m. Marjorie Hall Ross, Nov. 8, 1952; children: George Frederick, David Ross, John Andrew, Mary Elizabeth. Project engr. Chem. Constrn. Co., N.Y.C., 1948-56; sr. project engr. Am. Cyanamid Co., Wayne, N.J., 1956-67, mgr. materials handling, 1967-73, chief materials handling engr., 1973-82; chief engr. materials handling dept. Fenco Engrs., Inc., Toronto, Ont., Can., 1982—. Pack com. chmn. Fairfield County council Boy Scouts Am., 1967-69, troop com. chmn., 1971-73, com. mem. at large, 1974-77. Served with USAAF, 1942-45. Registered Profl. Engr., N.Y., N.J., Ont. Mem. Internat. Material Mgmt. Soc. (internat. v.p. 1977-79, dir. 1979-82, treas. Toronto chpt. 1983-85, 87-88, pres. 1988—), joint ASME-IMMS handbook com. 1980-85, Am. Inst. Chem. Engrs., Tau Beta Pi. Presbyterian. Patentee field hydrometallurgy. Home: 500 Underwood Crescent, Oakville, ON Canada L6L 5P1 Office: 2235 Sheppard Ave E, Willowdale, ON Canada M2J 5A6

VAN HEESWYCK, PIETER ERIC, airline executive; b. Den Bosch, Brabant, The Netherlands, Apr. 25, 1926; s. Ernest Hubert and Maria (Marynen) Van H.; m. Anneke Karreman, June 25, 1945. Comml. trainee KLM Royal Dutch Airlines, The Hague, 1947-51; regional mgr. KLM Royal Dutch Airlines, Sydney, Australia, 1951-77; gen. mgr. KLM Royal Dutch Airlines, Teheran, Iran, 1977-79, Manila, 1979-81, Bahrain, 1981-85, Bangkok, 1985—. Served with Dutch Air Force, 1944-47. Decorated knight Order Orange Nassau (The Netherlands); recipient Romulo medal UN Assn., Manila, 1979. Fellow Australian Inst. Travel. Roman Catholic. Lodge: Rotary. Office: KLM Royal Dutch Airlines, PO Box 1134, Bangkok Thailand

VANHOEBROUCK, JULES, management professional; b. Kolwezi, Shaba, Zaire, Nov. 8, 1950; s. Frans and Quintens B. VanH.; m. Corinne Dewever, Jan. 12, 1978; 1 child, Laurent. Hon. degree, U. Louvain, Belgium, Intern Trade Inst., Brussels. Asst. mgr. Norton and Wright, Brussels, 1978-80; purchasing mgr. Foraky, Brussels, 1980-85; br. mgr. Entrepose Montalev, Belgium, Luxemburg, 1986—. Club: World Trade Ctr. Internat. (intern). Lodge: Lions. Home: Ave Croix de Guerre 199, 1120 Brussels Belgium Office: Entrepose-Montalev, Ave Defre 269, 1180 Brussels Belgium

VAN HORN, JAMES HENRY, marketing professional; b. Chgo., Nov. 20, 1931. B.A., Pa. State U., 1954; postgrad. Johns Hopkins U., 1956-61. Sr. prin. engr. Litton Industries, New Rochelle, N.Y., 1960-64; mgr. communications div. Gen. Dynamics, Rochester, 1964-68; mgr. communications ITT, N.Y.C., 1968-70, tech. dir. ITTE, Brussels, Belgium, 1971-80, dir. bus. devel., 1980-88, br. head com. architecture Shape Tech. Ctr. NATO, The Hague, The Netherlands, 1988—; v.p. Space Age Survival, Inc., Balt., 1958-61. Contbr. articles to profl. jours.; patentee in field. Vice chmn. Republicans Abroad, 1985-86. Mem. Armed Forces Communications Electronics Assn. (pres. 1979), IEEE (sec.-treas. 1964-68). Republican. Office: STC Box 174, 2501 CD Den Hague The Netherlands

VAN HOWE, ANNETTE EVELYN, real estate agent; b. Chgo., Feb. 16, 1921; d. Frank and Susan (Linstra) Van Howe; B.A. in History magna cum laude, Hofstra U., 1952; M.A. in Am. History, SUNY-Binghamton, 1966; m. Edward L. Nezelek, Apr. 3, 1961. Editorial asst. Salute Mag., N.Y.C., 1946-48; asso. editor Med. Econs., Oradell, N.J., 1952-56; nat. mag. publicist Nat. Mental Health Assn., N.Y.C., 1956-60; exec. dir. Diabetes Assn. So. Calif., Los Angeles, 1960-61; corporate sec., v.p., editor, public relations dir. Edward L. Nezelek, Inc., Johnson City, N.Y., 1961-82; mgr. condominium, Fort Lauderdale, Fla., 1982-83; dir. Sky Harbour East Condo, 1983-88; substitute tchr. high schs., Binghamton, N.Y., 1961-63. Bd. dirs. Broome County Mental Health Assn., 1961-65, Fine Arts Soc., Roberson Center for Arts and Scis., 1968-70, Found. Wilson Meml. Hosp., Johnson City, 1972-81, Found. SUNY, Binghamton; trustee Broome Community Coll., 1973-78; v.p. Broward County Commn. on Status of Women, 1982—; bd. dirs. Ft. Lauderdale Women's Council of Realtors, 1986—, Broward Arts Guild, 1986; grad. Leadership Broward Class III, 1985, Leadership Am., 1988; trustee Unitarian-Universalist Ch. of Ft. Lauderdale, 1982—. Mem. AAUW (legis. chair Fla. div. 1986-87), Am. Med. Writers Assn., LWV (dir. Broome County 1969-70), Alumni Assn. SUNY Binghamton (dir. 1970-73), Am. Acad. Polit. and Social Sci., Nat. Assn. Female Execs., Am. Heritage Soc., Nature Conservancy, Nat. Hist. Soc., Ft. Lauderdale Women's Council Realtors (corr. sec.), Alpha Theta Beta, Phi Alpha Theta, Phi Gamma Mu. Clubs: Binghamton Garden, Binghamton Monday Afternoon, Acacia Garden (pres.); 110 Tower; Tower Forum; Downtown Council. Editor newsletter Mental Health Assn., 1965-68, newsletter Unitarian-Universalist Ch., weekly 1967-71, History of Broome County Meml. Arena, 1972. Home: 2100 S Ocean Dr Fort Lauderdale FL 33316 Office: 2230 SE 17th St Fort Lauderdale FL 33316

VAN HUFFELEN, GERRIT GIJSBERT, data processing executive; b. Hague, Zuid-Holland, The Netherlands, Oct. 7, 1944; s. Gerrit and Jacoba Maria (Cornelisse) van H.; m. Adriana van Oosten, Mar. 8, 1968 (div. Apr. 1975); children: Franck Anton, Jolijn. Degree in Mgmt. Info. Systems, Novi, Maarsen, The Netherlands, 1983. Cons. Colpapier, Mydrecht, The Netherlands, 1979-80; project mgr. Vereniging Van Artsen en Automobilisten Life Ins., Utrecht, The Netherlands, 1980-83, AEGON Ins., The Hague, 1983-84; cons. Post Telefonic and Telegraphic Inc., Groningen, The Netherlands, 1984, Algemeen Burgelijk Pensioen Fonds Ins. Co., Heerlen, The Netherlands, 1984, NN Ins., The Hague, 1985-86, Bull, Amersfoort, The Netherlands, 1986, ABP, Heerlen, The Netherlands, 1986—. Clubs: W.S.V. Heusden, Gloria Maris (Den Bosch). Home: Trompstraat 5, 5151 NA Drunen The Netherlands Office: Bureau van Huffelen, Trompstraat 5, 5151 NA Drunen The Netherlands

VAN ITTERSUM, BOUDEWIJN FRANCISCUS, stock exchange executive; b. Bloemendaal, Netherlands, June 7, 1939; s. Paul A.L.A. and Henriette F. (van Lennep) Van I.; m. Karin R.W. Van der Ven, Oct. 28, 1967; children—Adrienne, Emilie, Clarien. D.Econ. Scis., U. Amsterdam, 1965. Economist, fgn. dept. Ministry of Fin., The Hague, Netherlands, 1967-70, head dept. monetary policy, 1971-76, dir domestic fin. policies, 1976-77, dir. fgn. fin. relations, 1977-81; asst. exec. dir. IMF/World Bank, Washington, 1970-71; chmn. Amsterdam Stock Exchange, 1981—; v.p. Internat. Fedn. Stock Exchanges, Paris, 1985-87, pres., 1987—; dir. European Investment Bank, Luxemburg, 1977-81, Netherlands Credit Ins. Co., Amsterdam, 1977-81; vice chmn. Assn. Bank and Securities Industry, Amsterdam, 1981—; mem. banking council Netherlands Bank, Amsterdam, 1981—; mem. supervisory bd. Kas Assoc., 1981—. Contbr. articles to profl. jours. Served to 1st lt. Royal Netherlands Air Force, 1965-67. Office: Amsterdam Stock Exchange, PO Box 19163, Amsterdam 1000GD The Netherlands

VAN KAMMEN, EVERT, internist; b. Soest, Netherlands, Dec. 22, 1941; s. Daniel Paul and Christina P.H. (Rinse) Van K.; m. Lucretia Margaretha Van Kerkwijk, May 2, 1970; children—Daniel P., Marieke. MD, U. Utrecht (Netherlands), 1967, specialist in internal medicine, 1973, PhD, 1976. Intern, Univ. Hosp., Utrecht, 1965-67, resident, 1969-72; fellow in pharmacology Rudolf Magnus Inst., Utrecht, 1968; practice medicine specializing in hematology, 1973—; cons. internal medicine, surgery dept. Univ. Hosp., Utrecht, 1973-74, cons. internal medicine, hematology dept., 1974-76; cons. Refaja Hosp., Dordrecht, Netherlands, 1976—. Author: Sex Hormones in Uraemic Males, 1976, Geschiedenis Van de Tbc-bestrijding in Dordrecht, 1987. Mem. council Oud-Dordrecht, 1983—. Mem. Koninklijke Nederlandse Maatschappij tot bevordering der Geneeskunst, Netherlands Soc. for Clin. Sci., Dutch Soc. for Hematology, N.Y. Acad. Scis., Landelijke Specialisten Vereniging der KNMG. Office: Refaja Hospital, Van der Steenhovenplein 1, 3317 NM Dordrecht The Netherlands

VAN KREGTEN, ANTHONY GERARD LODEWYK WILLEM, JR., aerospace engineer; b. Middelburg, Netherlands, Dec. 7, 1906; s. Anthony Gerard Lodewyk Willem and Anna Hermanna (Rompelman) Van K.; came to U.S., 1953, naturalized, 1959; m. Lucille Plantenga, Sept. 26, 1935; children—Ronald, Fitzgerald. B.S., Holland Poly. U., Arnhem, 1930, M.S. in Aero. Engring., 1942. Mem. staff preliminary design Fokker Aircraft, Holland, 1931-45; asst. prof. aero. div. Delft (Holland) U., 1945-53; staff engr. Lockheed Aircraft Corp., Burbank, Calif., 1953-57, research specialist Lockheed Missile and Space Co., Sunnyvale, Calif., 1957-66; staff cons. engr., Lockheed Missile and Space Co. and Lockheed Ga. div., San Jose, Calif., 1966—; v.p. Pacific Tech. Inst., San Jose. Lic. aircraft pilot. Fellow AIAA (asso.); mem. ASTM, Am. Ordnance Assn., Nat. Aeronautic Assn., Aircraft Owners and Pilots Assn., Airmen's Assn. Santa Clara. Presbyn. Author: Directions Aircraft Design, 1953; Reliability Engineering Missile Systems, 1961; contbg. author Tech. Engring. Ency., 1948—; patentee antitank missile, 1965. Home: 258 Cronin Dr Santa Clara CA 95051 Office: Lockheed Missle & Space Co & Lockheed Ga div 100 N Winchester Blvd Suite 380 San Jose CA 95128

VAN LAAR, MYRTLE JUNE, children's librarian; b. Leota, Minn.; d. Lambertus and Sadie (Boermans) Van L. B.A. in Edn., Calvin Coll., 1949; A.M. in Art Edn., U. Mich., 1955, A.M. in L.S., 1965. Cert. tchr. and librarian, Md. Elem. tchr. Christian Schs., Grand Rapids, Mich., 1949-60; tchr. Washington Christian Sch., Silver Spring, Md., 1960-63; library assoc. Silver Spring Pub. Library, 1963-64; curriculum ctr. dir. Calvin Coll., Grand Rapids, 1965-68; children's age-level specialist Hyattsville br. Prince George's County Meml. Library System, 1968—; library chmn. Washington Christian Reformed Ch., Washington, 1983-88. Sec. Washington Christian Sch. Bd., Silver Spring, 1978-79, mem. edn. com., 1976-78. Mem. ALA. Mem. Christian Reformed Ch. Club: Laurel Art Guild.

VAN LANDINGHAM, LEANDER SHELTON, JR., lawyer; b. Memphis, July 15, 1925; s. Leander Shelton Van L.; m. Henrietta Adena Stapf, July 5, 1959; children—Ann Henrietta, Leander Shelton III. B.S. in Chemistry, U. N.C., 1948, M.A. in Organic Chemistry, 1949; J.D., Georgetown U., 1955. Bar: D.C. 1955, Md. 1963, Va. 1976. Patent adviser Dept. Navy, Washington, 1953-55; sole practice comml. law and patent, trademark and copyright law, Washington met. area, 1955 . Served to lt. USNR, 1943-46, 51-53. Mem. Am. Chem. Soc., Sci. Assn., Fed. Bar Assn., ABA, D.C. Bar Assn., Va. Bar Assn., Md. Bar Assn., Am. Patent Law Assn., Am. Judicature Soc., Sigma Xi, Phi Alpha Delta. Home: 10726 Stanmore Dr Potomac MD 20854

VAN LANDINGHAM, SAMUEL LEIGHTON, environmentalist, geologist, consultant, researcher; b. Iraan, Tex., Aug. 25, 1935; s. Grady Richard and Winnie (Fry) Van L.; m. Becky Jean Ball, Dec. 28, 1967. BS in Geology, Tex. Tech U., 1958; AB in Botany, U. Kans., 1960, MA in Botany, 1963; PhD in Biology, U. Louisville, 1966. Geologist Nelson Creek Mining Co., Rapid City, S.D., 1963; teaching asst. U. Louisville, 1963-66; asst. prof. biology Northeast La. U., Monroe, 1967-70; aquatic biologist Mich. Dept. Natural Resources, Lansing, 1972-73; research diatomist, research assoc. Calif. Acad. Scis., San Francisco, 1973-78; cons. environmentalist and geologist, Cin., 1970—; cons., expert witness AT&T Co., Pillsbury, Madison and Sutro, San Francisco, 1974-75; cons. U.S. EPA, Cin., 1972-82, Dames & Moore, Cin., 1974, U.S. Geol. Survey, Menlo Park, Calif., 1975-77, State of Calif., Sacramento, 1975-76, NUS Corp., Pitts., 1977, State of Miss., Ocean Springs, 1977, U. Laval, Quebec, Que., Can., 1982, Aquatic Analysts, Portland, Oreg., 1985. Author, editor: Geology of World Gem Deposits, 1985; Economic Evaluation of Mineral Property, 1983; Catalogue of the Fossil and Recent Genera and Species of Diatoms, 8 vols., 1967-79; author: Guide to the Identification, Environmental Requirements and Pollution Tolerance of Blue Green Algae, 1982; Jessup fellow Acad. Natural Scis. of Phila., 1962; McHenry fellow Acad. Natural Scis. of Phila., 1963; NSF grantee, 1969-70, 73-78. Mem. Geol. Soc. Am., Soc. Ind. Profl. Earth Scientists (cert. geologist 1982, earth scientist), Bay Area Diatom Group, Ariz.-Nev. Acad. Sci., Los Angeles Self Realization Fellowship. Zen Buddhist. Current work: Biological water quality appraisal and surveillance; tertiary non-marine stratigraphy of the Great Basin; ecology, paleoecology, and stratigraphy of non-marine algae; non-marine diatom index fossils; economic evaluation of diatomite deposits. Subspecialties: Limnology; Paleontology.

VAN LEEUWEN, DIRK WILLEM, banker; b. Arnhem, Gelderland, The Netherlands, Nov. 17, 1945; s. Jozef H. and Johanna M. (Kamphorst) Van L.; m. Johanna E. Keuper, Dec. 29, 1969; children: Jannetje C., Jozef H., Johanna M., Johannes. LLD, Utrecht (The Netherlands) U., 1971; ordinand, Southwark Ordination Course, London, 1982. Controller Marlo Spaanplaten, Lochem, The Netherlands, 1968-69; exec. trainee Amsterdam-Rotterdam Bank, Amsterdam, The Netherlands, 1969-72, asst. to bd. mem., 1972-73, sr. v.p., 1984-87, sr. v.p. internat. and corp. banking, 1987—; area mgr. Amsterdam-Rotterdam Bank, Zoetermeer, The Netherlands, 1973-76; dep. gen. mgr. Amsterdam-Rotterdam Bank, London, 1977-82, European Asian Bank, Singapore, 1976-77; mem. exec. com. European Bank Latin Am., Brussels, 1982-84; chmn. Amsterdam-Rotterdam Bank voor Belgie Fin., Antwerp, Belgium, 1986—; bd. dirs. Amsterdam-Rotterdam Bank Overseas, Curaçao, Netherlands Antilles. Editor: Enchiridion Copula Torum, 1972; contbr. articles to profl. jours. Chaplain English Ch., Haarlem, The Netherlands, 1984—; bd. dirs. Open Ankh Group of Hosps., Soesterberg, The Netherlands, 1986—. Mem. Christian Dem. Appeal Party. Anglican. Clubs: Cercle Gaulois, Het Beschreven Blad. Home: Sonnehoeck, Schotersingel 163, 2023 AD Haarlem The Netherlands Office: Amsterdam-Rotterdam Bank, Foppingadreef 22, Amsterdam ZO, The Netherlands

VAN LEUVEN, HOLLY GOODHUE, social scientist, consultant, researcher; b. Salem, Mass., Dec. 2, 1935; d. Nathaniel William and Elizabeth VanClowes (Crowley) Goodhue; m. John Jamison Porter, II, Oct. 16, 1954 (div. 1974); children: Donald J. II, Nathaniel G., Alison A. Dionne, Erin E.; m. Robert Joseph VanLeuven, Dec. 31, 1976. BA with honors, Western Mich. U., 1971, MA with honors, 1975. Exec. dir. Community Confrontation and Communication Assocs., Grand Rapids, Mich., 1969-73; coordinator tng., research Nat. Ctr. for Dispute Settlement, Washington, 1973; tng. dir. Forest View Psychiat. Hosp., Grand Rapids, 1974; case coordinator Libner, Van Leuven, & Kortering, P.C., Muskegon, Mich., 1982-87; pres. Genesis Cons. Group, Muskegon, Mich., Phoenix, 1987—; talk show host Sta. WTRU-TV, Muskegon, 1985; cons. U.S. Dept. Justice, Washington, 1969-73, No. Ireland Dept. Community Relations, Belfast, 1971; jury selection cons. various law firms in Midwest, 1975—. Contbr. articles to profl. jours. Bd. dirs. Planned Parenthood Western Mich., Grand Rapids, 1964-72, Jr. League Grand Rapids, 1955—, YFCA, Muskegon, 1981-83, Girl Scouts U.S., 1988—; chmn. Student Showcase, Inc., Muskegon, 1983—; candidate for Mich. State Rep. 97th Dist., Muskegon, 1978; pres. Planned Parenthood Assn., Muskegon, 1980. Mem. Am. Sociol. Assn., Am. Soc. Trial Cons. Clubs: Muskegon Country, Century; Women's City (Grand Rapids). Lodges: Zonta, Compass. Home: 966 Mona Brook Rd Muskegon MI 49441

VAN LOO, EDWARD VALENTIJN, automotive company executive; b. Borgerhout, Belgium, Nov. 23, 1934; s. Jules and Johanna (Hutsebaut) Van L.; m. Godelieve Elizabeth Durlinger, July 18, 1959; children—Werner, Ines. Econ. Humanities, St. Henricus Inst., 1946-52. Rep., Gen. Motors Continental, Antwerp, Belgium, 1955-67, dist. mgr., 1967-73, sales mgr., 1973-78, mktg. mgr., 1978-84, dir. mktg. div. GM Continental, 1984—;also dir. mktg. div. GM España. Served to lt. col. Belgian Air Force, 1977—. Mem. Belgian-Luxemburg C. of C., Madrid. Lodge: Rotary. Office: GM España, 91 Paseo De La Castellana, 28046 Madrid Spain

VAN LOOCK, CLAUDE CONRAD R.M., book dealer; b. Tournai, Hainaut, Belgium, Mar. 23, 1945; s. Albert and Solange (Thiebaut) Van L.; 1 child, Sophie. Owner Librairie Van Loock, Brussels, 1970—. Editor: Rassenfosse (E. Rouir), 1985, Felicien Rops (E. Rouir), 1987. Mem. Syndicat Belge De La Librairie Ancienne Et Moderne (v.p. 1985—). Office: Librairie Van Loock, 51 Rue Saint Jean, 1000 Brussels Belgium

VANMARCKE, ERIK HECTOR, civil engineering educator; b. Menen, Belgium, Aug. 6, 1941; came to U.S., 1965, naturalized, 1976; m. Louis Eugene and Rachel Louisa (van Hollebeke) V.; m. Margaret Maria Delesie, May 25, 1965; children: Lieven, Ann, Kristien. BS, U. Louvain, Belgium, 1965; MS, U. Del., 1967; PhD in Civil Engring, MIT, 1970. From instr. to prof. civil engring. MIT, Cambridge, 1969-85; Gilbert W. Winslow Career Devel. prof. MIT, 1974-77, dir. civil engring. systems group, 1976-80; prof. civil engring. Princeton U., 1985—; cons. Office Sci. and Tech. Policy, 1978-80; vis. scholar in engring. Harvard U., 1984-85; cons. various govt. agencies and engring. firms. Author: Random Fields: Analysis and Synthesis, 1983, editor: Internat. Jour. Structural Safety, 1981—. Mem. ASCE (Raymond C. Reese research award 1975, Walter L. Huber research prize 1984), Am. Geophys. Union, Seismol. Soc. Am., Internat. Soc. Soil Mechanics and Found. Engring., Sigma Xi. Home: 50 Brooks Bend Princeton NJ 08540 Office: Room E311 Engring Quadrangle Princeton U Princeton NJ 08544

VAN MEEL, JACOBUS MARCUS, psychologist; b. Amsterdam, The Netherlands, Sept. 28, 1931; s. Jacobus Van Meel and Isabella Heeffer; m. Annelies Jansen, Oct. 31, 1968. PhD, U. Leiden, 1960. Docent, research fellow U. Leiden, The Netherlands, 1956-71; assoc. prof. dept. psychiatry SUNY Downstate Med. Ctr., Brooklyn, 1971-72; prof. devel. psychology Tilburg U., The Netherlands, 1972—, dean faculty of psychology, 1977-79. Author: Children with Learning Difficulties, 4th ed., 1980, Psychology of Gestures, 1986; editor: (with others) Psychologists about the Child, 5 vols., 1976—. Dutch Orgn. of Pure Research grantee, 1963, Dutch Orgn. Research in Edn. grantee, 1971-74. Mem. Netherlands Inst. Psychology, Internat. Soc. for Study of Behavioral Devel., Soc. Research in Child Devel., Ned Tydschr Psychology (mem. editorial bd. 1973—). Home: Zandstraat 28, 5131AC Alphen NB The Netherlands Office: Tilburg U, Hogeschoollaan 225, 5037GC Tilburg The Netherlands

VANMEER, MARY ANN, publisher, writer, researcher; b. Mt. Clemens, Mich., Nov. 22; d. Leo Harold and Rose Emma (Gulden) VanM.; stepmother Ruth (Meek) VanM. Student Mich. State U., 1965-66, 67-68, Sorbonne U., Paris, 1968; B.A. in Edn., U. Fla., 1970. Pres. VanMeer Tutoring and Translating, N.Y.C., 1970-72; freelance writer, 1973-79; pres. VanMeer Publs., Inc., Clearwater, Fla., 1980—, VanMeer Media Advt., Inc., Clearwater, 1980—; exec. dir., founder Nat. Ctrs. for Health and Med. Info., Inc., Clearwater, 1982—; pres. Health and Med. Trends, Inc. 1987—. Author: Traveling with Your Dog, U.S.A., 1976; How to Set Up A Home Typing Business, 1978; Freelance Photographer's Handbook, 1979; See America Free, 1981; Free Campgrounds, U.S.A., 1982; Free Attractions, U.S.A., 1982, VanMeer's Guide to Free Attractions, U.S.A., 1984; VanMeer's Guide to Free Campgrounds, 1984; DUI Survival Manual, 1987; The 'How to Get Publicity for Your Business' Handbook, 1987; pub. Nat. Health and Med. Trends Mag., 1986—. Pub. info. chairperson, bd. dirs. Pinellas County chpt. Am. Cancer Soc., Clearwater, 1983-84, 86-88. Mem. Am. Booksellers Assn., Performing Arts, Concert, and Theatre, Author's Guild. Republican. Office: VanMeer Publs Inc PO Box 2138 Clearwater FL 34617 also: Nat Ctrs for Health and Med Info Inc PO Box 389 Clearwater FL 34617

VAN NAME, MARK LAWRENCE, computer consultant, writer; b. Haverhill, Mass., Mar. 14, 1955; s. Donald Louis and Nancy Ann (Bergeron) Van N.; m. Mary Anne Frazier, Aug. 18, 1976. B.S., Fla. State U., 1976; M.S., Pa. State U., 1977. Computer programmer II, Fla. State U., Tallahassee, 1975-76; teaching asst. Pa. State U., State College, 1976-77; computer scientist HRB-Singer, Inc., State College, 1977-78; mem. tech. staff Data Gen. Corp., Research Triangle Park, N.C., 1978-81; co-founder, pres. Blue Ridge Info. Systems, Inc., Raleigh, N.C., 1981-82; co-founder, v.p. research and devel. Foundation Computer Systems, Inc., Cary, N.C., 1982-86; co-founder, v.p. research and devel. Foresight Computer Corp., Cary, 1986-87; writer, computer cons., 1987— . Mem. Assn. for Computing Machinery, IEEE, Sci. Fiction Writers Am. Democrat. Contbr. short stories to mags. and articles on computers to profl. jours. Home: 10024 Sycamore Rd Durham NC 27703

VANNIASINGHAM, SAMUEL KANAGASABAPATHY, accountant; b. Singapore, Oct. 16, 1950; arrived in U.K., 1975; s. Nathan Kesagar and Mabel Gnanaratnam (Subramaniam) V.; m. Heather Christine Clark, August 5, 1981; children: Daniel James, David Joseph. Diploma in Acctg., Stamford Ctr., Singapore, 1972; degree Profl. Acctg., Polytech., London, 1977. Articled clk. Peat, Marwick, Mitchell, Singapore, 1974-75; part-time tchr. Adult Edn. Bd., Singapore, 1972-75; mgmt. trainee E. Russell Ltd., London, 1977-79, accounts mgr., 1980-85; mgmt. acct. MAT Transport Internat. Ltd., London, 1985-86, group mgmt. acct., 1986-87, group acct., 1988—. Sec. J.B. Taylors Ltd., Canvey Island, U.K., Nowbroad Ltd., Guildford, Surrey, U.K. Served to staff sergeant in nat. service Police dept., Singapore, 1968-75. Recipient Bravery commendation medal Police Force, Singapore, 1974. Fellow Chartered Assn., Mem. Brit. Inst. Mgmt., Singapore Cricket Assn. (test cricketer 1971-75). Methodist. Club: Hazelwood Squash (North London). Home: 17 Hyde Way, Edmonton, London N9 9RU, England Office: MAT Group Ltd, PO Box 251, Arnold House 36-41 Holywell Ln, London EC2P 2EQ, England

VAN NIEKERK, ANTON ALBERT, philosopher, educator; b. Brits, Republic South Africa, Dec. 4, 1953; s. Gert Hendrik and Elsie (Van Loggerenberg) Van N.; m.Amelia DuPreez, 1978; children: Gerhard, Bouwer, Albert. BTh, U. Stellenbosch, 1978, MA in Philosophy, 1980, D Phil, 1983. Lectr. in philosophy U. Stellenbosch, Republic South Africa, 1981-84, sr. lectr., 1985—. Author: To See the Invisible, 1986; co-author, editor: Modern Political Ideologies, 1987, What Comes after Apartheid?, 1987. Mem. South African Acad. Arts and Scis., Philos. Assn. So. Africa (mem. council 1985-86). Home: 4 Blenheim Rd, Stellenbosch 7600, Republic of South Africa Office: U Stellenbosch, Dept Philosophy, Stellenbosch 7600, Republic of South Africa

VAN OOSBREE, CHARLYNE SELMA NELSON, librarian; b. Alta, Iowa, Jan. 19, 1930; d. John Albin and Albertina (Rydstrom) Nelson; m. Anton Van Oosbree, Dec. 30, 1950 (dec. 1965); children: Tina Van Oosbree Taylor, Jon, David. BS in English, Iowa State U., 1970; MLS, U. Mo., 1973. Hosp. librarian Army Hosp., Ft. Leonard Wood, Mo., 1970-72; head sch. library Tng. Sch. for Boys, Boonville, Mo., 1973-76; head br. library Mid-Contninent Pub. Library, Independence, Mo., 1976-82; head base library Whiteman AFB, Mo., 1982-86; head base library Florennes AFB, Belgium, 1986-87; head base library Scott AFB, Ill., 1987—; mem. adv. council U. Mo. Sch. Library and Info. Sci., Columbia, 1978-80, sec., 1978-79; coordinator Writers' Group, Platte Woods, Mo., 1980-82. Contbr. articles to library publ., poems, articles to newspapers. Bd. mem. Tri-County Mental Health Assn., Kansas City, Mo., 1980-82, Park Hill Sch. Adv. Council, Kansas City, 1977-78, Synergy House, Parkville, Mo., 1976-77; mem. youth adv. council Whiteman AFB; counselor Widowed Persons Service, Kansas City, 1977-78. Named SAC Librarian of Yr., 1984; Mo. State Library scholar, 1972. Mem. ALA, Fed. Librarians Round Table, Beta Phi Mu. Home: 15 Lake Christine #11 Belleville IL 62221 Office: Base Library Scott AFB IL 62225

VAN OS, HENDRIK WILLEM, art history educator; b. Harderwijk, The Netherlands, Feb. 28, 1938. PhD, State U. Groningen, The Netherlands, 1969. Vis. mem. Inst. for Advanced Study, Princeton, N.J., 1969-70; asst. prof. art history State U. Groningen, 1971-74, prof., 1974—. Author: Maria's Demut une Verherrlichung in der sienesischen Malerei, 1969 (Carel van Mander prize 1969), Catalogue of Early Italian Paintings in Holland, 1969, 74, 78, Vecchietta and the Sacristy of the Siena Hospital Church, 1974, Sienese Altarpieces 1215-1460, 1984. Decorated comdr. ufficiale al merito della Republica Italiana; elected to Acad. degli Intronati, Siena, Acad. del Disegno, Florence. Mem. Comite Internat. d'Histoire de l'Art. Office: Inst for Art History, Oude Boteringestraat 81, 9712 GG Groningen The Netherlands

VAN PAEMEL, CHARLES MICHAEL, chemical company executive; b. Mt. Clemens, Mich., June 28, 1948; s. Frank Lewis and Evelyn (Malburg) Van P.; m. Laura Genevieve Diegel, Nov. 20, 1970; 1 child, Nicholas Michael. BS in Chemistry, Oakland U., Rochester, Mich., 1972, MS in Chemistry, 1973. Chemist Parke-Davis Inc., Detroit, 1972-73; with E.I. Du Pont de Nemours, 1973—; chemist Troy, Mich., 1973-76; product specialist auto finishes Southfield, Mich., 1976-77; supr. auto finishes devel. Toledo, 1977-78; mktg. mgr. indsl. finishes Wilmington, Del., 1978-80; bus. dir. finishes Du Pont Venezuela, Caracas, 1980-86; dir. finishes Europe Du Pont Belgium, Brussels, 1986-88; tech. mktg. mng. auto finishes Du Pont, Troy, Mich., 1988—. Contbr. articles to profl. jours. Served to cpl. USMC, 1968-70. NSF research grantee, 1971. Mem. Am. Chem. Soc. (Scholastic Achievement award 1972), Sigma Xi. Roman Catholic. Office: 940 Stephenson Hwy Troy MI 48007-7013

VAN PATTEN, JAMES JEFFERS, educator; b. North Rose, N.Y., Sept. 8, 1925; s. Earl F. and Dorothy (Jeffers) Van P.; B.A., Syracuse U., 1949; M.E., Tex. Western Coll., 1959; Ph.D., U. Tex., Austin, 1962; married. Asst. prof. philosophy and edn. Central Mo. State U., Warrensburg, 1962-64, asso. prof., 1964-69; asso. prof. vis. overseas U. Okla., Norman, 1969-71; prof. edn. U. Ark., Fayetteville, 1971—; visiting scholar, U. Mich., 1981, UCLA, 1987, U. Tex., Austin, 1987. Served with inf., U.S. Army, 1944-45. Decorated Purple Heart. Mem. Am. Ednl. Studies Assn., Mid South Future Soc., World Future Soc., Am. Philosophy Assn., Southwestern Philosophy of Edn. Soc. (pres. 1970), Ark. Edn. Assn. (pres. chpt. U. Ark.), Phi Delta Kappa (pres. chpt. U. Ark. 1976-77). Club: Kiwanis. Editor: Conflict, Permanency and Change in Education, 1976; contbr. articles to books, profl. jours.; founder Jour. of Thought. Home: 434 Hawthorn St Fayetteville AR 72701

VAN PELT, LLOYD FRANKLIN, veterinarian, educator; b. Brownsdale, Minn., June 23, 1930; s. Robert Luman and Tilda (Guttormson) Van P.; m. Constance Jean Rasmusson, Nov. 21, 1951; children—Lee Ann, Lynn Marie, Laura Jean. D.V.M., U. Minn., 1959. Diplomate Am. Coll. Lab. Animal Medicine. Dist. veterinarian Dept. Los Angeles County, South Gate, Calif., 1960-64; attending veterinarian Los Angeles County Harbor Gen. Hosp., Torrance, Calif., 1964-70, sr. veterinarian, 1970-72, chief veterinarian, 1972-74, dir. Veterinary Service, Los Angeles County Harbor/UCLA Med. Ctr., 1974-80; ptnr. Lincoln Ave. Animal Hosp., Orange, Calif., 1964-66; lectr. dept. pathology Sch. Medicine, UCLA, 1969-80; dir. Ctr. Exptl. Animal Resources, Northwestern U., 1980—, assoc. prof. dept. microbiology-immunology Med. and Dental Sch., 1981-87; site visitor Am. Assn. Accreditation of Lab. Animal Care, 1971—, mem. council on accreditation, 1977-80, trustee, 1981-87; cons. animal medicine VA Med. Ctr., Hines, Ill., 1982—, VA Lakeside Med. Ctr., Chgo., 1982—, Am. Dental Research Inst., Chgo., 1982—, Children's Meml. Hosp., Chgo., 1982—. Contbr. articles to sci. jours. Served AUS, 1949-52. Recipient Research grants, NIH, HEW, 1967-70. Mem. Am. Assn. Lab. Animal Sci. (Chgo. br.), Am. Soc. Lab. Animal Practitioners, AVMA, Ill. State Vet. Med. Assn., Northwestern Apple Computer Users Group. Republican. Lutheran. Current work: Clinical methods for the evaluation of male and female reproductive competence in laboratory monkeys, and insemination by intraperitoneal injection; effective animal care delivery and administration in the institutional setting. Subspecialty: Laboratory animal medicine.

VAN RAALTE, POLLY ANN, educator; b. N.Y.C., Sept. 22, 1951; d. Byron Emmanuel and Enid (Godnick) Van R.; student U. London, 1972; BA, Beaver Coll., 1973; MS in Edn., U. Pa., 1974, postgrad. in edn., 1975—; postgrad. in spl. edn. West Chester State Coll., 1975-77; student, Bank St. Coll.. Title I reading tchr. Oakview Sch., West Deptford Twp. Sch. Dist., Woodbury, N.J., 1974-75, Title I reading supr., summer 1975; lang. arts coordinator Main Line Day Sch., Mitchell Sch., Haverford, Pa., 1975-76; reading supr. Salvation Army, Phila., summer 1976; reading Huntingdon Jr. High Sch., Abington (Pa.) Sch. Dist., 1976-78; reading specialist No. 2 Sch., Lawrence Pub. Sch., Inwood, N.Y., 1978-87, high sch. reading specialist, Cedarhurst, N.Y., 88—; reading specialist Hewlett Elem. Sch., Hewlett-Woodmere Pub. Sch., Hewlett, N.Y., 1987-88; instr. reading and spl. edn. dept. Adelphi U., 1979—; cons. to sch. dists.; advisor Am. Biog. Inst., Inc.; speaker at reading convs. Coordinator, Five Towns Young Voter Registration, Hewlett, N.Y., summer, 1971; chmn. class fund Beaver Coll., also mem. internat. relations com. U. Pa. scholar, 1977-78. Mem. Internat. Reading Assn., Wis. Reading Assn., Nat. Council Tchrs. English, Nassau Reading Council, N.Y. Reading Assn., Council Exceptional Children, Nat. Assn. Gifted Children, Am. Assn. of the Gifted, Nat./State Leadership Tng. Inst. on the Gifted and Talented, Children's Lit. Assembly, N.Y. State English Council, Assn. Curriculum Devel., Am. Israel Pub. Affairs Com., New Leadership com. of Jewish Nat. Fund, Nat. Polit. Action Com, Am. Friends of Hebrew U. (torch com.), Technion Soc., Am. Friends David Yellin Tchr's. Coll., Am. Friends Ben Gurion U., Am. Friends Israel Philharmonic, Cooper-Hewitt Mus., Mus. Modern Art, Met. Mus. Art, Whitney Mus., Phila. Mus. Art, Smithsonian Inst., Friends of Carnegie Hall, Friends of Am. Ballet Theatre, U. Pa. Alumni Assn. N.Y.C., Pi Lambda Theta, Kappa Delta Pi (sec.). Club: Human Relations (sec.). Home: 26 Meadow Ln Lawrence NY 11559 Office: Hewlett Elem Sch Broadway and Herkimer St Hewlett NY 11557

VAN RAEMDONCK, CHARLES PHILIPPE, telecommunications executive; b. Brussels, Nov. 19, 1943; s. Mainy (Josette) van R.; m. Monique Rogival, Aug. 10, 1968; children: Thibault, Geoffroy, Stephanie. Degree in Comml. Engring., U. Louvain, Belgium, 1967. Asst. mgr. Compagnie Bruxelles Lambert, SA, Brussels, 1969-80; adminstrv. fin. mgr. Belgian Mech. Fabrication, SA, Grâce-Hollogne, Belgium, 1980-82; fin. mgr. Soc. Chimique Prayon-Rupel, SA, Engis, Belgium, 1983-87; dir. Soc. Worldwide Interbank Fin. Telecommunications (SWIFT), La Hulpe, Belgium, 1987—. Home: Chemin Demanet 7, 1330 Rixensart Belgium Office: SWIFT, Ave E Solvay 81, 1310 La Hulpe Belgium

VAN REENEN, JOHN LOUIS, steel distribution executive; b. Johannesburg, Transvaal, Republic South Africa, May 18, 1947; s. Fred John Augustus and Mercia Elizabeth (Tancred) Van R.; m. Janet Couper-Smith, June 25, 1971 (div. Sept. 1977); m. 2d, Michele Renee, Feb. 14, 1978; children—Andrew, Tracey, Samantha. C.A. (S.A.) in Acctg., U. Witwatersrand, 1971. Chartered acct., Republic South Africa. Articled clk. Geo. Mackenzie & Co., Johannesburg, 1966-72; fin. mgr. Messina (Tvl) Devel. Co. Ltd. Johannesburg, 1972-76; dir. Van Reenen & Nicholls (Pty) Ltd., Johannesburg, 1976—, dir. all group cos. Mem. Witwatersrand Agrl. Soc. (council 1984-85), Transvaal Soc. Chartered Accts., Young Pres. Orgn. Presbyterian. Clubs: Rand, Royal Johannesburg Golf (Johannesburg). Avocations: golfing; deep sea fishing; wine collecting. Home: 14 The Meadow Morningside, Sandton Republic of South Africa

VAN RIPER, PAUL PRITCHARD, political science educator; b. Laporte, Ind., July 29, 1916; s. Paul and Margaret (Pritchard) Van R.; m. Dorothy Ann Dodd Samuelson, May 11, 1964; 1 child, Michael Scott Samuelson. A.B., DePauw U., 1938; Ph.D., U. Chgo., 1947. Instr. Northwestern U., 1947-49, asst. prof. polit. sci., 1949-51; mgmt. analyst Office Comptroller Dept. Army, 1951-52; mem. faculty Cornell U., 1952-70, prof., 1957-70; chmn. gov. bd., exec. com. Cornell Social Sci. Research Center, 1956-58; prof., head dept. polit. sci. Tex. A&M U., 1970-77, prof., 1977-81, prof. emeritus, 1981—, coordinator M.P.A. program, 1979-81; vis. prof. U. Chgo., 1958, Ind. U., 1961, U. Strathclyde, Scotland, 1964, U. Mich., 1965, U. Okla., 1988, U. Utah, 1979. Author: History of the United States Civil Service, 1958, Some Educational and Social Aspects of Fraternity Life, 1961, (with others) The American Federal Executive, 1963, Handbook of Practical Politics, 3d edit. 1967. Mem. exec. com. Civil Service Reform Assn. N.Y., 1960-64; mem. hist. adv. com. NASA, 1964-66; Bd. dirs. Brazos Valley Community Action Agy., 1975-79. Served to maj. AUS, 1942-46. Decorated Croix de Guerre (France). Mem. Am. Polit. Sci. Assn., So. Polit. Sci. Assn., S.W. Polit. Sci. Assn. (exec. com. 1975-77), Am. Soc. Pub. Adminstrn. (nat. adv. com. 1957-60, Dimock award 1984), Internat. Personnel Mgmt. Assn., Phi Beta Kappa, Beta Theta Pi (v.p. 1962, gen. sec. 1963-65), Pi Sigma Alpha, Phi Kappa Phi, Sigma Delta Chi. Republican. Baptist. Home: 713 E 30th St Bryan TX 77803 Office: Dept Polit Sci Tex A and M Univ College Station TX 77843

VAN RUTTEN, PIERRE MARIE, French literary stylistics educator; b. Brussels, July 3, 1920; came to Can., 1962, naturalized, 1967; s. Georges A. and Madeleine (Kennes) van R.; m. Irma Gerbelotto, Aug. 29, 1970; children—Beatrice, Emmanuelle. Ph.D., U. Ottawa, Ont., Can., 1970. Asst. prof. U. Ottawa, 1965-70; assoc. prof. Carleton U., Ottawa, 1970-76, prof. French and comparative lit., 1976—; vis. prof. U. Urbino, Italy, 1978, U. Warsaw, Poland, 1985, U. Leningrad, USSR, 1987. Author: Le langage poetique de Saint John Perse, 1975; Eloges, 1977. Served to 1st lt., spl. ops. Belgian Army, 1942-45. Decorated comdr. Ordre de la Couronne, officer Ordre de Leopold, Croix de Guerre with palm (Belgium); recipient prix Christophe Plantin, Province Antwerp, Belgium, 1982. Mem. Can. Club, Can. Mediterranean Inst., MLA, Ottawa Art Assn. Avocation: painting. Home: 2237 Quinton St, Ottawa, ON Canada K1H 6V2

VAN SANDICK, LEONARD HENDRIK WILLEM, lawyer; b. Amsterdam, Feb. 4, 1933; s. Ivo and Eva (Schadee) Van S.; m. Florentina Maria van Rossem, June 22, 1964; children—Sjoerd Wildervanck, Willemijn, Johanna, Eveline, Ivo. Meester in de rechten, State U., Leyden, Netherlands, 1956. Assoc., van Rossem, Loeff & De Groot, Rotterdam, 1957-60; ptnr. Loeff & van der Ploeg, Rotterdam, 1961—, chmn. 1988—; mgr. local office Bow Valley Industries Ltd., Rotterdam, 1970—; mem. supervisory bd. Voyager Internat. Petroleum N.V., Curacao, Netherland Antilles, 1981-86, Ranchos California B.V., Rotterdam, 1981-85; mem. bd. Van Sandick Stichting, 1960—, Stichting Adminstr. Sigillo, 1972—; mem. supr. bd. Steeman Assurantiën, 1966-74; mem. internat. adv. bd. Atlantic Exchange Program; mem. adv. bd. Internat. and Comparative Law Ctr., Dallas. Coauthor: Scheepsraed, 1973; Dutch Business Law, 1978; Recht door Zee, 1980; Bank Secrecy, 1980; corr. editor Droit et Affaires, 1982, Internat. Banking Law, 1982, Oil & Gas: Law and Taxation Rev., 1982, Jour. Energy & Natural Resources Law, 1982, Internat. Legal Materials, 1985. Fulbright scholar, 1951-52. Mem. Netherlands Bar Assn., Rotterdam Bar Assn., Internat. Bar Assn. (chmn. banking com. 1984-88, council sect. on bus. law 1988), Inst. Transnat. Arbitration (mem. Eur. Council 1987—), ABA (assoc.), Am. Soc. Internat. Law, London Maritime Arbitrators' Assn. (supporting), Internat. Law Assn., Am. Arbitration Assn. (mem. panel 1982—). Volkspartij voor Vrijheid en Democratie. Home: Vredehofweg 52, 3062 ES Rotterdam The Netherlands Office: Loeff & van der Ploeg, Blaak 333, 3011 GB Rotterdam The Netherlands

VAN SCHAIK, TEUNIS, turbine services company executive, metallurgist; b. Assen, Netherlands, July 5, 1940; s. Gerrit and Bertha (Vermeulen) Van S.; m. Carla VandeGraaf, June 4, 1965; children—Marco, Bastian. Grad. Tech. High Sch., 1967. Asst. mgr. Werkspoor (V.M.F.), Amsterdam, Netherlands, 1961-68, mgr., 1969-73; prodn. mgr. Bergoss, Netherlands, 1969; tech. mgr. Elbar bv., Lomm, Netherlands, 1973-80, gen. mgr., 1980-83, pres. Elbar div., 1983—; dir. Indivers Cos.; cons. in field. Contbr. articles to profl. jours.; patentee in field. Mem. Am. Welding Soc., Internat. Inst. Welding (expert), Am. Soc. for Metals, Dutch Inst. Welding. Clubs: Lawn Tennis (chmn. 1971) (Amsterdam); Volleyball (chmn.) (Venlo). Avocations: volleyball; tennis. Home: Dennenlaan 11, Velden, Limburg 5941 CW The Netherlands Office: Elbar, Spiktweg 36, Lomm Limburg 5943AD The Netherlands

VAN SCHIJNDEL, MARTINUS ANTHONIUS ALOYSIUS, architect, educator; b. Hengelo, Overijssel, The Netherlands, June 21, 1943; s. Marinus Johannes and Gertruda Maria (Vogels) van S.; m. Henriëtte Madelon Elisabeth Ernst, Dec. 12, 1969; 1 child, Meike. Degree in bldg. engring., Uitgebreid Technisch Onderwys, Utrecht, The Netherlands, 1963; degree in archtl. design, Rietveld Acad., Amsterdam, 1967. Cert. architect, interior designer. Pvt. practice architecture, interior design and indsl. design Utrecht, 1969—; prof. U. Düsseldorf, Fed. Republic of Germany, 1987—; tchr. Aca. Architecture, Arnhem, The Netherlands, 1974-84. Indsl. designer: DELTA Vase, 1981; architect: Centraal Mus. Utrecht, 1986. Recipient 1st prize Arango Design Found., 1984, Bronze medal Salon des Artistes Décorateurs, Paris, 1985, Spl. Recognition award Arango Design Found., 1986, 1st prize Philips Lighting Corp., '1986. Mem. Internat. Fedn. Interior Designers, Union Internat. Architects, Fedn. Artists Assn., Soc. Indsl. Artists and Designers, European Com. Interior Designers. Home: Oudegracht 329, 3511 PC Utrecht The Netherlands Office: Geertestraat 2bis, 3511 XE Utrecht The Netherlands

VAN SWOL, NOEL WARREN, educator; b. N.Y.C., Dec. 30, 1941; s. Erwin Anton and Hildegard van S.; BA, Am. U., 1964; MA, Columbia U., 1967; MS, Syracuse U., 1972. Asst. underwriter Comml. Union Ins. Group Ltd., N.Y.C., 1964-66; tchr. social studies jr. high sch., Bklyn., 1966-67, Liberty (N.Y.) Cen. High Sch., 1967-69; instr. student personnel Sullivan County (N.Y.) Community Coll., 1969-70; tchr. social studies E. Syracuse-Minoa (N.Y.) High Sch., 1970—, coordinator social studies, 1976—; cons. to trainer of tchr. trainers project Syracuse U., 1971-74. Contbr. articles to profl. jours. Vice pres. Fremont (N.Y.) Taxpayers and Civic Assn., 1971; mem. Town of Fremont Rep. Vacancy Com., 1967, 73, 74, 78, 80, 81, 83; mem. Task Force Against Nuclear Pollution, Inc.; bd. dirs. Project Legal, 1983-84. Tchr. Leadership Devel. fellow, 1971, Freedoms Found. fellow, 1986, 87. Mem. Am. Hist. Assn., N.Y. State Hist. Assn., Am. Polit. Sci. Assn., Assn. Supervision and Curriculum Devel., Nat., N.Y. State, Cen. N.Y. Councils Social Studies, Social Studies Suprs. Assn., Orgn. Am. Historians, Soc. for History Edn., Upper Delaware Scenic River Assn., Upper Del. Coalition Concerned Citizens, Ind. Landholders Assn., Upper Del. Citizens Alliance, Am. Land Alliance, Western Sullivan County Taxpayers Assn., Phi Delta Kappa. Home: Route 97 Long Eddy NY 12760

VAN TIL, WILLIAM, educator, writer; b. Corona, N.Y., Jan. 8, 1911; s. William Joseph and Florence Alberta (MacLean) Van T.; m. Beatrice Barbara Blaha, Aug. 24, 1935; children: Jon, Barbara, Roy. B.A., Columbia, 1933; M.A., Tchrs. Coll., 1935; Ph.D., Ohio State U., 1946. Tchr. N.Y. State Tng. Sch. for Boys, 1933-34; instr. dept. univ. schs. Coll. Edn., Ohio State U., 1934-36, asst. prof., 1936-43, on leave, 1943-45; researchist, writer Consumer Edn. Study NEA, 1943-44; dir. learning materials Bur. Intercultural Edn., 1944-47; prof. edn. U. Ill., 1947-51; prof. edn., chmn. div. curriculum and teaching George Peabody Coll. Tchrs., Nashville, 1951-57; prof. edn., chmn. dept. secondary edn. N.Y. U., 1957-66, head div. secondary and higher edn., 1966-67; Coffman distinguished prof. edn. Ind. State U., 1967-77, emeritus, 1977; dir. univ. workshops Writing for Profl. Publs., 1978—; founder Lake Lure Press, 1983. Author: The Danube Flows Through Fascism, Economic Roads for American Democracy, The Making of a Modern Educator, Modern Education for the Junior High School Years, The Year 2000: Teacher Education, One Way of Looking At It, Education: A Beginning, Another Way of Looking At It, Van Til on Education, Secondary Education: School and Community, Writing for Professional Publication, rev., 1986; autobiography My Way of Looking At It, 1983; editor: Forces Affecting American Education, Curriculum: Quest for Relevance, ASCD in Retrospect, 1986; co-editor: Democratic Human Relations, Intercultural Attitudes in the Making, Education in American Life; adv. editor, Houghton Mifflin, 1964-70. Contbr. to numerous other publs. including Saturday Rev., Woman's Day, Parents; author articles, reviews and editorials; columnist: Ednl. Leadership, Contemporary Edn., Kappan; adv. bd. Profl. Educator, 1984—. Mem. Ill. Interracial Commn., 1949-51; moderator Nashville sch. desegregation meetings, 1955-57; adv. bd. jour. Teacher Edn., 1956-59; co-organized Nashville Community Relations Conf., 1956; cons. Phelps-Stokes Fund project, 1958-62; staff P.R. Edn. Survey, 1958-59, Iran Tchr. Edn. Survey, 1962, V.I. Edn. Survey, 1964, lectr. abroad, 1974. Recipient Centennial Achievement award Ohio State U., 1970; awards N.J. Collegiate Press Assn., 1962; N.J. Assn. Tchrs. English, 1962. Mem. John Dewey Soc. (v.p. 1957-60, acting pres. 1958-59, pres. 1964-66, award 1977, 86), Assn. Supervision and Curriculum Devel. (dir. 1951-54, 57-60, pres. 1961-62, chmn. rev. council 1972-73, resolutions com. 1982-85), United Educators (chmn. bd. educators 1969-77), Nat. Soc. Coll. Tchrs. Edn. (pres. 1967-68), Am. Edn. Studies Assn. (editorial bd. 1970-77), Asso. Orgn. Tchr. Edn. (adv. council 1967-73, chmn. issues tchr. edn. 1972-73), Nat. Soc. Study Edn. (editor Yearbook Issues in Secondary Edn. 1976), Kappa Delta Pi (laureate 1980—, chmn. book-of-yr. com. 1984-86). Home: Lake Lure Rural Route 31 Box 140 Terre Haute IN 47803 Office: Ind State U Terre Haute IN 47809

VAN UYTFANGHE, MARC JOZEF M., academic administrator, educator; b. Zele, East Flanders, Belgium, Feb. 28, 1948; s. Edmond P. Van Uytfanghe and Margaretha M. De Leenheer. Licentiate in classical philology, State U., Ghent, Belgium, 1970, PhD, LittD, 1979. Tchr. Pius X Coll., Zele, Belgium, 1970-71; sr. asst. lectr. dept. Postclassical and Medieval Latin State U. Ghent, 1971—; reader U. Antwerp (Belgium), 1987—. Author: Stylisation Biblique et Condition Humaine dans l'Hagiographie Mérovingienne, 1987. Laureate Royal Acad. Scis., Letters and Arts, Belgium, 1981. Mem. Soc. d'Histoire Religieuse de la France, Commn. Belge d'Histoire Ecclésiastique Comparative, Comité Nat. du Dictionnaire du Latin Médiéval, Found. Early Christian Studies. Roman Catholic. Home: Schoolstraat 45, B9140 Zele Belgium Office: Rijksuniversiteit Gent, Blandijnberg 2, B9000 Gent Belgium

VAN VALER, JOE NED, lawyer, land developer; b. Gas City, Ind., Mar. 13, 1935; s. Richard Carl and Wilma Amy (Kelly) Van V.; m. Constance Joy Richardson, June 25, 1960; children—Kimberly Joy, Kelli June, Lynn Louise, Joseph Jeffrey. A.B., Franklin Coll., 1959; LL.B., Ind. U., 1963. Bar: Ind. 1963, U.S. Dist. Ct. (so. dist.) Ind. 1963. Assoc. Van Valer & Williams and predecessor firms, 1963-65, ptnr., 1965-75, sr. ptnr., 1975—; pres. Home Owners Warranty Corp. of Central Ind., Indpls., 1984—, also dir.; pros. atty. 8th Jud. Dist., Franklin, Ind., 1967-74. Served with AUS, 1957-58. Mem. ABA, Indpls. Bar Assn., 8th Jud. Circuit Bar Assn., Nat. Assn. Home Builders (bd. dirs.), Home Builders Assn. Ind. (dir.), Builders Assn. Greater Indpls. (dir.). Republican. Methodist. Office: Van Valer & Williams 300 S Madison Ave PO Box 405 Greenwood IN 46142

VAN VESSEM, JAN COENRAAD, micro-electronics specialist, industrial consultant; b. Den Helder, Holland, Nov. 8, 1920; s. Jan and Vrouwtje Johanna (Dekker) V.; m. Janny Stork, Dec. 28, 1946; children—Erik-Jan, Miranda. B.S. in Chemistry and Physics, U. Utrecht, 1939, M.S. in Chemistry and Physics, 1942, Ph.D. in Chemistry and Physics, 1947. Tchr. Hilversum Coll., Holland, 1943-46; prodn. devel. engr. N.V. Philips, Eindhoven, Holland, 1946-54, chief engr., Nijmegen, Holland, 1954-62, dep. dir., 1962-72, mng. dir., Eindhoven, 1972-81; indsl. mgmt. cons., Waalre, Netherlands, 1982—; mem. supervisory bd. M.E.C.O., Den Bosch, 1981—; chief tech. advisor INDUMA, Helmond, 1982—; mem. adv. bd. HYMEC, Sittard, 1982—. Author: (with Lloyd P. Hunter) Handbook of Semiconductor Electronics, 2nd edit., 1962. Patentee on semicondr. mfg. Fellow IEEE. Avocations: painting; graphical arts, jazz. Home and Office: 19 Lissevenlaan, 5582 KB Waalre The Netherlands

VAN VINKENROYE DU WAYSAECK, FEDIA MAURICE GILLES, financial services executive; b. Brussels, Sept. 18, 1932; s. Maurice G. and Simone Barré, Van V.; m. Jutta (Stoltenberg); divorced; 1 child, Christophe. Student, Sorbonne U., 1948-49. Mgr. Editions and Publicité, Brussels, 1957-60; journalist Abpi, Brussels, 1961-68; asst. gen. mgr. Romanian Tourism Ministry, Brussels and Bucarest, 1963-73; gen. mgr., chief exec. officer Cogeco-Alsaver, Brussels, 1973-78, Hotel and Tourism Engring., Brussels, 1979—; gen. mgr. Engring. Cy ICDK, Brussels, 1981-85; sr. v.p., chief exec. officer Gold Mining and Mktg., Nairobi, Kenya, 1985—, United Fin. Services, Santiago, Chile, 1985—; sr. v.p., chief exec. officer Gold Mining and Mktg., Nairobi, Kenya, 1985—, Alpha Enterprises, Ltd., Rhodes, Greece, 1987—. Mag. editor: Diplomatic Courier, Ras Le Bol, Evasion, Semaine de Bruxelles. Sec. gen. Rassemblement de la Majorité-Rassemblement des Mécontents, Belgium, 1985—. Decorated Presdl. Citation of U.S., Presdl. Citation of Republic of Korea, Comdr. De L'Ordre Du Christ. Mem. European Brokers Assn. (sec. 1981—). Lodge: K.T. (Osmer Du Christ Comdr.).

VAN VLEDDER, LORRAINE MAY, public relations consultant; b. Johannesburg, Transvaal, South Africa, May 21, 1949; d. Wesley Edmund and Denise May San Garde; m. Andre Anton Van Vledder, Feb. 17, 1971 (div. 1978). Diploma in Home Econs., Damelin Coll., Johannesburg, S. Africa, 19. Food editor The Star Newspaper, Johannesburg, 1970-81; editor Professional Caterer, Johannesburg, 1981; group pub. relations officer Fedfood Group Food Mfrs., Johannesburg, 1981-83; dir. Elite Communications, Johannesburg, 1983, Hilton Roc Florist, Johannesburg, 1985-88; consumer promotions coordinator South African Sugar Assn., Durban, 1988—; owner, prin. On-Line Public Relations Co., Johannesburg, 1984-88; consumer promotions mgr. and home economist SA Sugar Assn., 1988—; cons. Machado Rainbow Trout, Machadodorp, S. Africa, 1983—; cons. to food cos. and restaurants. Author: Cooking with Angela Day, 1971; Entertaining with Angela Day, 1975. Mem. S. African Chefs Assn., Chaine Des Rotisseurs, Pub. Relations Inst. S. Africa, Food Stylists Guild (Bakers Dozen). Avocations: cooking, tennis, wine. Office: PO Box 1854, Durban 4000, Republic of South Africa

VAN WACHEM, LODEWIJK CHRISTIAAN, petroleum company executive; b. Pangkalan Brandan, The Netherland East Indies, July 31, 1931; m. Elisabeth G. Cristofoli, 1958; 3 children. Student Tech. U., Delft, The Netherlands. With Bataafsche Petroleum Maatschappij, The Hague, The Netherlands, 1953; mech. engr. Cia Shell de Venezuela, 1954-63; chief engr. Shell-BP Petroleum Devel. Co. Nigeria, 1963-66, mgr. engr., 1966-67, chmn., mng. dir., 1972-76; head tech. adminstrn. Brunei Shell Petroleum Co. Ltd., 1967-69, tech. dir., 1969-71; head production div. Shell Internat. Petroleum Maatschappij, The Hague, 1971-72, coordinator exploration and production, 1976-79; mng. dir. Royal Dutch Petroleum Co., until 1982, pres., 1982—; mem. presidium bd. dirs. Shell Petroleum N.V.; mng. dir. Shell Petroleum Co. Ltd., 1977; chmn. Shell Oil Co. USA; bd. dirs. Shell Can.; chmn. joint com. mng. dirs. Royal Dutch/Shell Group, 1985—. Recipient C.B.E., 1977, Knight Order Netherlands Lion, 1981. Home: Carel van Bylandtlaan 30, The Hague The Netherlands Office: Shell Oil Co 1 Shell Plaza Houston TX 77001 other: Carel van Bylandtlaan 30, The Hague Netherlands *

VAN WASSENHOVE, PATRICK, sales executive; b. Ostend, Belgium, Jan. 20, 1944; s. Frans and Elisa (Bekaert) Van W.; m. Christiane Bruyninckx, July 14, 1979; children: Marie-Lise, Yves, Frederic. BA in Biochemistry, U. Louvain, Belgium, 1967; BBA, U. Ghent, Belgium, 1968. Mgr. sales Synoglas N.V., Zele, Belgium, 1967—. Roman Catholic. Home: P Gorus St 9, B9140 Zele Belgium Office: Synoglas, Drukkerystraat 9, B9140 Zele Belgium

VAN WELL, GÜNTHER WILHELM, retired ambassador; b. Osterath, Germany, Oct. 15, 1922; s. Friedrich and Magda (Hulser) Van W.; m. Carolyn Stevens Bradley, Nov. 9, 1957; children—Kirsten, Mark. M.Econs., U. Bonn, Fed. Republic Germany, 1950, LL.M., %. Jr. barrister Dist. Ct.,

Dusseldorf, Fed. Republic Germany, 1950-51; 3d and 1st sec. Fgn. Office, Bonn, 1952-54, 59-62; 2d sec. UN Observer's Office, N.Y.C., 1954-59; cousellor Fed. Republic Germany embassy, Tokyo, 1963-67; dir. State Sec. Fgn. Office, Bonn, 1967-81; ambassador to UN and U.S.A. N.Y.C. and Washington, 1981-87; fellow Harvard U., Cambridge, Mass., 1961-62. Contbr. articles to profl. jours. Mem. German Soc. for Fgn. Policy, German Juristic Assn., Inst. for East-West Security Studies. Home: Steinstrasse 52, Boun-Bad Godesberg 5300, Federal Republic Germany Office: Embassy Fed Republic of Germany 4645 Reservoir Rd NW Washington DC 20007

VAN WINKLE, EDGAR WALLING, electrical engineer, computer consultant; b. Rutherford, N.J., Oct. 12, 1913; s. Winant and Jessie Walcott (Mucklow) Van W.; m. Jessie Stetler, Apr. 23, 1938; children—Barbara Van Winkle Clifton, Catrina Van Winkle Poindexter, Cornelia Van Winkle Carro. B.E.E., Rutgers U., 1936; M.S. in Indsl. Engring., Columbia U., 1943, P.E. in Indsl. Engring., 1966. Registered profl. engr., N.J. Elec. engr. A.B. Dumont Labs. Passaic, N.J., 1943-48; chief engr. Facsimile Electronics, Passaic, 1948-52; cons. Bur. Ships, Washington, 1952; asst. sr. staff scientist Bendix Corp., Teterboro, N.J., 1952-67; sr. staff scientist Conrac Corp., West Caldwell, N.J., 1967-78; pres. Empac, Inc., Rutherford, N.J., 1979—. Author profl. papers. Contbr. articles to profl. jours. Patentee in field. Ruling elder Presbyterian Ch., Rutherford, 1984—. Mem. IEEE (life, treas. artificial intelligence sect. North N.J. Chpt. 1982-84), Bendix Mgmt. Club (life), North N.J. Automatic Control Group (chmn. 1967-68), Met. Engring. Mgmt. (chmn. 1966-67), Mensa, Holland Soc., Delta Phi. Republican. Club: Upper Montclair Country. Current work: Artificial intelligence and robotics. Subspecialties: Artificial intelligence; Mathematical software.

VAN WYMEERSCH, CHARLES PAUL, educator; b. Liege, Belgium, May 7, 1946; s. Paul H. and Nelly F. (Meulemans) Van W.; m. Genevieve X. Byvoet, June 30, 1972; 1 dau. Laurence. Elec. Engr., Cath. U. Louvain, 1969, B.Econs., 1972; M.B. A., Cornell U., 1973. Research asst. Cath. U. Louvain, Belgium, 1971-72; attache Banque Bruxelles Lambert, 1973-76; prof. bus. fin. Namur U., Belgium, 1976—, chmn. dept. bus. econs., 1980—; dir. C. of C., Namur, 1982—, Internat. Trade & Invest Inst., 1981—. Author: Traite d'Analyse Financiere, 1982; editor: Traite pratique des comptes annuels, Guide des comptes annuels pour le Luxembourg. Sci. advisor Intercollegiate Ctr. for Mgmt. Sci. Office: Namur Univ, Dept Bus Economs, 8 Rempart de la Vierge, B5000 Namur Belgium

VAQUER, JEAN SÉBASTIEN, archaeologist; b. Carcassonne, Languedoc, France, Dec. 10, 1950; s. Sébastien and Jeanne (Gelin) V.; m. Lucile Sauniere, May 16, 1981. Lic., U. Montpellier, 1973, MA, 1975; postgrad., Ecole des Hautes Etudes en Scis. Sociales, Toulouse, France, 1983. Investigator Centre Nat. de la Recherche Scientifique, Toulouse, 1977—. Author: La ceramique chasséenne, 1975; co-author 5 books; contbr. numerous articles to profl. jours. Home: Le village Leuc, 11250 Saint Hilaire France Office: CNRS-EHESS, 56 rue du Taur, 31000 Toulouse France

VAQUERO SANCHEZ, ANTONIO, computer science educator; b. Pinos Puente, Granada, Spain, Aug. 30, 1938; s. Antonio Vaquero and Angustias Sánchez; m. Carmen Martin, Aug. 16, 1963; children: Ángeles, Carmen, Beatriz, Juan Ramón. BS, Inst. P. Sudrez, Granada, Spain, 1956; MS in Physics, U. Complutense, Madrid, 1961, PhD in Phys. Scis., 1967; D in Applied Math., Facility és Scis., Toulouse, France, 1967. Chief computer lab. Consejo Superior de Investigaciones Cientificas, Madrid, 1965-74; prof. Computer Sci. U. Autónoma, Barcelona, Spain, 1974-77, dir. Computer Sci. dept., 1974-77; prof. Computer Sci., vice dean U. Complutense, Madrid, 1977—, dir. Computer Sci. dept., 1985—; editor, cons. Internat. div. McGraw-Hill Pub. Co., 1983—; v.p. Assn. Española de Informática; mem. TC3 Internat. Fedn. Info. Processing, 1986—; pres. Fedn. Española de Sociedades de Informática. Author: Informática Diccionario, 1985, La Informática Aplicada a la Enseñanza, 1987; contbr. articles to profl. jours. Mem. IEEE (Computer Soc., former bd. dirs. Spanish com.), Assn. Computing Machinery, Inst. for Advanced Studies in Systems Research and Cybernetics (bd. dirs.). Home: Cyesa 8-9-I, 28017 Madrid Spain Office: U Complutense, Dept Info & Automatica, 28040 Madrid Spain

VARASTEH, SASSAN, management professional; b. Hamburg, Fed. Republic Germany, June 30, 1960; s. Said and Helga (Koehn) V.; m. Vivian Yih, Apr. 5, 1982; 1 child, Valerie Sara. BS, Babson Coll., Wellesly, Mass., 1981. Mktg. mgr. Corrobesch G.m.b.H., Hamburg, 1983-84; mng. dir. SAVA Internat., Hamburg, 1984—; cons. in field; bd. dirs. BEPTAL, Inc., Los Angeles. Club: Club of Clubs. Home: Rondeel 1, 2 Hamburg 60, Federal Republic of Germany Office: SAVA Internat,, Grosse Bleichen-8, 2 Hamburg 36, Federal Republic of Germany

VARDA, AGNES, screenwriter, director; b. Ixelles, Belgium, May 30, 1926; d. Eugene Jean and Christiane (Pasquet) V.; m. Jacques Demy, Jan. 8, 1962; children: Rosalie, Mathieu. Student Coll. de Sete, U. Paris, Ecole du Louvre. Ofcl. photographer Theatre Nat. Populaire, 1951-61; filmmaker, dir., 1954—, films include: La Pointe Courte, 1954; Cleo de 5 a 7, 1961; Le Bonheur, 1965; Les Creatures, 1966; Loin du Vietnam, 1967; Lions Love, 1969; Nausicaa, 1970; Daguerreotypes, 1975; L'Une Chante l'Autre Pas, 1976; Mur Murs, 1980; Documenteur, 1981; Vagabond, 1985; short films include: O Saisons, O Chateaux, 1957; L'Opera-Mouffe, 1958; Du Cote de la Cote, 1958; Salut les Cubains, 1963; Uncle Yanco, 1967; Black Panthers, 1968; Reponse de Femmes, 1968; Plaisir d'Amour en Iran, 1975; Ulysse, 1982; Les Dites Cariatides, 1984. Recipient Prix Melies, 1962; Prix Louis Dellue, 1965; David Selznick award 1965; Bronze Lion, Venice Festival, 1964; Silver Bear, Berlin Festival, 1965; 1st prize Oberhausen, Popular Univs. jury, 1970; Grand Prix Taormina, Sicily, 1977; Officer des Arts et des Lettres; Cesar award, 1984. *

VAREILLES, YVES, physician; b. Villeurganne, France, July 18, 1928; s. Michel and Marthe (Villeé) V.; m. May 29, 1957; children: Thierry, Anne, Elisabeth, Frederique, Chantal. Degree, U. Tours; MD, U. Lyon; Medecine du Travail, U. Strasbourg. Intern St. Luc Hosp., Lyon, France, 1954-56; medecin du travail Houilléres de Lorraine, St. Avold, France, 1958-64; gen. practice medicine Securite Soc. Miniere, Firminy, France, 1964—. Del., Cen. Democratic Soc., 1978; mcpl. conseiller, Firminy, 1987—. Served to lt. French armed forces, 1956-58. Decorated Reconnaisance medal. Roman Catholic. Office: Securite Soc Miniere, 34 Rue du Professeur Calmett, 42770 Firminy France

VARENNE, ANDRE GEORGES, cardiologist; b. Cabrespine, France, Nov. 27, 1926; s. Joseph and Angele (Lanet) V.; m. Huguette Comes, Dec. 11, 1954 (dec. 1987); children: Marie-Agnes, Elizabeth, Claire-Alexandra, Pierre-Andre. M.D., U. Lyon, 1955, cert. in cardiology, 1955. Resident, then asst. in medicine Hopital Pasteur, Nice, 1952-74, cons. cardiologist, 1974—; asst. prof. U. Nice Faculty Medicine, 1973—, dir. lab. cardiology, 1973—; cons. Monaco Cardio-Thoracic Ctr., 1987. Author, patentee in field. Served as officer M.C., French Army, 1952. Grantee French Govt., 1977-79, 80-82. Mem. French. Soc. Cardiologists, French Soc. Engrs. and Scientists, Soc. Electrics and Electronics, Italian Inst. Cardiology (hon.). Home: 6 rue Spitalieri, 06000 Nice France Office: Lab Cardiology Faculty Medicine, CHU Pasteur, 06031 Paris France

VARESE, STEFANO, anthropologist, educator; b. Genova, Liguria, Italy, July 27, 1939; s. Luigi and Giuseppina (Druetto) V.; m. Linda Marie Ayre, Apr. 9, 1975; children: Vanessa, André Luis. Diploma in History, Catholic U., Lima, Peru, 1964, BS in Ethnology, 1966, PhD in Anthropology, 1967. Prof., dept. anthropology San Marcos Nat. U., Lima, 1967-70; dir. Jungle Research Ctr., San Marcos Nat. U., Lima, 1966-68; dir. div. Amazon Native Communities, Lima, 1968-72; dir. research Popular Participation Study Ctr., Lima, 1972-74; prin. investigator Nat. Inst. Anthropology & History, Oaxaca, Mexico, 1975-79; dir. Reg. Unit Peoples Culture, Oaxaca, 1980-85; vis. scholar, prof. dept. anthropology and humanities ctr. Stanford U., Palo Alto, Calif., 1986—; prin. investigator Nat. System Sci. Research, Mexico, 1985—; cons. United Nations High Commr. for Refugees (Geneva), 1985—, UNESCO, Paris, 1977—; vis. prof. Stanford U., 1984-85; nat. investigator Ministry Edn. Mexico, 1985. Author: La Sal de los Cerros, 1974, Minoria Etnicas, comunidad Nacional, 1974, Indigenas y Educación en Mexico, 1983, Proyectos Etnicos y Proyectos nacionales, 1984; co-editor: Civilización, Jour. Culture & Politics. Jury mem. IVth Russell Tribunal on Human Rights, Rotterdam, London, 1981. Ford found. external fellow, 1987-88. Fellow Latin Am. Studies Assn.; mem. Anthrop. Cent. for Latin Am. Documentation, Ethnic Devel. Supporting Group (founder). Home: 3850 Holland Dr Santa Rosa CA 95404 Office: GADE, Apartado Postal 379, 68000 Oaxaca Mexico

VARET, MICHAEL A., lawyer; b. N.Y.C., Mar. 9, 1942; s. Guster V. and Frances B. (Goldberg) V.; m. Elizabeth R. Varet, June 3, 1973; 3 children. B.S. in Econs., U. Pa., 1962; LL.B., Yale U., 1965. Mem. firm Milgrim Thomajan & Lee P.C., N.Y.C., 1982—. Trustee Montefiore Med. Ctr., Bronx, N.Y., 1980—; bd. dirs. Sem. Library Corp. Jewish Theol. Sem., N.Y.C., 1983—, United Jewish Appeal-Fedn. Jewish Philanthropies of Greater N.Y., Inc., 1979-86, Mosholu Preservation Corp., Bronx, 1982—; bd. overseers Jewish Theol. Sem., 1982—, Jewish Publ. Soc. of Am., 1986—; mem. exec. com. Montefiore Med. Ctr., 1985—; mem. Council of Overseers United Jewish Appeal Fedn. of Jewish Philanthropies of Greater N.Y., Inc., 1986—. Served with USAR, 1966-72. Mem. ABA, N.Y. State Bar Assn., Assn. Bar City N.Y. (bd. dirs., exec. com. 1971-75), Internat. Fiscal Assn., Internat. Tax Planning Assn. Democrat. Jewish. Club: Yale (N.Y.C.). Office: Milgrim Thomajan & Lee PC 405 Lexington Ave New York NY 10174

VARGAS, LENA BESSETTE, nursing administrator; b. Hardwick, Vt., Dec. 26, 1922; d. Leon Alphonse and Dorilla Leah (Boudreau) Bessette; m. Jose Emilio Vargas, Sept. 3, 1949; children—Jose Emilio, Maria del Carmen, J. Ramon, Vicente Andres, Yolanda Teresa. B.S. in Nursing Edn., U. Vt., 1949. Instr. basic nursing Mary Fletcher Hosp., Burlington, Vt., 1947-49; clin. instr. St. Francis Hosp., Evanston, Ill., 1949-50; nurse participant streptomycin therapy research H.M. Biggs Meml. Hosp., Ithaca, N.Y., 1950-51; supr. ancillary personnel Providence Hosp., Washington, 1953-55, asst. dir. nursing, 1965—. Mem. council, del. cooperative congress Greenbelt Coop., Savage, Md., 1983—; bd. dirs. Providence Hosp. Fed. Credit Union, Washington, 1977-80, v.p. bd. dirs., 1983-85. Mem. AAUW (chmn. various coms.), Nat. League for Nursing, Christ Child Soc. Roman Catholic. Avocations: bridge, travel, real estate, horseback riding. Home: 10706 Keswick St Garrett Park MD 20896 Office: Providence Hosp 1150 Varnum St Washington DC 20017

VARGAS-CABA, ALFREDO, airline and hotel chain executive; b. Santiago, De Los Caballeros, Dominican Republic, Mar. 23, 1952; arrived in Fed. Republic Germany, 1979; s. Miguel Andrés and Maria Graciela (Caba) Vargas; m. Patricia Dumas, Jan. 6, 1984; children: Tiffany Sophie, Lorely Caroline. Licence Lettres, U. Besancon, France, 1974, postgrad., 1975-76. Lic. interpreter/translator. Ofcl. rep. Europe Ministry Tourism Dominican Republic, Geneva, 1976-79; dir. Europe Europe Ministry Tourism Dominican Republic, Frankfurt, Fed. Republic Germany, 1979-87; mgr. Germany, dir. Europe Dominicana Airlines, Frankfurt, Fed. Republic Germany, 1981—; 2nd sec. Embassy Dominican Republic, Bonn, Fed. Republic Germany, 1979-86; rep. Germany Premier Hotel Corp., Frankfurt, Fed. Republic Germany, 1986—; dir. sales Europe Premier Resorts and Hotel, Frankfurt, Fed. Republic Germany, 1987—. Author: Dominican Republic in Europe, 1978; contbr. articles to profl. jours. Gen. sec. Am. Field Service Dominican Republic, Exchange Program, Santiago, 1970-71; mem. nat. com. Am. Field Service Germany, Santo Domingo, Dominican Republic, 1976—; alt. del. World Tourism Orgn., Madrid, 1975, Gen. Assembly New Delhi, 1983, Sofia, Bulgaria, 1985, head del. Dominican Mission, Torremolinos, Spain, 1976. Am. Field Service scholar, Appleton, Wis., 1969, French U. scholar, Paris, Besancon, 1971-75. Mem. German-Dominican Soc. (mem. supporting bd. 1984—), German Travel Assn., Hotel Sales Mktg. Assn. Roman Catholic. Clubs: Corps Touristique, Porsche, Skal (Frankfurt). Home: Voelcker Strasse 24, D6000 Frankfurt M1 Federal Republic of Germany Office: Dominicana Airlines, Voelcker Str 24, D6000 Frankfurt M1 Federal Republic of Germany

VARGAS-SABORIO, BERNAL, Costa Rican diplomat; b. San Jose, Costa Rica, Aug. 12, 1944. Student U. Costa Rica, U. Manchester (Eng.); M.Social Sci., U. Chgo. With Costa Rican Directorate Gen. of Protocol, 1964-70; consul gen. 2d class, Chgo. and Midwest, 1970-73; minister-counselor, alt. rep. UN, 1973-75; minister plenipotentiary, alt. permanent rep., 1975-78; minister, consul gen. N.Y. and Eastern U.S., 1978-82; envoy to Can., 1982-84; UN dir. for Colombia, Venezuela and Ecuador, based in Bogota, 1984—; prof. social sci. Nat. U. Heredia, 1968-70; rep. numerous UN meetings and bodies. Author: The Emigration of Professional Personnel: The Brain Drain for Developing Countries to Developed Countries, 1973. Decorated comdr. Order Khmer Republic; grand officer Order Antonio Jose de Irisarri (Guatemala); grand officer Order Phoenix (Greece). Office: PO Box 6765, FDR Station New York NY 10150

VARGHA-KHADEM, FARANEH, neuropsychologist, researcher; b. Tehran, Iran, Jan. 16, 1949; d. Alimohammad and Rohanieh (Mohtadi) Vargha; m. Ramin Khadem, Sept. 20, 1969; children—Paryssa, Varqa, Ryyan. B.A., Concordia U., 1970; M.Sc., McGill U., 1972; M.A., U. Mass., 1977, Ph.D., 1979. Teaching asst. McGill U., Montreal, Que., Can., 1974-78, research asst., 1975-76; lectr. Concordia U., Montreal, 1979-81; postdoctoral fellow Montreal Children's Hosp., 1979-81; lectr. neurology and neurosurgery McGill U., Montreal, Que., 1981-83; lectr. developmental pediatrics U. London, 1983—; prin. clin. psychologist Hosp. Sick Children, London, 1987—; neuropsychol. cons. and expert witness on legal cases, 1983-85. Brit. Med. Research Council project grantee, 1983—; Govt. Que. postdoctoral fellow, 1979-82; Can. Council doctoral fellow, 1976-79; recipient Undergrad. award Que. Govt., 1968-70. Fellow Sigma Xi; mem. Soc. Research in Child Devel, Can. Assn. Studies on Baha'i Faith, Can. Psychol. Assn., European Brain and Behavior Soc. Home: 27 Hampstead Hill Gardens, London NW3, England Office: U London, Inst Child Health, Wolfson Ctr, Mecklenburgh Square, London WC1, England

VARGO, EDWARD PAUL, priest, English and literature educator; b. Lorain, Ohio, Aug. 10, 1935; s. Joseph and Julia (Dobos) V. A.A., Divine Word Coll., Conesus, N.Y., 1955; A.B., Divine Word Sem., Techny, Ill., 1957; A.M., U. Chgo., 1964, Ph.D., 1968. Ordained priest, Roman Catholic Ch., 1963. Instr. Divine Word Coll., Epworth, Iowa, 1965-66, assoc. prof., 1966-73, chmn. dept. English, 1966-73; assoc. prof. Fu Jen U., Taipei, Taiwan, 1974—, dean Coll. Fgn. Langs., 1984—, trustee, 1981-84, trustee Middle Sch., 1986—; dir. overseas tng. program Soc. Divine Word, Taipei, 1980-84, provincial consultor, 1981-87. Author: Rainstorms and Fire, 1973; editor Jour. Fu Jen Studies, 1974—; contbr. articles to profl. publs. U. Chgo. fellow, 1964, 66; Ford Found. fellow, 1967; recipient Nat. Sci. Council Research awards Republic China, 1985, 86, 87. Mem. MLA, Nat. Council Tchrs. English. Democrat. Roman Catholic. Avocation: hiking.

VARGUS, BRIAN STANLEY, sociologist, educator, political consultant; b. Vallejo, Calif., Aug. 2, 1938; s. Stanley John and Edna Nettie (Rabb) V.; m. Nanci Jean Reginelli, Aug. 29, 1964; children: Jilda, Rebecca, Abigail. B.A., U. Calif.-Berkeley, 1961, M.A., 1963; Ph.D., Ind. U., 1969. Instr., Bakersfield Coll., Calif., 1964-66, Ind. U., Bloomington, 1966-69; asst. prof. U. Pitts., 1969-75; prof. sociology Ind./Purdue U., Indpls., 1975—, dir. publ. opinion labs., 1975-86; pres. Opinion Research and Eval., Indpls., 1980—; cons. Bayh, Tabbert & Capehart, Indpls., 1984, Pub. Policy Cons., Bloomington, 1984, Ind. Bell, 1986—, Baker & Daniels, Indpls., 1985, Handley & Miller, Indpls, 1986, U.S. Dept. Justice, 1987, Clay County (Ind.) Prosecutor, 1987, Ind. Bell, 1986-87, Ind. Assn. Realtors, 1986-87; polit. analyst Sta. WISH-TV, Indpls., 1984—; polit. analyst, participant radio and TV programs; speaker in field. Author: Reading in Sociology, 3d edit., 1984, Tools for Sociology, 1985. Pres. bd. dirs. Greater Ind. Council on Alcholism, Nat. Council on Alcoholism, Indpls., 1982-84; bd. dirs. Indpls. Shakespeare Festival, 1988—; cons. Greater Indpls. Progress Com., 1982, Children's Mus., Indpls., 1984, 87, Gov.'s Task Force on Drunk Driving, Ind., 1984—. Fulbright fellow, 1973, Flynn fellow, 1981; recipient Disting. Service award Greater Council Alcoholism, 1984; recipient numerous research grants. Mem. Am. Sociol. Assn., Am. Assn. Pub. Opinion, Midwest Assn. Publ. Opinion Research. Methodist. Avocations: racquetball, reading, swimming. Home: 4084 Rocking Chair Rd Greenwood IN 46142 Office: Ind/Purdue U 425 Anges St Indianapolis IN 46220

VARIAN, JOHN PATRICK WERGE, hand surgeon; b. Dublin, Ireland, Apr. 30, 1942; s. Stephen Noel and Catalina Anna (Greene) Varian; m. Stella Beveen Lavan, Apr. 14, 1940; children—Sarah, Paul, Daniel. M.B.B.Ch., Trinity Coll., Dublin, 1965, M.A., 1966. Med. and surg. intern Sir Patrick Dun's Hosp., Dublin, 1965-66; surg. resident Bristol Tng. Sch., Eng., 1967-70; orthopedic resident Australian Orthopedic Tng. Sch., Sydney, 1970-73; cons. hand surgeon, Derby, Eng., 1973-81, Dublin, 1981—. Fellow Royal Coll. Surgeons (Eng.), Australian Coll. Surgeons; mem. Brit. Soc. Surgery of Hand (hon. treas. 1981—), French Soc. Surgery of Hand. Mem. Ch. of Ireland. Club: University. Avocations: fishing; sailing; golf; tennis. Home: 68 Eglinton Rd, Dublin 4 Ireland Office: Blackrock Clinic, Blackrock County Dublin Ireland

VARIS, MARTTI JOUKO HENRIK, manufacturing executive; b. Helsinki, Finland, June 26, 1945; s. Pentti K. and Aira M. (Haajanen) V.; m. Tea M. Hautala, 1969; children: Karri H.T., Markku J.P. MS, Helsinki Sch. Tech., 1971. Registered profl. engr. Project engr., prodn. mgr. Oy Wärtsilä Ab, Helsinki, 1970-80; pres. Evak Sanitär Ab, Bromölla, Sweden, 1981-84; dir. Oy E. Sarlin Ab, Helsinki, 1984—; bd. dirs. Sarlin Ltd., London, Europump Services Ltd., Bristol, Eng. Contbr. articles to profl. jours.; patentee in waste water tech. Served to 2nd lt. Artillery Finnish Armed Forces, 1964-65. Mem. Finnish Tech. Soc., Finnish Soc. Mech. Engrs. Lutheran. Office: Oy E Sarlin Ab, PO Box 750, SF-00101 Helsinki Finland

VARKONYI, PETER, Hungarian minister of foreign affairs; b. Budapest, Hungary, 1931; married; 2 children. Grad. Acad. Fgn. Affairs; PhD Eotvos Lorand U. of Sci., Budapest, 1970. Diplomatic missions to U.S., 1951, U.K., 1951, Egypt, 1957-58; head press dept. Hungarian Fgn. Ministry, 1958-61; pvt. sect. to Prime Minister of Hungary, 1961-65; dep. dept. head, central com. Hungarian Socialist Workers' Party, 1965-69, mem. central com., 1975—, sec. central com., 1982—; sec. of state as pres. Council of Ministers' Info. Office of Hungary, 1969-70; minister fgn. affairs Hungary, 1983—. Author: A magyar-amerikai allamkozi kapscolatok tortenete 1945-1948 (The History of Hungarian-American Inter-state Relations, 1945-48), 1970. Decorated Service medal of Merit, medal of Merit for Socialist Labor, Golden Labor Order of Merit, golden degree; also Egyptian and Finnish decorations. Office: Ministry of Fgn Affairs, Bem rakpoart 47, POB 423, H-1394 Budapest 62 Hungary

VARMA, THANKAM RAMA, college educator, consultant obstetrics and gynecology; b. Palghat, India, Oct. 2, 1937; came to Eng., 1965; d. Panicker Narayana and Meenakshi Kutty (Machat) Manambrakat; m. Rama Varmá, May 1, 1962; children: Meena, Sunil. M.B.B.S., Madras Med. Sch. (India), 1960; M.R.C.O.G., Royal Coll. Obstetricians and Gynecologists (Eng.), 1968; F.R.C.S., Royal Coll. Surgeons Edinburgh, 1968; Ph.D., Univ. London, 1975; F.R.C.O.G., Royal Coll. Obstetricians and Gynecologists, 1981. Sr. lectr., cons. gynecology and obstetrics St. Georges Med. Sch. and Hosp., London, 1976—, tchr., researcher, clin. work adminstrn., examiner; house physician to prof. medicine Gen. Hosp., Madras, 1960, house surgeon to prof. surgery, 1960-61, sr. house officer to prof. obstetrics and gynecology, 1961-62; sr. house officer K.G. Hosp., Madras, 1962-63, registrar, 1963-64; registrar to prof. obstetrics and gynecology Women and Children Hosp., Madras, 1964-65; sr. house surgeon St. Hild's Hosp., Hartlepool, Eng., 1965; sr. house officer St. Helier Hosp., Carshalton, 1967-68, registrar obstetrics and gynecology, 1968-70; sr. registrar, research fellow Westminster Med. Sch., Queen Mary's Hosp., Roehampton, Eng., 1970-73; sr. registrar St. George's Hosp., London, 1974-76; cons. in field. Contbr. articles to profl. jours. Recipient awards from Madras Univ. Balfour Meml. medal, Hon. Diwan Bahadue V. Ramabhadra Naidu medal, Nair Meml. medal, Lakshmanaswamy Mudaliar medal, Rangachari medal, Gangadharan Lakshminaraysnamma prize, Guraswami Mudalier prize, Govindarajulu prize, Raja of Panagal gold medal; awards Madras Med. Sch., Cert. of Honor, Rukmani Meml. Gold medal, Bradfield prize, Bhat prize, Lady Grant Duff Gold prize, Johnstone Gold medal. Fellow Royal Coll. Surgeons Edinburgh. Avocations: music; gardening; collecting stamps; growing indoor plants. Home: No 3 Woodcote Dr, Purley, Surrey CR2 3PD, England Office: St Georges Hosp and Med Sch, Blackshaw Rd, London SW17, England

VARNER, BARTON DOUGLAS, lawyer; b. Ida Grove, Iowa, May 2, 1920; s. Charles R. and Mary E. (Whinery) V.; m. Frances Elaine Seaton, May 9, 1943; children: Charles R., John A. Student, U. Nebr., 1938-42; LL.B., U. Mo. at Kansas City, 1951. Bar: Mo. 1951. Since practiced in Kansas City and Lake Ozark, Mo., ret. 1985; of counsel Gage and Tucker, Kansas City and Lake Ozark, 1985—; partner firm Gage and Tucker (and predecessors), 1955-85. Bd. mgrs. Kansas City YMCA, 1958-80, chmn., 1962; bd. dirs. Tuscumbia Rural Fire Dept. Served with USNR, 1942-45. Mem. ABA, Kansas City Bar Assn., Nebr. Alumni Assn. Kansas City (pres. 1960), Miller County Hist. Soc. (pres. 1988—, bd. dirs., counsel), Make Today Count (counsel), Delta Sigma Pi, Delta Theta Phi. Methodist (steward 1964-66, trustee 1968-69). Club: Kansas City (Kansas City, Mo.). Home: Rural Route 1 PO Box 204 Tuscumbia MO 65082 Office: Mut Benefit Life Bldg Kansas City MO 64108

VARNER, CHARLEEN LAVERNE MCCLANAHAN (MRS. ROBERT B. VARNER), educator, administrator, nutritionist; b. Alba, Mo., Aug. 28, 1931; d. Roy Calvin and Lela Ruhama (Smith) McClanahan; student Joplin (Mo.) Jr. Coll., 1949-51; B.S. in Edn., Kans. State Coll. Pittsburg, 1953; M.S., U. Ark., 1958; Ph.D., Tex. Woman's U. 1966; postgrad. Mich. State U., summer, 1955, U. Mo., summer 1962; m. Robert Bernard Varner, July 4, 1953. Apprentice county home agt. U. Mo., summer 1952; tchr. Ferry Pass Sch., Escambia County, Fla., 1953-54; tchr. biology, home econs. Joplin Sr. High Sch., 1954-59; instr. home econs. Kans. State Coll., Pittsburg, 1959-63; lectr. foods, nutrition Coll. Household Arts and Scis., Tex. Woman's U., 1963-64, research asst. NASA grant, 1964-66; asso. prof. home econs. Central Mo. State U., Warrensburg, 1966-70, adviser to Colhecon, 1966-70, adviser to Alpha Sigma Alpha, 1967-70, 72, mem. bd. advisers Honors Group, 1967-70; prof., head dept. home econs. Kans. State Tchrs. Coll., Emporia, 1970-73; prof., chmn. dept. home econs. Benedictine Coll., Atchison, Kans., 1973-74; prof., chmn. dept. home econs. Baker U., Baldwin City, Kans., 1974-75; owner, operator Diet-Con Dietary Cons. Enterprises, cons. dietitian, 1973—. Mem. Joplin Little Theater, 1956-60. Mem. NEA, Mo., Kans. state tchrs. assns., AAUW, Am., Mo., Kans. dietetics assns., Am., Mo., Kans. home econs. assns., Mo. Acad. Scis., AAUP, U. Ark. Alumni Assn., Alumni Assn. Kans. State Coll. of Pittsburg, Am. Vocat. Assn., Assn. Edn. Young Children, Sigma Xi, Beta Sigma Phi, Beta Beta Beta, Alpha Sigma Alpha, Delta Kappa Gamma, Kappa Kappa Iota, Phi Upsilon Omicron. Methodist (organist). Home: Main PO Box 1009 Topeka KS 66601

VARNER, ROBERT BERNARD, educator, counselor; b. Ellsworth, Kans., May 31, 1930; s. Bernard Lafayette and Leota (Campbell) V.; B.S., Kans. State U., Pittsburg, 1952; M.S., U. Ark., 1959; postgrad. Mich. State U., summer 1955, U. Mo., summer 1962, (grantee) U. Kans., 1972-73; m. Charleen LaVerne McClanahan, July 4, 1953. Athletic coach, social sci. tchr. Joplin (Mo.) Sr. High Sch., 1956-63; head social sci. dept. R.L. Turner High Sch., Carrollton, Tex., 1963-66; asst. athletic coach, jr. high sch. social sci. tchr. Warrensburg, Mo., 1966-70; coach, social sci. tchr., Emporia, Kans., 1970-72; asst. cottage dir., counselor Topeka Youth Ctr., 1973—; substitute tchr. Topeka Pub. Schs., 1974—. Recreation dir. Carrollton-Farmers Branch (Tex.) Recreation Center, 1964-66; city recreation dir., Warrensburg, Mo., 1966-68. Served with USN, 1953-54. Mem. NEA, Kans. State U.-Pittsburg Alumni Assn., U. Ark. Alumni Assn., Phi Delta Kappa, Sigma Tau Gamma. Democrat. Methodist. Club: Elks. Address: Main PO Box 1009 Topeka KS 66601

VARNEY, CARLETON BATES, JR., interior designer, columnist, educator, author; b. Lynn, Mass., Jan. 23, 1937; s. Carleton Bates and Julia (Raczkowskos) V.; m. Suzanne Maria Lickdyke, Dec. 25, 1969; children: Nicholas, Seamus, Sebastian. BA, Oberlin Coll., 1958; student, U. Madrid, 1957; MA, NYU, 1969; LHD (hon.), U. Charleston, 1987. Sch. tchr. 1958-59; asst. to pres. Dorothy Draper & Co., Inc., 1959-63, exec. v.p., 1963-66, pres., 1966—; dean Carleton Varney Sch. of Art & Design, U. Charleston, W.Va. Designer: chairs, 1964, decorative fabrics, 1964—, dinnerware and china, 1965—, crystal glassware, 1966—, table and bed linen, 1977—, ready to wear resort collection Cruzanwear, 1987, mens' wear furnishings for Rawlinson & Marking, London, 1987; interior designer: Dromoland Castle, Ireland, 1963, 88, Westbury Hotel, Belgium, 1964, N.Y. World's Fair, 1965, Clare Inn, Ireland, 1968, Greenbrier Hotel, White Sulphur Springs, W.Va., 1968, Westbury Hotel, San Francisco, 1973, Copley Plaza Hotel, Boston, 1976, Amway Grand Plaza Hotel, Grand Rapids, Mich., 1980, The Grand Hotel, Mackinac Island, Mich., 1978, Equinox House, Manchester, Vt.,

1984, Brazilian Ct. Hotel, Palm Beach, Fla., 1985, Waldorf Towers, N.Y.C., 1985, Dawn Beach Hotel, St. Maarten, 1985, Christian Broadcasting Conv. Ctr., 1986, Met. Opera House boutique, N.Y.C., 1985, (cruise ship) World Discoverer, 1984, Arrowwood Conv. Ctr., Purchase, N.Y., 1987, Boca Raton Hotel and Club, Fla., 1987, Speedway Club, Charlotte, N.C., 1987, Coccoloba Plantation, Anguilla, Brit. Virgin Islands, 1987, Villa Madeleine, St. Croix, Virgin Islands, 1987, Ashford Castle, Ireland, 1988, Adare Manor, Ireland, 1988, numerous others; designer: White House party for celebration Israel-Egypt Peace Treaty, 1979, charity movie premiers Lord Jim, 1965, Man for All Seasons, 1967, War and Peace, 1968 (Shelby Williams award for design achievement 1967); fashion benefit for Am. Found. for AIDS Research, 1988, log home for Pres. and Mrs. Carter, Ellijay, Ga., 1983; color cons. Carter Presdl. Library, 1986; trustee & curator: former presdl. yacht U.S.S. Sequoia, 1982; retail stores: Carleton Varney at the Greenbrier, White Sulphur Springs, W.Va., 1981, Carleton Varney at the Equinox, Manchester, Vt., 1985, Carleton Varney at Christiansted, St. Croix, Virgin Islands, 1986, Carleton Varney at the Mill, Christiansted, St. Croix, 1988; author: numerous books including You and Your Apartment, 1960, The Family Decorates a Home, 1962, Carleton Varney's Book of Decorating Ideas, 1970, Decorating With Color, 1971, Decorating For Fun, 1972, Carleton Varney Decorates Windows, 1975, Be Your Own Decorator, 1979, There's No Place Like Home, 1980, Down Home, 1981, Carleton Varney's ABC's of Decorating, 1983, Staying in Shape: An Insider's Guide to the Great Spas, 1983, Room by Room Decorating, 1984, Color Magic, 1985, Cabbage Roses, 1988; syndicated columnist: Your Family Decorator, 1968—. Mem. Nat. Soc. Indsl. Designers. Clubs: N.Y. Athletic; Shannon Rowing (Ireland); Millbrook Golf and Tennis (N.Y.). Office: Dorothy Draper & Co Inc 60 E 56th St New York NY 10022

VARNOLD, CECIL BURL, township official; b. Maquon, Ill., Mar. 14, 1912; s. James Martin and Nellie Mae (Smith) V.; m. Ellouise Lorraine Ronesela Conner, Oct. 14, 1943; children—Paul Martin, Richard Mark, Charles Burdette. Rd. commr. Maquon Twp. (Ill.), Maquon, 1939-47, 71-77; owner, operator Varnold Found. & Erection Co., Maquon, 1947-66. Mem. Ill. Assn. Twp. and County Ofcls., Taxpayers Fedn., Internat. Union Operating Engrs. Republican. Methodist. Clubs: Masons, Shriners. Home: PO Box 155 Maquon IL 61458

VARTY, E. KENNETH, French educator; b. Calke Village, Derbyshire, Eng., Aug. 18, 1927; s. Ernest and Doris (Hollingworth) V.; m. Hety Benninghoff; children: Anne, Catherine. BA with hons., U. Nottingham, Eng., 1951, PhD, 1954; DLitt., U. Keele, Eng., 1987. Asst. lectr. U. Coll., N. Staffordshire, Eng., 1953-56, lectr., 1956-61; lectr. French U. Leicester, Eng., 1961-66, sr. lectr., 1966-68; Stevenson prof. French U. Glasgow, Scotland, 1968—; vis. prof. U. Jerusalem, 1977, U. Oxford, 1974, U. Cambridge, 1984. Editor/author: The Earliest Branches of the Roman de Renart, 1987; contbr. articles to profl. jours. Served with RAF, 1945-48. Named Chevalier Dans l'ordre des Palmes Académiques French Ministry Edn., 1987. Fellow Soc. Antiquarians of London; mem. Brit. Br. of Internat. Arthurian Soc., Internat. Reynard Soc. (pres. 1974), Soc. for French Studies (treas. 1969-71). Anglican. Home: 4 Dundonald Rd, Glasgow G12 9LJ, Scotland Office: U Glasgow Dept French, Glasgow Scotland

VARY, JAMES PATRICK, physics educator; b. Savanna, Ill., May 23, 1943; s. Willis L. and Ethice K. (McCabe) V.; m. Audrey Maria Zarba, June 11, 1966; children—William James, Brian Edward. B.S., Boston Coll., 1965; M.Ph., Yale U., 1968, Ph.D., 1970. Research assoc. MIT, Cambridge, 1970-72; asst. physicist Brookhaven Nat. Lab., Upton, N.Y., 1972-74, assoc. physicist, 1974-75; asst. prof. physics Iowa State U., Ames, 1975-77, assoc. prof., 1977-81, prof., 1981—; dir. nuclear theory program Ames Lab., 1977-82; vis. prof. Calif. Inst. Tech., 1986-87; Disting. vis. prof. Ohio State U., 1987—. Contbr. articles to sci. jours. Alexander von Humboldt fellow, 1979. Mem. Am. Phys. Soc., AAAS, Union of Concerned Scientists, Sigma Xi.

VASARELY, VICTOR, artist; b. Pecs, Hungary, 1908. Student medicine; Dr. honoris causa in Humanities, State U. Cleve., 1977. Mem. Budapest Bauhaus; moved to Paris, 1930. One-man shows include Rose Fried Gallery, N.Y.C., World House Gallery, N.Y.C., Met. Mus. Art, Montevideo, Hanover Gallery, London, Pace Gallery, Boston, Papal Palace, Avignon, France, 1985, French Inst., Budapest, 1985, Galerija S. Dubrovnik, Sombor, Yugoslavia, Jazz Acad., Budapest, 1985, Villeurbanne City Hall, France, 1985, Galerie der Stadt Esslingen am Neckar, Fed. Republic Germany, 1986, Musée Nat. des Beaux-Arts d'Alger, 1986, Heimatsmus. Gablitzhalle, Austria, 1986, Galerie Guigné, Paris, 1987, Maison de Culture de Berlin, 1987, Galerie Richard, Zurich, 1987, Galerie Abisz de Stuttgart, 1987, numerous others; major group exhbns. Paris Salons, Stadelijk Mus., Amsterdam, Documenta III Kassel, Carnegie Inst., Gallery Chalette, N.Y.C., Sidney Janis Gallery, N.Y.C., Guggenheim Mus., Sao Paolo, Rio de Janeiro, Montevideo, State Gallery Esslingen, French Embassy Thailand; rep. permanent collections Mus. Modern Art, N.Y.C., Mus. St. Etienne, Paris, Mus. Modern Art, Paris, Albright-Knox Gallery, Harvard U., Buenos Aires Mus., Montivideo Mus., Brussels Mus., Reykjavik Mus., Carnegie Inst., Stedelijk Mus., Sao Paulo Mus., Tate Gallery, London, Vienna Mus., Tel Aviv Mus., Guggenheim Mus., Rockefeller Found., Helsinki Mus., Dallas Mus., others; study, followed by sculpture for XXIVth Olympic Games, Seoul, Korea; subject numerous bibliographies. Decorated officer Legion of Honor, officer Nat. Order of Arts and Letters, France; grand ribbon honor Order Andre Bello, Venezuela; medal Order of Flag, Hungary; recipient Guggenheim Internat. award Merit, 1964; named to Order Arts and Letters France, 1965; named hon. citizen of New Orleans, 1966; prize 9th Biennal Minister Fgn. Affairs, Tokyo, 1967; grand prize 8th Biennal Art Sao Paulo, Brazil, 1965; cert. of distinction NYU, 1978; Art prize City of Goslar, 1978; décoration du chéquier de la Caisse d'Epargne Ecureuil, 1986; mem. Com. d'Honneur de Compétition Industrie, Paris, 1987; pres. d'Honneur du Prix Départemental d'Architecture contemporaine au Moulin de Guérard, Montreuil; Meédaille de la Ville de Clermont-Ferrand, 1987. Mem. France-Hungary Assn. (hon. pres. 1977—), Internat. Inst. Nuclear Engrs. (corres. mem.). Address: 83 rue aux Religues, 77410 Annet-sur-Marne Claye Souilly, France

VASARY, TAMAS, concert pianist, conductor; b. Aug. 11, 1933; ed. Franz Liszt U. Music, Budapest, under Lajos Hernadi, Jozsef Gat and Zoltan Kodaly; m. Hdiko Kovacs, 1967. First solo performance at age 8; tchr. theory Franz Liszt Acad.; recitalist Leningrad, Moscow and Warsaw; settled in Switzerland, 1958; London debut, 1961, N.Y.C., 1962; debut as condr. Menton Festival of Music, 1971; has since appeared in Europe, South Africa, S.Am., U.S., Can., India, Thailand, Hong Kong, Australia, Japan, Mex.; mus. dir. No. Sinfonia, Newcastle, 1979-82; recs. for Deutsche Grammophone include: 3 records works of Franz Liszt, 8 of Chopin, 3 of Rachmaninoff, one of Debussy and Mozart. Recipient Liszt prices, Queen Elizabeth of Belgium prize, Marguerite Longue prize, Paris, Chopin prizes Internat. Competition, Warsaw, Internat. Competition Brazil, Bach and Paderewski medals, London. Office: care Harold Holt Ltd, 31 Sinclair Rd, London W14 0NS, England Address: F-77410 Annet-sur Marne France *

VASCONCELOS, ANTONIO MANUEL, wine company executive; b. Oporto, Portugal, July 30, 1945; s. João and Maria Madalena (Macedo Pinto) V.; m. Maria Luisa Sottomayor, Apr. 18, 1970; children: Rita, Nuno. Grad. in econs., Oporto U., 1967. Sr. acct. Mabor, Oporto, 1972-80; dir. Martinez Gassiot and Co. Ltd., Gaia, Portugal, 1980-83, Cockburn Smithes and Cia Ltd., Gaia, 1983—. Mem. Port Wine Shippers Assn. (v.p. 1983-86), Assn. Portugese Economists. Roman Catholic. Clubs: Portuense (Oporto), C. Vela Atlântico. Office: Cockburn Smithes and Cia Ltd, Rua Das Coradas 13, 4400 Gaia Portugal

VASILESCU, ALEXANDRU, mechanical engineer, educator; b. Brosteni-Arges, Romania, Mar. 10, 1926; s. Anghel and Trandafira Vasilescu; m. Motrea Rohovschi, Sept. 24, 1960; 1 child, Mihail. Diploma in Engring., Poly. Inst. of Timisoara, 1951. Asst. prof. engring. U. Galati, Romania, 1951-53, lectr., 1953-65, sr. lectr., 1965-74, prof. fluid mechanics, 1975—; participant 3s Nat. Congress on Theoretical and Applied Mechanics, Bulgaria, 1977, 3d Internat. Symposium on Theory and Practice of Mechanisms, Romania, 1981. Author: Dimensional Analysis and the Theory of Similarity, 1969, The Similarity of Elastic Systems, 1974, Hydromechanics, 1962, contbr. numerous article to profl. jours. Home: 16 AP 54 Melodiei, 6200 Galati Romania Office: Faculty of Mechanics, Galati U, Blvd Republicii 47, Galati Romania

VASOLI, CESARE, historian, educator; b. Florence, Italy, Jan. 12, 1924; s. Sady amd Sara Irma (Tofanari) V.; m. Nidia Danelon, Aug. 6, 1956. PhD, U. Florence, 1947; D (hon.), U. Tours, France, 1982. Asst. prof. U. Florence, 1948-56, prof., 1956-62, 70—; prof. U. Cagliari, Italy, 1962-66, U. Bari, Italy, 1966-68, U. Genova, Italy, 1968-70. Author: La retorica e la dialettica dell'Umanesimo, 1968, Profezia e ragione, 1974, I miti e gli astri, 1976, La cultura delle corti, 1980, Immagini umanistiche, 1983. Budapest Acad. Scis. hon. fellow; Florence Acad. La Colombaria fellow, 1971, Napoli Acad. Pontaniana fellow, 1975, Arezzo Acad. Petrarca fellow, 1981. Home: Via Nazioni Unite 51, 50126 Florence Italy

VASSILIADES, ELIAS DEMETRIOS, urban architect; b. Athens, Greece, Nov. 27, 1946; s. Demetrios and Sia (Aninou) V.; m. Frosso Iossifoglu, Dec. 20, 1969; 1 child, Daphne. BArch, Cornell U., 1969; MArch, U. Pa., 1972, M in City Planning, 1972. Lic. architect/engr., Greece. Architect Beyer-Blinder-Bell, N.Y.C., 1969-70; planning cons. U. Geneva, 1971; self-employed new towns cons. Phila., 1971-72; housing cons. Temple U., Phila., 1972; jr. officer for pub. works Hellenic Navy Command, Athens, 1973-75; devel. mgr. Pitria Ltd. Internat. Cons., Athens, 1976-82; area mgr. Candillis-Gredeco Internat. Cons., Athens and Dubai (United Arab Emirates), 1983—; pvt. practice architecture and devel. Athens, 1976-80, 86—. Contbr. articles to profl. publs.; producer (audio-visual) Urban Design in Manhattan, 1969. Recipient various awards for photography; Fulbright scholar, 1965. Mem. Tech. Chamber of Greece, Am. Inst. Planning (assoc.), Gargoyle Soc. (hon.). Clubs: H.O.R.C. (Piraeus, Greece), N.A.O.V. (Voula, Greece). Home: Kazaiskaki 28, 166 73 Voula Greece Office: Candillis-Gredeco, PO Box 3807, Dubai 282955, United Arab Emirates

VASSILIOU, GEORGE VASSOS, government official of Cyprus, consulting company executive; b. Famagusta, Cyprus, May 20, 1931; s. Vassos George and Sophia Othonos (Yavopoulou) V.; D. Econs., U. Geneva, 1949; postgrad. Budapest U., 1957, London U., 1959-60; m. Androulla Georgiadou, Oct. 9, 1966; children: Sophia, Evelthon, Vassiliki. Market researcher Reed Paper Group, London, 1960-62; establisher Middle East Mktg. Research and Cons. Group, Nicosia, Cyprus, 1962—, chmn., chief exec. officer, 1962—; pres. Cyprus, 1988—; dir. Bank of Cyprus, Synek Fashionwear, Bellfoods, Village Hotel; vice prof. Cranfield Sch. Mgmt.; founder, prin. Middle East Ctr. for Mgmt. Studies; frequent speaker internat. confs. and seminars Middle East, 1972-82. Bd. dirs. Cyprus State Fair Authority, 1970-78; mem. Edn. Adv. Council. Fellow Royal Econ. Soc., Royal Statis. Soc.; mem. European Soc. Opinion and Mktg. Research, Market Research Soc., Indsl. Market Research Assn., Nicosia C. of C. (v.p. 1968-72). Author: Marketing in the Middle East, 1980; Marketing Handbook, 1986. Contbr. articles to various publs. Home: 9 Orhpeos St, Nicosia Cyprus Office: Academias Ave, MEMRB House, Nicosia 2098, Cyprus

VASSILOPOULOS, YERASSIMOS GEORGE, marketing and merchandising company executive; b. Athens, Greece, May 14, 1957; s. George and Natalia (Valsamakis) V. B in Bus., Higher Sch. Econs., Athens, 1980; MBA, Northwestern U., 1982. Merchandising mgr. V Giant Supermarket, Athens, 1984-87; gen. mgr. Bass & Bass Ltd., Athens, 1987—. Served with Greek Navy, 1982-84. Mem. Athens Coll. Alumni Assn., Athens C. of C. (export dept.). Office: Bass & Bass Ltd, 3 Codrou, Filothei, 15237 Athens Greece

VASTRUP, CLAUS, economist; b. Copenhagen, Mar. 24, 1942; s. Niels and Inger (Friis) V.; m. Lis Werdelin Petersen, Nov. 26, 1966; children: Jacob, Pernille. Degree in econs., U. Copenhagen, 1966; D of Econs., U. Aarhus, Denmark, 1983. Economist Denmark Nat. Bank, Copenhagen, 1966-69; asst. prof. U. Copenhagen, 1969-72; assoc. prof. econs. U. Aarhus, Denmark, 1972-83; prof. U. Aarhus, 1983—; Mem. Council Econ. Advisors, Copenhagen, 1986-88, chmn. 1988. Office: Inst Econs, Universitetsparken, 8000 Aarhus C Denmark

VATTAIRE, JACK GEORGE, Ministry of Industry official France; b. Mailly La 'ville Yonne, France, Aug. 25, 1915; s. Lucien and Marie (Maison) V.; student Ecole Polytechnique, 1936-38, Ecole de Physique et Chimie Industrielles, Paris, 1941-48; doctorat de droit, 1947; student Ecole des Langue orientales Vivantes, 1941-46, Ecole Nationale d'Administration, 1947-48, Dartmouth Coll., 1950-51. Engr., Artillerie Navale, 1938-48; dir. Service Economique et Financier, Ministry Industry, 1949-55; dir. service coordination investments European steel industry, 1956-57; founder, dir., gen. mgr. ASTEF, 1957-69, ASMIC, 1961-69, ACTIM, 1970-80; chief gen. inspection Ministry Industry, Paris, 1981—. Decorated Croix de Guerre; officer de la Legion d'Honneur; comdr. Ordre National du Merite. Mem. Assn. des Anciens Eleves de l'ecole Polytechnique, Association de Anciencs Eleves de l'Ecole National d'Administration (gen. sec. 1949-55). Club: Auto de France. Home: 96 Rue de Longchamp, 92200 Neuilly sur Seine France

VAUDREY, BARBARA, physician, surgeon; b. Walthamstow, Eng., Oct. 29, 1922; d. Reginald Guley and Katharine (Day) Lewis; m. Oliver Claude Vaudrey, July 10, 1954; children—Claude William, Joseph Henry, Caroline Ann. M.B., B.S., London U., 1953. House physician Barnet Gen. Hosp., Eng., 1953-54, house surgeon, 1954-55; gen. practice medicine, London, 1955-77, Suffolk, Eng., 1970—; asst. police surgeon Suffolk County Constabulary, 1974-87. Contbr. articles to profl. jours. Mem. Parish Council, Stoke Ash., 1972—, chmn., 1981-84; com. mem. Women's Inst. Stoke Ash, 1970-84, chmn., 1971-72; mem. Royal Brit. Legion, Eye, 1983—, pres., 1985. Served with Aux. Terratorial Service, 1942-46. Mem. Royal Coll. Gen. Practitioners (faculty bd. 1975-88), Med. Women's Fedn., Brit. Med. Assn. Anglican. Avocations: knitting; reading; church bell ringing; drawing; metal work.

VAUGHAN, DAVID JOHN, distribution company executive; b. Detroit, July 17, 1924; s. David Evans and Erma Mildred V.; A.B., U. Ill., 1950; postgrad. U. Chgo., U. Mo.; m. Anne McKeown Miles, Aug. 21, 1975; children by previous marriage—David John, Melissa Ann, Julia Crawford McLaughlin. Chemist, Midland Electric Colleries, 1950-52; pres. Varrco Distbg. Co., Peoria, Ill., 1953—; prin. David J. Vaughan, investment adv., Peoria, 1970—; investment adviser Fundamentalist Fund; instr. Carl Sandburg Coll., Peoria, 1968—; advisor Leelanau Found., Leelanau Meml. Found. Served to lt. USAAF, 1942-46, USAF, 1951-52; Korea. Registered investment adv. Mem. Alpha Tau Omega, Phi Eta Sigma, Phi Alpha Delta. Republican. Presbyterian. Clubs: Peoria Country, Northport Point (Mich.); Peoria Skeet, Racquet, Naples (Fla.). Lodges: Masons, Shriners, Jesters. Home: 4510 N Miller Ave Peoria IL 61614 Office: 4617 N Prospect Rd Peoria Heights IL 61614

VAUGHAN, HERBERT WILEY, lawyer; b. Brookline, Mass, June 1, 1920; s. David D. and Elzie G. (Wiley) V.; m. Ann Graustein, June 28, 1941. Student U. Chgo., 1937-38; SB cum laude, Harvard U., 1941, LLB, 1948. Bar: Mass. 1948. Assoc. Hale and Dorr, Boston, 1948-54, jr. ptnr., 1954-56, sr. ptnr., 1956-82, co-mng. ptnr., 1976-80; pres. Herbert W. Vaughan, P.C.; sr. ptnr. Hale and Dorr, 1982—. Fellow Am. Bar Found. (life); mem. Am. Law Inst., Am. Coll. Mortgage Attys., Am. Coll. Real Estate Attys., ABA, Mass. Bar Assn., Boston Bar Assn., Internat. Bar Assn., Standing Com., The Trustees of Reservations. Clubs: Bay, Badminton and Tennis, Union (Boston), Boston Econ.; Longwood Cricket (Brookline, Mass.).

VAUGHAN, JACK CHAPLINE, retired physicist, author; b. Sarasota, Fla., Dec. 17, 1912; s. Alfred Jefferson and Blossom Creighton (Chapline) V.; B.A. in Physics and Math., Tex. Christian U., 1967; postgrad. U. Tex., Arlington, 1967-68, Ark. Law Sch., 1934-35; m. Anne Gwin, Sept. 4, 1942 (div. Mar. 1955); children—Jack Chapline, Gwin Barnum Vaughan (dec.), Thomas A.J., Anne; m. Lanette Worthington, Mar. 12, 1965. Propr. cattle ranch, Chicot County (Ark.), 1950, Adams County (Miss.), 1945-52; specifications writer Navy carrier-based aircraft programs Douglas Aircraft Corp. Los Angeles, 1952-55; head specifications group TITAN intercontinental ballistic missile nosecone Research and Adv. Devel. Div., AVCO, Boston, 1956; analyst, writer research and devel. proposals LTV Aerospace Corp., Dallas, 1956-59, sr. analyst progress reporting and contractually required data submissions LTV-NASA-SCOUT launch vehicle program, 1959-74. Served to maj. inf. AUS, 1940-45. Mem. Am. Phys. Soc., Honourable Soc. of Cymmrodorion (Wales). Author: (all Vaughan's American Histories) Frontier Ambassador, 1957; Vaughan's Brigade Army of Tennessee, vols. 1-10, 1960-75; The British History of Geoffrey of Monmouth, 1975; Blossom Chapline and Alfred Vaughan 3d, 1975; The Chronicles of Wales, 1976; Martha Jane, 1977; William Vaughan. . .Renaissance Scholar; American Colonist, 1978; Gyges, Ancient Lydians, 1978; Conquest of the South (1861-1865), Part I, 1979; Welsh Colony of Virginia, 1980; Genesis, 1981; World War II, 2 vols., 1982; Florence Plantation, 1983; translator: (from Russian) Pre-Greek Etymology, 1973; miscellaneous translations (from Russian, Latin and Welsh) all in Vaughan's Eurasian Histories, vol. 1, Caucasians, 1984, vol. 2, Cimmerians and Cymry, 1985, vol. 3, Cumbrian Romano-Britons, 1986, vols. 4 through 6, A Dictionary of the Ancient British Language with an Ethnological-Historical-Genealogical Introduction, (3 vols.) 1987. Address: PO Box 7632 Little Rock AR 72217

VAUGHAN, RICHARD ALLEN, life insurance underwriter; b. Sherman, Tex., July 18, 1946; s. John W. and Margaret Ann (Fires) V.; m. Terence Hall Thompson, Jan. 12, 1968; children—Shannon, Elizabeth, Todd. Student U. Tex., 1964-68; BBA North Tex. State U., 1969. CLU. Mgr., Vaughan Dept. Stores, Sherman, 1968-73; assoc. Fallon Co., Sherman, 1973-76; sr. assoc. Fallon & Vaughan, CLUs, Sherman, 1976-87, A.G. Edwards & Sons Inc., 1987—; founder, dir. Consol. Printing, Inc.; instr. Life Underwriter Tng. Council, Washington. Bd. dirs. Grayson County (Tex.) chpt. Am. Cancer Soc., 1973-77, pres., 1976-77; bd. dirs. Salvation Army, 1975-77; mem. Sherman City Council, 1977-79. Qualifying and life named Agt. of Yr., Indpls. Life Ins. Co., 1975. Mem. Am. Soc. CLUs, Nat. Assn. Life Underwriters, Life Underwriters Assn. (dir.), Tex. Assn. Life Underwriters, Assn. for Advanced Life Underwriting, Mensa, Intertel, Greater Sherman C. of C. (bd dirs.1985-88), Sigma Alpha Epsilon. Baptist. Office: AG Edwards & Sons Inc PO Box 3104 Sherman TX 75090

VAUGHAN, SARAH LOIS, singer; b. Newark, Mar. 27, 1924; d. Asbury and Ada (Baylor) V.; m. Waymon Reed, 1978, 1 child, Deborah. Singer with orchestras led by Earl Hines, 1943-44, Billy Eckstein, 1944-45, John Kirby, 1945-46; solo performer and rec. artist, 1945—, numerous albums including Sarah Vaughan, Swingin' Easy, No Count Sarah, Send In the Clowns, The George Gershwin Songbook, One World, One Peace, 1984, The Man I Love. Recipient numerous Down Beat mag. awards, including Down Beat Hall of Fame, 1985 Grammy award,1983. Address: care Triad Artists Inc 10100 Santa Monica Blvd 16th Floor Los Angeles CA 90067 *

VAUGHAN-RICHARDS, ALAN, architect; b. Maidenhead, England, May 10, 1925; s. Arthur and Elizabeth Grace (Hamer) Richards; m. Gladys Ayo Vaughan, Apr. 2, 1959; children: Elizabeth Remi, Athur Deinde, Vanessa Apinke, Kenneth Olufemi. Diploma in Arch., Poly. London, 1950; Diploma in Tropical Arch., Archtl. Assn. London, 1955. Architect Iraq Devel. Bd., Baghdad, 1952-54; assoc. Architects Co.-Partnership, Lagos & London, 1955-61; prin. Alan Vaughan-Richards Architects, Lagos, Nigeria, 1961-71; dir. Ibru, Vaughan-Richards & Assocs., Lagos, 1971—; external examiner Ahmadu Bello Univ., Zaria, Nigeria, supr. Univ. Lagos Arch. Dept. Co-author: Building Lagos, 1977; editor: W.A. Builder & Architect, 1969; master planner Univ. Venin, Univ. Lagos, Akoka & Abeokuta campuses; contbr. articles to profl. jours.; master planner U. Benin, U. LAgos Akoka and Abeokuta campuses; designer sci. faculty complex Sports Centre and Senor Staff Residences Univ. Benin, Benin Teaching Hosp., Accident Centre Gen. Practice Clinic and residences, temp campus Idi-Araba, vice-chancellor's lodge and professorial residences Law Faculty Complex, student hostels and Sports Centre Univ. Lagos, Bendel State Govt. Secretariate Benin City, Murtala Muhammed Civic Centre, TV Prodn. Centre, offices, factories, residences. Fellow Royal Inst. Brit. Architects; mem. Nigerian Inst. Architects, Lagos Hist. Monuments Preservation Com. Avocations: swimming; reading; writing; carpentry. Home: 12 James George St, PO Box 2458, Lagos Nigeria Office: Ibru Vaughan-Richards & Assocs, 225 Apapa Rd PO Box 2458, Lagos Nigeria

VAUGHN, CHARLES LECLAIRE, psychologist, marketing and management consultant; b. Emporia, Kans., Oct. 5, 1911; s. Charles and Anna (Jones) V.; m. Kathleen Inez Thayer, Nov. 5, 1935; children: Michael Thayer, Charles Robert, Kathleen Virginia Vaughn Wright, Richard James. BS, Kans. State Tchrs. Coll., 1931; PhD, U. Chgo., 1936. Diplomate Am. Bd. Examiners in Profl. Psychology; lic. psychologist, Mass., Conn., N.Y. Asst. dir. market research Psychol. Corp., N.Y.C., 1946-60; sr. research assoc. Dunlap & Assocs., Stamford, Conn., 1960-61; dir. bus. research to dir. Office of Spl. Programs, Boston Coll., 1961-77; pres. Vaughan Co., Needham, Mass., 1977—; bd. dirs. Communicare, Inc., Lacy Sales Inst. Author: Franchising: Its Nature, Scope, Advantages and Development, 2d edit., 1979; also several vols. of Franchising Today, Marketing in the Defense Industries; contbr. articles to profl. jours. Mem. admintrv. bd., treas. Carter Meml. United Meth. Ch., Needham, Mass., treas., 1983-87. Served to lt. USNR, 1943-46. Recipient Spl. awards Internat. Franchise Assn., Spl. awards Boston chpt. Am. Mktg. Assn. Fellow Am. Psychol. Assn.; mem. N.Y. Psychol. Assn. (bd. dirs.), U.S. Golf Assn. (Eagle), Nat. Sr. Sports Assn., Sigma Xi, Kappa Delta Pi, Phi Delta Theta. Republican. Address: 41 Stratford Rd Needham MA 02192

VAUGHN, JOHN VERNON, banker, industrialist; b. Grand Junction, Colo., June 24, 1909; s. John S. and Alice Ann (Baylis) V.; m. Dorothy May Pickrell, Oct. 12, 1934; children: Dorothy (Mrs. Richard H. Stone), John Spencer. A.B., UCLA, 1932. Br. mgr. Nat. Lead Co., 1932-37; sales mgr. Sillers Paint & Varnish Co., 1937-46, pres., gen. mgr., dir., 1946-58; pres., chmn. Dartell Labs., Inc., 1959-70; vice chmn. bd. Crocker Nat. Bank and Crocker Nat. Corp., San Francisco, 1970-75; dir. Crocker Nat. Bank and Crocker Nat. Corp., 1969-85; hon. dir. Crocker Nat. Bank; cons. Coopers & Lybrand, 1975-85; chmn. bd. Recon Optical, Inc.; dir. Trust Services Am., Forest Lawn Corp., Am. Security & Fidelity Corp.; IT Corp. Chmn. San Marino Recreation Commn., 1956-58, La. Better Bus. Bur., 1959-61, Invest-in-Am., 1970-73; chmn. citizen's adv. Council Pub. Transp., 1965-67; commr. Los Angeles Coliseum Commn., 1971-74; trustee Calif. Mus. Found., 1968-79; bd. dirs. Orthopaedic Hosp., 1965-87, pres., 1974-78, chmn. bd., 1978-79; bd. dirs. YMCA, Los Angeles, 1965-77, Central City Assn., So. Calif. Visitors Council, 1970-76, NCCJ, Calif. Museum Sci. and Industry, United Way of Los Angeles, Am. Heart Assn.; mem. Los Angeles Adv. Bd., Friends of Claremont Coll., 1973-78, Los Angeles Beautiful, 1972-74; regent U. Calif., 1958-59; hon. trustee UCLA Found., 1967—, Forest Lawn Meml. Park, 1968—, Claremont Men's Coll., 1970-71, Pepperdine U., 1972—; regent, mem. bd. visitors Grad. Sch. Bus. Adminstrn. UCLA, 1971-85; mem. Chancellor's Assocs., Calif. State Univs. and Colls. Recipient Distinguished Service award U. Calif. at Los Angeles, 1965; Outstanding Community Service award, 1970; Alumnus of Year award, 1971; Brotherhood award NCCJ, 1971; Los Angeles Jaycees award merit, 1972; Most Distinguished Citizen Los Angeles Realty Bd., 1972; other honors. Mem. Los Angeles Area C. of C. (bd. dirs. 1961, pres. 1969, chmn. 1970), World Affairs Council (chpt. v.p., treas. 1970-85, hon. dir. 1985—), Iranian-Am. Chamber Industry and Commerce (pres. 1971-79), Paint, Varnish and Lacquer Assn. (past nat. v.p., past chpt. pres.), Town Hall Calif. (dir. 1973-75), Young Pres.'s Orgn., Beta Theta Pi (pres. 1960). Presbyn. Clubs: Mason, Jonathan (pres. 1964), Los Angeles Country, California, Los Angeles (dir. 1979-85); San Gabriel (Calif.); Country (dir. 1964-68); Pasadena Athletic. Lodge: Internat. Order St. Hubertus. Home: 454 S Orange Grove Blvd Pasadena CA 91105 Office: 225 S Lake Ave Pasadena CA 91101

VAUGHN, MARY, health care facilities exec.; b. Trafford, Ala., Apr. 20, 1930; d. Grover Webster and Vivian Lenora (Dorman) V.; student Birmingham Bus. Coll., 1952, Howard Coll., 1959, U. Ala., 1960, 62, Balboa Intermediate Care Facility, San Diego, 1969-76; certificate in therapeutic activities tng. Grossmont Adult Sch., 1975; m. James T. Lovvorn, Mar. 1952 (div. 1959). Owner, pres., treas. Balboa Manor Inc. and Balboa Manor Health Facility, San Diego, 1969-79. Charter pres. Quota Club of Birmingham (Ala.), 1967-68; lt. gov. 8th dist. Quota Internat., 1968-69; supr. adv. com. to Jim Bates, 4th Dist. Supr. San Diego County, 1973—; mem. San Diego County Com. on the Handicapped, 1979—; mem. support com. Community Video Center, pub. access TV, 1979—. Pres., bd. dirs. Girls Club San Diego, 1987-88. Recipient Safety award Indsl. Indemnity, 1973, 75, cert. of appreciation Jim Bates, 1975, 11th Woman award Women's Internat. Ctr., 1988; named Citizen of Month Congl. Service award, 1987; notary pub., cert. nursing home adminstr., Calif. Mem. Am. Health Care Assn., Am. Coll. Nursing Home Adminstrs., Am., Calif. nursing home assns., Com. of

100 of San Diego Klee Wyk Soc., San Diego Opera, Bus. and Profl. Women's Club (pres. Birmingham chpt. 1967-69), San Diego Mus. Natural History, San Diego Mus. of Man, Nat. Notary Assn. Republican. Methodist. Author: Exploring Mental Therapy. Home: 2804 C St San Diego CA 92102

VAUGHN, RUFUS MAHLON, psychiatrist; b. Ensley, Ala., Oct. 31, 1924; s. Rufus Samuel and Anna Martina (Fink) V.; children: Stephen Andrew, Alexander. Student, U. Mich., 1942-43, 46-47; A.B., Birmingham So. Coll., 1949; M.D., Med. Coll. Ala., 1953. Diplomate Am. Bd. Psychiatry and Neurology, Am. Bd. Forensic Psychiatry. Intern USPHS Hosp., San Francisco, 1953-54; resident in psychiatry Ind. U. Hosp., Indpls., 1954-56, U. Calif. Hosp. at Los Angeles, 1956-57; dir. psychiatry Student Health Service, U. Mass., Amherst, 1958-59; researcher Boston State Hosp., 1959-61; asso. prof. psychiatry U. Fla., Gainesville, 1961-70; dir. Palm Beach County Mental Health Ctr., West Palm Beach, Fla., 1970-71; med. dir. Lake Hosp. and Clinic, Lake Worth, Fla., 1971-73; dir. tng., research So. Fla. State Hosp., Hollywood, 1973-74, supt., 1974; chief Bur. Mental Hosp. Services, Fla. Div. Mental Health, Tallahassee, 1974-75; pvt. practice medicine specializing in forensic psychiatry West Palm Beach, 1975-87; sr. physician No. Fla. Evaluation and Treatment Ctr., Gainesville, 1982-87; clin. prof. psychiatry U. Miami, 1973-75; med. dir. USPHS Res., 1980—; clin. assoc. prof. psychiatry U. Fla., 1983-87. Served with USNR, 1943-46. Mem. Am. Acad. Psychiatry and Law, Am. Coll. Forensic Psychiatry. Home: 606 NW 36th Ave Gainesville FL 32609

VAUGHN, (OLIVE) RUTH, author, playwright; b. Wellington, Tex., Aug. 31, 1935; d. S.L. and Nora Norris (Knowles) Wood; BA, MA, U. Kans.; PhD, Am. U.; children—Billy, Ron. Author 40 books, including: Fun for Christian Youth, 1960, Dreams Can Come True, 1964, Portrait in a Nursery, 1965, What I Will Tell My Children About God?, 1966, Skits that Win, 1967, No Matter the Weather, 1968, Hey! Have You Heard?, 1969, Playlets and Skits, 1970, Baby's Album, 1973, Even When I Cry, 1975, Proclaiming Christ in the Caribbean, 1976, More Skits that Win, 1977, Celebrate with Words, 1979, What's a Mother to Say?, 1980, Write to Discover Yourself, 1980, To Be a Girl—To Be a Woman, 1982, My God! My God!, 1982; author 57 plays, including: The Living Last Supper, The Man on the Center Cross, Behold a New World!, Lions Can't Eat Truth, Morning Comes at Sunrise, Catherine Marshall's Christy, Eugenia Price's The Beloved Invader; musical stageplays include: God's Dream, To Touch a Rainbow, Once Upon a Hill: The Coward and the Cut-Throat, Please Be King!, Shadow of the Almighty; prof. drama/creative writing Bethany Nazarene Coll., 1968-76; resident playwright Denver 1st Ch. of Nazarene, 1976-83; pres. Ruth Vaughn Inc., 1983—; pvt. practice counseling; author numerous short stories and articles. Mem. Women in Communication Internat., Internat. Platform Assn., Pi Lambda Theta, Theta Sigma Phi. Republican. Nazarene.

VAUX, TIMOTHY ROBERT, chemical company executive; b. Sacramento, Calif., Oct. 21, 1945; s. Robert Francis and Helen Louise (Kitterman) V.; m. Kristene Marie Petrucci, June 10, 1972; children: Stephanie, Alison, Alexander. BS, Calif. State U., Fresno, 1968. With sales dept. Ciba-Geigy, Fresno, 1969-73; with sales and mktg. dept. Am. Cyanamid, Princeton, N.J., 1973-78; mktg. mgr. Cyanamid Can., Inc., Montreal, Que., 1978-80; gen. mgr. DuPont Can., Inc., Toronto, Ont., 1980-87; with mktg. dept. E.I. du Pont de Nemours & Co., Inc., Wilmington, Del., 1987—; bd. dirs, 1st vice chmn. Crop Protection Inst. Can., Ottawa, Ont. Author: Sales Orientation, 1981. Roman Catholic. Office: EI du Pont de Nemours & Co Inc WM4-180 Barley Mill Plaza Wilmington DE 19898

VAYRYNEN, PAAVO MATTI, government official Finland; b. Kermi, Finland, Sept. 2, 1946; s. Juho Eemeli and Anna Liisa (Kaijankoski) V.; M. Polit. Scis., U. Helsinki, 1970; m. Vuokko Kaarina Tervonen, 1968; children: Tiina, Taneli, Lotta. With Govt. of Finland, 1970—; M.P., 1970; polit. sec. to prime minister, 1970-71; vice chmn. Center Party, 1972-80, chmn., 1972—; mem. Nordic Council, 1975-76; minister of edn., 1976-77; minister of labor; minister of fgn. affairs, 1977-87 . Served to lt. Finnish Army. Evangelical Lutheran. Author: Speaking for the Poor, 1971; This is a Time of Change, 1974. Office: Keskustapuolue, Pursimiehenkatu 15, Helsinki Finland 00170 *

VAYRYNEN, RAIMO VEIKKO, political science educator; b. Kiuruvesi, Finland, Apr. 17, 1947; s. Veikko Armas and Tyyne Maria (Tikkanen) V.; m. Eira Hellevi Merilainen, July 24, 1967; children: Pekka, Mikko, Maria; m. Paivi Kristiina Hakala, July 1, 1983. D of Social Sci., U. Tampere, Finland, 1973. Dir. Tampere Peace Research Inst., 1972-78; prof. polit. sci. U. Helsinki, Finland, 1978—, assoc. dean Faculty of Social Scis., 1987—; vis. prof. Princeton (N.J.) U., 1986-87. Author: Conflict in Finnish-Soviet Relations, 1972, Nuclear Weapons and Great Powers, 1982; co-author: Transnational Corporations and Armaments, 1982; editor: The Quest for Peace, 1987. Mem. Internat. Peace Research Assn. (sec.-gen. 1975-79), Internat. Studies Assn. (v.p. 1987-88), Internat. Social Sci. Council (chmn. issue group on peace 1984—), Finnish Polit. Sci. Assn. (pres. 1983-86), Finnish UN Assn. (pres. 1980-83). Mem. Social Dem. Party of Finland. Home: Mayratie 6A, 00800 Helsinki Finland Office: U Helsinki, Aleksanterinkatu 7, 00100 Helsinki Finland

VAZ, JOSÉ ALFREDO MANITA, food products executive; b. Amadora, Lisbon, Portugal, Oct. 26, 1948; José Vicente and Maria Da Piedade (Fernandes Manita) V.; m. Madalena Clímaco De Sousa E Brito , Aug. 16, 1973; children: Filipa Sousa Brito, Inês Sousa Brito . BBA, Superior Inst. Econs., Lisbon, 1972; postgrad., Getúlio Vargas Found., Rio De Janeiro, 1983. Fellow Tech. U. Lisbon, 1972—; economist State Dept. Fgn. Investment, Lisbon, 1973-74; assessor to the bd. Portuguese Chain-Stores Leader, Lisbon, 1976-77; asst. mgr. Cen. De Cervejas, Lisbon, 1977-80, mgr., 1980-84, also bd. dirs., 1984—; chief of staff to Sec. of Lisbon, Lisbon, 1978; sec. State for Home Trade, Lisbon; bus. cons., Lisbon, 1976; mem. gen. assembly Cicer, Guiné-Bissau, 1983-85, Socaju, 1983-85. Mem. Sedes, Lisbon, 1980—. Served to 2d ltd. Portugese Navy, 1974-77. Mem. Economists Trade Union. Roman Catholic. Clubs: Automóvel Portugal, Internat. de Football. Home: Rua Prof Vieira De Almeida, 7-66-N, 1600 Lisbon Portugal

VAZIRI, NOSRATOLA DABIR, internist, nephrologist, educator; b. Tehran, Iran, Oct. 13, 1939; came to U.S., 1969, naturalized, 1977; s. Abbas and Tahera V. M.D., Tehran U., 1966. Diplomate: Am. Bd. Internal Medicine, Am. Bd. Nephrology. Intern Cook County Hosp., Chgo., 1969-70; resident Berkshire Med. Ctr., Pittsfield, Mass., 1970-71, Wadsworth VA Med. Ctr., 1971-72, UCLA Med. Ctr., 1972-74; prof. medicine U. Calif.-Irvine, 1979—, chief nephrology div., 1977—, dir. hemodialysis unit, 1977—, dir., 1980, vice chmn. dept. medicine, 1982—; mem. sci. adv. council Nat. Kidney Found., 1977—. Contbr. numerous articles to med. jours. Recipient Golden Apple award, 1977; named outstanding tchr. U. Calif-Irvine, 1975, 78, 79, 80, 82. Fellow ACP; mem. Am. Soc. Nephrology, Am. Paraplegia Soc., Alpha Omega Alpha. Home: 66 Balboa Coves Newport Beach CA 92663 Office: U Calif Div Nephrology Dept Medicine Room C351 Med Sci Irvine CA 92717

VEATCH, JOHN WILLIAM, speech pathologist; b. Mitchell, S.D., Dec. 9, 1923; s. William Homer and Helen Gwendolyn (Lowther) V.; m. Doris Lavelle Guthrie (dec. 1978); children: Dean, Joan; m. Winnifred Ann Sawin, Aug. 6, 1982; children: Shaun, Monicah. BA in Speech, Wash. State U., 1946, BEd, 1951; MA in Speech, U. Wash., 1950; DEd, U. Idaho, 1970. Pvt. practice speech pathology Spokane, Wash., 1950-79; pvt. practice speech pathology and ednl. cons. Tacoma, 1980—; pres., chief exec. officer and dir. research. Espial Inst., Tacoma, 1982—. Author (test profiles) Personal Stress Balance Profile, 1982, Info. Processing Style, 1984, The Deep Screening Profile of Tongue Thrusting Activity, 1985, The Tongue Thrust Screening Test, 1986, Learning Style Profile, 1986. Fellow Northwest Acad. Speech Pathology (pres. 1978-82, 86—); mem. Internat. Assn. Oral Myology, Am. Speech and Hearing Assn. Home: 4708 64th Ave W Tacoma WA 98466 Office: 4113 Bridge Port Way W Suite B Tacoma WA 98466

VEAZEY, JOHN HOBSON, physician; b. Van Alstyne, Tex., June 27, 1901; s. James and Malta Augusta (Blassingame) V.; m. Elizabeth May Chandler, Mar. 14, 1935; children: Samuel, James. Grad., Austin Coll., 1918-22; MD, U. Tex., 1926. Intern Sherman (Tex.) Hosp., 1926-28; pvt. practice medicine, Madill, Okla., 1929-35, Ardmore, Okla., 1935—; co-founder Med. Arts Clinic, Ardmore, 1952—; pvt. practice internal medicine, Ardmore, 1957—; chief staff Meml. Hosp., So. Okla., 1958—, chmn. dept. internal medicine, 1973, chmn. pattern. gift com., 1983, mem. staff Ardmore Hosp.; pres. Med. Arts Bldg. Co. Ardmore, Med. Arts Clinic of Ardmore. Co-chmn. profl. div. United Fund, 1969; trustee Presbyn. Ch. Recipient 50-Year cert. of appreciation Bd. Trustees U. Tex. Med. Br. Alumni Assn., 1976; hon. at homecoming banquet U. Tex. Med. Br., 1987. Mem. AMA (Physician's Recognition award 1976, 79, 82, 85), Okla. State Med. Assn. (council 1944-56, life) Carter-Love-Marshall Med. Soc. (pres. 1955, life), Ardmore C. of C. (bd. dirs., v.p.), Am. Soc. Internal Medicine. Lodge: Masons. Home: 2 Overland Rt Ardmore OK 73401 Office: 921 14th St NW Ardmore OK 73401

VECCHIO, ROBERT PETER, business management educator; b. Chgo., June 29, 1950; s. Dominick C. and Angeline V.; m. Betty Ann Vecchio; Aug. 21, 1974; children: Julie, Mark. BS summa cum laude, DePaul U., 1972; MA, U. Ill., 1974, PhD, 1976. Instr. U. Ill., Urbana, 1973-76; mem. faculty dept. mgmt. U. Notre Dame, 1976-86, dept. chmn., 1983—, Franklin D. Schurz Prof. Mgmt., 1986—. Mem. Acad. Mgmt., Am. Psychol. Assn., Assn. Consumer Research, Inst. Mgmt. Scis., Am. Statis. Assn., Am. Inst. Decision Scis., Midwest Acad. Mgmt., Midwest Psychol. Assn., Phi Kappa Phi, Delta Epsilon Sigma, Phi Eta Sigma, Psi Chi. Home: 16856 Hampton Dr Granger IN 46530 Office: U Notre Dame Dept Mgmt Notre Dame IN 46556

VECHT, ROMEO JACQUES, cardiologist; b. Ghent, Belgium, Sept. 30, 1935; came to Eng., 1954; s. Philip Sidney and Hetty (Bienenzucht) V.; m. Noemi Bollag, July 3, 1966; children—Nina Georgy, Philip Patrick, Joshua Andrew. M.B., Ch.B., U. Bristol, 1962. Accredited class I cardiologist Joint Com. on Higher Med. Tng., London. Registrar Hammersmith Hosp., London, 1968-69; sr. registrar Groote Schuur Hosp., Capetown, South Africa, 1969-70; research fellow Kantonsspital, Zurich Switzerland, 1970-71; sr. registrar St. Marys Hosp., London, 1972-78, hon. cons. cardiologist, 1980-86; cons. cardiologist Manor House Hosp., London, 1976—. Editor: Angioplasty, 1984. Fellow Am. Coll. Cardiology; mem. N.Y. Acad. Scis., Royal Coll. Physicians, Brit. Med. Assn., Brit. Cardiac Soc., Royal Soc. Medicine. Conservative. Jewish. Avocation: history. Home: 56 Clifton Hill, London NW8 England

VEDEL, TOM, computer company executive; b. Copenhagen, Denmark, July 23, 1955; s. Ernst and Annie V.; m. Britta Nielsson. MS in Economy, Copenhagen, 1984. Mktg. asst. mgr. ISS Linned Service, Copenhagen, 1983-85; mktg. mgr. DDC Internat., Lyngby, Denmark, 1985—. Home: Praestetoften 5, DK-4735 Mern Denmark Office: DDC Internat, Lundtoftevej 1C, DK-2800 Lyngby Denmark

VEGA, BENJAMIN URBIZO, retired judge; b. La Ceiba, Honduras, Jan. 18, 1916. AB, U. So. Calif., 1938, postgrad., 1939-40; LLB, Pacific Coast U. Law, 1941. Bar: Calif. 1947, U.S. Dist. Ct. (so. dist.) Calif. 1947, U.S. Supreme Ct. 1958. Assoc. Anderson, McPharlin & Connors, Los Angeles, 1947-48, Newman & Newman, Los Angeles, 1948-51; dep. dist. atty. County of Los Angeles, 1951-66; judge Los Angeles, County Mcpl. Ct., East Los Angeles Jud. Dist., 1966-86, retired, 1986; leader faculty seminar Calif. Jud. Coll. at Earl Warren Legal Inst., U. Calif-Berkeley, 1978. Mem. Calif. Gov.'s Adv. Com. on Children and Youth, 1968; del. Commn. of the Califs., 1978; bd. dirs. Los Angeles-Mexico City Sister City Com.; pres. Argentine Cultural Found., 1983. Recipient award for outstanding services from Mayor of Los Angeles, 1973, City of Commerce, City of Montebello, Calif. Assembly, Southwestern Sch. Law, Disting. Pub. Service award Dist. Atty. Los Angeles County. Mem. Conf. Calif. Judges, Mcpl. Ct. Judges' Assn. (award for Outstanding Services), Los Angeles County, Am. Judicature Soc., World Affiars Council, Pi Sigma Alpha. Home: 101 California Ave Apt 1207 Santa Monica CA 90403

VEGA, JOSE MANUEL, mathematics professor; b. Madrid, Jan. 2, 1952; s. Samuel Vega and Amelia De Prada; m. Maria-Paz Diez-Rollan, July 28, 1983; children: Maria del Mar, Jose Manuel, Maria Paz. BS in Aero. Engring., ETSI Aeronauticos, Madrid, 1974, PhD in Aeronautical Engring., 1977; MA in Math., Universidad Complutense, Madrid, 1976. Teaching asst. math. Universidad Politecnica, Madrid, 1975-78; research cons. Northwestern U., Evanston, Ill., 1978-79; asst. prof. Universidad Politecnica, Madrid, 1979-81, assoc. prof., 1981-87, prof., 1987—. Contbr. articles to profl. jours. Mem. Am. Math. Soc. Roman Catholic. Office: ETSI Aeronauticos, Cardenal Cisneros 3, 28040 Madrid Spain

VEGA, LUIS VICTOR, university professor; b. Astorga, Leon, Spain, Aug. 21, 1943; s. Luis and Victoria (Reñon) V.; m. Rosa Alcocer, Aug. 17, 1968 (div. 1979); children: Leire, Susana. PhD, Univ. Complutense, Madrid, 1974. Sch. master La Laguna (Spain) High Sch., 1969-73; lectr. Univ. La Laguna, 1974-76, assoc. prof., 1976-78; prof. titular Univ. Nacional Educacion Distancia, Madrid, 1979, prof., 1984—; bd. dirs., chmn. Dept. Logic and Philosophy of Sci. Univ. Nacional Educacion Distancia, 1985—; cons. editorial bd. context Univ. Leon, 1984, theory Univ. Pais Vasco, San Sebastian, 1986. Editor: Lecturas de Logica, I, 1981, II, 1984; author: Analisis Logico, 2 vols., 1987; contbr. articles to profl. jours. Research grantee Ministerio Educacion Y Ciencia, 1980-84, Comision Asesora Interministerial de Ciencia Y Tecnologia, 1986-89. Mem. Sociedad Española de Historia de la Ciencia. Agnostic. Office: U Nacional Edn Distancia, ciudad Universitaria, 28040 Madrid Spain

VEGELIUS, JAN HILDING OLOF ALBERT, statistics educator and researcher; b. Steneby, Sweden, June 17, 1941; s. Hilding Johan and Elsa (Hansson) V.; m. Ebba Cecilia Carstelius, June 11, 1977; children: Johan Robert, Henrik Anders, Elsa Kristina. B.A., Göteborg U. (Sweden), 1965, M.A., 1965; Ph.D., Uppsala U. (Sweden), 1976. Tchr. dept. math. Goteborg U., 1965-69; tchr. dept. psychology Uppsala U., 1969-76, tchr. dept. stats., 1976— , sr. tchr., 1981—, docent, 1976—, research asst., 1979—. Author: On Various G-index Generalizations and Their Applicability Within the Clinical Domain, 1976; E-Correlation Coefficient Articles, 1978; Sveriges landskapsblommor och deras historia, 1981; Visor från Dal, 1984, Den Sägenspunna Släkten-om Håbolssläkten från Dalsland, 1987; contbr. numerous articles to internat. jours. Served with Air Def. Command, Swedish Army, 1961-62. Mem. Local Union of Internat. Order of Good Templars (dir. 1973—), Dalslands Hembygdsförbund, Svenska Statistikersamfundet, Håbolssläkt-föreningen (chmn. 1984—), Dalvisans Vänner (chmn. 1985—), Union Univ. Tchrs. Lutheran. Home: Himmelsvagen 19, S-75300 Storvreta Sweden Office: Dept Statistics, Box 513, S-75120 Uppsala 20 Sweden

VEITCH, BOYER LEWIS, printing company executive; b. Phila., Oct. 20, 1930; s. Samuel Lewis and Agnes May (Bell) V.; A.B., Lafayette Coll., 1953; postgrad. Wharton Evening Sch. Acctg. and Fin., U. Pa., 1957-59; m. Emmeline Barbara Smith, Nov. 22, 1952; children—William S., Nancy B., Thomas C. Advt. dir. Ware Bros. Co., Phila., 1956-62, v.p., 1962-69; salesman Zabel Bros. Co., Phila., 1969-75; chmn., pres. Veitch Printing Corp., Lancaster, Pa., 1975—. Trustee Lafayette Coll., Easton, Pa., 1981-86, 87—; vice chmn. coll. relations com., chmn. ann. fund, 1982-86, mem. fin. com., 1987—; bd. dirs., 2d v.p. Boys' and Girl's Club, Lancaster, 1980—; dir.Boy's Club Lancaster Found., Gt. Valley Civic Assn., 1969-79; trustee Fulton Opera House Found., 1985—, treas., 1985—; chmn. citizens for Schulze Com., Pa. 5th Congressional Dist., 1972-78; vestryman, sr. Warden St. Peter's Ch. of Gt. Valley, 1972-78. Served with CIC, U.S. Army, 1954-56. Recipient Bronze Hope Chest award Nat. Multiple Sclerosis Soc., 1982. Mem. Printing Industries Am., Graphic Arts Assn. (dir. 1980—, 2d vice chmn. 1986—), Susquehanna Litho Club (dir. 1976-80, pres. 1979-80), Lancaster Assn. Commerce and Industry, Aircraft Owners and Pilots Assn., SAR, Lafayette Coll. Alumni Assn. (dir. 1974-78, pres. 1978-80), NAM, Pa. Economy League, Nat. Fedn. Ind. Bus., Phi Kappa Psi (past pres. and dir. chpt. alumni assn.). Republican. Episcopalian. Lodge: Rotary. Clubs: Hamilton, Wash Day, Lancaster Country, Dawtaw Country, Avalon Yacht, Lancaster Aero. Home: 408 BB Sams Dr Dataw Island SC 29920 Home: 65 E 17th St Avalon NJ 08202 Office: Veitch Printing Corp 1740 Hempstead Rd Lancaster PA 17601

VEITCH, PATRICK LEE, opera administrator; b. Beaumont, Tex., Mar. 26, 1944; s. Melvin Wood and Sarah Irene Turner (Barton) V.; B.A., North Tex. State U., 1967; cert. Not for Profit Mgmt. Columbia U., 1978; m. Kathleen Norris, Dec. 27, 1979; 1 dau., Alexandra Norris. Acct. exec. Ketchum, MacLeod & Grove, N.Y.C., 1967-70; dir. publications Manhattan Coll., N.Y.C., 1970-73; dir. mktg. Met. Opera, N.Y.C., 1973-81; gen. mgr. The Australian Opera, Sydney, 1981—; lectr. arts mgmt. Columbia U., 1978-80, N.Y. U., 1979-80; cons. in field. Mem. Theatrical Proprietors and Entrepreneurs Assn. Australia (dir. 1981—). Address: PO Box R-223, Royal Exchange, 2000 New South Wales Australia also: 480 Elizabeth St, Surry Hills NSW 2010, Australia Office: Australian Opera, PO Box 291, Strawberry Hills NSW 2012, Australia *

VEIZER, JÁN, geology educator; b. Pobedim, Czechoslavakia, June 22, 1941; came to Can., 1973; s. Viktor and Brigita (Brandstetter) V.; m. Elena Ondrus, July 30, 1966; children: Robert, Andrew Douglas. Prom. Geol., Comenius U., Bratislava, Czechoslovakia, 1964, RNDr, 1968; CSc, Slovak Acad. Sci., Bratislava, Czechoslovakia, 1968; PhD, Australian Nat. U., Canberra, 1971. Asst. lectr. Comenius U., 1963-66; research scientist Slovak Acad. Sci., 1966-71; vis. asst. prof. UCLA, Los Angeles, 1972; vis. research scientist U. Göttingen (Germany), 1972-73; research scientist U. Tübingen (Germany), 1973; from asst. to full prof. U. Ottawa (Can.), 1973—; prof. Ruhr U., Bochum, Fed. Republic of Germany, 1988—; cons. NASA, Houston, 1983-86; vis. prof. and scholar Northwestern U., Evanston, Ill., 1983-87; vis. fellow Australian Nat. U., 1979; vis. prof. U. Tübingen, 1974; Lady Davis professorship Hebrew U., Jerusalem, 1987. Contbr. articles to profl. jours., chpts. to books. Served to j.lt. Med., 1965-66, Czechoslavakia. Named Research Prof. Yr., 1987; Humboldt fellow, 1980, Killam Research fellow Can. Council, 1986-88. Fellow Royal Soc. Can., Geol. Assn. Can. (Past-Pres. award 1987), Geol. Soc. Am.; mem. Geochem. Soc. Am. Roman Catholic. Club: Ski, Skying (Ottawa). Office: U Ottawa Dept Geology, Derry Lab, Ottawa, ON Canada K1N 6N5 also: Ruhr U Inst Geologie, Lehrstuhl Sedimentgeologie, 4630 Bochum Federal Republic of Germany

VELARDE, ROBERT M., nursing, hospital administrator, educator; b. Tampa, Fla., Oct. 28, 1950; s. Jesus Manuel and Angela (Velasco) V. AS in Nursing, Hillsborough Community Coll., Tampa, 1972; BS in Nursing, Samford U., 1975; M.Pub.Adminstrn., Golden Gate U., 1980. RN, Fla., Ala.; cert. in nursing adminstrn. advanced Am. Nurses Assn.; cert. surg. technologist Assn. Surg. Technologists. Surg. technologist attendant Centro Espanol Hosp., Tampa, 1965-72, nursing supr., 1972-74, asst. adminstr. patient services, 1975-85, adminstr., chief exec. officer, 1985-87; charge nurse emergency room Brookwood Med. Ctr., Birmingham, Ala., 1974-75; health occupations instr. Armwood High Sch., Seffner, Fla., 1988—; mem. blue ribbon task force to Fla. Bd. Nursing, 1982-83; mem. adv. bd. Fla. Nursing News. Active Tampa ARC. Recipient award from bd. dirs. Centro Espanol Hosp., 1977; Contbns. to Nursing award Minority Nurses Assn., 1979. Mem. Hillsborough County Vocat. Assn., Nursing Educators Assn. Tampa, Health Occupations Students Am., Am. Orgn. Nurse Execs., Tampa Bay Orgn. Nurse Execs., Am. Nurses Assn., Fla. Nurses Assn., Nurses House, Inc., Sigma Theta Tau (chpt. v.p. 1983-84). Democrat. Methodist. Home: 2618 W Saint John St Tampa FL 33607

VELARDO, JOSEPH THOMAS, molecular biology and endocrinology educator, scientist; b. Newark, Jan. 27, 1923; s. Michael Arthur and Antoinette (Iacullo) V.; m. Forresta M. Monica Power, Aug. 12, 1948 (dec. July 1976). A.B., No. Colo. U., 1948; S.M., Miami U., 1949; Ph.D., Harvard U., 1952. Research fellow in biology and endocrinology Harvard U., Cambridge, Mass., 1952-53, research assoc. in pathology, ob-gyn and surgery sch. medicine, 1953-55; asst. in surgery Peter Bent Brigham Hosp., Boston, 1954-55; asst. prof. anatomy and endocrinology sch. medicine Yale U., New Haven, 1955-61; prof. anatomy, chmn. dept. N.Y. Med. Coll., N.Y.C., 1961-62; cons. N.Y. Fertility Inst., 1961-62; dir. Inst. for Study Human Reprodn., Cleve., 1962-67; prof. biology John Carroll U., Cleve., 1962-67; mem. research and edn. divs. St. Ann Obstetric and Gynecologic Hosp., Cleve., 1962-67; head dept. research St. Ann Hosp., Cleve., 1964-67; prof. anatomy Stritch Sch. Medicine Loyola U., Chgo., 1967—, chmn. dept. anatomy, 1967-73; cons. Internat. Basic and Biol.-Biomed. Curricula, Lombard, Ill., 1979—. Author: (with others) Histochemistry of Enzymes in the Female Genital System, 1963, The Ovary, 1963, The Ureter, 1967, rev. edit., 1981; editor, contbr. Endocrinology of Reproduction, 1958, Essentials of Human Reproduction, 1958; cons. editor, co-author: The Uterus, 1959, Hormonal Steroids, Biochemistry, Pharmacology and Therapeutics, 1964; co-editor, contbr.: Biology of Reproduction, Basic and Clinical Studies, 1973; contbr. articles to profl. jours. Served with USAAF, 1943-45. Decorated Bronze star with 2 oak leaf clusters; recipient award Lederle Med. Fac. Awards Com., 1955-58; named hon. citizen of Sao Paulo Brazil, 1972, U.S. del. to Vatican, 1964. Fellow AAAS, N.Y. Acad. Scis., Gerontol. Soc., Pacific Coast Fertility Soc. (hon.); mem. Am. Assn. Anatomists, Am. Soc. Zoologists, Am. Physiol. Soc., Endocrine Soc., Soc. Endocrinology (Gt. Britain), Soc. Exptl. Biology and Medicine, Am. Soc. Study Sterility (Rubin award 1954), Internat. Fertility Assn., Pan Am. Assn. Anatomy, Midwestern Soc. Anatomists (pres. 1973-74), Mexican Soc. Anatomy (hon.), Sigma Xi, Kappa Delta Pi, Phi Sigma, Gamma Alpha, Alpha Epsilon Delta. Club: Harvard (Chgo.). Office: 607 E Wilson Rd Lombard IL 60148-4062

VELASCO, JOSE ANTONIO, cardiologist; b. Valencia, Spain, July 31, 1937; s. Luis and Maria Teresa (Rami) V.; m. Maria Isabel Grima, June 22, 1941; children: Isabel, Luis, Jose A. MD, U. Valencia, 1962, PhD, 1973. Intern Tuberculosis Sanatorium, Portaceli, Spain, 1962-63; resident Spl. Lungenklinik, Hemer, Fed. Republic Germany, 1963-64, Asthma Klinik, Lipspringe, Fed. Republic Germany, 1964-65, U. Hosp., Mainz, Fed. Republic Germany, 1965-66; asst. cardiology dept. Hosp. Gen. Valencia, 1967-78, sub.-chief, 1978-86, chief, 1987—; temporary adviser WHO, 1974-78, rehab. adviser, 1984—. Author: Ergometric Testing, 1973, Cardiac Rehabilitation, 1978; contbr. numerous articles to profl. jours. Mem. Internat. Soc. Cardiology (council cardiac rehab. 1980—), Spanish Soc. Cardiology, European Soc. Cardiology, Spanish Heart Found. (bd. dirs. 1986—). Roman Catholic. Home: Marques del Turia 7, 46005 Valencia Spain Office: Hosp Gen, Conde Savvatierra 39, 46004 Valencia Spain

VELASCO, MANUEL, pharmacology educator; b. Santa Bárbara, Barinas, Venezuela, Nov. 28, 1943. MD, Cen. U. Venezuela, Caracas, 1968; postgrad., Emory U., 1971-74. Resident-intern Hosp. Maternidad Concepción, 1967-68; instr. dept. pharmacology Cen. U. Venezuela, 1968-70, asst. prof., 1970-75, prof. agregado, 1975-78, assoc. prof., 1975-83, prof., 1983—, head sect. arterial hypertension service cardiology univ hosp., 1986, chmn. dept. pharmacology, 1987—, attending physician cardiology service, 1978—; mem. Nat. Council for Sci. and Technol. Research, 1982—; pres. organizing com. XII Latin Am. Congress Pharmacology and III Interam. Congress Clin. Pharmacology, 1988. Editor: (books) Arterial Hypertension, 1977, 80, Clinical Pharmacology and Therapeutics, 1983, Risks Conveyed by Antihypertensive Treatment, 1985; (jours.) Archivos Venezolanos de Farmacologiia, 1982—, Revista de la Facultad de Medicine, Cen. U. Venezuela, 1985—; ad hoc reviewer Hypertension, Jour. Cardiovascular Pharmacology, Act Cienti Venezolana. Mem. Soc. Venezolana de Farmacologia, Soc. Venezolana de Ciencias Fisiológicas, AAAS, Am. Fedn. Clin. Research, Am. Fedn. Clin. Pharmacology, Am. Soc. Clin. Pharmacology and Therapeutics, Inter-Am. Soc. Hypertension, Soc. Interam. de Farmacología Clínica y Terapéutica (pres. 1984-88). Address: Apartado Postal 76-333, El Marques, Caracas 1070-A, Venezuela

VELASQUEZ, ANA MARIA, languages educator; b. Callao, Lima, Peru, Nov. 18, 1947; came to U.S. 1980; d. Victor and Yolanda (Reinoso) V.; m. Scott Mathew Nakada, Mar. 19, 1981. Bachelor's Degree, San Marcos U., Lima, 1969; student French Paris VI U., 1971-72, student English Prince George Coll., 1983-84, student Quechua Yachay Wasi Coll., Lima, 1986. Cert. tchr., Peru. Educator San Jose de Cluny, Lima, 1968-71; translator Aubert & Duval, Paris, 1972-76; linguistic coordinator Ser. de Maquiniaria, Lima, 1977-80; educator, cons. INLINGUA, Washington, 1981-83, CACI, Inc., Arlington, Va., 1982-84; dir. AKTA Internat., Silver Spring, Md., 1984—. Author: Pronunciacion Basica Universal, 1974; South American Dialects, 1977; Abbreviated Telephone Communications System, 1984; Teaching Languages to Adults, 1985; Languages 365 Days, 1986. Coordinator literacy campaign, Puno, Peru, 1969. Mem. Internat. Platform Assn., Am. Assn. Applied Linguistics, Mensa. Republican. Roman Catholic. Avocations: chess, skiing. Home and Office: 12404 Lima Dr Silver Spring MD 20904

VELAYATI, ALI AKBAR, Iranian minister of foreign affairs, pediatrician; b. Tehran, Iran, June 25, 1945; s. Ali and Zobeideh Asghar; m. Shirin Khoshnevissan children—Maysam, Mohammad, Ali Asghar. Dr. Pediatrics, Tehran, 1974. Assoc. prof. Faculty Health Scis., Tehran, 1974-79; vice minister Ministry of Health, Tehran, 1979-80; rep. to Parliament, Tehran, 1980-81; minister of foreign affairs Iran, Tehran, 1981—. Author: Infectious Diseases, 3 vols., 1979; also articles. Mem. central com. Islamic Republic Party, Tehran, 1982—. Mem. Iranian Pediatrics Assn. Office: Ministry of Fgn Affairs, Teheran Iran *

VELDE, JOHN ERNEST, JR., business executive; b. Pekin, Ill., June 15, 1917; s. John Ernest and Alga (Anderson) V.; m. Shirley Margaret Walker, July 29, 1940 (dec. 1969); 1 dau., Drew; m. Gail Patrick, Sept. 28, 1974 (dec. July 1980); m. Gretchen Swanson Pullen, Nov. 7, 1981. A.B., U. Ill., 1938. Pres. Velde, Roelfs & Co., Pekin, 1955-60; dir. Herget Nat. Bank, 1948-75, Kroehler Mfg. Co., 1974-81; pres. Paisano Prodns., Inc., 1980—. Trustee Pekin Pub. Library, 1948-69, Pekin Meml. Hosp., 1950-69; chmn. Am. Library Trustee Assn. Found., 1976; trustee Am. Library Assn. Endowment, 1976-82, Everett McKinley Dirksen Research Center, 1965-74; chmn. trustees, bd. dirs. Center Ulcer Research and Edn. Found., 1977-82; mem. bd. councilors Brain Research Inst. UCLA, 1977-82; trustee Center for Am. Archeology, Evanston, 1978-83; mem. Nat. Commn. on Libraries and Info. Sci., 1970-79; mem. adv. bd. on White House Conf. on Libraries, 1976-80; trustee Joint Council on Econ. Edn., 1977-83; bd. dirs. U. Ill. Found., 1977-83, Omaha Pub. Library Found., 1985—; vice chmn. U. Ill. Pres.' Council, 1977-79, chmn., 1979-81, mem. fin. resources council steering com., 1976-78; mem. adv. council UCLA Grad. Sch. Library and Info. Sci., 1981-82; pres. Ill. Valley Library System, 1965-69; dir. Lakeview Center for Arts and Scis., Peoria, Ill., 1962-73; mem. Nat. Book Com., 1969-74. Served as lt. (j.g.) USNR, World War II. Mem. Am. Library Trustee Assn. (regional v.p. 1970-72, chmn. internat. relations com. 1973-76), Kappa Sigma. Clubs: Chgo. Yacht, Internat. (Chgo.); California (Los Angeles); Outrigger Canoe (Honolulu); Thunderbird Country (Rancho Mirage, Calif.); Chaine des Rotisseurs, Chevaliers du Tastevin; Circumnavigators (N.Y.C.); Omaha Country; Old Baldy (Saratoga, Wyo.), Eldorado Country (Indian Wells, Calif.), Morningside (Rancho Mirage, Calif.). Home: 8405 Indian Hills Dr Omaha NE 68114 also: 40-231 Club View Dr Rancho Mirage CA 92270

VELDMAN, JOHANNES, economics, history educator; b. The Hague, The Netherlands, Sept. 23, 1957; s. Johannes Veldman and Marie Christine Driessen; m. Vera Johanna Zielstra, Feb. 26, 1986. D in History, Econs., U. Leidett, The Netherlands. Tchr. history, econs., statis. expert Tinberger Coll., The Hague, 1987—; mem. examination bd. Tenedex, The Hague, 1987-88. Author, editor: Export, 1988; contbr. articles to profl. jours. Mem. Social Democratic Party. Home: Bussumsestreet 146, 2574 JP The Hague The Netherlands Office: Tinberger Coll, Stokroosstraat 165, The Hague The Netherlands

VELEZ, CARLOS, atomic energy agency administrator; b. San Sebastian, Spain, Nov. 26, 1927; came to Mex., 1942; s. Pedro and Damiana (Ocon) V.; m. Maria Tirado, June 16, 1956; children: Marisela, Maria Eugenia. Licencie es Scis., U. Paris, 1949; Ingenieur Radioelectricien, Ecole Superieure D'Dlectricite, Paris, 1951; MS in Engring., U. Mich., 1956, PhD in Nuclear Engring., 1959. With. Mexican Light and Power, Mexico City, 1952-66, dep. chief planning, 1961-66; head. dept. nuclear engring. Fed. Electricity Commn., Mexico City, 1966-71; mgr. devel. Nat. Inst. Nuclear Energy, Mexico City, 1971-75; 1st exec. dir. Electric Research Inst., Mexico City, 1975-76; gen. dir. Nat. Inst. Nuclear Energy, Mexico City, 1976-77; dep. dir. gen. Internat. Atomic Energy Agy., Vienna, 1980-86; gen. dir. Nat. Inst. Nuclear Research, Mexico City, 1987—; advisor Nat. Commn. Nuclear Energy, Mexico City, 1959-65; lectr. nuclear engring. Nat. Poly. Inst., Mexico City, 1965-74; lectr. physics Met. Autonomous U., Mexico City, 1974-75. Contbr. articles to profl. jours. Mem. Acad. Engring., Acad. Sci. Research, Mexican Soc., Sigma Xi. Home: Tiro al Pichón 138, 11910 Mexico City Mexico Office: Instituto Nacional de, Investigaciones Nucleares, Km 36 1/2, Carretara México-Toluca, Salazar Edo de México MEXICO

VELICHKO, VLADIMIR MAKAROVICH, Soviet government official; b. 1937. Trained as mech. engr. Mem. Communist Party Soviet Union, 1962—; from foreman to dir. of machine bldg. plan; 1st dep. minister Ministry Power Engring., Moscow, 1975-83, minister, 1983—; minister Ministry Heavy, Power and Transport Machine Bldg., Moscow, 1987—. Address: Ministry Heavy Power and, Transport Machine Bldg, Moscow USSR *

VELINOV, MITOV IVAN, Bulgarian supreme court executive, researcher; b. Lisetz, Bulgaria, Jan. 2, 1931; s. Velin Mitov and Vasilka Davidkova (Angelova) Nikova; m. Maria Georgieva Karadimova, May 31, 1959; children—Vasilka, Galina. Grad. in Law, Sofia U., 1956, also M.S. in Law. Jurist diplomate. Chief judge Regional Ct., Zlatograd, Bulgaria, 1957-59; mem. judge Cist. Ct., Smolian, Bulgaria, 1959-61; assoc. prof. Sofia U., Bulgaria, 1961-85, chief of chair in civil law, 1971—, mem. acad. council; cons. Legislation Council, Sofia, 1971-73; chief legal dept. Council of Ministers, Sofia, 1973-75; vice minister Ministry of Justice, Sofia, 1975-81; pres. Supreme Ct. Peoples Republic of Bulgaria, Sofia, 1981—; dep. Nat. Assembly; mem. Legis. Council, Sofia, 1973—. Editor in chief: Sotzialistichesko Pravo, Sofia; author books and publs. on civil law; editor various handbooks and references in field. Decorated Order Peoples Republic of Bulgaria, various medals. Mem. Union of Jurists in Bulgaria (pres. 1986—), Bulgarian C. of C. (arbitrator arbitartion ct.). Mem. Bulgarian Communist Party. Office: 2 Vitosha Blvd, Sofia Bulgaria

VELIOTES, NICHOLAS ALEXANDER, professional association executive, former ambassador and assistant secretary of state; b. Oakland, Calif., Oct. 28, 1928; s. Alexander and Irene (Kiskaskis) V.; m. Patricia Jane Nolan, July 17, 1953; children: Christopher, Michael. BA, U. Calif.-Berkeley, 1952, MA, 1954; postgrad., Princeton U., 1969-70. Teaching asst. U. Calif.-Berkeley, 1952-54; commd. officer U.S. Fgn. Service, 1955; held various Fgn. Service posts Italy, India, Laos, Israel, Jordan, Egypt; Asst. Sec. of State Near East/South Asia, 1981-83; ambassador to Jordan 1978-81, ambassador to Egypt, 1983-86; pres. Assn. Am. Pubs., 1986—. Served with U.S. Army, 1946-48. Recipient Sec. of State and Presdl. Disting. Service awards. Mem. Council on Fgn. Relations, Am. Acad. Diplomacy, VFW.

VELK, ROBERT JAMES, consulting psychologist; b. Chgo., Feb. 27, 1938; s. Jerry E. and Sylvia B. (Wladar) Vlk; m. Vera A. Kraml, Nov. 25, 1961; children—Robert Frank, Cheryl Anne. B.B.A., Northwestern U., 1963, M.B.A., 1968; M.A., Rutgers U., 1980, Ph.D., 1983. Asst. mgr. product decorations Meyercord Co., Carol Stream, Ill., 1959-65, nat. account mgr., 1965-68; assoc. Kepner Tregoe, Inc., Princeton, N.J., 1968-70, Western region mgr., 1970-72, dir. mktg. N.Am. ops., 1972-73; pres. Creative Leadership Inc., Princeton, 1973-83; pres. Cognitive Sci. Corp., Ft. Collins, Colo., 1983—. Author: Information and Imagination, 1978; Thinking About Thinking, 1978. Mem. Am. Psychol. Assn., Am. Soc. Tng. and Devel., Nat. Soc. Performance and Instrn., Cognitive Sci. Soc. Clubs: Christian Businessmen's Com. of Central Jersey (chmn. 1974-75), Gideon's. Office: Cognitive Sci Corp PO Box 1487 Fort Collins CO 80522

VENARD, DAVID, banker, consultant, educator; b. Hinsdale, Ill., Nov. 27, 1955; m. Diane L. Levy, Aug. 5, 1979. BS in Acctg. summa cum laude, Bradley U., 1977. CPA, Ill. Supr. Ernst & Whinney, Chgo., 1977-84; sr. v.p. and chief fin. officer Parkway Bank & Trust Co. and First State Bancorp, Inc., Harwood Heights, Ill., 1984—; 1st State Bank Chgo., Parkway Bank Schaumburg, Ill.; pres. Dane Assocs., Inc., Buffalo Grove, Ill., 1982—, Horizon Systems, 1983—; dir., treas. The Perfect Nut Co., Chgo.; chmn., pres. Chgo. Food Specialties, Ltd., 1988—. Editor, author course manual Bank Operations, Accounting and Auditing, and Bank Profitability, 1983-85. Bd. dirs., treas. Horwitz-Slavin Meml. Cancer Research Found., Northbrook, Ill., 1978-84. Mem. Am. Inst. CPAs (tech. adv. 1984-86), Ill. CPA Soc. (instr. 1982-85, specialized com. banking 1981—), Chgo. Fin. Microcomputer Users Group (dir. 1985-86), Delta Upsilon Internatl. (bd. dirs., asst. treas. 1983-85, treas. 85-86), Bradley Delta Upsilon (bd. dirs., pres. 1977-84, treas. 1984—). Republican. Jewish. Club: River (Chgo.). Office: Parkway Bank & Trust Co 4800 N Harlem Ave Harwood Heights IL 60656

VENCOVSKY, EUGEN JOSEF, psychiatrist, educator; b. Prostejov, Czechoslovakia; m. Blanka Fiedlerova. VMD, Med. Faculty of Charles U., 1933, Dr. Sc., 1963; Dr.med.h., U. Berlin, U. Crakow. Intern Medicine Faculty, Prague, 1933-39; resident Psyhciat. Hosp., Pilsen, 1939-45; dir. U. Psychiat. Clin., Pilsen, 1946-76, staff, 1977-78; prof., sr. staff Research Lab. Psychiat. Clin., Prague, 1974-78; profl. cons. psychopharmacotherapie U. Psychiat. Clin., Pilsen, 1978; examiner Postgrad. Psychiat. Sch., Prague, 1965; psychiatrist West Bohemia, 1965-79. Author: Paraptrenia, 1951, History of Czechoslovakian Psychiatry, 1957, Textbook of Psychiatry, 1976, Clinical Psychopharmacology, 1980, Reading About Psychiatry, 1982., 100 Years of Czech Psychiat. Clinic in Prague, 1987. Decorated Order Polonia Restituta, Purkinje Order. Fellow Royal Soc. Medicine, Royal Acad. Medicine, Soc. Med. Psychology, Swiss soc. Psychiats.; mem. N.Y. Acad. Scis., Med. Club Pilsen, Purkinje Med. Assn. (hon.), Czechoslovak Psychiat. Soc. (hon.), Psychiat. Soc. Poland, Psychiat. Soc. Hungary, Psychiat. Soc. USSR, Psychiat. Soc. Bulgaria, Psychiat. Soc. Fed. Republic Germany, Psychiat. Soc. Yugoslavia. Address: Drevena 3, CS-301 12, Pilsen Czechoslovakia

VENDER, CARL STANLEY, mining engineer and mine surveyor; b. Great Falls, Mont., Jan. 26, 1948; s. Fred and Zelma (Cunnington) V.; m. Mildred Ann Wickstrom, May 26, 1970; children—Charles, Bradley, Michael. A.A. No. Mont. Coll., 1969. Registered profl. surveyor, Mont., N.D. Rodman Mont. Hwy. Dept., Helena, 1969-70; engr. Knife River Coal, Bismarck, N.D., 1971—. Mem. N.D. Soc. Profl. Surveyors (state officer 1979-84, newsletter editor 1979—), Nat. Soc. Profl. Surveyors (chmn. com. 1983—), Internat. Soc. for Mine Surveyors (dir.), Am. Congress Surveying and Mapping (chmn. com. 1983—), Soc. Mining Engrs., Mont. Assn. Profl. Surveyors. Club: Toastmasters Internat. Office: Knife River Coal 1915 N Kavaney Dr Bismarck ND 58501

VENDITTO, JAMES JOSEPH, chemical engineer; b. Dobbs Ferry, N.Y., Nov. 13, 1951; s. Vincenzio Rocco and Maria Nichola (Cassetti) V.; children—Vincent James, Joseph Ryan. BSChemE, U. Okla., 1973. Registered profl. engr., Tex. Engr.-in-tng., Victoria, Tex., 1973-74; field engr. Halliburton Services, Alice, Tex., 1974-75, dist. engr., Mission, Tex., 1975-77, regional service sales engr., New Orleans, 1977-80, asst. div. engr., Corpus Christi, Tex., 1980-83, supt. stimulation dept., 1983, div. engr., 1983—; cons. in field; researcher high temperature fracturing fluids, chem. stimulation S. Tex. sandstones. Devel. new API cemeting temperatures and new refracturing tech. for oil and gas industry; contbr. articles to profl. jours. Active United Way; coach little league and soccer. Mem. Am. Inst. Chem. Engrs., Soc. Petroleum Engrs., AIME, Am. Petroleum Inst., Internat. Platform Assn., Nat. Soc. Profl. Engrs., Tex. Soc. Profl. Engrs. Republican. Roman Catholic. Club: Pharaoh Country. Lodge: KC. Home: 2211 Live Oak St Portland TX 78374 Office: 1220 First City Bank Tower FCB119 Corpus Christi TX 78477

VENIT, WILLIAM BENNETT, electrical products company executive, consultant; b. Chgo., May 28, 1931; s. George Bernard and Ida (Schaffel) V.; m. Nancy Jean Carlson, Jan. 28, 1956; children: Steven Louis, Aprilann. Student U. Ill., Champaign, 1949. Sales mgr. Coronet, Inc., Chgo., 1952-63, pres., chmn. bd. dirs., 1963-74; pres., chmn. bd. dirs. Roma Wire Inc., Chgo., 1971-74; pres. bd. dirs. Swing Time, Inc., Chgo., 1985—, chmn. bd. dirs., 1986—; pres. Wm. Allen Inc., Chgo., 1972-74; pres., chmn. bd. dirs. William Lamp Co., Inc., William Wire Co., Inc., 1974-76; pres., chmn. bd. dirs. MSWV, Inc., 1981—, pres. bd. dirs. 1985—; pres. Trio Steel Inc., Chgo.; spl. cons. MacKinney Co., Robert Shields Co., Pasadena, Calif.; cons. Nu Style Lamp Shade. Served with Q.M.C., AUS, 1949-52. Mem. Mfr. Agt. Club, Chgo. Lamp and Shade Inst. (bd. dirs.). Home: 323 Suwanee Ave Sarasota FL 34243 Office: 5512 W Lawrence Ave Chicago IL 60630 also: 323 Suwanee Ave Sarasota FL 33508

VENKATARAMAN, KRISHNASWAMY, UN executive; b. Mayuram, India, May 15, 1935; s. M. K. Krishnaswamy Iyer and Pichuiyer Chellammal; M.A., Madras (India) U., 1955; postgrad. (U.K. fellow) Cambridge (Eng.) U., 1964-65; Ph.D., Jawaharlal Nehru U., New Delhi, 1978; m. Padma Venkataraman, July 4, 1962; children—Meera, Shobana. With Indian Adminstrv. Service, 1957-79; chmn. Agro-Industries Corp., Madras, 1978-79; dir. Indian Ministry Industry, New Delhi, 1969-74; sr. tech. adv. UN Indsl. Devel. Orgn., Vienna, Austria, 1979—; active IAS, Tamil Nadu, Madras, Vellore, other locations, 1957-68; dir. Indian Ministry Industry, New Delhi, 1969-74; active UN Indsl. Devel. Orgn., 1974-78; chmn. Agro-Industries Corp., Madras, 1978-79; trainer/lectr. on tech. for devel.; mem. Indian coms. on research and devel. in pvt. sector, 1972-74; mem. Indian dels. to UN meetings, 1970-73. Recipient Norton prize Madras U., 1955. Mem. Indian Inst. Public Adminstrn. (life; sec. Madras br. 1967-68, 78-79, mem. governing council 1972-76). Author books, papers and UN reports, including States' Finances in India (Allen and Unwin), 1968; Power Development in India: Financial Aspects, 1972; editor: Public Grievances, 1969; Personnel Assessment, 1970. Office: PO Box 400, A1400 Vienna Austria

VENKATARAMAN, RAMASWAMY IYER, president of India; b. Rajamadam, India, Dec. 4, 1910; s. Ramaswami Iyer V.; m. Janaki Venkataraman, 1938; 3 daus. M. in Econs., Madras U., LLD (hon.); LLD (hon.) Nagarjuna U., U. Burdwan. Advocate, Madras High Ct. 1935, Supreme Ct., 1951; detained during Quit India Movement, 1942-44; mem. Provisional Parliament, 1950-52, mem. Lok Sabha, 1952-57, 77—; sec. Congress Party, 1953-54; mem. standing fin. com., estimates com., pub. accts. com., privileges com.; Minister for Industry and Labour, leader House, Govt. Madras, 1957-67, mem. union planning commn., 1967-71; chmn. Nat. Research and Devel. Corp.; Minister of Fin. and Industry, 1980-82, Minister of Def., 1982-84; del. to ILO, 1958, v.p., chmn. Council of States, India, 1984-87, pres. 1987—; UN Gen. Assembly, 1952-61. Mng. editor Labour Law Jour., 1971—. Address: Office of Pres, New Delhi India *

VENKATARAMIAH, AMARANENI, environ. physiologist; b. Atmakur, India, Aug. 16, 1928; came to U.S., 1969, naturalized, 1987; s. A. and A. (Lakshvamma) Rangaiah; m. Swarajyam Kurra, June 9, 1949; children: Sulochana, Rao, Bharadwaj, Kumar, Sujatha. B.S. in Biology and Chemistry, Andhra U., Waltair, India, 1955; M.A. in Zoology, Sri Venkateswara U., Tirupati, India, 1957, Ph.D. in Eco-Physiology, 1965. Lectr. Andhra Loyola Coll., Vijayawada, India, 1957-61, Sri Venkateswara U., 1965-66; research fellow Council of Sci. and Indsl. Research, New Delhi, India, 1966-67; head physiology sect. Gulf Research Lab., Ocean Springs, 1969-86; adj. prof. biology U. So. Miss., Hattiesburg, 1978—. Contbr. articles to profl. jours. Dept. Army grantee, 1970-77; Dept. Energy grantee, 1978-82; other grants. Mem. AAAS, Am. Soc. Zoologists, Gulf Estuarine Research Soc., Miss. Acad. Scis., Inc., World Mariculture Soc. Patentee in field. Current Work: Physiological ecology of marine animals with emphasis on osmoregulation and metabolic problems, crustacean aquaculture, toxicological effects of discharges from the ocean thermal energy conversion plants on marine animals. Subspecialties: Comparative physiology; Ocean energy conversion. Home: 219-1/2 Halstead Rd PO Box 1068 Ocean Springs MS 39564

VENTER, DANIEL CHRISTIAAN, food manufacturing executive; b. Johannesburg, Republic South Africa, Oct. 31, 1947; s. Hendrik Johannes and Rose (Matthysen) V.; m. Madelein Dreyer, July 4, 1970; children: Anel, Hendrik. B of Commerce, Univ. Pretoria, Republic South Africa, 1968, MBA, 1972. Computer programmer Asea Electric Corp., Pretoria, 1970-72; various mgmt. positions Unilever Ltd., Durban and Johannesburg, Republic South Africa, 1972-83; exec. dir. Kanhym Ltd., Johannesburg, 1983—. Chmn. sch. com. Benoni area, Johannesburg, 1984-85, Rapportryers Soc., Benoni, 1979-80. Mem. South African Inst. Mgmt., South African Meat Packers Assn. (vice chmn. 1986—). Mem. Christian Reformed Ch. Home: 8 Robinson St, Benoni Transvaal 1500, Republic of South Africa Office: Kanhym Investments Ltd, PO Box 16474, Doornfontein Transvaal, Republic of South Africa

VENTER, PIETER JACOBUS, broadcasting executive; b. Coligny, South Africa, Aug. 10, 1933; arrived in Namibia, 1969; s. Hermann August Wilhelm and Hester Maria (Wiese) V.; m. Ena Fouche Nel, July 2, 1955; children—Madele, Hesta, Augusta. B.A., U. Potchefstroom, 1953; Higher Edn. Diploma, Tchr.'s Tng. Coll., 1954. Tchr. Coligny Transvaal Edn. Dept., South Africa, 1955-58, tchr., Lichtenburg, 1959-61; asst. program organizer South Africa Broadcasting Corp., Transvaal, 1962-64, organizer sch. radio, 1964-66, asst. regional mgr., Eastern Cape, South Africa, 1966-69, regional mgr., Namibia, 1969-78; exec. chmn. South West Africa Broadcasting Corp., Namibia, 1979—. Chmn. South West Africa Namibia Sports Council, 1974-79; pres. South West Africa Nat. Rifle Assn., Namibia, 1973-82. Republican. Mem. Dutch Reformed Ch. Club: Windhoek Country. Office: SW Africa Broadcasting Corp, PO Box 321, Johan Albrech & Pettenkofer Sts, Windhoek 9000, Namibia

VENTOSA, JOSÉ M. ROSICH, educational administrator, educator; b. Barcelona, Spain, Sept. 26, 1933; s. Felix G. and Maria (Rosich) V.; m. Nieves V. Franques, Feb. 14, 1959; children: Josefelix, Alfonso, Juan Pablo, Alejandro, Celia. BS, Collegio San Miguel, Barcelona, 1950; D. Indsl. Engring., Escuela Técnica Superior de Ingenieros Industriales, Barcelona, 1958. Mgmt. cons. Consortium d'Organisateurs Conseils, Barcelona, 1958-61; expert regional mgmt. Internat. Labour Office (UNO), Cen. Am., 1961-64; dir. bus. edn. ctr. EPISE, Barcelona, 1965—; tchr. mgmt. Escuela Superior de Administración, Direccion de Empresas, Barcelona, 1965. Author: Contabilidad Analítica de Explotaciin, 1966, Técnicas de Mando y Relaciones Humanas, 1975, Fundamentals of Office Computers, 1972, Curso Básico de Valores Mobiliarios, 1973. Mem. Assn. Tchrs. Mgmt., Internat. Council Corr. Edn., Am. Soc. Tng. Dirs., Assn. Espanola de Dirs. Personnel, Assn. Formación y desarrollo en la Empresa (treas. 1981-83). Roman Catholic. Club: Tenis Barcino (Barcelona). Home: Rosellon 171, 08036 Barcelona Spain Office: Ensenanza Programada EPISE, Muntaner 430, 08006 Barcelona Spain

VERANO, ANTHONY FRANK, banker; b. West Harrison, N.Y., Jan. 4, 1931; s. Frank and Rose (Viscome) V.; m. Clara Cosentino, July 8, 1951; children—Rosemarie, Diana Lynn. Student, Am. Inst. Banking, 1956-60, Bank Adminstrn. Inst., U. Wis., 1962-64, RCA Programmers Sch., 1965, Burroughs Programmers Sch., 1965, N.J. Bankers Data Processing Sch., 1966-68, others. With County Trust Co., White Plains, N.Y., 1949-61; sr. auditor County Trust Co., 1960-61; with State Nat. Bank Conn., Bridgeport, 1961—; auditor State Nat. Bank Conn., 1962-79, exec. auditor, 1979—; exec. auditor Conn. Bank & Trust Co., 1983—; v.p., auditor Gateway Bank, Newtown, Conn., 1987—; tchr. bank auditing Am. Inst. Banking, 1976-78. Mem. adv. bd. Norwalk Community Coll., 1968—. Served with USN, 1951-52. Mem. Bank Adminstrn. Inst. (dir. Stamford chpt. 1967-68, sec. Western Conn. chpt. 1968-69, treas. 1969-70, v.p. 1970-71, pres. 1971-72), Am. Accounting Assn., Inst. Internal Auditors. (chartered bank auditor 1970). Home: 59 Bugg Hill Rd Monroe CT 06468 Office: Gateway Bank 191 S Main St Newtown CT 06470

VERBIEST, HENK, neurosurgeon; b. Rotterdam, Netherlands, July 16, 1909; s. Cornelis Eugenius and Mary Catherine (Peters) V.; m. Jose Henriette Hage, Sept. 26, 1953; children: Marie Jose, Nelly Marjolein. M.D., Leiden U., 1934, Ph.D., 1939. Tng. neurologist Leiden U., 1934-38; tng. neurosurgeon Paris Hopital de la Pitieé , 1938-39, Utrecht U., 1940-41, Amsterdam U., 1941-42; head neurosurg. dept. Utrecht U., Netherlands, 1942—, reader in neurosurgery, 1949, prof., 1963-80, vice dean Med. Faculty, 1972-76. Decorated comdr. Order of Merit (Italy), knight Order of Lion (Netherlands), Cross of Honour in the Order of the House of Orange; recipient Winkler medal, 1955, Gold medal Pavia U., 1982. named mem. hon. faculty Baylor U., 1967; hon. Houstonian, 1967. Mem. Netherlands Royal Acad. Scis., Netherlands Soc. Neurol. Surgeons (founding mem.), Internat. Soc. Study Lumbar Spine (pres. 1976-77, charter mem.), Cervical Research Soc., World Fedn. Neurol. Surgery (hon. life pres. 1977), Congress Soc. de Neurochir. Langue Française (pres. 1979). Editor Neurochirurgie, 1977, Acta Neurochirurgica, 1958. Adv. editor Jour. Neurosurgery, 1964; founder, chief editor Jour. Neuro-othopedics. Contbr. articles to med. jours. and books. Home: 32 Wilhelminapark, 3581 NH Utrecht The Netherlands Office: 101 Catharijnesingel, 3511 GV Utrecht The Netherlands

VERBON, HARRIE ADRIANUS, economics educator; b. Utrecht, The Netherlands, Jan. 21, 1951; s. Harrie Adrian and Anna Gijsberta (Van Zoelen) V.; m. Juliana Maria Huisman, Nov. 1, 1978. MA, Free U., Amsterdam, 1976, PhD, 1988. Asst. prof. Free U., 1973-76; research assoc. constrn. monetary model Dutch Cen. Bank, Amsterdam, 1979-82; asst. prof. econs. U. Amsterdam, 1982—. Author book on evolution of pub. pension schemes; contbr. articles to profl. jours. Mem. Pub. Choice Soc., Internat. Soc. Pub. Fin. Home: Fazantenkamp 380, 3607 XC Maarsen The Netherlands Office: U Amsterdam - Micro, Jodenbreestraat 23, 1011 NH Amsterdam The Netherlands

VERBRUGGE, BETTY LOU, county official; b. Dakota City, Iowa, Jan. 15, 1927; d. Myron and Bernice Sarah (Soppeland) Doty; m. Durand Daniel Verbrugge, Oct. 25, 1945; children: Judy, Gary. BA in Polit. Sci./Social Sci., Ft. Wright Coll., 1978. Cert. emergency med. technician; cert. intravenous therapy technician. Chief dep. Pend Oreille County, Newport, Wash., 1964-73, treas., 1973—. Mem. Nat. Assn. County Treas. (bd. dirs. 1978, hisitorian 1980—), Wash. State Treasurers Assn. (pres. 1977-78), Wash. Assn. County Ofcls. (pres. 1982-83, bd. dirs. 1978-84). Club: Soroptimist (pres. 1968-70, sec. Dist. 3, 1970-72, bd. dirs. 1972-78, treas. Northwestern region 1974-78), Pend Oreille County Emergency Med. Technician Assn. (sec./treas. 1982-86, pres. 1988). Lodge: Noble Grange (musician). Avocations: music, reading, bird watching, hiking, gardening.

VERBRUGGEN, HENRY WILLEM, marketing and business consultant; b. Helmond, Netherlands, June 21, 1941; s. Wilhelm Heinrich and Francina (Van Veghel) V.; B.B.A., Netherlands Inst. Bus. Studies, 1964; m. Maria Dymphina Kuypers, July 24, 1968; children: Martijn Willem, Rogier Hein. Area sales mgr. Carnation, Brussels, 1964-68; product mgr., sales and merchandising mgr. M & M/Mars, Brussels, 1969-74; mktg. and bus. cons., Brussels, 1975—; dir. Gamma Mktg. and Brokerage, Brussels, 1980—; v.p. Union Cycliste Internationale; pres. Fédération Internationale du Cyclisme Professionnel. Roman Catholic. Home and Office: Route d'Ohain 16 a, 1338 Lasne Belgium

VERDI, NEJAT HASAN, financial executive; b. Istanbul, Turkey, Feb. 14, 1913; s. Fazil Ibrahim and Fatma (Nigar) V.; M.Comml.Sci., Comml. Acad., Calw, Germany, 1933; m. Liselotte Annemarie Auer, Apr. 1, 1950; children—Aylin, Murat, Nilufer. Partner Verdi Ticaret ve Sanayi A.S., Istanbul, Turkey, 1927—, chmn. bd., also chmn. bd. subs., 1950—. Bd. dirs. Am. Hosp., Istanbul, 1967-81; chmn. Am. Hosp. and Nursing Sch. Com., 1967-81. Named Hon. Ambassador of New Orleans, in Istanbul, 1957. Clubs: Propeller of N.Y. (pres. 1952-60), Moda Yacht, Golf. Home: Hûsrev Gerede Cadd 75/7, Zorlu Apartman, Teskiviye, 80200 Istanbul Turkey Office: Verdi Ticaret ve Sanayi, Cumh Cadd 26 A, Pegasus Evi Harbiye, 80224 Istanbul Turkey

VERDIER, QUENTIN ROOSEVELT, personnel consultant; b. Mancelona, Mich., Mar. 19, 1921; s. John Walter and Louise (Hills) V.; m. Margaret Elizabeth Wells, Nov. 13, 1943; children: Margaret Louise, Quentin Wells, Nanette Marie Bloom. AB in Pub. Adminstrn., Kalamazoo Coll., 1943, MA in Pub. Adminstrn., 1947; postgrad., Am. U., 1948-51; PhD in Human Resource Devel., Columbia Pacific U., 1985. Cert. employment cons., personnel cons., forensic vocat. expert; lic. employment agt., Wis. Asst. personnel officer U.S. Savs. Bonds div. U.S. Treasury Dept., Washington, 1951-58; div. chief office of personnel Internat. Coop. Adminstrn./Agy. for Internat. Devel., Washington State Dept., 1959-63; dep. chief pub. adminstrn. div. U.S. Ops. Mission/Agy. for Internat. Devel., Saigon, South Vietnam, 1963-65; asst. dir. tng. Inst. Govt. Affairs U. Wis. Extension, Madison, 1966-67; pres., chief ops. officer AvailAbility of Madison, Inc., 1967—, also chmn. bd. dirs.; mem. adv. panel Nat. Forensic Ctr., Princeton, 1983—; intern Group XIII, Nat. Inst. Pub. Affairs, 1948-49. Author City Employee Handbook-Better Pub. Service, 1947; editor hist. pamphlet series Understanding Backgrounds, 1964; contbr. articles to profl. jours. Bd. dirs. Capital Community Citizen's Assn., Madison, 1967; pres. Country Heights Homeowners Assn., Oregon, 1969. Served with U.S. Army Air Corps, 1943-46. Recipient Wm G. Howard prize in polit. sci., 1946; Upjohn fellow Kalamazoo Coll., 1946-47. Mem. Nat. Assn. Personnel Cons., Am. Soc. Personnel Adminstrn., Wis. Assn. Personnel Cons., Am. Arbitration Assn. (arbitrator, mem. panel Chgo. regional office), U.S.A. Tug-of-War Assn. (sec., parliamentarian 1978), Am. Assn. Ret. Persons, Nat. Forensic Ctr., Wis. Acad. Scis., Arts and Letters, Nat. Geographic Soc., Smithsonian

Instn., Nat. Assn. Retired Credit Union People, Internat. Platform Assn., Internat. Exec. Service Corps, Friendship Force. Clubs: Fox Run Health, Toastmasters (dist. 36 gov.). Lodges: Masons (32 degree), Rotary.

VERECONDI, SCORECCI UMBERTO MARIA ALVIN, finance company executive; b. Milan, Italy, Sept. 20, 1938; s. Giuseppe and Anna (Cramer) Verecondi Scortecci; m. Mariqa Benedetta de Micheli, Apr. 24, 1971 (div.). Diploma, di Maturita Classica, 1959; Scienze Plitishe, U. degli Studi Genova, Italy, 1969. Sales export mgr. Carlo Erba SpA, Milan, 1965-67; asst. dir. R.E. Aga Khan Consortium, Sardinia, 1967-71; account exec. Merrill Lynch & Co., N.Y.C., Milan, 1971-78; export dir. G. Visconti di Modrone SpA, Milan, 1978-80, Conficda SpA Inst. Fiduciario, Milan, 1980-82; exec. fin. dir. Unione Fiduciaria SpA, Milan, 1982-84; securities and invetment mgr. Citicorp Investment Bank, Milan, 1984—. Served with Italian Air Force, 1963-64. Mem. Assn. Italiana Analisti Finanziari, Ordine dei Giornalisti. Roman Cathic. Clubs: Cubino-Dadi (Milan); Soc. dell Unione (Venice). Home: Via Pietro Cossa 5, 20122 Milano Italy Office: Citicorp Investment Bank, Foro Buonaparte 16, 20121 Milano Italy

VEREEN, WILLIAM JEROME, uniform manufacturing company executive; b. Moultrie, Ga., Sept. 7, 1940; s. William Coachman and Mary Elizabeth (Bunn) V.; m. Lula Evelyn King, June 9, 1963; children—Elizabeth King, William Coachman. B.S. in Indsl. Mgmt, Ga. Inst. Tech., 1963. With Riverside Mfg. Co., Moultrie, 1967—; v.p., then exec. v.p. Riverside Mfg. Co., 1970-77, pres., 1977-84, pres., treas., chief exec. officer, 1984—; also dir.; v.p., dir. Moultrie Cotton Mills, 1969—; exec. v.p. Riverside Industries, Inc., Moultrie, 1973-77; pres. Riverside Industries, Inc., 1977-84, chief exec. officer, 1984—, also dir.; v.p., dir. Riverside Uniform Rentals, Inc., Moultrie, 1971-80, pres., 1980-84, chief exec. officer, dir., 1984—; pres. Riverside Mfg. Co. (Ireland) Ltd., 1977—, Right Image Corp.; pres. Riverside Mfg. Co. GmbH, Rep. of Germany, 1979—, chief exec. officer, dir. 1984; pres., treas., chief exec. officer G.A. Rivers Corp., 1984—, Riverside Mfg. Co. (U.K.) Ltd., 1985—; advisor textile and apparel tariffs and quotas U.S. Dept. State Bd; bd. dirs. U.S. Bus. and Indsl. Council, C&S Nat. Bank of Colquitt County. Bd. dirs. Moultrie-Colquitt County (Ga.) Devel. Authority, 1973—, Moultrie-Colquitt County United Givers, 1968-75, Moultrie YMCA, 1968—, Colquitt County Cancer Soc., 1969-73; trustee Community Welfare Assn. Moultrie, 1970—, Pineland Sch., Moultrie, 1971—, Leadership Ga., 1972—, Ga. Council Econ. Edn.; trustee Am. Apparel Edn. Found. Served to capt. USMCR, 1963-67. Decorated Bronze Star, Purple Heart. Mem. Internat. Apparel Fedn. (bd. dirs.), Am. Apparel Mfrs. Assn. (dir., exec. com., edn. found. com., 2d vice chmn.), Nat. Assn. Uniform Mfrs. and Distbrs. (dir.), Young Presidents Orgn., Am. Apparel Edn. Found. (v.p., trustee), Sigma Alpha Epislon. Presbyterian (chmn. bd. deacons). Clubs: Elks, Kiwanis. Home: 21 Dogwood Circle Moultrie GA 31768 Office: PO Box 460 Moultrie GA 31768

VEREKETIS, CONSTANTIN KIMON, gas distribution company executive; b. Smyrna, Oct. 27, 1908; s. Kimon Constantin and Maria (Psychopoulou) V.; M.Law, Law U. Bucharest, Romania, 1940; m. Smaragda Kalassounda, June 2, 1963 (dec. 1983). With Concordia SA Petroleum Co. (Petrofina group), Ploesti and Bucarest, Romania, 1930-58; supply mgr. Greek State Refinery, Athens, 1958-60; with Petrogaz, Athens, 1960-83, dir., gen. mgr., 1965—, mng. dir., pres., 1984—; pres. Kosmogaz, Athens, 1980—, Mercantile SA, Athens, 1972—, Pyrogaz SA, Athens, 1968—, Petronaus, Athens, 1968—, Drago Fina, S.A., Athens, 1960—, Betofil SA, Athens, 1978-85; v.p. FINA Petroleum Co., Athens, 1978-86; pres. Greek Gas Distbn. Industries, Athens, 1972-86, hon. pres. 1986. Author: (novel) Marilena; also short stories and plays Served with arty., 1940-41. Mem. Assn. Greek Industries. Greek Orthodox. Clubs: Yacht of Greece; Athens; Tennis; Automobil. Lodge: Rotary (gov. 1982-83). Home: 7 Semitelou, 115 28 Athens Greece Office: 57 Acadimias St, 106 79 Athens Greece

VERGATI, BEN, advertising agency executive, writer; b. Dallas, Oct. 17, 1942; s. Benedict Vergati and Juanita Clara (Fincher) Hines; m. Marilee Johnson, Mar. 17, 1979; children:, Michael Benjamin, Eric Trenton. Student N. Tex. State U., Denton, 1965-69. Copywriter, The Bloom Agy., 1975-76, Crume & Assocs., Inc., Dallas, 1972-75, copy chief, 1976-77, v.p., creative dir., 1977-79, sr. v.p., creative dir., 1979-82, exec. v.p., exec. creative dir. Crume & Assocs, Dallas, 1982-85; founder, pres. Vergati & Assocs, Duncanville, Tex., 1986—; judge CLIO awards show, 1979, regional ADDY awards, 1983; cons. E. Tex. State U.; lectr. in field. Bd. dirs. Hope Cottage, Dallas, 1985—, (v.p. 1986) Animal Rehab. Ctr., Midlothian, Tex., 1983-85. Recipient 2 CLIO statuette awards 10 CLIO awards of excellence, 7 N.Y. Art Dirs. Club awards of excellence; 5 Nat. ADDY awards, 6 regional ADDY Gold medals, 5 regional ADDY Merit medals, 2 Obie awards, 5 N.Y. One Show awards of excellence, 1 Advt. Club ANDY award of Excellence, 5 ANDY awards of distinction, 3 Communications Arts awards of excellence, 27 Dallas Advt. League gold medals, 9 Dallas Advt. League Silver medals and 7 Bronze medals, 2 Dallas Soc. Visual Communications gold medals, 1 silver, 2 bronze Internat. Advt. Festival N.Y. Gold medal, Newspaper Advt. Bur. Athena award of Excellence; 9 Nat. Advt. Agy. Network Gold medals, 13 silver medals, 10 bronze medals; named Print Copywiter of SW Adweek Mag., 1988; numerous others. Mem. Dallas Soc. Visual Communications. Presbyterian. Office: Vergati & Assocs 931 Springwood Ln Duncanville TX 75137

VERGER, FERNAND HENRI, educator, scientific researcher; b. Paris, Apr. 24, 1929; s. Pierre Fernand and Henriette (Decourt) V.; m. Anne Marie Richez, Nov. 6, 1954; children: Françoise, Pierre. Licence, Sorbonne, 1950, Diplôme d'Etudes Supérieures, 1951, Doctorat d'Etat, 1969; Doctorat en Géographie, Faculté des Lettres, Poitiers, 1960. Attaché de recherches, Centre National de la Recherche Scientifique, Paris, 1956-59; chef de travaux, Université, Poitiers, France, 1959-61; maître asst. Ecole Normale Supérieure, Montrouge, France, 1961-69, prof., 1969—; dir. Ecole Pratique des Hautes Etudes, Sorbonne, Paris, 1966—; prin. investigator NASA, 1972-73, 75-77. Author: Marais et Wadden du Littoral Français, 1969; L'Observation de la Terre par les Satellites, 1982. Lauréat Academie des Sciences, Paris, 1973; recipient prix Fournier Société de Géographie, Paris, 1969. Mem. Comité National de la Recherche Scientifique (pres. 1975-80, 87—), Action Thematique Programmée Télédétection Spatiale (pres. 1979-85), Conseil d'Administration G.I.P. Reclus (pres. 1985—). Office: Ecole Normale Superieure, 45 Rue D Ulm, 75230 Paris Cedex 05 France

VERHAAREN, HAROLD CARL, lawyer; b. Salt Lake City, Apr. 11, 1938; m. Cynthia Mary Hughes, Nov. 25, 1964; children—Scott Harold, Steven Robert, Jill, Brent Carl, Brian Hughes. J.D., U. Utah, 1965. Bar: Utah 1965, U.S. Supreme Ct. 1978. Law clk. to chief justice Utah Supreme Ct., 1964-65; pres., bd. dirs. Mazuran, Verhaaren & Hayes, P.C., Salt Lake City; judge pro tem Small Claims Ct. Salt Lake County, 1978—. Chmn. Mt. Olympus Planning Dist., 1971-85; active Boy Scouts Am., 1967—. Recipient Silver Beaver award Boy Scouts Am. Mem. ABA, Utah Bar Assn., Salt Lake County Bar Assn., Am. Judicature Soc., Am. Arbitration Assn., Delta Theta Phi, Phi Kappa Phi, Phi Eta Sigma. Mormon. Office: 260 Parkview Plaza 2180 S 1300 E Salt Lake City UT 84106

VERHAGEN, PATRICK, cement company executive; b. Brussels, Belgium, Sept. 8, 1947; s. Paul and Vera (Harthoorn) V.; m. Luz Elena Iturralde Castello, July 26, 1980; children: Nicole, Harold. Diploma in Engring., Fed. Inst. Tech., Zurich, Switzerland, 1974; program Mgmt. Devel., Harvard U., 1982. Trainee Dundee Cement Co., 1974; cons. Holderbank Mgmt. and Cons. Ltd., Switzerland, 1975, 77, 80, sr. mgmt. cons., 1985; asst. plant mgr. Cementos Lima SA, Peru, 1976-77; v.p. ops. Cementos Selva Alegre C.E.M., Ecuador, 1978-79, Cementos Caribe C.A., Venezuela, 1981-84; sr. v.p. ops. Ciments D'Obourg SA, Mons, Belgium, 1986—; bd. dirs. Cobex S.A., Mons, Obourg Calcaire, Tournai, Belgium, Ciments D'Haccourt, Liège, Obourg Fin. S.A., Luxembourg. Mem. Centre Nat. Recherches Sci. et Tech. Pour L'Ind. Cim. (v.p. 1987), Delegation Patronale a la Commn. Paritaire, Com. Etudes Tech. Ind. Ciment. Club: Royal Golf du Hainaut (Mons). Office: Ciments D Obourg SA, Rue des Fabriques 2, B-7048 Mons, Hainaut Belgium

VERHOFSTADT, GUY MAURICE MARIE-LOUISE, government official Belgium; b. Dendermonde, Belgium, Nov. 4, 1953; s. Marcel and Gaby V.; m. Dominique Verkindere. Degree, Royal Sec. Mod. Sch., Gent, Belgium, 1970; licenciate in law, State U. Gent, 1975. Pres. LVSV, Gent, 1972-79; town concillor City of Gent, 1976-82; polit. sec. PVV, Brussels, 1977-82; 1st substitute Belgium Parliament - Chamber Reps., Brussels, 1978-82; pres. PVV-Jouth, Brussels, 1979-82, PVV, Brussels, 1982-85; mem. Belgium Parliament - Chamber Reps., 1985—; vice-prime minister Belgium, Brussels, 1985-88. Office: Cabinet, Law Rd 26, 1040 Brussels Belgium

VERIE, CHRISTIAN JACQUES, physicist, educator; b. Marrakech, Morocco, June 17, 1935; s. Pierre Arthur and Simone Rose (Husser) V.; m. Martine Nataf, Dec. 29, 1970; 1 son, Boris. M.S. in Physics, Sorbonne U., Paris, 1959; Ph.D. in Solid State Physics, Orsay U., Paris, 1963, Doctorat d'Etat, 1967. Mem. staff Centre National de la Recherche Scientifique, 1962—; maitre de recherche lab. solid state physics, Meudon-Bellevue (Paris), 1972-82; on sabbatical MIT, 1980-81; dir. Lab. Solid State Physics and Solar Energy, Valbonne (Nice), France, 1982—, 1st. class dir. research, 1987 ; prof. U. Nice; cons. in field. Served with French Army, 1963-64. Mem. French Soc. Physics, Am. Phys. Soc. Roman Catholic. Author, patentee in field. Home: 12 BD Marechal Leclerc, 06600 Antibes France Office: CNRS, Rue B Gregory Parc Sophia Antipolis, 06560 Valbonne France

VERIGAN, TERRENCE, marketing company executive, marketing and operations consultant; b. Seattle, May 18, 1948; s. Donald Calvin and Mary (Voigt) V.; m. Kathy Jeannette Higgins, Aug. 28, 1970. BA, U. New Orleans, 1971, postgrad., 1972-74; postgrad. Law Sch. Loyola U., New Orleans, 1980-82. Tchr., Jefferson Parish Schs., Metairie, La., 1971-75; sr. sales rep. Xerox Corp., Metairie, 1975-79; owner Terry Verigan, Cons., Metairie, 1979-83; market analyst AT&T, Metairie, 1983-84, sales mgr., 1984-86; dir. mktg., SE Health Plan, Baton Rouge, 1986-87, Delta Health, New Orleans, 1987-88; owner, Mktg. Mgmt. Resources, 1987—; spl. lectr. Inst. Politics Loyola U., New Orleans, 1979, La. Close Up Found., 1983. Rep. Dist. 8 Jefferson Parish Pub. Sch. Bd., Metairie, 1977-82, chmn. exec. com., 1979, chmn. ins. com., 1980, v.p., 1981; mem. Jefferson Parish exec. com. Republican Party of La., 1977-83. Recipient Community Leader of the Yr. award U. New Orleans, 1981; award of Excellence for Br. Leadership AT&T, 1983; Mgmt. Excellence award AT&T, 1984; Inst. Politics Loyola U., fellow, 1975. Mem. New Orleans C. of C., Omicron Delta Kappa, Kappa Delta Pi (pres. 1969-70), Phi Delta Kappa. Roman Catholic. Club: Plimsoll. Home and Office: Mktg Mgmt Resources 4009 W Esplanade Ave Metairie LA 70002

VERILHAC, DIDIER ROBERT, stationery manufacturing executive; b. Le Coteau, France, Jan. 11, 1944; s. Henri and Marie (Lombard) V.; m. Marie Magdeleine Cardinet; children: Stephanie, Christophe, Carole. Degree in engring., license es sci., Inst. Genie Chimique, Faculte des Sci., Toulouse, France, 1967; grad. mgmt. program, Inst. d'Adminstrn. des Enterprises, Paris, 1968. Chem. engr. Procon Inc. (U.O.P.), Paris, Chgo., 1969-69; comml. mgr. Papeteries Verilhac Freres, Vizille, France, 1979—. Office: Papeteries Verilhac Freres, F38220 Vizille France

VERITY, C. WILLIAM, JR., federal official; b. Middletown, Ohio, Jan. 26, 1917; m. Margaret Wymond; 3 children. BA, Yale U., 1939. Various mgmt. positions 1940-65; pres., chief exec. officer Armco Inc., Middletown, 1965-71, 72-82; chmn. U.S. C. of C., 1980-81, Presdl. Task Force on Pvt. Initiatives, Washington, 1981-83; co-chmn. U.S.-U.S.S.R. Trade and Econ. Council, 1977-84; mem. Presdl. Adv. Council on Pvt. Sect or Initiatives, 1983—; sec. Dept. of Commerce, Washington, 1987—. Served with USN, 1942-46. Office: Dept of Commerce 14th & Constitution Ave NW Washington DC 20230

VERJAT, ALAIN MASSMANN, language educator; b. Paris, Nov. 1, 1943; s. Jacques and Janine (Massmann) V.; m. Teresa Rey Canales, Aug. 2, 1966; children: Natalia, Sara. Licentiate, U. Barcelona, Spain, 1970, PhD, 1973. Tchr. secondary sch. Barcelona schs., 1974-76; prof. Romance languages, headmaster U. Autònoma Barcelona, Bellaterra, Spain, 1976-81; headmaster U. Barcelona, 1981—; dir dept. Romance languages U. Barcelona, 1982-87; Groupe of the Imaginary Researcher, 1978-87. Contbr. articles to scholarly jours. Mem. Ctr. Researches Imaginarye, Soc. Études Romantiques, Soc. Littératures ComparÉes, Assn. Profs. Filologia Francesa (pres. 1982—). Home: Peasseig de la Creu 14, 08190 Sant Cugat Del Valles Spain Office: U Barcelona, Dept Filologia Romanica, Gran Via de les Cortes, 08007 Barcelona Spain

VERMEERSCH, PIERRE MARIE, ancient history, physical geography educator; b. Gent, Belgium, Mar. 31, 1938; s. Joseph Vermeersch and Marie Dossche. PhB, Cath. U., Leuven, Belgium, 1958, DSc in Geography, 1971; student in theology, Cath. Sem., Gent, 1963. Ordained priest Roman Cath. Ch., 1963. Research assoc. Nat. Fund Sci. Research, Belgium, 1965-75; assoc. prof. Cath. U., Leuven, 1975-81, prof., 1981—, dir. Lab. for Prehistory, 1977—; dir. Belgian Middle Egypt Prehist. Project, 1975. Author: L'Elkabien, 1979. Home: Justus Lipsius Coll, Minderbroedersstraat 15, B-3000 Leuven Belgium Office: Lab for Prehistory, Redingenstraat 15 bis, B-3000 Leuven Belgium

VERMEERSCH, RAPHAEL FRANCOIS, stock brokerage company executive; b. Petegem, Belgium, Jan. 7, 1942; s. Louis Emmanuel and Irene (Verhougstracte) V.; m. Agnes Lejeune, Aug 2, 1964; 1 child, Frank. Student, pub. schs., Ghent, Belegium. Electrician Regie Telegraphe Telephone, Brussels, 1960-61, technician, 1962-65, supr., 1966-70; engr. lease ITT World Communications, Brussels, 1970-76; asst. v.p. Drexel Burnham Lambert, Brussels, 1976-78, v.p., 1979-81, corp. v.p. internat. communications, 1982—. Served with Belgian Army, 1959-60. Mem. Telecommunications Mgrs. Assn. Belgium (asst. v.p. 1985). Offcie: Drexel Burnham Lambert, 5 Blve de L'Empereur, 1000 Brussels Belgium

VERMEULE, CORNELIUS CLARKSON, III, museum curator; b. Orange, N.J., Aug. 10, 1925; s. Cornelius Clarkson, Jr. and Catherine Sayre (Comstock) V.; m. Emily Dickinson Townsend, Feb. 2, 1957; children—Emily D. Blake, Cornelius Adrian Comstock. Grad., Pomfret Sch., 1943; A.B., Harvard, 1949, M.A., 1951; Ph.D., U. London, Eng., 1953. Instr. fine arts, then asst. prof. U. Mich., 1953-55; asst. prof. classical archaeology Bryn Mawr (Pa.) Coll., 1955-57; curator classical art Mus. Fine Arts, Boston, 1957—; acting dir. Mus. Fine Arts, 1972-73; assoc. curator coins Mass. Hist. Soc., 1965-71, curator, 1971—; lectr. fine arts Smith Coll., 1960-64, Boston U., Harvard, Wellesley Coll.; vis. prof. Yale, 1969-70, 72-73; Thomas Spencer Jerome lectr. U. Mich., 1975-76; vis. prof. Boston Coll., 1978—; pres. Internat. Com. to Save Jewish Catacombs of Italy, 1980-84, chmn., 1984—. Author: (with N. Jacobs) Japanese Coinage, 1948, 2d edit., 1972, Bibliography of Applied Numismatics, 1956, The Goddess Roma, 1959, 2d edit., 1974, Dal Pozzo-Albani Drawings, 1960, European Art and the Classical Past, 1964, Drawings at Windsor Castle, 1966, Roman Imperial Art in Greece and Asia Minor, 1968, Polykleitos, 1969, Numismatic Art in America, 1971, (with M. Comstock) Greek Etruscan and Roman Bronzes, 1972, (with N. Neuerburg) Catalogue of the Ancient Art in the J. Paul Getty Museum, 1973, Greek and Roman Sculpture in Gold and Silver, 1974, Greek and Roman Cyprus, 1976, (with M. Comstock) Sculpture in Stone, 1976, Greek Sculpture and Roman Taste, 1977, Roman Art: Early Republic to Late Empire, 1978, (with A Herrmann) The Ernest Brummer Collections, Vol. II, 1979, Greek Art: Socrates to Sulla, 1980, The Jewish Experience in Roman Art, 1981, Masterpieces of Greek and Roman Sculpture in America, 1982, Greek Art: Prehistoric to Perikles, 1982, Numismatic Studies, 1983, Alexander the Great Conquers Rome, 1985, The Cult Images of Imperial Rome, 1986, Numismatic Art of the Greek Imperial World, 1987, Philatelic Art in America, 1987. Trustee Cardinal Spellman Philatelic Mus., 1980—. Served to 1st lt. AUS, 1943-47. Recipient Bicentennial medal Boston Coll., 1976; Fulbright fellow, 1951-53; Guggenheim fellow, 1968. Fellow Am. Numis. Soc. (life), Royal Numis. Soc., Soc. Antiquaries, Am. Acad. Arts and Scis.; mem. Coll. Art Assn. (life), Archaeol. Inst. Am. (life), German Archaeol. Inst., Holland Soc. N.Y., Colonial Lords of Manors in Am. Republican. Episcopalian. Club: Tavern (medalist 1986) (Boston). Home: 47 Coolidge Hill Rd Cambridge MA 02138 Office: Museum Fine Arts Boston MA 02115

VERMILYEA, ROSS ORRIN, management consultant; b. Winnipeg, Man., Can., July 12, 1945; s. Orrin H. and Eleanor M. (Ross) V.; m. Estelle N. Gawley, Aug. 14, 1970;. BSc in Elec. Engring., U. Man., 1967; MBA, U. Western Ont., London, 1972. Registered profl. engr.; cert. mgmt. cons. Project engr. Can. Gen. Electric Co., Montreal, Que., 1967-70; market analyst elec. div. Canron Ltd., Montreal, 1972-75; asst. to pres. Brown Boveri Can. Ltd., Montreal, 1975-77; mgr. mktg. Can. Kenworth Co., Ottawa, Ont., 1977-82; pres. Vermilyea & Assocs., Toronto, Ont., 1982—. Inventor electronic device. Mem. Inst. Cert. Mgmt. Cons. Ont., Assn. Profl. Engrs. Ont., Indsl. Mktg. Research Assn. Can., Bus. Profl. Advt. Assn. (chpt. pres. 1977-78). Office: Vermilyea & Assocs, 55 University Ave Suite 309, Toronto, ON Canada M5J 2H7

VERNICOS, GEORGE, economist, city official; b. Athens, Feb. 11, 1950; s. Alexander and Marina V. m. Sept. 30, 1974 (div. Apr. 1980); 1 child, Marina. M.A., U. Athens, 1974; postgrad. U. London, 1975. Dir., ptnr. Vernicos Yachts SA, Athens, 1976-81, pres., 1981—; v.p. Vernicos Shipping Co. Ltd., Athens, 1979—. Bd. dirs. Hellenic Register Shipping, 1983—, Bus. Reconstrn. Authority Greece, 1984—; leader Anti-dictator Student Movement Greece, 1971-74; sec. gen. Greek European Movement of Youth, 1969-72; sec. gen. Hellenic Democratic Youth, 1975-77; mem. Athens City Council, 1982—; pres. Chagiconstas Orphanage Inst., Athens, 1986—. Mem. Greek Yacht Brokers and Cons. Assn. (sec. gen. 1982—), Panhellenic Assn. Boat Importers (sec. gen. 1983—), Pub. Material Mgmt. Orgn. (bd. dirs. 1982-85), Hellenic Chamber of Shipping (bd. dirs. 1984—). Greek Orthodox. Office: Vernicos Yacht, 12 Diadochou Pavlou, 16675 Athens Greece

VERNICOS, NICOLAS A., shipping company executive; b. Sifnos, Cyclades, Greece, Apr. 2, 1945; s. Alexander N. and Marina A. (Kanaki) V.; m. Iro P Vetopoulos, Jan. 12, 1969 (div. 1971); m. Barbara Stratos, Dec. 4, 1977; children: Marina Alexia, Sofia, Irini Amalia. Degree, Athens Coll., Psychico, Greece, 1964; MSc in Econs., Athens Grad. Sch. Econs., 1970. Dir. N.E. Vernicos Shipping Co., Ltd., Piraeus, Greece, 1970—, Vernicos Yachts S.Am., Glyfada, Greece, 1977—; pres. Vernicos Maritime S.Am., Piraeus, Greece, 1977—; dir.— Hellenic Shipyards S.Am., Skaramanga, Greece, 1985—; mem. Greek delegation shipping com. UN Conf. on Trade and Devel., Geneva, 1984—, OECD, Paris, 1984—. Mem. Hellenci Chamber Shipping (exec. com. 1980—), Piraeus Chamber Commerce and Industry (bd. dirs. 1986—). Club: Piraeus Marine (v.p. 1981-86). Home: Tritonos 1, 16671 Kavouri Greece Office: Vernicos Maritime Co Ltd, 35-39 Akti Miaouli, 18510 Piraeus Greece

VERNICOS-EUGENIDES, NICOLAS MICHEL, shipping company executive; b. Sifnos, Greece, Apr. 14, 1920; came to Switzerland, 1954; s. Michel Nicolas and Kalliopi (Decavallas) Vernicos. B.Econs., U. Gothenburg (Sweden), 1941. Pres., Home Lines, Inc., Panama, 1954—, Home Lines Inc., Monrovia, Liberia, 1981—; gen. mgr. Société de Gestion Evge, La Tour de Peilz, Switzerland, 1954—; pres. TransSuez, Inc., Monrovia, 1976—, Scandinavian Near East Agys. Greece, 1980—; mem. Lloyd's Underwriters, 1971—; mem. Greek com. Germanische Lloyd, 1979—; mem. Greek com. Bur. Veritas, 1974—. Chmn. bd. dirs. Eugenides Found., Athens, 1981—; mem. com. Found. Coudenhove-Kalergi, Lausanne, Switzerland, 1982—. Decorated comdr. Royal Order of Phoenix (Greece), 1963; Order of Vasa 1st class (Sweden), 1958; comdr. Order of Lion of Finland, 1958; grand officer Order of Merit (Italy), 1964; Cross of Merit (Fed. Republic of Germany), 1960, Cross of Merit 1st class (Lower Saxony). Greek Orthodox. Office: Société de Gestion Evge, 74 Route de St Maur, 1814 La Tour de Peilz Switzerland

VERNON, ARTHUR E., pharmacist; b. Ashland, Ohio, Sept. 21, 1944; m. Susan Elberty, 1967; children: Elizabeth Anne, Andrew Elberty. BS in Pharmacy, Ohio No. U., 1967, postgrad., 1967-84. Registered pharmacist, Ohio. Co-owner Reynolds Drugs, Orrville, Ohio, 1967—. Com. mem. Trinity United Meth. Ch., 1967-84; active Orrville United Way, 1970-84; pres. Orrville Hist. Mus., 1974-85; bd. dirs. Orrville C. of C., 1970—, Orrville YMCA, Heart Health Wayne County, 1988; active Orrville Revitalization Campaign; mem. Orville Shade Tree Commn., Orrville All-Weather Track Com., 1986-88, Orrville Devel. Council, 1987—. Mem. Am. Pharm. Assn., Ohio State Pharm. Assn., Wayne Pharm. Assn. (pres.), Nat. Woodcarvers Club. Clubs: U.C. Investment, Farnsworth Trout. Lodge: Internat. Orgn. Odd Fellows. Avocations: conservation, reforestation for wildlife, ecology, art, carving. Home: 1185 N Crownhill Rd Orrville OH 44667 Office: 120 N Main St Orrville OH 44667

VERNON, DARRYL MITCHELL, lawyer; b. N.Y.C., May 4, 1956; s. Leonard and Joyce (Davidson) V.; m. Lauren Lynn Bernstein, Aug. 21, 1982. BA in Math., Tufts U., 1978; JD, Yeshiva U., 1981. Bar: N.Y. 1982, U.S. Dist. Ct. (so. and ea. dists.) N.Y. 1982, U.S. Ct. Appeals (2d cir.) 1987. Assoc. Hochberg & Greenberg, N.Y.C., 1981-82; ptnr. Greenberg & Vernon, N.Y.C., 1982-83; pres. Law Offices of Darryl M. Vernon, N.Y.C., 1983—. Samuel Belkin scholar Yeshiva U., 1979. Mem. ABA (young lawyers div., tax sect., exec. com. animal rights sect. 1985—, animal law report, urban, state and local govt. law sect.), N.Y. State Bar Assn. (real property law sect.), Assn. of Bar of City of N.Y. (real property legis. com. 1985—), Am. Soc. for Prevention of Cruelty to Animals, Animal Legal Def. Fund, N.Y. Lawyers Basketball League. Jewish. Home: 115 Fourth Ave New York NY 10003 Office: 261 Madison Ave New York NY 10016

VERNON, LAWRENCE GORDON, librarian; b. Belize, Belize, May 19, 1937; s. Angus Vernon and Anna Drucilla (Elliott) Vernon Gabourel; m. Crystal Yvonne Gibson, July 18, 1959; children—Marlon, Dylan, Karen. Assoc., Brit. Library Assn. Corr. Course, London, 1959-63. Library asst. Nat. Library Service, Belize, 1956-58, jr. asst. librarian, 1958-66, asst. librarian, 1966-76, sr. librarian, 1976-78, chief librarian, 1978—. Co-author: Among my Souvenirs, 1966. Sec. bd. govs. Excelsior Community High Sch., Belize City, Belize, 1979; vice-chmn. Council of Vol. Social Services, 1986; chmn. Belize Scholarship Com., 1983. Mem. Belize Library Assn. (treas. 1978). Methodist.

VERNON, SIDNEY, physician, publisher, author; b. N.Y.C., Nov. 12, 1906; s. Hyman and Lillian (Zonenberg) V.; m. Rosalie Silverstein, (dec. Oct. 1983); children—Kenneth, Sheridan. B.S., CCNY, 1926; M.D., L.I. Coll. Hosp., 1930. Intern, Bellevue Hosp., N.Y.C., 1930-31; resident Backus Hosp., Norwich, Conn., 1931-32; gen. practice medicine, Willimantic, Conn., 1932-41, 1952—; commd. 1st lt. U.S. Army, 1941, advanced through grades to lt. col., 1946; med. officer U.S. Army, 1941-50; chief surgery Arrowhead, Two Harbor Hosp., Minn., 1950-51; chief surgeon Army Hosp., Waltham, Mass., 1947, Ft. Monmouth, N.J., 1948-49, Air Force Hosp., Hempstead, N.Y., 1950 Author: How to Understand People, 1982; Reach for Charisma, 1984. Contbr. 75 articles to profl. jours. Decorated Bronze Star. Recipient Hon. Laymans award Community Assn. Health Phys. Edn. and Recreation. Fellow ACS, Internat. Coll. Surgery; mem. Am. Coll. Sports Medicine, AMA, Am. Bd, Abdominal Surgery (bd. govs.), Willimantic C. of C. (chmn. community council phys. fitness 1958-61), Am. Pain Soc., Internat. Assn. Pain., Inflammation Club Upjohn Pharm. Jewish. Lodge: B'nai Brith (pres. 1939-40).

VERONESI, UMBERTO, surgeon; b. Milan, Italy, Nov. 28, 1925; m. Susy Razon, Apr. 13, 1961; children—Paolo, Marco, Alberto, Pietro, Giulia, Silvia. Grad. Milan U., 1951. Dir. gen. Nat. Cancer Inst., Milan, 1975—; prof. pathology Perugia U. (Italy), from 1957; prof. surgery Milan U., from 1961; chmn. Melanoma Group, WHO, Milan, 1967. Author: Surgical Anatomy, 1961; Clinical Oncology, 1973; dir. Jour. Clin. and Exptl. Oncology. Recipient Nat. award Am. Cancer Soc., 1977, Gold medal Italian Ministry Health, 1978, Lucy Wortham James Clin. Research award Soc. Surg. Oncology, 1982. Mem. Internat. Union Against Cancer (pres. 1978-82), European Orgn. for Research in Cancer Treatment (pres. 1985). Office: Istituto Nazionale Tumori, Via Venezian 1, 20133 Milan Italy

VEROUGSTRAETE, JEAN MARIE, paper company executive; b. Ghent, Belgium, July 3, 1933; married; children: Anne, Regine, Chantal. Grad. in Law, State U. Ghent, 1955. With personnel services dept. Union des Papeteries, La Hulpe, Belgium, 1958-60; sec. gen. Papeteries du Pont-de-Warche, Malmédy, Belgium, 1960-65, S.A. Intermills and subs., La Hulpe, 1966-76; mng. dir. S.A. Editions and Imprimerie Duculot, Gembloux, Belgium, 1977—; pres., chmn. S.A. Intermills (now SOFIPAC SA), La Hulpe, 1980—. Served as res. officer Belgian mil., 1956-58. Home: Rue de Moriensart 4, 1341 Ceroux Mousty Belgium Office: SOFIPAC SA, rue François Dubois 2, 1310 La Hulpe Belgium

VERRAL, CHARLES SPAIN, author; b. Highfield, Ont., Can., Nov. 7, 1904; s. George William and Kate Elizabeth (Peacocke) V.; grad. Upper Can. Coll., 1923; student Ont. Coll. Art, Toronto, 1923-26; m. Jean Willis Mithoefer, Mar. 19, 1932; 1 son, Charles Spain. Comml. artist, N.Y.C., 1927-30; editor, art dir. Clayton Publs., N.Y.C., 1930-35; free-lance writer, 1935-60; writer, asso. editor Golden Press Dictionary, N.Y.C., 1960-61; writer, staff editor Harper Ency. Sci., N.Y.C., 1961-62; writer, editor Reader's Digest Assn., N.Y.C., 1962-74; free-lance writer, 1974—; sport columnist Youngperson, illustrated news jour., 1983—; co-author: Street and Smith Publs. mag. series, Bill Barnes (under name George L. Eaton), 1934-43; continuity writer United Features Syndicate newspaper strip Hap Hopper, 1941-47; radio script writer Mandrake the Magician, 1940-41. Mem. Authors Guild, Arts and Letters Club Toronto, Mystery Writers Am. Episcopalian. Author: Captain of the Ice, 1953; Champion of the Court, 1954; Mighty Men of Baseball, 1955; Wonderful World Series, 1956; Mystery of the Missing Message, 1959; Winning Quarterback, 1960; Jets, 1962; Robert Goddard, Father Space Age, 1963; Babe Ruth, Sultan of Swat, 1976; Casey Stengel, Baseball's Great Manager, 1978; others; editor: True Stories of Great Escapes, 1977; Treasury of Great Books, 1980; contbr. articles and short stories to numerous mags. and anthologies. Home and Office: 79 Jane St New York NY 10014

VERRETT, SHIRLEY, soprano; b. New Orleans, May 31, 1931; d. Leon Solomon and Elvira Sugustine (Harris) V.; m. Louis Frank LoMonaco, Dec. 10, 1963; 1 dau., Francesca. A.A., Ventura (Calif.) Coll., 1951; diploma in voice (scholarship 1956-61), Juilliard Sch. Music, 1961; Mus.D. (hon.), Coll. Holy Cross, Mass., 1978. mem. adv. bd. Opera Ebony. Recital debut Town Hall, N.Y.C., 1958; appeared as Irina in Lost in the Stars, 1958; orchestral debut Phila. Orch., 1960; operatic debut in Carmen, Festival of Two Worlds, Spoleto, Italy, 1962; debuts with Bolshoi Opera, Moscow, 1963, N.Y.C. Opera, 1964, Royal Opera, Covent Garden, 1966, Maggio Fiorentino, Florence, 1967, Met. Opera, 1968, Teatro San Carlos, Naples, 1968, Dallas Civic Opera, 1969, La Scala, 1970, Vienna State Opera, 1970, San Francisco Opera, 1972, Paris Opera, 1973, Opera Co. Boston, 1976; guest appearances with all major U.S. symphony orchs.; toured Eastern Europe and Greece with La Scala chorus and orch., 1981; TV debut on Ed Sullivan Show, 1963; TV performances include: Great Performances series, live performance of Macbeth at La Scala; rec. artist, RCA, Columbia, ABC (Westminster), Angel Everest, Kapp and Deutsche Grammophon. voice student with John Charles Thomas, Lotte Lehmann. Recipient Marian Anderson award, 1955, Nat. Fedn. Music Clubs award, 1961, Walter Naumberg award, 1958, Blanche Thebom award, 1960; John Hay Whitney fellow, 1959; Ford Found. fellow, 1962-63; Martha Baird Rockefeller Aid to Music Fund fellow, 1959-61; grantee William Matteus Sullivan Fund, 1959; grantee Berkshire Music Opera, 1956; recipient Achievement award Ventura Coll., 1963, Achievement award N.Y. chpt. Albert Einstein Coll. Medicine, 1975; 2 plaques Los Angeles Sentinel Newspaper, 1960; plaque Peninsula Music Festival, 1963; Los Angeles Times Woman of Yr. award, 1969. Mem. Mu Phi Epsilon. Address: care Columbia Artists Mgmt Inc 165 W 57th St New York NY 10019 *

VERRILL, CHARLES OWEN, JR., lawyer; b. Biddeford, Maine, Sept. 30, 1937; s. Charles Owen and Elizabeth (Handy) V.; m. Mary Ann Blanchard, Aug. 13, 1960; children: Martha Anne, Edward Blanchard, Ethan Christopher, Elizabeth Handy, Matthew Lawton, Peter Goldthwait. AB, Tufts U., 1959; LLB, Duke U., 1962. Bar: D.C. 1962. Assoc. Weaver & Glassie, 1962-64; assoc. Barco, Cook, Patton & Blow, 1964-66, ptnr., 1967; ptnr. Patton, Boggs & Blow, 1967-84, Wiley, Rein and Fielding, Washington, 1984—; lectr. Duke Law Sch., 1970-73; adj. prof. internat. trade law Georgetown U. Law Ctr., Washington, 1978—; conf. chmn. The Future of the Internat. Steel Industry, Bellagio, Italy, 1984, 87, 88, The U.S. Agenda for the Uruguay Round, Airlie House, Warenton, Va., 1986, The Polish Joint Venture Law, Cracow, Poland, 1987. Local dir. Tufts U. Ann. Fund, 1965-69; mem. Duke Law Alumni Council, 1972-75; trustee Internat. Law Inst., 1981—, chmn. bd. trustees, 1983-87. Recipient Service citation Tufts U. Alumni Assn., 1968. Mem. ABA, D.C. Bar Assn., Order of Coif, Theta Delta Chi, Phi Delta Phi. Clubs: Metropolitan (Washington); Tarratine (Dark Harbor, Maine); Chevy Chase (Md.). Home: 8205 Dunsinane Ct McLean VA 22101 Office: 1776 K St NW Washington DC 20006

VERRILL, F. GLENN, advertising executive; b. N.Y.C., Dec. 17, 1923; s. Ralph Francis and Rose (Verner) V.; m. Jean Demar, Aug. 25, 1946; children: Gary, Joan. A.B., Adelphi Coll., 1949; A.M., Harvard U., 1950. With Batten, Barton, Durstine & Osborn, Inc., 1952—, v.p., 1964; creative dir. Batten, Barton, Durstine & Osborn, Inc. (Burke Dowling Adams div.), Atlanta, 1965-70; exec. v.p., gen. mgr. Batten, Barton, Durstine & Osborn, Inc. (Burke Dowling Adams div.), 1970-71, pres., 1971—, also dir. parent co. Author: Advertising Procedure, 1983, rev. edit., 1986, 88. Mem. adv. bd. U. Ga.; bd. overseers Coll. Bus. Adminstrn., Ga. State U.; bd. dirs. Atlanta Humane Soc., pres., 1980-81; chmn. Advanced Advt. Inst. Atlanta, 1981; mem. Peabody award com., 1984—. Served with USAAF, 1943-46. Mem. Am. Assn. Advt. Agys. (nat. dir. 1973—). Episcopalian. Clubs: Atlanta Athletic, Cherokee, Harvard (Atlanta). Home: 2600 W Wesley Rd NW Atlanta GA 30327 Office: 3414 Peachtree Rd NW Atlanta GA 30326

VERRON, DOMINIQUE, pediatrician; b. Troyes, Aube, France, July 24, 1953; s. Jean and Yvette (Maillet) V.; m. Hugues Malbreil, Dec. 22, 1983. Degree in biochimie, 1971, MD, 1977. Practice medicine specializing in pediatrics Ramonville, St. Agne, France. Home and Office: 4 Chemin de Poucìquot, 31520 Ramonville, Saint Agne France

VERRY, WILLIAM ROBERT, mathematics researcher; b. Portland, Oreg., July 11, 1933; s. William Richard and Maurine Houser (Braden) V.; m. Bette Lee Ronspiess, Nov. 20, 1955 (div. 1981); children: William David, Sandra Kay Verry Londregan, Steven Bruce, Kenneth Scott; m. Jean Elizabeth Morrison, Oct. 16, 1982; step-children: Lucinda Jean Hale, Christine Carol Hale Fortner, Martha Jean Johnson, Brian Kenneth Lackey, Robert Morrison Lackey. BA, Reed Coll., 1955; BS, Portland State U., 1957; MA, Fresno State U., 1960; PhD, Ohio State U.-Columbus, 1972. Instr. chemistry Reedley (Calif.) Coll., 1957-60; ops. research analyst Naval Weapons Center, China Lake, Calif., 1960-63; ordnance engr. Honeywell Ordnance, Hopkins, Minn., 1963-64; sr. scientist Litton Industries, St. Paul., 1964-67; project mgr. Tech. Ops., Inc., Alexandria, Va., 1967-70; research assoc. Ohio State U., Columbus, 1970-72; prin. engr. Computer Sci. Corp., Falls Church, Va., 1972-77; mem. tech. staff MITRE Corp., Albuquerque, 1977-85; C3 program dir., assoc. prof. math. sci. Clemson U., S.C., 1985-87; mem. research staff Riverside Research Inst., Rosslyn, Va., 1987—. Founder, minister Christian Love Ctr. Mem. Ops. Research Soc. Am. Home: 6905 Valley Brook Dr Falls Church VA 22042-4024 Office: 1815 N Fort Myer Dr Arlington VA 22209

VERSACE, GIANNI, fashion designer; b. Reggion Calabria, Italy, Dec. 2, 1946; s. Antonio and Francesca Versace. Student, pub. sch., Italy. Designer: Complice, Genny and Callaghan, Milan, Italy, 1972-78; 1st signature women's wear collection, Milan, Italy, 1978—, menswear collection; founder 1st of 80 exclusive boutiques, Milan, 1979—; developer namesake fragrance, Italy, France, Switzerland, Austria and U.S.A., 1981—; costume desginer for ballets Leib und Leid, Josephlegende, Dyonisos, for opera Don Pasquale (La Scala), 1984. Recipient Golden Eye award for best fashion designer of women's wear for fall-winter, 1982-84, Cutty Sark award, 1983. Home: Via Della Spiga 25, 20121 Milan Italy Office: Gianni Versace Boutique 816 Madison Ave New York NY 10021 *

VERSCHUEREN, JEF (JOZEF FRANCISCA), linguist, researcher; b. Hoogstraten, Antwerp, Belgium, Apr. 30, 1952; s. Jacobus and Maria (Deckers) V.; m. Annie Maria Leo Verhaert, July 13, 1974; children:Jacob Martin Nicolaas, Rebecca Anna Maria, Xandra Kristien. Licentiate, U. Antwerp, 1974; MA in Linguistics, U. Calif.-Berkeley, 1976, PhD in Linguistics, 1980. Asst. U. Antwerp, 1974-75; research fellow Belgian Nat. Fund Sci. Research, Brussels, Antwerp, 1976-82, research assoc., 1982—; Author: What People Say They Do with Words, 1985; International News Reporting, 1985, A Comprehensive Bibliography of Pragmatics, 1987; editor Jour. Pragmatics, 1978-83, Pragmatics & Beyond, 1980—. Recipient Harkness fellow Commonwealth Fund N.Y., 1975-77. Mem. Linguistics Soc. Am., Societas Linguistica Europaea, Internat. Pragmatics Assn. (founder, gen. sec.). Home: Lange Leemstraat 297, B-2018 Antwerp Belgium Office: U Antwerp, Dept Germanic Philology, Universiteitsplein 1, B2610 Wilrijk Belgium

VERSCHUEREN, MAURITS VIKTOR, chemical company executive; b. Mechelen, Antwerp, Belgium, May 7, 1938; s. Frans and Elisabeth (De Vos) V.; m. Rosa Elisa De Vleeshouwer, Oct. 14, 1961; children—Christel, Ingrid. Grad. in Latin, math. H. Drievuldigheidscollege, Louvain, Belgium, 1951-57; student mgmt. techniques Ealing Tech. Coll., London, 1965-66; B.S. in Pub. Relations, European Inst. Mgmt., Geneva, 1977. Personnel adminstr. Procter & Gamble, Mechelen, Belgium, 1961-65; European corp. pub. relations Singer Bus. Machines, Nijmegen, Holland, 1965-73; European pub. relations and employee relations Addressograph Multigraph, Brussels, Belgium, 1973-77; corp. dir. strategic plans H.R.D. Cordis Dow, Miami, Fla., 1977-79, dir. European adminstrn. Cordis Dow, Brussels, Belgium, 1977—, also dir. Served to sgt. maj. Belgian Army, 1959-60. Mem. Profl. Union Pub. Relations Execs. and Cons., Belgian Ctr. Pub. Relations, European Ctr. Pub. Relations, Am. Soc. Tng. and Devel. Roman Catholic. Home: Augustijnenstraat 11/201, 2800 Mechelen, Antwerp Belgium Office: CD Medical Internat Ltd, 7 Ave Tedesco, 1160 Brussels Belgium

VERSIC, RONALD JAMES, research co. exec.; b. Dayton, Ohio, Oct. 19, 1942; s. Charles and Volunta Henrietta (Sherman) V.; B.S., U. Dayton, 1964; M.A., Johns Hopkins U., 1968; Ph.D., Ohio State U., 1969; m. Linda Joan Davies, June 11, 1966; children—Kathryn Clara, Paul Joseph. Sr. physicist GAF Corp., Binghamton, N.Y., 1969-70; program mgr. Systems Research Labs., Dayton, 1970-71; sr. scientist The Standard Register Co., Dayton, 1971-76; dir. research and devel. Monarch Marking Systems, Inc., Dayton, 1976-79; v.p. Ronald T. Dodge Co., Dayton, 1979—. Mem. Citizens' Housing Com., Oakwood, Ohio, 1978—, Precinct 1 Republican committeeman, Oakwood Ward, 1973-83. Named disting. outstanding lt. gov. Ohio Dist. Optimist Internat., 1975-76. Mem. Kettering-Moraine Mus. and Hist. Soc., Am. Chem. Soc., Oakwood Sister Cities, Soc. Photog. Scientists and Engrs., Am. Def. Preparedness Assn., Am. Inst. Physics, Am. Assn. Physics Tchrs., Am. Crystallographic Assn., AAAS, Air Force Assn. Ohio Acad. Sci., Newcomen Soc. N.Am., Inventors Council Dayton (founder and pres. 1982-84), Ohio Inventors Assn. (sec. 1985—), Nat. Congress Inventor Orgn. (exec. dir. 1985-87), Soc. Photo-Optical Instrumentation Engrs., Dayton Art Inst., Nat. Rifle Assn., Sigma Xi. Roman Catholic. Clubs: Johns Hopkins, Kettering Optimist (past pres.), Dayton Execs., Yugoslav of Greator Dayton, Engrs. of Dayton (bd. govs.), Walter P. Chrysler, Inc. Contbr. articles to profl. jours.; patentee in microencapsulation. Home: 1601 Shafor Blvd Dayton OH 45419 Office: PO Box 9488 Dayton OH 45409

VER STEEG, CLARENCE LESTER, historian, educator; b. Orange City, Iowa, Dec. 28, 1922; s. John A. and Annie (Vischer) Ver S.; m. Dorothy Ann De Vries, Dec. 24, 1943; 1 child, John Charles. AB, Morningside Coll., Sioux City, Iowa, 1943; MA, Columbia U., 1946, PhD, 1950. Lectr., then instr. history Columbia U., N.Y.C., 1946-50; mem. faculty Northwestern U., Evanston, Ill., 1950—, prof. history, 1959—, dean grad. sch., 1975-86; vis. lectr. Harvard U., 1959-60; mem. council Inst. Early Am. History and Culture, Williamsburg, Va., 1961-64, 68-72, chmn. exec. com., 1970-72; vis. mem. Inst. Advanced Study, Princeton, N.J., 1967-68; chmn. faculty com. to recommend Master Plan Higher Edn. in Ill., 1962-64; mem. Grad. Record Exam. Bd., 1981-86, chmn., 1984-86; bd. dirs. Ctr. for Research Libraries, 1980-85, Council Grad. Schs. in U.S., 1983-87; pres. Assn. Grad. Schs., 1984-85; mem. steering com. Grad. Research Project, Consortium on Financing Higher Edn., 1981-85; mem. working group on talent Nat. Acad. Scis., 1984-87; mem. Higher Edn. Policy Adv. Com. to OCLC, Online Computer Library Ctr., 1984-87. Author: Robert Morris, Revolutionary Financier, 1954, A True and Historical Narrative of the Colony of Georgia, 1960, The American People: Their History, 1961, The Formative Years, 1607-1763, 1964, (Brit. edit.), 1965, The Story of Our Country, 1965, (with others) Investigating Man's World, 6 vols., 1970, A People and a Nation, 1971, The Origins of a Southern Mosaic: Studies of Early Carolina and Georgia, 1975, World Cultures, 1977, American Spirit, 1982, rev. edit., 1985; editor: Great Issues in American History, From Settlement to Revolution 1584-1776, 1969; editorial cons.: Papers of Robert Morris, vols. I-VI, 1973—; contbr. articles to profl. jours. Served with USAAF, 1942-45. Decorated Air medal with 3 oak leaf clusters; 5 Battle Stars; Social Sci. Research Council fellow, 1948-49, George A. and Eliza Gardner Howard Found. fellow, 1954-55, Huntington Library research fellow, 1955, Am. Council Learned Socs. sr. fellow, 1958-59, Guggenheim fellow, 1964-65, NEH sr. fellow, 1973. Mem. AAUP, Am. Hist. Assn. (nominating com. 1965-68, chmn. 1967-68, Albert J. Beveridge prize 1952), Orgn. Am. Historians (editorial bd. Jour. Am. History 1968-72), So. Hist. Assn. (nominating com. 1970-72), Assn. Grad. Schs. in U.S. (pres. 1985). Presbyterian. Home: 2619 Ridge Ave Evanston IL 60201 Office: Northwestern U Evanston IL 60208

VERSTREKEN, LOUIS ARMAND, surgeon; b. Lier, Belgium, Aug. 23, 1929; s. Andre Jozef and Ria Anna (Plasschaert) V.; m. Therese Maria Boon, Jan 10, 1959; children: Andre, Jan, Annemarie, Paul, Wim. MD, Cath. U., Louvain, Belgium, 1954. Intern and resident in gen. surgery St. Rafael Clinic, Cath. U., Louvain, 1954-59; resident Royal Nat. Orthopedic Hosp., London, 1959; practice medicine specializing in surgery Lier, 1959—; instr. St. Elisabeth Nurses Sch., Lier, 1961—. Mem. Internat. Coll. Surgeons, Belgisch Chirurgisch Genootschap, Vlaamse Vereninging Gastroenterologie. Roman Catholic. Home: Bril 27, B2500 Lier Belgium

VERSTRINGHE, MARC EMILE SIDONIE, restauranteur, consultant; b. Bruges, Belgium, Dec. 18, 1934; came to Eng., 1957., s. Honore and Suzanne (Scherrens) V.; m. Carole Anita Finnimore, Nov. 4, 1967; children—Simon Marc, James Dominic. Diploma Ecole Moyenne, Saint Bernardus Inst., Knokke, Belgium, 1951; Advanced Mgmt. Program, Swansea U., Wales, 1972. Apprentice, Norfolk Hotel, Knokke, Zoute, Belgium, 1951-54; maitre d'hotel Lygon Arms, Broadway, Eng., 1957-59; mng. dir. Sutcliffe Catering Group, London, 1960-75; founder, chmn. Catering & Allied Services Internat., London and Amsterdam, 1975—; mem. bd. of ICA dir. de Blank Restaurants. Chmn. trustees and mgmt. com. Advanced Mgmt. Programme Internat., Oxford, Eng. Decorated chevalier Confrerie des Chevaliers du Tastevin, France, 1978. Fellow Inst. Dirs. London, Hotel Catering and Instnl. Mgmt. Assn.; mem. Guild of Sommeliers. Conservative. Clubs: Ampic. Lodge: Carbon. Office: Catering & Allied Services Internat Ltd, 12-15 Hanger Green, London W5 3EL, England

VERTUEL, MONIQUE MERYSE, physician; b. Alger, Algeria, July 27, 1950; arrived in France, 1962; d. Paul Gabriel and Louise (Scannapieco) V. MD, U. Montpellier, France, 1977. Intern Montpellier, 1976; resident psychiatric clinic, Quissac, France, 1977; gen. practice medicine Montpellier, 1978-87. Roman Catholic. Home and Office: Le Point 2000, Ave Villeneuve Angouleme, 34070 Montpellier, Languedoc France

VERWOERDT, ADRIAAN, psychiatrist; b. Voorburg, Netherlands, July 5, 1927; came to U.S., 1953, naturalized, 1958; s. Christopher and Juliana Margaretha (Busch) V.; children: Christopher Earl, Mark Adrian. M.D., Med. Sch. of Amsterdam, 1952. Diplomate: Pan Am. Med. Assn. Rotating intern Touro Infirmary, New Orleans, 1953-54; resident in psychiatry Duke U. Med. Center, Durham, N.C., 1954-55, 58-60; fellow in psychiat. research Duke U. Med. Center, 1960-61, asst. prof. psychiatry, 1963-67, assoc. prof., 1967-71, prof., 1971—, dir. geriatric psychiatry tng. program, 1966-78; dir. psychiat. residency tng. John Umstead Hosp., Butner, N.C., 1968-80; dir. Geropsychiatry Inst. (John Umstead Hosp.), Butner, N.C., 1980-86. Author: Communication with the Fatally Ill, 1966, Clinical Geropsychiatry, 1976; Contbr. articles to profl. jours. Served as capt. M.C. U.S. Army, 1955-57. NIMH Career Tchr. Tng. grantee, 1964-66. Fellow Am. Psychiat. Assn.; mem. Am. Geriatrics Soc., Am. Psychoanalytic Assn. Office: Duke U Med Center Durham NC 27710

VERZOSA, PURIFICACION LAHOZ, physician; b. Vigan, Luzon, Philippines, Sept. 27, 1914; d. Gaudencio and Anselma (Jaramillo) Lahoz; m. Candelario Villanueva Verzosa, Dec. 24, 1938; children: Fidelis, Mercedes, Angelica, Pilar, Candelario, Alexis, Roberto, Emmeline. Doctor of Medicine, Univ. Philippines, Manila, 1938; MA in Social Adminstrn., Philippine Women's U., Manila, 1951. Clin. fellow in orthomolecular psychiatry. Resident physician Vigan Christian Hosp., Philippines, 1938-40; med. officer Caliraya (Philippines) Hydroelectric Project Nat. Power Corp., 1939-41; sch. physician St. Theresa's Coll., St. Bridget Sch., Holy Spirit Convent, Quezon City, Philippines, 1955-72; practice medicine specializing in nutrition Quezon City, 1938—; indsl. physician Beta Constrn. Co., Philippine Contractors Assn., 1948-51; cons. Am. Biologics Inc.; speaker Philippine Rotary clubs. Subject of numerous articles in mags., newspapers; heard on radio and appeared on TV, 1978-79; contbr. articles to med. jours. Fellow Acad. Orthomolecular Medicine; mem. Nat. Research Council Philippines, Philippine Med. Assn., Philippine Med. Women's Assn., Philippine Bariatric Assn., Philippine Diabetic Soc., Acad. Orthomolecular Psychiatry, Calif. Orthomolecular Med. Soc., Internat. Acad. Preventive Medicine. Home and Office: 26 Ilang-Ilang St, Quezon City 3001, Philippines

VESCOVI, SELVI, pharmaceutical company executive; b. N.Y.C., June 14, 1930; s. Antonio and Desolina V.; B.S., Coll. William and Mary, 1951; m. Elma Pasquinelli, Oct. 17, 1954; children—Mark, James, Anne. Salesman, Upjohn Co., N.Y.C., 1954-59, sales supr.,1959-62, product mgr. U.S. domestic pharm. dir., 1962-65, mgr. mktg. planning internat. div., 1965-71, v.p. Europe, 1971-74, group v.p. Europe, 1975-77, exec. v.p. Upjohn Internat., Inc., Kalamazoo, Mich., 1978-85, pres., gen. mgr., 1985—, v.p. parent co., 1978—. Served to 2d lt. M.C., U.S. Army, 1951-53. Mem. Internat. Pharm. Mfrs. Assn. Republican. Roman Catholic. Office: Upjoh Internat 7000 Portage Rd Kalamazoo MI 49001

VESELY, ALEXANDER, consulting engineer, failure analysis consultant; b. Ladmovce, Czechoslovakia, Dec. 7, 1926; came to U.S., 1949; s. Joseph and Margaret (Lefkovitz) V.; m. Harriet Lee Roth, Aug. 11, 1957; 1 child, David Seth. BS in Civil Engring., Carnegie Mellon U., 1952; postgrad. John Marshall Law Sch., 1955; MS in Civil Engring., Ill. Inst. Tech., 1957. Registered profl. engr., Ind., W.Va.; registered land surveyor, Ind. Staff engr., Amoco Oil Co., Whiting, Ind., 1952-62; mgr. engring. Borg Warner Chem. Co., Washington, W.Va., 1962-77; assoc. engr. Mobil Research & Devel. Corp., Princeton, N.J., 1977-83; cons. engr. D.G. Peterson & Assocs. Inc., Greenfield, Mass., 1983-87; prin. Alexander Vesely & Assocs, 1987—; assoc. prof. Community Coll., Parkersburg, W.Va., 1965-67; chmn. Engrs. Week Com., Parkersburg, 1973. Pres. B'nai Israel Congregation, Parkersburg, 1976; bd. dirs. Bros. of Israel Congregation, Trenton, N.J., 1978-83. Served with U.S. Army, 1952-54. Carnegie Mellon U. scholar, 1950-52. Mem. Nat. Soc. Profl. Engrs. (pres. Parkersburg chpt. 1973-74), Am. Inst. Plant Engrs., ASCE, Tau Beta Pi (life). Republican. Jewish. Club: Scrabble, Chess, Bridge. Avocations: ping-pong; tennis; swimming. Home: 48 Hillcrest Dr Northampton MA 01060 Office: 48 Hillcrest Dr Northampton MA 01060

VESTAL, ADDISON ALEXANDER, estate manager; b. Whitewright, Tex., May 30, 1905; s. Rolla C. and Lora A. (Robinson) V.; B.A., Baylor U., 1927; M.S., Columbia, 1928; m. Lillian Cooper, July 3, 1937; children—William A., Gwen Vestal Farnham, Richard C. Estate mgr. R.K. Mellon & Sons, Pitts., 1938—; past chmn. bd. Blue Danube, Inc., Oil City, Pa. Pres., Ingomar (Pa.) Little League Baseball, 1945-81. Bd. dirs. Albert Schweitzer Hosp., Deschapelles, Haiti, Grant Found., Pitts.; trustee Laughlin Children's Center, Sewickley, Pa., 1957-87. Home: Sherwood Oaks Mars PA 16046 Office: 525 William Penn Pl Pittsburgh PA 15219

VESTAL, TOMMY RAY, lawyer; b. Shreveport, La., Sept. 19, 1939; s. Louie Wallace and Margaret (Golden) V.; m. Patricia Marie Blackwell, Jan. 24, 1981; children: Virginia Ann Yancy, John Wallace Vestal, Douglas William Yancy. BSME, U. Houston, 1967, JD, 1970. Bar: Tex. 1970, U.S. Patent Office 1972, U.S. Ct. Appeals (D.C. cir.) 1975. Patent atty. Am. Enka Corp., Asheville, N.C., 1970-71, Akzona Inc., Asheville, 1971-84, Akzo Am., Inc., Asheville, 1985-86; sr. patent atty. Fibers div. BASF Corp., Enka, N.C., 1986-87, div. patent counsel, 1987—. Mem. ABA, Am. Intellectual Property Law Assn., Carolina Patent, Trademark and Copyright Law Assn. (bd. dirs. 1983-85, 2d v.p. 1985-86, 1st v.p. 1986-87, pres. 1987-88), Asheville C. of C. (chmn. legal affairs com.), Phi Alpha Delta. Republican. Lutheran. Lodge: Kiwanis (pres. 1982). Home: 244 Bent Creek Ranch Rd Asheville NC 28806 Office: BASF Corp Div Fibers Sand Hill Rd Enka NC 28728

VESTERFELT, COLIN EDWARD ANSON, investment executive, consultant; b. Belleville, Ont., Can., May 23, 1947; came to U.S., 1965; s. James Peter and Evelyn Elizabeth (Anson) V.; m. Rondee Allene Holmes, Jan. 31, 1969; children—Kirste, Ian, Carly, Devra, C. Christian, Candice, Jamie. B.S., Brigham Young U., 1969, M.A., 1974, M.B.A., 1981; postgrad. U. Utah, Salt Lake City, 1978-79. Cert. psychologist, Alta. Counselor, Glenwood State Hosp., Iowa, 1971-73; counselor Latter Day Saints Social Services, Calgary, Alta., Can., 1973-74; program adminstr., psychologist Alta. Mental Health, Medicine Hat, Alta., 1974-78; pres. Can Am Assocs., Orem, Utah, 1978—; sr. fin. advisor Music Tchrs. Supply, Omaha, 1978—; supr. new product devel. and fin. analysis Timp Industries, Pleasant Grove, Utah, 1982-83. Author: (with Karen Ireland) Five Year Projection for Handicapped, 1978. Contbr. articles to profl. jours. Mem. exec. bd., treas. Alta. Union of Provincial Employees, Edmonton, 1976-78; co-chmn. Joint Consultation Com., chmn. Profl. Affairs Com., Province of Alta., Edmonton, 1976-78; council chmn. Boy Scouts Am., Orem, 1984—. Skagg's scholar, 1980; Exxon scholar, 1981; Grad. Sch. Mgmt. scholar Brigham Young U., 1982. Mem. Am. Assn. Mental Deficiency, Psychologists Assn. Alta., Canadian Psychol. Assn., Am. Psychol. Assn., Brigham Young U. Mgmt. Soc. Mormon. Home: 227 W 2000 N Orem UT 84057

VETTER, ELAINE, advertising agency executive; b. Freeport, N.Y., Oct. 23, 1938; d. Otto and Lillian (Pedersen) Buhler; m. William Vetter, Aug. 31, 1957 (div.); 1 child, Robert. A.A.S., SUNY-Farmingdale, 1958. Traffic mgr. Campbell-Ewald Advt., N.Y.C., 1962-68; traffic mgr. A C & R Advt., Inc., N.Y.C., 1968-78, asst. account exec., 1978-79, account exec., 1979-84, v.p., creative coordinator, 1984—. Office: AC&R Advt Inc 16 E 32d St New York NY 10016

VETTER, UDO, mathematician; b. Braunschweig, Fed. Republic Germany, Oct. 6, 1938; s. Günter and Berna (Schleef) V.; m. Christa Lorentz, May 12, 1964; children: Claus, Susanne, Jürgen, Jan, Dennis. Grad., U. Münster, Fed. Republic Germany, 1963; habilitation, U. Hannover, Fed. Republic Germany, 1968. Dozent U. Hannover, 1969-71; prof. U. Claustal, Fed. Republic Germany, 1971-77; full prof. U. Osnabrück, Fed. Republic Germany, 1977—. Author: Algebra, 1970, Determinantal Rings, 1987; contbr. articles to profl. jours. Mem. Deutsche Mathematiker-Vereinigung, Am. Math. Soc. Home: Bussardstrasse 21, D2842 Lohne Federal Republic of Germany Office: U Osnabrueck, Driverstrasse 21, D2848 Vechta Federal Republic of Germany

VETTORAZZI, GASTON, toxicologist; b. Trent, Italy, Feb. 5, 1928; s. Rudolph and Mary (Dal Canale) V.; M.D., U. Milan, 1954; M.S., La. State U., 1970, Ph.D., 1972. Diplomate Acad. Toxicological Scis. m. Mary-Francis Armental Segade; children—Ariane, Lara. Scientist in tropical medicine Ecuador, 1955-60; head sci. dept. Am. Sch., also prof. clin. chemist Sao Paulo (Brazil) U., 1961-68; assoc. researcher in food toxicology La. State U., 1968-72; sr. toxicologist, exec. sec. to JECFA and JMPR, Internat. Program on Chem. Safety, WHO, Geneva, Switzerland, 1972-88; dir. Internat. Toxicology Info. Ctr., San Sebastian, Spain, 1988—, Vettorazzi Assocs., San Sebastian, 1988—; prof. exptl. toxicology U. Milan (Italy), 1975; vis. prof. dept. pathology U. Rio de Janeiro. Recipient Internat. Soc. Regulatory Toxicology and Pharmacology award. Mem. Am. Soc. Toxicology, Nat. Acad. Medicine Argentina, European Soc. Toxicology, Inst. Food Technology, Internat. Soc. Ecotoxicology and Environ. Safety, N.Y. Acad. Scis., Am. Coll. Toxicology, Nat. Acad. Medicine Buenos Aires (hon.), Sigma Xi, Phi Kappa Phi, Gamma Sigma Delta. Author books and profl. articles on gen., food and pesticides toxicology; mem. editorial bd. sci. jours. Office: Internat Info Toxicology Ctr, Paseo Miraconcha 8, E-20007 San Sebastian Spain

VEVERKA, DONALD JOHN, lawyer; b. Chgo., July 20, 1935; s. John Edward and Irene Cecelia (Wasil) V.; m. Mary Almjeld, May 27, 1967; children—Tanya, Holly, Marc. B.S., Loyola U., Chgo., 1957; J.D., DePaul U., 1963. Bar: Ill. 1963, U.S. Dist. Ct. (no. dist.) Ill. 1963, U.S. Ct. Appeals (7th cir.) 1963, U.S. Supreme Ct. 1968. Asst. state's atty. civil appeals sect. Cook County State's Attys. Office, 1963-67; asst. atty. gen. appeals sect. Ill. Atty. Gen. Office, 1967-68; house counsel Kenilworth Ins. Co., 1968-69; ptnr. Bradshaw, Speranza, Veverka & Brumlik, 1969-72; spl. asst. atty. gen., 1970-72; ptnr. Speranza & Veverka, Chgo., 1972-73, 74—; officer Henehan Donovan Isaacson Speranza & Veverka, Ltd., Chgo., 1973-74; bd. dirs., officer DePaul Law Council, 1972-83; mem. Ill. Supreme Ct. Com. on Pattern Jury Instrns. Assoc. bd. dirs. LaGrange Community Meml. Hosp., 1979, officer, 1982-85, pres. 1986-87; bd. dirs. West Suburban YMCA, 1981—; trustee Village of LaGrange Park (Ill.), 1981—. Served to 1st lt. U.S. Army, 1967-69; capt. Res. Mem. ABA (faculty mem. Nat. Inst. Appellate Advocacy 1980, Ill. chmn. young lawyers com. on jud. selection 1971-72), Ill. State Bar Assn. (mem. com. on corrections reform 1974, also past mem. speakers bur., young mems. conf.), Bar Assn. Seventh Fed. Circuit (Ill. chmn. meetings com. 1976), DePaul Alumni Assn. (governing bd. 1975-82), Phi Alpha Delta, Blue Key. Roman Catholic. Clubs: YMCA Men's (LaGrange, Ill.); Athletic (Chgo.). Author: How To Buy or Sell Your Home Without a Lawyer, 1982; also articles. Home: 709 N Park Rd LaGrange Park IL 60525 Office: 180 N Michigan Ave Chicago IL 60601

VEYSEY, ARTHUR ERNEST, reporter, administrator, biographer; b. Boulder, Colo., Sept. 28, 1914; s. Ernest Charles and Lillian (Larson) V.; m. Florence Jones, 1937 (dec. 1940); 1 dau., Priscilla Joan; m. Gwendolyn Morgan, 1946. B.A., U. Colo., 1935; L.H.D., Ill. Benedictine Coll., 1986. Reporter Denver Post, 1935-37, Scottsbluff (Neb.) Star-Herald, 1937-41, Omaha World-Herald, 1941-43; war corr. Southwest Pacific, Chgo. Tribune, 1943- 45, fgn. corr., 1946-50, chief London bur., 1950-75; gen. mgr. Cantigny Trust, 1975-86. Author: Death in the Jungle, 1966, (with Gwen Morgan) Halas by Halas, 1979, Poor Little Rich Boy, Biography of Col. R.R. McCormick. Bd. dirs. The Forest Found. Recipient Norlin award U. Colo., 1986, Margaret Landon award, 1986. Club: Lake Zurich Golf. Address: 10 Cumberland Terr, Regent's Park, London NW1, England

VEZER, ARPAD, electrical engineer; b. Budapest, Hungary, June 5, 1957; s. Mihály and Ilona V.; Zsofia Zoltán V.; m. 15, 1983; children: Arpad Jr., Estella. BS in Elect. Enging., K. Kando Coll., Budapest, 1979. Cert. sr. devel. engr., Hungary. Maintenance engr. Hungarian TV, Budapest, 1979-83, maintenance, devel. engr., 1983-85, devel. engr., 1985—. Served with Hungarian mil., 1979-81. Mem. Orgn. Internat. Radio and TV, Hungarian Assn. Tech. and Sci. Home: Jozsef U 170, 1161 Budapest Hungary Office: Hungarian TV, Szabadsagter 17, 1810 Budapest Hungary

VIALLANEIX, PAUL, retired French literature educator; b. Gumont, France, July 4, 1925; s. Baptiste and Yvonne (Rioux) V.; m. Nelly Marié a Roux, Aug. 18, 1951. Agregation des lettres, Ecole Normale Superieure, Paris, 1950; Dr es lettres, U. Paris Sorbonne, 1959; MA, Cambridge (Eng.) U., 1969. Prof. French lit. U. Clermont-Ferand (France), 1952-85, Ecole Normale Superieure, Paris, 1952-75; dir. Réforme, Paris, 1984—; overseas fellow Churchill Coll., Cambridge U., 1969-73; vis. fellow St. Anthony's Coll., Oxford U., 1974-80. Contbr. essays to profl. jours. Served with French Army, 1943-44. Decorated officier des Palmes Academiques, commandeur des Arts et Lettres. Home: 14 Rue de L'Estrapade, 75005 Paris France Office: Reforme, 53-55 Ave du Maine, 75014 Paris France

VIAN, REGINALD DONALD, company group chairman; b. London, Mar. 25, 1933; s. Reginald and Alice Rose (Scott) V.; m. Sylvia Phillips, Aug. 14, 1954; children: Rosemary, Julia, Nicola. Student schs., London. Chmn. The E.C.L. Group of Cos., Belfast, Douglas, Isle of Man, Dublin, Ireland, London, N.Y.C., 1970—. Office: ECL Group of Cos Ltd, St Martins House, Waterloo Rd, Ballsbridge, Dublin 4 Ireland

VIART, GUY PASCAL, export manager; b. Arras, France, May 16, 1957; s. Micheline and Denis (Brasseur) V.; m. Brigitte Marie Theret, Aug. 19, 1977; children—Marc, Sophie. Baccalaureat with Honors, Lycee Robespierre, France, 1975; D. in Enging., Enstimd, France, 1975; grad. in Bus. Mgmt. Bus. Inst. Lille, 1986; grad. in Human Anatomy, Pitie-Salpeiriere Hosp., Paris, 1986 . Research & Devel. mgr. FICAL, Loison/Lens, France, 1980-83, export mgr., 1983-85, project mgr. in production restructuration, USINOR Wire Group, 1985-86; tech. mgr. SOFAMOR, Berck/mer., France, 1986—; auditor internat. orgn. OIPEEC, 1981-85; tchr. biomaterials, U. Medcine of Lille, France, 1986—; Author: (Invention) New Wire Galvanization, 1982; New Rope Design, 1983, New internal fixator for spine, 1987, New table for spinal surgery, 1988. Town councillor, Capelle-Fremont Pas De Calais, 1983. Mem. Departmental Council Confederation Gen. Des Cadres, Coirel-Dubousset (mem. tech. documentation resp 1987), Sand Yachting (administrv. mgr. French fedn. 1987). Roman Catholic. Home: CD 49, 62690 Capelle-Fremont France Office: SOFAMOR BP 139, 62604 Berck/mer France

VIBAT, EDISON MUNAR, architect; b. Tayug, Pangasinan, Philippines, Nov. 8, 1931; s. Severino Kagaoan Vibat and Albina (Baltazar) Munar; m. Natividad Barrios Santos, Sept. 8, 1955; children: Nanette, Edwin, Milagros, Edison Jr., Reina, Lorna. BS in Architecture, Mapua Inst. Tech., Manila, 1954; postgrad., USDA Grad. Sch., Washington, 1967. Pvt. practice architecture Manila, 1955-60; staff architect, job capt. Good, Long & Assocs., Harrisburg, Pa., 1964-65; architect U.S. AID, Kabul, Afghanistan, 1965-67; sr. architect Ministry of Works, Freetown, Sierra Leone, 1967-72; sr. architect spl. projects/tng. UN, N.Y.C., 1972-76; archtl. cons. Ministry of Works, Mbabane, Swaziland, 1976-78; chief architect, mgr. prodn. enging. Howard, Needles, Tammen & Bergendoff, Internat., Seattle and Manila, 1979-80; mgr. archtl. projects, coordinator A-E services Zuhair Fayez & Assocs., Jeddah and Riyadh, Saudi Arabia, 1980-83; pres., mng. architect E.M. Vibat & Assocs., Manila, 1983—; architect A.J. Luz & Assocs., Manila, 1955-60, Adrian Wilson & Assocs., Los Angeles and Manila, 1960-61, Ghana Housing Corp., Accra, 1961-63; sr. mng. ptnr., Garcia Vibat & Assocs., Manila, 1987—. cons., mgr. creation of new nat. solid waste commn. Office of the Pres., Manila, 1987. Served to 2d lt. Philippine Inf., 1952-54. Mem. United Architects Philippines (corp. chmn. publicity and documentation com., vice-chmn. profl. practice com. 1985). Roman Catholic. Office: Strata 100 Bldg, Emerald Ave, Pasig Metro Manila, Philippines

VICK, MARIE, retired educator; b. Saltillo, Tex., Jan. 22, 1922; d. Alphy Edgar and Mollie (Cowser) Pitts; B.S., Tex. Woman's U., Denton, 1942, M.A., 1949; m. Joe Edward Vick, Apr. 5, 1942; children: Mona Marie, Rex Edward. tchr. Harlingen (Tex.) High Sch., 1959-62, Harlingen Bonham Elem. Sch., 1958-59, San Angelo (Tex.) Sr. High Sch., 1957-58, San Angelo (Tex.) Jr. High Sch., 1950-52, instr. Tex. Woman's U., Denton, 1948-50; tchr. Monroe Jr. High Sch., Omaha, 1947-48, Crozier Tech. High Sch., Dallas, 1946-47, Santa Rita Elem. Sch., San Angelo, 1943-45, Coahoma (Tex.) High Sch., 1942-43; prof. health sci. Coll. Edn., U. Houston, 1962-80. Artist in oil, watercolor and acrylic. Recipient Cert. of Achievement, Tex. Commn. Intercollegiate Athletics for Women, 1972, Research Service award Tex. Cancer Control Program, 1978-79, Plaudit award Nat. Dance Assn., 1982, Disting. Service award Pan Am. U., 1983, Service citation Am. Cancer Soc., Cert. of Appreciation, Tex. div. Am. Cancer Soc., 1980; Favorite Prof. honoree Cap and Gown Mortar Bd., U. Houston, 1974. Mem. AAHPER (dance editor 1971-74), Am. Sch. Health Assn., AAHPERD, NEA, So. Assn. Health, Phys. Edn. Coll. Women (sec. dance sect. 1970-73), Tex. State Tchrs. Assn. (sect. chmn. 1964-65), Tex. Assn. Health, Phys. Edn. and Recreation (chmn. dance sect. 1968-69), Tex. Assn. Coll. Tchrs., Tex. Women's U. Nat. Alumnae Assn. (life), Tex. Women's Pioneer Club, Am. Assn. Ret. Persons (chmn. legis. com. Huntsville chpt.), Nat. Ret. Tchrs. Assn., Tex. Assn. Ret. Tchrs., Univ. Houston Assn. Ret. Profs., Tex. Women's Univ. Alumnae Assn. Walker County Ret. Tchrs. Assn. (legis. com.), Kelta Kappa Gamma (fin. com.). Democrat. Baptist. Author: A Collection of Dances for Children, 1970; Health Science in the Elementary School, 1979; contbr. articles to profl. jours. Home: RR #6 PO Box 681A Huntsville TX 77340-9806

VICKER, RAY, writer; b. Wis., Aug. 27, 1917; s. Joseph John and Mary (Young) V.; m. Margaret Ella Leach, Feb. 23, 1944. Student, Wis. State U., Stevens Point, 1934, Los Angeles City Coll., 1940-41, U.S. Mcht. Marine Officers' Sch., 1944, Northwestern U., 1947-49. With Chgo. Jour. Commerce, 1946-50, automobile editor, 1947-50; mem. staff Wall St. Jour., 1950-83; European editor Wall St. Jour., London, Eng., 1960-75. Author: How an Election Was Won, 1962, Those Swiss Money Men, 1973, Kingdom of Oil, 1974, Realms of Gold, 1975, This Hungry World, 1976, Dow Jones Guide to Retirement Planning, 1985; also numerous articles. Served with U.S. Merchant Marine, 1942-46. Recipient Outstanding Reporting Abroad award Chgo. Newspaper Guild, 1959; Best Bus. Reporting Abroad award E. W. Fairchild, 1963, 67; hon. mention, 1965; Bob Considine award, 1979; ICMA Journalism award, 1983. Mem. Sigma Delta Chi. Roman Catholic. Clubs: Overseas Press (Reporting award 1963, 67) (N.Y.C.); Press (Chgo.), Adventurers (Chgo.). Home and Office: 1209 Avenida Sevilla 2B Walnut Creek CA 94595

VICKERMAN, ANDREW, economic advisor; b. Rhiwbina, Cardiff, Wales, Oct. 30, 1954; s. Ferdindand and Joyce (Hill) V.; children: Jody Sarah, David Gareth. BA, Cambridge U., Eng., 1977, MA, 1981, PhD, 1984. Teaching asst. Cambridge U., 1977-79, tutor Queens Coll., 1980-82, 1980-82; researcher Inst. Social Studies, Hague, The Netherlands, 1979-80; lectr. U. Papua New Guinea, 1983-85, head econs. dept., 1985; econ. advisor to prime minister Papua New Guinea govt., Papua, 1985—; researcher Social Sci. Research Council, 1977-81, Inst. Social Studies, the Netherlands, 1979-80, Inst. Applied Social and Econ. Research, Papua New Guinea. Author: The Fate of the Peasantry, 1986; contbr. articles and book revs. to profl. jours. Office: Dept Prime Minister, PO Box 6605, Boroko Papua New Guinea

VICKERS, DAVID LEROY, materials executive; b. Detroit, Jan. 15, 1942; s. Vay Aldon and Vada Ann (Gaw) V.; m. Tomiye Tado, Apr. 22, 1961; children: David L. Jr., Steven T. BS in Indsl. Tech., Tenn Tech. U., 1967; MBA in Fin., Calif. State U., Long Beach, 1972. Chief indsl. engr. Pacific Tube Co., Commerce, Calif., 1967-73; dir. mfg. Ameron Inc., Monterey Park, Calif., 1973-84; exec. v.p. H.G. Fenton Material Co., San Diego, 1984—; bd. dirs. Pre-Mixed Concrete Co., San Diego, Sorrento Ready Mix Co., San Diego, A-1 Soils Co., San Diego, East County Materials, Inc.; officer Western Salt Co., San Diego; instr. U. of Hawaii, Honolulu, 1976-79, Loyola Marymount U., Los Angeles, 1970-74. Bd. dirs. Mission Valley YMCA, San Diego, 1985—. Served with USN, 1959-63. Mem. Inst. Indsl. Engrs. (sr.), So. Calif Work Simplification Assn. (bd. dirs., pres. 1968-74), The Execs. Assn. (bd. dirs. San Diego chpt.), San Diego Employers Assn. (bd. dirs., pres. 1988—). Republican. Methodist. Office: HG Fenton Material Co 7220 Trade St Suite 300 San Diego CA 92112

VICKERS, DOUGLAS, psychology educator; b. Tidworth, Wiltshire, Eng., Feb. 17, 1940; emigrated to Australia, 1967; s. Douglas and Ellen (Ramage) V.; m. Yvonne Victoria Jouty, May 1, 1965; children—Marc, Anne. M.A., Edinburgh U., 1961; B.A., Cambridge U., 1963, Ph.D., 1967. Lectr. psychology Adelaide U. (South Australia), 1967-72, sr. lectr., 1973-79, reader in psychology, 1980—. Author: Decision Processes in Visual Perception, 1979; contbr. articles to profl. jours. Australian Research Grant Com. research grantee Adelaide U., 1969-76, 81—; Sci. and Tech. fellow French Govt., Centre Nat. de la Recherche Sci. Marseilles, 1980; U. Adelaide spl. research grantee, 1981, 83, 85, 86, 87. Mem. Internat. Assn. Study of Attention and Performance (adv. council 1978-82), Australian Psychol. Soc., Internat. Soc. Psychophysics. Office: U Adelaide, Psychology Dept, North Terrace, Adelaide South Australia 5000, Australia

VICKERY, EUGENE LIVINGSTONE, retired physician, writer ; b. Fairmount, Ind., Nov. 27, 1913; s. Lee Otis and Grace (Hawkins) V.; B.S. with distinction, Northwestern U., 1935, M.B., 1940, M.D., 1941; m. Millie Margaret Cox, Dec. 21, 1941; children—Douglas Eugene, Constance Michelle Anita Sue, Jon Livingstone. Intern Evanston (Ill.) Hosp., 1940-41; pvt. practice medicine, Lena, Ill., 1946-84; chmn. med. records com. Freeport Meml. Hosp., 1954-64, sec. staff, 1964-67, chairman credentials com., 1964-69, v.p. staff, 1967-69, chief staff, 1969-71, chmn. constn. and bylaws com., 1971-80; mem. staff St. Francis Hosp.; local surgeon Ill. Central R.R.; health officer Lena, 1948-84; mem. Stephenson County Bd. Health, 1966-75, v.p., 1969-75; mem. peer rev. policy com. No. Ill. Found. Med. Care. Mem. Lena Sch. Bd., 1951-54; mem. Lena Library Bd., 1958-62; med. dir. Civil Def., rural Stephenson County, Ill., 1961-70; mem. exec. bd. Blackhawk Area council Boy Scouts Am., recipient Silver Beaver award Nat. Council, 1968, Distinguished Eagle award Nat. Council, 1977, mem. nat. council, 1971—; bd. dirs. Stephenson County unit Am. Cancer Soc. Served from 1st lt. to maj. AUS, 1941-46. Decorated Legion of Merit; recipient Lena Community Service award, 1972; named Ill. Family Physician of Yr., 1981; recipient Silver Wreath, Nat. Eagle Scout Assn., 1982. Mem. Stephenson County (pres.), Ill. (chmn. med.-legal council 1976-79) med. socs., AMA, Am. (mental health com. 1981), Ill. (chmn. bd. dirs., pres. 1979) acads. family physicians, Assn. Mil. Surgeons U.S., Assn. of Professions (dir., v.p.), Am. Numis. Assn., Nat. Rifle Assn., Ill. Gun Collectors Assn., Arctic Inst. N.Am., Am. Legion, Phi Beta Kappa. Republican. Mem. Evang. Free Ch. Lion. Clubs: Apple Canyon, Masons (32 deg.), Shriners. Author: Dad Calls Me Jack; Adventures in Rhyme; Life Goes On; author Weekly poetry column Vic's Verse. Contbr. articles to numis. and med. publs. Home and Office: 602 Oak St Lena IL 61048

VICKREY, ROBERT REMSEN, artist; b. N.Y.C., Aug. 20, 1926; s. Claude Claire and Caroline (McKim) V.; m. Marjorie Elizabeth Alexander, Sept. 18, 1950; children: Remsen Scott, Elizabeth Nicole, Wendy Caroline, Alexander Sean. Studied with Victoria Huntley; B.A., Yale U., 1947, B.F.A., 1950; student, Art Students League. Co-author: New Techniques in Egg Tempera, 1973, author: Robert Vickrey-Artist at Work, The Affable Curmudgeon, 1979; one-man shows, Midtown Galleries, N.Y.C., 1954-58, 62, 63, 69, 70, 72, Columbia (S.C.) Mus. Art, 1959, Davison Art Ctr., Wesleyan U., 1966, Va. Mus. Fine Arts, 1965, retrospective, U. Ariz. Mus. Art, 1973, San Diego Fine Arts Gallery, 1973; exhibited in nat. group shows; represented in permanent collections, Whitney Mus., Corcoran Gallery of Art, Washington, Lakeland (Fla.) Mus., Mus. Modern Art, Rio de Janeiro, Brazil, Sara Roby Found., Parrish Art Mus., Southampton, Isaac Delgado Mus., Dallas Mus., Munson-Williams-Proctor Inst., Utica, N.Y., Met. Mus. Art, NAD, Butler Inst. Am. Art, New Britain Mus. Am. Art, Gallery of Modern Art, Birmingham Mus., Spelman Coll., Newark Mus., many others; illustrator mag. covers, books. Recipient award Edward Austin Abbey mural competition, 1949, top prize Fla. Internat. Art Exhbn., 1952, 2d prize Internat. Hallmark competition, 1955, Am. Artist mag. citation, 1956, Winsor and Newton award Am. Water Color Soc., 1956, S.J. Wallace Truman prize Nat. Acad. ann., 1958, Salmagundi Club award Audubon Artists, 1971, spl. prize Internat. Biennial of Sport in Fine Arts, Mus. Contemporary Art, Madrid, 1973, numerous others. Mem. Audubon Artists, Am. Water Color Soc., Nat. Acad. Office: Kennedy Galleries 40 W 57th St New York NY 10022

VICTOR, MICHAEL GARY, physician, lawyer; b. Detroit, Sept. 20, 1945; s. Simon H. and Helen (Litsky) V.; m. Karen Sue Hutson, June 20, 1975; children—Elise Nicole, Sara Lisabeth. Bars: Ill. 1980, U.S. Dist. Ct. (no. dist.) Ill. 1980, U.S. Ct. Appeals (7th cir.) 1981; diplomate Am. Bd. Law in Medicine. Pres., Advocate Adv. Assocs., Chgo., 1982—; assoc. in medicine Northwestern U. Med. Sch., Chgo., 1982—; sole practice law, Barrington, Ill., 1982—; dir. emergency medicine Loretto Hosp., Chgo., 1980-85 , chief. sect. of emergency medicine St. Josephs Hosp., Chgo., 1985-87; v.p. Med. Emergency Services Assocs., Buffalo Grove, Ill; v.p. MESA Mgmt. Corp.; sec., treas. MESA Edn. and Research Found.; sec., treas. Mgmt. and Care Services Inc.; bd. dirs., Vital Med. Labs. Inc., 1987-88. Author: Informed Consent, 1980; Brain Death, 1980; (with others) Due Process for Physicians, 1984, A Physicians Guide to the Illinois Living Will Act. Recipient Service awards Am. Coll. Emergency Medicine, 1973-83. Fellow Am. Coll. Legal Medicine, Chgo. Acad. Legal Medicine; mem. Am. Coll. Emergency Physicians (pres. Ill. chpt. 1980, med.-legal-ins. council 1980-81, 83-84), ABA, Ill. State Bar Assn., Am. Soc. Law and Medicine, Assn. Trial Lawyers Am., Chgo. Bar Assn. (med.-legal council 1981-83), AMA, Ill. State Med. Soc. (med.-legal council 1980-86, 88), Chgo. Med. Soc. Jewish. Home and Office: 1609 Guthrie Circle Barrington IL 60010

VICTOR, RICHARD STEVEN, lawyer; b. Detroit, Mich., Aug. 3, 1949; s. Simon H. and Helen (Litsky) V.; m. Denise L. Berman, Nov. 26, 1978; children: Daniel, Ronald, Sandra. Bar: Mich. 1975, U.S. Dist. Ct. (ea. dist.) Mich. 1975. Assoc. Law Offices of Albert Best, Detroit, 1975; ptnr. Best & Victor, Oak Park, Mich., 1976-80; sole practice Oak Park, 1981-85; ptnr. Law Offices of Victor, Robbins and Bassett (formerly Victor and Robbins), Brimingham, Mich., 1986—; instr. in family law Oakland U., Rochester, Mich., 1976—. Author: (column) Legally Speaking, Stepfamily Bull., 1984—; tech. advisor "Whose Mother Am I?" Aaron Spelling Prodns./ABC Movies. Mem. community adv. bd. Woodland Hills Med. Ctr., 1981—; v.p. Bloomfield (Mich.) Sq. Homeowners Assn., 1985—, pres. 1988; chmn. legis. com. Birmingham Schs. PTA, 1987—. Mem. ABA (guest lectr. sem. 1988), Mich. Bar Assn. (treas. family law sect. 1987-88, sec. 1988—, chmn. continuing legal edn. com. family law sect. 1988—, Appreciation award from family law sect. 1987, 88), Oakland County Bar Assn. (chmn. lawyer's admission com. 1981, unauthorized practice of law 1982, oldtimer's night 1984-85, speakers bur. 1985), Family Law Council (chmn. legis. com. 1985-86, chmn. seminar series for continuing edn., treas. 1987-88, sec. 1988—), Oakland/Livingston Legal Aid Soc. (honor roll 1984), Stepfamily Assn. Am. Inc. (bd. dirs., legal counsel 1984—, bd. dirs. Southeast Mich. chpt. 1981—), Grandparents' Rights Org. (founder, bd. dirs. 1983—). Jewish. Lodge: B'nai B'rith Barristers. Office: Law Offices of Victor & Robbins 555 S Woodward Ave Suite 600 Birmingham MI 48011

VICTORA, CESAR GOMES, epidemiology educator; b. São Gabriel, Brazil, Mar. 28, 1952; s. Fernando Machado and Carmen Maria (Gomes) V.; m. Magda Floriana Damiani, Dec. 16, 1974; children: Gabriel, Julia. MD, Fed. U., Rio Grande do Sul, 1976; PhD in Epidemiology, Sch. Hygiene, London, 1983. Instr. Fed. U., Pelotas, Brazil, 1977-80, asst. prof., 1980-84, assoc. prof., 1984—; overseas assoc. London Sch. Hygiene, 1984—. Contbr. articles to profl. jours. Cons. Unicef, Brasília, 1987—. Nat. Research Council scholar, 1980-83, Overseas Students Scheme scholar, 1980-83. Mem. Internat. Epidemiol. Assn., Brazilian Assn. Population (research award 1981), Brazilian Assn. Pub. Health. Home: Anchieta 4718, 96015 Pelotas Brazil Office: Fed U Pelotas, CP 464, 96001 Pelotas Brazil

VICTORIA, ANTON SALVADOR, sales executive; b. Negombo, Sri Lanka, Oct. 1, 1946; s. Joseph Louis and Mary Audry (Fernando) V. Dep. Elec. Engr., Tech. Coll., Colombo, 1967; E.E., City and Guilds, London, 1969. Lectr. Coll. Tech., Kurunegala, 1970-74; sales engr. Quipment Constrn. Co., Colombo, 1974-76; sales mgr. Dieselsmotor Engring. Co., Colombo, Sri Lanka, 1974—. Pres. Civil Service Internat. Negombo, 1978; mem. bd. mgmt. Sri Lanka Red Cross Soc., Colombo, 1980—; asst. dist. commr. Sri Lanka Boy Scout Assn., Negombo. Home: 15/D Sri Wickrama Rajasinghe Rd, Negombo Sri Lanka Office: Diesel & Motor Engring Co Ltd, 65 Jetawana Rd, Colombo 14, Sri Lanka

VICTORIO-GUANIO, MA LUISA B, ophthalmologist; b. Pasig, Philippines, Dec. 10, 1922; d. Isidro Jualong and Balbina B. (Baylon) Victorio; m. Alberto S. Guanio, May 1, 1946; children: Gil, Edna, Quintin, Luis, Marcia, Lisa, Domingo, Eleanor. MD, U. Sto Tomas, Manila, 1944. Diplomate Philippines Bd. Ophthalmology. Med. officer PCAUI U.S. Liberation Forces, San Juan Rizal, 1945, Pasig Periculture Ctr., 1946-48; med. examiner Philippine Am. Life Ins. Corp., Manila, 1949—; civilian med. trainer otolarynhology V Luna Gen. Hosp., Quzan City, Philippines, 1954-60; gen. practice medicine specializing in ophthmalogy and otolanyngology Pasig, 1960—. Active Community Environ. Health Awareness Program, 1975—. Fellow Philippines Acad. Ophthalmology and Otolaryngology (life); mem. Philippine Soc. Ophthalmology (life), Pasig Med. Soc. (life, pres. 1984-85, Silver Jubilee award 1973), Rizal Med. Soc. (life), Philippine Med. Assn. (life), Philippine Med. Women's Assn. (life, pres. 1974-75, Leadership award 1975), Pasig Paternos Taguig (life, pres. 1974-75), Minenva Assn. Profl. (v.p. 1959). Roman Catholic. Home and Office: 6 Dr Sixto Antonio Ave, Pasig Metro Manilla 1600, Philippines

VICTORY, KAMARAN, investment executive, consultant; b. Tehran, Iran, Feb. 26, 1962; arrived in Can., 1976; s. Amir Hooshang and Malihe (Katirai) V. B in Commerce & Fin., U. Toronto, Ont., Can., 1984, MBA, 1985. Asst. treas. internat. investments Baha'i World Ctr., Haifa, Israel, 1985-87; chief fin. officer Shance Constrn. Inc., Toronto, 1983—, also bd. dirs.; chief exec. officer, mng. dir. Ikeli Ltd., Suva, Fiji, 1986—; cons. Continental Bd. Counsellors Australasia, Sydney, Australia, 1987—; nat. treas. Nat. Spiritual Assembly of Fiji, Suva, 1987—. Baha'i. Office: Ikeli Ltd, PO Box 13596, Suva Fiji

VIDAL, JACQUES GEORGES, orthopedic surgeon; b. Montpellier, France, Oct. 10, 1928; s. Joseph and Helene (Gaussel) V.; m. Michele Ginestie, June 22, 1960; children: Jean-Christophe, Sophie Laurence. MD, Faculty Medicine, Montpellier, 1958. Intern Hosp. Montpellier, 1952-58, surg. asst., 1958-61, prof. orthopedics, 1961-68, chief orthopedic surg. service, 1968—; prof. orthopedic surgery Faculty Medicine, Montpellier, 1968—, adminstr., 1982—; pres. Ctr. Orthopedic Maguelone, Palavas, France, 1982—. Contbr. articles to profl. jours.; inventor prostheses and mobility devices. Decorated Chevalier des Palmes Academiques, 1985. Mem. Nat. Counsel Univs., Internat. Soc. Orthopedic and Trauma Surgery, Internat. Coll. Surgeons, French Soc. Orthopedic and Trauma Surgery (pres. 1965), Belgian Soc. Orthopedic Surgery. Roman Catholic. Home: 22 Cours Gambetta, 34000 Montpellier France Office: Hosp Lapeyronie, 555 Rt de Ganges, 34059 Montpellier France

VIDAL, RICARDO CARDINAL, cardinal Roman Catholic Church; b. Mogpoc, Lucena, Philippines, Feb. 6, 1931. ordained 1956. Consecrated bishop Titular Ch. Claterna, 1971; archbishop Lipa, Philippines, 1973-82, Cebu, Philippines, 1982—; proclaimed cardinal 1985. Address: Chancery, PO Box 52, Cebu City 6401, Philippines *

VIDAL-NAQUET, PIERRE EMMANUEL, classicist, historian; b. Paris, July 23, 1930; s. Lucien Jules Daniel and Marguerite Valèrie (Valabrègue) V.-D.; m. Geneviève Gisèle Railhac; children: Denis, Jacques, Vincent. Lic. lès lettres, U. Paris, Sorbonne, 1952; LLD, U. Nancy, France, 1974; D honoris causa, U. Libre, Brussels, 1987. Prof. Lyceé Orlèans, France, 1955-56; asst. prof. U. Calais, 1956-61, U. Lille, 1961-62; attaché de recherche CNRS, Paris, 1962-69; maitre de conf. U. Lyons, 1964-66; sous dir. d'etudes Ecole Pratique de Haute Etude, Paris, 1966-69; dir. d'etudes Ecole des Hautes Etudes en Sci. Sociale, Paris, 1969—; elected mem. Com. Nat. du CNRS, Paris, 1982, Com. Nat. des Univs., Paris, 1986. Author: Torture Cancer of Democracy, 1967, (with J.P. Vernant) Tragedy and Myth in Ancient Greece, 1981, The Black Hunter, 1986. Mem. Com. Maurice Audin Amnesty Internat., Paris, 1987—. Named comdr. Order of Phoenix, Greek Govt., 1986; recipient Eschilo d'Oro award Inst. Nat. rer il drama autice, 1986. Mem. Hellenic Soc. London, Cen. de Recherche Comparees sur les Soc. Ancienne (bd. dirs. 1985). Home: 11 rue du Cherche Midi, 75006 Paris France Office: Cen de Recherce Comparees, 10 rue Monsieur le Prince, F 75006 Paris France

VIDMAN, LADISLAV, classical philologist, researcher; b. Kladno, Czechoslovakia, Feb. 20, 1924; s. Ladislav and Božena (Tomičková) V.; m. Anežka Schmidtová, Aug. 24, 1961; children: Ludmila, Anežka. PhD, Charles U., 1949; grad., Czechoslovak Acad. Scis., 1959. Researcher in classical philology Czechoslovak Acad. Scis., Prague, 1953—; collaborator Cen. Inst. Ancient History and Archaeology, German Dem. Republic Acad. Scis., Berlin, 1962—; mem. internat. com. Acad. Verlag, Berlin, 1972—. Author: Fasti Ostienses, 1957, 2d edit., 1982, Etude sur la correspondence de Pline le Jeune avec Trajan, 1960, Sylloge inscriptionum religionis Isiacae et Sarapiacae, 1969, Isis und Sarapis bei den Griechen und Romern, 1970. Psáno do kamene - Antická epigrafie (Written On Stone - Ancient Epigraphy), 1975, Corpus inscriptionum Latinarum VI 6, 2, Index cognominum, 1980, From Olympus to Pantheon - Ancient Religion and Morality, 1986; mem. editorial bd. Rev. Phililogus, 1977—; contbr. articles to profl. jours. Mem. Jednota Klasickych Filologo (sec. 1972—), Comité Internat. Congrès Epigraphiques, Deutsches Aschäologisches Inst. (corr.), Assn. Internat. Épigraphie Grecque et Latine. Roman Catholic. Home: Sidlistni 210, 16500 Prague Czechoslovakia Office: Czechoslovak Acad Scis, Kabinet Pro Studia Recka, Lazarska 8, 12000 Prague 2 Czechoslovakia

VIDUSSO, GIORGIO GIUSEPPE, musical director; b. Trieste, Venezia-Giulia, Italy, Oct. 7, 1926; s. Giuseppe and Bianca (Galante) V. Student, Music Sch. U., Bologna, Italy, 1944; MusB, Trieste, 1949. Pianist various locations, 1943-53; programs editor Radio Trieste, 1950-56; mus. mgr. RAI, Trieste, Rome and Milano, 1956—, Accademia Filarmonica Romana, Rome, 1966-84; mus. mgr. Fesival of Spoleto, 1973-78; supt. Teatro Comunale-Maggio Musicale Fioretine, Florence, 1986—. Contbr. articles to profl. jours. Office: Teatro Comunals di Firenze, Teatro Comunale Via Solferino 15, 50123 Florence Italy

VIDYARTHI, SUNIL KUMAR, chemical executive, researcher; b. Patsa, Bihar, India, Nov. 14, 1951; arrived in Can., 1969; s. Indra Kant and Chadrawati (Devi) Mishra; m. Asha Jha, Dec. 6, 1976; children: Neil Kant Mishra, Kapil Jay Mishra. BS with honors, Patna U., Bihar, 1966, MS,

1968; PhD, U. B.C., Vancouver, 1973; MBA, Concordia U., Montreal, Que., Can., 1987. Lectr. Magadh Mahila Coll., Patna, Bihar, 1969; project leader Domtar Research Ctr., Senneville, Que., 1975-79; sr. scientist Noranda Research Ctr., Pointe Claire, Que., 1979-80; sr. chemist Exxon Bldg. Products Can., LaSalle, Que., 1980-83, mgr. research, devel. insulation, 1983-85, mgr. tech. transfer, 1985-87, mgr. insulation bus. devel., 1987—; founding dir. Value Scis., Beaconsfield, Que. Contbr. numerous articles to profl. jours.; patentee chemicals, building materials. Recipient three gold medals Patna U., fellow Nat. Research Council Can., 1973-75. Mem. Chem. Inst. Can. (chmn. 1985-86, vice chmn. 1984-85), Chem. Engring. Soc. Can. (vice chmn. 1980). Home: 453 Coronet Ave, Beaconsfield, PQ Canada H9W 2E8 Office: Exxon Bldg Products Can, 100500 Côte de Liesse, Lachine, PQ Canada H8T 3E3

VIEHE, KARL WILLIAM, educator, consulting firm executive; b. Allentown, Pa., Aug. 12, 1943; s. John Sage and Margaret (Higgs) V. MA in Econs., Am. U., 1968, JD, Howard U., 1981; MLT, Georgetown U., 1982. Bar: D.C., U.S. Ct. Internat. Trade, U.S. Tax Ct., U.S. Ct. Appeals (4th and D.C. cirs.). Tchr. math. and Russian St. Alban's Sch., Washington, 1967-68; pres., chief exec. officer Investment Futures Group, Washington, 1968—; assoc. prof. math. and stats., U. D.C., Washington, 1970—; chmn. bd. dirs. Nat. Ednl. Trust, Washington, 1971—; internat. advt. dir. Washingtonian Mag., 1972-75; adj. prof. Grad. Sch. Bus., Am. U., Washington, 1972—; assoc. prof. law, chmn. mgmt. program Fla. Inst. Tech., 1983-85; of counsel Ebert & Bowytz, 1983—; Bar: D.C., U.S. Dist. Ct., D.C., U.S. Ct. Appeals, D.C. (4th cir., fed. cir.), U.S. Ct. Internat. Trade, U.S. Supreme Ct.; adj. prof. Grad. Sch. Bus. Adminstrn. George Washington U., 1986—; vis. prof. Internat. Devel. Law Inst., Rome, 1987—. Mem. Am. Econ. Assn., Am. Fin. Assn., ABA, D.C. Bar Assn., Am. Arbitration Assn. (comml. panel, internat. panel). Avocations: painting, piano, photography, tennis, golf. Home: 4397 Embassy Park Dr NW Washington DC 20016 Office: 2000 L St NW Suite 504 Washington DC 20036

VIEILLARD-BARON, BERTRAND LOUIS, engineer, corporation official; b. Tunis, Tunisia, Aug. 31, 1940; s. Henri Marie and Antoinette (Penet) V-B.; grad. French Ecole Polytechnique, 1962, French Ecole du Génie Maritime, 1965; m. Béatrice Michaud, Aug. 4, 1964; children: Emmanuel, Loic, Anne, Hubert, Mayeule. Metall. engr. for nuclear reactor Indret, France, 1965-70, 70-71; dir. research ctr. Le Creusot, France, 1971-75, corp. dir. research and devel., Creusot-Loire, Paris, 1975-84; mng. dir. French Research Inst. for Shipbldg., 1984—; pres. French Com. for Non Destructive Testing, French Inst. Mgmt. Research; adviser French Adminstrn. Naval Techs. Mem. French Shipbuilders Assn. (bd. dirs.), IFREMER (chmn. tech. com.). Home: 33 de Lattre, 78150 Le Chesnay France Office: 47 Rue de Monceau, 75008 Paris France

VIEIRA, JOAO BERNARDO, president Guinea-Bissau, military officer; b. Bissau, Guinea-Bissau, Apr. 27, 1939. Mil. trainee People's Republic China, 1960. Commd. officer Partido para a Independencia da Guine e Cabo Verde, 1961, advanced through grades to maj.-gen. 1983; mil. officer Catio region So. Guinea-Bissau, 1961-64, mem. Polit. Bur. Central Com. of Party, mil. comdr. so. front, 1964-65, mem. war council, 1965-67, Bur.'s del. on so. front, 1967-70, mem. Party's Exec. Com. for Combat, 1971-73, mem. Permanent Secretariat of Party, from 1973, pres. People's Nat. Assembly, state commr. armed forces, 1973-78, chief commr. Council State Commrs., 1978—, chmn. Nat. Council Guinea of Party, from 1979, pres. revolutionary council, head of state, supreme comdr. armed forces, 1980—, minister of def. and interior, from 1982, pres. Repub. Guinea-Bissau Council of State, 1983—. Recipient Amilcar Cabral medal, 1976, Colinas do Boe medal, 1984. Address: Office of Pres, Bissau Guinea-Bissau *

VIEMEISTER, PETER EMMONS, business executive; b. Mineola, N.Y., Feb. 15, 1929; s. August Louis and Janet (Emmons) V.; B.M.E. (Grumman scholar), Rensselaer Poly. Inst., 1950; S.M. (Sloan Fellow), Mass. Inst. Tech., 1969; m. Suzanne Neelands, 1951 (div. 1965); children—Clay N., Read L., Susan B., Katherine A.; m. 2d, Cynthia Lee Grubbs, 1983; 1 child, Benjamin T. With Lippincott & Margulies, N.Y.C., 1945; with Grumman Aircraft, Bethpage, N.Y., 1946-57, mgr. bus. planning, 1960-65, asst. to pres. and chmn. bd., 1965-69; pres. Grumman Data Systems Corp., Bethpage, 1969-73; chmn. bd. Computility, Inc., Boston, 1971-73; v.p. Grumman Corp., 1973-79; dir. Grumman Allied Industries, 1975-79, Paumonack Leasing Corp., 1976-79; adj. assoc. prof. Dowling Coll., 1972-73. Chmn. Empire State Coll. Found., 1975-78; trustee Huntington (Dist. 3) Public Schs., 1964-66; bd. dirs. Energy Research Inst. S.C., 1977-81; treas. Bedford Meml. Found., 1982—; chmn. Bedford City/County Mus., 1983—; trustee Lynchburg Coll., 1984—; adv. com. Inst. Energy Analysis, Oak Ridge, 1980-84. Mem. Sigma Xi, Tau Beta Pi. Author: The Lightning Book, 1961; Psychosystems, 1973. Inventor behavior simulator. Office: Solaridge Bedford VA 24523

VIENER, JOHN DAVID, lawyer; b. Richmond, Va., Oct. 18, 1939; s. Reuben and Thelma (Kurtz) V.; m. Karin Erika Bauer, Apr. 7, 1969; children: John David Jr., Katherine Bauer. BA, Yale U., 1961; JD, Harvard U., 1964. Bar: N.Y. State 1965, U.S. Supreme Ct. 1970, U.S. Dist. Ct. (so. dist.) N.Y. 1974, U.S. Tax Ct. 1975. Assoc. Satterlee, Warfield & Stephens, N.Y.C., 1964-69; sole practice N.Y.C., 1969-76; founder, bd. dirs., gen. counsel Foxfire Fund Inc., 1968-88; sr. ptnr. Christy & Viener, N.Y.C., 1976—; gen. counsel, bd. dirs. Landmark Communities, Inc., 1970—, NF&M Internat., Inc., 1976—, Singer Fund, Inc., 1979—; gen. counsel Nat. Cancer Found. Cancer Care, 1982-85, Am. Continental Properties Group, 1978—, Troster, Singer & Co., 1970-77; bd. dirs. Gen. Financiere Immob. et Commer. S.A., 1985—; spl. counsel fin. instns., investment banking and securities concerns; real estate and tax advisor to fgn. instns. Mem. ABA, N.Y. State Bar Assn., Assn. Bar City N.Y. Clubs: Harmonie (N.Y.C.); Manursing Island (Rye, N.Y.). Home: 45 E 62d St New York NY 10021 also: Rye NY 10580 Office: Christy & Viener 620 Fifth Ave New York NY 10020

VIERS, VALDYNE MARIE, nurse; b. Spokane, Wash., Sept. 8, 1947; d. Edward B. and Nellie (Moors) V. BSN, U. Wash., 1969; MS in Nursing, Tex. Women's U., 1977; PhD in Nursing, U. Tex. at Austin, 1986. Staff CCU-ICU nurse Sibley Meml. Hosp., Washington, 1969-71, Scott and White Hosp., Temple, Tex., 1971-72; immunizations and epidemiology nurse Tex. Dept. Health, Austin, 1972-74, nursing specialist for medicare and licensure, 1984-87; adminstrv. dir. research Hermann Hosp., Houston, 1987—; instr. nursing Angelina Coll., Lufkin, Tex., 1974-77; dir. spl. care nursing Meml. Hosp., Nacogdoches, Tex., 1977-78; dir. med. nursing Med. Ctr. Hosp., Nacagdoches, 1978-79; asst. prof. nursing Stephen F. Austin State U., Nacgdoches, 1979-82; asst. clin. prof. nursing U. Tex., Houston, 1987—; assoc. clin. prof. nursing Tex. Women's U., Houston, 1987—; mem. nurse research council Tex. Med. Ctr., Houston Research Adminstrs.' Council. Contbr. articles to profl. jours; presenter in field. Bd. dirs. Nacogdoches City/County Humane Soc. Named one of Outstanding Young Women in Am., 1978; F.A. Davis Nursing fellow, 1983-84. Mem. Tex. Med. Ctr. Nurse Research Council, Houston Research Adminstrs. Council, Am. Nurses Assn., Tex. Nurses Assn., U. Tex. Space Health and Sci.-Tech. Forum, Sigma Theta Tau, Phi Kappa Phi. Home: 4103 Leeshire Dr Houston TX 77025 Office: Hermann Hosp-Robertson Pavilion 6411 Fannin St Room 537 Houston TX 77030-1501

VIERTL, REINHARD KARL WOLFGANG, statistician, educator, consultant; b. Hall i Tirol, Austria, Mar. 25, 1946; s. Johann Andreas and Hildegard (Waltl) V.; m. Dorothea Elisabeth Pittner, June 24, 1972; children: Nikolaus, Philipp. Dipl. Ing., U. Tech., Vienna, Austria, 1972, Dr. Tech., 1974. Asst. U. Tech., Vienna, 1972-79, dozent, 1979-80, prof., 1982—; research fellow, vis. lectr., U. Calif.-Berkeley, 1980-81; vis. lectr. U. Klagenfurt, Austria, 1981-82; dir. Research Projects, Vienna, 1978-84; cons. gov. orgns., Vienna, 1983-84. Author, co-author, editor books on reliability, math.; contbr. articles to profl. jours. Head Nat. Conf. Sci. Personal, Vienna, 1981-82; mem. Austrian Council of Research, Vienna, 1981-82. Served with Basic Tng. Artillery, Austria, 1974. Max Kade Found. fellow, 1980. Fellow Inst. Statisticians; mem. Austrian Math. Soc., Austrian Statis. Soc., Austrian Bayes Soc. (head, founder), Internat. Statis. Inst., German Statis. Soc., Bernoulli Soc. for Probability. Roman Catholic. Office: Univ Tech, Wiedner Hauptstr 8-10, 1040 Vienna Austria

VIESER, MILFORD AUGUST, financial executive; b. Newark, Jan. 2, 1903; m. Vera Kniep; 1 son, William Milford. Ed., Pace U.; LL.D., Fairleigh Dickinson U. Chmn. finance com. Mut. Benefit Life Ins. Co., 1960-70, dir., 1960-72, now hon. dir.; past dir. U.S. Savs. Bank, Newark, Triangle Industries, Inc., Holmdel, N.J.; dir. 1st Fidelity Bancorp. of N.J., 1st Fidelity Bank of N.J., Am. Capitol Bond Fund, Inc., Am. Capitol Convertible Securities, Inc., Am. Capitol Devel. Fund, Houston. U.S. del. Housing Com. of Econ. Commn. for, Europe, 1957; mem. Fed. N.J. Tercentenary Celebration Commn., 1960; hon. co-chmn. Newark 300th Anniversary Corp.; former chmn. N.J. Hist. Soc., N.J. Am. Revolution Bicentennial Celebration Commn.; Mem. N.J. Republican Finance Com., former chmn.; del. Rep. Nat. Conv., 1956, 64; Hon. dir. Regional Plan Assn.; trustee, vice chmn. St. Barnabas Med. Center; trustee Newark Mus. Recipient Outstanding Citizen of N.J. award Advt. Club N.J., 1968. Fellow Royal Soc. Arts and Commerce (London); mem. Greater Newark C. of C. (past pres.), Mortgage Bankers Assn. of N.J. (pres. 1952). Conglist. Clubs: Essex (Newark); Baltusrol Golf (Springfield, N.J.); Tarratine Yacht (Dark Harbor, Maine); Nassau (Princeton, N.J.). Home: 8 Shore Edge Ln Short Hills NJ 07078 also: Dark Harbor ME 04848

VIGIL, CHARLES S., lawyer; b. Trinidad, Colo., June 9, 1912; s. J.U. and Andreita (Maes) V.; m. Kathleen A. Liebert, Jan. 2, 1943; children: David Charles Edward, Marcia Kathleen. LL.B., U. Colo., 1936. Bar: Colo. 1936. Dep. dist. atty. 3d Jud. Dist. Colo., 1937-42, asst. dist. atty., 1946-51; U.S. atty. Dist. Colo., 1951-53; pvt. practice law Denver.; Dir., sec. Las Animas Co. (Colo); ARC. Author: Saga of Casimiro Barela. Bd. dirs. Family and Children's Service Denver, Colo. Humane Soc., Animal Rescue and Adophan Soc., 1987, Auraria Community Center; mem. Bishop's com. on housing; Dem. candidate U.S. Congress, 1988. Served as ensign to lt. (s.g.) USCG, 1942-46. Recipient award of civil merit Spain, 1960, award of civil merit Colo. Centennial Expn. Bd., 1976; award Colo. Chicano Bar Assn., 1979. Mem. Internat. Law Assn., ABA, Fed. Bar Assn., Colo. Bar Assn. (bd. govs.), So. Colo. Bar Assn., Hispanic Bar Colo. (bd. dirs.), Am. Judicature Soc., Internat. Bar Assn., Inter-Am. Bar, V.F.W. (comdr.), Am. Legion (comdr.), Nat. Assn. Def. Lawyers, Am. Trial Lawyers Assn., Lambda Chi Alpha, Elk, Eagle, Cootie. Clubs: Lions, Denver Athletic, Columbine Country, City of Denver, Trinidad Country. Home: 1085 Sherman St Denver CO 80203 Office: 485 Capitol Life Ctr 225 E 16th Ave Denver CO 80203

VIGIL, DAVID CHARLES, lawyer; b. Bklyn., Jan. 29, 1944; s. Charles S. and Kathleen A. (Liebert) V. B.A., U. Colo., 1966; J.D., U. N.Mex., 1969. Bar: Colo. 1969, U.S. Dist. Ct. Colo. 1969, U.S. Ct. Appeals (10th cir.) 1969, U.S. Supreme Ct. 1974. Sole practice, Denver, 1969-80; ptnr. Vigil & Vigil, Denver, 1980—. Nat. Inst for Trial Advocacy grantee, 1983. Mem. Colo. Bar Assn. (ethics com. 1973-79), Denver Bar Assn. (jud. selection and benefits com. 1975—, chmn. 1988—), Assn. Trial Lawyers Am., Assn. Trial Lawyers Colo., Colo. Hispanic Bar Assn. (bd. dirs. 1986—, treas. 1988), Cath. Lawyers Guild, NITA Advocates Assn. Democrat. Roman Catholic. Clubs: City of Denver; Columbine County (Littleton, Colo.). Lodge: Elks. Office: Vigil & Vigil Colo State Bank Bldg Suite 1715 Denver CO 80202

VIGNA, CARMELO, philosopher; b. Rosolini, Siracusa, Italy, Nov. 26, 1940; s. Sebastiano and Giuseppa (Calvo) V.; m. Mirella Zanette, Aug. 27, 1966; children: Sebastiano, Giovanni. Laurea, U. Cattolica, Milan, Italy, 1963. Prof. U. Venice, Italy, 1981—; pres. Course in Philosophy, Venice, 1984-87. Author: (books) Ragione e Religione, 1971, Filosofia e Marxismo, 1975, Le Origini del Marxismo Teorico in Italia, 1977; author/editor: (books) A. Gramsci, 1979, La Ragione e la Dialettica, 1981, Teorie della Felicità, 1986, La Qualità de l'uomo, Milano, 1988. Mem. Soc. Filosofica Italiana Sezione Veneziana (pres. 1986—). Roman Catholic. Office: U Venice Dept Philosophy, Dorsoduro 960, 30123 Venice Italy

VIGNAL, PHILIPPE, gynecologist, obstetrician; b. Fianarantsoa, Democrat Madagascar, Nov. 25, 1951; s. Pierre and Ginette (Caulet) V.; m. Claudine Paulhac, July 7, 1972 (div. 1986); children: Lea, Marion, Mathilde. MD, U. René DesCartes, Paris, 1979. Intern Hosp. La Region Paris, 1975-80; liberal practitioner ob/gyn Paris, 1980—. Author: la Grossesse-Les Conseils Du Dr Vignal, 1984. Club: Stade Francais (Paris). Home: 14 Ave T Gautier, 75016 Paris France Office: 14 Ave de Messine, 75008 Paris France

VIGNAT, JEAN-PIERRE, psychiatrist; b. Lyon, France, Feb. 9, 1940; s. Eugene and Angele (Ventura) V.; m. Anne Fayolle, June 9, 1966; Frederique, Sophie, Geraldine. MD, Faculty of Medicine, Lyon, 1966. Externe Hosp. of Lyon, 1960-62; intern Hosp. Saint-Jean-de-Dieu, Lyon, 1963-68, attache de psychotherapie, 1969, med. asst., 1969-70, chief dept. psychiatry, 1971—; asst. Faculte de Medecine, Lyon, 1966-67; coordinator Groupe Francais d'Epidemiologie Psychiatrique, Lyon, 1983. Author: Le Viellard, l'Hospice et la Mort, 1970, L'identite du Psychothèrapeute, 1984; editor Jour. l'Hygiene et Sante Publique, 1964, Revue Française de Psychiatrie, 1983; contbr. articles to profl. jours. Served with French Army, 1967-68. Mem. Soc. Francaise de Gerontologie, Soc. Psychologie Medicale, Confederation Soc. Regionales Psychiatrie, Groupe Francaise d'Epidemiologie Psychiatrique (sec.-gen.), Soc. Rhone-Alpes Psychiatrie (sec.-gen.). Office: Hosp Saint-Jean-De-Dieu, 290 Rt de Vienne, 69373 Lyon Cedex 08 France

VIHAVAINEN, TIMO JUHANI, historian; b. Sulkava, Finland, May 9, 1947; s. Paavo Johannes and Lea (Inkeri) V.; m. Maija Liisa Nuopponen, June 11, 1973; children: Marja, Rosa, Juhani. Grad., U. Helsinki, Finland, 1970, Licentiate of Philosophy, 1983. Research fellow U. Helsinki, 1977—; working group sec. Finnish-Soviet com. Sci.-Tech. Cooperation, Helsinki, 1980—. Co-author: Venäjän ja Neuvostoliiton Historia, 1986, Suomen Historian Pikkujättiläinen, 1987; contbr. articles, essays on history and lit. to learned jours. and newspapers. Mem. Suomen Historiallinen Seura. Lutheran. Home: Vanhaistentie 14-0-168, 00420 Helsinki Finland Office: Inst Hist Research and Documentation, Vuorikatu 6A 4, 00100 Helsinki Finland

VIKLUND, WILLIAM EDWIN, banker; b. Bklyn., June 12, 1940; s. Edvin Oscar and Anna Ingegard (Kvarnstrom) V.; m. Joyce Eleanor Larson, Apr. 14, 1962; children—Mark William, David Andrew, Andrea Lynn. B.A., L.I. U., Bklyn., 1960. Vice-pres. Anchor Savs. Bank, Bklyn., 1966-72; sr. v.p. Bankers Trust Co., N.Y.C., 1972-80; pres. L.I. Savs. Bank, Syosset, N.Y., 1980—; trustee The Reserve Funds. Contbr. articles to profl. jours. Mem. N.Y. Real Estate Bd. Republican. Lutheran. Club: Westhampton (N.Y.) Country. Office: Long Island Savs Bank 50 Jackson Ave Syosset NY 11791

VIKØR, KNUT SIGURDSON, historian, educator; b. Orkdal, Norway, June 10, 1952; s. Sigurd and Kari (Hammer) V. Degree, U. Oslo, 1974; postgrad., U. Bergen, Norway, 1979. Research assoc. dept. hist. U. Bergen, 1983-86, Scandinavian Inst. Asian Studies, Copenhagen, 1987-88; asst. dir. Ctr. for Middle Eastern and Islamic Studies, U. Bergen, 1988—. Co-editor: Språkundertrykking, 1981; contbr. articles to profl. jours. Mem. Norwegian council for Middle Eastern Studies, Ctr. d'études pour l'histoire de Sahara. Home: Osv 179, N-5050 Nesttun Norway Office: Ctr. for Middle Eastern and Islamic Studies, Allégt 32, N-5007 Bergen Norway

VILAIN, JEAN MARIE, physician; b. Mortagne, France, May 2, 1943; s. Gaston and Yvette (Gravelle) V.; m. Anne-Marie Auroy, Aug. 5, 1967; children: Emmanuel, Jerome. MD, Faculte de Bordeaux, France, 1972, C.E.S., 1976. Externe CHU de Bordeaux, 1968-71; intern Hosp. de Jonzac, France, 1971-72; gen. practice medicine St. Genis de Saintonge, France, 1972—, Cen. de Secours de St. Fort sur Gironde, France, 1972—; correspondant de Hosp. d Jonzac, Clinique SG Anne-Jonzac, Clinique Richelieus St., Polyclinique Royan. Served to lt. French Army, 1970-71. Mem. Societe Francaise de Medecine Generale, Confederation des Syndicats medicaux Francaise. Club: Aero. Lodge: Rotary. Home: St Fort Sur Gironde, 17240 St-Genis-De-Santiago France

VILCEK, JAN TOMAS, medical educator; b. Bratislava, Czechoslovakia, June 17, 1933; came to U.S., 1965, naturalized, 1970.; s. Julius and Friderika (Fischer) V.; m. Marica F. Gerhath, July 28, 1962. M.D., Comenius U., Bratislava, 1957; C.Sc. (Ph.D.), Czechoslovakia Acad. Sci., Bratislava, 1962. Fellow Inst. Virology, Bratislava, 1957-62, head of lab., 1962-64; asst. prof. microbiology NYU Med. Ctr., N.Y.C., 1965-68, assoc. prof., 1968-73, prof., 1973—, head biol. response modifiers, 1983—; lectr. Chinese Acad. Med. Sci., Beijing, 1981, 83, Osaka U., 1987-88; chmn. nomenclature com. WHO, 1981-86, cons. biol. standardization com., 1982—; adv. com. Cancer Soc., 1981—, chmn., 1983; expert French Ministry of Health, 1983—; mem. sci. adv. bd. Max Planck Inst., Munich, 1987—. Author: Interferon, 1969; editor: Regulatory Functions of, 1980; editor-in-chief Jour. Archives of Virology, 1975-86; editor Interferons and the Immune Systems, 1984; mem. editorial bd.: Virology, 1979-81, Archives of Virology, 1986—, Infection and Immunity, 1983-85, Antiviral Research, 1984—, Jour. Interferon Res., 1980—, Jour. Immunological Methods, 1986—, Natural Immunity and Cell Growth Regulation, 1986—, Jour. Immunology, 1987—, Lymphokine research, 1987—, Jour. Biol. Chemistry, 1988—, 151 Atlas of Sci.: Immunology, 1988—; contbr. articles to profl. jours. Recipient Research Career Devel. award USPHS, 1968-73; grantee in field USPHS, numerous other orgns. Mem. AAAS, Soc. Gen. Microbiology, Am. Soc. Microbiology, Am. Assn. Immunologists, Am. Soc. Virology (charter mem), Internat. Soc. Interferon Research. Office: NYU Med Ctr 550 1st Ave New York NY 10016

VILCHES-O'BOURKE, OCTAVIO AUGUSTO, accounting company executive; b. Havana, Cuba, Aug. 15, 1923; came to U.S., 1962, naturalized, 1967; s. Bartolome and Isabel Susana (O'Bourke) Vilches; CPA, U. Havana, 1949, JD, 1951, PhD in Econ. Scis., 1953; m. Alba Del Valle Junco, July 24, 1954; 1 son, Octavio Roberto. Owner, Octavio Vilches & Assos., Havana, 1949-61; comptroller United R.R. of Cuba, 1950-53; cons. econ. affairs Cuban Dept. Labor, Havana, 1953; auditor Cuban Dept. Treasury, 1952-59; pres. Roble Furniture, Inc., San Juan, P.R., 1963-65, owner, Hato Rey, P.R., 1963—; pres. Mero Constrn. Corp., San Juan, 1973. Mem. Circulo Cubano P.R., Colegio Contadores Publicos en el Exilio, Colegio Abogados en el Exilio, Cuban Nat. Bar Assn.; Nat. Soc. Pub. Accts. Republican. Roman Catholic. Club: American (Miami, Fla.). Home: 146 Turquesa St Guaynabo PR 00920 Office: Condominio El Centro II Suite 1402 Hato Rey PR 00920

VILES, NICHOLAS JOHN, mechanical engineer; b. London, Eng., Jan. 17, 1962; s. William John and Antonia Mary (Southworth) V.; m. Deirdre Angela Viles, Apr. 27, 1985. BS in Mech. Engring., Southampton U., Eng., 1983. Project engr. English Electric Valve Co., Chelmsford, Eng., 1979-84; mgr. research and devel. Marr Engring., Leeds, Eng., 1984-85; mgr. product test equipment Marr Engring., Leeds, 1985-87, prodn. mgr., 1987—. Patentee in field. Mem. Inst. Mech. Engrs. Home: 13 B Chudleigh Mews, Chudleigh Rd, Harrogate, North Yorkshire HG1 5NP, England Office: Marr Engring, Globe Rd, Leeds LS1 15QL, England

VILGRAIN, PIERRE E., company executive; b. Nancy, France, June 7, 1922; s. Robert M. and Lucile Edith (Joucla-Pelous) V.; m. Micheline H. Jeannequin, Mar. 11, 1947; children—Francois, Marie-Edith Vilgrain Rey-Jouvin, Edouard, Elizabeth. Ed. St. Lawrence Coll., Instn. Frilley. Pres., Grande Semoulerie De L'Quest a Gond Pontouvre (France), Tenstar Aquitaine a Bordeaux (France); gen. dir., adminstr. Grands Moulins De Paris; dir. Compagnie Francaise Commerciale et Financiere, Sofida France, Sofida Belgium, S.A. Cerealis Geneve, Vie De France Corp. USA, Le Dictionnaire Robert. Decorated Croix-de-Guerre (France); recipient Presdl. Citation (U.S.A.). Clubs: Automobile de France, Yacht de France, Cercle du Bois de Boulogne, St-Cloud Country (pres.). Office: Grands Moulins De Paris, 15 rue Croix-des-Petits-Champs, 75001 Paris France

VILJANTO, JOUKO ALEKSI, pediatric surgeon, educator; b. Sortavala, Finland, Jan. 27, 1933; s. Mikko and Klaudia (Spiridonov) V.; m. Raili Mirja Torila, June 20, 1959; 1 child, Tanja. Legitimated physician, U. Turku, Finland, 1958, D.Med.Sci., 1964, Specialist in surgery, 1966, Specialist in pediatric surgery, 1970. Asst. in med. chemistry U. Turku, 1960-63, asst. in surgery, 1963-66, docent exptl. surgery, 1969-71, docent surgery, 1971-76, docent surgery and pediatric surgery, 1976-88; specialist surgeon Turku U. Central Hosp., 1966-68, pediatric surgeon, 1968-76, assoc. chief pediatric surgery, 1976-88, assoc. prof. surgery, 1988—. Contbr. articles on exptl. and clin. studies on wound healing, 1960—. Chmn. Turun Lääkärikeskus ja Laboratoriot Oy, 1977-88. Decorated Ordinis Leonis Finlandiae 1st class; WHO scholar, 1967; Research Council for Medicine grantee, 1974-79, 84-85. Mem. Finnish Surg. Assn., Scandinavian Assn. Pediatric Surgeons, Docent Assn. Turku U. (sec. 1976-78), Finnish Assn. Pediatric Surgeons (sec. 1978-80), Scandinavian Surg. Assn. Avocation: research in wound healing. Office: Turku U, Central Hosp, Dept Pediatrics, 20520 Turku 52 Finland

VILKKI, PANU ILMARI, pediatric surgeon, educator; b. Viitasaari, Finland, May 16, 1927; s. Joel Adiel and Suoma Eliisa (Kallo) V.; m. Liisa Fredriika Vestala, July 1, 1952 children—Jaana, Mikko (dec.), Juha, Vesa. M.D., Turku U., 1951, Ph.D., 1956. Asst. chief surgery U. Hosp. Turku, Finland, 1963-67, chief pediatric surgery, 1967—, lectr. 1967—; pediatric surgeon Univ. Children's Clinic, Helsinki, 1963; researcher Biochem. Inst., Helsinki, 1952-54, 60-61; vis. scientist NIH, Bethesda, Md., 1959-60, 78; chmn. council Lansetti Surg. Cons., Ltd., 1961-87; examiner pediatric surgery Nat. Bd. Finland, 1963—. Contbr. articles to profl. jours. Chmn. Red Cross, Turku, 1966-67; fgn. sec. Med. Students Orgn., Turku, 1949-50. Child Accident Prevention Com., Finland, 1980—. NIH, USPHS grantee, 1961; Commonwealth Fund N.Y. grantee, 1967; recipient NIH New Centennial medal, 1987. Mem. Finnish Med. Assn., Assn. Pediatric Surgeons Finland (chmn. 1976-79), Brit. Assn. Pediatric Surgeons, German Assn. Pediatric Surgeons, Scandinavian Assn. Pediatric Surgeons, Finnish Surg. Assn., Finnish Pediatric Assn., Finnish Orthopedic Assn., others. Lutheran. Lodges: Fraternitas 68, Syrak. Avocations: sailing; beekeeping. Office: Turku Univ, Central Hosp, Kiinanmyllynkatu 4, SF 20520 Turku Finland

VILLA, PAOLA, economics educator; b. Carate, Italy, June 1, 1949; s. Giovanni and Corinna (Masera) V. BA in Polit. Sci., U. Cattolica, Milan, Italy, 1974, PhD in Econs., 1984. Asst. prof. econs. U. Cattolica, 1974-80, researcher, 1981-87; assoc. prof. U. Trento, 1988—; cons. Commn. European Communitites, Brussels, 1984—. Author: The Structuring of Labour Markets, 1986; contbr. articles to profl. publs. Grantee Ente per Studi Monetari Bancari, Rome, 1976, Found. Luigi Einaudi Tourin, Italy, 1978, Cambridge (Eng.) U. research maintenance grantee, 1980; Clothworkers' Research studentship, Cambridge, 1979. Mem. Internat. Working Party on Labour Market Segmentation, Assn. Italiana Economisti del Lavoro. Roman Catholic. Office: U Cattolica, Largo Gemelli 1, 20123 Milan Italy

VILLADSEN, VILLADS, museum director; b. Copenhagen, Feb. 5, 1945; s. Jens Gustav and Gerda Villadsen; m. Kathrine Langballe. Magister, U. Copenhagen, 1975. Lectr. Inst. Art History U. Copenhagen, 1976-79; dir. Randers (Denmark) Art Gallery, 1979-85, The Royal Mus. Fine Art, Copenhagen, 1985—. Contbr. articles on art and architecture to profl. jours. Mem. Nivaagaard Malerisamling (bd. dirs. 1985), Den Hirschsprungske Samling (bd. dirs. 1985), Willumsenmuseet (bd. dirs. 1985). Office: Statens Museum for Kunst, Solvgade 48-50, DK-1307 Copenhagen K Denmark

VILLAGRAN, JOSE ARTURO, architect; b. Guatemala, Guatemala, May 13, 1948; s. Jose Arturo and Dora (Miller) V.; m. Vanessa Chocano, June 21, 1952 (div. June 1986); 1 child, Jose Arturo. BArch, San Carlos U., Guatemala, 1976. Draftsman Comosa, Guatemala, 1970; designer Architect Antonio Meléndez, Guatemala, 1971-73; freelance designer Guatemala, 1974-76; architect, ptnr. Architect Antonio Prado, Guatemala, 1976-82; pvt. practice architect Guatemala, 1983—. Mem. bd. dirs. Faculty Architecture, Guatemala, 1970-71. Home: 14 St 3-27 Zone 10, Guatemala City Guatemala Office: Ave Reforma 15-54 Zone 9, Guatemala City Guatemala

VILLANOVA, MELISSA HOPE, corporate executive; b. Boston, Mar. 2, 1922; d. Douglas Nathan and Margaret (Colby) F.; m. James Brooks Scott, Oct. 12, 1950; children: Beverly, Harold. BS, Hillsdale Coll., 1949; MS, Syracuse U., 1949; PhD, Harvard U., 1955. Mem. faculty Ohio State U., Columbus, 1949-53; mem. faculty U. So. Calif, Los Angeles, 1953-83; prof. U. So. Calif., Los Angeles, 1968-83, chmn. dept., 1968-75; with Linley Corp., 1983—, now chmn.; communications cons. Procter & Gamble; communication cons. Oak Industries Inc.; communications cons. Pitney bowes Inc., Ohio Bell Telephone. Author: (with Bahm and Okey) Literature for Listening. Bd. dirs. Los Angeles chpt. ARC. Served with USNR, 1945-46. Mem. Speech Communication Assn., Internat. Communication Assn., Western States Speech Assn. (editor jour. 1958-61), Los Angeles C. of C. Democrat.

Methodist. Club: Jonathan. Lodges: Elks; K.C. Home: Werik Office Bldg 936 Wisconsin St Suite B San Francisco CA 94107

VILLANUEVA, ANTONIO, surgeon, educator; b. Puentedeume, Spain, June 20, 1934; s. Ulpiano Villanueva and Candida Diaz; m. Pilar Alvarez-Santullano, May 10, 1976; children: André, Ana. M.D., Coll. Medicine (Spain), 1959, Ph.D., 1961. Intern Univ. Hosp., Santiago, Spain, 1959-61, instr. surgery, 1961-64, assoc. prof., 1965-82; asst. etranger Clinique Universitaire, Strasbourg, France, 1961-62; vis. prof. Radcliffe Infirmary, Oxford, Eng., 1963; fellow surgery Baylor U., Houston, 1964-66; with Coll. Medicine, Santiago, 1965—, prof., 1982—; head dept. cardiovascular surgery Santiago Hosp., 1979—. Contbr. articles to profl. jours. Recipient Baltar Found. prize U. Santiago, 1960; San Nicolas Found. Prize Royal Acad. Scis., 1960; Spain Nat. award in Medicine, 1960. Fellow N.Y. Acad. Scis., Internat. Coll. Angiology; mem. Coll. Francais de Pathologie Vasculaire, D.A. Cooley Cardiovascular Soc., M.E. DeBakey Internat. Cardiovascular Soc., Spanish Assn. Cardiovascular Surgery. Avocations: jazz piano player; music; sports; tennis. Home: Montero Rios 12, Santiago de Compostela Spain Office: Facultad de Medicina Universidad, Santiago de Composte Spain

VILLANUEVA, ARMANDO, Peru government official. Prime minister Peru, Lima, 1988—. Address: Office Prime Minister, Lima Peru *

VILLANUEVA, DARIO, academic educator; b. Villalba, Galicia, Spain, June 5, 1950; s. Francisco Villanueva and Maria Prieto; m. Ermitas Penas Varela, Mar. 28, 1950; children: Beatriz, José Francisco. MA in Romance Philology, U. Santiago de Compostela, Spain, 1972; D in Hispanic Philology, Autonomous U. Madrid, 1976. Asst. prof. U. Santiago de Compostela, Spain, 1972-75; prof. tutor Univ. Nat. de Edn., Pontevedra, Spain, 1975-77; assoc. prof. U. Santiago de Compostela, Spain, 1975-86, prof. theory of lit., 1987—; sec. Facultad de Filologia, 1978-83, dean, 1987—; dir. collection Ediciones Taurus, Madrid, 1984—; pres. Comision de Doctorado de la Univ., 1987—; vis. prof. Middlebury Coll., Vt., 1987—. Author: El Jarama de Sanchez Ferlosio, 1973, Estructura y Tiempo Reducido En La Novela, 1977; editor: La Novela Lirica, 1983, 2 vols. Named Disting. Vis. Fgn. Scholar Mid-Am. State Univs. Assn., 1982. Mem. Asociación Internacional de Hispanistas, Sociedad Española de Semiótica, Twentieth Century Spanish Assn. Am., Internat. Comparative Lit. Assn. Clubs: Real Aero (Santiago de Compostela); Nautico (Noya-Portosin, Spain). Home: Montero Rios 36-6 A, 15706 Santiago de Compostela Spain Office: Facultad de Filologia, Plaza de Mazarelos, 15703 Santiago de Compostela Spain

VILLANUEVA, DAVID ABADILLA, interior designer; b. Antipolo, Pontevedra, Negros Occidental Philippines, Aug. 29, 1963; s. Antonio Belo Villanueva and Lourdes (Dominguez) Abadilla. Degree, La Consolacion Coll., Bacolod City, Philippines, 1987. Designer jd Ilonggo, Bacolod City, 1984—. Mem. House of Negros. Home: Negros Occidental, Antipolo 6100, Philippines Office: 90-E San Juan St, Bacolod City, Negros Occidental 6100, Philippines

VILLANUEVA, ROBERTO T., investment company executive; b. Manila, Mar. 7, 1920; s. Manuel B. and Eugenia (Bosch) V.; m. Corazon Grau, Oct. 28, 1943; children: Roberto Jr., Luis, Eduardo. Grad. in commerce-law, U. Santo Tomas, Manila, 1940. Assoc. editor Manila Chronicle, Manila, 1945-47, gen. mgr., 1947-52; chmn. Binalbagan-Isabela Sugar Co., Manila, 1949-62; pres. Manila Electric Co., 1949-60, chmn., 1961-62; pres. Trans-Philippines Investment Corp., Manila, 1962-88, AGP Indsl. Corp., Manila, 1970-84; chmn. Atlantic, Gulf and Pacific Co. of Manila, Inc., 1971—; bd. dirs. Far East Bank and Trust Co., Manila, Lepanto Consol. Mining Co., Manila, Shearson Lehman Internat. Investments Inc.; chmn. Roberto Villanueva Inc., Manila, Hoechst Far East Mktg. Corp., Manila, Exquisite Form Industries Inc., N.Y.C.; chmn. adv. bd. Trans-Philippines Investment Corp., Manila, Pvt. Devel. Corp. of Philippines, Manila. Named Industry Leader Bus. Writers Assn. of Philippines, 1956, Businessman of Yr. Bus. Writers Assn. of Philippines, 1962, Mgmt. Man of Yr. Personnel Mgmt. Assn. Philippines, 1985; recipient World Bus. award Stanford Research Inst. Internat., 1983. Fellow Am. Inst. Mgmt., Internat. Acad. Mgmt.; mem. Conf. Bd. N.Y. (sr. mem.), Philippines-U.S. Bus. Council (chmn. 1986—), Asian Inst. Mgmt. (co-chmn. 1987—). Lodge: Knight of the Holy Sepulcher. Home: No 42 Banaba Rd, Forbes Park, Makati Metro Manila Philippines Office: Atlantic Gulf & Pacific Co, Ag & P Engr's Ctr, Sen Gil J Puyat Ave, Makati Metro Manila 2800, Philippines

VILLAROSA, CELIA JESSICA LIM, management consultant; b. Manila, June 28, 1953; d. Jesus Lim and Araceli Laperal Ricafort; m. Leovigildo Madi Villarosa; 1 child, Christine. BS in Edn. and Journalism, Lyceum of Phillipines, Manila, 1973; MA in Edn., Lyceum of Phillipines, 1977; PhD in Counseling Psychology, De La Salle U., Manila, 1985. Assoc. prof., sr. researcher career materials devel. project De La Salle U., 1974-75; mgr. office administrn. and manpower The Borromeo Group Cos., Manila, 1975-80; mgr. administrn., personnel and purchasing Manila Gas Group Cos., 1980-83; mgmt. cons., dir. United Human Resources Mgmt., Inc., Manila, 1983-86; mng. dir. Internat. Mgmt. Cons., Manila, 1986-87; dir. tng. Century Park Sheraton, Manila, 1987—; cons. orgnl. devel. to various cos., 1982-86, mgmt. to various corps., 1986—. Author: Career Development of the Filipina Executive, 1987. V.p. Philippine Assn. U. Women, Manila, 1974; career counselor civic groups, Manila, 1980—. Mem. Personnel Mgmt. Assn. Philippines (resource speaker 1979—), Philippine Soc. Tng. and Devel. (resource speaker 1983), Philippine Mktg. Assn. Roman Catholic. Club: Toastmasters (administrv. v.p. 1986-87, ednl. v.p. 1987—, Best Impromptu Speaker 1985); German (Manila). Lodge: Elks. Home: 12 Kamagong cor Talisay Rd, Mahogany Homes, St Martin Subdiv, Bagumbayan Taguig, Met Manila Philippines Office: Century Park Sheraton, Vito Cruz cor Adriatico, Manila Philippines

VILLARREAL, CARLOS CASTANEDA, engineer; b. Brownsville, Tex., Nov. 9, 1924; s. Jesus Jose and Elisa L. (Castaneda) V.; m. Doris Ann Akers, Sept. 10, 1948; children: Timothy Hill, David Akers. B.S., U.S. Naval Acad., 1948; M.S., U.S. Navy Postgrad. Sch., 1950; LL.D. (hon.), St. Mary's U., 1972. Registered profl. engr. Commd. ensign U.S. Navy, 1948, advanced through grades to lt., 1956; comdg. officer U.S.S. Rhea, 1951, U.S.S. Osprey, 1952; comdr. Mine Div. 31, 1953; resigned 1956; mgr. marine and indsl. operation Gen. Electric Co., 1956-66; v.p. mktg. and adminstrn. Marquardt Corp., 1966-69; head Urban Mass Transit Adminstrn., Dept. Transp., Washington, 1969-73; commr. Postal Rate Commn., 1973-79, vice chmn., 1975-79; v.p. Washington ops. Wilbur Smith and Assocs., engring. design and cons. firm, 1979-84, sr. v.p., 1984-86, exec. v.p., 1987—, also bd. dirs.; lectr. in field; mem. industry sector adv. com. Dept. Commerce; mem. sect. 15 adv. com. Dept. Transp., 1983-86. Contbr. to profl. jours. Mem. devel. com. Wolftrap Farm Park for the Performing Arts, 1973-78; mem. council St. Elizabeth Ch., 1982-86, chmn. fin. com.; mem. bd. edn. St. Elizabeth Sch.; bd. dirs. Assoc. Catholic Charities, 1983-86; mem. fin. com. Cath. Charities, U.S.A. Decorated knight Sovereign Mil. Hospitaller Order St. John of Jerusalem of Rhodes and Malta, 1981; recipient award outstanding achievement Dept. Transp. Mem. Am. Pub. Transit Assn., IEEE, Soc. Naval Architects and Marine Engrs., Soc. Am. Mil. Engrs., Am. Rds. and Transp. Builders Assn. (chmn. pub. transp. adv. council), Transp. Research Bd., Am. Cons. Engrs. Council (vice chmn. internat. com.), ASCE, NSPE (pres. D.C. Soc. 1986-87), Washington Soc. Engrs., Internat. Bridge, Tunnel and Turnpike Assn. Republican. Roman Catholic. Clubs: University (Washington), Army- Navy (Washington); University (Cin.). Office: 1100 Connecticut Ave NW Suite 750 Washington DC 20036

VILLAT, CLAUDE MAX, banker; b. Aarau, Switzerland, June 10, 1946; s. Marcel Charles and Anne Marie (Gloor) V. Major degree in commerce U. Aarau (Switzerland), 1965; cert. Swiss Merc. Sch., London, 1967. Stock exchange dealer Swiss Bank Corp., Lausanne, Switzerland, 1965-67; investment advisor, v.p. Nordfinanz-Bank Zurich, Switzerland, 1968-77; with comml. mktg. AVP Sogenal Zurich, 1977-79; dir., sr. v.p. fin. services Bankers Trust A.G., Zurich, 1979—; chmn. Pensionfund BTAG, Zurich, 1980—; mem. Swiss Stock Exchange, 1981—; chmn. Roi Ford GmbH Munchen (formerly M.C.D. GmbH Munchen), Munich, Ger., 1980—. Club: AMEX (Zurich). Office: Bankers Trust AG, Dreikonigstrasse 6, 8022 Zurich Switzerland

VILLAVERDE, XAVIER, architect; b. Buenos Aires, Argentina, Nov. 4, 1957; s. Manuel Evaristo and Marta Gloria (Bisio) V. B, San Martin de Tours, Buenos Aires, 1975; Architect, U. Buenos Aires, 1981. Registered architect, Buenos Aires. Architect Studio Villaverde, S.A., Buenos Aires, 1987—. inventor spray applicator. Clubs: C.U.B.A., Boating.

VILLAX, IVAN (JOÃO), research chemist; b. Magyarovar, Hungary, Apr. 16, 1925; Portuguese citizen, 1959; s. Edmond (Odon) and Marianne (Manninger) V.; grad. in Chem. Engring., Poly. Univ. Budapest, 1948; postgrad. research fellow U. Clermont-Ferrand, France, 1950-51; m. Diane de Lancastre Houssemayne Du Boulay, Feb. 8, 1958; children: Peter, Guy, Sofia, Miguel. Asst. Centre de Recherches Agronomiques, Clermont-Ferrand, France, 1949-51; dir. research Instituto Pasteur of Lisbon, Portugal, 1952-60; pres. Hovione-Sociedade Quimica, Lda., Lisbon, 1959—; mem. bd., research dir. Fermentfarma SpA., Corsico (Milano), Italy, 1960-67; dir. Hovione (H.K.) Ltd., Hong Kong, Hovione Japan Ltd., Tokyo, Hovione Inter Ltd., Zurich, Hovione (Macau) Soc. Quimica Lda., Macau. Mem. Am. Chem. Soc., Am. Soc. Microbiology. Roman Catholic. Club: Gremio Literario (Lisbon). Patentee field of organic chemistry and microbiology; contbr. sci. papers to profl. publs. Office: Quinta S Pedro Sete, Casas, 2670 Loures Portugal

VILLELLA, EDWARD JOSEPH, ballet dancer, choreographer; b. L.I., N.Y., Oct. 1, 1936; s. Joseph and Mildred (DeGiovanni) V.; m. Janet Greschler (div. Nov. 1980); 1 child, Roddy; m. Linda Carbonetta, Apr. 1981; children: Christa Francesca, Lauren. BS in Marine Transp., N.Y. State Maritime Coll., 1957; LHD (hon.), Boston Conservatory, 1985; hon. degree, Skidmore Coll., Fordham U., Nazareth Coll., Siena Coll. Mem. N.Y.C. Ballet, 1957, soloist, 1958-60, prin. soloist, 1960-83; artistic dir. Ballet Okla., Oklahoma City, 1983-86, Miami (Fla.) City Ballet, 1986—; vis. artist U.S. Mil. Acad. at West Point, 1981-82; vis. prof. dance U. Iowa, 1981. Dancer N.Y. City Ballet, from 1957; guest appearance as dancer London, 1962, Royal Danish Ballet Co., 1963, Boston Ballet, 1968, 69, Miami Ballet, 1968-69, N.Y.C. Opera, 1969, White House, London, 1971; appearances on TV shows including Ed Sullivan Show, Bell Telephone Hour, Mike Douglas Show, (TV spl.) Harlequin, 1975 (Emmy award), summer theatres, festivals, U.S. and abroad, 1957—; artistic coordinator, Eglevsky Ballet Co. (now AndréEglevsky State Ballet of N.Y.), N.Y.C., 1979-84; choreographer, Eglevsky Ballet Co., N.Y.C., 1980-84, N.J. Ballet, 1980—; artistic dir., Ballet Okla., Oklahoma City, 1984-86; lectr. in field. Mem. Nat. Council on Arts, 1968-74; chmn. Commn. for Cultural Affairs City N.Y., 1978; bd. visitors N.C. Sch. for the Arts. *

VILLOTTI, RICCARDO, medical manufacturing and health care company executive; b. Rome, June 19, 1930; s. Dante and Adele (Petrongari) V.; Organic Chemistry Degree, U. Rome, 1955; postgrad. (research fellow) U. Detroit, 1957-60. NIH research fellow, sr. chemist Syntex S.A., Mexico City, 1960-61; group leader Research Lab., Farmitalia, Milan, Italy, 1961-62; group leader Syntex Research Lab., Mexico City, 1962-63; area mgr. Internat. div. Syntex Corp., Palo Alto, Calif., 1963-66; mng. dir. Syntex Farmaceutici, Milan, 1966-70; sr. dir. mktg. and prodn. Recordati S.p.A., Milan, 1970-80; v.p. Pierrel S.p.A., Milan, 1981—; mem. exec. com. Nutritional Found. of Italy. Fulbright fellow, 1957. Mem. Italia Nostra, Italian Assn. Cancer Research, Am. Chem. Soc. Roman Catholic. Contbr. articles to Italian and fgn. profl. jours. Home: 1 Via Principe Amedeo, 20121 Milan Italy Office: 96 Bisceglie, 20152 Milan Italy

VILPPONEN, TAPIO ROY, public relations executive; b. Rauma, Finland, May 31, 1913; s. Armas and Alexandra (Kannelkoski); m. Toini Pyykkö (div. 1965); m. Rita Rif, 1965; children: Malo Mikael, Nemo Rafael. Studies with, E. Pakkala, Helsinki. Editor Pohjois Savo, Kuopio, Finland, 1930-36; copywriter Sek Advt. Agy., Helsinki, 1936-40; advt. mgr. Suomifilmi Movie Prodns., Helsinki, 1940-50; chief designer Socieda Arquitetura Corona, Sao Paulo, Brazil, 1950-54; arts mgr. Mainos TV, Helsinki, 1960-77; exec. dir. PR Relations Internat., Helsinki, 1977—. Author: El Zorro Del Castelrey; editor-in-chief Loo mag., Echo Internat. Rev., Me, Uutisaitta. Recipient 4 Finnish Oscar awards, 1942-51, Gold medal Finnish Motion Picture Acad., 1950. Mem. Brit. Royal TV Soc., Assn. Interior Architecture, Finnish Advt. (assoc.), Filmjournalists R.Y. (first chmn.), Hearing Impaired Architects Network. Home and Office: PR Rela Internat, Uudenmaankatu 32 A5, 00120 Helsinki Finland

VINARDI, JOSEPH JOHN, lawyer; b. Dawson, N. Mex., June 16, 1908; s. P. Anton and Constance (Bellezza) V.; m. Margaret Ann Schumann, Nov. 4, 1911; children—Gwendolyn Mary Lynn, Catherine Ann Vinardi Dickey, John J. Ph.B., Creighton U., 1930, J.D., 1932. Bar: Nebr. 1932, U.S. Dist. Ct. Nebr. 1932, U.S. Ct. Appeals (8th cir.) 1936. Ptnr. Gross, Welch, Vinardi, Kauffman and Day, Omaha, 1932—. Bd. dirs. United Omaha, 1963—; campaign mgr. various Republican campaigns for fed. and state offices, 1946-80. Served to maj. inf. U.S. Army, 1942-46. Recipient Freedom Found.'s award, 1950; Alumni Merit award Creighton U., 1978. Mem. ABA. Nebr. Bar Assn., Omaha Bar Assn., Am. Judicature Soc. Roman Catholic. Office: 800 Commerical Federal Tower 72d at Mercy Rd Omaha NE 68124

VINCENS, LOUIS-FRANÇOIS, surgeon; b. Treignac, France, June 11, 1939; s. Robert and Marie-Françoise (Maurin) V.; m. Catherine Laire, Apr. 3, 1970; 1 child, Xavier. MD, U. Clermont-Ferrand, France, 1968, student urology, 1971. Hosp. extern Clermont-Ferrand, France, 1959-63; hosp. intern Clermont-Ferrand, 1965-68, asst. hosp. clin. chief, 1969-71, practice medicine specializing in surgery, 1971—; gen.-pres., dir. Clinique des Domes, Clermont-Ferrand, 1987; expert Arreal Tribunal, Riom, 1975. Mem. French Assn. Urology. Roman Catholic. Lodge: Rotary. Home: Gregoire de Tours 8, 63000 Clermont-Ferrand France Office: 37 Gonod, 63000 Clermont-Ferrand France

VINCENT, BRUCE HAVIRD, oil and gas company executive, financial consultant; b. Laramie, Wyo., Nov. 7, 1947; s. Dale Leon and Mildred Sara (Havird) V.; children: Jennifer Jean, Bryce Havird. BA in Bus. Adminstrn., Duke U., 1969; MBA in Fin., U. Houston, 1976. Asst. v.p. First City Nat. Bank, Houston, 1975-77, v.p., group mgr. energy dept., 1977-80; exec. v.p., chief operating officer, bd. dirs. Peninsula Resources Corp., Corpus Christi, Tex., 1980-82; ptnr. investment banking Johnson & Vincent, Houston, 1982-85; pres., chief exec. officer Tangent Oil and Gas, Inc., Houston, 1985-86; exec. v.p., chief operating officer, chief fin. officer Energy Assets Internat. Corp., Houston, 1986—, also bd. dirs. Served to lt. USN, 1969-72. Mem. Ind. Petroleum Assn. of Am., Tex. Mid-Continent Oil and Gas Assn., Tex. Ind. Producers and Royalty Owners Assn., Internat. Assn. Fin. Planning. Episcopalian. Home: 1710 Milford Houston TX 77098 Office: Energy Assets Internat Corp 1221 Lamar Suite 1500 Houston TX 77010

VINCENT, CLARK EDWARD, sociologist; b. Otis, Colo., May 13, 1923; s. Ralph Ellory and Lillian May (Auld) V.; m. Roseann Wagoner, Dec. 27, 1955; children: Evelyn J. Vincent Stansbury, Timothy T., Thomas N., Walter W. A.B., U. Calif. at Berkeley, 1949, M.A., 1950, Ph.D. (NIMH fellow, Univ. fellow), 1952. From instr. to asst. prof. family sociology U. Calif. at Berkeley, 1952-59; asso. prof. State U. Iowa, 1959-60; scientist administr. NIMH, 1960-64, mem. research rev. com. applied research br., 1975-77; prof. sociology Bowman Gray Sch. Medicine, 1964—; dir. Behavioral Scis. Center, 1966-74, Marital Health Clinic, 1972-77, chmn. dept. med. social scis. and marital health, 1974-75; Cons. to tng. and manpower resources br. NIMH, 1964-65, 75-76, AID, Dept. State, 1969-71; spl. cons. to com. on family life Nat. Council Chs. Christ in U.S., 1963-66; mem. family life edn. com. Am. Coll. Obstetricians-Gynecologists. Author: Unmarried Mothers, 1961, Sexual and Marital Health, 1973; Asso. editor: Social Problems, 1961-64, 67-69, Jour. Marriage and Family, 1965-69, 75-78, Jour. Marriage and Family Counseling, 1975-78, Jour. Sex and Marital Therapy, 1974-79; Editorial bd.: Jour. Spl. Edn, 1967-78, Jour. of Divorce, 1977-81; Compiler, editor: Readings in Marriage Counseling, 1957, Human Sexuality in Medical Education and Practice, 1968; co-editor, compiler: Psychosocial Aspects of Medical Training, 1971; Contbr. numerous articles to profl. publs. Co-founder, bd. dirs. Sex Edn. and Information Council U.S., 1964-70, 72-74; bd. dirs. Nat. Council Illegitimacy, 1967-70; nat. chmn. Groves Conf. Marriage and the Family, 1962-63, bd. dirs., 1963-67. Recipient Clark E. Vincent scholarly award Calif. Assn. Marriage and Family Counselors, 1975; Medallion of Merit Wake Forest U., 1978; Sperry award N.C. Family Life Council, 1978. Fellow Am. Assn. Marriage and Family Therapists (past v.p., exec. bd., pres. 1973-74, Disting. Pioneer award 1978), Am. Sociol. Assn. (chmn. family sect. 1973-74), Soc. Sci. Study Sex; mem. Nat. Council Family Relations (chmn. counseling sect. 1961-62, exec. bd. 1962-65, pres. 1964-65), Sigma Xi. Home: 14 High Cloud Trail Sedona AZ 86336

VINCENT, DAVID RIDGELY, information executive; b. Detroit, Aug. 9, 1941; s. Charles Ridgely and Charlotte Jane (McCarroll) V.; m. Margaret Helen Anderson, Aug. 25, 1962 (div. 1973); children—Sandra Lee, Cheryl Ann; m. Judith Ann Gomez, July 2, 1978; 1 child, Amber; stepsons—Michael Jr., Jesse Joseph Flores. B.S., B.A., Calif. State U.-Sacramento, 1964; M.B.A., Calif. State U.-Hayward, 1971. Sr. ops. analyst Aerojet Gen. Corp., Sacramento, 1960-66; controller Hexcel Corp., Dublin, Calif., 1966-70; mng. dir. Memorex, Austria, 1970-74; sales mgr. Ampex World Ops., Switzerland, 1974-76; dir. product mgmt. NCR, Sunnyvale, Calif., 1976-79; v.p. Boole & Babbage Inc., gen. mgr. Inst. Info. Mgmt., Sunnyvale, Calif., 1979-85; pres. The Info. Group, Inc., Santa Clara, Calif., 1985—. Trustee Republican Nat. Task Force; deacon Union Ch., Cupertino, Calif.; USSF/NCAA soccer referee. Author: Perspectives in Information Management, Information Economics, 1983, Handbook of Information Resource Management, 1987; contbr. monographs and papers to profl. jours. Home: 2803 Kalliam Dr Santa Clara CA 95051 Office: PO Box Q Santa Clara CA 95055-3756

VINCENT, EDWARD PORTER, sales and service company executive; b. Franklin, Pa., Dec. 31, 1928; s. Arthur Porter and Leila F. (Watson) V.; B.S. in Chemistry, Grove City Coll., 1952; P.M.D., Harvard U., 1966; m. Sophie Harwood, Oct. 16, 1954; children—Mark P., Gregory S., Shawn E. Asst. supt. furnace dept. PPG Industries, Creighton, Pa., 1952-57; mgr. tech. sales Refractory div. Kaiser Aluminum and Chem. Corp., Oakland, Calif., 1957-66; exec. v.p. E.S.M., Inc., Valencia, Pa., 1966-69; v.p. mktg. Zedmark, Inc., Valencia, 1969-75, now dir.; pres. E.P. Vincent, Inc., Gibsonia, Pa., 1975—; engring. cons. to industry, 1975—; incorporator Vincent Assos., retail sales microcomputers, operating 5 retail outlets in Allegheny and Butler Counties, 1980. Bd. dirs., pres. Butler County Mental Health Assn., 1977-79. Mem. Am. Ceramic Soc. Republican. Clubs: Butler Country, Masons, Shriners. Home: 1221 North Dr Butler PA 16001 Office: 7204 McKnight Rd Pittsburgh PA 15237

VINCENT, GEOFFREY ALAN, financial executive; b. Melbourne, Australia, Feb. 11, 1941; s. Eric and Caroline Frances (Grieve) V.; B.Commerce in Acctg., Melbourne U., 1961, B.A., 1965; m. Lesley Carolyn McKenzie, Jan. 28, 1966 (div.); children—Mark Ian Vincent, Andrew David, Melinda Jane; m. Denise Margot Nugara, Sept. 18, 1987. Acct., Australian Mining & Smelting Ltd., Rum Jungle, No. Terr., 1965-67; adminstrv. mgr. Rio Tinto Brick Co., Melbourne, 1967-68; successively chief acct., treas., then controller Bougainville Copper Ltd., Melbourne and Papua New Guinea, 1969-76; exec. dir. Australian Soc. Accts., Melbourne, 1976-82; dir. fin. Monsanto Australia Ltd., Melbourne, 1982-86; dir. fin. Black & Decker Holdings Ltd., 1986-88, gen. mgr. fin. State Bank Victoria, 1988—. Sec. Brighton br. Liberal Party, 1975-78; pres. Apex Community Service Orgn., 1969-73. Recipient Queen Elizabeth medal, 1977; Order of Australia for services to acctg., 1981. Asso. Australian Soc. Accts., Inst. Chartered Secs. and Adminstrs. Mem. Ch. of Eng. Clubs: Kingston Heath Golf (Melbourne); Athenaeum; Royal Brighton Yacht. Home: 75 New St, Brighton 3186 Australia Office: 385 Bourke St, Melbourne 3000, Australia

VINCENT, HAL WELLMAN, marine corps officer, investor; b. Pontiac, Mich., Sept. 27, 1927; s. Harold and Glenda (Wellman) V.; m. Virginia Bayler, June 9, 1951; children: David B., Dale W., Deborah K. Vincent Minder. Student, Navy V-5 program Western Mich. Coll./Colgate U., 1945; BS, U.S. Naval Acad., 1950; postgrad., Marine Officers Basic Sch., 1950, Flight Sch., 1952, Test Pilot Sch., 1955, Navy Fleet Air Gunnery Sch., 1958, Air Force Fighter Weapons Sch., 1959, Marine Corps Command and Staff Coll., 1964, Indsl. Coll., 1969, Marine Air Weapons Tng. Unit, 1972. Commd. 2d lt. U.S. Marine Corps, 1950, advanced through grades to maj. gen., 1974; rifle and machinegun platoon comdr. Camp Lejeune, N.C., 1951; fighter pilot El Toro, Calif. and, Korea, 1953-54; test pilot (Flight Test Div.), Patuxent River, Md., 1955-57; ops. officer, squadron asst. and fighter pilot El Toro, 1958-59; conventional weapons project officer (Naval Air Weapons Test Center), China Lake, Calif., 1960-62; squadron ops. and exec. officer El Toro and Japan, 1962-64; aviation specialist Marine Corps amphibious warfare presentation team and staff officer Quantico, Va., 1965-66; comdg. officer (2d Marine Aircraft Wing fighter-attack squadron), Beaufort, S.C., 1967-68; exec. officer (Marine Aircraft Group), Vietnam, 1969; logistics staff officer (Fleet Marine Force Pacific), Hawaii, 1970-72; comdg. officer (Marine Aircraft Group), Yuma, Ariz., 1972-73; chief of staff (3d Marine Aircraft Wing), El Toro, 1973-76; dep. chief. of staff plans and policy, to (Comdr. in Chief Atlantic), Norfolk, Va., 1976-78; comdg. gen. (2d Marine Aircraft Wing), Cherry Point, N.C., 1978-80; dep. comdg. gen. (Fleet Marine Force Atlantic), Norfolk, 1980-82; ret. 1982, investor, 1982—; flight test pilot; preliminary pilot, evaluator new mil. aircraft. Contbr. numerous articles on tactics and conventional weapons delivery, flight test stability and control to various mil. publs. Decorated Legion of Merit with 2 gold stars, D.F.C., Bronze Star with combat V, Air medal with star and numeral 14, Joint Services Commendation medal U.S.; Honor medal 1st class; Cross of Gallantry with gold star Republic of Vietnam). Mem. SAR, Soc. Exptl. Test Pilots, Marine Corps Assn., Early Pioneer Naval Aviators, Marine Corps Aviation Assn., Mach 2 Club. Clubs: Army-Navy Country, Army-Navy Town.

VINCENT, LLOYD DREXELL, university president; b. DeQuincy, La., Jan. 7, 1924; s. Samuel and Lila (Dickerson) V.; m. Johnell Stuart, Aug. 30, 1947; children: Drexell Stuart, Sandra. Student, Rice U., 1946-47, 49-50; B.S., U. Tex., Austin, 1952, M.A., 1953, Ph.D., 1960; postdoctoral Inst. for Ednl. Mgmt., Harvard U., 1987. Asst. prof. U. Southwestern La., 1953-55, assoc. prof., 1956-58; instr. Tex. A&M U., 1955-56; Danforth Found. tchr. study grantee, NSF Sci. faculty fellow. U. Tex., 1958-59; research scientist Tex. Nuclear Corp., Austin, 1959-60; prof., dir. physics dept. Sam Houston State U., 1960-65, asst. to pres., 1965-67; pres. Angelo State U., San Angelo, Tex., 1967—; Co-owner, mgr. ACME Glass Corp., Baytown, Tex., 1947-49; physics cons. Columbia U. Tchrs. Coll., U.S. AID, India, summer 1966; dir. W.Tex. Utilities Co., 1978—; vice chmn. Council Presidents of Public Sr. Colls. and Univs. Tex., 1980-81; chmn. Council Presidents of Lone Star Athletic Conf., 1981-82, 86-87; mem. NCAA Pres.'s Commn., 1987—. Bd. dirs. West Tex. Rehab. Center, 1977—; bd. visitors Air U., Maxwell AFB, Ala., 1981-86. Served to 2d lt. USAAF, 1942-45. Named Citizen of Year San Angelo C. of C., 1975. Fellow Tex. Acad. Sci.; mem. Am. Phys. Soc., Am. Assn. State Colls. and Univs. (state rep. 1972-74, mission of univ., pres. and chancellors to Malaysia 1986), Am. Assn. Physics Tchrs. (sect. chmn. 1965-67, mem. nat. del. to USSR and China 1983), Assn. Tex. Colls. and Univs. (bd. dirs. 1981-85), So. Assn. Colls. and Schs. (mem. commn. on colls. 1985—), Sigma Xi, Sigma Pi Sigma. Democrat. Baptist. Club: Rotary. Office: Angelo State U Office of Pres San Angelo TX 76909

VINCENT, ROBERT KELLER, geophysicist, geological consulting company executive; b. Bunkie, La., Feb. 6, 1941; s. Edward and Frances L. (Keller) V.; B.A. cum laude, La. Tech. U., 1963, B.S. cum laude in Physics, 1963; M.S. in Physics, U. Md., 1966; postgrad. M.I.T., 1968; Ph.D. in Geology, U. Mich., 1973; m. Dinah Kay Mannerud, June 19, 1978; 1 child, Robert Anthony; stepchildren—Kimberley Jane, Hilary Beth, Cory Erwin; children by previous marriage—Derek Andrew, Heather Louise, David Christopher. Engr., Tex. Instruments, Inc., summers, 1963-65; research assoc. Willow Run Labs., U. Mich., Ann Arbor, 1970-72; research geophysicist Environ. Research Inst. Mich. (formerly Willow Run Labs.), 1972-74; founder, pres. Geospectra Corp., Ann Arbor, 1974—, chmn. bd., 1974—, cons. to oil and mining cos., 1974—; founder BioImage Corp.; pres., dir. Promethean Technologies, Inc., 1986—; cons. to NASA Planetary Radar Working Group, 1977-79, U.S. Army Expert Working Group, 1978-80. Contbr. over 60 tech. pubs. to profl. jours. Served to capt. USAF, 1966-70. Mem. Am. Geophys. Union, Am. Inst. Physics, Optical Soc. Am., AAAS, Am. Soc. Photogrammetry (chmn. geol. scis. com. 1981-82), Am. Assn. Petroleum Geologists, Mich. Tech. Council (chmn. 1984-85), Nat. Acad. Scis. (com. practical applications of remote sensing from space), Sigma Xi, Omicron Delta Kappa, Phi Kappa Phi. Methodist. Club: Masons. Contbr. articles to sci. jours. Home: 1645 Morehead Dr Ann Arbor MI 48103 Office: 333 Parkland Plaza PO Box 1387 Ann Arbor MI 48106

VINES, WILLIAM JOSHUA, business executive, farmer, grazier; b. Terang, Victoria, Australia, May 27, 1916. Student Haileybury Coll., 1928-32; grad. Royal Mil. Staff Coll., 1945. With wool dept. Australian Estates Co. Ltd., 1932-36, sta. auditor, 1936-38; sec. Alexander Fergusson Pty. Ltd., 1938-47; sales dir. assoc. co. Goodlass Wall Ltd., 1945-48; mng. dir. Lewis Berger & Sons (Victoria) Pty. Ltd., 1948-55, Lewis Berger & Sons (Australia) Pty. Ltd., 1952-55; group mng. dir. Lewis Berger & Sons Ltd., London, 1955-61; dir. Lewis Berger (later Berger, Jenson & Nicholson Ltd., London and Australia), 1961-74; mng. dir. Internat. Wool Secretariat, London, 1961-69, dir., 1961-79; owner Old Southwood Sta., Tara, Queensland, Australia, 1965-82; chmn. Dalgety Australia Ltd., 1969-80, dir., 1969-84, mng. dir., 1970-76, dir. Dalgety N.Z. Ltd., 1969-80, dir. Dalgety Ltd., London, 1969-80, dir. Dalgety Australia Holdings Ltd., 1984—, Dalgety Farmers Ltd., 1984—; chmn. Thorn Elec. Industries Australia Ltd., 1969-74; dir. Comml. Union Assurance Co. Australia Ltd., 1969-78, P. & O. Australia Holding Pty. Ltd., 1969-71; chmn. Wiggins Teape Ltd. Australia, 1969-72; dir. Wiggins Teape Ltd., London, 1969-78; chmn. Carbonless Papers (Wiggins Teape) Pty. Ltd., 1970-78; founding chmn. Australian Wool Commn., 1970-72; dir. ANZ Banking Group Ltd., 1976-89, dep. chmn., 1981-82, chmn., 1982-89; owner Cliffdale Sta., Currabubula, New South Wales, Australia, 1982—; dir., chmn. Associated Pulp & Paper Mills Ltd., 1972-83; dep. chmn. Tubemakers of Australia Ltd., 1970-86; dir. CRA Ltd., 1976-84, Port Phillip Mills Ltd., 1971—; parttime mem. exec. Commonwealth Sci. and Indsl. Research Orgn., 1973-78: mem. Commonwealth Govt. Econ. Adv. Group, 1976-86. Chmn. Sir Robert Menaies Meml. Trust; chmn. council Hawkesbury Agrl. Coll.; Australian counsellor Conf. Bd. Served to Maj. Australian Army, 1940-45. Mentioned in dispatches; decorated companion Order St. Michael and St. George for service to wool industry, 1969, Companion Order of Australia, 1987; invested Knight Bachelor, 1977. Address: Cliffdale, Currabubula NSW 2342, Australia other: 38 Bridge Street, Sydney NJW 2000, Australia

VINK, FRANS, publishing company executive; b. Tongelre, Netherlands, July 4, 1918; immigrated to Belgium, 1919; s. Jacobus Bartholomeus and Hermanna Maria (Droste) V.; m. Elizabeth Johanna Hoste, May 7, 1941; children—Frans Peter, Johan Barth, Gilles Paul. Degree in Comml. Engring., U. Libre de Brussels, 1940. With Philips S.A.B., Brussels, 1940-41; Union Chimique Belge, S.A., Brussels, 1941-44; sec. gen. Uitgeverij J. Hoste, Brussels, 1944-55, mng. dir., 1955—, pres., 1983—. Mem. Internat. Fedn. Newspaper Pubs. (pres. 1980-84), Belgische Vereniging van Dagbladuitgevers (pres. 1980-82), Centre d'Info. sur les Media (pres. 1974, 80-83). Club: Rotary (pres. 1970-72). Office: Uitgeverij J Hoste NV, Emile Jacqmainlaan 105, B1000 Brussels Belgium

VINKEN, PIERRE JACQUES, publishing executive, neurosurgeon; b. Heerlen, Netherlands, Nov. 25, 1927; s. Jan Willem and Marie (Hendriks) V.; M.D., U. Utrecht, 1955, postgrad. in psychiatry, neurology and neurosurgery, U. Amsterdam, 1957-63; hon. Dr., U. Paris, 1981; children—Paul Simon, Heleen, Charlotte, Lisa, Jan. Staff neurosurgeon Univ. Clinic, Amsterdam, 1964 69; cons. neurosurgeon Boerhaave Clinic, Amsterdam, 1964-72; pres., chief editor Excerpta Medica Found., Amsterdam and Princeton, N.J., 1962-88 ; mng. dir. Elsevier Pub. Co., Amsterdam, 1972-78; pres. Elsevier Pub. Co., Amsterdam, 1979—; adv. council AMRO-Bank, Amsterdam; dir. Wereldhave Investment Co., The Hague, Pierson Heldring Pierson, Amsterdam, Logica, Rotterdam; chmn. Bazis Fdn. Hsop. Info. System, Leyden, 1987—; prof. med. database informatics U. Leyden, 1975—; mem. Nat. Sci. Policy Council, The Hague, 1983—; chmn. Netherlands del. Intergovtl. Unisist Conf., Paris, 1970; mem. Netherlands Unisist Commn., 1971-79. Chmn. Netherlands Commn. Bibliography and Documentation, 1972-81; pres. Internat. Congress Patient Counselling, 1976-79. Mem. Neurol. Soc. India (hon.), French Neurol. Soc. (hon.), European Info. Providers Assn. (pres. 1980-83), Amsterdam Neurol. Soc. (hon.), Peruvian Soc. Psychiat. Neurology and Neurosurgey (hon.) Contbr. articles to sci. jours. Founder, editor-in-chief: Handbook of Clinical Neurology, 50 vols.; editor sci. books. Home: 142 Bentveldsweg, 2111 EE Aerdenhout The Netherlands Office: Elsevier NV, PO Box 470, 1000 AL Amsterdam The Netherlands

VINSON, BERNARD L(EONARD), personnel company executive; b. N.Y.C., May 31, 1919; m. Gloria Ann Konowitch, Oct. 17, 1948; children: Edward B., Marsha Lynn. BA, U. Mich., 1940, MA, 1941. Pres. Original TEMPO Services, East Meadow, N.Y., 1949—. Pres. Nassau County Conv. and Visitors Bur., N.Y., 1978, chmn., 1979—. Mem. Nassau County I.D.A., 1987—; pres. Hofstra U. Bd., 1975—. Served to lt. comdr. USN, 1941-46. Mem. L.I. Mid-Suffolk Bus. Assn. (pres. 1986—). Republican. Clubs: U. Mich. (N.Y.C.), Princeton (N.Y.C.); Hofstra Univ. (Hempstead, N.Y.); Chmn.'s (Mineola, N.Y.); Gov.'s (West Palm Beach). Lodges: Masons, Shriners, Elks, Scottish Rites. Home: 100 Bayview Ave Great Neck NY 11021 Office: Original TEMPO Services Corp 1900 Hempstead Turnpike East Meadow NY 11554

VIPPER, YURI B., literature educator, scholar; b. Moscow, Dec. 5, 1916; s. Boris R. and Maria (Shenkova) V.; m. Nina Alexeeva, Nov. 5, 1947. Cert. in French lit., U. Paris Sorbonne, 1938; MA, Latvian State U., Riga, 1941; D in Philology, USSR Ministry of High Edn., 1968. Lectr. Inst. Philosophy, Lit. and History, Moscow, 1941, Pedagogical Inst., Tashkent, USSR, 1941-42; lectr. Moscow State U., 1945-47, asst. prof., 1947-62, sr. researcher, 1962-64; sr. researcher Inst. World Lit., Moscow, 1965-77, head dept. history of world lit., 1978—; corr. mem. Acad. of Scis. of USSR, 1979, academician, 1987. Author: Formation of Classicism in French Poetry, 1967, Poetry of the Pleiad, 1976; mem. editorial bd. Bull. of Acad. of Scis., Moscow, 1987—; asst. editor, History of World Lit., 1983-87, editor in chief, 1988—, also contbr. Recipient diploma Supreme Council Russian Soviet Federative Socialist Republic, Moscow, 1978, Badge of Honor, Presidium of Supreme Council of USSR, 1986. Mem. Writers' Union of USSR, Internat. Comparative Lit. Assn. (v.p. 1979-84), Internat. Fedn. Modern Langs. and Lits. (v.p. 1984—). Office: Inst World Lit, Vorovsky St 25a, 121069 Moscow USSR

VIRGO, JOHN MICHAEL, economist, researcher, educator; b. Pressburry, Eng., Mar. 11, 1943; s. John Joseph and Muriel Agnes (Franks) V.; m. Katherine Sue Ulmrich, Sept. 6, 1980 (div. 1979); 1 child, Debra Marie. BA, Calif. State U., Fullerton, 1967, MA, 1969; MA, Claremont Grad. Sch., 1971, PhD, 1972. Instr. econs. Whittier (Calif.) Coll., 1970-71, Calif. State U., Fullerton and Long Beach, 1971-72, Claremont (Calif.) Grad. Sch., 1971-72; asst. prof. econs. Va. Commonwealth U., Richmond, 1972-74; assoc. prof. mgmt. So. Ill. U., Edwardsville, 1975-83, prof., 1984—; chief exec. officer, founder Internat. Health Econ. & Mgmt. Inst., Edwardsville, 1983-87. Author: Legal & Illegal California Farmworkers, 1974; author, editor: Health Care: An International Perspective, 1984, Exploring New Vistas in Health Care, 1985, Restructuring Health Policy, 1986. Served with USN, 1965-68. Mem. Internat. Hosp Fedn., Am. Econ. Assn., Am. Hosp. Assn., Am. Soc. Assn. Execs., Royal Econ. Soc., Atlantic Econ. Soc. (founder, exec. v.p., mng. editor jour. 1973-87), Allied Social Scis. Assn. (chmn. exec. confs. 1982-84), AMA, So. Econ. Assn. Democrat. Roman Catholic. Club: Sunset Hills (Edwardsville). Home: 315 Edwards Dr Edwardsville IL 62025 Office: So Ill U PO Box 1101 Edwardsville IL 62026-1101

VIRIYARUNGSARIT, SANTI, editor, publisher, columnist; b. Nakornpathom, Thailand, Aug. 1, 1946; s. Su and Ungmui V.; m. Sumolkree Chandra Kunjara, Nov. 13, 1975; children—Tanit, Pakanee and Parita (twins), Kawin. B. in Pub. Relations, Chulalongkorn U., 1973. Polit. news editor Thairath Daily, Bangkok, Thailand, 1972-76, social editor, 1976—; mng. dir. Media Associated, Bangkok, 1981—; cons. pub. relations Maboonkrong Complex, Bangkok, 1983-87. Editor: Computer Dictionary, 1984, 25 Thai Millionaire Life, 1984; exec. editor: (jour.) Money and Banking, 1982; (mag.) Modern Office, 1984. Chmn. pub. relations com. Thairath Found., Bangkok, 1983—; mem. bd. com. Communication Arts Alumni Chulalongkorn U., Bangkok, 1984-85; bd. dirs. Prommit Hosp., Bangkok, 1984—. Decorated comdr. 2nd and 3d class Most Exalted Order of White Elephant; knight comdr. 2d class Most Noble Order Crown of Thailand. Mem. Journalist Assn. Thailand, Reporter Assn. Thailand. Avocations: tennis; swimming; reading. Home: 42/38 Sci Chokchairuammit, Vipavadeerungsit Rd, Bangkok 10900, Thailand Office: Media Associated Co Ltd, 42/37 Soi Chokchairuammit, Vipavadeerungsit Rd, Bangkok 10900, Thailand

VIRNOT, URBAIN MARIE, manufacturing company executive; b. Wasquehal, Nord, France, Sept. 29, 1925; came to Switzerland, 1962; s. Urbain Gerard and Marie-Antoinette (Piat) V.; m. Chantal-Edmee Segard, Apr. 26, 1956; children: Urbain, Olivier, Nicolas, Bruno, Jean-Dominique. Commercial studies, Ecole de Hautes Etudes Commerciales, Paris, 1947. Gen. mgr. Cartonneries Mécaniques du Nord, Gravelines, France, 1947-52, Eyquem S.A., Paris, 1952-62; exec. v.p. SIM S.A., Morges, Switzerland, 1962-83, pres., 1983—; pres. SIM Portuguesa Lda, Braga, Portugal, 1983—. Home: 4 Ave de Plan, 1110 Morges Switzerland Office: SIM Internat SA, 1110 Morges Switzerland

VISCA, ARTURO SERGIO, president Uruguay National Academy of Letters; b. Montevideo, Uruguay, May 4, 1917; s. Arturo Pablo and Maria Magdalena Visca; m. Blanca Isabel Gimenez, Feb. 15, 1947; children: Blanca Mercedes, Ines Magdalena. B. in Medicine, U. de la Republic, Montevideo, Grad., Faculty of Humanities. Mem., Nat. Acad. Letters, Montevideo, 1969—, pres., 1973—. Author: Antologia del cuento uruguayo, 1962, 1968, Biblioteca Nacional del Uruguay, Tres narradores urugauyos, 1962, Conversando con Zum Felde, 1969, Aspectos de la narrativa criollista, 1972, Ensayos sobre literatura uruguaya, 1975, Un hombre y su mundo, 1978, Correspondencia intima de Delmira Agustina y Tres versiones de Lo Inefable, 1978, La mirada critica y otros ensayos, 1979. Recipient Nat. Prize of Lit., Uruguay, Gran. Nat. Prize Lit. Mem. Argentine Acad. Letters, Academia Norteamerican de la Lengua Española. Chilean Acad. Lang. Home: Galicia 2304, Montevideo Uruguay Office: Nat Acad Letters, 10 de Mayo, 1445 Piso lo Montevideo Uruguay other: Biblioteca Nacional del Uruguay, 18 de Julio 1790, Montevideo Uruguay

VISCHER, ERNST, chemical company executive; b. Basel, Switzerland, July 28, 1917; s. Ernst and Louise Vischer; m. Anne-Marie Wadler, Apr. 21, 1949. Ph.D. in Chemistry, U. Basel, 1944. Research chemist Imperial Chem. Industries, London, 1948-51; chemist pharm. research CIBA Ltd., Basel, 1952—; chmn. pharm. CIBA-Geigy Ltd., Basel, 1970—, mem. corp. exec. com., 1972—, dep. chmn. bd., 1980-87. Mem. European Fedn. Pharm. Industries Assns. (v.p. 1978-80), Internat. Fedn. Pharm. Mfrs. Assns. (pres. 1980-82). Home: Lange Gasse, CH4052 Basel Switzerland Office: Ciba-Geigy Ltd, CH4002 Basel Switzerland

VISCHER, JOHANN JACOB, architect; b. Basel, Switzerland, Feb. 1, 1950; s. Johann Jakob and Clara Erika (Messer) V. Diploma Arch. ETH Fed. Inst. Tech., Zurich, Switzerland, 1978. Designing architect, trainee Lockwood Greene Engrs., N.Y.C., 1975; architect Vischer Architects, Basel, 1979; freelance Vischer & Weber Architects, Basel, 1980; co-ptnr. Vischer & Oplatek Architects, Basel, 1981—. Served with Pioneers, 1971-80. Fellow Soc. Former Poly. Students; mem. Swiss Soc. Architects and Engrs., Register Swiss Architects and Engrs. Liberal Democrat. Office: Vischer & Oplatek Architects SIA, 86 Lange Gasse, CH4052 Basel Switzerland

VISENTINI, BRUNO, manufacturing company executive; b. Treviso, Italy, Aug. 1, 1914; s. Gustavo and Margherita (Tosello) V.; ed. U. Padua; m. Ernesta Caccianiga, July 5, 1941; children—Gustavo, Margherita, Stefano, Olga. Vice chmn. Inst. for Indsl. Reconstrn., 1950-72; chmn. Giorgio Cini Found., Venice, 1977; chmn., pres. Olivetti C., S.p.A., 1964-74, vice chmn., 1976-79, chmn., 1978-83, chief exec. officer, 1979-82; lectr. comml. law U. Rome, U. Urbino. Chmn., Italian Com. for Venice, 1970—; mem. UNESCO adv. com. for Venice, 1970; under sec. Ministry of Fin., 1945-46, minister of fin., 1974-76, budget and econ. planning ministry, 1979; dep. Italian Parliament, 1972-76, senator, 1976—; mem. European Parliament for Rome, from 1979; leader Partito Repubblicano Italiano (PRI), 1980—. Contbr. articles to profl. jours. Office: Partito Repubblicano Italiano, Piazza dei Caprettari 70, 00186 Rome Italy *

VISMARA, GIULIO, educator; b. Milan, Lombardy, Italy, Apr. 2, 1913; s. Achille and Giovanna (Gagliardi) V.; m. Lelia Marro, July 19, 1944; children—Elisabetta, Paola, Maria, Luigia, Giorgio Maria. LL.D., Faculty Law, Milan, 1935; Dr.h.c. (hon.), U. Montpellier, France, 1974, U. Lyon, France, 1981, U. Paris, 1984. Charged prof. U. Parma, 1938-40, U. Messina, 1940-41, U. Bari, 1941-43, Cath. U., Milano, Italy, 1943-47; prof. U. Urbino, 1945-55; prof. U. Pavia, Italy, 1955-63; prof. history Italian law U. Milano, 1963—. Author: Episcopalis audientia, 1937; Storia dei patti successori, 1941; Impium Foedus-Bisanzio e l'Islam, 1950; Edictum Theoderici-Fragmenta gaudenziana, 1968, Scritti di storia giuridica, vols. 1-7, 1987-88. Recipient Medaglia d'Oro Benemeriti Della Cultura, Ministro Pubblica Istruzione, 1971. Roman Catholic. Home: Via Pellegrini 14, 20122 Milan Italy Office: Istituto di storia del diritto, Italianovia Festa del Perdono 7, 20122 Milan Italy

VISSER, JAN DIRK, international trade executive; b. Rotterdam, Holland, Apr. 28, 1926; Drs. Econs., Erasmus U., 1951. Gen. dir. Conet B.V., Enschede, 1967—. Mem. C. of C. and Industry Twente and Salland (pres. 1982—). Home: Noord-Esmarkerrondweg 128, 7531 HA Enschede The Netherlands Office: Conet BV, PO Box 1201, Oldenzaalsestraat 500, Enschede, 7500 BE Enschede The Netherlands

VISWANATHAN, RAMASWAMY, physician, educator; b. Coimbatore, India, Aug. 20, 1949; came to U.S., 1972; s. Thiruvalangadu and Bhavani Krishnamurthy Ramaswamy; m. Kusum Ramakrishna, June 15, 1980; children: Vikram, Vivek. MB, BS, U. Madras, 1972. Diplomate Am. Bd. Psychiatry and Neurology. Med. intern Bklyn.-Cumberland Med. Center, 1972-73; resident in internal medicine L.I. Jewish-Hillside Med. Ctr.-Queens Hosp. Ctr. Affiliation, N.Y.C., 1973-74; resident in psychiatry SUNY Health Sci. Ctr., Bklyn., 1974-77, fellow in psychosomatic medicine, 1976-78, fellow in research tng. in psychiatry, 1977-79, mem. staff, 1978—, assoc. dir. med.-psychiat. liaison service, 1981-83, 84—, acting dir., 1983-84, med. dir. Phobia Clinic, 1982—, clin. asst. prof. psychiatry, 1979-87, clin. assoc. prof. psychiatry, 1987—, instr. in medicine, 1979—; cons. Bklyn. VA Med. Ctr., 1986—; practice medicine, specializing in psychiatry, psychosomatic medicine, behavior therapy, hypnosis and sex therapy, Bklyn., 1978—; mem. staff Kings County Hosp., Kingsboro Psychiat. Ctr.; lectr. to profl. and lay groups; coordinator course on life-threatening illness, dying and death, SUNY Health Sci. Ctr., 1984—, med. interviewing course, 1985—, mem. com. cancer edn. and preventive oncology, 1983—. Contbr. articles to profl. jours. Mem. ACP, AMA, Am. Psychiat. Assn., Bklyn. Psychiat. Soc. (councillor, pres. elect 1988—), Assn. Advancement of Behavior Therapy, Am. Psychosomatic Soc., Soc. Liaison Psychiatry (bd. dirs. 1986—, sec. 1987-88), Soc. for Sex Therapy and Research, Soc. Exploration Psychotherapy Integration, Am. Assn. Psychiatrists from India (founder, life mem., exec. com. 1979-85). Office: SUNY Health Sci Ctr 450 Clarkson Ave Box 127 Brooklyn NY 11203

VITA-FINZI, CLAUDIO, university educator; b. Sydney, New South Wales, Australia, Nov. 21, 1936; s. Paolo and Nadia (Touchmalova) V.-F.; m. Penelope Jean Angus, May 1, 1969; 1 child, Leo. BA, Cambridge U., Eng., 1958, PhD, 1962. Research fellow St. John's Coll., Cambridge U., 1961-64; lectr. Univ. Coll., London, 1964-74, reader, 1974-87, neotectonics prof., 1987—. Author: The Mediterranean Valleys, 1969, Recent Earth History, 1973, Archaeological Sites, 1978, Recent Earth Movements, 1986. Fellow Royal Geog. Soc. (Back award 1971), Geol. Soc. London. Home: 22 S Hill Park, London NW3 2SB, England Office: Univ Coll London, Gower St, London WCIE 6BT, England

VITALE, GERALD LEE, credit union executive; b. Chgo., Apr. 3, 1950; s. Le Roy Allen and Gilda Leanora (Rasori) V. BS in Psychology, Loyola U., Chgo., 1972. Credit mgr. Mellon Fin., Chgo., 1973-76, Kemper Ins. Co., Chgo., 1976-78; pres. Tribune Employees Credit Union, Chgo., 1978—; pres. NCR Credit Union User Group, Dayton, Ohio, 1984—. Counselor Youth Motivation Chgo. Commerce and Industry, 1980—; active Rep. Nat. Com., GOP Action Com., North Am., NCR Confedn., U.S. English, 43d ward Regular Reps., Chgo. Mem. Nat. Assn. Credit Union Service Orgn., Midwest Assn. Credit Unions, Nat. Platform Union, Pres. Assn., Credit Union Exec. Soc., Am. Individual Investors Soc., Credit Union Exec. Soc., Am. Mgmt. assn., U.S. English and N.Am. Confedn. of NCR Users, Am. Platform Assn., Midwest Assn. Credit Unions. Republican. Roman Catholic. Club: Barclay. Home: 1636 N Wells #2410 Chicago IL 60614 Office: Tribune Credit Union 435 N Michigan Chicago IL 60611

VITALIE, CARL LYNN, pharmacist, lawyer, educator; b. Clinton, Ind., Aug. 31, 1937; s. Paul Gilman and Martha Irrydell (Heidrick) V. D. Pharm., U. So. Calif., 1961, JD, 1965; postgrad., UCLA, 1977. Lic. pharmacist, Calif., Nev., Tex.; diplomate Am. Bd. Diplomates in Pharmacy. Community pharmacy practice various pharmacies, So. Calif., 1961-65; staff atty. Am. Pharm. Assn., Washington, 1965-66; staff pharmacist Sav-On Drugs, Inc., Anaheim, Calif., 1966-69, asst. dir. indsl. and pub. relations, 1969-71, dir. pharmacies, 1971-74, v.p. pharmacy ops., 1974-85; v.p. pharmacy div. The Vons Cos., Inc., El Monte, Calif., 1985-88; asst. prof. sch. pharmacy U. of the Pacific, Stockton, 1988—; lectr. pharmacy law and ethics U. So. Calif., Los Angeles, 1968-70; U.S. liaison Internat. Pharm. Students Fedn., 1959-62; mem. Calif. Bd. Pharmacy, 1968-76; bd. dirs. Bloomfield Leasing Corp., Chgo., 1985-87; researcher Earthwatch. Co-author: (with Nancy J. Wolff) Establishment and Maintenance of Membership Standards in Professional Societies of Pharmacists, 1967; mem. editorial adv. bd. Legal Aspects of Pharmacy Practice, 1978-80; also contbr. articles to profl. jours. Served with USAF, 1961-62, Calif., W.Va. Air N.G., 1962-68. Mem. ABA, Va. State Bar Assn., State Bar Assn. Calif., Am. Mgmt. Assn., Soc. for Advancement of Mgmt., Am. Soc. Pharmacy Law, Am., Calif. Pharm. Assns., Nat. Assn. Bds. Pharmacy, Acad. Gen. Practice Pharmacy, Town Hall Calif., Delta Theta Phi, Phi Delta Chi. Lodge: Masons. Home: 504 Northbrook Ct #4 Stockton CA 95207 Office: U of the Pacific Sch Pharmacy Stockton CA 95211

VITEK, JAMES ALLEN, nuclear engineer; b. Youngstown, Ohio, Mar. 30, 1958; s. John Paul and Eleanor Merrie (Sinclear) V. BE in Chem. Engring., Youngstown State U., 1983; MS in Nuclear Engring., Bettis Atomic Lab Nat. Research Found., 1984. Nuclear plant engr. Westinghouse, Idaho Falls, Idaho, 1983—, engring. officer of the watch, 1984, from engring. duty officer, to nuclear plant engr. of tng. to nulcear plant engr. of ops., 1985, quality control engr., 1986, nuclear plant engr. of tng., 1986—, sr. tng. asst., 1986, naval reactors engr., 1987, shift supr., 1988. Assoc. staff mem. Campus Life, Youngstown Ohio, 1976-82. Mem. NSPE, Am. Nuclear Soc., Am. Inst. Chem. Engrs., Idaho Soc. Profl. Engrs. (Engring. Deans Council pres. 1982-83), Omega Chi Epsilon (v.p. 1982-83). Republican. Mem. United Ch. Christ. Home: 4970 Mohawk Pocatello ID 83204 Office: Westinghouse Electric NRF PO Box 2068 Idaho Falls ID 83401

VITGER, JOHN ROLF, psychiatrist; b. Berlin, May 3, 1927; came to Denmark, 1943; s. Erhard and Alexandra (Christensen) V.; m. Jill Ulla Hovmand, Jan. 31, 1933; children: Rolf, Tune, Anne, Monique. Diploma in medicine, U. Copenhagen, 1957, degree in psychiatry, 1969. Cert. in psychiatry and psychoanalysis. Resident in chir., med. and oftalm. dept. Denmark, 1957-62; resident in psychiatry Glostrup, Denmark, 1962-64; resident in neurochir. and neurology dept. Copenhagen, 1964-66; resident in psychiatry Rigshospitalet, Copenhagen, 1966-70; clin. asst. in psychiatry Rigshospitalet, 1970-73; chief med. in psychiatry Montebello, Helsingør, Denmark, 1973-84, Psychotherapeutic Clinic Montebello, Helsingør, Denmark, 1984—; bd. dirs. Inst. Psychoanalytic Psychotherapy, Helsingør. Mem. Danish Psychiat. Soc. (head psychotherapy com. 1982-86), Danish Psychoanalytic Soc. (pres. 1981-85), Danish Soc. Psychoanalytic Psychotherapy (pres. 1985—). Home: Ørnholmvej 24, DK 3070 Snekkersten Denmark Office: Psychotherapeutic Clinic Montebello, Gurrevej 90, DK 3000 Helsingør Denmark

VITKOWSKY, VINCENT JOSEPH, lawyer; b. Newark, Oct. 3, 1955; s. Boniface and Rosemary (Ofack) V.; m. Mary Gunzburg, May 16, 1981; 1 child, Vincent Jr. BA, Northwestern U., 1977; JD, Cornell U., 1980. Bar: N.Y. 1981, N.Y. Dist. Ct. (so. and ea. dists.) N.Y. 1981. Assoc. Hart and Hume, N.Y.C., 1980-84, Kroll, Tract, Harnett, Pomerantz & Cameron, N.Y.C., 1984-86, Finley, Kumble, Wagner, Heine, Underberg, Manley, Meyerson & Casey, N.Y.C., 1987; of counsel Nixon, Hargrave, Devans & Doyle, N.Y.C., 1988—; lectr. industry and bar groups. Mem. ABA, Assn. Bar of City of N.Y., Internat. Bar Assn., Lawyers Alliance for Nuclear Arms Control, Internat. Amigo of Orgn. Am. States, Arms Control Assn. Democrat. Club: Cornell (N.Y.C.). Home: 24 Radio Pl No 25 Stamford CT 06906 Office: Nixon Hargrave Devans & Doyle 30 Rockefeller Plaza New York NY 10112 also: One Thomas Circle Washington DC 20005

VITT, DAVID AARON, medical manufacturing company executive; b. Phila., Aug. 3, 1938; s. Nathan and Flora B.; m. Renee Lee Salkever, Oct. 20, 1963; children: Nadine Lori, Jeffrey Richard. BS, Temple U., 1961. Sales engr. Picker X-Ray Corp., Phila., 1961-65; sales engr. Midwest Am., Chgo., 1965-67, product mgr., 1967-68, product mgr. regional sales, 1968-70; dir. mktg. Valtronic & Living Wills, Bronx, N.Y., 1970-74; v.p. Siemens Med. Systems Inc., gen. mgr. dental div., Iselin, N.J., 1974-86, past corp. v.p.; chief exec. officer, pres. Pelton & Crane, Charlotte, N.C., 1986—; industry rep. to Am. Nat. Standards Inst.; mem. exec. com. Jr. Achievement, Charlotte. Bd. dirs. Fund for Dental Health; apptd. mem. Charlotte Mecklenburg Community Relations Com. Served in USAR, 1961-68. Mem. Am. Mgmt. Assn. (bd. dirs. N.J. chpt.), Am. Mktg. Assn., Am. Dental Trade Assn. (bd. dirs.), Dental Mfrs. Am. (past pres.), Am. Acad. Dental Radiology. Republican. Lodge: Masons (32 deg.). Office: Pelton and Crane PO Box 241147 200 Clanton Rd Charlotte NC 28224

VITT, SAM B., independent media service executive; b. Greensboro, N.C., Oct. 23, 1926; s. Bruno Caesar and Gray (Bradshaw) V.; m. Marie Foster, Oct. 30, 1955; children: Joanne Louise, Michael Bradshaw, Mark Thomas. A.B., Dartmouth Coll., 1950. Exec. asst. TV film CBS, N.Y.C., 1950-52; broadcast media buyer Benton & Bowles, Inc., N.Y.C., 1952-54, Biow Co., N.Y.C., 1954-55; asso. account exec. Biow Co., 1955-56; broadcast media buyer Doherty, Clifford, Steers & Shenfield, Inc., N.Y.C., 1956-57; media supr. Doherty, Clifford, Steers & Shenfield, Inc., 1958-59, v.p. media supr., 1960, v.p., asso. media dir., 1960, v.p., media dir., 1960-63, v.p. in charge media and broadcast programming, 1963-64; v.p., exec. dir. media-program dept. Ted Bates & Co., Inc., N.Y.C., 1964-66; sr. v.p., exec. dir. media-program dept. Ted Bates & Co., Inc., 1966-69; dir. Advt. Info. Services, Inc., 1964-65; founder, pres. Vitt Media Internat., Inc., N.Y.C., 1969-81, chmn., chief exec. officer, 1982—; advt. dir. Banking Law Jour., 1955-69; lectr. in field, 1967—; lectr. advt. media N.Y. U., 1973, 74, Am. Mgmt. Assn., 1974, 75, Assn. Nat. Advertisers, 1967, 69, 70, Advt. Age Media Workshop, 1975. Media columnist: Madison Ave, 1963-68; editorial cons.: Media/Scope, 1968-69; contbg. editor: Handbook of Advertising Management, 1970; contbr. to: Advertising Procedure, 1969, rev. edit., 1973, 5th, 6th, 7th edits., 1977, Exploring Advertising, 1970; contbr. editor to Nation's Bus., Broadcasting, Variety, Anny, TV/Radio Age, Sponsor, Printer's Ink; producer rec. album The Body in the Seine; cover story guest editor: Media Decisions, 1967. Dir. N.Y.C. Comml. Devel. Corp., 1966-69; mem. com. Nat. UN Day Com., 1973, vice chmn., 1974, assoc. chmn., 1975, co-chmn., 1976-77; bd. dirs. UN Assn. Am., 1977; bd. dirs., chmn. Research Inst. Hearing and Balance Disorders Ltd., 1979—; mem. Pres. Reagan's Joint Presdl., Congl. Steering Com., 1982; mem. advt. adv. com. The Acting Com., 1984; chmn. radio-TV reps. div. Greater N.Y. Fund, 1962, chmn. consumer pub. div., 1963; bd. govs. N.Y. Young Republican Club, 1957-58; editor Directory, 1956-57. Served as lt. (j.g.) USN, 1944-46. Recipient Media award sta. WRAP, Norfolk, Va., 1962, award of Merit Greater N.Y. Fund, 1963, Gold Key Advt. Leadership award Sta. Reps. Assn., 1967, ann. honors Ad Daily, 1967, certificate of merit Media/Scope, 1967, 1969 Creative Pub. Statement Concerning Advt. award; named one of 10 Best Dressed Men in Advt. Community Gentlemen's Quar., 1979. Mem. Am. Assn. Advt. Agys. (broadcast media com. dir. corr. 1958-63, media operating com. on consumer mags. 1964-65), Internat. Radio and TV Soc. (timebuying and selling seminar com. dir. 1961-62), Internat. Radio and TV Found. (faculty seminar 1974), Nat. Acad. Arts Sci. (mem. com. dir.), Media Dirs. Council, Sigma Alpha Epsilon. Presbyterian. Clubs: Manor Park Beach (Larchmont, N.Y.); N.Y. Athletic (N.Y.C.); Roxbury Run (Denver, N.Y.). Home: 3 Roosevelt Ave Larchmont NY 10538 Office: Vitt Media Internat Inc 1114 Avenue of the Americas New York NY 10036

VIVERA, ARSENIO BONDOC, allergist; b. Cebu City, Philippines, Oct. 29, 1931; s. Arsenio R. and Ramona del Mar (Bondoc) V.; A.A., Cebu Coll., U. Philippines, 1950, M.D., 1954. Intern, Philippines Gen. Hosp., 1954-55; resident in medicine Beekman-Downtown Hosp., N.Y.C., 1955-57, Detroit Meml. Hosp., 1957-58; resident in allergy Robert A. Cooke Inst. Allergy, Roosevelt Hosp., N.Y.C., 1958-59, fellow in allergy, 1959-61; sr. cons. scientist Philippines Nat. Inst. Sci. and Tech., Manila, 1961-62; practice medicine specializing in allergy, N.Y.C.; chief allergy dept. attending physician N.Y. Polyclinic Med. Sch. and Health Center, 1972-77, adj. prof., 1972-77; clin. attending physician Robert A. Cooke Inst. Allergy, 1969—; asst. attending physician N.Y. Infirmary, N.Y.C., 1969—; chief allergy, attending St. Vincent's Hosp. and Med. Center, N.Y.C., 1977—. Diplomate Am. Bd. Allergy and Immunology. Fellow Am. Acad. Allergy, Am. Coll. Allergists, Am. Assn. Clin. Immunology and Allergy; mem. N.Y. Allergy Soc., AMA, Am. Assn. Cert. Allergists, N.Y. Acad. Scis., Am. Geriatric Soc., N.Y. State, N.Y. County med. socs. Office: 681 Lexington Ave 5th Floor New York NY 10022

VIVILLE, CHARLES, urology surgeon; b. Metz, France, Jan. 14, 1929; s. Gaston and Marie-Louse Viville; m. Anita Mohn, June 5, 1956; children: Isabelle, Christine, Stephane, Anne Laurence. MBBS, U. Strasbourg, France, 1960. Resident Centre Hospitalier Univeritaire de Strasbourg, 1962-66; chef de service d Urologie Clinque Bethesda, Strasbourg, 1966—. Contbr. articles to profl. jours. Served to lt. French Med. Corps, 1956-58. Mem. Assn. Francaise Urologie, Soc. Francaise Urologie, Soc. Belge Urologie, Alpine Surg. Soc. Home: 5 Rue Gen Le Jeune, 67000 Strasbourg France Office: Rue Goethe, 67000 Strasbourg France

VLACHOS, PETER GEORGE, economics educator; b. Dayton, Ohio, Apr. 4, 1944; s. George Peter and Thelma Lucille (Ridenour) V. B.A., U. Cin., 1966, M.A., 1967, Ph.D., 1969. Econ. affairs officer UN, Bangkok, 1975; assoc. prof. econs. and quantitative methods U. Hawaii, Honolulu, 1969-83; prof. Shanghai Inst. Internat. Econ. Mgmt., 1984—; staff planner City and County of Honolulu Dept. Gen. Planning, 1986; staff planner Hawaii State Dept. Land and Natural Resources, 1987—; cons. in field; vis. prof. Waseda U., Tokyo, 1973, Aoyama Gakuin Daigaku, Tokyo, 1977, Xavier U., Cin., 1973, 77. Editor: Journal Readings in Managerial Economics, 1975. Contbr. articles to profl. jours. Vol. Atherton br. YMCA, Honolulu, 1971-84; mem. Neighborhood Bd. 8, Neighborhood Commn., Honolulu, 1979-81. Recipient various grants U. Hawaii, U. Cin., Saudi Arabian Govt. Mem. Am. Econ. Assn., Western Econ. Assn., Hawaii Edn. Assn., AAUP, NEA. Eastern Orthodox.

VLAHAC, MARY ANN RITA, market research consultant, small business owner; b. Bridgeport, Conn., June 11, 1954; d. John S. and Catherine R. (Landor) V.; m. James Thomas Westerman, May 13, 1978; 1 child, Christopher James. A.S., Housatonic Community Coll., 1974; B.S., U. Conn., 1976; M.B.A., U. Bridgeport, 1980; student U. New Haven. Market research Remington Arms/duPont, Bridgeport, 1976-79; sr. market research staff Pitney Bowes, Stamford, Conn., 1979-86; mktg. research mgr. People's Bank, Bridgeport, 1986—; v.p. mktg. Mar-Kris Trading Co., Stratford, Conn., 1985—; owner Gewgaw, Stratford, 1980—; ptnr. Glass & Crafts, Bridgeport, 1980—. Stained glass artist. Adv., Housatonic Community Coll., 1985-86. Mem. U. Conn. Alumni Assn., U. Bridgeport Alumni Assn., Housatonic Community Coll. Alumni Assn., Conn. Crafts Guild, Stratford Hist. Soc. Avocations: art, music, classic film, acting, writing. Home: 545 Windsor Ave Stratford CT 06497

VLAJKOVIC, RADOVAN, Yugoslavian government official; b. Budjanovci, Vojvodina, 1922; married; 2 children. With Workers' Movement, 1940, Nat. Liberation Struggle, 1941; mem. Communist Party Yugoslavia, 1943—; former sec. regional and city com. in Pancevo and Novi Sad; former pres. Provincial Council of Fed. Trade Unions for Vojvodina, 1958; mem. central com. League Communists of Serbia, 1959-68, mem. presidency of central com., 1966—; pres. of the presidency SAP Yugoslavia, 1974-81, mem. of the presidency, 1986—. Fought in war of nat. libration, 1941-45. Decorated Partisan Meml. medal, numerous others. Office: Office of the Member of, the Presidency of the SFR, Of Yugoslavia, Belgrade Bulevar Lenjina 2 Yugoslavia

VLASOV, ALEKSANDR VLADIMIROVICH, Soviet government official; b. 1932. Grad., Irkutsk Metall. Mining Inst., 1954. Party positions Komsomol, 1954-65, mem. Communist Party, USSR, 1956—, Oblast sec., 2d Oblast sec. Communist Party com., Yakut, USSR, 1965-72, mem. Central Com., 1972-75, dep. Supreme Soviet, 1974—, 1st Oblast sec. Communist Party Central com., Chechen-Ingush, from 1975, candidate mem. Central Com., 1976-81, mem., 1981—, minister internal affairs, 1986—. Decorated Order of Lenin. Address: Ministry Internal Affairs, Moscow USSR *

VLERICK, ANDRE, economics educator; b. Kortrijk, West Flanders, Belgium, Sept. 11, 1919; s. Alfons and Afra (Van Elstraete) V.; m. Cecile Sab, Dec. 29, 1945. Bachelor Degree in Thomistic Philosophy, U. Louvain, 1941, LL.D., 1942, M. in Econs., 1943; research student in Econs. U. Cambridge, 1946, Harvard Internat. Seminar, 1953. Pub. adminstr. Belgian Adminstrn. for Econ. Coop., 1948-53; prof. econs. U. Ghent (Belgium), 1953—, founder, dir. Seminar Applied Econs., 1953, Centre Productivity and Research, 1953; hon. prof. Escuela de Adminstrn. de Empresas, Barcelona, 1969—; hon. fellow Berkeley Coll., Yale U., dir. Kredietbank, Brussels, 1953—, vice-chmn., 1974—, chmn., 1980—; chmn. bd. N.V. Investco, Brussels, 1957—, dir., hon. chmn., 1982—; chmn. Les Provinces Reunies, 1981—, S.A. Philips Belgium, 1981—; dir. S.A. Tessenderlo-Chemie, BASF Antwerp S.A., Degussa S.A. Antwerp; vis. prof. numerous univs.; cons., lectr. in field. Contbr. numerous articles to profl. jours. Minister-sec. state regional economy, Eyskens-Merlot-Cools, 1968-72; minister fin. Eyskens-Cools, 1972-73; mem. Belgian Senate, 1971-77, chmn. fin. commn., 1974-77; co-founder, bd. dirs. European Found. for Mgmt. Devel.; co-founder, bd. dirs. Found. for Industry, U. Brussels, Inst. Adminstrn., U. Brussels; mem. econ., polit. and social scis. commn. Nat. Fund for Sci. Research, Brussels; bd. dirs. Interuniv. Coll. for Doctoral Studies in Mgmt.; bd. dirs. Fondation Universitaire, chmn., 1979-82. Decorated commdr. Order of Leopold; grand cross Order of Orange-Nassau; grand officer Order of Merit (Grand Duchy of Luxemburg). Mem. Vlaams Economisch Verbond (bd. dirs.), Economische Raad voor Oost-Vlaanderen (co-founder), Westvlaamse Economische Raad, Vlaams Institut voor Ruimtelijke Ordening (co-founder). Roman Catholic. Home: Ketelpoort 23, 9000 Ghent Belgium also: Ave Louise 479, 1050 Brussels Belgium Office: Kredietbank NV, Arenbergstraat 7, 1000 Brussels Belgium *

VOCELKA, KARL GERHARD, university dozent; b. Vienna, Austria, May 23, 1947; s. Karl J. and Helene (Banar) V.; m. Sylvia E. Zeidler, Mar. 17, 1976 (div. 1986). PhD, U. Vienna, 1971. Univ. asst. U. Vienna, 1972-78, univ. dozent, 1978—; vis. prof. Viennese dept. Stanford U., 1980-87, Midwest Consortium for Studies Abroad, Vienna, 1987—. Author: Rudolf II u seine Zeit, 1986, K.U.K. Karikaturen, 1986, Trümmerjahre Wien, 1985, Verfassung oder Konkordat, 1978. Recipient Akademie der Wissensch Böhlau prize, Vienna, 1982, Sandoz prize, 1985, Förderungs prize, Vienna, 1988. Mem. Inst. Österreichische Geschichtsforschung. Socialist. Home: Ledderergasse 33/12, A-1080 Vienna Austria Office: Inst Osterreichische, Geschichsforschung, Dr Karl Luegerring 1, A-1010 Vienna Austria

VO CHI CONG, government official; b. Tam Ky district, Quangnam Danang Province, Vietnam, Aug. 7, 1913. Active Communist Youth Movement, 1930-34; joined Indochinese Communist Party, 1935, sec. local party cell, 1936, sec. dist. party com., 1939; sec. Provisional Party Com., Quangnam Danang Province, 1940; head uprising com. to seize power Quang Nam-Da Nang, 1945; then commissar regt. 9, dep. head personnel com. 5th mil. zone, 1946; adviser Party Representation Bd. and mem. regional party com. Northeast Kampuchea, 1951; party sec. Quang Nam-Da Nang Province, 1952; mem. land reform com. Viet Bac, 1954; dep. party sec. and sec. 5th zone party com. 1955; dep. sec. Party Cen. Com., 1961; party rep. Nat. Front for the Liberation of South Vietnam 1962; also v.p. of the Presidium Front Cen. Com.; dep. sec. and party sec. 5th zone and commissar 5th mil. zone 1964; dep. head representation com. Party Cen. Com., 1975; dep. 6th Nat. Assembly, 1976; also vice-chmn. Council of Ministers and Minister of Agr. 1978, dep. 7th Nat. Assembly and vice-chmn. Council of Ministers, 1981; mem. Party Cen. Com., 1982; also mem. polit. bur. and secretariat 1982; vice-chmn. Council of Ministers, 1986; now chmn. State Council. Office: State Council, Office of Chmn, Hanoi Socialist Republic of Vietnam *

VODERBERG, KURT ERNEST, machinery sales company executive; b. Rendsburg, Germany, Apr. 8, 1921; s. Max Henry and Margarethe (Siedel) V.; m. Louise Collier, May 21, 1948 (div. 1969); children—Paul, John, Mary Beth, Jill; m. 2d, Sophie Dufft, Sept. 5, 1969. B.S. in M.E., Ill. Inst. Tech., 1943; postgrad. Northwestern U., 1944-45. Registered profl. engr., Ill. Asst. master mechanic Danly Machine Co., Cicero, Ill., 1943-47; pres. Dynamic Machine Co., Chgo., 1947-75, pres. Dynamic Machinery Sales, Inc., Chgo., 1975—, pres. Paramount Machinery Sales Co., Chgo., 1982-85. Mem. Ill. Soc. Profl. Engrs., Soc. Mfg. Engrs., Tool and Die Inst., Chgo. Assn. Commerce and Industry (mem. com.). Lutheran. Clubs: Michigan Shores, American Turners, Glenbrook Shrine. Lodge: Masons. Patentee in field. Home: 1440 Sheridan Rd Apt 706 Wilmette IL 60091 Office: 1800 N Rockwell St Chicago IL 60647

VOGE, JEAN PAUL, telecommunication engineer and manager, educator; b. Casablanca, Morocco, Feb. 21, 1921; s. Louis and Germaine (Marage) V.; m. Genevieve Delattre, June 1, 1951; children—Christophe, Bertrand. Grad. Coll., St. Chamond, 1937, Ecole Polytech., Paris, 1942, Ecole Telecommunications, Paris, 1944. Engr., dept. head Nat. Ctr. for Telecommunication Research, Paris, 1944-57, gen. engr., 1957—; mem. Intelsat Bd., Washington, 1964-70; dir. Ecole Telecommunications, Paris, 1968-76; del. dir., spl. advisor Postal and Telecommunications Ministry, Paris, 1976—; pres., chmn. bd. dirs. Institut de' l'Audiovisuel et des Télécommunications en Europe, Montpellier, France, 1977-88; chmn. Forum Européen des Télécommunications, Brussels, 1986—; prof. Brussels U., 1964-86, Ecole des Telecommunications, Paris, 1948—, Ecole de l'Aviation Civile, Paris, 1948—. Author several books on radio and space scis. and info. and communication soc. Recipient Gold medal Assn. pour les Etudes et la Recherche Astronautique, 1963, Gold medal Institut Recherches Economiques et Sociales sur les Telecommunications, 1981; decorated commandeur Legion d'honneur, officer Palmes Academiques, commendeur Ordre du Merite (France); officer Order Leopold (Belgium). Fellow IEEE (pres. France sect. 1972-81); mem. Internat. Union Radio Scis. (pres. 1975-79), Internat. Council Sci. Unions, Internat. Inst. Communications (trustee 1980-87), French Commn. UNESCO Paris. Home: 5 Ave A Bartholome, 75015 Paris France Office: Ministry PTT, 20 Avenue de Segur, 75700 Paris France

VOGEL, H. VICTORIA, educator, psychotherapist. B.A., U. Md., 1968; M.A., NYU, 1970, 75; M.Ed., Tchrs. Coll. Columbia U., 1982, postgrad., 1982—. Tchr., Montgomery County (Md.) Jr. High Sch., 1968-69; with High Sch. div. N.Y.C. Bd. Edn., 1970—, tchr., guidance counselor, psychotherapist in pvt. practice; counseling cons. psychodiagnosis and devel. studies, 1984—; art/play therapist Hosp. Ctr. for Neuromuscular Disease and Devel. Disorders, 1987—; employment counselor-adminstr. N.Y. State Dept. Labor Concentrated Employment Program, 1971-72. Mem. Am. Psychol. Assn., Am. Orthopsychiat. Assn., Am. Soc. Group Psychotherapy and Psychodrama (publs. com. 1984—), Am. Assn. for Counseling and Devel., N.Y.C. Art Tchrs. Assn., Art/Play Therapy, Assn. Humanistic Psychology (exec. sec. 1981), Tchrs. Coll. Adminstrv. Women in Edn., Phi Delta Kappa (editor chpt. newsletter 1981-84, exec. sec. Columbia U. chpt. 1984—, chmn. nominating com. for chpt. officers 1986—, research rep. 1986—), Kappa Delta Pi.

VOGEL, HANS-JOCHEN, German politician; b. Gottingen, Germany, Feb. 3, 1926; m. Ilse Leisnering, 1951 (div. 1972); 3 children; m. 2d Liselotte Sonnenholzer Biersack, 1972. Ed. U. Munich, U. Marburg; Dr.jur. Asst. Bavarian Justice Ministry, 1952-54; lawyer Traunstein Dist. Ct., 1954-55; Bavarian State Chancellery, 1955-58; mem. Munich City Council (W.Ger.), 1958-60; chief burgomaster of Munich, 1960-72; minister for regional planning, bldg. and urban devel. of W.Ger., 1972-81, minister of justice, 1974; chief burgomaster of Berlin, 1981; leader of Socil Dem. Party, 1982-87, chmn., 1987—. Author: Stadt im Wandel, 1971; Die Amtskette, 1972. Vice pres. Organizing Com. for Munich Olympic Games, 1972. Decorated Grosses Bundesverdientskreuz, Bayerischer Verdienstorden; Order Brit. Empire, also others including decorations from France, Italy. Office: Sozialdemokratische Partei, Deutschlands, Ollenhauerstr 1, 5300 Bonn Federal Republic of Germany *

VOGEL, HOWARD STANLEY, lawyer; b. N.Y.C., Jan. 21, 1934; s. Moe and Sylvia (Miller) V.; m. Judith Anne Gelb, June 30, 1962; 1 son, Michael S. B.A., Bklyn. Coll., 1954; J.D., Columbia U., 1957; LL.M. in Corp. Law, NYU, 1969. Bar: N.Y. 1957, U.S. Supreme Ct. 1964. Assoc. Whitman & Ransom, N.Y.C., 1961-66; with Texaco Inc., 1966—, gen. atty., 1970-73, assoc. gen. counsel, 1973-81, gen. counsel Texaco Philanthropic Found. Inc., 1979-82, gen. counsel Jefferson Chem. Co., Texaco Chems. Can. Inc., 1973-82, assoc. gen. tax counsel, White Plains, N.Y., 1981—. Pres., dir. 169 E. 69th Corp., 1981—. Served to 1st lt. JAGC, U.S. Army, 1958-60. Mem. ABA, Assn. Bar City N.Y., Fed. Bar Council, Assn. Ex-Mems. of Squadron A (N.Y.C.). Club: Princeton (N.Y.C.). Home: 169 E 69th St Apt 9-D New York NY 10021 Office: 2000 Westchester Ave White Plains NY 10650

VOGEL, ROBERT, real estate developer; b. Hamburg, Fed. Republic Germany, June 8, 1919; s. Max P. and Anna M. (Freudendahl) V.; children: Tom, Jicky. Student, Hamburg High Sch. Mng. dir. Handesgesellschaft MbH, Hamburg, 1943—; gen. ptnr. Robert Vogel Kommanditges, Hamburg, 1955—, Anna M.M. Vogel Kommanditgesellschaft; mng. dir. Avis Immobilien GmbH, Hamburg, 1982—, Uccello Immobilien GmbH, Hamburg, 1982. Pres. Liberal party, 1987—; mem. parliament Hamburg, 1987—. Decorated chevalier Ordre de la Couronne (Belgium). Clubs: Norddt Regattaverein, Anglo-German. Office: Esplanade 37, Hamburg 36 Federal Republic of Germany

VOGEL, ROBERTA BURRAGE, psychologist; b. Georgetown, S.C., June 13, 1938; d. Demosthenes Edwin and Vivian Helen (Besselliеu) Burrage; BA, Temple U., 1960, MA, 1962; PhD, Mich. State U., 1967; cert. Ackerman Inst. Family Therapy, N.Y.C., 1981; children by previous marriage—Duane Stephen, Shoshana Lynn. Instr. Mich. State U., East Lansing, 1966-67, asst. prof., 1967-68; group leader, mem. staff Ctr. for Learning and Change, N.Y.C., 1970-75; staff psychologist, supr. group therapy North Richmond (S.I.) Community Mental Health Ctr., 1971-72; asst. prof. Coll. S.I., City U. N.Y., 1972-74, assoc. prof., 1974—, dir. spl. programs, 1979—, ednl. cons. Office Student Affairs and Spl. Programs, 1981—, chairperson dept. student devel./SEEK program, 1984—; dir. clin. services Black Psychology Inst., N.Y.C., 1978-81; evaluator sci. proposals NSF, Washington, 1981—; cons. Steinway Family and Child Devel. Ctr., 1984—, edn. com. Mayor's Commn. on Black New ;Yorkers, 1987. Bd. dirs. Martin Luther King Jr. Heritage House, 1972; bd. dirs. treas. New Morning Day Care Ctr., 1975-77; mem. adv. bd. S.I. br. Urban League, 1980—, chmn. edn. com., 1981-84, mem. task force on edn. N.Y. br., 1981-82; chair adv. bd. S.I. br. N.Y. Urban League, 1984-88 ; mem. S.I. Human Rights Adv. Council, S.I. Mediation Council. NIH research fellow, 1964-65; cert. psychologist, N.Y. State. Mem. N.Y. Assn. Black Psychologists (dir. 1975-81, pres. 1982-83), Am. Psychol. Assn., N.Y. Soc. Clin. Psychologists, Assn. Black Psychologists, Richmond County Psychol. Assn., S.I. Mental Health Soc. (bd. dirs. 1987—), Tri-State Assn. Ednl. Opportunity, N.Y. Urban League NAACP, Nat. Council Negro Women. Home: 173 St Pauls Ave Staten Island NY 10301 Office: Coll Staten Island 715 Ocean Terr Room H-13 Staten Island NY 10301

VOGELSGESANG, WOLFGANG MARIA, bookbinder, restaurateur; b. Landau, Pfalz, Germany, June 16, 1932; s. Karl and Emma (Reichel) V.; grad. Spranger-Gymnasium, 1948; m. Gisela Volckamer von Kirchensittenbach; children: Hartwig, Winfried, Birgit, Guntram. Referent, Christlich-Soziale Union, 1964; with Werkstätte für Bucheinband; pres. libraries bd. Internat. Youth Library, Munich, 1973—. Mem. Munich City Council, 1969—. Home: 6 Faistenlohestrasse, D8000 Munich 60 Federal Republic of Germany Office: 2 Marienplatz, D8000 Munich 2, Federal Republic of Germany

VOGL, OTTO, polymer science and engineering educator; b. Traiskirchen, Austria, Nov. 6, 1927; came to U.S., 1953, naturalized, 1959; s. Franz and Leopoldine (Scholz) V.; m. Jane Cunningham, June 10, 1955; children: Eric, Yvonne. Ph.D., U. Vienna, 1950; Dr. rer. nat. h.c., U. Jena, 1983. Instr. U. Vienna, 1948-55; research asso. U. Mich., 1953-55, Princeton U., 1955-56; scientist E.I. Du Pont de Nemours & Co., Wilmington, Del., 1956-70; prof. polymer sci. and engring. U. Mass., 1970-83, prof. emeritus, 1983—; Herman F. Mark prof. polymer sci. Poly. U., Bklyn., 1983—; guest prof. Kyoto U., 1968, 80, Osaka U., 1968, Royal Inst. Stockholm, 1971, 87, U. Freiburg, Germany, 1973, U. Berlin, 1977, Strasbourg U., 1976, Tech. U. Dresden, 1982; guest Soviet Acad. Sci., 1973, Polish Acad. Sci., 1973, 75, Acad. Sci. Rumania, 1974, 76; cons. in field. Chmn. com. on macromolecular chemistry Nat. Acad. Sci. Author: Polyaldehydes, 1967, (with Furukawa) Polymerization of Heterocyclics, 1973, Ionic Polymerization, 1976, (with Simionescu) Radical Co and Graftpolymerization, 1978, (with Donaruma) Polymeric Drugs, 1978, (with Donaruma and Ottenbrite) Polymers in Biology and Medicine, 1980, (with Goldberg and Donaruma) Targeted Drugs, 1983, (with Immergut) Polymer Science in the Next Decade, 1987; contbr. articles to profl. jours. Recipient Fulbright award, 1976, Humboldt prize, 1977, Chemistry Pioneer award, 1985, Gold medal City of Vienna, Austria, 1986, Exner medal, 1987; Japan Soc. Promotion of Sci. sr. fellow, 1980. Mem. Am. Chem. Soc. (chmn. div. polymer chemistry 1974, chmn. Conn. Valley sect. 1974), Am. Inst. Chem., AAAS, Austrian Chem. Soc., Japanese Soc. Polymer Sci., Nat. Acad. Sci. German Democratic Republic, Austrian Acad. Sci. Home: 349 Oxford Rd New Rochelle NY 10804 Office: Poly Univ NY Brooklyn NY 11201

VOGT, NIKOLAUS FRANZ, astronomer, educator; b. Breslau, Germany, Aug. 25, 1940; s. Gunther and Helene (Ramnitz) V.; student in Physics and Astronomy, U. Bonn, 1959-65; diploma in Physics, U. Bonn, 1965; Ph.D. in Astronomy, U. Bochum, 1969; Dr. Habil. in Astronomy, 1982; m. Patricia Geisse J., Aug. 25, 1976; children—Katia, Thomas, Stefan. Asst. prof., Astron. Inst., U. Bonn, W. Ger., 1965-66; asst. prof. Astron. Inst., Bochum, W. Ger., 1966-73; staff astronomer European So. Obs., La Silla, Chile, 1973-80; astronomer Astron. Inst. Munich, W.Ger., 1981-83; prof. astronomy Cath. U., Santiago, Chile, 1984—. Mem. Internat. Astron. Union, Astronomische Gesellschaft, Am. Astron. Soc. Condr. research in astrophysics; contbr. sci. articles to profl. publs. Office: U Catolica, Dept Astronomy, Casilla, 6014 Santiago Chile

VOGÜÉ, ADALBERT DE, monk, researcher; b. Paris, Dec. 4, 1924; Melchior and Geneviève (Brincard) de V. ThD, Cath. Inst., Paris, 1959. Joined Benedictine Order, 1944. Prof. theology Coll. St. Anselmo, Rome, 1966-75; researcher in monastic history, dir. western monasticism sect. Dizionario Degli Istituti Di Perfezione, Rome, 1970—. Author: La Règle de S. Benoît, 1971-77, Les Règles des Saints Pères, 1982, Le Maître, Eugippe et S. Benoît, 1984; editorial bd.: Studia Monastica, Montserrat, Spain, Monastic Studies, Montreal, Que., Can., 1983—; contbr. articles to profl. jours. Home and Office: Abbaye de la, Pierre-qui-Vire, 89830 Saint Léger Vauban France

VOHRA, PRAN, librarian; b. Delhi, India, Feb. 2, 1930; arrived in Can., 1969; s. K.C. and R.D. Vohra; m. Sha Vohra; children: Pradeep, Praveen. MA, Punjab U., New Delhi, 1960; MLS, Delhi U., Delhi, 1964, U. Western Ont., London, Can., 1972. Mem. account staff Office Acct. Gen. Centra Revenue, New Delhi, 1957-61; librarian World Affairs, New Delhi, 1961-63; head librarian St. Stephen's Coll., Delhi, 1964-70; librarian Ont. Edn., Toronto, Can., 1970-72, Ont. Housing Corp., Toronto, 1972-73; head librarian Wascana Campus Sask. Inst. Applied Sci. and Tech., Regina, Can., 1973—; indexer, book reviewer various jours. Zone rep., shop steward Sask. Govt. Employees Union. Mem. Can. Library Assn., Sask. Library Assn., India-Can. Assn., Internat. Soc. Krishna Conscious (life). Hindu. Home: 3406 25th Ave, Regina, SK Canada S4S 1L8 Office: SIAST Wascana Campus, 4635 Wascana Pkwy, Regina, SK Canada S4P 3A3

VOIGT, JOHN JACOB, telecommunications executive; b. Atlantic City, Apr. 2, 1942; s. Jacob Joseph and Mary Margret (Camp) V.; grad. Lawrenceville Sch., 1960; student U. Pitts., 1960-61; B.S. in Econs., Wharton Sch. Fin. and Commerce U. Pa., 1963, postgrad., 1964; m. Glenna Fitzsimons, Sept. 22, 1961; children—Bridget Glenna, John Jacob Jr. Pres., Nat. Accessories Co., Phila., 1970—; chmn. ICCI, ICCI Europe Ltd., Brussels, The Dynoptics Corp., Lausanne, Switzerland, 1984—, also bd. dirs.; pres., treas., dir. The Inteleplex Corp.; pres. Howard Butcher Trading Corp., Phila., 1976—; chmn. IMS Corp., Geneva, Switzerland, 1987—; dir. Atlantic Metal Finishing Co., Butcher Foods Inc., Cont. Quality Industries, IHESA, San Pedro Sula, Honduras, Sterling Group Ltd., London, Torreya Fin. Corp., Palm Beach, Fla.; cons. Compagnie Generale d'Electricite, Paris, Matra Group, Paris; v.p. Iben Petterson A/S, Copenhagen. Bd. govs. Betty Bacharach Hosp., 1976—; mem. vestry, sr. warden Ch. of Epiphany, Ventnor, N.J., 1975—. Republican. Clubs: Union League Phila., Princeton N.Y.C.; Atlantic City Country; Seaview Country; Ocean City Yacht; U. Pa. (N.Y.C.). Lodges: Order of St. John Jerusalem, Knights of Malta. Home: 2215 Burroughs Ave Linwood NJ 08221 Office: 30 Ave Van Bever, Brussels 1180, Belgium

VOINEA, RADU P(OLICARP), civil engineer; b. Craiova, Romania, May 24, 1923; s. Policarp and Gabriela Voinea; married; children: Ruxandra, Serban. Sr. lectr. Inst. Civil Engring., Bucharest, 1951-62; prof. Polytech. Inst., Bucharest, 1962—, pro-rector, 1964-67, rector, 1972-81; chmn. Romanian Acad., 1984—; prof. emeritus, scientist emeritus S.R. Romania; rector U. Bucharest;. Author: (with A. Beles) Lectures on the Strengths of Materials, 1958, (with V. Valcovici and S. Balan) Theoretical Mechanics, 1959, 3d edit., 1968, (with M.C. Atanasiu) Analytical Methods in the Theory of Mechanisms, 1964, (with D. Voiculescu and V. Ceausu) Mechanics, 1975, 2d edit., 1983, (with D. Vaoiculescu and F.P. Simion) Solid-State Mechanics with Applications in Engineering, 1988. Mem. Nat. Commn. Tensometry (chmn.), Romanian Council Sci. and Tech., PUGWASH (pres.), European Acad. Arts Sci. and Humanities. Office: Institutul Politehnic, Splaiul Independentei 313, Bucharest Romania

VOINOVICH, VLADIMIR NIKOLAYEVICH, freelance writer; b. Dushanbe, Tadzhikistan, USSR, Sept. 26, 1932; s. Nikolay Pavlovich and Rosa (Goikhman) V.; m. Valentina Voinovich; children: Marina, Pavel; m. Irina Braude, 1970; 1 child, Olga. Student, Pedagogical Inst., Moscow, 1959. Freelance writer 1962—; vis. fellow Princeton U., 1982-83. Author: The Life and Extraordinary Adventures of Private Ivan Chonkin, 1977, Ivankiad, 1977, Pretender to the Throne, 1981, Moscow-2042, 1987, others. Served with Soviet Air Force, 1951-55. Ford Found. grantee, 1982. Mem. Bavarian Acad. Fine Arts, Mark Twain Soc. (hon.). Home: Hans Carossa Strasse 5, 8035 Stockdorf Federal Republic of Germany

VOISINET, JAMES RAYMOND, mortgage banker; b. Buffalo, June 18, 1931; s. Walter E. and Hildegarde M. (Opitz) V.; m. Virginia M. Waud, Sept. 14, 1957; children: James Raymond, Sarah, Anne. BME, Cornell U., 1951; BA in Econs. cum laude, St. Lawrence U., 1954. Ptnr. Weber, Loes, Weber Assos., Buffalo, 1956-62; dir. mktg. Gold Bond div. Nat. Gypsum Co., Charlotte, N.C., 1962-72; v.p. merchandising Gold Bond div. Nat. Gypsum Co., Dallas, 1973-74, corp. v.p., 1974-84, corp. pres., chief operating officer, 1984-86; pres., chief exec. officer J.R. Voisinet Investments, Dallas, 1986-87; pres., chief exec. officer Troy & Nichols Mortgage Co., Monroe, La., 1987—, also bd. dirs.; bd. dirs. Stockton Savs. Assn., Dallas. Mem. devel. bd. U. Tex., Dallas; past dir. U.S. C. of C. Served to 1st lt. U.S. Army, 1954-56. Republican. Roman Catholic. Clubs: Dallas, Northwood. Home: 3228 Deborah Dr Monroe LA 71201 Office: Troy & Nichols Mortgage Co Box 4025 Monroe LA 71211

VOKHIWA, HAMILTON SHADRICK, editor; b. Mulanje, Malawi, July 25, 1941; s. Shadrick Vokhiwa and Harriet (McLean) Pangani; m. Rose Mulomba; 7 children. Grad. high sch., Blantyre, Malawi; diploma in journalism, Internat. Press Inst., Nairobi, Kenya, Thomson Found., Cardiff, UK. Reporter Malawi News, Blantyre, 1965-72; sub-editor Daily Times, Blantyre, 1972-75, sr. sub-editor, 1975-76, asst. editor, 1976-85, editor, 1985-87; company librarian Blantyre Print and Pub. Co. Library, Blantyre, 1988—. Fellow Internat. Press Inst., Thomson Found. Presbyterian. Office: Blantyre Print & Pub Co Library, Ginnery Corner Private Bag 39, Blantyre Malawi

VOLCKER, PAUL A., economist, former federal official, banker; b. Cape May, N.J., Sept. 5, 1927; s. Paul A. and Alma Louise (Klippel) V.; m. Barbara Marie Bahnson, Sept. 11, 1954; children: Janice, James. AB summa cum laude, Princeton U., 1949, LLD (hon.), 1982; MA, Harvard U., 1951; postgrad. in econs., U. London, 1951-52; LLD (hon.), Adelphi U., 1980, U. Notre Dame, 1980, Fairleigh Dickinson U., 1981, U. N.H., 1982, Dartmouth Coll., 1983, NYU, 1983, Lamar U., 1983; DBA, Bryant Coll., 1983. Economist Fed. Res. Bank N.Y., 1952-57; pres. Fed. Res. Bank of N.Y., 1975-79; economist Chase Manhattan Bank, N.Y.C., 1957-61, v.p., dir. planning, 1965-68; with Dept. Treasury, Washington, 1961-65, 69-74, dep. under sec. monetary affairs, 1963-65, under sec., 1969-74; chmn. bd. govs.

Fed. Res. Bd., Washington, 1979-87; chmn. James D. Wolfensohn Co., N.Y.C., 1988—; prof. Woodrow Wilson Sch. of Pub. and Internat. Affairs, 1988. Sr. fellow Woodrow Wilson Sch. Pub. and Internat. Affairs, 1974-75. *

VOLPÉ, ROBERT, endocrinologist; b. Toronto, Ont., Can., Mar. 6, 1926; s. Aaron G. and Esther (Shulman) Volpe; m. Ruth Vera Pullan, Sept. 5, 1949; children: Catherine, Elizabeth, Peter, Edward, Rose Ellen. M.D., U. Toronto, 1950. Intern U. Toronto, 1950-51, resident in medicine, 1951-52, 53-55, fellow in endocrinology, 1952-53, 55-57, sr. research fellow dept. medicine, 1957-62, McPhedran fellow, 1957-65, asst. prof., 1962-68, assoc. prof., 1968-72, prof., 1972—, dir. div. endocrinology and metabolism, 1987—, chmn. Centennial Com., 1987-88; attending staff St. Joseph's Hosp., Toronto, 1957-66; active staff Wellesley Hosp., Toronto, 1966—; dir. endocrinology research lab. Wellesley Hosp., 1968—, physician-in-chief, 1974-87; dir. Endocrinology div. U. Toronto, 1987—. Author: Systematic Endocrinology, 1973, 2d edit, 1979, Thyrotoxicosis, 1978, Auto-immunity in Endocrine System, 1981, Autoimmunity and Endocrine Disease, 1985; also over 220 research articles, especially on immunology of thyroid disease; past editorial bd.: Jour. Clin. Endocrinology and Metabolism, Clin. Medicine, Clin. Endocrinology, Annals Internal Medicine. Served with Royal Can. Naval Vol. Res., 1943-45. Recipient Goldie medal for med. research U. Toronto, 1971, Gold medal Jap. Endocrine Soc., 1986; Med. Research Council Can. grantee, 1955—. Fellow Royal Coll. Physicians (Can.), Royal Soc. Medicine, A.C.P. (gov. for Ont. 1978-83); mem. Can. Soc. Endocrinology and Metabolism (past pres., Sandoz prize lectr. 1985), Toronto Soc. Clin. Research (Baxter prize lectr. 1984), Can. Soc. Clin. Investigation, Am. Thyroid Assn. (pres. 1980-81), Assn. Am. Physicians, Endocrine Soc., Am. Fedn. Clin. Research, Can. Soc. Nuclear Medicine (Jamieson prize lectr. 1980), AAAS, N.Y. Acad. Sci., European Thyroid Assn. (corr.), Latin Am. Thyroid Assn. (corr.); hon. mem. Soc. Endocrinology and Metabolism of Chile. Clubs: Donalda, Alpine Ski, U. Toronto Faculty. Home: 3 Daleberry Pl, Don Mills, ON Canada M3B 2A5 Office: Wellesley Hosp, Toronto, ON Canada M4Y 1J3

VOLPERT, HOWARD ALAN, department store executive; b. Syracuse, N.Y., May 7, 1934; s. Myron and Marian G. (Berman) V.; grad. Syracuse U., 1959; m. Judith Ann Schmidt, July 27, 1969; children: Molly Anne, Adam Raphael. Exec. trainee, asst. buyer, buyer Open Dey Bros. Home Store, 1961-65; buyer, store mgr. Burdines Federated Dept. Store, Hollywood, Fla., 1970-76, mdse. mgr. Dadeland div., 1965-67, gen. mgr., 1967-69, now v.p., regional mgr. Burdines Central Fla., Orlando, also dir.; chmn., chief exec. officer Volpert Realty, Inc., Longwood, Fla.; bd. dirs. Sun Bank, Orlando Bus. Jour. Bd. dirs., head mchts. div. Combined Jewish Appeal; bd. dirs. Loch Haven Art Center, also chmn. fin. com.; bd. dirs. U. Central Fla., Mid Life Found., Seminole County United Way, John Young Sci. Ctr., Hebrew Day Sch., Statue of Liberty Found., Fla. Citrus Bowl, Fla. Symphony Orch., Am. Heart Assn.; vice chmn United Fund., Univ. Nat. Endowment Fund. Served as capt. AUS, 1959-61. Mem. Hollywood Fashion Center Mchts. Assn. (pres.), Hollywood C. of C. (past pres.), Greater Orlando C. of C. (bd. dirs.), Res. Officers Assn., Zeta Beta Tau (trustee). Club: Sweetwater Country (bd. dirs.). Lodges: Masons, Rotary. Home: 203 River View Dr Sweetwater Club Longwood FL 32779 Office: Volpert Realty Inc 155 East Lake Brantley Rd Longwood FL 32779

VOLPI, FRANCO, philosophical writer; b. Vicenza, Veneto, Italy, Oct. 4, 1952; s. Mario and Teresa (Chilovi) V.; m. Ruth Barbara Otte, June 18, 1982; 1 child, Laura. Student, U Cologne, (W.Ger.), 1972, 73-74; Ph.D., U. Padua, 1975; postgrad. U. Vienna, 1975-76. Sci. researcher U. Padua (Italy), 1977—, U. Louvain (Belgium), 1980-81; prof., U. Padua, 1987—. Author: Heidegger e Brentano, 1976; Heidegger e Hegel, 1977; Filosofia Pratica, 1980; Heidegger e Aristotele, 1984; Ars majeutica, 1985, Lexikon der Philosoph Werke, 1988; translator Heidegger (Wegmarken); contbr. articles to internat. philos. revs.; editorial bd. Philosophischer Literaturanzeiger, W.Ger., 1975—, Husserl-Studies, Netherlands, 1983—, Heidegger Studies, W.Ger., 1987—. Mem. Deutsche Gesellschaft fü r Phanomenologische Forschung, Soc. Filosó fica Italiana, Schopenhauer-Gesellschaft Heidegger-Gesellschaft. Home: Via Mameli 21, 36100 Vicenza Italy Office: Inst Filosofia, Via Accademia 5, 35139 Padova Italy

VOLYMER, YURIY MIKHAYLOVICH, Soviet government official; b. Viazemskiy, Khabarovsk, USSR, Aug. 28, 1933; married; 1 son. Grad., High Merchant Marine Engring. Sch., Vladivostock, USSR, 1957; student, Acad. Nat. Economy. With Far Ea. Shipping Co., Vladivistock, 1957-68; dep. pres. Primorsk Shipping Co., Nakhodka, 1969-75, pres., 1975-78; pres. Far Ea. Shipping Co., 198-86; minister of merchant marine USSR, Moscow, 1986—. Address: USSR Ministry Merchant Marine, 1/4 Ul Zhdanova, 103759 Moscow USSR *

VON ALBRECHT, MICHAEL, classicist, educator; b. Stuttgart, Württemberg, Fed. Republic of Germany, Aug. 22, 1933; s. Georg and Elise (Kratz) von A.; m. Ruth Krautter, July 24, 1959; children: Christiane, Martin, Dorothea. MA in Music, Staatliche Hochschule f. Musik, Stuttgart, 1955; PhD in Classics, U. Tübingen, Fed. Republic of Germany, 1959; postgrad., Studienstiftung des Deutschen Volkes, Paris, 1959-60; habilitation classics, U. Tübingen, Fed. Republic of Germany, 1963. Asst. prof. classics U. Tübingen, 1959-63; assoc. prof. U. Heidelberg, Fed. Republic of Germany, 1963-64, prof., 1964—; hon. mem., v.p. Ovidianum, 1972; vis. prof. U. Amsterdam, 1977-78, U. Tex., Austin, 1984, U. Fla., Gainesville, 1986; vis. mem. Inst. for Advanced Study, Princeton, N.J., 1980-81. Author: Silius Italicus, 1963, Master Roman Prose, 1988, Goethe und das Volkslied, 1972, Roemische Poesie, 1976, Rom: Spiegel Europas, 1988; editor: Musik in Antike und Neuzeit, 1987; contbr. articles to profl. jours. Mem. Mommsen-Gesellschaft, Am. Philol. Assn., Acad. Properziana, Acad. Latinitati Fovendae. Office: U Heidelberg Seminar Klassische, Philologie Marstallhof 4, D6900 Heidelberg Federal Republic of Germany

VON BAUER, ERIC ERNST, investment banking executive; b. LaHabra Heights, Calif., Apr. 12, 1942; s. Kurt Ernst and Margaret Ross (Porter) V.; m. Joyce Ruth Schmidt, Dec. 29, 1973; children—Suzanne Lynn, Katherine Jean. Student Occidental Coll., Los Angeles, 1960-63; M.B.A., U. Chgo., 1973; postgrad. U. Chgo. Law Sch., 1973. Registered rep. Piedmont Internat. Ltd. subs. Piedmont Capital Corp., Frankfurt, W.Ger., 1968-71; fin. adv. trust dept. 1st Nat. Bank Chgo., 1971-72; sec.-treas., controller, Am. Med. Bldgs. Inc., Milw., 1973-75; sr. managing cons. Mgmt. Analysis Ctr., Inc., Chgo., 1975-79; v.p., gen. mgr. corp. fin. adv. services div. Continental Ill. Nat. Bank, Trust Co., Chgo., 1979-82; pres., chief exec. officer The Capital Strategy Group, Inc., Chgo., 1982—; dir., pres. Chgo. chpt. N.Am. Soc. Corp. Planning, 1981-84; faculty mem. Keller Grad. Sch. Mgmt., Chgo., 1987—; guest lectr. U. Chgo. Grad Sch. Bus. Bd. dirs. Chgo. chpt. Reading is Fundamental, 1972-73; dist. adv. com. Fremont (Ill.) Unified Sch. Dist. Served to 1st lt. C.E. U.S. Army, 1964-67. Decorated Army Commendation award. Mem. Assn. Corp. Growth, Midwest Planning Assn., Friends of Small Bus., Am. Mgmt. Assn. C. of C. (dir. Chgo. jr. chpt. 1971-73). Presbyn. Club: Rotary (Chgo.) Author: Knowing Your Product Line Profitability: Key to Greater Strategic Success, 1984; co-author: Zero Base Planning, Budgeting, 1977; contbr. articles to profl. publs. Home: 28 Carlisle Rd Hawthorn Woods IL 60047 Office: Capital Strategy Group 20 N Wacker Dr Chicago IL 60606

VON BRAUN, ECKART HEINRICH, geologist; b. Hirschberg, Silesia, German Dem. Republic, Jan. 8, 1926; s. Constantin Kurt and Ilse Anna (du Mesnil) von B.; m. Rosmarie Elisabeth Hohl, June 24, 1960; children—Rainer, Dorothea, Jutta. Abitur, A. Thaer Gymnasium, Hamburg, 1946; student U. Mainz, 1946-48; Dr.Phil., U. Basel, Switzerland, 1953. Field geologist, Deilmann Bergbau GmbH, Bentheim, Germany, 1953-55; field geologist Tex. Gulf Sulphur Co., Houston, 1955-58; state geologist Bundesanstalt für Geowissenschaften und Rohstoffe, Hannover, Fed. Republic Germany, 1958-74; programme specialist UNESCO, Paris, 1974-86. Author: Uranprospektion 1956-1962, 1965; contbr. articles to profl. jours. Sec., Internat. Geol. Correlation Programme, UNESCO, 1974-86. Mem. Deutsche Geologische Gesellschaft, Schweizerische Geologische Gesellschaft, Vereinigung Schweizerischer Petrol-Geologen. Home: Wiesenweg 7, 3004 Isernhagen KB Federal Republic of Germany

VON BREDOW, WILFRIED, political science educator; b. Heinrichsdorf, Fed. Republic Germany, Jan. 2, 1944; s. Christoph and Anja (von Oettingen) von B.; m. Monika Schlesier; 1 child, Fenimore. PhD, Bonn (Fed. Republic Germany) U., 1968. Asst. Seminar Fuer Politische Wissenschaft U. Bonn, 1969-72; prof. polit. sci. Philipps U., Marburg, Fed. Republic Germany, 1972—, v.p., 1975-77; vis. profl. Trinity Coll. U. Toronto (Ont., Can.), 1986-87. Contbr. numerous articles to profl. jours. Served to lt. inf. German Army, 1962-64. Home: Altes SchulhausGoett, D-3551 Lahntal Federal Republic of Germany Office: Philipps U, W-Roepke St 6, D355 Marburg Federal Republic of Germany

VON BUEDINGEN, RICHARD PAUL, urologist; b. Rochester, N.Y., Sept. 14, 1938; s. Wilmer Edward and Clara Elma von B.; B.S., U. Wis., 1960, M.A. in Philosophy, 1961, M.D., 1965; m. Bari Luwe Solesky, Nov. 26, 1966; children—Kirsten Karla, Christian Karl. Commd. ensign U.S. Navy, 1964, advanced through grades to capt., 1975, intern, U.S. Naval Hosp., St. Albans, N.Y., 1965-66, resident in internal medicine, in plastic and thoracic surgery, in urology affiliate programs Naval Regional Med. Ctr., Oakland, Calif., and U.S. Hosp., Oakland, U. Calif. San Francisco, Stanford U., 1969-73, resident in pediatric urology, 1973, scientist astronaut trainee Naval Aerospace Med. Inst., Pensacola, Fla., 1966-67, group flight surgeon Marine Corp Air Sta., Beaufort, S.C., 1967-69, chief urology Naval Regional Med. Ctr., Long Beach, Calif., 1973-75, asst. clin. prof. urology, U. Calif., Irvine, 1973-75, resigned, 1975; pvt. practice urology, Aiken, S.C., 1975—; bd. trustees, chief of surgery HCA Aiken Regional Med. Ctrs., 1985—. Fellow Internat. Coll. Surgeons, ACS; mem. AMA, Am. Urol. Assn., S.C. Med. Assn. (com. on continuing edn. 1981-83), S.C. Urol. Assn., So. Med. Assn., Soc. Govt. Urologists, Aiken County Med. Soc., Am. Cancer Soc. (chmn. com. profl. edn. in S.C. 1980-82, nat. award for contbns. to profl. edn. 1982), Am. Diabetes Assn. (state bd. dirs., med. edn. com.), Am. Fertility Soc., Am. Lithotripsy Soc. Club: Whiskey Rd. Fox Hounds (Master of Fox Hounds). Contbr. articles to profl. publs. Home: 217 Easy St Aiken SC 29801 Office: 210 University Pkwy Suite 2300 Aiken SC 29801

VON DER ESCH, HANS ULRIK, lawyer; b. Nurnberg, Germany, Jan. 27, 1928; s. Hans Joachim and Kerstin Marianne (Sandstedt) von der E.; m. Marianne Hedvig Margaretha Celsing, Aug. 23, 1975; children: Ulrik, Fredrik; 1 child by previous marriage: Alexandra Louise. MBA U. Gothenburg, 1951; LLB, U. Stockholm, 1954. Bar: Sweden 1966. With Dist. Ct. Service, Nykoping and Stockholm, 1954-57; pres.'s asst. Bonniergroup, Stockholm, Hamburg, Geneva and N.Y.C., 1957-63, atty., Stockholm, 1963-66; sole practice, Stockholm, 1966—; ptnr. Advokatfirman Landahl, 1972—; chmn., dir. numerous Swedish and fgn. cos. Served with Swedish Army, 1946-48. Decorated Swedish Sign of Distinction; Finnish Golden Order of Merit; Norwegian Badge of Honor; Knight of the Order of St. John in Sweden. Mem. ABA, Swedish Lawyers Assn. (div. dir. 1974-79, del. 1979-88), Swedish Army and Air Force Res. Officers League (pres 1975-78), Swedish Parachute Assn. (pres. 1966-68), Royal Swedish Aero Club (bd. dirs. 1966-78, gen. counsel 1967-78, v.p. 1983-88), Internat. Bar Assn., Internat. Fiscal Assn., Lawyer-Pilots Bar Assn. Club: Nya Saellskapet (Stockholm). Mem. Swedish Ch. Contbr. articles on aviation. Holder world class record Class C light aircraft 1000-1750 kgs, piston engine, speed record over recognized course: Sal (Rep. of Cape Verde-Funchal (Madeira) 224.06 km/hr. Home: 25 Strandvägen, 11456 Stockholm Sweden Office: Cardellgatan 1, PO Box 5209, 102 45 Stockholm Sweden

VON DER PORTEN, PETER GERHARD, treasurer; b. Kingston, Jamaica, Nov. 6, 1946; s. Gerhard P. and Dorothea (Eisenmenger) von der P.; m. Wendy Roxanne Taylor; children: Fern, David, Suzanne, Mary. B in Engring., McGill U., Montreal, 1968; MBA, U. Western Ont., 1970. Budget mgr. Finning Ltd., Vancouver, B.C., 1971-74; service mgr. Finning Tractor & Equipment, Vancouver, B.C., 1974-77, area parts mgr., 1978-81; treas., officer Finning Ltd., Vancouver, B.C., 1981—; v.p. Shaughnessy Property Owners Assn. Bd. dirs. United Way, Vancouver, 1983-85. Scholar McGill U., 1965. Mem. Assn. Profl. Engrs. of B.C., Cash Mgmt., Fin. Execs. Inst. (treas. Vancouver chpt.). Office: Finning Ltd, 555 Great Northern Way, Vancouver, BC Canada V5T 1E2

VON DER PORTEN, ROBERT GERHARD, automotive executive; b. Kingston, Jamaica, May 20, 1951; married. 2 children. BA in Econs., U. Western Ont., London, 1972; MBA, U. Western Ont., 1974. Cons. Peat, Marwick and Ptnrs., Toronto, Ont., 1974-76; fin. analyst Reed Paper, Toronto, 1976-77; mgr. planning Speedy Muffler King/Walker, Toronto, 1977-81; dir. fin. Speedy Muffler King N.Am., Toronto, 1981-84; v.p. fin. Tenneco Automotive Retail, Toronto, 1984—.

VON DEWITZ, VICTOR BOTHO JOBST, diesel engine manufacturing company executive; b. Gumbinnen, East Prussia, Germany, Jan. 16, 1942; arrived in Eng., 1974; s. Berndt and Albertine (von Grueber) von D.; m. Ingrid M. Larsson, July 8, 1967; children: Carina, Susanne, Michael. Arbitur, Walldorf Sch, Benefeld, Fed. Republic Germany. Salesman Jung VW, Hamburg, Fed. Republic Germany, 1967-69; buyer Deutz Svenska, Stockholm, 1969-73, parts mgr., 1969-74; parts mgr. Deutz Engines Ltd KHD, London, 1974-83; mng. dir. Diesel Power Ltd., London, 1983—; bd. dirs. Factorprime Ltd., London, DF Aggregate Handels GmbH, Celle, Fed. Republic Germany. Chmn. Friends of Douglas House, London, 1986—. Served with German Army, 1965-66. Clubs: Internat. Sporting, Intermediate Sports (London). Home: 18 Arlington Rd, Richmond Surrey TW10 7BY, England Office: Diesel Power Ltd, 12 Mitcham Industrial Estates, Mitcham Surrey CR4 2AD, England

VON DOHNANYI, CHRISTOPH, musician, conductor; b. Berlin, Sept. 8, 1929; s. Hans and Christina (Bonhoeffer) D.; m. Anja Silja, Apr. 21, 1979; children: Julia, Benedikt, Olga. Student, Sch. law, Munich, Ger., Musikhochschule, Ger., Fla. State U., Berkshire Music Ctr. Coach, conductor Frankfort Opera, Ger.; gen. music dir. Lubeck, Kassel, Ger.; dir. West German Radio Symphony Cologne; gen. music dir., artistic dir. Frankfort Opera, Ger.; artistic dir., prin. condr. Hamburg State Opera, Ger., 1978-84; music dir. designate Cleve. Orch., 1982-84, music dir., 1984—; guest condr. in U.S. and Europe. Numerous recs. including 5 symphonies of Mendelssohn with Vienna Philharm., opera Lulu, Petrouchka Suite, Wozzeck. Recipient Richard Strauss prize, Munich; Bartok prize, Hungary; Goethe-Plaket award City of Frankfort. Home: Grosse-Theater-Strasse 34, D-2000 Hamburg 36 Federal Republic of Germany Office: The Cleve Orch 11001 Euclid Ave Cleveland OH 44106 *

VON EHRENFRIED, MANFRED HANS, II, scientist, business executive; b. Dayton, Ohio, Mar. 30, 1936; s. Manfred Hans and Carriebelle Metia (Romans) von E.; m. Alice Jane Edmonds, June 6, 1959 (div. 1980); m. 2d, Dayle Ann Thompson, June 11, 1982; children—Manfred III, Kevin, Heidi. B.S. in Physics, U. Richmond, 1960; grad. Fed. Exec. Inst., 1976. Tchr. physics, math. and sci. Colonial Heights, Va. High Sch., 1960-61; projects Mercury, Gemini, Apollo and Skylab mainline and mission mgr., NASA mission control ctr. flight controller, asst. flight dir., human factors test subject, high altitude aircraft crew mem. NASA, 1961-71; earth resources applications dept. mgr. EG&G Wolf Research Co., Riverdale, Md., 1971-72; project and dept. mgr. TRW, 1973-75; chief test and evaluation Nuclear Regulatory Commn., 1975-77; owner, prin. von Ehrenfried & Assocs., Leesburg, Va., 1977-79; prin. cons. Internat. Energy Assocs. Ltd., Washington, 1979-82; pvt. practice space, aviation and nuclear cons., Washington, 1982—; co-founder, bd. dirs. Washington Space Bus. Roundtable, 1985—. Co-founder & V.P. Technical & Administrative Services Corp. (TADCORPS) NASA Space Station Support Contractor, 1983—. Named Eagle scout Boy Scouts Am., 1952; recipient Sustained Superior Performance award NASA, 1965; and Outstanding Performance award NASA 1964; and Outstanding Performance award Nuclear Regulatory Commn., 1977. Mem. Am. Soc. Indsl. Security (cert. protection profl.), Exptl. Aircraft Assn. Republican. Lutheran. Contbr. articles in field to profl. jours.

VON ERDMANNSDORFF, WOLF-DIETRICH PAUL, sales executive; b. Berlin, May 1, 1927; s. Otto Bernhard Heinrich and Irmgard Anita (Albert) von E.; m. Sigrid Alice Charlotte Ursula Eberhardt, Feb. 21, 1958; children: Andreas, Anita, Magnus, Corinno. B Com., LLB, U. South Africa, Pretoria, 1953; diploma volkswirt, U. Tübingen, Fed. Republic of Germany, 1955, D in Polit. Sci., 1958. Clerk in econ. affairs German Embassy and Fgn. Office, Bonn, Pretoria, Fed. Republic of Germany, Republic of South Africa, 1951-54; with foreign dept. Demag A.G., Duisburg, Fed. Republic of Germany, 1956-60; sales mgr. Dinglerwerke A.G., Zweibrücken, Fed. Republic of Germany, 1960-67; sales dir. Stahl-u.Röhrenwerk Reisholz, Düsseldorf, Fed. Republic of Germany, 1967-72; comml. mgr., indsl. plants Gutehoffnungshütte A.G., Oberhausen, Fed. Republic of Germany, 1972-75; sales mgr., now sales coordinator Pierburg Autogerätebau (merged into Pierburg GmbH), Neuss, Fed. Republic of Germany, 1976—. Author: Entwicklungsland Ethiopien, 1956. Mem. Assn. German Automobile Industry for Fgn. Economy. Home: Koppenburgstr 99, D4200 Oberhausen Federal Republic of Germany Office: Pierburg GmbH, Leuschstrasse 1, D4040 Neuss Federal Republic of Germany

VON EYE, ALEXANDER ARTHUR, psychologist; b. Leipzig, Germany, Sept. 16, 1949; s. Werner H. and Jutta I. (Mohring) von E.; m. Donata Gosswein, Oct. 26, 1973; children—Maxine, Valerie, Julian. Diploma in Psychology, U. Trier, Fed. Republic Germany, 1974, Dr.phil., 1976, Dr.phil. habil., 1981. Asst. prof. U. Trier, 1974-77; asst. prof. U. Erlangen-Nurnberg, Nurnberg, 1977-79, Erlangen, 1979-81; sr. research scientist Max Planck Inst. for Human Devel. and Edn., Berlin, 1981-86; prof. human devel. Pa. State U., University Park, 1986—; cons. St. Josephshaus, Kleinzimmern, Fed. Republic Germany, 1978-86; hon. prof. psychology Tech. U., Berlin, 1985. Editor: (with others) Preventive Psychology, 1982, Semantic Dimensions, 1983, Individual Development and Social Change, 1984. Contbr. over 100 articles to profl. jours. Stiftung Volkswagenwerk grantee U. Trier, 1979. Mem. Internat. Biometric Soc., German Psychol. Soc., Am. Statis. Assn., Am. Psychol. Assn., Psychonomic Soc. Office: Pa State U Coll Health and Human Devel S 110 Henderson South University Park PA 16802

VON FIEANDT, DORRIT MARGARETA, ceramic artist; b. Helsinki, Finland, Nov. 5, 1927; d. John Rafael and Anna Elisabet (Finnlund) Flinkenberg; m. Berndt Johan von Fieandt; children: Kim, Monika, Benita. Degree in ceramic arts, H.S. of Applied Arts, Finland, 1948. Freelance ceramic artist, Helsinki, 1949-53, 65—; guest artist Arabia, Helsinki, 1986—. Represented in individual and group exhbns., Finland and Europe, 1967-87. Recipient prize for culture City of Helsinki, 1982. Mem. Finnish Orgn. for Indsl. Design and Applied Art, Zonta Helsinki I. Home: Merikatu 7A, 00140 Helsinki Finland

VON FRAUNHOFER, JOSEPH ANTHONY, metallurgical engineer, educator; b. London, Eng., Nov. 9, 1940; came to U.S., 1978; s. Hans and Jessie Josephine (Schoen) von F.; m. Anne Marsom, Sept. 7, 1962 (div. 1979); children—Nicola Anne, Michael Anthony. B.S., U. London, Eng., 1963, M.S., 1967; Ph.D., Council Nat. Acad. Awards, London, 1969. Chartered chemist; chartered engr. Sci. officer Brit. Rail Research Div., London, 1963-64; scientist Harris Plating Ltd., London, 1964-65; sr. officer research div. Gas Council, London, 1965-70; sr. lectr., dept. chmn. Inst. Dental Surgery, U. London, 1970-78; prof. biomaterials sci. U. Louisville., 1978—. Author: Potentiostat and Its Applications, 1972, Concise Corrosion Science, 1974, Paint Formulation, 1981, Protective Paint Coatings for Metals, 1976, Concise Paint Technology, 1977, Instrumentation in Metal Finishing, 1975. Basic Metal Finishing, 1976, Statistics in Medical, Dental and Biological Studies, 1976, Scientific Aspects of Dental Materials, 1975; contbr. sci. articles to profl. publs. Fellow Royal Soc. Chemistry, Instn. Corrosion Sci. and Tech. (sec. 1977-78), Acad. Dental Materials; mem. Instn. Metallurgists. Contbr. articles, chpts. to profl. publs. Home: 1845 Douglas Blvd Louisville KY 40205 Office: U Louisville Health Scis Ctr Dental Sch Louisville KY 40292

VON HASSEL, KAI-UWE, former government official; b. Gare, Tanzania, Apr. 21, 1913; s. Theodor and Emma (Jebsen) von H.; m. Elfriede Frolich (dec.); children—Joachim (dec.), Barbara Weisse; m. Monika Weichert, June 30, 1972; 1 child, Jan Friedrich. Abitur Real Gymnasium, Flensburg, 1933, Dr. Phil. h.c., U. Ankara, 1985. Mayor, Town of Glucksburg, Germany, 1947-63; prime minister State of Schleswig-Holstein, 1954-63; fed. minister def., Bonn, Fed. Republic Germany, 1963-66; speaker Fed. Parliament, Bonn, 1969-72, dep. speaker, 1972-76; speaker Parliamentary Assembly Western European Union, Paris, 1977-80; mem. Parliament Assembly Council of Europe, Strassbourg, 1977-80; mem. European Parliament, Strassbourg, 1979-84. Author: Verantwortung fur die Freiheit, 1966; Waafrika wa leo (book in Swahili), 1942. Pres. bd. Inst. Tropical and Subtropical Agr., Witzenhausen, 1957—; bd. dirs. Konrad Adenauer Found., Bonn., 1962—; pres. Hermann Ehlers Found., Kiel, 1968—; pres. German-Iranian Assn., Bonn, 1975—; bd. dirs. German Fin. Co. for Investment in Developing Countries. Recipient Grand Cross of Merit, Fed. Republic of Germany, 1956; Order of Brit. Empire, 1965; numerous internat. awards and honors. Home: Lyngsbergstrasse 39 B, D5300 Bonn 2 Federal Republic of Germany Office: Deutscher Bundestag-Bundeshaus, 5300 Bonn 1 Federal Republic of Germany

VON KARAJAN, HERBERT, conductor; b. Salzburg, Austria, Apr. 5, 1908; s. Ernst and Martha von K.; children: Isabel, Arabel. Student, Morzarteum, Salzburg; grad. as condr., Vienna Coll. Music, 1929. Conducting debut in The Marriage of Figaro, Ulm, Germany, 1929; condr. opera, Ulm, 1929-34; gen. dir. music, Aachen, Germany, from 1935; debut with Vienna State Opera, 1937, artistic dir., 1957-64; debut in Tristan and Isolde, Berlin State Opera, 1938; staatskapellmeister, 1941-44; condr., Prussian State Orch., until 1944; a founder, London Philharmonia Orch., 1948, permanent condr., from 1950; dir. concerts Gesellschaft der Musikfreunde, Vienna, from 1949; lifetime dir. concerts Berlin Philharm. Orch., 1955—; artistic supr., Orchestre de Paris, 1969-71; instr. Internat. Condrs.' Course, Berlin; also guest condr. concerts Vienna Symphony Orch., 1930-34; rec. artist with Deutsche Grammophon, Polydor Internat., Electric and Mus. Industries Ltd., London; numerous worldwide guest appearances including La Scala and Lucerne (Switzerland) Festival, numerous orchestral tours; in recent years with Berlin Philharm. and Vienna Singverein; U.S. tour, 1976, 82, Japan tour, 1977; condr. Salzburg Festival, 1951—; dir. and condr. films of operas and concerts, 1965—. recipient Mozart Ring, Vienna, 1957, Art prize City of Lucerne, 1969; Franco-German prize Aix-en-Provence, France, 1970; also Grammy awards named Hon. Citizen City of Berlin, 1973. Roman Catholic. Office: Berlin Philharm Orch, Matthaikirchstrasse 1, D-1000 Berlin 30, Federal Republic of Germany also: Festspielhaus, A-5010 Salzburg Austria *

VON KNORRING, ANNE-LIIS, physician, psychiatrist; b. Falun, Sweden, Dec. 22, 1945; d. Edvard and Aino (Aenlo) Raal; m. Lars Ingemar von Knorring, Jan. 8, 1967; children: Marika, Björn. MD, Umeå (Sweden) U., 1973, D in Medicine, 1983. Lic. physician Med. Bd., Sweden. Resident dept psychiatry Umeå Mental Hosp., 1973-74; resident child and adolescent psychiatry Umeå U., 1974-77, resident psychiatry, 1977, resident pediatrics, 1977-78, asst. head physician dept. child and adolescent psychiatry, 1980-83, asst. lectr. dept. psychiatric med. faculty, 1983-85, head physician dept. child and adolescent psychiatry, 1985—, assoc. prof. dept. child and adolescent psychiatry, 1986—. Author sci. books and papers. Mem. Swedish Soc. Alcohol and Drug Research (bd. dirs. 1986—), Swedish Med. Assn., Swedish Com. for the Prevention and Treatment of Depression, Swedish Assn. Child and Adolescent Psychiatry, Swedish Assn. Psychiatry, Scandinavian Assn. Biol. Psychiatry. Office: Umeå U, Dept Child, and Adolescent Psychiatry, S90185 Umeå Sweden

VON KNORRING, LARS INGEMAR, psychiatrist; b. Örebro, Sweden, Nov. 3, 1945; s. Sixten and Mai (Ahl) von K.; m. Anne-Liis Raal, Jan. 8, 1967; children: Marika, Björn. Degree, U. Gothenburg, 1966, U. Umeå, 1972; student, U. Umeå, 1975, D of Psychiatry, 1976. Intern Lycksele, Skelleftea, Umeå, 1968-75; from resident to head physician dept. psychiatry Umeå U., 1973-79, assoc. prof. psychiatry, 1976—. Editor Nordisk Psykiatrisk Tidsskrift, 1984—, various books, 1977—; contbr. articles to profl. jours. Mem. Swedish Med. Assn., Swedish Med. Soc., Swedish Assn. for Forensic Psychiatry, Scandinavian Assn. of Psychopharmacology, Internat. Assn. for the Study of Pain, Swedish Com. for the Prevention and Treatment of Depression, Swedish Assn. for Alcohol and Drug Research, Am. Soc. Biological Psychiatry, others. Home: Sofiehemsvagen 65C, S-90239 Umeå Sweden Office: Umeå U, Dept Psychiatry, S-90185 Umeå Sweden

VON KOHORN, BARON RALPH STEVEN, retired investment banker, author; b. Chemnitz, Ger., Dec. 14, 1919; s. Baron Oscar and Valerie (Wirth) von K.; ed. U. So. Calif., U. Mich.; m. Jillian Annette Bussell, Feb. 25, 1967;

children by previous marriage—Karen Janne, Kirk Steven. Dep. chmn. various world wide bus. orgns., 1945-62; ret., immigrated to N.Z., 1963; settlor von Kohorn Family Trust controlling Genrock Group of Cos., N.Z. and Australia. Founding sr. v.p., dir. Am. C. of C., 1965-74; bd. dirs. Am. Edn. Found. (Fulbright), 1965—, Kennedy Meml. Fellowship, 1972—, East-West Center, Honolulu, 1972-78; selector Eisenhower Fellowships, 1966-68, 78, 81, 86; trustee Wellington Visual Arts Trust, 1968-72; vice chmn., life mem. Wellington (N.Z.) Planetarium Soc., 1968-73, Inst. Advanced Motorists, Wellington, 1969-73; trustee, dir. N.Z. Sports Found., 1977-85, gov., 1986—; trustee Found. for Newborn Child, 1977—; trustee N.Z. Oral History Archives, 1981—; nat. treas. N.Z. Water Safety Council, 1979-87, Small Boat Safety Com., 1977—. Recipient Graham Hayter trophy, 1973, 74, 78, 79; Lane Bryant Internat. Vol. award, 1969; Water Safety award Minister of Internal Affairs, 1987, Minister of Transport Merit award, 1987; Outstanding Vol. Service award Wellington, N.Z., 1987; Tribute of Appreciation award U.S. Govt., 1987. Fellow Inst. Dirs. (London), N.Z. Inst. Mgmt. (counselor); mem. Royal Yachting Assn. (London) (life), Past Commodores Assn. N.Z. (pres.), Internat. Order Past Commodores (internat. v.p. 1982—), N.Z. Am. Assn. Clubs: Wellesley (Wellington), Tattersalls (Sydney), Univ., Civil Service, Royal N.Z. Yacht, Royal Port Nicholson Yacht (life mem.), Mana Cruising (life mem., past commodore). Author: What You Always Wanted to Know about Single Sideband Radio and Never Dared to Ask, 1976; VHF/FM Marine Radio, 1977; Columbia Cruises South, 1977; Columbia Cruises North, 1978; Management of a General Ancillary Licence for Clubs, 1978; Your Guide to Marine Search and Rescue, 1980; co-author, cartographer: A Cruising Man's Guide to the Marlborough Sounds, 1979; A Cruising Guide-Cape Palliser to Marlborough Sounds and Tasman Bay, 1982; The Sounds Crusing Guide, including Cape Palliser to Farewell Spit, 1986, The Cohorn Clan, 1987. Home: Herbert Gardens, 186 The Terrace, Wellington New Zealand Office: PO Box 491, Wellington New Zealand

VON LANG, FREDERICK WILLIAM, librarian, genealogist; b. Scranton, Pa., May 6, 1929; s. Frederick William and Carrie Della (Brundage) von L.; m. Ilsabe von Wackerbarth, July 12, 1960; children: Christoph, Karl Philipp. B.S., Kutztown U., 1951; M.L.S., Syracuse U., 1955. Librarian Broughal Jr. High Sch., Bethlehem, Pa., 1951-52; asst. librarian Bethlehem Pub. Library, 1952-55, Enoch Pratt Free Library, Balt., 1956-66; library dir. Lehigh County Community Coll. Library, Allentown, Pa., 1966-73, Auburn (Maine) Public Library, 1973-77; dir. St. Joseph (Mo.) Public Library, 1977-79, Hibbing (Minn.) Public Library, 1980—. Assoc. editor: Genealogisches Handbuch des in Bayern immatrikulierten Adels, Vol. 4, 1954. Treas., mem. exec. bd. Friends of Bethlehem Pub. Library; treas., mem. steering com. Auburn City Bicentennial Com.; mem. exec. bd. Northampton County Assn. for Blind, Pa.; ofcl. del. Mo. Gov.'s Conf. on Libraries and Info. Scis. Mem. ALA (councilor from Maine Library Assn. 1974-77), Maine Library Assn. (fed. coordinator A.L.A.), S.A.R., Maine Soc. Mayflower Descendents, Soc. Colonial Wars in Maine, Huguenot Soc. Maine, Bradford Family Compact., Beta Phi Mu. Lutheran. Clubs: Masons (32 deg.), KT, Shriners, Order Eastern Star, Elks, Rotary. Home: 2129 W 3d Ave Hibbing MN 55746 Office: 2020 E 5th Ave Hibbing MN 55746

VON LEDEN, HANS VICTOR, surgeon; b. Ger., Nov. 20, 1918; s. Peter Paul and Elizabeth (Freter) von L.; M.D., Loyola U., Chgo., 1941; m. Mary Louise Shine, Jan. 10, 1948; children—Jon Eric, Lisa Maria. Intern, Mercy Hosp.-Loyola U. Clinics, Chgo., 1941-42; resident Presbyn. Hosp., Chgo., 1942-43; fellow otolaryngology and plastic surgery Mayo Found., Rochester, Minn., 1943-44, 1st asst. Mayo Clinic, 1945; practice head and neck surgery, Chgo., 1947-61, Los Angeles, 1961—; clin. asso. Loyola U. Sch. Medicine, 1947-51; asso. prof. otolaryngology Cook County Grad. Sch. Medicine, 1948-58; from asst. to asso. prof. otolaryngology Northwestern U. Med. Sch., 1952-61; asso. prof. surgery head and neck UCLA, 1961-66; prof. biocommunications U. So. Calif., 1966—; cons. laryngology Juilliard Sch. Music and Drama, N.Y.C., 1969—, Calif. Bd. Med. Quality Assurance, 1985—; mem. staff Beverly Hills Med. Ctr., Santa Monica (Calif.) Hosp.; cons. staff White Meml. Med. Center, Rancho Los Amigos Hosp., Calif.; hon. staff Lenox Hill Hosp., N.Y.C.; cons. otolaryngology and plastic surgery U.S. Navy, 1947—; mil. adv. staff Ill. Office CD, 1954-61; cons. Federal Republic Germany, 1960—. Pres. Inst. Laryngology and Voice Disorders, 1959-65, med. dir., 1966—; exec. v.p., med. dir. William and Harriet Gould Found., 1955-61; co-chmn. Internat. Voice Conf., 1957; v.p. Voice Found. Am., 1969-76; vis. prof., guest lectr. various univs. U.S. and fgn. countries. Served as lt. M.C., USNR, 1945-46; sr. surgeon USPHSR, 1967-77; cons. USN, 1947—, Navy League. Recipient bronze plaque, gold medal Ill. Med. Soc., 1954, 60; gold medal Italian Red Cross, 1959; Bucranio, U. Padua, 1958, 60; Casselberry award Am. Laryngol. Assn., 1962, Gutzmann medal U. Berlin, 1980, other awards for contbns. to med. sci., edn.; Theodore Roosevelt Meml. award; decorated companion Mil. Order Fgn. Wars, comdr. Mil. Order World Wars, Naval Order U.S., Order of Merit First Class (Germany), knight Royal Order St. John, knight grand cross with collar Mil. and Hosp. Order St. Lazarus, knight grand cross Order St. John the Baptist, Orden Signum Fidei, knight comdr. Internat. Constantinian Order, gran oficial Orden Pro Juventute, Red Cross of Merit (Portugal), others. Diplomate Am. Bd. Otolaryngology, Internat. Bd. Surgery. Fellow ACS, Internat. Coll. Surgeons (pres. U.S. sect. 1971-72, gov. 1972-80; hon.), Am. Speech and Hearing Assn. (sci. awards 1960, 62, 65), Am. Acad. Facial Plastic and Reconstructive Surgery (dir. 1964-76), Am. Acad. Ophthalmology and Otolaryngology (cert. of merit 1953, award of honor 1959), Academia Peruana de Cirugia (hon.), AAAS, Am. Soc. Head and Neck Surgeons, Collegium Medicorum Theatri (sec. 1969-84, hon. pres. 1984—); mem. AMA (Hektoen award 1961, cert. of merit 1962, sci. achievement award 1981), Calif., Los Angeles County (councilor 1969-74, v.p. 1974-75, sec.-treas. 1975-76, pres.-elect 1976-77, pres. 1977-78, trustee 1978-80, chmn. bd. trustees 1980-82) med. assns., Soc. Mil. Otolaryngology (hon.), Am. Council Otolaryngology (dir. 1973-76), Am. Fedn. Clin. Research, Soc. Exptl. Biology and Med. Soc. Mil. Surgeons, Soc. Med. Cons. to Armed Forces, Pan-Am. Assn. Otolaryngology and Bronchoesophagology (sec.-gen. 1966-80, pres. 1980-82, councilor 1982—), Sigma Xi; hon. mem. socs. oto-rhino-laryngology Germany, Japan, Mexico, Colombia, Argentina, Chile, Peru, Panama, El Salvador, Denmark, Greece. Republican. Roman Catholic. Clubs: Army-Navy (Washington); Mariner (San Francisco). Author sci. textbooks and articles; producer med. motion pictures. Home: 259 Tilden Ave Los Angeles CA 90049 Office: 10921 Wilshire Blvd Los Angeles CA 90024

VON MARSCHALL, BARON WALTHER, diplomat; b. Freiburg, Germany, May 29, 1930; s. Baron Fritz and Nora (Kübler) von. M. LLD, U. Freiburg, Fed. Republic of Germany, 1960; grad. fgn. service exam., Ministry for Affairs, Bonn, Fed. Republic of Germany, 1961; postgrad., Royal Coll. Defence Studies, London, 1975. Attaché German Fgn. Service, Bonn, 1958-61, 3d sec., 1961-63, 2d sec., 1963-66, counsellor 1st class, 1976-79; 1st sec. German Embassy, Jakarta, Indonesia, 1967-69; ambassador Dhaka, Bangladesh, 1979-85, Rangoon, Burma, 1985—; counsellor German Diplomatic Mission, Phnom Penh, Cambodia, 1969-74. Author: Zum Problem der völkerrechtlichen Anerkennung der beiden dt. Regierungen, 1959. Mem. Evang. Ch. Office: Embassy, Fed Republic of Germany, 32 Natmuk Rd, PO Box 12, Rangoon Burma

VON MERING, OTTO OSWALD, educator; b. Berlin, Germany, Oct. 21, 1922; came to U.S., 1939, naturalized, 1954; s. Otto O. and Henriette (Troeger) von M.; m. Shirley Ruth Brook, Sept. 11, 1954; children: Gretchen, Karin, Gregory. Grad., Belmont Hill Sch., 1940; B.A. in History, Williams Coll., 1944; Ph.D. in Social Anthropology, Harvard U., 1956. Instr. Belmont Hill Sch., Belmont, Mass., 1945-47, Boston U., 1947-48, Cambridge Jr. Coll., 1948-49; research asst. lab. social relations Harvard U., 1950-51, Boston Psychopathic Hosp., 1951-53; Russell Sage Found. fellow N.Y.C., 1953-55; asst. prof. social anthropology U. Pitts. Coll. Medicine, 1955-60, assoc. prof., 1960-65, prof. social anthropology, 1965-71; prof. child devel. and child care U. Pitts. Coll. Allied Health Professions, 1969-71; prof. anthropology and family medicine U. Fla., 1971-76, prof. anthropology in ob-gyn, 1979—, prof. anthropology and gerontology, 1986—; lectr. Sigmund Freud Inst., Frankfurt, Germany, 1962-64, Pitts. Psychoanalytical Inst., 1960-71, Interuniversity Forum, 1967-71; cons. mental hosps.; tech. adviser Maurice Falk Med. Fund; Fulbright vis. lectr., 1962-63; Richard-Merton guest prof. Heidelberg U., Germany, 1962-63; vis. prof. Dartmouth, 1970-71; Am. Anthrop. Assn. vis. lectr., 1961-62, 71-74; dir. Tech. Assistance Resource Assos., U. Fla., 1979-84; supr. grad. study program Ctr. Gerontologic Studies, U. Fla., 1983-85, assoc. dir., 1985-86, dir., 1986—; mem. coordinating com. Geriatric Edn. Ctr., Coll. of Medicine, U. Fla.; chair, mem. adv. bd. Internat. Exchange Ctr. on Gerontology State U. System of Fla., 1987—;. Author: Remotivating the Mental Patient, 1957, A Grammar of Human Values, 1961, (with Mitscherlich and Brocher) Der Kranke in der Modernen Gesellschaft, 1967, (with Kasdan) Anthropology in the Behavioral and Health Sciences, 1970; also articles.; Commentary editor: Human Organization, 1974-76; Corr. editor.: Jour. Geriatric Psychiatry; mem. editorial bd.: Med. Anthropology, 1976-84. Recipient Fulbright-Hayes Travel award, 1962-63; Research grantee Wenner-Gren Found., N.Y., 1962-63; Research grantee Am. Philos. Soc., 1962-63; Research grantee Maurice Falk Med. Fund, 1970-71; Spl. fellow NIMH, 1971-72; Service Research grantee Dept. Health and Human Services, 1979-83; family health research grantee Walter Reed Army Inst. Research, 1987—. Fellow Am. Anthrop. Assn. (mem. James Mooney award com. 1978-81), AAAS, Am. Gerontol. Soc., Royal Soc. Health, Acad. Psychosomatic Medicine, Am. Ethnological Soc., Soc. Applied Anthropology, Royal Anthrop. Inst.; mem. Assn. Am. Med. Colls., Am. Fedn. Clin. Research, Am. Public Health Assn., British Soc. Gerontology, World Fedn. Mental Health, Internat. Assn. Social Psychiatry (regional counselor). Office: U Fla Gainesville FL 32611

VONNEGUT, KURT, JR., writer; b. Indpls., Nov. 11, 1922; s. Kurt and Edith (Lieber) V.; m. Jane Marie Cox, Sept. 1, 1945 (div. 1979); children: Mark, Edith, Nanette; adopted nephews: James, Steven and Kurt Adams; m. Jill Krementz, 1979, 1 child, Lily. Student, Cornell U., 1940-42, U. Chgo., 1945-47; MA in Anthropology, U. Chgo., 1971. Reporter Chgo. City News Bur., 1946; pub. relations with Gen. Electric Co., 1947-50; free-lance writer N.Y.C., 1950-65, 74—; lectr. writers workshop U. Iowa, Iowa City, 1965-67; lectr. in English Harvard U., Cambridge, Mass., 1970; disting. prof. CCNY, 1973-74. Author: (novels) Player Piano, 1951, Sirens of Titan, 1959, Mother Night, 1961, Cat's Cradle, 1963, God Bless You, Mr. Rosewater, 1964, Slaughterhouse-Five, 1969, Breakfast of Champions, 1973, Slapstick, or Lonesome No More, 1976, Jailbird, 1979, Deadeye Dick, 1982, Galápagos, 1985, Bluebeard, 1987; (collected stories) Welcome to the Monkey House, 1968; (play) Happy Birthday, Wanda June, 1970; (TV script) Between Time and Timbuktu or Prometheus-5, 1972; (essays) Wampeters, Foma and Granfalloons, 1974; (Christmas Story with illustrations by Ivan Chermayeff) Sun Moon Star, 1980; (autobiographical collage) Palm Sunday, 1981; also short stories, articles, revs. Served with inf. AUS, 1942-45. Guggenheim fellow, 1967-68. Mem. Nat. Inst. Arts and Letters (recipient Lit. award 1970). Address: care Donald C Farber 99 Park Ave 25th Floor New York NY 10016-1503

VONNOH, GIGI L(ICHTENSTEIN), newspaper editor; b. N.Y.C., Mar. 8, 1936; d. Alfred Boyd and Ilai (Bingham) Lichtenstein; m. Pen W. Reed, Nov. 30, 1957 (div. 1963); children—Pen W., Kent B.; m. 2d, George E. Vonnoh, Apr. 8, 1965. Student schs. Summit, N.J. Photo-journalist The Reporter, Florida Keys, Fla., 1965-70; reporter Free Press, Key Largo, Fla., 1970-74; reporter Keynoter, Marathon, Fla., 1974-79; photographer Sundial, Marathon, 1974-79; editor The Graham Star, Robbinsville, N.C., 1979—; dir. journalism class Stecoah, N.C., 1982; cons. Keys News, Marathon, 1970-79, Beta Club, Robbinsville, 1982-84, The Robin, Robbinsville, 1980-83. Trustee Graham County Mus. History, Robbinsville, 1982-83; bd. dirs. Graham County United Way, 1979-84; chmn. Am. Heart Assn., Robbinsville, 1979-84. Mem. Fla. Press Assn., N.C. Press Assn., Graham County C. of C. (dir. 1982-83). Republican. Lutheran-Episcopal. Clubs: Women's (pres. Marathon 1970-78), Hosp. Aux. (pres. Marathon 1972-76), Graham County Woman's. Home: 101 Shepard Creek Rd Robbinsville NC 28771 Office: Graham Star 129 By Pass Robbinsville NC 28771

VON OVERBECK, ALFRED EUGENE, educator of law, director; b. Bern, Switzerland, Mar. 8, 1925; married; 2 children. Licence en Droit, U. Fribourg, Switzerland, 1948, Docteur en Droit, 1961; Dr. honoris causae, U. Robert Schuman, 1986. Bar: Switzerland 1952. Practice 1952-56; sec., 1st sec. Permanent Bur. Hague Conf. on Pvt. Internat. Law, 1956-65, Swiss del., 1972—; prof. pvt. internat. law, comml. law and civil procedure U. Fribourg, 1965; pres. U. Fribourg, Switzerland, 1971-75, Conf. of Swiss U. Rectors, Switzerland, 1978-81; dir. Swiss Inst. Comparative Law, Lausanne, 1980—; head of seminars and lectures on pvt. internat. law U. Zurich, Switzerland, 1962-66; guest prof. U. Glasgow, U.K., 1967, U. Geneva, Switzerland, 1976-79, U. Neuchatel, Switzerland, 1967-68; vis. prof. U. Calif., Berkeley, fall 1973, Wuhan U., Peking U., 1988; vis. fellow Australian Nat. U., 1975; lectr. Hague Acad. of Internat. Law , 1961, 71, 82, Internat. Faculty of comparative Law, 1988q; arbitrator Internat. Ctr. for Settlement Investment Disputes, Washington. Contbr. numerous articles on pvt. internat. law to profl. jours. Mem. Inst. Internat. Law, Internat. Acad. Estate and Trust Law, Internat. Law Assn. (past pres. Swiss br.), Swiss Soc. Internat. Law (council), Deutsche Gesellschaft für Volkerrecht (v.p. 1973-77) The Netherlands Acad. Scis. (fgn.), Oesterreichische Akademie Wissenschaften (corr.). Home: Le Manoir, 1162 Saint-Prex Switzerland Office: Swiss Inst Comparative Law, Dorigny, 1015 Lausanne Switzerland

VON POHLE, CHARLES LAWRENCE, physician; b. Balt., Aug. 28, 1899; s. William Richard and Ida May (Peregoy) von P.; m. Laura Maxine Ross, Mar. 21, 1906; 1 child, Carlos Ross. AB in Sci., Columbia Union Coll., 1924; MD, Loma Linda U. Diplomate Nat. Bd. Med. Examiners. Practice, Chandler, Ariz., 1933-42, 46-56; chief-of-staff S.S. Dist. Hosp., Mesa, Ariz., 1947-48; bd. dirs. Ariz. Boys Ranch, Chandler, 1953-55; dir. U.S. Ops. Mission, Guatemale, 1956-63; program administr. Nat. Health Edn., Chad, 1963-65, 68. Contbr. articles on health and sanitation, 1942-65. Mem. adv. bd. Chandler Golden Age Ctr., 1977—; trustee Chandler Sch. Bd., 1938-42. Served to col. AUSMC, 1942-46. Decorated Legion of Merit, Order of Quetzal, Condor de Los Andes, Cruz de Boyaca. Mem. Ariz. State Med. Soc., Maricopa County Med. Soc. Adventist. Republican. Clubs: White Mountain Country (Pinetop, Ariz.), San Marcos Resort (Chandler). Lodge: Rotary Internat. (past pres., Paul Harris fellow 1984).

VON RAFFLER-ENGEL, WALBURGA, linguist, kinesicist, educator; b. Munich, Germany, Sept. 25, 1920; came to U.S., 1949, naturalized, 1955; d. Friedrich J. and Gertrud E. (Kiefer) von R.; m. A. Ferdinand Engel, June 2, 1957; children: Lea Maxine, Eric Robert von Raffler. D.Litt., U. Turin, Italy, 1947; M.S., Columbia U., 1951; Ph.D., Ind. U., 1953. Freelance journalist 1949-58; mem. faculty Bennett Coll., Greensboro, N.C., 1953-55, Morris Harvey Coll., Charleston, W.Va., 1955-57, Adelphi U., CUNY, 1957-58, NYU, 1958-59, U. Florence, Italy, 1959-60, Istituto Post Universitario Organizzazione Aziendale, Turin, 1960-61, Bologna Center of Johns Hopkins U., 1964, Vanderbilt U., Nashville, 1965—; prof. linguistics Vanderbilt U., 1977-85, prof. emerita, sr. research assoc. Inst. Pub. Policy Studies, 1985—, dir. linguistics program, 1978-86; chmn. com. on linguistics Nashville U. Ctr., 1974-79; Italian NSF prof. Psychol. Inst. U. Florence, Italy, 1986-87; prof. NATO Advanced Study Inst., Cortona, Italy, 1988; prof. linguistics Shanxi U., Peoples Republic China, 1985; vis. prof. U. Ottawa, Ont., Can., 1971-72, Inst. for Lang. Scis., Tokyo, 1976; grant evaluator NEH, NSF, Can. Council; manuscript reader Ind. U. Press, U. Ill. Press, Prentice-Hall; cons. Trinity U., Simon Frazer U. Author: Il prelinguaggio infantile, 1964, The Perception of Nonverbal Behavior in the Career Interview, 1983, 2d edit., 1985; co-author: Language Intervention Programs 1960-74, 1975; editor, co-editor 12 books; author film and videotape; contbr. over 300 articles to profl. and popular publs. Recipient grants from Am. Council Learned Socs., grants from NSF, grants from Can. Council, grants from Ford Found., grants from Kenan Venture Fund, grants from Japanese Ministry Edn., grants from NATO, grants from Finnish Acad., grants from Meharry Med. Coll., grants from Internat. Sociol Assn., grants from Internat. Council Linguists, grants from Tex. A&M U., grants from Vanderbilt U., grants from others. Mem. AAUP, Internat. Linguistics Assn., Linguistic Soc. Am. (chmn. Golden Anniversary film com. 1974) Internat. Sociol. Assn. (session chmn. profl. conf. 1983), Internat. Assn. for Applied Linguistics (com. on discourse analyses, sessions chmn. 1978), Lang. Origins Soc. (exec. com. 1982—, chmn. internat. congress, 1987), Internat. Sociol. Assn. (research com. for sociolinguistics, session co-chmn. internat. conf. 1983), Internat. Assn. for Study of Child Lang. (v.p. 1975-78, chmn. internat. conf. 1972), Inst. for Nonverbal Communication Research (workshop leader 1980-81), Tenn. Conf. on Linguistics (pres. 1976), Southeastern Conf. on Linguistics (hon. mem. 1985), Semiotic Soc. Am. (organizing com. Internat. Semiotics Inst. 1981), Kinesics Internat. (pres. 1988). Office: Vanderbilt U Box 26B Nashville TN 37235

VON SCHUBERT, ANDREAS, wine and agrl. exec.; b. Berlin, June 23, 1922; s. Carl and Renata (Harrach) von S.; student State Vocat. Inst., Trier, 1947-49, Nat. Viniculture Inst., Geisenheim, 1949-57; m. Gloria Horstmann, Mar. 15, 1951; children—Ellinor, Carl, Andrea. Owner estate Maximin Grünhaus, Trier, 1952—; pres. Assn. Shareholders Steel Works, Dillingen-Saar, 1950—; fin. com. Steel Worls Dillinger Hütte, 1960—; supervisory bd. Saar Industrie Bank, Neunkirchen, 1965—; mng. com. State Labor Office and Chamber Agr. Rheinland Pfalz, 1960—; mem. Dist. Assembly Trier, 1952-72; lay assessor Ct. of Aldermen, Trier, 1975-84; trustee State Vocat. Inst. Viniculture, Trier, 1950—; adv. bd. Port Authority Trier. Served with German Army, 1941. Decorated knight Order St. John; Paul Harris fellow Rotary Internat., 1974. Mem. Winegrower and Farmers Assn. Rheinland Pfalz, Agrl. Profl. Assn. Rhine, Fed. Union Agrl. Grads. (mng. com.), German Agrl. Soc. (wine commn.), German French Soc. Trier (pres. 1961—), Soc. Christian Jewish Coop., Chamber Music Assn. Mem. consistory Protestant Ch. Rhineland; mem. synod Protestant Ch. Germany. Club: Trier Rotary (pres. 1965-66). Address: Guünhaus bei, D5501 Trier Federal Republic of Germany

VON SCHULLER-GOETZBURG, VIKTORIN WOLFGANG, economist, consultant; b. Vienna, July 1, 1924; s. Viktorin Stefan and Paula Judith (Binder) von S-G.; M.S., U. Paris, 1948; Ph.D., U. Vienna, 1954; M.B.A., Vienna Bus. Sch., 1957. Asst. prof. Vienna Bus. Sch., 1954-58; internat. fellow Stanford Research Inst., Menlo Park, Calif., 1959-60; head econs and mktg. research IBB, Vienna and Fiduciaire Internationale, Paris, 1960-67; with SRI Internat., Zurich, 1968—, mgr. environ. and spl. studies Chem. Industries div. Europe, 1978-87, mgr. environ. and spl. studies Process Industries div., 1987—; cons. B.A.U., Dutch Ministry of Environment, EEC Commn., Euratom, I.A.R.C., UNEP. Smith-Mundt fellow, 1959. Mem. European Indsl. Mktg. Research Assn., European Chem. Mktg. Research Assn., Austrian Chem. Soc., German Chem. Soc., Austrian Assn. Graduated Economists. Clubs: Ancient Order St. George, Gesellschaft der Musikfreunde, Austrian Touring. Contbr. articles to profl. jours. Home: 3 Nibelungengasse, A-1010 Vienna Austria Office: 37 Pelikanstrasse, CH8001 Zurich Switzerland

VON STIETENCRON, HEINRICH H., educator; b. Ronco, Switzerland, June 18, 1933; s. Georg Eduard von S. Dr.phil., U. Munich, 1965; Dr.habil., U. Heidelberg, 1970. Asst. prof. South Asia Inst., Heidelberg, 1970-73; prof., head Seminar für Indologie u. Vgl. Religionswiss, U. Tubingen, W.Ger., 1973—, dean Fakultät für Kulturwissenschaften, 1981-82; vis. prof. Temple U., Phila., 1983. Author: Indische Sonnenpriester, 1966; Ganga und Yamuna, 1972; Co-author: The Cult of Jagannath and the Regional Tradition of Orissa, 1978; Christentum und Weltreligionen, 1984. Editor: Der Name Gottes, 1975; Angst und Gewalt, 1979; Dämonen und Gegengötter, 1984; Theologen und Theologien in verschiedenen Kulturkreisen, 1986; Purana Research Publs., Tübingen, vol. I; Sanskrit Indices and Text of the Brahma Purana, 1987. Contbr. articles to profl. jours. Mem. Deutsche Morgenländische Gesellschaft, Deutsche Vereinigung für Religionsgeschichte (pres. 1980—), Deutsche Gesellschaft fúr Asienkunke (exec. com. 1982—), Wiss Gesellschaft für Theologie (hon.), South Asian Religious Art Studies (adv. bd.), Institüt für Historische Anthropologie (chmn. 1984—). Office: U Tubingen, Seminar für Indologie, Munzgasse 30, D-7400 Tübingen Federal Republic of Germany

VON SYDOW, AKE CHRISTIAN, marketing executive; b. Waxholm, Sweden, Sept. 5, 1926; s. Christian F.C.H. and Margit (Lowenborg) von S.; m. Margit Lorvall, June 21, 1952; children: Carl, Martin, Daniel. MSc, Royal Inst. Tech. Stockholm, 1952; postgrad. MIT, 1952-53. Sales engr. STAL-Turbine Co., Finspong, Sweden, 1953-59, mng. dir. STAL-LAVAL (UK) Ltd., London, 1959-66; mktg. dir., STAL-LAVAL Turbine Co., Finspong, Sweden, 1966-81; v.p. ASEA AB, Vaesteras, Sweden, 1981-88; sr. v.p. ASEA Brown Boveri AB, 1988—; columnist local newspaper, 1984—. Contbr. articles on indsl. power generation to profl. jours. Served to maj. Swedish Army Res., 1972—. Conservative. Lutheran. Lodge: Rotary (pres. 1973-74). Home: 19 Asgatan, S72463 Vaesteras Sweden Office: ASEA Brown Baveri AB, S72183 Vaesteras Sweden

VON SYDOW, MAX (CARL ADOLF), actor; b. Lund, Sweden, Apr. 10, 1929; s. Carl Wilhelm and Greta (Rappe) von S.; m. Christina Olin, Aug. 1, 1951; children: Clas Wilhelm, Per Henrik. Student, Royal Dramatic Theatre Acad. Stockholm, 1948-51. Appearances with Mcpl. Theatre of Norrköping-Linköping, 1951-53, Mcpl. Theatre of Hälsingborg, 1953-55, Mcpl. Theatre of Malmö, 1955-60, Royal Dramatic Theatre Stockholm, 1960-74, 1988; appeared in plays including: Peer Gynt, Henry IV, The Tempest, Le misanthrope, Faust, Ett Dromspel, La valse des toreadors, Les sequestres d'Altona, After the Fall, The Wild Duck, The Night of the Tribades, 1977, Duet for One, 1981; films include: Bara en mor, 1949, Miss Julie, 1950, Det sjunde inseglet, 1957, Ansiktet (The Face), 1958, The Seventh Seal, 1956, The Magician, 1958, The Virgin Spring, 1959, The Wedding Day, 1960, Through a Glass Darkly, 1961, The Mistress, 1962, The Wonderful Adventures of Nils, 1962, Winter Light, 1963, 4 X 4, 1965, The Hour of the Wolf, 1968, The Shame, 1969, A Passion, 1968, The Greatest Story Ever Told, 1963, Hawaii, 1965, The Reward, 1965, The Quiller Memorandum, 1966, The Kremlin Letter, 1971, Night Visitor, 1971, The Emigrants, 1972, The Exorcist, 1973, The New Land, 1973, Steppenwolf, 1973, Heart of a Dog, 1975, Three Days of the Condor, 1975, Cadaveri Eccelenti, 1976, Voyage of the Damned, 1976, The Desert of the Tartars, 1976, Flash Gordon, 1980, Death Watch, 1980, Victory, 1980, The Flight of the Eagle, 1981, Conan the Barbarian, 1982, She Dances Alone, 1982, Le Cercle des Passions, 1982, Never Say Never Again, 1983, Dune, 1984, Dreamscape, 1984, Emerald, 1985, Hannah and her Sisters, 1986, The Second Victory, 1986, Oviri, 1986, Duet for One, 1986, Pelle the Conqueror, 1987, The Wolf at the Door, 1987; TV appearances include: Diary of Anne Frank, 1967, The Last Civilian, 1983, Samson and Delilah, 1984, The Belarus File, 1984, Christopher Columbus, 1985, The Last Place on Earth, 1985; dir. Katinka, 1988. Served with Swedish Quartermaster Corps, 1947-48. Recipient Royal Found. Cultural award, 1954. Office: care Paul Kohner Inc 9169 Sunset Blvd Los Angeles CA 90069 *

VON WECHMAR, BARON RUEDIGER EBERHARD, German diplomat; b. Berlin, Nov.15, 1923; s. Irnfried and Ilse von Wechmar; m. Rosemarie Warlimont, Mar. 15, 1947; children: Stephanie, Alexander; m. 2d, Susanne Woldenga, Nov. 16, 1961; 1 dau., Yvonne. Reporter German News Agy., also fgn. corr. UP, 1946-58; press officer German counsulate gen., N.Y.C., 1958-63; fgn. corr. German TV in Vienna, 1963-68; dep. counsul gen., N.Y., 1968-69; dept. govt. spokesman, Bonn, 1969-72; state sec. for info. and govt. spokesman, 1972-74, 77-78; ambassador, permanent rep. of W.Ger. to UN, N.Y.C., 1974-81; pres. UN Security Council, pres. UN Gen. Assembly, 1980-81; ambassador to Italy, 1981-83, to London, 1983—. Mem. adv. council Friedrich Naumann Found. Served to 1st lt. German Army, 1941-45; prisoner-of-war Am. Army, 1943-46. Recipient various decorations from fgn. countries. Mem. German Fgn. Affairs Soc., Aspen Inst. Humanistic Studies (sr. fellow). Mem. Free Democratic Party.

VON WEIZSACKER, RICHARD **See WEIZSACKER, RICHARD VON**

VON WRIGHT, GEORG HENRIK, philosopher, educator; b. Helsinki, June 14, 1916; s. Tor von Wright and Ragni Elisabeth Alfthan; m. Baroness Maria Elisabeth von Troil, 1941; 2 children. Ed. U. Helsinki, Cambridge U.; D. honoris causa, Helsinki U., Liverpool U., Lund U., U. Turku, Tampere U., Buenos Aires U., Salta U., St. Olaf Coll. Lectr. in philosophy U. Helsinki, 1943-46, prof. philosophy, 1946-61; prof. philosophy Cambridge U., 1948-51, Tarner lectr. Trinity Coll., 1969; hon. fellow Trinity Coll., Cambridge; vis. prof. Cornell U., 1954, 58, U. Calif., 1963, U. Pitts., 1966, U. Karlsruhe, 1975; Gifford lectr. U. St. Andrews, 1959-60; research fellow Acad. Finland, 1961-86; Andrew D. White prof.-at-large Cornell U., 1965-77; chancellor of Abo Acad., 1968-77; Woodbridge lectr. Columbia U., 1972; Nellie Wallace lectr. U. Oxford, 1978. Author: The Logical Problem of Induction, 1941; A Treatise on Induction and Probability, 1951; An Essay in Modal Logic, 1951; Logical Studies, 1957; The Varieties of Goodness, 1963; Norm and Action, 1963; The Logic of Preference, 1963; An Essay in Deontic Logic, 1968; Explanation and Understanding, 1971; Causality and Determinism, 1974; Freedom and Determination, 1980; Wittgenstein, 1982; Philosophical Papers, I-III, 1983-84. Recipient Wihuri Found. Internat. prize 1976, Alexander von Humbolt Found research award, 1986. Fellow

Finnish Soc. Sci., Royal Swedish Acad. Sci.; mem. Philos. Soc. Finland (pres. 1962-73), Internat. Union History and Philosophy of Sci. (pres. 1963-65), Inst. Internat. de Philosophie Paris (pres. 1975-78), Brit. Acad., Royal Danish Acad. Sci., Norwegian Acad. Sci. and Letters, European Acad. Arts, Sci. and Humanities, World Acad. Arts and Scis.; hon. fgn. mem. Am. Acad. Arts and Scis. Address: 4 Skepparegatan, Helsinki Finland

VON ZELEWSKY, ALEXANDER F., chemistry educator; b. Zurich, Switzerland, July 17, 1936; s. Othmar J. and Therese V. (Erb) von Z.; m. Hedwig L. Ebner, Oct. 4, 1960; children—Katja, Thomas. Diploma in Chemistry, Swiss Fed. Inst. Tech., 1960, Ph.D., 1964. Fellow Miller Inst., Berkeley, Calif., 1965-67; asst. Swiss Fed. Inst. Tech., Zurich, Switzerland, 1967-69; prof. Univ. Fribourg, Switzerland, 1969—, dir. inst., 1969—, dean. faculty sci., 1974-75; v.p. sci. council NSF, Switzerland, 1981—, v.p., 1985—; pres. Swiss Com. on Chemistry, 1985—. Contbr. articles to profl. jours. Mem. Am. Chem. Soc., Royal Chem. Soc. London, Swiss Chem. Soc. Office: Univ Fribourg, Faculty Sci, Perolles, CH1700 Fribourg Switzerland

VON ZERSSEN, GERD DETLEV, psychiatrist, researcher; b. Altona, Hamburg, Germany, Oct. 30, 1926; s. Otto Hermann and Irmgard Johanna (Zillgenz) von Z.; m. Takako Kojima; 1 child, Clemens. Diplom-Psychologe, U. Hamburg, Fed. Republic Germany, 1952, MD, 1953; habilitation, U. Heidelberg, Fed. Republic Germany, 1966. cert. prof. psychiatry, neurology. Extern various city hosps., Hamburg, 1953-58; extern, research fellow Med. Univ. Hosp., Hamburg, 1958-60; extern Neurol. Univ. Hosp., Hamburg, 1960-61; research fellow Psychiat. Univ. Hosp. Burghoelzli, Zurich, Switzerland, 1961-62; research asst. Psychiat. Univ. Hosp., Heidelberg, 1962-66; head psychiat. dept. Max-Planck Inst. Psychiatry, Munich, Fed. Republic Germany, 1966-85, head psychiatric evaluation research, 1986—; cons. Psychiat. Planning Com., Munich, 1967-71, Psychiat. Planning Com., Bonn, Fed. Republic Germany, 1971-75. Author: Clinical Self-Rating Scales, 1976; co-author: Course of Schizophrenia, 1986, Course of Affective Disorders, 1987. Served as pvt. German Army, 1944-45. Recipient Anna-Monika prize Dortmund, Fed. Republic Germany, 1985. Mem. German Assn. Psychiatry Neurology, German Psychoanalytic Assn., German Assn. Anthropology Human Genetics, German Assn. Med. Informatics Stats. Lutheran. Office: Max-Planck Inst Psychiatry, 2 Kraepelinst, D-8000 Munich 40, Bavaria Federal Republic of Germany

VOORBIJ, JOHANNES BENEDICTUS, literary and linguistic computing educator; b. Gouda, Zuid-Holland, The Netherlands, Mar. 9, 1954; s. Cornelis Albertus and Antoinette Josefina Theresia (Caspers) V. BA, State U. Groningen, The Netherlands, 1975, MA, 1980. Research asst. Dept. Medieval Studies, State U. Groningen, 1978-80, research fellow, 1980-86, researcher, 1986—; lectr. Dept. Literary and Linguistic Computing, State U. Utrecht, The Netherlands, 1986—. Author, editor: (collection of articles) Vincent of Beauvais and Alexander the Great, 1986; editor chpt. in book; contbr. articles to profl. jours. Travel grantee Ministry Cultural Affairs, Recreation and Welfare, Italy, Vatican City, 1981, 82, Faculty of Arts U. Groningen, Belgium, France, Fed. Republic Germany, U.K., 1980-83, Netherland Orgn. for Advancement of Pure Sci., Poland, Austria, Czechoslovakia, Fed. Republic Germany, 1983, 84, Can., 1988. Office: Vakgroep Computer, en Letteren, U Utrecht Achter de Dom 24, Utrecht 3512JP, The Netherlands

VORIS, WILLIAM, educational administrator; b. Neoga, Ill., Mar. 20, 1924; s. Louis K. and Faye (Hancock) V.; m. Mavis Marie Myre, Mar. 20, 1949; children: Charles William II, Michael K. BS, U. So. Calif., 1947, MBA, 1948; PhD, Ohio State U., 1951; LLD, Sung Kyun Kwan U. (Korea), 1972, Eastern Ill. U., 1976. Teaching asst. Ohio State U., Columbus, 1948-50; prof. mgmt. Wash. State U., Pullman, 1950-52; prof., head dept. mgmt. Los Angeles State Coll., 1952-58, 60-63; dean Coll. Bus. and Pub. Adminstrn., U. Ariz., Tucson, 1963-71; pres. Am. Grad. Sch. Internat. Mgmt., Glendale, Ariz., 1971—. Ford Found. research grantee Los Angeles State Coll., 1956; prof. U. Tehran (Iran), 1958-59; Ford Found. fellow Carnegie Inst. Tech., Pitts., 1961; prof. Am. U., Beirut, Lebanon, 1961, 62; cons. Hughes Aircraft Co., Los Angeles, Rheem Mfg. Co., Los Angeles, Northrop Aircraft Co., Palmdale, Calif., Harwood Co., Alhambra, Calif., ICA, Govt. Iran. Served with USNR, 1942-45. Fellow Acad. Mgmt.; mem. Ariz. Acad., Beta Gamma Sigma, Alpha Kappa Psi, Phi Delta Theta. Author: Production Control, Text and Cases, 1956, 3d edit., 1966; Management of Production, 1960. Research in indsl. future of Iran, mgmt. devel. in Middle East. Home: Thunderbird Campus Glendale AZ 85306

VORKAS, ANDREAS PAVLOU, surgeon; b. Nicosia, Cyprus, June 21, 1940; s. Paul and Chrystalleri (Kaniklides) V.; m. Lena Jane Vorkas; 1 child, Pavlos Andrea. MD, U. Athens, 1965; DO, U. London, 1978. Intern Aberdeen U. Hosp.; dir. eye dept. Larnarca (Cyprus) Hosp., 1971-84; mgr. pvt. hosp. Lanarca, 1986—; owner, mgr. Vosimcon Trading Co., Larnarca, 1986—; practice medicine specializing in eye surgery Lanarca. Contbr. articles to profl. jours. Fellow Royal Coll. Surgeons, Royal Soc. Medicine, Am. Acad. Ophthalmology, Royal Coll. Ophthalmology; mem. Greek Ophthalmol. Soc. Rally Party. Orthodox Ch. Address: Vosimcon, Timayia 77, PO Box 406, Lanarca Cyprus

VORMELAND, ODDVAR, Norwegian government official, former educational administrator; b. Hof, Solør, Hedmark, Norway, Feb. 28, 1924; s. Ola and Gyda (Hval) V.; m. Sigrun Røed, June 23, 1949; children—Hilde, Live. Student Elverum Laererskole (Norway), 1946-48; M.A., U. Oslo, 1951, Ph.D., 1967. Tchr. Taasen Sch., Oslo, 1951-55; ednl. psychologist Municipality of Oslo, 1955-59; univ. research fellow U. Oslo, 1959-64; dep. supt. Oslo Pub. Sch. System, 1964-71, dir. edn., 1971-84; dir. gen. Ministry of Ch. and Edn., Oslo, 1984—. Author: Elementary Education in Mother Tongue and Mathematics, 1966; Has Our Elementary School a Future, 1979; contbr. articles to profl. publs., 1949—; editor: The School as a Working Place, 1983. Postgrad. fellow UCLA, 1977-78. Mem. Tchr. and Mgmt. Orgns., Nat. Assn. Sch. Dirs. (chmn. 1982-84), Nat. Assn. Sch. Psychologists (chmn. 1957-60), Council Nat. Elem. Edn. (chmn. 1974-77). Lutheran. Lodge: Masons (speaker 1978-84). Office: Ministry of Ch and Edn, PO Box 8119 Dep N-0032, Oslo 1 Norway

VOROTNIKOV, VITALIY IVANOVICH, Soviet political official; b. 1926. Student Kuibyshev Aviation Inst. Technologist, later sec party com., chief controller of plant, 1942-44, 47-60; dep. Kuibyshev Dist. Com., 1961-67; chmn. Kuibyshev Exec. Com. of Dist. Soviet of Workers Deps., 1967-71; dep. to USSR Supreme Soviet, from 1970; 1st sec. Voronezh Dist. Com. of CPSU, 1971-75, mem. Central Com., 1971—, politburo, 1983—; 1st dep. chmn. Council of Ministers of RSFSR, 1975-76, chmn., 1983—; ambassador to Cuba, 1980-82. Decorated Order of October Revolution. Mem. USSR-Angola Friendship Soc. (chmn. 1976-79). Office: Chmn RSFSR, Council of Ministers, Moscow USSR *

VORSTER, DE WET STOCKSTROM, consultant, child and adolescent psychiatrist; b. Chgo., Nov. 18, 1928; s. de Wet and Paula Guether (Stockstrom) V.; m. Iona Jean Reid, Apr. 6, 1954; children—Ian de Wet, Mark Andrew, Wendy Kay, Timothy Neil, Gregory Stuart. MB ChB., U. Cape Town Med. Sch., 1953; Diploma Psychiatry, McGill U. (Can.), 1959; Diploma Psychol. Medicine, Royal Coll. Medicine, 1959. Intern, Gen. Hosp., Port Elizabeth, South Africa, 1954-55; resident Montreal Gen. Hosp., 1955-57, Wash. U. Student Health Ctr. and Guidance Clinic, St. Louis, 1957-58; registrar Kingseat Hosp., Aberdeen, Scotland, 1958-59; clin. med. officer Soweto Clinics, Johannesburg, South Africa, 1960; cons. psychiatry Gen. Hosp. and Child Clinics, Johannesburg, 1961-69; cons. child psychiatry Staines Child Psychiatry Clinics, Guildford Hosp., U.K., 1969-75, Child and Family Services, Mt. Gould Hosp., Plymouth, Eng., 1975—. Contbr. articles to profl. jours. Fellow Royal Coll. Psychiatry; mem. South African Med. Assn., Soc. Reproductive and Infant Psychology, Maternity and Neonate Div. Royal Coll. Medicine, Assn. Child Psychiatry (chmn. SW 1977—), Brit. Med. Assn. (chmn. 1984, 85), Am. Psychiat. Assn., Assn. Family Therapy. Mem. Ch. Eng. Avocations: choir; snow skiing; travel; classical music. Home: Santa Maria Wrangaton Rd, South Brent, Devon England Office: Mt Gay Hosp, Child and Family Service, Plymouth, Devon England

VORWERK, E. CHARLSIE, artist; b. Tennga, Ga., Jan. 28, 1934; d. James A. and Hester L. (Davis) Pritchett; A.B., Ga. State Coll. for Women, 1955; m. Norman T. Vorwerk, Feb. 9, 1956; children—Karl, Lauren, Michael. Billboard design artist Vanesco Poster, Chattanooga, 1955; cartographic draftsman TVA, Chattanooga, 1955; fashion illustrator Loveman's, Chattanooga, 1956; freelance comml. artist, 1957—; pvt. art instr. children and adults, all media, 1966—; art instr. continuing edn. Bapt. Coll. Charleston, S.C., 1979-82. Mem. Bd. Archtl. Rev., Summerville, 1976—; chmn. YMCA Flowertown Festival Art Exhibit, 1972-88; mem. women's bd. St. Paul's Episcopal Ch. 1968-84; active Boy Scouts Am., Girl Scouts U.S.A.; vol. Mental Health Clinic, 1972-74, others; coordinator Washington Park Picolo-Spoleto Art Exhibit, 1983-88, also exhibit chmn. for low country artists. Mem. Charleston Artists Guild, League of Charleston Artists, Minature Art Soc. Fla., Beaufort Art Assn., Am. Art Soc., Italian Art Acad. Illustrator: Tales and Taradidales; St. Paul's Epitahs; Captain Tom, others. Address: 315 W Carolina Ave Summerville SC 29483

VOS, JAN, crop physiologist; b. Netherland, 1948. Engring. degree, Agrl. U., Wageningen, Netherlands, 1974, Doctorate, 1981. Research officer The Netherlands Orgn. for Applied Sci. Research, Wageningen, 1974-79, Govt. Seed Testing Sta., Wageningen, 1979-81, Ctr. for Agrobiol. Research, Wageningen, 1981-87; sr. lectr. Agrl. U., Wageningen, 1987—. Office: Wageningen Agrl U, Haarweg 333, 6709 RZ Wageningen The Netherlands

VOS, JAN HENDRIK, sociologist; b. Gouda, Netherlands, Apr. 30, 1943; s. Martinus Cornelis and Cornelia (Vermeulen) V.; m. Rebekka Auguste Ong, July 14, 1942; children—Marc Paul, Michael, Mei Li, Nathan, David, Daniel. Candidates Sociology, U. Utrecht, Netherlands, 1964, Dr. Cultural Anthropology, 1969. Univ. counselor U. Eindhoven, Netherlands, 1969-71; ednl. cons. Dutch Govt., Utrecht, 1971-74; ednl. and orgn. cons. Holland Tng. Services, Arnhem, Netherlands, 1974—; dir. Christian Life Sch., Hague, 1975—, Dunamis, Arnhem, 1985-88, World Vision Nederland, 1987—. Editor numerous mags., 1975—. Contbr. articles to profl. jours. Bd. dirs. World Vision of Europe, London, 1984, Far East Broadcasting Corp., Netherlands, 1984, Middle East Media, Cyprus, 1985, Operation Mobilization, Rotterdam, 1976. Lutheran. Avocations: video; photography; audio recording. Home: Parkstraat 14A, Arnhem 6828 JH, The Netherlands Office: Holland Tng Services, Parkstraat 14, Arnhem 6800 AJ, The Netherlands

VOSKANYAN, GRANT MUSHEGOVICH, Soviet government official; b. 1924. Grad., Erevan Pedagogical Inst. Mem. Communist Party Soviet Union, 1946—; head dept. edn. Kirovakan City, until 1959, sec. dept. edn., 1959-64; 1st sec. Kirovakan City Com. Armenian Communist Party, 1965-67, mem. cen. com., 1966-71, 76—, mem. Apparat, 1967-73, head dept. party orgn. work with cen. com., 1973-75, candidate mem. bur., 1973-75, sec., mem. bur. cen. com., 1975—; now dep. chmn. Presidium, USSR Supreme Soviet. Address: USSR Supreme Soviet, Office Dep Chmn, Moscow USSR *

VOSS, AUGUST EDUARDOVICH, politician; b. Saltykovo, Omsk region, USSR, Oct. 30, 1916. Student, Communist Party Soviet Union Higher Party Sch. Tchr.-Tng. Inst., Acad. of Social Scis. Party official Latvia, 1945-49; head dept. sci. and culture Cen. Com. Communist Party of Latvia, 1953-54, party official, 1954-60, sec., 1960-66, first sec., 1966-84; chair Soviet of Nationalities USSR Supreme Soviet, 1984—, dep. to, 1966—; chair Com. for Pub. Edn., Sci. and Culture, Soviet Union and Latvian Supreme Soviet; mem. CPSU Cen. Com., 1971—. Served with Soviet Army, 1940-45. Decorated Order of Lenin and others. Office: The Kremlin, Moscow USSR *

VOTAPKA, RICHARD BRUCE, civil engineer; b. Queens, N.Y., Sept. 4, 1948; s. Richard William and Pauline Joan (Marshall) V.; B.S., Northeastern U., 1971; registered profl. engr., Fla.; m. Linda Louise Kauffman, Dec. 9, 1972; children—Kenneth, Kevin, Keith, Kathryn. Jr. design engr. Bessemer and Lake Erie R.R., Greenville, Pa., 1971-72, asst. track supr., Butler, Pa., 1972-73; design engr. GHQ, Inc., Merritt Island, Fla., 1973-75; acting city engr., engr. III, City of Vero Beach, Fla., 1975-77; project engr. Beindorf & Assocs., Inc., Vero Beach, 1977-87; v.p. Peterson & Votapka, Inc., Vero Beach, 1987—. Councilman, City of Sebastian (Fla.), 1981-83; trustee Humana Hosp., Sebastian, 1982-85; lay leader Sebastian Meth. Ch., 1983-86; cubmaster pack 589, Boy Scouts Am., 1985—; vice chmn. Indian River County Environ. Control Hearing Bd., 1985-88; v.p. Pelican Island Elem. Sch. PTA, 1985-86; mayor City of Sebastian, Fla. Mem. NSPE, ASCE (Engr. of Yr. award Cape Canaveral br. 1978), Fla. Engring. Soc., Soc. Am. Mil. Engrs., Am. Water Works Assn., Fla. Soc. Profl. Land Surveyors. Home: 873 SE Lance St Sebastian FL 32958 Office: Peterson & Votapka 1237 S Hwy 1 Vero Beach FL 32962

VOUGA, FRANCOIS, theologian, educator; b. Neuchâtel, Switzerland, Oct. 25, 1948; s. Paul-Henri and Jacqueline (Rochat) V.; m. Anne Fontaine Downs, June 6, 1983; children: Paul Etienne, Maren Elisabeth. ThD, U. Genève, 1985. Asst. N.T. U. Lausanne, Switzerland, 1973-74; pastor Eglise Nat. Protestant, Genève, 1975-82; maître-asst. Faculté libre de théologie, Montpellier, France, 1982-85, prof. N.T., 1985-86, assoc. prof., 1986-88; prof. for N.T. Kirchliche Hochschule Bethel, Bielefeld, Fed. Republic Germany, 1986—. Author: Le cadre historique et l'intention théologique de Jean, 1977, L'épître de Jacques, 1984, Jésus et la Loi selon la tradition synoptique, 1988; contbr. articles to profl. jours. Mem. Conseil Communal, Morges, Switzerland, 1969-70. Mem. Studiorum Novi Testamenti Societas, Wissenschaftliche Gesellschaft für Theologie. Mem. Socialist Party. Home: An der Rehwiese 42, D4800 Bielefeld Federal Republic of Germany Office: Kirchliche Hochschule Bethel, Remterweg 45, D4800 Bielefeld Federal Republic of Germany

VOULTSOS-VOURTZIS, PERICLES COUNT, composer, conductor, educator, author, former honorary consul Grenada; b. Athens, Greece, Jan. 26, 1910; came to U.S., 1921, naturalized, 1932; s. Christos C. and Aspasia (Kambouroglou) Voultsos-V.; m. Countess Helene Fioravanti, Oct. 26, 1946; 1 son, Basil.; children by previous marriage: Chris, George. Student in mech. engring, NYU, 1927; postgrad., N.Y. Coll. Music, 1934; tchr.'s diploma; Mus.B., U. Chgo., 1939; M.A., Staley Coll., Brookline, Mass., 1949; Ed.D., Calvin Coolidge Coll., Boston, 1956, Litt.D. (hon.), 1958; Ph.D. in Musicology, Milano Accademia, 1960; LL.D. (hon.), Emporia Coll., 1961. Mem. faculty N.Y. Coll. Music (now affiliated with NYU), N.Y.C., 1937-67; dir. Am. Conservatory of Music, 1930—; hon. prof. Nat. Conservatory, Athens; Nat. chmn. Greek sect. All-Am. origins Citizens for Eisenhower-Nixon, 1952; Permanent observer to UN (N-G-O) Inst. Humaniste, Paris, France, 1952; royal envoy plenipotentiary and extraordinary for King Peter of Yugoslavia, 1964; ambassador good will to Greece, Gov. Burns and people, Fla., 1965; ambassador good will to Greece of Gov. Smith and people, Tex., 1970; personal ambassador of King Ntare V of Burundi, to U.S., 1969; brig. gen. gov. staff La., a.d.c. to gov. La., 1965, 73; hon. consul of Grenada, 1976-79; hon. atty. gen. of La.; diplomate N.Y. Coll. Music (now Coll. Music NYU.), 1934. Composer many musical compositions; author lit. hist. works. N.Y.U. R.O.T.C. Served with SSS, World War II. Recipient Key to City San Francisco; Decorated medal in name of Congress Pres. Truman, 1945, Silver medal City of Paris (France), 1953, Golden Key City of Athens (Greece), 1972; decorated grand collar, grand master Sovereign Greek Order St. Dennis of Zante, Grand Cross Vasco Nunez de Balboa (Panama), Grand Cross Carlos Manuel de Cespedes (Cuba), Grand Cross Honneur et Merite (Haiti), Grand Cross Petion et Bolivar Grand Cross Prince Rwagasore (Burundi), Grand Cross Order Karyena (Burundi), Grand Cross of Rukinzo (Burundi), Petion et Bolivar Order of Karageorge (Yugoslavia), grand cross Order of St. Sava (Yugoslavia), Order of St. Andrew Constantinople, Grand Cross Order of Saints Peter and Paul, Antioch, grandcross Holy Sepulchre, grand officer Order of Crown, grand officer White Eagle (Yugoslavia), grand cross Ordre du Merite Empire Centrafricane, grand officer Order of Crown Order of Education, Haiti, chevalier St. Agatha, commandeur Order of Polonia Restituta Poland, chevalier Ordre du Monisaraphon Cambodia; grand cross St. Mark; chevalier Ordre du Sahametrei (Cambodia); Gold Cross of Merit (Poland); Medalha do Pacificador (Brazil); Order of Sant' Agata (San Marino); decorations and crosses of merit from Red Cross of govts. Greece, Japan, Spain, Portugal, Cuba, numerous others; named hon. citizen Zante, Greece, hon. citizen New Orleans, hon. citizen Lynn, Mass., hon. citizen Little Rock, hon. citizen Miami Beach, Fla., Col. ADC to Gov. Ky., 1987; awarded Gold medal City of Mesolongi (Greece), Gold medal City of Athens; Chevalier Legion d'Honneur, France, July 1957; Societe D'Entre Aide France. Mem. Am. Mil. Engrs. Soc., N.Y. Acad. Scis., AAAS, Soc. Fgn. Consuls, SAR., Soc. of Fils de la Revolution Americaine (Paris), Am. Internat. Inst. (pres.), Am. Soc. Greek Order St. Dennis of Zante, Nat. Legion Greek-Am. War Vets. in Am. (nat. comdr.), N.Y. State Vets. Arty. Corps, La Confrerie du Tastevin. Clubs: Hellenic (N.Y.C.), Army and Navy (N.Y.C.), Columbia (N.Y.C.), University (N.Y.C.); Army and Navy (Washington). Home: 739 W 186th St New York NY 10033

VOUTSAS, ALEXANDER MATTHEW, aeronautical aerospace engineering executive; b. N.Y.C., Mar. 26, 1923; s. Manthos Anthony and Mary (Pittika) Voutsadakis; m. Anastasia Sistovary, Sept. 17, 1957 (div.); children—Alexander Matthew, John. BAE in Aero-Engring., Rensselaer Poly. Inst., 1944; M.S., U.S. Naval Midshipman's Sch., Northwestern U., 1945, A.M.P., Harvard U. Grad. Bus. Sch., Boston, 1969; PhD in Engring., 1986. Registered profl. mech. engr., Calif., Greece. Research aerodynamicist NASA Ames Labs., Moffett Field, Calif., 1945-46; design aerodynamicist XP-92, F-102 aircraft design Gen. Dynamics Corp., San Diego, Calif., 1947-48; chief design aerodynamicist Hermes A-3 Intercontinental Ballistic Missile, Gen. Electric Co., Schenectady, N.Y., 1948-51; design aerodynamcist Rigel Missle, Grumman Aircraft Corp., Bethpage, N.Y., 1952-52; chief design project aerodynamicist Terrapin ionospheric rocket Republic Aviation, Hicksville, N.Y., 1952-56; asst. dept. head systems engring. inertial guidance hardware system devel. Atlas and Titan Ballistic Missiles Am. Bosch Arma Corp., Garden City, N.Y., 1956-61; mgr. mktg. communications aerospace systems ITT-Fed. Electric Corp., Paramus, N.J., 1962-67; cons. aerospace indsl. devel. and mktg., N.Y.C. and Greece, 1967-69; presdl. tech. adviser Motor Oil Hellas Ltd., N.Y.C. and Athens, 1969-73; pres. A. Voutsas Assocs., cons.; aero. engring. exec. Hellenic Aerospace Industry Ltd., Athens, Greece, 1981—; Contbr. tech. papers to internat. space symposia, articles, research papers to profl. jours,; inventor, patentee in field, including ultrasonic C-scan theory equipment for detection materials uniformity and med. applications, 1944; designed first ring-wing manned air vehicle Gen. Dynamics Corp., 1947-48; credited with first Delta Wing aero design at two to five times speed of sound, Gen. Electric; aero. designer first Am. 2-stage ballistic rocket with V-2 rocket boosters Gen. Electric; credited for first clipped delta canard wing controls on first submarine launched ballistic missile Grumman Aircraft; inventor, developer theory hardware of 3-D vibrating string accelerometer goniometer, later adopted for lunar gravity meter on APOLLO 17 Space Mission. Bd. dirs. Am. Acad. Greece, 1976-78; mem. U.S. Naval Bur. Ordnance Com., Washington. Served to lt. j.g. USNR, 1944-46. Decorated St. Andrews medal Patriarch of Orthodoxy, Istanbul, Turkey, 1969. Fellow Brit. Interplanetary Soc., Inst. Aero. Scis. (assoc.), AIAA, Am. Inst. Aeronautics and Astronautics (assoc.); mem. Am. Ordnance Assn. (propulsion com. 1961—), Nat. Space Inst. Navy League U.S. (v.p. Greece 1978-83). Clubs: Bembridge Sailing (Isle of Wight); Hellenic Yacht (Piraeus, Greece). Lodge: Rotary Internat. (Athens). Office: 21 Kalliga, Athens 114 73, Greece

VOYCHECK, GERALD LOUIS, social worker; b. Wilkes-Barre, Pa., Mar. 10, 1944; s. Martin Vojcik and Lottie (Lukashefska) V. BA, Quincy Coll., 1968; MA, Sangamon State U., 1981; postgrad., So. Ill. U., 1981-82. Tchr. St. James Trade Sch., Springfield, Ill., 1968-71; evening librarian Springfield Coll., 1968-69; cataloger St. Francis Convent, Springfield, 1971-72; worker child care Lt. Joseph P. Kennedy, Palos Park, Ill., 1972-73; technician mental retardation Good Shepherd Manor, Momence, Ill., 1973-75; asst. adminstr. Bro. James Ct., Springfield, 1975-76, adminstr., 1976-79, social worker, 1979—; exec. dir. Springfield Devel., 1985-86; instr. Lincoln Land Community Coll., Springfield, 1981—; interpreter Ill. Dept. Mental Health, Springfield, 1986. Vol. Acquired Immune Deficiency Disease, sexual assault counseling. Mem. Nat. Assn. Social Workers (registered), Franciscan Bros. Holy Cross (sec. 1973-76, bd. dirs. 1985—). Republican. Roman Catholic. Home: Rural Rt 1 Springfield IL 62707 Office: Brother James Ct Sangamon Ave Rd Springfield IL 62707

VOZAK, FRANK REDIN, III, social worker, educator; b. Alton, Ill., May 12, 1952; s. Frank Henry and Margarita (Redin) V.; m. Terrie Adrienne Rymer, June 30, 1985. B.S. in Social Work, St. Louis U., 1974, cert. environ. studies, 1974, cert. peace studies, 1975, M.S.W., 1975, cert. social worker, 1979. Diplomate Clin. Social Work; cert. assoc. addictions counselor, Ill., Clin. social work Edward J. Hines Jr. VA Hosp., Hines, Ill., 1977—; social work officer U.S. Army Med. Dept., 1975-77; instr. field work Jane Addams Sch. Social Work, U. Ill., Chgo., 1980—; social work cons. R.D. Traffic Sch., Inc., Aurora, Ill., 1984-85 . adult leader Order of Arrow, Boy Scouts Am. Maj. USAR, 1977—; vol. psychotraumatologist disaster services Mid Am. chpt. ARC, 1985—. Mem. Nat. Assn. Social Workers, Acad. Cert. Social Workers, Social Workers in Emergency Medicine (rec. sec. 1983-87, pres. 1987—), Nat. Eagle Scout Assn., Psychosocial Clinicians in Emergency Medicine, Ill. Terminal R.R. Hist. Soc., Nat. Model R.R. Assn., Ill. Ry. Mus., Elmhurst Model R.R. Club, Gulf Mobile & Ohio Hist. Soc., Oak Park Soc. Model Engrs. (sec. 1983—), Am. Youth Hostels, St. Louis U. Alumni Assn., Alton, Hines & Pacific R.R. Hist. Soc., Alpha Sigma Nu. Unitarian. Office: Edward J Hines Hosp Social Work Service VA Hines IL 60141

VOZNESENSKY, ANDREI, author, poet; b. Moscow, USSR, May 12, 1933; s. Andrei and Antonina (Pastuschina) V.; student Moscow Archtl. Inst., 1951-57; m. Zoja Boguslavskaja, 1964; 1 child. Author: (poems) The Parabola, 1960, Mosaics, 1960; The Triangled Pear, 1962; The Achillean Heart, 1966; Selected Poems, 1967; The Shadow of Sound, 1970; Glance, 1972; Set the Bird free!, 1974; Violoncello oak-leaf, 1975; Stained-glass panel Master, 1976; Temptation, 1978; Unaccountable, 1981; Antiworlds and the Fifth Ace (in English), 1966; Dogalypse (in English), 1972; Story Under Full Sail (in English), 1974; Nostalgia for the Present (in English), 1978; Selected Poems, 1979; (plays) Antiworlds, 1965; Save Your Faces, 1970; Juno, 1981; Perchance, 1981; co-author (poetry and prose anthology) Metropol, 1979. Recipient Internat. award for disting. achievement in poetry, 1978; USSR State award in lit., 1978. Mem. Soviet Writers' Union (bd. dirs.), Bayerischen Kunst Acad., Am. Acad. Arts and Letters, French Poetry Acad. Malarme. Home: Kotelnitcheskaya nab 1/15, BL W Apt 62, 109240 Moscow USSR Office: ul Nizhny-Krasnoselskaya 45, Moscow USSR *

VRANEK, JOHANNES O., jeweler; b. Berlin, Sept. 30, 1926; s. Franz and Caroline (Ungar) V.; m. Ingeborg Schäfer; children: Johannes, Metha. Grad. high sch., Berlin. Goldsmith F. Vranek & Söhne, Berlin, 1945-49; goldsmith designer F. Vranek & föhne, Berlin, 1949-55; co-owner F&H Vranek OHG, Detmold, Fed. Republic of Germany, 1955—. Author: Edelsteine; contbr. articles to profl. jours. Recipient 27 awards for jewelry design London Mus., 1969-85. Mem. Internat. Diamonds Exchanges. Roman Catholic. Clubs: Golf, Film (Detmold); Magic Circle.

VRANITZKY, FRANZ, federal chancellor of Austria; b. Vienna, Oct. 4, 1937; s. Franz and Rosa V.; m. Christine Kristen. Grad. Vienna Acad. of Trade and Commerce. With Austrian Nat. Bank, Fed. Res. Bd., 1961-70; personal asst. to Minister for Finance, Austria, 1970-76; dep. chmn. mng. bd. Creditanstalt Bankverein, 1976-81; chmn. mng. bd. Laenderbank, 1981-84; Fed. Minister Fin., Austria, 1984-86, Federal Chancellor, 1986—. Mem. Socialist Party of Austria. Past mem. Austrian Nat. Basketball Team. Office: Office of the Chancellor, Ballhausplat 2, 1014 Vienna Austria *

VRANKEN, JAN P.F., sociologist; b. Vucht, Limburg, Belgium, July 7, 1944; s. Joannes Bartel and Maria Catherina Vranken; m. Alice Maria Ghislaine Geelissen, Aug. 11, 1966; children: Jan, Wim. Lic. polit. and soc. scis., Catholic U. of Leuven, Belgium, 1966; D polit. and soc. scis., U. Antwerpen, Belgium, 1977. Asst. U. Antwerpen, Belgium, 1968-72, 1st asst., 1972-78, research leader, 1978-88, prof., 1988—; head dept. sociology, social policy U. Antwerpen, Belgium, 1984—. Author of over thirty books on poverty, migrant workers, and welfare state including Understanding Poverty, 1984, Anti-Poverty Policy in the E.C., 1984, Growth to Limits, 1987, Introduction to Sociology, 1988; editor Flemish Sociological Rev., 1986—. Mem. Internat. Sociol. Assn., Internat. Inst. Sociol. Home: Quinten Matsyslei 5, B2018 Antwerp Belgium Office: Univ Antwerpen, Prinsstraat 13, B2000 Antwerp Belgium

VRBIK, JAN, mathematics educator; b. Brno, Czechoslovakia, Sept. 23, 1945; emigrated to Can., 1968; s. Jan and Libuse (Pinkasova) V.; m. Josefina Docot, Sept. 27, 1983; children: Paul, Irene Maria. M.Sc., Charles U., Prague, Czechoslovakia, 1968; M.Sc., U. Calgary, Can., 1971, Ph.D., 1977. Cons. U. Calgary, 1975-81; sr. scientist PRI, Calgary, 1981-82; assoc. prof. math. Brock U., St. Catharines, Ont., Can., 1982—. Contbr. numerous articles on elasticity, statistics to sci. publs. Mem. Am. Math. Soc. Office: Brock U, Dept Math, Saint Catharines, ON Canada L2S 3A1

VREDENBREGT, JACOB GERARD, anthropology educator; b. Schiedam, Netherlands, Nov. 20, 1926; s. Jan and Elizabeth Maria (Demmenie) V.; adopted children—St. Mariam, Andalusia Mariam. Doctorandus, State U. (Leiden, Holland), 1960, D., 1968. Planter Dutch Plantation Cie, E. Java, Indonesia, 1951-56; research fellow Netherlands Orgn. Pure Research, The Hague, 1962-65; asst. prof. Leiden State U., Holland, 1966-68; correspondent Netherlands Radio and T.V., Hilversum, Holland, 1968-70; guest prof. U. Indonesia, Jakarta, 1970—; cons. Inst. Agama Islam Negeri, Indonesia, 1979-81. Author: De Baweanners in hun moederland enin Singapore, 1968, Metode Penelitian Masyarakat, 1978, Pengantar Metodologi untul ilmuilmu empiris, 1985, Aan het einde van de middag, 1984, De opstand, 1986, De Deftige Kolonie en andere Verhalen, 1988. Mem. Royal Inst. Linguistics and Anthropology, Vereniging van Letterkundi-gen. Avocations: photography; lepidopterology. Home: Ciputat 15411, Kebon Duren, Jakarta Indonesia

VRHOVEC, JOSIP, Yugoslavian government official; b. Zagreb, Croatia, Yugoslavia, 1926. Ed., Faculty Econs., Inst. Social Scis., Zagreb, M.Sc. With Nat. Liberation Movement, 1941; mem. League Communist Youth, 1941; mem. League of Communists, Yugoslavia, 1944; formerly editor, fgn. affairs columnist, then editor-in-chief Vjesnik u srijedu, weekly and Vjesnik daily, also permanent and spl. corr., 1952-59; exec. com. Central Com. of Leugue of Communists of Croatia, 1969-74; mem. presdl. council, central com., chmn. com. for ideological and theoretical questions, 1974-78, pres. council polit. sch. Josip Bro Tito, 1974-78; pres. presidency Central Com., Croatia, 1982-84; fed. sec. fgn. affairs Yugoslavia, 1978-82, mem. presidency of Yugoslavia from Croatia, 1984—. Contbr. numerous works in social scis. and internat. relations. Served with Nat. Liberation Army, Yugoslavia, 1943; mem. Yugoslavian Res., numerous Yugoslav and fgn. decorations. Office: Predsjednistvo SFR, Jugoslavije Bul Lenjina 6, Novi Beograd Yugoslavia *

VROUSOS, CONSTANTIN, radiologist, educator; b. Alexandria, Egypt, Aug. 11, 1934; arrived in France, 1952; s. Emmanuel Constantin and Helene (Carcallis) V.; m. Evelyne Grob, March 25, 1958; children: Helene, Emmanuelle, Alexis, Anne. Degree in Neuropsychiatry, U. Strasbourg, 1961, MD, 1965, degree in Radiology, 1968; study Radio-Isotopes, U. Paris, 1967. Diplomate med. Resident Strasbourg Hosp., 1961; radiology asst. Strasbourg Hosp. Med. Sch., 1965, Grenoble Hosp., France, 1969; prof. Grenoble Med. and Pharm. Sch., 1970; radiotherapy dept. head Grenoble Hosp., 1970—; chmn. Comprehensive Cancer Ctr., Nat. Federation of Cancer Depts.; dean Grenoble Sch. of Med. Author: Cervix and Endometrial Cancers, 1985, Non-Hodgkin's Lymphomas, 1985, Palliative Care, 1987. Orthodox. Lodge: Rotary. Office: Radiotherapy Dept CHURG, BP 217 X, 38043 Grenoble Cedex France

VU, JEAN-PIERRE, consultant; b. Thai Binh, Vietnam, Aug. 11, 1934; s. Xan Ngo Vu and Hoang T. Nguyen; m. Josephine Brece, Oct. 1, 1960; children: Cecile, Denis A., Catherine. BS in Agrl., U. Wis., 1958, MS in Agrl. Econs., 1959; MBA, Internat. U., Manila, 1982, PhD, 1983. Coop. expert Nat. Agrl. Credit Office, Saigon, Vietnam, 1959-61; asst. to retail mgr. Standard Vacuum Oil Co., Saigon, 1961-62; asst. planning mgr. Esso Standard Eastern, Saigon, 1966-71; project economist Asian Devel. Bank, Manila, 1971-79, sr. project economist, 1979-83, sr. cons. services specialist, 1983—. Served to lt. Republic Vietnam Army, 1962-66. Roman Catholic. Home: 26 Jackson St, Greenhills W, San Juan 1500, Philippines

VUCKOVICH, CAROL YETSO (MRS. MICHAEL VUCKOVICH), librarian; b. East Liverpool, Ohio, Sept. 23, 1940; d. Stephen A. and Louise (Sever) Yetso; B.S., Geneva Coll., 1966; M.L.S., U. Pitts., 1968; m. Michael Vuckovich, Sept. 24, 1970. Computation analyst Crucible Steel div. Colt Industries, Midland, Pa., 1958-62; library dir. Community Coll. Beaver County, Monaca, Pa., 1968—, instr. human anatomy and physiology, 1970—. Mem. Am. Library Assn., Pa. Library Assn., Spl. Libraries Assn., Am. Inst. Biol. Scis., Am. Anti-Vivisection Soc., Nat. Wildlife Fedn., Coll. and Research Libraries. Home: 21 Elm St Midland PA 15059

VUITTON, HENRY-LOUIS, designer; b. Asnieres, Seine, France, Aug. 10, 1911; s. Gaston-Louis and Renee (Versillé) V.; m. Josette Rateau, Oct. 15, 1935; children: Colette (Mrs. Jacques Novatin), Philippe-Louis (dec.), Daniele (Mrs. Philippe Masson). Student, Cours Saint-Louis, Paris. Comml. dir. Vuitton et Vuitton, Paris, 1945-75, pres. bd. mgrs., 1975-77; pres. bd. insps. Louis Vuitton (S.A.); hon. pres. Chambre Syndicale Nationale des Fabricants d'Articles de Voyage, 1977—; hon. v.p. Fedn. Nat. des Industries de la Maroquinerie et Articles de Voyage, 1977—; sec. Ct. of Arbitration, Conseil Nat. du Cuir, 1977—; v.p. Preparatory Interunion Com. of Adv. Sects.; hon. v.p. Natl. Fedn. of Mfg. Léather and Travel Article Inds., 1977—. Author: La Malle aux Souvenirs. Decorated officer Order Nat. of Merit France; Grande Medaille d'Or du Travail; recipient Silver medal City of Paris. Office: Louis Vuitton SA, 30 rue la Boetie, 75008 Paris France *

VUJANOVIC, BOZIDAR, engineer, educator; b. Smederevo, Yugoslavia, Sept. 8, 1930; s. Dragutin and Kosara (Matic) V.; grad. U. Belgrade, Yugoslavia, 1955, Ph.D., 1963; m. Olivera Milatovic, Aug. 15, 1954; children—Milica, Dragutin. Asst. prof. U. Belgrade, 1957-63; assoc. prof. U. Novi Sad, Yugoslavia, 1963-67, prof. applied mechanics, 1972—, head dept. mechanics, 1980—; research assoc. U. Ky., 1967-69; vis. prof. U. Tsukuba, Japan, 1977-78, Vanderbilt U., Nashville, 1984. Mem. Yugoslav Soc. Mechanics (pres. 1986—, mem. exec. council), Tensor Soc. (Japan), Sigma Xi. Contbr. articles to profl. jours. Home: 17 Fruskogorska, 21000 Novi Sad Yugoslavia Office: Univ Novi Sad, Dept Mechanics, Velijka Vlahovica, 21000 Novi Sad Yugoslavia

VUKOVIC, DRAGO VUKO, electronic engineer; b. Dubrovnik, Yugoslavia, Sept. 9, 1934; s. Vuko and Katica (Simunovic) V.; m. Marija Kakarigji, May 15, 1956; children—Katija, Snjezana, Sanja. Diploma engr., Faculty of Electrotehnics, Zagreb, 1961; M.S., Faculty of Econs., Zagreb, 1977. Supervising engr. Elektrojug, Dubrovnik, Yugoslavia, 1961-62; lighting designer Arhitekt, Dubrovnik, 1963-64; designer, supr. Biro za izgradnju, Dubrovnik, 1964-71, mng. dir., 1971-74; leader architect team Atelier LAPAD, Dubrovnik, 1974—; tchr., head electrotechnical div. Nautical Coll., Dubrovnik, 1963-67; cons. engr. Dubrovnik, Cavtat, Dubrovnik, 1968-75; collaborator Faculty of Architecture, Zagreb, 1974—. Contbr. in field. Served to capt. Yugoslavian Air Force, 1962-63. Recipient Town Planning & Architecture award Yugoslav Competition Com., Titograd, 1978; Plaque Assn. Visual Artists and Applied Arts of Croatia, 1982. Mem. Assn. Visual Artists of Applied Arts of Croatia, Soc. Ind. Geodesists, Civil Engrs. and Architects. Clubs: Radio Club (Dubrovnik); Am. Radio Relay League Inc, Am. Biog. Inst. Research Assn. Office: Atelier LAPAD, L Rogovskog 10, 50000 Dubrovnik Yugoslavia

VUORISTO, OSMO JALMARI, museum administrator, educator; b. Helsinki, Finland, Feb. 13, 1929; m. Edit Helena Korpinen, Mar. 14, 1954; children—Osmo Kalevi, Pekka Juhani. M.A., Univ. Helsinki, 1960, Ph.Licentiate, 1977, Ph.Doctor, 1978. Dir. No. Karelia Mus., Joensuu, Finland, 1954-58; curator Nat. Mus. of Finland, Helsinki, 1958-72, head sect. museology, 1973-78, dir., 1979—; docent ethnology Univ. Helsinki, 1979—. Author: Suomalaiset haarikka-astiat/Die Trinkgefä sse vom haarikka-Typ in Finnland, 1978; also articles and films. Active Council Mus. Affairs, 1974-81, Council Handicraft Mus. of Finland, Jyvaskyla, 1982—. Fellow Finnish Antiquites Soc.; corr. mem. Hungarian Ethnol. Soc., mem. Finnish Lit. Soc., Finnish Mus. Assn. Home: Kontulankaari 3 G 161, 00940 Helsinki Finland Office: Nat Mus Finland, Mannerheimintie 34, Box 913, 00101 Helsinki Finland

VURALHAN, ERCAN, minister of national defense; b. Malatya, Turkey, 1943; Married; 1 child. Grad., Am. High Sch., Tarsus, Turkey, 1961, U. Ankara, Fac. of Polit. Scis., 1965. Various diplomatic and consular posts 1965-77; dep. chief Mission of the Turkish Embassy, The Hague, The Netherlands, 1977-81; dep. head of Adminstrv. Dept. Ministry of Fgn. Affairs, 1981-83, head of Adminstrv. Dept., 1983-87; Turkish ambassador Saudi Arabia, 1987; minister nat. def. Ankara, Turkey, 1987—. Office: Ministry of Nat Def, Ankara Turkey *

VYAS, GIRISH NARMADASHANKAR, virologist, immunohematologist; b. Aglod, India, June 11, 1933; came to U.S., 1965, naturalized, 1973; s. Narmadashankar P. and Rukshmani A. (Joshi) V.; m. Devi Ratilal Trivedi, Apr. 3, 1962; children—Jay, Shrikrishna. B.Sc., U. Bombay, 1954, M.Sc., 1956, Ph.D., 1964. Postdoctoral fellow Western Res. U., 1965-66; mem. faculty U. Calif., San Francisco, 1967—; prof. lab. medicine U. Calif., 1977—; WHO cons., S.E. Asia, 1980; cons. in field; mem. com. viral hepatitis NRC, 1974-76; mem. task force blood processing Nat. Heart and Lung Inst., 1972-73; sci. program com. Am. Assn. Blood Banks, 1971-76; com. immunoglobulin allotypes WHO, 1974—; mem. U.S. del. immunologists to, Romania and Hungary, 1980; mem. FDA com. on blood and blood products, 1985; cons. to VA on med. research, 1985; cons. UN Devel. Program in India, 1986; delivered Dr. R.G. Dhayagude Meml. oration, 1986; chmn. symposium on DNA Probes in transfusion practice Internat. Transfusion Congress, London, 1988; chmn. symposium on Transfusion Associated Infections and Immune Response, San Francisco, 1988;. Author: Hepatitis and Blood Transfusion, 1972, Laboratory Diagnosis of Immunological Disorders, 1975, Membrane Structure and Function of Human Blood Cells, 1976, Viral Hepatitis, 1978, Use and Standardization of Chemically Defined Antigens, 1986; also research papers. Recipient Julliard prize Internat. Soc. Blood Transfusion, 1969; named Outstanding Immigrant in Bay Area Communities Mayor of Oakland, Calif., 1969; Fulbright scholar France, 1980. Mem. Am. Soc. Hematology, AAAS, Am. Assn. Immunologists, Am. Soc. Clin. Pathologists. Democrat. Hindu. Office: U Calif Lab Med M-523 San Francisco CA 94143

VYAS, RAM CHANDRA, mathematics educator; b. Jodhpur, Rajasthan, India, July 14, 1928; s. Sardarmal and Suraj Kaur Vyas; m. Chand Bohra; children—Sadhana, Ajay, Kalpana, Veena, Neena. B.A., Dungar Coll., 1948, M.A., 1950, LL.B., 1953; Ph.D., U. Jodhpur, 1975. Lectr. Govt. Rajasthan, 1952-62; asst. prof. U. Jodhpur, 1962-84, assoc. prof. math., 1984—, head math. dept. Faculty Engring., 1983—. Author: Intermediate Dynamics, 1957; Textbook on Differential and Integral Calculus Studies, 1959; also articles. Pres. Jodhpur U. Coop. Store, 1982—; chief warden Jodhpur U. Engring. Group Hostels, 1984—. Mem. Am. Math. Soc., Indian Math. Soc. Avocation: tennis. Home: U Bungalow III-B Agy, Jodhpur Rajasthan 34001, India Office: U Jodhpur, Dept Math Faculty Engring, Jodhpur 342001, India

VYVERBERG, ROBERT WILLIAM, mental health superintendent; b. Dubuque, Iowa, Dec. 23, 1940; s. William Pifer and Virginia Thelma (Rutger) V.; m. Mari Ann Jacobs, Nov. 6, 1982; children by previous marriage: Robert William, Benjamin Rutger. BEd, Ill. Wesleyan U., 1963; MS, Ill. State U., 1964; EdD, No. Ill. U., 1972. Dir. counseling services Crown High Sch., Carpentersville, Ill., 1964-67; dir. outcare services, children and adolescent unit H. Douglas Singer Mental Health Center, Rockford, Ill., 1969-72, dir. psychiat. rehab. and extended care services, 1972-82; region coordinator Services to Elderly, 1978-83; clin. dir. Children's and Adolescent Services, 1982-84, adminstrv. dir., 1982-84; supt. Zeller Mental Health Ctr., 1984—; lectr. crisis theory and crisis intervention No. Ill. U., 1970-84, instr. group counseling and psychotherapy, 1973; cons. Juvenile Justice Personnel Devel. Center, U. Wis., 1977. Mem. Nat. Rehab. Assn., Am. Assn. Counseling and Devel., Am. Rehab. Counselors Assn., Am. Mental Health Counselors Assn., Internat. Assn. Psycho-Social Rehab. Services, Assn. Mental Health Adminstrs. Methodist. Home: 4420 Lynnhurst Dr Peoria IL 61615 Office: Zeller Mental Health Ctr 5407 N University Peoria IL 61614

WAAGE, DONALD LANGSTON, public relations executive, banker; b. Minn., Jan. 30, 1925; s. John A. and Amanda O. (Andreas) W.; m. Lori deBrossoit, Sept. 8, 1946; children—Donn, Suzanne Friedman, Bruce, Eric. B.S., St. Cloud U., 1949; M.A., Am. U., 1962. Reporter, St. Cloud Daily Times, Minn., 1951-54; asst. mgr. fin. and taxation dept., sec. fin. com. C. of C. of U.S., Washington, 1954-60; asst. to bd. dirs., dir. congl. and pub. relations FDIC, Washington, 1960-62; sr. editor fin. reports and pub. Investors Diversified Services, Inc., Mpls., 1962-67; v.p. advertising and pub. relations North Am. Life and Casualty Co., Mpls., 1967-69; dir. fin. and pub. relations Josten's Inc., Mpls., 1969-72; v.p. Am. Survey Research Corp., Mpls., 1972-77; regional dir. Hwy. Users Fedn., Washington, 1977-83; exec. v.p., ptnr. Coughlan, Trepanier, Waage Assocs., Minnetonka, Minn., 1983—; cons. World Bank, Washington, 1965-70, Republican Nat. Com., Washington, 1974-77; dir. Summit Bank, Bloomington, Minn., 1968-80. Author Mil. history monograph, 1952; contbr. articles on banking to profl. jours. Vice chmn. Mpls. Symphony Orch. fund drive, 1964; chmn. Minnetonka Rep. fund drive, 1970-74; deacon Westminster Presbyn. Ch.; trustee Am. Univ., Washington, 1966-72. Served to maj. with U.S. Army, 1950-53. Mem. Minn. Press Club, French-Am. C. of C. Club: Wayzata Country; Twin City Polo; Exchequer (first chancellor, founder) (Washington).

WAAS, GEORGE LEE, lawyer; b. N.Y.C., July 12, 1943; s. George and Anne Waas; m. Harriet I. Waas, July 18, 1971; children—Elaine Beth, Amy Michelle. B.S. in Journalism, U. Fla., 1965; J.D., Fla. State U., 1970. Bar: Fla. 1970, U.S. Supreme Ct., 1973. Asst. atty. gen. State of Fla., 1970-71; staff atty. Fla. League of Cities, 1971; asst. to sec. and dir. labor Fla. Dept. Commerce, 1971-73; assoc. dir. continuing legal edn. Fla. Bar, 1973-74; asst. dean, instr. Coll. Law, Fla. State U., 1974-75; atty. Fla. Dept. Transp., 1975-77; asst. gen. counsel Fla. Dept. Health and Rehab. Services, 1977-80; ptnr. Slepin, Slepin, Lambert & Waas, 1981-86; counsel state elections Fla. Dept. of State, 1986-87; asst. atty. gen. State of Fla., Tallahassee, 1987—. Bd. dirs. Big Bend Muscular Dystrophy Assn., 1980-83, pres., 1983; mem. Leon County Cultural Resources Commn., 1985-87. Mem. Fla. Govt. Bar Assn. (pres. 1976-77), Fla. Bar (exec. council adminstrv. law sect. 1981—, chmn. 1985-86). Democrat. Jewish. Clubs: Capital Tiger Bay (dir. 1974-80) (Tallahassee); Masons. Contbr. articles to profl. jours. Home: 3797 Sally Ln Tallahassee FL 32312 Office: The Capitol Suite 1501 Tallahassee FL 32399

WACHNOVETZKY, FREDDY, chemical engineer, consultant; b. Mexico City, Mexico, May 25, 1958; s. Bernardo and Anna (Rudman) W. Chem. Engr., Universidad Nacional Autonoma De Mexico, 1982; MBA, Instituto Tech. De Estudios Superiores de Monterrey, Mexico, 1982. Mgr. maintenance engring. Corporacion Indsl. Mexicana S.A., Naucalpan, Mexico, 1981-83, 85-86; tchr. phys. chemistry, thermodynamics Universidad Nacional Autonoma de Mexico, 1981-84; tech. and mgmt. cons. Infotec, Mexico City, 1983-85; plant mng. CIMSA, Naucalpan, Mexico, 1987—; tchr. talmudial philosophy and ethics TOV Internat., Mexico City, 1988—; prodn. planning mgr. Ojos y Accesories SA, Naucalpan, Mexico, 1987—; sci. dir. Centro Educativo Albatros, Herradura, Mexico, 1981-84, Universidad Nuevo Mundo, Herradura, 1981-84; dir. Emek & Bethyacov Schs., Mexico City, 1985-87. Author: Fundamentos Basicos De Cinetica Quimica Y Catalisis Enzimatica, 1984. Mem. Asociaciones Autonomas Del Personal, Chem. Engring. Expert Panel for Specifying Equipment. Avocations: squash, tennis, soccer, reading, philosophy. Office: CIMSA, Esfuerzo Nacional #11, Alce Blanco Frac Naucalpanedo, 53370 Mexico City Mexico

WACHOWSKI, THEODORE JOHN, radiologist; b. Chgo., Nov. 20, 1907; s. Albert and Constance (Korzeniewski) W.; B.S., U. Ill., 1929, M.D., 1932; m. Barbara F. Benda, June 1, 1931; 1 son, Ted J. Waller. Intern, resident in radiology, asso. radiologist U. Ill. Hosps., 1931-67; clin. prof. radiology U. Ill., 1949-67; radiologist Copley Meml. Hosp., Aurora, Ill., 1935-77, Loretto Hosp., Chgo., 1941-48; practice medicine specializing in radiology, Wheaton, Ill., 1975-83; ret., 1983. Mem. Radiol. Soc. N.Am. (pres. 1960, Gold medal 1969), Am. Coll. Radiology (pres. 1963, Gold medal 1969), Ill., Kane County med. socs., AMA, Am. Roentgen Ray Soc., Chgo. Radiol. Soc. (past pres., Gold medal 1982). Republican. Club: Glen Oak Country. Contbr. articles to profl. jours. Home: 101 Tennyson Dr Wheaton IL 60187

WACHS, KATE MARY, psychologist; b. Chgo., Aug. 27, 1951; d. Charles Herbert and Rose Ann W. BA magna cum laude, Rosary Coll., 1974; MA, U. S.D., 1976, PhD, 1980. Licensed psychologist, Ill., Mich. Asst. clin. psychologist Lewis & Clark Mental Health Ctr., Yankton, S.D., 1977-78; intern clin. psychology Rush Presbyn. St. Luke's Med. Ctr., Chgo., 1978-79, house staff in psychology, 1979-80; psychologist Bay Med. Ctr., Bay City, Mich., 1980-83; pvt. practice psychology Mich., 1983-86, Chgo., 1984—; pres. IntiMate Introduction Service, Inc., Advanced Degrees Introductions, Inc.; columnist Chgo. Life Mag., 1984—, Women In Mgmt. Newsletter, 1984-86, Amplifier, 1986—; editor articles for local and nat. pubs.; guest on local and nat. radio and TV programs, 1982—. Mem. Assn. for Media Psychology (bd. dirs. 1985—), Am. Psychol. Assn. (bd. dirs. Div. 46 1986—, chmn. ethics/guidelines com. 1986-87, chmn. membership com. 1987—, liaison to Pub. Info. Com. 1987—), Am. Pain Soc., Women in Mgmt. (Women Achievement award entrepreneurial contbns. 1987). Office: 1030 N State Suite 7C Chicago IL 60610

WACHSMAN, HARVEY FREDERICK, neurosurgeon, lawyer; b. Bklyn., June 13, 1936; s. Ben and Mollie (Kugel) W.; m. Kathryn M. D'Agostino, Jan. 31, 1976; children: Dara Nicole, David Winston, Jacqueline Victoria, Lauren Elizabeth, Derek Charles, Ashley Max, Marea Lane, Melissa Roseanne. B.A., Tulane U., 1958; M.D., Chgo. Med. Sch., 1962; J.D., Bklyn. Law Sch., 1976. Bar: Conn. 1976, N.Y. 1977, Fla. 1977, D.C. 1978, U.S. Supreme Ct. 1980, Pa. 1984, Md. 1986, Tex. 1987; diplomate: Nat. Bd. Med. Examiners; cert., Am. Bed. Legal Medicine, Am. Bd. Profl. Liability Attys. cert. civil trial advocate, Nat. Bd. Trial Advocacy; diplomate Nat. Bd. Med. Examiners. Intern surgery Kings County Hosp. Ctr., Bklyn., 1962-63; resident in surgery Kingsbrook Med. Ctr., Bklyn., 1964-65; resident in neurol. surgery Emory U. Hosp., Atlanta, 1965-69; practice medicine specializing in neurosurgery Bridgeport, Conn., 1972-74; ptnr. firm Pegalis & Wachsman, Great Neck, N.Y., 1977—, Wachsman & Wachsman, Great Neck, 1976—; adj. prof. Bklyn. Law Sch., U.S. Fla. Coll. Medicine. Author: American Law of Medical Malpractice, Vol. I, 1980, American Law of Medical Malpractice, Vol. II, 1981, American Law of Medical Malpractice, Vol. III, 1982, Cumulative Supplement to American Law of Medical Malpractice, 1981, 82, 83, 84, 85; mem. editorial bd.: Legal Aspects of Med. Practice, 1978-82. Fellow Am. Coll. Legal Medicine (mem. bd. govs. 1986, chmn. edn. com. 1983—, chmn. 1985 nat. meeting, New Orleans), Am. Acad. Forensic Scis., Royal Soc. Medicine, Royal Soc. Arts (London), Roscoe Pound Found. of Assn. Trial Lawyers Am.; mem. Am. Soc. Law and Medicine, ABA, Congress Neurol. Surgeons, Assn. Trial Lawyers Am., Soc. Med. Jurisprudence, N.Y. Bar Assn., Conn. Bar Assn., Fla. Bar Assn., D.C. Bar Assn., N.Y. Acad. Scis., N.Y. Trial Lawyers Assn., Conn. Trial Lawyers Assn., Fla. Acad. Trial Lawyers, Md. Trial Lawyers Assn., Tex. Trial Lawyers Assn., Pa. Trial Lawyers Assn., Nassau County Bar Assn., Fairfield County Med. Soc., Nassau-Suffolk Trial Lawyers Assn. Club: Cosmos (Washington). Home: 55 Mill River Rd Brookville NY 11771 Office: 175 E Shore Rd Great Neck NY 11023

WACHTMEISTER, H. ALARIK, former steel company executive; b. Carlskrona, Sweden, May 11, 1922; s. Alarik and Margit (Stockenberg) W.; grad. Centre d'Etudes Industrielles, Geneva, 1951; m. Brita Kinch, July 15, 1950; children—C. Alarik, Anne D. H.E. Product mgr. foil Aluminum Co. Can., Ltd., Montreal, Que., 1951-55; mgr. steel sales Sandvik Can., Ltd., Montreal, 1955-58; export sales mgr. Nyby Bruks AB, Sweden, 1958-62; sales dir. Granges Nyby AB, Sweden, 1962-70, dir. fgn. subsidiaries, 1970-74, v.p., 1975-79; v.p. Nyby Uddeholm AB, Eskilstuna, Sweden, 1979-84. Author nat. security matters. Served to lt. Swedish Navy, 1941-47; to lt. comdr. Res., 1959-88. Decorated Order of St. John. Lutheran. Clubs: Rotary, Naval Officers (Stockholm); United Services (Montreal). Home: Wallakra Gard, 260 30 Vallakra Sweden

WACHTMEISTER, WILHELM H. F., Swedish diplomat; b. Vanas, Sweden, Apr. 29, 1923; s. Gustaf and Margaretha (Trolle) W.; m. Ulla Leuhusen, 1947; children—Ann, Christina, Erik. LL.D., U. Stockholm, Sweden, 1946. Attache Swedish Ministry for Fgn. Affairs, 1946-47; attache Swedish Embassy, Vienna, Madrid and Lisbon, 1947-50; 2d sec. Swedish Ministry Fgn. Affairs, Stockholm, Sweden, 1950-55; 1st sec. Swedish Embassy, Moscow, 1955-58; personal asst. to UN Sec. Gen., 1958-61; head UN sect. Fgn. Ministry, Stockholm, 1962-65, dep. under-sec. polit. affairs, 1965-66; ambassador to Algeria Swedish Embassy, 1966-67; under-sec. for polit. affairs Swedish Embassy, Stockholm, 1968-74; Swedish ambassador to U.S. Swedish Embassy, Washington, 1974—; dean diplomatic corps in Washington. Mem. Soc. Cincinnati (France). Club: Metropolitan (Washington). Home: 3900 Nebraska Ave NW Washington DC 20016 Office: Embassy of Sweden 600 New Hampshire Ave NW Washington DC 20037

WACKER, FREDERICK GLADE, JR., manufacturing company executive; b. Chgo., July 10, 1918; s. Frederick Glade and Grace Cook (Jennings) W.; m. Ursula Comandatore, Apr. 26, 1958; children: Frederick Glade III, Wendy, Joseph Comandatore. B.A., Yale U., 1940; student, Gen. Motors Inst. Tech., 1940-42. With AC Spark Plug div. Gen. Motors Corp., 1940-43; efficiency engr. 1941-43; with Ammco Tools, Inc., North Chicago, Ill., 1947-87; pres. Ammco Tools, Inc., 1948-87, chmn. bd., 1948—; founder 1954; since pres., chmn. bd. Liquid Controls Corp., North Chicago; chmn. bd. Liquid Controls Europe, Zurich, Switzerland, 1985—; ltd. ptnr. Francis I. DuPont & Co., N.Y.C., 1954-70; mem. exec. council Conf. Bd., 1971—. Condr. Freddie Wacker and His Orch., 1955-69, orch. has appeared on TV and radio, recs. for Dolphin and Cadet records. Bd. govs. United Republican Fund Ill.; trustee Lake Forest Acad., 1956-71, Warren Wilson Coll., 1973-81, Chgo. chpt. Multiple Sclerosis Soc.; bd. govs. Lyric Opera Chgo., 1963-66; bd. advisers Nat. Schs. Com., 1966—; mem. adv. council Trinity Evang. Div. Sch., 1977—; bd. dirs., vice chmn. Rockford Inst., 1983-87; bd. govs. GMI Engring. and Mgmt. Inst., 1983—; bd. regents Milw. Sch. Engring., 1981—. Served to lt. (j.g.) USNR, 1943-45. Mem. Chief Execs. Forum, Young Pres. Orgn. (chmn. Chgo. chpt. 1965-66), Sports Car Club Am. (pres. 1952-53), Ill. Mfrs. Assn. (bd. dirs. 1966—, chmn. bd. 1975), Chgo. Pres. Orgn. (pres. 1972-73), Automotive Hall of Fame (life, dir. 1976—), Soc. Automotive Engrs., World Bus. Council, Waukegan C. of C. (dir. 1965-68), Chgo. Fedn. Musicians (life). Presbyterian. Clubs: Chgo., Racquet (Chgo.) (pres. 1960-61), Casino (Chgo.), Mid-Am. (Chgo.), Shoreacres, Onwentsia (Lake Forest), N.Y. Yacht. Home: 1600 Green Bay Rd Lake Bluff IL 60044 Office: Wacker Park North Chicago IL 60064

WACKER, MARGARET MORRISSEY, communications executive; b. Washington, Dec. 12, 1951; d. Warren Ernest Clyde and Ann Romeyn (MacMillan) Wacker. B.A., Carnegie Mellon U., 1974. Promotion specialist Millipore Corp., Bedford, Mass., 1974-77, corp. communications mgr., 1982—, dir. communications Lab. Products div., 1981-82; dir. advt. IVAC div. Eli Lilly Co., San Diego, 1977-79, dist. sales mgr., Los Angeles, 1979-80; bus. unit mgr. Sage div. Orion Research, Cambridge, Mass., 1980-81; counselor to handicapped individuals in bus. Mem. Internat. Assn. Bus. Communicators. Democrat. Episcopalian. Avocations: painting; sewing. Home: The Brook House Atrium 99 Pond Ave Unit 322D Brookline MA 02146 Office: Millipore Corp 80 Ashby Rd Bedford MA 01730

WACKER, WARREN ERNEST CLYDE, physician, educator; b. Bklyn., Feb. 29, 1924; s. John Frederick and Kitty Dora (Morrissey) W.; m. Ann Romeyn MacMillan, May 22, 1948; children: Margaret Morrissey, John Frederick. Student, Georgetown U., 1946-47; M.D., George Washington U., 1951; M.A. (hon.), Harvard, 1968. Intern George Washington U. Hosp., 1951-52, resident, 1952-53; resident Peter Bent Brigham Hosp., Boston, 1953-55; Nat. Found. Infantile Paralysis fellow 1955-57; investigator Howard Hughes Med. Inst., Boston, 1957-68; mem. faculty Harvard Med. Sch., Boston, 1955—; assoc. prof. medicine Harvard Med. Sch., 1968-71, Henry K. Oliver prof. hygiene, 1971—, dir. univ. health services, 1971—, acting master Mather House, 1974-75, acting master Kirkland House, 1975-76, master Cabot House, 1978-84; vis. scholar St. Mary's Hosp. Med. Sch., 1964; vis. prof. U. Tel Aviv, 1987; dir. Applied Mgmt. Systems, Burlington, Mass., Millipore Corp., Bedford, Mass. Author: Magnesium and Man, 1981; sec., editorial adv. bd.: Biochemistry, 1962-76; assoc. editor: Magnesium; contbr. articles to med. and sci. jours. Bd. dirs. Harvard Community Health Plan, Boston, 1973-84, mem. fin. com., 1984-86, corp. 1986—; bd. dirs. Bishop Rhinelander Found., Cambridge, 1973-76, 78-84 ; pres. bd. overseers Peter Bent Brigham Hosp., Boston, 1979-84; trustee Brigham and Women's Hosp., Boston., Risk Mgmt. Found.; mem. corp. Mt. Auburn Hosp., Cambridge; mem. mgmt. bd., med. bd. MIT, 1985—. Served to 1st lt. USAAF, 1942-45. Decorated Air medal, D.F.C.; named Disting. Alumnus, George Washington U., 1963; recipient Cert. of Merit, Soc. Magnesium Research, 1985. Mem. Am. Chem. Soc., Am. Soc. Biol. Chemistry, Am. Soc. Clin. Investigation, AMA, Mass. Med. Soc., A.C.P., Am. Coll. Health Assn. (pres. 1981, Boynton award 1986), Biochemistry Soc. (London), Am. Coll. Nutrition, Sigma Xi, Alpha Omega Alpha. Democrat. Episcopalian. Clubs: Harvard (Boston); Cosmos (Washington). Home: 91 Glen Rd Brookline MA 02146 Office: 75 Mt Auburn St Cambridge MA 02138

WADA, EITARO, biogeochemist; b. Tokyo, Sept. 21, 1939; s. Torakichi and Kachiko (Katoh) W.; m. Setsuko Tanabe, May 3, 1967; children—Tohru,

Akane, Hiroshi. B.S., Tokyo U. Edn., 1962, M.S., 1964, Ph.D., 1967. Research assoc. U. Tokyo, 1967-76; vis. scientist U. Tex., Port Aransas, 1974-75; chief Mitsubishi-Kasei Inst. Life Scis., Tokyo, 1976—; instr. Sch. Meteorology, Chiba, Japan, 1967-68. Co-author: Marine Biochemistry, 1971; Heavy Nitrogen, 1980. Author/editor: Story of the Sea, 1984. Author jour. Nature, 1981; assoc. editor Oceanographic Soc. Japan, Tokyo, 1974. Pres. Sengoku Children's Assn., Kawasaki, Knaagawa, Japan, 1984, Bd. Isotopenpraxis (German Democratic Republic), 1987—. Recipient Okada price Oceanographic Soc. Japan, 1974. Mem. Geochem. Soc. Japan, Oceanographic Soc. Japan, Internat. Vereinigung fur Theoretische und Angewandte Limnology, Japanese Soc. Soil Sci. and Plant Nutrition. Buddhist. Avocation: travel. Home: 2-31-1 Suge-Sengoku, Tama-ku Kawasaki 214, Japan Office: Mitsubishi-Kasei, Inst Life Scis, 11 Minamiooya Machida, Tokyo 194, Japan

WADDELL, DAVID ALAN GILMOUR, historian, educator; b. Edinburgh, Scotland, Oct. 22, 1927; s. David and Helen (Gilmour) W.; m. Barbara Box, Mar. 17, 1951; children: Louise, Clive, Adrian. MA, U. St. Andrews, Scotland, 1949; PhD, U. Oxford, Eng., 1954. Lectr. history Univ. Coll. of the West Indies, Mona, Jamaica, 1954-59; lectr. history U. Edinburgh, 1959-63, sr. lectr. history, 1963-68; prof. modern history U. Stirling, Scotland, 1968—. Author: British Honduras, 1961, The West Indies And The Guianas, 1967, Gran Bretaña y La Independencia de Venezuela y Colombia, 1983; contbr. articles to hist. jours. Fellow Royal Hist. Soc.; mem. Scottish Soc. of the History of Medicine (pres.). Office: U Stirling, Stirling Scotland FK9 4LA

WADDINGTON, BETTE HOPE (ELIZABETH CROWDER), violinist, educator; b. San Francisco, July 27, 1921; d. John and Marguerite (Crowder) Waddington; BA in Music, U. Calif. at Berkeley, 1945, postgrad.; postgrad. (scholarship) Juilliard Sch. Music, 1950, San Jose State Coll., 1955; MA in Music, San Francisco State U., 1953; violin student of Joseph Fuchs, Melvin Ritter, Frank Gittelson, Felix Khuner, Daniel Bonsack, D.C. Dounis, Naoum Blinder, Eddy Brown; life cert. music and art Calif. Jr. Coll. Violinist Erie (Pa.) Symphony, 19510, Dallas Symphony, 1957, St. Louis Symphony, 1958—. Cert. gen. elem. and secondary tchr., Calif.; life cert. jr. coll. librarian. Toured alone and with St. Louis Symphony U.S., Can., Middle East, Japan, China, Europe; concert master Pa. Symphony, Redwood City and San Mateo, Calif., Grove Music Soc., N.Y.C., St. Louis Symphony, 1958—. Mem. Am. Musicians Union (St. Louis and San Francisco chpts.), U. Calif., San Francisco State Univ. Alumni Assn., San Francisco Musicians Union, Am. String Tchrs. Assn., San Jose State Univ. Alumni Assn., Sierra Club (life), Alpha Beta Alpha. Avocations: travel, art and archeology history, drawing, painting. Office: St Louis Symphony Orch Powell Hall Grand Ave and Delmar Blvd Saint Louis MO 63103

WADE, DALE BROOKINS, dentist, educator; b. Columbus, Ohio, July 25, 1940; s. Robert Edward and Louise (Roby) W.; m. Jan Schwiebert, June 22, 1963; children: Geoffrey Edward, Andrew Brookins. MS, Ohio State U., 1969, DDS, 1965. Diplomate Am. Bd. Orthodontics. Asst. clin. prof. Ohio State U., Columbus, 1969—; practice orthodontics, Columbus, 1969—. Editor Great Lakes Orthodontic Soc., 1980-86, Found. for Orthodontic Research; contbr. articles to profl. jours. Life mem. Upper Arlington Civic Assn., Columbus, 1980; scoutmaster Troop 180, Cen. Ohio council Boy Scouts Am., 1984—; mem. Pierre Fauchard Acad. Served as lt. USN, 1965-67. Fellow Acad. Internat. Dental Studies, Internat. Coll. Dentists; mem. Edward Angle Soc., Columbus Dental Soc. (pres. 1981), Gt. Lakes Orthodontic Soc. (1st v.p.), Ohio State U. Orthodontic Alumni Found. (pres. 1972), Am. Legion, Omicron Kappa Upsilon. Lodge: Sertoma (N.W. chpt. pres. 1976). Avocations: camping, skiing, photography, jogging, golf. Home: 3120 S Dorchester Rd Columbus OH 43221 Office: 3220 Riverside Dr Columbus OH 43221

WADE, HENRY WILLIAM RAWSON, educational administrator; b. London, Jan. 16, 1918; s. Henry Oswald and Eileen Lucy (Rawson-Ackroyd) W.; m. Marie Osland-Hill, Oct. 15, 1943 (dec. 1980); children: John Michael Ackroyd, Edward Henry Rawson, Marjorie Grace Hope Browne. BA, U. Cambridge, Eng., 1939. With His Majesty's Treasury, 1940-46; lectr. U. Cambridge, 1947-59, reader, 1959-61, master, 1976—, Rouse Ball prof. English law, 1978-82; prof. English law U. Oxford, Eng., 1961-76. Author: Towards Administrative Justice, 1963, Legal Control of Government, 1972, Constitutional Fundamentals, 1980, Administrative Law, 1988, (with Sir R. Megarry) The Law of Real Property, 1984; contbr. articles to profl. jours. Named to Queen's Counsel, 1968, Knight Bachelor The Queen, 1985. Fellow Brit. Acad. (v.p. 1981-83). Club: Oxford and Cambridge United Univ. (London). Office: British Acad, 20-21 Cornwall Terrace, London NW1 4QP, United Kingdom

WADE, JOHN WEBSTER, law educator, lawyer; consultant; b. Little Rock, Mar. 2, 1911; s. John William and Sarah Vista (Webster) W.; m. Mary Moody Johnson, June 1, 1946; children—John Webster, Mary R. Wade Shanks, William J., Ruth E. Wade Grant. B.A., U. Miss., 1932, J.D. 1934; LL.M., Harvard U., 1935, S.J.D., 1942. Bar: Miss. 1934, Tenn. 1947. Asst. prof. law U. Miss., 1936-38, assoc. prof., 1938-40, prof., 1940-47; prof. Vanderbilt U. Sch. Law, 1947-71, dean, 1952-72, Disting. prof. law, 1971-81, dean and Disting. prof. emeritus, 1981—; vis. prof. U. Tex., 1946-47, Columbia U., 1964-65, U. Mo., 1976-77, Coll. William and Mary, 1981-82, Cornell U., fall 1972, U. Mich., Fall 1982, Pepperdine U., 1983-84, Memphis State U., 1986, U. Hawaii, 1987; uniform laws commr. from Tenn., 1961—, v.p. Nat. Conf. Commrs. Uniform State Laws, 1977-79; reporter Restatement (Second) of Torts, 1970-81; speaker in field. Trustee Rhodes Coll., Memphis. Served to capt. USMCR, 1943-45. Decorated Bronze Star; recipient William L. Prosser award for outstanding contbn. of devel. of tort law, 1980. Mem. ABA, Miss. Bar Assn., Tenn. Bar Assn., Nashville Bar Assn., Assn. Bar City N.Y., Order of Coif (nat. pres. 1973-76), Am. Law Inst. (council 1960-70, 82—). Author: Cases and Materials on Restitution, 2d edit., 1966; Cases and Materials on Torts, 7th edit., 1982; contbr. numerous articles on torts, restitution and other topics to law revs. and other law publs. Office: Vanderbilt U Sch Law Nashville TN 37240

WADE, ROBERT HIRSCH BEARD, international consultant, former educational association official; b. Tamaqua, Pa., Oct. 5, 1916; s. Edgar Gerber and Florence Annabelle (Hirsch) W.; m. Eleanor Marguerite Borden, Sept. 14, 1946; 1 son, Gregory Borden. A.B. magna cum laude, Lafayette Coll., 1937; diplome d'etudes universitaires, Bordeaux U., 1938; Ph.D., Yale U., 1942. Instr. French, Yale U., 1939-42; chief Far Eastern analyst Office Naval Intelligence, 1946-54; asst. Office Nat. Security Council Affairs, Dept. Def., Washington, 1954-56; dir. Office Nat. Security Council Affairs, Dept. Def., 1956-61; spl. asst. to asst. sec. state for ednl. and cultural affairs 1962; dir. multilateral and spl. activities Bur. Ednl. and Cultural Affairs, Dept. State, 1962-64; U.S. permanent rep. to UNESCO, with rank of minister, 1964-69; asst. dir. U.S. Arms Control & Disarmament Agy., Washington, 1969-73; exec. dir. Fgn. Student Service Council, Washington, 1974-77; dir. Washington office Am. Assembly Collegiate Schs. Bus., 1977-85; internat. cons. 1986—; Mem. U.S. del. to UNESCO Gen. Confs., 1962, 1964, 1966, 68; dep. U.S. mem. exec. bd. UNESCO, 1964-69; mem. U.S. Nat. Commn. for UNESCO, 1977-83, vice chmn., 1978-79. Author, editor: Management for XXI Century, 1982. Trustee Am. Coll. in Paris, 1967-78, chmn. bd., 1967-69. Served to lt. USNR, 1942-46, PTO. Recipient Merit Citation award Nat. Civil Service League. Fellow Am. Fgn. Service Assn., Acad. Internat. Bus.; mem. Friends of Vieilles Maisons Francaises, Phi Beta Kappa, Kappa Delta Rho. Republican. Christian Scientist. Clubs: Union Interalliee (Paris), Racing (Paris); Chevy Chase (Washington). Home and Office: 3049 W Lane Keys NW Washington DC 20007

WADE, THOMAS EDWARD, electrical engineer, researcher; b. Jacksonville, Fla., Sept. 14, 1943; s. Wilton Fred and Alice Lucyle (Hedge) W.; m. Ann Elizabeth Chitty, Aug. 6, 1966; children—Amy Renee, Nathan Thomas, Laura Ann. B.S.E.E., U. Fla.-Gainesville, 1966, M.S.E.E., 1968, Ph.D., 1974. Interim asst. prof. U. Fla.-Gainesville, 1974-76; prof. elec. engring. Miss. State U., Starkville, 1976-85, dir. microelectronics research lab., 1978-85, assoc. dean. U. South Fla., Tampa, 1985—, dir. Engring. Indsl. Experiment Sta., exec. dir. Ctrs. for Engring. Devel. and Research, mem. presdl. faculty adv. com. for research and tech. devel., 1986—, mem. fed. demostration project com. for contracts and grants, 1986—; dir. Fla. Ctr. for Microelectronics Design and Test, 1986—; solid state circuit specialist Applied Micro-Circuits Corp., San Diego, 1981-82; sr. scientist NASA Marshall Space Flight Ctr., Huntsville, Ala., 1983; scientist Trilogy Semiconductor Corp., Santa Clara, Calif., 1984; cons. in field. Author: Polyimides for VLSI Applications, 1984, (U.S. Army handbook) Modern VLSI Circuit Fabrication Processess, 1984, Photosensitive Polyimides for VLSI Applications, 1986; contbr. articles to profl. jours. Vol., United Fund, Miss. State U., 1983-85. Recipient Outstanding Engring. Teaching award Coll. Engring. U. Fla., 1976, Cert. of Recognition NASA, (4 times) 1981-86, Outstanding Research award Sigma Xi, 1984. Mem. NSPE, IEEE (sr. mem.; guest editor periodical 1982, gen. chmn. Internat. VLSI Multilevel Interconnection Conf. annually 1984—; chmn. acad. affairs com. CHMT Soc. 1984-86, gen. chmn. univ./govt./industry microelectronics symposium, 1981), Am. Soc. Engring. Edn. (gen. chmn. engring. research council ann. meeting 1987, bd. dirs. 1987—, chmn. adminstrv. com. 1987), AAAS, Internat. Soc. Hybrid Microelectronics, Soc. Photo Optical Instrumentation Engring., Univ. Faculty Senate Assn. of Miss. (organizer 1985), Am. Vacuum Soc., Am. Phys. Soc., Am. Inst. Physics, Nat. Council Univ. Research Adminstrn., Soc. Research Adminstrs. (external relations com. for SRA), Fla. Engring. Soc. (v.p. edn. com.), Soc. Am. Inventors, Tampa Bay Internat. Super Task Force (vice chmn. edn. com. 1988), Sigma Xi (v.p. 1985), Tau Beta Pi (chpt. pres. 1969, 71, nat. outstanding chpt. award), Eta Kappa Nu (pres. 1968), Sigma Tau, Omicron Delta Kappa (v.p. 1974), Fla. Blue Key (v.p. 1972, sec, 1971), Epsilon Lambda Chi (founder 1970). Club: Rotary (Paul Harris Fellow 1987, perfect attendance award 1986—). Home: 5316 Witham Ct Tampa FL 33647

WADE, (SARAH) VIRGINIA, tennis player; b. Bournemouth, Eng., July 10, 1945; grad. Sussex U. Winner women's singles U.S. Open, 1968, doubles, 1973, 75; women's singles Australian Open, 1972, women's doubles, 1973; women's singles Italian Open, 1971; women's singles Rothmans Brit. Hard Ct. Championship, 1972; winner Dewar Cup, 1969, 73, 74, 75, 76; women's singles Green Shield Welsh Open, 1971; women's doubles Brit. Hard Ct. Championship, 1967, 74; mixed doubles South African Open, 1972; mem. winning Wrightman Cup team, 1965, 74, winning Fedn. Cup Team, 1967, 74; champion women's singles Wimbledon, 1977. Decorated Order Brit. Empire. Home: Sittingbourne, Sharsted Ct, Kent England Office: IMG 1 Erieview Plaza Cleveland OH 44199 also: care US Tennis Assn 52 E 42nd St New York NY 10017 *

WADE, WARREN THOMAS, publishing company executive; b. Jamaica, N.Y., Sept. 19, 1935; s. George Fred and Ursula Loretta W.; student L.I. U., 1954-56, night coll., C.W. Post Coll., 1956-66; m. Catherine Mary Lertola, May 18, 1969; children—Christine Marie, Mary Therese. With Leo Burnett Advt., N.Y.C., 1956-59; salesman Campbell Soup Co., L.I., 1959-65; nat. mail order mgr. House Beautiful mag., N.Y.C., 1965-71; bus. mgr. Bride's mag., N.Y.C., 1971—. Mem. 5-yr. curriculum planning com. local grade school, parish council local ch.; publicity dir. parish council. Served with USNR, 1954-62. Republican. Club: Sea Cliff Yacht. Home: 134 Weeks Rd East Williston NY 11596 Office: 350 Madison Ave New York NY 10017

WADHWA, YASH PAL, environmental engineer; b. Delhi, India, Oct. 4, 1946; came to U.S., 1969, naturalized, 1982; s. Rikhi Ram and Ram Devi (Grover) W.; m. Usha Rani Chugh, Jan. 25, 1972; children: Ajay Raj, Ravi Kumar. BSCE, U. Delhi, 1969; MSCE, U. Pitts., 1971. Registered profl. engr., Wis., Ill., N.Y. Project engr., mgr. Larsen Engrs./Architects, Rochester, N.Y., 1971-79; pres. Larsen Engrs., S.C., Milw., 1983—; sr. project mgr. DKI Group Engr., Milw., 1979-83; bd. dirs. Larsen Engrs./ Architects, Rochester; mgmt. del. to Republic of China, 1983. Account exec. United Way of Greater Milw., 1984-86; project bus. cons. Jr. Achievement, Inc., Milw., 1985—. Mem. ASCE (chmn. mgmt. tech. com. Wis. sect. 1986—), Wis. Soc. Profl. Engrs. (pres. Milw. South chpt. 1987—), Project Mgmt. Inst. (pres. midwest chpt. 1987—). Democrat. Hindu. Club: Toastmasters. Home: 920 W Brentwood Ln Glendale WI 53217 Office: Larsen Engrs SC 735 W Wisconsin Ave Milwaukee WI 53233

WADLEIGH, CECIL HERBERT, plant physiologist, resource conservationist; b. Gilbertville, Mass., Oct. 1, 1907; s. Hazen Carl and Lucy (Whitehead) W.; m. Clarice Lucile Bean, Sept. 1930; children—Evelyn Estelle, Carolyn Priscilla, Stanley Firth, Elaine Lucile. B.S., U. Mass., Amherst, 1930; M.S., Ohio State U., Columbus, 1933; Ph.D., Rutgers U., New Brunswick, N.J., 1935; D.Sc. (hon.), U. Mass., Amherst, 1974. Asst. prof. plant physiology U. Ark., Fayetteville, 1936-41; plant physiologist U.S. Salinity Lab., Riverside, Calif., 1941-51; head physiologist sugar plants div. U.S. Dept. Agr., Beltsville, Md., 1951-54, head physiologist soil-plant relations, 1954-55, dir. Soil and Water Conservation Research, 1955-70, sci. advisor, 1971; Mem. White House panel on Indus River Basin of Pakistan, 1961-63; mem. com. hydrology White House Office Sci. and Tech., 1961-62; mem. com. water resources research White House Office Sci. and Tech., 1963-68, com. environ. quality, 1967-69; ofcl. del. U.S. Dept. Agr. Brookings Instn. Conf. for Sci. Execs. in Govt., Williamsburg, Va., 1959; ofcl. rep. Dept. Agr. 2d White House Conf. on Conservation, 1963, Bi-lateral Conf. Environ. Protection, Pilsen, Czechoslovakia, 1973; tech. cons. Lake Verret Watershed Protection Project, La., 1972-76. Contbr. over 100 articles to profl. jours. Recipient Disting. Service award U.S. Dept. Agr., 1967; Hugh Hammond Bennet award Soil Conservation Soc. Am., 1976; named to Sci. Hall Fame, U.S. Dept. Agrl., 1987. Mem. Nat. Acad. Scis., Am. Soc. Plant Physiologists (pres. 1951-52), Am. Soc. Hort. Sci.; fellow Am. Soc. Agronomy, Soil Sci. Soc. Am., Soil Conservation Soc. Am. Home: 5621 Whitefield Chapel Rd Lanham MD 20706

WADLEY, M. RICHARD, consumer products executive; b. Lehi, Utah, Sept. 3, 1942; s. Merlyn R. and Verla Ann (Ball) W.; m. Kathleen Frandsen, Mar. 25, 1965 (div. Aug. 1984); children: Lisa Kathleen, Staci Lin, Eric Richard. BS, Brigham Young U., 1967; MBA, Northwestern U., 1968. Brand asst. packaged soap and detergent div. Procter & Gamble Co., Cin., 1968-69, asst. brand mgr. packaged soap and detergent div., 1970-71, brand mgr. Dawn detergent, 1972-73, copy supr. packaged soap and detergent div., 1974-75, brand mgr. Tide detergent, 1975-77, assoc. advt. mgr. packaged soap and detergent div., 1977-81; corp. product dir. Hallmark Cards, Inc., Kansas City, Mo., 1982-83, corp. product dir. Ambassador Cards div., 1983-85; v.p., gen. mgr. feminine protection div. Tambrands Inc., Lake Success, N.Y., 1986-88; pres. dairy/cheese div. Bongrain, Inc., N.Y.C., 1988—. Bd. dirs. L.I. Friends of the Arts, 1986—. Served with U.S. Army NG, 1960-67. Recipient scholarship Northwestern U., 1967-68; named An Outstanding Sr. Grad. Coll. Bus. Brigham Young U., 1967. Mem. Brigham Young U. Alumni Assn. (bd. dirs. 1984-85), Beta Gamma Sigma. Republican. Office: Bongrain Inc 32 Derby Rd Fort Washington NY 11050 also: Bongrain Inc 23 E 73d St New York NY 10021

WADLIN, MARTHA STEDMAN, social services administrator; b. Chgo., Jan. 21, 1937; d. John Stedman and Mary Jane (Laughlin) Denslow; m. Calvin H. Van O'Linda, June 1956 (dec. Sept. 1965); 1 child: Christopher Allen; m. James Edmund Wadlin, June 1976. Student, Northeast Mo. State U., 1959-60. Student wives advisor Kirksville (Mo.) Coll. Osteopathic Medicine, 1962-64; newswoman Sta. KTVO, Kirksville, 1967-68; sales rep. Leiter Designer Fabrics, Kansas City, Mo., 1969-71; office mgr. Ruby Green Seed House, Kirksville, 1971-72; coordinator, asst. dir. Northeast Mo. Comprehensive Health, Kirksville, 1972-74; asst. dir. Northeast Mo. Area Agy. on Aging, Kirksville, 1974-80, exec. dir., 1980—. Editor: (jour.) Leisure Activities for Mature Persons, 1974-80. Mem. Mo. Alliance of Area Agys. on Aging (pres. 1984, 85), Nat. Assn. Area Agys. on Aging (bd. dirs. 1985—, pvt. sector com., membership com.), Soc. Nonprofit Orgns. (charter), Mid-Am. Council on Aging (publicity com. 1978, 79), Nat. Council on Aging. Democrat. Episcopalian. Office: NE Mo Area Agy on Aging 705 E LaHarpe PO Box 1067 Kirksville MO 63501

WADMAN, WILLIAM WOOD, III, health physicist, consulting company executive, consultant; b. Oakland, Calif., Nov. 13, 1936; s. William Wood, Jr., and Lula Fae (Raisner) W.; M.A., U. Calif., Irvine, 1978; children—Roxanne Alyce Wadman Hubbing, Raymond Alan (dec.), Theresa Hope Wadman Foster; m. Barbara Jean Wadman; stepchildren: Denise Ellen Varine, Brian Ronald Varine. Radiation safety specialist, accelerator health physicist U. Calif. Lawrence Berkeley Lab., 1957-68; campus radiation safety officer U. Calif., Irvine, 1968-79; dir. ops., radiation safety officer Radiation Sterilizers, Inc., Tustin, Calif., 1979-80; prin., pres. Wm. Wadman & Assocs. Inc., 1980—; pres. Intracoastal Marine Enterprises Ltd., Martinez, Calif.; mem. team No. 1, health physics appraisal program NRC, 1980-81; cons. health physicist to industry; lectr. dept. community and environ. medicine U. Calif., Irvine, 1979-80, Orange Coast Coll. Active Cub Scouts; chief umpire Mission Viejo Little League, 1973. Served with USNR, 1955-63. Recipient award for profl. achievement U. Calif. Alumni Assn., 1972, Outstanding Performance award U. Calif., Irvine, 1973. Mem. Health Physics Soc. (treas. 1979-81, editor proc. 11th symposium, pres. So. Calif. chpt. 1977, Professionalism award 1975), Internat. Radiation Protection Assn. (U.S. del. 4th Congress 1977), Am. Nuclear Soc., Am. Public Health Assn. (chmn. program 1978, chmn. radiol. health sect. 1979-80), Campus Radiation Safety Officers (chmn. 1975, editor proc. 5th conf. 1975), ASTM. Club: UCI Univ. (dir. 1976, sec. 1977, treas. 1978). Contbr. articles to tech. jours. Home: 3687 Red Cedar Way Lake Oswego OR 97035 Office: 1000 E William St Suite 100 Carson City NV 89701

WAERN, JONAS CARL, former Swedish palace executive; b. Stockholm, July 23, 1915; s. Olof and Gerd Anna Sofia (Rehn) W.; m. Lissie Margrete Ehnstrom, Sept. 28, 1939; children—Stina, Olof, Peder, Lotta. Fil. Kand., U. Stockholm, 1976. Co brigade UN, Kongo, Zaire, 1961-62, Co. bn., Cyprus, 1964; a.d.c. to Swedish King, Royal Court, Stockholm, 1957-73, lord in waiting, 1974-86; gov. Gripsholm Castle and Stromsholm Palace, 1975-83; cons. Palace of Drottningholm, 1983-85. Author: Katanga, 1980; contbr. articles to profl. jours. Lodges: Rotary. Home: Damtorp, 170 11 Drottningholm Sweden

WAERN, YVONNE, psychologist, educator, researcher; b. Helsinki, Finland, July 21, 1935; d. Torbjörn Rosenblad and Nina Konstaninovna (Medvedjeff) Westren-Doll; m. Karl-Gustaf Waern, June 23, 1956; children: Annika, Nina-Helene. MS, U. Stockholm, 1957, PhD, 1964, 71. Lectr. U. Stockholm, 1957-71, researcher, 1971—, assoc. prof. psychology, 1976—. Author: Kunskap och Tankeprocesser, 1973, Tänkande Pågår, 1984, Cognitive Processes in Human Computer Interaction, 1988; contbr. articles to profl. jours. Mem. Am. Assn. Computing Machinery, Am. Ednl. Research Assn., Human Factors Soc., European Assn. for Research in Learning and Instrn., European Assn. Cognitive Ergonomics. Home: Skogsvagen 26, S-137 55 Vasterhaninge Sweden Office: U Stockholm Dept Psychology, S-106 91 Stockholm Sweden

WAERN-BUGGE, PEDER, management consulting company executive; b. Sundsvall, Sweden, Aug. 23, 1932; s. Thorild F.W. and Eivor (Ehlin) W.; m. Anita S.M. Persson, Dec. 1, 1934; children: Christian, Hans, Elisabet. MSc in Engring., Royal Inst. Tech., Stockholm, 1958; mktg. economist, Lulea Coll., Sweden, 1970. Research assoc. Royal Inst. Tech., Stockholm, 1958-60; project engr. ASSI, Piteå, Sweden, 1960-63, tech. dir., 1963-67, research mgr., 1967-77; corp. research dir. STORA, Falun, Sweden, 1977-83; cons., owner PWB Cons., Stockholm, 1983—; mem. research council Swedish Pulp and Paper Research Inst., Swedish Packaging Inst.; bd. dirs. Swedish Packaging Fedn. Served to 2d lt. Swedish Air Force, 1953-58. Mem. Swedish Pulp and Paper Engrs. Assn., Tech. Assn. Pulp and Paper Industry, Can. Pulp and Paper Assn. Lodge: Rotary (Piteå) (pres. 1973-74). Home: Vasterkroken 2, 18134 Lidingo Sweden Office: PWB Cons, Riddargatan 70, 11457 Stockholm Sweden

WAESELYNCK, FRANÇOIS, advertising executive; b. Dunkirk, France, Apr. 18, 1930; m. Monique Stoehr; 1 child, Antoine. Commd 2d lt. light inf. French Army, Baden-Baden, Fed. Republic Germany, 1950-52; market researcher Calor Household Equipment, Lyon, France, 1953-55, ORIC Market Research Inst., Paris, 1956-59; personnel mgr. Lever Factories, Lille, France and Algiers, Algeria, 1960-66; div. mgr. Unilever, Paris, 1967-69; with European tng. purchasing dept. Unilever, Hamburg, Fed. Republic Germany, London and Rotterdam, The Netherlands, 1970; media dir. Lintas Paris, 1971-75; chmn., chief exec. officer Initiative Media Paris, 1975—. Mem. Internat. Advt. Assn. Club: Cercle de l'Union Interalliée (Paris). Office: Initiative Media Paris, 21 rue Henri Rochefort, 75017 Paris France

WAGENER, KLAUS PAUL, physics educator; b. Halle/Saale, Ger., July 27, 1930; s. Ewald and Margarete (Ladendorf) W.; Ph.D., U. Goettingen, 1959, dipl. in physics, 1956; docent phys. chemistry Tech. U. Berlin, 1964; m. Gisela Jander, Aug. 31, 1957; children—Jens, Dirk, Silke, Ulf, Bjoern, Birte, Karen; m. Angela de Luca Rebello. Asst., U. Goettingen (Ger.), 1958; research asso. U. Zurich, 1959-61; dept. head Hahn-Meitner Inst. Nuclear Research, Berlin, 1964-67; asso. prof. U. Calif., La Jolla, 1966-67; prof. biophysics Tech. U. Aachen (W. Ger.), 1969—; dir. Inst. Phys. Chemistry, Nuclear Research Center, Juelich, Ger., 1968-78; active in sci. devel., Brazil, 1969; corr. faculty Pontificia Universidade Catolica, Rio de Janeiro, 1972. Contbr. articles to profl. jours.; editor Radiation and Environ. Biophysics, 1974. Home: Rua Dos Oitis 44, 22 453 Rio De Janeiro Brazil Office: PO Box 1913, 5170 Juelich Federal Republic of Germany

WAGENHALS, GERHARD, economist; b. Stuttgart, Germany, May 5, 1948; s. Paul and Lore (Sprandel) W.; m. Doris Lä pple, July 29, 1982. Diploma U. Tü bingen, 1976, Ph.D., 1980, Dr. rer. pol. habil. 1984. Dr. habilitatus, U. Heidelberg, 1976-80; vis. scholar U. Pa., Phila., 1980-82; asst. U. Heidelberg, 1982-88, Hochschuldozent, 1988—; privatdozent econs., 1984—. Author: Measurement of Inequality, 1981; The World Copper Market, 1984; contbr. articles to profl. jours. Mem. Econometric Soc., Am. Econ. Assn. Home: Silbershohl 18, D6901 Dossenheim Federal Republic of Germany Office: Univ Heidelberg, Grabengasse 14, D6900 Heidelberg Federal Republic of Germany

WAGGENER, RONALD EDGAR, radiologist; b. Green River, Wyo., Oct. 6, 1926; s. Edgar Fleetwood and Mary Harlene (Hutton) W.; m. Everina Ann Stalker, Aug. 1, 1948; children—Marta, Nancy, Paul, Daphne. Student, Colo. A&M U., 1944; student, Oreg. State U., 1945; B.S., U. Nebr., 1949, M.S., 1952, Ph.D., 1957, M.D. cum laude, 1954, postgrad., 1955-58; postgrad., St. Bartholomew's, London, 1956-57. Intern U. Nebr. Hosp., 1954-55, resident, 1955-56, 57-58; instr. radiology U. Nebr., Omaha, 1958, asst. prof., 1959-61, assoc. prof., 1962-80, clin. assoc. prof., 1981—; radiation therapist U. Nebr., 1959-65; radiation therapist Nebr. Meth. Hosp., Omaha, 1965-70, chmn. cancer com., 1964—, dir. cancer and radiation therapy, 1970—, dir. dept. radiology, 1977-81, dir. cancer fellowship program, 1977—; pres. Highland Assocs. Ltd., Omaha, 1960—, R.A. Enterprises, Inc., Omaha, 1960—; mem. cancer com. Children's Meml. Hosp., Omaha, 1970—. Contbr. articles to profl. jours. Served with C.E., U.S. Army, 1944-46. AEC fellow, 1952-53; Am. Cancer Soc. fellow, 1956-57. Fellow Am. Coll. Radiologists; mem. Midlands Soc. Therapeutic Radiology, (founder, pres. 1970-71), Nebr. Med. Assn., Am. Cancer Soc., Nebr. Radiology Soc. (pres. 1963-64), AMA, Am. Soc. Therapeutic Radiology, Radiol. Soc. N.Am., Faculty Radiologists Gt. Britain, Brit. Inst. Radiology, Am. Radium Soc., Soc. Nuclear Medicine, Am. Assn. Cancer Research, Thoroughbred Owners and Breeders Assn., Horsemen's Benevolent and Protective Assn., Sigma Xi, Alpha Omega Alpha, Phi Nu. Home: 1227 S 109th St Omaha NE 68144 Office: 8303 Dodge St Omaha NE 68114

WAGGONER, LELAND TATE, insurance company executive; b. Greensboro, Ga., Feb. 5, 1916; s. Andrew B. and Blanche (Proffitt) W.; m. Florence Adelaide Gee, Feb. 15, 1942; children: Frederick Charles, Leonora Blanche. AB, Maryville Coll., 1938; MBA with honors, NYU, 1972; CLU, 1941; LLD (hon.), Maryville Coll., 1987. Mgr. Mut. of N.Y., Boston, 1946-54; v.p. Western sect. Mut. of N.Y., San Francisco, 1954-57; v.p. sales Life Ins. Co. N.Am., Phila., 1957-63, Home Life Ins. Co., N.Y.C., 1963-69; sr. v.p., dir. Home Life Ins. Co., 1969-81; pres. Home Life Equity Sales Corp., 1970-81, Creative Mktg., Inc., 1981—; chmn. Va. Life Ins. Co. of N.Y., 1983—; exec. vis. prof. Ga. State U., 1981—; instr. Stanford Grad. Sch. Bus. Adminstrn., 1957; Past mem. bd. CLU Inst.; mem. agy. officers round table Life Ins. Mktg. and Research Assn.; life ins. pub. relations council Inst. Life Ins.; adv. bd. N.Y. State Ins. Dept.; past mem. agy. officers roundtable. Author: You Can See the World in Forty Days!; contbg. author: other booklets. Life Ins. Sales Mgmt. Handbook; Sr. editor: CLU Jour, 1946—; co-editor: The Life Insurance Policy Contract; cons. editor, contbg. author: Life and Health Insurance Handbook; interviewed for: Am. Coll.'s Oral History of Life Ins. Bd. dirs. and exec. com. Am. Bible Soc.; past bd. dirs. Maryville Coll., U. Tampa, Foster Parents Plan. Served to lt. comdr. USNR, 1942-45. Recipient Leland T. Waggoner distinguished lecture series in life and health ins. established at Ga. State U.; L. T. Waggoner room of Am. Colls. Grad. Center named for him.; N.J. Room of Am. Coll. Grad. Center named in his honor. Mem. Tenn Soc. Episcopalian. Clubs: Capital City (Atlanta); Baltusrol Golf. Lodge: Rotary. Home: 83 Slope Dr Short Hills NJ 07078 Office: 1120 Ave of the Americas New York NY 10036

WAGMAN, ROBERT JOHN, journalist; b. Chgo., Nov. 11, 1942; s. Albert Alan and Rosamond (Horner) W.; m. Carol Ann Mueller, Jan. 30, 1965; children: Jennifer, Robert, Patricia, Marilyn. A.B., St. Louis U., 1966, M.A., 1968, J.D., 1971. Analyst Dun & Bradstreet, 1965-67; with CBS News, 1967-71, 74-77; asst. to dean St. Louis U. Sch. Law, 1971-74; Washington bur. chief N.Am. Newspaper Alliance, 1977-80, Ind. News Alliance, 1980-82; columnist Newspaper Enterprise Assn., 1980—. Author: co-author: Hubert Humphrey, The Man and His Dream, 1978, Citizens Guide to the Tax Revolt, 1979, Asbestos: The Silent Killer, 1982, Lord's Justice, 1985, Instant Millionaires, 1986, The Nazi Hunters, 1988. Recipient Thomas Stokes award in journalism, 1977. Office: Suite 610 1110 Vermont Ave NW Washington DC 20005

WAGNER, ALAN BURTON, chemical company executive; b. Balt., June 8, 1938; s. Robert Ellsworth and Anna Margaret (Schnitzlein) W.; B.Engring. Sci. (scholastic leadership award) Johns Hopkins, 1960; M.M.E., Case-Western Res. U., 1962, Ph.D. in Bus. Mgmt., 1965; m. Lynn Felton Wynant, June 26, 1964; children—Brian Alan, David Scott, Elizabeth Lynn. Mgr. orgn. planning and devel. Internat. Minerals & Chem. Corp., Libertyville, Ill., 1964-67, dir. indsl. relations, 1967-70, v.p. div. orgn. and indsl. relations, 1970-73, corp. v.p. adminstrn., 1973-78; v.p. IMC Coal Corp., Lexington, Ky., 1977-79; pres., dir. Taylor Tot Products, Inc., Frankfort, Ky., 1979-80, Fed. Mining Co., 1980-82, Wagner Mgmt. Corp., 1982—; prin., dir. Hilliard-Lyons, Wagner Assoc., Ky. Metals, Inc., Carolina Metal, Inc., Fla. Metals, Inc.; dir. Crescent Industries Inc., So. Elkhorn Coal Corp.; lectr. in field. Trustee, Union Coll. Fellow Alfred P. Sloan Nat. Found.; mem. Chgo. Assn. Commerce and Industry, Chem. Industries Council of Midwest, ASME, Am. Mgmt. Assn., ASHRAE, (Homer Addams award), AAAS, Ky. Coal Assn. (dir.), Lexington C. of C., Sigma Xi, Omicron Delta Kappa. Clubs: Knollwood (Lake Forest, Ill); Greenbrier, Lafayette (Lexington). Home: 1523 Lakewood Ct Lexington KY 40502 Office: 110 W Vine St Lexington KY 40507

WAGNER, CARL ERNEST, physicist, manager; b. Berkeley Twp., N.J., July 10, 1940; s. Lawrence Frederick and Dorothy Estelle (Ayars) W.; m. Barbara Jean Carter, Apr. 8, 1979; children—Laura Christine, David Nicholas. S.B., MIT, 1961, Sc.D., 1970. Research and teaching asst. MIT, Cambridge, 1962-69; physicist U.S. Naval Research Lab., Washington, 1970-75; sr. scientist Sci. Applications, Inc., LaJolla, Calif., 1975-81, also cons.; chief physicist Inesco, Inc., La Jolla, 1981-84; sr. physicist TRW, Redondo Beach, Calif., 1984-87; prin. scientist Jaycor Inc., San Diego, 1987—; adj. prof. Calif. State U., Long Beach, 1986; cons. Energy Applications & Systems, Inc., Carlsbad, Calif., 1984. Contbr. articles to profl. jours. Alfred P. Sloan scholar MIT, 1957; U.S. Intercollegiate Chess Champion, 1967. Mem. Am. Phys. Soc., Am. Assn. Artificial Intelligence, Sigma Xi. Presbyterian.

WAGNER, DOROTHY MARIE, court reporting service executive; b. Milw., June 8, 1924; d. Theodore Anthony and Leona Helen (Ullrich) Wagner; grad. Milw. Bus. U., 1944; student Marquette U., U. Wis., Milw. Stenographer, legal sec., Milw., 1942-44; hearing reporter Wis. Workmen's Compensation Dept., 1944-48; ofcl. reporter to judge Circuit Ct., Milw., 1952-53; owner, operator ct. reporting service Dorothy M. Wagner & Assocs., Milw., 1948—; guest lectr. ct. reporting Madison Area Tech. Coll., 1981—. Recipient Gregg Diamond medal Gregg Pub. Co., 1950. Mem. Nat. (registered profl. reporter, certificate of proficiency), Wis. shorthand reporters assns., Am. Legion Aux., Met. Milw. Assn. Commerce. Roman Catholic. Home: 214 Williamsburg Dr Thiensville WI 53092 Office: 135 Wells St Suite 400 Milwaukee WI 53203

WAGNER, GUSTAV ALFRED, retired medical educator; b. Hannover, Fed. Republic of Germany, Jan. 10, 1918; s. Gustav and Anna Wagner; m. Inge Winiarz, Dec. 6, 1941; 1 child, Klaus-Dieter. MD, U. Berlin, 1944. Resident physician Mcpl. Dermatol. Hosp., Hannover, 1946-51; asst. prof. U. Dermatol. Hosp., Kiel, Fed. Republic of Germany, 1951-64; prof. medicine German Cancer Research Ctr., Heidelberg, Fed. Republic of Germany, 1964-86. Author/editor over 50 books and 300 jours. articles. Recipient Ernst von Bergmann medal Chamber German Physicians, 1980. Mem. numerous profl. orgns. Lodge: Lions. Home: Blutenweg 64, 6905 Schriesheim Baden Wurtt Federal Republic of Germany Office: German Cancer Research Ctr, Im Neuenheimer Feld 280, 6900 Heidelberg, Baden Wurtt Federal Republic of Germany

WAGNER, HELMUT ERWIN, business adminstration educator; b. Augsburg, Fed. Republic Germany, Feb. 7, 1936; s. Erwin F. and Therese (Zott) W.; m. Christa Stocks, Oct. 10, 1964; 1 child, Isabell. Diploma, U. Munich, 1959; DBA, U. Muenster, 1964, Habilitation, 1970. Asst. prof. U. Munich, 1959-60; faculty assoc. Harvard U., 1960-61; asst. prof. U. Muenster, 1962-66, U. Mannheim, 1966-70; docent U. Erlangen, Nuernberg, 1970-71; prof. U. Muenster, 1971—; dean U. Muenster, 1979-79 (pres. of convent 1976-78, prorector 1986—). Author: several books and articles in field. Lodge: Lions (pres. 1978-80). Office: Univ Muenster, Am Stadtgraben 13-15, D 4400 Muenster Federal Republic of Germany

WAGNER, JOCHEN BERNHARD, private investigator; b. Mainz, Fed. Republic Germany, Apr. 18, 1950; s. Jakob R. and Anna Maria (Blum) W.; m. Rosi M. Vetter, 1978. JD, Johannes-Gutenberg U., Mainz, 1976. Pres. Detektei Blum GmbH, Mainz, Detekta-Detektiv GmbH, Munich. Office: Detektei Blum GmbH, Kaiserstr 88, D 6500 Mainz 1 Federal Republic of Germany

WAGNER, JOSEPH CRIDER, ret. univ. adminstr.; b. North Manchester, Ind., Feb. 19, 1907; s. Arthur Augustus and Grace (Crider) W.; A.B., Manchester Coll., 1929, LL.D., 1961; M.A. in Econs., U. Mich., 1936; postgrad. U. Wis., 1930, U. Chgo., 1931-32, Columbia, 1935; m. Geraldine B. Garber, June 30, 1933; 1 dau., Joene Henning. Tchr. Hartford City (Ind.) High Schs., 1929-35, prin., 1936-37, supt. schs., 1937-45; supt. schs., Crawfordsville, Ind., 1946; bus. mgr., treas. Ball State U., Muncie, Ind., 1946-61, v.p. for bus. affairs, 1961-73, v.p. emeritus, 1973—, treas., prof., gen. bus. adminstrn.; lectr. Mem. Ind. Common Sch. Bldg. Commn., 1960—. Active United Fund of Delaware County. Trustee Ind. Heart Found., Manchester Coll.; mem. ins. trust of Am. Assn. Ret. Persons and Nat. Ret. Tchrs. Assn.; bd. dirs. Muncie YMCA, Ind. State Tchrs. Retirement Fund. Mem. gen. bd. edn., nat. cons. in fin. Methodist Ch. in U.S. Mem. Ind. Schoolmen's Club (pres. 1949), Ind. State Tchrs. Retirement Fund (bd. trustees 1975, pres. 1987-88), Internat. Platform Assn., Am. Assn. Ret. Persons (ins. trust), Tau Kappa Alpha, Delta Pi Epsilon, Phi Delta Kappa, Sigma Alpha Epsilon. Mason, Rotarian (past pres.). Contbr. articles to profl. and religious jours. Home: 629 Forest Ave Muncie IN 47304 Office: Ball State U 2000 University Ave Muncie IN 47303

WAGNER, JUDITH BUCK, investment advisory firm executive, banker; b. Altoona, Pa. Sept. 25, 1943; d. Harry Bud and Mary Elizabeth (Rhodes) B.; m. Mark S. Foster, June 17, 1967 (div. 1977); m. Joseph E. Wagner, Mar. 15, 1980; 1 child, Elizabeth. BA in History, U. Wash., 1965; grad. N.Y. Inst. Fin., 1968. Chartered fin. analyst; registered Am. Stock Exchange; registered N.Y. Stock Exchange; registered investment advisor. Security analyst Morgan, Olmstead, Kennedy & Gardner, Los Angeles, 1968-71; research cons., St. Louis, 1971-72; security analyst Boettcher & Co., Denver, 1972-75; pres. Wagner Investment Counsel, 1975-84; chmn. Wagner & Hamil, Inc., Denver, 1983—; chmn., bd. dirs. The Women's Bank, N.A., Denver, 1977—, organizational group pres., 1975-77; chmn. Equitable Bankshares Colo., Inc., Denver, 1980—; bd. dirs. Equitable Bank of Littleton, 1983—, pres., 1985; bd. dirs. Colo. Growth Capital, 1979-82; lectr. Denver U., Metro State, 1975-80. Author: Woman and Money series Colo. Woman Mag., 1976; moderator 'Catch 2' Sta. KWGN-TV, 1978-79. Pres. Big Sisters Colo., Denver, 1977-82, bd. dirs., 1973—; bd. fellows U. Denver, 1985—; bd. dirs. Red Cross, 1980, Assn. Children's Hosp., 1985, Colo. Health Facilities Authority, 1978-84, Jr. League Community Adv. Com., 1979—, Brother's Redevel., Inc., 1979-80; mem. Hist. Paramount Found., 1984, Denver Pub. Sch. Career Edn. Project, 1972; mem. investment com. YWCA, 1976—; mem. adv. com. Girl Scouts U.s.; mem. agy. relations com. Mile High United Way, 1978-81, chmn. United Way Venture Grant com., 1980-81; fin. chmn. Schoettler for State Treas., 1986; bd. dirs. Downtown Denver Inc., 1988—. Recipient Making It award Cosmopolitan Mag., 1977, Women on the Go award, Savvy mag., 1983, Minouri Yasoni award, 1986, Salute Spl. Honoree award, Big Sisters, 1987; named one of the Outstanding Young Women in Am., 1979; recipient Woman Who Makes A Difference award Internat. Women's Forum, 1987. Fellow Fin. Analysts Fedn.; mem. Women's Forum of Colo. (pres. 1979), Women's Found. Colo., Inc. (bd. dirs. 1986—), Denver Soc. Security Analysts (bd. dirs. 1976—, v.p. 1980-81, pres. 1981-82), Leadership Denver (Outstanding Alumna award 1987), Pi Beta Phi (pres. U. Wash. chpt. 1964-65). Office: Wagner & Hamil Inc 410 17th St #840 Denver CO 80202

WAGNER, JULIA A(NNE), retired editor; b. Alexandria, Va., Feb. 15, 1924; d. Luigi and Domenica (Di Giammarino) Coppa; Widowed. B.A., George Washington U., 1948, M.A., 1950. With U.S. Govt., Washington, 1941-55, publs. editor, 1951-55; editorial asst. Dell Pub. Co., N.Y.C., 1956-59, mng. editor, 1959-72, editor-in-chief, 1973-87. Mem. Am. Fedn. Astrologers. Democrat. Roman Catholic.

WAGNER, LOUISE HEMINGWAY BENTON, educational company executive; b. Chgo., July 29, 1937; d. William and Helen (Hemingway) Benton; student Skidmore Coll., 1955-57; B.A. in English, Finch Coll., 1960; m. Ralph C. Wagner, May 23, 1979. Pub. relations asst. Look mag., N.Y.C., 1960-62, Compton Ency., Chgo., 1962-63; mktg. services Ency. Brit. Press, Chgo., 1963-66; dir. exhibits Ency. Brit. Ednl. Corp., Chgo., 1966-70, v.p. mktg. services, 1970-83, chmn. bd. dirs., 1983-87, vice chmn. 1988—. Bd. dirs. Chgo. Lying-In Hosp., Cradle Soc., Evanston, Ill., Reading is Fundamental, Chgo.; mem. women's bd. U. Chgo.; governing mem. Orchestral Assn. Chgo., Art Inst. Chgo. Mem. ALA, Assn. for Edn. Communication Tech. Episcopalian. Clubs: Racquet, Mid-Am., Arts (Chgo.); Country of Fairfield (Conn.); Thorngate Country (Deerfield, Ill.). Office: Ency Brit Edn Corp 310 S Michigan Ave Chicago IL 60604

WAGNER, PAUL ALEXANDER, III, communications company executive; b. Poughkeepsie, N.Y., June 21, 1946; s. Paul and Paula E. (Shaw) W.; m. Helga Katarina Maurer, June 22, 1974. B.A., Columbia U., 1968; M.A., NYU, 1971. Editor publs. Western Electric Co., N.Y.C., 1969-73; instr. NYU, N.Y.C., 1972-73; dir. corp. planning Edison Electric Inst., N.Y.C., 1973-78; dir. pub. affairs Continental Forest Industries, Greenwich, Conn., 1979-80; mgr. corp. affairs Am. Broadcasting Cos., Inc., N.Y.C., 1980-83; dir. pub. relations CBS Fox Video, N.Y.C., 1984-87; v.p. pub. affairs Orion pictures Corp., 1987—; cons. in field. Mem. bus. adv. council White House Conf. on Aging, 1981. Served with U.S. Mcht. Marine, 1969. Columbia Pres.' scholar, 1967; J.W. Hill Found. fellow, 1970-76. Mem. Pub. Relations Soc. Am. (chmn. edn. com. 1976-77), MLA, Mensa, Nat. Captioning Inst. (corp. adv. council 1985—), Acad. Home Video Arts and Scis. (bd. govs. 1985—). Episcopalian. Club: Princeton (N.Y.C.). Avocations: yacht racing; squash. Home: 2H Weavers Hill Greenwich CT 06830 Office: Orion Pictures 540 Madison Ave New York NY 10022

WAGNER, PAUL ANTHONY, JR., educator; b. Pitts., Aug. 28, 1947; s. Paul A. and Mary K. Wagner; children: Nicole S., Eric P., Jason G. BS, NE Mo. State U., 1969; EdM, U. Mo., 1972, MA in Philosophy, 1976, PhD in Philosophy of Edn., 1978. Internal expeditor electromotive div. Gen. Motors, La Grange, Ill., 1970-71; instr. Moberly (Mo.) Jr. Coll., 1972-73, U. Mo., Columbia, 1973-78, Mo. Mil. Acad., 1978-79; prof. edn. and philosophy U. Houston-Clear Lake 1979—, prof., dir. Inst. Logical and Cognitive Studies, 1982—; dir. Tex. Ctr. for Study Profl. Ethics in Teaching, 1988—; research assoc. Ctr. for Moral Devel., Harvard U., 1985-86; vis. scholar Stanford U., Palo Alto, Calif., 1981; cons. to various sch. dists., 1979—. Contbr. articles on sci. edn. and philosophy of edn. to profl. jours. Mem. editorial bd. Jour. of Thought, 1981—, Focus on Learning, 1982-85; editorial cons. Instrnl. Scis., 1981-83. Editorial assoc. Brain and Behavioral Scis., 1986—. Mem. Human Rights Commn., Columbia, Mo., 1976-79, vice chmn., 1978-79; Sunday sch. tchr. Mary Queen Cath. Ch., Friendswood, Tex., 1979—. Served as sgt. Mo. N.G., 1970-76. Recipient Cert. of Appreciation, City of Columbia, Mo., 1978; named Atrium Circle disting. research prof., 1982, Chancellor's disting. service prof.; K.E. Graessle scholar, 1968; Mo. Peace Studies Inst. grantee, 1977. Mem. Am. Philos. Assn., Assn. Philosophers in Edn. (exec. bd., bd. dirs.), Philosophy of Edn. Soc., Am. Ednl. Studies Assn., Brit. Soc. for Philosophy of Sci., Philosophy of Sci. Assn., S.W. Philosophy of Edn. Soc., Tex. Ednl. Founds. Soc., Tex. Network for Tchr. Tng. in Philosophy for Children (bd. dirs.), Tex. Ctr. for Ethics in Edn. (bd. dirs. 1988—), S.W. Assn. Educators of Tchrs. of Sci., Correctional Edn. Assn., Tex. Ednl. Found. Soc. (pres. 1986—), Tex. Assn. Coll. Tchrs., Informal Logic Assn., Phi Delta Kappa, Kappa Delta Pi. Roman Catholic. Club: Clearlake Circle (Houston, chair 1979-85) Avocations: running, racquetball, reading, opera, ballet. Office: U Houston 2700 Bay Area Blvd PO Box 338 Houston TX 77058 also: Harvard U 312 Larsen Hall Appian Way Cambridge MA 02138

WAGNER, RICHARD, baseball club executive; b. Central City, Nebr., Oct. 19, 1927; s. John Howard and Esther Marie (Wolken) W.; m. Gloria Jean Larsen, May 10, 1950; children—Randolph G., Cynthia Kaye. Student, pub. schs., Central City. Gen. mgr. Lincoln Baseball Club, Nebr., 1955-58; mgr. Pershing Mcpl. Auditorium, Lincoln, 1958-61; exec. staff Ice Capades, Inc., Hollywood, Calif., 1961-63; gen. mgr. Sta. KSAL, Salina, Kans., 1963-65; dir. promotion and sales St. Louis Nat. Baseball Club, 1965-66; gen. mgr. Forum, Inglewood, Calif., 1966-67; asst. to exec. v.p. Cin. Reds, 1967-70, asst. to pres., 1970-74, v.p. adminstrn., 1975, exec. v.p., 1975-78, gen. mgr., 1977-83, pres., 1978-83; pres. Houston Astros Baseball Club, 1985-87; spl. asst. Office of Baseball Commr., 1988—; pres. RGW Enterprises, Inc., Phoenix, 1978—. Served with USNR, 1945-47, 50-52. Named Exec. of Yr., Minor League Baseball, Sporting News, 1958. Mem. Internat. Assn. Auditorium Mgrs. Republican. Methodist.

WAGNER, SAMUEL ALBIN MAR, records management executive, educator; b. Brighton, Colo., Feb. 23, 1942; s. Jacob Doer and Leota Garnet (Wilson) W.; m. Donna Dee Person, Mar. 20, 1987; children: Andrea, Kurt, Autumn, Jan, Arthur. BA in History, U. Colo., 1964, MA in History, 1965; STB (MTS) in History of World Religions, Harvard U., 1968. Cert. records mgr. Sr. asst. archivist Cornell U., Ithaca, N.Y., 1971-73; editor Brighton Blade Ft. Lupton Press, Brighton and Ft. Lupton, Colo., 1973-77; city archivist City of Providence, 1978-80; state records analyst Wyo. State Archives, Cheyenne, 1979-83; records mgr. Ft. Collins (Colo.) Police Dept., 1984-87; pres. Records Mgmt. Cons., Ft. Collins, 1985—; pub. records adminstr. State R.I., Providence, 1987—; bd. dirs. Records Inc., Cheyenne; instr. Chapman Coll., Cheyenne, 1981-87, Colo. State U., 1985-87. Author: Brighton Reflections: Bicentennial Years, 1976, Adams County: Crossroads of the West, 1977, Directory of Automated Records Management Systems, 1987, Crossroads of the West: A History of Brighton and the Platte Valley, 1987; editor: The Fort Lupton Story, 1976; contbr. numerous articles to profl. jours. county historian Adams County, Brighton, 1976-77; mem. Brighton Human Relations Commn., 1977-78; bd. dirs. Brighton Bicentennial Com., 1975-76, Brighton Centennial Com., 1986-87, R.I. Pub. Records Adv. Council, 1987—, R.I. Hist. Records Adv. Bd, 1987—. Recipient Hist. Preservation award Adams County Hist. Soc., 1978; Ethnic Heritage Project grantee Colo. Humanities Council, 1977; Ford Found. fellow, 1964. Mem. Microcomputer/PC Industry Action Com. (chmn. 1984-86, editor Software Dir. 1985—, Dir. Automated Records Systems 1986—), Assn. Records Mgr. Adminstrs. (pres. No. Colo. chpt. 1984-85, v.p. ocean state chpt. 1987—, chmn. various coms., Mem. of Yr. 1985), Inst. Cert. Records Mgrs. (regional coordinator, exam proctor 1982—), Soc. Am. Archivists, Assn. Info. and Image Mgmt., Nat. Assn. Govt. Archives and Records Adminstrs. Democrat. Unitarian. Home: 18 Ogden St Providence RI 02906 Office: Pub Records Adminstrn 83 Park St Providence RI 02903 Home: 231 Hobbs Ave Cheyenne WY 82009

WAGNER, THOMAS ALFRED, chemical engineer; b. Noerdlingen, Fed. Republic Germany, May 31, 1953; s. Alfred and Agnes (Guenther) W. Diploma in engring., FH Aalen, Fed. Republic Germany, 1979. Process engr. Siemens AG, Munich, 1979-82, process engr. dry etching, 1982-86, mgr. process engring. and dry etching, 1986—, cons. of computeruse and integration in the dept., 1988—. Home: Hermanstr 19, D8900 Augsburg Federal Republic of Germany Office: Siemens AG, ZFA PTE 133, Otto Hahn Ring 6, D8000 Munich 83, Federal Republic of Germany

WAGNER TIZON, ALLAN, former minister of foreign relations of Peru; b. Lima, Peru, Feb. 7, 1942. Grad., Universidad Católica del Perú, Universidad Nacoinal Mayor de San Marcos de Lima; postgrad. Academia Diplomatica del Perú. Held numerous internat. diplomatic positions and various positions in Ministry of Fgn. Relations, to 1985, Minister of Fgn. Relations, 1985—; prof. Academia Diplomática del Perú . Decorated Orden Al Mé rito por Servicios Distinguidos de la Repú blica del Perú ; Orden Francisco de Miranda de la República de Venezuela; Orden Cruzeiro do Sul de la Repú blica Rederativa del Brasil; Orden al Mérito de la República Argentina. Office: Ministerio de, Relaciones Exteriores, Lima 1 Peru *

WAGONER, DAVID EVERETT, lawyer; b. Pottstown, Pa., May 16, 1928; s. Claude Brower and Mary Kathryn (Groff) W.; children—Paul R., Colin H., Elon D., Peter B. B.A., Yale U., 1950; LL.B., U. Pa., 1953. Bar: D.C. 1953, Pa. 1953, Wash. 1953. Law clk. U.S. Ct. Appeals (3d cir.), Pa., 1955-56; law clk. U.S. Supreme Ct., Washington, 1956-57; ptnr. Perkins & Coie, Seattle, 1957—. Mem. sch. com. Mcpl. League Seattle and King County, 1958—, chmn., 1962-65; mem. Seattle schs. citizens coms. on equal ednl. opportunity and adult vocat. edn., 1963-64; mem. Nat. Com. Support Pub. Schs.; mem. adv. com. on community colls., to 1965, legislature interim com. on edn., 1964-65; mem. community coll. adv. com. to state supt. pub. instrn., 1965; chmn. edn. com. Forward Thrust, 1968; mem. Univ. Congl. Ch. Council Seattle, 1968-70; bd. dirs. Met. YMCA Seattle, 1968; bd. dirs. Seattle Pub. Schs., 1965-73, v.p., 1966-67, 72-73, pres., 1968, 73; trustee Evergreen State Coll. Found., chmn. 1986; trustee Pacific NW Ballet, v.p. 1986. Served to 1st lt. M.C., AUS, 1953-55. Fellow Am. Coll. Trial Lawyers; mem. English Speaking Union (v.p. Seattle 1961-62), ABA (chmn. appellate advocacy com.), Wash. State Bar Assn., Seattle-King County Bar Assn., Nat. Sch. Bds. Assn. (bd. dirs., chmn. Council Big City Bds. Edn. 1971-72), Chi Phi. Office: Perkins and Coie 1201 Third Ave 40th Floor Seattle WA 98101-3099 Office: Perkins and Coie Washington Bldg Seattle WA 98101

WAGSHAL, JEROME STANLEY, lawyer, philatelic consultant; b. Washington, June 20, 1928; s. Philip and May (Wolf) W. BA with distinction, George Washington U., 1950; LLB, Yale U., 1953. Bar: U.S. Dist. Ct. D.C. 1953, U.S. Ct. Appeals (D.C. cir.) 1953, U.S. Supreme Ct. 1958, N.Y. 1970. Instr. U.S. Naval Sch. of Naval Justice, 1953-57; trial atty. Dept. of Justice Antitrust Div., 1957-68; v.p., gen. counsel Ecol. Sci. Corp., 1968-69; ptnr. Dickstein, Shapiro & Galigan and successor firms, 1970-73; founding ptnr. Pearce & Wagshal, Washington, 1973-75; sole practice, Washington, 1975. Contbr. articles to legal and philatelic jours. past v.p. Georgetown Citizens Assn. Served to lt., USNR, 1953-57. Recipient Ashbrook Cup, 1970, Chase Cup, 1987, Neinken award, 1987, U.S. Philatelic Classics Soc., Schreiber Cup, Am. Philatelic Soc., 1970. Mem. ABA, D.C. Bar, Order of Coif, Phi Beta Kappa, Omicron Delta Kappa, Pi Gamma Mu, Phi Eta Sigma, Delta Sigma Rho. Clubs: Yale (N.Y.C.); City Tavern (Washington). Office: 3256 N St NW Washington DC 20007

WAGSTAFF, ROBERT HALL, lawyer; b. Kansas City, Mo., Nov. 5, 1941; s. Robert Wilson and Katherine Motter (Hall) W. A.B., Dartmouth Coll., 1963; J.D., U. Kans., 1966. Bar: Kans., Alaska, U.S. Ct. Appeals (9th cir.), U.S. Supreme Ct. Asst. atty. gen. State of Kans., 1966-67; asst. dist. atty. Fairbanks (Alaska), 1967-69; ptnr. Boyko & Walton, Anchorage, 1969-70; sr. ptnr. Wagstaff et. al., Anchorage, 1970—. Pres. U.S. Aerobatic Found., Oshkosh, Wis., 1986—. Mem. Alaska Bar Assn. (bd. govs. 1985—, pres. 1987-88), Lawyer-Pilots Bar Assn. (regional v.p.), ACLU (nat. bd. dirs. 1972-78). Office: 912 W 6th Ave Anchorage AK 99501-2024

WAGSTAFF, ROBERT WILSON, bottling company executive; b. Independence, Kans., Nov. 16, 1909; s. Thomas E. and Jane M. (Wilson) W.; m. Katherine Hall, Nov. 28, 1936; children—Katherine Tinsman, Robert Hall, Thomas Walton. A.B., Kans. U., 1930; LL.B., Harvard, 1933. Atty. Sinclair Refining Co., Kansas City, Mo., 1935-45; gen. counsel, later vice chmn., chief exec. officer Vendo Co., Kansas City, Mo., 1947-61; pres. Coca-Cola Bottling Co. Mid-Am., Inc., Shawnee Mission, Kans., 1961-77; chmn. Coca-Cola Bottling Co. Mid-Am., Inc., 1961-88; pres. Mid-Am. Container Corp., Lenexa, 1969-77, chmn., 1977-88; chmn. bd. Fed. Res. Bank Kansas City, Mo., 1970-74; dir. chmn. Kans. Nat. Bank and Trust Co.; dir. Am. Royal, pres., 1981-82; dir. Los Angeles Coca-Cola Bottling Co. Bd. dirs. Kansas City Crime Commn., Am. Royal; pres. St. Luke's Hosp., Kansas City, Mo., 1965-79, now vice chmn.; trustee Kans. Public Employee Retirement System, 1975-79; chancellor Episcopal Diocese W. Mo., 1956-71. Office: care Kans Nat Bank 4200 W 83d St Prairie Village KS 66208

WAHBA, AMAL SAAD, construction company executive; b. Cairo, Dec. 18, 1940; s. Saad Wahba Wassef and Afifa (Zaki Abd-El-Messieh); m. Ismail Hassan Fahmy, Mar. 27, 1969; 1 child, Tarek Ismail Fahmy. BArch with distinction, Cairo U., 1962. Designer Devel. and Popular Housing Co., Cairo, 1962-69, first designer, sect. head, dept. head, 1976—; archtl. designer Bur. D'Etudes Techniques, Alger, Algeria, 1969-76. Prin. works include: Supreme Ct. Bldg., Guiza, Egypt, Egyptian-Kuwait housing complex, 1987, El Manasterly Housing Complex, 1984. Home: 2 Okasha, Dokki Guiza Arab Republic of Egypt Office: Devel and Popular Housing Co. 4 Latin America, Cairo Arab Republic of Egypt

WAHBA, NAZMI KAMEL, economic analyst, accountant, consultant; b. Qaliub, Qaliubeia, Egypt, Feb. 16, 1943; s. Kamel Wahba and Galila Girgis (Sorial) Tadros. B.Sc. in Commerce, Faculty of Commerce, Cairo, 1964, M.A. in Econ. Acctg., 1974, Ph.D. in Econ. Acctg., 1986. Auditor, Central Orgn. of Acctg., Cairo, 1965-75, head econ. plan sect., 1979—; lectr. U. Mousol, Iraq, 1976-78; acctg. cons. several pvt. orgns., Cairo, 1978—. Author: Economic Policies, 1982, also several reports. Mem. Syndicate of Accts., Auditors and Economists, Am. Econ. Assn. Coptic Orthodox. Home: Yehia St Number 8, Qaliub Elbalad Arab Republic of Egypt Office: Central Orgn of Acctg, Madinat Nasr, Cairo Arab Republic of Egypt

WAHI, PURSHOTTAM LAL, cardiologist; b. Sargodha, Punjab, India, Dec. 4, 1928; s. Sh. Bindra Ban Wahi and Devki Devi; m. Pushpa, Nov. 26, 1958; 2 children. MBBS, Punjab U., 1951, MD, 1956. Asst. registrar Med. Coll. Amritsar, Punjab, India, 1956-57; registrar medicine Med. Coll. Amritsar, Patiala, India, 1957-60; asst. prof. medicine Med. Coll. Amritsar, Amritsr, Punjab, India, 1960-62; asst. prof. medicine Postgrad. Inst. Med. Edn. and Research, Chandigarh, India, 1962-64, assoc. prof., 1964-68, prof, sr. cardiologist, 1968-73, prof., head dept. cardiology, 1973—, sub dean, 1980-83, dean, 1983-85, dir., 1985—; mem. expert adv. panel cardiovascular diseases WHO, 1981—; dean faculty med. scis. Punjab U., 1986—; mem. planning and monitoring bd., 1986; mem. Punjab State Council Sci. and Tech.; mem. Sci. and Tech. Council U. Tech. Chandigarh; mem. Inst. Body, Sanjay Gandhi Postgrad.; mem. Inst. Med. Scis., Lucknow; mem. governing council Northeastern Indira Gandhi; mem. Regional Inst. Health and Med. Scis., Shillong, 1987; mem. acad. planning bd., Kurukeshetr U., 1987—; mem. bd. studies in medicine Guru Nanak Dev. U., Amritsar, 1986-88. Contbr. articles to med. jours. Mem. governing body Chittarangan Nat. Cancer Inst., Calcutta. U.S. AID fellow U. Va., Johns Hopkins Med. Ctr., Nat. Heart Inst., Royal Postgrad. Med. Sch., London, Hammersmith Hosp., 1965; recipient Amalnanda Das Gold medal, 1976, Padma Shri, 1983, Glaxo Oration Nat. Acad. Med. Scis., 1985, award Amrut Mody Research Found., 1985, B.C. Roy Nat award, 1986. Fellow Internat. Coll. Nutrition (chmn. cardiovascular council 1986-87), Coll. Chest Physicians, Am. Coll. Cardiology, Acad. Med. Scis.; mem. Internat. Soc. and Fedn. Cardiology Working Group Pulmonary Hypertension, Council Cardiac Metabolism, Cardiology Soc. India (v.p. 1967-82, 86-87), Council Nat. Acad. Med. Scis. (mem. council 1986—). Club: Postgrad. Inst. of Med. Edn. and Research. Home: House No 37, Sector 4, Chandigarh 160012, India Office: Postgrad Inst Med Edn and Research, 160012 Chandigarh India

WAHL, JACQUES HENRI, banking executive; b. Lille, France, Jan. 18, 1932; s. Abraham M. and Simone (Kornbluth) W.; m. Inna Cytrin, Mar. 1, 1945; children: Alexandre, Muriel, Cedric. Law student, U. Lille, 1952; economics student, U. Paris, 1953-56; polit. sci. student, Inst. d'etudes politiques, Paris, 1954; pub. adminstrn. student, Ecole Nationale d'Administral, Paris, 1956-61. Inspecteur de Finances Ministry of Fin. Treas. Dept., Paris, 1961-65, spl. asst. to ministers of economy and fin., 1965-68; asst. sec. Treas. Dept. Paris, 1971-73; exec. dir. IMF-IBRD and fin. minister French Embassy, Washington, 1973-78; sec. gen. of presidency French Republic,

1978-81, inspector gen. fin., 1981; pres., chief. operating officer Banque Nationale de Paris, Paris, 1982; chmn. bd. Banque Nationale de Paris, Luxembourg, 1983; chmn. bd. dirs. French Am. Banking Corp., N.Y.C., 1983. Decorated Chevalier de la Legion d' Honneur, Officier de l' Ordre Nat. du Méite.

WAHL, JAMES E., consultant; b. Regina, Sask., Can., Aug. 22, 1953; s. George J. and Irene (Laturnus) W.; m. Heather MacLean. BSc in Microbiology, U. Calgary (Can.), 1976; MBA, U. Western Ont. (London), 1982. Technologist Petro Can., Calgary, Alta., 1977-80; pres. Ithacan Mgmt. Cons., Ltd., Calgary, 1982-86; prin. Wahl and Assocs., Calgary, 1986—; dir., sr. officer Morningside Resources, Ltd., Calgary, 1986—. Home: 711 33A St NW, Calgary, AB Canada T2N 2X2

WAHL, PAUL, publisher, author; b. Union City, N.J., Jan. 17, 1922; s. Frank Joseph and Anne (Frechen) W. Grad. high sch., Bogota, N.J. Acct. Am. Cyanamid Co., N.Y.C., 1943-44, Wright Aero. Corp., Paterson, N.J., 1944-46; ptnr. Wahl Arms Co., Bogota, N.J., 1948-68; propr. Wahl Co., Bogota, N.J., 1962-68; ptnr. Frank J. Wahl Co., Bogota, N.J., 1969—; pres. Paul Wahl Corp., Bogota, N.J., 1986—. Author: Gun Traders Guide, 1953-78, Arms Trade Yearbook, 1955, 56, Single Lens Reflex Guide, 1959, Subminiature Technique, 1960, Press/View Camera Technique, 1962, The Candid Photographer, 1963, Carbine Handbook, 1964, (with D.R. Toppel) The Gatling Gun, 1965, New Carbine Handbook, 1988, Gatling, 1988, Big Gun Catalog, 1988; cons. editor Popular Sci. mag., 1976-80; contbr. feature articles to other major nat. mags.; designer Gatling Gun Centennial medal, 1961, Grant and Lee Commemorative medals, 1962. Mem. Nat. Assn. Sci. Writers, Authors League Am., Am. Soc. Mag. Photographers, Authors Guild, Aviation/Space Writers Assn., Nat. Writers Union, Am. Def. Preparedness Assn., Nat. Rifle Assn., Am. Med. Writers Assn., Soc. Photographic Scientists and Engrs., Internat. Motor Press Assn. Club: Nat. Press. Office: Paul Wahl Corp PO Box 500 Bogota NJ 07603-0500

WAHLBERG, KARL-ERIK HILDING, psychology educator; b. Tornio, Finland, Mar. 3, 1949; s. Hugo Hilding and Anne Alise (Numminen) W.; m. Leena Maija Paronen, Aug. 4, 1973; children: Anne-Marie Charlotta, Thomas Erik. MA, U. Turku, Finland, 1978, PhD, 1983. Research asst. U. Turku, 1976-78; psychologist U. Hosp. Oulu, Finland, 1978-82, lectr. psychology, 1982—; supr. family therapy Child Guidance Clinic, Raahe, Finland, 1982—, Oulu, 1984—; trainer family therapy Mental Health Orgn. Finland, 1983-86, U. Oulu, 1986—, U. Lappland, Tornio, 1986—. Contbr. articles to profl. jours. Served to ensign Finnish infantry, 1969-70. Recipient Alma and K.A. Snellman Found. award, 1984, Emil Aaltonen Found. award, 1984, 86, Oulu Found. award, 1986, U. of Oulu award, 1986; named Leading Psychologist Finnish Adoptive Mem. Family Study. Mem. Family Therapy Assn., Finnish Psychol. Soc. Lutheran. Home: Rajapyykintie 12, SF-90650 Oulu Finland Office: U Oulu, Dept Psychiatry, SF-90270 Oulu Finland

WAHLER, PETER, science educator; b. Schweinfurt, Fed. Republic of Germany, Apr. 11, 1947; s. Michael and Love Wahler. Diploma in Sociology, U. Munich, 1973. Lectr. youth tng. programs various orgns., Bavaria, Fed. Republic of Germany, 1973-74; sci. lectr. Deutschen Jugendinst Inst., Munich, 1974—. Contbr. articles to profl. jours. Mem. German Soc. Sociology (Family and Youth sect.). Office: German Youth Inst, Freibadstr 30, 8000 Munich #90 Federal Republic of Germany

WAHLGREN, ERIK, emeritus foreign language educator; b. Chgo., Nov. 2, 1911; s. Oscar G. and Marion I. (Wilkins) W.; m. Dorothy Sly, Nov. 9, 1939 (div. 1951); children: Nils, Arvid; m. Beverly Pont, Dec. 18, 1952 (div. 1969); children: Siri Wahlgren Grochowski, Thor; m. Helen Gilchrist-Wottring, July 2, 1971; 2 stepchildren. Ph.B., U. Chgo., 1933, Ph.D., 1938; M.A., U. Neb., 1936. Mem. faculty UCLA, 1938—, prof. Scandinavian langs., 1955-70, prof. Scandinavian and Germanic langs., 1970-77, prof. emeritus, 1977—, vice chmn. dept. Germanic langs., 1963-69; dir. U. Calif. study centers at Univs. Lund (Sweden) and Bergen (Norway), 1972-74; lectr. Uppsala U., also vis. prof. Stockholm Sch. Econs., 1947-48; exchange instr. U. B.C., summer 1940; vis. prof. Augustana Coll., summer 1946, U. Calif. at Berkeley, 1968, U. Wash., 1970, Portland State U., 1979-80; U.S. mem. Commn. Ednl. Exchange U.S.-Sweden, 1973-74; sr. fellow, cons. Monterey Inst. Fgn. Studies, 1977-78; adv. NEH, 1978—; advisor Oreg. Gov.'s Commn. on Fgn. Langs. and Internat. Study, 1981-83; German lang. dir. Army Specialized Tng. Program, 1943-44. Author: The Kensington Stone: A Mystery Solved, 1958, The Vikings and America, 1986; also several other books, translations and numerous articles on Scandinavian philology.; appeared various documentary films. Mem. Mayor's Community Adv. Com., 1964-73. Am.-Scandinavian Found. fellow Sweden, 1946-47, recipient Gold medal, 1975; grantee to Scandinavia Am. Philos. Soc., 1954-55; Guggenheim Meml. Found. fellow Scandinavia, 1961-62; recipient pub. citation Icelandic Community Los Angeles, 1964; decorated knight Royal Swedish Order of Polar Star, knight Order Lion of Finland, knight Icelandic Order of Falcon. Fellow Internat. Inst. Arts and Letters (life); mem. Swedish Cultural Soc. Am. (dir. 1940-48, pres. Los Angeles 1941-46), MLA So. Calif. (exec. bd. 1950-53), MLA Assn. Am. (chmn. Scandinavian sect. 1955, 67), Am.-Scandinavian Found. (pres. Los Angeles chpt. 1958-60), Soc. Advancement Scandinavian Study (assoc. editor 1947-57, 70-73, assoc. mng. editor 1957-69), Am. Assn. Tchrs. German (nat. exec. council 1957-59, 60-63), Finlandia Found., Medieval Acad. Am., Am. Swedish Hist. Mus., Swedish-Am. Hist. Soc. Calif., Nordic Heritage Mus. (Viking ship com.), World Affairs Council Oreg., Wash., Seattle Swedish Club, Oreg. Internat. Council, Tau Kappa Epsilon, Delta Sigma Rho, Delta Phi Alpha. Home and Office: 1121 Wilder Ave Apt 1500-B Honolulu HI 96822

WAHLGREN, OLOF GUSTAF CHRISTERSON, newspaper editor; b. Stockholm, Sept. 21, 1927; s. Christer Fredrik Olof and Jeanne Louise Charlotte (Nyblaeus) W.; B.A., U. Lund, 1951, M.A., 1954, Dr.(ph), 1957; m. Ulla Britt Andersson, July 15, 1955; children—Rebecca, Suzanne, Christer. Mem. staff Sydsvenska Dagbladet, morning paper, Malmö , 1953-87 , dep. dir., 1963-67, chief editor, 1967-87 , mng. dir., 1967-78; mng. dir. Kvällsposten, eve. paper, Malmö , 1963-78; dir. Sydsvenska Dagbladet AB & Kvällsposten AB, 1949-87 , chmn., 1978-87 ; Vice pres. Malmö Mcpl. Com. Art, 1968-76. Initiator, chmn. United Liberal Party movement in So. Sweden, 1964-69. Decorated knight 1st class Order Vasa; comdr. Finnish Order Lion, Icelandic Order Falcon; Order of Merit, Fed. Republic Germany; officer Italian Order Merit; knight Danish Order Dannebrog; officer French Legion of Honor; Knight of Polish Order Polonia Restituta. Mem. Swedish Newspaper Assn. (pres. South Sweden div., dir. 1967-87, hon. chmn. 1987), Internat. Press Inst. (chmn. Swedish nat. com. 1972-82, v.p. 1974-76, pres. 1976-78, hon. mem. 1979), Internat. Fedn. Newspaper Pubs. (exec. bur. com. 1974-84, sec. gen. 1978-84, hon. mem. 1984), World Press Freedom Com. (v.p. 1976-78). Clubs: Travellers (Malmö), Rotary. Author: Contreclock through France. Home: 5 b Nicoloviusgatan, S-21757 Malmö Sweden Office: 19 Krusegatan, Malmö Sweden

WAIHEE, JOHN DAVID, III, governor of Hawaii, lawyer; b. Honokaa, Hawaii, May 19, 1946; m. Lynne Kobashigawa; children: John David, Jennifer. B.A. in History and Bus., Andrews U., 1968; postgrad., Central Mich. U., 1973; J.D., U. Hawaii, 1976. Bar: Hawaii 1976. Community edn. coordinator Benton Harbor (Mich.) Area Schs., 1968-70, asst. dir. community edn., 1970-71; program evaluator, adminstrv. asst. to dirs., planner Honolulu Model Cities Program, 1971-73; sr. planner Office Human Resources City and County of Honolulu, 1973-74, program mgr. Office Human Resources, 1974-75; assoc. Shim, Sigal, Tam & Naito, Honolulu, 1975-79; ptnr. Waihee, Manuia, Yap, Pablo & Hoe, Honolulu, 1979-82; mem. Hawaiian Ho. of Reps., 1980-82; lt. gov. State of Hawaii, Honolulu, 1982-86, gov., 1986—. Del. 1978 Constnl. Conv.; del. Hawaii Dem. State Conv., 1972,74, 76, 78, 82; dir. and past pres. Kalihi-Palama Community Council; mem. steering com. Goals for Hawaii Orgn., past chmn. land use goals com., past co-chmn. outreach com.; past bd. dirs. Hawaii Sr. Citizens Travel Bd.; past mem. State Council on Housing and Constrn. Industry; mem. Kalihi-Palama Hawaiian Civic Club; past bd. dirs. Legal Aid Soc. of Hawaii, Alu Like. Mem. Hawaii Bar Assn. (chmn. unauthorized practice of law com. 1979, chmn. legis com. 1980), ABA, U. Hawaii Law Sch. Alumni, Filipino C. of C. Lodge: Kalakaua Lions. Office: Office of Gov 5th Fl State Capitol Honolulu HI 96813

WAIN, JOHN BARRINGTON, author; b. Stoke-on-Trent, Eng., Mar. 14, 1925; s. Arnold A. and Anne Wain; m. Eirian James, 1960; 3 sons. M.A., Oxford U.; D.Litt. (hon.) U. Keele, 1985, U. Loughborough, 1985. Lectr. English lit. U. Reading, 1947-55; freelance writer, lit. critic, 1955—; Churchill vis. prof. U. Bristol, 1967; vis. prof. Centre Exptl. U., Vincennes, France; George Elliston lectr. on poetry, U. Cin.; prof. poetry Oxford U., 1973-78, fellow Brasenose Coll., 1973—; dir. 1st Poetry at the Mermaid Festival, London, 1961. Poetry includes: Mixed Feelings, 1951; Weep Before God, 1961; Letters to Five Artists, 1969; Poems 1949-1979, 1981; novels include: Hurry on Down, 1953; The Contenders, 1958; Strike the Father Dead, 1962; The Smaller Sky, 1967; The Pardoner's Tale, 1978; Young Shoulders (Whitebread award), 1982; non-fiction publs. include: The Living World of Shakespeare, 1964; A House for the Truth, 1972; Samuel Johnson (Heinemann award 1975), 1974; Professing Poetry, 1977; author short stories; editor books on poets, poetry. Decorated companion Order of Brit. Empire; recipient Somerset Maugham award, 1958; James Tait Black Meml. prize, 1974; Whitbread award for fiction, 1982; 1st holder Fellowship in Creative Arts, Brasenose Coll., Oxford U., 1971-72; hon. fellow St. John's Coll., Oxford, 1985—. Office: Century Hutchinson Ltd, 62-65 Chandos Pl, London WC2, England *

WAINESS, MARCIA WATSON, legal administrator; b. Bklyn., Dec. 17, 1949; d. Stanley and Seena (Klein) Watson; m. Steven Richard Wainess, Aug. 7, 1975. Student, UCLA, 1967-71, 80-81, Grad. Sch. Mgmt. Exec. Program, 1988, grad. Grad. Sch. Mgmt. Exec. Program, 1988. Office mgr., paralegal Lewis, Marenstein & Kadar, Los Angeles, 1977-81; office mgr. Rosenfeld, Meyer & Susman, Beverly Hills, Calif., 1981-83; adminstr. Rudin, Richman & Appel, Beverly Hills, 1983; dir. adminstrn. Kadison, Pfaelzer, Los Angeles, 1983-87; exec. dir. Richards, Watson and Gershon, Los Angeles, 1987—; faculty mem. UCLA Legal Mgmt. & Adminstrn. Program, 1983, U. So. Calif. Paralegal Program, Los Angeles, 1985; mem. adv. bd. atty. asst. tng. program, UCLA, 1984—. Mem. ABA (chmn. Displaywrite Users Group 1986, legal tech. adv. council litigation support working group 1986-87), State Bar Calif., Los Angeles County Bar Assn. (exec. com. law office mgmt. sect.), Assn. Profl. Law Firm Mgrs., Assn. Legal Adminstrs. (asst. regional v.p. Calif. 1987-88, regional v.p. 1988-89, pres. Beverly Hills chpt. 1985-86, membership chmn. 1984-85, chmn. new adminstrn. sect. 1982-84). Office: Richards Watson and Gershon 333 S Hope St 38th Floor Los Angeles CA 90071

WAINIO, MARK ERNEST, loss control specialist; b. Virginia, Minn., Apr. 18, 1953. BA, Gustavus Adolphus Coll., 1975. Cert. safety profl., assoc. loss control mgmt., assoc. risk mgmt., CPCU. Carpenter ABI Contracting Inc., Virginia, 1975-77; co-owner Mesabi Builders, Albuquerque and Eveleth, Minn., 1977-79; sr. engring. rep. Aetna Life & Casualty, Albuquerque, 1979-86; loss control specialist CNA Ins. Cos., Albuquerque, 1986—. Mem. Am. Soc. Safety Engrs., CPCU. Home: 5525 Sonata Dr NE Albuquerque NM 87111 Office: CNA Ins Companies 8500 Menaul NE Albuquerque NM 87112

WAITE, DARVIN DANNY, accountant; b. Holdenville, Okla.; s. Delmer Charles and Lorraine (Young) W. BSBA, U. Ark., 1954. CPA, Ill. Auditor USDA, N.Y.C., New Orleans, 1963-69; auditor commodity exchange authority USDA, Chgo., 1969-75; sr. auditor U.S. Commodity Futures Trading Commn., Chgo., 1975—. Served with U.S. Army, 1948-51, NG, 1954-56, USAFR, 1956-62. Mem. Am. Inst. CPA's, Assn. Govt. Accts. (Chgo. chpt.), Ill. CPA Soc., Chgo. Met. CPA. Chpt. Republican. Lutheran. Home: 101 Wallace St Bartlett IL 60103 Office: US Commodity Futures Trading Commn Sears Tower Chicago IL 60606

WAITE, LAWRENCE WESLEY, physician; b. Chgo., June 27, 1951; s. Paul J. and Margaret E. (Cresson) W.; m. Courtnay M. Snyder, Nov. 1, 1974; children: Colleen Alexis, Rebecca Maureen, Alexander Quin. BA, Drake U., 1972; DO, Coll. Osteo. Medicine and Surgery, Des Moines, 1975; MPH, U. Mich., 1981. Diplomate Nat. Bd. Osteo. Examiners. Intern Garden City Osteo. Hosp., Mich., 1975-76; practice gen. osteo. medicine, Garden City, 1979-82, Battle Creek, 1982—; assoc. clin. prof. Mich. State U. Coll. Osteo. Medicine, East Lansing, 1979—; dir. med. edn. Lakeview Gen. Osteo. Hosp., Battle Creek, Mich., 1983-87; cons. Nat. Bd. Examiners Osteo. Physicians and Surgeons, 1981—. Writer TV program Cross Currents Ecology, 1971; editor radio series Friendship Hour, 1971-72. Bd. dirs., instr. Hospice Support Services, Inc., Westland, Mich., 1981-86; mem. profl. adv. council Good Samaritan Hosp., Battle Creek, 1982-83; bd. dirs. Neighborhood Planning Council 11, Battle Creek, 1982—; mem. population action council Population Inst., 1984—; exec. bd. officer Battle Creek area Urban League, 1987—. Served to lt. comdr. USN, 1976-79. State of Iowa scholar, 1969. Mem. Aerospace Med. Assn., AMA, Am. Osteo. Assn., Am. Pub. Health Assn., Am. Acad. Osteopathy, Bermuda Hist. Soc. (life). Episcopalian. Avocations: geography, medieval history, genealogy. Home: 140 S Lincoln Blvd Battle Creek MI 49015 Office: 3164 Capital Ave SW Battle Creek MI 49015

WAITE, PAUL J., climatologist, educator; b. New Salem, Ill., June 21, 1918; s. Wesley Philip and Edna Viola (Bartlett) W.; m. Margaret Elizabeth Cresson, June 13, 1943; children: Carolyn, Lawrence. BE, Western Ill. State U., 1940; MS, U. Mich., 1966. State climatologist Nat. Weather Service, Des Moines, Madison, 1956-73; meteorologist Nat. Weather Service, 1973-74, 1948-51, 1952-56; dep. project mgr. NOAA, Houston, 1974-76; state climatologist Iowa Dept. Agr., Des Moines, 1976—; adj. prof. geography, geology Drake U., Des Moines, 1970-74, 1976-88; asst. dir. Iowa Weather Service, Des Moines, 1959-70, dir. 1970-73; U.S. Dept. Commerce collaborator Iowa State U., Ames, 1959-73; cons. climatologist, 1988—. Contbr. articles to profl. jours. and chpts. to bks. Served to 1st lt. USAF, 1942-46, 1951-52, Korea. Recipient NASA Group Achievement Award, 1979. Fellow Iowa Acad. Scis. (Disting. Service award 1983, pres. 1986-87); mem. Am. Assn. State Climatologist (pres. 1977-78), Am. Meteorol. Soc., Nat. Weather Assn. Republican. Club: Toastmasters (Des Moines) (pres. 1980). Lodge: Masons. Avocations: hiking; gardening; photography. Home: 6657 NW Timberline Dr Des Moines IA 50313

WAITMAN, B. A., investment banking company executive; b. Ft. Collins, Colo., May 17, 1946; d. Henry and Lydia (Frickel) Kerbel; 1 child, Craig A. Adminstrv. asst. Fleishcer & Co., Phoenix, 1970-78; legal adminstr. Shank, Irwin & Holmes, Denver, 1978-80; v.p. Franchise Fin. Corp. Am., Phoenix, 1980-86, sr. v.p., 1986—. Republican. Baptist. Office: Franchise Fin Corp Am 500 Financial Ctr 3443 N Central Ave Phoenix AZ 85012

WAJDA, ANDRZEJ, film director; b. Swalki, Poland, Mar. 6, 1926; ed. Acad. Fine Arts, Cracow, and Film Acad., Lodz; m. Beata Tyszkiewicz (div.); 1 child; m. Krystyna Zachwatowic, 1975. Asst. staff mgr., 1953; film dir., 1954—; stage mgr. Teatr Stary, Cracow, 1973—; films include (in Polish): Generation, 1954, I'm Going to the Sun, 1955; Canal, 1956; Ashes and Diamonds, 1957; Lotna, 1959; Innocent Sorcerers, 1959; Samson, 1960; Servian Lady Macbeth, 1961; Love at 20, 1961; Ashes, 1965; Gates of Paradise, 1967; Everything for Sale, 1968; Jigsaw Puzzle, (for TV); Hunting Flies, 1969; Landscape after Battle, 1970; The Birch Wood, 1970; Pilatus (TV), 1971; Master and Margaret (W. German TV), 1972; Wedding, 1972; The Promised Land, 1975; The Shadow Line, 1976; Death Class, 1965; Man of Marble, 1977; Rough Treatment (UK), 1978; Orchestral Conductor, 1979; Man of Iron, 1981, Danton, 1982, Love in Germany, 1985; dir. plays Hatful of Rain, 1959, Hamlet, 1960, Two on the Seesaw, 1960, Wesele, 1962, The Demons, 1963, Play Strindberg, 1969, The Devils, 1961, Sticks and Bones (Moscow), 1972, Der Mittmacher, 1973, November Night, 1974, The Danton Affairs, 1975, The Demons, 1964, Idot, 1975, When Reason Sleeps, 1976, The Emigrants, 1976, Conversation with the Executioner, 1977, The Danton's Affair, 1978, Down the Years, Down the Days, 1978, Man of Marble, 1977, Hamlet, 1980, Man of Iron, 1981, Danton, 1982, Antygone, 1984, Crime and Punishment, 1984; scenography for Hatful of Rain, The Demons, 1975, November Night. Decorated Order Banner of Labor (2d class), Officer Cross of Order Polonia Restituta, Order Builders People's Poland; Order of Kirll and Methodius 1st Class (Bulgaria); recipient Polish State prize for Generation; Silver Palm, Cannes Film, 1957; Fipresci prize, 1957; Silver prize San Sebastian, 1973; State prize, Sri Lanka, 1963; Grand Prix Moscow Film Festival, 1975; Internat. prize Chgo. Festival, 1975; Valladolid prize, 1976; 1st prize for best dir. XVIII Film Festival, Cartagena, Colombia, 1978; prize Com. Polish Radio and TV; Cannes Film Festival award, 1978, 81; Cesar award, 1982; Brit. Acad. award for services to film, 1982; Onassis prize, 1982; Louis Delluc prize, 1982; Inamori Found. award, 1987. Mem. Union Polish Arts and Designers (hon.), Polish Film Assn. (pres. 1978—). Home: ul Haukego 14, 01-540 Warsaw Poland Office: Film Polski, ul Mazowiecka 6/8, Warsaw Poland *

WAKABAYASHI, MINORU, structural engineer; b. Tokyo, Aug. 13, 1921; m. Toshiko Nakano, May 31, 1947; children: Keiko, Yohko. B of Engring., U. Tokyo, 1946, D of Engring., 1957. Assoc. prof. Kyoto (Japan) U., 1959-64, prof., 1964-85, prof. emeritus, 1985—, dir. Disaster Prevention Research Inst., 1979-81; dir. gen. Gen. Bldg. Res. Corp. Japan, Suita, 1985—. Author: Steel Structures, 1985, Earthquake Resistant Buildings, 1986; also research papers. Mem. Archtl. Inst. Japan, Japan Concrete Inst., Am. Concrete Inst., ASCE, Internat. Assn. for Bridge and Structural Engring. Home: 518 Manhaim Yoshida-Kawaharacho, Kyoto 606, Japan Office: Gen Bldg Research Corp Japan, 5-8-1 Fujishrodai, Suita, Osaka 565, Japan

WAKAE, MASAMI, mathematics educator; b. Sumida, Tokyo, Japan, June 27, 1934; s. Ryutaro and Mume (Ohta) W.; m. Keiko Aihara, May 28, 1969; children: Michiyo, Tomoko. BS, Tokyo U. Edn., 1958; MS, U. Ill., 1961, PhD, 1966. Asst. prof. math. U. Ariz., Tucson, 1966-67; asst. prof. U. Man., Winnipeg, Can., 1967-69, assoc. prof., 1969; prof. Soka U., Tokyo, 1971—, dir., 1975-87, councillor, 1975—, dean, 1976—, trustee, 1986—. Author: Mathematics, 1976, Survey on Mathematics, 1984; contbr. articles to profl. jours. Dir. Nichiren Shoshu Internat., Tokyo, 1978—. Grantee NSF, U.S.A., 1966; grantee Nat. Research Council, Can., 1967-69. Mem. Am. Math. Soc., N.Y. Acad. Scis., Can. Math. Congress, Japanese Math. Soc., Math. Assn. of Am., Sigma Xi, Pi Mu Epsilon. Nichiren Shoshu Soka Gakkai. Office: Soka Univ, 1-236 Tangi-machi, Hachioji, Tokyo 192, Japan

WAKAMATU, NOBUYUKI, environmental engineer; b. Tokyo, Feb. 22, 1949; parents: Kouhei and Yasuko (Tukasa) W. Grad., Kwanto-Gakuin U., Yokohama, Japan, 1971. Lic. Architect. Engr. Yasui Architect and Engrs., Osaka, Japan, 1971-79, chief engr., 1979—. Mem. Soc. Heating, Air Conditioning and Sanitary Engrs. of Japan. Home: Midoriga-oka Kitamachi 13-8, Kawachi-nagano, 586 Osaka Japan Office: Yasui Architect and Engrs, Shimamachi 2-7, Higashi-ku, 540 Osaka Japan

WAKE, GRAEME CHARLES, mathematics professor; b. Eketahuna, Wellington, New Zealand, Jan. 25, 1943; s. Alan Walter and Constance Daphne (Evans) W.; m. Elizabeth Aidney Brundell, Dec. 11, 1965; children: Stephen, Timothy, Jeanette. BS, Victoria U., Wellington, 1963, MS, 1964, PhD, 1967. Teaching fellow Victoria U. of Wellington, 1965-67, lectr. math., 1967-72, sr. lectr. math., 1973-79, reader in math., 1980-85, acad. dean scis., 1983-84; sr. scholar Brasenose Coll. Oxford U., Eng., 1970-71; sr. vis. fellow U. Leeds, Eng., 1976-77; prof. math. Massey U., Palmerston North, New Zealand, 1986—. Contbr. more than 50 articles to profl. jours. Fellow Inst. for Math. and its Applications; mem. Soc. for Indsl. and Applied Math., New Zealand Math. Soc. (pres. 1978-85), Wellington Coll. Bd. Govs., Assn. U. Tchrs. (chmn. 1974-75). Mem. Labour Party. Anglican. Home: 125 Dittmer Dr, Palmerston North, Wellington 5320, New Zealand Office: Dept Math and Stats, Massey U, Palmerston North, Wellington 5301, New Zealand

WAKEHAM, JOHN, parliamentarian; b. England, June 22, 1932; s. Walter John and Eva Rose (Webb) W.; m. Anne Roberta Bailey, 1965 (dec. Oct. 1984); children: Jonathan, Benedict, David; m. Alison Bridget Ward, July 19, 1985. Grad., Charterhouse Sch., Surrey. Asst. govt. whip London, 1979-81, Lord Commr. to the Treasury, 1981, parliamentary Undersec. of State for industry, 1981-82, Minister of State, Treasury, 1982-83, govt. chief whip, 1983-87; Lord Privy Seal and leader House of Commons, London, 1987-88, Lord Pres. of council, leader, 1988—. Author: The Case against Wealth Tax, 1968, A Personal View, 1969. Conservative. Clubs: Carlton, St. Stephen's, Constitutional, Buick's; Royal Yacht Squadron. Office: House of Commons, London England

WAKEMAN, FREDERIC EVANS, JR., historian; b. Kansas City, Kans., Dec. 12, 1937; s. Frederic Evans and Margaret Ruth (Keyes) W.; m. Carolyn Huntley, Dec. 31, 1974; children—Frederic Evans III, Matthew Clark, Sarah Elizabeth. B.A., Harvard Coll., 1959; postgrad., Institut d'Etudes Politiques, U. Paris, 1959-60; M.A., U. Calif.-, Berkeley, 1962, Ph.D., 1965. Asst. prof. history U. Calif.-, Berkeley, 1965-67, assoc. prof., 1968-70, prof., 1970—, dir. Ctr. Chinese Studies, 1972-79; humanities research prof., vis. scholar Corpus Christi Coll., U. Cambridge, Eng., 1976-77, Beijing U., 1980-81, 85; acad. adviser U.S. Ednl. Del. for Study in China.; chmn. Joint Com. Chinese Studies Am. Council Learned Socs./Social Sci Research Council; sr. adviser Beijing office Nat. Acad. Scis.; pres. Social Sci. Research Council, 1986—. Author: Strangers at the Gate, 1966, History and Will, 1973, The Fall of Imperial China, 1975, Conflict and Control in Late Imperial China, 1976, Ming and Qing Historical Studies in the People's Republic of China, 1981, The Great Enterprise, 1986. Harvard Nat. scholar, 1955-59; Tower fellow, 1959-60; Fgn. Area fellow, 1963-65; Am. Council Learned Socs. fellow, 1967-68; Guggenheim fellow, 1973-74; NRC fellow, 1985. Mem. Am. Hist. Assn., Assn. Asian Studies. Home: 205 E 22d St New York NY 10010 Office: Inst East Asian Studies University of California Berkeley CA 94720

WAKEMAN, JOHN, editor, writer; b. London, Sept. 29, 1928; s. Frederick and Edith (Mayo) W.; m. Hilary Paulett, Mar. 15, 1957; children: Harry, Matthew, Tully, Theo, Rhiannon. Librarian various pub. libraries, London, 1946-57; acting dir. pub. relations Bklyn. Pub. Library, 1957-59; editor Wilson Library Bulletin, N.Y.C., 1959-61; freelance writer London, 1962-65; freelance editor, writer Norwich, Eng., 1965—; co-founder, co-editor The Rialto, Norwich, 1984—. Editor: World Authors: 1950-70, 1975, supplement, 1980, World Film Directors, 1987; author numerous poems; contbr. articles to periodicals. Served as cpl. RAF, 1947-49. Mem. Labour Party. Home and Office: 32 Grosvenor Rd, Norwich NR2 2PZ, England

WAKERLIN, GEORGE EARLE, educator, medical administrator; b. Chgo., July 1, 1901; s. George and Emma (Kenzig) W.; m. Ruth Billings Coleman, 1952; children—Susan, George Earle. B.S., U. Chgo., 1923; Ph.D., 1926; M.D., Rush Med. Coll., 1929; M.S., U. Wis., 1924. Surg. house officer Johns Hopkins Hosp., 1928-29, med. house officer, 1929-30; asst. in pharmacology U. Chgo., 1923, asso. in physiology, 1925-26, fellow, 1926-28; instr. pharmacology U. Wis., 1923-25; asst. prof. physiology and pharmacology U. Louisville, Ky. 1931-32; asst. prof. and acting head dept. physiology and pharmacology U. Louisville, 1932-33, asso. prof. and head dept., 1933-35, prof. and head dept., 1935-37; prof. and head dept. physiology U. Ill. Coll. of Medicine, 1937-58; asst. dean U. Ill. Coll. of Medicine (Rush-Presbyn. div.), 1945-46; med. dir. Am. Heart Assn., 1958-66; adj. prof. physiology Coll. Phys. and Surg., Columbia, 1959-66; prof. medicine U. Mo. Sch. Medicine, Columbia, 1966-71; prof. medicine emeritus U. Mo. Sch. Medicine, 1971—; free lance med. writer 1973—; state coordinator Mo. Regional Med. Program, 1966-68, dir. planning, 1968-71, central dist. cons., 1971-73. Author: A Laboratory Textbook of Human Physiology, parts I, II and III, 1937-52; Contbr. numerous articles to med. and sci. publs. Chmn. pub. health com. City Club of Chgo., 1940-45, chmn. med. and sci. com. Ill. Div. Am. Cancer Soc., 1945-50. mem. exec. com, 1945-58; pres. Chgo. Nutrition Assn., 1949-50. Served with Chem. Warfare Res. U.S. Army. as 1st lt., 1924-35; Med. Corp. Res. USN; as sr. lt. 1935-45. Recipient Disting. Alumni award U. Chgo., 1965, Gold medal Am. Heart Assn., 1966; grantee Markle Found., 1942-50; grantee Markle Found. War Prodn. Bd., 1943-45; grantee Markle Found. Office Naval Research, 1946-49; grantee Markle Found. Am. Found. for High Blood Pressure, 1948-49; grantee Markle Found. Nat. Heart Inst., 1949-58; grantee Markle Found. Chgo. Heart Assn., 1950-58; grantee Markle Found. Am. Heart Assn., 1951-58. Fellow Am. Public Health Assn., A.C.P., AAAS; mem. Am. Physiol. Soc. (distinguished mem., past chmn. circulation sect.), Am. Soc. Pharmacology and Exptl. Therapeutics, Soc. Exptl. Biology and Medicine, Central Soc. Clin. Research, Nat. Soc. Med. Research (dir. 1966-69), AAUP, Boone County Med. Soc., Mo. Med. Assn., Inst. Medicine of Chgo., Am. Heart Assn. (hon. fellow council clin. cardiology 1966—), AMA, So. Med. Assn., Sociedad Espanola de Cardiologica (hon.), Societe de Nephrologie (hon.), Phi Beta Kappa, Sigma Xi, Alpha Omega Alpha, Alpha Sigma Phi, Alpha Kappa Kappa. Home and Office: 231 El Bonito Way Millbrae CA 94030

WAKIL, ABDUL, government official; b. Kabul, Afghanistan, 1945. Student, Kabul U. Sec. gen. Fgn. Ministry Govt. of Afghanistan, then minister of fin.; then ambassador Govt. of Afghanistan, England, Vietnam; minister fgn. affairs Govt. of Afghanistan, 1986—; mem. People's Dem. Party Afghanistan, 1964—, mem. cen. com., 1977—; mem. Revolutionary Council Afghanistan. Office: Ministry Fgn Affairs, Kabul Afghanistan *

WAKIL, SHEIKH PARVEZ, sociologist, educator; b. Gujrat, Punjab, Pakistan, Dec. 16, 1935; s. Sheikh Abdul and Bint-ul (Fatah) W.; m. Farkhanda Akhtar Shah, Sept. 30, 1960; children—Salman, Gibran, Khayyam. Ed. Govt. Coll., Lahore, Pakistan, U. of Punjab, Wash. State U. Sr. lectr. sociology Punjab U., 1964; prof. sociology U. Sask., Saskatoon, 1964—; vis. faculty mem. Wayne State U., Detroit, 1970-71; advisor Govt. Canada, Govt. Pakistan Ministry Edn., 1976; assoc. dir. research (internat.) Northwest Inst. Research, Erie, Pa., 1976-78; exec. dir. internal ops. Keystone U. Research Corp., 1983—; bd. dirs. SGK-W Research Group, Detroit, 1985—; mem. Can. Commn. for UNESCO, 1983-86. Bd. dirs. South Asia Council. Author: Marriage and Family in Canada, 1976. Editor: Marriage, Family & Society, 1975; South Asia: Perspectives and Dimensions, 1977; contbr. articles to profl. jours. Pres. Pakistan-Can. Cultural Assn., 1965-70, 85-86; pres. Islamic Assn. Sask., 1972-73; bd. dirs. Can. Asian Studies Assn., 1973-81, 86—. Named Most Outstanding Pakistani Student in U.S. by Am. Friends of Middle East, 1962; U.S. Dept. State and Govt. of Pakistan grantee of Interuniv. Profs.' Exchange Program, 1959-64; Can. Council Research grantee, 1967-69, 83-86. Mem. Can. Sociology and Anthropology Assn., Can. Bar Assn., Am. Sociol. Assn., Vanier Inst. Family, Nat. Council Family Relations, Internat. Sociol. Assn. Lodge: Rotary. Avocations: photography; astronomy. Home: 1310 Elliott St, Saskatoon, SK Canada S7N 0V8 Office: Univ Sask, Saskatoon, SK Canada S7N 0W0

WALASZEK, ADAM, historian, educator; b. Krakow, Poland, June 14, 1951; s. Jozef and Maria (Kozakiewicz) W.; m. Joanna Bielecka; 1975; 1 child, Maria. MA in History, PhD in History, Jagiellonian U., Krakow, 1982. Asst. Jagiellonian U., 1979-81, asst. prof., 1981—. Author: Return Migration from the United States to Poland After World War II, 1983, Polish Immigrants in American Industry 1880-1930; editor: B. Dolanski, Memoirs, 1982; contbr. articles to profl. jours.; participating in Cleve. project coordinated by D. Hoerder, 1988. Recipient Kosciuszko Found. scholarship, N.Y.C., 1979-80, U. Wis. scholarship, Stevens Point, 1986, grant Immigration History Research Ctr., Mpls., grant Wayne State U., Detroit, 1986. Mem. Immigration History Soc., Polish Hist. Soc. Roman Catholic. Office: Inst Badan Polonijnych, Rynek GL 34, 31 010 Crakow Poland

WALASZEK, EDWARD JOSEPH, pharmacology educator; b. Chgo., July 4, 1927; married; two children. B.S., U. Ill., 1949; Ph.D. in Pharmacology, U. Chgo., 1953. Research fellow U. Edinburgh, 1953-55; asst. prof. neurophysiology and biochemistry U. Ill., 1955-56; asst. prof. pharmacology U. Kans. Sch. Medicine, Kansas City, 1957-59; assoc. prof. U. Kans. Sch. Medicine, 1959-62, prof., 1962—, chmn. dept., 1964—; USPHS spl. research fellow 1956-61; Mem. health study sec. med. chemistry NIH, 1962-66, mem. health study sect. on research career devel. award, 1966-70, mem. health study sect. on pharmacology-toxicology, 1974-78, research career award, 1963; mem. com. teaching of sci. Internat. Council Sci. Unions; mem. adv. council Internat. Union Pharmacology, 1972—, chmn. sect. teaching, 1975—; chmn. bd. Computer Assisted Teaching Systems Consortium. Editorial bd.: Med. Biology, 1974, Arch. int. Pharmacodyn, 1977. Recipient vice-chancellor's award U. Kans., 1974; medal Polish Pharm. Industry for Service to Pharmacology, 1976; Bela Issekutz medal Hungarian Acad. Scis., 1979. Fellow Am. Coll. Clin. Pharmacologists, AAAS, Am. Chem. Soc., Soc. Pharmacology, Soc. Neurosci.; mem. Finnish Acad. Sci. and Letters (fgn.), Sigma Xi, Alpha Omega Alpha, Rho Chi. Office: U Kans Dept Pharmacology Sch Medicine Kansas City KS 66103

WALCHER, ALAN ERNEST, lawyer; b. Chgo., Oct. 2, 1949; s. Chester R. and Dorothy E. (Kullgren) W.; m. Penny Marie Walcher; children: Dustin Alan, Michael Alan. B.S., U. Utah, 1971, cert. in internat. relations, 1971, J.D., 1974. Bar: Utah 1974, U.S. Dist. Ct. Utah 1974, U.S. Ct. Appeals (10th cir.) 1977, Calif. 1979, U.S. Dist. Ct. (cen. dist.) Calif. 1979, U.S. Ct. Appeals (9th cir.) 1983. Sole practice, Salt Lake City, 1974-79; ptnr. Costello & Walcher, Los Angeles, 1979-85, Walcher & Scheuer, 1985-88, Ford & Harrison, 1988—; judge pro tem Los Angeles Mcpl. Ct., 1986—; dir. Citronia, Inc., Los Angeles, 1979-81. Trial counsel Utah chpt. Common Cause, Salt Lake City, 1978-79. Robert Mukai scholar U. Utah, 1971. Mem. Soc. Bar and Gavel (v.p. 1975-77), ABA, Los Angeles County Bar Assn., Century City Bar Assn., Assn. Bus. Trial Lawyers, Phi Delta Phi, Owl and Key. Club: Woodland Hills Country (Los Angeles). Home: 17933 Sunburst St Northridge CA 91325 Office: Ford & Harrison 1095 Century City N Bldg 10100 Santa Monica Blvd Los Angeles CA 90067 also: Costello & Walcher 2029 Century Park East #1700 Los Angeles CA 90067-3003

WALCOTT, DEREK ALTON, poet, playwright; b. Castries, St. Lucia, West Indies, Jan. 23, 1930; s. Warwick and Alix W., m. Fay Moston, 1954 (div. 1959); 1 son; m. Margaret Ruth Maillard, 1962 (div.); 2 daus.; m. Norline Metivier. B.A., U. West Indies, Kingston, Jamaica, 1953. Former tchr. St. Lucia, Grenada, Jamaica; lectr. Harvard U., Columbia U., Yale U., Rutgers U.; now vis. prof. English, Boston U.; founder, playwright Trinidad Theatre Workshop. Author: (poetry) In A Green Night, 1962, Selected Poems, 1964, Castaway, 1965, The Gulf, 1969, Another Life, 1973, Sea Grapes, 1976, The Star-Apple Kingdom, 1980, The Fortunate Traveler, 1982, Midsummer, 1984, Three Plays, 1986, Collected Poems 1948-84, 1986, The Arkansas Testament, 1987; (plays) Henry Christophe: A Chronicle, 1950, Henry Dernier, 1951, Ione, 1957, Dream on Monkey Mountain & Other Plays, 1971, numerous others. Recipient Jamaica Drama Festival prize, 1958, Guinness award, 1961, Royal Soc. Lit. award, 1964, Obie award, 1971, Nat. Writers prize Welsh Arts Council, 1979, MacArthur Found. award, Queen Elizabeth II Gold Medal for Poetry, 1988; Rockefeller Found. grantee, 1957, 58; Eugene O'Neill Found. fellow, 1969. Address: 165 Duke of Edinburgh Ave, Diego Martin Trinidad *

WALCZAK, PAWEL GRZEGORZ, mathematician, educator; b. Lodz, Poland, Aug. 25, 1948; s. Henryk and Barbara Gabriela (Walczak) W.; m. Zofia Maria Zabierowska, Apr. 8, 1972; children: Blazej, Szymon, Maria. MSc, U. Lodz, 1971; PhD, Polish Acad. Sci., Warsaw, 1974, habilitation, 1983. Mem. adj. faculty Polish Acad. Sci., Warsaw, 1974-84; v.p. Lodz br., Polskie Towarzystwo Matematyczne, 1985—; asst. prof. math. U. Lodz, 1984—; vice head Inst. Math. U., 1987—; vis. prof. Inst. Math and Stats., U. São Paulo, Brazil, 1986. Author: (in Polish) Differential Geometry, 1980; also articles. Editor procs.: Differential Geometry, 1984. Mem. Polskie Towarzystwo Matematyczne, Am. Math. Soc. Roman Catholic. Avocations: chess, classical music. Home: Przelajowa 3, PL 94044, 868508 Lodz Poland Office: U Lodz Inst Math, Banacha 22, PL 90238, Lodz Poland

WALD, BERNARD JOSEPH, lawyer; b. Bklyn., Sept. 14, 1932; s. Max and Ruth (Mencher) W.; m. Francine Joy Weintraub, Feb. 2, 1964; children—David Evan, Kevin Mitchell. B.B.A. magna cum laude, CCNY; J.D. cum laude, NYU, 1955. Bar: N.Y. 1955, U.S. Dist. Ct. (so. dist.) N.Y. 1960, U.S. Dist. Ct. (ea. dist.) N.Y. 1960, U.S. Ct. Appeals (2d cir.) 1960, U.S. Supreme Ct. 1971. Mem. Herzfeld & Rubin, P.C. and predecessor firms, N.Y.C., 1955—. Mem. ABA, N.Y. State Bar Assn., Assn. Bar City N.Y., N.Y. County Lawyers Assn. Office: 40 Wall St New York NY 10005

WALD, FRANCINE JOY WEINTRAUB (MRS. BERNARD J. WALD), physicist; b. Bklyn., Jan. 13, 1938; d. Irving and Minnie (Reisig) Weintraub; student Bklyn. Coll., 1955-57; B.E.E., CCNY, 1960; M.S., Poly. Inst. Bklyn., 1962, Ph.D., 1969; m. Bernard J. Wald, Feb. 2, 1964; children—David Evan, Kevin Mitchell. Engr., Remington Rand Univac div. Sperry Rand Corp., Phila., 1960; instr. Poly. Inst. Bklyn., 1962-64, adj. research asso., 1969-70; lectr. N.Y. Community Coll., Bklyn., 1969, 70; instr. sci. Friends Sem., N.Y.C., 1975-76, chmn. dept. sci., 1976—. NDEA fellow, 1962-64. Mem. Am. Phys. Soc., Am. Assn. Physics Tchrs., Assn. Tchrs. in Ind. Schs., N.Y. Acad. Scis., Nat. Sci. Tchrs. Assn., AAAS, Sigma Xi, Tau Beta Pi, Eta Kappa Nu. Home: 520 LaGuardia Pl New York NY 10012

WALD, GEORGE, biochemist, educator; b. N.Y.C., Nov. 18, 1906; s. Isaac and Ernestine (Rosenmann) W.; m. Frances Kingsley, May 15, 1931 (div.); children: Michael, David; m. Ruth Hubbard, 1958; children: Elijah, Deborah. B.S., NYU, 1927, D.Sc. (hon.), 1965; M.A., Columbia U., 1928, Ph.D., 1932; M.D. (hon.), U. Berne, 1957; D.Sc., Yale U., 1958, Wesleyan U., 1962, McGill U., 1966, Amherst Coll., 1968, U. Rennes, 1970, U. Utah, 1971, Gustavus Adolphus U., 1972; D.H.L., Kalamazoo Coll., 1984, U. Leon, Nicaragua, 1984. NRC fellow at Kaiser Wilhelm Inst. Berlin and Heidelberg, U. Zurich, U. Chgo., 1932-34; tutor biochem. scis. Harvard U., 1934-35, instr. biology, 1935-39, faculty instr., 1939-44, asso. prof. biology, 1944-48, prof., 1948—, Higgins prof. biology, 1968-77, prof. emeritus, 1977—; vis. prof. biochemistry U. Calif., Berkeley, summer 1956; Nat. Sigma Xi lectr., 1952; chmn. divisional com. biology and med. scis. NSF, 1954-56; Guggenheim fellow, 1963-64; Overseas fellow Churchill Coll., Cambridge U., 1963-64; participant U.S.-Japan Eminent Scholar Exchange, 1973; guest China Assn. Friendship with Fgn. Peoples, 1972; v.p. Permanent Peoples' Tribunal, Rome, 1980—. Co-author: General Education in a Free Society, 1945, Twenty Six Afternoons of Biology, 1962, 66, also sci. papers on vision and biochem. evolution. Recipient Eli Lilly prize Am. Chem. Soc., 1939; Lasker award Am. Pub. Health Assn., 1953; Proctor medal Assn. Research in Ophthalmology, 1955; Rumford medal Am. Acad.; Arts and Scis., 1959; Ives medal Optical Soc. Am., 1966; Paul Karrer medal in chemistry U. Zurich, 1967; co-recipient Nobel prize for physiology, 1967; T. Duckett Jones award Helen Hay Whitney Found., 1967; Bradford Washburn medal Boston Mus. Sci., 1968; Max Berg award, 1969; Priestley medal Dickinson Coll., 1970. Fellow Nat. Acad. Sci., Am. Acad. Arts and Scis., Am. Philos. Soc. Home: 21 Lakeview Ave Cambridge MA 02138 Office: Harvard Univ Biol Labs Cambridge MA 02138

WALDECK, JACQUELINE ASHTON, author; b. Chgo.; d. John and Maria Teresa (Arneri) Ashton; m. William George Waldeck, Sept. 20, 1947 (div. June 1964). BA, U. Colo., 1948; postgrad. Tex. Agrl. & Mech. U., 1970. Staff and vol. writer Montrose Daily Press, Colo., 1949-66; feature editor Fiesta Mag., Boca Raton, Fla., 1971-76; free-lance writer, historian, pub., lectr., Boca Raton, 1971—. Author: Boca Raton from Pioneer Days, 1980, Boca Raton: A Romance, 1981, Boca Raton Pioneers and Addison Mizner, 1984; also numerous mag. articles. Sec. Tri-County Mental Health Assn., Montrose, 1964-65; pub. relations chmn. Montrose County chpt. ARC, 1950-63; bd. dirs. Friends Boca Raton Mus. Art, 1983-84; mem. Friends Boca Raton Library, Friends Caldwell Play House, Boca Raton, 1983—. Mem. Nat. League Am. Pen Women (br. v.p. 1984-88, Nat. Biennial award for non-fiction article 1984), Nat. Soc. Arts and Letters (chpt. bd. dirs. 1983-88, pub. relations chmn. drama, music, dance, arts and letters contests 1984-88), Fla. Hist. Soc., Boca Raton Hist. Soc., Greater Boca Raton C. of C. Avocations: dancing, psychology, anthropology, international relations, history. Home: 398 W Camino Real Apt 1 Boca Raton FL 33432

WALDECK, JOHN WALTER, JR., lawyer; b. Cleve., May 3, 1949; s. John Walter Sr. and Marjorie Ruth (Palenschat) W.; m. Cheryl Gene Cutter, Sept. 10, 1977; children: John III, Matthew, Rebecca. BS, John Carroll U., 1973; JD, Cleve. State U., 1977. Product applications chemist Synthetic Products Co., Cleve., 1969-76; assoc. Arter & Hadden, Cleve., 1977-85, ptnr., 1986-88; ptnr. Porter, Wright, Morris and Arthur, Cleve., 1988—. Chmn. Bainbridge Twp. Bd. Zoning Appeals, Chagrin Falls, Ohio, 1984—; trustee. Greater Cleve. chpt. Lupus Found. Am., Cleve., 1978—, sec., 1979-86; bd. dirs. Geauga County Mental Health Bd., Chardon, Ohio, 1988—. Mem. ABA (real property sect.), Ohio State Bar Assn. (real property sect.), Greater Cleve. Bar Assn. (real property sect.). Democrat. Roman Catholic. Club: 13th St. Racquet. Home: 18814 Rivers Edge Dr W Chagrin Falls OH 44022 Office: Porter Wright Morris & Arthur 1700 Huntington Bldg Cleveland OH 44115

WALDEN, AMELIA ELIZABETH (MRS. JOHN WILLIAM HARMON), writer; b. N.Y.C.; d. William A. and Elizabeth (Wanner) W.; m. John William Harmon, Feb. 9, 1946 (dec. 1950). B.S., Columbia U., 1934; cert., Am. Acad. Dramatic Arts. Author: Gateway, 1946, Waverly, 1947, Sunnycove, 1948, Skymountain, 1950, A Girl Called Hank, 1951, Marsha, On-Stage, 1952, Victory for Jill, 1953, All My Love, 1954, Daystar, 1955, Three Loves Has Sandy, 1955, The Bradford Story, 1956, I Found My Love, 1956, My Sister Mike, 1956, Palomino Girl, 1957, Flight Into Morning, 1957, Today is Mine, 1958, Queen of the Courts, 1959; duo of novels An American Teacher: Where Is My Heart?, 1960; How Bright the Dawn, 1962, A Boy to Remember, 1960, Shadow on Devils Peak, 1961; trilogy The American Shakespeare Festival: When Love Speaks, 1961; So Near the Heart, 1962, My World's the Stage, 1964, My Dreams Ride High, 1963, To Catch A Spy, 1964, The Spy on Danger Island, 1965, Race the Wild Wind, 1965, The Spy with Five Faces, 1966, In Search of Ophelia, 1966, A Spy Called Michel-E, 1967, A Name for Himself, 1967, The Spy Who Talked Too Much, 1968, Walk In A Tall Shadow, 1968, A Spycase Built For Two, 1969, Same Scene, Different Place, 1969, The Case of the Diamond Eye, 1969, Basketball Girl of the Year, 1970, What Happened to Candy Carmichael?, 1970, Valerie Valentine is Missing, 1971, Stay to Win, 1971, Play Ball, McGill, 1972, Where was Everyone when Sabrina Screamed?, 1973, Go, Phillips, Go, 1974, Escape on Skis, 1975, Heartbreak Tennis, 1977; Amelia Walden collection personal, profl. papers, original manuscripts, research data established at, U. Oreg., Eugene, 1982, pioneer young adult novel. Home: 89 N Compo Rd Westport CT 06880

WALDEN, PHILIP MICHAEL, recording company executive, publishing company executive; b. Greenville, S.C., Jan. 11, 1940; s. Clemuil Barto and Carolyn Hayes (McClendon) W.; m. Peggy Hackett, Sept. 13, 1969; children: Philip Michael, Amantha Starr. A.B. in Econs., Mercer U., 1962. Pres. Phil Walden Artists & Promotions, 1961, Walden Artists & Promotions, 1963-69, Phil Walden & Assos., 1965—, Capricorn Records, Inc., 1969—, Rear Exit and No Exit Music Pub. Co., 1969—. Campaign chmn. Macon Muscular Dystrophy Assn., 1975; chmn. Macon Heritage Found.; mem. In-Town Macon Neighborhood Assn.; Mem. nat. finance com. Jimmy Carter for Pres.; mem. Com. for Preservation of the White House; mem. nat. adv. bd. NORML; bd. dirs. Brandywine Conservancy; mem. Presdl. Inaugural Com., 1977; trustee Ga. Trust for Historic Preservation.; founder Otis Redding Scholarship Fund, Mercer U., Phil Walden scholarship. Served to 1st lt. Adj. Gen. Corps AUS, 1963-65. Recipient Gold and Platinum Record awards, pub. awards; Big Bear award Mercer U., 1975; Martin Luther King, Jr. Humanitarian award, 1977; Human Relations award Am. Jewish Com., 1978. Mem. Common Cause, Middle Ga. Hist. Soc., Nat. Assn. Rec. Arts and Scis., Rec. Industry Assn. Am. (dir.), Nat. Assn. Rec. Merchandisers, Phi Delta Theta Alumni Assn. Clubs: Gov.'s of Ga, Pres.'s of Mercer U, River North Golf and Country, Sea Pines, Elks. Home: PO Box 23288 Nashville TN 37205 Office: 115 2d Ave N Nashville TN 37201

WALDEN, RICHARD HENRY, plastic surgeon; b. N.Y.C., Aug. 5, 1913; s. Henry W. and Eva (Birke) W.; D.D.S., N.Y. U., 1938; M.D., L.I. Coll. Medicine, 1943; m. Dale Walden; children—Richard Henry, Kenneth, Peter, Terri Ann. Intern, Kings County Hosp., 1938-39, resident, 1939-40, 43-45; practice medicine specializing in plastic surgery and maxillofacial surgery; pres. L.I. Plastic Surg. Group P.C., 1968—; attending plastic surgeon Winthrop U. Hosp., Mineola, N.Y.; attending plastic surgeon Mercy Hosp., Rockville Center, N.Y.; assoc. prof. plastic and maxillo facial surgery SUNY, Stony Brook, 1975—; dir. N. Shore Univ. Hosp. Cleft Palate Center. Served to capt. M.C., U.S. Army, 1945-47. Mem. Am. Soc. Maxillofacial Surgeons (pres. 1977-78), Am. Assn. Plastic Surgeons, Am. Soc. Plastic and Reconstructive Surgery, Am. Cleft Palate Assn., Nassau County Med. Soc., Nassau Surg. Soc. (pres. 1965), Nassau Acad. Medicine (trustee, pres. 1988). Republican. Contbr. articles to profl. jours. Home: 19 Victorian Ln Brookville Long Island NY 11545 Office: 999 Franklyn Ave Garden City NY 11503

WALDHÄUSL, WERNER KLAUS, physician; b. Leipzig, Germany, Sept. 27, 1937; s. Friedrich Wilhelm and Therese Auguste (Falke) W.; M.D., U. Vienna, 1962; m. Marianne Hann-Kirchberger, 1965; children—Martin, Bernhard, Christoph. Instr. dept. exptl. pathology U. Vienna (Austria) Med. Sch., 1963-65, instr. dept. internal medicine, 1965-68; research asso. div. endocrinology and metabolism U. Mich. Med. Sch., Ann Arbor, 1968-70; with dept. internal medicine U. Vienna Med. Sch., 1970—, head div. clin. endocrinology and diabetes, mellitus, 1975, assoc. prof. internal medicine, 1978—, vice chmn. dept. internal medicine, 1985, chmn., 1987; E.F.F. Copp lectr., Los Angeles, 1983; Claude Bernard lectr., Rome, 1986. Recipient Stosius prize, 1970, 72; Sandoz prize, 1975; F. von Brü cke prize, 1976. Mem. European Soc. Clin. Investigation, Am. Diabetes Assn., Endocrine Soc., European Assn. Study Diabetes (v.p. 1982-84), Internat. Diabetes Fedn. (sci. sec. 10th congress). Contbr. articles on internal medicine, endocrinology and metabolism to med. jours. Home: 10 Dollinergasse, A 1190 Vienna Austria Office: 14 Lazarettgasse, 1 Med Klinik, A 1090 Vienna Austria

WALDHEIM, KURT, president of Austria, former sec.-gen. UN, diplomat; b. 1918; ed. Consular Acad. Vienna (Austria), U. Vienna; D.Jurisprudence; hon. degrees: LL.D., Fordham U., 1972, Carleton U., Ottawa, Can., 1972, U. Chile, Santiago, 1972, Rutgers U., 1972, Jawarharlal Nehru U. (India), 1973, U. Bucharest (Rumania), 1973, Wagner Coll., 1973, Cath. U. Am., 1974, Wilfrid Laurier U. (Can.), 1974, Cath. U. Leuven (Belgium), 1975, Charles U. (Czechoslovakia), 1975, Hamilton Coll., 1975, U. Denver, 1976, U. Philippines, 1976, Am. U., 1977, Kent State U., 1977, U. Warsaw, 1977, Moscow State U., 1977, Mongolian State U., 1977, U. Atlanta, Humboldt U. Berlin, U. S.C., U. Keele (Eng.), 1980, U. Notre Dame, South Bend, Ind., 1981. Entered Austrian Fgn. Service, 1945; served Ministry Fgn. Affairs; mem. Austrian del. to Paris, London and Moscow for negotiations on Austrian State Treaty, 1945-47; 1st sec. Austrian Embassy, Paris, 1948-51; head personnel div. Ministry Fgn. Affairs, 1951-55; permanent Austrian observer to UN, 1955-56; minister to Can., 1956-58; ambassador to Can., 1958-60; dir. gen. for polit. affairs Ministry Fgn. Affairs, 1960-64; permanent rep. to UN, 1964-68, 1964-68, chmn. outer space com. UN, 1965-68, 70-71; fed. minister for fgn. affairs Austria, 1968-70; candidate for presidency Republic of Austria, 1971; permanent rep. Austria to UN, 1970-71; sec.-gen. UN, 1971-82; pres. of Austria, 1986—; now guest prof. diplomacy Georgetown U., Washington; chmn. Inter Action Council. Recipient Karl Renner prize City of Vienna, 1978. Author: Der Österreichische Weg, 1971; The Austrian Example, 1973; Un Metier Unique au monde, 1977; Der schwierigste Job der Welt, 1978; Challenge of Peace, 1980; Building the Future Order, 1980. Address: Office of President, Hofburg Adlerstiege, 1014 Vienna Austria *

WALDMAN, JAY CARL, lawyer; b. Pitts., Nov. 16, 1944; s. Milton and Dorothy (Florence) W.; m. Roberta Tex Landy, Aug. 28, 1969. B.S., U. Wis., 1966; J.D., U. Pa., 1969. Bar: Pa. 1970, D.C. 1976, U.S. Supreme Ct. 1976. Assoc., Rose, Schmidt, Dixon & Hasley, Pitts., 1970-71; asst. U.S. atty. western dist. Pa., Pitts., 1971-75; dep. asst. U.S. Atty. Gen., Washington, 1975-77; counsel Gov. of Pa., Harrisburg, 1978-86; sr. ptnr., Dilworth, Paxson, Kalish & Kauffman, Phila., 1986—. Dir. Thornburgh for Gov. campaign., Pa., 1977-78; commr. Pa. Convention Ctr. Authority, 1986—. Fellow Am. Bar Found.; mem. ABA, Fed. Bar Assn., Union League Phila. Republican. Office: 2600 Fidelity Bldg Philadelphia PA 19109

WALDMAN, JULES LLOYD, editor, publisher; b. N.Y.C., Dec. 24, 1912; s. Harry A. and Anna Waldman; m. Agnes Tolnay, Sept. 24, 1949; children: Kathleen Ellen, Kenneth Lloyd. BA, Columbia, 1932 (state scholarship, 4 yrs.), postgrad., 1934-35. Mem. staff Bklyn. Daily Eagle, L.I. Daily Press, 1932-35; dir. staff pianist Radio Caracas, Venezuela, 1941-45; dir. bookstore chain Caracas, 1941-59; editor Clave mag., 1950-60; founder Caracas Daily Jour., 1945, editor, 1945-75, dir., 1975—, chmn. bd., 1982—; corr. N.Y. Times, 1945-65, Time mag., 1945-48; dir., prof. Centro Venezolano-Americano, Caracas, 1945—; prof. journalism Central U. Venezuela, 1948-50. Author: Venezuelan Sketches, 1988; pub.: Speaking of Venezuela, 1947, Caracas Everday, 1947; columnist, contbr. to mags. and newspapers. Established ann. Nat. Good Neighbor awards, Venezuela, 1947. Decorated Order Andres Bello, Order Liberator Simon Bolivar; recipient Municipal ant Nat. Newspaper prize, 1948, Order Francisco Miranda award Pres. Venezuela, 1968, Gold Key Municipal Council Caracas, 1968, Order of Merit, 1958; named Friend of Venezuela. Mem. Alumni Assn. Columbia U. in Venezuela (pres.), Venezuelan Newspaper Pubs. Assn. (bd. dirs.), Interamerican Press Assn. Club: Overseas Press (pres. Venezuela chpt.). Home: Quinta Montamar, Calle Gloria Junko Country Club, Caracas Venezuela Office: Daily Jour, Apartado 1408, Caracas Venezuela

WALDMAN, REBECCA (COOPER), art dealer; b. Phila., July 11, 1947; d. Frank N. Cooper and Bernice (Silverstein) Lewis; m. Michael J. Waldman, June 27, 1982. BA NYU, 1969, MA 1971, postgrad. Owner Gallery Rebecca Cooper, Washington, 1974-79; pres. Rebecca Cooper, Inc., N.Y.C., 1980—; sec. bd. assocs. Am. Craft Mus., lectr. Collectors Circle, 1985, 86; nat. patron Am. Fed. Art.; mem. jr. com. N.Y.C. Ballet, Princess Grace Found.; assoc. Mus. Modern Art, Met. Mus. Mem. Whitney Circle of Friends, Assocs. of Gruggenheim Mus.

WALDSCHMIDT, MICHEL, mathematics educator; b. Nancy, France, June 17, 1946; s. Pierre and Henriette (Trotot) W.; m. Anne Weber, July 26, 1968; children: Alexis, Hélene. Lic. math., U. Nancy, 1967, diplome d'etudes approfondies, 1968, agregation de math., 1969; these d'Etat, U. Bordeaux, France, 1972. Asst. U. Bordeaux, 1968-71; attaché de recherches CNRS Bordeaux, 1971-72; chargé d'enseignement U. d'Orsay, 1972-73; maitre de confs. U. P. et M. Curie (Paris VI), 1972-77, prof., 1977—; mem. Conseil Superieur des Corps Univs., 1980-82, Com. Nat. de la Recherche Sci., 1983-86; dir. Equipe de Theorie des Nombres CNRS, 1977-80, Equipe de Recherches Problemes Diophantiens, 1982—. Author: Nombres Transcendants, 1974, Nombres Transcendants et Groupes Algebriques, 1979, Transcendence Methods, 1979; mem. editorial bds. several math. publs. Recipient Medaille Albert Chatelet, 1974, Foundation Peccot award Coll. de France, 1977, Medaille d'Argent, Ctr. Nat. de la Recherche Sci., 1978, Prix Marquet, Acad. des Sci., Paris, 1980. Mem. Soc. Math. de France, Am. Math. Soc., Assn. Française pour l'Avancement des Scis. (pres. math. sect. 1983-84). Office: Inst Henri Poincare, 11 rue Pierre et, Marie Curie, 75231 Paris France

WALDVOGEL, GUY E., service company executive; b. Geneva, Oct. 15, 1936; s. Paul H. and Helene (DuBois) W.; m. Pierette Vontobel; children: Muriel, Christian, Ariane. BS in Chemistry, ETH, Zurich, 1961; PhD, ETH, 1965; PDM, Harvard U., 1969. Chemist Hoffmann La Roche, Basel, Switzerland, 1965-73; pres. Giuadan, Geneva, 1973-81, Alusuisse of Am., N.Y.C., 1981-83; group exec. v.p. Soc. Gen. Surveillance, Geneva, 1983—; Trustee, ETH, 1974-82. Office: Soc Gen de Surveillance SA, 1 pl des Alpes Case Postale 898, CH 1211 Geneva 1, Switzerland

WALENDOWSKI, GEORGE JERRY, business management specialist, accounting educator; b. Han-Minden, W.Ger., Mar. 25, 1947; came to U.S., 1949; s. Stefan and Eugenia (Lewandowska) W. A.A., Los Angeles City Coll., 1968; BS, Calif. State U.-Los Angeles, 1970, MBA, 1972. Cert. community coll. instr. acctg. and mgmt., Calif. Acct., Unocal (formerly Union Oil Co. Calif.), Los Angeles, 1972-76, data control supr., 1976-78, acctg. analyst, 1978-79; sr. fin. analyst Hughes Aircraft Co., El Segundo, Calif., 1979-83, fin. planning specialist, 1983-86; instr. bus. math. Los Angeles City Coll., 1976-80, instr. acctg., 1980—, mem. acctg. adv. com., 1984, 87; bus. mgmt. specialist, 1986—. Contbr. articles to profl. jours. Softball co-organizer Precious Blood Ch., Los Angeles, 1979. Recipient Outstanding Achievement awards, 1980, 87, Superior Performance award Hughes Aircraft Co., 1987. Mem. Internat. Platform Assn., Acad. Mgmt., Am. Acctg. Assn., Nat. Assn. Accts. (Robert Half Author's trophy Los Angeles chpt. 1980, cert. of appreciation 1980, 83, mem. Author's Circle 1980), Planning Forum (recognition award Los Angeles chpt. 1983), Am. Econ. Assn., Internat. Platform Assn., World Inst. Achievement, Beta Gamma Sigma. Republican. Roman Catholic. Home: 426 N Citrus Ave Los Angeles CA 90036 Office: Hughes Aircraft Co 2141 E Rosecrans El Segundo CA 90245

WALES, HUGH GREGORY, emeritus marketing educator, business executive; b. Topeka, Feb. 28, 1910; s. Raymond Otis and Nola V. (Chestnut) W.; m. Mary Alice Fulkerson, June 11, 1938; m. Helen Scott Valentine, Apr. 29, 1988. A.B., Washburn Coll., 1932; M.B.A., Harvard U., 1934; Ph.D., Northwestern U., 1944; D.Sc., Washburn Municipal U., 1968. Dean men N.W. Mo. State Tchrs. Coll., 1935-38, dean students, head dept. econs., 1938-39; dean students, dir. summer sch., vets. bur., head dept. econs. Washburn U., 1939-46; assoc. prof. marketing U. Ill., 1946-53, prof., 1953-70, prof. emeritus, dir. micro-precision projects, 1970—; prof. marketing and mgmt., head dept. Roosevelt U., 1970-75; pres. Decisions, Evaluations & Learning, Internat. Assocs.; vis. prof. marketing U. South Africa, Pretoria, 1962; lectr. U. Stellenbosch, South Africa, 1973, 75, 76; cons. South African Govt., Pretoria, 1974; participant internat. confs.; bus., marketing research cons.; internat. pres. Micro-precision Miniaturization Inst., 1970—, dir., program chmn., Chgo., 1970—. Author: Changing Perspectives in

Marketing, 1951, Marketing Research, 1952, 4th edit., 1974, Marketing Research-Selected Literature, 1952, Cases and Problems in Marketing Research, 1953, (with Robert Ferber) Basic Biblography in Marketing Research, 1956, 3d edit., 1974, Motivation and Market Behavior, (with Ferber), 1958, Advertising Copy, Layout, and Typography, (with Gentry and M. Wales), 1958, (with R. Ferber) The Champaign-Urbana Metropolitan Area, (with Engel and Warshaw) Promotional Strategy, 1967, 3d edit., 1975, (with Dik Twedt and Lyndon Dawson) Personality Theory in Marketing Research: A Basic Bibliography, 1976, (with Sharon Abrams) English as a Second Language in Business, 1978, (with Luck, Taylor and Rubin) Marketing Research, 1978; numerous others, works transl. several langs.; Contbr. (with Luck, Taylor and Rubin) articles to profl. jours. Pres. Civic Symphony Soc., 1964-65. Mem. Am. Econ. Assn., Am. Marketing Assn. (sec., acad. v.p.), Am. Watchmakers Inst. (dir. research and edn. 1963-66), Nat. Assn. Watch and Clock Collectors (chpt. pres. 1981, 83), Arizonans for Nat. Security (chmn. visual aids com. 1979—), Internat. Alliance Theatrical Stage Employees and Moving Picture Machine Operators, Internat. Platform Assn., Internat. TV Assn., Assn. Edn. Internat. Bus., Soc. Internat. Devel., Am. Statis. Assn., Nat. Assn. for Mgmt. Educators., Acad. Mgmt., We the People United (treas.), Tempe Repubican Men's Club, Tempe Bus. and Profl. Men's Club. Clubs: Ariz. Breakfast. Lodge: Rotary. Home: 2021 S LaRosa Dr Tempe AZ 85282

WALESA, LECH, Polish trade union activist; b. Popowo, Poland, Sept. 29, 1943; s. Boleslaw and Feliksa W.; student Tech. State Vocat. Sch., Lipno, Poland; hon. degrees: Ph.D., Aliance Coll., Pa., 1981, MacMurray Coll., Ill., 1982, U. Notre Dame, 1982, Providence Coll., 1982; m. Miroslawa Danuta, 1969; children: Bogdan, Slawomir, Przemyslaw, Jaroslaw, Magdalena, Anna, Maria Victoria, Brygida. Electrician, Lenin Shipyard, Gdansk, 1966-76, 80—, chmn. strike com., 1970, 80; co-founder, chmn. Nat. Coordinating Com. of Independent Trade Union Solidarity, 1980, held in detention, 1981-82. Author: A Way of Hope, 1987. Named Man of the Year Time mag., 1981, The Fin. Times, 1980, Free World Prize (Norway), 1982, Le Point, 1081, Le Soir l'Express, 1981, Die Zelt, 1981, Die Welt 1980; recipient Nobel prize for peace, 1983, Internat. Integrity award, 1986. Home: ul Pilotow 17D/3, Gdansk-Zaspa Poland Office: Komisja Krajowa NSZZ Solidarnosc, ul Grunwaldzka 103, P 80-244 Gdansk Poland

WALI, MOHAN KISHEN, environmental science and forestry educator; b. Kashmir, India, Mar. 1, 1937; came to U.S., 1969, naturalized, 1975; s. Jagan Nath and Somavati (Wattal) W.; m. Sarla Safaya, Sept. 25, 1960; children: Pamela, Promod. BS, U. Jammu and Kashmir, 1957; MS, U. Allahabad, India, 1960; PhD, U. B.C., Can., 1970. Lectr. S.P. Coll., Sringar, Kashmir, 1963-65; research fellow U. Copenhagen, 1965-66; grad. fellow U. B.C., 1967-69; asst. prof. biology U. N.D., Grand Forks, 1969-73, assoc. prof., 1973-79, prof., 1979-83, Hill research prof., 1973, dir. Forest River Biology Area Field Sta., 1970-79, Project Reclamation, 1975-83, spl. asst. to univ. pres., 1977-82; staff ecologist Grand Forks Energy Research Lab., U.S. Dept. Interior, 1974-75; prof. Coll. Environ. Sci. and Forestry, SUNY, Syracuse, 1983—, dir. grad. program environ. sci., 1983-85; vice chmn. N.D. Air Pollution Adv. Council, 1981-83; co-chair IV Internat. Congress on Ecology, 1986. Editor: Some Environmental Aspects of Strip-Mining in North Dakota, 1973, Prairie: A Multiple View, 1975, Practices and Problems of Land Reclamation in Western North America, 1975, Ecology and Coal Resource Development, 1979; sr. editor Reclamation Rev., 1976-80, chief editor, 1980-81; chief editor Reclamation and Revegetation Research, 1982—; contbr. articles to profl. jours. Recipient B.C. Gamble Disting. Teaching and Service award, 1977. Fellow Nat. Acad. of Scis. India, 1986; mem. Ecol. Soc. Am. (chmn. sect. internat. activities 1980-84), Brit. Ecol. Soc., Can. Bot. Assn. (dir. ecology sect. 1976-79, v.p. 1982-83), Torrey Bot. Club, AAAS, Am. Soc. Agronomy, Am. Inst. Biol. Sci. (gen. chmn. 34th ann. meeting), Internat. Assn. Ecology, Internat. Soc. Soil Sci., N.D. Acad. Sci. (chmn. editorial com. 1979-81), Sigma Xi (nat. lectr. 1983-85, pres Syracuse chpt. 1984-85, Outstanding Research award U. N.D. chpt. 1975). Office: SUNY Coll Environ Sci & Forestry Syracuse NY 13210

WALK, RICHARD DAVID, psychology educator; b. Camp Dix, N.J., Sept. 25, 1920; s. Arthur Richard and Elsie (Roberts) W.; m. Lois MacDonald, Apr. 1, 1950; children: Joan MacDonald, Elizabeth Walk Robbins, Richard David Jr. AB, Princeton U., 1942; MA, U. Iowa, 1947; PhD, Harvard U., 1951. Research assoc. Human Resource Research Office, George Washington U., Washington, 1952-53, from assoc. prof. to prof., 1959—; asst. prof. Cornell U., Ithaca, N.Y., 1953-59; vis. prof. MIT, Cambridge, 1965-66, London Sch. Econs., U. London, 1981. Author: Perceptual Development, 1981; editor: (with H.L. Pick Jr.) Perception and Experience, 1978, Chinese edit., 1987, Intersensory Perception and Sensory Integration, 1981; contbr. articles to profl. jours., chpts. to books. Served to lst lt. U.S. Army, 1942-45, ETO, 1951-52. Mem. Am. Psychol. Assn., Soc. for Research in Child Devel., Psychonomic Soc., Brit. Psychol. Assn. (fgn. assoc.), Behavioral and Brain Scis. (assoc.), Sigma Xi. Democrat. Episcopalian. Club: Princeton Terrace (N.J.). Home: 7100 Oakridge Ave Chevy Chase MD 20815 Office: George Washington Univ Dept of Psychology Washington DC 20052

WALKER, ALAN, minister; b. Sydney, Australia, June 4, 1911; s. Alfred Edgar and Violet Louise (Lavis) W.; MA, U. Sydney, 1943; DD (hon.) Bethany Bibl. Sem., Chgo., 1956; m. Winfired Garrard Channon, Mar. 26, 1938; children—Lynette, Bruce, David, Christopher. Ordained to ministry Meth. Ch., 1935; minister, Cessnock, New South Wales, 1939-44; supt. Waverley Meth. Mission, 1944-53; leader mission to nation, Australia, 1953-56; supt. Cen. Meth. Mission, Sydney, 1958-78; dir. world evangelism World Meth. Council, 1978—; vis. prof. evangelism Boston Sch. Theology, 1957. Chmn. Australian Nat. Goals and Directions Movement, 1981—. Author: Coaltown: A Sociological Survey of Cessnock, 1945, The Whole Gospel for the World, 1957, The Many Sided Cross of Jesus, 1965, Break-Through, 1969, God, The Distributor, 1973, Life Begins At Christ, 1980, Standing Up to Preach, 1983, Life in the Holy Spirit, 1986. Decorated knight bachelor, 1981, officer Order Brit. Empire, 1954: recipient Inst. De La Vie award, Paris, 1978, World Meth. Peace award (with wife), 1986. Home: 14 Owen Stanley Ave, Beacon Hill 2100 Australia Office: 1 Angel Pl, Sydney 2000, Australia

WALKER, DEREK HUGH, diversified service business executive; b. Chelmsford, Essex, Eng., Aug. 17, 1926; s. Hugh Conrad and May Victoria (Watson) W.; m. Daphne Marianne Bird, June 23, 1951; children: Malcolm Charles, Alison Jane. Grad., Bishop Stortford Coll., Hertfordshire, Eng., 1943. Sta. engr. Skyways Ltd., Kuwait, 1947-48; sr. prototype engr., asst. to gen. mgr. DeHavilland Aircraft Co., Leavoden, Eng., 1949-52; mgmt. trainee DeHavilland Aircraft Co., Hatfield, Eng., 1952-53; project mgr. DeHavilland Aircraft Co., Stevenage, Eng., 1953-55; joint gen. mgr. airspeed div. DeHavilland Aircraft Co., Christchurch, Eng., 1955-61; asst. mng. dir. DeVilbiss Internat., Eng. and France, 1961-64; indsl. relations adviser Rank Orgn., London, 1964-67, group personnel controller, 1967-78; mng. dir. Walker Brooks & Ptnrs. Ltd., Maidenhead, Eng., 1978—; mktg. dir. Engring. Info. Co. Ltd., London, 1984—; mktg., pub. relations rep. Computer and Mgmt. Services, Surrey, Eng., 1985—. Contbr. articles to profl. jours. Active Confederation Brit. Industry, 1984—. Served to tech. officer RAF, 1944-48. Fellow Companion Inst. Personnel Mgmt. (v.p. 1975), Inst. Dirs., Royal Soc. Arts, Brit. Inst. Mgmt. Mem. Conservative Party. Anglican. Clubs: 41 (Maidenhead) (founder, chmn. 1966), Phyllis Ct. (Henley-on-Thames, Eng.). Home: Fieldon House, Berry Hill, Taplow, Maidenhead, SL6 0DA England Office: Walker Brooks & Ptnrs Ltd, Feldon House, Berry Hill, Taplow, Maidenhead, SL6 0DA England

WALKER, DEWARD EDGAR, JR., anthropologist, educator; b. Johnson City, Tenn., Aug. 3, 1935; s. Deward Edgar and Matilda Jane (Clark) W.; m. Candace A. Walker; children: Alice, Deward III, Mary Jane, Sarah, Daniel. Student, Eastern Oreg. Coll., 1953-54, 56-58, Mex. City Coll., 1958; BA in Anthropology with honors, U. Oreg., 1960-61, PhD in Anthropology, 1964; postgrad., Wash. State U., 1962. Asst. prof. anthropology George Washington U., Washington, 1964-65; asst. prof. anthropology Wash. State U., Pullman, 1965-67, research collaborator, 1967-69; assoc. prof., chmn. dept. sociology and anthropology, U. Idaho, Moscow, 1967-69; prof. U. Colo., Boulder, 1969—, research assoc. in population processes program of inst. behavioral sci., 1969-73, assoc. dean Grad. Sch., 1973-76; affiliate faculty U. Idaho, 1971—. Co-editor Northwest Anthropol. Research Notes, 1966—, editor, Plateau Vol: Handbook of North American Indians, 1971—; contbr. articles to profl. jours. Served with U.S. Army, 1954-62. Fellow NSF, 1961, NDEA, 1961-64. Fellow Am. Anthropol. Assn. (assoc. editor Am. Anthropologist 1973-74), Soc. Applied Anthropology (life, exec. com. 1970-79, treas. 1976-79, chmn. High Plains Regional sect. 1980-82, cons., expert witness tribes of N.W., editor Human Orgn. 1970-76); mem. AAAS, Am. Acad. Polit. Social Scis., Northwest Anthropol. Conf. Home: PO Box 4147 Boulder CO 80306 Office: U Colo Dept Anthropology Box 233 Boulder CO 80309

WALKER, ELJANA M. DU VALL, civic worker; b. France, Jan. 18, 1924; came to U.S., 1948; naturalized, 1954; student Med. Inst., U. Paris, 1942-47; m. John S. Walker, Jr., Dec. 31, 1947; children—John, Peter, Barbara. Pres., Loyola Sch. PTA, 1958-59; bd. dirs. Santa Calus shop, 1959-73; treas. Archdiocese Denver Catholic Women, 1962-64; rep. Cath. Parent-Tchr League, 1962-65; pres. Aux. Denver Gen. Hosp., 1966-69; precinct committeewoman Arapahoe County Republican Women's Com., 1973-74; mem. re-election com. Arapahoe County Rep. Party, 1973-78, Reagan election com., 1980; block worker Arapahoe County March of Dimes, Heart Assn., Hemophilia Drive, Muscular Dystrophy and Multiple Sclerosis Drive, 1978-81; cen. city asst. Guild Debutante Charities, Inc. Recipient Distinguished Service award Am.-by-choice, 1966; named to Honor Roll, ARC, 1971. Mem. Cherry Hills Symphony, Lyric Opera Guild, Alliance Franciase (life mem.), ARC, Civic Ballet Guild (life mem.), Needlework Guild Am. (v.p. 1980-82), Kidney Found. (life), Denver Art Mus., U. Denver Art and Conservation Assns. (chmn. 1980-82), U. Denver Women's Library Assn., Chancellors Soc, Passage Inc. Roman Catholic. Clubs: Union (Chgo.); Denver Athletic, 26 (Denver); Welcome to Colo. Internat. Address: 6185 S Columbine Way Littleton CO 80121

WALKER, ELVA MAE DAWSON, consultant health, hospitals, aging; b. Everett, Mass., June 29, 1914; d. Charles Edward and Mary Elizabeth (Livingston) Dawson; m. John J. Spillane Jr. R.N., Peter Bent Brigham Hosp., Boston, 1937; student Simmons Coll., 1935, U. Minn., 1945-48; m. Walter Willard Walker, Dec. 16, 1939 (div. 1969). Supr. nursery Wesson Maternity Hosp., Springfield, Mass., 1937-38; asst. supr. out-patient dept. Peter Bent Brigham Hosp., Boston, 1938-40; supr. surgery and out-patient dept. Univ. Hosps., Mpls., 1945. Chmn. Gov.'s Citizens Council on Aging, Minn., 1960-68, acting dir., 1962-66, Econ. Opportunity Com. Hennepin County, 1964-69; v.p., treas. Nat. Purity Soap & Chem. Co., 1968-69, pres., 1969-76, chmn. bd., 1976—; cons. on aging to Minn. Dept. Pub. Welfare, 1962-67; mem. nat. adv. Council for Nurse Tng. Act, 1965-69, Com. Status on Women in Armed Services, 1967-70; dir. Nat. Council on the Aging, 1963-67, sec., 1965-67, 1986-88; dir. Planning Agy. for Hosps. of Met. Mpls., 1963—, United Hosp. Fund of Hennepin County, 1955—, Nat. Council Social Work Edn., 1966-68; vice chmn. Hennepin County Gen. Hosp. Adv. Bd., 1965-68; sec. Hennepin County Health Coalition, 1973; chmn. bd. dirs. Am. Rehab. Found, 1962-68, vice chmn., 1968-70, chmn. Minn. Bd. On Aging, 1988—, Sr. Resources, 1985-87, Nat. Retiree Vol. Council, 1986—; pres. bd. trustees Northwestern Hosp., 1956-59, Children's Hosp. Mpls., 1961-65; dir. Twin Cities Internat. Program for Youth Leaders and Social Workers, Inc., 1965-67; mem. community adv. council United Community Funds and Council Am., Inc., 1968, Nat. Assembly Social Policy and Devel., Inc., 1968—; mem. priorities determination com. United Fund Mpls., 1971; vice chmn. govt. specifications com. Soap and Detergent Assn., 1972-76, vice-chmn. indsl. and instn. com., 1974-76, chmn., 1976-78, bd. dirs., 1974—; candidate for Congress, 3d Minn. Dist., 1966; trustee Macalester Coll., Archie D. and Bertha H. Walker Found.; chmn. St. Mary's Jr. Coll. Bd., 1970-74, 78-80; pres. U. Minn. Sch. Nursing Found., 1958-70. Mem. Am. Pub. Welfare Assn., Mpls. Med. Research Found., Minn. League Nursing (pres. 1971-73), Jr. League Mpls. Democrat. Presbyterian. Home: 3655 Northome Rd Wayzata MN 55391 Office: Nat Purity Soap & Chem Co 110 SE 5th Ave Minneapolis MN 55414

WALKER, EUNICE MIRIAM ARNAUD, government official, writer; b. Monett, Mo.; d. Emile and Pauline (Barriquand) Arnaud; student S.W. Mo. State U.; B.A., U. Ark.; postgrad. George Washington U., 1956; m. Joseph Edward Walker (div.); children—Diane Leigh Walker Smith, Carole Cecile Walker Baker; m. 2d, William Roy Little. Reporter, feature writer The Monett (Mo.) Times, The Kansas City (Mo.) Star; publs. writer Woodrow Wilson Centennial Celebration Commn., Washington, 1957; pub. relations writer Senator Joseph S. Clark, Washington, 1958-59; asst. pub. relations Ho. of Reps. Com. on Sci. and Astronautics, 1959-61; info. specialist ACDA, Washington, 1961-65, policy reports officer, 1965-70; pub. info. officer U.S. Dept. Agr., Washington, 1970-76; free lance writer, 1956—. Mem. LWV, Nat. League Am. Penwomen, Nat. Press Club, Nat. Fedn. Press Women, Assn. Agr. Coll. Editors, Nat. Hist. Soc., Am. Hist. Soc., Nat. Archives, Smithsonian Assocs., Nat. Women's Polit. Caucus, Nat. Trust Historic Preservation, Am. Hort. Soc., Huguenot Soc., Lambda Tau (treas.), Kappa Delta Pi. Club: City Tavern (Washington). Episcopalian. Democrat. Author: Woodrow Wilson, 1958; contbr. articles to various publs.; sponsor civic improvements. Home: 1515 32d St NW Washington DC 20007

WALKER, EVELYN, retired educational television executive; b. Birmingham, Ala.; d. Preston Lucas and Mattie (Williams) W.; AB, Huntingdon Coll., 1927, student Cornell U., 1927-29, spl. courses U. Ill., 1955, MA, U. Ala., 1963; LHD, 1974. Speech instr. Phillips High Sch., Birmingham, 1930-34; head speech dept. Ramsay High Sch., Birmingham, 1934-52; chmn. radio and TV, Birmingham Pub. Schs., 1944-75, head instructional TV programming services, 1969-75; Miss Ann, broadcaster children's daily radio program, Birmingham, 1946-57; producer Our Am. Heritage radio series, 1944-54; TV staff producer programs shown daily Ala. Pub. TV Network, 1954-75; past cons. Gov.'s Ednl. TV Legislative Study Com., 1953; nat. del. Asian-Am. Women Broadcasters Conf., 1966; past chmn. Creative TV-Radio Writing Competition. Mem. Emerita Nat. Def. Adv. Com. on Women in Services; past TV-radio co-chmn. Gov.'s Adv. Bd. Safety Com.; past TV chmn. Festival of Arts; past audio-visual chmn. Ala. Congress, also past mem. Birmingham council P.T.A.; media chmn. Gov.'s Commn. on Yr. of the Child; bd. dirs. Women's Army Corps Found. Recipient Alumnae Achievement award Huntingdon Coll., 1958; Tops in Our Town award Birmingham News, 1957; Air Force Recruiting plaque, 1961; Spl. Bowl award for promoting arts through Ednl. TV., 1962; citation 4th Army Corps., 1962; cert. of appreciation Ala. Multiple Sclerosis Soc., 1962; Freedoms Found. at Valley Forge Educator's medal award, 1963; Top TV award A.R.C., 1964; Ala. Woman of Achievement award, 1964; Bronze plaque Ala. Dist. Exchange Clubs, 1969; cert. of appreciation Birmingham Bd. Edn., 1975; Obelisk award Children's Theatre, 1976; 20-Yr. Service award Ala. Ednl. TV Commn.; key to city of Birmingham, 1966; named Woman of Yr., Birmingham, 1965; named Ala. Woman of Yr., Progressive Farmer mag., 1966; hon. col. Ala. Mem. Am. Assn. Ret. Persons, Ala. Assn. Ret. Tchrs., Huntingdon Coll. Alumnae Assn. (former internat. pres.), Former Am. Women in Radio and TV, Ala. Hist. Assn., Arlington Hist. Assn. (dir., pres. 1981-83, bd. dirs. Arlington Antebellum Home and Gardens), Magna Charta Dames (past state sec.-treas.), DAR (former pub. relations com. Ala., TV chmn., state program chmn. 1979-85, state chmn. Seimes Microfilm com. 1985-88, state chmn. Motion Picture, Radio TV com. 1988—), Colonial Dames 17th Century (chmn. pub. relations com.), U.S. Daus. 1812 (past state TV chmn.), Daus. Am. Colonists (past 2d v.p. local chpt., state chmn. TV and radio), Ams. Royal Descent, Royal Order Garter, Plantagenets Soc. Am., Salvation Army Women's Aux., Symphony Aux., Humane Soc. Aux., Eagle Forum, Nat. League Am. Pen Women, Com. of 100 Women (bd. dirs.), Royal Order Crown, Women in Communications (past local pres., nat. headliner 1965), English Speaking Union, Birmingham-Jefferson Hist. Soc., Delta Delta Delta (mem. Golden Circle). Methodist. Clubs: Downtown, Birmingham Country, The Club. Home: 744 Euclid Ave Mountain Brook Birmingham AL 35213

WALKER, FRANCIS JOSEPH, lawyer; b. Tacoma, Aug. 5, 1922; s. John McSweeney and Sarah Veronica (Meechan) W.; m. Julia Corinne O'Brien, Jan. 27, 1951; children—Vincent Paul, Monica Irene Hylton, Jill Marie Nudell, John Michael, Michael Joseph, Thomas More. B.A., St. Martin's Coll., 1947; J.D., U. Wash., 1950. Bar: Wash. Asst. atty. gen. State of Wash., 1950-51; sole practice, Olympia, Wash., 1951—; gen. counsel Wash. Cath. Conf., 1967-76. Served to lt. (j.g.) USNR, 1943-46; PTO. Home: 2723 Hillside Dr Olympia WA 98501 Office: 203 E 4th Ave Suite 301 Olympia WA 98501

WALKER, FREDA ANNE ELIZABETH, psychologist; b. Wellington, New Zealand, Dec. 11, 1944; d. John and Olga (Khouri) W.; m. Louis Samuel Leland, Jr.; Oct. 20, 1972; 1 child, Daniel. BA, Victoria U., Wellington, 1965, BA with honors, 1966, MA, 1966; PhD in Psychology, Otago U., Dunedin, New Zealand, 1983. Psychologist Justice Dept., Wellington, 1967-69, psychologist, acting head dept. regional service, 1970-72; grad. selection officer British European Airways, London, 1969-70; head psychology dept. Cherry Farm Group Hosps., Dunedin, 1972-77; sr. clin. psychologist, head dept. Charry Farm Group Hosps., Dunedin, 1978-86; pvt. and guidance cons. Santa Barbara County, Calif., 1977-78; cons. psychologist St. Alban's Psychiatric Hosp., Radford, Va., 1985-86; prin. clin. psychologist Otago Hosp. Bd., Dunedin, 1986—. Contbr. articles to profl. jours. Mem. New Zealand Psychol. Soc. (assoc. 1979, pres. 1987—), mem. Nat. Assn. Hosp. Psychologists (exec. 1975-77, 1983-84), New Zealand Psychol. Soc. (membership sec. 1971-72, chairperson clin. div. 1973-74, assoc. 1979, pres. 1988—), New Zealand Rehab. Assn., New Zealand Inst. Health Adminstrs., Dunedin Wine and Food Soc.(former co-pres.). Club: Lebanese. Office: Otago Hosp Bd, Pvt Bag, Dunedin New Zealand

WALKER, GAIL JUANICE, electrologist; b. Bosque County, Tex., Sept. 3, 1937; d. Hiram Otis and Hazel Ruth (Carmichael) Gunter; cert. Shults Inst. Electrolysis, 1971; children—Lillian Ruth, Deborah Lynn. In quality control Johnson & Johnson, San Angelo, Tex., 1962-70; owner, pres., electrologist Ariz. Inst. Electrolysis, Scottsdale, 1979—; ednl. cons. Gail Walker's Internat. Sch. Electrolysis, Tokyo, 1980; area corr. Hair Route mag., 1981; participant continuing edn. program in electrology Shelby State Coll., 1981. Editor Electrolysis World. Cert., Pvt. Bus. and Tech. Schs., State of Ariz. Mem. Ariz. Assn. Electrologists (pres. 1980—), Am. Electrolysis Assn., Internat. Guild Profl. Electrologists, Nat. Fedn. Ind. Businessmen, Ariz. Assn. Electrologists (organizer 1980). Republican. Baptist. Club: Order of Eastern Star.

WALKER, GEORGE KONTZ, lawyer, educator; b. Tuscaloosa, Ala., July 8, 1938; s. Joseph Henry and Catherine Louise (Indorf) W.; m. Phyllis Ann Sherman, July 30, 1966; children: Charles Edward, Mary Neel. B.A., U. Ala., 1959; LL.B., Vanderbilt U., 1966; M.A., Duke U., 1968; LL.M., U. Va., 1972; postgrad. (Sterling fellow), Law Sch. Yale U., 1975-76. Bar: Va. 1967, N.C. 1976. Law clk. U.S. Dist. Ct., Richmond, Va., 1966-67; assoc. Hunton, Williams, Gay, Powell & Gibson, Richmond, 1967-70; practice law Charlottesville, Va., 1970-71; asst. prof. Wake Forest U. Law Sch., Winston-Salem, N.C., 1972-73, assoc. prof., 1974-77, prof., 1977—; vis. prof. Marshall-Wythe Sch. Law Coll. William and Mary, Williamsburg, Va., 1979-80, U. Ala. Law Sch., 1985; cons. Naval War Coll., 1976—. Author: International Law for the Naval Commander, 1985; contbr. articles to profl. jours. Served with USN, 1959-62; capt. USNR. Woodrow Wilson fellow, 1962-63. Mem. ABA, Va. Bar Assn., N.C. Bar Assn., Am. Soc. Internat. Law (exec. council 1988—), Am. Judicature Soc., Maritime Law Assn., Order of Barristers, Phi Beta Kappa, Sigma Alpha Epsilon, Phi Delta Phi. Democrat. Episcopalian. Club: Piedmont. Home: 3321 Pennington Ln Winston-Salem NC 27106-5439 Office: Wake Forest U Sch Law PO Box 7206 Winston-Salem NC 27109-7206

WALKER, GORDON REDFORD, tegestologist, international broker and specialist in oriental rugs; b. Glasgow, Scotland, June 19, 1932; s. George Robert and Mary Duff (Scott) W.; children from previous marriage: Louise Margaret, Kate Mary; m. Alma Madge Platts, Feb. 14, 1971. MA, U. Glasgow, 1952. Account exec. The London Press Exchange, 1957-60, account dir., 1960-62; dir. LPE Internat., London, 1962-64; mng. dir. LPE South Africa-Zimbabwe-Malawi, Johannesburg, South Africa, 1964-69; exec. v.p. Latin Am. ops. Leo Burnett Inc., various locations Mexico, P.R., South Am., 1969-71; mng. dir. Scott-Walker Ltd., Bath, Eng., 1971—, Walker Coulthard Ltd., Johannesburg, 1974-79. Author: 2800 Hours Company Time, 1972. Fellow Inst. Dirs.; mem. Inst. Practitioners in Advt., Internat. Advt. Assn. Club: Bristol-Clifton (Eng.) Golf. Home: The Lochan House, Breach Hill, Chew Stoke, Avon BS18 8YB, England Office: Scott Walker Ltd, 18 Green St, Bath, Avon BA1 2J2, England

WALKER, GRAHAM HERBERT, investment company executive; b. Rosetown, Sask., Can., Aug. 24, 1931; s. George Keys and Anne Viola (Sled) W.; children—Michael, Alison, Sandra, Erin. Can. Salesman Houston Willoughby, Regina, Sask., 1955-67, v.p., 1967-74, pres., 1974-80, chmn., chief exec. officer, 1980-83; dep. chmn., dir. Pemberton Houston Willoughby, Inc., Regina, 1985—; bd. dirs. Cairns Homes, Ltd., Regina, Sask., Saskatchewan Oil and Gas Corp., Regina, Co-Enerco, Calgary; Bd. dirs. Atlantic Council Can., CKCK Children's Fund, Regina, YMCA, Regina. Mem. C. of C. Clubs: Optimist, Assiniboia (Regina, Sask.). Home: 2007 E Cunning Crescent, Regina, SK Canada S4V 0M7 Office: Pemberton Houston Willoughby Inc, 2105 11th Ave, Regina, SK Canada S4P 3Z9

WALKER, HERBERT BROOKS, sculptor, museum director; b. Bklyn., Nov. 30, 1927; s. Robert Sanford Walker and Lillian Gahagan; m. Joan Allen, Sept. 1951 (div. 1969); children: Noel Gahagan, H. Brooks; m. Mercedes Spada, May 1980; children: Paolo Walter, Timothy Robert. BFA, Yale U., 1951. Photographer Gahagan Dredging, Caracas, Venezuela, 1953-54; with materials prodn. Standard Oil Co., Abadan, Iran, 1957-59; dir. Walker Mus., Fairlee, Vt., 1960—; free-lance sculptor Fairlee, Vt., 1960-70, Avesa, Italy, 1970—. Photographer: (book) Gaudi, 1958. Democrat. Club: Men's (Fairlee) (pres. 1962). Home: Avesa, 37127 Verona Italy Office: Walker Mus Fairlee VT 05045

WALKER, ILSE, zoologist; b. Winterthur, Zürich, Switzerland, Nov. 29, 1930; arrived in Brazil, 1976; d. Friedrich and Martha (Schaerer) Walker. MS in Zoology, U. Zürich, 1955, PhD in Zoology, 1958. Researcher U. Zürich, 1958, U. Bern, Switzerland, 1964, Tex. A&M U., 1964-65, Cornell U., Ithaca, N.Y., 1965-66; lectr. U. East Africa, Dar-es-Salaam, Tanzania, 1966-70, Imperial Coll., London, 1970-76; sr. research scientist Inst. Nat. Pesquisas Amazônia, Manaus, Brazil, 1976—; prof. in ecology, evolution theory 1976—. Contbr. articles to profl. jours. Mem. Swiss Zool. Soc., Brazilian Limnological Soc., Brazilian Assn Theoretical Biology (v.p.), Soc. Brasileira Progresso da Ciência. Office: Inst Nat Pesquisas Amazônia, Dept Ecologia, Aleixo Caixa Postal 478, 69011 Manaus Brazil

WALKER, JERRY VANZANT, lawyer; b. Casa Grande, Ariz., Dec. 12, 1925; s. Gerald Lee and Mildred (McMeans) W.; m. Virginia Lee Ridenhower, Dec. 18, 1948; children: Jerry Vanzant, Lucinda Lee. B.S., Tex. A&M U., 1949; LL.B., U. Tex., 1952. Bar: Tex. 1952. Since practiced in Houston; ptnr. Fulbright & Jaworski, 1952-86; vis. prof. med. jurisprudence Baylor Coll. Medicine; pres. Houston Jr. Bar Assn., 1960. Served with AUS, 1944-46. Fellow Am. Coll. Trial Lawyers; Mem. Am. Bar Assn. (com. admiralty and maritime law 1979-82, commn. med. profl. liability 1975-80, vice chmn. sect. ins., negligence and compensation 1976-79, vice chmn. sect. litigation 1979-80), State Bar Tex. (chmn. tort and compenation sect. 1966-67), Houston Bar Assn. (chmn. inter-profession relations with physicians com. 1970-74), Houston Assn. Def. Counsel (1st v.p. 1971), Tex. Assn. Def. Counsel, State Bar Tex. (dir. 1960-61), Internat. Assn. Ins. Counsel (pres. 1975-76), Def. Research Inst. (exec. com., dir. 1974-77, vice chmn. com. to improve adminstrn. civil justice 1976-77), Am. Bar Found., Tex. Bar Found., Houston Bar Found., Maritime Law Assn. U.S. (com. Comité Maritime Internat.), Houston C. of C. (life). Republican. Presbyterian. Clubs: Houston Country. Home: 101 Westcott St 1706 Houston TX 77007 Office: Houston Nat Bank Bldg 5757 Memorial Dr Suite 210 Houston TX 77007

WALKER, JESSIE, writer, photographer; b. Milw.; d. Stuart Richard and Loraine (Freuler) Walker; m. Arthur W. Griggs, Feb. 5, 1984; B.S., Medill Sch. Journalism, Northwestern U., also M.S. First major feature article appeared in The Am. Home mag.; contbr. numerous articles to nat. mags. including Am. Heritage's Americana, Better Homes and Gardens, McCall's, House and Garden, Good Housekeeping, others; midwest editor Am. Home mag.; contbg. editor Better Homes & Gardens; cover photographer Country Living, 1984, 85. Recipient Dorothy Dawes award for distinguished journalistic coverage in home furnishing, 1976, 77; named Headliner of Yr. North Shore Women in Communication, 1988. Mem. Am. Soc. Interior Designers (press mem.), Women in Communications. Author: How to Plan a Trend Setting Kitchen, 1962; How to Make Window Decorating Easy, 1969;

Shaker Design-150-year-old Modern, 1972; Good Design—What Makes It Last?, 1973; Junking Made Easy, 1974; Poster Power, 1976; For Collectors Only, 1977; Bishop Hill-Utopian Community 1978; also articles. Photographer cover photo Better Homes & Gardens, Sept. 1982, Oct. 1980, House Beautiful, Dec. 1981, Country Living, Jan., Feb., Sept., Nov., 1983, Jan., 1984, Dec., 1985, May, 1986, Jan., Feb., May, 1987, Mar. 1988. Address: 241 Fairview Rd Glencoe IL 60022

WALKER, JEWETT LYNIUS, clergyman, church official; b. Beaumont, Tex., Apr. 7, 1930; s. Elijah Harvey and Ella Jane (Wilson) W.; B.A., Calif. Western U., 1957; M.A., Kingdom Bible Inst., 1960; B.R.E., St. Stephens Coll., 1966, D.D., 1968; LL.D., Union Bapt. Sem., 1971; grad. Nat. Planned Giving Inst., 1981; m. Dorothy Mae Croom, Apr. 11, 1965; children—Cassandra Lynn, Jewett L., Kevin, Michael, Ella, Betty Renne, Kent, Elijah H. Ordained to ministry A.M.E. Zion Ch., 1957; pastor Shiloh A.M.E. Zion Ch., Monrovia, Calif., 1961-64, Martin Temple A.M.E. Zion Ch., Los Angeles, 1964-65, 1st A.M.E. Zion Ch., Compton, Calif., 1965-66, Met. A.M.E. Zion Ch., Los Angeles, 1966-73, Logan Temple A.M.E. Zion Ch., San Diego, 1973-74, Rock Hill A.M.E. Zion Ch., Indian Trail, N.C., 1974-79, Bennettsville A.M.E. Zion Ch., Norwood, N.C., 1979-86, Price Meml. A.M.E. Zion Ch., Concord, N.C., 1986—; sec. dept. home missions, brotherhood pensions and relief A.M.E. Zion Ch., Charlotte, N.C., 1974; mem. exec. bd. ch. and soc. Nat. Council Chs.; mem. World Meth. Council, del. 14th World Conf. Trustee, Clinton Coll., Rock Hill, Lomax-Hannon Coll., Greenville, Ala., Union Bapt. Theol. Sem., Birmingham, Ala.; bd. mgrs. McCrorey br. YMCA; pres. Am. Ch. Fin. Service Corp., Carolina Home Health Service Inc., Methodist Life Ins. Soc. Inc., bd. trustees State N.C. Coll. Found., Inc., 1987, del. Presbyn. Partners in Ecumenism Nat. Council Chs. Christ, 1986, pres., 1988—; del. Presbyn. Ch. U.S. Gen. Assembly, 1985. Fellow Nat. Assn. Ch. Bus. Adminstrs., Ch. Bus. Adminstrn., Presbyn. Ch. Bus. Adinstrn. Assn.; mem. NAACP (life). Clubs: Shriners, Masons (33 deg.). Author articles. Home: 910 Bridle Path Ln Charlotte NC 27211 Office: 4501 Walker Rd Charlotte NC 28211

WALKER, JOHN, Spanish educator, writer; b. Dumbarton, Scotland, Aug. 8, 1933; came to Can., 1967; s. James Charleton and Sarah (Leyden) W.; m. Irene Connolly, Aug. 6, 1960; children—James Patrick, Clare Helen, John Vincent. B.A. with honors, U. London, 1970 Ph.D., 1975; M.A. with honors, U. Glasgow, 1962. Lectr. Spanish, Brock U., St. Catharines, Ont., Can., 1967-69; asst. prof. Spanish, Queen's U., Kingston, Ont., 1969-72, assoc. prof., 1972-77, prof., 1977—, head dept., 1981-84; manuscript reader; grant adjudicator. Author: Cunninghame Graham and Scotland, 1980; Metaphysics and Aesthetics in the Works of Eduardo Barrios, 1983, A Critical Guide to La Vorágine, 1988. Editor: South American Sketches of R.B. Cunninghame Graham, 1978; Scottish Sketches of R.B. Cunninghame Graham, 1982; Temas criollos de R.B. Cunninghame Graham, 1984; North American Sketches of R.B. Cunninghame Graham, 1986. Contbr. numerous articles to scholarly jours. Can. Council grantee, 1970, 73, fellow, Argentina, 1976-77; SSHRCC fellow, 1984-85, grantee, 1983, 87-88. Mem. Internat. Assn. Hispanists, MLA, Can. Assn. Hispanists (award 1975), Latin Am. Studies Assn, also others. Avocations: soccer; music. Home: 244 Avenue Rd, Kingston, ON Canada K7M 1C7 Office: Queen's U, Kingston, ON Canada K7L 3N6

WALKER, JOHN SUMPTER, JR., lawyer; b. Richmond, Ark., Oct. 13, 1921; s. John Sumpter, Martha (Wilson) W.; m. Eljana M. duVall, Dec. 31, 1947; children—John Stephen, Barbara Monika Ann, Peter Mark Gregory. B.A., Tulane U., 1942; M.S., U. Denver, 1955, J.D., 1960; diploma Nat. Def. U., 1981. Bar: Colo. 1960, U.S. Dist. Ct. Colo. 1960, U.S. Supreme Ct., 1968, U.S. Ct. Appeals (10th cir.) 1960, U.S. Tax. Ct., 1981. With Denver & Rio Grande Western R.R. Co., 1951-61, gen. solicitor, 1961—; dir., pres. Denver Union Terminal Ry. Co.; cent. city asst. Guild Debutante Charities, Inc. Served with U.S. Army, 1942-46. Decorated Bronze Star. Mem. ABA, Colo. Bar Assn., Arapahoe County Bar Assn., Alliance Francaise (life), Order of St. Ives, U. Denver Chancellors' Soc., Cath. Lawyers Guild, Passage Inc. Republican. Roman Catholic. Club: Denver Athletic. Home: 6185 S Columbine Way Littleton CO 80121 Office: 986 One Park Central PO Box 5482 Denver CO 80217

WALKER, JONATHAN LEE, lawyer; b. Kalamazoo, Mar. 8, 1948; s. Harvey E. and Olivia M. (Estrada) W. B.A., U. Mich., 1969; J.D., Wayne State U., 1977. Bar: Mich. 1977, U.S. Dist. Ct. (ea. dist.) Mich. 1982. Assoc. firm Moore, Barr & Kerwin, Detroit, 1977-79; ptnr. firm Barr & Walker, Detroit, 1979-82; assoc. firm Richard M. Goodman, P.C., Detroit, 1983-87; hearing officer Mich. Civil Rights Commn., Detroit, 1983—; sole practice, Detroit, 1988—; participant Detroit Bar Assn. Vol. Lawyer Program. Bd. dirs. Community Treatment Ctr.-Project Rehab., Detroit, 1983—; mem. scholarship com. Latino en Marcha Scholarship Fund, Detroit, 1984; treas. youth assistance program Citizens Adv. Council. Mem. State Bar Mich. Found., Wayne County Mediation Tribunal, Inc. (mediator), Am. Arbitration Assn. (arbitrator), Nat. Lawyers Guild, Mich. Trial Lawyers Assn., Assn. Trial Lawyers Am., State Bar Mich. (chmn. com. on underrepresented groups in law 1983-85, com. judicial qualifications 1985-86), Trial Lawyers for Pub. Justice (founder 1981, Amicus com. 1985-86), Ctr. for Auto Safety. Office: 1028 Buhl Bldg Detroit MI 48226

WALKER, KENNETH LANE, business executive; b. Helston, Cornwall, Eng., Feb. 26, 1936; s. Herbert Arthur and Verona Sophie (Thomas) W.; m. Isabella Mary Moffat, July 25, 1964. BA in English with honors, Oxford U., 1960. Dist. officer H.M. Colonial Office, London, 1960-61; acct. Beecham Group, London, 1961-65; chief acct. Mono Containers Ltd., London, 1965-67, fin. dir., 1967-77; fin. dir. Kode Internat. PLC, Swindon, Wiltshire, 1977-85; mgmt. cons. 1985—. Served with RAF, 1955-57. Mem. Inst. Dirs. (chmn. Wiltshire Ctr. 1982—), Inst. Cost Mgmt. Accts. (assoc.). Conservative. Mem. Ch. of Eng. Club: City Livery (Embankment, London). Home and Office: Whitley Grange, Whitley near Melksham SN128QN, England

WALKER, KENNETH RICHARD, economist, educator; b. Otley, Yorks, Eng., Oct. 17, 1931; s. Arthur Bedford and Olive (Thornton) W.; m. June Abercrombie Collie, July 28, 1959; children: Neil George Arthur, Ruth Abercrombie. BA in Econs., U. Leeds, Eng., 1953; PhD in Econs., U. Oxford, Eng., 1959. Asst. lectr. polit. economy U. Aberdeen, Scotland, 1956-59; research fellow Sch. Oriental and African Studies, U. London, 1959-61, lectr. in econs., 1961-65, reader in econs., 1965-72, prof. econs., 1972—. Author: Planning in Chinese Agriculture, 1965, Grain Procurement and Consumption in China, 1984; mem. editorial exec. com.: The China Quar., 1965—; contbr. articles to profl. jours. Home: 4 Harpenden Rd, Saint Albans, Herts AL3 5AB, England Office: U London Sch Oriental/African, Studies Malet St, London England

WALKER, LANNON, foreign service officer; b. Los Angeles, Jan. 17, 1936; s. James Orville and Esther W.; m. Arlette Daguet, July 14, 1954; children: Rachelle, Anne. B.S., Georgetown U., 1961. Fgn. service officer Dept. State, 71961; polit. officer Dept. State, Rabat, Morocco, 1962-64; prin. officer Dept. State, Constantine, Algeria, 1964-66; assigned Exec. Secretariat Dept. State, 1966-69; econ. counselor Dept. State, Tripoli, Libya, 1969-70; dep. chief mission Dept. State, Yaounde, Cameroon, 1971-73; adminstrv. counselor Dept. State, Saigon, Viet Nam, 1973-74; dep. chief mission Dept. State, Kinshasa, Zaire, 1974-77; dep. asst. sec. African Affairs Dept. State, Washington, 1977-82; spl. adviser African affairs Dept. State, 1983-84, dep. insp. gen., 1984-85, ambassador to Senegal, 1985-88; employed in pvt. sector 1982-83. Served with USAF, 1953-58. Mem. Am. Fgn. Service Assn. (chmn. 1966-69). Roman Catholic. Home: 5911 Overlea Rd Bethesda CA 20016 Office: US Ambassador to Senegal care US State Dept Washington DC 20520

WALKER, LESLIE GRESSON, psychology educator, clinician; b. Glasgow, Scotland, May 17, 1949; s. Edward William and Elizabeth Mary Milne (McCormick) W.; m. Mary Birnie Durno, Sept. 6, 1974; children: Andrew Antony, Richard Birnie Durno. MA with first class honors, U. Aberdeen, 1971, PhD, 1975; Diploma in Clin. Psychology, Brit. Psychol. Soc., 1976. Clin. psychologist Grampian Health Bd., Scotland, 1971-76; lectr. U. Aberdeen, Scotland, 1976—; cons. Imperial Chem. Industries, 1986—. Co-author: Models for Psychotherapy: A Primer, 1982. Mem. Scottish Home and Health Dept., 1979-85. Fellow Brit. Psychol. Soc. (assoc.); mem. Nat. Com. Scientists in Professions Allied to Medicine (clin. psychology sub-com.), Brit. Soc. Exptl. and Clin. Hypnosis, Brit. Assn. Behavioural Psychotherapy, Assn. Child Psychology and Psychiatry, Grampian Div. Psychiatry (hon.). Mem. Ch. Scotland. Office: Aberdeen U Med Sch, Foresterhill, Aberdeen AB9 2ZD, Scotland

WALKER, MARGARET LINZEL, government official; b. Washington, Feb. 22, 1921; d. Frank A. and Verna (Diecks) Linzel; B.A., Stetson U., DeLand, Fla., 1942; divorced; 1 son, Paul L. With Treasury Dept., 1961-81, chief stats. and research staff Bur. Mint, 1970-79, chief program evaluation div., 1979-81, also mgr. fed women's program. Recipient Meritorious Service award Treasury Dept., 1975, Sec's award, 1975; Disting. Alumni award Stetson U., 1977. Mem. Federally Employed Women, Treasury Dept. Hist. Assn., Pi Beta Phi. Presbyterian. Club: Stetson U. Alumni.

WALKER, MICHAEL CLAUDE, finance educator; b. Sherman, Tex., June 8, 1940; s. Andrew Jackson and Alice Lorene (Curry) W.; m. Martha Ellen Hindman, Sept. 10, 1966; children: Stephanie Elizabeth, Rebecca Elaine, Priscilla Eileen. BA, Austin Coll., 1965; MA, Ohio State U., 1966; PhD, U. Houston, 1971. Instr. U. Houston, 1969-70; asst. prof. Ga. State U., Atlanta, 1971-75; assoc. prof. U. Okla., Norman, 1975-78; prof., head dept. fin., ins. and real estate North Tex. State U., Denton, 1978-85; prof., head dept. fin. U. Cin., 1985—, Virgil M. Schwarm prof. fin. and investments, 1988—. Co-editor: Cases in Financial Institutions, 1979; contbr. articles to profl. jours. Served with AUS, 1958-61. Recipient Leonard P. Ayers fellowship award, 1973. Mem. Am. Fin. Assn., Fin. Execs. Inst., Fin. Mgmt. Assn., So. Fin. Assn. (bd. dirs. 1983-85, sec.-treas. 1986-88, v.p. 1988—), Southwestern Fin. Assn. (bd. dirs. 1986-88), Beta Gamma Sigma, Omicron Delta Epsilon. Methodist. Office: Univ Cin Finance Dept Mail Location 195 Cincinnati OH 45221

WALKER, OLIVER MALLORY, mortgage banker, realtor; b. Alpine, Ala., Sept. 1898; s. Samuel and Ella Belle (Mallory) W.; student U. Ala., 1917, Marion (Ala.) Mil. Inst., 1917-18; B.S., U.S. Naval Acad., 1922; m. Elizabeth Powell Dunlop, June 11, 1932; children—Elizabeth Dunlop Walker Edgeworth, Ann Mallory Walker Gaffney, O. Mallory. Advt. salesman Am. Bur. Trade Extension, 1922, advt. mgr., 1923; organizer Washington Concrete Products Corp., 1924, sales mgr., 1924-30, v.p., 1930-43; sec., dir. Union Market Terminal, Washington, 1928-35; organizer, pres. Walker & Dunlop, Washington and Balt., 1935—; now chmn. bd.; dir. mem. exec. com. Title Guarantee Co., Balt., 1941-75; pres. Am. Standard Life Ins. Co., 1953-58; lectr., speaker mortgage financing. Pres., Washington Real Estate Bd., 1949-50; pres. mortgage council Nat. Assn. Real Estate Bds., 1954-55, chmn. com. real estate econs. 1956-60. Chmn. bd. zoning appeals, Montgomery County, Md., 1943-47. Trustee, pres. Whitehall Country Sch., 1944-46; trustee Landon Sch., 1950-52, Naval Acad. Found., 1968-79. Recipient Realtor of Yr. award Washington Bd. Realtors, 1967. Mem. Mortgage Bankers Assn. Am. (gov. 1952-60, v.p. 1960—, dir. 1961-69, Certified Mortgage Bankers award 1974, dir.). Clubs: Metropolitan, Chevy Chase, Army and Navy (Washington); Army and Navy Country (Arlington, Va.); Rehoboth Beach Country; Balboa (Mazatlan, Mexico). Author: Servicing Mortgage Loans, 1951. Co-author: Quar. Mortgage Market Reports, Nat. Assn. Real Estate Bds., 1955-65. Home: The Towers Apt 214W 4201 Cathedral Ave NW Washington DC 20016 Office: Walker and Dunlop 1156 15th St NW Washington DC 20005

WALKER, P(ERCIVAL) DUANE, health care industry infomation systems executive, consultant; b. McKeesport, Pa., June 5, 1931; s. Percy Theodore and Bertha I. (Westerberg) W.; B.S., Pa. State U., 1953; M.B.A., N.Y. U., 1969; m. Doris Jane McClymont, Dec. 12, 1959; children—Jeannine Cherie, Andrea Lee, Edward Duane. Systems engr. IBM Corp., Pitts., 1955-58; cons. corporate controller's staff Westinghouse Elec. Co., Pitts., 1958-59; mgr. mgmt. adv. services Price Waterhouse & Co., Pitts., 1959-62; successively mgr. market analysis-programming systems, mgr. info. systems planning and arch., mgr. bus. systems planning IBM Corp., Poughkeepsie and White Plains, N.Y., 1962-74; sr. v.p. mgmt. systems Humana, Inc., Louisville, 1974-82; founder, pres. PDW, Inc., 1982-84; founder, chmn. bd., chief exec. officer Internat. Med. Exchange, 1984-87; founder Dewey Walker & Assocs., 1987—; mem. adv. com. First Profl. Bank Los Angeles; dir. Gateway Med. Systems, Inc., Atlanta; dir., chmn. compensation com. Kurfees Coatings, Inc., Louisville; lectr., speaker univs., nat. profl. soc. meetings. Pa. State v.p. Jaycees, 1957; chmn. Hire the Physically Handicapped, 1957, Fund for the Arts, Louisville, 1976; dir. Jr. Achievement; mem. athletic com. Ky. Country Day Sch.; mem. Louisville Schs. and Bus. Coordinating Council, 1979-80; mem. Leadership Louisville, 1979-80; com. vice chmn. Boy Scouts Am., 1981. Named a Disting. Alumni Pa. State U.; named one of 87 People to Watch in 1987 by Louisville Mag. Mem. Soc. Mgmt. Info. Systems, Am. Inst. Indsl. Engrs., Kappa Delta Rho. Presbyterian. Clubs: Penn State Alumni, Penn State of Ky., Nittany Lions, Pitts. Playhouse, N.Y. U., Harmony Landing Country, Jefferson (Louisville). Home: 1309 N Buckeye Ln Goshen KY 40026 Office: Internat. Med Exchange 9000 Wessex Pl Suite 201 Louisville KY 40222

WALKER, PETER EDWARD, Secretary of State for Wales; b. England, Mar. 25, 1932; s. Sydney and Rose W.; m. Tessa Pout, 1969; 3 sons, 2 daus. Student, Latymer Upper Sch. Mem., nat. exec. Conservative Party, 1956—; nat. chmn. Young Conservatives, 1958-60; parliamentary candidate for Dartford Conservative Party, 1955, 59; parliamentary pvt. sec. Leader of House of Commons, 1963-64; opposition front bench spokesman fin. and econs., 1964-66, transport, 1966-68, local govt., housing and land, 1968-70; minister of housing and local govt. 1970; sec. of state environment, 1970-72, trade and industry, 1972-74; opposition spokesman trade, industry and consumer affairs, 1974, def., 1974-75; minister of agr., fisheries and food 1979-83, sec. of state for energy, 1983-87, sec. of state for Wales, 1987—. Author: The Ascent of Britain, 1977, Trust the People, 1987. *

WALKER, RAYMOND FRANCIS, business and financial consulting company executive; b. Medicine Lake, Mont., Nov. 9, 1914; s. Dennis Owen and Rose (Long) W.; m. Patricia K. Blakey, May 15, 1951; children: Richard A., Mark D., Maxie R. Forest, Victoria L. Le Huray, Suzanne J. Buhl, Tracy A. Grad. pub. schs.; student, Edison Vocat. Sch., 1935-39. Truck mgr. Pacific Food Products, Seattle, 1939-42; machinist Todd Shipyard, Seattle, 1943-45; owner Delbridge Auto Sales, Seattle, 1945-48; pres. Pacific Coast Acceptance Corp., 1949-60; v.p. West Coast Mortgage, Seattle, 1960-67, United Equities Corp., Seattle, 1965-69; pres. Income Mgmt. Corp., Seattle, 1970—; v.p. Internat. Mint and Foundry, Redmond, Wash., 1983—; cons. Life Ins. Co. Am., Consumer Loan Service. Mem. Nat. Assn. Security Dealers. Methodist. Lodge: Elks. Home: 777 W Sequim Bay Rd Sequim WA 98382

WALKER, RICHARD IAN BENTHAM, artist; b. Croydon, Surrey, Eng., Mar. 18, 1925; s. Norman and Margaret W.; student (Art scholar) Canford Sch., 1939-43, Queen's Coll., Oxford (Eng.) U., 1943-44, Croydon Sch. Art, 1945-48; art tchr.'s diploma London U., 1949; art tng. Slade Sch. Art, London, 1949. Portrait and landscape painter, illustrator; group shows include: Royal Acad., London, Paris Salon, Royal Soc. Portrait Painters, Royal Soc. Brit. Artists; one-man shows: St. Hilda's Coll., Oxford U., 1958, Fairfield Halls, Croydon, 1967, Mall Galleries, London, 1978, Alpine Gallery, London, 1981; represented in permanent collections: Royal Coll. Music, London, Mus. London, Middlesex Hosp. (Eng.), Brompton Hosp., London; exhibited in Royal Acad. at age 13; portraits include Leopold Stokowski, 1973, Herbert Howells, 1977, Douglas Bader, 1981; tchr. painting Croydon (Eng.) Sch. Art, 1947-50; lectr. art adult edn. courses, 1949-57. Served with RAF, 1943-45. Recipient Founder's Prize Royal Drawing Soc. Mem. Soc. Graphic Fine Art, United Soc. Artists, Armed Forces Art Soc. Home and Studio: 72 Coombe Rd., Croydon,, Surrey CRO 5SH England

WALKER, RONALD FREDERICK, scientific manager; b. London, Apr. 28, 1946; s. Frederick Sidney and Florence (Seipp) W.; m. Doreen ELizabeth Mary Turner, Apr. 29, 1978. Grad., North East London Poly., 1968; PhD, U. London, 1972. Chartered chemist, Eng. Research asst. Ministry of Tech., Waltham Abbey, Eng., 1966-67; research cons. North East London Poly. Consultancy Service, London, 1972-73; research assoc. U. London, 1973-75; sect. leader Health and Safety Exec. Dept., London, 1975-84, sci. mgr., 1984—. Contbr. numerous research publs. Fellow Royal Soc. of Chemistry (chartered). Anglican. Home: 44 Woodhill Crescent, Kenton HA3 OLY, England Office: Lab of the Gov Chemist, Queens Rd Teddington, Middlesex TW11 OLY, England

WALKER, RONALD H., executive search company executive; b. Bryan, Tex., July 25, 1937; s. Walter Hugh and Maxine (Tarver) W.; m. Anne Lucille Collins, Aug. 8, 1959; children: Lisa, Marjorie, Lynne. B.A., U. Ariz., 1960. With Allstate Ins. Co., Pasadena, Calif., 1964-67, Hudson Oxygen Therapy Sales Co., Los Angeles, 1967-69; asst. to sec. interior 1969-70; staff asst. to Pres. U.S., dir. White House Advance Office, 1970-72; spl. asst. to Pres. 1972-73; dir. Nat. Park Service, Washington, 1973-75; cons. Saudi Arabia, 1975; assoc. dir. World Championship Tennis, 1975-77; pres. Ron Walker & Assocs., Inc., Dallas, 1977-79; sr. officer, mng. dir. Korn/Ferry Internat., Washington, 1979—. Trustee Nat. Outdoor Leadership Sch., Nat. Fitness Found.; mem. Pres.'s Commn. on Bicentennial U.S. Constn., 1985—; trustee Ford's Theater; mem. Friends of Nancy Hanks Ctr.; chmn. 50th Presdl. Inauguration; mgr. 1984 Rep. Nat. Conv. Served with U.S. Army, 1961-64. Recipient Disting. Citizen award U. Ariz., 1973, Outstanding Service award Dept. Interior, 1975. Mem. Phi Delta Theta. Republican. Methodist. Office: Mng Dir Korn/Ferry Internat 900 19th St NW Suite 200 Washington DC 20006

WALKER, RONALD R., writer, newspaper editor, government official; b. Newport News, Va., Sept. 2, 1934; s. William R. and Jean Marie (King) W.; m. O. Diane Mawson, Apr. 16, 1961; children—Mark Jonathan, Steven Christopher. B.S., Pa. State U., 1956; postgrad. (Nieman fellow) Harvard U., 1970-71. Reporter, news editor, sr. editor, editorial page editor, mng. editor San Juan Star (P.R.), 1962-73, Washington columnist, 1982-84, city editor, 1984-87; instr. journalism Pa. State U., State College, 1973-74; asst. prof. Columbia U. Grad. Sch. Journalism, N.Y.C., 1974-76; editor The Daily News, V.I., 1976-77; press sec. Gov. V.I., 1978-79; adminstrv. asst. Rep. James H. Scheuer, U.S. Congress, 1980-82, special asst., Resident Commr. Jaime B. Fuster, U.S. Congress, 1987—. Served with U.S. Army, 1957-59. Mem. Soc. Nieman Fellows. Contbr. articles to nat. mags. and jours.

WALKER, SALLY BARBARA, glass company executive; b. Bellerose, N.Y., Nov. 21, 1921; d. Lambert Roger and Edith Demerest (Parkhouse) W.; diploma Cathedral Sch. St. Mary, 1939; A.A., Finch Jr. Coll., 1941. Tchr. interior design Finch Coll., 1941-42; draftsman AT&T, 1942-43; with Steuben Glass Co., N.Y.C., 1943—, exec. v.p., 1959-62, exec. v.p. ops., 1962-78, exec. v.p. ops. and sales, 1978-83, exec. v.p., 1983—. Mem. Fifth Ave. Assn. Republican. Episcopalian. Clubs: Rockaway Hunting, Lawrence Beach, U.S. Lawn Tennis, Colony, English-Speaking Union. Home: 116 E 66th St New York NY 10021 Office: 715 Fifth Ave New York NY 10022

WALKER, SANDRA, mezzo-soprano; b. Richmond, Va., Oct. 1, 1946; d. Phillip Loth and Mary Jane W.; m. Melvin Brown, May 17, 1975; 1 child, Noel Christian Brown. Mus.B., U. N.C., 1969; student, Manhattan Sch. Music, 1971-72. artist-in-residence Ky. Opera Assn., 1980. Recorded: Ned Rorem's song cycle King Midas on Desto Records, 1974; debut San Francisco Opera, 1972, re-engaged 1986, Chgo. Lyric Opera, 1973, re-engaged 1988, Washington Opera Soc., 1973, Phila. Lyric Opera, 1973, Teatro Communale, Florence, Italy, 1985, Met. Opera, N.Y.C., 1986, re-engaged 1989, Opernhaus Zurich, 1987, Stadt Theater Wiesbaden, 1987; leading mezzo soprano N.Y.C. Opera, 1974—, Stadt Theater, Würzburg, Germany, 1980-82, Stadt Theater Gelsenkirchen, W.Ger., 1983-85, Stadt Theater Essen, W.Ger, 1984, Frankfurt Opera, W.Ger., 1985; soloist Orchestra Santa Cecilia Academia, Rome, 1987, New Orch. Paris, 1988; singer in major U.S. and European music festivals Tanglewood, Caramoor, Spoleto-U.S.A. and Spoleto Festival of Two Worlds in, Italy; soloist, Am. Symphony, San Francisco Symphony, 1980; appeared in: PBS nat. telecasts Manon, The Ballad of Baby Doe, Saint of Bleeker Street, 1981, on Great Performances: in The Consul and Eugene Onegin, 1986; Met. Opera nat. broadcast Samson, 1986; orchestral appearances with Nat. Symphony, Washington, St. Louis Symphony, Chgo. Symphony, Richmond (Va.) Symphony. Recipient Nat. Endowment for Arts Affiliate Artist grant sponsored by Va. Opera Assn. and Sears Roebuck Co., 1978. Office: care Columbia Artists Mgmt Inc 165 W 57th St New York NY 10019

WALKER, TIMOTHY CRAIG, transportation executive; b. Huntington, W.Va., Jan. 16, 1945; s. John Paul and Marjorie Frances (Withers) W. BA, Northwestern U., 1967; BFT, Am. Grad. Sch. Internat. Mgmt., 1968. Mgmt. trainee to dir. OIM/internat. mktg. ops. NCR Corp., Dayton, Ohio, 1968-79; v.p. mktg. Do-Ray Lamp Co., Inc., Colorado City, Colo., 1979-87; v.p. mktg. Truck-Lite Co., Inc., Jamestown, N.Y., 1984—, bd. dirs., 1985—; recruiter Am. Grad. Sch. Internat. Mgmt., 1971—; Bd. dirs. Valley Human Resources, United Way agy., 1980-84, Goodwill Industries of Pueblo, Colo., 1983-84; mem. transp. com. Pueblo (Colo.) Area C. of C., 1981-84; mem. Working Group for U.S. Dept. Commerce MOSS Talks. Recipient Pres.'s award (1st alumnus) Am. Grad. Sch. Internat. Mgmt., 1976, award for excellence in internat. advt., 1968; mem. Automotive Hall of Fame. Mem. Transp. Safety Equipment Inst. N.Am. (chmn. mktg. and statis. com. 1980-82), Internat. Platform Assn., European Transport Maintenance Council, Heavy Duty Bus. Forum, Heavy Duty Mfrs. Assn. (bd. govs. 1987—). Republican. Presbyterian. Club. 500 Automotive Execs. Home: PO Box 1263 Jamestown NY 14702 Office: Truck-Lite Co PO Box 387 Jamestown NY 14702

WALKER, VINCENT HENRY, lawyer, government official; b. Lowell, Mass., Oct. 14, 1915; s. Daniel Henry and Annie Jane (Gookin) W.; m. Irene Iris Johnson, Nov. 16, 1946; children: Patricia Anne (Mrs. John Armstrong III), Johnnie Melinda. J.D., Boston Coll. Law, 1939; B.C.S., Benjamin Franklin U., 1951. Bar: Mass. 1940, Fed. Tax Ct. 1952, U.S. Supreme Ct. 1965, D.C. 1980. Partner firm 1940-42; gen. mgr., counsel, joint venture land and subdiv. devels. and sales South and Southwestern U.S., 1946-60; FHA regional atty. Southeastern U.S. and Virgin Islands; then regional atty. FHA Washington Hdqrs. for Mid Atlantic region, 1960; asst. for zone ops. Southwestern U.S., 1960-61; AID State Dept. contract specialist, chief comml. contracts br., adviser to Govt. of Sudan for contract negotiations, developed conversion of AID contracts to automatic data processing system in Vietnam AID Office of Contract Services, Washington, 1961-69; internat. trade policy specialist, chief trade policy br., dir. (acting) indsl. resources div. AID Office of Procurement, 1969-72; internat. trade specialist, agrl. commodities mgr., procurement support div. Office of Commodity Mgmt., AID, 1972-75; contract specialist, interagy. rep., mem. interagy. procurement policy com. Office Contracts Mgmt., 1975-85; ind. legal, fin. cons. 1985—. Author and interagy. collaborator AID govt. and world-wide legal and regulatory publs., export program directives, notices to U.S. industry, internat. posts and orgns., 1970-85; author: pub. Agrl. Commodity Supply, Price, Trends, Report, 1972-75; photog. works published various media in U.S. and fgn. countries, 1970—. Hon. mem. bd. dirs. Am. Opera Scholarship Soc.; mem. men's com. Internat. Eye Found.; contbr. incorporating atty. Lowell Light Opera Guild, 1942. Served to lt. comdr. USNR, Overseas, 1942-46. Named hon. citizen City of Lexington (Ky.), 1970. Mem. Lowell, Middlesex County, Mass., D.C. bar assns., Nat. Trust for Historic Preservation, Smithsonian Assos., Wolf Trap Assos. Home: 9908 Julliard Dr Bethesda MD 20817

WALKER, WALTER LADARE, lawyer; b. Newton County, Mo., Oct. 6, 1927; s. Walter Joseph and Mae (Patterson) W.; m. Marilyn Louise Land, June 24, 1951; children—Marcia Lynn, Charlotte Ann. A.A., Joplin Jr. Coll., 1946; J.D., U. Mo.-Columbia, 1953. Bar: Mo. 1953, U.S. Dist. Ct. (we. dist.) Mo. 1955. Sole practice, Neosho, Mo., 1953—; municipal judge City of Neosho, 1957-66. Bd. dirs. Masonic Home of Mo., St. Louis, 1969-73, pres., 1972-73; pres. Neosho R5 Sch. Bd., 1985-86. Served with U.S. Army, 1946-47, 50-51. Decorated Purple Heart. Mem. Newton-McDonald Counties Bar Assn. (pres. 1957-59), Disabled Am. Veterans, Am. Legion (commander 1956), Delta Theta Phi. Republican. Lodges: Masons (Grand Master Mo. 1973-74, Shriners, Lions (pres. 1971-72). Home: 1301 Benton Ave Neosho MO 64850 Office: PO Box 487 Neosho MO 64850

WALKER, WILLIAM GEORGE, marketing professional; b. Edinburgh, Scotland, Mar. 31, 1942; s. George Stenhouse and Mary Herriot Watt (McLennan) W.; m. Anne Crossman, Dec. 26, 1970 (div. Oct. 29, 1986); children: Alastair, Andrew, Douglas. BSc in Elec. Engring. with first class honors, U. Edinburgh, Scotland, 1963; MBA, Scottish Bus. Sch., Edinburgh, 1982. Design engr. Nuclear Enterprises Ltd., Edinburgh, 1963-65; project engr. Nuclear-Chgo. Corp., Des Plaines, Ill., 1965-68; product mgr. Intertechnique S.A., Paris, 1968-70; mng. dir. Ohio-Nuclear Ltd., Staines, Eng., 1970-78; proprietor Gen. Med. Systems Co., Edinburgh, 1978-83; mng. dir. Internat. Med. Dynamics Ltd., Edinburgh, 1983-86; mktg. dir. Reditronics Ltd., Jersey, Channel Islands, 1986-87; dir. European corp. devel. Dynatech Corp., Edinburgh, 1987—. Inventor, patentee in field. Fellow Brit. Inst. Mgmt. Mem. Scottish Nat. Party. Presbyterian. Club: Caledonian. Home: Red Carr House, FK0 5QE Blairogie by Stirling Scotland

WALKUP, JOHN FRANK, electrical engineer, educator; b. Oakland, Calif, Feb. 7, 1941; s. Francis Milton and Mabel Doreen (Lishman) W.; m. Patricia Ann Hagbom, June 26, 1965; children: Mary Kathleen, Amy Christine, Rebecca Joy. BA, Dartmouth Coll., 1962, BEE, 1963; MS, Stanford U., 1965, Engr., 1969, PhD, 1971. Registered profl. engr., Tex. Research asst. Stanford Electronics Labs., Stanford U., 1963-71; asst. prof. elec. engring. Tex. Tech. U., Lubbock, 1971-76, assoc. prof., 1976-81, prof., 1981-85, P.W. Horn prof., 1985—, assoc. dean engring., 1982-83; cons. in field. Author articles, book chpts. Recipient Goodrich prize Dartmouth Coll., 1963; Halliburton award for excellence in teaching Tex. Tech U., 1980; Pres.'s award for excellence in teaching, 1981; AT&T Found. award for teaching, 1985; Rushing faculty research award, 1986. Fellow Optical Soc. Am., IEEE; mem. Soc. Photo-Optical Instrumentation Engrs., Am. Soc. Engring. Edn., Sigma Xi.

WALL, ARTHUR FREDERIK, building contracting company executive; b. Cedar Rapids, Iowa, July 2, 1927; s. Arthur John and Randi Aletta (Bruas) W.; m. Ulla Viola Simonsen, May 29, 1973. B.A., U. Iowa, 1951. Treas., Wall & Co., Cedar Rapids, 1949-55, v.p., 1955-61, pres., 1961—. Served with USAF, 1945-46. Lutheran. Lodge: Cedar Rapids Danish Brotherhood (pres. 1978-82), Danish Brotherhood (pres. Iowa-Minn. dist. 1984-85). Avocations: fraternal lodges; organizing; building. Home: 362 E Post Rd SE Cedar Rapids IA 52403 Office: Wall & Co 1220 6th St SW Cedar Rapids IA 52404

WALL, JEAN MARIE, lawyer; b. Jersey City, Apr. 16, 1936; d. Joseph Edward and Marie (Kilian) Destler; 1 child, Elizabeth Anne. B.A. cum laude, St. Lawrence U., 1957; M.A., Middlebury Coll., 1962; J.D., San Fernando Valley Coll. Law, 1977. Bar: Calif. 1977. Sole practice, Glendale, Calif., 1977—. Mem. Friends of Los Angeles County Art Mus. Mem. ABA, Calif. Bar Assn., Glendale Bar Assn., Glendale C. of C. (membership com.), Phi Beta Kappa, Pi Sigma Alpha. Roman Catholic. Lodge: Rotary (internat. service chmn.). Office: 210 N Central Ave Suite 205 Glendale CA 91203

WALL, JOSEPH FRAZIER, historian, educator; b. Des Moines, July 10, 1920; s. Joseph Frazier and Minnie Ellen (Patton) W.; m. Beatrice Mills, Apr. 16, 1944; children—April Ane, Joseph Frazier, Julia Mills. B.A., Grinnell Coll., 1941, LL.D. (hon.), 1978; M.A., Harvard U., 1942; Ph.D., Columbia U., 1951; LL.D. (hon.), Simpson Coll., 1978, Luther Coll., 1982. Faculty Grinnell (Iowa) Coll., 1947-78, 80—, prof. history, 1957-78, James Morton Roberts honor prof., 1960-61, Parker prof., 1961-78, Earl Strong Disting. prof., 1972-78, chmn. dept. history, 1954-57, 58-60, chmn. div. social studies, 1956-57, 59-60, chmn. div. history, philosophy and math., 1965-66, chmn. faculty, 1966-69, dean coll., 1969-73, Rosenfield prof. pub. affairs, 1980-85; prof. history, chmn. dept. SUNY, Albany, 1978-80; spl. assignment to asst. oral history project Columbia, 1957; sr. research Fulbright scholar U. Edinburgh, Scotland, 1957-58; Fulbright prof. U. Gothenburg, Sweden, 1964-65, U. Salzburg, Austria, 1987-88. Author: (with Robert Parks) Freedom, 1955 (ann. Iowa Civil Liberties Union award 1956), Henry Watterson; Reconstructed Rebel, 1956 (hon. mention John A. Dunning prize 1956), Andrew Carnegie, 1970 (Bancroft prize 1971), Iowa, 1978, Policies and People, 1979, Skibo, 1985. Served to lt. USNR, 1942-46. Mem. Am. Assn. Univ. Profs., Iowa Assn. Univ. Profs. (chmn. 1955-56), Am. Hist. Assn., Orgn. Am. Historians (exec. bd. 1974-77), Soc. Am. Historians, Phi Beta Kappa, Sigma Delta Chi. Democrat. Home: 2000 Country Club Dr Grinnell IA 50112

WALL, LLOYD L., geological engineer; b. Jerome, Idaho, Feb. 2, 1936; s. Lloyd and Ola (Buck) W.; m. Myrna Bradshaw, Aug. 25, 1954; children: Jeffrey B., Julie, Neil S., Charlene, Gail, Matthew W., Suzzane, Michael L., Connie. AS, Coll. Eastern Utah, 1956; BS in Geology, Brigham Young U., 1958. Pres., owner Cons. Geologist, Salt Lake City and Brigham City, 1958—; plant mgr. Thiokol, Brigham City, Utah, 1958-66; mgr. ops. Sealcraft, Salt Lake City, 1966-68; mgr. programs Eaton-Kenway, Bountiful, Utah, 1968-76; pres., owner HydraPak, Inc., Salt Lake City, 1976—; pres. Kolt Mining Co., Salt Lake City, 1979—. Developer largest rocket motor vacuum casting system in free world, only high pressure water reclamation system for solid propellant rocket motors in free world, only acceptable seal mfg. process for NASA Space Shuttle rocket motor. Vol. tchr. Alta Acad., Salt Lake City, 1983—. Served as sgt. N.G., 1954-62. Mem. Geol. Soc. Am., Utah Geol. Assn. Republican. Mormon. Home: 2180 East Clayborne Ave Salt Lake City UT 84109

WALL, PATRICK DAVID, educator, scientist; b. Nottingham, Eng., Apr. 5, 1925. MA, U. Oxford, Eng., 1947; B.M., B.Ch., Middlesex Hosp. Med. Sch., London, 1948; D.M., U. Oxford, 1959; MD (hon.), U. Siena, 1987. Instr. in physiology Yale U., New Haven, 1948-50; asst. prof. anatomy U. Chgo., 1950-53; instr. physiology Harvard U., 1953-55; assoc. prof. biology MIT, Cambridge, Mass., 1957-59, prof. physiology, 1959-67; prof. anatomy U. London, 1967—; vis. prof. Hebrew U., Jerusalem, 1972—; editor Pain-Internat. Assn. for the Study of Pain, 1975—. Contbr. articles to profl. jours. Recipient Gunn award, 1987, Bonica medal Internat. Assn. Study Pain. Fellow Royal Coll. of Physicians (Sherrington medal 1987). Mem. Labour Party. Office: U Coll London, Gower St, London WC1E 6BT, England

WALL, ROBERT WILSON, JR., former utility executive; b. Monticello, Ark., June 11, 1916; s. Robert Wilson and Thursa (Cotham) W.; m. Joyce Esther Hoffman, Sept. 27, 1943; children: Mary Lynn Wall Sykes, Kathy Ann Wall Theros. B.A., U. Miss., 1938, J.D., 1940; grad. exec. program bus. adminstrn., Columbia U., 1974. Bar: Miss. bar 1940. With FBI, 1940-41, 47-53, spl. agt. in charge Miami (Fla.) office, 1951-53; with U.S. Fgn. Service, 1941-46; legal attache embassy U.S. Fgn. Service, Mexico City, 1944-46; personnel dir. Phillips Petroleum Co., Caracas, Venezuela, 1946-47; with Fla. Power & Light Co., Miami, 1953-81; v.p. Fla. Power & Light Co., 1963-73, sr. v.p., 1973-81; asst. chmn. Nat. Alliance Businessmen, 1966-70; bd. dirs. Southeastern Legal Found.; adv. bd. U. Miami Sch. Bus. Adminstrn. Div. chmn. United Fund Dade County, 1964-67; bd. dirs. Miami Better Bus. Bur., 1955-62, Goodwill Industries Miami, 1964-66, Miami council Girl Scouts Am., 1971-72. Mem. Am. Bar Assn., Am. Soc. Corp. Secs., Am. Arbitration Assn. (panel 1987), Soc. Former Spl. Agts. FBI, Miss. Bar Assn., Greater Miami C. of C. (dir. 1963, exec. com. 1964), Blue Key, Phi Delta Theta, Phi Delta Phi, Omicron Delta Kappa. Republican. Home: 16 Kituhwa Trail Brevard NC 28712

WALLACE, ANDERSON, JR., lawyer; b. Cleve., Sept. 24, 1939; s. Anderson and Agatha Lee (Culpepper) W.; m. Sally Smith; 1 child, Anderson. Student Ga. Inst. Tech., 1957-58; B.A., George Washington U., 1962, J.D., 1964, LL.M., 1966. Bar: Tex. 1968, U.S. Dist. Ct. (no. dist.) Tex. 1968, U.S. Ct. Claims 1968, U.S. Tax Ct. 1968, U.S. Ct. Appeals (5th cir.) 1968, U.S. Supreme Ct. 1971, U.S. Ct. Appeals (11th cir.) 1981. Program mgmt. asst. NASA, Washington, 1962-64; atty. U.S. Dept. Treasury, Washington, 1964-66; tax atty. Price Waterhouse & Co., Atlanta, 1966-67; tax ptnr. Jackson, Walker, Winstead, Cantwell & Miller, Dallas, 1967-84; dir. in charge tax dept. Baker, Mills & Glast, P.C., Dallas, 1984—; instr. Sch. Law So. Meth. U. Trustee S.W. Mus. Sci. and Tech., Dallas, 1974—, Girls Found Dallas Inc. Chmn. Inst. on Employee Benefits, Southwestern Legal Found., 1976. Mem. ABA. Office: 500 LTV Center 2001 Ross Ave Dallas TX 75201

WALLACE, GLADYS BALDWIN, librarian; b. Macon, Ga., June 5, 1923; d. Carter Shepherd and Dorothy (Richard) Baldwin; B.S. in Edn., Oglethorpe U., 1961; MLS, Emory U., 1966; Edn. Specialist, Ga. State U., 1980; m. Hugh Loring Wallace, Jr., Oct. 14, 1941; (div. Sept. 1968); children—Dorothy, Hugh Loring III. Librarian public elem. schs., Atlanta, 1956-66; librarian Northside High Sch., Atlanta, 1966-87; mem. High Mus. Art. Ga. Dept. Edn. grantee, 1950; NDEA grantee, 1963, 65. Mem., The Cousteau Soc., Atlanta Botanical Garden, Am. Assn. Retired Persons, Atlanta Symphony Orch. League, Madison-Morgan Cultural Center, Ga. Conservancy, Ga. Genealogical Soc.; Oglethorpe U. Nat. Alumni Assn., Emory U. Alumni Assn., Ga. State U. Alumni Assn., Atlanta Hist. Soc., Ga. Trust for Historic Preservation. Club: Northside Athletic (Atlanta). Home: 136 Peachtree Memorial Dr NW North Carolina Atlanta GA 30309

WALLACE, HAROLD LEW, historian, educator; b. Montgomery, Ind., Nov. 9, 1932; s. Lewis Alfred and Winifred Maria (Summers) W.; m. Janice June Inman, June 22, 1957; children: Stefanie Ann, Stacy Elizabeth, Jason Lew. A.B., Ind. U., 1961, M.A. (Univ. grantee), 1964, Ph.D., 1970. Tchr. history and English Mooreseville (Ind.) High Sch., 1961-63; teaching asst. Ind. U., 1963-64, univ. fellow, 1964-65; asst. prof., then assoc. prof. history Murray (Ky.) State U., 1965-71; prof. history, head social sci. div. No. Ky. U., Highland Heights, Ky., 1971—, dir. oral history program, 1980—; mem. continuing seminar community edn. Ball State U. and Mott Found., 1973—; mem. adv. bd. Ky. Oral History Commn., 1981—; vis. prof. Ky. Inst. for European Studies, Bregenz, Austria, summer 1987. Author: Coal in Kentucky, 1975; Contbr. articles to profl. jours.; Editorial bd.: U. Ky. Press, 1971—; cons., reviewer: Oceana Press, Inc, 1973—. Mem. advisory com. pub. documents, State of Ky.; Bd. dirs. Coll. Programs for No. Ky. Sr. Citizens. Served with USNR, 1952-56. Recipient Service award State Ind., 1957; Eli Lilly fellow, 1962, 63; Harry S. Truman research scholar, 1965, 71; grantee Murray State U., 1967, 71; grantee No. Ky. State U., 1973, 76, 78; grantee Mott Found., 1973; grantee Gen. Electric, 1982-83; Smithsonian fellow, 1983; grantee So. Regional Edn. Bd., 1986. Mem. Am., So. hist. assns., Orgn. Am. Historians, Polit. Sci. Acad., AAUP, Center Study Democratic Instrn., Mensa, Intertel, Sierra Club, Alpha Epsilon Delta, Phi Delta Kappa, Phi Alpha Theta. Home: 22 Orchard Terr Cold Springs KY 41076 Office: No Ky State U Highland Heights KY 41076

WALLACE, HELEN SARAH, international affairs researcher; b. Manchester, Eng., June 25, 1946; d. Edward and Joyce (Robinson) Rushworth; m. William Wallace, Aug. 24, 1968; children: Harriet, Edward. BA with honors, Oxford U., Eng., 1967; cert. in European studies, Coll. Europe, Bruges, Belgium, 1968; PhD, U. Manchester, 1975. vis. prof. Coll. Europe, Bruges, 1976—. Lectr. U. Manchester Inst. Sci. and Tech., 1974-78; policy planner Fgn. and Commonwealth Office, London, 1979-80; sr. lectr. Civil Service Coll., London, 1978-79, 80-85; dir. West European program Royal Inst. Internat. Affairs., London, 1985—. Author, editor numerous books and articles on European community. Office: Royal Inst Internat Affairs, 10 St James's Sq, London SW1, England

WALLACE, HERBERT NORMAN, lawyer; b. Syracuse, N.Y., Oct. 19, 1937; s. Louis H. and Betty (Wagner) W.; m. Frances Adele Groobman, June 1, 1963 (div. Sept. 1976); children: Craig, Julie; m. Frances Mae Souza, Nov. 15, 1977; 1 child, John. BA, Davis & Elkins Coll., 1959; JD, Syracuse U., 1962. Bar: N.Y. 1962, U.S. Dist. Ct. (no. dist.) N.Y. 1982. Asst. atty. gen. State of N.Y., Albany, 1963-66; asst. atty. gen in charge of Poughkeepsie (N.Y.) office State of N.Y., Poughkeepsie, 1966-79; counsel to banking com. N.Y. State Senate, Albany, 1979-84, counsel to Senator Rolison, 1984—; sole practice Poughkeepsie, N.Y., 1979-86; ptnr. Wallace & Moore, Poughkeepsie, 1986—. Mem. Poughkeepsie Rep. Com., 1977—;. Mem. N.Y. State Bar Assn., Dutchess County Bar Assn. Jewish. Home: 65 Cardinal Dr Poughkeepsie NY 12601 Office: 276 Main Mall Poughkeepsie NY 12601

WALLACE, JOHN CLEMENTS, metal company executive; b. Pitts., July 4, 1920; s. George R. and Jaquetta (Clements) W.; m. Carolyn Cresson, May 26, 1951 (dec. May 1956); 1 dau., Helen L.; m. Mary Willson, June 14, 1958; children: John Clements, Melissa W. B.E., Yale, 1942. Draftsman with Bessemer & Lake Erie R.R. Co., 1946-48; design engr. Lima Hamilton Corp., 1946-51; from chief engr. to v.p., gen. mgr. Hunt Spiller Mfg. Corp., Boston, 1951-57; v.p. mfg. Walworth Co., N.Y.C., 1957-58; v.p., gen. mgr. 1958-59, pres., 1959-60; sr. v.p., dir. John Wood Co. (metal fabrications), N.Y.C., 1960-71; dir. Anthes Imperial Ltd., 1967-69, Multiplex Co., 1966-70; pres. Struthers Nuclear & Process Co. div. (Struthers Wells Corp.), 1971, pres., dir. corp., 1972—. Served from ensign to lt. USNR, 1942-46. Mem. Yale Engring. Assn. Clubs: Union League (N.Y.C.); Short Hills (N.J.); Conwango (Warren, Pa.); Duquesne (Pitts.). Home: 500 3d Ave W Warren PA 16365 Office: 1003 Pennsylvania Ave W Warren PA 16365

WALLACE, JOHN EDWARD, artist, educator; b. St. Louis, Dec. 29, 1929; s. John Edward and Blanche C. (Beck) W.; m. Margaret Whitehurst Grimes, May 30, 1964; children—Carolyn Rose, Bernard Hulce, Jerome Hulce. B.F.A., Washington U., 1953; M.F.A., Ind. U., 1957; student Skowhegan Sch. Painting & Sculpture, 1953. Asst. prof. fine arts St. Louis Jr. Coll. Dist., 1965-68; prof. fine arts, Prairie State Coll., Chicago Heights, Ill., 1968-79, chmn., 1971-74; vis. artist Truro Ctr. for the Arts, 1976-78, Stamford Mus., 1982, Silvermine Art Guild, 1982; assoc. prof. art dept. Western Conn. State U., Danbury, 1981-87; chmn., 1987—; exhibited one-man shows Decatur Art Mus. Ill. 1954, St. Louis Artists Guild, 1959, Roswell (N.Mex.) Mus. and Art Ctr., 1968, Green Mountain Gallery, N.Y.C., 1979, Provincetown Group Gallery, Mass., 1987; exhibited group shows City Art Mus. St. Louis, 1950, 52, 54, Pa. Acad. Fine Arts, Phila., 1952, Denver Mus. Fine Arts, 1952, Bklyn. Mus., 1953 Cin. Art Mus., 1955, Dallas Mus. Fine Arts, 1955, IIT Inst. Design, 1954. USIA traveling exhbn., 1957-59, Skowhegan Ann. Exhbn. N.Y.C., 1966, 67, 68, 69, Bertrand Russell Centenary Exhbn., Nottingham, Eng., 1973, Provincetown Art Assn. Mus., 1978, 86, Stamford Mus., Conn., 1983, Artists' Choice Mus., N.Y.C., 1985, Washington Art Assn., Conn., 1985, Blue Mountain Gallery, N.Y.C., 1986; executed mural South Solon (Maine) Meeting House, 1954; sculpture panel Aquatic House, St. Louis Zool. Gardens, 1959; chmn. New Directions for Studio Teaching, 59th Ann. Coll. Art Assn. Am., 1971. Margaret Tiffany Balke fellow in mural painting, Skowhegan Sch. Painting and Sculpture, 1954; resident fellowship in painting Huntington Hartford Found., 1960; artist-in-residence, fellowship grant Roswell Mus. and Art Center, 1968; research grantee Conn. State U., 1986, 87. Mem. Coll. Art Assn. Am. Address: 25 Taunton Lake Rd Newtown CT 06470

WALLACE, KENNETH ALAN, investor; b. Gallup, N.Mex., Feb. 23, 1938; s. Charles Garrett and Elizabeth Eleanor (Jones) W.; A.B. in Philosophy, Cornell U., 1960; postgrad. U. N.Mex., 1960-61; m. Rebecca Marie Odell, July 11, 1980; children—Andrew McMillan, Aaron Blue, Susanna Garrett, Megan Elizabeth. Comml. loan officer Bank of N.Mex., Albuquerque, 1961-64; asst. cashier Ariz. Bank, Phoenix, 1964-67; comml. loan officer Valley Nat. Bank, Phoenix, 1967-70; pres. WWW, Inc., Houston, 1970-72; v.p. fin. Hometels of Am., Phoenix, 1972-77, Precision Mech. Co., Inc., 1972-77; ptnr. Schroeder-Wallace, 1977—; mng. ptnr. Pala Partners, San Diego; pres. Blackhawk, Inc., Phoenix, 1977—; pres., dir. Kloron Corp., Johannesburg, South Africa, Blackhawk, Inc., Phoenix; exec. v.p. South African BMX; dir. Schroeder Constrn. Co., Inc., Phoenix; v.p., dir. C.G. Wallace Co., Albuquerque, Apache County Sand Corp., Sanders, Ariz.; ptnr. New Dynasty Mining Corp., Vancouver, FWS, Phoenix, Univ. Sq. Assocs., Flagstaff, Ariz., Banador, Mijas, Spain, Sunset Properties, Manzanillo, Mex.; bd. dirs. World Trading and Shipping, N.Y.C.; gen. ptnr. Diamond W Ranch, Ltd., Sanders, Ariz., Wallco Enterprises, Ltd., Mobile, Ala.; mng. gen. ptnr. The Village at University Heights, Flagstaff. Loaned exec. Phoenix United Way, 1966, Tucson United Way, 1967; mem. Valley Big Bros., 1970—; bd. dirs. Phoenix Big Sisters, 1985-87; mem. Alhambra Village Planning Com.; fin. dir. Ret. Sr. Vol. Program, 1973-76; mem. Phoenix Men's Arts Council, 1968—, dir., 1974-75; mem. Phoenix Symphony Council. Campaign committeeman Republican gubernatorial race, N.Mex., 1964; treas. Phoenix Young Reps., 1966; bd. dirs. Devel. Authority for Tucson, 1967. Mem. Soaring Soc. Am. (Silver badge), Am. Rifle Assn. (life), Nat. Mktg. Assn. (Mktg. Performance of Year award 1966), S.W. Profl. Geog. Assn., Nat. Assn. Skin Diving Schs., Pima County Jr. C. of C. (dir. 1967), Phoenix Little Theatre, Phoenix Musical Theatre, S.W. Ensemble Theatre (dir.), Alpha Tau Omega. Mason (Shriner). Clubs: Univ., Plaza (Phoenix); Kona Kai (San Diego). Office: Schroeder-Wallace PO Box 7703 Phoenix AZ 85011

WALLACE, MARTHA REDFIELD, management consultant; b. Omaha, Dec. 27, 1927; d. Ralph J. and Lois (Thompson) Redfield. BA, Wellesley Coll., 1949; MA in Internat. Fin., Tufts U., 1950; LittD (hon.), Converse Coll., 1975; LLD (hon.), Occidental Coll., 1975, Pace U., 1975, Manhattan Coll., 1977. Instr. in econs., asst. to dean Fletcher Sch. Econs., Tufts U., 1950-51; economist Dept. State, Washington, 1951-53; with RCA Internat., 1954-55; mem. editorial staff Fortune mag., 1955-57; with IBM, 1960-61; asst. dir. corp. devel. Time, Inc., 1963-67; dir., bd. dirs. Henry Luce Found., Inc., N.Y.C., 1967-83; pres. Redfield Assocs., N.Y.C., 1983—; bd. dirs. Am. Express Co., Bristol-Myers Co., Chem. N.Y. Corp.; bd. dirs. N.Y. Stock Exchange, 1977-83, mem. surveillance com., 1985—; mem. Conf. Bd., 1974—, Nat. Com. on U.S.-China Relations, 1975—, Temporary Commn. on City Fins., 1975-77, Brit.-N.Am. Com., 1976—, Trilateral Commn., 1978-84; chmn., trustee Trust for Cultural Resources of City N.Y., 1977-81; mem. Adv. Com. on Adminstrn. of Justice, 1981-82; mem. social services vis. com. dept. polit. sci. MIT, 1986-88; mem. vis. com. dept. social scis. U. Chgo., 1980-84; treas. Nat. Com. for United States-China Relations, 1987—; mem. adv. com. Fletcher Sch. Law and Diplomacy, Tufts U.; mem. Sr. Bus. Adv. Council, Pres.'s Council and Adv. Group. Trustee Williams Coll., 1974-86, trustee emeritus, 1986—, citizens budget commn., 1976—, Internat. House, Greater N.Y. Councils, Boy Scouts Am.; bd. dirs. Am. Council on Germany, Greater N.Y. Fund/United Way, 1974-86, Legal Aid Soc., Regional Plan Assn., 1985-88, Citizens Crime Commn. N.Y.C., Inc., 1983—, N.Y.C. Partnership, 1980-85, Council Fgn. Relations, Inc., 1972-82; chmn. N.Y. Rhodes Scholars Selection Com., 1983-86, membership council Whitney Mus.; mem. Bretton Woods Com., 1987; bd. visitors Fletcher Sch. Law and Diplomacy, 1987—, mem. Wilson Council of Wilson Ctr., Washington. Wellesley Coll. Durant scholar, 1949. Mem. Am. Judicature Soc. (bd. dirs. 1978—, v.p., exec. com. 1978-81, chmn. 1981-83), Council on Founds. (bd. dirs. 1971-77), Found. Ctr. (bd. dirs. 1971-77), Japan Soc. (bd. dirs. 1975—, chmn. 75th Anniversary Fund 1982-83), Am. Council on Germany (bd. dirs. 1980—), World Resources Inst., Asia Soc. (mem. pres.'s council, mem. Asian agenda adv. group), N.Y. Racing Assn. (bd. dirs. 1976—), Acad. Polit. Scis., Saratoga Reading Rooms, Inc., Fairbank Ctr. for East Asian Studies, Phi Beta Kappa Assocs., Phi Beta Kappa. Clubs: River, Bd. Room, Economic, Wellesley. Home and Office: 435 E 52d St New York NY 10022

WALLACE, MARY ANN, development company executive; b. Reno County, Kans., Feb. 19, 1939; d. Ivan Lewis and Vina Sue (Smith) Newell; m. Alexander Wallace III, Feb. 17, 1968 (div. June 1982); 1 child, Alexander IV. BS, Wichita State U., 1961. Property mgr. 650 S. Grand Bldg. Co., Los Angeles, 1961-68; v.p. Milner Devel., Santa Monica, Calif., 1981-83; chief fin. officer Milner Devel., Los Angeles, 1983—; cons. Kitty Prodns., Los Angeles, 1978—; cons., v.p. Am. Mut. Prodns., Redlands, Calif., 1975—. V.p. Sister Servants of Mary Guild, Los Angeles, 1970-77; treas. Hosp. of Good Samaritan Aux., Los Angeles, 1969-75; press sec. Orphanage Guild Jrs., Los Angeles, 1974. Named Downtown Working Angel, Downtown Businessmen's Assn., Best Fund Raiser, Sister Servants of Mary Guild, 1974-76. Mem. Los Angeles World Affairs Council, Los Angeles Women in Bus., Nat. Art Assn. Republican. Roman Catholic. Club: Los Angeles Country (Beverly Hills, Calif.). Home: 3921 Woodcliff Rd Sherman Oaks CA 91403

WALLACE, MICHAEL ARTHUR, aerospace executive; b. Wichita, Kans., Nov. 22, 1951; m. Christine Campbell, May 30, 1981; children: Morgan Elizabeth, Allie Nicole. BS, U. Kans., 1973; MBA, Wichita State U., 1986. Acct. exec. Merrill Lynch, Wichita, Kans., 1976-77; mgr. sci. systems devel. Boeing Mil. Airplanes, Wichita, 1979-86, mgr. mkt. devel., 1986—. Competitor World Bobsled Championships, Cervinia, Italy, 1975. Mem. Wichita Area C. of C., Mensa.

WALLACE, RAYMOND P(AUL), patent engineer, consultant; b. Dunn, Wash.; s. John L. and Olive E. M. (Lindley) W.; AB, U. Calif., 1941, MA, 1947; DLitt, Western U., 1950; PhD, Kensington U., 1980. Teaching asst. U. Calif., 1942, nuclear engr. Radiation Lab., 1942-50, chief patent engr., 1950-53; chief patent engr., head patent dept. Mycalex Corp. Am., 1953-55; head patent dept., research div. Curtiss-Wright Corp., 1957-61, patent dept., 1961-75; cons., 1975—. Registered profl. engr., Calif. Recipient Atomic Energy Citation from War Dept., 1945. Mem. Heraldry Soc. Eng. (life), IEEE (sr., life mem.), N.J. Patent Law Assn., Sigma Xi (life), Phi Sigma, Psi Chi. Author: The Three Small Republics, 1947, Contribution to the History of Neutral Moresnet, 1948, The Royal House of Liechtenstein, 1951, Ethnogeny of Easter Island and Its Kings, 1951, Midget Lands, 1987, Cardboard Kingdoms, 1987. Contbr. articles to profl. publs. Responsible for inventions in atomic energy devel. Home: 77 Orange Rd Montclair NJ 07042

WALLACE, WILLIAM HARVELL, JR., state planner, community and economic developer; b. Eastaboga, Ala., Dec. 11, 1939; s. William Harvell and Bettye Lou (Wingo) W. B.S. in Bus. Adminstrn., Auburn U., 1965. Cartographer, Aero. Chart and Information Center, St. Louis, 1965-69; planning dir. East Ala. Regional Planning & Devel. Commn., Anniston, 1970-72; state planner Ala. Devel. Office, Montgomery, 1973-82; sect. chief econ. devel. Dept. Econ. and Community Affairs, Montgomery, 1982—; mem. adv. com. Ala. Rail Services, Montgomery, 1974—, Gov.'s Pvt. Industry Council, 1982—, So. Appalachian Regional Coal Team, 1976—, adv. bd. Fed.-State Coal Team, 1976—, Ala. Occupational Information Coordinating Com., 1985-87. Served with USAF, 1960-63. Mem. Am. Soc. Pub. Adminstrs. Baptist. Home: 170 Canyon Rd Wetumpka AL 36092 Office: State of Ala 3465 Norman Bridge Rd Montgomery AL 36105-0939

WALLACH, EVAN JONATHAN, lawyer, international law educator; b. Superior, Ariz., Nov. 11, 1949; s. Albert A. and Sara Florence (Rothaus) W. B.A., U. Ariz., 1973; J.D., U. Calif.-Berkeley, 1976; LL.B. in Internat. Law, Cambridge U., Eng., 1981. Bar: Nev. 1977, U.S. Dist. Ct. Nev. 1977, U.S. Supreme Ct. 1984. Assoc. firm Lionel Sawyer & Collins, Las Vegas, 1976-82, ptnr., 1983—; gen. counsel and pub. policy advisor to U.S. Sen. Harry M. Reid, Washington, 1987-88; instr. internat. law U. Nev., Las Vegas, 1981—. Gen. counsel Nev. Democratic Party, 1980-84, 88—; coordinator Nevadans for Mondale, 1983-84, Nevadans for Gore, 1987-88; del. Dem. Nat. Conv., San Francisco, 1984; alt. Dem. Nat. Conv., Atlanta, 1988; state dir. campaign in Nev. and Ariz. Gore for Pres., 1988. Served with U.S. Army, 1969-71; Vietnam. Decorated Bronze Star, Air medal. Mem. ABA, Phi Beta Kappa. Jewish. Club: Oxford-Cambridge (London). Office: Lionel Sawyer & Collins 300 So 4th St Suite 1700 Las Vegas NV 89101

WALLACH, PHILIP C(HARLES), public relations executive; b. N.Y.C., Nov. 17, 1914; s. Edgar Smith and Rix (Roth) W.; m. Magdalena Charlotta Falkenberg, Mar. 14, 1950. Student, NYU. Editor, writer Hearst Publs., N.Y.C., 1938-42; editor Shell Oil Co., N.Y.C., 1943-46; editor, dir. pub. relations W.R. Grace & Co., N.Y.C., 1946-54; dir. pub. relations and advt. H.K. Porter & Co., N.Y.C., 1954-58; pres. Wallach Assocs., Inc., N.Y.C., 1958-85; v.p. investor relations Occidental Petroleum Co., Los Angeles, 1985—; v.p. Occidental Internat. Corp., New York, 1987—. Pres. St. Paul Guild, N.Y.C., 1959-68, dir., 1964-72; pres. Catholic. Inst. of Press, N.Y.C., 1959-61, 61-63, 63-65; co-founder Air Force Assn., Washington, 1946; nat. committeeman Republican party, N.Y., 1945-60; mem. Repub. Nat. Com., Greenwich, Conn., 1982—; dir., mem. exec. com. U.S. Pakistan Econ. Council. Served with USAF, 1942-43. Mem. Pan Am. Soc., English Speaking Union, Bolivian Soc., Peruvian Soc., Chilean Soc. Home: 84 Lower Cross Rd Greenwich CT 06831 Office: Occidental Internat Corp 1230 Ave of Americas New York NY 10020

WALLANDER, JAN RICKARD, banker; b. Stockholm, Sweden, June 8, 1920; s. Sven and Elna (von Zweigbergk) W.; m. Ann-Charlotte Westergren, Aug. 26, 1941 (div. 1982); children—Anna Rogberg, Malin Wallander-Olsson, Fanny Borgstrom; m. Birgitta Celsing, Sept. 7, 1983. With Indsl. Inst. for Econs. and Social Research, 1945-48, pres., 1953-61; research mgr. Indsl. Council for Social and Econ. Studies, 1950-51, pres., 1951-53; pres. Sundsvallsbanken, 1961-70; pres. Svenska Hadelsbanken, Stockholm, 1971-78, chmn., 1978—. Contbr. articles to profl. publs. Chmn. bd. Tidnings AB Marieberg, Jan Wallander Found., Wenner-Gren Ctr., Found., Svenska Handelsbanken Pension Fund, Pension Soc. SHB; vice chmn. bd. Ericcsson, Beyer Industries AB; bd. dirs. Inst. Banking Research, Peter and Birgitte Celsing Found., AB Iggesungs Bruk, AB Industrivarden, Mo och Domsjo AB, Swedish Intercontinental Airways SILA, AB Aerotransport, Tore Browaldh Found., Econ. Planning Orgn., Marcus Wallenberg Found., World Wildlife Fund Swedan, The Swedish Assn. for Share Promotion; past mem. Nat. Bd. Univ. and Coll.; past chmn. bd. AB IRO, 1978-84, Swedish Securities Register Ctr., 1971-84. Decorated knight comdr.'s cross Royal Order of Vasa. Home: Klockberga, S-170 11 Dottningholm Sweden Office: Svenska Handelsbanken, Kungstradgardsgatan 2, S-103 28 Stockholm Sweden

WALLENBERG, PETER, banker, investor; b. Stockholm, May 29, 1926; s. Marcus Wallenberg and Dorothy Mackay; divorced; 3 children. LLM, U. Stockholm; hon. degree, Stockholm Sch. Econs., Augustana Coll., Sioux Falls, S.D. Various positions Atlas Copco Group, 1953-67; dep. mng. dir. Atlas Copco AB, 1970-74, chmn., 1974; 1st vice-chmn. Skandinaviska Enskilda Banken, Stockholm, 1984—; Chmn. STORA, Papyrus Ltd.; bd. dirs. ASEA, Brostroms, Electrolux Corp., Telefon AB, L.M. Ericsson Corp.; v.p. ICC, Paris; pvt. investor Wallenberg Found. Mem. Fedn. Swedish Industries (vice chmn.). Office: Skandinaviska Enskilda Banken, 10640 Stockholm Sweden *

WALLER, JOHN HENRY, author, international consultant; b. Paw Paw, Mich., May 8, 1923; s. George and Marguerite (Rowland) W.; m. Barbara Steuart Hans, Sept. 2, 1947; children—Stephanie Robinson, Gregory, Maria. B.A., U. Mich., 1946. Vice consul U.S. Fgn. Service, Iran, 1947-53, 2d sec., Khartoum, Sudan, 1960-62, spl. asst. to ambassador, New Delhi, 1955-57, 68-71; polit. analyst State Dept., Washington, 1962-68; insp. gen. CIA, Washington, 1976-80; free-lance author, Washington, 1968—. Author: (pen name John Rowland) Hostile Co-existence, History of Sino-Indian Relations, 1988, Gordon of Khartoum: The Saga of a Victorian Hero; (pen name John MacGregor) Tibet, A Chronicle of Exploration, 1970. Contbg. editor Mil. History Mag., Leesburg, Va., 1985—. Contbr. articles to popular history to profl. jours. Recipient Career Service award Nat. Civil Service League, 1979, 80, Disting. Intelligence medal CIA, 1980. Mem. Washington Inst. Fgn. Affairs, Middle East Inst. Club: Cosmos (Washington).

WALLER, ROBERT MORRIS, health care products company executive, international trade consultant; b. Flint, Mich., Jan. 3, 1944; s. Ashton Carr and Nell Kathryn (Morris) W.; m. Sharon L. Spratt, July 24, 1965; children—Robert M., Jennifer Anne. B.S. in Bus. Adminstrn., Northwestern U., 1966; M.B.A. with high honors, Hotchkiss scholar, Lake Forest (Ill.) Grad. Sch. Mgmt., 1984. Area ops. mgr. Am. Hosp. Supply Corp., Evanston, Ill., 1970-72, dir. distbn., 1972-74, v.p. ops., 1974-77, v.p. hosp. services, 1977-82; pres. AHSECO internat. sub., Am. Hosp. Supply Corp., Evanston, 1982-87; pres. distbn. div. Baxter Healthcare, Inc., 1987—. Contbr. articles to profl. jours. Mem. Internat. Mgmt. and Devel. Inst., Washington, 1984—; apptd. by Sec. Commerce to Ill. Dist. Export Council, 1985, exec. commn. India, U. S. Bus. Council, 1985—; deacon Presbyn. Ch., Deerfield, Ill., 1974; guest lectr. Northwestern U., 1980-82, U. Colo. 1987-88. Home: 1365 Elm Tree Rd Lake Forest IL 60045 Office: One Baxter Pkwy Deerfield IL 60015

WALLESTAD, PHILIP WESTON, physician; b. Madison, Wis., May 14, 1922; s. John Oscar and Dorothy Francis (White) W.; B.A., U. Wis., 1947, M.D., 1954; m. Edith Stolle, Jan. 15, 1949 (div. Mar. 1967); children—Kristin Eve, Ingrid Birgitta, Erika Ann; m. 2d, Muriel Annette Moen, June 22, 1968; children—Thomas John, Scott Philip. Intern, Calif. Lutheran Hosp., Los Angeles, 1954, resident in surgery, 1955-56; gen. practice medicine, Fredonia and Port Washington Wis., 1957-72, Libby, Mont., 1972-74; staff physician VA Hosp., Fort Harrison, Mont., 1974-77, Tomah, Wis., 1977-78, VA Hosp., Iron Mountain, Mich., 1978-88. Mem. Moral Majority, Conservative Caucus. Served with AUS, 1943-46; ETO; lt. col. USAF Res., 1979-82. Mem. Exptl. Aviation Assn., Am. Legion, DAV, Air Force Assn., Am. Security Council, Conservative Caucus, Am. Def. Preparedness Assn., U. Wis. Alumni Assn., Nat. W Club, NRA. Republican. Presbyterian Ch. (elder). Club: Rotary. Home: 1005 Bluff St Kingsford MI 49801 Office: VA Hosp Center H Iron Mountain MI 49801

WALLFISCH, LORY, pianist, harpsichordist, music educator; b. Ploesti, Romania, Apr. 21, 1922; came to U.S., 1947, naturalized, 1953; d. Samson and Carola Florin; m. Ernst Wallfisch, Nov. 12, 1944 (dec. May 1979); 1 child, Paul. Student, Royal Conservatory of Music, Bucharest; pvt. piano studies with Florica Muzicescu. Pianist WAllfisch Duo, appearing in Europe, U.S., Israel and North Africa, 1947-79; pvt. tchr. Romania, Switzerland and U.S., 1938-60; prof. music Smith Coll., Northampton, Mass., 1964—; performer, condr., master classes S.Am., 1982; performer, condr. master classes S.Am., 1982, Australia, 1983; participant Casals, Edinburgh, York, Venice, Besancon and Menuhin festivals; TV appearances; rec. artist Vox/Turnabout, DaCamera, Musical Heritage, Advance and Concert Hall Soc. labels; founder, pianist George Enescu Chamber Players. Contbr. articles to mags. Mem. European Piano Tchrs. Assn., Mass. Music Tchrs. Assn., Friends of Kennedy Ctr., Northampton Fedn. Musicians, George Enescu Soc. U.S. (founder). Home: Barrett Pl Northampton MA 01060 Office: Smith Coll Sage Hall Northampton MA 01060

WALLGREN, GEORG RABBE, surgeon; b. Helsinki, Finland, Nov. 28, 1920; s. Georg-Wilhelm and Rea (Strahle) W.; m. Karin Synnove Molander, Apr. 1, 1950; children: Georg-Wilhelm, Jean-Peter, Jeanette, Christoffer. MD, U. Helsinki, 1948. Resident in surgery Kotka (Finland) Gen. Hosp., 1949-53; surgeon Univ. Children's Hosp., Helsinki, 1953-56; asst. chief surgeon Aurora Hosp., Helsinki, 1956-79, chief surgeon, 1979-83; surgeon Eira Hosp., Helsinki, 1984—; prin. med. officer Fennia Ins. Co., Helsinki, 1978-85, Svensk-Finland Ins. Co., Helsinki, 1978—. Contbr. articles to profl. jours. Decorated several war medals for disting. service; recipient ASLA-Fulbright scholarship Colo. Gen. Hosp., Denver, 1957; named Medicinalråd Pres. Koivisto of Finland, 1984. Mem. Brit. Assn. Pediatric Surgeons, German Pediatric Surgery Assn., Scandinavian Assn. Pediatric Surgeons (gen. sec. 1964-80, pres. 1980-86, hon. 1986), Sulamaa Soc. (chmn. 1980-82, hon. 1986). Lutheran. Club: Nylandska Jakt. Lodges: Masons, Rotary. Home: Parkgatan 11-A-13, 00140 Helsinki Finland Office: Eira Hosp, Skeppareg 29, 00140 Helsinki Finland

WALLGREN, SVEN EINAR, manufacturing company executive; b. Ystad, Sweden, Sept. 17, 1929; s. Sven F. and Anna-Lisa (Bjurstrom) W.; m. Lena Sandlund, June 16, 1956 (dec.); children: Henrik, Johan, Britta, Per. MBA Stockholm Sch. Econs., 1953. Sales mgr. packing machines AB Akerlund & Rausing, 1958; mng. dir. Akerlund & Rausing Verpackung GmbH, Fed. Republic Germany, 1960-68; dir. match div. Swedish Match, 1968-73; exec. v.p. Esselte AB, Stockholm, 1973-74, pres., chief exec. officer, 1974—; dir. Esselte Group, Skandinavisha Enskilda Banken, 1983—, Tarkett AB, 1984—, Swedish Match AB, 1985—, Stockholm Stock Exchange, 1985—, AB Marabov, 1988—; mem. Swedish adv. bd. Fellow Royal Acad. Engring. Scis.; mem. Confedn. Swedish Industry (dir., chmn. 1983-85), Internat. C. of C., Swedish-Am. C. of C., Swedish-Finnish C. of C., Deutsch-Schwedishe C. of C., Swedish Industry and Commerce Trust Fund. Club: Stockholm Merchants' (chmn.). Home: 21 Skyttevagen, S 133 36 Saltsjobaden Sweden Office: Esselte Bus Systems Inc 71 Clinton Rd Garden City NY 11530

WALLIN, ÅKE HERMAN OLOF, advertising agency executive; b. Växjö, Sweden, Aug. 19, 1917; s. Thorsten and Alice (Nilsson) W.; Fil.Kand., U. Gothenburg, 1941; m. Ingegerd Hanna Kristina Öhrn, June 23, 1942; children—Annika, Marie, Suzanne. Editor, Flyg mag., Stockholm, 1942-46; public relations and advt. mgr. Manufaktur AB, Malmö Yllefabriks AB, Malmö, Sweden, 1946-53; mng. dir. Wallin Reklam AB Advt. Agy., Malmö, 1953—. Pres., Skånes Tourist Assn., 1980-84; mem. Malmö Com. Bd., 1969—; pres. Liberal Party of Malmö, 1980-83; bd. dirs. for hosps. in Malmö, 1968-85, pres. 1986—; City Commr. Malmö, 1986—. Served with Swedish Royal Air Force, 1939-45. Recipient Malmö Fire Brigade Gold medal, 1976; Swedish Employers Assn. Gold medal, 1977, 88. Mem. Malmö Advt. Assn. (v.p. 1960-65), Malmö Employers Assn. (pres. 1965—), Swedish Employers Assn. (v.p. 1972—), Internat. Advt. Assn., Malmö Market Assn., others. Liberal. Club: Swedish Publicity. Author: Flying Airpolice, 1944; Sand in the soul, 1945; Texts for the Swedish Broadcasting, 1943-46. Home: 24 Riddaregatan, 216 15 Malmo Sweden Office: 21 Timmermansgat, 216 19 Malmo Sweden

WALLIN, GARY PHILLIP, marketing and direct mail company executive; b. Newark, Nov. 8, 1940; s. Irving and Rose (Greenberg) W.; B.S., Upsala Coll., 1962; m. Irma Holtzman Wallin children—Ian Robert, Amy Gwen, Michael Adam, Justin Scott, Amanda Adrienne. Engr., Welch Communications Corp., Dover, N.J., 1962-64; asst. to v.p. Edison Electronics, Boonton, N.J., 1965; service mgr. Motorola, Inc., Franklin Park, Ill., 1965-69; owner, pres. Comex Systems, Inc., Comex, Inc., Manchester, N.H., 1969-84; pres. The Mail and Mktg. Store, Inc., Manchester, 1987—; bd. dirs. Metrobank, Inc., Roan Ventures, Inc., Microweigh Systems, Inc., Teleocator Network Am.; cons. in field; Patentee in field of digital communications. Commr. Manchester Airport Authority. Justice of the peace, Manchester, 1971—; bd. dirs., v.p. Am.-Israel Pub. Affairs Com.; bd. dirs. Council Jewish Fedns., Child and Family Services N.H., United Way Greater Manchester; exec. com. Am. Israel Pub. Affairs Com.; pres. Temple Israel, Jewish Fedn. Greater Manchester, Federated Arts Greater Manchester; assoc. chmn. nat. young leadership cabinet United Jewish Appeal; dir. local temple. Mem. IEEE, Radio Club Am., Electronic Industries Assn., AAAS, Soc. Am. Magicians, Internat. Brotherhood Magicians (sec. 1964), Hundred Club N.H. Clubs: Manchester Country. Patentee in field. Home: 11 Crestview Rd Manchester NH 03104

WALLIN, JACK ROBB, research plant pathology educator; b. Omaha, Nov. 21, 1915; s. Carl O.A. (Wallin) and Elizabeth Josephine (Smith) W.; m. Janet Mary Melhus, Sept. 25, 1937; children: Jack I.M., Robb M. B.S., Iowa State U., 1939, Ph.D., 1944. Research asst. prof. Iowa State U., Ames, 1944-47; research prof., research plant pathologist U.S. Dept. Agr., Agr. Research Service/Iowa State U., 1947-75; prof. plant pathology, researcher U.S. Dept. Agr., Agrl. Research Service U. Mo., Columbia, 1975—; U.S. rep. World Meteorol. Orgn., Geneva, 1959-61; mem. aeriobiology com. Nat. Acad. Sci., NRC, Washington, 1976-80. Patentee (in field). Recipient 1st Peterson award Internat. Soc. Biometeorology, 1966. Mem. Internat. Assn. Aerobiology, Am. Phytopathol. Soc. (sec. treas. N. Central div. 1964-65), Internat. Soc. Plant Pathology, Mo. Acad. Sci. (chmn. agrl. div. 1976-81). Republican. Presbyterian. Lodge: Rotary. Home: Route 5 Fulton MO 65261 Office: US Dept Agrl Research Service U Mo 312 Curtis Hall Columbia MO 65201

WALLIN, JUDITH KERSTIN, pediatrician, educator; b. Paris, Apr. 23, 1938; came to U.S., 1938; d. Theodore Bror and Ella Charlotte (Butler) Wallin. BS in Chemistry, Elizabethtown (Pa.) Coll., 1960; MD, Temple U., 1964. Diplomate Am. Bd. Pediatrics. Diplomate Am. Bd. Pediatrics. Intern Bellevue Hosp., N.Y.C., 1964-65, resident specializing in pediatrics, 1965-67, attending pediatrician, 1967—; instr. pediatrics, NYU, 1967-71, asst. prof. clin. pediatrics, 1971-74, assoc. prof., 1974—. Trustee Elizabethtown Coll., 1988—. Recipient Educate for Service through Profl. Achievement award, O.F. Stambaugh Alumni award Elizabethtown Coll., 1978. Home: 300 E 33d St New York NY 10016 Office: Bellevue Hosp Dept Pediatrics 27th St and 1st Ave New York NY 10016

WALLIN, WINSTON ROGER, manufacturing company executive; b. Mpls., Mar. 6, 1926; s. Carl A. and Theresa (Hegge) W.; m. Maxine Houghton, Sept. 10, 1949; children: Rebecca, Brooks, Lance, Bradford. BBA, U. Minn., 1948. With Pillsbury Co., Mpls., 1948-85, v.p. commodity ops., 1971-76, exec. v.p., 1976, pres., chief operating officer, 1977-84, vice chmn. bd., 1984-85; chmn. bd., pres., chief exec. officer Medtronic, Inc., Mpls., 1985—, also bd. dirs.; bd. dirs. Soo Line Corp., Bemis Co. Bd. dirs. Sci. Mus., Abbot Northwestern Hosp.; trustee Carleton Coll., Mpls. Soc. Fine Arts. Served with USN, 1944-46. Mem. Mpls. Grain Exchange (bd. dirs. 1977—). Clubs: Minneapolis, Minikahda, Interlachen. Home: 7022 Tupa Circle Edina MN 55435 Office: Medtronic Inc 7000 Central Ave NE Minneapolis MN 55432

WALLING, GEORGIA, psychotherapist b. Cedarhurst, N.Y.; d. William English and Anna (Strunsky) W.; student U. Paris, 1931-32, Vassar Coll., 1932-34; BA, Rollins Coll., 1935; MA, Columbia U., 1937, MS in Social Work, 1947. Cert. clin. social worker. Caseworker, Family Service Soc., Atlanta, 1948-49, Bklyn. Bur. Social Service, 1951-53, Inwood House, N.Y.C., 1954-58; sr. psychiat. casework therapist Childrens Village, Dobb's Ferry, N.Y., 1959-60; asso. staff mem. Postgrad Center for Mental Health, N.Y.C., 1960-65; pvt. practice psychotherapy and psychoanalysis, N.Y.C. Mem. Nat. Assn. Social Workers, N.Y. State Soc. Clin. Social Work Psychotherapists, Postgrad. Psychoanalytic Soc., Acad. Cert. Clin. Social Workers, Nat. Accreditation Assn. for Psychoanalysis.

WALLIS, ERNEST MARTIN, shoe company executive; b. Hamburg, Germany, Aug. 7, 1921; s. Alfred and Janina (Abarbanel) W.; brought to U.S., 1936, naturalized, 1942; student Heinrich Herz Real Gymnasium, Hamburg, 1936; grad. Holderness Sch., Plymouth, N.H., 1937; A.B., Coll. City of N.Y., 1941; m. Joan Oettinger, Jan. 13, 1947; children—Jeffrey Allan, David Andrew, Deborah Joy. Mgr., Specialty Importing Co., Inc., Cambridge, Mass., 1946-48; v.p. Embo Casual Footwear Corp., Boston, 1948-63; pres. Marlboro Footwear Co., 1963-65; regional sales mgr. Eversharp Pen Co., 1965-68; pres. Wallis Sales Inc., Miami, Fla. Treas., Parents of Blind Children, Inc.; chmn. shoe div. Boston Evening Clinic and Hosp.; del. Mass. Council Orgns. for the Blind, Boston. Served as technician 5th grade, 267th F.A. Bn., AUS, 1942-45, ETO. Decorated Bronze Star, Am. Service medal, European, African, Middle Eastern Service medal with 4 stars, World War II Victory Medal. Mem. Boston Power Squadron (dir. lt. comdr., pub. relations officer), Dale Carnegie Internat. (v.p. Boston chpt.), 210 Assos. (Boston), AIM. Clubs: Pleasant Park Yacht, Newton Yacht; Ocean Reef (Key Largo, Fla.); Racquet (Harbor Island, Fla.). Editor: Boston Light. Home: 900 Bay Dr Miami Beach FL 33141 Office: 4380 E 11th Ave Hialeah FL 33013

WALLMAN, CHARLES JAMES, former money handling products executive, author; b. Kiel, Wis., Feb. 19, 1924; s. Charles A. and Mary Ann (Loftus) W.; student Marquette U., 1942-43, Tex. Coll. Mines, 1943-44; B.B.A., U. Wis., 1949; m. Charline Marie Moore, June 14, 1952; children—Stephen, Jeffrey, Susan, Patricia, Andrew. Sales promotion mgr. Brandt, Inc., Watertown, Wis., 1949-65, v.p., 1960-70, exec. v.p., 1970-80, v.p. corp. devel., 1980-83, past dir.; written formal paper to the inst. "The 48ers of Watertown", presented orally at Symposium U. Wis.-Madison (Inst. for German-Am. Studies), 1986, written formal paper Business, Industry and the German Press in Early Watertown, Wis., 1853-65, presented orally at symposium U. Wis.-Madison Inst. for German-Am. Studies, 1987; guest speaker dept. German, U. Wis.-Madison, 1987. Former mem. exec. bd. Potawatomi council Boy Scouts Am., also former v.p. council; former bd. dirs., pres. Earl and Eugenia Quirk Found., Inc. Trustee, Joe Davies Scholarship Found.; bd. dirs. Watertown Meml. Hosp. Served with armored inf. AUS, 1943-45; ETO. Decorated Bronze Star. Mem. Am. Legion, E. Central Golf Assn. (past pres.), Wis. Alumni Assn. (local past pres.), 12th Armored Div. Assn., Watertown Hist. Soc. (bd. dirs.), Am. Ex-Prisoners of War, Inc., Phi Delta Theta. Republican. Roman Catholic. Club: Watertown County (past dir.). Lodges: Rotary (former bd. dirs.), Elks (past officer). Author: Edward J. Brandt, Inventor, 1984. Home: 700 Clyman St Watertown WI 53094

WALLMAN, GEORGE, hospital and food services administrator; b. N.Y.C., Apr. 10, 1917; s. Joseph and Celia (Kascawal) W.; m. Benita B. Kaufman, June 11, 1941. Student public schs., N.Y.C. Dir. food and banquet services Normandy Hotel, Hollywood, Calif., 1945-47; dir. food services Med. Center, N.Y.C., 1947-64; menucologist and cons. to hosps. 1964-67; dir. food services Montefiore Hosp., Pitts., 1967—; cons. public schs., homes and hosps. for aged, 1947—, cons. new food products various cos., 1967—; mem. Cancer Rehab. Project, U. Pitts., 1973—; lectr. on food to various profl. orgns., 1947—. Lectr.: program Exercise is Not Enough, Sta. NBC-TV, 1976; narrator, CBS Evening News; show Hosp. Gourmet, 1974; Contbg. editor, feature writer: Today's Chef, 1978—. Mem. Nat. Restaurant Assn., Am. Hosp. Assn., Am. Fedn. Musicians. Home: 1420 Centre Ave Pittsburgh PA 15219 Office: Montefiore Hosp Fifth Ave at Darragh Pittsburgh PA 15213

WALLMANN, JEFFREY MINER, author; b. Seattle, Dec. 5, 1941; s. George Rudolph and Elizabeth (Biggs) W.; B.S., Portland State U., 1962; m. Helga Reidun Eikefet, Dec. 1, 1974. Pvt. investigator Dale Systems, N.Y.C., 1962-63; asst. buyer, mgr. public money bidder Dohrmann Co., San Francisco, 1964-66; mfrs. rep. electronics industry, San Francisco, 1966-69; dir. public relations London Films, Cinelux-Universal and Trans-European Publs., 1970-75; editor-in-chief Riviera Life mag., 1975-77; cons. Marketeer, Eugene, Oreg., 1978—; books include: The Spiral Web, 1969, Judas Cross, 1974, Clean Sweep, 1976, Jamaica, 1977, Deathtrek, 1980, Blood and Passion, 1980; Brand of the Damned, 1981; The Manipulator, 1982; Return to Conta Lupe, 1983; The Celluloid Kid, 1984; Business Basic for Bunglers, 1984, Guide to Applications Basic, 1984; (under pseudonym Leon DaSilva) Green Hell, 1976, Breakout in Angola, 1977; (pseudonym Nick Carter) Hour of the Wolf, 1973, Ice Trap Terror, 1974; (pseudonym Peter Jensen) The Virgin Couple, 1970, Ravished, 1971; (pseudonmy Jackson Robard) Gang Initiation, 1971, Present for Teacher, 1972, Teacher's Lounge, 1972; (pseudonym Grant Roberts) The Reluctant Couple, 1969, Wayward Wives, 1970; (pseudonym Gregory St. Germain) Resistance #1: Night and Fog, 1982, Resistance #2: Maygar Massacre, 1983; (pseudonym Wesley Ellis) Lonestar on the Treachery Trail, 1982, numerous others in the Lonestar series; (pseudonym Tabor Evans) Longarm and the Lonestar Showdown, 1986; (psyeudonym Jon Sharpe) Trailsman 58: Slaughter Express, 1986, numerous others in Trailsman series; also many other pseudonyms and titles; contbr. articles and short stories to Argosy, Ellery Queen's Mystery Mag., Alfred Hitchcock's Mystery Mag., Mike Shayne's Mystery Mag., Zane Grey Western, Venture, Oui, TV Guide; also (under pseudonym William Jeffrey in collaboration with Bill Pronzini) Dual at Gold Buttes, 1980, Border Fever, 1982, Day of the Moon, 1983. Mem. Mystery Writers of Am., Sci. Fiction Writers Am., Western Writers Am., Crime Writers Assn., Eugene Bd. Realtors, Nat. Assn. Realtors.

WALLNER, FRIEDRICH, philosopher, educator; b. Weiten, Austria, July 21, 1945; s. Alois Pehm and Theresia W.; m. Rosemarie Micka, Apr. 12, 1973; children: Christian, Monika. MA, U. Vienna, Austria, 1969, PhD, 1972, Habilitation, 1981. Secondary tchr. Bundesoberstufenrealgymnasium, Wiener Neustadt, Austria, 1969-87; asst. prof. philosophy U. Vienna, 1981-87, prof., 1987—; speaker Wittgenstein Conf., Kirchberg, Austria, 1977-86; lectr. sci confs. Europe and N.Am., 1981—; organizer Popper Conf., Vienna, 1983; speaker advanced tng. for tchrs. Austrian Ministry Edn., 1983—. Author: Philosoph. Probl. d. Physik, 1982, Grenzen d. Spr.u.d. Erkenntnis, 1983, Wittgensteins phil. Lebensw. als Einheit, 1983, K. Popper. Philos. u. Wissenschaft, 1985 (book series) Philosophica, 1985—. Recipient Innitzerpreis Roman Cath. Ch., Vienna, 1984, Körnerpreis Pres. of Austria, 1985, sci. stipend City of Vienna, 1986. Mem. Kant Soc., Hegel Soc., Soc. German Philosophers, Soc. Austrian Philosophers. Roman Catholic. Home: Renngasse 10, A 2604 Theresienfeld Austria Office: U Vienna Inst fur, Sensengasse 8, A 1090 Vienna Austria

WALLOP, MALCOLM, U.S. senator; b. N.Y.C., Feb. 27, 1933; s. Oliver M. and Jean (Moore) W.; children: Malcolm, Amy, Paul, Matthew; m. French Wallop. B.A., Yale U., 1954. Owner, operator Canyon Ranch, Big Horn, Wyo.; mem. Wyo. Ho. of Reps., 1969-73, Wyo. Senate, 1973-77; mem. U.S. Senate from Wyo., 1976—, mem. coms. on energy and natural resources, fin., small bus.; ofcl. observer from Senate on arms control negotiations; mem. Commn. on Security and Cooperation in Europe. Served to lt. U.S. Army, 1955-57. Mem. Wyo. Stockgrowers Assn., Am. Nat. Cattleman's Assn., Am. Legion. Republican. Episcopalian. Office: 237 Russell Senate Bldg Washington DC 20510

WALLRAFF, HANS GÜNTER, freelance writer; b. Burscheid, Fed. Republic of Germany, Oct. 1, 1942; s. Josef and JOhanna Wallraff; m. Birgit Böll; 2 daughters. Book dealer 1957-61, factory worker, 1963-66. Author: Wir brauchen Dich. Als Arbeiter in Deutschen Grossbetrieben, 1966, 13 unerwünschte Reportagen, 1969, Von einem, der auszog und das fürchten lernte, 1970, Unser Faschismus nebenan, Der Aufmacher Der Mann der bei BILD Hans Esser war, 1977, Zeugen der Anklage Die Bildbeschreibung wird fortgesetzt, 1979, Ganz Unter, 1987; (play) Nachspiele, 1968; (with Bernt Engelmann) Ihr da oben- wir da unten; (with Echart Spoo) Unser Faschismus nebenan, Griechenland gestern- ein Lehrstück für morgen, 1975; (with Bernd Kuhlmann) Wie hätten wir's denn gerne. Mem. PEN. Home: Thebaerstr 20, D-5000 Cologne Federal Republic of Germany Office: Zentrum Buddesrepublic, Deutschland, 6100 Darmstadt Sandstr 10, Bonn Federal Republic of Germany *

WALLROCK, JOHN, insurance executive, consultant; b. Stanmore, Eng., Nov. 14, 1922; s. Samuel and Marie Kate (Hines) W.; m. Audrey Louise Ariow, May 19, 1967; children: Marina Louise, Camilla Gabrielle, Giles Edward. Cert. Bradfield Coll. Dir. J.H. Minet & Co., Ltd., London, 1955-72, chmn., 1972-80; chmn. Minet Holdings, Ltd., London, 1972-82; chmn. S. Katherines Ins. Co., London, 1972-82, Conocean Internat. Cons. Group, 1983—; bd. dirs. Fred S. James Inc., Chgo., 1975-78, Corroon & Black Ins., N.Y.C., 1979-82, Tugu Ins. Co., Hong Kong, 1976-82; underwriting mem. Lloyd's of London, 1950-84. Served to lt. Royal Navy, 1940-60. Recipient Freeman of City of London award, 1965. Fellow Corp. Ins. Brokers; mem. White Ensign Assn. (council mgmt. 1972-82), Honorable Co. Master Mariners, Nautical Inst. Clubs: East India, Royal London Yacht. Home: 27 Tai Tam Rd, Belgravia Heights Hong Kong Office: Conocean Internat Cons Group, Admiralty Centre Tower I, Suite 804A, 18 Harcourt Rd, Hong Kong Hong Kong

WALLS, ANDREW FINLAY, religious research administrator; b. Apr. 21, 1928; s. Andrew Finlay Walls and Florence Johnson; m. Doreen Mary Harden, Apr. 4, 1953; children: Christine, Andrew. BA in Theology with honors, U. Oxford, Eng., 1948, MA, 1952, LittB, 1954. Librarian Tyndale House, Cambridge, Eng., 1952-57; lectr. theology Fourah Bay Coll., Sierra Leone, 1957-62; head religion dept. U. Nigeria, Nsukka, 1962-65; sr. lectr. church history U. Aberdeen, Scotland, 1966-70, head religious studies dept., 1970-85; dir. Ctr. Study Christianity in Non-Western World U. Aberdeen, U. Edinburgh, Scotland, 1982—; vis. prof. various univs., sec. Scottish Inst. Missionary Studies, 1967—. Editor: Jour. Religion Africa, 1967-86, Bull. Scottish Inst. Missionary Studies, 1967—, Quar. bibliography World Mission, 1972—; contbr. articles to profl. jours. Councillor Aberdeen, 1974-80; chmn. Council Mus. Galleries Scotland, 1977-81, Disablement Income Group, Scotland, 1977-81; trustee Nat. Mus. Scotland, 1985-87. Served with RAF, 1948-50; officer Order of British Empire, 1987. Fellow Soc. Antiquaries Scotland; mem. Brit. Assn. History Religions (pres. 1976-79), Internat. Assn. Mission Studies (gen. sec. 1974-76), African Studies Assn. U.K., Deutsche Gesellschaft für Missionswissenschaft. Mem. Labour Party. Methodist. Home: 58 Stanley St, Aberdeen AB1 6UR, Scotland Office: Univ Edinburgh Ctr Study, Christianity Non-Western World, New Coll, Mound Pl, Edinburgh EH1 2LU, Scotland

WALLS, CARMAGE, newspaper publisher; b. Crisp County, Ga., Oct. 28, 1908; s. Benjamin Gaff and Anna (Byrd) W.; m. Odessa Dobbs (div.); children: Carmage Lee, Mark Thomas (dec.), Dinah Jean; m. Martha Ann Williams, Jan. 2, 1954; children: Byrd Cooper, Lissa Williams. Ed. pub. schs., Fla. Bus. mgr. Orlando (Fla.) Newspaper, Inc., 1934-40; pub. Macon (Ga.) Telegraph News, 1940-47; pres. Gen. Newspapers, Inc., Macon, 1945-59, So. Newspapers, Inc., Montgomery, Ala., 1951-69; also dir.; pub. Montgomery (Ala.) Advt.-Jour., 1963-69; chmn. bd., dir. Galveston Newspapers, Inc., Tex.; owner Walls Investment Co., Houston. Pres. Macon Area Devel. Commn., 1943-44, Macon C. of C., 1945; trustee Birmingham-So. Coll., 1971-7. Mem. So. Newspaper Pubs. Assn., Sigma Delta Chi. Episcopalian. Clubs: Houstonian, Warwick (Houston); Bob Smith Yacht (Galveston). Home: 623 Shartle Circle Houston TX 77024 Office: 1050 Wilcrest Dr Houston TX 77042

WALLSTRÖM, WESLEY DONALD, banker; b. Turlock, Calif., Oct. 4, 1929; s. Emil Reinhold and Edith Katherine (Lindberg) W.; student Modesto Jr. Coll., 1955-64; certificate Pacific Coast Banking Sch., U. Wash., 1974; m. Marilyn Irene Hallmark, May 12, 1951; children: Marc Gordon, Wendy Diane. Bookkeeper, teller First Nat. Bank, Turlock, 1947-50; v.p. Gordon Hallmark, Inc., Turlock, 1950-53; asst. cashier United Calif. Bank, Turlock, 1953-68, regional v.p., Fresno, 1968-72, v.p., mgr., Turlock, 1972-76; founding pres., dir. Golden Valley Bank, Turlock, 1976-84; pres. Wallström & Co., 1985—. Campaign chmn. United Crusade, Turlock, 1971; chmn., founding dir. Covenant Village, retirement home, Turlock, 1973—, treas. Covenant Retirement Communities West; founding pres. Turlock Regional Arts Council, 1974, dir., 1975-76. Served with U.S. N.G., 1948-56. Mem. Nat. Soc. Accts. for Coops., Ind. Bankers No. Calif., Am. Bankers Assn., U.S. Yacht Racing Union, No. Calif. Golf Assn., Turlock C. of C. (dir. 1973-75), Stanislaus Sailing Soc. (commodore 1980-81), Republican. Mem. Covenant Ch. Clubs: Turlock Golf and Country (pres. 1975-76, v.p., 1977, dir. 1977, 83). Lodges: Masons, Rotary. Home: 1720 Hammond Dr Turlock CA 95380 Office: Wallstrom & Co 2925 Niagara Turlock CA 95380

WALMAN, JEROME, psychotherapist, consultant; b. Charleston, W.Va., June 19, 1937; s. Joe and Madeline Minnie (Levy) W.; student W.Va. U., Boston U., Berkley Sch. Music, Boston; m. Mary Joan Granara, Sept. 5, 1960. Producer, composer, writer mus. compositions at Carnegie Hall, Broadway theatre, 1962, 63; practicing psychotherapist in spl. hypnosis and music therapy, 1964—; designer Jerome Walman Systems Applied Hypnosis, 1969; marriage and family counselor; lectr., dir. tng. programs on memory improvement and speed reading; dir., producer TV show Enterprises Unlimited, 1978—; producer, composer I Murdered Mary, N.Y.C., 1976, Last Call, N.Y.C., 1977, TV Mag., 1978; lectr. East-West Center, N.Y.C., 1978, Actors Tng. and Acting Therapy Center Am., Westwinds Learning Ctr., The Learning Exchange, 1986; cons. Dept. Def., NYU; personal image cons.; wine and food cons., dir. Cooking for Relaxation and Weight Control; wine and food critic; restaurant cons.-publicist; condr. courses in wine appreciation and food; editor Punch In Internat. Electronic Travel, Wine and Restaurant newsleter. Mem. Music Therapy Internat., Meditation and Mental Devel. Center N.Y., Memory Improvement and Concentration Center Am. Author papers on hypnosis, psychic phenomena and memory, music therapy, biofeedback and meditation application; featured in various publs. including Fortune, Gentleman's Quar., Cosmopolitan, Leaders mag., Mademoiselle; editor Punch in Internat. Wine, Restaurant and Travel Electronic Newslette; reviewer. Address: 400 E 59th St Apt 9F New York NY 10022

WALRATH, HARRY RIENZI, clergyman; b. Alameda, Calif., Mar. 7, 1926; s. Frank Rienzi and Cathren (Michlar) W.; A.A., City Coll. San Francisco, 1950; B.A., U. Calif. at Berkeley, 1952; M.Div., Ch. Div. Sch. of Pacific, 1959; m. Dorothy M. Baxter, June 24, 1961; 1 son, Gregory Rienzi. Dist. exec. San Mateo area council Boy Scouts Am., 1952-55; ordained deacon Episcopal Ch., 1959, priest, 1960; curate All Souls Parish, Berkeley, Calif., 1959-61; vicar St. Luke's, Atascadero, Calif., 1961-63, St. Andrew's, Garberville, Calif., 1963-64; asso. rector St. Luke's Ch., Los Gatos, 1964-65, Holy Spirit Parish, Missoula, Mont., 1965-67; vicar St. Peter's Ch., also headmaster St. Peter's Schs., Litchfield Park, Ariz., 1967-69; chaplain U. Mont., 1965-67; asst. rector Trinity Parish, Reno, 1969-72; coordinator counciling services Washoe County Council Alcoholism, Reno, 1972-74; adminstr. Cons. Assistance Services, Inc., Reno, 1974-76; pastoral counselor, contract chaplain Nev. Mental Health Inst., 1976-78; contract mental health chaplain VA Hosp., Reno, 1976-78; mental health chaplain VA Med. Ctr., 1978-83, staff chaplain, 1983-85, chief, chaplain service, 1985—, also triage coordinator for mental health; dir. youth Paso Robles Presbytery; chmn. Diocesan Commn. on Alcoholism; cons. teen-age problems Berkeley Presbytery; mem. clergy team Episcopal Marriage Encounter, 1979-85, also Episc. Engaged Encounter. Mem. at large Washoe dist. Nev. area council Boy Scouts Am., scoutmaster troop 73, 1976, troop 585, 1979-82, asst. scoutmaster troop 35, 1982—, assoc. adviser area 3 Western region, 1987—; lodge adviser Tannu Lodge 346, Order of Arrow, 1982-87; South Humboldt County chmn. Am. Cancer Soc. Trustee Community Youth Ctr., Reno. Served with USNR, 1944-46. Decorated Pacific Theater medal with star, Am. Theater medal, Victory medal, Fleet Unit Commendation medal; recipient dist. award of merit Boy Scouts Am., St. George award Episc. Ch.-Boy Scouts Am., Silver Beaver award Boy Scouts Am., 1986, Founders' award Order of the Arrow, Boy Scouts Am., 1985; performance awards VA-VA Med. Ctr., 1983, 84; named Arrowman of Yr., Order of Arrow, Boy Scouts Am. Cert. substance abuse counselor, Nev. Mem. Ch. Hist. Soc., U. Calif. Alumni Assn., Nat. Model R.R. Assn. (life), Sierra Club Calif., Missoula Council Chs. (pres.), Alpha Phi Omega. Democrat. Club: Rotary. Home: 580 Huffaker Ln E Reno NV 89511 Office: VA Med Ctr 1000 Locust St Reno NV 89520

WALSCHAP, HUGO, diplomat; b. Antwerp, Belgium, Apr. 26, 1926; s. Gerard Jacob Walschap; m. Hermine van Hasselt, 1950; children: Gerard, Yolande. MA in Polit. Sci., LLD, U. Brussels, 1948. Atty.-at-law Antwerp, 1948-51; with diplomatic service Ministry Fgn. Affairs, 1951-53; various diplomatic posts Ministry Fgn. Affairs, Peru, Thailand, France, U.S., 1953-69; ambassador to Venezuela, 1969-74, Columbia, 1976-80, Czechoslavakia, 1984-87; ambassador to Sweden Ministry External Affairs, 1987—; Belgian Roving Ambassador for Ea. Europe, 1980-84, Ambassador for Peace and Security, 1984; lectr. various U.S. univs., including UCLA, U. So. Calif., Brigham Young U. Contbr. articles to profl. jours. Fellow Club University Found. Brussels. Recipient nat. and fgn. decorations. Home: Rue St Bernard 76, 1060 Brussels Belgium Office: Ministry Fgn Affairs, Rue Quatre Bras 2, 1000 Brussels Belgium

WALSER, MARTIN, writer; b. Wasserburg-Bodensee, Mar. 24, 1927; s. Martin and Augusta (Schmid) W.; m. Kathe Jehle, 1950; 4 daus. Ed. Theologisch-Philosophische Hochschule, Regensburg, U. Tubingen. Writer, 1951—, publs. include: (short stories) Ein Flugzeug uber dem Haus, 1955; Lugengeschichten, 1964; (novels) Ehen in Philippsburg, 1957; Halbzeit, 1960; Das Einhorn, 1966; Fiction, 1970; Die Gallistl'sche Krankheit, 1972; Der Sturz, 1973; Jenseits der Liebe, 1976; Ein fliehendes Pferd, 1978; Seelenarbeit, 1979; Das Schwanenhaus, 1980; Brief an Lord Liszt, 1981; Brandung, 1985, Dorle und Wolf, 1987, Faget, 1988; (plays) Der Abstecher, 1961; Eiche und Angora, 1962; Uberlebensgross Herr Krott, 1963; Der schwarze Schwan, 1964; Die Zimmerschlacht, 1967; Ein Kinderspiel, 1970; Das Sauspiel, 1975; In Goethes Hand, 1982, Die Ohrfeige, 1986; (essays) Beschreibung einer Form, Versuch uber Franz Kafka, 1961; Erfahrungen und Leseerfahrungen, 1965; Heimatkunde, 1968; Wie und wovon handelt Literatur, 1973; Wer ist ein Schriftsteller, 1978; (poems) Der Grund zur Freude, 1978; (essay) Uber Tironie, 1981; Liebeserklarungen, 1983; Gestaendnis auf Raten, 1986. Recipient Group 47 prize, 1955, Hermann-Hesse prize, 1957, Schiller prize, 1980, G. Buechner prize, 1981. Address: Zum Hecht 36, 7770 Uberlingen-Nussdorf Federal Republic of Germany

WALSER, PETER, mining engineer; b. Linz, Upper Austria, Austria, May 22, 1943; s. Andreas and Elisabeth (Hagleitner) W.; m. Nora Lohmann, Oct. 13, 1970; children: Irgrid, Gudrun, Gerfried. BS, Mining U., Leoben, Austria, 1968, PhD, 1970. Site mgr. Bauxit Parnasse, Greece, 1969; exploration asst. Mining U., Leoben, 1970; exploration mgr. Sabina Mines Ltd., Can., 1971-72; mine mgr. GKB Fohnsdorf, Austria, 1972-76, Gold Mine Minerven, Venezuela, 1977-78; site mgr. Arge Bosruck Tunnel, Austria, 1979-80; mine mgr. WBH Tungsten Mine Mittersill, Austria, 1980-87, gen. mgr., 1987—. Mem. Sport Club Mittersill (pres. 1982—), Freunde der Montan U., Beg. Verein Üsterreich. Roman Catholic. Club: VDST (Leoben). Office: Wolfram Bergbau, A5730 Mittersill Austria

WALSH, CHARLES RICHARD, banker; b. Bklyn., Jan. 30, 1939; s. Charles John and Anna Ellen Walsh; B.S., Fordham U., 1960; M.B.A., St. John's U., 1966; D of Comml. Scis. (hon.), St. John's U., 1985; m. Marie Anne Goulden, June 24, 1961; children—Kevin C., Brian R., Gregory M. Credit and collection mgr. Texaco Inc., N.Y.C., 1961-67; mgr. credit research Trans World Airlines, N.Y.C., 1967-71; dir. br. ops. Avon Products Inc., N.Y.C., 1971-74; exec. v.p. Mfrs. Hanover Trust Co., Hicksville, N.Y., 1974—; dir., former chmn. bd. dirs. Eastern States Monetary Services, Lake Success, N.Y., 1978—. Sustaining mem. Republican Nat. Com., 1978—; mem. St. John's U. Adv. Bd., 1982—. Served with USAR, 1960, 61-62. Recipient Disting. Service award St. John's U., 1985. Cert. Soc. Cert. Consumer Credit Execs. Mem. N.Y. State Bankers Assn. (former dir., mem. gov. council, chmn. consumer banking div.), Am. Bankers Assn. (chmn. bank card div., mem. exec. com., former mem. communications council and chmn. edn. com.), Am. Mgmt. Assn., N.Y. Credit and Fin. Mgmt. Assn., Beta Gamma Sigma, Omicron Delta Epsilon. Republican. Clubs: Forest Estates (Oyster Bay, N.Y.). Home: 9 Blueberry Ln Oyster Bay NY 11771 Office: 100 Duffy Ave Hicksville NY 11801

WALSH, CORNELIUS STEPHEN, leasing company executive; b. N.Y.C., Dec. 27, 1907; s. William Francis and Frances (Murphy) W.; m. Edwyna Lois Senter, May 1, 1930; children—Jane Linda (Mrs. Walsh Weed), Richard Stephen, Suzanne Patricia. Student, Eastman-Gaines Sch., 1924-25. Assoc. with Dyson Shipping Co., Inc., 1925-27, Interocean Steamship Corp., 1928-30; sec. States Marine Corp., 1931-38, v.p., 1938-53, pres., 1953-65, dir., 1950-65; pres., dir. States Marine Corp. Del., 1946-65; chmn. Waterman Steamship Corp., N.Y.C., 1965—, Waterman Industries Corp., 1965—, Hammond Leasing Corp., 1967—; dir. Oliver Corp. Mem. Far East-Am. Council Commerce and Industry (dir.), Soc. Naval Architects and Marine Engrs. (asso.), Soc. of Four Arts (Palm Beach), Japan Soc. (hon. dir.), Am. Bur. Shipping. Clubs: Wall Street (N.Y.C.), Yacht (N.Y.C.), Met. Opera (N.Y.C.); Seawanhaka Corinthian Yacht (Oyster Bay, L.I., N.Y.); N. Am. Sta. Royal Scandinavian Yacht; Pine Valley Golf (Clementon, N.J.); Everglades (Palm Beach, Fla.), Bath and Tennis (Palm Beach, Fla.), Sailfish of Fla. (Palm Beach, Fla.). Home: 220 El Bravo Way Palm Beach FL 33480 Office: 120 Wall St New York NY 10005

WALSH, DENNIS MAXTON, travel agent, insurance consultant; b. Bradford, Yorkshire, Eng., Dec. 28, 1925; s. Walter and Edith (Gorrod) W.; divorced; 1 child, Moira Kay. From clk. to pres., owner Briggs & Hill, Bradford, 1947—; justice of peace City of Bradford, 1967. Pres. Bradford C. of C., 1985, 87; chmn. Assn. Yorkshire, Leeds, 1987, Bradford and Ilkley Coll., 1987—. Named Officer Most Excellent Order Brit. Empire Her Majesty the Queen, 1972. Fellow Inst. Travel and Tourism; mem. Nat. Assn. Ind. Travel Agents (pres.), World Ind. Network Travel Agents (pres.). Mem. Ch. of Eng. Office: Briggs & Hill, 20 Rawson Pl, Bradford England BD 1 3QN

WALSH, F. HOWARD, oil producer, rancher; b. Waco, Tex., Feb. 7, 1913; s. P. Frank and Maude (Gage) W.; m. Mary D. Fleming, Mar. 13, 1937; children: Richard F., F. Howard, D'Ann E. Walsh Bonnell, Maudi Walsh Roe, William Lloyd. B.B.A., Tex. Christian U., 1933, LL.D. (hon.), 1979. Self employed oil producer, rancher 1942—; pres. Walsh & Watts, Inc. Mem. Tex. Jud. Qualifications Commn., 1970-74; pres. Walsh Found.; v.p. Fleming Found.; hon. trustee Tex. Christian U.; guarantor Ft. Worth Arts Council (also hon. bd. mem.), Schola Cantorum, Ft. Worth Ballet, Tex. Boys' Choir, Ft. Worth Theatre, Ft. Worth Opera; bd. dirs. Southwestern Expdn. and Fat Stock Show, Ft. Worth. Named Valuable Alumnus, Tex. Christian U., 1967; recipient spl. recognition for support Univ. Ranch Tng. Program, Royal Purple (with wife) Tex. Christian U., 1979; Disting. Service award So. Bapt. Radio and TV Commn., 1972; tng. ctr. named in honor So. Bapt. Radio and TV Commn., 1976; Brotherhood citation NCCJ, 1978; named Patron of Arts in Ft. Worth, 1970; recipient Friends of Tex. Boys' Choir, 1981; donor Walsh Med. Bldg., Southwestern Bapt. Theol. Sem., land and bldgs. to Tex. Boys Choir, 1971, Wurlitzer Organ to Casa Manana, 1972; named Edna Gladney Internat. Grandparents, 1972; Tarrant County Jr. Coll. Library dedicated in honor, 1978; ballet season dedicated in honor by Ft. Worth Ballet Assn., 1978-79; benefactor ann. prodn. Littlest Wiseman, Christmas Gift to City of Ft. Worth; recipient appreciation award and citation Southwestern Bapt. Theol. Sem., 1981, B.H. Carroll Founders Southwestern Bapt. Theol. Sem., 1982; recipient (with wife) Sr. Citizen award, 1985. Mem. Tex.-Mid-Continent Oil and Gas Assn., West Central Tex. Oil and Gas Assn., North Tex. Oil and Gas Assn., Ind. Petroleum Assn., Tex. Ind. Producers and Royalty Owners, Am.-Internat. Charolais Assn., Tex. Christian U. Ex-Letterman's Assn. Baptist bd. sr. deacons. Clubs: Garden of Gods; Colorado Springs Country (Colorado Springs); Steeplechase, Fort Worth, Ridglea, Breakfast, Frog, Colonial Country, Shady Oaks Country, Century II, Petroleum, City, River Crest Country. Home: 2425 Stadium Dr Fort Worth TX 76109 Office: Walsh & Watts Inc 1007 InterFirst Ft Worth Bldg Fort Worth TX 76102 also: 1801 Culebra Colorado Springs CO 80907

WALSH, FRANCIS XAVIER, marketing and sales executive; b. Jersey City, Mar. 24, 1927; s. William J. and Agatha (Encowsky) W.; m. Gloria C. Bonomo, May 13, 1950; children: Kenneth X., Brian X. BS in Pharmacy, Rutgers U., 1950. Sales rep. E.R. Squibb & Sons, Princeton, N.J., 1952-59, sales tng. assoc., 1959-66; sales tng. and devel. mgr. Warren-Teed Pharms, Inc., Columbus, Ohio, 1966-68, dir. manpower devel., 1969; sales mgr. Consol. Biomed. Labs. subs. Rohm & Haas, Columbus, 1969-70, dir. mktg., 1970-78, v.p. sales, 1978-81, bd. dirs., 1975-81, sales and mktg. tng. cons. parent co., after 1981; dir. sales and mktg. MDS Health Group, Inc., 1984-88; now v.p. sales and mktg. Biosonics, Inc.; prin. Frank X. Walsh Assocs. Recipient Alumnus of Yr. award Rutgers Coll. Pharmacy, 1966. Served with USN, 1945-46, 51-52. Named to Hon. Order Ky. Colonels. Mem. Am. Soc. Tng. and Devel. (chmn. sales tng. div. 1970), Rutgers Coll. Pharmacy Alumni Assn. (pres. 1964-65), Rutgers U. Alumni Assn. (bd. govs. 1964, 65), N.J. Pharm. Assn. Roman Catholic. Lodge: Rotary. Office: 14000 D Commerce Pkwy Mount Laurel NJ 08054 Office: 355 Commerce Dr Amherst NY 14150

WALSH, HOWARD BENJAMIN, business consultant; b. Hampton, Iowa, Sept. 25, 1919; s. Benjamin George and Caroline (Heeren) W.; student mil. sci. U. Md., 1951-55; grad. Air War Coll., 1959, U.S. Navy Postgrad. Sch., 1966, U. So. Calif. Mgmt. Policy Inst., 1977; m. Barbara Mary Eales, June 1, 1945; children—Michael Benjamin, Mary Elizabeth. Commd. 2d lt. U.S. Army Air Force, 1940, advanced through grades to col., 1954; combat pilot 8th Air Force, World War II; exec. officer Hdqrs. U.S. Army Air Force, 1945-47; air attache U.S. embassy, Stockholm, 1947-51; NATO adv. Office Sec. Def., Washington, 1951-55; wing comdr. SAC, Dyess AFB, Tex., 1955-59; in sr. mil. posts NATO, Washington, France, Belgium, 1959-70, ret., 1970; exec. dir. Nat. Alliance Bus., Santa Barbara, Calif., 1971-82; bus. cons., 1982—. Trustee, Santa Barbara Art Inst., 1971-73, Direct Relief Internat., 1978-83; city commr. City of Santa Barbara, 1974-75; mem. U. So. Calif. Adv. Council, 1975-84; mem. CETA Manpower Planning Council, Santa Barbara County, 1975-79; mem. U. Calif. Gen. Affiliates (chmn. 1987-88), San Louis Obispo Trade Adv. Council Calif. Men's Colony, 1974-82; vice chmn. Pvt. Industry Council Santa Barbara County, 1979-82, chmn., 1982-84; bd. dirs. Interdenom, Ch. Camp, Camp Cachuma, Calif., 1975-80, ARC, 1976-87, Am. Freedom Coalition, 1988—; vice-chmn. ARC, 1981-87; bd. dirs. United Way, Santa Barbara County, 1976-82, pres., 1979-80; vestry mem. All Saints by the Sea Episcopal Ch., Montecito, Calif., 1977-81. Decorated Legion of Merit, D.F.C.(2), Air medal (4), Purple Heart, Meritorious Service medal (U.S.); knight Royal Order of Sword (Sweden); Croix de Guerre avec Palme (France); recipient commendation Calif. Assembly, 1973, Sec. of Army, 1946, of Air Force, 1965, of Labor, 1973, County of Santa Barbara, 1980, 83, Pres. U.S., 1978, 81; Disting. Citizens Community Service award Anti-Defamation League of B'nai B'rith, 1982. Mem. Council Fgn. Relations, Air Force Assn., Ret. Officers Assn., Am. Security Council. Republican. Clubs: Cosmopolitan, Channel City, Santa Barbara Ret. Officers (pres. 1976), Rotary (pres. local club 1980-81). Home: 48 Alston Pl Santa Barbara CA 93108

WALSH, JAMES DAVID, broadcasting company executive; b. Schenectady, Dec. 17, 1947; s. James A. and Dorothy (Sommer) W.; m. Mary Ellen Budge, Jan. 23, 1971; children: Jason P., Jeffrey J., Jennifer M. Student Northwestern Coll. Announcer, Sta. WFLY-FM, Troy, N.Y., 1971-72; account exec., announcer Sta. WABY, Albany, 1972-74; account exec. Sta. WPTR, Albany, 1974; founder Tri-City Comets Semi-Profl. Basketball, 1973-76; founder, gen. mgr., pres. Sta. WWWD, Schenectady, 1975—; pres. Walvon Communications, Inc., 1975—, W.V. Broadcasting, Inc., 1986-88; founder, gen. mgr., owner Sta. WVKZ-FM, Albany, 1987—. Dep. sheriff Schenectady County, 1980-85. Co-author: Greenburg's Guide to American Flyer Trains, 1980; co-editor: Updated Guide to American Flyer Trains. Recipient 18 gold and platinum records. Served with Army N.G., 1967-73. Mem. Train Collectors Assn., Am. Flyer Collectors Club, Internat. Platform Assn. Office: Sta WVKZ 433 State St Schenectady NY 12305

WALSH, JAMES HAMILTON, lawyer; b. Astoria, N.Y., May 20, 1947; s. Edward James and Helen Smith (Hamilton) W.; m. Janice Ausherman, Aug. 3, 1968; children—Tracy, Courtney, Eric. B.A. in Psychology, Bridgewater Coll., 1968; J.D., U. Va., 1975. Bar: Va. 1975, U.S. Dist. Ct. (ea. and we. dists.) Va. 1975, U.S. Ct. Appeals (4th cir.) 1976, U.S. Supreme Ct. 1982. Assoc. McGuire, Woods, Battle & Boothe (and predecessor firms), Richmond, Va., 1975-82, ptnr., 1982—; instr. Nat. Inst. Trial Adv.; spl. prosecutor U.S. Dist. Ct. (ea. dist.) Va., 1979, 84. Mem. staff Va. Law Rev. Served with U.S. Army, 1969-72. Mem. ABA (mem. antitrust sect. health care com., litigation sect.), Am. Trial Lawyers Assn., Va. State Bar (bd. govs. antitrust sect. 1984—, chmn. 1986—), Va. Bar Assn., Richmond Bar Assn., Order Coif, Phi Delta Phi. Episcopalian. Clubs: Willow Oaks, Bull and Bear (Richmond, Va.). Contbr. articles to profl. jours. Home: 3035 Stratford Rd Richmond VA 23225 Office: McGuire Woods Battle & Boothe 1 James Ctr Richmond VA 23219

WALSH, JAMES PATRICK, JR., insurance consultant, actuary; b. Ft. Thomas, Ky., Mar. 7, 1910; s. James Patrick and Minnie Louise (Cooper) W.; m. Evelyn Mary Sullivan, May 20, 1939. Comml. engr. degree, U. Cin., 1933. Acct. Firestone Tire & Rubber Co., also Gen. Motors Corp., 1933-36; rep. ARC, 1937, A.F.L., 1938-39; dir. Ohio Div. Minimum Wages, Columbus, 1939-42; asst. sec.-treas. union label trades dept. A.F.L., Washington, 1946-53; v.p. Pension and Group Cons., Inc., Cin., 1953—; Mem. Pres.'s Commn. Jud. and Congl. Salaries, 1953, Ohio Gov.'s Commn. Employment of Negro, 1940, Hamilton (O.) County Welfare Bd., 1955—, council long term illness and rehab. Cin. Pub. Health Fedn., 1957-68. Bd. dirs. U. Cin., 1959-67; bd. govs. St. Xavier High Sch., Cin.; trustee Brown Found., Newman Cath. Center, Cin. Served to lt. col. AUS, 1942-46; col. Res. ret. Decorated Legion of Merit, Commendation ribbon with two oak leaf clusters; named Ky. col., 1958, Ky. adm., 1968, Ohio commodore, 1985; recipient Disting. Alumni award U. Cin., 1969, Disting. Alumni award Covington Latin Sch., 1983, Insignis award St. Xavier High Sch., 1973, Americanism award Am. Legion, Kevin Barry award Ancient Order of Hiberians. Fellow Am. Soc. Pension Actuaries; mem. Am. Arbitration Assn. (nat. community disputes panel, employee benefit claims panel), Marine Corps Res. Officers Assn., Naval Res. Assn., Res. Officers Assn., Am. Legion, Q.M. Assn., VFW, Am. Mil. Retiree Assn., Nat. Assn. Uniform Services, English Speaking Union, Ohio Ret. Officers Assn. (past pres. council), Ret. Officers Assn. (past pres. Cin. chpt. 1973-74), Amvets, Air Force Assn., Ret. Officers Assn. (nat. bd. dirs. 1983—), Marine Corps League, Nat. Football Found. and Hall of Fame, Am. Fedn. State, County and Employees Union, Naval Order, Internat. Alliance Theatrical Stage Employees (past sgt. at arms), Internat. Hodcarriers, Bldg. and Common Laborers Union, Ins. Workers Internat. Union, Office Employees Internat. Union, Cooks and Pastry Cooks Local, Friendly Sons St. Patrick (past pres.), Covington Latin Sch. Alumni Assn. (past pres.), Soc. for Advancement Mgmt., Defense Supply Assn., Ancient Order Hibernians (past pres.), Assn. U.S. Army (trustee), Am. Ordnance Assn., Soc. Am. Mil. Engrs., Order of Alhambra, Internat. Assn. Health Underwriters, Allied Constrn. Industries, Navy League, Scabbard and Blade, Nat. Council of Cath. Men, Indsl. Relations Research Assn., Zoo Soc. of Cin., Millcreek Valley Assn., Alpha Kappa Psi. Republican. Roman Catholic. Clubs: C. Cin. (past pres.), Queen City, American Irish, Insiders, Touchdown, Blue Liners, Roundtable, Scuttlebuts, Newman, Bankers, Mil. (Cin.). Lodges: K.C. (4 deg.), Elks. Home: 5563 Julmar Dr Cincinnati OH 45238 Office: 309 Vine St Room 200 Cincinnati OH 45202

WALSH, JOHN, JR., museum director; b. Mason City, Wash., Dec. 9, 1937; s. John J. and Eleanor (Wilson) W.; m. Virginia Alys Galston, Feb. 17, 1961; children: Peter Wilson, Anne Galston, Frederick Matthiessen. B.A., Yale U., 1961; postgrad., U. Leyden, Netherlands, 1965-66; M.A., Columbia U., 1965, Ph.D., 1971. Lectr., research asst. Frick Collection, N.Y.C., 1966-68; asso. higher edn. Met. Mus. Art, N.Y.C., 1968-71; assoc. curator European paintings Met. Mus. Art, 1970-72, curator dept. European paintings, 1972-75, vice-chmn., 1974-75; adj. asso. prof. art history Columbia U., N.Y.C., 1969-72; adj. prof. Columbia U., 1972-75; prof. art history Barnard Coll., Columbia U., N.Y.C., 1975-77; Mrs. Russell W. Baker curator paintings Mus. Fine Arts, Boston, 1977-83; dir. J. Paul Getty Mus., Malibu, Calif., 1983—; vis. prof. fine arts Harvard U., 1979; mem. governing bd. Yale U. Art Gallery, 1975—; bd. Fellows Claremont U. Ctr. Grad. Sch., 1988—. Contbr. articles to profl. jours. Mem. county com. Democratic party, N.Y.C., 1968-71; mem. vis. com. Fogg Mus., Harvard U. Served with USNR, 1957-59. Fulbright grad. fellow The Netherlands, 1965-66. Mem. Coll. Art Assn., Am. Assn. Mus., Archaeol. Inst. Am. Club: Century Assn. (N.Y.C.). Office: J Paul Getty Mus PO Box 2112 Santa Monica CA 90406

WALSH, JOHN BRONSON, lawyer; b. Buffalo, Feb. 20, 1927; s. John A. and Alice (Condon) W.; m. Barbara Ashford, May 20, 1966; 1 child, Martha. AB, Canisius Coll., 1950; JD, Georgetown U., 1952. Bar: N.Y. 1953, U.S. Supreme Ct. 1958, U.S. Ct. Internat. Trade 1969, U.S. Ct. Customs and Patent Appeals 1973. Law clk. Covington & Burling, Washington, 1950-52, Galley & Locker, N.Y.C., 1952-53; trial atty. Garvey & Conway, N.Y.C., 1953-54; vol. atty. Nativity Mission, N.Y.C., 1953-54; ptnr. Jaeckle, Fleischmann, Kelly, Swart & Augspurger, and successor Jaeckle, Fleischmann & Mugel, Buffalo, 1955-60, 1976-80; ptnr. Walsh & Cleary, P.C., 1980—, J.B. Walsh & Assocs.; individual practice law, Buffalo, 1960-75; trial counsel Anti-trust div. U.S. Dept. Justice, Washington, 1960-61; spl. counsel on disciplinary proc. N.Y. Supreme Ct., 1960-76; appointee legal disciplinary coordinating com. State of N.Y., 1971; legis. counsel, spl. counsel to mayor Buffalo, 1969-75; counsel to sheriff Erie County, 1969-72; legis. counsel Niagara Frontier Transp. Authority; cons. Norfolk So. R.R., Ecology and Environment on Govtl. Affairs; guest lectr. univ. and profl. groups. Author: (TV series) The Law and You (Freedom Found. award, ABA award, Internat. Police Assn. award). Past pres. Ashford Hollow Found. Visual and Performing Arts; past trustee Dollar Bills, Inc., charitable youth orgn.; past co-producer Grand Island Playhouse and Players. Served with U.S. Army, 1945-46. Recipient Buffalo Jr. C. of C. Gold Key award for efforts to revitalize Erie County Bar Assn., 1962, Freedom Found. award for Law Day editorial, 1966. Fellow Am. Bar Found.; mem. ABA (del. internat. confs. Brussels 1963, Mexico City 1964, Lausanne, Switzerland 1964; merit award com. 1961-68; crime prevention and control com. 1968-70), N.Y. Trial Lawyers Assn., Am. Immigration Lawyers Assn., Am. Judicature Soc., N.Y. State Bar Assn., Erie County Bar Assn. (past sec.), Buffalo Bar Assn., Nat. Public Employer Labor Relations Assn., Am. Legion, Capitol Hill Club of Buffalo, Am. Assn. Airport Execs., N.Y. State Bus. Council (environ. law subcom., chmn. subcom.). Roman Catholic. Clubs: Buffalo Irish (bd. dirs.), Buffalo Athletic (past dir. and 1st v.p.), Buffalo Canoe, Buffalo City, Ft. Orange of Albany. Lodge: KC, Knights of Equity, Leoknights. Home: 193 Depew Ave Buffalo NY 14214 Office: Walsh & Cleary 210 Ellicott Sq Bldg Buffalo NY 14203

WALSH, LAWRENCE EDWARD, lawyer; b. Port Maitland, N.S., Can., Jan. 8, 1912; came to U.S., 1914, naturalized, 1922; s. Dr. Cornelius Edward and Lila May (Sanders) W.; m. Mary Alma Porter; children: Barbara Marie, Janet Maxine (Mrs. Alan Larson), Sara Porter (Mrs. Craig Miller), Dale Edward, Elizabeth Porter. A.B., Columbia, 1932, LL.B., 1935; LL.D., Union U., 1959, St. John's U., 1975, Suffolk U., 1975, Waynesburg Coll., 1976, Vt. Law Sch., 1976. Bar: N.Y. State 1936, D.C. 1981, Okla. 1981, U.S. Supreme Ct. 1951. Spl. asst. atty. gen. Drukman Investigation, 1936-38; dep. asst. dist. atty. N.Y. County, 1938-41; assoc. Davis Polk Wardwell Sunderland & Kiendl, 1941-43; asst. counsel to gov. N.Y. 1943-49, counsel to gov., 1950-51; counsel Pub. Service Commn., 1951-53; gen. counsel, exec. dir. Waterfront Commn. of N.Y. Harbor, 1953-54; U.S. judge So. Dist. N.Y., 1954-57; U.S. dep. atty. gen. 1957-60; partner firm Davis, Polk & Wardwell, 1961-81; counsel firm Crowe & Dunlevy, Oklahoma City, 1981—; ind. counsel Iran/Contra investigation, 1986—; dir. Kans. Gas and Electric Co., chmn. N.Y. State Moreland Commn. Alcoholic Beverage Control Law, 1963-64; pres. Columbia Alumni Fedn., 1968-69; dep. head with rank of ambassador U.S. delegation meetings on Vietnam, Paris, 1969; counsel to N.Y. State ct. on judiciary, 1971-72; 2d circuit mem. U.S. Circuit Judge Nominating Commn., 1978-80. Trustee emeritus Columbia U., Mut. Life Ins. Co., N.Y.; trustee William Nelson Cromwell Found. Fellow Am. Bar Found., Am. Coll. Trial Lawyers; mem. Am. Law Inst. (council), ABA (pres. 1975-76), N.Y. State Bar Assn. (pres. 1966-67), Oklahoma County Bar Assn., Okla. State Bar Assn., Internat. Bar Assn., Assn. of Bar of City of New York, N.Y. County Lawyers Assn.; hon. mem. Law Soc. Eng. and Wales, Can. Bar Assn., Mexican Bar Assn., Beta Theta Pi. Presbyterian. Clubs: N.Y. India House, The Century, Oklahoma City Golf and Country; Petroleum (Oklahoma City), Beacon (Oklahoma City). Home: 1902 Bedford Dr Oklahoma City OK 73116 Office: 1800 Mid-Am Tower Oklahoma City OK 73102

WALSH, LYNN DREWE, business and management educator; b. N.Y.C., May 8, 1946; s. John Martin and Adele Bertha (Hofmann) W.; 1 child, Matthew Adam. AB in English, North Cen. Coll., Naperville, Ill., 1968; MS in Counselor Edn., L.I. U., 1972; PhD in Organizational and Adminstrv. Studies in Higher Edn., NYU, 1984. Cert. tchr. secondary English, N.Y. Research asst. in chemistry North Cen. Coll., 1965-66; tchr. English, math. and sci. Marshall Jr. High Sch., Columbus, Ga., 1968-69; asst. to dir. continuing edn., adult studies evening div. and summer sch., C.W. Post Ctr., L.I. U., Greenvale, N.Y., 1969-71, asst. to v.p. for adminstrn., 1971-72; asst. to dean instrn., counselor Student Problem Solving Ctr., Nassau Community Coll., Garden City, N.Y., 1972-73; acad. adminstrv. assoc. SUNY, Old Westbury Coll., 1973-77, dir. instrnl. support, 1977-78, asst. v.p. for acad. affairs, 1978-81, acting v.p. for student devel., 1981-82, exec. asst. to pres. for instl. planning and devel., exec. dir. Old Westbury Found., 1982-84, assoc. v.p. for acad. affairs, and spl. asst. to pres. for planning, 1984-87, prof. bus. mgmt., 1987—; adj. asst. prof. higher edn. NYU, 1985—; mem. L.I. Regional Adv. Council on Higher Edn. Task Force on Acad. Affairs, 1973-87. Contbr. articles to profl. publs. Recipient Outstanding Contbn. to Student

Govt. award Student Govt. Assn., SUNY, Old Westbury Coll., 1981, citation for excellence in performance Dept. Counseling and Guidance, Grad. Sch. Edn., C.W. Post Ctr. L.I. U., 1972, Chancellor's award for excellence in profl. service SUNY, 1980, cert. of appreciation Grad. Student Orgn., NYU, 1987. Mem. Am. Assn. Higher Edn., Am. Assn. Univ. Adminstrs., Am. Ednl. Research Assn. (first chairperson grad. student div. J 1982-84, co-chairperson grad. student program com. for 1983 ann. meeting 1982—), Phi Delta Kappa, Phi Lambda Theta.

WALSH, PETER ALEXANDER, government official; b. Kellerberrin, Australia, Mar. 11, 1935; married; 4 children. With Western Australian Farmers' Union; mem. Australian senate, 1974, Shadow Ministry, 1977-83; minister for resources and energy 1977-83, minister assisting prime minister for pub. service, 1984-87, minister for fin., 1984—. Mem. Australian Labor Party. Home: Minister for Fin, Newlands St, Parkes Australian Capital Terrs, Australia *

WALSH, RICHARD GEORGE, agricultural economist; b. Seward, Nebr., Aug. 16, 1930; s. Thomas George and Francis Kathryn (Pape) W.; m. Patricia Burke Bard, 1976; children by previous marriage: Cathryn M., Susan E., Thomas R., Robert J. B.S., U. Nebr., 1952, M.A., 1955; Ph.D., U. Wis., 1961. From asst. prof. to prof. agrl. econs. U. Nebr., 1958-68; prof. dept. agrl. and resource econs. Colo. State U., Ft. Collins, 1968—; intergovt. exchange EPA, 1973-74; cons. FTC, 1965-66, 72, 78-79, U. P.R., 1967, Justice Dept., 1971, U.S. Forest Service, 1972, 82, 86, Bur. Land Mgmt., 1973, 85, Nat. Park Service, 1975-79; vis. prof. U. Md., 1965, Stanford Research Inst., 1971. Author: Economics of the Baking Industry, 1963, Market Structure of the Agricultural Industries, 1966, The Structure of Food Manufacturing, 1966, Organization and Competition in Food Retailing, 1966, Some Costs and Benefits of Strip Mining Western Coal, 1974, Efficiency of Wastewater Disposal in Mountain Areas, 1977, Value of Water to Recreation on High Mountain Reservoirs, 1980, Wilderness Resource Economics, 1982, Wild and Scenic River Economics, 1985, Recreation Economic Decisions: Comparing Benefits and Costs, 1986; also articles profl. jours. Bd. dirs. North Ft. Collins Sanitation Dist., 1971-73. Served to lt. (j.g.) USNR, 1952-54. Mem. Am. Econs. Assn., Am. Agrl. Econs. Assn. (Outstanding Published Research award 1964). Office: Dept Agrl and Resource Econs Colo State U Fort Collins CO 80523

WALSH, ROBERT ANTHONY, lawyer; b. Boston, Aug. 26, 1938; s. Frank and Emily Angelica (Bissitt) W.; m. Angela Rosalie Barile, Aug. 3, 1966; children: Maria, Robert II, Amy. SB, MIT, 1960; MS, Fla. Inst. Tech., 1967; JD, Suffolk U., 1971. Bar: Mass. 1971, Ill. 1976, U.S. Dist. Ct. Mass. 1972, U.S. Patent Office 1972, Can. Patent Office 1973, U.S. Supreme Ct. 1976, U.S. Ct. Appeals (Fed. cir.) 1982, U.S. Ct. Mil. Appeals 1983; registered profl. engr., Mass. Patent trainee, engr. Avco Research Lab., Everett, Mass., 1968-72; patent atty. GTE Labs., Waltham, Mass., 1972-73; group patent counsel Bell & Howell Co., Chgo., 1973-78; patent counsel ITT E. Coast Patents, Nutley, N.J., 1978-80, patent counsel internat., 1980-82; sr. patent counsel internat. ITT Corp., N.Y.C., 1982-86, dir. internat. patents, 1986-87; gen. patent counsel ITT Def. Tech. Corp., Nutley, 1987—; ednl. counselor admissions MIT, Northern, N.J., 1978—. Mem. Lakeland Hills YMCA, Mountain Lakes, N.J., Served to col. USAF, 1961-64, with Res. 1960—. Mem. ABA, Tri-State USAFR Lawyers Assn. (meritorious achievement award 1980), Internat. Patent Club (pres. 1988—), Am. Patent Law Assn., Chgo. Patent Law Assn., Air Force Assn., Res. Officers Assn., N.J. Patent Law Assn., Sigma Xi. Roman Catholic. Lodge: K.C. Home: 39 Arden Rd Mountain Lakes NJ 07046 Office: ITT Def Tech Corp Patent Dept 500 Washington Ave Nutley NJ 07110

WALSH, THOMAS JOSEPH, neuro-ophthalmologist; b. N.Y.C., Sept. 18, 1931; s. Thomas Joseph and Virginia (Hughes) W.; m. Sally Ann Maust, June 21, 1958; children—Thomas Raymond, Sara Ann, Mary Kelly, Kathleen Meghan. B.A., Coll. Fordham, 1954; M.D., Bowman Gray Med. Sch., 1958. Intern St. Vincent's Hosp., N.Y.C., 1958-59; resident ophthalmology Bowman Gray Med. Sch., Winston-Salem, N.C., 1961-64; fellow neuro-ophthalmology Bascom Palmer Eye Inst., Miami, Fla., 1964-65; practice medicine specializing in neuro-ophthalmology Stamford, Conn., 1965—; dir. neuro-ophthalmology service, asst. prof. ophthalmology and neurology Yale Sch. Medicine, New Haven, 1965-74; assoc. prof. Yale Sch. Medicine, 1974-79, prof., 1979—, also bd. permanent officers: dir. ophthalmology Stamford Hosp., 1978-83; mem. staff St. Joseph Hosp., Yale New Haven Hosp.; cons. to surgeon gen. army in neuro-ophthalmology Walter Reed Hosp., Washington, 1966—, VA Hosp., West Haven, 1965—, Silver Hill Found., New Canaan, Conn., 1974—; frequent lectr. various univs. Contbr. articles to various publs. Mem. adv. bd. Stamford Salvation Army, 1972—; mem. med. bd. Darien Nurses Assn., Conn., 1972—; surgeon Darien Fire Dept., 1969—. Served with AUS, 1959-61. Decorated Knight of Malta, 1983; Centennial fellow Johns Hopkins, 1976. Mem. AMA, Conn., Fairfield County med. socs., Acad. Ophthalmology, Oxford Ophthal. Congress, Acad. Neurology, Am. Assn. Neurol. Surgeons, Soc. Med. Cons. to Armed Forces. Club: Cosmos (Washington). Lodge: Lion. Office: 1100 Bedford St Stamford CT 06905

WALSMITH, CHARLES RODGER, psychologist, educator; b. Denver, May 19, 1926; s. Joseph Francis and Florence Ophelia (Brown-Smith) W.; B.A. (Chancellor's Ednl. scholar), U. Denver, 1956, M.A., 1962; postgrad. U. Wash., 1968-76; Ph.D., Stanton U., 1976; children—Karen Frances, Cynthia Ann, Erik Konrad. Research psychologist Personnel Tng. and Research Center, Maintenance Lab., USAF Lowery AFB, Denver, 1956; research asst. U. Colo. Med. Center, Denver, 1956-57, research asso., 1957-64; asst. prof. psychology North Park Coll., Chgo., 1965-66; sr. human engring. analyst, psychoacoustics Boeing Co., Seattle, 1965-68; instr. psychology dept. behavioral scis. Bellevue (Wash.) Community Coll., 1968-87, chmn. dept., 1968-75, 79-82, Phi Theta Kappa adviser, 1981-87, instr., chmn. dept. emeritus, 1987—. Resident trainer Gestalt Inst. of Can., Lake Cowichan, B.C., summers 1969-71, assoc., 1969—; dir. Gestalt Inst. of Wash., Bellevue, 1970—. Democratic precinct chmn., Renton, Wash., 1966-68; patron BCC Found. Served with USNR, 1944-46. Mem. Wash. State, Psychol. Assn., NEA, Wash. Edn. Assn., Inst. for Advancement of Health, Phi Beta Kappa, Psi Chi. Home: Gestalt House 14909 SE 44th Pl Bellevue WA 98006

WALSTON, LOLA INGE, dietitian; b. Chgo., Jan. 26, 1943; d. Willy and Ingeborg (Smith) Neumann; m. Steven Ward Walston, Aug. 5, 1967; children—Bradley, Scott. B.S., No. Ill. U., 1965; M.S., U. Iowa, 1967. Registered, lic. dietitian. Asst. dietary dir. Alaska Hosp. Med. Ctr., Anchorage, 1975-78; cons. dietitian Mercer County Hosp., Coldwater, Ohio, 1979; profl. service cons. Health Care and Retirement Corp. Am., Lima, Ohio, 1981-84; dietary dir. Estes Health Care Ctr., Montgomery, Ala., 1979-80, Mercy Meml. Hosp., Urbana, Ohio, 1984-86, Dairy & Nutrition Council Mid East, Dayton, Ohio, 1987—; cons. Sharonview Nursing Home, South Vienna, Ohio, 1987—; Miami Health Care Ctr., Troy, Ohio, Columbia House, Springfield, Ohio, SCOPE Nutrition Progarm for the elderly, Fairborn, Ohio, CLS Nutrition Program, Bellefontaine, Ohio, 1987—. Mem. com. Tecumseh council Boy Scouts Am., 1984, Tri-County Community Action Commn./CLS Nutrition, Bellefontaine, Ohio, 1987—. Mem. Am. Dietetic Assn., Ohio Dietetic Assn., Ohio Cons. Dietitians Health Care Facilities (chmn. 1982-84), Dayton Dietetic Assn., AAUW. Club: Hilltoppers (Fairborn, Ohio) (pres. 1982-83). Avocations: camping, sewing, knitting, crocheting, cooking.

WALSTON, RODERICK EUGENE, lawyer; b. Gooding, Idaho, Dec. 15, 1935; s. Loren R. and Iva M. (Boyer) W.; m. Margaret D. Grandey; children: Gregory Scott, Valerie Lynne. A.A., Boise Jr. Coll., 1956; B.A. cum laude, Columbia Coll., 1958; LL.B. scholar, Stanford U., 1961. Bar: Calif. 1961, U.S. Supreme Ct. 1973. Law clk to judge U.S. Ct. Appeals 9th Cir., 1961-62; dep. atty. gen State of Calif., San Francisco, 1963—, head natural resources sect, 1969—; spl. dep counsel Kings County, Calif., 1975-76. Contbr. articles to profl. jours.; bd. editors: Stanford Law Rev., 1959-61, Western Natural Resources Litigation Digest. Co-chmn. Idaho campaign against Right-to-Work initiative, 1958; Calif. rep. Western States Water Council, 1986—. Nat. Essay Contest winner Nat. Assn. Internat. Relations Clubs, 1956; Astor Found. scholar, 1956-58; Stanford Law Rev. prize, 1961. Mem. ABA (chmn. water resources com., 1988—, v. chmn. and conf. chmn., 1985-88), Contra Costa County Bar Assn., U.S. Supreme Ct. Hist. Soc., World Affairs Council No. Calif. Home: 19 Estabueno Dr Orinda CA 94563 Office: Calif Atty Gen's Office 350 McAllister St Suite 6000 San Francisco CA 94102

WALTER, PAUL, biochemist, educator; b. Davos, Switzerland, Apr. 14, 1933; s. Paul Donald and Grada (Schadee) W.; m. Helen Storkle, July 26, 1958; children—Philip, Nicole. Ph.D., ETH, Zurich, 1961. Postdoctoral fellow Brandeis U., Waltham, Mass., 1960-62; postdoctoral fellow U. Wis., Madison, 1962-65, asst. prof., 1965-67; privatdozent Univ. Berne (Switzerland), 1968, prof., 1970-75; prof. Univ. Basel (Switzerland), 1975—; dean med. faculty, 1987-88. Contbr. articles to profl. jours. Mem. Swiss Soc. Biochemistry (pres. 1980-83), Union Schweizerischer Gesellschaften fü r Exptl. Biology (pres. 1981-84), AAAS, Gesellschaft fü r Biologische Chemie, N.Y. Acad. Scis. Home: Nelkenrain 2, CH 4101 Oberwil Switzerland Office: U Basel Dept Biochemistry, Vesalianum Vesalgasse 1, CH-4-51 Basel Switzerland

WALTER, RALPH COLLINS, III, business executive; b. Hinsdale, Ill., Nov. 25, 1946; s. Ralph Collins and Ethel Marie (Eustice) W.; BA, Knox Coll., 1969; MA, Ind. U., 1972. Chartered fin. analyst. Instr., Ind. U. Bloomington, 1971-72; with A.G. Becker, Inc., Chgo., 1973-81, v.p., 1976-81; v.p. Dean Witter Reynolds Co., 1981-86; prof. fin. Northeastern Ill. U., Chgo., 1982-86, chmn. dept. fin., acctg. and law, 1983-86; v.p. The Chgo. Corp., 1986-88, sr. v.p., chief info. officer, 1988—. Trustee Northeastern Ill. U. Found., 1987—. Served to capt. U.S. Army, 1973. Woodrow Wilson fellow, 1969, Alfred P. Sloan scholar, 1966-69. Mem. Am. Econ. Assn., Am. Fin. Assn., Fin. Mgmt. Assn., Investment Analyst Soc. Chgo., Phi Beta Kappa. Home: 1251G West Fletcher Chicago IL 60657 Office: The Chgo Corp 208 S LaSalle Chicago IL 60604

WALTER, TERRY LYNN, consulting psychologist; b. Great Bend, Kans., Dec. 23, 1928; s. Clifton William and Helen Naudia (Rusco) W.; B.S., Kans. State U., 1952; M.Ed., U. Mo., 1969, Ph.D., 1979; m. Evelyn Margaret Evans, July 3, 1949; children—Marcia Jeanne, Sandra Alice, Michael Kent, Steven Craig. Chemist, Halliburton Oil Well Cement Co., Great Bend, 1945-47; research asst. U.S. Dept. Agr., Kans. State U., Manhattan, 1948-52; math. and sci. tchr. U. Md. Extension div., Eng., 1953-54; grade sch. tchr. Fairview Sch., Norton, Kans., 1955-56; cons. engr. Walter Cons. Engring. Service, Tribune, Kans., 1954—; pres. Asso. Personnel Technicians, Inc., cons. psychologists; owner, operator Mineral Exploration and Devel. Unltd., 1975—; grad. adminstrv. asst. dir. counseling bur. U. Mo., Columbia, 1968-69, counselor for testing, 1969—, instr. extension div., 1968—; asso. dir. Greeley Coop. Assn., Tribune, 1966-68. Bd. dirs. Wichita Guidance Center; chmn. bd. Christian Community Services, Inc., Wichita Guidance Center; bd. dirs. Am. Bapt. Conv. Served with USAF, 1952-54. Registered profl. engr., Kans. Mem. Am. Personnel and Guidance Assn., Am. Coll. Personnel Assn., Kans. Profl. Engrs., Am. Mgmt. Soc., Am. Soc. Personnel Adminstrs., Am. Psychol. Assn., Wichita Psychol. Assn., Alpha Kappa Lambda. Baptist (dir. Kans. conv. 1962-67). Patentee in field. Home: 6700 Abbotsford Pl Wichita KS 67206

WALTERS, ALAN ARTHUR, economist, educator; b. Leicester, Eng., 1926. B.Sc. in Econs., U. London, 1951; M.A., Oxford U., 1981; D.Lit. (hon.), U. Leicester, 1981; D.Soc.Sc. (hon.), U. Birmingham, 1984. Lectr. dept. econometrics and stats. U. Birmingham (Eng.), 1952-60, prof., 1961-68, head dept., 1961-68; Sir Ernest Cassel prof. econs. U. London, London Sch. Econs., 1968-75; prof. econs. Johns Hopkins U., Balt., 1975—; resident scholar Am. Enterprise Inst., Washington, 1983-84; vis. prof. Northwestern U., 1959-60, U. Va., 1966-67, MIT, 1967-68, Monash U. (Australia), 1971; Past cons. various central banks; mem. Commn. on London's Third Airport (Roskill), 1968-70; econ. adviser World Bank, 1976-80; adviser to Prime Minister, U.K., 1981-83, cons., 1983—. Author: (with R.W. Clower, G. Dalton and M. Harwitz) Growth Without Development, 1966; Integration in Freight Transport, 1968; The Economics of Road User Charges, 1968; An Introduction To Econometrics, 1968, 2d edit., 1969; Money in Bloom and Slump, 3d edit., 1971; Noise and Prices, 1975; (with P.R.G. Layard, and McGraw Hill) Microeconomic Theory, 1978; (with E. Bennathan) Port Pricing and Investment in Developing Countries, 1979, Britain's Economic Renaissance, 1986; editor: Money and Banking, 1970; contbr. articles to profl. publs. Decorated knight Order Brit. Empire; recipient Francis Boyer Lecture award Am. Enterprise Inst., 1983. Fellow Econometric Soc. Home: 2820 P St NW Washington DC 20007 Office: Am Enterprise Inst 1150 17th St NW Washington DC 20036 also: 21 Victoria Sq, London SW1W 0RB, England *

WALTERS, BARBARA, television journalist; b. Sept. 25, 1931; d. Lou and Dena (Selett) W.; m. Lee Guber, Dec. 8, 1963 (div. 1976); 1 dau., Jacqueline Dena; m. Merv Adelson, May 10, 1986. Grad., Sarah Lawrence Coll., 1953; LHD (hon.), Ohio State U., Marymount Coll., Tarrytown, N.Y., 1975, Wheaton Coll., 1983. Former writer-producer WNBC-TV; then with sta. WPIX and CBS-TV; joined Today Show, 1961, regular panel mem., 1963-74, co-host, 1974-76; newscaster ABC Evening News (now ABC World News Tonight), 1976. Contbr. to ABC programs Issues and Answers; appears on prime-time ABC entertainment spls.; co-host ABC TV news show 20/20; moderator syndicated TV program Not For Women Only. Author: How To Talk With Practically Anybody About Practically Anything, 1970. Contbr. to Reader's Digest. Hon. chmn. Nat. Assn. Help for Retarded Children, 1970. Recipient award of yr. Nat. Assn. TV Program Execs., 1975, Emmy award Nat. Acad. TV Arts and Scis., 1975; Mass Media award Am. Jewish Com. Inst. Human Relations, 1975; Hubert H. Humphrey Freedom prize Anti-Defamation League-B'nai B'rith, 1978; Matrix award N.Y. Women in Communications, 1977; Barbara Walters' Coll. Scholarship in Broadcast Journalism established in her honor Ill. Broadcasters Assn., 1975; named to 100 Women Accomplishment Harper's Bazaar, 1967, 71, One of Am.'s 75 Most Important Women Ladies' Home Jour., 1970, One of 10 Women of Decade Ladies' Home Jour., 1979, One of Am.'s 100 Most Important Women Ladies' Home Jour., 1983, Woman of Year in Communications, 1974; Woman of Year Theta Sigma Phi; Broadcaster of Yr. Internat. Radio and TV Soc., 1975; named one of 200 Leaders of Future Time Mag., 1974, One of Most Important Women of 1979 Roper Report, One of Women Most Admired by Am. People Gallup Poll, 1982, 84. Office: ABC News 1330 Ave of Americas New York NY 10019 *

WALTERS, DAVID MCLEAN, lawyer; b. Cleve., Apr. 4, 1917; s. William L. and Marguerite (McLean) W.; m. Betty J. Latimer, Mar. 25, 1939 (dec. 1983); 1 dau., Susan Patricia (Mrs. James Edward Smith). B.A., Baldwin-Wallace Coll., 1938; LL.B., Cleve. Sch. Law, 1943; J.D., U. Miami, 1950; L.H.D. (hon.), St. Thomas of Villanova U. Bar: Fed. bar 1950, Fla. bar 1950, D.C. bar 1950. Judge adminstrv. practices U.S. Dept. Justice, Washington, 1940-50; sr. law ptnr. firm Walters & Costanzo, Miami, Fla., 1950-80; of counsel firm Walters, Costanzo, Russell, Zyne & Newman, 1980—; ambassador to Vatican, 1976-77. Chmn. Fla. Harbor Pilot Commn., 1952-54; chmn. City of Miami Seaport Commn., 1953-54; spl. bond counsel, Dade County, 1957-58; gen. counsel Dade County Port Authority, 1957-58; vice-chmn. Nat. Democratic Finance Council, 1960-77; mem. Gov.'s Adv. Bd. on Health and Rehabilitative Service, 1976-77; sec.-treas. Inter-Am. Center Authority, 1960-74; chmn. Nat. Leukemia Soc., 1965-66, Archbishops Charities Drive, 1975-76; bd. adv. St. Thomas Law Sch., 1985—; personal rep. Pres. Reagan F.D.R. Meml. Commn., 1985; bd. dirs. Barry Coll.; chmn. bd. trustees Variety Children's Hosp.; pres. Miami Children's Hosp. Found.; trustee Gregorian Inst. Found., Rome. Served with CIC U.S. Army, 1943-46. Decorated Bronze Star medal., Knight St. Gregory the Great. Fellow Internat. Medicine Boston U Med. Sch. and Bd. Advs., 1985; mem. Am., Fla., Fed., D.C., Interam. bar assns., Am. Assn. Knights of Malta (v.p.), Omicron Delta Kappa. Democrat. Roman Catholic. Clubs: Ocean Reef, Serra, Sovereign Mil. Order Malta (master knight 1975—, exec. com. papaluisit to U.S. 1987). Home: 9202 SW 78th Pl Miami FL 33156 Office: 3000 SW 62d Ave Miami FL 33155

WALTERS, GOMER WINSTON, lawyer; b. Johnstown, Pa., Sept. 24, 1937; s. Philip Thomas and Margaret Elizabeth (Peat) W.; m. Jean Mary Jester, June 13, 1964 (divorced 1988); children—Bruce Joseph, Matthew Howel, Melinda Jean. B.E., Yale U., 1960; J.D., George Washington U., 1965. Bar: Ill. 1965, Pa. 1972, U.S. Dist. Ct. (no. dist.) Ill. 1965, U.S. Dist. Ct. (we. dist.) Pa. 1972, U.S. Dist. Ct. (no. dist.) Ohio 1973, U.S. Ct. Appeals (3 and 7th cirs.) 1981, U.S. Supreme Ct. 1982, U.S. Ct. Appeals (fed. cir.) 1982. Asso. Kirkland & Ellis, Chgo., 1965-70, ptnr., 1970-72; pat. atty. Westinghouse Electric Corp., Pitts., 1972-73; asso. Walsh, Case & Coale, Chgo., 1973-74, Lee & Smith, Chgo., 1975; ptnr. Haight, Hofeldt, Davis & Jambor, Chgo., 1975—; dir. R2 Corp., 1981-84, Vast Research Co., 1981-87; chmn.'s council Crow Canyon Archeol. Ctr., 1987—. Mem. ABA, Chgo. Bar Assn., Am. Intellectual Property Law Assn., Patent Law Assn. Chgo., Pitts. Patent Law Assn., Am. Judicature Soc., Assn. Trial Lawyers Am. Republican. Club: Chicago Athletic Assn. Office: Haight & Hofeldt 224 S Michigan Ave Suite 600 Chicago IL 60604

WALTERS, JEFFERSON BROOKS, musician, real estate broker; b. Dayton, Ohio, Jan. 20, 1922; s. Jefferson Brooks and Mildred Frances (Smith) W.; student U. Dayton, 1947; m. Mary Elizabeth Espey, Apr. 6, 1963 (dec. July 22, 1983); children—Dinah Christine Basson, Jefferson Brooks; m. 2d, Carol Elaine Clayton Gillette, Feb. 19, 1984. Composer, cornetist Dayton, 1934—; real estate broker, Dayton, 1948—; founder Am. Psalm Choir, 1965; apptd. deferred giving officer Kettering (Ohio) Med. Ctr., 1982—. Served with USCGR, 1942-45; PTO, ETO. Mem. SAR, Greater Dayton Antique Study Club (past pres.), Dayton Art Inst., Montgomery County Hist. Soc., Dayton Area Bd. Realtors. Presbyterian. Club: Masons (32 deg.). Condr., composer choral, solo voice settings of psalms and poetry Alfred Lord Tennyson; composer Crossing the Bar (meml. performances U.S. Navy band), 1961; composer The Yorktown Grand March (Good Citizenship medal SAR, 1988). Home: 4113 Roman Dr Dayton OH 45415 Office: Classics Realty 53 Park Ave Dayton OH 45419

WALTERS, PETER INGRAM, petroleum company executive; b. Birmingham, Eng., Mar. 11, 1931; s. Stephen and Edna F. (Redgate) W.; m. Patricia Anne Tulloch, 1960; 3 children. Student King Edward's Sch., Birmingham, Eng.; B.Com., U. Birmingham, D in Social Sci. (hon.), 1986. Joined Brit. Petroleum, 1954, v.p. BP N.Am., 1965-67, gen. mgr. supply and devel., 1969-70, regional dir. Western Hemisphere, 1971-72; dir. BP Trading Ltd., 1971-73, BP Chems. Internat., 1972, chmn., 1981; dep. chmn. The Brit. Petroleum Co. Ltd., 1980-81, mng. dir., 1973—; chmn. BP Am. Inc., N.Y.C.; v.p. Gen. Council of Brit. Shipping, 1974-76, pres., 1977-78; dir. Post Office, 1978-79, Nat. Westminister Bank. Created Knight, 1984; decorated comdr. Order of Leopold (Belgium), 1984. Mem. Soc. Chem. Industry (pres. 1978-80), Inst. Manpower Studies (pres. 1980-86). Office: British Petroleum Co Ltd, Britannic House, Moor Ln, London EC2 9BU, England *

WALTERS, VERNON ANTHONY, ambassador-at-large; b. N.Y.C., Jan. 3, 1917; s. Frederick J. and Laura (O'Connor) W. Student, St. Louis Gonzaga U., Paris, 1927-28, Stonyhurst Coll., Eng., 1928-34. Commd. 2d lt. U.S. Army, 1941, advanced through grades to lt. gen., ret., 1976; served in N. Africa, Italy, World War I; mil. attache Brazil, 1945-48; asst. to Gov. Harriman in Korea, 1950; accompanied Iran, 1951; asst. dep. chief staff SHAPE, Paris, 1951-56; staff asst. Pres. Eisenhower, 1956-60; mem. NATO standing group, Washington, 1956, 60; served in Vietnam 1967; aide Vice Pres. Nixon to S. Am., 1958; accompanied Pres. Nixon to Europe, 1969, 70; def. attache Am. Embassy, Paris, 1967-72; dep. dir. CIA, 1972-76; bus. cons., lectr. 1977-81; sr. advisor to sec. state Dept. State, Washington, 1981, ambassador-at-large, 1981-85; U.S. permanent rep. to UN 1985—; interpreter Pres. Roosevelt, Truman, Eisenhower, Nixon; participant IX Pan Am. Conf., Bogota, Columbia, 1948, Geneva, 1953, Bermuda, 1955, summit meetings. Author: Silent Missions. Decorated D.S.M. with oak leaf cluster; decorated U.S. Disting. Intelligence medal, Legion of Merit with oak leaf cluster, Bronze Star, Air medal U.S., Legion of Honor, Croix de Guerre France, Combat cross Brazil, Bronze medal valor Italy; recipient 3 Freedom Found. awards. Mem. VFW, Nat. Mil. Intelligence Assn. (pres.). Roman Catholic. Office: US Mission to the United Nations 799 United Nations Plaza New York NY 10017 *

WALTERSPIEL, OTTO HEINRICH, mining company executive; b. Munich, Sept. 7, 1927; s. Otto W. and Paula (Pesch) W.; m. Almuth Schaetz, 1957; children: Christoph, Mathias, Verena, Katharina. Diploma in agronomy, Tech U. Munich, 1950, D in Agriculture, 1952. Agronomist BASF Aktiengesellschaft, Ludwigshafen, Fed. Republic Germany, 1954-57, sales mgr., 1960-73, regional mgr., 1973-75; gen. mgr. Quimagra S.A., Mexico City, 1957-60; chmn. exec. bd. Kali und Salz AG, Kassel, Fed. Republic Germany, 1975—. Roman Catholic. Office: Kali und Salz AG, Friedrich Ebert Strasse 160, D3500 Kassel Federal Republic of Germany

WALTHALL, BENNIE HARRELL, geologist; b. Sayre, Ark., Mar. 12, 1925; s. Charles Clayton and Blanche Jewel (Hooks) W.; student So. Ark. U., 1942-44, 46-47; B.S., U. Tulsa, 1949, M.S., 1963; Ph.D., Columbia U., 1966; postgrad Grad. Sch. Bus. U. Tulsa, 1966; m. Marisa Mathilde Oggeri, Apr. 25, 1955; 1 dau., Dany Charmaine. Geol. draftsman, Sinclair Petroleum Co., 1949-51; jr. goephysicst Rogers Geophysical Co., Ethiopia, Tex. and Somalia, 1951-54; geologist, Sinclair Somal Corp., Somalia, 1954-59; geologist Sinclair Colombia Oil, Colombia, 1959-61; with Sinclair Oil & Gas, Tulsa, 1961-63; geologist Sinclair Oil & Gas Co., Alaska and Can., 1966-67; geologist Aramco, Saudi Arabia and London, 1968-78, sr. staff geologist, sr. edn. adv., 1978—. Served with AUS, 1944-46. Mem. Arabian Philatelic Assn. (treas. 1979, 81-82, pres. 1984-85), Arabian Natural History Soc. (pres. 1980-81), Geol. Soc. Am., Am. Assn. Petroleum Geologists, Can. Soc. Petroleum Geologists, Geol. Soc. London, Sigma Xi. Republican. Address: Box 2194 Aramco, Dhahran Saudi Arabia

WALTHER, MANFRED ODO, philosopher, educator; b. Berlin, May 24, 1938; s. Odo and Ilse (Petersdorff) W.; m. Gudrun Spennes, July 21, 1978; 1 child, Rebecca. PhD, U. Frankfurt, 1968. Asst. instr. U. Munster, Fed. Republic of Germany, 1964-66; projectionist HIS GmbH, Hannover, Fed. Republic of Germany, 1969-71; dozent U. Hamburg, Fed. Republic of Germany, 1971-74, prof. in didactics of Jurisprudence, 1975—, prof. in Philosophy, 1985—. Author: Metaphysik als Anti-Theologie, 1971; co-editor z. Hochschuldidaktik, 1971—, Fundamenta Juridica: Hannoversche Beiträge z. rechtswiss. Grundlagenforschung, 1986—, Politische Institutionen im gesellschaftl. Umbruch, 1988, Selbstbehauptung und Anerkennung: Beitr. z. Theorie d. Polit. b. Spinoza, Kant, Fichteu. Hegel; chief editor Studia Spinozana, 1985—. Home: Richard-Wagner St 19, 3000 Hannover 1 Federal Republic of Germany Office: Univ Hannover, Fachbereich Rechtswissenschaften, Hanomagstr 8, 3000 Hannover Federal Republic of Germany

WALTNER, HARRY GEORGE, JR., personnel executive; b. Kansas City, Mo., Feb. 2, 1906; s. Harry George and Minnie Lee (Ruland) W.; student U. Mo., 1923-24, U. Kansas City, 1924-27; m. Ruth Anna Laitner, June 28, 1927; children—Barbara Adams, Beverly Ruland, Lillian LeRoyce (Mrs. Warren Hardy Bascome), Harry George III. Admitted to Mo. bar, 1928; asso. Waltner & Waltner, 1928-32; asst. atty. gen. State of Mo., 1933-37; chief counsel, dir. Mo. Unemployment Compensation Com., 1937-44; social security specialist, ins. and social security dept. Standard Oil Co. (N.J.), 1945-50, asst. mgr. ins. and social security dept., 1950-55, social security adviser, 1955-58, Latin Am. adviser, 1958-63, Latin Am. benefit adviser employee relations dept., 1964-66; sr. employee benefits counselor Esso Inter-Am., Inc., 1966-71, cons. employee benefits and ins., 1971—. Cons. N.Y. Joint Legislative Com. on Unemployment Ins., 1948, N.Y. Joint Legislative Com. on Labor and Indsl. Conditions, 1949; mem. Disability Benefits Adv. Council to chmn. N.Y. Workmans Compensation Bd., 1949-60, Fed. Adv. Council on Employment Security to U.S. Sec. Labor, 1954-58; participant Am. Assembly Econ. Security, 1953. Paul Harris fellow Rotary Found. of Rotary Internat. Mem. Am. (com. pensions and other compensation), Mo., Kansas City bar assns., N.A.M. (employee health and benefits com. 1950-55, chmn. 1955-59), U.S. C. of C. (com. econ. security 1952-57), Pan-Am. Soc., Am. Pension Conf. (bd. govs. 1960-64) Internat. Soc. for Labor and Social Legislation, Am. Judicature Soc., Phi Alpha Delta, Delta Tau Delta, Rotarian. Clubs: Country of Coral Gables, Nat. Congl. Home: 1039 Hardee Rd Coral Gables FL 33146

WALTNER, JAMES DOUGLAS, pediatrician, educator; b. Yankton, S.D., Sept. 20, 1947; s. Glenn Hubert and Pauline Blanche (Hoffman) W. Student, U. S.D., 1965-68; MD, U. Tex., Dallas, 1972. Diplomate Am. Bd. Pediatrics. Pediatric intern Children's Med. Ctr., Dallas, 1972-73; resident in psychiatry Neuropsychiat. Inst., U. Mich., Ann Arbor, 1973-75; resident in pediatrics U. N.Mex. Sch. of Medicine/Bernalillo County Med. Ctr., Albuquerque, 1975-77, clin. asst. prof. pediatrics, 1978—; pvt. practice medicine specializing in pediatrics Espanola (N.Mex.) Pediatric Clinic, 1977-86; staff physician, med. dir. Los Lunas (N.Mex.) Hosp. and Tng. Sch.,

1986-87; physician adminstr. Coordinated Community In-Home Care, Santa Fe, 1987—, State N.Mex. Dept. Med. Assistance, Santa Fe, 1987—; chief of staff Espanola Hosp., 1980, trustee, 1980-85; med. dir. N.Mex. AIDS Services, Santa Fe, 1985—, mem. N.Mex. AIDS Task Force, 1983—. Contbr. articles to profl. jours. Fellow Am. Acad. Pediatrics; mem. AAAS, N.Mex. Med. Soc., N.Mex. Pediatric Soc., Am. Assn. Physicians for Human Rights, N.Mex. Assn. Physicians for Human Rights (pres. 1985-86). Recipient Upjohn Achievement award The Upjohn Co., Disting. Service award Espanola C. of C. 1980, Service and Edn. awards N.Mex. chpt. Am. Diabetes Assn., 1981. Fellow Am. Acad. Pediatrics; mem. AAAS, N.Mex. Med. Soc., N.Mex. Pediatric Soc., Am. Assn. Physicians for Human Rights, N.Mex. Assn. Physicians for Human Rights (pres. 1985-86). Home: 3603 Calle del Sol NE Albuquerque NM 87110 Office: Coordinated Community In-Home Care PERA Bldg Room 516 PO Box 2348 Santa Fe NM 87504-2348

WALTON, ANTHONY (TONY) JOHN, theater and film designer, book illustrator; b. Walton on Thames, Eng., Oct. 24, 1934; s. Lancelot Henry Frederick and Hilda Betty (Drew) W.; m. Julie Andrews, May 10, 1959 (div. 1968); 1 dau., Emma Kate. Student Oxford Sch. Tech. Art and Commerce, 1949-52, Slade Sch. Fine Art, London, 1954-55. Designer settings, costumes for theater prodns., London, off-Broadway, 1957-60, Broadway, 1961—; prodns. include: Sophisticated Ladies, Pippin, The Real Thing, Hurlyburly, House of Blue Leaves, Anything Goes, Front Page, I'm Not Rappaport, Social Security, 1987; ballets, principally San Francisco Ballet Co.; films include: Mary Poppins, A Funny Thing Happened on the Way to the Forum, Murder on the Orient Express, The Wiz, All That Jazz (Acad. award 1980), Prince of the City, Star 80, The Boyfriend and Heartburn, 1986, The Glass Menagerie, 1987; operas in Eng., Italy, U.S. Author: Adelie Penguin in Wonders, 1981. Illustrator: Wonders, 1981; The Importance of Being Earnest, 1973, Lady Windemere's Fan, 1973, Popcorn, 1972, God is a Good Friend, 1969, Witches Holiday, 1971, others. Served with RAF, 1952-54. Recipient Antoinette Perry award, 1972-73, 85-86, Drama Desk award, 1972-73, 85-86, Academy award, 1980, Tony award for scenic design, 1973, 1986, Emmy award, 1986. Mem. United Scenic Artists, Costume Designers Guild Calif., Acad. Motion Picture Arts and Scis. Office: care Martino Internat Creative Mgmt 40 W 57th St New York NY 10019

WALTON, ERNEST THOMAS SINTON, physicist; b. Dungarvan, County Waterford, Ireland, Oct. 6, 1903; s. J.A. Walton; MA, Methodist Coll., Belfast; MSc, Trinity Coll., Dublin; PhD, Cambridge U.; DSc (hon.), Queen's U., Belfast, Ireland, Gustavus Adolphus Coll., Minn., U. Ulster; m. Winifred Isabel Wilson, 1934; 4 children. Erasmus Smith's prof. natural and exptl. philosophy Trinity Coll., Dublin, 1947-74, fellow emeritus, 1974—. Recipient Overseas Research scholar, 1927-30, Sr. Research award, dept. sci. and indsl. research, 1930-34, Clerk Maxwell scholar, 1932-34, Hughes medal, Royal Soc., 1938, Nobel prize for physics, 1951. Home: 26 St Kevin's Park, Dartry Rd, Dublin 6 Ireland Office: Dept Physics, Trinity Coll, Dublin Ireland

WALTON, HERBERT WILSON, judge; b. Anaconda, Mont., Apr. 9, 1929; s. George Myrick and Neola Josephine (Wilson) W.; m. Barbara Lavon Pratt, Aug. 4, 1949; children—Michael Eugene, Constance Lynn, Herbert Steven, Cynthia Diane. A.B., U. Mo.-Kansas City, 1955, J.D., 1957. Bar: Kans. 1957, U.S. Dist. Ct. Kans. 1957. Asst. county atty. Johnson County (Kans.), 1957-60; probate judge Johnson County, 1960-65; judge Div. 1 10th Jud. Dist. Ct., 1965—; instr. bus. law U. Kans. Extension, 1963-71. Founding pres. Johnson County Scholarship Found.; active Kaw council Boy Scouts Am. Served with USN, 1947-48, 51-52. Mem. ABA, Kans. Jud. Council (chmn. pattern instrns. 1975—, chmn. family law adv. com., mem. com. on publs. on parentage act, protection from abuse and new divorce code), Johnson County Bar Assn., Kans. Bar Assn., Am. Judicature Soc., Assn. Family and Conciliation Cts., Kans. Dist. Judges Assn. (pres. 1973), U. Mo.-Kansas City Law Alumni Assn. (pres. 1973). Republican. Club: Olathe (Kans.) Optimists. Home: 405 Normandy Dr Olathe KS 66061 Office: Courthouse Olathe KS 66061

WALTON, MORGAN LAUCK, lawyer; b. Woodstock, Va., July 30, 1932; s. Morgan Lauck and Frances (Allen) W.; m. Jeannette Freeman Minor, Mar. 4, 1961; children: Morgan Lauck, Charles Lancelot Minor, Christoper Allen, Laura Cathlyn. BA, Randolph-Macon Coll., 1953; LLB, U. Va., 1959. Bar: Va. 1959, N.Y. 1959, U.S. Supreme Ct. 1963. Assoc. Donovan Leisure Newton & Irvine, N.Y.C., 1959-68, ptnr., 1968-84; sole practice Woodstock, Va., 1984—; gen. counsel Applied Concepts Corp., Edinburg, Va., 1987—. Contbr. articles to legal jours. Chmn. bd. trustees All Souls Unitarian Ch., N.Y.C., 1974-76, chmn. investment com., 1978-80; bd. dirs. Shenandoah Valley Music Festival, 1984-87, treas. 1986-87; trustee Randolph-Macon Acad., 1987—, Unitarian Universalist Ch. Shenandoah Valley, 1987—. Mem. ABA (chmn. Clayton Act com. antitrust sect. 1976-78, vice chmn. exemptions com. 1978-79), N.Y. State Bar Assn., Va. Bar Assn., Assn. of Bar of City of N.Y., Shenandoah County Bar Assn. (treas. 1987—), Order of Coif, Phi Beta Kappa. Clubs: Univ., Collectors (N.Y.). Lodge: Rotary. Home: Rt 2 Box 225 Woodstock VA 22664 Office: 405 Stoney Creek Blvd Edinburg VA 22824

WALTON, ROBERT CUTLER, theology educator; b. Jersey City; s. Donald James and Elizabeth (Reed) W.; m. Charlotte Wilhelmine Kollegger, Mar. 25, 1966; children: Alexander, Deborah, Christina. BA, Swarthmore Coll., 1954; BDiv, U. Harvard, 1958; MA, PhD, Yale U., 1961; cert., Göttingen U., 1957. Instr. Duke U., Durham, N.C., 1961-64; from asst. to assoc. prof. U. B.C., Vancouver, Can., 1964-71; prof. Wayne State U., Detroit, 1971-78; prof., dir. Westfälische-Wilhelms U. Münster, Fed. Republic Germany, 1978—. Author: Zwingli's Theocracy, 1967, European View of the Americas 1914-1918, 1972; editor: Studies in the Reformation, 1978. Mem. Detroit Com. on Fgn. Relations, 1974-78; mem. The Knights of the Hosp. of St. John at Jeruselem, Münster, 1983—. Mem. Soc. for Reformation Research (v.p. 1977-78, pres. 1978-79, co-editor editorial bd. 1978—), Pan-European Union (steering com. 1979-83), German-Am. Soc., Harvard Club Rhine-Ruhr. Club: Harvard (N.Y.C.). Home: Kapellenkamp 3, D4412 Ostbevern Federal Republic of Germany Office: U Munster Dept Theology, Universitatsstr 13-17, D4400 Munster Federal Republic of Germany

WALTON, ROBERT EDWARD, engineer; b. Chgo., July 11, 1923; s. William Charles and Martha (Walshon) W.; m. Edna Colson, June 9, 1945; children: Robert Edward, Martha C., James B., Nancy K.; m. Sandra A. Cidylo, Aug. 31, 1968. Student, Ind. U. Extension, 1942-43; BS, U. Tex., 1945. Registered profl. engr. in 34 states and Can. V.p., chief engr. Sweney Electric Co., Gary, Ind., 1951-55; pres. Walton-Abeyta and Assocs., Inc., Gary and Denver, 1955-77; v.p., mgr. bank properties div. Seattle 1st Nat. Bank, 1977-79; chmn., chief exec. officer Am. Resources Group, Inc., 1979-83, ret., 1983; bd. dirs. Quailmark Ltd., Monterey, Nashert Group, Inc.; commr. Arapahoe County Pub. Airport Authority; also investor. Served with USNR, 1942-46; USMC, 1946-51. Mem. Sigma Alpha Epsilon. Episcopalian. Clubs: Pinery Country, Metropolitan, Carmel Valley Golf and Country, Engineers (San Francisco). Home: 6400 N Ponderosa Way Parker CO 80134 Winter home: PO Box 22033 Carmel CA 93922

WALTON, SAM MOORE, discount retail chain executive; b. Kingfisher, Okla., 1920; m. Helen Walton; 4 children. BA, U. Mo., 1940. With J. C. Penney Co., Des Moines, 1938-42; franchise owner, operator Ben Franklin Stores, 1945-62; co-founder Wal-Mart Stores, Bentonville, Ark., 1962—, chmn., chief exec. officer, 1974—, chief exec. officer, 1974-88, also bd. dirs. Served with U.S. Army, 1942-45. Office: Wal-Mart Stores Inc 702 SW 8th St Bentonville AR 72712 •

WALTON, TERENCE MICHAEL, librarian; b. Norwalk, Conn., May 28, 1938; s. Charles Cameron and Mildred V. (Welch) W.; m. Geraldine Ryan Quinn, Jan. 3, 1964 (dec.); B.A., Ariz. State U., 1967; M.L.S., U. Hawaii, 1968. Asst. dir. adult edn. Ariz. Dept. Pub. Instrn., Phoenix, 1964-67; adult edn. coordinator Phoenix Coll., 1968-69; sr. reference librarian N.Y. Pub. Library, N.Y.C., 1969-70; head acquisitions Hunter Coll., CUNY, N.Y.C., 1970-75, U. Petroleum and Minerals, Dhahran, Saudi Arabia, 1975-77; assoc. dean Old Dominion U., Norfolk, Va., 1978-82; dir. Captiva Meml. Library, Captiva Island, Fla., 1983-87, coordinator Coll. Devel. and Mgmt., Lee County Library System, Ft. Myers, Fla., 1987—; adj. instr. Cath. U. Am., 1979-82; automation cons. U. Petroleum and Minerals, 1975-77, various libraries; adult edn. cons. Contbr. articles to profl. jours. NDEA fellow, 1964-67. Mem. Va. Council Higher Edn. (com. chmn. 1978-82), Va. Library Assn. (com. chmn. 1978-80), Tidewater Library Consortium (cons.), Southeastern Library Network (cons.), ALA, Library Info. Tech. Assn., Fla. Library Assn. Democrat. Roman Catholic. Home: PO Box 672 Captiva Island FL 33924 Office: Lee County Library System 11220-6 Metro Pkwy Fort Myers FL 33912

WALTZ, JOSEPH MCKENDREE, neurosurgeon, educator; b. Detroit, July 23, 1931; s. Ralph McKinley and Bertha (Seelye) W.; m. Janet Maureen Journey, June 26, 1954; children: Jeffrey McKinley, Mary Elaine, David Seelye, Stephen McKendree; m. Marilyn Liska, June 5, 1967; 1 child, Tristana McKendree. Student, U. Mich., 1950; B.S., U. Oreg., 1954, M.D., 1956. Diplomate Am. Bd. Neurol. Surgery. Surg. intern U. Mich. Hosp., 1956-57, gen. surg. resident, 1957-58, clin. instr. neurosurgery, 1960-63; neurosurg. assoc. St. Barnabas Hosp., N.Y.C., 1963—; assoc. dir. Inst. Neurosci., 1974—, dir. dept. neurol. surgery, 1977—; assoc. cons. neurosurgery Englewood (N.J.) Hosp., 1964—; assoc. prof. neurosurgery NYU Med. Center, 1974—; bd. dirs. Neurol. Surgery Research Found., 1978. Author papers on functional neurosurg. treatment of abnormal movement disorders cerebral palsy, others; cryothalamectomy-cryopulvinectomy and implantation brain pacemakers; chpt. in book on cryogenic surgery; contbr. chpts. to Cryogenic Surgery, Neurology, 1982, Advances in Neurology, 1983. Patentee 4-electrode quadrapolar computerized spinal cord stimulator. Mem. sci. adv. bd. Dystonia Med. Research Found., 1980—; trustee St. Barnabas Hosp., 1980—. Served to capt. M.C. AUS, 1958-60. Recipient bronze award Am. Congress Rehab. Medicine, 1967. Mem. Am. Paralysis Assn., World Soc. Stereotactic and Functional Neurosurgery, Congress Neurol. Surgeons, Nat. Ski Patrol, Soc. for Cryobiology, AMA, N.Y. State, Bronx County med. socs., N.Y. State Neurosurg. Soc., Phi Beta Pi. Home: Four B Island South 720 Milton Rd Milton Harbor Rye NY 10580 Office: St Barnabas Hosp 4422 3d Ave Bronx NY 10457

WAMBUZI, SAMUEL WILLIAM WAKO, chief justice Uganda; b. Uganda, Jan. 23, 1931; s. Erukana and Miriam (Naigaga) Kakungulu Wako; m. Gladys Bulyaba Nsibirwa, Jan. 7, 1956; children: Phillip William Wako, Samson Enoka Wambuzi, Veronica Gladys Naigaga Hansa, Miriam Sarah Musekwa. LLB, U. London, 1958; barrister at law, Lincoln's Inn, London, 1959; LLB (hon.), U. Hull, Eng., 1960. With dept. of pub. prosecutions Govt. of Uganda, 1960-61, crown prosecutor, 1961-62, crown counsel, 1962-63, sr. parliamentary counsel, 1963-64, 1st parliamentary counsel, 1964-69; judge High Ct. Uganda, 1969-72, acting chief justice, 1972-73, chief justice, 1973-75, 79-80, 86—; pres. Ct. Appeal for East Africa; judge of appeal Ct. of Appeal, Kenya, 1977-79; pres. Ct. of Appeal Uganda, 1986; legal cons. Sebalu & Lule, Kampala, Uganda, 1981-86; sec. De Lestang Commn., 1966; chmn. Uganda Armed Forces Pensions & Gratuities Appeals Bd., 1968-69, Uganda Armed Forces Pensions Assessment Bd., 1970—, Law Council, 1972; external examiner criminal procedure, civil procedure and evidence Makerere U., Kampala, 1971-75, 80—; mem. Common Market Tribunal, East African Community, 1972. Mem. bd. govs. Busoga Coll., Mwiri, Uganda; patron Busoga Coll. Mwiri Old Boys Assn., 1986. Mailing Address: PO Box 801, Kampala Uganda Office: High Court of Uganda, Kampala Uganda

WAN, ZHE-XIAN, mathematician, educator; b. Zhichuan, Shangdong, China, Nov. 7, 1927; s. Chenggui and Weijin (Zhou) W.; m. Shixian Wang, Feb. 7, 1957; children: Hong, Qing. BS, Tsinghua U., Beijing, China, 1948. Asst. Tsinghua U., Beijing, 1948-50; asst. Acad. Sinica, Beijing, 1950-52, asst. prof., 1952-64, assoc. prof., 1964-78, prof. math., 1978—. Author: Lie Algebras, 1964, Algebra and Coding Theory, 1975; co-author: Classical Groups, 1963 (award 1978), Finite Geometries and Block Designs, 1966, Non-linear Shift Register Sequences, 1978. Mem. Chinese Math. Soc., Am. Math. Soc. Office: Acad Sinica Inst Sci Systems, Zhongguancun, 100080 Beijing Peoples Republic of China

WANDERMAN, RICHARD GORDON, pediatrician; b. N.Y.C., Apr. 17, 1943; s. Herman L. and Helen L. (Cohn) W.; m. Judy Rosenberg, Nov. 2, 1980; children—Richard Gordon Jr., Gregory Lloyd, Adam Joseph; 1 stepdau., Shana Abraham. B.A., Western Res. U., Cleve., 1965; M.D., SUNY-Bklyn., 1969. Diplomate Am. Bd. Pediatrics. Intern, Kings County Hosp. Ctr., Bklyn., 1969-70, resident in pediatrics, 1970-71; resident in pediatrics L.I. Jewish-Hillside Med. Ctr., New Hyde Park, N.Y., 1971-72; practice medicine specializing in pediatrics, adolescent clin. ecology and allergy, Merrick, N.Y., 1972-74, Charleston, W.Va., 1974-78, Memphis, 1978—; pres., chmn. bd. DCT Enterprises, 1982—; mem. staff L.I. Jewish-Hillside Med. Ctr., 1972-74, Nassau County Med. Ctr., 1972-74, Hempstead Gen. Hosp., 1972-74, Charleston Area Med. Ctr., 1974-78, LeBonheur Children's Hosp., 1978—, St. Joseph Hosp., 1978—, St. Francis Hosp., 1978—, Bapt. Meml. Hosps., 1978—, Meth. Hosps., 1978—; asst. instr. pediatrics Downstate Med. Ctr., SUNY-Bklyn., 1970-71; clin. asst. prof. W.Va. U. Med. Sch., 1974-78, clin. assoc. prof., 1978; clin. assoc. prof. U. Tenn. Sch. for Health Scis., 1979—. Chmn. parent adv. com. Headstart Program, Kanawha, Boone and Clay counties, W.Va., 1977-78; Sunday Sch. tchr. Temple Israel Memphis, 1978-80; coach swim team Memphis Jewish Community Ctr., 1979-80, chmn. adolescent problems task force, 1980; mem. council Memphis chpt. Jewish Nat. Fund, 1981—; bd. dirs. Midsouth Area Jewish Nat. Fund, 1983-87. Mem. Am. Physician Fellowship, Inc., Tenn. Med. Assn., Memphis-Shelby County Med. Soc. (mem. grievance com.), Am. Acad. Environ. Medicine (mem. sch. and coll. health com. 1978), Am. Acad. Pediatrics (fellow adolescent medicine sect.), Tenn. Pediatric Soc., Soc. Clin. Ecology, Mensa, Les Amis du Vin, Zeta Beta Tau. Democrat. Office: 6584 Poplar Ave Suite 420 Memphis TN 38138

WANG, AI-NUNG, mathematics educator; b. Taipei, Taiwan, Nov. 2, 1952; s. Feng and Xueying (Lin) W.; m. Charlene Wang, Dec. 25, 1981; 1 child, Conway. BS, Taiwan U., 1974; PhD, U. Calif., Berkeley, 1981. Assoc. prof. mathematics Taiwan U., Taipei, 1982—; vis. asst. prof. Mich. Tech. U., Houghton, 1981-82. Served to ensign Chinese mil., 1974-76. Office: Taiwan U, Math Dept, Taipei 10764, Republic of China

WANG, AUGUST GABRIEL, psychiatrist; b. Torshavn, Denmark, Nov. 7, 1948; s. Einar Ole and Astrid (Petrine) W.; m. Kitty Joensen, July 22, 1972; children: Alexander, David Eskild. Degree in Bus., Tietgenskolen, 1984. Intern Landssjukrahusid, Torshavn, Faroe Islands, 1975-79; resident Amtshosp. NykØbing Sj., Denmark, 1979-80; clin. psychiatrist Odense (Denmark) U. Hosp., 1980-82, 84—; asst. prof. Inst. Psychiatry, Odense, 1982-84. Editor proceedings Trends in Scandinavian Psychiatry. Mem Danish Psychiatrists Assn. (bd. dirs. 1984—, newsletter editor 1984—). Liberal. Christian Brethren. Home: HP Simonsens Alle 24, 5250 Odense Denmark Office: Dept Psychiatry, Odense U Hosp, 5000C Odense Denmark

WANG, CHARLES PING, scientist; b. Shanghai, Republic of China, Apr. 25, 1937; came to U.S., 1962; s. Kuan-Ying and Ping-Lu (Ming) W.; m. Lily L. Lee, June 29, 1963. BS, Taiwan U., Republic of China, 1959; MS, Tsinghua U., Singchu, Republic of China, 1961; PhD, Calif. Inst. Tech., 1967. Mem. tech. staff Bellcomm, Washington, 1967-69; research engr. U. San Diego, 1969-74; sr. scientist Aerspace Corp., Los Angeles, 1976-86; pres. Optodyne, Inc., Compton, Calif., 1986—; adj. prof. U. Calif., San Diego, 1979—; pres. Chinese-Am. Engr. and Scientists Assn. So. Calif., Los Angeles, 1979-81; program chmn. Internation Conf. of Lasers, Shanghai, 1979-80; organizer and session chmn. Lasers Conf., Los Angeles, 1981-84, program chmn., Las Vegas, 1985. Editor in chief Series in Laser Tech., 1983—; contbr. articles to profl. jours.; inventor discharge excimer laser. Calif. Inst. Tech. scholar, 1965. Fellow Am. Optical Soc., AIAA (assoc., jour. editor 1981-83). Office: Optodyne Inc 1180 Mahalo Pl Compton CA 90220

WANG, CHEH CHENG, mechanical engineer; b. Chuan Chow, Fukien, China, Mar. 3, 1930; came to U.S., 1963, naturalized, 1976; s. Pi-Chen and Ling-Fung (Lee) W.; m. Esther Chun-Mei Chu, Aug. 12, 1967; children—Albert, Edward, Sophia. Diploma Engring., Nanking Inst. Tech., Peoples Republic of China, 1953; M.Sc., U. Calif.-Berkeley, 1965; Ph.D., U. Sheffield, Eng., 1976. Registered mech. engr., Wash. Lectr. Xian Inst. Aero. Engring., Peoples Republic of China, 1953-58; prin. designer V.K. Song & Co., Ltd., Hong Kong, 1959-62; asst. chief engr. Fulton Shipyard, Antioch, Calif., 1963-67; sr. mech. engr. Lockheed Shipbuilding, Seattle, 1967-68; chief mech. engr. Interactive Tech. Inc., Santa Clara, Calif., 1971-72; sr. staff engr. Central Engring. Labs., FMC Corp., Santa Clara, 1972-86; v.p. Pacific Applied Tech. Internat., Fremont, Calif., 1987—; founder 3E Software, 1986—; cons. in field. Contbr. articles to profl. jours. Mem. ASME (sec. Ditto, Santa Clara Valley sect. 1980-81), Am. Acad. Mechs., Soc. Indsl. and Applied Maths. Current work: Gear dynamics, applied numerical methods; computer aided engineering in solid mechanics areas; modeling and simulation of mechanical systems. Subspecialties: Mechanical engineering; Computer-aided design. Home: 1479 San Marcos Dr San Jose CA 95132

WANG, CHEN CHI, electronics company executive, real estate executive, finance company executive, food products executive; b. Taipei, Taiwan, China, Aug. 10, 1932; came to U.S., 1959, naturalized, 1970; s. Chin-Ting and Chen-Kim (Chen) W.; m. Victoria Rebisoff, Mar. 5, 1965; children: Katherine Kim, Gregory Chen, John Christopher, Michael Edward. B.A., Nat. Taiwan U., 1955; B.S.E.E., San Jose State U., 1965; M.B.A., U. Calif., Berkeley, 1961. With IBM Corp., San Jose, Calif., 1965-72; founder, chief exec. officer Electronics Internat. Co., Santa Clara, Calif., 1968-72, owner, gen. mgr., 1972-81, reorganized as EIC Group, 1982, now chmn. bd. and pres.; dir. Systek Electronics Corp., Santa Clara, 1970-73; founder, sr. partner Wang Enterprises, Santa Clara, 1974—; founder, sr. partner Hanson & Wang Devel. Co., Woodside, Calif., 1977-85; chmn. bd. Golden Alpha Enterprises, Foster City, Calif., 1979—; mng. ptnr. Woodside Acres-Las Pulgas Estate, Woodside, 1980-85; founder, sr. ptnr. DeVine & Wang, Oakland, Calif., 1977-83; Van Heal & Wang, West Village, Calif., 1981-82; founder, chmn. bd. EIC Fin. Corp., Redwood City, Calif., 1985—; chmn. bd. Maritek Corp., Corpus Christi, Tex., 1988—. Served to 2d lt., Nationalist Chinese Army, 1955-56. Mem. Internat. Platform Assn., Tau Beta Pi. Mem. Christian Ch. Author: Monetary and Banking System of Taiwan, 1955; The Small Car Market in the U.S., 1961. Home: 195 Brookwood Rd Woodside CA 94062 Office: EIC Fin Corp 2055 Woodside Rd Suite 100 Redwood City CA 94061

WANG, CHEN-KU, library administrator, educator; b. Peiping, China, July 18, 1924; s. Bing-fong Wang and Fong-gen Hsia; m. Shuo-fin Wang, Aug. 15, 1946; children: Pei-chi, shen-husing, Sheng-Wen. M.A., Peabody Coll. Tchrs., Nashville, 1959, LLD (hon.) Ohio State U., 1988. Prof. Nat. Taiwan Normal U., Taipei, 1960—; dir. Nat. Central Library, Taipei, 1977—; dir. Ctr. for Chinese Studies. Author: Selection and Acquisition of Library Materials, 1978. Named Knight Comdr. of Silvestri, Vatican; recipient Disting. Service award Chinese-Am. Librarians Assn., 1987.r, Office: Nat Central Library, 20 Chung-shan S Rd, Taipei 107, Republic of China

WANG, CHIA PING, physicist; b. Philippines, Sept. 1; came to U.S., 1963; s. Guan Can and Tah (Lin) W.; BS, U. London, 1950; MS, U. Malaya, 1951; PhD in Physics, Univs. Malaya and Cambridge, 1953; DSc in Physics, U. Singapore, 1972. Asst. lectr. U. Malaya, 1951-53; mem. faculty Nankai U., Tientsin, 1954-58, prof. physics, 1956-58, head electron physics div., 1955-58, mem. steering com. nuclear physics div., 1956-58; head electron physics Lanchow Atomic Project, 1958; mem. faculty Hong Kong U., also Chinese U. Hong Kong, 1958-63, prof. physics, 1959-63, acting head dept., 1959; research asso. lab. nuclear studies Cornell U., Ithaca, N.Y., 1963-64; assoc. prof. space sci. and applied physics Cath. U. Am., Washington, 1964-68; assoc. prof. physics Case Inst. Tech., Case Western Res. U., Cleve., 1966-70; vis. scientist, vis. prof. univs. Cambridge (Eng.), Leuven (Belgium), U.S. Naval Research Labs., U. Md., also MIT, 1970-75; research physicist radiation lab. U.S. Army Natick (Mass.) Research and Devel. Command, 1975—. Recipient Outstanding Performance award Dept. Army, 1980, Quality Increase award, 1980. Mem. Am. Phys. Soc., Inst. Physics London, N.Y. Acad. Scis., AAAS, Sigma Xi. Pioneer in fields of nuclear sub-structure, nucleon sub-unit structure, cosmic radiation, picosecond time to pulse-height conversion, thermal physics, lasers, microwaves; contbg. author: Atomic Structure and Interactions of Ionizing Radiations with Matter in Preservation of Food by Ionizing Radiation, 1982; contbr. numerous articles to profl. jours. Home: 28 Hallett Hill Rd Weston MA 02193 Office: US Army Natick Research & Devel Ctr Natick MA 01760

WANG, CHUNG-CHENG, neurosurgeon, researcher; b. Yantai, Shandong, Peoples Republic China, Dec. 20, 1925; s. Wang Xiang San and Wang Shung Shi; m. Han Yi-fang, 1952; children: Wang Xin, Wang Rui, Wang Jin. MD, Beijing Med. Coll., 1949. Resident doctor Tianjing (Peoples Republic China) Gen. Hosp., 1949-55; attending doctor Beijing Tongren Hosp., 1955-58, Beijing Xuanwu Hosp., 1958-78; prof. neurosurgery Capital Med. Coll., Beijing, 1978—; dir. Beijing Neurosurg. Inst., 1972—, researcher, 1977—; head dept. neurosurgery Beijing Xuanwu Hosp, Tiantan Hosp., 1972—, pres. 1972—; mem. expert adv. panel on neuroscis. WHO, 1981—. Author: Microneurosurgery, 1985, Angiography of Brain (also editor), 1965, (with others) Diagnosis And Treatment of Acute Head Injuries, 1960; chief editor: Neurosurgery I, II, III, 1974. Dep. The Nat. People's Congress, Beijing, 1978-82, The People's Congress Beijing, 1979—. Mem. Acad. Eurasiana Neurochirugica (hon. v.p.), Chinese Soc. Neurosurgery (chmn. 1986), Council Chinese Med. Assn., Internat. Brain Research Orgn. Office: Beijing Nerosurgical Inst, Tiantan Xili, Beijing People's Republic China

WANG, EDDY AN DI, civil engineer, consultant; b. Shanghai, Jiangsu, Peoples Republic of China, July 25, 1923; s. Cheng Rong Wang and Teng Fang Hu-Wang; m. Rui Fang Zhu, Sept. 5, 1948; children—Helen, Melon, Jing Lun. Student Nat. Conservatory of Music, Shanghai, 1942-45; B.S. in Civil Engring., St. John's U., Shanghai, 1946. Pvt. tchr. violin, Shanghai, 1943-46; calculating and design engr. Standard Vacuum Oil Co., Shanghai, 1947-51; chief structural group Beijin Archtl. Design Inst., Peoples Republic of China, 1951-58; dep. design chief engr. Research and Designing Inst. Rector Engring., Beijing, 1958-82; sr. engr. Shen Zhen Bldg. Sci. Ctr., Guang Dong Province, Peoples Republic of China, 1982—; lectr. in structural engring. Beijing Archtl. Design Inst. Tng. Ctr., 1952-53; design cons. Steel and Iron Research Acad. for Isotope Lab. Project, Beijing, 1962-63. Del. Sino-U.S. Nuclear Seminar, Hangzhou, Zhejiang Province, Peoples Republic of China, 1984, Guilin, Guangxi Province, Peoples Republic of China, 1985. Mem. Archtl. and Civil Engring. Soc., Nuclear Soc. China. Avocations: music; bridge. Home: Tong Xin Ridge Villa, Room 604, 3d Bldg, Sheung Po Rd, Shen Zhen, Guang Dong Peoples Republic of China Office: Shen Zhen Bldg Sci Ctr, Office Chief Engr, Sheung Po, Guang Dong People's Republic China

WANG, FRANCIS KAI-YUH, engineering and import company executive; b. Hofei, Anhwei, China, Dec. 3, 1935; came to Taiwan, 1950; s. Fu Tsu and Shui Wen W.; m. Margaret Tsung-Lin, Oct. 3, 1964; children—Austin Tse-Wen, Calvin Tse-Chung. B.M.E., Nat Taiwan U., 1959. Engr., Sung 1 Cotton Mill, Taipei, Taiwan, 1962-66; plant mgr. Lien Yu Industries Co. Ltd., Taipei, 1966-68; asst. mgr. machinery dept. United Exporters & Co. Ltd., Taipei, 1968-73; gen. mgr. EURO Ltd., Taipei, 1973-78, pres., 1978—. Served to 2d lt. Chinese Army, 1949-51. Mem. Soc. Mfg. Engrs. Club: Bankers (Taipei).

WANG, HOWARD WAI-KO, advertising executive; b. Hong Kong, Aug. 23, 1954; s. Chien-Yu and Chao-Yin (Tang) W. BS, U. Wis., 1976, MBA, 1978. Mktg. mgr. Citibank N.Am., Hong Kong, 1978-79; acct. mgr. TWK Kenyon & Eckhardt Ltd, Hong Kong, 1979-80, Leo Burnett Ltd., Hong Kong, 1980-82; account dir. Foote, Cone & Belding Ltd., Hong Kong, 1982, dir. account service, 1982-84, gen. mgr., 1984-86, mng. dir., 1987—; v.p., dir. mktg. Bank Am. NT&SA, Hong Kong, 1986-87; bd. dirs. Wilin Holdings Ltd., Hong Kong, Sigma Trading Ltd., Hong Kong. V.p. Lions Club South Kowloon, Hong Kong, 1984, hon. sec., 1983. Episcopalian. Home: 4 Broom Rd, Happy Valley Hong Kong Office: Bozell Jacobs Kenyon, and Eckhardt Ltd, 1101 Citicorp Ctr, 18 Whitfield Rd, Hong Kong Hong Kong

WANG, JIDA, sculptor; b. Beijing, Oct. 27, 1935; s. Shu Yi Wang and Chen Shin Chiu, m. Jin Gao, Apr. 27, 1971; children: Jin Ye, Jin Heh. Student, Cen. Inst. Fine Arts, Beijing, 1962, Grad., 1964. Prof. Innner Mongolia Normal U., Huhehaute, China, 1966-84; dep. dir. Standing Council Inner Mongolian Sculpture Acd. Soc., Huhehaute, 1984—. Prin. works include Hitching the Horses, Moon Flower, Wool, Heroes Guarding the Frontier. Recipient Honor Prize, Chinese Govt., 1977, Prize Chinese Minorities Fine Arts Works, Ministry Culture, 1982, Copper Prize, 6th Chinese Fine Arts Exhbn. Mem. Chinese Pottery and Porcelain Art Assn., Inner Mongolian

Sculpture Assn., Chinese Artists Assn., Am. Nat. Sculpture Soc. Home: 76-12 35 Ave Jackson Height NY 11372 Office: Inner Mongolian Artists Assn, 33 W Hu Hua Hao Te, Inner Mongolia People's Republic China

WANG, KUNG-LEE, economics consultant; b. Pei Tai-Ho, Hopei, China, Aug. 12, 1925; s. Cheng-Fu Wang and Funghin Liu; came to U.S., 1947; BA, Yenching U., 1947; MA, Brown U., 1950; MBA, Columbia U., 1958; MPA, Harvard U., 1965; m. Christine Wen, Aug. 15, 1959 (div.); 1 son, Christopher Ching-Yu. Acct. in charge fiscal mgmt. Bushwick Hosp., Bklyn., 1952-55; economist, civilian and mil. ops. analyst, internat. affairs C-E-I-R., Inc., Washington, 1955-60, cons. 1960-61; chief qualitative econs. analysis Bur. Mines, U.S. Dept. Interior, Washington, 1960-82; pres. KLW Internat., Inc., 1982—, Chi Am Metals & Energy, Inc., 1983-86; vice chmn. Chinatown Devel. Corp., 1983—, MLS Inc., 1986-87; dir. Internat. Data Applications Inc., 1969-71; econ. ops. advisor to ministry econs. affairs Republic of China, 1969-71; cons. ops. research office John Hopkins, Bethesda, Md., 1960-61; pres. U.S.-China Council Internat. Exchange Inc., 1988—; vice chmn. AmerAsia Inc., 1988—; ethnic advisor U.S. OEO, 1972-75. Pres., chmn. bd. dirs. Civic League of Brookmont, 1963-64; coordinator Chinese-Am. Leadership Council, 1971-73, pres. Rho Psi Found., Inc., 1966—; co-founder, div. Asian Pacific Am. Heritage Council, Inc., 1979—, pres., 1983-84; co-founder and nat. dir., Asian Am. Voters Coalition, 1985—; co-founder and dir., Nat. Chinese Am. Voters League, 1984—; founder, nat. pres. Orgn. Chinese Ams. Inc., 1973-77, nat. treas., v.p. fin., 1979-81, hon. mem. 1982; chmn. U.S.-China Capital Cities Friendship Council, 1987—. Nat. Inst. Pub. Affairs fellow, 1965. Mem. Am. Inst. Mining, Metall. and Petroleum Engrs. (charter pres. mineral econs. Washington sect. 1975-78, sect. Engr. of Yr. award 1976, sect. Mineral Economist of Yr. award 1984, nat. chmn. council econs. 1980-81), Am. Soc. Pub. Adminstrn., Kennedy Sch. Govt. Alumni Assn. of Harvard U. (dir. 1978-82), Am. Econs. Assn., Nat. Assn. Bus. Economists, Rho Psi. Mem. Chinese Christian Ch. Contbr. articles to profl. jours. Home: 1940 Dundee Rd Rockville MD 20850 Office: 11228 Georgia Ave Suite 9 Wheaton MD 20902

WANG, KUO-KAI GEORGE, technical marketing manager; b. Tainan, Taiwan, Sept. 19, 1951; came to U.S., 1975; s. Kai-Shung and Mei-Hwei W.; m. Menq-Yun Wu, Jan. 18, 1977; children: Charles, Albert. BS, Nat. Taiwan U., 1973; MS, SUNY-Stony Brook, 1976, PhD, 1979; MBA, U. Santa Clara, 1985; system design engr. dept. research and devel. Burroughs Corp., N.Y.C., 1979-81; staff engr. dept. strategic mktg., microprocessor div. Fairchild Corp., Santa Clara, Calif., 1981-84; product line mgr. dept. digital signal processing mktg. NEC Electronics, Inc., Mountain View, Calif., 1984—; product line mgr. Digital Signal Processing Mktg. Research in transient queueing theory and computer communication and digital electronics. Mem. IEEE Computer Soc., Communications Soc., Cybernetics Soc., N.Y. Acad. Scis., Sigma Xi. Home: 1425 Hawk Ct Sunnyvale CA 94087 Office: NEC Electronics Inc 401 Ellis St Mountain View CA 94043

WANG, LONG HUEI, microbiologist; b. Taichung, Taiwan, Sept. 5, 1940; s. Duey and Chao (Lin) W.; B.S., Nat. Taiwan U., 1964, M.S., 1967; Ph.D., Iowa State U., 1975; m. Chio-Huei Kan, Jan. 15, 1968; children—Hsien-Yih, Yih-Chuen. Mem. research staff Taiwan Sugar Research Inst., Tainan, 1967—, head dept. by-products utilization, 1982—. Recipient Outstanding Service award Taiwan Sugar Corp., 1980. Mem. Am. Soc. Microbiology, Soc. Indsl. Microbiology, Inst. Food Technologists, Chinese Agrl. Chemistry Soc., Biomass Energy Soc. of China, Sigma Xi. Editor reports. Office: 54 Sheng-Chan Rd, Tainan 70123, Republic China

WANG, MING CHANG, laser scientist, optical engineer; b. Chang Chun, Ji Lin, Peoples Republic of China, July 14, 1940; s. Xin Chuan Wang and Shu Hui Liu; m. Xiu Fen, Jan. 1, 1966; children: Xiao Zhuo, Ning. BS, U. Optics and Fine Mechanics, Chang Chun, 1963. Research asst. Inst. Optics and Fine Mechanics, Shanghai, Peoples Republic of China, 1963-78, research assoc., 1978-84, assoc. prof. optical engring., 1987—; vis. scholar U. Md., 1984-87. Author: Laser Physics, 1975; prin. researcher for devel. waveguide laser, 1979. Recipient Research and Devel. award Academia Sinica, 1979. Mem. Chinese Soc. Optics, Shanghai Soc. Laser. Home: 3416 Pulane Dr Hyattsville MD 20783 Office: Shanghai Inst Optics and Fine, Mechanics PO Box 8211, Shanghai Peoples Republic China

WANG, SING-WU, retired librarian; b. China, Dec. 24, 1920; s. Zhi-tang and Zhang W.; B.A., U. Zhejiang, China, 1944; M.A., Australian Nat. U., 1969; m. May, Nov. 20, 1947; children—Angela, Ruth, Kristina. Chief cataloguer of Chinese books, Nat. Central Library, Nanking, China, 1945-49; chief librarian Yang Ming Shan Inst. Library, Taipei, Taiwan, 1949-55; dir. Taiwan Provincial Library, Taipei, 1955-64; sr. specialist librarian Orientalia Sect., Nat. Library Australia, Canberra, 1964-73, chief librarian, 1973-85; exchange librarian Cleve. Public Library, 1959-60; examination passed Sch. Library Sci., Western Res. U., Cleve., 1959-60; asso. prof., prof. library sci., dept. social edn. Taiwan Normal U., Taipei, 1957-65; lectr. modern Chinese history, Coll. Chinese Culture, Yang Ming Shan, Taiwan, 1963-64; lectr. Chinese classics, dept. of Chinese, Australian Nat. U., Canberra, 1966; exec. dir., bd. dirs. Library Assn. of China, 1953-64, dir. library tng. assn., Taipei, 1956-58. Fellow, The China Acad., Yang Ming Shan, 1968—; recipient fgn. librarian program award, U.S. Dept. State, 1959-60, medal of the Order of Australia, 1986. Mem. ALA, Library Assn. Australia, Assn. for Asian Studies, Asian Studies Assn. Australia, E. Asian Librarians Group of Australia (newsletter editor, 1980-82; chmn. 1982-85, vice chmn. 1985-86). Baptist. Author: Introduction to the Classification of Books (in Chinese), 1955; On Library Services in Taiwan (in Chinese), 1963; The Organization of Chinese Emigration, 1848-1888, 1978; Chinese translator: Lincoln (Nathaniel Wright Stephenson), 1958; contbr. articles to publs. in English and Chinese, papers to confs. Australia and Taiwan (in English and Chinese). Home: 123 Namatjira Dr, 2611 Fischer Australia

WANG, STEPHEN, oil company executive; b. Havana, Cuba, Dec. 19, 1947; came to U.S., 1952, naturalized, 1962; s. Lincoln and Grace (Chiang) W.; A.B., Columbia Coll., 1968; B.S., Columbia U., 1970, M.B.A., 1971; m. Dulia Prima Co, Sept. 15, 1979; 1 child, Michael Clifton. Pres., Dining Systems, Inc., N.Y.C., 1973-76; dir. supply Buckeye Petrofuels Co., Radnor, Pa., 1976-79; v.p. Am. Refining Co., Villanova, Pa., 1979-83; v.p. Phoenix Petroleum Co., King of Prussia, Pa., 1983—. Mem. petroleum adv. bd. N.Y. Mercantile Exchange, 1980—. Mem. Oil Traders Assn. Republican. Office: Phoenix Petroleum Co King Prussia Bus Ctr 1009 W 9th Ave King of Prussia PA 19406

WANG, TSING-SHIH PETER, hotel executive, consultant; b. Singapore, Singapore, Apr. 9, 1952; s. En Pao Maurice and Chwee Keng (Wong) W.; m. Grace Maria-Jovita Rivera, Dec. 7, 1985. Student, Birmingham Poly., Eng., 1972-74; hotel diploma, Birmingham Coll. Food, Eng., 1974; chef diploma, Lusanne Swiss Hotel Sch., 1974. Chef Birmingham Children's Hosp., 1971, London Hilton, 1974; chef, maitre d'hotel Stratford Upon Avon (Eng.) Hotel, 1975-76; asst. food/beverage mgr. Goodwood Park Hotel, Singapore, 1977; exec. chef, catering mgr., dir. catering Singapore Airlines, 1977-85; project mgr. Hyatt Regency Singapore, 1985; dir. food-beverage Hyatt Kinabalu Internat., Kota, 1986, Hyatt Tianjin, China, 1987—; cons. mgr. Airlanka Catering, Sri Lanka, 1982; cons. interior decorator restaurants, Manila, 1984-85. Served with Singapore Army, 1969-71. Recipient Top Restaurant award Hotel Internat., 1985. Mem. Hotel Catering Instl. Adminstrn., Chaine Des Rotisserie. Methodist. Office: Hyatt Regency Tianjin, Jie Fang Rd, Tianjin Peoples Republic China

WANG, XINGWU, physics educator; b. Hangzhou, China, Feb. 19, 1953; came to U.S., 1982; s. Jinguang and Xiuying (Lin) W. BS, Harbin N. Eng. Inst., 1978; MS, Hangzhou U., 1981; PhD SUNY, Buffalo, 1987. Tchr., technician Hangzhou N. Sch., China, 1978-81; tchr. physics Hangzhou U., 1981-84; research asst. SUNY-Buffalo, 1984-87, research assoc., 1987—. Mem. Am. Phys. Soc. Home: 461 Braxmar Rd Buffalo NY 14150 Office: SUNY Dept Physics Buffalo NY 14260

WANG, ZENGQI, playwright, opera composer; b. Gaoyou County, Jiangsu, China, Mar. 15, 1920; s. Jusheng Wang; m. Shi Songqing, May 2, 1949; children: Lang, Ming, Chao. BA in Chinese Lit. and Lang., Nat. SW Associated U., China, 1943. Mid. sch. tchr. Kunming and Shanghai, 1943-47; researcher Wumen Hist. Mus., Peking, 1948-49; editor Beijing Lit. and Art, Beijing Singing Ballads, 1950-54, Folk Lit., Beijing, 1954-58; playwright Peking Opera Troupe of Beijing, 1962—. Author: Encounter by Chance, 1948, A Night Spent With Shepherd Boys, 1962, Short Stories by Wang Zengqi, 1982, Wild Jasmine, 1985. Recipient short stories award Chinese Writers' Assn., 1981, several other literary and opera awards. Mem. Chinese Writers Assn., Chinese Dramatists Assn., Beijing Dramatists Assn. Home: Building 9 12-1, Puhuangyu Rd, Beijing People's Republic of China

WANG, ZHONGDE, applied scientist; b. Nanjing, China, Mar. 19, 1937; s. Houyou Wang and Jinshu Liu; m. Manqinq He, Jan. 31, 1965; children: Zhiwei, Biao. Diploma in physics, Yunnan U., 1960. Research asst. Kunming Inst. Physics, 1960-78, assoc. research prof., 1978-80; vis. scholar U. Ariz., Tucson, 1980-82, research assoc., 1982-83; sr. engr. Kunming Inst. Physics, 1983-87; assoc. prof. Beijing U. Posts & Telecommunications, 1987-88, prof., 1988—. Reviewer, Math. Revs., 1984; contbr. numerous articles to profl. jours. Grantee, NSF, U.S., 1982, People's Republic of China Ministry Machinery, 1986, NSF, People's Republic of China, 1987. Mem. IEEE (sr.), Chinese Physics Soc., Chinese Inst. Electronics, Am. Math. Soc. Home: Beijing U Posts & Telecom, No 21111 Living Quarters, Beijing People's Republic of China Office: Beijing U Posts & Telecom, Box 93 Dept Elec Telecom, Beijing 100088, People's Republic of China

WANG, ZI-KUN, mathematics educator, university president; b. Jiangxi, China, Apr. 21, 1929; s. Chao-ji Wang and Shan-oi Guo; m. De-lin Dain, Aug. 18, 1958; children: Wei-min, Wei-zan. BA in Math., Wuhan U., People's Republic of China, 1952; PhD in Probability Theory, Moscow U., 1958. Instr. in math. Nankai U., People's Republic of China, 1952-55, prof. math., 1958-84; pres. Beijing Normal U., People's Republic of China, 1984—. Author: Theory of Stochastic Processes, 1965, Talks on Scientific Discovery, 1978, Birth-Death Proc., Markov Chains, 1980, Brownian Motion and Potentials, 1982; mem. editorial bd. Soc., Scientia, Sinica, Sci. Bulletin China. Recipient Sci. Conf. award, People's Republic of China, 1978, Excellent Popular Sci. Works prize, 1981, Nat. Sci. prize, 1982, Devel. Sci. Tech. prize, 1985. Mem. Nat. Math. Soc. China (mem. council), Assn. Sci. Tech. China (mem. com.), Higher Edn. Soc. China (mem. com.). Address: Beijing Normal U, Office of President, Beijing People's Republic of China

WANG BINGQIAN, Chinese state councilor; b. Li County, Hebei Province, 1925. Joined Chinese Communist Party, 1940; research staff, sec. Regional Fin. Dept., 1939-46, staff auditing com. Cen. Hebei Region, staff fin. and econ. office, sect. staff, 1946-48; dep. sect. chief auditing div. Fin. Dept., North China, 1948-49; sect. chief, div. chief, dep. dir., dir., vice minister, vice sec. party com., minister and sec. party com., from 1949, minister of fin., Cen. Govt., 1949-83; dir. budget dept. Ministry of Fin., 1963, vice minister of fin., 1973-80, minister of fin., 1980—, state councilor, 1983—; mem. 12th Cen., Com., Chinese Communist Party, 1982; pres. Acctg. Soc., 1980, hon. pres., 1985; gov. World Bank, 1980; Office: Ministry of Finance, Beijing People's Republic of China *

WANGCHUCK, HIS MAJESTY JIGME SINGYE, King of Bhutan; b. Bhutan, Nov. 11, 1955; s. King Jigme Dorji and Queen Asbi (Kesang) W.; student North Point, Darjeeling, Ugyuen Wangchuk Acad., Paro, also in Eng. Crown prince, 1972; succeeded to throne of Bhutan, 1972; crowned, 1974; chmn. Planning Commn. Bhutan, from 1972; also comdr.-in-chief armed forces. Address: Royal Palace, Thimphu Bhutan *

WANGCHUCK, PRINCESS SONAM CHHODEN, representative of His Majesty the King of Bhutan; b. Zurich, Switzerland, July 26, 1953; d. His Majesty King Jigme Dorji and Her Majesty Kesang (Choden) W.; m. Tsewang Jurmed Rixin, Oct. 15, 1979; children: Mila Singye, Meto Peldon. Student Heathfield Sch., Berkshire, U.K. Chmn. Royal Ins. Corp. of Bhutan, 1975—, Royal Civil Service Commn., 1982—, Druk Air Corp., 1981—, Royal Monetary Authority, 1982—; minister of fin., 1985—; pres. Nat. Women's Assn. of Bhutan, 1981—. Address: Ministry of Fin, Tashichho Dzong, Thimphu Bhutan

WANG FANG, government official. m. Liu Xin. Polit. commissar 94th div., 32d Army, 3d Field Army, 1949; dep. comdr. Hangzhou Air Def. Command, 1950; dep. dir. Pub. Security Dept. People's Govt. Zhejiang Province, 1951; polit. commissar Pub. Security Forces Zhejiang Province, 1954; mem. People's Govt. Zhejiang Province, 1955, dir. Pub. Security Dept., 1955; vice-gov. Zhejiang Province, 1964; branded counterrevolutionary revisionist and purged 1967; vice-chmn. Revolutionary Com. Zhejiang, 1977-79; mem. Standing Com. Zhejiang Province Communist Party, 1978, dep. sec., 1978-82; vice chmn. People's Congress Zhejiang Province, 1979-83; sec. Zhejiang Province Communist Party, 1982-83; mem. Chinese Communist Party Cen. Com., 1982; leading sec. Zhejiang Province Communist Party, 1983; state councilor State Council, 1988—; now also minister pub. sec. Address: State Council, Office of State Councilor, Beijing Peoples Republic of China *

WANGSAPRAWIRA, NADIMAN, industrial engineer; b. Bandung, Indonesia, Oct. 23, 1928; s. Mirun and Paisem W.; m. Menny Soehartini, July 23, 1954; children: Suryo Bandoro, Srihertanty Riza Perkasa, Sutknto, Anitas Jahria, Nurhadiwibowo, Evalatifah, Adam Prawirokusomo. Student, Acad. Journaistic, Jakarta, Indonesia, 1953. Chief engr. Jawa Unko Kaisha, Jakarta, 1943-45; supt. Dutch Oil Co., Jakarta, 1952-58; exec. dir. Firmayudhakarya, Sukabuma, Indonesia, 1963-85; comml. mgr. C.V. Makota Pelita, Jakarta, 1985—; chmn. Small Scale Industry, Sukabumi, 1982-85; comml. mgr. P.T. Jardam Group, Jakarta, 1985; sales mgr. P.T. Ciherangindah, Jakarta, 1985. Islamic. Home: 6/13 Jalan Cibatu Jati Cisaat, Sukabumi Indonesia Office: Firma Yudhakarya Trading Co, 6/13 Jacan Cibatujati Cisaat, Sukabumi Indonesia

WANG ZHEN, government official; b. Liuyang County, Hunan, People's Republic of China, 1908. Joined Chinese Communist Party, 1927; alt. mem. Chinese Communist Party Cen. Com., 1945-56; dep. comdr. Northwest China Mil. Region, 1952-54; mem. Nat. Def. Council, 1954-1966; promoted to col.-gen. 1955, minister state farms and reclamation, 1956-66; mem. Chinese Communist Party Cen. Com., 1956-85; vice premier 1975-80; mem. Politburo, Chinese Communist Party Cen. Com., 1978-85, mem. standing com. of the mil. commn., 1979-82; mem. Presidium, Congress of the Chinese Communist Party, 1982; vice-chmn. cen. adv. commn. Chinese Communist Party Cen. Com., 1985; v.p. People's Republic of China, 1988—. Decorated Order 1st August, Order Independence and Freedom, Order Liberation, all 1st class. Address: Chinese Communist Party, Vice Chmn Cen Adv Com, Beijing Peoples Republic of China *

WANK, GERALD SIDNEY, periodontist; b. Bklyn., Jan. 20, 1925; s. Joseph and Sadie (Ikowitz) W.; m. Gloria Baum, June 4, 1949; children: David, Stephen, Daniel. B.A., NYU, 1945, D.D.S., 1949; cert. in orthodontia, Columbia U., 1951, cert. in periodontia, 1956. Intern in oral surgery Bellevue Hosp., 1949-50; practice dentistry specializing in oral rehab. and periodontal prosthetics N.Y.C., Great Neck, N.Y., 1949—; instr. dept. periodontia, oral medicine NYU Dental Sch., 1956-63, asst. clin. prof. dept. periodontia, 1963-67, asst. prof. periodontia, oral medicine, former postgrad. dir. periodontal-prosthesis dept. fixed partial prosthesis, 1970—, clin. assoc. prof. periodontia and oral medicine, 1970-77, clin. prof., 1977—, postgrad. dir. periodontia, 1968-71; staff lectr. periodontology Harvard U. Sch. Dental Medicine, 1973-74; vis. lectr. Albert Einstein Coll. Medicine, N.Y.C. Community Coll. Sch. Dental Hygiene; sr. asst. attending staff North Shore Univ. Hosp., 1974-77, sr. asst. attending div. surgery, 1977—; cons. orthodontic panel N.Y. State, N.Y.C. depts. health; cons. periodontal prosthesis, Goldwater Meml. Hosp., N.Y.C.; former postgrad. instr. 1st Dist. Dental Soc. Postgrad. Sch.; lectr. various socs. N.Y. U.; mem. com. admissions N.Y. U. Coll. Dentistry, 1975—, chmn. fund raising, 1976—. Contbr. to: Practice of Periodontia, 1960, Dental Clinics of North America, 1972, 81, Manual of Clinical Periodontics, 1973; contbr. articles to profl. jours. Served to capt. USAF, 1953-55. Recipient Alumni Meritorious Service award N.Y. U., 1981, Coll. Dentistry Alumni Achievement award N.Y. U., 1983. Fellow Acad. Gen. Dentistry, N.Y. Acad. Dentistry, Internat. Coll. Dentists, Am. Coll. Dentists, Am. Acad. Oral Medicine (pres. N.Y. sect. 1971-72), Am. Pub. Health Assn.; mem. N.Y. Coll. Dentists (dir.), Dental Soc. N.Y.C. (dir. 1st dist., chmn. ethics com. 1985-86), Fedn. Dentaire Internat., Am. Assn. Dental Schs., N.Y. State Pub. Health Assn., AAUP, Pan Am. Med. Assn. (life), AAAS, ADA, Am. Acad. Periodontology, Sci. Research Soc. Am., Northeastern Soc. Periodontia, Am. Acad. Dental Medicine, Acad. Gen. Dentistry, Internat. Acad. Orthodontia, NYU Coll. Dentistry Alumni Assn. (dir., sec. 1973-74, v.p. 1974-75, pres. 1976-77), Am. Soc. Anesthesiology, Am. Assn. Endodontists, NYU Coll. Dentistry Dental Assocs. (charter), Acad. Oral Rehab. (hon.), First Dist. Dental Soc. (program chmn. 1984, chmn. continuing edn. 1983, sec., 1985, v.p. Eastern Dental Soc. br. 1986, pres.-elect 1987, pres. Eastern Dental Soc. br. 1988, bd. dirs.), NYU Gallatin Assos., Alumni Fedn. N.Y. U. (dir. 1976-81), Omicron Kappa Upsilon, Alpha Omega. Jewish. Clubs: Fresh Meadow Country (Great Neck, N.Y.); N.Y. U. (charter N.Y. U. Coll. Dentistry), Century (charter N.Y. U. Coll. Dentistry); Masons. Home and Office: 40 Bayview Ave Great Neck NY 11021 also: 14 E 60th St New York NY 10022

WANKE, GUNTHER, theology educator; b. Salzburg, Austria, Aug. 9, 1939; s. Adalbert Vinzenz and Ilse Barbara (Lehn) W.; m. Ulrike Katharina Fliegenschnee, Oct. 29, 1962; children: Michael, Daniel, Susanna. ThM, U. Vienna, 1962, ThD, 1964. Prof. U. Erlangen-Nürnberg, Fed. Republic Germany, 1976—, v.p., 1979-86. Author: Untersuchungen zur Sog Baruchschrift, 1971; editor: Zeitschrift für die Alttestamental Wissenschaft. Mem. Wissenschaftl Gesellschaft fur Theol. Lutheran. Home: Am Rothelheim 58, D8520 Erlangen Federal Republic of Germany Office: Univ Erlangen-Nurnberg, Kochstr 6, D8520 Erlangen Federal Republic of Germany

WANKLYN, CHRISTOPHER ANDREW, painter; b. Montreal, Que., Can., May 13, 1926; arrived in Morroco, 1954; s. David Angus and Hazel (Kennedy) W. BA, McGill U., 1948; MA, Sheffield U., 1949. One-man shows include: La Manoir Gallery, Rabat, Morocco, Nadar Galerie, Casablanca, Morocco, Mamounia Hotel, Marrakech, Morocco, other cities in Morocco. Home and Studio: BP 471, Marrakech Morocco

WAN LI, government official People's Republic China; b. Dongping, Shandong Province, 1917. Joined Chinese Communist Party, 1936; mem., dep. dir. industry devel. Southwest China Mil. and Adminstrv. Council, 1950; vice minister of Bldg. Constrn., 1952-56; dir. Urban Planning Bur., State Council, 1955-56; minister of Urban Constrn., 1956-58; sec. Communist Party, Beijing, 1958-66; vice-mayor Beijing, 1958-66; vice chmn. Beijing sect. Chinese People's Polit. Consultative Conf.; criticized and removed from office during Cultural Revolution, 1967; mem. Standing Com., Communist Party, Beijing Municipality, 1971-74; minister of Railways, 1975-77, criticized and removed from officer during Tian'anmen incident, later reinstated 1976; 1st sec. Chinese Communist Party, Anhui Province, 1977, chmn. Revolutionary Com., 1977-79, 1st polit. commissar Anhui Mil Dist., 1977-80; mem. 11th Cen. Com., Chinese Communist Party, 1977, mem. secretariat, 1980, mem. Politburo, 12th Cen. Com., 1982; chmn. standing com. Nat. People's Congress, 1988—; vice premier State Council, People's Republic China, 1980-88, minister State Agrl. Comm., 1980-82, acting premier during Zhao Ziyang's absence, 1982, 83; chmn. Nat. Com. Promoting Socialist Ethics, 1983; hon. pres. China Lit. Found. Recipient Gold Olympic Order, Internat. Olympic Com., 1986. Avocation: tennis. Office: Nat People's Congress, Chmn Standing Com, Beijing People's Republic China *

WANN, LAYMOND DOYLE, petroleum research scientist; b. Magazine, Ark., Apr. 25, 1924; s. Vernon Cecil and Emma (McCrary) W.; B.S. in Physics (Phi Eta Sigma scholar), Okla. State U., 1949, M.S., 1950; m. Betty Lou Brown, Nov. 6, 1948; children—Jacqueline, Lyndall Doyle. With Conoco Inc., Ponca City, Okla., 1951—, sr. research scientist, 1957-60, research group leader, 1960-81, asso. research dir., 1981—. Mem. Mcpl. Airport Bd., Ponca City. Served with AUS, 1942-46; ETO. Decorated Bronze Star. Mem. Am. Petroleum Inst. chmn. well logging subcom.), IEEE, Aircraft Owners and Pilots Assn., Seaplane Pilots Assn., VFW, Phi Kappa Phi, Pi Mu Epsilon, Sigma Phi Sigma. Republican. Episcopalian (vestryman). Contbr. articles on elec. and radioactive well-logging, elec. design to profl. jours. Patentee in field. Home: 1501 Monument Rd Ponca City OK 74601 Office: 1000 S Pine St Ponca City OK 74601

WANNER, PETER JOHN, chemical executive; b. London, Apr. 26, 1939; s. Johannes and Pauline Mary (Hamilton-Francis) W. MBA with honors, U. Zurich, 1968; postgrad., Stanford U., 1979. Asst. to v.p. for planning CIBA-GEIGY, Basel, Switzerland, 1969-76; mng. dir. CIBA-GEIGY, Nairobi, Kenya, 1977—; also bd. dirs. Ea. Africa CIBA-GEIGY, Nairobi. Contbr. numerous articles on econs. to profl. jours. Mem. Young Pres. Orgn. (com. Simba chpt. 1987). Lodge: Rotary. Home: PO Box 46057, Nairobi Kenya Office: CIBA Geigy, Koinange St, Nairobi Kenya

WAPINSKI, MAURICIO, food company executive; b. Monterrey, Mex., Aug. 21, 1955; s. Emanuel and Rebeca (Kleiman) W.; m. Janet Schwarz; children: Joanna, Deborah. B Indsl. Engring., U. Monterrey, 1977; MBA, U. Pa., 1979. Cons. Podolsky & Assocs., Mexico City, 1977-78, sr. cons., 1980-82; chief operating officer Kir Alimentos, Monterrey, 1982—; prof. ITESM, Monterrey, 1976-77; ednl. cons., Monterrey, 1982—. Mem. Wharton Sch. Bus. Alumni, Caintra. Home: Republica Dominicana 651, 64620 Monterrey Mexico Office: Kir Alimentos SA, Ave Conductores 600, 66490 Monterrey Mexico

WARBURTON, RALPH JOSEPH, architect, educator; b. Kansas City, Mo., Sept. 5, 1935; s. Ralph Gray and Emma Frieda (Niemann) W.; m. Carol Ruth Hychka, June 14, 1958; children: John Geoffrey, Joy Frances. B.Arch., MIT, 1958; M.Arch., Yale U., 1959, M.C.P., 1960. Registered architect, Colo., Fla., N.J., Md., Ill., N.Y., Va., D.C.; registered profl. engr., Fla., N.J., N.Y.; registered community planner, Mich., N.J. With various archtl. planning and engring. firms Kansas City, Mo., 1952-55, Boston, 1956-68, N.Y.C., 1959-62, Chgo., 1962-64; assoc. chief planning Skidmore, Owings & Merrill, Chgo., 1964-66; spl. asst. for urban design HUD, Washington, 1966-72, cons., 1972-77; prof. architecture, archtl. engring. and planning U. Miami, Coral Gables, Fla., 1972—, chmn. dept. architecture, archtl. engring. and planning, 1972-75, assoc. dean engring. and environ. design, 1973-74; adviser govt. Iran, 1970; advisor govt. France, 1973, govt. Ecuador, 1974; cons. in field, 1972—, lectr., critic design juror in field, 1965—; mem. chmn. Coral Gables Bd. Architects, 1980-82. Assoc. author: Man-Made America: Chaos or Control, 1963; editor: New Concepts in Urban Transportation, 1968, Housing Systems Proposals for Operation Breakthrough, 1970, Focus on Furniture, 1971, National Community Art Competition, 1971, Defining Critical Environmental Areas, 1974; contbg. editor: Progressive Architecture, 1974-84; editorial adv. bd.: Jour. Am. Planning Assn., 1983—, Planning for Higher Edn., 1986—; contbr. numerous articles to profl. jours.; mem. adv. panel, Industrialization Forum Quar., 1969-79. Mem. Met. Housing and Planning Council, Chgo., 1965-67; mem. exec. com. Yale U. Arts Assn., 1965-70; pres. Yale U. Planning Alumni Assn., 1983—; mem. ednl. adv. com. Fla. Bd. Architecture, 1975. Recipient W.E. Parsons medal Yale U., 1960; recipient Spl. Achievement award HUD, 1972, commendation Fla. Bd. Architecture, 1974, Fla. Trust Historic Preservation award, 1983, Group Achievement award NASA, 1976; Skidmore, Owings & Merrill traveling fellow MIT, 1958; vis. fellow Inst. Architecture and Urban Studies, N.Y.C., 1972-74; NSF grantee, 1980-82. Fellow AIA (nat. housing com. 1968-72, nat. regional devel. and natural resources com. 1974-75, nat. systems devel. com. 1972-73, nat. urban design com. 1968-73, bd. dirs. Fla. S. chpt. 1974-75), ASCE, Fla. Engring. Soc.; mem. Am. Inst. Cert. Planners (exec. com. dept. environ. planning 1973-74), Am. Soc. Engring. Edn. (chmn. archtl. engring. div. 1975-76), Nat. Soc. Profl. Engrs., Nat. Sculpture Soc. (allied profl. mem.), Nat. Trust Hist. Preservation (principles and guidelines com. 1967), Am. Soc. Landscape Architects (hon.) (chmn. design awards jury), Am. Planning Assn. (Fla. chpt. award excellence 1983), Internat. Fedn. Housing and Planning, Am. Soc. Interior Designers (hon.), Greater Miami C. of C. (chmn. new neighborhoods action com. 1973-74), Omicron Delta Kappa, Sigma Xi, Tau Beta Pi. Club: Cosmos (Washington). Home: 6910 Veronese St Coral Gables FL 33146 Office: 420 S Dixie Hwy Coral Gables FL 33146 also: U Miami Sch Architecture Coral Gables FL 33124

WARD, ALAN, writer, editor; b. Birmingham, West Midlands, Eng., Oct. 6, 1957; s. Stanley Ronald and Irene May (Ford) W. BSc with honors, Hatfield (Hertfordshire) Polytech., 1976-80. Research asst. Miles Labs., Slough, Bucks, 1980; info. officer Sterling-Winthrop Group, Surbiton, Surrey, Eng., 1981-82; sci. author, editor Adis Press Ltd., Auckland, New Zealand, 1982—. Contbr. articles to profl. jours. Office: Adis Press Ltd, Centorian Dr Mairangi Bay, Auckland New Zealand

WARD, ALBERT EUGENE, research center executive, archeologist, ethnohistorian; b. Carlinville, Ill., Aug. 20, 1940; s. Albert Alan and Eileen (Boston) W.; m. Gladys Anena Lea, Apr. 26, 1961 (div. Apr. 4, 1974); children—Scott Bradley, Brian Todd; m. Stefanie Helen Tschaikowsky, Apr. 24, 1982. A.A., Bethany Luth. Jr. Coll., Mankato, Minn., 1961; B.S., No. Ariz. U., 1968; M.A., U. Ariz., 1972. Lab. asst., asst. archeologist Mus. No. Ariz., Flagstaff, 1965-67; research archeologist Desert Research Inst., U. Nev., Las Vegas, 1968; research archeologist Archeol. Survey, Prescott Coll., Ariz., 1969-71, research assoc., 1971-73; research archeologist Ariz. Archeol. Ctr., Nat. Park Service, Tucson, 1972-73, research collaborator Chaco Ctr., Albuquerque, 1975; founder, dir. archeol. research program Mus. Albuquerque, 1975-76; founder, dir., 1976-79l pres. bd. dirs. Ctr. Anthrop. Studies, Albuquerque, 1976—; lectr. U. N.Mex. Community Coll., 1974-77, others; contract archeol. salvage and research projects in N.Mex. and Ariz. Editorial adv. bd. Hist. Archeology, 1978-80; editor publs. Ctr. Anthrop. Studies, 1978—. Contbr. articles to scholarly jours. Grantee Mus. No. Ariz., 1972, S.W. Monuments Assn., 1973, CETA, 1975-79, Nat. Park Service, 1978-79. Mem. Soc. Am. Archeology, Soc. Hist. Archeology, No. Ariz. Soc. Sci. and Art, Ariz. Archeol. and Hist. Soc., Archeol. Soc. N.Mex., Albuquerque Archeol. Soc., Am. Anthrop. Assn., S.W. Mission Research Ctr., Am. Soc. Conservation Archeology, Soc. Archeol. Scis., Southwestern Anthrop. Assn., N.Mex. Archeol. Council, Living Hist. Farms and Agrl. Mus. Assn. Republican. Lutheran. Office: Ctr Anthrop Studies PO Box 14576 Albuquerque NM 87191

WARD, ANTHONY JOHN, lawyer; b. Los Angeles, Sept. 25, 1931; s. John P. and Helen C. (Harris) W.; A.B., U. So. Calif., 1953; LL.B., U. Calif. at Berkeley, 1956; m. Marianne Edle von Graeve, Feb. 20, 1960 (div. 1977); 1 son, Mark Joachim; m. 2d, Julia Norby Credell, Nov. 4, 1978. Admitted to Calif. bar, 1957; asso. firm Ives, Kirwan & Dibble, Los Angeles, 1958-61; partner firm Marapese and Ward, Hawthorne, Calif., 1961-69; individual practice law, Torrance, Calif., 1969-76; partner firm Ward, Gaunt & Raskin, 1976—. Served to 1st lt. USAF, 1956-58. Mem. ABA, Blue Key, Calif. Trial Lawyers Assn., Lambda Chi Alpha. Democrat. Home: 2136 Via Pacheco Palos Verdes Estates CA 90274 Office: Pavilion A 21525 Hawthorne Blvd Torrance CA 90503

WARD, DAVID ERNEST, physician; b. Chatham, Kent, England, Mar. 25, 1947; s. Ernest and Hilda Grace (Fisher) W.; m. Jean Elizabeth Boyd, 1977 (div. 1986); m. Nicola Jane Flack, 1986. MB of Medicine and Surgery, Guy's Hosp., 1965; BSc, London U., 1967, MD, 1981. Diplomate, Am. Coll. Cardiologists, 1982. Resident St. Bartholomew's Hosp., London; sr. resident Brompton Hosp. and St. George's Hosp., London; Cardiology registrar St. Bartholomew's Hosp., London, 1976-79; sr. registrar cardiology Brompton Hosp., London, 1979-85; cons. physician, regional cardiothoracic unit St. George's Hosp., London, 1985. Author: Pacing for Tachycardia Control, 1983, Clinical Electropsysiology of the Heart, 1987; mem. editoril bd., Clin. Cardiology Jour., 1981; conbtr. over 150 articles to profl. jours. Recipient Freedom award City of London, 1984. Fellow Am. Coll. Cardiologists; mem. British Cardiac Soc., British Pacing and Electrophysiology Group (council mem. 1986—), Am. Heart Assn. (Council for Basic Sci.), N. Am. Soc. of Pacing and Electrophysiology, Royal Coll. of Physicians (lic. 1965, 73). Club: Worshipful Co. of Apothecaries (yeoman 1983). Home: 69 Harley St, London W1N 1DE, England Office: St Georges Hosp, Regional Cardiothoracic Unit, London SW17 0QT, England

WARD, DIANE KOROSY, lawyer; b. Cleve., Oct. 17, 1939; d. Theodore Louis and Edith (Bogar) Korosy; m. S. Mortimer Ward IV, July 2, 1960 (div. 1978); children: Christopher LaBruce, Samantha Martha; m. R. Michael Walters, June 30, 1979. AB, Heidelberg Coll., 1961; JD, U. San Diego, 1975. Bar: Calif. 1977, U.S. Dist. Ct. (so. dist.) Calif. 1977. Ptnr. Ward & Howell, San Diego, 1978-79, Walters, Howell & Ward, A.P.C., San Diego, 1979-81; mng. ptnr. Walters & Ward, A.P.C., San Diego, 1981— ; dir., v.p. Oak Broadcasting Systems, Inc., 1982-83; dir. Elisabeth Kubler-Ross Ctr., Inc., 1983-85; sheriff Ranchos del Norte Corral of Westerners, 1985-87; trustee San Diego Community Defenders, Inc., 1986-88. Pres. bd. dirs. Green Valley Civic Assn., 1979-80; trustee Palomar-Pomerado Hosp. Found., chmn. deferred giving, 1985—; trustee Episcopal Diocese of San Diego. Mem. ABA, Rancho Bernardo Bar Assn. (chmn. 1982-83), Lawyers Club San Diego, Profl. and Exec. Women of the Ranch (founder, pres. 1982—), San Diego Golden Eagle Club, Phi Delta Phi. Republican. Episcopalian. Club: Soroptimist Internat. (pres. chpt. 1979-80). Home: 16503 Avenida Florencia Poway CA 92064 Office: Walters & Ward 11665 Avena Pl Suite 203 San Diego CA 92128

WARD, EVAN, JR., pharmacist; b. Selma, Ala., Sept. 13, 1942; s. Evan and Hattie Mae (Hunter) W.; children from previous marriage—Donna Janine, Jennifer Lynn, Christopher Evan; m. Rita M. Lacey, Sept. 3, 1983; children—Nicholas Cameron, Dustin Roman. B.S., Fla. A&M U., 1965. Pharmacist, Triangle Prescription, Atlanta, 1966-70; pharmacist, asst. mgr. Walgreen Drugs, Atlanta, 1968-70; pharmacist, pres. Medics Drug Marts, Inc., Atlanta, 1970—; exec. v.p., founder W&W Pharms., Atlanta, 1982-84; cons. Sadie Mays Nursing Home, Atlanta, 1973-77; staff pharmacist McClendon Hosp., Atlanta, 1976-79; mem. adv. com. State Ga., 1984—. Mem. United Negro Coll. Fund, 1985, Nat. Urban League, 1985. Recipient Bus. Man of Year award Atlanta Bus. League, 1970, Cert. Appreciation award CETA, 1980. Mem. Ga. Pharm. Assn., Nat. Assn. Retail Druggists, Fla. A&M Sch. Pharmacists Alumni Assn. (pres. 1973, Pharmacist of Year 1973), Fla. A&M Alumni Assn. (Disting. Service award 1984), C. of C., Kappa Alpha Psi. Baptist. Office: Medics Drug Marts Inc 75 Peidmont Ave NE Atlanta GA 30303

WARD, FRANK BENJAMIN, corporate executive; b. Nashville, Tenn., June 9, 1947; s. Eugene Charles and Helen Felicita (McDonald) W.; m. Linda Ann Newman, Oct. 1, 1977. BS, U. Ala., Tuscaloosa, 1969, MA, 1971. Exec. asst. Am. Nat. Bank, Chattanooga, 1971; mktg. rep. Wilson Learning Corp., Mpls., 1972-76, v.p. banking div., 1976-78, v.p. eastern region, 1978-81; pres., chief exec. officer Corp. Performance Systems, Boston, 1981—; cons., Citibank, N.Y.C., AT&T, Morristown, N.J., 1st Nat. Bank Chgo., Wang, Harris Trust, Credit Suisse First Boston, Chem. Bank, Bankers Trust Co., Shearson Lehman Bros., Nat. Westminster Bank; adviser Marquis Who's Who, Chgo., 1984—; lectr. on tactical planning, mktg. of corp. fin. and capital markets U.Va. Contbr. articles to profl. jours. Club: Downtown Athletic (N.Y.C.). Office: Corp Performance Systems 727 Atlantic Ave Boston MA 02111

WARD, GEORGE TRUMAN, architect; b. Washington, July 24, 1927; s. Truman and Gladys Anna (Nutt) W.; B.S., Va. Poly. Inst., 1951, M.S., 1952; postgrad. George Washington U., 1966; m. Margaret Ann Hall, Sept. 10, 1949; children—Carol Ann Ward Dickson, Donna Lynne Ward Hale, George Truman, Robert Stephen. Archtl. draftsman Charles A. Pearson, Radford, Va., 1950; head archtl. sect. Hayes, Seay, Mattern & Mattern, Radford and Roanoke, 1951-52; with Joseph Saunders & Assos., Alexandria, Va., 1952-57, asso. architect, 1955-57; partner Vosbeck-Ward & Assos., Alexandria, 1957-64, Ward/Hall Assocs., Fairfax, Va., 1964—; dir. Crestar Bank, Washington, United Va. Bank/Greater Washington Region. Pres. PTA Burke (Va.) Sch., 1970-71; mem. bd. mgrs. Fairfax (Va.) County YMCA, 1964-76; chmn. adv. com. Coll. Architecture, Va. Poly. Inst., 1984—; bd. dirs. Va. Tech. Found., Inc.; pres. Springfield Rotary Found., 1978-79; vice chmn. county adv. bd. Salvation Army, 1978-79, 86-87; mem. Gen. Bd. Va. Bapts.; bd. visitors Va. Poly. Inst., 1984-87. Served with AUS, 1946-47. Registered profl. architect, Va., Md., D.C., W.Va., Ohio, N.J., Del., Pa., Tenn., Ga., N.C., N.Y., Tex. Paul Harris fellow. Recipient Disting. Service award Va. Tech. Alumni Assn., 1988. Mem. AIA (corp., charter Octagon Soc.), Interfaith Forum on Religion, Art and Architecture, Va. Assn. Professions, Va. C. of C., No. Va. Angus Assn. (pres. 1987-88), Tau Sigma Delta, Omicron Delta Kappa, Phi Kappa Phi, Pi Delta Epsilon, Ut Prosim. Baptist (deacon, moderator). Mason (Shriner, K.T.), Rotarian (charter mem., pres. Springfield 1973-74). Home: Glenara Farm Rt 1 Box 30 Marshall VA 22115 Office: 12011 Lee Jackson Meml Hwy Fairfax VA 22033

WARD, HILEY HENRY, journalist, educator; b. Lafayette, Ind., July 30, 1929; s. Hiley Lemen and Agnes (Fuller) W.; m. Charlotte Burns, May 28, 1951 (div. 1971); children: Dianne, Carolee, Marceline, Laurel; m. Joan Bastel, Aug. 20, 1977. BA, William Jewell Coll., 1951; MA, Berkeley (Calif.) Bapt. Div. Sch., 1953; MDiv, McCormick Theol. Sem., Chgo., 1955; summer, evening student, Northwestern U., 1948, 54, 56-57; PhD, U. Minn., 1977. News asst. Christian Advocate, 1953-55; editor jr. publs. David C. Cook Pub. Co., 1956-59; editor Record, Buchanan, Mich., 1960; religion editor Detroit Free Press, 1960-73; asst. prof. journalism Mankato (Minn.) State Coll., 1974-76; assoc. prof. journalism Wichita (Kans.) State U., 1976; prof. journalism Temple U., Phila., 1977—, dir. news-editorial sequence, journalism dept., 1977-80, chmn. dept., 1978-80; instr. journalism Oakland U., Rochester, Mich., evenings 1963-66. Author: Creative Giving, 1958, Space-Age Sunday, 1960, Documents of Dialogue, 1966, God and Marx Today, 1968, Ecumania, 1968, Rock 2000, 1969, Prophet of the Black Nation, 1969, The Far-out Saints of the Jesus Communes, 1972, Religion 2101 A.D., 1975, Feeling Good About Myself, 1983, Professional Newswriting, 1985, My Friend's Beliefs: A Young Reader's Guide to World Religions, 1988; editor: Media History Digest, 1979—; exec. editor: Kidbits, 1981-82; contbr. articles to profl. jours., feature articles to newspapers; also short stories and poems. Recipient citation Religious Heritage Am., 1962, Leidt award Episc. Ch., 1969; Religious Pub. Relations Council fellow, 1970. Mem. Religion Newswriters Assn. (pres. 1970-72), Am. Soc. Mag. Editors. Home: PO Box 399 1263 Folly Rd Warrington PA 18976 Office: Temple U Dept Journalism Philadelphia PA 19122

WARD, JACQUELINE REGINA (PAN), painter; b. Nice, France, Sept. 20, 1923; naturalized U.S. citizen, 1961; d. Edouard and Regina Clorinda (de Beytia) Monziols; student in France, Belgium, Chile; m. Theodore A. J. Ward, June 18, 1955. Mezzo-soprano Concerts Palais de Chaillot, others, France, 1949-53; one-woman shows: Galerie L. Tarbes, 1975, Galerie Dubernet, Tarbes, France, 1977, 80, 82, Gallery Ruhl, Nice, 1978; exhibited in group shows: Salon de l'Automne, Paris, 1972-73, Selected Contemporary Art, Geneva, 1974, State Gallery Ankara and I.C. Bankasi, Istanbul (both Turkey), 1977, Riom Mus. Women Painters of Today, 1977, Monte Carlo Women Creators, 1975, Gallery San Marco, Rome, 1977, London Gallery Blaise Preston Ltd., 1979-80, Gallery Dubernet, 1977-87, Nice Gallery, 1979, Exposition Peintres Contemporains, Paris, 1980, Academie Europé enne des Beaux Arts exhbns. in Que., Can., 1981, Tokyo, 1982, Museo de Bellas Artes, Santiago, Chile, Grand Palais Centennial, Paris, 1984, Musee J. Cheret, 1976-83, Internat. Group Exhbn., Geneva-Luxembourg-Belgium-France, 1985, Jacob Javits Hall, N.Y.C., 1986; represented in permanent collections: Nice, France, Ashmolean Mus., Oxford, Eng., Escolapio Sch., Jaca, Spain, Mus. Ch. Mons, France, Mus. de Ovar, Portugal, Galeria Augusta, Barcelona, Spain, Oscar and Peter Johnson Ltd., London, Gallery Dubernet, Tarbes, France. Decorated La Cruz de Caballero; recipient prix Cote d'Azur, 1972, 73, 74, Deauville Landscape, 1974, City of Rome, 1972-74, medal Newspaper La Depeche, 1975, Silver medal Ovar Mus., 1975, Prix d'Honneur Contemporary Art, Vichy, 1976, Bronze medal La Foret Mus., Tokyo, 1985; decorated cross golden palmas with merit Queen Fabiola Belgium. Mem. Soc. Grand Palais Paris Salon Des Independants. Home and Studio: 14 Rue Gauguin, 6500 Tarbes France

WARD, JAMES MICHAEL, historian; b. Washington, Aug. 6, 1953; s. John Lawrence Carberry and Margaret Cecilia (Brand) W. B.A., U. Md., 1974; M.A., NYU, 1978, Ph.D., 1983, cert. NYU Grad. Sch. of Bus. Adminstrn., 1985. Historian, pub. relations Colonial Dames Am., N.Y.C., 1979-81; freelance editor Garland Pub., Inc., N.Y.C., 1979-84; vis. asst. prof. of fine arts Trinity Coll., Hartford, Conn., 1984-85; freelance writer Seaport Mag., N.Y.C., 1984-85; freelance editor Rambusch Decorating Co., N.Y.C., 1983; lectr. Cooper-Hewitt Mus., 1987; art historian Garland Pub., Inc., 1980-81. Author: The Artifacts of R. Buckminster Fuller, 4 vols., 1985; editor Wunderman Worldwide and Saatchi & Saatchi, DFS Compton, 1987-88; writer Sotheby's Internat. Realty, N.Y.C.; contbr. articles to hist. mags. N.Y. State Council on the Arts grantee, 1982-83. Mem. Soc. of Architectural Historians N.Y. Chpt. (treas. 1982-85), The Coll. Art Assn. Avocations: photography; ocean liner history. Home: 1261 Park Ave Apt 11 New York NY 10029

WARD, JOE HENRY, JR., lawyer; b. Childress, Tex., Apr. 18, 1930; s. Joe Henry and Helen Ida (Chastain) W.; m. Carlotta Agnes Abreu, Feb. 7, 1959; children—James, Robert, William, John. BS in Acctg., Tex. Christian U., 1952; JD, So. Meth. U., 1964. Bar: Tex. 1964, Va. 1972, D.C. 1972; CPA, Tex. Mgr. Alexander Grant & Co., CPA's., Dallas, 1956-64; atty. U.S. Treasury, 1965-68; tax counsel U.S. Senate Fin. Com., 1968-72; sole practice, Washington, 1972-83; asst. gen. counsel, tax mgr. Epic Holdings, Ltd. and Crysopt Corp., 1983-87; sole practice, Washington, 1987—. Served to lt. USNR, 1952-56. Mem. ABA, Am. Inst. CPA's, Am. Assn. Atty.-CPA's. Club: Univ. (Washington). Home: 2639 Mann Ct Falls Church VA 22046 Office: 1730 K St NW Suite 304 Washington DC 20006

WARD, JOSEPH JORGENSON, publishing executive; b. Cedar City, Utah, Sept. 5, 1946; s. Parker Matheson and Thelma Leora (Jorgenson) W.; m. Rosemary Truman, Dec. 19, 1967 (div. 1972); children: Darren Joseph, Jason Truman; m. Diane Chamberlain, Apr. 7, 1973; children: Sasha Danielle, Justin Chamberlain. BS in Acctg., U. Utah, 1970; grad. advanced mgmt. program, Harvard U., 1984. Asst. gen. mgr. Little Am. Hotels, Salt Lake City, 1967-73; v.p., internat. dir. Sentry Ins. Co., Stevens Point, Wis., 1973-79; pres., chief exec. officer Europe and South Pacific Time Life Books, London, 1979—, chmn. dir., 1985—; v.p. internat. Time Life Books, Alexandria, Va., 1987—; dir. Time Life Internat. Ltd., London, 1986—; supervisory dir. Time Life Internat. BV, Amsterdam, The Netherlands, 1987—; also bd. dirs. 10 subs. cos. France, Fed. Republic Germany, Italy, Australia; dir. Mail Order Pubs. Authority, London, 1987. Served with USAR, 1970-78. Mem. Assn. Mail Order Pubs. (bd. dirs. 1987). Mormon. Home: 29 Campden Hill Sq, London W8 7JY, England Office: Time Life Books Europe, 153-157 New Bond St, London W1 0AA, England

WARD, LLEWELLYN O(RCUTT), III, oil producer; b. Oklahoma City, July 24, 1930; s. Llewellyn Orcutt II and Addie (Reisdorph) W.; m. Myra Beth Gungoll, Oct. 29, 1955; children: Casidy Ann, William Carlton. Student, Okla. Mil. Acad. Jr. Coll., 1948-50; BS, Okla. U., 1953. Registered profl. engr., Okla. Dist. engr. Delhi-Taylor Oil Corp., Tulsa, 1955-56; ptnr. Ward-Gungoll Oil Investments, Enid, Okla., 1956—; owner L.O. Ward Oil Ops., Enid, 1963—; v.p. 1420 Lahoma Rd. Inc., Enid, 1967—, also bd. dirs.; mem. Okla. Gov.'s Adv. Council on Energy; rep. to Interstate Oil Compact Commn.; bd. dirs. Community Bank and Trust Co. Enid. Chmn. Indsl. Devel. Commn., Enid, 1968—; active YMCA; mem. bd. visitors Coll. Engring., U. Okla.; mem. adv. council Sch. Bus., trustee Phillips U., Enid, Univ. Bd., Pepperdine, Calif.; Okla. chmn. U.S. Olympic Com., 1986—; chmn. bd. Okla. Polit. Action Com., 1974—, Bass Hosp.; Rep. chmn. Garfield County, 1967-69; Rep. nat. committeeman from Okla.; bd. dirs. Enid Indsl. Devel. Found., Pepperdine (Calif.) U.; trustee Phillips U., Enid. Served with C.E., U.S. Army, 1953-55. Named to Order of Ky. Cols. Mem. Am. Inst. Mining and Metall. Engrs., Ind. Petroleum Assn. Am. (area v.p., bd. dirs.), Okla. Ind. Petroleum Assn. (pres., bd. dirs.), Nat. Petroleum Council, Enid C. of C. (v.p., then pres.), Alpha Tau Omega. Methodist. Clubs: Toastmasters (pres. Enid chpt. 1966), Am. Bus. (pres. 1964). Lodges: Masons, Shriners, Rotary. Home: 900 Brookside Dr Enid OK 73701 Office: 502 S Fillmore Enid OK 73701

WARD, RICHARD HURLEY, university administrator; b. N.Y.C., Sept. 2, 1939; s. Hurley and Anna C. (Mittasch) W.; children from a previous marriage: Jeanne M., Jonathan B.; m. Michelle Ward, June 15, 1987. BS, John Jay Coll. Criminal Justice, 1968; M in Crim., U. Calif.-Berkeley, 1969, D in Crim., 1971. Detective, N.Y.C. Police Dept., 1962-70; coordinator student activities John Jay Coll., N.Y.C., 1970-71, dean students, 1971-75, v.p., 1975-77; vice chancellor, prof. criminology U. Ill., Chgo., 1977—; U.S. del. People to People Citizen Ambassador Program in China, 1983; leader U.S. del. People to People S.E. Asia, 1987; del. to China, Eisenhower Found., 1985; English lang. coordinator Internat. Course Higher Specialization Police Forces, Messina, Italy, 1981, 83, Madrid, 1984, course dir., 1982, 85; chmn. Joint Commn. on Criminology and Criminal Justice Edn. and Standards, 1975-80; vis. prof. Zagazig U., Egypt, Egyptian Police Acad., 1986; host, coordinator for Terrorism and Organized Crime Conf., U. Ill., 1986, 87; host, co-sponsor (with Police Tng. Acad. of Egypt) conf. Internat. Responses to Terrorism: New Initiatives, Cairo, 1988; U.S. del., co-leader for police specialization Crime Prevention and Criminal Justice Del. to China, 1984; team leader del. to Taiwan, 1985. Author: (with others) Police Robbery Control Manual, 1975; Introduction to Criminal Investigation, 1975, An Anti-Corruption Manual for Administrators in Law Enforcement, 1979; (with Robert McCormack) Quest for Quality, 1984; gen. editor Foundations of Criminal Justice, 46 vols., 1972-75; editor: (with Austin Fowler) Police and Law Enforcement, Vol. I, 1972; Police and Law Enforcement, Vol. II, 1975; The Terrorist Connection: A Pervasive Network; (newsletter) CJ Internat., 1985—; (with Harold Smith) International Terrorism: The Domestic Response.. Mem. Near West Side Community Conservation Council, 1982—; varsity baseball coach U. Ill., Chgo., 1980-82; varsity baseball coach John Jay Coll. Criminal Justice, N.Y.C., 1971-72. Served to cpl. USMC, 1957-61. Recipient Leonard Reisman award John Jay Coll. Criminal Justice, 1968, Alumni Achievement award, 1978; Richard McGee award U. Calif.-Berkeley Sch. Criminology, 1971; Justice Dept. fellow U. Calif.-Berkeley, 1968-69; Danforth Found. fellow, 1971. Mem. Acad. Criminal Justice Scis. (pres. 1977-78, Founder's award 1985), Am. Soc. Pub. Adminstrn., Internat. Assn. Chiefs of Police (chmn. edn. and tng. sect. 1974-75), Am. Assn. for Higher Edn., Am. Acad. for Profl. Law Enforcement (nat. bd. dirs. 1978-84), Sigma Delta Chi. Home: 918 S Bishop Chicago IL 60607 Office: U Ill at Chicago Box 6998 Chicago IL 60680

WARDEN, JOHN L., lawyer; b. Evansville, Ind., Sept. 22, 1941; s. Walter Wilson and Juanita (Veatch) W.; m. Phillis Ann Rodgers, Oct. 27, 1960; children—Anne W. Clark, John L., W. Carson. A.B., Harvard U., 1962; LL.B., U. Va., 1965. Bar: N.Y. 1966, U.S. Ct. Appeals (2d cir.) 1966, U.S. Dist. Ct. (so. and ea. dists.) N.Y. 1967, U.S. Ct. Appeals (10th cir.) 1971, U.S. Supreme Ct. 1972, U.S. Ct. Appeals (D.C. cir.) 1980. Assoc., Sullivan & Cromwell, N.Y.C., 1965-73, ptnr., 1973—. Fellow Am. Coll. Trial Lawyers; mem. Am. Law Inst., ABA, N.Y. State Bar Assn., Assn. of Bar of City of N.Y., N.Y. County Lawyers Assn. Republican. Episcopalian. Clubs: Knickerbocker, Down Town Assn. (N.Y.C.); Bedford (N.Y.) Golf and Tennis. Editor-in-chief Va. Law Review, 1964-65. Office: Sullivan & Cromwell 125 Broad St New York NY 10004

WARDHANA, GUNAWAN, personnel director, consultant, solicitor; b. Cepu, Cen. Java, Indonesia, Aug. 19, 1940; s. Karta Wardhana and Philipina Dorothea van Aagten; m. Latifa Sylvia Basrewan, Dec. 5, 1963; children: Davy Erwin, Heidy Irawati, Indry Kartika. LLD, U. Indonesia, 1961. Adminstrv. mgr. Masurai Concern, Jambi, Indonesia, 1959-61; mgr. fire safety and security Morrison Knudsen of Asia, Inc., Palembang, Indonesia, 1961-63; supt., personnel and adminstrn. mgr. Gesuri Lloyd, Palembang, Indonesia, 1963-72; site mgr. Airfast Services Indonesia, Jakarta, Palembang, 1972-77; mgr. personnel, gen. and legal affairs Bouraq Indonesia, Jakarta, 1977; dir. personnel Jakarta Mandarin Hotel, 1978-81; personnel mgr. P.T. Bayer Indonesia, Jakarta, 1981-83; personnel officer Standard Chartered Bank, Jakarta, 1984-85; mgr. human resources Lane Moving & Storage, Jakarta, 1985—; bd. dirs. P.T. Tusi, Jakarta, P.T. Indogulf Raya, Jakarta. Contbr. to various books on labor law, personnel tng. manuals. Mem. Indonesian Personnel Mgrs. Assn. (law com. 1978—), Indonesian Employees Assn. (coordinator South Jakarta chpt. 1985—). Moslem. Home: Kemanggisan Ilir III/80, Jakarta 11480, Indonesia Office: Lane Moving & Storage, Cilandak Comml Estate 408, Jakarta 12560, Indonesia

WARD-JACKSON, ADRIAN ALEXANDER, fine art expert; b. London, June 6, 1950; s. William Alexander and Catherine Elizabeth (Trew) W.J. Educated, Westminster, Vienna, 1967-70. Research asst. to Konrad Oberhuber Albertina Mus., Vienna, 1967-70; expert prints and drawings dept. Christie's, London, 1970-71; dir. P & D Colnaghi Ltd., London, 1971-75; chmn. Adrian Ward-Jackson Ltd., London, 1976—. Panel mem., mem. adv. panel Weltkunst Found., Zurich, Switzerland, 1981—, Ballet Rambert Sch., London, 1986—; bd. dirs. Ballet Rambert, 1984—, dep. chmn., 1986-87, co-chmn., 1987-88; bd. dirs. Mercury Theatre Trust Ltd., London, 1984—, dep. chmn., 1986-87, co-chmn., 1987; bd. govs. Royal Ballet, London, 1985—, bd. dirs., 1987—; bd. dirs Creative Dance Artists Trust, London, 1985—, Theatre Mus. Assn., London, 1987—, Soc. Brit. Theatre Designers, 1988—; trustee Aphrodisias Trust, London, 1985-86, Benesh Inst. Endowment Fund, London, 1987—, Dancers Resettlement Fund, London, 1987—; mem. ballet subcom. Royal Opera House, London, 1986-87; panel mem. Internat. Dance House Study Group, London, 1986—; council mem. Benesh Inst. Choreology, London, 1986—; council mem., dep. chmn. Aids Crisis Trust, London, 1987—; trustee Royal Opera House Trust, 1987—; dir. ballet bd. Royal Opera House, 1987—. Mem. Contemporary Art Soc. (exec. com. 1987—, dep. chmn. 1988—), Contemporary Art Soc. Projects Ltd. (dir. 1988—). Club: Turf (London). Office: 120 Mount St, London W1Y 5HB, England

WARD-MCLEMORE, ETHEL, research geophysicist, mathematician; b. Sylvarena, Miss., Jan. 22, 1908; d. William Robert and Frances Virginia (Douglas) Ward; B.A., Miss. Woman's Coll., 1928; M.A., U. N.C., 1929; postgrad. U. Chgo., 1931, Colo. Sch. Mines, 1941-42, So. Meth. U., 1962-64; m. Robert Henry McLemore, June 30, 1935; 1 dau., Mary Frances. Head math. dept. Miss. Jr. Coll., 1929-30; instr. chemistry, math. Miss. State Coll. for Women, 1930-32; research mathematician Humble Oil & Refining Co., Houston, 1933-36; ind. geophys. research, Tex. and Colo., 1936-42, Ft. Worth, 1946—; geophysicist United Geophys. Co., Pasadena, Cal., 1942-46; tchr. chemistry, physics, Hockaday Sch., Dallas, 1958-59, tchr. math., 1959-60; tchr. chemistry Ursuline Acad., Dallas, 1964-67, Hockaday Sch., 1968-69; geophys. cons., Dallas, 1957-77; bd. dirs. Geol. Info. Library of Dallas. Mem. Am. Math. Soc., Math. Assn. Am., Am. Geophys. Union (40 yr. Mem. Research Silver Pin award 1988), Seismol. Soc. Am., Soc. Exploration Geophysicists (50 yr. Gold cert. 1986), AAAS, Soc. Indsl. and Applied Math., Am. Chem. Soc., Inst. Math. Statistics, Tex Acad. Sci. (Appreciation cert. 1985), Dallas Geophys. Soc. (hon. life 1986, Disting. Service award 1988), Sigma Xi. Contbr. various articles to profl. jours.; author: China, 1983; also annotated bibliographies of sedimentary basins, 1981, 83. Home: 11625 Wander Ln Dallas TX 75230

WARE, MITCHELL, lawyer; b. Chgo., Dec. 27, 1933; s. Robert A. and Bertha (Peete) W.; m. Patricia R. Ford, Oct. 26, 1955 (div. Dec. 1967); children: Pamela Marie, Mitchell Gregory Robert; m. Nancy J. Herrmann, Dec. 20, 1973; 1 son, Michael Paul. BA, St. Ambrose Coll., 1955; JD, DePaul U., 1967. Bar: Ill. bar 1967. Narcotic agt. Ill. Div. Narcotic Control, 1960-66; law clk. U.S. Dist. Ct., 1966-67; TV news reporter WBBM-TV, Chgo., 1967-68; partner firm Mazza, Mazzio & Ware, Chgo., 1967-77; supt. Ill. Div. Narcotic Control, 1968-69, Ill. Bur. Investigation, Springfield, 1970-72; dep. supt. Chgo. Police Dept., 1972-78; sr. ptnr. firm Jones, Ware & Grenard, 1978—; div. dir. Regional Transp. Authority, 1978-83; mem. Pres. Nixon's Nat. Commn. Marijuana and Drug Abuse, 1971-73; prof. criminal law DePaul U., 1967-71; lectr., 1971-74. Author: Operational Handbook for Narcotic Law Enforcement Officers, 1975. Area chmn. Boy Scouts Am., 1969-71, exec. bd., 1972-82; trustee Fed. Defender Program; bd. dirs. Easter Seal Soc., Michael Reese Hosp. Served with AUS, 1955-57. Mem. Chgo. Bar Assn. (criminal law com. 1967-69), ABA, Ill. Bar Assn., Nat. Bar Assn., Fed. Bar Assn., Cook County Bar Assn., Am. Judicature Soc., Sisters of Blessed Sacrament Alumni Assn. (chmn. 1969—), Phi Alpha Delta. Office: Jones Ware & Grenard 180 N LaSalle St Suite 800 Chicago IL 60601

WARING, ALAN GEORGE, language educator; b. Liverpool, Eng., Dec. 12, 1929; s. Alfred and Isabelle (Battersby-Reid) W.; m. Patricia Joy Cunliffe, July 28, 1955; children: Caroline Mary Isabelle, Julian Paul. BA with honors, U. Manchester, Eng., 1952. Lang. specialist Fgn. and Commonwealth Office, London, 1953-57; lectr. Russian U. Leeds, Eng., 1957-65; head dept. Russian and Slavic Studies U. Sheffield, Eng., 1965—; cons. various bus., indsl., cultural orgns., London; adviser to govt. agys., Sheffield and London. Author: Russian Science Grammar, 1967, Comprehensive Russian, 1986. Mem. USSR Assn. (chmn. regional br. Great Britain 1986). Office: Sheffield U, Western Bank, Sheffield S10 2TN, England

WARING, JOHN ALFRED, research writer, lecturer, consultant; b. San Francisco, Dec. 30, 1913; s. John A. and Mary (Wheeler) W. Student pub. schs. Yachting, marine editor Chgo. Tribune, 1934-47; editor Kellogg Messenger, Kellogg Switchboard & Supply Co., Chgo., 1945-49; research cons. Baxter Internat. Econ. Research Bur., Inc., investment counselling, N.Y.C., 1951-52; research asst. mktg. research dept. Fuller, Smith & Ross, Inc., advt., N.Y.C., 1953; research writer, cons. Twentieth Century Fund, N.Y.C., 1953-54; research cons. Ford Motor Co., Dearborn, Mich., 1955; chief researcher Internat. Fact Finding Inst., Lawrence Orgn., public relations cons., N.Y.C., Washington, 1957-58; lectr. on energy, tech. and history

World Power Conf., Montreal, 1958, First Energy Inst., Am. U., Washington, 1960, Nat. Archives, Washington, 1962, Smithsonian Mus. History and Tech., Washington, 1968; guest lectr. social responsibility in sci. U. Md., 1972, guest lectr. sci. and environment, 1974; lectr. Internat. Conf. on Energy and Humanity, Queen Mary Coll., U. London, 1972, World Energy Conf., Detroit, 1974, History of Sci. Soc., Norwalk, Conn., 1974; research cons. PARM Project, Nat. Planning Assn., Washington, 1961-62; cons. Sci., Tech. and Fgn. Affairs Seminar, Fgn. Service Inst., Dept. State, 1965; vis. lectr. social implications of sci. for N. Am. U. Alta., Edmonton (Can.), 1981; lectr. Carnahan Conf. Harmonizing Tech. with Soc., U. Ky., Lexington, 1987; cons. U.S. energy statistics Smithsonian Instn., U.S. Bur. Census, 1960—; research cons. Program of Policy Studies in Sci. and Tech., George Washington U., 1967-68; del. U.S. commn. UNESCO Conf., San Francisco, 1969; inaugural lectr. Future of Sci. and Soc. in Am. Seminar U.S. Civil Service Commn., Washington, 1970; editorial cons. Nat. Acad. Engring., Washington, 1971; research cons., analyst Seminar Sch., Indsl. Coll. Armed Forces, Ft. Lesley J. McNair, Washington, 1958-74; researcher Office Plans and Programs, U.S. Army Med. Dept., Washington, 1975-76; asst. editor Def. Systems Mgmt. Rev. mag. Def. Systems Mgmt. Coll., Ft. Belvoir, Va., 1977-78; ret., 1979. Mem. Soc. History of Tech. (charter), History Sci. Soc., Technocracy, AAAS, Washington Acad. Scis., Washington Soc. Engrs. (sec. 1977), Phi Beta Kappa Assn. in D.C., Internat. Soc. Gen. Semantics, N.Y. Acad. Sci. Contbr. chpts. to books; compiler statis. tabulations. Home: 1320 S George Mason Dr Arlington VA 22204

WARIOBA, JOSEPH SINDE, prime minister, first vice president of Tanzania; b. Ikizu, Musoma, Mara, Tanzania, Sept. 3, 1940; s. Sinde Warioba; m. Evelyn Grace Ojjiki, 1969; children—Kipi, Jotham Mugabo, June Mwinuki, Christopher Keremba. LL.B. with honors, Univ. Coll. of Dar es Salaam, Tanzania, 1966. State atty. Atty. Gen.'s Chambers, Dar es Salaam, 1966-68; city solicitor City Council Dar es Salaam, 1968-70; divisional dir. Ministry Fgn. Affairs, Dar es Salaam, 1971-75; asst. atty. gen. Ministry Justice, Dar es Salaam, 1975-76, atty. gen., 1976, minister for justice, from 1983; prime minister, first v.p. Tanzania, Dar es Salaam, 1985—; del. UNESCO Conf., Paris, 1966, Refugee Conf., Addis Ababa, Ethiopia, 1967, Law of Treaties Conf., Vienna, Austria, 1968-69, OAU Council of Ministers, Addis Ababa, 1968, Human Rights Conf., Tehran, Iran, 1968, UN Gen. Assembly, intermittently, 1971-81, OAU Summits, intermittently, 1972-84, Law of Sea Confs., 1971-82. Mem. study group Tanzanyika African Nat. Union, 1967-74. Mem. Chama Cha Mapinduzi. Address: Office of Prime Minister, and First Vice Pres, Magogoni St, 3021 Dar es Salaam Tanzania other: PO Box 980, Dodoma Tanzania *

WARMAN, ERNEST A., research company executive, computer scientist; b. Peterborough, U.K., Nov. 13, 1935; s. Ernest Frederick and Ivy Irene (Newton) W.; m. Pauline Betty Punter, Apr. 11, 1959; children—Trina, Julie, Natalie. Higher Nat. Cert., Peterborough Tech. Coll., 1958; Cert. Engring., I.M.E., London, 1966; M.Tech., Brunel U., London, 1972, Ph.D., 1977. Tech. computer mgr. Perkins Engines, Peterborough, 1977; mng. dir. Productivity Internat., Inc., Peterborough 1978; prin. Inbucon, London, 1980; mng. dir. K Four Ltd., Peterborough, 1981—; dir. Cad Cam Publs.; reviewer E.E.C., Brussels; cons. D.O.I., London. Author numerous publs. Bd. govs. Peterborough County Sch., 1976. Recipient Silver Core award Internat. Fedn. Info. Processing, Geneva, 1983. Mem. Instn. Mech. Engrs., Instn. Prodn. Engrs., Brit. Computer Soc., Eurographics (founding mem.), Cad Cam Assn. (founding mem.), Assn. Computing Machinery. Office: K Four Ltd, 170 Park Rd, Peterborough PE1 2UF, England

WARNATH, MAXINE AMMER, organizational psychologist, educator; b. N.Y.C., Dec. 3, 1928; d. Philip and Jeanette Ammer; m. Charles Frederick Warnath, Aug. 20, 1952; children—Stephen Charles, Cindy Ruth. B.A., Bklyn. Coll., 1949; M.A., Columbia U., 1951, Ed.D., 1982. Lic. psychologist, Oreg. Various profl. positions Hunter Coll., U. Minn., U. Nebr., U. Oreg., 1951-62; asst. prof. psychology Oreg. Coll. Edn., Monmouth, 1962-77; assoc. prof. psychology, chmn. dept. psychology and spl. edn. Western Oreg. St. Coll., Monmouth, 1978-83, prof. 1986—, dir. organizational psychology program 1983—; pres. Profl. Perspectives, Salem, Oreg., 1987—; cons., dir. Orgn. Research and Devel., Salem, Oreg., 1982—, seminar leader Endeavors for Excellence program. Author: Power Dynamism, 1987. Mem. Oreg. Psychol. Assn. (pres. 1980-81, pres.-elect 1979-80, legis. liaison 1977-78), Am. Psychol. Assn. (com. pre-coll. psychology 1970-74), Western Psychol. Assn. Office: Orgn Research and Devel 708 Rural Ave S Salem OR 97302

WARNE, WILLIAM ELMO, irrigationist; b. nr. Seafield, Ind., Sept. 2, 1905; s. William Rufus and Nettie Jane (Williams) W.; m. Edith Margaret Peterson, July 9, 1929; children—Jane Ingrid (Mrs. David C. Beeder), William Robert, Margaret Edith (Mrs. John W. Monroe). A.B., U. Calif., 1927; D.Econs., Yonsei U., Seoul, 1959; LL.D., Seoul Nat. U., 1959. Reporter San Francisco Bull. and Oakland (Calif.) Post-Enquirer, 1925-27; news editor Brawley (Calif.) News, 1927, Calexico (Calif.) Chronicle, 1927-28; editor, night mgr. Los Angeles bur. A.P., 1928-31, corr. San Diego bur., 1931-33, Washington corr., 1933-35; editor, bur. reclamation Dept. Interior, 1935-37; on staff Third World Power Conf., 1936; assoc. to reviewing com. Nat. Resources Com. on preparation "Drainage Basin Problems and Programs, 1936, mem. editorial com. for revision, 1937; chief of information Bur. Reclamation, 1937-42; co-dir. (with Harlan H. Barrows) Columbia Basin Joint Investigations, 1939-42; chief of staff, war prodn. drive WPB, 1942; asst. dir. div. power Dept. Interior, 1942-43, dept. dir. information, 1943; asst. commr. Bur. Reclamation, 1943-47; apptd. asst. sec. Dept. Interior, 1947, asst. sec. Water and Power Devel., 1950-51; U.S. minister charge tech. cooperation Iran, 1951-55, Brazil, 1955-56; U.S. minister and econ. coordinator for Korea, 1956-59; dir. Cal. Dept. Fish and Game, 1959-60, Dept. Agr., 1960-61, Dept. Water Resources, 1961-67; v.p. water resources Devel. and Resources Corp., 1967-69; resources cons. 1969—; pres. Warne & Blanton Pubs. Inc., 1985—, Warne Walnut Wrancho, Inc., 1979—; Disting. Practitioner in Residence Sch. Pub. Adminstrn., U. So. Calif. at Sacramento, 1976-78; adminstr. Resources Agy. of Calif., 1961-63; Chmn. Pres.'s Com. on San Diego Water Supply, 1944-46; chmn. Fed. Inter-Agy. River Basin Com., 1948, Fed. Com. on Alaskan Devel., 1948; pres. Group Health Assn., Inc., 1947-51; chmn. U.S. delegation 2d Inter-Am. Conf. Indian Life, Cuzco, Peru, 1949; U.S. del. 4th World Power Conf., London, Eng., 1950; mem. Calif. Water Pollution Control Bd., 1959-67; vice chmn. 1960-62; mem. water pollution control adv. bd. Dept. Health, Edn. and Welfare, 1962-65, cons., 1966-67; chmn. Calif. delegation Western States Water Council, 1965-67. Author: Mission for Peace—Point 4 in Iran, 1956, The Bureau of Reclamation, 1973, How the Colorado River Was Spent, 1975, The Need to Institutionalize Desalting, 1978; prin. author: The California Experience with Mass Transfers of Water over Long Distances, 1978. Served as 2d lt. O.R.C., 1927-37. Recipient Distinguished Service award Dept. Interior, 1951; Distinguished Pub. Service Honor award FOA, 1955; Order of Crown Shah of Iran, 1955; Outstanding Service citation UN Command, 1959. Mem. Nat. Acad. Pub. Adminstrn. (chmn. standing com. on environ. and resources mgmt. 1971-78), Nat. Water Supply Improvement Assn. (pres. 1978-80, Lifetime Achievement award 1984), Sigma Delta Chi, Lambda Chi Alpha. Clubs: Sutter (Sacramento); Nat. Press (Washington); Explorers (N.Y.C.). Home: 2090 8th Ave Sacramento CA 95818

WARNER, CHARLES WILLIAM, JR., real estate broker, developer; b. Columbus, Ohio, Apr. 11, 1928; s. Charles William and Elsie (Burns) W.; m. Marjorie Lucille Dillin, July 20, 1952; children—Belinda Mae, Charles William III. B.Mus., Ohio State U., 1951. With Don M. Casto Orgn., Columbus, Ohio, 1951-69; pres. Chuck Warner & Assocs., Columbus, 1969—. Chancel choir dir. Northwest United Meth. Ch., Columbus, 1963-75, Northwest Evang. Christian Ch., 1975—. Mem. Nat. Assn. Realtors, Ohio Assn. Realtors, Columbus Bd. Realtors, Mansfield Bd. Realtors, Am. Fedn. Musicians. Evangelical Christian. Office: Chuck Warner & Assocs 5900 Sanmill Rd Dublin OH 43017

WARNER, DAVID, actor; b. Manchester, Eng., July 29, 1941; s. Herbert Simon Warner. Ed. Royal Acad. Dramatic Art. Joined Royal Shakespeare Co., 1963; numerous appearances in theatrical prodns., Eng., 1963—; (films) include Tom Jones, 1963, Morgan—A Suitable Case for Treatment, 1966, Work is a Four Letter Word, 1967, The Bofors Gun, 1968, The Ballad of Cable Hogue, 1970, Straw Dogs, 1971, A Doll's House, 1972, The Omen, 1975, Cross of Iron, 1976, The Disappearance, 1977, The Thirty Nine Steps, 1978, Nightwing, 1979, Time after Time, 1979, The Island, 1980; (TV appearances) include Clouds of Glory, 1977, Holocaust, 1977, (TV movies) include SOS Titanic, 1979, Masada, 1981, Charlie, 1984. Address: care Leading Artists Ltd, 60 Saint James's St, London SW1 England *

WARNER, JOHN HILLIARD, JR., technical services, military systems and software company executive; b. Santa Monica, Calif., Mar. 2, 1941; s. John Hilliard and Irene Anne (Oliva) W.; m. Helga Magdalena Farrington, Sept. 4, 1961; children: Tania Renee, James Michael. BS in Engring., UCLA, 1963, MS in Engring., 1965, PhD in Engring., 1967. Mem. staff Marquardt Corp., Van Nuys, Calif., 1963; mem. faculty West Coast U., Los Angeles, 1969-72; mem. staff TRW Systems Group, Redondo Beach, Calif., 1967-70, sect. mgr., 1970-73; mem. staff Sci. Applications Internat. Corp., San Diego, 1973-75, asst. v.p., 1975-77, v.p., 1977-80, corp. v.p., 1980-81, sr. v.p., 1981-87, sector v.p., 1987—, also bd. dirs.; cons. Rand Corp., Santa Monica, 1964-66. Contbr. articles to profl. jours. Mem. Am. Inst. Aeros. and Astronautics, Assn. of U.S. Army, Air Force Assn., Am. Def. Preparedness Assn., Am. Security Council, Armed Forces Communications & Electronics Assn., Navy League of U.S., Sigma Nu. Methodist. Office: Sci Applications Internat Corp 10260 Campus Point Dr San Diego CA 92121

WARNER, JOHN MCVICKER, construction company executive; b. Melbourne, Australia, Mar. 22, 1930; s. Richard McVicker and Ada Clare (Robinson) W.; m. Judith Elizabeth Longney, Jan. 5, 1955; children—Paul McVicker, Amanda, Mark Richardson. Diploma of Architecture, Royal Melbourne Inst. Tech., 1956. Sales mgr. Picton Hopkins & Son, P/L, Melbourne, 1948-56, 57-67; store architect Myer Emporium, Melbourne, 1956-57; gen. mgr. Thermalock P/L, Melbourne, 1967-69; mng. dir. Assoc. Insulation Holdings P/L, Sydney, Australia, 1972-86; ret. 1988. Fellow Royal Australian Inst. Architects. Liberal. Mem. Ch. of England. Club: Melbourne Cricket. Home: 4 Laing Ave, Killara NSW 2071, Australia

WARNER, JOHN WILLIAM, senator; b. Washington, Feb. 18, 1927; s. John William and Martha Stuart (Budd) W.; m. Elizabeth Taylor, 1976 (div. 1982); children by previous marriage: Mary Conover, Virginia Stuart, John William IV. B.S., Washington and Lee U., 1949; LL.B., U. Va., 1953. Law clk. to U.S. judge 1953-54, spl. asst. to U.S. atty., 1956-57; asst. U.S. atty. Dept. Justice, 1957-60; ptnr. Hogan & Hartson, 1960-68; undersec. of navy 1969-72, sec. of navy, 1972-74; adminstr. Am. Revolution Bicentennial Adminstrn., 1974-76; U.S. senator from Va. 1979—. Served with USNR, 1944-46; to capt. USMCR, 1949-52. Mem. Bar Assn. D.C. Republican. Episcopalian. Club: Metropolitan. Home: Atoka Farm PO Box 1320 Middleburg VA 22117 Office: Office of the Senate 421 Russell Senate Bldg Washington DC 20510

WARNER, MARTIN MICHAEL, philosophy educator; b. Epsom, Surrey, U.K., Sept. 27, 1940; s. Hugh Compton and Nancy le Plastrier (Owen) W.; m. Veronica Smith, July 28, 1972. M.A., Oxford U., 1962; B.Phil., 1965. Lectr. philosophy U. Coll. North Wales, Bangor, 1965-69, U. Warwick, Coventry, U.K., 1969—, program dir. Ctr. for Research in Philosophy and Literature, 1985-87. Contbr. articles, critical notices and revs. to profl. lit.; editorial adv. bd. Philosophy and Lit., 1982—. Mem. Royal Inst. Philosophy (mem. council 1981—, exec. com. 1982—), Soc. for Applied Philosophy (exec. com. 1983—), Aristotelian Soc., Mind Soc. Office: U Warwick, Dept Philosophy, Coventry CV4 7AL, England

WARNER, NANCY ELIZABETH, pathologist; b. Dixon, Ill., July 8, 1923; d. Henry Chester and Lucile (Mertz) W. B.S., U. Chgo., 1944, M.D., 1949. Intern U. Chgo. Clinics, 1949-50, asst. resident in pathology, 1950-53; resident in pathology Cedars of Lebanon Hosp., Los Angeles, 1953-54; asst. pathologist Cedars of Lebanon Hosp., 1954-58, asso. dir. div. labs., 1965-66; asst. prof. pathology U. Chgo., 1958-59, asso. prof., 1959-65; dir. U. Chgo. (Lab. Surg. Pathology), 1959-65; asso. prof. U. Wash. Sch. Medicine, Seattle, 1966-67; asso. prof. pathology U. So. Calif. Sch. Medicine, 1967-69, prof. pathology, 1969—, chmn. dept., 1972-83, asso. dean for academic affairs, 1977—; attending physician Med. Center, U. So. Calif. and U. So. Calif. Norris Cancer Hosp.; chief pathologist Womens Hosp. Los Angeles County/U. So. Calif. Med. Center, 1968-72, dir. labs. and pathology, 1972-83; cons. Barlow Sanatorium and Hosp., 1968—. Fellow Coll. Am. Pathologists, Am. Soc. Clin. Pathologists; mem. AAAS, AMA, U. Chgo. Alumni Assn., D.A.R., Daus. Founders and Patriots, Am. Assn. Pathologists, Calif. Soc. Pathologists, Am. Assn. Anatomists, Endocrine Soc., Los Angeles Soc. Pathologists, Am. Soc. Cytology, Microcirculatory Soc., European Soc. Microcirculation, Internat. Acad. Pathology, Los Angeles Acad. Medicine, Colonial Dames Am., Nat. Soc. Magna Charta Dames, Nat. Soc. U.S. Daus. 1812, Gen. Soc. Mayflower Descs., Sigma Xi, Alpha Omega Alpha. Office: Univ Southern Calif Sch Medicine 1441 Eastlake Ave Los Angeles CA 90033

WARNER, RAWLEIGH, JR., oil company executive; b. Chgo., Feb. 13, 1921; s. Rawleigh and Dorothy (Haskins) W.; m. Mary Ann deClairmont, Nov. 2, 1946; children: Alison W. Pyne, Suzanne W. Parsons. Grad., Lawrenceville (N.J.) Sch., 1940; A.B. cum laude, Princeton U., 1943. Sec., treas. Warner Bard Co., Chgo., 1946-48; with Continental Oil Co., 1948-53; asst. treas. Continental Oil Co., Houston, 1953-54; treas. Socony-Vacuum Overseas Supply Co., 1953-55; asst. treas. Mobil Overseas Oil Co., 1955-56; mgr. econs. dept., then mgr. Middle East dept. Socony Mobil Oil Co. Inc., 1956-59; regional v.p. Mobil Internat. Oil Co., 1959-60, exec. v.p., 1960-63, pres., 1963-64; exec. v.p., dir. Mobil Oil Corp. (formerly Socony Mobil Oil Co., Inc.), 1964, pres., 1965-69, chmn. bd., chief exec. officer, 1969-86; chmn. Mobil Corp., 1976-86; dir. Caterpillar Tractor Co., Chem. Bank-Chem. N.Y. Corp., Am. Tel. & Tel. Co., Am. Express Co., Allied-Signal Inc., Squibb Corp. Mem. bus. council Pres.'s Commn. on Arts and Humanities; trustee Solomon R. Guggenheim Found., Mayo Found. Served to capt. F.A. AUS, 1943-46. Decorated Purple Heart, Bronze Star, Silver Star. Mem. Am. Petroleum Inst. Republican. Presbyn. Clubs: Augusta (Ga.) Nat. Golf; Links (N.Y.C.); New Canaan Country; Blind Brook (Port Chester, N.Y.); Jupiter Island (Hobe Sound, Fla.); Chicago; Seminole (North Palm Beach, Fla.). Home: 24 Riverview Rd Hobe Sound FL 33475 Office: Mobil Corp 150 E 42d St New York NY 10017

WARNER, TEDDY FLEMING, lawyer; b. Findlay, Ohio, Jan. 3, 1932; s. Freeman Dininger and Marjorie (Fleming) W.; m. Carolyn Jean Warner, June 12, 1958; children—Wendy Ann, Randall Scott. A.A., Phoenix Coll., 1955; B.A. with distinction, Ariz. State U., 1956; J.D., U. Ariz., 1959. Bar: Ariz. 1959, U.S. Dist. Ct. Ariz. 1959, U.S. Supreme Ct. 1971. Ptnr. Warner Angle Roper & Hallam P.C. and predecessors, Phoenix, 1962—; sr. ptnr., pres., 1982—; lectr. legal econs. and pro bono legal services to poor programs. Bd. dirs. Phoenix and Valley of Sun YMCA, 1970-84, pres., 1977; bd. dirs. Sagauro-Grand Canyon chpt. March of Dimes/Birth Defects Found., 1968-82, chmn., 1972-73, state chmn., 1974-82, mem. nat. council chpt. vols., 1979-82; bd. dirs. Vol. Bur., 1975; life mem. Fiesta Bowl Com., 1979-84; chmn. bd. trustees Ariz. Perinatal Trust, 1980—; mem. Ariz. Acad.; bd. visitors Ariz. State U. Sch. Law, 1979—; mem Ariz. Supreme Ct. Com. on Fitness and Character, 1983—. Served with USAF, 1951-54. Fellow Am. Bar Found., Ariz. Bar Found. (founding, Pro Bono Service award 1987); mem. Maricopa County Bar Assn. (pres., dir. 1981), Maricopa County Bar Found. (charter), State Bar Ariz. (chmn. com. on del. legal services com.), ABA (ho. of dels. 1981—, delivery legal services com.), Ariz. State Law Soc., Law Coll. Assn. U. Ariz., Phi Delta Phi, Delta Sigma Phi. Republican. Clubs: Ariz. Country, Ariz. (sec., dir. 1971-73), Pinetop Country, Phoenix Country. Office: 3550 N Central Ave Suite 1700 Phoenix AZ 85012

WARNER, THEODORE KUGLER, JR., lawyer; b. Phila., Sept. 13, 1909; s. Theodore Kugler and Anna (Allen) W.; m. Dorothy Wark Hoehler, Nov. 23, 1935; children—Betsy Ann (Mrs. Douglas R. Bulcher), Peter Joyce. A.B., U. Pa., 1931, LL.B. cum laude, 1934. Bar: Pa. 1934. With Pa. R.R., Phila., 1934-70; chief tax counsel Pa. R.R., 1952-58, dir. taxation, 1958-68, v.p. taxes, 1968, v.p. accounting and taxes, 1968-69, v.p. corp. adminstrn., 1969-70; pres. Can. So. Ry., 1968-70; v.p. Pitts. & Lake Erie R.R., 1968-70; officer, dir. other Penn Central cos. 1968-70; counsel Duane, Morris & Heckscher, Phila., 1970-71, Harper & Driver, 1975—; lectr. on consol. returns various tax forums. Bd. suprs., Easttown Twp., Pa., 1962-70, chmn., 1966-70. Mem. Nat. Tax Assn. (pres. 1965-66), Am. Law Inst. (life mem.), Am., Pa. bar assns., Order of Coif, Tau Kappa Epsilon. Republican. Lutheran. Clubs: Aronimink Golf Club, Radnor Hunt, Union League. Lodge: Masons (33 deg., mem. com. on masonic homes 1970-84, chmn. 1975-77, 81-83, Franklin medal 1983). Home: 39 Old Covered Bridge Rd Newtown Square PA 19073 Office: Ave of Arts Bldg Philadelphia PA 19107

WARNICK, CHARLES TERRY, research biochemist; b. Brigham City, Utah, Jan. 29, 1943; s. Charles W. and Blanche (Richards) W.; m. Sandra Hathaway, Sept. 2, 1970; children: Derek, Darren, Bryan, Amber, Ashlee. BS, Brigham Young U., 1965; PhD, U. Utah, 1971. Postdoctoral fellow U. Alta., Edmonton, Alta., Can., 1970-72; research assoc. U. Utah, Salt Lake City, 1972-74, research instr., 1974-79, asst. research prof., 1979-81; asst. prof. biochemistry Latter-day Saints Hosp. and U. Utah, Salt Lake City, 1981—, cons. clin. labs., 1985—, also dir. research lab. Contbr. articles to profl. jours. Fellow NASA, 1965, Nat. Cancer Inst. Can., 1970; grantee NIH, 1978, Utah Heart Assn., 1982. Mem. AAAS, Am. Chem. Soc., N.Y. Acad. Sci. Mormon. Office: Latter-day Saints Hosp Research Lab 325 8th Ave Salt Lake City UT 84143

WARNKEN, VIRGINIA MURIEL THOMPSON, social worker; b. Anadarko, Okla., Aug. 13, 1927; d. Sam Monroe and Ruth L. (McAllister) Thompson; A.B., Okla. U., 1946; M.S.W., Washington U., 1949; m. Douglas Richard Warnken, Sept. 16, 1957; 1 son, William Monroe. Med. social cons. Crippled Children's Services, Little Rock, 1950-54; supr. VA Hosp., Little Rock, 1954-55; asst. prof. U. Tenn. Sch. Social Work, Nashville, 1955-57; dir. social services N.Y. State Rehab. Hosp., Rockland County, 1957-58; asst. prof. U. Chgo. Sch. Social Service Adminstrn., 1958-59; free lance editor, 1960—; instr. evening div. Coll. of Notre Dame, Belmont, Calif., 1967-68; asso. Mills Hosp., San Mateo, Calif., 1978—; med. aux. Community Hosp., Pacific Grove, Calif., 1980—. Com. mem. C. of C. Miss Belmont Pageant, 1971-84, co-chmn., 1975-78. U.S. Children's Bur. scholar, 1947-49. Mem. Assn. Crippled Children and Adults (dir. 1952-55), Assn. Mentally Retarded (dir. 1953-55), Am. Assn. Med. Social Workers (practice chmn. 1954-55), Nat. Assn. Social Workers (dir. 1962-66), Acad. Cert. Social Workers, Am. Assn. Med. Social Workers, Nat. Rehab. Assn., Am. Psychol. Assn., Am. Orthopsychiat. Assn., Council Social Work Edn. Democrat. Presbyterian. Clubs: Carmel Valley Golf and Country, Peninsula Golf and Country, Monterey Golf and Country (Palm Desert, Calif.). Author: Annotated Bibliography of Medical Information and Terminology, 1956. Address: 1399 Bel Aire Rd San Mateo CA 94402

WARNOCK, CURTLON LEE, lawyer, consultant; b. Mpls., Nov. 30, 1954; s. Lowell Wayne and Peggy Joan (Teague) W.; married, 1979; children: Curtlon Lee II, Joshua Douthit, Vanessa Ann. Student, Baylor U., 1973-77, JD, 1979. Bar: Tex. 1979, U.S. Dist. Ct. (so. dist.) Tex. 1981, U.S. Supreme Ct. 1986. Assoc. Culpepper & Conway, Houston, 1979-81; atty. Pogo Producing Co., Houston, 1981-86; sr. atty. Meridian Oil Inc., Houston, 1986—. Editor newspaper First Amendment, 1978. Mem. Com. for Pub. Info. Radio Show, Waco, Tex., 1978; bd. dirs., cons. Acad. Devel. Service, Inc., Houston, 1979—; counselor Baylor U. Law Sch., Waco, 1980; bd. dirs. Hugh O'Brien Youth Found., Houston, 1982-83. Nat. Merit scholar, Baylor U., 1973. Mem. ABA, Houston Bar Assn., Tex. Bar Assn., Houston Young Lawyers, Houston Jaycees (bd. dirs., legal counsel 1979-82). Republican. Baptist. Home: 410 River Forest Ct Houston TX 77079 Office: Meridian Oil Inc 2919 Allen Pkwy Suite 1000 Houston TX 77210

WARREN, BRUCE ALBERT, pathology educator, adminstrator; b. Sydney, New South Wales, Australia, Nov. 2, 1934; s. Arthur Roy and Albertha Lydia (Davis) W.; m. Diana Mary King, Aug. 14, 1964; children—Deborah Lynette, Dawson Grant. B.Sc. in Medicine, Sydney U., 1957, M.B.B.S., 1959; D.Phil., Oxford U., 1964, D.Sc., 1984. Intern, resident Sydney Hosp., 1959-61; researcher Oxford U., Eng., 1962-64, lectr., 1966-68; from asst. prof. to assoc. prof. U. Western Ont., Can., 1968-74, prof. pathology, 1974-80; clin. prof. pathology Prince Henry Hosp., U. New South Wales, 1980-83, prof. pathology, head anatomical pathology, 1983—. Co-author: Basic Histology, 1983; editor: Atheroembolism, 1986, Pathology, 1988—; contbr. articles to profl. jours. Mem. editorial bd. Haemostasis, 1975-83, Cancer Letters, 1977-84. Research grantee Med. Research Council Can., 1969-73, Ont. Heart Found., 1972-79, Nat. Cancer Inst. Can., 1968-80, Ont. Ministry Health, 1977-80; Brit. Commonwealth scholar, 1962-64. Fellow Royal Microscopical Soc. (life), Royal Soc. Medicine, Royal Coll. Pathologists of Australasia, Royal Coll. Pathologists; mem. Brit. Med. Assn., AAAS (life), Royal Soc. New South Wales (pres. 1981-82, v.p. 1982-85). Anglican. Clubs: Sr. Common Room, Univ. New South Wales; The Athenaeum (London). Home: 8 Arcadia St, Coogee NSW 2034, Australia Office: Dept Anatomical Pathology, The Prince Henry Hosp, Little Bay NSW 2036, Australia

WARREN, HOLLAND DOUGLAS, research physicist; b. Wilkes County, N.C., July 31, 1932; s. Henry Harrison and Nannie (Shaver) W.; m. Nancy Wall, May 21, 1955; children—Douglas Alan, Jill Jeneen, Karen Kay. B.S. in Math, Wake Forest U., 1959; M.S. in Physics, U. Va., 1961, Ph.D., 1963. Research assoc. U. Va., summers 1960-62; devel. physicist Celanese Corp., Charlotte, N.C., 1963-64; sr. physicist Babcock & Wilcox Co., Lynchburg, Va., 1964-69, research specialist, 1969-87, adv. engr., 1987—. Contbr. numerous articles to profl. jours. Served with USN, 1951-55. Mem. Am. Phys. Soc., Am. Nuclear Soc. (Va. sect.), Phi Beta Kappa, Kappa Mu Epsilon. Republican. Baptist. Research on theoretical and exptl. devel. of self-powered instrumentation for application inside the cores of nuclear power plants (incore instrumentation); patentee in field. Office: Babcock & Wilcox Co PO Box 10935 Lynchburg VA 24506-0935

WARREN, KENDRA S., information systems engineer; b. Champaign, Ill., Aug. 28, 1954; d. Kenneth E. and Pat E. (Miduri) W.; m. James Robert Russell, Apr. 27, 1984. B.A. in Anthropology, Wright State U., 1975; postgrad. in info. mgmt. Wright State U., 1984—; studies in program mgmt. Defense Systems Mgmt. Coll., 1987; also certs. from various U.S. Air Force and computer vendor tng. classes. Investigator, Smith & Schnacke, Attys. at Law, Dayton, Ohio, 1973-76; claims investigator State Farm Fire & Casualty, Dayton, 1976-79; computer programmer U.S. Air Force, Wright-Patterson AFB, Ohio, 1981-85, computer systems analyst, 1985-87, computer security and communications analyst, 1987; chief Systems Engring. Br., Reliability and Maintainability Info. System Program Mgmt. Office, 1987—. Author application software packages for use in vol. activities. Coordinator disaster vols. ARC, Dayton, 1979-84, chmn. disaster services, 1984-86, chmn. computer systems com., 1985—; precinct capt., mem. central com. Montgomery County Republican Party, Ohio, 1977-79, ward leader, mem. exec. com., 1979-81, also active election campaign coms., 1974-82; bd. dirs. Wright-Patterson AFB chpt. ARC, 1983—. Recipient citation for service Ohio Ho. of Reps., 1982, Disting. Service award Greater Dayton Jaycees, 1984; named One of Outstanding Young Women Am., 1983; scholar NSF Summer Linguistics Inst., No. Ariz. U., Flagstaff, 1971. Mem. Nat. Assn. Female Execs., Assn. Women in Computing. Home: 962 Ferndale Ave Dayton OH 45406 Office: USAF Logistics Command LMSC/SMI Tech Data Div Patterson AFB OH 45433

WARREN, LAWRENCE DALE, insurance and trade companies executive; b. Scottsburg, Ind., Jan. 4, 1944; s. Lionel G. and Edna Marie (Hollin) W.; student Purdue U., 1961-65; m. Esther Sibal, Aug. 7, 1976; children—Alana Kay, Douglas Dale, Kirsten, Kourtney. Owner, pres. Products Unltd., Inc., Houston, 1967-69; ter. mgr. W. R. Grace & Co., Houston, 1970-76; owner L. Warren & Co., Houston, 1965—; owner, pres. Warren Internat., Inc., 1976—, pres. Ledak, Inc., 1984—; dir. Delta Gulf Industries, Houston, Continental Casing Inc. Mem. Producers Council, Inc. (pres. 1975-76), Constrn. Specifications Inst. (membership chmn. 1973-74), Million Dollar Round Table, Internat. Platform. Assn. Republican. Methodist. Home: 506 Magic Oaks Dr Spring TX 77388 Office: 5616 Spring-Cypress Rd Spring TX 77379

WARREN, RICHARD WAYNE, obstetrician and gynecologist; b. Puxico, Mo., Nov. 26, 1935; s. Martin R. and Sarah E. (Crump) W.; B.A., U. Calif., Berkeley, 1957; M.D., Stanford, 1961; m. Rosalie J. Franzola, Aug. 16, 1959; children—Lani Marie, Richard W., Paul D. Intern, Oakland (Calif.) Naval Hosp., 1961-62; resident in ob-gyn Stanford Med. Center (Calif.), 1964-67; practice medicine specializing in ob-gyn, Mountain View, Calif., 1967—; mem. staff Stanford and El Camino hosps.; pres. Richard W. Warren M.D., Inc.; assoc. clin. prof. ob-gyn Stanford Sch. Medicine. Served with USN, 1961-64. Diplomate Am. Bd. Ob-Gyn. Fellow Am. Coll. Ob-Gyn; mem. AMA, Calif. Med. Assn., San Francisco Gynecol. Soc., Peninsula Gynecol. Soc., Am. Assn. Gynecologic Laparoscopists, Assn. Profs. Gynecology and

Obstetrics, Royal Soc. Medicine. Contbr. articles to profl. jours. Home: 102 Atherton Ave Atherton CA 94025 Office: 2500 Hospital Dr Mountain View CA 94040

WARREN, ROBERT PENN, writer, poet, educator; b. Guthrie, Ky., Apr. 24, 1905; s. Robert Franklin and Anna Ruth (Penn) W.; m. Emma Brescia, Sept. 12, 1930 (div. 1950); m. Eleanor Clark, 1952; children: Rosanna, Gabriel Penn. B.A. summa cum laude, Vanderbilt U., 1925; M.A., U. Calif., 1927; postgrad., Yale, 1927-28; B.Litt. (Rhodes scholar), Oxford U., 1930; Litt.D., U. Louisville, Colby Coll., U. Ky., Swarthmore Coll., Harvard U., Yale U., Fairfield U., Wesleyan U., Southwestern Coll. at Memphis, U. South, U. New Haven, Johns Hopkins U., Ariz. State U., Dartmouth Coll., Monmouth Coll., 1971, NYU, 1983, Oxford U., 1963; L.H.D., Kenyon Coll.; LL.D., U. Bridgeport. Mem. Fugitive Group of Poets, 1923-25; asst. prof. English, Southwestern Coll., Memphis, 1930-31; acting asst. prof. Vanderbilt U., 1931-34; asst. prof. La. State U., 1934-36, asso. prof., 1936-42; prof. English, U. Minn., 1942-50; prof. playwrighting Yale U., 1951-56, prof. English, 1961-73, prof. emeritus, 1973—; chair of poetry Library of Congress, 1944-45, cons. in poetry, 1986; mem. staff Writer Conf. U. Colo., 1936, 37, 40, Olivet Coll., 1940; vis. lectr. U. Iowa, 1941; Jefferson lectr. NEH, 1974. Author: novel World Enough and Time, 1950; poem Brother to Dragons, new version, 1979; novel Band of Angels, 1955, Segregation, 1956; poems Promises, 1957; Selected Essays, 1958; poems The Cave, 1959; poetry You, Emperors and Others, 1960, The Legacy of the Civil War, 1961; novel Wilderness, 1961, Flood, 1964; Who Speaks for the Negro, 1965, Selected Poems New and Old, 1923-1966, 1966; poems Incarnations, 1968; poetry Audubon: A Vision, 1969, Homage to Theodore Dreiser, 1971; Author of: Meet Me in The Green Glen; Author: Or Else-Poem/Poems 1968-74, 1975, Democracy and Poetry, 1975, Selected Poems: 1923-75, 1977; novel A Place To Come To, 1977; Now and Then: Poems 1976-79, Being Here: Poems, 1978-79, 80, Rumor Verified, Poems, 1981, Chief Joseph of the Nez Perce, a poem, 1983, New and Selected Poems 1923-1985, 1985; editor or co-editor other books; a founder and editor: The So. Rev., 1935-42. Poet laureate of U.S., 1986—; recipient Houghton Mifflin Lit. Fellowship award, 1936, Levinson prize Poetry: A Mag. of Verse, 1936, Caroline Sinkler prize Poetry Soc. S.C., 1936, 37, 38, Guggenheim fellow in writing, 1939-40, 47-48, Shelley prize for poetry, 1942, Pulitzer prize for fiction, 1947, Robert Meltzer award Screen Writers Guild, 1949, Sidney Hillman award, 1957, Pulitzer prize in poetry, 1957, 81, Edna St. Vincent Millay prize Am. Poetry Soc., 1958, Nat. Book award for poetry, 1958, Irita Van Doren Lit. award N.Y. Herald Tribune, 1965, Bollingen prize in poetry Yale U., 1967, Van Wyck Brooks award for poetry, 1970, Nat. medal for Lit., 1970, award for Lit., U. S.C., 1973, Emerson-Thoreau award Am. Acad. Arts and Scis., 1975, Copernicus prize Am. Acad. Poets, 1975, Harriet Monroe award for poetry, 1979, Presdl. Medal of Freedom, 1980, Common Wealth award, 1980, Gold medal for poetry Am. Acad. and Inst. Arts & Letters, 1985, Prize fellowship McArthur Found., 1981, Nat. Medal of Arts, 1987. Mem. Am. Acad. Arts and Letters, Acad. Arts and Scis., Am. Philos. Soc., Acad. Am. Poets (chancellor). Home: 2495 Redding Rd Fairfield CT 06430

WARREN, RUSSELL JAMES, financial consulting company executive; b. Cleve., July 28, 1938; s. Harold Fulton and Agnes Elmina (Hawkswell) W.; BS, Case Western Res. U., 1960; MBA, Harvard U., 1962; m. Doris Helen Kenyeres, June 6, 1964. With Ernst & Whinney, Cleve., 1962-87, partner in charge merger and acquisition services, 1976-87; pres. The TransAction Group, Inc., 1987—. Co-author: Implementing Mergers and Acquisitions in the Financial Services Industry, 1985; assoc. editor Jour. Corp. Growth, 1986-87, mem. editorial bd., 1988—; contbg. editor Jour. Buyouts and Acquisitions, 1984-86; contbg. author venture capital financing study conducted in five selected countries for Asian Devel. Bank, Malaysia, Indonesia, Pakistan, Sri Lanka, Thailand, 1986. Trustee, Case Western Res. U., 1980—; dir. Univ. Tech., Inc.; mem. bd. zoning appeals City of Lyndhurst, 1978—, chmn., 1980-82. CPA, Ohio. Mem. Am. Inst. CPAs, Ohio Soc. CPAs, Assn. for Corp. Growth (v.p. Cleve. chpt. 1983-86, pres. 1986-87), Cleve. Com. on Fgn. Relations, Newcomen Soc. Clubs: Mayfield Country, Catawba Island (Port Clinton, Ohio), Cleve. Athletic; Harvard (N.Y.C.); Put-in-Bay (Ohio) Yacht. Lodge: Jesters. Office: The TransAction Group 1666 Hanna Bldg Cleveland OH 44115-2001

WARREN, SHERI LYNN, news company executive; b. Rock Island, Ill., May 22, 1959; d. Jerry Roger and Kay Constance (Smith) W. BS in Journalism, U. Ill., 1981. Reader mail corr., researcher CBS Mag.-Woman's Day, N.Y.C., 1981-82, editorial asst. to editor-in-chief, 1982, art dept. coordinator, asst. art dir., 1983; communications coordinator Kable News Co., Inc., N.Y.C., 1984-85, advt. and promotion mgr., 1985-86; dir. promotions and communications Curtis Circulation Co., Inc., Hackensack, N.J., 1985—. Recipient Scripps-Howard award, 1980, Hugh Hefner Mag. award, 1981. Mem. Nat. Assn. Female Execs., Women in Communications, Advt. Women N.Y., Reps., Execs. and Distbrs., Internat. Newsstand Circulation Execs. Assn., Fidelity Council Ladies Aux. (recording sec.). Democrat. Roman Catholic. Avocations: photography, backgammon, sports, music. Home: 277 Driggs Ave Brooklyn NY 11222 Office: Curtis Circulation Co Inc 433 Hackensack Ave Hackensack NJ 07601

WARREN, WILLIAM CLEMENTS, lawyer, educator; b. Paris, Tex., Feb. 3, 1909; s. Archibald Levy and Elma (Clements) W.; m. Diana June Peel Willock, Jan. 13, 1945; children—Robert Peel, Larissa Eve, William Liversidge. A.B., U. Tex., 1930, A.M., 1931; LL.B., Harvard U., 1935; LL.D. (hon.), L.I. U., 1955, Columbia U., 1981; Dr. rer. pol., U. Basle, 1965. Bar: Ohio 1937, N.Y. 1952, D.C. 1959. Assoc. Davis, Polk & Wardwell, N.Y.C., 1935-37; assoc. Holiday, Grossman & McAfee, Cleve., 1937-42; assoc. Milbank, Tweed, Hadley & McCloy, N.Y.C., 1942-47; prof. law Western Res. U., Cleve., 1937-42; mem. faculty Columbia Law Sch., N.Y.C., 1946-82, Kent prof. law, 1959-77, Kent prof. emeritus, 1977—, dean, 1952-70, dean emeritus, 1970—; ptnr. Roberts & Holland, N.Y.C., 1957—; dir. Bankers Securities Corp., Guardian Life Ins. Co. Am., Sandoz, Inc., Sandoz United States, Inc., Sterling Nat. Bank & Trust Co. N.Y.C., CSS Industries, Aston-Martin LaGonda Group, Aladan Corp., Westward Communications; mem. N.Am. adv. bd. Swissair. Served as lt. col. U.S. Army, 1943-46. Decorated Bronze Star (2), Legion of Merit; comdr. Order of the Crown (Italy); recipient Medal for execellence Columbia Law Sch. Alumni Assn., 1969. Mem. ABA, Am. Judicature Soc., Am. Law Inst., Assn. of Bar of City of N.Y., N.Y. County Lawyers Assn., N.Y. State Bar Assn., Inst. Internat. Edn. (trustee), Order Moral Scis. (fgn. corr.), Accademia delle Scienze dell' Instituto di Bologna (fgn. corr. mem.; Order Moral Scis. 1971). Presbyterian. Clubs: Broad Street, Century Assn., Cosmos, Links, Metropolitan, Univ. Co-author: U.S. Income Taxation of Foreign Corporations and Nonresident Aliens, 1966; Cases and Materials on Accounting and the Law, 1978; Cases and Materials on Federal Wealth Transfer Taxation, 1982; Cases and Materials on Federal Income Taxation, Vol. I, 1972, supplement, 1983, Vol. II, 1980; pres., dir. Columbia Law Rev. Home: 325 Crest Rd Ridgewood NJ 07450 Office: 30 Rockefeller Plaza New York NY 10112

WARREN, WILLIAM ZIEGLER, lawyer, businessman, investor, consultant, engineer, accountant; b. Lebanon, Pa., Apr. 18, 1935; s. Lester Henry and Kathryn Sarah (Ziegler) W. B.S. in Engring. Sci., Pa. State U., 1963; M.S. in Mgmt. Sci. and Applied Physics, Cornell U., 1966; J.D., U. Md., 1971; cert. in Acctg. U. Calif.-Berkeley, 1983. Bar: Pa. 1971, U.S. Dist. Ct. (ea. dist.) Pa. 1972, U.S. Patent Office 1973, U.S. Supreme Ct. 1975, U.S. Ct. Appeals (fed. cir.) 1982. Engr.-in-tng. Western Electric Co., Laureldale and Reading, Pa., 1962; research teaching asst. Cornell U., Ithaca, N.Y., 1963-65; sci. systems analyst Armstrong World Industries, Lancaster, Pa., 1966-68; engr. guided missile systems Vitro Labs, Silver Spring, Md., 1968-69; sole practice, Bethel, Pa., 1969—; cons., software developer, real estate broker; instr. bus. adminstrn. Pa. State U., Schuylkill Haven, 1973. Author software package: Comput-Appraise (TM), 1984. Served with U.S. Army, 1957. Recipient Carnegie scholarship, Pa. State U., 1960, Engring. award, 1961; Am. Jurisprudence award U. Md., 1969. Sr. mem. Am. Inst. Indsl. Engrs.; mem. Pa. Bar Assn., ABA, Fed. Bar Assn., Cornell Soc. Engrs., Inst. Mgmt. Scis., Ops. Research Soc. Am., Pi Mu Epsilon, Sigma Pi Sigma, Sigma Tau, Tau Beta Pi. Republican. Home and Office: RD 1 Box 1091 Bethel PA 19507

WARRIER, RAMA CHANDRASEKHARA, information systems specialist, geologist; b. Trivandrum, Kerala, India, May 11, 1936; s. Rama and Amma (Saraswathy) W.; m. Radha Warrier, Mar. 15, 1946; children: Brinda, Indulekha, Chandra Chuda. BS, U. Kerala, 1956; M in Tech., U. Saugar, 1960; MBA, U. Delhi, 1974; cert., Ashridge Mgmt. Coll., 1986-87. Mgr. mines, geologist Sri Ram Mining Co., North Kanara, India, 1960-61; geologist Nat. Coal Devel. Corp., Ranchi, India, 1961, Minerals & Minerals Ltd., Ranchi, 1961-63, Hindustan Steel Ltd., Ranchi, 1963-65; sr. geologist Cement Corp. India Ltd., New Delhi, 1965-71; groundwater specialist Action for Food Prodn., New Delhi, 1971-75; geologist Algerian Nat. Oil Co., Algiers, 1975-81; supr. info. systems Abu Dhabi (United Arab Emirates) Nat. Oil Co., 1981—. mem. mng. com. Yamuna Group Housing Soc., New Delhi, 1974-75; founder, sec., pres., editor news bull. Indian Assn. Algiera, Algiers, 1977-80. Mem. Mining, Geol. and Metall. Inst. India (life), Indian Inst. Pub. Adminstrn. (life), Am. Assn. Petroleum Geologists, Soc. Petroleum Geologists, United Arab Emirates Computer Soc. Club: India Social Ctr. (Abu Dhabi). Office: Abu Dhabi Nat Oil Co, PO Box 898, Abu Dhabi United Arab Emirates

WARRING, DOUGLAS FRANKLIN, education educator, program director; b. Braham, Minn., Aug. 16, 1949; s. Herbert Franklin and Maxine (Anderson) W.; m. Sally Winifred Latimer, July 25, 1981; children: Jana, Leah, Andrew. BA, Bethel Coll., 1971; MA in Teaching, Coll. St. Thomas, 1975; PhD, U. Minn., 1983. Lic. social studies tchr., secondary sch. prin., Minn. Instr. bus. Inver Hills Community Coll., Inver Grove Heights, Minn., 1980-83; instr. psychology Concordia Coll., St. Paul, 1983; asst. prof. psychology U. Minn., Waseca, 1982-84; asst. prof. edn. Coll. St. Thomas, St. Paul, 1984—, dir. tchr. edn., 1985—. Mem. Curriculum Com., Bloomington, Minn., 1985—; vice chair Planning, Evaluation and Reporting Com., Bloomington, 1985-87, chair, 1988. Served with USAR. Named one of Outstanding Young Men of Am., 1985. Mem. NEA, Am. Psychol. Assn., Am. Assn. Tchr. Edn. (exec. bd. Minn. chpt. 1985—, nat. resolutions com. 1988—), Minn. Edn. Assn., Minn. Community Edn. Assn., Am. Ednl. Research Assn., Minn. Human Relations Assn., Am. Legion., Met. Wrestling Officials Assn. (v.p. 1982-86), Assn. Supervision and Curriculum Devel., Phi Delta Kappa. Home: 9625 13th Ave S Bloomington MN 55425 Office: Coll St Thomas 2115 Summit Ave Saint Paul MN 55105

WARSHAVSKY, SUZANNE MAY, lawyer; b. N.Y.C., July 22, 1944; d. Charles Finke and Charlotte (Ceaser) Goldman; m. Mordechai Warshavsky, June 7, 1964; children—Oren Jay, Adam Stuart, Claire Faye. A.B., Vassar Coll., 1965; J.D. cum laude NYU, 1968. Bar: N.Y. 1968, U.S. Dist. Ct. (so. and ea. dists.) 1972, U.S. Ct. Appeals (2d cir.) 1972, U.S. Supreme Ct. 1973. Assoc., Dewey, Ballantine, Bushby, Palmer & Wood, N.Y.C., 1968-73; assoc. Milgrim Thomajan Jacobs & Lee, P.C., N.Y.C., 1973-76; ptnr. Warshavsky, Hoffman & Cohen, P.C., N.Y.C., 1976—. Arbitrator, Civil Ct. of N.Y.C., 1975-86. Mem. ABA, N.Y. State Bar Assn. (pub. health com. 1972-77), Assn. of Bar of City of N.Y. (profl. and judicial ethics com. 1976-79), N.Y. Women's Bar Assn. (bd. trustees 1988—, chair com. on profl. ethics & discipline 1986—, judiciary com. and com on bus. and tax laws 1985—), Am. Arbitration Assn. (panel comml. arbitrators 1976-77, mem. com. on judiciary), Mag. Pubs. Assn. (legal affairs com. 1985-87). Home: 158 Gates Ave Montclair NJ 07042 Office: Warshavsky Hoffman & Cohen PC 500 Fifth Ave New York NY 10110

WARSHAW, ALLEN CHARLES, lawyer; b. Phila., Aug. 27, 1948; s. Julius and Miriam (Nepove) W.; m. Shirley A. Nes, Aug. 23, 1970; children—Christopher James, Andrew Charles. B.A., U. Pa., 1970; J.D., Villanova U., Pa., 1970-73. Bar: Pa. 1973, Calif. 1978; U.S. Ct. Appeals (3d cir.) 1975, U.S. Dist. Ct. (ea. and mid. dists.) Pa. 1974, U.S. Supreme Ct. 1977. Dep. atty. gen. Pa. Office Atty. Gen., Harrisburg, 1973-85, chief litigation sect., 1979-85, exec. dir. atty. gen., dir. commonwealth agys. legal services, 1985-86; assoc. Duane, Morris and Heckscher, Harrisburg, 1986—. Mem. staff U. Villanova Law Rev., 1973. Coach Lower Paxton Soccer Assn., Harrisburg, 1979—. Mem. Order Coif. Home: 3201 Twinn Ave Harrisburg PA 17109 Office: Duane Morris Heckscher 240 N 3d St PO Box 1003 Harrisburg PA 17108

WARSHAWSKY, ALBERT, controller; b. Asbury Park, N.J., Oct. 2, 1935; s. Harry and Eva (Holland) W.; B.B.A., U. Mich., 1957, M.B.A., 1958; m. Felicia Dawn Jacob, Aug. 14, 1966; children—David Sereno, Leah Vanessa. Sr. acct. Apfel & Englander, C.P.A.s, N.Y.C., 1959-65; mgr. Price Waterhouse & Co., N.Y.C., 1965-79; controller Marymount Manhattan Coll., N.Y.C., 1979—. Served with USMCR, 1958. Mem. Am. Inst. C.P.A.s, N.Y. State Soc. C.P.A.s, Nat. Assn. Accts., Beta Alpha Psi, Alpha Epsilon Pi. Home: 200 E 78th St New York NY 10021 Office: 221 E 71st St New York NY 10021

WARTER, GERARD, ophthalmologist; b. Strasbourg, France, Oct. 17, 1930; s. Arcadius and Sophie (Adlersberg) W.; m. Anne Bonnetain; children: Alexandra, Sophie. MD, diploma in opthalmology, 1957. Attending in opthalmology Hopital de Paris, 1960—; cons. in neuro-opthalmology Hopital de la Pitie, 1960-66. Contbr. articles to profl. jours. Bd. dirs. Orgn. Handicapped Children and Adults, Paris, 1980—, Research Orgn. on Infantile Psychosis, Paris, 1980—. Mem. Societe Francaise d'Opthalmologie. Club: Mont Saint Leger (Calvados, France). Office: 22 Rue Monsieur la Prince, 75006 Paris France

WARTHEN, JOHN EDWARD, construction, leasing and finance executive; b. Cedar City, Utah, May 8, 1922; s. Mark Tew and Emma (Simkins) W.; student Branch Agrl. Coll. So. Utah, Cedar City, 1940-41; m. Norma Jane Hansen, June 22, 1943; children—Russel Edward, John Merrill, Judith Lally, Linda Fahringer, Carla Jean Thompson, Lauri Janette Sherratt. Pres., mgr. St. George Service, Inc. (Utah), 1945-61, Warthen Constrn. Co., Las Vegas, 1961—, Warthen Buick, 1961—; pres., gen. mgr. Diversified Investment & Leasing Corp., Las Vegas. Councilman, City of St. George, 1950-54. Trustee, treas. Latter Day Saint Br. Geneal. Library, Las Vegas, 1964-76 ; co-founder Ctr. for Internat. Security Studies; past dist. dir. Freeman Inst.; past nat. dir. Liberty Amendment Com.; past chmn. Citizens for Pvt. Enterprise, Las Vegas; mem. Council Inter-Am. Security, Americanism Ednl. League; past fin. chmn. Boy Scouts Am.; past state chmn. Nev. Dealer Election Action Com.; mem. Nev. Devel. Authority, Pres.'s Club Brigham Young U. Mem. Ludwig Von Misses Inst. Econs. (charter), SAR (Good Citizenship award nat. soc.). Mormon (bishop 1957-61). Clubs: Rotary, Kiwanis. Home: 2475 E Viking St Las Vegas NV 89121 Office: 3025 E Sahara Ave Las Vegas NV 89104

WARTINGER, MANFRED, export executive; b. Linz, Austria, May 28, 1952; s. Rudolf and Emilie (Stuhr) W.; m. Susanna Fontanilla, April 2, 1982; 1 child, Natalia. BA, U. Linz, Austria, 1975. Planning asst. Knorr/CPC, Wels, Austria, 1975-76; mktg. asst. Fischer Skis, Ried, Austria, 1976-80; mktg. mgr. Anger Spectacles, Linz, 1980-82; orgn. mgr. Rosenbauer, Linz, 1982-84; export mgr. Messrs. Haas/PEZ Internat., Linz, 1984—. Home: Flemingstr 4, 4600 Wels Austria Office: Messrs HAAS, Eduard Haas Str 25, 4050 Traun Austria

WARUIMBO, STANELY WANGENDO, accountant; b. Nairobi, Kenya, Aug. 30, 1948; s. Josphat and Peris (Muthoni) W.; m. Anne Njeri Kuria, Dec. 31, 1977; children: Joe, Muthoni. BS in Bus. Adminstrn., U. Wis., Superior, 1969; postgrad., Northeastern U., Boston, 1970. Cert. internal auditor. Mgr. Standard Bank, Nairobi, 1971-72; chief auditor Kenya Shell Ltd., Nairobi, 1973-77; chief acct. Mobil Oil Kenya, Nairobi, 1978-81; chief auditor Kenya Tea Devel. Authority, Nairobi, 1982—; hon. auditor E. African Mgmt. Assn., 1976-77. Mem. Kenya African Nat. Union. Mem. Inst. Cost and Mgmt. Accts., Kenya Inst. Mgmt. Home: PO Box 54037, Nairobi Kenya Office: Kenya Tea Devel Authority, PO Box 30213, Nairobi Kenya

WARWICK SMITH, GEORGE, commercial arbitrator; b. Charters Towers, Queensland, Australia, Oct. 3, 1916; s. Arthur and Mary Olive (Gaul) W.; m. Joan Haynes, Dec. 27, 1944; children: Sandra, Karen, Simon. BA, U. Queensland, Brisbane, 1939; M in Commerce, U. Melbourne, Australia, 1957. Ofcl. dept. trade Australian Govt., Canberra, 1939-64, permanent head dept. territories, 1964-70, permanent head dept. interior, 1970-73; ambassador to multinat. trade negotiations Australian Govt., Geneva, 1973-76; Australian dir. works, sec. dept. constrn. Australian Govt., Canberra, 1976-80; chmn. Phosphate Mining Co. Christmas Island, Sydney, Australia, 1981-84; pres. dep. chmn. Coal Trading Co. Proprietary Ltd., Sydney, 1981-84; free-lance arbitrator comml. disputes Sydney, 1985—. Councillor Australian Nat. U., Canberra, 1967-68; bd. dirs. Canberra Girls Grammar Sch., 1962-73, chmn., 1971-73. Named Comdr., Order Brit. Empire Her Majesty the Queen, 1968. Inst. Arbitrators Australia. Club: Australian. Home: 69 Roslyn Gardens, Elizabeth Bay NSW 2011, Australia

WASCHKA, RONALD WILLIAM, independent oil and gas producer; b. Memphis, Sept. 2, 1932; s. Frederick William and Hazel Celeste (Guidroz) W.; B.A., U. Miss., 1960; M.A., Memphis State U., 1970, Ph.D., 1977; m. Patricia Janet Sinclair Hanney, July 27, 1963; children—Michael, John, Anne Marie, Helen Marissa. Service asst. Memphis State U., 1970, teaching asst., 1972-75; with Legis. Reference Service, Library of Congress, Washington, 1955; founder, owner Ronald Co., Inc., Memphis, 1963-81; ind. oil and gas producer, Germantown, Tenn., then Ft. Worth, 1972—. Com. mem. Boy Scouts Am., Germantown, 1975-81. Served with USAF, 1955-59, Tenn. Air N.G., 1963-69. Mem. Res. Officers Assn., Am. Petroleum Inst., Ind. Producers Assn. Am., Am. Econ. History Assn., Am. Hist. Assn., Orgn. Am. Historians, So. Hist. Assn. Republican. Roman Catholic. Clubs: Petroleum (Ft. Worth); Padre Isles Country (Corpus Christi); Sturgeon Bay Yacht (Wis.); Summit. Lodge: Rotary (Paul Harris fellow 1985). Died Feb. 6, 1987. Home: 2108 Oak Knoll Dr Colleyville TX 76034 Office: 210 W 6th St Suite 1202 Fort Worth TX 76102

WASHBURN, JERRY MARTIN, accountant, information systems company executive; b. Powell, Wyo., Dec. 31, 1943; s. Roland and Lavon (Martin) W.; divorced; children: Garth, Gavin, Kristina. BS in Acctg. Brigham Young U., 1969. CPA, Wash., Idaho, Oreg. Staff acct. Arthur Andersen & Co., Seattle, 1969-70, sr. auditor, Boise, Idaho, 1971-73, audit mgr., Boise and Portland, Oreg., 1976-79; v.p. controller Washburn Musicland, Inc., Phoenix, 1980-82; mgr., ptnr. Washburn Enterprises, Phoenix, 1977—; pres. Total Info. Systems, Inc., Phoenix, 1984—; founding dir. Internat. and Commerce Bank, Phoenix, 1985—. Mem. Inst. Internal Auditors (pres. Boise chpt. 1974, bd. dirs. Boise and Portland chpts. 1975-77), Am. Mgmt. Soc., Am. Inst. CPAs, Wash. Soc. CPAs, Idaho Soc. CPAs. Republican. Office: Total Info Systems Inc 4201 N 24th St Suite 150 Phoenix AZ 85016

WASHBURN, JOHN ROSSER, medical-surgical supply company executive, financial/investment consultant; b. Hopewell, Va., July 24, 1943; s. Winthrop Doane and Mary Virginia (Overstreet) W.; m. Judith Ann Rosen, May 16, 1971 (div. Feb. 1982); m. Tana Jean Demro, July 9, 1982; children—Eric Joseph Harrison, Amanda Ashley. Student Louisburg Jr. Coll., 1963, Va. Commonwealth U., 1963-64, U. Richmond Extension, 1967-69, Williams Coll., 1985, Stanford U., 1986-87. Asst. mgr. Liberty Loan Corp., Richmond, Va., 1965-67; loan interviewer Central Fidelity Bank, Richmond, 1967-69; regional credit/sales supr. Moores Bldg. Supplies, Inc., Roanoke, Va., 1969-74; corp. credit mgr. Owens & Minor, Inc., Richmond, 1974—; fin., investment cons. JA-GO Enterprises, Richmond, 1982—, Washburn Enterprises, 1984—; instr., lectr. investment, fin., credit mgmt., 1970—. Active Nat. Republican Congl. Com., 1980—, YMCA, 1979—, Am. Mus. Nat. History, 1982—, U.S. Def. Com., 1981—; mem. Credit Research Found. Mem. Internat. Platform Assn., Nat. Assn. Credit Mgmt. (Appreciation cert for outstanding service 1980-81, pres. Central Va. sect. 1979-80, chmn. legis. com. 1977-79, dir. 1983—), Am. Mgmt. Assn., Nat. Wildlife Fedn. Episcopalian. Clubs: Congressional (Washington); Hopewell (Va.) Yacht. Lodge: Moose. Office: Owens & Minor Inc 2727 Enterprise Pkwy Richmond VA 23229

WASHINGTON, NAPOLEON, JR., insurance agent, clergyman; b. Ft. Baker, Calif., Apr. 12, 1948; s. Napoleon and Annie D. (Carter) W.; A.A., Merced Coll., 1976; student Stanislaus State Coll., 1976-77; grad. Billy Graham Sch. Evangelism, 1987; m. Nadine Reed, Nov. 6, 1968; children—Gregory D., Kimberlee N., Geoffrey N. Lic. Baptist minister. Agt., Met. Life Ins. Co., Merced, Calif., 1970-72, sr. sales rep., 1972-83; broker Gen. Ins. Brokers, Merced, 1973—; owner Washington Assocs. Fin. Services; tchr. salesmanship Merced Coll., 1979—. Chmn. bd. trustees St. Matthew Baptist Ch., 1978—, ordained deacon, lic. minister, assoc. minister, 1982—; vice-chmn. Merced County Pvt. Industries Council, 1981-83; mem. ins. adv. council City of Merced Schs.; vocat. mgr. New Hope Found., Dos Palos, Calif., 1984-85. Served with U.S. Army, 1968-70. Recipient Nat. Quality award Nat. Assn. Life Underwriters, 1979, Nat. Sales Achievement award, 1979, Health Ins. Quality award, 1977; mem. Million Dollar Round Table, 1973, 74, 75, 76, 77, 78; teaching cert. Calif. community colls. Mem. Nat. Assn. Life Underwriters, Calif. Assn. Life Underwriters (dir. 1975-76), Merced County Assn. Life Underwriters (pres. 1976-77), Merced County Estate Planning Council (dir.), Merced County Pvt. Industries Council, NAACP, Phi Beta Lambda. Democrat. Club: Rotary (dir. 1974-76). Home: 1960 Cedar Crest Dr Merced CA 95340 Office: 935 W 18th St Merced CA 95340

WASHINGTON, PATRICIA LEATREAL, educator, consultant; b. Md., Apr. 30, 1947; d. William Howard and Dorothy Lee Long; m. Robert Levi Reed, July 4, 1967 (dec. 1969); m. Lindsay Washington, Oct. 2, 1976; 1 child, Ryan Lewis. M.A. in Adminstrn. and Supervision, Morgan State U., 1977. Tchr. Balt. City Pub. Schs., 1967-69, 72-81, tchr. gifted children, 1981—; tchr. pvt. sch., Balt., 1969-72, cons. in sci. to gifted and talented elem. students, 1982-85, teaching writing across the curriculum; instructional specialist to gifted and talented students Balt. City Pub. Schs., 1985—, Balt. Acad. Scis; dir. of gifted and talented students Fountain Acad. Author curriculum unit: William Shakespeare, 1984, Drug Abuse Education, 1985, Computer Programming for Gifted Students, 1987. Dir-at-large Provinces Civic Assn., 1978-80. Recipient Tchr. of Yr. award NEA, 1971; Funds for Ednl. Excellence grantee, 1986. Mem. NEA, State Md. Internat. Reading Assn., Olympics of the Mind Assn., Nat. Assn. Gifted Children, Phi Delta Kappa. Democrat. Baptist. Club: Bridge (v.p. 1980-84). Lodge: Eastern Star. Avocations: tennis; swimming; chess; ice skating; coin collecting.

WASHINGTON, REGINALD LOUIS, cardiologist, pediatrician, educator, administrator, author; b. Colorado Springs, Colo., Dec. 31, 1949; s. Lucius Louis and Brenette Y. (Wheeler) W.; m. Billye Faye Ned, Aug. 18, 1973; children: Danielle Larae, Reginald Quinn. BS in Zoology, Colo. State U., 1971; MD, U. Colo., 1975. Diplomate Nat. Bd. Med. Examiners, Am. Bd. Pediatrics, Pediatric Cardiology. Intern in pediatrics U. Colo. Med. Ctr., Denver, 1975-76, resident in pediatrics, 1976-78, chief resident, instr., 1978-79, fellow in pediatric cardiology, 1979-81, asst. prof. pediatrics, 1982-1988, assoc. prof. pediatrics, 1988—; staff cardiologist Children's Hosp., Denver, 1981—; mem. admissions com. U. Colo. Sch. Medicine, Denver, 1985-89; bd. dirs. Rocky Mountain Heart Found. for Children, Children's Health Care Assn., bd. dirs., treas. RMS, Inc. Adv. bd. dirs. Equitable Bank of Littleton, Colo., 1984-86. Recipient Mosby award in Pediatrics, U. Colo. Med. Ctr., 1975. Fellow Am. Acad. Pediatrics (cardiology subsect.), Am. Coll. Cardiology, Am. Heart Assn. (exec. com. 1988—, Torch of Hope 1987, editorial bd. Pediatric Experiences, 1988—), Soc. Critical Care Medicine; mem. Am. Acad. Pediatrics/Perinatology, N.Am. Soc. Pediatric Exercise Medicine (pres.), Colo. Heart Assn. (bd. dirs., exec. com. 1987—, grantee 1983-84). Democrat. Roman Catholic. Club: Denver Athletic. Home: 7423 Berkeley Circle Castle Rock CO 80104 Office: Dept Pediatric Cardiology 1056 E 19th Ave Denver CO 80218

WASIEK, KRZYSZTOF, computer science engineer; b. Warsaw, Poland, Mar. 26, 1944; s. Jan and Zofia Halina (Skowronska) W.; m. Anna Zofia Modlinska, Apr. 12, 1969; children: Joanna Magdalena, Jan Krzysztof, Marta Zofia. MSc in Elec. Engring., Warsaw Inst. Sci. and Tech., 1968. Head dept. computer control systems Inst. Computers, Warsaw, 1968-74; head dept., dep. main designer Research and Devel. Ctr. Computers, Warsaw, 1974-82; co-owner, dir. Polsystem, Warsaw, 1982-86; owner, dir. Microformat Computer, 1986—; Polish rep. to various organs of Council Mut. Econ. Aid European Socialist Countries, 1974-82. Contbr. numerous articles to profl. jours. Chmn. Solidarity trade union, 1980-81. Recipient diploma Minister Higher Edn. and Tech., Warsaw, 1978, Com. for Sci. and Tech., Warsaw, 1985. Mem. Polish Soc. Computers (charter), Assn. Polish Mech. Engrs. and Technicians, Polish Cath. Intellectuals Club. Club: Warsaw Ski. Avocations: downhill skiing, tennis, music. Home and Office: Sozopolska 1, Apt 111, 02-758 Warsaw Poland

WASIK, VINCENT A., investment banking and transportation executive; b. Dearborn, Mich., Oct. 5, 1944; s. Stanley W. and Irene F. Wasik; m. Donna M. Shubat, July 2, 1966; 1 dau., Jodi Lynn. B.A. cum laude, Mich. State U.,

1966, M.B.A., 1967. With RCA Corp., 1969-80; various mgmt. postiions Hertz Corp., 1970-74; v.p., gen. mgr. Hertz Corp. (Hertz Europe), 1974-77; exec. v.p., gen. mgr. Hertz Corp. (Rent A Car div.), 1977-80; pres., chief exec. officer Travel and Tourism Group, Holland Am. Line U.S.A., Inc., Stamford, Conn., 1980-83, Wesray Corp., Harding Resources, Inc., 1983-84; pres. Fidelco Capital Group, 1984—; pres., chief exec. officer Nat. Car Rental, Inc., 1986—; also bd. dirs. Nat. Car Rental Inc.; bd. dirs. Modernfold, Inc., MCR Inc., Westfort Mgmt. Resources, Inc. Served to 1st lt. U.S. Army, 1967-69. Decorated Army Commendation medal; recipient Silver award for leadership Chgo. Tribune, 1966. Mem. Am. Mgmt. Assn. Republican. Home: 3 Deerwood Rd Westport CT 06880 Office: 225 Millburn Ave Millburn NJ 07041 also: Nat Car Rental System Inc 7700 France Ave S Minneapolis MN 55435 also: One Station Pl Metro Ctr 5th Floor Stamford CT 06902

WASIOLEK, EDWARD, language educator; b. Camden, N.J., Apr. 27, 1924; s. Ignac and Mary (Szczesniewska) W.; m. Emma Jones Thomson, 1948; children: Mark Allan, Karen Lee, Eric Wade. B.A., Rutgers U., 1949; M.A., Harvard, 1950, Ph.D., 1955; postgrad., U. Bordeaux, France, 1950-51. Teaching fellow Harvard U., Cambridge, Mass., 1953-54, research fellow Russian Research Ctr., 1952-54; instr. English Ohio Wesleyan U., 1954-55; asst. prof. U. Chgo., 1955-60, assoc. prof. English and Russian, 1960-64, prof. Russian and comparative lit., 1964-69, Avalon prof. comparative lit. and Russian, 1969-76, Disting. Services prof. of English, comparative lit., and slavic studies, 1976—, chmn. comparative lit. program, 1965-83, chmn. dept. Slavic langs. and lit., 1971-77; vis. prof. Slavic and comparative lit. Harvard, 1966-67. Author: (with R. Bauer) Nine Soviet Portraits, 1955, Crime and Punishment and the Critics, 1961, Dostoevsky: The Major Fiction, 1964, The Notebooks for Crime and Punishment, 1967, The Brothers Karamazov and the Critics, 1967, The Notebooks for the Idiot, 1968, The Notebooks for the Possessed, 1968, The Notebooks for A Raw Youth, 1969, The Notebooks for the Brothers Karamazov, 1970, The Gambler, with Paulina Suslova's Diary, 1972, Tolstoy's Major Fiction, 1978, Critical Essays on Tolstoy, 1986. Served with USNR, 1943-46. Recipient Quantrell teaching prize U. Chgo., 1961; Laing Press prize, 1972; Research fellow USSR, 1963; Guggenheim fellow, 1983-84. Mem. Modern Lang. Assn., Phi Beta Kappa, Lambda Chi Alpha. Home: Butterfield Ln Flossmoor IL 60422 Office: Univ Chicago Chicago IL 60637

WASMUTH, CARL ERWIN, physician, lawyer; b. Pitts., Feb. 16, 1916; s. Edwin Hugo and Mary Blanche (Love) W.; m. Martha Conn, Aug. 25, 1939; children—Carl Erwin; m. Gertrude White Ruth, June 19, 1984. BS, U. Pitts., 1935, MD, 1939; LLB, Cleve.- Marshall Law Sch., 1959. Bar: Ohio bar 1959; diplomate: Am. Bd. Anesthesiology. Intern Western Pa. Hosp., Pitts., 1939-40; fellow anesthesiology Cleve. Clinic Found., 1949-51, mem. Emeritus staff, 1987—; pvt. practice medicine Dry Run, Pa., 1942-45, Scottdale, Pa., 1945-49; mem. dep. anesthesia Cleve. Clinic, 1951—, head dept., 1967-69; asso. prof. law Cleve.-Marshall Law Sch., 1959-66; adj. prof. Cleve. Marshall Law Sch., 1966-73. Author: Anesthesia and the Law, 1961, Law for the Physician, 1966, Law and the Surgical Team, 1968; Editor: Legal Problems in the Practice of Anesthesiology, 1973; contbg. editor: Hale's Anesthesiology; editorial bd.: Med. World News; Contbr. articles to profl. jours. Trustee Cleve.- Marshall Law Sch., chmn., 1969-71; bd. dirs. Scottdale Hosp. Found; chmn. bd. govs. Cleve. Clinic, 1969-77; trustee Cleve. Clinic Found., 1969-76, v.p., 1973-76; trustee Cleve. Clinic Ednl. Found., 1969-76, v.p., 1973-76; chmn. bd. trustees, pres. Cleve. Marshall Ednl. Found., 1972-81; bd. overseers Coll. Law, Cleve. State U., 1972-76; vis. com. Coll. Law, Case-Western Res. U., 1973-76; trustee United Torch Services; trustee Santa Cruz Med. Found., 1977, pres., 1978; bd. govs. Ohio World Trade Center; trustee Cancer Center Cleve., Ohio Coll. Podiatric Medicine, 1976, Am. Coll. Legal Medicine Research Found., 1984—; mem. U. Ariz. Found., 1978, World Congress Med. Law, 1967—, Keynoter 3d World Congress, 1971; sec. Commn. Med. Malpractice, HEW, 1972-73. Named Distinguished Eagle Scout Nat. Council Boy Scouts Am., 1977; named Outstanding Citizen Eagle Cuyahoga council, 1976; Citizen of Year Cleve. Area Bd. Realtors, 1976. Fellow Am. Coll. Anesthesiologists, Am. Coll. Legal Medicine (pres. bd. govs. 1966-69), A.C.P., Am. Coll. Chest Physicians, Law Sci. Acad.; mem. Am. Soc. Anesthesiologists (dir., pres. 1968, speaker ho. of dels.), Ohio Soc. Anesthesiologists (dir. 1960-69), Cleve. Soc. Anesthesiologists (pres. 1963), Internat. Anesthesia Research Soc., World Fedn. Soc. Anesthesiologists (vice chmn. Am. delegation 1967), Acad. Anesthesiology (chmn. program com. 1967), Am., Ohio med. assns., N.Y. Acad. Scis., Nat. Acad. Sci., NRC, Com. Cadaver Utilization, Cleve. Acad. Medicine, AAAS, Transplantation Soc. (charter), Am., Ohio, Cuyahoga County, Cleve. bar assns., Phi Rho Sigma, Delta Theta Phi. Clubs: Masons (Pa.) (32 deg., Shriner), Lions (Pa.) (past pres. local clubs), Union, Cleveland, Midday (Ariz.), Old Pueblo (Ariz.), Tucson (Ariz.), Country of Green Valley (Ariz.); Pleasant Valley Country (Scottdale, Pa.). Home: 901 N Hickory St Scottdale PA 15683 Office: The Cleve Clin Found 9500 Eclid Ave Cleveland OH 44106

WASS, HANNELORE LINA, educator; b. Heidelberg, Germany, Sept. 12, 1926; came to U.S., 1957, naturalized, 1963; d. Hermann and Mina (Lasch) Kraft; m. Irvin R. Wass, Nov. 24, 1959 (dec.); 1 child, Brian C.; m. Harry H. Hisler, Apr. 13, 1978. B.A., Tchrs. Coll., Heidelberg, 1951; M.A., U. Mich., 1960, Ph.D., 1968. Tchr. W. Ger. Univ. Lab. Schs., 1958-60; mem. faculty U. Mich., Ann Arbor, 1958-60, U. Chgo. Lab. Sch., 1960-61, U. Mich., 1963-64, Eastern Mich. U., 1965-69; prof. ednl. psychology U. Fla., Gainesville, 1969—; cons., lectr. in thanatology. Author: The Professional Education of Teachers, 1974; Dying-Facing the Facts, 2d edition, 1987; Death Education: An Annotated Resource Guide, 1980; Death Education: An Annotated Resource Guide, vol. 2, 1984; Helping Children Cope With Death, 2d edit., 1984; Childhood and Death, 1984. Founder, editor Death Studies, 1977—; cons. editor Ednl. Gerontology, 1977—, cons. editor Death, Aging, and Health Care, Hemisphere Pub. Corp. and Harper and Row; contbr. articles to profl. jours. Mem. Am. Psychol. Assn., Gerontol. Soc., Internat. Work Group Dying, Death and Bereavement (bd. dirs.), Assn. Death Edn. and Counseling (bd. dirs.). Methodist. Home: 6014 NW 54 Way Gainesville FL 32606 Office: U Fla 1418 Norman Hall Gainesville FL 32611

WASSER, HENRY, educator, university administrator; b. Pitts., Apr. 13, 1919; s. Nathan and Mollie (Mendelson) W.; m. Solidelle Felicité Fortier, Aug. 20, 1942; children: Michael Frederick (dec.), Eric Anthony (dec.), Frederick Anthony, Felicity Louise. B.A., M.A., Ohio State U., 1940; Ph.D., Columbia U., 1951. Teaching fellow George Washington U., 1940-42; analyst USAAF intelligence, 1941-43; chemist Goodyear Synthetic Rubber Co., 1943-45; tutor, assoc. prof. City Coll., CUNY, 1946-66; prof. English, dean faculties Richmond Coll., CUNY, 1966-73; v.p. for acad. affairs Calif. State U., Sacramento, 1973-74; prof. English Coll. S.I., CUNY, Richmond, 1974—; dir. Center for European Studies, Grad. Sch. CUNY, 1979—; Fulbright prof. U. Salonika, Greece, 1955-56; seminar assoc. Columbia U., 1961—, co-chair, 1982—, Colloquium on Higher Edn., Yale, 1974-75; Fulbright prof. Am. lit. U. Oslo, 1962-64, dir., prof. Am. Inst., 1963-64; vis. prof. U. Sussex, Eng., 1972; lectr. in field, Sweden, Norway, Eng., Germany, Poland, Yugoslavia, Italy. Author: The Scientific Thought of Henry Adams, 1956, (with others) Higher Education in Western Europe and North America: A Selected and Annotated Bibliography, 1979, American Literature and Language: A Selected and Annotated Bibliography, 1980; editor: (with Sigmund Skard) Americana Norvegica; Norwegian Contributions to American Studies, 1968, (with others) The Compleat University, 1983, Problems of the Urban University: A Comparative Perspective, 1984, Impact of Changing Labor Force on Higher Education, 1987; mem. bd. editors History of European Ideas, 1986—; contbr. articles to newspapers and profl. jours. Faculty trustee CUNY, 1981-86, trustee emeritus, 1986—; bd. dirs. Scandinavian Seminar, 1978-86, sec., 1980-86, vice chmn., 1983-86. Recipient Am. Scandinavian Found. award, 1969, 71, German Acad. Exchange Service award, 1973, 80, Swedish Info. Service award, 1979, Norwegian Ministry of Culture award, 1983, NEH award, 1984, Foscolo medal U. Pavia, Italy, 1986, German Marshall Fund award, 1985, 87, Atheneum medal U. Paria, Italy, 1988. Mem. Am. Studies Assn. (pres. Met. N.Y. chpt. 1961-62, mem. nat. exec. council 1968-74), Melville Soc. Am. (historian 1969-74), MLA, Am. Scandinavian Found. (fellow 1971), Internat. Assn. Univ. Profs. English, Assn. Upper Level Colls. and Univs. (2d v.p. 1971-72), Assn. for World Edn. (internat. council), Phi Beta Kappa (sec. City Coll. chpt. 1957-62, 64-67). Home: 333 E 34th St #16C New York NY 10016 also: 5517 Fieldston Rd Bx New York NY 10471 Office: CUNY Grad Sch and Coll of Staten Island Staten Island NY 10314

WASSERMAN, MARVIN, sales and marketing company executive; b. Bklyn., Feb. 16, 1931; s. William and Mary (Moskowitz) W.; m. Anita Strain, Jan. 1, 1956 (div. Aug. 1972); children: Steven, Neil, Mark; m. Mary M. McColgan, Aug. 7, 1981. AA, Glendale (Calif.) Coll., 1955; student, U. Calif. Los Angeles, 1964. Resident engr., sr. designer Pacific div. Bendix Corp., North Hollywood, Calif., 1955-62, sr. engr. systems div., Ann Arbor, Mich., 1962-64; configuration control coordinator Mich. div. Ling-Temco-Vought, Warren, 1964; sr. gen. engr. liaison Brown Engrng. Co., Inc., Huntsville, Ala., 1964-66; sr. tech. asst. IBM Fed. Systems div. Space Systems Center, Huntsville, 1966-67; sr. engring. specialist ARINC Research Corp., Ridgecrest, Calif., 1967-68; prin. devel. engr. Honeywell, Inc., Marine Systems Center, West Covina, Calif., 1968-69; sr. value engr. Aerojet ElectroSystems Co., Azusa, Calif., 1969-74; mgr. value engring. Byron Jackson Pump div. Borg Warner Corp., Vernon Calif., 1974-75; value engr. Ingersoll Rand Co. Proto Tool Div., Fullerton, Calif., 1975-77; v.p. Orosico, Inc., 1976-77; account mgr. McGraw-Hill Pub. Co., Westminster, Calif., 1977-78, regional mgr. Mid-West/Can. region, Chgo., 1978-80; mktg. mgr. aerospace Pyle-Nat., Chgo., 1980; owner, chief exec. officer The Listening Post, 1981—, A Boodstore & More, 1988—; instr. Grad. Sch. Mgmt., UCLA Extension. Com. chmn.Tennessee Valley council Boy Scouts Am., 1966-67, mem. awards com., Ridgecrest, 1967-68, mem. spl. projects com., Cypress, Calif., 1969-71. Loaned exec. Jr. Achievement fund raising campaign, 1975. Served with USAF, 1951-52. Mem. Soc. Am. Value Engrs. (Editorial award 1966-67, Value Engr. of Yr. award 1967, nat. dir. 1967-71, pres. Orange County chpt. 1970-71, nat. v.p. S.W. region 1971-74), Am. Soc. Performance Improvement (gen. chmn. nat. conf. 1976, v.p. So. Calif. chpt.). Jewish. Contbr. articles to profl. jours. Home: 4555 El Monte Dr Saginaw MI 48603 Office: A Bookstore & More, Cirlce Mall #7065 2811 Jefferson Ave Midland MI 48640

WASTBERG, OLLE M., newspaper association executive, consultant, politician; b. Stockholm, May 6, 1945; s. Erik and Greta (Hirsch) W.; m. Inger Claesson, Feb. 21, 1968; children—David, Elias. BA, U. Stockholm, 1972. Tchr. polit. sci. U. Stockholm, 1967-68; journalist polit. dept. Expressen, 1968-71; research fellow Bus. and Soc. Research Center, 1971-76; pres. Akieframjandet, 1976-82; mem. Parliament, 1976-82; pres. Swedish Newspaper Promotion Assn., 1983—; dir. Stockholm Stock Exchange, 1977-82, 88—; mem. govt. coms. on S. Africa consumer politics and stock market. Author books on African problems, immigration politics and econ. topics; contbr. articles to profl. jours. Polit. sec. Liberal Youth Sweden, 1966, v.p., 1968-71; bd. Liberal Party, 1972—, pres. exec. com., 1982-83. Recipient Gold medal Swedish Mktg. Group, 1982. Bd. dirs. Friends Hebrew U. of Jerusalem and Youth for Understanding. Home: Bellmangatan 6, 11720 Stockholm Sweden Office: Norrmalustorg 1, 11146 Stockholm Sweden

WASTENSON, MAGNUS HUGO, marketing professional; b. Stockholm, Mar. 28, 1948; s. Einar Hugo and Britt Mari-Anne (Palmgren) W.; student in Mktg. and Internat. Econs., Schartau Bus. Sch., Stockholm, 1968; M.B.A., Gothenburg Sch. Econs. and Bus. Adminstrn., 1971. Mktg. and planning mgr. Sandvik AB, head office Sandviken, Sweden, and German subs. head office, Dusseldorf, W. Ger., 1972-75; sr. cons. AB Saljkonsult Borje Lindberg AB. Stockholm, 1975-78; mktg. dir. Scandinavia PA Internat. Mgmt. Cons., ops. in Sweden, Denmark, Finland, and Norway, Stockholm, 1978-84; pres. Errpege Sweden-Internat. Bus. Systems AB, Stockholm, 1984-87. Swedish Trade Commr. export scholar, Dusseldorf, 1971-72. Mem. Swedish Mktg. Assn., Swedish M.B.A. Assn. Home: 2 Iversonsgatan, 11430 Stockholm Sweden Office: Box 3061, 17203 Suundbyberg Sweden

WASWO, RICHARD ARTHUR, English educator; b. Washington, Oct. 26, 1939; arrived in Switzerland, 1976; s. Arthur and Mildred Beulah (Slaybaugh) W.; m. Ann Lardner, Aug. 22, 1964. AB, Stanford U., 1961; MA, Harvard U., 1962, PhD, 1970. Asst. curator The Houghton Library, Cambridge, Mass., 1963; instr. humanities San Francisco State Coll., 1964-65; instr. English Lang. Edn. Council, Tokyo, 1966-67; asst. prof. English San Jose (Calif.) State Coll., 1967-70, U. Va., Charlottesville, 1970-76; asst. prof. English U. Geneva, 1976-82, prof., 1982—; vis. research fellow Merton Coll., Oxford, Eng., 1986-87. Author: The Fatal Mirror, 1972; Language and Meaning in the Renaissance, 1987; editor: On Poetry & Poetics, 1985. U. Va. Sesquicentinnial Assoc., 1974-75. Woodrow Wilson fellow, 1961-62. Mem. Renaissance Soc. Am., Internat. Soc. History Rhetoric, Coll. D'Anglicistes Romands (pres. 1979-80), Swiss Assn. U. Tchrs. English (v.p. 1985—), Phi Beta Kappa. Office: U Geneva,, Faculte Des Lettres, 1211-4 Geneva Switzerland

WATANABE, DANIEL HIROSHI, microbiologist; b. Los Angeles, Aug. 6, 1929; s. Takeo and Tai (Iwasaki) W.; BS, Pa. State U., 1957; MA, U. Calif., Berkeley, 1959; PhD, SUNY Upstate Med. Center 1973; m. Akiko Ito, May 16, 1963; children: Fujio M., Midori A. Asst. prof. Coll. Osteo. Medicine and Surgery, Des Moines, 1972-74; research asst. prof. N.Y. Med. Coll., Valhalla, 1974-78; research asst. prof. Baylor Coll. Medicine, Houston, 1978-84; instr. Houston Community Coll. system, 1982—; cons. on biotech. and med. meeting planning; exec. dir. Interface Internat. Confs. Pres., Japanese Am. Citizens League, Houston, 1982-84, Japan Am. Soc. of Houston, 1987—; 1st pres. Japan Am. Cultural Exchange Soc., Syracuse, 1972-73; 1st chmn. Asian Am. Festival Com. Houston, 1980; bd. dirs. Houston Ctr. for Humanities, 1983—, Council Asian-Am. Orgns., 1982—. Served with AUS, 1949-52; Japan. Recipient Merit cert. City Houston, 1981. Mem. Am. Soc. Microbiology, AAAS, Assn. Advancement Med. Instrumentation, Japan-Am. Soc. Houston (dir. 1982—), Japan Am. Soc. Houston (pres. 1987—). Sigma Xi. Office: W Resources 7418 Aqua Houston TX 77072

WATANABE, FUMIO, insurance executive; b. Mar. 28, 1917; married. Grad., Tokyo U., 1939. With Tokyo Fire and Marine Ins. Co., Ltd., 1939—, pres., 1978-88, chmn., 1988—; dir. Mitsubishi Bank, Ltd., Japan Airlines, Daido Fire and Marine Ins. Co., Ltd. Home: 1904 Shitasakunobe, Takatsuku, Kawasaki 213, Japan Office: Tokyo Fire and Marine Ins Ltd, 2-1 Marunouchi, 1-chome Chiyoda-ku, Tokyo Japan *

WATANABE, KOUICHI, pharmacologist, educator; b. Manchuria, Japan, Aug. 26, 1942; s. Tetsuya and Mine W.; m.; children—Toshikazu, Yoshihiro, Motohiro. B.S., Tokyo Coll. Pharmacy, 1966; M.S., Osaka U., 1968; Ph.D., 1971; LPIBA, 1986; DSci. (hon.) Internat. U. Found., 1987. Vis. fellow reprodn. research br. Nat. Inst. Child Health and Devel., NIH, Bethesda, Md., 1971-73; vis. scientist dept. pharmacology Coll. Medicine, Howard U., Washington, 1973-75, asst. prof., 1975-83; asst. prof. pharmacology U. Hawaii, 1983—; mgr. Fiujimoto Diagnostics Inc., Osaka, Japan. Contbr. articles to sci. jours. Am. Cancer Soc. grantee, 1980-81. Mem. Am. Soc. Pharmacology and Exptl. Therapeutics, N.Y. Acad. Scis., Am. Soc. Hypertension (charter). Subspecialties: Chemotherapy; Molecular pharmacology. Current work: Mechanism of action of various antineoplastic agts. on calmodulin. Vinca alkaloids found to be calmodulin inhibitors. Suggested that amounts of calmodulin or its binding proteins may be endogenous regulators of antineoplastic action or transport of these drugs. Home: 8-2-10 Minamirin-Kahn, Yamato -City, Kanagawa Japan Office: TKK Internat Div Taiyo Keiei Kanri Co Ltd, 1-22-27, Taiyo BLD, Hyakunincho, Shinjuku-ku, Tokyo Japan

WATANABE, MARK DAVID, pharmacist; b. Santa Monica, Calif., Dec. 7, 1955; s. Jack Shigeru and Rose Nobuko (Iida) W. BA in Chemistry, U. Calif., Irvine, 1977, BS in Biol. Sci., 1978; PharmD, U. Calif., San Francisco, 1982, PhD in Pharm. Chemistry, 1988. Lic. pharmacist, Calif., Oreg., Hawaii, Tex. Pharmacy intern various locations, San Francisco, 1979-82; pharmacist Kaiser Permanente, San Francisco, 1981-87; research asst. U. Calif., San Francisco, 1980-87; clin. scis. research fellow in psychiatric pharmacy U. Tex., 1987—. Regents scholar U. Calif., San Francisco, 1979-82; recipient Excellence in Teaching award Long Found., San Francisco, 1984. Mem. Am. Pharm. Assn., Tex. Pharm. Assn., Am. Soc. Hosp. Pharmacists, Am. Assn. Colls. of Pharmacy, Amnesty Internat. Unitarian Universalist. Clubs: Sierra, Mensa. Home: 4400 Horizon Hill Blvd #1411 San Antonio TX 78229 Office: U Tex Health Sci Ctr Dept Pharmacology San Antonio TX 78284

WATANABE, MASAO, history of science researcher and educator; b. Tokyo, Jan. 7, 1920; s. Yasuo and Satoe W.; m. Hiroko Ishihara, Dec. 1948; children—Nozomu, Tomo-o, Makoto. B.Eng., U. Tokyo, 1941, D.Sc., 1962; D.Litt., Tokyo U. Edn., 1961. Assoc. prof. U. Tokyo, 1944-47, prof., 1968-80; prof. emeritus, 1987—; assoc. prof., prof. Tokyo Woman's Christian Coll., 1950-59, 59-62; prof. Chuo U., Tokyo, 1962-68; prof. Niigata U., Japan, 1980-85; prof. Tokyo Denki U., 1985-88; prof. emeritus, 1987—, prof. history of sci. Internat. Christian U., Tokyo, 1988—; vis. scholar Harvard-Yenching Inst., U.S.A., 1955-56; Fulbright research scholar Harvard U., 1963-64; vis. fellow Trinity Coll., Oxford, Eng., 1976. Author: Science in the History of Modern Culture, 1963; The Japanese and Modern Science, 1976; Science across the Pacific, 1976. Editorial com. Annals of Sci., Eng., 1982—. Served as lt. Japanese Navy, 1942-44. Research grantee Harvard-Yenching Inst., 1955-56, Fulbright Com., 1963-64, Japan Soc. for Promotion Sci., 1976, 84, Australian Acad. Sci., 1984. Mem. Académie Internationale d'Histoire des Sciences (corr.), Brit. Soc. for History Sci., History of Sci. Soc. U.S.A., History of Sci. Soc. Japan, Japan Assn. for Philosophy of Sci. (coms.). Club: Internat. House (Tokyo). Avocations: hiking; classical music. Home: 16-3 1-chome Higashi-cho, Koganei-shi, Tokyo 184, Japan Office: Internat Christian U, Osawa, Mitaka-shi, Tokyo 181, Japan

WATANABE, MEIJI, architect, educator; b. Shimizu, Shizuoka, Japan, Nov. 3, 1935; s. Kunizo and Toshi W.; m. Yasuko Iguchi, Dec. 15, 1962; 1 child, Akiko. BArch, Kanto Gakuin U., Yokohama, Japan, 1958; MArch, Ill. Inst. Tech., 1962. Designer Mies Van Der Rohe Archtl. Office, Chgo., 1962-64, Kasumigaseki Planning Com., Tokyo, 1964-67; pres. Meiji Watanabe & Assocs., Tokyo, 1970—; prof. Kanto Gakuin U., 1981—; vis. prof. U. So. Calif., 1967; vis. critique Pratt Inst., Bklyn., 1982, Hong Kong U., 1984; cons. City of Yokosuka; moderator water front seminar, City of Yokohama, 1986. Designer Toyota dealership, Tokyo, Yamaha Internat., Los Angeles, Yamaha Can., Harapan Motor Sakti Industry, Jakarta, Indonesia; translator archtl. publs. Mem. Japan Architects Assn., Internat. Culture Ctr. Club: Yomiuri Tennis Garden (Kawasaki City). Office: Meiji Watanabe & Assocs, 30-4 Sakuragaoka-cho #502, Shibuya-ku, Tokyo 150, Japan

WATANABE, MORIYUKI, automotive company executive; b. Nov. 7, 1922; m. Senri Watanabe. Grad., U. Tokyo, 1945. With Mazda Motor Co., 1946—, chmn., 1984—. Home: 10 Koyo Naka-machi 5-chome, Minami-ku, Hiroshima 734 Japan Office: Mazda Motor Corp, 3-1 Sinchi Kuchu-ocho, Akigun, Hiroshima Japan *

WATANABE, RUTH TAIKO, music historian, library science educator; b. Los Angeles, May 12, 1916; d. Kohei and Iwa (Watanabe) W. B.Mus., U. So. Calif., 1937, A.B., 1939, A.M., 1941, M.Mus., 1942; postgrad., Eastman Sch. Music, Rochester, N.Y., 1942-46, Columbia U., 1947; Ph.D., U. Rochester, 1952. Dir. Sibley Music Library Eastman Sch. of Music, Rochester, N.Y., 1947-84; prof. music bibliography Eastman Sch. of Music, 1978-85, historian, archivist, 1984—; adj. prof. Sch. Library Sci. State U. Coll. at Geneseo, 1975-83; coordinator adult edn. program Rochester Civic Music Assn., 1963-75; mem. adv. com. Hochstein Music Sch.; lectr. on music, book reviewer, 1966—; program annotater Rochester Philharmonic Orch., 1959—. Author: Introduction to Music Research, 1967, Madrigali—II Verso, 1978; editor: Scribners New Music Library, vols. 2, 5, 8, 1973, Treasury of Four Hand Piano Music, 1979; contbr. articles to profl. jours., contbr. symphony orchs. of U.S., 1986, internat. music jours. Mem. overseers vis. com. Baxter Sch. Library Sci., Case Western Res. U., 1979-85. Mem. AAUW (Pa.-Del. fellowship. 1949-50, 1st v.p. Rochester 1964-65, mem. N.Y. state bd. 1965-66, mem. nat. com. on soc.'s reflection on arts 1967-69, nat. com. Am. fellowships awards 1969-74, br. pres. 1969-71, hon. co-chair Capitol Fund Drive, 1986—), Internat. Assn. Music Libraries (2d v.p. commn. on conservatory libraries, commn. research libraries), Am. Musicol. Soc., Music Library Assn. (v.p. 1968-70, citation 1986), Music library Assn. (mem. editorial bd. 1967—), Music Library Assn. (pres. 1979-81), ALA, Music Library Assn./Internat. Assn. Music Libraries (joint com., 1986-87), Civic Music Assn. Rochester, Riemen Scheider Bach Inst. (hon.), Phi Beta Kappa, Phi Kappa Phi, Mu Phi Epsilon (gen. chmn. nat. conv. 1956, nat. librarian 1958-60, recipient citation 1977), Pi Kappa Lambda (sec. 1978—, treas. 1980—), Delta Phi Alpha, Epsilon Phi, Delta Kappa Gamma (parliamentarian 1986—). Club: Soroptimist (chmn. North Atlantic Conf. 1961, pres. 1964-66), Univ. (Rochester). Home: 111 East Ave Apt 610 Rochester NY 14604 Office: Eastman Sch Music Rochester NY 14604

WATANABE, TAKENOBU, architect; b. Yokohama, Kanagawa, Japan, Jan. 10, 1938; s. Takeo and Motoko W.; m. Yoko Saton, Feb. 7, 1973; children: Sinya, Tetshya. Bachelor's degree, Tokyo U., 1962, M of Technology in Architecture, 1964. Lic. arch. Pres. Takenoba Watanabe Architect & Assocs., Tokyo, 1970—. Author: Big City, Small Room, 1974, Thoughts on Way of Living, 1983; translator: Prodigious Builders, 1981, The Skyscraper, 1988. Mem. Japan Inst. Architects, Japan Arch. Inst., Japan Film Pen Club, Japanese Poets Assn. Home: 2-21-16 Shimo-Ochiai Shinjuku-ku, Tokyo 161, Japan Office: Takenobu Watanabe Architects & Assocs, 4-10-14 Takadanobaba Shinjuku-ku, Tokyo Japan

WATANABE, TSUNEO, newspaper executive; b. Tokyo, May 30, 1926; s. Heikichi and Hanako (Yanai) W.; m. Astuko Nabeshima, May 25, 1954; 1 child, Mutsumi. B.A., U. Tokyo, 1949. With Yomiuri Shimbun, Tokyo, 1952—, chief Washington news bur., 1968-72, assoc. mng. editor, polit. editor, Tokyo, 1975-77, dep. mng. editor, 1977-79, exec. editor, 1979-80, chmn. editorial bd., 1979-87, sr. exec. dir., 1980-87.Author: A Study of Political Party Factions, 1958; Inside the White House, 1971; Watergate: Background and Foreground, 1973; Practical Wisdom of Politics, 1976. Served as pvt. Japanese Army. Club: Japan Nat. Press (dir. 1984—, editor-in-chief 1985—, sr. v.p. 1987) (Tokyo). Home: 12-6 Gobancho Chiyoda-ku, 102 Tokyo Japan Office: Yomiuri Shimbun, 1-7-1 Otemachi, Chiyoda-ku, 100-55 Tokyo Japan

WATARI, SUGIICHIRO, manufacturing company executive; b. Yamagata, Japan, Mar. 28, 1925; s. Yoshihiro and Aki (Tanaka) W.; m. Katsuko Inadome, Apr. 25, 1954; 1 child, Naohiro. BA, Tokyo U., 1948. Sr. v.p. Toshiba Corp., Tokyo, 1980-82, exec. v.p., 1982-84, sr. exec. v.p., 1984-86, pres., 1986-87, advisor to the bd., 1987—. Home: Kamiyoga Town Home, Room #310, 18 16 Kamiyoga 3 chome Setagaya ku, Tokyo 105, Japan Office: Toshiba Corp, 1-1 Shibaura 1-chome, Minato-ku, 105 Tokyo Japan

WATERFIELD, GILES ADRIAN, museum administrator; b. Guildford, Surrey, Eng., July 24, 1949; s. Anthony Henry and Honor Mary (Northen) W. BA, Oxford U., 1971; MA, U. London, 1975. Dir. edn. Royal Pavilion, Brighton, Eng., 1976-79; dir. Dulwich Picture Gallery, London, 1979—. Author, editor: Collection for a King, 1983; author: Soane and After, 1987. Mem. Georgian Group Com., London, 1986, So. Regional com. Nat. Trust, 1985—. Club: Travellers'. Office: Dulwich Picture Gallery, College Rd Dulwich, London SE21 7AD, England

WATERS, WAYNE ARTHUR, conference and travel service agency executive; b. Ft. Wayne, Ind., Mar. 9, 1929; s. Roy Edwin and Mary Catherine (Housel) W. m. Helen Marie Gump, Nov. 18, 1950; children: Bradley Wayne, Jeffry Scott, Ann Kathryn. Owner, mgr. Grain and Dairy Farm, Ft. Wayne, 1947-54; auto salesman Haynes & Potter, Auburn, Ind., 1956-58; asst. v.p. Lincoln Nat. Life, Ft. Wayne, 1958-83; pres. Conf. and Travel Services Inc., Ft. Wayne, 1983—; bd. dirs. Meeting World, 1979-81, 87. Contbr. articles to profl. jours. and mags. Fellow Internat. Biog. Assn.; named Boss of Yr. Am. Bus. Women. Assn., 1972, Boss of the Yr. Ft. Wayne Jaycees, 1987, Entrepreneur of the Yr. Arthur Young and Venture Mag., 1986. Mem. Soc. Co. Meeting Planners (bd. dirs. 1973-74, pres. 1975-76, Leadership award 1974), Ins. Conf. Planners (bd. dirs. 1979-81, pres. 1982), Am. Soc. Travel Agts., Soc. Incentive Travel Execs., Cruise Line Internat. Assn., Meeting Planners Internat., Internat. Platform Assn., The Travel Council, Ft. Wayne C. of C. (air service council 1984—, Small Bus. Person of Month 1984). Republican. Mem. Ch. of the Brethren. Clubs: Orchard Ridge Country (Ft. Wayne), Summit. Office: Conf and Travel Services Inc 1300 S Clinton Suite One Fort Wayne IN 46802

WATERS, WILLIAM ERNEST, microelectronics executive; b. Toronto, Ont., Can., Aug. 18, 1928; s. Charles Lacy and Margaret (Boulden) W.; B.A.Sc., U. Toronto, 1950; m. Evelyn Elizabeth Phillips, Jan. 18, 1952; children—Kenneth Geoffrey, Brian Gregory, Kimberly William. Gen. mgr. Hoskins Alloys of Can. Ltd., Toronto, 1953-59; pres. Waters Metal Products Ltd., Toronto, 1960—, Waters Metal Products, Inc., Buffalo, 1960-69, Watmet Inc., Niagara Falls, N.Y., 1968—, Microtectonics, Inc., Buffalo,

1968-71. Served with RCAF, 1946-52. Mem. Engring. Inst. Can., Ont. Assn. Profl. Engrs., Canadian Soc. for Elec. Engring., Internat. Soc. Hybrid Microelectronics, Mfrs. Agts. Nat. Assn. (dir. 1973-77), Beta Theta Pi. Clubs: Niagara Falls Golf and Country, Port Colborne, Rotary. Home: 5060 Woodland Dr Lewiston NY 14092

WATHEN, JULIAN PHILIP GERARD, banker; b. Cromer, Norfolk, Eng., May 21, 1923; s. Gerard Anstruther and Melicent Louis (Buxton) W.; m. Priscilla Florence Wilson, July 3, 1948; children: Simon, Lucy, Henrietta. Grad. high sch., Harrow, Eng. With Barclays Bank Co., 1948-84; local dir. Barclays Bank Co., Ghana, 1961-65; gen. mgr. Barclays Bank Co., London, 1965-74; vice chmn. Barclays Bank Co. PLC, London, 1974-84; bd. dirs. Mercantile and Gen. Reinsurance, London. Chmn. Hall Sch. Charitable Trust, London, 1977—; vice chmn. London House for Overseas Grads., London, 1983—. Served to capt. Brit. infantry, 1942-47. Fellow Inst. Bankers; mem. Royal Africa Soc. (pres. 1983—). Conservative. Anglican. Club: Travellers (London) (chmn. fin. com. 1986-87). Home: Woodcock House, Owlpen, Dursley GL11 5BY, England

WATKINS, CURTIS WINTHROP, artist; b. Pontiac, Mich., Apr. 9, 1946; s. Robert James and Arvella Marquitta (Chenoweth) W.; student Ann Arbor Art Center, 1964-66, Kendall Sch. Design, 1966-68, Kraus Hypnosis Center, 1966, 70, Arons Ethical Hypnosis Tng. Center, 1977; m. Gayle Lynn Blom, Dec. 19, 1975; 1 dau., Darcy Ann. Illustrator, instr. Ann Arbor Art Center, 1969-71; owner, dir. Hypno-Art Research Center and Studio, Howell, Mich., 1971—; research on visualization process of subconscious by doing art work under hypnosis; lectr. hypnosis convs. and schs.; one-man shows include: LeVern's Gallery, 1969, Rackham Gallery, 1973, Hartland Gallery, 1974, Platt Gallery, 1975, Detroit Artists Guild Gallery, 1975, Golden Gallery, 1977, Cromaine Gallery, 1982, Driggett Gallery, 1982, Mill Gallery, 1983, Walnut Street Gallery, 1983, Merrill Gallery, 1986, Corbino Gallery, 1986; group shows include Mich. All-State Show, 1980, Mich. State Fine Arts Exhibit, 1980, Washington Internat., 1981, Lansing Art Gallery (Mich.), 1981, Capitol City Arts Show, 1981, Mich. Ann., 1981, Mich. Ann., 1982-83; bd. dirs. 9th Ann. Hartland Art Show, 1975, Livingston Arts and Crafts Assn., 1977-79, Hartland Art Council, 1974-78. Recipient numerous awards of excellence in art. Mem. Internat. Soc. Artists, Assn. Advance Ethical Hypnosis, Am. Assn. Profl. Hypnologists, Internat. Soc. Profl. Hypnosis, Internat. Platform Assn. Presbyterian. Home and Studio: 1749 Pinckney Rd Howell MI 48843

WATKINS, FELIX SCOTT, printing company executive; b. Sutton, W.Va., Nov. 27, 1946; s. Felix Sutton and Helena Sara (Cogar) W.; student W.Va. Inst. Tech.; m. Vivian L. Watkins, June 20, 1970; children—Jeffrey Scott, Jamie Leigh. Salesman, Kingsport Press (Tenn.), 1971-73; sales mgr. George Banta Co., N.Y.C., 1973-74; production mgr. Fuller Typesetting, Phila., 1974-75; account exec. Rocappi, Pennsauken, N.J., 1975-78; pres. Photo Data, Inc., Washington, 1978—. Founding mem. Print Polit. Action Com. Mem. Washington Club Printing House Craftsmen, Washington Printing Guild (dir. masters printers div.), Printing Industries of Met. Washington (chmn. govt. affairs com.), Printing Industries of Am. (mem. Chmn.s' Club). Home: 9521 Orion Ct Burke VA 22015 Office: 12104-J Indian Creek Ct Beltsville MD 20705

WATKINS, HAYS THOMAS, railroad executive; b. Fern Creek, Ky., Jan. 26, 1926; s. Hays Thomas Sr. and Minnie Catherine (Whiteley) W.; m. Betty Jean Wright, Apr. 15, 1950; 1 son, Hays Thomas III. BS in Acctg., Western Ky. U., 1947; MBA, Northwestern U., 1948; LLD (hon.), Baldwin Wallace Coll., 1975, Alderson Broaddus Coll., 1980, Coll. of William and Mary, 1982, Va. Union U., 1987. C.P.A. With C. & O. Ry. Cleve., 1949-80, v.p. fin., 1964-67, v.p. adminstrv. group, 1967-71, pres., chief exec. officer, 1971-73, chmn. bd., chief exec. officer, 1973-80; with B. & O. R.R., 1964-80, v.p. finance, 1964-71, pres., chief exec. officer, 1971-73, vice chmn. bd., chief exec. officer, 1973-80; chmn., chief exec. officer Chessie System, Inc., 1973-80; pres. and co-chief exec. officer CSX Corp. (merger of Chessie System, Inc. and Seaboard Coast Line Industries, Inc.), Richmond, Va., 1980-82, chmn. bd., chief exec. officer, 1982—; bd. dirs. Black & Decker Mfg. Co., Westinghouse Electric Corp., Signet Banking Co., Richmond, Fredericksburg & Potomac R.R.; chmn. Ctr. for Inovative Tech., Va., 1987. Vice rector bd. visitors Coll. William and Mary, 1984-87, rector, 1987—; trustee Johns Hopkins U. Mus. Arts Assn. (Cleve. Orch.), Richmond Symphony Orch; mem. Va. Bus. Council. Served with AUS, 1945-47. Named Man of Yr., Modern R.R. mag., 1984; recipient Excellence in Mgmt. award Industry Week mag., 1982. Mem. Nat. Assn. Accts., Am. Inst. C.P.A.'s. Clubs: Commonwealth (Richmond, Va.); Country of Va. (Richmond). Home: 22 Lower Tuckahoe Rd W Richmond VA 23233 Office: CSX Corp 901 E Cary St Richmond VA 23219

WATKINS, JOHN CHESTER ANDERSON, newspaper publisher; b. Corpus Christi, Tex., Oct. 2, 1912; s. Dudley Warren and Ruth (Woodruff) W.; m. Helen Danforth, Nov. 20, 1943 (div. 1959); children: Fanchon Metcalf, Robert Danforth, Stephen Danforth, Jane Pierce; m. Izetta Jewel Smith, Feb., 1960. Litt.D., Bryant Coll.; D.J., Roger Williams Coll., 1983. Reporter, makeup editor, aviation editor Dayton (Ohio) Jour. and Herald, 1934-35; reporter, aviation editor, mil. corr. Balt. Sun, 1935-41; asst. to pub., assoc. pub. Providence Jour.-Bull., 1945-54, pub., 1954-79; chmn. Providence Jour. Co., 1961-85, chmn. emeritus, 1985—; chmn. bd. dirs. Copley/Colony Inc., Calif.; also bd. dirs. Colony Communications; pres. Interam. Press Assn., 1971-72; also mem. adv. council. Served as fighter pilot USAAF, 1941-45; operations officer 325th Fighter Group MTO. Decorated D.F.C., Air medal with 9 oak leaf clusters; knight comdr. Order of Merit Italy), R.I. Heritage Hall of Fame. Fellow New Eng. Acad. Journalists (Yankee Quill award); mem. Air Force Assn., Am. Soc. Newspaper Editors, New Eng. Daily Newspaper Assn. (pres. 1966-68). Clubs: Army-Navy Country (Washington); Hope, Agawam Hunt (Providence); Cruising Am; N.Y. Yacht (N.Y.C.); Spouting Rock Beach Assn., Ida Lewis Yacht (Newport, R.I.); La Jolla (Calif.) Beach and Tennis. Home: PO Box 1085 Providence RI 02901 Office: Providence Jour Co 75 fountain St Providence RI 02902

WATKINS, LEWIS BOONE, artist; b. Beckely, W.Va., July 24, 1945; s. Fred Boone and Margaret Theodoris (Laurie) W.; m. Marinda Ann Hogan, Aug. 18, 1979; children—Mary Sheridan, Marinda Laurie. B.S., W.Va. State Coll., 1978; postgrad. U. South Fla., 1979-82. Artist in residence Boxwood Gallery, Brooksville, Fla., 1978-79; instr. of gifted, Hernando County, Fla., 1979-81; artist in residence Casa Serena Gallery, Brooksville, 1981—; vis. artist W. Va. State Coll., Samford U., St. Leo Coll., U. Tampa (Fla.); works include numerous lithograph print edits., sculpture represented in permanent collections Fla. State Mus., U. Fla., Gainesville, Vatican Mus., Vatican City, Italy, W.Va. Fine Arts and Cultural Ctr., Charleston, Nat. Fine Arts Mus., Santiago, Chile, Nat. Art Gallery, Chile, St. Petersburg Fine Art Mus., also numerous pvt. collections; sculptures include Hernando Heritage Sculpture, 1981, Crosses of Life, 1982, Youth of Today, 1983; Am. Farmer Meml. Sculpture, Bonner, Kans., 1986. Bd. advisors Hernando County YMCA (Fla.); pres. Boxwood Art Guild, 1978; treas. Hernando County Young Republicans, 1981. Recipient various awards including Ambassador Artistic Achievement award State of W.Va., 1981; Outstanding Achievement award State of Fla., 1982; proclamation declaring Lewis Watkins Day, Hernando County, Fla., 1981; cert. of Recognition in Art, State of Ga., 1983, award for sculpture, Tampa, Fla., 1984, Pub. Service award City of Atlanta, 1984. Mem. Hernando Heritage Mus. Assn. (bd. dirs.), Hernando County C. of C.

WATKINS, SAMUEL RAYBURN, association executive; b. Benton, Ky., Apr. 21, 1923; s. Gipp and Keron (Wyatt) W.; student Tufts U., 1942-43; B.S. in History, Econs. and Journalism, Murray State U., 1944; M.S. in Mass Communications, History and Econs., U. Ill., 1951; m. Evelyn W. Ellis, Mar. 6, 1954; children—Julia Ellis, Samuel R. Night editor S.I. (N.Y.) Advance, 1946-48; instr. journalism U. Ill., 1948-49; editor, pub. Tribune-Democrat, Benton, 1948-54; adminstrv. sec. Louisville Area C. of C., 1950-55; pres. Assoc. Industries of Ky., Louisville, 1955-85; exec. v.p. Ky. Safety Council, 1980—. Pres. Nat. Labor-Mgmt. Found., 1970—; mem. Pres.' Com. on Employment of Physically Handicapped, 1968-72; mem. Ky. Labor Mgmt. Adv. Council, 1979-88; vice chmn. Ky. Employer Com. Support Guard and Res., 1979-88, chmn., 1985-88. Served to lt. USNR, 1942-46. Recipient Disting. Alumnus award Murray State U., 1979. Mem. Am. Soc. Assn. Execs. (past pres., chartered assn. exec.), Govt. Research Assn., Kappa Delta Pi, Tau Kappa Alpha, Sigma Delta Chi. Clubs: Louisville Pendennis, Louisville Boat. Author: Management Success Patterns, 1965; How to Be A Good Supervisor, 1969; Management Strategy in Labor Relations, 1970. Home: 2704 Poplar Hill Ct Louisville KY 40207 Office: 200 W Chestnut St Louisville KY 40202

WATLINGTON, ROSALIND THAYER, violinist, educator; b. Montclair, N.J., Feb. 11, 1925; d. Eugene Willard and Alys Waring (Stites) Garges; B.A., Maryville (Tenn.) Coll., 1946; spl. cert. in violin Royal Schs. Music, London, 1962; m. Francis W. H. Watlington, Apr. 3, 1948; children—Francis W., Diana Thayer Watlington Ruetenik. Violinist, Bermuda Oratorio Soc. Orch., Hamilton, 1960-61, Bermuda Philharmonic Soc., Hamilton, 1961—, Gilbert and Sullivan Soc. Prodns., Bermuda, 1972—; tchr. violin, viola, Pembroke, Bermuda, 1973—. Trustee Menuhin Found. (Bermuda); patron Bermuda Festival, 1975-85 . Mem. Am. String Tchrs. Assn., Amateur Chamber Music Players, Bermuda Philharm. Soc., Bermuda Soc. Art, Am. Soc., English Speaking Union. Bermuda Music and Dramatic Soc. Presbyterian. Home: Coralita, 6 Hidden Ln off Pitts Bay Rd, Pembroke HM06, Bermuda

WATSON, ABBIE I., retired public health nurse; b. Greenville, Mich., July 27, 1905; d. Alfred T. and Effie (Henry) Watson; R.N., Harper Hosp. Sch. Nursing, Detroit, 1929; B.S. in Public Health Nursing, Wayne U., 1947; M.S. in Nursing Edn., Western Res. U., 1948. Clinic nurse outpatient dept. Harper Hosp., 1930-33; staff nurse, supr. Vis. Nurse Assn., Detroit, 1933-35, 38-42; supr. Tulare County Health Dept., Visalia, Calif., 1935-38; adminstrv. chief nurse, capt. Army Nurse Corps, AUS, 1942-46; exec. dir. Instructive Vis. Nurse Assn., Richmond, Va., 1948-57; dir. bur. pub. health nursing Instructive Vis. Nurse Assn. and City of Richmond, 1952-57; dir. bur. public health nursing pub. health div. Health and Hosp. Corp. of Marion County, Indpls., 1957-61; chief bur. pub. health nursing Public Health Dept. D.C., 1961-65; dir. pub. health nursing Met. Health Dept., Nashville, 1965-72. Mem. nursing services com. D.C. chpt. ARC, 1960-61; spl. services dept. D.C. Tb Assn., 1961—; club rep. Festival U.S.A. Winter Haven Bicentennial Com. Fellow Am. Public Health Assn. (past vice chmn., past research chmn. public health nursing sect. So. br.), Am. Sch. Health Assn., Royal Soc. Health (London); mem. Am. Nurses Assn., Nat. League Nursing (past chmn. program planning com. public health nursing biennial conv.), D.C. Public Health Assn. (1st v.p., chmn. constn. and by-laws com.), Polk County Fedn. Women's Clubs (pres. 1981-82). Club: Woman's of Winter Haven (rec. sec., pres. 1978-81). Contbr. articles to profl. publs. Address: 1001 Carpenter's Way F116 Lakeland FL 33809

WATSON, ALEXANDER FLETCHER, ambassador; b. Boston, Aug. 8, 1939; s. Fletcher G. and Alice Victoria (Hodson) W.; m. Judith Dawson Tuttle, June 23, 1962; children: David F., Caitlin H. BA, Harvard U., 1961; MA, U. Wis., 1969. Consular officer Am. embassy, Santo Domingo, Dominican Republic, 1962-64, Madrid, 1964-66; internat. relations officer Dept. State, Washington, 1966-68, 73-75, spl. asst., 1975-77, dir. Office of Devel. Fin., 1978-79; polit. officer Am. embassy, Brasilia, Brazil, 1969-70; prin. officer Am. Consulate, Salvador, Brazil, 1970-73; dep. chief of mission Am. embassy, La Paz, Bolivia, 1979-81; dep. chief of mission Bogota, Colombia, 1981-84, Brasilia, Brazil, 1984-86; U.S. ambassador to Lima, Peru, 1986—. Decorated Order of San Carlos, Govt. of Colombia, 1984, Order of the Condor, Govt. of Bolivia, 1985, Labor Justice Order of Merit, Govt. Brazil, 1987. Mem. Am. Fgn. Service Assn., Smithsonian Instn. Club: Lima Golf; Internat. (Washington). Home and Office: Am Embassy APO Miami FL 34031

WATSON, ARTHUR CHRISTOPHER, retired diplomat; b. Kunming, Yunnan, China, Jan. 2, 1927; s. Alexander James and Mary Louise (Griffiths) W.; m. Mary Cecil Earl Candler, June 26, 1956; children: Mary Clare Turner Candler, Timothy Hardie Candler, Elizabeth Sarah. BA, U. Cambridge, Eng., 1948, MA, 1950. Dist. office Colonial Service, Uganda, 1951-63; prin. Commonwealth Relations Office, Eng., 1963-64; 1st sec. Brit. High Commn., Karachi, Pakistan, 1964-67, Fgn. and Commonwealth Office, London, 1967-71; commr. Diplomatic Service, Anguilla, 1971-74; gov. Diplomatic Service, Turks and Caicos Islands, 1975-78; high commr. Diplomatic Service, Brunei, 1978-83; gov. Montserrat, 1985-87; ret. 1987. Served to sub lt. Brit. Royal Navy, 1946-48. Decorated companion Order St. Michael and St. George. Mem. Royal Commonwealth Soc. Home: Holmesdale Oval Way, Gerrards Cross SL9 8QB, England

WATSON, ARTHUR DENNIS, government official; b. Brownsville, Pa., May 11, 1950; s. John Leslie and Margaret Teresa (Mastile) W.; m. Kathleen Frances Zaccardo, July 16, 1983. BSBA, U. Richmond, 1972; MS in Bus.-Govt. Relations Am. U., 1977, MA in Lit., 1979; PhD in English and Lit. Cath. U., 1987. Statistical asst. U.S. Postal Service Hdqrs., Washington, 1972-73, economist assoc., 1974-77, mktg. analyst, 1977; rate analyst U.S. Postal Rate Commn., Washington, 1977-79, public affairs officer, 1979-82; spokesman, public affairs officer ICC, Washington, 1982—; pres. Arthur D. Watson and Co., Springfield, Va., 1983—. Washington corr. Linn's Stamp News, Sidney, Ohio, 1983-84; contbr. articles to profl. jours.; reader Washington Ear, WETA-FM side channel, 1977. Served with USCG, 1972-78. Recipient Meritorious Service medal. Mem. Nat. Assn. Govt. Communicators, Pub. Relations Soc. Am., Am. Bus. Communication Assn., Am. U. Grad. Bus. Assn., USS Natoma Bar Assn., Pub. Relations Soc. Am., Thomas Hardy Soc. Am. Roman Catholic. Avocations: classical music, running, model building, travel. Home: 5420 Gainesville Rd Springfield VA 22151 Office: ICC 12th and Constitution Ave NW Washington DC 20423

WATSON, SIR BRUCE DUNSTAN, mining company executive; b. Stanthorpe, Queensland, Australia, Aug. 1, 1928; s. James Harvey and Edith Mary (Crawford) W.; m. June, Dec. 30, 1952; three children. B.Elec. Engring., U. Queensland, 1949, B. Commerce, 1957. Engr., Tasmanian Hydro Electricity Commn., 1950-54, Townsville Regional Electricity Bd., 1954-56; with M.I.M. Holdings Group Cos., 1956—, engr. Copper Refineries Pty., Ltd., Townsville, 1956-69, Mount Isa Mines, Ltd., 1970-73, group indsl. relations mgr. M.I.M. Group, Brisbane, Queensland, 1974-75; 1st gen. mgr. Agnew Mining Co., Western Australia, 1975-77; dir. M.I.M. Holdings Ltd., Brisbane, 1977, mng. dir., 1980, mng. dir., chief exec. officer, 1981-83, chmn., chief exec. officer, 1983—; Nat. Australia Bank Ltd. Bd. dirs. Australian Adminstrv. Staff Coll.; dir. ASARCO Inc. Named knight bachelor in Queen's birthday honours, 1985. Mem. Australia Mining Industry Council, supervisory bd. Metallgesellschdtt AG. Lodge: Lions. Office: MIM Holdings Ltd, 410 Ann St, Brisbane Queensland 4000, Australia

WATSON, DAVID COLQUITT, electrical engineer, educator b. Linden, Tex., Feb. 9, 1936; s. Colvin Colquitt and Nelena Gertrude (Keasler) W.; m. Flora Janet Thayn, Nov. 10, 1959; children: Flora Janeen, Melanie Beth, Lorrie Gaylene, Cherlayn Gail, Nathan David, Amy Melissa, Brian Colvin. BSEE, U. Utah, 1964, PhD in Elec. Engring. (NASA fellow), 1968. Electronic technician Hercules Powder Co., Magna, Utah, 1961-62; research fellow U. Utah, 1964-65, research asst. microwave devices and phys. electronics lab., 1964-68; sr. mem. tech. staff ESL, Inc., Sunnyvale, Calif., 1968-78, head dept. Communications, 1969-70; sr. engring. specialist Probe Systems, Inc., Sunnyvale, 1978-79; sr. mem. tech. staff ARGO Systems, Inc., Sunnyvale, 1979—; mem. faculty U. Santa Clara, 1978—, San Jose State U., 1981—. Contbr. articles to IEEE Transactions, 1965-78; co-inventor cyclotron-wave rectifier; inventor gradient descrambler. Served with USAF, 1956-60. Mem. IEEE, Phi Kappa Phi, Tau Beta Pi, Eta Kappa Nu. Mormon. Office: Argo Systems Inc 884 Hermosa Ct Sunnyvale CA 94086

WATSON, DONALD CHARLES, cardiothoracic surgeon, educator; b. Fairfield, Ohio, Mar. 15, 1945; s. Donald Charles and Pricilla H. Watson; m. Susan Robertson Prince, June 23, 1973; children—Kea Huntington, Katherine Anne, Kirsten Prince. B.A. in Applied Sci. Lehigh U., 1968, B.S. in Mech. Engring., 1968; M.S. in Mech. Engring., Stanford U., 1969; M.D., Duke U., 1972. Diplomate Am. Bd. Thoracic Surgery, Am. Bd. Surgery. Intern in surgery Stanford U. Med. Ctr., Calif., 1972-73, resident in cardiovascular surgery, 1973-74, resident in surgery, 1976-78, chief resident in heart transplant, 1978-79, chief resident in cardiovascular and gen. surgery, 1978-80; clin. assoc. surgery br. Nat. Heart and Lung Inst., 1974-76, acting sr. surgeon, 1976; assoc. cardiovascular surgeon dept. child health and devel. George Washington U., Washington, 1980-84, asst. prof. surgery, asst. prof. child health and devel., 1980-84, attending cardiovascular surgeon dept. child health and devel., 1984—; assoc. prof. surgery, assoc. prof. pediatrics U. Tenn.-Memphis, 1984—, chmn. cardiothoracic surgery, 1984—; mem. staff Le Bonheur children's Med. Ctr., Memphis, chmn. cardiothoracic surgery, 1984—; mem. staff William F. Bowld Med. Ctr., Memphis, Regional Med. ctr. at Memphis, Baptist Meml. Med. Ctr., Memphis; cons. in field; instr. advanced trauma life support; profl. cons., program reviewer HHS. Contbr. chpts., numerous articles, revs. to profl. publs. Served to lt. comdr. USPHS, 1974-76. Smith Kline & French fellow Lehigh U., 1967; NSF fellow Lehigh U., 1968; univ. interdepartmental scholar and univ. scholar Lehigh U., 1968. Fellow Am. Coll. Cardiology, Am. Coll. Chest Physicians (forum cardiovascular surgery, council critical care), Southeastern Surg. Congress, Am. Acad. Pediatrics (surgery sect.), ACS; mem. Assn. Surg. Edn., Am. Assn. Thoracic Surgery, Soc. Thoracic Surgeons, So. Thoracic Surg. Assn., Am. Thoracic Soc., Assn. Acad. Surgery, Internat. Soc. Heart Transplantation, Am. Fedn. Clin. Research, Found. Advanced Edn. in Scis., Andrew G. Morrow Soc., Council on Cardiovascular Surgery of Am. Heart Assn., Soc. Internat. di Chirig, AAAS, N.Y. Acad. Sci., AMA, NIH Alumni Assn., Stanford U. Med. Alumni Assn., Duke U. Med. Alumni Assn., Duke U. Alumni Assn., Stanford U. Alumni Assn., Lehigh U. Alumni Assn., Smithsonian Assocs., Sierra Club, U. Tenn. Pres.'s Club, LeBonheur Pres.'s Club, U.S. Yacht Racing Assn., Pilots Internat. Assn., Nat. Assn. Flight Instrs., Aircraft Owners and Pilots Assn., Order Ky. Cols., Phi Beta Kappa, Tau Beta Pi, Pi Tau Sigma, Phi Gamma Delta. Republican. Presbyterian. Club: Memphis Racquet. Avocations: sailing; racquet sports; flying. Office: U Tenn 956 Court Ave Room E 232 Memphis TN 38163

WATSON, DONALD RALPH, architect, author; b. Providence, Sept. 27, 1937; s. Ralph Giles W. and Ethel (Fletcher) Pastene; m. Marja Palmqvist, Sept. 8, 1966 (div. Jan. 1984); children: Petrik, Elsie; m. Judith Criste, Jan. 3, 1986. A.B., Yale U., 1959, B.Arch., 1962, M.Ed., 1969. Lic. architect Nat. Council Archtl. Registration Bds. Architect Peace Corps, Tunisia, 1962-64; archtl. cons. Govt. of Tunisia, 1964-65; pvt. practice architecture Trumbull, Conn., 1969—; cons. UN, Bhutan, 1976, World Bank, North Yemen, 1979, Dept. of Energy, 1979, Nat. Acad. Scis., 1982. Author: Designing and Building a Solar House, 1977, Energy Conservation Through Building Design, 1979, Climatic Design, 1983. Bd. dirs. Save the Children Fedn., 1979-82. Recipient Honor Design award Conn. Soc. Architects, 1974; recipient Honor Design award region AIA, 1978, 84, 1st award Owens Corning Energy Conservation Bldg. Design Program, 1983, Excellence in Housing award Energy Efficient Bldg. Assn., 1988; ACSA/AMAX research fellow, 1967-69; research fellow Rockefeller Found., 1978. Fellow AIA; mem. Am. Solar Energy Soc. (editor). Home: 54 Larkspur Dr Trumbull CT 06611

WATSON, FORREST ALBERT, lawyer, bank executive; b. Atlanta, May 7, 1951; s. Forrest Albert and Virginia Doris (Ritch) W.; m. Marlys Wise, Oct. 16, 1983; 1 child, Annaliese Marie Elizabeth. AB, Emory U., 1973; JD, U. Ga., 1975; postgrad., Mercer U., 1979-80, U. London, 1988—. Bar: Ga. 1975, U.S. Dist. Ct. (mid. dist.) Ga. 1976, U.S. Tax Ct. 1976, U.S. Ct. Appeals (5th cir.) 1977, U.S. Supreme Ct. 1980. Assoc. Banks, Smith & Lambdin, Barnesville, Ga., 1976-78; ptnr. Watson & Lindsey, Barnesville, 1978-82; gen. counsel United Bank Corp., Barnesville, 1981—, v.p., chief exec. officer, 1982—; gen. counsel Lamar State Bank, Barnesville, 1976-84, judge Small Claims Ct. Lamar County, Ga., 1976, City Ct. Milner, Ga., 1977; lectr. IBM, 1984-85; atty. City of Meansville, Ga., 1976, City of Milner, 1977. Assoc. editor Ga. Jour. Internat. Law, 1975. Gen. counsel Lamar County Devel. Authority, Barnesville, 1977; bd. dirs. Legaline Inc., Atlanta, 1983-85. Mem. ABA, Ga. Bar Assn., Cir. Ct. Bar Assn., Flint Circuit Bar Assn. Lutheran. Home: Po Box 347 Barnesville Rd Zebulon GA 30295 Office: United Bank Corp 314 Thomaston St Barnesville GA 30204

WATSON, SIR FRANCIS (JOHN BAGOTT), art director; b. Aug. 24, 1907; s. Hugh Watson Blakedown and Helen Marian Bagott Dudley; m. Mary Rosalie Gray, 1941 (div. 1969); 1 adopted child. BA, Cambridge (Eng.) U., 1929. Registrar Courtauld Inst. Art, 1934-38; asst. keeper, then dep. dir. Wallace Collection, 1938-63; dep. surveyor The Queen's Works of Art, 1947-52, The King's Works of Art, 1952-63; surveyor The Queen's Works of Art, 1963-72, advisor, 1972—; trustee Whitechapel Art Gallery, 1949-74; chmn. Furniture History Soc., 1966-74, Walpole Soc., 1970-74; Slade prof. fine art, Oxford (Eng.) U., 1969-70; Wrightsman prof. NYU, 1970-71; vis. lectr. U. Calif., 1970; Kress prof. Nat. Gallery, Washington, 1975-76. Author: Canaletto, 1949 (2d edit. 1954), (with others) Southill, A Regency House, 1951, Wallace Collection: Catalogue of Furniture, 1956, Louis XVI Furniture, 1959 (French edit. 1963), The Choiseul Gold Box, 1963, (with others) Great Family Collections, 1965, The Guardi Family of Painters, 1966, (with others) Eighteenth Century Gold Boxes, 1966, The Wrightsman Collection Catalogue, Vols. 1 and 2: Furniture, 1966, The Wrightsman Collection Catalogue, Vols. 3 and 4: Furniture, Goldsmith's Work and Ceramics, 1970, The Wrightsman Collection Catalogue, Vol. 5: Paintings and Sculpture, Giambattista Tiepolo, 1966, Fragonard, 1967, Chinese Porcelains in European Mounts, 1980, Mounted Oriental Porcelain in the Getty Musuem, 1982, Mounted Oriental Porcelain, 1986; contbr. numerous articles to profl. jours. Decorated officer Order of Merit, Govt. of Italy, 1961; recipient Gold medal NYU, 1966; Smithsonian Regent fellow, 1983-84. Club: Beefsteak. Home: West Farm House, Corton, Wiltshire England

WATSON, GEORGE HENRY, JR., broadcast executive, journalist; b. Birmingham, Ala., July 27, 1936; s. George Henry and Grace Elizabeth (Carr) W.; m. Ellen Havican Bradley, July 13, 1979; children—George H., III, Ellen Havican. B.A., Harvard U., 1959; M.S., Columbia U., 1960. Reporter Washington Post, 1960-61; corr. ABC News, 1962-75, Moscow bur. chief, 1966-69, London bur. chief, 1969-75, v.p., Washington bur. chief, 1976-80; v.p., mng. editor Cable News Network, 1980; v.p. news ABC News, N.Y.C., 1981-85; v.p., Washington bur. chief ABC News, 1985—, exec. in charge ABC News Viewpoint, 1981-85. Served with U.S. Army, 1958. Recipient Peabody award, 1982, DuPont Columbia award, 1983, nat. news Emmy award, 1984. Mem. Radio Television News Dirs. Assn., Soc. Profl. Journalists, Nat. Press Club, Overseas Press Club (award for best television documentary 1971, citation for excellence 1974), Washington Press Club. Club: Fed. City. Office: ABC News 1717 De Sales St NW Washington DC 20036

WATSON, GLENN R., lawyer; b. Okla., May 2, 1917; s. Albert Thomas and Ethel (Riddle) W.; m. Dorothy Ann Mosiman, Feb. 25, 1945; 1 dau., Carol Ann. Student, East Central State Okla., 1933-36; LL.B., Okla. U., 1939. Bar: Okla. 1939, Calif. 1946. Pvt. practice law Okla., 1939-41; ptnr. Richards, Watson & Gershon, Los Angeles, 1946—; city atty. Industry, Calif., 1958-65, 78-83, Commerce, Calif., 1960-61, Cerritos, Calif., 1956-64, Victorville, Calif., 1962-63, Carson, Calif., 1968—, Rosemead, Calif., 1960-76, Seal Beach, Calif., 1972-78, South El Monte, Calif., 1976-78, Avalon, Calif., 1976-80, Artesia, Calif., 1976—. Served with USNR, 1942-46. Mem. Los Angeles County, Am. bar assns., Am. Judicature Soc., Lawyers Club of Los Angeles (past pres.), Los Angeles World Affairs Council, La Canada C. of C. (past pres.), Order of Coif, Phi Delta Phi, Delta Chi. Home: 800 W 1st St Los Angeles CA 90012 Office: Richards Watson & Gershon 333 S Hope St Los Angeles CA 90071

WATSON, JAMES DEWEY, molecular biologist, educator; b. Chgo., Apr. 6, 1928; s. James Dewey and Jean (Mitchell) W.; m. Elizabeth Lewis, 1968; children: Rufus Robert, Duncan James. B.S., U. Chgo., 1947, D.Sc., 1961; Ph.D., Ind. U., 1950; D.Sc., 1963; LL.D., U. Notre Dame, 1965; D.Sc., L.I. U., 1970, Adelphi U., 1972, Brandeis U., 1973, Albert Einstein Coll. Medicine, 1974, Hofstra U., 1976, Harvard U., 1978, Rockefeller U., 1980, Clarkson Coll., 1981, SUNY, 1983; D.Sc. (hon.), U. Buenos Aires, Argentina, 1986; D.Sc., Rutgers U., 1988. Research fellow NRC, U. Copenhagen, 1950-51; Nat. Found. Infantile Paralysis fellow Cavendish Lab., Cambridge U., 1951-53; sr. research fellow biology Calif. Inst. Tech., 1953-55; asst. prof. biology Harvard, 1955-58, asso. prof., 1958-61, prof., 1961-76; dir. Cold Spring Harbor Lab., 1968—. Author: Molecular Biology of the Gene, 1965, 2d edit., 1970, 3d edit., 1976, 4th edit., 1986, The Double Helix, 1968, (with John Tooze) The DNA Story, 1981; (with others) The Molecular Biology of the Cell, 1983; (with John Tooze and David Kurtz) Recombinant DNA: A Short Course, 1983. Hon. fellow Clare Coll., Cambridge U.; Recipient (with F. H. C. Crick) John Collins Warren prize Mass. Gen. Hosp., 1959; Eli Lilly award in biochemistry Am. Chem. Soc., 1959; Albert Lasker prize Am. Pub.

Health Assn., 1960; with F.H.C. Crick Research Corp. prize, 1962; with F.H.C. Crick and M.H.F. Wilkins Nobel prize in medicine, 1962; Presdl. medal of freedom, 1977. Mem. Royal Soc. (London), Nat. Acad. Scis. (Carty medal 1971), Am. Philos. Soc., Danish Acad. Arts and Scis., Am. Assn. Cancer Research, Am. Acad. Arts and Sci., Am. Soc. Biol. Chemists. Home: Bungtown Rd Cold Spring Harbor NY 11724 Office: Cold Spring Harbor Lab PO Box 100 Cold Spring Harbor NY 11724

WATSON, KITTIE WELLS, speech communication educator; b. Newburgh, N.Y., July 31, 1953; d. Cody Usry and Bettie Richards (Todd) Watson. AA, Gainesville Jr. Coll., 1973; BS, U. Ga., 1975; MA, Auburn U., 1977; PhD, La. State U., 1981. Cert. tchr., Ga. Grad. teaching asst. Auburn U. (Ala.), 1975-77, instr., 1977-79; instr. Tulane U., New Orleans, 1979-81, asst. prof. speech communication, 1981-85, assoc. prof., 1985—, also acting head dept. speech communication, 1981-83, chmn. dept., 1982-84, assoc. dir. Inst. for Study Intrapersonal Processes; staff writer and reviewer Prentice-Hall, Wm. C. Brown, Addison Wesley pub. cos.; exec. v.p. SPECTRA Communication Assocs., pres. SPECTRA Creations; co-owner operator Rainbow River Studios. Mem. editorial bd. several jours. Author: Instructional Objectives and Evaluation, 1980, Effective Listening, 1983, Groups in Process, 3d edit., 1987; contbr. numerous articles to scholarly jours.; creator audio and video tapes: Watson-Barker Listening Test; Willing Yourself to Listen. Mem. Am. Council for Career Women, task force nat. tchr. cert. examination Ednl. Testing Service, recipient Mortar Bd. Teaching Excellence award Tulane U., 1982; Achiever award Am. Council for Career Women, 1987; Ralph Nichols Research award, 1988; inducted Listening Hall Fame 1988. Mem. Inst. Study of Intrapersonal Processes (assoc. dir.), Speech Communication Assn., Internat. Communication Assn., Am. Soc. Tng. and Devel. (v.p. profl. devel.), So. Speech Communication Assn., Eastern Speech Assn., Am. Soc. Tng. and Devel., Internat. Listening Assn. (1st. v.p., mem.-at-large, chmn. research com., Research award 1985, Ralph Nichols Research award 1988), Delta Delta Delta. Home: 701 Jefferson Ave Metairie LA 70001 Office: Tulane U Dept Communications Newcomb Hall New Orleans LA 70118

WATSON, LELAND HALE, theatrical lighting designer, educator, critic; b. Charleston, Ill., Feb. 18, 1926; s. Dallas V. and Hazel Emma (Dooley) W. B.A., State U. Iowa, 1948; M.F.A., Yale U., 1951. Instr. Utah State Agrl. Coll., Logan, 1948-49, Bklyn. Coll., 1952- 54; with CBS-TV, N.Y.C., 1951-55, Polakov Studio Design, N.Y.C., 1957-62; mem. faculty U. Houston, 1968-71; asst. prof. C.W. Post Coll., L.I.U., 1971-75; guest lectr. Syracuse (N.Y.) U., 1974-75; assoc. prof. Purdue U., 1975-81, prof., 1981—; guest lectr. Butler U., Indpls. Lighting designer, Cin. Ballet, 1977-80; lighting designer Broadway Productions, Diary of Anne Frank, View From the Bridge; off-Broadway prodns., The Blacks, Suddenly Last Summer; operas, N.Y.C., Houston, Phila., Balt., Vancouver, Wash., Milw., dance cos.; Seattle's World's Fair, 1962; 26 Broadway prodns., indsl. shows, Washington Arena.; co-author: Theatrical Lighting Practice, 1954; former columnist, sr. contbg. editor: Lighting Dimensions mag.; columnist Lighting Design and Application mag.; contbr. articles to mags. Served with AUS, 1944-45. Decorated Purple Heart; recipient Obie award for Machinal; rcipient Show Bus. award, 1959. Mem. United Scenic Artists, Internat. Alliance Theatrical and Stage Employees, U.S. Inst. Theatre Tech. (pres. 1980-82, Fellows award, Founders award 1982, Career Achievement award 1986), Soc. Brit. Theatre Designers, Internat. Assn. Lighting Designers, Am. Soc. Lighting Dirs., Illuminating Engring. Soc., Assn. Brit. Theatre Technicians, Theatrical Protective Union #1, Canadian Soc. TV Lighting Dirs., Phi Beta Kappa. Methodist. Address: 2400 State St Lafayette IN 47905

WATSON, MORRIS EDWARD, plastic company executive; b. Auckland, N.Z., Feb. 28, 1945; s. Edward Henry and Betty Sarah (Wilson) W.; ed. Auckland Tech. Inst.; m. Marion Isobel Burnett, May 6, 1967; children—Kim, Richard, Toni. Factory mgr. Nuon Industries Ltd., Auckland, 1966-69; mng. dir. Premier Plastics Ltd., Auckland, 1969—. Mem. Plastics Inst. N.Z. Clubs: Royal N.Z. Yacht Squadron, Panmure Yacht. Home: 11 Hames Terr, Auckland New Zealand Office: 32 Ethel St, Sandringham, Auckland New Zealand

WATSON, PAUL LESTER, accountant; b. Manchester, Conn., Aug. 20, 1945; s. Robert Victor and Lois May (Foster) W.; m. Patricia June Asel, June 24, 1967; children: Tonya, Gregory. AS, Manchester Community Coll., 1967; BS, Cen. Conn. State Coll., 1975. CPA, Conn. Cost acct. Case Bros., Inc., Manchester, 1966-67; staff acct. A. J. Hirschfeld & Co., West Hartford, Conn., 1971-77; sr. staff acct. Jerome I. Baskin & Co., Manchester, 1977-81; mgr. Sheptoff, Reuber, Nicola & Co., Glastonbury, Conn., 1981-85; owner Paul L. Watson, CPA, Coventry, Conn., 1985—. Treas. First Congl. Ch. of Coventry (Conn.); bd. dirs. Human Growth Services of Coventry; treas. The Hale Donation. Served with U.S. Army, 1968-71; Korea. Fellow Conn. Soc. CPA's; mem. Am. Inst. CPA's. Republican. Lodge: Rotary. Office: Paul L Watson CPA 1699 Boston Turnpike Coventry CT 06238

WATSON, ROBERT FRANCIS, lawyer; b. Houston, Jan. 9, 1936; s. Louis Leon and Lora Elizabeth (Hodges) W.; m. Marietta Kiser, Nov. 24, 1961; children—Julia, Melissa, Rebecca. B.A., Vanderbilt U., 1957; J.D., U. Denver, 1959. Bar: Colo. 1959, U.S. Dist. Ct. (no. dist.) Tex. 1967, U.S. Supreme Ct. 1968, Tex. 1973, U.S. Ct. Appeals (5th cir.) 1973, U.S. Dist. Ct. (so. dist.) Tex. 1980, U.S. Ct. Appeals (11th cir.) 1981. Law clk. U.S. Dist. Ct. Colo., 1960-61; trial atty. SEC, Denver, 1961-67, asst. regional adminstr., Ft. Worth, 1967-72, regional adminstr., 1972-75; ptnr. Law, Snakard & Gambill, P.C., Ft. Worth, 1975—; counsel City of Ft. Worth Police Investigation Commn., 1975; spl. counsel Office Atty. Gen. State Ariz., 1977-78. Mem. Ft. Worth Crime Commn., 1987—; pres. bd. trustees Trinity Valley Sch., Ft. Worth; adv. dir., pres. Lena Pope Home for Dependent and Neglected Children, Ft. Worth. Mem. ABA, State Bar Tex., Tarrant County Bar Assn., Colo. Bar Assn., Tex. Bar Found., Am. Counsel Assn., Fed. Bar Assn., Am. Judicature Soc., Phi Delta Phi. Republican. Presbyterian. Clubs: Ft. Worth, Shady Oaks Country (Ft. Worth). Contbr. articles to profl. jours. Office: Suite 3200 Tex Am Bank Bldg Fort Worth TX 76102

WATSON, WILLIAM KEITH ROSS, scientist; b. Lowestoft, Eng., Nov. 8, 1930; s. William Ross and Elizabeth Margaret (Wood) W.; came to U.S., 1953, naturalized, 1957; student Corpus Christi Coll., 1950-53; B.A., Cambridge (Eng.) U., 1953; M.A., U. Calif. at Berkeley, 1955, Ph.D., 1957; children—Christine Margaret, Cynthia Kathryn, Carolyn Elizabeth. Research asso., lectr. U. Calif. at Berkeley, 1957; Sloane fellow Calif. Inst. Tech., 1957-59; asst. prof. U. So. Calif., Los Angeles, 1959-61; asst. prof. physics U. Calif. at Riverside, 1961-64; v.p. Winston Research Corp., Los Angeles, 1962-63, dir., 1962-67; v.p. Highland Research Corp., Riverside, 1963-64, pres., 1964-66; corporate staff Astrodata, Inc., 1964-66; v.p. research Medical Electronics div. Becton Dickinson & Co., East Rutherford, N.J., 1966-69; dir. CALSEIA, Neuro-Psychiat. and Health Care Services, S.W. Energy Mgmt.; chmn. bd. Biomex Internat. Corp.; v.p., dir. research and devel. Internat. Thera peutics Inc., 1986—; sr. cons. Technicolor Corp. Sci.; cons. Abbott Labs., 1972-76, Kay Labs., 1972-76, U.S. Navy, 1976—, Dept. Energy, 1977—; solar cons. Calif. Gov.'s Office, 1980—. Mem. sci. adv. U.S. Senate Com. Energy and Natural Resources, 1977—, U.S. Dept. Def., 1977—, U.S. Senate Fin. Com., 1980—. Adv., Calif. Central Republican Com.; sci. advisor Carter Presdl. Campaign, 1976-76; mem. adv. bd. Energetics Systems Inc., Washington, 1981—; chmn. So. Calif.-San Diego County Desalination Com., 1983—; coordinator UN Decade of Water Global Communication Forum Mex., 1983; chmn. internat. symposium WHO, San Diego, 1986; introductory speaker US/Air 88, San Diego, 1988. Fulbright scholar, 1953. Fellow Am. Math. Soc.; mem. Am. Phys. Soc., Am. Inst. Aeros. and Astronautics, Bassetlaw Young Conservative Assn. (sec. 1950-52), Internat. Solar Energy Soc., Calif. Solar Energy Assn. (dir. 1975-80), Sigma Xi. Club: Rancho Santa Fe Tennis. Contbr. articles to sci. publs. Patentee med. instruments and renewable energy resources. Home: PO Box 1537 Rancho Santa Fe CA 92067

WATT, DAVID CAMPBELL, psychiatrist; b. London, Mar. 23, 1920; s. Duncan Campbell and Margaret (Birch) W.; m. Helen Elizabeth Short, Mar. 9, 1946. BSc, Glasgow (Scotland) U., 1940; DPM, London U., 1949; MD, Glasgow (Scotland) U., 1951; FRC in Psychiatry, Royal Coll. psychiatrists, Eng., 1971. Cons. psychiatrist dept. med. genetics Churchill Hosp., Oxford, Eng. Home: 7 Churchway Stone, Aylesbury, Buckinghamshire HP17 8RG, England

WATT, JAMES D., financial consultant; b. N.Y.C., Dec. 20, 1946; s. Douglas Benjamin and Ray (Mantel) W.; m. Maria Guarisco; children: Alexandra Bateman, Peter Douglas. B.A. in English, Iona Coll., 1969. Former asso. editor Scholastic Mags., N.Y.C.; pres. Re-Inovations Ltd., N.Y.C., 1974-76; account exec. Merrill, Lynch, Pierce, Fenner & Smith, N.Y.C., 1977-78; account exec. Oppenheimer & Co., N.Y.C., from 1978, now sr. v.p., fin. cons. Tchr., vol. with Pres. Johnson's War on Poverty Program, Elmsford, N.Y., 1965-66; contbr. J.O.B. program, N.Y.C. Republican. Roman Catholic. Home: 14 Green Ln Chappaqua NY 10514

WATT, ROGER JOHN, vision science researcher; b. London, Nov. 26, 1954; s. Ian and Pamela (Dudley) W.; m. Helen Marion Jeffs, Apr. 29, 1978; children: Sarah, Samuel. BA, U. Cambridge, Eng., 1977; PhD, Keele U., Staffordshire, Eng., 1980. Research fellow Durham (Eng.) U., 1980-81; research assoc. U. London, 1981-83, U. Cambridge, 1983-84; scientist Med. Research Council, Cambridge, 1984-88; research fellow U. Stirling, Scotland, 1988—; hon. fellowship University Coll., U. London, 1987. Author: Visual Processing, 1988; editor (jour.) Spatial Vision, 1984—; contbr. articles to profl. jours. Greystone scholar U. Cambridge, 1975-76. Ch. of Eng. Office: U Stirling, Dept Psychology, Stirling FK9 4LA, Scotland

WATT, RONALD WILLIAM, public relations executive; b. Cleve., Oct. 10, 1943; s. Archie Gordon and Molly (Champa) W.; m. Elizabeth K. Strasshofer, May 15, 1965 (div. Dec. 1973); children: Cheryl Marie, Laurie Michelle; m. Simona Catherine Yesbak, Dec. 21, 1973; children: Ronald William Jr., Amanda Catherine. BJ, Bowling Green State U., 1965. Reporter Sta. WSPD-TV and Radio, Toledo, 1965-66; mgr. pub. relations Toledo-Lucas County Port Authority, Toledo, 1966-68; account exec. Flournoy & Gibbs, Toledo, 1968-73; v.p. Edward Howard and Co., Cleve., 1973-79; pres. Watt-Jayme Pub. Relations, Cleve., 1979-81; pres., chief operating officer Watt, Roop & Co., Cleve., 1981 87, chmn., chief exec. officer, 1987—. Mem. Leadership Cleve., 1987—; chmn. Red Cross Centennial Cleve., 1981; co-founder Browns Buddies Program, Rainbow Babies, Childrens Hosp., Cleve., 1981; bd. dirs. Youth Opportunities, Inc., 1984—, Downtown Cleve. Bus. Council, 1987—, Nat. Conf. of Christians and Jews Cleve. chpt., 1988—, Citizens League of Cleve., 1988—. Named one of Outstanding Young Men Am., 1971. Mem. Nat. Media Conf. (bd. dirs. 1985—), Pub. Relations Soc. Am. (pres. Greater Cleve. chpt. 1981-82, 4 Silver Anvil awards 1969, 73, 87, accredited), Cleve. Advt. Club (bd. dirs. 1985—, v.p. activities 1988), Cleve. Press Club (bd. dirs. 1986—), Greater Cleve. Press Club (co-chmn. centennial 1987). Republican. Roman Catholic. Clubs: Canterbury Golf (Shaker Heights, Ohio); Firestone Country (Akron, Ohio); Hermit (Cleve.); Clifton (Lakewood, Ohio). Office: Watt Roop & Co 525 Nat City Bank Bldg Cleveland OH 44107

WATTERS, JAMES I(SAAC), chemistry and mathematics educator; b. Broadus, Mont., Apr. 4, 1908; s. James O. and Hilda C. (Erickson) W.; m. Louise G. Chambers, Aug. 28, 1938; children—Louise Emilie, Molly Marie, James Norman, Kathryn Verne. Student, U. Fla., 1926-28, U. Calif. at Berkeley, 1928-29; B.S., U. Minn., 1931, Ph.D., 1943. Tchr. Anoka pub. schs., 1931-38; instr. Cornell U., Ithaca, N.Y., 1941-43; chief analytical chemistry on atom bomb project U. Chgo., 1943-45; assoc. prof. U. Ky., 1945-48; assoc. prof. Ohio State U., Columbus, 1948-58, prof. chemistry, math. and phys. scis., 1958—; summer cons. U.S. AID, Punjab U., 1965, Annamalai U., 1966, Ujjain U., 1967; all India. Editor: Analytical Chemistry of Atomic Energy Project, 1951; Contbr.: chpts. to Treatise on Analytical Chemistry; also articles on polarography and spectrophotometry to tech. jours. Mem. Am. Chem. Soc., AAAS, Sigma Xi, Zeta Psi, Phi Lambda Upsilon. Lutheran. Home: 1470 Ridgeview Rd Columbus OH 43221

WATTS, FRASER NORMAN, psychologist; b. Coventry, England, May 5, 1946; s. Charles Norman and Audrey Margaret (Buckler) W. BA, Oxford (Eng.) U., 1968; MSc, London U., 1970, PhD, 1975. Lectr. Inst. Psychiatry London U., 1970-75; prin. psychologist King's Coll. Hosp., London, 1975-81; sr. scientist applied psychology unit Med. Research Council, Cambridge, Eng., 1981—. Author: (with D.H. Bennett) Theory and Practice of Psychiatric Rehabilitation, 1983; (with M.G. Williams) Psychology of Religious Knowing, 1988; (with others) Cognitive Psychology and Emotional Disorders, 1988; editor: New Developments in Clinical Psychology, 1985; (with G. Parry) Skills and Methods in Mental Health Research, 1988, Cognition and Emotion, Brighton, Eng., 1987—. Fellow British Psychological Soc. (chmn. div. clin. psychology 1983-84, pres. 1988—, council 1982—). Social Liberal Dem. Party. Mem. Ch. of Eng. Home: 81 Church Rd Hauxton, Cambridge CB2 5HS, England Office: Applied Psychology Unit, 15 Chaucer Rd, Cambridge CB2 2EF, England

WATTS, HELENA ROSELLE, military analyst; b. East Lynne, Mo., May 29, 1921; d. Elmer Wayne and Nellie Irene (Barrington) Long; m. Henry Millard Watts, June 14, 1940; children—Helena Roselle Watts Scott, Patricia Marie Watts Foble. B.A., Johns Hopkins U., 1952, postgrad., 1952-53. Assoc. engr., Westinghouse Corp., Balt., 1965-67; sr. analyst Merck, Sharp & Dohme, Westpoint, Pa., 1967-69; sr. engr. Bendix Radio div. Bendix Corp., Balt., 1970-72; sr. scientist Sci. Applications Internat. Corp., McLean, Va., 1975-84; mem. tech. staff The Mitre Corp., McLean, 1985—; adj. prof. Def. Intelligence Coll., Washington, 1984-85. Contbr. articles to tech. jours. Mem. IEEE, AAAS, Nat. Mil. Intelligence Assn., U.S. Naval Inst., Assn. Old Crows, Mensa, N.Y. Acad. Sci. Republican. Roman Catholic. Avocations: photography; gardening; reading. Home: 4302 Roberts Ave Annandale VA 22003 Office: The Mitre Corp W442 7525 Colshire Dr McLean VA 22102

WATTS, JOHN RANSFORD, university administrator; b. Boston, Feb. 9, 1930; s. Henry Fowler Ransford and Mary Marion (Macdonald) W.; m. Joyce Lannon, Dec. 2, 1975; 1 child, David Allister. AB, Boston Coll., 1950, MEd, 1965; MFA, Yale U., 1953; PhD, Union Grad. Sch., 1978.Prof., asst. dean Boston U., 1958-74; prof., dean of fine arts Calif. State U., Long Beach, 1974-79; dean and artistic dir. The Theatre Sch. (Goodman Sch. of Drama), DePaul U., Chgo., 1979—; gen. mgr. Boston Arts Festivals, 1955-64; adminstr. Arts Programs at Tanglewood, 1966-69; producing dir. Theatre Co. of Boston, 1973-75. Chmn., Mass. Council on Arts and Humanities, 1968-72; dir., v.p. Long Beach (Calif.) Pub. Corp. for the Arts, 1975-79; mem. theatre panel, Ill. Arts Council, 1981—. Served with U.S. Army, 1953-55. Mem. Mass. Ednl. Communications Commn., Am. Theatre Assn., Nat. Council on Arts in Edn., Met. Cultural Alliance, League Chgo. Theatres, Chgo. Internat. Theatre Festival, Phi Beta Kappa. Club: St. Botolph (Boston), Cliffdwellers (Chgo.). Office: De Paul U The Theatre Sch (Goodman Sch of Drama) 2135 N Kenmore Chicago IL 60614

WATTS, KEITH WILLIAM, electric utility executive; b. Yeppoon, Queensland, Australia, Dec. 1, 1932; s. Charles William McKenzie and Minnie Elizabeth (Blanning) W.; m. Dorothy Jane Fisher, Dec. 9, 1961; children: Jennifer, David. Diploma mech. and elec. engring., U. Queensland, Brisbane, Australia, 1953, B in Engring. with honors, 1969; MBA, Deakin U., Geelong, Victoria, 1985. Chartered elec. engr. Apprentice elec. engr. The Capricornia Regional Elec. Bd., Rockhampton, Queensland, 1948-54, engr., 1954-59; area engr. Gladstone, Queensland, 1959-66; area supervising engr. Rockhampton, Queensland, 1970-75; mgr. Mackay (Queensland) Regional Elec. Bd., 1975-77; gen. mgr. Mackay Elec. Bd., 1977-87, Capricornia Electricity Bd., Rockhampton, 1988—; convener com. on domestic utilisation tech. Electricity Supply Assn. Australia, 1986; mem. consultative council Queensland Electricity Supply Industry, 1977; dir., dep. chmn. Mackay Region Apprentice Employment Ltd., 1985; dir. Mackay Regional Devel. Bur. Inc., 1986; councillor Capricornia Inst. Advanced Edn., Rockhampton, 1987. Contbr. articles to profl. jours. Chmn. community gifts com. Good Sheperd Lodge Devel. Fund Appeal, Mackay, 1982, Whitsunday Anglical Sch. Devel. Fund Appeal, Mackay, 1987; parochial councillor St. Ambrose Anglican Parish, Anglican Diocese North Queensland, Mackay, 1977-87. Recipient Citation for Meritorious Service, Rotary Found., Australia, 1979. Fellow Instn. Engrs. Australia (chmn. 1981), Australian Inst. Mgmt. (chmn. 1978-79), INst. Dirs. Australia; mem. Australian Soc. Sugar Cane Technologists, Alumni Assn. U. Queensland, Australian Def. Assn., Deakin MBA Soc., Australian Adminstrv. Staff Coll. Assn. Clubs: United Service Inst., Returned Services League, Rockhampton, U. Queensland Staff and Grads. Lodge: Rotary (pres. Rockhampton club 1972-73), Masons. Office: Capricornia Electricity Ctr, Fitzroy and Alma St, Rockhampton, Rockhampton Queenland 4700, Australia also: Capricornia Electricity Ctr, P O Box 308, Rockhampton Queensland 4700, Australia

WATTS, LOU ELLEN, educator; b. Conway, S.C., Sept. 23, 1940; d. Bernie Louis and Dallie Ellen (Lemons) Overhultz; m. Ervin William Watts, Feb. 3, 1963; children: William Ashley. B in Music Edn., La. State U., 1962; postgrad. U. Ga., 1965; MEd, U. Ariz., 1987. Cert. elem. tchr., music tchr., Ind., Ga., La., Ariz. Music tchr. Westchester Twp. Sch., Chesterton, Ind., 1963-64; music cons. Clayton County Sch., Jonesboro, Ga., 1964-66; elem. and chorus tchr. Tucson Unified Sch. Dist., 1979—, intermediate head div. tchr., music cons., 1983-84, chorus dir., 1979-84, music tchr. mid. sch., 1987—; teacher, cons. archaeology, 1983—. Author (tchr./student manuals): Archaeology is More Than a Dig; contbr. articles to profl. jours. Pres., fine arts chmn., cons. Sahuaro Jr. Women's Club, Tucson, 1970-74; state consumer chmn., music award chmn. Ariz. Fedn. of Women's Club, 1970-72; mem. Tucson Panhellenic Council, 1971-72; project chmn. Southwest Children's Exploratory Ctr., Tucson. Tucson Enrichment Fund grantee, 1983—. Recipient Clubwoman of the Year Ariz. Fedn. Jr. Women's Club, 1972. Mem. NEA, Nat. Audubon Soc., Nat. Sci. Tchr. Assn., Music Educators Nat. Conf., Ariz. Edn. Assn., Ariz. Sci. Tchr.'s Assn. (Search for Excellence in Sci. award 1985), Tucson Edn. Assn., DAR, So. Ariz. Arabian Horse Assn., Delta Kappa Gamma, Sigma Alpha Iota. Home and Office: 8740 E Summer Terr Tucson AZ 85749

WAUGH, AUBERON ALEXANDER, critic, journalist; b. Dulverton, Somerset, Eng., Nov. 17, 1939; s. Evelyn and Laura (Herbert) W.; m. Teresa Onslow, Jan. 7, 1961; children—Margaret Sophia Laura, Alexander Evelyn Michael, Daisy Louisa Dominica, Nathaniel Thomas. Scholar in Classics, Downside; scholar in English, Christ Church, Oxford U. Editorial writer Daily Telegraph, London, 1960-63; columnist Cath. Herald, London, 1963-64, Daily Mirror, London, 1963-67; polit. corr. Spectator, London, 1967-70, chief fiction reviewer, 1970-73, 76 ; and lit. editor Private Eye, London, 1970-86; columnist News of the World, London, 1969-70, Sun, London, 1969-70, London Times, 1970, New Statesman, 1973-75; chief fiction reviewer Evening Standard, London, 1973-80, Daily Mail, London, 1981-86, Sunday Telegraph, 1981—; editor Lit. Rev., 1986—; chief book reviewer The Independent, 1986—. Author: The Foxglove Saga, 1960; Path of Dalliance, 1963; Who are the Violets Now'9 , 1965; Consider the Lilies, 1968, Britain's Shame, 1969; Country Topics, 1974; Four Crowded Years, 1976; In the Lion's Den, 1979; The Last Word—The Trial of Jeremy Thorpe, 1980; Auberon Waugh's Yearbook, 1981, Waugh on Wine, 1986, others. Pres. Brit. Croatian Soc., London, 1973—. Named Critic of Yr., Nat. Press, London, 1976, 78; Columnist of Yr., Granada TV, 1979. Roman Catholic. Club: Beefsteak. Home: Combe Florey House, Combe Florey, Taunton, Somerset TA4 3JD, England *

WAUTIER, JEAN LUC, hematologist; b. Colombelles, Calvados, France, Nov. 10, 1942; s. Marcel Jean and Léonie Benoite (Eliat) W.; m. Marie Paule Pepin, July 19, 1967; children: Jean Baptiste, Pauline. MD, U. Caen, France, 1971; degree in hematology, U. Paris, 1973, D of Biol. Scis., 1979. Asst. Hosp. St. Louis, Paris, 1972-75; cons. Hosp. Lariboisière, Paris, 1976-78, med. dir. Ctr. Transfusion, 1979—; sr. investigator Nat. Inst. Med. Research, Paris, 1980—; prof. hematology U. Paris VII, 1988—; mem. Consultative Med. Com., Paris, 1983. Co-author: Sang et Vaisseaux, 1987, 3 sci. films; editor: Nouvelle Revue Francaise d'Hematologie, 1983—; contbr. articles to profl. jours. Mem. exec. com. Assn. Personnels Sportifs Adminstrns. Paris, 1984. Recipient O. Lemonom price Paris Acad. Scis., 1983. Fellow Royal Soc. Medicine; mem. Internat. Soc. Hematology, French Soc. Hematology, Soc. Clin. Hemorheology, N.Y. Acad. Scis., Internat. Soc. Thrombosis Hemostasis. Club: Réalisme Efficacité Espérance Liberté (Paris). Office: Hosp Lariboisiere Ctr Transfusion, 2 Rue Ambroise Pare, 75010 Paris France

WAWRZYNIAK, STEPHEN DAVID, mfg. co. exec.; b. St. Joseph, Mo., Oct. 21, 1949; s. Michael Joseph and Kathryn Maxine (Cook) W.; B.B.A., Mo. Western State Coll., 1973, B.S. in Psychology, 1973; m. Melneta Elizabeth Maschek, June 25, 1975; children—Shannon, Tammy, Lisa, Karrie. Quality control insp. Carnation Co., St. Joseph, 1973-74, plant sanitarian, plant safety coordinator, 1974-76; exec. dir. quality control Doane Products, Joplin, Mo., 1976-82; exec. dir. tech. services, 1982-84; v.p. tech. services, 1984—. Served with U.S. Army, 1969-70. Lic. and cert. comml. pesticide applicator Mo., Iowa, Calif., Va., AL. Mem. Am. Soc. Quality Control (sr.mem., section chmn. 1980-81, reg. councilor adminstr. applications div. 1984-85), Inst. Food Technologists (profl. mem.), Am. Soc. Animal Sci., Am. Oil Chemists Soc., Am. Assn. Cereal Chemists, Pet Food Inst., Assn. Am. Feed Control Ofcls., Ducks Unltd., Mo. Pest Control Assn., Joplin, Mo. Sr. Volunteer Program (bd. dir. ombudsman program), Nat. Rifle Assn. Republican. Baptist. Clubs: Joplin Rifle and Pistol; Masons, Shriners. Home: 2602 S Kingdale Joplin MO 64804-1343 Office: PO Box 879 Joplin MO 64801

WAX, RAY VAN, state agency administrator; b. Sterling, Okla., June 7, 1944; s. Sam Van Wax and Betty Louise (Lucas) Landers; m. Linda Ann Willcutt, Dec. 31, 1972; children: Cody, Tiffany. Student, Pierce Coll., 1972-74, U. Wash., 1974, U. Ala., 1976. Safety inspector State Wash. Dept. Labor and Industry, Olympia, 1973-83; sr. safety inspector State Wash. Dept. Labor and Industry, Tacoma, 1983-84, mgr. safety regulations program, 1984—; cons. Wax Safety Services, Graham, Wash., 1980—. Editor numerous safety and health standards publs.; contbr. articles to profl. jours. Served with USN, 1962-68. Mem. Am. Soc. Safety Engrs., Am. Nat. Standards Insts. (coms.), World Safety Orgn. Home: 24214 64th Ave E PO Box 353 Graham WA 98338 Office: Wash Dept Labor/Industries Div Indsl Safety/Health 805 Plum St SE Box 207 Olympia WA 98504

WAXMAN, DAVID, physician, university consultant; b. Albany, N.Y., Feb. 7, 1918; s. Meyer and Fannie (Strosberg) W.; m. Jane Waxman; 6 children. B.S., Syracuse U., 1942, M.D., 1950. Intern Grace Hosp., Detroit, 1950-51; resident in medicine, fellow in cardiology U. Kans. Coll. Health Scis. and Hosp., Kansas City, 1958-61; instr. internal medicine U. Kans. Coll. Health Scis. and Hosp., 1961-64, asst. prof. internal medicine, 1964-69, assoc. prof., 1969-77, prof., 1977—, dir. dept. medicine outpatient service, 1970-74, asst. dean, 1970-71, assoc. dean for student affairs, 1971-72, dean of students, 1972-74, vice chancellor for students, 1974-76, vice chancellor, 1976-77, exec. vice chancellor, 1977-83, spl. cons. to chancellor for health affairs, 1983—; nat. cons. to surgeon gen. USAF. Contbr. articles to med. jours. Mem. Kans. State Bd. Healing Arts, 1984—. Served with USAFR, maj. gen. Res. ret. Decorated D.S.M. with one oak leaf cluster, Legion of Merit. Fellow ACP; mem. Kans. Med. Soc., Jackson County Med. Soc., Wyandotte County Med. Soc., Soc. Med. Cons. to the Armed Forces, Soc. Internists, Alpha Omega Alpha. Office: U Kans Coll of Health Scis and Hosp 39th and Rainbow Blvd Kansas City KS 66103

WAYLAND, L. C. NEWTON, public health pediatrician; b. Plainview, Tex., May 4, 1909; s. Levi Clarence and Connie Onita (Newton) W.; student Wayland Coll., Plainview, 1925-26, West Tex. State Tchrs. Coll., 1926-30; A.B., Stanford U., 1932, M.D., 1936; postgrad. U. Calif. Med. Sch., Children's, Gen. hosps., Los Angeles; m. Helen Hart, June 18, 1938 (div. 1966); children—Newton, Elizabeth, Constance. Intern, San Francisco City and County Hosp., Stanford Service, 1936; house officer San Mateo County Hosp., 1937, Children's Hosp., Los Angeles, 1938; dir. child health Santa Barbara (Calif.) County Health Dept., 1938-44; dir. health Santa Barbara City Schs., 1944-74; dir. health Santa Barbara City Coll., 1946-74; pvt. practice medicine specializing in pediatrics, 1955-70; ret. mem. pediatric staffs Santa Barbara Gen., St. Francis, Cottage, Goleta Valley hosps.; ret. med. cons. Calif. State Dept. Rehab., 1974-78; emeritus mem. med. staff Calif. State Prison at Soledad. Past non-nurse dir. exec. com., sch. nursing sect. Nat. Orgn. Pub. Health Nurses; past mem. adv. com. Calif. Dept. Edn. on Pub. Sch. Health; mem. Pub. Citizen Inc. Past 1st bd. dirs. Get Oil Out!; mem. vol. staff. Santa Barbara Zool. Gardens. Recipient award Calif. Sch. Nurses Orgn., 1965, 71. Fellow Am. Pub. Health Assn., Am. Sch. Health Assn. (past pres. Calif. div.); mem. NEA (ret.), Calif. Tchrs. Assn. (ret.), Calif. Med. Assn. (ret.), Santa Barbara County Med. Soc. (ret.), Am. Acad. Pediatrics, Los Angeles pediatric socs. (ret.), World Council Chs., Nat. Council Chs. (founding mem. laymen's commn.), No. Calif. Ecumenical Council, UN Assn. (past pres. Santa Barbara chpt.), Ams. for Democratic Action, NAACP, ACLU, Calif. Congress Parents and Tchrs. (hon. life), Scholastic Socs. South, Nat. Audubon Soc., Save the Redwoods League,

Wilderness Soc., Isaac Walton League, Nat. Parks Assn., Sierra Club, So. Christian Leadership Conf., Cousteau Soc., Planned Parenthood Fedn. Am., Environ. Protective Assn., Fellowship Reconciliation, Inst. for Am. Democracy, Com. for Improvement Med. Care, SANE, Nat. Indian Youth Council, Nat. and Internat. Wildlife Assn., Common Cause, Episcopal Peace Fellowship, Fund for Peace, Nat. and Internat. Nature Conservancy, Friends of the Earth, Green Peace, Gray Panthers, Defenders of Wildlife, Internat. Physicians for Prevention of Nuclear War, Leadership Circle of Physicians for Social Responsibility, Nat. Urban League, Religious Coalition for Abortion Rights, Nat. Abortion Rights Action League, Freedom from Hunger Found., Alliance for Survival, Inst. Aerobic Research, Ctr. War/Peace Studies, Am. Farmland Trust, Rural Advancement Fund, NOW, ERA, So. Poverty Law Center, United World Federalists, Zero Population Growth, Negative Population Growth, Amnesty Internat., Council for Livable World, Clergymen and Laymen Concerned, Am. Fedn. Scientists, Planning and Conservation League Calif., Am. Indian Fund, Humane Soc. U.S., Assn. for Vol. Sterilization, Council on Econ. Priorities, N. Am. Congress on Latin Am., Coalition for a New Fgn. Policy, Met. Opera Assn., Nat. Council on Aging, The Africa Fund., Ams. United for Separation of Ch. and State, Am. Friends Service Com., Nat. Assn. for R.R. Passengers, Calif. Tax Reform Assn., Nat. Com. for Peace in Cen. Am., LWV, Santa Barbara Citizens Planning Assn., Internat. Ctr. for Devel. Policy, Simon Wiesenthal Ctr., Am.-Israeli Civil Liberties Coalition, Internat. Platform Assn., Ctr. for Def. Info., OXFAM, Children's Aid Internat., Ctr. for Law in Pub. Interest, World Wildlife Fund, WAND, Children of War, Solar Lobby, Rainforest Action Network, Educators for Social Responsibility, PAX Ams., Nat. Cathedral Assn., People for the Am. Way, Cath. for Free Choice, N.Y. Acad. of Scis., Nat. Assn. World Health, YMCA, mem. hon. steering com. Ron Dellum's Nat. Adv. Bd., numerous others. Democrat. Episcopalian. Contbr. articles to ednl. and other profl. jours. Home: 1807 Paterna Rd Santa Barbara CA 93103

WAYMAN, PATRICK ARTHUR, astronomer; b. Bromley, Eng., Oct. 8, 1927; came to Ireland, 1964; s. Lewis John and Mary (Palmer) W.; m. Mavis McIntyre Smith Gibson, June 19, 1954; children: Russell, Karen, Sheila. BA, Cambridge U., Eng., 1948, MA, 1952, PhD, 1952. Sr. sci. officer Royal Greenwich Obs., Sussex, Eng., 1952-62, head dept., 1962-64; sr. prof. astronomy sect. Dublin (Ireland) Inst. for Advanced Studies, 1964—, now dir. obs. Contbr. articles to profl. jours. Mem. Royal Astron. Soc. (assoc.), Royal Irish Acad., Internat. Astron. Union (gen. sec. 1979-82, editor publ. 1979-82). Anglican. Home and Office: Dunsink Observatory, Dublin 15, Ireland

WAYMIRE, ROBERTA ARLENE, construction company executive; b. Wimbledon, N.D., June 20, 1936; d. Gaylord and Huldah Evelyn (Ekstrand) Thorne; student Brigham Young U., 1953-54; m. Kenneth L. Waymire, Feb. 26, 1955; children—Thorne L., Kent L. Reporter, Democrat Herald, Albany, Oreg., 1955-56; with Waverly Constrn. Co., Inc., Tigard, Oreg., 1964—, v.p., 1982—. Mem. Portland Metro Homebuilders Assn. Republican. Home and Office: 8735 SW Curry Dr #B Wilsonville OR 97070

WAYNE, JANE ELLEN, author; b. Phila., Apr. 6, 1936; d. Jesse Allen and Eleanor Mae (Brundle) Stump; student Grove City Coll., 1956, N.Y. U., 1956, Am. Acad. Dramatic Arts, 1957; m. Ronald R. Wayne, May 26, 1958 (div. 1967); 1 dau., Elizabeth Jo. Mem. promotion staff NBC, N.Y.C., 1957-65; mgr. V.I.P. div. N.Y. World's Fair, 1966; v.p. Abbot & Abbot Corp., N.Y.C., 1974-87; creator Beauty and Poise pvt. classes for bus. women, 1963-66. Mem. The Author's Guild, Sigma Delta Phi. Republican. Author: The Life of Robert Taylor, 1977; Kings of Tragedy, 1977; Tiffany, 1979; Lividia, 1979; The Love Gap, 1979; Kings of Tragedy II, 1982; Kings and Queens of Tragedy, 1983; The Barbara Stanwyck Story, 1985, Gable's Women, 1987, Joan Crawford's Men, 1988, Gary Cooper's Women, 1988; contbr. to Nat. Enquirer, Star mag. Home: 17-85 215th St Bayside Terrace NY 11360

WAYNE, KYRA PETROVSKAYA, author; b. Crimea, USSR, Dec. 31, 1918; came to U.S., 1948, naturalized, 1951; d. Prince Vasily Sergeyevich and Baroness Zinaida Fedorovna (Fon-Haffenberg) Obolensky; m. George J. Wayne, Apr. 21, 1961; 1 child, Ronald George. B.A., Leningrad Inst. Theatre Arts, 1939, M.A., 1940. Actress, concert singer, USSR, 1939-46; actress, U.S., 1948-51; enrichment lectr. Royal Viking Line cruises, Alaska-Can., Greek Islands-Black Sea, Russia/Europe, 1978-79, 81-82, 83-84, 86-87. Author: Kyra, 1959; Kyra's Secrets of Russian Cooking, 1960; The Quest for the Golden Fleece, 1962; Shurik, 1971; The Awakening, 1972; The Witches of Barguzin, 1975; Max, The Dog That Refused to Die, 1979 (Best Fiction award Dog Writers Assn. Am. 1980); Rekindle the Dreams, 1979, Quest for Empire, 1986. Founder, pres. Clean Air Program, Los Angeles County, 1971-72; mem. women's council KCET-Ednl. TV. Served to lt. Russian Army, 1941-43. Decorated Red Star, numerous other decorations USSR; recipient award Crusade for Freedom, 1955-56; award Los Angeles County, 1972. Mem. Soc. Children's Book Writers, Authors Guild, P.E.N., UCLA Med. Faculty Wives (pres. 1970-71, dir. 1971-75) UCLA Affiliates (life), Los Angeles Lung Assn. (life), Friends of the Lung Assn. (pres. 1988), Idyllwild Sch. Music, Art and Theatre Assn. (trustee 1987). Home: 234 S Rimpau Blvd Los Angeles CA 90004

WAYNE, ROBERT ANDREW, lawyer; b. Newark, Oct. 4, 1938; s. David Michael and Charlotte (Chesler) W.; m. Charlotte Fainblatt, Aug. 14, 1969; children—Andrew Mark, Gary Howard, Deborah Jill. B.A., Princeton U., 1960; J.D., Columbia U. 1963. Bar: N.J. 1964, U.S. Dist. Ct. N.J. 1964, U.S. Dist. Ct. (ea. and so. dists.) N.Y. 1966, U.S. Ct. Apls. (3d cir.) 1967, N.Y. 1981, U.S. Ct. Apls. (2d cir.) 1984, U.S. Supreme Ct. 1984, U.S. Claims Ct., 1984, U.S. Tax Ct. 1984. Assoc., Shanley & Fisher, Newark, 1964-69, ptnr., 1969-71; ptnr. Robinson, Wayne & LaSala, Newark, 1971—. Mem. Democratic County Com., Livingston, N.J., 1971-74. Served with AUS, 1963-69. Mem. ABA, N.J. Bar Assn., Essex County Bar Assn., Monmouth County Bar Assn., Fed. Bar Assn., Am. Coll. Real Estate Lawyers. Jewish. Office: Robinson Wayne & LaSala Gaetway I Newark NJ 07102

WAYNE, VICTOR SAMUEL, cardiologist; b. Melbourne, Australia, Jan. 7, 1953; s. Mark Isaac and Anita (Selzer) W.; m. Karen Susan Eisinger; children: Fairlie, Stephanie. BS with honors, Monash U., 1976. Diplomate Australian Soc. Ultrasound in Medicine. Intern, resident med. officer, registrar Alfred Hosp., Melbourne, 1976-79, cardiology registrar, 1980-81; advanced cardiology fellow St. Vincent Hosp., Worcester, Mass., 1982-83; instr. medicine U. Mass., Worcester, 1982-83; cardiologist St. Francis Xavier Cabrini Hosp., Epworth Hosp., Melbourne, 1983—; vis. physician, cardiologist Alfred Hosp., Monash U., Melbourne, 1983—. Grantee Nat. Heart Found., Alfred Hosp., 1982. Fellow Royal Australasian Coll. Physicians, Am. Coll. Chest Physicians, Internat. Acad. Chest Physicians and Surgeons, N.Y. Acad. Scis., Am. Coll. Cardiology, Internat. Coll. Angiology; mem. Cardiac Soc. Australia and New Zealand, Australian Soc. Echocardiography. Jewish. Club: Nat. Golf of Australia. Home: 16 Dunraven Ave Toorak, Melbourne Victoria 3144, Australia Office: Cabrini Med Ctr, Isabella St Malvern, Melbourne Victoria 3144, Australia

WAYTE, ALAN, lawyer; b. Huntington Park, Calif., Dec. 30, 1936; s. Paul Henry and Helen Lucille (McCarthy) W.; m. Beverly A. Bruen, Feb. 19, 1959 (div. 1972); children: David Alan, Lawrence Andrew, Marcia Louise; m. Nancy Kelly Wayte, July 5, 1975. AB, Stanford U., 1958, JD, 1960. Ptnr. Adams, Duque & Hazeltine, Los Angeles, 1966-85, Dewey, Ballantine, Bushby, Palmer & Wood, Los Angeles, 1985—. Mem. Los Angeles County Bar Assn. (chmn. real property sect. 1977-78), Calif. Bar Assn. (chmn. real property sect. 1981-82), Am. Coll. Real Estate Lawyers, Am. Coll. Mortgage Attys., Anglo-Am. Real Property Inst., Los Angeles Philharmonic Assn. (exec. com., bd. dirs. 1973—). Clubs: Chancery, California (Los Angeles); Valley Hunt (Pasadena). Home: 1484 Cambridge Rd San Marino CA 91108 Office: Dewey Ballantine Bushby et al 333 S Hope St Los Angeles CA 90071

WEADOCK, DANIEL P., corporate executive; b. N.Y.C., June 21, 1939; m. Florence Towey, Oct. 5, 1961; children: Daniel, Bryan, Kevin, Ann, Kathleen. B.S. in Fin, Fordham U., 1967. With central bookkeeping Chase Manhattan Bank, 1957-61; with ITT, 1961—, spl. asst. to office of pres., 1969-75; dir. ops. ITT Africa and Middle East, Brussels, 1975-79; pres. ITT Africa and Middle East, 1979; v.p. ITT, 1979-83; pres. ITT Europe Inc., Brussels, 1983—; exec. v.p. ITT, 1983—, group exec.-Europe; pres. ITT-Europe, Inc. Office: ITT World Hdqtrs 320 Park Ave New York NY 10022

WEADON, DONALD ALFORD, JR., international lawyer; b. Brisbane, Australia, Sept. 15, 1945; arrived U.S., 1946; s. Donald Alford and Ellen Martha (Salisbury) W. B.A., Cornell U., 1967; J.D., U. Calif.-San Francisco, 1975; M.B.A., Harvard U. Bus. Sch. Adj. Program, Iran Ctr. for Mgmt. Studies, Tehran, 1976. Bar: Calif. 1976, D.C. 1988. Assoc. law firm Hancock, Rothert & Bunshoft, San Francisco, 1977-80; jr. ptnr. law firm Bryan, Cave, McPheeters & McRoberts, Washington, 1980-83; ptnr., head internat. dept. Anderson Baker Kill & Olick, Washington, 1983-84; sr. ptnr. Weadon, Dibble & Rehm, 1984-88, Weaden, Rehm and Assocs., 1988—; speaker, cons. U.S. Dept. Commerce, 1980-83; cons. Internat. Mktg. Assn., 1980—; Scientific Apparatus Mfg. Assn., 1983—, Valve Mfrs. Assn., 1983—; internat. counsel Am. Electronics Assn., 1986—. Contbr. articles to profl. jours. Served to lt. comdr. USNR, 1968-72. Mem. ABA (chmn. China trade law com. 1982—, chmn. software and tech. data com. 1983—). Episcopalian. Clubs: Olympic, Savage. Office: Weadon Rehm & Assocs 1301 Pennsylvania Ave NW Suite 500 Washington DC 20004

WEARY, THOMAS SQUIRES, lawyer; b. Junction City, Kans., Feb. 15, 1925; s. Ulysses S. and Ina Belle (Kirkpatrick) W.; m. Helen Stephenson, Sept. 25, 1967. A.B. cum laude, Harvard U., 1946, J.D., 1950. Bar: Pa. 1951, U.S. Supreme Ct. 1963. ptnr. Saul, Ewing, Remick & Saul, Phila., 1967—; chief exec. officer Invisible Fence Co., Inc., Wayne, Pa., 1979—; arbitrator Am. Arbitration Assn. Bd. dirs., v.p., gen. counsel Acad. Vocal Arts, Phila.; bd. dirs. World Affairs Council Phila., mem. exec. com., treas.; bd. dirs. Diversified Community Services, Phila. Served to lt. (j.g.) USNR, 1943-49. Recipient Legion of Honor award Chapel of Four Chaplains, Phila., 1982. Mem. Interlex Group (founding ptnr.), Phila. Bar Assn., Pa. Bar Assn., Internat. Law Office Assn., ABA. Presbyterian. Clubs: Racquet, Harvard (dir.) (Phila.); Merion Cricket (Haverford, Pa.); Edgemere (Pike County, Pa.). Office: 3800 Centre Sq West Philadelphia PA 19102

WEATHERHEAD, ALBERT JOHN, III, business executive; b. Cleve., Feb. 17, 1925; s. Albert J. and Dorothy (Jones) W.; m. Celia Scott, Jan. 1, 1975; children: Dwight S., Michael H., Mary H. AB, Harvard U., 1950, postgrad. 1951. Prodn. mgr. Yale & Towne, Stamford, Conn., 1951-54, Blaw-Knox, Pitts., 1954-56; plant mgr. Weatherhead Co., Cleve., 1957-59, gen. mgr., 1959-61, v.p., gen. mgr., 1962-66, gen. sales mgr., 1962-63, v.p. mfg., 1964-66; v.p., dir. Weatherhead Co. of Can., Ltd. 1960-63, pres., chief exec. officer, dir., 1964-66; treas. Weatherchem Corp., 1971-82, pres., dir., 1971—; pres. Weatherhead Industries, 1987—, also bd. dirs., 1987—; bd. dirs. Weatherhead Co., Protane Corp., L.P.G. Leasing Corp., Leasepac Corp., Leasepac Can., Ltd., Creative Resources, Inc. Author: The New Age of Business, 1965. Mem. Harvard U. com. on univ. resources; trustee Case Western Res. U., mem. resources com., council on research involving human subjects, trustee Michelson-Morley Centennial Celebration, mem. Univ. Sch. alumni council, trustee Univ. Sch., hon. trustee for life Univ. Sch., 1988—; mem. vis. com. Ohio U., Athens; v.p. nat. adv. com. Rollins Coll., Winter Park, Fla.; adv. trustee Pinecrest Sch., Ft. Lauderdale, Fla.; mem. capital campaign steering com. Laurel Sch.; trustee Vocat. Guidance and Rehab. Services, Hwy. Safety Found., Arthritis Found.; v.p. Weatherhead Found.; bd. dirs. New Directions Inc., Glenwillow, Ohio; col. CAF. Served with USAAF, 1943-46. Mem. Am. Newcomen Soc., Beta Gamma Sigma (hon.). Clubs: Union (Cleve.); Country (Shaker Heights, Ohio); Ottawa Shooting (Freemont, Ohio); Ocean (Delray, Fla.); Everglades (Palm Beach, Fla); Codrington (Oxford, Eng.). Home: 19601 Shelburne Rd Shaker Heights OH 44118 Office: 25700 Science Park Dr Beachwood OH 44122

WEATHERSTONE, DENNIS, trust company executive; b. London, Nov. 29, 1930; s. Henry Philip and Gladys (Hart) W.; m. Marion Blunsum, Apr. 4, 1959; children—Hazel, Cheryl, Gretel, Richard Paul. Student, Northwestern Poly., London, 1946-49. Sr. v.p. Morgan Guaranty Trust Co. N.Y., N.Y.C., 1972-77, exec. v.p., 1977-79, treas., 1977-79, vice chmn., 1979-80, chmn. exec. com., 1980-86; pres. Morgan Guaranty Trust Co. N.Y. (name changed to J.P. Morgan & Co., Inc.), N.Y.C., 1987—; bd. dirs. Gen. Motors Corp. Mem. Assn. Reserve City Bankers. Office: JP Morgan & Co Inc 23 Wall St New York NY 10015 *

WEATHERUP, ROY GARFIELD, lawyer; b. Annapolis, Md., Apr. 20, 1947; s. Robert Alexander and Kathryn Crites (Hesser) W.; m. Wendy Gaines, Sept. 10, 1977; children: Jennifer, Christine. AB in Polit. Sci., Stanford U., 1968, JD, 1972. Bar: Calif. 1972, U.S. Dist. Ct. 1973, U.S. Ct. Appeals (9th cir.) 1975, U.S. Supreme Ct. 1980. Assoc. Haight, Brown & Bonesteel, Los Angeles, Santa Monica and Santa Ana, Calif., 1972-78, ptnr., 1979—; Moot Ct. judge UCLA, Loyola U., Pepperdine U.; arbitrator Am. Arbitration Assn. Mem. Calif. Acad. Appellate Lawyers, ABA, Town Hall Calif., Los Angeles County Bar Assn. Republican. Methodist. Home: 17260 Rayen St Northridge CA 91325 Office: Haight Brown & Bonesteel 201 Santa Monica Blvd Santa Monica CA 90406

WEATHERUP, WENDY GAINES, insurance agent, writer; b. Glendale, Calif., Oct. 20, 1952; d. William Hughes and Janet Ruth (Neptune) Gaines; m. Roy Garfield Weatherup, Sept. 10, 1977; children—Jennifer, Christine. B.A., U. So. Calif., 1974; Lic. ins. agt. Ins. agt. Gaines Agy., Northridge, Calif., 1974—. Mem. Nat. Assn. Female Execs., U. So. Calif. Alumni Assn., Alpha Gamma Delta. Republican. Methodist. Avocations: photography; travel; writing novels; computers. Home: 17260 Rayen St Northridge CA 91325 Office: Gaines Agy 8448 Reseda Blvd Northridge CA 91324

WEAVER, ARTHUR LAWRENCE, physician; b. Lincoln, Nebr., Sept. 3, 1936; s. Arthur J. and Harriet Elizabeth (Walt) W.; BS (Regents scholar) with distinction, U. Nebr., 1958; MD, Northwestern U., 1962; MS in Medicine, U. Minn., 1966; m. JoAnn Versemann, July 6, 1980; children: Arthur Jensen, Anne Christine. Intern U. Mich. Hosps., Ann Arbor, 1962-63; resident Mayo Grad. Sch. Medicine, Rochester, Minn., 1963-66; practice medicine specializing in rheumatology and internal medicine, Lincoln, 1968—; mem. staff Bryan Meml. Hosp., chmn. dept. rheumatology, 1976-78, 82-85, vice-chief staff, 1984—; mem. courtesy staff St. Elizabeths Hosp., Lincoln Gen. Hosp.; mem. cons. staff VA Hosp.; chmn. Juvenile Rheumatoid Arthritis Clinic, 1970—; assoc. prof. dept. internal medicine U. Nebr., Omaha, 1976—; med. dir. Lincoln Benefit Life Ins. Co., Nebr., 1972—; mem. exam. bd. Nat. Assn. Retail Druggists; mem. adv. com. Coop. Systematic Studies in Rheumatic Diseases III. Bd. dirs. Nebr. chpt. Arthritis Found., 1969—; mem. tech. cons. panel for rheumatology Harvard Research Based Relative Value Study; trustee U. Nebr. Found., 1974—. Served to capt., M.C., U.S. Army, 1966-68. Recipient Outstanding Nebraskan award U. Nebr., 1958, also C.W. Boucher award; Philip S. Hench award Rheumatology, Mayo Grad. Sch. Medicine, 1966; diplomate Am. Bd. Internal Medicine, Am. Bd. Rheumatology. Fellow ACP (Nebr. council 1983—), Am. Rheumatism Assn. (com. on rheumatologic practice 1983-87, pres.-elect Central region 1983-84, pres. Central region 1984-85; exec. com. 1985-86, bd. dirs. 1987—, planning com. 1987—); mem. Am. Soc. Internal Medicine (coordinating com. physician payment reform 1988—), Nebr. Soc. Internal Medicine, Nebraska Rheumatism Assn., AMA, Nebr. Med. Assn., Lancaster County Med. Soc., Mayo Grad. Sch. Medicine Alumni Assn., Arthritis Health Professions Assn. (com. on practice 1984-87), Nat. Soc. Clin. Rheumatology (program chairperson 1987-88), Midwest Cooperative Rheumatic Disease Study Group, (chmn. exec. com. 1986—), Arthritis Found. (profl. del.-at-large 1987-88). Phi Beta Kappa, Sigma Xi, Alpha Omega Alpha, Pi Kappa Epsilon, Phi Rho Sigma. Republican. Presbyterian. Editorial bd. Nebr. Med. Jour., 1982—; contbr. articles to med. jours. Home: 4239 Calvert Pl Lincoln NE 68506 Office: 2121 S 56th St Lincoln NE 68506

WEAVER, CHARLES LYNDELL, JR., architect; b. Canonsburg, Pa., July 5, 1945; s. Charles Lyndell and Georgia Lavelle (Gardner) W.; m. Ruth Marguerite Uxa, Feb. 27, 1982; children: Charles Lyndell III, John Francis. B.Arch., Pa. State U., 1969; cert. in assoc. studies U. Florence (Italy), 1968. Registered architect, Pa., Md., Mo. With Celento & Edson, Canonsburg, Pa., part-time 1966-71; project architect Meyers & D'Aleo, Balt., 1971-76, corp. dir., v.p., 1974-76; ptnr. Borrow Assocs.-Developers, Balt., 1976-79, Crowley/Weaver Constrn. Mgmt., Balt., 1976-79; pvt. practice architecture, Balt., 1976-79; cons., project mgr. U. Md., College Park, 1979-80; corp. cons. architect Bank Bldg. & Equipment Corp., Am., St. Louis, 1980-83; dir. archtl. and engring. services Ladue Bldg. & Engring. Inc., St. Louis, 1983-84; v.p., sec. Graphic Products Corp.; pres. CWCM Inc. Internat., 1987—; vis. Alpha Rho Chi lectr. Pa. State U., 1983; vis. lectr. Washington U. Lindenwood Coll., 1987; panel mem. Assn. Univ. Architects Conv., 1983. Project bus. cons. Jr. Achievement, 1982-85; mem. cluster com., advisor Explorer Program, 1982-85. Recipient 5 brochure and graphic awards Nat. Assn. Indsl. Artists, 1973; 1st award Profl. Builder/Am. Plywood Assn., 1974; Honor award Balt. chpt. AIA, 1974; Better Homes and Gardens award Sensible Growth, Nat. Assn. Home Builders, 1975; winner Ridgely's Delight Competition, Balt., 1976. Mem. BBC Credit Union (bd. dirs. 1983-85), Vitruvius Alumni Assn., Penn State Alumni Assn., Alpha Rho Chi (nat. treas. 1980-82). Home and Office: 1318 Shenandoah Saint Louis MO 63104

WEAVER, DONNA RAE, college administrator; b. Chgo., Oct. 15, 1945; d. Albert Louis and Gloria Elaine (Graffis) Florence; m. Clifford L. Weaver, Aug. 20, 1966; 1 child, Megan Rae. BS in Edn., No. Ill. U., 1966, EdD, 1977; MEd, De Paul U., 1974. Tchr. Richards High Sch., Oak Lawn, Ill., 1966-71, Sawyer Coll. Bus., Evanston, Ill., 1971-72; asst. prof. Oakton Community Coll., Morton Grove, Ill., 1972-75; vis. prof. U. Ill. at Chgo., 1977-78; dean Mallinckrodt Coll., Wilmette, Ill., 1978-83; assoc. v.p. campus dir. Nat. Coll. Edn., Chgo., 1983—; cons. Nancy Lovely and Assocs., Wilmette, 1981-84, N. Cen. Assn., Chgo., 1982—;bd. dirs. El Valor Corp., 1985-87. Contbr. articles to Am. Vocat. Jour., Ill. Bus. Edn. Assn. Monograph, Nat. Coll. Edn.'s ABS Rev. Mem. New Trier Twp. Health and Human Services Adv. Bd., Ill., 1985-88; bd. dirs. Open Lands Project, 1985-87, Kenilworth Village House, 1986-87. Recipient Achievement award for Outstanding Performance in Edn., Women in Mgmt., 1981; Am. Bd. Master Educators charter disting. fellow. Office: Nat Coll Edn 18 S Michigan Ave Chicago IL 60603

WEAVER, ELLSWORTH ELIAS, political science educator; b. Los Angeles, July 12, 1903; s. Ellsworth J. and Eliza (Culley) W.; student Weber Coll., Ogden, Utah, 1925-27; B.S., U. Utah, 1937, M.S., 1938; Ph.D., N.Y. U., 1953; m. Bessie Mickelson, Aug. 30, 1939; children—John, Ruth, Jared, Mary Lou, Joe. Grad. asst. N.Y. U., 1937-40; lectr. U. Utah, 1947-48, asst. prof., 1948-53, field rep. Inst. Govt., 1948-61, dir., 1961-72, asso. prof., 1953-57, prof., 1957-72, prof. emeritus, 1972—, chmn. dept. polit. sci., 1966-68; cons. Interstate Assn. Public Lands Counties, 1970-80; mem. exec. com. Conf. Univ. Burs. Govtl. Research Cons. Utah Municipal League, 1950-58, 62—, Utah Assn. County Ofcls., 1950-68; mem. Local Govt. Survey Commn. State Utah, 1955-57; mem. Com. Local Govt. Utah Legislative Council, 1957-59. Sec., Weber County Democratic Com., 1928-31. Served with CCC, 1933-35, U.S. Army Res., 1940-47. Mem. Am. Soc. Pub. Adminstrn., Am., Western polit. sci. assns., Utah Acad. Sci., Arts and Letters, Govtl. Research Assn., Tau Kappa Alpha. Delta Phi. Mem. Ch. of Jesus Christ of Latter-day Saints. Author: Revised Ordinances Midvale City, 1951; Legislative Apportionment in Utah, 1951; Revised Ordinances Town of Loa, 1955. Mng. editor: Western Polit. Quar., 1956-71. Home: 1370 Gilmer Dr Salt Lake City UT 84105

WEAVER, JOHN CARRIER, university president emeritus; b. Evanston, Ill., May 21, 1915; s. Andrew Thomas and Cornelia Myrta (Carrier) W.; m. Ruberta Louise Harwell, Aug. 8, 1940; children: Andrew Bennett, Thomas Harwell. A.B., U. Wis., 1936, A.M., 1937, Ph.D., 1942; LL.D., Mercer U., 1972; L.H.D., Coll. St. Scholastica, 1973; Litt.D., Drury Coll., 1973. Mem. editorial and research staff Am. Geog. Soc. of N.Y., 1940-42; mem. research staff Office of Geographer, U.S. Dept. State, 1942-44; asst. prof. dept. geography U. Minn., 1946-47, assoc. prof., 1947-48, prof., 1948-55; prof. geography, dean Sch. Arts and Sci., Kans. State U., 1955-57; prof. geography, dean grad. coll. U. Nebr., 1957-61; v.p. research, dean grad. coll., prof. geography State U. Iowa, 1961-64; v.p. academic affairs, dean faculties, prof. geography Ohio State U., Columbus, 1964-66; pres., prof. geography U. Mo., 1966-70, U. Wis., 1971; pres. U. Wis. System, 1971-77, emeritus, 1977—; prof. geography U. Wis. Milw., Madison, Green Bay, 1971-78; hon. prof. geography U. Wis. at Oshkosh; Disting. prof. U. So. Calif., 1977-85, emeritus, 1985—; exec. dir. Center for Study of Am. Experience, 1978-81, Annenberg Disting. scholar, 1981-82; research cons. Midwest Barley Improvement Assn., Milw., 1946-50; expert cons. to Com. on Geophysics and Geography, Research and Devel. Bd., Washington, 1947-53; mem. adv. com. on geography Office Naval Research, NRC, 1949-52, chmn., 1951-52; vis. prof. U. Oreg., summer 1951, Harvard U., summer 1954; cons. editor McGraw-Hill series in geography, 1951-67; mem. adv. com. to sec. HEW, 1958-62; mem. Mid-Am. State U. Assn., 1959-70, chmn., 1959-61, 70-71; chmn. Council Grad. Schs. U.S., 1961-62; mem. Woodrow Wilson fellow selection com., 1961-70; mem. com. instl. coop. Univs. Western Conf. and Chgo., 1962-66, chmn., 1964-66; pres. Assn. Grad. Schs. in Assn. Am. Univs., 1963-64; Wilton Park fellow Brit. Fgn. Office, 1965, 67, 70, 74, 76; chmn. Nat. Task Force on Future of Pharmacy Edn., 1981-84. Author: Ice Atlas of the Northern Hemisphere, 1946, American Barley Production, A Study in Agricultural Geography, 1950, A Statistical World Survey of Commercial Production, (with Fred E. Lukerman) A Geographical Source book, 1953, The American Railroads, 1958, Minnesota and Wisconsin, 1961; illustrator: Quiet Thoughts, 1971; contbr. articles to books and profl. periodicals; contbg. editor: Geog. Rev, 1955-70. Mem. Mo. Commn. of Higher Edn., 1966-70; mem. White House Task Force on Priorities in Higher Edn., 1969-70, Edn. Commn. of States, 1971-77; Bd. dirs. Harry S. Truman Library Inst. Nat. and Internat. Affairs, 1967-70; trustee Nat. Com. on Accreditation, 1966-76, Johnson Found., Racine, Wis., 1971-77, 81-82, Am. Univs. Field Service, 1971-75, Nat. Merit Scholarship Corp., 1971-77, 80-82, Chadwick Sch., Palos Verdes Peninsula, 1987—; mem. citizens' stamp adv. com. to Postmaster Gen., 1981-85. Served as lt. (j.g.) USNR, 1944-46; assigned specialist Hydrographic Office, Office of Chief of Naval Ops. Washington. Recipient Vilas medal U. Wis., 1936, Letter Commendation from Chief of Naval Ops., 1946; Carnegie Found. adminstrv. fellow, 1957-58. Fellow Am. Geog. Soc. (governing council 1974—, John Finley Breeze Morse medal 1986), AAAS; mem Assn. Am. Geographers (council 1949-51, Nat. Research award 1955), Am. Geophys. Union, Arctic Inst. N.Am. (charter asso.), Am. Polar Soc., Internat. Geog. Union, Am. Pharm. Assn. (hon.), Am. Friends of Wilton Park (pres. 1980-81), Phi Beta Kappa, Sigma Xi, Phi Kappa Phi, Delta Sigma Rho, Phi Eta Sigma, Alpha Kappa Psi, Chi Phi. Congregationalist. Home: 2978 Crownview Dr Rancho Palos Verdes CA 90274

WEAVER, MARGUERITE (PEGGY) MCKINNIE, plantation owner; b. Jackson, Tenn., June 7, 1925; d. Franklin Allen and Mary Alice (Caradine) McKinnie; children: Lynn Weaver Hermann, Thomas Jackson Weaver III, Franklin A. McKinnie Weaver. Student, U. Colo., 1943-45, Am. Acad. Dramatic Arts, 1945-46, S. Meisner's Profl. Classes, 1949. Actress theatrical cos., Can., New Eng., N.Y.C., 1946-52; mem. staff Mus. Modern Art, N.Y.C., 1949-50; editor radio/TV Sta. WTJS-AM-FM, Jackson Sun Newspaper, 1952-55; columnist Bolivar (Tenn.) Bulletin-Times; owner Heritage Plantation, Hickory Valley, Tenn. Chmn. Ho. of Reps. of Old Line Dist. Hardeman Countyy, Tenn., 1985—; founder, hon. bd. dirs. Paris-Henry County (Tenn.) Arts Council, 1965—; charter mem. adv. bd. Tenn. Arts Commn., Nashville, 1967-74, Tenn. Performing Arts Ctr., Nashville, 1972—; chmn. Tenn. Library Assn., Nashville, 1973-74; regional chmn. Opera Memphis, 1979—; patron Met. Opera Nat. Council, N.Y.C., 1980—. Mem. Am. Women in Radio and TV, Internat. Platform Assn., DAR. Methodist. Clubs: Jackson Golf and Country, English Speaking Union, Summit (Memphis). Avocations: horseback riding, travel, theatre, visiting art museums, golf. Home: Heritage Hall Heritage Farms Hickory Valley TN 38042

WEAVER, R(ICHARD) DONALD, clergyman; b. St. Louis, Mar. 25, 1926; s. Robert Raymond and Ada Viola (Holz) W. B.S.C., St. Louis U., 1949; M.Div., Garrett Theol. Sem., 1952; postgrad. U. Chgo., 1951-53; M.A., Scarritt Coll., 1979. Ordained to ministry United Methodist Ch., 1951; pastor, Lizton and Salem (Ind.) Meth. Chs., 1951-53, Centenary Meth. Ch., Veedersburg, Ind., 1953-58, Indiana Harbor United Meth. Ch., East Chicago, Ind., 1958-73, 1st United Meth. Ch., Hobart, Ind., 1973-80, 1st United Meth. Ch., Crown Point, Ind., 1980-84, Angola United Meth. Ch. (Ind.), 1984-87, St. Matthew United Meth. Ch. (Ind.), 1987—; lectr. Calumet Coll., Whiting, Ind., 1967-84. Pres., United Way, 1974, Twin City Community Services, 1970, Lake County Mental Health Assn., 1963, 64; v.p. Referral and Emergency Services, 1977-78, Steuben County United Way; bd. dirs. No. Ind. Health Systems Agy., 1976-78, Vis. Nurse Assn. N.W. Ind.; pres. Ind. United Meth. Children's Home, 1980-82; mem. East Chicago Housing Commn., 1965. Served with AUS, 1944-46; ETO. Recipient Community Leadership award Twin City Community Services, 1971. Mem. Am. Soc. Ch. History, Assn. Sociology of Religion, Hymn Soc. Am., Religious Edn. Assn.

U.S. and Can., Religious Research Assn., Soc. Sci. Study Religion, Steuben County Ministerial Assn. (sec.), Clinton County Ministerial Assn. Club: Rotary. Home: 1555 N Main St Frankfort IN 46041 Office: 1951 Wilshire Dr Frankfort IN 46041

WEAVER, WILLIAM CLAIR, JR., human resources development executive; b. Indiana, Pa., Apr. 11, 1936; s. William Clair and Zaida (Bley) W.; m. Janet Marcelle Boyd, Sept. 18, 1963 (div. 1978); 1 child, William Michael; m. Donna June Hubbuch, Feb. 10, 1984. B Aero Engring., Rensselaer Poly. Inst., 1958; MBA, Washington U., ST. Louis, 1971; postgrad., Rutgers U. Registered profl. engr. Engr. aerodynamics N.Am. Aviation, Los Angeles, 1959-60; engr. flight test ops. Boeing/Vertol, Phila., 1963-66; engr. flight test project Lockhead Electronics, Plainfield, N.J., 1966-69; project engr. advanced systems, sr. staff engr. Emerson Electric Co., St. Louis, 1969-72; pres. Achievement Assocs., Inc., St. Louis, 1972—; founder, charter mem. Catalyst, 1978—; speaker in field. Contbr. articles to profl. jours. 1965-71; author: Winning Selling, 1983, Winning Manager, 1988. Mem. adv. com. Boy Scouts Am., Bridgeton, Mo., 1974. Served to capt. USAF, 1960-63. Mem. Nat. Soc. Profl. Engrs.,Am. Soc. Bus. and Mgmt. Cons., Am. Ordnance Soc., Am. Inst. Aeronautics and Astrounautics, Assn. MBA Execs., Air Force Assn., Am. Helicopter Soc., St. Louis C. of C., Mensa, Beta Gamma Sigma. Republican. Lutheran. Home and Office: 13018 Ray Trog Ct Saint Louis MO 63146

WEAVER, WINSTON ODELL, construction company executive; b. Harrisonburg, Va., Dec. 15, 1921; s. Marion Ralston and Annie (Shank) W.; m. Phyllis Livengood, July 18, 1942; children: Winston Odell, M. Steven, M. Gregory. Student, Eastern Mennonite Coll., 1939-41; B.A., Bridgewater Coll., 1947, L.H.D., 1975. With Rockingham Constrn. Co., Inc., Harrisonburg, 1946—; pres., gen. mgr. Rockingham Constrn. Co., Inc., 1956-82, chmn., 1982—; owner Mariann Meadows Farms; dir. Mennonite Broadcasts, Inc., Harrisonburg, 1957-67, v.p., 1962-67; adv. bd. Va. Nat. Bank, Harrisonburg, 1970-79, vice chmn., 1975-79; dir. First Nat. Bank, Harrisonburg, 1958-70, Sarasota Bank & Trust, N.A., 1984-87; chmn. World Vision U.S., 1986-87. Pres. Harrisonburg-Rockingham chpt. Mental Health Assn., 1960-61; chmn. Cancer Crusade, Harrisonburg, 1966; nat. alumni fund chmn. Bridgewater (Va.) Coll., 1966, 67, also trustee, mem. exec. com.; bd. dirs. World Vision U.S., 1978—, vice chmn., mem. exec. com., 1979—; mem. exec. com. World Vision Internat., Los Angeles, 1972—, sec., 1982, bd. dirs., 1964—, project dir. design and constrn. hosp., Cambodia, 1972-75; bd. visitors James Madison U., Harrisonburg, 1973-80; campaign chmn. Harrisonburg/Rockingham United Way, 1976, pres., 1977, bd. dirs., 1979-81; trustee, exec. com. Bridgewater Coll., 1963—. Recipient Distinguished Service awards Mental Health Assn., 1961, Distinguished Service awards Cancer Crusade, 1966; named Alumnus of Year Bridgewater Coll., 1968; Outstanding Service award World Vision Internat., 1970; Harrisonburg-Rockingham C. of C. Businessman of Year award, 1977; Paul Harris fellow Rotary Club. Mem. Am. Fedn. Small Bus. (dir. 1981-85), Internat. Platform Assn. Club: Capitol Hill (Washington). Lodge: Rotary Internat. (v.p. Harrisonburg 1974-75, pres. Harrisonburg 1975-76, Rotarian of Yr. 1987, Paul Harris fellow). Home: 875 Summit Ave Harrisonburg VA 22801 Office: Rockingham Constrn Co Inc PO Box 808 Harrisonburg VA 22801

WEBB, JAMES H., JR., government official; b. Arlington, Va., Feb. 9, 1946; married; 3 children. B.A., U.S. Naval Acad., 1975; J.D., Georgetown U., 1975. Asst. minority counsel House Com. on Veterans Affairs, Washington, 1977-78, chief minority counsel, 1979-81; vis. writer U.S. Naval Acad., 1979; writer 1981-84; asst. sec. res. affairs Dept. Def., Washington, 1984-87; sec. Dept. of the Navy, Washington, 1987—. Author: A Country Such as This (nominated for Pulitzer and Pen-Faulkner awards), others. *

WEBB, MICHAEL JOHN TOWNSEND, chartered surveyor, construction economist; b. Dublin, Ireland, July 29, 1942; s. John Henry and Betty Beaufoy (Pollard) W.; m. Melissa Dorothy Standford, July 29, 1966; children: Sarah Melissa, Kate Melissa, Emma Charlotte, Richard Michael. Chartered quantity surveyor Patterson Kempster & Shortall, Dublin, 1959-66, ptnr., 1968-86; sr. ptnr. Dublin and London, 1986—; quantity surveyor Burrell Hayward & Budd, London, 1966-68; Irish rep. standing joint com. Standard Method Measurement, London, 1976—, European Com. for Constrn. Econs. EEC, 1980—; bd. dirs. Avering PLC, Dublin. Contbr. articles to profl. publs. Pres. Nat. Youth Council, 1970-73; bd. dirs. Nat. Council for Acad. Awards, 1980—; external examiner Trinity Coll., Dublin, Limerick Coll. Art, others, 1980—; chief commr. Scout Assn. Ireland, 1981-85; mem. Nat. Econ. and Social Council, 1983—. Recipient Silver Elk award Scout Assn. Ireland, 1978, Silver Wolf award U.K. Scout Assn., 1985. Fellow Royal Instn. Chartered Surveyors (Irish rep. edn. com. 1979—), Chartered Inst. Arbitrators; mem. Soc. Chartered Surveyors (chmn. 1988). Clubs: Kildare St., Univ., Royal St. George (Dublin). Home: 2 Mount Salus, Dalkey County, Dublin Ireland Office: Patterson Kempster & Shortall, 24 Lower Hatch St, 2 Dublin Ireland

WEBB, THOMAS IRWIN, JR., lawyer; b. Toledo, Sept. 16, 1948; s. Thomas Irwin and Marcia Davis (Winters) W.; m. Polly S. DeWitt, Oct. 11, 1986; 1 child, Elisabeth Hurst. BA, Williams Coll., 1970; postgrad. Boston U., 1970-71; JD, Case Western Res. U., 1973. Bar: Ohio. Assoc. Shumaker, Loop & Kendrick, Toledo, 1973-79, ptnr., 1979—; dir. Comml. Aluminum Cookware Co., Yark Oldsmobile, Inc. Council mem. Village of Ottawa Hills, Ohio, 1978-85, planning commn., 1978-85, chmn. fin. com., 1978-82; adv. bd. Ohio Div. Securities, 1979—; bd. dirs. Kiwanis Youth Found. of Toledo, Inc. Mem. ABA, Ohio Bar Assn., Toledo Bar Assn., Northwestern Ohio Alumni Assn. of Williams Coll. (pres. 1974-83), Nat. Assn. Bond Lawyers, Healthcare Fin. Mgmt. Assn., Toledo-Rowing Found. (trustee 1985—), Order of Coif. Republican. Episcopalian. Clubs: Crystal Downs Country, Toledo Country, The Toledo (trustee 1984—, pres. 1987—); Wills Club of N.Y. Office: Shumaker Loop & Kendrick 1000 Jackson Toledo OH 43624

WEBER, ARNOLD R., university president; b. N.Y.C., Sept. 20, 1929; s. Jack and Lena (Smith) W.; m. Edna M. Files, Feb. 7, 1954; children: David, Paul, Robert. B.A., U. Ill., 1951; M.A., MIT, 1958, Ph.D. in Econs., 1958. Instr., then asst. prof. econs. MIT, 1955-58; faculty U. Chgo. Grad. Sch. Bus., 1958-69, prof. indsl. relations, 1963-69; asst. sec. for manpower Dept. Labor, 1969-70; exec. dir. Cost of Living Council; also spl. asst. to Pres. Nixon, 1971; Gladys C. and Isidore Brown prof. urban and labor econs. U. Chgo., 1971-73; former provost Carnegie-Mellon U.; dean Carnegie-Mellon U. (Grad. Sch. Indsl. Adminstrn.), prof. labor econs. and pub. policy, 1973-80; pres. U. Colo., Boulder, 1980-85, Northwestern U., Evanston, Ill., 1985—; vis. prof. Stanford U., 1966; cons. union, mgmt. and govt. agys., 1960—, Dept. Labor, 1965; mem. Pres.'s Adv. Com. Labor Mgmt. Policy, 1964, Orgn. Econ. Coop. and Devel., 1987, Exec. Com. of Council on Competitiveness; vice chmn. sec. labor task force improving employment services, 1965; chmn. research adv. com. U.S. Employment Service, 1966; assoc. dir. Office Mgmt. and Budget, Exec. Office of Pres., 1970-71; chmn. Presdl. Railroad Emergency Bd., 1982; trustee Com. for Econ. Devel., Joint Council on Econ. Edn.; bd. dirs. Chgo. Council Fgn. Relations, Burlington Northern, Inc., Inland Steel Co., Pepsico Inc., Super Valu Stores, Inc. Author: (with G.P. Shultz) Strategies for the Displaced Worker, 1966; Contbr. (with G.P. Shultz) articles to profl. jours. Served to lt. (j.g.) USCGR, 1952-54, PTO. Ford Found. Faculty Research fellow, 1964-65. Mem. Indsl. Relations Research Assn. (bus.-higher edn. forum), Am. Econ. Assn., Nat. Acad. Pub. Adminstrn., Consortium of Social Scis. Assns. (bd. dirs.), Comml. Club Chgo., Econ. Club Chgo., Phi Beta Kappa. Jewish. Office: Northwestern U Office of Pres 633 Clark St Evanston IL 60201 *

WEBER, BARBARA M., sales executive; b. Oneonta, N.Y., Apr. 27, 1945; d. Peter J. and Helen (Bettiol) Macaluso; m. Peter Biddle Weber, July 29, 1972. Student, SUNY, Cortland, 1963-67; AAS in Merchandising and Retail Mgmt., SUNY, Mohawk Valley. Service cons. N.Y. Telephone, Albany, N.Y., 1966-68; sr. service advisor N.Y. Telephone, Albany, 1970-73; data communications instr. AT & T, nationwide, 1968-70; equipment mgr. Rushmore & Weber, Albany, 1978-82; v.p. ops. Rushmore & Weber, 1983—, gen. mgr., v.p., 1987—, also bd. dirs. Republican. Roman Catholic. Club: Schuyler Meadows Country. Home: PO Box 236 Newtonville NY 12128 Office: Rushmore & Weber Inc 272 Wolf Rd PO Box 757 Latham NY 12110

WEBER, CLARENCE ADAM, educator, author; b. Winfield, Kans., May 2, 1903; s. William J. and Pearl L. (Hunter) W.; A.B., Ill. Coll., 1924; M.A., U. Ill., 1929; Ph.D., Northwestern U., 1943; m. Mary E. Beaty, Aug. 7, 1925; children—Jane Weber Ruck, Betty L. (Mrs. Charles A. Dewey). Head dept. math. and coach Oakland Twp. High Sch., Oakland, Ill., 1924-27; supt. schs. Hume, Galva, Cicero, Ill., 1927-44; asso. prof. edn. U. Conn., Storrs, 1945-46, dir. Fort Trumbull br., 1946-50, prof. edn., 1950-66, prof. emeritus, 1967—, chmn. dept. sch. adminstrn., 1966, dean Sch. Edn., 1960-61. Corporator Windham Meml. Hosp., Willimantic, Conn., 1966—. Recipient Distinguished Service award Ill. Coll., 1988. Mem. Am. Assn. Sch. Adminstrs., Phi Delta Kappa. Clubs: Masons, Rotary (dist. gov. 1965-66). Author: Organization and Administration of Public Education in Connecticut, 1951; Personal Problems of School Administrators, 1954; Fundamentals of Education Leadership, 1955; Industrial Leadership, 1956; Leadership in Personnel Management, 1970; Roots of Rebellion, 1970; What the People Ought to Know about School Administration, 1971; Welcome to the Rotary Club, 1971; Mary E. Weber, a biography, 1977; Diamonds in the Driveway, 1979; (with Jean Poull) Songs of Cajean, 1979, Let's Cut the Cost of College Education; Double Trouble (an autobiography), 1980. Home: Whitney Commons #110 1204 Whitney Ave Hamden CT 06517

WEBER, ERNESTO JUAN, university dean, counselor; b. Mexico City, Aug. 20, 1930; m. Vera Elisa Engels, Oct. 25, 1958; children: Frank, Ernesto Jr., Monica. BS in Mech. Engring., Calif. Inst. Tech., 1952; PhD in counseling, U. Iberoamericana, Mexico City, 1980. Gen. mgr. Schultz y Cia, S.A., Mexico City, 1961-68, owner, pres., 1968-76; prof. U. Iberoamericana, Mexico City, 1976-85, dean dept. human devel. and edn., 1982-84; gen. corp. dir. Grupo Indsl., Aloymex, Mexico, 1987—; dir. dept. psychology Centro Medico la Pascua, Mexico City, 1980-81; profl. counselor, Mexico City, 1976—; dir. Metron S.A. 1966-70, Sycmatica, S.A. de C.V., 1967-76, Ascomatica, S.A. de C.V., 1967-76 (all Mexico City). Author: Der Integrierte Mensch, 1988; patentee in automatic controls; contbr. articles to profl. jours. Recipient Achievement award United Inventors and Scientists, 1974; award Automatic Switch Co., 1976. Mem. Assn. de Profs. e Inv. de La U.I.A., Assn. Mex. de Terapia Familiar. Club: Assoc. Empresarial Mexicano-Suiza, A.C. Home: Lluvia 470, J del Pedregal, Mexico City 01900, Mexico Office: Aloymex SA, de CV Marconi 7, 54030 Tlalnepantla Mexico

WEBER, FRANK EARL, periodontist; b. New Albany, Ind., Aug. 30, 1932; s. Frank H. and Elizabeth W.; divorced; children—Gregory K., Frank H. B.A., U. Louisville, 1954, D.D.S., 1962; M.S., U. Ky., 1955; postdoctoral specialty Ind. U., 1962-64. Grad. asst. U. Ky., Lexington, 1954-55; ins. underwriter Am. States Ins. Co., Indpls., 1958-60; grad. asst. Ind. U. Sch. Dentistry, 1962-64; practice dentistry specializing in periodontics, Indpls., 1964—; faculty practitioner Ind. U. Sch. Dentistry, 1978—. Contbr. articles to profl. jours. Served with USAF, 1956-58. USPHS scholar, 1959-62; Daman Runyon Cancer Research grantee, 1959-62. Fellow Royal Soc. Health, Acad. Dentistry Internat., Acad. Gen. Dentistry; mem. ADA, Ind. Dental Assn., Indpls. Dist. Dental Soc., Internat. Platform Assn., Nat. Fedn. Ind. Bus., Am. Endodontic Soc., Westside Dental Study Club, Chgo. Dental Soc., Fedn. Advanced Ethical Hypnosis, Acad. Oral Medicine (Merit award 1962), Am. Legion (post comdr. Post 26, 1988-89), Omicron Kappa Upsilon, Phi Kappa Phi, Phi Delta (pres. 1961-62) Beta Delta, Omicron Delta Kappa, Delta Sigma Delta (life), Sigma Phi Epsilon (life). Lodge: Optimists (v.p. Westside Indpls. chpt. 1986-88). Avocations: piloting, golfing, fishing, hunting. Office: Northwest Medical Center 3500 Lafayette Rd Indianapolis IN 46222

WEBER, GEORGE RICHARD, accountant, author; b. The Dalles, Oreg., Feb. 7, 1929; s. Richard Merle and Maud (Winchell) W.; B.S., Oreg. State U., 1950; M.B.A., U. Oreg., 1962; m. Nadine Hanson, Oct. 12, 1957; children—Elizabeth Ann Weber Katooli, Karen Louise, Linda Marie. Sr. trainee U.S. Nat. Bank of Portland (Oreg.), 1950-51; jr. acct. Ben Musa, C.P.A., The Dalles, 1954; tax and audit asst. Price Waterhouse, Portland, 1955-59; sr. acct. Burton M. Smith, C.P.A., Portland, 1959-62; pvt. C.P.A. practice, Portland, 1962—; lectr. acctg. Portland State Coll.; expert witness fin. and tax matters. Sec.-treas. Mt. Hood Kiwanis Camp, Inc., 1965. Exec. counselor SBA; mem. fin. com., powerlifting team U.S. Powerlifting Fedn., 1984, ambassador People to People, China, 1987. Served with AUS, 1951-53. Decorated Bronze Star; C.P.A., Oreg. Mem. Am. Inst. C.P.A.s, Internat. Platform Assn. (fgn. relations Portland com. 1985—). Oreg. City Traditional Jazz Soc., Order of the Holy Cross Jerusalem, Order St. Stephen the Martyr, Order St. Gregory the Illuminator, Knightly Assn. St. George the Martyr., World Lit. Acad., Portland C.S. Lewis Soc., Beta Alpha Psi, Pi Kappa Alpha. Republican. Episcopalian. Clubs: Kiwanis, Portland Track, City (Portland); Multnomah Athletic; Sunrise Toastmasters. Author: Small Business Long-term Finance, 1962, A History of the Coroner and Medical Examiner Offices, 1963. Contbr. to profl. publs. and poetry jours. Home: 2603 NE 32d Ave Portland OR 97212 Office: 4380 SW Macadam Suite 400 Portland OR 97201

WEBER, GEORGE RUSSELL, microbiologist; b. Novinger, Mo., Dec. 29, 1911; s. William and Celia Iciphene (Helton) W.; B.S., U. Mo., 1935; Ph.D., Iowa State Coll., 1940; D.Sc. (hon.) in Pub. Health, Internat. Univ. Found., Malta, 1986; spl. evening student George Washington U., 1944-45, U. Cin., 1948-49; m. Margaret Carrington Cable, Apr. 19, 1947; children—Jeanine Marie, Michael Elwin. Asst. chemist, expt. sta. U. Mo., 1935-36; teaching fellow in bacteriology Iowa State Coll., 1936-38, asst., 1938-39, teaching asst., 1939-40, instr., 1940-42; bacteriologist USPHS, 1946, sr. asst. scientist, 1947, scientist, 1949, chief sanitizing agents unit, 1949-53; research microbiologist Nat. Distillers & Chem. Corp., 1953-63, research project leader, 1963-73, sr. research microbiologist, 1973-75, research asso., 1975, ret., 1977; lectr. in biology U. Cin., 1969-70. Dir. Ky. br. Nat. Chinchilla Breeders of Am., 1955-57, research chmn., 1958-64; pres. Greater Cin. Chinchilla Breeders Assn., 1957-58, 63-64. Served from 1st lt. to maj. AUS, 1942-46; lt. col. AUS (ret.). Recipient War Dept. citation for control of food poisoning and infection, 1946, Albert Einstein Internat. Acad. Bronze Medal for Peace, 1987. Fellow Am. Public Health Assn., Royal Soc. Health (Eng.); mem. AAAS, Am. Soc. Microbiology, Am. Inst. Biol. Scis., Ohio Acad. Sci., N.Y. Acad. Scis., Am. Soc. Profl. Biologists (v.p. 1957-58), Smithsonian Assos., Inst. Food Technologists, Research Soc. Am., Res. Officers Assn. U.S. (exec. council Cin. chpt. 1963-65, chpt. pres. 1966-67), Ret. Officers Assn., Mil. Order World Wars, others, Sigma Xi, Phi Kappa Phi. Patentee animal feed, biol. metal corrosion control. Home: 1525 Burney Ln Cincinnati OH 45230

WEBER, MOLLY SMITH, editor; b. Durham, N.C., Sept. 4, 1957; d. H. Ralph and Sally Ann (Simmons) Smith; m. Walter Charles Weber, July 13, 1985. BA in Psychology, Yale U., 1979; MA in Edn., Stanford U., 1980. Dir. aquatics SUNY, Purchase, 1980-81; sales rep. Prentice-Hall, Inc., Englewood Cliffs, N.J., 1981-83; sales rep. West Ednl. Pub., St. Paul, 1983-85, acquisitions editor, 1985—. Active Dem. Polit. Campaigns, 1987—; mem. Nat. Dem. Com. Mem. Am. Mgmt. Assn., NOW. Avocations: swimming, snow and water skiing, running, photography. Home: 309 E 70th Terr Kansas City MO 64113 Office: West Pub Co PO Box 411628 Kansas City MO 64141

WEBER, PATRICIA LOUISE BRADEN, marketing educator; b. Ft. Wayne, Ind., Oct. 31, 1945; d. Walter Frederick and Margaret June (Houk) Nagel, Jr.; m. Joseph Lou Braden, Aug. 23, 1969 (div. Feb. 1975); m. 2d, Walter Jacob Weber, Jr., July 20, 1981 (div. July 1988). B.S. in Bus. Adminstrn. with distinction, Ind. U., 1967, M.B.A., 1969, D.Bus.Adminstrn., 1973. Staff research assoc. div. research Sch. Bus. Adminstrn., Ind. U., Bloomington, 1967-70; adj. asst. prof. mktg. Coll. Bus., Eastern Mich. U., Ypsilanti, 1970, assoc. dean Coll. Bus., 1981-87; dir. Ctr. for Enterpreneurship, 1987—; mem. research faculty Grad. Sch. Bus. Adminstrn., U. Mich., Ann Arbor, 1970-81, asst. dir. div. research, 1980-81, adj. assoc. prof. mktg., 1974-81; subprogram coordinator Coastal Zone research Mich. Sea Grant Program, Ann Arbor, 1977-86; mem. steering com. Minority Tech. Council Mich., Ann Arbor, 1982-83; mem. resource adv. com. Mich. changing economy program Mich. Dept. Commerce, Lansing, 1975-76; mem. subcoms. on competitive position, econ. growth and diversification, and statis. data Mich. Econ. Action Council, Lansing, 1975-76; dir. many sponsored research projects, cons. to govt., industry, bus. firms and profl. groups, 1970—. Author: Technological Entrepreneurship, 1977; (with Ramesh Gurnani) Data Processing in the Tax Function, 1980; also numerous tech. reports and articles in profl. jours. Program advisor Mich. Council for Arts, Detroit, 1978; bd. dirs. Child and Family Services of Washtenaw, Ann Arbor, 1983—, chmn. devel. com., 1984—. Mem. AAAS, Am. Inst. for Decision Scis. (chmn. Mktg. Track, Midwest AIDS), Am. Mktg. Assn. (chpt. v.p., dir. 1976-80, chmn. program com. 1977-78, editor chpt. membership directory 1977, Marketeer 1975-77; chpt. cert. of recognition 1976-79), Am. Statis. Assn., Internat. Council for Small Bus. (research adv. com. 1974-75), Mich. Tech. Council (mem. state bd. dirs, chmn. bd. dirs. so. cen. 1986—, research adv. bd. 1982-84), Soc. Automotive Engrs. (assoc. mem.; co-chmn. socio-tech. com. 1982—, sessions chmn. internat. congress 1982), Greater Detroit C. of C. (econ. devel. strategic planning com. 1982—), Eastern Mich. U. Women's Assn. (pres.-elect 1983, pres. 1984), Mich. Hist. Soc., Ann Arbor Art Assn. (dir., treas. 1980-85), DAR, Alpha Gamma Delta, Beta Gamma Sigma, Omicron Delta, Alpha Lambda Delta. Home: 550 Cliffs Dr N 202C Ypsilanti MI 48198 Office: Ea Mich U Ctr for Entrepreneurship 121 Pearl St Ypsilanti MI 48197

WEBER, PAUL-EGON, consulting physicist; b. Jena, Germany, Nov. 8, 1913; came to U.S., 1953; naturalized, 1957; s. Paul Albin and Barbara Babette (Bouffier) W.; m. Gertrud Anna Brü ningsen, Nov. 1, 1947; children: Barbara Johanna, Elfriede Margareta, Norbert Paul, Dieter Erich. Ingenieur, Hoehere Tech. Staatslehranstalt Machinenwesen, Frankfurt on Main, Germany, 1935; Diplom Ingenieur, Fachhochschule Frankfurt on Main, 1983. Devel. engr. Am. Optical Co., Buffalo, 1953-54; research engr. Wollensak Optical Co., Rochester, N.Y., 1954-57; physicist Stromberg Carlson, Rochester, 1957-58; staff engr. AVCO Crosly Div., Cin., 1958-59; prin. engr. Bendix Corp., South Bend, Ind. and Ann Arbor, Mich., 1959-61; scientist Trion Instruments, Ann Arbor, 1961-65; pvt. cons., Ypsilanti, Mich., 1965-66; physicist Bell and Howell, Chgo., 1966-78; cons. physicist, Libertyville, Ill., 1979—. Internat. patentee in field. Contbr. articles to profl. jours. Recipient award for disting. work German Govt. 1945. Mem. Deutsche Gesellschaft fuer angewandte Optik, Optical Soc. Am., Am. Inst. Physics.

WEBER, WALTER WINFIELD, JR., lawyer; b. Ramsey, N.J., Feb. 7, 1924; s. Walter W. and Mary Elizabeth (Collins) W.; m. Margaret Gardner Wilson, May 12, 1951; children—Ellen, Anne. B.S., Va. Mil. Inst., 1947; LL.B., Columbia U., 1950. Bar: N.J. 1949, N.Y. 1952, U.S. Supreme Ct. 1966. Assoc., Weber, Muth and Weber, Ramsey, N.J., 1949-52, ptnr., 1953—; dir. Citizens First Bancorp, Inc., Glen Rock, N.J., and subs.; judge Upper Saddle River Mcpl. Ct., 1955-56. Mem. bd. of mgrs. Bergen Pines County Hosp., 1972-76, v.p., 1976. Served in U.S. Army, 1943-45. Mem. Bergen County Bar Assn., N.J. State Bar Assn. (chmn. pub. utility law sect. 1972-74). Republican. Dutch Reformed. Clubs: Arcola Country (Paramus, N.J.), Joe Jefferson (Saddle River, N.J.), Masons. Address: 1 Cherry Ln Ramsey NJ 07446

WEBLEY, SIMON, research association director; b. Bristol, Eng., Aug. 10, 1932; s. Charles Ewart and Kathleen Violet Alice (Forse) W.; m. Helen Edith Kelso Coulter, Sept. 27, 1958; children—Jonathan, Peter, Elizabeth. B.A., Trinity Coll., Dublin, Ireland, 1955; M.A. (hon.), 1961. Research economist Reed Internat. Found. for Bus. Responsibility, London, 1958-65, dep. dir., 1965-67; lectr. Medway Coll. Tech., Chatham, 1967-69; dir. Brit.-N.Am. Research Assn., London, 1969—; dir. research Brit.-N.Am. Com., 1969—; trustee Kennedy Meml. Trust, 1979—; bd. dirs. Tear Fund, 1976—, chmn. 1981-86. Author: Technology Transfer to Developing Countries, 1979; What Shall It Profit?, 1981; The Law of the Sea Treaty, 1982; Multinational Corporations and Codes of Conduct, 1984; Stiffening the Sinews of the Nations, 1986. Ch. warden, mem. Ditton Parish Council, Kent, Eng. Served with RAF, 1955-57. Mem. Ctr. for Polic Studies (bd. dirs.). Anglican. Club: Reform. Avocations: travel, Tudor houses. Office: British-North Am Research Assn, Grosvenor Gardens House, 35-37 Grosvenor Gardens, London SW1 WOBS, England

WEBSTER, BURNICE HOYLE, physician; b. Leeville, Tenn., Mar. 3, 1910; s. Thomas Jefferson and Martha Anne (Melton) W.; B.A. magna cum laude, Vanderbilt U., 1936, M.D., 1940; D.Sc., Holy Trinity Coll., 1971; D. of Humanities, Geneva. Theol. Coll., 1960, Ph.D., Fla. Research Inst., 1973; D of Therapeutic Philosophy, World U., 1985; m. Georgia Kathryn Foglemann, May 6, 1939; children—Brenda Kathryn, Phillip Hoyle, Adrienne Elise. Intern St. Thomas Hosp., Nashville, 1940-42, resident, 1942-43; practice medicine, specializing in chest disease, Nashville, 1943—; mem. staff St. Thomas, Bapt., Nashville Gen., Westside hosps.; clin. prof. allied health Trevecca Coll.; cons. VA Hosp.; assoc. in medicine Vanderbilt Med. Sch., 1943—; med. dir. Nashville Health Care Corp., Univ. Health Care Corp.; prof. anatomy Gupton-Jones Sch. Mortuary Sci., 1941-43, Homes. Inc., Tenn. Squire. Pres., Middle-East Tenn. chpt. Arthritis Found.; crusader Soc. Descendants Latin Kingdom of Jerusalem. Served to med. dir. USPHS. Decorated baliff grand cross Hospitaller Order St. John of Jerusalem; chevalier Sovereign Mil. Order Temple of Jerusalem recipient Disting. Service award Arthritis Found. Fellow Am. Coll. Chest Physicians, Am., Internat. colls. angiology, Royal Soc. Health, Internat. Biog. Assn. (life); mem. Am. Cancer Soc. (dir., past pres. Nashville), AMA, Am. Thoracic Soc., So. Med. Soc. (life), Tenn. Med. Assn., Nashville Acad. Medicine, SCV (surgeon-in-chief), Order St. John of Jerusalem, Royal Soc. Medicine, Tenn. Assn. Long Term Physicians (past pres.), Phi Beta Kappa, Alpha Omega Alpha, Delta Phi Alpha. Lodge: Order of Descendants of Ireland. Research in mycotic and parasitic diseases. Home: 2315 Valley Brook Rd Nashville TN 37215 Office: 2015 Patterson St Nashville TN 37203

WEBSTER, CHRISTOPHER WHITE, foreign service officer; b. Boston, Oct. 30, 1953; s. Henry deForest and Marion (Havas) W.; B.A. cum laude, Amherst Coll., 1975; M.A., Johns Hopkins U., 1977. Asst. comml. attache Am. embassy, Buenos Aires, 1977-79, econ. comml. officer, Georgetown, Guyana, 1979-81; desk officer for Jamaica and Guyana, Washington, 1982-84; econ. officer Office of Energy, Washington, 1984-86; fin. and devel. officer, Lisbon, Portugal, 1986—. Recipient Superior Honor award Dept. State, 1983. Lodge: Lions (pres.'s award 1981). Home and Office: Am Embassy Lisbon APO New York NY 09678

WEBSTER, GEORGE DRURY, lawyer; b. Jacksonville, Fla., Feb. 8, 1921; s. George D. and Mary Gaines (Walker) W.; m. Ann Kilpatrick; children: Aen Walker, George Drury, Hugh Kilpatrick. B.A., Maryville Coll., 1941, LL.D. (hon.), 1984; LL.B., Harvard U., 1948. Bar: Tenn. 1948, D.C. 1952, Md. 1976. Atty. tax div. Dept Justice, 1949-51; sr. partner Webster, Chamberlain & Bean, Washington; lectr. numerous tax. insts. Author: Business and Professional Political Action Committees, 1979, The Law of Associations, 1988. Trustee U.S. Naval Acad. Found., Annapolis, Md.; spl. U.S. ambassador, 1972. Served to lt. USNR, 1942-46. Mem. Am. Law Inst., Am. Bar Assn. Clubs: Chevy Chase (Md.); Metropolitan (Washington); Racquet and Tennis (N.Y.C.). Home: 5305 Cardinal Ct Bethesda MD 20816 also: Webster Angus Farms Rogersville TN 37857 Office: Webster Chamberlain & Bean 1747 Pennsylvania Ave NW Washington DC 20006

WEBSTER, HENRY DEFOREST, experimental neuropathologist; b. N.Y.C., Apr. 22, 1927; s. Leslie Tillotson and Emily (deForest) W.; m. Marion Havas, June 12, 1951; children: Christopher, Henry, Sally, David, Steven; m. Barbara Woodward. A.B. cum laude, Amherst Coll., 1948; M.D., Harvard U., 1952. Intern Boston City Hosp., 1952-53, resident, 1953-54; resident in neurology Mass. Gen. Hosp., 1954-56, research fellow in neuropathology, 1956-59; prin. investigator NIH research grants for electron microscopic studies of peripheral neuropathy 1959-69; mem. staffs Mass. Gen., Newton-Wellesley hosps.; instr. neurology Harvard Med. Sch., 1959-63, assoc. in neurology, 1963-66, asst. prof. neuropathology, 1966; assoc. prof. neurology U. Miami Sch. Medicine, 1966-69, prof., 1969; head sect. cellular neuropathology Nat. Inst. Neurol. and Communicative Disorders and Stroke, NIH, Bethesda, Md., 1969—; assoc. chief Lab. of Neuropathology and Neuroanat. Scis., 1975-84; chief Lab. Exptl. Neuropathology, 1984—; Distinguished scientist and lectr. dept. anatomy Tulane U. Sch. Medicine, 1973; Royal Coll. lectr. Can. Assn. Neuropathologists, 1982; chmn. Winter Conf. on Brain Research, 1985, 86;. Author: (with A. Peters and S.L. Palay) The Fine Structure of the Nervous System, 1970, 76; Contbr. articles to sci. jours. Recipient Weil award Am. Assn. Neuropathologists, 1960, Superior Service award USPHS, 1977, A. von Humboldt award Fed. Republic Germany, 1985. Mem. Am. Assn. Neuropathologists (v.p. 1976-77, pres. 1978-79), Internat. Soc. Neuropathology (councillor 1976-80, v.p. 1980-84, exec. com. 1980-84, pres. 1986—), Internat. Congress Neuropathology (sec. gen. VIII 1978), Peripheral

Nerve Study Group (ad hoc com. 1975—, chmn. 1977 meeting), Am. Neurol. Assn., Am. Acad. Neurology, Am. Soc. Cell Biologists, Am..Assn. Anatomists, Soc. for Neurosci., Latent Image Workshop, Phi Beta Kappa, Sigma Xi. Club: Ausable. Office: Nat Inst Health Bldg 36 Bethesda MD 20892

WEBSTER, JEFFREY LEON, graphic designer; b. Idaho Falls, Idaho, Nov. 23, 1941; s. Leon A. and Marjory M. (McAllister) W.; student Sch. Associated Arts, St. Paul, 1962; m. Judith Kess, Apr. 17, 1965; children—Eric J., Marjorie P. Sci. illustrator Mayo Clinic, Rochester, Minn., 1963-66; layout artist Brown & Bigelow, St. Paul, 1966; graphic designer U. Minn., Mpls., 1966-67, U. Calgary (Alta., Can.), 1967-68; sr. artist Control Data Corp., St. Paul, 1968-70; mem. Idaho State U. Meml. Lectureship Com.; graphic designer Idaho State U., 1970-78; owner, operator studio, Harmony, Minn.; design, advt. and mktg. cons. Mem. Idaho Civic Symphony Bd. Recipient Profl. citation Library Congress, 1976. Artist pub. ednl. exhibits. Home and Office: Rt 1 Harmony MN 55939

WEBSTER, NORMAN ERIC, editor, journalist; b. Summerside, P.E.I., Canada, June 4, 1941; s. Eric and Elizabeth (Paterson) W.; m. Pat Roop, 1966; children: David, Andrew, Derek, Gillian, Hilary. B.A., Bishop's U., Que., 1962; M.A., St. John's Coll., Oxford, Eng., 1964. Corr. Globe and Mail, Quebec, 1965; reporter Globe and Mail, Ottawa, 1966; editor Globe Mag., Toronto, 1967-68; corr. Globe and Mail, Peking, China, 1969-71; asst. to pub. Winnipeg (Man., Can.) Free Press, 1971-72; bur. chief Globe and Mail, Toronto, 1972-74, columnist Ont. affairs, 1974-78; European corr. Globe and Mail, London, 1978-81; asst. editor Globe and Mail, Toronto, 1981-83, editor-in-chief, 1983—. Author: Discovering Today's China, 1972, The Pope in Poland, 1979. Rhodes scholar, 1962; recipient Nat. Newspaper award for Peking corr., 1971. Office: Globe & Mail, 444 Front St W, Toronto, ON Canada M5V 2S9

WEBSTER, RICHARD BRADFORD, lawyer; b. Cambridge, Mass., Aug. 14, 1927; s. Walter Wright and Mabel Claire (Randall) W.; grad. Phillips Exeter Acad., 1944; B.A. magna cum laude, Harvard U., 1949, LL.B. cum laude, 1952; m. Kathanne Harter, Jan. 4, 1953; children—Claire, Susan, Lucy, Amy. Admitted to Mass. and N.Y. bars; asso. firm Cleary, Gottlieb, Steen & Hamilton, 1952—, mem. firm, Paris, 1963-64, Brussels, 1964—; dir. Outboard Marine Belgium S.A.; mem. law faculty Salzburg Seminar, 1980; dir. Commn. for Ednl. Exchange Between the U.S., Belgium and Luxembourg. Treas. Ams. Abroad for Kennedy, Paris, 1960; founder Ams. Abroad for Johnson and Humphrey, Brussels, 1964; bd. dirs. Salzburg Seminar Am. Studies, 1980—. Served with AUS, 1946-47. Mem. Mass., Boston bar assns., Am. Soc. Internat. Law, Assn. Belge pour le Droit Européen, Am. and Common Market Club (dir. 1964—), Harvard U. Law Sch. Assn. Europe (pres. 1977-80, gov. 1980—), Am. C. of C. in Belgium (dir.). Club: Cercle Royal Gaulois Artistique et Literaire (Brussels). Home: 26 ave Rene Lyr, 1180 Brussels Belgium Office: 23 rue de la Loi, 1040 Brussels Belgium

WEBSTER, STOKELY, painter; b. Evanston, Ill., Aug. 23, 1912; s. Henry Kitchell and Mary Ward (Orth) W.; m. Iva Kitchell, Aug. 23, 1933; 1 child, Stephanie T.; m. Audrey Lenz Coutant, May 1984. Student, Yale U., U. Chgo.; studied art with Lawton Parker, Paris and Wayman Adams, N.Y.C. Landscape painter, Chgo., 1932; textile designer, N.Y.C., 1934-35; exhibited portraits and landscapes, Corcoran Biennial Exhbn. Washington, Allied Artists and NAD, N.Y.C., Art Inst. Chgo., Ill. State Mus., Albany (N.Y.) Inst. Art, Salon des Indé pendants, Paris, Salon des Artistes Francais, Paris; rep. The Phillips Collection, Washington, Mus. City N.Y., Fitchburg (Mass.) Art Mus., Ill. State Mus., Nat. Collection Fine Arts, Smithsonian Instn., Washington, Mus. Arts and Scis., Daytona Beach, Fla., Morse Mus., Winter Park, Fla., Newark Mus., Mus. Fine Arts, St. Petersburg, Fla., Northwestern U. Spl. Collection, AT&T Co., Indpls. Mus. Art, Hecksher Mus., Huntington, N.Y., Parrish Mus., Southhampton, N.Y., High Mus., Atlanta, Albright Knox Art Gall., Buffalo; one-man shows James St. Lawrence O'Toole Gallery, N.Y.C., 1940, Albert Roullier Gallery, Chgo., 1940, Vallombreuse Gallery, Biarritz, 1970, Vallombreuse Gallery, Palm Beach, Fla., 1973, Hobe Sound (Fla.) Gallery, 1974, Eric Galleries, N.Y.C., 1975, 78, Meml. Gallery, Ormond Beach, Fla., 1983, Brevard Mus., Melbourne, Fla., 1984, Polk Pub. Mus., Lakeland, Fla., 1984, Cornell Fine Arts Ctr., Winter Park, Fla., 1984, Lee Scarfone Gallery, U. Tampa, 1985, Mus. Arts and Sci., Daytona Beach, Fla., 1986, Stetson U., Deland, Fla., 1986, Fairfield (Ct.) U., 1986. Recipient 1st Hallgartin prize NAD, 1941. Home: 10 Harbor Rd Southport CT 06490 Gallery: Chapellier Galleries Inc 815 Park Ave New York NY 10019

WECHSBERG, MANFRED INGO, chemical researcher; b. Maehr-Ostrau, Czechoslovakia, May 1, 1940; s. Josef and Helene (Pawlas) Wechsberg. Degree in engring., Tech. U., Vienna, Austria, 1965, PhD in Chemistry, 1966. Asst. prof. Tech. U., 1966; vis. researcher U. Washington, Seattle, 1967, Princeton (N.J.) U., 1968, U. Calif., Berkeley, 1969; chemist Bayer AG, Leverkusen, Fed. Republic Germany, 1970-76; head research dept. Chemie Linz AG, Austria, 1979—. Patentee in field. Bd. dirs. Soc. Austrian-German Culture, Linz, 1984—, European Conf. Human Rights and Self Determination, Bern, Bonn, Linz, 1987. Mem. Austrian Chem. Soc. (bd. dirs. 1985—). Clubs: Verein der Leichtathleten des OTB OO, Athletics (pres.). Lodge: Akademische Gildenschaft (pres. 1983—). Home: Im Blumengrund 9/35, A4020 Linz Austria

WECHSLER, GIL, designer, lighting; b. N.Y.C., Feb. 5, 1942; s. Arnold J. and Miriam (Steinberg) W. Student Rensselaer Poly. Inst., 1958-61; B.S., NYU, 1964; M.F.A., Yale U., 1967. Lighting designer Harkness Ballet, N.Y.C., 1967-69, Pa. Ballet, Phila., 1969-70, Stratford Shakespeare Festival, Ont., Can., 1969-78, Guthrie Theatre, Mpls., 1971, Lyric Opera Chgo., 1972-76, Met. Opera, N.Y.C., 1976—; guest lectr. Teatro Colon, Buenos Aires, Argentina, 1985, Yale U., New Haven, 1980; guest lighting designer Paris Opera, 1983, Am. Ballet Theatre, N.Y.C., 1980. Cons. editor Opera Quar., 1983—. Mem. U.S. Inst. for Theatre Tech., United Scenic Artists. Avocations: collecting ocean liner memorabilia, gardening, painting. Home: 1 Lincoln Plaza New York NY 10023 Office: Met Opera Lincoln Ctr New York NY 10023

WECHTER, NORMAN ROBERT, paint manufacturing executive; b. Chgo., Apr. 12, 1926; s. Charles S. and Emily (Miller) W.; m. Harriet Golub, Oct. 10, 1948; children: Robin, Clari. BSBA, Northwestern U., Chgo., 1950. Pres. Federated Paint Mfg. Co., Chgo., 1950—. Served with USN, 1944-46. Republican. Jewish. Home: 180 E Pearson Chicago IL 60611 Office: Federated Paint Mfg Co 1882 S Normal Ave Chicago IL 60616

WEDDERBURN, ALEXANDER JOHN MACLAGAN, theology educator; b. Edinburgh, Scotland, Apr. 30, 1942; s. Thomas Maclagan and Margaret Marshall (Scott) W.; m. Brigitte Felber, July 17, 1971; children: Fiona, Martin. BA, Oxford U., 1964, MA, 1967; BD, U. Edinburgh, 1967; PhD, Cambridge U., 1971; postgrad., U. Göttingen, Federal Republic of Germany, 1971-72. Ordained minister, 1975. Tutorial asst. U. St. Andrews, Scotland, 1972-74, lectr., 1974—. Author: Baptism and Resurrection, 1987; co-editor: The New Testament and Gnosis, 1983; contbr. articles to profl. jours.; dir. Scottish Jour. Theology, 1974-85, cons. editor 1985—. Mem. Soc. Biblical Lit., Studiorum Novi Testamenti Societas, Royal Soc. for the Protection of Birds. Home: 5 Clatto Pl, Saint Andrews Fife KY16 8SD, Scotland Office: U Saint Andrews, Saint Andrews Fife KY16 9JU, Scotland

WEDDERBURN, DOROTHY ENID COLE, educational administrator; b. London, Sept. 18, 1925; d. Frederick C. and Ethel C. Barnard. BA, Cambridge U., 1946, MA, 1950; DLitt (hon.), Warwick U., 1984. Research officer dept. applied econs. Cambridge U., 1950-65; lectr., prof. indsl. sociology Imperial Coll. Sci. and Tech., London, 1965-81; sr. research fellow 1981, hon. fellow, 1986; prin. Bedford Coll., London, 1981-85, Royal Holloway and Bedford New Coll., Egham, Surrey, Eng., 1985—; pro vice chancellor U. London, 1986—; hon. fellow Ealing (Eng.) Coll. Higher Edn., 1985. Author: White Collar Redundancy, 1964, Redundancy and the Railwayman, 1964, Enterprise Planning for Change, 1968, Old Age in Three Industrial Societies, 1968; co-author: The Aged in the Welfare State, 1965. Mem. Ct. of London U., 1981—. Mem. Fawcett Soc. (hon. pres. 1986—), Nat. Orgn. for Women's Mgmt. Edn. (hon. v.p. 1983—). Home: 65 Ladbroke Grove Flat 5, London W11 2PD, England Office: Royal Holloway and Bedford, New Coll Egham Hill, Egham Surrey TW20 0EX, England

WEDDERBURN, KENNETH WILLIAM (BARON WEDDERBURN OF CHARLTON), law educator; b. London, Apr. 13, 1927; s. Herbert John and Mabel Ethel (Holland) W.; m. Nina Salaman, 1951 (div. 1960); children: Sarah Louise, David Roland, Lucy Rachel; m. Dorothy Cole, 1962 (div. 1969); m. 3d Frances Ann Knight, Aug. 22, 1969; 1 son, Jonathan Michael. MA, Cambridge U., 1948, LLB, 1949; Hon. Dott. Giuta, Paria, 1987. Barrister, Middle Temple. Fellow, tutor in law Clare Coll., Cambridge U., 1952-64; lectr. in law U. Cambridge, 1953-64; prof. comml. law London Sch. Econs., U. London, 1964—. Author: The Worker and the Law, 3d edit. 1986; co-author: (with B. Aaron and others) Industrial Conflict, 1972; (with P. Davies) Employment Grievances on Disputes and Procedures, 1969; (with R. Lewis and B. Clark) Labour Law and Industrial Relations, 1983; (with B. Veneziani and S. Ghimpu) Dritto Del Laroto in Europa, 1987. Chmn. ind. rev. com. Trades Union Congress, 1976—. Fellow Brit. Acad. Created life peer, baron, 1977. Mem. Labour Party. Office: U London, London Sch Econs, Houghton St, London WC2 England

WEDEKIND, LOTHAR HENRY, editor; b. Dörigsen, Fed. Republic Germany, July 8, 1949; s. Heinz and Gerda (Ahlborn) W; m. Miryam Vence, Dec. 21, 1972; children: Nikolai, Aron, Sophia-Gabriela. BA, Marquette U., 1971; MA, Am. U., Washington, 1976. Assoc. editor Army Times Pub. Co., Washington, 1976-79; staff writer, editor Energy Info. Adminstrn., Washington, 1980-81; staff writer Atomic Indsl. Forum, Washington, 1981-84; chief editor Internat. Atomic Energy Agy., Vienna, Austria, 1984—; cons. Energy Info. Adminstrn., 1981-82, Utility Consulting Group, Washington, 1982-84, Pub. Utilities Reports, Rosyln, Va., 1983-84. Contbr. reports, articles and poems to profl. jours. mgr. Reston (Va.) Soccer Assn, 1983-84. Served with U.S. Army, 1971-75. Recipient News Writing award Va. State Press Assn., 1976, 77, Mag. Writing merit Internat. Reading Assn., 1978. Mem. UN Periodicals' Editors Group (chmn. 1986-87), Marquette Univ. Alumni Assn., Kappa Tau Alpha. Office: Internat Atomic Energy Agy, Wagramerstr 5, 1400 Vienna Austria

WEDER, RICARDO ALBERTO, science educator; b. Rosario, Santa Fe, Argentina, Feb. 8, 1948; s. Roberto and Geltrudi (Zaninovich) W.; m. Teresa Cisneros, June 10, 1974; children: Natalie Danitza, Ricardo Eugenio. MS, U. Louvain, Belgium, 1972, DSc, 1974. Researcher Interuniv. Inst. Nuclear Research, Belgium, 1974-76; research fellow Harvard U., Cambridge, Mass., 1976-77; instr. Math., research assoc. Physics Princeton, N.J., 1977-78; investigator Inst. de Investigaciones en Math. Aplicadas y en Sistemas U. Nat. Autónoma de Mexico, 1978—, prof. Math., 1978—; vis. scientist Eidgenössische Technische Hochsule, Zurich, 1976, Centre de Physique Theorique, Ctr. Nat. de la Recherche Sci., Marseille, France, 1984, ; vis. prof. U. Nat. de Rosario, 1981, U. d'Aix Marseille, France, 1981, U. Utah, Salt Lake City, 1985-86; sr. investigator Inst. de Investigaciones en Math. Aplicadas y en Sistemas, U. Nat. Autónoma de Mex., 1978—. Contbr. articles to profl. jours. Fellow System of Nat. Researchers Mex.; mem. Internat. Assn. Math. Physics, Am. Math. Soc., Soc. Math. Mex., Soc. Math. Appliquées et Indsl. Office: Inst Invesigaciones Math, Aplicadas y Sistemas, U Nat Aut de Mexico, Apartaco Postal 20-726, Mexico City Mexico

WEED, EDWARD REILLY, marketing executive; b. Chgo., Jan. 25, 1940; s. Cornelius Cahill and Adelaide E. (Reilly) W.; student Fordham U., 1959-61, Loyola U., 1961-62; m. Lawrie Irving Bowes, Feb. 2, 1969. Account exec. Leo Burnett Co., Chgo., 1961-71; pres. GDC Ad Inc., corporate officer advt. and sales promotion Gen. Devel. Corp., Miami, Fla., 1971-74; v.p., account supr. D'Arcy Mac Manus & Masius, Chgo., 1975; group v.p. mktg. Hart Schaffner & Marx (Hartmarx), Chgo.; pres. Hart Services, Inc., 1975-82; v.p. mktg. Tishman, 1983-86; v.p. mktg. Hannah Marine, 1986—; dir. First Nat. Bank So. Miami. Trustee, Latin Sch. Found., 1976—; bd. dirs. North Ave. Day Nursery, 1969-73, Santa for Poor, 1975-87, Off-the-Street, 1982-87, Chgo. Boys' and Girls' Clubs, 1983—. Served with Ill. N.G. Republican. Roman Catholic. Clubs: Tavern, Cliff Dwellers, Saddle and Cycle. Office: Hannah Kingery at Archer Lemont IL 60439

WEE KIM WEE, president of the Republic of Singapore, journalist; b. Singapore, Nov. 4, 1915; m. Koh Sok Hiong; 7 children. Ed. Raffles Instn.-Singapore. With Straits Times, various positions, 1930-41, dep. editor, 1959-73; journalist UPI, 1941-59; high commr. to Malaysia, 1973-78; dean of diplomatic corps in Kuala Lumpur, 1978-80; ambassador to Japan, 1980-84; ambassador Republic of Korea, 1981-84; chmn. Singapore Broadcasting Corp., 1984-85; pres. Republic of Singapore, 1985—; justice of the peace, 1966. Recipient Pub. Service Star, Singapore, 1963, Meritorious Service medal for diplomatic services, 1979. Address: Istansa, Singapore 0922 Singapore Office: Chancellor Nat U of Singapore, 10 Kent Ridge Crescent, Singapore 0511 Singapore

WEEKS, ARTHUR ANDREW, lawyer, educator; b. Hanceville, Ala., Dec. 2, 1914; s. A.A. and Anna S. (Seibert) W.; m. Carol P. Weeks; children: John David, Carol Christine, Nancy Anna. A.B., Samford U., 1936; LL.B., U. Ala., 1939, J.D., 1939; LL.M., Duke U., 1950; LL.D. (hon.), Widener U., 1980. Bar: Ala. 1939, Tenn. 1948. Sole practice Birmingham, Ala., 1939-41, 1946-47, 1954-61; dean, prof. law Cumberland U. Sch. Law, 1947-54; dean, prof. Samford U., 1961-72, prof. law, 1972-74; prof. law Cumberland Sch. Law, Samford U., 1984—; prof. law Del. Sch. Law of Widener U., Wilmington, 1974-82, dean, 1974-80, interim dean, 1982-83, dean emeritus, prof., 1983—. Served to capt. AUS, 1941-46. Mem. ABA, Tenn. Bar Assn., Ala. Bar Assn., Birmingham Bar Assn., Del. Bar Assn. (assoc.), Phi Alpha Delta, Phi Kappa Phi, Delta Theta Phi. Home: 1105 Water Edge Ct Birmingham AL 35244

WEEKS, PATSY ANN LANDRY, librarian, teacher; b. Luling, Tex., Mar. 3, 1930; d. Lee and Mattie Wood (Callihan) Landry; m. Arnett S. Weeks, Dec. 2, 1950; children—Patsy Kate, Nancy Ann, Janie Marie. B.S., Southwest Tex. State U., San Marcos, 1951; M.L.S., Tex. Woman's U., Denton, 1979. Tchr. art, reading, math. Grandview Ind. Sch. Dist., Tex., 1950-52; tchr. phys. edn. Beaumont Ind. Sch. Dist., Tex., 1953; tchr. art, coll. algebra Cisco Jr. Coll., Tex., 1957-58; tchr. remedial reading Taylor County Schs., Tuscola, Tex., 1965-66; tchr. remedial reading Anson Ind. Sch. Dist. Tex., 1971-73; librarian Bangs Ind. Sch. Dist., Tex., 1973-79, learning resources coordinator, 1979—; adv. com. Edn. Service Ctr., 1978-83; coordinator Reading is Fundmental Program, 1978-83. Bd. dirs. Anson Pub. Library, Tex., 1971-72. Exhibitor oil paintings, pastels at Tex. fairs (1st prize 1952, 60). Mem. ALA, Assn. Library Service to children (Caldecott award com. 1986), Am. Assn. Sch. Librarians, Intellectual Freedom Round Table, Tex. Library Assn. (mem. intellectual freedom and profl. responsibility com. 1979-81, mem. Tex. Bluebonnet award com. 1982-85, chair adv. com. 1987, chair children's round table 1987), Tex. Assn. Sch. Librarians (media prodns. award com. 1985-86), Tex. Assn. Improvement Reading, Teenage Library Assn. Tex. (chmn. audio-visual award com. 1984), Tex. Assn. Sch. Library Adminstrs., Tex. State Tchr. Assn. (life), Phi Delta Kappa, Kappa Pi, Alpha Chi, Beta Phi Mu, Delta Kappa Gamma. Baptist. Clubs: Bangs Progressive Women's (treas. 1974-76). Home: 110 Poco St Bangs TX 76823 Office: Bangs Ind Sch Dist PO Box 969 Bangs TX 76823

WEEKS, RICHARD RALPH, marketing educator; b. Champaign, Ill., Sept. 18, 1932; s. Frank Cook and B. Caroline (Pool) W.; m. Sue Ann Grunwald, Aug. 29, 1953; children: Kimberly Sue, Bret William. B.S., U. Ill., 1955; M.B.A., Washington U., St. Louis, 1960, D.B.A., 1966. Exec. sec., editor bull. Am. Assembly Collegiate Schs. Bus., St. Louis, 1960-64; exec. sec. Beta Gamma Sigma; also editor Beta Gamma Sigma Exchange, 1961-64; 1st ann. A.A.C.B.S. doctoral fellow in bus. adminstrn. 1964-65; dir. MBA program, asst. prof. mktg. Coll. Bus., Okla. State U., 1965-66, asst. dean, dir. MBA program, asso. prof. mktg., 1966-67; dean, prof. mktg. Walter E. Heller Coll. Bus. Adminstrn., Roosevelt U., 1967-70; dean Coll. Bus. Adminstrn. U. R.I., 1970-85, acting v.p. bus. and fin., 1976-77, provost for pub. policy, pub. service and mgmt., 1979-85, prof. mktg., 1970—; dir. Potter Hazlehurst Inc., Providence Gas Co., Providence Energy Co., Newport Am. Corp. Editor: Faculty Personnel, 9th edit, 1965; contbg. editor Ency. Bus. Information Sources, 1964; editorial adv. bd. Bus. and Soc, 1968-70. Bd. dirs. Chgo. Econ. Devel. Corp., 1968-70, v.p., 1969-70; bd. dirs. Chgo. Financial Devel. Corp., 1970, Progress Assn. for Econ. Devel., 1972-73; bd. dirs. Council on Postsecondary Accreditation, 1974-83, mem. exec. com., 1977-82, chmn., 1979-81; bd. dirs. Friends of Jamestown Philomenian Library, 1972-77, pres., 1974-76; mem. adv. bd. Intercollegiate Case Clearinghouse, 1976-79; pres. Friends of URI Library, 1986—. Served to capt. USAF, 1955-63. Fulbright grantee, 1986. Mem. Am. Mktg. Assn. (dir. acad. placement 1966, 68), Ea. Fin. Assn. (dir. 1974-77), Council Profl. Edn. Bus. (sec.-treas. 1960-64, exec. com. 1961-64), Nat. Assn. State Univs. and Land-grant Colls., Commn. on Edn. for Bus. Professions (sec. 1973-76, chmn. 1976-78), New Eng. Assn. Schs. and Colls. (sec.-treas. 1983-85), Am. Assn. Collegiate Schs. Bus. (various com., bd. dirs. 1976-85, pres. 1983-84), Greater Providence C. of C. (dir. 1979-82), Delta Sigma Pi, Alpha Kappa Lambda, Beta Gamma Sigma (various coms., pres. 1978-80), Mu Kappa Tau, Pi Sigma Epsilon, Phi Kappa Phi. Home: Brenton's Cove #6 Harrison Ave Newport RI 02840 Office: Coll of Bus Adminstrn U RI Kingston RI 02881

WEEKS, ROBERT EARL, advertising executive; b. Yazoo City, Miss., Sept. 17, 1925; s. Dennis H. and Mamie O. (Randolph) W.; children: Suzanne Lynn, Robin Denise, Linda, Robert Earl II, Lisa Ann. Student, Wilson Jr. Coll., 1947, Latin Am. Inst. Pub. Relations, 1950, DePaul U., 1952. Br. mgr. King Records Inc., Chgo., 1948-50; assoc. Pursell Pub. Relations, Chgo., 1950-65; insp. Chgo. Bd. Health, 1965-66; adminstrv. asst. to Alderman Robert H. Miller, Chgo., 1966-69; coordinator task force for community broadcasting Chgo. Digest mag., 1969-76; pres. Troubadour & Assocs., Ltd., Chgo., 1969—; pub. Troubadour Digest mag., 1976—; writer Cablecommunications Resource Ctr., Washington, 1972—. Author: Cable TV in Chicago, 1976; editor Chgo. Radio Guide, 1985. Active with South Side Community Art Ctr., Hyde Park Improvement Assn. Served with USAAF, 1944-46. Mem. Black Media Reps. (v.p. 1976), Ill. Arts Assn., Am. Soc. Profl. Cons., Pub. Relations Soc. Am. Democrat. Roman Catholic. Clubs: Clef Social, Publicity of Chgo. Home: 5325 S Cottage Grove Ave Chicago IL 60615

WEEMS, FRANK TAYLOR, hi-tech start up executive, engineering and construction company executive, manufacturing company executive, marketing executive; b. Birmingham, Ala., Dec. 26, 1924; s. Ben Carpenter and Gladys (Taylor) W.; m. Kirsten Lee Borgen, Sept. 10, 1949 (dec. Feb. 23, 1985); children: Barbara Lee, William Taylor, Robert Chipley. BS ChemE, U. Ala., 1944; SM ChemE, M.I.T., 1950. Sales engr. Dorr Co., 1948-52; tech. dir. Eimco Corp., 1952-55, regional mgr., 1955-62, mgr. indsl. sales, 1962-66, mktg. dir., 1966-68, v.p. mktg., 1968-70, pres., 1970-72; exec. v.p., pres. Air Quality Control Group, Envirotech Corp., Menlo Park, Calif., 1972-82; exec. v.p., dir. Mountain States Mineral Enterprises, Tucson, 1982—; pres., dir. A.H. Ross & Assocs., Inc., Toronto, Ont., Can., 1982-86; v.p., dir. Mountain States Synfuels Corp., 1983-86; pres., chief fin. officer, chief exec. officer Cochlea Corp., 1984—, also bd. dirs.; chmn. Cochlea S.A., Aubange, Belgium; bd. dirs. Granger Assocs., Santa Clara, Calif.; chmn. bd. Chem. Engring. Corp. of Tokyo, 1976-80, Bahnson Co. Inc., Winston Salem, N.C., 1976-81. Active Little League Baseball, Weston, Conn.; trustee Rowland Hall-St. Marks Sch., Salt Lake City. Served with USNR, 1943-46. NRC fellow. Mem. AIME, Am. Inst. Chem. Engrs., Mining and Metall. Soc., Tau Beta Pi, Theta Tau. Republican. Episcopalian. Clubs: Mining (N.Y.C.), Chemists (N.Y.C.); Alta (Salt Lake City); Los Altos Golf and Country; Old Pueblo (Tucson). also: 8166 E McLaren Dr Tucson AZ 85715 Office: Cochlea Corp 985 Timonthy Dr San Jose CA 95133

WEERTS, RICHARD KENNETH, music educator; b. Peoria, Ill., Oct. 7, 1928; s. Gerhard Nicholas and Ellen Marie (Lindeburg) W. BS, U. Ill., 1951; MA, Columbia U., 1956, EdD, 1960; MA, N.E. Mo. State U., 1973. Tchr. Lyndhurst (N.J.) Pub. Schs., 1956-57; dir. instrumental music Scotch Plains (N.J.) Pub. Schs., 1957-61; prof. music N.E. Mo. State U., Kirksville, 1961—. Author: Handbook for Woodwinds, 1965, Developing Individual Skills for the High School Band, 1969, How to Develop and Maintain a Successful Woodwind Section, 1972, Original Manuscript Music, 1973, Handbook of Rehearsal Techniques for Band, 1976. Dir. music First United Meth. Ch., Kirksville, 1970—. Served with U.S. Army, 1951-55. Mem. Nat. Assn. Coll. Wind and Percussion Instrs. (nat. exec. sec./treas. 1971—, editor jour. 1968—), Music Educators Nat. Conf., Phi Delta Kappa. Office: care NE Mo State U Div Fine Arts Kirksville MO 63501

WEG, JOHN GERARD, physician; b. N.Y.C., Feb. 16, 1934; s. Leonard and Pauline M. (Kanzleiter) W.; m. Mary Loretta Flynn, June 2, 1956; children: Diane Marie, Kathryn Mary, Carol Ann, Loretta Louise, Veronica Susanne, Michelle Celeste. BA cum laude, Coll. Holy Cross, Worcester, Mass., 1955; MD, N.Y. Med. Coll., 1959. Diplomate: Am. Bd. Internal Medicine. Commd. 2nd lt. USAF, 1958, advanced through grades to capt., 1967; intern Walter Reed Gen. Hosp., Washington, 1959-60; resident, then chief resident in internal medicine Wilford Hall USAF Hosp., Lackland AFB, Tex., 1960-64; chief pulmonary sect. Wilford Hall USAF Hosp., 1964-66, chief inhalation sect., 1964-66, chief pulmonary and infectious disease service, 1966-67; resigned 1967; clin. dir. pulmonary disease div. Jefferson Davis Hosp., Houston, 1967-71; from asst. prof. to assoc. prof. medicine Baylor U. Coll. Medicine, Houston, 1967-71; assoc. prof. medicine U. Mich. Med. Sch. Univ. Hosp., Ann Arbor, 1971-74; prof. U. Mich. Med. Sch. Univ. Hosp., 1974—; physician-in-charge pulmonary div., 1971-81, physician-in-charge pulmonary and critical care med. div., 1981-85; cons. Ann Arbor VA, 1971—, Wayne County Gen. hosps., 1971-84; mem. adv. bd. Washtenaw County Health Dept., 1973—; mem. respiratory and nervous system panel, anesthesiology Sect. Nat. Ctr. Devices and Radiol. Health, FDA, 1983—, chmn., 1985—. Contbr. med. jours., reviewer, mem. editorial bds. Decorated Air Force Commendation medal; travelling fellow Nat. Tb and Respiratory Disease Assn., 1971; recipient Aesculpaius award Tex. Med. Assn., 1971. Fellow Am. Coll. Chest Physicians (chmn. bd. govs. 1976-79, gov. Mich. 1975-79, chmn. membership com. 1976-79, prof.-in-residence 1972—, chmn. critical care council 1982-85), Am. Coll. Chest Physicians and Internat. Acad. Chest Physicians (exec. council 1976-82, pres. 1980-81), ACP (chmn. Mich. program com. 1974); mem. AAAS, Am. Fedn. Clin. Research, AMA, Am. Thoracic Soc. (sec.-treas. 1974-76), Am. Assn. Inhalation Therapy, Air Force Soc. Internists and Allied Specialists, Soc. Med. Consultants to Armed Forces, Internat. Union Against Tb, Mich. Thoracic Soc. (pres. 1976-78), Mich. Lung Assn. (dir., Bruce Douglas award 1981), Am. Lung Assn., Research Club U. Mich., Assn. Advancement Med. Instrumentation, Central Soc. Clin. Research, Am. Bd. Internal Medicine (subsplty. com. on pulmonary disease 1980-86, critical care medicine test com. 1985-87, critical care medicine policy com. 1986-87), Alpha Omega Alpha. Home: 3060 Exmoor St Ann Arbor MI 48104 Office: 1500 E Medical Ctr Dr B I H 245 Box 0026 Ann Arbor MI 48109

WEGENER, BERNHARD GÜNTER, psychologist; b. Berlin, Aug. 4, 1944; s. Dante Ughetti and Irene (Wegener) Wegener. Diploma theology, U. Bonn, Fed. Republic Germany, 1968; diploma psychology, U. Berlin, 1973, ThD, 1979, D in Psychology, 1988. Tchr. psychology secondary sch. Berlin, 1974, pvt. practice behavioral psycology, 1974—; mng. psychologist Am. Urban Gen. Hosp., Berlin, 1974—; interpreter Berlin High Ct., 1976-87; lectr. nurse tng., Berlin, 1976-85. Co-editor: Richte unsere Fusse auf den Weg des Friedens, 1980; contbr. articles to profl. jours. Roman Catholic. Office: Krankenhaus Am Urban, Dieffenbach St 1, 1000 West Berlin 30 Federal Republic of Germany

WEGENER, HERMANN HORST, psychologist, educator; b. Kiel, Fed. Republic Germany, June 6, 1921; s. Heinrich and Wally (Dorau) W.; m. Gisela Wiedemann; children: Horst Detlef, Rosemarie. DPhil, Kiel U., 1949, MD, 1951, cert. habilitation, 1957. Lectr. Tchr. Tng. Coll., Fed. Republic Germany, 1952-57; lectr. U. Kiel, Fed. Republic Germany, 1957-62, prof., dir., 1962—; dir. Univ. Inst. Psychology, Fed. Republic Germany, 1963—. Mem. Deutsche Gesellschaft Psychologie, Internat. Assn. Applied Psychology, Am. Assn. Mental Deficiency. Office: Univ Kiel, Olshausenstrasse 40-60, D2300 Kiel Federal Republic of Germany

WEGENER, MARK DOUGLAS, lawyer; b. Cedar Rapids, Iowa, Nov. 1, 1948; s. Virgil Albert and Jean Frances (Wilke) W.; m. Donna Chait, May 28, 1972; children—Tara, David, Marisa. B.A. cum laude, Central Coll., Pella, Iowa, 1970; J.D., Rutgers U., 1973. Bar: D.C. 1974, U.S. Dist. Ct. D.C. 1974, U.S. Ct. Appeals (D.C. cir.) 1974. Assoc. firm Howrey & Simon, Washington, 1973-79, ptnr., 1979—. Mem. Washington Mayor's Internat. Adv. Council, 1984—. Mem. ABA (anti-trust sect., litigation sect.), D.C. Bar Assn. Club: Army & Navy. Home: 7257 Spring Side Way McLean VA 22101 Office: Howrey & Simon 1730 Pennsylvania Ave NW Washington DC 20006

WEGLARZ, JAN, educator; b. Poznan, Poland, Sept. 24, 1947; parents Józef and Irena (Held) W. MSc in Math., Adam Mickiewicz U., Poznan, 1969; MSc in Control Engring., Tech. U., Poznan, 1971, PhD in Control Systems, 1974, Cert. in Ops. Research, 1977. Research teaching asst. Tech. U., Poznan, 1971-72, 1972-74, asst. prof., 1974-78, assoc. prof., 1978-83, prof., 1983—; deputy dir. Inst. Automatyki Tech. U., Poznan, 1981-87, dir., 1987—. Co-author: Operations Research for Computer Sci, 1983 (Minister of Sci. award 1984), Scheduling Under Resource Constraints, 1986; contbr. articles to profl. jours. Recipient Pietrzak award, 1983; hon. by sci. sec. of Polish Acad. Scis., 1980, dept. tech. scis. Polish Acad. Scis., 1978. Mem. Polish Acad. Scis. (com. automatics and robotics 1987—, com. computer sci. 1981—), Polish Computer Soc. (council mem. 1984—, founder), Polish Cybernetical Soc. (Gold Distinction award 1986, chief of ops. research Working Group), Assn. of European Operational Research Societies (council rep. of Poland 1982—). Roman Catholic. Office: Tech U Poznan, Piotrowo 3A, 60 965 Poznan Poland

WEHRLY, JOSEPH MALACHI, industrial relations executive b. County Armagh, Ireland, Oct. 2, 1915; s. Albert and Mary Josephine (Gribbon) W.; came to U.S., 1931, naturalized, 1938; student Los Angeles City Coll., evenings 1947-49; certificate indsl. relations U. Calif. at Berkeley Extension, 1957; m. Margaret Elizabeth Banks, July 3, 1946; children—Joseph Michael, Kathleen Margaret, Stephen Patrick. Mgr. interplant relations Goodyear Tire & Rubber Co., Los Angeles, 1935-42; dir. indsl. relations Whittaker Corp., Los Angeles, 1946-60, Meletron Corp., Los Angeles, 1960-61; asst. indsl. relations mgr. Pacific Airmotive Corp., Burbank, Calif., 1961-63; personnel mgr. Menasco Mfg. Co., Burbank, 1963-66; indsl. relations adminstr. Internat. Electronic Research, Burbank, 1966; dir. indsl. relations Adams Rite Industries, Inc., Glendale, Calif., 1966-75, cons., 1975-76; personnel mgr. TOTCO div. Baker Internat. Corp., Glendale, 1975-80; instr. indsl. relations and supervision Los Angeles Pierce Coll., 1949-76. Served with U.S. Army, 1942-46. Mem. Personnel and Indsl. Relations Assn., Mchts. and Mfrs. Assn. Republican. Roman Catholic. Home: 4925 Swinton Ave Encino CA 91436

WEHRY, GAËTAN BERNARD MARIE, banker; b. Jakarta, Indonesia, Jan. 29, 1938; s. Georges Jean Wehry and Genevie ve Adelaide (Marquess) Le Grouz de Saint-Seine; m. Marie-Christine de Albuquerque d'Orey, Sept. 11, 1965; children—Maude, Guillaume, Gé rault, Emmanuel. M. in Law and Econs., State U. Leiden, Netherlands, 1965. Sr. v.p. Banque Paribas, Paris, 1965-82; 1st exec. v.p. Banque Finindus, Paris, 1982-85, sr. advisor internat. affairs, 1986—; mng. dir. Robeco-France, 1986—; dir. Handelskredit Bank AG, Zurich, Switzerland, 1982—, Enterprise Cordesse, Paris, 1981—. Mem. Fgn. Banks Club (assoc.). Roman Catholic. Club: Automobile (Paris). Avocations: golf; tennis; gardening. Home: 9 Ave Bugeaud, 75116 Paris France Office: Robeco-France Cie, 49 Ave George V, 75008 Paris France

WEI, MILLET LUNCHIN, consulting engineer; b. Taiwan, July 1, 1937; came to U.S., 1962, naturalized, 1973; s. Yu Tzu and Mei (Cheng) W.; m. Betty Teresa Leung, June 3, 1967; children—Natalie Vennesa, Terence. B.S., Nat. Taiwan U., Taipei, 1960; M.S., U. R.I., Kingston, 1964; Ph.D., Carnegie-Mellon U., Pitts., 1967. Registered profl. engr., Pa. Research engr. Bethlehem Steel Co., Pa., 1967-73, project engr., 1973-74, cons. engr. tech. services, 1974-84, cons. engr. Cons. Engring. Div., Applied Tech. Dept., 1984-86, con. steel ops., 1986—. Contbr. articles to profl. jours. Patentee in field. Served to 2d lt. Chinese Marine Corps, 1960-61. Mem. Assn. Iron and Steel Engrs. (Kelly award 1981, 86), AIME, ASME, ASCE, Chinese Inst. Engrs. U.S.A. Republican. Roman Catholic. Club: Shepherd Hills Country (Wescosville, Pa.). Home: 6106 Fairway Ln Wescosville PA 18106 Office: 701 E 3rd St 1148 Steel Gen Office Bethlehem PA 18016

WEICKER, LOWELL PALMER, JR., U.S. senator; b. Paris, France, May 16, 1931; s. Lowell Palmer and Mary (Bickford) Paulsen; m. Claudia Testa Ingram, Dec. 21, 1984; children by previous marriage—Scot, Gray, Brian, Sonny, Mason Ingram, Lowell Palmer III, Andrew Ingram. Grad., Lawrenceville Sch., 1949; B.A. in Polit. Sci, Yale, 1953; LL.B., U. Va., 1958. Bar: Conn. 1960. Mem. Conn. Gen. Assembly, 1963-69; 1st selectmen Greenwich, Conn., 1964-68; mem. 91st Congress, 4th Dist. Conn., 1969-71; U.S. senator from Conn., 1971—; mem. Com. on Energy and Natural Resources, Com. on Appropriations, Com. on Labor and Human Resources; ranking mem. Com. on Small Bus., Labor and Human Resources subcom. on Handicapped, Appropriations subcom. of Labor, Health and Human Resources. Served with US Army, 1953-55. Republican. Episcopalian. Office: 225 Russell Senate Bldg Washington DC 20510 •

WEIDA, LEWIS DIXON, mktg. analyst/cons.; b. Moran, Ind., Apr. 23, 1924; s. Charles Ray and Luella Mildred (Dixon) W.; student Kenyon Coll., 1943, Purdue U., 1946; B.S., Ind. U., 1948; M.S., Columbia U., 1950. Mgr. statis. analysis unit Gen. Motors Acceptance Corp., N.Y.C., 1949-55; asst. to exec. v.p. Am. Express Co., 1955-82. Served with USAAF, 1943-46; PTO. Mem. Internat. Platform Assn. Democrat. Club: Masons. Home: 25 Tudor City Pl New York NY 10017

WEIDACHER, ALOIS SEBASTIAN, social science researcher; b. Prags, Italy, Jan. 19, 1941; arrived in Fed. Republic Germany, 1969; s. John and Anne (Gasser) W.; m. Helga Seidenschnur, Mar. 21, 1952; children: Andrea, Michael. Lic. in Theology, Jesuite Theol. Faculty, Louvain, Belgium, 1966; cert. in Oriental langs., Louvain U., 1967; diploma in sociology, Bielefeld (Fed. Republic Germany) U., 1974. Tchr. profl. and pub. secondary sch., Brixen, Italy, 1967-69, Bielefeld Profl. Sch., 1970-73; social sci. researcher German Research Inst. for Youth and Family, Munich, 1974—; chaplain Brixen Town Parish, 1967-69, Bielefeld Town Parish, 1970-74. Author books and articles. Roman Catholic. Home: Valeryst 140, 8044 Unterschleissheim Federal Republic of Germany Office: Deutsches Jugendinstitut, Freibadst 30, 8000 Munich 90 Federal Republic of Germany

WEIDEMANN, CELIA JEAN, social scientist, international development consultant; b. Denver, Dec. 6, 1942; d. John Clement and Hazel (Van Tuyl) Kirlin; m. Wesley Clark Weidemann, July 1, 1972; 1 child, Stephanie Jean. BS, Iowa State U., 1964; MS, U. Wis.-Madison, 1970, PhD, 1973; postgrad. U. So. Calif., Washington, 1983. Advisor, UN Food & Agr. Orgn., Ibadan, Nigeria, 1973-77; ind. researcher, Asia and Near East, 1977-78; program coordinator, asst. prof., research assoc. U. Wis., Madison, 1979-81; chief institutional and human resources U.S. Agy. for Internat. Devel., Washington, 1982-85, team leader, cons., Sumatra, Indonesia, 1984; dir. fed. econs. program Midwest Research Inst., Washington, 1985-86; pres. Weidemann Assocs., Arlington, Va., 1986—; cons. Internat. Ctr. for Research on Women, Kinshasa Zaire, 1986, U.S. Congress, Aspen Inst., Ford Found., World Bank, Nigeria, Gambia, Indonesia; cons. U.S. Agy. for Internat. Devel., Kenya, Jordan, Global Exchange, 1986-87. Author: Planning Home Economics Curriculum for Social and Economic Development; contbr. chpts. to books and articles to profl. jours. Am. Home Econs. Assn. fellow, 1969-73 (recipient research grant Ford Found. 1987—). Mem. Soc. Internat. Devel., Am. Sociol. Assn., U.S. Dirs. of Internat. Agrl. Programs, Assn. for Women in Devel. (pres.-elect 1988—, founder, bd. dirs.), Internat. Devel. Conf. (bd. dirs., exec. com.), Am. Home Econs. Assn. (Wis. internat. chmn. 1980-81), Internat. Fedn. Home Econs., Internat. Platform Assn., Pi Lambda Theta, Omicron Nu. Roman Catholic. Avocations: mountain trekking, piano/pipe organ, canoeing, photography, poetry. Home: 2607 N 24th St Arlington VA 22207

WEIDEMEYER, CARLETON LLOYD, lawyer; b. Hebbville, Md., June 12, 1933. BA in Polit. Sci., U. Md., 1958; JD, Stetson U., 1961. Bar: Fla. 1961, D.C. 1971, U.S. Dist. Ct. (mid. dist.) Fla. 1963, U.S. Ct. Appeals (5th cir.) 1967, U.S. Ct. Appeals (D.C. cir.) 1976, U.S. Supreme Ct. 1966, U.S. Ct. Appeals (11th cir.) 1982. Research asst. Fla. 2d Dist Ct. Appeals, 1961-65; ptnr. Kalle and Weidemeyer, St. Petersburg, Fla., 1965-68; asst. pub. defender 6th Jud. Cir., Fla., 1966-69, 81-83; ptnr. Wightman, Weidemeyer, Jones, Turnbull and Cobb, Clearwater, Fla., 1968-82. guest lectr., Stetson U., 1978-80; bd. dirs. 1st Nat. Bank and Trust Co., 1974-78, Fla. Bank of Commerce, 1973-77. Author: (handbook) Arbitration of Entertainment Claims; editor: Ad Lib mag., 1978-81; contbr. numerous articles to profl. jours.; performer This Is Your Navy Radio Show, Memphis, 1951-52; leader Polka Dots, The Jazz Notes, 1976—; mem. St. Paul Ch. Orch.; performer Clearwater Jazz Holiday, 1980, 81, co-chmn., 1981. Bd. advisors Musicians Ins. Trust. Served with USN, 1951-54. Mem. Musicians Assn. Clearwater (pres. 1976-81), Fla.-Ga. Conf. Musicians (sec., treas. 1974-76), ABA, Assn. Trial Lawyers Am., Fla. Acad. Trial Lawyers, Fla. State Hist. Soc., Greater St. Petersburg Musicians Assn., Am. Fedn. Musicians (internat. law com.; pres. so. conf. musicians 1979-80), Clearwater Genealogy Soc., Pa. Geneal. Soc., Am. Legion, German Am. Geneal. Assn. D.A.V. Fleet Res., Phi Delta Phi, Sigma Pi, Kappa Kappa Psi. Lodges: Masons, Egypt Temple Shrine, Scottish Rite, Moose, Sertoma (bd. dirs. Clearwater chpt. 1984-86). Home: 2261 Belleair Rd Clearwater FL 33546 Office: Legal Arts Bldg Suite 1 501 S Ft Harrison Ave Clearwater FL 34616

WEIGHTMAN, JUDY MAE, lawyer; b. New Eagle, Pa., May 22, 1941; d. Morris and Ruth (Gutstadt) Epstein; children: Wayne, Randall, Darrell. BS in English, California U. of Pa., 1970; MA in Am. Studies, U. Hawaii, 1975; grantee in internat. relations Chaminade U., 1976; JD, Richardson Sch. Law, 1981. Bar: Hawaii 1981. Tchr. Fairfax County Sch. (Va.), 1968-72, Hawaii Pub. Schs., Honolulu, 1973-75; lectr. Kapiolani Community Coll., Honolulu, 1975-76; instr. Olympic Community Coll., Pearl Harbor, Hawaii, 1975-77; lectr. Hawaii Pacific Coll., Honolulu, 1977-78; law clerk to atty. gen. Hawaii and Case, Kay and Lynch and Davis & Levin, 1979-81, to chief judge Intermediate Ct. Appeals, Honolulu, 1981-82; dep. pub. defender Office of Pub. Defender, Honolulu, 1982-84; staff atty. Dept. Commerce & Consumer Affairs, State of Hawaii 1984-86; pres., dir. Am. Beltwrap Corp., 1986—; dir. pre-admission program, asst. prof. William S. Richardson Sch. Law, 1987—. Mem. neighborhood bd. No. 25 City and County Honolulu, 1976-77; vol. Legal Aid Soc., Honolulu, 1977-78; bd. dirs. women's div. Jewish Fedn., Protection and Advocacy Agy.; parent rep. Wheeler Intermediate Adv. Council, Honolulu, 1975-77; Hawaii rep. Metropolis Studios; trustee Carl K. Mirikitani Meml. Scholarship Fund, Arts Council Hawaii, membership dir. ACLU, 1977-78, bd. dirs., Hawaii, 1988—; founder Hawaii Holocaust Project. Community scholar, Honolulu, 1980. Mem. ABA, Hawaii Women Lawyers, Assn. Trial Lawyers Am., Hawaii Bar Assn., Am. Judicature Soc., Richardson Sch. Law Alumni Assn. (alumni rep. 1981-82), Phi Delta Phi (v.p. 1980-81). Democrat. Jewish. Clubs: Hadassah, Women's Guild.

WEIGL, PETR, film director; b. Brno, Moravia, Czechoslovakia, Mar. 16, 1939; s. Alfred and Gertruda (Dorožinska) W. Student, Film Acad., Prague, Czechoslovakia, 1961. Dramaturg Czechoslovak TV, Prague, 1961-75, Nat. Theatre Ballet, Prague, 1976—. Numerous feature films include The Turn of the Screw, Night of Lead, Romeo and Juliet, Labyrinth of Power, The Passion of St. Sebastian, Poetic Reflections, Prix Italia, 1969, 72; nominee for Emmy awards, 1983, 87. Home: Anenská 2, 110 00 Prague 1 Czechoslovakia Office: TV 2000 Film Fernsehprod, Gallierweg 9, 6200 Wiesbaden Federal Republic of Germany

WEIGLE, JOERG-PETER, conductor; b. Greifswald, Rostock, German Dem. Rep., Mar. 28, 1953; s. Theodor and Hildegard (Mielke) W.; m. Christiane Weigle, June 8, 1955; children: Andreas, Barbara. Student, Hanns-Eisler U., Berlin, 1978. First conductor Philharmonic Orch., Neubrandenburg, German Dem. Rep., 1977-80; chief conductor Philharmonic Orch., Dresden, German Dem. Rep., 1986—, Rundfunkchor Leipzig, German Dem. Rep., 1980-88. Office: Drescher Philarmonie, Kulturpalast Altmarkt, Postfach, DDR-8012 Dresden German Democratic Republic

WEIHAUPT, JOHN GEORGE, university administrator, scientist; b. La Crosse, Wis., Mar. 5, 1930; s. John George and Gladys Mae (Ash) W.; m. Audrey Mae Reis, Jan. 28, 1961. Student, St. Norbert Coll., De Pere, Wis., 1948-49; B.S., U. Wis., 1952, M.S., 1953; M.S., U. Wis.-Milw., 1971; Ph.D., U. Wis., 1973. Exploration geologist Am. Smelting & Refining Co., Nfld., 1953, Anaconda Co., Chile, S.Am., 1956-57; seismologist United Geophys. Corp., 1958; geophysicist Arctic Inst. N. Am., Antarctica, 1958-60, Geophys. and Polar Research Center, U. Wis., Antarctica, 1960-63; dir. participating Coll. and Univ. program, chmn. dept. phys. and biol. sci. U.S. Armed Forces Inst., Dept. Def., 1963-73; assoc. dean for acad. affairs Sch. Sci., Ind. U.-Purdue U., Indpls., 1973-78; prof. geology Sch. Sci., Ind. U.-Purdue U., 1973-78; asst. dean (Grad. Sch., prof. geoscis. Purdue U.), 1975-78; prof. geology, assoc. acad. v.p., dean grad. studies and research, v.p. Univ. Research Found., San Jose (Calif.) State U., 1978-82; vice chancellor for acad. affairs U. Colo., Denver, 1982—; Sci. cons., mem. sci. adv. bd. Holt Reinhart and Winston, Inc., 1967—; sci. editor, cons. McGraw-Hill Co., 1966—; hon. lectr. U. Wis., 1963-73; geol. cons., 1968—; editorial cons. John Wiley & Sons, 1968; editorial adv. bd. Dushkin Pub. Group, 1971—. Author: Exploration of the Oceans: An Introduction to Oceanography; mem. editorial bd. Internat. Jour. Interdisciplinary Cycle Research, Leiden. Mem. Capital Community Citizens Assn.; mem. Madison Transp. Study Com., Found. for Internat. Energy Research and Tng.; U.S. com. for UN Univ.; mem. sci. council Internat. Center for Interdisciplinary Cycle Research; mem. Internat. Awareness and Leadership Council; mem. governing bd. Moss Landing Marine Labs.; bd. dirs. San Jose State U. Found. Served as 1st lt. AUS, 1953-55, Korea. Mt. Weihaupt in Antarctica named for him, 1966; recipient Madisonian medal for outstanding community service, 1973; Outstanding Cote Meml. award, 1974; Antarctic medal, 1968. Fellow Geol. Soc. Am., Explorers Club; mem. Antarctican Soc., Nat. Sci. Tchrs. Assn., Am. Geophys. Union, Internat. Council Corr. Edu., Soc. Am. Mil. Engrs., Wis. Alumni Assn., Soc. Study Biol. Rhythms, Internat. Soc. for Chronobiology, Marine Tech. Soc., AAAS, Univ. Indsl. Adv. Council, Am. Council on Edn., Expdn. Polaire France (hon.), Found. for Study Cycles, Assn. Am. Geographers, Nat. Council Univ. Research Adminstrs., Soc. Research Adminstrs., Man-Environ. Communication Center, Internat. Union Geol. Scis., Internat. Geog. Union, Internat. Soc. Study Time, Community Council Pub. TV, Internat. Platform Assn., Ind., Midwest assns. grad. schs., Western Assn. Grad. Schs., Council Grad. Schs. in U.S., Wis. Alumni Assn. of San Francisco. Clubs: Carmel Racquet (Rinconada Racquet); Kiwanis. Home: 23906 Currant Dr Golden CO 80401 Office: Univ of Colorado at Denver 1200 Larimer Campus Box 172 Denver CO 80204

WEIHRICH, HEINZ, management educator. came to U.S., 1959; s. Paul and Anna Weihrich; m. Ursula Weihrich, Aug. 3, 1963. BS, UCLA, 1966, MBA, 1967, PhD, 1973. Assoc. Grad. Sch. Mgmt. UCLA, 1968-73; from asst. to assoc. prof. Ariz. State U., Tempe, 1973-80; prof. mgmt. U. San Francisco, 1980—; internat. mgmt. cons. in field. Author: (with Harold Koontz and Cyril O'Donnell) Management, 7th edit., 1980, Japanese, Portuguese, Chinese and Indonesian edits., 8th edit., 1984, Singapore edit., 1985, Indonesian edit., 1986, Philippines edit., Bengali edit., Taiwan edit. 1985 (with Harold Koontz) 9th edit. 1988, Singapore edit. 1988, (with Harold Koontz and Cyril O'Donnell) Management: A Book of Readings, 5th edit., 1980, (with George Odiorne and Jack Mendleson) Executive Skills: A Management by Objectives Approach, 1980, (with Jeanette Gilsdorf) Instructor's Manual for Management, 1980, (with Harold Koontz) Measuring Managers--A Double-Barreled Approach, 1981, (with Harold Koontz and Cyril O'Donnell) Essentials of Management, 3d edit. 1982, Taiwan, Philippines, Chinese and India edits., 4th edit., 1986, Singapore edit., 1986, (with Richard D. Babcock) Instructor's Manual for Essentials of Management, 3d edit., 1982, (with Harold Koontz and Cyril O'Donnell) Elementos de Administracion, 3d edit., 1983, 4th edit. 1988, Instructor's Manual for Management, 8th edit., 1984, Management Excellence--Productivity through MBO, 1985, Singapore edit. 1986, Italian edit., Japanese edit, Greek edit., Administracion, 1985, (with Steven Funk) Test File for Essentials of Management, 1986, Management Basiswissen, 1986, Excelencia Administrativa (Mex.), 1987; editor: (with Jack Mendleson) Management: An MBO Approach, 1978; contbr. numerous articles and papers to profl. jours. Grantee Am. Mgmt. Assn., 1970. Fellow Internat. Acad. Mgmt., mem. Acad. Mgmt., Assn. Mgmt. Excellence (trustee 1985-87), Assn. Bus. Simulation Exptl. Learning, Acad. Internat. Bus., Beta Gamma Sigma, Sigma Iota Epsilon. Roman Catholic. Office: U San Francisco Ignatian Heights San Francisco CA 94117-1080

WEIKERT, RALF, conductor, music director; b. St. Florian, Austria, Nov. 10, 1940; s. Fritz W. and Sigrid (Girgensohn) W.; m. Heidi Weikert, Sept. 14, 1963; children: Sascha, Christian. Conductor's diploma, Acad. Music, Vienna, 1963. Coach, conductor Landestheater, Salzburg, Austria, 1963-66; dir. music Theater der Stadt, Bonn, Fed. Republic Germany, 1966-77; conductor Salzburg Festival, Europe, Japan, 1971—, Vienna State Opera, 1975—, Munich State Opera, Berlin State Opera, 1975—; dep.gen. music dir. Frankfurt Opera, Fed. Republic Germany, 1977-81; dir. music Mozarteum Orchester and Theatre, Salzburg, 1981-84; conductor Munich State Opera, 1981—; dir. music Opernhaus Zürich, 1983—; conductor Met. Opera, N.Y.C., 1987—. Conductor: CBS Masterworks: Rossini Tancredi, 1985; Atlantis-Verlag: Schoeck Lebendig begraben, 1986; EMI Records: James Morris-Portrait, 1987. Recipient Nicolai-Malco prize Danish Radio, 1965, Mozart-Interpretation prize Austrian Govt., 1966, Dr. Karl-Böhm prize Austrian Minister Edn., 1975. Office: Opernhaus Zürich, Falkenstrasse 1, CH-8008 Zurich Switzerland

WEIL, HERMAN, psychology educator; b. Regisheim, Alsace Lorraine, Dec. 15, 1905; came to U.S., 1938, naturalized, 1944; m. Bertha Weiler, July 26, 1931; 1 son, Gunther M. Ph.D. in Psychology, U. Marburg, Germany, 1929, state exam. in math., chemistry, physics, 1929, state exam. in edn., 1931; D.Pub. Service (hon.), U. Wis.-Milw., 1986. Instr., Realgymnasium for Girls, Hersfeld, Germany, 1931-33; instr., studienrat Philanthropin Realgymnasium, Frankfurt on Main, Germany, 1933-38; postdoctoral scholar U. Iowa, 1939; prof. sci. Nebr. Central Coll., 1939-40; prof. Milw. Sch. Engring., 1940-43; prof. edn. and psychology, head dept. Wis. State Coll., Milw., 1943-56; prof. psychology U. Wis., Milw., 1956-76; prof. emeritus U. Wis., 1976—, chmn. dept., 1956-61, chmn. honors program superior students Coll. Letters and Scis., 1960-74, asso. dean, 1967-71, faculty retirement counselor, 1973-75; vis. prof. Northwestern U., summers 1947, 48, 51; cons. Human Relations Workshop, U. Mich., summers 1952-56; dir. Workshops on Human Relations, Wis. State Coll., summers 1952-56; lectr. Milw. Downer Coll., 1943-47; cons. Dept. State, also U.S. Office Edn., Jugenheim, Ger., 1954; Disting. Service fellow Temple Emanu-El B'ne Jeshurun, 1976-78, 79-84, emeritus, 1984—, dean adult Jewish studies, 1978-79; Disting. scholar-in-residence Milw. Jewish Community Center, 1977-80. Author: In Quest of Excellence, 1975, University of Wisconsin-Milwaukee Faculty Retirement Guidebook, 1975, 2d edit., 1976; contbr. chpts. and sects. to books on psychol. subjects. Co-chmn. Wis. region NCCJ, 1952-72, mem. commn. on edn. orgns., 1955-60, nat. bd. dirs., 1977-84, nat. co-chmn. schs. and colls. com. observance of Nat. Brotherhood Week, 1957; mem. Gov.'s Commn. on Human Rights, 1953-56; counselor Milw. B'nai B'rith Hillel Found., 1950-60; pres. New Home Club, Inc., 1940-57, hon. pres., 1977-87; chmn. Milw. chpt. Am. Jewish Com., 1973-75, mem. nat. exec. com., 1973-80. Recipient citation of merit for work in human relations Milw. B'nai B'rith Councils, 1952, Brotherhood award Wis. region NCCJ, 1959, Citation award Internat. Inst. Milwaukee County, 1960, Disting. Merit citation NCCJ, 1973; Disting. Merit citation Wis. Soc. Jewish Learning, 1973; Disting. Service award U. Wis.-Milw. chpt. AAUP, 1975; Disting. Merit citation Coll. Letters and Sci., U. Wis.-Milw., 1976; Am. Jewish Com. Inst. Human Relations award, 1978; guest of honor Mayor and Senate, City of West Berlin, 1979. Mem. AAUP (pres. Wis. conf. 1973-74), Wis. Soc. Jewish Learning (past pres.), Wis. Psychol. Assn. (past pres.), Milwaukee County Psychol. Assn. (past pres.), Nat. Collegiate Honors Council (mem. exec. com. 1972-73), Ret. Faculty Assn. U. Wis.-Milw. (pres. 1977-79), Phi Kappa Phi (hon.). Jewish (past v.p., trustee temple). Home: 2027 E Lake Bluff Blvd Milwaukee WI 53211

WEIL, LEON JEROME, diplomat; b. N.Y.C., June 15, 1927; m. Mabel Selig, Apr. 8, 1952; children: Leon Jerome, Katherine A., Caroline E. A.B. cum laude, Princeton U. Ptnr. Herzfeld & Stern, N.Y.C., 1974-84, Steiner Rouse & Co., 1950-74; U.S. ambassador to Nepal, 1984-87; exchange ofcl. Am. Stock Exchange. Trustee Berkshire Sch., Sheffield, Mass., Outward Bound Inc., Greenwich, Conn., Robert Taft Inst. Govt., N.Y.C.; mem. Pres.'s Council on Phys. Fitness and Sports. Served with USN, 1945-46. Republican. Club: City Athletic (N.Y.C.). Home: 213 E 48th St New York NY 10017

WEIL, ROLF ALFRED, university president emeritus, economist; b. Pforzheim, Germany, Oct. 29, 1921; came to U.S., 1936, naturalized, 1944; s. Henry and Lina (Landauer) W.; m. Leni Metzger, Nov. 3, 1945; children: Susan Linda, Ronald Alan. B.A., U. Chgo., 1942, Ph.D., 1950; D. Hebrew Letters, Coll. Jewish Studies, 1967; L.H.D., Loyola U., 1970; D.H.L., Bowling Green State U., Ohio, 1986. Research asst. Cowles Commn. for Research in Econs., 1942-44; research analyst Ill. Dept. Revenue, 1944-46; mem. faculty Roosevelt U., Chgo., 1946—, prof. fin. and econs., also chmn. dept. fin., 1954-65, dean Coll. Bus. Adminstrn., 1957-64, acting pres., 1965-66, pres., 1966-88; lectr. Ind. U.; tax cons. to pres. Selfhelp Home for Aged, Chgo. Author articles on finance. Mem. Am. Economic Assn. Clubs: Cliff Dwellers, University, Mid-Am. (Chgo.). Office: Roosevelt U 430 S Michigan Ave Chicago IL 60605

WEILER, KURT WALTER, radio astronomer; b. Phoenix, Mar. 16, 1943; s. Henry Carl and Dorothy (Esser) w.; m. Geertje Stoelwinder, June 8, 1979; children—Corinn Nynke Yoon, Sanna Femke Lee. B.S., U. Ariz., 1964; Ph.D., Calif. Inst. Tech., 1970. Guest investigator Netherlands Found. for Radioastronomy, Groningen, 1970-74; sci. collaborator Inst. for Radioastronomy, Bologna, Italy, 1975-76; sr. scientist Max Planck Inst. for Radioastronomy, Bonn, W.Ger., 1976-79; program dir. NSF, Washington, D.C., 1979-85; radio astronomer Naval Research Lab., Washington, 1985—; Halley steering com. NASA, Washington, 1981-85. Author: WSRT Users Guide, 1973, 75. Contbr. over 100 articles to profl. jours. and mags. Mem. Am. Astron. Soc., Royal Astron. Soc., Internat. Astron. Union, Internat. Sci. Radio Union, Nederlandse Astronomen Club. Club: Jaguar, Nat. Capital. Home: 6232 Cockspur Dr Alexandria VA 22310 Office: Naval Research Lab Code 4131 Washington DC 20375-5000

WEILL, MICHAEL, architect; b. Paris, Aug. 31, 1914; s. Edouard and Edmee (Hirschmann) W. Diplome d'architecte, Ecole des Beaux Arts, 1942. With Lagneau, Weill, Architects, Paris, 1947-55; cons. architect S.E.T.A.P., Paris, Neuilly, 1955-82, pres., Meudon, 1982—. Decorated chevalier Legion d'Honneur, Croix de Guerre (France); comdr. Alphonso le Sage (Spain). Hon. fellow AIA; mem. Order des Architects, Academie d'Architecture, Union Internationale des Architectes (sec.-gen. 1970-78). Address: 1 rue des Pins, 92-100 Boulogne France

WEILL, SAMUEL, JR., automobile company executive; b. Rochester, N.Y., Dec. 22, 1916; s. Samuel and Bertha (Stein) W.; student U. Buffalo, 1934-35; m. Mercedes Weil, May 20, 1939 (div. Aug. 1943); children: Rita and Eric (twins); m. Cléanthe Kimball Carr, Aug. 12, 1960 (div. 1982); m. Jacqueline Natalie Bateman, Jan. 5, 1983. Co-owner, Brayton Air Coll., St. Louis, 1937-42; assoc. editor, advt. mgr., bus. mgr. Road and Track Mag., Los Angeles, 1951-53; pres. Volkswagen Pacific, Inc., Culver City, Calif., 1953-73, Porsche Audi Pacific, Culver City, 1953-73; chmn. bd. Minto Internat., Inc., London; v.p. fin. Chieftain Oil Co., Ovai, Calif. Recipient Tom May award Jewish Hosp. and Research Center, 1971. Served with USAAF, 1943-45. Home: 305 Palomar Rd Ojai CA 93023 Office: Chieftan Oil Co 306 E Matilija St Suite 201 Ojai CA 93023

WEILLER, PAUL ANNIK, diversified company executive; b. Neuilly/Seine, France, July 28, 1933; s. Paul Louis Weiller and Aliki (Diplarakos) Russell; m. Olimpia Emanuela Torlonia, June 26, 1965; children—Beatrice, Sibilla, Cosima, Domitilla. Baccaraureat, Ecole des Roches, France, 1951; B.Sc. in Mech. Engring., MIT, 1956. Shareholders rep. IMOSTAB Group, Dusseldorf, W.Ger., 1965—. Vice pres. Wallerstein Found., Ares, France, 1969—; vice pres., treas. Paul Louis Weiller Found., Geneva, 1975—. Served to lt. French Air Force, 1957-59. Decorated Croix Valeur Militaire. Greek Orthodox. Club: Traveller's (Paris). Home: 19 Quai Des Bergues, 1211 Geneva Switzerland Office: IMOGEST SA, 47 rue Vieille du Temple, Paris France

WEIMER, PETER DWIGHT, mediator, lawyer; b. Grand Rapids, Mich., Oct. 14, 1938; s. Glen E. and Clarabel (Kauffman) W.; m. Judith Anne Minor; children: Melanie, Kim. BA, Bridgewater Coll., 1962; JD, Howard U., 1969. Assoc. counsel Loporto & Weimer Ltd., Manassas, Va., 1970-75; chief counsel Weimer & Cheatle Ltd., Manassas, 1975-79, Peter D. Weimer, P.C., Manassas, 1979-82; pres., mediator Mediation Ltd., Manassas, 1981—; pres. Citation Properties, Inc., Manassas, 1971—; pres. Preferred Research of No. Va., Inc., 1985—. Address: PO Box 1616 Manassas VA 22110

WEINBERG, STEVEN, physicist, educator; b. N.Y.C., May 3, 1933; s. Fred and Eva (Israel) W.; m. Louise Goldwasser, July 6, 1954; 1 child, Elizabeth. B.A., Cornell U., 1954; postgrad., Copenhagen Inst. Theoretical Physics, 1954-55; Ph.D., Princeton U., 1957; A.M. (hon.), Harvard U., 1973; Sc.D. (hon.), Knox Coll., 1978, U. Chgo., 1978, U. Rochester, 1979, Yale U.,

1979, CUNY, 1980, Clark U., 1982, Dartmouth Coll., 1984; Ph.D. (hon.), Weizmann Inst., 1985; D.Litt. (hon.), Washington Coll., 1985. Research assoc., instr. Columbia U., 1957-59; research physicist Lawrence Radiation Lab., Berkeley, Calif., 1959-60; mem. faculty U. Calif.-Berkeley, 1960-69, prof. physics, 1964-69; vis. prof. MIT, 1967-69, prof. physics, 1969-73; Higgins prof. physics Harvard U., 1973-83; sr. scientist Smithsonian Astrophys. lab., 1973-83; Josey prof. sci. U. Tex.-Austin, 1982—; sr. cons. Smithsonian Astrophys. Obs., 1983—; cons. Inst. Def. Analyses, Washington, 1960-73, ACDA, 1973; mem. Pres.'s Com. on Nat. Medal of Sci., 1979-82, Council of Scholars, Library of Congress, 1983-85; sr. adv. La Jolla Inst.; chair in physics Collège de France, 1971; mem. NRC Com. on Internat. Security and Arms Control, 1981; dir. Jerusalem Winter Sch. Theoretical Physics, 1983—; mem. adv. council Tex. SSC High Energy Research Facility, 1987, Nat. Acad. Scis. Supercolliders Site Eval. com., 1987-88; Silliman lectr. Yale U., 1977; Richtmeyer lectr., 1974; Scott lectr. Cavendish Lab., 1975; Lauritsen Meml. lectr. Calif. Inst. Tech., 1979; Bethe lectr. Cornell U., 1979; de Shalit lectr. Weizman Inst., 1979; Einstein lectr. Israel Acad. Arts and Scis., 1984; Sloan fellow, 1961-65; Loeb lectr. in physics Harvard U., 1966-67; Cherwell-Simon lectr. Oxford U., 1983; Bampton lectr. Columbia U., 1983; Morris Loeb vis. prof. physics Harvard U., 1983—; Hilldale lectr. U. Wis., 1985; Clark lectr. U. Tex.-Dallas, 1986; Dirac lectr. U. Cambridge, 1986. Author: Gravitation and Cosmology: Principles and Applications of the General Theory of Relativity, 1972, The First Three Minutes: A Modern View of the Origin of the Universe, 1977, The Discovery of Subatomic Particles, 1982; co-author (with R. Feynman) Elementary Particles and the Laws of Physics, 1987; research and publs. on elementary particles, quantum field theory, cosmology; co-editor, Cambridge U. Press, monographs on math. physics; editorial bd., Progress in Sci. Culture, U. Chgo. Press, series on theoretical astrophysics; mem. sci. book com. Sloan Found., 1985—; adv. bd. Issues in Sci. and Tech., 1984-87; mem. editorial bd. Jour. Math. Physics, 1986—; bd. assoc. editors Nuclear Physics B. Bd. overseers SSC Accelerator, 1984-86; bd. advisers Santa Barbara Inst. Theoretical Physics, 1983-86. Recipient J. Robert Oppenheimer meml. prize, 1973, recipient Dannie Heineman prize in math. physics, 1977, Am. Inst. Physics-U.S. Steel Found. sci. writing award, 1977, Nobel prize in physics, 1979, Elliott Cresson medal Franklin Inst., 1979. Mem. Am. Acad. Arts and Scis. (council), Am. Phys. Soc. (past councilor at large, panel on faculty positions com. on status of women in physics), Nat. Acad. Sci. (supercollider site evaluation com. 1987—), Einstein Archives (adv. bd. 19888—), Internat. Astron. Union, Council Fgn. Relations, Am. Philos. Soc., Royal Soc. London (fgn. mem.), Am. Mediaeval Acad., History of Sci. Soc., Philos. Soc. Tex. Clubs: Saturday (Boston); Headliners, Tuesday (Austin); Cambridge Sci. Soc.

WEINBERGER, CASPAR WILLARD, former U.S. secretary of defense; b. San Francisco, Aug. 18, 1917; s. Herman and Cerise Carpenter (Hampson) W.; m. Jane Dalton, Aug. 16, 1942; children: Arlin Cerise, Caspar Willard. A.B. magna cum laude, Harvard, 1938, LL.B., 1941. Bar: Calif. Law clk. U.S. Judge William E. Orr, 1945-47; with firm Heller, Ehrman, White & McAuliffe, 1947-69, ptnr., 1959-69; mem. Calif. Legislature from 21st Dist., 1952-58; vice chmn. Calif. Rep. Cen. Com., 1960-62, chmn., 1962-64; chmn. Com. Cal. Govt. Orgn. and Econs., 1967-68; dir. fin. Calif., 1968-69; chmn. FTC, 1970; dep. dir. Office Mgmt. and Budget, 1970-72, dir., 1972-73; counsellor to the Pres., 1973; sec. HEW, 1973-75; gen. counsel, v.p., dir. Bechtel Power Corp., San Francisco, 1975-80, Bechtel, Inc., 1975-80, Bechtel Corp., 1975-80; sec. Dept. Def., Washington, 1981-87; with firm Rogers and Wells, 1988—; formerly staff book reviewer San Francisco Chronicle; moderator weekly TV program Profile, Bay Area, sta. KQED, San Francisco, 1959-68; Frank Nelson Doubleday lectr., 1974. Writer column on Calif. govt., 1959-68. Chmn. Pres.'s Com. on Mental Retardation, 1973-75; former mem. Trilateral Commn.; former mem. adv. council Am. Ditchley Found.; former bd. dirs. Yosemite Inst.; former trustee St. Luke's Hosp., San Francisco, Mechanics Inst.; former chmn. nat. bd. trustees Nat. Symphony, Washington; former bd. govs. San Francisco Symphony. Served from pvt. to capt., inf. AUS, 1941-45, PTO. Decorated Bronze Star; Grand Cordon of Order of the Rising Sun, 1988. Mem. ABA, State Bar Calif. Episcopalian (former treas. Diocese of Calif.). Clubs: Century (New York); Bohemian (San Francisco), Pacific Union (San Francisco), Harvard (San Francisco); Burlingame County. Office: Rogers and Wells 1737 H St NW Washington DC 20006 *

WEINBRENNER, GEORGE RYAN, aeronautical engineer; b. Detroit, June 10, 1917; s. George Penbrook and Helen Mercedes (Ryan) W.; B.S., M.I.T., 1940, M.S., 1941; A.M.P., Harvard U., 1966; m. Billie Marjorie Elwood, May 2, 1955. Commd. 2d lt. USAAF, 1939, advanced through grades to col., 1949; def. attaché Am. embassy, Prague, Czechoslavakia, 1958-61; dep. chief staff intelligence Air Force Systems Command, Washington, 1962-68; comdr. fgn. tech. div. U.S. Air Force, Wright-Patterson AFB, Ohio, 1968-74; comdr. Brooks AFB, Tex., 1974-75; ret., 1975; exec. v.p. B.C. Wills & Co., Inc., Reno, Nev., 1975-84; lectr. Sch. Aerospace Medicine Brooks AFB, Tex., 1975-84; chmn. bd. Hispaño-Technica S.A. Inc., San Antonio, 1977—; adv. dir. Plaza Nat. Bank, San Antonio; cons. Def. Dept., 1981, Dept. Air Force, 1975-84. Decorated D.S.M., Legion of Merit, Bronze Star, Air medal, Purple Heart; Ordre National du Merite, Medaille de la Resistance, Croix de Guerre (France). Fellow AIAA (asso.); mem. San Antonio C. of C., World Affairs Council, Air Force Assn. (exec. sec. Tex. 1976-82), Assn. Former Intelligence Officers (nat. dir.), Air Force Hist. Found. (dir.), U.S. Strategic Inst., Tex. Aerospace and Nat. Def. Tech. Devel. Council, Am. Astronautical Soc., Aerospace Ednl. Found. (trustee), Mil. Order World Wars, Am. Legion, Assn. Old Crows, Kappa Sigma. Roman Catholic. Clubs: Army-Navy, Univ. (Washington); Army-Navy Country (Arlington, Va.); St. Anthonys (San Antonio); Spl. Forces (London). Home: 7400 Crestway #903 San Antonio TX 78239 Office: PO Box 18484 San Antonio TX 78218

WEINER, EARL DAVID, lawyer; b. Balt., Aug. 21, 1939; s. Jacob Joseph and Sophia Gertrude (Rachanow) W.; m. Gina Helen Priestley Ingoglia, Mar. 30, 1962; children: Melissa Danis Balmain, John Barlow. A.B., Dickinson Coll., 1960; LL.B., Yale U., 1968. Bar: N.Y. 1969. Assoc. Sullivan & Cromwell, N.Y.C., 1968-76, ptnr., 1976—; adj. lectr. Rutgers U. Sch. Law, 1987-88; bd. dirs. Hedwin Corp., Solvay Techs., Inc., The Acting Co., 1988—. Gov. Bklyn. Heights Assn., 1980-87, pres. 1985-87, mem. adv. com. 1987—; gov. The Heights Casino, 1979-84, pres., 1981-84; trustee Green-Wood Cemetery, 1986—, Bklyn. Bot. Garden, 1985—; bd. advisors Dickinson Coll., Carlisle, Pa., 1986—, chmn. 1988—; bd. advisors Hist. Districts Council, 1986—; mem. adv. com., East Rock Inst., 1988—. Served to lt. USN, 1961-65. Mem. ABA, N.Y. State Bar Assn., N.Y. City Bar Assn. Office: Sullivan and Cromwell 125 Broad St New York NY 10004

WEINGARTNER, PAUL ANDREAS, philosopher, educator; b. Innsbruck, Austria, June 8, 1931; s. Karland Maria Haselwanter Weigartner; m. Ursula Elfriede Steinhammer, Sept. 1, 1966; children: Thomas, Peter, Andreas, Veronika, Johannes. Tchr. diploma for elem. schs., Tchr. Tng. Coll., Innsbruck, 1952; PhD, U. Innsbruck, 1961; Dozent of Philosophy, U. Graz and U. Salzburg, 1965. Research asst. Inst. F. Wissenschaftstheorie, Salzburg, 1962-67; chmn. Inst. f. Wissenschaftstheorie, Salzburg, 1972—; chmn. dept. philosophy U. Salzburg, 1972-80, assoc. prof., 1970, full prof. philosophy, 1971—; regular referee Austrian Sci. Research Fund, Vienna, 1970—; lectr. in field. Author: Wissenschaftstheorie I and II, 1971, 76, 2d edit. 1978; editorial bd. various sci. jours.; contbr. 80 articles to profl. jours. Brit. Council research fellow U. London, 1961-62, Humboldt Stiftung research fellow, U. Munich, 1963-64; recipient Kardinal-Innitzer-Prize, 1966. Mem. Inst. of Gorres-Gessellschaft for Interdisciplinary Research, Assn. Symbolic Logic, Academie Internationale de Philosophie des Scis., others. Office: U Salzburg, Dept Philsophy, Franziskanergasse 1, A-5020 Salzburg Austria

WEINHOLD, VIRGINIA BEAMER, interior designer; b. Elizabeth, N.J., June 21, 1932; d. Clayton Mitchell and Rosemary (Behrend) Beamer; divorced; children: Thomas Craig, Robert Scott, Amy Linette. BA, Cornell U., 1955; BFA summa cum laude, Ohio State U., 1969; MA in Design Mgmt., Ohio State U., 1982. Freelance interior designer, 1969-72; interior designer, dir. interior design Karlsberger and Assos. Inc., Columbus, Ohio, 1972-82; assoc. prof. dept. indsl. design Ohio State U., 1982—; lectr. indsl. design Ohio State U., 1972, 79-80. Bd. visitors, mem. accreditation bd. Found. for Interior Design Edn. and Research. Mem. Inst. Bus. Designers (chpt. treas. 1977-79, nat. trustee 1979-81, nat. chmn. contract documents com. 1979-84, chpt. pres. 1981-83), Constrn. Specifications Inst., Interior Design Educator's Council, Illuminating Engring. Soc., asso. mem. AIA. Prin. works include Grands Rapids (Mich.) Osteo. Hosp., Melrose (Mass.) Wakefield Hosp., Christopher Inn, Columbus, John W. Galbreath Hdqrs., Columbus, Guernsey Meml. Hosp., Cambridge, Ohio, Trinity Epis. Ch. and Parish House, Columbus, Hale Hosp., Haverhill, Mass., others. Author: IBO Forms and Documents Manual, Interior Finish Materials for Health Care Facilities. Home: 112 Glen Dr Worthington OH 43085 Office: 128 N Oval Mall Columbus OH 43210

WEINIG, RICHARD ARTHUR, lawyer; b. Durango, Colo., Mar. 23, 1940; s. Arthur John and Edna (Novella) W.; m. Barbara A. Westerland, June 16, 1964. B.A. in Polit. Sci., Stanford U., 1962, postgrad. in Soviet Studies, 1962-65; J.D., U. Calif.-San Francisco, 1971. Bar: Alaska, 1971, U.S. Dist. Ct. Alaska 1971, U.S. Ct. Appeals (9th cir.) 1978, U.S. Supreme Ct. 1979. Assoc. Burr, Pease & Kurtz, Anchorage, 1971-73; assoc. Greater Anchorage Area Borough, 1973-75, Municipality of Anchorage, 1975-82; ptnr. Pletcher & Slaybaugh, Anchorage, 1982-88, Pletcher, Weinig, Lotteridge & Moser, 1988—. Active, Stanford U. Young Republicans, 1961-65, Alaska Rep. Com., 1971-83, Sierra Club, Mountaineering Club, Knik Canoyers and Kayakers of Alaska, Alaska Ctr. for Environ. Mem. ABA, Alaska Bar Assn., Anchorage Bar Assn., Nat. Rifle Assn. Republican. Presbyterian. Mem. editorial bd. Hastings Law Jour. Office: 480 W Tudor Rd Suite 101 Anchorage AK 99503

WEINLAND, STUART LOUIS, ceramic engineer, researcher; b. Dayton, Ohio, Sept. 25, 1940; s. Louis Albert and Mazel Clara (Schott) W. BS, Alfred U., 1962; MS, Miss. State U., 1965; postgrad., U. N.Mex., 1967. Assoc. ceramic engr. The Babcock and Wilcox Co., Alliance, Ohio, 1962-63; scientist Lockheed Missiles and Space Co., Sunnyvale, Calif., 1965-67; sr. engr. Martin Marietta Corp., Orlando, Fla., 1968-70; sr. sci. assoc. Lawrence Livermore (Calif.) Lab., 1976—. Contbr. articles to profl. jours.; patentee in field. Mem. Am. Ceramic Soc. Office: Lawrence Livermore Nat Lab 7000 E Ave L-369 Livermore CA 94550

WEINMANN, RICHARD ADRIAN, lawyer, arbitrator; b. N.Y.C., Oct. 15, 1917; s. Randolph and Mae (Korber) W.; m. Bert Millicent Landes, Dec. 26, 1946; children—Harriet Joan, Elaine Anita. LL.B., Bklyn. Law Sch., 1948; LL.M., NYU, 1953. Bar: N.Y. 1958, U.S. Dist. Ct. (so. dist.) N.Y. 1960, U.S. Dist. Ct. (ea. dist.) N.Y. 1960, U.S. Ct. Appeals (2d cir.) 1965, U.S. Supreme Ct. 1964. Ptnr. Sipser, Weinstock & Weinmann, N.Y.C., 1953-71; sole practice, N.Y.C., 1972—: guest lectr. seminars; mem. staff Cornell U. Sch. Indsl. and Labor Relations; panel arbitrator Am. Arbitration Assn. Suffolk and Nassau Counties Pub. Employment Relations Bds. N.Y. State; N.Y. State Bd. Mediation. Committeeman Nassau County (N.Y.), 1965—. Served with AUS, 1943-46. Mem. ABA, N.Y. State Bar Assn., N.Y. County Lawyers Assn., Am. Trial Lawyers Assn., Bar Assn. Nassau County, Indsl. Relations Research Assn., Union Lawyers Ednl. Conf. (legal adv. bd.), ACLU. Club: B'nai B'rith. Office: 292 Madison Ave New York NY 10017

WEINRICH, BRIAN ERWIN, mathematics educator; b. Passaic, N.J., Jan. 8, 1952; s. Erwin H. and Ann E. (Gall) W. B.S., Pa. State U., 1974, M.A., 1978; M.S., Shippensburg State U., 1983. Mathematician U.S. Dept. Agr., SEA-ARS, N.E. Watershed Research Ctr., University Park, Pa., 1974-80; instr. math and computer sci. Shippensburg (Pa.) U., 1980-84; asst. prof. math. and computer Sci. California U. (Pa.), 1984—; cons. in field. Author: (with A. S. Rogowski) Water Movement and Quality on Strip-Mined Lands: A Compilation of Computer Programs, 1984; contbg. author (Surface Mining) Edit, II, 1988; contbr. articles to profl. jours. Mem. Missions bd. Calvary Bapt. Ch., State College, Pa., 1975-80; visitation team Prince St. United Brethren Ch., Shippensburg, 1982-84; Bible study leader, asst. Sunday sch. tchr., Library Bapt. Ch., 1986—. U.S. Dept. Age, grantee, 1982—. Mem. Soc. for Indsl. and Applied Math., Math. Assn. Am., Am. Math. Soc. Republican. Home: 236 Water St West Newton PA 15089 Office: California U Dept Math and Computer Sci California PA 15419

WEINRICH, JOHNATHAN EDWARD, lawyer; b. N.Y.C., Sept. 17, 1949; s. John Edward and Anne (Murray) W.; children: Joy Teresa, Johnathan Joseph. BA, SUNY-Binghamton, 1974; JD, Vt. Law Sch., 1977. Bar: N.Y. 1978, U.S. Dist. Ct. (ea. and so. dist.) N.Y. 1978, U.S. Tax Ct. 1981, U.S. Ct. Appeals (2d cir.) 1980. Staff atty. Legal Aid Soc., N.Y.C., 1979-81; ptnr. Rutberg & Weinrich, N.Y.C, 1981-83; owner Johnathan E. Weinrich Law Firm, N.Y.C., 1983—. Editor Vt. Law. Rev., 1976-77. Legis. Counsel N.Y. City Councilman Ralph Colon, 1987—; Counsel Luis Nine Dem. Assn., Bronx, 1984; mem. Gov.'s Metro Task Force on Correctional Services, N.Y.C., 1984; sec. Com. to Re-elect Ralph C. Colon, 1987; trustee Vt. Law Sch., 1975-76. Mem. ABA, N.Y. State Trial Lawyers Assn., Assn. Trial Lawyers Am., Bklyn. Bar Assn., Kings County Criminal Bar Assn., Legal Aid Alumni Assn., N.Y. State Defenders Assn., N.Y. State Assn. Criminal Def. Attys. (charter 1987—). Democrat. Roman Catholic. Lodge: Masons. Address: 5 Beekman St Suite 801 New York NY 10038

WEINSTEIN, ALLEN, educator, historian, foundation administrator; b. N.Y.C., Sept. 1, 1937; s. Samuel and Sarah (Popkoff) W.; m. Diane Gilbert, June 14, 1969; children: Andrew Samuel, David Meier. BA, CCNY; MA, Yale U., PhD, 1967. Prof. Smith Coll., Northampton, Mass., 1966-81, Georgetown U., Washington, 1981-83; pres. R.M. Hutchins CSDI, Santa Barbara, Calif., 1984; prof. Boston U., 1985—; pres. The Ctr. for Democracy, Washington, 1985—. Author: Prelude to Populism, 1970, Freedom and Crisis, 1974, 3d edit., 1981, Perjury, 1978 (NISC award 1978), Between the Wars, 1978; editor: Am. Negro Slavery, 1968, 3d edit., 1981, HST and Israel, 1981; mem. editorial bd. The Washington Post, 1981; exec. editor The Washington Quar., 1982-83. Exec. dir. The Democracy Program, Washington, 1982-83; acting pres. Nat. Endowment for Democracy, Washington, 1983-84; chmn. edn. com. U.S. Inst. Peace, Washington, 1986—; mem. U.S. Observer del., Feb., 1986 Philippines election, co-author report; vice chmn. U.S. del. UNESCO World Conf. on Culture, 1982, UNESCO/IPDC meeting, 1983. Recipient Meade prize in history CCNY, 1960, Egleston prize Yale U., 1967, Binkley-Stephenson prize Orgn. Am. Historians, 1968, UN Peace medal, 1986; Fulbright lectr., Australia, 1968, 71; Commonwealth Fund lectr. U.S. History, U. London, 1981; Fourth of July Orator Faneuil Hall, Boston, 1987. Fellow Woodrow Wilson Ctr., NEH; mem. Soc. Am. Historians. Democrat. Jewish. Office: The Ctr for Democracy 1101 15th St NW Suite 505 Washington DC 20005

WEINSTEIN, GEORGE, accountant, management consultant; b. N.Y.C., Mar. 20, 1924; s. Morris J. and Sara (Broder) W.; m. Shirley Beatrice Greenberg, Sept. 1, 1945; children—Stanley Howard, Jerrald, Sara Belle. B.S., U. Ill., 1944, postgrad. Law Sch., 1944-55; M.B.A., NYU, 1947. Joined Morris J. Weinstein, Groothuis & Co., N.Y.C., 1944, ptnr., 1945-72; ptnr. Weinstein Assocs., N.Y.C. and Milw., 1973—; chmn. Weinstein Assocs. Ltd.; pres. dir. REIT Property Mgrs. Ltd., Milw.; pres. Hudson Valley Corp., WAL Ltd.; bd. dirs. Brit. Land of Am., chmn. exec. com.; bd. dirs. Regency Investors, John Stewart Axminster U.S.A., Ice Co. of Wis. Active United Jewish Appeal, Fedn. Jewish Philanthropies; bd. dirs., founder North Shore Hebrew Acad.; founder, past pres. Gt. Neck (N.Y.) Synagogue; chmn. Lake Park Synagogue; trustee M. Rainville trust; bd. dirs. Milw. Jewish Home, Jewish Nat. Fund, Milw. Hillel Acad. Mem. Am. Inst. Accts., N.Y. Soc. C.P.A.s, Hebrew Immigrant Soc., Tau Delta Phi (nat. treas.), Delta Sigma Phi. Clubs: President's of U. Ill., Westmoreland, Ambassadors of Yeshiva U., Milw. Athletic, Wisconsin of Milw.; Citrus (Orlando, Fla.). Lodge: Masons (past master). Address: 3900 N Lake Dr Milwaukee WI 53202 also: 1211 Gulf of Mexico Dr Longboat Key FL 33548

WEINSTEIN, GEORGE WILLIAM, ophthalmology educator; b. East Orange, N.J., Jan. 26, 1935; s. Henry J. and Irma C. (Klein) W.; m. Sheila Valerie Wohlreich, June 20, 1957; children: Bruce David, Elizabeth Joyce, Rachel Andrea. AB, U. Pa., 1955; MD, SUNY, Bklyn., 1959. Diplomate Am. Bd. Ophthalmology (bd. dirs. 1981—). Intern then resident in ophthalmology Kings County Hosp., Bklyn., 1959-63; asst. prof. ophthalmology Johns Hopkins U., Balt., 1967-70; head ophthalmology dept. U. Tex., San Antonio, 1970-80; prof., Jane McDermott Shott chmn. W.Va. U., Morgantown, 1980—; chmn. Long Range Planning com., 1986—. Author: Key Facts in Ophthalmology, 1984; editor: Open Angle Glaucoma, 1986; (jour.) Ophthalmic Surgery, 1971-81; contbr. articles to profl. jours. Served to lt. comdr. USPHS, 1963-65. Sr. Internat. fellow Fogarty Internat. Ctr. NIH, 1987. Mem. ACS (bd. govs. 1983-85, bd. regents 1987—), Assn. Univ. Profs. of Ophthalmology (pres. 1986-87), Am. Acad. Ophthalmology (pub. and profl. sec. 1981—, bd. dirs. 1980—, Honor award, Sr. Honor award), Alpha Omega Alpha (faculty 1987). Jewish. Home: 28 Lakeview Dr Morgantown WV 26505 Office: W Va U Coll Medicine Dept Ophthalmology Morgantown WV 26506

WEINSTEIN, HILLEL, electronics company executive; b. Tel Aviv, Nov. 1, 1935; s. Dov and Liza (Gorelik) W.; B.S. in Elec. Engring., N.Y. U., 1950; M.S., Poly. Inst. N.Y., 1962, Ph.D., 1965; m. Hanna Attias, June 25, 1956; children—Daphne, Thalia, Oren. Mem. tech. staff RCA Labs., Princeton, N.J., 1960-65; mgr. computer and info. scis., research div., then mgr. electronics area, info. systems div. Xerox Corp., Rochester, N.Y., 1965-68; pres. Sci. Data Systems Israel Ltd., Haifa, 1968—; dir. Water Technologies Ltd., T.M.B. Fertilizer Pumps Ltd. 1968-80, 82—; pres, chmn. Microkim Ltd., affiliate M/A-Com, Inc. (U.S.). Served with Israeli Army, 1954-56. Mem. IEEE, Israel Mgmt. Center, Sigma Xi, Tau Beta Pi, Eta Kappa Nu. Author, patentee in field. Home: 3 Tel Mane, Haifa Israel Office: PO Box 1797, Haifa 31016, Israel

WEINSTEIN, LEWIS H., lawyer; b. Vilna, Lithuania, Apr. 10, 1905; came to U.S., 1906; s. Jacob Menahem and Kuna (Romanow) W.; m. Selma Yeslawsky, Sept. 2, 1932 (dec. Apr. 1986); children: David J., Louise W. Dozois. AB magna cum laude, Harvard U., 1927, JD, 1930; DHL (hon.), Brandeis U., 1986; D Hebrew Laws (hon.), Hebrew Coll., Boston, 1987. Bar: Mass. 1930. Assoc., then ptnr. Rome & Weinstein, 1930-45; asst. corp. counsel Boston, 1934-45; ptnr. Foley, Hoag & Eliot, Boston, 1946-79; sr. ptnr. Foley, Hoag & Eliot, 1979-85, of counsel, 1985—; lectr. law Harvard, 1960-75; sr. vis. lectr. dept. city and regional planning MIT, 1960-68; occasional lectr. Practising Law Inst., N.Y.C., New Eng. Law Inst.-ABA, Am. Law Inst., Mass. Continuing Legal Edn.; past clk. Spencer Cos.; mem. faculty Nat. Inst. Trial Advocacy, Boulder, Colo.; mem. finance com., bd. dirs. B. & M. R.R., 1960-74; trustee Boston 5 Cent Savs. Bank, 1964-78; cons. U.S. Housing Authority, 1940-42. Contbr. articles to law and other jours.; author plays, biog. articles, also chpts. in legal books. Chmn. Mass. Emergency Housing Commn., 1946-47; chmn. Mass. Bd. Housing, 1947-48, Mass. Housing Council, 1948-52; mem. rent control and housing coms. Nat. Def. Commn., 1941-42; chmn. Nat. Jewish Community Relations Adv. Council, 1960-64, Armed Forces Adv. Com. Greater Boston, 1946-48; pres., Combined Jewish Philanthropies Greater Boston, 1954-57, gen. campaign chmn., 1957, now mem. exec. com.; past pres. Jewish Community Relations Council Met. Boston, 1952-54; former mem. nat. council Jewish Welfare Bd.; chmn. Conf. Presidents Maj. Am. Jewish Orgns., 1964-66; chmn. Nat. Conf. Soviet Jewry, 1968-70; mem. nat. com. Harvard Center for Jewish Studies; past lay rep. Nat. Assembly for Social Policy and Devel.; former mem. exec. com. City of Boston Civic Unity Com.; former mem. adv. council Mass. Dept. Edn.; Mass. Dept. Mental Health; mem. human rights com. also housing and urban renewal com. World Peace Through Law Center; former mem. exec. com., bd. dirs. New Eng. region, nat. bd. dirs. NCCJ; exec. com. Pres.'s Com. Equal Opportunity Housing, 1961-68; past chmn. Gov.'s Task Force to Establish Mass. Dept. Community Affairs; pres., 1965-66, now mem. exec. com. Council Jewish Fedn.; mem. nat. council Am. Jewish Joint Distbn. Com.; past v.p. Nat. Fedn. Jewish Men's Clubs.; hon. trustee United Israel Appeal; past trustee Social Law, Library Ct. House Boston; past v.p. Am. Jewish League for Israel; past trustee Mass. Fedn. Taxpayers' Assn.; past bd. overseers Hiatt Inst.; past mem. bd. overseers Lown Inst. Contemporary Jewish Studies, Heller Grad. Sch. Pub. Welfare; fellow Brandeis U.; past mem. vis. com., bd. overseers Middle Eastern Ctr. and Near Eastern Langs. and Civilizations, Harvard U.; mem. steering com. capital fund campaign, past class agt. , vice chmn. Coll. Law Sch. Class of 1930; mem. steering com. Divinity Sch. Fund for Christian-Jewish Relations; trustee Nat. Found. Jewish Culture, Meml. Found. Jewish Culture, Hebrew Rehab. Ctr. for Aged, Boston, 1955—, Beth Israel Hosp., 1956—, Inst. for Jewish Life; pres. Hebrew Coll., Boston, 1946-53, now trustee; mem. assembly Jewish Agy. for Israel; founding trustee Ency. Judaica Found.; mem. exec. Seminar program Aspen (Colo.) Inst., 1978; mem. Spl. Mass. Commn. To Investigate Corruption and Malfeasance in State and County Constrn., 1978-80. Served to col. AUS, World War II. Decorated Legion of Merit, Bronze Star with oak leaf cluster, Legion of Honor, Croix de Guerre with palm (France); recipient nat. citation NCCJ, Heritage award Yeshiva U., Nat. Community Service award Jewish Theol. Sem., FDR Day award Ams. Democratic Action, Mass., Harvard Ctr. Jewish Studies award, 1986; named Disting. Bostonian C.of C., 1988, Humanitarian of Yr., Alzheimer's Disease Mass. Assn., 1988. Fellow Am. Coll. Trial Lawyers, Am. Bar Found., Am. Assn. Jewish Edn.; mem. Am. Jewish Hist. Soc. (past mem. exec. council), Assn. U.S. Army (dir. Bay State chpt.), Boston Bar n. (past mem. council, chmn. real estate and eminent domain com.), Mass. Bar Assn. (past chmn. grievance com.), ABA (past mem. standing com. fed. judiciary), Mil Govt. Assn. (past. pres. Mass. chpt.), Phi Beta Kappa. Jewish (former temple trustee). Club: Union (Boston). Office: Foley Hoag & Eliot 1 Post Office Sq Boston MA 02109

WEINSTEIN, LEWIS J., lawyer; b. Irvington, N.J., Aug. 1, 1939; s. Morris William and Ruth G. (Gordon) W.; m. Doris. M. Maher, Aug. 6, 1972; children—Edward S., Robert G. A.B., Transylvania U., 1962; J.D., Rutgers U., 1966. Bar: N.J. 1967. Assoc. Fred Freeman, Newark, 1967-68, Kohn, Kirsch & Needle, Newark, 1968-69; sole practice, Maplewood, N.J., 1969—; med. staff atty. Irvington Gen. Hosp., 1968—. Pres. Harding Twp. Republican Club, New Vernon, N.J., 1982—; chmn. Harding Twp. Bd. Adjustment, New Vernon, 1982—, mem. Twp. Planning Bd., 1986—. Mem. N.J. State Bar Assn., Essex County Bar Assn., Am. Trial Lawyers Assn., Am. Soc. Hosp. Attys. Jewish. Home: Baxter Farm Rd Morristown NJ 07960 Office: 1878 Springfield Ave Maplewood NJ 07040

WEINSTEIN, LUIS N., psychiatrist, writer; b. Santiago, Mar. 21, 1931; s. Nicolas and Dora (Crenovich) W.; diploma in public health U. London, 1963; M.D., U. Chile, 1958; m. Maria Luisa Cayuela, Jan. 31, 1956; children—Luis, Jose, Marisa. Asso. prof. preventive medicine U. Chile, Santiago, 1958-73; dir., founder Center Socio Medical Anthropology Santiago, 1968-73; adviser in community psychiatry, Buenos Aires, 1974-76, Madrid, 1977; founder Center Public Health, Cespo, Santiago, 1978, Center Quillahue, Santiago, 1980, also co-dir., 1980—; founder Sch. Ruben Dario, Santiago, 1980, Tideh workshops for human devel., 1982; bd. dirs. Cuso, Found. for Internat. Devel., Can., 1986-87; advisor Canelo Adult Edn., 1987—. Editor: Man and Society, 1982—. Mem. semi-nat. psychol. welfare Cath. U. , 1987—. Brit. Council scholar, 1962-63; Fulbright vis. prof., Berkeley, 1968; Milbank Fund fellow, 1968-73; Ebert scholar, Buenos Aires, 1974, Madrid, 1977; Clacso scholar, Buenos Aires, 1975; Ebert scholar, Madrid, 1977. Mem. Am. Orthopsychiat. Assn., Soc. Ethics and Life Scis., Soc. Health and Human Values, Argentine Assn. Psychiatry, Chilean Assn. Psychiatry. Author: El Nino, la mirada y el otro, 1966, Ano Nuevo del Dos Mil, 1970, Salud Mental y Proceso de Cambio, 1975, Salud y Democratizació n, 1977, Salud y Autogestion, 1978, Fabulas Abiertas, 1979, Militancia en la Vida, 1980, Autoritarismo o Creatividad Social, 1982, Alamedas para la Renovació n, 1984, La racionalidad integrado y el dsattollo a la escala humana, 1986; contbr. articles to Dag Hammarsjkold Found, 1985-86. Office: Casilla 457-11, Correo 11, Santiago Chile

WEINSTEIN, MILTON CHARLES, educator; b. Brookline, Mass., July 14, 1949; s. William and Ethel (Rosenbloom) W.; m. Rhonda Kruger, June 14, 1970; children—Jeffrey William, Daniel Jay. A.B., A.M., Harvard U., 1970, M.P.P., 1972, Ph.D., 1973. Asst. prof. John F. Kennedy Sch. Govt., Harvard U., Cambridge, Mass., 1973-76, assoc. prof., 1976-80; prof. policy and decision scis. Harvard Sch. Pub. Health, Boston, 1980-86; Henry J. Kaiser prof. health policy and mgmt., 1986—; adj. prof. community and family medicine Dartmouth Med. Sch., Hanover, N.H., 1981—; cons. U.S. office Tech. Assessment, 1979—, U.S. HHS, 1979—, U.S. VA, 1984-86, U.S. EPA, 1983—, Smith Kline and French, 1984-87, Ciba-Geigy, 1987—, New Eng. Med. Ctr., 1986-87, Intermountain Health Care, 1987;mem. com. on priorities for new vaccine devel. Inst. Medicine. Author: Clinical Decision Analysis, 1980, Hypertension: A Policy Perspective, 1976; editorial bd.: Med. Decision Making, 1981—, Journal of Environmental Economics and Management, 1986—. NSF fellow, 1972. Mem. Soc. Med. Decision Making (trustee 1980-82, pres. 1984-85), Soc. Risk Analysis, Internat. Soc. Technology ASsessment in Health Care, Ops. Research Soc. Am., Phi Beta Kappa. Office: Harvard Sch Pub Health Dept Health Policy & Mgmt 677 Huntington Ave Boston MA 02115

WEINSTEIN, ROY, university dean, physics educator, researcher; b. N.Y.C., Apr. 21, 1927; s. Harry and Lillian (Ehrenberg) W.; m. Janet E. Spiller, Mar. 26, 1954; children: Lee Davis, Sara Lynn. B.S., MIT, 1951, Ph.D., 1954; Sc.D. (hon.), Lycoming Coll., 1981. Research asst. Mass. Inst. Tech., 1951-54, asst. prof., 1956-59; asst. prof. Brandeis U., Waltham, Mass., 1954-56; assoc. prof. Northeastern U., Boston, 1960-63, prof. physics, 1963-82, exec. officer, chmn. grad. div. of physics dept., 1967-69, chmn. physics dept., 1974-81; dean Coll. Natural Scis. and Math., prof. physics U. Houston, 1982—, dir. Inst. Beam Particle Dynamics, 1985—; assoc. dir., spokesman Tex. Ctr. for Superconductivity, 1987—; vis. scholar and physicist Stanford (Calif.) U., 1966-67, 81-82; bd. dirs. Perception Tech., Inc., Winchester, Mass., Omniwave Inc., Gloucester, Mass., Wincom Inc., Woburn, Mass.; cons. Visidyne Inc., Burlington, Mass., Stanford U., Houston Ptnrs., Cambridge (Mass.) Electron Accelerator, Harvard U., Cambridge, ; mem. adv. com., 1967-69, chmn. bd. dirs. Xytron Research Corp., 1986—; dir., mem. exec. com. Houston Area Research Ctr., 1984-87; 3d ann. faculty lectr. Northeastern U., 1966; chmn. organizing com. 4th ann. Internat. Conf. on Meson Spectroscopy, 1974, chmn. program com. 5th ann., 1977, mem. organizing com. 6th ann., 1980, 83; chmn. mgmt. group Tex. Accelerator Ctr., Woodlands, Tex., 1985—. Author: Atomic Physics, 1964, Nuclear Physics, 1964, Interactions of Radiation and Matter, 1964; editor: Nuclear Reactor Theory, 1964, Nuclear Materials, 1964; editor procs.: 5th Internat. Conf. on Mesons, 1977; contbr. numerous articles to profl. jours. Mem. Lexington (Mass.) Town Meeting, 1973-76, 77-84; vice chmn. Lexington Council on Aging, 1977-83. Served with USNR, 1945-46. NSF fellow Bohr Inst., Copenhagen, Denmark, 1959-60; NSF fellow Stanford, 1969-70; Guggenheim fellow Harvard, 1970-71; NSF research awards, 1961, 63, 64, 66, 68, 70-82, 82-88; Tex. research awards, 1986-87; Dept. Energy awards 1974, 77, 87, 88. Fellow Am. Phys. Soc.; mem. Am. Assn. Physics Tchrs., N.Y. Acad. Scis., Sigma Xi, Phi Kappa Phi (pres. chpt. 1977-78, nat. Triennial disting. scholar prize 1980-83), Pi Lambda Phi. Democrat. Unitarian. Club: Mason. Home: 4368 Fiesta Ln Houston TX 77004 Office: Univ Houston Coll Natural Sci and Math Houston TX 77004

WEINSTEIN, STANLEY, accountant; b. N.Y.C., Apr. 18, 1926; s. George and Bella (Schlufman) W.; m. Anita Cohen (div.); children—Harold, David; m. Betty Schwartz, 1981. B.B.A., CCNY, 1949. C.P.A., N.Y. Sr. ptnr. Mann Judd Landau, N.Y.C., 1954—; internat. mng. ptnr. Hodgson Landau Brands, N.Y.C., 1984—; C.P.A. adv. bd. Pace U., N.Y.C., 1974—, adj. assoc. prof., 1974—. Served as petty officer 3rd class U.S. Navy, 1944-46, PTO. Co-author SEC Compliance (Fin. Reporting and Forms). Dir. Macula Found., N.Y., 1983, Found. Studies of Hormone Related Cancers, 1983, Found. Interventional Cardiology, 1984, Hebrew Home for Aged, Riverdale, 1984. Mem. AICPA, N.Y. SSCPA, Am. Acctg. Assn. Clubs: Fenway (Scarsdale), Harmonie (N.Y.). Office: Mann Judd Landau 230 Park Ave New York NY 10169

WEINSTEIN, STEPHEN SAUL, lawyer; b. Newark, Jan. 13, 1939; s. Francis and Hanna (Posner) W.; m. Nancy Stein, June 27, 1962; children: Beth, Jill, Lisa, Michael. BS, Fairleigh Dickinson U., 1962; JD, American U., 1965. Bar: N.J. 1966, U.S. Dist. Ct. N.J. 1966, U.S. Supreme Ct. 1969, U.S. Ct. Appeals (D.C. cir.) 1977, U.S. Dist. Ct. (so. and ea. dist.) N.Y. 1980, U.S. Ct. Appeals (3d cir.) 1981, N.Y. 1981. Exec. asst. to Senator Harrison A. Williams Jr., U.S. Senate, 1963-65; law clk., 1965-66; asst. prosecutor County Morris, N.J., 1968-70; counsel Morris County Dem. Com., 1971, 73-88; mem. Stevens & Mathias, Newark, 1966-68, A.I. Harkavy, East Orange, N.J., 1966-69; pres. Stephen S. Weinstein, P.C., Morristown, N.J., 1968—. Trustee Sammy Davis, Jr. Liver Found., 1986—, Univ. Medicine and Dentistry N.J., 1976-84, mem. Dem. electoral coll. State of N.J., 1984, 88. Mem. Morris County Bar Assn. (trustee 1974-76, 79-82), Essex County Bar Assn., N.J. Bar Assn., Fed. Bar Assn., ABA, Assn. Trial Lawyers Am. (gov. 1981—), Pa. Trial Lawyers, Tex. Trial Lawyers Assn., Acad. Fla. Trial Lawyers, Nat. Dist. Attys. Assn., Trial Attys. N.J., Morris County 200 Club (trustee 1965-70), Practicing Law Inst. N.Y. (lectr.), Instn. Continuing Legal Edn. N.J. (lectr.), Scribes, Phi Alpha Delta. Office: 20 Park Pl Morristown NJ 07960

WEINSTOCK, LEONARD, lawyer; b. Bklyn., Aug. 18, 1935; s. Samuel Morris and Evelyn (Reiser) W.; m. Rita Lee Itkowitz, May 25, 1963; children—Gregg Douglas, Valerie Lisa, Tara Diane. B.S., Bklyn. Coll., 1956; J.D., St. John's U., Bklyn., 1959. Bar: N.Y. 1961, U.S. Supreme Ct. 1964, U.S. Ct. Appeals (2d cir.) 1963, U.S. Dist. Ct. (ea. and so. dists.) N.Y. 1963, U.S. Tax Ct. 1963. Assoc. Bernard Helfenstein law practice, Bklyn., 1962-63; supr. All State Ins. Co., Bklyn., 1963-64; atty. Hertz Corp., N.Y.C., 1964-65; ptnr. Nicholas & Weinstock, Flushing, N.Y., 1965-68; v.p., ptnr. Garbarini, Scher & DeCicco, P.C., N.Y.C., 1968—; lectr. Practicing Law Inst., N.Y.C., 1975—, N.Y. Trial Lawyers Assn., 1980—; arbitrator Nassau County Dist. Ct., Mineola, N.Y., 1979—, U.S. Dist. Ct. (ea. dist.) N.Y. 1986—; mem. Med. Malpractice Mediation Panel, Mineola, 1978—. Legal counsel Massapequa Soccer Club (N.Y.), 1981—; county committeeman Democratic Party, Massapequa Park, N.Y., 1979—. Served with U.S. Army, 1959-62. Mem. ABA, N.Y. State Bar Assn., Nassau County Bar Assn. (mem. med. jurisprudence ins. com. 1978), N.Y. Trial Lawyers Assn., Queens County Bar Assn. (mem. legal referral com. 1969). Avocations: stamp collecting, softball, racquetball. Home: 20 Massapequa Ave Massapequa NY 11758 Office: Garbarini and Scher PC 1114 Ave of Americas New York NY 10036

WEINSTOCK, LORD (ARNOLD), electric company executive; b. London, July 29, 1924; B.Sc. in Econs. U. London, 1945; D.Sc. (hon.), Salford, 1975, Aston, 1976, Bath, 1978, Reading, 1978; LL.D. (hon.), U. Leeds, 1978, U. Wales, 1985; D.Tech. (hon.), Loughborough U. Tech., 1981; DSc (hon.), U. Ulster, 1987. m. Netta Sobell, Oct. 23, 1949; children—Simon Andrew, Susan Gina. Jr. adminstrv. officer Admiralty, 1944-47; financier, property developer, 1947-54; with Radio & Allied (Holdings), Ltd., 1954-61; dir. General Electric Co., Ltd., of Eng., London, 1961-63, mng. dir., 1963—. Created knight, 1970; life peer, 1980; hon. fellow Peterhouse, Cambridge U., London Sch. Econs. and Polit. Sci. Fellow Royal Statis. Soc., Royal Coll. Radiologists (hon.). Office: Gen Electric Co Plc, 1 Stanhope Gate, London W1A 1EH, England

WEINY, GEORGE AZEM, physical education educator, consultant; b. Keokuk, Iowa, July 24, 1933; s. George Dunn and Emma Vivian (Kraushaar) W.; m. Jane Louise Eland, Sept. 29, 1956 (div. 1985); children: Tami L., Tomas A., Aaron A., Arden G.; m. Lori Arlene Rowe, Aug. 6, 1985; children: Austin George, Breck Philip. BA, Iowa Wesleyan Coll., 1957; MA, State U. Iowa, 1962; PhD, U. Beverly Hills, 1980. Phys. dir. YMCA, Keokuk, 1956-57; asst. dir. pub. relations Iowa Wesleyan Coll., Mt. Pleasant, Iowa, 1957-58; prin., tchr., coach Hillsboro (Iowa) High Sch., 1958-59; tchr., coach Burlington (Iowa) High Sch. and Jr. Coll., 1959-62, Pacific High Sch., San Bernardino, Calif., 1962-67; prof. phys. edn. Calif. State U., San Bernardino, 1967—; ednl. cons. Belau Modekngei Sch., West Caroline Islands, 1984-85; swim meet dir. Nat. Collegiate Athletic Assn., 1982-84, 86-88; tng. dir. for ofcls. So. Calif. Aquatics Fedn., 1967-78; asst. swim coach Calif. State U., Chico, 1979, scuba tour guide Dive Maui Resort, Hawaii, 1982-83; salvage diver U.S. Trust Territories, 1973; coach YMCA swim team, San Bernardino, 1962-77, 84-88. Editor: Swimming Rules and Case Studies, 1970-73; author: Snorkeling Fun for Everyone, 1982; contbr. articles to profl. jours. Mem. county water safety com. ARC, San Bernardino, 1968-80; bd. dirs. YMCA, San Bernardino, 1970-77; mem. Bicentennial Commn., San Bernardino, 1975-76. Served to sgt. U.S. Army, 1953-55, Iowa N.G., 1955-58. Recipient Outstanding Service award So. Calif. Aquatics Fedn., 1978. Mem. Profl. Assn. Diving Instrs. (cert.), Nat. Assn. Underwater Instrs. (cert.), Am. Assn. Health Phys. Edn. Recreation and Dance, Coll. Swim Coaches Assn., Am. Swim Coaches Assn. (cert.), Nat. Interscholastic Swim Coaches Assn. Club: Sea Sons Dive (Rialto, Calif.) (pres. 1982-83, sec. 1983-88). Home: PO Box 30393 San Bernardino CA 92413 Office: Calif State U 5500 University Pkwy San Bernardino CA 92407

WEIR, ALEXANDER, JR., utility consultant; b. Crossett, Ark., Dec. 19, 1922; s. Alexander and Mary Eloise (Field) W.; m. Florence Forschner, Dec. 28, 1946; children—Alexander III, Carol Jean, Bruce Richard. B.S. in Chem. Engring., U. Ark., 1943; M.Ch.E., Poly Inst. Bklyn., 1946; Ph.D., U. Mich., 1954; cert., U. So. Calif. Grad. Sch. Bus. Adminstrn., 1968. Analyst, chemist Am. Cyanimid and Chem. Corp., summers 1941, 42; chem. engr. Am. Cyanimid Co., Stanford Research Labs., 1943-47; with U. Mich., 1948-58; research assoc., project supr. Engring. Research Inst., U. Mich., 1948-57; lectr. chem. and metall. engring. dept. U. Mich., 1954-56, asst. prof., 1956-58; cons. Ramo-Wooldridge Corp., Los Angeles, 1956-57, mem. tech. staff, sect. head, asst. mgr., 1957-60, incharge Atlas Missile Captive test program, 1956-60; various tech. adv. positions Northrop Corp. Corp. Office, Beverly Hills, Calif., 1960-70; prin. scientist for air quality So. Calif. Edison Co., Los Angeles, 1970-76, mgr. chem. systems research and devel., 1976-86, chief research scientist, 1986-88; cons. in field Playa del Rey, Calif., 1988—; rep. Am. Rocket Soc. to Detroit Nuclear Council, 1954-57; chmn. session on chem. reactions Nuclear Sci. and Engring. Congress, Cleve., 1955; U.S. del. AGARD (NATO) Combustion Colloquium, Liege, Belgium, 1955; Western U.S. rep. task force on environ. research and devel. goals Electric Research Council, 1971; electric utility advisor Electric Power Research Inst., 1974-78, 84-87; industry advisor Dept. Chemistry and Biochemistry Calif. State U., Los Angeles, 1981—. Author: Two and Three Dimensional Flow of Air through Square-Edged Sonic Orifices, 1954; (with R.B. Morrison and T.C. Anderson) Notes on Combustion, 1955; also tech. papers. Inventer Weir power plant stack scrubber. Bd. govs., past pres. Civic Union Playa del Rey, chmn. sch., police and fire, nominating, civil def., army liaison coms; mem. Senate, Westchester YMCA, chmn. Dads sponsoring com., active fundraising; chmn. nominating com. Paseco del Rey Sch. PTA, 1961; mem. Los Angeles Mayors Community Adv. Com.; asst. chmn. advancement com., merit badge dean Cantinella dist. Los Angeles Area council Boy Scouts Am. Mem. Am. Geophys. Union, Navy League U.S. (v.p. Palos Verdes Peninsula council 1961-62), N.Y. Acad. Scis., Sci. Research Soc. Am., Am. Chem. Soc., Am. Inst. Chem. Engrs., AAAS, Combustion Inst., Air Pollution Control Assn., U.S. Power Squadron, Sigma Xi, Phi Kappa Phi, Phi Lambda Upsilon, Alpha Chi Sigma, Lambda Chi Alpha. Club: Santa Monica Yacht. Office: 8229 Billowvista Dr Playa del Rey CA 92093

WEIR, EUGENE ARNOLD, industrial real estate executive; b. Baton Rouge, Sept. 15, 1926; s. Claude Arnold and Myrtis (Downing) W.; student La. State U., 1944-46, 47; B.S. in Archtl. Engring., Kans. State U., 1950, B.S. in Architecture, 1951; m. Nancy Jean Fitzgerald, Apr. 3, 1954; children—Eugene Marcus, Jefferson Arnold, Nancy Kathryn. Constrn. aide Fed. Housing Adminstrn., Birmingham, Ala., 1950; with Ethyl Corp., Baton Rouge, 1951—, dir. corp. real estate, 1974-83, dir. corp. real estate and service dept., 1983—. Mem. Va. Mus.; bd. dirs. Baton Rouge Art Gallery, Central Richmond Assn. Served with USNR, 1944-46. Mem. AIA, Va. Soc. Architects, Indsl. Devel. Research Council, Internat. Assn. Corp. Real Estate Execs. (dir. 1977-81), Am. Inst. Corp. Asset Mgmt. (vice chmn. bd. govs.), Internat. Platform Assn., Kans. State U. Alumni Assn., Sigma Tau, Tau Sigma Delta, Kappa Alpha. Episcopalian. Clubs: Brandermill Country, Engineers of Richmond. Home: 3303 Fortune's Ridge Rd Midlothian VA 23113 Office: 330 S 4th St Richmond VA 23119

WEIR, GILLIAN CONSTANCE, concert organist, harpsichordist; b. Martinborough, N.Z., Jan. 17, 1941; d. Cecil Alexander and Clarice M. Foy (Bignell) W. Grad. Royal Coll. Music, London, 1965; D.Mus. (hon.), U. Victoria of Wellington, N.Z., 1983 . Concert appearances with leading Brit. Orchs. and Boston Orch., Seattle Orch., Australian ABC Orch., Wurttemberg Chamber and other fgn. orchs.; appeared at major internat. festivals including Edinburgh, Flanders, Aldeburgh, Bath, Proms, Europalia; appeared at concert halls including Royal Festival Hall, Royal Albert Hall, Lincoln Ctr. N.Y., Sydney Opera House; numerous radio and TV appearances in Brit. and world-wide including Royal Festival Hall Jubilee; adjudicator internat. competitions; artist in residence numerous univs. including Washington U., St. Louis, U. Western Australia, others; vis. lectr. Royal No. Coll. Music, Manchester, Eng., 1974—; speaker BBC programs on music and performance. Recipient Turnovsky award, 1985. Contbr. articles to profl. jours.; recs. include major series French baroque music for Argo; TV documentary film on career, 1982, BBC TV programs The King of Instruments, 1987. Fellow Royal Coll. Organists (hon., mem. council 1977—, mem. exec. 1981-85), Royal Canadian Coll. Organists (hon.); mem. Inc. Soc. Musicians, Sigma Alpha Iota (hon.). Office: care Rawstron-Still Internat, Mgmt Ltd, 113 Church Rd, London SE19 2PR, England also: care Phillip Truckenbrod PO Box 69 Hartford CT 06107-0069

WEIR, PETER FRANK, lawyer; b. Stuttgart, Ger., Mar. 26, 1933; s. Robert Henry and Ruth Sophie W.; m. Jean M., Sept. 27, 1958; children—Bradford F., Elizabeth A. B.A., Williams Coll., 1955; LL.B., Harvard U., 1958; M.B.A., N.Y.U., 1967. Bar: N.Y. 1959, Ga. 1957. Assoc. Cole & Deitz, N.Y.C., 1959-66, ptnr., 1966—. Bd. dirs. Episcopal Ch. Found., 1982—, also treas., chmn. fin. com., mem. exec. com., mem. steering com. N.Y. Regional Council, 1975-81, chmn., 1979-81; bd. dirs., counsel Point O'Woods Assn., N.Y., 1976—, v.p., 1982—; alt. bd. dirs. Fire Island Assn., 1976-86; sec. and dir. Elderworks Found., 1982—. Bd. trustees Church Club of N.Y., 1988—; served with Air N.G., 1958-63. Mem. ABA, N.Y. State Bar Assn., N.Y. County Bar Assn., Assn. Bar City N.Y. Republican. Clubs: Church (trustee 1988—), Down Town Assn., Williams (N.Y.C.); Club at Point O'Woods; Hillsboro (Pompano Beach, Fla.). Home: 530 E 86th St Apt 11C New York NY 10028 Office: 175 Water St 10th Floor New York NY 10038-4924

WEIR, PETER LINDSAY, film director; b. June 21, 1944, Sydney; s. Lindsay Weir and Peggy Barnsley; m. Wendy Stites, 1966; 2 children. Ed. Scots Coll., Sydney, Vaucluse Boys High Sch., Sydney U. Worked in real estate until 1965; worked as stagehand in TV, Sydney, 1967; dir. film sequences in variety show, 1968; dir. amateur univ. revs., 1967-69; dir. for Film Australia, 1969-73; made own short films, 1969-73, ind. feature film dir., writer, 1973—. Films include: Cars that Ate Paris, 1973; Picnic at Hanging Rock, 1975, The Last Wave, 1977, The Plumber, 1978, Gallipoli, 1980, The Year of Living Dangerously, 1982; Witness, 1985, The Mosquito Coast, 1986. Decorated Order of Australia, recipient various film awards. Home: 56 Sunrise Rd, Palm Beach NSW 2108, Australia Address: Australian Film Commn, West St, Sydney New South Wales, Australia *

WEIR, ROBERT H., lawyer; b. Boston, Dec. 7, 1922; s. Abraham and Beatrice (Stern) W.; A.B., Harvard U., 1944, LL.B., 1948; m. Ruth Hirsch, July 2, 1954 (dec. Nov. 1965); children—Anthony, David, Michael H.; m. 2d, Sylvia T. Frias; children—Nicole F., Daniella F. Admitted to Mass. bar, 1948, Wash. bar, 1952, Calif. bar, 1957; spl. asst. to atty. gen. U.S. Dept. Justice, Seattle, 1948-53, Washington, 1953-56; practiced in San Jose, also Palo Alto, Calif., 1957—. Instr. taxation of real estate U. Calif. at San Jose and San Francisco, 1957—; lectr. U. So. Calif. Tax Inst. Mem. prison com. Am. Friends Service Com. Bd. dirs. San Jose Light Opera Assn., Inc. Served with U.S. Army, 1942-45. Mem. Am., Santa Clara County bar assns., State Bar Calif., Am. Judicature Soc. Author: Advantages in Taxes, 1960. Tax columnist Rural Realtor, Chgo., 1959—. Speaker taxation annual meetings Nat. Assn. Real Estate Bds., 1958-60. Author: Taxes Working for You, 1966; How to Make the Most of Depreciation Write Off. Contbr. articles to profl. jours. Address: PO Box 5764 San Jose CA 95150

WEISBERG, AARON, internist, gastroenterologist, consultant, research, educator; b. Bklyn., July 21, 1915; s. Joseph and Yetta (Weisberg) W.; m. Ruth Hannah Mintz, Feb. 7, 1949; children—Harlene Edith, Sharon Esta Weisberg Shapiro. B.A. in Chemistry, NYU, 1935; M.D., Cin. Eclectic Med. Coll., 1939. Diplomate Am. Bd. Internal Medicine. Intern Coney Island Hosp., Bklyn., 1939-41, resident, 1941-42, attending physician, 1946-74, attending physician emeritus, 1974—; dir. medicine Carson C. Peck Meml. Hosp., Bklyn., 1954-70; chief of medicine Meth. Hosp. Bklyn., 1970-74, cons. in medicine and gastroenterology, 1974-86, hon. staff, 1986—; attending staff mem. in medicine and gastroenterology Tampa VA Hosp., 1974—, St. Petersburg (Fla.) Gen. Hosp., 1974—, Palms Pasadena Hosp., St. Petersburg, 1974—; med. dir. Sperry Gyroscope, Clearwater, Fla., 1975-84; clin. asst. prof. internal medicine and gastroenterology and clin. asst. prof. comprehensive medicine U. South Fla., 1975—; cons. gastroenterology Bay Pines (Fla.) VA Hosp. Contbr. numerous articles on cardiology, gastroenterology and cancer to profl. jours.; mem. editorial staff: Colon and Rectal Surgery, 1980—. Served to capt. M.C. U.S. Army, 1942-46. Recipient Gold Medal award Coney Island Hosp., 1972, Silver cert. Meth. Hosp., 1974. Fellow ACP, Am. Coll. Gastroenterology, Internat. Acad. Proctology, Royal Soc. Medicine, Am. Coll Nutrition; mem. Am. Fedn. Clin. Research (sr.), Am. Soc. Gastrointestinal Endoscopy, AMA, Pan Am. Soc., Occupational Med. Assn., Am. Chem. Soc., Am. Heart Assn., Phi Lambda Kappa. Clubs: NYU (N.Y.C.); Seminole Country and Golf. Research on cancer, thymus gland lymphocytes immunity. Office: 6499 38th Ave N Saint Petersburg FL 33710

WEISBERG, DAVID CHARLES, lawyer; b. N.Y.C., June 25, 1938; s. Leonard Joseph and Rae M. (Kimberg) W.; m. Linda G. Kerman, Aug. 27, 1975; children: Leonard J., Risa B. AB, U. Mich., 1958; LLB, Harvard U., 1961. Bar: N.Y. 1962, U.S. Dist. Ct. (so. and ea. dists.) N.Y. 1965, U.S. Supreme Ct. 1970. Assoc. firm Dreyer & Traub, Bklyn., 1962, Lee Franklin, Mineola, N.Y., 1962-65; sole practice, Patchogue, N.Y., 1965-67, 77-80; ptnr. Bass & Weisberg, Patchogue, 1967-77, Davidow, Davidow, Russo & Weisberg, Patchogue, 1981-82, Davidow, Davidow, Weisberg & Wismann, 1982—; assoc. justice and justice Village of Patchogue, 1968-70, village atty., 1970-85; spl. asst. dist. atty. Suffolk County, Patchogue, 1970-85; assoc. estate tax atty., appraiser N.Y. State Dept. Taxation and Fin., Hauppauge, N.Y., 1975-85. Law chmn. Suffolk County Democratic Com., N.Y., 1975-85; bd. dirs. Temple Beth El of Patchogue. Mem. Assn. Trial Lawyers Am., N.Y. State Trial Lawyers Assn., Nassau-Suffolk Trial Lawyers Sect., N.Y. State Bar Assn., Suffolk County Bar Assn. Lodges: Lions (pres. Medford 1978-79, 2d v.p. 1984-85), Masons. Office: Davidow Davidow Weisberg & Wismann 110 N Ocean Ave Box 350 Patchogue NY 11772

WEISBERGER, JOSEPH ROBERT, justice Rhode Island supreme court; b. Providence, Aug. 3, 1920; s. Samuel Joseph and Ann Elizabeth (Meighan) W.; m. Sylvia Blanche Pigeon, June 9, 1951; children: Joseph Robert, Paula Ann, Judith Marie. A.B., Brown U., 1942; J.D., Harvard U., 1949; LL.D., R.I. Coll., Suffolk U., Mt. St. Joseph Coll.; D.C.L., Providence Coll.; D.H.L., Bryant Coll. Bar: Mass 1949, R.I. 1950. Practice with Quinn & Quinn, Providence, 1951-56; solicitor Glocester, R.I., 1953-56; judge R.I. Superior Ct., Providence, 1956—; presiding justice R.I. Superior Ct., 1972-78; adj. prof. U. Nev., 1986—; mem. faculty Nat. Jud. Coll.; vis. lectr. Providence Coll., Suffolk Law Sch., Roger Williams Coll.; Chmn. New Eng. Regional Conf. Trial Judges, 1962, 63, 65; chmn. New Eng. Regional Commn. Disordered Offender, 1968-71, R.I. Com. Adoption on Rules Criminal Procedure, 1968-72, Gov. of R.I. Adv. Com. Corrections, 1973, Nat. Conf. State Trial Judges ABA, 1977-78; exec. com. Appelate Judges Conf. ABA, 1979—, vice chmn., 1983-85, chmn., 1985-86; bd. dirs. Nat. Center for State Cts., 1975—. Chmn. editorial bd.: Judges Jour, 1973-75. Pres. R.I. Health Facilities Planning Council, 1967-70; chmn. Gov. R.I. Council Mental Health, 1968-73; moderator Town of East Providence, 1954-56; mem. R.I. Senate, 1953-56, minority leader, 1955-56; vice chmn. bd. trustee R.I. Hosp., St. Joseph's Hosp. Served to lt. comdr. USNR, 1941-46. Inducted into R.I. Hall of Fame, 1980. Fellow Am. Bar Found.; mem. ABA (mem. ho. of dels., task force on criminal justice standards 1977-79), R.I. Bar Assn., Am. Judges Assn. (gov.), Inst. Jud. Adminstrn., Am. Judicature Soc. (bd. dirs.), Am. Law Inst., Phi Beta Kappa. Clubs: K.C., Knight of St. Gregory. Home: 60 Winthrop St East Providence RI 02915 Office: RI Supreme Ct 250 Benefit St Providence RI 02903

WEISER, NORMAN SIDNEY, publishing executive; b. Mpls., Oct. 1, 1919; s. Simon and Rosa (Davidson) W.; m. Ruth Miller, Mar. 23, 1943 (dec. July 1986); children: Judith Ann, Richard Alan. BA, Northwestern U., 1939. Reporter Radio Daily, 1938-42; reporter, editor Billboard Mag., 1947-52; pub. Down Beat Mag., 1952-59; v.p. United Artists, 1959-62, 64-68, 20th Century Fox, 1962-64; v.p., dir. (European ops. Paramount Music Div.), 1968-69; v.p., gen. mgr. Chappell Music Co., N.Y.C., 1969-73; pres. Chappell Music Co., 1973-77; sr. v.p., dir. Polygram Corp. U.S.; mem. mgmt. com., v.p. Internat. Polygram Pub. Div.; pres. Sesac, Inc., 1978-81; v.p., gen. mgr. Largo Music Corp., 1981-85; chmn. bd., chief exec. officer WMC Entertainment Corp., 1985; pres. Am. Acad. of Comedy Hall of Fame, N.Y.C., 1987—. Author: Writers' Radio Theater, 1940, Writers' Radio-TV Theater, 1942, Under The Big Top, 1947, History AAF, World War II, 1947; lyricist 40 songs. Bd. dirs. Parkinson Found.; mem. corp., bd. dirs. UNICEF. Served to capt. USAAF, 1943-47. Decorated Purple Heart, Commendation medal Sec. War; recipient Ben Gurion award, 1975. Mem. ASCAP (dir.), Nat. Music Pubs'. Assn. (v.p., dir.), Country Music Assn. (chmn. bd.). Club: Friars. Lodge: B'nai Brith. Home and Office: 58 W 58th St Apt 14E New York NY 10019

WEISINGER, RONALD JAY, mortgage banker; b. Youngstown, Ohio, Feb. 13, 1946; s. David S. and Sterna (Woolf) W.; m. Wendy Doris Cowen, Dec. 19, 1976. BS, Carroll Coll., 1968. Dir. cash dept. Nat. United Jewish Appeal, N.Y.C., 1975-78; exec. dir. Jewish Fedn. Pinellas County, Inc., Clearwater, Fla., 1978-80; pres. Capital Investment Co. Am., Inc., West Palm Beach, Fla., 1980-82; v.p. Worldwide Merc. Trading Co., Inc., West Palm Beach, 1982-83; v.p. W.J. Miller Mortgage Co., Inc., West Palm Beach, 1983; prin. VIP Mortgage Trust Co., VIP Mgmt. and Realty, Inc., West Palm Beach, 1984—; chmn. bd. dirs. VIP Title Services, Inc.; fin. cons. residential and comml. mortgages, real estate mgmt. and sales, comml. leasing; mfr. ATV's internationally; Carribbean Basin financier. Mem. Nat. Republican Congl. Com., 1980—; sponsor Rep. Party of U.S. Jewish.

WEISL, EDWIN L., JR., foundation executive, lawyer; b. N.Y.C., Oct. 17, 1929; s. Edwin L. and Alice (Todriff) W.; m. Barbara Butler, June 12, 1974; 1 child, by previous marriage, Angela Jane. A.B., Yale, 1951; LL.B., Columbia, 1956. Bar: N.Y. 1956, D.C. 1968. Assoc. Simpson Thacher & Bartlett, N.Y.C., 1956-64; mem. firm Simpson Thacher & Bartlett, 1964-65, 69-73; adminstr. parks, recreation and cultural affairs, commr. parks City of N.Y., 1973-75; asst. atty. gen. of U.S. in charge of land and natural resources division 1965-67, asst. atty. gen. in charge civil div., 1967-69; asst. spl. counsel, preparedness investigating com. U.S. Senate, 1957-58; former pres. Internat. Found. for Art Research. Dir. N.Y. State Democratic campaign, 1964; mem. The 1001, World Wildlife Fund; mem. vis. com. dept. European paintings Met. Mus. Art; bd. dirs. Robert Lehman Found., Washington Internat. Horse Show Assn., Ltd.; mem. corp. Presbyn. Hosp., N.Y.C.; bd. dirs. Old Master Exhbn. Soc. of N.Y. Served to lt. (j.g.) USNR, 1951-53. Clubs: Yale (N.Y.C.); Explorers, Warrenton Hunt. Office: 50 E 77th St New York NY 10021

WEISS, ARMAND BERL, economist; b. Richmond, Va., Apr. 2, 1931; s. Maurice Herbert and Henrietta (Shapiro) W.; B.S. in Econs., Wharton Sch. Fin., U. Pa., 1953, M.B.A., 1954; D.B.A., George Washington U., 1971; m. Judith Bernstein, May 18, 1957; children: Jo Ann Michele, Rhett Louis. Cert. assn. exec. Officer, U.S. Navy, 1954-65; spl. asst. to auditor gen. Dept. Navy, 1964-65; sr. economist Center for Naval Analyses, Arlington, Va., 1965-68; project dir. Logistics Mgmt. Inst., Washington, 1968-74; dir. systems integration Fed. Energy Adminstrn., Washington, 1974-76; sr. economist Nat. Commn. Supplies and Shortages, 1976-77; tech. asst. to v.p. System Planning Corp., 1977-78; pres., chmn. bd. Assns. Internat., Inc., 1978—; v.p., treas. Tech. Frontiers, Inc., 1978-80; sr. v.p. Weiss Pub. Co., Inc., Richmond, Va., 1960—; v.p. Condo News Internat., Inc., 1981; v.p., bd. dirs. Leaders Digest Inc., 1987—; sec., bd. dirs. Mgmt. Services Internat. Inc., 1987—; adj. prof. Am. U., 1979-80; vis. lectr. George Washington U., 1971; assoc. prof. George Mason U., 1984; chmn. U.S. del., session chmn. NATO Symposium on Cost-Benefit Analysis, The Hague, Netherlands, 1969, NATO Conf. on Operational Research in Indsl. Systems, St. Louis, France, 1970; pres. Nat. Council Assns. Policy Scis., 1971-77; chmn. adv. group Def. Econ. Adv. Council, 1970-74; resident asso. Smithsonian Instn., 1973—; expert cons. Dept. State, GAO; undercover agt. FBI, 3 yrs. Del. Pres.'s Mid-Century White House Conf. on Children and Youth, 1950; scoutmaster Japan, U.S., leader World Jamborees, France, Can., U.S., 1945-61; U.S. del. Internat. Conf. on Ops. Research, Dublin, Ireland, 1972; organizing com. Internat. Cost-Effectiveness Symposium, Washington, 1970; speaker Internat. Conf. Inst. Mgmt. Scis., Tel Aviv, 1973, del., Mexico City, 1967. Mem. bus. com. Nat. Symphony Orch., 1968-70, Washington Performing Arts Soc., 1974—; bus. mgr. Nat. Lyric Opera Co., 1983—; mem. mktg. com. Fairfax Symphony Orch., 1984—; exec. com. Mid Atlantic council Union Am. Hebrew Congregations, 1970-79, treas., 1974-79, mem. nat. MUM com., 1974-79; mem. dist. com. Boy Scouts Am., 1972-75; bd. dirs. Nat. Council Career Women, 1975-79. Fellow AAAS, Washington Acad. Scis. (gov. 1981—, v.p. 1987-88); mem. Ops. Research Soc. Am. (chmn. meetings com. 1969-71; chmn. cost-effectiveness sect. 1969-70), Washington Ops. Research/Mgmt. Sci. Council (editor newsletter 1969—, sec. 1971-72, pres. 1973-74, trustee 1975-77, bus. mgr. 1976—), Internat. Inst. Strategic Studies (London), Am. Soc. Assn. Execs. (membership com. 1981-82, cert.), Inst. for Mgmt. Sci., Am. Econ. Assn., Wharton Grad. Sch. Alumni Assn. (exec. com. 1970-73), Am. Acad. Polit. and Social Sci., Nat. Eagle Scout Assn.,

Am. Legion, Navy League of the U.S., Greater Wash. Soc. Assn. Execs., Fairfax County C. of C., Alumni Assn. George Washington U. (governing bd. 1974-82, chmn. univ. publs. com. 1976-78, Alumni Service award 1980), Alumni Assn. George Washington U. Sch. Govt. and Bus. Adminstrn. (exec. v.p. 1977-78, pres. 1978-79), George Washington U. Doctoral Assn. (sr. v.p. 1968-69). Jewish (pres. temple 1970-72). Club: Wharton Grad. Sch. Washington (sec. 1967-69, pres. 1969-70). Co-editor: Systems Analysis for Social Problems, 1970, The Relevance of Economic Analysis to Decision Making in the Department of Defense, 1972, Toward More Effective Public Programs: The Role of Analysis and Evaluation, 1975. Editor: Cost-Effectiveness Newsletter, 1966-70, Operations Research/Systems Analysis Today, 1971-73, Operation Research/Mgmt. Sci. Today, 1974-87; Feedback, 1979—, Condo World, 1981; assoc. editor Ops. Research, 1971-75; publisher: IEEE Scanner, 1983—, Spl. and Individual Needs Tech. Newsletter, 1987—, Jour. Parametrics, 1984-88. Home: 6516 Truman Ln Falls Church VA 22043

WEISS, HERBERT KLEMM, aeronautical engineer; b. Lawrence, Mass., June 22, 1917; s. Herbert Julius and Louise (Klemm) W.; m. Ethel Celesta Gitner, May 14, 1945; children—Janet Elaine, Jack Klemm (dec.). B.S., MIT, 1937, M.S., 1938. Engr. U.S. Army Arty. Bds., Ft. Monroe, Va, 1938-46; engr. U.S. Army Arty. Bds., Camp Davis, N.C., 1938-46, Ft. Bliss, Tex., 1938-46; chief WPN Systems Lab., Ballistic Research Labs., Aberdeen Proving Grounds, Md, 1946-53; chief WPN systems analysis dept. Northrop Aircraft Corp., 1953-58; mgr. advanced systems devel. mil. systems planning aeronutronic div. Ford Motor Co., Newport Beach, Calif., 1958-61; group dir., plans devel. and analysis Aerospace Corp., El Segundo, Calif., 1961-65; sr. scientist Litton Industries, Van Nuys, Calif., 1965-82; cons. mil. systems analysis 1982—; Mem. Sci. Adb. Bd. USAF, 1959-63, sci. adv. commn. Army Ball Research Labs., 1973-77; advisor Pres.'s Commn. Law Enforcement and Adminstrn. Justice, 1966; cons. Office Dir. Def., Research and Engrng., 1954-64. Contbr. articles to profl. jours. Patentee in field. Recipient Commendation for meritorious civilian service USAF, 1964. Fellow AAAS, Am. Inst. Aeros. and Astronautics (assoc.); mem. Ops. Research Soc. Am., IEEE, Inst. Mgmt. Scis. Republican. Presbyterian. Club: Cosmos. Home: PO Box 2668 Palos Verdes Peninsula CA 90274

WEISS, HOWARD JACOB, management science educator; b. Phila., Sept. 18, 1950; s. Ernest D. and Charlotte M. (Silverman) W.; m. Lucia Beck, Aug. 17, 1975; children—Lisa, Ernest. B.Sc., Washington U., St. Louis, 1972; M.S., Northwestern U., 1973, Ph.D., 1975. Asst. prof. Western Ill. U., Macomb, 1975-76; asst. prof. Temple U., Phila., 1976-81, assoc. prof. dept. mgmt., 1981-87, prof., 1987—; cons. USI, Inc., N.Y.C., Matlack, Inc., Lansdowne, Pa., Resources for Future with U.S. Dept. Energy, Mobil Oil Co., Pa. Dept. Transp. Author: (with Ben Lev) Introduction to Mathematical Programming, 1982. Mem. Ops. Research Soc. Am./Inst. Mgmt. Sci., Ops. Research Soc. Phila. (pres. 1977-78). Subspecialties: Operations research (engineering); Industrial engineering. Current work: Research interests in operations management, inventory, bulk service queues, job shop scheduling. Office: Temple U Dept Mgmt Sch Bus Adminstrn Philadelphia PA 19122 Home: 2157 Woodlawn Ave Glenside PA 19038

WEISS, KIM FLEMMING BO, data processing executive, publishing executive; b. Copenhagen, Apr. 2, 1949; s. Flemming Carsten and Ruth Karen Marie (Hansen) W.; m. Jonna Jensen, July 19, 1984; children: Isabella Laura Patricia, Alexandra Gabriella Elona. PhD in Theology, U. Copenhagen, 1970. Investment banker Investco Aktieselskab, Copenhagen, 1970-72; tax and investment advisor Monte-Carlo, Monaco, 1973-76; pub. Carlton Press, Copenhagen, 1977—; software planner Weiss Data Anpartsselskab, Copenhagen, 1986—; advisor tax legis. Republic of Nauru, 1979. Author: How to Play Backgammon, 1976, Tax Haven Manual, 1975-79. Recipient medal of honor Consulate Gen. Senegal, 1984. Clubs: Royal Danish Yacht, Scandinavian Backgammon (Copenhagen) (chmn. 1976—). Home: Noerregade 22, DK 1165 Copenhagen K Denmark Office: PO Box 2081, DK 1013 Copenhagen K Denmark

WEISS, PAUL, philosopher, educator; b. N.Y.C., May 19, 1901; s. Samuel and Emma (Rothschild) W.; m. Victoria Brodkin, Oct. 27, 1928 (dec. Dec. 1953); children: Judith, Jonathan. B.S.S., CCNY, 1927; A.M., Harvard U., 1928, Ph.D. (Sears Travelling fellow), 1929; L.H.D., Grinnell Coll., 1960, Pace Coll., 1969, Bellarmine Coll., 1973, Harverford Coll., 1974. Instr., tutor philsophy Harvard U., also instr. Radcliffe Coll., 1930-31; assoc. in philosophy Bryn Mawr (Pa.) Coll., 1931-33, assoc. prof., 1933-40, prof., 1940-46, chmn. dept., 1944-46; Guggenheim fellow 1938; vis. prof. Yale U., 1945-46, prof. philosophy, 1946-62, Sterling prof. philosophy, 1962-69, Sterling prof. emeritus, 1969—; Heffer prof. philosophy Catholic U. Am., 1969—; fellow Ezra Stiles Coll.; vis. prof. Philo. Hebrew U., Jerusalem, 1951, Orde Wingate lectr., 1954; Rockefeller-Rabinowitz grantee for study, in Israel and India, 1954; lectr. Aspen Inst., 1952, Chancellor's Forum, U. Denver, 1952, Japan, 1981; Powell lectr. U. Ind., 1958; Gates lectr. Grinnell Coll., 1960; Matchette lectr. Purdue U., 1961, Wesleyan Coll., 1963; Aquinas lectr. Marquette U., 1963; Townsend Harris medalist, 1963; Rhoades lectr. Haverford Coll., 1964; Phi Beta Kappa lectr., 1968-69; resident scholar State U. N.Y., 1969, 70; vis. prof. U. Denver, spring 1969; Eliot lectr. Marquette U., 1970; William De Vane medalist Yale, 1971; Aquinas lectr. St Marys, 1971; medalist City Coll., 1973, Hofstra U., 1973; B.Means lectr. Trinity Coll.; Ann. McDermott Lectr. U. Dallas, 1983. Author: Reality, 1938, Nature and Man, 1947, Man's Freedom, 1950, Portugese transl., 1960; Modes of Being, 1958, Our Public Life, 1959, World of Art, 1961, Hebrew transl., 1970; Nine Basic Arts, 1961, History: Written and Lived, 1962, Religion and Art, 1963, The God We Seek, 1964, Philosophy in Process, 11 vols., 1955-88, The Making of Men, 1967, Sport: A Philosophic Inquiry, 1969, Japanese transl., 1985, Beyond All Appearances, 1974, Cinematics, 1975, First Considerations, 1977, You, I and the Others, 1980, Privacy, 1983; Toward a Perfected State, 1986; co-author: Right and Wrong: A Philosophical Dialogue Between Father and Son, 1967, 1971, Approaches to World Peace, 1944, Perspectives on a Troubled Decade, 1950, Moral Principles of Action, 1952, Personal Moments of Discovery, 1953, Perspectives on Peirce, 1965, Dimensions of Job, 1969, Mid-Century American Philosophy, 1974, Philosophy of Baruch Spinoza, 1980, Existence and Actuality, 1984; co-editor Collected Papers of Charles S. Peirce, 6 vols; founder, editor Rev. of Metaphysics, 1947-63; editorial bd. Judaism; contbr. to profl. periodicals. Bd. govs. Hebrew U., Jerusalem; advisor Luce Found.; bd. dirs. Internat. Olympic Union. Mem. Assn. for Symbolic Logic (councillor 1936—), Am. Philos. Assn. (co-pres. 1966), Conf. on Sci. Philos. and Religion (founding mem.), C. S. Peirce Soc. (founding mem., pres.), Metaphys. Soc. Am. (founder, pres. 1951, 52, councillor 1953-58), Philos. Soc. for Study of Sport (founder, pres. 1973), Am. Friends of Hebrew U., Philos. Edn. Soc., Inc. (founder, v.p.), Société Européenne de Culture, Academie Internationale de Philosophie de l'Art, Am. Assn. Middle East Studies, Phi Beta Kappa. Clubs: Aurelian, Elizabethan, Washington Philosophic. Address: 2000 N St NW Washington DC 20036

WEISS, SAMUAL, hotel and restaurant company executive; b. Rock Springs, Wyo., Dec. 25, 1924; s. Morris and Alta Weiss; m. Barbara R. Coggan; children—Cathy, Marcy, Karen. B.A. cum laude, U. Mich., 1948; LL.B., Harvard U., 1951. Asst. v.p. Cuneo Press, Inc., Chgo., 1951-68; exec. v.p., treas., dir. Holly's Inc., Grand Rapids, Mich., 1968—; exec. v.p., dir. Holly Enterprises, Inc., Grand Rapids, 1969—, Holly Grills of Ind., South Bend, 1970—, Fare Devel. Corp., Grand Rapids, 1974—. Co-chmn. U.S. Olympic com. Mich., 1976-80; bd. control Intercollegiate Athletics U. Mich., 1982—. Served to 2d lt. USAAF, 1942-46. Mem. Nat. Assn. Corp. Real Estate Execs. (founding), Nat. Restaurant Assn., U. Mich. Alumni Assn. (dir.). Clubs: Peninsular (Grand Rapids). Home: 3645 Oak Terrace Ct SE Grand Rapids MI 49508 Office: PO Box 9260 255 Colrain St SW Grand Rapids MI 49509

WEISS, SHERMAN DAVID, lawyer; b. Detroit, Dec. 26, 1929; s. Abraham and Eva (Lieberman) W.; m. Lorraine Gloria Moss, Apr. 5, 1952; children—Roger Kevin, Diane Leslie, Linda Beth. Student U. Ill., 1947-48; B.S.C., Roosevelt U., 1951; J.D., Chgo.-Kent Coll. Law, 1957. Bar: Ill. 1958, U.S. Dist. Ct. (no. dist.) Ill. 1958, U.S. Ct. Appeals (7th cir.) 1965. Mem. Deutsch & Kurlan, Chgo., 1959-60, Brody and Gore, Chgo., 1960-62, Arnstein, Gluck, Weitzenfeld and Minow, Chgo., 1963-65; asst. sec., asst. v.p. Walter E. Heller Internat. Corp., Chgo., 1965-75, Imperial Leather & Sportswear, Ltd., Los Angeles, 1975-76; exec. v.p. Roth Carpet Mills, Santa Monica, Calif., 1977-78; sole practice, Los Angeles, 1979—; sr. research rep. Greenwich Assocs., 1985—; cons. fin. and bus. mgmt.; adj. prof. law John Marshall Sch. Law, Chgo., 1976-77. Bd. dirs. Met. YMCA Chgo., 1961-64; gen. counsel Leukemia League Ill., 1960-70. Served with U.S. Army, 1952-54. Mem. Ill. Bar Assn., ABA. Jewish. Case editor Chgo.-Kent Law Rev., 1956-57. Home: 5057 Kester Ave #205 Sherman Oaks CA 91403

WEISS, STEPHEN STEWART, electric insulation company executive; b. Birmingham, Eng., Mar. 18, 1945; s. Eric and Greta (Kobaltsky) W.; m. Liliane Lijn; children: Mischa, Sheba. BA, Pomona Coll., 1968. Trader mineral ore Naylor Benzon Ltd., London, 1968-70; founder, chief exec. Co-optic Ltd., London, 1970-76; mng. dir. Ericsten Investment Ltd., London, 1976—, East London Mica Ltd., 1979—. Editor creative photography, 1973-76; editor, pub. Young British Photographers, Real Britain Postcards, 1973-76; exhibited in various one-man photgraphy shows. Arts Council Great Britain grantee, 1974. Mem. British Elec. and Alied Mfrs. Assn. Home: 28 Camden Sq, London NW1 9XA, England Office: East London Mica Ltd, Ringwood Rd, London E17 8PP, England

WEISSBARD, SAMUEL HELD, lawyer; b. N.Y.C., Mar. 3, 1947; m. Wendy L. Fields; children from a previous marriage: Andrew Joshua, David S. BA, Case Western Res. U., 1967; JD with highest honors, George Washington U., 1970. Bar: D.C. 1970, U.S. Supreme Ct. 1974. Assoc. Fried, Frank, Harris, Shriver & Kampelman, 1970-73, Arent, Fox, Kintner, Plotkin & Kahn, 1973-78; prin. Weissbard & Fields, P.C., 1978-83; shareholder, v.p. Wilkes, Artis, Hedrick & Lane, Washington, 1983-86; ptnr. Foley & Lardner, Washington, 1986—. Editor-in-chief George Washington U. Law Rev., 1969-70. Bd. dirs. Luther Rice Soc. George Washington U., 1985—. Recipient John Bell Larner medal, 1970. Mem. ABA, D.C. Bar Assn., Order of Coif. Office: Foley & Lardner 1775 Pennsylvania Ave NW Washington DC 20006

WEISSENBERG, ALEXIS, pianist, harpsichordist; b. Sofia, Bulgaria, July 26, 1929; came to U.S., 1946; Student piano and composition with, Wladigueroff; also with, Olga Samaroff at Juilliard Sch. Music, Arthur Schnabel and Wanda Landowska. Numerous appearances throughout Europe, S.Am., U.S., Japan, Am. debut with N.Y. Philharmonic; soloist with, Berlin, Vienna, Japan, Czech philharmonics, Phila., Cleve., Minn., Royal Danish, Boston orchs., Chgo., Pitts. symphonies, Orchestre de Paris, also Ravinia, Blossom, Tanglewood and Salzburg festivals; rec. artist, RCA, Angel. Recipient 1st prize Internat. Leventritt competition and Phila. Youth competition, 1946. Address: care Columbia Artists Mgmt Inc 165 W 57th St New York NY 10019 *

WEISSER, JOHN DIETMAR, geologist; b. Altlandsberg, Aug. 17, 1933; s. Heinrich and Elisabeth (Dormann) W.; m. Maria Fenge, Apr. 6, 1962; children—Martin, Christiane, Anne, Katharina. Abitur, Gym. Berlin, 1953; Ph.D., U. Bonn, 1961. Asst. geologist U. Bonn, Fed. Republic Germany, 1957-61; mining geologist Sachtleben, Meggen, Fed. Republic of Germany, 1961-63; research geologist Sch. of Mines, Clausthal, Fed. Republic Germany, 1965—; chief geologist Sachtleben, 1969—; chief geologist Internat. Mining Dept. Metallgesellschaft AG, Frankfurt, Fed. Republic Germany, 1982-86, also v.p. exploration; Prof Econ. Geology, U. Heidelberg, 1986—. Contbr. articles to profl. jours. Mem. ARC (Berlin). Mem. Soc. Econ. Geologists, German Geol. Soc. Lodge: Lions (Frankfurt). Home: Dietmar Weisser Kolberger, WEG 31, 6380 Bad Homburg Federal Republic of Germany Office: Metallgesellschaft AG, Internat Mining Div, Reuterweg 14, 6000 Frankfurt Main 1 Federal Republic of Germany

WEISSMAN, BARRY LEIGH, lawyer; b. Los Angeles, May 30, 1948; s. Sidney and Eleanor (Siegel) W.; m. Beverly Jean Blumenfeld, Sept. 12, 1982. B.A., U. Calif.-Davis, 1970; J.D., U. Santa Clara, 1973. Bar: Calif. Supreme Ct. 1973, U.S. Dist. Ct. (cen. dist.) Calif. 1976, U.S. Supreme Ct. 1977, U.S. Ct. Appeals (D.C. cir.) 1978. Sole practice law, Beverly Hills, Calif., 1974-84; ptnr. Valentini, Fini, Ferraro, Gallavotti & Weissman, Brentwood, Calif., from 1984; now ptnr. Kroll & Tract, Los Angeles; judge pro tem Los Angeles Mcpl. Ct., 1975—; arbitrator Am. Arbitration Assn.; examiner State Bar Calif., 1976-80; mem. adv. commn malpractice ins., Calif. State Senate. Mem. ABA (mem. spl. com. on prepaid legal services, co-chmn. editorial bd. gen. practice sect.'s publs.), Beverly Hills Bar Assn., Century City Bar Assn. (bd. govs., chmn., editor Century City Bar Jour.), Beverly Hills C. of C. (co-chmn. legal justice com.), Colorado River Assn., Western Los Angeles Regional C. of C. (dir., chmn. com. on energy prodn. and conservation). Office: Kroll & Tract 3435 Wilshire Blvd Los Angeles CA 90010

WEISSMAN, JOEL MICHAEL, lawyer; b. Bklyn., Feb. 12, 1950; s. Jerome and Bessie (Rapaport) W.; m. Alexandra Lee Redmond; children: Robert, Bradley. BA in Psychology, Bridgewater State U., 1968-72; JD, Stetson U., 1976. Bar: Fla. 1976, U.S. Dist. Ct. (so. dist.) Fla. 1976, U.S. Ct. Appeals (5th and 11th cirs.) 1981, U.S. Supreme Ct. 1981. Asst. state atty. Palm Beach County, Fla., 1976-79; assoc. Christisen, Jackin & Meyers, 1979-80, Sales & Weissman, P.A., 1980-83; sole practice, Palm Beach, 1984—. Mem. ABA, Assn. Trial Lawyers Am., Fla. Acad. Trial Lawyers, Fla. Acad. Marital Lawyers, Palm Beach County Bar Assn. Jewish. Home: 11741 Cottonwood Ave Palm Beach Gardens FL 33410 Office: 250 Australian Ave Suite 1000 West Palm Beach FL 33401

WEISSMAN, RONEE FREEMAN, tour agency owner, speech pathologist; b. N.Y.C., Apr. 16, 1951; d. Jonas Herbert and Marion (Rosen) Freeman; B.A. magna cum laude, Queens Coll., 1973, M.A. in Speech Pathology, 1978; m. Eugene Weissman, Jan. 28, 1973; children—Ilana Nicole, Adam Scott. Tchr. high sch. speech, theatre and English, N.Y.C., 1973-75; speech pathologist Byram Hills (N.Y.) Sch. Dist., part-time, 1979-80, E. Ramapo Sch. Dist., Rockland, N.Y., 1981-82; speech pathologist Vis. Therapy Assocs., 1983-84; owner, v.p., dir. Weissman Teen Tours, Inc., Ardsley, N.Y., 1974—. Youth dir., Sunday sch. tchr. Temple Israel, New Rochelle. Speech and hearing handicapped cert., speech arts cert., N.Y.; lic. speech pathologist, N.Y. Mem. Am. Speech, Lang. and Hearing Assn. (cert. clin. competency), N.Y. State Speech, Lang. and Hearing Assn., Am. Camping Assn. (cert.), Westchester Assn. Women Bus. Owners, Sales and Mktg. Execs. of Westchester, Phi Beta Kappa, Kappa Delta Pi. Home and Office: 517 Almena Ave Ardsley NY 10502

WEISSMANN, CHARLES, molecular biologist; b. 1931; diploma U. Zurich; Dir. Molecular Biology Inst.; past pres. Schweizerische Gesellschaft fü r Zell-und Molekularbiologie; chmn. sci. bd. Biogen, 1984-86; pres. Ernst Hadorn-Stiftung, Zurich, 1986—. Recipient Ruzicka prize in chemistry; Otto Warburg prize; H.P. Heineken prize; Sir H. Krebs medal; Scheele medal, Krebspreis Schweizerische Krebsliga, 1987, Jung-Preis Für Medizin, Hamburg, 1988. Mem. European Molecular Biology Orgn., Am. Acad. Arts and Scis., Deutsche Akademie der Naturforscher Leopoldina, Royal Soc. (fgn.), Weizmann Inst. Sci. (bd. govs. 1985—), ZMB Heidelberg (sci. adv. bd. 1988—). Office: Universitat Zurich Honggerberg, Molecular Biology Inst I, CH-8093 Zurich Switzerland

WEISSMANN, HEIDI SEITELBLUM, radiologist, educator; b. N.Y.C., Feb. 4, 1951; d. Louis and June (Joseph) Seitel Bloom; m. Murray H. Weissmann, June 16, 1973; 1 dau., Lauren Erica. B.S. in Chemistry magna cum laude, Bklyn. Coll., CUNY, 1970; M.D., Mt. Sinai Sch. Medicine, N.Y.C., 1974. Diplomate Nat. Bd. Med. Examiners. Intern Montefiore Med. Ctr., Bronx, N.Y., 1974-75, resident in diagnostic radiology, 1975-78 ; fellow in computerized transaxial tomography and ultrasonography N.Y. Hosp.-Cornell U. Med. Ctr., N.Y.C., 1978-79; instr. in radiology and nuclear medicine Albert Einstein Coll. Medicine and Montefiore Med. Ctr., Bronx, 1979-80, asst. prof. radiology and nuclear medicine, 1980-84, assoc. prof. nuclear medicine, 1984—, assoc. prof. radiology, 1986—; adj. attending physician Montefiore Med. Ctr., 1979-87; chmn. Nuclear Medicine Grand Rounds: Greater N.Y., 1980—; physician coordinator Nuclear Medicine Technologist In-Service Tng. Program, 1982-86; cons. NIH, 1984-86, NIH Diagnostic Radiology, 1985-86. Assoc. editor Nuclear Medicine Ann., 5 vols., 1979-84, editor, 3 vols., 1985—; contbr. chpts. to books, articles to jours.; reviewer Jour. of Radiology, 1981—, mem. editorial adv. bd., 1985-86, assoc. editor, 1986—; reviewer. Jour. of Nuclear Medicine, 1981—, Am. Jour. of Roentgenology, 1986—, Gastroenterology, 1986—, Western Jour. of Medicine, 1985—; contbr. audiovisual programs and films. Recipient Saul Horowitz, Jr., Meml. award (Disting. Alumnus award), Mt. Sinai Sch. Medicine, 1980, Pres.' award, Am. Roentgen Ray Soc., 1979, Berta Rubinstein, M.D., Resident award, 1978, others. Mem. Radiol. Soc. N.Am. (mem. subcom. for nuclear medicine of program com., 1981, 82, 83, chmn. 1984, 85, 86), Soc. Nuclear Medicine (trustee 1983-87, 88—, sec.-treas. Correlative Imaging Council 1979-82, exec. bd. 1982-84, pres. 1984-86, mem. acad. council 1980—, task force on interrelationship between nuclear medicine and nuclear magnetic resonance 1983—, gov. Greater N.Y. chpt. 1983-85, treas., 1985-86, 86-87, 2d ann. Tetalman award of Edn. and Research Found. 1982, mem., vice chmn. coms. and subcoms.), Soc. Gastrointestinal Radiologists, Am. Inst. Ultrasound in Medicine, N.Y. Acad. Scis., Assoc. Alumni Mt. Sinai Med. Ctr., Nuclear Radiology Club (chmn. 1983—). Phi Beta Kappa.

WEITZ, JOHN, fashion designer; b. Berlin, May 25, 1923; came to U.S., 1940, naturalized, 1943; s. Robert and Hedy (Jacob) W.; m. Susan Kohner, Aug. 30, 1964; children: Paul John, Christopher John; children by previous marriage: Karen Weitz Curtis, Robert. Student, Hall Sch., London, 1936, St. Paul's Sch., London, 1936-39; certificate, Oxford-Cambridge Sch., 1938. Founder John Weitz Designs, Inc., N.Y.C., 1954—. Designer various cos., until 1954; Author: Value of Nothing (Best Seller list 1970), Man in Charge, (Best Seller list 1974), Friends in High Places, 1982. Bd. dirs. Allen-Stevenson Sch., N.Y.C., Phoenix House, Raoul Wallenberg Com., William J. Donovan Found., Vets. of O.S.S., Council of Fashion Designers of Am., Leo Baeck Inst., Ednl. Found. for the Fashion Industries; mem. pres.' council Mus. of City of N.Y. Served to capt. M.I., AUS, 1943-46, ETO. Decorated First Class Cross Order of Merit (Fed. Republic Germany); recipient Sports Illustrated award, 1959, NBC Today award, 1960, Phila. Mus. award, 1960, Caswell Massey awards 1963-66, Harpers Bazaar medallion, 1966, Moscow diploma, 1967, Coty award, 1974, Cartier Design award, 1981, Mayor's Liberty medal, N.Y.C., 1986, Cutty Sark Career Achievement award, 1986; named to Internat. Best Dressed List Hall of Fame, 1971,. Mem. Vets. of OSS (bd. dirs.). Clubs: Union, Skeeters@ 21, (N.Y.C.); Special Forces, Marks, Old Pauline (London) (v.p.); Chevaliers de Tastevin, Beach (Palm Beach); Vintage Sports Car, USN Acad. Sailing Squadron, SAg Harbor Yacht, East Hampton Yacht, PEN Am. Ctr. Office: 600 Madison Ave New York NY 10022

WEITZMAN, ARTHUR JOSHUA, educator; b. Newark, Sept. 13, 1933; s. Louis I. and Cecele W.; m. Catherine Ezell, Aug. 8, 1982; children: Peter A., Anne E. B.A., U. Chgo., 1956, M.A., 1957; Ph.D., NYU, 1964. Instr. English, Bklyn. Coll., 1960-63; asst. prof. Temple U., Phila., 1963-69; assoc. prof. Northeastern U., Boston, 1969-72; prof. Northeastern U., 1972—; field editor G.K. Hall Pub. Co. Editor: Letters Writ by a Turkish Spy (G.P. Marana), 1970; founder, co-editor: The Scriblerian, 1968—; co-editor: Milton and the Romantics, 1980-81; contbr.: revs. and articles to profl. jours. and newspapers including Los Angeles Times, Boston Globe, Miami Herald. NEH fellow, 1972-73; Mellon fellow, 1976; research grantee Temple U.; research grantee Northeastern U. Mem. MLA, Am. Soc. 18th Century Studies, Conf. Editors Learned Jours. Jewish. Home: 4 Bellis Ct Cambridge MA 02140 Office: Dept English 400 Holmes Northeastern U Boston MA 02115

WEIZSACKER, RICHARD VON (RICHARD VON WEIZSACKER), president of West Germany; b. Stuttgart, Apr. 15, 1920; m. Marianne von Kretschmann, Oct. 10, 1953; children—Robert, Andreas, Marianne, Fritz. Ed. Oxford U., DCL (hon.), 1988; ed. Grenoble U., Goettingen U.; Dr. jur. (hon.) D Weizman Inst. Grenoble, Tel Aviv, Locven, Belgium, Istanbul, Socre, Bolivia, Göttingen, Harvard U. Mem. CDU, 1954—, mem. fed. exec. com., 1966—, chmn. commn. on basic policy issues, chmn. regional group Berlin, 1981-83, fed. dep. chmn., 1983-84; mem. German Bundestag, 1969-81, v.p., 1979-81, dep. chmn. Christian Democratic Union/Christian Socialist Union Parliamentary party, 1973-79; mem. Ho. of Reps., Berlin, 1979, 81-84; governing mayor, Berlin, 1981-84; pres. Federal Republic Germany, 1979-81, pres., 1984—. Recipient Theodor Hup prize Naumann Stifftung, Bonn., 1983, Romano Guardini prize for music, 1987. Office: Office of Pres, Villa Hammerschmidt, Bonn Federal Republic of Germany

WEJCHERT, ANDRZEJ, architect; b. Gdansk, Poland, May 21, 1937; arrived in Ireland, 1964; s. Tadeusz and Irena (Moigis) W.; m. Danuta Kornaus, Nov. 16, 1965; children: Agnieszka, Michael. Degree in engrng. architecture, Warsaw (Poland) Poly., 1961. Architect Design Office of Pub. Bldgs., Warsaw, 1959-64, Risteruccі Agence, Paris, 1964; prin. A. Wejchert-Architect, Dublin, Ireland, 1964-74; ptnr. A&D Wejchert Architects, Dublin, 1974—; assessor European Archtl. Heritage Yr., Ireland, 1976; external examiner Sch. Architecture, U. Coll., Dublin, 1982-85. Architect bldgs. including, U. Coll. Dublin, Tech. Parks, Limerick, Ireland and Dublin, Town Ctr., Blanchardstown, Ireland. Recipient 1st pl. award for design of New U., 1964, diploma Europa Nostra, 1982, 1st pl. award Nat. Trust Ireland, 1984; archtl. works named Bldg. of Yr. Plan Archtl. Mag., 1980, 84, 87. Fellow Royal Inst. Architects Ireland (registered, council 1976—, gold medal 1977, commendation 1985); mem. Royal Inst. Brit. Architects. Office: 10 Lad Ln, Dublin 2, Ireland

WELCH, DAVID WILLIAM, lawyer; b. St. Louis, Feb. 26, 1941; s. Claude LeRoy Welch and Mary Eleanor (Peggs) Penney; m. Candace Lee Capages, June 5, 1971; children: Joseph Peggs, Heather Elizabeth, Katherine Laura. BSBA, Washington U., St. Louis, 1963; JD, U. Tulsa, 1971. Bar: Okla. 1972, Mo. 1973, U.S. Dist. Ct. (ea. dist.) Mo. 1974, U.S. Ct. Appeals(8th cir.) 1977. Contract adminstr. McDonnell Aircraft Corp., St. Louis, 1965-66; bus. analyst Dun & Bradstreet Inc., Los Angeles, 1967-68, atty. U.S. Dept. Labor, Washington, 1972-73; ptnr. Moller Talent, Kuelthau & Welch, St. Louis, 1973-88, Lashly, Baer and Hamel, St. Louis, 1988—. Author: (handbook) Missouri Employment Law, 1986; contbr. book chpt. Missouri Bar Employer-Employee Law, 1985. Mem. City of Creve Coeur Ethics Commn., Mo.; bd. dirs. Camp Wyman, Eureka, Mo., 1982—, sec., 1987-88, 2d v.p., 1988—. Mem. ABA, Fed. Bar Assn., Mo. Bar Assn., Okla. Bar Assn., St. Louis Bar Assn., Regional Commerce and Growth Assn., Mo. C. of C. Democrat. Mem. Christian Ch. Lodge: Kiwanis (bd. dirs. local chpt. 1979—, sec. 1982-83, v.p. 1983-84, named Man of Yr. 1985). Home: 536 N Mosley Rd Saint Louis MO 63141 Office: Lashly Baer and Hamel 714 Locust St Saint Louis MO 63101

WELCH, HERBERT EUGENE, electronics corporation executive, educator; b. Gainsville, Tex., Aug. 22, 1933; s. John Arthur and Virginia Pearl (White) W.; m. Nedra Jo Thorn, Sept. 15, 1951; children—Randy Eugene, Pamela Denise Welch Alcorn. B.S. in Physics, Tex. Tech. U., 1965, M.S. in Physics, 1968, Ph.D. in Physics, 1969. Sr. staff engr. Collins Radio, Dallas, 1969-72; dir. engrng. Rockwell Internat., Dallas, 1972-80, Chgo., 1980-81, dir. product devel., Dallas, 1981-82; v.p. United Telecom/U.S. TEL, Dallas, 1982-84; v.p., gen. mgr. Andrew Corp., Plano, Tex., 1984-85; chmn. bd. dirs., chief exec. officer Teling Systems Inc., 1988—; adj. assoc. prof. of elec. engrng. U. Tex., Arlington, 1974—. Patentee in field. Contbr. articles to engrng. jours. Named Disting. Alumnus Tex. Tech. U., 1988. Mem. IEEE (chmn. nominating com., 1980-81, Dallas sect. 1979-80, exec. vice chmn. 1978-79, mem. steering com. 1982, edn. chmn. 1976-77), Am. Soc. of Engrng. Edn. (Rockwell Internat. Corp. rep. 1978—), Nat. Mgmt. Assn. (charter), Am. Phys. Soc., AAUP, AAAS, Internat. Platform Assn., Sigma Pi Sigma, (sec., treas. 1964, pres. 1966, faculty prize for best student paper 1964), Inst. of Cert. Profl. Mgrs., Am. Mgmt. Assn. Democrat. Baptist. Club: Engineers (Dallas). Office: Teling Systems Inc 1651 Glenville Dr Richardson TX 75081

WELCH, JOHN FRANCIS, JR., electrical manufacturing company executive; b.'Peabody, Mass., Nov. 19, 1935; s. John Francis and Grace (Andrews) W.; m. Carolyn B. Osburn, Nov. 21, 1959; children—Katherine, John, Anne, Mark. B.S. in Chem. Engrng, U. Mass., 1957; M.S., U. Ill., 1958, Ph.D., 1960. With Gen. Electric Co., Fairfield, Conn., 1960—, v.p., 1972, v.p., group exec. components and materials group, 1973-77, sr. v.p., sector exec., consumer products and services sector, 1977-79, vice chmn., exec. officer, 1979-81, chmn., chief exec. officer, 1981—; also dir. Gen. Electric Fin. Services. Chmn. Nat. Acad. Engrng. Office: Gen Electric Co 3135 Easton Turnpike Fairfield CT 06431 *

WELCH, MARY-SCOTT, writer; b. Chgo.; d. William Scott and Myrtle (Ferrin) Stewart; A.B. in English, U. Ill.; m. Barrett F. Welch (dec.); children: Farley, Laura Stewart, Margaret, Mary Barrett. Books include: Your First Hundred Meals, What Every Young Man Should Know, The Family Wilderness Handbook, Networking: The Great New Way for Women to Get

Ahead; former mem. staff Esquire-Coronet mag., Pageant mag., Look mag.; contbg. editor Glamour mag.; columnist Seventeen mag., McCall's mag., Vogue mag.; contbr. to mags. including Ladies Home Jour., Redbook, Ms., Modern Maturity, Working Woman, Woman's Day. Bd. advisors Inst. Women and Work, Cornell U. Served with USNR. Mem. Authors Guild, Authors League, Women in Communications, Women's Inst. Freedom of Press, NOW (adv. bd.; past coordinator rape prevention com. N.Y.C.), Phi Beta Kappa, Kappa Kappa Gamma, environ. and civil liberties orgns. Home and Office: 30 Waterside Plaza New York NY 10010

WELCH, PETER THOMAS, toiletries company executive; b. Stockport, Cheshire, Eng., June 2, 1936; s. Frances Percival and Ruth (Clark) W.; m. Joanna Christine Mitford, June 8, 1963; children: Nicola, Catherine, Lisa, John. BA, Trinity Coll., Dublin, Ireland, 1961, MA, 1969. Research and devel. exec. Reckitt and Colman Ltd., Hull, Eng., 1961-63; mktg. mgr. Reckitt and Colman Ltd., Venezuela, 1963-68; dir. Latin Am. div. Reckitt and Colman Ltd., London, 1970-74, dir. comml. planning, 1974-75; sr. cons. Inbucon Ltd., London, 1968-70; mng. dir. Schwarzkopf Ltd., Aylesbury, 1975-77; owner, mng. dir. Entermark Ltd., Princes Risborough, Eng., 1977-80; mng. dir. Cadogan Investments Ltd., London, 1980-81; dir. Cossons Internat. Ltd., Manchester, Eng., 1981-86, Cussons Group Ltd., Manchester, 1986—. Mem. Inst. Mktg. Office: Cussons Group Ltd, 60 Whitworth St, Manchester M1 6LU, England

WELCH, THOMAS C., manufacturing executive; b. Glendale, Calif., Aug. 23, 1926; s. Thomas Perry and Martha (Abraham) W.; m. R. Virginia, Aug. 6, 1949; children: Michael, Stephen, Dennis, Tom, Patrick, Kevin. BS, UCLA, 1949. V.p., gen. mgr. clock div. Sunbeam Appliances, Chgo., 1969-74, v.p. clock and home care div., 1974; pres. Hanson Scale Co., Chgo., 1974-77, Sunbeam Leisure Products Co., Neosho, Mo., 1975—; bd. dirs. Glenview (Ill.) State Bank, 1968-74. Bd. pres. United Fund, Neosho, 1979-80; bd. dirs. Neosho Industries Inc., 1980—. Served with USN, 1944-46. Republican. Roman Catholic. Lodge: Rotary. Home: 58 Swanage Circle Bella Vista AR 72714 Office: Sunbeam Leisure Products Co 4101 Howard Bush Dr Neosho MO 64850

WELCH, WALTER ANDREW, JR., lawyer; b. Dec. 13; s. Walter Andrew and Myrtle Marie (Kunzmann) W. BSAS, So. Ill. U., 1974; grad. U.S. Naval Justice Sch., 1974, J.D. Pepperdine U., 1980, U.S. Dept. Justice Legal Edn. Inst., 1985. Bar: Calif., N.J., U.S. Ct. Customs and Patent Appeals, U.S. Tax Ct., U.S. Ct. Mil. Appeals, U.S. Claims Ct., U.S. Ct. Appeals (3d, 4th, 5th and 9th cirs.), U.S. Dist. Ct. (so. and cen. dists.) Calif., U.S. Dist. Ct. N.J.; lic. comml. pilot FAA. Sole practice, Los Angeles and Washington, 1981—; adj. prof. aviation law So. Ill. U.; real estate broker, Calif., 1981—, Va. 1984—; vis. asst. prof., 1986—. Contbr. articles to legal revs. Served with USMC, 1974-77. Grantee and fellow Pepperdine U. Sch. Law, 1978-80. Mem. AIAA, Lawyer-Pilot's Bar Assn., Assn. Naval Aviation, Marine Corps Aviation Assn., Fed. Bar Assn., Assn. Trial Lawyers Am., ABA, Christian Legal Soc., Calif. State Bar (del. conv. 1981—). Office: PO Box 9606 Marina del Rey CA 90291

WELDON, GEORGE FRANCIS DARYL, management consultant; b. London, Dec. 9, 1946; s. Francis William Charles and Diana Geraldine (Anderson) w.; m. Jane Margaret Knapman, June 27, 1981; children: Claire Elizabeth, Sarah Jane. MA in Natural Scis., Oxford U., 1968; MBA, Carnegie-Mellon U., 1973. Mgmt. trainee Clarks Shoes, Eng., 1969-71, distbn. mgr., 1973-75; mgmt. cons. Touche Ross & Co., Eng., 1975-78, ptnr., 1978—, nat. dir. mktg., 1985-87, ptnr. in charge gen. mgmt. consultancy div., 1987—. Mem. London Region Council Confedn. of Britain Industry, Eng., 1987—. Club: Oxford and Cambridge (London). Office: Touche Ross & Co, Hill House 1 Little New St, London EC4A 3TR, England

WELDON, NIALL GERARD, retired airline executive; b. Dublin, Ireland, Oct. 11, 1922; s. Thomas and Mary (Kelly) W.; m. Lily Shiels, Nov. 22, 1950; children: Barry, Mary, Elizabeth, Ann, Janine, Karen, Ian, Declan. B of Commerce with honours, Univ. Coll., Dublin, diploma in pub. adminstrn. Asst. to sec. Bord Na Mona, Dublin, 1943-47; with Aer Lingus, 1947-88; asst. to dist. mgr. Aer Lingus, London, 1948-50; pensions and staff records officer Aer Lingus, Dublin, 1951-55, services supt., 1956-59, asst. services mgr., airport mgr., 1959-65, personnel mgr., 1966-67, gen. sales mgr., 1967-68, sec., gen. mgr. corp. affairs, 1968-88; chmn. bd. dirs. Jurys Hotel Group, Dublin; chmn. bd. Beaumont Hosp. Fellow Inst. Irish Secs. and Asminstrs., Irish Inst. Transport; mem. Inst. Personnel Mgmt. Roman Catholic. Club: Skerries Golf (Dublin). Home: Lauragh Channel Rd, Rush, 6 Dublin Ireland Office: Aer Lingus plc, Dublin Airport, Dublin Ireland

WELGE, MARTIN KONRAD, business administration educator, researcher, consultant; b. Detmold, Northrhine Westfalia, Fed. Republic of Germany, Sept. 22 1943; s. Konrad and Theresia (Dohle) W.; m. Hannelore Offenbacher. Diplom-Kaufmann, U. Cologne, Fed. Republic of Germany, 1969, Dr. rer. pol., 1973, Dr. rer. pol. habil., 1978; postgrad. Stanford U., 1969-70. Asst. prof. U. Cologne, 1973-78; assoc. prof., 1978-80; prof. bus. adminstrn. U. Hagen, Fed. Republic of Germany, 1980-84, prof. bus. adminstrn. U. Essen, Fed. Republic of Germany, 1984-87; prof. bus. policy U. Dortmund, Fed. Republic of Germany, 1987—; vis. prof. European Inst., Brussels, 1980-81; sr. cons. Heinle, Wischer & Ptnr., Stuttgart, W.Ger., 1978—, TOV Rheinland, Cologne, 1982—, OECD, Paris, 1985—. Author: Profit-Center-Organization, 1975; Management in Deutschen Multinationalen Unternehmungen, 1980; (series) Unternehmungsführung: Vol. 1: Planung, 1985, Vol. 2: Organisation, 1987, Vol. 3: Controlling, 1988; co-author: Beyond Theory Z, 1984; contbr. articles to nat. and internat. jours. Served to lt. W. Ger. Armed Forces 1963-65. Scholar Deutscher Akademischer Austauschdienst, 1969, Fritz-Thyssen-Stiftung, 1975. Mem. European Internat. Bus. Assn. (country rep.), Verband der Hochschullehrer für Betriebswirtschaft, Acad. Mgmt.nt. Bus. Mem. Free Democratic Party. Home: Birkmannsweg 34, D-4300 Essen 1, Federal Republic of Germany Office: Universität Dortmund, Lehrstuhl für Unternehmungsführung, PO Box 50 05 00, D-4600 Dortmund 50, Federal Republic of Germany

WELIN, WALTER, financial advisor; b. Lund, Sweden, Sept. 20, 1908; s. Lars and Adele (Hellegren) W.; m. Ulla Olsson, Nov. 25, 1950; 1 child, Lars. Grad. Econs. and Fin., U. Lund, MA in Polit. Sci. 1943, student grad. law sch. 1945. Dir. dept. The Royal Swedish Patent Office, Stockholm, 1948-74; fin. advisor/cons. in pvt. practice, Lund. Club: St. Knut Guild. Mem. N.Y. Acad. Sics., Nat. Geographic Soc. Address: Siriusgatan 25 S-223, 57 Lund Sweden

WELLEMIN, JOHN HENRY, small business owner; b. Prague, Czechoslovakia, Feb. 4, 1925; arrived in Eng., 1939; s. Francis and Martha (Popper) W; m. Ursala Hess, July 24, 1954; children: Carey, Alison. Salesman Brit-Over Ltd., London, 1948-52; tech. salesman Gaston Marbaix Ltd., London, 1952-57; area sales mgr. Stuart Davis Ltd., Coventry, Eng., 1957-59; with sales, service and mktg. depts., various mgmt. positions Rank Xerox Ltd., London, 1959-80; prin. John H. Wellemin, Pinner, Eng., 1980—; cons., lectr., course leader Mgmt. Ctr. Europe, Brussels, 1981—, Stiftelsen Institutet for Foretags Utveckling, Beras, Sweden, 1983-87, Dunn & Bradstreet, London, 1985—, Brit. Inst. Mgmt., Corby, Eng., 1986—, Eli Lilly, Xerox USA, Tetrapak, Switzerland and numerous others cos. Author: Professional Service Management, 1984, A Career in Professional Service Engineering, 1987; contbr. articles to profl. jours. Home and Office: 9 Winchester Dr, Pinner HA5 1DB, England

WELLER, THOMAS HUCKLE, physician, emeritus educator; b. Ann Arbor, Mich., June 15, 1915; s. Carl V. and Elsie A. (Huckle) W.; m. Kathleen R. Fahey, Aug. 18, 1945; children: Peter Fahey, Nancy Kathleen, Robert Andrew, Janet Louise. A.B., U. Mich., 1936; M.S., 1937, LL.D. (hon.), 1956; M.D., Harvard, 1940; Sc.D., Gustavus Adolphus U., 1975, U. Mass., 1985; L.H.D., Lowell U., 1977. Diplomate Am. Bd. Pediatrics. Teaching fellow bacteriology Harvard Med. Sch., 1940-41, research fellow tropical medicine, pediatrics, 1947-48, instr. comparative pathology, tropical medicine, 1948-49, asst. prof. tropical pub. health Sch. Pub. Health, 1949-50, assoc. prof., 1950-54, Richard Pearson Strong prof. tropical pub. health, 1954-85, prof. emeritus, 1985—, head dept., 1954-81; intern bacteriology and pathology Children's Hosp., Boston, 1941; intern medicine Children's Hosp., 1942, asst. resident medicine, 1946, asst. dir. research div. infectious diseases, 1949-55; mem. commn. parasitic diseases Armed Forces Epidemiol. Bd., 1953-72, dir., 1953-59; charge parasitology, bacteriology, virology sections Antilles Dept. Med. Lab., P.R. Author sci. papers. Served to maj. M.C. AUS, 1942-46. Recipient E. Mead Johnson award for devel. tissue culture procedures in study virus diseases Am. Acad. Pediatrics, 1953; Kimble Methodology award, 1954; Nobel prize in physiology and medicine, 1954; George Ledlie prize, 1963; Weinstein Cerebral Palsy award, 1973; Stern Symposium honoree, 1972; Bristol award Infectious Diseases Soc. Am., 1980; Gold medal and diploma of honor U. Costa Rica, 1984. Fellow Am. Acad. Arts and Scis.; mem. Harvey Soc., AMA, Am. Soc. Parasitologists, Am., Royal socs. tropical medicine and hygiene, Am. Pub. Health Assn., AAAS, Am. Epidemiological Soc., Nat. Acad. Scis., Am. Pediatric Soc., Assn. Am. Physicians, Soc. Exptl. Biology and Medicine, Am. Assn. Immunologists. Soc. Pediatric Research, Phi Beta Kappa., Sigma Xi, Alpha Omega Alpha. Home and Office: 56 Winding River Rd Needham MA 02192

WELLES, ERNEST I., chemical company executive; b. N.Y.C., Aug. 5, 1925; s. Henry and Lena (Halberg) W.; B.S. cum laude, Coll. City N.Y., 1946, B.S., Sch. Edn., 1949, M.S., 1953; Sc.D. (hon), London Inst., 1973 . Chemist, Lucius Pitkin, Inc., N.Y.C., 1944-45; research chemist Nuodex Products Co., Elizabeth, N.J., 1946-50; group leader Foster D. Snell, Inc., N.Y.C., 1950-51; asst. tech. dir. Permatex, Inc., Bklyn., 1951-52; chief chemist Dexter Chem. Corp., N.Y.C., 1952-67; product mgr. textile chem. sales Quaker Chem. Corp., Conshohocken, Pa., 1967-74; dir. mktg., textile chem. sales Hart Products Corp., Jersey City, 1974; mktg. dir. Leatex Chem. Co., Phila., 1974-78; v.p. mktg. Eaton Labs., Inc., 1978-85; mgr. sales div. Pure-Kem, Inc., Paterson, N.J., 1985—. Fellow Am. Inst. Chemists; mem. Am. Chem. Soc. (sr.), Am. Assn. Textile Chemists and Colorists, Am. Assn. Textile Technologists, Am. Oil Chemists Soc., Salesmen's Assn. Chem. Industries. Club: Masons. Patentee in field. Home: PO Box 1140 Bryn Mawr PA 19010 Office: 295 Governor St Paterson NJ 07501

WELLES, JOHN GALT, museum director; b. Orange, N.J., Aug. 24, 1925; s. Paul and Elizabeth Ash (Galt) W.; m. Barbara Lee Chrisman, Sept. 15, 1951; children: Virginia Chrisman, Deborah Galt, Barton Jeffery, Holly Page. BE, Yale U., 1946; MBA, U. Pa., 1949. Test engr. Gen. Electric Co., Lynn, Mass., 1947; labor relations staff New Departure div. Gen Motors Corp., Bristol, Conn., 1949-51; mem. staff Mountain States Employers Council, Denver, 1952-55; head indsl. econs. div. U. Denver Research Inst., Denver, 1956-74; v.p. planning and devel. Colo. Sch. Mines, Golden, 1974-83; regional adminstr. EPA, Denver, 1983-87; exec. dir. Denver Mus. Natural History, 1987—. Sr. cons. Secretariat, UN Conf. Human Environment, Geneva, 1971-72; cons. Bus. Internat., S.A., Geneva, 1972; dir. KCFR Pub. Broadcasting of Colo. Inc., Denver, 1985—; chmn. Colo. Front Range Project, Denver, 1979-80. Contbr. articles to profl. jours., newspapers. Recipient Disting. Service award Denver Regional Council Govts., 1980, Barnes award EPA, 1987. Mem. Am. Econ. Assn., AAAS, World Future Soc., Tau Beta Pi, Blue Key. Republican. Episcopalian. Clubs: Arapahoe Tennis (pres. 1964-65); University (Denver). Office: Denver Mus Natural History City Park Denver CO 80205

WELLES, KELLY, advertising and marketing executive; b. Bellingham, Wash., June 10, 1948; d. Solon Richard and Elva Maria (Dibble) Boynton. Student, Sorbonne, Paris, 1966-67; BA, U. Wash., 1968; MA in Polit. Sci., New Sch. for Social Research, N.Y.C., 1974. Advt. copywriter Norton Simon Communication, N.Y.C., 1974-75; v.p., creative dir. Gordon & Shortt Advt., N.Y.C., 1976-79; exec. dir. advt. Paramount Pictures, N.Y.C., 1979-80; sr. copywriter, assoc. creative dir. William Esty Co., 1981-82; v.p., assoc. creative dir. Bozell & Jacobs Advt., N.Y.C., 1982-84; chmn., pres. Welles & Connaught, Inc., 1984-86; co-founder Future Resources inc., 1986—; mass media cons. to Ford Found., 1976. Author: Analysis of Folk in Third World Communications, 1976. Councillor French C. of C., 1983-84; dir. media task force Coordination Com. for UN, 1983—; dir. media adv. council Univ. for Peace, 1986—. Intern UN, Geneva, SHAPE and NATO, Paris, The Common Market, Internat. Ct. at the Hague, 1966; recipient Casebook Print award, 1975, The One Show award, 1976, Effie award, 1979. Mem. Advt. Women of N.Y. (dir., 1979-80), N.Y. Women in Communications (bd. dirs. 1982-83), Ad Net (bd. dirs. 1984—), Ad Net Pub. Service Cum., (chmn.), TV Acad. Arts and Scis. (Emmy award judge 1980), Fgn. Policy Assn. Home: 425 E 63rd St New York NY 10021

WELLES, NYDIA LELIA CÁNOVAS, psychologist; b. Buenos Aires, Argentina, Mar. 30, 1935; came to U.S., 1967, naturalized, 1977; d. Artemio Tomás and Pura (Martínez) Cánovas; B.A. in Elem. Edn., Nat. Coll. Edn., Evanston, Ill., 1976; M.A. in Counseling Psychology, Northwestern U., 1977, PhD in Counseling Psychology, 1986; m. Lorant Welles, Oct. 21, 1967; 1 son, Lorant Esteban. Tchr. in Argentina, 1954-64; pvt. practice psychology, Argentina, 1964-67; social worker Cath. Charities, Chgo., 1971-75; translator SRA, Chgo., 1975; test adminstr. Ednl. Testing Service, 1975-76; Latin Am. Services supr. Edgewater Uptown Community Mental Health Council, Chgo., 1978-80 ; research asst. Center Family Studies, 1978-79; mem. allocation com. campaign for human devel. Archdiocesis of Chgo., 1985—. Mem. Ill. Assn. for Hispanic Mental Health (co-founder), Phi Delta Kappa. Roman Catholic. Author papers in field.

WELLS, BEN HARRIS, retired beverage company executive; b. Saginaw, Mich., June 11, 1906; s. Ben W. and Florence (Harris) W.; m. Katherine Gladney, June 17, 1938; children: Katherine Graves, Ben Gladney. Student, Ind. U., 1922-25; A.B., U. Mich., 1929, M.A., 1931; L.H.D., Westminster Coll., 1979, U. Mo.-St. Louis, 1983. Tchr. John Burroughs Sch., St. Louis County, 1929-31, 33-38; critic, tchr. U. Mich. Sch. Edn., 1931-33; with Seven-Up Co., St. Louis, 1938-78; pres. Seven-Up Co., 1965-74, chmn., 1974-78; Chmn. Consumer Research Inst., 1970-77. Trustee John Burroughs Sch., 1954-61; pres. St. Louis Symphony Soc., 1970-78, chmn., 1978-84, v.p. 1985—; chmn. Com. for Arts Mo., 1976-84; mem. U. Mich. Devel. Council, 1979-85, Library Nat. Council, Washington U., St. Louis; pres. Laumeier Internat. Sculpture Park, St. Louis County, 1981-83; mem. community adv. bd. Sta. KWMU-Radio, U. Mo.; hon. life mem. Opera Theatre of St. Louis Bd.; bd. dirs. St. Louis council Boy Scouts Am., 1974-80, St. Louis United Way, 1974-80, St. Louis Arts and Humanities Commn., 1976-81, Community Found., 1977-87, St. Louis Conservatory and Schs. for Arts, 1979—, 1st St. Forum, 1979—, Winston Churchill Meml. and Library, Fulton, Mo., 1979—, Music Assocs. of Aspen (Colo.), 1979—, Am. Symphony Orch. League, 1986—; bd. dirs. emeritus Civic Progress; mem. U. Mich. Devel. Council, 1979-85. Recipient Mo. Arts award, 1984. Mem. St. Louis Symphony Orch. (hon. life), Am. Fedn. Musicians (hon. mem. musicians local), Phi Beta Kappa, Sigma Chi. Clubs: Media, St. Louis, Bellerive Country, Bogey, Noonday, University, Racquet (St. Louis). Lodge: Rotary. Office: 560 Trinity at Delmar Saint Louis MO 63130

WELLS, DAMON, JR., investment company executive; b. Houston, May 20, 1937; s. Damon and Margaret Corinne (Howze) W.; B.A. magna cum laude, Yale U., 1958; B.A., Oxford U., 1964, M.A., 1968; Ph.D., Rice U., 1968. Owner, chief exec. officer Damon Wells Interests, Houston, 1958—. Bd. dirs. Child Guidance Center of Houston, 1970-73, Jefferson Davis Assn., 1973-81; trustee Christ Ch. Cathedral Endowment Fund, 1970-73, 84-88, Kinkaid Sch., 1972-86, Kinkaid Sch. Endowment Fund, 1981-86; mem. Sr. Common Room, Pembroke Coll., Oxford U., 1972—; trustee Camp Allen retreat of Episc. Diocese of Tex., 1976-78; founding bd. dirs. Brit. Inst. U.S., 1979-80; mem. pres.' council Tex. A&M U., 1983—. Fellow Jonathan Edwards Coll., Yale U., 1982—; hon. fellow Pembroke Coll., Oxford U., 1984—. Mem. English-Speaking Union (nat. dir. 1970-72, v.p. Houston br. 1966-73), Council Fgn. Affairs, Phi Beta Kappa, Pi Sigma Alpha. Episcopalian. Clubs: Coronado, Houston Country, Houston; Yale (N.Y.C.); United Oxford and Cambridge U. (London); Cosmos (Washington). Author: Stephen Douglas: The Last Years, 1857-1861, 1971. Home: 3435 Westheimer Rd Houston TX 77027 Office: River Oaks Bank Bldg Suite 806 2001 Kirby Dr Houston TX 77019

WELLS, FAY GILLIS, writer, lecturer, broadcaster; b. Mpls., Oct. 15, 1908; d. Julius Howells and Minnie Irene (Shafer) Gillis; student Mich. State Coll., 1925-28; m. Linton Wells, Apr. 1, 1935 (dec. 1976); 1 son, Linton Wells, II. Free-lance corr. in USSR for N.Y. Herald Tribune and AP, 1930-34, aviation mags., 1930-36; fgn. corr. N.Y. Herald Tribune, 1935-36, spl. Hollywood corr., 1937-38, syndicated boating columnist, 1960-62; contbr. book revs. Saturday Review, 1939-42; dep. chief of mission for U.S. Comml. Co., Portuguese W. Africa, 1942-46; White House corr. Storer Broadcasting Co., 1964-77; aircraft pilot, 1929; designer yacht interiors Alta Grant Samuels, 1958-62; now co-chmn. Internat. Forest of Friendship; hon. co-chmn. Nat. Air Heritage Council; mem. com. to select 1st journalist in space, 1985—. Recipient Sherman Fairchild Internat. Air Safety Writing award, 1965, Amelia Earhart medal, 1967, Golden Age of Flight award Nat. Air and Space Mus.-Dept. Transp., 1984, award Internat. Conf. Women Engrs. and Scientists, 1984. Mem. 1967. Mem. Aviation/Space Writers Assn., Am. Women in Radio and TV (pres. Washington chpt. 1968-69, CBS Charlotte Friel award 1972), Radio-TV Corrs. Assn., White House Corrs. Assn., Aircraft Owners and Pilots Assn., The Ninety-Nines (charter mem.; Most Valuable Pilot, Washington chpt. 1975), OX5 Aviation Pioneers (Outstanding Woman of Year award 1972), Internat. Soc. Woman Geographers, Broadcast Pioneers, Zonta Internat., Nat. Bus. and Profl. Womens Clubs, Nat. League Am. Pen Women, Nat. Aero. Assn. (named elder statesman 1984). Clubs: Georgetown, Overseas Press (founding mem. 1939), Am. Newspaper Women's, Nat. Press, Internat. Forest Friendship (co-gen. chmn. 1976—). Home: 4211 Duvawn St Alexandria VA 22310

WELLS, FRANCES JEAN, economist; B. Washington, Oct. 28, 1937; d. Oris Vernon and Frances (Ingram) Wells; B.A., Wellesley Coll., 1959; M.B.A., N.Y. U., 1971. With comml. banking dept. Bankers Trust Co., N.Y.C., 1959-63; program dir. devel. fund Wellesley Coll., 1963-67, dir. spl. fund programs, 1967-69; analyst in money and banking econs. div. Congl. Research Service, Library of Congress, Washington, 1973-77, specialist in money and banking, 1977-88, specialist in econ. policy, 1988—. Mem. Am. Econs. Assn., Am. Fin. Assn. Home: 1600 N Oak St Apt 418 Arlington VA 22209 Office: Library of Congress Congl Research Service Washington DC 20540

WELLS, HERMAN B., university chancellor; b. Jamestown, Ind., June 7, 1902; s. Joseph Granville and Anna (Harting) W. Student, U. Ill., 1920-21; BS, Ind. U., 1924, AM, 1927, LLD, 1962; postgrad., U. Wis., 1927-28, LLD (hon.), 1946; LLD (hon.), Butler U., Rose Poly. Inst., DePauw U., 1939, Wabash Coll., 1942, Earlham, 1948, Valparaiso U., 1953, Miami U., Tri-State Coll., 1959, U. Louisville, 1961, Franklin Coll., Anderson Coll., 1962, Ball State Tchrs. Coll., Washington U., 1963, U. Notre Dame, St. Joseph's Coll., U. Calif., Ind. State Coll., 1964, Drury Coll., 1968, Columbia, 1969, Chgo. Circle Campus U. Ill., 1973, Howard U., 1976, U. S.C., 1980, L.H.D., 1963, Marian Coll., 1970; hon. doctorate in edn., Coll. Edn., Bangkok, 1968. Asst. cashier First Nat. Bank, Lebanon, Ind., 1924-26; asst. dept. econs. U. Wis., 1927-28; field sec. Ind. Bankers Assn., 1928-31; sec., research dir. Study Commn. for Ind. Financial Instns., 1931-33; instr. econs. Ind. U., 1930-33, asst. prof., 1933-35; supr. div. of banks and trust cos., div. of research and statistics Ind. Dept. Financial Instns., 1933-35; sec. Commn. for Ind. Financial Instns., 1933-36; prof. adminstrn. Sch. Bus. Adminstrn. Ind. U., 1935-72, dean, 1935-37, acting pres., 1937-1938, pres., 1938-62, univ. chancellor, 1962—; interim pres. Ind. U., 1968; chmn. Ind. U. Found., 1937-62, 69-72, vice chmn., 1975—, pres., 1962-69, chmn. exec. com., 1969—; chmn. Fed. Home Loan Bank of Indpls., 1940-71; dir. Ind. Bell Telephone Co., 1951-72, Chemed Corp., 1970—, Lilly Endowment, Inc., 1973—; Spl. adviser on Liberated Areas, U.S. Dept. State, 1944; cons. U.S. delegation San Francisco Conf. for Am. Council on Edn., 1945; Mem. Allied Missions for Observation Greek elections, rank of Minister, 1946; adviser on cultural affairs to mil. gov. U.S. Zone, Germany, 1947-48; del. 12th Gen. Assembly of UN, 1957; adviser Ministry Edn., Pakistan, 1959; head U.S. delegation SEATO Prep. Commn. on Univ. Problems, Bangkok, 1960; mem. UN com. experts to rev. activities and orgn. UN Secretariat, 1960-61, Nat. Citizen's Commn. Internat. Cooperation, Com. Econ. Devel., 1958-61; chmn. legislature's cons. higher edn. State N.Y., 1963-64; mem. Pres.'s Com. U.S. Soviet Trade Relations, 1965; mem. rev. com. on Haile Sellassie I U., Addis Ababa, 1966-75; mem. pres.'s Spl. Com. on Overseas Vol. Activities, 1967; mem. Nat. Commn. on U.S.-China Relations, 1969; tech. adv. bd. Milbank Meml. Fund, 1973-78; Ex-pres. Nat. Assn. State Univs., State U. Assn.; exec. com. Am. Council on Edn. (chmn. council), 1944-45; mem. 1st bd. regents Am. Savs. & Loan Inst. Grad. Sch. Savs. and Loan.; Trustee Edn. and World Affairs, 1963-71, chmn., 1963-70; trustee Howard U., 1956-75, Am. U. at Cairo, 1957-75, Ind. Inst. Tech. (emeritus), Earlham Coll. (hon.), Carnegie Found. for Advancement Teaching, 1941-62; former mem. adv. council Am. Sch. of Madrid; mem. nat. com. on govt. fin. Brookings Instn.; bd. visitors Tulane U.; chmn. Aerospace Research Applications Center, Ind. U., 1962-72; nat. bd. dirs. Goodwill Industries Am., 1962-69; bd. dirs. James Whitcomb Riley Meml. Assn. (v.p.), Sigma Nu Ednl. Found., 1946—, Arthur R. Metz Foundation, Learning Resources Inst., 1959-65, Council on Library Resources, Historic Landmarks Found. Ind., 1974—; chmn. adv. com. Acad. in Pub. Service, 1976—. Author: (with others) Report of Study Commission for Indiana Financial Institutions, 1932, Being Lucky: Reminiscences and Reflections, 1980, articles in mags. Recipient Distinguished Service award Ind. Jr. C. of C., 1938; 1st ann. award N.Y. Alumni chpt. Beta Gamma Sigma, 1939; Gold medal award Internat. Benjamin Franklin Soc., 1959; Comdrs. Cross of Order of Merit Germany, 1960; Radio Sta. WHAS Ind. Man of Year, 1960; Man of Year awards Indpls. Times, 1961; Man of Year awards Ind. Optometric Assn., 1961; comdr. Most Exalted Order White Elephant, 1962; knight comdr. 2d class Most Noble Order Crown, 1968; Thailand; Nat. Interfrat. Conf. award, 1962; Hoosier of Year award Sons of Ind. in N.Y., 1963; Interfrat. Service award Lambda Chi Alpha, 1964; Robins of Am. award, 1964; Distinguished Service Sch. Adminstrn. award Am. Assn. Sch. Adminstrs., 1965; Ind. Arts award, 1977; Liberty Bell award, 1978; Hon. mem. United Steelworkers Am., Dist. 30, Nat. Exchange Clubs, DeMolay Legion of Honor, 1975; hon. v.p. AM. Sunday Sch. Union. Fellow Internat. Coll. Dentists (hon.), Am. Coll. Dentists (hon.), Am. Acad. Arts and Scis.; mem. Am. Philos. Soc., Am. Assn. Sch. Adminstrs., Royal Soc. Art London (Benjamin Franklin fellow), NEA (ex-pres. div. higher edn.), Am. Econ. Assn., Internat. Assn. Univs. (gov., v.p. 1955-60), AAUP, Am. Research Inst. for Arts (chmn. bd. 1975-77), Nat. Commn. on Humanities (vice chmn. 1964-65), Ind. Acad. Social Scis. (past pres.), Ind. Soc. of Chgo., Ind. Soc. Pioneers, Ind. Hist. Soc. (dir. 1968—), Ind. Acad., Ind. Tchrs. Assn., Mortar Bd., Blue Key, Phi Beta Kappa, Phi Mu Alpha, Kappa Delta Pi, Beta Gamma Sigma, Alpha Kappa Psi, Kappa Kappa Psi, Sigma Nu (regent 1968-70). Methodist (trustee). Clubs: Mason (33 deg.), Kiwanian (hon.), Rotarian (hon.), Athenaeum; Columbia (Indpls.), Athletic (Indpls.); Century Assn. (N.Y.C.), University (N.Y.C.); University (Chgo.); Cosmos (Washington). Home: 1321 E 10th St Bloomington IN 47401 Office: Ind Univ Bryan Hall Office of Chancellor Bloomington IN 47405 *

WELLS, HERSCHEL JAMES, physician, former hospital administrator; b. Kirkland, Ark., Feb. 23, 1924; s. Alymer James and Martha Thelma (Cross) W.; m. Carmen Ruth Williams, Aug. 5, 1946; children: Judith Alliece (Mrs. W.J. Jarecki), Pamela Elliece (Mrs. G. D. McKinven), Joanne Olivia (Mrs. E.M. Meyer). Student, Emory U., 1941-42, U. Ark., 1942-43; M.D., U. Tenn., 1946. Rotating intern, then resident internal medicine Wayne County Gen. Hosp. (and Infirmary), Eloise, Mich., 1946-50; dir. infirmary div. Wayne County Gen. Hosp. (and Infirmary), 1955-65, gen. supt., 1965-74; dir. Wayne County Gen. Hosp. (Walter P. Reuther Meml. Long Term Care Facility), 1974-78; rev. physician DDS, SSA, Traverse City, Mich., 1978—. Served to maj. M.C. AUS, 1948-55. Fellow Am. Coll. Nursing Home Adminstrs.; mem. A. M.A., Mich., Wayne County med. socs., Am. Fedn. Clin. Research, Mich. Assn. Professions, Alpha Kappa Kappa, Pi Kappa Alpha. Club: Mason (Shriner, 32 deg.). Home: PO Box 305 Mesick MI 49668 Office: PO Box 712 Traverse City MI 49684

WELLS, JESSIE ELISABETH, biostatistician; b. Dunedin, New Zealand, Sept. 7, 1946; d. Colin Archibald Gunn and Margaret Dorothy (Weir) McKenzie; m. Arthur Russell Wells, May 18, 1968; children: Robin Morgan, Jessie Anne. BSc with honours, U. Canterbury, 1968, PhD, 1970. Registered psychologist. Postdoctoral fellow psychology dept. U. Toronto, 1970-72, asst. prof., 1971-72; lectr. psychology dept. Massey U., Palmerston North, New Zealand, 1973-78; researcher Health Planning and Research Unit, Christchurch, New Zealand, 1978-80; biostatistician Christchurch Sch. Med., Otago U., Christchurch, New Zealand, 1980—; mem. research com. Alcoholic Liquor Adv. Council, Wellington, New Zealand, 1980-84; reviewer/referee New Zealand Med. Jour., 1982—; grant referee Med. Research Council New Zealand, 1985—. Contbr. articles to profl. jours., chpts. to books. Helen MacMillan Brown Bursary sr. scholar U. Canterbury, 1964, 65, 67; New Zealand U. Grants Com. scholar, Christchurch, 1968, 70, Toronto, 1970-71. Mem. New Zealand Stats. Assn., Pub. Health Assn. Australia and New Zealand (epidemidogy sec.). Home: 19

Owens TCE, Christchurch 4, New Zealand Office: U Otago Christchurch Sch Medicine, PO Box 4345, Christchurch New Zealand

WELLS, JOEL REAVES, JR., bank holding company executive; b. Troy, Ala., Nov. 14, 1928; s. Joel Reaves and Julia (Talley) W.; m. Betty Stratton, June 27, 1953; children: Linda, Martha, Joel. B.S.B.A., U. Fla., 1950, J.D., 1951. Bar: Fla. Ptnr. Maguire, Voorhis & Wells, Orlando, Fla., 1956-75; pres. Major Realty Co., Orlando, 1972-75; exec. v.p. Sun Banks, Inc., Orlando, 1975-76, pres., 1976—, chief exec. officer, 1982—; chmn. Sun Banks of Fla., Inc., Orlando, from 1982; now also pres., dir. SunTrust Banks, Inc., Atlanta; bd. dirs. parent co. Sun Bank, N.A., Sun Century of Broward, Ft. Lauderdale. Mem. Fla. Council of 100, from 1975; pres. Central Fla. Devel. Com., 1965; chmn. Mcpl. Planning Bd., Orlando, 1962, 63; pres. United Appeal Orange County, 1960. Recipient Disting. Service award Orlando Jaycees, 1960. Mem. Orlando C. of C. (pres. 1970). Methodist. Clubs: Rotary (pres. 1966-67), Univ., Citrus, Country (Orlando). Office: SunTrust Banks Inc PO Box 4418 25 Park Pl Atlanta GA 30308 *

WELLS, MELISSA FOELSCH, foreign service officer; b. Tallinn, Estonia, Nov. 18, 1932; emigrated to U.S., 1936, naturalized, 1941; d. Kuno Georg and Miliza (Korjus) Foelsch; m. Alfred Washburn Wells, 1960; children: Christopher, Gregory. BS in Fgn. Service, Georgetown U., 1956. Consular officer Trinidad, 1961-64; econ. officer mission OECD, Paris, 1964-66; econ. officer London, 1966-71; internat. economist Dept. State, Washington, 1971-73; dep. dir. maj. export projects Dept. Commerce, 1973-75; comml. counselor Brazil, 1975-76; ambassador to Guinea-Bissau and Cape Verde, 1976-77; U.S. rep. to ECOSOC, UN, N.Y.C., 1977-79; resident rep. UNDP, Kampala, Uganda, 1979-81; dir. IMPACT program UNDP, Geneva, 1982-86; ambassador to Mozambique, 1987—. Mem. Am. Fgn. Service Assn. Office: US Ambassador to Mozambique care Dept State Washington DC 20520

WELLS, PATRICIA BENNETT, business administration educator; b. Park River, N.D., Mar. 25, 1935; d. Benjamin Beekman Bennett and Alice Catherine (Peerboom) Bennett Breckinridge; A.A., Allan Hancok Coll., Santa Maria, Calif., 1964; B.S. magna cum laude, Coll. Great Falls, 1966; M.S., U. N.D., 1967, Ph.D., 1971; children—Bruce Bennett, Barbara Lea. Fiscal acct. USIA, Washington, 1954-56; public acct., Bremerton, Wash., 1956; statistician U.S. Navy, Bremerton, 1957-59; med. services accounts officer U.S. Air Force, Vandenberg AFB, Calif., 1962-64; instr. bus. adminstrn. Western New Eng. Coll., 1967-69; vis. prof. econs. Chapman Coll., 1970; vis. prof. U. So. Calif. systems Griffith AFB, N.Y., 1971-72; assoc. prof., dir. adminstrn. mgmt. program Va. State U., 1974-81; assoc. prof. bus. adminstrn. Oreg. State U., Corvallis, 1974-81, prof. mgmt., 1982—, univ. curriculum coordinator, 1984-86, dir. adminstrv. mgmt. program, 1974-81, pres. Faculty Senate, 1981; cons. process tech. devel. Digital Equipment Corp., 1982. Pres., chmn. bd. dirs. Adminstrv. Orgnl. Services, Inc., Corvallis, 1976-83, Dynamic Achievement, Inc., 1983—; bd. dirs. Oreg. State U. Bookstores, Inc., 1987—. Cert. adminstrv. mgr. Pres. TYEE mobile home park. Fellow Assn. Bus. Communication (mem. internat. bd. 1980-83, v.p. Northwest 1981, 2d v.p. 1982-83, 1st v.p. 1983-84, pres. 1984-85); mem. Am. Bus. Women's Assn. (named Top Businesswoman in Nation 1980, Bus. Assoc. Yr. 1986), Assn. Info. Systems Profls., Adminstrv. Mgmt. Soc., AAUP (chpt. sec. 1973, chpt. bd. dirs. 1982, 84-87, pres. Oreg. conf. 1983-85), Am. Vocat. Assn. (nominating com. 1976), Associated Oreg. Faculties, Nat. Bus. Edn. Assn., Nat. Assn. Tchr. Edn. for Bus. Office Edn. (pres. 1976-77, chmn. public relations com. 1978-81), Corvallis Area C. of C. (v.p. chamber devel. 1987-88, pres. 1988—, Pres.' award 1986), Sigma Kappa. Roman Catholic. Lodge: Rotary. Contbr. numerous articles to profl. jours. Office: Oreg State U Coll Bus 418C Bexell Corvallis OR 97331

WELLS, PETER BOYD, lawyer; b. Austin, Tex., Sept. 30, 1915; s. Peter Boyd and Eleanor (Henderson) W.; m. Betty Louise Perkins, May 26, 1951; children—Peter Boyd, Elizabeth Wells Howell. B.A., U. Tex., 1936; LL.B., Harvard U., 1940. Bar: Tex., 1941. Assoc., Benckenstein, Wells & Duncan, Beaumont, Tex., 1946-58; sole practice, Beaumont, 1958-61; ptnr. Wells, Duncan & Beard, Beaumont, 1961-70, Wells, Peyton, Beard, Greenberg, Hunt & Crawford, Beaumont, 1970—; speaker estate planning. Former treas. Tex. Hist. Found. Served to maj. inf., AUS, 1941-45; ETO. Decorated Bronze Star; cert. in estate planning and probate law. Mem. ABA, Tex. Bar Found., Tex. Philos. Soc., Phi Beta Kappa, Phi Kappa Psi. Presbyterian. Clubs: Tower, Beaumont, Beaumont Rotary, Knights of San Jacinto, Sons Republic of Tex. Home: 2570 Long St Beaumont TX 77702 Office: Wells & Peyton 624 Petroleum Bldg PO Box 3708 Beaumont TX 77704

WELLS, PETER SCOVILLE, management consultant; b. N.Y.C., Apr. 25, 1938; s. Jonathan Godfrey and Eleanore Denning (Scoville) W.; student U. Va., 1956-58, Columbia U., 1959-61; m. Patricia Ann Trent, Dec. 8, 1973; 1 son by previous marriage, Peter Scoville. Asst. to controller Laird & Co., N.Y.C., 1961-63; asst. to partner charge ops. Goldman Sachs, N.Y.C., 1963-64; mgr. new bus. dept. B.J. Herkimer Co., N.Y.C., 1964-67; divisional policy and procedures adminstr. Paine, Webber, Jackson & Curtis, Inc., N.Y.C., 1967-70, asst. to exec. cashier, 1970-73, asst. v.p., mgr. employment services, adminstr. equal employment opportunity, 1973-80; personnel officer, exec. recruiter N.Y. Stock Exchange, 1980-86; mgr. employment. N.Y. Stock Exchange, sr. v.p. Wesley Brown & Bartle, 1986-87; v.p., dir. Alliance Mktg., Inc, 1987—. Bd. dirs. Harlem Interfaith Counseling Service. Cons. human affairs Gracie Sq. Hosp. Served with AUS, 1958. Mem. N.Y.C. C. of C., SAR, Phi Kappa Psi. Home: 449 E 78th St New York NY 10021 Office: 152 Madison Ave New York NY 10016

WELLS, RICHARD A., electronics company executive; b. Houston, June 9, 1943; s. Odell A. and Murrie B. (Scallorn) W.; m. Sue Ellen Juel, Aug. 23, 1964; children: Anne Elizabeth, Robert Martin. BA, U. Tex., 1964; MS, U. Ill., 1969. Flight controller IBM/NASA, Houston, 1964-67; mem. faculty U. Ill., Urbana, 1967-70; with Gould Inc., Boston, 1970-72, Cleve., 1972-77; founder, pres., chief exec. officer KMW Systems, Austin, Tex., 1977—; bd. dirs. Ultra Systems Design Inc., Austin. Contbr. articles to profl. jours. Trustee Laguna Gloria Art Found., Austin, 1984—; mem. Austin Econ. Devel. Commn., 1987, Technology Industry Legis. Task Force, 1986—. Mem. Nat. Computer Graphics Assn., Assn. of Computing Machinery, Austin C. of C. (bd. dirs. 1988—), Mensa. Clubs: Lost Creek, Hills/Lakeway (Austin). Office: KMW Systems Corp 100 Shepherd Mountain Plaza Austin TX 78730

WELLS, WILLIAM STEVEN, marketing communications consultant, syndicated cartoonist; b. Detroit, Aug. 19, 1945; s. Ronald and Eleanor (Vancea) W.; m. Mary Rudolph, Nov. 27, 1969; children: Adam, David. AB, Hamilton Coll., 1967. Journalist New Haven Register, Providence Jour., Detroit Free Press, 1968-75; exec. asst. to Mich. Gov. William Milliken, Lansing, 1975-76; account exec. Fleishman-Hillard, Inc., St. Louis, 1976-78; v.p., mgr. Doremus & Co., Mpls., 1978-80; sr. v.p., mng. dir. Hill & Knowlton, Inc., Mpls., 1980-84; pres. Wells and Co., 1984-87; chmn., chief exec. officer Wells and Miller, Mpls., 1988—; co-author syndicated bus. cartoon strip Executive Suite, United Features Syndicate. Contbr. articles to profl. jours. Served with USNR, 1968-69. Mem. Nat. Investor Relations Inst., Issues Mgmt. Assn. Republican. Clubs: Mpls., Edina Country, Minn. Squash Raquets Assn. Office: Wells and Miller 250 Thresher Square W 700 S Third St Minneapolis MN 55415

WELS, RICHARD HOFFMAN, lawyer; b. N.Y.C., May 3, 1913; s. Isidor and Belle (Hoffman) W.; m. Marguerite Samet, Dec. 12, 1954; children: Susan, Amy. A.B., Cornell, 1933; LL.B., Harvard U., 1936; postgrad., U. Ariz., 1944. Bar: N.Y. 1936. Spl. asst. dist. atty. N.Y. Co., 1936-37; asso. Handel & Panuch, N.Y.C., 1937-38; mem. legal staff, asst. to chmn. SEC, Washington, 1938-42; spl. asst. atty. gen. U.S. and spl. asst. U.S. atty., 1941-42; spl. counsel Com. Naval Affairs, U.S. Ho. of Reps., 1943, Sea-Air Commn., Nat. Fedn. Am. Shipping, 1946; trustee, sec. William Alanson White Inst. Psychiatry, N.Y.C., 1946—; vice. chmn., dir. Am. Parents Com.; mem. Moss & Wels, 1946-57, Moss, Wels & Marcus, 1957-68, Sulzberger, Wels & Marcus, 1968-72, Moss, Wels & Marcus, 1972-78, Sperry, Weinberg, Wels, Waldman & Rubenstein, 1979-84, Wels & Zerin, 1985—; gen. counsel Bowling Proprs. Assn. Am., 1956-67, N.Y. State Bowling Proprs. Assn., Am. Acad. Psychoanalysis; commr. Interprofl. Comn. on Marriage and Div.; lectr. Practising Law Inst.; dir. H-R Television, Inc., Belgrave Capital Corp., Broadcast Data Base, Inc., Belgrave Securities Corp.; chmn. bd. govs. Islands Research Found.; bd. govs., chmn., trustee Daytop Village, Inc.; chmn. bd. trustees Bleuler Psychotherapy Center; trustee N.Y. State Sch. Psychiatry, Margaret Chase Smith Library, Skowhegan, Maine. Co-author: Sexual Behavior and the Law; bd. editors Family Law Quar.; contbr. articles to profl. jours. Vice chmn. Am. Jewish Com., now mem. nat. exec. bd. Served from ensign to lt. USNR, 1942-46; mem. staff Under Sec. Forrestal, 1943-44; in 1944-46, P.T.O. Mem. ABA (fin. officer, mem. council Am. family law sect.), N.Y. State Bar Assn. (chmn. family law sect.), N.Y. City Bar Assn., Am. Acad. Matrimonial Lawyers (gov.), Am. Legion, Naval Order U.S., Mil. Order World Wars, Fed. Bar Assn., Res. Officers Assn., Assn. I.C.C. Practitioners, Fed. Communications Bar Assn., Pi Lambda Phi, Sphinx Head. Clubs: Harmonie (gov.), Harvard, Cornell (N.Y.C.); Nat. Lawyers (Washington); Sunningdale Country (Scarsdale, N.Y.), Statler (Ithaca, N.Y.). Home: 480 Park Ave New York NY 10022 Office: Wels & Zerin 55 E 59th St New York NY 10022

WELSH, JOHN BERESFORD, JR., lawyer; b. Seattle, Feb. 16, 1940; s. John B. and Rowena Morgan (Custer) W. Student U. Hawaii, 1960, Georgetown U., 1960; BA, U. Wash., 1962, LLB, 1965. Bar: Wash. 1965. Staff counsel Joint Com. on Govtl. Cooperation, 1965-66; asst. atty. gen. Dept. Labor and Industries, 1966-67; atty. Legis. Council, acting as counsel to Pub. Health Com., Labor Com., Pub. Employees Collective Bargaining Com., Com. on State Instns. and Youth Devel., State of Wash., 1967-73; sr. counsel Wash. Ho. of Reps., counsel to Ho. Com. on Social and Health Services, Olympia, 1973-86; counsel Ho. Com. Human Services and Ho. Com. Health Care, 1987—; legal cons. Gov.'s Planning Commn. Vocat. Rehab., 1968, Gov.'s Commn. on Youth Involvement, 1969; envoy from Gov. Wash. to investiture of Prince of Wales, London, 1969; faculty Nat. Conf. State Legislatures, Denver, 1977, New Orleans, 1977; faculty, chmn. legis. issues com., 1986, mem. steering com., long range planning com. Council of State Govts. Clearinghouse on Licensure, Enforcement and Regulation, 1984, 86—, Council of State Govts. com. on suggested state legis., 1988—. Hon. prof. health adminstrn. Eastern Wash. U., 1982. Mem. Wash. Bar Assn., Govtl. Lawyers Assn., Nat. Health Lawyers Assn., Société des Amis du Musée de l'Armée, Paris, English Speaking Union, Assn. Belge Napoleonienne, Souvenir Napoleonien (Paris), Napoleonic Soc., Phi Delta Phi. Office: State of Washington House of Reps Olympia WA 98504

WELSH, JUDSON BOOTH, banker; b. Rochester, N.Y., Oct. 22, 1945; s. Frederic Sager and Helen (Groves) W. BA in Econs., St. Lawrence U., 1964-67; M in Internat. Mgmt., Thunderbird Grad. Sch. Internat. Mgmt., 1972-73. Statistician, Eastman Kodak, Ltd., London, 1966; ter. rep. Eastman Kodak Co., Rochester, 1970-73; asst. v.p. Chem. Bank Internat., 1973-77, founder Chem. Bank Rep. Office, regional rep. W. Africa, Abidjan, Ivory Coast, 1977-79; asst. v.p. 1st Nat. Bank of Boston, 1980-86; founderBoston Bank Cameroon, 1979-81; fin. cons., gen. mgr. Flightways, 1982-83 ; asst. v.p. Africa div., Fidelity Bank Phila., London, 1986—; dir. Buildis S.A., Geneva; founder Buildis, Sarl, Abidjan; fin. cons. Banque National d'Epargne et du Credit, Abidjan, 1984-85; leader seminars for W. African nations; advisor West Africa chpt. Internat. Exec. Service Corps. Served to lt. USN, 1967-70, Vietnam. Decorated D.S.M. (Vietnam). Mem. Am. Mgmt. Assn., Airplane Owners and Pilots Assn. Acad. Polit. Sci., Table Round Abidjan (charter). Author internat. credit seminar. Home: 31 Fitzjames Ave, London W14, England Office: Fidelity Bank Phila/Africa div, 1 Bishopsgate, London EC2 N3AB, England

WELSH, WILMER HAYDEN, music educator, composer, organist; b. Cin., July 17, 1932; s. Wilmer Wesley Welsh and Dorothy Mary (Exon) Hamilton; m. Constance Teri DeBear, June 30, 1957 (div. 1982); children: Benjamin Hayden, Stephen Andrew. B.S., Johns Hopkins U., 1953; artist diploma Peabody Conservatory Music, 1953, B.Music, 1954, M.Music, 1955. Asst. prof. music Winthrop Coll., Rock Hill, S.C., 1959-63; assoc. prof. music Davidson Coll., N.C., 1963-72, prof. music, 1972—, chmn. dept. music 1981-87, composer in residence, 1987—; organ recitalist specializing in Am. music from Colonial period to present; subject doctoral dissertation, 1985. Composer symphonies, concertos, operas, music for ch. festivals; performances throughout world. Contbr. articles to profl. jours. Grantee Ford Found., 1959, Nat. Endowment Arts, 1969, N.C. Arts Council, 1985; recipient Thomas Jefferson award McConnell Found., 1976. Mem. Am. Guild Organists, AAUP, Music Educators Nat. Conf., Coll. Music Soc., Am. Music Ctr., The Sonneck Soc. Republican. Episcopalian. Avocations: writing; antiques; gardening; swimming. Home: 510 South St Davidson NC 28036 Office: Davidson Coll PO Box 358 Davidson NC 28036

WELSHANS, MERLE TALMADGE, management consultant; b. Murphysboro, Ill., June 17, 1918; s. Arthur Isaac and Martha Ellen (Blair) W.; B.Ed., So. Ill. U., 1940; M.A., Washington U., St. Louis, 1947, Ph.D., 1951; m. Mary Katherine Whitenbaugh, June 2, 1942; children—Elizabeth Margaret Van Steenbergh, Arthur Edmund, Janice Ann. Asst. v.p. Merc. Mortgage Co., Olney, Ill., 1940; exec. officer, dept. bus. adminstrn. George Washington U., 1950-54; prof. fin. Grad. Sch. Bus. Adminstrn., Washington U., 1954-69; v.p. fin. Union Electric Co., St. Louis, 1969-83; mgmt. cons., 1983—; dir. Prudential-Bache Investment Co., Olympic Trust Co. Trustee St. Louis Sch. Pharmacy; chmn. bd. trustees Deaconess Hosp. Found. Served to capt. U.S. Army, 1942-45. Decorated Bronze Star medal. Mem. Fin. Mgmt. Assn. (dir.), Am. Econ. Assn., Am. Fin. Assn., Am. Soc. Fin. Analysis, Alpha Kappa Phi, Beta Gamma Sigma, Artus. Methodist. Author: (with R.W. Melicher) Finance, 7th edit., 1988; cons. economist, editor Fin. Newsletter, 1965-69. Address: 14360 Ladue Rd Chesterfield MO 63107

WELT, PHILIPPE, photography director; b. Paris, Mar. 28, 1946; s. Maurice and Henriette (Nicolas) W. Student, Ecole De Vaugirand, Paris, 1967. Freelance camera asst. 1968-78, freelance dir. photography, 1978—. Dir. photography: films Atelier Laranne (Gold Ninewe award for photography 1982), Fourth Cheri (award for phototography 1987). Named Best Cameraman of the Yr. Media Mag., 1985, 86. Home: 16 Rue Des Volontaires, 75015 Paris France

WELTENS, BERT, linguist; b. Heer, Limburg, The Netherlands, July 23, 1957. BA, U. Nijmegen, The Netherlands, 1978, MA, 1981. Research asst. U. Reading, Eng., 1981-82; researcher U. Nijmegen, 1982—, lectr., 1987—. Author: The Grammar of English Dialect, 1984; editor: Language Attrition in Progress, 1986; editor: Dialect and Education, 1988; contbr. articles to profl. jours. The Brit. Council grantee, 1981-82. Office: Dept Applied Linguistics, Erasmusplein 1, 6525 HT Nijmegen The Netherlands

WELTERS, GERALD ERYK, mathematics educator; b. Maastricht, Netherlands, July 20, 1947; came to Spain, 1952; s. Otto Reinhold and Erika Emilie (Dyhdalewicz) W. Licenciado en ciencias, U. Barcelona, 1970; Drs. in Wiskunde, U. Amsterdam, 1977; D.Math., U. Utrecht, Netherlands, 1981. Wetensch medewerker Math. Instituut, U. Utrecht, Netherlands, 1978-81; catedrático interino Facultad de Matemáticas, U. Barcelona, 1981-85, prof. titular, 1985-86, catedrático, 1986—. Mem. Wiskundig Genootschap, Am. Math. Soc., Societé Mathématique de France. Home: Ciudad de Balaguer, 43 Pral 2A, 08022 Barcelona Spain Office: Univ Barcelona, Facultad de Matematicas, Dept Algebra Y Geometria, Gran Via 585, 08007 Barcelona Spain

WELTY, ELMER ELIAS, lawyer, retired army officer; b. Pandora, Am. Legion, Res Sept. 3, 1906; s. Elias and Elizabeth (Amstutz) W.; m. Dorothy Tolford, June, 1929; 1 dau., Nancy Lee; m. 2d, Gertrude Kintzer, June, 1936 (div. 1946); children—Linda Ann, Rebecca Lou, Richard Edward; m. 3d, Lyla Rogers, Feb. 23, 1946. Student, Ohio No. U., 1924-26, LL.D. (hon.), 1982; grad. Fgn. Affairs Study Course, Yale U., 1945. Bar: Ohio 1928, Japan 1949. Served with Ohio Nat. Guard, 1926-33; commd. 2d lt. U.S. Army, 1933, advanced through grades to col. 1949, ret. 1978; served in CBI, 1943-45, with Gen. Hdqrs. staff, Tokyo, 1946-49; solicitor City of Lima (Ohio), 1929-33; pros. atty., Logan County, Ohio, 1940; ptnr. Welty, Shimeall and Kasari Internat., Tokyo, 1949-78, of counsel, Pompano Beach, Fla., 1978—. Decorated Bronze Star, China medal. Mem. ABA, Ohio Bar Assn., Dai Ichi Bar Assn., Am. Soc. Internat. Law, Interamerican Bar Assn., World Peace Through Law (charter mem.), Am. Legion, Res Officers Assn., Ret. Officers Assn., Mil Order of World Wars, Am. C. of C. in Japan (pres. 1952-53, dir. 1950-60) Am. Club of Tokyo (past pres., bd. of govs. 1948-64). Republican. Clubs: Bohemian (San Francisco); Explorers (N.Y.C.); Outriggers (Honolulu). Lodge: Elks (past exalted ruler). Address: 43 Avista Circle Saint Augustine FL 72084-3806

WELTY, EUDORA, author; b. Jackson, Miss.; d. Christian Webb and Chestina (Andrews) W. Student, Miss. State Coll. for Women; B.A., U. Wis., 1929; postgrad., Columbia Sch. Advt., 1930-31. Author: A Curtain of Green, 1941, The Robber Bridegroom, 1942, The Wide Net, 1943, Delta Wedding, 1946, The Golden Apples, 1949, The Ponder Heart, 1954, The Bride of the Innisfallen, 1955, The Shoe Bird, 1964, Losing Battles, 1970, One Time, One Place, 1971, The Optimist's Daughter, 1972 (Pulitzer prize 1973), The Eye of the Story, 1978, The Collected Stories of Eudora Welty, 1980, One Writer's Beginnings, 1985; contbr.: New Yorker. Recipient creative arts medal for fiction Brandeis U., 1966, Nat. Inst. Arts and Letters Gold Medal, 1972, Nat. Medal for Lit., 1980, Presdl. Medal of Freedom, 1980, Commonwealth medal, 1984, Nat. Medal of Arts, 1987. Mem. Am. Acad. Arts and Letters. Home: 1119 Pinehurst St Jackson MS 39202 *

WEN, GUO-CHUN, mathematician, educator; b. Hangzhou, Zhejiang, People's Republic of China, Sept. 29, 1930; s. Shao and Lin-shi Wen; m. Fu Fang, May 1, 1962; children: Wen Xin, Wen Jian-xin. Grad., Peking U., Beijing, 1955, postgrad. degree, 1959. Tchr. math. dept. Peking U., 1959-79; lectr. Inst. Math. Peking U., 1979-80, assoc. prof., 1980-85, prof., 1985—; chmn. math. dept. Yantai U., Shandong, 1985—; vis. prof. Free U. Berlin, Fed. Republic Germany, 1986; guest prof. Free U., Berlin, 1986; reviewer Math. Reviews, 1984. Author: Conformal Mappings and Boundary Value Problems, 1985, Linear and Nonlinear Elliptic Complex Equations, 1986; contbr. articles to prof. jours.; mem. editorial bd. Jour. Complex Variables, 1982—. Mem. China Math. Soc., Am. Math. Soc. Home: Peking U, #210 Bldg 48 Zhongguanyuan, Beijing People's Republic of China Office: Peking U Inst Math, Beijing People's Republic of China

WEN, TIEN KUANG, real estate executive; b. Meihsien, China, Feb. 11, 1924; M.A., Columbia U., 1950, LLD Marquis Found., 1988; m. Chong Chook Yew, Dec. 24, 1946; children—Ming Kang, Sui Han, Chiu Chi, Hsia Min. Sec., Chinese C. of C., Chinese Mining Assn., 1952-55; Chinese mgr. Banque de L'Indochine, Kuala Lumpur, 1958-71; chmn. Selangor Properties Ltd., Kuala Lumpur, 1963—. Chmn., Malayan Public Library Assn., 1957—, others; CD World U. Conf., 1984, hon. chmn. Tung Shin Hosp., justice of peace. Decorated D.P.M.P., Sultan of Perak, 1966; P.S.M., King, 1984. Mem. Basketball Assn. (hon.chmn.), Table Tennis Assn. (hon. chmn.), Kayin Assn., (hon. chmn.), Kwantung Assn. (gov. com.). Home: 33A Jalan Balau, Damansara Heights, Kuala Lumpur Malaysia Office: 6A Jalan Batai, Damansara Heights, Kuala Lumpur Malaysia

WENDEBORN, RICHARD DONALD, manufacturing company executive; b. Winnipeg, Man., Can.; came to U.S., 1976; s. Curtis and Rose (Lysecki) W.; m. Dorothy Ann Munn, Aug. 24, 1957; children: Margaret Gayle, Beverly Jane, Stephen Richard, Peter Donald, Ann Elizabeth. Diploma, Colo. Sch. Mines, 1952; grad., Advanced Mgmt. Program, Harvard, 1975. With Canadian Ingersoll-Rand Co., Montreal, 1952—; gen. mgr., v.p., dir. Canadian Ingersoll-Rand Co., 1968, pres., 1969-74, chmn. bd., 1975—; exec. v.p. Ingersoll-Rand Co., Woodcliff Lake, N.J., 1976—; bd. dirs. IR Can., IR Holdings-U.K., Calif. Pellet Mill; mem. Can. Govt. Oil and Gas Tech. Exchange Program with USSR, 1972—, Minerals and Metals Mission to Peoples Republic China, 1972—. Mem. Resource Fund Colo. Sch. Mines. Recipient Disting. Achievement medal Colo. Sch. Mines, 1973. Mem. Machinery and Equipment Mfrs. Assn. Can. (dir. 1974—, past chmn.), Tau Beta Pi. Home: 34 Grist Mill Ln Upper Saddle River NJ 07458 Office: Ingersoll-Rand Co 200 Chestnut Ridge Rd Woodcliff Lake NJ 07675

WENDEL, FAYE F., coin equipment manufacturing executive; b. Newark, Sept. 16, 1928; d. John Thomas and Sara Rose (Agliozzo) Fiorenza; m. Daniel C. Wendel, Nov. 26, 1949; children—Catherine C., Daniel C. III, Wayne J. Sec., P. Ballantine & Sons, Newark, 1946-49; head hostess, asst. to mgr. Bambergers-Carriage House Restaurant, 1971-74; sec. Peter Wendel & Sons, Inc., Irvington, N.J., 1961-78; sec. Wendel Industries, Inc., Union, N.J., 1978-80, pres., 1980—; pres. D.C. Wendel Corp., 1982—. Tchrs. aide St. Ann Sch.; asst. treas. Ladies Aux. St. Rose of Lima Ch., 1963. Mem. Short Hills Assn., Twig Group of Overlook Hosp., Rotary Assn., Am. Soc. Profl. and Exec. Women. Clubs: Republican, Short Hills Racquet. Home: 33 Quaker Rd Short Hills NJ 07078 Office: 1012 Greeley Ave N Union NJ 07083

WENDELBERGER, JAMES GEORGE, statistician, consultant; b. Milw., Mar. 13, 1953; s. Joseph Martin and Elizabeth (Neimon) W.; m. Joanne Marie Roth; 1 child, Barbara Ann. B.S. with distinction in Math. and Physics, U. Wis.-Madison, 1976, M.S. in Stats, 1978, Ph.D., 1982. Research assoc. Space Sci. and Engrng. Ctr., U. Wis.-Madison, 1982-83; sr. research scientist Gen. Motors Research Lab., 1983-87, quantitative analysis mgr. Urban Sci. Applications, Inc., 1987-88, gen. mgr. retail div. Urban Sci. Applications, Inc., 1988—. Mem. Inst. Math. Stats., Soc. Indsl. and Applied Math., Am. Statis. Assn., AAAS, Math Assn. of Am., Inst. Mgmt. Sci., Nat. Geog. Soc., The PlanetarySoc., Sigma Xi. Subspecialties: Statistics; Mathematical software. Current work: Consulting research statistician. Home: 5000 West Utica Rd Utica MI 48087-4239 Office: Urban Sci Applications 200 Renaissance Ctr Suite 1230 Detroit MI 48243

WENDELL, DAVID TAYLOR, investment counselor; b. Hackensack, N.J., Dec. 8, 1931; s. Edward Nelson and Eunice (Taylor) W.; m. Mary Beal, Apr. 9, 1955 (dic. Mar. 1980); children—Karen, Erica; m. Sharman Maria Parker, July 18, 1981. A.B. cum laude, Harvard Coll., 1953; M.B.A., Harvard U., 1958. Chartered fin. analyst. Security analyst Nat. Shamut Bank, Boston, 1958-59; sr. v.p. David L. Babson & Co. Inc., Boston, 1959-79; chmn., chief exec. officer David Wendell Assocs., Inc., Bath, Maine, 1979—; econ. and investment cons. Yeager, Wood & Marshall, Inc., N.Y.C., 1981—; investment cons. Loring, Wolcott & Coolidge, Boston, 1980—. Contbr. articles to profl. jours. Co-chmn. tax re-evaluation planning com., Concord, Mass., 1972-74; Served with U.S. Army, 1951-54, ETO. Recipient Honor cert. Valley Forge Freedoms Found., 1975, Disting. Service in Investment Edn. award Investment Edn. Inst., 1975. Mem. Boston Econ. Club (pres. 1976), Boston Security Analysts Soc. Club: Algonquin (Boston). Avocations: sailing; skiing; travel. Office: PO Box 171 97 Commercial St Bath ME 04530

WENDER, IRA TENSARD, lawyer; b. Pitts., Jan. 5, 1927; s. Louis and Luba (Kibrick) W.; student Swarthmore Coll., 1942-45; m. Phyllis M. Bellows, June 24, 1966; children: Justin B., Sarah T.; children by previous marriage: Theodore M., Matthew G., Abigail A., John B. JD, U. Chgo., 1948; LLM, N.Y. U., 1951.Atty. Lord, Day and Lord, N.Y.C., 1950-52, 54-59; asst. dir. internat. program in taxation Harvard Law Sch., 1952-54; lectr. N.Y. U. Sch. Law, N.Y.C., 1954-59; partner Baker and McKenzie, Chgo., 1959-61, founding ptnr. N.Y.C. office, 1961-71; sr. ptnr. Wender, Murase & White, 1971-82, of counsel, 1982-86; chmn. C. Brewer and Co., Ltd., Honolulu, 1969-75; pres., chief exec. officer A.G. Becker Paribas Inc., 1978-82; chmn., chief exec. officer Sussex Securities Inc., 1983-85; of counsel Patterson, Belknap, Webb & Tyler, N.Y.C., 1986-87, ptnr., 1988—; dir. REFAC Tech. Devel. Corp., N.Y.C., IU Internat. Corp., Wilmington, Del., Scopas Tech. Co., Inc., N.Y.C., Southwest Realty Ltd., Dallas. Bd. mgrs. Swarthmore Coll.; trustee Brearley Sch., N.Y.C., 1980-85, Putney (Vt.) Sch., 1985—; active Council on Fgn. Relations. Mem. Am., N.Y. State bar assns., Assn. Bar City N.Y. Author: (with E.R. Barlow) Foreign Investment and Taxation, 1955. Office: Patterson Belknap Webb & Tyler 30 Rockefeller Plaza New York NY 10112

WENDERLEIN, MATTHIAS, gynecologist; b. Nuremburg, Fed. Republic Germany, Aug. 27, 1941. MD, ULM Univ., 1970; Diploma in Psychology, Erlangen U., 1971. Curriculum advisor Fed. Ministry of Health, Bonn, People's Rep. Germany; dir. Clinic for Psychosomatic Disease and Sexual Medicine, 1985—, vice chmn. dept. ob-gyn., 1986—, prof., 1983. Contbr. articles to profl. jours. Office: Univesitäts-Frauenklinik, PrittzwitzstrBe 43, 7900 Ulm Federal Republic of Germany

WENDLAND, KARL-LUDOLF, psychiatrist, neurologist, educator; b. Hannover, Niedersachsen, Fed. Republic of Germany, July 23, 1929; s. Richard Konrad Hans and Wilhelmine Johanna Elisabeth (Lanckau) W. MD, Georg August U., Göttingen, Fed. Republic of Germany, 1956;

diploma in psychology, Christian Albrechts U., Kiel, Fed. Republic of Germany, 1962, privatdozent, 1970. Asst. physician Nervenklinik Christian Albrechts U., 1958-63, 65-70, asst. physician Hygiene Inst., 1964, asst. med. dir. Abteilung Psychiatrie, 1971—. Contbr. articles to profl. jours. Mem. Deutsche EEG Gesellschaft, Deutsche Gesellschaft für Psychiatrie und Nervenheilkunde, Marburger Bund. Mem. Evangelical Lutheran Ch. Office: Christian Albrechts U, Nervenklinik Niemannsweg 147, 2300 Kiel 1, Federal Republic of Germany

WENDLINGER, ROBERT MATTHEW, communications and training consultant; b. N.Y.C.; s. Harry and Rose (Pollock) W.; B.S., Columbia U., 1952; m. Dalis Peralta, 1955 (div. 1973); children: David, Marcella, Marta; m. Joan Hays Cole, June 23, 1984. Script editor Radio Free Europe, N.Y.C., 1950-52; asso. editor Ind. Film Jour., N.Y.C., 1953-57; gen. mgr. Kermit Rolland and Assos., Princeton, N.J., 1957-59; exec. asst. in charge editorial services United Hosp. Fund of N.Y., N.Y.C., 1959-60; mgr. info. sect. Com. for Air and Water Conservation, Am. Petroleum Inst., N.Y.C., 1966-67; with Bank of Am. NT & SA, San Francisco, 1967-78, asst. v.p. communications, 1972-78; pres. Communications Cons. and Services, Berkeley, Calif., 1978—; mem. grad. faculty St. Mary's Coll., Moraga, Calif., 1975-78; mem. Astron Corp. Fellow Am. Bus. Communication Assn.; mem. Indsl. Communication Council (past pres.). Author: (with James M. Reid, Jr.) Effective Letters: A Program in Self-Instruction, 1964, 3d edit., 1978; contbr.; Everbody Wins; TA Applied to Organizations, 1973; Affirmative Action for Women, 1973; McGraw-Hill Ency. Professional Management, 1978.

WENDT, HENRY, III, pharmaceutical company executive; b. Neptune City, N.J., July 19, 1933; s. Henry II and Rachel L. (Wood) W.; m. Holly Peterson, June 23, 1956; children: Henry IV, Laura. AB, Princeton U., 1955. With Smith, Kline & French Labs, Phila., 1955-70, v.p. mktg., gen. mgr., 1970-71; pres., chief operating officer Smith Kline Corp., Phila., 1971-76, also bd. dirs.; chief exec. officer Smith, Kline, Beckman Corp., Phila., 1982—, pres., 1982, chmn.; bd. dirs. ARCO; dir. Asia-Pacific ops. Louis A. Allen Assn., 1967-70. Contbr. articles to profl. jours. Bd. dirs. Phila. Contributionship; trustee Phila. Mus. Art; mem. adv. council dept. East Asian studies Princeton U. Mem. The Bus. Roundtable, ARCO (bd. dirs.). Club: Phila. Merion Cricket. Office: Smith Kline Beckman Corp 1 Franklin Plaza Philadelphia PA 19101 *

WENDT, MICHAEL, veterinarian, educator; b. Hannover, Fed. Republic of Germany, Nov. 25, 1956; s. Kurt and Maria-Luise (Frey) W. Lic. vet. practitioner, Vet. High Sch., Hannover, 1981; DVM, 1984. Practice vet. medicine Trittau, Fed. Republic of Germany, 1982-83; vet. collaborator, lectr. Vet. High Sch., Hannover, 1983—; lect. Internat. Pig Vet. Congress, Barcelona, Spain, 1986; vet. specialist on swine diseases Vet. Chamber, Hannover. Contbr. articles to vet. jours. Mem. Deutsche Veterinar-medizinische Gesellschaft. Club: Alt-Germania (Hannover). Home: Pasteurallee 6A, 3000 Hannover Federal Republic of Germany Office: Tierarztliche Hochschule, Bischofsholer Damn 15, 3000 Hannover Federal Republic of Germany

WENG, GEORGE JUENG-CIOUS, engineering educator; b. Taiwan, Oct. 8, 1944; s. Wan-Chung and Kuan-chia (Hsieh) W.; m. Shu-yu Huang, Oct. 26, 1949; children—Bruce, Joyce. B.S., Taiwan U., 1967; M.Phil., Yale U., 1971, Ph.D., 1974. Research fellow Delft (Netherlands) U. Tech., 1973-74; postdoctoral fellow Yale U., UCLA, 1974-76; sr. research engr. Gen. Motors Research Lab., Warren, Mich., 1976-77; asst. prof. mechanics and materials sci. Rutgers U., New Brunswick, N.J., 1977-80, assoc. prof., 1980-84, prof., 1984—. Contbr. articles to profl. jours.; editor Acta Mechanica, 1985—; assoc. editor Journal of Engineering Materials and Technology; transl. ASME, 1984—; editorial bd. Internat. Jour. of Plasticity, 1984—. NSF grantee, 1978, 80, 83, 86; U.S. Dept. Enrgy grantee, 1980. Mem. Am. Acad. Mechanics, ASME, AIME, Soc. Rheology, Sigma Xi. Subspecialties: Solid mechanics; Mechanics of Materials. Current work: Micromechanics of plastic deformation of metals, creep at elevated temperature, mechanics of composite materials. Home: 116 Berkley Ave Belle Mead NJ 08502 Office: Coll Engring Rutgers U Piscataway NJ 08855

WENGER, VICKI, interior designer; b. Indpls., Aug. 30, 1928. Ed. U. Nebr., Internat. Inst. Interior Design, Parsons in Paris. Pres., Vicki Wenger Interiors, Bethesda, Md., 1963-71, Washington, 1982—, pres. Beautiful Spaces Inc., Washington, 1982—; chief designer Creative Design, Capitol Heights, Md., 1969-84; lectr. Nat. Assn. Home Builders, 1983—; mem. programs com. D.C. Assn. Home Builders, 1983—. Author-host: (patented TV interior design show) Beautiful Spaces 1984. Designer Gourmet Gala, March of Dimes, Washington, 1986-88; designer decorator showcase Nat. Symphony Orch., Washington, 1983-88, Am. Cancer Soc., Washington, 1983. Mem. Am. Soc. Interior Designers (profl. mem. 1973—; mem. nat. bd. 1973-75, nat. examining com. 1977-78, pres. Md. chpt. 1976, mem. president's barrier free com. 1980), Nat. Trust Hist. Preservation, Smithsonian Instn. (sponsor), Friends of Corcoran Mus. (sponsor), Friends of Kennedy Ctr., Friends of Vieilles Maisons Françaises. Democrat. Presbyterian. Club: Pisces (Washington). Office: Vicki Wenger Interiors 3227 N St NW Suite 303 Washington DC 20007

WENGERD, SHERMAN ALEXANDER, geologist, educator; b. Millersburg, Ohio, Feb. 17, 1915; s. Allen Stephen and Elizabeth (Miller) W.; m. Florence Margaret Mather, June 12, 1940; children: Anne Marie Wengerd Riffey, Timothy Mather, Diana Elizabeth Wengerd Roach, Stephanie Katherine Wengerd Allen. AB, Coll. Wooster, 1936; MA, Harvard U., 1938, PhD, 1947. Registered profl. engr., N.Mex.; registered geologist, Calif.; lic. pilot, FAA. Geophysicist, Shell Oil Co., 1937; mining geologist, Ramshorn, Idaho, 1938; Austin teaching fellow Harvard U., 1938-40; research petroleum geologist Shell, Mid-continent, 1940-42, 45-47; prof. geology U. N.Mex., 1947-76; ret., 1976; disting. prof. petroleum geology, 1982; research geologist, 1947—, Petroleum Ind., 1976—; past co-owner Pub. Lands Exploration, Inc., Corona and Capitan Oil Cos.; ltd. ptnr. Rio Petro Oil Co., Dallas. Served to lt. comdr. USNR, 1942-45; capt. Res., ret. Recipient Disting. Alumnus citation Coll. Wooster, 1979. Author chpts. in textbooks and encys., articles in geol. bulls., newsletters. Fellow Geol. Soc. Am., Explorers Club of N.Y.; mem. Four Corners Geol. Soc. (hon. life mem., pres. 1953), N.Mex. Geol. Soc. (hon. life mem.), Am. Assn. Petroleum Geologists (nat. editor 1957-59, pres. 1971-72, chmn. adv. council 1972-73, Presdl. award 1948, hon. life mem.), Am. Petroleum Inst. (acad. mem., exploration com. 1970-72), Am. Inst. Profl. Geologists (state sect. pres. 1970, nat. editor 1965-66), Am. Soc. Photogrammetry, Marine Tech. Soc. (charter mem.), Internat. Assn. Sedimentology, Soc. Econ. Paleontologists and Mineralogists (dir. found. 1982-86), Aircraft Owners and Pilots Assn., Pilots Internat. Assn., OX5 Aviation Pioneers (life), Thomas L. Popejoy Soc., Sigma Xi, Sigma Gamma Epsilon, Phi Kappa Phi. Home: 1040 Stanford Dr NE Albuquerque NM 87106

WENIG, LYNNE GAYE, management consultant; b. N.Y.C., June 29, 1937; arrived in Australia, 1958, naturalized, 1970; divorced; children: Janette Lea, Leonard Mark. AAS, N.Y. Tech. Coll., 1957; tchr. tng., Melbourne Secondary Tchrs. Coll., Australia, 1964; student in mgmt., Melbourne U., 1978; BA, LaTrobe U., Melbourne, 1982. Tchr. Richmond Girls High Sch., Melbourne, 1963-67; lectr. Caulfield Inst. Tech., Melbourne, 1968-71, sr. lectr., 1972-80; head mgmt. dept. Chisholm Inst. Tech., Melbourne, 1981-83; pub. Women Australia mag., Melbourne, 1983-84; mng. dir. Lynne Wenig & Assocs., Melbourne, 1984—; pub. Exec. Woman's Report, Melbourne, 1987—; assoc. Research & Planning Inc., Cambridge, Mass., 1980—. Author: The Modern Typist's Handbook, 1972, English for Office Skills, 1981, Pitman Handbook for Typing and Keyboarding, 1988; contbr. articles to profl. jours. V.p. Victoria Inst. Colls. Staff Assn., Melbourne, 1977-79, 81-83, Fedn. Coll. Academics, Melbourne, 1978-79; mem. standing com. on tng. for advanced tech. Australian Nat. Tng. Council, 1983-86; dep. chair council Canberra (Australia) Coll. Advanced Edn., 1986—. Victoria Inst. Colls. fellowship, 1971; Ian Potter Found. fellow, Melbourne, 1975; Mmgt. scholar Commonwealth Devel. Bank, Melbourne, 1978; Myer Found. scholar, Melbourne, 1980. Mem. Australian Inst. Mgmt., Women in Mgmt. (pres. 1983), Australian Inst. Tng. and Devel., Am. Soc. for Tng. and Devel., Internat. Inst. Systems Profls., Melbourne U. Bus. Schs. Assn., Australian Nat. Tng. Council (mem. advanced tech. standing com.). Office: Lynne Wenig & Assocs, 118 Queen St, 3000 Melbourne, Victoria Australia

WENNERHOLM, HUGO AXEL CHRISTIAN, trade association administrator; b. Stockholm, Apr. 18, 1929; s. H. Axel L. and Signy (Adamsen) W.; m. Eva Axelson; children: Charlotte, Anna, Hedvig. Degree in law, Stockholm U., 1955. Sec. Stockholm Retail Trade Fedn., 1957-60, mng. dir., 1961-65; mng. dir. SW Paint Trade Fedn., Stockholm, 1966—. Contbr. articles to profl. jours. Mem. Parliament, 1982-85; dep. mayor Stockholm, 1983—. Served to capt. Swedish mil. Conservative. Lutheran. Lodge: Rotary (past pres. Stockholm). Home: Lidov 25, 11525 Stockholm Sweden

WENSSING, HORST FRIEDRICH, civil engineer; b. Iserlohn, W. Ger., Feb. 15, 1930; s. Josef and Milly (Schmidt) W.; diplom engr. Tech. U. Aachen, 1956; m. Waltraud Klumpp, Oct. 13, 1962; children—Birgitta, Horst. Chief supt. constrn., mgr. tech. dept. Walter Hohler Constrn., Dortmund, 1956-63; joint venture mgr., chief supt. Niko Lafrentz/Walter Latuske/Walter Hohler, Schwerte, 1961-62; cons. civil engr., Iserlohn, 1964—; gen. mgr. IGI-Ingenieur-Cons GmbH, Iserlohn, 1977-81; owner, operator Photogrammetric Survey Consulting Co., Iserlohn, 1982—. Mem. Assn. Indsl. Engrs., Architects and Engrs. Assn., Alliance German Engrs. Clubs: Lions (pres. 1982-83). Contbr. articles to profl. jours. Home: 46 Tiefendorf, 5800 Hagen Federal Republic of Germany Office: 48/48a Langestrasse, 5860 Iserlohn Federal Republic of Germany

WENTWORTH, THEODORE SUMNER, lawyer; b. Bklyn., July 18, 1938; s. Theodore Sumner and Alice Ruth (Wortmann) W.; AA, Am. River Coll., 1958; JD, U. Calif., Hastings Coll. Law, 1962; m. Sharon Linelle Arkush, 1965 (dec. 1987); children—Christina Linn, Kathryn Allison. Admitted to Calif. bar, 1963; assoc. Adams, Hunt & Martin, Santa Ana, Calif., 1963-66; partner Hunt, Liljestrom & Wentworth, Santa Ana, 1967-77; pres. Solabs Corp.; chmn. bd., exec. v.p. Plant Warehouse, Inc., Hawaii, 1974-82; prin. Law Offices of Theodore S. Wentworth, specializing in personal injury, product liability and profl. malpractice litigation, Irvine, Calif. Pres., bd. dirs. Santa Ana-Tustin Community Chest, 1972; v.p., trustee South Orange County United Way, 1973-75; pres. Orange County Fedn. Funds, 1972-73; bd. dirs. Orange County Mental Health Assn. Diplomate Nat. Bd. Trial Advocacy. Mem. State Bar Calif., ABA, Orange County Bar Assn. (dir. 1972-76), Am. Trial Lawyers Assn. (judge pro tem superior ct. attys. panel), Calif. Trial Lawyers Assn. (bd. govs. 1968-70), Orange County Trial Lawyers Assn. (pres. 1967-68), Am. Bd. Trial Advocates, Lawyer-Pilots Bar Assn., Am. Bd. Trial Advs., Aircraft Owners and Pilots Assn. Clubs: Bahia Corinthian Yacht, Balboa Bay (Newport Beach, Calif.); Lincoln (Orange County); Corsair Yacht (Catalina, Calif.). Research in vedic prins., natural law, metaphysics. Office: 2112 Business Center Dr Suite 220 Irvine CA 92715

WENTZ, DENNIS KEITH, physician, educator; b. Napoleon, N.D., Sept. 1, 1935; s. Edwin J. and Bertha Louise (Kaz) W.; B.A., North Central Coll., Naperville, Ill., 1957; M.D., U. Chgo., 1961; grad. exec. program health systems mgmt., Harvard U., 1975; m. Anne Colston, Sept. 28, 1968. Intern, U. Md. Hosp., 1961-62, resident, 1962-64, 66-67; fellow in gastroenterology Scott and White Clinic, Temple, Tex., 1964-66; asst. dean U. Md. Med. Sch., 1971-77; assoc. dir. clin. affairs U. Md. Hosp., 1974-77; asst. vice chancellor acad. affairs U. Tenn. Center Health Scis., Memphis, 1977-80; dir. med. services, assoc. dean clin. affairs Vanderbilt U. Sch. Medicine and Hosp., 1980-84, assoc. dean for grad. and continuing med. edn., 1984-88, asst. prof. medicine, 1971—, assoc. prof. med. adminstrn., 1980—; bd. dirs. div. continuing med. edn. AMA, Chgo., 1988—. Bd. dirs., treas. Memphis Orch. Soc.; bd. dirs. Salvation Army, Nashville, Nashville Opera Assn. Served to lt. comdr. M.C., USNR, 1977-79. Mem. AMA, Am. Coll. Physician Execs., Am. Acad. Med. Dirs., Am. Assn. Med. Systems and Informatics, Am. Soc. Cytology, Am. Soc. Internal Medicine, Meeting Planners, Internat. Profl. Conv. Mgmt. Assn., Soc. Med. Coll. Dirs. of Continuing Edn. (pres. 1987-88), So. Med. Assn., Tenn. Med. Assn., Nashville Acad. Medicine. Episcopalian. Clubs: Maryland (Balt.); Gibson Island (Md.). Author articles in field. Home: 4390 Chickering Ln Nashville TN 37215 Office: AMA 535 N Dearborn Chicago IL 60610

WENZ, MICHAEL FRANK, JR., nuclear engineer; b. Arlington, Va., Dec. 9, 1953; Michael Frank and Theo (Lambert) W. B.S. in Nuclear Engring., U. Va., 1975, B.S. in Applied Math., 1975, M.E. in Nuclear Engring., 1977. Nuclear engr. Naval Reactors, Naval Sea Systems Command, Washington, 1977-84; asst. to Naval Reactors rep. Norfolk Naval Shipyard, Nuclear Propulsion Directorate, Naval Sea Systems Command, 1984-87 nuclear engr. Naval Reactors, 1987—. Mem. Am. Nuclear Soc., Tau Beta Pi. Home: 5601 Seminary Rd Apt 2407 Falls Church VA 22041 Office: Naval Reactors Naval Sea Systems Command Code 08 Washington DC 20362

WEOBLEY, CHRISTOPHER PHILIP, computer company executive; b. Gillingham, Kent, Eng., Jan. 13, 1953; s. Philip Henry and Margarita Jean (Bently) W.; m. Julie Anne Collins, June 1, 1974; 1 child, Sarah Victoria. Matriculated secondary sch., Gillingham. Test technician Marconi Avionics, Rochester, Eng., 1973-79, computer engr. Data Gen. Ltd., London, 1979-83; founder, chief exec. officer, sales mgr. S.I.M. Ltd., London, 1983—. Mem. Conservative Party. Home: 22 Hamelin Rd, Gillingham Kent ME7 3ER, England Office: SIM Ltd, Lanterns Ct, Unit A-2, Mill Harbour London E14, England

WEPSTER, ALEXANDRA SPOOR, small business owner; b. Amsterdam, Dec. 19, 1924; d. Dio J.P. Huysmans and Maria Catharina (Buys) Spoor; m. Arnout Wepster, Feb. 21, 1949; children: Corine, Alexander, Steven. BA, Mt. Holyoke Coll., 1946; summer study, NYU, 1944; student, U. Mich., 1945, U. Amsterdam, The Netherlands, 1947-49. Owner, dir. Alexandra Antiquités, Zevenhuizen, The Netherlands, 1981—; lectr. in field. Contbr. articles to profl. jours. Mem. Verenigde Nederlandse Antiquairs. Club: Am.-Netherlands Club (sec., membership chair, philanthropic chair, and other positions since 1955), Rotterdam.

WERBELOW, LAWRENCE GLEN, chemistry educator, researcher; b. Ross, Calif., Dec. 19, 1948; s. Arnold Glen and Helen Corrine (Freeburg) W.; m. Catherine Elizabeth Fouques, Dec. 28, 1979; children: Prisca, Guilhem, Neil. B.Sc., Humboldt State U., 1970; Ph.D., U. B.C., 1974; D.Sc., U. Provence, Marseille, France, 1979. Research assoc. U. Utah, Salt Lake City, 1974-78; vis. prof. U. Provence, Marseille, 1978-79, Mont. State U., Bozeman, 1979-80; prof. chemistry N.Mex. Inst. Mining and Tech., Socorro, 1980—; vis. scientist Los Alamos Nat. Lab., 1980—; vis. prof. U. Paris, 1987, U. Lausanne, 1989 . Contbr. chpts. to books, articles to profl. jours. Nat. Research Council Can. fellow, 1974; Am. Chem. Soc. grantee, 1980; NSF grantee, 1980; NATO grantee, 1982; Research Corp. grantee, 1983; Dept. Energy grantee, 1985, CNRS grantee, 1980-87. Mem. Internat. Soc. Magnetic Resonance. Subspecialties: Nuclear magnetic resonance (chemistry); Nuclear magnetic resonance (biotechnology). Current work: Time-dependent aspects of nuclear paramagnetism; creation and dissipation of transient multipolar spin order; quantum theory angular momentum. Home: 907 Michigan St Socorro NM 87801 Office: N Mex Inst Mining and Tech Dept Chemistry Socorro NM 87801

WERDELIN, HANS, company executive; b. Copenhagen, Oct. 26, 1938. MSME, Royal Tech. U., Denmark, 1963. Pres. Sophus Berendsen A/S, Copenhagen, 1977—; chmn. bd. dirs. Det Danske Traelastkompagni, Copenhagen, 1984—, Riso Natio nat. Lab., Roshilde, Denmark; bd. dirs. Nordisk Insulin, Copenhagen, Magasin du Nord, Th Wellel and Vett, Copenhagen. Home: Richelieus Alle 4, 2900 Hellerup Denmark Office: Sophus Berendsen A/S, Klausdalsbrovej 1, 2860 Soborg Denmark

WERNER, EWALD AUGUST, metal physicist; b. Leoben, Styria, Austria, Mar. 17, 1956; s. Ewald August and Erna (Genser) W.; m. Anita Steiner, Sept. 22, 1984; children: Roman Johann, Robert Ewald. Diploma in engring., Montan U., Leoben, 1980; PhD, Montan U., 1984. Researcher Inst. of Solid State Physics Austrian Acad. Scis., Leoben, 1979-84; postdoctoral fellow Swiss Fed. Inst. Tech., Zurich, Switzerland, 1984-86; asst. physicist Inst. Metal Physics U. Montan, 1986—; tchr. Inst. Math. Montan U., 1977-84, 86—. Contbr. articles to profl. jours. Served to 2d lt. inf. Austrian Army, 1974-75. Mem. Austrian Math. Soc. Roman Catholic. Club: Austrian Alpine (Trofaiach). Office: Montan Univ, Franz Josef Strasse 18, A8700 Leoben Austria

WERNER, HELMUT, business executive; b. Cologne, Germany, Sept. 2, 1936; m. Erika Werner; children—Jens, Britta. Abitur Beethoven-gymnasium, 1956; diploma U. Cologne, 1961. With Englebert & Co., GmbH, Aachen, Fed. Republic Germany, 1961-67, sales mgr., 1969-70; gen. product mgr. Uniroyal Europe, Liege, Belgium, 1970-78, mng. dir., 1978-79; exec. bd. Continental AG, Hannover, Fed. Republic Germany, 1979-81, chmn., 1982—; exec. bd. Daimler Benz AG, Stuttgart. Office: Continental AG, Konigsworther Platz 1, D3000 Hanover 1, Federal Republic of Germany

WERNER, JONATHAN MARK, lawyer; b. San Pedro Sula, Honduras, Nov. 10, 1953; s. Joseph Raymond and Joan Marie (Kearney) W.; m. Norma Isabel Kattán, May 10, 1986; 1 child, Jonathan Mark Jr. JD, Nat. Aut. U., Honduras, 1978; LLM, Tulane U., Honduras, 1980; diplomate, Hague Internat. Acad. Law, Honduras, 1980; postgrad., La. State U., Honduras, 1979. Bar: Honduras 1978. Ptnr. Werner Law Firm, San Pedro Sula, 1978-87; dir. Cia. de Creditos, S.A./div. Bank of Boston, San Pedro Sula, 1975—; sec., dir. MARCASA, Tegucigalpa, Honduras, 1983—; counsel Banco La Capitalizadora Hondurena, S.A., San Pedro Sula, Honduras, 1982—, Textiles de Honduras, S.A., San Pedro Sula, Honduras, 1981—. Bd. dirs. Fundació n para la Investigació n y Desarrollo Empresarial, 1985-86; v.p. Fundació n Instituto Sunpedrano de Educació n Especial; coordinator for Honduras, Caribbean Basin Project, C. of C. of New Orleans, 1984-85. Mem. Inter Am. Bar Assn., Am. Fgn. Law Assn., Internat. Bar Assn., Am. Soc. Notaries, Societas Petitorum Magistrorum, Honduran Am. C. of C. (pres. 1984, bd. dirs. 1983—), Assn. Am. C. of C. of Latin Am. (bd. dirs.), Fundacion Instituto Sampedrano de Educació n Especial (v.p., founding mem.), Phi Delta Phi. Roman Catholic. Clubs: Casino Country (San Pedro Sula); Bankers (Miami, Fla.). Home: 21 Ave S O #88 Col Trejo, San Pedro Sula Honduras Office: Bufete Werner, PO Box 500, San Pedro Sula Honduras

WERNER, OTMAR, philologist, educator; b. Bamberg, Fed. Republic Germany, Sept. 9, 1932; s. Valentin and Margarete (Magerlein) W.; m. Waldtraut Glinka, May 13, 1967; 1 child, Peter Jörg. State exam, U. Erlangen, 1957, DPhil, 1959. Univ. asst. U. Erlangen (Fed. Republic Germany), 1960-68; prof. German philology U. Tübingen (Fed. Republic Germany), 1968-75; prof. comparative Germanic philology and Scandinavian U. Freiburg i. Br. (Fed. Republic Germany), 1975—. Author, translator, editor books and articles, 1961—. Home: Wittentalstrasse 12, D7801 Stegen Federal Republic of Germany Office: U Freiburg i Br, Werthmannplatz 3, D7800 Freiburg Federal Republic of Germany

WERNIK, URI, clinical psychologist; b. Dresden, Fed. Republic of Germany, Apr. 15, 1945; s. Reuben and Giza (Rosenblum) W.; m. Irene Groffsky; children: Haran, Edan, Sahar. BA, Hebrew U., Jerusalem, 1968, MA cum laude, 1972; D in Psychology, U. Ill., 1979. Dir. rehab. program Eitanim Psychiat. Hosp., Jerusalem, 1972-76, dir. unit for autistic adolescents,, 1979-81; dir. sex therapy clinic, Misgav Ladach Hosp., Jerusalem, 1979—; clin. psychologist Bezalel Acad. Art and Design, Jerusalem, 1979—. Author: Open Minded Sex, 1987; contbr. articles to profl. jours. Served to maj. Res. forces of Israel Def. Forces, 1968—. Fellow Israeli Psychol. Assn., Israeli Assn. Clin. Hypnosis, Israel Soc. Sex Therapy; mem. Am. Psychol. Assn. Home: 26 Rachel Imenu, Jerusalem 93228, Israel

WERTHEN, HANS LENNART OSCAR, business executive; b. Ludvika, June 15, 1919; s. Oscar F. and Mabel (Evans) W.; m. Britta Ekstrom, 1950; 3 children. Ed. Falu Laroverk, Falun, Royal Inst. Tech., Stockholm. Asst. prof. Royal Inst. Tech., Stockholm, 1942-46, chief TV research, 1947-51; chief TV Research Lab., AGA AB, 1952-56; v.p. (Eng.) Norrkopings Elektrotekniska Fabrikers AB (NEFA) (Phillips), 1956-59; v.p. L.M. Ericsson Telephone Co., Stockholm, 1960, sr. v.p., 1963-67, chmn., 1981—; pres. AB Electrolux, 1967-74; group exec. chmn., 1974-81, chmn., 1981—; chmn. Granges AB, 1977—; bd. dirs. Fedn. Swedish Industries, 1980—. Decorated knight comdr. Royal Oder Vasa (Sweden); Order White Rose (Finland); recipient John Ericson medal, 1982. Avocations: history; music; mountain climbing. Address: AB Electrolux, 105 45 Stockholm Sweden other: LM Ericson Telephone Co, S-12625 Stockholm Sweden

WERTHMUELLER, ERNST, manufacturing executive; b. Aarau, Switzerland, Aug. 5, 1949; s. Albert and Marie (Paulin) W.; m. Lilo Schenker, Aug. 1, 1970; children: Tamara Deborah, Nanda Surangi Lakmini. BS in Engring., HTL Zurich, 1974; Degree in Mktg., Univ., 1979; Program for Exec. Devel., Harvard U. and Lausanne U., Switzerland, 1987. Devel. engr. Wez AG, Oberenfelden, Switzerland, 1968-73; product devel. Symalit Co. Ltd., Lenzburg, Switzerland, 1974-78, sales rep. Europe, 1978-79; sales rep. worldwide Symalit Co., Ltd., Lenzburg, Switzerland, 1979-80; sales mgr. Symalit Co., Ltd., Leneburg, Switzerland, 1980-87, bus. mgr. overseas, 1987—; confidential clk. Symalit Co., Ltd., 1980—; lectr. in field. Author: Managing Corrosion with Plastics, 1983. Mayor Mcpl. Council, Holziken, Switzerland, 1975. Served with Swiss Army, 1968. Ref. Home: Bergstrasse 181, 5043 Holziken Switzerland Office: Symalit Co Ltd, Lenzhard, 5600 Lenzburg Switzerland

WESBERRY, JAMES PICKETT, clergyman; b. Bishopville, S.C., Apr. 16, 1906; s. William McLeod and Lillian Ione (Galloway) W.; m. Ruby Lee Perry, Sept. 5, 1929 (dec. Dec. 1941); 1 child, James Pickett; m. Mary Sue Latimer, June 1, 1943 (dec. Sept. 7, 1982); m. Alice Margaret Spratlin, Oct. 15, 1983. A.B., Mercer U., 1929, M.A., 1930, D.D., 1957; B.D., Newton Theol. Inst., 1931; M. Sacred Theology, Andover Newton Theol. Inst., 1934; postgrad., Harvard U., 1931, Union Theol. Sem., N.Y.C., summers 1935, 65, Yale U., 1946, So. Bapt. Theol. Sem., 1957, Princeton U., 1958, Mansfield Coll., Oxford U., 1979; LL.D., Atlanta Law Sch., 1946; L.H.D., LaGrange Coll., 1962; Litt. D., Bolen-Draughan Coll., 1967. Ordained to ministry Bapt. Ch., 1926; pastor Soperton, Ga., 1928-30, Medford, Mass., 1930-31, Kingstree, S.C., 1931-33, Bamberg, S.C., 1933-44; pastor Morningside Bapt. Ch., Atlanta, 1944-75; pastor emeritus Morningside Bapt. Ch., 1975—; engaged in evangelism, counseling, editing, publishing and chaplaincies 1975—; mem. exec. com. So. Bapt. Conv., 1959-65, 74-86, mem. chaplains commn., 1973-79, chmn. adminstrv. com., 1974-79; pres. Ga. Bapt. Conv., 1956-57, 57-58, rec. sec., 1970—; prof. Mercer U. extension, Atlanta, 1944-53; pres. Highview Nursing Home, Atlanta, 1947-60, chaplain, 1975—; pres. Nat. Youth Courtesy Found., 1971—; staff corr. Christian Century, 1951-58; editor column The People's Pulpit; columnist Atlanta Times, 1964-65; chaplain Yaarab Temple, 20 yrs.; chaplain Grand Lodge of Ga. Author: Prayers in Congress, 1949, Every Citizen Has A Right to Know, 1954, Baptists in South Carolina Before the War Between the States, 1966, Rainbow Over Russia, 1962, Meditations for Happy Christians, 1973, Evangelistic Sermons, 1974, When Hell Trembles, 1974, The Morningside Man (Wesberry's biography by James C. Bryant), 1975, Bread in a Barren Land, 1982, The Lord's Day, 1986; editor: Sunday Mag., 1975—; editor: Basharet, 1976-77; asst. editor, 1977—, editor emeritus, 1978—. Chmn. Ga. Lit. Commn., 1953-74; acting chaplain U.S. Ho. Reps., July-Aug., 1949; mem. Gov.'s Citizens Penal Reform Commn., 1968, Fulton County Draft Bd., 1968-71; bd. dirs. Atlanta Fund Rev. Bd., 1964-70, Grady Met. Girls Club, 1969-72, hon. bd. dirs., Atlanta Union Mission, 1972—, Dogwood Assn. Festival, 1970-71; trustee Mercer U., 1944-49, 54-57, 72-74, mem. pres.'s council, 1974-88, also mem. adv. com. Sch. Pharmacy; trustee Atlanta Bapt. Coll., 1964-72, Truett McConnell Coll., Cleveland, Ga., 1960-65; mem. pres.'s council Tift Coll., Forsyth, Ga., 1976—; bd. mgrs. Lord's Day Alliance U.S., 1971—, exec. dir., 1975—. Elected Man of the South Dixie Bus. mag., 1972; named to South's Hall of Fame, 1972. Mem. Atlanta Area Mil. Chaplains Assn. (hon.), SAR (state chaplain 1981), Royal Order Scotland. Clubs: Atlanta Harvard, Atlanta Athletic, Atlanta Amateur Movie, Half Century of Mercer U. (pres.). Lodges: Kiwanis, Masons (Shriner), Lions. Home: 1715 Merton Rd NE Atlanta GA 30306 Office: Suite 107 Baptist Center 2930 Flowers Rd S Atlanta GA 30341

WESENBERG, JOHN HERMAN, association executive; b. Davenport, Iowa, Jan. 16, 1927; s. Herman B. and Nell (Watterson) W.; m. Alice Jane McMahill, Sept. 10, 1949; children: Anne, John, Sue, James. Student, Iowa State U., 1944-45, 47, Amherst Coll., 1946; B.A., U. Iowa, 1951, M.A., 1952; postgrad., Northwestern U., 1952-55, Mich. State U., 1956-67. Research asso. Bur. Bus. and Econ. Research, U. Iowa, 1949-52; asst. mgr. Danville (Ill.) C. of C., 1952-54; exec. v.p. Belleville (Ill.) C. of C., 1954-57; sec. Retail Mchts. and Central Dist. Bur., Des Moines, 1957-62; exec. v.p. Greater Des Moines C. of C., 1963-80; sec. Greater Des Moines Com., 1963-80; sr. exec.

v.p. Greater Albuquerque C. of C., 1980-82, Met. Tulsa C. of C., 1982—; trustee Employee Stock Ownership Plan, Internat. Bank, Washington, 1977-80, 83-84; lectr. Inst. Orgn. Mgmt., Mich. State U., 1959-67, 69-70, U. Colo., 1970, 75, 81, 85, 87, Syracuse U., 1971, U. Santa Clara, Calif., 1972, 74-75; lectr. Tex. Christian U., 1971, 73, U. Del., 1973-76, 80, U. Ga., 1973, 86, U. Notre Dame, 1975, 81, So. Meth. U., 1975-76, 81, 84, 85, 87, Mills Coll., 1976, San Jose Coll., 1981, U. Okla., 1984, 86, 88. Co-chmn. Des Moines Mail Users Council, 1963-68; sec.-treas. Des Moines Housing Corp., Baseball, Inc., 1963-80; sec. Des Moines Devel. Corp., Des Moines Industries, Inc., 1963-80, Community Improvement, Inc., 1968-80, Greater Des Moines Community Found., 1968-80; treas. Greater Des Moines Shippers Assn., 1971-80; trustee Fringe Benefits, Inc., Washington, 1969-82; mem. exec. com. Iowa Council on Econ. Edn., 1978-80; mem. planning com. Grand View Coll., 1976-80; mem. adv. council, region VIII SBA, 1973-80; Mem. bd. regents Inst. Orgn. Mgmt., Mich. State U., 1962-67, chmn., 1965-66; bd. regents U. Colo., 1977-80, So. Meth. U., 1980-81; vice chmn. nat. bd. regents Inst. for Orgn. Mgmt., 1978-79, chmn., 1979-80; trustee U. Albuquerque, 1980-82. Served with USAAF, 1944-46. Mem. Am. C. of C. Execs. (dir. 1965-73, 84—, pres. 1971-72), C. of C. U.S. (dir. 1979-81), Iowa C. of C. Execs. (dir. 1960-66, pres. 1964), Okla. C. of C. Execs. (dir. 1983-86, pres. 1986), Am. Retail Execs. Assn. (dir. 1961-63), Ill. Mfrs. Assn. (exec. com. So. div. 1955-57), St. Louis Indsl. Council (v.p. 1957), Okla. C. of C. and Industry (mem. exec. com., bd. dirs. 1986) Industries for Tulsa (sec. 1986—), Am. Arbitration Assn., Nat. Assn. Housing and Redevel. Ofcls., Internat. Downtown Exec. Assn., Iowa Bd. Internat. Edn., Mountain States Assn. (v.p. 1980-81), Beta Theta Pi (gen. sec. 1974-80, trustee 1974-80). Club: Des Moines. Home: 6718 E 65th Pl Tulsa OK 74133 Office: Met Tulsa C of C 616 S Boston Tulsa OK 74119

WESKER, ARNOLD, playwright, director; b. Stepney, London, May 24, 1932; s. Joseph and Leah Perlmutter) W.; m. Doreen Cecile Bicker, 1958; 4 children. Student pub. schs., London. Worked as furniture maker's apprentice, carpenter's mate, booksellers asst. RAF, 1950-52; plumber's mate, farm labourer, seed sorter, kitchen porter and pastry cook; chmn. Brit. Ctr. of Internat. Theatre Inst., 1978-82; pres. Internat. Com. of Playwrights, 1979-83. Recipient bursary Arts Council, 1959, Encyclopedia Britinica award, 1959, 61, Goldie award, 1987, Spectator and Critics Gold medal Madrid, 1961, 73. Dir. Centre Forty Two, 1961-70; author, dir. (plays): The Four Seasons, Cuba, 1968, The Friends, Stadsteatern, Stockholm, 1970, London, 1970, The Old Ones, Munich, Their Very Own and Golden City, Aarhus, 1974, Love Letters on Blue Paper, Nat. Theatre, London, 1978, Oslo, 1980, Annie Wobbler, Birmingham, 1983, London, 1984; dir. The Entertainer (Osborne), Theatre Clwyd, 1983, Yardsale RSC Actor's Festival, 1985, Whatever Happened to Betty Lemon and Yardsale, London, 1987; author plays: The Kitchen, 1957, The Wesker Trilogy—Chicken Soup with Barley, 1958, Roots, 1959, I'm Talking About Jerusalem, 1960, Chips with Everything, 1962; (TV) Menace, 1963, Their Very Own and Golden City (Marzotto prize), 1964, The Four Seasons, 1965, The Friends, 1970, The Old Ones, 1972, The Journalists, 1972, The Wedding Feast, 1974, Shylock, 1975, Love Letters on Blue Paper, 1976, Caritas, 1981, Sullied Hand (one act), 1981; (collected essays and lectures): Fear of Fragmentation, Distinctions, 1985, Words as Definitions of Experience, Journey into Journalism, 1977; (stories) Six Sundays in January, Love Letters on Blue Paper, 1974, Say Goodbye You May Never See Them Again, 1974, Said the Old Man To the Young Man, 1978; Fatlips, children's book, 1978, The Journalists, triptych, 1979, Collected Plays and Stories, 5 vols., 1979; (cycle of one woman plays) Annie Wobbler, 1983, Four Portraits , 1984, Yardsale, 1985, Whatever Happened to Betty Lemon, 1986, The Mistress, 1988; (filmscript) Lady O, 1983; (TV play) Breakfast 1983; Thieves in the Night, 4 90-minute plays for TV, 1985; When God wanted a Son, 1986, Badenheim 1939 (from a novel by Aharon Appelfeld), 1987, Lady Othello (from original film script), 1987; (one act plays for young people) Little Old Lady and Shoeshine. Address: 37 Ashley Rd, London N19 3AG, England

WESLAGER, CLINTON ALFRED, historian, writer; b. Pitts., Apr. 30, 1909; s. Fred H. and Alice (Lowe) W.; m. Ruth G. Hurst, June 9, 1934; children: Ruth Ann (Mrs. George G. Tatnall), Clinton Alfred, Thomas Hurst. B.A., U. Pitts., 1933; L.H.D. (hon.), Widener U., 1986. Vis. prof. Am. history Wesley Coll., 1969, U. Del., 1971-73; Vis. prof. Am. history Brandywine Coll., 1970-82, prof. emeritus, 1983—; pres. Archeol. Soc. Del., 1942-48, Eastern States Archeol. Fedn., 1954-58. Author: Delaware's Forgotten Folk, 1943, Delaware's Buried Past, 1944, Delaware's Forgotten River, 1947, The Nanticoke Indians, 1948, Brandywine Springs, 1949, Indian Place-Names in Delaware, 1950, Red Men on the Brandywine, 1953, Richardsons of Delaware, 1957, Dutch Explorers, Traders and Settlers, 1961, Garrett Snuff Fortune, 1965, English on the Delaware, 1967, Log Cabin in America, 1969, The Delaware Indians, A History, 1972, Magic Medicines of the Indians, 1973, The Stamp Act Congress, 1976, The Delaware Indian Westward Migration, 1978, The Delawares, A Critical Bibliography, 1978, The Nanticoke Indians, Past and Present, 1983, Swedes and Dutch at New Castle, 1987, New Sweden on the Delaware, 1988; editor: Historic Red Clay Valley, Inc, 1961-69. Pres. trustees Richardson Park Sch., 1953-57. Recipient award of merit Am. Assn. State and Local History, 1965, 68, Christian Lindback award for excellence in teaching, 1977, Archibald Crozier award Archeol. Soc. Del., 1978, Trustees award Hist. Soc. Del., 1987, Medal of Distinction U. Del., 1988. Fellow Archeol. Soc. N.J., Holland Soc. N.Y.; mem. AAUP, Hist. Soc. Pa., Soc. Pa. Archaeology, Sigma Delta Chi. Lodge: Masons. Home: Old Public Rd Hockessin DE 19707

WESNES, KEITH ANDREW, drug research facility administrator; b. London, Sept. 12, 1950; s. Andreas Ludwig and Marjorie Myrtle (Hallows) W.; 1 child, Anna Letitia Marjorie. BS in Exptl. Psycholgy with first class honors, Reading (Eng.) U., 1973, PhD in Human Psychopharmacology, 1979. Research assoc. psychology dept. Reading (Eng.) U., 1976-79, research fellow psychology dept., 1979-83, sr. research fellow psychology dept., 1983-85, hon. research fellow psychology dept., 1985-86; hon. research fellow dept. pharmacology Guy's Hosp Med. Sch., London, 1985-86; dir. So. Clin. Psychopharmacology, Guildford, Surrey, 1983-86; mng. dir. Cognitive Drug Researoh Ltd., Reading, 1986—; cons. scientist Rothmans Internat., Basildon, Essex, Eng., 1985-86, also other pharm. cos. Contbr. numerous articles to profl. jours. Recipient numerous research grants. Fellow Royal Statis. Soc.; mem. Brit. Psychol. Soc., Brain Research Assn., Brit. Assn. Psychopharmacology, European Coll. Neuropsychopharmacology, Exptl. Psychology Soc. Clubs: Reading U. Rugby Football (pres. 1983—), Old Readingensians Rugby Football (v.p. 1986—). Office: Cognitive Drug Research Ltd, 13 The Grove, Reading, Berkshire RG1 4RB, England

WESOLOW, ADAM (SIGMUND ADAM WESOLOWSKI), thoracic-cardiovascular surgeon; b. Saugus, Mass., Feb. 6, 1923; s. Joseph and Adamina (Ploharska) W.; m. Wanda B. Kirbi, Oct. 7, 1945; children: Carl Adam, Paul David, Joan Marie, Adam John, Edward Alan. Student, Harvard U., 1941-44; M.D., Tufts U., 1948, M.S. in Surgery, 1951; Sc.D., Alliance Coll. Intern in surgery Johns Hopkins Hosp., 1948-49; Charleton research and tng. fellow Tufts U. Coll. Medicine, 1949-51; resident in surgery Ziskind Surg. Research Lab., New Eng. Med. Center, Boston, 1949-52, Kings County Hosp., N.Y.C., 1954-56; sr. registrar thoracic surgery Guy's Hosp., London, 1956-57; mem. faculty SUNY Downstate Med. Center, Bklyn., 1957—; clin. prof. surgery SUNY Downstate Med. Center, 1964—; chmn. dept. surgery Meadowbrook Hosp., E. Meadow, N.Y., 1964-66; dir. cardiovascular research lab. Mercy Hosp., Rockville Centre, N.Y., 1966-78; chief thoracic-cardiovascular surgery Mercy Hosp., 1974-78; chmn. dept. surgery Hosp. St. Raphael, New Haven, 1978-79; chief thoracic surgery VA Med. Ctr., Togus, Maine, 1980-88; founding pres. Nassau-Suffolk Regional Med. Program, 1968-70; mem. U.S. Nat. Com. Engring. in Medicine and Biology, 1967; chmn. com. on device legis. Aoc. Vascular Surgery-Internat. Cardiovascular Soc., 1966; founding chmn., sec. U.S. com. cardiovascular devices Internat. Standards Orgn., 1972, chmn. subcom 2 on cardiovascular implants U.S. tech. adv. group, 1973; chmn. Gordon Research Conf. Biomaterials, 1973; mem. disting. faculty Okla. Cardiovascular Inst., 1981. Author 2 books, chpts. in books, numerous articles in field. Served to capt. M.C. AUS, 1952-54. Recipient Medicus Man of Year award Polish-Am. Med. and Dental Assn., 1974, Clemson award First World Biomaterials Congress, Vienna, Austria, 1980, Jacob Markowitz award, Boston, 1988; research scholar ACS, 1956-59. Mem. Am. Coll. Surgery, Soc. Univ. Surgeons, Vascular Surgeons Soc., Internat. Cardiovascular Soc., Soc. Thoracic Surgery, Am. Assn., Thorasic Surgery, Royal Coll. Medicine, Royal Soc. Health, ASTM (chmn. subcom. cardiovascular materials and devices 1984—), Am. Soc. Artificial Internal Organs (a founder, pres. 1966), Assn. Advancement Med. Instrumentation (chmn. subcom. vascular prostheses 1969), Soc. Biomaterials (a founder, pres. 1976), Nat. Acupuncture Research Soc.; hon. mem. Cardiovascular Soc. Chile, Assn. Polish Surgeons, Polish-Am. Med. Soc. Home: 665 Lowell St Lynnfield MA 01940

WESOLOWSKI, ADOLPH JOHN, electrical engineer; b. Chelsea, Mass., June 4, 1916; s. Joseph A. and Adamina (Ploharska) W.; B.S., Harvard U., 1938; postgrad. Pa. State U., 1958-59; M.S. in Engring., Ariz. State U., 1964; m. Eleanor Louise Currier, June 3, 1939 (div. 1967); children—Mary Eleanor (Mrs. Harold A. Downing), Eleanor Louise (Mrs. John Tennyson), Joseph Walter, Allen Joseph, Frank James, Steven Michael; m. Gabrielle Bourgon, 1968. Turbine engr. Gen. Electric Co., Lynn, Mass., 1938-41; field engr., Boston, 1941-45, motor design engr., Lynn, 1945-50, chief aircraft generator engr., Lynn, also Erie, Pa., 1950-59; sr. design engr. AiResearch Mfg. Co., Phoenix, 1959-66; project engr. Garrett Mfg. Ltd., Rexdale, Ont., Can., 1966-68, Leland Airborne Products, Vandalia, Ohio, 1968-70; chief engr. Dyna Corp., Dayton, Ohio, 1970-75; pres. World Wide Artifacts Inc., 1975—; cons. engr. electro-mech. design. Registered profl. engr., Mass. Mem. IEEE (chmn. aerospace energy conversion com. 1962-64), Internat. Aerospace Elec. Conf. (chmn. 1964), Phoenix C. of C., Greater Erie C. of C., Ohio Archaeol. Soc., Central States Archaeol. Soc., Artifact Soc. (founder). Club: Point of Pines Yacht (past fin. sec.) (Revere, Mass.). Patentee in field. Home: 10355 E Cholla Scottsdale AZ 85260

WESOLOWSKI, ZBIGNIEW, acoustician, scientific facility administrator; b. Lubosz, Poland, Jan. 7, 1933; s. Lucjan and Prakseda (Leske) W.; m. Hanna Nochowicz, June 27, 1958; children: Pawel, Marta. MSc, Tech. U. Polish Acad. Scis., Warsaw, Poland, 1957, PhD, 1963, Habilitation, 1966. Researcher Tech. U., 1955-62; researcher Inst. Fundamental Tech. Research of Polish Acad. of Scis., 1975-79, dep. dir., head aeroacoustics dept., 1980—. Author: Dynamic Problems of Non-Linear Elasticity, 1972, Acoustics of Elastic Body, 1987. Mem. Gesellschaft für die Angewandte Matematik und Mechanik (governing bd. 1979-80). Home: Starej Basni 12/38, 01-853 Warsaw Poland Office: Polish Acad Scis, Swietokrzyska 21, 00-079 Warsaw Poland

WESSE, DAVID JOSEPH, university official; b. Chgo., May 5, 1951; s. Herman Theodore and Lorraine Joan (Holland) W.; m. Deborah Lynn Smith, Oct. 11, 1975; children: Jason David, Eric Joseph. AA, Thornton Coll., 1971; postgrad., Purdue U., 1971-72; BS, Ill. State U., 1973; MS, Loyola U., 1983. Adminstrv. mgr. Donnelley Directory Corp., Chgo., 1974-76, Loyola U., Chgo., 1976-79, Joint Commn. on Accreditation Hosps., Chgo., 1979-81; adminstrv. dir., asst. sec. Northwestern U., Evanston, Ill., 1981—. Pres., bd. dirs. Riverdale Library Dist., 1975, Riverdale Youth Commn., 1975. Recipient Service Recognition award Riverdale Library Dist., 1975. Mem. Adminstrv. Mgmt. Soc. (bd. dirs. Chgo. chpt. 1983-88, pres. 1986-87, mem. bd. regents 1986-88), Nat. Assn. Coll. and Univ. Bus. Officers (com. mem. 1986-87), Lambda Epsilon. Lutheran. Home: 207 S Washington St Wheaton IL 60187 Office: Northwestern U 633 Clark St Evanston IL 60208

WESSEL, PETER LORENTZ, telecommunication systems engineer; b. Oslo, Norway, Nov. 22, 1938; s. Jan and Liv (Christiansen) W.; m. Karen Marie Bjornstad, Jan. 15, 1977; children—Ruth Charlotte, Jan Christopher. S.B. in E.E., MIT, 1966; grad. Norwegian Sch. Mgmt., Oslo, 1973; diploma North European Mgmt. Inst., Oslo, 1974. Project mgr. Radionette A/S, Oslo, 1966-72; project mgr. Tanbergs Radiofabrikk A/S, Oslo, 1972-79; system engr. A/S Elektrisk Bur., Asker, Norway, 1979—; mem. council Electronics Research Lab., Norwegian Inst. Tech., Trondheim, 1966-72; chmn. bd. SEAS A/S, Moss, Norway, 1980. Contbr. articles in field to profl. jours.; patentee in field. Served with Norwegian Air Force, 1957-62. Mem. IEEE, Norwegian Soc. Chartered Engrs., Norwegian Mktg. Assn., Sigma Xi, Tau Beta Pi, Eta Kappa Nu. Conservative. Home: Johs Hartmannsvei 12, 1364 Hvalstad Norway Office: A/S Elektrisk Bur, Bergerveien 12, 1360 Nesbru Norway

WESSEL, WESSEL, executive search consulting company executive; b. Amsterdam, The Netherlands, Apr. 28, 1920. Account exec. various advt. agys., Amsterdam, 1947-57; mng. dir. J. Walter Thompson Co., Amsterdam, 1957-67; ptnr., sr. cons. Wessel, Coenen & Ptnrs., Amsterdam, 1967—. Mem. Assn. Cons. for Exec. Recruitment and Selection (bd. dirs. 1982-86, chmn. 1982-85). Office: De Lairessestraat 19, 1071 NR Amsterdam The Netherlands

WESSELS, DAVID JOSEPH, priest, political scientist; b. St. Louis, Mar. 22, 1945; arrived in Japan, 1970; s. Bernard Henry and Frances Bernadine (Krampe) W. AB in Philosophy, St. Louis U., 1968; MA in Govt., Georgetown U., 1970; Sacrae Theologiae Licentiatus, Sophia U., Tokyo, 1976; PhD in Polit. Sci., Yale U., 1981. Ordained priest Roman Catholic Ch., 1976. Instr. Internat. Coll. Sophia U., 1972-73, 75, asst. faculty fgn. studies, 1972-81; lectr. Yale Coll., New Haven, Conn., 1978; Yale Coll., 1981-85, assoc. prof., 1985—; lectr. faculty fgn. studies Sophia U.; cons. UN Univ., Tokyo, 1981-82, 84, 86; vis. researcher Georgetown U., Washington, 1987; vis. scholarCtr. Study Human Rights, Columbia U., 1987. Author: Human Rights and Contemporary World Politics, 1981, The International Politics of Peace, 1986; mem. editorial bd. Jour. Internat. Studies, 1981—; contbr. articles to profl. jours. Mem. Internat. Polit. Sci. Assn., Japan Assn. Internat. Relations, Peace Studies Assn. Japan, Internat. Studies Assn., Am. Polit. Sci. Assn. Roman Catholic. Office: Sophia U, 7-1 Kioicho, Chiyoda-ku, Tokyo 102, Japan

WESSELS, WESSEL HENDRIK, psychiatrist, educator; b. Vrede, Republic South Africa, Oct. 9, 1933; s. Wessel Hendrik Uys and Maria Magdalena Jacomina (Rudolph) W.; m. Marianne Muller, Mar. 10, 1956; children: Mariette, Anthon Michael, Marius Rudolph. MB ChB, U. Pretoria, 1959; diploma in psychol. medicine, U. Witwatersrand, Republic South Africa, 1968; MD, U. Orange Free State, Republic South Africa, 1972. Intern Pretoria Gen. Hosp., 1959-60; resident Tara Moross Ctr. and Sterkfontein Hosp., Johannesburg and Krugersdorp, Republic South Africa; practice medicine specializing in family medicine Nylstroom, Republic S. Africa, 1960-64; med. officer psychiatry Witrand Hosp. and Tower Hosp., Potchefstroom and Ft. Beaufort, Republic S. Africa, 1964-66; registrar in psychiatry Tara Moross Ctr. and Sterkfontein Hosp., Johannesburg and Krugersdorp, Republic S. Africa, 1967-69; lectr. U. Orange Free State, Bloemfontein, Republic S. Africa, 1969-73, sr. lectr., 1974-76, assoc. prof., 1977-80; prof., chmn. dept. psychiatry U. Natal, Durban, Republic S. Africa, 1981—; mem. Med. Research Council South Africa, mem. exec. council, 1987—. Author: Basic Psychiatry for Nurses, 1978, Psychiatry, Art or Science, 1983; contbr. articles to nat. internat. jours. Mem. Found. Simon Van Der Stel, 1974—, mem. Kwa Zulu-South Africa Liaison Sub-Com., 1981—. Recipient citation for contbn. to transcultural psychiatry Soc. Neurology and Psychiatry, Taiwan, Republic of China, 1983. Fellow South African Inst. Psychotherapy (sec. 1977-78); mem. Soc. Psychiatrists South Africa (pres. 1985-87), South African Sports Medicine Assn. (founding mem.), Med. Assn. South Africa (mem. regional council 1980), So. African Soc. Biol. Psychiatry (chmn. 1978-81), So. African Assn. Med. Edn. (regional editor 1983—). Mem. Dutch Reform Ch. Home: 5 Ernest Whitcutt Rd, Cowies Hill, 3610 Natal Republic of South Africa Office: Med Sch U Natal, 719 Umbilo Rd, 4001 Durban Republic of South Africa

WESSENIUS, STEN HENRY, pianist, educator; b. Orebro, Sweden, July 26, 1926; s. August Gunnar and Hildur (Engstrom) W.; studied piano with Olof Wibergh, Sven Brandel, Robert Riefling, Martha Mayer-Reinach; m. Ester Runa Carlsson, May 21, 1961; 1 son, Dag Magnus. Tchr. piano, violin, and music classes, various schs. in Sweden, 1954-63; tchr. piano Kommunala Musikskola, Stockholm, 1963—; pianist various concerts Sweden, W. Ger., Norway, also radio and TV. Mem. Svenska Pianopedagogforbundet, Svenska Facklararforbundet. Author: Compendium of Piano Pedagogy, 1965. Home: 33A5 Hornsgatan, 116 49 Stockholm Sweden

WESSLINK, MICHAEL JOHN, brewing company executive; b. Sydney, New South Wales, Australia, July 7, 1947; s. John Vincent and Mary Josephine (McMahon) W.; m. Helen Joy Hamilton, Sept. 22, 1975; children: Sarah, Jane, Fiona Mary. BS in Chem. Engring. with honors, Sydney U., 1968; MBA, U. New South Wales, Sydney, 1974. Ops. research asst. Tooheys Ltd., Sydney, 1969-71, plant brewer, 1971-72, devel. asst., 1972-74, mgr. plant, 1976-80; mgr. fin. Wynn Winegrowers Pty. Ltd., Melbourne, Australia, 1974-76; sec. group co. Castlemaine Tooheys Ltd., Brisbane, 1980-83; gen. mgr. comml. products Castlemaine Perkins, Brisbane, 1983-85; chief exec. Bond Brewing Western Australia Ltd. (formerly Swan Brewery Co. Ltd.), Perth, 1985—. Served with Australian Army Res., 1967-72. Clubs: Cruising Yacht Australia (Sydney), Royal Perth Yacht, Western Australia Turf. Office: Bond Brewing Western Australia Ltd, 25 Baile Rd Canning Vale, Perth 6155, Australia

WEST, BYRON KENNETH, banker; b. Denver, Sept. 18, 1933; s. Willis Byron and Cecil Bernice (Leathers) W.; m. Barbara Huth, June 25, 1955. AB, U. Ill., 1955; MBA, U. Chgo., 1960. With Harris Bank, Chgo., 1957—, investment analyst, 1957-62, v.p., 1966-76; group exec. Harris Bank Internat. Banking Group, Chgo., 1974-76, head banking dept., exec. v.p., 1976-80, pres., 1980; chmn. bd., chief exec. officer Harris Bankcorp, Inc., Chgo., 1984—, also bd. dirs.; chmn., chief exec. officer Harris Trust and Savs. Bank, Chgo., 1985—; bd. govs. Midwest Stock Exchange; chmn. Chgo. Clearing House; bd. dirs. Motorola, Inc. Trustee U. Chgo., Rush-Presbyn.-St. Luke's Med Center; mem. governing bd. Chgo. Orchestral Assn.; bd. dirs. U. Ill. Found. Served with USN, 1955-57. Mem. Res. City Bankers Assn., Christian Laymen of Chgo., Phi Beta Kappa. Republican. Clubs: Skokie Country (Glencoe, Ill.); Pine Valley (N.J.); Univ., Chgo., Commonwealth, Comml., Econ. (Chgo.). Home: 200 Forest St Winnetka IL 60093 Office: Harris Bankcorp Inc 111 W Monroe St PO Box 755 Chicago IL 60690 *

WEST, CLAUDE OTIS, department store executive; b. Minden, La., Aug. 26, 1927; s. Herman O. and Gladys (Tatum) W.; B.A., La. State U., 1949; postgrad. N.Y. U. Sch. Retailing, summers 1953, 54; m. Leatrice Mae David, Sept. 3, 1946; children—Sandra Lee (Mrs. James M. Jackson), Peggy Ann (Mrs. Charles Waters), Claudia Jane (Mrs. Stephen Lee). Asst. mgr. West Bros., Springhill, La., 1949-51, asst. mgr., Bastrop, La., 1951-52, Stuttgart, Ark., 1952-53, Homer, La., 1953, buyer gen. office, DeRidder, La., 1953-56, buyer, v.p. West & Co. of La., Inc., Minden, 1956-65, pres., 1965—; pres. Gibson Products Co. of Camden, Inc. (Ark), 1964—, Gibson Products Co. of Greenwood Inc. (Miss.), 1965—, West's-Gibson Products Co., Inc., Minden, 1966—, Gibson's Shopping Center of Benton, Inc. (Ark.), 1968—; developer West Plaza Shopping Center, Minden; dir. Peoples Bank, Minden. Mem. Minden City Airport Commn., 1969-79; pres. West Found., 1983—; pres. Bossier-Webster Fair & Forrest Festival, 1959; v.p. Minden Parents League, 1969; comdr. Am. Legion Post, 1962; pres. Am. Legion Club, Inc., 1964, Minden Edn. Found., 1966-67; bd. dirs. Glenbrook Sch., 1970-73, Minden Econ. Devel. Corp.; exec. bd. Norwela council Boy Scouts Am.; mem. La. State U. Found., Sports Found. Served with USNR, 1945-46. Recipient Minden Disting. Service award, Young Man of Year, 1961; Minden Man of Yr. award, 1975. Mem. Minden C. of C. (pres. 1960, chmn. long range planning com. 1968-69), Lambda Chi Alpha. Baptist (deacon). Mason. Clubs: Lions, Pine Hills Country, Minden Ambassadors, Minden Tennis and Aquatic (dir. 1968-69), Louisi-Anne Booster, Shreveport. Home: 1110 Madison Ave Minden LA 71055 Office: West Plaza Shopping Center Minden LA 71055

WEST, HERBERT BUELL, foundation executive; b. Birmingham, Apr. 19, 1916; s. Edward Hamilton and Clarine (Buell) W.; A.B., Birmingham-So. Coll., 1936; m. Maria Selden McDonald, Nov. 29, 1946; children—Maria Newill, Herbert Buell, William McDonald, Maria Selden, Jane Hamilton. Writer, v.p., account supr. Batten, Barton, Durstine & Osborn, Inc., N.Y.C., 1936-66; dir., mem. distbn. com. N.Y. Community Trust, N.Y.C., 1967—; pres., dir. Community Funds, Inc., 1967—. James Found., Inc., 1968—, Fairfield Coop. Found., 1984—. Pres., chmn. bd. Am. br. Internat. Social Service, 1966-72, v.p., 1972-83, bd. dirs., 1972—; trustee United Community Funds and Council Am., 1968-71, Fay Sch., Southborough, Mass., 1970-80; trustee NYU Med. Center, 1973—, mem. exec. com., 1979-84; chmn. bd. trustees, chmn. exec. com. The Found. Center, 1975-81; warden St. Luke's Episcopal Ch., Darien, Conn., 1976-79; chmn. joint com. United Way/Community Found. Cooperation, 1987—, com. mem. Greater N.Y. Fund/United Way, 1976-84; bd. dirs. Welfare Research, Inc., 1972—, chmn. bd. dirs., 1978-84; bd. dirs., mem. exec. com. Nat. Charities Info. Bur., Inc., 1978—; bd. dirs. Council on Found., 1980-87, vice chmn., 1984-87; bd. dirs. Am. Council Nationalities Service, 1983—; pres. A Better Chance in Darien (Conn.), 1980-83, bd. dirs., 1983-85. Served to maj. Adjutant Gen. Corps, AUS, 1941-46. Decorated Legion Merit. Mem. N.Y. Regional Assn. of Grantmakers (v.p., dir. 1979-82). Episcopalian (mem. nat. exec. council 1961-68). Clubs: Century Association, University. Mem. Interphil (London). Home: 28 Driftway Ln Darien CT 06820 Office: NY Community Trust 415 Madison Ave New York NY 10017

WEST, JAMES HAROLD, accounting company executive; b. San Diego, Oct. 11, 1926; s. Robert Reed and Clara Leona (Moses) W.; m. Norma Jean, 1953 (div.); 1 son, Timothy James; m., Jerel Lynn Smith, Nov. 16, 1976; 1 son, James Nelson. B.S., U. So. Calif., Los Angeles, 1949. C.P.A., Calif. Ptnr., McCracken & Co., San Diego, 1950-61; mgr. Ernst & Ernst, San Diego, 1961-64; pres. West Johnston Turnquist & Schmitt, San Diego, 1964—. Bd. govs. ARC, Washington, 1981-87; pres., bd. dirs. Combined Arts and Edn. Council, San Diego, 1980-83, Francis Parker Sch., 1988—; bd. dirs. San Diego Hosp. Assn., 1981—; treas. Pioneer Hook & Ladder, San Diego, 1966—; trustee Calif. Western Sch. Law, 1985—; bd. advisors U. So. Calif. Sch. Acctg., 1985—. Served with AUS, 1945-46; PTO. Mem. Calif. Soc. C.P.A.s (bd. dirs. 1963-64), Am. Inst. C.P.A.s. Republican. Clubs: University (San Diego); Capital Hill (Washington). Lodge: Masons. Home: 3311 Lucinda St San Diego CA 92106 Office: West Johnston Turnquist & Schmitt 2550 5th Ave San Diego CA 92103

WEST, JOHN CARL, lawyer, former ambassador; b. Camden, S.C., Aug. 27, 1922; s. Shelton J. and Mattie (Ratterree) W.; A.B., The Citadel, 1942; LL.B. magna cum laude, U. S.C., 1948; m. Lois Rhame, Aug. 29, 1948; children—John Carl, Douglas Allen, Shelton Anne. Bar: S.C. 1947. Ptnr. West, Holland, Furman & Cooper, Camden, 1947-70, West, Cooper, Bowen, Beard & Smoot, Camden, 1975-77; mem. S.C. Senate, 1954-66; lt. gov. State of S.C., 1966-70, gov., 1971-75; ambassador to Kingdom of Saudi Arabia, 1977-81; individual practice law, Hilton Head Island, S.C., 1981—; disting. prof. Middle East studies U. S.C., 1981—; dir. Donaldson, Lufkin & Jenrette, Whittaker Corp., Circle S Industries, Inc. Trustee Presbyn. Coll., So. Center Internat. Studies. Served to maj. AUS, 1942-46. Decorated Army Commendation medal; comdr. Order of Merit (W. Ger.). Mem. Phi Beta Kappa. Democrat. Presbyterian (elder). Address: PO Drawer 13 Hilton Head Island SC 29938 *

WEST, MACDONALD, real estate executive; b. Bournemouth, Eng., July 15, 1943; came to U.S., 1968; s. Joseph Stanley and Maisie Siswick (Hollom) W.; diploma London U. Coll. Estate Mgmt., 1968; M.B.A., Columbia U., 1970; m. Charlotte Denise Duvall, Nov. 1, 1980. Trainee surveyor Navy Works Dept., Admiralty, London, 1960-64; sr. asso. Robinson & Roods, London, 1965-68; dir. cost control Nat. Liberty Corp., Valley Forge, Pa., 1970-71; v.p., dir. Philipsborn Cos., Coral Gables, Fla., 1972-76, Allen Morris Co., Miami, Fla., 1976—; sr. v.p., chief exec. officer Allen Morris Constrn. Co., 1978—, also sr. v.p. asset mgmt. div. Deacon, Univ. Bapt. Ch., Coral Gables, 1977—. Fellow Royal Instn. Chartered Surveyors; mem. Am. Soc. Real Estate Counselors (v.p., gov.), Urban Land Inst., Nat. Assn. Indsl. and Office Parks, Indsl. Assn. Dade County, Miami Bd. Realtors. Republican. Clubs: Miami, Bankers (Miami)Brickell; Lodge: Rotary (dir.) (Coral Gables). Home: 5325 Orduna Dr Coral Gables FL 33146 Office: 1000 Brickell Ave Miami FL 33131

WEST, MORRIS LANGLO, novelist; b. Melbourne, Australia, Apr. 26, 1916; s. Charles Langlo and Florence Guilfoyle (Hanlon) W.; m. Joyce Lawford; children: Christopher, Paul, Melanie, Michael. Author: Gallows on the Sand, 1955, Kundu, 1956, Children of the Sun, 1957, The Crooked Road (English title: The Big Story), 1957, The Concubine, 1958, Backlash (English title: The Second Victory), 1958, The Devil's Advocate (Nat. Brotherhood award Nat. Council Christians and Jews 1960, James Tait Black Meml. award 1960), 1959 (William Hienemann award Royal Soc. 1960, filmed 1977), The Naked Country, 1960, Daughter of Silence, 1961, play, 1961; The Shoes of the Fisherman, 1963, The Ambassador, 1965, Tower of Babel, 1968, (with R. Francis) Scandal in the Assembly, 1970, The Heretic, A Play in Three Acts, 1970, Summer of the Red Wolf, 1971, the

Salamander, 1973, Harlequin, 1974, The Navigator, 1976, Proteus, 1979, The Clowns of God, 1981, The World is Made of Glass, 1983. Served to lt. Australian Imperial Forces, 1939-43, PTO. Recipient Internat. Dag Hammarskjold prize (grand collar of merit), 1978. Fellow Royal Soc. Lit., World Acad. Arts and Sci. Clubs: Royal Prince Alfred Yacht (Sydney, Australia), Elanora Golf (Sydney, Australia). Office: Rosenman Colin Freund Lewis and Cohen 575 Madison Ave New York NY 10022 *

WEST, RHEA HORACE, JR., educator; b. Loudon, Tenn., Oct. 5, 1920; s. Rhea Horace and Verna (Quillen) W.; B.S. in Accounting, U. Tenn., 1947; postgrad. (Sloan fellow, M.I.T. fellow), M.I.T., 1959-60, 63, Case Inst. Tech., summer 1960; Ph.D., U. Ala., 1964. Asso. prof. mgmt. Wake Forest Coll., 1950-51; budget and reports analyst AEC, Oak Ridge, 1951-55; teaching fellow U. Ala., Tuscaloosa, 1956-57; asst. prof. mgmt. U. Ark., Fayetteville, 1957-59; Sloan teaching intern M.I.T., Cambridge, 1959-60; asso. prof. econs. Carson-Newman Coll., Jefferson City, Tenn., 1960-65; prof. mgmt. Ga. State Coll., 1965-70; prof. mgmt., dir. grad. studies Auburn (Ala.) U., 1970-75; acad. dean Cooper Inst., Knoxville, Tenn., 1976-82; chmn. dept. bus. Winston-Salem (N.C.) State U., 1982—; mgmt. cons.; cons. Cape Kennedy and Huntsville (NASA), Lockheed Aircraft Co., U.S. CSC, others; exec. v.p. Enviro South. Active Center for Study Democratic Instns., Atlanta High Mus. Art; mem. men's com. Internat. Debutantes Ball, N.Y.C., 1976—; supr. registration U. Tenn., 1946-50. Served with AUS, 1943-46. Mem. Am. Accounting Assn., Am. Mgmt. Assn., Am. Soc. Personnel Adminstrn. (nat. dir. industry edn. com. 1958-60), Inst. Mgmt. Scis., Soc. Advancement Mgmt., Acad. Mgmt., Soc. Sloan Fellows, Opelika Arts Assn., Acad. Polit. Sci., Am. Acad. Polit. and Social Scis., AAUP, Am. Legion, Opelika C. of C., Am. Ordnance Assn., Smithsonian Assos., Am. Acad. Arts and Scis., AAAS, AIAA, Am. Inst. Decision Scis., Am. Judicature Soc., N.Y. Acad. Scis., Internat. Platform Assn., UN Assn. U.S., Newcomen Soc. N.Am., East Tenn. Personnel and Guidance Assn., Sigma Iota Epsilon, Alpha Kappa Psi (dist. dir. 1965—), Alpha Phi Omega, Kappa Phi Kappa (pres. 1969-70), Alpha Iota Delta, Phi Beta Lambda. Baptist. Clubs: Mass. Inst. Tech., Harvard Faculty, Kiwanis (pres. 1965). Book rev. editor Personnel Adminstr., 1960—. Contbr. numerous articles and book revs. to profl. publs. Home: 4819 Skyline Dr Knoxville TN 37914

WEST, TERENCE DOUGLAS, furniture company design executive; b. Twin Falls, Idaho, Sept. 12, 1948; s. Clark Ernest and Elsie Erma (Kulm) W. B.S., San Jose State U., 1971. Indsl. designer Clement Labs., Palo Alto, Calif., 1970-74, U.S. Govt., Washington, 1974-78; dir. design Steelcase, Inc., Grand Rapids, Mich., 1978—. Com. mem. San Jose Urban Coalition, 1971-72; Fulbright commn. on Design and Design Edn. in Great Britain. Contbr.: Behaviour and Information Technology, 1987; also articles to profl. jours., patentee sensor seating. Mem. Archtl. League of N.Y., Nat. Trust for Hist. Preservation, Inst. Bus. Designers, Am. Soc. Interior Designers Industry Found. Interior Edn. and Research, Indsl. Designers Soc. Am., Design Mgmt. Inst. Democrat. Lutheran. Home: 9655 Ravine Ridge SE Caledonia MI 49316 Office: Steelcase Inc PO Box 1967 Grand Rapids MI 49501

WESTBERG, JOHN AUGUSTIN, lawyer; b. Springfield, Mass., Oct. 12, 1931; s. Carl Joseph and Elizabeth Rebecca (Glassmire) W.; B.A., Coll. William and Mary, 1955; J.D., U. Va., 1959; m. Mina Lari, Aug. 11, 1976; children—Christine, Steven, Jennifer, Saman. Admitted to N.Y. bar, 1960, D.C. bar, 1969, U.S. Supreme Ct. bar, 1968; asso. firm Lord, Day and Lord, N.Y.C., 1959-64; legal adv. AID, Washington, 1964-65, regional legal adv. for Middle East, Am. Embassy, Teheran, Iran, also AID affairs officer, 1965-68; founder John A. Westberg & Assos., Inc., Teheran, 1968, pres., 1968-79; partner Wald, Harkrader & Ross, London and Washington, 1981-87. Mem. N.Y. County Democratic Com., 1963. Mem. Internat. Bar Assn., Am. Bar Assn., Am. Soc. Internat. Law, Assn. Bar City N.Y., D.C. Bar, Iran Am. C. of C. (bd. govs. 1973-77). Club: Cosmos. Contbr articles to bus. and law jours. Home: 4306 Westover Pl NW Washington DC 20016 Office: 4306 Westover Pl Washington DC 20016

WESTBO, LEONARD ARCHIBALD, JR., electronics engineer; b. Tacoma, Wash., Dec. 4, 1931; s. Leonard Archibald and Agnes (Martinson) W.; B.A. in Gen. Studies, U. Wash., 1958. Electronics engr. FAA, Seattle Air Route Traffic Control Center, Auburn, Wash., 1961-72; asst. br. chief electronics engring. br. 13th Coast Guard Dist., Seattle, 1972-87. Served with USCG, 1951-54, 1958-61. Registered profl. engr., Wash. Mem. Aircraft Owners and Pilots Assn., IEEE, Am. Radio Relay League. Home: 10528 SE 323d St Auburn WA 98002 Office: 10528 SE 323d St Auburn WA 98002

WESTBY, CARL MARTIN, JR., clergyman, educator; b. Aberdeen, S.D., Jan. 24, 1928; s. Carl Martin and Ruth Gudrun (Lundly) W.; m. Elaine Ruth Solomonson, Aug. 22, 1959; children—Joel Carl, Rebekah Kay, Nathan Andrew, Deborah Ann. B.A., St. Olaf Coll., Northfield, Minn., 1951; M.A., U. Mont., Missoula, 1954; B.D., Luther Theol. Sem., St. Paul, 1961. Cert. tchr., Mont.; ordained to ministry Am. Lutheran Ch., 1961. Tchr. high sch., Red Lodge, Mont., 1954-55; mem. adminstrv. staff U. Mont., Missoula, 1955-58; youth worker Our Saviour's Luth. Ch., Mpls., 1958-61; pastor Fujieda Luth. Ch., Fujieda, Shizouka-Ken, Japan, 1963-66; student worker Ichigaya Luth. Student Ctr., Tokyo, 1967-69; pastor St. Paul Internat. Lutheran Ch., Tokyo, 1969—; historian Exec. Com. of the Japan Luth. Mission of the Am. Lutheran Ch., 1964-66, vice chmn., 1968-70; chmn. bd., supr., worker Tokyo English Life Line, 1971—; chmn., treas. Tokyo Ecumenical Counsel, 1980—. Active Boy Scouts Am., U.S. and Japan, 1950-73; trustee Am. Sch. Japan, Tokyo, 1975-84, bd. dirs., 1985—. Served with U.S. Army, 1946-47. Mem. Internat. House of Japan, Am. C. of C. in Japan, Phi Alpha Theta, Alpha Phi Omega. Republican. Home: Homat Kojimachi 401, 1-12-2 Kojimachi, Tokyo 102, Japan Office: Saint Paul Internat Luth Ch, 1-2-32 Fujimi, Chiyoda-ku, Tokyo 102, Japan

WESTBY, TOV OLE JACOB, computer company executive; b. Sarpsborg, Norway, Dec. 13, 1960; s. Thor Harald and Idun Adfrid (Jacobsen) W. B.System Devel-Analytics, More and Romsdal Distriktshogskole, 1981, micro computer design degree, 1982. Founder, co-owner, jr. exec., product mgr., dir. West Computers A/S, Molde, Fed. Republic Germany and Oslo, 1983—; gen. mgr. Westby Trading & C.O., Fredrikstad and Molde, 1979—; chmn. Nortech Engring. Als, Molde, 1985—; dir. West Mannes, Bodx, Norwegian Petroleum A/S, New Aalesund, Svalbard, Norway. Served with Royal Norwegian Air Force, 1982-83. Recipient Mktg. award Norwegian Mktg. Assn., 1985. Mem. Norwegian Computers. Assn., Norwegian Def. Assn. Mem. Norwegian Conservative Party. Avocations: technical venture projects; skiing; hunting; boat racing; literature. Office: West Computers A/S, Drammensveien 43, Oslo 2 Norway

WESTER, KEITH ALBERT, film and television recording engineer; b. Seattle, Feb. 21, 1940; s. Albert John and Evelyn Grace (Nettell) W., m. Judith Elizabeth Jones, 1968 (div. Mar. 1974); 1 child, Wendy Elizabeth. AA, Am. River Coll., Sacramento, 1959; BA, Calif. State U., Los Angeles, 1962; MA, UCLA, 1965. Lic. multi-engine rated pilot. Prodn. asst. KCRA-TV, Sacramento, 1956; announcer KSFM, Sacramento, 1960; film editor, sound rec. technician Urie & Assocs., Hollywood, Calif., 1963-66; co-owner Steckler-Wester Film Prodns., Hollywood, 1966-70; owner Profl. Sound Recorders, Studio City, Calif., 1970—, Aerocharter, Studio City, 1974—. Mem. Acad. Motion Picture Arts Scis. (Sound Branch exec. bd.), Acad. of Television Arts & Scis. (Emmy award, An Early Frost, 1986), Cinema Audio Soc. (sec. 1985—, Sound award 1987), Soc. Motion Picture and Television Engrs., Internat. Sound Technicians, Local 695, Assn. Film Craftsmen (sec. 1967-73, treas. 1973-76), Screen Actors Guild. Clubs: Aircraft Owners & Pilots Assn., Am. Radio Relay League. Home: 4146 Bellingham Ave Studio City CA 91604 Office: Profl Sound Recorders 22440 Clarendon Woodland Hills CA 91367

WESTER, PER OLOV, medical educator; b. Skövde, Sweden, May 22, 1929; s. Manfred Erik and Alice Margreta (Monteleone) W.; m. Marta Maria, Feb. 10, 1930; children: Jan, Per, Ann. Specialist internal medicine, Karolinska Inst., Stockholm, 1967, cardiology, 1970, endocrinology, 1975. Asst. physician Karolinska Inst., Stockholm, 1959-67, asst. prof., 1967-77; prof. Umea (Sweden) Univ. Hosp., 1977—; chmn. stroke adv. group World Health Orgn., 1987. Contbr. approx. 300 articles on internal medicine, cardiology, endocrinology and metabolism. Fellow Am. Coll. Nutrition; mem. Swedish Soc. Cardiology, Internat. Coll. Nutrition (governing bd. 1985), Swedish Soc. Hypertension (chmn. 1983), Scandinavian Soc. Cerebrovascular Disease (chmn., founder 1979). Home: Kvarnvagen 1 E, 90249 Umea Sweden Office: Umea Univ Hosp, Med Dept, 90185 Umea Sweden

WESTER, RURIC HERSCHEL, JR., lawyer; b. Ruskin, Fla., Aug. 9, 1930; s. Ruric Herschel and Mabel Olivia (Curry) W.; m. Joan Hisae Momohira, Oct. 12, 1951; children—Mary, John William, George Warham, Ruric Herschel, Mark, Luke. B.A. cum laude in Polit. Sci., St. Mary's U., San Antonio, 1973; J.D., 1976. Bar: Tex. 1976. Enlisted U.S. Air Force, 1948, served to maj., ret., 1970; owner, operator Fujiya Japanese Restaurant, San Antonio, 1970—; sole practice, Seguin, 1976-79; atty. Lippe & Wester, Seguin, 1979-84; asst. county atty. Guadalupe County, Tex., 1983-84; ptnr. Wester & Roush, Austin, 1984-85, Wester & Wester, Austin, 1985—; instr. polit. sci. St. Mary's U., San Antonio, 1978, bus. law Tex. Lutheran Coll., Seguin, 1980. County chmn. Guadalupe County Republican Party, 1980-84; mem. Seguin Planning Commn., 1983-84; del. Rep. State Conv., Tex., 1972-84, Nat. Conv., 1984. Mem. Tex. Bar Assn. (chmn. dist. subcom. on admissions 1979-85), Conservation Soc. Sequin (bd. dirs. 1965-85), Phi Delta Phi, Pi Gamma Mu. Methodist. Lodges: Lions (bd. dirs. 1976-78), Masons. Home: 1811 E Court St Seguin TX 78155 Office: 1101 S Capitol Tex Hwy Bldg H Austin TX 78746

WESTERBERG, GUNNAR OLOF, investor; b. Halmstad, Halland, Sweden, June 27, 1920; s. N.O. Gottfrid and Ellen H.E. (Brauns) W.; m. Christine M. Reinius, Apr. 26, 1945; children—Elisabeth, Goran, Nils. M.S. in Mech. Engring., Royal Inst. Tech., 1947; postgrad. U. Wis., 1949. Engr. Nordiska Maskinfilt AB, Halmstad, 1947-50, mng. dir., 1950-69; div. pres. Europe, Albany Internat., N.Y., 1969-74, exec. v.p., 1974-76, vice chmn., 1976-83; pres. Securities Atlanta Ltd., Zurich, 1983—; dir. Fedn. Textile Industry of Sweden, Stockholm, 1955-69. Mem. State Planning Bd., Halmstad, 1965-69, State Labour Bd., 1965-69; consul (hon.) for Republic of Finland, 1953-69. Served to capt. Swedish Res. Decorated knight Royal Order of Vasa, (Sweden); knight Order of Lion of Finland. Mem. Soc. Swedish Engrs., Swiss Am. C. of C., Swiss Inst. Internat. Studies, Finnish-Swedish C. of C. (bd. dirs. 1952-69) Clubs: Club Baur au Lac, Le Mirador Country, World Wildlife Fund. Lodge: Rotary. Home: Aussichtstrasse 21, Herrliberg, CH-8704 Zurich Switzerland Office: Securities Atlanta Ltd, Dufourstrasse 101, CH-8704 Zurich Switzerland

WESTERDAHL, CHRISTER LENNART, archaeologist, ethnologist, museum curator; b. Stockholm, Nov. 13, 1945; s. Herbert Lennart and Margit Anna Charlotta (Svensson) W.; m. Anna Kristina Drake, Oct. 18, 1985. Matriculation, Bandhagen gymnasium, Stockholm, 1965; MA, Stockholm U., 1969; postgrad Umeå U., 1984—. Freelance journalist, 1969-73; freelance archaeologist and ethnologist, 1969—; curator Mus. of Örnsköldsvik, 1980—. Author: Kulturhistoria och grottor, 1982, Förhistoria nolaskogs, 1985, Samer nolaskogs, 1986, "Et satt som likna them uti theras Öfriga lefnadsart", 1987, Norrlandsleden I, 1987, II, 1988; editor, prin. contbr.: S.W. Greenland, 1974, Gotska Sandön, 1977; prin. editor, contbr. Spetsbergen--Land i norr; contbr. numerous articles to profl. jours. Served with Swedish Army. Recipient Harold Hvarfner award Cen. Swedish Mus. of Ethnology, 1983; scholar Berit Wallenberg Found., 1983, 88, Kempe Found., 1971-87. Mem. Soc. Marine Archaeology (founder, chief editor Transactions), Nature and Soc. (founder), Swedish Speleological Soc. Avocation: outdoor activities. Home: Järvstagatan 14 G, S-89161 Örnsköldsvik Sweden Office: Mus of Örnsköldsvik, Läroverksgatan, S-89133 Örnsköldsvik Sweden

WESTERDAHL, JOHN BRIAN, nutritionist, health educator; b. Tucson, Dec. 3, 1954; s. Jay E. and Margaret (Meyer) W. AA, Orange Coast Coll., 1977; BS, Pacific Union Coll., 1979; MPH, Loma Linda U., 1981. Registered dietitian. Nutritionist, health educator Castle Med. Ctr., Kailua, Hawaii, 1981-84, health promotion coordinator, 1984-87, asst. dir. health promotion, 1987-88, dir. health promotion, 1988—; talk show host Nutrition and You, Sta. KGU-Radio, Honolulu, 1983—; nutrition com. mem. Hawaii Heart Assn., Honolulu, 1984—; mem. nutrition study group Govs. Conf. Health Promotion and Disease Prevention for Hawaii, 1985. Named One of Outstanding Young Men Am., 1984, One of 10 Outstanding Young Persons in Hawaii, 1988. Mem. AAAS, Am. Coll. Sports Medicine, Am. Dietetic Assn., Am. Pub. Health Assn., Hawaii Nutrition Council (v.p. 1983-86, pres. elect 1988—), Hawaii Dietetic Assn., Seventh-day Adventist Dietetic Assn., Soc. for Nutrition Edn., Soc. Pub. Health Edn., Assn. for Fitness in Bus., Nat. Wellness Assn., N.Y. Acad. Scis., Am. Coll. Nutrition, Nutrition Today Soc. Republican. Seventh Day Adventist. Office: Castle Med Ctr 640 Ulukahiki St Kailua HI 96734

WESTERHOFF, HAROLD E., social agency executive; b. Hawthorne, N.J., Sept. 14, 1915; s. Jacob J. and Margaret (Laggner) W. Student, N.Y.U., U. Pa. Formerly with office comptroller Eclipse-Pioneer div. Bendix Aviation Corp.; mem. Internat. Soc. Christian Endeavor; past pres. N.J. Union, head exec. conf., v.p. charge Middle Atlantic region, also mem. exec. com., former gen. sec. and treas.; trustee, former gen. s World's Christian Endeavor Union, leader numerous convs. and confs. of orgn.; v.p. for fiscal affairs Greer-Woodycrest Children's Services, Hope Farm, Dutchess County, N.Y., 1966-81; fin. cons. Greer Inst. of Group Care Consultants, 1978—; mem. bd. edn. Hope Farm Union Free Sch. Dist. Former mem. hdgrs. com. Ohio Alcohol Edn. Council; former mem. exec. council All-American Conf. to Combat Communism., Pres. bd. edn., Hawthorne, N.J. Served with AUS, World War II. Decorated Bronze Star. Mem. Dutch Reformed Ch. Clubs: Optimist, Lions. Address: 209 GreerCrest Millbrook NY 12545

WESTERHOFF, HEINZ, thermodynamic engineer; b. Hagen, Fed. Republic Germany, May 12, 1928; s. August and Alma Westerhoff; m. Gertrud Keppler, May 30, 1954; children: Monika, Brigitte. Diploma in engring., Technische Hochschule, Aachen, Fed. Republic Germany, 1955. Engr. indsl. furnace system Siemens, Mülheim a d Ruhr, Fed. Republic Germany, 1955-56, 1957-60; engr. indsl. furnace system Power Plant Fortuna, Cologne, Fed. Republic Germany, 1956-57; engr. indsl. furnace system Reining Heisskühlung, Mülheim a d Ruhr, 1960-64, exec. pres., 1965—. Home: Jakobstr 36, D4330 Mulheim an der Ruhr 1, Federal Republic of Germany Office: Reining Heisskuhlung, Box 130245, D4330 Mulheim a d Ruhr 13, Federal Republic of Germany

WESTFALL, RICHARD MERRILL, chemist, research administrator; b. Denver, Dec. 17, 1956; s. Robert Raymond and Madelyn Evastine (Cornwell) W. Student, U. Colo., 1976-80. Mem. lab. staff NOAA, Boulder, Colo., 1978-79, Solar Energy Research Inst., Golden, Colo., 1979-80; dir. research Galactic Products, Denver, 1981-82; pres., dir. research CEL Systems Corp., Arvada, Colo. and Schertz, Tex., 1982—; process chemist, engr. Tex. Med. Instruments, Schertz, 1986-87. Inventor electrolytic growth tin and other metals, and process, 1980-82; patentee in field. Mem. AIAA, Air Force Assn. Home: 4838 Stuart St Denver CO 80212

WESTON, CARYL RAE, business educator, writer; b. Oamaru, N.Z., Dec. 18, 1941; d. Percival Claude and Catherine L. (Hancox) W. B.Comm. with honors, U. Melbourne, 1966; B.Jurisprudence, Monash U., 1972, LL.B., 1972, Ph.D. in Econs., 1972. Teaching fellow/sr. teaching fellow, faculty econs. Monash U., Melbourne, Australia, 1966-69; research fellow econs. La Trobe U., Melbourne, 1970-73, lectr., 1974, sr. lectr. econs., 1974-84; prof. banking and mgmt. Massey U., Palmerston North, N.Z., 1985—; cons. to govt. and the banking, fin. and futures industry. Author: Domestic and Multinational Banking, 1980; Gold: A World Survey, 1983; Strategic Materials, 1984; International Trade Finance, 1985; Managing Foreign Exchange Risk, 1985; Combating Commercial Crime: A Casebook, 1987; also articles. Found. editor Massey Jour. Asian and PacificBus. Mem. coms. for design and constrn. sports stadia. Ian Roach Found. fellow, 1983-84; recipient Silver medal Royal Lifesaving Soc., N.Z., 1956-57. Mem. Econ. Soc. Australia, Western Econs. Assn., Can. Econs. Assn. Avocations: badminton; driving. Office: Massey U, Pvt Bag, Palmerston North New Zealand

WESTON, DAWN THOMPSON, artist, researcher; b. Joliet, Ill., Apr. 15, 1919; d. Cyril C. and Vivian Grace Thompson; student (scholar) Penn Hall Jr. Coll., Chambersburg, Pa., 1937-38; B.S., Northwestern U., 1942, postgrad. in reading and speech pathology, 1960-61, M.A. in Edni. Adminstrn., 1970; postgrad. U. Ill., 1964; student Art Inst. Chgo., 1954, Pestalozzi-Froebel, Chgo., 1955, Phila. Inst. for Achievement Human Potential, 1963; m. Arthur Walter Weston, Sept. 10, 1940; children—Roger Lance, Randall Kent, Cynthia Brooke. Therapist, USN Hosp., Gt. Lakes, Ill., 1940-45; tchr. Holy Child and Waukegan (Ill.) High Schs., 1946-54; elem. and jr. high art dir. Lake Bluff (Ill.) Schs., 1954-58; pioneer ednl. dir. Grove Sch. for Brain-Injured, Lake Forest, Ill., 1958-66, now life mem. corp., chmn. bd., 1984-87; one-woman shows: Evanston Woman's Club, Northwestern U., Deerpath Gallery, Lake Forest; The Hein Co., Waukegan; numerous group shows, 1939-76. Represented in permanent collections: ARC, Victory Meml. Hosp., Waukegan, Sierra Assos., Chgo., numerous pvt. collections U.S., Can., Japan, Africa; works include: Poisonous Plants of Midwest set of etchings for Country Gentleman mag., 1956, Clouds mural, 1981; ind. researcher on shifting visual imagery due to trauma, 1982—. Mem. Presdl. Gold Chain, Trinity Coll., 1979. Named Citizen of Yr., Grove Sch., 1978, room at sch. named in her honor, 1982; cert. tchr./adminstr., Ill. Mem. Art Inst. Chgo., Deerpath Art League, Pi Lambda Theta. Methodist (del. Ann. Conf. 1982-88). Research on uneven growth, 1969—. Home and Office: 349 E Hilldale Pl Lake Forest IL 60045

WESTON, GARFIELD HOWARD, food company executive; b. Toronto, Apr. 28, 1927; s. Willard Garfield and Reta Lila (Howard) W.; m. Mary Ruth Kippenberger, Aug. 8, 1959; 6 children. Ed. Sir William Borlase Sch., Marlow, Oxford, Eng., 1941-1944 New Coll., Oxford U., 1944-1945, Harvard U., 1951-54, Weston Biscuit Co., Australia, 1954-60; vice chmn. Assoc. Brit. Foods, London, 1960-67, chmn., 1967—, chmn. Fortnum and Mason, PLC, London 1980. Office: Assoc Brit Foods Plc, Bowater House, 68 Knightsbridge, London SW1X 7LR England

WESTON, WILLARD GALEN, diversified holdings executive; b. Eng., Oct. 29, 1940; married, 1966; 2 children. LLD honoris causa, U. Western Ont. Chmn., pres. George Weston Ltd. and Wittington Investments Ltd. (holding co. of other Weston cos.); chmn. Holt Renfrew & Co. Ltd., Loblaw Cos. Ltd., Weston Foods Ltd., Weston Resources Ltd., Brown Thomas Group Ltd. (Ireland); dir. George Weston Holdings Ltd. (Eng.), Associated British Foods plc (Eng.), Can. Imperial Bank of Commerce; vice chmn. Fortnum & Mason plc (Eng.). Pres. The W. Garfield Weston Found.; chmn. The Weston Can. Found.; bd. dirs. Lester B. Pearson Coll. Pacific, United World Colls., Operation Raleigh, Can.; life mem. Royal Ont. Mus., Art Gallery Ont. Clubs: Badminton and Racquet Toronto, York (Toronto), Toronto; Lyford Cay (Nassau). Office: George Weston Ltd, 22 St Clair Ave E, Suite 1901, Toronto, ON Canada M4T 2S3

WESTRA, PIETER EGBERT, librarian; b. Groningen, The Netherlands, May 23, 1937; s. Pieter and Tryntje (Meima) w.; m. Hendrina Fredrika Ferreira, Aug. 24, 1968; children: Pieter Willem, Isabel, Willem Ferreira. BA in Library Sci., U. Pretoria, South Africa, 1959, MLS, 1978. Library asst. Transvaal Province Library, Pretoria, 1957-59, librarian, 1960; sen. librarian State Library, Pretoria, 1961-75, asst. dir., 1976-80; dir. South African Library, Cape Town, 1981—. Author: Public Lending Right in Theory and Practice, 1979, Liber Amicorum Pro Balkema, 1983; editor Quarterly Bulletin of South African Library, 1981—; contbr. numerout articles to scholarly jours. Sec. Genootskap Nederland South Africa, Pretoria, 1972-80; pres. Van Ewyck Found., Cape Town, 1983—. Fellow: South African Inst. Library and Info. Sci.; mem. South African Acad. (assoc.). Clubs: Nederlandse (Cape Town); City and Civil Service (Cape Town). Home: 18 Uitvlugt, Pinelands Cape Town 7405, Republic of South Africa Office: South African Library, Queen Victoria St, PO Box 496, Cape Town 8000, Republic of South Africa

WESTRAN, ROY ALVIN, insurance company executive; b. Taft, Oreg., Apr. 30, 1925; s. Carl A. and Mae E. (Barnhart) W.; m. Dawn M. Oeschger, Oct. 18, 1952; children: Denise, Thomas, Michael, Dawna. B.B.A., Golden Gate Coll., 1955, M.B.A., 1957. Mem. sales staff C.A. Westran Agy., Taft, 1946-49; underwriter Fireman's Fund Group, San Francisco, 1949-52; ins. mgr. Kaiser Aluminum Chem. Co., Oakland, 1952-66; pres., dir. Citizens Ins. Co., Howell, Mich., 1967—; chmn. bd. 1st Nat. Bank, Howell; pres. Am. Select Ins. Co., Columbus, Ohio, 1967-85, dir., 1967—; pres. Beacon Ins. Co. Am., Westerville, Ohio, 1967-85, dir., 1967—; pres., dir. Citizens' Man, Inc.; v.p., dir. Hanover Ins. Co., Massachusetts Bay Ins. Co.; bd. dirs. Oakland Kaiser Fed. Credit Union, 1957-60, Calif. Compensation Fire Co. Mem. ins. adv. council Salvation Army, San Francisco, 1957-60; chmn. drive United Way, Livingston County, 1980; bd. dirs., mem. exec. com. Portage Trails council Boy Scouts Am., 1970-72; trustee, mem. exec. com. Child and Family Services Mich., 1972-75; past bd. dirs. McPherson Health Ctr., Howell; bd. dirs. Cleary Coll., 1984-85; mem. adv. council Olivet Coll., 1984—. Served with U.S. Army, 1943-46. Mem. Ins. Inst. Am., Mich. C. of C. (past dir.), Am. Soc. Ins. Mgmt. (past pres.), Soc. CPCU's (nat. pres. 1968-69), Traffic Safety Assn. Detroit (trustee 1967—), Traffic Safety for Mich. Assn. Office: Citizens Ins Co of America 645 W Grand River Howell MI 48834

WETHERALL, ROBERT SHAW, librarian; b. Jesup, Ga., Aug. 18, 1944; s. Robert and Elizabeth (Shaw) W; m. Cynthia Jane Campbell, July 31, 1976; children—Robert G., Gerritt C. B.A. in History, U. Del., 1966, M.A. in History, 1968; M.L.S., Drexel U., 1973. Cert. profl. librarian, N.J. Librarian Cumberland County Library, Bridgeton, N.J., 1973 76; asst. dir., 1976-80, dir., 1981—; mem. Cumberland County Audio-Visual Aids Commn., Bridgeton, 1981—; pres. South Jersey Regional Library Coop., Inc., 1986—. Served with USAF, 1968-72. Mem. N.J. Library Assn., ALA. Lodge: Rotary (Bridgeton). Office: Cumberland County Library 800 E Commerce St Bridgeton NJ 08302

WETSTEIN, LEWIS, cardio-thoracic surgeon, cardiac researcher, electrophysiologist, educator; b. N.Y.C., June 23, 1947; s. Benjamin and Rose (Finkilstein) W.; m.; 1 dau., Jennifer Sandra. B.A., Queens Coll., 1968; M.D., Autonoumous U., Barcelona, Spain, 1973. Diplomate: Am. Bd. Surgery, Am. Bd. Thoracic Surgery. Intern L.F. Jewish Hosp.-Hillside Med. Center, 1973-75; resident in surgery Kings County Hosp.-Downstate Med. Center, 1975-80; asst. instr. surgery Downstate Med. Ctr., Bklyn., 1975-80; instr. surgery U. Pa., Phila., 1980-82, research assoc., 1980-82; asst. prof. surgery Med. Coll. Pa., Phila., 1982-84; assoc. prof. surgery div. thoracic and cardiac surgery Med. Coll. Va., 1984-87; cons. VA Hosp., Phila., 1982-84; chief thoracic surgery McGuire VA Hosp., 1984-87; cons. for cardiothoracic affairs Surgeon Gen. of Air Force, 1985—. Assoc. editor Cardiology Emergency Decisions, Cardiology Product News, Hosp. Physician, Cardiac Chronicle. Contbr. articles to profl. jours. Served as maj. USAFR, 1976—. Recipient postdoctoral research service award NIH, 1980-82, spl. investigatorship award Am. Heart Assn., 1983-85, research adv. group award VA, 1985-86, New Investigator award NIH, 1986—. Fellow Assn. Acad. Surgery, ACS, Am. Coll. Cardiology, Am. Coll. Chest Physicians, Soc. Thoracic Surgeons, Soc. Univ. Surgeons. Jewish. Office: 4 Bridge Plaza Dr Manalapan NJ 07726

WETTE, EDUARD WILHELM, mathematician; b. Radevormwald, Germany, Feb. 4, 1925; s. Eduard and Anna Auguste (Finkensieper) W.; self-taught; m. Anna Maria Elisabeth Mohrhauer, Dec. 28, 1950; 1 dau., Adelheid Margaretha Elisabeth. Ind. researcher; mem. adv. council Internat. Logic Rev., Bologna, Italy, 1975. Served with 405 Regt., 1944-45. Recipient prize Bonn U., 1968. Mem. Assn. Symbolic Logic, Am. Math. Soc., Math. Assn. Am., History of Sci. Soc., Soc. History of Tech., N.Y. Acad. Scis., Centro Superiore di Logica e Scienze Comparate. Author articles on finite contradictions within pure arithmetic; anti-relativistic morphometric representation of the motions' totality; intrafinite recursive world calculus. Home: 14 Blumenstrasse, D5608 Radevormwald Federal Republic of Germany Office: PO Box 4115, Hennef 41, D5202 Uckerath Federal Republic of Germany

WETTER, FRIEDRICH CARDINAL, cardinal Roman Catholic Church; b. Landau, Speyer, Germany, Feb. 20, 1928. ordained 1953. Consecrated bishop Speyer, 1968; archbishop Munich and Freising, Fed. Republic Germany, 1982—; proclaimed cardinal 1985. Address: Postfach 360, D-8000 Munich 33 Federal Republic of Germany *

WETTIG, GERHARD, political scientist; b. Gelnhausen, Hesse, Germany, Feb. 17, 1934; s. Hermann and Kathe (Leiske) W.; m. Heide Wallowy, Apr. 12, 1962; children: Andreas, Friedmunt, Tobias, Hannes. PhD, U. Gottingen, Fed. Republic of Germany, 1961. Research asst. Evangelische Studiengemeinschaft, Heidelberg, Fed. Republic of Germany, 1961-62; mem.

research staff German Soc. Fgn. Affairs, Bonn, Fed. Republic of Germany, 1962-66; mem. sr. research staff Fed. Inst. for Ea. and Internat. Studies, Cologne, Fed. Republic of Germany, 1966-74, dep. head fgn. policy research, 1974-88, dir. security studies, 1986—; head dept. Inst. East-West Internat. Politics, Cologne, 1988—. Author: Entmilitarisierung und Wiederbewaffnung in Deutschland, 1943, 55, 67, Broadcasting and Detente, 1977; co-editor Umstrittene Sicherheit, 1982, Krieg und Frieden im Sowjetischer Sicht, 1986. Jour. Aussenpolitik, 1984—; mem. German editorial bd.: Comparative Strategy jour., 1987—. Home: Ringstrasse 51, D5000 Cologne 71, Federal Republic of Germany Office: Fed Inst Ea and Internat Studies, Lindenbornstrasse 22, 5000 Cologne 30 Federal Republic of Germany

WETTSTEIN, FREDERICK ALBERT, III, psychological researcher; b. Pompton Plains, N.J., Aug. 19, 1943; s. Frederick Albert, II and Cecelia Veronica (Carberry) W.; student Rutgers U., 1964; m. Marianne, Dec. 25, 1961. With Am. Cyanamid Co., Wayne, N.J., 1970—, psychol. researcher, 1971—, also oceanographic experiments; explorer world deserts; arctic areas. Active SNCC, Ch. Universal Brotherhood. Served with AUS, 1963. Mem. Am. Mgmt. Assn. Republican. Roman Catholic. Author: Patterns, 1970. Home: 63d St Bloomingdale NJ 07403

WETZEL, ALBERT JOHN, university executive, systems analyst, former air force officer, cons.; b. New Orleans, Dec. 29, 1917; s. Albert John and Emelie (Willoz) W.; B.Engring., Tulane U., 1939; M.S., Johns Hopkins U., 1950; postgrad. UCLA, George Washington U., 1952, 1956, Armed Forces Staff Coll., 1955; grad. Command and Gen. Staff Coll., Advanced Flying Sch. (Jet); m. Helen Elizabeth Zurad, Sept. 7, 1946; children—Albert John, Elizabeth Ann, Joan Clark, Edward Russel. Commd. 2d lt. C.E., U.S. Army, 1941, advanced through grades to col. USAF, 1956; exptl. test pilot, 1943-45; fighter pilot, 1945-47; tech. staff officer Armed Forces Spl. Weapons Project, Washington, exec. asst. to dir. of guided missiles, office of Sec. of Def., 1952-55; service in Europe, Asia, Middle East; wing comdr. SAC, 1955-57; dir. Titan ICBM and Gemini Space Program, 1957-62; exec. dir. USAF Council, 1962-63; dir. strategic programs, def., research and engring. Office Sec. of Def., 1963-65, ret., 1965; dir. research and sponsored programs, then dir. univ. devel. Tulane U., 1965-76, v.p. alumni and univ. affairs, 1976-80, sr. adviser to pres., 1980-81, asst. to pres., 1981—, adj. prof. mgmt. and engring. mgmt., 1965—; mem. rocket and space panel Pres.'s Sci. Adv. Com., 1965-71; bd. dirs. Gulf South Research Inst., Inst. Def. Analysis, Washington; del. Nat. Conf. Advancement Research. Bd. dirs. Walter Clark Teagle Found. (N.Y.C.), also exec. com., Crippled Children's Hosp., New Orleans, La. Council Music and Performing Arts, Council. Devel. French in La.; trustee Delgado Jr. Coll.; pres. bd. dirs. New Orleans Catholic Found.; bd. dirs. Girl Scouts U.S.A.; exec. com. local Boy Scouts Am.; commr. La. Ednl. TV Authority. Decorated Legion of Merit, Command Pilot, Armed Forces and Air Force Commendation Medal. Registered profl. engr., Ohio. Fellow AIAA; mem. AAAS (sci. mem.), Greater New Orleans Area C. of C. (v.p.), Oak Ridge Assn. Univs., Air Force Assn., Eagle Scout Assn., Navy League U.S., Sigma Xi, Kappa Sigma, Tau Beta Pi, Omicron Delta Kappa. Clubs: Internat. House, Bienville, Plimsoll (New Orleans); Univ. (N.Y.C.); Army-Navy (Washington). Lodges: Rotary, Order of St. Louis, Order Holy Sepulchre of Jerusalem (Knight Comdr.). Contbr. articles on aeros., strategic mil. weapons and strategy, instl. devel., planned gifts programs and univ. advancement to profl. jours. Home: 7 Richmond Pl New Orleans LA 70115 Office: Tulane U New Orleans LA 70118

WETZELL, OTTO WOLFGANG, engineering educator; b. Niebuell, Fed. Republic Germany, Nov. 10, 1932; s. Friedrich and Hilde (Buchka) W.; m. Helen Krikelas; children: Richard Friedrich, Christina. Diploma in Engring., Tech. Univ. Hannover, Fed. Republic Germany, 1959, D in Engring., 1965; MS, Stanford U., 1960. Cons. engr. Köper-Medau-Wetzell, Hannover, 1965-68; prof. engring. Fachhohschule Münster, Fed. Republic Germany, 1968—. Author: Techn. Mechanik, 4 Volumes, 1972-75; editor: EDV-Handbuch für Bauingenieure, 5 Volumes, 1979-83, Bautechn. Zahlentafeln, 23d edit., 1987; EDV für Bauingenieure, 1985-88. Club: MAIV (Münster) (pres. 1986-87). Home: Parkallee 19, D4400 Munster Federal Republic of Germany Office: Fachhochschule Munster, Corrensstrase 25, D4400 Munster Federal Republic of Germany

WEWER, DEE J., artist, educator, creative arts therapist; b. Mobile, Ala., Apr. 27, 1948; d. Gene B. and Juanita (Schmeckenbecher) Wewer. B.S., U. So. Miss., 1969; M.A., Am. U., 1974; postgrad. Georgetown U., 1981-82; Ph.D., Union Grad. Sch., 1986. With Dixie Press, Biloxi, Miss., 1968-70; tchr. St. Martin Public Sch., Biloxi, 1970; editor newspaper of Nat. War Coll., Ft. McNair, Washington, 1971-73; press and scheduling asso. and coordinator Nat. Fedn. State Chairmen, Office of Chmn., Republican Nat. Com., Washington, 1972-73; cons. Nat. Women's Edn. Fund, Nat. Women's Polit. Caucus, 1973-74; gen. mgr., treas. Printing Services Unltd., Washington, 1975; instr. Inst. Politics, Harvard U., Boston, 1976; media dir./prodn. mgr./creative group head Bailey, Deardourff & Assos., Washington, 1975-76; dir. mktg./account supr. Weitzman & Assocs., Washington, 1976-78; dir. mktg. Britches of Georgetown, Washington, 1978-79; instr. Coll. Bus. and Mgmt., U. Md., College Park, 1980-83; v.p. public affairs AMF Head Sports Wear, Columbia, Md., 1979-81; exec. v.p. Sport-Obermeyer, Aspen, Colo., 1982-85; creativity coach, painter, writer, cons., 1985—; instr. Colo. Mountain Coll., 1985—; paintings represented by Aspen Artists Gallery, R Collection, Los Angeles, Santa Fe Ambiance Gallery,Boulder, Colo., Sheehan & Assocs., Balt.; owner Wewer Studios. Represented in permanent collection Aspen Art Mus. Charter mem. Aspen Initiative.Recipient Creative Design Distinction, Andy, Printing Industries Am., 1981; Distinctive Merit award Advt. Club of N.Y., 1980, Art Dirs. Club of Met. Washington, 1980; Clio awards, 1979; named Outstanding Working Woman, Glamour mag., 1978, Outstanding Tchr., Colo. Mountain Coll.; Nat. Newspaper Nat. Creativity award, 1974. Mem. Ski Industries of Am., Women in Advt. and Mktg., Am. Women in Radio and TV, Am. Mgmt. Assn., Advt. Club, Art Dirs. Club, NOW. Studio: Wewer Studios 228 Teal Ct Aspen CO 81611

WEXNER, LESLIE HERBERT, retail apparel chain executive; b. Dayton, Ohio, 1937. BS with honors, Ohio State U., 1959, HHD (hon.), 1986; LLD (hon.), Hofstra U., 1987. Founder, pres., chmn. bd. The Limited, Inc., fashion chain, Columbus, 1963—; dir., mem. exec. com. Banc One Corp., Sotheby's Holdings Inc.; mem. bus. adminstrn. adv. council Ohio State U. Bd. dirs. Columbus Urban League, 1982-84, Hebrew Immigrant Aid Soc., N.Y.C., 1982—; trustee Columbus Symphony Orch.; co-chmn. Internat. United Jewish Appeal Com.; nat. vice chmn. United Jewish Appeal; bd. dirs., mem. exec. com. Am. Jewish Joint Distbn. Com., Inc.; trustee Columbus Jewish Fedn., 1972, Capitol South Community Urban Redevel. Corp., Columbus Mus. Art; chmn. Columbus Capital Corp. for Civic Improvement. Named Man of Yr. Am. Mktg. Assn., 1974. Mem. Young Presidents Orgn., Sigma Alpha Mu. Club: B'nai B'rith. Office: The Limited Inc 2 Limited Pkwy Box 16000 Columbus OH 43216

WEYAND, CARLTON DAVIS, composer, music publisher, designer; b. Buffalo, Feb. 19, 1916; s. William George and Mary E. (Davis) W.; m. Annemarie M. Nos, July 19, 1947. Student Millard Fillmore Coll., 1937, Syracuse U., 1939, Bryant Stratton, 1973. Singer-entertainer stage/radio, 1924-40; barge capt., Erie Canal, N.Y., 1936, 39; contractor Weyand Bldg., Buffalo, 1947-54; self-employed designer, Buffalo, 1954-67; pub. Weyand Music, Depew, N.Y., 1967—; musician-piano arranger, Depew, 1967—; owner Da-Car Recording Co., 1967—. Composer, pub. Moon Over the River, 1940, My Old Hometown, 1942, The 80's Song Folio, 1977, Grey Mood Tonight, 1978, Song for Freedom, 1978, Piano Classics Collection, 1988; composer Bicentennial Suite, 1787—, collection piano classics and preludes, 1988; pub. A Father for Christmas, 1983 (Hazel Adair, Werner Janssen), 1984, To Seal Our Love (Werner Janssen, Lockenbie), 1984; composer, publisher Yesterday, A Love Ago, 1980, Change of Heart, 1980, Now I Know, 1980, Empty Sea, 1980; collaborator, pub. Thanks, Mr. Handel (Werner Janssen, W. Brandin), 1988; performed as singer at Maxine Theatre, 1930, Marble Arch Theatre, London, 1944; performed under psuedonym Tex Davis, 1936. Sec., Pan Am. Club, Buffalo, 1951. Served with USAF, 1941-47; ETO. Recipient Electric Motor Control award Niagara Mohawk Power Corp., Buffalo, 1964. Fellow AIA; mem. ASCAP, Nat. Acad. Popular Music, N.Y.C., 1987, Am. Biog. Inst. (research bd. advisors, (hon.) 1987), Nat. Music Pubs. Assn., Internat. Platform Assn., Songwriter's Guild. Republican. Lutheran. Club: Frohsinn Singing Soc. (Buffalo) (tenor 1948-54). Avocations: oil-painting, sketch drawing, Roman history. Home: 297 Rehm Rd Depew NY 14043

WEYERHAEUSER, GEORGE HUNT, forest products company executive; b. Seattle, July 8, 1926; s. John Philip and Helen (Walker) W.; m. Wendy Wagner, July 10, 1948; children: Virginia Lee, George Hunt, Susan W., Phyllis A., David M., Merrill W. BS with honors in Indsl. Engring., Yale U., 1949. With Weyerhaeuser Co., Tacoma, 1949—, successively mill foreman, br. mgr., 1949-56, v.p., 1957-62, exec. v.p., 1962-66, pres., 1966—, also chief exec. officer, bd. dirs., chmn., 1988—; bd. dirs. Boeing Co., SAFECO Corp., Chevron Copr.; mem. adv. bd. sch. of bus. adminstrn. U. Wash., the Bus. Council, Bus. Roundtable, Wash. State Bus. Roundtable. Office: Weyerhaeuser Co Tacoma WA 98477

WEYGAND, LAWRENCE RAY, insurance company executive; b. South Haven, Mich., Jan. 5, 1940; s. Ray and Lorraine (Berkins) W.; B.A., Drake U., 1962, postgrad., 1962-63; m. Paula West, May 2, 1987; 1 son, Chad C. Comml. multi-peril ins. underwriter Aetna Casualty & Surety Co., Mpls., also Indpls., 1964-66, Safeco Ins. Co., Denver, 1966-69; pres., chmn. bd. Weygand & Co., ins. agts., brokers and consultants, Denver, 1969—; pres. Homeowners Ins. Agy., Inc., Scottsdale, Ariz., Homeowners Ins., Inc., Denver, Weygand & Co. of Ariz., Inc., Scottsdale, Transatlantic Underwriters, Inc.; owner U.S. Insurors, Inc., Ariz. Dealers Ins. Services, Inc., Colo. Dealers Ins. Services, Inc., Denver, Storage Pak Ins., Inc.; owner, pres. mng. gen. agy. serving Colo., Ariz., Nev., Utah and N.Mex.; asst. to Gov. State of Iowa, 1961-62. Mem. bus. community adv. council Regis Coll., 1976—. Mem. Ind. Ins. Agts. Colo. (chmn. fair and ethical practice com.), Ind. Ins. Agts. Am., Profl. Ins. Agts. Colo., Profl. Ins. Agts. Am., Alpha Tau Omega. Republican. Congregationalist. Clubs: Denver Athletic. Home: 10703 E Crestline Ave Englewood CO 80110 Home: 8415 E San Candido Dr Scottsdale AZ 85258 Office: 1582 S Parker Rd Denver CO 80231 Office: 3200 N Hayden St Scottsdale AZ 85258

WEYLAND, ALPHONSE JOSEPH, ambassador; b. Luxembourg, Luxembourg, Apr. 24, 1943; s. Adolphe and Marie (Kox) W.; m. France Munmowen, 1969 (div. 1983); children: Serge, Philippe. D of Law, Law Faculty Paris, Luxembourg, 1967; diploma, Inst. Polit. Sci., Paris, 1967. Dep. permanent rep. to EEC Diplomatic Service of Luxembourg, 1976-80; ambassador to United Nations Diplomatic Service of Luxembourg, N.Y.C., 1983-84; ambassador to EEC Diplomatic Service of Luxembourg, Brussels, 1986-88; dir. fgn. trade Fgn. Ministry, Luxembourg, 1980-83. Recipient Grand Cross, Spain; named Grand Officer, Holland, Grand Officer, Italy. Lodge: Rotary (hon.). Home: 22 Val du Bois, Kraainem, 1050 Brussels Belgium Office: ECC, 73 Ave de Kontelberg, 1040 Brussels Belgium

WEYSSER, JOHN LOUIS GALLUS, consulting mining engineer; b. Nutley, N.J., Feb. 12, 1910; s. John Robert Gallus and Helen (Konstan) W.; B.S., Lehigh U., 1931, E.M., 1937; m. Ethel Miriam Bullock, Apr. 23, 1931. Instr. mining engring. Pa. State U., 1931-34; research mining engr. Lehigh Nav. Coal Co. (Pa.), 1934-39, cost engr. 1938-39; asst. prof. mining engring. U. Ill., 1939-41; tech. adviser Office Prodn. Mgmt., 1941-42, War Prodn. Bd., Washington, 1942-43; chief coal mining sect. WPB, Washington, 1943-45; project mgr. Lehigh Nav. Coal Co., 1946-48; gen. mgr. Lehigh Materials Co., 1948-51; cons. mining engr., 1951—; v.p. Pierce Mgmt. Corp., Scranton, Pa., 1959-67; co-gen. mgr. Dai Han Coal Corp., Seoul, Korea, 1959-64; cons. Def. Solid Fuels Adminstrn., Washington, 1951, various mining cos., 1951-53, UN Korean Reconstrn. Agy., Dai Han Coal Corp., Korea, 1953-54, ICA, Washington, 1955; minerals adviser Govt. of Pakistan, 1956-57; coal industry adviser Republic of Korea, 1964-67, Turkish Coal Enterprise mine devel. project, Zonguldak, Turkey, 1969-70. Recipient Premier's citation for contbn. to econ. devel. Republic of Korea, 1963. Active Boy Scouts Am., 1936-39. Recipient citation Sec. of War, 1943. Registered profl. engr., Ky., Pa. Mem. AIME (Legion of Honor award 1979), Ill. Mining Inst., Rocky Mountain Coal Mining Inst., Am. Soc. Engring. Edn., Nat., Pa. socs. profl. engrs., Lehigh U. Alumni Assn., Korean Mining Inst. (hon.), Sigma Gamma Epsilon (hon.), Theta Xi. Republican. Episcopalian. Lion. Club: Seoul Country (hon.). Author: Mine Transportation, 1952; Pennsylvania Anthracite Mining Guidance Standards, 1954. Contbr. articles profl. jours. Originator long hole anthracite mining method. Home: 1501 Hartwick Dr Sun City Center FL 33570

WHALEN, MARGARET L., accountant; b. Jerome, Ariz., Sept. 18, 1944; d. Salvador Pina and Mercedes (Lopez) Rodriguez; m. Ronald Lee Ledesma, June 29, 1963; children—Ronnette M.; m. Daniel Peter Whalen, Aug. 26, 1972; children—Tara L., Daniel Peter, Salvador. Student Calif. State U.-Los Angeles, 1978-79, E. Los Angeles Coll., 1966-72, U. Calif.-Riverside, 1962-63. C.P.A., Calif. Accounts payable clk. Byron Jackson, Vernon, Calif., 1965-66; accounts payable clk., to acctg. analyst Holly div. LSI, South Gate, Calif., 1966-69; staff acct. Maginnis, Bell, Knechtel & McIntyre, C.P.A.s, Pasadena, 1969-76; staff acct. Bell, Goehner & Isham, Pasadena, 1976-78; prin. Whalen's Bookkeeping & Tax Service, Glendora, Calif., 1978-81, Margaret L. Whalen, C.P.A. Azusa, Calif., 1981—. Mem. Am. Inst. C.P.A.s, Calif. Soc. C.P.A.s, Enrolled Agts. Republican. Roman Catholic. Club: Jerome Verde Valley (pres.). Home: 136 S Sandalwood Pl Glendora CA 91740 Office: 1197 W Arrow Hwy Azusa CA 91702

WHALING, FRANK, religious studies educator, clergyman; b. Pontefract, Yorkshire, Eng., Feb. 5, 1934; s. Frederick and Ida (Johnson) W.; m. Patricia Hill, Aug. 6, 1960; children—John Prem Francis, Ruth Shanti Patricia. B.A. in History, Christ's Coll., Cambridge U., 1957, B.A. in Theology, Wesley House, Cambridge U., 1959, M.A., Cambridge U., 1961; Th.D. in Comparative Religion, Harvard U., 1973. Ordained to ministry, Methodist Ch. Minister, Methodist Ch., Birmingham, Eng., 1960-62; minister, coll. mgr. Methodist Ch., Faizabad and Banaras, India, 1962-66; minister Methodist Ch., Eastbourne, Eng., 1966-69; teaching fellow Harvard U., Cambridge, Mass., 1971-72, vis. prof., 1979; spl. tchr. to sr. lectr. in religious studies Edinburgh (Scotland) U., 1973—; spl. lectr., vis. prof. U. Ind., 1975, Dartmouth Coll., 1982, Peking U., 1982, 87, Witwatersrand U., S. Africa, 1984, Calcutta U., 1985; dir. Edinburgh-Farmington Project, Edinburgh and Oxford, 1977-81; cons. Radio Scotland, Glasgow, 1980—; dir. Edinburgh-Cook Project, Edinburgh and Gloucester, 1981-83. Author: An Approach to Dialogue: Hinduism & Christianity, 1966; The Rise of the Religious Significance of Rāma, 1980; John and Charles Wesley: Selected Writings, 1981; Religions of the World, 1985; Christian Theology and World Religions: A Global Approach, 1986; The World's Religious Traditions: Current Perspectives in Religious Studies, 1984; Contemporary Approaches to the Study of Religion: The Humanities, 1984; Contemporary Approaches to the Study of Religion: The Social Sciences, 1985; Religion in Today's World, 1987; contbr. articles and revs. to profl. jours.; cons. 26 vol. series World Spirituality, 1981—. Mem. council Shap Working Party, London, 1973—; mem. Internat. Ctr. Integrative Studies, N.Y.C., 1974—; chmn. to pres. Scottish Working Party on Religion in Edn., Edinburgh, 1975—; mem. council Christian Edn. Movement in Scotland, Dunblane, 1979—; chmn. Scottish Churches China Group, 1986—, Edinburgh Inter-Faith Assn., 1987—; dir. Edinburgh Cancer Heop Ctr., 1988—. Recipient Theyer Honor award, Harvard U., 1971; Maitland fellow, Cambridge U., 1969, Fulbright fellow, Harvard U., 1981; Brit. Acad. to Chinese Acad. Social Scis. Exchange fellow, 1982, 87; Brit. Council grantee, Moray grantee, Commonwealth Inst. grantee, Carnegie grantee, Farmington grantee, Cook grantee. Fellow Royal Asiatic Soc., World Lit. Acad.; mem. Brit. Assn. History Religions (com. officer 1980-84), Theology Soc., Indian Religions Soc., Internat. Biog. Assn., Am. Biog. Inst., Internat. Hall of Leaders, World Inst. Achievement, World Lit. Acad., Internat. Assn. Buddhist Studies, Religion and Theology Soc., Brit. Fulbright Soc., Farmington Council, Soc. Authors. Home: 29 Ormidale Terr, Murrayfield, Edinburgh EH12 6EA, Scotland Office: U Edinburgh, The Mound, Edinburgh EH1, Scotland

WHAM, WILLIAM NEIL, publisher; b. N.Y.C., Dec. 28, 1934; s. William and Jessie (Neill) W.; m. Lynn McCorvie, Mar. 6, 1966; children: McCorvie, Avery. B.S., Syracuse U., 1956. Salesman Mut. N.Y., N.Y.C., 1959-61; regional sales mgr. Doubleday Pub. Co., N.Y.C., 1961-64, Reinhold Pub. Co., N.Y.C., 1964-68; sales mgr. United Bus. Publs., N.Y.C., 1968; pres., pub. jours. Internat. Scientific Communications, Inc., Fairfield, Conn., 1968—. Founder: (with Kenneth S. Halaby) sci. jours. Am. Lab., Internat. Lab., Am. Biotech. Lab., Am. Clin. Products Rev., Internat. Biotech. Lab., Lab. Products Tech., Am. Lab. News. Served with AUS, 1956-58. Home: 157 Pinewood Trail Trumbull CT 06611 Office: Internat Scientific Communications Inc 30 Controls Dr Shelton CT 06484-0870

WHARTON, WILLIAM POLK, consulting psychologist; b. Hopkinsville, Ky.; s. William Polk and Rowena Evelyn (Wall) W.; m. Lillian Marie Andersen, Mar. 11, 1944; 1 child, Christine Evelyn Wharton Leonard. B.A., Yale U., 1934; M.A., Tchrs. Coll., 1949; Ph.D., Columbia U., 1952. Diplomate Am. Bd. Profl. Psychology, Am. Bd. Psychotherapy; Lic. psychologist, Pa. Research advt. promotion, advt. sales Esquire Inc., N.Y.C., 1934-40; dir. counseling, prof. edn., counseling psychologist Allegheny Coll., Meadville, Pa., 1952-74; dir. Ednl. Guidance Clinic, Meadville, 1958-74; pvt. practice cons. psychologist Meadville, 1974—; cons. U.S. Army Edn. Ctr., Ft. Meade, Md., 1960-61; research adv. council Ednl. Devel. Ctr., Berea, Ohio, 1971-72; cons. to pres. Alliance Coll., Cambridge Springs, Md., 1975-76. Mem. editorial bd. Psychotherapy, 1966-68; reviewer Jour. Coll. Student Personnel, 1984-88; contbr. articles to profl. jours. Chmn. MH/MR Bd. Crawford County Pa., Meadville, 1970-73; com. chmn., Drug and Alcohol Council Crawford County Pa., Meadville, 1973-76; ethics com. chmn. North West Pa. Psychol. Assn., 1975-78; del. Pa. Mental Health Assn. Crawford County, 1978-79. Served to lt. col. U.S. Army, 1941-46, Res. Psychotherapy Research Group vis. fellow, 1961-62. Fellow Pa. Psychol. Assn.; mem. Am. Psychol. Assn. (Disting. Contbn. award 1985), Am. Personnel & Guidance Assn., Nat. Vocat. Guidance Assn., Pa. Coll. Personnel Assn. (chmn. 1956-57), Phi Beta Kappa. Phi Delta Kappa, Kappa Beta Pi. Home and Office: 415 N Main St Meadville PA 16335

WHATLEY, JACQUELINE BELTRAM, lawyer; b. West Orange, N.J., Sept. 26, 1944; d. Quirino and Eliane (Gruet) Beltram; m. John W. Whatley, June 25, 1966. BA, U. Tampa, 1966; JD, Stetson U., 1969. Bar: Fla. 1969, Alaska 1971. Assoc. Gibbons, Tucker, McEwen Smith & Cofer, Tampa, Fla., 1969-71; sole practice, Anchorage, 1971-73; ptnr. Gibbons, Tucker, Miller, Whatley & Stein, P.A., Tampa, 1973-81, pres., 1981—. Bd. dirs. Travelers Aid Soc.; trustee Humana Women's Hosp., Tampa, Keystone United Meth. Ch., 1986—. Mem. ABA, Fla. Bar Assn., Alaska Bar Assn., Tenn. Walking Horse Breeders and Exhibitors Assn. (v.p. 1984-87, dir. for Fla. 1981-87), Fla. Walking and Racking Horse Assn. (bd. dirs. 1988—, pres. 1980-82). Republican. Methodist. Club: Athena (Tampa). Home: PO Box 17595 Tampa FL 33682 Office: 101 E Kennedy Blvd Tampa FL 33602

WHEATON, JOHN SOUTHWORTH, distribution company executive; b. Balt., Dec. 26, 1928; s. Ezra Almon and Ruth Adelaide (Otis) W.; m. Joy Lorraine Thuressen, Dec. 16, 1950; children: Sandra, Jason, Christopher. B.A., Stanford U., 1951; M.B.A., Columbia U., 1953. Mgr. fin. TRW, Inc., Redondo Beach, Calif., 1956-60; v.p. ops. Bissett-Berman Corp., Santa Monica, Calif., 1960-71; v.p. ops. control Foremost-McKesson, Inc., San Francisco, 1971-74; v.p. planning and analysis McKesson Corp., San Francisco, 1974-86, exec. v.p. adminstrn., 1986—; bd. dirs. Armor All, Irvine, Calif., Pharm. Card Systems, Scottsdale, Ariz. Bd. dirs. Assn. Corp. Growth, San Francisco. Served to lt. USNR, 1953-56. Club: Olympic. Office: McKesson Corp One Post St San Francisco CA 94104

WHEELER, ELTON SAMUEL, financial executive; b. Salinas, Calif., Oct. 25, 1943; s. Luther Elton and Naomi E. (Beatty) W.; B.S., Calif. State U., 1966; m. Patricia Lynne McCleary, Sept. 2, 1967; children—Pamela Kathleen, Leslie Elizabeth-Anne, Deborah Suzanne, Jonathan Samuel. Acct., Coopers & Lybrand, Oakland, Calif., 1967-70; controller Adams Properties, Inc., San Francisco, 1970-71, treas., 1972-75, v.p., chief fin. officer, 1976-77; v.p., chief fin. officer Adams Capital Mgmt. Co., San Francisco, 1977-79, pres., chief exec. officer, 1979-87; pres., chief exec. officer, dir. Calif. Real Estate Investment Trust, 1980—; Served with USMCR, 1966-72. C.P.A., Calif. Mem. Nat. Assn. Real Estate Investment Trusts, Inc. (treas., bd. govs.), Am. Inst. CPAs, Calif. Soc. CPAs. Club: Olympic. Office: 850 Montgomery St Suite 100 San Francisco CA 94133

WHEELER, RAYMOND LESLIE, aerospace engineer; b. London, Oct. 25, 1927; s. Edmund Francis and Ivy Geraldine (Fryer) W.; m. Jean McInnes, Mar. 22, 1950; children: Lesley, Jennifer, Douglas. BS in Engring., Southampton U., 1949; MS, Imperial Coll., 1952. Chartered engr., Eng. Apprentice Westland Aerospace, Ltd. (formerly Saunders-Roe Ltd.), East Cowes, Isle of Wight, U.K., 1945-52, sr. stressman, 1952-62, chief stressman, 1962-65, chief structural designer, 1965-68, chief designer, 1966-72, tech. dir., 1972-85, dir. bus. devel., 1986—. Contbr. articles to sci. publs.; patentee air cushion vehicle field. Bd. govs. Isle of Wight Coll. Arts, 1980—; chmn. bd. govs. Whippingham Primary Sch., Isle of Wight, 1982—, Isle of Wight Area Bd. Young Enterprise, 1984—. Fellow Royal Aero. Soc., Royal Instn. Naval Architects. Methodist. Home: 106 Old Rd, East Cowes Isle of Wight PO 32 6AX, England Office: Westland Aerospace Ltd, East Cowes Isle of Wight PO32 6RH, England

WHEELER, RURIC E., educator; b. Clarkson, Ky., Nov. 30, 1923; s. Mark H. and Mary (Sullivan) W.; A.B., Western Ky. U., 1947; M.S., U. Ky., 1948, Ph.D., 1952; m. Joyce Ray, May 31, 1946; children—Eddy Ray, Paul Warren. Instr. math. U. Ky., 1948-52; asst. prof. statistics Fla. State U., 1952-53; asso. prof. math. Samford U., 1953-55, prof., head dept., 1955-65, chmn. div. natural scis., 1965-67, asst. to acad. dean, 1967-68; dean Howard Coll. Arts and Scis., 1968-70, v.p. acad. affairs, 1970-87, univ. professor, 1987—; cons. in field; dir. NSF Inst., 1961, Ala. Vis. Scientist Program, 1962-67. Mem. Birmingham Manpower Area Planning Council, 1972-75. Trustee Gorgas Found., 1968—; mem. Jefferson County Ednl. Consortium, 1981—, pres. 1986-88; mem. Commn. to Upgrade Jefferson County Schs., 1982-86. Served to lt. USAAF, 1943-46. Mem. Am. Edn. Assn., Am. Math. Soc., Am. Math. Assn. (chmn. S.E. sect. 1966-67), Nat. Council Tchrs. Math., Assn. Math. Tchrs. Ala. (pres. 1963), Assn. So. Bapt. Colls. and Schs. (sec. 1973, v.p. 1974, pres. 1975, deans sect.), Ala. Acad. Sci. (pres. 1967-69), Am. Assn. Higher Edn., Assn. Ala. Coll. Adminstrs. (exec. com. 1976—, pres. 1978-79), Am. Assn. U. Adminstrs. (exec. com. Ala. sect. 1972-74, v.p. 1974-76, pres. 1976-77), Am. Conf. Acad. Deans, So. Conf. Deans Faculties and Acad. Vice Presidents (pres. 1982), Conf. Acad. Deans of So. States (pres. 1985-86). Baptist (deacon). Rotarian (pres. 1982). Author: Modern Math, An Elementary Approach, 1966, 7th edit., 1988, alt. edit., 1981; Fundamental Concepts of Math, 1968, 2d edit., 1976; Modern Math for Business, 1969, 4th edit., 1986; A Programmed Study of Number Systems, 1972; Finite Mathematics, 1974, 3d edit., 1985; Intuitive Geometry, 1975; Mathematics, an Everyday Language, 1979; Student Activities Manual, Elementary Mathematics, 1984; Mathematicas un Lenguaje Cotidiano, 1982, Activities Manual for Elementary School Teachers, 1988, Introduccion a los Conjuntos Numericos, 1976. Home: 1347 Badham Dr Birmingham AL 35216

WHEELER, THOMAS FRANCIS, data processing executive; b. Norristown, Pa., Jan. 27, 1937; s. Thomas Francis and Dorothy Marie (Kane) W.; m. Margaret Anne Raleigh, April 4, 1964; children: Thomas A., Michael T., Margaret T. BA, Villanova U., 1960; postgrad., Cath. U. Am., 1960-61. Physics, math. tchr. St. Pius X High Sch., Pottstown, Pa., 1962-63; computer programmer IBM Corp., Endicott, N.Y., 1963-68, mgr. programming, 1968-74; asst. to v.p. systems devel. IBM Corp., Poughkeepsie, N.Y., 1974-75; design mgr. communications and distributed systems IBM Corp., Kingston, N.Y., 1975-78; cons. for engring., programming, tech. IBM Corp., Armonk, N.Y., 1978-81; mgr. systems architecture IBM Corp., White Plains, N.Y., 1981-84; v.p. advanced systems Gen. Elec. Calma, San Diego, 1984-87; pres. Daplus Co., 1987—; mem. steering com. for engring. mgmt. edn. San Diego State U., 1985—; lectr. Mfg. Tech. Inst., 1981-84, devel. mgmt. tng. 1981-84; frequent speaker; mem. adv. com. U. Calif. San Diego Sch. Engring., 1986—. Author numerous research papers; contbr. articles to tech. jours. Various positions Boy Scouts Am., Binghamton, N.Y., Poughkeepsie, N.Y., White Plains N.Y., Dallas, 1961-84; mem. fin. com. campaign Sen. James Buckley, N.Y., 1976. Recipient Silver Beaver award Boy Scouts Am., Poughkeepsie, 1978. Mem. IEEE (computer soc., Disting. Lectr. award 1985), AAAS, N.Y. Acad. Sci., World Future Soc., Assn. of Computing Machinery, San Diego C. of C., Am. Electronic Assn. (chmn. edn. com. 1987—, air space Am. protocol com.). Republican. Roman Catholic. Lodge: Kiwanis. Office: Gen Electric Calma Advanced Systems 9805 Scranton Rd San Diego CA 92121

WHELAN, JAMES ROBERT, magazine editor-in-chief, investment consultant; b. Buffalo, July 27, 1933; s. Robert and Margaret (Southard) W.; children: Robert J., Heather Elizabeth. Student, U. Buffalo, 1951-53, U.

R.I., 1955-57; B.A., Fla. Internat. U., 1974; Nieman fellow, Harvard U., 1966-67. Staff corr., fgn. corr., country mgr., div. mgr. UPI, Buffalo, 1952-53, Providence, 1955-57, Boston, 1957-58, Buenos Aires, Argentina, 1958-61, Caracas, Venezuela, 1961-66, San Juan, P.R., 1966, 68; regional dir. corp. relations, then v.p. ops. ITT World Directories, ITT, San Juan, 1968-70; Latin Am. corr. Scripps-Howard Newspaper Alliance, Washington, 1970-71; mng. editor Miami (Fla.) News, 1971-73; free-lance writer 1973-74; pres., editor, pub. Hialeah (Fla.) Pub. Co., 1975-77; v.p., editorial dir. Panax Corp., Washington, 1977-80; v.p., editor Sacramento Union, 1980-82; editor, pub. Washington Times, 1982-84; mng. dir. CBN News, 1985-86; pres. Capital Communications Internat., 1986—; guest lectr. Boston U., U. Miami, Central U., Venezuela, Cath. U., Andres Bello, Caracas; guest lectr. Fla. Internat. U., U. Tex., Austin; guest prof. U. Fla., 1973; exec. v.p., editor-in-chief Conservative Digest mag. Author: Through the American Looking Glass: Central America's Crisis, 1980, Allende: Death of a Marxist Dream, 1981, Catastrophe in the Caribbean: The Failure of America's Human Rights Policy in Central America, 1984, The Soviet Assault on America's Southern Flank, 1988. Bd. dirs. Christian Community Service Agy., Miami, 1973, Hialeah-Miami Springs (Fla.) C. of C., 1976-77, Wolf Trap Found., 1984-87; bd. dirs. Nat. Council for Better Edn.; chmn. print media div. United Way campaign, Sacramento, 1981; bd. govs. Council on Nat. Policy, Washington, 1981-87; del. Commn. of Californias, 1981; pres. Council for Inter-Am. Security Ednl. Inst., 1986—; mem. spl. task force on pub. safety Greater Washington Bd. Trade; mem. Nat. Commn. on Free and Responsible Media, 1983-84; bd. dirs. Nat. Bus. Consortium for Gifted and Talented Children, 1985-87; bd. govs. Internat. Policy Forum, 1985—; mem. Presdl. Bd. Fgn. Scholarships (Fulbright Commn.), 1986—, exec./planning com., 1987—. Served with Signal Corps U.S. Army, 1953-55. Recipient Golden Press award Am. Legion Aux., 1977; citation of excellence Overseas Press Club, 1971; Unity award Lincoln U., 1976; Golden Press award Am. Legion Aux., Fla., 1977. Mem. Am. Soc. Newspapers Editors, Nat. Press Club, Overseas Press Club, Sigma Delta Chi. Clubs: University (Washington); Georgetown, Cosmos; Harvard (N.Y.C.). Home: 1201 S Eads St Arlington VA 22202 Office: Conservative Digest Mag 1210 National Press Bldg Washington DC 20045

WHELAN, JOSEPH L., neurologist; b. Chisholm, Minn., Aug. 13, 1917; s. James Gorman and Johanna (Quilty) W.; m. Gloria Ann Rewoldt, June 12, 1948; children: Joe, Jennifer Whelan Connolly. Student, Hibbing Jr. Coll., 1935-38; BS, U. Minn., 1940, MB, 1942, MD, 1943. Diplomate Am. Bd. Psychiatry and Neurology. Intern Detroit Receiving Hosp., 1942-43; fellow neurology U. Pa. Hosp., Phila., 1946-47; resident neurology U. Minn. Hosps., Mpls., 1947-49; chief neurology service VA Hosp., Mpls., 1949; spl. fellow electroencephalography Mayo Clinic, Rochester, Minn., 1951; practice medicine specializing in neurology Detroit, 1949-73, Petoskey and Gaylord, Mich., 1973—; asst. prof. Wayne State U., 1957-63; chief neurology services Grace Hosp., St. John's Hosp., Bon Secour Hosp., Detroit; cons. neurologist No. Mich. Hosps., Charlevoix Area Hosp., Community Meml. Hosp., Cheboygan, Ostego Meml. hosp., Gaylord; instr. U. Minn. Med. Sch., 1949; cons. USPHS, Detroit Bd. Edn. Contbr. articles to profl. jours. Founder, mem. ad hoc Com. to Force Lawyers Out of Govt.; chmn. Reagan-Bush Campaign, Kalkaska County, Mich., 1980. Served to capt. AUS, 1943-46. Fellow Am. Acad. Neurology (treas. 1955-57), Am. Electroencephalography Soc.; mem. Assn. Research Nervous and Mental Diseases, Soc. Clin. Neurologists, Mich. Neurol. Assn. (sec.-treas. 1967-76), AMA, Mich. Med. Assn., No. Mich. Med. Soc., AAAS, N.Y. Acad. Sci. Republican. Roman Catholic. Club: Grosse Pointe (Mich.). Address: Oxbow 9797 N Twin Lake Rd NE Mancelona MI 49659

WHIDDEN, STANLEY JOHN, physiologist, physician; b. N.Y.C., Oct. 10, 1947; s. Stanley Graham and Maybell (Van Houten) W. AS, Delgado Coll., 1969; BS, Southeastern La. U., 1971, MS, 1973; PhD, Auburn U., 1979; MD, U. Auto. De Ciudad Juarex, Mex., 1984; postgrad. Hyperbaric Physicians Ctr., NOAA, Nat. Def. U. , 1986. Asst. head ops. Nuclear Sci. Ctr., Auburn U., Ala., 1976-78; lectr. physiology U. Wis.-Madison, 1978-79; asst. prof. U. New Orleans, 1979-80; postdoctoral fellow shock physiology La. State U. Med. Ctr., New Orleans, 1980-82; research, med. staff JESM Baromed. Inst., New Orleans, 1984-86; asst. prof. research La. State U. Med. Ctr., New Orleans, 1988—. Contbr. chpt. to books: Handbook of Shock and Trauma, 1983, Phsyiological Basis of Decompression Sickness, 1987. Served to maj. USAR, 1966—. Named to Hon. Col., La. Gov. Staff, 1985; named one of Outstanding Young Men of Am., 1986; fellow NASA, 1987. Mem. AAUP, AAAS, Am. Physiology Soc., Soc. Neurosci. Am. Chem. Soc., Aerospace Med. Assn., Aerospace Physiol. Soc., Am. Vet. Physiology and Pharmacology Soc., Am. Burn Assn., N.Y. Acad. Sci., Shock Soc., Undersea Med. Soc. Republican. Club: Spl. Forces assn. (New Orleans) (pres. 1983-84). Current work: Underlining cardiovascular and metabolic responses during shock with resuscitation and hyperbaric medical treatment. Subspecialties: Physiology (medicine); Space medicine. Named one of Outstanding Young Men in Am., 1986. Office: LSUMC Dept Physiology 1901 Perdido St New Orleans LA 70122

WHIGHAM, THOMAS EDMONDSON, lawyer; b. Opp, Ala., Dec. 8, 1952; s. Julian Bertie and Mildred (Edmondson) W.; m. Sally Ann Oyler, Apr. 4, 1981; children: Thomas Edmondson Jr., Bert Michael. AA, U. Fla., 1974, BA, 1977; JD, Nova U., 1980. Bar: Fla. 1981, U.S. Dist. Ct. (mid. dist.) Fla. 1981, U.S. Ct. Claims 1981, U.S. Ct. Appeals (11th cir.) 1981, U.S. Supreme Ct., 1984. Ptnr. Stenstrom, McIntosh, Julian, Colbert & Whigham, P.A., Sanford, Fla., 1980—; designated atty. Personal Injury and Wrongful Death Fla., Bar Designation Program, 1985. Committeeman Seminole County Dem. Party, Sanford, 1978; del. Fla. Dem. Conv., Orlando, 1978; mem. Sch. Dividend Program, 1983—, Sanford Bd. Adjustments and Appeals, 1984-86, Seminole county Farm Bur., 1983—; Seminole High Sch. Booster, 1971—, Gator Boosters, 1981—; mem. adv. com. Sanford Youth Club, 1988. Mem. ABA, Fla. Bar Assn., Seminole County Bar Assn. (treas. 1985-86, chmn. law week 1988), Assn. Trial Lawyers of Am., Acad. Fla. Trial Lawyers, Ducks Unltd., Nat. Wildlife Fedn., Fla. Wildlife Fedn., Audubon Soc., Alpha Tau Omega, Phi Alpha Delta. Democrat. Baptist. Club: Cen. Fla. Gator Orlando. Lodge: Optimist (pres. Sanford club 1979-1980), Rotary. Office: Stenstrom McIntosh et al 200 W First St Suite 22 Sanford FL 32771

WHIPP, RICHARD THOMAS, history, strategic change researcher; b. London, Sept. 29, 1954; s. Samuel Richard and Jesse (Cass) W.; m. Anne Elizabeth Smith, July 8, 1978. BA with honors, Cambridge U., 1977; MA, Warwick U., Coventry, Eng., 1979, Cambridge U., 1981; PhD, Warwick U., 1983. Research fellow Work Orgn. Research Ctr., Aston U., Birmingham, Eng., 1982-84, sr. research fellow, 1984-85; prin. research fellow Ctr. for Corp. Strategy and Change, Warwick U., 1985—. Author: Innovation and the Auto Industry, 1986; contbr. articles to profl. jours. Mem. Brit. Univ. Indsl. Relations Assn. Office: Warwick U, Sch Indsl and Bus Studies, Coventry CV4 7AL, England

WHIPPLE, ELEANOR BLANCHE, educational administrator, social worker; b. Bellingham, Wash., June 7, 1916; d. Charles William and Susan Blanche (Campbell) W.; B.A. in Sociology, U. Wash., 1938, M.S.W., 1949; Ph.D., U. Santa Barbara, 1982; m. Robert Auld Fowler, Oct. 1, 1938 (div. 1947); children—Lawrence William, Jeanice Marie Fowler Roosevelt. Lic. clin. social worker. Founder, dir. Camp Cloud's End, Deception Pass, Wash., 1939-42; therapist Family Counseling Service, Seattle, 1949-58; pvt. practice counselling, Burbank, Calif., 1958-60; social service dir. Hollygrove Children's Residential Treatment Center, Hollywood, Calif., 1960-66, exec. dir., 1966-81; adj. faculty Biola U., La Mirada, Calif., 1972-80; dean Grad. Sch. Calif. Christian Inst., Orange, 1981-85, pres., 1985—. V.p., bd. dirs. Christian Fellowship for the Blind, Inc. Mem. Nat. Assn. Social Workers (chartered), Assn. Christian Therapists, Acad. Cert. Social Workers, N.Am. Assn. Christians in Social Work (bd. dirs., disting. service award). Contbr. articles in field to profl. publs. Home: 1105 Mound Ave Apt 9 South Pasadena CA 91030 Office: Calif Christian Inst 1744 W Katella Ave Orange CA 92667

WHIPPLE, GEORGE STEPHENSON, architect; b. Evanston, Ill., Sept. 21, 1950; s. Taggart and Katharine (Brewster) W.; m. Lydia Buckley, May 30, 1981; children: Katherine Elizabeth, John Taggart. B.A., Harvard U., 1974; student Boston Architectural Ctr., 1975-76. Vice-pres., Call Us Inc., Edgartown, Mass., 1970-74; pres. Cattle Creek Assocs., Carbondale, Colo., 1976—, Earthworks Constrn., Carbondale, 1978-87; pres., Whipple and Brewster Corp., Aspen, 1988—. Chmn., Redstone Hist. Preservation Commn., Colo. Mem. Rocky Mountain Harvard Club. Office: 121 S Galena Suite 203 Aspen CO 81611

WHIPPLE, KENNETH, automotive company executive; b. 1934. BS, MIT, 1958. With Ford Motor Co., Dearborn, Mich., 1958—, system and data processing mgr. fin. and ins. ops, 1966-69, mgr. mgmt. services dept. fin. staff, 1969-71, system analyst mgr. fin. staff, 1971-74, asst. controller internat. fin. staff, 1974-75, v.p. fin. and ins. subs., 1975-77, exec. v.p. fin. and ins. subs., 1977-80, pres. fin. and ins. subs., 1980-84, v.p. corp. strategy anaysis, 1984-86, v.p., 1986—; now also chmn. Ford of Europe, Inc. Office: Ford Motor Co The American Rd Dearborn MI 48121 also: Ford of Europe Inc, Eagle Way, Brentwood, Essex CM13 3BW, England *

WHIPPS, EDWARD FRANKLIN, lawyer; b. Columbus, Ohio, Dec. 17, 1936; s. Rusk Henry and Agnes Lucille (Green) W.; children: Edward Scott, Rusk Huot, Sylvia Louise, Rudyard Christian. B.A., Ohio Wesleyan U., 1958; J.D., Ohio State U., 1961. Bar: Ohio 1961, U.S. Dist. Ct. (so. dist.) Ohio 1962, U.S. Dist. Ct. (no. dist.) Ohio 1964, U.S. Ct. Claims 1963, U.S. Supreme Ct. 1963, Miss. 1965, U.S. Ct. Appeals (6th cir.) 1980. Assoc. George, Greek, King & McMahon, Columbus, 1961-66; ptnr. George, Greek, King, McMahon & McConnaughey, Columbus, 1966-79, McConnaughey, Stradley, Mone & Moul, Columbus, 1979-81, Thompson, Hine & Flory, Columbus, 1981—. Host: TV programs Upper Arlington Plain Talk, 1979-82; TV program Briding Disability, 1981-82, Lawyers on Call, 1982—, U.A. Today, 1982-86, The Ohio Wesleyan Experience, 1984—. Mem. Upper Arlington (Ohio) Bd. Edn., 1971-80, pres., 1978-79; mem. bd. alumni dirs. Ohio Wesleyan U., 1975-79. Mem. Columbus Bar Assn., Ohio State Bar Assn., ABA, Assn. Trial Lawyers Am., Ohio Acad. Trial Lawyers, Franklin County Trial Lawyers Assn., Am. Judicature Soc., Columbus Bar Found., Columbus C. of C., Upper Arlington Area C. of C. (trustee 1978—), Creative Living Inc. (founder, trustee 1969—), Delta Tau Delta (nat. v.p. 1976-78). Republican. Clubs: Lawyers, Barristers, Columbus Athletic, Columbus Touchdown, Downtown Quarterback, Ohio State U. Faculty (Columbus). Home: 3771 Lyon Dr Columbus OH 43220 Office: Thompson Hine & Flory 100 E Broad St Suite 1700 Columbus OH 43215

WHISKER, CHARLES JEWELL, art director; b. Londonderry, Northern Ireland, Oct. 18, 1949; s. Charles John and Ethel (Jewell) W.; m. Mariad McKillen, Aug. 1, 1982; children: India Chalia, Domino Sewell Isis. Student, Ulster Coll. Art & Design, Belfast, Ireland, 1966-71; BA, U. South Wales, Cardiff, 1972. Sch. tchr. London, 1974-80; dept. head Crawford Mcpl. Coll. Art, Cork, Ireland, 1980-81; lectr. Nat. Coll. Art, Dublin, 1981-86; art dir. Windmill Ln. Pictures, Dublin, 1986—; painter. Home: Carpenterstown House Castlenock, Dublin Ireland Office: Windmill Ln Pictures, Windmill Ln, Dublin Ireland

WHISSON, MICHAEL GEORGE, dean, anthropology educator; b. Croydon, England, June 10, 1937; arrived in South Africa, 1965; s. Herbert James and Katherine May (Halliday) W.; m. Adrienne Merle Fincham Pannell, Sept. 21, 1968; children: David George, Rebecca Katherine. BA with honors, St. Catherine's Coll.-Cambridge U., 1960, PhD, 1963. Research fellow East African Inst. Social and Economic Research, Makerere, Uganda, 1960-62; lectr. U. B.C., Vancouver, Can., 1963-64; dir. research Discharged Prisoners Aid Soc., Hong Kong, 1964-65; lectr. U. Cape Town, South Africa, 1965-78; prof. anthropology Rhodes U., Grahamstown, South Africa, 1978—, dean of arts, 1987—. Author: Change and Challenge, 1965, Under the Rug, 1965; contbr. numerous articles to profl. jours. Lay minister Ch. of the Province South Africa, Cape Town and Grahamstown, 1967—; councillor Grahamstown Cathedral and Diocese, 1982—, provincial Synod rep., 1982—. Fellow Royal Anthropol. Inst. Mem. Anglican Church. Home: 20 Worcester St, Grahamstown 6140, Republic of South Africa Office: Rhodes University, Office of Dean of Arts, Grahamstown 6140, Republic of South Africa

WHISTLER, LAURENCE, artist, writer, poet; b. Eng., Jan. 21, 1912; s. Henry And Helen (Ward) W.; m. Jill Furse, 1939 (dec. 1944); 2 children; m. Theresa Furse, 1950 (div.); 2 children; m. Carol Dawson, 1987. BA, Oxford U., Eng., MA, 1985. Work on glass includes engraved ch. windows and panels at Sherborne Abbey, Guards' Chapel, London, St. Hugh's Coll., Oxford, Salisbury Cathedral, Thornham Parva, Suffolk, others; exhbns. include Agnews, Bond Street, 1969, Marble Hill, Twickenham, 1972, Ashmolean, 1976; author: (prose) Sir John Vanbrugh, 1938, The English Festivals, 1947, Rex Whistler, His Life and His Drawings, 1948, Pictures on Glass, 1972, The Image on the Glass, 1975, Scenes and Signs on Glass, 1985, others; (poems) The World's Room, 1949, The View From This Window, 1956, Audible Silence, 1961, To Celebrate Her Living, 1967, Enter, 1987. Served to capt. The Rifle Brigade, 1939-45. Decorated Order Brit. Empire, 1955, comdr. Order Brit. Empire, 1973; recipient King's Gold medal for Poetry, 1936, Atlantic award for Lit., 1945; hon. fellow Balliol Coll., Oxford U., 1974. Mem. Guild of Glass Engravers (pres. 1975-80). Home and Office: Iscoed, Ferryside, Dyfed England

WHITAKER, CORINNE COOPER, financial executive, artist; b. Stamford, Conn., Aug. 31, 1934; d. Samuel and Natalie Gordon; B.A. (Durant scholar), Wellesley Coll., 1956; postgrad. N.Y. Inst. Fin., 1972-73, U. Houston, 1974; children—Nanette Cooper McGuinness, Robin Cooper Feldman. Sr. account exec. Eppler, Guerin & Turner, Inc., Houston, 1972-76; fixed income liaison Loeb, Rhodes & Co., Los Angeles, 1976-77; cons. Edward T. Watkins & Co., Houston, 1977; account exec., asso. v.p. Bateman Eichler Hill Richards, Los Angeles, 1977-79; chmn. bd., chief adminstrv. officer Don C. Whitaker, Inc., Los Angeles, 1980-84; pres. Hillcreast Cons., Inc., 1984—; mem. Pacific Stock Exchange; organized seminars, courses in field; seminar coordinator Investment Dynamics series, Houston, 1975. Bd. dirs. women's div., nat. publicity chmn. Aerospace Med. Assn., 1964; lectr. African art, docent leader Rice U. Media Center Art to Schs. Program, 1974-75; mem. bus. and industry com. women's council Los Angeles Area C. of C., 1978. Recipient John Masefield award Wellesley Coll., 1956, Katherine Lee Bates award, 1956; Vol. Service award N.Y. Med. Coll., Flower and Fifth Ave. Hosps., 1958; Rookie of Yr. award Eppler Guerin & Turner, 1973, award of excellence, 1976, named to Millionaires Club 1973-75; commendation Houston Jr. C. of C., 1975; named to Century Club, Bateman Eichler Hill Richards Inc., 1978. Mem. Norton Simon Mus., Friends of Photography, Fellows of Contemporary Art, Soc. for Contemporary Photography, Nat. Mus. of Women in Arts (charter), Los Angeles Floor Brokers Assn. (founder), Phi Beta Kappa. Clubs: Wellesley Coll. Alumnae (chmn. spl. gifts div. Washington area 1964).

WHITAKER, RONALD MARTIN, engineer; b. Fullerton, Nebr., Jan. 30, 1933; s. Leonard Bert and Margaret Mary (Seely) W.; student Central Tech. Community Coll., Hastings, Nebr., 1977, Franklin U., Columbus, Ohio, 1981 Ohio U., Lancaster; m. Janet Louise Spitz, Apr. 12, 1955; children—Mark David, Jeffrey Keith, Wendy Elaine. Mgr. Spitz Foundry Inc., Hastings, Nebr., 1965-78, Crosier Monastery, 1978; plant engr. Lattimer Stevens Co., Columbus, Ohio, 1978-80, v.p. engring., 1980-85, methods engr., 1985-86; facilities engr. Winters Industries div. Whittaker Corp., Canton, Ohio, 1986-87' facilities engr., 1986, sr. mfg. engr., 1987—; instr. Engr. Ctr., Ft. Belvoir, Va., 1953. Scoutmaster Overland Trails council Boy Scouts Am., Grand Island, Nebr., 1970-78, dist. camping dir., 1975-78, Order of Arrow advisor, 1976-78; extraordinary minister Roman Cath. Ch. Served with C.E. U.S. Army, 1953-55. Decorated Combat Infantryman's Badge, others; cert. mfg. engr.; registered profl. engr. Mem. NSPE, Soc. Mfg. Engrs. (chmn. sr. mem.), Am. Foundrymen's Soc. (sr.), Nat. Rifle Assn. (endowment mem., cert. firearms instr.), Nebr. Rifle and Pistol Assn. (life mem.), Nat. Reloaders Assn. (life), Central Ohio Council Internat. Visitors, Am Legion, Nat. Eagle Scout Assn., Am. Photog. Soc. Republican. Editorial cons. Plant Engineering mag. Home: 3042 Chaucer Dr NE North Canton OH 44721-3611 Office: Winters Industries Div Whittaker Corp 4125 Mahoning Rd NE Canton OH 44721

WHITAKER, THOMAS KENNETH, university chancellor, former president Royal Irish Academy; b. Rostrevor, Ireland, Dec. 8, 1916; s. Edward and Jane (O'Connor) W.; m. Nora Fogarty; children—Kenneth, Gerald, Raymond, David, Catherine, Brian. M.S. in Econs., U. London, 1953; D.Econ.Sc., Nat. U. Ireland, Dublin, 1962; LL.D. (hon.), U. Dublin, 1976, Queen's U. Belfast, No. Ireland, 1981; D.Sc. (hon.), U. Ulster, 1983. Sec. Irish Dept. Fin., 1956-69; gov. Central Bank Ireland, 1969-76; dir. A. Guinness & Sons, 1976-84, Bank of Ireland, 1976-85; chancellor Nat. U. Ireland, Dublin, 1976—; pres. Royal Irish Acad., 1985-87, Econ. and Social Research Inst., Dublin, 1970-87; chmn. council Dublin Inst. Advanced Studies, 1980—. Author: Financing by Credit Creation, 1947; Interests, 1983; Editor, contbg. author: Economic Development, 1958. Senator Irish Parliament, Dublin, 1977-82. Decorated comdr. Legion of Honor (France). Roman Catholic. Avocations: fishing; golf.

WHITCOMB, BARBARA ANN, food industry executive; b. Newark, Oct. 2, 1951; d. Andrew Walter and Ann Barbara (Chulick) Liyana; 1 dau., Joy. B.S. in Mgmt., Rensselaer Poly. Inst., 1973; M.B.A., U. Wis., 1975. C.P.A., Tenn.; cert. mgmt. acct. Acctg. supr. Koehring Co., Appleton, Wis., 1973-75, market analyst, 1975; fin. systems analyst Dobbs-Life Savers, Inc., Memphis, 1976-77, mgr. adminstrv. procedures, 1977-80; dir. adminstrv. control Dobbs Houses, Inc., Memphis, 1980-82, dir. ops. services, 1982-83; div. ops. mgr. Frito-Lay, Inc., Memphis, 1983-84, Mgr. sales ops., Dallas, 1984-85; mgr. expense analysis, Dallas, 1985-86. mgr. mktg. performance analysis, 1986—. Mem. Am. Inst. C.P.A.s, Inst. Mgmt. Acctg., Nat. Assn. Accts. Home: 1109 Highedge Dr Plano TX 75075 Office: SIPO Box 660634 Dallas TX 60634

WHITE, ADRIAN MICHAEL STEPHEN, banker; b. nr. Kent, Eng., Aug. 15, 1940; s. Malcolm Royston and Joan May (Richards) W.; m. Elaine M. Dorion, 1966; children: Malcolm, Catherine. Grad., McGill U., Montreal, 1964. Chartered accountant, Que., Ont. With Coopers & Lybrand, chartered accountants, 1962-66; acting treas. Rothesay Paper Corp., 1965; asst. treas. Genstar Ltd., 1967-71; treas. Brinco Ltd.; also Churchill Falls (Labrador) Corp., 1971-75; treas. Algoma Steel Corp., Ltd., Sault Ste. Marie, Ont., 1975-80; v.p., chief fin. officer Little Long Lac Gold Mines Ltd., Toronto, Ont., 1980-81; v.p. Bank of Montreal, Toronto, 1981-88; chief fin. officer Curragh Resources Group, Toronto, 1988—; fin. columnist Indsl. Mgmt. mag. Bd. dirs. Drs. Hosp. Found., 1986. Mem. Fin. Execs. Inst. (chmn. Can. internat. fin. com.), Internat. Fiscal Assn., Canadian Tax Found. Address: 72 Sir Williams Ln, Islington, ON Canada M9A 1V3

WHITE, BENJAMIN STEVEN, mathematician, researcher; b. Boston, Sept. 29, 1945; s. Norman Kenneth White and Mildred Ruth (Silverman) Segal; m. Helen Katherine Frazer, June 12, 1966; children—Adam Frazer, Ethan Abraham. S.B., MIT, 1967; M.A., U. Ariz., 1968; Ph.D., Courant Inst., NYU, 1974. Sr. mathematician Raytheon Co., Newport, R.I., 1969-70; systems analyst Time-Sharing Resources, N.Y.C., 1970-71; vis. mem. Courant Inst., NYU, 1974-75; instr. applied math. Calif. Inst. Tech., Pasadena, 1975-78; mem. tech. staff Jet Propulsion Lab., Pasadena, 1978-81; corp. research Exxon Research and Engring. Co., Annandale, N.J., 1981—, head applied math. group, 1986—; instr. NYU, Bronx, 1971-72; v.p. Perceptive Systems, Inc., Pasadena, 1981. Contbr. articles to profl. jours. Mem. Soc. for Indsl. and Applied Math., Am. Math. Soc., AAAS, N.Y. Acad. Scis. Democrat. Home: 345 Shunpike Rd Chatham Township NJ 07928

WHITE, BETTY MAYNARD, social worker; b. N.Y.C., May 22, 1922; d. William and Madge (Hooks) Maynard; B.A., Hunter Coll., 1964; M.S.W., Columbia U., 1969; m. Charles E. White, Sept. 8, 1941; 1 son, Charles B. Case worker Bur. Child Welfare, Jamaica, N.Y., 1964-69; supr. foster care Spl. Services for Children, Jamaica, 1969-73, case supr. application sec., family services, group services, 1973-83, supr. III, borough coordinator for Manhattan and Bronx, Office Home Care Services, Div. Med. Rev., 1983-84, dir. div. Med. Rev., 1984; pvt. practice, 1986—. Mem. Nat. Assn. Social Workers, Acad. Cert. Social Workers, Hunter Coll. Alumni Assn. Democrat. Roman Catholic. Home: 117-30 170th St Saint Albans NY 11434 Office: Spl Services for Children 165-15 Archer Ave Jamaica NY 11433

WHITE, MRS. C. B. See **JAMES, P(HYLLIS) D(OROTHY)**

WHITE, ETHYLE HERMAN (MRS. S. ROY WHITE), artist; b. San Antonio, Apr. 10, 1904; d. Ferdinand and Minnie (Simmang) Herman; ed. pvt. schs., instrs.; m. S. Roy White, Mar. 3, 1924 (dec.); children: Mrs. William Marion Mohrle, Patsyruth Wheeler. Exhibited numerous one-man, group shows, Tex.; represented pub. collections in U.S., pvt. collections in Switzerland, Germany, Sweden. Del. Internat. Com. Centro Studi E. Scambi Internationali. Mem. Anahuac Fine Arts Group, San Antonio, Beaumont, Galveston, Houston art leagues, Daus. Republic Tex., UDC, Pastel Soc. Tex., Watercolor Soc., Nat. League Am. Pen Women, Dallas Tex. Sumie Soc. of Am., Baytown (Tex.) Porcelain Guild. Episcopalian. Mem. Order Eastern Star. Clubs: Fine Arts (Anahuac); Artist and Craftsmen (Dallas). Author, illustrator: Arabella. Author: Poet's Hour. Home: PO Box 176 Anahuac TX 77514

WHITE, F(REDERICK) CLIFTON, public affairs consultant; b. Leonardsville, N.Y., June 13, 1918; s. Frederick H. and Mary (Hicks) W.; A.B., Colgate U., 1940; postgrad. Cornell U., 1945-47; hon. degree Hillsdale Coll., 1974; m. Gladys Bunnell, June 22, 1940; children—F(rederick) Clifton, A. Carole White Green. Pres., F. Clifton White & Assos., Inc., Greenwich, Conn., 1961; pres. Pub. Affairs Analysts Inc., N.Y.C., 1970-77; pres. DirAction Services, Inc., Greenwich, 1966-70, chmn. bd. 1971—; pres. Pub. Affairs Counsellors, Inc., N.Y.C., 1957-60; instr. social sci. Cornell U., Ithaca, N.Y., 1945-50; lectr. polit. sci. Ithaca Coll., 1949-51. Chmn. bd. Internat. Found. for Electoral Systems; del Pres.'s Hwy. Safety Council, 1953; exec. dep. commr. N.Y. State Bur. Motor Vehicles, 1952-55, acting commr., 1955; mem. adv. council on presdl. selection Brookings Instn., Washington, 1971—; mem. pub. membership inspection team USIA, 1972—; mem. Aid Election Observation Team, Costa Rica, 1986; chmn. Presdl. Commn. on Broadcasting to Cuba, 1982 dir. Pub. Affairs Council, Washington, 1958—; dir. John M. Ashbrook Ctr. Pub. Affairs, disting. vis. prof. Ashland Coll.; sr. advisor Republican Nat. Chmn., 1983-84. Del. Republican Nat. Conv., 1952, 56, 60, hon. del., 1972; del., chmn. Conv. Coms. Nat. Young Rep. Conv., 1949, 51, 53, 55; pres. N.Y. State Young Reps., 1950-52; spl. asst. N.Y. State Rep. State Chmn., 1950-52; dir. orgn. Nat. Nixon-Lodge Vols., 1960, Nat. Draft Goldwater Com., 1963; nat. dir. Goldwater for Pres. Com., 1963, 64, Citizens for Goldwater-Miller, 1964; campaign mgr. Buckley for Senate, N.Y., 1970; cons. to chmn. Com. to Reelect the Pres., 1972; polit. dir. for Ronald Reagan, Rep. Conv., 1980; sr. adv. Reagan-Bush Presdl. Campaign, 1980; mem. exec. com. Pres.-Elect's Transition Team, 1980; bd. dirs. Ctr. for Democracy at Boston U., Nat. Republican Inst. for Internat. Affairs. Served to capt. USAAF, 1942-45. Decorated Air medal with 3 oak leaf clusters, D.F.C. Mem. Inst. Fiscal and Polit. Edn. (chmn.), Am. Assn. Polit. Cons. (pres. 1970-74), Internat. Assn. Polit. Cons. (dir. 1970-74, pres. 1978), Am. Polit. Sci. Assn., Am. Acad. Polit. and Sci. Assn., Acad. Polit. Sci., SAR, Am. Acad. Polit. and Social Sci. (adv. commn. intergovtl. relations 1976-78), Public Members Assn., Internat. Found. for Electoral systems (chmn. 1988). Presbyterian (elder). Clubs: Union League (N.Y.C.); Capitol Hill (Washington); Apawamis (Rye, N.Y.); Ashland (Ohio). Lodge: Masons (32 deg.). Author: (with Joseph Eley) You Should Be a Politician, 1959; (with William J. Gill) Suite 3505, 1967; (with Charles Spiegler) Yes, We Can, 1972; (with William J. Gill) Why Reagan Won, 1981. Office: PO Box 1605 Greenwich CT 06830

WHITE, GEORGE EDWARD, pedodontist; b. Jamestown, N.Y., July 31, 1941; s. Gordon Ennis and Margaret (Appleyard) W.; AB, Colgate U., 1963; DDS, SUNY, Buffalo, 1967; PhD, MIT, 1973; DBA, Century U., 1982. Assoc. prof., chmn. dept. oral pediatrics Tufts U. Sch. Dental Medicine, Boston, 1973—; chief dept. oral pediatrics New Eng. Med. Center Hosp., Boston, 1973-80; practice pedodontics, Boston; lectr. M.I.T., 1975-80; cons. Abcor, Inc. Nat. Inst. Dental Research grantee, 1973—. Fellow Am. Acad. Pedodontics, Acad. Gen. Dentistry; mem. Internat. Assn. Dental Research, Fedn. Dentaire Internationale, AAAS. Author: Dental Caries: A Multifactorial Disease, 1975, To Stand Alone, 1979; co-author: Maxillofacial Orthopedics: For the Growing Child, 1983; founder, editor-in-chief Jour. Pedodontics, 1976; editor: Clin. Oral Pediatrics, 1979; contbr. articles to profl. jours. Office: Tufts U Sch Dental Medicine Dept Pediatric Dentistry 1 Kneeland St Boston MA 02111

WHITE, GILBERT F(OWLER), geographer; b. Chgo., Nov. 26, 1911; s. Arthur E. and Mary (Guthrie) W.; m. Anne Elizabeth Underwood, Apr. 28, 1944; children: William D., Mary, Frances. B.S., U. Chgo., 1932, S.M., 1934, Ph.D., 1942; LL.D. (hon.), Hamilton Coll., 1951, also Swarthmore

Coll., Earlham Coll., Richmond, Ind., Mich. State U., Augustana Coll.; Sc.D. (hon.), Haverford Coll.; hon. degree, Northland Coll. Geographer Miss. Valley Com. of P.W.A., 1934, Nat. Resources Bd., 1934-35; sec. land and water com. Nat. Resources Com. and Nat. Resources Planning Bd., 1935-40; with Exec. Office Pres., Bur. Budget, 1941-42; asst. exec. sec. Am. Friends Service Com., 1945-46; relief adminstr. in France, 1942-43; interned Baden-Baden; sec. Am. Relief for India, 1945-46; pres. Haverford Coll., 1946-55; prof. geography U. Chgo., 1956-69; prof. geography, dir. Inst. Behavioral Sci., U. Colo., Boulder, 1970-78; Gustavson disting. prof. emeritus Inst. Behavioral Sci., U. Colo., 1979—; dir. Natural Hazards Info. Ctr., 1978-84; exec. editor Environment mag., 1983—; vis. prof. Oxford U., 1962-63; cons. Investigations Lower Mekong Basin, 1961-62, 70; U.S. mem. UNESCO adv. com. on arid zone research, 1954-55; mem. mission Am. Vol. Agys. Relief Germany, 1946; vice chmn. Pres.'s Water Resources Policy Commn., 1950; mem. com. natural resources Hoover Commn., 1948; chmn. UN Panel Integrated River Basin Devel., 1956-57; chmn. com. water Nat. Acad. Scis., 1964-68; chmn. Task Force Fed. Flood Control Policy, 1965-66; sci. adv. to adminstr. UN Devel. Program, 1966-71; chmn. adv. bd. Energy Policy Project, 1972-74; chmn. Am. Friends Service Com., 1963-69; chmn. com. on man and environment IGU, 1969-76; chmn. steering com. High Sch. Geography com., 1964-70; mem. Tech. Assessment Adv. Council, 1974-76; chmn. environ. studies bd. NRC, 1975-77; pres. Sci. Com. on Problems of Environment, 1976-82; chmn. bd. Resources for Future, 1973-79; co-chmn. U.S.-Egypt Joint Consultative Com. on Sci. and Tech., 1981-86; mem. adv. group on greenhouse gases World Meteorol. Orgn., Internat. Council of Scientific Unions, UN Environ. Program., 1986. Author: Human Adjustment to Floods; Science and Future of Arid Lands, 1960, Social and Economic Aspects of Natural Resources, 1962, Choice of Adjustment to Floods, 1964, Strategies of American Water Management, 1969; co-author: Drawers of Water, 1972, Assessment of Research on Natural Hazards, 1975, Flood Hazard in the United States, 1975, The Environment as Hazard, 1978, also various govt. reports, 1937-45; editor: Natural Hazards: Local, National and Global, 1974, Environmental Aspects of Complex River Development, 1977; co-editor: Environmental Issues, 1977, The World Environment, 1972-1982, 1982, Environmental Effects of Nuclear War, 1983. Recipient Daly medal Am. Geog. Soc., 1971, Eben award Am. Water Resources Assn., 1972, alumni medal U. Chgo., 1979, Outstanding Achievement award Nat. Council for Geog. Edn., 1981, Sasakawa UN Environ. prize, 1985, Tyler prize, 1987. Mem. Assn. Am. Geographers (pres., Outstanding Achievement award 1955, 74, Anderson medal 1986), Nat. Acad. Scis. (commn. natural resources 1973-80, chmn. 1977-80, Environ. award 1980), Internat. Council Sci. Unions (steering com. on study of environ. consequences of nuclear war 1983-87), Soviet Geog. Soc. (hon.), Royal Geog. Soc. (hon.), USSR Acad. Scis. (fgn.), Phi Beta Kappa, Sigma Xi. Mem. Soc. Friends. Club: Cosmos (Washington). Home: 624 Pearl St Apt 302 Boulder CO 80302

WHITE, SIR (VINCENT) GORDON LINDSAY, textile company executive; b. May 11, 1923; s. Charles and Lily May (Wilson) W.; m. Virginia Anne White, 1974; 3 children. Grad., De Aston Sch., Linconshire. Chmn. Welbecson Ltd., 1947-65; dept. chmn. Hanson Trust Ltd., 1965-73; chmn. Hanson Industries N.Am., Iselin, N.J., 1983—; mem. spl. commn. Hanson's Trust's opportunities overseas, 1979-83. Mem. Council for Police Rehab. Appeal, 1985—; bd. dirs. Shakespeare Theatre, Golger Library, Washington, 1985—; bd. dirs., chmn. internat. com. Congl. Award, 1984—; gov. BFI, 1982-84. Served with British mil., 1940-46. St. Peter's Coll. hon. fellow, 1984; recipient Nat. Vol. Leadership award, Congl. award, 1984, Aims of Industry Free Enterprise award, 1985. Clubs: Spl. Forces; Brook, Explorer's (N.Y.C.); Mid-Ocean (Bermuda). Office: Hanson Industries NAm 100 Wood Ave S Iselin NJ 08830 also: 410 Park Ave New York NY 10022 *

WHITE, HOWARD ASHLEY, emeritus university president; b. Cloverdale, Ala., Sept. 28, 1913; s. John Parker and Mabel Clara (Hipp) W.; m. Maxcine Elliott Feltman, June 17, 1952; children—Ashley Feltman, Howard Elliott. Diploma, David Lipscomb Coll., 1932; B.A., Tulane U., 1946, M.A., 1950, Ph.D., 1956. Ordained to ministry Ch. of Christ, 1933; minister Carrollton Ave. Ch. of Christ, New Orleans, 1941-52; assoc. prof. history David Lipscomb Coll., Nashville, 1953-56; prof., chmn. dept. David Lipscomb Coll., 1956-58; chmn. social sci. dept. Pepperdine U., Malibu, Calif., 1958-65; dean grad. studies Pepperdine U., 1965-67, dean undergrad. studies, 1967-70, exec. v.p., 1970-78, pres., 1978-85, pres. emeritus, 1985—. Mem. Am. Hist. Assn., So. Hist. Assn., Orgn. Am. Historians, Phi Alpha Theta, Phi Delta Kappa. Clubs: Calif, Lincoln, Regency, Rotary. Home: 24440 Tiner Ct Malibu CA 90265 Office: Pepperdine U 24255 Pacific Coast Hwy Malibu CA 90265

WHITE, JACK RONALD, electronic engineer; b. Beeville, Tex., Sept. 23, 1943; s. Gene Wallace and Janet Marjorie (Copeland) W.; m. Junko Imaizumi, June 17, 1973; children: John Christopher, Jennifer Anne. BEE, U. Calif.-Santa Barbara, 1970. Electronics tech. Dynalectron Corp., Point Mugu, Calif., 1964-65, Electro Optical Inc., Santa Barbara, 1965-70; electronic engr. Pacific Missile Test Ctr., Point Mugu, 1970—. Patentee in field; author: The Invisible World of the Infrared, 1984, Satellites of Today and Tomorrow, 1985, How Computers Really Work, 1986, The Hidden World of Forces, 1987. Served with USN, 1961-64. Recipient Design award EDN Mag, 1975, Spl. Achievement award Dept. Def., 1981, Outstanding Performance award Dept. Def., 1983. Mem. Soc. Children's Book Writers. Republican. Home and Office: 2641 Truman St Camarillo CA 93010

WHITE, JAMES EDWARD, geophysicist; b. Cherokee, Tex., May 10, 1918; s. William Cleburne and Willie (Carter) W.; m. Courtenay Brumby, Feb. 1, 1941; children: Rebecca White Vanderslice, Peter McDuffie, Margaret Marie White Curren, Courtenay White Forte. B.A., U. Tex., 1941, M.A., 1946; Ph.D., MIT, 1949. Dir. Underwater Sound Lab., MIT, Cambridge, 1941-45; scientist Def. Research Lab., Austin, Tex., 1945-46; research assoc. MIT, 1946-49; group leader, field research lab. Mobil Oil Co., Dallas, 1949-55; mgr. physics dept. Denver Research Center, Marathon Oil Co., 1955-69; v.p. Globe Universal Scis., Midland, Tex., 1969-71; adj. prof. dept. geophysics Colo. Sch. Mines, Golden, 1972-73, C.H. Green prof., 1976-87, prof. emeritus, 1986—; L.A. Nelson prof. U. Tex., El Paso, 1973-76; Esso vis. prof. U. Sydney, Australia, 1975; vis. prof. MIT, 1982, U. Tex.-Austin, 1985; del. U.S.-USSR geophysics exchange Dept. State, 1965; mem. bd. Am. Geol. Inst., 1972; mem. space applications bd. Nat. Acad. Enging., 1972-77; exchange scientist Nat. Acad. Sci., 1973-74; del. conf. on oil exploration China Geophys. Soc.-Soc. Exploration Geophysicists, 1981. Author: Seismic Waves: Radiation, Transmission, Attenuation, 1965, Underground Sound: Application of Seismic Waves, 1983, (with R.L. Sengbush) Production Seismology, 1987; editor: Vertical Seismic Profiling (E.I. Galperin), 1974; contbr. articles to profl. jours. Fellow Acoustical Soc. Am.; mem. Soc. Exploration Geophysicists (hon., Maurice Ewing medal 1986, Halliburton award 1987), Sigma Xi. Unitarian. Club: Cosmos. Office: Dept Geophysics Colo Sch Mines Golden CO 80401

WHITE, JUDY MARY, writer, publisher; b. Sydney, New South Wales, Australia, Jan. 7, 1933; d. William Sparke and Evelyn Jean (Mackeller) Crossing; m. Michael Francis White, Feb. 3, 1956; children: Antony, Peter, Wendy, Scott, Camilla, Mark, Edward. B in Econs., U. Sydney, 1956; MLitt, U. New England, Australia, 1984; MA (hon.), U. Newcastle, Australia, 1988. Author, pub. Seven Press, Scone, Australia, 1981—. Author: Belltrees, 1981, Tocal, 1986. Archivist Royal Agrl. Soc., Sydney, 1976—; gov. Elizabethan Theatre Trust, Sydney, 1983—; historian Australian Bicentenary, 1987, com. mem., 1985. Mem. Royal Australian Hist. Soc., Nat. Trust Australia. Mem. National Party. Anglican. Club: Royal Sydney Golf Club. Home: Belltrees, Scone New South Wales 2337, Australia Office: Seven Press, PO Box 387, Scone New South Wales 2337, Australia

WHITE, KATHERINE PATRICIA, lawyer; b. N.Y.C., Feb. 1, 1948; d. Edward Christopher and Catherine Elizabeth (Walsh) W. BA in English, Molloy Coll., 1969; JD, St. John's U., 1971. Bar: N.Y. 1972, U.S. Dist. Ct. (ea. and so. dists.) N.Y., 1973, U.S. Supreme Ct. 1976. Atty. Western Electric Co., Inc., N.Y.C., 1971-79, AT&T Co., Inc., N.Y.C., 1979-83, AT&T Communications, Inc., N.Y.C., 1984—; adj. prof. law N.Y. Law Sch., N.Y.C., 1987-88, Fordham U. Sch. of Law, 1988—. Vol. Sloan Kettering Inst., 1973, North Shore U. Hosp., 1975, various fed., state and local polit. campaigns; judge N.Y. State Bicentennial Writing Competition, N.Y.C., 1977-78; chmn. Com. to Elect Supreme Ct. Judge, N.Y.C., 1982. Mem. Am. Corp. Counsel Assn., N.Y. State Bar Assn. (young lawyers com., bus. and banking law com. real estate law sect., corp. counsel sect.), Nassau County Bar Assn. (membership com., environ. law com., real estate sect., young lawyers sect.), Assn. of Bar of City of N.Y. (adminstrv. law com. 1982-85, young lawyers com. 1976-79, judge nat. moot ct. competition 1979—), Cath. Lawyers Guild for Diocese of Rockville Ctr. (pres. 1980-81), St. John's U. Sch. Law Alumni Assn. (pres. L.I. chpt. 1986-88), Women's Nat. Republican Club (bd. govs. 1988-81). Clubs: Metropolitan, Wharton Bus. Sch. N.Y. (N.Y.C.). Home: 5 Starlight Ct Babylon NY 11704 Office: AT&T Communications Inc 32 Ave of the Americas New York NY 10013

WHITE, KENNETH JAMES, lawyer; b. Bryan, Ohio, Apr. 16, 1948; s. James Foster and Doris E. (Hatfield) W.; m. Diane G. Frechette, Sept. 20, 1969; children: James Renald, David Kenneth. B.S. cum laude in Journalism, Bowling Green State U., 1970; J.D. cum laude, U. Toledo, 1974. Bar: Ohio 1974, U.S. Dist. Ct. (no. dist.) Ohio 1974, U.S. Ct. Appeals (6th cir.) 1983. Law clk. to pres. judge U.S. Dist. Ct., Toledo, Ohio, 1974-76; ptnr. Spengler, Nathanson, McCarthy & Durfee, Toledo, 1976-84; ptnr. Jacobson, Maynard, Tuschman & Kalur, 1985—. Articles editor U. Toledo Law Rev. 1973-74. Author: (with others) Appellate Practice, Ohio Legal Center Institute, 1981. Mem. ABA, Ohio Bar Assn., Toledo Bar Assn. Home: 468 Patriot Dr W Waterville OH 43566 Office: Jacobson Maynard Tuschman & Kalur 9th Floor 4 Seagate Toledo OH 43604

WHITE, MERIT PENNIMAN, engineering educator; b. Whately, Mass., Oct. 25, 1908; s. Henry and Jessie (Penniman) W.; m. Jarmila Jaskova, 1965; children—Mary Jessie, Irene Helen, Elisabeth Cecelia, Ellen Patricia. A.B. cum laude, Dartmouth Coll., 1930, C.E., 1931; M.S., Calif. Inst. Tech., 1932, Ph.D. magna cum laude, 1935. With U.S. Dept. Agr., 1935-37; postdoctoral fellow Harvard U., 1937-38; research asso. Calif. Inst. Tech., 1938-39; asst. prof. Ill. Inst. Tech., 1939-42; cons. OSRD, 1942-45, War and Navy Depts., 1945-47; prof., head civil engring. dept. U. Mass., 1948—, Commonwealth head of dept., 1961-77, Commonwealth prof., 1977—. Contbr. articles to engring. jours. Recipient Pres.'s certificate of merit, 1948. Fellow ASME; mem. Inst. Mech. Engrs., ASCE (life), Phi Beta Kappa, Sigma Xi, Tau Beta Pi. Home: Whately MA 01093 Office: U Mass Amherst MA 01003

WHITE, NORMAN ARTHUR, engineer, energy company executive, educator; b. Hetton-le-Hole, Durham, Eng., Apr. 11, 1922; s. Charles Brewster and Lillian Sarah (Finch) W.; m. Joyce Marjorie Rogers, Dec. 16, 1944 (dec. July 1982); children: Howard Russell, Lorraine Avril; m. Marjorie Iris Rushton, May 14, 1983. BS in Enging., U. London, 1949, PhD in Econs., 1973; MS, U. Philippines, 1955; grad. Advanced Mgmt. Program, Harvard U., 1968. Chartered engr. Research engr., product devel. mgr. Royal Dutch/Shell Group, 1945-64, gen. mgr. spl. product div., 1964-68, chief exec. new enterprises div., 1968-72, chmn./dir. Shell Oil and Mining operating cos., 1963-72; dir., chmn. exec. com. Tanks Oil & Gas Ltd., London, 1974-85; prin. exec. Norman White Assocs., 1972—; spl. adv. Hambros Bank Ltd., London, 1972-76; corp. adv. Placer Devel. Ltd., Vancouver, B.C., Can., 1973-78; oil advisor Tanks Consol. Investments plc, Nassau, The Bahamas, 1974-85; dir. Environ. Resources Ltd., 1973-87; dep. chmn. Strategy International, Ltd., 1976-82; vice chmn. Transat Energy, Inc., Washington, 1977—; chmn. KBC Advanced Tech., 1979—, Am. Oil Field Systems plc, 1980-85; dep. chmn. Brit. Can. Resources Ltd., Calgary, 1980-83; chmn. Ocean Thermal Energy Conversion Systems Ltd., 1982—, Tesel-Gearhart plc., 1983-85, Process Automation & Computer Systems Ltd, 1985—, Andaman Resources, 1986—, also bd dirs.; vis. prof. Manchester Bus. Sch., 1971—, Henley Adminstrv. staff Coll., Henley-on-Thames, Eng., 1976—; vis. lectr. Royal Coll. Def. Studies, 1981-84; bd. dirs. Henley Centre for Forecasting, dep. chmn. 1974-87; bd. dirs. Concorde Energy plc. (formerly Petranol); mem. Brit. nat. com. World Energy Conf., 1977—, mem. conservation commn., 1979—; chmn. Brit. nat. com. World Petroleum Congresses, 1987—, treas., 1983—. Author: Financing the International Petroleum Industry, 1978, Oil Substitution - World Outlook to 2020, 1983; contbr. articles to profl. jours. Mem. senate U. London, 1974-87; mem. governing bd. King Edward VI's Royal Grammar Sch., Guildford, 1976—; mem. parliamentary and sci. com. House of Commons, 1977-83 and 1987. Fellow Inst. Mech. Engrs. (mem. council 1981-85, 87, chmn. engring. mgmt. div. 1981-85), Instn. Mining and Metallurgy, Inst. Energy, Inst. Petroleum (mem. council 1975-81, v.p. 1978-81), Royal Soc. Arts, Brit. Inst. Mgmt., Royal Inst. Internat. Affairs; mem. Am. Soc. Petroleum Engrs., Can. Inst. Mining, Freeman City of London, Liveryman, Worshipful Co. Engrs., Worshipful Co. Spectacle Makers. Clubs: Athaenaeum, Harvard Bus.; St. George's House (Windsor Castle) (assoc.). Home: Green Ridges, 6 Downside Rd, Guildford Surrey GU4 8PH, England Office: 9 Park House, 123-125 Harley St, London W1N 1HE, England

WHITE, PATRICK, author; b. London, May 28, 1912; s. Victor and Ruth (Withycombe) W.; B.A., Kings Coll., Cambridge U., 1935. Author: Happy Valley, 1939, The Living and the Dead, 1941, The Aunt's Story, 1948, The Tree of Man, 1955, Voss, 1957, Riders in the Chariot, 1961, The Burnt Ones, 1964, The Solid Mandala, 1966, The Vivisector, 1970, The Eye of the Storm, 1973, The Cockatoos, 1974, A Fringe of Leaves, 1976, The Twyborn Affair, 1979, Memoirs of Many in One, 1986; (self-portrait) Flaws in the Glass, 1981; (plays) The Ham Funeral, 1947, The Season at Sarsaparilla, 1961, A Cheery Soul, 1962, Night On Bald Mountain, 1962, Big Toys, 1977, Signal Driver, 1981, Netherwood, 1983; (screenplay) The Night The Prowler, 1978. Served with RAF, World War II. Recipient Nobel prize in lit., 1973. Home: 20 Martin Rd, Centennial Park, Sydney New South Wales 2021, Australia *

WHITE, PAUL DUNBAR, lawyer; b. LaGrange, Ky., Oct. 20, 1917; s. Isham Forrest and Florence (Harris) W.; m. Marion Loutenas Stallworth, Sept. 2, 1949; children: Paulette, Ronald. A.B., Ky. State Coll., 1940; LL.B., Western Res. U., 1950. Bar: Ohio 1950, U.S. Supreme Ct. 1972. Supr. Ind. State Boys Sch., 1940-41; group worker spl. projects Karamu, Cleve., 1941-43; visitor Cuyahoga County Agy., 1946-47; individual practice law Cleve., 1950-51; police prosecutor City of Cleve., 1951-59, 1st asst. prosecutor, 1960-63, dir. law, 1967-68; judge Cleve. Mcpl. Ct., 1964-67; assoc. Baker & Hostetler, Cleve., 1968-70; ptnr. Baker & Hostetler, 1970—; mem. State of Ohio Bd. Examiners, 1972-78. Trustee NCCJ, Cleve., 1972-86; trustee Ohio Law Opportunity Fund, 1975-87, Cleve. Urban League, 1975-78, Dyke Coll., Cleve., 1976-86; bd. commrs. Cleve. Met. Park, 1975-78. Served with U.S. Army, 1943-46. Mem. ABA, Ohio Bar Assn., Greater Cleve. Bar Assn. (trustee 1976-79, del. 8th Jud. Dist. Ohio conf. 1985—), Nat. Bar Assn., Soc. Benchers (Case Western Res. U.), Norman S. Minor Bar Assn. Home: 16210 Telfair Ave Cleveland OH 44128 Office: Baker & Hostetler 3200 National City Ctr Cleveland OH 44114

WHITE, REX NAMOND, educational administrator; b. Gilmer, Tex., Jan. 27, 1930; s. Robert Nathaniel and Dollie Mae (Dunagan) W.; student Kilgore Jr. Coll., 1947-49; B.S., East Tex. State U., 1950, M.Ed., 1955; m. Gloria Green, June 4, 1955; children—Kevin Clyde, Brent Nathaniel, Shelly. Elem. tchr., Campus Ward Sch., Longview, Tex., 1950-51, Foster Elem. Sch., Longview, 1953; tchr., coach New London (Tex.) Jr. High Sch. and Sr. High Sch., 1953-55, tchr. advanced math. and physics, coach, 1955-65; prin. West Rusk County Jr. High Sch., New London, 1965-67; supt. Tatum Ind. Sch. Dist., Tatum, Tex., 1967-73; tchr. advanced math. Robert E. Lee High Sch., Tyler, Tex., 1973-77; prin. James S. Hogg Middle Sch., Tyler, 1977—. Mem. NEA, Nat. Middle Sch. Assn. (bd. dirs. 1987), Tex. Tchrs. Assn., Tex. Assn. Secondary Sch. Prins., East Tex. Middle Sch. League, Tex. Middle Sch. Assn. (pres.-elect 1986-87, pres. 1987—). Baptist. Club: Optimists. Lodge: Rose City Kiwanis. Office: James S Hogg Middle Sch 920 S Broadway Tyler TX 75701

WHITE, ROBERT J., educator, neurosurgeon, neuroscientist; b. Duluth, Minn., Jan. 21, 1926; married, 1950; children: Robert, Christopher, Patricia, Michael, Daniel, Pamela, James, Richard, Marguerite, Ruth. B.S., Coll. St. Thomas, U. Minn., 1951, Ph.D. in Neurosurg. Physiology, 1962; M.D., Harvard, 1953; D.Sc. (hon.), John Carroll U., 1979, Cleve. State U., 1981. Intern surgery Peter Bent Brigham Hosp., Boston, 1953-54; resident Boston Children's Hosp. and Peter Bent Brigham Hosp., 1954-55; fellow neurosurgery Mayo Clinic, 1955-58; asst. to staff 1958-59, research asso. neuro physiol., 1959-61; mem. faculty Case Western Res. U. Sch. Medicine, 1961—, prof. neurosurgery, 1966—, co-dir. neurosurgery, 1972, co-chmn. neurosurgery, 1973—; dir. neurosurg. and brain research lab. Cleve. Met. Gen. Hosp., 1961—; neurosurgeon Univ. Hosps.; also sr. attending neurosurgeon VA Hosp., 1961—; lectr. USSR, 1966, 68, 70, 72, 73, 78, 79, People's Republic China, 1977, 81; advisor to Vatican authorities on bioethics; mem. adv. com. for Biotech. Applied to Man of the Pontifical Acad. Scis. Gen. editor: Internat. Soc. Angiol. Jour, 1966; editor: Western Hemisphere Jour. Resuscitation, 1971—, Surg. Neurology, Resuscitation, Jour. of Trauma; co-editor: Surg. Neurology, 1973—; Contbr. numerous articles to profl. jours. Served with AUS, 1944-46. Recipient Mayo Clinic Research award, 1958; Med. Mut. Honor award, 1975; L.W. Freeman award PF, 1977. Mem. ACS (com. on trauma task force), Harvey Cushing Soc., Soc. Univ. Surgeons, Am. Physiol. Soc., Soc. Univ. Neurosurgeons (pres. 1978-79), Ohio Neurosurg. Soc. (pres. 1975), Northeast Ohio Neurosurg. Soc. (pres. 1971), Soc. Exptl. Biology, Internat. Soc. Cybernetic Medicine (mem. internat. bd. 1971—), Internat. Soc. Surgery, Soc. Neurol. Surgeons, Neurosurg. Soc. Am., A.C.S., AMA, Acad. Medicine Cleve. (dir., pres. 1978-79). Address: 3395 Scranton Rd Cleveland OH 44109

WHITE, ROBERT JOSEPH, JR, real estate developer; b. Athol, Mass., Dec. 29, 1943; s. Robert Joseph and Bertha Elizabeth (Litchfield) W.; B.A., U. Mass., 1965; M.Ed., Boston U., 1968; M.A. in Math., Northeastern U., 1971; postgrad. Harvard U. Bus. Sch., 1976. Math. tchr., career edn. coordinator Boston Public Schs., 1966—; owner, mgr. White Real Estate, Boston and Brookline, Mass., 1974—, pres., 1972—; gen. partner Real Estate Syndicator, 1981-82; pres. Whiden Devel. Corp., 1981-82, Whiden Devel. Co., 1982—, Glen Grove Devel. Corp., Boston; owner Devon on the Commons, Boston, 1982—, Davios Italian Restaurant, Boston, 1982—, Dover Sea Grill, Boston, 1982—; pres. Triton Devel. Corp., Aptos, Calif., 1985-86. cons. condominium conversion; instr. real estate investment Boston U., Boston Coll. Donor, Boston Summerthing; youth activities coordinator Boston YMCA; spring day coordinator Jamaica Panel Civic Assn.; mem. Republicans to Enhance Am. Com. Recipient cert. for outstanding civic contbns. City of Brookline, 1977, 79. Mem. Greater Boston Area Rental Housing Assn., Brookline Property Owners Assn., Boston Tchrs. Union, Nat. Wildlife Fedn., Religious Heritage of Am. Republican. Roman Catholic. Club: Rotary. Contbr. articles on real estate to newspapers. Home: 478 Jamaicaway Boston MA 02130

WHITE, ROY BERNARD, theater executive; b. Cin., July 30, 1926; s. Maurice and Anna (Rudin) W.; m. Sally Lee Ostrom, June 17, 1951; children: Maurice Ostrom, Barbara Dee, Daniel Robert. B.A., U. Cin., 1949; student, U. Miami, Fla., 1946-47. Mem. sales staff Twentieth Century Fox Films, Cin., 1949-52; with Mid-States Theatres, Cin., 1952—; pres. Mid-States Theatres, 1962—; mem. Nat. Assn. Theatre Owners, N.Y.C., 1962—; dir. Nat. Assn. Theatre Owners, 1966-70, nat. pres., 1971-73, exec. com., 1971—, chmn. bd., 1973-75; Mem. film adv. panel Ohio Arts Council, 1974—; bd. dirs. Will Rogers Meml. Fund, Found. Motion Picture Pioneers, Inc.; mem. media arts panel Nat. Endowment for Arts, 1979—. Served with USAAF, 1944-45. Named Exhibitor of Year Internat. Film Importers and Distbrs. Am., 1973. Mem. Am. Film Inst. (trustee 1972-75, exec. com. 1972-75), Fedn. Motion Picture Pioneers (v.p.), Alpha Epsilon Pi, Phi Eta Sigma. Clubs: Masons, Queen City Racquet, Crest Hills Country, Amberley Village (Ohio) Tennis (pres. 1972-73), Bankers; Quail Creek Country (Naples, Fla.). Home: 4401 Gulf Shore Blvd N #1605 Naples FL 33940

WHITE, RUTH BENNETT, nutritionist, educator, writer; b. Howe, Okla., Aug. 18, 1906; d. Ambrose L. and Sarah A. (Blevins) Bennett; m. Carl Milton White, Aug. 5, 1928; children—Sherril White Spencer, Caroline White Buchanan. B.A. with honors, Okla. Baptist U., 1928; M.S. (fellow), U. Iowa, 1930; postgrad. Cornell U., 1930-34, Columbia, 1955-56. Teaching fellow Okla. Baptist U., 1925-26; prin. Jr. High Sch., Heavener, Okla., 1926-27; research fellow in chemistry of food, Cornell U., 1930-31; surveyor of diets, research fellow N.Y. State 4-H Club camps, summer 1931-34; instr. nutrition Coll. Home Econs., Cornell U., Ithaca, N.Y., 1931-34; tchr. pub. schs., N.Y.C., 1956-58 Fort Lee (N.J.) High Sch., 1959-60; pub. lectr. foods and nutrition, 1931—; nutrition specialist for community programs Cornell U. N.Y. State Extension, 1931-34, Ankara, Turkey, 1960-61, Lagos, Nigeria, 1962-64; mem. Nat. Commn. on Revision of Home Econs. Curriculum, Fed. Republic of Nigeria, 1962-64. Author: If Food Could Talk, 1932; You and Your Food (text), 4th edit., 1976; Food and Your Future (text), 1972, 3d edit., 1985. Contbr. articles on nutrition to profl. jours. and newspapers. Mem. Leonia (N.J.) Bd. Edn., 1950-54. Recipient Disting. Alumni Achievement award Okla. Baptist U., 1975; named Woman of the Year, San Diego dist. Calif. Home Econs. Assn., 1973, 74; Woman of Achievement award Pres.'s Council Womens Service, Bus. and Profl. Clubs San Diego, 1973, 74. Mem. Am. Home Econs. Assn. (award for profl. contbns. in writng textbooks on food & nutrition 1984), Calif., Channel Islands home econs. assns., Internat. Fedn. Home Econs. (mem. council 1970-76), AAUW (del. nat. conv. 1984), Soc. Nutrition Edn., Nat. League Am. Pen Women, Pi Lambda Theta, Pi Kappa Delta. Democrat. Address: 2550 Treasure Dr Santa Barbara CA 93105

WHITE, RUTH MIRIAM WEIHS (MRS. PAUL WHITE), trade and fin. co. exec.; b. Vienna, Austria; d. Hugo and Ilka (Herzog) Weihs; came to U.S., 1947, naturalized, 1952; B.A. in Bus. Adminstrn., St. John's U., Shanghai, China, 1947; postgrad. N.Y.U., Coll. City N.Y.; m. Paul White, Sept. 18, 1949. Exec. sec. to chmn. bd. Pan Am. Trade Devel. Corp., N.Y.C., 1947-49, mgr., 1949-53, asst. v.p., 1953-58, v.p., 1958-75, sr. v.p., 1975—; also pres. Indsl. Crystal Corp.

WHITE, SANDRA R., account representative, chemist; b. Houston, Oct. 18, 1948; d. Earl Douglas and Joleta (Phillips) Lively; m. Gerald Robert White, Sept. 30, 1983; children by previous marriage—Laurie Joanna, Jamie Racquel. Student San Jacinto Coll., 1966-68; B.S. in Chemistry, Sam Houston State U., 1970; MBA Houston Bapt. U. Grad. Sch. Bus., 1987. Chemist, Sorbotec, Inc., Houston, 1971-72, Champion Papers, Inc., Pasadena, Tex., 1974-75, Core Labs, Inc., Houston, 1981-82; account rep. Foxboro Co., Houston, 1982-88, sr. control systems engring. techologist SIP Engring. Inc., Houston, 1988—; moon rock chemist at Lunar Receiving Lab., Johnson Space Ctr., Brown & Root-Northrup, Houston, 1970-71; salesman Tex. Real Estate Commn., 1972—; mem. Act for Eight Community TV, Cousteau Soc. Charter mem. Nat./State Leadership Tng. Inst. on Gifted and Talented, Ventura, Calif. 1979—; mem. Houston Mus. Natural Sci., Houston Contemporary Arts Mus. Sam Houston State U. undergrad. research fellow in organic chemistry, 1969-70. Mem. Soc. Women Engrs., Nat. Assn. Female Execs., Am. Chem. Soc. (sr. mem.), Instrument Soc. Am., Nat. Mus. for Women in the Arts (charter), Nat. Assn. Corrosion Engrs., Instrument Soc. Am. (sr., bd. dirs. standards practices com. 1987, Standards and Practices com. liason). Republican. Methodist. Club: Christian Women's. Home: 5155 Cripple Creek Houston TX 77017 Office: SIP Engring PO Box 34311 Houston TX 77234

WHITE, STEPHEN JOHN, advertising executive; b. London, July 23, 1948; s. George Edward and Doreen W.; m. Helen Catherine Mackeonis, Apr. 6, 1971; children: Claire, Victoria. Trainee Sullivan, Stauffer, Colwill & Bayles-Lintas, London, 1965-70; mgr. McCann-Erickson, London, 1970-79; dir. Wight Collins Rutherford Scott, London, 1979—. Mem. Inst. Practitioners in Advt., Communication, Advt. and Mktg. Found. Clubs: Royal Automobile Club, Vanderbilt (London).

WHITE, STEPHEN RICHARD, lawyer, educator; b. Pensacola, Fla., Apr. 14, 1948; s. Edward Timothy and Jane Helen (Zaruba) W.; m. Veronica DiBenedetto, Mar. 19, 1972; children—Christopher Stephen, John Patrick. B.A., Fla. State U., 1970, J.D., 1972; M.A., Yale U., 1974, M.Philosophy, 1975. Bar: Fla. 1973, U.S. Dist. Ct. (mid. dist.) Fla. 1980, U.S. Ct. Appeals (5th cir.) 1980, U.S. Ct. Appeals (11th cir.) 1983, U.S. Supreme Ct. 1980. Intake counselor Juvenile Ct. of Record, Pensacola, Fla., 1970; legal intern Office Atty Gen. Fla., Tallahassee, 1972, Legal Aid, Tallahassee, 1972; hot-line asst. Office Atty. Gen. Fla., Tallahassee, 1972-73; asst. state atty., Jacksonville, Fla., 1976-87; asst. prof. Appalachian State U., Boone, N.C., 1987—; tng. officer for State Atty.'s Office, 1984-86; spl. asst. atty gen., 1983-84; instr. Police Acad., Jacksonville, 1982-87; substitute instr. U. No. Fla., Jacksonville, 1983-84; lectr. on drugs Duval County Schs., Jacksonville, 1983-85, to statewide seminar of prosecutors regarding motion practice, 1986, for police in-service tng., 1986-87, on role of prosecutor Fla. Jr. Coll., 1986, research on prosecutorial decision making. Editor Fla. State U. Law Rev., 1972, Newsletter of Law, State Atty.'s Office, Jacksonville, 1983-84; contbr. to book and profl. jours. Served to capt., legal officer USAF, 1973. Mem. Am. Judicature Soc., Law and Soc. Assn., Jacksonville Bar Assn., Fla. Pros.

Attys. Assn. (mem. edn. com.), Alpha Kappa Delta, Pi Sigma Alpha. Democrat. Roman Catholic. Home: 206 Hillandale Dr Boone NC 28607 Office: Appalachian State U Dept Polit Sci/ Criminal Justice Boone NC 28608

WHITE, STEVEN JAMES, electronics manufacturing company executive; b. Bryn Mawr, Pa., Aug. 31, 1951; s. Aubrey and Kate (Nicol) W. Student Stevens Inst. tech., 1969-73; BSEE, U. Wash., 1983. Design engr. Sundstrand Corp., Redmond, Wash., 1973-75; sr. design engr., 1977-79; project engr. resource Control, Redmond, 1975-77; chmn., chief exec. officer Tech. Arts Corp., Seattle, 1979—; grad. researcher dept. computer sci. MIT, 1988—; pres., dir. Fibre Graphics Corp, 1986—; pres. Tech. Arts, Seattle, cons. 1977-83. Patentee white scanner 3D measurement. Mem. IEEE, Tau Beta Pi. Office: Tech Arts Corp 15660 NE 36th St Suite 200 Redmond WA 98052

WHITE, SUSANNE TROPEZ, pediatrician, educator; b. New Orleans, Apr. 13, 1949; d. Maxwell Sterling and Ethel (Ross) Tropez; m. James Carnell White, Apr. 10, 1971; children—Lisa, Janifer, James Carnell. B.S., Bennett Coll., 1971; M.D., U. N.C., 1975, M.P.H., 1982. Diplomate Am. Bd. Pediatrics. Resident in pediatrics N.C. Meml. Hosp., Chapel Hill, 1975-76, 77-79; pediatrician Darnell Army Hosp., Ft. Hood, Tex., 1976-77; acting dir. pediatric day clinic Wake County Med. Ctr., Raleigh, N.C., 1979-82, dir. pediatric day clinic, 1982-88, dir. teens with tots clinic, 1980-88; asst. prof. pediatrics U. N.C. Chapel Hill, 1982-88, assoc. prof. pediatrics La. State U., New Orleans, 1988—; dir. div. pediatric emergency room, 1988—; pediatrician Shelly Child Devel. Ctr., Raleigh, 1981-88, child med. examiner program, Raleigh, 1979-88. Contbr. articles to profl. jours. Mem. Walnut Terr. Child Devel. Ctr., Raleigh, 1981-83, chmn., 1982-83; chmn. pastor of parish com. Longview Ch., Raleigh, 1982-84, 87-88. Faculty Devel. fellow U. N.C. Sch. Medicine, 1985-87, preventive medicine, 1979-82. Fellow Am. Acad. Pediatrics; mem. N.C. Pediatric Soc. (com. child abuse and neglect, adolescent pregnancy), Ambulatory Pediatric Assn., Adolescent Pregnancy Coalition United Way, Bennett Coll. Alumnae Assn., United Methodist Women. Democrat.

WHITE, TERRENCE HAROLD, university dean, sociologist, management studies; b. Ottawa, Ont., Canada, Mar. 31, 1943; s. William Harold and Shirley Margaret (Ballantine) W.; m. Susan Elizabeth Hornaday; children: Christine Susan, Julie Pamela. Ph.D., U. Toronto, 1972. Head dept. sociology and anthropology U. Windsor, Ont., Can., 1973-75; prof., chmn. dept. sociology U. Alta., Edmonton, 1975-80, dean faculty of arts, 1980—; pres. T.H. White Orgn. Research Services Ltd., Edmonton, 1975—; dir. Labatt's Brewing Alta., Edmonton, 1981—. Author: Power or Pawns: Boards of Directors, 1978, Human Resource Management, 1979; editor: Introduction to Work Science, 1981, QWL in Canada: Case Studies, 1983. Bd. dirs. Progressive Conservative Assn., Edmonton South, 1976-81, 1st v.p., 1981-85, pres., 1985—; bd. dirs. Tri-Bach Festival Found., Edmonton, 1981—, Alta. Ballet Co., 1985—, Edmonton Symphony Soc., Edmonton Conv. and Tourism Authority, Arch Enterprises; bd. govs. U. Alta., 1984—. Mem. Delta Tau Kappa, Alpha Kappa Delta. Club: Riverbend Racquet (Edmonton). Lodge: Rotary (pres. Edmonton South 1981-82). Home: 10520 31 Ave, Edmonton, AB Canada T6J 2Y3 Office: U Alta, PO Box 103 Sub 11, Edmonton, AB Canada T6G 2EO

WHITE, THOMAS LESTER, consulting engineer; b. Youngstown, Ohio, May 30, 1903; s. William Lester and Ethel Mary (Jackson) W.; m. Marion Elizabeth Evans, Sept. 24, 1930 (dec. July 1983); 1 dau., Harrietellen White McKendrick; m. Doris E. Zerella, Oct. 6, 1984. Tool designer, engr. Comml. Intertech Corp. (previously Comml. Shearing Inc.), Youngstown, 1924-26, chief engr., 1926-51, cons. engr., 1951-68, 68—; cons. engr. coal mines, metal mines, hwy., railroad and subway tunnels, Belgium, Portugal, India, Australia, S.Am., Can., others; lectr. various univs. and tech. orgns. Registered profl. engr., Ohio. Fellow ASME (life, past chmn. petroleum div.); mem. Am. Ry. Engring. Assn., Mahoning Valley Tech. Soc. (named outstanding person 1973). Baptist. Clubs: Kiwanis, Shriners, Masons. Author: (with R.V. Proctor and Karl Terzaghi) Rock Tunneling with Steel Supports, 1946; Earth Tunneling with Steel Supports, 1977. Contbr. articles to profl. jours. Address: 721 W Warren Ave Youngstown OH 44511

WHITE, W. ARTHUR, geologist; b. Sumner, Ill., Dec. 9, 1916; s. Millard Otto and Joy Olive (Atkins) W.; m. Alma Evelyn Simonton McCullough, June 21, 1941. B.S., U. Ill., 1940, M.S., 1947, Ph.D., 1955. With Ill. Geol. Survey, Urbana, 1943-79, geologist, 1955-58, head clay resources and clay mineral tech. sect., 1958-72, geologist, 1972-79, geologist emeritus, 1979—; pvt. cons. geologist Urbana, 1979—; prof. geology Fed. U. Rio Grande do Sul, Brazil, 1970. Contbr. articles to profl. jours. Fellow Geol. Soc. Am., Mineral. Soc. Am., AAAS; mem. Internat. Clay Mineral Soc., Am. Clay Mineral Soc., Ill. Acad. Sci., Mus. Natural History (assoc.), Nat. Geog. Soc., Am. Chem. Soc., Mental Health Soc., Colloid Chem. Soc., Geochem. Soc., Soc. Econ. Petrologists and Mineralogists, Sigma Xi. Home: 603 Colorado St Urbana IL 61801

WHITE, WILLIAM ALLEN, civil engineer; b. Joliet, Mont., Mar. 27, 1906; s. William McCord and (Compton) W.; m. Lucille Virginia Emmett, Mar. 10, 1934; children—Mack William, Virginia Frances. B.A. in Math, U. Mont., Missoula, 1930, M.A., 1937. Tchr. sci. and math. Joliet High Sch., 1932-34; civilian engr. U.S. Corps Engrs., 1934-42, 45-47; statistician Q.M.C., Washington, 1942-45; sec. Calif. Bd. Registration Profl. Engrs., Sacramento, 1948-55; exec. dir. Calif. Council Civil Engrs. and Land Surveyors, 1956-76; panelist Am. Arbitration Assn., 1975—; bd. dirs. Design Professionals Safety Assn., 1976—; trustee, sec. Civil Engrs. and Land Surveyors Trust, 1969—. Author manuals, papers, editor guides. Recipient Service to Profession award Engring. Council Sacramento Valley, 1968; also various citations, commendations. Life mem. ASCE (Surveying and Mapping award 1976), Am. Congress Surveying and Mapping; mem. Am. Soc. Assn. Execs. Republican. Baptist. Club: Joliet Masons. Address: 5505 8th Ave Sacramento CA 95820

WHITE, WILLIAM CLINTON, physician; b. Scottsville, Va., Nov. 22, 1911; s. Llewellyn Gordon and Caroline Rebecca (Rawlings) W.; m. Frances Evelyn Daniel, July 2, 1938; children—William Clinton, Elizabeth White Martin. B.S., Va. Mil. Inst., 1933; M.D., U. Va., 1937. Diplomate Am. Bd. Pathology. Intern, Walter Reed Gen. Hosp., Washington, 1937-39; resident in pathology U. Colo. Med. Ctr., Denver, 1949-53, assoc. prof., 1949-65; med. dir. Los Alamos Hosp., 1946-49; cons. U. Calif. Sci. Labs., Los Alamos, 1949-59; chmn. dept. pathology Denver Gen. Hosp., 1953-65; dir. med. edn. and research Pensacola Found. for Med. Edn. and Research (Fla.), 1965-78; bd. dirs., 1976—; cons. med. edn., emeritus dir. med. edn. Pensacola Edn. Program (Fla.), 1978—; co-founder, dir. Rocky Mountain Natural Gas Co.; dir. Midwest Nat. Gas Co. Bd. govs. Fellowship Concerned Churchmen, 1982-85, pres., 1983-85. Mem. Selective Service Bd., N.Mex., 1946-49; mem. adv. bd. on cancer to Gov. of Colo., 1960-65; mem. Community Hosp. Council, Fla. Bd. Regents, 1971-74; mem. vestry, chmn. fin. com., sr. warden Christ Ch.; active Salvation Army, Boy Scouts Am. Served to col., M.C., U.S. Army, 1938-46. Recipient cert. of appreciation SSS, 1951; citation of merit Bd. Health and Hosps., Denver, 1963. Mem. AMA, Am. Soc. Clin. Pathologists (counselor), Colo. Soc. Pathology (pres.), Internat. Acad. Pathology (hon. life), Colo. State Med. Soc., Denver Med. Soc., Escambia County Med. Soc. (hon. life), Los Alamos County Med. Soc. (pres.). Clubs: Andalusia Country (Ala.); Pensacola Country. Lodges: Rotary Internat., St. Andrew's Soc. (trustee 1981—), Masons, Shriners, K.T. Contbr. articles to profl. jours. Home: 615 Bayshore Dr Apt 101 Warrington FL 32507 Office: Rt 6 Box 251A Andalusia AL 36420

WHITE, WILLIAM SAMUEL, foundation executive; b. Cin., May 8, 1937; s. Nathaniel Ridgway and Mary (Loundes) W.; m. Claire Mott, July 1, 1961; children: Tiffany Loundes, Ridgway Harding. BA, Dartmouth Coll., 1959, MBA, 1960; LL.D. (hon.), Eastern Mich. U., 1975. With Barrett & Williams, N.Y.C., 1961-62; sr. assoc. Bruce Payne & Assos., N.Y.C., 1962-71; v.p. C. S. Mott Found., Flint, Mich., 1971-75; pres. C. S. Mott Found., 1976—, trustee, 1971—, also chmn. bd. dirs.; dir. U.S. Sugar Corp., Continental Water Corp. Mem. exec. com. Daycroft Sch., Greenwich, Conn., 1966-70; bd. dirs. Flint Area Conf., 1971-84; mem. citizens adv. task force U. Mich., Flint, 1974-79; chmn. Council of Mich. Founds., 1979-81, Flint Area Focus Council, 1987—; mem. Pres.'s Task Force on Pvt. Sector Initiatives, 1982; trustee GMI Engring. and Mgmt. Inst., 1982-86; dir. Council on Founds., 1985—. Served with U.S. Army, 1960-62. Office: Mott Found Bldg 503 S Saginaw St Flint MI 48502

WHITE, WILLIAM VANNOY, association executive; b. Lenoir, N.C., Mar. 24, 1924; s. Frank Boyd and Cornelia (Miller) W.; B.A., U. N.C., 1950; postgrad. U. Miss., 1950-51; m. Joan Robinson, Sept. 11, 1948; children—William Vannoy II, Cynthia Elma, Melinda Carol. Public health adviser USPHS, N.C., 1949, Miss., 1950-51, U. Ala. Med. Sch., 1952-53, dir. communicable disease program, Pa., 1954-57; chief cons. region III, HEW, P.R., V.I., 1957-61, chief family safety br., Washington, 1961-65, legis. liaison Bur. Disease Prevention and Environ. Control, 1966; exec. dir. Nat. Commn. on Product Safety, 1967-70; dir. Injury Data and Control Center, Bur. Product Safety, FDA, Washington, 1970-73, dir. Bur. Info. Edn., U.S. Consumer Product Safety Commn., Bethesda, Md., 1973-77; v.p. Shannondale Club Ltd., 1978, dir., 1978-79; pres., dir. Citizens of Shannondale, Inc., 1979-81; real estate broker, Charles Town, W.Va.; vis. prof. U. N.C., U. Mich., Columbia U., U. Minn., Purdue U.; dir. Nat. Safety Council, 1967-75; chmn. Nat. Info. Bd. dirs. The Old Opera House, Charles Town, 1977-81, 1st v.p., chmn. program bd., 1981, pres., 1983-84; sr. warden and trustee St. Andrew's Episcopal Ch., Mt. Mission, W.Va., 1978-86; v.p. Episc. Churchmen, Diocese of W.Va., 1981-83, pres., 1983-86; bd. dirs. Ednl. Broadcasting Authority, State of W.Va., vice chmn., 1983—. Served with USNR, 1942-46. Recipient Superior Service award HEW, 1959, Meritorious Service award Nat. Commn. on Product Safety, 1970, Merit award FDA, 1972. Mem. Sigma Nu, Phi Mu Alpha. Clubs: Thomas Jefferson Washington civitan clubs. Contbr. articles on consumer product safety to profl. publs. Home: Moon Ridge Route 2 PO Box 615 Harpers Ferry WV 24525 Office: PO Box 596 Charles Town WV 25414

WHITE, WILLIS SHERIDAN, JR., utilities executive; b. nr. Portsmouth, Va., Dec. 17, 1926; s. Willis Sheridan and Carrie (Culpepper) W.; m. LaVerne Behrends, Oct. 8, 1949; children—Willis Sheridan III, Marguerite Louise White Spangler, Cynthia Diane. B.S., Va. Poly. Inst., 1948; M.S., Mass. Inst. Tech., 1958. With Am. Electric Power Co. System, 1948—; asst. engr. Am. Electric Power Service Corp., N.Y.C., 1948-52, asst. to pres., 1952-54, office mgr., 1954-57, adminstrv. asst. to operating v.p., 1958-61; div. mgr. Am. Electric Power Service Corp. (Appalachian Power Co.), Lynchburg, Va., 1962-66; asst. gen. mgr. Am. Electric Power Service Corp. (Appalachian Power Co.), Roanoke, Va., 1966-67, asst. v.p., 1967-69, v.p., 1969, exec. v.p., dir., 1969-73; sr. exec. v.p. ops., dir. Am. Electric Power Service Corp., N.Y.C., 1973-75, vice chmn. ops., dir., 1975—; dir. Am. Electric Power Co., N.Y.C., 1972—, chmn. bd., chief exec. officer, 1976—; chmn., dir. AEP Energy Services, Inc., AEP Generating Co., Appalachian Power Co., Roanoke, Va., Columbus So. Power Co., Ind. Mich. Power Co., Ky. Power Co., Kingsport Power Co., Mich. Power Co., Ohio Power Co., Wheeling Power Co.; pres., dir. Ohio Valley Electric Corp., Ind.-Ky. Electric Corp., 1977—, Beech Bottom Power Co., Blackhawk Coal Co., Cedar Coal Co., Cardinal Operating Co., Castlegate Coal Co., Cedar Coal Co., Central Appalachian Coal Co., Central Coal Co., Central Ohio Coal Co., Central Operating Co., Franklin Real Estate Co., Ind. Franklin Realty Co., Central Operating Co., Colomet, Inc., Franklin Real Estate Co., Kanawha Valley Power Co., Mich. Gas Exploration Co., Ind. Franklin Realty, Price River Coal Co., Simco, Inc., So. Appalachian Coal Co., So. Ohio Coal Co., Twin Br. R.R. Co., W.Va. Power Co., Wheeling Electric Co., Windsor Power House Coal Co.; pres. Internat. Conf. on Large High Voltage Elec. Systems (CIGRE). Trustee, Battelle Meml. Inst.; bd. visitors Va. Poly. Inst. and State U. Served with USNR, 1945-46. Sloan fellow, 1957-58. Mem. IEEE, Nat. Coal Assn. (dir.), Nat. Coal Council (bd. dirs.), Assn. Edison Illuminating Cos. (exec. com.), NAM (dir.), Nat. Acad. Engring., Eta Kappa Nu. Methodist. Office: Appalachian Power Co 40 Franklin Rd Roanoke VA 24022 also: Battelle Meml Inst 505 King Ave Columbus OH 43201

WHITEHAND, JEREMY WILLIAM RICHARD, geographer, educator; b. Reading, Eng., Aug. 10, 1938; s. Percy Herbert and Stella Mildred (Frost) W.; m. Susan Mabel Frederick, July 12, 1968; children: Richard, Caroline, Nicholas. BA, U. Reading, 1960, PhD, 1965. Demonstrator in geography U. Newcastle-upon-Tyne, Eng., 1963-66; lectr. in geography U. Glasgow, Scotland, 1966-71; lectr. in geography U. Birmingham, Eng., 1971-85, sr. lectr. in geography, 1985-88, reader in urban geography, 1988—. Hon. editor jour. Area, 1977-80; contbr. articles to profl. jours. Grantee Social Sci. Research Council, 1980-81, Leverhulme Trust, 1987-88. Fellow Royal Geog. Soc. (editorial adv. com. 1981—); mem. Assn. Am. Geographers, Inst. Brit. Geographers (council mem. 1977-80, sec. editorial bd. spl. publs. 1981-85), Geog. Assn., Royal Scottish Geog. Soc. Home: 47 Selly Park Rd, Birmingham B29 7PH, England Office: U Birmingham, Dept of Geography, Birmingham B15 2TT, England

WHITEHEAD, JOHN ROBERT, airline executive; b. Johannesburg, Transvaal, Republic S. Africa, Mar. 3, 1948; s. Arnold and Jean Cooper (Mills) W.; m. Blondine Fardala, Aug. 18, 1973; children: Christopher John, Lydie Marie. Diploma in exporting, Auckland U., 1973. Comml. trainee Air New Zealand, Auckland, New Zealand, 1965-70; with passenger sales UTA French Airlines, Auckland, 1970-72, with cargo sales, 1972-74, mgr. cargo sales, 1974—. Contbr. articles to numerous profl. jours. Mem. X Export Inst. New Zealand, A.O.C. Cargo Subcom. (chmn. 1984-86), Cargo Investigation Panel. Club: Airline (Auckland). Office: UTA French Airlines, 57 Fort Street, Auckland New Zealand

WHITEHEAD, SIR JOHN (STAINTON), diplomat; b. Sept. 20, 1932; s. John William and Kathleen Whitehead; m. Mary Carolyn Hilton, 1964; 3 children. Student, Christ's Hosp.; MA, U. Oxford. With Her Majesty's Armed Forces, 1950-52, Oxford, 1952-55; with Fgn. Office, 1955-56, 61-64; 3d sec., later 2d sec. Her Majesty's Diplomatic Service, Tokyo, 1956-61; 1st sec. Her Majesty's Diplomatic Service, Washington, 1964-67; 1st sec. (econ.) Her Majesty's Diplomatic Service, Tokyo, 1968-71; with FCO, 1971-76, head personnel services dept., 1973-76; counsellor Bonn, 1976-80; minister Tokyo, 1980-84; dep. under-sec. of state FCO, 1984-86; ambassador to Japan 1986—. Decorated KCMG, 1986, CMG, 1976, CVO, 1978. Clubs: United Oxford and Cambridge U. Office: British Embassy, 1 Ichiban-cho, Chiyoda-ku, Tokyo 100 Japan also: Bracken Edge, High Pitfold, Hindhead, Surrey England *

WHITEHEAD, JOHN W., lawyer, organization administrator; b. Pulaski, Tenn., July 14, 1946; s. John M. and Alatha (Wiser) W.; m. Virginia Carolyn Nichols, Aug. 26, 1967; children: Jayson Reau, Jonathan Mathew, Elisabeth Anne, Joel Christofer, Joshua Benjamen. BA, U. Ark., 1969, JD, 1974. Bar: Ark. 1974, U.S. Dist. Ct. (ea. and we. dists.) Ark. 1974, U.S. Supreme Ct. 1977, U.S. Ct. Appeals (9th cir.) 1980, Va. 1981, U.S. Ct. Appeals (7th cir.) 1981. Spl. counsel Christian Legal Soc., Oak Park, Ill., 1977-78; assoc. Gibbs & Craze, Cleve., 1978-79; sole practice law Manassas, Va., 1979-82; pres. The Rutherford Inst., Manassas, Va., 1982—, also bd. dirs.; frequent lectr. colls., law schs.; past adj. prof. O.W. Coburn Sch. Law. Author: The Separation Illusion, 1977, Schools on Fire, 1980, The New Tyranny, 1982, The Second American Revolution, 1982, The Stealing of America, 1983, The Freedom of Religious Expression in Public High Schools, 1983, The End of Man, 1986, An American Dream, 1987, several others; contbr. numerous articles to profl. jours.; contbr. numerous chpts. to books. Served to 1st lt. U.S. Army, 1969-71. Named Christian Leader of Yr. Christian World Affairs Conf., Washington, 1986. Mem. ABA, Ark. Bar Assn., Va. Bar Assn. Office: The Rutherford Inst 9411 Battle St Manassas VA 22110

WHITEHORNE, ROBERT ALVIN, business educator; b. Portsmouth, Va., June 20, 1925; s. Stanford Laferty and Ruth (Speight) W.; B.E.E., Va. Poly. Inst., 1948, M.E.E., 1951; m. Margaret Kirby, Sept. 6, 1946; children—Lynn Whitehorne Sacco, Robert Alvin, Cynthia Leigh Moore. Engr., IBM Corp., Poughkeepsie, N.Y., 1950-54, lab. adminstr., Kingston, N.Y., 1954-56, dir. employee relations, Armonk, N.Y., 1956-72, resident mgr. Mid-Hudson Valley, Poughkeepsie, 1972-74; v.p.-personnel and orgn. planning Sperry & Hutchinson Co., N.Y.C., 1976-79; exec. v.p. Michelin Tire Corp., Grenville, S.C., 1974-76; dir. CODESCO, Inc., SPAN-America, Inc.; mem. faculty Coll. Bus. Adminstrn., U. S.C., Columbia, 1979-85; mem. faculty Coll. William and Mary, 1985—. Former trustee U. S.C. Bus. Partnership Found.; mem. plans for progress com. Pres.'s Commn. on Equal Employment Activity, 1963-68. Served with USMCR, 1944-46. Methodist. Club: Kingsmill. Home: 216 Fairfax Way Williamsburg VA 23185-6546 Office: Coll William and Mary Sch Bus Adminstrn Williamsburg VA 23187

WHITEHOUSE, JOHN COLIN, modern language educator, translator; b. Sheffield, Yorkshire, Eng., Sept. 24, 1932; s. John Cyril and Doris Lilian (Beckett) W.; m. Anne Marie Coyne, Aug. 3, 1957; 6 children. BA with honors, U. Sheffield, 1953, MA, 1965; PhD, U. Bradford, 1981. Lectr. Wigan Tech. Coll., 1956-58, Gloucester (Eng.) Tech. Coll., 1958-63; lectr. U. Bradford, Eng., 1963-75, sr. lectr., 1975—; examiner various nat. and internat. bodies. Author: Advanced Conversational French, 1969, Le Réalisme Dans Les Romans de Bernanos, 1968; contbr. articles to profl. jours. French Govt. scholar, Paris, 1953-54. Mem. Modern Humanities Research Assn., Soc. French Studies. Office: U Bradford, Dept Modern Langs, Bradford Yorkshire BD7 1DP, England

WHITEHOUSE-TEDD, CARL, retail video executive; b. Sollihill, West Midlands, Eng., Aug. 5, 1960; s. Eric Frederick and Joan Hilda (Bywater) W. Engring. apprentice Carter Indsl. Products Ltd., Birmingham, Eng., 1976-81, contracts engr., 1981-84; advt. mgr. Land of Video Ltd., London, 1984-85; br. mgr. Video Victoria (Scotland) Ltd., Glasgow, 1985—; chmn., chief exec. Dreamland Video Ltd., Glasgow, 1987—; chmn., mng. dir. Whitehouse Leisure (Holdings) Ltd., Glasgow, 1987—. Mem. British Inst. Mgmt., Inst. Technician Engrs. in Mech. Engring. Mem. Ch. of Eng. Home: 300 Mallard Crescent, Greenhills, East Kilbride G75 8UQ, Scotland Office: Video Victoria (Scotland) Ltd, 47 Kyle St, Glasgow G4 OJD, Scotland

WHITE-HUNT, KEITH, industrial development executive; b. Rowlands Gill, Eng., Sept. 6, 1950; s. Thomas William and Louisa (Robson) W-H.; m. Brenda Liddle, Jan. 1, 1970; children: Keith Brendan, John Roland, Daniel Thomas, Brooke Arran, Edward James. BA in Econ. Studies with honors, U. Exeter, United Kingdom, 1973; MS in Indsl. Mgmt., U. Bradford, Eng., 1975; DSc in Bus. Econs., U. Lodz, Poland, 1982. Cert. in edn., registered cons. in info. tech., registered cons. in export sales. Asst. prof. U. Bradford, 1973-77; assoc. prof. U. Sokoto, Nigeria, 1977-78, U. Stirling, Scotland, 1978-80; v.p. corp. devel. Lithgows Ltd., Scotland, 1980-83; deputy chief exec. & pres. N. Am. Yorkshire & Humberside Deve. Assn., Eng., 1983—; vis. prof. U. R.I., 1980—, Tech. U. of Lodz, 1980—, U. of Lodz, 1985—; bd. dirs. White-Hunt Industries Ltd., Eng. contbr. numerous articles to profl. jours. Recipient David Forsyth award U. Leeds, 1976, Amicus Poloniae award for Contbn. to Coop. Acad. Research in Poland, 1981. Fellow British Inst. of Mgmt., Inst. of Sales and Mktg. Mgmt., Inst. of Petroleum, Internat. Inst. of Social Econs., Inst. of Mktg.; mem. Inst. of Info. Scientists, Inst. of Wastes Mgmt. Lodge: Rotary. Home: 141 Pepper Ct Los Altos CA 94022 also: 102 Valley Dr, Ben Rhydding, Ilkley, West Yorkshire LS29 8PA, England Office: Yorkshire & Humberside Devel 435 Tasso St Suite 315 Palo Alto CA 94301 Office: Yorkshire & Humberside, Westgate House, 100 Wellington St, Leeds, West Yorkshire LS1 4LT, England

WHITEHURST, BROOKS MORRIS, chemical engineer; b. Reading, Pa., Apr. 9, 1930; s. David Brooks and Bessie Ann (Lowry) W.; B.S., Va. Poly. Inst. and State U., 1951; m. Carolyn Sue Boyer, July 4, 1951; children—Garnett, Anita, Robert. Sr. process asst. Am. Enka Corp., Lowland, Tenn., 1951-56; sr. process devel. engr. Va.-Carolina Chem. Corp., Richmond, Va., 1956-63; project engr. Texaco Inc., Richmond, 1963-66; mgr. engring. services Texasgulf, Inc., Aurora, N.C., 1967-80, mgr. spl. projects and long range planning, 1980-81; pres. Whitehurst Assocs., Inc., New Bern, N.C., 1981—; instr., lectr., cons. alternative sources of energy community colls. and univs.; presenter paper Solar World Forum, Brighton, Eng., 1981. Co-chmn. N.C. state supt. task force on secondary edn., 1974—; mem. N.C. Personnel Commn. for Public Sch. Employees; mem. N.C. state adv. com. on trade and indsl. edn., 1971-77; chmn. Gov.'s Task Force Vols. in the Workplace, 1981; chmn. State Adv. Council Career Edn., 1977—; gov.'s liaison for edn. and bus., 1978-79. Registered profl. engr., N.C. Recipient commendation Pres. U.S., 1981. Mem. Am. Inst. Chem. Engrs., Am. Inst. Chemists (dir. 1980-84; cert.), N.C. Inst. Chemists (pres. 1975-77), Nat. Soc. Profl. Engrs., N.C. Soc. Profl. Engrs., Royal Soc. Chemistry. Patentee in field. Home: 1983 Hoods Creek Dr New Bern NC 28562 Office: PO Box 3335 New Bern NC 28560

WHITEHURST, WILLIAM WILFRED, JR., mgmt. cons.; b. Balt., Mar. 4, 1937; s. William Wilfred and Elizabeth (Hogg) W.; B.A., Princeton, 1958; M.S., Carnegie Inst. Tech., 1963; m. Linda Joan Potter, July 1, 1961; children—Catherine Elizabeth, William Wilfred, III. Mathematician Nat. Security Agy., Fort George G. Meade, Md., 1961-63; mgmt. cons. McKinsey & Co., Inc., Washington, 1963-66; partner L.E. Peabody & Assos., Washington, 1966-69, exec. v.p., dir. L.E. Peabody & Assos., Inc., Lanham, Md., 1969-82, pres., dir., 1983-86, pres. W.W. Whitehurst & Assocs., Inc., Cockeysville, Md., 1986—. Served to lt. USNR, 1958-61. Mem. Operations Research Soc. Am., Inst. Mgmt. Scis., Washington Soc. Investment Analysts. Episcopalian. Clubs: University, Princeton (Washington); Princeton (N.J.) Quadrangle. Home and Office: 12421 Happy Hollow Rd Cockeysville MD 21030

WHITELAW, WILLIAM STEPHEN IAN (VISCOUNT), former member British House of Lords; b. June 28, 1918; s. W.A. Whitelaw; m. Cecilia Doriel, 1943; 4 children. Ed. Winchester Coll., Trinity Coll., Cambridge. M.P. from Penrith and Border Div. of Cumberland, House of Lords, London, England, 1955-83; PPS to Chancellor of Exchequer, 1957-58, to Pres. of BOT, 1956; asst. govt. whip, 1959-61; Lord commr. of Treasury, 1961-62; parliamentary sec. Minister of Labour, 1962-64; chief opposition whip, 1964-70; Lord pres. of Council, leader Ho. of Commons, 1970-72; sec. of state for No. Ireland, 1972-73, sec. of Employment, 1973-74; chmn. Conservative Party, 1974-75; dep. leader opposition, spokesman on home affairs, 1975-79; home sec., 1979-83; Lord pres. of Council, leader Ho. of Lords, London, 1983-88; vis. fellow Nuffield Coll., Oxford, Eng., 1970. Address: House of Lords, London SW 1 England *

WHITESIDE, DAVID POWERS, JR., lawyer; b. Tupelo, Miss., Jan. 1, 1950; s. David Powers and Delores Deen (Gerkin) W. m. Roseanna McCoy, June 2, 1972; children—David III, Lauren. B.A., Samford U., 1972; cert. Exeter Coll., Oxford U., England, 1974; J.D., Duke U., 1975; LL.M., U. Ala.-Tuscaloosa, 1980. Bar: Ala. 1975, U.S. Dist. Ct. (no. dist.) Ala. 1975, U.S. Ct. Appeals (5th cir.) 1975, U.S. Ct. Appeals (11th cir.) 1981, U.S. Supreme Ct. 1978. Assoc. Johnston, Barton, Proctor et al., Birmingham, Ala., 1975-81, ptnr., 1981—; gen. counsel, Personnel Bd. Jefferson County, Birmingham, 1981-86; legal counsel Jefferson County Citizens Supervisory Commn., Birmingham, 1982-85; lectr. Ala. Jud. Coll., 1985—. First. v.p. Birmingham Music Club, 1979-81; mem. Com. for a Better Ala., Birmingham, 1981-82. Recipient Mark Donahue Meml. award Ala. Sports Car Club, 1981-82; named to Outstanding Young Men of Am., 1982; Winner Palm Beach Hist. Races, 1984, Summit Point Hist. Races, 1987, Bahama Vintage Grand Prix, 1987. Mem. U.S. Ct. of Appeals Fifth Cir. Judicial Conf. (Host com. 1977), U.S. Ct. Fifth Cir. Judicial Conf., (del. 1978); U.S. Ct. Appeals 11th Cir. Judicial Conf. (del. 1982, 86), Newcomen Soc. N.Am., Birmingham Bar Assn. (editorial staff 1980-81), ABA (sect. on employment relations), Phi Alpha Theta, Omicron Delta Kappa. Episcopalian. Club: Mountain Brook. Lodge: Rotary. Home: 2840 Overton Rd Birmingham AL 35223 Office: Johnston Barton Proctor Swedlaw & Naff 1100 Park Place Tower Birmingham AL 35203

WHITESIDE, DEREK THOMAS, mathematics history researcher; b. Blackpool, Lancashire, Eng., July 23, 1932; s. Ernest and Edith (Watts) W.; children: Simon Thomas, Philippa Ann. BA, U. Bristol, Eng, 1954; PhD, U. Cambridge, Eng, 1961; DLitt (hon.), U. Lancaster, Eng, 1987. Sr. research fellow Leverhulme Found., Eng., 1959-61; fellow Dept. Sci. and Ind. Research, Eng., 1961-63; research asst. U. Cambridge, 1963-72, sr. research fellow Churchill Coll., 1970-75, asst. dir. research, 1972-76, reader history of math., 1976-87, prof. history of math. and exact scis., 1987—. Editor: Mathematical Papers of Isaac Newton, 1967-81. Served with Brit. Army, 1954-56. Recipient Koyré medal Acad. Internat. Hist. Sci., 1968, Sarton medal Am. Hist. Sci. Soc., 1977. Fellow Brit. Acad. Office: U Cambridge, Dept Pure Math and Math Stats, 16 Mill Ln, Cambridge CB2 1SB, England

WHITESIDE, ELIZABETH AYRES, lawyer; b. Columbus, Ohio, Feb. 24, 1960; d. Alba Lea and Virginia (Ayres) W. Student, Ind. U., 1978-80; BFA, U. Wis., Milw., 1982; JD, Ohio State U., 1985. Bar: Ohio, 1985, D.C., 1986, N.Y., 1988, U.S. Dist. Ct. (no. and so. dists.) Ohio, 1986, U.S. Ct. Appeals (6th and D.C. cirs.), 1986, U.S. Tax Ct., 1986. Dep. clk. Franklin County

Mcpl. Ct, Columbus, 1981; law clk. Chester, Hoffman & Willcox, Columbus, 1983-84, Porter, Wright, Morris & Arthur, Columbus, 1984; assoc. Squire, Sanders & Dempsey, Columbus, 1985-87, Shearman & Sterling, N.Y.C., 1987—. Mng. editor Ohio State U. Law Jour., 1984-85. Mem. ABA, D.C. Bar Assn., Ohio Bar Assn., N.Y. County Bar Assn., Columbus Bar Assn., Am. Judicature Soc., Phi Delta Phi. Republican. Methodist. Home: 260 W 52d St #5-K New York NY 10019 Office: Shearman & Sterling 599 Lexington Ave New York NY 10022

WHITE-WARE, GRACE ELIZABETH, educator; b. St. Louis, Oct. 5, 1921; d. James Eathel, Sr. and Madree (Penn) White; divorced; 1 son, James Otis Ware II (Oloye Kunle Adeyemon). BA in Edn., H.B. Stowe Tchrs. Coll., 1943. Mgr. advt. Superior Press, St. Louis, 1935-39; tri-owner, v.p. Carolina Oil Co., St. Louis, 1938-42; with pub. relations Triangle Press, St. Louis, 1939-47, sales promotion, 1939-47; account supr. overtime payroll Bell Tel. Labs., Inc., N.Y.C., 1943-46; tchr. Dunbar Elem. Sch., St. Louis, 1946-47, Garfield Elem. Sch., Chgo., 1948-49, Betsy Ross Elem. Sch., Chgo., 1950-51, Lincoln Sch., Richmond, Mo., 1951, Dunbar Sch., Kinlock, Mo., 1952, Gladstone Elem. Sch., Cleve., 1954-61, Quincy Elem. Sch., Cleve., 1961-78, W.H. Brett Elem. Sch., Euclid Park, Cleve., 1979-82; head tchr. Head Start program, 1965; adult edn. tchr. Cleve. Bd. Edn., 1965-82; program adminstr. Tutoring and Nutrition Project, Delta Sigma Theta, 1983—; tchr. TV Tonight Sch., lessons for adults, Cleve., 1972; tri-owner, v.p., social editor Style mag., St. Louis, 1947-49; owner/mgr. Wentworth Record Distbrs., Chgo., 1947-51; supr. accounts receivable div. Spiegel, Inc., Chgo., 1947-52; radio panelist Calling All Americans, Cleve., 1957-58; sec. bd. dirs. Hough Pub. Co., also Hough Area Devel. Corp., Cleve., 1968-69. Mem. child devel. parent bd. Greater Cleve. Neighborhood Centers Assn.; mem. fund raising com. Food First Program, co-chmn. woman's aux. Black Econ. Union, Cleve.; vice chmn. Cleve. com. Youth for Understanding Teenage Program; mem. Cleve. Council Human Relations; mem. Cleve. chpt. CORE; charter mem., fin. sec. Tots and Teens, Inc.; treas. Jr. Women's Civic League; mem. Cleve. bd. Afro-Am. Cultural and Hist. Soc.; women's aux. bd. Talbert Clinic and Day Care Center, Cleve.; adv. bd. Langston Hughes Library; mem. Forest City Hosp. Aux. Bd., also Women's Aux. Com. Forest City Hosp.; scholarship com. Women's Allied Arts Assn. Greater Cleve., 1972-74; mem. spl. com. Lake Erie council Girl Scouts U.S.A., 1982-84; co-coordinator Cuyahoga County Child Watch Project, 1982-83. Named Most Outstanding Vol. of Year, N.Y. Fedn. Settlements, 1944, Leading Tchr. of Community, Cleve. Call and Post, weekly newspaper, 1958; recipient Martha Holden Jennings scholar award Martha Holden Jennings Found., Cleve., 1966-67, Spl. Outstanding Tchrs. award, 1973; Outstanding Service award Black Econ. Union, 1970; Cert. of Appreciation, City of Cleve., 1973; Ednl. Service to Community award Urban League, 1986 Mem. Ohio, Cleve. edn. assns., Nat. Assn. Public Sch. Adult Edn., Nat. Assn. Minority Polit. women (treas. 1985-87), NAACP, Phillis Wheatley Assn., Moreland Community Assn., Nat. Council Negro Women, Top Ladies of Distinction (pres. Cleve. 1980-82), Phi Delta Kappa (1st v.p. Cleve. 1971-73, Outstanding Achievement award 1975), Delta Sigma Theta (pres. Cleve. 1969-73), Delta Kappa Gamma, Eta Phi Beta (regional treas. 1979-83, nat. treas. 1984-88). Democrat. Clubs: Novelette Bridge (pres. Cleve. 1973-77), Arewa Du-Du Bridge (treas. 1980—). Lodge: Kiwanis. Home: 14701 Milverton Rd Cleveland OH 44120-4227

WHITFIELD, DAVID RICHARD, model management executive; b. Pontiac, Mich., May 24, 1928; s. Awbery and Ruth Elizabeth (Mattison) W.; m. Lee Kusiak, Mar. 22, 1958; children: Pamela, Robin, Richard, Noelle. AA, Chgo. Acad. Fine Arts, 1950. Dir. Patricia Stevens, N.Y.C., 1956-57; pres. Patricia Stevens, Cleve., 1957-70; pres. David & Lee, Inc., Cleve., 1970-75, Chgo., 1976—. Pub. (mag.) Model's Life, 1987. Served to USN, 1946-48, PTO. Mem. Am. Model Mgrs. Assn. (pres. 1986—), DuPage Power Squadron. Republican. Methodist. Clubs: Burnham Park Yacht, Lake Michigan Yachting Assn. (Chgo.). Office: David & Lee Model Mgmt 70 W Hubbard St Chicago IL 60610

WHITFIELD, GRAHAM FRANK, orthopedic surgeon; b. Cheam, Surrey, Eng., Feb. 8, 1942; came to U.S., 1969, naturalized, 1975; s. Reginald Frank and Marjorie Joyce (Bennett) W. BSc, King's Coll., U. London, 1963, PhD, Queen Mary Coll., U. London, 1969; MD, N.Y. Med. Coll., 1976. Research scientist Unilever Research Lab., Eng., 1963-66; postdoctoral fellow dept. chemistry Temple U., 1969-71, instr., 1971-72, asst. prof., 1972-73; resident in surgery N.Y. Med. Coll. Affiliated Hosps., N.Y.C., 1976-78, resident in orthopedics, 1978-79, sr. resident in orthopedic surgery, 1979-80, chief resident, 1980-81; attending orthopedic surgeon Good Samaritan Hosp., West Palm Beach, Fla., 1981-87, John F. Kennedy Meml. Hosp., Lake Worth, Fla., 1981—. Recipient N.Y. Med. Coll. Surg. Soc. award, 1976. Mem. AMA, Fla. Med. Assn., Palm Beach County Med. Soc., Royal Inst. Chemistry (Eng.), So. Orthopedic Assn., Fla. Orthopedic Soc., Sigma Xi. Clubs: Poinciana, Beach (Palm Beach), Colette; Brit. Schs. and Univs., Soc. Sons of St. George (N.Y.C.); Govs. of Palm Beaches (West Palm Beach). Lodge: Rotary. Author: (with Joseph Cohn and Louis Del Guercio) Critical Care Readings, 1981; editorial bd., contbg. editor Hosp. Physician, 1978-82; cons. editor Physician Asst. and Health Practitioner, 1979-82; orthopedic cons. Conv. Reporter, 1980-82; assoc. editor in chief Critical Care Monitor, 1980-82; edit. bd. Complications in Orthopedics, 1986—; practice panel cons. in orthopedic surgery Infections in Surgery, 1982—. Home: 235 Queens Ln Palm Beach FL 33480 Office: 1870 Forest Hill Blvd West Palm Beach FL 33406

WHITLEY, JOHN, editor, food reviewer; b. Paris, May 15, 1938. BA, Leeds U., Eng., 1960. Asst. dir. CineFrance, Paris, 1956-58; free-lance reporter Algiers and Paris, 1956-62; reporter, sub. No. Echo, Darlington, Eng., 1962-66; mem. editorial staff Sunday Times, London, 1969—, reviews editor, 1987—. Office: The Sunday Times, 1 Pennington St, London E1, England

WHITLEY, JOHN STUART, educator; b. Halifax, Eng., Mar. 25, 1940; s. Samuel and Gladys (Farrar) W.; m. Lynn Victoria Fry, July 13, 1968; children: Anna Elizabeth, Erica Lynn, Stephen John. BA in English Lang. and Lit. with honors, Sheffield U., 1961, MA in English Lang. and Lit., 1962. Teaching fellow Dept. English, U. Mich., Ann Arbor, 1962-63, instr., 1963-64, vis. asst. prof., 1967-68, vis. prof., 1974; asst. lectr. English U. Sussex, 1964-66, lectr. English, 1966-80, reader in Am. Studies, 1980—, dean Sch. English and Am. Studies, 1978-82, chmn. Am. Studies, 1983-86. Author: William Golding: Lord of the Flies, 1970, F. Scott Fitzgerald, The Great Gatsby, 1976; editor: Charles Dickens American Notes, 1972, Ten Modern American Short Stories, 1969; contbr. articles to profl. jours. Mem. Labour Party, campaign for Nuclear Disarmament, Lewes Little Theatre. Fulbright awardee, U. Mich., 1962, English Speaking Union fellow, 1962. Mem. Brit. Assn. for Am. Studies (exec. com. 1982—), editor pamphlets series, 1984—), Int. U.S. Studies, Assn. U. Tchrs. Office: U Sussex, Falmer Brighton BN1 9ON, England

WHITLOCK, FOSTER BRAND, pharmaceutical company executive; b. Highland Park, N.J., Oct. 27, 1914; s. Frank Boudinot and Rosena (Foster) W.; m. Edna Gertrude Evans, Jan. 26, 1945; children: Charlane (Mrs. Mowery), Frances (Ms. Edmondson), Janet (Mrs. Wise), Brand. Student, Rutgers U., 1932-33, L.H.D. (hon.); student, U. Wis., 1934-36, Columbia U., 1954; LL.D. (hon.), Phila. Coll. Pharmacy. Engr., clk. RCA Communications, Inc., 1936-39; salesman Johnson & Johnson, New Brunswick, N.J., 1939-40; pres., dir. Johnson & Johnson, 1958-77, mem. exec. com., 1964-77, vice chmn., 1973-77; pres. Johnson & Johnson Internat., 1973-77; pres. Am. Found. Pharm. Edn., 1972-73; mem. Joint Commn. on Prescription Drug Use, 1976-79. Bd. dirs. Project HOPE.; Trustee, bd. govs. Rutgers U., 1968-77; pres. Rutgers U. Found., 1975-76; chmn. bd. Overlook Hosp., Summit, N.J., 1977-78; trustee Overlook Hosp. Found., 1975—, Robert Wood Johnson Found., 1979—. Served to capt. USAAF, 1942-46. Decorated Bronze Star medal. Mem. Pharm. Mfrs. Assn. (dir., chmn. 1973-74), Internat. Fedn. Pharm. Mfrs. Assns. (pres. 1974-76), S.A.R., Chi Psi. Presbyterian. Clubs: N.Y. Yacht (N.Y.C.); Ocean Reef (Fla.); Baltusrol Golf, Key Largo (Fla.) Anglers. Address: PO Box 727 Southwest Harbor ME 04679 Office: Suite 200 Plaza II One Johnson & Johnson Plaza New Brunswick NJ 08933

WHITMAN, CLEMENTINE MCGOWIN, university administrator, oil company executive; b. Jackson, Ala., Apr. 15, 1943; d. Douglas DeVaughn and Juanita (Spann) McGowin; m. R. Wayne Whitman, Apr. 12, 1968 (div. July 1978). B.S., U. Ala., 1965. Teaching fellow U. Ala.-Tuscaloosa, 1965-68, fiscal asst., 1968-70; adminstrv. asst. U. Ala. Sch. Medicine, Birmingham, 1970-79; exec. asst. to internal medicine chmn. U. Tex. Med. Sch. Houston, 1979-88, mem. employee relations com., 1979-88, sec. com., 1979-82, chmn. com., 1983-84, 85-86; mem. pres.'s employee relations adv. council, 1983-88 (chmn. 1987-88); exec. asst. to internal medicine chmn. U. Ark. Coll. Medicine, Little Rock, 1988—. Mem. U. Ala. Alumni Assn., U.S. Figure Skating Assn., Boat Owner's Assn. of U.S. Presbyterian. Club: Birmingham Figure Skating. Home: 2200 Andover Sq #1002 Little Rock AR 72207 Office: U Arkansas Coll of Medicine Dept of Internal Medicine 4301 W Markham Slot 640 Little Rock AR 72205

WHITMAN, KENNETH JAY, advertising executive; b. N.Y.C., May 4, 1947; s. Howard Jay and Suzanne Marcia (Desberg) W.; m. Linda Loy Meisnest, Nov. 25, 1968; 1 child, Tyler Ondine. Student, Berklee Sch. Mus., 1965-66, Hubbard Acad., 1968-70. Nat. dep. dir. Pub. Relations Bur., Los Angeles, 1970-75; pres. Creative Cons., Los Angeles, 1975-82; pres., creative dir. Whitman & Green Advt., Toluca Lake, Calif., 1982-86, Whitman-Olson, Toluca Lake, 1986—. Co-author: Strategic Advertising, 1986; editor Freedom news jour., 1971-79; contbr. newspaper column Shape of Things, 1971-79. Pres. Los Angeles Citizens Commn. Human Rights, 1971-75. Recipient Cert. of Design Excellence Print Regional Design Ann., 1985, 87, Award of Excellence Consolidated Papers, 1985, 1st place award Sunny Creative Radio, 2 Telly awards, 1988, Belding award Advt. Club Los Angeles. Mem. Bus. and Profl. Advt. Assn. (Award for Excellence 1987), Art Dirs. Club of Los Angeles, VSC (pres. 1964-65). Office: Whitman-Olson 10200 Riverside Dr Toluca Lake CA 91602

WHITMEE, PIERS ANTHONY BARRETT, management consultant; b. London, Oct. 17, 1932; s. James Oswald and Kathleen Emma (Barrett) W.; m. Susan Wilmot, July 3, 1960; children: James, Gavin, Bruce. BA, U. Cambridge, Eng., 1956, MA, 1978. Group personnel mgr. Tate and Lyle, London, 1956-70; dir. Berndtson Internat., London, 1970-79; mng. dir. Berndtson Internat., N.Y.C., 1979-81; dir. Welbeck Group, London, 1981—; bd. dirs. A.W. Assocs. Ltd., London, Robert Marshall Advt. Contbr. articles to profl. jours. Served to lt. Brit. Royal Navy, 1951-53. Recipient Coronation medal H.M. Queen, 1953. Mem. Royal Soc. Arts. Club: Oriental (London). Office: Welbeck Group Ltd, 25 Haymarket, London W1Y 4EN, England

WHITMORE, JACOB LESLIE, III, forester, researcher, consultant; b. Pontiac, Mich., Jan. 21, 1939; s. Jacob Leslie and Grace Mae (Wall) W.; m. Menandra Sabina Mosquera-Moreno, Jan. 7, 1965; children: Jacqueline Grace, Michelle Jacinta. B.S., U. Mich., 1961, M.F., 1968; postgrad. U. Wash., 1968-69. Forester, Am. Friends Service Com., San Martin, Puebla, Mex., 1962-64; instr., researcher silviculture and tree improvement Tropical Agrl. Research and Tng. Ctr., Turrialba, Costa Rica, 1974-76; research forester Inst. Tropical Forestry, USDA Forest Service, Rio Piedras, P.R., 1969-74, 76-80, internat. forester, Washington, 1980-87 ; prin. research silviculturist,1987—; U.S. del. Latin Am. Forestry Commn., Mex., 1980, Com. Forest Devel. in Tropics, Rome, 1983; USDA-Forest Service liaison to Peace Corps, 1982-85, Asia coordinator, 1981-82; program coordinator Man and Biosphere, 1980-81, research coordinator, 1985-87; sec. U.S. nat. com. IX World Forestry Congress, Mexico City, 1985; cons. AID, FAO, Peace Corps, others, 1969-87; staff mem. Timber Mgmt. Research, 1987—; mem. Orgn. Tropical Forestry Studies, 1986-87. Contbr. articles to profl. jours.; editor/author other publs. U. P.R. grantee, 1979; Block Drug Co. grantee, 1967; Orgn. Tropical Studies grantee, 1967; World Wildlife Fund Conservation grantee, 1987. Fellow Soc. Am. Foresters (mem. editorial bd. Jour. Forestry 1985-87); mem. Ecol. Soc. Am., Internat. Soc. Tropical Foresters (membership chmn. 1983-85), Internat. Union Forestry Research Orgn. (working party chmn. 1978-87, dep. coordinator, exec. bd. mem., 1987—), Orgn. Profl. Employees USDA (v.p. local chpt. 1984-86, council mem., 1986—). Roman Catholic. Clubs: Soc. Les Voyageurs (chief 1966), Trigon. Home: 3904 Ridge Rd Annandale VA 22003 Office: USDA Forest Service-Timber Mgmt Research 1621 N Kent St Rosslyn VA 22209

WHITMORE, KAY REX, photographic company executive; b. Salt Lake City, July 24, 1932; s. Rex Grange and Ferrol Terry (Smith) W.; m. Yvonne Schofield, June 6, 1956; children: Richard, Kimberly, Michele, Cynthia, Suzanne, Scott. Student, U. Utah, 1950-53, B.S., 1957; M.S., M.I.T., 1975. With Eastman Kodak Co., Rochester, N.Y., 1957—, engr. film mfg., 1957-67; with factory start-up Eastman Kodak Co., Guadalajara, Mex., 1967-71; various mgmt. positions film mfg. Eastman Kodak Co., Rochester, 1971-74, asst. v.p., gen. mgr. Latin Am. Region, 1975-79, v.p., asst. gen. mgr. U.S. and Can. Photog. Div., 1979-80, exec. v.p. and gen. mgr., 1981-83, pres., 1983—, also dir.; bd. dirs. The Chase Manhattan Corp., Chase Lincoln First Bank, Bus. Council State of N.Y., Indsl. Mgmt. Council. Bd. dirs. Nat. Council for Minorities in Engring., chmn.; trustee U. Rochester. Served with U.S. Army, 1953-55. Mem. Rochester C. of C. (bd. dirs.), Am. Soc. Quality Control. Mormon. Office: Eastman Kodak Co 343 State St Rochester NY 14650

WHITMORE, WILLIAM FRANCIS, missile scientist; b. Boston, Jan. 6, 1917; s. Charles Edward and Elizabeth Manning (Gardiner) W.; m. Elizabeth Sherman Arnold, Nov. 1, 1946; children: Charles, Edward, Thomas, Peter. S.B., Mass. Inst. Tech., 1938; Ph.D. (Univ. fellow), U. Calif.-Berkeley, 1941. Math. physicist Naval Ordnance Lab., 1941-42; instr. physics MIT, 1942-46; sr. staff mem. ops. evaluation group U.S. Navy, 1946-57, chief scientist spl. projects office, 1957-59; mem. chief scientist's staff missiles and space div. Lockheed Aircraft Corp., 1959-62; dep. chief scientist Lockheed Missiles & Space Co., Sunnyvale, Calif., 1962-64; asst. to pres. Lockheed Missiles & Space Co., 1964-69, chief scientist (ocean systems), 1969-83, cons., 1984—; spl. cons. evaluation bd. of USAAF, ETO, 1945; sci. analyst to comdg. gen. 1st Marine Wing, Korea, 1953, to asst. chief naval ops. for guided missiles, 1950-56; cons. adv. panel ordnance, transport and supply Dir. Def. Research and Engring., 1958-62; mem. adv. bd. for Naval Ordnance Labs., 1968-75, chmn., 1968-73; cons. marine bd. NRC, 1973—. Mem. vis. com., math. dept. M.I.T., 1971-78. Recipient Navy Meritorious Pub. Service citation, 1961; Sec. Navy certificate of commendations (3), 1960-66. Assoc. fellow Am. Inst. Aeros. and Astronautics; mem. Am. Math. Soc., Math. Assn. Am., Optical Soc. Am., Ops. Research Soc. Am., Nat. Rifle Assn. (life), Phi Beta Kappa, Sigma Xi. Club: Cosmos. Home: 14120 Miranda Ave Los Altos Hills CA 94022 Office: Lockheed Missiles and Space Co Box 504 Sunnyvale CA 94086

WHITNEY, JANE, foreign service officer; b. Champaign, Ill., July 15, 1941; d. Robert F. and Mussette (Cary) W. BA, Beloit Coll., 1963; CD, U. Aix, Marseille, France, 1962. Joined Fgn. Service, U.S. Dept. State, 1965, vice consul, Saigon, Vietnam, 1966-68, career counselor, 1968-70, spl. asst. Office of Dir. Gen., 1970-72, consul, Stuttgart, Fed. Republic Germany, 1972-74, Ankara, Turkey, 1974-76, spl. asst. Office of Asst. Sec. for Consular Affairs, 1976-77, mem. Bd. Examiners Fgn. Service, 1977-78, 79-81, consul, Munich, Fed. Republic Germany, 1978-79, Buenos Aires, Argentina, 1981-82, ethics officer Office of Legal Adviser, 1982-85, advisor Office of Asst. Sec. for Diplomatic Security, 1985-86, dep. prin. officer, consul, Stuttgart, 1986—. Recipient awards U.S. Dept. State, 1968, 70, 81, 85, 87. Democrat. Roman Catholic.

WHITNEY, MYRNA-LYNNE, logistics engineer; b. Montreal, Que., Can., May 27, 1942; came to U.S., 1949, naturalized, 1962; d. Edmund W. and Florence S. (Richardson) Prasloski; B.A. magna cum laude, Calif. State U.-Northridge, 1971; M.S., Central Mo. State U., 1975; m. Richard A. Whitney, Jan. 2, 1977. Sec., Rockwell Internat., Canoga Park, Calif., 1962-69, methods and procedures analyst, 1976-77, environ. health and safety engr., 1977-79, system safety engr., 1979-81, developer missile support plan, 1981-84, tech. asst. space shuttle program, 1984; logistics specialist Dept. Air Force, 1984—. Served with USAF, 1971-74; maj. Res., 1975—. Decorated USAF Meritorious Service medal, Air Force Commendation medal. Mem. Am. Soc. Safety Engrs., Soc. of Logistics Engrs., System Safety Soc., Reserve Officers Assn., Phi Kappa Phi. Office: Air Force Plant Rep Rocketdyne 6633 Canoga Ave Canoga Park CA 91303-2790

WHITNEY, RALPH ROYAL, JR., financial executive; b. Phila., Dec. 10, 1934; s. Ralph Royal and Florence Elizabeth (Whitney) W.; m. Fay Wadsworth, Apr. 4, 1959; children: Lynn Marie, Paula Sue, Brian Ralph. BA, U. Rochester, 1957, MBA, 1972. Spl. agt. Prudential Ins. Co., Rochester, N.Y., 1958-59; div. mgr. Prudential Ins. Co., Rochester, 1959-63; gen. agt. Nat. Life Vt., Syracuse, 1963-64; controller Wadsworth Mfg. Assocs. Inc., Syracuse, 1964-65, v.p., 1965-68, pres., 1968-71; pres. Warren Components Corp., Warren, Pa., 1968—; pres., mng. prin. ptnr. Hammond Kennedy & Co., N.Y.C., 1972—; chmn. IFR Systems Inc.; chmn., chief exec. officer Holbrook Patterson Inc., Grobot File Co. Am.; bd. dirs. Excel Industries Corp., Regency Electronics Inc. Mfg. Co., Displays Inc., Selas Corp. Am., D.M. Mossberg & Son Inc. Episcopalian. Clubs: N.Y. Yacht, Lotus (N.Y.C.); Century (Syracuse). Home: 100 Grays Ln #108 Haverford PA 19041

WHITNEY, ROBERT AVERY, management consultant, publisher; b. Buffalo, Nov. 7, 1912; s. John Boardman and Cora Edith (Avery) W.; m. Marie Therese Thone; children: Grace Ann, Marguerite, Barbara Griffith, Robert Avery, John David, Virginia Bradley. Student, Berlin U., 1931-32, U. Buffalo, 1933; A.B., Hobart Coll., 1935. Sales rep. Wilson & Co., Stamford, Conn., 1935-37; statistician Francis I. duPont, N.Y., 1937; eastern sales mgr. Simplicity Mag., N.Y.C., 1937-40; sales promotion and advt. mgr. Corning (N.Y.) Glass Works, 1940-43; chief of controlled materials plan div. WPB, 1942-43; promotion dir. McGraw Hill Pub. Co., N.Y., 1943-46; dir. Ency. Brit. Press, Chgo., also N.Y., 1946-47; exec. dir. Nat. Fedn. Sales Execs., N.Y.C., 1947-48; pres. Nat. Sales Execs., Inc., 1948-57, Mgmt. and Mktg. Inst., 1957—, Robert A. Whitney & Co., 1962—, Mgmt. By Commitment Inc., 1976—; spl. cons. to dir. RFC, Washington, 1944-45; cons. to dir. Office of War Mblzn. and Reconversion, Washington, 1945-46; adviser War Assets Adminstrn., Washington, 1944-45; founder, dir. First Internat. Distbn. Congress, Milan, Italy, 1956; mem. nat. industry adv. council to sec. of treasury; mem. nat. distbn. council to sec. of commerce; mem. industry adv. com. to U.S. Army and Air Force; mem. adv. com. ECA; dir. 1st White House Conf. Small Bus. and Distbn.; dir. Ritec Ltd., DLI Internat. Inc., Elderworks, 1st Internat. Distbn. Congress, Milan, 1956. Author: The Instant Manager, also 20 books on mgmt. Founder, chancellor 1st grad. sch. sales mgmt. and mktg. Rutgers U., 1951; trustee Hobart Coll., mem. alumni council; trustee Irvington House, NYU Hosp.; mem. adv. council Sch. Bus., NYU; bd. dirs. Am. Found. Religion and Psychiatry. Named to Hall of Fame of Distbn., 1953; recipient Outstanding Man in Mgmt. and Mktg. award, 1963; Citation award Hobart Coll., 1985. Mem. Nat. Planning Assn. (dir.), N.Y. Bd. Trade, Am. Mgmt. Assn., Inst. Dirs. (London), Am. Mktg. Assn., Internat. C. of C. (chmn. dist. com. U.S. council), Newcomen Soc., Kappa Alpha (nat. pres. 1963-64). Republican. Episcopalian. Clubs: N.Y. Sales Executives, Metropolitan, Canadian (N.Y.C.); Union League (Chgo.); Arts and Inst. Dirs. (London). Home: 34 Rock Spring Ave West Orange NJ 07052 Office: 3 Chemin des Raviers, 1958 Perly Geneva Switzerland

WHITNEY, STEPHEN, mathematics and computer science educator; b. Boston, June 8, 1950; came to Can., 1953; s. Eoin Laird and Marion (Roberts) W.; m. Karolle Duchesneau, Feb. 17, 1973; children—Corinne, Emily. Ph.D. in Math., Université Laval, Que., Can., 1977. Research asst. Def. Research Establishment, Valcartier, Can., 1970-72; sessional lectr. U. Alta., Edmonton, Can., 1975-76, 78, I. W. Killam Found. postdoctoral scholar, 1978; chargé de cours Université Laval, 1976-77, 80, 83-84; sr. lectr. U. Samoa, Apia, West Samoa, 1979, 81-82; prof. math., computer sci. Universite du Qué., Chicoutimi, Can., 1984—. Commn. des études, U. du Québec, Chicoutimi, 1987—. Author: (with W. S. Hatcher) Absolute Algebra, 1978; contbr. articles to profl. jours. Pres. Spiritual Assembly of the Baha'is of Chicoutimi, 1984-85, sec., 1985—; adminstr. Sagym Gymnastics Club, 1986—. Nat. Sci. and Engring. Research Council scholar U. Laval, 1972-75, 80, Fonds FCAC postdoctoral scholar, 1983-84. Mem. Am. Math. Soc., Association Mathématique du Québec, Assn. Computing Machinery, World Federalist Assn. of Can., Canadian Orgn. for Devel. Through Edn., Assn. Baha'i Studies. Office: U du Québec, Dept Des Scis Fondamentales, Chicoutimi, PQ Canada G7H 2B1

WHITNEY, THOMAS PORTER, author, translator; b. Toledo, Jan. 26, 1917; s. Herbert Porter and Louise (Metzger) W.; m. Marguerite Carusone, Sept. 21, 1974; children by previous marriages: John Herbert, Louise Whitney Christofferson, Julia Forrestel. Grad., Phillips Exeter Acad., 1934; AB summa cum laude, Amherst Coll., 1937; MA, Columbia U., 1940. Instr. social scis. Bennett Coll., 1940-41; social sci. analyst OSS, Washington, 1941-44; attache, chief econ. sect. U.S. Embassy, Moscow, USSR, 1944-47; staff corr. AP of Am., Moscow, USSR, 1947-53; fgn. news analyst AP of Am., N.Y.C., 1953-59; pres. Yulya Music, Inc.; propr. Whitney Book Shops Conn., 1975—; owner Thomas P. Whitney Racing Stable, 1975—; pres. Book Call, New Canaan, Conn., 1982—. Author: Has Russia Changed, 1960, Russia in My Life, 1962; editor: The Communist Blueprint for the Future, 1962, Khrushchev Speaks, 1963; editor, translator: The New Writing in Russia, 1964, In a Certain Kingdom, Twelve Russian Fairy Tales, 1972, The Young Russians, A Collection of Stories About Them, 1972; translator: One Day in the Life of Ivan Denisovich, 1963, Scarlet Sails, 1967, Prince Ivan, The Firebird and the Gray Wolf, 1968, The First Circle, 1968, Vasilisa the Beautiful, 1970, Forever Flowing, 1972, The Nobel Lecture on Literature, 1972, The Foundation Pit, 1973, The Gulag Archipelago, Vol. I, 1973, Vol. II, 1975, Children of the Street, 1979, Memoirs of General Peter Grigorenko, 1982, The Month Brothers, 1982; contbr. articles to popular mags. including Wall Street Jour., N.Y. Times. Trustee Julia A. Whitney Found., Washington, Conn., Hartley House, N.Y.C., 1984—. Mem. Overseas Press Club Am. (pres. 1958-59), ASCAP, PEN Am. Ctr. (mem. exec. bd. 1986—), Thoroughbred Owners and Breeders Assn. (trustee 1984—), Nat. Mus. Racing (trustee 1986—), Yaddo Corp. (dir. 1987—), Phi Beta Kappa, Alpha Delta Phi. Clubs: The Brook (N.Y.); Turf and Field, Thoroughbred of Am., Saratoga Reading Rooms. Address: Roxbury Rd Washington CT 06793

WHITSON, LISH, lawyer; b. Washington, Oct. 13, 1942; s. I. Lish and Clytie B. (Collier) W.; m. Barbara Lee Sullivan, Sept. 16, 1965; children—L. Richard, Kimberly S. B.A. in Philosophy, Pa. State U., 1965; J.D., U. Wash., 1972. Bar: Wash. 1973, U.S. Dist. Ct. (we. dist.) 1973, U.S. Supreme Ct. 1977. Assoc. Seattle-King County Pub. Defender Assn., 1972-76; assoc. Helsell, Fetterman, Martin, Todd & Hokanson, Seattle, 1976-81, ptnr., 1981—; dir. Am. Judicature Soc., Chgo., Seattle Pub. Def. Assn., 1982-86. Bd. mem., chmn. Downtown Emergency Service Ctr., Seattle, 1981—, Seattle Pub. Def. Assn.; trustee Seattle Youth Symphony Orch., bd. dirs., 1986—; bd. dirs. Allied Arts, 1988—. Mem. ABA, Seattle-King County Bar Assn. (pro bono com. chmn. 1981-84, bd. dirs. 1988—), Fed. Bar Assn., Assn. Trial Lawyers Am. Am. Judicature Soc. Club: Wash. Athletic. Office: Helsell Fetterman Martin Todd & Hokanson Washington Bldg Seattle WA 98101

WHITT, MICHAEL RAYBURN, lawyer, technology consultant; b. Miles City, Mont., Aug. 2, 1952; arrived in Can., 1952; s. Rayburn Harrell and Sylvia Gladys (Ekeland) W.; m. Sheila Dorcas Kernahan, July 21, 1973; 1 child, Katherine Siobhan. BA, U. Calgary, Alta, Can., 1973; LIB, U. B.C., Vancouver, 1978. Marine seismic worker We. Geophysical Co., Ala., 1970-73; assoc. Woods, Homme, Baker and Co., Calgary, 1978-81, James and Taylor, Calgary, 1981-82; ptn., sr. solicitor McMurchie Davison and Whitt, Calgary, 1982-86; founder, sr. solicitor Whitt and Co., Calgary, 1986—; bd. dirs. LSI Logic Corp. Can., council, 1985-87, Exmos Semiconductor Corp. treas., 1986—, Snowdance Resorts Inc., TMI Tech., Inc., v.p., counsel, 1987—; founder, pres. See First Can. Inc., also bd. dirs. Author: Time Management Systems, 1984. Treas. C.B.A. Intellectual Property Subsect., Calgary, 1986—; advisor Calgary Research and Devel. Assn. Incubator, Calgary, 1985—, World Job and Food Bank, Calgary, 1986—. Mem. Alta. Law Soc., Can. Bar Assn. (mem. subsect. exec. com.), Calgary Bar Assn. Mem. Progressive Conservative Party. Club: Glencoe. Office: Whitt and Co, Suite 1500-112 4th Ave SW, Calgary, AB Canada

WHITTAKER, JOHN DEAN, engineering management educator; b. Vancouver, B.C., Can., Apr. 25, 1940; s. John Dean and Theresa (Sadlier-Brown) W.; m. Patricia Rowland (div.); children: Justin, Jason, Annthea, Katy; m. Nancy Gibson; children: Michael, Carolyn, Diana, Steven, Virginia. BS, U. Alta., Edmonton, 1962; MS, MIT, Cambridge, Mass., 1963; PhD, City of London U., 1971. Registered profl. engr., Alta. Designer Whittaker, Laviolette & Co., Edmonton, 1964-67, Ove Arup & Ptnrs., London, 1967-68; asst. prof. Tech. U of Nova Scotia, Halifax, Can., 1970-73; expert UN devel. program Internat. Labor Orgn., Bombay, 1973-75; prof. U. Alta.,

Edmonton, 1975—; productivity advisor Internat. Labor Office, Ethiopia/Turkey, 1986. Author: (textbook) Economic Analysis for Engineers and Managers, 1986. Mem. Assn. Profl. Engrs., Geologists and Geophysicists of Alta., Inst. Mgmt. Scis., Can. Operational Research Soc., Operational Research Soc. Office: U Alberta, Edmonton, AB Canada T6G 2G8

WHITTEMORE, RONALD CLARENCE, computer program analyst; b. Saco, Maine, Apr. 3, 1938; s. Kenneth Edward and Bertha Dorkas (Grace) W.; m. Lillian Marie Therriault, Nov. 24, 1962; 1 child, Deborah Lorraine. BSBA, Hawthorne Coll., 1984. Computer programmer Cross Co., Hartford, Vermont, 1966-68; sr. programmer Joy Mfg., Claremont, N.H., 1968-73, Computac, West Lebanon, N.H., 1973-79; programming mgr. Datamann, Wilder, Vt., 1979—. Pres. Claremont Men's Softball League, 1980. Served with USN, 1956-60, USAF, 1961-65. Fellow Data Processing Mgmt. Assn.; mem. VFW, (past post comdr.). Republican. Roman Catholic. Clubs: White Mountain Chess (pres. 1971-80) (Claremont), Circle 8 Square Dance (bd. dirs. 1984-85). Lodge: KC. Avocations: running; chess; softball; reading; biking. Home: 6 Memorial Dr Claremont NH 03743 Office: Datamann 222 Hartford Ave Wilder VT 05088

WHITTIER, SARAJANE, social studies educator; b. North Manchester, Ind., Dec. 17, 1912; d. Charles and Ethel Clo (Free) Leckrone; m. C. Taylor Whittier, June 18, 1934; children: Chip, Tim, Cece, Penny. BA, U. Chgo., 1934, MA, 1946. Research sec. Oriental Inst., Chgo., 1935-39; tchr. pub. schs., Flossmoor, Ill., 1939-41, Sta. WSUN-TV, St. Petersburg, Fla., 1955-56, Sta. GWETA-TV, Washington, 1961-62; substitute tchr. pub. schs., Fla. and Md., 1962—. Co-author: Pasture Trails, 1941. Asst. monthly newsletter Supt.'s Digest, 1983-85. Pres., PTA, St. Petersburg, 1960's; Kans. chmn. Friends of J.F.K. Ctr., Topeka, 1969-75, Tex. chmn., San Antonio, 1975-82; guardian Camp Fire Girls, Chgo., 1936-41, bd. dirs. Camp Fire Kans., Tex., La. Gaithersburg, Md., 1958-64; Sunday sch. tchr. Christian Ch., Chgo., 1926-34, chmn. Westbank Forum Ch. Women United. St. Petersburg, 1950-57, pianist, San Antonio, 1975-82. U. Chgo. scholar, 1933-34. Mem. AAUW (past pres., life mem.). Republican. Club: Capital Speakers (Washington). Avocations: acting, music, directing little theatres, photography, world traveling. Home: 756 Fairlawn Dr Gretna LA 70056

WHITTINGHAM, DAVID GORDON, research scientist; b. Abergavenny, Gwent, Wales, June 5, 1938; s. Percy Phillip and Eurena Jane (Parry) W.; m. Nancy Gayle Wynne Saunders, July 15, 1967; children—Leah Katharine, Emma Wynne, Mary Alison. B.Sc., Univ. Coll., U. London, 1960; B.Vet.Med., Royal Veterinary Coll., U. London, 1962, Ph.D., 1967, D.Sc., 1979; M.A., Darwin Coll., Cambridge U., 1972. Diplomate Royal Coll. Veterinary Surgeons. Postdoctoral fellow Johns Hopkins U., Balt., 1966-67, U. Sydney (New South Wales, Australia), 1968-69; Beit fellow Cambridge U., 1969-71, asst. dir. research, 1971-74; scientist Med. Research Council, London, 1974-81, dir., 1981—; cons. WHO, Switzerland, 1977-79; mem. Internat. Cell Research Orgn., France, 1975—; mem. Genome Com., World Wildlife Orgn., 1980—. Contbr. numerous articles to sci. jours. Fulbright travelling fellow, 1963-66; Pa. Plan fellow, 1964-66; recipient George Porter prize, 1977, Samuel Weiner award U. Manitoba, Can., 1987. Fellow Royal Veterinary Coll. Surgeons, Royal Soc. Medicine, London Zool. Soc., Inst. Biology; mem. Brit. Vet. Assn. Mem. Ch. of England. Home: 16 Larpent Ave, Putney, London England Office: MRC Experimental Embryology, and Teratology Unit Med, Woodmansterne Rd, Carshalton Surrey SM5 4EF, England

WHITTINGTON, FLOYD LEON, Asian business consultant, retired oil company executive, foreign service officer, economist; b. Fairfield, Iowa, May 27, 1909; s. Thomas Clyde and Ora E. (Trail) W.; m. Winifred Carol McDonald, July 31, 1933; children: Susan Whittington West, Thomas Lee. A.B., Parsons Coll., 1931; M.A., U. Iowa, 1936; student, U. Minn., 1940, Northwestern U., 1941-42. Econs., speech instr. Fairfield High Sch., 1931-36, Superior (Wis.) High Sch., 1936-40; supr. tchr. tng. Superior State Tchrs. Coll., 1936-40; econs., finance instr. Carroll Coll., Waukesha, Wis., 1940-42; price exec. OPA, Wis. and Iowa, 1942-46; indsl. relations mgr. Armstrong Tire & Rubber Co., Des Moines, 1946-48; dir. price and distbn. div. SCAP, Tokyo, Japan, 1948-51; Far East economist ODM, Washington, 1951-52; asst. adviser to sec. on Japanese financial and econ. problems Dept. State, Washington, 1952-53; chief Far Eastern sect. Internat. Finance div.; bd. govs. FRS, Washington, 1953-56; officer charge econ. affairs Office S.E. Asian Affairs, Dept. State, 1956-57, dep. dir., 1957-58; became counselor of embassy Am. embassy, Bangkok, 1958; counselor, polit. officer Am. embassy, Djakarta, Indonesia, 1962-65; counselor of embassy for econ. affairs Seoul, Korea, 1965-66; v.p. Pacific Gulf Oil, Ltd., Seoul, 1966—; exec. v.p. S.E. Asia Gulf Co., Bangkok, 1967-72, Gulf Oil Co. Siam, Ltd., Bangkok, 1967-72; v.p. Gulf Oil Co.-South Asia, Singapore, 1970-72; now Asian bus. cons. Recipient Meritorious Civilian Service citation Dept. Army, 1950. Mem. Am. Econ. Assn., Am. Acad. Polit. Sci., World Affairs Council Seattle (pres.), Seattle Com. Fgn. Relations, Pi Kappa Delta, Theta Alpha Phi. Presbyterian. Clubs: Royal Bangkok (Thailand); Sports; Lakes (Sun City, Ariz.). Lodges: Masons; Shriners; Rotary. Address: 10344 Loma Blanca Dr Sun City AZ 85351

WHITTINGTON, VERLE GLENN, petroleum company executive; b. Fairfield, Iowa, Dec. 2, 1929; s. Harold William and Grace Marie (Wilson) W.; m. Pauline Curran, Oct. 31, 1952; children: Kathleen Ann, James Edd, Mark Steven, Carol Lynn, John Joseph, Michael Aaron. B.A., Parsons Coll., Fairfield, 1952; J.D., U. Iowa, 1955. With Shell Oil Co., 1955—; mgr. non-exempt employee relations and indsl. safety Shell Oil Co., N.Y.C., 1968-70; mgr. indsl. relations, employee relations orgn. Shell Oil Co., Houston, 1970-73; treas. Shell Oil Co., 1973-75, v.p. employee relations, 1975—; chmn. Conf. Bd.'s Human Resource Mgmt. Com.; bd. dirs. R&F Coal Co., Turris Coal Co., Triton Coal Co., Marrowbone Coal Co., Wolf Creek Coal Co., Shell Mining Co., Scallop Corp., Pike County Coal Co.; chmn. trustees Shell Pension Fund, Provident Fund. Bd. dirs., Jr. Achievement SE Tex.; mem. Houston Loaned Exec. Com.; sec./treas. Exec. Service Core Houston; trustee Nat. Ctr. Occupational Readjustment. Mem. ABA, Iowa Bar Assn., Houston Bar Assn., Labor Policy Assn. (chmn. exec. com., dir.), Unemployed Benefits Assn., Bus. Roundtable (exec. com. and employee relations com.), Petroleum Club Houston. Roman Catholic. Club: Elk. Club: River Plantation Country (Conroe). Home: 101 Biloxi Ct Conroe TX 77302 Office: Shell Oil Co One Shell Plaza PO Box 2463 Houston TX 77001

WHITTLESEY, FAITH RYAN, lawyer; b. Jersey City, Feb. 21, 1939; widow; children: Henry, Amy, William. B.A. cum laude, Wells Coll., 1960; J.D., U. Pa., 1963. Spl. asst. atty. gen. Pa. Dept. Justice, Phila., 1964-65; law clk. to judge U.S. Dist. Ct. (ea. dist.) Pa., 1965-66; spl. asst. atty. gen. Pa. Dept. Public Welfare, 1967-70; asst. U.S. atty. Ea. Dist. Pa., 1970-72; mem. Pa. Ho. of Reps., 1972-76; chmn., vice chmn. Delaware County Council, Media, Pa., 1976-81; mem. firm Wolf, Block, Schorr and Solis-Cohen, Phila., 1980-81; ambassador to Switzerland, Bern 1981-83; asst. to pres. for pub. liaison, mem. sr. staff The White House, Washington, 1983-85; ambassador to Switzerland 1985-88; ptnr. Myerson & Kuhn, N.Y.C., 1988—. Ford Found. grantee. Mem. Phi Beta Kappa. Office: Myerson & Kuhn 237 Park Ave New York NY 10017

WHITWORTH, CHARLES WALTERS, JR., English literature educator; b. Thomasville, Ga., Oct. 9, 1943; s. Charles Walters and Margaret Adeline (Upshaw) W.; m. Elisabeth Nelly Hélène Perrier, Sept. 26, 1970; children: Dimitri Christopher Lionel, Upshaw, Jessića Sara Elisabeth, Tristan Pascal André Charles. BA, Earlham Coll., 1965; postgrad., U. N.C., 1965-66; MA, U. Birmingham, 1971, PhD, 1978; Diplôma d'Etudes Approfondies, U. Montpellier, 1976. Inhalation therapist New Eng. Bapt. Hosp., Boston, 1968-70; instr. lit. Shorter Coll., Rome, Ga., 1972; lectr. U. Paul Valéry, Montpellier, France, 1972-74, asst. assoc., 1974-76; lectr. U. Birmingham, Eng., 1976—, assoc. fellow Shakespeare Inst., 1980—. author: (poems) Other Window, 1969; editor: (jour.) Cahiers Elisabéthains, 1976—, (plays) Three Sixteenth-Century Comedies, 1984; contbr. articles, revs. to profl. jours., poems, essays to lit. jours., newspapers. Mem. Amnesty Internat., Birmingham, 1979—, World Disarmament Campaign, London, 1984—. Humanities research grantee Brit. Acad., 1980, 84. Mem. MLA, Early English Text Soc., Assn. Univ. Tchrs., Internat. Arthurian Soc., Internat. Shakespeare Assn., Brit. Horn Soc., Poetry Book Soc., Brit. Theater Assn. Clubs: Warwickshire County Cricket; Birmingham Fencing. Office: U Birmingham, Dept Eng Lang & Lit, PO Box 363, Birmingham B15 2TT, England

WHONG, LONG WOON, internist; b. Pyeng Yang, North Korea, Feb. 11, 1908; s. Hyung Kun and Sin Kun (Woo) W.; m. Bo Ok Kim, Jan. 2, 1940; children: Young Min, Young Nam, Young Man. Student, Tokyo Comml. U., 1926-29; BS, Mt. Union Coll., 1933; MD, U. Pitts., 1937; postgrad., Tulane Med. Sch., 1938-39; MPH, Harvard U., 1946. Med. diplomate South Korea. Head med. dept., vice supt. to acting supt. Taegu (Republic of Korea) Presbyn. Hosp., 1940-59; practice medicine specializing in internal medicine Taegu, 1959—; bd. dirs. Pohang Presbyn. Hosp. Mem. council Korean Red Cross, Kyungbuk, 1964-74; pres. Taegu Family Welfare Assn., 1971-73, bd. dirs. 1970—. Mem. Korean Med. Assn. (bd. dirs. Kyungbun br., Taegu br.), Korean Internal Assn., Med. Assn. Kyungbuk Province (pres. 1961-63), Taegu Med. Assn. (pres. 1963-64), Korea Tuberculosis Assn. (mem. council Kyungbuk br. 1961-64), Korean Anti-Parasite Assn. (mem. council Kyungbuk br. 1961-65). Presbyterian. Lodge: Rotary (gov. dist. #376 1970-71). Home and Office: 50 2d St Buksungno, Taegu Republic of Korea

WIBAUX, FERNAND, French territory government official; b. Paris, July 21, 1921; s. René and Marcelle (Candelier) W.; m. Jacqueline Piezel (dec.); children: Michèle, Nicole, Jean; m. Jeanine Petrequin, Oct. 15, 1973. PhD in Law, U. Paris. Dir. cultural and social affairs Ministry Cooperation, 1974; chief staff Sec. for Cooperation, 1976; ambassador to Senegal, Cabo Verde, Guinea-Bissau and Gambia 1977-83, ambassador to Lebanon, 1983-85; high commissioner New Caledonia, 1985—. Decorated Comdr. Order of the Legion of Honor, Nat. Order of Merit, War Cross. *

WICE, DAVID HERSCHEL, clergyman; b. Petersburg, Va., Feb. 1, 1908; s. Henry and Rose (Cooper) W.; A.B., Washington and Lee U., 1927, M.A., 1928, D.D., 1948; Rabbi, Hebrew Union Coll., 1933, D.H.L., 1954; D.H.L., Gratz Coll., 1983; m. Sophie Salzer, Feb. 22, 1934; children—Carol Ruth Wice Gross, David Henry. Rabbi, Temple Israel, Omaha, 1933-41, Temple B'nai Jeshurun, Newark, 1941-47, Congregation Rodeph Shalom, Phila., 1947-81, emeritus, 1981—. Am. dir. World Union for Progressive Judaism, 1945-55, governing bd., exec. com., 1946, later chmn. exec. com., pres., 1973-80; mem. com. Central Conf. Am. Rabbis, 1945-47, 71-72, chmn. com. on structure and orgn., 1956-63, chmn. com. world Jewry, 1965, chmn. com. family, 1967—; pres. Phila. Bd. Rabbis, 1954-56; charter pres. Jewish Community Chaplaincy Service; pres. Marriage Council, 1961-64, also Planned Parenthood; co-chmn. com. on merger Family Service Assn. Am.-Child Welfare League Am., Nat. Conf. Christians and Jews, Phila.; mem. nat. bd. Council Religion Indep. Schs.; mem. forum 15, White House Conf. Children and Youth, 1970. Bd. dirs. Family Service Assn. Am., 1959—, v.p., 1963-65, pres., 1965-67; bd. dirs. Union Am. Hebrew Congregations New Ams., Council Jewish Edn., Fedn. Jewish Agys., Jewish Community Relations Council (all Phila.); co-chmn. bd. overseers Hebrew Union Coll.-Jewish Inst. Religion. Home: 135 S 19th St Apt 1510 Philadelphia PA 19103 Office: 615 N Broad St Philadelphia PA 19123

WICH, DONALD ANTHONY, JR., lawyer; b. Detroit, Apr. 13, 1947; s. Donald Anthony and Margaret Louise (Blatz) W. B.A. with honors, Notre Dame U., Ind., 1969, J.D., 1972. Bar: Fla. 1972, U.S. Dist. Ct. (so. dist.) Fla. 1972; U.S. Ct. Appeals (5th and 11th cirs.) 1982, U.S. Supreme Ct. 1976. Assoc. VISTA, Miami, Fla., 1972-74; atty. Legal Services, Miami, 1973-75; adj. prof. law U. Miami, Fla., 1974-75; ptnr. Sullivan, Bailey, Wich & Stockman, P.A., Pompano, and Ft. Lauderdale, Fla., 1976—; pres., dir. Legal Aid of Broward, Ft. Lauderdale, 1976-82. Mem. ABA, Lawyers Title Guaranty Fund (spl. bar counsel to Fla. Bar Grievance com., bro. chmn. Fla. Bar UPL com.), Am. Arbitration Assn., North Broward Bar Assn. (pres. 1983-84), Acad. Fla. Trial Lawyers Assn. (sustaining mem.), Broward County Trial Lawyers Assn. (pres. 1988-89, sustaining mem.), Broward Bar Assn. (chmn. legis. com. 1984-85, exec. com. 1986—, vice-chmn. bench-bar com.), Assn. Trial Lawyers Am., Tex. Trial Lawyers Assn., N.Y. Trial Lawyers Assn., Pompano Beach C. of C. (v.p. 1986-88, dir. 1984-87, Govtl. Affairs Chmn. 1983-84, Art Show chmn. 1984-85, Seafood festival chmn. 1986—), Notre Dame Frederick Sorin Soc. Lodge: Rotary (bd. dirs. 1987—). Office: Glendale Fed Bldg Sullivan Bailey Wich & Stockman PA 2335 E Atlantic Blvd Suite 301 Pompano Beach FL 33062

WICHT, PIETER HAROLD, management consultant; b. Port Elizabeth, East Cape, South Africa, Feb. 15, 1949; s. Johan Hendrik and Babeta (Hofmeyr) W.; divorced; children—Zita, Alethea, Jonathan, Clarrissa. M.B.A., U. Cape Town (South Africa), 1981. Chartered acct., S. Africa. Auditor Cecil Kiplin, Cape Town, 1967-75; fin. mgr. Sea Harvest, Saldanna Bay, South Africa, 1975-77; fin. controller Angus Hanken, Pretoria, South Africa, 1977-79; gen. mgr. Natyre, Johannesburg, South Africa, 1979-81; mng. dir. Interfashions, Cape Town, 1982-84; prin. cons. Touche Ross, Cape Town, 1984-86; fin. exec. Caltex Oil South Africa, 1986-88; prin. Wicht & Assocs., Rondebosch, South Africa 1988—; mem. recruitment com. Cape Town Bus. Sch., 1982-83. Fellow Inst. Cost and Mgmt. Accts. (pres. Cape br. 1984-88, nat. vice-chmn. 1987-88), Assn. Acctg. Technicians. Methodist Clubs: Kelvin Grove (Cape Town); Pretoria Country. Home: 8 Park Rd, Rondebosch Cape 7700, Republic of South Africa

WICKER, ED FRANKLIN, research plant pathologist; b. Upper Tygart, Ky., Aug. 21, 1930; s. Leslie and Bessie Mae (Hamilton) W.; m. Veneta Carol Law, Dec. 20, 1953; children—Cynthia, Sonja. B.S. in Forestry, Wash. State U., Pullman, 1959, Ph.D. in Plant Pathology, 1965. Research forester Intermountain Forest and Range Expt. Sta., USDA Forest Service, Spokane, Wash., 1959-63, plant pathologist, 1963-78; staff research plant pathologist USDA Forest Service, Washington, 1978-82; asst. dir. Rocky Mountain Forest and Range Expt. Sta., Fort Collins, Colo., 1982—; vis. scientist sch. botany Cambridge (Eng.) U., 1970-71. Contbr. articles to profl. jours. Served with USAF, 1950-54. Recipient Research award Govt. of Japan, 1974. Mem. Am. Phytopathol. Soc., Soc. Am. Foresters, Mycol. Soc. Am. Subspecialties: Plant pathology; Resource conservation. Current work: Biology, ecology, and control of dwarf mistletoes; biology of conifer stem rusts; biological control of forest tree diseases. Home: 4118 Attleboro Ct Fort Collins CO 80525 Office: 240 W Prospect St Fort Collins CO 80526

WICKEY, EDWARD LEWIS, proprietary school executive; b. N.Y.C., Oct. 20, 1942; s. Edward Lewis and Martha Elizabeth (Franke) W.; m. Faye Donna Delucia, Dec. 29, 1963 (div. 1970); 1 son, Keith Christopher; m. Karen Ann Swanner, Feb. 27, 1971 (div. 1976); children—Gina Michelle, Robert William (dec.); m. Nancy Ann Evans, Feb. 26, 1977. A.S. with honors, Grossmont Coll. Chief operating officer Bill Wade Sch., San Diego, 1969-75; admissions dir. San Diego Coll. Bus., 1975-79; chief exec. officer Bryman Schs., Dallas, 1979-80, Airco Tech. Inst., Houston, 1980-81, Gen. Industries, Houston, 1981—; chmn., chief exec. officer NTDS, Inc., Houston, 1983—; cons. San Diego County Orgn. Pvt. Edn., 1977-79. Served with AUS, 1959-62. Mem. Tex. Assn. Pvt. Schs., Nat. Assn. Truck Driving Schs. (pres.), Houston Assn. Pvt. Schs., Calif. Assn. Pvt. Edn., Nat. Assn. Accts., Nat. Rehab. Assn. Republican. Home: 10611 Village Trail Houston TX 77065

WICKHAM, JOHN ADAMS, JR., retired army officer; b. Dobbs Ferry, N.Y., June 25, 1928; s. John Adams and Jean Gordon (Koch) W.; m. Ann Lindsley Prior, June 18, 1955; children: Lindsley, John Adams, Matthew. B.S., U.S. Mil. Acad., 1950; M.A., Harvard U., 1955, M.P.A., 1956; grad., Nat. War Coll., 1967. Commd. 2d lt. U.S. Army, 1950, advanced through grades to gen., 1979; asst. prof. social scis. U.S. Mil. Acad., 1956-60; bn. comdr. 1st Cavalry Div., Republic of Vietnam, 1967; brigade comdr., chief of staff 3d Inf. Div., Fed. Republic of Germany, 1969-70; army mem. chmn.'s staff group Office of Chmn. Joint Chiefs of Staff, Washington, 1970-71; dep. chief of staff for econ. affairs Mil. Assistance Command, Republic of Vietnam, 1971-73; dep. chief, negotiator U.S. del. Four Party Joint Mil. Commn., Republic of Vietnam, 1973; sr. mil. asst. to Sec. Def. Washington, 1973-76; comdr. 101st Airborne Div. (Air Assault), Ft. Campbell, Ky., 1976-78; dir. Joint Staff Orgn. Washington, 1978-79; comdr. in chief UN Command, Republic of Korea-U.S. Combined Forces Command, Korea, 1979-82; vice chief of staff U.S. Army, Washington, 1982-83, chief of staff, 1983-87, ret., 1987; pres. Armed Forces Communications and Electronics Assn., Fairfax, Va., 1987—; bd. dirs. Nat. Safety Council, Cooper Inst. for Aerobic Research. Decorated D.S.M. (8), Silver Star (2), Legion of Merit (4), Bronze Star, Air medal (11), Purple Heart, Legion of Honor (France), Order of Mil. Merit (Rep. of Korea), Royal Order of Polar Star (Sweden), numerous other fgn. decorations. Mem. Assn. U.S. Army, 101st Airborne Assn., Council on Fgn. Relations, Army Mut. Aid Assn. Home: 1721 Chesterbrook Vale Ct McLean VA 22101 Office: Armed Forces Communications and Electronics Assn 4400 Fair Lakes Ct Fairfax VA 22033-3899

WICKI, DIETER, banker; b. Escholzmatt, Switzerland, June 11, 1931; s. Michael H.H. and Anna L. Wicki; m. Inge V. Schroth, May 26, 1958; 1 child, Norbert. Dr Rer Pol in Polit. Econs., U. Berne, Switzerland, 1958. Ptnr., owner Dr. D. Wicki Group Cos., Zurich, Switzerland, 1962-80; dir. Capital Adv. Ltd., Zurich, 1980-81; v.p., dir. McLeod Young Weir Internat. Ltd., London, 1981—; bd. dirs. T.R.V. Minerals Corp., Vancouver, B.C., Can., HPY Industries Ltd., Vancouver. Author: Der Finanzausgleich zwischen Staat und Gemeinden im Kanton Bern, 1958, Neue Chancen fuer Gewinne mit Zinspapieren, 1981, Kanadische Goldminenaktien, 1984; editor News Flash weekly letter, Goldminenaktien, 1982-86. Mem. Can. Securities Inst. (rep.). Home: Bellerivestrasse 65, CH-8008 Zurich Switzerland Office: McLeod Young Weir Internat, Schutzengasse 19, CH-8001 Zurich Switzerland

WICKMAN, BO GUNNAR GEORG, public relations executive; b. Stockholm, Apr. 7, 1933; s. Gunnar and Ingrid (Moquist) W.; m. Siv. Nilsson, Aug. 15, 1959 (div. 1980); children—Pia, Louise. Diploma Grad. Sch. Communications, Stockholm, 1958; diploma P.M.D., Harvard U. Bus. Sch., 1971. Cons., Stig Arbman AB, Stockholm 1960-63, Stb-Ogilvy, Stockholm, 1963-66; mgr. client services Intermarco-Farner, Stockholm, 1966-73, McCann-Erickson, Stockholm, 1973-75; dep. gen. mgr. Relationskonsult, Stockholm, 1975-87; sr. v.p. pub. relations WASA Ins., Stockholm, 1987—; cons. Philips, Stockholm, 1967-73, Coca-Cola Co., Sweden, 1973-80, SAAB Aircraft div., Sweden, 1976-82, Am. Express Co., London and Stockholm, 1979-87. Contbr. articles to mktg. and communications jours. Served to capt. Swedish Air Force Res., 1952-80. Mem. Psychol. Def. Assn., Swedish Pub. Relations Assn. (bd. dirs. 1981—). Club: Harvard Bus. Sch. (pres. Sweden 1981). Home: Trossvagen 13,, 13300 Saltsjobaden Sweden Office: WASA Ins Co, 10376 Stockholm Sweden

WICKWIRE, PATRICIA JOANNE NELLOR, psychologist, educator; b. Sioux City, Iowa; d. William McKinley and Clara Rose (Pautsch) Nellor; B.A. cum laude, U. No. Iowa, 1951; M.A., U. Iowa, 1959; Ph.D., U. Tex., Austin, 1971; postgrad. U. So. Calif., UCLA, Calif. State U., Long Beach, 1951-66; m. Robert James Wickwire, Sept. 7, 1957; 1 son, William James. Tchr., Ricketts Ind. Schs., Iowa, 1946-48; tchr., counselor Waverly-Shell Rock Ind. Schs., Iowa, 1951-55; reading cons., head dormitory counselor U. Iowa, Iowa City, 1955-57; tchr., sch. psychologist, adminstr. S. Bay Union High Sch. Dist., Redondo Beach, Calif., 1962—, dir. student services and spl. edn.; cons. mgmt. and edn.; mem. Calif. Interagency Mental Health Council, exec. bd., 1968-72; chmn. Friends of Dominguez Hills (Calif.), 1981—; mem. exec. bd. Beach Cities Symphony Assn., 1970-82. Lic. ednl. psychologist, marriage, family and child counselor, Calif. Mem. AAUW (exec. bd., chpt. pres. 1962-72), Los Angeles County Dirs. Pupil Services (chmn. 1974-79), Los Angeles County Personnel and Guidance Assn. (pres. 1977-78), Calif. Personnel and Guidance Assn. (exec. bd. 1984—, pres. 1988—), Assn. Calif. Sch. Adminstrs. (dir. 1977-81), Los Angeles County SW Bd. Dist. Adminstrs. for Spl. Edn. (chmn. 1976-81), Calif. Assn. Sch. Psychologist (dir. 1981—), Am. Psychol. Assn., Am. Assn. Sch. Adminstrs., Calif. Assn. for Measurement and Evaluation in Guidance (dir. 1981, pres. 1984-85), Am. Assn. Counseling and Devel., Assn. Measurement and Eval. in Guidance (Western regional editor 1987—, conv. chair 1986), Calif. Assn. Counseling and Devel. (exec. bd. 1984—, pres. 1988—), Internat. Career Assn. Network (chair 1985—), Pi Lambda Theta, Alpha Phi Gamma, Psi Chi, Kappa Delta Pi, Sigma Alpha Iota. Contbr. articles in field to profl. jours. Home and Office: 2900 Amby Pl Hermosa Beach CA 90254

WIDDRINGTON, PETER NIGEL TINLING, brewery, food company executive; b. Toronto, Ont., Can., June 2, 1930; s. Gerard and Margery (MacDonald) W.; m. Betty Ann Lawrence, Oct. 12, 1956; children: Lucinda Ann, Andrea Stacy. B.A. with honors, Queen's U., Kingston, Ont., 1953; M.B.A., Harvard, 1955. Salesman Labatt's Co., London, Ont., 1955-57; asst. regional mgr. So. Ont. region Labatt's Ont. Breweries Ltd., 1957-58; gen. mgr. Kiewel & Pelissiers, Winnipeg, 1961-62; regional mgr. Labatt's Ont. Breweries Ltd., 1958-61; gen. mgr. Labatt's Man. Breweries Ltd., Winnipeg, Man., 1962-65, Labatt's B.C. Breweries Ltd., Vancouver, B.C., 1965-68; pres. Lucky Breweries Inc., San Francisco, 1968-71; v.p. corp. devel. John Labatt Ltd., 1971-73, sr. v.p., 1973, pres., chief exec. officer, 1973-87, chmn., chief exec. officer, 1987—; bd. dirs. BP Can. Ltd., Toronto Blue Jays Baseball Club, Brascan Ltd., John Labatt Ltd., Can. Imperial Bank of Commerce, Ellis-Don Ltd., Laidlaw Transp. Ltd. Bd. dirs. The Fraser Inst., Vancouver; bd. govs. Olympic Trust Fund of Can. Home: Doncaster Ave, London, ON Canada N6G 2A4 Office: John Labatt Ltd, 451 Ridout St N, London, ON Canada N6A 5L3

WIDELL, CARL-OLAF, physicist; b. Lund, Sweden, July 28, 1935; s. Gustav and Rut (Nilsson) W.; m. Ulla Lohmin, Aug. 24, 1964; children: Carl, Sven, Olle. Fil Kand, Lund U., 1964. Health physicist Studsvik Energiteknik AB, Nykoping, Sweden, 1959-82, product mgr., 1982—; expert IAEA, Tehran, Iran, 1977-78; Swedish del. ISO/TC 85/SC2, 1962—, IEC/TC 45/SC 45 B and SC 45 A, 1982—. Contbr. articles on health physics and nuclear instrumentation to profl. jours. Mem. Health Physics Soc., Internat. Radiation Protewction Assn., Nordic Soc. for Radiation Protection, Hosp. Physicists Assn., Am. Nuclear Soc., Nordic Soc. Reliability Engrs., Fachverband fuer Strahlenscutz, Swedish Assn. Radiation Physics (bd. dirs.), Swedish Assn. Nuclear Tech., Swedish Assn. Radiobiology, Swedish Tech. Physicists Assn. Conservative. Lutheran. Home: Marmorv 23, S-611 44 Nykoping Sweden Office: Studsvik Energiteknik AB, S-611 82 Nykoping Sweden

WIDENER, GARY WAYNE, industrial manufacturing and distribution company official; b. Hot Springs, Ark., Feb. 9, 1946; s. Darrel and Mary M. (Rowton) W.; m. Judith Scott, Nov. 30, 1968. B.A. in Bus. Adminstrn., Avila Coll., Kansas City, Mo., 1976. Materials mgr. Litton Dental Products, Olathe, Kans., 1974-77, MIS mgr., 1977-78; internal auditor PACCAR, Inc., Kansas City, Mo., 1978-80, gen. mgr. Dynacraft div., Bellevue, Wash., 1980-87, corp. dir. purchasing, Bellevue, 1987—. Served with USN, 1966-73. Cert. purchasing mgr. Mem. Am. Prodn. and Inventory Control Soc. (chpt. pres. 1978-79; cert.). Home: 448 174th Pl NE Bellevue WA 98008 Office: PO Box 1518 Bellevue WA 98009

WIDERA, G. E. O., mechanical engineering educator, consultant; b. Dortmund, Germany, Feb. 16, 1938; came to U.S., 1950; s. Otto and Gertrude (Yzermann) W.; m. Kristel Kornas, June 21, 1974; children—Nicholas, Erika. B.S., U. Wis., 1960, M.S., 1962, Ph.D., 1965. Asst. prof., then prof. materials engring. dept. U. Ill.-Chgo., 1965-82, prof. mech. engring., 1982—, head dept., 1983—, acting head indsl. systems engring. dept., 1985-86, dir. off-campus engring. programs, 1987—; Gastdozent U. Stuttgart, W.Ger., 1968; vis. prof. U. Wis.-Milw., 1973-74, Marquette U., Milw., 1978-79; cons. Ladish Co., Cudahy, Wis., 1967-76, Howmedica, Inc., Chgo., 1972-75, Sargent & Lundy, 1970—, Nat. Bur. Standards, 1980; vis. scientist Argonne Nat. Lab., Ill., 1968. Editor: Procs. Innovations in Structural Engring., 1974, Pressure Vessel Design, 1982; assoc. editor: Pressure Vessel Tech., 1977-81, Applied Mechanics Revs., 1987—; editorial bd.: Pressure Vessels and Piping Design Technology, 1982; tech. editor: Pressure Vessel Technology, 1983—; co-editor: McGraw Hill Handbook of Metalforming, 1985, Design and Analysis of Plates and Shells, 1986. Standard Oil Co. Calif. fellow, 1961-63; NASA fellow, 1966; Nat. Acad. Scis. travel grantee, Russia, 1972; von Humboldt fellow, W.Ger., 1968-69. Fellow ASME (chmn. pressure vessel research com. 1982-87, chmn. design and analysis com. pressure vessel and piping div. 1980-83, chmn. jr. awards com. applied mechanics div. 1973-76, chmn. machine design div. of Chgo. sect. 1967-68, editor newsletter 1971-73, exec. com. Chgo., sect. 1970-73, mem. exec. com. and program chmn. pressure vessel and piping div. 1985—), ASCE (sec.-treas. structural div. of Ill. sect. 1972-73, chmn. div. 1976-77, chmn. peer review com., tech. council on research 1984, council on structural plastics), Soc. Mfg. Engrs. (sr. mem.), Am. Soc. for Engring. Edn., Nat Soc. Profl. Engrs., Gesellschaft für Angewandte Mathematik und Mechanik, Am. Acad. Mechanics, WRC (pressure vessel research com., chmn. task group on design procedures for shell intersections, 1983-87, chmn. subcom. on reinforced openings and external loads, 1987—). Research on mechanics of composite materials, plates and shells, asymptotic methods in elasticity, pressure vessels and piping, mechanics of deformation processing. Home: 3622 Russett Ln Northbrook IL 60062 Office: Univ of Ill at Chicago Dept of Mech Engring Box 4348 M/C 251 Chicago IL 60680

WIDERBERG, BO, film director, writer; b. Malmö, Sweden, June 8, 1930; s. Arvid Widerberg and Margaretha Gustafsson; m. Ann Mari Björklund, 1953 (divorced); m. Vanja Nettelbladt, 1957. Director: (films) The Pram, 1962, Raven's End, 1963, Love 65, 1965, Elvira Madigan, 1967, Adalen '31, 1969 (Best Fgn. Film U.S. Film Critics Guild), The Ballad of Joe Hill, 1971, Stubby, 1974, Man on the Roof, 1977, Victoria, 1979; author: Kyssas, 1952, Erotikon, 1957, En stuhl, Madame, 1961, Den gröna draken, Vision in svensk film. Office: care Svenska Filminstitutet, Kungsgatan 48, Stockholm C Sweden *

WIDJAJA, POERNOMO, packaging company executive; b. Wlingi, East Java, Indonesia, Nov. 22, 1954; S. Jusak Widjaja and Hanna Setiawati; m. Purnamasari, Jan. 27, 1975; 1 child, Iwan Kristono. Degree in Mech. Engring., Rajasa, Surabaya, Indonesia, 1977; degree in Elec. Engring., Surabaya Inst. Tech., 1979. Mfg. supr. PT Rajin Steel Pipe, Surabaya, 1974-75; mgr. PT Sarana Steel Co., Surabaya, 1975-77, PT Kahardjaja, Surabaya, 1977-79; mgr. sales Print & Pack AG, Zurich, Switzerland, 1979-80; nat. mgr. Print & Pack AG, Singapore, 1980-82; area mgr. Print & Pack AG, Indonesia, 1982-84; dir. operations PT Surya Multi Indopack, Surabaya, 1984-86, comml. dir., 1986—; bd. dirs. PT Purytek Tunggal Prima. Author: Total Quality Control in Packaging, 1984 (award 1985). Recipient Best Achievement award Surabaya Engr. Club, 1986; named Mgr. Year Indonesian Mgr. Assn., 1984. Fellow Indonesian Packaging Assn.; mem. Brit. Inst. Packaging, Indonesian Engr. Assn. Clubs: Patra, Technicum. Lodge: Rotary. Home: Manyar Tirtoyoso Selatan VII/6, Surabaya East Java 60118, Indonesia Office: PT Surya Multi Indopack, Rungkut Industri 14/4, Surabaya East Java 60293, Indonesia

WIEBE, MICHAEL EUGENE, microbiologist, cell biologist; b. Newton, Kans., Oct. 1, 1942; s. Austin Roy and Ruth Fern (Stucky) W.; m. Rebecca Ann Doak, June 12, 1965; 1 child, Brandon Clark. BS, Sterling Coll., 1965; PhD, U. Kansas, 1971. Research assoc. Duke U. Med. Ctr., Durham, N.C., 1971-73; asst. prof. Cornell U. Med. Coll., N.Y.C., 1973-81, assoc. prof., 1981-85; assoc. dir. research and devel. N.Y. Blood Ctr., N.Y.C., 1980-83, dir. Leukocyte products, 1983-84; sr. scientist Genentech Inc., South San Francisco, Calif., 1984—. Contbr. articles to profl. jours. Postdoctoral fellow NIH, 1971-73. Mem. AAAS, Am. Soc. for Microbiology, Am. Soc. Virology, Am. Soc. Tropical Medicine and Hygiene, Soc. of Exptl. Biology and Medicine, Tissue Culture Assn., N.Y Acad. Sci. Presbyterian. Home: 44 Woodhill Dr Redwood City CA 94061 Office: Genentech Inc 460 Point San Bruno Blvd South San Francisco CA 94080

WIEBES, CEES, political scientist; b. Rotterdam, Holland, The Netherlands, July 1, 1950; s. Anthonie and Martha (Stolk) W.; m. Sofia Everhartz. Cert., U. Amsterdam, 1971, cert. sociale acad., 1976, grad. internat. relations and law cum laude, 1983. Staff mem. Polit. Youth Council, Amsterdam, 1975-77; lectr. Dept. Internat. Relations, U. Amsterdam, 1983—. Author and co-author 3 books; contbr. articles to profl. jours. Research grantee U.S. Info. Agy., 1983-86, ZWO, 1985, Harry S. Truman Library, 1985; Can. Embassy travel grantee, 1983-86. Mem. Soc. for Historians on Am. Fgn. Relations. Mem. Labour Party. Home: Plantage Parklaan 27-I, 1018 SW Amsterdam The Netherlands Office: U Amsterdam Dept Internat. Relations, Oude Zijds Achterburgwal 237, 1012 DL Amsterdam The Netherlands

WIECHA, JOSEPH AUGUSTINE, linguist, educator; b. Chorzów II, Poland, Sept. 20, 1926; came to U.S., 1955, naturalized, 1958; s. Karol and Gertruda (Rudzki) W.; m. Mary Ruth Moore, 1953; children: Joseph Damian, Charles Francis, John Moore. B.A. with 1st class honors, Nat. U. Ireland, 1950; Ph.D. with highest distinction, N.Y. U., 1963. Instr. fgn. langs. U.S. Third Air Force, London, 1951-55; instr. German and Spanish U. Md., London, 1951-55; tchr. Spanish and math. Bklyn. Friends Sch., 1955-56; instr. German N.Y. U., N.Y.C., summer, 1958; lectr. German and humanities Harvard U., Boston, 1959-63; lectr. German lit. Colby Coll., summer 1963; prof. German SUNY, Oswego, 1963-69; chmn. dept. fgn. langs. and lit. SUNY, 1963-69, chmn. dept. Germanic and Slavic langs. and lit., 1969-72, Disting. Teaching prof., 1973—; chmn. SUNY (Fgn. Studies Center), 1972-73; lectr. and cons. methodology of teaching fgn. langs., since 1959—; condr. seminars teaching methodology fgn. langs. Nat. U. of Pedro Enriquez Ureña, Santo Domingo, 1973, U. Pisa, Italy, 1974, Moscow State Pedagogical Inst.; Fgn. Langs., USSR, 1976; vis. prof. U. Wroctaw, Poland, 1977; mem. Middle States Assn. Colls. and Schs., 1981—. Served as officer 2d Polish Corps Brit. Army, 1944-47. Decorated Bronze medal Polish Army, also; Brit. Def. medal; French Star; Star of Italy; recipient diploma of spl. recognition Universidad Nacional de Pedro Enriquez Ureña, 1973; Galileo medal U. Pisa, 1974; Ogden Butler fellow, 1958-59; Fels fellow, 1956-59; Kosciuszko Found. fellow, 1959. Mem. MLA, N.Y. State Assn. Fgn. Lang. Tchrs. (dir. 1975-78, Disting. Tchr. award 1975, Disting. Bd. Dirs. award 1978, Spl. Contbn. to Teaching Fgn. Langs. award 1979), Am. Assn. Tchrs. of German, Polish Inst. Arts and Scis. in Am., Delta Phi Alpha (hon.), Dobro Slovo (hon.). Home: 55 W 6th St Oswego NY 13126 Office: 224 Rich Hall SUNY Oswego NY 13126

WIED, GEORGE LUDWIG, physician; b. Carlsbad, Czechoslovakia, Feb. 7, 1921; came to U.S., 1953, naturalized, 1960; s. Ernst George and Anna (Travnicek) W.; m. Daga M. Graaz, Mar. 19, 1949 (dec. Aug. 1977). M.D., Charles U., Prague, 1945. Intern County Hosp., Carlsbad, Czechoslovakia, 1945; intern U. Chgo. Hosps., 1955; resident in ob-gyn U. Munich, Fed. Republic Germany, 1946-48; practice medicine specializing in ob-gyn West Berlin, 1948-53; asst. ob-gyn Free U., West Berlin, 1948-52; assoc. chmn. dept. ob-gyn Moabit Hosp., Free U., West Berlin, 1953; asst. prof., dir. cytology U. Chgo., 1954-59, assoc. prof., 1959-65, prof., 1965—, mem. bd. adult edn., 1964-68, prof. pathology, 1967—, Blum-Riese prof. ob-gyn, 1968—, acting chmn. dept. ob-gyn, 1974-75. Contbr. articles to profl. jours.; editor-in-chief Jour. Reproductive Medicine, Acta Cytologica, Analytical and Quantitative Cytology, Clinical Cytology; editor: Introduction to Quantitative Cytochemistry, Automated Cell Identification and Cell Sorting. Hon. dir. Chgo. Cancer Prevention Ctr., 1959-83; chmn. jury Maurice Goldblatt Cytology award, 1963—. Recipient Cert. of Merit, U.S. Surgeon Gen., 1952, Maurice Goldblatt Cytology award, 1961, George N. Papanicolaou Cytology award, 1970. Mem. Am. Soc. Cytology (pres. 1965-66), Mex. Soc. Cytology (hon.), Spanish Soc. Cytology (hon.), Brazilian Soc. Cytology (fgn. corr.), Indian Acad. Cytology (hon.), Latin-Am. Soc. Cytology (hon.), Japanese Soc. Cytology (hon.), German Soc. Cytology (hon.), Internat. Acad. Cytology (pres. 1977-80), Central Soc. Clin. Research, Chgo. Path. Soc., Chgo. Gynecol. Soc. (hon.). Am. Soc. Cell Biology, German Soc. Ob-Gyn. Bavarian Soc. Ob-Gyn. German Soc. Endocrinology. Swedish Soc. Medicine (hon.), Sigma Xi. Home: 1640 E 50th St Chicago IL 60615-3161 Office: Univ Chgo Hosps 5841 S Maryland Ave Chicago IL 60637

WIEDEMANN, CHARLES LOUIS, dentist; b. Belvidere, N.J., May 6, 1936; s. Charles and Clothilde Paulina (Fischer) W.; m. Jacqueline Burdzy, June 11, 1960; children—Lorraine Carol, Julie Patricia. B.A., Rutgers U., 1957; D.D.S., Fairleigh Dickinson U., 1962; postgrad. student Inst. for Grad. Dentists, 1968-69, U. Pa., 1974-75. Pvt. practice dentistry, Hackettstown, N.J., 1966—; mem., founder dental sect. staff Hackettstown Community Hosp., chief of dentistry, 1973-75, 77-78; dental dir. Heath Village Retirement Community, Hackettstown, N.J., 1970—; columnist Hackettstown Gazette, 1983-85; co-dir. Stargazer, Board of Ed, Online Mag. telecommunications systems, 1985-86; lectr. Morris County Coll., dental socs. Chmn. Bd. Health, Washington Twp., Morris County, N.J., 1975-78. Served to capt. Dental Corps, AUS, 1962-65. Recipient cert. Stuart L. Isler Found. for Preventive Dentistry, 1986. Fellow Acad. Gen. Dentistry, Am. Endodontic Soc. (Communicator of Yr. award 1983); mem. Am. Analgesia Soc., Internat. Analgesia Soc., Am. Dental Assn., N.J. Dental Assn. Warren-Sussex Dental Soc., Tri-County Dental Soc. Republican. Author: The Now Philosophy for Dentistry, 1972; Fantastic Facts About Dental Health, 1975, (computer software) The Format Machine, 1987. Editorial adv. panel Dental Econs. Jour., 1979-80; contbr. articles to profl. jours. Mem. Found. for Motivation in Dentistry (founder, bd. dirs. 1973-88). Club: Hackettstown Dental Study (co-founder, mem. 1974-88). Office: 110 Mill St Hackettstown NJ 07840

WIEDEMANN, CONRAD, literature educator; b. Karlsbad, Czechoslovakia, Apr. 10, 1937; s. Walther and Gertrude (von Powolny) W.; m. Ingrid Schrimpl, Sept. 5, 1965; 1 child, Katharina. PhD, J.W. Goethe U., Frankfurt, Fed. Republic Germany, 1965. Prof. U. Frankfurt, 1972-76, U. Giessen, Fed. Republic Germany, 1976—; vis. prof. U. Göttingen, 1975, U. Vienna, 1975-76, U. Jerusalem, 1981. Author: Johann Klaj, 1965; editor: Rom-Paris-London, 1988, (jour.) German-Roman Monatsschrift, 1978—, (reprint series) Deutsche Neudrucke Barock, 1978—. Fellow Wissenschaftskolleg zu Berlin. Evangelical. Office: Inst Neuere Deutsche Literatur, Otto Behaghelstr 10, D-6300 Giessen Federal Republic of Germany

WIEDEMANN, HANS-RUDOLF, pediatrician; b. Bremen, West Germany, Feb. 16, 1915; s. Otto and Helene (Wilmanns) W.; ed., U. Freiburg, 1935-36, U. Munich, 1937-38, U. Hamburg, 1938, U. Lausanne, 1938-39, U. Jena, 1939-40; m. Gisela von Sybel, May 16, 1942; children—Jurgen, Gisela, Rainer, Ingeborg, Volker, Elisabeth. With children's clinic U. Jena, 1940-45; head doctor children's clinic, Bremen, 1945-46, U. Bonn., 1946-52; prof. medicine U. Bonn, 1950-52; head children's clinic, Krefeld, 1952-61, U. Kiel, 1961-80; chmn. ann. meeting German Soc. Pediatrics, Kiel, 1977. Mem. German Soc. Pediatrics (hon.), German Soc. Social Pediatrics, German Soc. Children's Psychiatry, Swiss Soc. Hematology (corr.), Am. Pediatric Soc. (hon.), Austrian Soc. Pediatrics (hon.), French Soc. Pediatrics (corr.), Italian Soc. Pediatrics (corr.), Swiss Soc. Pediatrics (corr.), Hungarian Soc. Pediatrics (hon.), Chilean Soc. Pediatrics (hon.), Leopoldina. Club: Rotary. Author: (with others) Bone Dysplasias, 1974; The Characteristic Syndrome, 1982; editor-in-chief European Jour. Pediatrics, 1976-84, other pediatric jours.; co-author Lehrbuch der Kinderheilkunde, 1955-80; contbr. numerous articles to sci. jours. Home: 26 Caprivi Strasse, D2300 Kiel Federal Republic of Germany Office: 20 Schwanenweg, D2300 Kiel Federal Republic of Germany

WIEDEMANN, HERBERT, law educator; b. Berlin, Oct. 21, 1932; s. Wilhelm and Ilse (Glauning) W.; D.Jur., U. Munich, 1951, habil., 1963; m. Claudia Bü cklers, 1959; children—Andreas, Rainer, Margarete. Mem. faculty univs. Munich, Hamburg and Berlin, 1963-67; guest lectr. U. Calif., Berkeley, 1966, 78, 86; mem. faculty U. Cologne Law Sch., 1967—, prof. law, 1967—, univ. rector, 1979-81, dir. Inst. Labor and Comml. Law, 1967—; justice Ct. Appeals, Düsseldorf, 1986—. Mem. Acad. Scis. Dusseldorf. Author books, papers in field. Home: 15 Am Lehnshof, D5063 Overath-Immekeppel Federal Republic of Germany Office: U Cologne, Inst Arbeits und Wirtschaftscrecht, Albert us Magnus Platz, D500 Cologne 41, Federal Republic of Germany

WIEDOW, CARL PAUL, electromech. and geophys. instruments company executive; b. Pasadena, Calif., Dec. 3, 1907; s. Carl and Clara Minna (Matthes) W.; m. Mary Maletia Foulks, 1935 (div. Jan. 1946); m. Mary Louise Montesano, Nov. 27, 1947. A.B. in Math., Occidental Coll., 1933; M.S. in Physics, Calif. Inst. Tech., 1945, M.S. in Elec. Engring., 1946; Ph.D. in Elec. Engring., Oreg. State U., 1956. Registered profl. engr., Calif. Assoc. prof. electronics U.S. Naval Postgrad. Sch., Monterey, Calif., 1956-59; design specialist Gen. Dynamics Astronautics, San Diego, 1955-61, Ryan Aerospace div., San Diego, 1961-62; prof., head dept. physics Calif. Western U., San Diego, 1962-66; staff engr. Marine Advisors, La Jolla, Calif., 1966-67; chief of research Humphrey Inc., San Diego, 1967—; cons. engr. Elgin Nat. Watch Co., West Coast Micronics div., 1959-60, Gen. Dynamics Astronautics, San Diego, 1963-64, Havens Industries, San Diego, 1962-64, Solar, San Diego, 1964-66, Anka Industries, Chula Vista, Calif., 1979—. Counselor, judge Sci. Fair, San Diego, 1962—; acad. asst. NSF, 1966-68. Mem. Optical Soc. San Diego, AAUP, Sigma Xi, Sigma Tau, Sigma Pi Sigma, Pi Mu Epsilon. Clubs: Soc. Wireless Pioneers, Quarter Century Wireless Assn., Old Time Communicators.

WIEGAND, FREDERICK WILLIAM, JR., petroleum engineer; b. Austin, Tex., Dec. 22, 1945; s. Frederick William and Navene R. (Lee) W.; m. Patricia Ann Yesenik Jan. 24, 1970 (div. 1979); children—Gretchen Eileen, Carl Jonathan; m. Charlotte Harriet Watson, Oct. 15, 1983; children—Sandra, Bryan Frederick, Douglas. B.S. in Geology, U. Tex., 1969, B.S. in Petroleum Engring., 1969, M.S. in Petroleum Engring., 1970, postgrad. Thurgood Marshall Sch. Law. Registered profl. engr., Tex. Reservoir engr. Gulf Oil Co., Houston, 1970; reserve engr. State Tex., Austin, 1973-74; drilling engr. Esso Exploration Co., Houston, 1977-78; internat. cons., S. Am. and Middle East, 1978—; owner, pres. Wiegand Bros. Drilling Co., Inc., Lockhart, Tex. and Houston, 1978—. Pres. Young Adult Republicans, San Antonio, 1978. Served to 1st lt. U.S. Army, 1971-72; Vietnam; maj. C.E. (Res.), 1983—; mil. attache Honduras, 1987 . Mem. ABA, Am. Assn. Petroleum Geologists, Soc. Petroleum Engrs., Tex. Bar Assn., Houston Geological Soc., Phi Alpha Delta. Roman Catholic. Avocations: radio amateur, pilot, marksmanship. other: 51002 Academy #9 Houston TX 77005

WIEGANDT, RICHARD, mathematician, educator; b. Budapest, Sept. 19, 1932; s. Arthur and Julianna (Oszwald) W.; m. Ilona Pusztai; children: Peter, Thomas. D Rerum Naturalium, L. Eötvös U., Budapest, 1967; D of Math. Scis., Hungarian Acad. Scis., 1975. Cert. tchr. high sch. math. and physics. Tchr. M. Tancsics High Sch., Oroshaza, Hungary, 1955-61; sci. co-worker Math. Inst., Budapest, 1964-72, sci. chief co-worker, 1972-78, sci. advisor, 1978—, head dept. algebra, 1982—; vis. prof. UNESCO, U. Islamabad, Pakistan, 1970-72, Tech. U. Clausthal, Fed. Republic Germany, 1978, U. B.C., Vancouver, 1982, U. Fla., Gainesville, 1986. Author: Radical and Semisimple Classes of Rings, 1974; contbr. numerous articles to profl. jours. Mem. J Bolyai Math. Soc., Am. Math. Soc. Home: Orso Utca 50, H-1026 Budapest Hungary Office: Math Inst Hungarian Acad Sci, Realtanoda utca 13-15, H-1053 Budapest Hungary

WIEGERSMA, SJOERD, psychology researcher; b. Zuid-Beijerland, The Netherlands, July 31, 1940; s. Foppe and Geesje (Groenhof) W.; m. Albertje Buursma, Aug. 20, 1971; children: Foppe Mark, Trijntje Marianne. Grad. tchr. sem., Drachten, The Netherlands, 1961; diploma in psychology, State U. Groningen, The Netherlands, 1971; PhD, State U. Utrecht, The Netherlands, 1982. Tchr. spl. child care various cities, The Netherlands, 1961-65; researcher, mem. social sci. faculty State U. Utrecht, 1971—. Contbr. articles to profl. publs. Home: Melafier 8, 3831 VS Leusden Utrecht The Netherlands Office: Vakgroep Psychonomie, Heidelberglaan 2, 3508TC Utrecht The Netherlands

WIEGLER, BARRY ALLAN, management consulting company executive; b. Newark, June 17, 1938; s. Paul Louis and Marie B. W.; m. Deanna Mae Miller, Mar. 20, 1976; children: Laurie, David, Michael, Lisa, Shera. Student Santa Monica City Coll., 1956-59; BBA, Woodbury U., 1965; postgrad. in bus. adminstrn. Calif. State U.-Los Angeles, 1965-67. Cert. jr. coll. tchr., Calif.; cert. systems profl., cert. data processor. Asst. v.p. Security Pacific Nat. Bank, Los Angeles, 1961-69; mgr. fin. industry planning Computer div. Gen. Electric Co., Phoenix, 1969-71; dir. research and planning MSI Data Corp., Costa Mesa, Calif., 1971-72; v.p. Gottfried Cons., Inc., San Francisco, 1973-80, Los Angeles, 1980-81, sr. v.p., 1981-82; pres., co-founder Key Cons. Group, Inc., Santa Monica, Calif., 1982-88 , Sherman Oaks, Calif., 1988—; trustee chmn. bd.'s devel. and alumni relations com., mem. exec. com. Woodbury U.; instr., mem. curriculum adv. com. El Camino Coll., 1965-67. Served with USAFR, 1959-65. Clubs: Warner Center (Woodland Hills, Calif.). Author and nat. speaker on mgmt.; data processing columnist Pacific Banker mag.; developer productivity mgmt. processes. Office: Keys Cons Group Inc 15250 Ventura Blvd Suite 802 Sherman Oaks CA 91403

WIEHN, ERHARD ROY, sociologist; b. Saarbrucken, Germany, Aug. 1, 1937; s. Karl and Elisabeth (Petry) W.; m. Heide Mirjam Sebastian. Abitur humanist, Abendgymnasium, 1961; M.A., U. Tübingen, 1965; Dr. rer. soc., U. Konstanz, 1967. Asst. prof. U. Tübingen, 1965-66; prof. sociology U. Konstanz, 1974—; U. Konstanz commr. for Tel Aviv U.; fellow Netherlands Inst. Advanced Study, Wassenaar, 1971-72; vis. prof. Bielefeld, 1974, faculty dean, 1983-84. Mem. German Israel Soc. Konstanz (chmn.). Author numerous books; contbr. articles to profl. jours. Home: Mainaustrasse 4, 7750 Konstanz Federal Republic of Germany Office: U Konstanz, Dept Sociology, 7750 Konstanz Federal Republic of Germany

WIEHN, HELMUT, manufacturing company executive, engineer; b. Pirmasens, Fed. Republic of Germany, Aug. 10, 1930; s. Heinrich Wiehn; m. Irgard Köhler. Dip. Mech. Engring., Tech. U. Karlsruhe, Fed. Repubic Germany, 1955. Mem. exec. bd. Deutsche Babcock AG, Oberhausen, Fed. Republic Germany; now mng. dir. Deutsche Babcock Beteiligungs GmbH, Oberhausen, Fed. Republic Germany; chmn. supervisory bd. Vereinigte Kesselwerke AG, Düsseldorf, Turbon-Tunzini Klimatechnik GmbH, Bergisch Gladbach and Berlin; dep. chmn. supervisory bd. Deutsche Babcock Anlagen AG. Office: Deutsche Babcock AG, Duisburger Str 375, D-4200 Oberhausen 1 Federal Republic of Germany *

WIELAND, WILLIAM DEAN, health care consulting firm executive; b. Peoria, Ill., Feb. 15, 1948; s. George William and Virginia Lee (Delicath) W.; m. Joyce Lumia; 1 child, William Michael. BBA, Bradley U., 1971. Asst. adminstr. Galesburg (Ill.) Cottage Hosp., 1974-75; v.p. Anton & Damian, Iowa City, 1976-77; mgr. Clifton, Gunderson & Co., Peoria, 1977-80; v.p. OHMS Health Mgmt. Services, Columbus, 1980-84; dir., cons. VHA Cons. Services, Tampa, Fla., 1984—; cons. Vol. Hosps. Am. Cons. Service, Tampa, 1984—, OHMS Health Mgmt Services, Columbus, 1980-84; small bus. cons. Clifton, Gunderson & Co, 1977-80. Mem. Hosp. Mgmt. Systems Soc., Healthcare Fin. Mgmt. Assn., Soc. for Hosp. Planning & Mktg. Club: American Business (Peoria) (bd. dirs. 1978-80).

WIELECH, DENNIS DAVID, telecommunications company executive, financial consultant; b. Balt., Oct. 2, 1936; s. George Vitold Wielech and Sylvia Earlene (LaGue) Wielech Braithwaite; m. Victoria Teresa Grzymala, Sept. 8, 1962; children—Kathryn Denise, D. David. Student Balt. City Coll., 1952-55, Johns Hopkins U., 1964-67; cert. fin. planner Coll. for Fin. Planning, Denver, 1972. C.L.U. Fin. cons. Dennis D. Wielech & Assocs., Balt., 1966-82; v.p., dir. internat. mktg. Internat. Mobile Machines Corp., Phila., 1982-86; chmn. bd. Omnilink Internat. Corp., Glen Burnie, Md., 1986-87; pres. and chief exec. officer Applied Superconduction Techs., Inc., Annapolis, Md., 1987—. bd. dirs. MIT Enterprise Forum of Washington, D.C.-Balt., Inc. Mem. Republican Presdl. Task Force, Washington, 1983-84; mem. U.S. Senatorial Club, Washington, 1983-84. Mem. Am. Soc. C.L.U.s (pres. Balt. chpt. 1974-75), Nat. Assn. Corp. Dirs. (founding-Metro Washington, D.C.-Balt. chpt.), Balt. Assn. Fin. Planners (pres. 1970-75), Md. Assn. Life Underwriters (pres. 1977), Md. Assn. Health Underwriters (pres. 1976, Man of Yr. 1976). Roman Catholic. Home: Guilford House 4001 Greenway Baltimore MD 21218 Office: Flight Infolink Inc 7310 Ritchie Hwy Suite 601 Glen Burnie ND 21061

WIEMANN, MARION RUSSELL, JR., biologist, microscopist; b. Chesterton, Ind., Sept. 7, 1929; s. Marion Russell and Verda (Peek) W.; 1 child from previous marriage, Tamara Lee (Mrs. Donald D. Kelley. BS, Ind. U., 1959. Histo-research techician U. Chgo., 1959, research asst., 1959-62, research technician, 1962-64; tchr. sci. Westchester Twp. Sch., Chesterton, Ind., 1964-66; with U. Chgo., 1965-79, sr. research technician, 1967-70, research technologist, 1970-79; prin. Marion Wiemann & Assos., cons. research and devel., Chesterton, Ind., 1979—. Served with USN, 1951-53. Recipient Disting. Tech. Communicator award Soc. for Tech. Communication, 1974; named Sagamore of the Wabash Gov. Ind., 1985; McCrone Research Inst. scholar, 1968. Fellow World Literary Acad.; mem. Internat. Platform Assn., Field Mus. Natural History (assoc.), AAAS, Soil Sci. Soc. Am., Am. Soc. Agronomy, Crop Sci. Soc. Am., Internat. Soc. Soil Sci., VFW (charter mem., bd. dirs., post judge adv. 1986, apptd. post adj. 1986, Cross of Malta 1986). Club: Governors. Author: Tooth Decay, Its Cause and Prevention Through Controlled Soil Composition, 1985; contbr. articles to profl. jours. and newspapers. Address: PO Box E Chesterton IN 46304

WIEMER, ROBERT ERNEST, film and television producer; b. Highland Park, Mich., Jan. 30, 1938; s. Carl Ernest and Marion (Israelian) W.; m. Rhea Dale McGeath, June 14, 1958; children: Robert Marshall, Rhea Whitney. BA, Ohio Wesleyan U., 1959. Ind. producer 1956-60; dir. documentary ops. WCBS-TV, N.Y.C., 1964-67; ind. producer of television, theatrical and bus. films N.Y.C., 1967-72; exec. producer motion pictures and TV, ITT, N.Y.C., 1973-84; pres. subs. Blue Marble Co., Inc., Telemontage, Inc., Alphaventure Music, Inc., Betaventure Music, Inc. ITT, 1973-84; founder, pres., chief exec. officer Tigerfilm, Inc., 1984—; chmn., bd. dirs. Golden Tiger Pictures, Hollywood, Calif., 1988—; bd. dirs. Princeton-Am. Communications, Inc., 1986-88; exec. producer Emmy and Peabody award winning children's television show Big Blue Marble; writer, producer, dir. feature films: My Seventeenth Summer, Witch's Sister, Do Me a Favor, Anna to the Infinite Power, Somewhere, Tomorrow, Night Train to Kathmandu. Child actor, Jam Handy Orgn., Detroit, 1946-48. Deacon Dutch Reform Ch. in Am. Served to capt. USAF, 1960-64. Recipient CINE award, 1974, 76, 77, 79, 81. Mem. Nat. Acad. TV Arts and Scis., Info. Film Producers Assn. (Outstanding Producer award), Nat. Assn. TV Programming Execs., Am. Women in Radio and TV, N.J. Broadcasters Assn. Office: Tigerfilm Inc 6565 Sunset Blvd Hollywood CA 90028

WIENER, HARRY, pharmaceutical company executive, physician; b. Vienna, Austria, Oct. 29, 1924; s. Joseph and Beile W.; m. Charlotte Baran, May 1, 1982. B.S., Bklyn. Coll., 1945; M.D., L.I.U., 1949. With Pfizer Inc., N.Y.C., 1958—, dir. profl. info., 1958—. Served with M.C., AUS, 1953-55; Korea. Author: Generic Drugs--Safety and Effectiveness, 1973, Schizophrenia and Anti-Schizophrenia, 1977, Findings in Computed Tomography, 1979. Mem. AMA, N.Y. Acad. Medicine, Am. Med. Writers Assn. Developer Wiener numbers for calculation of phys. properties of hydrocarbons, 1947, proposer theory of human pheromones, 1966, genetics-environment symmetry in schizophrenia, 1976. Home: 429 E 52d St New York NY 10022 Office: 235 E 42d St New York NY 10017

WIENER, HESH (HAROLD FREDERIC WIENER), publisher, editor, consultant; b. Bklyn., July 20, 1946; s. Jesse Leonard and Regina (Rappaport) W. B.S. in Polit. Sci., MIT, 1969. Mem. staff systems devel. Data Gen. Corp., Southboro, Mass., 1969-70; dir. computer edn. project U. Calif., Berkeley, 1970-72; editor Computer Decisions Mag., Rochelle Park, N.J., 1973-78; editor, pub. Tech. News Am., N.Y.C., 1976—; pres. Tech. News of Am. Co., Inc., N.Y.C., 1982—; pub. Computer and Communications Buyer Newsletter, 1979—, Mainstream Newsletter, 1980-82, Infoperspectives Newsletter, 1982—, Storage Tech. Monitor, 1984-87; pub. U.S. edit. Computergram Internat. Newsletter, 1985—; cons. Hewlett-Packard Co., 1971-72, Xerox Corp., 1972-73; advisor NSF, 1975—. Corr. Computer Weekly, U.K., 1975-81, Computable, Amsterdam, 1976—, Computing Can., 1977-78, Ordinateurs, Paris, 1977—, Data News, Brussels, 1979-86, Informatics, U.K., 1981-85, Datanytt, Copenhagen, 1982—, Mgmt. Tech. mag., 1983-85; contbg. editor: Bus. and Society Rev., 1978-85, BusinessWeek Newsletter for Info. Execs., 1987—, Datamation Mag., 1983—; contbr. N.Y. Times Syndicate, Los Angeles Times Syndicate, N.Am. Newspaper Alliance Wireservice, Newsday, Manhattan, Inc., Rom Mag., Informatique (Paris), The Economist (London), Dun's Bus. Month, Software News, Digital News, Data Communications, Bus. Week Report for Info. Execs. Club: Overseas Press. Home: 246 6th Ave Brooklyn NY 11215 Office: Tech News Am 110 Greene St New York NY 10012

WIENER, ROBERT ALVIN, accountant; b. N.Y.C., Jan. 9, 1918; s. George and Rose Vivian (Fink) W.; m. Annabelle Kalbfeld, Jan. 1, 1941; children—Marilyn Wiener Grunewald, Marjorie Wiener Petit, Mark. B.C.S., NYU, 1938. C.P.A., N.Y., Ill. Sr. partner Robert A. Wiener & Co. (C.P.A.'s), N.Y.C., 1946-71; partner Alexander Grant & Co. (C.P.A.'s), N.Y.C., 1971-73; v.p., gen. auditor Seeburg Industries, Inc., N.Y.C., 1973-77; pvt. practice acctg. 1978-80, 84—; asst. prof. Pace Coll., 1956-77; lectr. Baruch Coll., 1947-77. Author: Insolvency Accounting, 1977. Served with AUS, 1943-46. Decorated Bronze Star. Mem. Am. Inst. C.P.A.s, N.Y. State Soc. C.P.A.s, Accts. Club Am., Fin. Execs. Inst., Inst. Internal Auditors, Assn. Insolvency Accts., Pi Lambda Phi. Clubs: Collectors (N.Y.C.), N.Y. U. (N.Y.C.). Home: 30 Waterside Plaza New York NY 10010

WIENER, SOLOMON, author, consultant, former city official; b. N.Y.C., Mar. 5, 1915; s. Morris David and Anna (Pinchuk) W.; B.S., Cornell, 1936; M. Pub. Adminstrn., N.Y.U., 1946; m. Gertrude Klings, Feb. 24, 1946; children—Marjorie Diane Wein, Willa Kay Ehrlich. Exam. asst. N.Y.C. Dept. Personnel, 1937-42, civil service examiner, 1946-55, asst. div. chief, 1955-59, div. chief, 1959-67, asst. dir. exams., 1967-70, dir. exams., 1970-72, asst. personnel dir. exams., 1972-75; author, cons., 1975—; tchr. Washington

Irving Evening Adult Sch., N.Y.C., 1949-60, tchr.-in-charge, 1960-67. Served with AUS, 1942-46; PTO. Decorated Bronze Star. Mem. Am. Soc. Pub. Adminstrn., Internat. Personnel Mgmt. Assn., Profl. Assn. for Mcpl. Mgmt. (exec. v.p. 1969-75), Res. Officers Assn., Am. Def. Preparedness Assn. Author: A Handy Book of Commonly Used American Idioms, rev. edit., 1981; Manual de Modismos Americanos Má s Comunes, rev. edit., 1981; A Handy Guide to Irregular Verbs and the Use and Formation of Tenses, 1959; Guí a Completa de Los Verbos Irregulares en Inglé s s y el Uso y Formació n de los Tiempos, 1959; Questions and Answers on American Citizenship, rev. edit., 1982; Clear and Simple Guide to Business Letter Writing, rev. edit., 1978; The College Graduate Guide for Scoring High on Employment Tests, 1981; The High School Graduate Guide for Scoring High on Civil Service Tests, 1981; How to Take and Pass Simple Tests for Civil Service Jobs, 1981; Officer Candidate Tests, 1985; co-author Practice for the Armed Forces Test, 1988; contbr. to ARCO ROTC Coll. Guide, 1988. Home: 523 E 14th St New York NY 10009

WIERNIK, PETER HARRIS, oncologist, educator; b. Crocket, Tex., June 16, 1939; s. Harris and Molly (Emmerman) W.; m. Roberta Joan Fuller, Sept. 6, 1961; children: Julie Anne, Lisa Britt, Peter Harrison. B.A. with distinction, U. Va., 1961, M.D., 1965; Dr. h.c., U. of Republic, Montevideo, Uruguay, 1982. Diplomate Am. Bd. Internal Medicine (subcom. on med. oncology 1981-87), Sub-Bd. Med. Oncology. Intern, Cleve. Met. Gen. Hosp., 1965-66, resident, 1969-70; resident Osler Service Johns Hopkins Hosp., Balt., 1970-71; sr. asst. surgeon USPHS, 1966, advanced through grades to med. dir., 1976; sr. staff assoc. Balt. Cancer Research Center, 1966-71, chief sect. med. oncology, 1971-76, chief clin. oncology br., 1976-82, dir., 1976-82, assoc. dir. div. cancer treatment, 1976-82; asst. prof. medicine U. Md. Hosp., Balt., 1971-74, asso. prof., 1974-76, prof., 1976-82; Gutman prof., chmn. dept. oncology Montefiore Med. Ctr., 1982—; head div. med. oncology Albert Einstein Coll., 1982—; assoc. dir. Albert Einstein Cancer Ctr., 1982—; cons. hematology and med. oncology Union Meml. Hosp., Greater Balt. Med. Center, Franklin Sq. Hosp.; bd. dirs. Balt. City unit Am. Cancer Soc., 1971-78, chmn. patient care com., 1972-75, mem. profl. edn. and grants com. N.Y.C. div., 1983—, mem. nat. clin. fellowship com., 1984—; mem. med. adv. com. Nat. Leukemia Assn., 1976—; chmn. adult leukemia com. Cancer and Leukemia Group B, 1976-82; prin. investigator Eastern Coop. Oncology Group, 1982—; chmn. gynecol. oncology com., 1986-88; sci. cons. Vt. Regional Cancer Ctr., 1987—. Editor: Controversies in Oncology, 1982, Supportive Care of the Cancer Patient, 1983, Neoplastic Diseases of the Blood, 1985; assoc. editor: Medical Oncology and Tumor Pharmacotherapy, 1987—; co-editor: Year Book of Hematology, 1986—; N.Am. editor Jour. Cancer Research and Clin. Oncology, 1986—; mem. editorial bd. Cancer Treatment Reports, 1972-76, Leukemia Research, 1976-86, Leukemia, 1986—, Cancer Clin. Trials, 1977—, Hosp. Practice, 1979—, sect. editor antineoplastic drugs Jour. Clin. Pharmacology, 1985—; co-editor Am. Jour. Med. Scis., 1976-81; also articles, chpts. in books. Recipient Z Soc. award U. Va., 1961, Byrd S. Leavell Hematology award U. Va. Sch. Medicine, 1965. Fellow AAAS, Am. Coll. Clin. Pharmacology, Internat. Soc. Hematology, Royal Soc. Medicine (London), ACP; mem. Am. Soc. Clin. Investigation, Am. Soc. Clin. Oncology (chmn. edn. and tng. com. 1976-79, 84, subcom. on clin. investigation 1980-82), Am. Assn. Cancer Research, Am. Soc. Hematology, Am. Fedn. Clin. Research, Am. Acad. Clin. Toxicology, Internat. Soc. Exptl. Hematology, N.Y. Acad. Sci., Am. Soc. Hosp. Pharmacy, Am. Soc. Clin. Pharmacology and Therapeutics, Am. Radium Soc. (program com. 1987—, exec. com. 1988), Phi Beta Kappa, Sigma Xi, Alpha Omega Alpha, Phi Sigma (award 1961). Home: 43 Longview Ln Chappaqua NY 10514 Office: Montefiore Med Ctr 111 E 210th St New York NY 10467

WIESCHENBERG, KLAUS, chemical company executive; b. Hannover, Ger., Mar. 2, 1932; came to U.S., 1959; s. Heinz and Ruth (Wilke) W.; Abitur, Hermann Billung Gymnasium, Celle, Ger., 1951; B.A., Fairleigh Dickinson U., Madison, N.J., 1974, M.B.A., 1977; m. Nona Bodareva, June 7, 1958; children—Michael, Axel, Natasha. Export/import corr. Deutsche Bank, Hannover, 1953; export corr. Hoechst AG, Frankfurt, Germany, 1954-55; various mktg. positions Am. Hoechst Corp., 1956-68, various fin. positions, 1969-78; v.p. planning corp. div., Somerville, N.J., 1978-85; v.p. Office of Pres. and Corp. Devel., 1985-87; v.p. corp. devel. Hoechst Celanese Corp., 1987—. Past pres. Toastmasters Internat., Charlotte, N.C., 1962. Mem. Comml. Devel. Assn. (chmn. membership com. 1984-86), Am. Mgmt. Assn., Planning Forum (v.p. N.Y. Met. chpt. 1986—). Republican. Eastern Orthodox. Home: 494 Steel Gap Rd Bridgewater NJ 08807 Office: Route 202 206 N Somerville NJ 08876

WIESE, TERRY EUGENE, sales and marketing executive; b. East St. Louis, Ill., Apr. 2, 1948; s. Herman and Opal F. (Terry) W.; m. Janet T. Kimmel, Apr. 1988; stepchildren: Meghan R. Kimmel, Kristen M. Kimmel. B.S. in Engring., U.S. Mil. Acad., 1973. Commd. 2d lt. U.S. Army, 1973, advanced through grades to capt., resigned, 1978; sales rep. McDonnell Douglas Automation Co., St. Louis, 1978-80, br./dist. mgr United Computing Systems, St. Louis, 1980-81; mgr. affiliate sales Uninet, Inc., Kansas City, Mo., 1981-82, dir. hdqrs. sales, 1982-83, dir. central area sales, Lenexa, Kans., 1983-84, dir. nat. accounts/central area sales, 1984, dir. field engring., 1984; dir. nat. accounts MCI Telecommunications, Washington, 1984-86; v.p. mktg. Instnl. Communications Co., McLean, Va., 1986—; v.p. market devel. No. Telecom Co., Richardson, Tex., 1987—, v.p. networks mktg., 1988—; telecommunications cons. United Way, 1982—. Author: ARTEPS for Nuclear Units, 1977; Lance Nuclear Missile ARTEP, 1978; Honest John Rocket ARTEP, 1978; ARTEP for Division/Brigade Elements, 1978. Pres. Aid Assn. for Lutherans, Collinsville, Ill., 1978-80; chmn. stewardship/budget com. Good Shepard Luth. Ch., Collinsville, 1979-81; chmn. United Way campaign, 1982-84. Mem. Am. Assn. Cost Engrs., Regional Commerce and Growth Assn. Republican. Home: 3305 Terry Dr Plano TX 75023 Office: No TelecomPalisades II 2435 North Central Expwy Richardson TX 75080

WIESEL, ELIE, writer, educator; b. Sighet, Transylvania, Sept. 30, 1928; came to U.S., 1956, naturalized, 1963; s. Shlomo and Sarah (Feig) W.; m. Marion Erster Rose, 1969; 1 child, Shlomo Elisha. Student, the Sorbonne, Paris, 1948-51; LittD (hon.), Jewish Theol. Sem., N.Y.C., 1967, Marquette U., 1975, Simmons Coll., 1976, Anna Maria Coll., 1980, Yale U., 1981, Wake Forest U., 1985, Haverford Coll., 1985, Capital U., 1986, L.I. U., 1986; LHD (hon.), Hebrew Union Coll., 1968, Manhattanville Coll., 1972, Yeshiva U., 1973, Boston U., 1974, Coll. of St. Scholastica, 1978, Wesleyan U., 1979, Brandeis U., 1980, Kenyon Coll., 1982, Hobart/William Smith Coll., 1982, Emory U., 1983, Fla. Internat. U., 1983, Siena Heights Coll., 1983, Fairfield U., 1983, Dropsie Coll., 1983, Moravian Coll., 1983, Colgate U., 1984, SUNY, Binghamton, 1985, Lehigh U., 1985, Coll. of New Rochelle, 1986, Tufts U., 1986, Georgetown U., 1986, Hamilton Coll., 1986, Rockford Coll., 1986, Villanova U., 1987, Coll. of St. Thomas, 1987, U. Denver, 1987, Walsh Coll., 1987, Loyola Coll., 1987, the Sorbonne, 1987; Phd (hon.), Bar-Ilan U., 1973, U. Haifa, 1986; LLD (hon.), Hofstra U., 1975, Talmudic U. Fla., 1979, U. Notre Dame, 1980; HHD (hon.), U. Hartford, 1985, Lycoming Coll., 1987; D of Hebrew Letters, Spertus Coll. Judaica, 1973. Disting. prof. Judaic studies CCNY, 1972-76; Andrew Mellon prof. humanities Boston U., 1976—; Henry Luce vis. scholar in Humanities and Social Thought, Whitney Humanities Ctr., Yale U., 1982-83; Disting. vis. prof. Lit. and Philosophy, Fla. Internat. U., 1982; chmn. U.S. Pres.'s Commn. on the Holocaust, 1979-80, U.S. Holocaust Meml. Council, 1980-86; hon. chmn. Nat. Jewish Resource Ctr., U.S. Com. to Free Vladimir Slepak, N.Y.C. Holocaust Meml. Commn., Am. Friends of Ghetto Fighter's House; hon. pres. Am. Gathering of Jewish Holocaust Survivors; bd. dirs. Nat. Com. on Am. Fgn. Policy, 1983—, Hebrew Arts Sch., HUMANITAS, Internat. Rescue Com., 1985—, Am. Assocs. Ben-Gurion U. of the Negev; bd. govs. Oxford Ctr. for Postgrad. Hebrew studies, Haifa U., Tel-Aviv U.; bd. trustees Yeshiva U., 1977—; colleague Cathedral St. John the Divine, 1975—; mem. adv. bd. Boston U. Inst. for Philosophy & Religion, Nat. Inst. Against Prejudice & Violence, Internat. Ctr. in N.Y.; mem. jury Neustadt Internat. Prize Lit., 1984; lectr. Andrew W. Mellon Ann. Lecture Series Boston U., 92d St. YMHA, YWHA Ann. Lectr. Series, ann. radio broadcast series Eternal Light for Jewish Theol. Sem. Am. Author: Night, 1960, Dawn, 1961, The Accident, 1962, The Town Beyond the Wall, 1964, The Gates of the Forest, 1966, The Jews of Silence, 1966, Legends of Our Time, 1968, A Beggar in Jerusalem, 1970, One Generation After, 1971, Souls on Fire, 1972, The Oath, 1973, Ani Maamin, 1973, Zalmen, or the Madness of God, 1975, Messengers of God, 1976, A Jew Today, 1978, Four Hasidic Masters, 1978, The Trial of God, 1979, Le Testament D'Un Poète Juif Assassiné (France's Prix Livre-Inter 1980, Bourse Goncourt, 1980, Prix des Bibliothècaires, 1981), 1985, Images from the Bible, 1980, Five Biblical Portraits, 1981, Somewhere A Master, 1982, Paroles d'Étranger, 1982, The Golem, 1983, The Fifth Son (Grand Prix de la'Littérature, City of Paris), 1985, Signes d'Exode, 1985, Against Silence (3 vols., ed. Irving Abrahamson), 1985, Job ou Dieu dans la Tempêe, 1986, A Song for Hope, 1987, The Nobel Speech, 1987 Tempete Twilight, 1988; editorial and adv. bds. Midstream, Religion and Lit. (U. Notre Dame), Sh'ma: Jour. of Responsibility, Forthcoming: Jewish Imaginative Writing, Hadassah Mag., Acad. of the Air for Jewish Studies; chmn. editorial bd. Holocaust and Genocide Studies: An Internat. Jour. Chmn. adv. bd. World Union Jewish Students, 1985—; comité d'Honneur Ligue International Contre le Racisme et l'Antisemitisme, 1985—; founder Nat. Jewish Ctr. Learning and Leadership; mem. adv. bd. Andrei Sakharov Inst.; mem. soc. fellows Ctr. Judaic Studies, U. Denver; bd. overseer Bar-Ilan U., 1970—. Recipient Prix Rivarol, 1963, Jewish Heritage award, Haifa U., 1975, Remembrance award, 1965, Prix du Souvenir, 1965, Nat. Jewish Book Council award, 1965, 73, Prix Médicis, 1968, Prix Bordin French Acad., 1972, Eleanor Roosevelt Meml. award, N.Y. United Jewish Appeal, 1972, Am. Liberties medallion Am. Jewish Com., 1972, Martin Luther King Jr. medallion, CCNY, 1973, Annual award for Disting. Service to Am. Jewry, Nat. Fedn. of Jewish Men's Clubs, 1973, Faculty Disting. Scholar award Hofstra U., 1974, Rambam award Am. Mizrachi Women, 1974, Meml. award N.Y. Soc. Clin. Psychologists, 1975, First Spertus Internat. award, 1976, Myrtle Wreath award Hadassah, 1977, King Solomon award, 1977, Liberty award HIAS, 1977, Jewish Heritage award, B'nai B'rith, 1966, Avoda award, Jewish Tchrs. Assn., 1972, Humanitarian award, B'rith Sholom, 1978, Joseph Prize for Human Rights, Anti-Defamation League, 1978, Zalman Shazar award State of Israel, 1979, Presdl. Citation, NYU, 1979, Inaugural award for Lit., Israel Bonds Prime Minister's Com., 1979, Jabotinsky medal, State of Israel, 1980, Rabbanit Sarah Herzog award Emunah Women of Am., 1981, Le Grand Prix Littéraire du Festival Internat. Deauville, 1983, Internat. Lit. prize for Peace, Royal Acad. Belgium, 1983, Lit. Lions award N.Y. Pub. Library, 1983, Jordan Davidson Humanitarian award Fla. Internat. U., 1983, Anatoly Scharansky Humanitarian award, 1983, Commandeur de la Légion d'Honneur award, 1984, Congressional gold medal, 1984, Voice of Conscience award Am. Jewish Congress, 1985, Remembrance award, Israel Bonds, 1985, Anne Frank award, 1985, Freedom of Worship medal FDR 4 Freedoms Found., 1985, Medal of Liberty award Statue of Liberty Presentation, 1986, Nobel Peace Prize, 1986, First Herzl Lit. award, First David Ben-Gurion award, Nat. UJA, Gov.'s award, Shaarei Tzedek, Internat. Kaplun Found. award Hebrew U. Jerusalem, Scopus award, 1974, Am.-Israeli Friendship award, Disting. Writers award Lincolnwood Library, 1984, First Chancellor Joseph H. Lookstein award Bar-Ilan U., 1984, Sam Levenson Meml. award Jewish Community Relations Council, 1985, Comenius award Moravian Coll., 1985, Henrietta Szold award Hadassah, 1985, Disting. Community Service award Mut. Am., 1985, Covenant Peace award Synagogue Council Am., 1985, Jacob Pat award World Congress Jewish Culture, 1985, Humanitarian award Internat. League Human Rights, 1985, Disting. Foreign-Born Am. award Internat. Ctr. N.Y., Inc., 1986, Freedom Cup award Women's League Israel, 1986, First Jacob Javits Humanitarian award UJA Young Leadership, 1986, Freedom award Internat. Rescue Com., 1987, Achievement award Artist and Writers for Peace in the Middle East, 1987, La Grande Médaille de Vermeil de la Ville de Paris, 1987, La Médaille de la Chancellerie de l'Université de Paris, 1987, La Médaille de l'Université de Paris, 1987, First Eitinger Prize, U. Oslo, 1987, Lifetime Achievment award Present Tense mag., 1987, Spl. Christopher award The Christophers, 1987, Achievement award State Israel, 1987, Sem. medal Jewish Theol. Sem. Am., 1987, Metcalf Cup and Prize for Excellence in Teaching, Boston U., 1987, Spl. award Nat. Com. on Am. Fgn. Policy, 1987, Grã-Cruz da Ordem Nacional do Cruzeiro do Sul, Brazil's highest distinction, 1987, Profiles of Courage award B'nai B'rith, 1987, Centennial medal U. Scranton, 1987, Citation from Religious Edn. Assn., 1987; honors established in his name: Elie Wiesel award for Holocaust Research, U. Haifa, Elie Wiesel Chair in Holocaust Studies, Bar-Ilan U., Elie Wiesel Endowment Fund for Jewish Culture, U. Denver, 1987. Fellow Jewish Acad. Arts and Scis., Am. Acad. Arts & Scis., Timothy Dwight Coll., Yale U.; mem. Fgn. Press Assn. (hon. life), Amnesty Internat., PEN, Writers & Artists for Peace in Middle East, Writers Guild of Am. East, The Author's Guild, Royal Norwegian Soc. Scis. and Letters, Phi Beta Kappa. Address: Boston U 745 Commonwealth Ave Boston MA 02215

WIESEL, TORSTEN NILS, neurobiologist, educator; b. Upsala, Sweden, June 3, 1924; came to U.S., 1955; s. Fritz Samuel and Anna-Lisa Elisabet (Bentzer) W.; 1 dau., Sara Elisabet. MD, Karolinska Inst., Stockholm, 1954; AM (hon.), Harvard U., 1967. Instr. physiology Karolinska Inst., 1954-55; asst. dept. child psychiatry Karolinska Hosp., 1954-55; fellow in ophthalmology Johns Hopkins U., 1955-58, asst. prof. ophthalmic physiology, 1958-59; asso. in neurophysiology and neuropharmacology Harvard U. Med. Sch., Boston, 1959-60; asst. prof. neurophysiology and neuropharmacology Harvard U. Med. Sch., 1960-64, asst. prof. neurophysiology, dept. psychiatry, 1964-67, prof. physiology, 1967-68, prof. neurobiology, 1968-74, Robert Winthrop prof. neurobiology, 1974-83, chmn. dept. neurobiology, 1973-82; prof. neurobiology Rockefeller U., N.Y.C., 1983—; Ferrier lectr. Royal Soc. London, 1972; NIH lectr., 1975; Grass lectr. Soc. Neurosci., 1976; lectr. Coll. de France, 1977; Hitchcock prof. U. Calif.-Berkeley, 1980; Sharpey-Schafer lectr. Phys. Soc. London; George Cotzias lectr. Am. Acad. Neurology, 1983. Contbr. numerous articles to profl. jours. Recipient Jules Stein award Trustees for Prevention Blindness, 1971, Lewis S. Rosenstiel prize Brandeis U., 1972, Friedenwald award Trustees of Assn. for Research in Vision and Ophthalmology, 1975, Karl Spencer Lashley prize Am. Philos. Soc., 1977, Louisa Gross Horwitz prize Columbia U., 1978, Dickson prize U. Pitts., 1979, Nobel prize in Physiology/Medicine, 1981. Mem. Am. Physiol. Soc., Am. Philos. Soc., AAAS, Am. Acad. Arts and Scis., Nat. Acad. Arts and Scis., Swedish Physiol. Soc., Soc. Neurosci. (pres. 1978-79), Royal Soc. (fgn. mem.), Physiol. Soc. (Eng.) (hon. mem.). Office: Rockefeller U York Ave and 66th Streets New York NY 10021 *

WIESENBERG, JACQUELINE LEONARDI, lecturer; b. West Haven, Conn., May 4, 1928; d. Curzio and Filmenia Olga (Turriziana) Leonardi; m. Russel John Wiesenberg, Nov. 23; children—James Wynne, Deborann Donna. B.A., State U. N.Y. at Buffalo, 1970, postgrad., 1970-73, 80—. Interviewer, examiner Dept. Labor, New Haven, 1948-52; sec. W.I. Clark Co., Hamden, Conn., 1952-55; acct. VA Hosp., West Haven, 1956-60; acct.-commissary U.S. Air Force Missle Site, Niagara Falls, N.Y., 1961-62; tchr. Buffalo City Schs., 1970-73, 79; acct. Erie County Social Services, Buffalo, 1971-73; lectr., 1973—. Contbr. articles to CAP, U.S. Air Force mag., 1954—. Capt., Nat. Found. March of Dimes, 1969—, com. mem. telethon, 1983-86; den mother Boy Scouts Am., 1961-68; chmn. Meals on Wheels, Town of Amherst, 1975-76; leader, travel chmn. Girl Scouts Am., 1968-77. Mem. Internat. Platform Assn., Am. Astrol. Assn., Western N.Y. Conf. Aging, Epsilon Delta Chi, Alpha Iota. Home: 14 Norman Pl Amherst NY 14226

WIESENTHAL, SIMON, association executive, engineer; b. Dec. 31, 1908; s. Hans and Rosa (Rapp) W.; grad. engr., Prague, Czechoslovakia; Dr.h.c., Hebrew Union Coll., N.Y.C., 1974, Hebrew Theol. Coll., Chgo., 1976, Washington U., St. Louis, 1981, Colby Coll., Waterville, Maine, 1982, John Jay Coll., N.Y.C., 1982; m. Cyla Muller, 1936. Individual practice architecture; head Jewish Center of Documentation; chmn. Jewish Central Com. U.S.A. Zone; chmn. Assn. Jews Persecuted by Nazi Regime; v.p. Union Internationale des Resistants et Deportes, Brussels; v.p. Fed. Assn. Jewish Communities Austria. Decorated medal of Freedom (Netherlands, Luxembourg); Gt. Medal of Merit (W. Ger.), Grand Cross of Merit; diploma of honor Resistance, UN, City of Los Angeles, State of Calif., Orgn. Jewish War Vets. U.S.A.; needle of honor Austrian Resistance; Merit award Decalogue Soc. Lawyers, Chgo., 1978; Jean-Moulin-Medaille, French Resistance; Kaj-Munk medal, Denmark; comdr. Order of Orange Nassau (Netherlands); comdr. Order of Republic (Italy); named hon. citizen of Dallas, 1979, of Louisville, 1979, of Miami Beach, 1983, of Shelby County and Memphis, 1984; Henrietta Szold award, 1979; Justice Louis D. Brandeis award, 1980; Gold medal of Am. Congress, Pres. Carter, 1980; Jerusalem medal, 1980; medal of Honor, Foundation Yad Vashem, Jerusalem; proclamation City of N.Y., 1981; comdr. Order of Merit (Luxembourg); David award Diaspora Jewry, 1981; Simon Wiesenthal Ctr. for Holocaust Studies, Yeshiva U., Los Angeles established, Apr. 1977; recipient Gold medal Union Jewish Congregations in Austria, Gt. medal Pres. of Fed. Republic of Germany, 1985, Grand Silver Hon. medal Mayor of Vienna, Austria, 1985; created Knight of Hon. Legion of France Pres. of France, 1986. Hon. mem. Inst. Recherches de Psychotherapie (France), Dutch Resistance, Danish Assn. Freedom Fighters; mem. Internat. Council of Yad Vashem (Jerusalem). Author: KZ Mauthausen, 1946; Head Mufti Head-Agent of the Axis, 1947; I Hunted Eichmann, 1961; Limitation, 1964; The Murderers Among Us, 1967; The Sunflower, 1969; Sails of Hope, 1973; The Case of Krystyna Jaworska, 1975; Max and Helen, 1982, Every Day Remembrance Day, 1986. Address: Salztorgasse 6/IV/5, 1010 Vienna Austria

WIESNER, JEROME BERT, engineering educator and researcher; b. Detroit, May 30, 1915; s. Joseph and Ida (Friedman) W.; m. Laya Wainger, Sept. 1, 1940; children: Stephen Jay, Zachary Kurt, Elizabeth Ann, Joshua A. B.S., U. Mich., 1937, M.S., 1938, Ph.D., 1950. Assoc. dir. U. Mich. Broadcasting Service, 1937-40; chief engr. Acoustical Record Lab., Library of Congress, 1940-42; staff Mass. Inst. Tech. Radiation Lab., 1942-45, U. of Calif. Los Alamos Lab., 1945-46; mem. faculty Mass. Inst. Tech., 1946-71, dir. research lab. of electronics, 1952-61, head dept. elec. engring., 1959-60, dean of sci., 1964-66, provost, 1966-71, pres., 1971-80, Inst. researcher and prof., 1980—; spl. asst. to Pres. on sci. and tech., 1961-64; chmn. Pres.'s Sci. Adv. Com., 1961-64; chmn. tech. assessment adv. council Office Tech. Assessment, U.S. Congress, 1976-79; Dir. Automatix, Damon Biotech., Cons. for Mgmt. Inc., The Faxon Co. Author: Where Science and Politics Meet, 1965, ABM—An Evaluation, 1969. Bd. govs. Weizmann Inst. Sci., MacArthur Found.; trustee Woods Hole Oceanographic Inst., Kennedy Meml. Trust; bd. of overseers Harvard U., 1987—. Fellow IEEE, Am. Acad. Arts and Scis.; mem. Am. Philos. Soc., AAUP, Am. Geophys. Union, Acoustical Soc. Am., Nat. Acad. Engring., Nat. Acad. Scis., MIT Corp. (life), Sigma Xi, Phi Kappa Phi, Eta Kappa Nu, Tau Beta Pi. Home: 61 Shattuck Rd Watertown MA 02172 Office: MIT 20 Ames St E15-207 Cambridge MA 02139

WIESNER, SHARON MARIE, investment banker, oil production executive; b. Omaha, July 16, 1938; d. Ralph Remmington and Evelyn Adeline (Morris) Von Bremer; m. Virgil James Wiesner, Apr. 4, 1959 (div. 1982); children—Scott James, Lydia Marie, Michelle Elizabeth. B.A., Creighton U., 1959; M.A., U. Nebr.-Omaha, 1964, postgrad., 1979-82. Owner, v.p. Wiesner Distbg. Co. Inc., Lincoln, Nebr., 1966-72, Wiesner Tire Co. Inc., Omaha, 1972-75; v.p. Fin. Inc., Omaha, 1975-82; with fin., sales oil Am. Internat. Sales Corp., Dallas, 1982-83; pres. Joint Capital Resources, Dallas, 1983—; Richland Petroleum seminar, 1987; Dresser Atlas Oil, Logging and Geol. Inst., 1987. Editor: Born Rich: A Historical Book of Omaha, 1978. Author: Slanting News, 1959; Critical Study of Iago's Motivation, 1964. Vice pres. Assistance League Omaha, 1973-78; fund raiser Opera Omaha; v.p. women's bd. Omaha Community Playhouse; v.p. Lincoln Symphony Guild, 1966-71; bd. dirs. Omaha Jr. Theatre, 1975-79. Named Outstanding Young Woman Jr. C. of C., Norfolk, Nebr., 1964; recipient Valuable Service awards Lincoln Gen. Hosp., Omaha Community Playhouse. Mem. Omaha Writers Group, The Quill, Landmarks Inc., Nat. Beer Wholesalers, AAUW, Omaha Symphony Guild (v.p. 1973-78), Omaha C. of C., Lincoln C. of C., Brownville Hist. Soc., Brownville Fine Arts Assn., Nebr. Kennel Club, Dalmatian Club Am., Minn.-St. Paul Dalmatian Club, Blue Ribbon Dog Breeders, Beta Sigma Phi, Omicron Delta Kappa, Phi Delta Gamma, Theta Phi Alpha (pres. 1958-59). Club: Womens (v.p. 1966-70). Avocations: painting; music; art; writing. Home and Office: Joint Capital Resources PO Box 12518 Dallas TX 75225

WIGAN, MARCUS RAMSAY, transportation research scientist; b. Horsham, Sussex, Eng., Sept. 3, 1941; s. Edmund Ramsay and Eileen (Power) W.; m. Jane Frances Geiringer, July 4, 1964 (dec. 1981); m. Christina Elger, Sept. 4, 1984; 1 child, Rebecca Jane. BA, Oxford U., 1963, D.Phil, 1967. Scientist Nat. Coal Bd. Operational Research Group, London, 1963-64; mem. staff Atomic Energy Research Establishment, Harwell, Eng., 1964-67; prin. sci. officer Transport and Rd. Research Lab., Crowthorne, Eng., 1967-74; prin. planner Greater London Council, 1974-76; chief scientist Australian Rd. Research Bd., Vermont, Victoria, 1976—; chmn. motorcycle helmet/visor com. Standards Assn. Australia, Sydney, 1982—; expert advisor standing com. on rd. safety Ho. of Reps., Canberra, Australia, 1977-78; mem. State Bicycle Com., Victoria, 1979—; mem. coms. NSF Transp. Research Bd., Washington, 1976—. Author: New Techniques for Transport Systems Analysis, 1977, Australian Personal Travel Characteristics, 1987, Knowledge Engineering Tools on Microsystems, 1987; contbr. articles to profl. jours.; assoc. editor Transp. Research, 1979—. Tech. advisor Autocycle Union Australia, 1979-80; mem. com. social or econ. implications Australian Computer Soc., 1986—. Served with RAFVR, 1963-67. Sr. vis. fellow U.K. Sci. and Engring. Research Council, Leeds, Eng., 1982, 83; recipient FIM Internat. Motorcycle Competition Lic., 1974-80. Mem. Inst. Physics, Brit. Computer Soc. Instn. Civil Engrs., Australian Computer Soc., Inst. Engrs. Australia, Chartered Inst. Transport. Home: 68 Castle St, Eaglemont Victoria 3084, Australia Office: Australian Rd Research Bd, 500 Burwood Hwy, Vermont Victoria 3133, Australia

WIGGINS, WALTON WRAY, publisher; b. Roswell, N.Mex., May 13, 1924; s. Miles Burgess and Mona Cecil (Brown) W.; grad. Motion Picture Cameraman Sch., Astoria, N.Y., 1945; m. Roynel Fitzgerald, Apr. 30, 1963; children—Walton Wray, Kimberly Douglas, Lisa Renee. Free-lance photojournalist for nat. mags., 1948-60; dir. public relations Ruidoso Racing Assn., Ruidoso Downs, N.Mex., 1960-69, v.p., 1967-68; founder, pub. Speedhorse Publs., Roswell, N.Mex. and Norman, Okla., 1969-78; owner/operator Wiggins Galleries Fine Art, 1978—; pres. Quarter Racing World, 1970-78, Am. Horse Publs., Washington, 1978; del. leader People to People, Internat. Served with U.S. Army, 1943-46. Recipient Detroit Art Dirs. award, 1955, Greatest Contbr. award Quarter Racing Owners Am., 1974. Mem. Overseas Press Club, Am. Soc. Mag. Photographers, Am. Horse Publs. Republican. Author: The Great American Speedhorse, 1978; Cockleburs and Cowchips, 1975; Alfred Morang-A Neglected Master, 1979; Ernest Berke-Paintings and Sculptures of the Old West, 1980; Juan Dell-The First Lady of Western Bronze, 1981; Go Man Go-The Legendary Speedhorse, 1982; The Transcendental Art of Emil James, 1988. Office: 104 Cedar-Aqua Fria Estates Ruidoso Downs NM 88346

WIGHTMAN, NANCY MATTHEWS, swim school adminstrator; b. Las Vegas, Nev., Jan. 18, 1941; d. Arthur Elmer Matthews and Wilma Rose (Gustin) Matthews Firth; m. Edward F. Wightman, Nov. 16, 1968. BA, U. Calif., Riverside, 1963; MA, Claremont Grad. Sch., 1969; postgrad. Union Coll., 1973. Teaching asst. Scripps Coll., Claremont, Calif., 1963-65; activities advisor, instr. Chico State Coll., Calif., 1965-67; residence dir. SUNY-Albany, 1967-69, quad coordinator, 1969-71; personnel dir. Environ. One Corp., Schenectady, 1972-73; dir. health, phys. edn. and recreation Troy-Cohoes YWCA, N.Y., 1973-78; pres. Swim Sch., Inc., Troy, 1978—; v.p. devel. U.S. Synchronized Swimming, Indpls., 1982-86, instr. trainer coaching cert., 1983—, v.p. fin. 1986—, judge; head coach Troy Sculpins, Inc. Synchronized Swim Team, Troy, 1974—. Co-author: Better Synchronized Swimming for Girls, 1981. Bd. dirs. ARC, Troy, 1974—, water safety instr. trainer, 1970—; mem. planning com. Robison Pool, Troy, 1984. Mem. U.S. Synchronized Swim. Democrat. Presbyterian. Avocations: sailing, swimming, crocheting, needlepoint. Office: The Swim Sch Inc 172 1st St Troy NY 12180

WIGINTON, JAY SPENCER, chemical company executive; b. Lubbock, Tex., Sept. 21, 1941; s. Clarence Elbert and Faye (George) W.; B.S., Tex. Tech. U., 1963, M.S., 1968; m. Billye Kay Freitag, Nov. 28, 1968; children—Lauren, Lindsay. Sales rep. West Tex. ter. Syntex Labs., Lubbock, 1968-70, regional sales rep., 1970-72, Far East regional mgr., Des Moines, 1972-73, dir. mktg., 1973-74; regional sales mgr. Zoecon Corp., Dallas, 1974-76, nat. accounts mgr. Custom div., 1976-78; gen. mgr. V.A. Snell & Co. div. Gt. Plains Chem. Co., San Antonio, 1978-83, Southwest regional mgr., 1983-84, dir. field devel., 1984-85; dist. mgr. Agri-Sales Assocs., Inc., 1985-87; regional mgr. Vet Brand, Inc., 1987—. Served with AUS, 1964-66; Vietnam. Mem. Tex. Grain and Feed Assn., Tex. Cattle Feeders Assn., Tex. Chem. Assn., Kappa Sigma. Mem. Christian Ch. (Disciples of Christ). Office: 2012 Northwest Military Hwy San Antonio TX 78213

WIGNER, EUGENE PAUL, physicist, educator; b. Budapest, Hungary, Nov. 17, 1902; came to U.S., 1930, naturalized, 1937; s. Anthony and Elisabeth (Einhorn) W.; m. Amelia Z. Frank, Dec. 23, 1936 (dec. 1937); m. Mary Annette Wheeler, June 4, 1941 (dec. Nov. 1977); m. Eileen C.P.

Hamilton, Dec. 29, 1979. Chem. Engr. and Dr. Engring., Technische Hochschule, Berlin, 1925; hon. D.Sc., U. Wis., 1949, Washington U., 1950, Case Inst. Tech., 1956, U. Chgo., 1957, Colby Coll., 1959, U. Pa., 1961, Thiel Coll., 1964, U. Notre Dame, 1965, Technische Universität Berlin, 1966, Swarthmore Coll., 1966, Université de Louvain, Belgium, 1967; Dr.Jr., U. Alta., 1957; L.H.D., Yeshiva U., 1963; hon. degrees, U. Liège, 1967, U. Ill., 1968, Seton Hall U., 1969, Catholic U., 1969, Rockefeller U., 1970, Israel Inst. Tech., 1973, Lowell U., 1976, Princeton U., 1976, U. Tex., 1978, Clarkson Coll., 1979, Allegheny Coll., 1979, Gustav Adolphus Coll., 1981, Stevens Inst. Tech., 1982, SUNY, 1982, La. State U., 1985. Asst. Technische Hochschule, Berlin, 1926-27, asst. prof., 1928-33; asst. U. Göttingen, 1927-28; Lectr. Princeton U., 1930, halftime prof. math. physics, 1931-36; prof. physics U. Wis., 1936-38; Thomas D. Jones prof. theoretical physics Princeton U., 1938-71; on leave of absence 1942-45; with Metall. Lab., U. Chgo., 1946-47; as dir. research and devel. Clinton Labs.; dir. CD Research Project, Oak Ridge, 1964-65; Lorentz lectr. Inst. Lorentz, Leiden, 1957; cons. prof. La. State U., 1971-85, ret., 1985; mem. gen. adv. com. AEC, 1952-57, 59-64; mem. math. panel NRC, 1952-54; physics panel NSF, 1953-56; vis. com. Nat. Bur. Standards, 1947-51. Author: (with L. Eisenbud) Nuclear Structure, 1958, The Physical Theory of Neutron Chain Reactors (with A.M. Weinberg), 1958, Group Theory and its Applications to the Quantum Mechanics of Atomic Spectre, 1931, English translation, 1959, Symmetries and Reflections, 1967, Survival and the Bomb, 1969. Decorated medal of Merit, 1946; recipient Franklin medal Franklin Inst., 1950, citation N.J. Tchrs. Assn., 1951, Enrico Fermi award AEC, 1958, Atoms for Peace award, 1960, Max Planck medal German Phys. Soc., 1961, Nobel prize for physics, 1963, George Washington award Am. Hungarian Studies Found., 1964, Semmelweiss medal Am. Hungarian Med. Assn., 1965, Nat. Sci. medal, 1969, Pfizer award, 1971, Albert Einstein award, 1972, Golden Plate medal Am. Acad. Achievement, 1974, Disting. Achievement award La. State U., 1977, Wigner medal, 1978, Founders medal Internat. Cultural Found., 1982, Medal of the Hungarian Central Research Inst., Medal of the Autonomous Univ. Barcelona, Am. Preparedness award, 1985; named Nuclear Pioneer Soc. Nuclear Medicine, 1977, Colonel Gov. of La., 1983. Mem. Royal Soc. Eng. (fgn.), Royal Netherlands Acad. Sci. and Letters, Am. Nuclear Soc., Am. Phys. Soc. (v.p. 1955, pres. 1956), Am. Math. Soc., Am. Assn. Physics Tchrs., Am. Acad. Arts and Scis., Am. Philos. Soc., Nat. Acad. Scis., N.Y. Acad. Scis. (hon. life mem.), Austrian Acad. Scis., German Phys. Soc., Franklin Inst., AAAS, Sigma Xi, Acad. Sci., Gottingen, Germany (corr.), Hungarian Acad. Sci. (hon.), Austrian Acad. Scis. (hon.), Hungarian L. Eötvös Phys. Soc. (hon.). Office: Princeton U Jadwin Hall Princeton NJ 08540

WIGNESAN, T., comparatist-aesthetician, researcher; b. Kuala Krai, Kelantan, Malaysia, July 14, 1933; s. Thuraiappah and Thangamuttu; children: Nachiketas. Maitrise enseignement Español, U. Paris VIII, 1973; D d'Etat ès Lettres et Scis. Humaines, U. Paris I, 1987. Journalist Straits Times Press Group, Kuala Lumpur (Malaysia) and Singapore, 1954, 64-65, Malayan Times, Kuala Lumpur, 1962; instr. European div. U. Md., Heidelberg, Fed. Republic Germany, 1960-61; schoolmaster Colegio Claret, Madrid, 1968-69; researcher-in-charge 1st class Nat. Ctr. Sci. Research, Ministry Nat. Edn., Paris, 1973—; researcher, instr. Inst. Gen. and Comparative Lit. U. Paris III, 1973-83, instr. doctoral program, 1981-83, researcher Ctr. Comparative Poetics, 1983-85; researcher philosophy of art and creation U. Paris I, 1986—; lectr. Commonwealth Inst., London, 1965. Author: (poetry) Tracks of a Tramp, 1961; editor: (anthology) Bunga Emas, 1964; author: Etude Comparée des Littératures Nationales et/ou Officielles de la Malaisie et de Singapour depuis 1941, 1988; contbr. articles to profl. jours. Fellow Royal Asiatic Soc. Gt. Britain and Ireland; mem. Royal Inst. Linguistics and Anthropology The Netherlands. Club: Les betes noires (Fresnes, France) (founding pres. 1986). Office: U Paris I, Inst Aesthetics, 162 rue St Charles, 75015 Paris France

WIGUNA, DJONNY, insurance company executive; b. Jakarta, Indonesia, Aug. 12, 1951; s. Djakaria and Anna (Setiawati) W.; m. Henny Kumalasari Tjenghar, May 12, 1979; children: Alvernia, Annette, Andrew. B in Acctg., U. Indonesia, Jakarta, 1977. With Inti Salim Corp., Jakarta, 1976—; gem mgr. Cent. Asia Ins. Co. Ltd., Jakarta, 1982, Cent. Asia Raya Life Ins. Co. Ltd., Jakarta, 1983, 1987—; pres., dir. Cent. Antar Jasa Broker Ltd., Jakarta, 1984, Indosurance Broker Utama Ltd., Jakarta, 1987; lectr. Atma Jaya Cath. U., Jakarta, 1985-86. Clubs: Jakarta Hilton Executive, Mega Indah Sports. Home: Jl Kemanggisan Utama II/126, Jakarta 11480, Indonesia Office: Cent Asia Raya Life Ins Co Ltd, Duta Merlin Complex Blk A 6 & 7, Jakarta 10130, Indonesia

WIIN-NIELSEN, AKSEL CHRISTOPHER, meteorologist educator; b. Juelsminde, Denmark, Dec. 17, 1924; emigrated to U.S., 1959; s. Aage Nielsen and Marie Christophersen; m. Bente Havsteen Zimsen, Dec. 5, 1953; children: Charlotte, Barbro Marianne, Karen Margrete. B.S. in Math, U. Copenhagen, Denmark, 1947, M.S. in Math, 1950; Fil. Lic. in Meteorology, U. Stockholm, Sweden, 1957, Ph.D. in Meteorology, 1960; Dr. Sc. (h.c.), U. Reading, 1981; DSc (honoris causa), U. Copenhagen, 1986. Staff meteorologist Danish Meteorol. Inst., 1952-55; research meteorologist Internat. Meteorol. Inst., U. Stockholm, 1955-58, asst. prof., 1957-58; exec. editor publ. Internat. Meteorol. Inst., U. Stockholm (Tellus), 1957-58; research meteorologist Air Weather Service, USAF; also staff mem. joint numerical weather prediction unit and lectr. George Washington U., 1959-61; research staff mem. Nat. Center Atmospheric Research, 1961-62, asst. dir., 1962-63; prof., chmn. dept. meteorology and oceanography U. Mich., 1963-71; prof. theoretical meteorology U. Bergen, Norway, 1971-72, U. Mich., 1972-74; dir. European Centre for Medium-Range Weather Forecasts, 1974-79; sec. gen. World Meteorol. Orgn., 1980-83; dir. Danish Meteorol. Inst., 1984-87; pres. Internat. Commn. for Dynamic Meteorology, 1971-79; chmn. working group on numerical experimentation, also mem. joint organizing com. Global Atmospheric Research Program, 1973-79; chmn. working group on earth scis., sci. adv. com. European Space Agy., 1977-79; sci. adv. com. Max Planck Inst. Meteorology, Hamburg, W. Ger.; v.p. Eumetsat Council, 1986-87; v.p. Council for European Ctr. for Medium-Range Weather Forecasts, 1985-86, pres., 1986-87; vis. scientist Nat. Ctr. Atmosphere Res., 1987; vis. prof. U. Mich., 1988, U. Copenhagan and Aarhus, 1988. Recipient Ohridski medal Sofia (Bulgaria) U., 1980; Buys-Ballot medal Acad. Sci., Netherlands, 1981; Wihuri prize, Finland, 1983; Rossby prize Swedish Geophys. Soc., 1985. Fellow Am. Meteorol. Soc.; mem. Am. Geophys. Union, Swedish, Norwegian geophys. socs., Royal Swedish Acad. Sci., Royal Meteorol. Soc. (hon.), Finnish Acad. Arts and Scis., European Geophysical Soc. (pres. 1988—),Danish Acad. Tech. Scis., Royal Danish Soc. Scis., Tau Beta Pi. Home: Solbakken 6, 3230 Grasted Denmark

WIJASURIYA, DONALD EARLIAN KINGSLEY, librarian; b. Kuala Lumpur, Malaysia, Nov. 22, 1934; s. James Robert Solomon and Florence Mabel Cecilia (De Silva) W.; B.A., U. Ceylon, 1959; A.L.A., Library Assn. U.K., 1962, F.L.A., 1965; Ph.D., Loughborough U., U.K., 1980; Assoc. of the Library Assn. of Australia (ALAA), Australian Library Assn., 1984; m. Annette Jayatilaka, Apr. 3, 1961; children—Rohan, Rienzie, Renan. Asst. librarian U. Malaya, Kuala Lampur, 1964-69, dep. librarian, 1970-72; dep. dir. gen., Nat. Library of Malaysia, Kuala Lumpur, 1972-83, acting dir. gen., 1983-86, dir. gen., 1987—. Recipient BCK Kedah Disting. Service Star, 1979, KMN Royal Order of Chivalry, 1979. Mem. Malaysian Library Assn. (pres. 1972, 73, 75), Congress of S.E. Asian Librarians (chmn. exec. bd. 1978-81), Australian Library Assn., UNESCO Nat. Assn. of Malaysia (hon. sec.), Library Assn. U.K., Internat. Fedn. of Library Assns. and Insts. (IFLA) regional standing com. for Asia and Oceania (chmn. 1988-89). Clubs: Nat. Subang Golf, Port Dickson Yacht. Co-author: Index Malaysiana, 1972, 74, 85; The Barefoot Librarian, 1975. Editor: Blueprint for School Library Development in Malaysia, 1979; The Need to Know, 1977; Access to Information, 1981; contbr. over 60 articles to profl. jours., Ency. of Library and Info. Sci., ALA Ency. Home: No 4 RD 5/3 Petaling, Jaya, Selangor Malaysia Office: Nat Library of Malaysia, Complex Bukit Naga, Damansara Heights, Kuala Lumpur Malaysia

WIJAYA, ANDI, clinical laboratory executive, clinical chemistry educator; b. Klaten, Central Java, Indonesia, July 2, 1936; s. Yantik and Kwan Eng (Sie) W.; m. Mariani Nursanti, Feb. 5, 1935; 1 child, Rini Mariani. MS in Pharmacy, Bandung Inst. Tech., Indonesia, 1963; PhD in Clin. Chemistry, U. Munster, West Germany, 1976; MBA, Kennedy Western U., U.S.A., 1986. Cert. clin. chemist. Researcher Pharm. Industry, Solo, Indonesia, 1963-66; dir. Pharmacist, Solo, Indonesia, 1966-68; asst. prof. Atmajaya U., Solo, Indonesia, 1968-73; exec. dir. Prodia Clin. Labs., Bandung, Indonesia, 1975—; assoc. prof. clin. chemistry Bandung Inst. Tech., 1980—, Pajajaran U., Bandung, Indonesia, 1983—; cons. Directory Lab. Services, Indonesian Ministry of Health, 1980-85. Mem. Indonesian Assn. Clin. Chemistry (founder, exec. bd. mem., Clin. Chemistry award 1986), Am. Assn. Clin. Chemistry, Clin. Ligand Assay Soc., Clin. Lab. Mgmt. Assn., Internat. Soc. Clin. Enzymology; fellow Nat. Acad. Clin. Biochemistry. Christian. Office: Prodia Clin Labs, Wastukencana 38, 40116 Bandung Indonesia

WIJAYA, RUSMIN, plantation executive; b. Prapat, Indonesia, Sept. 14, 1954; s. Suito and Sri Utami (Dewi) W.; m. Sri Leiny Kusno; children: Wiriadynata, Sri Novianty, Eric, Adi Wirianto. Diploma, Acton Coll., London, 1974. Pres., dir. Sumber Tani Agung Plantation, Ltd., Medan, Indonesia, 1974—; exec. dir. Tri Sukses Makmur Wijaya, Medan, Indonesia, 1986—; mgr. Jaya Motors, Prapat, 1970—. Office: Sumber Tani Agung, 26-C Perniagaan Baru, Medan 20111, Indonesia

WIJEMANNE, LIVY RAJASINGHE, communications executive; b. Colombo, Sri Lanka, Feb. 16, 1918; s. Bartholamew Reginald and Lalindra (Adhihetty) W.; m. Gertrude Dagmar Gladys Wettasingae, Oct. 16, 1947; children: Jayanthi Jayewardene, Roshan Corera, Karminie DeSilva, Dhanaraj. Student, Royal Coll., Colombo, 1927-36, Univ. Coll., Ceylon Law Coll., Colombo, 1936-48. English announcer Colombo Broadcasting Sta., 1944-49, controller, head broadcaster, 1949-50; head western programming. Radio Ceylon, Colombo, 1950-55, asst. dir. comml. broadcasting, 1955-60, additional dir. comml. broadcasting, 1960-68; dir. comml. service Sri Lanka Broadcasting Corp., Colombo, 1968-71, dir. English services, 1971-73; adminstrv. officer Mercantile Credit Ltd. Group, Colombo, 1974-77; advisor Nat. Savs. Bank, Colombo, 1977-78, Mahaweli Authority Sri Lanka, Colombo, 1978-84; chmn. Sri Lanka Broadcasting Corp., Colombo, 1984—; adminstrv. sec. Museaus Coll. V.p. Crippled Children's Aid Assn., Colombo, 1980—, HavelockTown Welfare Soc., Colombo, 1984—. Mem. Royal Commonwealth Soc. (pres. 1984—), Colombo Plan Internat. Soc. (pres. 1985—). Buddhist. Home: 10C Elibank Rd, Colombo 5 Sri Lanka Office: Sri Lanka Broadcasting Corp, Independence Sq, POB 574, Colombo 7 Sri Lanka

WIJEYEWARDENE, GEHAN, anthropologist, researcher; b. Colombo, Sri Lanka, Jan. 9, 1932; arrived in Australia, 1964; s. Earle and Mignon (Moonemalle) W.; m. Margarete Deitmer, June 24, 1957; children: Gisela, Ingrid, Kerstin. BA, Ceylon U., Sri Lanka, 1954, U. Cambridge, Eng., 1957; MA, U. Cambridge, Eng., 1960, PhD, 1961. Asst. lectr. U. Ceylon, Peradeniya, 1954-55; jr. research fellow Makerere U., Kampala, Uganda, 1957-60; lectr. U. Singapore, 1961-64; research fellow Australian Nat. U., Canberra, 1964-67, sr. research fellow, 1969-72, sr. fellow, 1972—; vis. prof. U. Wash., Seattle, 1967-68. Author: Place and Emotion, 1986; translator various books. Fellow Royal Anthopol. Inst.; mem. Australian Nat. U. Academic Staff Assn. (exec.). Office: Australian Nat U, 2601 Canberra Australia

WIKBORG, TORD BENKESTOK, printing company executive; b. Oslo, Norway, Nov. 2, 1919; s. Tord and Edith (Lyche) W.; m. Gerda Aagot Olsen, Apr. 11, 1948; children—Tove, Edith, Ole, Kristin. Craft cert. printing Harald Lyche & Co. A.s., Drammen, Norway, 1939-45, mgr. letterpress, 1945-62, mgr. add. offset/binding, 1962-67, mng. dir., 1967-86; bd. dirs. Grafiske Bedr. Landsfor., Oslo, 1960-82, chmn. bd., 1980-82. Contbr. articles to profl. jours. Recipient Extension award Lions Internat., Drammen/Chgo., 1973, 100% Distbn. Gov. award, 1973; hon. mem. award Markedsforingsforening, Drammen, 1975, Boktrykkerforeningen, Drammen, 1975. Lutheran. Home: Hotvetveien 50, 3018 Drammen Norway Office: Harald Lyche & Co As, Nedre Eikervei 14, 3000 Drammen Norway

WIKSTEN, BARRY FRANK, communications executive; b. Seattle, June 23, 1935; s. Frank Alfred and Alice Gertrude (Ensor) W.; m. Madeleine Schmeil, Nov. 23, 1979; children: Karen Anne, Eric Marshal, Kurt Edward. BA, Miami U., Oxford, Ohio, 1960; MA, Fletcher Sch. Law and Diplomacy, 1961. Dir. econ. programs U.S. Council, Internat. C. of C., N.Y.C., 1962-63; with TWA, N.Y.C., 1964-79, dir. fin. relations, 1972, v.p. pub. affairs, 1973, v.p. pub. relations, 1974-75, sr. v.p. pub. affairs, mem. airline policy bd., 1976-79; v.p. corp. adminstrn. Trans World Corp., 1979-82, also sec. corp. policy com., mem. consumer affairs com. and corp. compensation com.; sr. v.p. communications CIGNA Corp., Phila., 1982-84, sr. v.p. pub. affairs, 1984—. Served with USMC, 1954-57. Mem. Pub. Affairs Research Council (mem. conf. bd.), Am. Council Life Ins. (pub. relations program com.), Ins. Info. Inst. (spl. communications oversight com.), World Affairs Council Phila. (bd. dirs.). Clubs: Union League (N.Y.); The Athenaeum. Office: Cigna Corp One Logan Sq Philadelphia PA 19103

WILAYTO, HENRY JOHN, manufacturing company transportation executive; b. Nashua, N.H., Jan. 4, 1917; s. Alexander Matheuw and Genevieve (Michnevitch) W.; B.A. magna cum laude, Boston U., 1952; postgrad. Babson Coll., 1978—; m. Helen Mary Butchard, June 17, 1946; children—Anne-Marie Christine Wilayto Bishop, Philip Henry, Allan John, Kathryn Helen Wilayto MacDonald, Margaret Elizabeth Wilayto Gallagher. Field rep., asst. disaster dir. ARC, Boston, 1952; flight test facility bus. mgr. M.I.T., Concord, 1952-55; asst. to controller, purchasing agt. Allied Research Assos., Boston, 1955-57; purchasing agt. Lab. for Electronics, Boston, 1957-63; mgr. freight consolidation and analysis Honeywell Info. Systems, Billerica, Mass., 1963-82; pres. H.J.W. & Assos., internat. transp. cons., 1982-86; conducted purchasing, transp. and packaging panels and seminars; elder advocate Com. Mass. Exec. Office Elder Affairs, 1985; mem. Council for Vet.'s Affairs, Mass., 1987-88, Mass. Council Aging, 1987-88. Served with U.S. Army, 1940-48; PTO. Mem. New Eng. Purchasing Agts. Assn. (dir. 1960-65), Am. Defenders of Bataan and Corregidor (organizer, charter, life mem.; vice nat. comdr. 1964-67, exec. bd. 1982—, nat. sr. vice comdr. 1986-87, comdr. 1987-88), Soc. Packaging and Handling Engrs. (Merit and Service awards for conducting seminars 1972—), Nat. Com. for Internat. Documentation, Nat. Def. Transp. Assn. (co-chmn. ARC transp. com. New Eng. chpt.), VFW, DAV (life), Delta Nu Alpha (regional v.p. 1979-83). Democrat. Roman Catholic. Club: Elks. Contbr. articles to profl. jours. Office: HJW & Assos 31A Staffordshire Ln Concord Village Concord MA 01742

WILBER, LAURA ANN, audiologist; b. Memphis, May 26, 1934; d. Leon Austin and Ivah Edith (Ostrander) W. B.S. in Speech Correction, U. So. Miss., 1955; M.S. in Deaf Edn. (grad. fellow), Gallaudet Coll., 1958; Ph.D. in Audiology (grad. fellow), Northwestern U., 1964. Tchr. hard of hearing and deaf McKinley Elem. Sch., Bakersfield, Calif., 1955-57; speech therapist, coordinator spl. edn. U.S. Army Dependent Sch. System, Heidelberg, Ger., 1958-61; audiology research asst. Northwestern U., Evanston, Ill., 1961-64; asst. research audiologist UCLA, 1964-70; dir. Audiology Clinic, UCLA Hosp., 1968-69; asso. prof. dept. otorhinolaryngology, dir. hearing and speech services Albert Einstein Coll. Medicine, Bronx, N.Y., 1970-77; asst. prof. dept. rehab. medicine Albert Einstein Coll. Medicine, 1971-77; prof. audiology, dir. hearing clinics dept. communicative disorders Northwestern U., 1978-81, acting chmn. dept., head program audiology, 1981—; lectr., mem. faculty Calif. State U., Los Angeles, U. So. Calif., 1964-71; mem. working groups Am. Nat. Standards Inst., 1970—, chmn. com. on bioacoustics, 1984; noise expert N.Y.C. Eviron. Control Bd., 1972-78, mem. steering com. on noise subcom., 1971-78; U.S. rep. working groups in techniques for audiometry and threshold of hearing Internat. Standars Orgn., 1973—; chmn. Clinic Sch.-Council N.Y., 1972-73. Author: (with Feldman) Acoustic Impedance and Admittance; contbr. articles to profl. publs., chpts to books. Fellow Am. Speech-Lang.-Hearing Assn. (com. audiologic standards 1971—, subcom. electroacoustic characteristics 1973—, v.p. standards and ethics 1978-80, pres.-elect 1981, pres. 1982); mem. N.Y. State Speech and Hearing Assn. (v.p. hosp. and agys. 1975-76, pres. 1977-78), Calif. Speech and Hearing Assn., Acoustical So. Am., N.Y. Audiology Study Group (chmn. 1973-74), Dirs. Hosp. Speech and Hearing Programs Assn., Soc. Ear, Nose and Throat Advances in Children, Acad. Rehab. Audiology (pres. 1987), Am. Auditory Soc. (pres. 1980). Home: 422 Skokie Blvd Wilmette IL 60091 Office: Audiology and Hearing Impairment Program Frances Searle Bldg Northwestern U 2299 Sheridan Rd Evanston IL 60208

WILBERS, JOACHIM JOHANNES, gerontologist, researcher; b. Duisburg, Fed. Republic Germany, Mar. 28, 1959; s. Wilhelm and Hedwig (Scherhag) W. Diploma, U. Bonn, Fed. Republic Germany, 1983, PhD, 1985. Parliamentary asst. Sec. of State for Youth, Family and Health, Bonn, 1985-86; polit. advisor hdqtrs. Christian Dem. U., Bonn, 1986-87; researcher U. Heidelberg, Fed. Republic Germany, 1987—. Author: Die Kiv Von CDU/CSU, 1986; contbr. articles to profl. jours. Mem. Deutsche Gesellschaft Fur Gerontologie. Roman Catholic. Office: U Heidelberg, Inst fur Gerontologie, Akademiestrasse 3, 6900 Heidelberg Federal Republic of Germany

WILBUR, E. PACKER, investment company executive; b. Bridgeport, Conn., Sept. 9, 1936; s. E. Packer and Elizabeth (Wells) W.; m. Laura Mary Ferrier, Sept. 17, 1965; children—Alison Mary, Andrew Packer, Gillian Elizabeth. B.A., Yale U., 1959; M.B.A., Harvard U., 1965. Cons. McKinsey & Co. Inc., N.Y.C., 1964-67; dir. corp. planning Am. Express Co., N.Y.C., 1967-69; v.p. Van Alstyne Noel & Co., N.Y.C., 1969-70; exec. v.p., dir., mem. exec. com. Newburger Loeb & Co. Inc., N.Y.C., 1970-73; pres. E.P. Wilbur & Co., Inc., Southport, Conn., 1973—, Southport Fin. Corp., 1986—; chmn. bd. Criterion Mgmt., Inc., Lafayette, Ind., Trend Mgmt., Inc., Tampa, Fla., Fairfield Advisors, Inc., Southport, EPW Securities, Inc., Southport; gen. partner Grandland Realty Assos., English Oaks Apts., Pepper Hill Townhouses, Kemar Townhouse Assos., Autumn Woods Assos., Country Villa Assos., others; former allied mem. N.Y. Stock Exchange. Contbr. articles to fin. jours. Past bd. dirs. Inst. Govt. Assisted Housing, Washington; Mus. Art, Sci., Industry, Bridgeport, Wakeman Meml. Boys' Club, Southport, Greater Bridgeport Jr. Hockey League, Pequot Library, Southport, Northfield-Mt. Hermon Sch. Served with AUS, 1959-60. Clubs: Pequot Yacht (Southport), Pequot Running (Southport) (chmn.); Country Club of Fairfield. Home: 648 Harbor Rd Southport CT 06490 Office: 2507 Post Rd Southport CT 06490

WILCHEK, MEIR, biochemist; b. Warsaw, Poland, Oct. 17, 1935; arrived in Israel, 1949; s. Eliezer Nechemia and Rachel (Zaidenberg) W.; m. Esther Edlis, Mar. 14, 1960; children: Eliezer Yizhak, Yael Zvia, Hagit Zipora. BS, Bar-Ilon U., Ramat Gan, Israel, 1960; PhD, Weizmann Inst., Rehovot, Israel, 1965. Chief chemist Yeda Co., Rehovot, 1960-62; research assoc. Dept. Biophysics, Weizmann Inst., Rehovot, 1965-66, sr. scientist, 1968-71, assoc. prof., 1971-74, prof., 1974—, head, 1977-78, 83—; vis. fellow NIH, Bethesda, Md., 1966-67, research assoc., 1967-68; vis. scientist NIH, 1972, 74-75, Fogarty scholar, 1981-82; chief cons. Miles-Yeda (Bio Makor), Rehovot, 1960-87; mem. Israeli Acad. of Scis., 1988. Editor: Biochemical and Biophysical Methods, 1975—, Applied Biochemistry and Biotechnology, 1975—, Methods in Enzymology vols. 34 and 46, 1974, 77, Affinity Chromatography and Biological Recognition, 1983; contbr. articles to profl. jours. Recipient Rothschild prize in chemistry, Israel, 1984, Wolf prize for medicine, Israel, 1987—, Pierce prize, Rockford, Ill., 1987. Mem. Am. Soc. Biol. Chemist (hon.), Am. Chem. Soc., European Molecular Biology Orgn., Israel Biochem. Soc., Israel Chem. Soc., Israel Immunological Soc., Israeli Acad. Scis. Office: Weizmann Inst Sci, Rehovot Israel

WILCOCK, JOHN, television producer; b. Sheffield, Eng., Aug. 4, 1927; s. Richard Barker Wilcox and Edith Clara Gambling; divorced. Grad. high sch., Halifax, Eng. Reporter Sheffield Telegraph, 1944-48, The Daily Mail, London, 1948-50, The Daily Mirror, London, 1950-52, Liberty mag., Saturday Night mag., Toronto, Ont., Can., 1952-54; asst. travel editor N.Y. Times, N.Y.C.; producer The John and Joanna Show BM-Nomad, London. Author: The Village Square, 1957, Magical and Mystical Sites, 1977, Occult Guide to South America, 1978, Traveling in Venzuela, 1978; various travel books, 1960-81. Home: 206 Middle Rd Santa Barbara CA 93108 Office: BM-Nomad, London WC1 V3XX, England

WILCOX, COLLEEN BRIDGET, special education administrator; b. Rock Island, Ill., July 24, 1949; d. Wayne Eugene and Virginia Mae (Dewrose) W. B.S., U. Iowa, 1971; M.S., U. Ariz., 1974; PhD U. So. Calif., 1986; ednl. adminstrn. credential U. So. Calif. Asst. dir. parks and recreation City of Moline (Ill.), 1969-74; dir. speech pathology Instituto Guatemalteca Sequiridad, Peace Corps., Guatemala City, 1971-72; speech and lang. specialist Tucson Sch. Dist., 1974-75; aphasia tchr. specialist, itinerant specialist Los Angeles County Schs., 1975-77; program specialist in severe lang. disorder/aphasia Los Angeles County Supt. Schs., 1977-79, program adminstr./communication disorders, 1979-83, mem. budget standards com. 1979-82; mem. credential adv. bd., communications dept. Calif. State U., Los Angeles, 1978, asst. prof., 1977-83, chmn. sabbatical rev. com.; dir. spl. edn. Tucson Unified Sch. Dist., 1983-88; supt. No. Suburban Spl. Edn. Dist., Highland Park, Ill., 1988—; art dir. the Great Stampede, 1981-83; Bd. dirs. dept. developmental disabilities Assn. Retarded Citizens; bd. dirs. Tuscon Chpt. Diabetes Assn., 1988—, Pima Council on Developmental Disabilities; chmn. spl. edn. adv. council Pima Coll. Spl. Edn.; co-chair Mayor's Com. Constitution Celebration, 1986. Recipient Harriett Rutherford Johnstown award Pi Beta Phi, 1971; Barnes Drill award U. Iowa, 1971; lic. speech pathologist, cert. tchr. speech and hearing therapy, severely handicapped credential, learning handicapped credential, Calif.; cert. speech and lang. therapist, Ariz. Mem. Calif. Speech and Hearing Assn. (exec. council 1986—), Am. Speech and Hearing Assn. (cert. clin. competence in speech pathology, conv. com. 1979, com. on manpower 1982-83, Ariz. legis. councilor 1986—), Jr. League of Tucson (state polit. action delegate 1986), Council Exceptional Children (legis. com.), Pi Beta Phi Alumnae, Phi Delta Kappa. Co-author, illustrator: Let's Share, 1983, Super Soup, 1986, Understanding and Preventing AIDS, 1987. Home: 1900 Chestnut #207 Glenview IL 60025

WILCOX, JAMES KERMIT, III, banker; b. New Martinsville, W.Va., Nov. 29, 1954; s. James Kermit and June Jeannine (Bowers) W.; A.A., Somerset County Coll., 1975; B.A., Kean Coll. N.J., 1978, M.A. in Ednl. Adminstrn. and Supervision, 1983; m. Sharon Louise Reese, Dec. 9, 1978; 1 dau., Kimberley Reese. Cert. protection profl. With Savs. Bank Central N.J., Plainfield, 1976—, teller, 1979—, asst. treas./tng. officer, 1979—, asst. v.p., 1981-84; v.p., security officer First Atlantic Savs. and Loan, 1984—; mem. faculty Am. Inst. Banking, 1980—; instr. Savs. Banks' Assn. N.J., 1980—. Lt., North Plainfield Rescue Squad, 1976, sgt., 1977; trustee Grant Ave. Community Ctr., 1985—. Recipient Outstanding Service awards Somerset County Coll., 1975; Somerville-Raritan Exchange Club scholar, 1975. Mem. Assn. Supervision and Curriculum Devel., Am. Soc. for Indsl. Security, United Security Profls. Am., Cen. Jersey Security Assn. Lodge: Lions. Home: 307 Manning Ave North Plainfield NJ 07060 Office: 1 Cragwood Rd South Plainfield NJ 07080

WILCOX, LAIRD MAURICE, investigator, writer; b. San Francisco, Nov. 28, 1942; s. Laird and AuDeene Helen (Stromer) W.; student Washburn U., 1961-62, U. Kans., 1963-65; m. Eileen Maddocks, 1962 (div. 1967); children—Laird Anthony IV, Elizabeth Leone; m. 2d, Diana Brown, 1978; 1 dau., Carrie Lynn. With Fluor Corp., Ltd., 1960-62; mgr. office supply store U. Kans., 1963; editor Kans. Free Press, 1963-66; owner, operator Maury Wilcox Constrn. Co., Kansas City, Mo., 1967-70; carpenter foreman various employers, 1974—; semi-profl. genealogist, 1975-78; chief investigator Editorial Research Service, Kansas City, Mo., 1977—; assoc. faculty Baker U., 1986—; lectr. various fields. Dep. sheriff Wyandotte County, Kans., 1971-75. Fellow Augustan Soc., Acad. Police Sci.; mem. Internat. Brotherhood of Carpenters and Joiners of Am. (officer 1975-82, condr. carpenter's local 61 1977-82), Nat. Rifle Assn., Mensa, ACLU, Internat. Legion of Intelligence, Nat. Coalition Against Censorship, Free Press Assn., SAR, Soc. Mayflower Descs., Mil. Order Loyal Legion of U.S., Nat. Soc. Old Plymouth Colony Descs., St. Andrew Soc. Author: Guide To The American Left, 1970; Guide to The American Right, 1970; Psychological Uses of Genealogy, 1976; Astrology, Mysticism and The Occult, 1978; Directory of the American Right, 1981; Directory of the American Left, 1981; Directory of the Occult and Paranormal, 1981; Guide to the American Right, 1984; Guide to the American Left, 1984; editor Wilcox Report, 1979—, Civil Liberties Rev., 1986—, Master Bibliography on Terrorism, Assassination, Espionage and Propaganda, 1988, Selected Quotations for the Ideological Skeptic, 1988. Founder Wilcox Collection on Contemporary Polit. Movements, U. Kans. Libraries. Home and Office: PO Box 2047 Olathe KS 66061

WILCOXSON, MOZELLE TROUT, rancher, oil company executive, dietitian; b. Terral, Okla., Jan. 27, 1917; d. John Randolph T. and Lula Pearl (Timberlake) Trout; m. Luther Karl Wilcoxson, Dec. 30, 1938 (dec.); children—Johnnie, George, Karla, Thomas. B.S., U. Okla., 1939. Cert. tchr.

home econs., sociology, econs., polit. sci. Tchr. schs. Norman, Okla., 1937-38, Terral High Sch. (Okla.), 1939-42; owner, operator M & M Oil Co., Terral, 1958—; pres., chmn. bd. Trout Ltd., Jefferson County, Okla., 1961—; interior decorator Antiques and Designs, Dallas, 1980-84. Former mem. pub. relations com. Nat. Fedn. Republican Womens Clubs; pres. local Rep. Woman's Club, 1954-55. Mem. Presdl. Task Force, 1988,; former candidate for State Rep. Mem. Dallas Real Estate Bd. (broker agt.), Dallas Council on World Affairs, Delta Gamma. Methodist. Clubs: Strawhat Garden, N.Dallas Woman's, Preston Wood Country, N. Shore Womens. Lodge: Order Eastern Star (past matron). Home: 11544 E Rick's Circle Dallas TX 75230 Home: PO Box 637 Terral OK 93569

WILD, JOHN PAUL, radio astronomer; b. Sheffield, Eng., 1923; s. Bessie Arnold and Alwyn H. Wild; m. Elaine Poole Hull, 1948; 3 children. Educated Whitgift Sch., Croydon, Eng. and Peterhouse, Cambridge. Researcher in radio astronomy, especially of the sun, Radiophysics Div. of Commonwealth Sci. and Indsl. Research Orgn., CSIRO, Australia, 1947-77, chief of div., 1971-77, chmn., 1978-85; pres. Radio Astronomy Commn. of Internat. Astron. Union, 1967-70. Contbr. articles to profl. jours. Served as radar officer Royal Navy, 1943-47. Recipient Hale Prize for solar astronomy, Am. Astron. Soc., 1980; Edgeworth David medal, Hendryk Arctowski Gold medal Nat. Acad. Sci., Balthasar van der Pol Gold medal Internat. Union Radio Sci., Herschel medal Royal Astron. Soc., Thomas Rankin Lyle medal Australian Acad. Sci., Royal medal Royal Soc. London, 1980, Am. Astron. Soc., 1980; Grand Masters medal Guild Air Pilots and Navigators, 1982; Anzaas medal, 1984. Mem. Am. Philos. Soc. (fgn.), Am. Acad. Arts and Scis. (fgn. hon.), Royal Soc. Sci. Liege (corr.). Address: RMB 338, Sutton Rd, Via Queanbeyan New South Wales 2620, Australia also: CSIRO, PO Box 225, Dickson, Canberra 2602, Australia

WILD, STEPHEN KENT, insurance marketing company executive; b. Omaha, Nov. 18, 1948; s. Roger Charles and Marguerite Mae W.; m. Cheryl Katherine Sparano, June 5, 1971; children—Deric Justin, Drew Ian. Student Ottawa U., 1967-68, U. Nebr.-Omaha, 1968-71. Internal auditor Kirkpatrick, Pettis, Smith and Polian, Omaha, 1971-75; fin. planner First Fin. Planning Group, Omaha, 1975-80; mng. gen. agt. E.F. Hutton Life Ins. Co., Omaha, 1980-81; chmn. bd. Fin. Dynamics, Omaha, 1981—, Securities Am., Inc., 1984—; life ins. cons. Mem. Nat. Assn. Life Underwriters, Internat. Assn. Fin. Planners. Baptist. Home: 16561 Nina Circle Omaha NE 68130 Office: 7100 W Center Rd Suite 500 Omaha NE 68106-2798

WILDE, CHARLES BROADWATER, investment banker, oil company executive; b. Oakland, Calif., July 22, 1940; s. Willard Henry and Elizabeth M. (Broadwater) W.; A.B., U. Calif. at Berkeley, 1962; m. Molly Burnett, June 23, 1962 (div. July 1986); children—Charles Broadwater, Stephen Burnett; m. Dori Sternberg, Aug. 3, 1986. Salesman Procter & Gamble, San Francisco, 1963-64, dist. head salesman, 1964-65, unit mgr., 1965-67; account exec. Dean Witter, Reynolds, Inc., Hayward, Calif., 1967-70, asst. v.p., divisional syndicate mgr., 1972-74, v.p., nat. dir. tax advantaged investments, 1974-79; v.p. Winthrop Fin. Co., Inc., San Francisco, 1979-82; sr. v.p. Winthrop Securities Co., Inc., 1979-82; exec. v.p. Peregrine Oil & Gas Co., Burlingame, Calif., 1982-83, Western Dominion Capital Corp., Denver; exec. v.p., ptnr., dir. Splty. Shelter Inc., Walnut Creek, Calif., 1983-85; pres. GRZ & Assocs., 1983; sr. v.p. sales and mktg. Traweek Investment Co., Marina del Rey, Calif., 1983-87; pres. CEO CD & Assocs., Los Angeles, 1987—; dir. Allen & Dorward Advt., Jimmie Huega Ctr., Vail, Colo.; cons. indsl. solar energy conversions Dept. Energy; co-founder, dir., exec. v.p. Interflight Corp., Long Beach, Calif., 1970-72. Vice pres. Tahoe Pines Assn., 1968-71. Fin. chmn. No. Calif. com. for Brian Van Camp, candidate Calif. sec. state, 1974. Bd. dirs. Golden Bear Athletic Found.; pres. No. Calif. chpt. Nat. Multiple Sclerosis Soc., 1980. Mem. Big C Soc. (dir. 1972-77, fin. chmn. 1973-77), U. Calif. Young Alumni Assn. (dir. 1968-70). Clubs: Bohemian (San Francisco); Claremont Country (Oakland). Home: 13229-G Fiji Way Marina del Rey CA 90292 Office: 11150 Olympic Blvd Suite 1180 Los Angeles CA 90064

WILDEBUSH, JOSEPH FREDERICK, economist; b. Bklyn., July 18, 1910; s. Harry Frederick and Elizabeth (Stolzenberg) W.; A.B., Columbia, 1931, postgrad Law Sch., 1932; LL.B., Bklyn. Law Sch., 1934, J.D., 1967; m. Martha Janssens, July 18, 1935; children—Diane Elaine (Mrs. Solon Finkelstein), Joan Marilyn (Mrs. Bobby Sanford Berry); m. Edith Sorensen, May 30, 1964. Admitted to N.Y. State bar, 1934, Fed. bar, 1935; practice law, N.Y.C., 1934-41; labor relations dir. Botany Mills, Passaic, N.J., 1945-48; exec. v.p. Silk and Rayon Printers and Dyers Assn. Am., Inc., Paterson, N.J., 1948-70; exec. v.p. Textile Printers and Dyers Labor Relations Inst., Paterson, 1954-70; mem. panel labor arbitrators Fed. Mediation and Conciliation Service, N.Y. State Mediation Bd., N.J. State Mediation Bd., N.J. Pub. Employment Relations Commn., Am. Arbitration Assn.; co-adj. faculty Rutgers U., 1948—; lectr. Pres. Pascack Valley Hosp., Westwood, N.J., 1950-64, chmn. bd., 1964-67, chmn. emeritus, 1967—; pres. Group Health Ins. N.J., 1962-65, chmn. bd., 1965-80; dir. Group Health Ins. N.Y., 1950—. Served as maj. Engrs. Corps, AUS, 1941-43. Mem. N.Y. County Lawyers Assn., Am. Acad. Polit. and Social Sci., Indsl. Relations Research Assn., Ret. Officers Assn., Nat. Geog. Soc. Lutheran. Contbr. articles profl. jours. Home and Office: 37 James Terr Pompton Lakes NJ 07442

WILDENMANN, RUDOLF, political scientist, educator; b. Stuttgart, Germany, Jan. 15, 1921; s. Ernst and Luise (Moeck) W.; m. Rosmarie Thon, Feb. 2, 1973; 1 child, Valerie; children by previous marriage: Silke, Beryl, Boris. Dipl. rer. pol., U. Heidelberg, 1950, Dr. phil., 1952; Dr. habil., U. Cologne, 1962; D in Sociology, U. Bochum, 1986; D in Econs., U. Saarbruecker. Indsl. clk., Stuttgart, 1935-40; editor Deutsche Zeitung, 1952-56; dir. Inst. Civil Edn., Cologne, 1956-59; docent U. Cologne (W. Ger.), 1959-63; acad. adv. Fed. Chancellory, 1963-69; regular commentator German TV, 1964—; prof. polit. sci. U. Mannheim, 1964—, dean, 1966, 74, rector, 1967-69, 76-79; prof. polit. sci. Inst. European U., Florence, 1980-83; chmn. Ctr. for Surveys, Methods and Analysis, Mannheim, 1974-80; bd. dirs. European Inst., U. Mannheim, 1983-84, Inst. Social Scis., 1985-86, dir. research Ctr. Societal Devel., 1986—. Author various books; editor several publs. on social sics.; contbr. articles to profl. jours. Served with Army, 1940-41; prisoner of war, 1941-46. Mem. German Research Assn. (senator 1968-74), Deutsche Vereinigung Politische Wissenschaft, Deutsche Parlamentarische Gesellschaft, Internat. Polit. Sci. Assn., Am. Polit. Sci. Assn., Deutsche Gesellschaft für Soziologie, Deutsche Gesellschaft für Politikwissenschaft, Internat. Sociol. Assn., Internat. Soc. Polit. Psychology, Am. Acad. Polit. Sci. Club: Mannheim. Home: 6 Wilhelm Leuschnerstrasse, 68 Mannheim Federal Republic of Germany Office: Schloss U Mannheim, 68 Mannheim Federal Republic of Germany

WILDENSTEIN, DANIEL LEOPOLD, art gallery executive, historian; b. Verrieres-le-Buisson, France, Sept. 11, 1917; s. Georges and Jane (Levi) W.; m. Martine Kapferer, 1939 (div. 1968); children: Alec, Guy; m. Sylvia Roth, 1978. Licencie-es-lettres, Sorbonne, 1939. V.p. Wildenstein & Co., N.Y.C., 1943-59, pres., 1959-68, chmn. bd., 1968—; pres. Wildenstein Found., N.Y.C., 1964—; exec. dir. Wildenstein Arte, Buenos Aires, 1963—, Wildenstein & Co. Galleries, London; founder Am. Inst. in France, N.Y.C., 1947—; dir. Arts newspaper, Paris, 1959-62, Gazette des Beaux-Arts, 1951-56, 63—. Author: Edouard Manet, 2 vols., 1976-77, Claude Monet, 3 vols., 1975-79. Dir. activities Mus. Jacquemart-André, Mus. Chaalis, Paris. Decorated Comdr. des Arts et des Lettres, Comdr. de l'Ordre De Leopold II, Belgium; recipient Hallmark art award. Mem. French C. of C. in U.S. Home: 57 rue la Boetie, 75008 Paris France

WILDENTHAL, C(LAUD) KERN, physician, educator; b. San Marcos, Tex., July 1, 1941; s. Bryan and Doris (Kellam) W.; m. Margaret Dehlinger, Oct. 15, 1964; children—Pamela, Catharine. B.A., Sul Ross Coll., 1960; M.D., U. Tex. Southwestern Med. Ctr., Dallas, 1964; Ph.D., U. Cambridge, Eng., 1970. Intern Bellevue Hosp., N.Y.C., 1964-65; resident in medicine, fellow cardiology Parkland Hosp., Dallas, 1965-67; research fellow Nat. Heart Inst., Bethesda, Md., 1967-68; vis. research fellow Strangeways Research Lab., Cambridge, 1968-70; asst. prof. to prof. internal medicine and physiology U. Tex. Southwestern Med. Ctr., Dallas, 1970-76, prof., dean grad. sch., 1976-80, prof., dean Southwestern Med. Sch., 1980-86, prof., pres., 1986—; sci. cons. Strangeways Research Lab.; chmn. Basic Sci. Council, Am. Heart Assn. Author: Regulation of Cardiac Metabolism, 1976, Degradative Processes in Heart and Skeletal Muscle, 1980; contbr. articles to profl. jours. Bd. dirs. Tex. br. Am. Heart Assn., 1978—, The Dallas Opera, The Dallas Assembly. USPHS spl. research fellow, 1968-70; recipient Research Career Devel. award NIH, 1972; John Simon Guggenheim Meml. fellow, 1975-76. Mem. Am. Soc. Clin. Investigation, Am. Coll. Cardiology, Royal Soc. Medicine Gt. Britain, Am. Physiol. Soc., Internat. Soc. Heart Research (past pres. Am. sect.), Am. Fedn. Clin. Research (past pres. So. sect.), Assn. Am. Med. Colls., Assn. Am. Physicians, AMA, Dallas C. of C. Home: 4001 Hanover Dallas TX 75225 Office: U Tex Southwestern Med Ctr 5323 Harry Hines Blvd Dallas TX 75235

WILDER, ANNETTE BEDFORD (MRS. EUGENE WILDER), librarian; b. Natchez, Miss.; d. George Madison and Ella (Ford) Bedford; B.A., Miss. Woman's Coll., 1929; postgrad. Tulane U., 1932, U. So. Miss., 1940; M.A., Vanderbilt U., 1948; m. Eugene Wilder, July 10, 1919; 1 son, Eugene. Instr. French and Spanish, U. So. Miss., 1928-33, librarian Demonstration Sch., 1940-55, acquisitions librarian, asst. prof. library sci., 1955-60, reference librarian, 1960-64, reference librarian, assoc. prof., 1964-70. Pres., Hattiesburg Music Club, 1927-28; chmn. bd. dirs. Hattiesburg Civic Music Assn., 1927-29; v.p. Original Home and Garden Club, 1938-39; pres. Hattiesburg High Sch. PTA, 1938-39; bd. dirs. Garden Clubs of Miss., 1938-42; sec. bd. dirs. Hattiesburg Community Chest, 1942-43; chmn. bd. dirs. Hattiesburg council Girl Scouts Am., 1942; with Canteen Corps, ARC, 1942-45; pres. Womans Club, 1954-55; trustee Hattiesburg Pub. Library, 1955-75, chmn., 1958-61; bd. dirs. Miss. dist. YWCA, 1956-60; bd. dirs. Hattiesburg br. AAUW Scholarship Fund, 1953. Mem. Am., Southeastern, Miss. library assns., D.A.R. (regent John Rolfe chpt. 1955-57, registrar Norvell Robertson chpt. 1961-80), Daus. Am. Colonists (state regent 1964-67, So. regional chmn. 1967-70), Daus. Founders and Patriots Am. (state sec. 1952-60, state registrar 1970-74, councillor 1988—), Magna Charta Dames, Order Americans of Armorial Ancestry, Colonial Dames Am., Order First Families of Miss. 1699-1817, Miss. Geneal. Soc., Delta Kappa Gamma, Sigma Delta Pi, Pi Delta Phi, Kappa Delta Pi. Baptist. Address: 902 W Pine PO Box 785 Hattiesburg MS 39401

WILDER, JAMES D., geology and mining administrator; b. Wheelersburg, Ohio, June 25, 1935; s. Theodore Roosevelt and Gladys (Crabtree) W.; children: Jaymie Deanna, Julie Lynne. Graduated high sch., Wheelersburg. Lic. real estate agt. Portsmouth, Ohio; mgr. comml. pilots, fixed base operator Scioto County Airport, Ohio; mgr. and part owner sporting goods store, Portsmouth; cons. geologist Paradise, Calif., 1973-81; pres. Mining Consultants, Inc., Paradise, 1981-84; dir. Geology and Devel. Para-Butte Mining, Inc., Paradise, 1984-88, pres., 1988—. Served with U.S. Army, 1956-57. Home and Office: Para-Butte Mining Inc 1737 Drayer Dr Paradise CA 95969

WILDRICK, KENYON JONES, clergyman; b. Rahway, N.J., June 14, 1933; s. Stanley B. and Adele (Jones) W.; BA, Trinity Coll., Hartford, Conn., 1955, BD, Princeton U., 1958, ThM, 1962, DD, Trinity Coll., Conn., 1985; m. Nancy Ruth Mersfelder, Aug. 23, 1958; children—Catherine Ruth, Margaret Jeanne, Kenyon Douglas. Ordained to ministry Presbyterian Ch., 1958; asst. minister Community Congregational Ch., Short Hills, N.J., 1958-61, asso. minister, 1961-67, sr. minister, 1967—; campus ministry Middle Atlantic Conf., 1962-65. Bd. dirs. Milburn-Short Hills chpt. ARC, 1963-64; ch. and ministry com. N.J. Assn., 1965—; trustee Ctr. Theol. Inquiry, Princeton, N.J., 1985—; pres. bd. trustees Overlook Protestant Chaplaincy Program, 1973—; trustee Presbyn. Homes N.J., 1981—. Mem. Millburn Clergy Assn. (chmn. 1987—), Delta Phi. Club: Rotary (dir. Milburn Club 1973). Home: 79 Addison Dr Short Hills NJ 07078 Office: 200 Hartshorn Dr Short Hills NJ 07078

WILES, DAVID KIMBALL, teacher educator; b. Tuscaloosa, Ala., Feb. 23, 1942; s. Kimball and Hilda (Long) W.; m. Marilyn McCall, Jan. 31, 1964; children—Corey, Matthew. B.S. in Edn., Fla. State U., 1964; M.S. in Polit. Sci., U. Fla., 1967, Ed.D. in Adminstrn., 1969. Asst. prof. U. Toronto, Ont., Can., 1969-72; assoc. prof. Va. Poly. Inst., Blacksburg, 1972-74; prof. edn. Miami U., Oxford, Ohio, 1974-78, prof. edn. and pub. policy, SUNY-Albany, 1978—, Rockefeller Coll., U. Albany; dir. Edn. Adaptation Inc., Fla. Author: (with others) Practical Politics, 1981; Energy, Winter and Schools, 1979; Perspectives on Educational Research, 1971. Served to lt. U.S. Army, 1965-66, with Res. 1967-68. Grantee N.Y. State Edn. Dept., 1983, Spencer Found., 1982. Fellow Internat. Bibliog. Ctr., Am. Council Edn. Democrat. Avocations: body surfing, cross country skiing, reading, microcomputing. Home: Route 1 Box 322 Delmar NY 12054 Office: Edn Adaptations Inc 8220 Rt A-1-A S Saint Augustine FL 32086

WILEY, ALBERT LEE, JR., physician, engineer, educator; b. Forest City, N.C., June 9, 1936; s. Albert Lee and Mary Louise (Davis) W.; m. Janet Lee Pratt, June 18, 1960; children: Allison Lee, Susan Caroline, Mary Catherine, Heather Elizabeth. B of Nuclear Engring., N.C. State U., 1958, postgrad., 1958-59; MD, U. Rochester, N.Y., 1963; PhD, U. Wis., 1972. Diplomate Am. Bd. Nuclear Medicine, Am. Bd. Radiology. Nuclear engr. Lockheed Corp., Marietta, Ga., 1958; intern in surgery-medicine U. Va. Med. Sch., Charlottesville, 1963-64; resident in radiation therapy Sanford U., Palo Alto, Calif., 1964-65; resident and postdoctoral fellow U. Wis. Hosp., Madison, 1965-68; med. dir. USN Radiol. Def. Lab., San Francisco, 1968-69; staff physician Balboa Hosp., USN, San Diego, 1969-70; asst. prof. radiotherapy M.D. Anderson Hosp. U. Tex., Houston, 1972-73; prof. radiology, human oncology, med. physics U. Wis., Madison, 1970-88; prof., vice chmn. radiation oncology East Carolina U. Sch. Med., Greenville, N.C., 1988—; cons. U.S. Nuclear Regulatory Commn., 1981-82, Nat. Cancer Inst.; advisor, cons. numerous univs. and govt. agys.; mem. Wis. Radioactive Waste Bd., Gov.'s Council on Biotech., Wis. Com. on UN. Contbr. over 100 articles and abstracts on med. physics, nuclear medicine, biology and cancer to profl. jours. Rep. candidate for U.S. Congress from 2d Wis. dist., 1982, 1984; Rep. candidate for gov. State of Wis., 1986. Served to lt. comdr. USNR, 1968-70. Fellow Oak Ridge Inst. Nuclear Studies, N.C. State U., 1958-59. Fellow Am. Coll. Preventive Medicine; mem. IEEE, AMA, Am. Assn. Physicists in Medicine, Am. Soc. Therapeutic Radiation Oncologists, Health Physics Soc., Soc. Nuclear Medicine, VFW, Am. Legion, USN Ret. Res. Officers Assn., Tau Beta Pi. Lutheran. Home: 3235 Hwy 138 Stoughton WI 53589 Office: East Carolina U Med Sch Radiation Oncology Dept Greenville NC 27858

WILEY, SCOTT TAYLOR, investment banker; b. Teaneck, N.J., Nov. 26, 1949; s. Eugene Taylor and Elinor Starr (Sullivan) W.; A.B. with honors in Econs., Dartmouth Coll., 1971; M.B.A., U. Chgo., 1973; m. Joy Gwenn McArthur, June 24, 1972; children—Peter, Glen. Vice pres. Morgan Guaranty Trust Co. of N.Y., N.Y.C., 1973-81; pres. Copeland, Wickersham, Wiley & Co., N.Y.C., 1981—. bd. dirs. Premier Bank, N.Am., Vanderbilt Petroleum, Inc., Gulf Exploration Cons., Inc., Excaliber Resources, Inc.; dir. Premier Bank, N.A. Dallas Gas & Electric Inc. Mem. juvenile conf. com. Borough of Oradell (N.J.), 1975-79, mem. planning bd., 1979—. Mem. Nat. Assn. Petroleum Investment Analysts (dir. 1978—, treas. 1979, sec. 1980, pres. 1982), N.Y. Soc. Security Analysts, N.Y. Oil Analysts Group, Tex. Mid-Continent Oil and Gas Assn., Fin. Analysts Fedn. Clubs: Dartmouth of No. N.J. (trustee 1975-78, 81—, sec. 1976-78, 81); Dartmouth of N.Y. Home: 653 Center St Oradell NJ 07649 Office: 52 Vanderbilt St New York NY 10017

WILGARDE, RALPH L., hospital administrator; b. Phila., Jan. 8, 1928; B.A., U. Pa., 1949, M.B.A., 1954; M.Pub. Adminstrn., Cornell U., 1960. Adminstrv. asst. Jefferson Hosp., Phila., 1956-58; asst. adminstr. Frankford Hosp., 1960-64; dir. Irvington (N.J.) Gen. Hosp., 1964-66, Cottage Hosp., Grosse Pointe, Mich., 1966—. Served with AUS, 1950-52. Mem. Am. Hosp. Assn., Am. Coll. Hosp. Adminstrn. Home: 1217 Bishop Rd Grosse Pointe MI 48230 Office: 159 Kercheval Ave Grosse Pointe MI 48236

WILHELM, HANS ADOLF, consultant in chemistry, educator; b. Heilbronn, Germany, June 14, 1919. Diploma in Chemistry, U. Heidelberg (W. Ger.), 1949, Dr. rer. nat., 1951. Asst., stipendiat Internat. Wool Secretariat London, Heidelberg, 1951-52; chemist in research BASF Aktiengesellschaft, Ludwigshafen, W. Ger., 1952-55, leader research and devel. groups, 1956-67; lectureship Technische Hochschule, Aachen, W. Ger., 1969—; dir., owner Institut für Polymerberatung, Bad Rappenau-Heinsheim, W. Ger., 1971—. Contbr. Ullmanns Encyklopädie; also numerous articles to profl. jours. Holder over 1200 patents in field. Served to 1st lt. German Army, 1938-45. Recipient medal of Merit, Fachverband Schaumkunststoffe im GKI, 1975; book published in honor of 60th Birthday, 1979, Bundesverdienstkreuz, 1986. Mem. Gesellschaft Deutscher Chemiker, Am. Chem. Soc., Assn. Textile Chemists and Colorists, German Assn. Inventors, Soc. for Social Responsibility in Sci., Assn. Medieval History. Roman Catholic. Home: Nachtigallenweg 25, D6927 Bad Rappenau-Heinsheim Federal Republic of Germany Office: Inst für Polymerberatung, Nachtigallenweg 25, D6927 Bad Rappenau-Heinsheim Federal Republic of Germany

WILHELM, WILKIN MABEN, data processing executive; b. Freetown, Sierra Leone, June 20, 1945; m. Yvette Remie, May 8, 1971; 1 child, Gerald Matthew Khalid. MS In Computer Sci., Pacific So. U., 1983, PhD in Bus. Adminstrn., 1985. Sr. systems cons. Cent. Statistics Orgn., Manama, Bahrain, 1980-85; dir. info. ctr. Gen. Orgn. for Social Ins., Manama, 1985—. Mem. Brit. Computer Soc., Inst. Data Processing Mgmt., Assn., for Computing Machinery, Brit. Inst. Mgmt., Inst. Electrical and Electronic engrs. Home: #640, RD 3809, Block 338, Manama Bahrain Office: Social Insurance, PO Box 5319, Manama Bahrain

WILHITE, ROBERT KEITH, educational administrator; b. Alton, Ill., Aug. 9, 1947; s. Bob Lee and Carmen M. (Owens) W.; m. Carol Ann Skupien, Aug. 14, 1976. B.A., So. Ill. U., 1969; M.Ed., Loyola U., Chgo., 1976, Ed.D., 1982. Cert. tchr., sch. supr. and adminstr., Ill. English tchr. Edwardsville (Ill.) Jr. High Sch., 1969-70; lang. arts tchr. Mannheim Jr. High Sch., Melrose Park, Ill., 1972-78; reading specialist Wheaton (Ill.) Pub. Schs. 1978-82; curriculum supr. reading, lang. arts, kindergarten and career edn. Waukegan (Ill.) Pub. Schs. 1982-84, prin. Greenwood Sch., 1984-86; prin. Wayne Thomas Sch., Highland Park, Ill., 1986—; chmn. select curriculum com., Wheaton, 1979-82. Author: Techniques of Creative Writing, 1976, The Role of the Principal in Reading, 1982. Served with C.E., U.S. Army, 1970-72. Decorated Army Commendation medal. Mem. Internat. Reading Assn., Nat. Council Tchrs. of English, Assn. Supervision and Curriculum Devel., Ill. Reading Council, Secondary Reading League, Ill. Assn. Sch. Prins., Prins. Roundtable of No. Ill., Ill. Assn. Sch. Adminstrs., Nat. Assn. Elem. Sch. Prins. Office: Wayne Thomas Sch 2939 Summit Ave Highland Park IL 60035

WILK, DAVID I., lawyer, consultant; b. Lubbock, Tex., Feb. 1, 1957. BS magna cum laude, U. Tex., 1977; JD, U. Okla., 1981. Bar: Tex. 1981, U.S. Dist. Ct. (no. dist.) Tex. 1981, U.S. Tax Ct. 1982, U.S. Ct. Appeals (5th cir.) 1983. Assoc. Remmel & Rubin, Dallas, 1981-82; gen. cousel Entec Products Corp., Dallas, 1982-83; ptnr. Wilk & Flint, Dallas, 1983—; cons. Intermode Inc., Dallas, 1985—; instr. bus. law El Centro Coll., Dallas, 1983; selected Citizen Ambassador to Japan, 1988—; bd. dirs. The Reservation Desk Inc., Dallas, Accessories Unltd., Hong Kong and Dallas, Martin Miller, Inc., Emerald City Limousine, Dallas. Mem. ABA, Tex. Bar Assn., Dallas Bar Assn., Assn. Trial Lawyers Am., Tex. Young Lawyers Assn., Tax Lawyer Assn. (articles editor 1983-85). Club: Cipango (Dallas). Office: Wilk & Flint 3710 Rawlins LB22 Suite 911 Dallas TX 75219

WILKERSON, JAMES NEILL, lawyer; b. Tyler, Tex., Dec. 17, 1939; s. Hubert Cecil and Vida (Alexander) W.; children—Cody, Ike. A.A., Tyler Jr. Coll., 1960; B.B.A., U. Tex., 1966, LL.B., 1968. Bar: Tex. 1968, U.S. Dist. Ct. (we. dist.) Tex. 1974, U.S. Supreme Ct. 1973. Sole practice, Georgetown, Tex., 1977—; intr. Central Tex. Coll., Copperaas Cove, Tex., 1973-74; asst prof. law U.S. Mil. Acad., West Point, N.Y., 1971-73; pres. Ind. Living and Security Co., 1986—. Pres., Beautify Georgetown Assn., 1977-80, 81-82; pres. U. Tex. Young Reps., 1964-65; co-chmn. Bush for Pres., 1988, Reagan-Bush campaign, 1980; mem. Williamson County Rep. Com., 1977-81; chmn. Hist. Preservation Com., 1979-85. Served to col. USAR, 1968—. Decorated Bronze Star, Air medal. Mem. Williamson County Bar Assn. Methodist. Lodges: Sertoma (v.p. 1981-83, 87), Lions (pres. 1982-83). Office: PO Box 1090 Georgetown TX 78627

WILKERSON, WILLIAM HOLTON, banker; b. Greenville, N.C., Feb. 16, 1947; s. Edwin Cisco and Agnes Holton (Gaskins) W.; m. Ellen Logan Tomskey, Oct. 27, 1973; 1 child, William Holton Jr. A.B. in Econs., U. N.C., 1970. Asst. v.p. First Union Nat. Bank, Greensboro, N.C., 1972-77; v.p. Peoples Bank & Trust Co., Rocky Mount, N.C., 1977-79; sr. v.p. Hibernia Nat. Bank, New Orleans, 1979-86; exec. v.p. Peoples Bank and Trust Co., 1987—. Bd. advisor Jr. League, New Orleans, 1986; bd. dirs. Trinity Episcopal Sch., New Orleans, 1986, Community Ministries Inc., Rocky Mount, 1988—. Mem. Robert Morris Assoc., New Orleans C. of C., Omicron Delta Epsilon, Chi Beta Phi, Phi Sigma Phi. Republican. Episcopalian. Clubs: Boston, New Orleans Country (New Orleans), Benvenue Country (Rocky Mount). Avocations: golf; tennis.

WILKES, CHARLES D., distribution and marketing companies executive, consultant; b. Paris, Apr. 14, 1920 (parents Am. citizens); s. Charles and Carmen (Priou-Perdonnet) D-W. Student, Breguet Coll., Paris, 1938-40; B.S., Bur. des Temps Elementaires, Paris, 1947. Econ. commr., diplomat for French African countries ECA/Mut. Security Agy., Am. embassy, Paris, 1949-56; continental mgr. United Artists TV, N.Y.C., 1956-63; cons. Publicker, Phila., 1962-68, French European rep. Warner Bros. TV, Los Angeles, 1969-72; Europe, Mid East/Africa rep. N.T.A., Los Angeles, 1972-80; exec. and dir. several world wide cos., 1980—. Econ. commr. Econ. Surveys, 1946-49. Served to lt. USN, 1941-46, PTO. Decorated Air medal(s), Presdl. Unit citation (U.S.), Legion of Honor (France). Club: Cercle Union Interalliee (Paris). Office: World Trade Ctr, PO Box 306, 1215 Geneva Airport 15 Switzerland

WILKES, DELANO ANGUS, architect; b. Panama City, Fla., Jan. 25, 1935; s. Burnice Angus and Flora Mae (Scott) W.; m. Dona Jean Murren, June 25, 1960. B.Arch., U. Fla., 1958. Cert. Nat. Council Archtl. Registration Bds. Designer, Perkins & Will Partnership, Chgo., 1960-63; designer, job capt. Harry Weese, Ltd., Chgo., 1963-66; project architect Fitch Larocca Carrington, Chgo., 1967-69; architect Mittelbusher & Tourtelot, Chgo., 1970-71; assoc. Bank Bldg. Corp., Chgo., 1972-75; sr. assoc. Charles Edward Stade & Assocs., Park Ridge, Ill., 1975-77; sr. architect Consoer Morgan Architect, Chgo., 1977-83, mktg. coordinator, 1980-83; design cons. Chamlin & Assocs., Peru and Morris, Ill., 1969-82, dir. architecture, 1983-86, v.p. architecture, 1986—; archtl. cons. Sweet's div. McGraw Hill., Inc., Chgo. Mem. coordinating com. Dune Acres Plan Commn. (Ind.), 1983—; bldg.commr. City of Dune Acres, 1984—; chmn. Ind. party Dune Acres, 1987; elected trustee Dune Acres Toen Bd. 1988—, pres. Town Bd., 1988—; cons. Inst. of Crippled and Disabled, N.Y.C., 1978-83; guest lectr., field trip guide Coll. DuPage, Glen Ellyn, Ill., 1968-76; guest architect med. adv. com. to Pres.'s Com. for Handicapped, 1977, 78. Vice chmn. Westchester County Dem. Precinct, Porter County, Ind., 1986; chmn. selection com. Dem. Hdqrs., Porter County, 1986; mem. Dem. Cen. Com., Porter County, 1986; treas. Com. to elect Kovach to Council, Porter County, 1986; vice chmn. Duneland Dems., 1988. Mem. Businessmen for Pub. Interest, Folsom Family Assn. Am. (pres. 1978-82, v.p. 1982—, nominating chmn. 1983, host ann. meeting, Chgo. 1981), AIA, Chgo AIA (chmn. design awards display com. 1978-79, producer New Mem. Show 1979, chmn. pub. relations com. 1980), Art Inst. Chgo., Chgo. Lyric Opera Guild, Chgo. Assn. Commerce and Industry (display dir. 1979 meeting), Am. Soc. Interior Design (coordinator Info. Fair 1979), N.C. Geneal. Soc., New Eng. Hist. Geneal. Soc., Putnam County Hist. Soc., Soc. Colonial Wars, Gargoyle. Democrat. Unitarian. Author: Colonel Ebenezer Folsom, 1778-1789, North Carolina Patriot and Tory Scourge, 1975; editor Folsom Bull., 1977-80; producer documentary film The Angry Minority, Menninger Found., 1978. Home: 23 Circle Dr Dune Acres IN 46304 Office: Sweets div McGraw-Hill 230 W Monroe St Chicago IL 60606

WILKEY, MALCOLM RICHARD, ambassador; b. Murfreesboro, Tenn., Dec. 6, 1918; s. Malcolm Newton and Elizabeth (Gilbert) W.; m. Emma Secul Depolo, Dec. 21, 1959. AB, Harvard U., 1940, LLB, 1948; LLD (hon.), Rose-Hulman Inst. Tech., 1984. Bar: Tex. 1948, N.Y. 1963, U.S. Supreme Ct. 1952, U.S. Ct. Appeals (D.C. cir.) 1958. Partner Butler Binion Rice & Cook, 1948-54, 61-63; U.S. atty. So. Dist. Tex., 1954-58; asst. atty. gen. U.S. 1958-61; sec., asso. gen. counsel Kennecott Copper Corp., 1963-67, gen. counsel, sec., 1967-70; judge U.S. Ct. Appeals D.C. Circuit, 1970-85; U.S. ambassador to Uruguay 1985—; lectr. constl. and adminstrv. law London Poly., 1979, 80; lectr. Tulane U. Law Summer Sch., Grenoble, France, 1981, 83, San Diego Law Summer Sch., Oxford, Eng., 1983, Brigham Young U. Law Sch., 1984; vis. fellow Wolfson Coll., Cambridge U., Eng.,

1985. Del., Republican Nat. Conv., 1960. Served from 2d lt. to lt. col. AUS, 1941-45. Fellow Am. Bar Found.; mem. ABA (commn. on a nat. inst. of justice, chmn. drafting com. 1975-79), Assn. Bar City N.Y., Am. Law Inst. (adv. com. restatement fgn. relations law of U.S.), Jud. Conf. U.S. (com. on standards for admission to fed. cts. 1976-79), Phi Beta Kappa, Delta Sigma Rho, Phi Delta Phi (hon.). Office: Am Embassy, Montevideo Uruguay also: Dept of State US Ambassador to Uruguay Washington DC 20520

WILKIE, VALLEAU, JR., foundation executive; b. Summit, N.J., July 3, 1923; s. Valleau and Amelia Willetts (Parry) W.; m. Donna Hartwell, Oct. 28, 1985; children: Janice, Robert. A.B., Yale U., 1948; M.A., Harvard U., 1954. Instr. history Phillips Acad., 1948-59; headmaster Gov. Dummer Acad., Byfield, Mass., 1959-72; mem. bd. trustees Gov. Dummer Acad., 1960-72, dir. devel., 1972-73; exec. v.p. Sid W. Richardson Found., Ft. Worth, 1973—. Bd. dirs. S.W. Ednl. Devel. Lab., 1976-82, pres., 1981-82; mem. Council on Founds., Inc., 1980—, bd. dirs., 1981-87, chmn. bd., 1985-87; bd. dirs. Conf. of S.W. Founds., 1977-82, pres., 1981-82; bd. dirs. Found. Ctr., 1982—. Served to 1st lt. USAAF, 1942-45. Mem. Headmasters Assn., N.E. Assn. Schs. and Colls. (chmn. commn. on ind. secondary schs. 1967-70, pres. 1972-73), Delta Kappa Epsilon. Episcopalian. Address: 3409 Worth Hills Dr Fort Worth TX 76109

WILKINS, SIR GRAHAM JOHN, business executive; b. Mudford, Somerset, Eng., Jan. 22, 1924; s. George W. and Ann May (Clarke) W.; m. Daphne Mildred Haynes, 1945. B.Sc., Univ. Coll. of South West, Exeter. Mng. dir. Beecham Research Labs., 1961; chmn. Beecham Pharm. div.; dir. Beecham Group Plc, 1964, mng. dir. pharms., 1973; exec. vice chmn. Beecham Group Ltd., 1974-75, chmn., 1975-85, pres., 1985—; vice chmn. Medico-Pharm. Forum, 1972-73; dir. Courtaulds PLC, 1975, Hill Samuel & Co. Ltd., 1976—, Thorn Elec. Industries PLC, 1978—. Mem. Proprietary Assn. Great Britain (vice chmn. 1966-68); Assn. Brit. Pharm. Industry (pres. 1969-71), European Fedn. Pharm. Industries Assn. Office: Thorn Emi PLC, Thorn Emi House, Upper St Martins Ln, London WC2H 9ED, England *

WILKINS, JERRY LYNN, lawyer, oil producing company executive, clergyman; b. Big Spring, Tex., June 1, 1936; s. Claude F. and Grace L. (Jones) W.; children by previous marriage—Gregory, Tammy, Scott, Brett; m. Valerie Ann Nuanez, Aug. 1, 1986. B.A., Baylor U., 1958, LL.B., 1960. Bar: Tex. 1960, U.S. Dist. Ct. (no. dist.) Tex. 1960, U.S. Ct. Appeals (5th cir.); ordained to ministry, 1977. Sole practice, Dallas, 1960—; capt. Air America, Vietnam, 1967-68, Joint Church Aid, Biafra, 1969-70, TransInternat. Airlines, Oakland, Calif., 1977-79; gen. counsel First Tex. Petroleum, Dallas, 1982; owner Wooltex, Inc., Dallas, 1983—; owner, dir., legal counsel Intermountain Gas Inc., Dallas, 1983-84; bd. dirs. Engineered Roof Cons., Continental Tex. Corp., Arlington, Acklin Pain Research Inst., Inc., Irving, Tex., Silver Leaf Metals Internat. Inc., Silver Leaf Mining Inc.; bd. dirs., v.p. for legal affairs, underwriter Lloyds U.S. Inc.; bd. dirs., co-founder R.O.A.S., Inc., Maritime Internat., Inc., Maritime Oil Recovery, Inc., Moriah Oil Recovery Barges, Inc., Megas Homes Internat., Urex Internat.; mem. legal counsel, bd. dirs. U.S. Fiduciary Co. Inc., U.S. Fiduciary Trust Co. Inc.; cons. in field. Author: Gods Prosperity, 1980; So You Think You Have Prayed, 1980. Editor numerous books; contbr. articles to profl. jours. Bd. dirs., pres. Beasley For Children Found. Inc., Dallas, 1978—; mem. Republican Presdl. Task Force, Washington, 1984—; bd. dirs., pilot Wings for Christians, Dallas, 1976—, Wings for Christ, Waco, Tex., 1976—. Recipient Cert. of Appreciation Parachute Club of Am., 1966; cert. of record holder for high altitude sky diving State of Tex., 1966, 67; Cert. of Achievement, Tex. State Guard, 1968. Mem. ABA, Nat. Lawyers Assn., Plaintiff Trial Lawyers Assn., Internat. Platform Assn., Tex. Trial Attys. Assn., Assn. Trial Lawyers Am., Quiet Birdmen, Tex. Outdoor Writers Assn., Nat. Rifle Assn., Tex. Rifle Assn., Parachute Assn. Am., P51 Mustang Pilots Assn., Phi Alpha Delta. Clubs: U.S. Senatorial; U.S. Parachute (Monterey, Calif.). Avocations: shooting, hunting, fishing, flying, sports. Achievements: atty. (2 Tex. landmark cases) securing custody of female child for stepfather against natural parents, securing outside jail work program for convicted man, others. Office: PO Box 59462 Dallas TX 75229

WILKINS, MAURICE HUGH FREDERICK, biophysicist; b. Pongaroa, N.Z., Dec. 15, 1916; s. Edgar Henry and Eveline (Whittaker) W.; Ph.D., St. John's Coll., Cambridge, 1940; LL.D., U. Glasgow, 1972; m. Patricia Ann Chidgey, Mar. 12, 1959; children—Sarah Fenella, George Hugh, Emily Lucy Una, William Henry. Research with Manhattan Project, U. Calif., Berkeley, 1944; lectr. St. Andrews U., 1945; mem. faculty Kings Coll., London, 1946—, dep. dir. biophysics unit Med. Research Council, 1955-70, dir. biophysics unit, 1970-72, dir. neurobiology unit, 1972-74, prof. molecular biology, 1962-70, prof. biophysics, 1970-81, also dir. MRC cell biophysics unit (formerly Med. Research Council neurobiology unit), 1974-80. Decorated comdr. Brit. Empire; recipient Albert Lasker award Am. Pub. Health Assn., 1960, Nobel prize for physiology and medicine (with F.H.C. Crick and J.D. Watson), 1962; fellow King's Coll., 1973—. Fellow Royal Soc., 1959; mem. Brit. Biophys. Soc. (past chmn.), Am. Soc. Biol. Chemists (hon.), Brit. Soc. for Social Responsibility in Sci. (pres. 1969), Am. Acad. Arts and Scis. (fgn. hon.). Research, publs. on structure of nerve membranes and X-ray diffraction analysis of structure of DNA; devel. of electron trap theory of phosphorescence and thermo-luminescence; light microscopy techniques for cyto-chem. research, including use of interference microscope for dry mass determination in cells. *

WILKINS, WILLIAM S., insurance company executive; b. Wyandotte, Mich., Aug. 30, 1942; m. Karen Wilkins, June 14, 1969. A.S. in Engring., Henry Ford Coll., 1966; degree in bus. adminstrn. Wayne State U., 1970; completed exec. program Stanford U., 1986. Programmer, Uniroyal, Inc., Allen Park, Mich., 1966-70; v.p. D.P. Alexander Hamilton Life, Farmington, Mich., 1970-80, John Alden Life, Miami, Fla., 1980-82, pres., chief exec. officer, 1988—, also bd. dirs.; exec. v.p. Continental Life and Accident, Boise, 1982-85; Office: John Alden Life 7300 Corp Ctr Dr Miami FL 33126

WILKINSON, DAVID STANLEY, pathologist, consultant, researcher; b. Richmond, Va., Feb. 2, 1945; s. Herbert Carroll and Hattie Mae (Vaughan) W.; m. Judith Farish Pace, June 16, 1967; children—Jill Marie, Julie Lynne, Virginia Ann. B.S. in Chemistry, Va. Mil. Inst., Lexington, 1967; Ph.D. in Exptl. Oncology and Pathology, U. Wis.-Madison, 1971; M.D., U. Miami, 1978. Diplomate: Am. Bd. Pathology. Commd. 2d lt. U.S. Army, 1967, advanced through grades to maj., 1982; fellow McArdle Lab. Cancer Research U. Wis., 1967-71; asst. prof. biochemistry U. South Fla., Tampa, 1972-76; resident in pathology Walter Reed Army Med. Ctr., Washington, 1978-82; instr. pathology Uniformed Services U. of Health Scis., Bethesda, 1979-82; chief clin. pathology Eisenhower Army Med. Ctr., Ft. Gordon, Ga., 1982-84; assoc. prof. pathology, dir. clin. pathology div. George Washington U. Med. Ctr., 1984—; mem. clin. faculty Med. Coll. Ga. Augusta, until 1984; lectr. in field. Contbr. articles to profl. jours. Damon Runyon-Walter Winchell Cancer Fund grantee, 1973; Am. Cancer Soc. grantee, 1973; Nat. Cancer Inst. grantee, 1975. Fellow Am. Soc. Clin. Pathology, Am. Coll. Pathologists; mem. Am. Assn. Cancer Research. Soc. Exptl. Biology and Medicine, Am. Assn. Clin. Chemistry, Clin. Lab. Mgmt. Assn., Am. Assn. Med. Systems and Informatics. Republican. Club: VMI Keydet (Lexington, Va.). Office: George Washington Univ Hosp 901 23d St NW Washington DC 20037

WILKINSON, ENDYMION PORTER, scholar-diplomat; b. Lewes, Sussex, Eng., May 15, 1941; s. George Curwen and Pamela Algernon (Black) W.; B.A., King's Coll., Cambridge U., 1964, M.A., 1967; postgrad. Beijing Inst. Langs., 1964-66; Ph.D., Princeton U., 1970. Lectr. in history of Far East, U. London, 1970-74; acting head of del. EEC Del., Tokyo, Japan, 1974, head econ. and comml. dept. Del. of Com. of European Communities to Japan, 1974-79, prin. adminstr. external relations dept. EEC Commn., Brussels, 1979-82; counselor and dep. head EEC del. to S.E. Asia, 1982-88. Head Asia div. EEC Commn., Brussels, 1988—. Mem. Assn. of Asian Studies, Brit. Assn. for Chinese Studies. Author: The History of Imperial China, A Research Guide, 1973; Studies in Chinese Price History, 1980; Misunderstanding: Europe Versus Japan, Tokyo, 1980, English edition, 1981; translator from Chinese: Landlord and Labor in Late Imperial China, 1978; The People's Comicbook, 1973; author, commentator TV series, Tokyo, 1981.

WILKINSON, GEOFFREY, chemist, educator; b. Todmorden, Eng., July 14, 1921; s. Henry and Ruth (Crowther) W.; BSc, Imperial Coll., London, 1941, PhD, 1946; DSc (hon.), U. Edinburgh, 1977, U. Granada, 1977, Columbia U., 1979, U. Bath, 1980; m. Lise Schou, July 17, 1951; children: Anne Marie, Pernille Jane. With NRC, Can., 1943-46; staff Radiation Lab., U. Calif., Berkeley, 1946-50; mem. faculty MIT, 1950-51, chemistry dept. Harvard U., 1951-55; faculty Imperial Coll. Sci. and Tech., U. London, 1955—, now prof. emritus; Falk-Plaut vis. lectr. Columbia, 1961; Arthur D. Little vis. prof. MIT, 1967; Hawkins Meml. lectr. U. Chgo., 1968; 1st Mond lectr. Royal Soc. Chemistry, 1981; Chini lectr. Italian Chem. Soc., 1981. John Simon Guggenheim fellow, 1954; recipient award inorganic chemistry Am. Chem. Soc., 1966, Centennial Fgn. fellow, 1976, Royal Soc. Chemistry transition metal chemistry, 1972; Lavoisier medal French Chem. Soc., 1968; Nobel prize in chemistry, 1973; Hiroshima U. medal, 1978; Royal medal, 1981; Galileo medal U. Pisa, 1983. Fellow Royal Soc.; fgn. mem. Royal Danish Acad. Sci., Am. Acad. Arts and Scis., Nat. Acad. Scis., Spanish Sci. Research Council. Author: (with F.A. Cotton) Advanced Inorganic Chemistry: A Comprehensive Text, 5th edit., 1988; Basic Inorganic Chemistry, 2d edit., 1987. Office: Imperial Coll of Sci & Tech, Dept of Chemistry, London SW7 2AY, England

WILKINSON, JAMES ALLAN, lawyer; b. Cumberland, Md., Feb. 10, 1945; s. John Robinson and Dorothy Jane (Kelley) W.; m. Elizabeth Susanne Quinlan, Apr. 14, 1973; 1 child, Kathryn Barrett. BS in Fgn. Service, Georgetown U., 1967; JD, Duquesne U., 1978. Bar: Pa., U.S. Dist. Ct. (we. dist.) Pa. Legis. analyst Office of Mgmt. and Budget, Washington, 1972-73; dep. exec. sec. Cost of Living Council, Washington, 1973-74; sr. fin. analyst U.S. Steel Corp., Pitts., 1974-82; ptnr. Buchanan Ingersoll, Pitts., 1982—; adj. prof. U. Pitts. Sch. Law, 1988—. Author: Financing and Refinancing Under Prospective Payment, 1985; contbr. articles to profl. jours. Counsel Oversight Com. on Organ Transplantation, Pitts., 1986—; bd. dirs. Pitts. Symphony Soc., 1986—, We. Pa. Com. for Prevention of Child Abuse, 1987—. Served with USN, 1968-71. Mem. ABA, Am. Acad. Hosp. Attys., Am. Soc. of Law and Medicine, Nat. Assn. of Bond Lawyers, Nat. Health Lawyers Assn. Republican. Episcopalian. Clubs: Duquesne (Pitts.), Pitts. Athletic Assn. Home: 1201 Macon Ave Pittsburgh PA 15218 Office: Buchanan Ingersoll Profl Corp 600 Grant St 57th Floor Pittsburgh PA 15219

WILKINSON, PAUL, political scientist, educator; b. Harrow, Middlesex, Eng., May 9, 1937; s. Walter Ross and Joan Rosemary (Paul) W.; B.A. in Politics and Modern History, Univ. Coll., Swansea, Wales, 1959; M.A. in Politics, U. Wales, Cardiff, 1968; m. Susan Flook, Mar. 19, 1960; children—Rachel Margaret, John Paul, Charles Ross. Asst. lectr. in politics Univ. Coll., Cardiff, 1966-68, lectr., 1968-75, sr. lectr., 1975-78; vis. prof. Simon Fraser U., B.C., Can., 1973; reader U. Wales, 1978-79; prof. internat. relations, head dept. politics and internat. relations U. Aberdeen (Scotland), 1979—, assoc. Centre for Def. Studies; chmn. Research Found. for Study of Terrorism, 1986—; hon. fellow Univ. Coll. Swansea, 1986; spl. cons. CBS News, 1986—, ITN, London, 1986—. Served with RAF, 1959-65. Mem. Brit. Internat. Studies Assn., Polit. Studies Assn., Internat. Inst. Strategic Studies. Scottish Episcopalian. Author: Social Movement, 1971; Political Terrorism, 1974; Terrorism and the Liberal State, 1977, rev. edit., 1986; Terrorism vs. Liberal Democracy: The Problems of Response, 1976; Terrorism: Theory and Practice, 1979; Defence of the West, 1983; British Perspectives on Terrorism, 1981; The New Fascists, 1981, rev. edit., 1983 Terrorism and International Order, 1986; editor: Contemporary Research on Terrorism, 1987; editorial advisor Contemporary Rev., 1979—; mem. editorial bd. Conflict Quar.; editor: Key Concepts in International Relations series, 1979—; History of Political Violence series, 1979—, Jour. Terrorism Research. Office: U Aberdeen, Old Aberdeen Scotland

WILKINSON, RICHARD HANWELL, chemical pathologist, consultant; b. Dewsbury, Yorkshire, Eng., Feb. 27, 1921; s. Richard Arthur and Muriel Anita (Burton) W.; m. Kathleen Mary Garside, Mar. 31, 1945; children—Andrew Richard, Julia Mary. M.A., M.B., B.Ch., Cambridge U., Eng., 1945, M.D., 1952; D.M., Oxford U., Eng., 1963. Pathologist Royal Nat. Orthopaedic Hosp., London, 1949-50; chem. pathologist Hosp. for Sick Children, London, 1950-60; chem. pathologist Oxford Teaching Hosps., 1960-86, clin. lectr. biochemistry, 1963; lectr. London U., 1949-50, Oxford U., 1960-86; ret., 1986. Author: Chemical Micromethods in Clinical Medicine, 1959; also articles. Local chmn. Liberal Party, 1950—. Recipient numerous grants, 1949—. Fellow Royal Coll. Pathologists, Royal Soc. Medicine. Methodist. Avocation: sailing. Home: 86 Staunton Rd, Oxford OX3 7TR, England

WILKINSON, THOMAS ALLAN, engineering geologist; b. Fort Worth, Jan. 6, 1932; s. Joseph Ackinson and Grace (Wythe) W.; m. Rosalyn Sarah Schilz, Dec. 21, 1959; children—Chris Allan, Nachelle Marie, Tedric Gordon. B.S. in Geology, U. Okla., 1954, M.S. in Geology, 1956, postgrad., 1958-59. Registered geologist, Calif. Cert. Engring. Geologist, Calif. Engring. geologist Corps of Engrs., Kansas City, Mo., 1959-64, project geologist, Stockton, Mo., 1964-65, dist. geologist, Buffalo, 1965-71, chief geotech. br., 1971—; lectr. in geology Canisius Coll., Buffalo, 1971-72, Waterways Expt. Sta., Vicksburg, Miss., 1982—; cons. in engring. geology NRC, Bethesda, Md., 1978-82, Dept of Energy, Columbus, Ohio, 1984-87; v.p. The Leading Edge Tng. Consultants, Buffalo, 1987—. Contbr. articles to profl. jours. Pres. Willow Ridge PTA, Amherst, N.Y., 1976; umpire Little League Baseball, Amherst, 1978; sports photographer Sweet Home High Sch., Amherst, 1980—; lectr. various civic orgns., western N.Y., 1965—. Served to lt. U.S. Army, 1955-57. Kansas City Assn. Trustee Found. scholar, 1960-61. Mem. Assn. Engring. Geologists, Geol. Soc. Am., Internat. Soc. for Rock Mechanics, Soc. Am. Mil. Engrs. (bd. dirs. 1983-87), Sigma Xi. Republican. Unitarian. Current work: Manage engineers and geologists in geotechnical design of harbor, navigation, and flood control projects in New York, Pennsylvania, and Ohio. Subspecialty: Engineering geology. Office: US Army Engr Dist Buffalo 1776 Niagara St Buffalo NY 14207-3199

WILKS, JACQUELIN HOLSOMBACK, educator; b. Oakdale, La., Jan. 18, 1950; d. Jack and Ida Mae (Bass) Holsomback; B.S., La. Coll., 1972; M.A.T., Okla. City U., 1982; postgrad. So. Bapt. Theol. Sem., Louisville, 1974, S.E. Mo. State U., 1977; counseling cert. Central State U., Edmond, Okla., 1983; m. Thomas M. Wilks, Jan. 28, 1972; children—Thomas David, Bryan Emerson. Sec. to adminstr. Allen Parish Hosp., Kinder, La., 1968-69; tchr. horseback riding, swimming Triple D Guest Ranche, Warren, Tex., 1969; singer, speaker Found. Singers, including TV and radio appearances, record albums, 1970-71; tchr. English, reading Pine Bluff (Ark.) High Sch., 1972-74; tchr. kindergarten Doyle Elem. Sch., East Prairie (Mo.) R-2 Sch. Dist., 1974-75; tchr. 1st grad Bertrand (Mo.) Elem. Sch., 1975-76; tchr. 6th grade sci. A.D. Simpson Sch., Charleston, Mo., 1976-78; dir. admissions and fin. aid Mo. Bapt. Coll., St. Louis, 1978-80; fin. adminstr. Control Data Inst., Control Data Corp., St. Louis, 1980-81; bd. dirs. Computer Commn. Services Inc., 1986—; dir. tutorial services, instr. tutorial methods Okla. Bapt. U., 1981-83 instr. horsemanship St. Gregory's Jr. Coll., 1981; counselor Gordon Cooper Area Vocat. Tech. Sch., 1982-83, Shawnee Jr. High Sch. (Okla.), 1983-85; dir. Resource Ctr., instr. English, St. Gregory's Coll., Shawnee, Okla., 1985—; bd. dirs. Computer Commn. Services Inc., Tulsa; tutor for children under jurisdiction Juvenile Ct., Jefferson County, Ark., 1972-73, leader group counseling/therapy sessions, 1972. Choreographer, First Bapt. Ch. Youth Choir, Pine Bluff; v.p. St. Gregory's Coll. Therapeutic Horsemanship Program, 1981-82; Republican election judge. Recipient Kathryn Carpenter award La. Bapt. Conv., 1971; Real Scope award Realty World, St. Louis, 1980; lic. Realtor, Mo. Mem. Nat. Hist. Soc., Univ. Alliance Okla. Bapt. U., Nat. Assn. Fin. Aid Adminstrs., Nat. Assn. Admissions Counselors, Athenian Lit. Soc., Nat. Geog. Soc., Gamma Beta Phi, Kappa Delta, Phi Kappa Phi. Republican. Baptist. Clubs: Kathryn Boone Music, Civinette Booster. Home: Route 3 Box 143 Shawnee OK 74801 Office: St Gregory's Coll 1900 W MacArthur Shawnee OK 74801

WILLARD, H(ARRISON) ROBERT, electrical engineer; b. Seattle, May 31, 1933; s. Harrison Eugene and Florence Linea (Chelquist) W.; B.S.E.E., U. Wash., 1955, M.S.E.E., 1957, Ph.D., 1971. Staff asso. Boeing Sci. Research Labs., Seattle, 1959-64; research asso. U. Wash., 1968-72, sr. engr. and research prof. applied physics lab., 1972-81; sr. engr. Boeing Aerospace Co., Seattle, 1981-84; dir. instrumentation and engring. MetriCor Inc. (previously Tech. Dynamics Inc.), 1984—. Served with AUS, 1957-59. Lic. profl. engr., Wash. Mem. IEEE, Am. Geophys. Union, Phi Beta Kappa, Sigma Xi, Tau Beta Pi. Contbr. articles to tech. jours. Patentee in field. Office: 18800 142 Ave NE Suite 4 Woodinville WA 98072

WILLARD, JOHN GERARD, consultant, author, lecturer; b. Pitts., Nov. 20, 1952; s. Cornelius Merle and May E. (Hinds) W.; BA in Journalism, Duquesne U., Pitts., 1974; m. Lorraine L. Franze, Sept. 2, 1978; children: Mary Elizabeth, Kristen Anne, Lisa Lorraine. Producer, dir. air talent Sta. WDUQ-FM, Pitts., 1971-73; master control tech. dir. Sta. KDKA-TV, Pitts., 1973; cons. communications Better Bus. Bur., Pitts., 1974; asst. account exec. Marc & Co., Advt., Pitts., 1975; adminstr. employee benefit adminstrn. Rockwell Internat. Corp., Pitts., 1975-80, adminstr. relocation and corp. personnel procedures, 1980-81, mgr. corp. policy, 1981-82; pres. John G. Willard Cons., 1982—. Contbr. articles in field. Mem. Am. Mensa Ltd., Internat. Platform Assn., Smithsonian Nat. Instn., Nat. Rifle Assn. (markmanship instr.), Stage 62, Kappa Tau Alpha, Alpha Tau Omega. Office: 360 Middlegate Dr Bethel Park PA 15102

WILLARD, RALPH LAWRENCE, physician, former college president; b. Manchester, Iowa, Apr. 6, 1922; s. Hosea B. and Ruth A. (Hazelrigg) W.; m. Margaret Dyer Dennis, Sept. 26, 1969; children: Laurie, Jane, Ann, H. Thomas. Student, Cornell Coll., 1940-42, Coe Coll., 1945; D.O., Kirksville Coll. Osteo. Medicine, 1949; EdD (hon.), U. North Tex., 1985. Intern Kirksville Osteo. Hosp., 1949-50, resident in surgery, 1954-57; chmn. dept. surgery Davenport Osteo. Hosp., 1957-68; dean, prof. surgery Kirksville Coll. Osteo. Medicine, 1969-73; asso. dean acad. affairs, prof. surgery Mich. State U. Coll. Osteo. Medicine, 1974-75; dean Tex. Coll. Osteopathic Medicine, 1975-76, pres., 1981-85, prof. surgery, 1985—; v.p. med. affairs North Tex. State U., Denton, 1976-81; mem. Nat. Adv. Council Edn. for Health Professions, 1971-73, Iowa Gov.'s Council Hosps. and Health Related Facilities, 1965-68; chmn. council deans Am. Assn. Colls. Osteo. Medicine, 1970-73, pres., 1979-80. Served with USAAF, 1942-45; Served with USAF, 1952-53; col. USAFR, ret. Decorated D.F.C., Air medal with 4 oak leaf clusters, Meritorious Service medal, Legion of Merit. Fellow Am. Coll. Osteo. Surgeons; mem. Am., Tex. osteo. assns., Am. Acad. Osteopathy, Acad. Osteo. Dirs. Med. Edn., Aerospace Med. Assn., Am. Coll. Physician Execs., Assn. Mil. Surgeons U.S., Am. Acad. Med. Dirs., Soc. Air Force Flight Surgeons, Quiet Birdmen., Ft. Worth C.of C. (dir.). Democrat. Episcopalian. Clubs: Carswell Officers, Century II. Lodges: Rotary, Masons (Shriner), Order of Daedalians. Home: PO Box 9074 Fort Worth TX 76147 Office: Camp Bowie at Montgomery Fort Worth TX 76107

WILLBANKS, ROGER PAUL, publishing and book distributing company executive; b. Denver, Nov. 25, 1934; s. Edward James and Ada Gladys (Davis) W.; m. Beverly Rae Masters, June 16, 1957; children—Wendy Lee, Roger Craig. B.S., U. Denver, 1957, M.B.A., 1965. Economist, bus. writer, bus. forecaster Mountain States Telephone Co., Denver, 1959-66; dir. pub. relations Denver Bd. Water Commrs., 1967-70; pres. Royal Publs. Inc., Denver, 1971—, Nutri-Books Corp., Denver, 1971—, Inter-Sports Book and Video, 1986—. Editor Denver Water News, 1967-70, Mountain States Bus., 1962-66. Mem. Gov. of Colo.'s Revenue Forecasting Com., 1963-66. Served with U.S. Army, 1957-58. Recipient pub. relations award Am. Water Works Assn., 1970. Mem. Am. Booksellers Assn., Nat. Nutritional Foods Assn., Pub. Relations Soc. Am. (charter mem. health sect.), Denver C. of C., SAR. Republican. Lutheran. Clubs: Columbine Country, Denver Press, Auburn Cord Duesenberg, Rolls Royce Owners, Classic Car of Am., Denver U. Century (Denver). Address: Royal Publs Inc PO Box 5793 Denver CO 80217

WILLBRAND, MARY LOUISE, speech pathologist, educator; b. Tulsa, Aug. 16, 1936; d. Raymond Richard and Wilma (Collins) Scott; m. Richard D. Rieke, June 24, 1979; 1 dau., Amy Dawn. A.A. in Drama, Christian Coll., 1956; student Mary Washington Coll., 1955, Tulsa U., 1957; B.S., U. Mo., 1958, M.A., 1969, Ph.D., 1972; postgrad. Stanford U., 1969. Speech clinician pub. schs., Moberly, Mo., 1958-61, Columbia, Mo., 1961-65, Cerebral Palsy Center, Fayette, Mo., 1967; tchr. speech and drama summer enrichment program, Columbia Mo., 1963-65; lang. clinician Inst. Childhood Aphasia, Palo Alto, Calif., 1969; instr. speech pathology U. Mo., Columbia, 1969-71; dir. speech-lang. pathology and audiology U. Utah, Salt Lake City, 1976-81, prof. speech pathology, 1973—; cons. to sch. dists. Mo., Wyo., Utah, Tex. Author: (with M.J. Mecham) Language Disorders in Children, 1979, Treatment of Language Disorders, 1985; (with R.D. Rieke) Teaching Oral Communication in Elementary Schools, 1983. Contbr. numerous articles to profl. jours. Vice pres., bd. dirs. Montessori Sch., Columbia, 1969-71; mem. exec. council Nat. Charity League, Salt Lake City, 1974-77; mem. home-sch. bd. Rowland Hall-St. Marks Sch., Salt Lake City, 1975-77; v.p., bd. dirs. Boy's Club Early Childhood Edn. Center, Salt Lake City, 1980—. Coll. Humanities grantee U. Utah, 1975, research com. grantee, 1981-83. Mem. Utah Speech and Hearing Assn. (pres.), Am. Speech-Lang-Hearing Assn. (visitor edn. tng. bd. site). Home: 1485 Sigsbee Ave Salt Lake City UT 84103 Office: U Utah 1201 Behavioral Sci Bldg Salt Lake City UT 84112

WILLCOX, FREDERICK PRESTON, inventor; b. Los Angeles, Aug. 1, 1910; s. Frederick William and Kate Lillian (Preston) W.; m. Velma Rose Gander, 1935; 1 dau., Ann Louise. Grad. high sch. Self-employed research and devel. engr. and cons., 1939-51; govt. cons., 1949-50, 61-65; tech. v.p. Fairchild Camera & Instrument Corp., 1951-60; inventor, researcher, developer, New Canaan, Conn., 1960—. Holder over 90 patents in photog., graphic arts and data communications equipment, high speed teleprinters and typewriters; photography work exhibited Smithsonian Gallery. Served to maj. U.S. Army, 1940-45. Recipient Sherman Fairchild Photogrammetric award Am. Soc. Photogrammetry, 1951. Fellow AAAS; mem. Am. Soc. Photogrammetry and Remote Sensing, Soc. Photog. Scientists and Engrs., ASME, AIAA, Optical Soc. Am., Am. Def. Preparedness Assn. Episcopalian. Avocations: machine sculpture, photography. Home and Office: 565 Oenoke Ridge New Canaan CT 06840

WILLCOX, PETER JOHN, oil company executive; b. Coleford, Eng., Aug. 17, 1945; arrived in Australia, 1986; s. Arthur Frederick and Moira Josephine Willcox. BA with honors, Cambridge U., Eng., 1966; MA in Physics, Cambridge U., 1966; postgrad., Stanford U., 1983. With Iraq Petroleum Co., London and Abu Dhabi, Quatar, 1966-73, Amoco Prodn. Co., various internat. locations, 1973-85; exec. gen. mgr. BHP Petroleum Pty. Ltd., Melbourne, Australia, 1986-87, chief exec. officer, 1987—; bd. dirs. Woodside Petroleum. Mem. Australian Inst. Petroleum (bd. dirs.). Club: Oxford and Cambridge (Eng.); Melbourne. Office: BHP Petroleum Pty Ltd, 35 Collins St, Melbourne 3000, Australia

WILLE, ANDREAS WALTER, psychiatrist; b. Zürich, Switzerland, May 3, 1943; s. Walther Hermann and Lisa-Lotte (Boesch) W.; m. Elisabeth Brütsch, May 31, 1970; children: Lukas, Beat, Samuel. Md. U. Zürich, 1971. Cert. child and adolescent psychiatrist, psychotherapist. Head physician Kinderspital, Zürich, 1975-76; head physician Child Psychiatry Service, Zürich, 1976-81, sub-chief, 1981—; cons. psychiatrist Child-Hosp., Winterthur, 1976—; therapy supr. Sch. Psychologist, Winterthur, 1976—; med. examiner U. Zürich, 1983—; univ. lectr. Univ. Med.Facility, Zürich, 1985. Author: Encopresis, 1984; contbr. numerous articles to profl. jours. Mem. Swiss Soc. Child Psychol., Swiss Soc. Psychiatry, Swiss Soc. Psychotherapy, Swiss Soc. Psychotherapy, Swiss Med. Soc.

WILLEBRANDS, JOHANNES GERARDUS MARIA, archbishop, cardinal; b. Bovenkarspel, Netherlands, Sept. 4, 1909; s. Herman and Aafje (Kok) W.; Ph.D., U. Rome, 1937; D.Litt. (hon.), St. Louis U., 1968, St. Olaf Coll., 1976, Coll. St. Thomas, St. Paul, 1979; D. Rights (hon.), U. Notre Dame, 1970, Cath. U. Am., 1974; Th.D. (hon.), Cath. U., Louvain, Belgium, 1971, Theol. Acad. Leningrad, USSR, 1973, Assumption Coll., 1980, U. Oxford, Eng., 1987, Cath. U. Munich, 1987; hon. doctorate, Cath. U., Poland, 1985; LHD (hon.), Bellarmine Coll., 1987; LLD (hon.), Seton Hall U., 1987. Ordained priest, Roman Catholic Ch., 1934, bishop, 1964, cardinal, 1969; chaplain, Amsterdam, Netherlands, 1937-40; prof. philosophy Filosoficum of diocese Haarlem (Netherlands), 1940-60, dir. Filosoficum, 1945-60; sec. Secretariat for Promoting Christian Unity, Rome, 1960, pres., 1969—; archbishop of Utrecht (Netherlands), 1975-83. Address: Via dell'Erba 1, 00193 Rome Italy

WILLEMSEN, ARIE WOLTER, librarian; b. Terwolde, The Netherlands, Jan. 29, 1930; s. Evert Jan and Maria (van Mullem) W.; m. Françoise

Yvonne Carrière; children: Wolter, Francine. MA in History, U. Utrecht, The Netherlands, 1954, PhD in History, 1958. Librarian Koninklijke Bibliotheek, The Hague, The Netherlands, 1957-69, dep. chief librarian, 1969-86, chief librarian, 1986—; pres. Raad voor de Nederlandse Taal en Letteren, The Netherlands and Belgium, 1983—. Author: Het Vlaams Nationalisme, 1914-40, 1958, De Vlaamse Beweging 2 vols., 1830-1940, 1974-75, Hetinieuwe gebouw van de Koninklijke Bibliotheek, 1982; editor several periodicals. Recipient Orde Vlaamse Leeuw, 1981; named Officier Kroonorde België, Belgian Govt., 1975. Fellow Maatschappij der Nederlandse Leterkunde, Nederlands Historisch Genootschap, Nederlandse Vereniging van Bibliothecarissen. Partijlvan de Arbeid. Home: Victor Hugoplantsoen 8, Utrecht The Netherlands Office: Koninklijke Bibliotheek, Prins Willem Alexanderhof 5, 2595 BE The Hague The Netherlands

WILLES, MARK HINCKLEY, food industry executive; b. Salt Lake City, July 16, 1941; s. Joseph Simmons and Ruth (Hinckley) W.; m. Laura Fayone, June 7, 1961; children: Wendy Anne, Susan Kay, Keith Mark, Stephen Joseph, Matthew Bryant. AB, Columbia U., 1963, PhD, 1967. Mem. staff banking and currency com. Ho. of Reps., Washington, 1966-67; asst. prof. fin. U. Pa., Pitts., 1967-69; economist Fed. Res. Bank, Phila., 1967, sr. economist, 1969-70, dir. research, 1970-71, v.p., dir. research, 1971, 1st v.p., 1971-77; pres. Fed. Res. Bank of Mpls., 1977-80; exec. v.p., chief fin. officer Gen. Mills, Inc., Mpls., 1980-85, pres., 1985—. Office: Gen Mills Inc 1 General Mills Blvd Minneapolis MN 55426

WILLEY, ERNEST REGINALD, marketing and sales consultant, researcher; b. Truro, Cornwall, Eng., Feb. 23, 1918; s. Ernest Reginald and Florence Mabel (Glanville) W.; m. Hilda Joan Lee, Mar. 29, 1948; children—Stephen Ernest John, Linda Ruth, David James, Andrew Reginald. Student Tech. Coll., Truro, 1929-35. Salesman, Bennett Opie Ltd., London, 1946-48, sales mgr., 1948-58, mktg. and sales dir., Sittingbourne, Kent, 1958-83; co. dir. Castle Tea Co. Ltd., London, 1978-85; cons., Canterbury, Kent, 1983—; chmn. Progressive Mktg., Ltd., London, 1988—. Editor Regnal League mag., 1935-39. Chief organizer Central Civic Group Pub. Meetings, Truro, 1938. Served with Brit. Army, 1939-45; Europe and Malta. Mem. Inst. Cert. Grocers (Fin. award 1939), Brit. Inst. Mktg. (diploma 1949). Home: Etchinghurst Pilgrims Ln, Chilham, Canterbury Kent CT4 8AA England

WILLEY, JAMES PETERSON, design company business management consultant; b. Logan, Utah, May 9, 1950; s. Lynn Robison and Marie (Peterson) W.; m. Marci Ann Movitz, Mar. 11, 1971; children: April, James Scott, Michelle, Jeffrey David. BS, Utah State U., 1972; MBA, Fla. Inst. Tech., 1980. Commd. U.S. Army, 1972, advanced through grades to maj.; comdr. hdqrs. and Main Co. U.S. Army, Ft. Hood, Tex., 1974-76; comdr. 48th Maint. Co. U.S. Army, Baumholder, Fed. Republic Germany, 1976-77; sec., gen. staff U.S. Army, Heidelberg, Fed. Republic Germany, 1977-79; resigned U.S. Army, 1983; asst. prof. N.C. State U., Raleigh, 1979-83; pres. MLV Inc., Raleigh, N.C., 1983-84; v.p. fin. Evergreen Mgmt. Corp., Southern Pines, N.C., 1984-88; v.p., gen. mgr. Distbn. Services, Inc., Atlanta, 1988—; cons. Miller/Zell Inc., Atlanta, 1985-88, Adcom, Inc., Detroit, 1988—; S.A.F.E., Detroit, 1988—; chief fin. officer JHC Enterprises Inc., Southern Pines, Car-Ten, Inc., Memphis, Fluid Services, Inc., Louisville. Chmn. Southern Pines Boy Scout Com., Raleigh Boy Scout Com. Named Top Developer Jiffy Lube Internat. Inc., 1984, 85. Mem. Am. Mgmt. Assn., Am. Equipment Lessors, Pi Sigma Alpha (v.p. 1971-72), Delta Sigma Phi (faculty advisor 1980-83), . Sandhills (N.C.) C. of C. (corp. rep.). Republican. Mormon. Home: 3591 Morishop Cove Marietta GA 30064

WILLIAMS, ALFRED BLYTHE, business communication educator; b. Oakland City, Ind., Sept. 17, 1940; s. Ross Merl and Jesse Adell (Helsley) W. B.S. cum laude, Oakland City Coll., 1963; M.S., Ind. U., 1964; Ph.D., Ga. State U., 1974. Cert. tchr. bus. edn. and English, Ind. Tchr. Arlington High Sch., Indpls., 1964-65, Oakland City Coll., Ind., 1965-69; editor Southwestern Pub. Co., Cin., 1969-72, cons., 1981; adj. prof. Ga. State U., Atlanta, 1972-74; assoc. prof. bus. communications U. Southwestern La., Lafayette, 1975—, chmn. dept., 1986—; cons. John Wiley Pub. Co., N.Y., 1981-82. Author study guides. Editor Information Systems Bus. Communication Jour., 1983. Patron Lafayette Community Concerts, 1984; contbr. La. and Nat. Republican parties, Baton Rouge, Washington, 1983, 84. Mem. Assn. Bus. Communicators (bd. dirs. 1986—, Francis W. Weeks Merit award 1984), AAUP, La. Assn. Higher Edn., Sierra Club, Phi Delta Kappa, Delta Pi Epsilon. Methodist. Lodge: Kiwanis.

WILLIAMS, ANNIE JOHN, educator; b. Reidsville, N.C., Aug. 26, 1913; d. John Wesley and Martha Anne (Walker) W. AB, Greensboro Coll., 1933; MA, U. N.C., Chapel Hill, 1939; postgrad., Appalachian State U., summer 1944, Duke U., summer 1936, Cornell U., summer 1961. Tchr. math. Blackstone (Va.) Coll., 1934-35; tchr. Hoke High Sch., Raeford, N.C., 1935-37, Massey Hill High Sch., Fayetteville, N.C., 1937-42, Alexander Graham Jr. High Sch., Fayetteville, 1942-43, Carr Jr. High Sch., Durham, N.C., 1943-53; supr. math. N.C. Dept. Pub. Instrn., Raleigh, 1959-62; tchr. math. Durham High Sch., 1953-59, 62-78, ret., 1978; vol. in math. N.C. Sch. Sci. and Math., Durham, 1980—; adj. asst. prof. dept. math. and sci. edn. N.C. State U., Raleigh, 1966-73. Author: (with Brown and Montgomery) Algebra, First Course, 1963, Algebra, Second Course, 1963. Recipient cert. of recognition Dept. Math. and Sci. Edn. N.C. State U., 1979, Gov.'s award for outstanding vol. service, 1986; named Vol. of Yr., Key Vol. Program co-sponsored by Vol. Services Bur. and Durham Morning Herald, 1986. Mem. Nat. Council Tchrs. Math. (life, bd. dirs. 1957-60), Math. Assn. Am. (life), N.C. Council Tchrs. Math. (hon. life, W.W. Rankin Meml. award 1975), Internat. Platform Assn., DAR (N.C. chpt. chair Am. History Month 1980-82, corr. sec. 1982-84, chaplain 1984-86, Gen. Davie chpt.), Delta Kappa Gamma, Mu Alpha Theta (hon.). Methodist. Clubs: Pierian Lit. (sec. 1979-80, pres. 1980-81), Durham Woman's (co-chmn. internat. affairs dept. 1985-87). Home and Office: 2021 Sprunt Ave Durham NC 27705

WILLIAMS, ARTHUR, engineering consultant; b. Swindon, Eng., July 29, 1904; came to U.S., 1926, naturalized, 1942; s. Joseph and Emily (Chirgwin) W.; m. Ellen M.I. Cullingford, Apr. 8, 1929; children: Valerie (Mrs. Robert C. Norcross), Brian R. Student, Swindon Coll. Engring. Sch., 1921-26, Harvard U. Bus. Sch., 1955. Chief engr. Superheater Co., East Chicago, Ind., 1927-42; v.p. Superheater Co., 1946, Combustion Engring., Inc., 1949-58; v.p., sec. Submerged Combustion, Inc., 1958-65; cons. Selas Corp. Am., 1965-66; cons. engr., 1966—. Episcopalian. Address: Givens Estate Wesley Drive Villa 20-E Asheville NC 28803

WILLIAMS, BEN FRANKLIN, JR., lawyer, mayor; b. El Paso, Tex., Aug. 12, 1929; s. Ben Franklin and Dorothy (Whitaker) W.; m. Daisy Federighi, June 2, 1951; children: Elizabeth Lee, Diane Marie, Katherine Ann, Benjamin Franklin III. B.A., U. Ariz., 1951, J.D., 1956. Bar: Ariz. 1956. With Bd. Immigration Appeals, Dept. Justice, 1957, ICC, 1959; practice in Douglas, Ariz., 1956—; city atty. Douglas and Tombstone, 1962; atty. Mexican consul 1960; mayor of Douglas, 1980—; bd. dirs. Ariz. Pub. Service Co. Pres. Ariz. League Cities and Towns, pres. Douglas Sch. Bd., 1963, 69, 70; mem. bd. Ariz. Dept. Econ. Planning and Devel.; bd. dirs. Ariz.-Mex. Commn., Ariz. Acad. (Town Hall), Merabank & Ariz. Pub. Service Co.; ward committeeman Douglas Republican Com., 1962. Served to 1st lt. AUS, 1951-53. Mem. ABA, Internat. Bar Assn., Ariz. Bar Assn. (treas. 1963), Cochise County Bar Assn. (pres. 1959), Am. Judicature Soc., U. Ariz. Law Coll. Assn. (dir.), Ariz. Hist. Soc. (dir.), Sigma Nu, Phi Delta Phi, Blue Key. Episcopalian. Lodge: Elks. Home: 2100 9th St Douglas AZ 85607 Office: 1930 11th St Douglas AZ 85608

WILLIAMS, BETTY, peace activist; b. Belfast, No. Ireland, May 22, 1943; m. Ralph Williams, 1961 (div.); 2 children; m. James T. Perkins, 1983. LL.D. (hon.), Yale U.; L.H.D. (hon.), Coll. Siera Heights, 1977. Co-organizer (with Mairead Corrigan) of movement Women for Peace (now Community of Peace People), Belfast, 1976-80; co-founder (with Mairead Corrigan) mag. Peace by Peace. Co-recipient Nobel Prize for Peace for 1976 (awarded 1977), Norwegian People's Peace Prize, 1976, Carl von Ossietzky prize German Fed. Republic, 1976. Roman Catholic. Office: Orchardville Gardens, Finaghy, Belfast 10 Northern Ireland also: Peace People, 224 Lisburn Rd, Belfast BT9 6GE, Northern Ireland *

WILLIAMS, CECILIA LEE PURSEL, optometrist; b. Lewisburg, Pa., Nov. 15, 1948; d. Lee LaVerne and Geraldine May (Steininger) Pursel; student Lycoming Coll., 1966-68; B.S. (Women's Aux. of Pa. Optometrists scholar 1968-70, Pa. State grantee 1968-70), Pa. Coll. Optometry, 1970, O.D. (Women's Aux. of Pa. Optometrists scholar 1970-72, Pa. State grantee 1970-72), 1972; m. Richard Lee Williams, May 17, 1975; 1 son, Kent Lee. Research optometrist in soft lens materials Gumpelmayer Optik, Vienna, Austria, 1973; optometrist Sterling Optical Co. Contact Lens Center, Washington, 1974-79; pvt. practice optometry, Springfield, Va., 1980—. Recipient Clin. Efficiency award Pa. Coll. Optometry, 1972; lic. and/or cert. optometrist, D.C., Pa., N.Y., N.J., Va. Mem. Optometric Center of Nation's Capital (dir. 1977-80), Am. Optometric Assn., Va. Optometric Assn., No. Va. Optometric Soc., Nat. Honor Soc. for Optometry, Omega Delta. Home: 3600 Wilton Hall Ct Alexandria VA 22310 Office: 6795A Springfield Mall Springfield VA 22150

WILLIAMS, C(HARLES) K(ENNETH), poet, literature and writing educator; b. Newark, Nov. 4, 1936; s. Paul Bernard and Dossie (Kasdin) W.; m. Sarah Dean Jones, June, 1966 (div. 1975); 1 child, Jessica Anne; m. Catherine Justine Mauger, Apr. 15, 1975; 1 child, Jed Mauger. BA, U. Pa., 1958. Vis. prof. lit. Beaver Coll., Jenkintown, Pa., 1975, Drexel U., Phila., 1976, U. Calif., Irvine, 1978, Boston U., 1979-80, Bklyn. Coll., 1982-83; Mellon vis. prof. lit. Franklin and Marshall Coll., Lancaster, Pa., 1977; prof. writing Columbia U., N.Y.C., 1981-85; prof. lit. George Mason U., Fairfax, Va., 1982—; Halloway lectr. U. Calif., Berkeley, 1986. Author: Lies, 1969, I Am the Bitter Name, 1972, With Ignorance, 1977, Tar, 1983, Flesh and Blood, 1987; contbr. editor Am. Poetry Rev., 1972—. Sponsor People's Fund, Phila., 1967—. Recipient Nat. Book Critics Circle award in poetry, 1987; fellow Guggenheim Found., 1975, Nat. Endowment for Arts, 1985. Mem. PEN, Poetry Soc. Am. Home: 23 Rue des Petits Hotels, 75010 Paris France Office: George Mason U Dept English Fairfax VA 22030

WILLIAMS, COLIN HASELHURST, geography educator, researcher; b. Barry, Wales, Oct. 29, 1950; s. Islwyn and Margaret Irene (Haselhurst) W.; m. Meryl Elizabeth Thomas, Aug. 21, 1973; 1 child, Rhodri Samuel. BSc Econ. first class hons., U. Wales, 1972, PhD, 1978. Tutor, tchrs. asst. U. We. Ont., London, 1973-74; tutor Open U. Wales, 1974-76; lectr. N. Staffordshire (Eng.) Polytech., 1976-84; prin. lectr. geography N. Staffordshire (Eng.) Polytech., Stoke on Trent, 1984-88, prof., 1988—; vis. prof. Pa. State U., University Park, 1982-83; cons., researcher The Welsh Office, Cardiff, 1982—; research advisor Welsh Joint Edn. Com., Cardiff, 1987—. Editor: National Seperatism, 1982, Language in Geographic Context, 1988, Community Conflict, Nationalism and Partition, 1988, (jour.) Multilingul and Multicultural Devel. Discussion Papers in Geolinguists, 1980—; rev. editor: Jour. Mulitlingual and Multicultural Devel., 1981—. Preacher, Bretheren Assemblies, 1975—; active, Welsh Lang. Movement, 1969—. Recipient scholarship English Speaking Union, 1973-74, HSIF/ESRC Swedish U., 1982, Brit. Acad., 1980, 86-87, Can. Studies in U.K., 1979; Fulbright scholar, prof. Pa. State U., 1982-83; Swedish Inst. scholar U. Lund, 1988. Mem. Inst. Brit. Geography (polit. geography com. 1985—), Brit. Assn. Can. Studies. Home: 39 Crestwood Dr, Stone, Staffs ST15 OLW, England Office: N Staffordshire Polytech, Leek Rd, Stoke, Staffs ST4 2DE, England

WILLIAMS, EARL DUANE, accounting executive; b. Hiwasse, Ark., Mar. 2, 1929; s. James Martin and Goldie Faye (Reeves) W.; m. Dorothy Jean Rasner, May 3, 1952; children: Earl Duane, Ronald Lee. Acctg. mgr. Philco Ford, Palo Alto, Calif., 1966-69; instr. acctg. Foothill and Deanza Coll., Cupertino, Calif., 1967-69; controller, treas. Bekins Maintenance, Los Angeles, 1969-70; chief acct. Title Ins. & Trust Co., Los Angeles, 1970-72; controller Continental Devel. Co., El Segundo, Calif., 1972-76; v.p. fin. Computer Infomatrix, Inc., Los Angeles, 1976-77; pres. Nationwide Acctg. Service, Woodland Hills, Calif., 1972—; instr. acctg. Calif. Credential C.P.A.'s. Chmn. Liaison League Rehab. Group, 1973—; co-chmn. Re-election of Judge Sanches;com. mem. to re-elect Sen. Ed Davis; mem. com. re-election of Los Angeles County Sheriff; mem. West Hills Property Owners Assn. (bd. dirs.); mem. Los Angeles Philanthropic Found. Served with USAF, 1951-55. Recipient Cert. of Appreciation Vikings of Scandia, 1975, 76, 77, 78-87, Boy Scouts. Am., 1967. Mem. Nat. Assn. Accts., Controllers Assn., Internat. Footprint Assn. , Internat. Chili Soc., Nat. Soc. Pub. Accts., Calif. Assn. Ind. Accts., Nat. Soc. Tax Profls., Nat. Tax. Certificatio Bd., Navy League (life), Gold Pennant Gourmet (pres.), Woodland Hills C. of C. Republican. Lodges: Masons (32 degree), Elks. Clubs: Friars (Calif.), Los Angeles, Hollywood Press, Greater Los Angeles Press, Vikings of Scandia (chief 1984), Red Barons, Silver Dollar, Masquers, Town Hall Calif. Home: 23427 Strathern St West Hills CA 91304

WILLIAMS, EARL GLYNN, secondary school administrator; b. Hazard, Ky., July 12, 1949; s. James Clayton and Corrina (Schenkel) W.; m. Linda Day Davis, Aug. 15, 1970; children: Matthew, Shane, Angie. BS, Ball State U., 1973, MA, 1976; EdS, Ind. U., 1984, postgrad., 1984—. Cert. teaching adminstr., Ind. Tchr., coach Connersville (Ind.) High Sch., 1974-76; asst. prin. West Middle Sch., Martinsville, Ind., 1976-86, prin., 1986 . Bd dirs. local YMCA, Big Bros. and Big Sisters, Morgan County Task Force for Youth. Mem. N.Cen. Assn. Colls. and Univs. (program evaluator), Assn. Curriculum and Supervision Devel., Nat. Assn. Secondary Sch. Prins. (state exec. com., state mid. level com.), State Athletic Dirs. Assn., Phi Alpha Theta. Republican. Lodges: Lions, Elks. Office: 109 E Garfield St Martinsville IN 46151

WILLIAMS, EDDIE ERWIN, III, lawyer; b. Rocky Mount, N.C., Feb. 6, 1948; s. Eddie Erwin and Eula Meredith (Garland) W.; children: Jackson Hill, James Barnett. BA, Wofford Coll., 1970; JD, Vanderbilt U., 1973. Bar: Tenn. 1973, U.S. Dist. Ct. Tenn. 1974, U.S. Supreme Ct. 1979. Atty.-ptnr. Bryant, Price, Brandt, Jordan & Williams, Johnson City, Tenn., 1973-79; cir. ct. judge 1st Jud. Dist., Tenn., 1979-84; atty.-ptnr. Baker, Worthington, Crossley, Stansberry & Woolf, Johnson City, 1984—; faculty Tenn. Jud. Acad., 1982—; bd. of regents State of Tenn. Bd. dirs. Sequoyah Council Boy Scouts Am., United Way; regional chmn. Am. Cancer Crusade for Tenn.; exec. com., bd. dirs. East Tenn. State U. Found. Recipient Hon. Alumnus award East Tenn. State U. Mem. ABA, Tenn. Bar Assn. (Liberty Through Law award 1981), Internat. Acad. Trial Judges (fellow), Assn. Am. Trial Lawyers, Assn. Tenn. Trial Lawyers, Johnson City C. of C. (v.p., bd. dirs.), Rocky Mt. Hist. Assn. (trustee, v.p.). Republican. Episcopalian. Home: 811 Cloudland Dr Johnson City TN 37601 Office: Baker Worthington et al 207 Mockingbird Ln PO Box 3038 Johnson City TN 37602

WILLIAMS, EDWARD EARL, JR., educator, financial executive; b. Houston, Aug. 21, 1945; s. Edward Earl and Doris Jewel (Jones) W.; m. Susan M. Warren, June 28, 1983; children—Laura Michelle, David Brian. B.S. (Benjamin Franklin scholar, Jesse Jones scholar), U. Pa., 1966; Ph.D. (Tex. Savs. and Loan League fellow, NDEA fellow), U. Tex., 1968. Asst. prof. econs. Rutgers U., New Brunswick, N.J., 1968-70; asso. prof. fin. McGill U., Montreal, Que., Can., 1970-73; v.p., economist Service Corp. Internat., Houston, 1973-77; prof. adminstrv. sci. Rice U., Houston, 1978-82, Henry Gardiner Symonds prof., 1982—; chmn. bd. Service Tech. Internat., Inc., Houston, 1976—; chmn. bd., pres. Tex. Capital Investment Advisers, 1979—; chmn. bd. First Tex. Venture Capital Corp., 1983—; dir. Equus Capital Corp., Questech Inc., Yellow Cab Service Corp., Video Rental of Pa. Inc., Associated Bldg. Services Co.; investment com. Service Corp. Internat. Mem. Fin. Mgmt. Assn., Internat. Platform Assn., Beta Gamma Sigma, Alpha Kappa Psi. Author: An Integrated Analysis for Managerial Finance, 1970; Investment Analysis, 1974; Business Planning for the Entrepreneur, 1983; contbr. articles to profl. jours. Home: 12903 Forest Meadow Dr Cypress TX 77429 Office: Rice U Jesse H Jones Grad Sch Adminstrn Houston TX 77001

WILLIAMS, ELLIS, law enforcement officer, clergyman; b. Raymond, Miss., Oct. 27, 1931; s. Currie and Elise (Morrison) W.; student Union Bapt. Theol. Sem., 1963-64; BA in Criminology, Loyola U. South, New Orleans, 1972, MEd, 1974, M in Criminal Justice, 1981; m. Priscilla Norman, Jan. 9, 1954; children—Debra, Rita, Claude, Lathan, Glenn, Zelia. Patrolman, dept. police City of New Orleans, 1964-77, police sergeant, asst. platoon comdr., 1977-79, police lt., platoon comdr., 1979-86, div. comdr., 1986—; past v.p. La. Polygraph Bd.; assoc. minister Historic 2d Baptist Ch., New Orleans. Cert. fingerprint identification technician; cert. polygraphist Am. Polygraph Assn. Mem. Fraternal Order Police, Police Mut. Benevolent Assn., Internat. Assn. Identifications, La. Assn. Identification, Am. Polygraph Assn., La. Polygraph Assn., Cross Keys, Kappa Delta Pi. Democrat. Lodge: Masons. Home: 3108 Metropolitan St New Orleans LA 70126 Office: 715 S Broad St New Orleans LA 70119

WILLIAMS, ERIC JOSEPH, transportation executive; b. Havana, Cuba, Nov. 15, 1945; came to U.S., 1961; s. Eric and Frances (Waterhouse) W.; m. Maria Julia Williams, Mar. 30, 1984; children: Jason, Natasha. B.S. in Fgn. Service, Georgetown U., 1968. With Emery Worldwide, 1970—, sales rep., Miami, Fla., 1970-74, sales mgr., 1975-76, country mgr., Caracas, Venezuela, 1976-77, regional mgr. S.Am., Miami, 1977-81, dist. mgr. Latin Am.-Caribbean, Miami, 1981-84, div. gen. mgr. Latin Am.-Caribbean, 1984-86, dir. Latin Am.-Caribbean sector, 1986—; adult edn. tchr., Miami, 1973-75. Served to 1st lt. U.S. Army, 1968-70. Mem. Soc. Ams., Coral Gables C. of C., Georgetown U. Alumni Assn. (com.), Internat. Platform Assn. Episcopalian. Clubs: Coconut Grove Sailing (com. 1975-76), Biltmore Tennis. Home: 501 Raven Ave Miami Springs FL 33166 Office: Emery Worldwide 1150 NW 72d Ave Suite 530 Miami FL 33126

WILLIAMS, FRANCIS LEON, retired engineering executive, consultant; b. McGill, Nev., Sept. 19, 1918; s. Leon Alfred and Mazie Arabella (Blanchard) W.; m. Ailsa Bailey, Oct. 1944 (div.); children: Rhonda, Graham, Alison; m. Marita I. Fury, Feb. 23, 1974. Student, Calif. Inst. Tech., 1940-41, UCLA, 1946-47, Am. TV Labs., 1948; BME, Sydney U., Australia, 1952; postgrad., San Jose State Coll., 1958-60, Foothill Coll., 1961, Regional Vocat. Ctr., San Jose, Calif., 1962, Alexander Hamilton Inst., 1971-72, Lane Community Coll., 1978-85. Project engr., prodn. supr. Crompton, Parkinson, Australia Pty., Ltd., Sydney, 1949-50; field and sales engr. Perkins Australia Pty. Ltd., Sydney, 1951-54; chief mech. engr. Vicon Corp., San Carlos, Calif., 1955-60; design engr., group leader Lockheed Missiles and Space Co., Sunnyvale, Calif., 1960-70; prin. Astro-Tech Cons. Co., Los Altos, Calif., 1971-72; mech. designer Morvue and Morden Machines, Portland, Oreg., 1973-74; sr. mech. design engr. Chip-N-Saw div. Can-Car of Can., Eugene, Oreg., 1974-75; sales mgr. Indsl. Constrn. Co., Eugene, 1975-76, gen. mgr., 1977-78; ops. mgr. Steel Structures, Eugene, 1976-77; mech. design and project engr. Carothers Co., Eugene, 1978-80; chief engr. Bio Solar and Woodex Corps., Eugene and Brownsville, Oreg., 1980-83; cons. and design engr. Am. Fabricators, Woodburn, Oreg., 1983-84; design engr., draftsman Peterson Pacific Corp., Pleasant Hill, Oreg., 1984-85, Jensen Drilling Co., Glenwood, Oreg., 1985; design engr. Judco & Ball Flight Dryers, Inc., Harbor City, Calif., 1985-86; sr. v.p. The Richelsen Co., also cons.; advisor solid waste recovery County Bd. Commr.'s Office, Eugene, 1984-85. Contbr. articles to profl. jours.; patentee in field. Chmn. bldg. and grounds Westminster Presbyn. Ch., Eugene, 1984-86. Served with USAF, 1941-45. Democrat. Lodge: Elks. Home: 2324 Lillian St Eugene OR 97401

WILLIAMS, FRED ALTON (AL), JR., business educator, college administrator; b. Paris, Tex., June 13, 1923; s. Fred Alton and Mary Catherine (Gilliland) W.; BBA, U. Tex., Austin, 1950; m. Patsy Ruth Williams, Dec. 17, 1954; children: Marilyn Williams Dixon, Carol Williams Huska. Ptnr. Williams Air Activities, Civilian Flight Sch., Sales & Service, Tyler, Tex., 1946-52; ptnr., v.p. Williams Marine Co., Tyler, Holiday Marina-Resort, Inc., Lake Tawakoni, Tex., 1952-65; recruiter Dallas Fashion Merchandising Coll., 1965-70; exec. dir. Tyler Comml. Coll., 1970-76; dir. fin. aid and secretarial studies Northwood Inst. Tex., Cedar Hill, 1976-79, dir. ops. and fin. aid, instr., 1979—; cons. in field; coordinator workshops. Served with USAF, World War II; capt. Res. ret. Mem. Nat., Tex. assns. student fin. aid adminstrs., Kappa Sigma. Baptist. Home: 127 Rowland Pl Tyler TX 75701 Office: PO Box 58 Cedar Hill TX 75104

WILLIAMS, GENA KAY, automotive dealership executive; b. Fairfax, Va., Apr. 12, 1963; d. Leon Ellis and Vena Pearl (Hicks) W. BS, U. Ariz., 1981; postgrad. Hofstra U., 1983; student in Archtl. Drafting, ITT Tech. Inst., Sacramento, 1988—. Cert. mgmt acctg., internal auditor. Controller TGI Friday's, Tuscon, Ariz., Westbury, N.Y., 1980-83; auto dealer, bus. mgr. Williams, Inc., Hampton, Va., 1983—. ROTC scholar U. Ariz., Tucson, 1979. Mem. Peninsula Assn. Credit Execs., Nat. Assn. Female Execs., Am. Mgmt. Assn., Peninsula Women's Network, Intertel, Triple Nine Soc., Mensa. Republican. Presbyterian. Lodge: Rosicrucians, Martinist. Avocations: photography, skiing.

WILLIAMS, GEORGE ANTHONY RICHARD, journalist, editor; b. Wigan, Lancashire, Eng., Apr. 4, 1952; s. Richard and Barbara (Beresford) W. Chief reporter Northants Evening Telegraph, Kettering, Eng., 1970-74; asst. editor Coventry Evening Telegraph, West Midlands, Eng., 1974-78, Birmingham Post and Mail, West Midlands, 1978-79; editor Gulf Daily News, Manama, Bahrain, 1983—. Named Provincial Report Yr., 1973. Conservative. Mem. Ch. of Eng. Clubs: British (Bahrain), Awali Golf (Bahrain). Home: PO Box 29123, Manama Bahrain Office: Gulf Daily News, PO Box 5300, Manama Bahrain

WILLIAMS, HAROLD MARVIN, foundation official, former government official, former university dean, former corporate executive; b. Phila., Jan. 5, 1928; s. Louis W. and Sophie (Fox) W.; A.B., UCLA, 1946; LL.B., Harvard U., 1949; postgrad. U. So. Calif. Grad. Sch. Law, 1955-56; children—Ralph A., Susan J. Bar: Calif. 1950; practiced in Los Angeles, 1950, 53-55; with Hunt Foods and Industries, Inc., Los Angeles, 1955-68, v.p. 1958-60, exec. v.p., 1960-68, pres., 1968; gen., mgr. Hunt-Wesson Foods, 1964-66, pres., 1966-68; chmn. finance com. Norton Simon, Inc., 1968-70, chmn. bd., 1969-70, dir., 1959-77; dir. Times-Mirror Corp., Pan Am. World Airways, Am. Med. Internat.; prof. mgmt., dean Grad. Sch. Mgmt., UCLA, 1970-77; pres., dir. Special Investments & Securities Inc., 1961-66; chmn. SEC, Washington, 1977-81; pres., chief exec. officer J. Paul Getty Trust, 1981—; regent U. Calif., 1983—. Mem. Commn. for Econ. Devel. State of Calif., 1973-77; energy coordinator City of Los Angeles, 1973-74; public mem. Nat. Advt. Review Bd., 1971-75; co-chmn. Public Commn. on Los Angeles County Govt.; commn. to rev. Master Plan for Higher Edn., State of Calif., 1985-87. Served as 1st lt. AUS, 1950- 53. Mem. State Bar Calif. Office: 1875 Century Park E Los Angeles CA 90067

WILLIAMS, HENRY HARVEY, government official St. Vincent and Grenadines. Acting gov. gen. Kingstown, St. Vincent and the Grenadines, 1988—. Address: Office of Gov Gen, Kingstown Saint Vincent and Grenadines *

WILLIAMS, HOWARD WALTER, aerospace engineer; b. Evansville, Ind., Oct. 18, 1937; s. Walter Charles and Marie Louise (Bollinger) W.; m. Phyllis Ann Scofield, May 4, 1956 (div. Sept. 1970); m. Marilee Sharon Mulvane, Oct. 30, 1970; children: Deborah, Steven, Kevin, Glenn, Lori, Michele. AA, Pasadena City Coll., 1956; BSME, Calif. State U., Los Angeles, 1967; BSBA, U. San Francisco, 1978. Turbojet, rocket engr. Aerojet-Gen. Corp., Azusa, Calif., 1956-59, infrared sensor engr., 1959-60, rocket, torpedo engr., 1960-66; power, propulsion mgr. Aerojet-Gen. Corp., Sacramento, 1967-73, high speed ship systems mgr., 1974-78, combustion, power mgr., rocket engine mktg. mgr., 1979—. Author: (with others) Heat Exchangers, 1980, Industrial Heat Exchangers, 1985; co-inventor Closed Cycle Power System, 1969. Recipient Energy Innovations award U.S. Dept. Energy, 1985. Mem. AIAA (sr.; Best Paper 1966), Am. Soc. Metals (organizing dir. indsl. heat exchange confs. 1985—). Office: Aerojet TechSystems Co Aerojet Rd & Folsom Blvd Rancho Cordova CA 95670

WILLIAMS, JACK RAYMOND, civil engineer; b. Barberton, Ohio, Mar. 14, 1923; s. Charles Baird and Mary (Dean) W.; m. Mary Berneice Jones, Mar. 5, 1947 (dec.); children: Jacqueline Rae, Drew Alan. Student Colo. Sch. Mines, 1942-43, Purdue U., 1944-45; BS, U. Colo., 1946. Gravity and seismograph engr. Carter Oil Co., Western U.S. and Venezuela, 1946-50; with Rock Island R.R., Chgo., 1950-80, structural designer, asst. to engr. bridges, asst. engr. bridges, 1950-63, engr. bridges system, 1963-80; sr. bridge engr. Thomas K. Dyer Inc., 1980-82; v.p. Alfred Benesch & Co., 1982—. Served with USMCR, 1943-45. Fellow ASCE; mem. Am. Concrete Inst., Am. Ry. Bridge and Bldg. Assn. (past pres.), Am. Ry. Engring. Assn. Home: 293 Minocqua St Park Forest IL 60466 Office: 233 N Michigan Ave Chicago IL 60604

WILLIAMS, JACOB ADELAYO AYELANIMI, geneticist, plant breeder; b. Brass, Nigeria, Aug. 1, 1938; s. Daniel Adetunji and Sybil Munafa (Aprekuma) W.; student Kings Coll., Lagos, Nigeria, 1951-57, Univ. Coll. Ibadan, 1958-62; B.Sc. with honors, U. London, 1962; M.Sc.Hort., U. Calif., Davis, 1966, Ph.D. in Genetics, 1972; m. Abigael Olufemi Elemide, July 22, 1969; children—Adeniyi, Adetunji, Adejoke, Adewole. Sr. sci. master Anglican Grammar Sch., Igbara-Oke, Nigeria, 1962-63; demonstrator dept. botany U. Ife (Nigeria), 1963; research officer Cocoa Research Inst. Nigeria, Ibadan, 1963-68, sr. research officer, 1969-72, prin. research officer, 1972-76, asst. chief research officer, 1976, chief research officer, 1977-78, asst. dir. prodn. and substas., 1978-85; asst. dir. coffee research program, tech. cons. on coffee Standards Orgn. Nigeria, 1985—. Chmn. bd. govs. Ibadan Grammar Sch., 1977-80. Mem. Sci. Assn. Nigeria, W. African Sci. Assn., Agrl. Soc. Nigeria, N.Y. Acad. Scis., Genetics Soc. Nigeria (pres. 1977-78), Sigma Xi. Baptist. Club: Gambari Recreational (Onigambari, Ibadan). Contbr. articles and revs. to sci. jours. Office: PMB 5244, Ibadan Nigeria

WILLIAMS, JAMES HENRY, JR., mechanical engineer, educator, consultant; b. Newport News, Va., Apr. 4, 1941; s. James H. Williams and Margaret L. (Holt) Mithcell; children: James Henry III, Sky Margaret Melodie. Mech. designer (Homer L. Ferguson scholar), Newport News Apprentice Sch., 1965; S.B., MIT, 1967, S.M., 1968; Ph.D., Trinity Coll., Cambridge U., 1970. Sr. design engr. Newport News Shipyard, 1960-70; asst. prof. mech. engring. M.I.T., 1970-74, assoc. prof., 1974-81, prof., 1981—, duPont prof., 1973, Edgerton prof., 1974-76, head, 1974—; cons. engring. to numerous cos. Contbr. numerous articles on stress analysis, vibration, fracture mechanics, composite materials and nondestructive testing to profl. jours. Recipient Charles F. Bailey Bronze medal, 1961, Charles F. Bailey Silver medal, 1962, Charles F. Bailey Gold medal, 1963, Baker award M.I.T., 1973, Den Hartog Disting. Educator award, 1981. Mem. ASME, Am. Soc. Nondestructive Testing, Nat. Tech. Assn. Subspecialties: Theoretical and applied mechanics; Composite materials. Office: 77 Massachusetts Ave Room 3-360 Cambridge MA 02139

WILLIAMS, JAMES MERRILL, microbiologist; b. Grand Forks, N.D., Aug. 6, 1928; s. Merrill Leroy and Bertha M. (Zintel) W.; B.S., U. N.D., 1950; M.S., N.D. State U., 1952; m. Ruth A. Kirby, June 20, 1954; children—Peter J., Todd K. Bacteriologist, Rocky Mountain Lab., Hamilton, Mont., 1952-54, Mont. State Bd. Health, Helena, 1954-56, Anchor Serum Co., St. Joseph, Mo., 1956-58, St. Mary's Hosp., Rhinelander, Wis., 1958-60, Ancker Hosp., St. Paul, 1960-62; dir. biol. control Philips Roxane, 1962-68; dir. bacteriol. research Boehringer Ingelheim Animal Health, Inc., St. Joseph, 1968-78, dir. biol. research, 1978—; affiliate prof. U. Idaho, 1974—. Served with M.C., AUS, 1946-48. Mem. Am. Soc. Microbiology, U.S. Animal Health Assn., Am. Mgmt. Assn. Republican. Methodist. Clubs: Masons, Shriners. Research on staphylococcal mastitis, vibriosis, reproductive, respiratory disease. Patentee brucella canis vaccine. Office: 2621 N Belt St Saint Joseph MO 64502

WILLIAMS, JIMMIE LEE, criminal justice educator, security consultant; b. Joplin, Mo., July 8, 1943; s. Marion Thad and Lefa Ione (Busse) W.; m. Sharon Irene Kendrick, Aug. 1, 1961 (div. Sept. 1974); children—Christine Diane, Barbara Jean; m. Peggy Sue Callahan, Oct. 1, 1975; children—Jimmie Lee II, Patrick Sean, Jennifer Nicole. A.S. in Law Enforcement, Mo. So. State Coll., 1970, B.S., 1974; M.S. in Criminal Justice Adminstrn., Central Mo. State U., 1976. Juvenile officer Joplin Police Dept., 1967-75, 29th Jud. Dist., Joplin, 1975-76; asst. prof. criminal justice Mo. So. State Coll., Joplin, 1976; owner, mgr. Williams Cons. Co., Seneca, Mo., 1982—. Author: (with others) Transportation Security Personnel Training Manual, 3 vols., 1978. Mem. subcom. Handbook for Law Enforcement Officers (Mo. Criminal Code), 1979. Sec.-treas. Seneca Recreation Bd., 1979-84. Served with U.S. Army, 1965-67, Vietnam. Republican. Mem. Reorganized Ch. of Jesus Christ of Latter Day Saints. Club: Seneca Athletic (pres. 1977-78). Home: Rt 2 Box 270 Seneca MO 64865 Office: Mo So State Coll Newman and Duquesne Rds Joplin MO 64801

WILLIAMS, JOHN, guitarist; b. Melbourne, Australia, Apr. 24, 1941. Student Royal Coll. Music, London; studied guitar with father and Segovia at Accad. Chigiana, Siena. Numerous concerts, radio and TV appearances, worldwide; numerous solo records and records with leading orchs.; appeared with Julian Bream, Itzhak Perlman, Cleo Laine, others; founder with Brian Gascoigne The Height Below (ensemble), 1974; mem. group Sky, 1979-85; artistic dir. South Bank Summer Music, 1984-85. Office: care Harold Holt Ltd, 31 Sinclair Rd, London W14 England

WILLIAMS, JOHN TOWNER, composer, conductor; b. Flushing, N.Y., Feb. 8, 1932. Student, UCLA; pvt. studies with, Mario Castelnuovo-Tedesco, Los Angeles; student, Juilliard Sch.; pvt. studies with, Madame Rosina Lhevinne, N.Y.C.; hon. degree, Berklee Coll. Music, Boston, Northeastern U., Boston, Tufts U., U. So. Calif., Boston U., New Eng. Conservatory Music, Providence Coll.; others. Condr. Boston Pops Orch., 1980—. Composer: (film scores) I Passed for White, 1960, Because They're Young, 1960, The Secret Ways, 1961, Bachelor Flat, 1961, Diamond Head, 1962, Gidget Goes to Rome, 1963, The Killers, 1964, John Goldfarb, Please Come Home, 1964, None But the Brave, 1965, How to Steal a Million, 1966, The Rare Breed, 1966, Not With My Wife, You Don't, 1966, The Plainsman, 1966, Penelope, 1966, A Guide for the Married Man, 1967, Valley of the Dolls, 1967 (nominated Acad. award), Fitzwilly, 1968, Sergeant Ryker, 1969, The Reivers, 1969 (nominated Acad. award), Daddy's Gone A-Hunting, 1969, Goodbye Mr. Chips, 1970 (nominated Acad. award), The Story of A Woman, 1970, Fiddler on the Roof (Acad. award for musical adaptation), 1971, The Cowboys, 1972, The Poseidon Adventure, 1972 (nominated Acad. award), Images, 1972 (nominated Acad. award), Pete 'n' Tillie, 1972, The Paper Chase, 1973, The Long Goodbye, 1973, The Man Who Loved Cat Dancing, 1973, Cinderella Liberty, 1973 (nominated Acad. award), Tom Sawyer, 1973 (nominated Acad. award), Sugarland Express, 1974, Earthquake, 1974, The Towering Inferno, 1974, Conrack, 1974, Jaws, 1975 (Acad. award 1976, Grammy award, Golden Globe award), The Eiger Sanction, 1976, Family Plot, 1976, Midway, 1976, The Missouri Breaks, 1976, Raggedy Ann and Andy, 1977, Black Sunday, 1977, Star Wars, 1977 (Acad. award, 3 Grammy awards, Golden Globe award), Close Encounters of the Third Kind, 1977 (2 Grammy awards, nominated Acad. award), The Fury, 1978, Jaws II, 1978, Superman, 1978 (2 Grammy awards), Dracula, 1979, "1941", 1980, The Empire Strikes Back, 1980 (2 Grammy awards, nominated Acad. award), Raiders of the Lost Ark, 1981 (Grammy award, nominated Acad. award), E.T., 1982 (Acad. award for best original score, 3 Grammy awards, Golden Globe award), Monsignor, 1982, Return of the Jedi, 1983 (nominated Acad. award), Indiana Jones and the Temple of Doom, 1984 (nominated Acad. award), The River, 1984 (nominated Acad. award), Space Camp, 1986, The Witches of Eastwick, 1987; composer: (TV programs) Heidi, 1969 (Emmy award), Jane Eyre, 1971 (Emmy award), others; composer numerous concert pieces and symphonies including, Jubilee 350 Fanfare for the Boston Pops, 1980, theme to the 1984 Summer Olympic Games, Liberty Fanfare, 1987; performed numerous record albums with Boston Pops Orch. including Pops in Space, That's Entertainment (Pops on Broadway), Pops on the March, Pops Around the World (Digital Overtures), Aisle Seat, Pops Out of This World, Boston Pops on Stage, America, the Dream Goes On; collaborator: (with Jessye Norman) With A Song in My Heart, Swing, Swing, Swing; guest condr. major orchs. including London Symphony Orch., Cleve. Orch., Phila. Orch., Toronto Orch., Montreal Orch. Served with USAF. Recipient several gold and platinum records Rec. Industry Assn. Am. Address: Triad Artistic Inc 10100 Santa Monica Blvd 16th Floor Los Angeles CA 90067 also: Boston Pops Orch 301 Massachusetts Ave Boston MA 02115

WILLIAMS, JOSEPH DALTON, pharmaceutical company executive; b. Washington, Pa., Aug. 15, 1926; s. Joseph Dalton and Jane (Day) W.; m. Mildred E. Bellaire, June 28, 1973; children: Terri, Daniel. B.Sc. in Pharmacy, U. Nebr., 1950, D.Pharmacy (hon.), 1978; D.H.L., Albany Coll. Pharmacy, Union U., 1980, Rutgers U., 1987; D.Sc. (hon.), Phila. Coll. Pharmacy and Sci., Long Island U., 1988. Pres. Parke-Davis Co., Detroit, 1973-76; pres. pharm. group Warner-Lambert Co., Morris Plains, N.J., 1976-77; pres. Internat. Group, 1977-79; pres., dir. Warner-Lambert Corp., 1979-80, pres., chief operating officer, 1980-84, chief exec. officer, 1985, chmn., 1985—; dir. AT&T, J.C. Penney & Co. Bd. dirs. People to People Health Found.; trustee Columbia U. Served with USNR, 1943-46. Mem. Pharm. Mfrs. Assn., Am. Pharm. Assn., N.J. Pharm. Assn. Clubs: Links (N.Y.C.); Pine Valley (N.J.) Golf; Baltusrol Golf (Springfield, N.J.); Mid Ocean (Bermuda). Office: Warner-Lambert Co 201 Tabor Rd Morris Plains NJ 07950

WILLIAMS, JOSEPH EUGENE, clinical social worker, educator; b. Allentown, Pa., June 13, 1948; s. Joseph Adolph and Cecelia Florence (Zandarski) W. B.A., Moravian Coll., 1970; M.S.W., Ohio State U., 1973. Diplomate Clin. Soc. Work. Asst. youth dir. Allentown YMCA, 1970-71; unit social worker Wiley House, Bethlehem, Pa., 1973-76; adj. prof. Northampton Community Coll., Green Pond, Pa., 1977-83; prof. (part-time) Kutztown State U., Pa., 1979; assoc. prof. (part-time) Moravian Coll., Bethlehem, 1982—; community treatment program supr. Wiley House, 1976—; agy. rep. group case subcom. Community Council, Bethlehem, 1975; mem. Lehigh Valley Ind. Colls. and Social Work Edn., Bethlehem, 1981-82; field instr., Allentown, 1974-81; mem. com. spl. needs adv. Bethlehem Area Votech Ctr., 1984—, chmn., 1988— . Presenter at confs. Bd. rep. coll. union governing bd. and lab. program bds. Moravian Coll. Alumni Bd., 1974-76; vol. Lehigh County Vols. in Probation, Allentown, 1974-76; contbg. mem. Democratic Nat. Com., Washington, 1986. Recipient Outstanding Service award Bucks County Juvenile Ct., Pa., 1984. Mem. Nat. Assn. Social Workers (chmn. program com. 1981), Child Care Assn. of Pa., Acad. Cert. Social Workers (nat. clin. register). Democrat. Unitarian. Avocations: computer telecommunications; amateur radio; writing. Office: Wiley House 1650 Broadway Bethlehem PA 18015

WILLIAMS, KEN MICHAEL, logistics engineer; b. Charleston, W. Va., Mar. 7, 1944; s. R. Don and Ruth Norma (Berg) W.; m. Khanh Thi Tran, July 26, 1973; children: Xali Khanh, Donn Christopher. BA, Ohio State U., 1968; MA, Mich. State U., 1977; AA, Cerritos Coll., 1987. Cert. bus. and indsl. mgmt. tchr., Calif. Commd. U.S. Army, 1968, resigned, 1984; logistics specialist McDonnell Douglas, Long Beach, Calif., 1985; asst. material mgmt. officer Fed. Agy., Long Beach, 1986—; bd. dirs. TFW Scis., Long Beach; pres. Wms. Scis., Westminster, Calif., 1984-88; cons. Success Strategy Tng., Orange, Calif., 1985-88; logistics instr. Cerritos Coll., Norwalk, Calif., 1985—. Bd. dirs. Site Council Clegg Sch., Westminster, 1985—. Recipient Community Service award Camp Zama, 1978; numerous awards U.S. Army, 1968-84. Mem. Soc. Logistics Engrs. (chmn. 1987-88, vice-chmn. ops. 1986-87, newsletter editor 1985-86, chpt. chmn. 1987-88, Award of Excellence 1986, 87, Internat. Lodistics award 1987, Internat. Newsletter award 1987, Pres.' Honor Roll 1986, 87, Soc. Commendation 1987), Am. Prodn. Inventory Control Soc., Retired Officers Assn., VFW. Republican. Methodist. Lodges: Masons, Shriners. Home: 14082 Rondeau #1 Westminster CA 92683 Office: Div Material Mgmt Office 3700 Spring St Long Beach CA 90822

WILLIAMS, KOREN DEBI A., barrister; b. Nassau, New Providence, The Bahamas, Mar. 27, 1958; d. Carleton Winston and Katherina Eunice (Pinder) W.; m. Perry Michael Burrows, Mar. 3, 1987; 1 child, Seve Burrows. BL, U. Buckingham, Eng., 1979; Barrister of Laws, Council Legal Edn., London, 1980; ML, U. Calif., Berkeley, 1981. Bar: Bahamas, 1980. Barrister-at-law Messrs. Isaacs, Bethell, Barnett & Co., Nassau, 1981-82; legal counsel The Grand Bahama Port Authority, Ltd., Freeport Comml. and Indsl. Ltd., Grand Bahama Utility Co., Ltd., Freeport, The Bahamas, 1983-84, The Grand Bahama Devel. Co., Ltd., Freeport, 1983-84, Grand Bahama Airport Co., Ltd., Freeport, 1983-84; barrister-at-law Messrs. Graham, Thompson & Co., Nassau, The Bahamas, 1984-88, Messrs. K.D.A. Williams & Co., Nassau, 1988—; cons. Trade Devel. Bank, Nassau, 1987—. Mem. Bahamas Bar Assn., Hon. Soc. Inner Temple, Links and Friends. Anglican. Home: Eastern Rd, PO Box SS 5301, Nassau, New Providence The Bahamas Office: Messrs KDA Williams & Co, PO Box N10850, Nassau The Bahamas

WILLIAMS, LOUIS BOOTH, college president emeritus; b. Paris, Tex., Oct. 15, 1916; s. William Louis and Maggie Jo (Booth) W.; AA, Paris (Tex.) Jr. Coll., 1935; BBA, U. Tex., 1951; MBA, E. Tex. State U., 1961; LLD (hon.), Tex. Wesleyan U., 1976; m. Mary Lou Newman, Oct. 15, 1938; children: Joanne Williams Click, Louis Booth. Profl. local C. of C. exec., Austin, Navasota and Paris, Tex., 1938-44; mgr. Bireley's Beverages, Denison, Tex., 1946-49; asst. to pres. Paris Jr. Coll., 1949-52; personnel mgr. Paris Works, Babcock & Wilcox Co., 1952-67; pres. Paris Jr. Coll., 1968-83, pres. emeritus, 1983—; dir. Liberty Nat. Bank, Paris, McCuistion Regional Med. Ctr., vice chmn. Served with USNR, lt. comdr. ret. Recipient Silver Beaver award Boy Scouts Am., 1956; Paul Harris fellow Rotary Internat., 1974. Mem. Am. Assn. Community Jr. Colls., Tex. Assn. Colls. and Univs. (pres. 1981), Assn. Tex. Jr. Colls. (pres. 1976), Theta Kappa Omega, Delta Sigma Pi, Phi Theta Kappa (hon.). Democrat. Methodist. Lodge: Rotary (dist. gov. 1985-86). Author: The Organization, Administration and Functions of a Local Chamber of Commerce, 1937. Home: 3170 Laurel Ln Paris TX 75460 Office: Paris Jr Coll Clarksville St Paris TX 75460

WILLIAMS, LUTHER FRANCIS, educator, clergyman; b. Etowah, Tenn., May 14, 1932; s. Frelon Charles and Mattie Lee (Gentry) W.; A.S., Freed Hardeman Coll., 1957; B.S., Tenn. Wesleyan Coll., 1964; M.M. Math., U. S.C., 1967; Ed.D., U. Tenn., 1977; m. Barbara Ann Gibson, July 20, 1950; children—Carol Ann, Patricia Lynn, Barbara Kay. Ordained to ministry Church of Christ, 1951; minister Dublin Ch. of Christ, Ga., 1957-61; tchr. math. Meigs High Sch., Decatur, Tenn., 1961-66; instr. math. Cleveland State Community Coll., Tenn., 1968-74, 75-77, dir. instl. research, 1977-84, asst. dean health and life scis., 1984-87, dir. student info. systems and services, 1987—; minister Central Ch. of Christ, Athens, Tenn., 1969-72, Calhoun, Tenn., 1973-75, Etowah, Tenn., 1976-87. Chmn. bd. dirs. Cleveland State Christian Student Ctr., 1978-82; bd. dirs. Richmond-Tatum Christian Sch., 1979; elder Etowah Ch. of Christ, 1981-87; ednl. dir. Cen. Ch. of Christ, 1988—. Recipient Disting. Service to Edn. award Freed Hardeman Coll., 1984. Mem. E. Tenn. Edn. Assn. (research com. 1985-86), Southeastern Assn. Coll. Researchers, Nat. Council Instructional Adminstrn., Phi Delta Kappa. Republican. Home: Rt 5 Box 1283 Athens TN 37303 Office: PO Box 3570 Cleveland TN 37311

WILLIAMS, MELVIN DONALD, anthropologist, educator; b. Pitts., Feb. 3, 1933; s. Aaron and Gladys Virginia (Barnes) W.; m. Faye Wanda Strawder, June 20, 1958; children: Aaron Ellsworth, Steven Rodney, Craig Haywood. A.B., U. Pitts., 1955, M.A., 1969, Ph.D., 1973. Owner, operator Wholesale Periodical Distbn. Co., Pitts., 1955-66; instr. dept. sociology and anthropology Carlow Coll., 1969-71, asst. prof., 1971-75, chmn. dept. sociology and anthropology, 1973-75; assoc. prof. anthropology U. Pitts., 1976-79, adj. prof., 1979-82; prof. anthropology Purdue U., 1979-83, U. Md., College Park, 1983-88, U. Mich., Ann Arbor, 1988—; Olie B. O'Connor prof. Am. instns. Colgate U., 1976-77. Author: On the Street Where I Lived, Community in a Black Pentecostal Church; editor: Selected Readings in Afro-American Anthropology; contbr. articles to profl. publs. Co-chmn. project area com. Urban Redevel. Authority, Pitts., 1972—; co-dir. interdisciplinary family community project Western Psychiat. Inst. and Clinic, 1973-76; bd. dirs. Cath. Social Service of Allegheny County, Pa., 1973-76. Served with U.S. Army, 1957-58. NSF field tng. fellow in anthropology, 1967; grantee, 1969-72; Community Action Pitts. grantee, 1969-71; Social Sci. Research Council grantee, 1974-75; Lilly Endowment grantee, 1980-83, 85-86; NDEA Title IV fellow, 1969. Fellow Am. Anthrop. Assn.; mem. African Studies Assn., AAAS, AAUP, Am. Sociol. Assn., Assn. Study Afro-Am. Life and History, Soc. for Psychol. Anthropology. Home: 1119 N Lang Ave Pittsburgh PA 15208

WILLIAMS, MILLER, poet, translator; b. Hoxie, Ark., Apr. 8, 1930; s. Ernest Burdette and Ann Jeanette (Miller) W.; m. Lucille Day, Dec. 29, 1951 (div.); m. Rebecca Jordan Hall, Apr. 11, 1969; children: Lucinda, Robert, Karyn. B.S., Ark. State Coll., 1951; M.S., U. Ark., 1952; postgrad., La. State U., 1951, U. Miss., 1957; H.H.D. (hon.), Lander Coll. Instr. in English La. State U., 1962-63, asst. prof., 1964-66; vis. prof. U. Chile, Santiago, 1963-64; assoc. prof. Loyola U., New Orleans, 1966-70; Fulbright prof. Nat. U. Mexico, Mexico City, 1970; co-dir. grad. program in creative writing U. Ark., 1970-84, assoc. prof., 1971-73, prof. English and fgn. langs., dir. program in transl., 1973-87, prof., 1987—, dir. poetry-in-the prisons programs div. continuing edn., 1974-79, chmn. program in comparative lit., 1978-80; dir. U. Ark. Press, 1980—; fellow Am. Acad. in Rome, 1976—, adv. council Sch. Classical Studies, 1985—; first U.S. del. Pan Am. Conf. Univ. Artists and Writers, Concepcion, Chile, 1964; mem. poetry staff Bread Loaf Writers Conf., 1967-72; founder, exec. dir. Ark. Poetry Circuit, 1975. Author: K-2 (poems); A Circle of Stone, 1964, Recital, 1965, So Long At the Fair, 1968, The Only World There Is, 1971; (criticism) The Achievement of John Ciardi, 1968, The Poetry of John Crowe Ransom, 1971; (with John Ciardi) (criticism) How Does a Poem Mean?, 1974; (poems) Halfway From Hoxie: New & Selected Poems, 1973, Why God Permits Evil, 1977, Distractions, 1981, The Boys on Their Bony Mules, 1983; translator: (poems) Poems & Antipoems (Nicanor Parra), 1967, Emergency Poems (Nicanor Parra), 1972, Sonnets of Giuseppe Belli, 1981; editor: (poems) 19 Poetas de Hoy en Los Estados Unidos, 1966, (with John William Corrington) Southern Writing in the Sixties: Poetry, 1967, Southern Writing in the Sixties: Fiction, 1966, Chile: An Anthology of New Writing, 1968, Contemporary Poetry in America, 1972, (with James A. McPherson) Railroad: Trains and Train People in American Culture, 1976, A Roman Collection: An Anthology of Writing about Rome and Italy, 1980, Ozark, Ozark: A Hillside Reader, 1981, (criticism) Patterns of Poetry, 1986, (poetry) Imperfect Love, 1986; poetry editor La. State U. Press, 1966-68; founding editor: (poems) New Orleans Rev, 1968-69; contbg. editor: (poems) Translation Rev, 1978—; contbr. articles to profl. publs. Mem. ACLU. Recipient Henry Bellaman Poetry award, 1957; award in Poetry, Arts Fund, 1973; Prix de Rome, Am. Acad. Arts and Letters, 1976; Bread Loaf fellow in poetry, 1961; Amy Lowell Travelling scholar in poetry, 1963. Mem. MLA, South Central MLA, Am. Lit. Translators Assn. (v.p. 1978-79, pres. 1979-81), PEN, AAUP. Home: 1111 Valley View Dr Fayetteville AR 72701 Office: U Ark Press McIlroy House 201 Ozark St Fayetteville AR 72701

WILLIAMS, NANCY ELLEN-WEBB, social services administrator; b. Quincy, Ill., Aug. 1; d. Charles and Garnet Naomi (Davis) Webb; m. Jesse B. Williams, Apr. 11, 1959; children: Cynthia L. Williams Clay, Troy Andrea Williams Redic, Bernard Peter. BA, Quincy Coll., 1957; postgrad., Tenn. A&I U., 1961; M Pub. Adminstrn., U. Nev., Las Vegas, 1977; LHD (hon.), U. Humanistic Studies, 1986. Cert. peace officer, Nev. (chmn. Standards and Tng. Com., 1978-81). Tchr. Shelby County Tng. Sch., Memphis, 1957-61; dep. probation officer Clark County Juvenile Ct., Las Vegas, 1961-66, supervising probation officer, 1966-74, dir. probation services, 1974-80, dir. intake admissions, 1980-81, dir. Child Haven, 1981—; mem. Nev. Crime Commn., 1970-81. Author: When We Were Colored, 1986, Dinah's Pain and Other Poems of the Black Life Experience, 1988; contbr. poetry to various mags. Mem. exec. com. Clark County Econ. Opportunity Bd., Las Vegas, 1963-71; chmn. So. Nev. Task Force on Corrections, 1974-81; mem. Gov.'s Com. on Justice Standards and Goals, 1979-81; bd. dirs. U. Humanistic Studies, Las Vegas, 1984—. Recipient Friend of the Golden Gloves award Golden Gloves Regional Bd., 1981, Tribute to Black Women award U. Nev., Las Vegas, 1984. Fellow Am. Acad. Neurol. and Orthopedic Surgeons (assoc.); mem. AAUW, Nat. Council Juvenile Ct. Judges, Nat. Writers Assn. Democrat. Office: Child Haven 3401 E Bonanza Rd Las Vegas NV 89101

WILLIAMS, PAUL ROBERT, school system administrator; b. Portsmouth, Ohio, Aug. 30, 1937; s. Jesse Clinton and Lola Ethel (Harden) W.; m. Catherine Wilson, Sept. 4, 1959; children: Jacqueline Joy, John Scott. BS, Taylor U., 1961; MA, Mich. State U., 1969, PhD, 1980. Tchr. Chesaning (Mich.) Union Schs., 1961-70, curriculum coordinator, 1970-74; asst. supt. Durand (Mich.) Area Schs., 1974-75; supt. Caledonia (Mich.) Pub. Schs., 1975-80, Lakeview Sch. Dist., Battle Creek, Mich., 1980—. Contbr. articles to profl. jours. Chmn. Lakeview Downtown Devel. Authority, Battle Creek, Mich., 1983—; mem. exec. bd. Battle Creek Unltd., 1986; pres. Battle Creek Symphony, 1987—, United Way of Greater Battle Creek, 1986; mem. bd. mgrs. Mich. PTA, 1980-87; trustee Winshop Found., Battlecreek, 1986—; bd. dirs. Binder Park Zoo, Battle Creek. Recipient Ednl. Div. award Kent County United Way, 1979, Disting. Service award Mich. PTA, 1985, Campaign Chairperson award United Way of Greater Battle Creek, 1986, Econ. Fund. Devel. award Battle Creek Unltd., 1986. Mem. Mich. Assn. Sch. Adminstrs. (pres. regions 3 and 7 1980-86, governing council 1985—, chmn. interorganization com. 1985—, Service award 1986), Kent County Supt. Assn. (Disting. Service award 1980), Battle Creek C. of C. (bd. dirs. 1984—, vice chair 1987), Mich. State U. Coll. Edn. Alumni Assn. (pres. 1986—). Republican. Methodist. Lodge: Rotary (exec. bd. Battle Creek 1983—, pres.-elect 1988). Home: 256 E Hamilton Ln Battle Creek MI 49015 Office: Lakeview Sch Dist 15 Arbor St Battle Creek MI 49015

WILLIAMS, PAUL WHITCOMB, lawyer; b. Rochester, N.Y., July 12, 1903; s. Henry B. and Lillian Gray (White) W.; m. Minerva Fedyn Sawdon, Aug. 10, 1956. AB magna cum laude, Harvard U., 1925, LLB, 1929; student, Emmanuel Coll., Cambridge (Eng.) U., 1925-26; LLD, New Bedford Inst. Tech., 1958, Southeastern Mass. U., No. Dartmouth, 1975; LHD, Bard Coll., 1975. Bar: N.Y. 1931. Assoc. Cravath, de Gersdorf, Swaine & Wood, 1929-31; assoc. Cahill, Gordon & Reindel, N.Y.C., 1933-39, ptnr., 1939-42, 45-54, 58-77; asst. atty. U.S. Dist. Ct. (so. dist.) N.Y., 1931-33, atty., 1955-58; spl. counsel to Ins. Dept. State N.Y., 1951-52; spl. asst. atty. gen. in charge investigations State of N.Y., Saratoga and Columbia counties, 1952-54; justice Supreme Ct. State of N.Y., 1954; bd. dirs. Sterling Bancorp, Sterling Nat. Bank & Trust Co., N.Y.; chmn. minimum wage bd. Confectionery Industry, N.Y., 1947. Pres. Manhattan council Boy Scouts Am., 1952-56, mem. exec. bd. of Greater N.Y. councils, 1956—, pres., 1962-65, chmn. bd., 1965-67, hon. chmn. bd., 1967-77; chmn. bd. N.Y.C. div. Am. Cancer Soc., 1965-74, chmn. exec. com. nat. orgn., 1975-77, vice chmn. bd., 1977-79; chmn. exec. com. Am. Cancer Soc. Palm Beach Benefit, 1985—; chmn. bd. trustees Bard Coll., 1964-74, life trustee, 1974—; mem. bd. advisors St. Mary's Hosp., Palm Beach, 1985—; N.Y.C. Republican candidate for Congress, 8th N.Y. Dist., 1946. Served as lt. comdr. USNR, 1942-45. Decorated officer Order of Merit (France). Mem. Assn. Bar City N.Y. (chmn. sect. on trials and appeals 1949-51, 58-59, v.p. 1958-59), Harvard Law Sch. Assn. N.Y. (v.p. 1958-59), Pilgrims of U.S., Soc. Colonial Wars (Fla. gov. 1985—), Roundtable Palm Beach (pres. 1986—), N.Y. County Lawyers Assn., Am. Law Inst., Am. Judicature Soc., Inst. Jud. Adminstrn., Am. Bar Found., Am. Coll. Trial Lawyers, ABA, Fed. Bar Assn. (pres. Empire chpt. 1956-58), N.Y. State Bar Assn., Southwestern Legal Found., VFW, S.R. (pres. 1962-64), Mil. Order World Wars, Am. Legion, English Speaking Union, Soc. of the Four Arts, Phi Beta Kappa. Episcopalian. Clubs: Brook, N.Y. Young Rep. (pres. 1936), Harvard U., Univ. (N.Y.C.); Southampton, Shinnecock Hills Golf (Southampton, L.I.); L.I. (pres. 1974-77) (Eastport); Quantuck Beach (L.I.); Anglers (N.Y.); Everglades, Seminole Golf, Bath and Tennis, Old Guard Golfers (Palm Beach, Fla.). Lodge: Masons. Home: 12445 Plantation Ln North Palm Beach FL 33408

WILLIAMS, PHILIP COPELAIN, physician; b. Vicksburg, Miss., Dec. 9, 1917; s. John Oliver and Eva (Copelain) W.; B.S. magna cum laude, Morehouse Coll., 1937; M.D., U. Ill., 1941; m. Constance Shielda Rhetta, May 29, 1943; children—Philip, Susan Carol, Paul Rhetta. Intern, Cook County Hosp., Chgo., 1942-43, resident in ob-gyn, 1946-48; resident in gynecology U. Ill., 1948-49; practice medicine specializing in ob-gyn, Chgo., 1949—; mem. staff St. Joseph Hosp., Augustana Hosp., Cook County Hosp., McGaw Hosp.; clin. prof. Med. Sch. Northwestern U., Chgo. Bd. dirs. Am. Cancer Soc. Chgo. unit and Ill. div. Served with U.S. Army, 1943-45. Recipient Civic award Loyola U., 1970; Edwin S. Hamilton Interstate Teaching award, 1984; diplomate Am. Bd. Ob-Gyn, Fellow ACS, Internat. Coll. Surgeons; mem. AMA, Chgo., Ill. med. socs., AMA, Chgo. Gynecol. Soc. (treas. 1975-78, pres. 1980-81), Am. Fertility Soc., Inst. Medicine, N.Y. Acad. Scis., AAAS. Presbyn. Clubs: Barclay, Carlton, Plaza. Contbr. articles to profl. jours. Home: 1040 N Lake Shore Dr Chicago IL 60611 Office: 200 E 75th St Chicago IL 60619

WILLIAMS, PHILIP EUGENE, missionary, English educator; b. Weatherly, Pa., June 3, 1923; s. Ernest Lester and Edith Estelle (Grimm) W.; m. Mary Edith Tatem, June 28, 1947; children—Carolyn Joy, Edith Gay, Bonnie Tatem. A.B., Franklin and Marshall, 1947; M.Div. magna cum laude, Yale U., 1950; S.T.M., Union Theol. Sem., 1956; Ph.D., U. Pa., 1964. Ordained to ministry United Ch. Christ, 1950. Dir. Yale U. Internat. House, 1949-50; missionary to Japan, United Ch. Christ, N.Y.C., 1950—; prof. English, North Japan U., Sendai, 1958-78; prof. English, Doshisha U., Kyoto, Japan, 1978—; vis. prof. Ryukoku U., Kyoto, 1979—; dir. Nat. Council Chs., Tokyo, 1958-68; adj. prof. Ursinus Coll., 1968-78; vis. prof. Union Theol. Sem., N.Y.C., 1983. Author: Journey into Mission, 1957; Classics in Criticism, 1959; Invitation to American Literature, 1980, Brit. Lit., 1982, Am.Women Writers, 1987; Japan's Neighbor, China, 1982.

Trustee North Japan U., 1957-78, Union Theol. Sem., Tokyo, 1960—, Japan Am. Soc., Sendai, Japan, 1964-78; supr. Princeton Ednl. Testing Service, Sendai, 1969-78. Served with USNR, 1943-46. U. Pa. fellow 1963-64. Mem. MLA, English Lit. Soc. Japan, Am. Studies Assn. Japan, Am. Lit. Soc. Japan. Club: P.E.N. (Japan). Home: 258 Okamatsu-cho, Kami-kyo Ku, Kyoto 602, Japan Office: Doshisha U, Dept English, Kami-kyo Ku, Kyoto 602, Japan

WILLIAMS, PHILLIP WAYNE, securities and diversified company executive, former army officer, consultant; b. Birmingham, Ala., Nov. 1, 1939; s. Louie Alfred and A. Banks (Osborn) W.; (divorced); children—Phillip Wayne, Christopher N.; m. Ramsey Waddell, Mar. 19, 1988. B.S. in Math. and Physics, Florence State Coll. (Ala.), 1961; M. Adminstrv. Sci., U. Ala.-Huntsville, 1977; D. Pub. Adminstrn., Nova U., 1978. Dep. sheriff, Lauderdale County, Florence, 1960-61; commd. 2d lt. U.S. Army, 1961, advanced through grades to lt. col., 1977; served as comdr., staff officer, platoon, co., bn., project mgr. laser designators Redstone Arsenal, Ala., 1973-74, ret., 1982; chmn., pres. COMTEL-South, Inc., Huntsville, Ala., 1982-85, Joint Capital Securities, Inc., Joint Capital Services, cons. Applied Research, Inc., Huntsville, 1983—; cons. def. industries, 1983—. Bd. dirs. Better Bus. Bur. No. Ala., 1985. Decorated Legion of Merit, Bronze Star with V and 5 oak leaf clusters, Air Medal with V and no. 7, Army Commendation medal with V and 3 oak leaf clusters; Vietnam Gallantry Cross with Silver Star, Vietnam Gallantry Cross with Palm, Vietnam Tech. Service Medal 1st Class, Vietnam Honor Medal 1st Class, Vietnam Civic Action Medal. Mem. U.S. Armor Assn., Assn. U.S. Army, Blackhorse Assn., Am. Def. Preparedness Assn. (dir. 1982-84, regional v.p. 1985—), Am. Soc. Pub. Adminstrn. (pres. 1982-84). Office: Joint Capital Services 225 A Holmes Ave Huntsville AL 35801

WILLIAMS, RANDALL ALAN, orthopaedic surgeon; b. Chattanooga, Apr. 7, 1936; s. Fred Madison and Ethelyn (Smtih) W.; student U. Chattanooga, 1954-56; MD, Tulane U., 1960; m. Carol Magendie, Nov. 7, 1986; children: Laura W. Bergeron, E. Kelley. Intern, Charity Hosp., New Orleans, 1960-61, resident in orthopedic surgery, 1961, 63-67; instr. orthopaedic surgery Tulane U. Sch. Medicine, New Orleans, 1967-69, clin. asst. prof. orthopaedic surgery, 1978—; emergency med. advisor Jefferson Parish Sheriff's Office, 1974-86, Jefferson Levee Dist. Police, 1976-80; bd. dirs. Emergency Med. Services of S.E. La., 1978-80; examiner Am. Bd. Cert. in Orthotics and Prosthetics, 1967, 68, 69; NIH co-clinic chief Juvenile Amputee Clinic for U.S. and Can., New Orleans, 1967-73; chief scoliosis clinic Cripped Children's Program, State of La., New Orleans, 1967-73; cons. orthopaedic surgery VA Hosp., Pineville, La., 1967-70, Huey P. Long Charity Hosp., Pineville, 1967-70, Lallie Kemp Charity Hosp., Independence, La., 1967-69; emergency med. advisor Kenner (La.) Police Dept., 1974-86, Jefferson Levee Dist. Police, 1976-80; instr. cardiopulmonary resuscitation Am. Heart Assn. of La., 1977-86. Served with USAF, 1961-63. Diplomate Am. Bd. Orthopaedic Surgery. Fellow A.C.S., Am. Acad. Orthopaedic Surgeons, Internat. Coll. Surgeons; mem. So. Med. Assn., La. Orthopaedic Assn., Mid-Am. Orthopaedic Soc. (charter), North Am. Spine Soc., Greater New Orleans Orthopaedic Soc. Episcopalian. Contbr. articles to profl. jours. Home: 1016 La Fontaine Ocean Springs MS 39564

WILLIAMS, RAYMOND, writer educator; b. Gwent, Wales, Aug. 31, 1921; s. Henry Joseph and Gwendolene (Bird) W.; m. Joyce Mary Dalling, June 16, 1942; children—Merryn, Ederyn, Gwydion. M.A., Trinity Coll., Cambridge U., Litt.D.; D. Litt. (hon.), Open U., U. Wales, U. Kent. Tutor extra-mural dept. Oxford U., 1946-61; fellow Jesus Coll., Cambridge U., 1961—, reader in drama, 1967-74, prof. drama, 1974-83; mem. Arts Council, 1976-78; vis. prof. polit. sci. Stanford U., 1973, Open U., 1975; editor New Thinkers Library, 1962-70, Politics and Letters, 1946-47, May Day Manifesto, 1968. Author: Reading and Criticism, 1950; Drama from Ibsen to Eliot, 1952; Drama in Performance, 1954 (rev. edit. 1968); Culture and Society, 1958; Border Country, 1960; The Long Revolution, 1961; Communications, 1962, 2d edit. 1976; Second Generation, 1964; Modern Tragedy, 1966; Public Inquiry, 1967; Drama from Ibsen to Brecht, 1968; The English Novel from Dickens to Lawrence, 1970; A Letter from the Country, 1971; Orwell, 1971; The Country and the City, 1973; Television: technology and cultural form, 1974; editor: George Orwell, 1975; Keywords, 1976; Maxism and Literature, 1977; The Volunteers, 1978; (with Marie Axton) English Drama: forms and development, 1978; The Fight for Manod, 1979; Politics and Letters, interviews with New Left Review, 1979; Problems in Materialism and Culture, 1980; editor: Contact: the history of human communications, 1981; Culture, 1981; Writing in Society, 1983; Towards 2000, 1983; Loyalties, 1985. Address: Jesus Coll, Cambridge Univ, Cambridge England

WILLIAMS, RICHARD JAMES, food service executive; b. Goliad, Tex., Aug. 19, 1942; s. L. D. and Freida Irene (Watkins) W.; m. Shirley Ann Mihalik, July 11, 1967; children—Kenneth F., Dawn L. A.A., Santa Ana Jr. Coll. (Calif.), 1965. Area mgr. Jack in the Box Restaurant, San Diego, 1972-80; v.p. ops. Franchise Dirs., Inc., Bradley, Ill., 1980-81; area supr. Pizza Hut of Am., Inc., Lombard, Ill., 1981-83; regional dir. of food service Montgomery Ward Co., Chgo., 1983-84, v.p. ops. Golden Bear Restaurants, Mt. Prospect, Ill., 1983-84; franchise area dir. Wendy's Internat., Oakbrook Terrace, Ill., 1984-86; regional mgr. franchise ops. Godfather's Pizza, Inc., 1986—. Author: Anthology of American High School Poetry, 1959. Served with USMC, 1960-72. Decorated Silver Star, Bronze Star. Republican. Mem. Chs. of Christ. Home: 221 Wianno Ln Schaumburg IL 60194 Office: Godfather's Pizza Inc 9140 W Dodge Rd Omaha NE 68114

WILLIAMS, ROBERT STEWART, entertainment company executive; b. Uniontown, Pa., Sept. 10, 1944; s. Jack Christopher and Ann Gertrude Williams; m. Deborah Robertson, Sept. 11, 1975. children: John Christopher, Justin Scott, Whitney Bridget. Student St. John's Sch., Uniontown, Pa. Pres. Republic Personnel Service, Inc., Virginia Beach, Va., 1966-68, Nat. Personnel Services, Inc., Virginia Beach, 1966-69; chmn. bd., chief exec. officer Wil-Var Enterprises, Virginia Beach, 1969-75; pres., chief operating officer Spotlite Entertainment Enterprises, Ltd., N.Y.C., 1975—; pres., chmn. bd. and chief exec. officer Wilholl Communications, Inc., 1980—; chmn. bd., founding mem. P.C. Worldwide, 1982—. Named Theatrical Producer of Yr., 1980; recipient Performance Readers Poll award; named Producer of Yr., Neptune Internat., 1975-76. Republican. Roman Catholic. Home: 184 Laurel Hill Rd Mount Lakes NJ 07046 Office: Spotlite Enterprises Ltd 221 W 57th St New York NY 10019

WILLIAMS, RODNEY THOMAS, environmental engineer, educator; b. Charters Towers, Queensland, Australia, Dec. 21, 1944; s. Thomas and Dorothy (Riley) W.; m. Barbara Mary Henson, Dec. 13, 1969; children: Jeremy Thomas, Menindee Kathleen, Peter Alexander. BCE, U. Queensland, 1966, BSc in Math., 1969; M in Pub. Adminstrn., Calif. State U., Hayward, 1980. Engr. Brisbane City council, Australia, 1966-70; sr. san. engr. East Bay Mcpl. Utility Dist., Calif., 1971-75; dir. Commonwealth Dept. Environment, Canberra, Australia, 1975-76; exec. officer Gt. Barrier Ree Marine Park Authority, Townsville, Australia, 1976-81; environ. officer Queensland Electricity Commn., Brisbane, 1982—. Contbr. articles to profl. jours. Recipient Mgmt. award Commonwealth Govt., 1979. Mem. Inst. of Engrs. (environ. panel), ASCE, Internat. Union for Conservation of Nature (commn. on edn.). Home: 122 Victoria Ave, 4068 Chelmer Queensland Australia Office: Queensland Electricity Commn, PO Box 10, 4001 Brisbane Australia

WILLIAMS, RONALD DOHERTY, lawyer; b. New Haven, Apr. 6, 1927; s. Richard Hugh and Ethel W. (Nelson) W.; m. Laura Costarelli, Aug. 25, 1951; children—Craig F., Ronald D., Ellen A., Jane E. B.A., U. Va., 1951, LL.B., 1954. Bar: Conn. 1954. Assoc., Pullman, Comley, Bradley & Reeves, Bridgeport, Conn., 1954-60, ptnr., 1960—; atty. state trial referee, 1984—; Selectman, Town of Easton (Conn.), 1975-85, justice of the peace, 1977—, town atty., 1985—. v.p. Bridgeport Area Found.; mem. adv. com. U. Bridgeport Law Sch., 1982—; mem. statewide Grievance Com., 1985—. Served with AC, U.S. Army, 1945-46. Fellow Am. Coll. Trial Lawyers; mem. ABA, Conn. Bar Assn. (bd. govs. 1975-78), Bridgeport Bar Assn. (pres. 1975), Conn. Def. Lawyers Assn. (pres. 1984-85), Am. Bd. Trial Advs. Republican. Roman Catholic. Club: Algonquin (Bridgeport). Home: 14 Newman Dr Easton CT 06612 Office: 855 Main St Bridgeport CT 06604

WILLIAMS, RONALD JOHN, electrical engineer, educator; b. Blue Ash, Ohio, Dec. 14, 1927; s. John Wolfe and Ethel Virginia (Scheve) W.; B.S., Okla. A&M Coll., 1949; M.S., Okla. State U., 1963; Ph.D., Tex. A&M U., 1969; m. Patricia Whelan, Aug. 10, 1946; children: Carolyn Virginia (Mrs. Dan Roy Byrne), Eamonn Timothy. Asst. dean applied scis. Del Mar Coll., Corpus Christi, Tex., 1969-71, chmn. engring. tech., 1967-70, prof. engring. tech., 1968—; vis. prof. engring. tech. Tex. A&M U., 1971-72; dir. engring. tech. programs U. Ala., 1985-87; participant World Conf. on Edn. in Applied Engring. and Engring. Tech., Cologne, W.Ger., 1984, Internat. Conf. on Small Computers, Macau, 1985; cons. in field. NSF-Sci. Faculty fellow, 1964-65; named tchr. of year Tex. Jr. Coll., 1969, Piper prof., 1984; AEC trainee, 1965. Mem. IEEE (Centennial Medal 1984), Nat., Tex. (pres. Nueces chpt. 1983-84, chmn. state ethics com. 1984-85) Socs. Profl. Engrs., ACM, Am. Nuclear Soc., ASME, ASCE, AIAA, ISA, AIME, ASEE, ASSE, IIE, SAME, Soc. Mfg. Engrs., Sigma Xi, Eta Kappa Nu, Tau Beta Pi, Tau Alpha Pi. Democrat. Roman Catholic. Home: PO Box 6027 Corpus Christi TX 78466

WILLIAMS, RONALD OSCAR, systems engineer; b. Denver, May 10, 1940; s. Oscar H. and Evelyn (Johnson) W. B.S. in Applied Math., U. Colo. Coll. Engring., 1964, postgrad. U. Colo., U. Denver, George Washington U. Computer programmer Apollo Systems dept., missile and space div. Gen. Electric Co., Kennedy Space Center, Fla., 1965-67, Manned Spacecraft Center, Houston, 1967-68; computer programmer U. Colo., Boulder, 1968-73; computer programmer analyst def. systems div. System Devel. Corp. for NORAD, Colorado Springs, 1974-75; engr. def. systems and command-and-info. systems Martin Marietta Aerospace, Denver, 1976-80; systems engr. space and communications group, def. info. systems div. Hughes Aircraft Co., Englewood, Colo., 1980—. Vol. fireman Clear Lake City (Tex.) Fire Dept., 1968; officer Boulder Emergency Squad, 1969-76, rescue squadman, 1969-76, liaison to cadets, 1971, personnel officer, 1971-76, exec. bd., 1971-76, award of merit, 1971, 72, emergency med. technician 1973—; spl. police officer Boulder Police Dept., 1970-75; spl. dep. sheriff Boulder County Sheriff's Dept., 1970-71; nat. adv. bd. Am. Security Council, 1979—, Coalition of Peace through Strength, 1979—; mem. Republican Nat. Com., Nat. Rep. Senatorial Com. Served with USMCR, 1958-66. Decorated Organized Res. medal; recipient Cost Improvement Program award Hughes Aircraft Co., 1982, Systems Improvement award, 1982, Top Cost Improvement Program award, 1983. Mem. AAAS, Math. Assn. Am., Am. Math. Soc., Soc. Indsl. and Applied Math., AIAA, Armed Forces Communications and Electronics Assn., Assn. Old Crows, Am. Def. Preparedness Assn., Marine Corps Assn., Air Force Assn., Nat. Geog. Soc., Smithsonian Instn. (assoc.), Met. Opera Guild, Colo. Hist. Soc., Hist. Denver, Inc., Historic Boulder, Inc., Denver Art Mus., Denver Botanic Gardens, Denver Mus. Natural History, Denver Zool. Found., Inc., Am. Mensa Ltd., Denver Mile Hi Mensa. Republican. Lutheran. Club: Hour of Power Eagles (Garden Grove, Calif.). Home: 7504 W Quarto Ave Littleton CO 80123-4332 Office: Def Info Systems div Hughes Aircraft Co 8000 E Maplewood Ave Englewood CO 80111-4999

WILLIAMS, RUTH LEE, clinical social worker; b. Dallas, June 24, 1944; d. Carl Woodley and Nancy Ruth (Gardner) W. BA, So. Meth. U., 1966; M Sci.in Social Work, U. Tex., Austin, 1969. Milieu coordinator Starr Commonwealth, Albion, Mich., 1969-73; clin. social worker Katherine Hamilton Mental Health Care, Terre Haute, Ind., 1973-74; clin. social worker, supr. Pikes Peak Mental Health Ctr., Colorado Springs, Colo., 1974-78; pvt. practice social work Colorado Springs, 1978—; pres. Hearthstone Inn, Inc., Colorado Springs, 1978—; practitioner Jin Shin Jyutsu, Colorado Springs, 1978—; pres., bd. dirs. Premier Care (formerly Colorado Springs Mental Health Care Providers Inc.), 1986-87, chmn. quality assurance com., 1987—. Author, editor: From the Kitchen of The Hearthstone Inn, 1981, 2d rev. edit., 1986. Mem. Nat. Registry Health Care Providers in Clin. Social Work (charter mem.), Colo. Soc. Clin. Social Work (editor 1976), Nat. Assn. Soc. Workers (diplomate), Nat. Bd. Social Work Examiners (cert.), Nat. Assn. Ind. Innkeepers, So. Meth. U. Alumni Assn. (life). Home: 11555 Howell Rd Colorado Springs CO 80908 Office: 536 E Uintah Colorado Springs CO 80903

WILLIAMS, SHARON TAYLOR, interior designer; b. Waukegan, Ill., Aug. 23, 1948; d. John Issac and Ruth (Robertson) Williams; B.S. in Bus. Edn. and Interior Design, Western Ill. U., 1970; postgrad. U. Minn., 1975, 79; postgrad. U. Calif., Berkeley. Interior designer masterplan sales and interior design studio Dayton's Dept. Store, St. Paul, 1973-77; owner, pres., dir. interior design The S. Williams Design Group, Mpls., 1977—; mem. faculty dept. applied arts U. Wis.-Stout; mem. faculty U. Calif. pre-college acad. program, 1988—; mfrs. rep. contract and furnishings for instns. Recipient design and sales achievement award Dayton's Dept. Store, 1974. Fellow Internat. Biog. Assn.; mem. Am. Soc. Interior Designers, Mpls. Soc. Fine Arts, Mpls. Inst. Arts, Nat. Assn. Women Bus. Owners, Nat. Assn. Female Execs., Minn. Soc. AIA (interiors com.), Greater Mpls. C. of C., North Suburban C. of C., Alpha Omicron Phi. Methodist.

WILLIAMS, SHIRLEY VIVIEN TERESA BRITTAIN, political party official, research fellow; b. London, July 27, 1930; d. George Gordon and Vera Mary (Brittain) Catlin. M.A., Somerville Coll., Oxford, 1951; postgrad. (Smith-Mundt scholar), Columbia U., 1951-52; D.Ed. (hon.), Council for Nat. Acad. Awards, 1969; D.Polit. Economy (hon.), Leuven U., 1977; Litt.D. (hon.), Radcliffe Coll.-Harvard U., 1978; LL.D. (hon.), U. Leeds, Sheffield U., 1980; Dr.Pol.Econ. (hon.), U. Bath; m. Bernard Williams, July 2, 1955 (dissolved 1974); 1 dau., Rebecca Clare; m. Richard Neustadt, Dec. 19, 1987. M.P. for Hitchin, 1964-74, Hertford and Stevenage, 1974-79, Crosby, 1981-83; minister of state, edn. and sci., 1967-69, Home Office, 1969-70; sec. of state, prices and consumer protection, 1974-76, edn. and sci., 1976-79; paymaster gen., 1976-79; mem. nat. exec. com. Labour party, 1970-81, mem. U.K. Cabinet, 1974-79; pres. Social Democratic Party, 1982—; Godkin lectr. Harvard U., also fellow Inst. Politics, 1979-80; Rede lectr. Cambridge U., 1980; research fellow Policy Studies Inst., London, 1979-85; vis. fellow Nuffield Coll., Oxford, 1968-76; broadcaster Shirley Williams in Conversation, BBC-TV, 1979. Author: Politics Is for People, 1981; A Job To Live, 1985. Chmn. studies of youth unemployment OECD, 1979-83. Mem. Assn. Profl. Execs. Clerical and Computer Staff. Roman Catholic. Author publs. in field. Office: care Social Dem Party, 4 Cowley St, London SW1P 3NB, England

WILLIAMS, THOMAS RICE, bank executive; b. Atlanta, Sept. 14, 1928; s. George K. and Isabel (Rice) W.; m. Loraine Plant, Mar. 18, 1950; children: Janet, Susan, Thomas Rice Jr. B.S. in Indsl. Engring, Ga. Inst. Tech., 1950; M.S. in Indsl. Mgmt, MIT, 1954. Indsl. engr. Dan River Mills, Danville, Va., 1950-53; dir. indsl. engring. Riegel Textile Corp., Ware Shoals, S.C., 1954-59; v.p. Bruce Payne & Assocs., Inc., N.Y.C., 1959-64; asst. to pres. Patchogue-Plymouth Co., N.Y.C., 1964-65; from v.p. to exec. v.p. Nat. City Bank, Cleve., 1965-72; pres. First Nat. Bank Atlanta, 1972-76, chief exec. officer, chmn. bd., 1976-87; pres. First Atlanta Corp. (formerly First Nat. Holding Corp.), 1974-87, chmn. bd., 1976-87; pres. The Wales Group, Inc.; chmn. 1st Wachovia Corp., 1985-87; dir. Eastern Air Lines, Ga. Power, Nat. Service Industries, Inc., Nat. Life Ins. Co., ConAgra, Inc., Bell South Corp., Gerber Alley ; mem. devel. com. MIT Corp. Trustee Atlanta U. Center, 1977—, Alexander-Tharpe Scholarship Fund, 1975-76, Ga. Tech. Found., 1975—, Agnes Scott Coll., 1975-87, Atlanta Arts Alliance, 1976—, Emory U., Scottish Rite Hosp. for Crippled Children, Shepherd Spinal Ctr., So. Ctr. for Internat. Studies, NCCJ; bd. dirs. Fulton County unit Am. Cancer Soc., 1973—, Central Atlanta Progress; treas. United Way Met. Atlanta, 1975-77; adv. bd. Christian Council Met. Atlanta, 1977—; sec., treas. CED, Ala. Shakespeare Festival, Atlanta Music Fesitval Assn., Atlanta Opera Endowment, Inc; chmn. corp. campaign UNCF. Recipient Human Relations award Am. Jewish Com. Inst. of Human Relations, 1980, Atlanta Bus. League award 1987. Mem. Conf. Bd., Atlanta C. of C. (immediate past pres.), Gridiron Soc., Sigma Alpha Epsilon. Episcopalian. Clubs: Rotary (Atlanta) (dir. 1976-79), Capital City (Atlanta) (gov. 1977-80), Piedmont Driving (Atlanta), Commerce (Atlanta) (dir. 1976—, immediate past. pres.), Peachtree Golf (Atlanta); Union (Cleve.); Farmington Country (Charlottesville, Va.). Office: The First Nat Bank of Atlanta 1320 First Atlanta Tower 2 Peachtree St NW Atlanta GA 30383

WILLIAMS, THOMAS STAFFORD CARDINAL, archbishop of Wellington; b. Wellington, N.Z., Mar. 20, 1930; s. Thomas Stafford and Lillian Maude (Kelly) W. S.T.L., Pontifical U. de Propaganda Fide, Rome, 1960; B. Soc. Sc., Nat. U. of Ireland (Dublin), 1962; ordained priest Roman Catholic Ch., 1959; Archbishop of Wellington, 1979—; elevated to Sacred Coll. Cardinals, 1983.

WILLIAMS, TYLER EDWARD, JR., government official; b. Chgo., July 10, 1926; s. Tyler Edward and Anne (Salmon) W.; BS, Ill. Inst. Tech., 1951, MS, 1956; MEd, U. Va., 1972; postgrad. U. Iowa; m. Frances M. Reif, Aug. 27, 1949; children: Tyler Edward III, Michael, Thomas, Margaret, Gerard, Joseph (dec.), John, Mary Frances. Dept. supr. Oscar Mayer & Co., Chgo., 1949-52; indsl. engr. Am. Gage & Machine Co., Chgo., 1952-54; sr. indsl. engr. Bendix Aviation Corp., Davenport, Iowa, 1954-55; engr., engring. exec. Ordnance Corps, U.S. Army, Rock Island Arsenal, Ill., 1955-63, Office Sec., Commerce Dept., Washington, 1963-65, Office Comptroller Army, Army Dept., 1965-70, Safeguard System Office, Hdqrs. Army Dept., 1971-73; asst. dir. facilities and logistics Office Dep. Asst. Sec. Def., 1973-75; asst. controller, bd. govs. FRS, 1975-77; Office Asst. Sec. Conservation and Renewable Energy Dept. Energy, Washington, 1977-87; dir. instl. conservation program Designers and Planners, Arlington, Va., 1987—; professorial lectr. George Washington U. Commr., Fairfax County (Va.) Econ. Devel. Authority, 1975-83. Served from seaman to capt. USNR, 1944—. Registered profl. engr., Ind.; Fed. Mid-Career fellow U. Va., 1970-71. Mem. AAAS, Am. Soc. Mil. Comptrollers, Am. Soc. Engring. Edn., Assn. Energy Economists, U.S. Naval Inst. Contbr. articles to profl. and tech. jours. Home: 3312 Prince William Dr Mantua Hills Fairfax VA 22031 Office: Office Asst Sec Conservation and Renewable Energy US Dept Energy CE-231 Washington DC 20585

WILLIAMS, WALTER BAKER, mortgage banker; b. Seattle, May 12, 1921; s. William Walter and Anna Leland (Baker) W.; m. Marie Davis Wilson, July 6, 1945; children: Kathryn Williams-Mullins, Marcia Frances Williams Swanson, Bruce Wilson, Wendy Susan. BA, U. Wash., 1943; JD, Harvard U., 1948. With Bogle & Gates, Seattle, 1948-63, ptnr., 1960-63; pres. Continental Inc., Seattle, 1963—; bd. dirs. United Graphics Inc., Seattle, 1973-86, Fed. Nat. Mortgage Assn., 1976-77. Rep. Wash. State Ho. of Reps., Olympia, 1961-63; sen. Wash. State Senate, Olympia, 1963-71; chmn. Econ. Devel. Council of Puget Sound, Seattle, 1981-82; pres. Japan-Am. Soc. of Seattle, 1971-72; chmn. Woodland Park Zoo Commn., Seattle, 1984-85. Served to capt. USMC, 1942-46, PTO. Recipient Brotherhood Citation, NCCJ, Seattle, 1980. Mem. Mortgage Bankers Assn. of Am. (pres. 1973-74), Wash. Mortgage Bankers Assn. Republican. Congregationalist. Club: Rainier (pres. 1987-88) (Seattle). Lodge: Rotary (pres. local club 1984-85).

WILLIAMS, WALTER FRED, steel company executive; b. Upland, Pa., Feb. 7, 1929; s. Walter James and Florence (Stott) W.; m. Joan B. Carey, Aug. 26, 1950; children—Jeffrey F., Richard C., Douglas E. B.Civil Engring. summa cum laude, U. Del., 1951; postgrad., Harvard, 1969; D (hon.), Allentown Coll., 1983. With Bethlehem Steel Corp., Pa., 1951—, asst. chief engr. on staff v.p. operations, 1965-66, chief engr. constrn., 1966-67, chief engr. projects group engring. dept., then mgr. engring. in charge projects, design and constrn., 1967-68, asst. to v.p. engring., 1968, asst. v.p. shipbldg., 1968-70, v.p. shipbldg., 1970-75, v.p. steel operations, 1975-77, sr. v.p. steel operations, 1978-80, pres., chief operating officer, 1980-85, chmn., chief exec. officer, 1986—, also dir. Served to 1st lt. U.S. Army, 1951-53. Mem. Am. Iron and Steel Inst. (bd. dirs.), Nat. Assn. Mfrs. (bd. dirs.), Bus. Roundtable, Internat. Iron and Steel Inst. (bd. dirs.)., Conf. Bd. Methodist. Clubs: Saucon Valley Country (Bethlehem). Home: Saucon Valley Rd 4 Bethlehem PA 18015 Office: Bethlehem Steel Corp 8th Eaton Aves Bethlehem PA 18016

WILLIAMS, WALTER RANDOLPH, insurance executive; b. Cairo, Ill., May 20, 1939; s. Randolph and Catherine (White) W.; student U. Philippines, 1957-59; B.A., Chgo. Tchrs. Coll., 1964; postgrad. Coll. Fin. Planning., 1981—; m. Lisa R., Mar. 31, 1978; children—Walter R. Jr., Lorian E., J. Arthur, Shareeff J. Counselor, Chgo. Bd. Edn., 1965-68; sales rep. Met. Life, 1967-68; dist. mgr. Nat. Research Cons., Skokie, Ill., 1968-72; dist. mgr. Family Life, Wilmette, Ill., 1972-78; mktg. dir. Multi-Fin. Corp., Chgo., 1982-84, Capitol Life, others; exec. sales dir. Am. Bankers Life, Miami, Fla., 1983-84; regional v.p. Am. Investors Life Ins. Co., Chgo., 1984—; investment instr. Cosmopolitan C. of C., 1979-82; pres. Multi-Lines Fin., 1985—; fin. writer Chgo. Citizens News, 1983—; mem. econ. adv. bd. Kennedy-King Coll., Chgo., 1985—; regional dir. Mortgage Services Div. Inc., 1986—; cons. in field. Chmn., Ill. House Ins. Com. on Red-Lining-Rate Fixing, 1979. Served with USAF, 1956-59. Recipient Spl. award. Chgo. Jaycees, 1979. Mem. Nat. Assn. Term Life Underwriters, Internat. Life Ins. Assn., Internat. Assn. Fin. Planners. Club: Sno-Gophers Ski. Contbr. articles to profl. jours.; fin. editor Chgo. Mahogany Mag., 1980-81.

WILLIAMS, WILLIAM JOSEPH, insurance company executive; b. Cin., Dec. 19, 1915; s. Charles Finn and Elizabeth (Ryan) W.; m. Helen DeCourcy, May 26, 1941; children—Mary Frances Williams Clauder, William Joseph, Richard Francis, Carol Ann Williams Jodar, Sharon Mary Williams Frisbie, Thomas Luke. AB, Georgetown U., 1937; postgrad. in bus., Harvard U., 1938. With Western-So. Life Ins. Co., Cin., 1939-54, chmn. bd., 1979-84, pres., 1984—, now also chief operating officer, bd. dirs.; pres. N.Am. Mgmt. & Devel. Co., Cin., 1954-84; chmn. Cin. Reds Baseball Club, 1966-85; dir. Cin. Bengals, Columbus Mut. Ins., Ohio. Chmn. bd. Good Samaritan Hosp., Cin., 1984-86, Taft Mus., Cin., 1984-87; trustee, v.p. Cin. Art Mus.; trustee Cin. Inst. Fine Arts, Children's Home Cin.; bd. dirs. Georgetown U. Served to capt. U.S. Army, 1941-45. Decorated knight Order Knights of Malta, knight comdr. Holy Sepulchre; honored by NCCJ, 1979. Roman Catholic. Clubs: Queen City (pres. 1982-84), Commercial (pres. 1983), Cin. Country (Cin.); Camargo; Royal Poinciana Golf (Naples, Fla.). Home: 7801 Ayres Rd Cincinnati OH 45230 Office: Western & So Life Ins Co 400 Broadway Cincinnati OH 45202 *

WILLIAMS, WINTON HUGH, civil engineer; b. Tampa, Fla., Feb. 14, 1920; s. Herbert DeMain and Alice (Grant) W.; grad. Adj Gens. Sch., Gainesville, Fla., 1943; student U. Tampa, 1948; grad. Transp. Sch., Ft. Eustis, Va., 1949; B.C.E., U. Fla., 1959; grad. Command and Gen. Staff Coll., Ft. Levenworth, Kans., 1964, Engrs. Sch., Ft. Belvoir, 1965, Indsl. Coll. Armed Forces, Washington, 1966, Logistics Mgmt. Center, Ft. Lee, Va., 1972; m. Elizabeth Walser Seelye, Dec. 18, 1949; children—Jan, Dick, Bill, Ann. Constrn. engr. air fields C.E., U.S. Army, McCoy AFB, Fla., 1959-61, Homestead AFB, Miami, Fla., 1961-62; civil engr. C.E., Jacksonville (Fla.) Dist. Office, 1962-64, chief master planning and layout sect., mil. br., engring. div., 1964-70; chief master planning and real estate div. Hdqrs. U.S. Army So. Command, Ft. Amador, C.Z., 1970-75, spl. asst. planning and mil. constrn. programming Marine Corps Air Bases Eastern Area, Marine Corps Air Sta., Cherry Point, N.C., 1975-82; cons. engr., Morehead City, N.C., 1982—. Mem. Morehead City Planning Bd., 1982—; active Boy Scouts, C.Z.; mem. nat. council U. Tampa. Served with AUS, World War II, Korean War; ETO, Korea; col. Res. Decorated Breast Order of Yun Hi (Republic of China); presdl. citation, Meritorious Service medal (Republic of Korea); eagle scout with gold palm; registered profl. engr., Fla., N.C., C.Z. Fellow ASCE; mem. Res. Officers Assn. (life, v.p. C.Am. and S.Am.), Nat. Soc. Profl. Engrs., Profl. Engrs. N.C., Am. Soc. Photogrammetry, Prestressed Concrete Inst. (profl.), Soc. Am. Mil. Engrs. (engr.), Nat. Eagle Scout Assn., Nat. Rifle Assn. Am., Am. Legion (life), Order Arrow, Theta Chi. Presbyterian. Lion. Clubs: Fort Clayton Riding (pres.), Fort Clayton Golf, Gamboa Golf and Country, Balboa Gun, Am. Bowling Congress. Home and Office: 4408 Coral Point Dr Morehead City NC 28557

WILLIAMSON, EVANGELINE FLOANN, vocational rehabilitation corporate executive; b. Ft. Wayne, Ind., Nov. 29, 1934; d. David Samuel and Anna Florence (Baker) McNelly; m. Clark Murray Williamson, Dec. 20, 1957 (div. 1964); 1 child, Dawn Valerie (dec.). BA with distinction Transylvania U., 1956. Asst. dir. publs. ABA, Chgo., 1958-66; pres., owner Herringshaw-Smith, Inc., Chgo., 1966-77; internal cons. Monarch Printing Corp., Chgo., 1978-80, Callaghan & Co., Wilmette, Ill., 1980-82; v.p., co-owner Career Evaluation Systems, Inc., Chgo., 1983—; bd. dirs. MarTech Enterprises, Chgo. Author: From Typist to Typesetter, 1978; editor: Transylvania: Tutor to the West (John Wright), 1975; editor, designer: Silvermiths, Jewelers, Clock and Watchmakers of Kentucky, 1785-1900 (Marquis Boultinghouse), 1980; speaker in field; contbr. articles to profl. jours. Bd. dirs., treas. West Central Assn., Chgo., 1976-77; bd. dirs. Martha

Washington Hosp., Chgo., 1975-76, Mary Thompson Hosp., Chgo., 1977. Named to Nat. Disting. Registry in Med. and Vocat. Rehab., 1987. Mem. Am. Voc. Assn., Nat. Rehab. Assn., Am. Assn. for Counseling and Devel., World Future Soc., Niles C. of C. Republican. Mem. Christian Ch. Avocations: antique clock and furniture collecting, writing. Office: Career Evaluation Systems Inc 6050 W Touhy Ave Chicago IL 60648

WILLIAMSON, FLETCHER PHILLIPS, real estate broker; b. Cambridge, Md., Dec. 16, 1923; s. William Fletcher and Florence M. (Phillips) W.; student U. Md., 1941, 42; m. Betty June (Stoker), Apr. 6, 1943; 1 son, Jeffrey Phillips; m. 2d, Helen M. Stumberg, Aug. 28, 1972. Test engr. Engring. Lab., Glen Martin Co., 1942-43; salesman Corkran Ice Cream Co., Cambridge, 1946-50; real estate broker, 1950—; chmn. bd. Williamson Real Estate, Dorchester Corp., 1963-72; bd. dirs. WCEM, Inc., 1966-75; vice chmn. bd., dir. Nat. Bank of Cambridge, 1979—; dir. Cam-Storage Inc., Dorchester Indsl. Devel. Corp., Delmarva Bank Data Processing Ctr.; co-receiver White & Nelson, Inc. Bd. dirs. Delmarva council Boy Scouts Am.; past pres. Cambridge Hosp., United Fund of Dorchester County; bd. dirs. Del. Mus. Natural History, Dorchester County Pub. Library; bd. dirs., v.p. Game Conservation Internat. Served as ordnance tech. intelligence engr. AUS, 1943-46; ETO. Mem. Md. Real Estate Assn. (gov. 1956-66), Outdoor Writers Assn., Nat. Rifle Assn., Nat. Def. Preparedness Assn., Cambridge Dorchester C. of C. (dir. 1955—), Power Squadron (comdr. 1954-56), Dorchester County Bd. Realtors (pres.), Explorers Club, Soc. of S. Pole. Methodist. Clubs: Rolling Rock, Shikar Safari, Anglers, Chesapeake Bay Yacht, Camp Fire, Md., Georgetown. Lodges: Masons, Shriners.

WILLIAMSON, JOHN GLOVER, obstetrician and gynecologist; b. Belfast, No. Ireland, July 4, 1939; s. Richard John and Esther Charlotte (Glover) W.; m. Madeline Ruth Langford, Sept. 6, 1969; children—Anna, Richard, Katharine. B.A., Trinity Coll., 1963, M.A., 1967, M.A.O., 1971. House physician and surgeon Royal City of Dublin Hosp., 1963-64; registrar in gen. surgery Meath Hosp., Dublin, 1966-67; registrar in obstetrics and gynecology Rotunda Hosp., Dublin, 1969-70; sr. registrar in obstetrics and gynecology John Radcliffe Hosp., Oxford, Eng., 1971-75; assoc. lectr. clin. medicine Cambridge U., 1976—; cons. obstetrician and gynecologist Addenbrookes Hosp., Cambridge, 1976—; chmn. obstetrics com. Cambridge Health Dist., 1976-80; MB examiner Cambridge U., 1977—; dir. urodynamic assessment clinic Addenbrookes Hosp., 1978—, coordinator infertility service, 1983—, mem. med. exec. com., 1984—. Contbr. articles to profl. jours. Inventor med. instrument. Biggar Meml. scholar, 1960. Fellow Royal Coll. Obstetricians and Gynecologists, Royal Soc. Medicine (v.p.); mem. Gynecol. Vis. Soc. G.B. and Ireland, Cambridge Med. Soc., Internat. Continence Soc., Brit. Fertility Soc. Mem. Ch. of Eng. Clubs: Apothecaries Soc. Lodge: Rotary. Avocations: tennis; golf; gardening. Home: 8 Chaucer Rd, Cambridge CB2 2EB, England Office: Addenbrookes Hosp, Dept Gynecology, Level 2, Cambridge England

WILLIAMSON, JUANITA V., English educator; b. Shelby, Miss.; d. John M. and Alice E. (McAllister) W. BA, LeMoyne-Owen Coll., 1938; MA, Atlanta U., 1940; PhD, U. Mich., 1961. Asst. prof. English LeMoyne-Owen Coll., Memphis, 1947-56, prof., 1956—, Disting. Service prof., 1980; adj. prof. Memphis State U., 1975—, linguist, summer 1969, 73, 75; vis. prof. Ball State U., Muncie, Ind., 1963-64, U. Tenn., Knoxville, summer 1975; vis. prof. U. Wis., Milw., summer 73, linguist, summer 1966-67; linguist French Inst. Atlanta U., summer 1963, Hampton (Va.) Inst., summer 1964, U. Ark., Pine Bluff, summer 1981. Editor: A Various Language, 1971; contbr. articles to profl. jours. Mem. exec. com. United Way, Memphis, 1953-56; cons. Girl Scouts U.S., Memphis, 1956; bd. dirs. Integration Service, Memphis, 1952-58; mem. exec. com. hist. council United Ch. Christ, 1976. Recipient citation for excellence in edn. Memphis City Council, 1973; fellow Rockefeller Found., 1949-51, Ford Found., 1954; HEW grantee, 1964-68. Mem. MLA (program com., minority affairs com.), Nat. Council Tchrs. English (coll. sect. exec. com. 1976-79), Am. Dialect Soc. (exec. com. 1979-82), Conf. on Coll. Composition and Communication (exec. com. 1969-71), Delta Sigma Theta. Home: 1217 Cannon St Memphis TN 38106 Office: LeMoyne-Owen Coll 807 Walker Ave Memphis TN 38126

WILLIAMSON, NEIL SEYMOUR, III, aircraft company executive, retired Army officer; b. Dumont, N.J., Jan. 5, 1935; s. Neil Seymour and Mary Louise (Bittenbender) W.; m. Sue Carrole Cooper, Dec. 15, 1985; children: Deborah D., Leisa L., Neil S. IV, Dirk A., Wendy L. BS, U.S. Mil. Acad., 1958; MSME, U. Mich., 1963. Commd. 2d lt. U.S. Army, 1958, advanced through grades to col.; assoc. prof. dept. earth, space and graphic scis. U.S. Mil. Acad., West Point, N.Y., 1965-68; chief edn. sect. U.S. Army, Ft. McNair, D.C., 1970-71; analyst armor infantry systems group Pentagon U.S. Army, Washington, 1972-73, systems analyst requirements office Pentagon, 1974-75, program analyst, 1975-76; chief advanced systems concept office U.S. Army, Redstone Arsenal, Ala., 1976-77; comdr., dir. fire control & small caliber weapon systems lab. U.S. Army, Dover, N.J., 1977-78; project mgr. TOW U.S. Army, Redstone Arsenal, 1978-81; ret. U.S. Army, 1981; program mgr. Hughes Aircraft Co., El Segundo, Calif., 1981—. Decorated Bronze Star with one oak leaf cluster, Legion of Merit with one oak leaf cluster, Air medal with seven oak leaf clusters, Purple Heart. Mem. Soc. Automotive Engrs., Am. Def. Prepardness Assn., Army Aviation Assn. (pres. Tenn. Valley chpt. 1980), Am. Helicopter Soc., U.S. Armor Assn., Disabled Am. Vets. Office: Hughes Aircraft Co PO Box 902 El Segundo CA 90245

WILLIAMSON, NICOL, actor; b. Hamilton, Scotland, Sept. 14, 1938; s. Hugh and Mary (Storrie) W.; m. K. Jill Townsend, July 17, 1971 (div. 1977); 1 son. Student, Central Grammar Sch., Birmingham, Eng. Appeared with Dundee Repertory Theatre, 1960-61, Royal Ct. tour in Arden of Faversham, 1961, That's Us; joined Royal Shakespeare Co., 1962; appeared in Nil Carborundum, The Lower Depths, Women Beware Women, Ginger Man, London, 1963, A Cuckoo in the Nest, 1963, Waiting for Godot, London, 1964, Inadmissible Evidence (N.Y. Drama Critics award), London, N.Y.C., 1964-65, 81 (Evening Standard award), Diary of a Madman, London, 1967, Hamlet, London, N.Y.C., 1968-69, Uncle Vanya, 1971, Corialanus, 1973, Nicol Williamson's Late Show, 1973, Midwinter Spring, 1973-74, Twelfth Night, 1974-75, Macbeth, 1974, 82, also TV film, 1982; plays Rex, 1976, The Entertainer, N.Y.C., 1983, The Real Thing, 1985; dir. (plays) The Lark, Edmonton, Ont., Can., 1983; motion pictures include Six-Sided Triangle, Inadmissible Evidence, 1967, The Bofors Gun, 1967, Laughter in the Dark, 1968, The Reckoning, 1968, Hamlet, 1969 (Evening Standard Drama award), Jerusalem File, 1972, Black Widow, 1987; appeared in TV prodn. Arturo VI, 1972, I Know What I Meant, 1974, The Wilby Conspiracy, 1974, Robin and Marion, 1975, The Seven-Per-Cent-Solution, 1975, The Goodbye Girl, 1977, The Cheap Detective, 1978, The Human Factor, 1979, Excalibur, 1980, Venom, 1980, I'm Dancing as Fast as I Can, 1981, Christopher Columbus, 1985, Return to Oz, 1984, Lord Mountbatten-The Last Viceroy, 1984. also: care ICM, 388-396, Oxford W1X 3LD, England *

WILLIAMSON, STEPHEN VICTOR, state official; b. Tulare, Calif., May 20, 1950; s. Grady Edgar and June Bernice (Gragg) W. B.A., U. Calif.-Davis, 1971. Sr. coordinator U. Calif. Statewide Student Body Presidents Council-Student Lobby, 1971-73; cons. budget div. Calif. Dept. Fin., 1973-74, Systems Research Inc., Los Angeles, 1974-76, Calif. Research, Sacramento, Calif., 1976-78; dir. Calif. State Clearinghouse, Gov.'s Office Planning and Research, Sacramento, 1978-82; exec. com. State EDP Policy, 1983-84; mgr. info. systems Calif. Housing Fin. Agy., Sacramento, 1983-84; sr. mgr., mgmt. cons. Price Waterhouse, 1984—. Mem. Assn. Environ. Profls. (Achievement of Yr. award 1982), Assn. for Computing Machinery, Data Processing Mgmt. Assn., Assn. Systems Mgmt., Am. Soc. Pub. Adminstrs. (Sacramento chpt. exec. bd.), Chi Phi. Office: Price Waterhouse 455 Capitol Mall Sacramento CA 95814

WILLIAMSON, VIKKI LYN, finance executive; b. Huntington, W.Va., June 30, 1956; d. Ernest E. and Wanda C. (Cole) W. BA in Secondary Edn., English, Temple U., 1978; postgrad. in Acctg. and Fin., U. Cin., 1984—. CPA, Ohio; cert. tchr., Tenn., Ohio. Tchr. Springfield Christian Acad., Tenn., 1978-79; acctg. asst. Children's Hosp. Med. Ctr., Cin., 1979-84; asst. dir. fin. services U. Cin. Med. Ctr., 1984-85, dir. fin. services, 1985-88, dir. fin. and adminstrn., 1988—; instr. Miami U., Oxford, Ohio, 1984—; bd. dirs. Contemporary Dance Theatre, 1987—. Mem. Healthcare Fin. Mgmt. Assn., Am. Assn. Blood Banks, Ohio Assn. Blood Banks (fin. com. mem. 1986—), Assn. Women Adminstrs. (fin. com. mem. 1987—), U. Cin. Assn. Mid-Level Adminstrs. (bd. dirs. 1987—), Am. Inst. CPA's, Alpha Epsilon Theta, Beta Gamma Sigma, Delta Mu Delta. Office: U Cin Med Ctr Hoxworth Blood Ctr 3231 Burnet Ave ML #55 Cincinnati OH 45267

WILLIE, CAROLYN SYLVIA, microcomputer consultant, market research analyst; b. Camden, N.J., Mar. 23, 1941; arrived in Australia, 1982; d. Thomas Lamont and Carolyn (Woodmansee) Wilson; m. Roy Emil Willie Jr., Dec. 29, 1962. BA, U. Utah, 1963; MBA, U. B.C., Vancouver, Can., 1971. Research asst. Utah Dept. Health, Salt Lake City, 1963-65; mgr. dept. statis. research Blue Cross/Blue Shield, Salt Lake City, 1965-69; project dir. Opportunity Rehab. Workshop, Vancouver, 1971-72; asst. project dir. McDonald Research Assocs., Vancouver, 1972-73; research analyst B.C. Cen. Credit Unions, Vancouver, 1973-74; cons. U. B.C., 1974-79; project mgr. Market Facts, Brisbane, Queensland, Australia, 1982-84; cons. microsystems and mktg. to pvt. and govt. orgns., Brisbane, 1984—; exec. dir. Cinderbeach P/L, Brisbane, 1985—; lectr. dept. info. systems Queensland Inst. Tech., Brisbane, 1986—. Mem. Market Research Soc. Australia, Brisbane Combined Ashton-Tate Users Group, Lotus Users Group, Brisbane 16 Bit Computer Users Group, (founding pres.), Nat. Assn. Tng. Disabled in Office Work (hon. sec.). Clubs: Carawah Women's (charter); Bluewater Cruising Assn. (Vancouver). Avocations: amateur radio, sailing, orchids. Home and Office: 114 Mountjoy Terr, Manly, Brisbane Queensland 4179, Australia

WILLIG, BILLY WINSTON, metal processing executive; b. Temple, Tex., Mar. 11, 1929; s. Bruno William and Mary Sophia (Barth) W.; m. Lanelle Clyde Brooks, Sept. 11, 1951; children: Bruce Wayne, Jana Lynn. BS in Mech. Engring., U. Tex., 1951. Pres. Western Iron Works, San Angelo, Tex., 1950—; Bd. dirs. San Angelo Industries, Inc., pres. 1975-80; pres., bd. dirs. West Tex. Indsl. Devel. Corp., 1980—. Mem. Nat. Council Boy Scouts Am., pres. Area IV 1980-83; v.p. S. Cen. Region, 1984-87; nat. rep. Boy Scouts Am., 1986—; mem. adv. bd. Salvation Army, 1979—, chmn. 1984; v.p. Dist. VI Area PTA, 1983-85, sec. 1986-87; v.p. West Tex. C. of C., 1984-85; mem. Hwy. 87 Improvement com., 1983—, pres., 1983-88; bd. dirs. YMCA, 1977—, pres. 1980-82, exec. com. 1983—; chmn., bd. dirs. city council adv. com. San Angelo Pub. Housing Authority, 1985—, chmn. 1988—; chmn. Concho Valley Pvt. Industry Council, 1982—; trustee San Angelo Ind. Sch. Dist., 1966-84; trustee Tex. Assn. Sch. Bds., 1975-84, sec.-treas. 1982-83, bd. dirs. Tex. Sch. Services Found., 1982-84, chmn. Unemployment Compensation Trust, 1982-84. Recipient Silver Antelope award Boy Scouts Am., 1988. Recipient Silver Beaver award Boy Scouts Am., 1976; named Ex-Student of Yr., Angelo State U., 1984. Mem. Am. Foundrymen's Soc., Tex. Assn. Pvt. Industry Councils (bd. dirs. 1984—), San Angelo Mfrs. Assn. (pres. 1981—), Angelo State U. Ex-Students Assn. (bd. dirs. 1983-87, v.p. 1985-86, pres. 1986-87), San Angelo C. of C. (pres. 1978, mil. affairs. com. 1984—, chmn. hwy. com. 1986-87, Citizen of Yr. 1979). Presbyterian. Club: Concho Yacht (commodore 1969). Lodge: Rotary. (pres. 1980). Home: 1618 Shafter San Angelo TX 76901 Office: Western Iron Works Inc 21 E State St San Angelo TX 76903

WILLINGHAM, MARY MAXINE, fashion retailer; b. Childress, Tex., Sept. 12, 1928; d. Charles Bryan and Mary (Bohannon) McCollum; m. Welborn Kiefer Willingham, Aug. 14, 1950; children—Sharon, Douglas, Sheila. B.A., Tex. Tech U., 1949. Interviewer Univ. Placement Service, Tex. Tech U., Lubbock, 1964-69; owner, mgr., buyer Maxine's Accent, Lubbock, 1969—; speaker in field. Leader Campfire Girls, Lubbock, 1964-65; sec. Community Theatre, Lubbock, 1962-64. Named Outstanding Mcht., Fashion Retailor mag., 1971, Outstanding Retailer; recipient Golden Sun award Dallas Market, May 1985. Mem. Lubbock Symphony Guild, Ranch and Heritage Ctr. Club: Faculty Women's. Office: 10 Briercroft Ctr Lubbock TX 79412

WILLIS, GLENN HARRY, oil company executive; b. Magnolia, Ark., Apr. 18, 1922; s. Bernard B. and Irene (Thornton) W.; m. Louise McKinney, May 11, 1948; children: Stephen, Susan, Mary Lynn, Glenda. Oil buyer Standard Oil of Ind., New Orleans, 1950-55; oil buyer Clark Oil & Refining Corp., Dallas, 1955-56, v.p. crude oil supply and transp. dept., 1966-76; v.p., dir. Intercontinental Petroleum Corp., Inc., Dallas, 1976-77; pres., dir. Dorchester Petroleum Co., Dallas, 1977—, Dorchester Refining Co., Dallas, 1977—, Dorchester Pipeline Co., Dallas, 1977—, Dorchester Gas Corp., Dallas, 1977—; pres., chmn. bd. Dor-Texan Petroleum, Inc., 1981-86; exec. v.p. Clark Maritime, Inc.; pres. Am. Shield Refining Co., 1987—; bd. dirs. Southcap Pipeline Co., Chgo. Pipeline Co., Clark Pipeline Co., Arabian Shield Devel. Co. Active precinct worker Dem. party, 1956—. Served with AUS, 1940-45. Decorated Combat Infantryman's badge. Mem. Am. Inst. Mining Engrs. Clubs: Petroleum of Dallas, Dallas Athletic, Austin (Tex.). Home: 11084 Erhard Dr Dallas TX 75228 Office: 12700 Park Cental Dr Suite 415 Dallas TX 75251

WILLIS, HAROLD WENDT, SR., real estate developer; b. Marion, Ala., Oct. 7, 1927; s. Robert James and Della (Wendt) W.; student Loma Linda U., 1960, various courses San Bernardino Valley Coll.; m. Patsy Gay Bacon, Aug. 2, 1947 (div. Jan. 1975); children: Harold Wendt II, Timothy Gay, April Ann, Brian Tad, Suzanne Gail; m. Vernette Jacobson Osborne, Mar. 30, 1980 (div. 1984); m. Ofelia Alvarez, Sept. 23, 1984; children: Ryran Robert, Samantha Ofelia. Ptnr., Victoria Guernsey, San Bernardino, Calif., 1950-63, co-pres., 1963-74, pres., 1974—; owner Quik-Save, 1966—, K-Mart Shopping Ctr., San Bernardino, 1969—; pres. Energy Delivery Systems, Food and Fuel, Inc. San Bernardino City water commr., 1965—. Bd. councillors Loma Linda (Calif.) U., 1968-85, pres., 1971-74. Served as officer U.S. Mcht. Marine, 1945-46. Recipient Silver medal in 3000 meter steeplechase Sr. Olympics, U. So. Calif., 1979, 81, 82, 83; lic. pvt. pilot. Mem. Calif. Dairy Industries Assn. (pres. 1963, 64), Liga Internat. (2d v.p. 1978, pres. 1982, 83). Seventh-day Adventist (deacon 1950-67). Office: PO Box 5607 San Bernardino CA 92412

WILLIS, ISAAC, dermatologist, educator; b. Albany, Ga., July 13, 1940; s. R.L. and Susie M. (Miller) W.; m. Alliene Horne, June 12, 1965; children—Isaac Horne, Alliric Isaac. B.S., Morehouse Coll., 1961; M.D., Howard U., 1965. Diplomate: Am. Bd. Dermatology. Intern Phila. Gen. Hosp., 1965-66; fellow Howard U., Washington, 1966-67; resident, fellow U. Pa., Phila., 1967-69, assoc. in dermatology, 1969-70; instr. dept. dermatology U. Calif.-San Francisco, 1970-72; asst. prof. Johns Hopkins U. and Johns Hopkins Hosp., Balt., 1972-73, Emory U., Atlanta, 1973-77, assoc. prof., 1977-82; prof. Morehouse Sch. Medicine, Atlanta, 1982—; attending staff Phila. Gen. Hosp., 1969-70, Moffit Hosp., U. Calif., 1970-72, Johns Hopkins Hosp., Balt. City Hosp., Good Samaritan Hosp., 1972-74, Crawford W. Long Meml. Hosp., Atlanta, 1974—, West Paces Ferry Hosp., 1974—, others.; mem. grants rev. panel EPA, 1986—; mem. gen. medicine group IA study sect. NIH, 1985—; cons. in field; bd. dirs. Heritage Bank, Comml. Bank of Ga., chmn. audit com., 1988—. Served to col. USAR, 1983—. EPA grantee, 1985—. Author: Textbook of Dermatology, 1971—; Contbr. articles to profl. jours. Chmn. bd. med. dirs. Lupus Erythematosus Found., Atlanta, 1975-83; bd. dirs. Jacquelyn McClure Lupus Erythematosus Clinic, 1982—; bd. med. dirs. Skin Cancer Found., 1980—; trustee Friendship Bapt. Ch., Atlanta, 1980—. Nat. Cancer Inst. grantee, 1974-77, 78—; EPA grantee, 1980—, 82—. Fellow Am. Acad. Dermatolgy, Am. Dermtol. Assn.; mem. Soc. Investigative Dermatology, Am. Fedn. Clin. Research, AAAS, Am. Soc. Photobiology, Am. Med. Assn., Nat. Med. Assn., Internat. Soc. Tropical Dermatology, Pan Am. Med. Assn., Phi Beta Kappa, Omicron Delta Kappa. Clubs: Frontiers Internat., Sportsman Internat. Subspecialties: Dermatology; Cancer research (medicine). Office: NW Med Ctr Suite 342 3280 Howell Mill Rd NW Atlanta GA 30327 Home: 1141 Regency Rd NW Atlanta GA 30327

WILLIS, JERRY WELDON, educator; b. Tuscumbia, Ala., Jan. 27, 1943; s. Elbert Carter and Lavice Mae (McAlpin) W.; m. Dee Anna Smith, Mar. 28, 1987; 1 dau., Amy Elizabeth. B.A., Union U., 1966; Ph.D., U. Ala., 1970. Asst. prof. U. Guelph (Ont., Can.), 1972-74; asst. prof. U. Western Ont., London, 1974-76; asst. prof. U. B.C. (Can.), Vancouver, 1976-78; prof. edn. Tex. Tech U., Lubbock, 1978-87; dean Edn. and Home Econs. Miss. U. for Women, 1987-88; prof. and program coordinator Instrnl. Tech.-Ednl. Computing, E. Carolina U. Sch. of Edn., 1988—; pres. Willis Pub. Group. Mem. Am. Psychol. Assn., Assn. Ednl. Data Systems, Assn. Devel. of Computer Based Instructional Systems. Author: Peanut Butter and Jelly Guide to Computers, 1978 (Outstanding Computer Book, Am. Library Jour.); Nailing Jelly to a Tree, 1981; Computers for Everybody, 1981 (Outstanding Computer Book, Am. Library Jour.); Computers for People, 1982; Computers, Teaching and Learning, 1983; The Essential Commodore 128 User's Guide, 1986; The Essential Atari ST User's Guide, 1986; Super Calc 3: Learning, Mastering, and Using, 1986; Using Super Calc 4, 1987; Desktop Publishing with your IBM PC and Compatible, 1987; Educational Computing: An Introduction, 1986; Computer Simulations: A Guide to Educational Applications, 1986; also 24 other books and transls. in 8 langs. Home: 1704 E Sixth St Greenville NC 27858 Office: E Carolina Univ Sch of Edn Greenville NC 27858

WILLIS, JOHN FRISTOE, concertmaster, optometrist; b. St. Louis, Jan. 27, 1910; s. Prior Fristoe and Elva Cora (Moss) W.; m. Alice Alvana Overbay, Aug. 31, 1943; 1 child, John Thomas. AB, Washington U., St. Louis, 1932, postgrad., 1934; postgrad. U. So. Calif., 1939, Am. Conservatory Music, Chgo., 1952-55; OD, No. Ill. Coll. Optometry, 1948. violinist-soloist, Stas. KWK/WIL/KSD/KMOX, St. Louis, 1927-32; supr. music Prosser, (Wash.) Public Schs., 1935-36; prof. violin Fla. State Sch. for Deaf and Blind, 1937; violin soloist So. Calif. Symphony Orch., 1939, concertmaster, 1939-41; concertmaster Albert Coates Grand Opera Symphony, Los Angeles, 1939; pvt. practice optometry, Villa Park, Ill., 1955—. Violin soloist Chgo. Bus. Men's Symphony, 1956-61, 71-72, concertmaster, 1956—. Chmn. Save Our Sight program Lions Club, Villa Park, 1971, 75. Bd. dirs. Chgo. Bus. Men's Orch., 1972. Served with USNR, 1942-45. Recipient Albert Coates Masterly Violinist award, 1939. Mem. Am. Optometric Assn., Ill. Optometric Assn., VFW, SAR, Tau Kappa Epsilon. Lodge: Lions (chmn. scholarship com. 1985, 86, 87, 88, dir. 1984—, mem. fin. com. 1983-84, 85, 86, 87, 88) (Villa Park). Home: 106 E Kenilworth St Box 255 Villa Park IL 60181

WILLIS, JOHN PATRICK, chemist; b. Albany, N.Y., Mar. 10, 1947; s. John James and Mary Catherine (Varden) W.; B.S., Iona Coll., 1969; M.S., SUNY, Oswego, 1974; Ph.D., U. Conn., 1977; m. Tientje Jane Dirzuweit, July 22, 1972. Assoc. prodn. chemist Winthrop Labs., Rensselaer, N.Y., 1970-72; research chemist Uniroyal, Inc., Middlebury, Conn., 1977-79; postdoctoral researcher U. Minn., Mpls., 1979-80; mgr. chem. research Nova Biomed. Corp., Newton, Mass., 1980-83; founder, chmn. Ilex Corp., Marlboro, Mass., 1983-87; med. cons., 1987-88; founder T.J. Assocs., Biomed. Cons., Harvard, Mass., 1987—; v.p., chief operating officer Radiometer Am. Inc., Westlake, Ohio, 1988—. U. Conn. Research Found. fellow, 1976. Mem. adv. bd. Clin Lab. Practice, Mass. Dept. Pub. Health, 1986-87, 128 Entrepreneurs' Ctr., Waltham, Mass., 1986-88; . Fellow Am. Inst. Chemists; mem. Am. Chem. Soc., Electrochem. Soc., Am. Assn. Clin. Chemistry, N.Y. Acad. Scis., Sigma XI, Phi Kappa Phi, Phi Lambda Upsilon. Democrat. Roman Catholic. Research in bioelectrochemistry and organic electrochemistry; patentee in field.

WILLIS, LOUISE MCKINNEY, retired petroleum company executive; b. Cooper, Tex., Nov. 12, 1924; d. Charles Martin and Birdie Floy (Griffin) McKinney; m. Glenn Harry Willis, May 7, 1948; children: Stephen Eric, Susan Renee, Mary Lynn, Glenda Ann. Student U. Okla., 1946-47. Instrument repair technician Tinker Field AFB, Okla., 1943-46; transit check clk. Fed. Res. Bank, Oklahoma City, 1948-50; sec. Southwestern Power Co., Tulsa, 1950-51, U.S. Govt. Agy., New Orleans, 1951-53; dist. mgr. World Book Encyclopedia, Dallas, 1972-78; v.p. Dor-Texan Petroleum, Inc., Dallas, 1980-87, ret., 1987. Mem. Dallas Opera Guild, 1984-85; pres. Dallas PTA, 1965-66, hon. life mem., 1975—; pres. St. Andrews Study Club, Dallas, 1968-69, 87-88; chmn. Cotillion Park Bd., Dallas, 1964-66. Mem. Dallas C. of C. Baptist. Clubs: Petroleum, Dallas Athletic. Lodge: Order of Rainbow Girls (chmn. bd. dirs. 1973-76).

WILLMETH, ROGER EARL, lawyer; b. Atchison, Kans., Apr. 24, 1946; s. Marion Clair and Virginia Rosemary (Bryant) W.; m. Janice Hazel Matthews, Apr. 14, 1973; children: Jennifer Lynn, Melissa Anne. Student No. Ill. U., 1964-65, DePaul U., 1965-67; J.D., John Marshall Law Sch., Chgo., 1970. Bar: Ill. 1970, U.S. Ct. Mil. Appeals 1971, U.S. Ct. Appeals (9th cir.) 1978, Guam 1979, U.S. Dist. Ct. Guam, 1979, U.S. Supreme Ct. 1979, U.S. Dist. Ct. (cen. dist.) Ill. 1979. Asst. atty. gen. Territory of Guam, Agana, 1977-79, State of Ill., Springfield, 1979-81; gen. atty. 375th Air Base Group, U.S. Air Force, Scott AFB, Ill., 1981-84, atty., adviser communications command, 1984—; spl. asst. U.S. atty. So. Dist. Ill., 1983-84. Bd. dirs. Country Lake Estates Owners Assn. Served to capt. JAGC, USAF, 1970-77, lt. col. with USAF Res. Decorated Air Force Commendation medal; recipient Am. Jurisprudence award, 1970; Award of Excellence for Civil Litigation, Guam Atty. Gen., 1979; Outstanding Civilian Atty. of Yr. award Mil. Airlift Command, 1982, Air Force Civilian Meritorious Service Medal, 1984. Mem. Guam Bar Assn., U.S. Tennis Assn. Methodist. Club: St. Clair Tennis (O'Fallon, Ill.). Home: Rural Rt 4 #4 S Mulberry Rd Collinsville IL 62234 Office: HQ Air Force Communications/JA Scott AFB IL 62225

WILLMORE, LARRY NEAL, economist; b. Norfolk, Nebr., Mar. 14, 1944; s. Richard Lawrence and Nelda Elaine (Watson) W.; m. Ligia Maria Quiros-Paniagua, Nov. 8, 1976; children—Christopher, Andrew. B.A. in History, U. Nebr., 1968; M.A. in Internat. Affairs, Carleton U., Ottawa, Ont., Can., 1970, M.A. in Econs., 1971, Ph.D. in Econs., 1977. Vis. prof. U. Costa Rica, 1973-74; lectr. Carleton U., 1974-75; economist Govt. Can., Ottawa, 1975-77, Govt. Costa Rica, 1977-78; economist UN Econ. Commn. for Latin Am. and Caribbean, Santiago, Chile, 1978-82, Brasilia, Brazil, 1983-87, Mexico City, Mex., 1988—. Author: Market Structure, Firm Size and Brazilian Exports, 1985; also numerous articles in acad. jours. Paterson fellow Carleton U. Sch. Internat. Affairs, 1969; Queen Elizabeth II scholar Govt. of Ont., 1972; Can. Council fellow, 1972; thesis research grantee Internat. Devel. Research Centre, 1972. Mem. Am. Econ. Assn., Econometric Soc., Sociedade Brasileira de Econometria. Home: Loma de Vista Hermosa 343, 05100 Mexico City Mexico Office: UN Econ Commn for Latin Am and Caribbean, Apartado Postal 6-718, 06600 Mexico City Mexico

WILLMOTT, PETER, sociologist; b. Oxford, Eng., Sept. 18, 1923; s. Benjamin Merriman and Dorothy (Waymouth) W.; m. Phyllis Noble, July 31, 1948; children: Lewis, Michael. BSc in Sociology, London U., 1959. Researcher Inst. Community Studies, London, 1954-64, co-dir., 1964-78; dir. Centre for Environ. Studies, London, 1978-80; head cen. policy unit Greater London Council, 1981-83; sr. fellow Policy Studies Inst., London, 1983—; vis. prof. London Sch. Econs., U. London, 1983—. Author: (with others) Family and Kinship in East London, 1953, The Symmetrical Family, 1973; author: Social Networks, 1986, Friendship Networks, 1987. Mem. British Sociol. Assn. Office: Policy Studies Inst, 100 Park Village E, London NW1 3SR, England

WILLOCH, KÅRE, former prime minister of Norway; b. Oslo, Oct. 3, 1928; s. Haakon and Agnes (Saure) W.; grad. in Econs., U. Oslo, 1953; LL.D. (hon.), St. Olaf Coll., Minn., 1982; m. Anne Marie Jörgensen, 1954; 3 children. Counsellor, Fedn. Norwegian Industries, 1954-63; mem. Oslo City Council, 52-59; mem. Storting (Norwegian Parliament), 1957—, chmn. Conservative Party Group in Storting, 1970-81; minister of Trade and Shipping, 1963, 65-70; sec.-gen. Conservative Party, 1963-65, chmn., 1970-74; prime minister of Norway, 1981-86; mem. Nordic Council, 1970-86, pres., 1973; past mem. Norwegian del. to UN Gen. Assembly; chmn. Internat. Dem. Union, 1987—. Office: Hoyre, Stortingsgt 20, 0161 Oslo 1 Norway

WILLOUR, DAVID ROGER, banker; b. Wooster, Ohio, Feb. 28, 1939; s. Paul and Anabel (Clouse) W.; m. Judith Ann Fulcomer, Sept. 8, 1962; children: Geoffrey Thomas Lee, Douglas Dean. AB, Coll. Wooster, 1961; MBA, U. Pa., 1964; diploma Nat. Grad. Trust Sch., 1972. Corp. trust adminstr. Cen. Nat. Bank, Cleve., 1964-69; trust officer, then asst. v.p. Equibank N.A., Pitts., 1969-74; asst. v.p. Mellon Bank, N.A., Pitts., 1974-78, v.p., 1978-84, head trust employee benefit adminstrv. div., 1980, head new trust product devel. div., 1982, head trust mktg. and new ventures, 1983; v.p., head instnl. and employee benefits dept. Conn. Bank and Trust Co., Hartford, 1984-87, managing v.p., head instnl. fiduciary div., 1986—; also lectr. civic groups, bus. assns. profl. confs. Author papers in field. Vestryman, sec., chmn. fin. com. Fox Chapel (Pa.) Episcopal Ch., 1974-78; vestryman, chmn. membership com. St. John's Ch., West Hartford, 1988; active Pitts. Campaign for Wooster Coll. Mem. Am. Bankers Assn., Wharton Grad. Sch. Alumni Assn., Stock Transfer Assn. Cleve., Stock

Transfer Assn. Pitts., Estate Planning Council Pitts., Greater Pitts. Employee Benefit Council (vice chmn. 1977-82), Corp. Fiduciaries Assn. Western Pa. , Estate and Bus. Planning Council of Hartford, Conn., Assn. MBA Execs. Republican. Clubs: Cleve. Athletic, Rotary (Hartford) ; University, 514 (Pitts.); Hartford. Home: 44 Brenway Dr West Hartford CT 06117 Office: Conn Bank and Trust Co One Constitution Plaza Hartford CT 06115

WILMAN, HUGH, information technologist; b. North Wembley, Middlesex, Eng., Mar. 9, 1935; s. William Eric and Phyllis Prichard (Jones) W.; m. Anita Joy Evelyn Phillips, July 22, 1961; children: Judith Amanda, Bridget Elizabeth. Diploma in Elec. Engring., Northampton Coll. Advanced Tech., London, 1960; Diploma in Music, Middlesex Poly., 1979. Devel. engr. Standard Telephones & Communications, London, 1956-58; mathematician, telecommunications engr. Elliott Bros., Borehamwood, Herts, Eng., 1958-61; instrumentation engr. Unilever, London, 1961-65; tech. info. officer Instn. Elec. Engrs., London, 1965-71, head, library and info. services, 1971-75; phys. scis. and tech. specialist British Library, London, 1975-79, project innovator info. and reprographics tech., 1979—. Co-inventor digital book scanners, book photocopier and closed book copier for fragile books; patentee; contbr. articles to profl. jours. Mem. Instn. Elec. Engrs., Inst. Info. Scientists, British Computer Soc., Soc. Imaging Sci and Tech. Home: 76 Mount Grace Rd, Potters Bar, Herts EN6 1QZ, England Office: British Library, Great Russell St, London WC1B 3DG, England

WILMER, HARRY ARON, psychiatrist; b. New Orleans, Mar. 5, 1917; s. Harry Aron and Leona (Schlenker) W.; B.S., U. Minn., 1938, M.B., 1940, M.S., 1940, M.D., 1941, Ph.D., 1944; m. Jane Harris, Oct. 31, 1944; children—Harry, John, Thomas, James, Mary. Intern, Gorgas Hosp., Ancon, C.Z., 1940-41; resident in neurology and psychiatry Mayo Clinic, Rochester, Minn., 1945-49, cons. in psychiatry, 1957-58; physician Palo Alto (Calif.) Clinic, 1949-51; pvt. practice medicine, Palo Alto, 1951-55, 1958-64; prof. psychiatry U. Calif. Med. Sch., San Francisco, 1964-69; sr. psychiatrist Scott & White Clinic, Temple, Tex., 1969-74; prof. psychiatry U. Tex. Health Sci. Ctr., San Antonio, 1974-87; mem. staff Audie Murphy VA Hosp., San Antonio, part-time 1974-82; founder, dir. Internat. Film Festivals on Culture and Psychiatry, U. Tex. Health Sci. Center, 1972-80; founder, pres., dir. Inst. Humanities, Salado, Tex., 1980—; practice medicine, specializing in psychiatry, Salado, Tex., 1982—. Served to capt. M.C., USNR, 1955-57. Guggenheim fellow, Zurich, 1969-70; NRC fellow, Johns Hopkins Hosp., 1944-45. Fellow Am. Psychiat. Assn. (life, emeritus), Am. Coll. Psychiatrists, Am. Acad. Psychoanalysis; mem. AAAS, Internat. Assn. Analytical Psychology. Author: Huber the Tuber, 1942; Corky the Killer, 1945; This is Your World, 1952; Social Psychiatry in Action, 1958; First Book for the Mind, 1963; Vietnam in Remission, 1985, Practical Jung, 1987; (film) People Need People, 1961, Facing Evil, 1988. Home: 506 S Ridge Rd Mill Creek Salado TX 76571

WILMOT, ROBERT WILLIAM (ROBB WILMOT), business executive, electrical engineer; b. Jan. 2, 1945; s. Thomas Arthur William Wilmot and Frances Mary Hull; m. Mary Josephine Sharkey, 1969; 2 sons. BSc in Electrical Engring., Nottingham (Eng.) U., DSc (hon.), 1983. With Tex. Instruments, 1966-81; European tech. dir. Tex. Instruments, France, 1973-74; div. dir. USA Tex. Instruments, 1974-78, mng. dir., 1978-81, asst. v.p., 1980; mng. dir. Internat. Computers, 1981-83, chief exec., 1983-84, chmn., 1985; chmn. Wilmot Enterprises Ltd., 1984—; founder, co-chmn. Silicon Structures, ES2, 1985—; founder, chmn. Orgn. and System Innovations Ltd., OASIS, 1986—; founder, bd. dirs. MOVID Inc., 1987—; bd. dirs. Octagon Industries Ltd.; ptnr. Euroventurer U.K. and Ireland Program, 1987—; council mem. Ctr. of Bus. Strategy, London Bus. Sch. Decorated CBE, 1985. Office: The White House, Bolney Rd Lower Shiplake, Henley-on-Thames, Oxford RG9 3PA, England *

WILMOTH, GEOFFREY DAVID, civil servant, city planner; b. Bundaberg, Queensland, Australia, Nov. 4, 1946; s. Geoffrey Reginald and Norma Gordon (Ferrier) W.; m. Jill Lang, Feb. 14, 1970 (div. Feb. 1979); m. Vivian Kwang-Wen Lin, Sept. 14, 1979. Grad., Choate Sch., Eng., 1965; B in Econs. with 1st class honors, U. Queensland, 1969; M in Town and County Planning, U. Sydney, 1972; PhD in City and Regional Planning, U. Calif., 1983. Researcher Urbsearch Pty. Ltd., Sydney, 1968-69; geographer Clarke, Gazzard Planners Pty. Ltd., Gold Coast, Queensland, 1969-70; project mgr. Urban Systems Corp., Sydney, 1972-73; dir. strategy div. Australian Dept. Urban and Regional Devel., Canberra, 1973-75; dir. regional devel. div. Australian Dept. Nat. Devel., Canberra, 1978; lectr. San Francisco State U., 1978-80; head cen. policy div. New South Wales Dept. Environ. and Planning, 1982-86, head planning div., 1986—; gov. Planning Research Ctr., Sydney, 1982—; mem. Hunter Devel. Bd. Newcastle, New South Wales, Australia, 1984-86; chmn. Illawarra Planning Com., Wollongong, 1987—, Kosciusko Planning and Devel. Com., 1987—. Contbr. articles to profl. jours. Honors scholar U. Queensland, 1969. Mem. Australian Inst. Urban Studies (councilor 1984—, chmn. New South Wales br., 1985-86, chmn. internat. com., 1987—). Home: 80 Phillip St, Balmain Sydney New South Wales 2041, Australia Office: Dept Planning, 175 Liverpool St, Sydney New South Wales 2001, Australia

WILMS, HENRI ROGER, sales executive; b. Antwerp, Belgium, July 5, 1960; arrived in Switzerland, 1984; s. Jean Jacques Louis and Rosemarie (Fuchs) W.; m. Brigitte Lüönd; children: Patricia, Daria. LSA, St.-Henricus, Antwerp, Belgium; HTS, Don Bosco, Hoboken, Belgium. Sales supr. Landre & Glinderman, Antwerp, Belgium, 1980-84; service supr. Peyer Ag, Wollerau, Switzerland, 1985-86; sales mgr. Spectralab, Kilchberg, Switzerland, 1986—. Home: Turmmatt, CH-6418 Rothenthurm Switzerland Office: Spectralab, Brunnenmoosstr 7, 8802 Kilchberg Switzerland

WILMSHURST, MARTIN NEVILLE, restaurateur; b. Exeter, Devon, Eng., June 23, 1946; s. Neville Vincent and Dorothy Margaret (Bark) W.; m. Rita Iñes Marquez, Jan. 11, 1986; 1 child, Martin Ricardo. Grad., Truro Pub. Sch., Cornwall, Eng. Diploma in Hotel Mgmt. Purser Merchant Navy, Eng., 1964-73; coach courier Centralian Tours, Australia, 1973-74; caterer Deniliquin, Australia, 1974-77; camp and catering mgr. Queensland, Sodexho, Australia, 1977-81; camp specialist Bechtel Internat., Jubail, Saudi Arabia, 1982-83; catering mgr. Bechtel Internat., Ok Tedi, Papua, New Guinea, 1983-84; project mgr. catering Sodexho, Sheagum, Saudi Arabia, 1984-85; project mgr. Albert Abela, Colombia, S.Am., 1985-87; proprietor Incredible Edibles Restaurant, Deniliquin, 1987—. Justice of Peace New South Wales Justice Dept., Australia, 1980. Fellow Catering Inst. Australia; mem. Brit. Inst. Mgmt., Hotel Catering Institutional Mgmt. Assn., Deniliquin C. of C. (sec. 1977). Mem. Liberal Party. Mem. Ch. of Eng. Club: Dramatic (pres. 1977-78). Lodge: Lions (pres. Deniliquin chpt. 1976-77) (pres. Ok Tedi chpt. 1984). Home: 403 Harfleur St, Box 850, Deniliquin, New South Wales 2710, Australia Office: Incredible Edibles, 81 Hardinge St, Deniliquin, New South Wales 2710, Australia

WILSON, ABRAHAM, lawyer; b. Zhitomir, Ukraine, Nov. 19, 1922; came to U.S., 1923; s. Isaac and Katie (Garshoig) W.; m. Gloria Bachman, July 26, 1949 (div. Dec. 1965); 1 child, Chana; m. Christine Haftkowycz, July 23, 1966; children—Marko A., Raissa. B.S., Rutgers U., 1947, M.S. in Chemistry, 1950; Ph.D. in Chemistry, 1951; J.D. cum laude, Seton Hall U., 1974. Bar: N.J. 1974, U.S. Dist. Ct. N.J. 1974, (so. dist, ea. dist) N.Y. U.S. Patent Office 1975, U.S. Supreme Ct. 1984. Sr. scientist Colgate Palmolive Co., Jersey City, 1951-55; group leader phys. chem. research Am. Cyanamid Co., Bound Brook, N.J., 1955-56; counsel, asst. to pres. TPCO, Inc., South Brunswick, N.J., 1974-76; sole practice, Piscataway, N.J., 1976-86; ptnr., Sherman, Kuhn, Justin & Wilson, 1986—; instr. physical chemistry Rutgers U., 1951-56; gen. counsel Enzon, Inc., South Plainfield, N.J., 1981-87, outside counsel, 1987—. Patentee in field. Councilman Borough Govt., Millstone, N.J., 1959-61, mayor, 1962-64; bd. dirs. Piscataway Community TV Authority, 1986-88, chmn. 1986-88, Raritan Valley ARC, 1986—; mem. mayor's dept. Piscataway environ. commn., 1988—. Served as 2d lt. USAF, 1943-46, PTO. Recipient Sr. Research award Am. Cyanamid Co.; fellow Imperial Coll. Sci. Tech., London, 1961-62. Mem. Am. Chem. Soc., N.J. Bar Assn., N.J. Patent Bar Assn., Middlesex County Bar Assn., Am. Intellectual Property Assn. Democrat. Jewish. Office: Sherman Kuhn Justin & Wilson Raritan Ctr Plaza 1 Box 6315 Edison NJ 08818

WILSON, ALEXANDER MURRAY, retired mining company executive; b. Tulare, Calif., May 17, 1922; s. Alexander Murray and Grace (Creech) W.; m. Beverlee Elayne Forsblad, Jan. 4, 1948; children—Shelley, Kristin, Alexis. B.S. in Metall. Engring., U. Calif., Berkeley, 1948. With Bradley Mining Co., Stibnite, Idaho, 1948-51, Molybdenum Corp. Am., Nipton, Calif., 1951-54; with Utah Internat. Inc., San Francisco, 1954-87, pres., 1971-79, chief exec. officer, 1978-87, chmn. bd. dirs., 1979-87; mem. Kaiser Aluminum Retirement com., Internat. Adv. Bd., SRI; bd. dirs. The Clarkson Co., Fireman's Fund Corp. Bd. dirs. Smith-Kettlewell Eye Research Found. Served with AUS, 1944-46. Mem. Mining and Metall Soc. Am., Soc. Mining Engrs. Office: 550 California St San Francisco CA 94104

WILSON, ALVIN FREDERICK, automotive engr.; b. Cambridge, Ohio, June 6, 1929; s. Freeman D. and Phyllis R. (McGaughlin) W.; B.S.E., Ohio State U., 1952; 1 son, Kevin P. With Chrysler Corp., Detroit, 1952-69; with U.S. Suzuki Motor Corp., Brea, Calif., 1969—, then nat. mgr. consumer affairs and product liability litigation; now dir. legal div. Am. Suzuki Motor Corp. Mem. Soc. Automotive Engrs., Motorcycle Industry Council, Sporting Goods Mfrs. Assn. Calif., Def. Research Inst. Office: care Suzuki Motor Corp 3251 E Imperial Brea CA 92621

WILSON, SIR ANGUS (FRANK JOHNSTONE), writer, professor emeritus; b. Eng., Aug. 11, 1913; s. William Frederick and Maud Ellen (Caney) W. Grad., Westminster Sch., Oxford (Eng.) U.; LittD, U. Leicester (Eng.), 1977, U. East Anglia (Eng.) and U. Liverpool, 1979, U. Sussex, 1981, U. Sorbonne, 1984. Dep. supt. reading room British Mus.; vis. prof., lectr. various Am. Univs., U.K. Fgn. Service (Intelligence), 1942-45; prof. U. East Anglia, Eng., 1963-78. Author: Anglo Saxon Attitudes, 1956, As If By Magic, 1973, The World of Charles Dickens, 1970, The Strange Ride of Rudyard Kipling, 1977; many others. Named Comdr. Order British Empire, 1968, Chevalier de l'Ordre des Arts et des Lettres, 1972, Knight Her Majesty The Queen, 1980, Fgn. Hon. Memer Am. Inst. Arts and Letters, 1980. Mem. Powys Soc. (pres. 1970-80), Dickens Fellowship (pres. 1974-75), Kipling Soc. (pres. 1980-88), Royal Soc. Lit. (1982-88). Club: Ahtenaeum (London). Address: 7 Place de la Republique, Apt 61, 13210 Saint Remy de Provence France

WILSON, ANTHONY, English government official; b. Leeds, Yorkshire, Eng., Feb. 17, 1928; s. Charles Ernest and Martha Clarice (Mee) W.; m. Margaret Josephine Hudson, June 18, 1955; children—Duncan Henry, Victoria Margaret, Oliver Charles. Mem. staff John Gordon Walton, Leeds, Eng., 1949-52; with Price Waterhouse, London, 1952-84, ptnr., 1961-84; head U.K. Govt. Accountancy Service, 1984—; accountancy advisor to Her Majesty's Treasury, 1984—; mem. U.K. Acctg. Standards Com., 1984—, Auditing Practices Com., 1987—; mem. U.K. Govt. Adv. Com. on Prodn. Statis., London, 1972-84. Chmn. Dorset Opera Co. (Eng.), 1988. Served with Royal Navy, 1946-49. Decorated Knight Bachelor, 1988. Fellow Inst. Chartered Accts. in Eng. and Wales (council 1985—), Royal Soc. Arts; mem. Inst. Internal Auditors (assoc.), English Ceramic Circle, No. Ceramic Soc., S.W. Arts Mgmt. Com. Anglican. Clubs: Reform. Home: The Barn House, 89 Newland, Sherborne, Dorset DT9 3AG England Office: Her Majesty's Treasury, Parliament St, London W1G 1P, England

WILSON, BRANDON LAINE, advertising and public relations executive, writer, photographer; b. Sewickley, Pa., Oct. 2, 1953; s. Edgar C. and Mary Beth (Tuttle) W.; m. Kathryn Langton Ward, Oct. 3, 1974 (div. 1977). B.A., U. N.C., 1973; Cert. Am. Acad. Dramatic Arts, 1974; lic. in broadcasting 3d class, FCC. Asst. acct. exec. Hill & Knowlton Pub. Relations, Pitts., 1973; dir. video Seattle Repertory Co., 1975-76; cameraman UNC-TV Network, Chapel Hill, 1976-77; dir. advt. and TV Prodn. N.Am. Films, Eugene, Oreg., 1977-79; gen. mgr. Boulder Community Coops., 1980-81; pub. info. officer, asst. to mayor City of Barrow, Alaska, 1981-82; dir. advt. and promotion Anchorage Conv. and Visitors Bur., Anchorage, 1983-85; mgr. mktg. communications GTE, Honolulu, 1986-87; sr. copywriter Peck, Sims, Mueller Advt., Honolulu, 198-7-89; prin., pres., creative dir. Wilson and Assoc., 1987—. Prin. works (TV) include: The General Assembly Today, 1976-77, (films) Sasquatch, Mystery of the Sacred Shroud, Buffalo Rider; contbr. articles to nat. mags. and newspapers. Recipient Eagle Scout award Boy Scouts Am.; named one of Exceptionally Able Youth, 1970, one of Outstanding Young Men in Am., 1986, Men of Achievement U.K., 1987. Mem. Honolulu Advt. Fedn., Pub. Relations Soc. Am. (accredited), Cousteau Soc., Mensa. Mem. Soc. Friends.

WILSON, CARL ARTHUR, real estate broker; b. Manhasset, N.Y., Sept. 29, 1947; s. Archie and Florence (Hefner) W.; m. Mary Elizabeth Coppes; children: Melissa Starr, Clay Alan. Student UCLA, 1966-68, 70-71. Tournament bridge dir. North Hollywood (Calif.) Bridge Club, 1967-68, 70-71; computer operator IBM, Los Angeles, 1967-68, 70-71; bus. devel. mgr. Walker & Lee Real Estate, Anaheim, Calif., 1972-76; v.p. sales and mktg. The Estes Co., Phoenix, 1976-82, Continental Homes Inc., 1982-84; pres. Roadrunner Homes Corp., Phoenix, 1984-86, Lexington Homes, Inc., 1986, Barrington Homes, 1986—; adv. dir. Liberty Bank. Mem. Glendale (Ariz.) Citizens Bond Council, 1986-87, pres.'s council Am. Grad. Sch. Internat. Mgmt., 1985—; vice-chmn. Glendale Planning and Zoning Commn., 1986—, chmn., 1987—; mem. bd. trustees Valley of Sun United Way, 1987—. Mem. Nat. Assn. Homebuilders (bd. dirs. 1985—), Cen. Ariz. Homebuilders Assn. (adv. com. 1979-82, treas. 1986, sec. 1987, v.p. 1987—, bd. dirs. 1985—); mem. bd. adjustments City of Glendale, 1976-81, chmn., 1980-81, mem. bond council, 1981—; planning and zoning commr. City of Glendale, 1981—; mem. real estate edn. adv. council State Bd. Community Coll., 1981—; precinct committeeman, dep. registrar, 1980-81. Served with U.S. Army, 1968-70. Mem. Glendale C. of C. (dir. 1980-83), Sales and Mktg. Council (chmn. edn. com. 1980, chmn. council 1981—, Mame grand award 1981). Home: PO Box 10141 Phoenix AZ 85064

WILSON, CHRISTOPHER WHITWELL, protection services company executive; b. London, Sept. 20, 1915; s. Philip Whitwell and Alice Selina (Collins) W.; grad. Princeton U., 1937; m. Margaret Ryan, May 27, 1939; children—Pamela, Joan, Christopher, Anthony. Clk., Tri Continental Corp., 1933-35; analyst N.Y. Life Ins. Co., 1938-39; lend lease officer Brit. Petroleum Mission, 1939-45; head market research Caribbean, Standard Oil Co. N.J., Havana, Cuba, 1945-60; chmn., owner Caribbean Protective Services, Kingston, Jamaica, 1961-85; chmn. Caribbean Research Ltd., 1960-72; pres. C.W. Wilson & Assocs., Inc., 1985—. Councilor, presiding officer City of Belleair Beach, 1983-84; commr. of baseball, Jamaica, 1964-69. Mem. Am. Soc. Indsl. Security Jamaica Soc. Indsl. Security (past pres.), Jamaica Joint Indsl. Council Security Services (past pres.), Sales and Mktg. Execs. (past exec. dir. Jamaica chpt.), Runaway Bay Citizens Assn. (past pres.). Roman Catholic. Lodges: Rotary of St. Andrews (past pres.); Belleair Bluffs Rotary (bd. dirs., past pres.). Home: 111 17th St Belleair Beach FL 33535

WILSON, CLAUDE RAYMOND, JR., lawyer; b. Dallas, Feb. 22, 1933; s. Claude Raymond and Lottie (Watts) W.; m. Barbara Jean Cowherd, Apr. 30, 1960; 1 dau., Deidra Nicole. B.B.A., So. Meth. U., 1954, LL.B., 1956. C.P.A., Calif., Tex.; cert. tax law specialist, Tex. Bd. Legal Specialization. Asso. firm Cervin & Melton, Dallas, 1956-58; atty. Tex. & Pacific R.R. Co., Dallas, 1958-60; atty. office regional counsel IRS, San Francisco, 1960-63; sr. trial atty. office chief counsel IRS, Washington, 1963-65; partner firm Golden, Potts, Boeckman & Wilson, Dallas, 1965—. Mem. ABA, Dallas Bar Assn., State Bar Tex., Tex. Soc. C.P.A.s (dir. 1973—, sec. 1978-79, mem. exec. com. 1980-81, v.p. 1985-86, pres. 1989-90, pres. Dallas Chpt. Tex. Soc. CPA's 1983-84), Delta Sigma Phi, Delta Theta Phi. Republican. Episcopalian. Clubs: Dallas Gun, Willow Bend Hunt and Polo, Crescent. Lodges: Masons (Scottish Rite), Shriners, Jesters. Home: 4069 Hanover St Dallas TX 75225 Office: 1st Republic Bank Ctr Tower II Suite 2300 Dallas TX 75201

WILSON, COLIN HENRY, writer; b. Leicester, Eng., June 26, 1931; s. Arthur and Anetta W.; m. Joy Stewart; children: Sally, Damon, Rowan; 1 son from previous marriage: Roderick. writer in residence Hollins (Va.) Coll., 1966-67; vis. prof. U. Wash., Seattle, 1967, Rutgers U., New Brunswick, N.J., 1974. Author numerous books including novels: The Glass Cage, 1967, The Occult, 1971, The Black Room, 1971, The Space Vampires, 1975, Mysteries, 1978; 6 critical studies in the Outsider series; non-fiction: Access to Inner Worlds, 1982, The Criminal History of Mankind, 1983, (with Donald Seaman) Modern Encyclopedia of Murder, 1983, The Essential Colin Wilson, 1984, The Personality Surgeon, 1986, (with Damon Wilson) Encyclopedia of Unsolved Mysteries, 1987, Spiderworld, 1987, The Misfits, 1988, Beyond The Occult, 1988. Club: Savage.

WILSON, CONRAD RITCHIE, English instructor, writer, artist; b. Alexandria, Ind., Mar. 23, 1935; s. Everett Lee and Addie Mildred (Ritchie) W.; divorced; children: Lolita Louise, Marta Raquel Claudia, Anthony Alexander Carlos. Student, Mexico City Coll., 1953-54; BA in English, Ball State U., 1960; postgrad., Calif. State U., Long Beach, 1985. Cert. tchr., Ind. Chmn. Eng. dept. Nkubmi Internat. Coll., Kobwe, Zambia, 1965-67; instr. lang. U. Petroleum and Minerals, Dhahran, Saudi Arabia, 1968-73; instr. lang. Northrop Corp., Dhahran, 1973-77, Khamis Mushayt, Saudi Arabia, 1979-85; freelance writer fiction, non-fiction and travel articles. Hermosa Beach and Long Beach, Calif., 1978—.

WILSON, SIR DAVID CLIVE, British diplomatist; b. Alloa, Scotland, Feb. 14, 1935; s. William Skinner and Enid (Sanders) W.; m. Natasha Helen Mary Alexander, Apr. 1, 1967; children: Peter Michael Alexander, Andrew Marcus William. Student, Trinity Coll., Scotland, 1948-53; MA, Oxford U., Eng., 1958; PhD, London U., 1974. Served with various fgn. offices and Fgn. and Commonwealth Office Brit. Diplomatic Service, 1958-68; cabinet office polit. advisor Brit. Diplomatic Service, Hong Kong and London, 1977-81; editor The China Quarterly, London, 1968-74; gov. with Brit. Diplomatic Service Hong Kong, 1987—; with Fgn. and Commonwealth Office, London, 1981-87; vis. scholar Columbia U., N.Y.C., 1972. Served as 2d lt. with Brit. military, 1953-55. Home and Office: Govt House, Hong Kong Hong Kong

WILSON, DAVID MACKENZIE, museum administrator; b. Oct. 30, 1931; s. Joseph W.; Litt.D., St. John's Coll., Cambridge, Eng., 1950; postgrad. Lund U., Sweden, 1953-54; m. Eva Sjogren, 1955. Research asst. Cambridge U., 1954; asst. keeper Brit. Mus., London, 1954-64, dir., 1977—; reader archaeology Anglo Saxon period London U., 1964-71, prof. medieval archaeology, 1971-76; joint head dept. Scandinavian studies Univ. Coll. London, 1973-76. Office: Brit Mus, Great Russell St, London WC1B 3DG, England

WILSON, DOUGLAS EDWIN, lawyer; b. Sacramento, Apr. 23, 1917; s. Richard Matthew and Ruth (O'Brien) W.; A.B., U. of Pacific, 1940; J.D., U. Calif. at San Francisco, 1948; m. Helen Marie Lewis, Apr. 5, 1942; children—Sandra Jane (Mrs. Kenneth Arthur Olds), Kent Lewis, Jay Douglas. Admitted to Calif. bar, 1949; partner Forslund & Wilson, Stockton, 1949-83, Wilson & Wison, 1983—; U.S. magistrate Stockton, Eastern Dist. of Calif., 1962-76. Mem. San Joaquin County Retirement Bd., 1952-72. Served to capt. AUS, 1941-46. Recipient Silver Beaver award Boy Scouts, 1955, Distinguished Eagle Scout award, 1971. Mem. San Joaquin County, Calif. State bars, Am. Legion. Republican. Methodist. Mason (Shriner, K.T.), Elk, Rotarian. Club: Commonwealth (San Francisco). Home: 2134 Gardena Ave Stockton CA 95204 Office: 11 S San Joaquin Stockton CA 95202

WILSON, EDWARD JOHN, clergyman, spiritual and mental health counselor; b. Memphis, Mar. 16, 1946; s. Richard Clark Wilson and Helen Jane (Jordan) Burcl; m. Marilyn E. May, May 6, 1978 (div. 1983); 1 child, Elizabeth Claire. BS in Psychology, U. Houston, 1983, M.Ed. in Counseling Psychology, 1985; postgrad. Houston Grad. Sch. Theology; D.D. (hon.), Universal Life Ch., Modesto, Calif., 1981. Ordained to ministry Universal Life Ch., 1980. Prin. Wilson Vending Co., Houston, 1968-74; salesman Century 21 Westway Realty, Houston, 1974-75; sales mgr. Century 21 James L. Berry Realty, Houston, 1975-77; v.p. broker services Century 21 of Tex., Inc., Houston, 1977-80; pastor Universal Life Ch., Houston, 1980—; instr. Houston Bapt. U., 1983-85; exec. dir. Motivational Counseling and Hypnosis Ctr., Houston. Editor, pub. ULC News newsletter, 1984-87; editor, pub., contbg. author The Motivator newsletter, 1988—. Mem. Am. Assn. Counseling and Devel., Tex. Assn. Counseling and Devel., Houston Assn. Counseling and Devel., Am. Mental Health Counselors Assn., Tex. Mental Health Counselors Assn., Assn. for Humanistic Psychology, Mental Health Assn. of Houston, Am. Assn. Profl. Hypnotherapists, Assn. Counselor Edn. and Supervision, Assn. for Specialists in Group Work, Assn. Religious and Values Issues in Counseling, Nat. Assn. Clergy Hypnotists, Nat. Soc. Hypnotherapists, Nat. Assn. Religious Counselors, Assn. Ind. Ministers, Mensa. Republican. Club: Toastmasters (pres. Houston club 1982). Avocations: camping, photography, movies. Home: 1601 Hollyhurst Apt #B-10 Houston TX 77056 Office: Universal Life Church 2715 Bissonnet Suite 409 Houston TX 77005

WILSON, H(AROLD) FRED(ERICK), research scientist; b. Columbiana, Ohio, Aug. 15, 1922; s. Lloyd Ralph and Erma Rebecca (Frederick) W.; m. Alice Marjorie Steer, Aug. 20, 1949; children: Janice, Deborah, James, Kathleen. B.A., Oberlin Coll., 1947; Ph.D., U. Rochester, 1950. With Rohm & Haas Co., Phila., 1950-83; beginning as research scientist, successively lab. head, research supr., asst. dir., assoc. dir., dir. research Rohm & Haas Co., 1950-74, v.p., 1974-83, chief sci. officer, from 1981; now with Wilson Assocs., Cape May, N.J.; mem. U.S. nat. com. IUPAC, 1977-84, vice chmn., 1980-82, chmn., 1982-84, fin. com., 1979—, chmn., 1981—; chmn. I.R.I. Research Corp., 1980-82, dir., 1979-82. Served to 1st lt. USAAF, 1942-46. Decorated Air Medal. Mem. Am. Chem. Soc., AAAS, Soc. Chem. Industry, Dirs. Indsl. Research. Office: Wilson Assocs PO Box 2132 Cape May NJ 08204

WILSON, IAN HOLROYDE, management consultant, futurist; b. Pinner, England, June 16, 1925; came to U.S., 1954; s. William Brash and Dorothy (Holroyde) W.; m. Page Tuttle Hedden, Mar. 17, 1951 (div. Dec. 1983); children: Rebecca, Dorothy, Ellen, Holly, Alexandra. MA, Oxford U., 1948. Orgn. cons. Imperial Chem. Industries, London, 1948-54; various staff exec. positions in strategic planning, mgmt. devel. Gen. Electric Co., Fairfield, Conn., 1954-80; sr. cons. to maj. U.S. and internat. cos. SRI Internat., Menlo Park, Calif., 1980—; exec. in residence Va. Commonwealth U., Richmond, 1976. Author: Planning for Major Change, 1976; (with others) Business Environment of the 70's, 1970; mem. editorial bd. Planning Rev., Oxford, Ohio, 1973-81; Am. editor Long Range Planning Jour., London, 1981—. Chmn. Citizen's Long Range Ednl. Goals Com., Westport, Conn., 1967-70; mem. strategic process com. United Way of Am., Alexandria, Va., 1985—. Served to capt. Brit. Army, 1943-45, ETO. Mem. AAAS, Planning Forum, World Future Soc. Unitarian. Home: 165 Alpine Terr San Francisco CA 94117 Office: SRI Internat 333 Ravenswood Ave Menlo Park CA 94025

WILSON, J. TYLEE, business executive; b. Teaneck, N.J., June 18, 1931; s. Eric J. and Florence Q. W.; m. Patricia F. Harrington, July 17, 1970; children: Jeffrey J., Debra L., Christopher F. A.B., Lafayette Coll., 1953. Group v.p., dir. Chesebrough-Pond's Inc., 1960-74; pres., chief exec. officer RJR Foods, Inc., 1974-76; chmn., chief exec. officer R.J. Reynolds Tobacco Internat., Inc., Winston-Salem, N.C., 1976-78; exec. v.p. RJR Nabisco, Inc. (formerly R.J. Reynolds Industries Co. Inc.), Winston-Salem, 1976-79; pres. R.J. Reynolds Tobacco Internat., Inc., Winston-Salem, 1979-83; chmn., chief exec. officer RJR Nabisco, Inc. (formerly R.J. Reynolds Industries Co., Inc.), Winston-Salem, 1984-87; retired 1987; pres. J. Tylee Wilson Assocs., Jacksonville, 1987—; bd. dirs. Bell South Corp., Am. Heritage Life Ins. Co., Carolina Power & Light Co., Barnett Bank of Jacksonville, N.A., Avis Rent-A-Car Systems, Inc., Anchor Glass Container. Bd. visitors Wake Forest U.; trustee Jacksonville (Fla.) U.; bd. dirs. The Bus. Council, Jacksonville Symphony Assn. Served with U.S. Army, 1954-56. Clubs: Piedmont (Winston-Salem), Old Town (Winston-Salem); River (Jacksonville), Marsh Landing Country (Jacksonville), Epping Forest Yacht (Jacksonville, Fla.), Ponte Vedra; Fisher Island (Fla.); The Links (N.Y.C.), The Sky (N.Y.C.); Treasure Cay Yacht & Country (Abaco, Bahamas). Office: J Tylee Wilson Assocs 301 W Bay St Suite 2706 Jacksonville FL 32202-4425

WILSON, JAMES LAURENCE, real estate development executive, financial services consultant; b. Jamaica, N.Y., Mar. 20, 1945; s. William Henry and Beulah (Baylis) W.; m. Marilyn Murray, June 13, 1981; children—Leigh William, Robin Steele, Brennen Julian. BS, Union Coll., 1968. Dir. World Assocs., Inc., Ft. Lauderdale, Fla., 1970-77; div. head Royal Trust Bank, Miami, Fla., 1978-81; sr. lending officer S.E. Bank, Tampa, 1982-83; sr. v.p. Southcoast, Inc., shopping ctr. devel. co., Tampa, 1984—; pres., dir. Gulfcoast Capital Resource Corp., Tampa, 1984—. Mem. Mortgage Bankers Assn., Am. Bankers Assn., Econ. Soc. South Fla., Am. Inst. Banking, Internat. Council Shopping Ctrs. Republican. Clubs: Avila Golf and Country, Centre. Home: 5002 Barrowe Pl Tampa FL 33624 Office: Bayshore Investments 5002 Barrowe Pl Tampa FL 33624

WILSON, JOHN FOSTER, international health consultant; b. Nottingham, Eng., Jan. 20, 1919; s. George Henry and Leonora Carrick (Foster) W.; student Worcester Coll. Blind, 1932-37; B.A. with honours, Oxford U., 1940, M.A., 1941; m. Chloe Jean MacDermid, 1944; children—Claire Elizabeth, Felicity Jane. Founder, 1950, dir. Royal Commonwealth Soc. Blind, 1950-83, v.p., 1984; founder, pres. Internat. Agy. Prevention Blindness, 1975, hon. life pres., 1981; sr. cons. UN Devel. Programme, 1983—; cons. WHO. Named hon. fellow St. Catherine's Coll., Oxford U.; research fellow Fogarty Internat. Ctr., 1984; decorated knight batchelor, 1975; decorated comdr. Order Brit. Empire, 1965; recipient Helen Keller Internat. award, 1970, Lions Internat. Humanitarian award, 1978, World Humanity award, 1979, Albert Lasker Spl. Public Service award, 1979. Mem. Royal Commonwealth Soc. Author: Blindness in British African and Near East Territories, 1948, Ghana's Handicapped Citizens, 1960, Travelling Blind, 1962, World Blindness and its Prevention, 1979, Vol. II, 1983; also articles. Address: 22 The Cliff, Roedean, Brighton East Sussex, England

WILSON, KENNETH GEDDES, physics research administrator, educator; b. Waltham, Mass., June 8, 1936; s. E. Bright and Emily Fisher (Buckingham) W.; m. Alison Brown, 1982. A.B., Harvard U., 1956, DSc hon., 1981; Ph.D., Calif. Tech. Inst., 1961; Ph.D. (hon.), U. Chgo., 1976. Asst. prof., then prof. physics Cornell U., Ithaca, N.Y., 1963—, James A. Weeks chmn. in phys. sci., 1974—. Recipient Nobel prize in physics, 1982, Dannie Heinemann Prize, 1973, Boltzmann medal, 1975, Wolf Prize, 1980, A.C. Eringen medal, 1984, Franklin medal, 1983, Disting. alumni award Calif. Inst. Tech., 1981. Mem. Nat. Acad. Scis., Am. Philosophical Soc., Am. Acad. Arts and Scis.

WILSON, KRISTAL ANNE, bank officer; b. Ft. Dodge, Iowa, U.S., Mar. 9, 1960; arrived in Eng., 1984; d. Robert Arthur and Mary Ann (Lane) Foust; m. Eric Paul Wilson, June 12, 1982. BS, St. Olaf Coll., 1982. Mgmt. trainee to credit officer First Nat. Bank Hopkins, Mpls., 1982-85; credit analyst Bank of Boston, London, 1985-86; adminstrv. officer Continental Bank, London, 1986-88; pvt. banking officer Norwest Bank Minn. N.A., Mpls., 1988—; sec. Continental Cons. Co. Ltd., London, 1987-88. Congregationalist. Home: 6213 Creek Valley Rd Edina MN 55435 Office: Norwest Bank Minn NA Norwest Center Office 8th St & Marquette Ave Minneapolis MN 55479

WILSON, LAWRENCE GRAHAM, III, binational center executive; b. Mobile, Ala., June 6, 1944; came to Ecuador, 1969; s. Lawrence Graham and Mary Blanche (Williams) W.; m. Lesvia Irene Lima, Oct. 8, 1969 (div.); children—Wendy, Vanessa, Stephanie, Nicole. B.S. in Biology, Troy State U., 1966; Med. Technologist, Providence Hosp., Mobile, Ala., 1972. Tchr. biology Am. Sch. of Guayaquil, Ecuador, 1969-71; owner, mgr. Bioanalytical Lab., Guayaquil, 1973-76; owner, gen. mgr. Wilson Co. Ltd., Guayaquil, 1976-86; dir. Ecuadorean U.S. Cultural Ctr., Guayaquil, 1982—. Bd. dirs. Fulbright Commn., Guayaquil, 1975-83; a founder, bd. dirs. Interamerican Acad., Guayaquil, 1978, "Por Cristo" Med. Charity, 1984—; pres. bd. Am. Sch. of Guayaquil, 1984—. Served with USN, 1966-68. Mem. Am. Soc. Clin. Pathologists (assoc. mem.; registered med. technologist), Am. C. of C. (pres. 1982-83). Roman Catholic. Club: Nautico (Guayaquil). Avocations: metal detecting, fishing, coin collecting. Office: PO Box 5717, Guayaquil Ecuador

WILSON, LEONARD RICHARD, geologist, consultant; b. Superior, Wis., July 23, 1906; s. Ernest and Sarah Jane (Cooke) W.; m. Marian Alice DeWilde, Sept. 1, 1930; children—Richard Graham, Marcia Graham. Ph.B., U. Wis.-Madison, 1930, Ph.M., 1932, Ph.D., 1935. Research assoc. Wis. Geol. and Nat. Hist. Survey, Trout Lake, Wis., 1932-36; instr. to prof. geology Coe Coll., Cedar Rapids, Iowa, 1934-46; head dept. geology and mineralogy U. Mass., Amherst, 1946-56; leader Greenland Ice Cap Am. Geog. Soc., N.Y.C., 1953; prof. geology NYU, N.Y.C., 1956-57; prof. to George L. Cross research prof. geology and geophysics U. Okla., Norman, 1957-77, prof. emeritus, 1977—; geologist Okla. Geol. Survey, Norman, 1957-77, ret. 1977—; cons. in field; research assoc., mem. edn. bd. Mus. Nat. Hist., N.Y.C., 1956-77; curator paleobotany-micropaleontology Okla. Mus. Natural Hist., Norman, 1968—, Okla. Mus. Nat. Hist., Norman, 1968— . Contbr. articles to profl. jours. Editor proceedings Iowa Acad. Sci., 1936-46. Melhaup fellow Ohio State U., 1939-40; NSF grantee, 1959-65. Fellow AAAS, Geol. Soc. Am., Palynological Soc. India (Erdtman Internat. medal 1973); mem. Am. Assn. Petroleum Geologists, Am. Assn. Stratigraphic Palynologists (hon.), Nat. Assn. Geology Tchrs. (hon. life), Audubon Soc. (pres. Norman br. 1982-83), Explorers Club, Sigma Xi, Phi Beta Kappa, Phi Kappa Phi. Current work: Stratigraphic research in Paleozoic palynology as it relates to hydrocarbon maturation and associated strata. Subspecialties: Geology; Chronobiology.

WILSON, LEVON EDWARD, lawyer, law educator; b. Charlotte, N.C., Apr. 2, 1954; s. James A. and Thomasina Wilson. BSBA, Western Carolina U., 1976; JD, N.C. Cen. U., 1979. Bar: N.C. 1981, U.S. Dist. Ct. (mid. dist.) N.C. 1981, U.S. Tax Ct. 1981, U.S. Ct. Appeals (4th cir.) 1982. Sole practice Greensboro, N.C., 1981-85; asst. county atty. Guilford County, Greensboro, 1985-88; asst. prof. N.C. A.&T. State U., Greensboro, 1988—; pres. Trade Brokers Cons.; legal counsel, bd. dirs. Rhodes Assocs., Inc., Greensboro, 1982—; legal counsel Guilford County Sheriff's Dept., Greensboro, 1985-88. bd. dirs. Post Advocacy Detention Program. Recipient Service award Blacks in Mgmt., 1980. Mem. ABA, N.C. Bar Assn., Am. Bus. Law Assn., N.C. Assn. Police Attys., Greensboro Jaycees, Phi Delta Phi. Democrat. Methodist. Home: PO Box 21664 Greensboro NC 27420

WILSON, LOIS M., clergyman; b. Winnipeg, Man., Can., Apr. 8, 1927; d. Edwin Gardiner Dunn and Ada Minnie (Davis) Freeman; m. Roy F. Wilson, June 9, 1950; children: Ruth, Jean, Neil, Bruce. B.A., United Coll., Winnipeg, 1947, B.Div., 1969; Diploma in TV prodn., Ryerson Tech. Inst., 1974; D.Div. (hon.), Victoria U., Toronto, 1978, United Theol. Coll., Montreal, 1978, Wycliff Coll., 1983, Queens U., Kingston, 1984, U. Winnipeg, 1986, Mt. Allison U., 1988; LL.D., Trent U., Peterborough, 1984; D.C.L., Acadia U., 1984; D.Hum.L., Mt. St. Vincent, Halifax, 1984. Ordained to ministry United Church of Can., 1965. Minister United Church of Can., Thunder Bay, 1965-69, Hamilton, 1969-78, Kingston, 1978-80; moderator United Church of Can., 1980-82; pres. Can. Council of Chs., Toronto, Ont., 1976-79; co-dir. Ecumenical Forum Can., Toronto, Ont., 1983—; pres. World Council of Chs., Geneva, 1983—; mem. adv. council internat. devel. studies U. Toronto, 1987—; spokesperson Project Ploughshares, 1st and 2d UN Conf. on Disarmament, N.Y.C., 1978, 82; lectr. Vancouver Sch. Theology, 1980, Queens Theol. Coll., 1982-83; officer Human Rights Commn., Ont., 1973. Author: Like a Mighty River, 1981; contbr. articles to Internat. Rev. of Mission, other publs.; author publs. in field. Pres., Social Planning Council, Thunder Bay, 1967-68; pres. Can. Com. for Scientists and Scholars, Toronto, 1982; bd. dirs. Elizabeth Fry Soc., Hamilton, 1976-79, Amnesty Internat., 1978—, Can. Inst. for Internat. Peace and Security, 1984-88, Energy Probe, 1981-86; mem. Refugee Status Adv. Com., 1985—; bd. dirs. Can. Univ. Service Overseas, 1983-85; councillor Amnesty Internat., 1986—; bd. dirs. coop. program on intern devel. U. Toronto, 1986—. Decorated Order of Can., 1984 Queens Jubilee medal (Can.); named hon. pres. Student Christian Movement of Can., Toronto, 1976; recipient World Federalist peace award, 1985; Pearson peace medal UN Assn. of Can., 1985. Mem. Can. Assn. Adult Edn. (bd. dirs. 1986—), AUW (pub. rev. bd. 1986—), Friends of Can. Broadcasting (bd. dirs. 1986—), Civil Liberties Assn. (bd. dirs. 1986—). Office: care World Council Churches, 150 Route de Ferney, PO Box 66, 1211 Geneva 20, Switzerland

WILSON, MICHAEL HOLCOMBE, Canadian government official; b. Toronto, Ont., Can., Nov. 4, 1937; s. Harry Holcombe and Constance L. (Davies) W.; m. Margaret Catherine Smellie, Oct. 17, 1964; children: Cameron, Geoffrey, Lara. Student, Upper Can. Coll.; B. Comm., U. Toronto, 1959. With Harris & Partners Ltd., Toronto, 1961-63, 65-73; v.p. Harris & Partners Ltd., 1972; exec. v.p. following merger with Dominion Securities Ltd., 1973-79; mem. Can. Ho. of Commons, Ottawa, 1979—; minister of state for internat. trade Govt. Can., Ottawa, 1979-80; minister of fin. Govt. Can., 1984—. Campaign chmn. Can. Cancer Soc., 1972-75, pres., 1977-79; bd. dirs. Dellcrest Children's Home. Mem. Investment Dealers Assn. (chmn. Ont. dist. 1975-76), Kappa Alpha. Progressive Conservative. Anglican. Clubs: Toronto, Toronto Golf, Badminton and Racquet, Osler Bluff Ski, Can. of Toronto (dir. 1972-78, v.p. 1976-78). Office: House of Commons, Dept of Finance, Ottawa, ON Canada K1A 0A6

WILSON, ORME, JR., retired foreign service officer; b. N.Y.C., July 3, 1920; s. Orme and Alice (Barland) W.; m. Mildred Eddy Dunn, Feb. 16, 1950; children: Marshall, Elsie Dunn, Orme Ill. Student, St. Alban's Sch., Washington, 1929-33, St. Mark's Sch., Southborough, Mass., 1933-38; S.B. cum laude, Harvard, 1942; M.A., George Washington U., 1951; diploma, USAF War Coll., 1965. Jr. pilot Pan Am. World Airways, 1946-47, U.S. Army Map Service, 1950; joined Fgn. Service, 1950; vice consul Frankfurt/am/Main Germany, 1951-53; vice consul Southampton, Eng., 1953-54; 2d sec. Belgrade, Yugoslavia, 1958-61; 2nd then 1st sec. Athens, Greece, 1961-64; assigned Washington, 1955-57, 65-70; consul gen. Zagreb, Yugoslavia, 1970-74; adviser U.S. Mission to U.N., 1974-77; polit. counselor U.S. Mission to NATO, 1977-80; Bd. dirs. Laurel Race Course, Laurel, Md., 1968-84. Contbr. to Eastern Europe: Essays in Geographical Problems, 1970. Trustee Bishop Rhinelander Found. for Episcopal Chaplaincy Harvard and Radcliffe, 1967-71, 76-78, 80-83, hon. 1987—; adv. bd. visitors Mary Baldwin Coll., 1981—; pres. Friends of U. Va. Blandy Exptl. Farm, 1983-86, bd. dirs., 1983—, treas., 1986-87; bd. mgrs. Seamen's Ch. Inst. N.Y. and N.J., 1984—. Served to lt. USNR, 1942-46. Fellow Am. Geog. Soc.; mem. U.S. Tennis Assn. (Prentice Cup Com.), Thoroughbred Club Am., Va. Thoroughbred Assn. (dir. 1982—, treas. 1983-84, v.p. 1984—), Am. Horse Council. Episcopalian. Clubs: Mason. (N.Y.C.), Internat. Lawn Tennis of U.S.A. (N.Y.C.), Harvard (N.Y.C., Belgium), Brook (N.Y.C.), Racquet and Tennis (N.Y.C.); Metropolitan (Washington), Chevy Chase (Washington). Home: Westfield Farm White Post VA 22663

WILSON, PATRICIA JANE, educator, librarian, educational and library consultant; b. Jennings, La., May 3, 1946; d. Ralph Harold and Wilda Ruth (Smith) Potter; m. Wendell Merlin Wilson, Aug. 24, 1968. B.S., La. State U., 1967; M.S. U. Houston-Clear Lake, 1979; Ed.D., U. Houston, 1985. Cert. tchr., learning resources specialist (librarian), Tex. Tchr., England AFB (La.) Elem. Sch., 1967-68, Edward White Elem. Sch., Clear Creek Ind. Schs., Seabrook, Tex., 1972-77; librarian C.D. Landolt Elem. Sch., Friendswood, Tex., 1979-81; instr./lectr. children's lit. U. Houston 1983-86; with U. Houston/Clear Lake, 1984-87; cons. Hermann Hosp., Baywood Hosp., 1986-87. Trustee, Freeman Meml. Library, Houston, 1982-87, v.p., 1985-86, pres., 1986-87; mem. Armand Bayou Nature Ctr., Houston, 1980—; bd. dirs. Sta. KUHT-TV, 1984-87. Editor A Rev. Sampler, 1985-86; Author: HAPPENINGS: Developing Successful Programs for School Libraries, 1987; contbg. editor Tex. Library Jour., 1988—; contbr. articles to profl. jours. Mem. ALA, Am. Assn. Sch. Librarians, Internat. Reading Assn., Nat. Council Tchrs. English, (Books for You com. 1985—), Tex. Joint Council Tchrs. English, Antarctican Soc., Kappa Delta Pi, Alpha Delta Kappa, Phi Delta Kappa. Methodist. Club: Lakewood Yacht (Seabrook). Home and Office: 1118 Appleford Dr Seabrook TX 77586

WILSON, PERKINS, lawyer, linguist; b. Cin., Aug. 17, 1929; s. Russell and Elizabeth Baldwin (Smith) W.; A.B., Princeton U., 1951; J.D., U. Va., 1956; m. Mary Earle Mackall, June 8, 1957; children—Russell Perkins, William Mackall, Elizabeth Drake. Admitted to Ohio bar, 1956, N.Y. State bar, 1958, Va. bar, 1959; asso. firm Shearman & Sterling, N.Y.C., 1956-58, Hunton & Williams, Richmond, Va., 1958-62; atty. Reynolds Metals Co., Richmond, 1962-77; asst. atty. gen. State of Va., Richmond, 1979-82; of counsel Thompson & McMullan, Richmond, 1983—. Served with U.S. Army, 1951-53. Mem. ABA, Linguistic Soc. Am., Assn. Computational Linguistics, Soc. History Tech., Am. Assn. Tchrs. Italian, Am. Classical League, Va. Bar Assn., Richmond Bar Assn. (past chmn. corp. counsel sect.), Am. Assn. Tchrs. of German, Am. Assn. Tchrs. of French, Am. Assn. Tchrs. Spanish and Portuguese. Episcopalian. Clubs: Commonwealth, Country of Va. Author: Guide to French Noun Gender, 1978; Basic German Gender, 1986; Basic German Noun Plurals, 1987; Basic Spanish Gender, 1984; Basic French Gender, 1985; Basic Italian Gender, 1985; Basic Portuguese Gender, 1986, Basic Latin Nouns, 1988. Home: 204 Tuckahoe Blvd Richmond VA 23226 Office: Thompson & McMullan 100 Shockoe Slip Richmond VA 23219

WILSON, PETE, senator; b. Lake Forest, Ill., Aug. 23, 1933; s. James Boone and Margaret (Callaghan) W.; m. Betty Robertson (div.); m. Gayle Edlund, May 29, 1983. B.A. in English Lit., Yale U., 1955; J.D., U. Calif.-Berkeley, 1962; LL.D., Grove City Coll., 1983, U. Calif.-San Diego, 1983, U. San Diego, 1984. Bar: Calif. 1962. Mem. Calif. Legislature, Sacramento, 1966-71; mayor City of San Diego, 1971-83; U.S. Senator from Calif. 1983—. Trustee Conservation Found.; mem. exec. bd. San Diego County council Boy Scouts Am.; hon. trustee So. Calif. Council Soviet Jews; adv. mem. Urban Land Inst., 1985-86; founding dir. Retinitis Pigmentosa Internat.; hon. dir. Alzheimer's Family Ctr., Inc., 1985; hon. bd. dirs. Shakespeare-San Francisco, 1985. Recipient Golden Bulldog award, 1984, 85, 86, Guardian of Small Bus. award, 1984; ROTC scholar Yale U., 1951-55; named Legislator of Yr., League Calif. Cities, 1985; Man of Yr. award Nat. Guard Assn. Calif., 1986, Man of Yr. citation U. Calif. Boalt Hall, 1986. Mem. Nat. Mil. Family Assn. (adv. bd.), Phi Delta Phi, Zeta Psi. Republican. Episcopalian. Office: US Senate 720 Hart Senate Bldg Washington DC 20510 •

WILSON, PETER, contracts manager; b. Farnworth, Eng., Jan. 15, 1954; s. Margaret Wilson; m. Rebecca King, June 15, 1975 (div. Feb. 1981); m. Annette West, Mar. 30, 1988. Trainee site agt. Brosely Homes Ltd., Leigh, Eng., 1972-73; materials expediter Andrew Hamer & Son Ltd., Bolton, Eng., 1973-79; area rep. Express Wholesale Ltd., Manchester, Eng., 1979-80; prodn. mgr. Trailer Shop Industries, Weatherford, Tex., 1980-81; contracts mgr. Saud a Al-Twajri Est., Jubail, Saudi Arabia, 1981—; owner Hamlyn Properties, Bolton, 1983—; owner, dir. Zamora Ltd., Isle-of-Man, 1984—. Recipient cert. of honor Jubail Municipality, 1986, cert. of appreciation, 1987. Mem. Conservative Party. Methodist. Clubs: Jubail Rugby (capt. 1982-87), Brit. Sub-Aqua. Office: Saud A Al-Twajri Est, PO Box 852, Jubail 31951, Saudi Arabia

WILSON, PETER WADE, pharmaceutical company executive; b. Kenilworth, Warwickshire, Eng., Mar. 1, 1944; came to U.S., 1983; s. John Pearson and Nancy Wade (Harston) W.; m. Evelyne Ohayon; children: Joseph Robert, Edward John, David Peter. BS, Birmingham U., Eng., 1966; MBA, Harvard U. Bus. Sch., 1975. Systems analyst Rolls Royce, Ltd., Conventry, Eng., 1966-70; controller Sandvik France, Levallois, 1970-73; ops. dir. Massey Ferguson, Athismos, France, 1975-77; European controller Revlon Health Care Group, Paris, 1978-80; fin., adminstrv. dir. Lab. Armour Montagu, Levallois, France, 1980-83; gen. mgr. USV Can., Mississauga, Ont., 1983-86; v.p. internat. corp. devel. Connaught Labs., Ltd., Willowdale, Ont., 1986—. Mem. Inst. Prodn. Engrs., Toronto Bd. Trade. Conservative. Home: 14 Aldburn Rd, Toronto, ON Canada M6C 2K3 Office: Connaught Labs Ltd, 1755 Steeles Ave W, Willowdale, ON Canada M2R 3T4

WILSON, RAY CLARENCE, savings and loan executive; b. Houston, July 10, 1929; s. Rogers C. and Hattie (Schumacher) W.; AA, Blinn Coll., 1947; BBA, U. Tex., 1949, MBA, 1951; m. Lucy Ann Reid, Mar. 23, 1951; children: Reid Carroll, Cynthia Ann, Lisa Ann. Asst. mgr. mortgage loan dept. Richard Gill Co., San Antonio, 1951-54; loan insp. Nat. Life Ins. Co., Montpelier, Vt., 1954-58; regional supr. Jefferson Standard Life Ins. Co., Greensboro, N.C., 1958-63; v.p. Am. Nat. Ins. Co., Galveston, Tex., 1963-69, sr. v.p., 1969-72; pres. ANREM Corp., 1969-72; chmn. bd., mng. trustee Diversified Mortgage Investors, Boston, 1972-74; pres. Diversified Advisers, Inc., Coral Gables, Fla., 1972-74; chmn., chief exec. officer Rotan Mosle Mortgage Co., Houston, 1974-77, pres. Rotan Mosle Realty Investments, 1974-77; sr. v.p. Soc. for Savs., Hartford, Conn., 1977-78; exec. v.p. San Antonio Savs., 1978-84; pres. Real Estate Group, 1984—; dir. Mortgage Corp. Tex., Marathon Title Co., Thrift Mgmt. Corp. Tex.; bd. dirs. San Antonio Fed. Savs. Bank; lectr. Real Estate Inst. U. N.C., 1960-63, Mortgage Banking Seminar Mich. State U., 1961-68, So. Meth. U., 1969-71, Sch. Mortgage Banking, Northwestern U., 1964-66. Chmn. acquisitions and preservations com. Galveston Hist. Found., 1965-66; bd. dirs. Galveston YMCA, 1964-68; trustee Trinity Episcopal Sch., 1965-72. Mem. Am. Inst. Real Estate Appraisers, Urban Land Inst., Tex. Mortgage Bankers Assn. (dir. 1966-72), Mortgage Bankers Assn. Am., Phi Sigma Kappa. Republican. Episcopalian. Clubs: Oak Hills Country; Giraud. Home: 207 Sheffield Pl San Antonio TX 78213 Office: San Antonio Savs Assn 601 NW Loop 410 San Antonio TX 78216

WILSON, RICHARD LEE, political science educator; b. Worthington, Minn., Dec. 20, 1944; s. G. Roy and Dorothy Eileen (Johnson) W.; m. Carolyn Ann Dirks, Aug. 24, 1968 (div.); 1 child, Kevin Richard. BA, U. Chgo., 1966, postgrad., 1966-67; PhD, Johns Hopkins U., 1971; postdoctoral grad., Columbia U., 1988. Congl. aide 4th Congl. Dist. Md., 1971; asst. prof. polit. sci. U. Tenn., Chattanooga, 1971-76, assoc. prof., 1976-87, prof., 1988—; registrar at-large Hamilton County Election Commn., 1977-84; lectr. Robert A. Taft Inst. Govt., U. Tenn., Nashville, 1978, 79, 81; supr. state legis. and met. internship program U. Tenn., Chattanooga, 1972-86; vis. prof. Govt. Fgn. Affairs Coll., Beijing, 1986-87; Fulbright prof. Govt. Beijing U., 1988-89. Author: Tennessee Politics, 1976; contbr. chpts. to books. Chmn. Hamilton County Health Planning Adv. Council, 1975-79; bd. dirs. Ga.-Tenn. Regional Health Commn., 1978-82; active Tenn. State Health Coordinating Council, 1977-81; exec. com. State Health Coordinating Council, 1979-81. Named Outstanding Educator of Yr., Signal Mountain (Tenn.) Jaycees, 1973, Outstanding Prof. of Yr., SGA, 1985-86; recipient Polit. Edn. award NAACP, 1980, Excellent Prof. award Fgn. Affairs Coll., Beijing, 1987, NEH grant, 1988. Mem. So. Polit. Sci. Assn., Midwest Polit. Sci. Assn., Tenn. Polit. Sci. Assn., Nat. Soc. Internships and Exptl. Edn., SAR, China People's Friendship Assn., Aircraft Owners and Pilots Assn. Methodist. Office: U Tenn Dept Polit Sci Chattanooga TN 37403

WILSON, ROBERT FOSTER, lawyer; b. Windsor, Colo., Apr. 6, 1926; s. Foster W. and Anne Lucille (Svedman) W.; m. Mary Elizabeth Clark, Mar. 4, 1951 (div. Feb. 1972); children—Robert F., Katharine A.; m. Sally Anne Nemec, June 8, 1982. B.A. in Econs., U. Iowa, 1950, J.D., 1951. Bar: Iowa 1951, U.S. Dist. Ct. (no. and so. dists.) Iowa 1956, U.S. Ct. Appeals (8th cir.) 1967. Atty., FTC, Chgo., 1951-55; sole practice, Cedar Rapids, Iowa, 1955—; dir. Appollo Computer Tech., Veterans Pub. Safety. Democratic state rep. Iowa Legislature, Linn County, 1959-60; mem. Iowa Reapportionment Com., 1968; pres. Linn County Day Care, Cedar Repids, 1968-70; del. to U.S. and Japan Bilateral Session on Legal and Econ. Relations Conf., Tokyo, 1988. Served to sgt. U.S. Army, 1944-46. Mem. Am. Legion (judge advocate 1970-75), Iowa Trial Lawyers Assn., Assn. Trial Lawyers Am., Iowa Bar Assn., Linn County Bar Assn., Delta Theta Phi. Club: Cedar View Country. Lodges: Elks, Eagles. Home: 100-1st Ave NE Cedar Rapids IA 52401 Office: 810 Dows Bldg Cedar Rapids IA 52401

WILSON, ROBERT GODFREY, radiologist; b. Montgomery, Ala., Mar. 18, 1937; s. Robert Woodridge and Lucille (Godfrey) W.; B.A., Huntingdon Coll., 1957; M.D., Med. Coll. Ala., 1961; m. Dorothy June Waters, Aug. 31, 1957; children—Amy Lucille, Robert Darwin, Robert Woodridge II, Lucy Elizabeth. Intern, Letterman Gen. Hosp., San Francisco, 1961-62; resident in radiology U. Okla. Med. Center, Oklahoma City, 1965-68, clin. instr. in radiology, 1968—; practice medicine specializing in diagnostic and therapeutic radiology, nuclear medicine, Shawnee, Okla., 1968—; mem. med. staff Shawnee Med. Center, Mission Hill Meml. Hosp., Shawnee, 1968—. Served to capt. M.C., USAF, 1960-65. Diplomate Nat. Bd. Med. Examiners, Am. Bd. Radiology, Am. Bd. Nuclear Medicine. Mem. AMA, Okla., Pottawatomie County med. socs., Okla., Greater Oklahoma City radiol. socs., Am. Coll. Radiology, Soc. Nuclear Medicine, Radiol. Soc. N.Am. Methodist. Home: 26 Sequoyah Blvd Shawnee OK 74801 Office: 1110 N Harrison St Shawnee OK 74801

WILSON, ROBERT PETER, mining company executive; b. London, Sept. 2, 1943; s. Alfred and Dorothy Eileen (Matthews) W.; m. Shirley Elisabeth Robson, Feb. 7, 1975; children: Nicola Claire, Andrew James. BA in Econs., Sussex U., 1966. Asst. economist Dunlop Ltd., London, 1966-67; economist Mobil Oil Co. Ltd., London, 1967-70; fin. analyst The RTZ Corp., London, 1970-72; comml. dir. AM & S Europe Ltd. subs. RTZ Corp., Bristol, Eng., 1972-79, mng. dir., 1979-82; strategy mgr. The RTZ Corp., 1982-86, dir. planning & devel., 1987—, also bd. dirs. Home: Leigh House, Eriswell Crescent, Walton-on-Thames KT12 5DS, England Office: The RTZ Corp, 6 St James Sq, London SW1 4LD, England

WILSON, ROBERT WOODROW, radio astronomer; b. Houston, Jan. 10, 1936; s. Ralph Woodrow and Fannie May (Willis) W.; m. Elizabeth Rhoads Sawin, Sept. 4, 1958; children—Philip Garrett, Suzanne Katherine, Randal Woodrow. B.A. with honors in Physics, Rice U., 1957; Ph.D., Calif. Inst. Tech., 1962. Research fellow Calif. Inst. Tech., Pasadena, 1962-63; mem. tech. staff AT&T Bell Labs., Holmdel, N.J., 1963-76; head radio physics research dept. AT&T Bell Labs., 1976—. Recipient Henry Draper medal Royal Astron. Soc., London, 1977, Herschel medal Nat. Acad. Scis., 1977; Nobel prize in physics, 1978; NSF fellow, 1958-61; Cole fellow, 1957-58. Mem. Am. Astron. Soc., Internat. Astron. Union, Am. Phys. Soc., Internat. Sci. Radio Union, Nat. Acad. Scis., Phi Beta Kappa, Sigma Xi. Home: 9 Valley Point Dr Holmdel NJ 07733 Office: AT&T Bell Labs HOH L239 Holmdel NJ 07733

WILSON, RONALD KENNETH, bank executive; b. Port of Spain, Trinidad and Tobago, Aug. 20, 1943; s. Ronald Arnold and Una (James) W.; m. Lorinne Claudia Charles, July 6, 1981; children: Kieron Jude, Kyle. BA with hons., U. of West Indies, Trinidad, 1971; diploma, Mausica Tchrs. Coll. Tchr. I Ministry of Edn., Trinidad and Tobago, 1967, tchr. II, 1970-71; grad. master Dept. Edn., Turks and Caicos Islands, 1976-77; lectr. Mausica Tchrs.' Coll., Trinidad and Tobago, 1971-75; mgmt. trainee Workers' Bank of Trinidad and Tobago, Port of Spain, 1978, asst. corp. sec., 1978-83, mgr. corp. administrn., 1983-85, asst. gen. mgr., 1985—; Bd. dirs. United Trust Corp. of Trinidad and Tobago, Port of Spain, Riverside Plaza Consumers Coop., Port of Spain. Pres. Port of Spain Jaycees, 1983. Fellow Inst. Chartered Secs. and Adminstrs. (W.E. Wallace Meml. prize 1983); mem. Assn. Chartered Secs. and Adminstrs. Trinidad and Tobago (v.p. 1986-87), Brit. Inst. Mgmt., Caribbean Assn. Indigenous Banks (v.p., mem. exec. council West Indies chpt. 1986-87), Inst. Banking Trinidad and Tobago (mem. council 1985-87). Anglican. Home: 41 Irish Ave, La Horquette, Glencoe Trinidad and Tobago Office: Workers' Bank Trinidad and, Tobago Duncan St and, Independence Sq PO Box 927, Port of Spain Trinidad and Tobago

WILSON, THOMAS LEON, physicist; b. Alpine, Tex., May 21, 1942; s. Homer Marvin and Ogarita Maude (Bailey) W.; m. Joyce Ann Krevosky, May 7, 1978; children—Kenneth Edward Byron, Bailey Elizabeth Victoria. B.A., Rice U., 1964, B.S., 1965, M.A., 1974, Ph.D., 1976. With NASA, Houston, 1965—, astronaut instr., 1965-74, high-energy theoretical physicist, 1969—. Contbr. articles in field to profl. jours. Recipient Hugo Gernsback award IEEE, 1964; NASA fellow, 1969-76. Mem. Am. Phys. Soc., AAAS, N.Y. Acad. Scis., Am. Assn. Physicists in Medicine. Research on grand unified field theory, relativistic quantum field theory, quantum chromodynamics, supergravity, cosmology, astrophysics, deep inelastic scattering, authority on neutrino tomography, discover classical uncertainty principle. Subspecialty: relativity and gravitation. Patentee in field; originator olive branch as symbol of man's 1st landing on moon (on Susan B. Anthony and Eisenhower dollars). Home: 206 Woodcombe Dr Houston TX 77062 Office: NASA Johnson Space Center Houston TX 77058

WILSON, THOMAS WILLIAM, lawyer; b. Bklyn., Sept. 14, 1935; s. Matthew and Alice (McCrory) W.; m. Eileen Marie McGann, June 4, 1960; children—Jeanne Alice, Thomas William, David Matthew. A.B., Columbia U., 1957, LL.B., 1960. Bar: N.Y. 1962, U.S. Dist. Ct. (so. and ea. dists.) N.Y. 1962, D.C. 1972. Assoc. Mendes and Mount, N.Y.C., 1961-65, Haller & Small, N.Y.C., 1965-66; gen. counsel Prudential of Gt. Brit., N.Y.C., 1966-68; ptnr. Wilson, Elser, Edelman & Dicker, N.Y.C., 1968—. Contbr. articles to profl. jours. Served with U.S. Army, 1960-65. Mem. ABA, N.Y. State Bar Assn., Def. Research Inst. (editorial bd. profl. liability reporter). Office: Wilson Elser Moskowitz Edelman & Dicker 420 Lexington Ave New York NY 10170

WILSON, VINCENT JOSEPH, JR., writer, historian, publisher; b. Cleve., Apr. 24, 1921; s. Vincent Joseph and Genevieve Margaret (Vleck) W.; student Georgetown U., 1939-41; A.B. with honors, Ariz. State U., 1948; M.A., Claremont Grad. Sch., 1949; postgrad. Harvard U., 1949-50; m. Mary Jo Cavender, Sept. 30, 1944; children—Nicholas Cavender, Liza Jane. Instr., English dept. Mitchell Coll., New London Conn., 1950-53, chmn. dept.,

1953-55; corr. New London Day, 1952-55; editor Nat. Security Agy., Fort Meade, Md., 1956-62, sr. staff writer, 1963-71, chief historian, sr. editor, 1972-81, pub. Am. History Research Assn., 1962—; lectr. English, U. Md., 1959-67, George Washington U., 1963-65. Served to 1st lt. USAAF, 1943-46. Recipient Freedoms Found. at Valley Forge Washington medal, 1968, Honor award, 1974, Nat. Security Agy. Meritorious Service award, 1975. Mem. Am. Hist. Assn. Club: Cosmos (Washington). Author: The Book of the Presidents, 1962, 9th edit., 1985; The Book of Great American Documents, 1967, 76, 87; The Book of States, 1972, 79; The Book of the Founding Fathers, 1974, 86; The Book of Distinguished American Women, 1983; contbr. articles in field to various pubs. Home and Office: 1711 Gold Mine Rd PO Box 140 Brookeville MD 20833

WILSON, WALTER WILLIAM, lawyer; b. Newton, Kans., Dec. 8, 1947; s. Walter Garnet and Mary Elizabeth (Lynsky) W.; m. Judy Marie Anne Destouet, Jan. 26, 1976; children—Melissa Marie, Walter William. B.S., Woodbury Coll., 1972; J.D., Am. U., 1975. Bar: Mo. 1976, U.S. Dist. Ct. (we. dist.) Mo. 1976. Sole practice, St. Louis, 1976—. Bd. dirs. Ctr. for POW/MIA Accountability, Washington, 1982—; Orgn. for Americans Missing Abroad, St. Louis, 1976—; Counsel St. Charles County Bd. Edn., 1978-79, Mo. Parents and Children, St. Louis, 1982-83. Served with U.S. Army, 1967-68. Mem. ABA, Bar Assn. Met. St. Louis, Am. Soc. Internat. Law Inst., Inter-Am. Bar Assn., Internat. Bar Assn., Internat. Antitrust Soc., Union Internat. des Avocats. English Speaking Union (bd. dirs. St. Louis br.), Com. Fgn. Relations. Republican. Episcopalian. Club: Discussion (St. Louis) (bd. dirs.), Univ. Home and Office: 8 Spoede Ln Saint Louis MO 63141

WILSON, YVONNE CHANTILOUPE, family counselor; b. Mandeville, Jamaica, Mar. 26, 1944; d. Raphael Wilburn and Leila May (Mahoney) Chantiloupe; m. Robert Lee Wilson, Jr., Dec. 23, 1967 (div. 1978); children: Robert Lee III, Kurt Olaf; m. Godfrey Alexander Phillip, Aug, 29, 1985. AA, Laguardia Community Coll., 1977; BA, Calif. State U., San Bernardino, 1981; MA, Azusa Pacific U., 1983. Lic. marriage, family and child counselor. Social service counselor Casa De San Bernardino, 1978-80; mental health asst. County Mental Health, San Bernardino, 1980-84; instr. Adelphi Bus. Coll., San Bernardino, 1984-85; adminstrv. dir. owner Home Tutoring Service, Rialto, 1984-86; marriage, family counselor Psychology Ctr., San Bernardino, 1983—; pvt. practice marriage, family counseling San Bernardino, 1983—; social service practitioner Dept. Psych. Social. Services, Riverside, Calif., 1985-87; dir. in. services Inland Empire Residential Ctrs., Mentone, Calif., 1987—; bd. dirs. Sch.. Attendance Rev. Bd., Rialto Sch. Dist., 1978-85, Casa de Ayuda, San Bernardino, 1984-85; mem. adv. bd. Chaffey Coll., Alta Loma, Calif, 1983-84; cons. Daughters United Dept. Pub. Soc. Service, Riverside, 1986—. Mem. Calif. Assn. Marriage and Family Therapists, Calif. State U. Alumni Assn. (sec., treas. 1984-86.). Home: 150 E Morgan St Rialto CA 92376

WILTSE, DORN NORMAN, insurance executive; b. Caro, Mich., Sept. 20, 1911; s. Norman Anson and Evie Markham (McCartney) W.; student Eastern Mich. U., 1931-33; teaching cert. Central Mich. U., 1933-37; m. Gladys May Garner, Nov. 11, 1932; children—Dorr Norman, Saire Christina. Tchr., Tuscola County (Mich.) Public Schs. 1931-42; br. mgr. Mich. Mut. Ins. Co., Caro, 1942-75; city assessor, Caro, 1964—, also casualty ins. cons., Caro, 1975-79. Vice pres. Caro Devel. Corp., 1975-79, pres., 1983—; adv. bd. DeMolay Found. of Mich., 1965-67; founder, pres. Watrousville-Caro Area Hist. Soc., 1972-75, 78; pres. Caro Hist. Commn., 1975-79; chmn. bd. Caro Community Hosp. Endowment Found., 1982—; chmn. Caro Bicentennial Commn., 1975-76; mem. Com. to Elect Pres. Gerald R. Ford, 1975-76; mem. Indianfields-Caro-Almer Planning Commn., 1972-79; co-chmn. Mich. Sesquicentennial for Tuscola County, 1986-87. Tuscola County Citizen of Yr., Caro C. of C., 1975. Mem. Mich. Assessors Assn., Caro Masonic Bldg. Assn., Inc. (pres. 1974-79), Nat. Trust Hist. Preservation, Nat. Hist. Soc., Hist. Soc. Mich., Huguenot Soc. Mich., Saginaw Geneal. Soc., Mich. Archaeol. Soc. Democrat. Presbyterian (elder). Clubs: Caro Lions (pres. 1946), Mich. Nat. Quarter Century, Masons (past master), Shriners. Author: The First Hundred Years, 1978; The Hidden Years of the Master, 1976; The Wiltse Saga, 1980; A Look in Your Own Backyard, 1983. Home: 708 W Sherman St Box 143 Caro MI 48723 Office: 247 S State St Caro MI 48723

WILTSE, GLADYS MAY, social worker; b. Denmark Twp., Mich., July 2, 1908; d. Norman John and Alice May (Levis) Garner; B.A., Eastern Mich. U., 1948; postgrad. U. Mich., 1955-69; m. Dorr Norman Wiltse, Nov. 11, 1932; children—Dorr Norman, Saire Christina Wiltse Keckler. Tchr. public high sch., Mayville, Mich., 1927-30; Vassar (Mich.) High Sch., 1930-33; social worker Tuscola County (Mich.) Bur. Social Aid, 1937-40, supr., 1940-44; area rep. Mich. Dept. Social Welfare Thumb Area, 1944-48; tchr. Caro High Sch., 1955-73; mem. Tuscola Social Services Bd., 1952-85, chmn., 1954-68, vice chmn., 1968-79, 83-85; founder, sponsor Caro High Sch. History Club, 1958 73. Co-founder Watrousville-Caro Area Hist. Soc. and Museum, 1972. Recipient award of commendation Mich. Civil War Centnnial Graves Registration Com., 1965; Merit award Rotary Club, 1975; cert. appreciation Saginaw Inter-Tribal Assn., Inc., 1977; Outstanding Soc. Service award Watrousville-Caro Social Hist. Soc., 1982, numerous other awards. Mem. Mich. Counties Social Services Assn. (Meritorious award 1959, cert. commendation 1981), Caro Tchrs. Assn. (Life 1956-57), Ret. Tchrs.' Assn., Indianfields Questers (pres. 1974-76), Tuscola County Med. Care Facility Forget Me Not Club, Cass River Gem and Mineral Soc., Saginaw Geneal. Soc. Clubs: Caro Garden (pres. 1977-78), DAR, Nat. Soc. Colonial Dames XVII Century, Nat. Soc. Daus. of Barons Runnemede, Huguenot Soc. Mich., Order of Crown of Charlemagne in U.S.A., Nat. Soc. Old Plymouth Colony Descs., Nat. Soc. Daus. Colonial Wars, Order Three Crusades, 1096-1192, Nat. Soc. Sons and Daus. of Pilgrims. Dames of the Court of Honor, Ancient and Honorable Artillery Co., Nat. Soc. of Magna Charta Dames, Colonial Daus., of the XVII Century. Home: 708 W Sherman St PO Box 143 Caro MI 48723

WILTSHAW, DESMOND GREER, economist, educator; b. Newcastle under Lyme, Eng., Aug. 8, 1943; s. George and Brenda Mary Alexandra (Greer) W. BSc (Econ.), London Sch. Econs., 1966; MSc, Queen Mary Coll., 1968. Planning asst. Stoke-on-Trent (Eng.) City Planning Office, 1966-67; asst. researcher London Ministry Housing and Local Govt., 1968-69, Trent Poly., Nottingham, 1969—; sr. lectr. dept. town and country planning, 1969-87, dept. surveying, 1987—; vis. lectr. U. Nottingham, 1982—; research supr. House Builders Fedn. Birmingham, 1985-86. Contbr. articles to profl. jours. Mem. Internat. Transactional Analysis Assn. Office: Dept Surveying, Trent Poly Burton St, Nottingham NG1 4BU, England

WILTSHIRE, KENNETH WILLIAM, political science educator, Australian government administrator; b. Brisbane, Queensland, Australia, Dec. 11, 1944; s. Harry William and Beryl Muriel (Burdeu) W.; m. Gail Jocelyn Raymond, Apr. 27, 1968; one son, Christopher James. B.Econ. with honors, U. Queensland, Brisbane, 1968, Ph.D., 1981; M.Sc.Econ., London Sch. Econs., 1972. Research economist Queensland Govt., Brisbane, 1962-70; sr. lectr. U. Queensland, 1972-83, assoc. prof. polit. sci., 1983—; chmn. Australian Heritage Commn., Canberra, 1982-85; mem. exec. com. UNESCO Nat. Com. cons. in field. Author: An Introduction to Australian Public Administration, 1974; formulating Government Budgets, 1976; Administrative Federalism, 1977; Planning and Federalism, 1986, Privatisation: The British Experience, 1987, The History of the Professional Officers Association, 1987. Broadcaster Australian Broadcasting Commn., 1973—; polit. analyst Ten TV Network Australia, 1974—; mem. Inquiry Into Efficiency and Effectiveness of Brisbane City Council, 1979. Fellow Royal Australian Inst. Pub. Adminstrn.; mem. Inst. Pub. Adminstrn. Can., Royal Inst. Pub. Adminstrn. (U.K.), Convocation London Sch. Econs. (life). Office: U Queensland, St Lucia St, Brisbane Queensland 4067, Australia

WIMBERLY, BEADIE RENEAU (LEIGH), financial services executive; b. Fouke, Ark., Apr. 18, 1937; d. Woodrow Wilson and Grace B. (Winkley) Reneau; m. Benjamin Leon Price, 1954 (div. 1955); m. Elbert William Wimberly, Dec. 16, 1956; children—Stephanie Elaine Wimberly Davis, Jeffrey Scott, Lael Wimberly Carter Alston. Student William & Mary Coll., 1964-65, U. Md.-Ludwigsburg/Stuttgart, 1966-68, Northwestern State U. La., 1973-75, Cornell U., 1979, Leonard Sch. 1983. Cert. ins. agt.; registered gen. securities rep. SEC, registered investment adviser SEC. Internat. trainer of trainers North Atlantic council Girl Scouts, Fed. Republic Germany,

1965-69, 76-78; inventory master The Myers Co., Inc., El Paso, Tex., 1970; abstract asst. Vernon Abstract Co., Inc., Leesville, La., 1970-71; sec. to chief utilities and pollution control Dept. Army, U.S. Civil Service, Ft. Polk, La., 1971-72, asst. to post safety officer, 1972-73, administr. tech. Adj. Gen.'s Office, 1973-75, sr. library technician post libraries, 1975, personnel staffing specialist, Stuttgart, Fed. Republic Germany, 1976-79, voucher examiner Fin. and Acctg. Office, Ft. Polk, 1980-81; chief exec. officer Fin. Strategies, Inc., Leesville, La., 1981—, stockbroker, corp. exec., 1983—, mktg. exec., 1983—; labor cons. AFL/CIO, Ft. Polk, 1981—; sr. resident mgr. Anchor Nat. Fin. Services Inc.; dir., treas. Wimberly Enterprises, Inc. Bd. dirs. Calcasieu Parish council Boy Scouts Am., 1988—; treas. Vernon Parish Hist./Geneal. Soc., 1986-87; pres. Vernon Parish Helpline/Lifeline, 1985; charter mem. Nat. Mus. of Women in the Arts; mem. Vernon Parish Arts Council. Mem. Pilot Internat., Internat. Assn. Fin. Planners, Nat. Assn. Govt. Employees (v.p. Ft. Polk chpt. 1980-81), Internat. Platform Assn., C. of C., Assn. U.S. Army, Am. Assn. Fin. Profls., Nat. Women's Polit. Caucus, Am. Soc. Mil. Comptrollers, LWV-La. (state bd. dirs. 1986-87, treas. Leesville chpt. 1982-87), NOW (Ruston-Grambling chpt.). Republican. Baptist. Club: Toastmasters (named Competent Toastmaster, 1979). Lodge: Rotary (bd. mem.-at-large Leesville club 1988—). Office: Fin Strategies Inc 302 N 5th St Leesville LA 71444

WIMPRESS, GORDON DUNCAN, JR., foundation executive, educator; b. Riverside, Calif., Apr. 10, 1922; s. Gordon Duncan and Maude A. (Waldo) W.; m. Jean Margaret Skerry, Nov. 30, 1946; children—Wendy Jo, Victoria Jean, Gordon Duncan III. B.A., U. Oreg., Eugene, 1946, M.A., 1951; Ph.D., U. Denver, 1958; LL.D., Monmouth Coll., 1970; L.H.D., Tusculum Coll., Greenville, Tenn., 1971. Lic. comml. pilot. Dir. pub. relations, instr. journalism Whittier Coll., Calif., 1946-51; asst. to pres. Colo. Sch. Mines, Golden, 1951-59; pres. Monticello Coll., Alton, Ill., 1959-64, Monmouth Coll., Ill., 1964-70, Trinity U., San Antonio, 1970-77, vice chmn. bd. govs. Southwest Found. for Research and Edn., San Antonio, 1977-82; pres. SW Found. for Biomed. Research, San Antonio, 1982—; commr. Burlington No. R.R. Scholarship Selection Com.; bd. govs. Southwest Found. for Biomed. Research; chmn. Valero Energy Corp. Scholarship Commn., Military Affairs Council; bd. dirs. Southwest Research Inst., 1st RepublicBank, San Antonio. Author: American Journalism Comes of Age, 1950. Bd. dirs. Am. Inst. for Character Edn., ARC, Am. Heart Assn., San Antonio, Mission Rd. Devel. Ctr., Cancer Therapy and Research Found., Japan Am. Soc. San Antonio, San Antonio Oral Health Assn.; exec. cons. Donald W. Reynolds Found., Inc.; trustee Mind Sci. Found.; chmn. San Antonio Area Employer Support of Guard and Res.; mem. San Antonio Fiesta Commn.; trustee San Antonio Med. Found.; trustee Winston Sch., Sigma Phi Epsilon Edn. Found.; ruling elder United Presbyn. Ch., U.S.A.; mem. World Bus. Council. Served to 1st lt. AUS, 1942-45, ETO. Decorated Bronze Star. Mem. Aircraft Owners and Pilots Assn., Am. Acad. Polit. and Social Sci., Am. Assn. Higher Edn., Am. Council on Edn., Assn. Am. Colls., Council Advancement and Support Assn., MENSA, Nat. Pilots Assn., Pilots Internat. Assn., Inc., Quiet Birdmen, San Antonio Pilots Assn., Greater San Antonio C. of C. (bd. dirs., steering com. mil. affairs council), Assn. Former Intelligence Officers, Confederate Air Force, Pi Gamma Mu, Sigma Delta Chi, Sigma Delta Pi, Sigma Phi Epsilon (trustee found.), Sigma Upsilon, Newcomen Soc. N.Am. Clubs: Argyle, St. Anthony, San Antonio Country, the Dominion (bd. govs.), Ariel House, City (San Antonio), San Antonio Golf Assn. (v.p.). Lodge: Rotary (dist. gov. 1983-84, San Antonio). Office: Southwest Found for Biomed Research W Loop 410 at Military Dr PO Box 28147 San Antonio TX 78284

WINARSKI, DANIEL JAMES, mechanical engineer; b. Toledo, Dec. 16, 1948; s. Daniel Edward and Marguerite (Pietersien) W.; BS in Engring., U. Mich., 1970, PhD (NSF fellow), 1976; MS, U. Colo., 1973; m. Donna Ilene Robinson, Oct. 10, 1970; 1 son, Tyson York. Mech. engr. Libbey Owens Ford Co., Toledo, summers 1968, 69, 72; petroleum engr. Exxon Production Research, Houston, 1976-77; staff engr. mech. engring. sect. IBM, Tucson, 1977-84, adv. engr., 1984-86, systems engr., performance evaluator, 1986—; assoc. prof. dept. mechanics U.S. Mil. Acad., 1980—; instr. minority computer edn. No. Ariz. U., 1983-85. Served to 1st lt. U.S. Army, 1970-72; maj. Res., 1984. Recipient IBM Invention Achievement award, 1981, 82, 83, IBM Mfg. award, 1986; registered profl. engr., Ariz., Colo. Mem. ASME (pub. chmn. U. Mich. 1974), Sharlot Hall Mus., Mus. No. Ariz., Phi Eta Sigma, Pi Tau Sigma, Tau Beta Pi. Republican. Methodist. Club: So. Ariz. Designer adjustable artificial leg; patentee tape reel hub, tape loose-wrap check, tape reel sizing, tape reel-cartridge. Office: IBM Corp 67E/060-1 Tucson AZ 85744

WINATA, EVY, oil company executive; b. Jakarta, West-Java, Indonesia, Feb. 13, 1945; parents Lim Kang Sip and Lea Winata. Student, Krisnadwipayana U., Jakarta, 1965-67; cert., Asian Inst. Mgmt., Makati, Philippines, 1984. Sec. trade dept. Italian Embassy, Jakarta, 1967-68; sec. Messageries Maritimes, Jakarta, 1968, Schlumberger Oil Co., Jakarta, 1969-71; fin. mgr. Pvt. Co., Jakarta, 1971-76; adminstr., fin. dir. P.T. Atvaviola Inc., Jakarta, 1977—. Baptist. Home: Jalan Sindoro No 3, Jakarta Selatan West-Java 12980, Indonesia

WINBERG, CLAES ULRIK, management executive; b. Copenhagen, Sept. 23, 1925; s. Karl and Nellie (Moller) W.; M.S., Tech. U. Denmark, 1952; m. Ebba Kristina Bergenstrahle, Apr. 9, 1952; children—Ulrik, Flemming, Christer. Engr.. Husqvarna Vapenfabriks AB, Sweden, 1952-53; engr. Sundstrand Machine Tool Co., Rockford, Ill., 1953-55; sales engr., Sundstrand, Paris, 1955-57; export mgr. A/S Atlas, Copenhagen, 1957-60; pres. A/S Soren Wistoft & Co., Fabriker, Copenhagen, 1960-62; asst. mgr. AB Svenska Flaktfabriken, Stockholm, 1962-66; pres. Hexagon AB, Stockholm, 1966-71; v.p. AB Bofors, Sweden, 1971-72, pres., 1972-84; bd. dirs. Hasselfors AB, other cos. and orgns. Decorated comdr. Order of Vasa, comdr. Order of Vita Ros (Finland), King's medal. Mem. Royal Patriotic Soc. Home: Strandvagen 49, 11523 Stockholm Sweden

WINCHELL, WILLIAM OLIN, mechanical engineer, educator; b. Rochester, N.Y., Dec. 31, 1933; s. Leslie Olin and Hazel Agnes (Apker) W.; m. Doris Jane Martenson, Jan. 19, 1957; children: Jason, Darrell, Kirk. BME, GMI Engring. and Mgmt. Inst., 1956; MSc, Ohio State U., 1970; MBA, U. Detroit, 1976; JD, Detroit Coll. Law, 1980. Bar: Mich. 1981, U.S. Dist. Ct. (ea. dist.) Mich. 1981, U.S. Ct. Appeals (6th cir.) 1982, U.S. Supreme Ct. 1985, N.Y. 1988; registered profl. engr., Mich., N.Y. Cons. Gen. Motors Corp., Detroit and Warren, Mich. and Lockport, N.Y., 1951-87; sole practice Royal Oak, Mich., 1981-88; assoc. prof., chmn. dept indsl. engring. Alfred (N.Y.) U., 1987—. Mem. Royal Oak Long Range Planning Commn., 1980. Served to lt. commdr. USNR, 1956-76. Burton fellow Detroit Coll. Law, 1978. Fellow Am. Soc. Quality Control (v.p. 1985-88); mem. ABA, Mich. Bar Assn., Soc. Mfg. Engrs., Inst. Indsl. Engrs., Tau Beta Pi, Beta Gamma Sigma. Roman Catholic. Club: North Star Sail. Office: Alfred U Sch Engring Div Indsl and Mech Engring Alfred NY 14802

WINCHESTER, ALMA ELIZABETH TATSCH (MRS. CLARENCE FLOYD WINCHESTER), civic worker, radio writer and broadcaster; b. Fredericksburg, Tex.; d. Otto August and Meta (Hohenberger) Tatsch; spl. student Am. Conservatory Music (Chgo.), 1937-38; m. Clarence Floyd Winchester, Sept. 25, 1943. Singer Chgo. Civic Opera Jr. Chorus, 1937-38; writer radio script Evans Fur Co., Chgo., 1941-42; writer Sta. KTSA, San Antonio, 1942-43; women's dir., writer, broadcaster Sta. KNOE, Monroe, La., 1944-45; writer, music lead in Boyce Smith Show, Sta. WGN, Chgo., 1944; women's dir., writer, broadcaster Sta. WGGG, Gainesville, Fla., 1948-49; public relations Stokeley-Van Camp, Inc., Washington, 1954-55. Mem. Salvation Army Aux., Washington; mem. women's bd. Providence Hosp., Washington, Pan-Am. liaison com. Women's Orgns., Washington, to 1981; mem. Women's Internat. Religious Fellowship in cooperation with UNESCO, UNICEF, schs., embassies; past pres. City of Hope Med. Research chpt. 56, Washington. Mem. Los Picaros (hon.). Mem. Christian Ch. Home: 3900 Watson Pl NW A Bldg Apt #2-E Washington DC 20016

WINCHESTER, CLARENCE FLOYD, retired nutritionist; b. Chgo., Oct. 14, 1901; s. Leon Alpheus and Nina Pearl (Thompson) W.; B.S.. U. Calif. at Berkeley, 1924, M.S., 1935; Ph.D., U. Mo., 1939; m. Maxine Gertrude Kiefer, Sept. 15, 1924 (div. 1938); 1 dau., Maxine Claire (Mrs. Robert Cloon); m. 2d, Alma Elizabeth Tatsch, Sept. 25, 1943. Tchr. pub. schs., Los Angeles, 1924-28, Palo Verde, Calif., 1928-29, Fresno, Calif., 1929-31;

research scientist U. N.H., 1931-32, U. Calif. at Davis, 1932-37, U. Mo., 1937-46; asso. prof. U. Fla., 1946-49; agrl. research scientist, Beltsville, Md., 1949-61; nutritionist U.S. Dept. Interior, 1961-66; lectr. Howard U., Washington, 1966-75; nutrition cons., 1975-82. Served from 1st lt. to capt., U.S. Army, 1942-46. Fellow AAAS, Am. Inst. Chemists; mem. Am. Chem. Soc., Am. Inst. Nutrition, AAUP, Assn. Overseas Educators, Am. Soc. Animal Prodn.. Mil. Order World Wars, Sigma Xi, Gamma Sigma Delta, Alpha Chi Sigma, Gamma Alpha. Mason (32 deg.). Club: Cosmos (Washington). Home: 3900 Watson Pl NW Bldg A Apt 2E Washington DC 20016 Mailing: care of Donald Winchester 1100 Morton St Alameda CA 94501

WINDELS, PAUL, JR., lawyer; b. Bklyn., Nov. 13, 1921; s. Paul and Louise E. (Gross) W.; m. Patricia Ripley, Sept. 10, 1955; children: Paul III, Mary H., James H.R., Patrick D. A.B., Princeton U., 1943; LL.B., Harvard U., 1948. Bar: N.Y. 1949. Spl asst. counsel N.Y. State Crime Commn., 1951; asst. U.S. atty. Eastern Dist. N.Y., 1953-56; N.Y. regional adminstr. SEC, 1956-61, also spl. asst., U.S. atty. for prosecution securities frauds, 1956-58; lectr. law Am. Inst. Banking, 1950-57; assoc. Windels, Marx, Davies & Ives (and predecessor firms), 1961—. Author: Our Securities Markets-Some SEC Problems and Techniques, 1962. Trustee, pres. Bklyn. Law Sch.; trustee, past pres. Fed. Bar Council; trustee, treas. French Inst./ Alliance Française; chmn. French-Am. Monument Found.; mem. adv. bd. NYU Inst. French Studies; mem. Woods Hole Oceanographic Inst. Served from pvt. to capt. F.A. AUS, 1943-46, ETO; maj. Army. Res. Recipient Flemming award for fed. service; decorated chevalier Order French Acad. Palms; officer Nat. Order Merit France. Fellow Am. Bar Found.; mem. ABA, N.Y. State Bar Assn., Assn. of Bar of City of N.Y.; Assn. N.Y. County Lawyers Assn. Republican. Presbyterian. Office: 156 W 56th St New York NY 10019

WINDERMAN, LEE JAY, psychologist; b. Bklyn., Feb. 9, 1948; s. Abraham and Frances (Klein) W. B.A., Bklyn. Coll., 1970; M.A. (NIMH fellow), U. Calif.-Berkeley, 1974, Ph.D. (NIMH fellow), 1978. Univ. postdoctoral fellow pediatric psychology, div. behavioral pediatrics and child devel. U. Tex. Med. Br., Galveston, 1978-79; fellow in family therapy Galveston Family Inst., 1979-80, resident sr. faculty, dir. continuing edn. 1980-84, assoc. dir., 1984—; faculty Houston Family Inst., 1984—; pvt. practice, Houston, 1984—; cons. Hope Center for Youth, Houston, 1980—, Family Therapy Consortium, 1981—. Mem. Am. Psychol. Assn., Am. Acad. Behavioral Medicine, SW Psychol. Assn., Am. Assn. Marriage and Family Therapists, Tex. Assn. Marriage and Family Therapists (bd. dirs. 1985—), Nat. Council Health Service Providers. Office: 1020 Holcombe Blvd Suite 1200 Houston TX 77030

WINDHAM, EDWARD JAMES, bank executive, leasing company executive; b. Salt Lake City, Dec. 13, 1950; s. James Rudolph and Margaret Ann (Griffith) W.; m. Marilyn Ann Kenyon, Mar. 27, 1973; children: Ian James, Kendra Ann. Student, U. Calif., San Diego, 1969-70, 72-74, U. Calif., Santa Barbara, 1970-72. Cert. mortgage credit examiner HUD. Emergency med. technician Hartson's Mobile Intensive Care Unit, San Diego, 1973-76; salesman Bonanza Properties, Tustin, Calif., 1976; loan officer Medallion Mortgage, Santa Cruz, Calif., 1976-80; sr. loan officer Cen. Pacific Mortgage, Santa Cruz, 1980-83, v.p., 1983-86; ptnr. Winn Leasing Co., Santa Cruz, 1983—; v.p. Community West Mortgage, 1986—; cons. Contour Inc., San Jose, Calif., 1983-85. Pres. Evergreen Estates Homeowners Assn., Soquel, Calif., 1983-85. Recipient Best Havana Brown award S.W. region Cat Fanciers Assn., 1976,77. Mem. Nat. Assn. Rev. Appraisers and Rev. Underwriters (sr., cert.), Mortgage Bankers Assn., Calif. Mortgage Bankers Assn., Mensa, Intertel. Republican. Lodge: Masons (master Santa Cruz 1987). Home: 3907 Adar Ln Soquel CA 95073 Office: Community West Mortgage PO Box 939 Capitola CA 95010-0939

WINDSOR, ROBERT KENNEDY, association executive, consultant, inventor; b. Phila., Sept. 17, 1933; s. William Elmer and Margaret Kennedy (Wilson) W.; m. Mary Margaret Willis, June 25, 1955 (div. Mar. 1961); 1 son, David Kennedy. A.B., Bowdoin Coll., 1955; postgrad., Columbia U., 1961. Traffic supr. Bell Telephone Co. Pa., Phila., 1955-64; gen. mgr. Soc. Indsl. and Applied Maths., Phila., 1964-76; mng. partner Phoebus Co., Newcastle, Del., 1973-76; pres. Phoebus Co., 1976-80; partner Windsor & Knipe, Phila., 1968-76; exec. v.p. AAHPER and Dance, Reston, Va., 1980-81; exec. dir. Adminstrv. Mgmt. Soc., Willow Grove, Pa., 1981—; dir. Weather Energy Systems, Inc., AMSCO. Internat. sec. AMS Found. Served with Signal Corps U.S. Army, 1956-58; Res. 1958-67. Mem. Am. Mgmt. Assn., Am. Soc. Assn. Execs., Soc. Office Automation Profls. (dir.), Nat. Assn. Industry-Edn. Cooperation (dir.), Del. Valley Soc. of Assn. Execs., Golfing Soc. Scotland (exec. sec., dir.), Chi Psi.

WINER, JANE LOUISE, psychology educator; b. Albany, N.Y., Nov. 1, 1947; d. Harold and Elizabeth Gertrude (Jensen) W.; m. Monty Joseph Strauss, Nov. 4, 1978. B.A., SUNY-Albany, 1969, M.L.S., 1970; M.A., Ohio State U. 1971, Ph.D., 1973. Lic. psychologist, Tex.; registered psychologist Nat. Register Health Service Providers in Psychology. Asst. prof. psychology Tex. Tech U., Lubbock, 1975-81, assoc. prof., 1981-86, prof., 1986—; assoc. dean research Coll. Arts Scis., 1987—. Contbr. articles to profl. jours. NSF grad. trainee Ohio State U., 1970-73. Mem. Am. Psychol. Assn., Southwestern Psychol. Assn., Tex. Psychol. Assn., Assn. Counseling and Devel., Assn. Women in Sci. Democrat. Jewish. Research on vocat. psychology, including vocat. choice, person-environ. congruence, computer literacy and applications. Home: 7010 Nashville Dr Lubbock TX 79413 Office: Tex Tech Univ Coll Arts and Sci Office of Dean Lubbock TX 79409

WINER, WARREN JAMES, insurance executive; b. Wichita, Kans., June 16, 1946; s. Henry Charles and Isabel (Ginsburg) W.; m. Mary Jean Kovacs, June 23, 1968 (div. Feb. 1973); m. Jo Lynn Sondag, May 3, 1975; children: Adam, Lauren. BS in Math., Stanford U., 1968. With Gen. Am. Life Ins. Co., St. Louis, 1968-73, dir. retirement plans, 1973-76, 2d v.p., 1976-80; v.p., sr. actuary Powers, Carpenter & Hall, St. Louis 1980-84, sr. v.p., dir. pension div., 1984-85, pres., chief operating officer, 1985-86, lobbyist, commentator 1985—, pres., chief exec. officer, 1986—; pres. C&B Cons. Group, 1988—; mem. Actuarial Exam. Com., Chgo., 1973-74. Contbr. articles to profl. jours. Bd. dirs. Lucky Lane Nursery Sch. Assn., St. Louis 1978-83; co-v.p. PTA, Conway Sch., St. Louis, 1986-87, co-pres., 1987—; bd. dirs. pilot div. United Way, 1986-87. Fellow Soc. Actuaries; mem. Am. Acad. Actuaries, Enrollment of Actuaries (joint bd.), Am. Life Ins. Assn. (small case task force 1979-80), Life Office Mgmt. Assn. (ICPAC com. 1975-80), St. Louis Actuaries Club. Jewish. Clubs: St. Louis, Clayton (St. Louis). Office: Corroon & Black Cons Group 231 S Bemiston Suite 400 Saint Louis MO 63105

WINFORD, DONALD CHARLES, linguist, educator; b. San Fernando, Trinidad and Tobago, Apr. 18, 1945; s. Andrew and Olive (Hunte) W. BA in English, King's Coll., U. London, 1968; PhD in Linguistics, U. York, Eng., 1972. Lectr. U. W.I., St. Augustine, Trinidad and Tobago, 1972-84, chmn. dept. linguistics, 1974-75; sr. lectr., 1984—; assoc. prof. U. Tex., Austin, 1979; lectr. U. Tex., El Paso, 1982-83. Editor: (jour.) Caribbean Issues, 1974; contbr. articles to profl. jours. Mem. Internat. assn. for Applied Linguistics, Linguistic Assn. Am., Soc. Caribbean Linguistics (sec./treas. 1984—). Roman Catholic. Home: 1 Gordon St Lot 4, Saint Augustine Trinidad and Tobago Office: U WI Dept Linguistics, Saint Augustine Trinidad and Tobago

WING, ADRIEN KATHERINE, legal educator; b. Oceanside, Calif., Aug. 7, 1956; d. John Ellison and Katherine (Pruitt) Wing; m. Enrico A. Melson, Apr. 28, 1983; 1 child, Che-Cabral. A.B. magna cum laude, Princeton U., 1978; M.A., UCLA, 1979; J.D., Stanford Law Sch., 1982. Bar: N.Y. 1983, U.S. Dist. Ct. (so. and ea. dists.) N.Y. 1983, U.S. Ct. Appeals (5th and 9th circs.). Assoc. Curtis, Mallet-Prevost, Colt & Mosle, N.Y.C., 1982-86, Rabinowitz, Boudin, Stadard, Krinsky & Lieberman, 1986-87; assoc. prof. law U. Iowa, Iowa City, 1987—; mem. alumni council Princeton U., 1983-85, trustee Class of '78 Found., 1984-87. Mem. ABA Cocaon. young lawyers sect. 1985—), Nat. Conf. Black Lawyers (UN rep.), chmn. internat. affairs sect. 1982—), Internat. Assn. Dem. Lawyers (UN rep. 1984-87), Am. Soc. Internat. Law (exec. council 1986—), Black Alumni of Princeton U. Inc. (bd. dirs. 1982-87), Council on Fgn. Relations. Avocations: photography, jogging, writing, poetry.

WING, JAMES ERWIN, investment advisor; b. Grand Rapids, Mich., Sept. 21, 1958; s. Ray Erwin and Helen May (Dennis) W.; m. Dana Mason, Oct. 13, 1984. B.S., Babson Coll., 1980. Owner McNally-Wing Co., Wellesley, Mass., 1976-80; investment advisor E.F. Hutton, Chestnut Hill, Mass., 1980-85; investment adviser, v.p. Drexel Burnham Lambert, Boston, 1985—. Republican. Home: 585A Gray St Westwood MA 02090 Office: Drexel Burnham Lambert 1 Federal St 34th Floor Boston MA 02110

WING, KYLENE SCARBOROUGH (MRS. ROBERT L. WING), columnist; b. Charlotte, N.C.; d. Kyle and Tomi (Riggs) Scarborough; grad. Stevens Schs. for Models, 1946-47, Ben Bard Acad. Theatre, Hollywood, Calif., 1952, Nat. Acad. Broadcasting Washington, 1957, UCLA Extension, 1965, Free U. Berlin Otto-Suhrz Inst. Extension, 1966. m. Robert L. Wing, Jan. 16, 1943; children—Susan, Jayme. Columnist, Kylene's Kalifornia Kapers, Inverness, Fla., 1965-66, Kylene's Kontinental Kapers, Berlin, Germany, 1966-68; publicity chmn. Am. Women's Club Founder patron Huntington Hartford Theatre; mem. Concerned Friend Nat. League Families POW-MIA, U.S. Congl. Adv. Bd. Recipient letter of Appreciation USAF, 1973. Mem. Planetary Soc., Hollywood C. of C., Freedom Found. at Valley Forge, Los Angeles World Affairs Council. Presbyn. Clubs: German American Women's, American Women's, American Yacht (all Berlin); Los Angeles Riding and Polo; Air Force Officers Wives; Bel-Air Republican Women's. Address: 3405 Blair Dr Hollywood CA 90068

WINGARD, RAYMOND RANDOLPH, wood preservation, chemicals and forest products company executive; b. Goshen, Ala., Nov. 6, 1930; s. Raymond T. and Mary (Sanders) W.; student So. Meth. U., 1948-49, Birmingham-So. Coll., 1949-50, Harvard, 1973; m. Gainnell Harris, June 2, 1951; children—Renee, Kay, Beckie, Robin, Randy. With Koppers Co. Inc., 1951-60, 61-62 , area mgr., Montgomery, Ala., 1963-64, agy. mgr. Ala. Farm Bur. Service, Andalusia, 1962-63; mgr. R.R. sales and plannning Western region, Chgo., 1964-71, div. mgr., asst. v.p. R.R. sales and planning, 1971-74, asst. v.p., mktg. mgr., Pitts., 1974-75, v.p., mgr. human resources, 1975-80, v.p., mgr. mktg. dept., 1981-85, v.p., mgr. adminstrv. services and corp. planning, 1985—. Chmn., R-1 Sch. Dist. Adv. Council, Independence, Mo., 1960; pres. Independence Suburban Community Improvement League, 1959-60; mem. dist. 58 Bd. Edn., 1959-71; trustee Pitts. Council Internat. Visitors, 1978-84, pres., 1982-83; pres. Minority Engring. Edn. Effect, Inc., 1977-80; bd. dirs. Allegheny council Boy Scouts Am., Blue Cross of Pa., vice-chmn., 1986—. Served with AUS, 1950-51. Mem. Am. Wood Preservers Assn., Pitts. Personnel Assn., Ry. Tie Assn., Pa. State C. of C., YMCA, Western Ry. Club, Labor Policy Assn. Methodist. Club: Duquesne. Home: 8656 Peters Rd Mars PA 16046 Office: Koppers Bldg Pittsburgh PA 15219

WINGTI, PAIAS, former prime minister of Papua, New Guinea. Student U. Papua New Guinea. Joined Nat. Parliament, 1977, govt. whip and asst. speaker, 1977-78, opposition leader, 1985; leader People's Dem. Movement; minister transport and civil aviation, Papua New Guinea, 1979-80, former dep. prime minister, minister nat. planning; prime minister, 1987-88. Address: Office of Prime Minister, PO Box 6605, Boroko Papua New Guinea

WINIARCZYK, MAREK, humanities educator; b. Wroclaw, Poland, June 30, 1947; s. Gustaw and Maria (Tomaszuk) W. MA, Wroclaw U., 1970, PhD, 1976, D Habilitatus, 1982. Librarian U. Wroclaw, Poland, 1970-73, lectr. dept. fgn. lang., 1973-83, assoc. prof. classical lang., 1983—. Author: Starozytne wykazy ateistow, 1977, Diagorae Melii et Theodori Cyrenaei reliquiae, 1981; author dictionary: Sigla Latina, 1977; contbr. articles to profl. jours. Mem. Wrocvlawskie Towarzystwo Naukowe, Polskie Towarzystwo Filologiczne (chief of br. 1986—). Roman Catholic. Home: Kaz Jagiellonczyka 10/13, 50240 Wroclaw Poland Office: Wroclaw U, Biskupa Nankiera 2, 50139 Wroclaw Poland

WINICK, PAULINE, sports, communications executive; b. N.Y.C., Sept. 19, 1946; d. Morris and Frances (Fox) Leiderman; m. Bruce Jeffrey Winick, June 19, 1966 (div. 1977); children—Margot Scott, Graham Douglas. B.A., Bklyn. Coll., 1966; M.A., NYU, 1971; A.S., Miami-Dade Community Coll., 1977. Tchr. N.Y.C. Pub. Schs., 1966-66, 69-74, Bloomington (Ind.) Pub. Schs., 1968-69; producer Sta. WPLG-TV, Miami, Fla., 1975-79; dir. Office of Communications, Metro-Dade County, Miami, Fla., 1979-86; exec. asst. city mgr. City of Miami, 1986; proprietor Pauline Winick and Assocs., 1986—; v.p. for adminstrn. Miami Heat Basketball Team, 1988—. Bd. dirs. Fla. Close-Up, Miami, 1979—, Miami City Ballet, Anti-Defamation League, 1983, LWV, Miami, 1980, Dade Pub. Edn. Fund, 1987—; counselor Dade County Cultural Affairs Council; mem. exec. com. Leadership Miami Conf., 1980-82; bd. dirs. Found. for Excellence in Pub. Edn., 1987—; Miami Arts Exchange, 1987—, Jewish Fedn. TV, 1987—. Mem. Nat. Acad. TV Arts and Scis. (bd. govs. Miami chpt. 1986-88), Fla. Bar Assn. (mem. grievance com.). Home: 11420 SW 72d Ave Miami FL 33156 Office: 330 Greco Ave Coral Gables FL 33146 Office: The Miami Heat The Miami Arena Miami FL 33136-4102

WINKEL, JØRGEN, work physiologist, researcher; b. Copenhagen, Apr. 25, 1946; came to Sweden, 1976; s. Per and Regitze Terese (Keyper) W.; m. Eva Elisabeth Pavell, Apr. 19, 1984. B.Sc., Nat. Coll. Phys. Edn., 1968; M.Sc., U. Copenhagen, 1976; Ph.D., Karolinska Inst., 1986. Tchr. U. Copenhagen, 1970-71; tchr. Coll. Phys. Therapy, Copenhagen, 1971-76; tchr., researcher U. Lulea, 1976-80, head work physiology div. Dept. Human Work Scis., 1980-85; expert work physiology Nat. Bd. Occupational Safety and Health, Stockholm, 1983-85, researcher unit work physiology, 1985-87; researcher Nat. Inst. Occupational Health, 1987—; assoc. prof., U. Lulea, Sweden, 1987—. Mem. Internat. Soc. Biomechanics, Nordic Ergonomics Soc. Author: Applied Work Physiology, 1978; contbr. articles on foot complaints in prolonged sitting and the significance of leg activity; electromyographic studies of muscular load and fatigue in working life. Home: Torneagatan 50, S-164 79 Kista Sweden

WINKLER, EIKE-MEINRAD, psychologist, anthropologist, educator; b. Vienna, Austria, Oct. 3, 1948; s. Helmut and Ursula (Engler) W.; m. Brigitte Hoeller, May 16, 1962; 1 child, Iska-Ricarda. PhD in Psychology, U. Vienna, Austria, 1974, PhD in Anthropology, 1989. Research asst. Inst. for Human Biology, Vienna, Austria, 1973-74, univ. asst., 1974-78, asst. prof., 1982—; mem. numerous excavations and expeditions to Africa. Author: Expedition Mensch, 1982, Tell el Dab'a, 1988; contbr. articles to profl. publications. Office: Inst Human Biology, Althanstrasse 14, 1090 Vienna Austria

WINKLER, GUENTHER, educator; b. Unterhaus, Carinthia Austria, Jan. 15, 1929; s. Andreas and Agnes (Stampfer) W.; Dr.jur., U. Innsbruck, 1951, Dr.phil. (hon.), 1975, Dr. iur. (hon.) 1985. Lectr. U. Innsbruck (Austria), 1951-55, asst. reader, 1955-56; asst. reader Vienna (Austria) U., 1956-59, assoc. prof., 1959-61, prof. polit. and adminstrv. sci., Austrian constnl. and adminstrv. law, theory of law and state, 1961—, dean Law Faculty, 1965-66, rector of univ., 1972-73, prorector, 1973-75; chmn. Inst. Chinese Culture (Sun Yat-sen), Vienna, 1971—; chmn. Union German Constl. Law Tchrs., 1979-81. Decorated Great Cross of Honor, Commdr. of Order of Service Merit, Austria, 1971, 76, Commdr. of Service Merit of Lower Austria, 1986; Great Order of Brilliant Star, Republic of China, 1975, Great Cordon of Brilliant Star, 1976, Great Cordon of Order of Propitious Clouds, 1986; Great Commdr. of Order of Finnish Lion, Finland, 1976; Cordon of Order of Diplomatic Service Merit, Korea, 1973; Commdr. of Order of Great Lion, Senegal, 1975; Great Commdr. of Order of Saint Sylvester, Vatican, 1976. Mem. Internat. Assn. Adminstrv. Sci., Internat. Assn. for Polit. Sci., Internat. Assn. for Philosophy of Law and Social Philosophy, Internat. Law Assn., Institut du droit administratif (Belgium). Author: Der Bescheid, 1956; Die absolute Nichtigkeit von Verwaltungsakt, 1960, Wertbetrachtung im Recht und ihre Grenzen, 1969; Gesetzgebung und Verwaltung im Wirtschaftsrecht, 1970; Orientierungen im öffentlichen Recht, 1979; Die Wissenschaft vom Verwaltungsrecht, 1979; Sein und Sollen, 1980, Die Rechtspersönlichkeit der Universitäten, 1988; author: Forschungen aus Staat und Recht, 1967—. Home: Reisnerstrasse 22/5/11, A1030 Vienna Austria Office: U Vienna, Institut für Staats-und, Verwaltungsrecht, A1010 Vienna Austria

WINKLER, HEINRICH AUGUST, modern history educator; b. Koenigsberg, Germany, Dec. 19, 1938; s. Theodor and Brigitte (Seraphim) W.; m. Doerte Schnur, July 19, 1974. Abitur, Humboldt-Gymnasium, Ulm,

Baden-Wuerttemberg, 1957; PhD, Tuebingen U., Muenster, Heidelberg, Tuebingen, 1963; Habilitation, Free U., West Berlin, 1970. Asst. Free U., West Berlin, 1964-70; assoc. prof. Free U., West Berlin, Federal Republic of Germany, 1970-72; full prof. modern history U. Freiburg, Federal Republic of Germany, 1972—. Author: Preussischer Liberalismus und deutscher Nationalstaat, 1964, Mittelstand, Demokratie und Nationalsozialismus, 1972, Revolution, Staat Faschismus, 1978, Liberalismus und Antiliberalismus, 1979, Arbeiter und Arbeiterbewegung in des Weimarer Republik 1918-1933 (3 vols.), 1984, 85, 87; contbr. articles to profl. jours. Recipient Chester Penn Higby prize Jour. Modern History, 1976; scholar Princeton U., 1974-75, Woodrow Wilson Internat. Ctr., 1977-78; fellow German Kennedy Meml., 1967-68, 70-71, Wissenschaftskolleg zu Berlin, 1985-86. Mem. Assn. German Historians (exec. com. 1972-80), Berliner Wissenschaftliche Gesellschaft, Arbeitskreis für moderne Sozialgeschichte, Am. Hist. Assn. Home: Reckenbachstrasse 1, D7801 Stegen 2, Federal Republic of Germany Office: U Freiburg, History Seminar, Werthmannplatz, D7800 Freiburg Federal Republic of Germany

WINKLER, HOWARD LESLIE, investment banker, stockbroker; b. N.Y.C., Aug. 16, 1950; s. Martin and Magda (Stark) W.; m. Robin Lynn Richards, Sept. 12, 1976; 1 child, David Menachem. AA in Mktg., Los Angeles City Coll., 1973, AA in Bus. Data Processing, AA in Bus. Mgmt., 1981. Sr. cons. Fin. Cons. Inc., Los Angeles, 1972-81; asst. v.p. Merrill Lynch, Inc., Los Angeles, 1981-83; v.p. Drexel, Burnham, Lambert, Inc., Beverly Hills, Calif., 1983-84; pres. Howard Winkler Investments, Beverly Hills, Calif., 1984—; ptnr. N.W.B. Assocs., Los Angeles, 1988—; investment cons. Molecular Electronics Corp., Torrance, Calif., 1987—; bd. dirs. United Community and Housing Devel. Corp., Los Angeles. Mem. Rep. party Calif., 1985—, Rep. party Los Angeles County, 1985—, Rep. Senatorial Inner Circle, 1986—, Rep. Presdl. Task Force, 1985—. Nat. Rep. Senatorial Com., 1986—, Golden Circle Calif., 1986—, Comm. on Legislation and Civic Action Agudath Israel Calif., 1985—; commr. Los Angeles County Narcotics and Dangerous Drugs Commn., 1988—; program chmn. Calif. Lincoln Clubs Pac, 1987—. Served with U.S. Army, 1969-72, Southeast Asia. Recipient Community Service award Agudath Israel Calif., 1986, President's Community Leadership award, 1986, Disting. Community Service US. Senator Pete Wilson, 1986, Calif. Gov.'s Leadership award, 1986, Community Service award U.S. Congresswoman Bobbi Fiedler, 1986, Resolution of Commendation Calif. State Assembly, 1986, Outstanding Community Service Commendation Los Angeles County Bd. Suprs., 1986, Outstanding Citizenship award City of Los Angeles, 1986. Mem. Calif. Young Reps., Calif. Rep. Assembly, VFW, Jewish War Veterans. Office: Howard Winkler Investments 9033 Wilshire Blvd Suite 402 Beverly Hills CA 90211

WINKLER, LEE B., business consultant; b. Buffalo, Dec. 31, 1925; s. Jack W. and Caroline (Marienthal) W.; children by previous marriage—James, Stewart Gilbert, Nicole Borgenicht, Cristina Ehrlich, Richard Ehrlich Jr.; m. Maria Mal Verde. B.S. cum laude, NYU, 1945, M.S. cum laude, 1947. Mgr. Equitable Life Assurance Soc., N.Y.C., 1948-58; pres. Winkler Assos. Ltd., Beverly Hills, Calif., and N.Y.C., 1958—, Global Bus. Mgmt. Inc., Beverly Hills, 1967—; v.p. Bayly Martin & Fay Inc., N.Y.C., 1965-68, John C. Paige & Co., N.Y.C., 1968-71; cons. Albert G. Ruben Co., Beverly Hills, 1971—. Served with AUS, 1943-45. Decorated chevalier comdr. Order Holy Cross Jerusalem, also spl. exec. comdr., charge d'affaires, 1970; chevalier comdr. Sovereign Order Cyprus, 1970. Mem. Nat. Acad. TV Arts and Scis., Nat. Acad. Recording Arts and Scis., Beverly Hills C. of C., Phi Beta Kappa, Beta Gamma Sigma, Mu Gamma Tau, Psi Chi Omega. Office: 9000 Sunset Blvd Los Angeles CA 90069

WINLAW, IAN, financial consultant; b. Sydney, N.S.W., Australia, Jan. 7, 1939; s. Robert Murray and Marjorie (Elm) Strang; m. Pamela Mary Winlaw, May 2, 1963; children—Catherine, David, Andrew, Jennifer. B.Com., Victoria U. of Wellington, 1960; M.Com., U. N.S.W., 1973. Ptnr., Mann, Judd & Co., Sydney, N.S.W., 1960-73; owner Ian Winlaw & Co. Sydney, 1973—; dir. Finemore Holdings, Canberra, 1982—, Blackmorls Labs., Sydney, 1978—, Barlow Marine, Sydney, 1984—; dir. McDowell Pacific, Sydney, 1975—. Joint author: Australian Commercial Dictionary, 1964. Fellow Inst. Chartered Accts. Australia; mem. Inst. Dirs. Mem. Liberal Party. Anglican. Clubs: Avondale Golf, Royal Auto. Home: 14 Hampden Ave, Wahrooga, New South Wales 2076, Australia Office: 6700 MLC Centre, 19 Martin Pl, Sydney New South Wales 2000, Australia

WINNER, ANNE MOORE WINDLE, sch. psychologist; b. West Chester, Pa., Sept. 4, 1921; d. Ernest Garfield and Sylvia Louise (Moore) Windle; B.A. in Philosophy, Swarthmore (Pa.) Coll., 1942; postgrad. scholar, Pa. Sch. Social Work, 1945-46; M.A. in Psychology (scholar), Bucknell U., Lewisburg, Pa., 1961; cert. of advanced study in communication disorders Johns Hopkins U., 1974; EdD, Pa. State U., 1988; m. Drexel Winner, Apr. 15, 1944 (dec. 1967); children—Catherine Winner Salam, David R., Hanna Winner Dunleavy, Rebecca Winner Diehl. Sch. psychologist II, Balt. City Schs., 1963—; cons. psychologist problems of children, pets; Md. rep. Internat. Sch. Psychology Com., 1981-84. Mem. Md. Psychol. Assn. (officer 1975, 76), Balt. City Assn. Sch. Psychologists (pres. 1980-82), Pa. Assn. Sch. Psychologists, Md. Assn. Sch. Psychologists, Am. Psychol. Assn. (asso.), Golden Retriever Club Am. Quaker. Author articles in field. Address: 102 E Chestnut Hill Ln Reisterstown MD 21136

WINNER, MICHAEL ROBERT, film director, writer, producer; b. London, Oct. 30, 1935; s. George Joseph and Helen (Zloty) W. Degree in law and econs. with honors, Downing Coll., Cambridge (Eng.) U., 1956. Writer Fleet St. (newspapers), London, 1956-58. Engaged in film prodn. 1956—; dir. films Play it Cool, 1962, West 11, 1963, The Mechanic, 1972, Death Wish II, 1981; dir.; writer The Cool Mikado, 1962, You Must be Joking, 1965, The Wicked Lady, 1982; producer, dir. The System, 1963, I'll Never Forget What's 'isname, 1967, The Games, 1969, Lawman, 1970, The Nightcomers, 1971, Chato's Land, 1971, Scorpio, 1972, The Stone Killer, 1973, Death Wish, 1974, Won Ton Ton The Dog Who Saved Hollywood, 1975, Firepower, 1978, Scream for Help, 1983, Death Wish III, 1985; producer, writer, dir. films The Jokers, 1966, Hannibal Brooks, 1968, The Sentinel, 1976, The Big Sleep, 1977, Appointment With Death, 1987, A Chorus of Disapproval, 1988; producer plays Nights at the Comedy, Comedy Theatre, London, 1960, The Silence of St. Just, Gardner Centre, Brighton, 1971, The Tempest, Wyndhams Theatre, London, 1974, A Day in the Ukraine, Mayfair Theatre, London, 1978. Founder, chmn. Police Meml. Trust, 1984. Mem. Dirs. Guild Gt. Britain (council, trustee, chief censorship officer 1983). Office: Scimitar Films Ltd, 6-8 Sackville St, Piccadilly, London W1X 1DD, England

WINNINGSTAD, CHESTER NORMAN, computer company executive; b. Berkeley, Calif., Nov. 5, 1925; s. Chester Hafdan and Phyllis Amy (Whichello) W.; m. Dolores Constance Campbell, Mar. 24, 1948; children: Richard Norman, Dolores Steven, Joanne. BS, U. Calif., Berkeley, 1948; MBA, Portland State U., 1973; LLD, Pacific U., 1982. Engr. TV Calif., San Francisco, 1948-50, Lawrence Berkeley Labs., 1950-58; mgr. Tektronix, Beaverton, Oreg., 1958-70; chmn. Floating Point Systems Inc., Beaverton, 1970-86, vice chmn. 1986, chmn. 1987—; chmn. Lattice Internat., Inc., Portland, Oreg., 1984—; Aircraft at your Call, Hillsboro, Oreg., 1982—; bd. dirs. Optical Data, Inc. Patentee in field. Trustee Oreg. Mus. Sci. and Industry 1983-86. Served with USNR, 1942-44. Named Free Enterprise Man of Yr., Nat. Mgmt. Assn., 1981, Oreg. Bus. Leader of Yr., Assn. Oreg. Industries, 1984. Mem. IEEE (sr.). Clubs: University, Columbia Aviation Country. Office: Floating Point Systems Inc 3601 SW Murray Blvd Beaverton OR 97005

WINSTEIN, STEWART ROBERT, lawyer; b. Viola, Ill., May 28, 1914; s. Abraham and Esther (Meyer) W.; m. Dorothy Shock, Nov. 2, 1961; 1 son, Arthur R. AB, Augustana Coll., 1935; JD, U. Chgo., 1938; D (hon.) Marycrest Coll., 1987. Bar: Ill. Pnr. Winstein, Kavensky, Wallace & Doughty, Rock Island, Ill., 1939—. Trustee Marycrest Coll., Davenport, Iowa, 1980—; fin. officer State of Ill., 1963-70; del. Democratic Nat. Conv., 1968, 72 and mid-term conf., 1978, 88; Ill. Dem. State Central committeeman, 1970—; vice chmn. State of Ill. Dem. State Central Com., 1970-82; pub. adminstr. Rock Island County, 1974-78; commr. Met. Airport Authority, 1972—; chmn. bd., 1986—. Mem. ABA, Ill. Bar Assn., Rock Island County Bar Assn., Chgo. Bar Assn., Assn. Trial Lawyers of Am. Jewish. Contbr. articles to profl. jours.

WINSTON, ARTHUR WILLIAM, physicist, indsl. controls and microwave products co. exec.; b. Toronto, Ont., Can., Feb. 11, 1930; came to U.S., 1951, naturalized, 1959; s. Maurice and Alma (Freedman) W.; B.A.Sc., U. Toronto, 1951; PhD., M.I.T., 1954; m. Lily Baum, Sept. 4, 1949; children—Leslie, Pamela, David, Matthew. Physicist, NRC, Toronto, 1949-51; research asst. M.I.T., Cambridge, 1951-54; sr. engr. Schlumberger Corp., Houston, 1954-57; physicist Nat. Research Corp., Cambridge, 1957-59; chief scientist Allied Research Assos., Boston, 1959-61; pres. Space Scis., Inc., Waltham, Mass., 1961-65, Ikor Inc., Burlington, Mass., 1965-75, Wincom Corp., Lawrence, Mass., 1979-86; coordinator and prof., advanced tech. and engring., The Gordon Inst., 1986—; v.p. Omni-Wave Electronics Corp., Gloucester, Mass., 1976-78; dir. Granite State Controls, Inc.; adj. prof. Northeastern U., 1978—; mem. U.S. Dept. Commerce European Pollution Control Trade Mission, 1971; chmn. Electro Conf., 1960, MIT Boston Seminar Series, 1988—. Judge, Mass. State Sci. Fair, 1957—; chmn. internat. intercultural programs com. Lexington chpt. Am. Field Service, 1977—. Recipient cert. of appreciation U.S. Dept. Commerce, 1971, Inventor's award, 1986; Wallberg Meml. scholar, 1949; Assn. Profl. Engrs. scholar, 1949; others. Mem. Am. Phys. Soc., IEEE, AIAA, Am. Geophys. Union, Air Pollution Control Assn., AIME, Sigma Xi. Clubs: M.I.T., Appalachian Mountain. Contbr. numerous articles to profl. jours. Home: 7 Wainwright Rd Winchester MA 01890 Office: 15 Audubon Rd Wakefield MA 01880

WINSTON, HAROLD RONALD, lawyer; b. Atlantic, Iowa, Feb. 7, 1932; s. Louis D. and Leta B. (Carter) W.; m. Carol J. Sundeen, June 11, 1955; children: Leslie Winston Yannetti, Lisa Winston Barbour, Laura L. B.A., U. Iowa, 1954, J.D., 1958. Bar: Iowa 1958, U.S. District Ct. (no. and so. dists.) Iowa 1962, U.S. Tax Ct. 1962, U.S. Ct. Appeals (8th cir.) 1970, U.S. Supreme Ct. 1969. Trust Officer United Home Bank & Trust Co., Mason City, Iowa, 1958-59; mem. Breese & Cornwell, 1960-62, Breese Cornwell Winston & Reuber, 1963-73, Winston Schroeder & Reuber, 1974-79, Winston, Reuber & Swanson, P.C., Mason City, 1980—; police judge, Mason City, 1961-73. Author profl. publs. Past pres. Family YMCA, Mason City, Cerro Gordo County Estate Planning Council; active numerous local charitable orgns. Served to capt. USAF, 1955-57. Fellow Am. Coll. Probate Counsel; mem. ABA, Iowa Bar Assn. (gov., lectr. ann. meeting 1977, 78, 79), 2d Jud. Dist. Ba r Assn. (lectr. meeting 1981, 82), Cerro Gordo County Bar Assn. (past pres.), Am. Judicature Soc., Assn. Trial Lawyers Am. Republican. Presbyterian (elder). Clubs: Euchre and Cycle, Mason City Country, Masons, Kiwanis. Office: Winston Reuber & Swanson 119 2nd St NW Mason City IA 50401

WINSTON, REGINALD MICHAEL, statistician; b. Roseau, Dominica, Oct. 15, 1953; s. Maud Beresford Ferguson. Cert. in pub. adminstrn., U. West Indies, Mona, Jamaica, 1987, postgrad. Statis. asst. Ministry of Fin., Roseau, 1972—. Contbr. poems to profl. jours. Pres. Club for Disabled Children, Roseau, 1983—. Home: 35 Great Marlborough St, Roseau British West Indies Dominica Office: Ministry of Fin Statis Div, Bath Rd, Roseau British West Indies Dominica

WINSTON-SMITH, SAMUEL, investment banker; b. Adelaide, South Australia, Oct. 6, 1939; m. Judith Anne Marchant, Dec. 19, 1964; children—Simon, Franç oise, Louise, Justine. Diploma, St. Ignatius Coll., 1957. Trainee exec. Nestle Co. of Australia, Queensland, 1960-62; cons. agt. AMP Soc., Queensland, 1962-81; regional rep. Dominguez Barry Samuel Montagu Ltd., 1981—, exec. dir., regional dir. Dep. commr. French pavilion Expo 88. Named Hon. Consul of France, 1985—. Mem. Inst. Dirs.; past mem. Million Dollar Round Table. Roman Catholic. Clubs: Brisbane (pres. 1983-84), Tattersails, Royal Queensland Yacht Squadron (committeeman 1973), Queensland Turf. Avocation: sailing. Office: S Winston Smith Pyt Ltd, PO Box 606 GPO, Brisbane 4001, Australia

WINTELS, THEODORUS-GERTRUDIS, electrical engineer; b. Venray, Limburg, The Netherlands, Dec. 29, 1924; s. Theodorus-Gerard and Maria Hubertina (Verbeek) W.; m. Bertha Anna Bormans, Feb. 27, 1954 (dec. July 1980); children: Hanneke, Mark, Ton, Antoinette; m. Johanna Isabel Gieles, Oct. 8, 1982. Degree in Elec. Engring., Tech. High Sch., Eindhoven, The Netherlands, 1947. Coal mining engr. Oranje Nassau, Heerlen, Holland, 1947-67; ming. dir. Elec. Installation Co., 's Hertogenbosch, Holland, 1967-83, Testing Inst. SOBA BV., Sittard, Holland, 1982—; bd. dirs. Tech. Sch. Orgn., 'dHertogenbosch. Mem. Council Cert., den Haag, The Netherlands, 1986—. Decorated Cross of War, Govt. Netherlands, 1983, Cross of Merit, Red Cross, The Netherlands, 1948. Mem. Internat. Orgn. Indsl. Maintenance. Christian Dem. Party. Roman Catholic. Club: Chaine des Rotisseurs ('s Hertogenbosch). Home: Papendyk 31, 5386-EB Geffen The Netherlands Office: SOBA BV, Nolenslaan 126, 6136-GV Sittard The Netherlands

WINTER, ARTHUR, neurosurgeon; b. Newark, Sept. 7, 1922; s. Benjamin and Rose W.; m. Ruth N. Grosman, June 16, 1957; children: Robin, Craig, Grant. BA, Drew U., 1947; PCB cum laude, U. Montreal, 1948, MD, 1953. Intern U. Montreal Hosps., Can., 1952-53; resident Beth Israel Hosp., Newark, 1953-55; resident in neurol. surgery Baylor Med. Coll.-Tex. Med. Ctr., Houston, 1955-56, Albert Einstein Med. Ctr., N.Y.C., 1956-59; practice medicine specializing in neurol. surgery Livingston, N.J., 1960—; mem. attending staff St. Barnabas Med. Ctr., Hosp. Ctr. at Orange (N.J.), N.J. Orthopedic Hosp., VA Hosp.; cons. numerous hosps. and rehab. instns.; clin. instr. N.J. Coll. Medicine and Dentistry. Author: The Moment of Death, 1969, Surgical Control of Behavior, 1971, Life and Death Decisions; contbr. numerous articles to profl. jours.; developer Winter head dressing, microsurg. brain retractor, pupicon. Served with U.S. Army, 1943-46, ETO. Decorated Purple Heart, 3 battle stars; grantee Multiple Sclerosis Research Fund, 1974, N.J. Dept. Health, Beth Israel Hosp. Fellow Am. Acd. Neurol. and Orthopedic Surgeons, Am. Coll. Emergency Physicians, N.J. Acad. Medicine, Royal Soc. Health; mem. AMA, EEG Soc. (assoc.), AAAS, Congress of Neurol. Surgeons, Essex County Med. Assn., Soc. Neurosci., Am. Soc. Sterotactic and Functionary Neurosurgery. Office: 22 Old Short Hills Rd Suite 110 Livingston NJ 07039

WINTER, JOAN ELIZABETH, psychotherapist; b. Aiken, S.C., Feb. 24, 1947; d. John S. and Mary Elizabeth (Caldwell) Winter. BS, Ariz. State U., 1970; MSW, Va. Commonwealth U., 1977. Lic. clin. social worker, Va. Counselor Child Psychiatry Hosp., Phoenix, 1969-70, Ariz. Job Coll., Casa Grande, 1970-71; dir. Halfway House, Richmond, Va., 1971-73; state supr. resdl. treatment, Richmond, 1973-75; psychotherapist Med. Coll. Va., Richmond, 1975-76, Va. Commonwealth U., 1976-77; exec. dir. Family Research Project, Richmond, Va., 1979-81; dir. Family Inst. Va., Richmond, 1980—; examiner, approved supr. Bd. Behavioral Scis., Commonwealth of Va., 1982-86; mem. Avanta Network, Exec. Council and Faculty, Nat. Inst. of Drug Abuse, Research Adv. Com. Author: The Phenomenon of Incest, 1977, The Use of Self in Therapy: The Person and Practice of the Therapist, 1987, Family Life of Psychotherapists, 1987; contbr. articles to profl. jours. Diplomate Nat. Assn. Social Workers; mem. Am. Soc. Cert. Social Workers, Am. Family Therapy Assn., Am. Assn. Marriage and Family Therapy (approved supr.), Avanta Network Faculty. Address: 2910 Monument Ave Richmond VA 23221

WINTER, MARTIN, lawyer, builder; b. N.Y.C., Dec. 29, 1907; s. Louis and Rose W.; B.A., Columbia U., 1928; LL.B, Fordham U., 1930; m. Adele Godfrey, Feb. 2, 1941; children—Carolyn Bybee, Marjorie Krieger. Admitted to N.Y. State bar, 1933; trust dept. exec. Central Hanover Bank, N.Y.C., 1932-33; assoc. firm Seligsberg & Lewis, N.Y.C., 1933-35; founder, partner firm Chorosh & Winter, N.Y.C., 1935-77; builder housing projects, L.I., N.Y., 1947—; mem. faculty Columbia U.; lectr. Practicing Law Inst. Ofcl. adviser Mayor Lindsay's Office of S.I. Devel., 1966-72; chmn. bldg. com. Village Russell Gardens, Nassau County, N.Y. Mem. Regional Plan Assn., Nassau County Bar Assn. Club: North Shore Country (Glen Head, N.Y.). Author: Inside Staten Island, 1964.

WINTER, PETER MJCHAEL, physician, anesthesiologist, educator; b. Sverdlovsk, Russia, Aug. 5, 1934; came to U.S., 1938, naturalized, 1944; s. George and Anne W.; m. Madge Sato, Aug. 22, 1964; children: Karin Anne, Christopher George. B.A., Cornell U., 1958; M.D., U. Rochester, 1962. Intern U. Utah, Salt Lake City, 1962-63; resident in anesthesiology, pharmacology and respiratory physiology Mass. Gen. Hosp., Boston, 1963-65; USPHS fellow Harvard U. Med. Sch.; 1964-66; Buswell fellow dept.

physiology, asst. prof. SUNY, Buffalo, 1966-69; assoc. prof. dept. anesthesiology Sch. Medicine, U. Wash., Seattle, 1969-74; prof. Sch. Medicine, U. Wash., 1974-79; prof., chmn. dept. anesthesiology and critical care medicine U. Pitts. Sch. Medicine, 1979—; cons. Union Carbide Corp., NIH; med. officer Tektite II (underwater habitation project); anesthesiologist in chief Univ. Health Center Hosps., Pitts. Mem. editorial bd. Jour. Critical Care Medicine; editorial cons. Anesthesiology; contbr. chpts. to books, papers and abstracts on anesthesia, environ. phys. pharmacology and med. edn. to publs. Served with U.S. Army, 1953-56. Recipient NIH career devel. award, 1971. Mem. AMA, Am. Coll. Chest Physicians, Am. Soc. Anesthesiologists, N.Y. Acad. Scis., Undersea Med. Soc. Internat. Anesthesia Research Soc., Soc. Acad. Anesthesia Chairmen, Assn. Univ. Anesthetists. Club: Am. Alpine. Office: 1385 E Scaife Hall Univ Pittsburgh School Medicine Pittsburgh PA 15260

WINTER, THOMAS GUSTAV, physicist; b. N.Y.C., Jan. 14, 1946; s. Henry Ernest and Caroline G. (Kunkel) W.; m. Janis Rae Bruehl, June 11, 1967; 1 child, John Thomas. B.A. magna cum laude, Queens Coll. City N.Y., 1967; Ph.D., U. Wis.-Madison, 1972. Teaching asst. U. Wis.-Madison, 1967-70, research asst., 1970-72; univ. fellow Queen's U., Belfast, No. Ireland, 1972-73; research assoc. Rice U., Houston, 1973-76; asst. prof. physics Pa. State U., Wilkes-Barre, Pa., 1976-81, assoc. prof., 1981—, prof., 1987—; vis. assoc. prof. Kans. State U., 1983; sr. research assoc. Rice U., 1984. Referee Phys. Review, 1973—, Phys. Review Letters, 1986—, Jour. Physics, 1987—. Contbr. articles to profl. jours. U.S. Dept. Energy grantee, 1986—. Mem. Union Concerned Scientists, Fedn. Am. Scientists, Energy Com. Northeastern Pa. Econ. Devel. Council, Wyo. Valley Peace Com., Wilkes-Barre, Mem. Am. Physical Soc., Phi Beta Kappa. Clubs: Wyoming Valley Striders (Wilkes-Barre); N.Y. Rd. Runners. Home: 90 E Franklin St Shavertown PA 18708

WINTERER, WILLIAM G., hotel executive; b. St. Louis, July 7, 1934; s. Herbert O. and Dorothy (Sprengnether) W.; B.A., U. Fla., 1956; M.B.A., Harvard U., 1962; m. Victoria Thompson, Sept. 2, 1967; children—William, Andrew, Britton, Mark. Mgr. corporate fin. dept., partner Goodbody & Co., 1966-69; pres. Fla. Capital Corp., Greenwich, Conn., 1969-72; owner Griswold Inn, Essex, Conn., 1972—, Town Farms Inn, Middletown, Conn., 1978-85, Dock N' Dine at Saybrook Point, Old Saybrook, Conn., 1981-86; bd. dirs. Zimmer Corp., Bostwick Invest Co.; chmn. audit com. Custom Marine, Inc., 1986—; mem. adv. bd. United Bank and Trust. Life trustee, founding pres. Conn. River Found. at Steamboat Dock; trustee Ivoryton Playhouse Found., 1979-82; corporator Middlesex Hosp.; commissioner Conn. Hist. Commn., 1979-82; bd. dirs. Gov.'s Vacation Travel Council, 1976-79. Served with USCG Res. Mem. Conn. Restaurant Assn. (dir. 1973-77). Republican. Roman Catholic. Clubs: N.Y. Yacht, Seawanhaka Corinthian Yacht, Essex Yacht (bd. govs.), Pettipaug Yacht, Ocean Cruising; Harvard, Williams (N.Y.C.); Hartford; Old Lyme Beach; English Speaking Union, St. George's Soc. Home: Turtle Bay Essex CT 06426 Office: Main St Essex CT 06426

WINTERHOFF-SPURK, PETER ULRICH, psychology educator; b. Grimma, Saxony, German Democratic Republic, July 2, 1945; arrived in Fed. Republic Germany, 1951; Diploma in psychology, Phillips U., Marburg, Fed. Republic Germany, 1977; PhD, U. Mannheim, Fed. Republic Germany, 1983. Research asst. U. Mannheim, 1977-82, teaching asst., 1982-83, asst. prof. psychology, 1983—. Author: The Functions of Gaze and Smile While Requesting, 1983, Television, 1986, Empirical Psychology of TV, 1988, TV and World-Knowledge, 1988; co-editor Jour. Psychology of Media, 1988. Served in armed forces Fed. Republic Germany, 1965-69. Mem. German Psychol. Assn. Home: Hauptstrasse 71a, 6802 Ladenburg Federal Republic of Germany Office: U Mannheim, Schloss, 6800 Mannheim Federal Republic of Germany

WINTERS, THOMAS BERNARR, mechanical engineer, campground director; b. Ironton, Ohio, Sept. 18, 1931; s. Raymond Franklin and Adryenne Beryl (Lynd) W.; m. Dolores Jean Leis, Aug. 30, 1953. Attended Franklin U. With Westinghouse Electric Co., Columbus, Ohio, 1956-69; with Westreco, Marysville, Ohio, 1969—, design engr., 1969—; pres., chief exec. officer Winters Recreational Area, Raymond, Ohio, 1981—, also bd. dirs. Patentee icemaker, water delivery, defrost timer, others. Served with USNR, 1949-59. Methodist. Office: 20267 SR 347 Raymond OH 43067

WINTHER, KJELD CHRISTEN, hotel and restaurant owner; b. Copenhagen, Jan. 15, 1932; arrived in France, 1975; s. Edwin Rahr and Sofie (Moss) W.; m. Solveig Danborg, Oct. 22, 1955; children: Steen Aage, Charlotte, Henrik Edwin. Engr. Schou & Co., Copenhagen, 1958-61, Storm Vulcan, Dallas, 1961-64, Seest, Aarhus, Denmark, 1964-67; owner Winther Designs, Stilling, Denmark, 1967-75, l'Ancienne Gendarmerie, Lantosque, France, 1975—. Office: 1 Ancienne Gendarmerie, Le Rivet, F-06450 Lantosque France

WINTLE, CHRISTOPHER SIMON, music lecturer; b. London, Apr. 3, 1945; s. Francis Julian and Olivia (Ellis) W.; m. Sarah Elizabeth Thesiger, June 26, 1974; children: Alice Marina, Emily Miranda. BA in Mus. with honors, Oxford (Eng.) U., 1966, BMus, 1967. Lectr. music U. Southampton, Hampshire, Eng., 1969-70, U. Reading, Bershire, Eng., 1971-78; prin. lectr. Goldsmiths' Coll., U. London, 1978—. Mem. editorial bd. Music Analysis jour., 1982—, Cambridge Opera Jour., 1986—; contbr. articles to profl. jours. Princeton U. vis. fellow, 1974. Democrat. Home: 49 Stradell Rd, Putney, London SE24 9HL, England Office: U London Goldsmiths' Coll, New Cross, London SE14 6NW, England

WINTON, JEFFREY BLAKE, arbitrator; b. Chgo., Feb. 16, 1945; s. Stanley A. and Phyllis R. (Levin) W.; B.S., U. Ill., 1966, M.S. in Labor Relations, 1968; m. Shoshana Nahmani, 1976. With Midwest Stock Exchange, Chgo., 1968-70; dir. mediation services Office of State Sch. Supt., 1970-73; pres., chief exec. officer Radionic Industries, Inc. (formerly Radionic Transformers Corp.), Chgo., 1973—; pres. Jeffrey B. Winton & Assocs., Chgo., 1972—. Lectr. labor relations and mgmt. Northwestern U., 1974-78. Campaign aide Senator Adlai E. Stevenson, III, 1966, 70, 74; arbitrator, mediator Fact-Finder: Federal Mediation and Conciliation Service, Am. Arbitration Assn., Iowa Public Employment Relations Bd., Wis. Employment Relations Commn., Ind. Edn. Relations Bd., Nat. Mediation Bd., Ill. Pub. Employment Relations Bd., Ill. Tchr. Hearing Panel, Ill. Edn. Employment Relations Bd. Recipient Gold Key to City of Champaign, Ill., 1968. Mem. Nat. Acad. Arbitrators, Am. Arbitration Assn. (labor panel), Fed. Mediation and Conciliation Service (labor panel), Indsl. Relations Research Assn., Nat. Mediation Bd., Soc. Profls. in Dispute Resolution (v.p.), Chgo. Assn. Commerce. Contbr. articles to profl. publs. Office: Suite 100 2525 W Moffat Chicago IL 60647

WINTZ, JOSEPH ANTHONY, III, consulting engineer, researcher; b. Phila., July 25, 1946; s. Joseph Anthony, Jr. and Margaret Jeannette (Stoner) W.; m. Nina Leigh Fuhst, June 14, 1969; children—Joseph Anthony IV, Carey Leigh. B.S.C.E., U. Va., 1970; M.S., George Washington U., 1974. Registered profl. engr., D.C., Pa., Va., W. Va. Student asst. Va. Hwy. Research Council, Charlottesville, 1969-70; structural engr. Fortune, Downey & Elliott Ltd., Alexandria, Va., 1970-74; sr. structural engr. Bernard Johnson, Inc., Washington, 1974-75, Airways Engring. Corp., Washington, 1975-76; asst. chief engr. Brick Inst. Am., McLean, Va., 1976-84; pres., sr. cons. Joseph Wintz, Ltd., Falls Church, Va., 1984-88; sr. cons. Law Engring., Chantilly, Va., 1988—. Editor Proc. of 5th Internat. Brick Masonry Conf., 1982. Contbr. articles on masonry to profl. jours. Mem. Am. Soc. for Engring. Edn., Am. Concrete Inst., ASCE, ASTM, Brit. Masonry Soc., Constrn. Specifications Inst., Earthquake Engring. Research Inst., Internat. Council Bldg. Research, Studies and Documentation, Masonry Soc., Internat. Union Testing and Research Labs. for Materials and Structures, Nat. Soc. Archtl. Engrs., Nat. Inst. Bldg. Scis., NSPE, Nat. Acad. Forensic Engrs., Nat. Trust Hist. Preservation, N.Z. Nat. Soc. Earthquake Engrs. Current work: Properties and performance of masonry assemblages and materials, especially in their application to design, construction and maintenance of masonry systems in architectural structures. Subspecialty: Structural engineering. Home: 3250 Annandale Rd Falls Church VA 22042

WIONO, DJOKO, management consultant; b. Ambarawa, Java, Indonesia, Sept. 27, 1951; s. Soekarman and Siti (Sari) D.; m. Oktorina, July 6, 1980; children—Muhammad Ario Wibowo, Firman Achmad Royghaan. B.S. in Econs., U. Indonesia, 1980, grad. in philosophy, 1988. Quality assurance engr. Monsanto Pan Electronics, Jakarta, Indonesia, 1974-76; prodn. sr. supr., Jakarta, 1976-78; electronic educator Course & Study Group, Jakarta, 1977-80; elec. cons. PRW Architects, Jakarta, 1977-81, Mirazh Architects, Jakarta, 1980-81; dir. Cipta 81, Jakarta, 1981-84, Lutansuhi, 1987—; pres., dir. Interjayco, Jakarta, 1983-85; pres. Cipta Jasa Dynasty, Jakarta, 1984; chmn. Imperindo Hasta Eka, Jakarta, 1984 Coordinator alumni The Ship for Southeast Asian Youth, Jakarta, 1982-83; sec. Philosophy Found. Indonesia, 1984. Mem. Himpunan Ahli Elektronika Indonesia, Jaycees Internat. (internat. trainer 1981, senator 1982), Japan Jr. Chamber (hon. mem.), Indonesia Jaycees (nat. pres. 1982). Mem. Inst. for Strategic and Devel. Studies. Moslem. Home: Jl Cipinang Baru Bundar A-4, Jakarta Timur Indonesia Office: Jl Balitung III/8, Jakarta 12110, Indonesia

WIORKOWSKI, GABRIELLE KAY, data processing consultant; b. Tulsa, Nov. 10, 1943; d. Marshall Frank and Iva Ann (Johnson) Patterson; B.A. summa cum laude, St. Mary's U., 1971; M.S., U. Tex., Dallas, 1979; m. John J. Wiorkowski, June 4, 1966; 1 dau., Fleur. Adminstrv. asst. Stritch Sch. Medicine, Loyola U., Chgo., 1963-67; sr. programmer Corn Products Co., Chgo., 1967-68; mgr. data communications Jewel Co., Chgo., 1971-74; ind. data processing cons., Dallas, 1975—; lectr. U. Tex., Dallas, 1980—; mgr. data base mgmt. systems Sun Co. Inc., Dallas, 1981-83; DBA systems supr. Tex. Instruments, Inc., Dallas, 1983-85; sr. cons. Codd & Date Cons. Group, Dallas, 1985—. Mem. Richardson Assn. Gifted and Talented (treas. 1979-80), Assn. Computing Machinery, Nat. Computer Conf. (publs. chmn., steering com. 1977), Delta Epsilon Sigma, Pi Gamma Mu. Republican. Presbyterian. Author: DB2: Design Development Guide, 1988; author chpt. in book; contbr. articles to profl. jours. Home and office: 428 Bedford Dr Richardson TX 75080

WIPF, KARL ARTHUR, historian, educator; b. Winterthur, Switzerland, Apr. 11, 1938; s. Karl and Julia (Keller) W.; Ph.D., U. Zurich, 1972. Asst. philology U. Zurich, Switzerland, 1971-73, lectr. philol., theol. faculties, 1972—, asst. theol. faculty, 1975-78; chmn. Am. and prehistoric Europe sect. Inst. Canarium, Hallein, Austria, 1980—, v.p., 1983-86; corr. mem. El Mus. Canario, Canary Islands, 1980—; mem. Mus. Am. Indian (Heye Found.), N.Y.C., 1979—; guide for sci. tours, 1963—. Served with Swiss Army, 1958—. Mem. Swiss Soc. Richard Wagner (life), Soc. Comparative Studies Rock-Paintings Austria (editorial), Current Anthropology (Chgo.) (asso.), Swiss Americanists Soc. (Geneva) (life). Author: Elpis- -Reflections on the Conception of Hope in the Work of Goethe, 1974, Wanderer in the Night - Interpretations in History of Religion of Pre-Columbian Chronicles, 1980, The Myth of the Holy Grail, 1980, 81, The World Structure of the Nordic Peoples, part I, 1980, part II, 1982, Treasures of Old-High-German Poetry, 1985, The Theory of Myth, 1985, The Meistersinger, Part I, 1985, Part II, 1987, Religious Phenomena in Prehistoric Times, 1987, Mesoamerican Religious: Contemporary Cultures: Encyclopedia of Religion, 1987; co-editor: jour. Mexicon, 1979-82. Mem. Soc. Prehistory and Early History (Bonn, Fed. Republic Germany), Soc. of Am. Archaelogy, Am. Anthrop. Assn., Gesellschaft fur Vor, The Australian Rock Art Research Assn. . Home: 4-C Schulweg, CH-8500 Frauenfeld Switzerland

WIRAHADIKUSUMAH, UMAR, former vice president of Indonesia, retired army officer; b. Sumedang, West Java, Oct. 10, 1924; Commd. officer Indonesian Army, ret.; platoon comdr., Tasakmalaya, 1942; mem. PETA (Self Defence Forces), 1944; comdr. TKR (People's Security Army), Cicalengka, West Java, 1945; chief of staff of gen. div., Siliwangi, 1949; comdr. Mil. Command of Greater City of Djakarta, 1958, of Territory V/Java, 1965; comdr. Kostrad, 1966; army chief of staff, 1969-73; chmn. Audit Bd. (BPK), 1973-83; v.p. Indonesia, 1983-87. Played key role in crushing abortive Communist coup, 1965. Decorated 12 Indonesian medals; decorations from Fed. Rep. Germany, Netherlands, Yugoslavia, Rep. Korea, Belgium, and Malaysia. Office: Office of Vice Pres, Jakarta Indonesia *

WIREN, MATS T., surgeon, hospital administrator; b. Frösön, Jämtland, Sweden, Oct. 25, 1939; s. P. F. Ku and Margit M. T. (Jansson) W.; m. Inger M. Karlsson, June 5, 1965; children: Anna M.E., Per O.F., Kajsa M. Med. kand., U. Uppsala, 1961; MD, U. Umeå, 1966. With Sjukhuset Kir. Klinik, Örnsköldsvik, Sweden, 1966-70, Linköping, 1970-72; resident Sjukhuset Kir. Klinik, Härnösand, 1972-85, gen. surgeon, 1985—, head clinic, 1986—. Ombudsman local doctors union Ångermanl, 1984-85. Served to lt. col. UN Hosp., 1981-83. Mem. Swedish Surg. Assn., Swedish Orthopedics Assn., Swedish Jaycees. Lutheran. Lodge: Masons. Home: 17 Lidgatan, S-87161 Harnosand Sweden Office: Hosp Harnosand Surg Clinic, S-87129 Harnosand Sweden

WIRMARK, BO DAVID INGVAR, diplomat; b. Virserum, Småland, Sweden, Mar. 22, 1926; s. Oscar Gustafsson and Elsa Gustafsson (Petersson) W.; m. Wivni Johansen, 1953 (div. 1955); m. Alicia Bareche Corvinos, Oct. 24, 1962. BA, Uppsala U., 1950, MA, 1952. Editor Frisinnad Ungdom mag. Nat. Liberal Youth Orgn., Stockholm, 1952-54, gen. sec., 1954; nat. sec. Nat. Union Secondary Sch. Tchrs., Stockholm, 1954-58; gen. sec. World Assembly of Youth, Paris, 1958-59; cons. Council for Swedish Info., Brussels, 1959-64, Stockholm, 1964-67; gen. sec. Liberal Party, Stockholm, 1967-69; mem. Provincial Council, Stockholm, 1967-71, Swedish Parliament, Stockholm, 1971-73, 76-79; expert cons. Ministry Fgn. Affairs, Stockholm, 1976-79; ambassador Ministry Fgn. Affairs, Dar es Salaam, Tanzania, 1979-85, Mexico City, 1985—; cons. internat. affairs Swedish Savs. Banks Assn., Stockholm, 1969-79. Author: Do the Resources of the Earth Suffice, 1955, Problems of the Arab World, 1959, Marxism, Liberalism and the Problems of the Developing World, 1969, Europe and the Developing Countries, 1969, Saving for Development, 1970, Continent in Disequilibrium-Latin American Perspectives, 1973, The Rich and the Poor, 1975, Liberals about Development, 1978. Mem. Cen. Com. for Swedish Tech. Assistance, Stockholm, 1953-58; v.p. Liberal Internat., 1969-79; mem. nat. bd. Swedish Internat. Devel. Authority, Stockholm, 1970-79. Recipient La Croix d'Argent de Mérite Govt. of Poland in exile, 1959, Lórdre de la Couronne Govt. of Belgium, 1964. Lutheran. Home: Embajada de Suecia, Ap Postal 10-726, 11000 Mexico City Mexico

WIRSCHING, CHARLES PHILIPP, JR., brokerage house executive, investment executive; b. Chgo., Oct. 26, 1935; s. Charles Philipp and Mamie Ethel (York) W.; m. Beverly Ann Bryan, May 28, 1966. BA, U. N.C., 1957. Sales rep. Adams-Millis Corp., Chgo., 1963-67; ptnr. Schwartz-Wirsching, Chgo., 1968-70; sec., dir. Edwin H. Mann, Inc., Chgo., 1971-74; stockbroker Paine Webber, Inc., Chgo., 1975-85, account v.p., 1986—. Republican. Episcopalian. Home: 434 Clinton Pl River Forest IL 60305 Office: Paine Webber Inc 55 W Monroe Chicago IL 60603

WIRSIG, JANE DEALY, writer, editor; b. Boston, Aug. 22, 1919; d. James Bond and Anna B. (McQuillen) Dealy; B.A., Vassar Coll., 1941; M.S. (Vassar Coll. fellow 1941-42), Columbia U., 1942; m. Woodrow Wirsig, Dec. 11, 1942; children—Alan Robert, Guy Rodney, Paul Harold. Network radio newswriter CBS, 1942-43; free lance writer articles, short stories various mags., 1942—; editor Vassar Alumnae mag., 1952-53; editor, rewriter Companion in Paris, Woman's Home Companion, 1953-56; editor Wirsig, Gordon & O'Connor, Inc., Princeton, N.J., 1956-58; editorial cons. Ednl. Testing Service, Princeton, 1957-60, dir. publs., 1960-70, exec. dir. info. services and publs., 1971-74, sec. corp., 1974-80. Mem. exec. bd. George Washington council Boy Scouts Am., 1976-80. Mem. Am. Assn. Higher Edn., Greater Princeton C. of C. (dir. 1974-81, v.p. 1976-80, pres. 1980), Phi Beta Kappa. Club: Vassar (Central N.J. v.p. 1955-57). Home: 25 Gordon Way Princeton NJ 08540

WIRSIG, WOODROW, trade organization executive, magazine editor, business executive; b. Spokane, Wash., June 28, 1916; s. Otto Alan and Beulah Juliet (Marohn) W.; m. Jane Barbara Dealy, Dec. 11, 1942; children: Alan Robert, Guy Rodney, Paul Harold. Student, Kearney (Nebr.) State Tchrs. Coll., Los Angeles City Coll., UCLA, 1933-39; B.A., Occidental Coll., 1941; M.S., Columbia Grad. Sch. Journalism, 1942. Dir. Occidental Coll. News Bur., 1939-41; radio newswriter WQXR, N.Y.C., 1941-42; news writer, propaganda analyst CBS, 1942-43; rewrite man Los Angeles Times, 1943-44; asst. editor This Week mag., 1944-45; staff writer Look mag., 1946, asst. mng. editor, 1946-49, exec. editor, 1950-52; mng. editor Quick mag., 1949-50; asso. editor Newsweek mag., Ladies' Home Jour., 1952; editor Woman's Home Companion, 1952-56; editorial cons. Ednl. Testing Service, Princeton, 1957-67; TV cons. NBC-TV, ABC-TV; creator Nat. Daytime Radio Programs, 1957-60; radio documentary Companion; pres. communications firm Wirsig, Gordon and O'Connor, Inc., 1956-58; editor Printers' Ink mag., N.Y.C., 1958-65, Salesweek mag., 1959-60; editorial dir. Overseas Press Club ann. mag. Dateline, 1961, 62; creator, editorial dir. Calif. Life mag.; pres. Better Bus. Bur. Met. N.Y., Inc., 1966-77; also pres. Edn. Research Found.; pres. Bus. Advocacy Center, Inc., 1977—; creator Corp. Social Accountability Audit and Customer Services/Consumer Affairs Audit.; Cons. to Office Sec. HEW, 1965-66. Editor, contbr.: Your Diabetes (Dr. Herbert Pollack), 1951; Editor: Advertising: Today-Yesterday-Tomorrow; New Products Marketing; Cons. editor: Principles of Advertising; Contbr. nat. mags.; lectr.; syndicated columnist: other newspapers Los Angeles Times, 1964-65. Recipient gold medal Benjamin Franklin Mag. Awards, 1956. Mem. Soc. Consumer Affairs Profls. (pres. 1983), Newcomen Soc., Sigma Delta Chi, Phi Gamma Delta, Gamma Delta Upsilon, Archons. Democrat. Presbyterian. Clubs: Players, Overseas Press, Nat. Press, N.Y. Advt; City (N.Y.C.); Springdale Country (Princeton), Nassau (Princeton); University. Home and Office: 25 Gordon Way Queenston Common Princeton NJ 08540

WIRSZUP, IZAAK, mathematician, educator; b. Wilno, Poland, Jan. 5, 1915; came to U.S., 1949, naturalized, 1955; s. Samuel and Pera (Golomb) W.; m. Pola Ofman, July 19, 1940 (dec. 1943); 1 son Vladimir (dec. 1943); m. Pera Poswianska, Apr. 23, 1949; 1 dau., Marina (Mrs. Arnold M. Tatar). Magister of Philosophy in Math, U. Wilno, 1939; Ph.D. in Math, U. Chgo., 1955. Lectr. math. Tech. Inst. Wilno, 1939-41; dir. Bur. d'Études et de Statistiques Spéciales, Société Centrale d'Achat-Société Anonyme des Monoprix, Paris, France, 1946-49; mem. faculty U. Chgo., 1949—, prof. math., 1965-85, prof. math. emeritus, 1985—, prin. investigator Sch. Math. Project (sponsored by Amoco Found., also dir. resource devel. component), 1983—, dir. Internat. Math. Edn. Resource Ctr., 1988—; dir. NSF Survey Applied Soviet Research in Math. Edn., 1985—; Cons. Ford Found., Colombia, Peru, 1965, 66, Sch. Math. Study Group, 1960, 61, 66-68; participant, writer tchr. tng. material African Math. Program, Entebbe, Uganda, summer 1964, Mombasa, Kenya, summers 1965, 66; assoc. dir. Survey Recent Eastern European Math. Lit., 1956-68, dir., 1968-84; dir. NSF program application computers to mgmt., 1976-83; Cons. NSF-AID Sci. Edn. Program, India, 1969; mem. U.S. Commn. on Math. Instn., 1969-73. Contbr. articles to profl. jours.; Editor Math. books, transls., adaptions from Russian.; Adviser math.: Ency. Brit., 1971—. Recipient Lewellyn John and Harriet Manchester Quantrell award U. Chgo., 1958; resident master Woodward Ct., U. Chgo., 1971-85. Mem. N.Y. Acad. Scis., Am. Math. Soc., Math. Assn. Am., AAAS, Nat. Council Tchrs. Math. (chmn. com. internat. math. edn. 1967-69). Home: 5750 Kenwood Ave Chicago IL 60637 Office: U Chgo Dept Math 5734 University Ave Chicago IL 60637

WIRTH, RICHARD MARVIN, educator; b. Grosse Pointe, Mich., Aug. 26, 1929; s. Marvin Oscar and Marion (Maxfield) W.; B.Sc., Wayne State U., 1950, M.A., 1952; postgrad. U. Wis., Western State Coll. Colo., Ball State Tchrs. Coll. Tchr. drama and debate Warren (Mich.) Consol. Schs., 1951-87. Former organist and choir dir. St. John's Evang. United Ch. of Christ, lay minister, 1979; ordained minister of worship, 1982; former kapellmeister St. John-St. Luke United Ch. Christ; former master Co. of Lay Ministries. Mem. scholastic writing awards adv. com. SE Mich. Named Vol. of Week, United Found., 1963; recipient Silver Beaver award Boy Scouts Am., 1962; Disting. Educator award Mich. State Fair, 1964; Disting. Tchr. award Mich. Assn. Classroom Tchrs., 1969. Mem. Mich. (pres. dept. classroom tchrs., Tchr. of Yr. 1962, dir. area 6, parliamentarian 1972-80, dir.), Ky. (parliamentarian 1974), Kans., Okla. (parliamentarian 1979-80) Warren (editor Harbinger, past pres., sr. trustee) edn. assns., Mich. Student Congress (parliamentarian), Southfield Public Employees, Speech Assn. Am., Nat. Cath. Forensic League (parliamentarian 1979, 82), Nat. Council Tchrs. of English, Mich. League Credit Unions, Mich. League Practical Nurses (parliamentarian), Delta Sigma Rho. Editor of ednl. publs. Contbr. articles to profl. jours. Home: Box 283 Algonac MI 48001 Office: 2120 Russell Detroit MI 48207

WIRTH, TIMOTHY ENDICOTT, senator; b. Santa Fe, Sept. 22, 1939; s. Cecil and Virginia Maude (Davis) W.; m. Wren Winslow, Nov. 26, 1965; children: Christopher, Kelsey. B.A., Harvard U., 1961, M.Ed., 1964; Ph.D., Stanford U., 1973. White House fellow, spl. asst. to sec. HEW, Washington, 1967; asst. to chmn. Nat. Urban Coalition, Washington, 1968; dep. asst. sec. for edn. HEW, Washington, 1969; v.p. Great Western United Corp., Denver, 1970; mgr. Rocky Mountain office Arthur D. Little, Inc. (cons. firm), Denver, 1971-73; mem. 94th-99th Congresses from 2d Colo. Dist., 1975-87, mem. energy and commerce com., sci. and tech. com., budget com., chmn. subcom. telecommunications, fin. and consumer protection; U.S. senator from Colo. 1987—, mem. arms services com., energy and natural resources com., budget com., banking com. Mem. Gov.'s Task Force on Returned Vietnam Vets., 1970-73; mem. bd. visitors U.S. Air Force Acad., 1978—; advisor Pres.'s Commn. on the 80's, 1979-80; trustee Planned Parenthood, Denver Head Start. Recipient Disting. Service award HEW, 1969; Ford Found. fellow, 1964 66. Mem. White House Fellows Assn. (pres. 1968-69), Denver Council Fgn. Relations (exec. com. 1974-75). Office: US Senate Office Senate Members Washington DC 20510

WIRTHS, WALLACE RICHARD, industrial consultant; b. Englewood, N.J., July 7, 1921; s. Rudolph and Dorothy (Berls) W.; B.S., Lehigh U., 1942; postgrad. Fordham U. Law Sch., 1942-43; LL.D. (hon.), Upsala Coll., 1980; Asst. indsl. relations mgr. Aluminum Co. Am., Edgewater, N.J., 1943-54; pub. relations project mgr. Sylvania Elec. Products, Inc., N.Y.C., 1954-56; asst. to v.p. Westinghouse Electric Corp., Bloomfield, N.J., 1956-80; dir. Inter-Continental Enterprises, Bloomfield; v.p. Twin Ponds Excavating & Landscaping Corp., 1973-78; pres. Unique Homeowners Am.; pres. Wantage Galleries, Inc., Colesville, N.J.; pres. Wallace Richard Wirths and Assocs., 1983—; pres. The Oak Shoppe, Port Jervis, N.Y.; dir. Colonial Decorators. Mem. Nat. Council on Crime and Delinquency, 1966-79; mem. adv. council Tocks Island Region, 1966-77; mem. N.J. Employers Legis. Com., 1959-78; mem. com. on subliminal projection N.J. Legislature, 1962-63; mem. pres.' adv. council Bloomfield Coll., 1971-77, Upsala Coll.; mem. publs. com. Lehigh U., 1971-74; trustee Sussex County Big Bros., 1972-80, Nat. Trust for Historic Preservation, regional Health Planning Council N.J., 1978-82, Culver Brook Restoration Found., 1979-85, Sussex County Arts Council, 1983—, life mem.; del. Easter Seal Soc. N.J., 1978-82; Rep. committeeman, Sussex County, N.J., 1962—; mem. Sussex County Soil Conservation Dist., 1967—, Republican Pres. Task Force, 1984—, U.S. Congressional Adv. Bd., 1985—. Trustee Alexander Linn Hosp., Sussex, 1966-78, chmn. physician recruiting com.; mem. U.S. Congl. Adv. Bd., 1985—; commentator WSUS and WSUS TV. Served with USNR, 1950-54. Recipient Ortho Nat. Community Service award, 1976, Westinghouse Nat. award Community Service, 1976, N.J. State Assembly award for outstanding community service to state, 1978; named Soil Farmer of Yr., Sussex County, 1975, Big Bro. of Yr., 1978, Man of Yr., 1979; Ky. col. Mem. N.J. C. of C., Bloomfield C. of C., Trinidad and Tobago C. of C. U.S.A. (v.p.), Acad. Polit. Sci., Sussex County Hist. Soc. (life), N.J. Press Assn., N.J. Broadcasters Assn., N.J. Agrl. Soc., N.J. Hist. Soc., NAACP, Nat. Trust Historic Preservation, Illuminating Engring. Soc., Friends of Free China. Clubs: Rep.Congrl., Franklin Mineral Mus. (life), Sussex County Century, Governor's, U.S. Senatorial. Author: Candidly Speaking, 1982, Democracy, Panacea or Pandemonium, 1985, Sixty Seconds Candidly Speaking with Wally Wirths, 1985, Love Me, Hate Me, But Don't Turn Me Off, 1987, Saga of an American Family, 1987; editor The Candidly Speaking Report, 1986; author weekly newspaper column Candidly Speaking, 1969—. Donated 271 acre estate for Upsala Coll. campus, Sussex, N.J., 1978. Home: Wantage House RD 3 Sussex NJ 07461 Office: SlCompton Rd S2RD 3 Sussex NJ 07461

WIRYAWAN, NIZAM JIM, trading company executive; b. Jakarta, Indonesia, Nov. 9, 1942; s. Uceh and Lidia W.; LL.M., European Inst. Bus. Adminstrn., 1977; m. Zahrida Zainal; children—Lestari, Wahyu L. Consumer div. mgr. Bristol Myers/Mead Johnson, Jakarta, 1968-72; nat. mktg. mgr. S. C. Johnson & Son/J-Wax, Jakarta/Hong Kong, 1973-74; gen. sales mgr. Johnson & Johnson, Jakarta, 1975; gen. mgr. Golden Mississippi, Jakarta, 1976-79; dir., gen. mgr. Brink Molyn Paints, Jakarta, 1979-81; dir., gen. mgr. P. T. Brink Molyn Paints, Indonesia, 1979-81; mktg. dir. Borsumij Wehry, Jakarta, 1981—; mng. dir. Printemps Superstore, 1986—; guest lectr. Assn. Mktg. Profls. in Indonesia, 1977-79. Mem. Am. Mktg. Assn. (exec. bd.), Am. Inst. Mgmt. (exec. council), Brit. Inst. Mgmt. (London), Brit. Inst. Mktg. (Cookham, Eng.), Australian Mktg. Inst. Presbyterian. Club: Six

Continental. Home: 4 Tanah Tinggi VI, Jakarta Pusat Indonesia Office: Wisma Dharmala Sakti, 4th Floor, Sudirman 32, Jakarta Indonesia

WIRZ, JOST, advertising company executive; b. Zurich, Switzerland, Oct. 25, 1941; s. Adolf Eric and Ruth Marcelle (Egli) W.; m. Ruth Beatrice Wunderli, July 9, 1965; children: Tobias, Benno. MBA, Northwestern U., Chgo., 1967. Trainee BBDO Advt. Co., N.Y.C., 1963; media researcher Ogilvy and Mather, London, 1964-65; account supr. Adolf Wirz Inc. Advt., Zurich, 1967-70, chmn., 1975—; chmn. Wirz Holding Inc., Zurich, 1975—, Wirz Mgmt. Cons. Group Zurich, Zurich, 1975—; bd. dirs. Publitest Inc., Mktg. Research, Zurich, Ludwig Walser Design AG, Baden-Dattwil, Switzerland, Eibel and Brugger AG, Direct Mktg., Zurich. Contbr. articles to profl. jours.; mem. Media Commn. Zurich, 1987—. Recipient Jr. Achievement award Internat. Advt. Assn., World Congress, Paris, 1965. Mem. Bund Schweizer Werbeagenturen (vice chmn. 1978-87, chmn. 1987—), Schweizerische Werbewirtschaft (exec. bd. 1981—), European Assn. Advt. Agys. (council 1978—). Mem. Freisinnig-Demokratische Party. Lodge: Rotary (pres. 1984-85). Home: Uetlibergihalde 9, 8045 Zurich Switzerland Office: Adolf Wirz Inc Advt, Uetlibergstrasse 132, 8045 Zurich Switzerland

WIRZ, WILLY WALTER, manufacturing company executive; b. Solothurn, Switzerland, Jan. 7, 1936; s. Willy and Marie (Haupt) W.; children—Cornelia, Christoph Alfons, Madeleine Elisabeth. Ingenieurschule HTL diploma, 1958; student Von Roll PLC-Zurich, 1952-55. Prodn. chem. engr. Mettler Instruments PLC, Stafa, 1962-64; sales mgr. Analytic Kontron PLC, Zurich, 1964-69; research project leader SCM Corp., Zumikon-Zurich, 1969-71; chief chem. engr. Hasler PLC, Berne, Switzerland, 1971—; gen. mgr. Wintion PLC, Gerzensee, Berne. Author: pH and pCl Values, ISE Measuring Technology, 1974. Patentee in field. Mem. C. of C., STC Schweiz. Verband der Chemiker HTL, HIV Handels-und Industrieverein. Home: Mühledorf bei Kirchdorf, CH-3116 Berne Switzerland Office: CH-3115 Gerzensee Berne, Switzerland

WISDOM, GUYRENA KNIGHT, psychologist, educator; b. St. Louis, July 27, 1923; d. Gladys Margaret (Hankins) McCullin; AB, Stowe Tchrs. Coll., 1945; AM, U. Ill., 1951; postgrad. St. Louis U., 1952-53, 58, 62; Washington U., St. Louis, 1959-61; U. Chgo., 1966-67; Drury Coll., 1968; U. Mo., 1971-72; Fontbonne Coll., 1973; Harris-Stowe State Coll., 1974, 81-82. Tchr. elementary sch. St. Louis Pub. Sch. System, 1945-63, psychol. examiner, 1963-68, sch. psychologist, 1968-74, cons. spl. edn., 1974-77, supr. spl. edn. dept., 1977-79, coordinator staff devel. div., 1979-81; pvt. tutor, 1971-72; sch. psychologist, 1984-85; pvt. practice psychologist, St. Louis, 1985-88; ednl. assessment specialist St. Louis Regional Ctr. for the Developmentally Disabled, 1988—; instr. Harris Tchrs. Coll., St. Louis, 1973-74, Harris-Stowe Coll., 1979. Contbr. articles to profl. jours. Mem. Nat. Assn. Sch. Psychologists, Mo. Assn. Children With Learning Disabilities, Council for Exceptional Children, Mo. Tchrs. Assn., Assn. Supervision and Curriculum Devel., Pi Lambda Theta, Kappa Delta Pi. Roman Catholic. Home: 5046 Wabada St Saint Louis MO 63113

WISE, GARY LAMAR, electrical engineering and mathematics educator, researcher, investment researcher; b. Texas City, Tex., July 29, 1945; s. Calder Lamar and Ruby Lavon (Strom) W.; m. Mary Estella Warren, Dec. 28, 1974; 1 child, Tanna Estella. BA summa cum laude, Rice U., 1971; MSE, Princeton U., 1973, MA 1973, PhD, 1974. Postdoctoral research assoc. Princeton U., N.J., 1974; asst. prof. Tex. Tech U., Lubbock, 1975-76; asst. prof. U. Tex., Austin, 1976-80, assoc. prof., 1980-84, prof. elec. and computer engring. and math., 1984—; tech. reviewer Army Research Office, Durham, N.C., 1976, Air Force Office Sci. Research, Washington, 1980, 83—, Harper and Row Pubs., N.Y.C., 1982-83, NSF, 1984, 87; cons. Baylor Coll. Medicine, Houston, 1972; mem. control group League City Nat. Bank, 1978-82; speaker at numerous tech. confs. Contbr. chpts., numerous articles to profl. publs. Recipient award for outstanding contbns. to Coll. Engring., U. Tex. Engring. Found., 1979, 81; Air Force Office Sci. research grantee, 1976—; research contracts E-Systems, Inc., 1983-85; Carroll D. Simmons Centennial teaching fellow U. Tex., Austin, 1982-84. Mem. IEEE, Soc. Indsl. and Applied Math., Am. Math. Soc., Inst. Math. Stats., Math. Assn. Am., Eta Kappa Nu, Phi Beta Kappa, Tau Beta Pi. Methodist. Home: 8 Muir Lane Austin TX 78746 Office: U Tex Dept Elec and Computer Engring Austin TX 78712

WISE, GEORGE SCHNEIWEIS, university chancellor; b. Pinsk, Poland, Apr. 7, 1906; came to U.S., 1926, naturalized, 1939; s. Noah and Chaya (Rabinowitz) Schneiweis; m. Florence Rosenberg, Dec. 8, 1933. B.S. summa cum laude, Furman U., 1928, LL.D., 1973; M.A., Columbia, 1930, Ph.D., 1950, LL.D., 1981; Ph.D. (hon.), Hebrew U., 1957, Tel Aviv U., 1972, Bar Ilan U., 1976; LL.D., U. Miami, 1977, Yeshiva U., 1983; H.L.D., U. Fla., 1977. Assoc. dir. Bur. Applied Social Research, Columbia, 1949-52, lectr. sociology, 1950-52; vis. prof. U. Mexico, 1956; pres. Tel-Aviv U., 1963-71, Chancellor for life, 1971—; Disting. prof. emeritus of internat. affairs U. Miami, 1981—; Pres. Inter-Am. Paper Corp., Fabricas de Papel Tuxtepec, Mex., 1955-63; pres., chmn. Clal Israel Latin Am. Devel. Co., 1962-69; dir., exec. Israel Corp., Ltd.; dir. Indsl. Devel. Bank Israel, Israeli Paper Mills, Hadera. Author: Caudillo, 1951, Mexico de Aleman, 1952; editor: Middle East Perspectives: the next 20 years, 1981. Chmn. bd. govs. Hebrew U., 1953-62; chmn. Jewish Telegraphic Agy., 1951-55; trustee Mount Sinai Med. Center, Miami, 1977—, U. Miami, 1981. Decorated Order Aguila Azteca Govt. Mex., 1946. Fellow Am. Sociol. Soc.; mem. Israel Am. Soc. (pres.), Israel Am. C. of C. Clubs: Yale (N.Y.C.), Columbia U. (N.Y.C.); Univ. (Mex.); Bankers (Miami), Standard (Miami), Westview Country (Miami). Home: 5500 Collins Ave Miami Beach FL 33140 Office: 999 S Bayshore Dr Miami FL 33131 other: Tel Aviv Univ, Ramat Aviv, Tel Aviv 69978, Israel *

WISE, ROBERT, producer, director; b. Winchester, Ind., Sept. 10, 1914. Student, Franklin Coll., D.F.A. (hon.), 1968. Staff cutting dept. R.K.O., 1933, became sound cutter, asst. editor, film editor, 1939-43, dir., 1943-49; with 20th Century-Fox, 1949-52, M.G.M., 1954-57; free-lance 1958-73; Past mem. Nat. Council of Arts. Ind. producer/dir. various studios: motion pictures include The Curse of the Cat People, 1944, Mademoiselle Fifi, 1944, The Body Snatcher, 1945, A Game of Death, 1945, Criminal Court, 1946, Born to Kill, 1947, Mystery in Mexico, 1948, Blood on the Moon, 1948, The Set Up, 1949, Two Flags West, 1950, Three Secrets, 1950, The House on Telegraph Hill, 1951, The Day the Earth Stood Still, 1951, The Captive City, 1952, Something For the Birds, 1952, The Desert Rats, 1953, Destination Gobi, 1953, So Big, 1953, Executive Suite, 1954, Helen of Troy, 1955, Tribute to a Bad Man, 1956, Somebody Up There Likes Me, 1957, This Could Be the Night, 1957, Until They Sail, 1957, Run Silent, Run Deep, 1958, I Want to Live, 1958, Odds Against Tomorrow, 1959, West Side Story (Acad. award best dir. (with Jerome Robbins) and best picture), 1961, Two For the Seasaw, 1962, The Haunting, 1963, The Sound of Music, 1965 (Acad. award best dir., best picture), The Sand Pebbles, 1966, Star!, 1968, The Andromeda Strain, 1971, Two People, 1973, The Hindenburg, 1975, Audrey Rose, 1977, Star Trek-The Motion Picture, 1979; partner ind. film co., 1970—. Mem. Dirs. Guild (pres. 1971), Acad. Motion Picture Arts and Scis. (pres. 1985-87). Address: Robert Wise Prodns 315 S Beverly Dr Suite 214 Beverly Hills CA 90212-4301 *

WISE, WILMA MARK, credit bureau and employment agency executive; b. Frankfort, Ill., Mar. 13, 1926; d. Paul and Louise (Staedke) Mark; m. Perry Kenneth Wise, Sept. 5, 1948; children: Douglas Kent, Dennis Mark. Student Met. Bus. Coll., 1943-44; grad. exec. devel. program Ind. U. Grad. Sch. Bus., 1975. Owner, ptnr. Naperville Credit Bur. (Ill.), 1958-70; gen. mgr., v.p. First Suburban Services, Naperville, 1970-75; pres., gen. mgr. Wise Surburban Services, Inc., divs. Snelling and Snelling, Wise Credit Bur., Wise/TempForce, Naperville, Ill., 1975—. Mem., pres. Naperville Dist. No. 203 Career Edn. Adv. Council, 1971—; mem. exec. com. North Cen. Coll. Community Fund Drive, 1980—, chmn., 1984-85; mem. exec. com. DuPage County Pvt. Industry Council, 1983—; 1st pres. Ill. Bus. Week, 1984. Named Boss of Year, Am. Bus. Women's Assn., 1979. Mem. Ill. Assn. Personnel Cons. (bd. dirs. 1976-81) Ill. Collector's Assn. (bd. dirs. 1982—, v.p. 1983-84, pres. 1985-86), Am. Collector's Assn., Internat. Fellowship Cert. Collectors, Associated Credit Burs. Inc. (Internat. Key Leadership award 1979, Excellence award 1984), Associated Credit Burs. Ill. (bd. dirs. 1975—, pres. 1979-80), Women in Mgmt. (Woman of Achievement award 1982), Naperville C. of C. (bd. dirs. 1960-66), Downers Grove C. of C. (bd. dirs. 1972-75), Naperville Organ Soc. Luth. (mem. council 1978-84). Club: Cosmopolitan Dance (Naperville). Home: 7S410 Arbor Dr Naperville IL 60540 Office: 638-40 E Ogden Ave Twin Center Naperville IL 60540

WISKOW, DORIAN MILO, security company executive; b. Huddersfield, Yorksire, Eng., Dec. 13, 1960; s. Michael André and Margarete (Jackson) W.; m. Fiona Christine Sykes, Jan. 4, 1983 (div. Mar. 1988). Programmer Hyman Computer Systems Ltd., Manchester, Eng., 1979-80; cons. Hunter Douglas, Europe, Rotterdam, Holland, 1980-81; dir. Productive Computer Systems, Inc., Middletown, Conn., 1981-83; support specialist Sharp Electronics Ltd., Manchester, 1983-85; mktg. mgr. Videoscan Ltd., Macclesfield, Eng., 1985-87; tech. dir. Secure Solutions Ltd., Warrington, Eng., 1987—; bd. dirs. Secure Solutions Ltd., Warrington, Productive Computer Systems Ltd., London. Conservative. Office: Secure Solutions Ltd, St James Ct, Wilderspool Causway, WA4 6PS Warrington England

WISNER, CYNTHIA ANN, geologist; b. Carthage, Mo., July 7, 1957; d. James William and Billie Ann (Glaze) Schooler; m. David Lee Wisner, Feb. 12, 1983. BS in Geology, Baylor U., 1980; postgrad., Houston Bapt. U., 1986—. Geologist McClelland Engrs., Houston, 1980, Getty Oil subs. Texaco, Houston, 1981-85, Minatome Corp., Houston, 1985-86. Mem. Houston Geol. Soc., Am. Assn. Petroleum Geologists, Delta Gamma. Home: 9507 Wellsworth Houston TX 77083

WISNER, FRANK GEORGE, foreign service officer; b. N.Y.C., July 2, 1938; s. Frank Gardiner W. and Mary Knowles (Fritchey); m. Genevieve de Virel, July 2, 1969 (dec. 1974); 1 dau., Sabrina; m. Christine de Ganay, June 28, 1976; stepchildren: Caroline Sarkozy, Olivier Sarkozy, 1 son, David. B.A., Princeton U., 1961. Dep. dir. Pres.' Task Force Refugee Resettlement, Washington, 1976; dir. So. Africa U.S. Dept. State, Washington, 1976-77, dep. exec. sec., 1977-79; ambassador Am. embassy, Lusaka, Zambia, 1979-82; dep. asst. sec. Dept. State, Washington, 1982-86; U.S. Ambassador to Arab Republic of Egypt Cairo, 1986—. Recipient Meritorious Honor award Dept. State, 1973; recipient Mil. Medal of Honor Govt. of Vietnam, 1968, Social Selfare Medal of Honor, 1968. Mem. Council on Fgn. Relations. Episcopalian. Clubs: Metropolitan (Washington); Ivy (Princton, N.J.). Office: US Embassy Box 1 FPO New York NY 09527

WISSE, FREDERIK, produce exporter, export company executive; b. Dordrecht, The Netherlands, Sept. 26, 1947; arrived in Germany, 1983.; s. Frederik Jan and Elisabeth Apolonia (Groeneveld) W.; m. Inge Huse, Aug. 20, 1983. Grad. high sch., Dordrecht. Mktg. mgr. KLM Freight Sales Dept., Schiphol, The Netherlands, 1972-74, sales sec., 1974-76, mgr. inner sales, 1976-82; European rep. Maxim Brand, Inc., N.Y., 1982—; mgr., owner Fa. Maxim Brand, Rotterdam, The Netherlands, 1985—. Inventor closed horse stall for B747, 1977-78; initiator applying sci. post-harvest treatment soft-fruit, 1985-86. Pres. Ch. Youth Club, Dordrecht, 1965-67. Mem. German Evangelic Ch. Club: KLM Scalesman (Amstelveen). Home: Kornerstrasse 5, 4190 Kleve Federal Republic of Germany Office: Fa Maxim Brand, Vierhavensstraat 40, 3029 BE Rotterdam The Netherlands

WIST, ABUND OTTOKAR, biomedical engineer, radiation physicist, educator; b. Vienna, Austria, May 23, 1926; s. Engelbert Johannes and Augusta Barbara (Ungewitter) W.; m. Suzanne Gregson Smiley, Nov. 30, 1963; children: John Joseph, Abund Charles. BS, Tech U. Graz, 1947; MEd, U. Vienna, 1950, PhD, 1951. Research and devel. engr. Hornyphon AG, Vienna, 1952-54, Siemens & Halske AG, Munich, Germany, 1954-58; dir. research and devel. Brinkman Instruments Co., Westbury, N.Y., 1958-64; sr. scientist Fisher Sci. Inc., Pitts., 1964-69; mem. faculty U. Pitts., 1970-73; asst. prof. computer sci. Va. Commonwealth U., 1973-76, asst. prof. biophysics, 1976-82, asst. prof. physiology and biophysics, 1982-84, asst. prof. radiology, 1984—, founder, gen. chmn. Symposium Computer Applications in Med. Care, Washington, 1977-79, grad. faculty, 1988—. Author: Electronic Design of Microprocessor Based Instrumentation and Control Systems, 1986; contbr. numerous articles and chpts. to profl. jours. and books; patentee in electronic and lab. instrumentation. NASA/Am. Soc. Engring. Edn. faculty fellow, summer 1975; U.S. biomed. engring. del. People's Republic China, 1987. Mem. IEEE (sr.), ASTM, Am. Chem. Soc., N.Y. Acad. Scis., AAAS, Richmond Computer Club (founder, pres. 1977-79), Biomed. Engring. Soc., Am. Assn. Physics in Medicine. Roman Catholic. Home: 9304 Farmington Dr Richmond VA 23229 Office: 1101 E Marshall St PO Box 72 Richmond VA 23298

WISWALL, FRANK LAWRENCE, JR., admiralty lawyer; b. Albany, N.Y., Sept. 21, 1939; s. Frank Lawrence and Clara Elizabeth (Chapman) W.; m. Elizabeth Curtiss Nelson, Aug. 9, 1975; children by previous marriage: Anne W. Larson, Frank Lawrence III. B.A., Colby Coll., 1962; J.D., Cornell U., 1965; Ph.D. in Jurisprudence, Cambridge U., 1967. Bar: Maine 1965, N.Y. 1968, U.S. Supreme Ct. 1968, D.C. 1975, Va. 1978; lic. master small ocean passenger vessels, 1960—. Mem. firm Wiswall & Wiswall, Castine, Maine, 1965-72; atty. Burlingham, Underwood, Barron, Wright & White, N.Y.C., 1967-73; maritime legal adviser Republic of Liberia, 1968—, admiralty counsel, 1974-85; gen. counsel Liberian Services, Inc., N.Y.C. and Reston, Va., 1973-77; pres. Liberian Services, Inc., 1974-85, chief counsel, 1977—, vice-chmn. bd. dirs., 1988—; legal adviser Internat. Bank, Washington, 1972—; ptnr. firm Martin & Smith, Washington, 1975-78; counsel Martin & Smith, 1979-80; mem. legal com. Internat. Maritime Orgn., London, 1972-74, vice chmn. 1974-79, chmn., 1980-84; vis. lectr. Cornell Law Sch., 1969-76, 82; lectr. U. Va. Law Sch. and Center for Oceans Law and Policy, 1978-82; prof. law Cornell U., 1984; Johnsen prof. maritime law Tulane U., 1985; prof. law World Maritime U., Malmo, Sweden, 1986, 88; tutorial supr. internat. law Clare Coll., Cambridge, Eng., 1966, 67; del. Internat. Conf. Marine Pollution, London, 1973; del., chmn. drafting com. Internat. Conf. Carriage of Passengers and Luggage by Sea, Athens, 1974; del. Internat. Conf. on Safety of Life at Sea, London, 1974, 3d UN Conf. on Law of Sea, Caracas, Venezuela, 1974, 3d UN Conf. on Law of Sea (all subsequent sessions); del., chmn. com. final clauses Internat. Conf. on Limitation of Liability for Maritime Claims, London, 1976; del. UN Conf. Carriage of Goods by Sea, Hamburg, 1978, XIII Diplomatic Conf. on Maritime Law, Brussels, 1979; chmn. com. of the whole Internat. Conf. Carriage of Hazardous Substances by Sea, 1984; del. internat. conf. on Maritime Terrorism, Rome, 1988; counsel various marine casualty bds. of investigation, 1970—, harbormaster, Port of Castine, 1960-62; dep. chancellor Diocese of the Mid-Atlantic States Anglican Cath. Ch., 1988—. Author: The Development of Admiralty Jurisdiction and Practice Since 1800, 1970; contbr. articles to profl. jours. Recipient Yorke prize U. Cambridge, 1968-69. Fellow Royal Hist. Soc.; mem. Titulaire, Comite Maritime Internat., Maritime Law Assn. U.S. (chmn. com. on intergovtl. orgns. 1983-87, chmn. com. on CMI, 1987—), Ecclesiastical Law Soc., Selden Soc., Am. Socs. Legal History and Internat. Law, U.K., U.S. assns. average adjusters, ABA, Maine Bar Assn., Bar Assn. City N.Y. (admiralty com. 1971-79), Alpha Delta Phi, Phi Delta Phi. Clubs: United Oxford and Cambridge U, London; Century Assn. (N.Y.C.); Cosmos (Washington). Office: 11870-D Sunrise Valley Dr Reston VA 22091-3303

WITCHER, DANIEL DOUGHERTY, pharmaceutical company executive; b. Atlanta, May 17, 1924; s. Julius Gordon and Myrtice Eleanor (Daniel) W.; children: Beth S., Daniel Dougherty, J. Wright, Benjamin G.; m. Betty Lou Middaugh, Oct. 30, 1982. Student, Mercer U., 1946-47, Am. Grad. Sch. Internat. Mgmt., 1949-50. Regional dir. Sterling Drug Co., Rio de Janeiro and Sao Paulo, Brazil, 1951-56; gen. mgr. Mead Johnson & Co., Sao Paulo, 1956-60; area mgr. Upjohn Internat., Inc., Sao Paulo, 1960-64; v.p. Upjohn Internat., Inc., Kalamazoo, 1964-70, group v.p., 1970-73; pres., gen. mgr. Upjohn Internat., 1973-86; v.p. Upjohn Co., 1973-86; corp. v.p. Worldwide Human Health Bus., 1985-86, corp. sr. v.p., 1986—, also bd. dirs.; chmn. Upjohn Health Care Services, 1982—. Trustee Am. Grad. Sch. Internat. Mgmt., 1981—. Served with USN, 1943-46. Mem. Pharm. Mfrs. Assn. (chmn. internat. sect. 1981-82, 85-86). Republican. Episcopalian. Office: The Upjohn Co 7000 Portage Rd Kalamazoo MI 49002

WITENBERG, EARL GEORGE, psychoanalyst, psychiatrist; b. Middletown, Conn., Aug. 30, 1917; s. Nathan and Goldie (Ruderman) W.; B.A., Wesleyan U., 1937, M.A., 1939; M.D., U. Rochester, 1943; m. Mary Jane Hoffman, Apr. 4, 1948 (dec.); children—William, Susan; m. Carol J. Eagle, June 1, 1986. Intern, Strong Meml. Hosp., Rochester, N.Y., 1943-44; resident in psychiatry Bellevue Hosp., N.Y.C., 1946-48; clin. dir. Postgrad. Center for Psychotherapy, N.Y.C., 1948-49, med. coordinator, 1949-51; chmn. exec. com., fellow W.A. White Inst., 1960-63, dir. inst., 1963—; practice medicine specializing in psychiatry and psychoanalysis, N.Y.C., 1948—; asso. clin. prof. Albert Einstein Coll. Medicine, 1974-79. Served to lt. M.C., USNR, 1944-46. Fellow Am. Psychiat. Assn.; mem. Am. Acad. Psychoanalysis (pres. 1976-77, William Silverberg award 1977), Am. Coll. Psychoanalysts, AAAS, Sigma Xi, Phi Beta Kappa. Author: How Not to Succeed in Psychotherapy..., 1972; contbr. articles to med. jours., chpts. to books. Home: 215 E 68th St New York NY 10021 Office: 20 W 74th St New York NY 10023

WITHALM, CLAUDIO IMMANUEL, mathematics educator; b. Graz, Austria, Nov. 16, 1943; s. Berthold and Maria (Wikullil) W.; m. Annette Auer-Grumbach, Nov. 18, 1977; children by previous marriage—Gregor, Armin, Pia; children by present marriage—Aimée, Cyrill, Philipp, Tycho; 1 foster child, Christian (dec.). Dr.phil., U. Graz, 1972. Sci. asst. U. Graz, 1970-72, univ. asst., 1972-76, univ. dozent, 1976-84, tit. ao. univ. prof. math., 1984—, adminstr., 1970—. Contbr. articles to profl. jours. Mem. Austrian Math. Soc., N.Y. Acad. Scis., Orgn. Univ. Tchrs Graz. Home: Michelbachberg 61, Empersdorf, A8081 Graz Austria Office: U Graz Math Inst, Elisabethstrasse 16, A8010 Graz Austria

WITHAM, PHILLIP ROSS, biological scientist, consultant; b. Stuart, Fla., Apr. 11, 1917; s. Paul Witham and Lucille (Ross) Zeigler; m. Mabel Josephine Blasko, May 27, 1945; children—Chester Randolph, Steven Paul, Timothy Dean, Julie Ann. B. of Ind. Studies, U. South Fla., 1973; M. of Liberal Studies, U. Okla., 1976. Aviation machinest mate U.S. Navy, 1934-44, civilian, 1949-52; tollkeepr, civilian aviation mechanic Fla. Turnpike, Palm City, 1956-58; hydroponics supr. Pub. Health Found. for Blood Pressure and Cancer Research, Stuart, Fla., 1959-63; project leader Fla. Dept. Natural Resources, Stuart, 1963-87; research assoc., Rosensteil Sch. of Marine and Atmospheric Sci., 1987—; team mem. U.S. Fish and Wildlife Service and Nat. Marine Fisheries Service, St. Petersburg, Fla., 1979—, U.S. Corps Engrs., Jacksonville, Fla., 1982—; chmn. sci. bd. dirs. Nat. Save the Sea Turtle Foudn., 1987—; cons. in field. Author: (with others) Turtles: Extinction or Survival, 1974. Fellow Explorers Club; mem. Am. Soc. Zoologists, Ecol. Soc. Am., Am. Inst. Fisheries Research Biologists, Fla. Acad. Scis., Izaak Walton League. Lodge: Masons. Current work: Seaturtles, secondary interest in spiny lobsters; oceanic dispersal, growth and survival of head started (pen-reared) yearlings; management of turtle populations in highly developed area. Subspecialties: Marine biology; Behavioral ecology. Home: 1457 NW Lake Point Stuart FL 33494

WITHERSPOON, WALTER PENNINGTON, JR., orthodontist, philanthropist; b. Columbia, S.C., Sept. 3, 1938; s. Walter P. and Florence Evelyn (Jones) W.; m. Joyce Ann Smith, Sept. 6, 1970; 1 child, Annie Melissa. BS, U. S.C., 1960; DDS, U. N.C., 1964, MSO, 1969. Bd. qualified Am. Bd. Orthodontics. Pvt. practice in orthodontia, Columbia, 1969—; med. staff Bapt. Med. Ctr., Columbia, 1970—, Lexington County Hosp., West Columbia, 1974—. Höst Nite Line, Dove Broadcasting Co. Adv. bd. 1st Palmetto Bank and Trust, West Columbia, 1982; del. S.C. Rep. Com., 1983; bd. dirs. Southeastern Coll. Assemblies of God, Lakeland, Fla., 1984, Brookland Plantation Home for Boys, Orangeburg, S.C.; chmn. Lexington County Rep. Party; commr. Richland/Lexington Counties Commn. for Tech. Edn.; mem. S.C. Steering Com. Pat Robertson for Pres.; mem. Richland/Lexington Commn. for Tech. Edn. Served to lt. USN, 1964-66. Recipient Century Mem. award Boy Scouts Am., 1984. Mem. Greater Columbia Dental Assn. (pres. 1975-76), S.C. Dental Assn. (ho. of dels. 1971-73), ADA, S.C. Orthodontic Assn., Am. Assn. Orthodontists. Club: Sertoma (pres. 1975-76). Lodge: Am. Legion. Home: 250 Lancer Dr Columbia SC 29212 Office: 205 Med Circle West Columbia SC 29169

WITHERSPOON, WILLIAM, investment economist; b. St. Louis, Nov. 21, 1909; s. William Conner and Mary Louise (Houston) W.; student Washington U. Evening Sch., 1928-47; m. Margaret Telford Johanson, June 25, 1938; children—James Tomlin, Jane Witherspoon Peltz, Elizabeth Witherspoon Vodra. Research dept. A. G. Edwards & Sons, 1928-31; pres. Witherspoon Investment Co., 1931-34; head research dept. Newhard Cook & Co., 1934-43; chief price analysis St. Louis Ordnance Dist., 1943-45; head research dept. Newhard Cook & Co., 1945-53; owner Witherspoon Investment Counsel, 1953-64; ltd. partner Newhard Cook & Co., economist, investment analyst, 1965-68; v.p. research Stifel, Nicolaus & Co., 1968-81; lectr. on investments Washington U., 1948-67. Mem. Clayton Bd. of Edn., 1955-68, treas., 1956-68, pres., 1966-67; mem. Clayton Park and Recreation Commn., 1959-60; trustee Ednl. TV, KETC, 1963-64; mem. investment com. Gen. Assembly Mission Bd. Presbyterian Ch. U.S., Atlanta, 1976-79, mem. permanent com. ordination exams, 1979-85; bd. dirs. Ctr. for Theology and the Natural Scis., Berkeley, Calif., 1988—. Served as civilian Ordnance Dept., AUS, 1943-45. Chartered fin. analyst. Mem. St. Louis Soc. Fin. Analysts (pres. 1949-50). Club: Mo. Athletic (St. Louis). Home: 6401 Ellenwood Clayton MO 63105-2228

WITHOFS, LEON JOSEPH, pediatrician; b. Rocourt, Liege, Belgium, Apr. 13, 1945; s. Louis and Josee (Sauvage) W.; m. Marie Laure Creppe, July 29, 1969; children: Joana, Nadia, Shirley. MD, U. Liege, 1971. Lic. pediatrician. Practice medicine specializing in pediatrics Liege, 1976-80; pediatric echographist Clinique St. Vincent, Liege, 1980—. Mem. Am. Soc. Echocardiography. Home: 22 Rue D'Ans, B4420 Rocourt Leige, Belgium Office: Clinique St Vincent, Rue F Lefebvre, B4420 Rocourt Leige, Belgium

WITHUHN, WILLIAM LAWRENCE, museum administrator and curator, railroad economics consultant; b. Portland, Oreg., Aug. 12, 1941; s. Vernon Lawrence and Ruth Eleanor (Ferguson) W.; B.A., U. Calif.-Berkeley, 1963; M.B.A. with distinction, Cornell U., 1977, M.A., 1980, postgrad., 1980-82; m. Gail Joy Hartman, Nov. 22, 1964; children—James, Thomas, Harold. Commd. regular 2d lt. U.S. Air Force, 1963, advanced through grades to capt., 1967; indsl. engr., asst. dir. manpower and orgn., Travis AFB, Calif., 1964-65; global, polar, tactical, and instr. navigator worldwide, 1965-72; spl. ops. navigator, Vietnam, 1969-70; select lead navigator Mil. Airlift Command, 1970-72; ret., 1972; intern, then staff asst. U.S. Ho. of Reps., 1973-74; v.p. Va. & Md. R.R. Co., Cape Charles, Va., 1977-81; v.p. Md. & Del. R.R., Federalsburg, Md., 1977-81; sr. v.p. Ont. Midland R.R., Ont. Central R.R., Sodus, N.Y., 1979-83; v.p. Rail Mgmt. Services, Inc., Syracuse, N.Y., 1979-83, RSA Leasing Co., Syracuse, 1980-83; exec. v.p. Am. Coal Enterprises, Inc., Akron, Ohio, 1980-82; v.p., gen. mgr. Allegheny So. Ry., Martinsburg, Pa., 1982-83; adminstr. dept. history of sci. and tech. Nat. Museum Am. History, Smithsonian Instn., Washington, 1983—, supervising curator div. transp., 1983—, dep. chmn. dept. sci. and tech., 1984—; dir. Rail Mgmt. Services, Inc., Syracuse, N.Y., The Waring Group, Inc., transp. cons., Salisbury, Md.; cons. Pa. Hist. and Mus. Commn., 1982—. Decorated D.F.C. with cluster, Bronze Star, Air Medal with 11 clusters. De Karman fellow, 1979-80; Smithsonian fellow, 1980-81. Mem. Am. Inst. Indsl. Engrs., AAAS, History of Sci. Soc., Am. Hist. Assn., Soc. for History of Tech., Ry. and Locomotive Hist. Soc. (pres.), Am. Shortline R.R. Assn., Ry. Fuel and Operating Officers Assn., Theta Chi. Club: Cornell (Washington). Contbr. articles to profl. jours. Home: 6311 Barr's Ln Lanham MD 20706 Office: Nat Mus Am History Smithsonian Instn Room 5010 Washington DC 20560

WITSIL, ELIZABETH SMITH ALISON (MRS. WALTER EARLE WITSIL), former social worker; b. Wilmington, Del., Sept. 13, 1909; d. Alexander and Katharine Anna (Smith) Alison; A.B., Wilson Coll., 1931; postgrad. Columbia U., 1934-36; m. Walter Earle Witsil, Aug. 27, 1938 (dec. Feb. 1964); 1 child, Adah Elizabeth Witsil Unger; step-children—Walter Earle, Sarah Virginia Witsil Lloyd. Accounting clk. Remington Rand, Inc., Bridgeport, Conn., 1932-33; social case-worker Bridgeport Br.-New Eng. Home for Little Wanderers, 1933-36; social case worker Conn. Children's Aid Soc., Danbury, 1936-38; dir. membership, pub. relations and publicity YWCA, Bridgeport, 1964-75; dir. cultural tours and vols. Bridgeport Mus. Arts, Sci. and Industry, 1975-83. Mem. Bd. Fin. Fairfield (Conn.), 1955-79; mem. Fairfield Rep. Town Meeting, 1947-55; pres. bd. mgrs. Woodfield Maternity Home and Adoption Service, Bridgeport, 1954-57, mem. corp.; bd. dirs. Vis. Nurse Assn. Bridgeport, United Fund Council Eastern Fairfield County, Bridgeport Council Ch. Women, Child Guidance Center of Bridgeport, Conn. Conf. Social Work, Mountain Grove Cemetery Assn., Bridgeport; v.p. Fairfield Community Services; trustee Greater Bridgeport Symphony Soc., 1978—; mem. Sr. Citizens Tax Relief Com., Fairfield, 1980-

85, Sr. Citizens Life Center Study and Bldg. Com., 1981-84; bd. assos. U. Bridgeport; mem. Republican Women's Assn. Fairfield. Mem. AAUW, LWV, DAR, Bridgeport Hosp. Aux. (pres. 1961-63), Delta Kappa Gamma (hon.). Presbyterian (trustee, elder). Clubs: Contemporary (sec. 1957-64, pres. 1976), Wilson Coll. Home: 235 Millard St Apt C3 Fairfield CT 06430

WITTE, ELS, historian, educator; b. Antwerp, Belgium; s. Karel and Y. (Dumont) W. Lic. in Philosophy and History, State U. of Ghent, Belgium, 1966; PhD in Contemporary History, State U. of Ghent, 1970. Asp. fonds natr. de la Recherche Suistifique Brussels, Belgium, 1966-70; asst. prof. History State U. Ghert, Belgium, 1970-73; prof. Vrije U. Brussels, 1974-80, full prof., 1980—, dean of faculty Philosophy and Arts Depts., 1984—; Head of Bd. Ctr. Research Brussels Lang. Situation, Vrije U., 1978—; pres. Bd. of Flemisch Radio and TV Inst. (BRT). Author: Politike Geschiedenis van Belgie Sunds 1830, 1985; editor Reschiedenis van Vlaanderen, 1983, La Belgigue Politique de 1830 a nos youres, 1987. Active Sint-Joost-ten-Node Community Council, 1978-82; bd. dirs. Centre d' NIstoire Contemp., 1980—, Fond Nat. de la Recherche Seint, 1984—. Recipient Pro Cititate award Credit Communal, Brussels, 1968. Mem. Revue belge d' Histoire Contemporaire (sec. Ghent chpt. 1969—), Taal en Sociale Integratie (editor 1978—). Socialist. Home: Scailquin 37/12, B1030 Brussels Belgium Office: Vrije U Brussels, Pleinlaan 2, Brussels Belgium

WITTE, ERICH HELMUT HANS, psychologist, educator; b. Berlin, May 14, 1946; s. Erich Kühn and Ursula (Witte) Renner; m. Hannelore Kuntze, July 31, 1970; children: Nele, Daniel. Diploma, U. Hamburg, 1970, PhD, 1973, habilitation, 1977. Lectr. U. Hamburg, Fed. Republic of Germany, 1970-77, prof., 1977—. Author: Behavior in Group Situation, 1979, Significance Tests and Statistical Inference, 1980, Social Psychology, 1989; author and editor: Introduction into Psychology, 1977. Mem. Deutsche Gesellschaft für Psychologie, European Assn. Exptl. Social Psychology, Arbeitskreis Für Anwendungsorientierte Sozial Wissenschaft. Office: Psychol Inst I, Von Melle Park 6, D2000 Hamburg Federal Republic of Germany

WITTEN, DAVID MELVIN, radiology educator; b. Trenton, Mo., Aug. 16, 1926; s. Buford Isom and Mary Louise (Melvin) W.; m. Netta Lee Watkins, Dec. 23, 1950; children—David Melvin, II, Michael Lee. Student, Trenton Jr. Coll., 1943-44, 46-47; A.B., Washington U., St. Louis, 1950, M.D., 1954; M.S. in Radiology, Mayo Grad. Sch. Medicine, U. Minn., 1960. Diplomate: Am. Bd. Radiology. Intern Virginia Mason Hosp., Seattle, 1954-55; practice medicine specializing in family medicine Trenton, Mo., 1955-57; fellow in radiology Mayo Clinic/Mayo Found., Rochester, Minn., 1957-60; cons. in diagnostic roentgenology Mayo Clinic, 1960-70; instr. Mayo Grad. Sch. Medicine, Rochester, 1960-66; asst. prof. radiology Mayo Grad. Sch. Medicine, 1966-70; pvt. practice medicine specializing in radiology Aberdeen, Wash., 1970-71; clin. assoc. prof. U. Wash., 1970-71; prof. diagnostic radiology, chmn. dept. diagnostic radiology U. Ala., Birmingham, 1971-82; diagnostic radiologist in chief Univ. Hosp., Birmingham, 1971-82; prof., chmn. dept. radiology U. Mo., Columbia, 1982-87; pres. U. Ala. Health Services Found., 1973-75. Author: Atlas of Tumor Radiology - The Breast, 1969, Clinical Urography, 1977; contbr. numerous articles on radiology of breast cancer, urologic and gastrointestinal disease to profl. jours.; editorial bd.: Am. Jour. Roentgenology, 1976-87, Applied Radiology, 1978—, Urologic Radiology, 1979-87, Radiographics, 1983—. Served with USNR, 1944-46. Fellow Am. Coll. Radiology; mem. Radiol. Soc. N. Am., Am. Roentgen Ray Soc., AAAS, Soc. Genitourinary Radiology (pres. 1981-82), Assn. Univ. Radiologists, AMA, Mo. Radiol. Soc., Mo. State Med. Assn., Canadian Assn. Radiologists (hon.), Nat. Audubon Soc. Home: Route 3 Box 62B Columbia MO 65203 Office: University of Missouri Health Sciences Center 1 Hospital Drive Columbia MO 65201

WITTEN, THOMAS DAVID, health care executive; b. Washington, Dec. 6, 1943; s. Shurl George and Ruth Rollins W.; m. Brenda Jane Pope, Feb. 4, 1967. Salesman, J.M. Mathis Co., Durham, N.C., 1966-67; asst. mgr. Marriott Corp., Washington, 1967-68, food service dir., Easton, Md., 1968-75, food service dir., Kingsport, Tenn., 1975-76, dist. mgr. health care, southeast region, Atlanta, from 1976; pres. health care Canteen Co. div., Chgo., 1981-86; now pres. Food Mgmt. Group Internat., Miami; v.p., owner Nat. Tape Video, Atlanta. Talbot County chmn. Nat. Cancer Com., 1974; coach, exec. com., pres. Talbot Little League Football, 1971-75; bd. dirs. Chesapeake Rehab. Center; bd. advisers Chowan Coll., Murfreesboro, N.C. Served with N.C. NG, 1965-71. Mem. Am. Assn. Hosp. Food Service Dirs., Exec. Chefs Assn., Nat. Pilot Assn. Democrat. Roman Catholic. Clubs: Elks, Kiwanis (pres. Easton, lt. gov.-elect dist. 15, 1975). Home: 1910 Ardsley Dr Marietta GA 30062 Office: 1729 Killian Hill Rd LiL Burn GA 30247

WITTENBORN, JOHN RICHARD, psychology educator, clinical researcher, consultant; b. Ft. Gage, Ill., May 22, 1915; s. Richard Edward and Mabel (Mulholl) W.; m. Sarah Elizabeth Alwood, Apr. 29, 1938; children—Sarah Elizabeth, Gretchen Ann, Richard, Christopher Dirk. Ed.B., So. Ill. U., 1937; M.S., U. Ill., 1939, Ph.D., 1942. Instr. Yale U., New Haven, 1942-45, asst. prof., 1945-50, assoc. prof., 1950-54; clin. psychologist dept. univ. health, 1942-48; Univ. prof. psychology and edn. Rutgers U., New Brunswick, N.J., 1954—, dir. interdisciplinary research ctr., 1958-85; adv. com. psychopharmacology FDA, Washington, 1970-73; cons. pharm. industries. Author: Wittenborn Psychiatric Rating Scale, 1955, rev., 1964, Clinical Pharmacology of Anxiety, 1966, Placement of Adoptive Children, 1957, Guidelines for Clinical Trials of Psychotropic Drugs, 1977; assoc. editor Neuropsychobiology; editorial adv. bd. Human Psychopharmacology, Progress in Neuro-Psychopharmacology and Biol. Psychiatry; mem. editorial bd. Stress Medicine; mem. adv. bd. Jour. Nervous and Mental Disease; adv. editor Pharmacopsychoecologia. Branford Coll. fellow, 1944-54. USPHS fellow, 1948-50; recipient disting. teaching and research award Rutgers U., 1961; Devel. Sch. Psychology award N.J. Assn. Sch. Psychologists, 1973. Fellow Am. Coll. Neuropsychopharmacology (sec.-treas. 1964-72, pres. 1973, Paul Hoch Disting. Service award 1968), Collegium International Neuropsychopharmacologicum (v.p. 1982-87), Am. Psychol. Assn., Royal Belgian Soc. Mental Medicine (hon.), Belgium Coll. Neuropsychopharmacology (hon.), Brit. Assn. Psychopharmacology. Club: Cosmos (Washington). Office: Rutgers U Psychology Bldg New Brunswick NJ 08903

WITTEVEEN, SIBBLE JOZEF, data processing company executive; b. Bolsward, Friesland, The Netherlands, Sept. 28, 1956. Programmer Rai Documentatie Centrum, Amsterdam, 1978-79; system mgr. NOVA Automation B.V., Nieuwegein, 1980-82; cons. Database Cons. Europe B.V., Amsterdam, 1982-85, sect. leader, 1985—, dept. mgr., 1987—; EDP advisor Glaxo B.V., The Netherlands, 1985—. Office: Database Cons Europe, West Nederland bv, Prinsengracht 747, 1017 JX Amsterdam The Netherlands

WITTFOHT, HANS HEINRICH HERMANN, construction consultant; b. Wittingen, Germany, Nov. 26, 1924; s. Johann and Anna (Kleineberg) W.; Dipl.-Ing., Tech. Hochschule Karlsruhe, 1951, Dr.-Ing., 1963; Dr.-Ing. E.h., Tech. U. Stuttgart, 1979; m. Irma Redmann, July 29, 1950; children—Dörte, Jens. With Polensky & Zöllner Gesellschaft mbH & Co., Frankfurt am Main, Fed. Republic Germany, 1951—, dept. dir., 1959-68, mng. dir., 1968—, ptnr., 1970—, pres., 1980-87; pres. German Concrete Assn., 1985—; lectr., nat. and internat. congresses. Served with tank, arty. corps. German Army, 1942-45. Decorated Iron Cross I; recipient nat. Ehrenzeichen des VDI, 1977; internat. medal FIP, 1978; with Emil-Mörsch Denkmünze des Deutschen Beton-Vereins, 1981—; Golden medaille Gustave Magnel, 1984, Silver medal Ville de Paris, 1987, Kerensky medal, 1988; hon. fellow The Inst. pf Structural Engrs., 1986; also awards for bridge constrn. in nat., internat. competitions. Mem. German Concrete Soc. (chmn.), German Soc. Engrs. (bd. dirs.), Research Assn. Underground Transp. Facilities (bd. dirs.), Internat. Assn. Bridge and Structural Engring. (v.p. tech. com.), Fédération Internationale de la Précontrainte (pres., mem. presidium). Author: Kreisfoermig gekruemmte Träger, 1964; Triumph der Spannweiten, 1972; Building Bridges, 1984; contbr. numerous articles to profl. lit. Patentee in field of bridge bldg. Home: 26 Gimbacher Weg, 6233, Kelkheim D Federal Republic Germany Office: 61 Bahnhofstrasse, 6200 Wiesbaden 1 Federal Republic of Germany

WITTHÖFT, HARALD, historian; b. Lüneburg, Lower Saxony, Federal Republic Germany, July 6, 1931; m. Babett Freyse, Sept. 20, 1969; children: Bettina, Christiane. Matric, Johanneum, Lüneburg, 1951; final degree, Coll. Edn., Lüneburg, 1953; PhD in History, U. Göttingen, Fed. Republic Germany, 1959. State's examen history, geography, phys. edn., U. Göttingen, 1960. Historian Inst. for Sci. Film, Göttingen, 1960-62; asst. faculty econs. history U. Melbourne, Australia, 1962, acting lectr. faculty arts, 1963-64; historian Inst. Ednl. Film, Munich, Fed. Republic Germany, 1964-65; lectr. Coll. Edn., Lüneburg, 1965-70; prof. econ., social history, didactics U. Siegen, Fed. Republic Germany, 1970—. Author: Umrisse Einer Historischen Metrologie, 1979, Münzfuss, pondus Caroli, 1984; editor: Sachüberlieferung und Geschichte, 1984. Mem. Internat. Com. Hist. Metrology (gen. sec. 1983-85, pres. 1986—). Office: U Siegen FB 1, A-Reichwein Str, D5900 Siegen Federal Republic of Germany

WITTIG, RAYMOND SHAFFER, lawyer; b. Allentown, Pa., Dec. 13, 1944; s. Raymond Baety and Alice (Shaffer) W.; m. Beth Glover, June 21, 1975; children—Meaghan G., Allison G. B.A., Pa. State U., 1966, M.Ed., 1968; J.D., Dickinson Sch. Law, 1974. Bar: Pa. 1974, D.C. Ct. Apls. 1978. Research psychologist Intext Corp., Scranton, Pa., 1968; minority counsel, procurement subcom. and gen. oversight subcom. Small Bus. Com., U.S. Ho. of Reps., Washington, 1975-76, 77-78, counsel full Ho. Small Bus. Com. 1979-84; atty. Lipsen, Hamberger & Whitten, Washington, 1984-88; sole practice, Rockville, Md., 1988—. Served to capt. U.S. Army, 1969-71. Mem. Nat. Fedn. Ind. Bus., U.S. C. of C. (small bus. council), Nat. Order Barristers. Club: Capitol Hill. Home: 4618 Holly Ridge Rd Rockville MD 20853

WITTING, CHRIS J., electrical manufacturing executive; b. Cranford, N.J., Apr. 7, 1915; s. Nicholas and Anne (Begasse) W.; B.S., N.Y. U., 1941; grad. Am. Inst. Banking; student Fordham Law Sch.; D.Eng. (hon.), Clarkson Coll. Tech.; m. Grace Orrok, Oct. 8, 1938; children—Leland James, Anne Kristin, Nancy Jane, Chris J. Exec. asst. Guaranty Trust Co., 1933-36, N.Y. Trust Co., 1936-39; mgr. Price Waterhouse & Co., 1939-41; comptroller, treas. U.S.O. Camp Shows, Inc., 1941-46; mng. dir. Allen B. DuMont Labs., Inc., 1946-53; pres. Westinghouse Broadcasting Co., 1953-54, group v.p. and gen. mgr. consumer products group, Westinghouse Electric Corp., 1954-64; v.p. exec. asst. to chmn. and pres. Internat. Tel.& Tel. Corp., 1964-65; pres., chief exec. officer, dir. Crouse-Hinds Co., Syracuse, N.Y., 1965-75, chmn., chief exec. officer, 1975-82; vice chmn. bd. Cooper Industries Inc., Houston; bd. dirs. Continental Info. Systems Corp., Fay's Drug Co. Inc., Key Atlantic Bancorp, Key Bank of Cen. N.Y., KeyCorp, Albany, N.Y., Lipe-Rollway Corp.; bd. dirs., vice chmn. bd. Unity Mut. Life Ins. Co., Windsor Life Ins. Co. of Am.; chmn. Onondaga Venture Capital Fund Inc.; chmn. Pub. Auditorium Authority of Pitts. and Allegheny County, 1963-64; chmn. bd. trustees Syracuse U.; pres. Met. Devel. Found. of Syracuse & Cen. N.Y. Mem. Nat. Electric Mfrs. Assn. (chmn. bd. govs., bd. dirs.), Electronic Industries Assn. (bd. govs. 1961-62, dir. 1960-63), Nat. Planning Assn. (nat. council), Am. Mgmt. Assn. (mem. mktg. planning council), Elec. Mfrs. Club, Mfrs. Assn. Syracuse (dir.), Met. Devel. Assn. Syracuse and Onondaga County, N.Y. (dir.). Clubs: Athletic, Union League, Century, Onondaga Country, Athletic (Syracuse). Home: 518 Bradford Pkwy Syracuse NY 13224 Office: State Tower Bldg Syracuse NY 13202

WITTLINGER, TIMOTHY DAVID, lawyer; b. Dayton, Ohio, Oct. 12, 1940; s. Charles Frederick and Dorothy Elizabeth (Golden) W.; m. Diane Cleo Dominy, May 20, 1967; children: Kristine Elizabeth, David Matthew. B.S. in Math., Purdue U., 1962; J.D. with distinction, U. Mich., 1965. Bar: Mich. 1966, U.S. Dist. Ct. (ea. dist.) Mich. 1966, U.S. Ct. Appeals (6th cir.) 1968, U.S. Supreme Ct. 1971. Assoc. Hill, Lewis, Adams, Goodrich & Tait, Detroit, 1965-72, ptnr., 1973—, head litigation dept., 1976—; mem. profl. assistance com. U.S. Dist. Ct. (ea. dist.) Mich., 1981-82. Mem. house of deps. Episcopal Ch., N.Y.C., 1979—; vice chmn. Robert Whitaker Sch. Theology, 1983-87; sec. bd. trustees Episcopal Ch., Diocese of Mich., Detroit, 1983—; chair, sec. Grubb Inst. Behavioral Studies Ltd., Washington, 1986-87. Mem. State Bar Mich., ABA, Nat. Bd. Trial Advocacy (cert.), Engring. Soc. Detroit. Home: 736 N Glenhurst Birmingham MI 48009 Office: Hill Lewis Adams Goodrich & Tait 100 Renaissance Ctr 32d Floor Detroit MI 48243

WITTOUCK, ERIC, company executive; b. Brussels, Oct. 5, 1946; s. Michel Wittouck and Helena Princess Scherbatow; m. Brigitte Baiwir, Aug. 22, 1979; children: Amandine, Flore, Amaury. MA in Applied Econs., U. Louvain, 1970. Dir. Raffinerie Tirlemontoise S.A., Brussels, 1970-84, chmn., 1984-86; chmn. R.T. Holding S.A., Brussels, 1986—; chmn. Tiense Suiker Europe B.V., Rotterdam, The Netherlands, Tiense Suikar Europe B.V., Rotterdam, Winco B.V., Rotterdam; dir. various cos. Belgium and U.S. Mem. Assn. of the Nobility of the Belgian Kingdom (life), Russian Nobility Assn. in Am. (assoc.). Club: Royal Golf of Belgium. Home: 17 Dreve de Lorraine, B1180 Brussels Belgium Office: R T Holding SA, 182 Ave de Tervueren, B1150 Brussels Belgium

WITTROCK, MERLIN CARL, educational psychologist, educator; b. Twin Falls, Idaho, Jan. 3, 1931; s. Herman C. and Mary Ellen (Baumann) W.; m. Nancy McNulty, Apr. 3, 1953; children: Steven, Catherine, Rebecca. B.S. in Biology, U. Mo., Columbia, 1953, M.S. in Ednl. Psychology, 1956; Ph.D. in Ednl. Psychology, U. Ill., Urbana, 1960. Prof. grad. sch. edn. UCLA, 1960—, founder Ctr. Study Evaluation, 1966, chmn. div. ednl. psychology; fellow Center for Advanced Study in Behavioral Scis., 1967-68; vis. prof. U. Wis., U. Ill., Ind. U., Monash U., Australia. Author or editor: The Evaluation of Instruction, 1970, Changing Education, 1973, Learning and Instruction, 1977, The Human Brain, 1977, Danish transl., 1980, Spanish transl., 1982, The Brain and Psychology, 1980, Instructional Psychology: Education and Cognitive Processes of the Brain; Neuropsychological and Cognitive Processes of Reading, 1981, Handbook of Research on Teaching, 3d edit., 1986; editor-in-chief: Readings in Educational Research, 7 vols, 1977; assoc. editor: Ednl. Psychologist; contbr. articles to profl. jours. Served to capt. USAF. Ford Found. grantee; recipient Thorndike award for outstanding psychol. research, 1987. Fellow Am. Psychol. Assn. (mem. assn. council 1987—), AAAS; mem. Am. Ednl. Research Assn. (chmn. ann. conv., chmn. publs. 1980-83, assn. council 1986-88, bd. dirs., award for outstanding research 1986), Phi Delta Kappa. Office: UCLA 321 Moore Hall Los Angeles CA 90024

WOBER, YUSUF AHMED, government administrator; b. Harar, Ethiopia, Sept. 7, 1943; s. Ahmed Mohamed Wober and Fatuma Yusuf Tahir; m. Ferida Ahmed, Nov. 14, 1975; children: Adib, Hanan. BA in Econs., Addis Ababa (Ethiopia) U., 1968; MS in Transp. Sci., Northwestern U., 1972. Chief planning and programming Ethiopia Highway Authority, Addis Ababa, 1968-73; head transport and communications dept. Ethiopian Planning Commn., Addis Ababa, 1973-74; permanent sec. Ministry of Transport and Communications, Addis Ababa, 1975-76; Minister of Transport and Communications Addis Ababa, 1976-87; v.p. Council of State of Ethiopia 1987—; mem. internat. adv. com. Sub-Saharan Africa Transp. Program, 1987—; mem. Nat. Shengo (Parliament) Ethiopia. Author: (with others) Road Investment Programming in Developing Countries, 1976. Home: Kefitegna 23, Kebele 13 House #1938, Addis Ababa Ethiopia 41304 Office: Council of the State, Addis Ababa Ethiopia 1013

WODLINGER, MARK L., broadcast executive; b. Jacksonville, Fla., July 13, 1922; s. Mark H. and Beatrice Mae (Boney) W.; m. Connie Jean Bates, May 3, 1974; children: Mark, Jacqueline, Steve, Mike, Kevin. BS, U. Fla., 1943. Salesman Sta. WQUA, Moline, Ill., 1948; mgr. Sta. WOC-AM-FM-TV, Davenport, Iowa, 1949-58; v.p. Sta. WMBD-TV, Peoria, Ill., 1959-61; v.p., gen. mgr. Sta. WZZM-TV, Grand Rapids, Mich., 1962-63, Sta. KMBC-TV, Kansas City, Mo., 1963-69; pres. Intermedia, Kansas City, 1969-73; builder, owner comml. radio stas. Swaziland, Africa; operator Radio Malawi, Blantyre, and Marknews TV and Radio News Bur., Nairobe, Kenya, 1971-74; owner, pres. Sta. KBEQ, Kansas City, 1973-77; owner Sta. WCJX-FM, Miami, Sta. WIXI-FM, Naples and Ft. Myers, Fla.; pres., chmn. bd. Wodlinger Broadcasting Co., 1978—; owner TV-5, Houston, Hit Video USA, Satellite Music Network, Houston; dir. Sta. KCPT-TV, Kansas City, Sta. KCWV-FM, Leavenworth, Kans., Sta. KCWV, Kansas City, MidAm. Bank & Trust Co., Kansas City., City Bank of Kansas City, Info-Data, Kansas City, Commerce Nat. Bank, Naples. Bd. dirs. Kansas City Philharm., Kansas City Civic Council, Naples YMCA; mem. Conservancy, Naples Civic Assn. Served to lt. U.S. Navy, 1941-45. Mem. Nat. Assn. Broadcasters, Mo. Assn. Broadcasters, Broadcast Pioneers. Republican. Episcopalian. Clubs: Kansas City, University, Vanguard, Carriage, Port Royal, Naples Yacht, Houston Yacht, White Lake Yacht (Whitehall, Mich.). Lodge: Rotary. Home: 6439 Wenonga Rd Mission Hills KS 66208 also: 800 Galleon Dr Naples FL 33940 Office: 4350 Johnson Dr Shawnee Mission KS 66205

WOEHRLEN, ARTHUR EDWARD, JR., dentist; b. Detroit, Dec. 9, 1947; s. Arthur Edward and Olga (Hewka) W.; m. Sara Elizabeth Heikoff, Aug. 13, 1972; 1 child, Tess Helena. DDS, U. Mich., 1973. Resident in gen. dentistry USAF, 1973-74; gen. practice dentistry Redwood Dental Group, Warren, Mich., 1976—; instr. Sinai Hosp., Detroit, 1977—; chief of dentistry St. John's Hosp., Macomb Ctr., Mt. Clemens, Mich., 1982—; mem. dentistry staff Hutzel Hosp., Warren; reviewer Chubb Ins. Co. (malpractice claims); bd. mem. Mich. Acad. Gen. Dentistry (chmn. State of Mich. Continuing Dental Edn. Accreditation). Contbr. articles on dentistry to profl. jours. Served to capt. USAF, 1973-76. Fellow Internat. Coll. of Oral Implantologists; mem. ADA, Acad. Gen. Dentistry (master), Mich. Dental Assn., Acad. Gen. Dentistry, Am. Acad. Oral Medicine, Fedn. Dentaire Internationale, Acad. Dentistry for the Handicapped, Am. Acad. Oral Implantologists, Internat. Coll. Oral Implantologists, Macomb Dist. Dental Soc.; panel mem. Am. Arbitration Assn. Republican. Home: 25460 Dundee Huntington Woods MI 48070 Office: Redwood Dental Group 13403 E 13 Mile Rd Warren MI 48070

WOESSNER, MARK MATTHIAS, printing company executive; b. Berlin, Oct. 14, 1938; m. Liselotte Woessner; 2 children. Ed. high sch., Karlsruhe, Fed. Republic Germany. Asst. mgr. Bertelsmann Corp., Gütersloh, Fed. Republic Germany, 1968-72, pres. printing and mfg. div., 1976-83, pres., chief exec. officer, 1983—; tech. mgr. Mohndruck Printing Co., 1972-74. Contbr. reports to tech. jours. including Jour. U. Stuttgart. Office: Bertelsmann Corp, Car-Bertelsmannstrasse 270, 4830 Gütersloh Federal Republic of Germany *

WOESTENBURG, LAURENT CORNELIUS, publishing executive; b. Weelde, Antwerpen, Belgium, July 24, 1932; s. Jozef and Joanna (Gijsbregts) W.; m. Lea Moonen, Dec. 31, 1958. Lic. in German langs., Cath. U. Louvain, Belgium, 1957, aggregate in higher edn., 1958. Tchr. tech. schs., Antwerp, 1958-60; tchr. secondary edn. Lier, Belgium, 1959-61; editor J. Van In Pub. House, Lier, 1961-73, mng. dir., 1974—; part-time tchr. Med. Sch. Lier, 1961-66; lectr. faculty applied econ. scis. Univ. Faculteiten Sint-Ignatius, U. Antwerp, 1966—. Co-author: Wel en Wee in Weelde, 1978, Waarvan Akte, 1974, Ontwikkelingen rond Schoolboeken en België en Nederland, 1985; editor, co-author: Poppel in Goede en Kwade Dagen, 1979, Zoals ze Waren, 1979, Het Educatieve Boek, 1979, Ravels in Lief en Leed, 1980, Weelde Toen en Nu, 1982, De Drie van Het Noorden, 1987. Pres. Heemkundekring Nicolaus Poppelius history assn., Ravels, Cantorye Poppeliensis choir. Mem. Ednl. Pubs. Assn. Flanders (pres.), Assn. Christian Employers. Lodge: Order of Leopold II (officer 1986). Home: Beatrijs van Nazarethlaan 2, 2391 Ravels, Antwerp Belgium Office: Uitgeverij J Van In, Grote Markt 39, 2500 Lier, Antwerp Belgium

WOHLMUT, THOMAS ARTHUR, communications exec.; b. Perth, Australia, Feb. 19, 1953; came to U.S., 1957, naturalized, 1963; s. Arthur John and Georgina Elfreida (Pipek) W.; B.A. cum laude, UCLA, 1975; m. Debra Lynn Hansen, Aug. 1, 1979 1 child, Katherine Emily. TV prodn. asst. (All in the Family, Mary Tyler Moore Show, Carol Burnett Show, Emmy Awards Show), CBS, Hollywood, Calif., 1971-74; video disc producer I/O Metrics Corp., Calif., 1975-77; dir., writer Innovative Media Inc., Menlo Park, Calif., 1977-78; pres. Wohlmut Media Services, Sunnyvale, 1978—; cons. Bechtel Power Corp., Sunset Mag., Xerox-Diablo Systems, Pacific Gas & Electric Co., Elec. Power Research Inst., Advanced Micro Devices, Amdahl Corp., IBM-Rolm; lectr. in field. Mem. Internat. TV Assn. (past. pres. San Francisco chpt., v.p. for Alaska, Wash., Idaho, Oreg., Utah, Nev., No. Calif., Joyce Nelson award 1987), Soc. Visual Communicators, Internat. Interactive Communications Soc. (founder, 1st pres.), Am. Soc. Tng. and Devel., Am. Film Inst. Office: 2600 Central Ave Suite L Union City CA 94587

WOHLREICH, JACK JAY, lawyer; b. Newark, Feb. 8, 1946; s. Charles Carl and Erna D. (Epstein) W.; m. Jane Friedlander, June 21, 1969; children: Erin Michelle, Caleb Joshua. BA in Polit. Sci., Am. U., 1968, JD, 1971; postdoctoral, George Washington U., 1972. Bar: Md. 1972, D.C. 1972, U.S. Dist. Ct. Md. 1972, U.S. Dist. Ct. D.C. 1972, U.S. Ct. Appeals (4th cir.) 1973, U.S. Supreme Ct. 1975, Ill. 1976, U.S. Dist. Ct. (no. dist.) Ill. 1976. Asst. chief counsel FDA div. HHS, Washington, 1971-75; assoc. gen. counsel and chief of litigation Baxter Travenol Labs., Inc., Deerfield, Ill., 1975-86; assoc. gen. counsel Baxter Internat., Inc., Deerfield, Ill., 1986—; lectr. various insts. Contbg. editor Am. U. Law Rev., 1969-71. Asst. to candidate/advanceman Dem. Nat. Com., 1968, Kennedy for Pres. Com., Washington, 1968; chief of advance R. Sargent Shriver, 1970-71; staff asst. congl. leadership for future com., 1971; founding mem. Gaithersburg (Md.) Hebrew Congregation, 1974. Mem. ABA, Ill. Bar Assn., D.C. Bar Assn., Md. Bar Assn., Food and Drug Inst., Pharm. Mfgs. Assn., Health Industries Mfgs. Assn., Tau Epsilon Phi. Home: 175 Belle Ave Highland Park IL 60035 Office: Baxter Travenol Labs Inc One Baxter Pkwy Deerfield IL 60015

WOJCIECHOWSKI, FRANZ LAURENS, psychologist; b. Heerlen, Limburg, The Netherlands, May 25, 1951; s. Franz and Anna Maria Gertrude (Hendriks) W.; m. Petronella Wilhelmina Pluk, Sept. 4, 1986; 1 child, Martina Emilia Franciska. BA in Edn., Pedagogische Acad., Heerlen, 1972; BA in Psychology, Cath. U., Nijmegen, Netherlands, 1975, MA in Psychology cum laude, 1978, BA in Anthropology, 1980, MA in Anthropology cum laude, PhD in Clin. Psychology, 1984. Lic. clin. psychologist, psychotherapist. Instr. dept. psychology Cath. U., 1980-85; sr. clin. psychologist Canisius-Wilhelmina Hosp., Nijmegen, 1985-86; sr. clin. psychologist, cons. Acad. Hosp., U. Limburg, Maastricht, The Netherlands, 1986—; cons. Golden Hill Paugussett Tribe, Trumbull, Conn., 1982—. Author: Double Blind Research in Psychotherapy, 1984, The Paugussett Tribes, 1985; co-editor: Common Factors in Psychotherapy, 1985; editor-in-chief: De Kiva Jour., Amsterdam, Netherlands, 1986—; contbr. articles to profl. publs. Mem. Dutch Assn. Psychologists, Dutch Assn. for Behavior Therapy, Dutch Assn. for Hypnotherapy. Home: Gerendalsweg 23, 6307 PG Scheulder The Netherlands Office: U Limburg Acad Hosp, St Annadal 1, BX 6201 Maastricht, Limburg The Netherlands

WOJCIK, CASS, decorative supply company executive, former city official; b. Rochester, N.Y., Dec. 3, 1920; s. Emil M. and Casimira C. (Krawiecz) W.; student Lawrence Inst. Tech., 1941-43, Yale U., 1943-44, U.S. Sch. for European Personnel, Czechoslovakia, 1945; m. Lilliam Leocadia Lendzion, Sept. 25, 1948; 1 son, Robert Cass. Owner, Nat. Florists Supply Co., Detroit, 1948—, Nat. Decorative, Detroit, 1950—; co-owner Creation Center, Detroit, 1955-60; cons.-contractor hort.-bot. design auto show displays, TV producers, designers and decorators. Mem. Regional Planning and Evaluation Council, 1969—; city-wide mem. Detroit Bd. Edn., 1970-75; commr. Detroit Public Schs. Employees Retirement Commn., until 1975; mem. Area Occupational Ednl. Commn., Ednl. Task Force; chmn., grand marshal Ann. Gen. Pulaski Day Parade, Detroit, 1970, 71; mem. Friends of Belle Isle; mem. Nat. Arboretum Adv. Council, U.S. Dept. Agr., 1982-83; mem. pastoral council Archdiocese of Detroit, 1983-86; v.p. student affairs Barna Inst., Ft. Lauderdale, Fla.; vice chmn. 13th Congl. Dist. Rep. Party Mich., 1987—; elected to 1988 electoral coll. Served with U.S. Army, 1944-46. Decorated Bronze Star; recipient citation Polish-Am. Congress, 1971. Mem. S.E. Mich. Council Govts., Mich., Nat. sch. bd. assns., Big Cities Sch. Bd. Com., Nat. Council Great Cities Schs., Mcpl. Finance Officers Assn. U.S., Nat. Council Tchr. Retirement, Central Citizens Com. Detroit, Internat. Platform Assn., Mich. Heritage Council, Nat. Geog. Soc. Roman Catholic. Club: Polish Century (Detroit). Home: 451 Lodge Dr Detroit MI 48214

WOJTAK, RUTH MARIE, retail company executive; b. Kenosha, Wis., Sept. 25, 1956; d. Richard Stanley and Anne Theresa (Steplyk) W. Assoc. Applied Sci., Gateway Tech. Inst., 1976; B.A., U. Wis.-Parkside, 1980. Transp. aide Kenosha Achievement Ctr. (Wis.), 1977; lifeguard U. Wis.-Parkside, Kenosha, 1980, library clk., 1978-80; asst. mgr. K Mart Corp., Troy, Mich., 1980—. Mem. Am. Mgmt. Assn., Distributive Edn. Clubs Am. (parliamentarian 1976), Nat. Assn. Female Execs., U. Wis.-Parkside Alumni Assn., Career Guild. Roman Catholic.

WOJTILLA, GYULA, archivist; b. Budapest, Hungary, June 13, 1945; s. Gyula Wojtilla and Etelka Isztin; m. Agnes Salgó, Dec. 27, 1971; children: Gergely, Kinga. MA in History, MA in Indology, Budapest U., 1969; PhD in Linguistics, Acad. Sci., Budapest, 1972. Mem. research staff Hungarian Acad., Budapest, 1970-80; lectr. U. Delhi, India, 1980-83; head archives Hungarian Acad. Scis., Budapest, 1983—; examiner Cen. Bd. Lang. Examinations, Budapest, 1985-86. Author: (books) R. Tagore in Hungary, 1983, A List of Words in Sanskrit and Hungarian, 1984; contbr. numerous articles to profl. jours. Research fellow Banaras Hindu U., Benares, India, 1973-74. Mem. Linguistic Soc. India (life), Asiatic Soc. Bengal, Hungarian Soc. Ancient Studies, Hungarian Soc. Archivarists, Körösi Csoma Soc. Budapest (mem. exec. com.). Home: Pannonia 3, H-1205 Budapest Hungary

WOLANIN, SOPHIE MAE, tutor, lecturer, civic worker; b. Alton, Ill., June 11, 1915; d. Stephen and Mary (Fijalka) W. Student Pa. State Coll., 1943-44; certificate secretarial sci. U. S.C., 1946, B.S. in Bus. Adminstrn. cum laude, 1948; PhD, Colo. State Christian Coll., 1972. Clk., stenographer, sec. Mercer County (Pa.) Tax Collector's Office, Sharon, 1932-34; receptionist, social sec., nurse-technician to doctor, N.Y.C., 1934-37; coil winder, assembler Westinghouse Electric Corp., Sharon, 1937-39, duplicator operator, typist, stenographer, 1939-44, confidential sec., Pitts., 1949-54; exec. sec., charter mem. Westinghouse Credit Corp., Pitts., 1954-72, hdqrs. sr. sec., 1972-80, reporter WCC News, 1967-68, asst. editor, 1968-71, asso. editor, 1971-76; student office sec. to dean U. S.C. Sch. Commerce, 1944-46, instr. math., bus. adminstrn., secretarial sci., 1946-48. Publicity and pub. relations chmn., corr. sec. South Oakland Rehab. Council, 1967-69; U. S.C. official del. Univ. Pitts. 200th Anniversary Bicentennial Convocation, 1986; mem. nat. adv. bd. Am. Security Council; mem. Friends Winston Churchill Meml. and Library, Westminster Coll., Fulton, Mo.; active U. S.C. Ednl. Found. Fellow; charter mem. Rep. Presdl. Task Force, trustee; sustaining mem. Rep. Nat. Com.; permanent mem. Nat. Rep. Senatorial Com.; patron Inst. Community Service (life), U. S.C. Alumni Assn. (Pa. state fund chmn. 1967-68, pres. council 1972-76, ofcl. del. rep. inauguration Bethany Coll. pres. 1973); mem. Allegheny County Scholarship Assn. (life), Allegheny County League Women voters, AAUW (life), Internat. Fedn. U. Women, N.E. Historic Geneal. Soc. (life), Hypatian Lit. Soc. (hon.), Acad. Polit. Sci. (Columbia) (life), Bus. and Profl. Women's Club Pitts. (bd. dirs. 1963-80, editor Bull. 1963-65, treas. 1965-66, historian 1969-70, pub. relations 1971-76, Woman of Year 1972), Met. Opera Guild, Nat. Arbor Day Found., Kosciuszko Found. (assoc.), World Literacy Acad., Cambridge, Eng. (life); charter mem. Nat. Mus. Women in Arts, Statue Liberty Ellis Island Found. Inc., Shenago Conservancy (life); supporting mem. Nat. Woman's Hall of Fame; recipient numerous prizes Allegheny County Fair, 1951-56; citation Congl. Record, 1969; medal of Merit, Pres. Reagan, 1982; others. Mem. Liturgical Conf. N. Am. (life), Westinghouse Vet. Employees Assn., Nat. Soc. Lit. and Arts, Early Am. Soc., Am. Acad. Social and Polit. Sci., Societe Commemorative de Femmes Celebres, Nat. Trust Historic Preservation, Am. Counselors Soc. (life), Am. Mus. Natural History (asso.), Nat. Hist. Soc. (founding mem.), Anglo-Am. Hist. Soc. (charter), Nat. Assn. Exec. Secs., Internat. Platform Assn., Smithsonian Assos., Asso. Nat. Archives, Nat., Pa., Fed. bus. and profl. women's clubs, Mercer County Hist. Soc. (life), Am. Bible Soc., Polish Am. Numismatic Assn., Polonus Philatelic Soc., UN Assn. U.S., Polish Inst. Arts and Scis. Am. Inc. (assoc.), N.Y. Acad. Scis. (assoc.), Am. Council Polish Cultural Clubs Inc. Roman Catholic (mem. St. Paul Cathedral Altar Soc., patron organ recitals). Clubs: Jonathan Maxcy of U. S.C. (charter); Univ. Catholic of Pitts.; Key of Pa., Fedn. Bus. and Profl. Women (hon.); Coll. (hon.) (Sharon). Contbr. articles to newspapers; Am. corr. Polish radio and TV. Home: 5223 Smith-Stewart Rd SE Girard OH 44420

WOLCOTT, DEAN EDISON, insurance company executive; b. Syracuse, N.Y., 1929; married. BA, Syracuse U., 1950. Sales correspondent, Colo. Fuel & Iron Co., 1950-52; sales rep. Standard Brands, Inc., 1952-55; with Aetna Life & Casualty Co., 1955—, supr. Buffalo office, 1959-60, gen. agt. Utica office, 1960-64, assoc. gen. agt. Pitts. office, 1964-65, gen. agt. Pitts. office, 1965-70, sr. v.p. life div., 1970-81, sr. v.p. personal fin. security div., 1981—; also pres., bd. dirs. Aetna Life Ins. & Annuity Co. (subs.), Hartford, Conn. Served with U.S. Army, 1952-54. Office: Aetna Casualty & Surety Co 151 Farmington Ave Hartford CT 06156 *

WOLCOTT, JOHN WINTHROP, III, business executive; b. Balt., Dec. 3, 1924; s. John Winthrop, Jr. and Dorothy C. (Fraser) W.; m. Elizabeth Thelin Hooper, Apr. 24, 1948 (div. 1985); children: John Winthrop IV, Elizabeth T., Katherine C.; m. Karen E. Jones, Oct. 1, 1985. B.Indsl. Engring., Gen. Motors Inst., 1951. Registered profl. engr., Ohio. With Gen. Motors Corp., 1946-53, Weatherhead Co., Cleve., 1957-60; v.p. H.K. Porter Co., Inc., Pitts., 1960-64; pres. Ametek, Inc., N.Y.C., 1964-66; v.p. Am. Machine & Foundry Co., 1966-77, group exec. process equipment group, 1967-70; exec. v.p. ops. AMF, Inc., 1970-77; pres., chief exec. officer, dir. Transway Internat. Corp., N.Y.C., 1978-86, chmn. bd., 1982-86; adv. bd. LePercq, de Neuflize & Co., N.Y.C., 1986—. Served with USCGR, 1943-46. Mem. Soc. Automotive Engrs., Soc. Colonial Wars. Episcopalian. Clubs: Mt. Kisco Country Maryland (Balt.); Brook (N.Y.C.). Home: 14 Wolf Hill Rd Chappaqua NY 10514 Office: Le Percq de Nevflize & Co 345 Park Ave New York NY 10154

WOLDERLING, JOHANNES ALEX, manufacturing executive; b. Surabaya, Indonesia, Mar. 29, 1927; came to The Netherlands, 1946; s. Hendrik Carel Wolderling and Sophia Schwarz; widowed; children: Helen Margot, Ester Gabrielle. Student, Tech. Coll., Rotterdam, The Netherlands, 1948, Tech. U., Delft, 1950-53; BSME, U. Economics, Rotterdam, 1960-62. Engr. Royal Dutch Blast Furnaces and Steel Mills, IJmuiden, The Netherlands, 1948-53; engr. Amsterdam Rubber and Palm Oil Plantation Co., Sumatra, Indonesia, 1953-58, Royal Dutch Blast Furnaces and Steel Mills, IJmuiden, 1958-62; tech. prod. mgr. Bruynzeel lumber Co., Suriname, S. Am., 1962-66; orgn./ systems engr. Fokker Aircraft Co., Schiphol, The Netherlands, 1966-69; sales engr. civil aircraft Fokker Aircraft Co., Schiphol, 1969-73, area mgr. civil aircraft, 1973-79; sales dir. civil aircraft Fokker Aircraft Co., Amsterdam, The Netherlands, 1979-87; advisor Fokker Aircraft Co., Amsterdam, 1987—; mem. supervisory bd. Aviona Internat., Antwerp, 1988—.

WOLF, ANDREW, food manufacturing company executive; b. Budapest, Hungary, May 20, 1927; came to U.S., 1947, naturalized, 1952; s. Alfred and Magda Farkas. Diploma, Baking Inst. Tech., Budapest, 1942-45; B.S. in Mech. Engring., CCNY, 1955-62; postgrad. Ill. Inst. Tech., Chgo., 1962-64; M.B.A., U. Chgo., 1973. Pres., owner, Mignon Pastry Shops, N.Y.C., 1948-51, 1952-54; cons. Hanscom Bakeries, N.Y.C., 1954-55; dir. new products Arnold Bakers, N.Y. and Conn., 1955-60; dir. new products research and devel. Kitchens of Sara Lee, Deerfield, Ill., 1960-71, v.p. research and devel., 1971—; rep. Sara Lee Corp., Grocery Mfrs. Am. Tech. Com. for Food Protection, 1975—; spokesman Frozen Food Action Communications Team, Inc., radio and TV, 1982—. Contbr. articles to profl. jours. Patentee bakery equipment and methods. Served with U.S. Army, 1947-48, 1951-52. Recipient Hon. Tex. Citizenship award State of Tex., 1969; Bishop award Tex. Dept. Mental Health, 1972. Mem. White House Conf. on Food and Nutrition, 1959, Pres. Reagan's Task Force on Phys. Fitness and Nutrition, 1983. Mem. Am. Frozen Food Inst. (research and tech. services council, quality maintenance task force council), Am. Bakers Assn. (liaison com. U.S. Dept. Agr.), Inst. Food Technologists, Am. Soc. Bakery Engrs., Tau Beta Pi, Pi Tau Sigma. Home: 2785 Daiquiri Dr Deerfield IL 60015

WOLF, ARON S., psychiatrist; b. Newark, Aug. 25, 1937; B.A., Dartmouth Coll., 1959; M.D., U. Md., 1963; married; children—Jon, Lisa, Laurie. Intern, U. Md. Hosp., Balt., 1963-64; resident in psychiatry Psychiat. Inst., U. Md. Hosp., Balt., 1964-67, chief resident, 1966-67; practice medicine specializing in psychiatry, Anchorage, 1967—; dir. Springfield Hosp. Alcoholic Clinic, Balt., 1966-67; psychiat. cons. Levindale Hebrew Home and Infirmary, Balt., 1966-67, McLaughlin Yough Center, Anchorage, 1969-72; mem. staff Providence Hosp., chief psychiatry sect., 1977-81; mem. staff Humana Hosp., Alaska, Kodiak Island Hosp., Palmer Valley Hosp., Valdez Community Hosp., Bethel Community Hosp., Cordova Alaska Hosp.; mem. staff Charter North Hosp., exec. com., 1984-86; staff psychiatrist Langdon Psychiat. Clinic, 1970-71; partner Langdon Clinic, Anchorage, 1971—, clinic pres., 1981; med. dir. Cordova Community Mental Health Center, 1976-80, 84—; cons. Alaska Native Med. Center, 1975-77, Woman's Resource Center, Anchorage, 1977-81; instr. dept. psychology U. Alaska, Anchorage, 1968-75; assoc. clin. prof. psychiatry U. Alaska, Fairbanks, 1974-85, clin. prof., 1985—; assoc. clin. prof. U. Wash., 1974-85, clin. prof., 1985—, adj. prof.psychiatry Sch. Medicine U. N.Mex.; participant weekly mental health TV talk show, Anchorage, 1970—; guest lectr. to various profl. and civic groups, 1967—. Vice pres. Greater Anchorage Area Borough Sch. Bd., 1971-72, pres., 1973-74; pres. Chugach Optional Sch. Parent Adv. Bd., 1976-77; mem. med. adv. com. Alaska Kidney Found., 1977-82; mem. Alaska Gov.'s Mental Health Adv. Bd., 1976-84, chmn., 1983; mem. Gov's. Task Force on Criminally Committed Patients, 1980—; bd. dirs. Greater Anchorage Drug Mgmt. Group, 1972-73. Served with M.C., USAF, 1967-70. Recipient Wendell-Muncie award Md. Med. Soc., 1967; diplomate Am. Bd. Psychiatry and Neurology, Am. Bd. Forensic Psychiatry. Fellow Am. Psychiat. Assn. (pres. Alaska dist. br. 1975, sec. Alaska br. 1984-85, del. assembly 1975-81, 86, area III chmn. assembly procedures com. 1982—, nat. planning com. 1981, nat. membership com. 1981-86, chmn. confidentiality com., 1986—, recorder of assembly 1984-85, chmn. 1988, Alaska del., 1986—); mem. Am. Acad. Psychiatry and Law (mem. ethics com., 1987) , Am. Soc. Law and Medicine, Soc. Air Force Psychiatrists, ACLU, AMA (chmn. mental health com. 1971-75, medicine and law com. 1980-81), Alaska Med. Assn., N.Y. Acad. Scis. Contbr. articles on psychiatry to profl. jours. Home: 8133 Sundi Dr Anchorage AK 99502 Office: 4001 Dale St Anchorage AK 99508

WOLF, DAVID, lawyer; b. Boston, July 11, 1927; s. Ezekiel and Ray (Cohen) W.; m. Maxine Laura Bunnin, June 29, 1963; children—Eric E., Douglas R., James A. BA, U. Mass., 1949; LLB, Harvard U., 1952; postgrad., Northeastern U., 1952-55. Bar: Mass. 1952, U.S. Patent Office 1952, U.S. Ct. Customs and Patent Appeals 1955, U.S. Supreme Ct. 1958, U.S. Ct. Appeals (fed. cir.) 1983. Ptnr. Wolf, Greenfield & Sacks (P.C.), Boston, 1952—; bd. dirs. Emile Bernat & Sons Co. Watercolor artist; exhibited various local shows. Bd. dirs. Killington East Homeowners Assn., 1986—, Newton Country Players, 1964-67; mem. Am. Jewish Com. Recipient various awards for art. Mem. ABA (lectr. trademark trial adv. program 1986), Am. Patent Law Assn., Lic. Execs. Soc., U.S. Trademark Assn., Mass. Bar Assn., Boston Bar Assn., Boston Patent Law Assn. (pres. 1976), New Eng.-Israel C. of C. (v.p., bd. dirs. 1984-87), Alpha Epsilon Pi. Lodge: B'nai B'rith, Free Sons Israel. Office: Wolf Greenfield & Sacks PC Fed Reserve Plaza 600 Atlantic Ave Boston MA 02210

WOLF, FREDRIC M., educational psychologist; b. Canton, Ohio, Aug. 7, 1945; s. Wayne S. and Anita (Manheim) W.; m. Leora DeLelyes Lucas, Sept. 29, 1985; 1 child, Jacob M. B.S., U. Wis., 1967; postgrad. Law Sch. Georgetown U., 1967-68; M.Ed., Kent State U., 1977, PH.D., 1980. Instr. math. Cuyahoga Community Coll., Cleve., 1978-79; research assoc. behavioral scis. Northeastern Ohio U. Med. Coll., Rootstown, 1979-80; research assoc. med. edn. Ohio State U. Coll. Medicine, Columbus 1980-82, clin. asst. prof. pediatrics, 1981-82; asst. prof. postgrad. medicine U. Mich. Med. Sch., Ann Arbor, 1982-87; assoc. prof. 1987—. assoc. dir. edn. Mich. Diabetes Research and Tng. Ctr., Ann Arbor, 1982-84; acting dir. 1984-85; cons. Office Technology Assessment, U.S. Congress, 1987—; cons. Office Research U.S. Dept. Edn., 1986—; cons. Nat. Heart Lung and Blood Inst. NIH, Bethesda, Md., 1985; cons. NSF, Nat. Research Council, Nat. Acad. Scis . Author: Meta-analysis: Quantitative Methods for Research Synthesis, 1986; contbr. articles to profl. jours. Vol., Peace Corps, Latin Am., 1969-72. Grantee Mich. Dept. Pub. Health, 1984-86, Spencer Found., 1983-84, NIH, 1985—. Mem. AAAS, Am. Diabetes Assn., Am. Psychol. Assn., Am. Statis. Assn., Midwestern Ednl. Research Assn. (v.p. 1984-85, pres. 1986-87), Soc. Behavioral Medicine, Soc. Med. Decision Making, Sigma Xi. Avocations: bird watching, canoeing, tennis, squash, skiing. Office: U Mich Dept Postgrad Medicine Box 0201 Ann Arbor MI 48109-0201

WOLF, GYULA, agricultural engineer, educator; b. Bácsalmás, Hungary, Mar. 2, 1934; s. Gyula and Leona (Beck) W.; m. Anna Ságat, May 11, 1936; children: Csilla, Csaba. BS in Agril., U. Gödöllo, 1957. Head animal breeding br. State Farm, Komárom, Hungary, 1964-70; researcher Agrl. Coll., Kapsovár, Hungary, 1964-70; prof. animal sci. Agrl. U., Kapsovár, 1970—, head dept. dairy sci., 1979—. Author: Handbook of Cattle Breeders, 1981, Breeding Cattle, 1986. Mem. Nat. Acad. Agrl. Engrs. (head of working com. regional com. 1983—). Evangelic. Home: Rudnay 10, 7400 Kaposvar Hugary Office: Agrl Univ, Faculty Animal Sci, PO Box 16, 7401 Kaposvar Hungary

WOLF, JACK STANLEY, financial executive; b. Kansas City, Mo., Nov. 9, 1934; s. Joseph and Mary (Coppaken) W.; m. R. Marlene Kirkpatrick, July 29, 1969. B.A., U. Mo., 1956. C.L.U., 1972. Agt., sales mgr. Prudential Ins. Co. Am., Houston, 1967-78; mgr., gen. agt. Jack Wolf, C.L.U. Ins., 1972—; pres. Fin. Planning & Pension Cons., Houston, 1979—; gen. agy. mgr. Am. Gen. Life Ins. Co., 1980—. Served with U.S. Army, 1958-63. Recipient numerous awards various ins. cos., 1968—. Mem. East Ft. Bend C. of C., Million Dollar Round Table (life and qualifying), Tex. Leaders Round Table, Houston Assn. Life Underwriters, Gen. Agts. and Mgrs. Assn., Am. Soc. CLU's, Am. Contract Bridge League. U. Mo. Alumni Assn. (life). Jewish. Lodge: East Ft. Bend Kiwanis (past pres.). Home: 1443 Sugar Creek Blvd Sugar Land TX 77478 Office: 9894 Bissonnet Suite 700 Houston TX 77036

WOLF, JOSEPH, anthropologist; b. Prague, Czechoslovakia, Mar. 20, 1927; s. Joseph and Marie Wolf; B.A., Charles U., 1951, Ph.D., 1969; m. Eva Wolf, Dec. 23, 1971; children—Radomira, George, Thomas. Lectr., asst. prof. cultural anthropology and ethnology Charles U., Prague, 1960-73, Internat. U. 17th Nov., Prague, 1974-75; head dept. sci. tech. info. studies Inst. Edn.; expert in cultural anthropology Inst. Psychology, Czech Acad. Sci., Prague, 1976—. Recipient medal J.A. Comenius, 1970, awards Czechoslovak Sci. Tech. Soc., 1981. Mem. Czechoslovak Sociol. and Anthrop. Soc. (dir.), Czechoslovak Sci. Tech. Soc. (dir.), Nat. Geog. Soc., European Anthrop. Assn. Author: Introduction to the Study of Man, Culture and Society, 1965-70; Integral Anthropology, 1971; Last Witnesses of Prehistory, 1972; Ency. of Man, 1977; The Dawn of Man, 1978; Peoples of Five Continents, 1979; Anthropology of Aging, 1982; Ency. of Nations, Past and Present, 1984. Home: 5 V Cibulkach, 15000 Prague 5, Czechoslovakia

WOLF, MORRIS PHILIP, business communication educator, author; b. Bklyn., Apr. 28, 1929; s. Leo and Jeanne (Applebaum) W.; B.A., N.Y. U., 1949, M.A., 1951; Ph.D., U. Ga., 1959. Asst. prof. U. Ga. Centers, Columbus and Ft. Benning, 1953-54, dir. U. Ga. Center, Gainesville, 1954-56, Augusta Center, 1956-58; assoc. prof., asst. dean and dir. extended services Augusta Coll., 1959-60, prof., chmn. dept. English and speech, 1960-62; assoc. prof. bus. communication U. Houston, 1962-67, prof., 1970-74, chmn. dept. gen. bus. adminstrn., 1968-70, coordinator, 1970-74; ind. researcher, writer, 1974-82; assoc. prof. bus. communication, dept. office adminstrn. and bus. communication Coll. Adminstrn. and Bus., La. Tech. U., Ruston, 1982-87 ; cons. in field; profl. actor with programs broadcast from N.Y.C. on ABC, CBS, NBC including Adventures of Frank Merriwell, Aunt Jenny's Real Life Stories, The Eternal Light, Famous Jury Trials, The Goldbergs, The Greatest Story Ever Told, Hollywood Screen Test, Philco Playhouse, others; performer with Equity A touring stage prodns. The Heiress, Springboard to Nowhere, Little Women, Mr. and Mrs. North, On Borrowed Time, others; producer, performer on public service TV-radio programs, Augusta, 1956-61; narrator Augusta Choral Soc. Bicentennial Program, Song of Affirmation, 1975-77, others; lectr. in field. Served to capt. AUS and U.S. Army Res., 1951-64. Recipient Disting. Faculty award U. Houston Coll. Bus. Alumni Assn., 1967; Teaching Excellence award U. Houston, 1971. Fellow Am. Bus. Communication Assn. (past pres., publs. bd.); mem. Beta Gamma Sigma, Sigma Delta Omicron, Phi Kappa Phi. Author: (with Robert R. Aurner) Effective Communication in Business, 5th edit., 1967, sr. co-author, 6th edit., 1974, 7th edit., 1979, 8th edit., 1984; sr. co-author: (with Bette A. Stead) Easy Grammar: A Programmed Review, 1970; contbr. articles to profl. jours.; poems incl. Hypocrite, Scent of Lavender, 1951, Of Curricular Concern, 1951, Reconnaissance Patrol, 1957, others; plays incl.: Hatred, 1951; Continuum, 1952; I Want to Report A Suicide, 1956; Mirrors (radio drama), 1974. Home: 410 James St Ruston LA 71270

WOLF, PETER, mathematician of economics; b. Bamberg, Federal Republic of Germany; s. Johann and Barbara (Bauer) W.; m. Dorothea Nagel, Oct. 23, 1987. MS, Syracuse U., 1986; Diploma Wirtschaftsmathematiker, U. Ulm, 1987. With Univ. Clin. Hosp., U. Ulm, Federal Republic Germany, 1987—. Mem. Gesellschaft für Informatik. Roman Catholic. Home: Johannisstrasse 15, 7910 Neu-Ulm Federal Republic of Germany Office: U Ulm Clinical Hosp, Oberer Eselberg, 7900 Ulm Federal Republic of Germany

WOLF, URSULA, philosopher, educator; b. Karlsruhe, Fed. Republic Germany, Nov. 4, 1951; d. Herbert and Charlotte (Wachter) W. MA, U. Heidelberg, Fed. Republic Germany, 1974, PhD, 1978; habilitation, Freie U., Berlin, 1983. Asst. prof. Inst. Philosophy, Freie U., 1980-84, prof., 1984-87; prof. Fachbereich Philosophy, U. Frankfurt, Fed. Republic Germany, 1987—; translator Suhrkamp Verlag, 1978-80. Author: Möglichkeit und Notwendigkeit bei Aristoleles und heute, 1979, Das Problem des Moralischen Sollens, 1984, (with others) Logischsemantische Prodädeutik, 1983; editor: Eigennamen, 1985; contbr. articles to profl. jours. Office: Fachbereich Philosophie, Dantestr 4-6, D6000 Frankfurt Federal Republic of Germany

WOLFE, CLIFFORD EUGENE, architect; b. Harrington, Wash., Mar. 26, 1906; s. Delwin Lindsley and Luella Grace (Cox) W.; m. Frances Lillian Parkes, Sept. 12, 1936 (dec.); children—Gretchen Yvonne Wolfe Mason, Eric Von; m. Mary Theye Worthen. A.B. in Architecture, U. Calif.-Berkeley, 1933. Registered architect, Calif. Assoc. architect John Knox Ballantine, Architect, San Francisco, 1933-42; supervising architect, prodn. engr. G.W. Williams Co. Contractors, Burlingame, Calif., 1942-44; state-wide coordinator med. schs. and health ctrs. U. Calif.-Berkeley, San Francisco and Los Angeles, 1944-52; sec. council on hosp. planning Am. Hosp. Assn., Chgo., 1952-59; dir. planning dept. Office of York & Sawyer, Architects, N.Y.C., 1959-74; prin. Clifford E. Wolfe, AIA-E, Oakland, Calif., 1974—; assoc. designer State of Calif. Commn. for Golden Gate Internat. Exposition, San Francisco, 1938-39; cons. Fed. Hosp. Council, Washington, 1954-60; mem. Pres.'s Conf. on Occupational Safety, Washington, 1955; research architect Hosp Research and Ednl. Trust, Chgo., 1957-59; instr. hosp. planning Columbia U., N.Y.C., 1961-73. Author, editor manuals on hosp. planning, engring. and safety, 1954-58. Author: Ballad of Humphrey The Humpback Whale, 1985; contbr. poetry to Tecolote Anthology, 1983, The Ina Coolbrith Circle, 1985 (Grand prize Ina Coolbrith award 1986), Islandia, 1986. Hosp. planning research grantee USPHS, 1956. Mem. AIA (chmn. honor awards com. Chgo. chpt. 1958-59, chmn. activities com. N.Y. chpt. 1972-74, mem. emeritus East Bay chpt. 1974—). Address: 3900 Harrison St Apt 306 Oakland CA 94611

WOLFE, CORINNE HOWELL, retired social worker; b. El Paso, Tex., Dec. 15, 1912; d. David Emerson and Clara (Schultz) Howell; B.A., U. Tex., El Paso, 1933; M.S.W., Tulane U., 1944; LL.D. (hon.), N.Mex. State U., 1983; m. Howard Clark Wolfe, Jr., Feb. 29, 1936. Social worker Tex. Dept. Public Welfare, 1933-45, Family Service Assn., Ft. Worth, 1945-46, VA, Dallas, 1946-48; dir. staff devel. and tng. Social and Rehab. Service, HEW, Washington, 1948-72; prof. social work N.Mex. Highlands U., Las Vegas, 1972-82, ret., 1982; cons. social services, social work edn. Mem. adv. panel N.Mex. Community Corrections. Recipient Disting. Service award HEW, 1973; Outstanding Alumni award Tulane U., 1975, Father Reynolds Rivera Humanitarian award Bar Assn., 1987; named N.Mex. Vol. of Yr., 1983. Mem. Nat. Assn. Social Workers (Nat. Social Worker Yr. 1986), Council Social Work Edn. (Disting. Service award 1972), N.Mex. Alliance Mentally Ill, Northern N.Mex. Civil Liberties Union (chair), N.Mex. Human Services Coalition (co-chair), Council Social Work Edn., Am. Public Welfare Assn., Nat. and Internat. Conf. on Social Welfare, Santa Fe Living Treasure. Democrat. Methodist. Contbr. articles to profl. jours. Home: 2509 Avenida de Isidro Santa Fe NM 87505

WOLFE, DAVID K., lawyer; b. Lafayette, Ind., Feb. 6, 1922; s. Simon and Nora I. (Connaroe) W.; m. Charity Phillips, Aug. 19, 1958. Student, Purdue U.; JD with high distinction, U. Ariz., 1950. Bar: Ariz. 1950, U.S. Dist. Ct. Ariz. 1957, U.S. Ct. Appeals (9th cir.) 1957, U.S. Supreme Ct. 1978. Since practiced in Tucson, 1950—; sr. ptnr. Wolfe & Ostapuk, 1976—; judge pro tem domestic relation div. Pima County Superior Ct., Tucson, 1986—. Served with USAAF, 1943-45, USAF, 1950-52; maj. USAFR ret. Decorated D.F.C. with oak leaf cluster, Air medal with 4 oak leaf clusters. Fellow Am. Acad. Matrimonial Lawyers, Ariz. Bar Found.; mem. ABA (family law sect., pub. utility law sect., litigation sect.), State Bar Ariz. (com. profl. ethics 1960-72, bd. govs. 1961-64, com. on exams. and admissions 1961-72, chmn. 1968-72, 78-80, family law sect., award for service 1980), Inter.-Am. Bar Assn., Pima County Bar Assn. (pres. 1958), Judge Advs. Assn., Order of Coif, Alpha Delta, Phi Kappa Phi, Theta Xi. Democrat. Home: 3407 Arroyo Chico Tucson AZ 85716 Office: SW Savings Bldg 160 N Stone Ave Tucson AZ 85701

WOLFE, DAVID LOUIS, lawyer; b. Kankakee, Ill., July 24, 1951; s. August Christian and Irma Marie (Nordmeyer) W.; m. Gail Lauret Fritz, Aug. 25, 1972; children—Laura Beth, Brian David, Kaitlin Ann. B.S., U. Ill., 1973; J.D., U. Mich. 1976. Bar: Ill. 1976, U.S. Dist. Ct. (no. dist.) Ill. 1976. Assoc., Gardner, Carton & Douglas, Chgo., 1976-82, ptnr., 1983—. Contbr. articles to legal publs.; lectr. estate planning Aid Assn. for Lutherans SMART Program, Chgo., 1980—; lectr. Ill. Inst. Continuing Legal Edn., Chgo. Bar Assn., Lake Shore Nat. Bank, Ill. State Bar Assn. Recipient Recognition award Ill. Inst. Continuing Legal Edn., 1981-84. Mem. ABA (sects. on taxation, corp. banking and bus. law, forum com. on entertainment and sports industries, 1981—), Chgo. Bar Assn. (employee benefits com., sports law com., fed. tax com.), Nat. Football League Players Assn. (cert. contract advisor 1983—), Nat. Collegiate Athletic Assn. (cert. contract advisor), Chgo. Assn. Commerce and Industry (employee benefit subcommittee 1983—), Ill. State Bar Assn. (employee benefits sect. council, 1986—, recognition award 1983), Phi Kappa Phi, Beta Alpha Psi, Beta Gamma Sigma, Sigma Iota Lambda, Phi Eta Sigma.

WOLFE, DEBORAH CANNON PARTRIDGE, government education consultant; b. Cranford, N.J.; d. David Wadsworth and Gertrude (Moody) Cannon; 1 son, Roy. B.S., N.J. State Coll.; M.A., Ed.D., Tchrs. Coll., Columbia U.; postgrad., Vassar Coll., U. Pa., Union Theol. Sem., Jewish Sem. Am.; hon. doctorates, Seton Hall U., Coll. New Rochelle, Morris Brown U.; LL.D., Kean Coll., 1981; L.H.D., Stockton State Coll.; L.L.D., Centenary Coll. Former prin., tchr. pub. schs. Cranford, also Tuskegee, Ala.; faculty Tuskegee Inst., Grambling Coll., NYU, Fordham U., U. Mich., Tex. Coll., Columbia U.; supervision and adminstrn. curriculum devel., social studies U. Ill., summers; prof. edn., affirmative action officer Queens Coll.; prof. edn. and children's lit. Wayne State U., summer; now edn. chief U.S. Ho. of Reps. Com. on Edn. and Labor, 1962—; Fulbright prof. Am. lit. NYU; U.S. rep. 1st World Conf. on Women in Politics; chair non-govtl. reps. to UN (NGO/DPI exec. com.), 1983—; editorial cons. Macmillan Pub. Co.; cons. Ency. Brit.; adv. bd. Ednl. Testing Service; asso. minister First Bapt. Ch., Cranford, N.J.; mem. State Bd. Edn., 1964—; chairperson N.J. Bd. Higher Edn., 1967—; mem. nat. adv. panel on vocat. edn. HEW; mem. citizen's adv. com. to Bd. Edn., Cranford; mem. Citizen's Adv. Com. on Youth Fitness, Pres.'s Adv. Com. on Youth Fitness, White House Conf. Children and Youth, 1950, 60, White House Conf. Edn., 1955, White House Conf. Aging, 1960, White House Conf. Civil Rights, 1966, White House Conf. on Children, 1970, Adv. Council for Innovations in Edn.; v.p. Nat. Alliance for Safer Cities; cons. Vista Corps, OEO. Contbr. articles to ednl. publs. Bd. dirs. Cranford Welfare Assn., Community Center, 1st Bapt. Ch., Cranford, Community Center Migratory Laborers, Hurlock, Md.; trustee Sci. Service, Seton Hall U.; mem. Public Broadcasting Authority.; bd. regents Seton Hall U.; sec. Kappa Delta Pi Ednl. Found.; mem. adv. com. Elizabeth and Arthur Schlesinger Library, Radcliffe Coll.; trustee Edn. Devel. Center. Recipient Nat. Achievement award Nat. Assn. Negro Bus. and Profl. Women's Clubs, 1958; Woman of Year award Delta Beta Zeta; Woman of Year award Morgan State Coll.; Achievement award Atlantic region Zeta Phi Beta. Mem. Council Nat. Orgns. Children and Youth, Am. Council Human Rights (v.p.), NCCJ, Nat. Panhellenic Council (dir.), Nat. Assn. Negro Bus. and Profl. Women (chmn. speakers bur.), Nat. Assn. Black Educators (pres.), NEA (life), LWV, N.Y. Tchrs. Assn., Am. Tchrs. Assn., Fellowship So. Churchmen, AAUW (nat. edn. chmn.), AAUP, Internat. Reading Assn., Comparative Edn. Soc., Am. Acad. Polit. and Social Sci., Internat. Assn. Childhood Edn., Nat. Soc. Study Edn., Am. Council Edn. (commn. fed. relations), Assn. Supervision and Curriculum Devel. (rev. council), AAAS (chmn. tchr. edn. com.), Nat. Alliance Black Educators (pres.), NAACP, Internat. Platform Assn., Ch. Women United (UN rep., mem. exec. com.), UN Assn.-U.S.A. (exec. com.), Delta Kappa Gamma Edn. Soc. (chmn. world fellowship com.), Kappa Delta Pi (chmn. ritual com.), Pi Lambda Theta, Zeta Phi Beta (internat. pres. 1954, chmn. edn. found. 1974—). Home: 62 S Union Ave Cranford NJ 07016 Office: NJ State Bd Higher Edn 20 W State St Trenton NJ 08625

WOLFE, EDWARD CLARE, retired investment executive; b. Horton, Kans., Feb. 16, 1922; s. Roland John and Mary Clella (Braley) W.; m. Julia Teran, Apr. 12, 1965. Student pub. schs., Lincoln, Nebr. Tool and die maker, designer Boeing Co., Wichita, Kans. and Seattle, 1947-52, Torrington Mfg. Co., Van Nuys, Calif., 1952-60; registered rep. Dempsey-Tegeler & Co., Glendale, Calif., 1960-70, Mitchum Jones & Templeton, Pasadena, Calif., 1970-71, Wagenseller & Durst, Pasadena, Calif., 1971-72, Schumacher & Assocs., Glendale, Calif., 1975—; account exec., Universal Stock Transfer, Woodland Hills, Calif., 1976-78; loan officer Sutro Mortgage, Inc., Los Angeles, 1978-79. Served with USNR, 1944-46. Republican. Home: 21315 Kingsbury St Chatsworth CA 91311

WOLFE, ESTEMORE ALVIS, insurance company executive; b. Crystal Springs, Miss., Dec. 29, 1919; s. Henry and Vinia (Crump) W. BS, Jackson State Coll., 1947; postgrad. Fla. Meml. Coll., 1948-49, NYU, 1952-53; MEd, Wayne State U., 1951; MA, Purdue U., 1953; DEd, Boston U., 1958; LHD (hon.), Wilberforce U., 1959; LittD (hon.), Creighton U., 1961; LHD (hon.), Syracuse U., 1963; postgrad. Purdue U., 1964. Dir. med. technicians Detroit Tb Sanitorium, 1947-48; ednl. cons., mass media specialist Detroit Bd. Edn., 1948—; v.p., sec. Wright Mut. Ins. Co., Detroit, 1955—; v.p., sales dir. promotions Elramco Enterprises, Inc., Albany, N.Y., 1983—; mem. internat. adv. Hamilton Funding Corp.; dir. Ind. Prodns. Corp., also chmn. nat. edn. com. for educators; lectr., guest prof. Gt. Lakes Coll., Assumption Coll. (Can.), Wayne U., 1953-56, Jackson State Coll., Bethany Coll., U. Detroit, Wis. State U., Stevens Point, So. U. (La.); pres. nat. bd. Kids Kollege Jackson State U., 1987; writer column Detroit Times; cons. to pres. P. Lenud & Co. Mem. White House Conf. of Children and Youth, 1960; mem. Council on Aging, 1965-66; campaign chmn. devel. fund drive Jackson State Coll. 1970-71, trustee Devel. Found., 1984—; organizer, pres. Detroit chpt. Friends of AMISTAD, 1972, nat. v.p., 1972-73, nat. pres. and bd. dirs., 1973—; chmn. bd. trustees Detroit Met. Symphony Orch.; trustee Nat. Negro Archives Mus., Washington, Mich. council Arts, Scis. and Letters, Bethany (W.Va.) Coll., Meth. ch. Served with AUS, 1942-46. Recipient Nat. Human Relations award Clark U., 1969, citation Am. Airlines in recognition of contbns. to devel. air transp. and nat. air power, 1969, Presdl. citation for performance beyond call of duty, 1945, citation and plaque outstanding service and leadership City of Detroit, 1973, Achievement award Jackson State U. Alumni Assn., also Centennial medallion, also trophy Southeastern Mich. alumni chpt., 1984, plaque Kiwanis Clubs, 1978, Am. Heritage Found. award, 1980, key to City, Omaha; Estemore A. Wolfe Daymayoral proclaimation and key to City Cin., 1988; Pres.emeritus endowed scholarship award Nat. Friends of AMISTAD; numerous other plaques and citations for leadership in bus., civic orgns., edn. devel., CASE TWO award Council for Advancement and Support for Higher Edn., 1979, plaque U. Detroit, 1979, 2d Century award Jackson State U., 1979, Spirit of Detroit award Detroit City Council, 1980, Key to City of New Orleans, 1980, Outstanding Alumnus award Boston U., 1981, life membership plaque Friends of Amistad, 1981, Nat. Leadership award Friends of Amistad, 1986, plaque for hist. achievements Am. Heritage Found., 1984, Pearl Cross of Distinction, Central United Meth. Ch., Detroit, Freedom Bowl award Miller Brewing Co., 1985, cert. of Merit Mich. Senate, 1986, 15 more awards, 1984-86; Estemore A. Wolfe Day proclaimed in Davenport, Iowa, 1980; named hon. staff col. Gov. Miss., 1977. Mem. NAACP, Nat. Soc. Visual Edn., Nat. Geog. Soc., Am. Acad. Social and Polit. Sci., Nat. Ins. Assn., Detroit Fedn. Tchrs., Detroit Assn. Radio and TV, Detroit Assn. Film Tchrs., Internat. Platform Assn., Detroit Schoolmen's Club, Detroit Roundtable, Nat. Congress Parents and Tchrs., Orgn. Alumni Assn. Wayne State U. (pres.), Nat. Alumni Assn. Jackson State U. (pres. 1976—, regional dir.). Democrat. Lodge: Kiwanis (Lafayette Park pres. 1983, World Service plaque 1985, Disting. Club Pres. plaque 1985, Exemplary Service award 1985). Office: 2995 E Grand Blvd Detroit MI 48202

WOLFE, JAMES HASTINGS, political scientist, educator; b. Newport News, Va., Oct. 3, 1934; s. Walter John and Grace (Hastings) W.; m. Irmgard Pfender, June 10, 1965; children: Christine, Karin. BA, Harvard U., 1955; M.A., U. Conn., 1958; Ph.D., U. Md., 1962. Asst. prof. polit. sci. U. S.C., 1962-65; assoc. prof. U. Md., 1965-75; prof. polit. sci. U. So. Miss., 1975—; internat. affairs editor USA Today mag., 1981—; cons. State Dept., summers 1967, 79, 83, 85, 86. Served with AUS, 1955-57. Research fellow Alexander von Humboldt Found., 1964-65, 72-73. Mem. Internat. Studies Assn., Am. Soc. Internat. Law. Author: Indivisible Germany: Illusion or Reality?, 1963; co-author: Introduction to International Relations: Power and Justice, 1978, 3d edit., 1986. Contbr. articles to profl. jours. Home: 2600 Sunset Dr Hattiesburg MS 39402 Office: U So Miss Box 8261 Hattiesburg MS 39406

WOLFE, JAMES RONALD, lawyer; b. Pitts., Dec. 10, 1932; s. James Thaddeus and Helen Matilda (Corey) W.; m. Anne Lisbeth Dahle Eriksen, May 28, 1960; children: Ronald, Christopher, Geoffrey. B.A. summa cum laude, Duquesne U., 1954; LL.B. cum laude, NYU, 1959. Bar: N.Y. 1959. Assoc. Simpson Thacher & Bartlett, N.Y.C., 1959-69, ptnr., 1969—. Co-editor: West's McKinney's Forms, Uniform Commercial Code, 1965. Served to 1st lt. U.S. Army, 1955-57. Mem. ABA, N.Y. State Bar Assn., Assn. Bar City N.Y., Am. Judicature Soc., N.Y. Law Inst., Internat. Platform Assn. Republican. Roman Catholic. Home: 641 King St Chappaqua NY 10514 Office: Simpson Thacher & Bartlett 1 Battery Park Plaza New York NY 10004

WOLFE, JOHN ALLEN, geologist, consultant; b. Riverton, Iowa, June 3, 1920; s. Asa Allen and Alice (Thomas) W.; Geol. Engr., EM, Colo. Sch. Mines, 1947, MS, 1954; PhD, Columbia Pacific U., 1983; m. Adelfa Guamos, 1972; children: James Perry, Cynthia Wolfe Burke. Dir. exploration Ideal Cement Co., Denver, 1948-65; geol. cons., Philippines, Latin Am., 1965-68; pres. Mineral Resources Cons., Houston, 1968-72; ptnr. Schoenike, Wolfe & Assocs., Houston, 1970-75; pres. Taysan Copper, Inc., Manila, 1973—; v.p. Kenmare Minerals Inc., Manila, 1988—, also bd. dirs.; profl. lectr. Nat. Inst. Geol. Scis., U. Philippines, 1984—; lectr., cons. in field; mem. Colo. Mining Industry Devel. Bd., 1963-65. Fellow Geol. Soc. Am.; mem. AAAS, Am. Mining Congress (gov. 1963-65), Colo. Mining Assn. (pres. 1963), Am. Inst. Mining Engrs., Geol. Soc. Philippines (founding), Am. Geophys. Union, Assn. Geologists for Internat. Devel., Soc. Econ. Geologists, Am. Inst. Profl. Geologists. Republican. Author: Mineral Resources, a World Review, 1984. Contbr. articles to profl. jours. Home: care Taysan Copper Inc, MCCPO Box 1868, Makati Philippines Office: 6363 Richmond Ave Suite 210 Houston TX 77057

WOLFE, LAWRENCE IRVING, internist; b. Duluth, Minn., Mar. 31, 1924; s. Joseph and Edith (Kremen) W.; B.S., U. Minn., 1944, M.B., 1946, M.D., 1947; m. Charlotte Ione Avrick, Dec. 16, 1945; children—Jonathan, Douglas, Lori Allison. Intern, Ancker Hosp., St. Paul, 1947; postgrad. U. Minn. Hosp., Mpls., 1947-48; resident So. Pacific Gen. Hosp., San Francisco, 1948-50, Permanente Hosp., Oakland, Calif., 1950-51; pvt. practice specializing in internal medicine, San Carlos, Calif., 1951—; mem. staff Sequoia, San Mateo County Gen., Stanford-Palo Alto, Belmont Hills hosps.; faculty dept. medicine Stanford U., 1958—, now clin. asso. prof. Served with USNR, 1943-45, 1953-55. Diplomate Am. Bd. Internal Medicine, Pan Am. Med. Assn. Mem. Am., Calif. med. assns., San Mateo County Med. Soc., Am. Geriatrics Soc., Royal Soc. Medicine, A.C.P., Am., Calif. socs. internal medicine, Am. Heart Assn. Clubs: Stanford Faculty, Menlo Circus. Home: 180 Elena Ave Atherton CA 94025 Office: 1100 Laurel St San Carlos CA 94070

WOLFE, MAURICE G., manufacturing company executive; b. Chgo., May 11, 1931; s. Wolf and Rita (Rosenberg) Ghitzis; B.A., U. So. Calif., 1958; A.A., Los Angeles City Coll., 1955; m. Marilyn Thalheimer Frank, Jan. 11, 1978 (dec. Feb. 1986); 1 son, Mark D.; 1 stepdau., Heather Byer. Asst. sales mgr. Am. handicrafts Tandy Corp., Los Angeles, 1958; v.p. Vivitar Corp., Santa Monica, Calif., 1959-70; pres. Personapac Co., Los Angeles, 1970-71; mgmt. cons. Technicolor Corp., Pacific Coast Farms, 20th Century Plastics, Photo Plastics, Wein Corp., Los Angeles, 1971-75; pres. Great Am. Corp., Laguna Hills, Calif. 1975—. Served with U.S. Army, 1951-53. Mem. Printing Industry Am., Nat. Assn. Printers and Lithographers, Soc. Motion Picture and TV Engrs. Home: 28257 Paseo Andante San Juan Capistrano CA 92675 Office: 39965 Comercio Rancho Santa Margarita CA 92688

WOLFE, SUZANNE ROSEN, lawyer; b. N.Y.C., Aug. 29, 1934; d. Theodore and Jessie Olga (Solomon) Rosen; B.A., NYU, 1955; J.D., Cath. U. Am., 1964; postdoctoral U. Paris, 1964-65; m. Edward Inman Wolfe, III, May 11, 1953 (div.); children—Richard, Kenneth, Jessie, Charles; m. Laurent Nicolas Edward Martin, June 20, 1986. Individual practice law, Paris, 1966-71; gen. counsel World ORT Union, Geneva, 1971-80; atty. Meade Wasserman Schneider, internat. comml. law, Geneva and Paris, 1980-81; law practice, Paris and Geneva, 1981-82; sr. ptnr. law firm, Geneva, 1982—. Fellow Internat. Comml. Comparative Law, Pisa, Italy, 1965. Mem. Am. Internat. Bus. Lawyers, Am. Arbitration Assn., Internat. C. of C. (U.S. council), Swiss Arbitration Assn., Internat. Comml. Arbitration Commn., Chartered Inst. Arbitrators (v.p. Geneva Internat. Cultural Ctr. com.). Home: 6 rue Thalberg, 1201 Geneva Switzerland Office: 15 rue du Cendrier, 1201 Geneva Switzerland

WOLFE, TRACEY DIANNE, distributing company executive; b. Dallas, June 13, 1951; d. George F. Wolfe and Helen Ruth Cline Lemons; B.S. in Edn. and Social Sci., East Tex. State U., Commerce, 1973, M.S. in Elem. Edn., 1976; 1 son, Bronson Alan. Asst. to dir. student devel. East Tex. State U., 1973-74; corp. sec., v.p. Wolfe Distbg. Co., beer distbrs., Terrell, Tex., 1974—. Mem. Pilot Club Internat., Kappa Delta (alumnae v.p. 1978-79, alumnae treas. 1979-81, province pres. 1980-82). Republican. Methodist. C-lub: Pilot (Terrell). Home: 3316 Lakeside Dr Rockwall TX 75087 Office: 100 Metro Dr Terrell TX 75160

WOLFENSON, AZI U., electrical, mechanical and industrial engineer, consultant; b. Rumania, Aug. 1, 1933; came to Peru, 1937; s. Samuel G. and Polea S. (Ulanowski) W.; m. Rebeca Sterental, Jan. 10, 1983; children by previous marriage—Ida, Jeannette, Ruth, Moises, Alex. Mech., Elec. Engr., Universidad Nacional de Ingenieria, Peru, 1955; M.Sc. in Indsl. Engring., U. Mich., 1966; Indsl. Engr., U. Nacional de Ingenieria, Peru, 1967; Ph.D. in Engring. Mgmt., Pacific Western U., 1983, Ph.D. in Engring. Energy, Century U., 1985. Power engr. Peruvian Trading Co., 1956-57; gen. mgr. AMSA Ingenieros S.A., 1957-60; prof. Universidad Nacional de Ingenieria, Peru, 1956-72, dean mech. and elec. engring., 1964-66, dean indsl. engring., 1967-72; dir. SWSA Automotive Parts, Peru, 1954-77; project mgr. Nat. Fin. Corp., Cofide, 1971-73; Peruvian dir. Corporacion Andina de Fomento, CAF, 1971-73; rep. in Peru, CAF, 1973-74; pres. DESPRO cons. firm, 1973-76; exec. pres. Electroperu, 1976-80; cons. engr., 1964—; dir. Tech. Transference Studies, 1971-72. Mem. Superior Council Electricity, 1964-66; metal mech. expert for andean group, 1970-71; Nat. council Foreing Investment and Tech. Transfer, 1972-73; mem. Consultive Council Ministry Economy and Fin., 1973-74; pres. Peruvian Jewish Community, 1966-70, Peruvian Hebrew Sch., 1976-78; promoter, co-founder, gen. mgr. La Republica Newspaper, Peru, 1981; pres. PROA project promotion AG, Switzerland, 1982—; cofounder El Popular, 1983, El Nacional, 1985. Recipient awards Order Merit for Disting. Services, Peru, 1980, Disting. by City Council of Huancayo, 1980, Trujillo, 1978, Huaral, 1979, Piura, 1980, Disting. Contbn. award City of Lima, 1970, 71, Disting. Contbn. to Elec. Devel. in Peru, 1979; others; named 1979 Exec., Gente mag., recognition Israel Govt., 1967, Disting. Comision Integracion Electrica Regional, CIER, medal, 1984. Fellow Inst. Prodn. Engrs., Brit. Inst. Mgmt.; mem. Colegio Ingenieros Peru, Instituto Peruano de Ingenieros Mecanicos (pres. 1965-66, v.p. 1967, dir. 1969, 70, 76), Asociacion Electrotechnica del Peru, ASME, AIIE (sr.), MTM Assn., Am. Soc. Engring. Edn., Am. Inst. Mgmt. Sci., AAAS, Assn. Mgmt. Sci. (dir. 1968), Asociacion Peruana Avance Ciencia, Inst. Adminstrv. Mgmt., British Inst. Mgmt., others. Author: Work Communications, 1966, Programmed Learning, 1966, Production Planning and Control, 1968, Transfer of Technology, 1971, National Electrical Development, 1977, Energy and Development, 1979, El Gran Desafio, 1981, Hacia una politica alternativa, 1982, The Power of Communications: The Media, 1987. Contbr. articles to newspapers and jours. Clubs: Club der 200, FCL, Hebraica. Home: Haldenstrasse 24, 6006 Lucerne Switzerland

WOLFF, CLAUDE, textile engineer, educator; b. Strasbourg, Alsace, France, Aug. 22, 1935; s. Benjamin and Alice Wolff; m. Hirsch Huguette, Dec. 19, 1963; children: Helene, Philippe. Lic. es Scis. in Physics, D in Engring. Sci. Physics, U. Strasbourg, France, 1957, PhD, 1961, DSc, 1967. Physicist Lorraine - Escaut, Thionville, France, 1957; asst. instr. U. Strasbourg, France, 1958-61, asst. prof., 1961-69; prof. U. Brest, France, 1969-78, U. Mulhouse, France, 1978—; dir. Ecole Nat. Supérieure des Industries Textiles, Mulhouse, France. Editor: Polymers and Lubrication, 1975; author: Viscosité, 1980; author: (with others) Rheooptical Properties of Polymers, 1986; co-editor jour. Non-Newtonian Fluid Mechanics, 1974—. Served as sgt. French Air Force, 1962-63. Recipient Palmes Académiques Ministry Edn., Paris, 1982. Mem. Soc. Française de Physique, Groupe Français de Rhéologie, British Soc. Rheology, Soc. Rheology, Assn. Univ. de Mécanique. Office: Ecole Nat Sup Ind Textiles, 11 rue Alfred Werner, 68093 Mulhouse France

WOLFF, DEBORAH H(OROWITZ), lawyer; b. Phila., Apr. 6, 1940; d. Samuel and Anne (Manstein) Horowitz; m. Morris H. Wolff, May 15, 1966 (divorced); children—Michelle Lynn, Lesley Anne; m. Walter Allan Levy, June 7, 1987. B.S., U. Pa., 1962, M.S., 1966; postgrad., Sophia U., Tokyo, 1968; L.L.M., Villanova U., 1979. Tchr. Overbrook High Sch., Phila., 1962-68; homebound tchr. Lower Merior Twp., Montgomery County, 1968-71; asst. dean U. Pa., Phila., 1975-76; law clk. firm Stassen, Kostos and Mason, Phila., 1977-78; assoc. firm Spencer, Sherr, Moses and Zuckerman, Norristown, Pa., 1980-81; ptnr. Wolff Assocs., 1981—; lectr. law and estate planning, Phila., 1980—; Recipient 3d ann. Community Service award Phila. Mayor's Com. for Women, 1984; named Pa. Heroine of Month, Ladies Home Jour., July 1984. Founder Take a Brother Program; bd. dirs. Germantown Jewish Ctr.; high sch. sponsor World Affairs Club, Phila., 1962-68; mem. exec. com. Crime Prevention Assn., Phila., 1965—; bd. dirs. U. Pa. Alumnae Bd., Phila., 1965—; chmn. urban conf. Boys Club Am., 1987. Mem. ABA, Pa. Bar Assn., Phila. Bar Assn., Montgomery County Bar Assn., Phila. Women's Network, Bus. Women's Network (pres.). Club: Cosmopolitan (membership com. Phila.). Home and Office: 422 W Mermaid Ln Philadelphia PA 19118

WOLFF, FRITZ KONRAD, advertising agency executive; b. Freudenstadt, Germany, July 11, 1935; s. Konrad W. and Sofia (Faust) W.; m. Helga Wolff, Feb. 20, 1958 (dec. 1976); children: Thomas, Stefan, Susanne; m. Brigitte Wolff, Oct. 10, 1977. Trainee Pino AG, Freudenstadt, 1953-57, W. Eiselen, Ulm, Fed. Republic of Germany, 1952-57; copywriter Lintas Advt. Agy., Hamburg, Fed. Republic of Germany, 1957-59, Troost Advt. Agy., Duesseldorf, Fed. Republic of Germany, 1959-61; creative dir. Ted Bates Advt. Agy., Franfurt, Fed. Republic of Germany, 1962-65; mng. ptnr. Koenigsteiner Gruppe, Kronberg, Fed. Republic of Germany, 1965—, BBDO, Duesseldorf, 1981—, Koenigsteiner Gruppe/BBDO, 1981—. Recipient German Direct Mktg. award, 1985; named Hon. Consul for Antigua and Barbuda in Germany, 1988—. Mem. Art Dirs. Club Germany (recipient gold medal 1985). Home: PO Box 1354, D-6242 Kronberg Nr Frankfurt Federal Republic of Germany Office: Koenigsteiner Gruppe, 2 Minnholzweg, D-6242 Kronberg Federal Republic of Germany

WOLFF, HEINZ ARTHUR, architect; b. Braunschweig, Fed. Republic Germany, Apr. 14, 1909; s. Conrad and Marie (Schulze) W.; m. Hedwig Schuerkotter, Apr. 26, 1945; 1 child, Matthias. Diploma in Architecture, U. Braunschweig, 1932, D in Engring., 1935. Asst. chmn. constrns. Tech. U., Braunschweig, 1933-35; architect for airports No. Germany, 1935-40, Belgium and Italy, 1940-45, Cemetery for Fallen Soldiers, Rimini, 1945; architect town planning office Braunschweig, 1945-53; conservationist in charge monuments office No. Saxony, Fed. Republic Germany, 1953-72; pvt. practice architecture Hannover, Fed. Republic Germany, 1972—. Designer decorative pavements and facades, reliefs in concrete, fresco paintings, watercolors, organ-cases. Mem. Internat. Council Monuments and Sites, German Council for Bells, Soc. Friends of Organs. Lutheran. Home and Office: Sextrostr 27, D 3000 Hannover Federal Republic of Germany

WOLFF, HERBERT ERIC, banker, honorary counsul of Malaysia, former army officer; b. Cologne, Germany, May 24, 1925; s. Hugo and Juanna Anna (Van Dam) W.; m. Billy Rafael, Nov. 13, 1946 (dec. July 1987); children: Karen, Herbert E., Allen R. B.A., Rutgers U., 1953; B.S., U. Md., 1957; M.A., George Washington U., 1962; grad., U.S. Army War Coll., 1962, Harvard U., 1979. Commd. 2d lt. U.S. Army, 1945, advanced through grades to maj. gen.; served in Fed. Republic of Germany, Greece, Iran, Republic of Korea, Australia, New Guinea, The Phillipines, Japan and Socialist Republic of Vietnam; dep. dir. ops. NSA-CSS, Ft. Meade, Md., 1973-75; dep. corps. comdr. V. Corps U.S. Army, Frankfurt, Fed. Republic Germany; comdr. gen. U.S. Army Western Command U.S. Army, Hawaii, 1977-81; with First Hawaiian Bank, Honolulu, 1981—, sr. v.p., corp. sec., 1981—. Author: The Man on Horseback, 1962, The Tenth Principle of War, 1964, Public Support, 1964, The Military Instructor, 1968. Mem. exec. bd. Aloha council Boy Scouts Am.; bd. dirs. USO; mem. Silver Jubilee Commn. State of Hawaii; v.p. Hawaii Com. Fgn. Relations; bd. dirs. Pacific Asian Affairs Council; pres. Hawaii Army Mus. Soc. Decorated Bronze Star with V and 3 oak leaf clusters U.S. Army; decorated Air medal (24) U.S. Army, Joint Services comendation medal U.S. Army, Army Comendation medal U.S. Army, Purple Heart, Gallantry Cross with 2 palms, Gallantry Cross with palm and silver star Nat. Order 5th class S. Vietnam, Order Nat. Security Merit Choen-Su S. Korea, D.S.M. with oakleaf clusters (2), U.S. Army, Silver Star with oak leaf cluster U.S. Army, Legion of Merit with 3 oak leaf clusters U.S. Army, D.F.C. U.S. Army. Mem. Am. Bankers Assn., Am. Soc. Corp. Secs., Assn. U.S. Army (trustee), 1st Inf. Div. Assn., 1st Cav. Div. Assn., U.S. Army Mus. Soc. (trustee), Phi Kappa Phi. Clubs: Plaza, Waialae Country. Lodge: Rotary. Office: 1st Hawaiian Bank 165 S King St PO Box 3200 Honolulu HI 96813

WOLFF, LINDA M., personnel executive; b. Chgo., June 30, 1953; d. Calvin and Marian Wolff. BA in Psychology and Speech Communications, Northeastern Ill. U., 1976. Recruiter Trans Union Corp., Chgo., 1977-78; compensation adminstr. Am. Res. Corp., Chgo., 1978-79; sr. compensation specialist Bankers Life and Casualty Co., Chgo., 1979-80; dir. human resources and devel. IDC Services, Inc., Chgo., 1980-84; v.p. regional dir. human resources Burson-Marsteller, pub. relations, Chgo., 1984-87; regional mgr. human resources programs Nat. Advanced Systems, 1988—. Mem. Am. Soc. Personnel Adminstrn., Am. Compensation Assn., Soc. Human Resources Profls., Am. Soc. Tng. and Devel., Am. Mgmt. Assn.

WOLFF, PATRICK MARIE FRANÇOIS ALBERT, physician, consultant; b. Rosieres, Haute Loire, France, July 30, 1944; S. Jacques and Alice (Keil) W.; m. Hélène Bessiere, July 25, 1968 (dec. July 1985); children: Isabelle, Laurent, Sophie, Eric. MD, Faculty Medecine Montpellier, France, 1970. Instr. Faculty Medicine, Montpellier, 1965-75; hosp. externe Univ. Hosp., Montpellier, 1966-70; hosp. attache Regional Hosp., Montpellier, 1975-77; pvt. cons. Montpellier, 1973—. Contbr. articles to Resonance. Served with French med. corps, 1970-72. Mem. Trade Union Physicians (sec.-gen. 1988), Soc. Francaise Sénologie Pathologie Mammaire, Nat. Ctr. Sci. Research. Roman Catholic. Club: Photo. Home and Office: 1900 Ave Pére Soulas, 34090 Montpellier, Hérault France

WOLFF VON NATTERMOELLER, HANS JÜERGEN, film director, script writer, producer; b. Dresden, Germany, June 23, 1921; s. Hans Conrad Wolff and Maria (Weber) Wolff Von N.; m. Ingeborg Dorothea Bruhn, 1960; children by previous marriage: Daniela, Mario. Grad. high sch., Berlin; dipl. Maestro di Pittura (hon.), Seminario Internat. d'Arte Moderna e Contemporanea, 1982. Journalist Wiesbaden and Frankfurt, Germany, 1946; script writer Curt Oertel Film Studios, Wiesbaden, 1948; dir., script writer UFA Universum Film AG, 1953-62; head of prodns., 1st dir. ZDF, Germany, 1963; prodn. head ZDF, Mainz, Germany, 1969, prodn. head of staff, 1972-85; chief Internat. Film Union, Remagen, Germany, 1966; media cons., 1986—. Author 37 film scripts, dir. 43 films. Served to lt., Naval Reserve, 1941-46. Recipient Film prize Fed. German Rep., 1956, Grand Prix award Internat. Film Festival, Brussels, 1956, Internat. Film Festival award, Harrogate, Eng., 1957, Cultural Film award Fed. German Rep., 1957, Internat. Film Fair award, Hollywood, Calif., 1964, VIP award Ency. Corp., U.S.A., 1979, Gold medal Acad. of Art of Italy, 1980, Merit award Services to the Arts, 1981, Golden Centaur award Italian Acad., 1982, Gold medal Internat. Parliament, U.S.A., 1983, Grand prize of the Nations, Italy, 1983, Victory Statue of the World prize of Culture, Italy, 1984. Mem. Italian Acad. of Arts, Marquis Giuseppe Scicluna Internat. U. Found. Home and Office: 32 Tiergartenstr, 4000 Duesseldorf 1 Federal Republic of Germany

WOLFOWITZ, BRIAN LESTER, otorhinolarynogologist; b. Durban, Natal, Republic of South Africa, Mar. 17, 1942; s. Leon and Freda (Crouse) W.; m. Barbara Sheila Goldberg; children: Karen, David, Maxine. MD, Witwatersrand U., Johannesburg, Republic of South Africa, 1964, PhD, 1974. Registered Republic of South Africa Med. and Dental Council in Otorhinolaryngology. Otorhinolaryngologist Baragwanath Hosp., Johannesburg, 1968-73; practice medicine specializing in otorhinolaryngology Johannesburg, 1973—; lectr. anatomy dept. Witwatersrand U., 1966—, dept. otolaryngology, 1968-78. Contbr. articles to profl. jours. Fellow Royal Coll. Surgeons; mem. Am. Acad. Facial, Plastic and Reconstructive Surgeons, South African Soc. Otolaryngology. Jewish. Office: 51 Esselen Towers, Johannesburg, Transvaal Republic of South Africa

WOLFOWITZ, PAUL DUNDES, U.S. ambassador to Indonesia; b. N.Y.C., Dec. 22, 1943; s. Jacob and Lillian (Dundes) W.; m. Clare Selgin, Nov. 25, 1968; children: Sara Elizabeth, David Samuel, Rachel Dahlia. B.A. in Math, Cornell U., 1965; M.A., U. Chgo., 1967, Ph.D. in Polit. Sci, 1972. Lectr., asst. prof. Yale U., 1970-73; with U.S. Arms Control and Disarmament Agy., 1973-77, spl. asst. to dir., 1974-75, dep. asst. dir., 1976; spl. asst. for SALT, 1976-77; with Dept. Def., Washington, 1977-80; dep. asst. Sec. of Def., regional programs, program analysis and evaluation Office of Sec. of Def., 1977-80; vis. assoc. prof. Sch. Advanced Internat. Studies, Johns Hopkins U., 1980-81; dir. policy planning staff U.S. Dept. State, 1981-82, asst. sec. for East Asian and Pacific affairs, 1982-86; U.S. ambassador to Indonesia 1986—. Recipient Disting. Civilian Service medal U.S. Dept. Def., Disting. Honor award U.S. Dept. State. Office: Ambassador to Indonesia US Embassy Box 1 APO San Francisco CA 96356

WOLF-PHILLIPS, LESLIE ARTHUR, political scientist, educator; b. Worcester, England, Feb. 19, 1929; s. Walter George and Annie Elizabeth (Wilesmith) Phillips; m. Lisa Joan Wolf-Phillips, 1960 (div. 1986); children: Jonathan, Rebekah. BS in Polit. Sci. with first class honors, London Sch. Econs., 1958; LLM, U. Coll. London, 1970. From asst. lectr., to sr. lectr. in polit. sci. London Sch. Econs., 1960—; constitutional advisor to prime minister Pakistan, 1975-76; participant Internat. Seminar Constitution Writing, Washington, 1983, Seminar on Comparative Constitutions, Brasilia, Brazil, 1987. Author: Comparative Constitutions, 1968, Constitutions of Modern States, 1972. Served with Brit. Army, 1947-49. Mem. Assn. Univ. Tchrs., Nat. Union Journalists, Polit. Studies Assn. U.K., Royal Inst. Pub. Adminstrn., Hansard Soc. Parliamentary Govt. Labour Party. Home: 20 Teversham Rd, Fulbourn, Cambridge CBI 5EB, England Office: London Sch Econs, Houghton St, London WC2 2AE, England

WOLFRAM, THOMAS, physicist; b. St. Louis, July 27, 1936; s. Ferdinand I. and Audrey H. (Calvert) W.; m. Eleanor Elaine, May 22, 1965; children: Michael, Gregory, Melanie, Susan, Steven. BA, U. Calif., Riverside, 1959, PhD in Physics, 1963; MA in Physics, UCLA, 1960. Engr. Atomics International, Canoga Park, Calif., 1960-63; mem. tech. staff N.Am. Aviation Corp. Sci. Ctr., Thousand Oaks, Calif., 1963-68; group leader in solid state physics Rockwell Internat. Sci. Ctr., Thousand Oaks, 1968-72, dir. div. physics and chemistry, 1972-74; prof. physics, chmn. dept. physics and astronomy U. Mo., Columbia, 1974-83; dir. phys. tech. div. AMOCO Corp., 1983-87; v.p. mfg. and tech., gen. mgr. AMOCO Laser Co., 1987—; cons. in field. Editor: Inelastic Electron Tunneling Spectroscopy, 1978, research, numerous publs. in field. Recipient Disting. Prof. award Argonne Univs. Assn., 1977. Fellow Am. Phys. Soc. Office: Amoco Laser Co 1251 Frontenac Rd Naperville IL 60540

WOLFSON, SIR ISAAC, foundation executive; b. Sept. 17, 1897; s. Lord Wolfson; m. Edith Specterman, 1926 (dec. 1981); 1 son. Student, Queen's Park Sch., Glasgow, Scotland; DCL (hon.), U. Oxford, 1963; LLD (hon.), U. London, 1958, U. Glasgow, 1963, U. Cambridge, 1966, U. Manchester, 1967, U. Strathclyde, 1969, Brandeis U., 1969, U. Nottingham, 1971; PhD (hon.), U. Jerusalem, 1970. Joined The Great Universal Stores Ltd., 1932, joint chmn., then hon. life pres., 1987—; hon. pres. Weizmann Inst. Sci. Found., trustee Religious Ctr., Jerusalem; trustee Wolfson Found., 1955—; mem. Worshipful Co. of Pattenmakers. Mem. grand council Cancer

Research Campaign; patron Royal Coll. Surgeons. Fellow Weizmann Inst. Sci., Israel, St. Edmund Hall, Oxford, jews' Coll., Lady Margaret Hall, Oxford, Wolfson Coll., Oxford; recipient Einstein award, U.S., 1967, Herbert Lehmann award, U.S., 1968; named Freeman City of Glasgow, 1971. Office: The Great Universal Stores PLC, PO Box 1BZ, Universal House, London W1A 1BZ, England *

WOLFSON, ROBERT PRED, aerospace engineer; b. Miami, Fla., May 29, 1926; s. O. Philip and Nora Jacqueline (Pred) W.; m. Helene Clare Abrahm, Nov. 12, 1949; children: Philip Michael, Robert P. BE, Tulane U., 1948; postgrad., Pa. State U., 1962-64, Poly. Inst. Bklyn., 1965. Air conditioning engr. Equitable Equipment Co., New Orleans, 1948-49, Wood-Leppard Air Conditioning Co., Houston, 1949, Conditioned Air Corp., Miami, 1949-50, Lewco Co., Miami, 1950-54, Hill-York Corp., Miami, 1954-55; thermoelectric energy research engr. The Franklin Inst Labs. Research and Devel., Phila., 1955-59; thermoelectric research and devel. mgr. Tenn. Products & Chem. Corp., Nashville, 1959-61; photovoltaic power systems devel. engr., planetary quarantine mgr. Gen. Electric Co., Phila., 1961-71; sci. contamination specialist for Viking spacecraft Bionetics Corp., Hampton, Va., 1972; planetary quarantine project mgr., Mars/Earth back contamination research mgr., dir. energy programs Exotech. Inc., Gaithersburg, Md., 1972-80; project engr. The Aerospace Corp., El Segundo, Calif., 1980—. Contbr. articles to profl. jours. Served with USNR, 1944-46. Mem. IEEE, Wash. Acad. Scis. Home: 19 Laguna Ct Manhattan Beach CA 90266

WOLGA, JEAN IGOR, physician; b. Paris, Aug. 31, 1948; s. Jacques and Victoria (Tress) W.; m. Angele Michelle Vizzini, May 5, 1972; children: Nadine, Pierre-Emmanuel, Catherine, Nicolas. Dr Etat en Medecine, U. Grenoble, 1975, Attestation de Pediatrie, 1977; Diploma in Tropical Medicine and Health, U. Marseille, 1975; Diploma in Agrl. Medicine, U. Tours, 1978; Diploma in Leprosy, U. Montpellier, 1982. Resident Centre Hospitalier, Annemasse, France, 1973-78; gen. practice medicine Bapt. Mission Hosp., Ferkessedougou, Ivory Coast, 1976-77, 82-83, Novalaise, France, 1978-82, Grenoble, France, 1983—; cons. in tropical medicine Centre Hospitalier Univ., Grenoble, 1979—; instr. tropical medicine Faculty Medicine, U. Grenoble, 1978—; instr. gen. and family practice, 1986—; med. expert Ct. Appeals, Grenoble, 1980—. Author: Conseils aux Voyageurs, 1981 (Prix Medec 1982); contbr. articles to med. jours.; patentee African root for treating hepatitis. Mem. French Soc. Exotic Pathology, Swiss Soc. Tropical Medicine and Parasitology. Mem. Christian Evang. Ch. Home: chemin du Cerf Cidex 612, 38330 Saint Nazaire les Eymes France Office: 16 ave Jeanne d'Arc, 38100 Grenoble France

WOLKIN, PAUL ALEXANDER, lawyer, institute executive; b. Phila., Oct. 14, 1917; s. Alex and Anna (Friedman) W.; stepson Rebecca (Likalter) W.; m. Martha Kessler, June 25, 1944; children: Rachel, Adam. B.A., U. Pa., 1937, M.A., 1938, J.D., 1941. Bar: Pa. 1942, U.S. Supreme Ct. 1947. Law clk. U.S. Ct. Appeals (3d Cir.), Phila., 1942-44; atty. Fgn. Econ. Adminstrn., Washington, 1944-45; asso. gen. counsel French Supply Council, Washington, 1945-46; asst. legal adviser Dept. State, 1946-47; legis. draftsman Phila. Charter Commn., 1948-51; spl. asst. to Phila. Solicitor, 1951; partner firm Wolkin, Sarner & Cooper, Phila., 1951-66; counsel Sarner, Cooper & Stein, Phila., 1966-69, Hudson, Wilf & Kronfeld, Phila., 1971-78, Rawle & Henderson, 1980-81; asst. dir. Am. Law Inst., Phila., 1947-77; exec. v.p. Am. Law Inst., 1977—, sec., 1979—; exec. dir. com. on continuing profl. edn. Am. Law Inst.-ABA, 1963—; sec. permanent editorial bd. Uniform Comml. Code, 1962—; mem. com. specialized personnel Dept. Labor, 1964-69; dir. Public Service Satellite Consortium, 1980-84. Editor: The Practical Lawyer, 1955—; contbr. articles to profl. jours. Pres. Phila. Child Guidance Center, 1966-72. Fellow Am. Bar Found.; mem. Am. Law Inst., Jud. Conf. Third Cir. U.S., ABA (spl. com. on standards and codes 1974-80), Pa. Bar Assn., Phila. Bar Assn., Pa. Bar Inst. (bd. dirs. 1967-75), Order of Coif, Lawyers Club, Scribes (past pres.). Home: 1610 N 72d St Philadelphia PA 19151 Office: Am Law Inst 4025 Chestnut St Philadelphia PA 19104

WOLKOWSKI, LESZEK AUGUST, marketing specialist; b. Wilno, Poland, Jan. 14, 1941; s. John and Halina Teresa (Wankowicz) W.; m. Barbara M. Szlachcic, Mar. 22, 1968 (div.); 1 child, Grazyna Grace; m. 2d, Rosita Perez, June 16, 1981 (div.); m. 3d, Anna Krol, June 10, 1982 (div.); 1 child, Leszek August; m. 4th, Grace Baginski, July 3, 1986 (div.). Baccalaureate, Lycee Polonais de Paris, 1961; student, Cen. Sch. Econs., Warsaw, Poland, 1961-62, U. Warsaw, 1962-65, U. Paris, 1965-67; BA with honors, U. Ill., 1969; MA, Loyola U., Chgo., 1975; PhD in Comparative Internat. Edn. and Psychology, Loyola U., 1979. Instr. modern langs. Loyola U., Chgo., 1969-71; tchr. Notre Dame High Sch., Niles, Ill., 1971-76; instr. Skokie (Ill.) Coll., 1971-79; tchr. modern langs. and debate Adlai Stevenson High Sch., Lincolnshire, Ill., 1976-78; instr. English Roper IBG Corp., Wheeling, Ill., 1977-78; ins. agt. Mass. Life Ins. Co., Chgo., 1978; real estate broker Gen. Devel. Corp., Chgo., 1978; dist. mktg. dir. U.S. C. of C., Oak Brook, Ill., 1979—; dir. Poland-Austria Program, 1975, German Exchange Program, 1977. Produced Waldemar Kocon Am. Debut in Chgo., 1984. Recipient awards for effective mktg., 1980, 81, 82, Million Dollar Mktg. award, 1987. Mem. Polish-Am. Educators Assn., Loyola U. Chgo. Alumni Assn., Phi Delta Kappa. Office: 2000 Spring Rd Oak Brook IL 60521

WOLLAN, EUGENE, lawyer; b. N.Y.C., Nov. 2, 1928; s. Isidor and Mollie (Elterman) W.; m. Jean B. Sack, June 6, 1954 (div. 1974); children—Eric G., Jennifer J.; m. Marjorie Cama, Nov. 25, 1977; stepchildren—Valerie M. Rosenwasser, Jon J. Rosenwasser. B.A. cum laude, Harvard U., 1948, J.D., 1950. Bar: N.Y., 1950, U.S. Dist. Ct. (so. and ea. dists.) N.Y. 1953. U.S. Ct. Appeals (2d cir.) 1955, U.S. Ct. Mil. Appeals 1951, U.S. Supreme Ct. 1960. Assoc. Rein Mound & Cotton, N.Y.C., 1953-62, ptnr., 1963-87, Mound, Cotton & Wollan, 1987—. Mem. Joint Conf. Com. on Ct. Congestion. Served to col. USAR, 1951-81. Mem. Internat. Assn. Ins. Counsel, Defense Research Inst., Internat. Soc. Barristers, Assn. Internationale De Droit Des Assurances, N.Y.C. Bar Assn., N.Y. County Lawyers, Judge Advocates Assn. Clubs: Harvard (N.Y.C.), Met. Opera Guild (N.Y.C.), City Midday Drug and Chem. (N.Y.C.). Home: 200 E 71st St New York NY 10021 Office: Mound Cotton & Wollan 125 Maiden Ln New York NY 10038

WOLLEMBORG, LEO JOSEPH, newspaperman; b. Loreggia, Italy, Aug. 30, 1912; emigrated to U.S., 1939, naturalized, 1943; s. Leone and Alina (Fano) W.; m. Mafalda Cusi, Mar. 27, 1962; 1 son, Leo R. Ph.D. in Litt.; Ph.D. in History, U. Rome, Italy, 1933, Ph.D. in Law, 1936. Lectr. internat. relations Columbia Grad Sch., 1940-42; script writer, news editor Italian sect. OWI, 1942-43; Rome corr. Washington Post, 1953-70; Italian and Vatican corr. Los Angeles Times-Washington Post News Service, 1962-70; Rome corr. Phila. Bull., 1970-72, 78-82; Rome Corr. Progresso Italo-Americano, N.Y.C., 1982—; Rome corr. Freedom at Issue, 1978—; assoc. pub., polit. commentator Daily Am., Rome, 1972-76; Participant round table debates internat. affairs Italian TV, 1961—; contbr. on Italian affairs to Wall Street Journal, 1982—. Author: Tra Washingtone Roma, 1959, Italia al Rallentatore, 1966, Stelle, Strisce & Tricolore, 1983; Contbr. numerous articles to nat. mags., jours., newspapers. Served with AUS, 1943-47, ETO. Mem. Fgn. Press Assn. Rome. Address: 373 Via Nomentana, Rome Italy 00162

WOLLENBERG, SUSAN LESLEY FREDA, music educator; b. Lancashire, Eng., Apr. 28, 1949; m. L.S. Wollenberg, Aug. 31, 1969; children: Michael, Anne. BA with class I honours, Oxford U., 1969, DPhil, 1975. U. lectr. music Oxford (Eng.) U., 1972—; fellow, tutor in music Lady Margaret Hall, 1972—; fellow archivist 1986—; lectr. music Brasenose Coll., 1987—. Contbr. articles and revs. to musicological jours., symposia, encys., chpts. to books. Halstead postgrad. scholar Oxford U. Faculty Music, 1969-72. Mem. Royal Mus. Assn. Home: 131 Eynsham Rd, Botley Oxford OX2 9BY, England Office: Oxford U Faculty Music, Saint Aldates Oxford OX1 1DB, England

WOLLMAN, HARRY, medical educator; b. Bklyn., Sept. 26, 1932; s. Jacob and Florence Roslyn (Hoffman) W.; m. Anne Carolyn Hamel, Feb. 16, 1957; children—Julie Ellen, Emily Jane, Diana Leigh. A.B. summa cum laude (hon. John Harvard scholar 1950-53, hon. Harvard Coll. scholar 1953-54, Detur award 1951), Harvard, 1954, M.D., 1958. Diplomate: Am. Bd. Anesthesiology. Intern U. Chgo. Clinics, 1958-59; resident U. Pa., 1959-63, assoc. in anesthesia, 1963-65, mem. faculty, 1965—, prof. anesthesia, 1970—, prof. pharmacology, 1971—, Robert Dunning Dripps prof., chmn. dept. anesthesia, 1972-87; prin. investigator Anesthesia Research Center, 1972-78; program dir. Anesthesia Research Tng. Grant, 1972—; v.p. acad. affairs, dean sch. of medicine Hahnemann U., Phila., 1987—; Mem. anesthesia drug panel, drug efficacy study, com. on anesthesia Nat. Acad. Scis.-NRC, 1970-71, com. on adverse reactions to anesthesia drugs, 1971-72; mem. pharm. and toxicology tng. grants com. NIH, 1966-68, anesthesia tng. grants com., 1971-73, surgery, anesthesia and trauma study sect., 1974-78; chmn. com. on studies involving human beings U. Pa., 1972-76, chmn. clin. practice exec. com., 1976-80. Assoc. editor for revs.: Anesthesiology, 1970-75; Contbr. and editor books. NIH research traineeship fellow, 1959-63; Pharm. Mfg. Assn. fellow, 1960-61. Mem. Pa. Soc. Anesthesiologists (pres. 1972-73), Am. Physiol. Soc., Assn. U. Anesthetists (exec. council 1971-74, chmn. sci. adv. bd. 1975-77), Soc. Acad. Anesthesia Chairmen (chmn. com. on financial resources 1973-77, pres.-elect 1976-77, pres. 1977-78), Am. Soc. Anesthesiologists, Phila. Soc. Anesthesiologists, AMA, Pa. Med. Soc., Phila. County Med. Soc., Am. Dental Soc. Anesthesiology (adv. bd. 1985—), John Morgan Soc., Coll. Physicians Phila., Phi Beta Kappa, Sigma Xi. Republican. Unitarian. Home: 2203 Delancey Pl Philadelphia PA 19103 Office: Hahnemann U Broad and Vine St Mail Stop 490 Philadelphia PA 19102

WOLPER, MARSHALL, financial consultant; b. Chgo., Nov. 19, 1922; s. Harry B. and Bessie (Steiner) W.; m. Thelma R. Freedman, April 15, 1957 (div. Oct. 1968); m. Jacqueline N. Miller, Sept. 19, 1969 (div. Jan. 1976); m. Lucee I. G. Lee, Mar. 20, 1985; stepchildren—Robert Insinga, Cyndi Insinga Wolper. B.A. in Polit. Sci. and Econs., U. Ill., 1942. Chartered fin. cons. With Kent Products, Chgo., 1946; pres. Marshall Industries, Chgo., 1947-52; with Equitable Life Assurance Soc., 1953—, nat. honor agt., 1966, nat. sales cons., 1967—; sr. partner Wolper & Katz, 1958—; partner Wolper and Katz Thoroughbred Racing Stable, 1977-82; instr. life underwriting and pensions U. Miami, 1959—; pres. Marshall Wolper Co., 1963—; chmn. bd. M.W. Computer Systems, Inc., 1971-80; pres. Marshall Wolper Pension Sers. Inc., 1978-80, Wolper, Ross & Co., 1980—; lectr. life ins., employee benefit plans, pensions, estate planning to various univs. and spl. meetings; pres. Greater Miami Tax Inst., 1963, Estate Planning Council Greater Miami, 1969-70; faculty Practicing Law Inst., 1967—; mem. adv. com., lectr. Inst. on Estate Planning. Author: Medical Entities Taxed as Corporations, 1961, Tax and Business Aspects of Professional Corporations and Associations, 1968; contbr. articles to profl. jours. Bd. dirs. Dade County chpt. ARC, Profl. Selling Inst. Served to 1st lt. AUS, World War II, ETO. Decorated Bronze Star, Purple Heart; recipient Paragon award Equitable Life Assurance Soc., 1972; C.L.U. Mem. Am. Soc. C.L.U.s (pres. Miami chpt. 1963, inst. faculty 1963-65, dir. 1966-67, regional v.p. 1968), The Am. Coll. (joint com. on continuing edn. 1965—), Nat. Assn. Life Underwriters (lectr. 1963, 66, 81), Million Dollar Round Table (life mem., speaker 1962-81, exec. com. 1974-78, pres. 1977), Assn. Advanced Life Underwriting (lectr. 1966, pres. 1972), Am. Soc. Pension Actuaries (dir.), Nat. Assn. Pension Consultants and Adminstrs. (treas.). Home: 714 W DiLido Dr Miami Beach FL 33139 Office: 4770 Biscayne Blvd Miami FL 33137 also: 555 Madison Ave New York NY 10022

WOLSON, CRAIG ALAN, lawyer; b. Toledo, Feb. 20, 1949; s. Max A. and Elaine B. (Cohn) W.; m. Janis Nan Braun, July 30, 1972 (div. Mar. 1986); m. Ellen Carol Schulgasser, Oct. 26, 1986. BA, U. Mich., 1971, JD, 1974. Bar: N.Y. 1975, U.S. Dist. Ct. (so. and ea. dists.) N.Y. 1975, U.S. Ct. Appeals (2d cir.) 1975, U.S. Supreme Ct. 1978. Assoc. Shearman & Sterling, N.Y.C., 1974-81; v.p., asst. gen. counsel Thomson McKinnon Securities Inc., N.Y.C., 1981-85; v.p., sec. gen. counsel J.D. Mattus Co., Inc., Greenwich, Conn., 1985-88; also bd. dirs. J.D. Mattus Co., Inc., Greenwich; v.p., asst. gen. counsel Chem. Bank, N.Y.C., 1988—; dep. clk. Lucas County Courthouse, Toledo, 1968-69, 71-72. Articles and administrv. editor U. Mich. Law Rev., 1973-74. Mem. ABA, N.Y. State Bar Assn., Assn. of Bar of City of N.Y., Phi Beta Kappa, Phi Eta Sigma, Pi Sigma Alpha. Home: 13 Dingletown Rd Greenwich CT 06830 Office: Chemical Bank 277 Park Ave New York NY 10172

WOLSTENHOLME, ERIC FRANK, university professor, consultant; b. Wigan, Lancashire, England, June 28, 1944; s. Frank Simpson and Doris (Hart) W.; m. Elizabeth Ann Flint, July 23, 1966; children: Matthew, Tom, Susie. BSc in Engring., Nottingham U., England, 1966, PhD in Engring., 1968; M of Tech. Operational Research, Brunel U., England, 1970. Operational research scientist British Coal, Doncaster, England, 1968-74, purchasing mgr., 1974-76; prof. Bradford (England) U. Mgmt. Ctr., 1976—. Contbr. articles to prof. jours. Fellow Inst. Mining Engrs., Operational Reseach Soc., Chartered Engrs.; mem. System Dynamics Soc. Office: Bradford U Mgmt Ctr, Emm Ln, Bradford W Yorkshire, England

WOMER, JAN LINWOOD, clergyman; b. Beaver Falls, Pa., Dec. 13, 1939; s. L. Arthur and Emma (Mortensen) W.; m. Sharyn Elizabeth Edelblute, Sept. 6, 1967; children—Justin A.L., Colin C.E. B.A., U. Calif.-Riverside, 1961; M.Div., Pacific Luth. Theol. Sem., 1965; M.A., Ph.D., U. Oxford. Ordained to ministry Lutheran Ch., 1968. Prof. theology Nommensen U., Sumatra, Indonesia, 1971-75; pastor Mt. Calvary Luth. Ch., Cypress, Calif., 1975-80; asst. to bishop Pacific S.W. Synod, Luth. Ch. Am., Los Angeles, 1980-83; lectr. theology and fellow Mansfield Coll., U. Oxford, Eng., 1983—, acting prin., 1985-86, prin., 1986—; mem. co-opted staff Assembly Luth. World Fedn., Budapest, Hungary, 1984; del. nat. conv. Luth. Ch. Am., Seattle, 1980, Toronto, 1984, ecumenical officer Pacific S.W. Synod, Los Angeles, 1981-83, mem. cons. com. worship, Phila., 1978-82; lectr. Luth. Confs. Worship and Music, 1978-83; cons. Internat. Anglican-Luth. Dialogues, 1986—. Author: Morality and Ethics in Early Christianity, 1987; Author and editor: Ecclesia-Leiturgia-Ministerium, 1977. Contbr. articles to profl. jours. Pres. youth adv. bd. City of Concord, Calif., 1979-81. Mem. N.Am. Acad. Liturgy, Soc. Study Theology, Soc. Study Christian Ethics (U.K.), Soc. Christian Ethics (U.S.), Luth. Council Great Britain. Democrat. Clubs: United Oxford and Cambridge U, Oxford Soc., Oxford Union. Lodge: Rotary. Home: 3920 Winston Dr Moffman Estates IL 60195 Office: Mansfield Coll, Oxford OX1 3TF, England

WONDER, STEVIE (STEVLAND MORRIS), singer, musician, composer; b. Saginaw, Mich., May 13, 1950; m. Syreeta Wright, 1971 (div. 1972); children: Aisha, Keita, Mumtaz. Student pub. schs. in Detroit until age 12; then transferred to, Mich. Sch. for Blind. Solo singer, Whitestone Bapt. Ch., Detroit, 1959, rec. artist, Motown Records, Detroit, 1963-70; founder, pres. music pub. co., Black Bull Music, Inc., 1970—, Wondirection Records, Inc., 1982—; recs. include Fingertips, 1963, Uptight/Purple Raindrops, 1965, Someday At Christmas/The Miracles of Christmas, 1966, I'm Wondering/Everytime I See You I Go Wild, 1966, I Was Made To Love Her/Hold Me, 1967, Shoo-Be-Doo-Be-Doo-Da-Day/Why Don't You Lead Me To Love, 1968, You Met Your Match/My Girl, 1968, For Once In My Life, I Don't Know Why, My Cherie Amour, Yester-Me, Yester-You, Yesterday, Never Had a Dream Come True, Signed, Sealed, Delivered I'm Yours, Heaven Help Us All, I Wish (Grammy award 1977), Don't You Worry 'Bout a Thing, You Haven't Done Nothin', Boogie on Reggae Woman, (Grammy award 1975), Isn't She Lovely, Sir Duke, Another Star, As, You Are the Sunshine of My Life, (Grammy award 1974), Superstition, (Grammy award 1974), Higher Ground, Living For the City, (Grammy award 1975); albums include Uptight, 1966, Down To Earth, 1966, I Was Made To Love Her, 1967, Someday At Christmas, 1967, Stevie Wonder's Greatest Hits, 1968, Music of My Mind, 1972, Innervisions, 1973 (Grammy award 1974), Fulfillingness' First Finale (Grammy award 1975), Songs In the Key of Life, 1976 (Grammy award 1977), Stevie Wonder Live, Where I'm Coming From, 1972, Talking Book, 1972, Journey Through the Secret Life of Plants, 1979, Hotter than July, 1980, Woman in Red (Acad. award, Golden Globe award for single I Just Called to Say I Love You), 1984, In Square Circle (best soul/r&b album of yr., Down Beat mag. Readers' poll) 1986, Characters, 1987; appeared in films: Bikini Beach, 1964, Muscle Beach Party, 1964; frequent TV appearances include: Mike Douglas Show, guest host Saturday Night Live; named (Musician of Year, Down Beat mag. Rock/Blues Poll 1973-75, 77-78, Best Selling Male Soul Artist of Year, Nat. Assn. Rec. Merchandisers 1974), recipient (numerous Grammy awards also numerous awards for best singer/songwriter; Rock Music award 1977, Am. Music award 1978, Am. Video award for best rhythm and blues video for Ebony and Ivory 1982, Inducted Songwriters Hall of Fame 1982. Address: Black Bull Music 4616 Magnolia Blvd Burbank CA 91505 *

WONG, BENJAMIN WINGNIN, finance executive; b. Hong Kong, June 20, 1949; came to U.S., 1970; s. Ding Lun and Ling Sik (Lui) W.; m. Cecilia Y. Wong, Mar. 22, 1974; 1 child, Vivian. BS with high honors, U. Wis., Stevens Point, 1973; MBA with distinction, Northwestern U., 1974. Fin. analyst Chemed Corp., Cin., 1974-76, mgr. fgn. exchange, 1976-78, asst. treas., 1978-87; chmn., pres. New Asia Bank, Chgo., 1987—. Recipient Disting. Scholar award Northwestern U., 1974. Mem. Assn. MBA Execs. Club: Bankers. Home: 20 W 324 Redcliffe Downers Grove IL 60516 Office: New Asia Bank 222 W Cermak Chicago IL 60616

WONG, CHEE CHAN, chemical company executive; b. Singapore, Sept. 3, 1949; m. Loh Kwee Kim, Oct. 6, 1974; children—Chih Wei, Su-May. Student pub. schs., Singapore. Asst. to adminstrv. sec. Applied Chems., Singapore, 1969-72; office mgr. EcoLab, Singapore, 1972-76, mng. dir., 1976—. Address: 11 Sunrise Dr, Singapore Singapore Office: Ecolab Singapore, 7 Fourth Lokyang Rd, Singapore Singapore

WONG, CHIN WAH, quantity surveyor; b. Singapore, Mar. 4, 1954; s. Joon Kai and Jee Lan (Kam) W.; m. Edna Teo Beng Kuan, Oct. 28, 1986. BS in Bldg. with honors, U. Singapore, 1979. Contracts officer Jurong Town Corp., Singapore, 1979-85, exec. contracts officer, 1985—; quantity surveyor Mass Rapid Transit Corp., Singapore, 1985-88. Served to lt. arty. Singapore Armed Forces, 1972-75. Mem. Singapore Inst. Surveyors (Gold Medal 1979). Club: Jurong Country. Home: 10 Lakepoint Dr, Apt #12-49, Singapore 2264, Singapore Office: Jurong Town Corp, Singapore Singapore

WONG, DAVID T., biochemist; b. Hong Kong, Nov. 6, 1935; s. Chi-Keung and Pui-King W.; m. Christina lee, Dec. 28, 1963; children—Conrad, Melvin, Vincent. Student, Nat. U. Taiwan, 1955-56; B.S., Seattle Pacific Coll., 1960; M.S., Oreg. State U., 1964; Ph.D., U. Oreg., 1966. Postdoctoral fellow U. Pa., Phila., 1966-68; sr. biochemist Lilly Research Labs., Indpls., 1968-72, research biochemist, 1973-77, sr. research scientist, 1978—. Contbr. numerous articles to sci. jours. Mem. Am. Soc. Pharmacology and Exptl. Therapeutics, Internat. Soc. Neurochemistry, Am. Soc. Neurochemistry, Soc. Neurosci. (pres. Indpls. chpt. 1987—), Soc. Chinese Biochemists in Am., N.Y. Acad. Scis., Indpls. Assn. Chinese Ams. (pres. 1987), Sigma Xi. Research on biochemistry and pharmacology of neurotransmission; development of new type of antidepressant drug, Fluoxetine, a selective inhibitor of serotonin uptake and Tomoxetine, a selective inhibitor of norepinephrine uptake; studies of potentially useful substances which activate transmission of norepinephrine, dopamine, serotonin, acetylcholine and GABA-neurons; studies of natural products led to the discovery of carboxylic ionophores: Narasin, A28695 and A204, which increase transport of cations across biomembranes. Office: Lilly Research Labs Indianapolis IN 46285

WONG, FRANCISCO LEE, trading company executive; b. Manila, Dec. 3, 1941; s. Yao Wong and Wee (Chan) Lee; m. Rachel Yu, June 8, 1969; children: Gigi Carol, Mary Ann, Francisco Jr., Alan David, Henry Joseph, Kendrick Ken, Kelvin Karl. BSEE, Mapua Inst. Tech., Manila, 1965. Asst. to pres. Gen. Offset Press Printing Co., Quezon City, Philippines, Phils. & Container Corp. & United Packing COrp. of the Phils., Quezon City, 1962-68; gen. mgr., treas., bd. dirs. Handyware Philippines, Inc., Quezon City, 1968-75, pres., gen. mgr., bd. dirs., 1975—, chmn. bd., 1970-76; exec. v.p., gen. mgr. Propak Philippines, Inc., Quezon City, 1971-75, pres., gen. mgr., bd. dirs., 1977—. Mem. Printing Assn. of the Philippines, Packaging Inst. Philippines, Potato Chips and Snacks Food Assn. (assoc.), Philippine C. of C., Philippine Columbian Assn. Clubs: Wack Wack Golf and Country (Mandaluyong); Manila Polo; Lodges: Rotary, Elks. Home: 662 Richmond St, Mandaluyong Philipines Office: Handyware Philippines Inc, 47-49 Malasimbo St, 3008 Quezon City Philippines

WONG, JAMES BOK, economist, engineer, technologist; b. Canton, People's Republic of China; came to U.S., 1938, naturalized, 1962; s. Gen Ham and Chen (Yee) W.; m. Wai Ping Lim, Aug. 3, 1946; children: John, Jane Doris, Julia Ann. BS in Agr., U. Md., 1949, BS in Chem. Engring., 1950; MS, U. Ill., 1951, PhD, 1954. Research asst. U. Ill., Champaign-Urbana, 1950-53; chem. engr. Standard Oil of Ind., Whiting, 1953-55; process design engr., research engr. Shell Devel. Co., Emeryville, Calif., 1955-61; sr. planning engr., prin. planning engr. Chem. Plastics Group, Dart Industries, Inc. (formerly Rexall Drug & Chem. Co.), Los Angeles, 1961-66, supr. planning and econs., 1966-67, mgr. long range planning and econs., 1967, chief economist, 1967-72, dir. econs. and ops. analysis, 1972-78, dir. internat. techs., 1978-81; pres. James B. Wong Assocs., Los Angeles, 1981—; chmn. exec. com., dir. United Pacific Bank, 1982-84, 86—; tech. cons. various corps. Contbr. articles to profl. jours. Bd. dirs., pres. Chinese Am. Citizens Alliance Found. Served with USAAF, 1943-46. Named to Exec. Order Ohio Commodores. Mem. Asian Am. Edn. Commn., 1971-81; recipient Los Angeles Outstanding Vol. Service award, 1977. Mem. Am. Inst. Chem. Engrs., Am. Chem. Soc. VFW (vice comdr. 1959), Sigma Xi, Tau Beta Pi, Phi Kappa Phi, Pi Mu Epsilon, Phi Lambda Upsilon, Phi Eta Sigma. Home: 2460 Venus Dr Los Angeles CA 90046

WONG, JOSEPH YIK NANG, chemist; b. Hong Kong, Aug. 25, 1938; s. Wing-Suen and So-Mui (Lai) W.; m. Josephine Kwai-Yue, Dec. 3, 1971; children: Joanne Sau-Ting, Anthony Lui-Kong. BSc with honors, McGill U., 1962, PhD, 1968. Chemist Noranda Research Ctr., Montreal, Que., Can., 1968-69, Merck Frosst Labs., Montreal, 1969-70; chemist Govt. Lab., Hong Kong, 1971-76, sr. chemist, 1976—; hoklas assessor Hong Kong lab. accreditation system, Hong Kong Govt., 1986—. Mem. Chem. Inst. Can., Can. Soc. Chem. Engring., Govt. Lab. Chemists Assn. Hong Kong. Home: 64C Macdonnell Rd, 8th Floor, Hong Kong Hong Kong Office: Govt Lab, 12-16 Oil St North Point, Hong Kong Hong Kong

WONG, LOUIS K.C., retail company executive; b. Hong Kong, Nov. 22, 1936; s. Y.Y. and Lan (Luk) W.; m. 1975; children: Rebecca Ying, Mia Yin. BA, U. Hong Kong, 1962. Import mgr. J.D. Hutchinson & Co., Ltd., Hong Kong, 1962-64; gen. mgr. Fidelity Merc. Co., Ltd., Hong Kong, 1964—; mng. dir. Fidelity Merc. Co., Ltd., London, 1982—; mng. dir. Wholesome Co., Ltd., Taiwan, 1976—. Mem. Hong Kong Exporters Assn. (chmn. 1980-81, 1987-89). Office: Fidelity Merc Co Ltd, 65 Wong Chuk Hang Rd, Hong Kong Hong Kong

WONG, YI-TING, food products executive; b. Peking, May 27, 1920; s. Cho-Min and Lu-Chi (Wang) W.; m. Shuan-hui Fang; children: Henry, Katherine, James, Wendy. BA, Nat. Associated Southwestern U., Republic of China, 1942. Chief mining div. Taiwan Provincial Govt., Taipei, Republic of China, 1948-52; dir. 3d dept. Taiwan Supply Bur., Taipei, 1952-56; pres. Taiwan Coal Control Commn., Taipei, 1956-60; convenor Fgn. Exchange and Trade Commn., Taipei, 1960-66; dir. SEC, Taipei, 1966-67; vice minister Econ. Ministry, Taipei, 1967-81; dir. gen. Bd. Fgn. Trade, Taipei, 1969-79; chmn. bd. dirs. Taiwan Sugar Corp., Taipei, 1981—; chmn. bd. dirs. Life Guard Pharm. Co., Taipei, 1984—. Contbr. editorials to newspapers and mags. Mem. cen. com. Kuo Min Tang, Taipei, 1981. Mem. Mont Pelerin Soc., Chinese Engrs. Soc. U.S. (Disting. Service award 1982). Buddhist. Home: 5 Lane 35, Sec 4 Jen Ai Rd, Taipei Republic of China Office: Taiwan Sugar Corp, 25 Pao Ching Rd, Taipei Republic of China

WONG-DIAZ, FRANCISCO RAIMUNDO, lawyer; b. Havana, Cuba, Oct. 29, 1944; came to U.S., Nov. 1961; s. Juan and Teresa (Diaz de Villegas) Wong; m. Maria Victoria Campos, 1986; 1 child, Richard Alan. BA with honors, No. Mich. U., 1963; MA with highest honors, U. Detroit, 1967; PhD, MA, U. Mich., 1973; JD, U. Calif.-Berkeley, 1976. Bar: Calif. 1980, U.S. Dist. Ct. (no. dist.) Calif. 1985, Fla. 1987. Asst. prof. San Francisco State U., 1977; vis. scholar U. Calif. Berkeley Sch. Bus., Berkeley, 1983-84; prof. City Coll. San Francisco, 1975—, dept. chmn., 1978-85; sole practice, Kentfield, Calif., 1980—; assoc. dean Miami-Dade Coll., 1986; dir. Cutcliffe Consulting, Inc., Hawthorne, LaFamila Ctr., Inc., San Rafael, Calif., 1980-85, Small Bus. Inst., Kentfield, 1982-86. Bd. editors Indsl. Relations Law Jour., 1975-76; lector St. Sebastian's Ch., 1984—. Diplomat-scholar U.S. Dept. State, Washington, 1976; Horace C. Rackham fellow U. Mich., 1970; NEH fellow, summer 1981. Mem. ABA, Am. Polit. Sci. Assn., Cuban Am. Nat. Council, World Affairs Council (seminar leader San Francisco 1980). Pan-Am. Soc. Roman Catholic. Club: Commonwealth.

WONG SIU HING, JEAN PAUL, management consulting company executive, industrial relations specialist; b. Port Louis, Mauritius, Nov. 22, 1943; s. Joseph and Elizabeth Look Moy (Chan Chiang) W.; m. Rosemay Fee Yin Kwoon Kung Mun, Aug. 18, 1966; children: Tony Paul, Davy Paul, Nadia. Student, U. Mauritius, 1973-75. Customs and excise officer Customs & Exçise Dept., Port Louis, Mauritius, 1961-77; personnel mgr. Ireland Blyth, Ltd., Port Louis, 1977-84, coordinator human resources dept.,, 1984—; cons. personnel and indsl. relations depts. Personnel Mgmt. Cons., Port Louis, 1982—. Hubert H. Humphrey fellow U.S. Info. Agy. U. Minn., 1987-88; Inst. Internat. Edn. fellow. Mem. Brit. Inst. Mgmt., Mauritius Inst. Mgmt., Internat. Indsl. Relations Assn.; Assn. Personnel Mgrs. (co-founder). Roman Catholic. Home: Corner Redoute & Cross Sts, Port Louis Mauritius Office: Ireland Blyth Ltd, Dr Ferriere St, Port Louis Mauritius

WONNEBERGER, REINHARD, theology educator, computer scientist; b. Forchheim, Germany, Sept. 30, 1946; s. Arthur and Elfriede (Blasig) W.; m. Brigitte Goecke, Apr. 25, 1980; children: Sigrun, Henrike. I. Theol.Exam., Bayrische Landeskirche, Munich, Fed. Republic Germany, 1970; II. Theol. Exam., Badische Landeskirche, Karlsruhe, Fed. Republic Germany, 1975; Dr. theol., U. Heidelberg, Fed. Republic Germany, 1975. Asst. prof. theology and EDP, U. Heidelberg, 1972-76, U. Hamburg, Fed. Republic Germany, 1977-86; computer scientist Electronic Data Systems (Deutschland) GmbH, Rüsselsheim, 1986—. Author: Syntax und Exegese, 1979; Understanding BHS (Biblica Hebraica Stuttgartensia), 1984; German, 1985; Verheissung und Versprechen, 1986; Kompaktführer LaTex, 1987; also numerous articles; expert in linguistics, on ethics of EDP. Lutheran. Office: EDS, Eisenstrasse 56 (N15), 6090 Rüsselsheim Federal Republic of Germany

WOO, SAVIO LAU CHING, molecular medical geneticist; b. Shaghai, China, Dec. 20, 1944; came to U.S., 1966; s. Kwok-Cheung and Fun-sin (Yu) W.; m. Emily H. Chang, July 14, 1973; children—Audrey C. C., Brian Y.Y. B.Sc., Loyola Coll., Montreal, Can., 1966; Ph.D., U. Wash., 1971. Asst. prof. cell biology Baylor Coll. Medicine, Houston, 1975-78, assoc. prof., 1979-83, prof., 1984—, prof. Inst. Molecular Genetics, 1985—, dir. grad. tng. program cell and molecular biology, 1987—; assoc. investigator Howard Hughes Med. Inst., Coconut Grove, Fla., 1977-79, investigator, 1979—; organizer, 1st chmn. Gordon Conf. on Molecular Genetics, 1985; co-organizer Searle-UCLA Symposium, 1986; cons. Cooper Lab., Palo Alto, Calif., 1982-84, Zymos Corp., Seattle, 1982-86; sr. sci. advisor Molecular Therapeutics, Inc., West Haven, 1986—, Am. Soc Human Genetics, 1985—. Mem. editorial bd. DNA, 1983—, Molecular Neurobiology, 1986, Genomics, 1987—; contbr. over 100 sci. articles to prof. publs. Mem. bd. dirs. March of Dimes Birth Defects Found., Met. Houston chpt., 1979-87. Mem. NIH (study sect. on molecular biology 1983-85, merit award, 1988—), Nat. Inst. Child Health and Human Devel. (bd. sci. counselors 1988—), Am. Soc. Biol. Chemists, Am. Soc. Cell Biology, N.Y. Acad. Scis., Soc. Study Inborn Errors of Metabolism (D. Noel Raime meml. award 1983).

WOO, SAVIO LAU-YUEN, bioengineering educator; b. Shanghai, Peoples Republic of China, June 3, 1942; s. Kwok CHong and Fung Sing (Yu) W.; m. Patricia Tak-kit Cheong, Sept. 6, 1969; children: Kirstin Wei-Chi, Jonathan I-Huei. BSME, Chico State U., 1965; MS, U. Wash., 1966, PhD, 1971. Research assoc. U. Wash., Seattle, 1968-70; asst. research prof. U. Calif.-San Diego, La Jolla, 1970-74, assoc. research prof., 1974-75, assoc. prof., 1975-80, prof. surgery and bioengring., 1980—; prin. investigator VA Med. Ctr., San Diego, 1972—; cons. bioengr. Childrens Hosp., San Diego, 1973-80; cons. med. implant cos., 1978-85; vis. prof. biomechanics Kobe, Japan U., 1981-82; dir., chief exec. officer M&D Coutts Inst. for Joint Reconstrn. and Research, 1984—. Assoc. editor: Jour. Biochem. Engring., 1979-87, Jour. Biomechanics, 1978—, Jour. Orthopedic Research, 1983—; contbr. articles to profl. jours. Recipient Elizabeth Winston Lanier Kappa Delta Award, 1983, 85, award for excellence in basic sci. research Am. Orthopaedic Soc. Sports Medicine, 1983, 86, Wartenweiler Meml. Lectureship Internat. Soc. Biomechs., 1987; Citation award Am. Coll. Sports Medicine, 1988; Japan Soc. of Promotion of Sci. fellow, 1981; Research Career Devel. award NIH, 1977-82, Citation award AM. Coll. Sports Medicine, 1988. Mem. ASME (sec., chmn. biomechanics com., chmn. honors com. bioengring. div., mem. exec. com., 1983-88, sec. 1985-86, chmn. 1986-87), Western Orthopaedic Assn., Biomed. Engring. Soc. (bd. dirs. 1984-86), Am. Acad. Orthopedic Surgeons, Orthopaedic Research Soc. (exec. com. 1983-88, chmn. program com. 1985-86, pres. 1986-87), Am. Soc. Biomechs. (pres. 1985-86, exec. com. 1977-80, 84-87), Internat. Soc. Fractures Repair (bd. dirs. 1984—, v.p. 1987—). Home: 4455 Heritage Glen Ln San Diego CA 92310 Office: U Calif San Diego Div Orthopaedic Surgery M-030 La Jolla CA 92093

WOO, SHUK SING BETTY, social services administrator, social worker; b. Canton, Peoples Republic of China, Apr. 4, 1949; d. Shek Tong and So Jue (Wong) W. B of Social Work with distinction, McGill U., Quebec, Can., 1975, MSW, 1976; diploma in exec. mgmt., Chinese U., Hong Kong, 1985. Case worker Salvation Army, Hong Kong, 1971-72; social worker Lutheran World Fedn. Dept. World Service, Hong Kong, 1972-74; coordinator child care ctrs. Hong Kong Christian Service, 1976-80, asst. dir., 1980—; mem. (under the Hong Kong Govt.) working group on rev. child care services Social Welfare Dept., 1978, working group on development residential child care services Health and Welfare Br., 1985-87, Panel Assessors in Magistrate Cts., 1982—, coordinating com. foster care service Social Welfare Dept., 1984-6; lectr. in-service tng. courses for child care ctrs. personnel and social workers. Mem. Welfare Digest Editorial Bd., 1977-80, 84-86, chmn., 1980-84; mem. working group Cen. Adminstrv. Support in Welfare Services under the Hong Kong Council of Social Service, 1980-81, com. polit. system Spl. Ref. to Social Welfare, 1985, Ad Hoc Group on Report on Young Persons, "Effects of Age in Civil Law" 1986, mgmt. com. Family Services and Child Care Div., 1978-80, 83-85, chmn., 1985-87; mem. Working Group on Family as Unit Welfare Planning, 1979-80, organizing com. Milti-Disciplinary Against Child Abuse Conf., 1986—; chmn. Preparatory Group for Formation of Hong Kong Child Care Workers Assn., 1978-80 and numerous other coms. Mem. YMCA, Hong Kong Social Workers Assn., Mental Health Assn. of Hong Kong, Hong Kong Council of Early Childhood Edn. and Services (vice chmn.), Outstanding Young Persons Assn., Hong Kong Child Care Workers Assn. (cons. 1981), Child Care Cen. Com. Mem. China Christian Ch. Club: The Kowloon (Hong Kong). Office: Hong Kong Christian Service, 33 Granville Rd, Tsimshatsui Hong Kong

WOO, VICTOR CHI-PANG, ophthalmologist; b. Shanghai, People's Republic China, Sept. 25, 1943; arrived in Hong Kong, 1950; s. Keing Bai and Yu Sing (Chu) W.; m. Maisie Wong; children: Monique, Anthony. MBBS, Hong Kong U., 1969; DO, Royal Coll. Eng., 1973. Ophthalmic surgeon Drs. Woo, Tong & Ptnrs., Hong Kong, 1974—; co. dir. Hong Kong Optical Co., Ltd., 1974—; Chmn. Hong Kong Eye Bank Research Found., 1987. Mem. Hong Kong Ophthal. Assn. (chmn. 1975-78, vice chmn. 1986—). Office: 150 Prince Edward Rd, Rm 703, Kowloon Hong Kong Hong Kong

WOOD, CHARLES CRESSON, information systems security consultant, educator; b. Phila., Feb. 22, 1955; s. Charles Wistar and Margaret Davis (Ansley) W. B.S.E. with honors in Acctg., U. Pa., 1976, M.S.E. in Computer and Info. Sci., 1979, M.B.A. in Fin., 1979. C.P.A., Calif. Teaching fellow computer sci. U. Pa., Phila., 1976-79; system performance engr. Booz-Allen & Hamilton, Washington, 1976; systems designer Am. Mgmt. Systems, Washington, 1977; acct. Richard Eisner & Co., N.Y.C., 1978; security cons., analyst specializing in fin. info. systems, computer security and privacy, cryptography; cons. in computer systems security Stanford Research Inst., Menlo Park, Calif., 1979-83; sr. info. security cons. Bank of Am., San Francisco, 1984-85; mem. faculty Golden Gate U., 1984-88; founder, prin. cons. Info. Integrity Investments, 1984—. Contbg. editor: Computers and Security mag., 1983—. Author 2 books on computer security; contbr. 45 tech. articles on info. security to profl. jours. Founder and former pres. Found. for Alternative Research; past bd. dirs. Mid-Peninsula Peace Ctr. EDP Auditors' Assn., World Future Soc., Info. Systems Security Assn. Quaker. Office: 2040 Polk St #313 San Francisco CA 94109

WOOD, DAVID ALVRA, educator, pathologist; b. Flora Vista, N.Mex., Dec. 21, 1904; s. Evans and Blanche D. (Wormell) W.; m. Ora Belle Bomberger, May 15, 1937; children—Kate Douglas (Mrs. K.J. Bossart, Jr.), David A., John Archer, William Allen, Charles Evans. A.B., Stanford U., 1926, M.D., 1930. Faculty Stanford, 1930-51; prof. pathology (oncology) U. Calif. Sch. Medicine, 1951-72; prof. emeritus U. Calif. Sch. Med., 1972—; dir. Cancer Research Inst., 1951-72, research oncologist, 1972-74, cons., 1974—; Cons. pathology San Francisco area VA, 1949-66; cons. Nat. Cancer Inst., USPHS, 1956-70; participant Nat. Cancer Program Plan, chmn. screening population groups, 1971-74; spl. cons., co-chmn. adv. com. cancer control program Bur. State Services USPHS, 1959-64; mem. cancer adv. council, Calif., 1959—, chmn., 1966-71; mem. U.S. nat. com. Nat. Acad. Scis. to Internat. Union Against Cancer, 1961-63; U.S. nat. organizing com. to 10th Internat. Cancer Congress, 1967-70; mem. Am. Joint Com. on Colon, Rectum and Anus, 1962-84; research collaborator, med. dept Brookhaven Nat. Lab., Upton, N.Y., 1963-71; chmn. external adv. com. U. Chgo. Cancer Center, 1973-83; mem. fellowships selection com. Internat Agy. Research on Cancer, WHO, Lyon, France, 1970-73, Internat. Reference Center (stomach, esophagus) WHO, Tokyo, 1968-74; rep. Internat. Socs. Pathology at WHO meeting in, Turku, Finland, 1974; mem. cadre and chmn. subcom. Pathology Nat. Large Bowel Cancer Project, U. Tex., Houston, 1973-75. Editorial bd.: Cancer Excerpta Medica, Amsterdam, Netherlands, Jour. Soviet Oncology, 1981-85; Author profl. articles on dual pulmonary circulation of lungs, neoplastic diseases, med. edn., acute virus hepatitis. Served to capt. M.C. USNR, World War II. Recipient award and medal Am. Joint Com. Cancer Staging and End Result Reporting, 1969; Meritorious Service award SSS, 1972. Fellow Am. Coll. Radiology (hon.), Am. Geog. Soc., Royal Soc. Medicine (London); mem. Calif. Med. Assn. (chmn. cancer commn. 1958-60, vice chmn. 1960-63, sci. bd. 1963-71, chmn. cancer com. 1963-67), Am. Cancer Soc. (Bronze medal 1950, Nat. Service award 1972, pres. 1956-57, hon. life.), Armed Forces Inst. Pathology (sci. adv. bd. 1956-61, hon. cons. 1969), Internat. Acad. Pathology, Am. Soc. Cytology (hon.; chmn. awards com. 1958-65), Assn. Clin. Pathologists Gt. Britain (corr.), Coll. Am. Pathologists (pres. 1952-55, Sci. Products Found award 1958), Calif. Acad. Sci., James Ewing Soc. (Lucy Wortham James award 1970), Am. Assn. Cancer Insts. (pres. 1970-72), Am. Assn. Cancer Edn. (historian 1981—, Samuel C. Harvey lectr. 1973, Margaret Edwards medal 1987), Calif. Acad. Medicine, AMA (council vol. health agys. 1952-63, chmn. com. on continuing profl. edn. program of vol. health agys.), Am. Assn. Pathologists, Am. Assn. Cancer Reearch, Fedn. Am. Soc. Exptl. Biology, Arthur Purdy Stout Soc. Surg. Pathologists (hon.), Stanford Med. Alumni Assn. (pres. 1947, J.E. Wallace Sterling Disting. Alumnus award 1988), S.A.R., Sigma Xi, Phi Lambda Upsilon. Clubs: Commonwealth of Calif. (San Francisco), Pacific Union (San Francisco). Home: 54 Commonwealth Ave San Francisco CA 94118

WOOD, FERGUS JAMES, geophysicist, consultant; b. London, Ont., Can., May 13, 1917; came to U.S., 1924, naturalized, 1932; s. Louis Aubrey and Dora Isabel (Elson) W.; student U. Oreg., 1934-36; A.B., U. Calif.-Berkeley, 1938, postgrad., 1938-39; postgrad. U. Chgo., 1939-40, U. Mich., 1940-42, Calif. Inst. Tech., 1946; m. Doris M. Hack, Sept. 14, 1946; children—Kathryn Celeste Wood Madden, Bonnie Patricia Wood Ward. Teaching asst. U. Mich., 1940-42; instr. in physics and astronomy Pasadena City Coll., 1946-48, John Muir Coll., 1948-49; asst. prof. physics U. Md., 1949-50; assoc. physicist Johns Hopkins U. Applied Physics Lab., 1950-55; sci. editor Ency. Americana, N.Y.C., 1955-60; aero. and space research scientist, sci. asst. to dir. Office Space Flight Programs, Hdqrs., NASA, Washington, 1960-61; program dir. fgn. sci. info. NSF, Washington, 1961-62; phys. scientist, chief sci. and tech. info. staff U.S. Coast and Geodetic Survey (now Nat. Ocean Service), Rockville, Md., 1962-66, phys. scientist Office of Dir., 1967-73, research asso. Office of Dir., 1973-77; cons. tidal dynamics, Bonita, Calif., 1978—. Served to capt. USAAF, 1942-46. Recipient Spl. Achievement award Dept. Commerce, NOAA, 1970, 74, 76, 77. Mem. Sigma Pi Sigma, Pi Mu Epsilon, Delta Phi Alpha. Democrat. Presbyterian. Author: The Strategic Role of Perigean Spring Tides in Nautical History and North American Coastal Flooding, 1635-1976, 1978; Tidal Dynamics; Coastal Flooding and Cycles of Gravitational Force, 1986; contbr. numerous articles to encys., reference sources, profl. jours.; writer, tech. dir. documentary film: Pathfinders from the Stars, 1967; editor-in-chief: The Prince William Sound, Alaska, Earthquake of 1964 and Aftershocks, vols. 1-2A and sci. coordinator vols. 2B, 2C and 3, 1966-69. Home: 3103 Casa Bonita Dr Bonita CA 92002

WOOD, JACALYN KAY, educational consultant; b. Columbus, Ohio, May 25, 1949; d. Carleston John and Grace Anna (Schumacher) W. B.A., Georgetown Coll., 1971; M.S., Ohio State U., 1976; Ph.D., Miami U., 1981. Elem. tchr. Bethel-Tate Schs., Ohio, 1971-73, Columbus (Ohio) Christian Sch., 1973-74, Franklin (Ohio) Schs., 1974-79; teaching fellow Miami U., Oxford, Ohio, 1979-81; cons. intermediate grades Erie County Schs., Sandusky, Ohio, 1981— presenter tchr. inservice tng. Mem. council Sta. WVIZ-TV, 1981—; mem. exec. com. Perkins Community Schs., 1981-85; mem. community adv. bd. Sandusky Vols. Am., Sandusky Soc. Bank, vol. Firelands Community Hosp. Mem. Am. Businesswomen's Assn. (local pres. 1985), Assn. Supervision and Curriculum Devel., Internat. Reading Assn., Ohio Sch. Suprs. Assn. (regional pres. 1986, state pres. 1986-87), Phi Delta Kappa (local sec. 1985, 86). Baptist. Home: 320 Fremont Ave Apt #4 Sandusky OH 44870 Office: 2902 Columbus Ave Sandusky OH 44870

WOOD, JAMES, supermarket executive; b. Newcastle-upon-Tyne, Eng., Jan. 19, 1930; came to U.S., 1974; s. Edward and Catherine Wilhelmina (Parker) W.; m. Colleen Margaret Taylor, Aug. 14, 1954; children: Julie, Sarah. Grad., Loughborough Coll., Leicestershire, England. Chief food chain Newport Coop. Soc., S. Wales, U.K., 1959-62, Grays Food Coop. Soc., Eng., 1962-66; dir., joint dep. mng. dir. charge retailing Cavenham, Ttd., Hayes, Eng., 1966-80; pres. Grand Union Co., Elmwood Park, N.J., 1973-79; chief exec. officer, dir. Grand Union Co., from 1973, chmn. bd., 1979-80; chmn. bd., chief exec. officer Gt. Atlantic & Pacific Tea Co., Inc., 1980—; bd. dirs. Irma Fabrikerne A/S, Denmark, Schering-Plough Corp. Bd. govs. James Madison Coll., Harrisonburg, Va. Served with Brit. Army, 1948-50. Mem. Food Mktg. Inst. (bd. dirs.). Roman Catholic. Office: Great Atlantic & Pacific Tea Co Inc 2 Paragon Dr Montvale NJ 07645

WOOD, JAMES E., JR., religion educator, author; b. Portsmouth, Va., July 29, 1922; s. James E. and Elsie Elizabeth (Bryant) W.; m. Alma Leacy McKenzie, Aug. 12, 1943; 1 son, James Edward III. BA, Carson-Newman Coll., 1943; MA, Columbia U., 1949; BD, So. Bapt. Theol. Sem., 1947, ThM, 1948; PhD, So. Baptist Theol. Sem., 1957; postgrad., U. Tenn., 1943-44; cert. in Chinese, Yale U., 1949-50; Japanese diploma, Naganuma Sch. Japanese Studies, Tokyo, 1950-51, Oxford U., Eng., 1983; LLD hon., Seinan Gakuin U., Japan, 1983. Ordained to ministry So. Bapt. Ch., 1942. Pastor So. Bapt. chs., Tenn. and Ky., 1942-48; missionary to Japan 1950-55; prof. religion and lit. Seinan Gakuin U., Japan, 1951-55; prof. history of religions Baylor U., Waco, Tex., 1955-73, dir. honors program, 1959-64; dir. J.M. Dawson Inst. Ch.-State Studies Baylor U., 1959-73, 80—, chmn. interdeptl. grad. degree program in ch.-state studies, 1962-73, 80—, Simon and Ethel Bunn prof. ch.-state studies, 1980—, chmn. faculty-student Far Eastern exchange program, 1970-72; exec. dir. Bapt. Joint Com. on Public Affairs, Washington, 1972-80; mem. central panel Bapt. World Alliance Commn. on Religious Liberty and Human Rights, 1965-75, Commn. on Freedom, Justice and Peace, 1976-80, Commn. Human Rights, 1981—; chmn. Bapt. Com. on Bicentennial, 1973-76; mem. So. Bapt. Inter-Agy. Council, 1972-80, vice chmn., 1975-76, sec., 1976-77; vis. prof. So. Bapt. Theol. Sem., Louisville, 1974, Okla. Bapt. U., Shawnee, 1977, N.Am. Bapt. Sem., Sioux Falls, S.D., 1974, 79; vis. lectr. Ashland (Ohio) Theol. Sem., 1971; Vernon Richardson lectr. Univ. Bapt. Ch., Balt., 1975; lectr. Notre Dame U., 1980, Carver-Barnes lectr. Southeastern Bapt. Theol. Sem., 1981; Asian Found. lectr. Seinan Gakuin U., Japan, 1983; lectr. Campbell U., 1985, Brigham Young U., 1986, U. Kans., 1987; vice chmn. Nat. Com. for Amish Religious Freedom, 1960-68; mem. Nat. Com. for Restoration Blue Lake Lands to Taos Indians, 1963-70; cons. asst. secretariat on religious liberty World Council Chs., 1963-65. Author: A History of American Literature: An Anthology, 1952, (with others) Church and State in Scripture, History and Constitutional Law, 1958, The Problem of Nationalism, 1969, Nationhood and the Kingdom, 1977, Secular Humanism and the Public Schools, 1986; editor: Markham Press Fund, Baylor U. Press, 1970-72; founding editor: Jour. Ch. and State, 1959-73, 80—, mem. editorial council, 1973-80; mem. editorial bd. Religion and Pub. Edn., Religious Freedom Reporter; editor, contbr.: Church and State, 1960, Jewish-Christian Relations in Today's World, 1971, Baptists and the American Experience, 1977, Religion and Politics, 1983, Religion, the State, and Education, 1984, Religion and the State, 1985, Report from the Capital, 1975-80; area editor, contbr.: Ency. So. Bapts., 1982; contbr.: We Hold These Truths, 1964, The Teacher's Yoke, 1964, The Best of Church and State, 1948-75, Issues in Church and State, 1977, Taxation and the Free Exercise of Religion, 1978, First World Congress on Religious Liberty, 1978, The Church, The State and Human Rights, 1980, The Minister's Manual: 1982-83, Freedom of Religion in America, 1982, Government Intervention in Religious Affairs 1982, Dictionary of Theology, 1982, Religion, Education and the First Amendment, 1986, Taking Sides: Clashing Views on Controversial Political Issues, 1986, Church and State in American History, 1987, Global Outreach: Global Congress of the World's Religions, 1987, Dictionary of Christianity in America, 1988, Ecumenical Perspective on Church and State: Protestant, Catholic and Jewish, 1988, Readings in Church and State, 1988; contbr. numerous articles to profl. jours. Sponsor Ams. for Public Schs., 1963-68; bd. dirs. Waco (Tex.) Planned Parenthood, 1966-72, pres., 1971-72; sponsor Christians Concerned for Israel, 1968—, Tex. Conf. Chs. Consultation on Religion and Public Edn., 1971, Nat. Christian Leadership Conf. for Israel, 1978—; pres. Waco area ACLU, bd. dirs. Tex. unit, 1968-72; pres. Nat. Council Religion and Public Edn., 1979-83, exec. com., 1975—, bd. dirs., 1972—; chmn. exec. com. Council Washington Reps. on UN, 1977-80, mem. council exec. com., 1973-80; exec. com. Nat. Coalition on Public Edn. and Religious Liberty, 1973—; mem. religious liberty com. Nat. Council Chs. U.S.A., 1972—, also mem. com. internat. concerns on human rights; Am. rep. Chs. Montreux Colloquium on Helsinki Final Act, 1977; v.p. Waco Conf. Christians and Jews, Internat. Acad. for Freedom of Religion and Belief, 1987—; trustee Internat. Devel. Conf., 1974-80; adv. com. Am.-Israel Friendship League, 1977—; founder, chmn. Waco Human Rights Week, 1981—. Recipient Disting. Alumnus award Carson-Newman Coll., 1974; Religious Liberty award Alliance for Preservation of Religious Liberty, 1980; award Hadassah, 1981; Human Rights award Waco Conf. Christians and Jews, 1986; hon. Tex. col., 1969. Mem. Am. Soc. Ch. History, Am. Acad. Religion, Am. Soc. Internat. Law, N. Am. Soc. Ecumenists, NCCJ (ad. com. on ch. state and taxation 1979-85), ACLU, Phi Eta Sigma, Pi Kappa Delta, Alpha Psi Omega. Home: 3306 Lake Heights Dr Waco TX 76708 Office: Box 380 Baylor Univ Waco TX 76798

WOOD, JOHN WALTER, JR., advertising agency executive, international relations consultant; b. N.Y.C., July 7, 1941; s. John Walter Sr. and Suzanne (Cort) W.; m. Charlotte Mary Baron Cusack-Jobson; 1 son, William Duncan. BA first class, Trinity Coll., Ireland, 1962, MA; postgrad., London Sch. Econs.; MA with distinction in Internat. Relations, U. So. Calif., 1978; MA, Oxford U., 1986. Chief copy dept. C.P.V. Kenyon & Eckhardt, Ltd., London, 1965; assoc. creative dir. Pritchard Wood & Partner, London, 1965-68; chmn. Wood Brigdale & Co., London, 1968—; bd. dirs. Oxford Analytica Ltd; chmn. Trilateral Communications Ltd, 1986—; chmn. Republicans Abroad; bd. advisors Sch. Internat. Relations, U. So. Calif.; gov. Regents Coll., London. Author: The Instrument of Advertising, 1977; The Question of Costs, 1978; (with others) The Implementation of American Defense Policy in Western Europe, 1983. Chmn. Republicans Abroad, Eng.; advisor Fullbright Commn. Recipient various advt. awards, including Cannes Film, Venice Film, Cork Film, Hollywood Broadcast, N.Y. Broadcast festivals. Fellow Inst. Dirs.; mem. Anglo-Am. C. of C., Assn. Polit. Risk Analysis, Internat. Soc. Polit. Psychology, Westminster C. of C., Anglo-Dutch C. of C., Royal Inst. Internat. Affairs, Internat. Inst. Strategic Studies, Mind Assn., Aristotelian Soc. Clubs: Hurlingham, Oxford, Cambridge, Royal Automobile, Bucks London, Union, Shinnecock Yacht. Office: Wood Brigdale & Co Ltd, Kent House, Market Place, London W1, England

WOOD, LARRY (MARY LAIRD), journalist, author, university educator, public relations executive; b. Sandpoint, Idaho; d. Edward Hayes and Alice (McNeel) Small; children: Mary, Marcia, Barry. BA magna cum laude, U. Wash., 1938, MA with highest honors, 1940; postgrad., Stanford U., 1941-42, U. Calif., Berkeley, 1946-47; cert. in photography, U. Calif., Berkeley, 1971; postgrad. journalism, U. Wis., 1971-72, U. Minn., 1971-72, U. Ga., 1972-73; postgrad. in art, architecture and marine biology, U. Calif., Santa Cruz, 1974-76, Stanford Hopkins Marine Sta., Santa Cruz, 1977-80. Feature writer and columnist 1939—; prof. pub. relations and journalism San Diego State U., 1974, 75; vis. prof. journalism San Jose State U., 1976; assoc. prof. journalism Calif. State U., Hayward, 1978; prof. sci. and environ. journalism U. Calif. Berkeley Extension, 1979—. Contbr. over 3,000 articles on real estate, architecture, edn., oceanography, science, environment, bus. and travel for newspapers, nat. mags., popular sci. mags., nat. and internat. newspaper syndicates, inflight mags., city mags., travel and architecture mags. including Oakland Tribune, Seattle Times, San Francisco Chronicle, Parade, San Jose Mercury News, Christian Sci. Monitor, MonitoRadio, Sports Illus., Mechanix Illus., Popular Mechanics, Parents, House Beautiful, Oceans, Sea Frontiers, PSA Mag., AAA Westways, AAA Motorland, Hawaiian Airlines in Paradise, Linguapress, Travel & Leisure, Family Handyman, Chevron USA. Significant works include home and garden columnist and editor, 5-part series Pacific Coast Ports, 5-part series Railroads of the West, San Francisco Cultural Scene, Endangered Species, Megamouth New Species of Shark, Columbia Receding Glacier, Calif. Underwater Parks, Ebey's Landing Nat. Hist. Preserve, Los Angeles Youth Gangs, Hist. Carousels, Idaho's Big Lakes. Co-author over 20 books including: McGraw-Hill English for Social Living, 1944, Fawcett Boating Books, 1956-66, Fodor's San Francisco, 1982—, Fodor's California, 1984—, Charles Merrill Focus on Life Science, Focus on Physical Science, 1983, 87, Social Issues Research Inc.'s Earth Science, 1988, Woltors-Nordoff-Longman English Language Texts, 1988. Reviewer for Charles Merrill texts, 1983-84; book reviewer for Professional Communicator, 1987—. Nat. chmn. travel writing contest for U.S. univ. journalism students Assn. for Edn. in Journalism/Soc. Am. Travel Writers, 1979-83; judge writing contest for Nat. Assn. Real Estate Editors, 1982-84; mem. adv. bd. KRON/TV, 1986—. Numerous awards, honors, citations, speaking engagements including induction into Broadway Hall of Fame, Seattle, 1984, citations for environ. writing from Nat. Park Service, U.S. Forest Service, Bur. Land Mgmt., Oakland Mus. Assn., Oakland C. of C.; co-recipient Nat. Headliner award for Best Sunday Newspaper Mag. Mem. Pub. Relations Soc. Am. (charter mem. travel and tourism div.), Nat. Sch. Pub. Relations Assn., Environ. Cons. N.Am., Assn. Edn. in Journalism (exec. bd. nat. mag. div. 1978, panel chmn. 1979, 80), Women in Communications (nat. bd. officer 1975-77), Soc. Profl. Journalists (nat. bd. for hist. sites 1980—), Nat. Press Photographers Assn., Nat. Assn. Sci. Writers, Calif. Writers Club (officer 1967, 72), Am. Assn. Med. Writers, Soc. Am. Travel Writers, Internat. Oceanographic Found., Oceanic Soc., Calif. Acad. Environ. News Writers, U. Wash. Alumni (life, charter mem. ocean scis. alumni), U. Calif.-Berkeley Alumni (life), Stanford Alumni, Mortar Board Alumnae Assn., Phi Beta Kappa, Theta Sigma Phi. Home: 6161 Castle Dr Oakland CA 94611

WOOD, MARCUS JOHN, electronics company executive; b. Rugby, Eng., Jan. 3, 1950; s. Gilbert Allen and Jean Gardiner W.; m. Maureen Lynn Adie, July 14, 1972; children: Christopher Paul, Katherine Anne. BSc in Physics with honors, U. Dundee, Scotland, 1972, PhD, 1975. Engr. Marconi Electronic Devices Ltd., Billericay, Eng., 1975-78, group leader, 1979-82, tech. mgr., 1983-85; tech. mktg. mgr. M.M. Microwave Ltd., York, Eng., 1985-86; mgr. microwave components group Ferranti PLC, Dundee, 1987—. Contbr. articles to profl. jours. Office: Ferranti PLC, Dunsinane Ave, Dundee DD2 3PN, Scotland

WOOD, OLIVER GILLAN, JR., banking and finance educator; b. Greer, S.C., Apr. 27, 1937; s. Oliver Gillan and Grace (McBrayer) W.; m. Patricia Myers, Apr. 27, 1978; 1 child: Brian Jay; stepchildren: Mary Ross, Merrill Ross, Michael Ross. BBA, U. S.C., 1958, MA in Econs., 1963; PhD, U. Fla., 1965. Asst. prof. banking and fin. U. S.C., Columbia, 1965-68, assoc. prof. banking and fin., 1968-73, prof. banking and fin., 1973—; chmn. U. S.C. Press com. Author: Commercial Banking, 1978, (with others) Analysis of Bank Financial Statements, 1979, Introduction to Money and Banking, 1980, (with others) How to Borrow Money, 1981. Bd. dirs., founder Republic Nat. Bank, Columbia, 1975-87. Served to Capt. USNR, 1959-87. Mem. Am. Econs. Assn., Am. Fin. Assn., Fin. Mgmt. Assn., So. Fin. Assn., Eastern Fin. Assn., Beta Gamma Sigma (pres. 1972). Home: 3601 Boundbrook Ln Columbia SC 29206 Office: U SC Coll Bus Adminstrn Columbia SC 29208

WOOD, PHILOMENA TERESA, advertising executive; b. Warrington, Cheshire, Eng., Jan. 13, 1931; d. Thomas Patrick and May Veronica (Turner) Toole; m. Arthur Preston Wood, June 22, 1957; 1 child, Graeme Nicholas. Grad. pvt. sch., Cheshire. Clk. Wales Post Office, 1949-52; caterer small hotels, Wales, 1952-53; clk. FWW and Co., Ltd., Wales, 1953-56; asst. to publicity mgr. AEI Industries, Manchester, Lancashire, Eng., 1956-58;

clk./typist Engring. Cons., Manchester, 1958-65; classifed exec., gen. asst. Advt. Agy., Manchester, 1970-75; account exec., asst. dir. Arthur Wood Assocs., Manchester, 1975-80; dir. Arthur Wood Advt. Ltd., Manchester, 1980—. Club: Didsbury Golf. Home: 19 Valley Dr, Wilmslow, Cheshire SK9 3DN, England Office: Arthur Wood Advt Ltd, Dane Rd, Sale, Cheshire M33 1BP, England

WOOD, ROBERT HART, consulting civil engineer; b. Columbus, Miss., Dec. 9, 1910; s. Charles Lyon and Lena (Roden) W.; m. Esther Louise Drake, Sept. 21, 1940; children: Robert Hart, Charles Drake, Sarah Esther. B.S.C.E., Miss. State Coll., 1932; M.S.C.E., Purdue U., 1933. Registered profl. engr., Ky., Miss., Ind., Mich., Tenn., Ark., Ga., La. With Miss. Hwy. Dept., 1933-37, 38-40, 46; structural designer Va. Bridge Co., Birmingham, Ala., 1937-38; asst. chief engr., then asso. Hazelet & Erdal (cons. engr.), Louisville, 1946-56; partner Hazelet & Erdal (cons. engr.), 1956-81, spl. cons., 1981—. Author articles in field. Trustee Ridgewood Assn., 1954-58; mem. Louisville and Jefferson County Planning and Zoning Commn., 1954-57. Served to lt. col. AUS, 1940-46. Fellow ASCE (life); fellow Am. Cons. Engrs. Council (life), Am. Concrete Inst.; mem. Ky. Soc. Profl. Engrs. (life, Outstanding Engr. in Pvt. Practice award 1975-76), Cons. Engrs. Council Ky. (life; dir., past pres.), Internat. Assn. Bridge and Structural Engrs., Louisville Area C. of C. (charter), Hon. Order Ky. Cols., Sigma Xi, Tau Beta Pi, Phi Kappa Phi. Democrat. Presbyterian. Clubs: Pendennis (Louisville), Big Spring Country (Louisville). Home: 502 Ridgewood Rd Louisville KY 40207

WOOD, ROBERT RAY, fastener industry manufacturing executive; b. Coffeyville, Kans., Dec. 19, 1942; s. Robert Gould and Geraldine Rosalie (Newman) W.; B.S., U. Wyo., 1966; M.B.A., No. Ill. U., 1974; m. Nola Jean Freouf, June 7, 1964; children—Robert Dean, Todd Ray. With Ingersoll Milling Machine Co., Rockford, Ill., 1966-82, controller, 1972-76, v.p. fin., 1976-82, sec., 1982-84; pres. Ingersoll Cutting Tool Co., 1982-87; chmn., pres., chief exec. officer, Rockford Products Corp., 1987—; mem. audit com., dir. First Nat. Bank & Trust Co., Rockford; dir., mem. exec. com. First Community Bancorp. Asst. state chief Y-Indian guide program; past mem. mgmt. adv. bd. Rock Valley Coll.; bd. dirs. Civic League Winnebago County, 1975, Wesley Willows Retirement and Nursing Center, 1975-78; bd. dirs. YMCA, 1976—, treas., 1979—, 2 v.p., 1981, pres., 1982; recipient Vol. of Yr. award, 1975; pres. NW Community Nursery Sch., 1971; bd. dirs., treas. Rockford Community Trust; bd. dirs. treas. Blackhawk Area council Boy Scouts Am.; pres. Rockford United Way, 1986 bd. dirs. Boylan Edn. Found.; chmn. long-range planning com. Christ United Meth. Ch. Recipient Excalibur award Rockford Newspapers, 1984; Silver Beaver award Boy Scouts Am., 1985. Mem. Nat. Assn. Accts., Fin. Execs. Inst. (charter, 2d v.p. 1978-79, pres. 1979-80), Cutting Tool Mfrs. Assn. (Midwest pub. affairs chmn.), Pres. Assn. of Am. Mgmt. Assns., Young Presidents Orgn., Alpha Kappa Psi (chpt. pres. 1965). Club: Rockford Rotary (Service above Self award 1983). Home: 1610 Shaw Woods Dr Rockford IL 61107 Office: 505 Fulton Ave Rockford IL 61103

WOOD, ROBERT WARREN, lawyer; b. Des Moines, July 5, 1955; s. Merle Warren and Cecily Ann (Sherk) W.; m. Beatrice Wood, Aug. 4, 1979; 1 child, Bryce Mercedes. Student, U. Sheffield, Eng., 1975-76; AB, Humboldt State U., 1976; JD, U. Chgo., 1979. Bar: Ariz. 1979, Calif. 1980, U.S. Tax Ct. 1980. Assoc. Jennings, Strouss, Phoenix, 1979-80, McCutchen, Doyle, San Francisco, 1980-82, Broad, Khourie, San Francisco, 1982-85; assoc. Steefel, Levitt & Weiss, San Francisco, 1985-87, ptnr., 1987—; instr. in law U. Calif. San Francisco, 1981-82. Author: Taxation of Corporate Liquidations: A Complete Planning Guide, 1987, The Executive's Complete Guide to Business Taxes, 1988; author: (with others) California Closely Held Corporations: Tax Planning and Practice Guide, 1987; mem. editorial bd. Jour. Corporate Taxation, Taxation for Lawyers, Jour. Real Estate Taxation, Jour. Bank Taxation, Corporate Taxation, Journal of Taxation of S Corporations, S Corporations: The Journal of Tax, Legal and Business Strategies; contbr. articles to profl. jours. Mem. Calif. Bd. Legal Specialization (cert. specialist taxation). Republican. Office: Steefel Levitt & Weiss One Embarcadero Ctr 29th Floor San Francisco CA 94111

WOOD, ROBERTA SUSAN, foreign service officer; b. Clarksdale, Miss., Oct. 4, 1948; d. Robert Larkin and Dorothy Eloise (Shelton) Wood; B.A. with distinction, Southwestern U., Memphis, 1970; postgrad. Nat. U. Cuyo, Mendoza, Argentina, 1970-71; M.P.A., Harvard U., 1980. Joined U.S. Fgn. Service, 1972; service in Manila, Naples and Turin, Italy and Port-au-Prince, Haiti; mgmt. analyst Dept. State, Washington, 1980-84; U.S. consul gen., Jakarta, Indonesia, 1984-87, NATO Def. Coll., Rome, 1987-88; U.S. Consul Gen. Marseilles, France, 1988—. Fulbright scholar, 1970-71. Mem. Am. Fgn. Service Assn., Consular Officers Assn., Friends of Nat. Zoo, Friends of Kennedy Center, Planned Parenthood Washington, Phi Beta Kappa. Home and Office: Marseille American Embassy APO New York NY 09777

WOOD, SAMUEL EUGENE, college administer, psychology educator; b. Brotherton, Tenn., Aug. 16, 1934; s. Samuel Ernest and Daisy J. (Jernigan) W.; m. Helen J. Walker, June 2, 1956; children: Liane Wood Kelly, Susan Wood Benson, Alan Richard; m. Ellen Rosenthal Green, Sept. 8, 1977; stepchildren: Bart M. Green, Julie Alice Green. BS in English and Music, Tenn. Tech. U., 1961; M in Edn. Adminstrn., U. Fla., 1967, D in Edn., 1969. Asst. prof. edn. W.Va. U., 1968-70; asst. prof. edn. U. Mo., St. Louis, 1970-75, mem. doctoral faculty, 1973-75; dir. research Ednl. Devel. Ctr., Belleville, Ill., 1976-81; prof. psychology Meramec Coll., St. Louis, 1981—; pres. Higher Edn. Ctr., St. Louis, 1985—; exec. dir. Edn. Opportunity Ctrs., St. Louis, 1985—; bd. commrs. Pub. TV Com., St. Louis, 1985—; planning com. St. Louis Schs., 1985—; administr. German-Am. Student Exchange Program Internat. Bus. Students, 1985—; sponsor Higher Edn. Ctr. Internat. Edn. Council, 1985—; co-founder, pres. Higher Edn. Cen. Cable TV Channel, Sta. HEC-TV, St. Louis, 1986. Musician, composer with U.S. Navy Band, 1956-59; composer A Nautical Musical Comedy, A chilkds Garden of Verses in Song, 1979; numerous poems set to music; contbr. articles to ednl. and sci. jours. Served with USN, 1955-59. US Office Edn. grantee 1976-81, 85. Mem. Internat. Edn. Consortium (bd. dirs. 1985—), Phi Kappa Phi. Democrat. Baptist. Home: 5 Sona Ln Saint Louis MO 63141 Office: Higher Edn Ctr 928A N McKnight Rd Saint Louis MO 63132

WOOD, SHELTON EUGENE, educator, consultant; b. Douglas, Ga., May 20, 1938; s. Shelton and Mae Lillie (Pheil) W.; A.A., St. Johns U., 1958; B.A., U. Nebr., 1959; M.Ed., Coll. William and Mary, 1971; Ph.D., Sussex U., 1973; Ed.D., Nova U., 1975; M.A., Central Mich. U., 1977; m. Edna Louise Tanner, Aug. 25, 1958; children—Shelton John, Deirdre Louise. Area mgr. Marshall Fields Corp., Fla., 1957-58; transp. supr. Greyhound Corp., Jacksonville, Fla., 1959-62; commd. lt. U.S. Army, 1963, advanced through grades to lt. col., 1977; with Redstone Readiness Group, 1977-80; chief studies and analysis div. Korean Inst. for Def. Analysis, 1981-83; faculty St. Johns River Community Coll., 1984—. Active Boy Scouts Am., 1977—; lay leader United Meth. Ch., Falls Church, Va., 1977-79. Decorated Bronze Star with 2 oak leaf clusters, Air Medal with 3 oak leaf clusters, Purple Heart. Fellow Sussex Coll., 1969-70. Mem. Am. Soc. Trainers and Developers (pres. S.E. chpt. 1974-75), Am. Def. Preparedness Assn., NEA, Phi Kappa Delta, Phi Delta Kappa. Clubs: Masons, Shriners. Author: An Analysis of Incoming Freshmen at NSC, 1975; Choice of College Factors, 1976; 71 articles and reports in field of mil. tng., edn. and mgmt. Address: PO Box 820 San Mateo FL 32088

WOOD, WILLIAM MCBRAYER, lawyer; b. Greenville, S.C., Jan. 27, 1942; s. Oliver Gillan and Grace (McBrayer) W.; m. Nancy Cooper, Feb. 17, 1973; children: Margaret, Walter, Lewis. BS in Acctg., U. S.C., 1964, JD cum laude, 1972; LLM in Estate Planning (scholar), U. Miami, 1980. Bar: S.C. 1972, Fla. 1979, D.C. 1973, U.S. Tax Ct. 1972, U.S. Ct. Claims 1972, U.S. Supreme Ct. 1977. Intern ct. of claims sect., tax div. U.S. Dept. Justice, 1971; law clk. to chief judge U.S. Ct. Claims, Washington, 1972-74; ptnr. firm Edwards Wood, Duggan & Reese, Greer and Greenville, 1974-78; asst. prof. law Cumberland Law Sch., Samford U., Birmingham, Ala., 1978-79; faculty Nat. Inst. Trial Advocacy, N.E. Regional Inst., Hofstra U., 1979, 83-87, teaching team 5th intensive trial techniques course, 1983; ptnr. firm Shutts & Bowen, Miami, 1980-85; sole practice, Miami, 1985—. Contbg. editor: The Lawyers PC; Fla. editor: Drafting Wills and Trust Agreements; substantive com. editor ABA: The Tax Lawyer, 1983—; Pres. Piedmont Heritage Fund., Inc. 1975-78; del. State Rep. Grassroots Conv., 1985, Presdl. II Conv., 1987. Served with USAF, 1965-69, Vietnam. Decorated Air Force Commendation medal; recipient Am. Jurisprudence award in real propery and tax I, 1971; winner Grand prize So. Living Mag. travel photo contest, 1969. Mem. ABA (taxation sect.), S.C. Bar Assn., Fla. Bar Assn., D.C. Bar Assn., Greer C. of C. (pres. 1977, Outstanding leadership award 1976), Greater Greenville C. of C. (dir. 1977), Order Wig and Robe, Estate Planning Council South Fla., Omicron Delta Kappa. Episcopalian. Club: Bankers. Lodge: Masons, Rotary. Office: One Biscayne Tower Suite 1616 Miami FL 33131-1310

WOOD, WILLIAM RANSOM, former university president, city official, corporate executive; b. nr. Jacksonville, Ill., Feb. 3, 1907; s. William James and Elizabeth (Ransom) W.; m. Margaret Osborne, 1930 (dec. 1942); 1 son, William Osborne (dec. 1978); m. Dorothy Jane Irving, Mar. 18, 1944; children: Mark Irving, Karen Jane Parrish. A.B., Ill. Coll., 1927, LL.D., 1960; M.A., U. Iowa, 1936, Ph.D., 1939. Tchr., coach pubs. schs. Mich., Iowa, Ill., 1928-46; asst. Supt. Evanston Twp. Schs., Ill., 1948-50; specialist jr. colls. and lower divs. U.S. Office Edn., 1950-53; program planning officer (U.S. Office Edn.), 1953; dean statewide devel. higher edn. U. Nev., 1954-55, acting chmn. dept. English, 1955-56, acad. v.p., 1955-60, acting pres., 1958-60; pres. U. Alaska, 1960-73; mayor Fairbanks, Alaska, 1978-80; pres. Pacific Alaska Assocs., Ltd.; exec. v.p. Fairbanks Indsl. Devel. Corp., Festival Fairbanks '84; mem. staff study needs and resources higher edn. FAO, Libya, 1955; mem. study group off-duty ednl. program armed forces in Europe, U.S. Dept. Def., 1955; del. Am. Assembly Fgn. Relations, 1957-58; chmn. Nev. com. Fulbright scholarships, 1957-58; mem. chancellor's panel SUNY; mem. sci. group traveling to Antarctica, New Zealand, Australia. Editor: Looking Ahead, 1953, From Here On, 1954, All Around the Land, 1954, Youth and The World, 1955, To Be an American, 1957; author, editor: On Your Own, 1953; co-editor: Short Stories as You Like Them, 1940, Youth Thinks it Through, 1941, Just for Sport, 1943, Fact and Opinion, 1945, Short Short Stories, 1951, Study of Financing of Higher Education in Asia, 1968; poet: Not From Stone, 1983. Chmn. Alaska Am. Cancer Soc.; v.p. Alaska council Boy Scouts Am.; mem. bd. Rampart Dam adv. com.; mem. Gen. Med. Scis. Nat. Adv. Council, Alaska Higher Edn. Facilities Commn., 1967, Alaska Small Bus. Adv. Council, 1968, Satellite Communications Task Force; spl. asst. to mayor for trade and devel., Fairbanks North Star borough, 1984—; chmn. Greater Fairbanks Community Hosp. Found.; mem. White House Fellows Selection Panel, Nat. Adv. Council on Edn. Professions Devel.; chmn. Alaska Heart Assn.; mem. Alaskan Command Civilian Adv. Bd., 1962—; bd. dirs. U. Alaska Found., exec. dir. Fest. Fairbanks '84, 1981—. Served to lt. USNR, 1943-46; capt. USNR, ret. 1968. Recipient Outstanding Alaskan award, 1984, Alaskan of Yr. award, 1985, Centennial award Alexis de Tocqueville Soc., 1987. Fellow Arctic Inst. N. Am.; mem. Am. Geog. Soc., Assn. Higher Edn. (exec. com.), Nat. Univ. Extension Assn., N.W. Assn. Secondary and Higher Schs., Western Assn. Colls., Navy League, AAAS, Assn. Applied Solar Energy (adv. council 1959), Am. Assn. Land-grant Colls. and State Univs., Internat. Assn. Univ. Presidents (exec. com.). Methodist. Clubs: Explorers, Fairbanks Petroleum, Washington Athletic. Lodge: Rotary (gov. dist. 503 1985-86). Office: Pacific Alaska Associates Ltd 665 10th Ave Fairbanks AK 99701

WOODARD, DOROTHY MARIE, insurance broker; b. Houston, Feb. 7, 1932; d. Gerald Edgar and Bessie Katherine (Crain) Floeck; student N.Mex. State U., 1950; m. Jack W. Woodard; June 19, 1950 (dec.); m. Norman W. Libby, July 19, 1982. Partner, Western Oil Co., Tucumcari, N.Mex., 1950—; owner, mgr. Woodard & Co., Las Cruces, N.Mex., 1959-67; agt., dist. mgr. United Nations Ins. Co., Denver, 1968-74; agt. Western Nat. Life Ins. Co., Amarillo, Tex., 1976—. Exec. dir. Tucumcari Indsl. Commn., 1979—; dir. Bravo Dome Study Com., 1979—; owner Libby Cattle Co., Libby Ranch Co.; regional bd. dirs. N.Mex., Eastern Plains Council Govts., 1979—. Mem. Tucumcari C. of C. Club: Mesa Country. Home: PO Box 823 Tucumcari NM 88401

WOODBURY, FRANKLIN BENNETT WESSLER, metallurgical engineer; b. Joplin, Mo., Dec. 11, 1937; s. Samuel and Pauline Patricia (Bennett) W. AS, Joplin Jr. Coll., 1963; BS in Metall. Engring., U. Mo.-Rolla, 1966. Registered profl. engr., Mo., Minn. Assoc. engr. Uranium div. Mallingckrodt Chem., St. Charles, Mo., 1964; research fellow Gen. Motors Research Lab., Warren, Mich., 1966; asst. instr. metall. engring. U. Mo., Rolla, 1968-71; research metallurgist Twin Cities Research Ctr., Bur. Mines, Dept. Interior, Minn., 1971-80, staff engr. office of dir., div. mineral resources tech., Washington, 1980-81, participant deptl. exec. managerial devel. program, 1980-81, mgr. substitute materials research, 1981-82, mgr. advanced mining tech. div. conservation and devel. mining research, Washington, 1982-87, sr. staff engr. for minerals and metals, 1987—. Contbr. papers to profl. publs. and confs. Mem. sci. and tech. resource council, Minn. Legislature, 1977-80. Served with USAF, 1957-61. Named Engr. of Yr., Minn., 1978; NDEA grad. fellow, 1967-70. Mem. AIME (sec.-treas. Washington sect. 1984-85, 2d v.p. 1986-87), Nat. Soc. Profl. Engrs. (chmn. nat. task group on engring. mgmt. 1977-80, bd. govs. profl. engrs. in govt. 1976-86, rep. to organizing com. internat. conf. engring. mgmt. 1986—), Minn. Soc. Profl. Engrs. (exec. com. at-large 1978-80, chmn., vice chmn. coms.), Minn. Engring. Socs. Joint Task Com. on Engring. Edn. (chmn. 1977-80), Mo. Soc. Profl. Engrs., Va. Soc. Profl. Engrs. (pres. George Washington chpt. 1983-84, bd. dirs. 1982-86, v.p. for govt. 1984-86, pres.-elect 1987-88, pres. 1988—), Washington Soc. Engrs., Scientists and Engrs. Tech. Assessment Council Minn. (AIME rep. to bd. dirs. 1976-78, v.p. 1978-80), Am. Soc. Engring. Mgmt. (chmn. Nat. Capitol Area sect. 1985-86, nat. membership chmn. 1985-86 at. large dir. bd. dirs. 1986—), Am. Soc. for Metals, Sigma Xi, Tau Beta Pi, Alpha Sigma Mu. Roman Catholic. Club: KC.

WOODCOCK, GEORGE, author; b. Winnipeg, Man., Can., May 8, 1912; s. Samuel Arthur and Margaret Gertrude (Lewis) W.; m. Ingeborg Hedwig Elisabeth Linzer, Feb. 10, 1949. Student, Morley Coll., London; LL.D., U. Victoria, U. Winnipeg; D.Litt., Sir George Williams U., U. Ottawa, U. B.C. Broadcaster contbg. several hundred talks and scripts of plays and documentaries to CBC programs; editor of Now, 1940-47; profl. writer 1946—; first in Eng. to 1949 and afterwards in Can.; faculty U. Wash., 1954-55; asso. prof. English U. B.C., Vancouver, 1956-63; lectr. Asian studies U. B.C., 1963—; editor Canadian Lit., 1959-77. Author: The White Island, 1940, The Centre Cannot Hold, 1943, William Godwin, A Biography, 1946, The Incomparable Aphra: A Life of Mrs. Aphra Behn, 1948, The Writer and Politics, 1948, Imagine the South, 1947, The Paradox of Oscar Wilde, 1950, A Hundred Years of Revolution: 1848 and After, 1948, The Letters of Charles Lamb, 1950, The Anarchist Prince, 1950 (later trans. into French), Ravens and Prophets: Travels in Western Canada, 1952, Pierre-Joseph Proudhon, 1956, To the City of the Dead: Travels in Mexico, 1956, Incas and Other Men: Travels in Peru, 1959, Anarchism, 1962, Faces of India, 1964, Asia, Gods and Cities, 1966, The Greeks in India, 1966, A Choice of Critics, 1966, The Crystal Spirit, 1966 (Gov. Gen. award for Eng. Nonfiction), Kerala, 1967, Selected Poems, 1967, The Doukhobors, 1968, Canada and the Canadians, 1969, The Hudson's Bay Company, 1970, Odysseus Ever Returning, 1970, Gandhi, 1971 (U. B.C. medal), Dawn and the Darkest Hour: A Study of Aldous Huxley, 1972, Herbert Read, The Stream and the Source, 1972, The Rejection of Politics, 1972, Who Killed the British Empire?, 1974, Amor de Cosmos, 1975, Gabriel Dumont, 1975 (U. B.C. medal), Notes on Visitations, 1976, South Sea Journey, 1976, Peoples of the Coast, 1977, Thomas Merton, Monk and Poet, 1978, Faces from History, 1978, The Kestrel and Other Poems, 1978, The Canadians, 1979, The World of Canadian Writing, 1980, The George Woodcock Reader, 1980, The Mountain Road, 1981, Taking it to the Letter, 1981, Confederation Betrayed, 1981, Ivan Eyre, 1981, The Benefactor, 1982, Letter to the Past, 1982, Collected Poems, 1983; British Columbia, a Celebration, 1983, Orwell's Message: 1984 and the Present, 1984, Strange Bedfellows: The State and the Arts in Canada, 1985, The Walls of India, 1985, The University of British Columbia, 1986, Northern Spring, 1987, Beyond the Blue Mountain, 1987, The Social History of Canada, 1988, Caves in the Desert, 1988, The Marvenous Century, 1988. Recipient Gov. Gen.'s award, 1966, Molson prize, 1973; Can. Council Travel grantee, 1961, 63, 65; Guggenheim fellow, 1951-52; Canadian Govt. Overseas fellow, 1957-58; Can. Council Killam fellow, 1970-71; Can. Council Sr. Arts fellow, 1975, 78.

WOODFIELD, ANDREW RAYMOND, philosophy educator, author; b. London, Aug. 5, 1946; s. Ernest Raymond and Hilda Ellen (Shipp) W.; m. Mignon Ingred Elizabeth Korn, May 15, 1984; 1 child, Georgia Elena. MA, Oxford (Eng.) U., 1967, D Philosophy, 1975; MLitt, Edinburgh (Scotland) U., 1969. Lectr. Sheffield (Eng.) U., 1969-70, Merton Coll., Oxford, 1973-75; jr. research fellow Linacre Coll., Oxford, 1974-76; lectr. UCLA, 1975-76, U. Bristol, Eng., 1976—, Birkbeck Coll., London, 1985-86; vis. lectr. various univs. in U.S.A., Europe and Brazil, 1981—. Author: Teleology, 1976; editor: Thought and Object, 1982; contbr. articles to profl. jours. Research grantee British Acad., 1978; overseas grantee British Council, 1981, 82, 85. Mem. Aristotelian Soc., Am. Philos. Assn., Soc. Philosophy and Psychology. Office: U Bristol Dept Philosophy, 9 Woodland Rd, Bristol BS8 1TB, England

WOODHALL, JOHN ALEXANDER, JR., construction company executive; b. Peoria, Ill., Oct. 10, 1929; s. John Alexander and Marion Ellen (Solstad) W.; B.B.A., U. Minn., 1952; m. Donna Irene Simmons, Aug. 21, 1948; children—John Alexander, Susan, Cheryl, Douglas, Robert. Project supt. Central States Constrn. Co., Willmar, Minn., 1953-57, v.p., project mgr., 1957-60; v.p., area mgr. Allied Enterprises, Willmar, 1960-69; exec. v.p. Central Allied Enterprises, Inc., Canton, Ohio, 1969-74, chmn., chief exec. officer, 1974—. Vice chmn. Minn. Gov.'s Occupational Safety Health Adv. Council; bd. dirs., chmn. Minn. Safety Council, chmn., 1983; pres. W. Central Safety Council, 1979; bd. dirs. Nat. Safety Council, 1984—; dist. commr. Viking council Boy Scouts Am., 1969-71. Mem. Am. Mgmt. Assn., Am. Arbitration Assn., Associated Gen. Contractors Am. (dir.), Associated Gen. Contractors Minn. (pres. 1977), Pres.'s Assn. Lutheran. Clubs: Kiwanis (Willmar); Masons, Shriners, Mpls. Athletic. Home: 3201 Croydon Dr NW Canton OH 44718 also: 4 Belleview Blvd Apt 404 Belleair FL 34616 Office: Cen Allied Enterprises PO Box 1317 Willmar MN 56201 also: PO Box 80449 Canton OH 44708

WOODHEAD, ROBERT KENNETH, construction company executive; b. Wendell, Idaho, Feb. 11, 1925; s. Albert Arthur and Clara (Larson) W.; m. Dolores Lucille Calvert, Apr. 29, 1951; 1 dau., Linda D. B.A., U. Idaho, 1948, Ph.D., 1980. With Morrison-Knudsen Co. Inc., Boise, Idaho, 1948—; treas. Morrison-Knudsen Co. Inc., 1968—, v.p. adminstrn., 1969-72, v.p. corp. affairs, 1972-73, sr. v.p. corp. affairs, 1973-85, exec. v.p., chief fin. officer, 1985—; also dir.; dir. Nat. Steel and Shipbuilding, H.K. Ferguson Co., Emkay Devel., Broadway Ins. Co. Bd. dirs. U. Idaho Found. Served with USAF, World War II. Mem. Delta Chi. Club: Elk. Home: 4957 Mountain View Dr Boise ID 83704 Office: PO Box 7808 Boise ID 83729

WOODLEY, DAVID TIMOTHY, dermatology educator; b. St. Louis, Aug. 1, 1946; s. Raoul Ramos-Mimosa and Marian (Schlueter) W.; m. Christina Paschall Prentice, May 4, 1974; children: David Thatcher, Thomas Colgate. AB, Washington U., St. Louis, 1968; MD, U. Mo., 1973. Diplomate Am. Bd. Internal Medicine, Am. Bd. Dermatology, Nat. Bd. Internal Medicine. Intern Beth Israel Med. Ctr., Mt. Sinai Sch. Medicine, N.Y. Hosp., Cornell U. Sch. Medicine, N.Y.C., 1973-74; resident in internal medicine U. Nebr., Omaha, 1974-76; resident in dermatology U. N.C., Chapel Hill, 1976-78, asst. prof. dermatology, 1983-85, assoc. prof. dermatology, 1985-88; prof. medicine, co-chief div. dermatology Cornell U. Med. Coll., N.Y., 1988—; research fellow U. Paris, 1978-80; expert NIH, Bethesda, Md., 1980-82; cons. VA Med. Ctr., AHEC Med. Ctr., Fayetteville, N.C., 1983—. Contbr. chpts. to books and articles in field to profl. jours. Mem. Clean Water Action Project, Washington, 1982-83, mem. Potomac Albicore Fleet, Washington, 1982-83, Friends of the Art Sch., Chapel Hill, 1983—, Jungian Soc. Triangle Area, Chapel Hill, 1983—. Fellow Am. Acad. Dermatology; mem. Dermatology Found., Am. Soc. for Clin. Research, Soc. Investigative Dermatology, ACP (assoc.), Assn. Physican Poets, Am. Soc. for Clin. Investigation, 1988. Home: 195 Marilyn Ln Chapel Hill NC 27514 Office: U NC Med Sch Dept Dermatology Room 137 NC Meml Hosp Chapel Hill NC 27514

WOODRING, DEWAYNE STANLEY, association executive; b. Gary, Ind., Nov. 10, 1931; s. J. Stanley and Vera Luella (Brown) W.; m. Donna Jean Wishart, June 15, 1957; children: Judith Lynn (Mrs. Richard Bigelow), Beth Ellen. B.S. in Speech with distinction, Northwestern U., 1954, postgrad. studies in radio and TV broadcasting, 1954-57; M.Div., Garrett Theol. Sem., 1957; L.H.D., Mt. Union Coll., Alliance, Ohio, 1967; D.D., Salem (W.Va.) Coll., 1970. Asso. youth dir. Gary YMCA, 1950-55; ordained to ministry United Methodist Ch., 1955; minister of edn. Griffith (Ind.) Meth. Ch., 1955-57; minister adminstrn. and program 1st Meth. Ch., Eugene, Oreg., 1957-59; dir. pub. relations Dakotas area Meth. Ch., 1959-60, dir. pub. relations Ohio area, 1960-64; adminstrv. exec. to bishop Ohio East area United Meth. Ch., Canton, 1964-77; asst. gen. sec. Gen. Council on Fin. and Adminstrn., United Meth. Ch., Evanston, Ill., 1977-79; assoc. gen. sec. Gen. Council on Fin. and Adminstrn., 1979-84; exec. dir. Religious Conf. Mgmt. Assn., 1982—; mem. staff, dept. radio services 2d assembly World Council Chs., Evanston, 1954;vice chmn. commn. on entertainment and program North Central Jurisdictional Conf., 1968-726, chmn., 1972-76; mem. commn. on gen. conf. United Meth. Ch., 1972—, bus. mgr., exec. dir., 1976—, mem. div. interpretation, 1969-72; chmn. communications commn. Ohio Council Chs., 1961-65; mem. exec. com. Nat. Assn. United Meth. Founds., 1968-72; del. World Meth. Conf., London, Eng., 1966, Dublin, Ireland, 1976, Honolulu, 1981, Nairobi, 1986, exec. com. World Meth. Council, 1986—; bd. dirs. Ohio East Area United Meth. Found., 1967-78, v.p., 1967-76; chmn. bd. mgrs. United Meth. Bldg., Evanston, 1977-84; lectr., cons. on fgn. travel. Creator: nationally distbd. radio series The Word and Music; writer, dir.: television series Parables in Miniature, 1957-59. Adviser East Ohio Conf. Communications Commn., 1968-76; pres. Guild Assos., 1971—; Trustee, 1st v.p. Copeland Oaks Retirement Center, Sebring, Ohio, 1969-76. Recipient Cert. Meeting Profl. award, 1985. Mem. Am. Soc. Assn. Execs., Meeting Planners Internat., Conv. Liaison Council (bd. dirs.), Def. Orientation Conf. Assn. (dir.), Cert. Meeting Profls. (bd. dirs.), Nat. Assn. Exposition Mgrs. Home: 7224 Chablis Ct Indianapolis IN 46278 Office: One Hoosier Dome Suite 120 Indianapolis IN 46225

WOODROE, STEPHEN CLARK, lawyer; b. Charleston, W.Va., Oct. 28, 1940; s. William May and Isabel Tomasa (Clark); m. Marla Kathleen Reid, Oct. 2, 1976. BA magna cum laude, Harvard Coll., 1963; JD, U. Va., 1969. Bar: W.Va. 1969. Assoc. Campbell, Love, Woodroe & Kizer, Charleston, 1969-74, ptnr., 1974-76; ptnr. Love, Wise, Robinson & Woodroe, Charleston, 1976-80; asst. atty. gen. State of W.Va., Charleston, 1980-85; sole practice, Charleston, 1985—. Conv. del. 350th Anniversary Celebration Harvard U., 1986. Mem. W.Va. State Bar, W.Va. Bar Assn., Kanawha County Bar Assn., ABA, Am. Arbitration Assn., Am. Judicature Soc., Phi Delta Phi. Democrat. Episcopalian. Club: Farmington Country (Charlottesville). Lodge: Elks, Charleston Rotary. Home: 513 Linden Rd Charleston WV 25314 Office: Charleston Nat Plaza Suite 213 PO Box 3022 Charleston WV 25331

WOODROW, BARRY CHARLES, manufacturing executive; b. Poole, Dorset, Eng., Nov. 15, 1949; arrived in Iceland, 1984; s. Alan Charlie and Marjorie Lillian (Pollard) W.; m. Euphemia Dianne Summers, Aug. 2, 1975 (div. Jan. 1984); m. Anna Skúladóttir, Feb. 21, 1984; 1 child, Karen Emilía. BSc, U. Reading, 1970. Asst. chief chemist Nchanga Consol. Copper Mines, Kitwe, Zambia, 1971-74; works mgr. Consol. Lighting Ltd., Kitwe, 1974-79; mgr. tech. services Kenya Furfural Co. Ltd., Eldoret, 1979-82; project coordinator Colechurch Internat. Ltd., Makurdi, Nigeria, 1983-84; gen. mgr. Entek of Iceland Ltd., Reykjavik, 1984—; com. mem. Kenya Bur. of Standards, Nairobi, Kenya, 1981-82. Producer, dir. various stage plays 1973-79, 80-82. Chmn. Nkana Kitwe Arts Soc., 1977-79, hon. life mem., 1979; prodns. dir. Uasin Gishu Arts Soc., Eldoret, 1979-81. Fellow Brit. Soc. Commerce; mem. British Inst. of Mgmt., Iceland Assn. of Chartered Engrs. Office: Entek of Iceland Ltd, Sidumuli 33, IS-108 Reykjavik Iceland

WOODRUFF, LAURENCE DAVID, oil company executive; b. Detroit, Feb. 20, 1924; emigrated to Can., 1932; s. Norris Counsel and Mabel Marion (Fleming) W.; m. Elizabeth M. Wilcox, May 23, 1947; children: James Laurence Dudley, Norris David, Richard Wilcox. B.A. with honors, U. Toronto, 1946. With Shell Can., 1946-67, Shell Internat., London, 1968-70; exec. v.p. Can. Fuel Marketers, Toronto, Ont., 1970-72, pres., 1973-79; pres., dir. Can. Ultramar Ltd., Toronto, 1980-85, chmn., 1985—; dir. Ultramar PLC, London, Ultramar Oil & Gas (Can.) Ltd., Calgary, Alta., 1980—, T.I. Industries Ltd., London, Ont., 1985—. Office: Ultramar Can Inc, 1 Valleybrook Dr, Don Mills, ON Canada M3B 2S8

WOODRUFF, SIR MICHAEL FRANCIS ADDISON, surgeon; b. London, Apr. 3, 1911; s. Harold Addison and Margaret Ada (Cooper) W.; m. Hazel Gwenyth Ashby, 1946; 3 children. Ed. Wesley Coll., Melbourne, Queen's Coll.; M.B., B.S., U. Melbourne, Australia, 1937, M.D., 1940. Tutor in surgery, U. Sheffield, 1946-48; lectr. surgery U. Aberdeen, 1948-52; prof. surgery U. Otago, N.Z., 1953-55; prof. surgery U. Edinburgh, 1957-77, emeritus, 1977—; surgeon Edinburgh Royal Infirmary, 1957-77; former dir. Nuffield Transplantation Surgery Unit, Edinburgh; fgn. assoc. Acad. de Chirurgie, France, 1964. Author: (with A. Dean Smith) Deficiency Diseases in Japanese Prison Camps, 1951; Transplantation of Tissues and Organs, 1960; On Science and Surgery, 1976; F.R.C.S., 1947; The Interaction of Cancer and Host, 1980; (with Hedley Berry) Surgery for Dental Students, 4th edit., 1984; contbr. articles to profl. jours. Recipient Lister medal, 1969. Fellow ACS (hon.), Am. Surg. Soc. (hon.), Royal Soc.; mem. Am. Surg. Assn. (hon.), The Transplantation Soc. (pres. 1972-74), Deutsche Gesellschaft fur Chirurgie (corr.), Royal Coll. Physicians Edinburgh. Avocations: music; sailing. Address: 506 Lanark Rd, Juniper Green, Edinburgh EH 14 5DH, Scotland

WOODRUFF, VIRGINIA, television and radio host, producer; b. Morrisville, Pa.; d. Edwin Nichols and Louise (Meredith) W.; m. Raymond F. Beagle Jr. (div.); m. Albert Plaut II (div.); 1 child, Elise Meredith. Past student, Rutgers U. News corr. Sta. WNEW-TV Metromedia, N.Y.C., 1967; nat., internat. critic-at-large Mut. Broadcasting System, 1968-75; lectr. circ. Leigh Bur., 1969-71; byline columnist N.Y. Daily Mirror, N.Y.C., 1971; first Arts critic Teleprompter and Group W Cable TV, 1977-84; host/producer The First Nighter N.Y. Times Primetime Cable Highlight program, 1977-84; pres., chief exec. officer Starpower, Inc., 1984—; affiliate news corr. ABC Radio Network, N.Y.C., 1984-86; contbr. feature writer Vis à Vis, United AL internat. mag., 1988—, perennial critic Off-Off Broadway Short Play Festival, N.Y.C., 1984—. Contbg. media feature writer Vis à Vis mag., 1988—. Mem. celebrity panel Arthritis Telethon, N.Y.C., 1976. Selected episodes First Nighter program in archives N.Y. Pub. Library, Billy Rose Theatre Collection, Rodgers and Hammerstein Collection, Performing Arts Research Ctr. Mem. Drama Desk. Presbyterian. Office: Starpower 35 E 10th St New York NY 10003

WOODRUM, ROBERT LEE, public relations executive; b. Merkel, Tex., Mar. 3, 1945; s. Bill and Norma (Shea) W.; m. Linda Mary Larkin, July 20, 1968; children: Jennifer, Michael. B.A., Calif. State U., 1967; postgrad., U. Okla., 1974. Press sec. U.S. Senate, Washington, 1977-78; dir. pub. affairs U.S. Office Personnel Mgmt., Washington, 1979-80; pres. Corp. Communications, Washington, 1980-82; v.p. Norton Simon Inc., N.Y.C., 1982-83; with Nat. Football League, N.Y.C., 1983-84; exec. dir. Ritz Paris Hemingway Award; pres. Ritz Paris Internat., 1984-86; sr. v.p. The Home Group, Inc., 1986—. Advisor USIA, Washington, 1980; advisor ARC, 1983, White House Vets. Com., 1979-80. Served to lt. comdr. USN, 1968-77. Decorated Navy Achievement medal 2. Club: New York Athletic. Home: 120 Long Neck Point Rd Darien CT 06820 Office: 59 Maiden Ln New York NY 10038

WOODS, BOBBY JOE (BOB), transportation executive; b. Frederick, Okla., June 20, 1935; s. Vivin Richard and Mattie Marie (Malone) W.; m. O. Dell Smith, July 21, 1957; children: Donald B., Kathryn M., David R., Lynda J. Student, U. Calif., Berkeley, 1955-56; AA, Phoenix Coll., 1955; student, Glendale (Ariz.) Coll., 1968, 75. Credit mgr. Sam Boren Tire Co., Albuquerque, 1966-67; office mgr. Menke Transp., Albuquerque, 1967-68; dist. exec. Boy Scouts Am., Phoenix, 1968-76; pres. Southwest Prorate Inc., Phoenix, 1976—; owner Southwest Vehicle Title Service, Phoenix, 1985—. Commr. Boy Scouts Am., Ariz., N.Mex. Mem. Profl. Trucking Services Assn. (2d vice pres.). Republican. Mem. Evangelical Free Ch. Lodge: Lions (zone chmn. South Phoenix 1983-84, dep. dist. gov. 1984-85, dist. sight and hearing chmn. 1985-89, Sight and Hearing Found. state hearing chmn. 1987-89). Home: 918 W Cochise Phoenix AZ 85021 Office: Southwest Prorate Inc 8902 N Central Phoenix AZ 85020

WOODS, JOHN WITHERSPOON, banker; b. Evanston, Ill., Aug. 18, 1931; s. J. Albert and Cornelia (Witherspoon) W.; m. Loti Moultrie Chisolm, Sept. 5, 1953; children: Loti, Cindy, Corrie. BA, U. of South, 1954. With Chem. Bank, N.Y.C., 1954-69; v.p., head Chem. Bank (So. div.), 1965-69; chmn., chief exec. officer Am South Bancorp., 1972—, Am South Bank N.A., 1983—; dir. Protective Life Ins. Co., Birmingham, Ala., Power Co. Birmingham. Trustee So. Research Inst., Birmingham, Tuskegee Inst.; bd. dirs. Community Chest-United Way of Jefferson County, past pres.; past chmn. working com. of 35 Gov.'s Ednl. Reform Commn.; bd. dirs. Ala. Inst. Deaf and Blind Found.; co.-chmn, bd. dirs. Ala. Mgmt. Improvement Program, Inc. Served to 1st lt. USAF, 1955-57. Named to Ala. Acad. Honor. Mem. Birmingham Area C. of C. (pres. 1978, dir., exec. com.), Assn. Res. City Bankers, Assn. Bank Holding Cos. (bd. dirs.). Office: Am South Bank NA 1900 5th Ave N PO Box 11007 Birmingham AL 35288

WOODS, MARY JOAN, pediatric nurse practitioner; b. Vincennes, Ind., July 11, 1928; d. John Arthur and Maud Claribel (Davidson) Caniff; m. John Thomas Woods, Sept. 17, 1949; children—John Thomas, William Patrick, Richard, Michael, Elizabeth, Stephen, Jennifer, Cynthia. Diploma, Deaconess Hosp., 1949; cert. Sch. Nurse Practitioner, U. Evansville, 1974; cert. Pediatric Nurse Practitioner, Ind. U., 1976. Supr., Well Baby Clinic, Pub. Health Nursing Assn., Evansville, Ind., 1972; supr. Sweetser Clinic, Evansville, 1973; pediatric nurse practitioner, Evansville-Vanderburgh Health Dept., Evansville, Ind., 1973—; tchr. parenting class Welborn Clinic, Evansville State Hosp., Prevention Crisis Nursery, Friendship Ministries; instr. parenting class and CPR, ARC; lectr. U. Evansville, also Deaconess Hosp. Tchr. St. James Ch.; taskforce mem. Latchkey Program; organist St. James Cath. Ch. Fellow Nat. Assn. Pediatric Nurse Assocs. and Practitioners; mem. Ind. State Nurses Assn. (former state officer), DAR (vice regent Mary Anthony McGary chpt.), Univ. Evansville Women, Am. Guild of Organists. Republican. Roman Catholic. Home: Rural Route 6 Baseline Rd Box 339 Evansville IN 47711 Office: Civic Center Complex Health Dept Nursing Div Evansville IN 47708

WOODS, PENDLETON, college official; author; b. Ft. Smith, Ark., Dec. 18, 1923; s. John Powell and Mabel (Hon) W.; B.A. in Journalism, U. Ark., 1948; m. Lois Robin Freeman, Apr. 3, 1948; children—Margaret, Paul Pendleton, Nancy. Editor, asst. pub. mgr. Okla. Gas & Electric Co., Oklahoma City, 1948-69; dir. Living Legends of Okla., Okla. Christian Coll., Oklahoma City, 1969-82, project, promotion dir. Enterprise Square, 1988—; arbitrator Better Bus. Bur. Bd. dirs. Campfire Girls Council, Okla. Jr. Symphony (past pres.), Boy Scout Council, Central Park Neighborhood Assn., Zoo Amphitheater of Oklahoma City, Will Rogers Centennial Commn.; v.p. Okla. for Resource Preservation, Okla. Found. Epilepsy; pres. Keep Okla. Beautiful; past pres. Oklahoma City Mental Health Clin.; pub. relations chmn. Oklahoma County chpt. A.R.C.; past chmn. Western Heritage award Nat. Cowboy Hall of Fame; past pres. Variety Health Center; dir. Am. Freedom Council; exec. dir. Oklahoma City Bicentennial Commn.; mem. Okla. Disabilities Council. Served with AUS, World War II and Korean; col., state historian Okla. N.G.; chmn. Oklahoma City Independence Day Parade, mem. exec. com. Oklahoma City Centennial Commn. Named Outstanding Young Man of Year, Oklahoma City Jr. C. of C., 1953; recipient Silver Beaver award Boy Scouts Am., 1963, Silver medal award of Advt. Fedn. Am., Disting. Community Service award of Neighborhood Devel. and Conservation Ctr, Patrick Henry Patriotism medal of Mil. Order of the World Wars; also 3 honor medals Freedoms Found.; recipient Jefferson Davis medal United Daus. of the Confederacy. Mem. Soc. Asso. Indsl. Editors (past v.p.), Advt. Fedn. Am. (past dist. dir.; Silver Medal award), Central Okla. Indsl. Communicators (past pres., hon. life mem.), Okla. Jr. C. of C. (hon. life; past internat. dir.), Okla. Distributive Edn. Clubs (hon. life), Oklahoma City Advt. Club (past pres.), Okla. Zool. Soc., Okla. Geneal. Soc. (past pres.), Okla. City chpt. U. Ark. Almuni Assn. (charter pres.), Okla. Lung Assn. (pub. relations com.), Okla. County chpt. Am. Cancer Soc., Okla. Travel Industries Assn., Okla. Hist. Soc. (publ. editor), Okla. Heritage Assn. (publ. editor), Oklahoma City Beautiful (publ. editor), Oklahoma County Hist. Soc. (dir., pres.), 45th Inf. Div. Assn. (pres.), Mus. Unassigned Lands (chmn.), Mil. Order World Wars (regional comdr.), Okla. City (comdr.), Oklahoma City Hist. Preservation Commn., Sigma Delta Chi, Kappa Sigma (nat. commr. publs). Club: Lincoln Park Country (pres.), Author: You and Your Company Magazine, 1950; Church of Tomorrow, 1964; Myriad of Sports, 1971; This Was Oklahoma, 1979. Recorded Sounds of Scouting, 1969; Born Grown, 1974 (Western Heritage award Nat. Cowboy Hall Fame). Home: 541 NW 31st St Oklahoma City OK 73118

WOODS, ROBERT LAWRENCE, insurance company executive, consultant; b. Los Angeles, May 17, 1911; s. Walter A. and Alice (Strang) W.; A.B., U. Calif. at Los Angeles, 1933; C.L.U., Am. Coll. Life Underwriters, 1937; m. Dorothy Welbourn, Oct. 10, 1942; children—Robert Lawrence, Susan Welbourn Woods Barker. With Los Angeles agy. of Mass. Mut. Life Ins. Co., 1934—, asst. gen. agt., 1938-46, assoc. gen. agt., 1946-49, gen. agt. in partnership, 1949-57, sole gen. agt., 1957-73. Fund raising chmn. Los Angeles chpt. ARC, 1961, dir., 1960-63. Trustee Am. Coll., 1958-61, 71-79. Served to lt. col., inf., AUS, 1941-46. Recipient John Newton Russell award Nat. Assn. Life Underwriters, 1971, Will G. Farrell award Los Angeles Life Ins. Assns., 1974; named to Mgmt. Hall of Fame, Nat. Gen. Agts. and Mgrs. Conf., 1974. Mem. Am. Soc. C.L.U.'s (pres. Los Angeles 1953-54, nat. pres. 1959-60), Mass. Mut. Gen. Agts. Assn. (pres. 1959-60), Gen. Agts. and Mgrs. Assn. (pres. Los Angeles 1957-58, nat. pres. 1967-68), Phi Gamma Delta. Home: 720 N Oakhurst Dr Beverly Hills CA 90210 Office: 4401 Wilshire Blvd Los Angeles CA 90010

WOODS, WALTER ABNER, marketing executive, educator, consumer behavior researcher; b. Lingle, Wyo., Jan. 16, 1915; s. James Abner and Mazeppa (Israel) W.; m. Margaret C. Edmiston, June 15, 1955 (div. 1974); 1 dau., Dana Jeanne. A.B., U. Wyo., 1937; M.A., Syracuse U., 1942; Ph.D., Columbia U., 1952; student, Art Students League, N.Y.C., 1946-47. Research psychologist Art Sch., Pratt Inst., Bklyn., 1948-51; assoc. prof. psychology Richmond (Va.) Profl. Inst., 1952-55; v.p., sr. dir. research Nowland & Co., Greenwich, Ct., 1955-61; pres., sr. researcher Products & Concepts Research Inc. Sparta (N.J.), Brussels, Sydney, 1961—; prof. mktg. West Ga. Coll., Carrollton, 1971-85, emeritus, 1985—; vis. prof. mktg. Bogasici U., Instanbul, 1986-87; dir. Prognosis S.A., Brussels, 1963—; cons. in field. Author: Consumer Behavior, 1980. County chmn. Ford for Pres., Carroll County, Ga., 1976; coordinator Anderson for Pres. campaign, Ga., 1980. Served to lt. USNR, 1942-46. Recipient disting. mktg. service award Sales Execs. Club of N.Y., 1968; named Outstanding Educator of Am., 1973. Fellow Acad. Mktg. Sci.; mem. Am. Psychol. Assn., Am. Mktg. Assn., Internat. Assn. for Empirical Aesthetics, AAAS. Subspecialties: Behavior psychology; Cognition. Current work: Supra level purposes and motives in consuming behavior; motivation and perception in art experiencing. Developer: pesonality test Polychrome Index, 1954; color aptitude test, 1951; originator product concept research, 1957; co-developer positioning strategy, 1959. Home: 389 Smyrna Church Rd Carrollton GA 30117 Office: West Ga Coll Carrollton Ga 30118

WOODS, WALTER THOMAS, JR., physiologist, technical consultant; b. Nashville, Mar. 13, 1947; s. Walter Thomas and Evelyn Eugenia (Cooper) W.; children—Thomas Cooper, Kathleen Gage, Helen Frye. B.A., U. of the South, Sewanee, Tenn., 1969; M.A., Appalachian State U., 1971; Ph.D., Bowman Gray Sch. Medicine Wake Forest U., 1975. With dept. physiology and biophysics U. Ala., Birmingham, 1975—, asst. prof., 1979-84, assoc. prof., 1984—, with dept. medicine div. cardiovascular disease, 1974—, instr., 1976-83, assoc. prof., 1984—; founder Oracle Systems, Inc., Birmingham, Ala.; bd. dirs. Research for Oracle Systems, Inc., Birmingham; outside expert in cardiac electrophysiology Med. Research Council, Can., 1983—. Contbr. articles to profl. jours. NSF trainee, 1973-74; Am. Heart Assn. grantee, 1981; Lilly Research Labs. grantee, 1982; NIH grantee, 1983, U.S. Army Med. Research and Devel. Command grantee, 1983—. Fellow Council Circulation Am. Heart Assn., Am. Physiol. Soc. (cardiovascular sect.). Republican. Episcopalian. Club: Mt. Brook (Birmingham). Home: PO Box 7662A Birmingham AL 35253 Office: U Ala at Birmingham University Station Birmingham AL 35294 also: Oracle Systems Inc CADIe 1075 13th St S Suite 211 Birmingham AL 35205

WOODS, WENDY, reporter, editor; b. Newark, Nov. 16, 1952; d. Julian Jonathan and Eileen Margaret (Woods) A.; m. Nicholas Cobalt Gorski, May 29, 1983. Student Wilkes Coll., Wilkes-Barre, Pa., 1970-72; B.A. in Film, Syracuse U., 1976. News reporter Sta. WILK, Wilkes-Barre, 1971-72; reporter, anchor Sta. WIXT-TV, Syracuse, N.Y., 1975-81; corr. Cable News Network, San Francisco, 1981-82; news reporter Sta. KGO-TV (ABC), San Francisco, 1982-84; reporter Computer Chronicles (PBS TV show), 1984—. Editor in chief newsletter Newsbytes, 1983—(Best Online Publ. award Computer Press Assn. 1985). . Recipient best environ. reporting award Central N.Y. Environ. Assn., 1979; best reporting under deadline pressure award Syracuse Press Club, 1980, best investigative reporting award, 1981. Mem. Computer Press Assn. (pres. 1987, v.p. 1988).

WOODS, WILLIAM ELLIS, lawyer, pharmacist, association executive; b. Ballinger, Tex., Sept. 25, 1917; s. Cary Dysart and Gertrude Mae (Ellis) W.; m. Martha Brockman, May 28, 1954. B.S., U. Tex. Sch. Pharmacy, 1938; J.D., Sch. Law, 1953. Bar: Tex. bar 1954, U.S. Supreme Ct 1957. Dir. emergency med. service Tex. State Health Dept., 1942-43, USPHS, 1943-47; asst. dir. Nat. Pharm. Survey Office, 1947-48; with Eli Lilly & Co., 1948-51; first dir. U. Tex. Pharmacy Extension Service, Austin, 1953-54; sole practice Corpus Christi, Tex., 1954-58; asst. to exec. v.p. Nat. Pharm Council, N.Y.C., 1958-64; sec. Nat. Pharm Council, 1964-65; Washington rep., asso. gen. counsel Nat. Assn. Retail Druggists, 1964-76, exec. v.p., 1976-84, hon. past pres., 1984; mem. Joint Commn. Pharmacy Practitioners; chmn. Nat. Small Bus. Legis. Council, 1981; pres. Nat. Drug Trade Conf., 1981; del. U.S. Pharmacopoeial Convs., 1975, 80. Contbr. articles to pharmacy publs. Recipient Achievement Medal award Alpha Zeta Omega, 1975, Lubin Prof. Pharmacy award U. Tenn., 1982. Mem. ABA, Tex. Bar Assn., Law Sci. Acad., Phi Delta Phi. Methodist. Clubs: Internat., Capitol Hill, Nat. Assn. Execs. (Washington); Can. (N.Y.C.). Home: PO Box 1045 Easton MD 21601

WOODSIDE, BERTRAM JOHN, infosystem engineer; b. Danville, Pa., Apr. 20, 1946; s. Cyrus G. and Almerta T. (Kitchen) W.; m. Doreen Knowles; 1 child, Russell. BS, USAF Acad., 1968. Cert. purchasing mgr. Commissioned 2d lt. USAF, 1968, advanced through grades to capt., 1971, resigned, 1976; plant engr. Linde div. Union Carbide Corp., Pitts., 1976, distribution supt., 1977-78; region purchasing mgr. Linde div. Union Carbide Corp., Cleve., 1979-82, region tech. supr., 1983; process analyst Linde div. Union Carbide Corp., Lorain, Ohio, 1984-87, region mgr. process computer services, 1987—. Recipient D.F.C. with oak leaf cluster, 8 Air medals. Club: Bay Boat (Bay Village, Ohio) (sec. 1984-87). Office: Union Carbide Corp Box 1153 Lorain OH 44055

WOOD-SMITH, DONALD, plastic surgeon; b. Sydney, Australia, June 30, 1931; s. William Frederick and Vera Mary; M.B., B.S., Sydney U., 1954; m. Lelia Christine, June 14, 1975; children—Christina Margaret, Donald William, Phillip Raynor. Surg. resident Lewisham Hosp., Sydney, 1954-56, Royal Marsden Hosp. and Royal Coll. Surgeons, Engl., 1957-58; resident plastic surgery N.Y. U. Hosp. Med. Center, 1960-64, asst. and asso. attending surgeon, 1964—; vis. surgeon Bellevue Hosp., 1964—; chmn. plastic surgery Manhattan Eye Ear and Throat Hosp., 1975-77; asso. prof. plastic surgery NYU, 1977-84, prof., 1984—; surgeon, dir. plastic surgery Manhattan Eye Ear and Throat Hosp., 1977-84; cons. plastic surgeon N.Y. Eye and Ear Infirmary, chmn. dept. plastic and reconstructive surgery, 1984—. Diplomate Am. Bd. Plastic Surgery. Fellow ACS, Royal Coll. Surgeons of Edinburgh; mem. Am. Assn. Plastic Surgeons, Am. Soc. Plastic and Reconstructive Surgeons, Am. Soc. Maxillofacial Surgeons, Transplantation Soc., N.Y. Acad. Medicine, Brit. Assn. Plastic Surgeons. Republican. Club: N.Y. Athletic. Author: Nursing Care of the Plastic Surgery Patient, 1967; Cosmetic Facial Surgery, 1973; contbr. articles to med. jours. Office: 830 Park Ave New York NY 10021

WOODSON, RILEY D., consulting engineer; b. Penalosa, Kans., Nov. 29, 1908; s. Guy Malcolm and Grace Greenwood (Ogle) W.; B.S.M.E. cum laude, U. Kans., 1935; m. Virginia Marie Anderson, May 31, 1947; children—R. Donald, Marjorie Gayl Woodson Brownlee. With Black and Veatch Cons. Engrs., 1935—, partner, head power div., 1958-78, cons. power div., 1979—. Fellow ASME, Am. Inst. Cons. Engrs.; mem. IEEE, Am. Nuclear Soc., Nat. Soc. Profl. Engrs., Tau Beta Pi, Sigma Tau. Republican. Methodist. Club: Indian Hills Country. Patentee in field. Home: 2012 W 50th Terr Shawnee Mission KS 66205 Office: 11401 Lamar Overland Park KS 66211

WOODSON, STEPHEN WILLIAM, collection agency executive; b. Kansas City, Mo., May 31, 1950; s. William Albert and Patricia Marguerite (May) W.; A.A., Maple Woods Community Coll., 1977. Asst. mgr. Pub. Fin., San Pedro, Calif., 1973-74; asst. to v.p. MOAMCO, Mpls., 1974-75; pres. Met. Collection Services, Inc., North Kansas City, Mo., 1975-81, Regional Collection Services, 1981-84; collection cons. Blue Valley Fed. Savs. & Loan, 1975-86; pres. Transam. Collection Services, 1986—. Active Big Bros. and Sisters, Kansas City, Mo., 1977—; counselor Mo. Dept. Probation and Parole; pres. Job Readiness, Inc., 1983-86; mem. citizens adv. bd. Kansas City Alliance Bus. Task Force. Served with USN, 1967-70. Recipient Whitehall Found. Scholastic award, 1968. Mem. Internat. Traders Assn., Am. Collectors Assn., Northland C. of C. Democrat. Lutheran. Home: 6909 Fisk St Kansas City MO 64151 Office: PO Box 34687 Kansas City MO 64116

WOODWARD, BRYAN, electrical engineer, scientific diver; b. Gloucestershire, Eng., Feb. 11, 1941; s. Frederick Woodward and Grace Margaret (Reynolds) Woodward Fuller; m. Joy Elizabeth Dunning, Mar. 28, 1970; children: Faye Shelley, James Dunning. BS, U. London, 1964, MS, 1966, PhD, 1968, Diploma of Imperial Coll., 1966. Chartered engr. Sci. officer Royal Australian Navy, Sydney, 1967-68; research assoc. Guy's Hosp. Med. Sch., London, 1969-71; research scientist Australian AEC, Sydney, 1972-75; lectr., sr. lectr., now reader Loughborough (Eng.) U. Tech., 1975—; vis. scientist Ctr. Nat. Sci. Research, Marseille, France, 1982-83; external examiner U. London, U. Birmingham (Eng.) and U. Provence (France), 1982—; cons. Ameeco Hydrospace, Andover, Eng., 1982-86; chief examiner Engring. Council, London, 1986—. Author: Writing Technical Articles, 1988; contbr. sci. papers to jours. and proceedings. Recipient Gold medal for diving Duke of Edinburgh Scheme, London, 1971. Fellow Royal Geograph. Soc.; mem. Inst. Acoustics, Biol. Engring. Soc., Soc. Underwater Tech., Inst. Elec. Engrs. Office: U Tech Dept Electronic, Elec Engring, Loughborough Leicestershire LE11 3TU, England

WOODWARD, ISABEL AVILA, writer; b. Key West, Fla., Mar. 14, 1906; d. Alfredo and Isabel (Lopez) Avila; student Fla. State Coll. for Women, 1925, A.B. in Edn., 1938; cert. in teaching Spanish, U. Miami, 1961; summer study U. Fla., Eckerd Coll.; postgrad. St. Lawrence U., U. Miami; m. Clyde B. Woodward, June 6, 1944 (dec.); children—Joy Avis Ball, Greer Isabel Woodward Sucke. Tchr., Key West, 1927-42, remedial reading cons., 1941-42; reading tchr., asst. reading lab. and clinic St. Lawrence U., summer 1941; Spanish translator U.S. Office of Censorship, Miami, 1943; tchr. Central Beach Elem. Sch., Miami Beach, Fla., 1943-44, Silver Bluff Elem. Sch., 1943-50, Henry West Lab. Sch., Coral Gables, Fla., 1955-57, Dade Demonstration Sch., Miami, 1957-61; author 125 sch. radio lessons for teaching Spanish, Dade County Elem. Schs., 1961; tchr. Spanish Workshop for Fla.; speaker poetry and short story writing, 1977; guest lectr. on writing the short story Fla. Inst. Tech., Jensen Beach, 1981; freelance writer; contbr. to Listen Mag., Sunshine Mag., Lookout Mag., Christian Sci. Monitor, Miami Herald, Three/Four, Child Life, Wee Wisdom, Fla. Wildlife, Young World; sponsor Port St. Lucie Jr. Woman's Club, 1983. Recipient Honoris Causa award Alpha Delta Kappa, 1972-74, award Contra Costa Times, Calif., 1985; named one of 5 Outstanding Fla. Tchrs., 1972-74. Mem. Nat. League Am. Pen Women (1st v.p. Greater Miami br. 1974-76, historian 1978—, librarian 1978—, awards for writing 1973, 74, 77, 1st and 3d place state writing awards for adult and juvenile fiction 1983, state 1st prize short story 1985), AAUW, Alpha Delta Kappa, Psi Psi Psi. Address: 1950 Palm City Rd Apt 6-301 Stuart FL 34994

WOODWARD, JACK CARLTON, pottery company executive; b. Roseville, Ohio, July 26, 1923; s. Floyd Harris and Clara Marie (Ungemach) W.; B.B.A., lMeredith Coll., 1942; m. Janice Colleen Harper, Nov. 8, 1962; children—Jon, Jo Ellen, Sharon, Vickie, Jane. With Robinson Ransbottom Pottery Co., Roseville, 1937—, treas., 1970-72, exec. v.p., 1972-78, pres., gen mgr., 1978—, also dir. Mem. Republican Central Com., Zanesville, 1949-53. Served with U.S. Army, 1943-46. Mem. Pottery, China and Glass Assn., Southeastern Ohio Ceramic Assn., U.S. C. of C., Ohio C. of C., Zanesville Area C. of C. (dir. 1976). Presbyterian. Clubs: Elks, Masons (32 deg.), Eagles. Office: Roseville OH 43777

WOODWARD, JAMES KENNETH, pharmacologist; b. Anderson, Mo., Feb. 5, 1938; s. Audley J. and Doris Evelyn (Fields) W.; A.B. in Chemistry, B.S. in Biology, S.W. Mo. State Coll., 1960; postgrad. U. Kans. (USPHS fellow) 1960-62; Ph.D. (USPHS fellow), U. Pa. Sch. Medicine, 1967; m. Kathleen Ruth Winget, June 25, 1960; children—Audley J., Kimie Connette. Pharmacologist, Stine Lab., Newark, Del., 1963-65, research pharmacologist, 1967-71; sr. research pharmacologist Merrell-Nat. Labs., Cin., 1972-73, sect. head, 1973-74, head dept. pharmacology, 1974-78; head dept. pre-clin. pharmacology Merrell Research Center, Merrell Dow Pharms., Inc., 1978-83, assoc. dir. research adminstrn. Merrell Dow Research Inst., 1983-88, dir. biol. devel. Merrell Dow Research Inst., 1988—. USPHS post-doctoral fellow U. Pa., 1967. Pres., Golf Manor Recreation Commn., Cin., 1973-75. Mem. Phila. Physiol. Soc., AAAS. Democrat. Baptist. Patentee antisecretory compounds of imidazoline series. Home: 7700 Shadowhill Way Cincinnati OH 45242 Office: 2110 E Galbraith Rd Cincinnati OH 45215

WOODWARD, MADISON TRUMAN, JR., lawyer; b. New Orleans, Feb. 15, 1908; s. Madison Truman and Maude W.; m. Elvina Bernard, June 30, 1937 (dec. Sept. 26, 1964); children: Anne Carol Woodward Baker, Elizabeth H. Woodward Ryan, Lucie B. Woodward Cavaroc, Margaret E., Madison Truman III; m. Ethel Dameron, June 24, 1977. LL.B., Tulane U., 1927; postgrad., U. Mich., 1927-28. Bar: La. 1929. Since practiced in New Orleans; asso. firm Milling, Benson, Woodward, Hillyer, Pierson & Miller (and predecessors), 1929-36, mem. firm, 1937—. Author: Louisiana Notarial Manual, 1953, 2d edit., 1962, Supplement, 1973; contbr. articles to legal jours. Trustee Trinity Episcopal Sch., New Orleans, 1965-71; chmn. Victor Bernard Found., 1965—. Fellow Am. Bar Found., Am. Coll. Trial Lawyers, Am. Coll. Probate Counsel; mem. ABA (state del. 1982-87, ho. of dels. 1979-87, bd. of govs. 1987—), La. Bar Assn. (pres. 1973-74), New Orleans Bar Assn., Am. Law Inst., La. State Law Inst. (council 1957—, v.p. 1969-80, pres. 1980-81, vice chmn. 1982—), Nat. Conf. Bar Pres. (exec. council 1973-75), 5th Cir. Jud. Conf. (del. 1966—, lawyers adv. com. 1982-84), Am. Judicature Soc. (bd. dirs. 1973-76), La. Bar Found. (chmn. 1980-85), Valencia Inc. (gov. 1960-78, pres. 1963-64), U.S. Supreme Ct. Hist. Soc. (trustee 1985—), New Orleans C. of C., Garden Dist. Assn. (pres. 1964-65), Soc. Colonial Wars in La. (mem. council 1973—, gov. 1983-85), Order St. Lazarus (comdr. so. comandery 1986—), Pi Kappa Phi. Clubs: Pickwick (New Orleans), New Orleans Country (New Orleans), Plimsoll (New Orleans), Stratford (New Orleans), International House (New Orleans); City (Baton Rouge). Home: 1234 6th St New Orleans LA 70115 Office: 909 Poydras St LL&E Tower Suite 2300 New Orleans LA 70112

WOODWARD, ROBERT SIMPSON, IV, economics educator; b. Easton, Pa., May 7, 1943; s. Robert Simpson and Esther Evans (Thomas) W.; B.A., Haverford Coll., 1965; Ph.D., Washington U., St. Louis, 1972; m. Mary P. Hutton, Feb. 15, 1969; children—Christopher Thomas, Rebecca Marie. Brookings Econ. Policy fellow HEW, Washington, 1975-76; asst. prof. U. Western Ont. (Can.), London, 1972-77; asst. prof. Sch. Medicine, Washington U., St. Louis, 1978-86, assoc. prof., 1986—; pres. TeacherWorks Software, Inc., 1987— . Mem. adv. council Mo. Kidney Program, 1980-86, vice-chmn., 1983, chmn. 1984-85; coop. mem. Haverford Coll., 1968—. NDEA fellow, 1968-71; Kellogg Nat. fellow, 1981-84. Mem. Am. Econs. Assn., Am. Statis. Assn. Contbr. articles to profl. jours. Home: 7050 Westmoreland St University City MO 63130 Office: 4547 Clayton Ave Saint Louis MO 63110

WOOLDRIDGE, DAVID IAN, architect; b. Trinidad, W.I., Aug. 9, 1944; came to Can., 1962; s. Henry Frank and Elma Jeanne (Rauseo) W.; m. Beryl Marie Vincent (div.); 1 child, Talia Mae. B.Arch., Tech. U. N.S., Halifax, 1968. Registered architect, Ont. Draftsman George Wimpey Can., Toronto, Ont., 1968-71; office mgr. Sheldon D. Rosen, Toronto, 1972-78; prin. David Wooldridge Architects, Toronto, 1979—. Mem. Toronto Home Builders Assn., Ont. Assn. Architects, Royal Archtl. Inst. Can. Progressive Conservative. Roman Catholic. Club: Holiday Fitness (Toronto). Avocations:

tennis; golf; squash; current music; dancing. Office: 1131A Leslie St Suite 210, Don Mills, ON Canada M3C 2K9

WOOLDRIDGE, MICHAEL JAMES, engineering researcher; b. Coventry, Eng., July 15, 1933; arrived in Australia, 1967; s. Frederick Walter and Dorothy Elizabeth (Walder) W.; m. Mavis Anne Baber, Sept. 15, 1956 (div. 1983); children: Michael Clive, John Duncan, Ann Jacqueline; m. Carole Edwina Hyde, Dec. 29, 1983. BS in Physics with honours, U. Leeds (Eng.), 1954. Structural and stress analyst Hawker Siddeley Dynamics Ltd., Coventry, 1956-61, sect. and group leader, 1961-67; from sr. research scientist to prin. research scientist mech. engring. div. Commonwealth Scientific Indsl. Research Orgn., Melbourne, Australia, 1967-80, prin. research scientist energy tech. div., 1981-84, sr. prin. research scientist energy tech. div., 1984-87, sr. prin. research scientist bldg. constrn. and engring. div., 1988—; cons. Assn. Southeast Asian Nations-Australia Econ. Cooperation Program, 1984—; cons., del. Korea-Australia Energy Consultations, Seoul, 1987. Contbr. numerous articles to profl. jours. Scout leader Boy Scouts Eng., Conventry, 1953-62, Boy Scouts Australia, Melbourne, 1967-74; mem., sec. sch. council Bentleigh High Sch., Melbourne, 1972-77. Mem. Royal Aero. Soc., ASHRAE (mem. tech. coms., internat. best paper award 1980), Australian Inst. Refrigeration, Air Conditioning and Heating (mem. tech. coms.). Mem. Ch. of England. Clubs: Flinders Golf (Australia); Sandringham Golf (Melbourne) (capt. 1977-79). Home: 10 Victoria Ave, Somers 3927, Australia Office: CSIRO Div Bldg Constrn, and Engring Div, PO Box 56, Highett 3190, Australia

WOOLEY, GARY RICHARD, engineering company executive; b. New Orleans, Oct. 21, 1946; s. Harold Aloysius and Althea (Herman) W.; m. Diana Lynn Picklesimer, Oct. 28, 1967; children: Tanya Jill, Tamara Lynn, Todd Richard. BS, La. State U., 1969, MS, 1970, PhD (Dissertation fellow), 1972. Registered profl. engr., Tex. Mechanic, Shell Oil Co., summer 1966; prodn. engr. Chevron Oil Co., summer 1967, constrn. engr., summer 1968; field engr. surface equipment group Humble Oil & Refining Co., La. Offshore Dist., New Orleans, 1969; grad. teaching asst. engring. sci. dept. La. State U., Baton Rouge, 1969-72; sr. research engr. Arctic spl. projects, group leader Prodn. Research Center, Atlantic Richfield Co., Plano, Tex., 1972-78; v.p., dir. Enertech Engring. & Research Co., Houston, 1978-86; v.p., dir. Enertech Computing Corp., 1981-86; pres. Gary R. Wooley & Assocs., 1986—. Contbr. articles and papers to profl. lit. Mem. adminstrv. bd. Meth. Ch. NSF trainee, 1969-71. Mem. Soc. Petroleum Engrs.-AIME, ASME (vice chmn. drilling and prodn. com. 1975, chmn. rock mechanics com. 1976, tech. reviewer Applied Mechanics Rev. 1975-80), Sigma Xi, Phi Kappa Phi, Tau Beta Pi, Pi Tau Sigma. Republican. Clubs: Gymnastics Boosters of Houston, Aerobats Boosters (v.p. 1977), Westside Tennis, Lakeside Civic (Houston); Canyon Creek Country (Richardson, Tex.). Home: 10911 Tupperlake Dr Houston TX 77042 Office: Gary R Wooley & Assocs 3657 Briarpark Suite 105 Houston TX 77042

WOOLF, HARRY, historian, educator; b. N.Y.C., Aug. 12, 1923; s. Abraham and Anna (Frankman) W.; m. Patricia A. Kelsh; children: Susan Deborah, Alan, Aaron, Sara Anna. B.S., U. Chgo., 1948, M.A., 1949; Ph.D., Cornell U., 1955; D.Sc. (hon.), Whitman Coll., 1979, Am. U., 1982; LHD (hon)., Johns Hopkins U., 1983, St. Lawrence U., 1986. Instr. physics Boston U., 1953-55; instr. history Brandeis U., 1954-55; asst. prof. history U. Wash., 1955-58, assoc. prof., 1958-59, prof. history of science, 1959-61; Willis K. Shepard prof. history of sci. Johns Hopkins U., 1961-76, chmn. dept. history of sci., 1961-72, provost, 1972-76; dir. Inst. for Advanced Study, Princeton, N.J., 1976-87, prof., 1987—; trustee, sci. advisor Cluster C Funds Merrill Lynch, 1982—; mem. adv. council Sch. Advanced Internat. Studies, Washington, 1973-76; adv. bd. Smithsonian Research awards, 1975-79; trustee Asso. Univs., Inc., Brookhaven Nat. Labs., 1972-82; mem. vis. com. student affairs MIT, 1973-77, mem. corp. vis. com. dept. linguistics and philosophy, 1977-83, mem. corp. vis. com. dept. physics, 1979-85; mem. Nat. Adv. Child Health and Human Devel. Council NIH, 1977-80; mem. vis. com. Research Center for Lang. Scis., Ind. U., 1977-80; com. visitors Vanderbilt Grad. Sch., Nashville, 1977-79; adv. council dept. philosophy Princeton U., 1980-84, adv. council dept. comparative lit., 1982—; mem. adv. panel WGBH, NOVA, 1979—; bd. dirs. Westmark Internat., 1987—; mem. adv. council NSF, 1984—. Author: Transits of Venus, 1959, 81, Quantification, 1961, Science as a Cultural Force, 1964, Some Strangeness in the Proportion, 1980, The Analytic Spirit, 1981; contbr. articles, revs. to profl. publs.; Editor: Isis Internat, rev. devoted to history of sci. and its cultural influences, 1958-64; series editor The Sources of Science, 1964—; assoc. editor Dictionary of Scientific Biography, 1970-80; editorial bd. Interdisciplinary Sci. Revs, 1975—; editorial adv. bd. The Writings of Albert Einstein, 1977—. Trustee Hampshire Coll., Amherst, Mass., 1977-79; trustee Winterthur Mus., 1978-83; bd. govs. Tel-Aviv U., 1977—; trustee-at-large Univs. Research Assn., Inc., 1978—, chmn. bd., 1979—; mem. adv. council John F. Kennedy Inst. for Handicapped Children, 1979—; mem. Internat. Research and Exchanges Bd., 1980—; chmn. MX Missile basing adv. panel Office of Tech. Assessment, Congress of U.S., 1980-81; trustee Rockefeller Found., 1984—; bd. dirs. Alex. Brown Mut. Funds, Balt., 1981—; dir. at large Am. Cancer Soc., 1982-86; mem. sci. adv. bd. Wissenschaftskolleg zu Berlin, Ger., 1981-87; mem. adv. bd. Stanford Humanities Ctr., 1981-87; bd. dirs. W. Alton Jones Cell Sci. Ctr., 1982-85. Served with AUS, 1943-46. NSF sr. postdoctoral fellow Europe, 1961-62. Fellow AAAS (v.p. 1960), Acad. Internat. d'Histoire des Scis.; mem. History of Sci. Soc., Am. Philos. Soc., Council on Fgn. Relations, Am. Acad. Arts and Scis., Phi Beta Kappa, Sigma Xi, Phi Alpha Theta. Office: Princeton U Inst for Advanced Study Olden Ln Princeton NJ 08540

WOOLF, PRESTON G., beverage company executive, lawyer; b. Indpls., Oct. 10, 1906; s. Merritt Edgar and Bertha E. (Stone) W.; B.S., U. Fla., 1928; LL.B., Ind. U., 1932; grad. in material resources Indsl. Coll. Armed Forces; m. Phoebe Ann Cummins, Nov. 9, 1937 (dec. 1980); m. 2d, Betty Lee Deats, Jan. 2, 1982. Export mgr. Hurty-Peck & Co., Indpls., 1932-36, asst. sec., 1936-47, sec, 1947-76; asst. sec. Hurty-Peck & Co. of Calif., Orange, 1942-46, sec., 1946-76; pres. Am. Beverage and Supply Corp., Indpls., 1945-76, chmn. bd., 1976—; sec. Costa Rican Devel. Co., San Jose, Hurty-Peck Eastern, Inc., Union, N.J., Blanke-Baer Co., St. Louis, Gt. Am. Trading Corp., St. Louis, Mfrs. Fin. Corp., Indpls., Remi Foods Corp., Chgo., Universal Falvors Ill., Chgo., 1959-77; dir. Woolf Internat., Ltd., Hong Kong, 1961—, Ambesco de Mé xico, S.A. de C.V., New Mexico City, Universal Flavors Corp., Universal Flavors, Calif., Inc., Universal Flavors N.J., Inc., Universal Flavors Mo., Inc., 1959-77; spl. fgn. corr. Indpls. Star, 1959—; columnist chain S. Am. newspapers, 1960—; mem. world trade adv. com. U.S. Dept. Commerce, 1958-60, mem. Midwest regional com., 1960-67; co-sponsor Central Asian Studies Program, Oxford U., 1980—. Leader, Republican polit. study mission to Arabian world, 1966; leader Ind. Bankers and Indsl. Leaders study tour around world, 1967, to Africa, 1968, to China, 1976; cons. on Oriental affairs; mem. Trade Missions subcom. Council Fgn. Relations; mem. Ind. Fgn. Lang. Adv. Com.; pres. Indpls. Council World Affairs, 1958-60; dir. Internat. Bldg., Ind. State Fair, 1958-60; dir. Internat. Sch. Bus., Ind. U., 1961-67; mem. adv. council State Ind. Fgn. Lang. Program; 1st v.p. Ind. Econ. Edn. Found., 1965-77; chmn. Ind. Peoples World Affairs Com., 1961—; dir. Citizen's Com. for Free Cuba, 1965—; mem. bd. strategy Episcopal Diocese Indpls., 1961-66; co-sponsor Asian Studies Inst., Oxford, Eng., 1982—. Decorated Gold Cross Merit, 1st class (Fed. Republic W.Ger.); recipient citation Indpls. C. of C., 1960; Rabbi Stephen S. Wise Meml. citation Am. Jewish Congress, 1959. Mem. English-Speaking Union, Japan Soc., Asia Soc., U.S. C. of C. (world trade com.), Pan Am. Soc., AIM, Am. Bar Assn., Am. Security Council Washington, Inter-Am. Lawyers Assn. (founder 1935, pres. 1935-38), Am. Legion, Indpls. C. of C. (leader trade missions to Orient 1963, Latin Am. 1965), Delta Chi, Sigma Delta Chi, Sigma Delta Kappa. Republican. Episcopalian. Clubs: Rotary, Athletic, Press, Literary (Indpls.); Overseas Press (N.Y.C.); Am. (Hong Kong, Singapore); Fgn. Corrs. (Tokyo); Masons. Mem. record-breaking around-the-world Flight Pan Am. Airways, 1976, N. and S. Poles Expdn., 1977. Home: 14825 Allisonville Rd Noblesville IN 46060-4337 Office: 5700 W Raymond St Indianapolis IN 46241

WOOLLEY, KENNETH FRANK, architect; b. Sydney, Australia, May 29, 1933; s. Frank and Doris May (Mudear) W.; m. Cynthia Stuart; m. 2d Virginia Braden, 1980; 3 children. Student U. Sydney. Design architect Govt. Architect's Office, Sydney, 1955-56, 67-63; asst. architect Chamberlin, Powell & Bon, London, 1956-57; ptnr. Ancher Mortlock, Murray & Woolley, Sydney, 1964-69, dir., 1969-75; dir. Ancher Mortlock & Woolley Pty. Ltd., 1975—; vis. tutor, critic, prof. U. Sydney, U. New South Wales, New South Wales Inst. Tech.; mem. New South Wales Bd. Architects, 1960-72, New South Wales Bldg. Regulations Adv. Com., 1960-74, New South Wales Bd. Archtl. Edn., 1969-72, Royal Australian Inst. Architects Aboriginal Housing Panel, 1972-76. Maj. works include: Australian Embassy, Bangkok, Sydney Town Hall renovations, new offices and city sq., three student union bldgs., Univs. in N.S.W., numerous urban housing devel., radio stas., Vanuatu, Solomon Islands; mem. quality rev. com. Darung Harbour Redevel. Authority, 1985; contbr. articles to profl. jours. Recipient Sulman award, 1962; Bronze medal, 1962; Wilkinson award, 1962, 68, 83; Blacket award, 1964; others. Office: A Mortlock & Woolley Pty Ltd, 40 Collins St, 2010 Surrey, New South Wales Australia *

WOOTEN, BILLY MACK, health care centers adminstr.; b. San Angelo, Tex., Feb. 25, 1947; s. Billy S. and Maxine C. (Watson) W.; B.A. in Psychology, N.Mex. State U., 1969, M.A., 1976; B.A. in Social Work, St. Cloud (Minn.) State U., 1974; M.S. in Mental Retardation, Mankato (Minn.) State U., 1980; Ph.D. in Psychology, Columbia Pacific U., 1981; m. Linda Ruth Lundgren, Apr. 7, 1973; children—Joshua S., Joseph A. Mental health counselor Southwest Mental Health Center, Alamogordo, N.Mex., 1972-73; exec. dir. REM, Inc., Marshall, Minn., 1975-85; state adminstr. REM-Ind. Inc., 1985—; pres. Prairie Systems, Inc., 1983—; adj. prof. spl. edn., Mankato State U.; chmn. Services Industries, Inc.; cons. REM Cons. & Services, Inc., Mpls., Ind. Dept. Mental Health. Served with USAF, 1969-73; pvt. practice Behavior Analysts, 1978—. Served with USAF, 1969-73. Mem. Am. Assn. Mental Deficiency (vice chairperson psychology 1977-79, editor Region VIII Newsletter 1979—, Minn. sec.-treas.), Assn. Advancement of Behavior Therapy, Assn. Behavior Analysis, Minn. Assn. Behavior Analysis (membership chmn., pres. 1982-83). Democrat. Unitarian. Club: Kiwanis. Author: (with David C. Pfriem) An Introduction to Behavioral Techniques, 1979; A Rational Approach to Counseling the Mentally Retarded, 1981; contbr. articles to profl. jours. Home: 1121 Fairbanks Dr Carmel IN 46032 Office: 11711 N Meridian Suite 750 Carmel IN 46032

WOOTTEN, JOHN ROBERT, investor; b. Chickasha, Okla., Feb. 5, 1929; s. Henry Hughes and Ella Gayle (Ditzler) W.; B.S., Colo. A&M U., 1953; m. Mary Lou Schmausser, Mar. 15, 1952 (div.); children—Pamela Jean, Robert Hughes; m. 2d, Geraldine Ann Theisen, Aug. 14, 1982. Sec., S.W. Radio & Equipment Co., Oklahoma City, 1953-55; pres. Belcaro Homes, Inc., 1955-60, Bob Wootten Ford, Yukon, Okla., 1960-68, Bus. Data Systems, 1968-72; chmn., chief exec. officer 1st Nat. Bank, Moore, Okla., 1970-72; pres. Communications Enterprises, Inc., Liberal, Kans., 1967-79, Trebor Leasing Co., 1965-87, Okla. Sch. Book Depository, Inc., Oklahoma City, 1976-80, S.W. Sch. Book Depository, Inc., Dallas, 1976-86; chmn., chief exec. officer Exchange Nat. Bank Del City (Okla.), 1976-78; dir. S.W. Bancshares Corp., Oklahoma City. Pres., Okla. chpt. Am. Cancer Soc., 1966-67, Okla. chpt. Arthritis Found., 1973-76, Lyric Theater Okla., 1976-77; chmn. bd. trustees Bone and Joint Hosp., 1976-81; bd. dirs. Okla. Theater Center, Dallas Theater Center; trustee Oklahoma City U.; pres. Last Frontier council Boy Scouts Am., 1968-70, Silver Beaver award, 1971; Republican nominee for Lt. Gov. of Okla., 1966. Mem. Ind. Bankers Assn., Am. Bankers Assn., Tex. Bookmen's Assn., Okla. Bookmen's Assn., Tex. Assn. Sch. Adminstrs., Econ. Club Okla., Navy League. Republican. Episcopalian. Club: Oklahoma City Rotary (pres. 1963-64). Home: 6918 Tokalon Dr Dallas TX 75214

WOOTTON, HARRY, investment company executive; b. Chadderton, U.K., Apr. 1, 1918; s. Walter and Florence (Richards) W.; student Manchester Coll. Tech., 1937-39; m. Doris Cartwright, Nov., 1939; children—Judith Anne, Jacqueline Carol, John Stuart, Josephine Pamela. Apprentice, Met. Vickers, 1935-39; foreman Ferranti Ltd., 1939-40; prodn. engr. Nuswift Engring., 1941-43; indsl. valuer Wheatley Kirk Price & Co., 1945-55; founder Wootton Haslam and Co. Ltd., indsl. cons., Johannesburg, S. Africa, 1955-77; founder Map Centre Ltd., Johannesburg, 1959-76; founder Indsl. Applications, Johannesburg, 1960-77; owner, mng. dir. Hardor Investments (Pty.) Ltd., 1960—; mng. dir. East London Printers (Pty.) Ltd., 1960-79, Bartlam Investments (Pty.) Ltd., 1972—; owner, dir. Umvoti Villa Farms, Greytown, S.Africa, 1966—. Served as seagoing engr. Mcht. Navy, 1940-41. Home and Office: Umvoti Villa Farms, PO Box 211, Greytown 3500 Republic of South Africa

WORCESTER, ROBERT MILTON, market research company executive; b. Dec. 21, 1933; s. C.M. and Violet Ruth Worcester; m. Joann Ransdell, 1958 (div.); 2 children; m. Margaret Smallbone, 1982. BS, U. Kans., 1955. Mgmt. cons. McKinsey & Co., Kansas City, Mo., 1962-65; controller, asst. to chmn. Opinion Research Corp., London, 1965-68; mng. dir. Market and Opinion Research Internat. (MORI) Ltd., London, 1969—, chmn., 1973—; past pres. World Assn. for Pub. Opinion Research; cons. London Times, Economist newspapers; frequent radio and TV broadcasts and presentations to colls. and orgns. Editor: Consumer Market Research Handbook, 1971, 3d edit., 1986, (with M. Harrop) Political Communications, 1982, Political Opinion Polling: An International Review, 1983, (with Watkins) Private Opinions, Public Polls, 1986; columnist London Times; contbr. articles to tech. and profl. jours. Mem. Pilgrims' Soc., UNESCO Internat. Social Sci. Council, Ditchley Found. (program com.). Club: Reform. Address: 32 Old Queen St, London SW1 H9HP, England

WORDEN, KATHARINE COLE, sculptor; b. N.Y.C., May 4, 1925; d. Philip Gillette and Katharine (Pyle) Cole; student Potters Sch., Tucson, 1940-42, Sarah Lawrence Coll., 1942-44; m. Frederic G. Worden, Jan. 8, 1944; children—Rick, Dwight, Philip, Barbara, Katharine. Sculptor; works exhibited Royce Galleries, Galerie Francoise Besnard (Paris), Cooling Gallery (London), Galerie Schumacher (Munich), Selected Artists Gallery, N.Y.C., Art Inst. Boston, Reid Gallery, Nashville, Weiner Gallery, N.Y.C., Boston Athanaeum, House of Humor and Satire, Gabrovo, Bulgaria, 1983, Newport Bay Club, 1984; pvt. collections Grand Palais (Paris), Dakar and Bathurst, Africa; dir. Stride Rite Corp., 1980-85; occupational therapist psychopathic ward Los Angeles County Gen. Hosp., 1953-57; Headstart vol., Watts, Calif., 1965-67; tchr. sculpture Watts Towers Art Center, 1967-69; participant White House Women Doers Luncheon meeting, 1968; dir. Cambridgeport Problem Center, Cambridge, Mass., 1969-71; mem. Jud. Nominating Commn., 1976-79; bd. overseers Boston Mus. Fine Arts, 1980-83; trustee Communication Research Inst., Miami, Fla., 1960-69, chmn. bd., 1966-69; trustee Newport Art Mus., 1984-86, Newport Health Found., 1986—; bd. dirs. Boston Center for Arts, 1976-80, Child and Family Services of Newport County, 1983—. Mem. Common Cause (Mass. adv. bd. 1971-72, dir. 1974-75), Mass. Civil Liberties Union (exec. bd. 1973-74, dir. 1976-77). Home: 24 Ft Wetherill Rd Jamestown RI 02835

WORENKLEIN, JACOB J., lawyer; b. N.Y.C., Oct. 1, 1948; s. Abraham and Cela (Zyskind) W.; m. Marion Knopf, June 27, 1967; children: David, Daniel, Laura. BA, Columbia U., 1969; MBA, JD, NYU, 1973. Bar: N.Y. 1974. Assoc. Milbank, Tweed, Hadley & McCloy, N.Y.C., 1973-81, ptnr., 1982—, also firm exec. com., 1984-86, co-chmn. firm planning com., 1988—; chmn. Utility Leasing Conf., 1988. Contbr. articles to profl. jours. Pres. Old Broadway Synagogue, N.Y.C., 1978—; trustee Fedn. Jewish Philanthropies, N.Y.C., 1984-86; bd. of overseers, United Jewish Appeal-Fedn. Jewish Philanthropies, 1987—. Mem. ABA (electricity and utility financing com.), N.Y. State Bar Assn. (sec. action unit toward more effective legislature 1975), Assn. of Bar of City of N.Y., Fed. Energy Bar Assn., Down Town Assn., Phi Beta Kappa. Office: Milbank Tweed Hadley & McCloy 1 Chase Manhattan Plaza New York NY 10005

WORKMAN, CHARLES CLEVELAND, JR., management consultant; b. Lineville, Ala., Apr. 14, 1913; s. Charles Cleveland and Emma Franklin (Jones) W.; B.S., Auburn U., 1934; m. Jane Lucille Pinaire, Aug. 19, 1944 (dec.); 1 dau., Janet Susan Workman Baltzer; m. Bessie Kate Bradford, Mar. 23, 1968 (dec.); m. Shelby Gause Freeman, June 28, 1985. Trainee, Consol. Millinery Co. of Chgo., 1934-35, br. mgr., Miami, Fla. also Allentown, Pa., 1935-36; asst. dept. mgr. Stewart Dry Goods Co., Louisville, 1937; with IBM Corp., 1937-70, sales rep., Louisville, 1937-40, br mgr., Shreveport, La., 1946-49, Houston, 1950-54, mgr. Southeast dist., Atlanta, 1955-62, dir. mktg. Fed. Systems div., Washington, 1963, mgr. aerospace and dist. br., Atlanta, 1964-70; pres. Mgmt. Services, Inc., Atlanta, 1971-74; So. regional mgr. TLW Corp., Atlanta, 1974-76; mgmt. cons., Atlanta, 1977—; gen. ptnr. Midtown Investment Properties, Etowah Investment Properties, Dawson Investment Opportunity. Bd. dirs. Goodwill Industries, 1960-73, pres., 1972-73; various offices ARC, 1937-71, United Way, 1937-71; mem. U.S. Congressional Adv. Bd., Am. Security Council, 1980—. Served to lt. col. AUS, 1940-45. Mem. SAR, Nat. Assn. Accts., Nat. Sales Execs. Club. Republican. Presbyterian (deacon). Clubs: Kiwanis Internat., Cherokee Town and Country. Address: 9790 Huntcliff Trace Atlanta GA 30350

WORKMAN, GEORGE HENRY, engineering consultant; b. Muskegon, Mich., Sept. 18, 1939; s. Harvey Merton and Bettie Jane (Meyers) W.; Asso. Sci., Muskegon Community Coll., 1960; B.S.E., U. Mich., 1966, M.S.E., 1966, Ph.D., 1969; m. Vicki Sue Hanish, June 17, 1967; children—Mark, Larry. Prin. engr. Battelle Meml. Inst., Columbus, Ohio, 1969-76; pres. Applied Mechanics Inc., Longboat Key, Fla., 1976—; instr. dept. civil engring. Ohio State U., 1973, 82. Served with USN, 1961-64. Named Outstanding Undergrad. Student, Engring. Mechanics dept. U. Mich., 1965-66, Outstanding Grad. Student, Civil Engring. dept., 1968-69. Registered profl. engr., Ohio. Mem. Am. Acad. of Mechanics, ASME, ASCE, Nat. Soc. Profl. Engrs., Sigma Xi, Chi Epsilon, Phi Kappa Phi, Phi Theta Kappa. Congregationalist. Contbr. tech. papers to nat. and internat. confs. Home and Office: 3431 Bayou Court Longboat Key FL 34228

WORLEY, MARVIN GEORGE, JR., architect; b. Oak Park, Ill., Oct. 10, 1934; s. Marvin George and Marie Hyancinth (Donahue) W.; B.Arch., U. Ill., 1958; m. Maryalice Ryan, July 11, 1959; children—Michael Craig, Carrie Ann, Alissa Maria. Project engr. St. Louis area Nike missile bases U.S. Army C.E., Granite City, Ill., 1958-59, architect N.Cen. div. U.S. Army C.E., Chgo., 1960; architect Yerkes & Grunsfeld, architects, Chgo., 1961-65, asso., 1965; asso. Grunsfeld & Assos., architects, Chgo., 1966-85.; prin. Marvin Worley Architects, Oak Park, Ill., 1985—. Dist. architect Oak Park Elementary Schs., Dist. 97, 1973-80. Mem. Oak Park Community Improvement Commn., 1973-75; mem. exec. bd. Oak Park Council PTA, 1970-73, pres., 1971-72. Served with AUS, 1959. Mem. AIA (corporate), Chgo. Assn. Commerce and Industry. Office: 37 South Boulevard Oak Park IL 60302

WORLING, PETER METCALFE, pharmaceutical distribution executive; b. Nagrakata, Jalpaiguri, Doars, India, June 16, 1928; came to U.K., 1932; s. Alexander Davidson and Florence (Metcalfe) W.; m. Iris Isabella McBeath, Mar. 20, 1954; children—Bruce, Helen, Fiona. Pharm. chemist, Robert Gordons Coll., Aberdeen, Scotland, 1950; PhD Bradford U., 1988. Cert. pharmacist. Export sales exec. Carnegie's of Welwyn Ltd., Welwyn Garden City, Hertfordshire, Eng., 1950-53, home sales mgr., 1953-56; br. pharmacist Bradley & Bliss Ltd., Reading, Berkshire, Eng., 1956-65; br. mgr. Vestric Ltd., Ruislip, Middlesex, Eng., 1965-66, regional dir., Edinburgh, Scotland, 1966-73, mgr. dir. Runcorn, Cheshire, Eng., 1979-87, dir., 1973-79; chmn. Pharmagen Ltd., Runcorn, 1980—, Pharmed Ltd., 1982—, dir., A.A.H. Pharmaceuticals, Ltd., 1987—. Fellow Royal Pharm. Soc.; mem. Coll. of Pharmacy Practice, Nat. Assn. Pharm. Distbrs. (chmn. 1983-85), Proprietary Articles Trade Assn. (pres. 1984-85). Presbyterian. Home: Riverhurst 19 Eyebrook Rd, Bowdon Cheshire WA14 3LH, England Office: AAH Pharmaceuticals Ltd, West Ln Runcorn, Cheshire WA7 2PE, England

WÖRNER, MANFRED, international organization executive; b. Stuttgart, Germany, Sept. 24, 1934; s. Carl and Kläre W.; m. Elfie Reiusch, 1982. Student in law U. Heidelberg (W.Ger.), U. Paris; Ph.D. in Law, U. Munich (W.Ger.), 1961. Parliamentary adviser Baden-Württemberg State Assembly (W.Ger.), 1962-64; mem. German Bundestag, Bonn, W.Ger., from 1965, chmn. com. on def., 1976-80, minister of def., 1982-88; dep. chmn. Konrad Adenauer Found., 1970—. Dep. chmn. Christian Democratic Union parliamentary party, Bundstag, 1969-71, chmn. group of Bundestag deps. from Baden-Württemberg, 1970-82, chmn. working group on def. Christian Dem. Union/CSU parliamentary party, 1972-76, dep. chmn. party, 1980-82; mem. nat. exec. Christian Dem. Union, from 1973. Sec. gen. NATO, Brussels, 1988—. Office: care NATO, 1110 Brussels Belgium *

WORRALL, LESLIE, civic planner; b. Runcorn, Cheshire, Eng., Oct. 25, 1952; s. Ronald Stonewall and Joyce (Hewitt) W.; m. Linda Carol Worrall, Dec. 17, 1977. BA in Geography with hons., Hull U., Eng., 1974; M in Civic Design, Liverpool U., Eng., 1977, PhD in Regional Sci., 1987. Chartered planner. Researcher Telford (Eng.) Devel. Corp., 1977-80; prin. policy planner Wrekin Council, Telford, 1980—. Contbr. articles to profl. jours. U. Liverpool fellow, 1987—. Fellow Royal Stat. Soc.; mem. Royal Town Planning Inst., Regional Sci. Assn., Internat. Assn. Urban and Regional Statisticians, Local Authorities Research and Intelligence Assn. (hon sec. 1986-88, chmn. 1988—). Home: 2 Spafield Close, Shawbirch, Telford TF5 0NL, England Office: Wrekin Council Policy Unit, PO Box 213 Malinslee House, Telford TF3 4LD, England

WORRELL, RICHARD VERNON, orthopedic surgeon, college dean; b. Bklyn., June 4, 1931; s. John Elmer and Elaine (Callender) W.; B.A., NYU, 1952; M.D., Meharry Med. Coll., 1958; m. Audrey Frances Martiny, June 14, 1958; children—Philip Vernon, Amy Elizabeth. Intern Meharry Med. Coll., Nashville, 1958-59; resident gen. surgery Mercy-Douglass Hosp., Phila., 1960-61; resident orthopaedic surgery State U. N.Y. Buffalo Sch. Medicine Affiliated Hosps., 1961-64; resident in orthopaedic pathology Temple U. Med. Center, Phila., 1966-67; pvt. practice orthopaedic surgery, Phila., 1964-68; asst. prof. acting head div. orthopaedic surgery U. Conn. Sch. Medicine 1968-70; attending orthopaedic surgeon E.J. Meyer Meml. Hosp., Buffalo, Millard Fillmore Hosp., Buffalo, VA Hosp., Buffalo, Buffalo State Hosp.; clin. instr. orthopaedic surgery SUNY, Buffalo, 1970-74; chief orthopedic surgery VA Hosp., Newington, Conn., 1974-80; asst. prof. surgery (orthopaedics) U. Conn. Sch. Medicine, 1974-77, assoc. prof., 1977-83, asst. dean student affairs, 1980-83; prof. clin. surgery SUNY Downstate Med. Ctr., Bklyn., 1983—; dir. orthopedic surgery Brookdale Hosp. Med. Ctr., Bklyn., 1983-86; prof. of orthopaedics U. N.Mex. Sch. of Medicine, 1986—; dir. orthopaedic oncology U. N.Mex. Med. Ctr., 1987—; mem. med. staff U. N.Mex. Cancer Ctr., 1987—; chief orthopaedic surgery VA Med. Ctr., Albuquerque, 1987—; cons. in orthopaedic surgery Newington (Conn.) Children's Hosp., 1968-70; mem. sickle cell disease adv. com. NIH, 1982-86. Bd. dirs. Big Bros. Greater Hartford. Served to capt. M.C., U.S. Army Res., 1962-69. Diplomate Am. Bd. Orthopaedic Surgery, Nat. Bd. Med. Examiners. Fellow ACS, Am. Acad. Orthopaedic Surgeons; mem. Orthopaedic Research Soc., Internat. Soc. Orthopaedic Surgery and Traumatology, AMA, Royal Med Soc. (affiliate), Alpha Omega Alpha.

WORSHAM, EARL S., real estate investor, developer; b. Knoxville, Tenn., Nov. 15, 1932; s. Earl S. and Melba (Reagan) W.; m. Nancy Davidson, July 10, 1952 (div.); children—Lee, Elizabeth, Lyn; m. 2d, Anita Moiger, 1974; 1 child, Susan. Diploma Culver Mil. Acad., 1950; B.S. in Fin., U. Tenn., 1955; M.B.A., Am. U., 1957. Pres., chmn. Worsham Bros. Co., Inc., Tenn., Ga., Fla., 1952—, chmn. Westley-Swift Found., Atlanta, 1983—, The Westminster Group, Atlanta, 1973—; chmn. The Resource Ctr., Atlanta; developer, owner Hyatt Regency, Miami, Knoxville, Excelsior Hotel, Little Rock, also others. Active United Fund, Miami, Fla., Served with U.S. Army, 1955-57. Recipient Developer of Yr. award City of Miami, 1979, Dade County, 1979, City of Miami Reach, 1979. Mem. Urban Land Inst. Clubs: Miami; Cherokee Country (Knoxville); Anglers (N.Y.C.). Home: 1 Cherokee Rd Atlanta GA 30305 Office: Worsham Bros Co Inc 1401 W Paces Ferry Rd Atlanta GA 30327

WORTHINGTON, BARBARA CAVEDO, clinical psychologist; b. Richmond, Va., June 25, 1942; d. William Fitzgerald Cavedo and Edith Earline (Mann) Cavedo Gould; B.A. with high honors, Christopher Newport Coll., 1973; MA (Roper Grad. fellow, Williams fellow), U. Richmond, 1974; PhD, Va. Commonwealth U., 1978; m. Clarke Worthington III, Dec. 20, 1963; 1 son, Tyler Clarke. Psychol. intern VA Treatment Ctr., Med. Coll. of Va., Richmond, 1977-78; clin. child psychologist Child Guidance Clinic, Winston-Salem, N.C., 1978-80; pvt. practice clin. psychology, Winston-Salem, 1980—; ptnr. Triad Psychol. Assocs. Mem. bd. dirs. Winston-Salem/Forsyth County Battered Women's Services, 1980-82, youth adv. bd. Sawtooth Ctr. for Design. Mem. NOW (treas. Winston-Salem chpt. 1979), Forsyth Area Psychol. Assn., N.C. Psychol. Assn., Va. Psychol. Assn., Assn. Women in Psychology, Menninger Found., Am. Psychol. Assn. Democrat. Episcopalian. Contbr. articles to profl. publs. Home: 1850 Runnymeade Rd Winston-Salem NC 27104

WORTZ, CARL HAGLIN, III, business consultant; b. Ft. Smith, Ark., May 9, 1921; s. Carl H. Wortz and Ed Dell (Haglin) W.; grad. N.Mex. Mil.

Inst., 1940, Sparton Sch. Aeronautics, 1943; B.S. in Bus., U. Ark., 1947; m. Charlotte Wacker, June 29, 1943; 1 dau., Carolyn Jane. Former pres. Wortz Co.; pres. Wortz Assocs.; dir. Tex. Group. Served with AUS, 1943-46; CBI. Mem. Sigma Alpha Epsilon. Methodist. Club: International House (New Orleans). Office: PO Box 45565 Dallas TX 75245 Office: 260 Ledgerwood Rd Hot Springs AR 71901

WORTZEL, MURRAY N., periodicals librarian, educator; b. Bklyn., July 1, 1923; s. Alex and Anna (Weintraub) W. A.B., Stanford U., 1946; M.L.S., Columbia U., 1963, cert., 1974. Cashier, bookstore mgr. Columbia U. Sch. Social Work, N.Y.C., 1950-63; asst. to social sci. librarian Hunter Coll., N.Y.C., 1963-64, social sci. librarian, instr., Bronx, 1964-66; reference librarian, Herbert H. Lehman Coll., CUNY, Bronx, 1967-79, asst. prof., 1970-80, periodicals librarian, assoc. prof., 1981—; guest lectr. Baruch Coll. CUNY, 1979. Referee articles in social scis. for Spl. Libraries Jour., N.Y., 1970—. Served with U.S. Army, 1942-45. Faculty fellow Lehman Coll., CUNY, Bronx, 1965-66. Mem. Am. Library Assn. (numerous coms.), Spl. Libraries Assn. (chmn. social sci. div. 1974-75, book rev. editor 1982—, Disting. Service award 1987, sec.-treas. social sci. div. 1988—), Soc. Work Librarians Group (coordinator), Council Social Work Edn., Social Welfare History Group (co-chair), , AAAS, N.Y. Acad. Sci., Sigma Xi, Kappa Delta Pi. Avocation: music of Kurt Weill. Home: 401 1st Ave Apt 11C New York NY 10010

WOUK, HERMAN, writer; b. N.Y.C., May 27, 1915; s. Abraham Isaac and Esther (Levine) W.; m. Betty Sarah Brown, Dec. 9, 1945; children: Abraham Isaac (dec.), Nathaniel, Joseph. AB with gen. honors, Columbia U., 1934; LHD (hon.), Yeshiva U., 1954; LLD (hon.), Clark U., 1960; LittD (hon.), Am. Internat. Coll., 1979. Writer radio programs for various comedians N.Y.C., 1935; asst. writer weekly radio scripts comedian Fred Allen, 1936-41; Presdl. cons. to U.S. Treasury, 1941; vis. prof. English Yeshiva U., 1952-57; scholar-in-residence Aspen Inst. Humanistic Studies, 1973-74. Author (novels) Aurora Dawn, 1947, The City Boy, 1948, Slattery's Hurricane, 1949, The Caine Mutiny, 1951 (Pulitzer Prize award for fiction 1952), Marjorie Morningstar, 1955, Youngblood Hawke, 1962, Don't Stop the Carnival, 1965, The Winds of War, 1971, War and Remembrance, 1978, Inside, Outside, 1985 (Washingtonian Book award 1986), (dramas) The Traitor, 1949, The Caine Mutiny Court-Martial, 1953, (comedy) Nature's Way, 1957, (nonfiction) This is My God, 1959, (screenplays for TV serials) The Winds of War, 1983, War and Remembrance, 1986. Trustee Coll. of V.I., 1961-69; mem. adv. council Ctr. for U.S.-China Arts Exchange, 1981-87; bd. dirs. Washington Nat. Symphony, 1969-71, Kennedy Ctr. Prodns., 1974-75. Served to exec. officer U.S.S. Southard USNR, 1942-46, PTO. Recipient Richard H. Fox prize, 1934, Columbia U. medal for Excellence, 1952, Alexander Hamilton medal, 1980, U. Calif.-Berkeley medal, 1984; Golden Plate award Am. Acad. Achievement, 1986. Mem. Naval Res. Assn., Dramatists Guild, Authors Guild, Internat. Platform Assn. (Ralph Waldo Emerson award 1981), PEN. Jewish. Clubs: Bohemian (San Francisco); Cosmos, Metropolitan (Washington); Century Assn. (N.Y.C.). Office: care BSW Literary Agy 3255 N St NW Washington DC 20007

WOZENCRAFT, FRANK MCREYNOLDS, lawyer; b. Dallas, Apr. 25, 1923; s. Frank Wilson and Mary Victoria (McReynolds) W.; m. Shirley Ann Cooper, Nov. 25, 1960; children: Frank McReynolds, Ann Lacey, George Wilson. B.A. summa cum laude, Williams Coll., 1946; LL.B., Yale U., 1949. Bar: Tex. 1950. Law clk. to Justice Hugo L. Black, U.S. Supreme Ct., Washington, 1949-50; mem. firm Baker & Botts, Houston, 1950-60; partner Baker & Botts, 1960-66, 69—; dir. Rusk Corp.; asst. atty. gen. charge Office Legal Counsel, Dept. Justice, Washington, 1966-69; mem. legal adv. com. N.Y. Stock Exchange, 1978-83; Mem. Commn. Polit. Activity Govt. Employees, 1967; mem. Pres.'s Adv. Panel on Ins., 1967-68; vice chmn. Adminstrv. Conf. U.S., 1968-71, sr. fellow, 1982—; U.S. rep. Vienna Conf. on Law of Treaties, 1968. Mem. exec. bd. Sam Houston Area council Boy Scouts Am., 1959-66, 69—, v.p., 1974-79; past mem. adv. bd. Houston Mus. Fine Arts; past chmn. bd. Assn. Community TV; past mem. bd. govs. Public Broadcasting Service; trustee Hedgecroft Hosp., 1964-66, St. John's Sch., Houston, 1972-79; bd. dirs. Alley Theatre, 1961-66, 73-80. Served to capt. U.S. Army, 1943-46. Decorated Bronze Star. Mem. Am. Law Inst. (council), ABA (chmn. sect. adminstrv. law 1973-74, spl. com. open meetings legislation 1974-75), Houston Bar Assn., State Bar Tex. (chmn. sect. corp. banking and bus. law 1962-63), Philos. Soc. Tex. (v.p. 1987—), Order of Coif, Gargoyle, Phi Beta Kappa, Phi Delta Theta, Phi Delta Phi. Episcopalian. Clubs: Houston (pres. 1984-85), Houston Country; Chevy Chase (Md.); Univ. (Washington). Home: 51 E Broad Oaks St Houston TX 77056 Office: 3000 One Shell Plaza Houston TX 77002

WRAGG, LAISHLEY PALMER, JR., lawyer; b. Pitts., Oct. 11, 1933; s. Laishley Palmer and Irma Grace (Hill) W.; m. Marilyn Jean Smith, Apr. 26, 1957; children: Laishley P., Peter M.B. BBA, U. Mich., 1955; LLB cum laude, Harvard U., 1960; diploma in comparative legal studies Trinity Hall Coll., Cambridge U. (Eng.), 1961. Bar: N.Y. 1962, U.S. Supreme Ct. 1974, Conseil Juridique, France 1977. Assoc. Cravath, Swaine & Moore, N.Y.C., 1961-62, 1965-69, Paris, 1963-65, assoc. Curtis, Mallet-Prevost, Colt & Mosle, N.Y.C., 1969-70, ptnr., 1970—. Mem. U.S. Dept. State ad hoc com. on large constrn. projects; U.S. del. to 15th-20th sessions of UNCITRAL. Served to lt. USN, 1955-57. Mem. Assn. of Bar of City of N.Y., U. S. Council of Internat. C. of C. (com. on restrictive bus. practices), Inter-Am. Bar Assn., French Am. C. of C., France Am. Soc. (N.Y.C.). Republican. Presbyterian. Clubs: Am. Yacht (Rye, N.Y.); Hawks (Cambridge, Eng.), Ekwanok County (Manchester, Vt.); Automobile de France (Paris); Harvard of N.Y., Duquesne (Pitts.). Contbr. articles on law to profl. jours. Home: 123 E 75th St New York NY 10021 Office: 101 Park Ave New York NY 10178

WRANGLÉN, KARL GUSTAF (GÖSTA), applied electrochemistry educator, consultant; b. Örebro, Sweden, Mar. 19, 1923; m. Elevy Brodin, June 27, 1953; 1 son, Hans (dec.). Chem. Engr., Royal Inst. Tech., Stockholm, 1947, D.Engring., 1950, D.Tech., 1955. Guest worker Nat. Bur. Standards, Washington, 1950; research engr. various industries, Sweden, 1951-58; assoc. prof. applied electrochemistry and corrosion sci. Royal Inst. Tech., Stockholm, 1959-63, prof., 1963—, conferrer of hon. doctors, 1983; cons. Sandvik Steel Works, Sweden, 1963-85. Author: Electrocrystallization of Metals, 1955 (Japanese translation 1956); Corrosion and Protection of Metals, 1972 (translated into Japanese, Polish, Italian, German), 2d edit., 1985. Mem. Internat. Soc. Electrochemistry (dir. 1969-78, pres. 1975-76). Conservative. Lutheran. Office: Royal Inst Tech, 79 Valhallavägen, Stockholm S-10044, Sweden

WRAY, KARL, newspaper broker, former newspaper owner and publisher; b. Bishop, Tex., June 8, 1913; s. Ernest Paul and Gertrude (Garvin) W.; m. Flora-Lee Koepp, Aug. 11, 1951; children: Diana, Mark, Kenneth, Norman, Thomas. A.B., Columbia U., 1935. Auditor U.S. Dept. Agr., Washington, also Little Rock, 1935-37; salesman O'Mara & Ormsbee, Inc., N.Y.C., 1937-42; advt. mgr. Lompoc (Calif.) Record, 1947-54; owner, pub. San Clemente (Calif.) Daily Sun-Post, 1954-67, Coastline Dispatch, San Juan Capistrano, Calif., 1956-67, Dana Point (Calif.) Lamplighter, 1966-67; cons. Lear Siegler, Inc., Washington, 1967-68; pub. Daily Star-Progress, La Habra, Calif., 1969-74, Anaheim (Calif.) Bulletin, 1974-86. Mem. Calif. State Park Commn., 1960-64, vice chmn., 1961-62; mem. exec. bd. Orange County council Boy Scouts Am., 1961-64, 76-87; mem. citizens adv. com. Orange Coast Coll., 1963-66; bd. dirs. Calif. Newspaper Youth Found., 1978-84; pres. Freedom Bowl, Inc., Anaheim, Calif., 1981-84, chmn. bd., 1984-86, bd. dirs., 1986— . Served to capt. USMC, 1942-46. Mem. Calif. Newspaper Advt. Execs. Assn. (pres. 1952-53), Calif. Newspaper Pubs. Assn. (dir. 1960-64), Am. Theatre Critics Assn., Baseball Writers Assn. Am., Football Writers Assn. Am., Calif. Press Assn., San Juan Capistrano C. of C. (pres. 1966), San Clemente C. of C. (pres. 1956-57), La Habra C. of C. (dir. 1970-74), Anaheim C. of C. (dir. 1974-86). Presbyterian (elder). Address: 2420 S Ola Vista San Clemente CA 92672-4360

WREDE, JOHAN O. W., academic administrator; b. Helsinki, Finland, Oct. 18, 1935; s. Wilhelm Otto Casper and Eja (Westerlund) W.; m. Gunnel Julia Maria Cavonius; children: Henrik, Alexander, Matilda. Degree, U. Helsinki, Finland, 1960, fil. license, 1963, fil. doctorate, 1965. Dramaturge Finnish Broadcasting Corp., Helsinki, 1960-62; research asst. Finnish Acad., Helsinki, 1964-65, jr. fellow, 1965-68; docent U. Helsinki, Helsinki, 1968-69, prof., 1969—, dean Faculty of Arts, 1976-79, vice rector, 1983—. Contbr. over 200 articles to profl. jours. Recipient Hallberg prize Soc. Swedish Lit., 1966, Henrik Schück prize Swedish Acad., 1985; named life mem. Clare Hall, Cambridge, 1982—. Office: U Helsinki, Hallituskatu 11-13, 00100 Helsinki Finland

WRETLIND, KARL ARVID JOHANNES, nutritionist; b. Avesta, Sweden, Jan. 28, 1919; s. Johannes and Agnes (Gullberg) W.; M.D., Karolinska Inst., Stockholm, Sweden, 1949; D.Sc. (hon.), Rutgers U., 1980; m. Svea Astrid Lindewall, May 14, 1944; children—Bengt Magnus, Sophie Marie Louise. Asst. prof. pharmacology Karolinska Institutet, 1949-62; prof. nutrition Swedish NIH, Stockholm, 1962-70; prof. nutrition Karolinska Institutet, Stockholm, 1970-76; head Vitrum Inst. Human Nutrition, Stockholm, 1977-79, dir. Cutter-Vitrum Inst. Human Nutrition, Berkeley, Calif., 1979-80; vis. prof. dept. surgery, also Inst. Human Nutrition, Columbia Coll. Phys. and Surgs., N.Y.C., 1981; sci. adv. KabiVitrum Co., Stockholm. Chmn., Swedish Food Law Com., 1962-70. Decorated Swedish Royal Order Polar Star, comdr. Swedish Royal Order Vasa; recipient Bristol-Myers award nutrition research, 1986. Mem. Royal Acad. Engring. Scis. Sweden (gold medal 1979), Swedish Nutrition Soc., Swedish Soc. Physicians. Conservative. Lutheran. Club: Rotary. Author numerous articles on nutrition. Home: Floragatan 2, S11431 Stockholm Sweden Office: KabiVitrum, 11287 Stockholm Sweden

WRIGGINS, WILLIAM HOWARD, educator, former ambassador; b. Phila., Feb. 14, 1918; s. Charles Cornelius and Evelyn (Walker) W.; B.A. cum laude, Dartmouth Coll., 1940; cert. Ecole Libres des Sciences Politques, Paris, 1939; student U. Chgo. Grad. Sch., 1940-41; M.A., Yale U., 1948, Ph.D. (Sterling fellow 1951-52), 1952; m. Sarah Edith Hovey, Dec. 22, 1947; children—Diana, Charles Christopher, Jennifer. Relief adminstr. Am. Friends Service Com., 1942-46, 48, 49; mem. staff Yale U. Inst. Internat. Studies, 1950-51; mem. polit. sci. dept. Vassar Coll., 1952-55, 57-58; research fellow Rockefeller Found. study of politics in Ceylon, 1955-57; chief fgn. affairs div., legislative reference service Library of Congress, 1958-61; mem. policy planning council Dept. State, 1961-65; research asso. Wash. Center Fgn. Policy, SAIS, 1965-66; sr. staff mem. NSC, 1966-67; prof. govt., dir. So. Asian Inst. Columbia U., N.Y.C. 1967-77, prof. govt., 1980-86, Bryce prof. History Internat. Relations, 1987—; ambassador to Sri Lanka and Maldives, Colomo, 1977-80. Rhodes fellow St. Antony's Coll., Oxford, Eng., 1973-74. Mem. founding com. Sandy Spring (Md.) Friends Sch., 1959; bd. dirs. Am. Friends Service Com., 1958-60, Inst. Current World Affairs. Mem. Council Fgn. Relations, Am. Polit. Sci. Assn., Johns Hopkins Soc. Scholars, Assn. Asian Studies, Royal Asiatic Soc., Asia Soc. (exec. com., trustee, dir. 1972-77). Mem. Soc. of Friends. Club: Century. Author: Ceylon: Dilemmas of a New Nation, 1960; The Ruler's Imperative: Strategies for Political Survival in Asia and Africa, 1969; (with others) Population, Politics and the Future of Southern Asia, 1973; (with K.M. de Siva) The Life and Times f J.R. Jayewardene of Sri Lauba, 1988; Third World Strategies for Change: The Political Context of North-South Interdependence, 1978; contbr. research publs., others. Address: 5249 Sycamore Ave Bronx NY 10471

WRIGHT, A(RCHIBALD) NELSON, chemical company executive, researcher; b. Toronto, Ont., Can., May 22, 1932; s. Archibald S. and Ethel Agnes (Majury) W.; m. Chloe Anne Lafond, May 11, 1955 (dec. Feb. 1985); children—Percival N., Adrian E., Dawn E.; m. Hélène Vincent, June 13, 1987; 1 child, Nicolas Vincent. B.Sc., McGill U., 1953, Ph.D., 1957. Postdoctoral fellow Leeds U., Eng., 1957-59; research assoc. McGill U., Montreal, Que., 1959-63; chemist Gen. Electric Research & Devel. Ctr., Schenectady, 1963-67, mgr. photochemistry br./reaction and processes br., 1967-69, 69-73, mgr. planning resources, 1973-78; v.p. research and devel. Synergetics Industries Ltd., Montreal, 1978—, also dir. Co-author: Active Nitrogen, 1968. Patentee in field. Research fellow NRC Can., McGill U., 1954-57, W. R. Grace fellow, Leeds, Eng., 1957-59; recipient IR-100 award Indsl. Research, 1967. Mem. Chem. Inst. Can. (chmn. macromolecular sci. and engring. div. 1983-85), Soc. Plastics Engrs. (chmn. bd. dirs. vinyl div. 1988-89), Royal Soc. Chemistry, Am. Chem. Soc., Am. Physics Soc., AAAS, Sigma Xi. Unitarian. Avocations: Alpine and cross-country skiing; windsurfing; waterskiing; hiking; music; literature. Home: 41 Albert St, Agathe-des-Monts, PQ Canada J8C 1Z7 Office: Carlew Inc, 172 Clement, Ville La Salle, PQ Canada H8R 1T6

WRIGHT, CAROLE YVONNE, chiropractor, consultant; b. Long Beach, Calif., July 12, 1932; d. Paul Burt and Mary Leoan (Staley) Fickes; 1 dau., Morgan Michelle. D. Chiropractic, Palmer Coll., Davenport, Iowa, 1975. Instr. Palmer Coll., 1975-76; dir., owner Wright Chiropractic Clinic, Rocklin, Calif., 1978—, Woodland, Calif., 1980-81; dir., co-owner Ft. Sutter Chiropractic Clinic, Sacramento, 1985—; cons. in field; lectr., speaker on radio programs, at seminars. Contbr. articles to profl. jours. Co-chmn. Harold Michaels for Congress campaign, Alameda, Calif., 1972; dist. dir. 14th Congl. Dist., 1983—. Mem. Internat. Chiropractic Assn. Calif. (bd. dirs. 1978-81, pres. 1983-85), Palmer Coll. Alumni Assn. (Calif. state pres. 1981-83), Rocklin C. of C. (bd. dirs. 1979-81), Rocklin-Loomis Bus. and Profl. Women. Republican. Avocations: reading; travel. Home: 4270 Cavitt Stallman Rd Roseville CA 95661 Office: Wright Chiropractic Clinic 3175 Sunset Blvd Suite 105 Rocklin CA 95677

WRIGHT, CHARLES ALAN, law educator, author; b. Phila., Sept. 3, 1927; s. Charles Adshead and Helen (McCormack) W.; m. Mary Joan Herriott, July 8, 1950 (div. Jan. 1955); children—Charles Edward; m. Eleanor Custis Broyles Clarke, Dec. 17, 1955; children—Henrietta, Cecily; stepchildren—Eleanor Custis Clarke, Margot Clarke. A.B., Wesleyan U., Middletown, Conn., 1947; LL.B., Yale U., 1949. Bar: Minn. 1951, Tex. 1959. Law clk. U.S. Circuit Judge Clark, New Haven, 1949-50; asst. prof. law U. Minn., 1950- 53, assoc. prof., 1953-55; assoc. prof. law U. Tex., Austin, 1955-58; prof. U. Tex., 1958-65, McCormick prof., 1965-80, Bates chair, 1980—; Vis. prof. U. Pa., Phila., 1959-60, Harvard U., 1964-65, Yale, 1968-69; vis. fellow Wolfson Coll., Cambridge U., 1984; reporter study div. of jurisdiction between state and fed. cts. Am. Law Inst., 1963-69; mem. adv. com. on civil rules Jud. Conf. U.S., 1961-64, mem. standing com. on rules of practice and proc., 1964-76, 87—; cons., counsel for Pres., 1973-74; mem. com. on infractions NCAA, 1973-83, chmn., 1978-83; mem. permanent com. for Oliver Wendell Holmes Devise, 1975-83; mem. Commn. on Bicentennial of U.S. Constn., 1985—. Author: Wright's Minnesota Rules, 1954, Cases on Remedies, 1955, (with C.T. McCormick and J.H. Chadbourn) Cases on Federal Courts, 8th edit., 1988, Handbook of the Law of Federal Courts, 4th edit., 1983, (with H.M. Reasoner) Procedure-The Handmaid of Justice, 1965, Federal Practice and Procedure: Criminal, 2d edit., 1982, (with A.R. Miller) Federal Practice and Procedure: Civil, 1969-73, 2d edit. (with A.R. Miller and M.K. Kane), 1983—, (with A.R. Miller and E.H. Cooper) Federal Practice and Procedure: Jurisdiction and Related Matters, 1975-82, 2d edit., 1986—, (with K.W. Graham) Federal Practice and Procedure: Evidence, 1977—. Trustee St. Stephen's Episcopal Sch., Austin, Tex., 1962-66; trustee St. Andrew's Episcopal Sch., Austin, 1971-74, 77-80, 81-84, chmn. bd., 1973-74, 79-80; trustee Capitol Broadcasting Assn., Austin, 1966—, chmn. bd., 1969—; trustee Austin Symphony Orch. Soc., 1966—, mem. exec. com., 1966-70, 72-83, 86—; trustee Austin Choral Union, 1984—, Austin Lyric Opera Soc., 1986—. Hon. fellow Wolfson Coll., Cambridge U., 1986—. Mem. Am. Law Inst. (mem. council 1969—, 2d v.p. 1987-88, 1st v.p. 1988—), ABA (mem. commn. on standards jud. adminstrn. 1970-77), Am. Bar Found., Inst. Jud. Adminstrn., Am. Judicature Soc., Am. Acad. Arts and Scis., Philos. Soc. Tex., Order of Coif, Phi Kappa Phi, Omicron Delta Kappa. Republican. Episcopalian (sr. warden). Clubs: Country, Tarry House, Headliners, Hidden Hills, Metropolitan (Austin); Century, Yale (N.Y.C.). Home: 5304 Western Hills Dr Austin TX 78731

WRIGHT, CREIGHTON BOLTER, cardiovascular surgeon, educator; b. Washington, Jan. 29, 1939; s. Benjamin Washington and Catherine Adele (Bolter) W.; m. Carolyn Eleanor Craver, Jan. 29, 1966; children—Creighton Bolter, Benson, Kathryn, Elizabeth. B.A., Duke U., 1961, M.D., 1965. Diplomate Am. Bd. Thoracic Surgery, Am. Bd. Surgery, subbd. Gen. Vascular Surgery. Intern, Duke U., Durham, N.C., 1965-66; resident in surgery U. Va., Charlottesville, 1966-71; from asst. prof. to assoc. prof. George Washington U., 1974-76; assoc. prof., then prof. surgery U. Iowa, 1976-81; prof. clin. surgery U. Cin., also clin. prof. surgery Uniformed Services U., 1981—. Served to col. USAR, 1966—. Decorated Meritorious Service medal; recipient Kindred Resident Teaching award, 1967, Golden Apple Teaching award, 1975. Mem. Assn. Acad. Surgery (pres. 1980), Central Surg. Assn., Soc. Univ. Surgeons, Soc. Vascular Surgery, Internat. Soc. Cardiovascular Surgery, Muller Surg. Soc. (pres. 1985-87), Am. Assn. Thoracic Surgery, Soc. Thoracic Surgery, So. Thoracic Surg. Assn., Midwestern Vascular Surg. Soc., Alpha Omega Alpha, Sigma Chi. Editor: Vascular Grafting, 1983; (with others) Venous Trauma, 1983; contbr. articles to profl. jours., chpts. to books. Home: 1242 Edwards Rd Cincinnati OH 45208 Office: Services U 2139 Auburn Ave Cincinnati OH 45219

WRIGHT, DONALD KENNETH, public relations and journalism educator; b. Vancouver, B.C., Can., Feb. 11, 1945; came to U.S., 1970; s. Kenneth William Thomas and Rosemary Humphries (Edmonds) W.; B.A., Wash. State U., 1967; M.A., Calif. State U., 1971; Ph.D., U. Minn., 1974. Editor, Fresno (Calif.) Advertiser, 1970; adminstrv. asst. U. Minn., Mpls., 1971-73; mem. faculty U. Wyo., Laramie, 1973-74, U. Tex., Austin, 1974-77; prof. journalism U. Ga., Athens, 1977-82; prof., chmn. communication U. South Ala., Mobile, 1982—; cons. to bus. and industry and gov. inst. Mem. Soc. Profl. Jours., Internat. Pub. Relations Assn., Pub. Relations Soc. Am., Assn. Edn. Journalism, Sigma Delta Chi, Phi Kappa Phi. Presbyterian. Contbr. articles to profl. jours. Presbyterian. Home: 139 Batre Ln Mobile AL 36608 Office: U South Ala Chmn Communication Mobile AL 36688

WRIGHT, EDWARD STEWART, mechanical engineer, consultant; b. Englewood, N.J., Jan. 18, 1930; s. William H. and Mildred (Stewart) W.; m. Lenaire Jean Botting, Oct. 21, 1951; children—Jeffry, Jody, William. B.S. in Agr., Rutgers U., 1951; B.S. in Aero-Mech. Engring., Air Force Inst. Tech., 1960; M.S. in Aero-Engring., Princeton U., 1965. Commd. 2d lt. U.S. Air Force, 1951, advanced through grades to capt., 1963; chief systems analyst United Techs. Research Ctr., East Hartford, Conn., 1963-73, mgr. energy systems, 1973-79; mgr. components product planning Deere and Co., Moline, Ill., 1979-83, dir. govt. products, 1983—; pres. John Deere Techs. Internat., Inc.; pres. Wis. Internat. Engring. Ltd., Racine, 1975—; cons. Fed. Energy Office, Washington, 1973-74; cons. USAF on Strategic Def. Initiative, 1988. Author course Introduction to Gas Turbine, 1976-80. Contbr. articles to profl. jours. Fellow ASME (chmn. gas turbine div. 1975-79, v.p. council engring.); mem. Soc. Automotive Engrs. (chmn. Iowa, Ill. sect. 1984—), Am. Soc. Agrl. Engrs. Clubs: Short Hills Country (Moline); Baldwin Yacht (Old Saybrook, Conn.). Home: 917 48th St A Moline IL 61265

WRIGHT, GORDON PRIBYL, operations research educator; b. Crosby, Minn., May 18, 1938; s. Kenneth Eugene and Verla Emily (Pribyl) W.; m. Judith Ann Hill, Aug. 19, 1961; 1 dau., Teresa Ann. B.A., Macalester Coll., 1960; M.A., U. Mass., 1963; Ph.D., Case Western Res. U., 1967. Systems analyst Conn. Gen. Life Ins. Co., Bloomfield, 1960-61; instr. dept. math. U. Mass., 1961-63; statistician, mgmt. scis. group Goodyear Tire & Rubber Co., Akron, Ohio, 1963-64; instr., research asst., ops. research dept. Case Inst. Tech., Cleve., 1964-67; asst. prof. dept. indsl. engring. and mgmt. scis. Technol. Inst., Northwestern U., 1967-70; assoc. prof. mgmt. and statistics Krannert Grad. Sch. Mgmt. and Sch. of Sci., Purdue U., West Lafayette, Ind., 1970-75; assoc. dean Krannert Grad. Sch. Mgmt. and Sch. of Sci., Purdue U., 1979-84, dir. prof., 1982—, Krannert disting. prof., 1982—, dir. of research, 1985—, dir. doctoral programs, 1985 ; prof., chmn. mgmt., dir. profl. programs Krannert Grad. Sch. Mgmt., Purdue U., 1978-79; Basil Turner prof. mgmt. Purdue U., 1987—; vis. prof. bus. adminstrn. and stats. Amos Tuck Sch. Bus. Adminstrn., Dartmouth Coll., 1976-77; vis. prof. Bradley U.; vis. prof. mgmt. sci. Grad. Sch. Mgmt. UCLA, 1984-85; cons. Okamura Mfg. Co., Yokohama, Japan. Author: (with David G. Olson) Designing Water Pollution Detection Systems, 1974, (with Andrew B. Whinston and Gary J. Koehler) Optimization of Leontief Systems, 1975, (with Herbert M. Moskowitz) An Experiential Approach to Management Science, 1975, Introduction to Management Science, 1979, Statistics for Business and Economics, 1982, (with Frank M. Bass) Stochastic Brand Coice and Brand Switching: Theory Analysis and Description, 1980; contbr. (with Frank M. Bass) articles on ops. research and mgmt. to profl. jours. Served with USAF Res., 1961-67. Recipient Salgo-Noren Found. award for outstanding teaching in bus. adminstrn., 1975; NSF research grantee, 1968-70; Dept. Transp. research grantee, 1972-74; HEW research grantee, 1969-70; Sloan Found. research grantee, 1972-75; Fulbright scholar to Ger., 1986; Vis. Erskine fellowship U. Canterbury, New Zealand, 1985. Mem. Ops. Research Soc. Am., Inst. Mgmt. Scis., Sigma Xi, Beta Gamma Sigma. Home: 136 Seminole Dr West Lafayette IN 47906 Office: Krannert Sch Mgmt Purdue U West Lafayette IN 47907

WRIGHT, HELEN KENNEDY, editor, librarian; b. Indpls., Sept. 23, 1927; d. William Henry and Ida Louise (Crosby) Kennedy; m. Samuel A. Wright, Sept. 5, 1970; 1 child, Carl F. Prince II (dec.). BA, Butler U., 1945, MS, 1950; MS, Columbia U., 1952. Reference librarian N.Y. Pub. Library, N.Y.C., 1952-53, Bklyn. Pub. Library, 1953-54; cataloger U. Utah, 1954-57; librarian Chgo. Pub. Library; asst. dir. pub. dept. ALA, Chgo., 1958-62, editor Reference Books Bull., 1962-85; asst. dir. for new product planning, pub. services, 1985-87; asst. editor ALA Yearbook, 1987—. Contbr. to Ency. of Careers, Ency. of Library and Info. Sci., New Book of Knowledge Ency., Bulletin of Bibliography, New Golden Book Encyclopedia. Mem. Phi Kappa Phi, Kappa Delta Pi, Sigma Gamma Rho. Roman Catholic. Home: 1138 W 111th St Chicago IL 60643 Office: Am Library Assn 50 E Huron Chicago IL 60611

WRIGHT, JAMES C., JR., speaker of the U.S. House of Representatives; b. Ft. Worth, Dec. 22, 1922; s. James C. and Marie (Lyster) W.; m. Betty Hay, Nov. 12, 1972; children by previous marriage: Jimmy, Virginia Sue, Patricia Kay, Alicia Marie. Student, Weatherford Coll., also U. Tex. Partner trade extension and advt. firm; mem. Tex. Legislature, 1947-49; mayor Weatherford, Tex., 1950-54; mem. 84th-100th congresses, 12th Tex. Dist., majority leader, 1976-87; elected speaker of the House of Reps. 100th congress, 1987. Author: You and Your Congressman, 1965, The Coming Water Famine, 1966, Of Swords and Plowshares, 1968; Reflections of a Public Man, 1984; co-author: Congress and Conscience, 1970. Served with USAAF, World War II. Decorated D.F.C., Legion of Merit; named Outstanding Young Man Tex. Jr. C. of C., 1953. Mem. League Tex. Municipalities (pres. 1953). Democrat. Presbyterian. Address: US Ho Reps Washington DC 20515

WRIGHT, JANET H., management company executive; b. Lansing, Mich., May 5, 1936; d. Alfred E. and Olive (Woodry) H.; m. Paul E. Peterson, Dec. 20, 1959 (div. Dec. 1971); Andrew, Russell, Timothy; m. Thompson T. Wright, May 12, 1973; stepchildren—Robert, William, Debra, Holly, Diane, Donna, Thompson. Ed. Mich. State U., 1954-58. Cert. expn. mgr. Engaged in radio, TV and ice show prodn. and pub. relations, 1958-73; asst. dir. convs. Profl. Photographers Am., Des Plaines, Ill., 1975-78; pres. The Wright Orgn., Inc., Des Plaines, 1978—. Officer Des Plaines Sister Cities Internat., 1983-87; active Des Plaines Econ. Devel. Commn., 1987—; rec. sec. Des Plaines Sesquicentennial, 1984-85; judge U.S. Figure Skating Assn., 1978—; mem., recording sec. DuPage Figure Skating Club, 1984-88, v.p., 1988—. Mem. Nat. Assn. Expn. Mgrs. (bd. dirs. 1985—, chpt. pres. 1983, chpt. bd. dirs. 1979-84, nat. chmn. industry and govt. relations com. 1985-88), Meeting Planners Internat., Trade Show Bur., LWV (chpt. officer), P.E.O. (organizing chpt. pres. 1962), Profl. Conv. Mgrs. Assn. Avocation: figure skating. Office: The Wright Orgn 716 Lee St Des Plaines IL 60016

WRIGHT, JEANNE ELIZABETH JASON, advertising executive; b. Washington, June 24, 1934; d. Robert Stewart and Elizabeth (Gaddis) Jason; m. Benjamin Hickman Wright, Oct. 30, 1965; stepchildren: Benjamin, Deborah, David, Patricia. B.A., Radcliffe Coll., 1956; M.A., U. Chgo., 1958. Psychiat. social worker Lake County Mental Health Clinic, Gary, Ind., Psychiat. and Psychosomatic Inst., Michael Reese Hosp., Chgo., Jewish Child Care Assn., N.Y.C., 1958-70; gen. mgr. Black Media, Inc. (advt. rep. co.), N.Y.C., 1970-74; pres. Black Media, Inc. (advt. rep. co.), 1974-75, Black Resources, Inc., also pres., exec. editor Nat. Black Monitor, N.Y.C., 1975—; also syndicator weekly editorial features. Mem. planning com. First Black Power Conf., Newark, 1966, Second Black Power Conf., Phila., 1967, First Internat. Black Cultural and Bus. Expn., N.Y.C., 1971; nat. bd. dirs. Family Service Assn. Am., 1968-70; bd. dirs. Afro-Am. Family & Community Services, Inc., Chgo., 1971-75; founding council mem. Nat. Assault on Illiteracy Program, 1980—; pres. Metro-N.Y. chpt. Nat. Assn. Media Women Inc., 1986—. Recipient Pres.'s award Nat. Assn. Black Women Attys., 1977, 2d Ann. Freedom's Jour. award Journalism Students and Faculty of U. D.C.

Dept. Communicative and Performing Arts, 1979; named Disting. Black Woman in Industry Nat. Council Negro Women, 1981; recipient Spl. award Beta Omicron chpt. Phi Delta Kappa, 1982. Mem. Nat. Assn. Social Workers, AAAS, Acad. Cert. Social Workers, NAACP, Nat. Assn. Media Women (Nat. Media Woman of Yr. award 1984, 86, Founders award 1986), Newswomen's Club N.Y., Inc., U. Chgo. Alumni Assn., Alpha Kappa Alpha. Democrat. Clubs: Radcliffe, Harvard (N.Y.C.). Office: 410 Central Park W Penthouse C New York NY 10025

WRIGHT, JESSE GRAHAM, museum director; b. Sidney, Ohio, July 29, 1939; s. Jesse Graham and Bernadine (Thedieck) W.; m. Joan Foster, July 6, 1968; children: Graham, Foster. BA, Loyola U., Chgo., 1964; MA in English, Loyola U., 1965; MFA, U. Notre Dame, 1969. Asst. to artist Terry Netter N.Y.C., 1966-67; instr. St. Mary's Coll., Notre Dame, Ind., 1967-68; dir. South Bent (Ind.) Arts Ctr., 1968-70, Michael C. Rockefeller Arts Ctr. Gallery, N.Y.C., 1970-74, Canton (Ohio) Arts Ctr., 1974-77, J.B. Speed Art Mus., Louiseville, 1984-85; asst. prof. SUNY, Fredonia, 1970-74; pres., dir. Philbrook Art Ctr., Tulsa, 1977-84; v.p. Charles Webb Co., N.Y.C., 1986-87; founder The Wright Group, Louisville, 1987—; co-founder, treas.. co-chmn. exhibit com. Gallery Assn. N.Y. State, 1971-74. Author exhbn. catalogues: Wreck, a Tragic-Romantic American Theme, 1972, Florist Transworld Delivery Collection, 1973. Mem. Okla. Humanities Com., 1979-81, Tulsa Arts Commn., 1978-84, Tulsa airport sulpture com. CAA, 1979-84. Mem. Am. Assn. Mus., Okla. Mus. Assn. (pres. 1980-81), Tulsa C. of C. Republican. Episcopalina. Club: Audubon County. Home: 81 Valley Rd Louisville KY 40204 Office: The Wright Group 100 E Liberty St Suite 300 Louisville KY 40202 also: PO Box 70289 Louisville KY 40270

WRIGHT, JOHN GEORGE, JR., manufacturing company executive; b. Cleve., June 5, 1947; s. John George and Margaret Josephine (Laumer) W.; m. Isabelle H. Pasquier, Dec. 21, 1976; children—Daniel William, Marie-Christine, Nicholas Fernand. BS, Wharton Sch., U. Pa., 1969; MS summa cum laude, U. Minn., 1970; MBA, M.A.M., Claremont Grad. Sch., 1982, PhD, 1984. Mktg. rep. Columbia-Great Lakes Corp., Northridge, Chatsworth, Calif., 1970-73, corp. gen. mgr., 1973-80, v.p., 1980-87, pres., 1987—; pres. CGL Ribbons Pty Ltd., 1988—; also bd. dirs.; pres. Columbia France, S.A., 1987—; pres., chmn. bd. dirs. Columbia Cintas de Impresiones S.A., 1987—, CGL Holding, 1987. Mem. Data Processing Mgrs. Assn., U. Pa. Alumni Assn. (v.p., exec. com.), Beta Gamma Sigma, Delta Upsilon (life), Delta Sigma Pi (life). Office: Columbia-Great Lakes Corp 21823 Plummer St Chatsworth CA 91311

WRIGHT, JOHN ROBERT (JACK), horticulturist; b. Twin Falls, Idaho, July 13, 1940; s. Loyd Kenneth and Bessie Margaret (Roberts) W.; m. F. Elaine Jacobs, Aug. 2, 1959; children—Douglas Wayne, David Scott, Teresa Lynn. Mgr., Kimberly Nurseries, Inc., Twin Falls, 1967—, pres., prin., 1978—; founder, pres. Bonanza Investment Group, Twin Falls, 1974—, Smith & Wright Investment Group, Twin Falls, 1978—; ptnr. Liberty Enterprises Investment Group. Scoutmaster, Snake River Cub Scout council Boy Scouts Am., 1970-74; mem. City Council, 1984, pres. 1985-86, acting mayor City of Kimberly, 1986, police commr. City of Kimberly, 1986, City Library Bd., 1985, Park and Recreation Bd., 1985, Planning and Zoning Commn., 1984-85. Served with AUS, 1962. Mem. Twin Falls C. of C., Idaho Tree and Nursery Assn., Nat. Assn. Watch and Clock Collectors, Assn. Gen. Contractors. Republican. Christian. Club: Masons (32 deg.). Home: 824 N Main St Kimberly ID 83341 Office: Route 3 Twin Falls ID 83301

WRIGHT, JOSEPH ROBERT, JR., government administrator; b. Tulsa, Sept. 24, 1938; s. Joe Robert and Ann Helen (Cech) W. B.S., Colo. Sch. Mines, 1961; M.I.A., Yale U., 1964. Vice pres. Booz, Allen & Hamilton, 1965-71; dep. dir. Bur. Census, Dept. Commerce, 1971-72; dep. adminstr. mgmt. Social and Econ. Statis. Adminstrn., 1972-73, acting asst. sec. econ. affairs, 1973; asst. sec. adminstr. Dept. Agr., 1973-76; pres. Citicorp Retail Services Inc. and Retail Consumer Services Inc., N.Y.C., 1976-81, Retail Consumer Services, Inc., N.Y.C., 1977-81; dep. sec. Dept. Commerce, Washington, 1981-82; dep. dir. Office Mgmt. and Budget, Washington, 1982—; chmn. Pres.'s Council on Integrity and Efficiency, 1982—; fed. co-chmn. Coastal Plains Regional Commn., 1981-82, Four Corners Regional Commn., 1981-82, New Eng. Regional Commn., 1981-82, Old West Regional Commn., 1981-82, Ozarks Regional Commn., 1981-82, Pacific Northwest Regional Commn., 1981-82, Southwest Border Regional Commn., 1981-82, Upper Great Lakes Regional Commn., 1981-82; chmn. Pres.'s Council on Mgmt. Improvement, 1984—. Served to 1st lt. AUS, 1963-65. Named Govt. Exec. Yr., Govt. Computer News Mag., 1968. Mem. Young Pres. Orgn., Nat. Assn. Pub. Adminstrn., Assn. of Fed. Investigators, Colo. Sch. Mines Alumni Assn. Home: 3631 49th St NW Washington DC 20016 Office: Office Mgmt and Budget Old Exec Office Bldg 17th & Penns Washington DC 20503

WRIGHT, KATIE HARPER, educational administrator, journalist; b. Crawfordsville, Ark., Oct. 5, 1923; d. James Hale and Connie Mary (Locke) Harper; B.A., U. Ill., 1944; M.Ed., 1959; Ed.D., St. Louis U., 1979; m. Marvin Wright, Mar. 21, 1952; 1 dau., Virginia K. Jordan. Elem. and spl. edn. tchr. East St. Louis (Ill.) Pub. Schs., 1944-65, dir. Dist. 189 Instructional Materials Program, 1965-71, dir. spl. edn. Dists. 188, 189, 1971-77, asst. supt. programs, 1977-79; adj. faculty Harris/Stowe State Coll., 1980; cons. to numerous workshops, seminars in field; mem. study tour People's Republic of China, 1984. Mem. Ill. Commn. on Children, 1973-85, East St. Louis Bd. Election Commrs.; pres. bd. dirs. St. Clair County Mental Health Center, 1970-72, 87—; bd. dirs. River Bluff council Girl Scouts, 1979—, nat. bd. dirs., 1981-84; bd. dirs. United Way, 1979—, Urban League, 1979—; pres. bd. trustees East St. Louis Pub. Library, 1972-77; pres., bd. dirs. St. Clair County Mental Health Ctrs., 1987; adv. bd. Landmark Bank; charter mem. Coalition of 100 Black Women; mem. coordinating council ethnic affairs Synod of Mid-Am., Presbyn. Ch. U.S.A; charter mem. Metro East Links Group; charter mem. Gateway chpt. The Links, Inc. Recipient Lamp of Learning award East St. Louis Jr. Wednesday Club, 1965, Journalist award Sigma Gamma Rho, 1986; named woman of the yr. in edn. St. Clair County YWCA, 1987; Nat. Top Lady of the Yr., 1988; Outstanding Working Woman award Downtown St. Louis, Inc., 1967; Ill. State citation for ednl. document Love is Not Enough, 1974; Delta Sigma Theta citation for document Good Works, 1979; award Nat. Council Negro Women, 1983; Girl Scout Thanks badge, 1982; Community Service award Met. East Bar Assn., 1983; named Woman of Achievement, St. Louis Globe Democrat, 1974, Outstanding Adminstr. So. region Ill. Office Edn., 1975, named Woman of Yr. in Edn. St. Clair County YWCA, 1987. Mem. Am. Libraries Trustees Assn. (regional v.p. 1978-79, nat. sec. 1979-80), Ill. Commn. on Children, Mensa, Council for Exceptional Children, Top Ladies of Distinction (pres. 1987—), Delta Sigma Theta (chpt. pres. 1960-62), Kappa Delta Pi (pres. So. Ill. U. chpt. 1973-74), Phi Delta Kappa (Service Key award 1984, chpt. pres. 1984-85), Iota Phi Lambda, Pi Lambda Theta (chpt. pres. 1985—). Republican. Presbyterian. Club: East St. Louis Women's (pres. 1973-75). Contbr. articles to profl. jours.; feature writer St. Louis Argus Newspaper, 1979—. Home: 733 N 40th St East Saint Louis IL 62205

WRIGHT, KENNETH, lecturer; b. Stoke-on-Trent, Staffs, Britain, Apr. 1, 1938; s. Alec and Elsie (Worthington) W.; m. Margaret Elizabeth Bell, Aug. 4, 1967; children—Eleanor Jane, Edwin Ivan, Alison Elaine. B.A., Oxford U., 1959, D.Phil., 1962. Research asst. U. Computing Lab, Newcastle Upon Tyne, Eng., 1962-64, lectr., 1964—; vis. asst. prof. U. Toronto, Ont., 1971-72. Contbr. articles to profl. jours. Fellow Inst. of Math. and its Applications. Anglican. Avocations: violin; walking. Home: 19 Tynedale Terr Benton, Newcastle Upon Tyne NE12 8AY, England Office: U Newcastle Upon Tyne Computing Lab, Claremont Tower Claremont Rd, Newcastle Upon Tyne NE1 7RU, England

WRIGHT, KENNETH LYLE, psychologist; b. American Falls, Idaho, Sept. 11, 1911; s. Jesse Joshua and Martha Sophia (Dickenson) W. children—Anne Collins, Correlia Carmelette Brown, Sandra Lynne Sutherland. B.A., U. Wash., 1941; M.A., U. So. Calif., 1957; Ph.D., San Gabriel Coll., 1958. Coach State Tng. Sch. for Boys, Chehalis, Wash., 1941; dep. probation officer, Los Angeles County, Calif., 1954-56; vis. lectr. Whittier Coll. (Calif.), 1955-56; dist. sch. psychologist Anaheim Union High Sch. Dist. (Calif.); guidance counselor, vice prin. Orleans Am. High Sch., Dept. Army (France), also psychol. services and spl. edn. coordinator Dependent Edn. Group Hdqrs., Karlsruhe, W.Ger., 1959-62; edn. specialist U.S. Navy, San Diego, 1962-63; pvt. practice psychology, San Diego, 1963-64, 69—; psychol. cons. Clin. Bd. Speech Therapy, Children's Hosp., San Diego, 1963-64; vis. prof. U. Western Ont., lectr., sch. psychologist London Bd. Edn. (Ont., Can.), 1964-66; dir. psychol. services Niagara Falls Dist. Bd. Edn. (N.Y.), 1966-69; lectr. Syracuse U., 1968. Pres. Whittier Coordinating Council; a founder Can. Sch. Vol. Program; founder Niagara Inst. Human Devel., founder San Diego Forensic Soc., 1988 European Assns. Am. Personnel and Guidance and Speech and Hearing in Dependent Schs., chmn. Instl. Research Bd., 1987-88. Served with USNR, 1941-46. Recipient outstanding award San Diego County Assn. Retarded Children. Fellow San Diego Biomed. Research Inst. (past pres.); mem. Assn. Children with Learning Disabilities, Council Exceptional Children (past pres. Niagara Falls chpt.), Royal Soc. Medicine, Am. Psychol. Assn., Calif. Psychol. Assn., San Diego County Psychol. Assn., Am. Soc. Clin. Hypnosis, Calif. Soc. Clin. Hypnosis (sec.), San Diego County Soc. Clin Hypnosis (pres. 1975-76), San Diego Assn. Clin. Psychologists (past pres.), Instl. Research Bd. (chmn.), Mensa (10-yr. cert. as proctor). Club: Koha Kai. Lodge: Masons. Author: My Name Is Kim; The American Symbol; The Fantastic Journey with Visualization and Imagery; The Psychological Effects of Allergy; Allergy and Learning Disabilities in Children. Home: 751 Amiford Dr San Diego CA 92107 Office: 4070 Goldfinch San Diego CA 92103

WRIGHT, LAURENCE CASTO, orthodontist; b. Cleve., Aug. 31, 1927; s. Laurence P. and Ruth A. (Casto) W.; student Westminster Coll., 1948-51; B.S., Western Res. U., 1952, D.D.S., 1955; certificate in orthodontics, U. Buffalo, 1957; m. Joan Finley, June 23, 1951; children—David, James, Douglas, Jonathan. Individual practice dentistry specializing in orthodontics, Buffalo, 1957—, asso. with Dr. Walter H. Ellis, 1957-59; mem. J. Sutton Regan Cleft Palate Clinic; staff mem. Children's Hosp., Buffalo. Club, dist. and state pres. Y's Men's Internat., 1958-64, internat. pres., 1966-67; chmn. bd. mgrs. (N.E.) YMCA, 1971-72; pres. Buffalo Banjo Band, 1981; dir. campus ministries, Daemen Coll., Buffalo, 1987—. Served with AUS, 1946-48. Fellow Am. Coll. Dentists, Internat. Coll. Dentists (regent 1979-84); mem. U. Buffalo Orthodontic Alumni Assn. (pres. 1968-70), 8th Dist. Orthodontic Soc. (pres. 1973-74), Erie County (pres. 1981), N.Y. State dental socs., Western N.Y. Orthodontic Acad., ADA (nat. award in preventive dentistry 1974), Am. Assn. Orthodontics, Am. Cleft Palate Assn., Amherst C. of C., Delta Sigma Delta (treas., sec. 1962-85). Rotarian.

WRIGHT, LYNNE C., defense systems executive; b. Gadsden, Ala., Jan. 19, 1954; d. William Earl and Pauline (Hill) W. B.S., U. Ala., 1974, M.A., 1976, Ph.D., 1978. Inst. U. Ala., University, 1974-79; program mgr., systems analyst Analytic Services, Inc., Arlington, Va., 1979-83; div. mgr., chief scientist TITAN Systems, Inc., Vienna, Va., 1983-86; chief exec. officer, chmn. bd. SKW Corp., 1986—. Contbr. articles to profl. jours. First soprano soloist ch. choir, Falls Church, Va., 1969—, mem. fin. com., 1980—, sec. fin. com., 1983-84. Recipient Outstanding Tech. Service commendation U.S. Air Force, 1982; named Most Valuable Performer, TITAN Systems, Inc., 1984. Mem. Am. Math. Soc., Math. Assn. Am., Am. Astronautical Soc., Women in Math., Armed Forces Communications and Electronics Assn., Women in Aerospace. Mortar Bd., Phi Mu Epsilon, Delta Gamma (chmn. fashion bd. 1973). Baptist. Office: SKW Corp 1901 N Moore St Suite 1000 Arlington VA 22209

WRIGHT, MARY RUTH (MRS. WILLIAM KEMP WRIGHT), psychologist; b. St. Louis, Apr. 2, 1922; d. Leon Carl and Gwendolyn (Travis) Brown; R.N., Washington U., St. Louis, 1944; B.S., U. Houston, 1966, M.A., 1967; Ph.D., Union Grad. Sch., 1978; m. William Kemp Wright, Feb. 10, 1945; children—Gwendolyn, Veronica, Victoria, Jennifer. Instr. surgery Washington U. Sch. Nursing, 1944-45, U.S. Cadet Nurse Corps, USPHS, 1944; instr. pediatrics Children's Meml. Hosp., Chgo., 1945-46; teaching fellow U. Houston, 1965-66; instr. S. Tex. Jr. Coll., Houston, 1967-70; mental health cons. St. Joseph Mental Hosp., Houston, 1966-67; staff psychol. services Almeda Clinic, Houston, 1966-70; pvt. practice marriage and family counselor, Houston, 1970—; med.-psychol. researcher and writer, 1970—; psychologist Vasectomy Clinic, Houston Dept. Health, 1971-80; clin. asst. prof. psychology, dept. otorhinolaryngology and communicative scis. Baylor Coll. Medicine, Houston, 1979—. Recipient spl. award Security Agy., 1945. Mem. Am. Psychol. Assn., Am. Assn. Marriage and Family Counselors, Am. Assn. Sex Educators and Counselors, Internat. Council Psychologists, Nat. Council Family Relations, Nat. Assn. Social Workers, Mental Health Assn. Houston and Harris County (dir.). Contbr. articles to profl. jours. Home: 3671 Del Monte St Houston TX 77019 Office: 4200 Westheimer Suite 160 Houston TX 77027

WRIGHT, MICHAEL WILLIAM, wholesale food company executive; b. Mpls., June 13, 1938; s. Thomas W. and Winifred M. Wright; m. Susan Marie Guzy. B.A., U. Minn., 1961, J.D. with honors, 1963. Ptnr. Dorsey & Whitney, Mpls., 1966-77; sr. v.p. Super Valu Stores, Inc., Mpls., 1977-78, pres., chief operating officer, 1978—, chief exec. officer, 1981—, chmn., 1982—; bd. dirs., chmn. Fed. Res. Bank, Mpls.; bd. dirs. Deluxe Corp., Mpls., Honeywell, Inc., Food Mktg. Inst., Nat. Am. Wholesale Grocers Assn.; chmn. Minn. Bus. Partnership. Trustee U. Minn. Found. Served as 1st lt. U.S. Army, 1964-66. Office: Super Valu Stores Inc 11840 Valley View Rd PO Box 990 Minneapolis MN 55440

WRIGHT, NANCY HOWELL, interior designer; b. Detroit, Sept. 6, 1932; d. David Austin and Catherine (Bradley) Howell; BFA Ohio Wesleyan U.; student Parsons Sch. Design, 1977; m. Hastings Kemper Wright, June 19, 1954; children—Mark, Kenneth, Barbara, Donald. Interior decorator Country Manor of Branford (Conn.), 1971-75, design mgr., 1976—. Sec. Branford Art League, 1977; chmn. Harrison House Hist. House, Branford, Conn., 1983-84. Allied mem. Am. Soc. Interior Designers (award for best Conn. retail store design, 1980); mem. Delta Phi Delta. Republican. Episcopalian. Home: 35 Wood Rd Branford CT 06405 Office: 312 E Main St Branford CT 06405

WRIGHT, RICHARD DONALD, financial executive; b. Chester, Pa., Mar. 18, 1936; s. Richard H. and Anita C. (Howery) W.; B.S. in Bus. Adminstrn., Pa. State U., 1963; m. Joan Cooke, Oct. 24, 1959; children—Richard, Paul, Susan. Trainee, corp. fin. mgmt., internal auditor, corp. staff auditor RCA, Cherry Hill, N.J., 1963-66; with Smith Kline French Labs. div. Smith Kline Beckman Corp., Phila., 1966-83, mgr. budget, 1966-69, mgr. planning and control, 1969-70, mgr. fin. ops., 1970-72, controller mfg. ops., 1972-73, dir. fin. planning, 1973-74, controller pharm. ops., U.S., 1974-79; v.p., dir. Franklin Town Corp., pres. F.T. Mgmt. Corp. affiliate Smith Kline Corp., 1979-83; with Henkel and McCoy Inc., 1983—, Blue Bell, Pa.; controller, 1983-85, v.p., dir., 1985—, chief fin. officer, 1988—. Mem. Fin. Execs. Inst. (cert.), Planning Execs. Inst., Ocean County Bd. Realtors, Nat. Assn. Accts., Sigma Tau Gamma. Lectr. in field. Home: 104 Shadow Lake Dr Vincentown NJ 08088

WRIGHT, ROBERT F., petroleum products company executive. Previously exec. v.p. Amerada Hess Corp., N.Y.C., pres., chief operating officer, 1986—, also bd. dirs. Office: Amerada Hess Corp 1185 Ave of the Americas New York NY 10036 *

WRIGLEY, ELIZABETH SPRINGER (MRS. OLIVER K. WRIGLEY), found. exec.; b. Pitts., Oct. 4, 1915; d. Charles Woodward and Sarah Maria (Roberts) Springer; B.A. U. Pitts., 1935; B.S., Carnegie Inst. Tech., 1936; m. Oliver Kenneth Wrigley, June 16, 1936 (dec. July 1978). Procedure analyst U.S. Steel Corp., Pitts., 1941-43; research asst. The Francis Bacon Found., Inc., Los Angeles, 1944, exec., 1945-50, trustee, 1950—, dir. research, 1951-53, pres., 1954—, dir. Francis Bacon Library; mem. adv. council Royal Skakespeare Revels in the Ojai; mem. regional Fine Arts adv. council Calif. State Poly. U., Pomona. Mem. ALA, Calif. Library Assn., Renaissance Soc. Am., Modern Humanities Research Assn., Cryptogram Assn., Alpha Delta Pi. Presbyn. Mem. Order Eastern Star, Damascus Shrine. Editor: The Skeleton Text of the Shakespeare Folio L.A. (by W.C. Arensberg), 1952. Compiler: Short Title Catalogue Numbers in the Library of the Francis Bacon Foundation, 1958; Wing Numbers in the Library of the Francis Bacon Foundation, 1959; Supplement To Francis Bacon Library Holdings in the STC of English Books, 1967; (with David W. Davies) A Concordance to the Essays of Francis Bacon, 1973. Home: 4805 N Pal Mal Ave Temple City CA 91780 Office: Francis Bacon Library 655 N Dartmouth Ave Claremont CA 91711

WROBLOWA, HALINA STEFANIA, electrochemist; b. Gdansk, Poland, July 5, 1925; came to U.S., 1960, naturalized, 1970; M.Sc., U. Lodz (Poland), 1949; Ph.D., Warsaw Inst. Tech., 1958; 1 dau., Krystyna Wrobel-Knight. Chmn. dept. prep. studies U. Lodz, 1950-53; adj. Inst. for Phys. Chemistry, Acad. Scis., Warsaw, Poland, 1958-60; dep. dir. electrochemistry lab. Energy Inst., U. Pa., Phila., 1960-67, dir. electrochemistry lab., 1968-75; prin. research scientist Ford Motor Co., Dearborn, Mich., 1978—. Served with Polish Underground Army, 1943-45. Decorated Silver Cross of Merit with Swords. Mem. Electrochem. Soc., Internat. Electrochem. Soc., Mensa, Sigma Xi. Contbr. chpts. to books, articles to profl. jours., patent lit. Office: Ford Motor Co SRL S-2079 PO Box 2053 Dearborn MI 48322

WRONGMAN-OPONJURU, GOFFINE DECKTO, non-profit organization executive; b. Nyapea, West Nile, Uganda, Dec. 4, 1957; s. Celestino Bichala and Leonora Dokower Oponjuru; m. Janet Adupa Decktor; children: Jacqueline Decktor, Caroline Decktor, Jocelyne Decktor. Adminstrv. officer Save the Children Fund (UK), Kampala City, Uganda, 1979—, field adminstr., 1979-81, dir., 1970—. Mem. Am. Mgmt. Assn., Uganda Red Cross Soc. (life), St. Vincent de Paul Soc. Roman Catholic. Home: Archbishop Janan Luwum St, Plot 8 Apt 1 Luwum St, PO Box 3513, Kampala Uganda Office: PO Box 1124, Kampala Uganda

WU, CHI-HAUR, robotics engineer, educator b. Taipei, China, May 9, 1951; came to U.S., 1975, naturalized, 1985; s. Mu-Chiai and Po-Lun (Chang) W.; m. Miao-Ying Yeh, Jan. 22, 1977; 1 child, Alexander. B.S., Nat. Taiwan U. (China), 1973; M.S., Va. Poly. Inst. and State U., 1977; Ph.D., Purdue U., 1980. Sr. engr. Unimation Inc., Danbury, Conn., 1981-83, cons., 1983—; asst. prof. engrng. and computer sci. Northwestern U., Evanston, Ill., 1983-86, assoc. prof., 1986—. Engrng. Found. Research Initiation grantee, 1984; NSF grantee, 1985. Mem. IEEE, Robotics Internat. of Soc. Mfg. Engrs. (Outstanding Young Mfg. Engr. award 1985). Current work: Robotics, manipulators control and programming, robotic vision and sensory control, pattern recognition, integrated computer-control systems, limb control by brains and robots and industrial automation. Subspecialties: Robotics; Computer engineering.

WU, CHING-MU, mathematician; b. Tainan, Republic of China, May 16, 1929; s. Wen-kwei and Bii (Lin) W.; m. Nuan Shy, Dec. 26, 1954; children: Hwey-jen, Hwey-lee, Hwey-daw, Hwey-shen. BS, Nat. Taiwan U., 1953; PhD, Osaka City U., 1971. Asst. instr. to assoc. prof. Nat. Cheng-kung U., Tainan, Republic of China, 1953-65; assoc. prof., prof. Tunghai U., Taichung, Republic of China, 1965-72; research fellow Research Inst. Math. Scis. Nat. Kyoto U., Japan, 1969-71; prof., dir. grad. sch. math. Tamkang U., Tamsui, Republic of China, 1972-78; vis. prof. U. West Fla., Pensacola, 1978-80; chair prof. Tamkang U., Tamsui, 1980—. Served to 2d lt. Republic of China Army. Recipient Decoration for Disting. Educator Ministry Edn., 1983. Fellow Nat. Sci. Council of Republic of China (research grantee 1969—), United Bd. Christian Higher Edn. in Asia. Home: PO Box 1-64, Tamsui 25199, Republic of China Office: Tamkang U, Grad Sch Math, Tamsui 25137, Republic of China

WU, CHING-SHENG, physics educator; b. Nanjing, China, Nov. 11, 1929; came to U.S., 1954, naturalized, 1963; s. Shao-Ling Wu and Chen-Fang Pan; m. Lucia Zah-Chien Moh, Aug. 12, 1961; 1 child, Bryant C.Y. B.S., Nat. Taiwan U., China, 1954; M.S., Va. Poly. Inst., 1956; Ph.D., Princeton U., 1959. Sr. scientist Jet Propulsion Lab., Pasadena, Calif., 1959-69; vis. scientist Atomic Enery Research Establishment, Harwell, Eng., 1961-62; research prof. U. Md. Inst. Phys. Sci. and Tech., College Park, 1969—; vis. assoc. prof. MIT, 1966-67; vis. prof. Nat. Taiwan U., 1968-69, Fed. U. Rio Grande do Sul, Brazil, 1977, Imperial Coll. Sci. and Tech., U. London, 1977-78; vis. prof. Chinese Acad. Scis., Bejing, 1978, hon. prof., 1979—; cons. NASA, Washington, 1977-83; mem. adv. bd. Assn. Plasma Studies in Peoples Republic China, 1985—; invited lectr. numerous profl. confs., U.S. and abroad. Assoc. editor Jour. Geophys. Research, 1984-86; editorial bd. Sci. and Tech. Revs., 1986—. Contbr. numerous articles to profl. jours. Fellow Govt. China, Taiwan, 1949-53, Va. Poly. Inst. Research Found., 1954-55, N.Y. Acad. Sci., 1987; Guggenheim fellow, 1957-58; Wallace Meml. scholar, 1956-57; research grantee NASA, 1972-74, 74—, NSF, 1973-75, 86—, Office Naval Research, 1982—, Internat. Solar Terrestrial Program, 1982—; recipient Achievement citation NASA, 1969. Fellow Am. Phys. Soc., N.Y. Acad. Scis.; mem. Am. Geophys. Union, Internat. Union Radio Sci. (mem. U.,S. nat. com. of Commn. H), N.Y. Acad. Sci., Sigma Xi.

WU, DELON, cardiologist; b. Chang-Hua, Taiwan, Sept. 17, 1941; s. Su-Chang and Kwei-Jin (Hwang) W.; M.D., Nat. Taiwan U., 1966; m. Iou-Jih Hung, Oct. 18, 1968; 1 son, Lawrence. Intern, resident in medicine Cook County Hosp., Chgo., 1967-69; resident in medicine, fellow in cardiology U. Ill. Hosp., Chgo., 1969-73; asst. prof., then assoc. prof. U. Ill. Med. Sch., Chgo., 1973-78; prof. medicine Taipei Med. Coll., 1978-84; vice supt., dir. med. research and edn. Chang Gung Meml. Hosp., Taipei, 1978-82; prof. medicine U. So. Calif., Los Angeles, 1982-84; dean Chang Gung Med. Coll., 1987—. Fellow Am. Coll. Cardiology, Council Clin. Cardiology of Am. Heart Assn.; mem. Am. Fedn. Clin. Research. Author papers in field. Editorial referee med. jours. Home: No 1, Lane 44, Lin-Yi St, Taipei Republic China Office: 199 Tun-Hua N Rd, Taipei Republic of China

WU, HARRY PAO-TUNG, librarian; b. Chinan, Shantung, China, May 1, 1932; s. James Ching-Mei and Elizabeth Hsiao (Lu) W.; B.A., Nat. Taiwan U., Taipei, 1959; student Ohio State U., 1962; M.L.S., Kent State U., 1966; m. Irene I-Len Sun, June 23, 1961; children—Eva Pei-Chen, Walter Pei-Liang. Came to U.S., 1960. Archive and library asst. Taiwan Handicraft Promotion Center, Taipei, 1959-60; student asst. Kent State U. Library, 1960-61; reference librarian Massillon (Ohio) Pub. Library, 1964-65, acting asst. dir., 1965, asst. dir., head adult services, 1966; dir. Flesh Pub. Library, Piqua, Ohio, 1966-68; dir. St. Clair County Library System, Port Huron, Mich., 1968—; founder and dir. Blue Water Library Fedn., Port Huron, 1974—; pres. Mich. Library Film Circuit, Lansing, 1977-79; bd. dirs. Mich. Waterways council Girl Scouts U.S.A., Port Huron, 1985-86. Mem. Am., Mich. (chmn. library systems roundtable 1974-75) library assns., Am. Mgmt. Assn., Assn. Ednl. Communications and Tech., Detroit Suburban Librarians Roundtable. Clubs: Port Huron Internat. (pres. 1988), Rotary (dir. 1972-74, 88—). Home: 1518 Holland Ave Port Huron MI 48060 Office: 210 McMorran Blvd Port Huron MI 48060

WU, JONATHAN CHARNGHAU, accountant, consultant; b. Chungli, Republic of China, Feb. 12, 1953; came to U.S., 1980; s. Fupei and Lianmei (Liu) W.; m. Liming Han, Mar. 25, 1979. BS, Fujen U., Taipei, Republic of China, 1975; M in Mgmt., Northwestern U., 1982; MA, U. Ill., Chgo., 1985. CPA, Tex. Asst. to v.p. Shus Found., Taipei, 1977-78; ptnr. Bianko Co., Taipei, 1978-80; adj. lectr. Roosevelt U., Chgo., 1983-84; sr. fin. systems analyst Tex. Dept. Community Affairs, Austin, 1984-86, asst. dir. acctg. system, 1986-87, dir. data services, 1987; chief fin. officer Full Employment Council, Kansas City, Mo., 1987—; acctg. and tax systems cons., Austin, 1984—. Author, editor: Job Tng. Ptnrship. Act Fin. Mgmt. Manual, 1986, Food Science, 1978; also articles. Served to 2d lt. Chinese Air Force, 1975-77. Mem. Am. Inst. CPA's, Tex. Soc. CPA's, Inst. Mgmt. Accts. (cert.), Inst. Internal Auditors (cert.), Northwestern Mgmt. Assn. Home: 9410 NW 60th Parkville MO 64152 Office: Full Employment Council 1740 Paseo Kansas City MO 64108

WU, LINDA, editor, publisher; b. N.Y.C., May 21, 1944; d. George Y.L. and May (Cheng) W.; m. Frank J.H. Liu, June 25, 1967; divorced; children: Clifford, Craig. BA, Western Coll. for Women, 1966; postgrad., U. Leeds, London Sch. Econs., King's Coll., Eng., 1966-67. Editorial researcher Reader's Digest, N.Y.C., 1966; reporter China Post, Taipei, Republic of China, 1967-68, feature writer, page editor, 1968-70; founder, editor-in-chief ECHO Mag. Co., Taipei, 1970—, ECHO Pub. Co. Ltd., Taipei, 1976—; pres. ECHO Communications Co., Ltd., Taipei, 1985—, ECHO Internat. Co., Ltd., Taipei, 1987—. Editor-in-chief: Chinese Children's Stories, 1981 (Best Book award 1983), Chinese Rice Cookbook, 1983 (Best Book award 1984), ECHO's Children's Ency., 1985 (Best Book award 1985); Han Sheng mag., 1978—. Chmn. organizing com. Republic of China Children's Mus., Taipei, 1979-86. Fulbright-Hays scholar, 1966-67. Clubs: Women's Garden and Art (charter). Lodge: Zonta (charter mem. Taipei club). Office: ECHO Pub Co Ltd, 5-2 Pa Teh Rd, Sect 4 Ln 72, Taipei Republic of China

WU, PHILIP MAN CHI, surgeon; b. Hong Kong, Aug. 6, 1939; m. Lina Dominica Man Ping Shing, Dec. 10, 1966; children: Christine, Sarah. MB, BS, U. Hong Kong, 1965; FRCS, Edinburgh, 1972; DLO, Royal Coll. Surgeons and Physicians, London, 1976; FACS, Edinburgh, 1978. Intern in surgery Queen Mary Hosp., Hong Kong, 1965-66, med. and health officer surgery unit, 1966-72; med. and health officer ENT unit Queen Mary and Queen Elizabeth Hosp., Hong Kong, 1972-75, sr. med. and health officer, 1975-77, cons. ENT surgeon, 1977-79; cons., ENT surgeon H.K. Sanatorium & Hosp., Hong Kong, 1982—, Alice Ho Miu Ling Nethersole Hosp., Hong Kong, 1982—. Fellow Hong Kong Surg. Soc., ACS, Royal Coll. Surgeons U.K.; mem. Hong Kong Med. Soc., Hong Kong Otorhinolaryngological Soc. (pres. 1978-80). Clubs Hong Kong Country, Royal Hong Kong Jockey. Home: Baguio Villa, Blk 31, 2/F Hong Kong Hong Kong Office: 603 Manning House, 48 Queen's Rd Central, Hong Kong Hong Kong

WU, PO-SHUN, biochemical researcher; b. Taipei, Republic of China, July 26, 1947; came to U.S., 1969; s. Ann-Pan and Zuei-Mei (Lee) W.; m. Susan H.W. Chen, Apr. 1, 1981; 1 child, Martin Jason. BS, Nat. Taiwan U., Taipei, 1969; MS, U. Akron, 1972; PhD, Georgetown U., 1977. Research-fellow Albert Einstein Coll. Medicine, Bronx, N.Y., 1977-79, Calif. Inst. Tech., Pasadena, 1980-82; asst. prof. Calif. State U., Los Angeles, 1982; research scientist Pacific Med. Ctr., San Francisco, 1982-84; mgr. quality control Xoma Corp., Berkeley, Calif., 1984-85; mgr. tech. ops. Gene Labs Inc., San Carlos, Calif., 1985—. Contbr. articles to profl. jours. and chpts. to books. Mem. AAAS, Am. Chem. Soc., N.Y. Acad. Scis. Home: 1366 28th Ave San Francisco CA 94122 Office: Gene Labs Inc 505 Penobscot Dr Redwood City CA 94063

WU, TSE CHENG, chemist; b. Hong Kong, Aug. 21, 1923; s. Shau Chuan and Shui (Chan) W.; B.S., Yenching U., 1946; M.S., U. Ill., 1948; Ph.D., Iowa State U., 1952; m. Janet Ling, June 14, 1963; children—Alan, Anna, Bernard. Came to U.S., 1947, naturalized, 1962. Prodn. chemist, Yungli Industries, Tangku, China, 1946-47; research asso. Iowa State U., Ames, 1952-53; research chemist duPont Co., Waynesboro, Va., 1953-60; research chemist Gen. Electric, Waterford, N.Y., 1960-71; sr. research chemist Abcor, Inc., Wilmington, Mass., 1971-77; research assoc. Allied-Signal, Inc., Morristown, N.J., 1977—. Mem. Troy Arts Guild, 1968-71, Morris County Art Assn., 1981—. Recipient Gold medallion award for inventions Gen. Electric Co., 1967; Allied Corp. patent award, 1983. Eastman Kodak Research fellow, 1951-52. Mem. Am. Chem. Soc., Sigma Xi, Phi Kappa Phi, Phi Lambda Upsilon, Alpha Chi Sigma. Contbr. profl. jours. Patentee in polymer chemistry and organosilicon chemistry. Home: 14-E Dorado Dr Morristown NJ 07960 Office: Allied-Signal Inc Morristown NJ 07960

WU, WEN CHUAN, microbial geneticist, educator; b. Taoyuan, Taiwan, Republic of China, Apr. 24, 1931; s. Shiao Tzuon and Mao (Lee) Shieh; m. Yuyen Chen, Nov. 19, 1967; children—Yuan Chenn, Philip Chenn. B.Sc., Nat. Chung Hsing U., 1956; M.Sc., U. Atla. (Can.), 1966; Ph.D., Tokyo U. Agr., 1972. Fgn. research fellow in microbial genetics Nat. Inst. Genetics, Misima, Shizuoka, Japan, 1969-72; postdoctoral fellow in microbial genetics Faculty of Medicine, Meml. U. Nfld. (Can.), St. John's, 1972-75; assoc. prof. microbial genetics, dept. plant pathology Nat. Chung Hsing U., Taichung, Taiwan, Republic of China, 1975-80, prof., 1980—; vis. prof. Meml. U. Nfld., 1983, U. Guelph (Ont., Can.), 1983-84. Editor-in-chief: Plant Protection Bull., 1980-82, editorial com., 1978-83, 86—. Mem. editorial com. Chinese Jour. Microbiology and Immunology, 1981—. Served with Republic of China Marine Corps, 1957-58. Mem. Canadian Soc. Microbiologists, Genetics Soc. Can., Chinese Soc. Microbiology, Plant Protection Soc. Republic of China, Phytopathol. Soc. Japan, Sigma Xi. Home: 20-3 Minyi St, Taichung 40222, Republic of China Office: Nat Chung Hsing U, Dept Plant Pathology, Taichung 40227, Republic of China

WUCHTERL, KURT JOSEF, philosophy and mathematics educator; b. Kaplitz, Czechoslovakia, Jan. 15, 1931; arrived in Germany, 1946; s. Vinzenz Martin and Anna Maria (Schneider) W.; m. Gisela Magdalena Zeslawski, Mar. 11, 1960; children: Martina, Petra, Josef, Christine. PhD, U. Heidelberg, Fed. Republic of Germany, 1958; D Habilitation, U. Stuttgart, Fed. Republic of Germany, 1975. Cert. math. and physics tchr. Studienassessor Gymnasium, Ellwangen, Fed. Republic of Germany, 1960-63; studienrat, -oberrat Gymnasium, Ulm, Fed. Republic of Germany, 1963-71; gymnasialprof. Gymnasium, Schwäbisch-Gmünd, Fed. Republic of Germany, 1971-80; apl. professor for philosophy U. Stuttgart, 1981—. Author: Struktur und Sprachspiel bei Wittgenstein, 1969, Methoden der Gegenwartsphilosophie, 1977, 2d rev. edit., 1987, Philosophie und Religion, 1982, Lehrbuch der Philosophie, 1984, 2d rev. edit., 1986 Grundkurs: Geschichte der Philosophie, 1986; (with A. Huebner) Wittgenstein, 1979; four textbooks; contbr. articles on philosophy to profl. jours. Recipient 1st prize award Aristotelian Soc. Roman Catholic. Home: Isarstrasse 7, 7070 Schwäbisch-Gmünd Federal Republic of Germany Office: U Stuttgart, Univ Fac Philosophy, Friedrichstrasse 10/XI, 7000 Stuttgart Federal Republic of Germany

WUHL, CHARLES MICHAEL, psychiatrist; b. N.Y.C., Sept. 24, 1943; s. Isadore and Sali (Ackner) W.; m. Gail; children—Elise, Amy. M.D., U. Bologna, 1973. Diplomate Am. Bd. Psychiatry and Neurology. Intern, N.Y. Med. Coll., 1975-76, resident in psychiatry, 1976-77; fellow in child psychiatry Columbia Presbyn. Med. Center, 1977-78; practice medicine specializing in psychiatry and child psychiatry, Englewood, N.J., 1978—; attending staff, mem. faculty N.Y. Med. Coll.; psychiatrist NYU, also asst. clin. prof. psychiatry NYU Sch. Medicine. Contbr. to Psychosocial Aspects of Pediatric Care, 1978, World Book Ency., 1980—. Mem. Am. Psychiat Assn., AMA, Am. Acad. Child Psychiatry. Office: 163 Engle St Englewood NJ 07631

WUKASCH, DORIS LUCILLE STORK, educator, counselor; b. Somerville, Tex., Dec. 30, 1924; d. Edwin William and Clara Rofine (Fuchs) Stork; B.A. with high honors, U. Tex., 1944, M.Ed., 1969; m. Joe Eugene Wukasch, July 7, 1945 (div. 1971); children—Linda Thiering, Susan Wukasch Richter, Jean Wukasch Mihalik, Jonathan. Chemist Tex. Dept. Health, Austin, 1944-45; microbiologist Terrell Labs., Ft. Worth, 1946-47; exec. sec. Wukasch Architects and Engrs., Austin, 1954-66; editorial asst. Steck-Vaughn Pubs., Austin, 1966; rehab. caseworker, job counselor Mary Lee Sch., Austin, 1969-70; spl. tchr. career edn. Austin Ind. Sch. 1970-85. Instr. ARC, 1972—; vol. tchr. Austin State Sch., 1958-68, Papua New Guinea, 1986. Area chmn. Am. Cancer Soc., 1970; mem. Women's Archtl. Guild, 1954-71, pres., 1964; mem. Women in the Arts, 1987—, Smithsonian Assn., 1972—, Wycliffe Assos., 1973—, Summer Inst. Linguistics, 1986, Wycliffe Bible Translators, 1986; active Stephen Minister. HEW grantee, 1968-69. Cert. rehab. counselor. Mem. Nat. Rehab. Counselors Assn., Nat., Tex. State tchrs. assn., Nat. Trust Historic Preservation, Christian Bus. and Profl. Women's Council, AAUW, Phi Beta Kappa. Lutheran. Contbr. poems and articles to mags. and newspapers. Home: 2500 Inwood Pl Austin TX 78703

WUKETITS, FRANZ MANFRED, philosophy of science educator; b. Parndorf, Austria, Jan. 5, 1955; s. Franz and Erika (Wallentich) W. PhD, U. Vienna, 1978. Lectr. U. Vienna, 1979-80, prof. Inst. Philosophy, 1980—. Author 16 books; contbr. articles to sci. jours. Recipient Österreichischer Staatpreis Für Wissenschaftliche Publizistik, Ministry of Sci., Austria, 1982. Home: Hauptstrasse 111, 7111 Parndorf Austria Office: Inst Philosophy, Universitaetsstr, 1010 Vienna Austria

WULBRECHT ZADVINSKIS, DOREEN MARIE, entrepreneur, training consultant; b. Detroit, May 25, 1955; d. Donald John and Gladys Estell (Keichinger) W. B.A.E., Eastern Mich. U., 1977. Lic. real estate cons., Mich. With McBee Systems, Grand Rapids, Mich., 1978; with New Dimension in Edn., Houston, 1979-80, regional mgr., 1980; salesman Pitney Bowes, Grand Rapids, 1980-81; owner Wulbrecht Carpet Wholesalers, Grand Rapids, 1981-85; owner Fantasies Gift Store, 1986-88; asst. dir. W.A. Lettinga Entrepreneurial Ctr. Davenport Coll., 1988—; condr. seminars in field; lectr. in field; cons. in field. Contbr. articles to profl. jours. Vol. Arts Council Festival, Grand Rapids, 1984, supr., 1985. Recipient Top Salesperson award Pitney Bowes, 1980, 81; Top Producer, McBee Systems, 1978; Top Mgr., New Dimensions in Edn., 1979, Sales award, 1979. Mem. Nat. Speakers Assn. Republican. Roman Catholic. Avocations: reading; photography; biking. Home: 15023 154th St Grand Haven MI 49417 Office: Davenport Coll WA Lettinga Entrepreneurial Ctr 473 E Fulton Grand Rapids MI 49503

WULFF, HANS DIEDERICH, urologic surgeon; b. Kiel, Fed. Republic Germany, Nov. 23, 1937; s. Heinz Dietrich and Margarete W.; m. Helga Dolch, Oct. 6, 1967; children—Heike, Hauke. M.D., U. Saarlandes, 1964. Intern, resident in urology Urologic Clinic, Homburg/Saar, 1964-68; resident in urology Urologic Clinic, U. Mainz, 1968-70, sr. physician, prin. physician, 1970-73, asst. prof., 1971-73, asso. prof., 1973—; physician in charge Urologic Clinic, Herford (W. Ger.) Dist. Hosp., 1973—; lectr. in urology U. Munster, Fed. Republic Germany, 1977. Contbr. to med. textbooks and med. jours. Recipient prix Specia, 1963. Mem. Deutsche Gesellschaft fü r Urologie, Sudwestdeutsche Gesellschaft fü r Urologie, Berufsverband Deutscher Urologen. Home: 75 Waltgeristr, 4900 Herford Federal Republic of Germany Office: 70 Schwarzenmoorstr, 4900 Herford NRW Federal Republic of Germany

WULLAERT, PIERRE, physician; b. Segre, Maine et Loire, France, May 4, 1926; s. Léon and Marie-Louise (Saladin) W.; m. Jocelyne Fauret, June 21, 1958; children: Patrick, Annie. Diploma of sport medicine, U. Lyon, France, 1955, MD, 1956; diploma body injury evaluation, U. Paris, 1969. Dr. in charge Angers, 1957—; med. inspector for sports Sports Direction Dept. Maine et Loire, 1963-70, Sports Direction Région Pays de la Loire, 1970-87; tech. counselor French Sec. of State for Youngs and Sports, 1987—; med. adviser ins. cos., France, 1963—; chief sec. Nat. Syndicate Sport Physicians, France, 1968-77; dep. prof. Faculties of Medicine, Angers, Nantes, Tours, 1969—; attaché-cons. U. Hosp. Ctr., Angers, 1970—; med. expert Appeal Ct., Angers, 1970—; pres. Football Regional Med. Com., Pays de Loire, France, 1981—; heading dir. Sports Medecine Actualites, 1981—, merite cycliste 1983; v.p. Med. Experts of Appeal Ct. Assn., Angers, 1986—. Author: Guide Pratique Medecine du Sport, 1978, Dictionnaire de Medecine du Sport, 1987; pub. service column Le Concours Medical, 1985—. Scout-chief Les Eclaireurs de France, Paris, Angers, Segre, 1945-59; founder and camp master Internat. Camps for Youngers, France, Germany, 1951-59; bd. dirs. Lycée David d'Angers, 1972-78; tech. adviser Internat. Com. against oldness symptomatology, Royan, France, 1986—. Recipient Bronze medal Nat. Medecine Acad., 1969, Chevalier Ordre Nat. du Merite French State, 1976, Chevalier Ordre Palmes Academiques, 1977, Silver medal Youth and Sports, 1978. Fellow Internat. Fedn. Sport Medicine; Societe Française de Medecine du Sport (bd. dirs., Bronze medal 1979), Fedn. Française de Football (nat. med. com, Gold medal 1986), Societe de Medecine Soprtive de L'Ouest (founder, chief sec.). Home: 2 Pl Victor Bernier, Angers, Maine & Loire France 49000 Office: Cen Univ Hosp, 1 Ave de l'Hotel Dieu, 49040 Angers France

WUORI, PAUL ADOLF, engineering educator; b. Kauniainen, Finland, Aug. 1, 1933; s. Bruno Adolf and Anna Maria (Nyberg) W.; m. Anne Mari Pihlström, Aug. 17, 1963; children: Eva Maria, Johan Henrik. MS in Engring., Helsinki U. of Tech., Espoo, Finland, 1960, Lic. of Tech., 1969, D in Tech., 1972. Lab engr. Helsinki U. of Tech., Espoo, 1960-67, acting prof., 1967-73, prof. in hydraulic machines, 1973-76, 85—, dean dept. mech. engring., 1976-79, pres., 1979-85; cons. in field. Patentee in field; author: European Journal of Engineering Education, 1987. Served to lt. Finnish Air Force Res., 1959-60. Named Commdr. of the Order of the white rose of Finland, 1983. Mem. European Soc. for Engring. Edn. (mem. adminstrv. council 1979-87, pres. 1985-86), Finnish Acad. Tech. Scis. Lutheran. Club: Helsinki Yacht Soc. Lodges: Ind. Order Odd Fellows, 5 Grankulla (chmn. 1974-75). Home: Tallbackavägen 12, 02700 Grankulla Finland Office: Helsinki Univ of Tech, Otakaari 4 A, 02150 Espoo Finland

WURDEMAN, LEW EDWARD, data processing corporation consultant; b. Colorado Springs, Colo., Oct. 31, 1949; s. Robert Martin and Shirley Gladys (Reetz) W. Student U. Tex., El Paso, 1967-69, U. Minn., 1969-72. Adminstr. Control Data Corp., Bloomington, Minn., 1969-81, product specialist, 1981-83, systems mgr., 1983-84, cons., 1984—. Republican. Lutheran. Clubs: German Shepherd Dog of Mpls., German Shepherd Dog of Am. Avocations: dog breeding, training, computers, photography. Home: 5827 210th ST W Farmington MN 55024-9617 Office: Control Data Corp PO Box 1305 BLCW1X Minneapolis MN 55440

WURR, PETER REINHARD, management and marketing consultant; b. Neumuenster, Germany, June 23, 1943; s. Alwin and Erna Johanna (Milahn) W.; m. Sonja-Petra Czybulka, Aug. 3, 1984; children: Peter Philipp, Julia Katharine. BA, U. Cologne, 1964; postgrad. in psychology, U. Goettingern, 1964-65, U. Freiburg, 1964-65. Apprentice Dresdner Bank AG, Cologne, Fed. Republic Germany, 1960-62; sales rep. Remington-Rand Univac GmbH, Frankfurt, Bonn, Fed. Republic Germany, 1966-68; br. mgr. Mohawk Data Scis. GmbH, Hanover, Fed. Republic Germany, 1969-72; gen. mgr. CIT-Transac GmbH, Frankfurt, 1975-77; founder, pres. PRW-Unternehmensberatung GmbH, Koerdorf/Taunus, Fed. Republic Germany, 1978—. Co-author: Yearbook Office Automation, 1985, 86, Marketing for Computers and New Media, 1985, Dictionary of Computer Sciences, 1987; author: Men Who Wrote Computer History; editor Office Mgmt., 1982—; corr. Datamation mag., 1985; editor-in-chief IT-Market, 1987—. Mem. ADI, Assn. German EDP Users (bd. dirs. 1970-72, 82-85), German Journalists Assn., German-Am. C. of C. Home and Office: Neuwagenmuehle, 5429 Koerdorf/Taunus Federal Republic of Germany

WURZBACHER, GERHARD, sociology educator; b. Zwickau, Saxony, Germany, July 31, 1912; s. Paul and Hedwig (Künze) W.; m. Annelore Bock, Sept. 18, 1939; children: Frank, Heike, Wulf, Hartmut. Degree in Pedagogique, U. Leipzig, Germany, 1936; Dr. in History, U. Berlin, Germany, 1939; Habilitation in Sociology, U. Hamburg, Fed. Republic Germany, 1952. Lectr., asst. Acad. for Econs. and Politics, Hamburg, 1948-52; research leader UNESCO Inst. for Social Scis., Cologne, Fed. Republic Germany, 1952-54; prof. sociology Pedagogical High Sch., Hannover, Fed. Republic Germany, 1954-56, U. Kiel, Fed. Republic Germany, 1956—; Fulbright prof. U. S.C., Columbia, 1956; prof. sociology and social anthropology U. Erlangen-Nuremberg, Fed. Republic Germany, 1965-80, with Interdisciplinary Research Ctr. for Social Scis., 1980—. Author several books on sociology; contbr. articles to profl. jours. Advisor Fed. Ministry Family, Youth and Health, Fed. Republic Germany, Protestant Ch. Germany, Council Against Drug Addiction, German Sports Orgn., all 1957-75. Named 1st Class Bundesverdienstkreuz, 1982. Home: Am Heckacker 24, D8501 Kalchreuth, Bavaria Federal Republic of Germany Office: Sozialwissenschaftliches Forschungszentrum, d U Erzangen-Nuremberg, Fingasse 7-9, D8500 Nuremberg, Bavaria Federal Republic of Germany

WUSSAR-NARH, FRANCIS, wholesale and distribution company executive, consultant; b. Big Ada, Accra, Ghana, May 14, 1944; s. John Nartey and Comfort (Korkor) Ankama Wussar; m. Victoria Mensah, May 5, 1974; children—George, Hilda, Yvonne, Edwin, Solomon. B.Sc. in Adminstrv. Acctg., U. Ghana, 1971. Auditor United Africa Co. Ghana Ltd., Accra, 1971-76, sr. auditor, 1985—; acct. Guiness Ghana Ltd., Kumasi, 1976-85; chief exec. Luhuesey Enterprises, Kumasi, Ghana, 1980-85. Mem. Ghana Inst. Mgmt., Ghana Inst. Fin. Planners and Adminstrs., Inst. Chartered Accts., Ghana. Methodist. Club: Wesley Men's Fellowship (Kumasi). Lodges: Masons, Rotary. Avocation: swimming. Home: Ahodwo Rd Box 8721, Kumasi Ghana

WU XUEQIAN, vice premier State Council, People's Republic of China; b. Shanghai, China, 1921; m. Bi Ling. Joined Chinese Communist Party, 1939; dep. dir. internat. liaison dept. New Dem. Youth League, 1949-52, mem. cen. com., 1953, dir., 1953-56; mem. nat. com. Fedn. Dem. Youth, 1953, dir., until 1958, vice chmn., 1958-64; sec. gen. del. to 6th Festival World Fedn. Dem. Youth, Moscow, 1957; dep. from Anhui Province to 3d Nat. People's Congress, 1964-67; mem. 5th Chinese People's Polit. Consultative Conf., 1978; dep. fgn. minister People's Republic of China, 1982, minister fgn. affairs, 1982-88, state councilor State Council, 1983-88, vice premier, and head of tourism, 1988—; mem. 12th Cen. Com., Chinese Communist Party, 1982—, mem. politburo, 1985—. Address: Ministry of Foreign Affairs,, Beijing People's Republic of China *

WYATT, JOE BILLY, university chancellor; b. Tyler, Tex., July 21, 1935; s. Joe and Fay (Pinkerton) W.; m. Faye Hocutt, July 21, 1956; children: Joseph Robert, Sandra Faye. B.A., U. Tex., 1956; M.A., Tex. Christian U., 1960. Systems engr. Gen. Dynamics Corp., 1956-65; mgr. Digital Computer Lab., 1961-65; dir. computer ctr., assoc. prof. computer sci. U. Houston, 1965-72; dir. Office Info. Tech. Harvard U., 1972-76, sr. lectr. computer sci., 1972-82, v.p. adminstrn., 1976-82; chancellor Vanderbilt U., Nashville, 1982—; mem. faculty Kennedy Sch. of Harvard U., 1972-82; bd. dirs. Hosp. Corp. Am., 1984—, Sonat Inc., 1984—. Author (with others) Financial Planning Models for Colleges and Universities, 1979; editor-in chief: Jour. Applied Mgmt. Systems, 1983; contbr. articles to profl. jours.; patentee in field of data processing. Trustee Harvard U. Press, 1976-83, pres., 1975-76, chmn. bd., 1976-79; trustee EDUCOM, Princeton, N.J., 1973-81; bd. dirs. Nashville Inst. Arts, 1982-83; chmn. adv. com. IST, NSF, 1978-85; vice chmn. bd. Mass. Tech. Devel. Corp., Boston, 1977-83; mem. policy bd. Nat. Assn. Ind. Colls. and Univs., 1980-82; fellow Gallaudet Coll., 1981-83. Recipient award for exemplary leadership CAUSE, Hilton Head, S.C., 1982, Nat. Tree of Life award Jewish Nat. Fund, 1988; named Outstanding Tennessean Gov. of Tenn., 1986; mem. alumni bd. dirs. Harvard Bus. Sch., 1982—. Mem. Assn. Computing Machinery (pres. Dallas, Ft. Worth chpt. 1963-65), IEEE, Univs. Research Assn. (bd. trustees 1988—), So. Univs. Research Assn., Inc. (chmn. council pres. 1988—), Aircraft Owners and Pilots Assn., Assn. Am. Univs. Research Com., Sigma Xi, Beta Gamma Sigma, Phi Beta Kappa (hon.). Methodist. Club: Harvard (N.Y.C.). Office: Vanderbilt U Office of Chancellor 211 Kirkland Hall Nashville TN 37240 *

WYATT, KATHRYN ELIZABETH BENTON, psychologist, educator; b. Danville, Va., May 11, 1928; d. Joseph Nelson and Margaret (Davis) Benton; B.A., Randolph Macon Woman's Coll., Lynchburg, Va., 1949; M.Ed., U. Va., 1952; M.A., U. N.C., Greensboro, 1974, Ph.D., 1977; m. Landon Russell Wyatt, Aug. 30, 1952; children—Margaret Wyatt Scott, Landon Russell, III, Elizabeth Wyatt Ashe. Instr., then asst. prof. psychology Stratford Coll., Danville, 1949-74, chmn. dept., 1963-74; prof. psychology Danville Community Coll., 1977—. Mem. Danville Sch. Bd.; deacon, tchr. 1st Bapt. Ch., Danville; pres. so. region Va. Sch. Bds. Assn. Mem. Am. Psychol. Assn., Soc. Research Child Devel., Southeastern Psychol. Assn., Va. Psychol. Assn., Va. Acad. Sci. Clubs: Friends Danville Pub. Library (pres.), The Wednesday Club (pres.), Gabriella, Wayside Garden, Shakespeare. Author articles in field. Home: 301 Magnolia St Danville VA 24541 Office: Danville Community Coll Danville VA 24541

WYATT, OSCAR SHERMAN, JR., energy company executive; b. Beaumont, Tex., July 11, 1924; s. Oscar Sherman Sr. and Eva (Coday) W.; m. Lynn Wyatt; children: Carl, Steven, Douglas, Oscar Sherman III, Brad. BS in Mech. Engring., Tex. Agrl. and Mech. Coll., 1949. With Kerr-McGee Co., 1949; with Reed Roller Bit Co., 1949-51; ptnr. Wymore Oil Co., 1951-55; founder Coastal Corp., Corpus Christi, Tex., 1955; now chmn., chief exec. officer. Coastal Corp., Houston. Served with USAAF, World War II. Home: 1620 River Oaks Blvd Houston TX 77019 Office: The Coastal Corp 9 Greenway Plaza E Houston TX 77046

WYCKOFF, ALEXANDER, stage designer, educator; b. Leonia, N.J., Aug. 17, 1898; s. James Talmage and Wilhelmina (Ludwig) W.; 1 child, Peter Talmage. Student, Columbia Coll., 1916-17, 19, Carnegie Inst. Tech., 1920. Designer, H. Robert Law Studios, N.Y.C., 1920-21, 24-25; instr., designer drama dept. Carnegie Inst. Tech., Pitts., 1921-24; dir. Memphis Little Theatre, 1927-30; art dir. U. Mich., Ann Arbor, 1932-41, 50; supr. design Phila. Mus. Sch., 1933-43; writer, illustrator, stage designer, Leonia, N.J., 1950-69, Tustin, Calif., 1971—; art dir. pageant Rensselaer Poly. Inst., 1924, U.S. Govt., Yorktown, Va., 1931, Joint City/Producers Corp., Alexandria, Va., 1949; art dir. Cin. Art Theatre, 1925-26. Author: (with Edward Warwick and Henry Pitz) Early American Dress, 1964; editor: Arts of Design-Dunlap, 1965; author/illustrator: 19th Century Dress, 1966-81, 1600 World Dress, 1982-83, Sketchbook of Aboriginal Dress, Western Hemisphere, Post-Glacial to 1866 A.D., 1987. Pres., bd. dirs. Leonia players Guild, N.J., 1920-53, Leonia Pub. Library, 1962-69, Wyckoff House Found. (hon.); vol. advisor Performing Arts, Tustin High Sch., Calif., 1975—. Served with U.S. Army, 1917-18. Mem. Nat. Theatre Conf. (founding, bd. dirs.). Address: 12937 B Newport Ave Tustin CA 92680

WYCOFF, CHARLES COLEMAN, retired physician, anesthesiologist; b. Glazier, Tex., Sept. 2, 1918; s. James Garfield and Ada Sharpe (Braden) W.; m. Gene Marie Henry, May 16, 1942; children: Michelle, Geoffrey, Brian, Roger, Daniel, Norman, Irene, Teresa. AB, U. Calif., Berkeley, 1941; MD, U. Calif., San Francisco, 1943. Diplomate Am. Bd. Anesthesiology. Founder The Wycoff Group of Anesthesiology, San Francisco, 1947-53; chief of anesthesia St. Joseph's Hosp., San Francisco, 1947-52, San Francisco County Hosp., 1953-54; asst. prof. anesthesiology Columbia U., N.Y.C., 1955-63; creator residency tng. program in anesthesiology St. Joseph's Hosp., San Francisco, 1950, San Francisco County Hosp., 1954; practice anesthesiology, tchr. Presbyn. Med. Ctr., N.Y.C., 1955-63; clin. practice anesthesiology St. Francis Meml. Hosp., 1963-84; councilor at large Alumni Faculty Assn. Sch. Medicine U. Calif., San Francisco, 1979-80. Producer, dir. films on regional anesthesia; contbr. articles to sci. jours. Scoutmaster Boy Scouts Am., San Francisco, 1953-55. Served to capt. M.C., U.S. Army, 1945-47. Republican. Home: 870 Joost Ave San Francisco CA 94127

WYCOFF, ROBERT E., petroleum company executive; b. Tulsa, 1930; married. B.S.M.E., Stanford U., 1952, M.S.M.E., 1953. With Atlantic Richfield Co., Los Angeles, 1953—, various engring. and mgmt. positions, 1957-70, mgr. western region Internat. div., 1971-73, v.p., resident mgr. Alaska region N.Am. Producing div., 1973-74, corp. planning v.p., 1974-77, sr. v.p. planning and fin., 1977-80, exec. v.p., 1980-84, chief corp. officer, 1984, vice chmn., 1985, pres., chief operating officer, 1986—, also dir.; bd. dirs. 1st Republic Bank Corp. Mem. ASME, Am. Petroleum Inst. Office: Atlantic Richfield Co 515 S Flower St Los Angeles CA 90071

WYLLER, THOMAS CHRISTIAN, political scientist, educator; b. Stavanger, Norway, Sept. 16, 1922; s. Trygve and Anne Kathrine (Dons) W.; children from previous marriage: Trygve, Tom Ketil; children from current marriage: Torgeir, Vegard. MA, U. Oslo, 1951, PhD, 1958. Assoc. prof. polit. sci. U. Oslo, 1958-65, prof., 1965—. Author in field. Home: Nordstrandv 9, Oslo Norway Office: U Oslo, Oslo Norway

WYMAN, WILLIAM ROBERT, academic administrator; b. Edmonton, Alta., Can., Dec. 4, 1930; s. Robert Andrew and Dora (Joberns) W.; m. Dorothy Taylor, Sept. 4, 1954; children—Timothy, Robyn, Leslie. B.Comm., U. B.C., 1956. Chmn. bd., dir. Pemberton Houston Willoughby Inc., Vancouver, B.C., Can., 1982—; analyst Can. Life Assurance Co., Toronto, Ont., Can., 1956-57, Hall Securities Ltd., Vancouver, B.C., Can., 1957-60; registered rep. Richardson Securities Can., 1960-65; mgr. research dept. Pemberton Securities Ltd., 1962, retail dept. mgr. and dir., 1965-69, v.p., 1969-71, sr. v.p., 1971-75, pres., chief exec. officer, 1975-82; chancellor U. B.C.; mem. policy com. Bus. Council on Nat. Issues; bd. govs. Employers Council B.C. Mem. Conf. Bd. (sr.), Investment Dealers Assn. Can. (past chmn.), Vancouver Bd. Trade (past chmn.), Can. C. of C. (past chmn.). Anglican. Clubs: Capilano Golf and Country; Hollyburn Country; Vancouver. Office: Box 49160, 4 Bentall Ctr, Vancouver, BC Canada V7X 1K6 *

WYMOR, LARRY LOWELL, textile executive; b. Cleve., Jan. 14, 1936; s. Emanuel and Marie P. (Blank) W.; m. Elinor M. Fox; children: Marcia G., Steven J. BBA, Case Western Res.U., 1958, LLB, 1961. Ptnr. Burke, Haber & Berick, Cleve., 1961-81; pres. Cleve. Cotton Products Co., 1981—; sr. v.p. The Tranzonic Cos., Cleveland, 1981—; exec. com., bd. dirs. Internat. Assn. of Wiping Cloth Mfrs., Washington. Mem. exec. com. Park Synagogue, Cleve., 1981—; bd. dirs. Mayfield Ednl. Excellence Found., Cleve., 1986—; bd. dirs. Menorah Park Ctr., Cleve., 1984—. Named Man of Yr., Park Synagogue Men's Club, 1978, named Centerite of Yr., Park Synagogue, 1981. Lodge: B'nai B'rith (pres. dist. 2 Cin. 1986-87, vice chmn. internat. youth orgn., chmn. nat. leadership cabinet, Gold Key award Youth Commn. 1985). Office: Cleve Cotton Products Co PO Box 6500 Cleveland OH 44101

WYNGAARDEN, JAMES BARNES, physician; b. East Grand Rapids, Mich., Oct. 19, 1924; s. Martin Jacob and Johanna (Kempers) W.; m. Ethel Vredevoogd, June 20, 1946 (div. 1977); children: Patricia Wyngaarden Fitzpatrick, Joanna Wyngaarden Gandy, Martha Wyngaarden Krauss, Lisa Wyngaarden Rolland, James Barnes Jr. Student, Calvin Coll., 1942-43, Western Mich. U., 1943-44; MD, U. Mich., 1948; DSc (hon.), U. Mich. and Med. Coll. of Ohio, 1984, Tel Aviv U., 1987; PhD (hon.), U. Ill., Chgo., 1985; DSc (hon.), George Washington U., 1985. Diplomate: Am. Bd. Internal Medicine. Intern Mass. Gen. Hosp., Boston, 1948-49; resident Mass.

Gen. Hosp., 1949-51; vis. investigator Pub. Health Research Inst., N.Y.C., 1952-53; investigator NIH, USPHS, Bethesda, Md., 1953-56; asso. prof. medicine and biochemistry Duke Med. Sch., 1956-61, prof., 1961-65; vis. scientist Inst. de Biologie-Physiochemique, Paris, 1963-64; prof., chmn. U. Pa. Med. Sch., 1965-67; physician-in-chief Med. Service Hosp. U. PA., Phila., 1965-67; Frederic M. Hanes prof., chmn. dept. medicine Duke Med. Sch., 1967-82; physician-in-chief Med. Service Duke U. Hosp., Durham, N.C., 1967-82; chief of staff Duke U. Hosp., Durham, 1981-82; dir. NIH, Bethesda, MD, 1982—; mem. staff Duke, VA, Durham County hosps.; cons. Office Sci. and Tech. Exec. Office of Pres., 1966-72; Mem. Pres.'s Sci. Adv. Com., 1972-73; mem. Pres.'s Com. for Nat. Medal of Sci., 1977-80; mem. adv. com. biology and medicine AEC, 1966-68; mem. bd. sci. counselors NIH, 1971-74; mem. adv. bd. Howard Hughes Med. Inst., 1969-82; mem. adv. council Life Ins. Med. Research Fund, 1967-70; adv. bd. Sci. Yr., 1977-81; vice chmn. Com. on Study Nat. Needs for Biomed. and Behavioral Research Personnel, NRC, 1977-81. Author: (with W.N. Kelley) Gout and Hyperuricemia, 1976; (with J.B. Stanbury) The Metabolic Bases of Inherited Disease, 1966; (with O. Sperling, A. DeVries) Purine Metabolism in Man, 1974; editor: (with L.H. Smith Jr.) Cecil Textbook of Medicine, 1982, 85; Mem. editorial bd.: Jour. Biol. Chemistry, 1971-74, Arthritis and Rheumatism, 1959-66, Jour. Clinical Investigation, 1962-66, Ann. Internal Medicine, 1964-74, Medicine, 1963— ; editor: (with J.B. Stanbury, D.S. Fredrickson) The Metabolic Basis of Inherited Disease, 1960, 66, 72, 78, 83, (with O. Sperling and A. DeVries) Purine Metabolism in Man, 1974, (with L.H. Smith, Jr.) Cecil Textbook of Medicine, 16th edit., 1982, 17th edit., 1985, 18th edit., 1988 (with L.H. Smith Jr.) Rev. of Gen. Internal Medicine: A Self-Assessment Guide, 2d edit., 1982, 3d edit., 1985. Bd. dirs. Royal Soc. Medicine Found., 1971-76, The Robert Wood Johnson Found. Clin. Scholar Program., 1973-78. Served with USNR, 1943-46; sr. surgeon USPHS, 1951-56, rear adm. USPHS, 1982—. Recipient Borden Undergrad. Research award U. Mich., 1948, N.C. Gov.'s award for sci., 1974, Disting. Alumnus award Western Mich. U., 1984, Robert Williams award Assn. Profs. Medicine, 1985; Dalton scholar in medicine Mass. Gen. Hosp., 1950; Royal Coll. Physicians fellow, 1984. Mem. Am. Rheumatism Assn., Am. Fedn. Clin. Research, So. Soc. Clin. Investigation (pres. 1974, founder's medal 1978), ACP (John Phillips Meml. award 1980), Am. Soc. Clin. Investigation, AAAS, Am. Soc. Biol. Chemists, Assn. Am. Physicians (councillor 1973-77, pres. 1978), Endocrine Soc., Nat. Acad. Scis., Royal Acad. Scis. Sweden, Am. Acad. Arts and Sci., Inst. Medicine, Sigma Xi. Democrat. Presbyterian. Club: Interurban Clinical (Balt.). Office: Nat Inst of Health Bldg 1 Rm 124 Bethesda MD 20892

WYNNE, ARTHUR VINCENT, JR., press clipping bureau executive; b. Orange, N.J., Oct. 4, 1933; s. Arthur Vincent and Majorie E. (Stout) W.; B.A., U. Mich., 1955; M.B.A., U. Chgo., 1962; m. Sandra Anne Gerow, Apr. 21, 1982; Ann Walters, Sept. 24, 1960; children—Arthur Vincent III, Bradley Allen, Cathy. With Burrelle's Press Clipping Service, 1955—, midwest sales mgr., 1958-60, nat. sales mgr., N.Y.C., 1960-75, partner, 1961—; pres. Internationale Fedn. Press Clipping Bureaux, Paris, 1965-70, New Eng. Newsclips, Framingham, Mass., 1970—; dir. Hudson City Savs. Bank, Paramus, N.J. chmn., past pres. N.Am. Conf. Press Clipping Services, N.Y.C. Pres. Republican Club, Livingston, 1966; councilman Livingston, N.J., 1967-71; mayor Livingston, 1968; trustee Newark Acad. Served to 1st lt. USAAF, 1956-58. Named Livingston Young Man of Year, 1966; recipient Disting. Service award Publicity Club N.Y., 1964. Mem. Public Relations Soc. Am., Employers Assn. N.J. (pres. 1976-78), Livingston Jaycees, N.J. Press Assn. Sigma Chi. Presbyterian. Club: Publicity of New York. Home: 90 Carriage House Rd Bernardsville NJ 07924 Office: 75 E Northfield Rd Livingston NJ 07039

WYNNE, CAREY HOWARD, JR. (JEAN-PIERRE SOLÒMON), history and religion educator; b. Pine Bluff, Ark., Mar. 16, 1950; s. Carey Howard and Gertie (Lamb) W. A.B., Morehouse Coll., 1970; A.M., U. Chgo., 1972; postgrad., 1972-73; D.D. (hon.), Universal Ch. Faculty assoc. U. Chgo. Div. Sch., 1972-74; assoc. religion dept. history Morehouse Coll., Atlanta, 1973—; cons. U.S. News and World Report, others; advisor Morehouse Coll.; cons. Msgr. A. Lanzoni, dept. head Secretariat of State, The Vatican, also to Pope John Paul II; Episcopal convenor Synod of Bishops, The Vatican, 1984. Exec. sec. Democratic party Fulton County; active Butler St. YMCA, Atlanta U. Ctr. Community Chorus; tenor soloist. Recipient J.J. Starks Best Man of Affairs award Morehouse Coll., 1970; Rockefeller Protestant fellow, 1970; Lyndon Baines award U. Tex.-Austin, 1970; Ford Found. fellow, 1971-75. Mem. Am. Soc. Ch. History, Internat. Patristics Council, Am. Acad. Religion, Songwriters, Resources and Services (Music Union), Internat. Religious Assn., Inc., Phi Alpha Theta. Democrat. Roman Catholic (mem. Faith Community of St. Charles Lwanga). Contbr. to books, profl. jours.; author: The Tradition: Sacerdotium and Regnum and the Two Beckets, 1972; The Spiritual Significance of Pope John Paul II, San Vittorino, Italia, 1978; On the Rhythm of Soul Truth, 1982; What Are Visions and Values without God?, 1983; On Rhythms of Liberation Notes, 1984; Arius and the Castle of Misty Blue, 1985; composer musical score, For Thine is the Kingdom, The Power, and the Glory, Forever, Amen, 1982; composer Obedience, 1983; God: The Almighty Power, 1984; The Love of God, 1985, The Beatitudes, 1986.

WYNNE, JOHN MACDONALD, JR., financial company executive; b. Sacramento, Sept. 12, 1945; s. John MacDonald and Helen (Gurley) W. A.B., Dartmouth Coll., 1967; M.B.A., Harvard U., 1969. Mem. research faculty Harvard U., Boston, 1969-72; spl. asst. Exec. Office Human Services, Commonwealth Mass., Boston, 1972-74; project dir. Am. Justice Inst., Sacramento, 1974-77; cons. ABT Assocs., Cambridge, Mass., 1977-78, Dickenson, O'Brien & Assocs., San Francisco, 1978-79, 81; ptnr. Service Mgmt. Group, Paris, 1979-80; pres. Wynne Assocs., Boston, 1981-83; pres. Techsoft Inc., Chestnut Hill, Mass., 1983-85, Market Tech., Cambridge, 1985-86; pres. First Kendall Corp., Cambridge, 1986—, also bd. dirs. Author: Prison Employee Unionism, 1977. Div. research fellow Harvard Bus. Sch., Boston, 1971. Bd. dirs. Social Service Ctrs., Inc., 1984—. Clubs: Harvard (Boston); The Country (Brookline, Mass.); Univ. (San Francisco). Office: First Kendall Corp One Kendall Sq Cambridge MA 02139

WYNSTRA, NANCY ANN, lawyer; b. Seattle, June 25, 1941; d. Walter S. and Gaile E. (Cogley) W. B.A. cum laude, Whitman Coll., 1963; LL.B. cum laude, Columbia U., 1966. Bar: Wash. 1966, D.C. 1969, Ill. 1979, Pa. 1984. With appellate sect., civil div. U.S. Dept. Justice, Washington, 1966-67; TV corr.-legal news Sta. WRC, NBC and Sta. WTOP, CBS, Washington, 1967-68; spl. asst. Corp. Counsel, D.C., Washington, 1968-70; dir. planning and research D.C. Superior Ct., Washington, 1970-78; spl. advisor White House Spl. Action Office for Drug Abuse Prevention, Washington, 1973-74; fellow Drug Abuse Council, 1974-75; gen. counsel Michael Reese Hosp. and Med. Center, Chgo., 1978-83; exec. v.p., gen. counsel Allegheny Health Services, Inc., Pitts., 1983—; cons. to various drug abuse programs, 1971-78. Mem. ABA, Nat. Health Lawyers Assn. (bd. dirs. 1985—), Am. Soc. Hosp. Attys., others. Presbyterian. Contbr. articles to profl. jours. Office: Allegheny Gen Hosp 320 E North Ave Pittsburgh PA 15208

WYNTER, HECTOR LINCOLN, b. Camaguey, Cuba, July 27, 1926; s. Percival George and Lola Maud (Reid) W.; teaching cert. Havana U., 1946; M.A. in Modern Langs. (Rhodes scholar), Oxford U., 1952; diploma in edn. London U., 1953; UN fellow, 1953; m. Jacqueline Antrobus, Sept. 1, 1956 (div. 1969); children—Astrid, Brian, Colin; m. 2d, Diana Ayee, Dec. 31, 1969; children—Sara-Jean, Lincoln, Mark. Sr. Spanish master Calabar High Sch., Jamaica, 1945-49, lectr. adult edn., 1953-55; dep. registrar U. W.I., 1955-59, prof. adult edn., 1959-65, secondment as registrar, 1964-65; dir. projects Assn. Caribbean Univs., 1972-74; editor Gleaner Publs., Kingston, Jamaica, 1974-85; dir. Gleaner Co.; bd. dirs. Caribbeana Council of Washington, UNESCO, Paris, non-resident ambassador, 1981—, chmn. exec. bd., 1974-76, minister of cabinet, 1967-72, senator, 1962-72, ambassador to Trinidad and Tobago, 1963-64; former chmn. Jamaica Labour Party; chmn. Bustamante Inst. Pub. and Internat. Affairs, 1984—. Served as cadet under-officer Jamaica Cadet Force, 1942-44. Decorated Order of Jamaica, 1981. Home: 5 Monterey Dr, Kingston 5 Jamaica Office: Bustamante Inst Pub Internat, Affairs, 11 Worthington Ave, Kingston 5 Jamaica *

WYRSCH, JAMES ROBERT, lawyer, educator; b. Springfield, Mo., Feb. 23, 1942; s. Louis Joseph and Jane Elizabeth (Welsh) W.; m. B. Darlene Wyrsch, Oct. 18, 1975; children—Scott, Keith, Mark, Brian, Marcia. B.A., U. Notre Dame, 1963; J.D., Georgetown U., 1966; LL.M., U. Mo., Kansas City, 1972. Bar: Mo. 1966, U.S. Ct. Appeals (8th cir.) 1971, U.S. Supreme Ct. 1972, U.S. Ct. Appeals (10th cir.) 1974, U.S. Ct. Appeals (5th cir.) 1974, U.S. Ct. Mil. & Appeals 1978, U.S. Ct. Appeals (6th cir.) 1982, U.S. Ct. Appeals (11th cir.) 1984, U.S. Ct. Appeals (7th cir.) 1986. Assoc., Koenigsdorf, Wyrsch and Ramsey, and predecessors, Kansas City, Mo., 1970-71, of counsel, 1972-77, ptnr., 1978—; adj. prof. U. Mo., 1981—; mem. com. instrns. Mo. Supreme Ct., 1983—. Served as capt. U.S. Army, 1966-69. Mem. Am. Arbitration Assn. (panel arbitrators), ABA, Mo. Bar Assn. (vice chmn. criminal law com. 1978-79), Kansas City Bar Assn. (chmn. anti-trust com. 1981), Assn. Trial Lawyers Am., Nat. Assn. Criminal Def. Attys., Mo. Assn. Criminal Def. Attys. (sec. 1982), Phi Delta Phi. Democrat. Roman Catholic. Contbr. in field. Home: 811 Hearnes St Blue Springs MO 64015 Office: Koenigsdorf Wyrsch & Ramsey 1006 Grand Ave Suite 1050 Kansas City MO 64106

WYRTZEN, JAMES CHARLES, psychotherapist; b. N.Y.C., Aug. 27, 1942; s. James and Malvina Wyrtzen; BA, Moravian Coll. and Theol. Sem., 1964, MDiv, 1967; DMin, N.Y. Theol. Sem., 1981; Pastoral Care Cert. Insts. of Religion and Health, N.Y.C., 1970, Pastoral Counseling Certificate, 1973; m. Marcia Metz, Aug. 17, 1975; children: Christy, Andrew Mark, David Christopher. Ordained to ministry United Methodist Ch., 1966; pastor Westhampton Beach (N.Y.), United Meth. Ch., 1967-70, Whitestone (N.Y.) United Meth. Ch., 1970-73; dir. Whitestone Counseling Center, 1973-76, also staff therapist Yorkville (N.Y.) Counseling Center, South Nassau (N.Y.) Family Counseling Inst.; pvt. practice psychotherapy, N.Y.C., 1973—; exec. dir. Center for Creative Living, Allendale, N.J., 1976-88, pres., 1976-88, sr. staff therapist, 1988—; dir. tng. Blanton, Peale Grad. Inst. of the Insts. Religion and Health, 1988—. Pres., Hampton Council Chs., 1969-70. Recipient Cora Dosta Moses Homeltics prize Moravian Theol. Sem., 1967. Lic. marriage and family counselor, N.J., Calif. Mem. Am. Assn. Marriage and Family Counselors, Am. Group Psychotherapy Assn., Alumni Assn. Insts. Religion and Health (v.p. 1985-87, pres. 1987-88), Am. Assn. Pastoral Counselors (v.p., pres. elect 1988—, assoc. sec.-treas. 1983-87, mem. exec. com. 1983-87, bd. govs. 1983-87). Democrat. Home: 2-20 34th St Fair Lawn NJ 07410 Office: Ctr for Creative Living 37 E Allendale Ave and Franklin Turnpike Allendale NJ 07401 also: 16 E 79th St Suite 44 New York NY 10021

WYSOCZYNSKI, DONALD THOMAS, tool and diemaking company executive; b. Grand Rapids, Mich., Feb. 9, 1931; s. Charles Anthony and Anna Francis (Antosczak) W.; m. Ruth Marlene Chicklon, Jan. 24, 1953; children: James Allen, Thomas Lee, Gerald Paul. Student, Grand Rapids Jr. Coll., 1948-50. Apprentice Fischer Body div. Gen. Motors Corp., Grand Rapids, 1955-57, Leese Tool and Die, Grand Rapids, 1957-66; tool engr. Grand Rapids Metalcraft, 1966-72; design engr. Slagboom Tool and Die Co., Grand Rapids, 1973-77; div. mgr. Trojan Tool div. Douglas and Lomason Co. Inc., Carrollton, Ga., 1977-87; prin. Die-Tech Design, Carrollton, 1987—. Past bd. dirs. Cath. War Vets. U.S.A.; formerly active Grand Valley council Boy Scouts Am. Served with USN, 1952-54. Recipient Silver Beaver award Boy Scouts Am.; St. George medal for scouting work Grand Rapids Roman Cath. Diocese. Republican. Lodges: Kiwanis (bd. dirs.), Moose (fellow 1984, past lodge sec.), Elks (Carrollton) (bd. dirs.). Home and Office: 109 Wilson Circle Carrollton GA 30117

WYSS, KURT, advertising consultant; b. Zurich, Switzerland, Aug. 17, 1943; m. Ruth Elisabeth Weideli, Oct. 26, 1968; children—Mirjam, Eveline. Dipl. Werbeassistent, 1968; Eidg. dipl. Werbeleiter, 1973, Swiss Ctr. for Mktg., Advt. and Communication, 1973. Mgr., co-ptnr., Wyss & Gloor, Zurich, 1973-87, owner, mgr., 1987—. Mem. Schweizerischer Verkaufs-und Marketingleiter Club, Vereinigung fü r Werbekommunikation, Schweizer Werbewirtschaft, Bund Schweizer Werbeagenturen, Internat. Assn. Ind. Advt. Agys. Home: Rutlistrasse 24, CH-8308 Illnau Zurich Switzerland Office: Wyss & Ptnr AG, Dubendorf Str 4, 8051 Zurich Switzerland

WYSZYNSKI, VALENTINE ANTHONY, sound design engineer; b. Chgo., Dec. 24, 1941; s. Anthony Marion and Genevieve Ann (Stabosz) W.; m. Joy Anne Halvorsen, Oct. 5, 1966 (div.); children: April Suzanne, Brian Matthew, Charlotte Lillian; m. Elizabeth DeWitt, May 1978 (div.); children: Tonia Rae, Brian Lee. Student U.S. Air Force Inst., 1965-68, Nat. Tech Schs., 1968-70; BSEE, N.Mex. State U., 1980, BS in Music Engring. and Drama Tech., 1981. With U.S. Post Office, Lyons, Ill., 1959-64, Circle News, Joliet, Ill., 1971-73; dist. mgr. So. N.Mex. region Combined Ins. Co. of Am., Chgo., 1973-76; sound design engr. drama dept. N.Mex. State U., University Park, 1977-81; ptnr., gen. mgr. Desert Distbg., Las Cruces, N.Mex., 1978-84; editor, photographer Coomes Advt./Entertainment Guide, Las Cruces, 1981-84; gen. mgr. Heartline Prodns., Wood Dale, Ill., 1984—; sound design engr. Candlelight Dinner Playhouse, Summit, Ill., 1985; sales engring. cons. Kayak Mfg. Corp., Westmont, Ill., 1985-86; mgr. advt., mktg. dir. Star-Sentinel Pub., Melrose Pk., Ill., 1987—; ptnr., gen. mgr. Press Express, Inc., Chandler, Ariz., 1988—; mgr., lead guitarist The Majestics, 1959-64, The 1st Nat. Bank, 1968-73. Composer original music for N.Mex. State Univ. prodns. Equus, 1977, Children of a Lesser God, 1979 (Tony award N.Mex. State 1980). Served to staff sgt. USAF, 1964-70. Mem. Soc. Broadcast Engrs., Soc. Electronic Musicians, U.S. Inst. Theatre Tech., Satellite Antenna Specialists Am., Jaycees (life Romeoville, Ill. chpt., editor Monitor mag. 1969-71, Spoke of Yr. award 1970, Editor of Yr. award 1971), VFW. Democrat. Roman Catholic. Avocations: music, photography, creative writing, crafts design, camping. Office: PO Box 178 Higley AZ 85236

WYZNER, EUGENIUSZ, diplomat; b. Chelmno, Poland, Oct. 31, 1931; s. Henryk and Janina (Czaplicka) W.; m. Elzbieta Laudanska, June 27, 1961; 1 child, Jaroslaw. Student, U. Warsaw, Poland, 1952; LLM, U. Warsaw, 1954; postgrad., Hague (The Netherlands) Acad. of Internat. Law, 1958. With Ministry Fgn. Affairs, Poland, 1952-54; sec. of the neutral supervisory com. Ministry Fgn. Affairs, Korea, 1954-55; mem. staff Ministry Fgn. Affairs, Warsaw, 1956-61; ambassador to Geneva 1973-78; dir. dept. internat. orgns. Ministry Fgn. Affairs, Warsaw, 1978-81; permanent rep., ambassador to security council UN, N.Y.C., 1981-82; chmn. UN Disarmament Commn., 1982; undersec. gen. conf. services and spl. assignments UN Disarmament Commn., N.Y.C., 1982—. Vice chmn. preparatory com. Internat. Conf. on Human Rights, chmn. com. on periodic reportson human rights, 1965-68; chmn. sub-com. of UN Com. on Peaceful Uses of Outer Space, 1967-82; pres. Rev. Conf. of Parties to Treaty on Prohibition of Nuclear Weapons, 1977; mem. Polish delegation of UN Gen. Assembly, UN Programme Planning and Budgeting Bd, 1984—; chmn. UN Publs. Bd., 1982—. Decorated Cross of Polonia Restituta Polish Council of State, 1969, 77, Golden Cross of Merit, 1964. Mem. Internat. Inst. Outer Space Law (bd. trustees 1974—, Citation 1977), Internat. Peace Acad. (bd. dirs. 1983—), Internat. Congress Inst. (bd. dirs. 1987—),. Office: care/United Nations Office of the Under-Sec-Gen New York NY 10017

XANTHOPOULOS, DIOMEDES, jeweler; b. Athens, Greece, May 2, 1926; s. Constantin and Elly (Stavrianos) X.; m. Angelique Papagianopoulos, Oct. 2, 1955; children: Maria-Elly, Celia. Degree in Econs., Univ. Econ. and Comml. Studies, Athens, 1947. Jeweler in family enterprises Athens, 1953—. Contbr. articles to econ. jours. Served as res. officer Royal Hellenique Navy, 1947-53. Decorated Silver Cross; recipient Medal of Resistance During German Occupation World War II, 1983. Clubs: Golf of Athens, Cercle d'Athenes. Lodges: Masons (32 degree), Rotary (past pres.). Home: 15 Voulis St, 105 63 Athens Greece Office: Xanthopoulos Jeweler, 4 Voukourestiou St, 105 64 Athens Greece

XENAKIS, IANNIS, composer, architect, engineer; b. Athens, Greece, May 29, 1922; s. Clearchos Xenakis and Fotini Pavlou; m. Françoise Gargouil, 1953; 1 daugher. Student, Athens Polytechnic Inst., Ecole Normale de Musique, Paris, Paris Conservatoire; student engring. Collaborated with architect Le Corbusier, 1947-60; innovator mass concept of music, Stochastic Music, Symbolic Music; designer Philips Pavilion, Brussels World Fair, 1958, sonic, sculptural and light composition Polytope for French Pavilion, Expo 1967 Montreal, music and light spectacle Persepolis on ruins and mountain, Persepolis, Iran, Polytope de Cluny, Paris, 1972; musical compositions include: Metastasis, 1954, Pithoprakta, 1956, Achorripsis, 1957, Symos, 1959, Analogiques, 1962, Amorsima-Morsima, 1962, Straté, 1963, Eonta, 1963, Akrat, 1965, Terretektorh, 1966, Nuits, 1968, Nomos Gamma, 1968, Persephassa, 1969, Antikhthon, 1971, Aroura, 1971, Linaia-Agon, 1972, Eridanos, 1973, Cendrées, 1974, Erikhthon, 1974, Gmeeoorh, 1974, Noomena, 1974, Empreintes, 1975, Phlegra, 1975, Psappha, 1975, N'Shima, 1975, Khoaï, 1976, Retours- Windungen, 1976, Epeï, 1976, Dmaathen, 1976, Akanthos, 1977, Kottos, 1977, Jonchaies, 1977, Le Diatope, 1978, Polytope at Mycenae, 1978, Pleiades, 1978, Aïs, 1980, Nekuïa, 1981, Komboï, 1981, For the Whales, 1982, Shaar, 1983, Tetras, 1983, Lichens, 1984, Naama, 1984, Thalein, 1984, Keqrops, 1986, Honos, 1986, Akea, 1986 and others; author: Musiques fornelles, 1963, Formalized Music, 1970, Musique Architecture, 1970, Xenakis- les Polytopes, 1975, Arts/Sciences: Alloys, 1979; contbr. articles top profl. jours. Served with Greek Resistance, World War II, condemned to death, exile in France. Home: 9 rue Chaptal, 75009 Paris France *

XENOULIS, ALEXANDER CONSTANTINE, nuclear chemist, researcher; b. Volos, Thessaly, Greece, Aug. 22, 1940; s. Constantine Pericles and Maria (Segopoulou) X.; m. Catherine Douka, Oct. 28, 1977. BA, Nat. U., Athens, Greece, 1964; PhD, Washington U., St. Louis, 1972. Teaching, research assoc. Ga. Inst. Tech., Atlanta, 1972-74; researcher Oak Ridge (Tenn.) Nat. Lab., 1972-74, Nuclear Research Ctr. Demokritos, Athens, 1974-81; dir. phys. dept. Nuclear Research Ctr. Demokritos, 1981-85, sr. researcher, 1985—. Contbr. articles to profl. publs. Served to 2d lt. Greek Army, 1963-65. Mem. Greek Chem. Soc. (bd. dirs. 1975-77). Greek Orthodox. Home: 19th Km Leoforou Parnithos, 13671 Aharnai, Attiki Greece Office: Nat Research Ctr, Demokritos, GR-153 10 (01) 65 18 770 Aghia Paraskevi Greece

XI, ZE-ZONG, history educator; b. Shanxi, China, June 9, 1927; s. Ren-Yin and Mu-Dan (Li) X.; m. Liu-Yun Shi, Apr. 28, 1956; children—Yun-Ping, Hong. B.S., Zhong-Shan U. (China), 1951. Editor, Sci. Press, Beijing, China, 1951-56; instr. Hist. Natural Sci. Research Inst., Beijing, 1957-78, assoc. prof., 1978-81, prof., 1981—, dir., 1983—. Author: Cosmology in Chinese History, 1975; contbr. articles to profl. jours. Mem. Chinese Astron. Soc., Chinese Soc. History Sci. and Tech. (v.p.), Internat. Astron. Union, Am. Astron. Soc., Internat. Acad. History Sci. (corr.). Home: Li-Shi Alley 43, Beijing Peoples Republic of China Office: Inst History Natural Sci, Gong Yuan Xi Jie, Beijing Peoples Republic of China

XIANG, LONGWAN, mathematics educator, higher education reseacher; b. Shanghai, China, Feb. 4, 1941; s. Zhejun (C.C.) Hsiang and Zhou Fang; m. Jiang Fu, Jan. 20, 1968; children: Xiang Yuchen, Xiang Yuming. Grad., diplomate of math., Fudan U., Shanghai, 1963. Asst. tchr. Xi'an Jiaotong U., Xi'an, People's Republic of China, 1963-78, lectr., 1978-80, assoc. prof., head differential equation group, 1982-84; assoc. prof., head differential equation and control Shanghai Jiaotong U., 1984—, vice-chmn., Applied Mathematics Dept., 1988—; vis. scholar Columbia U., N.Y.C., MIT, Cambridge, Mass. and speaker rythym of Tang poetry poem Harvard U., Boston, Mass., Princeton (N.J.) U., 1980-82. Author: (text) Advanced Mathematics, 1979. Recipient Outstanding Tchrs. award, Xi'an Jiaotong U., 1978, First prize for tchrs. Shanghai Jiaotong U., 1985; research fellow Higher Edn. Inst. Shanghai Jiaotong U., 1985—. Mem. Chinese Math. Soc., Soc. Industry and Applied Math., Shanghai Oversea Returned Scholar Assn. (dir. and dep. sec.-gen. 1987—). Office: Shanghai Jiaotong U Dept Applied Math, 1954 Huashan Rd, Shanghai People's Republic of China

XIAO, SHUTIE, mathematics educator; b. Wuhan, Hubei, China, Dec. 9, 1929; s. Zhengchang and Fenyu (Zhou) Xiao; m. Efang Wang, Aug. 31, 1956; children: Renmeng, Rengiu. Degree, Peking U., Beijing, 1955. Lectr. dept. math. Peking U., 1955-79, assoc. prof. dept. math., 1979-82; prof. dept. applied math. Tsinghua U., Beijing, 1983—; chmn. Com. of Undergrad. Texts on Applied Math., Beijing, 1985—. Editor: International Workshop on Applied Differential Equations, 1985. Recipient Progress of Sci. and Tech. award State Ednl. Commn., 1986. Mem. The Standing Com. of Chinese Math. Soc., Soc. Indsl. and Applied Math. U.S. Home: Tsinghua U, #6-302, Southwest Bldg 12, Beijing Peoples Republic of China Office: Tsinghua U, Dept Applied Math, Beijing Peoples Republic of China

XIE, DAO-YUAN, library director; b. Liuan, Anhui, People's Republic China, Nov. 16, 1924; s. Yun-gao Xie and Man-hua Xu; m. Shi Yushan, Nov. 20, 1953; children: Shan, Chuan, Dong. BA in Journalism, Yenching U., Beijing, 1950. Sec. Communist Party Com. Yenching U., Beijing, 1951-52; dep. sec. Community Party Com. Beijing U., Beijing, 1952-66; mem. univ. council Beijing U., 1952-66, dir. teaching, research section on Lenin-Marxism studies, 1952-66, dir. library, 1978-83; dep. dir. Nat. Library China, Beijing, 1983—. Author: Building of Modern Libraries In China, 1983, 2d edit. 1985. Home: 37/301 Yandong Yuan, Peking U, Beijing People's Republic China Office: Nat Library of China, Bai Shi Quao 39, Beijing People's Republic of China

XIE, GANQUAN, mathematician, computer information scientist, educator; b. Changsha, Hunan, People's Republic of China, July 2, 1943; s. Shuming and Liusumen Xie; m. Jianhua Li, Oct. 1, 1969; children: Feng Linda, Lee. BCS, Hunan U., Changsha City, 1966; PhD, SUNY, 1984. Asst. prof. Hunan Computer Research Inst., 1967-80; vice-chmn. Soc. Computational Math., Hunan, 1979-81; postdoctoral research Courant Inst. Math., N.Y.C., 1984-; prof., dir. Hunan Computer Research Tech. Inst., 1987—; mem. council Polit. Consulate Com. Hunan Province, 1987—, Chinese Computatuioal Math. Soc., 1979-81. Mem. editorial com. Jour. Computational Math., Beijing, 1987; inventor in field. Nat. Sci. Found. grantee, 1986-87. Mem. Soc. Indsl. Applied Math. Home: Hunan Computer Research Tech, Changsha West River, Yuelu Hill 410012, People's Republic of China Office: Hunan Computer Research Tech Inst, 15 S Yuelu Rd, Yuelu Hill, Changsha 410012, People's Republic of China

XIE, QIMEI, United Nations official; b. Beijing, Jan. 10, 1923; m.; 2 children. BA, Cen. U. Nanjing, China, 1947. Mem. council Chinese People's Inst. Fgn. Affairs, 1968-73; counsellor and minister counsellor Chinese Liaison Office and Chinese embassy, Washington, 1973-81; dep. dir. then dir. Dept. Internat. Orgns. and Confs., Ministry Fgn. Affairs, 1981-84; ambassador and dep. permanent rep. UN, N.Y.C., 1984-85, under-sec. gen. dept. tech. cooperation for devel., 1985—. Office: UN Office Under Sec Gen 1 UN Plaza DC1-1220 New York NY 10017

XIN, YUAN-LONG, mathematician, educator; b. Shanghai, Peoples Republic China, Feb. 23, 1943; s. Shen-Chu and Chue-Zhen (Chow) X.; m. Yun-Ping Fang; 1 child, Xin Lei. Grad., Fudan U., Shanghai, 1965. Teaching asst. Fudan U. Inst. Math., 1965-78, lectr., 1978-84, assoc. prof., 1985-86, prof. math., 1987—; vis. prof. SUNY, Stony Brook, 1979-80, Institut des Hautes Etudes Scientifiques in France, 1983, Max-Planck Inst. Math. in Germany, 1984;. Recipient awards Nat. Sci. Congress, 1978, advance prize Chinese Nat. Com. Sci. and Tech., 1984, natural sci. prize Nat. Com. Edn., 1985, Peoples Republic of China, 1978-85. Office: Fudan Univ, Inst Math, Shanghai Peoples Republic of China

XU, GUANGSHAN, mathematician, educator; b. Harbin, Heilongjiang, People's Republic of China, July 30, 1940; s. Runchang Xu and Yiying Tian; m. Xuemin Dou, Nov. 27, 1971; 1 child, Ning. Student, Chinese U. Sci. and Tech., Beijing, 1958- 63. Assoc. prof. Inst. Math. Academia Sinica, Beijing, 1982-86, prof., 1986—, head dept. number theory, 1987—. Mem. Chinese Math. Soc., Am. Math. Soc. Home: 940-505, Zhong Guan Cun, Beijing Peoples Republic of China Office: Inst Math Acad Sinica, Zhong Guan Cun, Beijing Peoples Republic of China

XU, PEICHENG, English educator; b. Long Li County, Guizhou, Peoples Republic of China, Aug. 7, 1943; s. Quanji Xu and Quiaomei Luo; m. Jing Ran, Nov. 20, 1969 (dec. June 1983); children—Xu Ming; m. Ning Zhang, Sept. 28, 1984; children—Zhang Leting, Zhang Letian. Student, Guiyang Tchrs. Coll., 1960-62, Guizhou U., 1962-64. English asst. Guiyang Tchrs. Coll., 1964-77, english instr., 1978—; dep. dir. teaching sect. fgn. lang. dept. Guizhou Normal U., 1980-87; vis. scholar U. Mich., 1985-86; assoc. prof, chmn. dept. fgn. langs. non-majors Guizhou Normal U., 1987—. Translator: Jaws, 1983, The Lottery, 1985. Mem. Fgn. Lang. Assn. Guizhou, Translators Soc. Guizhou, MLA. Avocations: watching football games; fishing; table tennis. Office: Fgn Lang Dept, Guizhou Normal U, Guiyang Peoples Republic of China

XU, XU-DIAN, historian, educator; b. Beijing, Oct. 30, 1917; s. Shiziang and Xixhang (Meng) X.; m. Ruby Wang, May 17, 1944; children: Li, Wei. AB, Yanjing U., Beijing, 1940. Researcher Palace Mus., Beijing, 1940-45; lectr. Yanjing U., 1945-47, Fujian Christian U., Fuchou, Peoples Republic of China, 1947-50; assoc. prof. Shandong Christian U., Jinan, Peoples Republic of China, 1950-51; prof. Shandong U., Jinan, 1951—, chmn. labor unit dept. history, 1960-64; research guide U. Oreg., 1978-79. Author: Modern Chinese History, 1977, History of the Boxer Movement, 1981, Essays on the Histrory of the Boxers, 1983; contbr. articles to profl. jours. Chmn. Sept. 3d Party to Aid Democracy and Sci., 1975-86; mem. People's Polit. Consultative Conf., Jinan, 1983—. Mem. Teaching and Researching Group in Modern Chinese History (bd. dirs 1960-86), Assn. for Study of Boxer Movement (vice-chmn. 1980-86), Research Group in Modern Chinese History (bd. dirs. 1965-68, 78-84), Assn. Asian Studies U.S.A. Home: The First Dormitory, Old Campus, Jinan Shandong Peoples Republic of China Office: Shandong U Dept Hist, Jinan Peoples Republic of China

XU, YE JI, educator; b. Su Zhou, Peoples Rep China, June 12, 1935; parents Qian Jin Xu and Hua Ge; m. Mei Qin Yu, Dec. 31, 1966; 1 child Yu Gong. BA, Fudan U., Shanghai, Peoples Rep. China, 1957. Asst. prof. Fudan U., Shanghai, 1957-77, lectr., 1977-84, prof., 1984—. Contbr. articles to profl. jours. Mem. Math. Soc. of the Rep. of China, Statis. Soc. of the Rep. of China, Am. Math. Soc. (reciprocity mem.). Home: Second Dorm Fudan Univ, Shanghai 5-201, People's Republic of China Office: Fudan Univ, Shanghai People's Republic of China

XUEREB, PAUL, government official; b. Rabat, Malta, July 21, 1923; s. Adeodate Xuereb and Maria Dolores Busuttil; m. Edwidge Muscat; 1 child, Maria. Student, Flores Coll., Valletta, Malta, City Literacy Inst. U. London, 1946-49, Regent Street Poly. U. London, 1946-49. Clk. engring. dept. Brit. Imperial Dockyard, 1946; supr. accounts dept. Peter Robinson, Ltd., London, 1946-50; clk. Dept. Inland Revenue, London, 1950; mng. dir. Fardex Trade Devel. Co., Ltd., Malta, 1950; lit. editor, asst. editor publ. The Voice of Malta, Malta Labour Party Orgn., 1959-64; gen. mgr. Malta Labour Party Pub. House, 1964-71; elected M.P. Republic of Malta, 1962, 66, 71, 76, 81; apptd. parliamentary sec. Office of Prime Minister, 1971; portfolio mgr. Minister of Trade, Industry, Agriculture and Tourism, 1971—; resigned Republic of Malta Ho. of Reps., 1983, nominated speaker ho. reps. by govt., 1986; apptd. by prime minister to acting pres. Republic of Malta, 1987, now pres.; chmn. Mid-Med Bank Ltd., Medigrain Ltd., 1976-82; former chmn. Investment Finance Bank Ltd., Trade Licensing Bd.; nominated chmn. Malta Devel. Corp.; bd. dirs. Air Malta Co. Ltd., Mdina Weave; mem. disciplinary bd. Malta Labour Party. Author numerous short stories, novels, and hist. guide books. Decorated Africa Star, War medal, Victory medal (Malta). Office: Pres of Republic of Malta, The Palace, Valletta Malta *

YADAVALLI, SRIRAMAMURTI VENKATA, physicist, researcher; b. Secunderabad, India, May 12, 1924; came to U.S., 1948, naturalized, 1963; s. Sankara Somayajulu and Durgamba (Boddupalli) Y.; B.S., Andhra U., 1942, M.S., 1945; M.S., U. Calif., Berkeley, 1949, Ph.D., 1953; m. Suzan Sunel, Apr. 26, 1952. Research engr. Inst. Engring. Research, U. Calif., Berkeley, 1952-53; mem. tech. staff, cons. engr. Electric Co., Syracuse, 1953-59; N.Y. and Palo Alto, Calif., sr. math. physicist, staff scientist Stanford Research Inst., Menlo Park, Calif., 1959-77; pres., dir. research Shastra, Inc., Palo Alto, 1977—. Mem. IEEE (sr.), Am. Phys. Soc., AAAS, N.Y. Acad. Scis., Soc. Engring. Sci., AIAA, Sigma Xi. Contbr. articles to profl. jours. Home: 868 Thornwood Dr Palo Alto CA 94303 Office: Shastra Inc PO Box 1231 Palo Alto CA 94302

YADLIN, RIVKA, researcher; b. Haifa, Israel, Apr. 24, 1934; d. Akiva and Shoshana (Weisman) Tolochinsky; m. Yehoshua Yadlin; children: Naama, Shlomit. Tchr. cert., Realy Tchrs. Coll., 1954; BA in Middle Eastern Studies, Hebrew U., 1952, PhD, 1987. Tchr. Arabic Harei-Ephraim Regional Kibbutz Sch., Israel, 1957-58; researcher Shiloah Research Ctr., Tel-Aviv, 1962-70; lectr. Sch. for Overseas Students Hebrew U., 1977-82, research fellow Truman Inst., 1975—; affiliate L. Davis Inst. for Internat. Relations, 1986—; cons. various govt. agencies, Israel, 1975-82, cultural institutions, 1975-82; affiliate Vidal Sassoon Internat. Ctr. for Study of Anti-Semitism, 1985-87; lectr. in field. Asst. editor Middle East Record, 1961; editor: An Egyptian Portrait, 1985, An Arrogant Oppressive Spirit, 1988; contbr. articles to profl. jours. Active Jewish Agy and World Zionist Orgn., N.Y.C., 1959-62, 71-75. Served as sgt. Israeli Mil., 1955-57. Jewish. Office: Truman Inst, Mount Scopus, Jerusalem 91905, Israel

YAEGER, BILLIE PATRICIA, advertising sales executive; b. Boston, Mar. 17, 1949; d. Harold Stern and Marie Frances (Levenson) Y. Student, Logos Bible Coll. Office mgr., NE rep. Ticketron, Inc., Boston, 1968-73; owner, mgr. Performance King, Natick, Mass., 1973-74, House of Portraits, Lakeland, Fla., 1974-75; employment counselor Snelling & Snelling, Lakeland, 1975-77; advt. sales account exec. The Ledger/N.Y. Times, Lakeland, 1977—. Recipient Chmn. of Bd. award N.Y. Times, 1984-85, 10 Yr. Service award The Ledger/N.Y. Times, 1987, Commendation award Fla. Dept. Law Enforcement, 1986; named Salesperson of Yr. The Ledger, 1987. Mem. Nat. Assn. Female Execs. Republican. Avocations: photography, writing, waterskiing.

YAGER, JOHN WARREN, lawyer, banker; b. Toledo, Sept. 16, 1920; s. Joseph A. and Edna Gertrude (Pratt) Y.; m. Dorothy W. Merki, July 25, 1942; children: Julie M., John M. AB, U. Mich., 1942, JD, 1948. Bar: Ohio 1948. Sole practice Toledo, 1948-64; trust officer Toledo Trust Co., 1964-69; v.p., trust officer First Nat. Bank, Toledo, 1969—; sec. First Ohio Bancshares, Inc., 1980-85. Pres. Toledo Met. Park Dist., 1971-85, Neighborhood Health Assn., 1974-75, councilman, Toledo, 1955-57, 60-61, mayor, 1958-59; bd. dirs. Toledo-Lucas County Library, 1968-70, Riverside Hosp., Downtown Toledo Assn.; past pres. Toledo Legal Aid Soc., Toledo Council Chs., Toledo Mcpl. League, Econ. Opportunity Planning Assn., Toledo, Com. on Relations with Toledo, Spain. Served to maj. USMC, 1942-46, 50-52. Decorated Bronze Star; named one of 10 outstanding young men Toledo, 1952, 54, 55. Mem. Ohio Bar Assn., Toledo Bar Assn., Toledo Estate Planning Council, Delta Tau Delta. Club: Belmont Country (Toledo). Home: 29301 Bates Rd Perrysburg OH 43551-3808 Office: First Nat Bank Toledo 606 Madison Ave Toledo OH 43604

YAGI, SAKAE, chemical engineer; b. Tokyo, July 26, 1904; s. Kyutaro and Yasuko Yagi; B.S., U. Tokyo, 1928; D.Eng., Tokyo Inst. Tech., 1943; m. Yoshiko Mizuta, 1932 (dec. 1973); children—Tomoko Yagi Kikuchi, Hajime, Junko Yagi Kawai, Masako Yagi Hirano; m. 2d, Etsuko Hoshino, May 22, 1976. Asso. prof. chem. engring. Tokyo Inst. Tech., 1936-43, prof., 1943-53; prof. U. Tokyo, 1943-65, emeritus, 1965—; exec. v.p. Chiyoda Chem. Engring. & Constrn. Co., 1965-77; chmn. bd. Chiyoda Internat. Corp., Seattle, 1977-79; cons. chem. engr., 1977—; chmn. com. safety guards nuclear reactor installations Japanese Govt., 1957-63. Recipient Gold medal Rice U., Houston, 1962, award Chem. Soc. Japan, 1962. Mem. Soc. Chem. Engrs. Japan (pres. 1961-63, hon. mem. 1973—), Atomic Energy Soc. Japan (pres. 1969-71, hon. mem. 1971—), Am. Inst. Chem. Engrs., Nat. Acad. Engring. (fgn. asso.), Buddhist. Club: Tokyo-South Rotary. Author: Industrial Furnaces, 1956, Chemical Process Engineering, 1971; also articles. Home: 2-5-10 Kakinokizaka, Meguro-ku, Tokyo 152 Japan

YAGI, YASUHIRO, steel company executive; b. Feb. 15, 1920; married. Grad., Tokyo U., 1943. With Kawasaki Steel Corp., 1943—, exec. dir., 1974-77, mng. dir., 1977-79, v.p., 1979-88, pres., 1988—; v.p. Nikon Tekko Associated. Mem. Japan Metals Acad. (council). Home: 29-15 Minami Nagasaki, 4-chome Toshima-ku, Tokyo 171, Japan Office: Kawasaki Steel Corp, 2-3 Uchisaiwaicho 2-chome, Chiyoda-ku, Tokyo Japan *

YAGO, BERNARD CARDINAL, archbishop; b. Pass, Ivory Coast, July 1916. Ordained priest Roman Catholic Ch., 1947. Archbishop of Abidjan (Ivory Coast), 1960; elevated to Sared Coll. of Cardinals, 1983; pres. Ivory Coast Episcopal Conf. Mem. Secretariat Christian Unity. First native mem. of ch. hierarchy from Ivory Coast. Address: Archeveche, 01 BP 1278, 23 Blvd Ceozel, Abidjan Ivory Coast *

YAGODA, DAVID VITAL, real estate investor and consultant; b. N.Y.C., Sept. 12, 1927; s. Meyer and Sarah (Freilich) Y.; student Yeshiva Coll., 1945-47, CCNY, 1947-48; LL.B., Bklyn. Law Sch., 1950; m. Grace S. Udell, Nov. 23, 1967; children—Janet L., Barbara A. Exec., Premier Toy Corp., N.Y.C., 1950-67; pres. Meysar Realty Corp., N.Y.C., 1967—, David Yagoda, Inc., N.Y.C., 1980—; v.p. MYM Realty Corp., N.Y.C., 1970—; partner, chief exec. officer Four Star Holding, N.Y.C., 1978—. Trustee, Gt. Neck (N.Y.) Synagogue, 1969—, pres., 1975-77; trustee Boys Town of Jersualem, 1986—, Yeshiva U., 1987—; vice chmn. bd. trustees Stern Coll. for Women, 1987—; mem. Gt. Neck Democratic Com., 1972-81; pres. Gt. Neck Dem. Club, 1980-84 trustee North Shore Hebrew Acad., 1976—. Mem. Real Estate Bd. N.Y. Club: B'nai B'rith. Home: 150 E 69th St New York NY 10021 Office: 1501 Broadway New York NY 10036

YAHAGI, TSUNEO, consulting company executive, educator; b. Tokyo, Feb. 27, 1942; s. Toshio and Kimiko Y.; B.S., Keio U., Tokyo, 1965; M.B.A. with honor, Stanford U., 1974, Ph.D., 1981; m. Reiko Shinjo, Apr. 7, 1967; children—Tamako, Naohisa, Tomozo. With Mitsubishi Corp., Tokyo, 1965-72; exec. v.p. Fuji Die Co., Tokyo, 1972-84, exec. rep. U.S., 1976-81; exec. ptnr. TechnoFront Inc., Tokyo, 1985—; asso. prof. Grad. Sch. Bus. Keio U., Yokohama, Japan, 1982—. Trustee, AFS Internat./Intercultural, N.Y.C., 1976-80, AFS Japan Assn., 1965—. Recipient award Am. Assembly Collegiate Sch. Bus., 1979. Mem. Strategic Mgmt. Soc. Contbr. articles to profl. jours. Home: 1-1-10 Chidori, Ota-ku, Tokyo 146 Japan Office: 1960 Hiyoshi Honmachi, Kohoku-ku Yokohama Japan

YAHIRO, TOSHIKUNI, diversified company executive; b. Tokyo, Feb. 1, 1915; s. Shunsuke and Kikuyo Yahiro. B of Econs., Tokyo U. Commerce, 1940; m. Akiko Kato, Feb. 4, 1948; 1 child, Kuniko. With Mitsui & Co. Ltd., Tokyo, 1940—, dep. gen. mgr. 2d chem. dept., 1963-67, gen. mgr., plastics and chem. depts., 1967-71, bd. dirs., 1972-74, exec. mng. dir., 1974-76, sr. exec. mng. dir., 1976-77, exec. v.p., 1977-79, pres., 1979-85, chmn. bd. dirs., 1985—; vice chmn. Keidanren, Tokyo, 1986—, chmn. com. fgn. trade, 1984—; vice chmn. Japan Fgn. Trade Council, Inc., Tokyo, 1982—; pres. Japan-Portugal Soc., 1983—. Decorated Madarski Konik, Bulgaria, 1985, Gran-Cruz da Ordem do Infante Don Henrique, Portugal, 1986, Comdr. of the Order of Merit of the Polish People's Republic, Poland, 1987, Grand Gordon of the Order of the Sacred Treasure by the Emperor, Japan, 1987. Avocations: golf, kabuki. Home: #704 2-28 Ropongi, 7 chome, 106 Minato-ku, Tokyo Japan Address: Mitsui & Co Ltd 2 1 Otemachi, 1 chome chiyoda ku, 100 Tokyo Japan

YAKIMOFF, NAUM ASSENOFF, neuroscientist; b. Sofia, Bulgaria, Oct. 21, 1943; s. Assen Naumoff Yakimoff and Liliana Todorova (Kuleva) Yakimova; m. Marussia Yordanova Tasseva, May 10, 1973; children: Assen, Liliana.. Degree in physics, Bulgarian Acad Sci., Sofia, 1968; PhD, Soviet Acad. Sci., Leningrad, 1973. Reserach fellow Inst. Physiology, Bulgarian Acad. Scis., 1971-78, assoc. prof. psychophysiology, 1978—, bd. dirs. acad. trade union com., 1981—. Author: The Brain, 1984, (Popular Sci. award 1985); sec. Acta Physiol. et Pharmacology Bulgarian Jour., 1974—; contbr. over 70 articles to profl. publs. Named to Order of Cyrillus and Methodius, State Council of Bulgaria, 1987. Mem. Bulgarian Physiol. Soc., Bulgarian Phys. Soc., Bulgarian Neurosci. Soc. Home: Han Asparuh #46, 1000 Sofia Bulgaria Office: Bulgarian Acad Sci, Inst Physiol Bldg 23, 1113 Sofia Bulgaria

YAKIR, JOSEPH, engineering and manufacturing company executive, consultant; b. Haifa, Israel, Dec. 1, 1929; s. Jacob Chayim and Ester (Glickstein) Toker; children: Ron, Dan, Nilly. BS, U. Mich., 1954. Design engr. Higgins Inc., New Orleans, 1954-56; head design dept. Israeli Navy, Haifa, 1957-63; head projects Somerfin S.A., Glasgow, Scotland, 1963-66; pres. IMCO Industries Ltd., Tel-Hanan, Israel, 1966—. Contbr. articles to various publs.; inventor floatable drilling rig, 1955. Served to lt. comdr. Israeli Navy, 1948-63. Mem. Soc. Naval Architects, Assn. Israeli Engrs. Jewish. Office: IMCO Industries Ltd, PO Box 189, Tel-Hanan Israel

YAKOVLEV, ALEKSANDR NIKOLAYEVICH, Soviet government official; b. Dec. 2, 1923. Ed., Yaroslavl Pedagogical Inst., 1946. Mem. Communist Party Soviet Union, 1944—, mem. Yaroslavl dist. com., 1946-48; chief lectr. Yaroslavl Party Sch., 1948-50; dep. head dept. sci. and culture Cen. Com. Communist Party Soviet Union, 1953-56, in apparatus of, 1960-62, instr. dept. propoganda and agitation, 1962-64; candidate mem., then mem. Politburo Cen. Com. Communist Party Soviet Union, Moscow, 1987—, head radio and TV broadcasting propoganda dept., 1964-65, 1st dep head, acting head, 1965-73, mem. cen. auditing com., 1971-76, head propoganda dept., 1985—, sec. responsible for propoganda, 1986—; ambassador to Can. 1973-83. Served with Soviet Army, 1941-43. Office: Communist Party Soviet Union, Politburo, Moscow USSR *

YAKU, TAKEO, computer scientist, educator; b. Tokyo, Oct. 21, 1947; s. Masao and Teru (Nagashima) Y. BSc, Jiyu Gakuen Coll., Tokyo, 1970; MSc, Waseda U., Tokyo, 1972, DSc, 1977. Vis. lectr. Tokai U., Hiratsuka, Japan, 1975-76, 85—, asst. prof., 1976-79, assoc. prof., 1979-85; vis. lectr. Waseda U., 1979—; assoc. prof. Tokyo Denki U., Hatoyama, Japan, 1985—. Author: (with others) Micro Computer Handbook, 1985, (with others) Structured Editors, 1987; contbr. articles to profl. jours. Mem. Am. Math. Soc., Assn. Computing Machinery. Club: IRS (Tokyo). Home: 3-10-17 Yagisawa, Hoya-Shi 202, Japan Office: Tokyo Denki U, Ishizaka 925, Hatoyama-Machi, Saitama 350-03, Japan

YALOURIS, NICHOLAS, archaeologist; b. Smyrna, Asia Minor, Aug. 2, 1918; s. Philemon and Anastasia (Zormalia) Y.; grad. dept. philosophy U. Athens, 1940; Ph.D., U. Basel (Switzerland), 1949; m. Athanasia Bogri, May 4, 1963; children—Marc-Pierre, Helen-Anastasia. Researcher, Musé e d'Art et d'Histoire, Geneva, 1949-50; officer Greek Archaeol. Service, 1951-81; dir. antiquities Western Peloponnes, 1952-66, dir. Greek antiquities, 1970-71, dir. Nat. Archaeol. Mus., 1973-80, gen. insp. Service, 1977-81; prof. U. Athens, 1977-78; sr. research fellow Greek and Roman antiquities Met. Mus. Art, N.Y.C., 1969; lectr. Coll. Year in Athens, 1964—; excavations include ancient Elis, Temple of Apollo Epikourios at Bassae, also sites in Achaia, Elis, Messenia; mem. Inst. Advanced Studies, Princeton, N.J., 1968-69. Served with Greek Army, 1938-41, 45. Fulbright scholar, 1955-56; scholar Warburg Inst., London, 1958. Mem. Greek Archaeol. Soc., German Archaeol. Inst., Austrian Archaeol. Inst., Lexicon Iconographicum Mythologiae Classicae (pres.); hon. mem. Internat. Com. of Olympic Games, Archaeol. Inst. Am. Author: Athena als Herrin der Pferde, 1950, The Sculptures of the Parthenon, 1960, The Sculptures of the Temple of Zeus in Olympia, 1969, Olympia, Altis and Museum, 1972, Pegasus, The Art of the Legend from Prehistoric to Modern Times, 1975, The Sculpture of the Temple of Asclepiosiin Epidanuros, 1988; also guidebooks, articles in field.

YALOW, ROSALYN SUSSMAN, medical physicist; b. N.Y.C., July 19, 1921; d. Simon and Clara (Zipper) Sussman; m. A. Aaron Yalow, June 6, 1943; children: Benjamin, Elanna. A.B., Hunter Coll., 1941; M.S., U. Ill., Urbana, 1942, Ph.D., 1945; D.Sc. (hon.), U. Ill., Chgo., 1974, Phila. Coll. Pharmacy and Sci., 1976, N.Y. Med. Coll., 1976, Med. Coll. Wis., Milw., 1977, Yeshiva U., 1977, Southampton (N.Y.) Coll., 1978, Bucknell U., 1978, Princeton U., 1978, Jersey City State Coll., 1979, Med. Coll. Pa., 1979, Manhattan Coll., 1979, U. Vt., 1980, U. Hartford, 1980, Rutgers U., 1980, Rensselaer Poly. Inst., 1980, Colgate U., 1981, U. So. Calif., 1981, Clarkson Coll., 1982, U. Miami, 1983, Washington U., St. Louis, 1983, Adelphi U., 1983, U. Alta. (Can.), 1983, Columbia U., 1984, SUNY, 1984, Tel Aviv U., 1985, Claremont (Calif.) U., 1986, Mills Coll., Oakland, Calif., 1986, Cedar Crest Coll., Allentown, Pa., 1988, Drew U., Madison, N.J., 1988, Lehigh U., 1988; L.H.D. (hon.), Hunter Coll., 1978, Sacred Heart U., Conn., 1978, St. Michael's Coll., Winooski Park, Vt., 1979, Johns Hopkins U., 1979; D. honoris causa, U. Rosario, Argentina, 1980, U. Ghent, Belgium, 1984; D. Humanities and Letters (hon.), Columbia U., 1984; D. Philosophy (hon.), Bar-Ilan U., Israel, 1987. Diplomate: Am. Bd. Scis. Lectr., asst. prof. physics Hunter Coll., 1946-50; physicist, asst. chief radioisotope service VA Hosp., Bronx, N.Y., 1950-70, chief nuclear medicine, 1970-80, acting chief radioisotope service, 1968-70; research prof. Mt. Sinai Sch. Medicine, CUNY, 1968-74, Disting. Service prof., 1974-79, Solomon A. Berson Disting. prof.-at-large, 1986—; Disting. prof.-at-large Albert Einstein Coll. Medicine, Yeshiva U., 1979-85, prof. emeritus, 1986—; chmn. dept. clin. scis. Montefiore Med. Ctr., Bronx, 1980-85; cons. Lenox Hill Hosp., N.Y.C., 1956-62, WHO, Bombay, 1978; sec. U.S. Nat. Com. on Med. Physics, 1963-67; mem. nat. com. Radiation Protection, Subcom. 13, 1957; mem. Pres.'s Study Group on Careers for Women, 1966-72; sr. med. investigator VA, 1972—; dir. Solomon A. Berson Research Lab., VA Hosp., Bronx, N.Y., 1973—. Co-editor: Hormone and Metabolic Research, 1973-79; editorial adv. council: Acta Diabetologica Latina, 1975-77, Ency. Universalis, 1978—; editorial bd.: Mt. Sinai Jour. Medicine, 1976-79, Diabetes, 1976, Endocrinology, 1967-72; contbr. numerous articles to profl. jours. Bd. dirs. N.Y. Diabetes Assn., 1974. Recipient VA William S. Middleton Med. Research award, 1960; Eli Lilly award Am. Diabetes Assn., 1961; Van Slyke award N.Y. met. sect. Am. Assn. Clin. Chemists, 1968; award A.C.P., 1971; Dickson prize U. Pitts., 1971; Howard Taylor Ricketts award U. Chgo., 1971; Gairdner Found. Internat. award, 1971; Commemorative medallion Am. Diabetes Assn., 1972; Bernstein award Med. Soc. State N.Y., 1974; Boehringer-Mannheim Corp. award Am. Assn. Clin. Chemists, 1975; Sci. Achievement award AMA, 1975; Exceptional Service award VA, 1975; A. Cressy Morrison award N.Y. Acad. Scis., 1975; sustaining membership award Assn. Mil. Surgeons, 1975; Distinguished Achievement award Modern Medicine, 1976; Albert Lasker Basic Med. Research award, 1976; La Madonnina Internat. prize Milan, 1977; Golden Plate award Am. Acad. Achievement, 1977; Nobel prize for physiology medicine, 1977; citation of esteem St. John's U., 1979; G. von Hevesy medal, 1978; Rosalyn S. Yalow Research and Devel. award established Am. Diabetes Assn., 1978; Banting medal, 1978; Torch of Learning award Am. Friends Hebrew U., 1978; Virchow gold medal Virchow-Pirquet Med. Soc., 1978; Gratum Genus Humanum gold medal World Fedn. Nuclear Medicine or Biology, 1978; Jacobi medallion Assn. Alumni Mt. Sinai Sch. Medicine, 1978; Jubilee medal Coll. of New Rochelle, 1978; VA Exceptional Service award, 1978; Fed. Woman's award, 1961; Harvey lectr., 1966; Am. Gastroenterol. Assn. Meml. lectr., 1972; Joslin lectr. New Eng. Diabetes Assn., 1972; Franklin I. Harris Meml. lectr., 1973; 1st Hagedorn Meml. lectr. Acta Endocrinologica Congress, 1973; Sarasota Med. award for achievement and excellence, 1979; gold medal Phi Lambda Kappa, 1980; Achievement in Life award Ency. Brit., 1980; Theobald Smith award, 1982; Pres.'s Cabinet award U. Detroit, 1982; John and Samuel Bard award in medicine and sci. Bard Coll., 1982; Disting. Research award Dallas Assn. Retarded Citizens, 1982; numerous others. Fellow N.Y. Acad. Scis. (chmn. biophysics div. 1964-65), Am. Coll. Radiology (asso. in physics), Clin. Soc. N.Y. Diabetes Assn.; mem. Nat. Acad. Scis., Am. Acad. Arts and Scis., Am. Phys. Soc., Radiation Research Soc., Am. Assn. Physicists in Medicine, Biophys. Soc., Soc. Nuclear Medicine, Endocrine Soc. (Koch award 1972, pres. 1978), Am. Physiol. Soc., (hon.) Harvey Soc., (hon.) Med. Assn. Argentina, (hon.) Diabetes Soc. Argentina, (hon.) Am. Coll. Nuclear Physicians, (hon.) The N.Y. Acad. Medicine, (hon.) Am. Gastroent. Assn., (hon.) N.Y. Roentgen Soc., (hon.) Soc. Nuclear Medicine, Phi Beta Kappa, Sigma Xi, Sigma Pi Sigma, Pi Mu Epsilon, Sigma Delta Epsilon. Office: VA Med Ctr 130 W Kingsbridge Rd Bronx NY 10468

YALOWITZ, JEROME MYER, clinical psychologist; b. Chgo., Oct. 24, 1922; s. Joseph and Mary (Shure) Y.; B.S., U. Ill., 1948, M.S., 1949; divorced; children—Rhoda L., Kenneth G., Jean B. Clin. psychologist Manteno (Ill.) State Hosp., 1949-51; chief psychologist E. Moline (Ill.) State Hosp., 1952-54, Peoria (Ill.) State Hosp., 1954-73; coordinator services for elderly Region 1B, Ill. Dept. Mental Health, also dir. Comprehensive Geriatric Treatment Service, Zeller Mental Health Center, Peoria, 1973-86; chief psychologist Painway Program Pekin (Ill.) Meml. Hosp., 1986— . Served with AUS, 1943-46. Recipient Francis J. Gerty award State of Ill., 1969, 74, 79, 82. Mem. Am. Psychol. Assn., Midwestern Psychol. Assn., Ill. Psychol. Assn. (council 1966-74), Central Ill. Soc. Health Service Providers in Psychology (v.p. 1980-82), Peoria Area Assn. Psychologists (pres. 1956-57, 75-76). Jewish. Editor, Ill. Psychologist, 1966-71. Home: 419 Clybourn Ct Peoria IL 61614 Office: Pekin Meml Hosp Court and 14th St Pekin IL 61554

YAMADA, AKIHIRO, English language and literature educator; b. Nagoya, Japan, Jan. 31, 1929; s. Etsujiro and Yuki (Takeuchi) Y.; B.A., Faculty of Letters, Nagoya U., 1952; M.A. (Brit. Council scholar), Shakespeare Inst., U. Birmingham, 1962, Ph.D. (Brit. Council fellow), 1976; m. Yasuko Uchida, Feb. 3, 1957; children—Akiko, Akira. Asst., Mie U., Tsu, Japan, 1952-60, lectr., 1960-62, asst. prof., 1962; asst. prof. Shinshu U., Matsumoto, Japan, 1962-70, prof. English, 1970-88, dir. faculty library, 1971-74, mem. univ. senate, 1978-80; prof. emeritus, 1988; prof. Meisel U., Hino-Shi, Tokyo. Japanese Minstry of Edn. grantee, 1954-55, 64-66, 68-73, 78—; Fulbright fellow, 1966-67; Folger Shakespeare Library fellow, 1967; Brit. Acad./Japan Soc. for Promotion of Sci. fellow, 1982; recipient 2d prize Editol. Soc. Japan, 1981. Mem. Malone Soc. Eng., Internat. Shakespeare Assn., Shakespeare Soc. Japan, English Lit. Soc. Japan, Soc. for Textual Scholarship. Author: Bibliographical Studies in Elizabethan Dramatic Texts, An Introduction, 1969; George Chapman: The Widow's Tears, 1975; Books and the Age of Shakespeare, 1979, Audiences and Readers: The Rise of Elizabethan Theatre and the Rise of the Company of Stationers of London, 1986; Bibliotheca Shakespeariana, Unit 8: Printing and the Book Trade, 1986, W. Shakespeare: King Richard the Third, 1987. Home: 7 10 Hodokubo 2 Chome, Hino Shi, Tokyo 191, Japan Office: Grad Sch of Humanities, Meisei U, Hino-shi, Tokyo 191, Japan

YAMADA, MAKIKO, business educator, executive advisor; b. Negishi, Taito-ku, Tokyo, Mar. 7, 1938; d. Shoji and Midori (Kaiho) K.; m. Ryosuke Suzuki, Apr. 29, 1961 (div. 1966); children—Ayako, Makoto; m. 2d, Susumu Yamada, Sept. 7, 1973. B.A., Rikkyo U., Tokyo, 1960; M.A., NYU, 1970. Research asst. prof. U. Chgo., 1974; dir. Japan Productivity Ctr., Tokyo, 1976—; pres. YMS Planning Co., Ltd., 1986-87, Inst. Pub. and Indsl. Communications, Tokyo, 1987—; prof. Sanno Coll., Kanagawa, Japan, 1976-82; asst. prof. Musashi U., Tokyo, 1976-82; vis. prof. Salomon Bros. Ctr., N.Y.C., 1982; assoc. prof. Internat. U. of Japan, Niigata, 1982-87, research assoc. The U.S.-Japan Relations Ctr., 1987—; cons. Japan Tobacco Incorp., Tokyo, 1974-75, various Japanese and Am. cos., 1981—. Author: Troubled Personnel Management in Japan, 1986; Lobbying in U.S. Congress, 1982; Business Climate in U.S., 1981; American Professional, 1979 (best seller 1980), American Business Elite, 1976 (best seller 1977). Vis. scholar Fed. Bar Assn., Washington, 1978; adv. com. for Indsl. Devel., Kanagawa, Japan, 1981, Com. fro Urban Devel. of Tokyo, 1987—. Attended Internat. Communication Conf., Eleanor Roosevelt Found., U.S., 1969; Walgreen fellow U. Chgo., 1972; Research Fund winner Nat. Inst. Research Advancement, Tokyo, 1981. Mem. Acad. Assn. Organizational Sci., Bus. History Soc. Japan. Office: #501 Bancho Hime, 1 Nibancho Chiyoda-Ku, Tokyo 102, Japan

YAMADA, SHINICHI, computer scientist, educator; b. Nagoya, Japan, Jan. 10, 1937; s. Umekichi and Nami (Kawashima) Y.; m. Atsuyo Yamamoto, Oct. 10, 1964; 1 child, Atsushi. BS, U. Tokyo, 1959, DSc, 1988; SM, Harvard U., 1970. System analyst Nippon Univac Co., Tokyo, 1959-70, tech. advisor, 1970—; lectr. Keio U., Tokyo, 1980—, Waseda U., Tokyo, 1982—; observer Inst. New Generation Computer Tech., 1983—. Author: Sciences of Information Processing, Micro-Prolog Collection, Kowalski Logic for Problem Solving; translator, editor Univac Tech. Rev. Jour. Mem. editorial staff Info. Processing Soc. Japan, 1983—. Mem. IEEE, Am. Math. Soc., Math. Soc. Japan, Assn. Symbolic Logic, Assn. Computing Machinery. Democratic Liberal. Buddhist. Clubs: Harvard of Japan, Gakushi-kai. Avocations: fishing, goh, bonsai. Home: 2-21-9 Nakahara, Mitaka-Shi, Tokyo 181, Japan Office: Nihon Unisys Ltd, 2-17-51 Akasaka, Minato-ku, Tokyo 107, Japan

YAMAGATA, KENJI, physician; b. Tokyo, Dec. 30, 1946; s. Kenkichi, and Hiroko (Goto) Y.; m. Aiko Hirose, Aug. 31, 1975; children—Akira, Yuri, Hiroshi. B.S., U. Tokyo, 1972; M.D., Loma Linda U., 1976. Diplomate Am. Bd. Internal Medicine. Clin. asst. resident Loma Linda U., Calif., 1976-80; chmn. internal medicine Kobe Adventist Hosp., Japan, 1981—, chmn. in-service edn., 1983—; cons. Five-Day Plans Against Smoking, Kobe, 1980—. Author: SDA and Modern Japanese Society, 1972, SDA and Politics, 1973; The Meaning of Suffering, 1986; contbr. articles to profl. jours. Mem. ACP, Japanese Soc. Internal Medicine, N.Y. Acad. Scis., Japanese Med. Assn., Japan Christian Med. Assn. Clubs: Japan Xylophone Assn., Seidon Computer. Home: 4-1 8 chome Arinodai Kita-ku, Kobe 651-13 Japan Office: Kobe Adventist Hosp, 4-1 8 chome Arinodai Kita-ku, Kobe 651-13 Japan

YAMAGUCHI, HIROSHI, publisher; b. Okayama, Japan, July 15, 1928; s. Sakuma and Tsuyuko Y.; m. Kazuko, Mar. 20, 1930; 1 child, Takeshi. Student, Doshisha U., Kyoto, Japan, 1949. Reporter Okayama

(Japan) Newspaper, 1950-57; reporter Zaikai biweekly mag., Tokyo, 1957-70, editor, 1970-74, pres., 1974-80, chmn., 1980-84; pub. Aji no Techo monthly gourmet mag., Tokyo, 1984—; columnist Japan Times, Tokyo, 1981—; chmn. Bunka Tsushin-sha, Tokyo, 1987—. Author: The Downfall of Japan, 1978, Logic of Prosperity and Decline, 1979, Split of the Liberal Democratic Party, 1983. Buddhism. Lodge: Kiwanis. Home: CI Mansion Komaba A-1303, 4-27-32 Ikejiri Setagaya-ku, Tokyo Japan Office: Shuwa Gaien Residence No 608, 2-6-6 Jingumae Shibuya-ku, Tokyo Japan

YAMAJI, HIROSHI, business executive; b. Horie-Tadotsu Nakatado, Kagawa, Japan, July 6, 1944; s. Yamaji and Yamaji (Matsuda) Chiyoko; div. Grad. Zentsuji Daiichi sch. With all Nippon Airways Co., Ltd., 1965—, in charge of passengers, Tokyo, 1971-76, supr. handling, Osaka, 1976-80, supr. cabin service, 1980-83, supr. handling, Saporo, 1983—. Avocations: traveling. Home: 3-3-34 Suimeidai, Hyogo Prefecture, Kawanishi-City 66601, Japan Office: All Nippon Airways Co Ltd, Osaka Internat Airport, Itami 563, Japan

YAMAKAWA, DAVID KIYOSHI, JR., lawyer; b. San Francisco, Jan. 25, 1936; s. David Kiyoshi and Shizu (Negishi) Y. B.S., U. Calif.-Berkeley, 1958, J.D., 1963. Bar: Calif. 1964, U.S. Supreme Ct. 1970. Prin. Law Offices of David K. Yamakawa Jr., San Francisco, 1964—. Dep. dir. Community Action Agy., San Francisco, 1968-69; dir. City Demonstration Agy., San Francisco, 1969-70; mem. adv. council Calif. Senate Subcom. on the Disabled, 1982-83; chmn. community residential treatment system adv. com. Calif. Dept. Mental Health, 1980-85; mem. San Francisco Human Rights Commn., 1975—; pres. Legal Assistance to the Elderly, 1981-83 ; 2d v.p. Nat. Conf. Social Welfare, 1983—; v.p. Region IX, Nat. Mental Health Assn., 1981-83; bd. dirs. Mt. Zion Hosp. and Med. Ctr., 1983—; bd. dirs. United Neighborhood Ctrs. of Am., 1977-83; ARC of the Bay Area, 1988—; chmn. bd. trustees United Way Bay area, 1983-85; bd. dirs. Children's Home Soc. Calif., 1985—; chief fin. officer Assisi Nature Council/USA, 1988—; v.p. Friends of Legal Assistance to the Elderly, 1984—; vice chmn. Friends of the San Francisco Human Rights Commn., 1985—; bd. dirs. Ind. Sector, 1986—, Keep Libraries Alive, 1986—, La Madre de los Pobres, 1982—, Nat. Concilio of Am., 1987—; pres. Council Internat. Programs, San Francisco, 1987—. Recipient John S. Williams Outstanding Planning and Agy. Relations vol. award United Way of the Bay Area, 1980, Mortimer Fleishhacker Jr. Outstanding Vol. award, United Way, 1985; Spl. Recognition award Legal Assistance to the Elderly, 1983, commendation Bd. Suprs. City and County of San Francisco, 1983, cert. Honor, Bd. Suprs. City and County San Fracnsico, 1985; San Francisco Found. award, 1985; Octobe 10, 1985 proclaimed as David Yamakawa Day in San Francisco, 1985. Mem. ABA (Liberty Bell award 1986). Office: 582 Market St Suite 410 San Francisco CA 94104

YAMAKAWA, HIROMI, polymer chemist, educator; b. Akashi, Hyogo-ken, Japan, Dec. 3, 1931; s. Riichi and Tsugiko (Matsumoto) Y.; m. Emiko Kajiura, Mar. 15, 1964. B.S., Kyoto U., Japan, 1954, M.S., 1956, Ph.D., 1959. Japan Soc. for Promotion of Sci. postdoctoral fellow Kyoto U., Japan, 1959-61; research assoc. James Franck Inst., U. Chgo., 1961-63; instr. dept. polymer chemistry Kyoto U., 1963-64, assoc. prof., 1964-86, prof., 1986—; vis. fellow dept. chemistry Dartmouth Coll., Hanover, N.H., 1971-72. Author: Modern Theory of Polymer Solutions, 1971; mem. editorial adv. bd. Macromolecules, 1987—; exec. editor Polymer Jour., 1988—; contbr. articles to profl. jours. Mem. Soc. Polymer Sci. Japan (award in polymer sci. 1969), Phys. Soc. Japan, Chem. Soc. Japan, Am. Phys. Soc., Am. Chem. Soc. Office: Kyoto U, Dept Polymer Chemistry, Kyoto 606 Japan

YAMAKAWA, KIKUO, English philology educator; b. Aomori, Japan, Jan. 2, 1919; s. Kichisaburo and Hisa (Sato) Y.; m. Tatsuko Narita; children—Kyoko, Shuji. Student Tokyo Sch. Fgn. Langs., 1936-40. Tchr. English, Soma Middle Sch., Nakamura, Fukushima, Japan, 1940-42, Third Tokyo Mcpl. Middle Sch., 1942-45, Aomori Prefectural Middle Sch., 1945-47; asst. prof. Tokai Sci. Coll., Shimizu, Shizuoka, Japan, 1947-50; docent Hitotsubashi U., Tokyo, 1950-52, asst. prof., 1952-64, prof., 1964-82; prof. English philology Fukuoka U. (Japan), 1982—. Author: The Development and Characteristics of English Verbals, 1963; contbr. articles on hist. studies of English syntax to profl. jours., 1949-87; co-editor: Seibido's Dictionary of English Linguistics, 1973; Kenkyusha's New English-Japanese Dictionary, 5th edit., 1980; Kenkyusha's New Collegiate English-Japanese Dictionary, 5th edit., 1985. Recipient English Lit. Soc. Japan award, 1948. Mem. Japan Assn. Coll. English Tchrs. (councillor 1970—), Japan Soc. Stylistics (bd. dirs. 1973—), Japan Soc. Mediaeval English Studies (councillor 1985—). Home: 3-12-20 Higashi-cho Kichijoji, Musashino, Tokyo 180, Japan Office: Fukuoka U, 8-19-1 Nanakuma, Jonan-ku, Fukuoka 814 01, Japan

YAMAKI, MASAO, dentist, educator; b. Osaka, Japan, June 14, 1934; s. Shigeji and Shige (Shirakawa) Y.; m. Hiromi Yamashita, Dec. 18, 1963; children: Hiroshi, Mariko. D.D.S., Tokyo Med. and Dental U., 1960; D. Med. Sci., Kyoto U., 1965. Research fellow Eastman Dental Ctr., Rochester, N.Y., 1965-66, research assoc., 1966-67; instr. Hiroshima U. (Japan), 1967-68, assoc. prof., 1968-77, prof., 1977—. Author: Advanced Textbook of Dental Materials, 1983. Mem. Japanese Soc. Dental Materials and Devices. Home: 1362-129 Katsugi, Kabe-cho, Hiroshima 731-02, Japan Office: Hiroshima U School Dentistry, Dept Dental Materials, 1-2-3-Kasumi-cho, Hiroshima 734, Japan

YAMAMOTO, JOE, psychiatrist, educator; b. Los Angeles, Apr. 18, 1924; s. Zenzaburo and Tomie (Yamada) Y.; m. Maria Fujitomi, Sept. 5, 1947; children: Eric Robert, Andrew Jolyon. Student, Los Angeles City Coll., 1941-42, Hamline U., 1943-45; B.S., U. Minn., 1946, M.B., 1948, M.D., 1949. Asst. prof. dept. psychiatry, neurology, behavioral sci. U. Okla. Med. Center, 1955-58, asst. prof., 1958-60; assoc. prof. dept. psychiatry U. So. Calif. Sch. Medicine, Los Angeles, 1961-69; prof. U. So. Calif. Sch. Medicine, 1969-77, co-dir. grad. edn. psychiatry, 1963-70; prof. UCLA, 1977—; dir. Psychiat. Outpatient Clinic, Los Angeles County-U. So. Calif. Med. Center, 1958-77; dir. adult ambulatory care services UCLA Neuropsychiat. Inst., 1977-88, chief Lab. for Cross Cultural Studies. Contbr. articles in field to profl. jours. Served to capt., M.C. U.S. Army, 1953-55. Fellow Am. Psychiat. Assn., Pacific Rim Coll. Psychiatrists, Am. Acad. Psychoanalysis (trustee, mem. exec. com., pres. 1978-79), Am. Coll. Psychiatrists, Am. Assn. for Social Psychiatry (trustee 1981-84, v.p. 1984-86); mem. So. Calif. Psychoanalytic Inst. and Soc. (pres. 1972-73), Soc. for Study of Culture and Psychiatry, Group for Advancement Psychiatry, Kappa Phi, Alpha Omega Alpha. Office: UCLA Neuropsychiat Inst 760 Westwood Plaza Los Angeles CA 90024-1759

YAMAMOTO, KEISHIRO, auditor; b. Tokyo, June 6, 1920; s. Masuzo and Hana Yamamoto; m. Yoko Yamamoto; children: Teruo, Haruo, Kazuo. BA in Econs., Keio U., Tokyo, 1943. Pres. Nisshion Spinning Co., Ltd., Tokyo, 1973-79, chmn., 1979-80, statutory auditor, 1980-85; statutory auditor Toho Rayon Co., Ltd., Tokyo, 1981-87; standing dir. Japan Fedn. Employers' Assn., Tokyo, 1974-79, Fedn. Econ. Orgn., Tokyo, 1974-79; bd. dirs. Japan Com. for Econ. Devel., Tokyo, 1974-85. Auditor Mori Meml. Found. Served with Japanese Army, 1944-45. Mem. Japan Statutory Auditor Assn. (advisor). Mem. Liberal Dem. Pary. Buddhist. Clubs: Kanto, Nihon Kogyo. Home: 2-2-17 Kamiaso, Aso-ku, Kawasaki 215, Japan

YAMAMOTO, KENICHI, automotive executive; b. Hiroshima, Japan, Sept. 16, 1922; married; 2 children. BS in Mech. Engring., Tokyo U., 1944. Registered profl. engr., Tokyo. Mgr. designing dept. tech. div. Mazda Motor Corp., Aki-gun, Japan, 1956-63, mgr. rotary engine research and devel. div., 1963-78, mng. dir., gen. mgr. research and devel., 1978-80, mng. dir., gen. mgr. advanced tech., 1980-82, sr. mng. dir., 1982-84, pres., 1984-87, chmn., 1987—. Recipient Man of Yr. award Automotive Industries mag. 1986. Mem. Soc. Mech. Engrs. (award 1970). Office: Mazda Motor Corp, Shinchi, 3-1, Fuchu-cho, Aki-gun 730-91, Japan

YAMAMOTO, MASAYUKI, rural architect; b. Toyonaka, Osaka, Japan, Mar. 23, 1944; s. Shinichi and Hatue Y.; m. Utako Takizawa, Apr. 13, 1981; 1 child, Machiko. B in Engring., Tokyo U., 1967. Archtl. diplomate. Architect Madoka Architects Inc., Tokyo, 1967-73; chief researcher Community Devel. Ctr., Tokyo, 1974—; cons. Norin Chukin Bank, Tokyo, 1973—; chmn. Agrl. Promotion Com., Chofu, Tokyo, 1985—. Columnist Front of Urbanization, 1980-81. Mem. Tokyo Archtl. Soc., Comml. Assn. Kagurazaka Tokyo (officer 1985—). Home: 403-43 Akagishitamachi, Shinjuku-ku, Tokyo 162, Japan Office: Community Devel Ctr, 1-1-12 Uchikanda, Chiyoda-ku, Tokyo 101, Japan

YAMAMOTO, MIKIO, public health and human ecology researcher and educator; b. Shimizu, Japan, May 13, 1913; s. Masaji and Uta (Yamamoto) Y.; m. Masa Azuma, Mar. 13, 1949; children—Masatoshi Yamamoto, Izumi Nishikawa. M.D., Tokyo Imperial U., 1939; D.Med. Sci., Tokyo U., 1951. Prof. Juntendo U., Tokyo, 1956-73; prof. Teikyo U., Tokyo, 1973-84, vis. prof., 1984—; mem. govt. council on population problems, Tokyo, 1965-81; pres. Inst. Comprehensive Health Care, Tokyo, 1984—; v.p. Internat. Union for Health Edn., Paris, 1969-73, 76-79; chmn. Health Edn. com. Japan Med. Assn., 1975-83; bd. dirs. Internat. Fed. Preventive and Social Medicine, Rome, 1984—; founder Japanese Soc. Comprehensive Health Care, Tokyo, 1970—. Author, editor 29 books, 1953-85; also articles. Mem. populations council Japanese Govt., Tokyo, 1965-81; mem. council Kanagawa Prefectural Govt., Yokohama, Japan, 1969—; mem. editorial bd. Shizuoko Shimbun, Shizuoka, Japan, 1984—; mem. nat. com. Diagnosis of Pneumoconiosis, Tokyo, 1952-83. Served to lt. comdr. Japanese Navy, 1939-46. Recipient Silver medal French Med. Acad., 1973; Blue Ribbon medal Japanese Govt., 1977; Spl. award Ministry of Labour, Tokyo, 1973; Service award Kanagawa Prefectural govt., 1983. Fellow Japanese Soc. Health and Human Ecology; mem. Internat. Union Health Edn., (v.p. 1969-73, 76-79), Am. Pub. Health Assn., Japanese Soc. for Hygiene (hon.). Internat. Epidemiological Soc., N.Y. Acad. of Sci. Avocation: painting. Home: Inamuragasaki 1-14-2, Kamakura, Kanagawa Prefecture 248 Japan Office: Inst of Comprehensive Health Care, Kudan Minami 4-8-21, Tokyo 102 Japan

YAMAMOTO, SHIGERU, educator; b. Kyoto, Japan, July 12, 1929; s. Seiichi and Fusae (Maki) Y.; B.A., U. Kyoto, 1955, M.A., 1958; m. Toshi Kataoka, Mar. 27, 1959. Asst., lit. faculty U. Kyoto, Japan, 1961-62; instr. Kyoto Prefectural U., 1962-64, asst. prof., 1964-81, prof. lit., 1981—, dean, 1986—. Ednl. Ministry of Japan and Kyoto Prefecture grantee, 1974-75. Mem. Soc. for Near Eastern Studies in Japan, Japanese Soc. Western History, Soc. Hist. Research (Kyoto). Contbr. articles to profl. jours.; mem. editorial staff Acta Sumerologica. Home: 15-11 Higashidacho Kamitakano, Sakyoku, Kyoto 606 Japan Office: 1 Hangicho Shimogamo, Sakyoku Kyoto 606 Japan

YAMAMOTO, SHOZO, biochemist; b. Osaka, Japan, May 12, 1933; s. Matusjiro and Teruko (Nakamura) Y.; m. Ikuko Tsubaki, May 12, 1963; children—Toshitaka, Yoritaka, Yukiko. M.D., Osaka U., 1960; Ph.D., Kyoto U., 1967. Intern, Osaka Univ. Hosp., 1960-61; research assoc. Kyoto U., 1964-72, lectr., 1972-75, assoc. prof., 1975-78; research fellow Harvard U., 1967-69; prof. Sch. Medicine, Tokushima U., 1979—. Mem. editorial bd. Prostaglandins, 1977—; co-editor Oxygenases and Oxygen Metabolism, 1982; co-editor: Advances in Prostaglandin, Thromboxane, and Leukotriene Research, vol. 15. Mem. Japanese Biochem. Soc., Vitamin Soc. Japan, Japan Soc. Clin. Chemistry. Home: 24-59 Nakatsuura, Hachiman-cho, Tokushima 770, Japan Office: Tokushima Univ Sch Medicine, Dept Biochemistry, Kuramoto-cho, Tokushima 770 Japan

YAMAMOTO, SOBEH, metal plating company executive; b. Tokyo, Oct. 12, 1926; s. Soichiro and Tsuneko (Tsurusawa) Y.; m. Yoshiko Shimamoto, May 10, 1953; children: Kaoru, Susuke. BS in Chemistry, Tokyo Met. U., 1957. Cert. cons. engr. Staff engr. indsl. research inst. Tokyo Met. U., 1950-62; tech. dir. Nippon Electroplating Works, Ltd., Kawaguchi, Japan, 1962-71; pres. Japan Plating Lab., Inc., Yamato, 1971-88, chmn., 1988—; examiner Cons. Engr. Exam. Com., Tokyo, 1979-83; mem. Japan Indsl. Standards Com., Tokyo, 1967—. Author, editor: Practice in Electroplating, 1970; co-author: (handbook) Surface Finishing of Metals, 1969; contbr. articles to profl. jours. Fellow: The Metal Finishing Soc. Japan (bd. dirs. 1984—), Am. Electroplaters' and Surface Finishers' Soc., Inc.; mem. Japan Cons. Engrs. Assn. Buddhist. Club: Hadano Country, Tomei-Koyama Country. Lodge: Rotary. Home: 3-2-22 Kinuta, Setagaya 157, Japan Office: Japan Plating Lab Inc, 4-2-23 Fukami-Nishi, Yamato, Kanagawa 242, Japan

YAMAMOTO, TADASHI, international exchange center president; b. Tokyo, Japan, Mar. 11, 1936; s. Haruji and Toyoko (Hasegawa) Y.; m. Chiyoko Aikawa, Dec. 17, 1966; children—Taro, Jiro, Saburo, Shiro. B.A., St. Norbert Coll. (Wis.), 1960; M.B.A., Marquette U., Milw., 1962. Asst. to pres. Shin-Etsu Chem., Tokyo, 1962-69; exec. sec. Japan Council for Internat. Understanding, Tokyo, 1964-69; pres. Japan Ctr. for Internat. Exchange, 1969—; pres., chmn. bd. JCIE, Inc./U.S.A., N.Y.C., 1976—; Japanese dir. Trilateral Commn., Tokyo, 1973—; exec. dir. U.S.-Japan Adv. Commn., 1983-84; mem. exec. adv. com. Asian Community Trust, 1979—; cons. Children's TV Workshop, 1973—. Translator: Crisis in the Classroom, 1973; School for the 70's and Beyond: A Call to Action, 1976; co-editor: The Shimoda Report, 1982; Korea and Japan, 1978. Recipient Japan Found. award for promoting internat. exchange, 1974. Roman Catholic. Home: 5-28-13 Shimomeguro, Meguro-ku, Tokyo 153 Japan Office: Japan Ctr for Internat Exchange, 4-9-17 Minami-Azabu, Minato-ku, Tokyo 106 Japan

YAMAMOTO, TAKUMA, manufacturing executive; b. Kumamoto, Japan, Sept. 11, 1925. BEE, U. Tokyo, 1949; LHD (hon.), U. Honolulu, 1986. With Fujitsu Ltd., Tokyo, 1949—, bd. dirs., 1975—, mng. dir., 1976—, exec. dir., 1979—, pres., rep. dir., 1981—. Mem. Communication Industries Assn. Japan (vice chmn. 1986—), Japan Electronic Industry Devel. Assn. (chmn. 1987—). Office: Fujitsu Ltd, 6-1 Marunouchi 1-Chome, Chiyoda-ku, Tokyo 100, Japan

YAMAMOTO, TOSHIHIDE, physician, endocrinologist; b. Osaka, Japan, Aug. 4, 1937; s. Eiji and Kanako (Kanoh) Y.; m. Setsuko Suzuki, Mar. 20, 1965; children—Hiroshi, Kenji. M.D., Osaka U., 1964, Doctor Med. Sci., 1974. Intern, resident in medicine R.I. Hosp., Providence, 1967-69; research fellow Boston City Hosp., Harvard Med. Sch., 1969-71; jr. physician Osaka U. Hosp., 1971-72; dir. endocrine lab. Ctr. Adult Diseases, Osaka, 1972-77; dir. profl. service Kishiwada Tokushukai Hosp., Kishiwada, 1977-82; exec. dir. Tokushukai Med. Corp., Osaka, 1982—. contbr. articles to profl. jours. Mem. Japanese Soc. Internal Medicine, Japanese Soc. Endocrinology. Office: Tokushukai Med Corp, Yodokoh Bldg, 6th Floor, Minami Honmachi 4-36 Higashi-ku, Osaka 541 Japan

YAMAMOTO, YUICHI, manufacturing company executive; b. DaLian, China, Sept. 15, 1940; s. Tatsumo and Yoshiko Y.; m. Kyoko Yamamoto, Apr. 27, 1970; children—Takehiro, Tomohiro. B.A., Keio U., 1963; M.A., Sophia U., 1972. Sales mgr. George I. Purdy & Co., Ltd., Tokyo, 1963-65; adminstrv. asst. Clark Bros. Co. Ltd., Tokyo, 1965-66; with Dresser Japan Ltd., Tokyo, 1967—, rep. dir., 1973-76, rep. dir., pres., 1977—; bd. dirs. SDC Corp., Tokyo, Niigata Worthington Co. Ltd., Tokyo, Niigata Masoneilan Co. Ltd., Tokyo, Niigate Ashcraft Keiki Co. Ltd. Avocations: Tennis; shakuhachi (bamboo flute). Home: 6-13 Shimorenjaku 3-chome, Mitaka City 181, Japan Office: Dresser Japan Ltd, 818 Shin Tokyo Bldg, 3-1 Marunouchi 3 chome, Chiyodaku 100, Tokyo Japan

YAMAMURA, KOHTAROH, industrial health scientist, educator; b. Hakodate, Hokkaido, Japan, Apr. 29, 1933; s. Yasaburo and Uki Yamamura; m. Kyohko Yamamura; children: Takashi, Asako. B of Medicine, Hokkaido U., 1958, MD, 1959, PhD, 1969. Intern, then residen; psychiatrist Watanabe Hosp., Hokodate, 1956-64; prof. Div. of Medicine Dept. of Health Hokkaido U., 1964-69; chief scientist Research Inst. of Labour Sci. of Japan Nat. Ry., Tokyo, 1969-75, Tokyo Met. Inst. of Neurosci., Fuchu, 1975-78; assoc. prof. Dept. Pub. Health Sappro Med. Coll., Hokkaido, 1978-83; prof. Dept. of Hygiene Asahikawa Med. Coll., Hokkaido, 1983—; mem. Japan Environ. Agy. (traffic noise com.), 1978-80. Editor Japanese Jour. Indsl. Health, 1987—; contbr. articles to profl. jours. Fellow Japan Assn. Indsl. Health; mem. Acoustical Soc. Am. Home: 3-2-2 Midoriqaoka, Asahikawa Japan Office: Asahikawa Med Coll, 4-5-3-11 Nishikagura, Asahikawa 078, Japan

YAMANA, HIDEAKI, surgeon; b. Fukuoka, Japan, Jan. 5, 1949; s. Sansetsu and Mieko (Sadanaga) Y.; M.D., Kurume U., 1973, D.Med. Sci., 1980; m. Kazuko Takao, Mar. 16, 1976; 1 child, Hidekazu. Asst., first dept. of surgery, Kurume (Japan) U. Sch. Medicine, 1973—, asst. prof., 1986— . Recipient honor research prize, First Dept. Surgery, Kurume U. Sch. Medicine, 1980. Mem. Japan Surg. Soc., Japanese Assn. Thoracic Surgery, Japanese Soc. Gastroenterol. Surgery, Japanese Soc. Gastroenterology, N.Y. Acad. Scis., Collegium Internationale Chirurugiae Digestivae, Internat. Soc. Diseases Esophagus. Liberal. Buddhist. Clubs: Kyushu Doctors' Rugby Football, Kokura High Sch. Rugby Old Boy. Contbr. articles to Japanese med. jour. Home: 3-190-7 Sasayamamaci, Kurume 830 Japan Office: 67 Asahimachi, Kurume 830, Japan

YAMASHITA, NAOKI, chemical engineer; b. Tokyo, Mar. 5, 1943; s. Heishirou and Misao (Suzuki) Y.; m. Megumi Yoshimoto, Dec. 6, 1970; children—Ayumi, Eri. B.S., Tokyo U., 1966. Chem. engr. Ube Industries Ltd., Japan, 1966-77, chem. rep., N.Y.C., 1977-79, asst. mgr. Engring. div., Tokyo, 1979-82, mgr., 1982—. Mem. Am. Inst. Chem. Engrs., Am. Chem. Soc. Avocations: golf; go; badminton; Shogi (Japanese chess). Office: Ube Industries Ltd Engring Div, 1-12-32 Akasaka, Minato-ku, Tokyo 107, Japan

YAMASHITA, TSUKASA, educator, architect; b. Kumamoto, Kyushu, Japan, Apr. 20, 1934; s. Arataro and Chiwa Y.; m. Asako Murakami, Dec. 15, 1962; children: Kaura, Taro, Sakura. BS, Waseda U., Tokyo, 1957; MArch, Yale U., 1964. Registered architect, Japan. Designer, draftsman Paul Rudolph Architect, N.Y.C., 1964; asst. prof. U. Kans., Lawrence, 1965; asst. prof. Kogakuin U., Tokyo, 1966, prof., 1979, dean, 1980, 1987—, dir. library, 1984, 1987—; pres. Tsukasa Yamashita Archtl. Firm, Tokyo, 1967—. Prin. works include Hakone Internat. Conf. Ctr., 1972 (one of best 4 1972), Archtl. Inst. Japan New Head Office, 1980 (award of Excellance 1980), Ctr. Plaza, Koyo Town, 1982 (Design award J.C.P.A. 1982), ASAO Cultural Ctr., 1985 (Best Architecture 1985). Mem. com. Amenity Town Planning, Kawasaki, Kanagawa, 1986. Recipient Grand Prix award Biennale of Internat. Architecture and City, 1983, Rose Morgan Professorship U. Kans., 1974; Fulbright scholar, 1964. Mem. Archtl. Inst. Japan, Japan Inst. of Architecture. Home: 503 Yoyogi New Hight, 2 41 Yoyogi Shibuya-Ku, Tokyo 151, Japan Office: Kogakuin U Dept Architecture, 1 24 Nishishinjuku, Tokyo 160, Japan

YAMAZAKI, SHOZO, accountant; b. Sendai, Miyagi-Prefecture, Japan, Sept. 12, 1948; s. Toshio and Toshiko (Sugita) Y.; m. Hiroko Nanaumi, Feb. 23, 1975; 1 child, Yumi. B in Econs., Tohoku U., Sendai, Japan, 1972; postgrad., U. Pa., 1983. CPA, Japan. Auditor Tohmatsu Awoki & Co., Tokyo, 1970—, audit mgr., 1980-83; mgr. Touche Ross & Co., Sao Paulo, Brazil, 1975-80; dir. Touche Ross & Cia/Tohmatsu Awoki & Cia, Sao Paulo, 1984-85; ptnr. Tohmatsu Awoki & Sanwa, Tokyo, 1983—. Mem. Japanese Inst. CPA. Home: 31-3-1503, Honcho, Wako, Saitama Prefecture 351-01, Japan Office: Tohmatsu Awaoki & Sanwa, 13-23 Shibaura 4-chome Minato-K, Tokyo 108, Japan

YAMBRUSIC, EDWARD SLAVKO, lawyer, consultant; b. Conway, Pa., Mar. 9, 1933; s. Michael Misko and Slavica Sylvia (Yambrusic) Y. B.A., Duquesne U., 1957; postgrad. Georgetown U. Law Ctr., 1959-61; J.D., U. Balt., 1966; cert. The Hague (Netherlands) Acad. Internat. Law, 1967, 69, diploma Ctr. Study and Research of Internat. Law and Internat. Relations, 1970; Ph.D. in Pub. Internat. Law, Cath. U. Am., 1984. Bar: Md. 1969, U.S. Ct. Customs and Patent Appeals 1972, U.S. Supreme Ct. 1972. Copyright examiner U.S. Copyright Office, Library of Congress, Washington, 1960-69, atty. adviser Office Register of Copyrights, 1969—; pvt. practice internat. and immigration law, 1969—; legal counsel Nat. Ethnic Studies Assembly, 1976—, Soc. Fed. Linguists, 1980. Pres. Nat. Confedn. Am. Ethnic Groups, Washington; nat. chmn. Croatian-Am. Bicentennial Com.; nat. chmn. Nat. Pilgrimage of Croatian-Ams. to Nat. Shrine of Immaculate Conception, Washington; v.p. Croatian Acad. Am. Served to capt. U.S. Army, 1957-59. Duquesne U. Tamburitzans scholar, 1953-57; Hague Acad. Internat. Law fellow, 1970. Mem. ABA, Md. Bar Assn., Internat. Law Assn., Internat. Fiscal Assn., Am. Soc. Internat. Law, Croatian Cath. Union Am., Croatian Frat. Union Am. Republican. Roman Catholic. Author: Treaty Interpretation: Theory and Reality, 1987; contbr. articles to ofcl. newsletter Nat. Confedn. Am. Ethnic Groups, also legal jours. Home and Office: 4720 Massachusetts Ave NW Washington DC 20016

YAMIN, MICHAEL GEOFFREY, lawyer; b. N.Y.C., Nov. 10, 1931; s. Michael and Ethel Y.; m. Martina Schaap, Apr. 16, 1961; children: Michael Jeremy, Katrina. AB magna cum laude, Harvard U., 1953, LLB, 1958. Bar: N.Y. 1959, U.S. Dist. Ct. (so. dist.) N.Y., U.S. Dist. Ct. (ea. dist.) N.Y., U.S. Ct. Appeals (2d cir.) 1966, U.S. Supreme Ct. 1967. Assoc. Weil, Gotshal & Manges, N.Y.C., 1958-65; sr. ptnr. Colton, Hartnick, Yamin & Sheresky, N.Y.C., 1966—. Bd. trustees Gov.'s Com. Scholastic Achievement, 1976—; chmn. Manhattan Community Bd. 6, 1986-88, mem., 1974—; mem. Mahattan Borough Bd., 1986-88; bd. trustees Rockland County Soc. Prevention of Cruelty to Children, 1979—. Served as lt. USNR, 1953-55, Korea. Mem. ABA, N.Y. State Bar Assn., Assn. Bar City N.Y., Fed. Bar Counsel, Am. Fgn. Law Assn., Internat. Law Assn., Societe de Legislation Comparee, Internat. Bar Assn. Clubs: Harvard Faculty (Cambridge, Mass.); Harmonie, Harvard (N.Y.C.) (trustee N.Y. Found. 1981—, sub-chmn. schs. and scholarships com. 1972—, bd. mgrs. 1985-88). Home: 206 E 30th St New York NY 10016 Office: 79 Madison Ave New York NY 10016

YANAGIDA, YUKIO, lawyer; b. Toyama, Japan, Jan. 22, 1933; s. Kensho and Yoshie Y.; LLB, Waseda U., 1956, LLM, 1958; LLM, Harvard U., 1966; m. Keiko Hirai, Feb. 6, 1968; children: Tamae, Kazuhiro. Sr. ptnr. firm Yanagida & Nomura, Tokyo, 1972—. Mem. Tokyo Bar Assn., Japan Fedn. Bar Assn. Buddhist. Office: 1310 North Tower, Yurakucho Denki Bldg 7-1, Yukakucho 1-chome Chiyoda-ku, Tokyo 100, Japan

YANAI, MASASHI, parking garage company executive; b. Amagasaki, Hyogo, Japan, Mar. 12, 1919; s. Rinzoh and Toku (Ikebe) Y.; m. Setsuko Tsuge, Oct. 16, 1947; children: Yohko, Junichi. BCS, Kansei Gakuin Comml. Coll., Nishinomiya, Japan, 1940. Clk. several sects. Yanmar Diesel Engine Co., Ltd., Osaka, Japan, 1940-54, chief several sects. and divs., 1954-70, dir., 1970-76; pres. Kyowa Agrl. Machinery Co., Ltd., Okayama, Japan, 1976; exec. v.p. Seirei Indsl. Co., Ltd., Okayama, 1976-80; pres. Yaesu Parking Co., Ltd., Tokyo, 1980—. Mem. Yamaoka Scholarship Soc. (councilor 1980—), All Nippon Underground Shopping Ctr. Fedn. Buddhist. Home: 5-27-22-404 Kyodo, Setagaya-Ku, Tokyo 156, Japan Office: Yaesu Parking Co Ltd, 2-1-1 Yaesu, Chuo-Ku, Tokyo 104, Japan

YANAI, SHINICHI, ambassador; b. Niigata, Japan, Mar. 1, 1925; s. Junji and Toshiko (Tetsuka) Y.; m. Sumiko Minami, May 2, 1960. Grad. law sch., Tokyo U., 1950. Minister Deligation of Japan to Orgns. for Econ. Cooperation and Devel., Paris, France, 1976-79; gen. dir. Econ. Corp. Bur., Tokyo, 1979-81; ambassador Republic of Pakistan, Islamabad, Pakistan, 1982-84; dep. minister Foreign Affairs, Tokyo, 1985-87. Office: Embassy of Japan, 18-11 Chunghak-dong, Chongo-Ku, Seoul Republic of Korea

YANCEY, WALLACE GLENN, insurance company executive; b. Langdale, Ala., Sept. 8, 1930; s. Wallace Odell and Nellie Leigh (Roughton) Y.; m. Betty Jo Carden, June 1, 1956; children—Angela, Susan, Reed. B.S. in Bus. Adminstrn., Auburn U., 1956. Sales rep. Arkwright Mut. Ins. Co. (formerly Arkwright-Boston Ins. Co.), Birmingham, Ala., 1957-59; sales rep. Arkwright Mut. Ins. Co. (formerly Arkwright-Boston Ins. Co.), Atlanta, 1960-61; br. mgr. Arkwright Mut. Ins. Co. (formerly Arkwright-Boston Ins. Co.), N.Y.C., 1961-64; regional sales mgr. Arkwright Mut. Ins. Co. (formerly Arkwright-Boston Ins. Co.), Atlanta, 1964-68; v.p. mktg. Arkwright Mut. Ins. Co. (formerly Arkwright-Boston Ins. Co.), Waltham, Mass., 1975-79, sr. v.p., 1979—; v.p., gen. mgr. Hobbs Group, Inc. (formerly Hobbs Brook Agy., Inc.), Waltham, 1969-75; pres., chief exec. officer Hobbs Group, Inc. (formerly Hobbs Brook Agy., Inc.), Waltham, 1975—, HPR Mut. Ltd., Bermuda, Arkwright Mgmt. Corp, Hamilton, Bermuda; exec. v.p. Arkwright Mut. Ins. Co., Waltham, 1988—. Comdr. Acton Minutemen, Mass., 1978-79; bd. dirs. Acton Youth Hockey Assn., 1973-75. Served with USN, 1948-52, Korea. Republican. Congregationalist. Home: 110 Whitman St Stow MA 01775 Office: Arkwright Mut Ins Co 225 Wyman St Waltham MA 02154

YANG, CHEN NING, physicist, educator; b. Hofei, Anhwei, People's Republic of China, Sept. 22, 1922; naturalized, 1964; s. Ke Chuan and Meng Hwa Lo; m. Chih Li Tu, Aug. 26, 1950; children: Franklin, Gilbert, Eulee. BS, Nat. S.W. Assoc. U., China, 1942; PhD, U. Chgo., 1948; DSc (hon.), Princeton U., 1958, Bklyn. Poly. Inst., 1965, U. Wroclaw, Poland, 1974, Gustavus Adolphus Coll., 1975, U. Md., 1979, U. Durham, Eng., 1979, Fudan U., 1984, Eldg. Technische Hochschule, Switzerland, 1987. Instr., U. Chgo., 1948-49; mem. Inst. Advanced Study, Princeton U., 1949-55, prof., 1955-66; Albert Einstein prof. SUNY, Stony Brook, 1966—; dir. SUNY (Inst. Theoretical Physics), 1966—. Trustee Rockefeller U., 1970-76, Salk Inst., 1978—, Ben Gurion U., 1980—. Recipient Albert Einstein Commemorative award in sci., 1957, Nobel prize for physics, 1957, Rumford prize, 1980, Nat. medal of sci., 1986, Liberty award, 1986. Mem. Am. Phys. Soc., Nat. Acad. Scis., Brazilian Acad. Scis., Venezuelan Acad. Scis., Royal Spanish Acad. Scis., Am. Philos. Soc., AAAS (bd. dirs. 1975-79), Sigma Xi. Office: SUNY Physics Dept Stony Brook NY 11794

YANG, CHING MAI, educator; b. Kiang-su Province, China, Jan. 15, 1921; s. Shao Yun and Yao (Zun) Y.; postgrad. Harvard U., 1958-60, (hon. fellow English dept.) U. Wis., 1968-69; m. Hsueh Hung Chang, Aug. 2, 1938; children—Shih Chi, Shih Ching, Shih Ying, Shih Ping. Instr. in English, Taipei Inst. Tech., 1947-54; asso. prof. Taiwan Normal U., 1954-61, prof., 1961-64, chmn. dept. English, 1964-68, dir. Grad. Inst. English, 1969-76; chmn. fgn. lang. dept., dean Coll. Arts and Letters, Nat. Central U. Taiwan, 1976-82; prof. Grad. Inst. English, Taiwan Normal U., 1982—. Recipient medal and citation for 40 yrs. disting. service in edn. Govt. of Republic of China, 1987. Contbr. articles to profl. jours.; author: Essentials of the English Tense, 1954; The OE Relative Particle, 1962; Teaching English as a Foreign Language and English for Science and Technology, 1978; others. Office: Grad Inst English, Taiwan Normal U, Taipei 10613, Taiwan

YANG, HU-SHAN, ambassador; b. Hopei, Peoples Republic of China, 1927. Degree, Peking U., 1952. Head div. Fgn. Ministry, Peoples Republic of China, 1972-80; advisor and dep. del. to gen. assembly UN, N.Y.C., 1972-73, 1981-84; del. com. on disarmament UN, Geneva, 1980; alt. rep. security council UN, N.Y.C., 1981-84, counsellor Chinese mission, 1981-84, mem. com. contbns., 1983-84; ambassador to Libya Tripoli, 1985—. Office: Embassy Peoples Republic, of China, Gargaresh M 86 POB 5329, Tripoli 5329, Libya other: care Fgn Ministry, Beijing Peoples Republic of China

YANG, LING LING, psychiatrist, educator; b. Changsha, Republic of China, Sept. 2, 1933; d. Ji-Ye and Shu (Zhao) Y.; m. Chengye Zuo, Apr. 30, 1954; 1 child, Yang Zuo. MD, Hunan Med. Coll., 1956. Resident in psychiatry Hunan Med. Coll., Changshe, 1956-60, clin. psychiatrist, 1961-78; from asst. prof. dept. psychiatry to prof. Hunan Med. Coll., Changsha, 1978—, chmn. dept. psychiatry, 1984-87. Author: Child Intelligence, 1981, Mental Retardation, 1984, Psychiatric Diagnosis, 1980. contbr. articles to profl. jours. Fellow Chinese Psychiatric Assn.; mem. Hunan Psychiatric Assn., Chinese Psychol. Assn., Internat. Neurophysical Soc. Home: Campus apt Wen Yi Cun #4 304, #2 Affiliated Hosp Hunan Med Coll, Changsha Hunan Peoples Republic of China Office: #2 Affiliated Hosp, Hunan Med Coll, Changsha Hunan Peoples Republic of China

YANG, LO, mathematician; b. Nantoong, Jiangsu, China, Nov. 10, 1939; s. Jing-yuan and Jing-juan (Chew) Y.; m. Che-yuan Hwang, Mar. 31, 1967; children: Yan Yang, Bing Yang. Bachelor's, Peking (now Beijing) U., 1962; PhD, Inst. Math. Academia Sinica, Beijing, 1966. With Inst. Math. Academia Sinica, 1967-76, assoc. prof. math., 1977-78, prof., 1979—, dep. dir., 1982-86, dir., 1987—; vis. prof. Cornell U., Ithaca, N.Y., 1979, Purdue U., West Lafayette, Ind., 1980; mem. Mittag-Leffler Inst., Stockholm, 1983, Inst. Advanced Study, Princeton, N.J., 1984-85, judging com. Nat. Com. Degrees, China, 1982—, NSF China, 1986—. Author: Theory of Value Distribution and It's New Research, 1983 (1st prize Chinese Sci. Books); contbr. articles to profl. jours. V.p. All China Youth Fedn., Beijing, 1979—; mem. Chinese People's Polit. Consultative Conf., Beijing, 1983—; vice chmn. World Youth Summit, Hiroshima, Japan, 1985. Recipient Nat. Sci. Congress State Council prize, Beijing, 1978, Chinese Natural Scis. State Council prize, 1982. Mem. Chinese Math. Soc. (sec.-gen. 1983—), China Assn. Sci. and Tech. (com. 1986—), Inst. Math. (bd. dirs. 1987—), China Internat. Conf. Ctr Sci. and Tech. (council). Office: Inst Math Academia Sinica, 100080 Beijing Peoples Republic of China

YANG, PETER QUAY, international maketing company executive; b. Shanghai, China, Nov. 19, 1922; s. Sih-Zun and Joan (Tong) Y.; B.F.A., R.I. Sch. Design, 1950; M.F.A., Cranbrook Acad. Art, 1951; m. Lucy Ting, Apr. 6, 1957. Staff designer Gen. Motors Corp., Detroit, Mich., 1951-54; project designer W. B. Ford Design Corp., Detroit, 1954-55; pres. Yang-Gardner Assocs., Inc., N.Y.C., 1955-75; instr. product design Pratt Inst., N.Y.C., 1958-60; chmn. Colemanco Ltd., Hong Kong, 1975—. Mem. U.S. Pres. Com. on Employment of the Handicapped, 1967-78. Mem. Indsl. Designer's Soc. Am. (dir. 1969-72), Internat. Micrographic Congress (pres. 1980), Marquis Biog. Library Soc. (adv. com.), Am. C. of C. Hong Kong, Image Processing Assn. Rotarian. Patentee Unilock systems. Home: 51 Stubbs Rd, Apt 7B Hong Kong Office: Coleman Bus Systems (HK) Ltd, Room 902-B Watson's Estate, Watson's Rd, North Point Hong Kong

YANG, SONG-YU, research biochemist; b. Wu-Xi, Jiangsu, China, Oct. 27, 1938; came to U.S. 19, naturalized 19; s. Rong-Geng Zong and Su-Fei Yang; m. Xue-Ying He, Jan. 1965; children—Ying-Zi, Yu-Xiao. M.D., Peking Med. Coll., 1960; M.S., CCNY, 1983; Ph.D., CUNY, 1984. Med. diplomate Peking Med. Coll. Instr. Peking Med. Coll., 1960-75; asst. prof. Academia Sinica, Shanghai, China, 1975-80; teaching asst. CCNY, 1981-84; research assoc. Research Found. of CUNY, 1984—. Author: Biology of Cancer, 1978; contbr. articles to profl. jours. Recipient L.J. Curtman Prize CCNY, 1984. Mem. Am. Chemistry Soc., Am. Soc. Biol. Chemists, AAAS, Chinese Med. Assn., N.Y. Acad. Scis., Sigma Xi. Office: Dept Chemistry CCNY Convent Ave at 138 St New York NY 10031

YANG, WILOX, physicist; b. Canton, China, May 25, 1922; s. Shaw Hong and Ah Han (Lee) Y.; m. Constance Lee Bycofski, Jan. 20, 1960 (dec. June 1964); m. Janet D. Smith, Mar. 23, 1966; children—Eleanor, Lisa, Lori. B.Sc., Huachung U., Wuchang, China, 1947; M.Sc., Poly. Inst. N.Y., 1963, Ph.D., 1974. Mem. staff Princeton-Penn Accelerator, Princeton (N.J.) U., 1962-69; mem. staff high energy physics research U. Pa., Phila., 1969-75; engring. physicist Fermilab, Batavia, Ill., 1975—. Mem. Am. Phys. Soc., N.Y. Acad. Sci., Sigma Xi. Democrat. Club: Sigma Xi. Contbr. articles to profl. jours. Home: 30 W 113 Lindenwood Ct Warrenville IL 60555 Office: Fermi Nat Accelerator Lab PO Box 500 Batavia IL 60510

YANG SHANGKUN, president People's Republic of China; b. Shuangjiang City, Sichuan, People's Republic of China, 1907; m. Li Bozhao, 1931 (dec. 1985). Student, Shanghai U., Sun Yat-sen U., Moscow, 1927-30. Mem. Chinese Communist Party, from 1926, Cen. Exec. Com., from 1932; head propaganda dept., sec. Chinese Communist Party orgn. All-China Fedn. Trade Unions, Shanghai, after 1931; former editor Red China newspaper; dir. polit. dept. 1st Red Army, 1932; former sec. north bur. Chinese Communist Party Cen. Com., sec., 1943, former dir. Gen. Office,, former dep. sec.-gen., former alt. mem. Secretariat,; mem. Standing Com. Nat. People's Congress, 1965; 2d Party sec. 1979-80; vice-chmn. Guangdon Provincial Revolutionary Com., 1979, chmn., 1979-80; 1st sec. Guangzhou Municipality Communist Party, 1979-80; mem. standing com. Chinese People's Polit. Consultative Conf., 1979-83; mem. Chinese Communist Party 11th Cen. Com., 1979—; vice-gov. Guangdong Province, 1979-80; 1st sec. Party Com., Guangdong Mil. Dist., 1980; dep. for Guangdong Province 5th Nat. People's Congress, from 1980, mem. Presidium, 3d session, 1980, vice-chmn., sec.-gen., 1980-83; sec.-gen. Mil. Commn., Chinese Communist Party Cen. Com., 1981-82; permanent chmn., sec.-gen. 4th session 5th Nat. People's Congress, from 1981, mem. Presidium, sec.-gen., 1982; mem. Politburo Chinese Communist Party Cen. Com., 1982, permanent vice-chmn. Mil. Commn.,, from 1982; vice-chmn. Cen. Mil. Commn., 1983, 88—; pres. People's Republic of China, 1988—. Address: Office of Pres, Beijing Peoples Republic of China *

YANISH, ELIZABETH YAFFE, sculptor; b. St. Louis; d. Sam and Fannie May (Weil) Yaffe; student Washington U., 1941, Denver U., 1960; pvt. studies; m. Nathan Yanish, July 5, 1944; children—Ronald, Marilyn Ginsburg, Mindy. One-woman shows: Woodstock Gallery, London, 1973, Internat. House, Denver, 1963, Colo. Women's Coll., Denver, 1975, Contemporaries Gallery, Santa Fe, 1963, So. Colo. State Coll. Pueblo, 1967, others; exhibited in group shows: Salt Lake City Mus., 1964, 71, Denver Art Mus., 1961-75, Oklahoma City Mus., 1969, Joslyn Mus., Omaha, 1964-68, Lucca (Italy) Invitational, 1971, others; represented in permanent collections: Colo. State Bank, Bmh Synagogue, Denver, Denver Womens Coll., Har Ha Shem Congregation, Boulder, Colo., Faith Bible Chapel, Denver, others. Chmn. visual arts Colo. Centennial-Bicentennial, 1974-75; pres. Denver Council Arts and Humanities, 1973-75; mem. Mayor's Com. on Child Abuse, 1974-75; co-chmn. visual arts spree Denver Pub. Schs., 1975; trustee Denver Center for the Performing Arts, 1973-75; chmn. Concerned Citizens for Arts, 1976; pres. Beth Israel Hosp. Aux., 1985-87; organizer Coat Drive for the Needy, 1982-87; bd. dirs. Srs., Inc. Recipient McCormick award Ball State U., Muncie, Ind., 1964, Purchase award Colo. Women's Coll., Denver, 1963, Tyler (Tex.) Mus., 1963, 1st prize in sculpture 1st Nat. Space Art Show, 1971; Humanities scholar Auraria Libraries, U. Colo., Denver. Mem. Artists Equity Assn., Rocky Mountain Liturgical Arts, Allied Sculptors Colo., Allied Arts Inc. Hist. Denver, Symphony Guild, Parks People, Beth Israel Aux. Jewish. Home: 131 Fairfax St Denver CO 80220

YANKOWSKI, CARL JAMES, consumer packaged goods executive, marketing consultant; b. Butler, Pa., July 22, 1948; s. Mitchel Carl and Helen Margaret (Miseyka) Y.; m. Patricia Pamela Petraglia, June 11, 1977. B.S.E.E., MIT, 1971, B.S. in Mgmt., 1971. Mktg. asst. Procter & Gamble, Cin., 1971-75; product mgr. Memorex Corp., Santa Clara, Calif., 1976-77; group dir. mktg. Pepsi Cola Co., Purchase, N.Y., 1977-81; gen. mgr. mktg. Gen. Electric Co., Bridgeport, Conn., 1981-83; pres., chief exec. officer Cadbury-Schweppes div., Stamford, Conn., 1983-88; dir. Sodamate Holdings Ltd., London, 1988—; v.p. mktg. Polaroid Corp. Recipient Exec. Devel. Program selection Gen. Electric Co., Fairfield, Conn., 1983. Mem. S.W. Fairfield County Indsl. Assn., Stamford Hist. Soc. Republican. Roman Catholic. Clubs: Stamford Yacht; Porsche of Am. (Va.). Avocations: classic autos; squash; gardening; antiques; woodworking. Home: 78 Hoyclo Rd Stamford CT 06903

YANNAS, IOANNIS VASSILIOS, polymer science and engineering educator; b. Athens, Apr. 14, 1935; s. Vassilios Pavlos and Thalia (Sarafoglou) Y.; m. Stamatia Frondistou (div. Oct. 1984); children: Tania, Alexis. AB, Harvard U., 1957; SM, MIT, 1959; MS, Princeton U., 1965, PhD, 1966. Asst. prof. mech. engring. MIT, Cambridge, 1966-68, duPont asst. prof., 1968-69, assoc. prof., 1969-78, prof. polymer sci. and engring., 1978—, prof., dept. materials sci. and engring., 1983—; prof. Harvard-MIT Div. Health Scis. and Tech., Cambridge, 1978—; vis. prof. Royal Inst. Tech., Stockholm, 1974. Mem. editorial bd. Jour. Biomed. Materials Research, 1986—; contbr. over 100 tech. articles; 9 patents in field. Recipient Founders award Soc. for Biomaterials, 1982, Fred O. Conley award Soc. Plastics Engrs., 1982, award in medicine and genetics Sci. Digest/Cutty Sark, 1982, Doolittle award Am. Chem. Soc., 1988; Fellow Pub. Health Service, Princeton U., 1963, Shriners Burns Inst., Mass. Gen. Hosp., Boston, 1980-81. Fellow Am. Inst. Chemists; mem. Inst. Medicine of Nat. Acad. Scis. Office: MIT Bldg 3-336 77 Massachusetts Ave Cambridge MA 02139

YANNOPOULOS, MARINOS, banker; b. Athens, Greece, Aug. 7, 1953; s. Stamatios and Emilia (Gerolymbou) Y.; m. Evagelia Nikolopoulou, Dec. 9, 1978; children: Maria-Eleni, Alexia, Andreas. Student, Athens Coll., 1972; BA in Econs., Deree-Pierce Coll., Athens, 1975; MA, U. Sussex, Eng., 1976; MBA, Manchester (Eng.) Bus. Sch., 1978. Lead auditor Esso Europe Inc., Rome, 1978-80; treas. Esso Greece, Athens, 1980-83; dealer money mkt. Chase Manhatan Bank, N.Y.C., 1983-84, dealer fgn. exchange, 1984-86; country mgr. treasury Chase Manhatan Bank, Milano, Italy, 1986—. Mem. Assn. Tesorieri Inst. Creditizie, Forex Club Italiano, Borsa de Milano. Christian Orthodox. Club: Athens Tennis. Office: Chase Manhattan Bank, Piazza Meda 1, 20121 Milan Italy

YANO, KATSUMI, engineer; b. Sakai, Osaka, Japan, May 30, 1928; s. Toyojiro and Kayako Yano; m. Yoko Iyotani, Oct. 18, 1956; children: Miyako Tsukiyama, Tomo Iyotani. B in Engring., Osaka (Japan) U., 1953. Registered architect, structural engineer. Structural engr. Nikken Sekkei Ltd., Osaka, Japan, 1953-55; structural engr. Nikken Sekkei Ltd., Tokyo, 1955-65, mgr. structural engring., 1965-75, mgr. design, 1975-77, dir., 1977-85, sr. mng. dir., 1985—; mem. archtl. council Japan Ministry of Constrn., 1982-87. Author: Structural Design, 1981, Examples of Structural Calculation I, 1979. Mem. Japan Structural Cons. Assn. (chmn. 1981—), Archtl. Inst. Japan (bd. dirs. 1983-85, Design award 1971, Achievement award 1967), Japan Inst. Architects. Lodge: Rotary. Home: 4-10-21 Minamiyukigaya, Ohta-ku, Toyko 145, Japan Office: Nikken Sekkei, 1-4 Koraku, Bunkyo-ku, Tokyo 112, Japan

YANO, MITSUO, banker; b. Nishinomiya, Hyogo, Japan, Jan. 5, 1941; s. Konosuke and Sei (Suita) Y.; m. Fuyuko Tsukamoto, Sept. 26, 1945; children: Mitsuei, Mitsunobu, Yoshiei. BBA, Kobe (Japan) U., 1963. Gen. mgr. The Sanwa Bank, Ltd., Kashiwa, Chiba, Japan, 1982-84; gen. mgr. Tokyo, 1984-86, Chgo., 1986—. Clubs: Union League (Chgo.), River Forest C.C. (Elmhurst, Ill.). Office: The Sanwa Bank Ltd 39 S LaSalle St Chicago IL 60603

YANO, SHINTARO, engineering executive, educator; b. Fukuoka, Kyuushuu, Japan, Dec. 8, 1926; s. Yoshiyuki and Aki Yano; m. Akiko Yano, Oct. 25, 1955; 1 child, Kenichi; Mech. Engr., Taga Tech. Coll., Japan, 1947; Ph.D. (hon.) Osaka U., 1962; Cons. Eng. (hon.) Sci. and Tech. Agy. of Japan, 1959. Chief mech. div. Kyushu Electric Power Co., Japan, 1958-63; chief engring. devel. div. Kajima Corp., Tokyo, 1964-67, vice dir. overseas constrn. div., 1967-70, vice dir. environmen devel. dept., 1971-76, supervisory engr., 1977-86; advisor Nippon Koei Co., Ltd., Tokyo, 1987—; prof. dept. sci. and engring. Nippon U., 1964—; prof. Musashi Inst. Tech., 1965—; water resource agy. advisor for Indonesia, 1965, 67, Republic of China, 1968-69, Republic of Korea, 1969; mgr. group of inspection for USSR pipe line, 1975; UN rep. for Japan, 1983; mem. resources com. Sci. and Tech. Agy., Transp. Econ. Research Ctr. Contbr. articles to profl. jours. Decorated Purple Ribbon medal (Japan). Japan Soc. Civil Engrs. Home: 3-28-10 Imagawa Suginami-Ku, Tokyo 167 Japan Office: Nippon Koei Co Ltd, 5-4 Kojimachi, Chiyoda-Ku, Tokyo 102, Japan

YANOFF, MYRON, ophthalmologist; b. Phila., Dec. 21, 1936; s. Jacob and Lillian S. (Fishman) Y.; m. Karin Michele Lindblad, Aug. 8, 1980; 1 dau., Alexis A.; children by previous marriage: Steven L., David A., Joanne M. A.B., U. Pa., 1957; M.D., 1961. Prof. ophthalmology and pathology U. Pa. Med. Sch., Phila.; William F. Norris and George E. de Schwinitz prof. ophthalmology, chmn. dept., dir. Scheie Eye Inst., 1977-88; chmn., prof. ophthalmology Hahnemann U., 1988—. Author: Ocular Pathology; also articles. Served to maj. M.C. USAR. Mem. Am. Ophthalmologic Soc., Verhoeff Soc., Am. Acad. Ophthalmology. Office: Hahnemann U Feinstein Bldg Dept Ophthalmology Broad & Race Sts Philadelphia PA 19102

YANYALI, NUSRET, corporation executive; b. Aug. 22, 1928; s. Cemil Musa and Hadiye (Arifzade)Y.; m. Ayse Nihal Diner, Apr. 10, 1951; 1 child, Yavuz. CPE, U. Mich., Ann Arbor, 1955; DBA, Galatasaray Advanced Econs. and Trade Inst., Istanbul, 1966. Office mgr. TPAO Turkish Petroleum Corp., Ankara, 1955-62; purchasing mgr. Goodyear Tires AS, Istanbul, 1962-64, Mobil Oil & Gas Cos. in Turkey, Istanbul, 1964-80; coordinator Yanyali Prodn. & Mktg. Enterprises, Istanbul, 1980—; mng. dir. Dost Food & Farming AS, Inc., Istanbul, 1982—; dir. Latinlord Ltd., London, 1983—. Named to IBC Roll of Honor for Outstanding Contbn. in Mktg. and Bus. Adminstrn.; recipient MWW Recognition for Outstanding Achievement award, ABI Service award, ABI Internat. Cultural diploma of Honor. Mem. Istanbul C. of C., BIHTD Internat. Exec. Service Corps, Istanbul. Club: Levent Tennis Assn. (Istanbul). Permanent Address: Yeni Levent Blok 19/49, Konakler, 80620 Istanbul Turkey Office: Dost Ortaklar AS, Dergiler Sokak 18, Kat 1, 80300 Istanbul Turkey

YAO, JOHN CHENG YU, industrial goods distributing company executive, management consultant; b. Shanghai, China, May 11, 1946; came to Hong Kong, 1950; m. Maria Irene Da Graca, May 13, 1972; children—Desiree, Peter. Cert. of Bus. Adminstrn., Chu Hai Coll., 1968; diploma in Mgmt. Studies, U. Hong Kong, 1973; MBA U. Hong Kong, 1987. Supr., Price Waterhouse & Co., Hong Kong, 1965-71; fin. controller Am. Engring. Corp., Hong Kong, 1971-78; group acct. Sime Darby (HK) Ltd., Hong Kong, 1978-80; gen. mgr. Winfield Group, Hong Kong, 1980; dir. Wytaly Co. Ltd., Hong Kong, 1980—; dir. Diesel Equipment Distributors Ltd., Hong Kong; cons. The Guangzhou Econ. & Tech. Exploring Zone, People's Republic China, 1985. Contbr. articles to music jour. Mem. Brit. Inst. Mgmt., Hong Kong U. Mgmt. Alumni Soc. (sec. 1983-85, vice chmn. 1985-86). Lodge: Rotary. Home: 6 Cleveland St, Flat D 6/F, Hong Kong Hong Kong Office: Wytaly Co Ltd, 4/F E Point Bldg, 92 Gloucester Rd, Hong Kong Hong Kong

YAO YILIN, Chinese government official; b. Jiangsi Province, China, 1917. Sec.-gen. N. China Bur. Central Com., Chinese Communist Party, 1937-46; mem. fin. and econ. com. N. China People's Govt., 1948-49, dir. dept. industry and commerce, 1948-49; vice minister trade, 1949-52; mem. provisional bd. dirs. All-China Fedn. Coops., 1950; mem. Central Com. to check Austerity Program, 1951; vice minister commerce, 1952-58; mem. nat. com. All-China Fedn. of Supply and Mktg. Coops., 1954; dep. for Jiangxi to 1st Nat. People's Congress, 1954-59; vice minister, 1st minister commerce, 1958; alt. mem. 8th Central Com. Chinese Communist Party, 1958; dep. dir. bur. fin. and trade adminstrn. office State Council, 1959; mem., pres. All-China Conf. Advanced Producers, 1959; mem. standing com. 3d Chinese People's Polit. Consultative Conf., 1959; dep. dir. fin. and trade work dept. Chinese Communist Party Central Com., 1959-67, dir. dept., 1964-67; minister of commerce, 1960-67; accused of counter-revolutionary revisionism, 1967; alt. mem. 10th Central Com. Chinese Communist Party, 1973-77; vice minister fgn. trade, 1973-78; mem. presidium 11th Nat. Congress Chinese Communist Party, 1977; vice premier, 1978—; minister of commerce, 1978-79, minister 4th Ministry Machine Bldg., 1979-80; sec.-gen. State Fin. and Econs. Commn., 1979-81; dir. gen. office Chinese Communist Party, 1979, dep. sec. gen. Central Com., 1979-82, mem. secretariat 11th Central Com., 1980-85; minister in charge State Planning Commn., 1980-83, 87—; alt. mem. politburo 12th Central Com., 1982-85, mem., 1986—, mem. Standing Com., 1987—; sec. secretariat Chinese Communist Party, 1982. Address: Office of Vice Premier, care State Council, Beijing People's Republic China *

YAP, ALVIN TAN, construction company executive; b. Cebu, Philippines, Feb. 1, 1960; s. Gregorio and Susana Uy (Tan) Y. Sudent, Univ. San Carlos, Cebu City, 1978—. Field mgr. Mario Yap Constrn. Co., Cebu, 1982—; gen. mgr. Alacrity Enterprises, Cebu, 1984—. Chmn. Visayas-Mindanao Table Tennis Tournament, Cebu, 1986; asst. troop leader Cebu Eastern Coll. Boy Scouts, 1976-77; pres. Cebu Progressive Youth Club, 1984-86; treas. Amity Table Tennis Group, 1982-83; chmn. table tennis div. CEBU Inter-Family Youth Assn., 1988—. Mem. CEBU Table Tennis Assn. (treas. 1982-86). Jehovah's Witness. Office: Alacrity Enterprises, 191 Manalili St, Cebu 6401, Philippines

YAP, HIAN POH, mathematician, educator; b. Fu Chien, Republic China, Dec. 4, 1938; arrived in Singapore, 1956; s. Khoi Kak and Kim Tang (Chua) Y.; m. Peh Bee Guat; children: Siong Yew, Tiong Peng. BS, Nanyang U., Singapore, 1963; MS, U. Singapore, 1967, PhD, 1969. Asst. lectr. math. U. Singapore, 1966-68; postdoctoral fellow U. Alta., Edmonton, Can., 1970-71; lectr. U. Singapore, 1969-76, sr. lectr., 1977-80; sr. lectr. Nat. U. Singapore, 1981-85, assoc. prof., 1986—; vis. fellow U. Waterloo, Ont., Can., 1973, U. Calgary, Alta., 1980-81; vis. prof. MIT, Cambridge, Mass., 1974. Author: Some Topics in Graph Theory, 1986; editor: Graph Theory Singapore 1983, 1984; editor Graphs and Combinatorics Jour., 1985—; contbr. over 40 papers to math. jours. Mem. Singapore Math. Soc., Am. Math. Soc., London Math. Soc., Australian Math. Soc., Southeast Asian Math. Soc. Home: 77 Phoenix Garden, Singapore Singapore 2366 Office: Nat Univ Singapore, 10 Kent Ridge Crescent, Singapore Singapore 0511

YAP, KIE-HAN, engineering executive; b. Yogyakarta, Java, Indonesia, Sept. 16, 1925; s. Hong-Tjoen and Souw-Lien (Tan) Y.; m. Kiauw-Lan The, Mar. 7, 1954; children—Tjay-Hok, Tjay-Yong. Ir, Tech. U. Delft, Netherlands, 1953. Dir., Research Inst. Mgmt. Sci., U. Delft, 1955-61; dir., founder CBO Mgmt. and Tech. Systems Ctr., Rotterdam, Netherlands, 1961—; lectr. various univs., Western Europe and U.S., 1961—. advisor internat. orgns., 1961—. Contbr. articles to profl. jours. Mem. Royal Inst. Engrs. Netherlands. Home: Hoyledesingel 14, Rotterdam 3054 EK The Netherlands

YAP, MEOW FOO, psychiatrist; b. West Malaysia, Apr. 15, 1918; s. Yong Chan and Choon (Chin) Y.; M.B., B.S., U. Hong Kong, 1946, M.D., 1959; postgrad. (Colombo Plan fellow), Inst. Psychiatry London, 1956-59, diploma in psychol. medicine, 1959; m. Wai Leng Wong, May 4, 1948; 1 dau., Charmaine Lai Meng. Med. officer Singapore Med. Services, 1947-61; med. supt., sr. cons. psychiatrist Woodbridge Hosp., Singapore, 1961-71, also past bd. visitors; cons. Samaritans of Singapore. cons. pvt. psychiatrist, Singapore, 1971-77, 78—; cons. psychiatrist Mental Health Services Western Australia, Perth, 1977-78; lectr. U. Singapore, 1960-71. Past bd. visitors Changi Prison Hosp.; past exec. com. Singapore Assn. Retarded Children. Served to capt. Chinese Army, 1944-45. Fellow Internat. Biog. Assn. (U.K.); mem. Singapore Psychiatrist Assn., Acad. Medicine Singapore, Singapore Assn. Mental Health (past v.p.), Soc. Clin. Hypnosis, Soc. Pvt. Practitioners. Contbr. articles to profl. publs. Office: Orchard Bldg, 1 Grange Rd #04-11, Singapore 0923 Singapore

YAQUB-KHAN, SAHABZADA, Pakistani foreign minister; b. Dec. 1920; student Royal Indian Mil. Coll. and Indian Mil. Acad., Debra Dun, 1932-40, Pakistan Army Command and Staff Coll., Quatta, Ecole Superieure de Guerre, Paris, 1953-54, Imperial Def. Coll., London. Commd. officer Indian Army, 1940-47; commd. officer Pakistan Army, 1947, advanced through grades to lt. gen., 1969; vice chief gen. staff Pakistan Army, 1958; comdr. armored div.; comdt. Army Staff Coll.; chief gen. staff Pakistan Army, corps comdr., comdr. Eastern Zone, 1969-71; gov., martial law adminstr. of East Pakistan (now Bangladesh); ret., 1971; Pakistan ambassador to France, 1972, 80-82, ambassador to Ireland, 1972-73, ambassador to U.S.A., ambassador to Jamaica, 1973-77, ambassador to Moscow, 1979-80; fgn. minister Govt. of Pakistan, Islamabad, 1982-87, 88—. Office: Ministry of Fgn Affairs, Islamabad Pakistan *

YARBOROUGH, WILLIAM GLENN, JR., retired military officer, forest farmer, defense and international business executive; b. Rock Hill, S.C., June 21, 1940; s. William Glenn and Bessie (Rainsford) Y.; m. Betsy Gibson, Jan. 24, 1969; children—Bill, Clinton, Frank, Elizabeth. BS, U. S.C., 1961, MBA, 1969; postgrad. Command and Gen. Staff Coll., 1970, Naval War Coll., 1979, Colgate-Darden Grad. Bus. Sch., U. Va., 1983. U.S. Army, advanced through grades to col., 1980; co. and troop comdr. and squadron staff officer, Viet Nam, Europe, 1961-71, strategist, Washington, 1971-73, chief of assignments, Office Personnel Mgmt., Mil. Personnel Ctr., Washington, 1973-76; comdr. 1st Squadron, 1st Cavalry, Europe, 1976-78; chief of staff and spl. asst. to chief of staff 1st Armored Div., Europe, 1978; br. chief Office of Chief of Staff, Washington, 1979-80; exec. to dep. commanding gen. Material Devel. and Readiness Command, Washington, 1980-81; exec. asst. sec. for research, devel. and acquisition, Washington, 1981-85. Decorated Silver Star, Bronze Star medal with 4 oak leaf clusters and V device, Purple Heart. Mem. Assn. U.S. Army, Am. Legion, Armed Forces Communications and Electronics Assn., U.S. Army Armor Assn., SAR, Am. Def. Preparedness Assn., Purple Heart VFW Soc. Clubs: Army-Navy, Army Navy Country.

YARBOROUGH, WILLIAM PELHAM, retired army officer, writer, lecturer, consultant; b. Seattle, May 12, 1912; s. Leroy W. and Addessia (Hooker) Y.; m. Norma Mae Tuttle, Dec. 26, 1936; children: Norma Kay (dec.), William Lee, Patricia Mae. B.S., U.S. Mil. Acad., 1936; grad., Command and Gen. Staff Coll., 1944, Brit. Staff Coll., 1950, Army War Coll., 1953. Commd. 2d lt. U.S. Army, 1936, advanced through grades to lt. gen., 1968; various assignments U.S., Philippines and ETO, 1936-42; exec. officer Paratroop Task Force, N. Africa, 1942; comdr. 2d Bn., 504th Par. Inf. Regt., 82d Airborne Div., Sicily invasion, 1943, 509th Parachute Inf., Italy and France, 1943-44; comdg. officer 473 Inf., Italy, 1945; provost marshal 15th Army Group, ETO, 1945, Vienna Area Command and U.S. Forces, Austria, 1945-47; operations officer, gen. staff Joint Mil. Assistance Adv. Group, London, Eng., 1951-52; mem. faculty Army War Coll., 1953-56, 57; dep. chief Mil. Assistance and Adv. Group, Cambodia, 1956-57; comdg. officer 66th CIC Group, Stuttgart, Germany, 1958-60, 66th M.I. Group, Stuttgart, 1960; comdg. gen. USA Spl. Warfare Center; also comdt. U.S. Army Spl. Warfare Sch., Ft. Bragg, 1961-65; sr. mem. UN Command Mil. Armistice Commn., Korea, 1965; asst. dep. chief staff DCSOPS for spl. operations Dept. Army, Washington; chmn. U.S. delegation Inter-Am. Def. Bd., Joint Brazil U.S. Def. Commn., Joint Mexican-U.S. Def. Commn.;

Army mem. U.S. sect. permanent Joint Bd. on Def., Can.-U.S. Def. Commn., Washington, 1965; asst. chief of staff intelligence Dept. Army Washington, 1966-68; comdg. gen. I Corps Group, Korea, 1968-69; chief staff, also dep. comdr.-in-chief U.S. Army, Pacific, Hawaii, 1969-71; ret. (U.S. Army), 1971. William P. Yarborough collection papers and artifacts donated to, Mugar Meml. Libraries, Boston U.; Author: Trial in Africa, 1976, Bail Out Over North Africa, 1980. Bd. dirs. Humanities Found., N.C. State U.; mem. citizens adv. group Comprehensive Cancer Center, Duke U.; bd. dirs. Princess Mother's Found., Thailand. Fellow Company Mil. Historians, Explorers Club; mem. Am. African Affairs Assn. (chmn.), Assn. Former Intelligence Officers, Assn. U.S. Army, Assn. Grad. U.S. Mil. Acad., Ends of Earth Soc., N.C. Japan Ctr. of N.C. State U. Club: Kiwanis. Home: 160 Hillside Rd Southern Pines NC 28387

YARLING, CHARLES BYRON, process engineer; b. El Paso, Tex., May 8, 1945; s. Byron Hendricks and Clara Catherine (Wingo) Y.; BA in Math., U. Tex., 1968, BSEE, 1976. Field service engr. Welex, Beaumont, Tex., 1976-77; design engr. Accelerators, Inc., Austin, Tex., 1977-78; staff process engr. ion implantation Motorola, Mesa, Ariz., 1979-85; field process specialist Applied Materials, Santa Clara, Calif., 1985—. Served with U.S. Army, 1968-70. Decorated Purple Heart, Army Commendation medal; recipient Motorola Engring. award, 1980, Silver Quill award, 1983. Author 7 tech. pubs. in field. Mem. IEEE, Am. Vacuum Soc., Motorola Sci. and Tech. Soc., Pi Lambda Phi (nat. council 1973-76). Office: 3050 Bowers M/S 3002 Santa Clara CA 95054-3201

YASEEN, LEONARD CLAYTON, consultant; b. Chicago Heights, Ill., June 27, 1912; ed. U. Ill.; m. Helen M. Fantus, July 29, 1934; children—Roger, Barbara. Ret. chmn. bd. Fantus Co. ; trustee Hirshhorn Mus. (Smithsonian Inst.); founder Yaseen Studies in Modern Art, Met. Mus. Art, N.Y.C., Yaseen Lectures Neuberger Mus.; former dir. Witco Chem. Co. Bd. dirs. Purchase Coll. Found. Author: Plant Location, 1956; A Guide to Facilities Location, 1971; Direct Investment in the United States, 1974; Industrial Development in a Changing World, 1975; The Jesus Connection, 1985. Clubs: Century, Sky. Home: 2 Bay Ave Larchmont NY 10538

YASSA, GUIRGUIS FAHMY, infosystems specialist; b. Khartoum, Sudan, Oct. 1, 1930; came to U.S., 1969, naturalized, 1976; s. Fahmy and Brinsa Bissada (Nakhla) Y.; m. Laila Naguib Nosseir, Sept. 6, 1959; children—Elham, Medhat, Magdi, Laura. B.Engring. with distinction, Cairo U., 1951, M.Sc. in Surveying, 1964, diploma stats., 1966; Govt. Netherlands fellow, Internat. Inst. Aerial Survey, Delft, 1956; Ph.D., Cornell U., 1973. Successively topographic engr., photogrammetric engr., head photogrammetric sect. Survey of Egypt, 1951-67; sr. lectr. Internat. Inst. Aerial Survey, 1967-69; teaching asst. Cornell U., 1969-72; systems analyst, dir. mapping Robinson Aerial Surveys Co., Newton, N.J., 1973-79; tech. analyst Warner Computer Systems Co., Teaneck, N.J., 1979-80; sr. analyst ops. Chase Manhattan Bank, N.Y.C., 1980—. Mem. Am. Soc. Photogrammetry (Talbert Abrams award 1974), ASCE, Sigma Xi. Author papers in field. Home: RD 7 Box 344 Sussex NJ 07461 Office: Chase Manhattan Bank 1 New York Plaza New York NY

YASSINE, KHAIR NIMER, archaeologist; b. Amman, Jordan, May 29, 1934; s. Nimer Othman Yassine and Ramziah Suluman Malhas; m. Eileen Paul Jones (div. 1974); 1 child, Lisa; m. Rabha Naji Masri, Jan. 21, 1950; children: Lina, Rami. BA, Ain Shams U., Cairo, Egypt, 1959; MA, U. Pa., Phila., 1966; PhD, U. Chgo., 1974. Mus. curator Dept. Antiquities, Amman, Jordan, 1963-66; tchr. U. Jordan, Amman, 1974-79; chmn. dept. archaeology Jordan U., 1979-82; research asst. U. Pa., Phila., 1982-83; prof. U. Kuwait, 1984-85, U. Jordan, Amman, 1985—; bd. dirs. Tell El Mazar Excavation Project, Jordan Valley Survey Project; cons. Nat. Mus., Amman, 1963-68, Univ. Mus., Amman, 1974—. Author: Archaeology of Jordan, 1979, Tell el Mazar, vol. 1, 1984; editor jour. Arab Museum, 1985—. Fulbright scholar U. Pa., 1982. Mem. Arab Historian Orgn. Home: PO Box 410403, Amman Jordan Office: Univ of Jordan, Dept Archaeology, Amman Jordan

YASUE, KUNIO, physicist, applied mathematician; b. Okayama, Japan, Sept. 27, 1951; s. Teruyoshi and Kotoe (Hiramatsu) Y.; m. Saeko Takayanagi, Apr. 18, 1976; children—Ayako, Kanako. BS Tohoku U., Japan, 1974; MS Kyoto U., 1976; PhD Nagoya U., 1979. Researcher, U. Geneva, 1978-82; chief researcher Toshiba Research and Devel. Ctr., Kawasaki, Japan, 1982-84; asst. prof. Notre Dame Seishin U., Okayama, 1984—; dir. research inst. for informatics and sci. Notre Dame Seishin U., Okayama. Contbr. articles to profl. jours. Ministry Edn. Japan grantee, 1985. Mem. Internat. Neural Network Soc., Am. Math. Soc. Buddhist. Club: Daito Ryu (Master Sagawa). Home: 1 12 7 Tsugura cho, Okayama 700, Japan Office: Notre Dame Seishin U, 2 16 9 Ifuku cho, Okayama 700, Japan

YASUGI, MARIKO, mathematics educator; b. Tokyo, Oct. 29, 1937; d. Ryuichi and Yasuko (Obata) Y. BA, U. Tokyo, 1960, MS, 1962, DSc, 1966; postgrad. U. Ill., 1963-66. Lectr. U. Bristol, Eng., 1966-68; postdoctoral fellow Carnegie-Mellon U., Pitts., 1968-70; asst. prof. math. Dalhousie U., Halifax, N.S., Can., 1970-72; assoc. prof. math. Shizuoka U., Japan, 1972-77, U. Tsukuba, Ibaraki, Japan, 1977-86; prof. math. Kyoto Sangyo U., Japan, 1986—. Contbr. articles to math. jours. Recipient Saruhashi prize Assn. for Bright Future for Women Scientists, Tokyo, 1985. Mem. Assn. for Symbolic Logic, Am. Math. Soc., Math. Soc. Japan, Japan Assn. for Philosophy of Sci. (com.), Assn. Software Sci. Avocations: aerobics, weight training. Home: 302 Doeru-Shugakuin, Yamabana-Morimotocho 12, Kyoto Sakyoku 606, Japan Office: Faculty Sci Kyoto Sangyo U, Kita-ku, Kyoto 603, Japan

YASUTOMI, KIYOYUKI, trading company executive; b. Tokyo, Sept. 30, 1928; d. Shigeto and Aiko Tanaka. BA, Hokkaido (Japan) U., 1952; MA, U. Chgo., 1954, postgrad., 1955; postgrad., Colombia U., 1956. Pres. Kiyo, Inc., Tokyo, 1965-77; pres. M.E.I. Japan, Inc., Tokyo, 1978—, also bd. dirs.; bd. dirs. Far East Fine Arts, Inc., Tokyo. Home: 2-26-14 Higashi, Yukigaya, Ohta-ku, Tokyo 145, Japan Office: MEI Japan Inc, Sanyo Blv 6-F, Shinjuku-ku, Tokyo Japan

YATES, ALDEN PERRY, engineering and construction company executive; b. Los Angeles, July 12, 1928; s. John Perry and Sybill Norma (Kerr) Y.; m. Dawn Blacker, Dec. 16, 1950; children: Stephen, Michael, Karen, Jeffrey, Russell, Patricia. B.S.C.E., Stanford U., 1951. Field engr. Bechtel Corp., San Francisco, 1953-70; v.p. Bechtel Power Corp., San Francisco, 1970-75; v.p., dep. div. mgr. Internat. Bechtel, Inc., Kuwait City, Kuwait, 1975-78, Bechtel Overseas Corp., London, 1978-80; pres. Bechtel Petroleum, Inc., Houston, 1980-83, Bechtel Group, Inc., San Francisco, 1983—; dir. 1st City Bancorp. of Tex., Inc.; chmn., dir. Bechtel Western Power Corp., Bechtel Eastern Power Corp., Bechtel Inc., Bechtel Nat. Inc., Bechtel Civil Inc. Served to lt. j.g. USCG, 1951-53. Republican. Clubs: Pacific Union (San Francisco); San Francisco Golf. Office: Bechtel Group Inc Box 3965 50 Beale St San Francisco CA 94119 also: Bechtel Western Power Corp 12440 E Imperial Hwy Box 60860 Norwalk CA 90060 *

YATES, DANIEL LOUIS, management consultant; b. Berchem, Antwerp, Belgium, Dec. 2, 1952; s. Edward James and Rosa Magdalena (Huylebroeck) Y.; m. Irene Philma Eklim-Jaboh, Nov. 24, 1981; 1 child, Gary Edward Eklim. EDP Audit, U. Faciliteiten Sint Ignatius Antwerpen, 1984; EDP Functional Design, Cath. U. Leuven, Belgium, 1987. Registered mgmt. cons. Materials requirements planning controller Fluor Belgium N.V., Antwerp, 1974-76, Lummus CE Gmbh, Speyer, Fed. Republic Germany, 1976-77, Foster Wheeler GB, Abadan, Iran, 1978-79, Williams Bros., Sharjah, United Arab Emirates, 1979; mgmt. cons. trainer Alexander Proudfoot Group Cos., Brussels, Paris, London, 1979-80; sr. cons. IMPAC Ltd., London and Dublin, Ireland, 1980-82; internal auditor, cons. Stella Artois Belgium, Enugu, Nigeria, 1982-83; sr. cons. Syn-Cronamics Internat. Ltd., London, 1984-86; mng. dir. YSA Mgmt. Services, London and Brussels, 1986—; registered mem. panel experts The Crown Agts. for Overseas Govts. and Adminstrns., London, 1984. Hon. sec. Brit.-Belgian Social Club, Antwerp, 1983; founder, mem. Antwerp Brit. Conservative Party, 1986. Served with Brit. Armed Forces, 1971-74. Fellow Inst. Mgmt. Specialists, Inst. Sales and Mktg. Mgmt.; mem. Inst. Mgmt. Cons. (assoc.), Brit. Inst. Mgmt., Assn. Productivity Specialists, Internat. Inst. Accts. Mem. Ch. Eng. Clubs: PKE, Chibmans. Lodge: Royal Brit. Legion. Home: Ter Beke 14, B-2520 Edegem Antwerp, Belgium Office: YSA Mgmt Services, 3 Munster Mews, 323 Lillie Rd, London SW6 7LJ, England

YATES, PETER, director, producer; b. July 24, 1929; s. Robert L. and Constance Yates; m. Virginia Pope; 3 children. Student, Royal Acad. of Dramatic Art. Entered film industry 1956. Films directed: Summer Holiday, 1962, One Way Pendulum, 1964, Robbery, 1966, Bullitt, 1968, John and Mary, 1969, Murphy's War, 1970, The Hot Rock, 1971, The Friends of Eddie Coyle, 1972, For Pete's Sake, 1973, Mother, Jugs and Speed, 1975, The Deep, 1976; dir., producer Breaking Away, 1979, (nominated Acad. award 1980), Eyewitness, 1980, Krull, 1982, The Dresser, 1983 (nominated Acad. award 1984), Eleni, 1985, The House on Carroll Street, 1986, Suspect, 1987; theatre dir. The American Dream, 1961, The Death of Bessie Smith, 1961, Passing Game, 1977, Interpreters, 1985. Address: care Mr Sam Cohn ICM Inc 40 W 57th St New York NY 10019

YATSEVITCH, GRATIAN MICHAEL, retired army officer, diplomat, engineer; b. Kiev, Russia, Nov. 16, 1911; s. Michael Gratian and Margaret (Thomas) Y.; A.B., Harvard U., 1933, M.A., 1934, postgrad. (J.B. Woodworth fellow), 1935-40; m. Barbara Stewart Franks, July 2, 1973; children by previous marriage—Gael Yatsevitch McKibben, Peter, Kara, Gratian. Mining engr. Zlot Mines Ltd., also Beshina Gold Mines Ltd. of London in Yugoslavia, 1935-40, mgr. gold mine, 1936-40; commd. 2d lt. field arty.-U.S. Army, 1933, advanced through grades to col., 1951; chief cannon and aircraft armament br. devel. prodn. cannon, Office of Chief of Ordnance, 1940-45; mil. attache, Moscow, 1945-46; U.S. del. Allied Control Commn., Sofia, Bulgaria, 1946-47; mil. attache, Sofia, 1947-49; attache and spl. asst. to U.S. Ambassador, Turkey, 1952-53, Iran, 1957-63; sr. staff officer, Washington, 1950-52, 53-57; ret., 1969; hon. chmn. Star Trading and Marine Co., Washington; econ. cons. Middle E. Decorated Legion of Merit with oak leaf cluster. Clubs: Met. (Washington); Carlton, Lansdowne (London); Camden Yacht. Contbr. articles on arty. and mineral. subjects to mags. Home: Easterly Shermans Point Camden ME 04843 Office: Suite 450 1050 17th St NW Washington DC 20036

YAU, STEPHEN SIK-SANG, computer scientist, electrical engineering educator; b. Wusei, Kiangsu, China, Aug. 6, 1935; came to U.S., 1958, naturalized, 1968; s. Pen-Chi and Wen-Chum (Shum) Y.; m. Vickie Liu, June 14, 1964; children: Andrew, Philip. B.S. in Elec. Engring, Nat. Taiwan U., China, 1958; M.S. in Elec. Engring, U. Ill., Urbana, 1959, Ph.D., 1961. Research asst. elec. engring. lab. U. Ill., Urbana, 1959-61; asst. prof. elec. engring. Northwestern U., Evanston, Ill., 1961-64, asso. prof., 1964-68, prof., 1968-88, prof. computer scis., 1970-88, Walter P. Murphy prof. Elec. Engring. and Computer Sci., 1986-88, also chmn. dept. computer scis., 1972-77; chmn. dept. elec. engring. and computer sci. Northwestern U., 1977-88; prof. computer and info. sci, chmn. dept., dir. Software Engring. Research Ctr. U. Fla., Gainesville, 1988—; Conf. chmn. IEEE Computer Conf., Chgo., 1967; symposium chmn. Symposium on feature extraction and selection in pattern recognition Argonne Nat. Lab., 1970; gen. chmn. Nat. Computer Conf., Chgo., 1974, First Internat. Computer Software and Applications Conf., Chgo., 1977; Trustee Nat. Electronics Conf., Inc., 1965-68; chmn. organizing com 11th World Computer Congress, Internat. Fedn. Info. Processing, San Francisco, 1989. Editor-in-chief Computer mag., 1981-84; contbr. numerous articles on computer sci., elec. engring. and related fields to profl. pubs. Recipient Louis E. Levy medal Franklin Inst., 1963, Golden Plate award Am. Acad. of Achievement, 1964. Fellow IEEE (mem. governing bd. Computer Soc. 1967-76, pres. 1974-75, dir. Inst. 1976-77; Richard E. Merwin award Computer Soc. 1981, Centennial medal 1984, Extraordinary Achievement 1985, Outstanding Contbn. award Computer Sci. Soc. 1985), AAAS, Franklin Inst.; mem. Assn. for Computing Machinery, Soc. for Indsl. and Applied Math., Am. Soc. for Engring. Edn., Am. Fedn. Info.-Processing Socs. (mem. exec. com. 1974-76, 79-82, dir. 1972-82, chmn. awards com. 1979-82, v.p. 1982-84, pres. 1984-86; chmn. Nat. Computer Conf. Bd. 1982-83), Sigma Xi, Tau Beta Pi, Eta Kappa Nu, Pi Mu Epsilon. Home: 2609 Noyes St Evanston IL 60201 Office: U Fla Computer and Info Sci Dept Room 301 Computer Sci and Engring Bldg Gainesville FL 32611

YAW, CHARLES EDWARD, quality control manager; b. Battle Creek, Mich., Nov. 12, 1938; s. Victor Lenard and Brittie (Parker) Y.; m. Phyllis Thayer, Apr. 16, 1961 (div. Oct. 1965); children: Shelly, Cyntha; m. Audrey M. Howell, May 12, 1967; children: Chalres E. II, Debra A., Robert J. BS in Quality Control Engring., Kellogg Community Coll., 1960. Quality control leader Tex. Aluminum, Mojave, Calif., 1967-72; shift supr. Cadillac Plastics, Kalamazoo, 1972-73; shift foreman Swanson Pipe Co., Phoenix, 1973-76; electrician's asst. Thermoliac Systems, Phoenix, 1976-77; mgr. quality control Ariz. Aluminum Co., Phoenix, 1977—; bd. dirs. 47 Place, Phoenix, Almex, Phoenix. Mem. ASTM, Am. Soc. Quality Control (cert.). Democrat. Roman Catholic. Home: 5137 W Vogel Glendale AZ 85302 Office: Easco Aluminum 249 S 51 Ave PO Box 6736 Phoenix AZ 85005

YAWORSKY, GEORGE MYROSLAW, physicist, technical and management consultant; b. Aug. 4, 1940; s. Myroslaw and Mary (Yaworsky) Y.; m. Zenia Maria Smishkewych, Sept. 9, 1972; 1 dau., Maria Diana. B.S. in Physics, Rensselaer Poly. Inst., 1962, M.B.A., 1977, Ph.D. in Physics, 1979; M.S. in Physics, Carnegie-Mellon U., 1964. Physicist Republic Steel Research Ctr., Independence, Ohio, 1966-68; tech. and mgmt. cons. in ops. research, mktg. analyses, computer modeling, sci. programming and other areas to state govt., pvt. cos., 1972-81; internat. tech. assessment and analysis cons. EG&G, Inc., Rockville, Md., 1981-82; program dir.-computer integrated mfg. Eagle Research Group, Arlington, Va., 1982-83; prin. investigator high volume mfg. Sci. Applications, Inc., McLean, Va., 1983-84; cons. computer integrated mfg., materials sci., tech. transfer and mgmt., 1984—; mem. U.S. del. to Coordinating Com. for Multilateral Export Controls, Paris, 1982. Contbr. articles to profl. jours. Recipient Physics Teaching award Rensselaer Poly. Inst., 1971; John Huntington scholar; Rensselaer Alumni scholar. Mem. N.Y. Acad. Scis., Robotics Internat. of Soc. Mfg. Engrs. (sr.), Computer and Automated Systems Assn. of Soc. Mfg. Engrs. (sr., chmn. Greater Washington chpt. 1985—), Am. Phys. Soc., Am. Assn. Physics Tchrs., Am. Prodn. and Inventory Control Soc., AAAS, Rensselaer Alumni Assn., Am. Assn. for Artificial Intelligence, Robotic Industries Assn., Internat. Platform Assn., Sigma Xi. Office: 2000 S Eads St Arlington VA 22202

YAZKULIYEV, BALLY YAZKULIYEVICH, Soviet government official; b. 1930. Grad. Tchrs. Inst. in Tashauz, 1949, Pedagogical Inst., Khardzhou, 1952, CPSU Central Com. Party Higher Sch., 1962. Tchr., 1949-52; held Komsomol posts, 1952-60; held state, Party, trade union and econ. posts, 1962-71; mem. auditing com. CP Turkmenistan, 1966-71; chmn. Oblast Exec. Com. of People's Depts. in Tashauz, 1971-73; dep. to Supreme Soviet Turkmen SSR, 1971—; mem. Central Com., 1971—, candidate mem. Bur. Central Com., 1975, Bureau Central Com. CP Turkmenistan, 1975—; chmn. Turkmen Republican Trade Union Council, 1973-75; chmn. Council of Ministers and Fgn. Minister Turkmen SSR, 1975-78; mem. Central Auditing Com. CPSU, 1976-81; chmn. Presidium of Supreme Soviet Turkmen SSR, 1978—; dep. chmn. Presidium of USSR Supreme Soviet, 1979—; candidate mem. Central Com. CPSU, 1981—. Address: USSR Soviet Presidium, The Kremlin, Moscow USSR *

YAZOV, DMITRI TIMOFEEVICH, Soviet military official; b. 1923. Grad., M.V. Miltary Acad., 1956, Mil. Acad. Gen. Staff, 1967. Entered Soviet Army, 1941, served at front, 1941-45, various command posts, 1945-76; 1st dep. comdr. troops Far Ea. Mil. Dist. 1976-79; comdr. Cen. Group Forces Czechoslovakia, 1979-80; dep. to USSR Supreme Soviet, 1979—; comdr. troops Cen. Asian Mil. Dist. 1980—; mem. cen. com., mem. bur. cen. com. Kazakh Communist Party, 1981—; candidate mem. cen. com. Communist Party Soviet Union, 1981—; dep. minister def. Moscow, 1987, minister def., 1987—. Address: Ministry of Def, Moscow USSR *

YCASIANO, ARISTEO TANTOCO, textile manufacturing company executive; b. Manila, Aug. 12, 1916; s. Francisco Roxas and Lagrimas Martinez (Tantoco) Y.; m. Elisabeth Kaiho Scheerer, June 11, 1939 (dec. Oct. 1983); children—Francis, Robin, Dennis, Philip. B.S. in Indsl. Tech., Ateneo de Manila, 1938. Research asst. Bur. Sci., Manila, 1938-39; chief chemist United Dairies, Inc., Manila, 1939-41, La Tondena Distillery, Manila, 1945-47; mem. faculty Avaneta Inst. Agr., Manila, 1947-49; research chemist Ramie Devel. corp., Manila, 1949-53; chief research and devel. Philippine Packing Corp., Manila, 1954-57; sr. v.p., gen. mgr. Ramie Textiles, Inc., Manila, 1957—, also dir.; chmn. adv. com. to Philippine Textile Research Inst., Manila, 1978-81. Sch. chmn. Namfrel, Valenzuela, Philippines, 1984; mem. exec. Boy Scouts of Philippines, Valenzuela chpt., 1976-78; v.p., adviser C. of C. and Industry of Valenzuela, 1974-77. Research and devel. processes ramie fiber contributed to industry growth in Philippines. Mem. Nat. Research Council of Philippines, Employers Confedn. of Philippines. Lodges: Rotary (pres. 1976-78), K.C. (grand knight 1981-82). Avocations: jogging; swimming. Office: Ramie Textiles, Inc, Bagbaguin, Valenzuela, Manila Philippines

YDE, JENS, banker; b. Thisted, Denmark, Jan. 8, 1943; s. Carl and Elna (Hedeholm) Y.; m. Karen Bodil Andersen; children: Lars, Lise, Soeren. Asst. A/S H&L Bank, Thisted, Denmark, 1960-68, asst. mgr., 1968-79, mgr., 1979—. Mem. The Conservative Party (local chmn. 1978-80), Thisted Community High Sch. (bd. dirs. 1973—), Thisted Tourist Assn. (bd. dirs 1980—). Office: A/S H&L Banken, Jernbanegade 7A, 7700 Thisted Denmark

YEAGER, ANSON ANDERS, columnist, former newspaper editor; b. Salt Lake City, June 5, 1919; s. Charles Franklin and Elise Marie (Thingelstad) Y.; m. Ada May Bidwell, Sept. 10, 1944; children—Karen Ann, Anson Anders, Harry H., Terry Douglas, Ellen Elise. B.S., S.D. State U.-Brookings, 1947; LL.D., Dakota State Coll., Madison, S.D., 1972. Printer's devil, linotype operator Faith Ind. and Gazette (S.D.), 1935-38; printer S.D. State U., 1940-41; staff writer Argus Leader, Sioux Falls, S.D., 1947-55, Sunday editor, 1955-60, exec. editor, 1961-77, assoc. editor, 1978-84, editor editorial page, 1961-84, columnist, 1984—, author editorials and column of commentary; lectr. dept. journalism U. S.D., 1953-55. Contbr. World Book Ency., 1966—. Bd. dirs. Sioux Falls Devel. Found., 1967; dir. Sioux council Boy Scouts Am., Sioux Falls, 1967-72, v.p., 1970-72; bd. dirs. Boys' Club of Sioux Falls, 1966-68. Served to capt. U.S. Army, 1942-46, 50-52; lt. col. Res. (ret.). Decorated Army Commendation medal; recipient Editorial Excellence award William Allen White Found., 1976; Disting. Alumni award S.D. State U., 1980; Ralph D. Casey Minn. award for Disting. Service in Journalism U. Minn., 1981, Eminent Service award East River Elec. Power Coop., 1984, Mass Communications award S.D. State U., 1985, Disting. Service award S.D. Press Assn., 1988. Mem. Sioux Falls Area C. of C. (dir. 1967-70), Am. Soc. Newspaper Editors, S.D. AP Mng. Editors (Newsman of Yr. award 1978, Les Helgeland Community Service award 1985), Sigma Delta Chi. Republican. Methodist. Lodge: Rotary.

YEAMANS, GEORGE THOMAS, library science and telecommunications educator, consultant; b. Richmond, Va., Nov. 7, 1929; s. James Norman and Dolphine Sophia (Manhart) Y.; m. Mary Ann Seng, Feb. 1, 1958; children—Debra, Susan, Julia. A.B., U. Va., 1950; M.S.L.S., U. Ky., 1955; Ed.D., Ind. U., 1965. Asst. audio-visual dir. Ind. State U., Terre Haute, 1957-58; asst. film librarian Ball State U., Muncie, Ind., 1958-61, film librarian, 1961-69, assoc. prof. library sci., 1969-72, prof., 1972—; cons. Pendleton (Ind.) Sch. Corp., 1962, 67, Captioned Films for the Deaf Workshop, Muncie, Ind., 1963, 64, 65, Decatur (Ind.) Sch. System, 1978; adjudicator Ind. Media Fair, 1979-88. Author: Projectionists' Programmed Primer, 1969, rev. edit., 1982; Mounting and Preserving Pictorial Materials, 1976; Tape Recording, 1978; Transparency Making, 1977; Photographic Principles, 1981; Computer Literacy—A Programmed Primer, 1985; contbr. articles to profl. jours. Campaign worker Wilson for Mayor, Muncie, Ind., 1979. Served with USMC, 1950-52. Recipient Citations of Achievement, Internat. Biog. Assn., Cambridge, Eng., 1973, Am. Biog. Assn., 1976, Mayor James P. Carey award for achievement for disting. contbns. to Ball State U. and City of Muncie, 1988. Mem. NEA (del. assembly dept. audiovisual instrn. 1967), Am. Film Inst., ALA, Audio-Visual Instrn. Dirs. Ind. (exec. bd. 1962-68, pres. 1966-67), Ind. Assn. Ednl. Communications and Tech. (dist. dir. 1972-75), Assn. Ind. Media Educators (chmn. auditing com. 1979-81), Internat. TV Assn., Am. Film Inst., Phi Delta Kappa. Republican. Unitarian. Club: Catalina (Muncie). Home: 4507 W Burton Dr Muncie IN 47304 Office: Ball State U Muncie IN 47306

YEANG, KENNETH KING-MUN, architect; b. Penang, Malaysia, Oct. 6, 1948; s. Cheng-Hin and Yeut-Kuen (Chung) Y.; m. Priscilla Pit-Ling, Nov. 18, 1986. AA, Archtl. Assn. Sch., London, 1972; PhD, Cambridge U., 1981. Prin. T.R. Hamzah & Yeang SDN BHD Architects, Malaysia, 1976—. Principle works include Malaysia Roof-Roof House, 1984, Malaysian IBM Plaza, 1987; author: Tropical Verandah City, 1987, Tropical Urban Regionalism, 1987. Mem. Malaysia Inst. Architects (pres. 1983-87), Commonwealth Assn. Architects (v.p. 1983-87, Sir Robert Matthew award 1987), Architects Regional Council Asia (chmn. bd. dirs. 1987-88). Club: Royal Selangor Golf (Kuala Lumpur). Lodge: Baldwin Lowick. Office: TR Hamzah & Yeang SDN BHD, #8 Jalan 1, Taman Sri Ukay, 68000 Ampang Selangor Malaysia

YEE, CHE FONG, international trade expert; b. Selangor, Malaysia, July 14, 1942; s. Yee Choy and Lum (Foong) Y.; m. Lin Kwee, Nov. 11, 1967; children: Tuck Meng, Tuck Sun, Mei Ping. BA in Econs. with honors, U. Malaya, 1964. Sr. official Ministry Trade and Industry, Malaysia, 1965-74, head internat. trade, 1975-76; CFTC regional trade expert Dept. Trade, Canberra, 1981—; chief del. of Malaysia to GATT MIN (Tokyo Round), 1976-80; rep. of Malaysia to UNCTAD and GATT, 1976-80; minister econs. Permanent Mission to UN, Geneva, 1976-80; cons. UNDP, 1981, UNCTAP, 1986, 87. Decorated Order of Chivalry (Malaysia). Buddhist. Home: 37 Laycock Pl, Holt, Canberra 2615, Australia Office: Dept Fgn Affairs and Trade, Barton, Canberra 2600, Australia

YEE, PHILLIP KOON HIN, engineer; b. Honolulu, Feb. 19, 1916; s. Sheong and Shee (Leong) Y.; m. Maybelle W.Y. Lee, May 6, 1939; children—Curtis Q.H., Gary Q.L., Stephen Q.S. B.S. in Civil Engring., U. Hawaii, 1938. Registered profl. engr., Hawaii. Sports cartoonist Honolulu Star-Bull., 1934-45; planning draftsman Territorial Planning Bd., Honolulu, 1938-39; civil engr. U.S. Engrs. Office, Honolulu, 1940-41, head water supply sect., 1941-45; asst. supt. Suburban Water System, City and County Honolulu, 1945-60; engr. P. Yee & Assocs. Inc., Honolulu, 1960—; pres. Ala Moana Investment Corp., Honolulu, 1960-65, Intercontinental Corp., Honolulu, 1965-70; dir. Phillip K.H. Yee & Assocs., Honolulu. Mem. Cons. Engrs. Council Trade Mission IV, S.E. Asia, 1968; mem., citizen ambassador People to People waste water mgmt. delegation People's Republic of China, 1983. Recipient Cert. of Appreciation, U.S. Dept. Commerce, Washington, 1968. Mem. Cons. Engrs. Council, Am. Security Council, U.S. Congl. Adv. Bd. (state advisor). Astarian, Ashtar Command. Club: Engring. Assocs. (Honolulu). Home: 1885 Paula Dr Honolulu HI 96816 Office: Phillip KH Yee & Assocs Inc 243 Liluokalani AVe Honolulu HI 96815

YEGANEH, ALI, film director, cinematographer; b. Bijar, Iran, Aug. 11, 1952; s. Oasat and Moulouk (Najafian) Y. MFA, So. Meth. U., 1977; PhD in Philosophy, U. Paris, Nanterre, France, 1983. Freelance film dir., cinematographer 1977—. Dir. documentaries include Illustration, Agoraphobia, Isolation; (fiction) Oxygen, 1980.

YEGGE, ROBERT BERNARD, lawyer, educator; b. Denver, June 17, 1934; s. Ronald Van Kirk and Fairy (Hill) Y. A.B. magna cum laude, Princeton U., 1956; M.A. in Sociology, U. Denver, 1958, J.D., 1959. Bar: Colo. 1959, D.C. 1978. Partner firm Yegge, Hall and Evans, Denver, 1959-78; with Nelson & Harding, 1979—; prof. U. Denver Coll. Law, 1965—, dean, 1965-77, dean emeritus, 1977—; asst. to pres. Denver Post, 1971-75. Author: Colorado Negotiable Instruments Law, 1960, Some Goals; Some Tasks, 1965, The American Lawyer: 1976, 1966, New Careers in Law, 1969, The Law Graduate, 1972, Tomorrow's Lawyer: A Shortage and Challenge, 1974, Declaration of Independence for Legal Education, 1976. Mng. trustee Denver Center for Performing Arts, 1972-75; chmn. Colo. Council Arts and Humanities, 1968-80, chmn. emeritus, 1980—; mem. scholar selection com. Henry Luce Found., 1975—; Active nat. and local A.R.C., chmn. Denver region, 1985—; Trustee Denver Symphony Soc., Inst. of Ct. Mgmt.; trustee, vice chmn. Nat. Assembly State Arts Agys.; vice chmn. Mexican-Am. Legal Edn. and Def. Fund, 1970-76. Recipient Disting. Service award Denver Jr. C. of C., 1965; Harrison Tweed award Am. Assn. Continuing Edn. Adminstrs., 1985. Mem. Law and Soc. Assn. (life, pres. 1965-70), ABA (chmn. lawyers conf. 1987—, chmn. accreditation commn. for legal assistant programs 1987—), Colo. Bar Assn. (bd. govs. 1965-77), Denver Bar Assn., D.C. Bar Assn., Am. Law Inst., Am. Judicature Soc. (bd. dirs. 1968-72, 75—, Herbert Harley award 1985), Am. Acad. Polit. and Social Sci., Am. Sociol. Soc., Assn. Am. Law Schs., Order St. Ives, Phi Beta Kappa, Beta

Theta Pi, Phi Delta Phi, Alpha Kappa Delta, Omicron Delta Kappa. Home: 4209 W 38th Ave Denver CO 80212

YEH, CHI-TUNG, civil engineer, educator; b. Kaohsiung, Taiwan, Dec. 18, 1936; s. Fu-Yung and Arh-Fong (Shih) Y.; Ph.D. in Civil Engring., U. Wash., 1970; m. Fu-Mei, Sept. 10, 1961; children—I-jun, Chiu-In, Wen-jin, In-chao, Jin-Chin. Chief of design div. Taiwan Area Freeway Constrn. Bur., 1970-76; head dept. constrn. engring. and tech. Nat. Taiwan Inst. Tech., 1976-79; commr. Kaohsiung City Planning Commn., Kaohsiung (Taiwan) City Govt., 1979-82; dir. Grad. Inst. Civil Engring., Tamkang U., Tamsui, Taipei County, Taiwan, 1981-84; cons. C.T. Yeh & Assos., Architects and Engrs.; pres. St. John's and St. Mary's Inst. Tech., 1985—. Mem. Chinese Inst. Engrs. (outstanding young engr. award, 1975), Chinese Inst. Civil and Hydraulic Engring., Chinese Architect Assn. Author book in Chinese: Method of Construction and Technology, 1978. Home: 4th Floor, No 8-1, Lane 560, Kuang-Fu S Rd, Taipei Republic of China Office: 16 Hsien-Hsiao Li, Tamsui,, Taipei County Republic of China

YEH, WALTER HUAI-TEH, educator, composer; b. Shanghai, China, Jan. 7, 1911; came to U.S., 1944, naturalized, 1955; s. Ziang Tsung and Pei-Yu (Huang) Y.; A.B., St. John's U. (China), 1933; grad. summa cum laude Nat. Conservatory of Music (China), 1935; M.A. and Mus. M., Eastman Sch. Music, U. Rochester, 1945; A.M., Harvard, 1948, researcher, 1951-54; Ph.D., U. Rochester, 1949; m. Moong Yue, Aug. 8, 1942; children—Peter Wen-chun, Arthur Cho-chun. Prof. flute Nat. Conservatory of Music, China, 1940-44; prof. music, chmn. joint music dept. Allen U and Benedict Coll., Columbia, S.C., 1954-81, prof. music Allen U., 1954-85, chmn. humanities div. Allen U., 1957-60, 63-79, chmn. div. fine arts and drama Benedict Coll., 1968-71, 72-74, interim pres. Allen U., 1973. Bd. dirs. Columbia Lyric Theatre, 1972-75. Fellow Internat. Inst. Arts and Letters. Club: Rotary. Composer: Concerto Grosso in F for Oboe, String Quartet and Harp with String Orchestra, 1944; Symphony in D, 1944; Chinese Suite, 1945; Chinese Symphony, 1948; (madrigal) Come Away, Come Away, Death!, 1957; The Cuckoo Chorus, 1958; Hymn for Peace, 1960; And Ruth Said: Intreat Me Not to Leave Thee, 1962; The Solitary Reaper, 1964; She Never Told Her Love, 1965; This Glorious Christmas Night, 1967; Gloria Patri and Kyrie, 1968; The Pattering Rain, 1968; The Lord's Prayer, 1969; We Shall Overcome, 1970; A Tombstone Epitaph, 1971; Alleuia, May Peace Be on Earth, 1972; Farewell for Ever!, 1972; All Glory, Praise and Honor, 1973; Echoes from on the Great Wall, 1974; He Who Loves God Loves All People, 1975; Last Night, 1975; Oh Slide and Stamp!, 1976; For Dust Thou Art, and Unto Dust Shalt Thou Return, 1977; Think! Think! Think!, 1977; Long, Long Ago, 1977; Farewell Alma Mater Dear! God Be With You Till We Meet Again, 1977; Concerto Ecclesiastico, 1979; Orientalia string quartet, 1980; A Song for the Chinese People, 1981; A Japanese Song, 1982; Doxology in Chinese Style, 1983; Oriental Theme and Variations for String Quartet or String Orch., 1985; Author: An Application of Ancient Chinese Medical Practices to Modern Disease: VD-HIV (AIDS), Cancer, etc with Nature-made, Controlled and Variable Quasi-live Virocine, 1986. Home: 710 Heidt St Columbia SC 29205

YELENICK, MARY THERESE, lawyer; b. Denver, May 17, 1954; d. John Andrew and Maesel Joyce (Reed) Y. B.A. magna cum laude, Colo. Coll., 1976; J.D. cum laude, Georgetown U., 1979. Bar: D.C. 1979, U.S. Dist. Ct. D.C. 1980, U.S. Ct. Appeals (D.C. cir.) 1981, N.Y. 1982, U.S. Dist. Ct. (so. and ea. dists.) N.Y. 1982. Law clk. to presiding justices Superior Ct. D.C., 1979-81; assoc. Chadbourne & Parke, N.Y.C., 1981—. Editor Jour. of Law and Policy Internat. Bus., 1978-79. Mem. Phi Beta Kappa. Democrat. Roman Catholic. Home: 310 E 46th St New York NY 10017 Office: Chadbourne & Parke 30 Rockefeller Plaza New York NY 10112

YENDO, MASAYOSHI, architect; b. Yokohama, Japan, Nov. 30, 1920; s. Masanao and Ima (Nakamura) Y.; m. Fumi Matsuzaki, Dec. 25, 1956; children—Masahiko, Yoshihiko. B.S. in Architecture, Waseda Univ., 1945. With Murano Architect Office, Osaka, 1946-49; pres. M. Yendo Assoc. Architects and Engrs., Tokyo, 1952—. Important works include: 77th Bank Head Office, 1957; Keio Dept. Store, 1960; Yamaguchi Bank Head Office, 1962; Kashoen Hotel, 1962; Yaizu Plant Yamanouchi Pharm. Co., 1967; Coca-Cola Head Office (Japan), 1971; Yakult Head Office, 1972; Heibonsha Head Office, 1972; Tokyo Am. Club, 1972; Taiyo Fishery Co., Ltd. Head Office, 1973; Seiyu Store Kasugai Shopping Ctr., 1975. Recipient Bldg. Contractors Soc. prize, 1965; Minister of Edn. award of art, 1966. Fellow AIA (hon. 1987); mem. Japan Architects Assn. (pres. 1982-86), Archtl. Inst. Japan (councilor, award 1966). Club: Tokyo Am. Office: M Yendo Assocs Architects & Engrs, 5-6 Ginza 8-chome, Tokyo 104 Japan

YESSIOS, CHRIS IOANNIS, architect, educator; b. Edessa, Greece, Aug. 10, 1938; came to U.S., 1968, naturalized, 1979; s. Ioannis C. and Aikaterini (Papachristou) Y.; m. Alexandra Varsamis, Sept. 1, 1971; children: Yiannis, Katerina, Dorina, Christina. Diploma in Law, Aristotelian U., Thesaloniki, Greece, 1962, diploma in Architecture, 1967; Ph.D., Carnegie-Mellon U., 1973. Tech. dir., ptnr. Gorgoi Workshop for Interior Designs and Popular Crafts, Athens and Thessaloniki, Greece, 1960-62, with various archtl. and planning firms, 1962-73, pvt. practice architecture specializing in single family houses and apt. bldgs., Thessaloniki and Columbus, Ohio, 1974—; teaching asst. dept. urban affairs U. Pitts., 1968; teaching and research assoc. dept. architecture Carnegie-Mellon U., 1969-71, lectr., 1971-73; asst. prof. architecture Ohio State U., 1973-79, assoc. prof. architecture and computer-aided design, 1979-83, prof., 1983—, cons. in computer-aided design and computer graphics techiques for practice architecture and planning, 1975—. Research publs. and presentations in field; author user manuals of implemented systems. Recipient Best Research Paper Contest citation 15th Design Automation Conf., Las Vegas, Nev., 1978, Mayor's prize for Vernacular Theme Mayor Thessaloniki, 1962; IBM grantee, 1982-85; NSF grantee, 1986—. Mem. Greek Inst. Architects, Tech. Chamber Greece, Environ. Design and Research Assn., Design Methods Group, Assn. Computer Aided Design in Architecture (pres. 1983-84), Assn. Computing Machinery, Spl. Interest Group for Computer Graphics, Spl. Interest Group for Design Automation, Nat. Computer Graphics Assn., Anatolia Coll. Alumni Assn., Carnegie-Mellon U. Alumni Assn. Greek Orthodox. Current Work: Development of innovative techniques for use of computer (primarily computer graphics) in environmental design (computer-aided architectural design). Subspecialties: Graphics, image processing, architectural/void modeling, expert systems, and pattern recognition; Computer-aided design. Home: 4740 Shire Ridge Rd E Columbus OH 43026 Office: Dept Architecture Ohio State U 190 W 17th Ave Columbus OH 43210

YETGINER, ORHAN, manufacturing company executive; b. Samsun, Turkey, Mar. 3, 1935; s. Ihsan and Hamdiye Yetginer; m. Sibel Çulha, Sept. 14, 1978; 1 child, Gülin. MSME, Tech. U. Istanbul, Turkey, 1961; MBA, Mich. State U., 1973. Product mgr. Gümüs Motor Factory, Istanbul, Turkey, 1961-62; mil. service, tchr. Turkish Navy, Istanbul, 1962-64; researcher Tech. U. Istanbul, 1964-66; propr. Engring. Co., Samsun, 1966-70; specialist Koç Holding A.S., Istanbul, 1973-76; gen. mgr. Ersu Meyve ve Gida Sanayii A.S., Istanbul, 1976-77, Kav Orman Sanayii A.S., Istanbul, 1977—. Mem. Am. Soc. Heating Refrigerating and Air-Conditioning Engrs. (assoc.). Moslem. Home: I Levent Sümbül Sokak 21, Istanbul Turkey Office: Kav Orman Sanayii AS, Istiklâl Cad 347/3, Beyoğlu, Istanbul Turkey

YETT, FOWLER REDFORD, mathematics educator; b. Johnson City, Tex., Oct. 18, 1919; s. James William, Sr. and Rebecca Jane (Stribling) Y.; B.S. in Chem. Engring. (Univ. scholar), U. Tex., Austin, 1943, M.A. in Math., 1952; Ph.D., Iowa State U., 1955; m. Mary Sue Lyttle, June 17, 1945 (div. 1977); children—Jane Marie, Rebecca YettRoot, Mary Wester Yett Coutts. Research chemist, research chem. engr. Manhattan Project, U. Chgo., 1943-44, Richland, Wash., 1944-45, Dow Chem. Co., Freeport, Tex., 1945; owner, mgr. Camera Supplies of Houston, 1946-49; teaching fellow math. U. Tex., Austin, 1949-52, asst. prof., 1956-65; instr. math. Iowa State U., Ames, 1952-55; asst. prof. math. Long Beach (Calif.) State Coll., 1955-56; prof. math. U. So. Ala., Mobile, 1965—, chmn. dept., 1965-68; sr. research engr. N.Am. Aviation, Inc., Downey, Calif., summers 1956-57, 59; faculty research asso. Boeing Co., Seattle, summer 1958; pres. Dr. Fowler Redford Yett & Daus., Inc., Dr. Yett's Oil Co., Dr. Yett's Royal Chinese Herb Co. Active all Lyndon Baines Johnson election campaigns, 1937-68. Recipient Excellence in Teaching awards U. Tex., Austin, 1958, U. So. Ala., Mobile, 1975. Mem. Am. Math. Soc.; life mem. Tau Beta Pi, Omega Chi Epsilon, Phi Lambda Upsilon, Phi Eta Sigma, Pi Mu Epsilon. Methodist (tchr. Sunday sch. 1970-71). Home: 660 N Merritt Dr Mobile AL 36609 Office: Math Dept U So Ala Mobile AL 36688

YEUNG, CHAP-YUNG, pediatrics educator; b. Hong Kong, Dec. 29, 1936; s. Him and Lai-Yin (Pang) Y.; m. Helen Kwan-sik Chiu; children—Rae Sukman, Jane Suk-Cheung. M.B., B.S., U. Hong Kong, 1961. Cons. pediatrician Queen Elizabeth Hosp., Hong Kong, 1970-72; asst. prof. pediatrics McMaster U., Can., 1972, assoc. dir. neonatal services, 1974-76; cons. Scarborough Centenary Hosp., Ont., Can., 1977-80, Govt. of Hong Kong, 1980—; prof., chair dept. pediatrics U. Hong Kong, 1980—; hon. adviser Assn. Child Health and Devel., 1985—, Spastics Assn. Hong Kong, 1985—, Beijing-Hong Kong Acad. Exchange Ctr.; v.p. Hong Kong Coll. Physicians, 1987—. Commonwealth med. scholar, 1966-68; Commonwealth fellow, Melbourne, 1970. Fellow Royal Coll. Physicians Can., Royal Coll. Physicians Edinburgh and Glasgow; mem. Assn. Maternal and Neonatal Health (pres. 1984—), Internat. Coll. Pediatricians, Brit. Pediatric Assn., Can. Med. Assn., Hong Kong Med. Assn. Home: 350 Victoria Rd, #C-9, Hong Kong Hong Kong Office: U Hong Kong, Queen Mary Hosp, Dept Pediatrics, Hong Kong Hong Kong

YEUNG, CHUN SING ANDY, bank executive; b. Hong Kong, Aug. 27, 1955; s. Yee Hing and Kam Lin (Tse) Y.; m. Mo Ching Agnes Ip; 1 child, Hoi Lam Helena. MBA, Calif. Coast U., 1988. Remittance clk. Bank Am. NT & SA, Hong Kong, 1973-77; supr. Chase Manhattan Bank, Hong Kong, 1977-80, prodn. controller, 1980-81, money transfer dept. mgr., 1981-83; ops. and systems mgr. Chase Manhattan Trust Co., Hong Kong, 1983-87; mgr. ops., controller, v.p. BT Brokerage (Asia) Ltd., Hong Kong, 1987—. Fellow Brit. Soc. Commerce, Inst. Commerce; mem. Assn. Cost Exec. Accts. (assoc.), Brit. Inst. Mgmt., Inst. Adminstrv. Accts. (assoc.), Inst. Adminstrv. Mgmt. Club: Pacific. Home: 38 Cloud View Rd, Evelyn Towers 3/F Flat G Hong Kong Office: Chase Manhattan Bank, 30/F Admiralty Ctr, Tower 1 Hong Kong

YEUNG, PHILIP KIN CHOD, electronic manufacturing company executive; b. People's Republic of China, Nov. 2, 1949; s. Lin Chin and Tai Min Yeung; m. Mei Foon Lam, Mar. 30, 1977; children: Allan, Doris. MBA, U. East Asia, Macau, 1986. Chief acct. China Translation and Printing Services Ltd., Hong Kong, 1969-73; chief fin. officer, dep. mng. dir. Kras Asia Ltd., Kowloon, Hong Kong, 1973—; also bd. dirs. Kras Asid Ltd., Kowloon, Hong Kong. Mem. Brit. Inst. Mgmt., Inst. Mktg. Home: Suite 3012, Block E, Kornhill Garden, Quarry Bay Hong Kong

YEVTUSHENKO, YEVGENIY ALEKSANDROVICH, poet; b. Zima, Irkutsk Region, USSR, July 18, 1933; student Gorky Literary Inst., 1951-54; m. Bella Akhmadulina, 1954; m 2d, Galina Semyonova; m. 3d, Jan Butler, 1978; 1 child. Geol. expeditions to Kazakhstan, 1948, The Altai, 1950; author: (verse) includes Scouts of the Future, 1952, The Third Snow, 1955, The Highway of Enthusiasts, 1956, Zima Junction, 1956, The Promise, 1959, Conversation with a Count, Moscow Goods Station, At the Skorokhod Plant, The Nihilist, The Apple, 1960-61, A Sweep of the Arm, 1962, Tenderness, 1962, A Precocious Autobiography, 1963, Cashier, Woman, Mother, On the Banks of the Dnieper River, A Woman and A Girl, Do the Russians Want War?, Bratskaya Hydro-Electric Power Station, 1965, A Boat of Communication, 1966, Poems Chosen by the Author, 1966, Collection of Verses, 1967, That's What Is Happening to Me, 1968, It's Snowing White, 1969, I am of Siberian Stock, 1971, Stolen Apples, 1972, A Father's Hearing, 1976, From Desire to Desire, 1976, Love Poems, 1977, People of the Morning, 1978, Heavy Soils, 1978, Winter Station, 1978, The Face Behind the Face, 1979, Ivan the Terrible, 1979, Ivan the Fool, 1979; books of poetry: Longbow and Lyre, 1959, Poems of Several Years, 1959; (play) Under the Skin of the Statue of Liberty, 1972; (novel) Wild Berries, 1981; mem. editorial bd. Yunost mag.; appeared in film Ascent, 1979; dir. film Kindergarten, 1984. Recipient USSR Com. for Def. of Peace award, 1965, USSR State prize, 1984; decorated Order of Red Banner of Labour. Office: Union of USSR Writers, ul Vorovskogo 52, Moscow USSR *

YIANNOPOULOS, ATHANASSIOS NICHOLAS, legal educator; b. Thessaloniki, Greece, Mar. 13, 1928; came to U.S., 1953, naturalized, 1963; s. Nicholas A. and Areti T. (Alvanos) Y.; m. Mirta Valdes, May 9, 1982; children—Maria, Nicholas, Alexander. LL.B., U. Thessaloniki, 1950; M.C.L., U. Chgo., 1954; LL.M. (Walter Perry Johnson fellow in law), U. Calif., Berkeley, 1955, J.S.D., 1956; J.D., U. Cologne, W. Ger., 1961. Bar: Greece 1958. Mem. faculty La. State U., Baton Rouge, 1958-79; W.R. Irby prof. law Tulane U. Law Sch., New Orleans, 1979—; in charge revision La. Civil Code, Law Inst., 1962—. Author: Civil Law Property, 2d edit, 1980, Personal Servitudes, 2d edit, 1978, Predial Servitudes, 1983; (with T. Schoenbaum) Admiralty and Maritime Law, 1984; editor: Louisiana Civil Code, annually 1980—; contbr.: articles to various periodicals Ency. Brit. Pres. Baton Rouge Symphony Assn., 1972-73; bd. dirs. Music Soc., 1961-79. Served to 2d lt. Greek Army, 1950-53. Mem. Order of Phoenix, Phi Alpha Delta. Mem. Greek Orthodox Ch. Club: Baton Rouge City. Office: Tulane U Sch Law New Orleans LA 70118

YI KUN-MO, premier of Democratic People's Republic of Korea. Mem. Korean Workers Party, Cen. People's Com.; premier Govt. of Dem. People's Republic of Korea, 1987—. Office: Office of Premier, Pyong Yang Democratic People's Republic of Korea *

YILMA, ADAMU BELAY, manufacturing executive; b. Addis Ababa, Ethiopia; s. Belay and Kibasework Adamu; m. Kidan Yemane; children: Yared, Estedar, Menilik. BBA, Addis Ababa U., 1971. Asst. mktg. specialist Livestock & Meat Bd., Addis Ababa, 1971-74; adminstrv. officer Ctr. Interpreneurship & Mgmt., Addis Ababa, 1974-75; head adminstrn. tng. Ethopian Printing Corp., Addis Ababa, 1975-78, gen. mgr., 1978-86; gen. mgr. Nat. Leather & Shoe Corp., Addis Ababa, 1986—; chmn. bd. dirs. Ethiopian Pulp & Paper Co., 1979-86. Bd. dirs. Nat. Lottery Aminstrn., 1980—. Mem. Addis Ababa C. of C. (bd. dirs. 1983-85, pres. 1985-87), Ethiopian C. of C. (v.p. 1985-87). Office: Nat Leather & Shoe Corp, Addis Ababa, Shoa Ethiopia

YILMAZ, AHMET MESUT, minister of foreign affairs; b. Istanbul, Turkey, Nov. 6, 1947; s. Hasan and Güzide (özbarlas) Y.; m. Berna Müren; children: Yavuz, Hasan. Student, Siyasal Bilgiler Fakültesi, Turkey. Minister of state, govt. spokesman Republic of Turkey, Ankara, 1983-86, minister of culture and tourism, 1986-87, minister of foreign affairs, 1987—. Served to 2d lt. Turkish Gendarmerie, 1975. Mem. Anavatan Partisi (Motherland Party). Clubs: Galatasaray, Büyük, Anadolu.

YING, SHUH-PAN, acoustician, physicist, consultant, researcher; b. Shaohsing, China, July 12, 1929; came to U.S., 1960, naturalized, 1972; s. Hok-Song and Yen-Yun (Fan) Y.; m. Tienchu Chen, Sept. 23, 1956; children—Ramona, John, William. B.S. in Physics, Nat. Taiwan U., Republic of China, 1959; M.S. in Physics, U. Mass., 1962; Ph.D. in Physics, U. Mich., 1969. Registered profl. engr., N.Y., Mich., N.C. Sr. research engr. Southwest Research Inst., San Antonio, 1970-76; project mgr., prin. cons. Gilbert/Commonwealth, Jackson, Mich., 1976-84, sect. mgr., project mgr., cons., 1984—. Patentee pulsed acoustic image tube. Author tech. papers. Served to capt. Chinese Air Force, 1947-55. Fellow Acoustical Soc. Am. (com. mem. 1978—); mem. Am. Nat. Standards Inst. (chmn. sub-com. 1978—), Am. Phys. Soc., Am. Soc. Nondestructive Testing, Nat. Soc. Profl. Engrs. (chpt. v.p. 1982-83), Phi Kappa Phi. Club: Toastmasters (pres. 1981). Current work: Acoustical technology applied to machinery diagnosis, human effects in sound, and non-destructive testing. Subspecialties: Acoustics; Nondestructive testing. Home: 3378 Vrooman Rd Jackson MI 49201

YING RUOCHENG, actor; b. Beijing, China, June 21, 1929; s. Chienli Ignatius and Baozhen (Cai) Y.; student Quinghua U., Beijing, 1946-50; m. Wu Shiliang, July 17, 1950; children: Ying Ziaole, Ying Da. Actor, Beijing People's Art Theatre, 1950-76, from 1978; editor China Reconstructs, 1976-78; prin. actor numerous films; actor Kublai Khan in TV mini series Marco Polo, 1982, films include: Dr. Bethune, Measure for Measure, Intimate Friends, Teahouse, The Last Emperor, 1987; transl., dir. plays: The Star Turns Red, As it Happened, The Coffee House Politician, The Sugar Cane Plantation, Measure by Measure, 1981; Fulbright Asian prof. in residence, U. Missouri, Kansas City, 1982. Mem. All China Theatre Assn. (dir. Beijing br.). Transl., editor: Stanislavsky Produces Othello, 1954. Home: 10 Qianchang Hutong, East City, Beijing Peoples Republic of China Office: Beijing People's Art Theatre, Beijing Peoples Republic of China *

YIREN, RONG, bank executive; b. Wuxi, Jiangsu, Peoples Republic China, May 1, 1916; s. Deshen Rong; m. Yang Jian Qing, 1936; children: Zhi He, Zhi Pin, Zhi Jian, Zhi Wan. BA, St. John's U., 1937; D. of Letters (hon.), U. Hofstra, 1986. Mgr. Mow Sing Flour Mills, Wuxi, 1937-49; v.p. Foh Sing Flour Mills, Shanghai, Peoples Republic China, 1947-55; pres. Sung Sing Textile Printing and Dying Co., Shanghai, 1950-55; vice mayor City of Shanghai, 1957-66; vice minister Ministry of Textile Industry, Beijing, Peoples Republic China, 1959-66; chmn. China Internat. Trust and Investment Co., Beijing, 1979—; exec. dir. Bank of China, Beijing; vice chmn. Soong Chingling Found., Beijing, 1983—; mem. bus. adv. com. Internat. Fin. Corp., 1986—; hon. chmn. China Nat. Com. for Pacific Econ. Cooperation, 1987—; lectr. in field. Contbr. articles to profl. jours. Vice chmn. nat. com. Chinese Polit. Consultative Conf., 1978-83; vice chmn. standing com. 6th and 7th Nat. People's Congress, Peoples Republic China, 1983-88, 88—; hon. advisor China Soccer Assn., Beijing, 1984—; chmn. bd. trustees Jinan U., Guangahou, Peoples Republic China, 1985—; hon. chmn. bd. trustees Jiangnan U., Wuxi, 1985—. Recipient The Appeal of Conscience award, 1986. Mem. All China Assn. Industry and Commerce (vice chmn. 1953-87, hon. chmn. 1987—), China Softball Assn. (hon. chmn. 1986—). Office: China Internat Trust/Invest Corp, 19 Jianguomennai Dajie, Beijing Peoples Republic China

YLI-JOKIPII, PENTTI OLAVI, geography educator; b. Jalasjarvi, Finland, Feb. 7, 1941; s. Väinö Gabriel and Laimi Susanna (Hakkola) Yli-J.; m. Hilkka Mirjami Pekonen, Mar. 2, 1969; children: Kaisa, Markus. BSc, U. Helsinki, Finland, 1964, MSc, 1965, PhD, 1967. Assoc. prof. U. Helsinki, 1968-69, 71-73; prof. econ. geography Turku (Finland) Sch. Econs., 1973-74; prof. geography U. Turku, 1974—, now dean faculty sci.; vis. scholar Mich. State U., 1970. Author papers, articles, books on econ. geography, geography and regional planning. Mem. Geog. Soc. Finland (pres. 1979), Finnish Nat. Com. Internat. Geog. Union (pres. 1983—). Office: U Turku, Dept Geography, 20500 Turku Finland

YLINEN, JAAKKO KRISTIAN, architect; b. Helsinki, Finland, May 18, 1936; s. Arvo Albin and Lea Maria (Hietarinta) Ylinen; m. Maija Vappu Suomalainen, Dec. 4, 1967; 1 child, Kristian. MArch, Helsinki U. Tech., 1962, Licentiate Tech., 1968. Ptnr. Mansikka, Salonen & Ylinen, Architects, Helsinki, 1963-67, Salonen & Ylinen, Architects, Helsinki, 1967-68, Kaupunkisuuunnittelu Ltd., Helsinki, 1969—; sr. asst. architecture Helsinki U. Tech., 1964-69; lectr. architecture, 1971-77. Contbr. articles to profl. jours. Mem. State Council Architecture, Finland, 1968-71, chmn. 1971-73; vice-chmn. State Council for Arts, Finland, 1971-73, bd. dirs. Bldg. Info. Instn., Helsinki, 1975-78. Mem. Finnish Assn. Architects, Finnish Assn. Cons. Engrs. Home: Katajanokankatu 3A 6, SF 00160 Helsinki Finland Office: Kaupunkisuunnittelu Ltd, Toolonkatu 11A, SF00100 Helsinki Finland

YOCKEY, ANTHONY SCOTT, financial placement agent, consultant, compute softwar consultant; b. Fremont, Ohio, Mar. 14, 1956; s. Layton E. and Carol S. Yockey; m. Penny L. Rife, Aug. 25, 1979; children: Kathleen S., Angela D., Cassandra L. Student, U. Toledo, 1974-75, Davis Jr. Coll., Toledo, 1980-81. Pres. Anthony S. Yockey Enterprises Inc., Toledo, 1977—; owner, mgr. Nat. Fin. Corp., Toledo, 1979-82, Progressive Pub. Group, Toledo, 1984-88, Trans-Continental Services, Toledo, 1985-87; pres., chief exec. officer Yockey, Jordan & Yockey, Inc., Toledo, 1987—, v.p. Comprehensive Fin. Services div., 1987—, v.p. Comprehensive Fin. Group, 1987. Republican. Methodist. Home: 610 Colburn St Toledo OH 43609-3304 Office: Yockey Jordan & Yockey PO Box 4095 Toledo OH 43609

YODER, GENE FRANCIS, geologist; b. Washington, Iowa, May 17, 1934; s. Glenn Clayton and Elizabeth Margaret (Bauer) Y.; student U. Iowa, 1952-56; B.S. in Geology, Western State Coll. of Colo., 1959; m. Marilyn L. Scott, June 19, 1954; children—Christy Moore, Jene, Beth, David. Jr. geologist Pinnacle Exploration, Inc., Gunnison, Colo., 1956-60; asst. store mgr. oil field supply Franklin Supply Co., Moab, Utah, 1960-63; sr. geologist, mine supt. Homestake Mining Co., Kenedy, Tex., Casper, Wyo., Gunnison, Colo., and La Sal, Utah, 1963-74; land mgr. metals div. Union Carbide Corp., Grand Junction, Colo., 1974—; uranium cons., 1974. Mem. Grand Junction dist. adv. council Bur. Land Mgmt. Served with U.S. Army, 1954-56. Mem. Am. Mining Congress (public lands com. 1976—), Am. Assn. Petroleum Landmen (chmn. mining and geothermal com. 1979), Rocky Mountain Assn. Mineral Landmen, N.Mex. Mining Assn., Colo. Mining Assn., AIME, Soc. Mining Engrs. Republican. Lutheran. Home: 2813 Mesa Ave Grand Junction CO 81501 Office: PO Box 1029 Grand Junction CO 81502

YODER, JOHN CHRISTIAN, business executive, lawyer; b. Newton, Kans., Jan. 9, 1951; s. Gideon G. and Stella H. Yoder; B.A., Chapman Coll., 1972; J.D., U. Kans., 1975; M.B.A., U. Chgo., 1976. Bar: Kans. 1975, Ind. 1976, U.S. Supreme Ct. 1981, D.C. 1985. Asst. prof. bus. Goshen Coll. (Ind.), 1975-76; pvt. practice law, Hesston, Kans., 1976-77; assoc. dist. judge 9th Jud. Dist., Newton, Kans., 1977-80; chmn. bd., v.p., dir. Jay Energy Devel. Co., 1978-81; chmn. bd. Stone Mill Wichita, Inc., 1977-80, Stone Mill Bakeries, Inc., 1977-81; jud. fellow U.S. Supreme Ct., Washington, 1980-81; spl. asst. to chief justice U.S. Supreme Ct., Washington, 1981-83; dir. Asset Forfeiture Office, Dept. Justice, Washington, 1983-84; gen. counsel Sterling Investment Resources Inc., Wichita, Kans., 1987—; chmn. bd., pres. Eon Resources, Inc., 1981-87; pres. Bus. Resources Group, Inc., Washington, 1984-87; sr. v.p. Sino Am. Transport, Ltd., Washington, 1987—; exec. v.p., dir. Patriot Life Ins. Co., 1985; chmn. Gattlin Inc., Albuquerque, 1986—; dir. Kinderhook Oil & Gas, Inc., Sanders & Co., U.S. Petroleum Corp. Bd. dirs. Showalter Villa, Hesston, 1977-80, Substance Abuse Bd. Harvey County, 1977-80. Mem. ABA, Kans. Bar Assn., Ind. Bar Assn., Harvey County Bar Assn., D.C. Bar Assn., Fed. Bar Assn., U.S. C. of C. (council on trends and perspectives 1981—). Republican. Mennonite. Home: Rt 3 Box 109 Harpers Ferry WV 25425 Office: 1511 K St NW Suite 1000 Washington DC 20005

YODMANI, SONGSUDA KITTIKACHORN, writer; b. Bangkok, Thailand, Dec. 17, 1943; d. Field Mashal Thanom and Lady Chongkol (Krabuenyuth) Kittikachorn; m. Suvit Yodmani, May 2, 1969; children—Suvongse, Pongsak, Chakra. B.Architecture (Hon.), Chulalongkorn U., Bangkok, 1963-67; M.C.P., Harvard U., 1973. Lectr., Chulanlongkorn U., 1972-73; private practice architecture, 1973-79; free lance writer, 1979—. Author: Yai Goes Abroad, 1983; Home and School, 1985; The Queen's Visit to America, 1985. Contbr. numerous articles on edn. and social justice to mags. Mem. com. Social Welfare Council Mother's Day Celebration, Bangkok, 1983—; mem. fund raising com. Kidney Found, Support Found. Mem. PEN Club of Thailand, Harvard Club of Thailand (mem. exec. com.), Architects' Assn. Avocations: painting, swimming, reading. Office: 99 Ranong II Rd, Bangkok Thailand

YOERGER, ROGER RAYMOND, agricultural engineer, educator; b. LeMars, Iowa, Feb. 17, 1929; s. Raymond Herman and Crystal Victoria (Ward) Y.; m. Barbara M. Ellison, Feb. 14, 1953; 1 child, Karen Lynne; m. Laura M. Summitt, Dec. 23, 1971; stepchildren—Daniel L. Summitt, Linda Summitt Canull, Anita Summitt Smith. B.S., Iowa State U., 1949, M.S., 1951, Ph.D., 1957. Registered profl. engr., Ill., Pa., Iowa. Instr., asst. prof. agrl. engring. Iowa State U., 1949-56; assoc. prof. agrl. engring. Pa. State U., 1956-58; prof. agrl. engring. U. Ill., Urbana, 1959-85; head agrl. engring. dept. U. Ill., 1978-85, prof. emeritus agrl. engring., 1985—. Contbr. articles to profl. jours. Patentee in field. Mem. Ill. Noise Task Force, 1974—. Fellow Am. Soc. Agrl. Engrs.; mem. Am. Soc. Engring. Edn., AAAS, Phi Kappa Phi (dir. fellowships, dir. 1971-83, pres. elect. 1983-86, pres. 1986—). Roman Catholic. Lodges: Rotary, Moose. Home: 107 W Holmes Urbana IL 61801 Office: 1304 W Pennsylvania Ave Urbana IL 61801

YOKELY, RONALD EUGENE, mechanical engineer, research corporation executive; b. High Point, N.C., Feb. 7, 1942; s. Clarence Eugene and Grayce (Waddy) Y.; B.S. in Mech. Engring., N.C. State U., Raleigh, 1963; m. E. Joanne Williams, July 6, 1963; children—Rhonda Lynette, Rene Michelle. Test engr. McDonnell Aircraft Corp., St. Louis, 1963-67; sect. mgr. simulation products div. Singer Co., Houston, 1967-73; engring. mgr. Aeronutronic Ford Corp., Houston, 1973-76; sr. v.p. Onyx Corp., Bethesda, Md., 1976-78; pres., treas. Acumenics Research & Tech., Inc. subs. Hadron, Inc., Fairfax., Va., 1978—; corp. v.p. Hadron, Inc., Fairfax, 1983—; cons. FAA, 1975-76. Registered profl. engr., Tex. Mem. AIAA, IEEE, Nat. Soc. Profl. Engrs., AAAS, , Omega Psi Phi. Episcopalian. Co-author: Microcomputers—A Technology Forecast and Assessment to the Year 2000, 1980, Japanese transl., 1981. Home: 10894 Lake Windermere Dr Great Falls VA 22066 Office: 9990 Lee Hwy Fairfax VA 22030

YOKEN, MELVIN BARTON, French educator; b. Fall River, Mass., June 25, 1939; s. Albert Benjamin and Sylvia Sarah (White) Y.; m. Cynthia Stein, June 20, 1976; children—Andrew Brett, David Ryan, Jonathan Barry. B.A., U. Mass., 1960, Ph.D., 1972; M.A.T., Brown U., 1961; student, U. Montreal, summers 1982—. Instr. French, Southeastern Mass. U., North Dartmouth, 1966-72, asst. prof., 1972-76, assoc. prof., 1976-81 prof., 1981—, dir. French Inst., French summer study program, 1981—; vis. prof. Wheaton Coll., 1987, translator New Bedford Superior Ct., New Bedford, Mass., 1985—, Fall River Superior Ct., Fall River, Mass., 1985—; mem. nominating com. Nobel prize for lit., 1972—. Pres., Friends of Fall River Public Library, 1972-80, pres. bd. dirs., 1972-80; pres. New Bedford Public Library, 1980-82, Am. Field Service, 1985—. Recipient Disting. Service award City Fall River, 1974, 80, Golden Poetry award, 1985, Excellence in Teaching French award, 1984, 85; Gov.'s citation, 1986; Govt. of Que. grantee, 1981-85, Can. Embassy grantee, 1986,87. Mem. MLA (life), Am. Assn. Tchrs. French (life), Am. Council Tchrs. Fgn. Langs., Middlebury Amicale (life), Northeast MLA (coordinator 1987—), New Eng. Fgn. Lang. Assn., Mass. Fgn. Lang. Assn. (dir. 1984—), N.Y. State Assn. Fgn. Lang. Tchrs., Internat. Platform Assn., Fall River C. of C. Author: Claude Tillier, 1976, Speech is Plurality, 1978, Claude Tillier (1801-44): Fame and Fortune in His Novelistic Work, 1978, Entretiens Québécois I, 1986, Entretiens Québécois II, 1988, Letters of Robert Molloy, 1988. Avocations: traveling, languages, baseball, postcards, meteorology books Home: 261 Carroll St New Bedford MA 02740 Office: Southeastern Mass U North Dept French Old Westport Rd Dartmouth MA 02747

YOKOBORI, TAKEO, scientist; b. Tochigi-ken, Japan, Nov. 20, 1917; s. Syotaro and Yayoi (Kobori) Y.; B. Engring., U. Tokyo, 1941, Sc.D., 1956; m. Miyoko Uzuka, Aug. 20, 1945; 1 son, Toshimitsu. Asso. prof. mech. engring. Tohoku U., 1955-57, prof., 1957-81, prof. emeritus, 1981—; prof. Kogakuin U., 1981—; founder, dir. Research Inst. Strength and Fracture for Materials, 1964-81; mem. Sci. Council Japan, 1966-85. Recipient Japan Acad. Sci. prize, 1971; guest U.S.S.R. Acad. Scis., 1971. Mem. Internat. Congress on Fracture (pres. 1965-73, founder pres. 1973—), Internat. Cooperative Fracture Research Inst. (pres. 1974—), Japanese Soc. Strength and Fracture of Materials (pres. 1966—), Japan Soc. Mech. Engrs. (hon.), Japan Inst. Metals (hon.), Japan Soc. Biomaterials (founding pres. 1978—), Japan Soc. Materials Sci., Nat. Acad. Engring. U.S. (fgn. assoc.), Author: The Strength, Fracture and Fatigue of Materials, 1965; An Interdisciplinary Approach to Fracture and Strength of Solids, 1968; Methodologies and Fundamentals of Fracture of Matter and Solids, 1978. Home: 31-15 Aoyama 1 chome, Sendai Japan

YOKOGAWA, KIYOSHI, engineer, researcher; b. Saiki, Ohita, Japan, Sept. 28, 1946; arrived in Kure, 1974; s. Suekichi and Hatsuko (Suzuki) Y.; m. Masako Hirokaga, Apr. 29, 1972; children: Jun, Chisaki. BS in Engring., Kyoto U., 1969, MS in Engring., 1971; D in Engring., Hokkaido U., 1985. Registered profl. engr. Asst. prof. The Iron and Steel Tech. Coll., Amagasaki, Hyogo, Japan, 1971-74; researcher Govt. Indsl. Research Inst. Chugoko, Ministry of Internat. Trade and Industry, Kure, Hiroshima, 1974-80; sr. researcher Govt. Indsl. Research Inst. Chugoko, MITI, Kure, Hiroshima, 1980—; cons. Nat. Space Devel. Agy. Japan, Tokyo, 1986—. Contbr. articles to profl. jours.; patentee in field. Mem. The Japan Inst. Metals (Metallographic Photograph prize 1976), The Iron and Steel Inst. Japan. Home: Agachuo 5-10-40-101, Kure, Hiroshima 737, Japan Office: Govt Indsl Research Inst Chugoku, MITI, Hiro-Suehiro 2-2-2, 737-01 Kure, Hiroshima Japan

YOKOM, DIANE ELAINE, retail design consultant; b. Detroit, Aug. 11, 1949; d. Robert William and Dorothy Mae (Leddick) Y.; m. John Richard Houghtaling, June 29, 1985. BS in Interior Design, Mich. State U., 1971. Designer Morse Shoe, Canton, Mass.; then designer Creative Atmospheres, Boston, Yokom Design, Boston, The Architects Collaborative, Cambridge, Mass.; then retail design cons. The Rouse Co., Columbia, Md., Durango, Colo.; lectr. The Rouse Co., 1983—, Melvin Simon and Assocs.; photographer workshops, seminars, shops and developers, 1985—; mfr. Sugarplum Stockings, Durango, 1986. Author: Retail Design Idea Book, 1985; (instrnl. videotape) Visual Merchandising-10 Steps to Success; designer The Chocolate Rule, 1980— (Silver medal 1980). Recipient Merit award Communication Arts, 1980, Merit award Art Dirs. Club Boston, 1978, 80. Mem. Nat. Trust for Hist. Preservation, Save the Children Found. Office: 375 Broadway #105 Laguna Beach CA 92651

YOKOYA, YUMI, manufacturing company executive; b. Tanabe, Wakayma, Japan, Mar. 30, 1929; s. Taka Y.; m. Sachiko, Oct. 28, 1954; children: Hirokazu, Noriko. B.Tech., Chiba Inst. Tech., 1953. With Nissan Motor Co. Ltd., Tokyo, 1953-85. Served with Japanese Air Force. Home: 4-11-21 Serigaya Konan-Ward, Yokohama Kanagawa 233, Japan Office: Kanto Seiki Co Ltd, 1910 Nissin-Cho, 2-chome, Omiye, Saitama 331, Japan

YOKOYAMA, MORIO, metal trading executive; b. Osaka, Japan, Feb. 27, 1938; s. Kiyoshi and Fumiko Yokoyama; m. Etsuko Norizoe, Nov. 8, 1964; children: Ikuko, Lisa. BA, Keio U., Tokyo, 1960. Rep. Kawasaki Steel Corp., N.Y.C., 1965-67, Los Angeles, 1968-69; pres. Taisei Internat. Corp., Osaka, 1970—. Mem. Japan Steel Importers Assn. (vice chmn. 1986). Club: Arima Royal Golf. Lodge: Rotary (Osaka). Home: 4-11-17 Mikage Yamate, Kobe Japan Office: Taisei Internat Corp, 1-13-1400 Umeda, Kitaku, Osaka Japan

YONDA, ALFRED WILLIAM, mathematician; b. Cambridge, Mass., Aug. 10, 1919; s. Walter and Theophelia (Naruscewicz) Y.; B.S., U. Ala., 1952, M.A. in Math., 1954; m. Mary Jane McManus, Dec. 19, 1949 (dec.); children—Nancy, Kathryn, Elizabeth, John; m. Peggy A. Terrel, June 22, 1975. Mathematician rocket research Redstone Arsenal, Huntsville, Ala., 1953, U.S. Army Ballistic Research Labs., Aberdeen (Md.) Proving Grounds, 1954-56; instr. math. U. Ala., Tuscaloosa, 1954, Temple U., Phila., 1956-57; asso. scientist, research and devel. div. Avco Corp., Wilmington, Mass., 1957-59; sr. mem. tech. staff RCA, Camden, N.J., 1959-66; mgr. computer analysis and programming dept. Raytheon Co. space and information systems div., Sudbury, Mass., 1966-70, mgr. software systems lab., 1969-70, prin. engr. missiles systems div., 1970-73; mgr. systems analysis and programming GTE Sylvania, 1973-77, mgr. software engring. Atlantic ops., 1977-82, sr. mem. tech. staff Communications Systems div., 1983—. Pres., Milford Area Assn. Retarded Children, 1970-74; vice-chmn. fin. com. Town of Medway, 1973; bd. dirs. Blackstone Valley Mental Health and Retardation Area Bd., 1970-76; trustee Medway Libraries, 1973-82, chmn., 1974-81. Served with USAAF, 1943-46. Hon. fellow Advanced Level Telecommunications Tng. Center, New Delhi, India, 1981. Registered profl. engr. Mem. AAAS, IEEE, Math. Assn. Am., N.Y. Acad. Scis., Sigma Xi, Phi Eta Sigma, Pi Mu Epsilon (pres. Ala. chpt. 1953-54), Sigma Pi Sigma. Contbr. articles to profl. jours. Home: 12 Sunset Dr Medway MA 02053 Office: GTE 77 A St Needham MA 02194

YONEKURA, YOSHIHARU, physician; b. Otsu, Japan, Apr. 30, 1948; s. Yoshio and Kazu (Hayashi) Y.; m. Yoshie Itami, Sept. 25, 1978; children—Kumiko, Yuriko, Kazuo. M.D., Kyoto U., 1973, D. Med. Sci., 1980. Medical diplomate. Resident Kyoto U. Hosp., Japan, 1973-76, asst. prof., 1980—; vis. asst. scientist Brookhaven Nat. Lab., Upton, N.Y., 1980-82. Mem. Soc. Nuclear Medicine, Radiol. Soc. N.Am., IEEE. Office: Dept Nuclear Medicine, Kyoto U Sch Medicine, Sakyo-Ku, Kyoto 606 Japan

YONEZAWA, SHIGERU, telecommunications official; b. Toyama Prefecture, Japan, Feb. 1, 1911; s. Yosochichi and Kimiko Yonezawa; m. Tokuko; children—Janichi, Kenji. Master's degree Tokyo Imperial U., 1933; D.Engring., 1942; D.Engring. (hon.), King Monkut Inst. Tech., Thailand. Pres., Nippon Tel. & Tel. Co., 1965-77; pres. Assn. Telecommunications; mem. Council Sci. and Tech. of Cabinet of Japanese Govt., 1973—; mem. Japan Sci. Council, 1959-65; chmn. Inst. Econs. and Telecommunications; dir. Fedn. Econ. Orgns. Author: Microwave Communication, Technical Innovation and Telecommunications, My Personal History. Recipient Mainichi Indsl. prize; Spl. prize Assn. Communications; decorated 1st class Order of Merit (Japan). Fellow IEEE (Founders medal); mem. Nippon Indsl. Club. Lodge: Rotary. Office: 1-12-1 Shin-Yurakucho Bldg, Chiyodaku, Tokyo Japan

YONG, AMOS WILDER, trade, design and contracting, computer service company executive; b. Shanghai, China, Oct. 30, 1937; s. John Kong Ling and Evelyn Thia Chin (Hwang) Y.; m. Daisy Lam, Aug. 22, 1959; children—Amos Wilder, Jr., Emeline May, Angeline Jane. B.A., Calif. State U., 1968. With Union Bank Calif., 1954-64, Bullock's Inc., 1964-66, Systems Info. Co., 1966-67, Buffum's Inc., 1968-69; dir. Gulf Thai Ltd., Bangkok, Thailand, 1969-70; fin. rep. NCR, Hong Kong, 1970-71; gen. mgr. Dataprep Ltd., Hong Kong, 1971-72; chmn., mng. dir. Amda Ltd., Kowloon, Hong Kong, 1972—; chmn. bd. dirs. Hong Kong World Relief Ltd.; chmn. bd. mgrs. Alliance Indsl. Adminstrn. Evening Inst.; bd. advisors Far East Nat. Bank, Los Angeles; mng. dir. Wada Machinery Ltd; bd. dirs. Trans World Radio Ltd. Bd. dirs. United Christian Coll., Hong Kong, Sch. for Christ Found., Hong Kong, Research Inst. Christian Educators, Hong Kong. Mem. Assn. Computing Machinery, IEEE, Chinese Lang. Computer Soc., Hong Kong Computer Soc., Am. C. of C. in Hong Kong, Am. Mgmt. Assn. Internat., Am. Inst. Mgmt. Club: Kiwanis (dir. 1977). Home: Townhouse 80, Sunderland Estate, 1 Hereford Rd, Kowloon Hong Kong Office: 706 President Comml Ctr, 602 Nathan Rd, Kowloon Hong Kong

YONKERS, WILLIAM FREDERICK, manufacturing company executive; b. Evanston, Ill., Aug. 15, 1942; s. William A. and Elizabeth (Freudenreich) Y.; B.S. in Physics, Fairleigh Dickinson U., 1967; M.S. in Engring., Stevens Inst. Tech., 1971; M.B.A. in Corp. Fin., U. Pa., 1972; m. Susan Ennis McCurdy, Apr. 14, 1978; children—William Robert, Amanda Crawford. Hydrodynamic test engr. Davidson Lab., Hoboken, N.J., 1968-71; sr. fin. analyst Ford Motor Co., Dearborn, Mich., 1973-75; mgr. fin. reporting Info. Processing div. Xerox Corp., El Segundo, Calif., 1975-76, mgr. consolidation and reporting Bus. Devel. Group, Rochester, N.Y., 1977, mgr. program and pricing rev. Info. Products group, Greenwich, Conn., 1978, mgr. opns. analysis Office Products div., Stamford, Conn., 1979, mgr. shareholder relations, 1980-84; mgr. Office Corp., sec. 1984-88; exec. v.p., corp. sec. NGA Printing Co., Balt., 1988—. NSF fellow, 1968. Mem. Am. Inst. Physics, SAR, Sigma Xi, Beta Gamma Sigma. Republican. Clubs: Exchange, New Canaan Field. Home: 304 Somerset Rd Baltimore MD 21210 Office: NGA Printing Co 1100 Wicomico St Suite 705 Raleigh Indusl Ctr Baltimore MD 21230

YOO, DAL, physician, educator, medical researcher; b. Kwang-Ju, Korea, Nov. 20, 1943; came to U.S., 1967, naturalized, 1972; s. Bong Soo and Yang Hee (Kim) Y.; m. Charlotte M. Nordanlycke, Apr. 14, 1974 (div. 1987); children—Derek Torgny, Nora Ottilia. BS, Seoul Nat. U., 1963, MD, 1967. Diplomate Am. Bd. Internal Medicine, Am. Bd. Hematology, Am. Bd. Med. Oncology, Intern St. Luke's Hosp., Newburgh, N.Y., 1967-68, asst. resident in internal medicine, 1968, resident in anatomic pathology, 1968-69; resident Thomas Jefferson U. Hosp., 1969-70, George Washington U. Hosp., 1970-71, fellow in hematology and oncology, 1971-72, 74-75, assoc. clin. prof. medicine, 1975—; fellow in blood banking and immunohematology ARC, Washington, 1975; practice medicine specializing in internal medicine, hematology and med. oncology, Washington, 1975—; sr. attending physician Washington Hosp. Ctr., 1975—; chief hematology-oncology sect. Providence Hosp., Washington; mem. active staff Capitol Hill Hosp.; mem. courtesy staff Washington Adventist Hosp., Holy Cross Hosp. Contbr. articles to profl. jours. Served to maj. U.S. Army, 1972-74. Fellow ACP; mem. Med. Soc. D.C., Washington Blood Club, Washington Soc. Oncology, Am. Soc. Hematology, Am. Soc. Clin. Oncology. Presbyterian. Research on clin. and lab. hematology and medical oncology. Home: 9725 Conestoga Way Potomac MD 20854 Office: Providence Hosp 1160 Varnum St NE Suite 212 Washington DC 20017 also: 950 Pennsylvania Ave SE Suite 370 Washington DC 20003

YOO, YOUNG HYUN, librarian; b. Hongsong, South Korea, July 15, 1927; s. Bock Don and In Nye (Park) Y.; LL.B., Korean U., 1957; M.S. in L.S., George Peabody Coll., 1958; LL.M., Seoul Nat. U., 1960; M.C.L. in Am. Practice, George Washington U., 1977; m. Sun Gyu Im, Oct. 23, 1958; children—Elizabeth M., Sarah T., Daniel D., Alice W. Chief Western books dept. Dongguk U., Seoul, 1948-59; lectr. library sci. dept. Yonsei U., Seoul, 1958-60; lectr. library sci. Seoul Nat. U., 1961-62; lectr. civil and criminal law Nat. Communications Coll., Seoul, 1962-63; lectr. English law Korea U., Seoul, 1961-62; lectr. library workshops Yonsei U. and Seoul Nat. Univ., 1959-62; law librarian Coll. Law, Seoul Nat. U., 1959-63; reference librarian Oriental div. Library of Congress, Washington, 1963-68, subject analyst East Asian publs. of law, politics and social scis. processing dept., 1968—; cons. computerized bibliographical system, human relations area files Yale U., 1967-72. Mem. Kings Park West Civic Assn., Fairfax, Va., 1974—; counillor Korean Library Assn., 1961-63; spl. advisor Far Eastern Research and Publs. Center, 1970-80. Served with USMC, 1950-53. ICA grantee, 1957-58. Mem. U.S. Library of Congress Profl. Staff Assn., ALA, George Washington Law Assn., Korean Legal Center, Criminal Law and Criminology Soc. Korea, Korean Library Assn. Democrat. Author: An Analysis of Criminal Law of Korea, 1392-1910, 1960; Glossary of Library Science, 1962; A Glance over Welfare States: United States, 1962; On Bibliographical Control, 1962; Retrieval of Legal Sources, 1963; English-Korean Dictionary Romanized, 1962; Source Materials on Korean Economy, 1966; (juvenile lit.) Two Korean Brothers, 1970; Wisdom of the Far East: A Dictionary of Proverbs, Maxims and Famous Classical Phrases of the Chinese, Japanese and Koreans, 1972; Towards World Peace Through Legal Controls in the Air and Outer Space, 1973; (translator into Korean) Dewey Decimal Classification, 1960, An Introduction to Library Science, 1961. Home: 10204 Bessmer Ln Fairfax VA 22032 Office: Processing Dept Library of Congress 1st and Independence Ave SE Washington DC 20540

YOON, HOIL, lawyer; b. Tokyo, Nov. 22, 1943; came to U.S. from Korea, 1970; s. Hakwon and Hoik (Lee) Y.; m. Giyun Kim, June 1, 1968; children—Shinwon E., Eunice J., Grace J., James S. LL.B., Seoul Nat. U., 1965, LL.M., 1967; J.D., Notre Dame U., 1973. Bar: Korea 1967, Ill. 1973, D.C. 1981, U.S. Supreme Ct. 1977, N.Y. 1988. Judge, Seoul Civil Dist., Korea, 1970; assoc. Baker & McKenzie, Chgo., 1973-79, ptnr., 1979-87; ptnr. Baker & McKenzie, N.Y.C., 1987—; panelist Am. Arbitration Assn. N.Y.C., 1982—; mem. Korean Comml. Arbitration Bd., 1982—; lectr. Columbia U. Sch. of Law, N.Y.C., 1985—. Contbr. articles to legal jours. Bd. dirs. Korean-Am. Community Services, Inc., 1982— , U.S.-Korea Soc., Inc., 1984—. Served to capt. Korean Air Force, 1967-69. Recipient Presdl. decoration Republic of Korea, 1984. Mem. ABA (chmn. subcom. on Korea 1983-84), Bar Assn. D.C., Chgo., N.Y. Bar Assns., Seoul Bar Assn., Korean Bar Assn. Home: 4 Gate House Rd Scarsdale NY 10583 Office: Baker & McKenzie 805 3d Ave New York NY 10022

YOON, JONG SIK, geneticist, educator; b. Suwon, Korea, Jan. 25, 1937; came to U.S., 1962, naturalized, 1976; s. Ki and Pil (Kang) Y.; m. Kyung-Soon Ahn, Sept. 10, 1962; children—Edward, Mimi, Sunny. B.S., Yonsei U., Seoul, Korea, 1961; M.A., U. Tex.-Austin, 1964, Ph.D., 1965. Research scientist U. Tex.-Austin also Houston, 1965-68; asst. prof. Yonsei U., 1968-71; research scientist U. Tex.-Austin, 1971-78; assoc. prof. Bowling Green State U., 1978-83, prof. genetics, 1983—, dir. Nat. Drosophila Species Resource Ctr., 1982—. Presbyterian. Contbr. articles to profl. jours. Home: 4 Picardie Ct Bowling Green OH 43402 Office: Bowling Green State U Dept Biol Scis Bowling Green OH 43403

YOPCONKA, NATALIE ANN CATHERINE, computer specialist, educator; b. Taylor, Pa., July 21, 1942; d. Michael Joseph and Natalie Ann Lucille (Panek) Yopconka; B.S., U. Md., 1965; M.B.A., George Washington U., 1976; MA in Edn., Human Devel. George Washington U., 1988; postgrad. numerous courses. Mgmt. analyst, adminstrv. trainee, computer programmer U.S. Dept. Commerce, Maritime Adminstrn., Washington, 1965-67; computer programmer, computer specialist Dept. Labor, Washington, 1967-78; instr. computer sci. Assn. for Computing Machinery, Washington, 1978; instr. computer sci. Montgomery Coll., Takoma Park and Rockville, Md., 1979; sr. programmer analyst Dynamic Data Processing, Inc., Silver Spring, Md., 1979; instr. Nat. Bus. Sch., Inc., Alexandria, Va., 1980; cons. McLeod Corp., Washington, 1980; lectr. computer sci., coop. coordinator U. Md., College Park, 1980-81; sr. adminstrv. applications analyst programmer, Data Transformation Corp., Washington, 1981; sr. systems analyst Singer Link Simulation Systems div., Silver Spring, 1981-82; self-employed accessory designer, 1982-83; market researcher Washington Fin. Service, 1982-83; lectr. computer info. and systems sci. U. D.C., Rockville, Md., 1983; prof computer programming and mgmt. info. systems Benjamin Franklin U., Washington, 1983; researcher Info. U.S.A., Potomac, Md., 1983-85; self-employed admissions rep. Brook-Wein Bus. Inst., Washington, 1985; pvt. distbr., Hyattsville, Columbia, Md., 1979—; course developer, instr. Grad. Sch. USDA, Balt., 1986-87; pvt. cons. Columbia, Md., 1987—. Mem. Takoma Park Disability Com.; Mayor's Com. on Energy, Housing and Planning, 1980-81; mem. choir Our Lady of Sorrows Cath. Ch., 1977-82. Mem. EDP Auditors Assn., Assn. for Computing Machinery (edn. com., instr. 1978-79, edn. com. 1980-81, profl. devel. com. 1982-83), Data Processing Mgmt. Assn., Balt. Washington Info. System Educators (consortium com. 1984-85, program com. for 1986 regional tng. conf. 1985-86), Nat. Bus. Edn. Assn., Electronic Connectors Study Group, Am. Automobile Assn., IEEE Computer Soc. (mem. various coms.), Integrated Software Fed. Users Group, Columbia-Balt. User Group, Assn. of Supervision and Curriculum Devel., Md. Assn. for Supervision and Curriculum Devel., Am. Biog. Inst. Research Assn., Phi Delta Gamma (scholarship com. 1977-78, social com. 1980-81, hospitality com. 1982-83). Clubs: Cath. Alumni, Howard County Newcomers, Fed. Poets. Home and Office: 6099 Majors Ln Apt 8 Columbia MD 21045

YORK, JANET BREWSTER, nurse, family and sex therapist; b. N.Y.C., Mar. 5, 1941; d. Edward Cox and Janet Stone Brewster; A.A. with honors, Briarclif Coll., 1961; R.N. with highest honors, U. Iowa, 1965; B.A. summa cum laude, Marymount Manhattan Coll., 1975; M.A. with honors, N.Y. U., 1978; m. Albert Thompson York, Mar. 31, 1962 (dec.); children—Clifton Gaston, Torrance Brewster; 1 adopted child, Justin Brigham. Nurse, Manhattan Eye, Ear and Throat Hosp., N.Y.C., 1966-74; nurse, counselor Washington Free Clinic, 1969-71; family therapist Ackerman Family Inst., N.Y.C., 1976-80; sex therapist N.Y. Med. Coll., Flower Fifth Ave Hosp., N.Y.C., 1976-80; individual practice family and sex therapy, N.Y.C., 1978—; supervisory staff grad. edn. program in human sexuality N.Y.U. Med. Center, 1982—. Bd. dirs. Spence/Chapin Adoption Agy. Fellow Internat. Council of Sex Edn. and Parenthood, Am. U., 1981. Mem. Am. Soc. for Sex Therapy and Research, Am. Assn. Sex Edn., Counseling and Therapy, Soc. for Sci. Study Sex, Sex Info. and Edn. Council U.S., Am. Assn. Marriage and Family Therapists. Clubs: Lawrence Beach, Rockaway Hunting, N.Y.U, Millbrook. Contbr. articles to profl. jours.; also videotape Death as a Part of Life. Home: 155 E 72d St New York NY 10021

YORK, JOHN CHRISTOPHER, lawyer, investment banker; b. Evansville, Ind., Apr. 27, 1946; s. James Edward and Madge (Wease) Y.; m. Judith Anne Carmack, Aug. 24, 1968; children—George Edward Carmack, Charlotte Bayley, Alice Mercer. B.A., Vanderbilt U., 1968; J.D., Harvard U., 1971. Bar: Ill. 1971, U.S. Dist. Ct. (no. dist.) Ill. 1971. Assoc. firm Mayer Brown & Platt, Chgo., 1971-74; sr. v.p., sec., prin. JMB Realty Corp., Chgo., 1974-84; pres. Robert E. Lend Co. Inc., 1984—, Packard Properties Inc., 1984—; counsel Bell, Boyd & Lloyd, Chgo., 1986—; bd. dirs. Riverside Corp., Chgo., McKeever Electric Supply Co., Columbus, Ohio. Bd. dirs. Landmarks Preservation Council of Ill., 1972—, Streeterville Corp., 1986-87, Washington Sq. Health Found., 1985—, Henrotin Hosp., 1976—; mem. vestry St. Chrysostom's Ch., 1980—. Mem. ABA, Chgo. Bar Assn., Lambda Alpha Internat. Republican. Episcopalian. Clubs: Chgo., Casino, Racquet, Saddle and Cycle. Home: 1242 Lake Shore Dr Chicago IL 60610 Office: Robert E Lend Co Inc 737 N Michigan Ave Chicago IL 60611

YORK, MICHAEL OTTO, author, museum custodian, reporter; b. Buffalo, Sept. 15, 1939; s. Otto and Myrth (Brooks) Y.; m. Nancy Williams, June 3, 1966. BA, U. Calif., 1961; MA, San Francisco State U., 1970. Asst. buyer The Broadway, Los Angeles, 1963-65; teaching asst. San Francisco State U., 1966; reporter The Murray Hill News, N.Y.C., 1970—; mus. custodian Amsterdam Ctr. for Eurindic Studies, Netherlands, 1981—. Author: The Rome Festival Calendar, 1986. Mem. San Francisco Mus. Fine Arts (bd. dirs. 1981—), Brit. Mus. Home: Tellus et les Etoiles, Aups France 8363 Office: Amsterdam Ctr for Eurindic, Studies, Reguliersgracht 33, Amsterdam The Netherlands 1017 LK

YORK, SUSANNAH, actress; b. London, Eng., Jan. 9, 1942; m. Michael Wells, 1960; children: Sasha, Orlando. Attended, London's Royal Acad. Dramatic Art. Made acting debut in repertory; entered TV in 1959; TV appearances include: Jane Eyre, TV spl. for NBC, 1971; TV films: Slaughter on St. Teresa's Day, Fallen Angels, Golden Gate Murders, 1979, Prince Regent, A Christmas Carol, Second Chance, We'll Meet Again, 1980; motion pictures include: Tunes of Glory, Freud, Tom Jones, They Shoot Horses, Don't They? (Acad. award nominee), A Man for All Seasons, The Killing of Sister George, Oh What a Lovely War, The Battle of Britain, Brotherly Love, Zee & Company, Happy Birthday, Wanda June, Images, The Maids, Gold, Eliza Fraser, Conduct Unbecoming, Heaven Save Us from Our Friends, Sky Riders, The Silent Partner, Superman I, The Shout, Superman II, Falling in Love, Alice, The Awakening, Loophole, Bluebeard, The Falcons Malteser; stage appearances include Hedda Gabbler, Penthesilea, The Human Voice, Fatal Attraction, The Applecart, The Women, Lyric for a Tango; books include Lark's Castle, In Search of Unicorns. Office: care Jeremy Conway, 109 Jermyn St, London W1, England

YOSELOFF, THOMAS, publisher; b. Sioux City, Iowa, Sept. 8, 1913; s. Morris and Sarah (Rosansky) Y.; m. Sara Rothfuss, Apr. 30, 1938; children: Julien David, Mark Laurence; m. Lauretta Sellitti, Apr. 23, 1964; 1 dau., Tamar Rachel. A.B., U. Iowa, 1934; Litt.D. (hon.), Bucknell U., 1982; L.H.D. (hon.), Fairleigh Dickinson U., 1982. Pres., chmn. bd. Rosemont Pub. & Printing Corp., 1969—; chmn. Associated Univ. Presses, 1969—, Golden Cockerel Press, London, 1979—. Author: A Fellow of Infinite Jest, 1946, (with Lillian Stuckey) Merry Adventures of Till Eulenspiegel, 1944, Further Adventures of Till Eulenspiegel, pub. 1957, The Time of My Life, 1979; Editor: Seven Poets in Search of an Answer, 1944, Voyage to America, 1961, Comic Almanac, 1963, The Man from the Mercury, 1986. Pres. Center for War/Peace Studies, 1977—. Recipient award of merit Bucknell U., 1975, award of merit U. Del., 1987. Mem. Phi Beta Kappa, Sigma Delta Chi, Delta Sigma Rho. Home: 68 Cedar Dr Colts Neck NJ 07722 Office: 440 Forsgate Dr Cranbury NJ 08512

YOSHIDA, KENICHI, senior fund manager; b. Kyoto, Japan, Oct. 1, 1958; arrived in Eng., 1983; s. Chuichiro and Atsuko (Honda) Y.; m. Lesley Jane McCaughan, May 4, 1985; 2 children: Keina, Rie. BSBA, Boston U., 1981. Exec. Nomura Securities, Tokyo, 1981-83; exec. Nomura Internat., London, 1983-87, mgr., 1987-88; mgr. Warburg Asset Mgmt., London, 1988, Warburg Investment Mgmt., Japan, 1988—. Office: Warburg Asset Mgmt, 33 King William St, London EC4R 9AS, England

YOSHIDA, NORIHIRO, mathematician; b. Fukuoka-Ken, Japan, Aug. 11, 1938; s. Yoshikatsu and Harue (Yamamoto) Y. Student, Tokyo U. Fgn. Studies, 1963-64; BSc, U. Tokyo, 1970. Exec. dir. Soc. Advancement of Culture U. Tokyo, 1964-68; promoter Interfield Edn. Dept., Tokyo, 1978-82; researcher Human Devel. Inst., Tokyo, 1982-84; phon-in Dr., lectr. Borgnan Sci. Acad., Tokyo, 1984-86; mgr. Borgnan Human Devel. Inst., Tokyo, 1986—; sec.-gen. Soc. Advancement of Sci., 1984—. Mem. Accelerated Teaching and Ednl. Research Group, Soc. Reading Sci. Books, Japan Math. Soc., Am. Math. Soc., Soc. Teaching Japanese as Fgn. Lang. Home: 2-15-2 206 Akabanekita, Kita-ku, Tokyo 115, Japan Office: Borgnan Human Devel Inst, 1-25-3 Higashi-Ikebukuro, Toshima-ku, Tokyo 170, Japan

YOSHIDA, SEIICHI, plant physiologist, educator; b. Tokyo, Sept. 7, 1926; s. Hiromoto C. and Yoshika Y.; B.Sc., Tokyo U., 1952, D.Sc., 1961; m. Akiyo Kondo, Nov. 18, 1952; children—Yuichi, Junko. Lectr., Tokyo U., 1962-65; mem. faculty Tokyo Met. U., 1965—, prof. plant physiology, 1976-88; research asso. McGill U., Montreal, Que., Can., 1961-62. Mem. Japanese Soc. Plant Physiologists, Bot. Soc. Japan, N.Y. Acad. Scis. Author papers in field; editor Plant and Cell Physiology, 1975-78, 85—; editor Bot. mag., 1956-68, editor-in-chief, 1984. Home: 2-30-24 Sengoku, Bunkyo-ku, Tokyo 112 Japan Office: 2-1-1 Fukazawa, Setagaya-ku, Tokyo 158 Japan

YOSHIMURA, JUNZO, architect; b. Tokyo, Sept. 7, 1908; m. Takiko Ohmura, 1944; 1 child, Takako. Grad. Tokyo Acad. Fine Arts (now Tokyo U. Arts), 1926. Registered 1st class architect, Japan. Mem. staff Antonin Raymond, Architect, Tokyo, also Pa., 1931-42; individual practice architecture, Tokyo, 1943—; asst. prof. Tokyo U. Arts, 1944-62, prof., 1962-70, prof. emeritus, 1970—; pres. Junzo Yoshimura Architect, Tokyo, 1970—. Architect basic design Imperial Palace Japan, 1963, bldg. Aichi Prefectural U. of Arts, 1970, Nara Internat. Mus., 1973, Japan House, N.Y.C., 1971, Norwegian Embassy, Tokyo, 1978. Recipient Parson medal Parson Sch. Design, 1956, award Japanese Acad. Art, 1975; decorated 3d Order Merit (Japan). Mem. AIA (hon.), Archtl. Inst. Japan (Archtl. Inst. prize 1956), Japan Architects Assn., Sociadad de Arqutectos Mexicanos (hon.). Office: Junzo Yoshimura Architect, 8-6 Mejiro 3-chome, Toshima-ku, Tokyo 171 Japan *

YOSHITANI, YUTAKA, engineering educator; b. Tokyo, Aug. 30, 1928; s. Senkichi and Aiko Y.; m. Kazuko Ohkura, June 22, 1958; children: Makoto, Ken. BS in Engring., Tokyo U., 1952, PhD, 1981; MS, MIT, 1960. With tech. devel. dept. Fuji Iron & Steel Co., Tokyo, 1958-70; with engring. div. Nippon Steel Co., Tokyo, 1970-80; prof. mech. engring. Nagaoka U. Tech., Japan, 1980—. Author: Towards Japanese Style Technology, 1980; inventor in field. Tech. advisor Niigata Pri, 1985, Nagaoka Technopolice, 1985, Nagaoka City, 1985. Mem. Mech. Engring. Soc., Iron & Steel Inst. (Yamakawa award 1980), Soc. Instrument and Control Engrs., Japan Robotics Soc., Assn. Indsl. Robotics. Home: 4-26-19 Deneuchofu, Otaka, Tokyo 145, Japan Office: Tech U Nagaoka, Fukasawa 1769-1, Nagaoka, Niigata 940-21, Japan

YOSHIYAMA, HIROKICHI, electrical machinery manufacturing company executive; b. Kobe, Japan, Dec. 1, 1911; s. Kyosuke and Rei Yoshiyama; grad. Elec. Engring. Dept., Tokyo U., 1935; m. Michi Samejima; children—Emiko Yoshiyama Takekoshi, Yuriko Yoshiyama Saito. With Hitachi, Ltd., Tokyo, 1935—, dir., 1961-87, exec. mng. dir., then sr. exec. mng. dir., 1964-69, exec. v.p., 1969-71, pres., 1971-81, chmn., 1981-87; cons. bd. dirs., 1987—; commr. Space Activities Commn., Sci. and Tech. Agy., 1985—. Recipient medal of honor with blue ribbon, 1973, First Class of the Order of the Sacred Treasure, 1982. Mem. Assn. for Promotion Internat. Trade (Japan) (v.p. 1978—), Japan Elec. Mfrs. Assn. (pres. 1974-76), Japan Machinery Fedn. (v.p. 1978—), Keidanren (Fedn. Econ. Orgns.) (vice chmn. 1980-86). Home: 17-15-103, 3-chome Uehara, Shibuya-ku, Tokyo Japan Office: Hitachi Ltd, 6 Kanda-Surugadai, 4-chome, Chiyoda-ku, Tokyo 101 Japan

YOSHIZAKI, YASUHIRO, educator; b. Oita-ken, Japan, Feb. 4, 1943; s. Hikojiro and Keiko (Ishibashi) Y.; B.A., Kyushu U., 1965, M.A., 1967; M.A. in English, Stephen F. Austin State U., Nacogdoches, Tex., 1972; m. Kuniko Ikeda, Mar. 30, 1966; 1 child, Izumi. Instr., Kinjogakuin U., Omori, Nagoya, 1969-70; teaching asst. Stephen F. Austin State U., 1970-72; mem. faculty Kitakyushu U., 1972—, asso. prof. English and comparative lit., 1973-84, prof., 1984—; vis. scholar U. Calif., Berkeley, 1975-76. Kimura Found. grantee, 1975. Mem. Assn. Asian Studies, Assn. Tchrs. Japanese, Japanese Comparative Lit. Assn., English Lit. Soc. Japan, Am. Lit. Soc. Japan, Kyushu Am. Lit. Soc. Mem. United Ch. of Christ. Author: Bibliography of William Faulkner in Japan, 1932-1972, 1975; Studies in Japanese Literature and Language, A Bibliography of English Materials, 1979; Faulkner's Theme of Nature, 1982. Office: Kitakyushu U, 4 Kitagata Kokura, Kitakyushu 802 Japan

YOST, ROBERT LLOYD, international affairs consultant, retired foreign service officer; b. Kirkland, Wash., Sept. 8, 1922; s. Bartley Francis and Irma (Cleopha) Y.; m. June Horsley, Sept. 2, 1945; children: Barbara June, Elizabeth Anne, John Bartley. B.A. in Econs., UCLA, 1942; postgrad., Harvard U., 1952-53; M.S. in Internat. Relations, George Washington U., 1968. Commd. fgn. service officer Dept. State, 1946; 3d sec. Madrid, 1946-49; vice consul Antwerp, Belgium, 1949-52; consul Leopoldville, 1953-55; research specialist Dept. State, Washington, 1958-58; officer-in-charge OEEC affairs 1958-59; consul, prin. officer Cebu, P.R., 1959-62; 1st sec., fin. adviser U.S. del. to OECD Paris, 1962-65; also U.S. mem. com. invisible transactions and alt. U.S. rep. bd. mgmt. European Monetary Agreement; spl. asst. to asst. sec. of State for European Affairs, 1965-67; assigned to Nat. War Coll., 1967-68; counselor, dep. chief mission Am. embassy Addis Ababa, Ethiopia, 1968-72; ambassador to Burundi, Bujumbura, 1972-74; dep. insp. gen. Fgn. Service, Washington, 1974-78; ambassador to Dominican Republic, Santo Domingo, 1978-82; internat. affairs cons. 1982—. Served with AUS, 1942-46. Mem. Am. Fgn. Service Assn., Acad. Polit. Sci., Am. Acad., Nat. War Coll. Alumni Assn., World Affairs Council of No. Calif., Fedn. for Am. Immigration Reform. Club: Commonwealth. Address: 117 Mountain Valley Oakland CA 94605

YOST, WILLIAM ARTHUR, III, corporation lawyer; b. Greensburg, Pa., Apr. 7, 1935; s. William Arthur Jr. and Virginia (Penny) Y.; m. Katherine Luedke, Apr. 20, 1963; children: Virginia, Alexander. AB, Haverford Coll., 1957; LLB, Yale U., 1960. Bar: Wis. 1960, Tex 1984. Assoc. Erbstoeszer, Cleary & Zabel, Milw., 1960-61; atty. Allis-Chalmers Co., Milw., 1961-68, Pabst Brewing Co., Milw., 1968-70, Ft. Howard Paper Co., Green Bay, Wis., 1970-72; corp. counsel, sec., v.p. adminstrn. Will Ross Inc., Milw., 1972-78; pres. Yost, Krombach & Schmitt, S.C., Cedarburg, Wis., 1978-83; v.p. legal and sec. Pearle Health Services Inc., Dallas, 1983—, also bd. dirs.; guest lectr. in internat. law So. Meth. U., Dallas, 1987—. Sec. Wis. Arthritis Found., Milw., 1978-83, bd. dirs., 1985—; bd. dirs. St. John's Home, Milw., 1975-83, pres. 1983; bd. dirs. Milw. chpt. ARC, 1963-70, 72-78, Town North YMCA, Dallas, 1987—. Mem. ABA, Internat. Bar Assn., Tex. Bar Assn., Wis. Bar Assn., Dallas Bar Assn., Am. Corp. Counsel Assn., Am. Soc. Corp. Secs. Republican. Episcopalian. Clubs: Yale (N.Y.C.); Town (Milw.); T-Bar Racquet (Dallas). Office: Pearle Health Services Inc 2534 Royal Ln Dallas TX 75229

YOSTE, CHARLES TODD, lawyer; b. Vicksburg, Miss., Nov. 11, 1948; s. Harry M. and Charlene (Todd) Y. B.S., Miss. State U., 1971; J.D., U. Miss., 1976. Bar: Miss. 1976, U.S. Dist. Ct. Miss. 1976, U.S. Ct. Appeals, 1982. Sole practice, Starkville, Miss., 1976—; city atty. Starkville, Miss., 1979-85, pros. atty., 1977-79, city judge, 1981-82. Candidate for Congress 2d dist. Miss., 1980. Served to capt. U.S. Army, 1971-73. Recipient Outstanding Young Man award Starkville Jaycees, 1980. Mem. ABA, Miss. Bar Assn., Am. Trial Lawyers Assn., Miss. Trial Lawyers Assn., Starkville C. of C. (pres. 1982), Am. Legion. Republican. Roman Catholic. Lodge: Rotary. Home: 902 S Montgomerery St Starkville MS 39759 Office: PO Box 488 Starkville MS 39759

YOU, JONG SOUE, economics educator, consultant; b. Korea, Nov. 11, 1941; came to Can., 1971; s. Min Kyu and Keum Soon (Kim) Y.; m. Kyoung-Ja Chung, Aug. 30, 1970; children—John, Carolyn. B.A., Seoul Nat. U., Korea, 1964, M.A., 1966; Ph.D., SUNY-Binghamton, 1972. Asst. prof. Ea. Wash. State U., Cheney, 1970-71; assoc. prof. Algoma U. Coll., Sault Ste Marie, Ont., Can., 1971—, chmn. dept. econs., 1976—, mem. bd. govs., 1985—; cons. Can.-Am. Fin. Cons., Sault Ste Marie, 1984—; vis. research fellow Carlton U., 1978-79, Korea Inst. of Energy and Resources, 1982. Author: Security of Long-Term Supply of Coal for Korea and Canada's Coal Resources, 1983; contbr. articles to profl. jours. Fulbright travel grantee, 1966. Mem. Am. Econ. Assn., Can. Econs. Assn. Club: Sault Ste Marie Golf. Avocations: down-hill skiing; golf. Office: Algoma U Coll, Sault Sainte Marie, ON Canada P6A 2G4

YOUN, CHANG E., manufacturing company executive; b. Jinju, Kyungsang Nam-Do, Korea, Nov. 16, 1939; s. Byung Min Youn and Il Nam Cho; m. Mi Jae Bang, Apr. 3, 1966; children: Ji Myung, Ji Ho. B., Seoul Nat. U., 1964; postgrad. Internat. Mktg. Inst., Australia, 1974. Chief, Gold Star Co., Ltd., Seoul, 1964-68; mgr. Gold Star Telecomm Co., Ltd., Seoul, 1969-74; mng. mgr. Lucky-Goldstar Internat., Seoul, 1974-79; pres. Kanglim Industries Co. Ltd., Chongwon, Korea, 1979—, Kanglim Co. Ltd., Chongwon, 1982—. Served with Korean Marines, 1960-63. Unido fellow, 1973-74. Avocation: mountain climbing. Office: Kanglim Co Ltd, PO Box Yoido 745, Seoul Republic of Korea also: Hyondo Indsl Complex, Chongwon Chungbuk Republic of Korea

YOUN, SO YOUNG, electrical engineer; b. Seoul, Korea, Nov. 20, 1941; came to U.S., 1972; s. Tai Ku Youn and Kil (Soon) Kim; m. Young Mee Youn, Apr. 12, 1972; 1 dau., H. Grace. B.S. in Elec. Engring., Yonsei U., Seoul, 1965; M.S. in Elec. Engring., U. Mo., 1975; M.S. in Computer Engring., So. Meth. U., 1980. Research assoc. Yonsei U., 1965-67; fellow UN (I.T.U.), Geneva, 1969-71; engr. Mostek Corp. subs. United Technologies, Carrollton, Tex., 1980-83; sr. engr. Fairchild Semiconductor Div., Mountain View, Calif., 1984-85; prin. CMOS prodn. engr. solid state div. research and devel. Honeywell Inc., Plymouth, Minn., 1985-86; sr. engr. Monolithic Memories Inc., 1986—. Mem. IEEE (Electron Devices Soc.), IEEE (Solid State Circuit Soc.), IEEE VLSI subcom. 1982-83). Home: 4937 Flat Rock Circle San Jose CA 95136

YOUNES, JEAN M., cardiologist; b. Tunis, Tunisia, May 2, 1945; s. Jules and Mathilde (Marec). Y.; m. Marianne B. Lenkel, June 20, 1971; children: Jennifer, Jessica, Jeremy. MD, U. Paris, 1970. Diplomate in cardiology. Intern, resident Paris hosps., 1969-72; practice medicine specializing in cardiology Paris, 1972—. Office: 13 rue de Tretaigne, 75018 Paris France

YOUNG, LORD (DAVID IVOR), secretary of state for trade and industry; b. England, Feb. 27, 1932; s. Joseph and Rebecca Y.; m. Lita Marianne Shaw, 1956; 2 daus. Student, Christ's Coll., Finchley; LLB with honors, Univ. Coll., London. Bar: admitted solicitor 1956. Exec. Great Universal Stores Ltd., 1956-61; chmn. Eldonwall Ltd., 1961-75, Mfrs. Hanover Property Services Ltd., 1974-84; dir. Town & Country Properties Ltd., 1972-75; chmn. British ORT, 1975-80, pres., 1980-82; mem. adminstrv. com. World ORT Union, 1980-84; dir. Ctr. for Policy Studies, 1979-82, mem. mgmt. bd., 1977; mem. English Indsl. Estates Corp., 1980-82; chmn. Manpower Services Commn., 1982-84, indsl. advisor, 1979-80, spl. advisor, 1980-82; minister without portfolio 1984-85, sec. of state for employment, 1985-87, sec. of state for trade and industry, 1987—; chmn. Internat. Council of Jewish Social and Welfare Services, 1981-84; hon. FRPS, 1981. Mem. NEDC. Clubs: Savile; West Sussex Golf. Address: care 88 Brook St, London W1 England *

YOUNG, ALEXANDER STUARD, JR., lawyer; b. Washington, Aug. 27, 1921; s. Alexander Stuard and Gertrude Louise (Parsons) Y.; m. Mary Elizabeth Primm, Oct. 25, 1945; children: Alexander Stuard III, A. Suzanne Young Wieland, A. Steven, A. Stanley. BS in Econs, U. Pa., 1942; JD, Georgetown U., 1950. Bar: D.C. 1950, Pa. 1951, U.S. Supreme Ct 1953. Commd. 2d lt. U.S. Army Air Force, 1942; advanced through grades to col. U.S. Air Force, 1966; service in N. Africa and Italy, 1943-45; sta. at Hdqrs. Washington, 1946-50, 51-52; ret. 1952; with Mil. Intelligence Res., Phila., 1953-56; dist. comdr. OSI Res., 1956-65; assoc. firm Stradley, Ronon, Stevens & Young, Phila., 1950-51, 52-56; partner Stradley, Ronon, Stevens & Young, 1957—; dir. Vestaur Securities, Inc. Author: The Rights and Liabilities of Shareholders—United States, 1977, also articles; editorial asst. in transl.: W. Ger. Fgn. Investment Co. Laws, 1971, W. Ger. Domestic Investment Co. Laws, 1981; contbr.: chpt. to Practical Guide for Investments in the U.S, 1979, 2d edit., 1982. Bd. dirs., sec.-treas. Binder Schweitzer Amazonian Hosp. Found., Inc., N.Y.C., 1961-70; mem. Branford (Conn.) Electric Ry. Assn., 1969—, Pop Warner Little Scholars, Phila., 1975—; bd. dirs. World Affairs Council of Phila., 1984-88, adv. bd. 1988—. Decorated Bronze Star, Air Force Commendation ribbon. Mem. Am. Bar Assn., Pa. Bar Assn., Phila. Bar Assn., D.C. Bar Assn., Asia-Pacific Lawyers Assn., Inter-Am. Bar Assn., Internat. Bar Assn. (mem. council bus. law sect. 1986—), Fed. Bar Assn., Am. Law Inst., Am. Judicature Soc., Internat. Fiscal Assn., Nat. Lawyers Club, Union Internat. des Avocats, Phi Alpha Delta, Lambda Chi Alpha. Republican. Episcopalian. Clubs: Inst. Dirs. (London), Pen and Wig (London); Officers Open Mess of McGuire (N.J.) AFB; Penn; Union League (Phila.); Army-Navy (Washington). Lodge: Masons. Office: 2600 One Commerce Sq Philadelphia PA 19103-7098

YOUNG, BARNEY THORNTON, lawyer; b. Chillicothe, Tex., Aug. 10, 1934; s. Bayne and Helen Irene (Thornton) Y.; m. Sarah Elizabeth Taylor, Aug. 31, 1957; children: Jay Thornton, Sarah Elizabeth, Serena Taylor. B.A., Yale U., 1955; LL.B., U. Tex., 1958. Bar: Tex. 1958. Assoc. Thompson, Knight, Wright & Simmons, Dallas, 1958-65; partner Rain, Harrell, Emery, Young & Doke, Dallas, 1965-87; mem. firm Locke Purnell Rain Harrell (A Profl. Corp.), 1987—; dir. Horchow Mail Order, Inc., Jones-Blair Co. Mem. adv. council Dallas Community Chest Trust Fund, Inc., 1964-66; bd. dirs. Mental Health Assn. Dallas County, Inc., 1969-72; trustee Hockaday Sch., Dallas, 1971-77, Dallas Zoolog. Soc., 1986—; trustee Lamplighter Sch., Dallas, 1976—, chmn. bd. trustees, 1983-86; trustee St. Mark's Sch., Dallas, 1970—, pres., 1976-78; trustee The Found. for the Callier Ctr. and Communication Disorders, 1988—, Friends of the Ctr. for Human Nutrition, 1988—; bd. dirs. Trammell Crow Family Found., 1984-87; mem. Yale Devel. Bd., 1984—. Fellow Tex. Bar Found.; mem. Am., Tex., Dallas bar assns., Am. Judicature Soc., Order of Coif, Phi Beta Kappa, Pi Sigma Alpha, Phi Gamma Delta, Phi Delta Phi. Clubs: Dallas, City, Dallas Country, Dallas County Republican Men's (bd. dirs. 1977-79), Petroleum (all Dallas); Yale (Dallas, N.Y.C.). Home: 6901 Turtle Creek Blvd Dallas TX 75205 Office: Locke Purnell Rain Harrell Suite 2200 2200 Ross Ave Dallas TX 75201-6776

YOUNG, B.J. BOND, national/international marketing executive; b. Dowagiac, Mich., Mar. 26, 1948; d. Charles W. and Agnes Mary Ann (Hampel) Sarabyn; m. Alexander Young, Oct. 9, 1982. Student, Northwood Inst. Pvt. practice mktg. communications N.Y.C., Chgo., Washington, 1967-78; ptnr. Bond & Polos Communications Cons., Chgo., 1974-78; advt. mgr. H. Wilson Co. div. Ebsco, South Holland, Ill., 1978-81, dir. mktg., 1981-84; pres., owner On Target Solutions, Ft. Lauderdale, Fla., 1984—. Active fed. and state polit. campaign mgmt. Recipient various profl. awards. Mem. Internat. Platform Assn. Home: 619 Orton Ave #601 Fort Lauderdale FL 33304 Office: 300 SW 2nd St Suite #9 Fort Lauderdale FL 33312

YOUNG, CHARLES EDWARD, university chancellor; b. San Bernardino, Calif., Dec. 30, 1931; s. Clayton Charles and Eula May (Walters) Y. A.A., San Bernardino Coll., 1954; A.B., U. Calif.-Riverside, 1955; M.A., U. Calif.-Riverside, Los Angeles, 1957, Ph.D., 1960; D.H.L. (hon.), U. Judaism, Los Angeles, 1969. Congl. fellow Washington, 1958-59; adminstrv. analyst Office of the Pres., U. Calif., Berkeley, 1959-60; asst. prof. polit. sci. U. Calif., Davis, 1960; asst. prof. polit. sci. UCLA, 1960-66, assoc. prof., 1966-69, prof., 1969—, asst. to chancellor, 1960-62, asst. chancellor, 1962-63, vice chancellor, adminstrn., 1963-68, now chancellor.; dir. UMF Systems, Inc., Intel Corp., Am. Savs. and Loan Assn., Fin. Corp. Am.; Cons. Peace Corps., 1961-62, to Ford Found. on Latin Am. Activities, 1964-66. Mem. Nat. Com. on U.S.-China Relations; mem. chancellor's assos. UCLA; past chair. Assn. Am. Univs.; mem. adminstrv. bd. Internat. Assn. Univs.; bd. govs. Found. Internat. Exchange Sci. and Cultural Info. by Telecommunications, The Theatre Group Inc.; v.p. Young Musicians Found.; bd. dirs. Los Angeles Internat. Visitors Council, Greater Los Angeles Energy Coalition; trustee UCLA Found. Served with USAF, 1951-52. Named Young Man of Year Westwood Jr. C. of C., 1962. Office: UCLA 405 Hilgard Ave Los Angeles CA 90024 *

YOUNG, DAVID REGINALD, managing director; b. Jersey City, N.J., Nov. 10, 1936; s. Francis Herbert and Winifred Ann (Brady) Y.; m. Suannah Lee Kelly, May 24, 1969; children: Bradden Hamilton, Catherine Longworth, Christina Molloy, David Kelly DePauw, Jonathan Cameron Childs. BS in Physics, Wheaton Coll., Ill., 1959; MA in Law, Oxford U., Eng., 1963; LLD, Cornell U., Ithaca, N.Y., 1964; PhD, Oxford U., Eng., 1982. Assoc. Milbank Tweed Hadley and McCloy, N.Y.C., 1965-70; asst. to Henry Kissinger Nat. Security Council, Washington, 1970-73; dir. Oxford (Eng.) Analytica Ltd., 1975—; lectr. in politics Queen's Coll., Oxford. Contbg. editor America in Perspective, 1986. Served to cap. U.S. Army, 1959-61. Mem. Royal Inst. Internat. Affairs, Internat. Inst. for Strategic Studies., Am. Bar Assn. Club: Oxford (Cambridge). Home: The West Wing Baldon House, Marsh Baldon Oxfordshire England OX5 9LS Office: Oxford Analytica Ltd, 91A High Street, Oxford England OX1 4BJ

YOUNG, DOROTHY THERESSA, educator; b. Cleve., Jan. 14, 1929; d. James Anthony and Josephine Juanita (Page) Y. B.A., Western Res. U., 1950; postgrad., Bryn Mawr Coll., 1955; student Inst. Edn., U. London, 1964, 65, Royal Sch. Church Music (Eng.), 1964, 65, St. John's Coll. (Eng.), 1966, Matlock Coll. Edn. (Eng.), 1967, Downe House (Eng.), 1970, Kodaly Course, Esztergom (Hungary), 1971, Royal Acad. Dance (London), 1971, Centre de Danse Internat. Rosella Hightower (France), 1972, Internat. Ballet Sem. (Denmark), 1972, 74, Internationaler Sommerkurs Fur Tanz (Switzerland), 1973-75. Cert. tchr. N.Y.C., N.Y. Tchr. Cleve. Bd. Edn., 1957-61, N.Y.C. Bd. Edn., 1962—. Mem. St. Thomas Ch., N.Y. Mem. Met. Mus. Art, Mus. Modern Art, N.Y. Zool. Soc., Am. Mus. Natural History, South St. Seaport Mus. Episcopalian. Club: Bryn Mawr. Avocations: dance; karate; music; cooking. Office: PS 116 Manhattan 210 E 33d St New York NY 10016

YOUNG, EDWIN S. W., federal agency official; b. Honolulu, Nov. 13, 1943; s. Hoon Kwan and Clara (Lee) Y.; m. Joan Tay, May 19, 1978. BA, U. Hawaii, 1966; MBA, U. Utah, 1975; MS, U. So. Calif., 1983. Asst. gen. mgr. Royal Men's Shops, Inc., Honolulu, 1973-75; mgmt. analyst U.S. Gen. Acctg. Office, Denver and Honolulu, 1976-83; audit mgr. U.S. Air Force Audit Agy., Los Angeles, 1983-84, 87—; commd. fgn. service officer Dept. State, 1984, with Office of Insp. Gen., Office Policy and Program Rev., Washington, 1984-87, USAF Audit Agy. rep. to World Affairs Council So. Calif., Norton AFB, 1987—. U.S. govt. rep. Pacific and Asian Affairs Council, Honolulu, 1978-83; community coordinator, com. chmn. Kailua Neighborhood Bd., Honolulu, 1978-83; area rep. Urban Mass Transit Authority, Honolulu, 1978-83; active John F. Kennedy Ctr. for Arts, Corcoran Gallery Art. Served to capt. USAF, 1966-72. Recipient Commendation award U.S. Gen. Acctg. Office, 1980, Commendation award U.S. Air Force Audit Agy., 1983, Commendation award Air Force Acctg. and Fin. Ctr., 1984. Mem. Assn. Govt. Accts., Soc. Mil. Comptrollers, Inst. Internal Auditors, Nat. Geog. Soc., Chinese C. of C., World Affairs Council, Smithsonian Inst. Roman Catholic. Avocations: photography, skiing, swimming, sailing, snorkeling.

YOUNG, FRANCIS ALLAN, psychologist; b. Utica, N.Y., Dec. 29, 1918; s. Frank Allan and Julia Mae (McOwen) Y.; m. Judith Wadsworth Wright, Dec. 21, 1945; children—Francis Allan, Thomas Robert. B.S., U. Tampa, 1941; M.A., Western Res. U., 1945; Ph.D., Ohio State U., 1949. Instr. Wash. State U., Pullman, 1948-50; asst. prof. Wash. State U., 1950-56, assoc. prof., 1956-61, prof. psychology, 1961—, dir. primate research center, 1957—; vis. prof. ophthalmology U. Oreg., Portland, 1964; vis. prof. pharmacology U. Uppsala (Sweden) Med. Sch., 1971; vis. prof. optometry U. Houston, 1979-80. Editor: (with Donald B. Lindsley) Early Experience and Visual Information Processing in Perceptual and Reading Disorders, 1970. Named Disting. Psychologist State of Wash., Wash. Psychol. Assn., 1973; recipient Paul Yarwood Meml. award Calif. Optometric Assn., 1978; Apollo award Am. Optometric Assn., 1980; Nat. Acad. Sci.-NRC sr. postdoctoral fellow in physiol. psychology U. Wash., 1956-57; research grantee NSF, 1950-53; research grantee USAF, 1965-72; research grantee NIH, 1960-78. Fellow Am. Acad. Optometry, Am. Pychol. Assn. ((pres. Div. 31) 1974-75)); mem. Common Cause, Ams. Dem. Action, Assn. Research in Vision and Ophthalmology, Internat. Soc. Myopia Research (sec.-treas. 1978—), AAAS, Psychonomic Soc., Wash. State Psychol. Assn. (exec. sec. 1965-77), Western Psychol. Assn.; Mem. N.Y. Acad. Scis.; mem. Sigma Xi, Psi Chi (nat. pres. 1968-70). Home: NW 344 Webb St Pullman WA 99163 Office: Wash State U Pullman WA 99164

YOUNG, FRANCIS BALDWIN, JR., pharmacist; b. Charlotte, N.C., July 24, 1952; s. Francis Baldwin and Martha (Bately) Y.; BS in Pharmacy, N.D. State U., 1976. Intern pharmacy City Drug Store, Mohall, N.D., 1975-76; pharmacist Ronholm Drug, Jamestown, N.D., 1976-81; pharmacist, mgr. Revco Drug Store Inc., Big Spring, Tex., 1981-83; pharmacist, owner The Medicine Shoppe, Belton, Tex., 1984—; cons. pharmacist Hi Acres Nursing Center, Jamestown, 1978-81, 83—; mem. Girling Health Care Adv. Bd., 1984—. Columnist Am. Jour. Med. Philately, 1975—. Named Outstanding Jaycees of Month, 1977, 78, 79, 80. Mem. Tex. Pharm. Assn., Nat. Assn. Retail Druggist, Am. Topical Assn., Jamestown Jaycees (Presdl. award of honor 1979, Disting. Service award 1980, named as N.D. Outstanding Project chmn. 1979-80). Roman Catholic. Lodge: KC (Outstanding Knight of Month award 1987). Office: The Medicine Shoppe 502 E Central Ave Belton TX 76513

YOUNG, GARRY GEAN, consulting engineer; b. Ft. Smith, Ark., Sept. 7, 1951; s. Lee Leonard and Lola Belle (Bartlett) Y.; m. Patricia Ann Farmer, June 24, 1977; children—Kathryn Elizabeth, Emily Anne. B.S. in M.E., U. Ark., 1974, M.S., 1975. Registered profl. engr., Ark., D.C. Prodn. engr. Ark. Power & Light Co., Little Rock, 1975-79; fellow Adv. Com. on Reactor Safeguards, Washington, 1979-80, reactor engr., 1980-81; lead licensing engr. United Energy Services Corp., Atlanta, 1981-85; pres., cons. engr. Young Engring. Services Inc., Little Rock, 1986—. Author tech. papers. Youth leader, Sunday Sch. tchr. Knollwood Bapt. Ch., Burke, Va., 1980-81; co-dir. children's ch. First Bapt. Ch. of Pelham, Ala., 1982-83. Mem. ASME, Am. Nuclear Soc. (chmn. Ark. sect. 1987-88), Health Physics Soc., Pi Tau Sigma. Home: 4100 Sam Peck Rd Little Rock AR 72212 Office: Young Engring Services One City Ctr 400 W 7th St Suite 201 Little Rock AR 72201

YOUNG, GEORGE HAYWOOD, JR., business executive, retired army officer; b. Pine Bluff, Ark., Jan. 21, 1921; s. George Haywood and Sarah (Mercer) Y.; B.S. with honors, The Citadel, 1942; postgrad. Command and Gen. Staff Coll., 1946, Armed Forces Staff Coll., 1955, Indsl. Coll. Armed Forces, 1962; M.S., U. So. Calif., 1958; M.B.A., George Washington U., 1962; m. Jeanne Marie Collins, Feb. 5, 1946; children—Cornelia Collins, George Haywood III. Commd. 2d lt. U.S. Army, 1942, advanced through grades to brig. gen., 1966; served ETO, World War II, in 3 combat amphibious landings and 6 campaigns; staff mem. Joint Brazil-U.S. Mil. Commn., Rio de Janeiro, 1946-49; bn. officer 3d Inf. Div., Ft. Benning, 1949-50, Korea, 1950-52; mem. Army Dept. Gen. Staff, Washington, 1952-54, 58-61, Ft. Monroe, 1954-56; chief plans br., dep. chief staff logistics U.S. Army Europe, 1962-64; comdg. officer 1st Brigade, 3d Inf. Div., Germany, 1964-66; chief staff U.S. Army Communications Zone, Europe, 1966-67; dep. chief staff plans and ops. U.S. Army Viet Nam, 1967; asst. div. comdr. Americal Div., 1967-68; comdg. gen. Da Nang Support Command, Viet Nam, 1968, 24th Inf. Div., Germany, 1968-70; dir. U.S. Army Materiel Command, Washington, 1970-71; ret., 1971; corp. dir. indsl. relations Vendo Corp., Kansas City, Mo., 1972-79, v.p. govt. affairs, 1979-81; pres. Milton Corp., Leavenworth, Kans., 1982—. Pres., German-Am. Fedn. Germany, 1969-70; Alpine dist. commr. Boy Scouts Europe, 1969-70. Decorated D.S.M., Silver Star with oak leaf cluster, Legion of Merit with 3 oak leaf clusters, Bronze Star with V and 2 oak leaf clusters, Purple Heart with oak leaf clusters, Air medal with 22 oak leaf clusters, Army Commendation ribbon with 2 oak leaf clusters, Combat Infantry badge with star; Order Mil. Merit (Brazil); Order Merit Fifth Class (Viet Nam); Cross of Gallantry (Viet Nam); recipient Internat. Disting. Service award Kiwanis; Stadt Schweinfurt award; named hon. senator Augsburger Carneval Verein. Mem. Kans. Hist. Soc., Internat. Relations Council, Mil. Order World Wars. Clubs: Army Navy Country (Arlington, Va.); Army-Navy (Washington); Ft. Leavenworth (Kans.) Golf and Country. Home: 207 Vine St Leavenworth KS 66048

YOUNG, GERALD LEONARD, SR., farm equipment manufacturing executive; b. Billings, Mont., June 18, 1937; s. Leonard V. and Gladys (Laughery) Y.; m. Georgia M. Hartman, Mar. 5, 1982; children: Gerald L. Jr., Robert C. Student, Eastern Mont. Coll.; BA, Mont. State U., 1962. Territory mgr. Cert. Labs., Dallas, 1968-72, Midland Implement, Billings, 1972-75; ops. mgr. Renn U.S. div. Anthes Industries, Billings, 1975-80; gen. mgr. Renn U.S. div. Anthes Industries, Ft. Benton, Mont., 1980-84; dir. mktg. Renn div. Anthes Industries, Edmonton, Alta., Can., 1984-85, gen. mgr., 1985-87; v.p., gen. mgr. Renn-Verter, Edmonton, Alberta, Can., 1987—; corp. officer Anthes Industries Mississaqua, Ont., Can., 1985-86, Strathcond Resource, Edmonton, 1986—. Served with USN, 1954-58, Korea. Republican. Lodge: Elks. Home: 5908 177th St, Edmonton, AB Canada T6M 1H8 Office: Renn-Vertec Inc, 9303 51st Ave, Edmonton, AB Canada T6E 4W8

YOUNG, GORDON ELLSWORTH, composer, organist; b. McPherson, Kans., Oct. 15, 1919; s. Benjamin Warden and Rose Esther (Johnson) Y. Mus.B., Southwestern Coll., 1940, Mus.D., 1960; attended, Curtis Inst. Music, 1944-46. Organist First Meth. Ch., Tulsa, 1940-44; Organist First Presbyn. Ch., Lancaster, Pa., 1944-48, Detroit, 1952-72; concert artist.; Music tchr.; mem. faculty Tex. Christian U., 1950-52. Composer numerous organ, choir, solo voice and instrumental works. Recipient Special Tribute award State of Mich. Mem. ASCAP (several awards). Republican. Presbyn. Office: Box 256 Detroit MI 48231

YOUNG, HOWARD HOW-WAH, company executive; b. Hong Kong, Mar. 30, 1948; m. Joyce Cheng; 2 children. Shipping exec. Swire Shipping Agys., Ltd., Hong Kong, 1968-80; mng. dir. Swire Travel, Ltd., Hong Kong, 1980-86; gen. mgr. John Swire & Sons (China), Ltd., Beijing, 1986—. Active Hong Kong Urban Council, 1978-86. Named one of Ten Outstanding Young Persons Hong Kong Jaycees, 1978. Lodge: Rotary (Hong Kong). Office: John Swire & Sons Ltd, 4/F Swire House, Hong Kong Hong Kong

YOUNG, JAMES OLIVER, dentist, communication company executive; b. Parris Island, S.C., Apr. 19, 1945; s. William Oliver and Ruth Cherokee (Risner) Y.; m. Virginia Evelyn Koontz; children—Amy Robyn, Jenny Elizabeth, Thomas William. B.S., Southeast State U., Okla., 1967; D.D.S., Baylor U., 1972. Practice dentistry, Ardmore, Okla., 1972—; v.p. Cherokee Telephone Co., Calera, Okla., 1963—; pres. Communication Equipment Co., Calera, 1984—. Trustee Ardmore Devel. Authority, 1980-85; bd. dirs. Ardmore Community Concerts Assn., 1980-85. Named one of Outstanding Young Men Am., 1981. Fellow Acad. Gen. Dentistry, Acad. of Dentistry Internat.; mem. ADA, Okla. Dental Assn., Ind. Dentists of So. Okla. (pres. 1986), Okla. C. of C. (bd. dirs. 1984-85). Democrat. Methodist. Lodge: Masons. Avocations: skiing; sailing. Home: 2207 Ridgeway St Ardmore OK 73401 Office: 221 2d Ave NW Ardmore OK 73401

YOUNG, JESS WOLLETT, lawyer; b. San Antonio, Sept. 16, 1926; s. James L. and Zetta (Alonso) Y.; m. Mary Alma Keeter, Apr. 17, 1954; children—Zetta, Imogen. BA, Trinity U., San Antonio, 1957; LLB, St. Mary's U., 1958. Bar: Tex. 1957, U.S. Dist. Ct. (we. dist.) Tex. 1960, U.S. Dist. Ct. (so. dist.) Tex. 1961, U.S. Tax Ct. 1970, U.S. Ct. Appeals (5th cir.) 1981, U.S. Supreme Ct. 1981. Ptnr. Thompson, Thompson, Young & Jones, San Antonio, 1958-63, Mousund, Ball & Young, San Antonio, 1965-73; v.p., dir. Moursund, Ball & Young, Inc., San Antonio, 1973-78; pres., dir. Young & Richards, Inc., San Antonio, 1978-81, Young, Murray & Richards, Inc., San Antonio, 1981-82, Young & Murray, Inc., 1983-87, sole practice, 1987—; county judge, Bexar County (Tex.), 1964; city atty. City of Olmos Park (Tex.), 1965-70, City of Poteet (Tex.), 1975-76; spl. county judge, Bexar County, 1967. Mem. Tex. State Dem. Exec. Com., 1970-72, Tex. State Rep. Exec. Com., 1984—; Rep. Precinct committeeman, 1984—; Dem. precinct committeeman, San Antonio, 1964-76. Served with USNR, 1944-46. Mem. ABA, Tex. Assn. Def. Counsel, Tex. Assn. Bank Counsel, San Antonio Bar Assn., Delta Theta Phi. Episcopalian. Clubs: San Antonio Petroleum, San Antonio Gun (dir. 1958-63, 80-82). Home: 321 Thelma Dr San Antonio TX 78212 Office: 1017 N Central Pkwy Suite 155 San Antonio TX 78232

YOUNG, JOAN CRAWFORD, advertising executive; b. Hobbs, N.Mex., July 30, 1931; d. William Bill and Ora Maydelle (Boone) Crawford; m. Herchelle B. Young, Nov. 23, 1971 (div.). B.A., Hardin Simmons U., 1952; postgrad. Tex. Tech. U., 1953-54. Reporter, Lubbock (Tex.) Avalanche-Jour., 1952-54; promotion dir. KCBD-TV, Lubbock, 1954-62; account exec. Ward Hicks Advt., Albuquerque, 1962-70; v.p. Mellekas & Assocs., Advt., Albuquerque, 1970-78; pres. J. Young Advt., Albuquerque, 1978—. Bd. dirs. N.Mex. Symphony Orch., 1970-73, United Way of Greater Albuquerque, 1985—. Recipient Silver medal N.Mex. Advt. Fedn., 1977. Mem. N.Mex. Advt. Fedn. (dir. 1975-76), Am. Advt. Fedn., Greater Albuquerque C. of C. (dir. 1984). Republican. Author: (with Louise Allen and Audre Lipscomb) Radio and TV Continuity Writing, 1962. Home: 3425 Avenida Charada NW Albuquerque NM 87107 Also: 303 Roma NW Albuquerque NM 87102

YOUNG, JOHN A., JR., oil company executive; b. Newport, R.I., Aug. 29, 1909; s. John Albion and Ellen Spooner (Gladding) Y.; m. Helen Moseley Mackintosh. Ph.B., Brown U., 1932, M.Sc., 1934, postgrad., 1935-37; postgrad. Harvard U., 1937-39, Ph.D., 1946. Cert. petroleum geologist. Instr. in geology Mich. State Coll., East Lansing, 1939-44; asst. prof. geology Syracuse U., (N.Y.), 1946-47; geologist Sun Oil Co., McAllen, Tex., 1944-46, asst. dist. geologist, 1947-50, sr. staff geologist, Phila., 1950-70; with Tax Shelter Adv. Service, Narberth, Pa., 1970-73, sr. v.p., dir., 1970-73; sr. v.p. exploration and prodn. Omni-Exploration, Inc., Radnor, Pa., 1974-83. Author numerous reports. Fellow Geol. Soc. Am.; mem. Am. Assn. Petroleum Geologists, Houston Geol. Soc. Home: PO Box 436 Devon PA 19333 Office: 4 E Lancaster Ave Paoli PA 19301

YOUNG, JOHN ALAN, electronics company executive; b. Nampa, Idaho, Apr. 24, 1932; s. Lloyd Arthur and Karen Eliza (Miller) Y.; m. Rosemary Murray, Aug. 1, 1954; children: Gregory, Peter, Diana. B.S. in Elec. Engring, Oreg. State U., 1953; M.B.A., Stanford U., 1958. Various mktg. and finance positions Hewlett Packard Co. Inc., Palo Alto, Calif., 1958-63, gen. mgr. microwave div., 1963-68, v.p. electronic products group, 1968-74, exec. v.p., dir., 1974-77, pres., 1977—, chief exec. officer, 1978—; bd. dirs. Wells Fargo Bank, Chevron Corp. Chmn. ann. fund Stanford, 1969-73, nat. chmn. corp. gifts, 1973-77; Bd. dirs. Mid-Peninsula Urban Coalition, 1972-80, co-chmn., 1976-80; mem. adv. council Grad. Sch. Bus., Stanford U., 1968-73, 75-80, univ. trustee, 1977-86, chmn. Pres.'s Commn. Indsl. Competitiveness, 1983; chmn. Nat. Jr. Achievement, 1983-85. Served with USAF, 1954-56. Mem. Am. Electronics Assn. (founder, chmn. council on competitiveness, 1986), Policy Com. Bus. Roundtable, Bus. Council. Office: 3000 Hanover St Palo Alto CA 94304

YOUNG, JOHN ANDREW, lawyer; b. Corpus Christi, Tex., Nov. 10, 1916; s. Phillip Marvin and Katherine Julia Y.; m. Jane Fife Gallier, Jan. 21, 1950 (dec. 1977); children—Gaffney, Nancy, John, Robert, Patty. B.A., St. Edward's U., Austin, Tex., 1938, LL.D., 1961; student Tex. U. Sch. Law, 1939-41. Bar: Tex. 1940, U.S. Supreme Ct. 1955, U.S. Ct. Appeals (D.C. cir.) 1979, U. D.C. 1978. Chief prosecutor Dist. Atty's. Office, Corpus Christi, 1946-50; county atty. Nueces County (Tex.), Corpus Christi, 1950-51, county judge, 1952-56; mem. 1957-79 Congresses from 14th Tex. dist.; sole practice Washington, 1979—; legal and legis. cons. The Coastal Corp., Houston, 1979—. Contbr. numerous articles and treatises to newspapers and legal jours. Served to lt. cmdr. USN, 1941-45. Recipient Distinguished Service award City of Corpus Christi, 1971, Distinguished Service medal U.S. Fish & Wildlife Service, 1967; numerous plaques of appreciation, 1965-77. Mem. ABA, D.C. Bar Assn., Tex. Bar Assn., Maritime Law Assn. of U.S., Corpus Christi C. of C. (plaques 1965, 76), Delta Theta Phi. Clubs: Chesapeake Country, (Lusby, Md.), Old Dominion Yacht (Alexandria, Va.), Nat. Democratic (Washington). Lodges: K.C., Elks, Eagles, Moose, VFW, DAV, Am. Legion. Home: 1705 N Albemarle St McLean VA 22101 Office: 1899 L St Suite 500 Washington DC 20036

YOUNG, JOHN HARDIN, lawyer; b. Washington, Apr. 25, 1948; s. John D. and Laura Virginia (Gwathmey) Y. A.B., Colgate U., 1970; J.D., U. Va., 1973; postgrad., Hague Acad. Internat. Law, Netherlands, 1973; B.C.L., Oxford U., (Eng.), 1976. Bar: Va. 1973, D.C. 1974, Pa. 1979, U.S. Dist. Ct. (ea. dist.) Va. 1974, U.S. Dist. Ct. (ea. dist.) Pa. 1978, U.S. Dist. Ct. D.C. 1974, Internat. Trade Ct. 1974, U.S. Ct. Appeals (4th, Fed. and D.C. cirs.), U.S. Supreme Ct. 1977. Intern U.S. Senator William B. Spong, Jr., Washington, 1968; asst. atty. gen. complex litigation Commonwealth of Va., Richmond, 1976-78; trial counsel U.S. Dept. Labor, Washington, 1981-82; sole practice Washington, 1983-88; ptnr. Porter, Wright, Morris & Arthur, Washington, 1988—; U.S. rep. UN Internat. Law Seminar, Geneva, 1974; mem. adv. bd. Antitrust Bull., Jour. Reprints Antitrust and Econs.; mem. U.S. Sec. State's Adv. Com. Pvt. Internat. Law, 1987—; lectr. continuing legal edn. Contbr. articles to profl. jours. Mem. ABA (council 1986—, adminstrv. law sect., chmn. trade regulation and competition com. 1983-86), Am. Law Inst., Hon. Soc. Middle Temple, Phi Alpha Theta, Phi Delta Phi. Episcopalian. Home: 5146 Woodmire Ln Alexandria VA 22311 Office: Porter Wright Morris & Arthur 1233 20th St NW Washington DC 20036

YOUNG, JOHN HENDRICKS, lawyer; b. Pelham, N.Y., Aug. 12, 1912; s. John Hendricks and Elizabeth (Chatterton) Y.; m. Fredrika Cosden Ritter, Feb. 8, 1967; children: John Hendricks, Anne Payne, Judith S. (Mrs. Richard Geiger). Grad., Phillips Acad., 1930; BA, Yale U., 1934, JD, 1937. Bar: N.Y. 1938. Asso. firm Carter, Ledyard & Milburn, N.Y.C., 1937-42, 45-47, mem. firm, 1947-82, counsel, 1982-84; counsel Hughes Hubbard & Reed, N.Y.C., 1985—; Lectr. taxation Practising Law Inst. N.Y., Inst. Continuing Legal Edn., Ga.; dir. Whitney Industries, Inc. Contbr. articles to profl. jours. Trustee Cornelius Vanderbilt Whitney Found. Served to lt. USNR, 1942-45, PTO. Decorated Bronze Star with combat V. Mem. Assn. Bar City N.Y. (lectr.), N.Y. Bar Assn., Internat. Bar Assn. (mem. council bus. law sect. Eng.), ABA, Am. Branch Internat. Law Assn., Lawasia (Australia chpt.), Asia Pacific Lawyers Assn. (Republic of Korea chpt.), World Peace through Law Center, World Assn. Lawyers (hon. chmn. sect. on taxation), Union Internat. des Avocates (Belgium), Am. Soc. Internat. Law, Internat. Fiscal Assn. (exec. council U.S. br.), Tax Forum, Am. Law Inst. (tax adv. group), N.Y. Law Inst., Internat. Fiscal Assn. (Netherlands). Clubs: Metropolitan (N.Y.C.), Yale (N.Y.C.). Office: Hughes Hubbard & Reed 801 Brickell Ave Suite 1100 Miami FL 33131 Also: 1 Wall St New York NY 10005

YOUNG, MARGARET ALETHA MCMULLEN (MRS. HERBERT WILSON YOUNG), social worker; b. Vossburg, Miss., June 13, 1916; d. Grady Garland and Virgie Aletha (Moore) McMullen; B.A. cum laude, Columbia Bible Coll., 1949; grad. Massey Bus. Coll., 1958; M.S.W., Fla. State U., 1965; postgrad. Jacksonville U., 1961-62, Tulane U., 1967; m. Herbert Wilson Young, Aug. 19, 1959. Dir. Christian edn. Eau Claire Presbyn. Ch., Columbia, S.C., 1946-51; tchr. Massey Bus. Coll., Jacksonville, Fla., 1954-57, office mgr., 1957-59; social worker, unit supr. Fla. div. Family Services, St. Petersburg, 1960-66, dist. casework supr., 1966-71; social worker, project supr., program supr. Project Playpen, Inc., 1971-81, pres. bd., 1982-83, cons., 1986—; mem. council Child Devel. Ctr., 1983—; mem. transitional housing com., Religious Community Services, 1984—. Mem. Acad. Cert. Social Workers, Nat. Assn. Social Workers (pres. Tampa Bay chpt. 1973-74), Fla. Assn. for Health and Social Services (pres. chpt. 1971), Nature conservancy, Fla. Assn. for Children Under Six. Democrat. Presbyn. Rotary Ann (pres. 1970-71). Home: 330 Roebling Rd N Belleair FL 34616

YOUNG, MARGARET BUCKNER, civic worker, author; b. Campbellsville, Ky.; d. Frank W. and Eva (Carter) Buckner; B.A., Ky. State Coll., 1942; M.A., U. Minn., 1946; m. Whitney M. Young, Jr., Jan. 2, 1944 (dec. Mar. 1971); children—Marcia Elaine, Lauren Lee. Instr., Ky. State Coll., 1942-44; instr. edn. and psychology Spelman Coll., Atlanta, 1957-60; dir. Philip Morris, Inc., N.Y. Life Ins. Co. Alternate del. UN Gen. Assembly, 1973. Mem. pub. policy com. Advt. Council. Trustee Lincoln Center for Performing Arts; chmn. Whitney M. Young, Jr. Meml. Found.; trustee Met. Mus. Art; bd. govs. UN Assn., 1975-82; bd. visitors U.S. Mil. Acad., 1978-80. Author: The First Book of American Negroes, 1966; The Picture Life of Martin Luther King, Jr., 1968; The Picture Life of Ralph J. Bunche, 1968; Black American Leaders-Watts, 1969; The Picture Life of Thurgood Marshall, 1970; pub. affairs phamphlet. Home: 330 Oxford Rd New Rochelle NY 10804 Office: 100 Park Ave New York NY 10017

YOUNG, MARJORIE WILLIS, writer, journalist, lecturer; b. Mansfield, Ohio; d. John Edgar and Mary Adelle (Reiter) Willis; student agr. Cornell U., 1924; student Art Students League, 1925-27, Cooper Union, 1925-27, Columbia U., 1927, 43, Sorbonne, U. Paris, 1928-30, Japanese Lang. Sch., Tokyo, 1934-35, N.Y. U., 1944; m. James Russell Young, Oct. 2, 1934; 1 son, Willis Patterson. Columnist in Far East, Internat. News Service, 1938-41; feature writer King Features Syndicate, 1939, Saturday Pictorial Rev., 1941-45; asst. tech. dir. motion picture Behind the Rising Sun, 1943; research dept. Believe It or Not, 1946-48; feature editor and columnist The Sunday Star, Wilmington, Del., 1946-48; promotion dir. David McKay Pub. Co., 1945-48; lectr. Nat. Concert and Artists Corp., 1942-43; feature writer Anderson (S.C.) Independent, 1949-73; feature writer Anderson Daily Mail, 1949-73, asso. editor The New South, ann. spl. edit. of Daily Mail, 1966-73; editor The Safety Jour., Anderson, 1953—; program moderator Decorating for a Holiday, Sta. WAIM-TV, 1953-55, safety program moderator WAIM-TV, 1953—, program moderator How to Cut and Sew, 1954-55, travel feature program WAIM-WCAC-FM, 1973-82; travel editor Quote mag., 1977-80; editor Vets. of Safety news page, What's What monthly; dir. Capitol City Communications, Inc. Spl. scroll dir. Chinese War Orphans Relief, 1941-45; publicity dir. Crusade for Children, State of Del., 1948; publicity chmn. S.C. Indsl. Nurses Assn., 1953; dir. S.C. 4-H Club TV Safety Program, 1953; coordinator Ann. S.C. State Landmark Conf., 1979. Bd. dirs. Anderson Heritage, Inc. Recipient various awards for safety activities including Disting. Service award S.C. Occupational Safety Council, 1973. Mem. U. S.C. Caroliniana Soc., Writers Assn. Am., Am. Women in Radio and TV, Nat. Recreation Assn., S.C. Recreation Soc. (v.p. and program dir. 1954-56), Anderson County Hist. Soc. (pres. 1978-80), Am. Soc. Safety Engrs., Vets. Safety Internat., (pres. 1979), DAR, Colonial Dames of the XVII Century. Episcopalian. Clubs: Am. News Women's, Nat. Press (Washington); Overseas Press of Am.; Cornell Women's (N.Y.C.). Author: Decorating for Joyful Occasions, 1952; It's Time for Christmas Decorations, 1957; Fodor's Tour Guide of South Carolina, 1966-68, Tour Guide of Georgia, 1966-67; Japanese American Cook Book, 1972; The Cateechee Trail, 1975; South Carolina's Women Patriots of the American Revolution, 1975; Mystery of the Ivory Eagle, 1980. Editor: Textile Leaders, 1963. Home: 2003 Laurel Dr Anderson SC 29621 Office: Safety Jour PO Box 4189 Anderson SC 29622

YOUNG, MICHAEL RICHARD, lawyer; b. Wiesbaden, Fed. Republic Germany, May 12, 1956; came to U.S., 1957; s. Richard Barton and Janet (Crawford) Y.; m. Leslie Anne Carroll, Aug. 11, 1984. BA magna cum laude, Allegheny Coll., 1978—; JD, Duke U., 1981—. Bar: N.Y. 1982, U.S. Dist. Ct. (so. and ea. dists.) 1982. Assoc. Willkie Farr & Gallagher, N.Y.C., 1981—. Research and mng. editor Duke Law Jour., 1980-81. Mem. N.Y.C. Bar Assn. (com. on legal edn. and admission to bar 1983—), Phi Beta Kappa. Home: 390 1st Ave Apt MH New York NY 10010 Office: Willkie Farr & Gallagher One Citicorp Ctr 153 E 53d St New York NY 10022

YOUNG, PETER COLIN, environmental science educator, administrator; b. Walsall, Staffordshire, Eng., Dec. 5, 1939; s. John William and Naomi Bessie (Crane) Y.; m. Wendy Anne Lowe, Aug. 31, 1963; children—Timothy John, Melanie Clare, Jeremy Peter. B of Tech., Loughborough U., Leicestershire, Eng., 1962, MS, 1964; MA, Cambridge (Eng.) U., 1970, PhD, 1970. Chartered aero. engr., Eng. Engr., Brit. Aircraft Corp., Warton, Eng., 1958-63; control and systems engr. Naval Weapons Ctr., China Lake, Calif., 1968-70; lectr. control and systems U. Cambridge, 1970-75; professorial fellow Australian Nat. U., Canberra, 1975-81; prof., head dept. environ. sci. U. Lancaster, Eng., 1981-87, dir. Centre for Research on Environ Systems, 1987—; dir. quantitative environ. sci. and tech. U. Lancaster Devel. Co., 1982—; IBM vis. prof. U. Ghent, Belgium, 1980. Author: Environmental Water Quality, 1982, Recursive Estimation, 1984/84; editor: Modelling in Biotechnology, 1983; contbr. numerous articles to profl. jours. Whitworth fellow U.K. Dept. Edn. and Sci., 1965, fellow Clare Hall, Cambridge U., 1970-75, Royal Soc. Arts, 1983. Fellow Cambridge Philos. Soc.; mem. Instn. Elec. Engrs., Royal Aero. Soc., Instn. Mech. Engrs., Australian Statis. Soc., Brit. Hydrological Soc. Home: Green Meadows, Stanmore Dr, Lancaster, Lancashire LA1 5BL, England Office: Univ Lancaster, Dept Environ Scis, Lancaster, Lancashire LA1 4YQ, England

YOUNG, PETER RICHARD, manufacturing company executive; b. Newcastle, Eng., Dec. 25, 1944; s. Kenneth Henry and Marian Heather (Phillips) Y.; m. Avrial Eugenie Young, Nov. 30, 1973; children: Desia G., Roxzan I., Phillippa N., Kyle R. BSc, U. Bristol, 1966, PhD, 1969. Mgr. overseas investment Fisons Ltd., London, 1970-74, gen. mgr., Toronto, 1974-79, v.p. fin., Bedford, Mass., 1979—; chmn. Haake Buchler Instruments Inc., Saddle Brook, N.J., 1981—. Fellow Inst. Cost and Mgmt. Accts.; mem. Can. Inst. Chemists, Brit. Inst. Mgmt., Royal Inst. Chemistry. Anglican. Clubs: Oriental (London); Harare (Zimbabwe); Nat. (Toronto). Home: 53 Tarbell Spring Rd Concord MA 01742 Office: 2 Preston Ct Bedford MA 01730

YOUNG, ROBERT AARON, art dealer; b. N.Y.C., Dec. 7; s. Jack and Ruth (Rosenberg) Y.; m. Ethel Greenbaum, Sept. 30, 1956; children—Aaron, Claudia. B.S., Syracuse U., 1954. Exec. v.p. Harvey Probber Furniture, N.Y.C., 1958-63; prin. Robert Aaron Young, Inc., Art Dealer and Pub., N.Y.C., 1963—; founder Ctr. for African Art. Producer video tapes on art related subjects. Founding soc. Lenox Hill Hosp.; mem. Am. Ballet Theatre.

YOUNG, ROBERT ANTHONY, automotive executive; b. Grantham, Lincolnshire, Eng., Feb. 24, 1930; came to Hong Kong, 1966.; s. Edward James and Edith Anne (Nicholls) Y.; m. Barbara Dable, Mar. 23, 1954; children: P. Young, A.W.J. Young. Grad., King's Sch., 1948. Sales mgr. African Lakes Corp., Malawai, 1955-59; br. mgr. Automobile Palace, Banger, N. Wales, 1959-63; sales mgr. United Africa Corp., Freetown, Sierra Leone, 1963-66; gen. mgr. Crown Motors, Ltd., Hong Kong, 1966-71, mng. dir., 1971—; motors dir. Inchcape Pacific, Ltd. subs. Crown Motors Group, Hong Kong, 1986—. Mem. (assoc.) Yacht Brokes, Designers and Surveyors Assn., Inst. Diagnostic Engrs. Clubs: 2 Yacht, World Trade Ctr., Royal Hong Kong Jockey. Home: House E Kellett Villas 51, Mount Kellett Rd The Peak, Hong Kong Hong Kong Office: Crown Motors Ltd, 1063 Kings Rd, Crown Motors Bldg, Quarry Bay Hong Kong

YOUNG, WILLIAM LEE, management consultant; b. Ankara, Turkey, Aug. 25, 1954; s. William Lee and Marion Elisabeth (Peers) Y.; m. Amanda Barclay. BS, Queen's U., Kingston, Ont., 1977; MBA, Harvard U., Cambridge, Mass., 1981. Cert. profl. engr. Design engr. Imperial Oil, Toronto, Ont., Can., 1977-79; v.p. Bain & Co., London, 1981—; bd. dirs. Northumberland Mines Ltd., Toronto, Ont., Can.; ptnr. Bain Internat., Boston, 1986—; joint mng. dir. Westbourne Mgmt. Group Ltd. Mem. Ont. Assn. Profl. Engrs. Clubs: Rideau, Harvard. Office: Bain & Co, 143 Hillsdale Ave East, Toronto, ON Canada

YOUNG, WILLIAM LEWIS, mathematics educator; b. Buffalo, July 27, 1929; s. Charles William Young and Ada Laura (Lynch) Stremble. B.S., Hartwick Coll., 1951; M.A., Pa. State U., 1962; M.S. SUNY-Buffalo, 1978, M.L.S., 1979. Instr. SUNY-Buffalo, 1960-65; asst. prof. State Coll., Fredonia, N.Y., 1965-67; ops. analyst Calspan, Buffalo, 1967-69; prof. math. dept. Erie Community Coll., Orchard Park, N.Y., 1969—, coordinator math. and computer sci., 1982-84; v.p. faculty fedn., 1974-77. Pres. Aurora Hist. Soc., East Aurora, N.Y., 1975-79, trustee, 1974-82; chmn. Millard Fillmore House Council, East Aurora, 1976-81. Served to 1st lt. USAF, 1951-57. Ohio Coll. Library Ctr. research fellow, 1979. Mem. Assn. Computing Machinery, IEEE. Home: 806 Luther Rd East Aurora NY 14052 Office: Erie Community Coll 4140 Southwestern Blvd Orchard Park NY 14127

YOUNGER, GEORGE KENNETH HOTSON, British secretary of state defense; b. Stirling, Scotland, Sept. 22, 1931; s. Viscount Younger of Leckie and Evelyn Margaret McClure; m. Diana Rhona, 1954; children: James, Joanna, Charles, Andrew. Grad. with honors in Modern History, Oxford U. Dir., George Younger & Son Ltd., 1958-68, J.G. Thomson & Co. Ltd., Leith, 1962-66, Maclachlans Ltd., 1968-70, Tennant Caledonian Breweries Ltd., 1977—; M.P. for Ayr, 1964—; Scottish Conservative whip, 1965-67; Parliamentary under-sec. state for devel. Scottish Office, 1970-74; minister of state for def., 1974, sec. of state for Scotland, 1979-86; sec. state def., 1986—; chmn. Conservative Party in Scotland, 1974-75; mem. Queen's Body Guard for Scotland. Served with Argyll and Sutherland Highlanders Regular and Territorial Army, 1950-65. Recipient Terr. Decoration. Mem. Royal Co. of Archers. Mem. Ch. of Scotland. Club: Caledonian (London). Office: House of Commons, Westminster, London, SW1 England

YOUNGER, KENNETH WAYNE, human resources and management consultant; b. Jacksonville, Fla., Oct. 26, 1951; s. Ralph B. Jr. and Henrietta (Wingate) Y.; m. Nancy Lynn Ford, June 5, 1971; children: Kenan, Lynden. BA, Carson-Newman Coll., 1972; MS, Okla. State U., 1974, PhD, 1975. Asst. prof. psychology and computer sci. Calumet Coll., Whiting, Ind., 1975-76; asst. prof. psychology Carson-Newman Coll., Jefferson City, Tenn., 1976-79; project mgr. mgmt. devel. Arthur Andersen & Co., Chgo., 1979-80; v.p. Drake Beam Morin Inc., Chgo., 1980-82; mng. ptnr. Savard Younger Cons. Group, Chgo., 1982-87; pres. The Younger Mgmt. Group, Indpls., 1988—; guest lectr. Recipient Outstanding Sci. Achievement award U.S. Navy, 1969, Meritorious Research award Okla. Psychol. Assn., 1973, Outstanding Faculty Service award Carson-Newman Student Found., 1977; NSF scholar, 1967, Regents scholar State of Fla., 1969. Mem. Greater O'Hare Assn. Industry and Commerce, U.S. Jaycees (Outstanding Young Am. 1981), Tenn. Squires, Phi Kappa Phi. Baptist. Office: Younger Mgmt Group 5987 E 71st St Suite 210 Indianapolis IN 46220-4051

YOUNG LIVELY, SANDRA LEE, nurse; b. Rockport, Ind., Dec. 31, 1943; d. William Cody and Flora Juanita (Carver) Thorpe; m. Kenneth Leon Doom, May 4, 1962 (div. 1975); children—Patricia, Anita, Elizabeth. A.S., Vincennes U., 1979, student, U. So. Ind., 1987—. Nursing aide, nurse Forest Del Nursing Home, Princeton, Ind., 1975-80; charge nurse Welborn Bapt. Hosp., Evansville, Ind., 1979-80, 82-83; staff nurse Longview Regional Hosp., Tex., 1980-82; dir. home health Roy H. Laird Meml. Hosp., Kilgore, Tex., 1984-86; med. post-coronary nurse Mercy Hosp., Owensboro, Ky., 1987, Dept. of Corrections charge nurse, Branchville Trg. Ctr., Tell City, Ind, 1987— ; staff nurse, asst. dir. Leisure Lodge Home Health, Overton, Tex., 1983-84. Grantee Roy H. Laird Meml. Hosp., 1986. Mem. Nat. Assn. Female Execs., Menniger Found., Vincennes U. Alumni Assn., Smithsonian Inst. Avocations: writing, research, cake decorating, house plants. Home: 435 S Lincoln Ave PO Box 431 Rockport IN 47635 Office: Branchville Tng Ctr Dept of Corrections PO Box 500 Tell City IN 47586

YOUNGMAN, WILLIAM STERLING, lawyer; b. Boston, May 25, 1907; s. William Sterling and Helen Isabel (Yerxa) Y.; m. Elsie Hooper Perkins, Apr. 17, 1937; children: William Sterling, 3d, Robert, Elsie Youngman Hull. Student, Middlesex Sch., 1919-25; A.B. magna cum laude, Harvard U., 1929, J.D. magna cum laude, 1932; LL.D. (hon.), Middlebury Coll., 1978. Bar: Mass. 1934, U.S. Supreme Ct. 1939, D.C. 1941, N.Y. 1951, N.H. 1969. Law sec. to Judge Learned Hand, N.Y.C., 1932-33; with law firm Palmer, Dodge, Barstow, Wilkins & Davis, Boston, 1933-38; counsel Nat. Power Policy Commn., Washington, and; chief counsel power div. PWA, 1939-40; gen. counsel FPC, 1940-1941; exec. v.p. and dir. China Def. Supplies, Inc., 1941-42, pres., 1942-45; gen. counsel in U.S., Nat. Resources Commn. of China, 1944-47; partner Corcoran and Youngman, 1941-49; pres. C.V. Starr & Co., Inc., 1949-68; chmn. bd. Am. Home Asssurance Co., Ins. Co. of State of Pa., 1952-69, Am. Internat. Assurance Co., Ltd., Hong Kong, 1958-67, Philippine Am. Life Ins. Co., 1958-68, Am. Internat. Underwriters Corp., 1959-68, Am. Internat. Reins. Co., 1967-68, Am. Internat. Group, 1968; Vice chmn. Council for Latin Am., 1967-69. Trustee emeritus Middlebury Coll.; Mem. Council Fgn. Relations. Clubs: Metropolitan, Chevy Chase (Washington); St. Botolph (Boston); Harvard, River, Down Town Assn. (N.Y.C.); Varsity (Harvard U.), Manchester (Mass.) Yacht; Essex County (Mass.). Home: 480 Indian Harbor Rd John's Island Vero Beach FL 32963

YOUNKIN, C. GEORGE, archivist; b. Great Bend, Kan., Oct. 13, 1910; s. Charles Franklin and Nannie Sylvia (Wilson) Y.; student Washburn U., 1932-35, Southeastern U., Washington, 1936-37; m. Ruth Ward, Dec. 27, 1939 (dec. 1980); children—Karen (Mrs. John R. Postma), Eleta (Mrs. Stephen B. McElroy), Cheryl (Mrs. Thomas R. Gamble), Chip G. With U.S. Dept. Agr., Washington, 1935-51; with Nat. Archives, Ft. Worth, 1951-75, regional archivist for Ark., La., N.Mex., Okla. and Tex., 1968-75; ret., 1975; pres. S.W. Archives Cons., 1975—; archive cons. Kiowa Hist. and Research Assn., Carnegie, Okla. Mem. council exec. com. and historian Boy Scouts Am., Ft. Worth, 1975—; mem. Gov.'s Adv. Com. on Aged for Tarrant County, 1976-80; mem. Tarrant County Hist. Commn.; trustee Ch. of Good Shepherd, 1980-83. Served with AUS, 1943-45. Recipient Silver Beaver award Boy Scouts Am., 1966, Order of Arrow, Boy Scouts Am., 1966; pub. service award GSA, 1967, spl. service award Fed. Bus. Assn., 1967, Cross and Flame award United Meth. Ch. and Boy Scouts Am., 1988. Fellow Tex. State Geneal. Soc.; mem. Soc. S.W. Archivists (sec.-treas. 1971-80), Internat. Council Archives, Soc. Am. Archivists (regional activities com.), Nat. Trust Historic Preservation, Kiowa Tia-Piah Soc. Carnegie (Okla.), Westerners Internat., Western History Assn., Tex. Hist. Assn. Dir., Llano Estacado Heritage Quar., 1974-82. Home and Office: 3501 Quail Ln Arlington TX 76016

YOUNKIN, GREGORY WAYNE, data processing executive; b. Buffalo, N.Y., May 28, 1953; s. George W. and Nancy L. (Greenwald) Y. Student, U. Wis. Ctr., Fond du Lac, 1973-75; BS in Secondary Edn. with high honors, U. Wis., Oshkosh, 1977; A in Programming, MPTI, 1982. Data processing mgr. PCA of Juneau, Wis., 1982-85; programmer/analyst dept. health and social services State of Wis., Madison, 1986-87, systems programmer dept. health and social services, 1987—. Lodge: Lions (sec. Juneau 1986—). Home: PO Box 152 Juneau WI 53039

YOUST, DAVID BENNETT, career development educator; b. Buffalo, May 14, 1938; s. Howard Page and Agnes (Bennett) Y.; B.S., SUNY-Albany, 1959; M.S., Syracuse (N.Y.) U., 1961; Ph.D., Mich. State U., 1969; cert. career counselor Nat. Bd. Counselor Cert.; m. Faye Phillips; children—Stacy, Shawna, Liesl, Genny, Elizabeth. Tchr. sci. North Syracuse schs., 1959-61; adminstr. student personnel Mich. State U., 1961-63; counselor, prin., program dir. Rochester (N.Y.) schs., 1963-70; sr. research technologist Eastman Kodak Co., Rochester, 1970-72; asst. dean Nat. Tech. Inst. for the Deaf, Rochester Inst. Tech., 1972-74; mem. faculty Empire State Coll., SUNY, Rochester, 1974-78; exec. dir. Career Devel. Council, Corning, N.Y., 1978-84; mgr. tng. engring. and innovation Corning Glass Works, N.Y., 1984—; cons., prin. Career Devel. Mgmt.; adj. faculty Corning Community Coll., Elmira Coll. Bd. dirs. 171 Cedar Arts Center. Mem. Nat. Career Devel. Assn. (Merit award 1970, 84), Am. Ednl. Research Assn., Assn. Measurement and Evaluation in Guidance, Am. Assn. Counseling and Devel., Am. Soc. Tng. and Devel. Republican. Author guide, articles in field; mem. editorial bd. Career Devel. Quar. Home: 12 Pinewood Cir Corning NY 14830-3618 Office: Corning Glass Works MP PS 2 Corning NY 14831

YOUTCHEFF, JOHN SHELDON, physicist; b. Newark, Apr. 16, 1925; s. Slav Joseph and Florence Catherine (Davidson) Y.; A.B., Columbia, 1949, B.S., 1950; Ph.D., U. Calif. at Los Angeles, 1953; m. Elsie Marianne, June 17, 1950; children—Karen Janette, John Sheldon, Mark Allen, Heidi Mary Anne, Lisa Ellen. Ops. analyst Gen. Electric Co., Ithaca, N.Y., 1953-56, cons. engr. Missile & Space Div., Phila., 1956-64, mgr. advanced reliability programs, 1964-72; mgr. reliability and maintainability Litton Industries, College Pk., Md., 1972-73; program mgr. U.S. Postal Service Hdqrs., Washington, 1973—; instr. U. Pa., 1965-66, Villanova U., 1957—. Served to lt. USAAF, 1943-46; to comdr. USNR, 1946—. Registered profl. engr., Calif., D.C. Fellow AAAS, British Interplanetary Soc., Am. Inst. Aero. and Astronautics (asso.); mem. IEEE (sr.), Ops. Research Soc., Research Soc. Am., Am. Math. Soc., Am. Physics Soc., Am. Chem. Soc., Am. Astron. Soc., Am. Geol. Soc., Nat. Soc. Profl. Engrs., Engring. and Tech. Socs. Council Del. Valley (speakers bur.), Res. Officers Assn., Am. Legion. Roman Catholic. Clubs: Explorers (N.Y.C.), Optimists Internat. (pres. Valley Forge chpt. 1970-71). Holder 3 U.S. patents; contbr. articles to profl. jours. and proc. Home: 543 Midland Ave Berwyn PA 19312 Office: L'Enfant Plaza Washington DC 20260

YOZAWITZ, ALLAN, neuropsychologist; b. Bklyn., Jan. 8, 1949; s. Louis and Sylvia Claire Y.; m. Arlene Susan Greenfield, Jan. 20, 1973; children—Elissa Gayle, Justin Mark. B.S., Poly. Inst. Bklyn., 1970; M.A., Queens Coll. CUNY, 1973; Ph.D., CUNY, 1977. Asst. research scientist biometrics N.Y. State Dept. Mental Hygiene, N.Y.C., 1970-77; trainee clin. neuropsychology Montefiore Hosp. and Med. Center, Bronx, N.Y., 1974-75; cons. gerontology sect. N.Y. State Psychiat. Inst., N.Y.C., 1975-76; dir. neuropsychology lab. Hutchings Psychiat. Center, N.Y. State Office Mental Health, Syracuse, 1977—; asst. prof. Med. Coll. SUNY Health Sci. Center, Syracuse, 1979—; adj. asst. prof. psychology Syracuse U., 1979—; cons. Syracuse Devel. Center, 1979-83, Benjamin Rush Center, Syracuse, 1980-88; pvt. practice, Syracuse, 1979—; apptd. to profl. adv. bd. N.Y. State Head Injury Assn., 1984, apptd. exam. cons. N.Y. State Bd. for Psychology, 1987, apptd. N.Y. State Bd. Psychology, 1988; examiner Am. Bd. Profl. Psychology, Am. Bd. Clin. Neuropsychology. Contbr. articles to profl. jours; cons. editor Jour. Clin. and Exptl. Neuropsychology; mem. editorial bd. Neuropsychology Rev.; reviewer profl. jours. NIMH grantee, 1974-77, 79-82. Mem. AAAS, Am. Psychol. Assn. (charter mem. div. clin. neuropsychology 1979—), Internat. Neuropsychol. Soc. (task force on edn., accreditation and credentialing 1979, dir. continuing edn. 1985), N.Y. State Psychol. Assn., N.Y. Acad. Scis., Soc. Neuroscience, Syracuse Alliance Support Assns. for the Neurologically Disabled (founding mem. 1985). Subspecialties: Neuropsychology; Psychiatry. Current work: Cognitive rehabilitation of psychiatric patients based on neuropsychological diagnosis, computer software design for cognitive rehabilitation, theories of neuropsychological basis of psychiatric disorder. Home: 150 Brookside Ln Fayetteville NY 13066 Office: Hutchings Psychiat Center Neuropsychology Lab Syracuse NY 13210

YU, BO-LIN, psychologist, educator; b. Changsha, Hunan, People's Republic China, Nov. 11, 1938; d. Qing-xian and Mei-qing Y.; m. Shu-ren Wang, May 22, 1966; 1 child, Jing Wang. Grad., Beijing U., 1962; postgrad., Chinese Acad. Scis., Beijing, 1962-66. Researcher U. Mich., Ann Arbor, 1981-82; prof. psychology Chinese Acad. Scis., 1986—; prof. Beijing Normal U., 1985-87. Author: Color Vision Research, 1979, Introduction of Psychology, 1986, Experimental Psychology, 1987; contbr. articles to profl. jours. Recipient awards Chinese Acad. Scis., 1979, 80. Mem. Chinese Psychol. Soc., Chinese Standardization Assn., Beijing Lighting Soc. Office: Inst Psychology, Chinese Acad Scis, Beijing Peoples Republic China

YU, CESAR YANTUM, physician, pharmacologist, educator; b. Manila, Mar. 28, 1930; s. See Lay and Sia Teck Y.; m. Sandra Go, Apr. 28, 1957; children: Sabrina Go, Lawrence Go, Vincent Go. AA, Santo Tomas U., Philippines, 1952, BS in Zool., 1956, MD, 1958; postgrad., U. Philippines, 1984. Diplomate Philippine Acad. Family Medicine Bd., Philippine Mil. Surgeon Bd., Philippine Med. Bd. Intern Santo Tomas U. Hosp. and North Gen. Hosp. (now Jose Reyes Meml. Hosp.), Manila, 1957-58; resident Santo Tomas U. Hosp, Manila, 1958-60, staff mem. dept. pediatrics, 1958-60; med. cons. Met. Hosp., Manila, 1968—; clin. preceptor UST Coll. of Medicine, Manila, 1970-73; med. cons. U. Philippines Gen. Hosp., Manila, 1975-80; asst. prof. in pharmacology Philippines Muslim Christian Coll. of Medicine (now Rizal Coll. of Medicine), Manila, 1983—. Author: (with others) Fundamentals o Family Medicine, 1977. Served to lt. col. Philippine Med. Corp, 1977. Recipient Presdl. Humanitarian award, 1968. Fellow Philippine Acad. Family Physician (nat. v.p. 1979-81), Philippine Assn. Mil. Surgeons; mem. Manila Med Soc. (life, chpt. pres. 1979-82), Philippine Med. Assn., Philippine Inventor Soc., Philippine Pediatric Soc., Philippine Assn. Geriatric and Gerontology (bd. dirs. 1984—), Philippine Soc. for Microbiology and Infectious Diseases, Philippine Soc. of Exptl. and Clin. Pharmacology. Roman Catholic. Lodges: Mason (worshipful master 1980, grand inspector 1985—), Kasilawan. Home: 18 Kabignayan St, Quezon City Philippines Office: Met Hosp, 1357 Masangkay St, Manila Philippines

YU, CHENG WOU, human genetics educator; b. Kwangtong, China, Apr. 10, 1942; came to U.S., 1969, naturalized, 1983; s. Jang Jong and Feng Tze (Pang) Y.; m. Kathy Lin Ling, May 20, 1972; children—Ivy I-Hua, Victor I-Bing. B.S. in Agronomy, Nat. Taiwan U., Taipei, 1965; M.S. in Plant Sci., Mont. State U., 1971, Ph.D. in Genetics, 1975. Diplomate Am. Bd. Med. Genetics. Postdoctoral fellow Johns Hopkins Med. Sch., 1975-77; sr. assoc. Emory U. Med. Sch., 1977-79; asst. prof. La. State U. Med. Ctr., 1979-83, assoc. prof., 1983-84; dir. lab. Calif. Prenatal Diagnosis Inst., San Jose, Calif., 1984-88, also dir.; assoc. prof. U. Calif. Med. Sch., San Francisco, 1988—; dir. cytogenetic and prenatal detection lab., Valley Children's Hosp., Fresno, Calif., 1988—; Contbr. 40 articles to profl. jours. Recipient So. Med. Assn. Research award, 1980, Biomed. Research award La. Med. Sch., 1980; Bd. of Regents La. State U. research grantee, 1982. Mem. AAAS, Am. Soc. Human Genetics, Tissue Culture Assn., Am. Soc. Genetics, Assn. Cytogenetic Technologists. Home: 414 Crystalline Dr Fremont CA 94539

YU, PAUL NANGAN, physician, educator; b. Kiangsi, China, Nov. 7, 1915; came to U.S., 1947, naturalized, 1952; s. Y.S. and L.H. (Yang) Y.; m. Iling Tang, June 4, 1944; children: Pauline R., Diane C., Lorraine M., Corrine M. M.D., Nat. Med. Coll., Shanghai, China, 1939. Intern First Red Cross Hosp., Shanghai, 1938-39; asst. and chief resident in medicine Central Hosp., Chungking, China, 1940-43; asst. resident in medicine Strong Meml. Hosp., Rochester, N.Y., 1947-48; practice medicine specializing in cardiology Rochester, 1952—; asst. prof. medicine U. Rochester Med. Sch., 1954-59, asso. prof., 1959-63, prof., 1963-69, Sarah McCort Ward prof., 1969—; head cardiology unit U. Rochester Med. Center and Strong Meml. Hosp., Rochester, 1957-82. Author: Pulmonary Blood Volume in Health and Disease; Editor: (with J.F. Goodwin) Progress in Cardiology, (1972—) Modern Concepts of Cardiovascular Disease, 1976-78. Brit. Council scholar, U.K. Mem. Assn. Am. Physicians, Am. Clin. and Climatol. Assn., Assn. Univ. Cardiologists, Am. Coll. Cardiology, ACP, Am. Physiol. Soc., Am. Heart Assn. (pres. 1972-73), Sigma Xi, Alpha Omega Alpha. Home: 651 Claybourne Rd Rochester NY 14618

YU, YAN LI, biochemist, educator; b. Beijing, Nov. 27, 1951; s. Xi Lu Yu and Gui Lan Yuan; m. Zong Min Li, Mar. 15, 1979; 1 child, Li Jing. BS, Ji Lin U., Chang Chun Ji Lin, 1977. Research asst. Lab. Photosynthesis, Inst. Botany, Acad. Sinica, Beijing, 1977-86; asst. prof. Lab. Photosynthesis, Inst. Botany, Acad. Sinica, 1986—. Contbr. articles to profl. publs. Recipient Important Achievement Sci. and Tech. award, Acad. Sinica, 1980, Advancement Sci. and Tech. award, 1986. Mem. China Assn. Sci. and Tech., Chinese Soc. Plant Physiology, Chinese Soc. Biophysics. Office: Acad Sinica Inst Botany, 141 Xi Zhi Men Wai Da Jie, Beijing 100044, Peoples Republic of China

YUCEL, EDGAR KENT, lawyer, consultant; b. Ankara, Turkey, Aug. 18, 1927; came to U.S., 1948, naturalized, 1958; s. Mustafa Muammer and Refika (Sunkitay) Y.; m. Martha Ellen Diggs, Sept. 8, 1954; 1 child, Edgar Kent. B.S., Galatasaray Lyceum, Istanbul, Turkey, 1948; M.A., U. Ala., 1953, postgrad., 1953-56; J.D., U. Minn., 1962. Bar: Minn. 1962, U.S. Dist. Ct. Minn. 1969. Instr. polit. sci. and econs. U. Ala., Tuscaloosa and Huntsville, 1953-56; project engr. So. Assoc. Engrs., Huntsville, 1956-59, supervising engr. Sperry Univac Co., St. Paul, 1959-62; sr. atty. 3M Co., St. Paul, 1962-69, asst. gen counsel, 1969-81, spl. counsel, 1981—; seminar lectr. St. John's U., Collegeville, Minn., 1976; adj. faculty grad. sch. Coll. St. Thomas, St. Paul, 1986; pro bono atty. So. Minn. Regional Legal Services, St. Paul, 1983—. Patentee marking tape. Trustee, gov. Health Central Inc., Mpls., 1972-78; v.p., sec., bd. dirs. Life Scis. Found., Mpls., 1973—; pres. Turkish Cultural Soc., Mpls., 1965-67; vice consul ad honorem Republic of Costa Rica, Mpls., 1964—; del. Internat. Labour Orgns., Tripartite, 1987. Mem. ABA, Minn. Bar Assn., Corp. Counsel Assn. (bd. dirs. 1964-67, pres. 1967-68), Licensing Execs. Soc., Soc. Univ. Patent Adminstrs., Minn. Patent and Trademark Law Assn., Am. Arbitration Assn. (arbitrator 1984—). Clubs: Minneapolis, Minn. Alumni (Mpls). Home: 4712 Merilane Minneapolis MN 55436 Office: 3M Co Patent Counsel 3M Ctr 220-11W-01 Saint Paul MN 55144

YUCHENGCO, ALFONSO TIAOQUI, telephone company executive; b. Manila, Philippines, Feb. 6, 1923; s. Enrique Tiaoqui and Tay (Hao) Y.; B.S. in Commerce, Far Eastern U., 1946; m. Paz SyCip, July 31, 1943 (div.); children—Helen Yuchengco Dee, Susanne, Annabelle Yuchengco Puey, Mona Lisa, Yvonne, Alfonso, Albert, Alfonso III. Chmn. bd. Eastern Gen. Reins. Corp., Manila, 1962, Malayan Overseas Ins. Corp., Taipei, Taiwan, 1966, Rizal Comml. Banking Corp., Makati, 1967, Pan-Malayan Mgmt. and Investment Corp., Makati, 1967, Philippine Rock Products, Inc., Makati, 1967, Dole Philippines, Inc., Standard Fruits (Philippines) Inc., Philippine Fuji Xerox Corp., BA Finance Corp., Makati, Zamboanga Wood Products, Inc., Makati, 1970, Philippine Long Distance Telephone Co., Makati, 1970—; pres. Malayan Group of Ins. Cos.; dir. Pan Malayan Ins. Corp., Manila, 1963, Daiwa Securities Internat., Hong Kong, Asian Hull Syndicate, Hong Kong, Checkered Farms, Inc., 1st Nationwide Assurance Corp., Makati, Pacific Meml. Plan, Pacific Fund, Inc.; chmn. exec. com. House of Investments, Inc., Indsl. Finance Corp., Gt. Pacific Life Assurance Corp.; chmn. adv. bd. Philippine Pacific Capital Corp. Bd. dirs. Internat. Ins. Seminar; past bd. dirs. Philippine Fire Protection Assn., Barrio Book Found. Named Ins. Man of Year, Bus. Writers Assn. Philippines, 1955; Outstanding Alumnus, Ins. Leader, Far Eastern U. Mem. Philippine Ins. Inst., Philippine Inst. C.P.A.s, Philippine Chamber Ins. and Surety (past pres.), Manila Jaycees (past pres.), Philippines C. of C. (past dir. and chmn. fin. com.), Filipino Life Ins. Assn. (past pres.). Clubs: Baguio Country, Casino Español, Club Filipino, Manila Polo, Manila Yacht, Wack-Wack Golf and Country, Manila Golf. Home: 29 Tamarind Rd, Makati 3116 Philippines Office: Philippine Long Distance Telephone Co, Legazpi St, PO Box 952, Makati, Metro Manila Philippines *

YUEN, KENG HONG PETER, physician; b. Hong Kong, June 13, 1951; s. Wai and Sou Ying (Liu) Y.; m. Wai Chu Lau, Nov. 28, 1976; children: Selene, Selwyn, Sheila. MBBS, U. Hong Kong, 1975. House officer United Christian Hosp., Hong Kong, 1975-76, Queen Elizabeth's Hosp., Hong Kong, 1976; med. and health officer Lady Trench Polyclinic, Hong Kong, 1976-77; gen. practice medicine Kwai Shing Estate, Hong Kong, 1977—; med. cons. Jr. Police Officer's Assn., Hong Kong, 1977—, Pioneer Life Saving Club, Hong Kong, 1978-81, Lik On Guard Force, Ltd., Hong Kong, 1985—, Lonsdale & Kirkby Ins., Ltd., 1986—;. Author: A Unified View of Art, 1988. Fellow Hong Kong Coll. Gen. Practitioners; mem. Mensa. Office: Shop 23 2/F Shopping Ctr, Kwai Shing West Estate, Hong Kong Hong Kong

YUJI, MASUDA, economist, educator; b. Choshi, Chiba, Japan, July 3, 1938; s. Takeshi and Tsune M.; m. Michiko, Mar. 15, 1972; children—Yoko, Hiroshi, Yasushi. B. in Western History, Waseda U., Tokyo, 1963, M. in Econs., 1967; B. in Econs., Tokyo U., 1965. Sr. economist Japan Soc. for the Promotion of Machine Industry, Econ. Research Inst., Tokyo, 1967—; prof. Osaka City U. Econ. Research Inst., 1983-87; prof. Tokyo-Keizai U. Faculty Bus. Adminstrn., 1987—. Author: Aerospace Industry, 1979, Advanced Technology Industry, 1980, New Stream of Technological Innovation, 1983, New Age of Information/Communication, 1985, The Perspective for Knowledge Society, 1986. Econ. Policy Soc. Japan, Peace Study Soc. Japan. Home: 2-15-31-905 Takanawa, Minato-ku 108 Tokyo Japan Office: Tokyo-Keizai U, Minamicho 1-7, Kokubunji-City 185, Japan

YUKINORI, KUWANO, electronics company executive; b. Ongagun, Fukuoka, Japan, Feb. 14, 1941; s. Shigenori and Masue K.; m. Yoko Tokunaga, May 3, 1968; 1 child, Kootaro. B in Engring., Kumamoto U., Japan, 1963; PhD, Osaka U., Japan, 1982. Researcher, research ctr. Sanyo Electric Co., Ltd., Osaka, 1963-78, sect. mgr., research ctr., 1978-84, dept. mgr., research ctr., 1984—, gen. mgr., functional material research ctr., 1987—. Author: Amorphous, 1985, Solar Cells and It's Applications, 1985; author, editor: Electronic Elements, 1986. Recipient Minister's award, 1980, Richard M. Fulrath award, Ceramic Soc. USA, 1983, Chem. Soc. Japan award, 1986. Mem. Japan Soc. Applied Physics, IEEE of Japan, Japan Soc. Ceramics. Home: 2-55-10 Amanogahara, Katano, Osaka 176, Japan Office: Sanyo Electric Co Ltd, Functional Material Research Ctr, 1-18-13 Hashiridani, Hirakata, Osaka 573, Japan

YU KUO-HWA, prime minister Taiwan, Republic of China; b. Chekiang, China, Jan. 10, 1914; s. Cho-Ping and Eir-Ying (Hu) Y.; BA, Tsinghua U., 1934; postgrad. Harvard U., 1944-46, London Sch. Econs., 1946-47; D.Comm. (hon.), St. John's U., 1973; m. Toong Metsung, June 1946; children: Frank, Philip. Sec. to pres. Nat. Mil. Council, 1936-44; alt. exec. dir. IBRD, 1947-50, IMF, 1951-55; pres. Central Trust China, 1955-61; mng. dir. China Devel. Corp., 1959-67; chmn. bd. Bank of China, 1961-67, China Ins. Co. Ltd., 1961-67; alt. gov. IBRD, 1964-67, gov. for Republic of China, 1967-69; minister of fin., 1967-69; gov. Central Bank Republic China, 1969-84; minister of state, 1969-84; chmn. Council Econ. Planning and Devel., 1977-84; gov. IMF 1969-80, Asian Devel. Bank, 1969-84; mem. Cen. Standing Com., Kuomintang, 1979—; prime minister, 1984—. Office: Office of the Premier, 1 Chung Hsiao East Rd Sect 1, Taipei 10023, Taiwan

YUN, CHONGSUN THOMAS, dentist; b. Seoul, July 23, 1934; came to U.S., 1951, naturalized, 1968; s. Tchi-Chang Yun and Jin Sil Sohn; B.A., U. Maine, 1958; D.D.S. (Prosthetics award), NYU, 1962; m. Jeannie Myunghae Hong, Sept. 19, 1970; children—Juliana Inkyung, Jonathan Inkoo. Intern, L.I. Coll. Hosp., 1962-63, mem. attending staff, 1963-67; gen. practice dentistry, N.Y.C., 1963—; instr. NYU Coll. Dentistry, 1963-65; mem. attending staff Roosevelt Hosp., N.Y.C., 1968-70. Bd. dirs. Korean Sch. of N.Y., 1982-87; elder Korean Presbyn. Ch. of Westchester, chairperson christian edn. com. of ch., 1985-87. Recipient Humanitarian award Korean Lang. Sch. N.Y., 1976. Fellow Acad. Gen. Dentistry, Internat. Coll. Applied Nutrition; mem. ADA, Am. Prosthodontic Soc., First Dist. Dental Soc., Korean Dental Assn. Eastern U.S.A. (pres., bd. dirs. 1987—), Korean Dental Assn. (citation 1978), Kyung Ki Alumni Assn. N.Y. (pres. 1974-76), U.S.-China Friendship Soc., Japanese Med. Soc. Am., Omicron Kappa Upsilon. Home: 41 Overlook Dr Chappaqua NY 10514 Office: 400 Madison Ave New York NY 10017

YUN, DANIEL DUWHAN, physician, foundation administrator; b. Chinjoo, Korea, Jan. 20, 1933; came to U.S., 1959, naturalized, 1972; s. Kapryong and Woo Im Yun; B.S., Coll. Sci. and Engring., Yon-Sei U., 1954, M.D., 1958; student U. Pa., 1963; m. Rebecca Sungja Choi, Apr. 13, 1959; children—Samuel, Lois, Caroline, Judith. Intern, Quincy (Mass.) City Hosp., 1960; resident and fellow Presbyn.-U. Pa. Med. Ctr., Phila., 1961-65; med. dir. Paddon Meml. Hosp., Nfld., Labrador, Can., 1965-66; dir. spl. care unit Rolling Hill Hosp., Elkins Park, Pa., 1967-79; founder, pres. Philip Jaisohn Meml. Found., Inc., Elkins Park, Pa., 1975—, also med. dir., trustee; clin. prof. medicine U. Xochicalco, 1978. Mem. Bd. Asian Studies Found., U.S. Senatorial Bus. Adv. Bd.; mem. home safety com. Mayor's Commn. on Services to Aging, Phila.; trustee United Way of Southeastern Pa., co-founder Republican Presdl. Task Force; mem. U.S. Congl. Adv. Bd.; cons. on Korean affairs Phila. City Council; hon. mem. adv. council Peaceful Unification Policy of Korea; chmn. bd. Korean-Am. Christian Broadcasting of Phila.; mem. Phila. Internat. City Coordinating Com. Recipient Phila. award-Human Rights award, 1981, Disting. Community Service award Phila. Dist. Atty., 1981, medal of Merit Presdl. Task Force, 1981, Medal of Nat. Order, Republic of Korea, 1984, Nat. Dong Baek medal Republic of Korea, 1987, award City Council Phila., 1987; named to Legion of Honor, The Chaple of Four Chaplains. Mem. Am. Soc. Internal Medicine, Am. Coll. Cardiology, Am. Heart Assn. (mem. council on clin. cardiology), AMA, Pa. Med. Soc., Philadelphia County Med. Soc., Royal Soc. Health, Am. Coll. Internat. Physicians, World Med. Assn., Fedn. State Med. Bds., Am. Law Enforcement Officers' Assn., Am. Fedn. Police, Internat. Culture Soc. Korea (hon.), Am. Soc. Contemporary Medicine and Surgery. Home: 3903 Somers Dr Huntingdon Valley PA 19006 Office: 60 E Township Line Rd Elkins Park PA 19117

YUN, JAMES MYUNG JU, international business executive; b. Kyungpuk, Korea, Sept. 28, 1938; s. Ungpal and Kwanjo (Hong) Y.; B.A., SUNY, New Paltz, 1963; postgrad. Cornell U., 1964; M.B.A., Fairleigh Dickinson U., 1973; postgrad. Harvard U. Bus. Sch.; m. Susan M. Acker, Dec. 18, 1965; children—Jamie, Cheryl, Adrienne, David. Asst. dir. pharmacology USV Pharms., Yonkers, N.Y., 1965-67; mgr. tech. documentation Schering Corp., Bloomfield, N.J., 1967-74; dir. project mgmt. Hoechst Roussel Co., Sommerville, N.J., 1974-76; dir. sci. communications, dir. research adminstrn. and planning Purdue Frederick Co., Norwalk, Conn., 1976-79, dir. sci. communication, 1976-79, exec. dir. research and devel., 1979-82, new product mktg. dir., 1982-85, mktg. v.p., 1985-86; chmn. Wilton (Conn.) Internat. Group, 1987—. Sec.-treas. Glenwood Terr. Homeowner's Assn., 1974; pres. Wilton Assn. Gifted Children, 1979-81; fin chmn. Black Rock Congregated Ch., 1980—, elder, 1988. Served to 2d lt. Republic of Korea Army, 1959-60. Mem. Am. Chem. Soc., Am. Soc. Info. Sci., Drug Info. Assn., Project Mgmt. Inst., Pharm. Mfrs. Assn., N.Am. Soc. Strategic Planning, Soc. Research Adminstrn., Kyungpuk High Sch. Assn. (pres. 1972) Republican. Home: 79 Sturges Ridge Rd Wilton CT 06897 Office: Wilton Internat Group Wilton CT 06897

YUN, PETER SUBUENG, economics educator; b. Yong-Wol, Korea, June 7, 1936; s. Sea Young and Soon Oak (Kim) Y.; m. Sandy J. Forsythe, June 21, 1970; children: Amy Rebecca, Peter Jung. B.A., U. Ga., 1966, Ph.D., 1975; M.A., U. Okla., 1968. Asst. prof. econs. Clinch Valley Coll., Wise, Va., 1974-79, assoc. prof., 1979-86, prof., 1986—; chmn. bus. div., 1979-86. Pres., Universal Bus. Services, Wise, 1981—; dir. Va. Gov's. Sch for the gifted Clinch Valley Coll., 1987—. Invest-in-America grantee, 1979, 80; recipient Outstanding Alumni award Emmanuel Coll., 1984. Mem. Am. Econ. Assn., So. Econ. Assn. Home: PO Box 2620 Wise VA 24293 Office: Clinch Valley Coll PO Box 16 Wise VA 24293

YUNG, CHEUK WO, dermatologist; b. Hong Kong, Jan. 17, 1949; came to U.S., 1969; s. Hau S. and Bun C. (Mui) Y.; m. Betsy K. Poon, May 30, 1977; children: Sophia, Steve. BS, Columbia U., 1972; MD, NYU, 1977. Diplomate Am. Bd. Dermatology. Intern Maimonides Med. Ctr., Bklyn., 1977-78; resident Cin. Med. Ctr., 1978-79; resident U. Chgo. Med. Ctr., 1979-80; chief resident, 1980-81, instr., 1981-82, clin. asst. prof., 1985—; practice medicine specializing in dermatology, Orland Park, Ill., 1982-86, Chgo., 1986—; cons. Oak Forest Hosp., Ill., Palos Community Hosp., Holy Cross Hosp., Chgo. Contbr. articles to profl. jours. Bd. dirs. Chinatown Planning Council, N.Y.C., 1971. Fellow Am. Acad. Dermatology; mem. AMA, Ill. Med Soc., Chgo. Med. Soc. Home: 13629 Idlewild Dr Orland Park IL 60462 Office: 7123 W Archer Ave Chicago IL 60638

YUNGWIRTH, FRANCIS PETER, mining company executive; b. Bruno, Sask., Can., June 29, 1951; s. Francis X. Yungwirth and Florence C. Krentz; m. Claudette D. Dubiel, May 17, 1975; children: Grace A., Francis C., Dale P., Claudette M. BS in Mining Engring., U. Sask., 1973, LLB, 1976. Registered profl. engr., Ont. Mine engr. Hudson Bay Mining & Smelting, Flin Flon, Man., 1976-78; mine evaluation engr. Hudson Bay Mining & Smelting, Toronto, Ont., 1978-80; asst. mine supt. Hudson Bay Mining & Smelting, Flin Flon, 1980-81, mine supt., 1981-85, chief engr. of mines, 1985-86; v.p. Moneta Porcupine Mines, Inc., Timmins, Ont., 1986—; bd. dirs. Moneta Porcupine Mines Inc.; com. mem. Adv. Counsel Mining Appointment, Man., 1983-86; sec. metal mining div. Can. Inst. Mining, Montreal, 1987—; co-chmn. of metal mining sect. Can. Inst. Mining Ann. Gen. Meeting, Toronto, 1987. Chmn. Adult Village Man. Winter Games, Flin Flon, 1986. Govt. of Sask. scholar, 1969. Mem. Law Soc. Upper Can., Assn. Profl. Engrs. Ont., Can. Inst. Mining & Metallurgy, Can. Bar Assn.

YUNICH, DAVID LAWRENCE, consumer goods consultant; b. Albany, N.Y., May 21, 1917; s. Max A. and Bess (Fellman) Y.; m. Beverly F. Blickman, June 11, 1941; children—Robert Hardle, Peter B. A.B., Union Coll., 1939, LL.D., 1964; postgrad., Harvard Grad. Sch. Bus. Adminstrn., 1939-40. Mdse. councilor L. Bamberger & Co., Newark, 1947-48; pres., dir. L. Bamberger & Co., 1955-62; v.p. Macy's, N.Y., 1941-51; sr. v.p. Macy's, 1951-62, pres., 1962-71; vice chmn. bd. R. H. Macy & Co. Inc., 1971-73, dir., 1958-73; chmn. Met. Transp. Authority, 1974-1977; bd. dirs. Prudential Ins. Co. Am., Prudential Found., NYNEX Corp., 1970-88, J.U.T. Group Inc., 1969-87, Bermans The Leather Experts, Channel Home Ctrs., W. R. Grace & Co., E. River Savs. Bank, Fidelity Group of Mut. Funds, Perdue Farms, Inc., Fibers Industries, Inc., Mfrs. Hanover Trust Co., Inc., 1968-73. Chmn. Mayor's Council Econ. and Bus. Advisers, N.Y.C., 1973-74; mem. N.Y. State Banking Bd., 1968-74; dir. Regional Plan Assn.; chmn. Gov.'s Commn. Financing Mass Transp., 1970-72; mem. Grace Commn.; pres. Greater N.Y. council Boy Scouts Am., 1972-1976; trustee Union Coll., 1965-72, Skidmore Coll., 1966-73, Albany Med. Coll., 1967-74, Carnegie Hall Corp., Saratoga Performing Arts; bd. dirs. Ednl. Broadcasting Corp., 1960-68, Nat. Jewish Hosp., Denver, 1960-68; bd. govs., trustee Rutgers U., New Brunswick, N.J., 1958-62. Decorated chevalier confrerie de Chevaliers du Tastevin. Mem. N.Y. Chamber Commerce and Industry (chmn. bd. 1971-74), Retail Dry Goods Assn. (pres. 1964-69), Am. Public Transp. Assn. (v.p.), Nat. Retail Mchts. Assn. (dir.), Am. Mgmt. Assn. (dir. 1958-68). Clubs: Harvard Bus. Sch., Harvard, Recess, Univ., Econ. (N.Y.C.); Blind Brook, Scarsdale (Westchester); Saratoga Golf and Polo (Saratoga Springs, N.Y.); Sandy Lane Golf (Barbados, W.I.). Home: Five Birches Cooper Rd Scarsdale NY 10583 Office: 1114 Ave of Americas New York NY 10036

YUNIS, JORGE JOSE, geneticist, pathologist, educator; b. Sincelejo, Colombia; m. Mary Brogmus. M.D., Central U., Madrid, Spain, 1956. Gen. practice medicine Barranquilla, Colombia, 1957-59; resident in clin. pathology U. Minn., Mpls., 1959-62, resident in anatomical pathology, 1962-64, mem. faculty, 1965—, prof., 1969—, dir. grad. studies of lab. medicine, 1969-74, dir. grad. studies of pathology, 1972-74, chmn. human genetics com. for health scis., 1972-77; vis. prof. numerous univs. Author: Human Chromosome Method, 1965, 75, Biochemical Methods in Red Cell Genetics, 1969, Molecular Pathology, 1975, New Chromosomal Syndromes, 1977, Molecular Structure of Human Chromosomes, 1977; contbr. more than 200 articles to profl. jours. Named Clin. Prof. of Yr., Harvard Med. Sch., 1987; honored by Colombian Parliament, Bogota, 1986. Mem. Leukemia Soc. Am. (trustee 1983-88), Colombian Acad. Medicine. Office: Univ Minnesota Hosps Med Sch Box 198 Minneapolis MN 55455

YUNUSOV, MAHMADYUSUF KAMAROVICH, mathematician, educator; b. Dushanbe, Tajik, USSR, Dec. 1, 1949; s. Yunusov Kamar and Miskol (Caramatulloeva) Y.; m. Akobirova Sabohat, Aug. 7, 1960; children: Firdous, Mahvash. Diploma in math., Moscow State U., 1970; candidate of scis., Acad. Scis., Moscow, 1975. Lectr. Tajik State U., Dushanbe, 1970-71, 1981—; head dept. Acad. Scis., Dushanbe, 1975-81. Author profl. monograph, contbr. articles to jours. Served Soviet Army. Laureate of Comsomol Cen. Com., 1978. Home: 17 Lenin St, Dushanve, Tajik SSR 734025, USSR

YURT, ROGER WILLIAM, medical educator, physician; b. Louisville, June 8, 1945; s. Albert William and Mary Louise (McGrath) Y.; m. Joan A. Terry, Sept. 3, 1971; children: Jennifer, Daniel, Gregory. BS in Biology, Loyola U., New Orleans, 1967; MD, U. Miami, 1972. Diplomate Nat. Bd. Med. Examiners. Intern Parkland Meml. Hosp.-Southwestern Med. Sch., U. Tex.-Dallas, 1972-73, resident in surgery, 1973-74; postdoctoral fellow in medicine Robert B. Brigham Hosp.-Harvard U. Med. Sch., Boston, 1974-77; postdoctoral trainee NIH, 1975-77; resident in surgery, then chief resident in surgery N.Y. Hosp.-Cornell Med. Ctr., N.Y.C., 1977-79, acting dir. Burn Ctr., dir. research, 1982-83, dir. Trauma Ctr., 1984—, assoc. prof. surgery, 1982—, vice chmn. dept. surgery Cornell U. Med. Coll., 1987—; clin. asst. prof. surgery Uniformed Services U. of Health Sci., Bethesda, Md., 1980-82; clin. asst. prof. gen. surgery Health Sci. Ctr., U. Tex.-San Antonio, 1981-82; chmn. burn com., mem. bd. dirs. Regional Emergency Med. Services of N.Y., 1982-84, mem. trauma ctr. adv. com., 1984—, N.Y. Bklyn. ACS Com. Trauma; dir. Mulhearn Research Lab., N.Y.C., 1982—. Editor: Infections in Surgery, 1981—; contbr. articles to med. jours. Served to maj. M.C., U.S. Army, 1979-82. Grantee United Health Found., 1968-69, NIH, 1984-87; fellow Sch. Medicine, U. Miami, summer 1969-71, USPHS, 1973-75; Irma Hirschl Trust Career Scientist award, 1984—. Mem. Surg. Infection Soc. (charter, chmn. membership com., sec. 1987—), Assn. Acad. Surgery, Soc. Univ. Surgeons, Internat. Surg. Soc., Am. Assn. for Surgery of Trauma, Ea. Assn. for Surgery of Trauma, Alpha Omega Alpha, Omicron Delta Kappa. Roman Catholic. Office: 525 E 68th St Room F-1919 New York NY 10021

YUSPEH, ALAN RALPH, lawyer; b. New Orleans, June 13, 1949; s. Michel and Rose Fay (Rabenovitz) Y.; m. Janet Horn, June 8, 1975. B.A., Yale U., 1971; M.B.A., Harvard U., 1973; J.D., Georgetown U., 1978. Bar: D.C. 1978. Mgmt. cons. McKinsey & Co., Washington, 1973-74; adminstrv. asst., legis. asst. Office of U.S. Senator J. Bennett Johnston, Washington, 1974-78; atty. Shaw, Pittman, Potts & Trowbridge, Washington, 1978-79, Ginsburg, Feldman, Weil and Bress, Washington, 1979-82; gen. counsel Com. on Armed Services-U.S. Senate, Washington, 1982-85; ptnr. Preston, Thorgrimson, Ellis & Holman, 1985—. Editor Law and Policy in Internat. Business jour., 1978-79; assoc. editor Pub. Contract Law jour., 1987—. Served to 1st lt. USAR, 1971-77. Mem. ABA (vice chmn. com. major systems, sect. pub. contract law 1984—). Club: Fed. City, Army and Navy (Washington). Home: 2332 Bright Leaf Way Baltimore MD 21209 Office: Preston Thorgrimson Ellis & Holman 1735 New York Ave NW #500 Washington DC 20006

YUSUF, SHAIKH MOHAMMAD, medical educator; b. Eminabad, Gujranwala, Punjab, Pakistan, Jan. 7, 1919; s. Shaikh Qadir Bakhsh and Meharunnisa Y.; m. Iqbal Begam; children: Shahwar, Iftikhar, Rehana, Farzana, Tehseen. Fellow in Sci., Islamia Coll., Lahore, 1936; MBBS, U. Lahore; M of Philosophy, Jinnah Postgrad., Karachi, 1961; PhD, Ind. U. Med. Ctr., 1963. Med. officer Provincial Civil Hosps., various cities, 1942-53; demonstrator Nishtar Med. Coll., Multan, Punjab, 1953-55; asst. prof. pharmacology, therapeutics Nishtar Med. Coll., Multan, 1955-66; prof. Liaquat Med. Coll., Jamshoro, Sind, 1966-68, Dow Med. Coll., Karachi, Sind, 1968-71, Jinnah Postgrad. Med. Ctr., Karachi, 1971-78, Army Med. Coll., Rawalpindi, Punjab, 1978—; bd. dirs. Cen. Drug Licensing and Registration, Islamabad; mem. Nat. Formulary Com., Islamabad, 1972-75. Editor: (fortnightly jour.) Medical News; hon. mem. editorial bd. Medical Progress, New Zealand, 1984, Medicine Digest Asia, Singapore, 1984; contbr. articles to profl. jours. Mem. Pakistan Med. Assn. (sec. 1957-59), Pakistan Pharmacology Soc. (treas. 1966-71, pres. 1980—). Home: 27-B RR Camp, Rawalpindi Cantt Pakistan Office: Dept Pharmacology & Therapy, Army Med Coll, Rawalpini, Punjab Pakistan

ZAAIMAN, REGINALD BRANDT, librarian, administrator; b. Zastron, Republic of South Africa, Aug. 3, 1922; s. Gert Thomas and Gertruida Elizabeth Johanna (Brandt) Z.; m. Linda du Toit, June 29, 1959 (div. 1977); 3 children. BA, U. Stellenbosch, 1944. Socius South African Library Assn., 1959; head info. scis. Iscor, Pretoria, Republic of South Africa, 1959-76; prof. info. scis., head dept. library and info. services U.S. Africa, Pretoria, Republic of South Africa, 1976-84, 85-87; dir. State Library, Pretoria, Republic of South Africa, 1987—; editor South African libraries, 1980-85; mem. Com. Nat. Info. Policy, 1980-86, South African Inst. for Library and Info. Sci., 1945—, Nat. Library Adv. Council, 1967-82, Nat. Adv. Council Librarinaship and Info. Affairs, 1982-86, Adv. Com. for Info. and Documentation CSIR, 1963-86, Working Group Unit for Library and Info. Sci. Research, 1981-87, Working Group for Research Project on Curricularisation of Library and Info. Edn., 1986—. Author: Differences in educational programmes for librarians and information officers, 1984, The information society in South Africa, 1985, The use of libraries for the development of South Africa, 1988. South African Inst. for Library and Info. Sci. fellow 1959. Mem. South African Library Assn. (pres. 1968-70). Home: 177 Smith St, Pretoria 0002, Republic of South Africa Office: State Library, PO Box 397, Pretoria 0001, Republic of South Africa

ZABALETA, NICANOR, harpist; b. San Sebastian, Guipuzcoa, Spain, Jan. 7, 1907; s. Pedro Zabaleta and Isabel Zala S.; m. Graciela Torres, Feb. 22, 1952; children: Pedro, Estella. Grad., Madrid Royal Conservatory, 1920. Harpist in numerous concerts worldwide, various music festivals including those in West Berlin, Lucerne, France, Edinburgh, Scotland, Osaka, Japan, Paris, Prague, Venice, Italy; producer numerous records including (with Y. Menuhin) Music for Violin and Harp, (with the Madrid Nat. Orch.) Concierto de Aranjuez, (with the Berlin Philhamonic and the Vienna Philharmonic) Mozart's Flute and Harp Concerto, (with English Chamber Orch) Bach/Handel Concertos, (solo) Bach Program, Spanish Harp Music from the 16th to the 18th Centuries, others; publ. Six Variations Faciles Sur Un Theme Suisse Pour la Harpe ou le Forte Piano, 1959, Dussek-Sonata for Harp in C minor, 1959, 16th to 18th Century Spanish Harp Music, 1959. Home: Villa Izar, Aldapeta, 20009 San Sebastian Spain

ZABEL, JERRY, manufacturing company executive; b. Feldafing, Fed. Republic Germany, Jan. 5, 1947, came to U.S., 1949, naturalized, 1955; s. Sam and Sara (Turetz) Z.; m. Diane L. Silverman, Feb. 16, 1969; children—Steven, Rachel, Brian, Tracy. BBA, Roosevelt U., 1974, MBA, 1978. Cert. in prodn. and inventory mgmt. Factory mgr. Hart Schaffner & Marx, Chgo., 1969-74; planner Abbott Labs., North Chicago, Ill., 1974-79; mgr. Addressograph Multigraph, Mt. Prospect, Ill., 1979-80; dir. Internat. Jensen, Schiller Park, Ill., 1980-85; mgr. mfg. FelPro, Skokie, Ill., 1985—; instr. Webster Coll., Fort Sheridan, Ill., 1981, Columbia Coll., Fort Sheridan, 1978-81. Patentee in field. Served with U.S. Army, 1965-68, Vietnam. Decorated. Mem. Am. Prodn. and Inventory Control Soc. (profl. cert. materials mgmt. 1982, cert. prodn. inventory mgmt. 1987), Internat. Material Mgmt. Soc., Cosmopolitan C. of C. (Cert. of Appreciation 1974). Home: 1203 Devonshire Buffalo Grove IL 60089

ZACCONE, SUZANNE MARIA, sales executive; b. Chgo., Oct. 23, 1957; d. Dominic Robert and Lorretta F. (Urban) Z. Grad. high sch., Downers Grove, Ill. Sales sec. Brookeridge Realty, Downers Grove, 1975-76; sales cons. Kafka Estates Inc., Downers Grove, 1975-76; adminstrv. asst. Chem. Dist., Inc., Oakbrook, Ill., 1976-77; sales rep., mgr. Anographics Corp., Burr Ridge, Ill., 1977-85; pres., owner Graphic Solutions, Inc., Downers Grove, 1985—. Mem. Women in Mgmt., Nat. Assn. Female Execs., Sales and Mktg. Execs. of Chgo., Women Entrepreneurs of DuPage County. Avocations: reading, sailing, cooking, needlepoint, scuba diving. Office: Graphic Solutions Inc 5117 Main St Downers Grove IL 60515

ZACHER, ALLAN NORMAN, JR., clergyman, psychologist, lawyer; b. Decatur, Ill., May 23, 1928; s. Allan Norman and Eleanor (Shaw) Z.; student Washington U. Sch. Bus. and Pub. Adminstrn., St. Louis, 1946, 48-50; J.D., Washington U., 1952, Ph.D., 1971; M.Div., Va. Theol. Sem., 1955; S.T.M., Eden Theol. Sem., 1966; m. Estelle Medalie, July 19, 1952 (dec. Mar. 1982); children—Allan Norman III, Mark, John; m. Deborah Bradley, Dec. 27, 1985. Bar: Mo. 1952; ordained to ministry Episcopal Ch., 1955. Assoc. Fred B. Whalen, St. Louis, 1950-52; asst. rector Truro Episcopal Ch., Fairfax, Va., 1955-58; canon counselor Christ Ch. Cathedral, St. Louis, 1958-64; dir. Pastoral Counseling Inst., St. Louis, 1958—; vicar Grace Episcopal Ch., St. Louis, 1958-63; vis. lectr. Eden Sem., St. Louis U., Washington U.; chmn. dept. Christian social relations Diocese of Mo., 1959-63, mem. council, 1969-63; pvt. practice clin. psychology, St. Louis, 1971—; cons. to family life, assoc. joint family life com. Nat. Council Episcopal Ch., 1962-65; labor arbitrator Fed. Mediation and Conciliation Service, 1959—. Pres. mem. steering com. St. Louis Group Psychotherapy Forum, 1962-65; mem. St. Louis Bd. Edn., 1963-69; pres. Northside Neighborhood Council, St. Louis, 1959-61; treas. Mo. Council Family Relations. Chmn. psychodrama and religion round table, 1st Internat. Congress of Psychodrama, Milan, Italy, 1964, 2d Internat. Congress, Barcelona, Spain, 1966. Bd. dirs. Grace Hill House, St. Louis, chaplain, 1958-63. Served with AUS, 1946-48, Kent fellow, 1968; Community Mental Health Research fellow, 1968; cert. trainer and practitioner in psychodrama and group psychotherapy Am. Bd. Examiners; lic. clin. psychologist, Mo., Ill.; mem. Nat. Register Health Service Providers in Psychology. Fellow Am. Acad. Matrimonial lawyers; mem. St. Louis (family law com.), Am. (family law com. on marriage and family counseling conciliation), Mo. (family law com.), Fed. bar, assns., Am. Soc. Group Psychotherapy and Psychodrama, Episcopal Soc. for Racial Unity (nat. bd.), Am. Assn. Pastoral Counselors (diplomate; mem. funding bd. 1963-65), Am. Assn. Marriage Counselors, Mo. Psychol. Assn., Soc. St. Louis Psychologists (past pres.), Assn. for Clin. Pastoral Edn., Soc. for Religion in Higher Edn. Contbr. articles to religious, psychol. and legal publs. Home: 16 Hortense Pl Saint Louis MO 63108 Office: 8420 Delmar Blvd Saint Louis MO 63124

ZACHERT, VIRGINIA, psychologist, educator; b. Jacksonville, Ala., Mar. 1, 1920; d. R.E. and Cora H. (Massee) Z. Student, Norman Jr. Coll., 1937; A.B., Ga. State Woman's Coll., 1940; M.A., Emory U., 1947; Ph.D., Purdue U., 1949. Diplomate: Am. Bd. Profl. Psychologists. Statistician Davison-Paxon Co., Atlanta, 1941-44; research psychologist Mil. Contracts, Auburn Research Found., Ala. Poly. Inst.; indsl. and research psychologist Sturm & O'Brien (cons. engrs.), 1958-59; research project dir. Western Design, Biloxi, Miss., 1960-61; self-employed cons. psychologist Norman Park, Ga., 1961-71, Good Hope, Ga., 1971—; research assoc. med. edn. Med. Coll. Ga., Augusta, 1963-65, assoc. prof., 1965-70, research prof., 1970-84, research prof. emeritus, 1984—, chief learning materials div., 1973-84, mem. faculty senate, 1976-84, mem. acad. council, 1976-82, pres. acad. council, 1983, sec., 1978; mem. Ga. Bd. Examiners of Psychologists, 1974-79, v.p., 1977, pres., 1978; mem. adv. bd. Comdr. Gen. ATC USAF, 1967-70; cons. Ga. Silver Haired Legislature, 1980, senator, 1987—, pres. protem, 1987. Author: (with P.L. Wilds) Essentials of Gynecology-Oncology, 1967, Applications of Gynecology-Oncology, 1967. Del. White House Conf. on Aging, 1981. Served as aerologist USN, 1944-46; aviation psychologist USAF, 1949-54. Fellow Am. Psychol. Assn., AAAS; mem. AAUP (chpt. pres. 1977-80), Sigma Xi. (chpt. pres. 1980-81). Baptist. Home: 1126 Highland Ave Augusta GA 30904-4628 Office: Med Coll Ga Dept Ob-Gyn Augusta GA 30912

ZACHMANN, WILLIAM FRANCIS, computer/communications industry market research company executive; b. Cleve., Oct. 19, 1942; s. Kurt Wilhelm and Jean (O'Konski) Z.; B.A., Harvard U., 1966; m. Elizabeth Ann Loftus, June 7, 1980. Programmer/analyst Cambridge Computer Assocs. (Mass.), 1967-69; systems research officer First Nat. Bank Boston, 1969-74; dir. research Forum Corp., Boston, 1974-75; coordinator personnel adminstrn. Harvard U., Cambridge, 1976-77; mgr. tech. support CallData Systems, Boston, 1977-79; v.p. tech. assessment Internat. Data Corp., Framingham, Mass., 1979-83; v.p. corp. research Internat. Data Corp., Framingham, Mass., 1983-87, sr. v.p., 1987—. Mem. City Mgrs. Adv. Com. on Cable TV, Cambridge, 1979-83. Mem. IEEE, Assn. for Computing Machinery. Clubs: Harvard (Boston); Harvard Faculty (Cambridge). Author: Keys to Application Development Productivity, 1981; contbg. editor Computer Industry Report, 1982—, Communications and Distributed Resources Report, 1983-87 , PC World mag., 1987—; columnist On Communications mag., 1984-86, Software News mag., 1984-86, Computerworld mag., 1986—, Infoworld mag., 1987—, Micromarketworld mag., 1985-87. Home: PO Box 2805 160 Standish St Duxbury MA 02331 Office: 5 Speen St Framingham MA 01701

ZACHRISSON, CARL UDDO, political scientist, educator; b. San Francisco, Dec. 4, 1940; s. Carl Uddo and Erma Christiana (Luce) Z.; m. Adele Lee Hall, Dec. 30, 1971; children: Carl Frederick, Christopher Dawes. B.A., Stanford U., 1962; Lic. es Sci. Politiques, Grad. Inst. Internat. Studies, U. Geneva (Switzerland); D.Phil., Oxford U. (Eng.), 1972. Instr. to asst. prof. polit. studies Pitzer Coll., Claremont, Calif., 1967-74; assoc. prof. internat. relations Pomona Coll., Claremont, 1974-81; from asst. prof. to prof. govt. and internat. relations Claremont Grad. Sch., 1972—; dir. West Coast Region, Inst. Internat. Edn., San Francisco, 1983—; pres. Internat. Studies Assocs. Inc., 1981-83; lectr. USIS, West Africa, 1972; dir. Edn. Abroad, Pomona and Scripps Colls., 1973-81; v.p. So. Calif. div. UN Assn., 1976-79; bd. dirs. Council Internat. Ednl. Exchange, 1978-81, So. Calif. Global Edn. task force, 1978-81. Treas. Calif. Council UN U., 1979-81; bd. dirs. Internat. Visitors Ctr., San Francisco, 1986—, San Francisco-Abidjan Sister City Com., 1986—; mem. Am. Com. U.S.-Soviet Relations; mem. San Francisco Com. on Fgn. Relations, 1984—; pres. bd. trustees Internat. Exchange Network of No. Calif., 1985-88; chmn. bd. trustees Town Sch. Boys, 1986-88; sr. warden St. Mary the Virgin Episcopal Ch., San Francisco, 1986-88. Mem. African Studies Assn., Am. Polit. Sci Assn., Am. Soc. Internat. Law, Nat. Assn. Fgn. Student Affairs, Soc. Internat. Edn., Tng. and Research, Soc. Internat. Devel. Clubs: Bohemian, Oxford Union Soc.; Norfolk Country (Conn.). Author: (with R. Tebbets) Educating for International Competence, 1984; (with T. Brown) Foreign Student Resource Guide for Home Country Employment, 1988.

ZACKHEIM, MARC ALLEN, child psychologist, editor; b. N.Y.C., Oct. 12, 1950; s. Seymour David and Blanche (Kalt) Z.; m. Elisa Freiden, Mar. 14, 1978 (div.). AA, U. Fla., 1970, BA with high honors, 1972; MS, Fla. State U., 1974, PhD, 1977. Lic. psychologist, Fla., Ill., Ind., Ala. Intern, Duke U. Med. Ctr., Durham, N.C., 1976; postdoctoral fellow in psychology Fla. State U., 1978; resident in psychology Rush-Presbyn. St. Luke's Med. Ctr., Chgo., 1979; attending child psychologist Assocs. in Adolescent Psychiatry, Chgo., 1979-85, dir. tng., 1981-85; v.p. Assocs. in Clin. Psychology, 1985—; faculty Auburn (Ala.) U.; attending child psychologist Riveredge Hosp., Forest Park, Ill., 1979—; cons. editor Ednl. and Psychol. Research. Contbr. articles to profl. jours., including Readings, A Jour. Am. Orthopsych. Assn. USPHS fellow, 1973-76. Apptd. Ill. Guardianship and Advocacy Commn., 1988—. Mem. Am. Psychol. Assn., State of Ill. Human Rights Auth., Ill. Psychol. Assn., Midwest Psychol. Assn., Fla. Psychol. Assn., S.E. Psychol. Assn., Chgo. Assn. for Psychoanalytic Psychology, Acad. Psychosomatic Medicine. Home: 1322 W Chase Ave Chicago IL 60626 Office: Riveredge Hosp 8311 Roosevelt Rd Forest Park IL 60130 also: 10330 Roosevelt Rd Suite 303 Westchester IL 60153

ZACKS, ROGER WILLIAM, orchestral musician; b. Detroit, Oct. 1, 1958; s. Norman and Florence (Safran) Z.; m. Annette Jansen, Dec. 21, 1987. MusB, Northwestern U., 1979; MusM, New Eng. Conservatory, Boston, 1982. Prin. trumpet Landestheater Orchester Detmold, Fed. Republic of Germany, 1983; assoc. prin. trumpet Hessiche Staatstheater Orchester, Kassel, Fed. Republic of Germany, 1983-87; co-prin. trumpet Duisburg Sinfoniker of Deutsche Oper Am Rhein, Fed. Republic of Germany, 1987—. Jewish. Home: Schillerstrasse 14, 4100 Duisburg 14 Federal Republic of Germany

ZADEH, LOTFI A., educator; b. Baku, Russia, Feb. 4, 1921; s. Rahim A. and Fania (Koriman) Asker; came to U.S., 1944, naturalized, 1956; B.S., U. Teheran (Iran), 1942; M.S., M.I.T., 1946; Ph.D., Columbia U., 1949; m. Fay Sand, Mar. 21, 1946; children—Stella, Norman. Mem. faculty Columbia U., 1946-59, prof. elec. engring., 1957-59; mem. Inst. Advanced Study, Princeton, N.J., 1956; prof. elec. engring. U. Calif., Berkeley, 1959—, chmn. dept., 1963-68; vis. prof. M.I.T., 1962, 68. Mem. U.S. commn. 6, Internat. Sci. Radio Union, 1960-63; mem. tech. adv. bd. U.S. Postal Service. Guggenheim fellow, 1967-68. Fellow IEEE (Edn. medal 1973, Centennial award 1984), AAAS; mem. Nat. Acad. Engring. Author: (with C. A. Desoer) Linear System Theory, 1963; also articles; editor: (with E. Polak) System Theory, 1968; Fuzzy Sets and Systems; assoc. editor Jour. Math. Analysis Applications; editorial bd. Info. Scis., Jour. Info. and Optimization Scis., Math. Modeling, Jour. Optimization Theory and Applications, Policy Analysis Info. Systems, Fuzzy Math., Info. Systems, Networks, Jour. Gen. Systems, others; editor Jour. Computer and System Scis. Home: 904 Mendocino Berkeley CA 94707 Office: Univ of Calif Berkeley Computer Sci Div Room 561 Evans Hall Berkeley CA 94720

ZADER, GUSTAVE CHARLES, management executive; b. McKeesport, Pa., Feb. 18, 1917; s. Stanley N. and Stella (Myers) Z.; B.S., Davis-Elkins Coll., 1940, Pd.D., A.M., W.Va. U., 1948; Ph.D., N.Y. U., 1959; m. Margaret Katherine Parsons, Dec. 28, 1940; children—Sheila Anne Zader Staggs, Gustave Charles, William Thomas Parsons, John Raymond, James Robert. Tchr. math. and sci., coach athletics pub. schs. W.Va., 1940-43; tchr. courses in pupil personnel Ednl. Adminstrn. Extension div. U. S.C., 1948-50; instr. to prof. math. and edn. The Citadel, Charleston, S.C., 1946-55; v.p. Coll. of Gt. Falls (Mont.), 1960-62; dir. univ. relations Loyola U., Chgo., 1962-64; pres. Mt. St. Scholastica Coll., 1964-67; exec. dir. Sacramento State Coll., 1967-68; prof. edn. adminstrn. Oklahoma City U., 1968-72, dir. research and community services, 1968-69, dean Sch. Bus., 1969-72; prof. edn., dir. Center Grad. Studies, Va. Poly. Inst. and State U., Reston, 1972-77; pres. Margus, Inc., 1977—. Chmn. Okla. Urban Planning Council, Okla. Environ. Council, Okla. Econ. Research Council; mem. Task Force To Draft Goals for Okla., Oklahoma City-Tulsa Diocesan Bd. Christian Edn., Coordinating Council Okla. Consortium on Research; v.p. Okla. Council on Econ. Edn.; dir. Oklahoma City Community Credit Assn., Okla. Internat. Trade Assn., SW Alliance for Latin Am. Bd. dirs. Community Concerts; chmn. Arlington Com. of 100. Served with USNR, World War II, Korea. Recipient Key to City, Denver; citation for service Gov. Ind.; WTHI-TV award for outstanding community service Terre Haute. Mem. Chi Beta Phi, Delta Sigma Pi. Club: Rotary. Home: 106 Interpromontory Rd Great Falls VA 22066

ZADOW, JOHN GREIG, government agency administrator, researcher; b. Melbourne, Victoria, Australia, Apr. 28, 1941; s. Harold Louis and Gladys Alexandra (Greig) Z.; m. Betty Josephine Rockliff, Aug. 10, 1963 (div. 1988); children: Kirsten, Simon; m. Susan Michelle Collins, June 14, 1988. BSc with hons., U. Melbourne, 1961, MS, 1973; D in Applied Sci., Victoria Inst. Colls., Melbourne, 1981. Research chemist Taubmans Indsl. Coatings, Melbourne, 1958-64, Australian Paper Mfrs., Melbourne, 1964-67; scientist Dairy Research Lab. Commonwealth Sci. and Indsl. Research Orgn., Highett, Victoria, 1967-86, head of lab., 1986—. Contbr. articles to profl. jours. Recipient Silver medal Australian Soc. Dairy Tech., 1978, Australian Jour. Dairy Tech. award Australian Soc. Dairy Tech., 1986. Mem. Dairy Industry Assn. Australia (corp.), Inst. Food Technologists (assoc.), Australian Inst. Food Sci. and Tech. (assoc.), Internat. Dairy Fedn. (group experts). Club: Black Rock (Victoria) Yacht. (sail com. 1985-88). Home: 21a Kershaw St, Mordialloc, Victoria 3195, Australia Office: Commonwealth Sci & Indsl Research, Orgn, Dairy Research Lab, PO Box 20, Highett, Victoria 3190, Australia

ZADOW, SUSAN MICHELLE, librarian; b. Townsville, Queensland, Australia, Aug. 19, 1947; d. Stewart Horton Delbridge and Patricia Margaret (Henderson) Preston; m. Peter James Collins, Aug. 9, 1969 (div. 1984); 1 child, Matthew Stewart; m. John Greig Zadow, June 15, 1988. Grad., Library Assn. Australia, Melbourne, 1967; Diploma in Data Processing, Royal Melbourne Inst. Tech., 1976; Cert. in Farm Mgmt., Glenormiston (Australia) Agrl. Coll., 1978. Library asst. BP Australia, Melbourne, 1966-67; library officer Commonwealth Sci. and Indsl. Research Orgn. div. Forest Products, S. Melbourne, 1967-73; librarian CSIRO Dairy Research Lab., Highett, 1973—. Contbr. articles, papers, reports to tech. publs. Mem. Library Assn. Australia, Dairy Industry Assn. Australia. Club: Black Rock Yacht (Victoria). Home: 21a Kershaw St, Mordialloc Victoria 3195, Australia Office: CSIRO Dairy Research Lab, PO Box 20, 3190 Highett Victoria Australia

ZAEB, JAHAN, dairy executive; b. Sahiwal, Punjab, Pakistan, Aug. 16, 1955; s. Tajuddin and Surraya Taj Zaeb; m. Bushra Zaeb, Feb. 27, 1981; children—Saira, Umer Jahan. B.S., Govt. Coll., Sahiwal, 1974; diploma in diary engring. Jutland Technol. Inst., Aarhus, Denmark, 1978. Dir. Green Dairies Ltd., Sahiwal, 1975-78, mng. dir., 1978-80, dir., 1975—; chief exec., mng. dir. Pakistan Dairies Ltd., Sahiwal, 1980—; dir. Green Enterprises Ltd., Sahiwal, Green Fields Ltd., Sahiwal; dairy adviser Agrl. Devel. Bank of Pakistan, Islamabad, 1981-83. Melvin Jones fellow Lions Clubs Internat. Found., 1984; recipient Best Businessman of Sahiwal award Aiwan-E Sakafat, 1984. Fellow Pakistan Dairy Assn. (exec. mem.); mem. Pakistan Inst. Mgmt. (life), Lahore C. of C. and Industry, Fed. Dairy Devel., Tetrapak Consumers Assn. Pakistan. Bd. Mem. Pakistan Muslim League. Muslim. Clubs: Gymkhana (Lahore); Sahiwal (mem. exec. com.). Lodge: Lions (pres. Sahiwal 1983—). Avocation: reading financial and dairy papers. Home: Green House, Liaquat Rd, Sahiwal, Punjab Pakistan Office: Pakistan Dairies Ltd, Multan Rd, Sahiwal, Punjab Pakistan

ZAFAR, KHALID MASOOD, tea and spices company executive; b. Calcutta, India, May 4, 1937; arrived in Pakistan, 1949; s. M. Hamid and Sughra (Asad) Z.; m. Anisa Akram, May 18, 1962; children: Nanzeen, Imran, Mahjabeen. BA, U. Punjab, Lahore, Pakistan, 1956; MPA, U. Karachi, Pakistan, 1958. Bus. improvement officer Bata Shoe Co., Lahore, 1960-64; sales supt. Pakistan Internat. Airlines, Karachi, 1964-68; sr. sales officer Exxon Chems., Karachi, 1968-73; dir. supr. Ont. Hosp. Assn., Toronto, Can., 1974-77; mgr. adminstrn. and personnel Aga Khan Hosp. Project, Karachi, 1978-80; corp. sec., gen. mgr. mktg. Brooke Bond, Karachi, 1980—, sales dir., 1988—. Mem. Internat. Advt. Assn. (v.p. Pakistan chpt.), Mktg. Assn. Pakistan, Employers Fedn. Pakistan (rep.). Home: 54/II 23d St DHAV, Karachi Pakistan Office: Brooke Bond Pakistan Ltd, PO Box 2705, Karachi Pakistan

ZAGAMI, ANTHONY JAMES, lawyer; b. Washington, Jan. 19, 1951; s. Placidino and Rosemary Zagami; m. Natalie Ann Manganello, July 19, 1980; 1 child, Brian. AA, Prince Georges Community Coll., 1971; BS in Bus. and Pub. Adminstrn., U. Md., 1973, postgrad., 1974; JD, George Mason U., 1977. Bar: D.C. 1978, U.S. Dist. Ct. D.C. 1979, U.S. Ct. Appeals (D.C. cir.) 1979, U.S. Supreme Ct. 1983. Asst. to sec. of majority U.S. Senate, Washington, 1977-78, staff asst. to Sec. of Senate, 1978-81; gen. counsel joint com. on printing U.S. Congress, Washington, 1981—. Chmn. legal adv. com. U.S. Senate Employees Fed. Credit Union Bd. Dirs.; counsel U.S. Senate Staff Club. Mem. ABA, Phi Alpha Phi. Home: 9021 Adelphi Rd Adelphi MD 20783 Office: US Congress Joint Com Printing Hart Senate Office Bldg Room SH-818 Washington DC 20510

ZAGAR, LAWRENCE THOMAS, financial executive; b. Aliquippa, Pa., Apr. 17, 1921; s. Anthony and Mary (Padavich) Z.; B.S., St. Vincent Coll., Latrobe, Pa., 1944, postgrad. Southwestern U., Los Angeles, 1953, UCLA, 1955-60; Ph.D. (hon.), 1974; m. Sylvia Louise Puskarich, May 11, 1946; 1 son, Terence Richard. Controller, Cath. Youth Orgn., Archidocese of Los Angeles, 1947-51; cost acct. Solar Mfg. Corp., 1953; cost acct. Ducommun Metals & Supply Co., Los Angeles, 1954-56, mgr. profit improvement dept., 1957-60, project control mgr., 1958-60, corp. budget mgr., 1960-62; mgr. fin. planning and controls Riverside Cement Co., Los Angeles, 1962-63; v.p. fin. Medallion Printers & Lithographers, Los Angeles, 1963-64, also dir.; asst. sec.-treas., controller Pacific Western Industries, Inc., Los Angeles, 1965-66, asst. sec., 1966-67; sec.-treas. Simi Valley Rock Products, Inc., 1965-70, Glenn E. Walker Corp., Walnut, Calif., 1965-67, Mountain Rock Products, Upland, Calif., 1965-67; pres. Furnishings Complete, Los Angeles, 1967-69; chief adminstrv. officer Jules Strongbow Enterprises, Inc., Los Angeles, 1968-70; v.p. Fin. Communications Clearing House, Los Angeles, 1970-71, pres., 1971-85, pres. emeritus, 1985—, also dir.; mem. U.S. Senatorial Bus. Adv. Bd., 1980-84, 87—; Joint Presdl./Congl. Steering Com., 1980-84; spl. adv. U.S. Congressional Adv. Bd., 1984-87. Mem. Calif. Athletic Commn.; mem. So. Calif. Golden Gloves Com., 1948-68; bd. dirs. Boxers and Wrestlers Fund, Inc.; bd. govs., chmn. fin. com. Vols. of Am., Los Angeles, 1978—; mem. pres.'s council Calif. State Poly. U., 1980—. Served from pvt. to 1st lt. USMC, 1942-46, comdg. officer, 1951-53, maj., 1954. Recipient Letterman of Distinction award St. Vincent Coll., 1984. Mem. St. Vincent Alumni Assn. Republican. Roman Catholic. Author articles in field. Home: 4360 W 4th St Los Angeles CA 90020 Office: 3691 Bandini Blvd Los Angeles CA 90023

ZAGÓRSKI, KRZYSZTOF HUBERT, sociologist; b. Czestochowa, Poland, May 27, 1841; arrived in Australia, 1983; s. Juliusz M. and Anna (Kamienska) Z.; m. Janina Frentzel, July 2, 1966; 1 child, Natalia. MA, Warsaw (Poland) U., 1964, PhD, 1968; habilitation, Polish Acad. Sci., Warsaw, 1978. Asst. prof. Warsaw U., 1964-68; head research sect. Cen. Statictical Office, Warsaw, 1968-76; research fellow Polish Acad. Scis., 1976-83; sr. research fellow Australian Nat. U., Canberra, 1983—; vis. lectr. Va.

Poly. Inst., Blacksburg, 1978. Author: Development, Social Structure and Social Mobility, 1978, Social Mobility into Post-Industrial Society, 1984; author other books and articles. Dep. chmn. inst. br. Solidarnosc, Warsaw, 1980-83. Mem. Internat. Sociol. Assn., Regional Sci. Assn. Office: Australian Nat U, Canberra 2601, Australia

ZAGREANU, IOAN, cardiologist, educator; b. Puin, Cluj, Romania, Dec. 16, 1921; s. Matei and Eleonora (Plaian) Z.; m. Lucia Marza, Oct. 6, 1949; 1 child, Liana. M.D., Faculty of Medicine, Cluj, 1946; Ph.D. in Cardiology, Inst. Medicine and Pharmacy, 1964, Docent, 1974. Intern various clinics, Cluj, 1945-47; specialization First Med. Clinic, Cluj, 1947-51; teaching asst., 1951-59, asst. prof., 1967-70; assoc. prof. Fifth Med. Clinic, Cluj, 1970-77, prof., 1977—, head dept., 1976—. Author: The Modern Auscultation of the Heart, 1974, Clinical Electrocardiography, 1976, Essential Pulmonary Arterial Hypertension, 1978, Angina Pectoris, 1983. Mem. Union of Soc. Med. Scis. (sec. 1972—), French Soc. Cardiology (corr.). Romanian Communist. Home: Nuferilor Nr 1, Cluj-Napoca 3400 Romania Office: Fifth Med Clinic, Str Tabacarilor Nr 11, Cluj-Napoca Romania

ZAHN, PAUL HUGH, writer, consultant; b. Hermosa Beach, Calif., Feb. 26, 1944; s. Howard and Florence (Trout) Z.; m. Sylvie Eugenie Vervroegen, Oct. 27, 1973. BSc, U. Oreg., 1966, MSc, 1968; diploma, Control Data Inst., Long Beach, Calif., 1971. Asst. advt. mgr. Stoody Co., Whittier, Calif., 1970-71; account exec., copywriter Parker-Rumrill, Brussels and Europe, 1972-73; European advt. mgr. Automated Bldg. Co. Components, Brussels, 1972-73; freelance copywriter, publ. relations cons. 1974-75, freelance journalist specializing in comml., indsl. and fin. matters, 1975-81; external relations officer Soc. for Worldwide Interbank Fin. Telecom, Brussels, 1981-84; mktg. exec. Sperry Internat. Banking Ctr., Brussels, 1984-86; freelance writer, cons. Brussels, 1986—; cons. European Communications Group, Belgium, 1986—; ptnr. Viking Tech. Inc.,Brussels. Served with U.S. Army, 1968-71, Vietnam. Decorated Bronze Star medal. Mem. Brussels Fgn. Press Assn. (bd. dirs.). Home: Ave des Grenadiers 8, 1050 Brussels Belgium

ZAHN, RUDOLF KARL, biochemist, educator; b. Bad Orb, Germany, Feb. 6, 1920; s. Jakob Simon and Maria Margarethe (Noll) Z.; grad. summa cum laude in Medicine, Johann Wolfgang Goethe Universitat, Frankfurt, Dr. med., PhD (hon.) U. Zagreb, 1988 ; m. Gertrud Daimler, Feb. 17, 1942; children—Matthias A.A., Isabel M. Rockefeller fellow Harvard U., 1949-50; mem. faculty dept. pharmacy U. Pa., Phila., 1950; chief kidney lab. dept. physiology, sci. assoc. dept. biochemistry U. Frankfurt (W. Ger.), 1950-56, docent, 1956-61, assoc. prof. physiology and biochemistry, 1961-67; chmn., dir. Inst. Biochemistry, Johannes Gutenberg U., Mainz, W. Ger., 1967—; prof. Rudjer Boskovic, Zagreb, Yugoslavia; head Joint Venture Lab. Marine Molecular Biology, Rovinji, Yugoslavia and Mainz, W. Ger., 1971—; prof. med. biochemistry U. Kurume-Fukuoka (Japan), 1981; cons. Bundesminister Forschung u. Technologie; full mem. Acad. Sci. and Literature; chmn. Commn. Molecular Biology, 1973—. Mem. Gesellschaft für Biologische Chemie, Deutsche Gesellschaft für Klinische Chemie, Deutsche Gesellschaft für Elektronenmikroskopie, Deutsche Gesellschaft für Biophysik, European Assn. Cancer Research, Gesellschaft für Freunde des Deutsche-Amerikanischen Akademischen Austauschs, N.Y. Acad. Scis., Paul Ehrlich Gesellschaft für Chemotherapie, Internat. Soc. Research in Med. Edn., Medizinische Gesellschaft Mainz, Gesellschaft für Genetik Munchen, Deutsche Pharmakologische Gesellschaft, European Environ. Mutagen Soc., AAAS, Deutsche Gesellschaft für Gerontologie, Gesellschaft deutscher Chemiker. European editor Mechanisms Aging Development; editor Research Molecular Biology, Acad. Sci. Lit., Mainz; chmn., organizer Karl August Forster lectures on Programmed Biosynthesis, 1968—; contbr. articles to profl. jours. Office: Physiologische-Chemisches Inst, Johannes Gutenberg U, Duesberg Weg, 6500 Mainz Federal Republic of Germany

ZAHRA, ANTHONY GEORGE, travel company executive; b. Sliema, Malta, Apr. 10, 1945; s. Anthony George and Ersilia (Sammut) Z.; m. Jacqueline Panton, Jan. 4, 1974; 1 child, Nicholas. Student, Stella Maris Coll., Gzira, Malta. Chief exec. Alpine Rent-A-Car Ltd, San Gwann, Malta, 1969—, Alpine Travel Ltd., San Gwann, 1971—, Alpine Holding Ltd., San Gwann, 1973—, Alpine Ins. Brokers Ltd., San Gwann, 1973—, Maltatours (U.K.) Ltd., London, 1974—, Comtec Service Ltd., Sliema, Malta, 1975—, Allfreight Ltd., Fgura, Malta, 1978—, Alfonso Ltd., St. Julian's, Malta, 1985—, Intratours (U.K.) Ltd., London, 1986—. Mem. Assn. Malta Travel Agents, Assn. British Travel Agents, Inst. Dirs., C. of C. Home: The Panthers Cisk Ln, San Pawl tat-Targa Malta

ZAIDI, SHABIH HAIDER, otolaryngologist, educator; b. Ajmer, Rajrutana, India, Oct. 7, 1944; s. Nasir Hussain and Zakira (Hussain) Z.; m. Zohra Hasan, Jan. 20, 1973; children: Ali, Zehra, Sarah. MBBS, Dow Med. Coll., Karachi, Pakistan, 1966; Diploma in Oto-Laryngology, U. London, 1971. House surgeon Dow Med. Coll. Hosp., 1967-68, house physician, 1968, asst. prof. otolaryngology, cons., 1972-77, assoc. prof., 1977-83, prof., chief surgeon otolaryngology, 1983—; sr. house officer North Middlesex Group Hosps., London, 1968-69, Nottingham (Eng.) Gen. Univ. Hosp., 1969-70; registrar, clin. tutor Edinburgh (Scotland) Univ. Royal Infirmary Hosp., 1970-71; sr. registrar Midland Group Hosps., Birmingham, Eng., 1971-72; prof., chmn. Chandka Med. Coll., Larkana, Pakistan, 1983-85; prin., dean, prof. Sind Med. Coll., Karachi, 1985-86; prof. Dow Med. Coll., Karachi, 1987; prof., chmn. Jinnah postgrad. med. ctr., Karachi, 1988; cons. surgeon Medicon Gen. Hosp., Karachi, 1979-87, also chmn. bd.; mem. Gov.'s Commn. on Med. Edn., Karachi, 1986. Co-author: A Short Book of Entomological Disease, 1984; joint editor: Pakistan Jour. of Otolaryngology, 1985; contbr. articles to profl. jours. Recipient Pres.'s shield Pres. of Pakistan, 1985. Fellow Royal Coll. Surgeons of Edinburgh, ACS, Internat. Coll. Surgeons, Pakistan Soc. Otolaryngology (v.p. 1987, shield of merit 1983-86); mem. Japanese Soc. Laryngectomees. Islam. Club: Karachi Gymkhana. Home: 7-B 9th Zamzama St, Clifton, Karachi Pakistan Office: Medicon Gen Hosp, 13-C Block 4 FB Area, Karachi, Sind Pakistan

ZAIKOV, LEV NIKOLAYEVICH, Soviet government official; b. 1923. Ed., Leningrad Econ. Engring. Inst. Mem. Communist Party Soviet Union, 1957—; metal worker, shop supt., prodn. chief at a plant, 1941-61; dir. of a plant Leningrad, 1961-71; gen. dir. of a sci. prodn. assn. 1971-76; chair exec. com. Leningrad City Soviet, 1976—; dep. to USSR Supreme Soviet, Moscow, 1979—; mem. cen. com. Communist Party Soviet Union, Moscow, 1981—, sec., 1985—, mem. Politburo, 1986—. Office: Communist Party Soviet Union, Politburo, Moscow USSR *

ZAIN AZRAAI, Malaysian Ministry of Finance Administrator; b. Malaysia, 1936; grad. with honors in Politics, Philosophy and Econs., Oxford U., 1956; postgrad. London Sch. Econs.; m. 1967; 2 daus. Asst. sec. in polit. div. Ministry Fgn. Affairs, Malaysia, 1959-62, mem. Malayan High Commn. in London, 1962; served with Malaya's Permanent Mission to UN, 1962-66; spl. asst. to sec.-gen. Ministry of Fgn. Affairs prin. asst. sec. Ministry Fgn. Affairs, 1966, later undersec. for polit. affairs; prin. pvt. sec. to Prime Minister of Malaysia, 1971; ambassador to U.S. and Mex., 1976-83; exec. dir. World Bank, 1976-83; ambassador to UN, 1984—; instr. internat. relations U. Malaya, Malaysian Armed Forces Staff Coll. Trustee, Malaysian Nat. Art Gallery, also chmn. Office: Khazanah Malaysia, Ministry of Fin Block 9, Julan Dut, 50592 Kuala Lumpur Malaysia

ZAISER, ERNEST MATHEW, aircraft company executive; b. Uniontown, Pa., Dec. 5, 1926; s. Ernest Mathew and Kathryn Bertha (Swyoski) Zaiser; m. Janet Louise Watson, Aug. 4, 1951; children—John Watson, Carl Edward, Paul Martin, Martha Janet. B.S. in Mech. Engring., Yale U., 1947. Chief preliminary design engr. Hamilton Standard, Windsor Locks, Conn., 1947-63, mktg. mgr., 1963-66; with McDonnell Douglas Aircraft, 1966—, mgr. internat. mktg., St. Louis, 1966-69, gen. mgr. F-4 tech. services, Nagoya, Japan, 1969-74, rep. dir., mng. dir. McDonnell Douglas-Japan, Tokyo, 1974-78, v.p. ops. F-15 tech. services, Nagoya, 1978—, dir. F-4 tech. services, St. Louis, 1969-74; auditor McDonnell Douglas-Japan, Tokyo, 1978—. Bd. dirs. Nagoya Internat. Sch., 1969-72, chmn., 1970. Served with USN, 1944-46. Mem. Internat. House of Japan. Clubs: American (Tokyo). Office: 5-13 Nishiki 1 chome, McDonnell Douglas F, 15 Tech Services, Nissho-Iwai Bldg, Nakaku Nagoya 460 Japan

ZAISER, SALLY SOLEMMA VANN, retail book company executive; b. Birmingham, Ala., Jan. 18, 1917; d. Carl Waldo and Einnan (Herndon) Vann; student Birmingham-So. Coll., 1933-36, Akron Coll. Bus., 1937; m. Foster E. Zaiser, Nov. 11, 1939. Acct., A. Simionato, San Francisco, 1958-65; head acctg. dept. Richard T. Clarke Co., San Francisco, 1966; acct. John Howell-Books, San Francisco, 1967-72, sec., treas., 1972-83, 84-85, dir., 1982-85; sec. Great Eastern Mines, Inc., Albuquerque, 1969-81, dir., 1980-85. Braille transcriber for ARC, Kansas City, Mo. 1941-45; vol. worker ARC Hosp. Program, São Paulo, Brazil, 1952. Mem. Book Club Calif., Calif. Hist. Soc., Soc. Lit. and Arts, Gleeson Library Assocs. (dir. 1984-87, editor GLA newsletter 1984-87), Nat. Notary Assn., Theta Upsilon. Republican. Episcopalian. Club: Capitol Hill. Home: 355 Serrano Dr Apt 4-C San Francisco CA 94132 Office: 434 Post St San Francisco CA 94102

ZAJDLER, ARTUR, urban architect; b. Sosnowiec, Silesia, Poland, Nov. 21, 1933; came to Can., 1978, naturalized, 1981; s. Artur W. and Stefania W. (Flak) Z.; m. Maria Kristina Krakowiak, Apr. 8, 1967; children—Artur Mark, Caroline Maria. M.S. in Architecture, Tech. U., Gdansk, Poland, 1959, Diploma in Town Planning, 1963. Registered architect, Alta. Project architect Veli Paatela Architect, Helsinki, Finland, 1965-66, Atelier for Master Plan of East Coast Agglomeration, Gdansk, 1966-69; chief project architect Invest Project, Gdansk, 1969-72; chief resident architect pub. bldgs. div. Nat. Theatre Constrn., Lagos, Nigeria, 1972-78; project architect Hugh McMillan Architect, Calgary, Alta., Can., 1978-80; architect Alta. Mortgage & Housing Corp., Edmonton, 1980-86; project mgr. Alta. Pub. Works Supply and Services, Edmonton, 1986—; prin. Artur Zajdler, Architect, Edmonton, 1981—; hon. sec. Assn. Polish Architects, Gdansk, 1970-71. Recipient 2d prize Adminstrn. Centre for Polish Ocean Lines Nat. Competition, 1968, 1st prize Assn. Polish Architects Housing Competition, 1970, 1st prize Housing Estate in Gdynia Nat. Competition, 1971, letter of acknowledgement Gen. Contractor for Nat. Arts Theatre, Lagos, 1976. Mem. Alta. Assn. Architects (Banff session com. 1987-88), Royal Archtl. Inst. Can. Lutheran. Avocations: photography; biographical research; swimming; cycling; cross country skiing. Home: 12328 51A Ave, Edmonton, AB Canada T6H ON4 Office: Alta Pub Works Supply Services, Project Mgmt Div, 21st Floor College Plaza, 8215 112th St, Edmonton, AB Canada T6G 5A9

ZAJICEK (ZEE), BARBARA JEANNE, health care association executive; b. Peoria, Ill., Jan. 12, 1932; d. Gale Edward and Thelma Beatrice (Drury) Allen; student pub. schs.; m. Albert F. Zajicek, July 5, 1973 (dec.); children: Gregg Hahn, Lisa Hahn, Dana Hahn. Office supr., then exec. asst. to pres. Larry Smith & Co., Northfield, Ill., 1970-74, 76-78; asst. to pres., leasing agt. Devel. Control Corp., Northfield, 1974-76; bus. mgr. EMSCO, Ltd., Des Plaines, Ill., 1978-85; v.p./asst. sec.-treas. Midwest Med. Mgmt., 1982-85; exec. dir. Fla. chpt. Am. Coll. Emergency Physicians, Orlando, 1985—. Mem. Emergency Medicine Mgmt. Assn. (past pres., exec. dir. 1985-88), ASAE, FSAE, Meeting Planners Internat., Republican. Lutheran. Home: 3689 Jericho Dr Casselberry FL 32707-6203 Office: Fla Chpt Am Coll Emergency Physicians 5824 S Semoran Blvd Orlando FL 32822-4812

ZAKAKIS, DIMITRIOS PAUL, shipping company executive, shipowner; b. Athens, Greece, Apr. 8, 1945; s. Paul Pandelis and Polymnia (Vamvakas) Z.; m. Angelique-Theodosios Moschopoulos, Sept. 12, 1972; children: Paul, Polymnia. Grad., Mcht. Marine Acad., Hydra, Greece, 1965. 2d officer Valmas Bros. Shipping Co., Piraeus, Greece, 1970-72, chief officer, 1972-75, marine master, 1976-77; mng. dir. Endeavour Shipping, Piraeus, Greece, 1977-85, pres., 1986—. Served with Royal Hellenic Navy, 1968-70. Mem. Mcht. Marine Acad. Grads. Assn. Greek Orthodox. Club: U.S. Propeller. Home: 12 Singrou St, 15232 Halandri Greece Office: Endeavour Shipping Co, 2 Afendouli St, 18536 Piraeus Greece

ZAKHEM, SAM HANNA, diplomat; b. Beirut, Nov. 25, 1935; s. Hanna Y. and Matilda (Khozami) Z.; m. Marilyn Rosina Gillis; children: John Stuart, Charles Samir, James Paul. BA in Econs., Am. U., Cairo, 1957; MBA, U. Detroit, 1959; MA in Polit. Sci., U. Colo., 1968, PhD, 1970; postgrad., Wayne State U., Detroit, 1960-62. Prof. polit. sci. U. Colo., Denver, 1968-72; dir. ctr. for internat. students U. Denver, 1972-73; research analyst Heritage Found., Washington, 1973-74; dir. corp. relations Rocky Mountains Orthodontics, Denver, 1976-82, v.p. corp. relations, 1982-86; ambassador to Bahrain, Manama, 1986—; rep. Colo. Ho. of Reps., Denver, 1974-78; senator Colo. State Senate, 1979-83. Named Am. by Choice, State of Colo., 1972, Citizen of Yr., VFW, 1974; recipient George Washington Freedom medal Freedom Found. Valley Forge, 1978. Republican. Eastern Orthodox. Home: 2691 S Zurich Ct Denver CO 80219 Office: American Embassy Bahrain, PO Box 26431, Manama Bahrain

ZAKS, PATRICK ALAIN, physician, photographer; b. Paris, Oct. 4, 1949; s. Sylvain and Claudine (Goldrei) Zaks; divorced; children: Nadine Nicole, Gaël Gilles. BS in Math., Louis-le-Grand, France, 1967; MD, 1977; cert. d'Etudes Spécialisées en Stérilité, U. Paris V, 1978. Fellow U. Calif., San Francisco, 1974; cons., prof. pub. health various state and pvt. orgns., Paris, 1975—; researcher Cochin Hosp., Paris, 1975-78. Recipient Silver medal Acad. Soc. Arts and Letters in Paris, 1986. Office: 42 Rue Campo-Formio, 75013 Paris France

ZALAZAR, DANIEL (EDUARDO), educator, editor; b. San Juan, Argentina, Jan. 15, 1928; came to U.S., 1967; s. Daniel Zaragoza and Maria Julia (Orihuela) Z.; m. Geraldine Korb, Jan. 20, 1973. Prof. Philosophy, Universidad Nacional de Cuyo, Mendoza, Argentina, 1956; PhD, U. Pitts., 1970. Dean faculty humanities U. San Juan, San Juan, Argentina, 1965-66, pres., 1972-73; prof. philosophy Nat. U. San Juan, 1974-76; chmn. dept. fgn. langs. and lits. Indiana U. of Pa., 1978-79, assoc. prof., 1976-88; founding editor Hispanic Jour., 1979-85; participant confs. in Latin Am. thought and lit., 1970, 71, 72, 82, 83. Author: Ensayos de interpretacion literaria, 1976, 79, Libertad y creacion en los ensayos de Alejandro Korn, 1974, La Evolución de las ideas de Domingo F. Sarmiento, 1986; co-author: Universidad Nacional de San Juan, Estudio de factibilidad, 6 vols., 1973; contbr. articles to publs. Andrew Mellon fellow, 1968-69; winner 1st place Nat. Argentine Competition, Nat. Found. of Arts, 1972. Mem. AAUP, Instituto Internacional de Literatura Iberoamericana, Latin Am. Studies Assn., MLA, Latin Am. Indian Lits. Association (founding), Editores de Publicaciones Periódicas Norteamericanas OAS, Instituto Cuyano de Cultura Americana (hon. Mendoza, Argentina), Biblioteca Franklin (bd. San Juan).

ZALDASTANI, OTHAR, structural engineer; b. Tiflis, Georgia, USSR, Aug. 10, 1922; came to U.S., 1946; naturalized, 1956; s. Soliko Nicholas and Mariam Vachnadze (Hirsely) Z.; m. Elizabeth Reily Bailey, June 22, 1963; children: Elizabeth, Anne, Alexander. Diplome D'Ingenieur, Ecole Nationale des Ponts et Chaussees, Paris, 1945; Licencie es Sciences, Sorbonne, Paris, 1946; M.S. in Soil Mechanics, Harvard U., 1947, D.Sc. in Aerodynamics, 1950. Registered profl. engr., Mass., R.I., Tenn., Mo., N.H. Mem. faculty Harvard U., Cambridge, Mass., 1947-50; ptnr. Nichols, Norton and Zaldastani, Boston, 1952-63; pres. Nichols, Norton and Zaldastani, Inc., Boston, 1964-76, Zaldastani Assocs., Inc., Boston, 1976—; Gordon McKay vis. lectr. structural mechanics Harvard U., 1961; trustee, 1st v.p. Mass. Constrn. Industry Bd., 1973-76; mem. Mass. Designer Selection Bd., 1976-80. Contbg. author: Advances in Applied Mechanics, vol. 3, 1953. Patentee sound absorbing block, prestressed concrete beam and deck system. Trustee Wheelock Coll., Boston, 1975-81, mem. corp., 1984—; trustee Boston U. Med. Ctr., 1976—; trustee Brooks Sch., North Andover, Mass., 1986—. Recipient awards from various orgns. and agys. including Prestressed Concrete Inst., Cons. Engrs. Council New Eng., Am. Inst. Steel Constrn., Concrete Reinforcing Steel Inst., Dept. Transp., Am. Concrete Inst. Fellow ASCE (Ralph W. Horne award), Am. Concrete Inst., AIAA (assoc. fellow); mem. Georgian Assn. in the U.S. (pres. 1958-65), Sigma Xi. Clubs: Harvard, Harvard Faculty (Cambridge), Somerset (Boston); Country (Brookline, Mass.); Rolling Rock (Ligonier, Pa.). Home: 70 Suffolk Rd Chestnut Hill MA 02167 Office: Zaldastani Assocs Inc 7 Water St Boston MA 02109

ZALESKI, MAREK BOHDAN, immunologist; b. Krzemieniec, Poland, Oct. 18, 1936; came to U.S., 1969, naturalized, 1977; s. Stanislaw and Jadwiga (Zienkowicz) Z. M.D., Sch. Medicine, Warsaw, 1960, Dr. Med. Sci., 1963. Instr. dept. histology Sch. Medicine, Warsaw, 1955-60; asst. prof. Sch. Medicine, 1960-69; research asst. prof. (Henry C. and Bertha H. Buswell fellow) dept. microbiology SUNY, Buffalo, 1969-72; assoc. prof. SUNY, 1976-78, prof., 1978—; vis. scientist Inst. Exptl. Biology and Genetics, Czechoslovak Acad. Sci., Prague, 1965; Brit. Council's scholar, research lab. Queen Victoria Hosp., East Grinstead, Eng., 1966-67; asst. prof. dept. anatomy Mich. State U., East Lansing, 1972-75, assoc. prof., 1975-76. Contbg. author: Transplantation and Preservation of Tissues in Human Clinic, 1966, The Man, 1968, Cytophysiology, 1970, Principles of Immunology, 1978, Medical Microbiology, 1982, Molecular Immunology, 1984; Co-author: Immunogenetics, 1983, co-editor: Immunobiology of Major Histocompatibility Complex, 1981; co-transl.: (J. Tischner) Spirit of Solidarity, Marxism and Christianity: The Quarrel and the Dialogue in Poland; editorial com. Immunol. Investigations; contbr. articles to med. jours. Mem. adv. com. for Internat. Rescue Com., Amnesty Internat., Raul Wallenberg Com. USA. NIH grantee, 1976—; NEH grantee, 1985-87. Mem. Polish Anat. Soc., Transplantation Soc., Internat. Soc. Exptl. Hematology, Ernest Witebsky Center Immunology, Am. Assn. Immunologists, Buffalo Collegium of Immunology, N.Y. Acad. Scis., Solidarity and Human Rights Assn. Roman Catholic. Office: SUNY Dept Microbiology Buffalo NY 14214

ZALESKI, ZBIGNIEW, psychology educator; b. Rogoziniec, Poland, Apr. 29, 1947; s. Pawel and Emilia (Krapiec) Z.; m. Wiesia Migas, Feb. 15, 1976; children: Sebastian, Kamil. MS, Cath. U., Lublin, Poland, 1972, PhD, 1978. Asst. prof. Cath. U., Lublin, 1974-79, assoc. prof., 1979—; psychologist Lublin Sch. Dist., 1973-74; psychotherapist Students Health Ctr., Lublin, 1974-80; cons. Psychol. Counselling Ctr., Lublin, 1982-84; vis. research prof. U. Calif., Los Angeles, 1984-85; assoc. prof. Calif. State U., Long Beach, 1985—. Author: Motivational Function of Goals in Human Activity, 1987; contbr. articles to profl. jours. Active Solidarity Union, Lublin, 1980-81. Mem. Polish Psychol. Assn. (v.p. Lublin chpt. 1984-87). Roman Catholic. Home: Jankowskiego 1, 20-734 Lublin Poland Office: Cath Univ of Lublin, Al. Raclawickie 14, 20-950 Lublin Poland

ZALTA, EDWARD, otorhinolaryngologist; b. Houston, Mar. 2, 1930; s. Nouri Louis and Marie Zahde (Lizmi) Z.; m. Carolyn Mary Gordon, Oct. 8, 1971; 1 child, Ryan David; children by previous marriage: Nouri Allan, Lori Ann, Barry Thomas, Marci Louise. BS, Tulane U., 1952, MD, 1956. Diplomate Am. Bd. Quality Assurance and Utilization Rev. Physicians. Intern Brooke Army Hosp., San Antonio, 1956-57; resident in otolaryngology U.S. Army Hosp., Ft. Campbell, Ky., 1957-60; practice medicine specializing in otolaryngology Glendora, West Covina and San Dimas, Calif., 1960-82; ENT cons. City of Hope Med. Ctr., 1961-76; mem. staff Foothill Presbyn.; past pres. Los Angeles Found. Community Service, Los Angeles Poison Info. Ctr., So. Calif. Physicians Council, Inc.; founder pres., chmn. bd. CAPP CARE, INC.; chmn. bd. MDM; founder Inter-Hosp. Council Continuing Med. Edn. Author: (with others) Medicine and Your Money; contbr. articles to profl. jours. Pres. bd. govs. Glendora Unified Sch. Dist., 1965-71; mem. Calif. Cancer Adv. Council, 1967-71, Commn. of Californias, Los Angeles County Commn. on Economy and Efficiency. Served to capt. M.C. AUS, 1957-60. Recipient Award of Merit Order St. Lazarus, 1981. Mem. AMA, Calif. Med. Assn., Los Angeles County Med. Assn. (past pres.), Am. Acad. Otolaryngology, Am. Council Otolaryngology, Am. Assn. Preferred Provider Orgns. (past pres.), Am. Coll. Utilization Rev. Physicians, Kappa Nu, Phi Delta Epsilon. Republican. Jewish. Clubs: Glendora Country, Centurion, Sea Bluff Beach and Racquet; Center (Costa Mesa, Calif.); Pacific Golf (San Juan Capistrano, Calif.). Home: Three Morning Dove Dr Laguna Niguel CA 92677 Office: 17390 Brookhurst Ave Fountain Valley CA 92708

ZAMECK, HARVEY JASON, lawyer; b. Detroit, Oct. 19, 1943; s. Aaron and Mary (Silverstein) Z.; m. Diane Roslyn Smaller, Aug. 30, 1970; children—Allison Nicole, Stephanie Dawn. B.S.Ed., Wayne State U., 1964; J.D. (Clyde DeWitt scholar), U. Mich., 1968. Bar: Mich. 1968. Assoc. Keywell and Rosenfeld, Detroit, 1968-70; sole practice, Southfield, Mich., 1970—. Mem. ABA, Detroit Bar Assn., Am. Trial Lawyers Assn., Comml. Law League, Oakland County Bar Assn. Jewish. Home: 30740 Woodstream Ct Farmington Hills MI 48018 Office: 15999 W 12 Mile Southfield MI 48076

ZAMER, BELINDA ROSE, psychologist, educator; b. Washington, Oct. 26, 1953; d. Fred Elias and Yvonne Rose (Habib) Z. AA, Prince George's Coll., Largo, Md., 1973; BA, Cath. U. Am., 1974; MA, George Washington U., 1976, EdD, 1983. Asst. dir., sr. therapist Navy Dept., Washington, 1976-78; employee relations staff EPA, Washington, 1978-82, psychologist, 1982-84; asst. prof. George Washington U., 1983—; instr. Central Mich. U., Washington, 1984—, U. Md., College Park, 1984, John Hopkins U., U. So. Calif., NVA and Marymount U.; cons. WHO, NIMH Study Ctr., Washington; instr. U. Va., Marymount U, U. So. Calif. Bd. dirs. Prince George's Mental Health Assn., Cheverly, Md., 1974; exec. adv. bd. County Council Mental Health, Upper Marlboro, Md., 1975; bd. dirs. NIMH, Adelphi, Md., 1975. Catholic U. Bd. Trustees fellow, 1975, Health and Human Services of Washington grantee, 1976. Mem. AAUW, Nat. Council Exec. Women, Literacy Council Prince George County, Prince George's County Bus. and Profl. Women (exec. bd. 1983), So. Prince George's Bus. and Profl. Women, Alexandria Bus. and Profl. Women, Phi Beta Kappa (v.p. 1975-76), Psi Chi (v.p. 1976).

ZAMES, GEORGE DAVID, electrical engineer, educator; b. Poland, Jan. 7, 1934; s. Sam Simha and Leona Z.; m. Eva Eisenfarb, July 21, 1964; children: Ethan, Jonathan. B.Eng., McGill U., 1954; Sc.D. in Elec. Engring, MIT, 1960. Asst. prof. MIT, 1960-62, 63-65, Harvard U., 1962-63; sr. scientist NASA, Cambridge, Mass., 1965-71; vis. prof. Technion, Haifa, Israel, 1972-74; prof. elec. engring. McGill U., Montreal, 1974—, Macdonald chair. elec. engring., 1983—. Assoc. editor: So. Indsl. and Applied Math Jour. on Control, 1968-84, Systems and Control Letters, 1981-84, Internat. Math. Assn. Jour. Math. Control and Info., 1983—, Math. of Control Signals and Systems, 1987—; contbr. articles to profl. jours. Recipient classic paper citation Inst. Sci. Info., 1981; Athlone fellow Imperial Coll., London U., 1954-56; Nat. Acad. Scis. Resident Research Assoc., 1966-67; Guggenheim fellow, 1967-68; Killam fellow, 1984-86; sr. fellow Can. Inst. Advanced Research, 1984—; recipient Brit. Assn. medal, McGill U., 1954; Outstanding Paper award Am. Automatic Control Council, 1968; Control Sci. Field award IEEE, 1985, Outstanding Paper awards Control Systems Soc., 1977, 80, 82, 86. Fellow IEEE; mem. Sigma Xi. Home: 4996 Circle Rd, Montreal, PQ Canada H3W 1Z7 Office: Dept Elec Engring, McGill Univ, 3480 University St, Montreal, PQ Canada H3A 2A7

ZAMORA, JULIO CESAR, information services executive; b. Panama City, Republic of Panama, July 4, 1944; s. Tomas and Marina (Medina) Z. BS, Nat. Inst., Panama City, 1963; BBA, U. Ariz., 1977; MA in Internat. Mgmt., Am. Grad. Sch. Internat. Mgmt., 1979. Mgr. bus. and sales Up with People Inc., Tucson, 1979-81; mgr. Reuters Ltd., Panama City, 1981—. Mem. Assn. Panama de Ejecutivos de Empresa. Roman Catholic. Club: Altos del Lago (Panama City). Home: Calle Santiago #H, 431 Villa Caceres, Panama City Republic of Panama Office: Reuters Ltd, PO Box 2523 Zona 9A, Panama City Republic of Panama

ZAMORA-MADARIA, EDUARDO, physician, educator; b. La Redondela, Huelva, Spain, Apr. 19, 1933; s. Eduardo Zamora and Lucia Madaria Vesga; m. Alejandra Manosalbas, May 24, 1963. MD, U. Seville, 1949-55. Med. instr. U. Seville, Spain, 1956-64; titular prof. U. Seville, 1966-75, prof. internal medicine, 1986—; prof. internal medicine U. Córdoba, Spain, 1975-77, U. Badajoz, Spain, 1977-78, U. Cádiz, Spain, 1977-86; dir. sch. internal medicine U. Cádiz, 1978-86, vicerector, 1980-84. Mem. editorial bd. Anales de Medicina Internat. Madrid, 1983—; contbr. articles to profl. jours. Served to capt. med. corps Spanish mil., 1957-63. U. Zürich fellow, 1965. Mem. European Soc. Clin. Investigation, Nat. Soc. Internal Medicine, Nat. Soc. Endocrinology, Nat. Bd. Endocrinology Madrid, Soc. Internal Medicine of Andalucia (v.p. 1985-87, pres. 1987). Roman Catholic. Home: Asuncion 47 1 C, 41011 Seville Spain Office: Facultad de Medicina, Fedrianis/n, Seville Spain

ZAMPELAS, MICHAEL HERODOTOU, accountant; b. Nicosia, Cyprus, Mar. 19, 1937; s. Herodotos and Maria (Michael) Z.; m. Loukia Rodhitou, Sept. 8, 1958; children—Koula, Maria, Irene. F.C.A., Inst. Chartered Accts. in Eng. and Wales, 1960-65. Sr., Maiden Penny Quick & Co., London, 1960-66; mgr. Price Waterhouse, Nicosia, 1966-68; ptnr. Ioannou, Zampelas & Co., 1968-70; chmn., mng. ptnr. Coopers & Lybrand/Ioannou, Zampelas & Co., 1970—. Loan commr. Govt. of Cyprus, Nicosia, 1982—; chmn. bd. dirs. Cyprus Forest Industries Ltd., 1983—, Cyprus Ports Authority, 1986-

88. Author: Cyprus-The Way for Businessmen and Investors, 1984, 2d edit., 1987; co-author Developing Cyprus into a Financial and Commercial Centre, 1987. Fellow Inst. Chartered Accts. in Eng. and Wales; mem. Inst. C.P.A. of Cyprus (pres. 1978-80), Cyprus-Am. Assn., Cyprus-Austrian Assn., Inst. Dirs. London. Christian Orthodox. Club: London-Am. Lodges: Rotary, Lions, Masons. Office: Coopers & Lybrand/Ioannou Zampelas & Co, 3 Themistocle, 3 Themistocles Dervis St, POB 1612, Nicosia Cyprus

ZAMPIELLO, RICHARD SIDNEY, metals and trading company executive; b. New Haven, May 7, 1933; s. Sidney Nickolas and Louise Z.; B.A., Trinity Coll., 1955; M.B.A., U. Bridgeport, 1961; m. Helen Shirley Palsa, Oct. 10, 1961; 1 son, Geoffrey Richard. With Westinghouse Elec. Corp., Pitts., 1955-64; exec. v.p. Ullrich Copper Corp., subs. Foster Wheeler, Kenilworth, N.J., 1964-71; sr. v.p. Gerald Metals, Inc., Stamford, Conn., 1971-85; group v.p. Diversified Industries Corp., St. Louis, 1985—; pres. Plume and Atwood Brass Mill div. Diversified Industries Corp., Thomaston, Conn., 1985—. Mem. ASME, Soc. Mfg. Engrs., AIME. Clubs: Yale, Mining (N.Y.C.); Lake Waramug Country (Washington, Conn.), Washington Country. Home: Woodbury Rd Washington CT 06793 Office: 235 E Main St Thomaston CT 06787 also: Diversified Industries Inc 101 S Hanley Rd Clayton MO 63105

ZAMYATIN, LEONID MITROFANOVICH, Soviet diplomat and journalist; b. Nizhni Devitsk, Voronezh Region, Russia, Mar. 9, 1922; married; 1 child. Ed., Moscow Aviation Inst. and Higher Diplomatic Sch. Mem., Communist Party, 1944—, mem. Central Com., 1976—; Ministry Fgn. Affairs staff, U.S.S.R., 1946-50, first sec. Sec. Ministry Fgn. Affairs, 1950-52, asst. head third European dept. Ministry Fgn. Affairs, 1952-53, first sec. Counsellor on Polit. Questions, U.S.S.R. Mission to UN, 1953-57, Soviet dep. rep. preparatory com., later bd. govs. Internat. Atomic Energy Agy., 1957-59, Soviet rep., 1959-60, dep. head Am. countries dept. Ministry Fgn. Affairs, 1960-62, head press dept., 1962-70, mem. Collegium of Ministry, 1962-70, dir.-gen. TASS News Agy., 1970-78, govt. minister, 1972—; mem. Com. Fgn. Relations, Soviet Nationalities, 1974—; chief dept. info. Central Com., Communist Party, 1978-86; Soviet Ambassador to U.K., 1986—. Dep. to U.S.S.R. Supreme Soviet, 1970—. Decorated Lenin prize, 1978; Order of Lenin (2); numerous decorations from U.S.S.R. Address: Soviet Embassy, 13 Kensington Palace Gardens, London W8 4QX England

ZANDER, JOSEF, gynecologist; b. Juelich, Germany, June 19, 1918; s. Karl and Gertrud (Mueller) Z.; M.D., U. Tuebingen, 1946; M.D. (hon.) U. Innsbrück, Austria, 1986; postgrad. Kaiser Wilhelm Inst. Biochemistry, 1947-49; m. Lotte Stockhausen, Aug. 9, 1956; children—Karl, Gabriele, Ferdinand, Jan, Susanne, Katharina. Tng. in ob-gyn, univs. Marburg and Cologne med. schs., 1949-56; research asso. biochemistry U. Utah, 1956-57; mem. faculty U. Cologne Med. Sch., 1958-64; prof. ob-gyn, chmn. dept. U. Heidelberg Med. Sch., 1964-69; prof., chmn. 1st dept. ob-gyn, U. Munich Med. Sch., 1970-87. Fellow ACS; hon. fellow, Am. Coll. Obstetrics and Gynecology, Am. Gynecol. Soc., Felix Rutledge Soc., mem. German Soc. Endocrinology, Endocrine Soc. U.S., Am. Soc. Pelvic Surgeons, German Acad. Natural Scientists Leopoldina, Bavarian Acad. Scis.; hon. mem. German, Hungarian, Bavarian, Italian and Austrian ob-gyn socs. Roman Catholic. Club: Rotary. Author, editor books, jours. in field. Office: 11 Maistrasse, 8000 Munich 2 Federal Republic of Germany

ZANDJANI, TUBAGUS CHAIRUL AMACHI, accountant; b. Tasikmalaya, West Jawa, Indonesia, Jan. 31, 1949; s. Tubagus Yahya and Lasmini Z.; m. Indrawani Soetami, Sept. 9, 1972; children: Yusuf Khudri, Abu Nasri, Ratu Safia. M of Acctg. and Econs., U. Indonesia, 1972. CPA, tax cons. Acct. P.T. ITCI Wayer Hauser, Jakarta, 1972-74; controller P.T. Morgan Gillette Group, Jakarta, 1974-75; auditor, tax cons. Arthur, Young & Co., Jakarta, 1975-76; ptnr. Drs. Tb. Ch. Amachi Zandjani, 1977—; lectr. U. Indonesia Econs. Dept., 1971—. contbr. to several books on Indonesian econ. Mem. Internat. Fiscal Assn. of Netherlands, Indonesian Tax Cons. Assn., Indonesian Acct. Assn., Indonesian Pub. Acct. Assn., Am. Acct. Assn. Mem. Golkar party. Moslem. Office: Drs Tb Ch Amachi Zandjani, Jl Danau Tondano 8C-10C, 10210 Jakarta Indonesia

ZANELLA, AFRICA GARCIA, marketing, international executive; b. Africa, Feb. 1, 1949; married; children: Ariadne, Katrina. B in Commerce, U. New South Wales, Australia, 1972, M in Commerce, 1977. Lectr. Australian Inst. Mgmt., 1988—. Fellow Am.-Cham Australia; mem. Am. Ins. Assn., Singapore C. of C., Mktg. and Sales Assn., UN Cons. Group, Sietar. Home: 35 Tambourine Bay Rd, Lane Cove New South Wales 2067, Australia Office: Brazil Intal Mktg Hdqrs, 140 Xavier Ferreira, Auxiliadora, Poa Irs Brazil

ZANES, GEORGE WILLIAM, marketing research firm executive, marketing/research consultant; b. Laconia, N.H., May 13, 1926; s. Robert Lewis and Mina (Edgerly) Z.; m. Anne Schuetz, Dec. 21, 1957 (div. 1970); children—Laura, David; m. Ruth Weissman, June 17, 1970; stepchildren—Glenn, Lee. B.S., U. N.H., 1952. Dir. indsl. relations I.P.C. Inc., Bristol, N.H., 1953-56; dir. spl. projects Am. Research Bur. Inc., Beltsville, Md., 1957-60; dir. spl. projects Alfred Politz Research Inc., N.Y.C., 1960-62; v.p. Simulmatics Corp., N.Y.C., 1962-63; group research mgr. Foote Cone & Belding Inc., N.Y.C., 1963-65; v.p. Trendex Inc., N.Y.C., 1965-67; pres. Zanes & Assocs. Inc., Ft. Lee, N.J., 1967-80, chmn., chief exec. officer, 1980—, also bd. dirs.; pres. The Mktg. Research Workshop Inc., Ft. Lee, 1974—, also bd. dirs.; bd. dirs. Ad Net, Inc. Mem. Ft. Lee Rent Leveling Bd., 1972-73. Served to staff sgt. Inf., U.S. Army, 1944-47, ETO, capt. Res. ret. Mem. Am. Mktg. Assn., Am. Mgmt. Assn., Mktg. Research Assn., Council Am. Survey Research Orgns., Q.R.C.A., Acacia. Home: 7000 East Blvd Guttenberg NJ 07093 Office: Zanes & Assocs Inc 1350 15th St Fort Lee NJ 07024

ZANI, FREDERICK CAESAR, guidance counselor; b. Medford, Mass., June 9, 1929; s. John and Catherine (Voluletti) Z.; B.S. in Edn. cum laude, Salem State Coll., 1954; M.Ed., Boston U., 1959, cert. in advanced grad. studies, 1967; Ph.D. (hon.), World U. Roundtable, 1986; Lic. psychologist; m. Dorothy Ann Menezes, Feb. 20, 1960; children—Gregory Robert, Elizabeth Ruth. Tchr., 1954-60; tchr., Gloucester, Mass., public schs., 1960-65; guidance counselor, Attleboro, Mass. public schs., 1965—. Mem. Mass. Assn. Children with Learning Disabilities (v.p. Attleboro chpt. 1969-70), Attleboro, Mass. tchrs. assns., NEA, Attleboro Mental Health Center, Boston Children's Hosp. Med. Center Parent Orgn. for Exceptional Children, Internat. Platform Assn., Christian Edn. Assn. Mem. Assembly of God Ch. Contbr. articles to jours. Home: 709 Holmes Rd North Attleboro MA 02760

ZANONE, VALERIO, Italian government official; b. Jan. 22, 1936. Grad. in arts and philosophy, Turin U. Mem. Italian Liberal Party, 1955—, gen. sec., 1976-85; mem. Nat. Council, Rome, 1969—, Cen. Directorate, Rome, 1971—; mem. chamber deps. Constituency Turin and Constituency Verona, Italy, 1976—; minister ecology Italy, Rome, 1985-86, minister industry and trade, 1986-87, minister def., 1987—. Address: Ministry of Def, Via Vittorio Veneto 33, 00100 Rome Italy *

ZANOT, CRAIG ALLEN, lawyer; b. Wyandotte, Mich., Nov. 15, 1955; s. Thomas and Faye Blanch (Sperry) Z. AB with distinction, U. Mich., 1977; JD cum laude, Ind. U., 1980. Bar: Ind. 1980, U.S. Dist. Ct. (so. dist.) Ind. 1980, U.S. Dist. Ct. (no. dist.) Ind. 1981, U.S. Ct. Appeals (6th cir.) 1985, U.S. Dist. Ct. (ea. dist.) Mich. 1987. Law clk. to presiding justice Allen County Superior Ct, Ft. Wayne, 1980-81; ptnr. Davidson, Breen & Doud P.C., Saginaw, Mich., 1981—. Mem. ABA, Mich. Bar Assn., Ind. Bar Assn., Saginaw County Bar Assn. Roman Catholic. Home: 2085 Marlou Ct Saginaw MI 48603 Office: Davidson Breen & Doud PC 1121 N Michigan Ave Saginaw MI 48602

ZANOTTI, LUCIANO, aerospace company executive; b. Bologna, Italy, June 26, 1932; s. Armando and Olivia (Morotti) Z.; m. Giuliana Rossi, 1983. DSc, Bologna U., 1969. Librarian, then dir. Interdisciplinary Tech. Documentation Research Ctr., Bologna, 1960-70; founder Societa Italiana Termoimpianti, SRL, Milan, 1970; pres. Aerea SpA, Milan, 1974—, PMA-Soc. for Strategy of Quality SRL, Milan, 1981—; mng. dir. Internova-Soc. Advance Tech. Systems and Materials SRL, Milan, 1981; pres. Manens Intertecnica, SRL, Verona, 1971—. Author papers, revs. in field. Bd. dirs. Intermcpl. Coop. Soc. Small Farmers, Zola Predosa, 1973—. Served as 2d lt. Italian Army, 1959-60. Recipient 1st prize essay student class Union Mfrs., Como, 1966. Fellow Inst. Advancement Research and Studies Electronics and Data Processing (founder); mem. Am. Mgmt. Assn. Internat., Italian Assn. for Computing Automation, Italian Soc. Med. Ultracoustic Physics (sec., treas.), Italian Math. Union, Italian Phys. Soc., Italian Electrotech. and Electronics Soc., Italian Union Armed Forces Officers Res., Iniziativa Italia Entrepreneur Assn. (pres. 1985). Roman Catholic. Home: Casella Postale 139, 40100 Bologna Italy Office: 24 corso Vittorio Emanuele 11, 20122 Milan Italy

ZANTUA, ANTONIO PRADO, physician; b. Camaligan, Camarines Sur, Philippines, May 10, 1933; s. Amando Hernandez and Carmen (Prado) Z.; m. Paz Cabrera Lizaso, June 26, 1963; children: Maria Cecilia, Mary Jane, Omar Anthony, Maria Paz. MD, U. Sto Tomas, Manila, Philippines, 1958. Mcpl. health officer Dept. Health, Camarines Sur, 1959-64; chief of clinic Zantua Gen. Hosp., Digos, Davao del Sur, 1964-65; asst. med. dir. and chief of clinics Maria Rios Meml. Hosp., Malilipot, Albay, 1974-75, Zantua Gen. Hosp., Legazpi City, 1975-76; med. dir. Our Lady of Lourdes Hosp., Virac, Catanduanes, 1976-81, Our Lady of Pñnafrancia Hosp., Virac, Catanduanes, 1981—; chmn. Provincial Hosp. Council, Catanduanes, 1986-87. Editor in chief: Rural Health Digest, 1962-64, Bicol Today, Bicol Region, 1975-76; editor, publisher Island Reporter, 1968-72; editorial cons.: Youth Power, TINGRAW, READY. Mem. Catanduanes Med. Soc. (pres. CMS 1979-801, pres. PHA Cantanduanes Chpt. 1976-87); pres. Catanduanes Pvt. Hosp. Assn.; dir. Bicol PHA 1976—, Philippine Med. Assn. (exec. council mem. 1980-81), Bicol Dist. Councilor, PMA, 1980-81. Roman Catholic. Lodges: Kiwanis (pres. 1977-78), Lions (press relations officer 1964-65). Home: Francia Virac, 5001 Catanduanes Philippines Office: Our Lady of Peñafrancia Hosp, Francia Virac, 5001 Catanduanes Philippines

ZANUSSI, KRZYSZTOF, film director, scriptwriter; b. June 17, 1939; s. Jerzy and Jadqiga A.; ed. Warsaw and Cracow univ., Lodz Higher Film Sch. Dir numerous short feature films; films include Death of a Provincial, 1967; Structure of Crystals, 1972; Family Life, 1972; Illumination, 1972; The Catamount Killing (U.S.), 1973; Womens Decision (OCIC prize West Berlin Internat. Film Festival 1975), 1974; Camouflage (Spl. prize Teheran Internat. Film Festival 1977; Grand prize Polish Film Festival 1977), 1977; Spiral (prize of journalists Polish Film Festival 1978; Cannes 1978; OCIC prize), 1978; Wege in der Nacht (W. Ger.), 1979; Constant Factor (best dir. award Cannes), 1980; Contract (Distbn. prize Venice Film Festival), 1980; From a Far Country (Italy, Great Britain); Imperative (W.Ger., France); Year of the Quiet Sun (U.S., W.Ger. (Golden Lion Venice Film Fest), 1984; The Power of Evil (France, Italy, OCIC prize Montreal), 1985; Wherever You Are, 1988; TV films: Face to Face, 1967; Gdansk Lions, Credit, 1968, Mountains at Dark, 1970, Role, 1971, Behind the Wall, (Grand priz San Remo Internat. Film Festival 1972), 1971, Nachtdienst, 1975, Anatomiestunde, 1975, Haus der Frauen, 1978; Versuchung, 1981, Unaproachable 82, Blaubart, 1984, Grand Prix Venezia TV. Mem. Erlöschene Zeiten, Mia Varsavia, Polish Film Assn. (vice chmn. 1971-81). Author: Nowele Filmowe, 1976; Scenariusze Filmowe, 1978; Sei Film, 1979; Rigorista, 1982. Address: 8 rue Richepance, 75001 Paris France other: care Polski Film, ul Mazowiecka 6/8, 00-048 Warsaw Poland

ZAPF, HUBERT JOSEF, English educator; b. Fichtelberg, West Germany, May 6, 1948; s. Albin Georg and Lydia (Babo) Z.; m. Jacoba Anna Tulp, Nov. 12, 1982; children: Jakob, Eleonor, Ruth-Maria. MA, U. Dayton, 1972; PhD, U. Paderborn, West Germany, 1980; habil., U. Paderborn, 1987. Asst. prof. U. Wurzburg, West Germany, 1972-77; lectr. U. Coll. at Buckingham, Eng., 1977-78; asst. English lit. U. Paderborn, West Germany, 1979—. Author: Saul Bellow, 1981, Theory of Modern English Drama, 1988; contbr. articles to profl. jours. Mem. German Soc. English Romanticism, German Soc. Am. Studies. Roman Catholic. Home: Wegelange 53, 4799 Borchen 2 Federal Republic of Germany Office: Univ Paderborn, Dept English, Warburger Strasse 100, 4790 Paderborn Federal Republic of Germany

ZAPF, OTTO WOLFGANG, industrial designer; b. Rossbach, Sudetenland, Czechoslovakia, Aug. 10, 1931; s. Otto and Helene (Moll) Z.; m. Roselie Wendel; children: Florian, Carolina. Grad. high sch., Kronberg, Fed. Republic Germany. Prin. Zapf Design, Konigstein, Fed. Republic Germany, 1956—. Recipient Bundespreis Guteform Leuchtsäule, 1972, Gold award Inst. Office System of Bus. Designers, 1978. Mem. Deutcher Werkbund. Lutheran. Clubs: Ea. Sailing (Greenport, L.I.); Tennis (Königstein). Home: Olmuhlweg 33B, D6240 Koningstein, Hessen Taunus Federal Republic of Germany Office: Zapf Design, Herzog-Adolph Strasse 5, D6240 Konigstein, Hessen Taunus Federal Republic of Germany also: Zapf Design Main Rd Box 842 Orient, Long Island NY 11957

ZAPOLEON, MARGUERITE WYKOFF, labor economist, consultant, lecturer, author; b. Cin., Aug. 18, 1907; d. Fred Clark and Elizabeth (Voth) Wykoff; B.A., engring. degree, U. Cin., 1928; postgrad. Geneva Sch. Internat. Studies, 1927, N.Y. Sch. Social Work, 1928-29, London Sch. Econs. and Polit. Sci., 1932; M.A., Am. U., 1938; m. Louis B. Zapoleon, Oct. 2, 1937 (dec. Dec. 1969). Began career as vocation counselor Cin. Pub. Schs., 1929-35; chief of counseling div. D.C. Employment Center, 1935-39; specialist occupational info. and guidance service U.S. Office Edn., 1939-43; tng. specialist Hdqrs. ASF, 1943-44; chief employment opportunities br. Women's Bur., Dept. Labor, 1944-51, spl. asst. occupational outlook service Bur. Labor Statistics, 1951-55, spl. asst. to dir. Women's Bur., 1955-60; cons. on labor econs. and vocat. guidance, 1960—; lectr., workshop leader, instr. vocat. guidance and occupational research colls., univs., AAUW adult counseling project, 1965; adv. com., panel asso. Assn. Appraisers Earning Capacity, 1964-70; mem. tech. coms., recorder employment sect. White House Conf. on Aging, 1971. Bd. dirs. Am. Soc. Econometric Appraisers, 1967-70; bd. dirs. Friends of Everglades, Broward County, chmn. 1972—; bd. dirs. Environ. Council of Broward County, 1979-87; trustee Fla. Council Aging, 1973-75. Mem. Nat. Vocat. Guidance Assn. (trustee 1945-51), Council Guidance and Personnel Assn. (v.p. 1947-48), Alliance for Guidance Rural Youth (2d v.p. 1952-60), Am. Personnel and Guidance Assn. (del. Assembly 1951-60), Am. Econ. Assn., Nat. League Am. Pen Women, AAAS, Am. Statis. Assn., Nature Conservancy (rec. sec. Fla. chpt. 1972-78), Fla. Wildlife Fedn., Fairchild Gardens, Cousteau Soc., Am. Forestry Assn., Kappa Kappa Gamma (alumni achievement award 1968). Presbyterian. Author: (with Louise Moore) Reference and Related Information: Vocational Guidance for Girls and Women, 1941; Community Occupational Surveys, 1942; The College Girl Looks Ahead to Her Career Opportunities, 1956; Occupational Planning for Women, 1961; Girls and Their Futures, 1963, rev. edit., 1978; Wrongful Death of Housewife and Mother, 1965; Economic Aspects of Counseling Adult Women, 1966; Everyone Needs a Mountain, 1985, Cincinnati Citizens: Elizabeth and M. Edith Campbell Women of Cincinnati, 1870-1970, vol. III, 1986 ; also author of numerous govermental pamphlets on occupations and vocational guidance edn. and tng.; contbr. articles to profl. jours.; editor Vocat. Guidance Quar., 1953-54. Home: 816 SE Riviera Isle Fort Lauderdale FL 33301

ZARB, FRANK GUSTAVE, investment company executive; b. N.Y.C., Feb. 17, 1935; s. Gustave and Rosemary (Antinora) Z.; m. Patricia Koster, Mar. 31, 1957; children: Krista Ann, Frank, Jr. B.B.A., Hofstra U., 1957, M.B.A., 1962, L.H.D., 1975. Trainee Cities Service Oil Co., N.Y.C., 1957-62; gen. partner Goodbody & Co., N.Y.C., 1962-69; exec. v.p. CBWL-Hayden Stone, Inc. (investment banking), N.Y.C., 1969-71; asst. sec. U.S. Dept. Labor, Washington, 1971-72; exec. v.p. Hayden Stone, Inc., N.Y.C., 1972-73; assoc. dir. Office of Mgmt. and Budget, Washington, 1973-74; asst. to Pres., U.S., 1974-77; adminstr. Fed. Energy Adminstrn., Washington, 1974-77; adv. U.S. Congress and State of Alaska, 1977-78; gen. ptnr. Lazard Freres & Co., N.Y.C., 1977—; director Securities Investor Protection Corp, Washington, 1988—; dir. Energy Fund, Hay Systems, Inc., Lazard Asia Ltd., Comml. Credit Co. Author: The Stockmarket Handbook, 1969, Handbook of Financial Markets, The Municipal Bond Handbook. Bd. dirs. Nat. Council for U.S.-China Trade, Council for U.S. and Italy; trustee Gerald R. Ford Found.; chmn. bd. trustees Hofstra U., 1986-87. Recipient Disting. Scholar award Hofstra U., 1974. Mem. Am. Soc. Pub. Adminstrn. (hon. life), Council Fgn. Relations, Securities Investor Protection Corp. Office: Lazard Freres & Co One Rockefeller Plaza New York NY 10020

ZAREMBA, THOMAS EDMUND MICHAEL BARRY, educator; b. Detroit, May 6; s. Edmund Julius Thiel and Ethel Grace (Barry) Z. Ed. Oakland U., Rochester, Mich., U. Detroit, Wayne State U. Tchr., Center Line (Mich.) Public Schs., Livonia (Mich.) Public Schs.; instr. biol. scis. Wayne State U., Detroit. Mem. Mich. Eye Bank, Internat. Friends Van Cliburn, Met. Opera Guild, Friends of Detroit Symphony Orch., Founders Soc., Detroit Inst. Arts, Internat. Platform Assn., Detroit Sci. Ctr., Friends for Orch. Hall, Orch. Hall Assocs.; bd. dirs. Van. Cliburn Found, Inc., Detroit Grand Oprea Assn. Mem. AAAS, Nat. Funeral Dirs. Assn., Mich. Funeral Dirs. Assn., Am. Film Inst. (sponsor), Wayne State U. Alumni Assn., Oakland U. Alumni Assn. Roman Catholic. Club: Scarab (life), Players (Detroit). Office: 217 Farnsworth St Detroit MI 48202 Office: 5980 Cass Ave Detroit MI 48202

ZARIKIAN, ESTEBAN, industrialist; b. Athens, Greece, Oct. 12, 1914; arrived in Venezuela, 1930; s. Zareh and Eva (Epremian) Z.; m. Sada Sahagian; children: Zareh, Surpik, Marco. Pres. C.A. Telares de Marcay, Caracas, Venezuela, 1954-68, Texfin C.A., Caracas, Venezuela, 1968—, Viviendas y Edificaciones S.A., Caracas, Venezuela, 1988—; bd. dirs. Olivio & Bakirgian, Manchester, Eng., Banco el Caribe, Caracas, Banco Union, Caracas, Banco Hipotecario Unido, Caracas, Hotel Tamanaco, Caracas. Recipient Francisco de Miranda 1st class award. Clubs: Laguna Beach (Caraballeda, Venezuela); Valle Arriba Golf (Caracas). Address: Grupo Telares Maracay, Edf Don Raul, Esquina Abanico, Caracas 1010, Venezuela

ZARNOWSKA, ANNA MARIA, historian, educator; b. Warsaw, Poland, June 28, 1931; d. Arkadiusz and Janina (Kaleta) Rozwadowski; m. Janusz Zarnowski, Sept. 20, 1952; 1 child, Witold. MA, U. Warsaw, 1954, PhD, 1962. Asst. U. Warsaw, 1959-63, sr. asst., 1964-74, asst. prof. history, 1975-85, assoc. prof., 1985—. Author: Genesis of 1906 Scission in Socialist Party, 1965 (Jour. Polityka award 1966), Working Class in Poland 1870-1914, 1974 (Jour. Polityka award 1975), Workers of Warsaw, 1985 (Jour. Polityka award 1986). Mem. Internat. Tagung Historiker Arbeiterbewegung (rep. Warsaw U. 1980—). Home: Krasinskiego 26, 01 769 Warsaw Poland Office: U Warsaw Dept History, Krakowskie Przedmiescie 26/28, 00 927 Warsaw Poland

ZARNOWSKI, JANUSZ, historian, research educator; b. Warsaw, Poland, Apr. 26, 1932; s. Waclaw and Maria (Holc) Z.; m. Anna Maria Rozwadowska, Sept. 20, 1952; 1 child, Witold. MA, U. Warsaw, 1954; PhD, Inst. History, Warsaw, 1961, Dr. Habilitation, 1964. Jr. asst. U. Warsaw, 1954-55; with Inst. for History Polish Acad. Scis., 1956—; assoc. prof., head research group Inst. for History, 1973-80, dep. dir., 1973-76, prof., head research group, 1981—. Author: Polish Intelligentsia 1918-1939, 1964 (Polityka prize 1965), Polish Socialists 1935-39, 1965, Polish Society 1918-1939, 1973 (Polityka prize 1974), November 1918 (in English), 1984; editor Dictatorships in East-Central Europe, 1918-39 (in English), 1983. Mem. Inernat. Assn. Contemporary History of Europe, Internat. Commn. Study of Slavs (bd. dirs. 1985). Home: Krasinskiego 26, 01-769 Warsaw Poland Office: Inst for History, Rynek St Miasta 29/31, 00-272 Warsaw Poland

ZARSE, LEIGH BRYANT, architect, architectural engineer; b. Wauwatosa, Wis., Sept. 26, 1930; s. Alfred Henry and Cecile (Moreau) Z.; student U. Wis., Milw., 1948-50, Ohio State U., 1950-52; B. Archtl. Engring., U. Ill., 1954; m. Hannelore Schilling, June 30, 1973. Partner, Zarse & Zarse, Inc., Milw., 1957-84, pres., 1967-84; structural project engr. Milw. Met. Sewerage Dist., 1984—; mem. municipal planning com. City Club of Milw., 1965—, sec. bd. dirs., 1971. Served to maj. USAFR, 1954-57. Registered architect and profl. engr., Wis.; certified multi-disaster design protection specialist CD Preparedness Agy. Mem. AIA (Top Honor award 1963), ASCE, Am. Concrete Inst., Engrs. and Scientists of Milw., Aircraft Owners Pilots Assn., Alpha Rho Chi, Sigma Delta Omega (pres. local chpt. 1949-50). Designer numerous local, state and fed. govt. bldgs., including: 1500 seat amphitheater for Gen. McCormack, Lackland AFB, San Antonio, 1954, 40 schs. in S.E. Wis., 1957—, Kenosha (Wis. City Hall, 1971, St. Francis (Wis.) City Hall, 1963, Hales Corners (Wis.) City Hall, 1968, FAA and Weather Bur. Bldg. at Gen. Billy Mitchell Field, Milw., 1970, MMSD Hdqtrs. Office Bldg., 1987, Jones Island Maintenance Facility, 1988. Home: 1812 Mountain Ave Wauwatosa WI 53213

ZARUTSKIE, PAUL WALTER, reproductive endocrinologist, obstetrician/gynecologist.; b. Darby, Pa., May 4, 1951; s. Michael Andrew and Nita (Tatusko) Z. BS, Duke U., 1972; MD, Hahnemann Med. Coll., 1976. Diplomate Am. Bd. Obstetrics and Gynecology, Reproductive Endocrinology. Resident Duke U. Med. Ctr., Durham, N.C., 1976-79, chief resident, 1979-80; clin. fellow reproductive endocrinology Brigham and Women's Hosp., Boston, 1980-82; instr. ob-gyn Harvard U., Boston, 1980; asst. prof. U. Pitts., 1982-84; asst. prof. U. Wash., Seattle, 1984—, clin. dir. in vitro fertilization program, 1984—; co-dir. Andrology Lab., 1987-88; dir. Spl. Infertility Programs. Contbr. articles to profl. jours. Med. adv., bd. trustees Resolve Puget Sound. Fellow Am. Coll. Ob-gyn; mem. Am. Fertility Soc., Am. Andrology Soc., Bayard Carter Soc., Alpha Omega Alpha, Sigma Xi. Office: U Wash Dept Ob-Gyn RH-20 1959 NE Pacific St Seattle WA 98195

ZARWYN, BERTHOLD, physical scientist; b. Vienna, Aug. 22, 1921; came to U.S., 1949, naturalized, 1955; s. Joseph and Bronislava Regina (Unger) Z.; M.E., Gliwice, Poland, 1946; Sc.D., Munich (W. Ger.) U., 1947; Ph.D., N.Y.U., 1954; Engring. Sc.D., Columbia, 1963. Project engr. Curtiss-Wright Corp., Woodridge, N.J., 1951-55; staff scientist AMF Corp., N.Y.C., 1955-57; chief scientist Link Aviation Co., Binghamton, N.Y., 1957-58; head research staff Am. Bosch-Arma Corp., Garden City, N.Y., 1958-63; corp. cons. Cutler-Hammer Corp., Deer Park, N.Y., 1963-65; chief engr. Bell Aerosystems Corp., Niagara Falls, N.Y., 1965-66; sr. cons. Mitre Corp., Bedford, Mass., 1966-68; spl. asst. to commanding gen., acting chief engr. Hdqrs. U.S. Army Materiel Command, Arlington, Va., 1968-71, chief phys. scis. br., U.S. Army Devel. and Readiness Command, Alexandria, Va., 1971-75, phys. scientist U.S. Army Harry Diamond Labs., Washington, 1975-78; chief system analysis br. U.S. Army Electronic Research and Devel. Command, Adelphi, Md., 1978-79, chief tech. div., 1979-81, asst. tech. dir., 1981-85; spl. asst. to dep. chief of staff for tech. and program mgmt. U.S. Army Lab. Command, Adelphi, 1985-87, pres. Pan-Tech. Corp., 1987—; adj. faculty, lectr., cons. in field; dir. Film Microelectronics Co. Inc., Burlington, Mass., 1965-67. Mem. IEEE, Am. Phys. Soc., N.Y. Acad. Scis., Sigma Xi. Editorial bd. Bavarian Soc. Engrs., 1947-49; translation panel Russian Jour. Applied Math. and Mechanics with Pergamon Inst., 1956-57. Inventor nuclear gyroscope, microwave holography, other items. Home and Office: Pan-Tech Corp 9727 Mt Pisgah Rd Apt 801 Silver Spring MD 20903

ZAU, YEN CHUNG TOMMY, electronic co. exec.; b. Shanghai, China, Sept. 11, 1935; s. Pao Fu and May Ching (Chen) Z.; ed. Bradford Durfee Coll. Tech., 1958; m. Lillian Ting Yuk Ying, Sept. 6, 1958; children—Tommy, Timothy, Mark. Lectr., Hong Kong Tech. Coll., 1959-64; mng. dir. Micro Electronics Ltd., Hong Kong, 1964-69; mng. dir. Electronic Devices Ltd., Hong Kong, 1969—; lay assessor Magistrates Cts. chmn. electronics industry tng. bd. vocat. tng. council; mem. electronic gases subcom. Fire Services Dept. Mem. Chinese Mfrs. Assn. Hong Kong (vice chmn.), Fedn. Hong Kong Industries (chmn. electronics group 1-2, chmn. Hong-Kong/China Indsl. Coop. com.), Hong Kong Mgmt. Assn. (com. mem. Chinese Exec. Club, com. mem. Bus. Enterprises Mgmt. Ctr., prodn. mgmt. com.), Fedn. Industries of Tsuen Wan (vice chmn.), Am. C. of C. in Hong Kong (mem. electronic com.) Home: 240 Prince Edward Rd 5A, Kowloon Hong Kong Office: 5F 100 Kwai Cheong Rd, Kwai Chung NT, Kowloon Hong Kong

ZAVELSON, LESTER SANFORD, business management consultant; b. Cleve., July 10, 1915; s. Abraham Phillip and Sophia (Miller) Z.; m. Maxine Lois Abrams, Dec. 26, 1938; children—Thomas M., Daniel Lee. B.B.A., Ohio State U., 1937. Exec. v.p. Ind. Towel Supply Co., Mansfield, Ohio, 1938-78; pres., chmn. bd. Reed Road, Inc., Mansfield, 1978—; ptnr. Mansfield Assocs., 1960—; columnist Laundry Digest, Chgo., 1980—. Bd. dirs. Hospice, Score, ARC, Mansfield Cancer Found., Richland County Red Cross; mem. Richland County Recreation Bd.; mem. local Democratic exec. com., 1960-88; pres. Temple Emanuel, 1980-87; bd. dirs. Ohio Penal Insts., Richland County Red Cross, 1974—. Recipient Ty award Mktg. Club, 1976.

Mem. Mktg. Club N. Central Ohio (past pres., dir.), Ohio State U. Alumni Assn. (past pres.), Clubs: Exchange (past pres., dir.), University, International Trade of Ohio. Lodges: Shriners, Masons, Elks. Home: 666 W Andover Rd Mansfield OH 44907 Office: PO Box 1562 210 W Longview Ave Mansfield OH 44901

ZAVOLI, SERGIO, journalist, radio/TV executive; b. Ravenna, Italy, Sept. 21, 1923; s. Edgardo and Clara (Paracciani) Z.; m. Rosalba Calderoni; 1 dau., Valentina. Entered RAI as spl. corr., 1948, dir. radio news, 1961-62, spl. corr., for TV news, 1962, vice dir. Telegiornale, 1969, pres. RAI-TV, Rome, 1980—. Recipient Nat. and internat. prizes including Prix Italia, Marconi, Salsmaggiore, TV Festival of Cannes. Contbr. articles to profl. jours. Office: Radiotelevisione Italiana, Via Mazzini 14, I 00195 Rome Italy *

ZAVRŠKI, JOSIP, musician; b. Zagreb, Croatia, Yugoslavia, Feb. 12, 1917; s. Vjekoslav and Katarina (Škalic) Z.; m. Alojzija Grozdanic, June 1955; children: Velebit, Dinarka. Student, Acad. Music Art, Zagreb, 1952; student in music entertainment, Orf Instrumentarium, Fredeburg, 1978. Cons. Jadran Film, Zagreb, 1947-51; prof. music Tchr. Sch., Zagreb, 1951-55; condr. Croation Nat. Teatre, Zagreb, 1955-66; free lance artist; cons. Republic Inst. for Edn. and Culture, Zagreb, 1961-62; lectr. Inst. for Cuture, Zagreb, 1963-83. Author: Methodological Instructions for Music Teachers and Childrens Choir Condustors, 1951, History of Music, 1963, Theory of Music, 1973; condr. various radio and TV programs, Zagreb, 1949-61. Recipient award Mayor of Zagreb, 1969, award Pres. of Yugoslavia, Belgrade, 1969. Mem. Union Artists in Music Entertainment (presidentship 1962-72, award 1975, 87), Union Artists in Serious Music (presidentship 1981-87). Roman Catholic. Home: Ilica 65, 41000 Zagreb, Croatia Yugoslavia

ZAWADA, EDWARD THADDEUS, JR., physician, educator; b. Chgo., Oct. 3, 1947; s. Edward Thaddeus and Evelyn Mary (Kovarek) Z.; m. Nancy Ann Stephen, Mar. 26, 1977; children—Elizabeth, Nicholas, Victoria. B.S. summa cum laude, Loyola U., Chgo., 1969; M.D. summa cum laude, Loyola-Stritch Sch. Medicine, 1973. Diplomate Am. Bd. Internal Medicine, Am. Bd. Nephrology, Am. Bd. Nutrition. Intern UCLA Hosp., 1973, resident, 1974-76; asst. prof. medicine UCLA, 1978-79, U. Utah, Salt Lake City, 1979-81; assoc. prof. medicine Med. Coll. Va., Richmond, 1981-83; assoc. prof. medicine, physiology, pharmacology U. S.D. Sch. Medicine, Sioux Falls, 1983-86, Freeman prof., chmn. dept. Internal Medicine, 1987—, also chief div. nephrology and hypertension, 1981—, chmn. internal medicne, 1987—; chief renal sect. Salt Lake VA Med. Ctr., 1980-81; asst. chief med. service McGuire VA Med. Ctr., Richmond, 1981-83. Contbr. articles to profl. publs. Editor: Geriatric Nephrology and Urology, 1984. Pres. Minnehaha div. Am. Heart Assn., 1984—, pres.-elect Dakota affiliate, 1987—. VA Hosp. System grantee, 1981-85, 85-88. Fellow ACP, Am. Coll. Chest Physicians, Am. Coll. Nutrition; mem. Internat. Soc. Nephrology, Am. Soc. Nephrology, Am. Soc. Pharmacology and Exptl. Therapeutics. Democrat. Roman Catholic. Club: Westward Ho Country (Sioux Falls). Avocations: golf; tennis; skiing; cinema; music. Home: 1608 Cedar Ln Sioux Falls SD 57103 Office: U SD Sch Medicine 2501 W 22d St Sioux Falls SD 57105

ZAWODNY, JANUSZ KAZIMIERZ, international relations educator; b. Warsaw, Poland, Dec. 11, 1921; came to U.S., 1948, naturalized, 1955; s. Kazimierz and Wanda (Pukk) Z.; B.S., State U. Iowa, 1950, M.A. in Internat. Relations, 1951; Ph.D. in Polit. Sci. (Social Sci. Research Council fellow), Stanford U., 1955; m. LaRae Koppit; 1 son, Roman Janusz. Instr., then asst. prof. Princeton U., 1955-58; fellow Center Advanced Study Behavioral Scis., Stanford U., 1961-62; prof. Washington U., 1963-65; asso. prof. U. Pa., 1962-63, prof. internat. relations, 1965-75; Avery prof. internat. relations Claremont Grad. Sch. and Pomona Coll., 1975-82; fellow Inst. Social and Behavioral Pathology, U. Chgo., 1977-88; cons. Exec. Office of Pres.; staff Nat. Security Council, 1979—; mem. Inst. for Advanced Study, Princeton, 1971-72. Sr. asso. mem. St. Antony's Coll., Oxford (Eng.) U., 1968-69; research asso. Harvard U. Center Internat. Affairs, 1968; U.S. Dept. State Scholar-Diplomat Seminar, summer 1973. Served with Polish Underground Forces, 1940-44, Brit. Army, 1945-48. Decorated Virtuti Militari, grand officer Polonia Restituta, Cross of Valor, Gold and Silver Crosses of Merit with Swords; recipient Gold medal Medicus Assn. N.Y., 1980; Lit. Prize, Kultura, Paris, 1980. Ford Faculty fellow, 1956, 58-59, 68-69; grantee Am. Council Learned Socs., Am. Philos. Soc., 1967-68. Author: Nothing But Honor:The Uprising of Warsaw, 1944, 1978, 80; Man and International Relations: Contributions of the Social Sciences to the Study of Conflict and Integration, 2 vols., 1967; Guide to the Study of International Relations, 1967; Death in the Forest: The Story of the Katyn Forest Massacre (translated into Japanese, German, French, Norwegian, Italian, Polish), 1962, 71, 80, 88; also articles. Contbr. to Am. Scholar, 1962, Internat. Ency. Social Scis., 1968. Home: 23703 Margaret Rd Brush Prairie WA 98606

ZAYAC, IVAN BOHDAN SIMON, architect; b. Lviv, Austria (now Ukrainian SSR), Oct. 6, 1910; s. Julian and Falina Knight Radwan von Pawencki Z.; came to U.S., 1948, naturalized, 1955; M.L., U. Jan. Kasimierz (Poland), 1932, M. Diplomatic Scis., 1934; diploma in music Lviv Conservatory of Music, 1933; postgrad. in law Sorbonne, U. Paris, 1946-48; postgrad. in architecture Ecole Superieure Nationale des Beaux Arts, Paris, 1947-48, Cooper Union, 1953; m. Elsa Schoenberg, May 3, 1947 (dec. Aug. 1981); 1 dau., Maria Falina; m. Stephanie Dorosh, May 7, 1984. Judge, pres. of ct., asst. prof. law, Poland, 1935-44; law counselor Allgemeine Electrizitä t Gesellschaft, Bratislava, Czechoslovakia, 1944-45; with various archtl. firms, N.Y.C., 1950-53; with Eggers and Higgins Co., N.Y.C., 1953-57, Philip C. Johnson and Assocs., N.Y.C., 1957-60, Edward Durell Stone and Assocs., N.Y.C., 1963-70, I.M. Pei and Partners, N.Y.C., 1971-74; cons. Edward Larrabee Barnes Assocs. P.C., N.Y.C.; prin. Ivan Zayac, Architect, Forest Hills, N.Y., 1974—; art critic Svoboda daily, Suchasnist monthly; lectr. to profl. socs. Sec. Ukrainian Relief Com., 1940-43. Fellow Ukrainian Engrs. Soc. (hon. mem. 1985—, past chpt. pres.); mem. N.Y. Acad. Scis., AAAS, Shevchenko Scientific Soc., Ukrainian Acad. Art and Scis., Ukrainian Artists Assn., World Congress Free Ukrainians (past div. chmn.), Ukrainian Nat. Assn. (dir. 1977-80), Selfreliance Assn. Am. Ukrainians (past dir.), Assn. Ukrainian Foresters and Lumbermen (hon.). Ukrainian Orthodox. Designer Ukrainian Cultural Center, Mus. Ukrainian Art, Hunter, N.Y., numerous houses. Contbr. articles to profl. jours. Home and Office: 68-49 Exeter St Forest Hills NY 11375

ZEA AGUILAR, LEOPOLDO, Mexican university educator, writer; b. México, June 30, 1912; s. Leopoldo Zea and Lu Aguilar; m. Elena Prado Vertiz, 1943 (div.); 6 children; m. Maria Elena Rodriquez Ozán, 1982. Editor review Tierra Neuva, 1940; prof. Escuela Nacional Preparatoria, 1942-47, Escuela Normal de Maestros, 1944-45, Faculty of Philosophy and Letters, U. Nacional Autónoma de México, 1944; mem. El Colegio de México, 1940; pres. Com. foré History of Ideas, Panamerican Inst. Geography and History; chief dept. univ. studies Sec. Pub. Edn., 1953-54; research work, 1954—; mem. Soc. Europé enne de Culture, 1953—; dir. gen. cultural relations Fgn. Office; v.p. hist. com. Pan Am. Inst. Geography and History, 1961—; dir. Faculty of Philosophy and Letters, 1966-70, prof. emeritus, 1971—; dir. gen. cultural broadcasting, 1970—; co-ordinator co-ordination and diffusion Center for Latin Am. Studies. Publications include El Positivismo en México, 1943, Apogeo y Decadencia del Positivismo en México, 1944, Ensayos sobre Filosofca en la Historia, 1948, Dos Etapas del Pensamiento en Hispanoamérica, 1949, La Filosofca como Comromiso, 1952, América como Conciencia, 1952, Conciencia y posibilidad del Mexicano, 1952, El Occidente y la Conciencia de México, 1953, La Conciencia del Hombre en la Filosofía, 1952, América en la conciencia de Europa, 1952, La Filosofía en México 1955, Esquema para una Historia de las ideas en América, 1956, Del Liberalismo a la Revolución en la Educacion Mexicana, 1956, América en la Historia 1957, La Cultura y el Hombre de nuestros días, 1959, Latinomérica y el Mundo, 1960, Ensayos sobre México y Latinamérica, 1960, Democracias y Dictaduras en Latinoamérica, 1960, America Latine e la Culture Occidentalé, 1961, El Pensamiento Latino-americano 1963, Latinamérica en la formacion de nuestro tiempo, 1965, Antologia de la Filosofía Americana Contemporánea, 1968, Latin America and the World, 1969, Dependencia y Liberación en la Cultura Lationoamericana, 1974, Cultura y Filosofía en Latino-América, 1976, Dialéctica de la Conciencia Americana, 1976, Latinamérica Tercer Mundo, 1977, Filosofía de la Historia Americana, 1978, Simón Bolívar, 1980, Latinomaérica en la Encrucijada de la Historia, 1980, Sentido de la Difusión Cultural Lationoamerica, 1981. Recipient Nat. prize for sci. and arts, 1980; decorations from Italy, France, Perú, Yugoslavia. Avocations: music; art. Office: Ciudad Univ, Planta Baja, Torre de Humanidades I, Mexico City Mexico also: Prol Amores 1874, Deputy 401, Col del Valle, Mexico City 12 Mexico *

ZECHA, ANDREW HOWARD, international holding company executive; b. Sukabumi, Indonesia, Mar. 8, 1927; came to U.S., 1946; s. Aristides William Lauw and Kim See (Lim) Z.; m. Helen Joan Lee, June 7, 1950; children—Angelyn, Anthony. B.Sc., Lycoming Coll. (Pa.), 1949; M.B.A., M.A., Columbia U., 1950; LL.B., U. Indonesia, 1954; Ph.D., MIT, 1956; LL.D. (hon.), U. Kristen, Indonesia, 1960. Chief exec. officer Lawsim Zecha & Co., Jakarta, Indonesia, 1950-54; mng. dir. Muller and Phipps Ltd., Jakarta, 1956-64; dean bus. sch. U. Singapore, 1965-72; sr. ptnr., mng. dir. Zecha Cons., Singapore, 1972-76; dean Grad. Bus. Sch., Wilmington Coll., Del., 1976-78; mem. exec. con. Alexander Proudfoot/APC Co., West Palm Beach, Fla., 1978-81; planning dir., dir. internat. div. Syncom Inc., Buffalo, 1981-84; mng. dir., pres. Intrafin Co. Ltd., Hongkong/U.S.A., 1984—; acting dean bus. sch. Universitas Kristen, 1953-54; pres. Bus. Research, Jakarta, 1959-64; bd. dirs. Pub. Utilities Bd., Singapore, 1967-70; chmn. Singapore Inst. Mgmt., 1967-71; cons. People's Republic China, 1984—; Establisher, exec. v.p. Mahkota Coll./Boston U. in Kuala Lampur, Malaysia, 1988. Founder, 1st pres. Assn. Asian Bus. Schs., 1969-71. Republican. Roman Catholic. Avocations: tennis; traveling; reading. Office: Intrafin Co Ltd, Fairmont House 20th Floor, Hong Kong Hong Kong Office: Mahkota Coll, Jalan Parlimen, 50480 Kuala Lumpur Malaysia

ZECHA, AUSTEN VICTOR LAUW, advertising and marketing executive; b. Jakarta, Indonesia, Jan. 1, 1940; s. Aristede W. L. and Kim S. L.; m. Linda O'Reilly, Dec. 20, 1969; children: Alexander, Adam, Christian, Alia. Ed., Eaglebrook Sch., Deerfield, Mass., Phillips Acad., Andover, Mass.; BA, Stanford U., 1961, MA, 1962. Reporter The Straits Times, Kuala Lumpur, 1962; S.E. Asian advisor to Robert F. Kennedy, 1964-66; communications advisor Exxon Corp., N.Y.C., 1966-69; internat. relations advisor Mobil Oil Corp., N.Y.C., 1969-71; founder AMC-Melewar Zecha group agys., Zecha Assocs. Ltd. (now Advt. Mktg. Communications Ltd.), Hong Kong, 1971-74; founder, chief exec. officer PTM Communications, Kuala Lumpur, 1974-76, Melewar Zecha Communications Agy. group, 1976—; lectr. Asian Inst. Mgmt., Manila, Inst. Pub. Relations, Malaysia. Recipient Religious Leadership award Presbyn. Ch. Malaysia, 1981. Mem. Assn. Accredited Advt. Agys. Malaysia, Inst. Pub. Relations Malaysia, Pacific Asia Travel Assn. (allied assoc. council, mktg. authority). Clubs: Skal of Kuala Lumpur, Lake, Port Dickson Yacht, Bankers. Home: 6 Dalaman Tunku, Kenny Hill, 50480 Kuala Lumpur Malaysia Office: Wisma AMC, 1 Jalan Sri Semantan Satu, Damansara Heights, 50490 Kuala Lumpur Malaysia

ZECHLIN, RUTH, composer; b. Groszhartmannsdorf, Germany, June 22, 1926; d. Hermann and Friedel (Tillich) Oschatz; student composition and organ Conservatory of Music, Leipzig, 1943-49; 1 dau. Asst., Conservatory of Music, Leipzig, 1949-50; univ. lectr. Conservatory of Music, Berlin, German Dem. Republic, 1950-69, prof. composition, 1969-86; compositions include chamber music, symphonic works, concertos, oper, ballet; harpsichordist, rec. artist. Recipient Goethepriize of Berlin, 1962, Kunstprize of German Democratic Republic, 1965, Nationalprize, German Democratic Republic, 1972, 82. Mem. Acad. of Arts German Democratic Republic. Evangelical Lutheran.

ZEEMAN, JOAN JAVITS, writer, inventor; b. N.Y.C., Aug. 17, 1928; d. Benjamin Abraham and Lily (Braxton) Javits; m. John Huibert Zeeman III, Mar. 20, 1954; children—Jonathan, Andrea Zeeman Deane, Eloise Zeeman Scharff, Phoebe, Merrily Margaret. B.A., Vassar Coll., 1949; M.Ed., U. Vt., 1976. Pub. relations exec. Benjamin Sonnenberg, N.Y.C., 1949-51; freelance writer, 1952—. Trustee TheatreWorks(formerly Performing Arts Repertory Theatre), N.Y.C., 1953-83, Profl. Childrens Sch., N.Y.C., 1980—. Author: The Compleat Child, 1964. Lyricist musical plays: Young Abe Lincoln, 1961; Hotel Passionato, 1965; song lyricist: Santa Baby, 1953. Patentee Alphocube. Mem. ASCAP, Dramatists Guild. Club: Vassar (sec. 1978-84, v.p. 1984-86) (Westchester, N.Y.). Home: 230 Palmo Way Palm Beach FL 33480 Office: 520 Hommocks Rd Larchmont NY 10538

ZEFFIRELLI, FRANCO, theater and film director; b. Florence, Italy, Feb. 12, 1923; s. Ottorino Corsi and Alaide Cipriani. Attended, U. Architecture, Florence. Actor in Crime and Punishment, 1946, Euridyce, 1947; appeared in film Onorevole Angelina, 1948; set designer for various prodns. of Luchino Visconti, 1949-52, A Streetcar Named Desire, The Three Sisters; dir. (films) The Taming of the Shrew, 1966, Romeo and Juliet, 1967, Brother Sun, Sister Moon, 1971, Filumena, 1977, The Champ, 1979, Endless Love, 1981, I Pagliacci, 1981, La Traviata, 1982, Cavalleria Rusticana, 1986, Otello, 1986, The Young Toscanini, 1988, (ballet) Swan Lake, 1985; TV dir. Giorni Di Distruzione, 1966, Fidelio conducted by Leonard Bernstein, 1970, Missa Solemnis of Beethoven conducted by Wolfgang Sawallisch in Basilica of St. Peter in presence of Pope Paul VI, 1970, Jesus of Nazareth (epic film), 1976; numerous operas including Cenerentola, La Scala, 1953, I Pagliacci, 1959, Cavalleria Rusticana, 1959, Lucia Di Lammermoor, Covent Garden, 1959, La Boheme, La Scala, 1963, Falstaff, Met. Opera, 1964, Tosca, Covent Garden, 1965, Norma, Paris Opera, 1965, Anthony and Cleopatra, Met. Opera, 1966, Otello, Met. Opera, 1972, Don Giovanni, Staatsoper, Vienna, 1972, Un Ballo in Maschera, La Scala, 1972, Otello, La Scala, 1976, Carmen, Staatsoper, Vienna, 1978, La Traviata, 1979, 83; theater dir. Romeo and Juliet, Old Vic Co., London, 1960, Othello, Stratford-on-Avon, Eng., 1961, Camille, Winter Garden Theatre, N.Y.C., 1962, Who's Afraid of Virginia Woolf?, Festival del Teatro, Venice, and Paris, 1963, Romeo and Juliet, Verona, Italy, Paris, Vienna, Austria, Rome and Milan, Italy, Moscow and Leningrad, 1964, Hamlet, 1964, After The Fall, 1965, Much Ado About Nothing, Old Vic Theatre, 1965, La Lupa, Florence, Rome, Vienna, Zurich, Switzerland, Paris, London and Moscow, 1965, A Delicate Balance, 1966, Black Comedy, 1967, Venti Zecchini D'Oro, 1968, Due Piu Due Non Fanno Quattro, 1969, Sabato, Doemnica, Lunedi, Nat. Theatre, London, 1973, The Dead City, Italy, 1975, Lorenzaccio, Comedie Française, Paris, 1976, Filumena Marturano, Lyric Theatre, London, 1977; author: Zeffirelli by Zeffirelli, 1986. Recipient Liberty award, 1986. Mem. Dirs. Guild Am. Roman Catholic. also: 448 Via Appia Pignatelli, Rome I-00178, Italy *

ZEGARELLI, EDWARD VICTOR, researcher, dental educator; b. Utica, N.Y., Sept. 9, 1912; s. Frank Anthony and Maria Josephine (Ambroselli) Z.; m. Irene Marie Ceconi, June 17, 1939; children: Edward V., David J., Philip E., Peter J. A.B., Columbia U., 1934, D.D.S., 1937, D.Sc. (hon.), 1983; M.S., U. Chgo., 1942. Diplomate: Am. Bd. Oral Medicine. Staff Sch. Dental and Oral Surgery, Columbia U., 1937—, asst. instr., then successively instr., asst. prof., asso. prof., head diagnosis and roentgenology, 1947-58, chmn. com. dental research, 1956—, Dr. Edwin S. Robinson prof. dentistry, 1958, prof. dentistry, dir. div. stomatology, 1958—, acting dean, 1973, dean, 1974-78, dean emeritus, 1979—; chmn. sect. hosp. dental services Columbia-Presbyn. Med. Center; dir. and attending dentist dental service Presbyn. Hosp., 1974-79, also mem. exec. com. of med. bd., 1974-76; police surgeon N.Y.C., 1968—; cons., dentist-in-residence VA, Washington; Weisberger Meml. lectr. Harvard U., 1969, Mershon Meml. lectr., 1970, Ralph L. Spaulding Meml. lectr., 1972; deans com. Montrose VA Hosp.; cons. East Orange, Kingsbridge VA hosps., Westchester Med. Ctr., Valhalla, N.Y., USPHS, Phelps Meml. Hosp., Tarrytown, N.Y., Vassar Bros. Hosp., Poughkeepsie, Bur. Medicine, FDA, Council on Dental Therapeutics; area cons. VA; cons.-lectr. U.S. Naval Dental Sch., Bethesda, Md., 1970—; pres. N.Y. State Bd. Dental Examiners, 1970-71; chmn. exam. rev. com. N.E. Regional Bd. Dental Examiners, 1969—; Samuel Charles Miller Meml. lectr., 1976; mem. council deans Am. Assn. Dental Schs., 1973-79; mem. postgrad. edn. com. N.Y.C. Cancer Com.; mem. profl. edn. and grants com. N.Y.C. div. Am. Cancer Soc., 1963-73; now bd. dirs.; chmn. panel on drugs in dentistry Nat. Acad. Scis., NRC, FDA; mem. N.Y. State Health Research Council, N.Y. Commn. on Health Manpower; chmn. bd. govs. (dental) Gen. Health Ins., N.Y.C. Contbg. author: The Thyroid, Medical Roentgenology, Current Pediatric Therapy, Cancer of Head and Neck; author: (with others) Pharmacotherapeutics of Oral Disease, 1964, Clinical Stomatology, 1966, Diagnosis of Diseases of Mouth and Jaws, 1969, 2d edit., 1978; also articles on mouth, jaw bone disease. Bd. dirs. Hist. Soc. Tarrytowns, 1983, United Way Tarrytowns, 1983, YMCA of Tarrytowns, 1984, Phelps Meml. Hosp. Hospice Agy, 1986. Recipient Austin Sniffen medal 9th Dist. Dental Soc., 1961; Columbia U. Dental Alumni Research award, 1963; Jarvie-Burkhart medal N.Y. Dental Soc., 1970; Samuel J. Miller medal Am. Acad. Oral Medicine, 1976; Henry Spenadel award 1st Dist. Dental Soc., 1979; Man of Yr. award C. of C. Tarrytowns and Irvington, 1983; Man of Achievement award Americans for Italian Migration, 1984; named Disting. Practitioner mem. Nat. Acads. Practice, 1986. Fellow Am. Coll. Dentists (William J. Gies medal 1981), N.Y. Acad. Dentistry, Internat. Coll. Dentists, 9th Dist. Dental Soc.; mem. Am. Acad. Oral Pathology, Am. Assn. for Cancer Edn. (charter), Am. Assn. Dental Examiners (Dentist Citizen of Yr. award 1978), Orgn. Tchrs. Oral Diagnosis, N.Y. Acad. Scis., N.Y. Dental Soc. (chmn. council sci. research 1956-71), Greater N.Y. Acad. Prosthodontics (hon.), Guatemala Dental Soc. (hon.), Am. Dental Assn. (mem. council dental therapeutics 1963-69, vice chmn. 1969), Columbia Dental Alumni Assn., William Jarvie Research Soc., Internat. Assn. Dental Research, AAAS, Nat. Italian-Am. Found., Sigma Xi (chpt. pres. 1974-76), Omicron Kappa Upsilon (sec. treas. Columbia chpt. 1944-57, pres. 1959-60), Sigma Phi Alpha., Knight Malta. Lodge: Rotary (pres. 1985-86) (Tarrytown). Home: 120 Gory Brook Rd North Tarrytown NY 10591 Office: 630 W 168th St New York NY 10032

ZEHEL, WENDELL EVANS, surgeon; b. Brownsville, Pa., Mar. 6, 1934; s. Michael and Emma (Evans) Z.; B.A., Washington and Jefferson Coll., 1956; M.D., U. Pitts., 1960; postgrad. in bioengring. Carnegie-Mellon U., 1968-75; m. Joan Leasure, Nov. 1, 1958; children—Lori Ann, Wendell Charles. Intern, Shadyside Hosp., Pitts., 1960-61; resident in surgery U. Pitts., VA Hosp., 1963-66, Wilmington (Del.) Med. Center, 1966-68; practice medicine, specializing in surgery, Pitts., 1968—; surgeon St. Clair Hosp., Pitts., 1968—. Served with USAF, 1961-63. Diplomate Am. Bd. Surgery. Fellow A.C.S.; mem. Assn. Advancement of Med. Instrumentation. Home: 553 Harrogate Dr Pittsburgh PA 15241 Office: 1000 Bower Hill Rd Pittsburgh PA 15243

ZEHENDER, MANFRED KARL HEINZ, cardiologist; b. Bad Kreuznach, Fed. Republic Germany, Oct. 28, 1957. MD, U. Mainz, 1984. Research fellow U. Limburg, Maastricht, The Netherlands, 1984-85, U. Pa., Phila., 1985; cardiologist U. Freiburg, Fed. Republic Germany, 1986—; presenter in field. Author: Programmed Stimulation, Antiarrhythmic Agents, Silent Myocardial Ischemia Pacemaker; contbr. more than 100 articles to profl. jours. Deutsche Forschungsgemeinschaff grantee. Mem. Deutsche Gesellschafft für Herz und Kreislaufforschung (grantee). Home: Herrengarten 27, 6552 Ebernburg Federal Republic of Germany

ZEIDLER, EBERHARD HEINRICH, architect; b. Braunsdorf, Germany, Jan. 11, 1926; immigrated to Can., 1951; s. Paul Albert and Dorothea (Dabbert) Z.; m. Phyllis Jane Abbott, Jan. 26, 1957; children—Margaret, Robert, Kate, Christina. Cand. Arch., Bauhaus, Weimar, W.Ger., 1948; Dipl.Ing., Technische U. Karlsruhe (W.Ger.), 1949; LL.D., McMaster U., Hamilton, Ont., 1982; D in Engring. (hon.) Tech. U. Nova Scotia, Can. Designer, Prof. Egon Eierman, Karlsruhe, 1949-50; assoc. prof. Lindner Osnabruck, W.Ger., 1950-51; assoc. in charge design Blackwell & Craig, Toronto, 1951-54; prtnr. Blackwell, Craig, Zeidler, Toronto, Ont., Can., 1954; sr. ptnr. Zeidler Roberts, Toronto, 1954—; com. mem. Can. Inst. Advanced Research, Toronto, 1982—; adj. prof. U. Toronto, 1983. Author: Healing the Hospital, 1974; Multifunctional Architecture in Urban Context, 1984. Mem. City of Toronto Planning Bd., 1972-75; bd. dirs. Branksome Hall Sch., Toronto, 1980-86. Recipient Massey medals Gov. Gen. Can., 1982, award Urban Land Inst., 1983, Lifetime Acheivement award, Toronto Arts Soc., 1987. Fellow AIA (honour award 1981), Royal Archtl. Inst. Can. (Gold medal, 1986); mem. Royal Can. Acad. Arts (acadamican 1973—). Anglican. Clubs: Badminton and Racquet, Royal Can. Yacht (Toronto). Office: Zeidler R Partnership/Architects, 315 Queen St W, Toronto, ON Canada N5V 2X2

ZEIDLER, WOLFGANG WALTHER HEINRICH, law educator, judge. Degree in law, Johanneum Hamburg/U. Hamburg, Fed. Republic Germany. Criminal, civil and adminstrv. ct. judge Hamburg, 1953-64; asst. del. to Fed. Constl. Ct. Karlsruhe, Fed. Republic Germany, 1955-58; research fellow Harvard U. Sch. Law, Cambridge, Mass., 1959-60; with civil service Hamburg, 1965-67; assoc. judge Fed. Constl. Ct., 1967-70; pres. Fed. Supreme Adminstrv. Tribunal, Berlin, 1970-75; v.p., presiding judge 2d chamber Fed. Constl. Ct., 1975-83, pres., 1983-87; pres. Bundesverfassungsgerichts, Karlsruhe, 1987—; vis. prof. U. Bologna, Italy, 1987-88. Contbr. articles to profl. jours. Named Hon. Prof. U. Mainz, Fed. Republic Germany, 1978. Office: Bundesverfassungsgericht, Schlossbezirk 3, Postfach 1771, 7500 Karlsruhe Federal Republic of Germany

ZEIER, HANS JAKOB, biology educator; b. Lucerne, Switzerland, Mar. 27, 1939; s. Hans and Margrit (Stutz) Z.; m. Elisabeth Marchand, May 8, 1976; children: Priska, Max, Dominique. BA, Kantonsschule Luzern, 1959; Sekundarlehrerdiplom, Kanton Luzern, Staatsexamen, 1962; PhD, U. Zurich, Switzerland, 1965. Asst. Inst. Brain Research U. Zurich, 1963-67; research assoc. psychology dept. MIT, Cambridge, Mass., 1967-69, lectr. Swiss Fed. Inst. Tech., Zurich, 1969-83, prof., 1983—; vis. prof. Univ. Fribourg, Switzerland, 1981-85; adv. bd. mem. Swiss Sci. Council, Bern, 1977. Author: Wörterbuch der Lerntheorien, 1976; co-author: Gehirn und Geist, 1980; editor: Lernen und Verhalten, 1984. Mem. Community Council, Dübendorf, Switzerland, 1984. Mem. Am. Psychol. Assn., European Brain and Behaviour Soc., Internat. Brain Research Orgn., Soc. for Psychophysiological Research, Union Schweizerischer Gesellschaften Exptl. Biologie. Mem. Christlichdemokratische Volkspartei. Office: Swiss Fed Inst Tech, Turnerstrasse 1, CH-8092 Zurich Switzerland

ZEIF, RICHARD ALLEN, lawyer; b. New Haven, July 7, 1929; s. Samuel Morris and Shirley F. (Fodor) Z.; grad. N.Y.U., 1950, postgrad., 1953; LLB Bklyn. Law Sch., 1952; m. Gloria A. Feldman, Aug. 19, 1956; children: Sasha, Andrew, Juliet. Admitted to N.Y. bar, 1952; ptnr. firm Nierenberg, Zeif & Weinstein, N.Y.C., 1952—; sec. Negotiation Inst., 1966—; mem. faculty New Sch., 1974-83; past adj. prof. New Eng. Sch. Law; cons., lectr. in field. Founder Democratic Reform Movement, N.Y.C., 1958. Served with AUS, 1952-55. Contbr. articles to profl. jours. Decorated Meritorious Service medal; recipient 1st Human Rights award N.Y. State Div. Human Rights, 1971; designated Academico Honoris Causa, Mex. Acad. Internat. Law, 1971. Fellow Am. Acad. Polit. and Social Scientists; mem. ABA (chmn. African law com. 1975-80), Internat. Fedn. Tng. and Devel. Orgns. (bd. dirs.), Explorers Club (chmn. fgn. relations com. 1974). Clubs: N.Y. Athletic, KP. Editor: Art of Negotiating Newsletter, 1980—. Office: 230 Park Ave Suite 460 New York NY 10169

ZEIGER, DELBERT LEE, human services program adminstr.; b. Compton, Calif., Jan. 5, 1941; s. John Q. and Lois M. (Smith) Z.; B.A., Calif. State U., Los Angeles, 1964; M. Pub. Adminstrn., U. So. Calif., 1973; m. Pamela Earl, Aug. 26, 1962; children—Julie, Jennifer. Social worker San Bernardino County (Calif.) Dept. Public Social Services, 1966-68, ednl. tng. specialist, 1969, social service supr., 1970-71, program asst. to dep. dir., 1971-72, Ont. dist. supr., 1972-77, San Bernardino dist. mgr., 1977-79; program mgr. Yolo County (Calif.) Dept. Social Services, 1979-80, dir. Social Services div., 1980-84, sr. social worker, 1984—; guest lectr., field instr., social services dept. Chaffey Coll. Co-chmn. Victor Valley Community Action Program; mem. San Bernardino County Dependency Prevention Commn.; coach Sunshine Soccer League, 1976; bd. dirs., mem. exec. com., treas. Mental Health Assn. San Bernardino, 1977-79; mem. dir.'s adv. bd. Ret. Sr. Vol. Program, City of San Bernardino, 1979; bd. dirs. Planned Parenthood of Yolo County, 1980. Recipient Key Man award Associated In Group Donors United Givers, 1971; Outstanding Service award City of Ontario, 1976. Mem. Am. Mgmt. Assn., San Bernardino, Apple Valley Victorville (sec., treas. 1966-68) jr. chambers commerce. Home: 1610 Edwin Ave Woodland CA 95695 Office: 120 W Main St Woodland CA 95695

ZEILINGER, ELNA RAE, educator; b. Tempe, Ariz., Mar. 24, 1937; d. Clayborn Eddie and Ruby Elna (Laird) Simpson; B.A. in Edn., Ariz. State U., 1958, M.A. in Edn., 1966, Ed.S., 1980; m. Philip Thomas Zeilinger, June 13, 1970; children—Shari, Chris. Bookkeeper, First Nat. Bank of Tempe, 1955-56; with registrar's office Ariz. State U., 1956-58; jr. high tchr., recreation dir. City of Tempe, tchr. Thew Sch., Tempe, 1958-61, elem. tchr. Mitchell Sch., 1962-74, intern prin., 1976, personnel intern, 1977; specialist in gifted edn. Tempe Elem. Schs., 1977-78; elem. tchr. Holdeman Sch., Tempe, 1988—; grad. asst. ednl. adminstrn., Iota Workshop coordinator Ariz. State

U., 1978; presenter Ariz. Gifted Conf., 1978-81; condr. survey of gifted programs, 1980; reporter public relations Tempe Sch. Dist., 1978-80, Access com. for gifted programs, 1981-83. Freedom Train com. Ariz. Bicentennial Comm., 1975-76. Named Outstanding Leader in Elem. and Secondary Schs., 1976' Ariz. Cattle Growers scholar, 1954-55; Elks scholar, 1954-55; recipient Judges award Tempe Art League, 1970, Best of Show, Scottsdale Art League, 1976. Mem. Council Exceptional Children, Ariz. Assn. Gifted and Talented, Ariz. Sch. Adminstrs., Tempe Hist. Assn. (liaison 1975), Scottsdale Artists League, Tempe Art League, Am. Bus. Women's Assn. (Woman of Yr. 1983), Phi Kappa Phi, Pi Lambda Theta, Kappa Delta Pi, Phi Delta Kappa, Kappa Delta. Democrat. Congregationalist. Club: Eastern Star. Author: Leadership Role of the Principal in Gifted Programs: A Handbook, 1980; Classified Personnel Handbook, 1977, also reports and monographs. Home: 610 E Colgate St Tempe AZ 85283 Office: Tempe Elem Schs 1326 W 18th St Tempe AZ 85281

ZEISET, JAMES A., aeronautical engineer; b. Goshen, Ind., Nov. 2, 1944; s. Alvin V. and Dorothy I. Zeiset. Pres. Monarch Mfg., Inc., 1976—; exec. dir. U.S. Hangliding Assn., Pearblossom, Calif., 1988—. Office: US Hang Gliding Assn PO Box 500 Pearblossom CA 93553

ZEITLIN, GERALD MARK, electrical engineer; b. Phila., May 7, 1937; s. David Edward and Charlotte (Freedman) Z.; m. Frances Loretta Scherr, May 17, 1983. BEE, Cornell U., 1960; MSEE, U. Colo., 1969. Electronic engr. Nat. Security Agy., Ft. Meade, Md., 1962-64, Westinghouse Georesearch Lab., Boulder, Colo., 1966-69; owner Sunrise Books, Estes Park, Colo., 1969-71; asst. research computer sci. U. Calif., San Francisco, 1972-78; assoc. devel. engr. U. Calif., Berkeley, 1978-82; sr. systems engr. EEG Systems Lab., San Francisco, 1982-86; computer cons., expert systems design Pacific Bell, San Francisco, 1986-87; systems analyst Pacific Bell, San Ramon, Calif., 1987—. Contbr. articles to profl. jours. Served to 1st lt. U.S. Army, 1960-62. Summer Faculty fellow NASA-Am. Soc. Engring. Edn., Ames Research Ctr., 1981. Mem. IEEE, Computer Soc. IEEE, Assn. Computing Machinery, Info. Systems Security Assn. Democrat. Jewish. Home: 196 Caldecott Ln #212 Oakland CA 94618 Office: Pacific Bell 2600 Camino Ramon Rm 3C590 San Ramon CA 94583

ZEITLIN, MAURICE, sociology educator, author; b. Detroit, Feb. 24, 1935; s. Albert J. and Rose (Goldberg) Z.; m. Marilyn Geller, Mar. 1, 1959; children: Michelle, Carla, Erica. BA cum laude, Wayne State U., 1957; MA, U. Calif.-Berkeley, 1960, PhD, 1964. Instr. anthropology and sociology Princeton (N.J.) U., 1961-64, research assoc. Ctr. Internat. Studies, 1962-64; asst. prof. sociology U. Wis.-Madison, 1964-67, assoc. prof., 1967-70, prof., 1970-77, dir. Ctr. Social Orgn., 1974-76; prof. sociology UCLA, 1977—, also research assoc. Inst. Indsl. Relations; vis. prof. polit. sci. and sociology Hebrew U., Jerusalem, 1971-72. Author: (with R. Scheer) Cuba: An American Tragedy, 1963, 1964, Revolutionary Politics and the Cuban Working Class, 1967, 1970, The Civil Wars in Chile, 1984, Landlords and Capitalists, 1988; Latin Am. editor Ramparts mag., 1967-73; editor-in-chief: Political Power and Social Theory, 1980—; editor: (with J. Petras) Latin America: Reform or Revolution?, 1968, American Society, Inc., 1970, 1977, Father Camilo Torres: Revolutionary Writings, 1972, Classes, Class Conflict, and the State, 1980, How Mighty a Force?, 1983, Insurgent Workers: The Origins of Industrial Unionism, 1987. Chmn. Madison Citizens for a Vote on Vietnam, 1967-68; chmn. Am. Com. for Chile, 1973-75; mem. exec. bd. U.S. Com. for Justice to Latin Am. Polit. Prisoners, 1977-84; mem. exec. com. Calif. Campaign for Econ. Democracy, 1983-86. Ford Found. fellow, 1965-67, 70-71; Guggenheim fellow, 1981-82; NSF grantee, 1981, 82; recipient Project Censored award Top Censored Story, 1981; named to Ten Best Censored list, 1978. Mem. Am. Sociol. Assn. (governing council 1977-80), Internat. Sociol. Assn. (editorial bd. 1977-81), Latin Am. Studies Assn., Orgn. Am. Historians. Democrat. Jewish. Office: UCLA Haines 237 405 Hilgard Ave Los Angeles CA 90024

ZEKIYAN, BOGHOS LEVON, literature educator; b. Istanbul, Turkey, Oct. 21, 1943; s. Andon and Sofi (Mazlemian) A. Lic. in Philosophy, Pontificia U., Gregoriana, 1962, lic. in Theology, 1966, specialization in Theology, 1968; PhD, U. Istanbul, 1973. Tchr. high sch. Pangalti Lisesi, Istanbul, 1971-74; tchr. high sch. Collegio Moorat-Raphael, Venice, Italy, 1974-85, dir., prin., 1982-85; prof. Armenian lang. and lit. U. degli Studi di Venezia, 1976—; editor in chief Hay-Endanik, Venice, 1974-82, Bazmavep Revue d'Etudes Arméniennes, Venice, 1980-85; sect. head Centro Studi e Documentazione della Cultura Armena, Milan, 1976-82; sci. sec. Acad. Armena Sancti Lazari, Venice, 1974-81. Author: L'interiorismo agostiniano, 1981, Humanism, 1982; contbr. articles to profl. publs. Mem. Soc. Armenian Studies, Assn. Internal des Etudes Arméniennes (bd. dirs. 1983—), Research on Armenian Architecture, Assn. for Study and Promotion of Armenian Lang. (founder). Roman Catholic of Armenian Rite. Office: U Venice, S Polo 2035, 30125 Venice Italy

ZELENKA, JAN, journalist, broadcasting company executive; b. Usti nad Orlichi, Dec. 5, 1923; married; 4 children. Ed. Charles U., Prague. Dir.-gen. Czechoslovak. TV, 1969—; dep. to House of the People, Fed. Assembly, 1971—; chmn. adminstrn. Council Internat. Radio and TV Orgn., 1971-73; mem. central com. Communist Party of Czechoslovakia, 1981—. Recipient Gold Dove 1st prize for TV film Great Concert, Internat. Leipzig TV Festival, 1971, Czechoslovak prize for Journalism, 1979; decorated Order of 25th Feb. 1948, 1949, Order of Labour, 1973, Order of Victorious February, 1983. Contbr. articles to profl. jours. Address: Ceskoslovenska Televize, Kavcihory, Prague 4 Czechoslovakia

ZELENY, JINDŘICH, philosopher, educator; b. Bitovany, Czechoslovakia, Nov. 13, 1922; s. Jindřich and Marie (Machová) Z.; m. Jiřina Topičvá, Oct. 21, 1946; children: Hana, Zdeňka. PhD, Charles U., Prague, 1948. Assoc. prof. philosophy Charles U., 1954-67, prof., 1967—; dep. dir. Inst. for Philosophy, Czechoslovakian Acad. Scis., Prague, 1981-85, also corr. mem. Author: The Logic of Marx, 1980, Dialektick der Rationalität, 1986, also 4 books on epistemology. Mem. Czechoslovakian Philos. Soc. (v.p. 1970-81), Internat. Fedn. Philos. Socs. (mem. steering com. 1983—), Internat. Gesellschaft für Dialektische Philosophie (mem. presidium 1981—). Home: Soukenicka 29, 11000 Prague Czechoslovakia Office: Czech Acad Scis Inst for, Philosophy Jilska 1, 11000 Prague Czechoslovakia

ZELEZNY, WILLIAM FRANCIS, retired physical chemist; b. Rollins, Mont., Sept. 5, 1918; s. Joseph Matthew and Birdie Estelle (Loder) Z.; m. Virginia Lee Scarcliff, Sept. 14, 1949. BS in Chemistry, Mont. State Coll., 1940; MS in Metallurgy, Mont. Sch. Mines, 1941; PhD in Phys. Chemistry, State U. Iowa, 1951. Scientist NACA, Cleve., 1951-54; metallurgist div. indsl. research Wash. State Coll., Pullman, 1954-57; scientist atomic energy div. Phillips Petroleum Co., Idaho Falls, Id., 1957-66, Idaho Nuclear Corp., Idaho Falls, 1966-70; mem. staff Los Alamos (N.Mex.) Sci. Lab., 1970-80; instr. metallurgy State U. Iowa, Iowa City, 1948-49; asst. prof. metallurgy Wash. State Coll., 1956-57; instr. U. Idaho, Idaho Falls, 1960-68. Contbr. articles to profl. jours.; patentee in field. Bd. dirs. Biol. Sta. Univ. Mont., Polson, Mont., 1984—. Served with AUS, 1944-46. Mem. Am. Chem. Soc. (sec. N.Mex. sect. 1978-79), Microbeam Analysis Soc., Am. Soc. Metals, Am. Inst. Mining Metall. and Petroleum Engrs., Sigma Xi, Alpha Chi Sigma. Democrat. Methodist. Home: PO Box 37 Rollins MT 59931

ZELIBOR, JOSEPH LOUIS, JR., research microbiologist; b. Coronado, Calif., Oct. 20, 1953; s. Joseph Louis and Mavie Rita (Ames) Z. Assoc. Sci., No. Va. Community Coll., 1974; B.S., Purdue U., 1976; Ph.D., U. Md., 1988. Sci. cons. Systems Integration & Research, Inc., Arlington, Va., 1975-76, dir. sci. research, 1976-77; research microbiologist U.S. Geol. Survey, Reston, Va., 1977-83, safety officer, 1978-83; faculty research assoc. U. Md., College Park, 1983-86. Contbr. articles to profl. jours. Inventor in field. Served with USN, 1971-72. Grantee ERDA, 1977, U.S. Geol. Survey, 1983-85. Mem. AAAS, Am. Chem. Soc., Am. Soc. Microbiology, Sigma Xi. Office: U Md Dept Microbiology College Park MD 20742

ZELL, DOLORES PFAFFENDORF, government relations, educational administrator; b. Miami, Fla., July 13, 1944; d. George and Pearl (Watford) Pfaffendorf; B.S. in Edn., William Carey Coll., 1969; M.A. in Coll. Personnel Administrn., U. Miami, 1971, doctorate, 1986; m. Don Richard Zell, Aug. 16, 1969. Placement dir. William Carey Coll., Hattiesburg, Miss., 1967-69; asst. dir. Pearson Hall, U. Miami (Fla.), 1969-70; customer service rep. Burdines, Miami, 1970-76; tchr. A.L. Lewis Elem Sch., Miami Public Schs., 1970-75, area coordinator sch. vol. program, 1975-77, tchr. R.R. Moton Elem. Sch., 1979-80, Coral Reef Elem. Sch., 1979; asst. prin. Opa Locka Elem. Sch., Dade County (Fla.) Public Schs., 1980-81, Vineland and Bel Aire Elem. Sch., 1983-85, Redland Elem., 1986-87; exec. dir. Fla. Job. Tng. Coordinating Council, 1988—; legis. aide state rep. Dexter Lehtinen, Fla., 1981—; adj. prof. Fla. Internat. U., Miami-Dade Community Coll. Coordinator Lehtinen legis. campaign, 1978, 80. Tchr. Sunday Sch., Bapt. Ch.; officer Young Democrats; legis. chmn. Dade County Sch. Adminstrs. Assn.; mem. S. Dade Democratic Club,Am. Bus. Women's Assn., Assn. Elem. Sch. Prins., Assn. Supervision and Curriculum Devel., Internat. Reading Assn., Nat. Sch. Vol. Program, Inc., S. Dade Reading Council, Phi Delta Kappa. Club: Briar Bay. Contbr. articles in field to profl. jours. Home: 13323 SW 103 Pl Miami FL 33176 Office: 18 House Office Bldg The Capitol Tallahassee FL 32301

ZELLER, FRANCIS JOSEPH, college dean; b. Chgo., July 31, 1943; s. Charles Joseph Paul and Erma (Kile) Z.; m. Frances Joan McGrath, Aug. 3, 1968; children—Patrick, Brian. B.A. in English, Lewis U., 1967; M.A., No. Ill. U., 1970, Ed.D., 1983. Tchr., chmn. English dept. Schaumburg Dist. 54, Ill., 1967-70; asst. bus. mgr. Park Ridge Sch. Dist. 64, Ill., 1970-71; bus. mgr. Barrington Sch. Dist. 224, Ill., 1971-73; dean bus. services Ill. Valley Community Coll., Oglesby, 1973—. Exec. mem. Boy Scouts of Am., Peoria, Ill., 1983—; mem. Peoria Diocesan Pastoral Council, 1983—. Mem. Internat. Assn. Sch. Bus. Ofcls. (bd. dirs. 1985—, chmn. legal aspects com.), Ill. Assn. Sch. Bus. Ofcls., Ill. Assn. Community Coll. Bus. Adminstrs. (bd. dirs. 1984—), NEA, Delta Sigma Pi. Roman Catholic. Lodge: Rotary. Avocations: cross country skiing; tennis; hunting; distance bicycling. Office: Ill Valley Community Coll 2578 E 350th Rd Oglesby IL 61348

ZELLER, PAUL WILLIAM, lawyer; b. Eunice, La., Sept. 17, 1948; s. Andrew Albert and Margaret Lucille (Fontenot) Z.; m. Marlene Linda Parrillo, Dec. 17, 1966; children—Paul William, Jr., Jonathan Randolph, Amanda Louise, Joshua Andrew. B.A., La. State U., 1969; J.D., U. Va., 1972. Bar: N.Y. 1973, U.S. Dist. Ct. (so. dist.) N.Y. 1974, U.S. Ct. Appeals (2nd cir.) 1974. Assoc., Debevoise and Plimpton, N.Y.C., 1972-81; asst. corp. counsel Reliance Group, Inc., N.Y.C., 1981-83; asst. v.p. Reliance Group Holdings, Inc., N.Y.C., 1982, v.p., asst. gen. counsel, 1983, v.p., dep. gen. counsel, 1984—; bd. dirs. Empire Gas Corp. Bd. of editors, U. Va. Law Review, 1970-72. Mem. Assn. Bar City of N.Y., Phi Delta Phi. Democrat. Roman Catholic. Office: Reliance Group Holdings Inc 55 E 52d St New York NY 10055

ZELLING, HOWARD EDGAR, justice Supreme Court of South Australia; b. Adelaide, South Australia, Australia, Aug. 14, 1916; s. Edgar Proctor and Florence May (Merritt) Z.; m. Sesca Ross Anderson, Jan. 21, 1950. LL.B., U. Adelaide, 1938, honors LL.B., 1941, D. Univ., 1983. Created Queen's Counsel, 1962; bar: South Australia 1938. Lectr. constl. law U. Adelaide, 1947-62, examiner, 1947-81, lectr. Faculty of Econs., 1952-60; acting justice Supreme Ct. South Australia (Australia), Adelaide, 1969, justice, 1969—; pres. Law Council of Australia, 1966-68; chmn. Law Reform Com. of South Australia, 1968—. Contbr. articles to legal and other jours., 1948-84; author numerous law reform reports, 1968—. Procurator Presbyterian Ch. South Australia, 1945-60. Decorated comdr. Order Brit. Empire, officer Order of Australia. Club: Adelaide. Lodge: Grand Lodge South Australia (grand master 1972-76). Home: 43 Edwards St, South Brighton, South Australia 5048, Australia Office: Supreme Ct, South Australia, Victoria Sq, Adelaide 5000 Australia

ZELNICK, CARL ROBERT, journalist; b. N.Y.C., Aug. 9, 1940; s. David Isadore and Lillian (Ostrow) Z.; m. Pamela Margaret Sharp, Dec. 30, 1967; children: Eva Michal, Dara Yael, Marni Ruth. B.S., Cornell U., 1961; LL.B., U. Va., 1964. Bar: N.Y. 1965, D.C. 1966. Law asso. H. Charles Ephraim, Washington, 1981-82; corr./columnist Anchorage Daily News, 1968-76; Assoc. editor Environmental Law Reporter, 1971-72; spl. corr. Christian Sci. Monitor, 1973-77; corr./bur. chief Nat. Pub. Radio, Washington, 1972-76; exec. editor Frost/Nixon Interviews, Washington, 1976-77; dir. news coverage ABC-TV, Washington, 1977-81; dep. bur. chief ABC News, Washington, 1981-82; Moscow bur. chief, corr. ABC News, 1982-84; corr. ABC News, Israel, 1984-86; ABC News Pentagon corr. Washington, 1986—. Contbr. articles to newspapers and mags. Served with USMC, 1964-65. Recipient Gavel awards Am. Bar Assn., 1969, 74, Du Pont award Columbia U. Sch. Journalism, 1984, Emmy award, 1984. Mem. Council on Fgn. Relations, Radio and TV Corrs. Assn., Internat. Inst. for Strategic Studies, Phi Epsilon Pi, Pi Delta Phi. Jewish. Clubs: Fed. City, Washington Press. Office: ABC News 1124 Connecticut Ave Washington DC 20036

ZEMAITIS, ALGIRDAS JONAS ALEXIS, international organization official; b. Salniskiai Manor, Lithuania, Mar 9, 1933; came to U.S., 1949, naturalized, 1954; s. Vincentas Petras and Bronislava (Rusecki-Ruseckas) Z. Prince de Druck; m. Vanda Jadvyga Kibort-Kybartas, Apr. 5, 1956; children: Alexis-Pius-Kestutis, Maria-Birute, Rita-Vilia, Paulus-Algirdas, Julia-Dalia.; grad. student U. Bonn, Fed. Republic Germany, 1954-56, BA (hon.) Balliol Coll., Oxford (Eng.) U., 1959, MA, 1964; v.p. Union-Chretienne-Democrate d'Europe Cen. S/J, Paris, 1955-59; asst. to pres., sr. economist Borg-Warner Internat. Corp., Chgo., 1959-61; dir. gen. Market Facts ROC Internat., Chgo., 1962-63; internat. economist Sears, Roebuck & Co., Chgo., 1963-66; sr. internat. trade officer AID, U.S. Dept. of State., Washington, 1966-68; economist FAO, UN, Rome, 1968-75, country project officer, 1975-83, dep. rep. in the Sudan, Khartoum, 1983-86. Contbr. articles to profl. jours. Chmn., Bonn Komite Litauisches Welt Gemeinschaft, Bonn, 1954-56; del. Internat. Christian Democratic Movement, Europe and Latin Am., 1955-66. Served with AUS, 1952-54. Decorated Papal Knight Grand Officer, Equestrian Order Holy Sepulchre of Jerusalem. Mem. various profl. and acad. socs. Home: Collegio Lituano, 20 Via Casalmonferrato, 00182 Rome Italy Office: FAO, 00100 Rome Italy

ZEMANEK, HEINZ, computer scientist; b. Vienna, Austria, Jan. 1, 1920; s. Ferdinand and Theresia (Renner) Z.; m. Maria Assumpta Lindebner, Aug. 12, 1950; children: Georg, Benedicta. Dipl. Ing., U. Tech. Vienna, 1944, Dr. techn., 1951; Dr. (hon.), U. Linz, Austria, 1982; Dr. Ing. (hon.), U. Erlangen, Fed. Republic Germany, 1986. Telecommunications researcher German Air Force, 1943-45; engaged in bus. 1945-47; mem. faculty U. Tech. Vienna, 1947—, prof. telecommunications and computer sci., 1964—; with IBM Corp., 1961-85, dir. IBM Lab., Vienna, 1961-75. Author: Information Theory, 1959; Calendar and Chronology, 1978, 4th edition, 1987; co-author: Computers, 1971; editor profl. jours. Internat. commnr. for Austria, Boy Scouts, 1949-53. Decorated Grosses Goldenes Ehrenzeichen Verdienste (Austria), 1974, Goldenes Ehrenzeichen Verdienste (Vienna), 1986; Heinz Zemanek Prize established in his honor Austrian Computer Soc., 1985; recipient Stefan medal Electro tech. Soc. Austria, 1969; Prechtl medal U. Tech. Vienna, 1978; Computer Pioneer medal IEEE, 1986; Ov Plaquette German Mus., Munich, 1988; IBM fellow, 1975-85. Mem. West Berlin Acad. Arts, Austrian Computer Soc. (past pres.), Austrian Acad. Scis., Vienna Cath. Acad.; corr. mem. Spanish Acad. Scis.; hon. mem. Internat. Fedn. Info. Processing (pres. 1971-74), Computer Soc. Japan, Computer Soc. S. Africa. Home: Blutgasse 3, Vienna A-1010 Austria Office: PO Box 251, A-1011 Vienna Austria

ZEMPELIN, HANS GUENTHER, chemical company executive; b. Wiesbaden, Fed. Republic Germany, June 8, 1926; s. Otto and Hanna (Imgart) Z.; m. Liselotte A. Boden. DCL, U. Heidelberg, Fed. Republic Germany, 1952. Adv. Glanzstoff AG, Wuppertal, Fed. Republic Germany, 1956-61; mgr. personnel Glanzstoff AG, Oberbruch, 1961-67, mgr. plant, 1967-70; mem. exec. bd. Enka AG, Wuppertal, 1970-75, pres., 1975-85, chmn. (non-exec.), 1985—; mem. supervisory council Akzo NV, Arnhem, The Netherlands, 1987, Strabag Bau-AG, Cologne, Fed. Republic Germany, 1984, Dahlbusch AG, Gelsenkirchen, Fed. Republic Germany, 1984. Recipient Commandeur Oranje-Nassau Queen of The Netherlands, Grosses Bundesverdienskreuz Pres. Fed. Republic of Germany, 1987. Mem. German Fedn. Employers (exec. com. 1986). Lodge: Rotary. Home: Wettiner Str 49 a, D 5600 Wuppertal Federal Republic of Germany Office: Enka AG, Kasinostrasse, D 5600 Wuppertal Federal Republic of Germany

ZENATTI, ARLETTE HÉLENE, psychologist, researcher; b. Paris, Feb. 23, 1931; d. Emile and Lucie (Bloch) Z. PhD in Psychology, U. Paris, 1967, State Doctorate, 1978. Pianist 1953 69; prof. Nat. Conservatory Music, Le Mans, France, 1964-70; researcher Nat. Ctr. Sci. Research, Paris, 1970—. Author: Le Développement Génétique de la Perception Musicale, 1969, L'enfant et son Environnement Musical, 1981; contbr. articles to profl. jours. Recipient first prize Nat. Superior Conservatory Music, Paris, 1953, 1960, 1962,Bronze medal Nat. Ctr. Sci. Research, 1968. Mem. French Psychology Soc., Council Research Music Edn., Soc. Research Psychology Music. Home: 9 Allee des Roches, 94370 Sucy en Brie France Office: Ctr Nat Recherche Sci, 15 Quai Anatole France, 75700 Paris France

ZENDLE, HOWARD MARK, software development researcher; b. Binghamton, N.Y., June 8, 1949; s. Abraham and Evelyn (Hershowitz) Z. BA in Physics, SUNY-Binghamton, 1972, MA, in Physics, 1976; MS, in elec. engring. Syracuse U., 1987. With IBM, Owego, N.Y., 1974—, staff programmer, 1978-83, mgr. microprocessor applications software, 1979-81, mgr. tactical avionics software, 1981-82, adv. programmer, 1983-86, sr. programmer, 1986—. Sec., Men's Club Beth David Synagogue, Binghamton, 1984-85, v.p., 1986-88; bd. dirs. Jewish Community Ctr., Binghamton, 1983-86. Recipient Informal awards IBM, 1975, 78, 81, 83. Mem. Assn. for Computing Machinery, IEEE. Republican. Club: Central Electric Railfan's Assn. Lodge: Masons. Avocations: railfanning, research into history of industrial development in America.

ZENIYA, TORU, automotive service company executive; b. Tokyo, June 22, 1930; s. Kuranosuke and Takako Z.; m. Tokuko Kagami, Mar. 10, 1956; children—Nobuko, Ikuko, Shigeko. Diploma, Tokyo City U., 1949, Chuo U., Tokyo, 1954; grad. tech. seminar Dunwoody Indsl. Inst., Mpls., 1960. Serviceman Nissan Motor Co., Tokyo, 1953-55; dir. Zeniya Automobile Co., Tokyo, 1956-68, pres., 1968—. Pres. Awaji Primary Pub. Sch. PTA, Chiyodaku, Tokyo, 1976, Rensei Jr. High Sch. PTA, Chiyodaku, 1980. Internat. Coop. Adminstrn. Program scholar U.S. Mem. Tokyo Automobile Service Promotion Assn. (bd. dirs. 1985-86, award 1980), Tokyo Automobile Service Commerce and Industry Guild (bd. dirs. 1985-86). Democrat. Buddhist. Lodge: Chiyoda Auto Guild. Avocation: golf. Home: 2-11 Awajicho, Kanda, Chiyoda-ku, Tokyo 101, Japan Office: Zeniya Jidosha Kogyo, 2-7 Awajicho Kanda, Chiyoda-ku, Tokyo 101, Japan

ZENO-ZENCOVICH, LIVIO, international organization official; b. Trieste, Italy, Oct. 22, 1913; s. Vincent and Cornelia (Magrini) Z.-Z; m. Beatrice Lennox Gordon, Aug. 31, 1948; children: Alexander, Vincent. PhD, U. Rome, 1936. Polit. commentator BBC, London, 1941-46; pvt. sec. to Italian fgn. minister Italian Ministry of Fgn. Affairs, Rome, 1947-51; asst. dir. pub. info. NATO, London and Paris, 1951-53; chief editor daily newspaper La Voce Repubblicana, Rome, 1956-57; asst. dir. UN, Rome, 1958-62; ctr. dir. UN, Beirut, 1962-67, Cairo, 1967-71. Author: Biography of Count Sforza, 1975, Pocket History of the European Community, 1979, also numerous essays. Fellow Deputazione di Storia Patria, Trieste, 1984—. Mem. Italian Rep. Party. Roman Catholic. Home: Viale Miramare 215, 34136 Trieste Italy

ZERFOSS, LESTER FRANK, mgmt. cons., educator; b. Mountaintop, Pa., Nov. 2, 1903; s. Clinton and Mabel (Wilcox) Z.; B.A. cum laude, Pa. State U., 1926, M.Ed., 1934, Ed.D., 1958; m. Harriet Mildred Cary, Dec. 21, 1928 (dec. Dec. 1978); children—Patricia Ann (Mrs. Thomas Sibben), Clinton Cary, Robert Williamson; m. Irma J. Allen, July 12, 1980. Coll. tchr., pub. sch. adminstr., Pa., 1928-41; supr. design, devel. Gen. Motors Inst., 1942-46; head supervisory devel. Detroit Edison Co., 1946-52; corporate tng. dir. Am. Enka Corp. (N.C.), 1952-59, dir. indsl. relations, mgmt. services, 1959-66, mgmt. cons. tech., mgmt. devel., 1966-73; prof. psychology, dir. mgmt. devel. programs U. N.C. at Asheville, 1966-74, prof. mgmt. and developmental psychology, chmn. dept. mgmt., 1974-76 emeritus prof. mgmt., 1976—; pres. L.F. Zerfoss Assos., Inc., Mgmt. Consultants, 1976—; cons. on mgmt. devel. State of N.C. Mem. N.C. Personnel Bd., 1966-72, Southeastern Regional Manpower Adv. Com., 1966-71, N.C. Community Coll. Adv. Council, 1966—. Trustee, exec. bd., chmn. instructional com. Brevard Coll.; trustee Mountain Manpower Corp. Recipient Disting. Prof. award U. N.C., 1976. Mem. Am. Mgmt. Assn. (lectr. mgmt. devel. pres.'s assn.), Nat. Soc. Advancement Mgmt. (profl. mgr. citation 1962), Am. Soc. Tng. and Devel., Phi Delta Kappa (Disting. Service award 1982), Kappa Phi Kappa, Iota Alpha Delta, Kappa Delta Pi, Delta Sigma Phi. Contbg. author Training and Development Handbook, 1967, Management Handbook for Plant Engineers, 1978, Psychology in Action, 1978; author: Developing Professional Personnel in Business, Industry and Government, 1968, (with Irma Zerfoss) All God's Children Got Wings, 1987; contbr. to Personnel Administration in the Collegium, 1982; contbr. articles to profl. jours. Home and Office: PO Box 386 Liberty SC 29657

ZERLANG, MARTIN, literature educator; b. Hørsholm, Denmark, Sept. 1, 1952; s. Poul and Elsebet (Garde-Hansen) Z.; divorced; children: Line, Maja. MA, U. Copenhagen, Denmark, 1977. Asst. prof. U. Aalborg, Denmark, 1983-85, U. Copenhagen, 1985—. Author: Bøndernes Klassekamp, 1976, En Selvskrreven Historie, 1982; author, editor Dansk Litteraturhistorie, 1985; editor Kultur og Klasse; contbr. articles to profl. jours. Mem. Assn. De Estudios De Literaturas y Sociedades De Am. Latina. Home: Jakob Dannefordsvej 7, 1973 Frederiksberg C Denmark Office: U Copenhagen, Njalsgade 80, 2300 Copenhagen Denmark

ZERLAUT, GENE ARLIS, chemist; b. Bailey, Mich., June 23, 1930; s. George David and Glenna Mae (Palm) Z.; student Western Mich. U., 1948-49; B.S., U. Mich., 1956; m. Cecelia Gail McGukin, Mar. 4, 1961; children—Scott Michael, Christopher Robert. Chemist, U.S. Army Ballistic Missle Agy., Huntsville, Ala., 1958-60; aerospace technologist, chemist NASA, Huntsville, 1960-62; sr. chemist, mgr. polymer chemistry research Ill. Inst. Tech. Research Inst., Chgo., 1962-73; pres., tech. dir. DSET Labs., Inc., Phoenix, 1973—. Coach, Little League Baseball, 1974-76; bd. dirs., vice chmn. bd. Solar Energy Research and Edn. Found., 1978-79; commr. Ariz. Solar Commn., 1979-83. Served with U.S. Army, 1956-58. Recipient Invention awards NASA, 1968, Innovation award, 1973. Mem. Solar Energy Industries Assn. (bd. govs. 1976, v.p. 1978-79, exec. com. 1979-81, bd. dirs. 1981-86), Am. Inst. Chemists (dir. 1975), ASTM (nat. chmn. solar energy conversion com. 1978-83, award of merit 1987), Am. Council Ind. Labs., Am. Inst. Aeros. and Astronautics, Am. Nat. Standards Inst. (mem. solar energy standards coordinating com. 1979-83, tech. adv. group on plastics, 1974—,), Internat. Solar Energy Soc., Internat. Standards Orgn. (chmn. U.S. tech. adv. com. on solar energy), Soc. Plastics Engrs., Fedn. Paint Socs. Patentee in field. Contbr. articles to profl. jours. Research in spectral solar radiometry and accelerated environ. testing. Home: 346 W Pine Valley Dr Phoenix AZ 85023 Office: Box 1850 Black Canyon Stage I Phoenix AZ 85029

ZERNA, WOLFGANG, civil engineer, educator; b. Berlin, Oct. 11, 1916; s. Paul August and Olga Maria (Pomrenke) Z.; diploma in Engring., U. Berlin, 1940; D. Eng., U. Hannover, 1947; Dr.-Ing.E.h. Stuttgart U., 1974; m. Margit Elisabeth Kirski, Aug. 31, 1954. Engr., Polensky & Zollner, Cologne, 1950-52; chief engr. Philipp Holzmann AG, Frankfurt am Main, 1953-57; prof. civil engring. Tech. U., Hannover, 1958-67; prof. Ruhr-Univ., Bochum, 1968—; cons. in field. Mem. Am. Concrete Inst. Author: (with A.E. Green) Theoretical Elasticity, 1968, Spannbetonträger, 1987. Contbr. articles to profl. jours. Home: 3 Am Wittenstein, 4320 Hattingen Federal Republic of Germany Office: 150 Universitatsstr, 4630 Bochum 1 Federal Republic of Germany

ZERZAN, CHARLES JOSEPH, JR., physician; b. Portland, Oreg., Dec. 1, 1921; s. Charles Joseph and Margaret Cecelia (Mahony) Z.; B.A., Wilamette U., 1948; M.D., Marquette U., 1951; m. Joan Margaret Kathan, Feb. 7, 1948; children—Charles Joseph, Michael, Kathryn, Paul, Joan, Margaret, Terrance, Phillip, Thomas, Rose, Kevin, Gregory. Commd. 2d. lt., U.S. Army, 1940, advanced through grades to capt., 1945, ret., 1946, re-enlisted, 1951, advanced through grades to lt. col., M.C., 1965; intern Madigan Gen. Hosp., Ft. Lewis, Wash., 1951-52; resident in internal medicine Letterman Gen. Hosp., San Francisco, 1953-56, Walter Reed Gen. Hosp., Washington, 1960-61; chief of medicine Rodriquez Army Hosp., 1957-60, U.S. Army Hosp., Fort Gordon, Calif., 1962-65; chief gastroenterology Fitzsimmons Gen. Hosp., Denver, 1965-66; chief profl. services U.S. Army Hosp., Ft. Carson, Colo., 1967-68; dir. continuing med. edn. U. Oreg., Portland, 1968-73; partner Permanente Clinic, Portland, 1973—; assoc. clin. prof. medicine

U. Oreg., 1973—; individual practice medicine, specializing in gastroenterology, Portland, 1968—; staff Northwest Permanente, P.C.; dir., 1980-83. Mem. Portland Com. Fgn. Relations, 1986—. Decorated Legion of Merit, Army Commendation medal with oak leaf cluster. Diplomate Am. Bd. Internal Medicine. Fellow A.C.P.; mem. Am. Gastroenterol. Assn., Oreg. Med. Assn. (del. Clackamas County, membership task force), Ret. Officers Assn. Republican. Roman Catholic. Home: 6364 SE McNary Rd Milwaukie OR 97222 Office: 10200 SE Sunnyside Rd Clackamas OR 97015

ZETTERLING, MAI ELISABETH, film director, actress, author; b. May 24, 1925; m. Tutte Lemkow, 1944; 1 son, 1 dau.; m. 2d David Hughes 1958 (div. 1977). Ed. Royal Theatre Sch. Drama, Stockholm. Staff of Nat. Theatre, Stockholm, 1943-45; under contract film dir. to Sandrews of Sweden; Swedish stage appearances include: St. Mark's Eve, The Beautiful People, Shadow and Substance, Twelfth Night, Merchant of Venice, Les Mouches, House of Bernada; London stage appearances include: The Wild Duck, The Doll's House, Point of Departure and Restless Heart, The Seagull, Creditors; acted in films: Frenzy, 1944. Frieda 1947, The Bad Lord Byron, 1948, Quartet, 1948, Knock on Wood, 1954, A Prize of Gold, 1955, Seven Waves Away, 1956, Only Two Can Play, 1962, The Main Attraction, 1962, The Bay of St. Michael, 1963; film dir. BBC TV Documentaries; dir., co-writer films: The War Game (1st prize Venice Film Festival 1963), 1963; (feature films) Loving Couples, 1965, Night Games, 1966, Dr. Glas, 1968, The Girls, 1968, Flickorna, 1968; (films) Vincent the Dutchman, We Have Many Names, 1975, The Moon Is a Green Cheese, 1976, The Native Squatter, 1977, Lady Policeman, 1979, Of Seals and Men, 1979; (feature film Eng.) Scrubbers, 1983; co-dir. Visions of Eight, 1973; dir., writer (feature film Sweden) Amorosa, 1986; author: (with David Hughes) The Cat's Tale, 1965, Night Games (novel), In the Shadow of the Sun (short stories), 1975, Bird of Passage (novel), 1976, Rains Hat (children's book), 1979, Ice Island (novel), 1979, All Those Tomorrows (autobiography), 1985. Address: care Douglas Rae Mgmt Ltd, 28 Charing Cross Rd, London W1 England *

ZEVI, BRUNO, architectural historian and critic; b. Rome, Jan. 22, 1918; s. Guido and Ada (Bondi) Z.; m. Tullia Calabi, Dec. 26, 1940; children—Adachiara, Luca. Classical studies Liceo Tasso, Rome, 1934-37; M.Architecture, Harvard U., 1942; D.Architecture, Faculty Architecture, Rome, 1945; hon. degree Architecture, U. Buenos Aires, 1951; hon. prof. Universidad Nat. del Cuzco, 1977; LHD (hon.) U. Mich., 1986. Prof. archtl. history U. Venice (Italy), 1948-63, U. Rome, 1964-79. Author: Architecture as Space, 1957; The Modern Language of Architecture, 1978; Bruno Zevi on Modern Architecture (Andrea O. Dean), 1983. Editor: L'architettura monthly mag., 1955—; columnist L'Espresso weekly publ., 1955—. Fellow AIA (hon.); mem. Internat. Com. Archtl. Critics (pres. 1979—), Italian Inst. Architecture (v.p 1959—), Royal Inst. Brit. Architects (hon.), Accademia Nazionale di San Luca (Rome). Socialist. Jewish. Club: Tennis (Rome). Office: Via Nomentana 150, 00162 Rome Italy

ZEYBEKOGLU, ILHAN I., architect; b. Odemis, Turkey, Mar. 22, 1939; came to U.S., 1968; s. Ismail and Suphiye (Soyer) Z.; Diploma in Architecture, U. Stuttgart (Germany), 1965; M.Arch., Harvard U., 1969; m. Annie Aleskovsky, Nov. 17, 1979; children—Ilhan, Erol. Designer Rolf Gutbrod, Frei Otto, Architects, Stuttgart, 1965-68; asst. prof. architecture Harvard U., 1969-75; pres. Zeybekoglu, Bokhari & Assos. Inc., Cambridge, Mass., 1974-81, Ilhan Zeybekoglu Assos., Architects and Planners, 1981-84; prin. Archiplan, Architects and Planners, London, 1985-86; pres. Zeybekoglu Nayman Assocs, Inc., Architects, Urban Designers, Cambridge, 1986—. Mem. AIA, Boston Soc. Architects, Turkish Chamber Architects. Archtl. works: Visitor Center, Brigantine Nat. Wildlife Service, Oceanville, N.J., Yanbu (Saudi Arabia) Indsl. City, Harvard Bus. Sch. Glass Hall renovation (Archtl. Record Interiors award 1980), Islamic Devel. Bank (1st prize internat. design competition), 1985. Home: 452 Beacon St Boston MA 02115 Office: Zeybekoglu Nayman Assocs Inc 10 River St Cambridge MA 02139

Z'GRAGGEN, JOHN ANTON, religious organization director, researcher; b. Schattdorf, Switzerland, June 24, 1932; arrived in Papua New Guinea, 1963.; s. Alois and Josephina (Herger) Z. MA, C.U.A., Washington, 1962; PhD, A.N.U., Canberra, Australia, 1969. Catholic priest Divine Word Missionaries, Madang, Papua New Guinea, 1961—; mem. Anthropos Inst., St. Augustin, 1970-85; dir. Divine Word Inst., Madang, 1983—. Author: numerous pubs. on lang. of Madang Dist., 1962-84. Research grant Swiss Nat. Funds, Berne, 1971, 80, UNESCO, Paris, 1985. Office: Research Ctr Divine Word Inst, PO Box 483, Madang Papua New Guinea

ZHANG, CUN-QUAN, mathematician; b. Shanghai, China, Aug. 4, 1952; came to Can., 1982; s. Ren-Gui and Yun-Yu (Tang) Z.; m. Hui-Min Yang, Jan. 20, 1982; PhD, Simon Fraser U., BC, 1987. M.Sc., Qufu Tchrs. Coll., Shandong, China, 1982. asst. prof., W.Va. U., 1987—. Worker, technician Wuhu Light Industry Machine Bldg. Factory, Wafu, Anhui, China, 1977-78; asst. researcher Inst. System Sci., Chinese Acad. Scis., Beijing, 1981; asst. prof., Simon Fraser U., 1986-87. Contbr. articles to profl. jours. Mem. Chinese Ops. Research Soc., Chinese System Scis. Soc., Chinese Graph Theory Soc., Am. Math. Soc., Can. Math. Soc. Office: West Virginia Univ Dept Math Morgantown WV 26506

ZHANG, JIN HAO, mathematician, educator; b. Jiang Su, People's Republic of China, Dec. 1, 1942; s. Si-Wei Zhang and Pi-Kun Wu; m. Ning LIng Xia, Feb. 23, 1973; 1 child, Zhen Hui. Grad., Fudan U., Shanghai, Republic of China, 1965. Asst. prof. Fudan U., 1965-67; lectr. Fudan U., Shanghai, 1977-87, assoc. prof., 1987—; technician Wujing Chem. Plant, Shanghai, 1967-77. Contbr. articles to profl. jours. Grantee Fudan Sci. Found., 1986, Nation Sci. Found., 1987. Mem. Chinese Math. Soc., Am. Math. Soc. Office: Fudan U Dept Math, Handan Rd 220, 201903 Shanghai People's Republic China

ZHANG, SHI-SHENG, mathematician; b. Qu'jing, Yunnan, Peoples Republic of China, Dec. 25, 1935; s. Hai-qing Chang and He-nan Wang; m. Zhou Li-hui, Feb. 11, 1959; children: Chagn-jun, Chang-ying, Chang-hui. BS, Sichuan U., Chengdu, Peoples Republic of China, 1958. Teaching asst. Sichuan U., Chengdu, 1958-62, asst. prof. math., 1983, prof., 1987—; prof. math. Xuzou Tchrs. Coll., Peoples Republic of China, 1984-85, Guizou Normal U., Gui'yang, Peoples Republic of China, 1986. Author: Fixed Point Theory, 1984, Integral Equations, 1987; contbr. articles to profl. jours. Grantee, Nat. Natural Sci. Found. of China, B0ijing, 1984, 88, award Sichuan Com. of Sci., Chengdu, 1986, 87. Mem. Chinese Math. Soc., Am. Math. Soc., Probability and Statis. Soc. China. Office: Sichuan U Dept Math, Chengdu 610064, Peoples Republic of China

ZHANG, SHUNIAN, mathematics educator, researcher; b. Shanghai, China, Aug. 29, 1940; s. Lianfang and Rixiang (Sun) Z.; m. Xinglin Zhang, May 1, 1964; children—Hao, Liang. Grad. Anhui U., Hefei, Anhui, China, 1962. Asst. dept. math. Anhui U., Hefei, Anhui, China, 1962-78, lectr., 1978-84, assoc. prof., 1984—; research assoc. U. Toronto, Ont., Can., 1980-82; lectr. Anhua U., 1982-84; vis. assoc. prof. So. Ill. U., Carbondale, 1984-86; prof. Anhui U., 1986—. Author: Annals of Differential Equations, 1985. Named hon. citizen of Okla., 1985. Mem. Math. Soc. China, Am. Math. Soc. Avocation: stamp collecting. Office: Anhui U., Dept Math, Hefei Anhui People's Republic of China

ZHANG, ZHONGFU, mathematician, educator; b. Henan, People's Republic of China, June 7, 1938; s. Guangxue Zhang and Mian Li; m. Feng Daoxian, Sept. 5, 1965; children: Yan, Hui, Chao, Ming. BS, Lanzhou U., People's Republic of China, 1962. Teaching asst. Lanzhou Railway Coll., People's Republic of China, 1962-78, lectr., 1978-85, prof., 1985—. Author: Basic Knowledge of Management Mathematics, 1987; contbr. numerous articles to profl. jours. (province and ministry 1st prize, 1985, 86); editor Jour. Math. Teaching and Research, Gansu, 1983, Journ. Lanzhou Railway Coll., Gansu, 1985; reviewer Math. Reviews, USA, 1985; examiner Math. and Physics Jour., Wuhan, 1984. Mem. China Graph Theory Soc., China Combined Math. Soc., Gansu Math. Soc. (mem. exec. com.), Gansu Ops. Research Soc. Home: Lanzhou 730071, People's Republic of China Office: Lanzhou Railway Coll, Lanzhou, Gansu 730071, People's Republic of China

ZHANG, ZICUN, economist; b. Apr. 5, 1918; m. Zhang Wenya, 1944; 2 children. Educated Qinghua U., Beijing, U. Cambridge. Instr. dept. econs. Qinghua U., 1940-43; economist stats. div., research dept. IMF, 1947-48; sr. econ. affairs officer econ. stability sect. UN, 1948, chief developing areas sect., 1955, dep. dir. Centre for Devel. Planning, Projections and Policies, 1963, dir. Div. Pub. Adminstrn. and Fin., 1973, sr. adviser Dept. Tech. Coop. for Devel., 1980; dep. dir. Fin. Research Inst., People's Bank of China, 1980; exec. dir. for China, IMF, 1980-85. Author: Cyclical Movements in the Balance of Payments, 1949; contbr. articles to profl. jours. Home: 36 Kilmer Rd Larchmont NY 10538 *

ZHANG AIPING, former state councilor People's Republic of China; b. Da County, Sichuan Province, 1908; m. Li Youlan. Joined Chinese Communist Party, 1928; alt. mem. Cen. Exec. Com., Soviet Republic of China, 1934; dir. polit. dept. 3d Red Army Corps, Long March, 1934-35; acting comdr. Cavalry Regiment Mil. Commn., Chinese Communist Party, 1936; led 4th Column of 6th Detachment, New 4th Army, 1938, comdr. Huaibei Corps, 1939, dep. comdr. 3d div., 1941; chief of staff 3d Field Army, 1948-54; comdr. 7th Army Corps, 1952-54; vet. of army and party cadre; mem. mil. cadre in East China, 1949-54; dep. chief of gen. staff People's Liberation Army, 1954-67, 77-82; alt. mem. 8th Cen. Com. Chinese Communist Party, 1958; criticized and ousted from office in Cultural Revolution, 1967; chmn. Sci. and Technol. Commn. for Nat. Def., 1975-82; mem. 11th Cen. Com. Chinese Communist Party, 1977, mem. Standing Com., 5th Nat. People's Congress, 1978-82, mem. Presidium, 12th Cen. Com., 1982; vice-premier, 1980-82; minister of def., 1982-88; state councillor, 1982-88. Address: State Council, Beijing People's Republic of China *

ZHANG JIE, writer; b. Beijing, Apr. 27, 1937; m. Y.Y. Sun; 1 child, Tang Di. Student, People's U., Beijing. Author: Leaden Wings, 1981 (trans. into German, French, English, Swedish, Norwegian, Finish, Dutch, Danish, Brazilian, Spanish, Russian, Portugese), The Ark, 1981 (also trans.), numerous short story collections. Recipient 3 nat. awards for short stories, 1978, 79, 83, 1 nat. award for novelette, 1983-84, 1 nat. award for novel, 1983-1985. Mem. Chinese Assn. Writers, Beijing Polit. Cons. Conf., Internat. PEN. Communist. Office: Beijing Writers' Assn, Beijing Peoples Republic of China

ZHAO, BAO-XU, political science educator, educational administrator; b. Beijing, Nov. 18, 1922; s. Bo-Shan Zhao and Wen-Jin Zhang; m. Si-Kou Chen, May 4, 1946; children: Chen, Qing, Yang. BA, Peking U., 1948. Teaching asst. Peking U., Beijing, 1948-52, lectr., 1952-60, assoc. prof., 1960-83, prof., 1983—, chmn. dept. internat. politics, 1960-66, 78-83, dir. Inst. Afro-Asian Studies, 1973-86; disting. vis. scholar Inst. East Asian Studies, U. Calif., Berkeley, 1981-83; dir. Res. Ctr. Social Devel. of Contemporary China, 1988—; vis. prof. Free Univ. Berlin, 1983-84; v.p. Cen. Acad. Socialism, Beijing, 1985-87. Author: The Revival of Political Science in China, 1983, Contemporary Chinese Poitics, 1985; chief editor: Introduction to Political Science, 1982. Mem. Internat. Polit. Sci. Assn. (exec. council 1985—), Chinese Polit. Sci. Assn. (exec. council 1980—), Chinese Assn. Global Ethnic Studies (v.p. 1978—), Chinese Soc. Asian and African Studies (council mem. 1986—), Chinese Assn. Internat. Understanding (council mem. 1980—), Bejing Assn. Polit. Sci. and Pub. Adminstrn. Studies (pres. 1988—). Office: Peking U, Dept Internat Politics, 100871, Beijing Peoples Republic China

ZHAO, HONGZHOU, physicist, educator, researcher; b. Wen County, Henan, China, Apr. 22, 1941; s. Tongwen and Caizi (Yang) S.; m. Liying Li, Oct. 1, 1974; 1 child, Yu. Student, Nankai U., Tianjin, 1959-64, Peking U., 1964-66. Research Inst. Physics, Beijing, 1974-82; researcher, vice-prof. Inst. High-Energy Physics, Beijing, 1982-85; dir., prof. China Inst. of Sci. of Sci., Beijing, 1985-87, v.p. China Acad. Mgmt. Scis., 1987—; hon. prof. Ctr. for Sci. of Sci., Beijing, 1985—. Author: Theory of Science Capacity, 1984 (award of excellence 1986), Review of Big Science, 1988, Science and Revolution, 1988, Science and Potential Science (in press); mem. editorial bd. Scientometrics, Technology Analysis and Strategic Management. Mem. China Assn. for Sci. of Sci. and Sci. Policy (v.p. 1986—), China Assn. Personnel and Talents. Home: Jia 2, Sha Tan Bei Jie, Beijing People's Republic of China Office: China Inst of Sci of Sci, Jia 2, Sha Tan Bei Jie, 100009 Beijing People's Republic of China

ZHAO, XIN-AN, physicist; b. People's Republic of China, Jan. 28, 1941; s. Zu-You and Ru-Ju (Wang) Z.; m. Ya-Qin, Jan. 28, 1968. BS, Fudan U., Shanghai, People's Republic of China, 1965. Research assoc. Shanghai Inst. Metallurgy Acad. Scis. of China, 1965-84, 88—; vis. assoc. Calif. Inst. Tech., Pasadena, Calif., 1984-87. Mem. Chinese Inst. Electronics, Material Research Soc., The Böhmische Phys. Soc. Home: 1774 22 N Sichuan Rd, Shanghai People's Republic of China Office: Shanghai Inst Metallurgy, 865 Changning Rd, Shanghai 200050, People's Republic of China

ZHAO ZIYANG, government official People's Republic of China, b. 1919, Huaxian County, Henan Province, China; m. Liang Boqi; 5 children. Joined Chinese Communist Party, 1938; mem. standing com. South China Subbureau, Chinese Communist Party Cen. Com., 1950, sec. gen., 1952-54, dir. Rural Work Dept., 1953-55, 3d sec., 1954-55; mem. People's Council, Guangdong Province, 1955, dep. sec. Communist Party, 1955-56, sec., 1957-61, 73-74, 2nd sec., 1961-65, 1st sec., 1965, 74-75, vice chmn. Revolutionary Com., 1972-74, chmn. 1975; polit. commissar Guangdong mil. dist. People's Liberation Army, 1964; sec. Cen.-South bur. Chinese Communist Party Cen. Com., 1965-67; criticized and ousted from office in Cultural Revolution, 1967; vice chmn. Nei Monggol Revolutionary Com., 1971; sec. Chinese Communist Party Nei Monggol, 1971; chmn. Guangdong Revolutionary Com., 1972; mem. 10th Cen. Com., Chinese Communist Party, 1973, alt. mem. Politburo, 11th Cen. Com., 1977-79, mem., 1979, mem. Standing Com. of Politburo, 1980—, mem. Politburo 12th Cen. Com., 1982—, sec. gen., 1982, gen. sec., 1987—, first vice chmn. mil. affairs commn., 1987—; 1st sec. Communist Party, Sichuan Province, 1975-80; chmn. Sichuan Revolutionary Com., 1975-79; exec. chmn. 5th Nat. Com., Chinese People's Polit. Consultative Conf., vice chmn., 1978; 1st polit. commissar Chengdu mil. dist. People's Liberation Army, 1976-80; vice premier then premier of State Council, 1980-87; minister Commn. for Econ. Reconstrn., from 1982. Address: Chinese Communist Party, Office of Gen Sec, Beijing People's Republic of China *

ZHENG TUOBIN, government official. Trade counselor Chinese Embassy, Moscow, 1960-64; dep. dir. dept. Ministry of Foreign Trade, 1972, dir. third dept., 1973-77; vice minister of foreign trade 1978-81, minister of fgn. trade, 1981-82, vice minister fgn. econ. relations and trade, 1982-85, dep. sec. party group fgn. econ. relations and trade, 1983—, minister fgn. econ. relations and trade, 1985—; leader trade dels. to Europe, N. Am., Asia; mem. 12th cen. com. Chinese Communist Party, 1982; dep. dir. com. for commemorating 40th anniversary of UN. Office: Ministry Fgn Econ Relations, and Trade, Beijing Peoples Republic of China *

ZHENGYU, NI, international association judge; b. Wujiang, Jiangsu, Peoples Republic China, July 28, 1906; s. Diming Ni and Langfen Dzang; m. Fengzhen Ni; 1 child, Naixian. BA, Chitz U., Shanghai; B in Laws, Soochow U., Shanghai; JD, Johns Hopkins U.; LLD (hon.), Osmania U., Hyderbad, India. Prof. law Soochow U., Shanghai, 1948-54; legal counsel ambassador office Ministry Fgn. Affairs, Beijing, 1956-84; judge Internat. Ct. Justice, The Hague, The Netherlands, 1985—; lectr. law sch. Soochow U., Great China U., Cahaoyang Law Coll., Chongqing, Peoples Republic China, Soochow-Shanghai Union of Coll. Law and Commerce, Chongqing, 1930-45; mem. internat. prosecution section Internat. Mil. Tribunal for the Far East, Tokyo, 1946-48, internat. law commn., UN, 1982-84, nat. com. Chinese People's Consultative Council, 1959-84; legal counsel Chinese del. 27th UN Gen. Assembly, 1972, Chinese del. sea bed com. UN, 1972-73, Chinese del. 3d Conf. Law and the Sea, Caracas, Venezuela, 1974, Geneva, 1975, 82, N.Y.C., 1977, 81. Contbr. articles to profl. jours. Mem. Chinese Soc. Internat. Law (bd. dirs. 1980—), Chinese Soc. Oceanography (hon. pres. 1985—). Office: care/Internat Ct Justice, Peace Palace, 2517 KJ The Hague The Netherlands

ZHIVKOV, TODOR KHRISTOV, President of Bulgaria; b. Pravets, Bulgaria, Sept. 7, 1911; student Secondary Graphical Sch. and High Sch., Sofia; grad. Sofia Polygraphic Sch., 1932; m. Mara Malleeva (dec.); children: Ludmilla, Vladimir. Printer; joined Young Communist League, 1928, head, 1934-41, joined Bulgarian Communist Party, 1932, head, 1934-41; active organizer partisan movement in Sofia Dist. during anti-fascist struggle in Bulgaria; candidate mem. Cen. Com. of Bulgarian Communist Party, 1945, full mem., 1948; 1st sec. Sofia Mcpl. Com., 1948-49; alt. mem., party sec. Bulgarian Communist Party, 1950, mem. polit. bur. Cen. Com., 1951—, 1st sec., 1954-81, gen. sec., 1981—; dep. Nat. Assembly of People's Republic of Bulgaria, 1945—, mem. presidium, 1946-62; prime minister, chmn. Council of Ministers of Bulgaria, 1962-71; pres. State Council, 1971—. Author many works from 1937-77, 25 vols. including vols. on Bulgarian economy, on arts, sci. and culture, others. Address: Office of Chairman State Council, Durzhaven Suvet, Sofia Bulgaria *

ZHOU, GUOZHEN, fine arts educator; b. Hunan, China, July 11, 1931; s. Wanlong and He (Zhao Xiu) Z.; children from previous marriage: Shi, Fang. Student, Suzhou Art Sch., People's Republic of China, 1950-51; B, Cen. Acad. Art, Beijing, 1954. Ceramic artist Ceramic Research Inst., Jin De Zheng, People's Republic China, 1954-76; lectr. Ceramic Research Inst., Jin De Zheng, 1976-82, prof., 1982—. Author: Zhou guo shen Ceramics Art, 1985 (1st prize 1986); sculptor Snow Leopard, 1982 (1st prize 1984), Black Monkey, 1985. Rep. JingXi Province People's Cong., 1978—, vice chmn. standing com., 1987. Mem. Chinese Artists Assn. (vice chmn. Jiang Xi br. 1986—), Sculptors Soc. Jiang Xi Province (pres. 1985—). Office: Jingdezhen Ceramic Inst, Jing De Zhen, Jiangxi Province People's Republic of China

ZHOU, ZUO LING, mathematics educator, researcher; b. Shenyang, Peoples Republic of China, Apr. 19, 1938; s. Lian Fang (Zhang) Z.; m. Bingqin Wang, Feb. 20, 1976; 1 child, Lei. Grad., Beijing U., 1962. Student math. dept. Beijing U., 1956-62; asst. lectr. math. Zhongshan U., Guangzhou, 1962-81; lectr. Jinan U., Guangzhou, 1981-84; lectr., prof. computer sci. dept. Zhongshan U., Guangzhou, 1984—; part-time prof. The Research Ctr. of Nonlinear Systems, Nanjing U., 1987—. Contbr. over 20 articles to math. jours.; mem. editorial bd. Chinese Quar. Jour. Math., 1985—; reviewer Math. Revs., 1986—. Recipient 3 awards Guangdong Province, 1981, 82, 86, Ministry of Edn. award, Beijing, 1986; grantee Found. of Zhongshan U. Advanced Research Ctr., Hong Kong, 1985—. Mem. Chinese Math. Soc., Am. Math. Soc. Office: Zhongshan U Dept Computer Sci, Guangzhou Peoples Republic of China

ZHU, TONG BO, English language and literature educator, translator, specialist in modern western literary criticism; b. Hengyang, China, Feb. 6, 1938; s. Hua Ting and De Fen (Ding) Zhu; m. Kuang Hui, Feb. 11, 1967; children—Xiao Fan, Xiao Yong. A.B. cum laude, ZhongShan U., Guangzhou, 1959; vis. scholar Harvard U., 1980-81; sr. vis. scholar Cambridge U., Eng., 1981-82. Instr. English, Sichuan U., Chengdu, 1959-65, lectr. English, 1966-76, dir. grad. studies English and Am. lit., 1977—, assoc. prof. English and lit. 1983-88, prof. English and Am. Lit., 1988—; chmn. dept., 1984—, dir. Ctr. for Am. Studies, 1984—. Author: Robert Frost and his Poetic Writing, 1983; Modern Western Criticism: a Historical Outline, 1985. Editor: Modern English and American Criticism, 1982; Modern English and American Prose, 1978; co-translator A Dictionary of Modern Critical Terms (ed. by Roger Fowler), 1987, The Ascent of Man (by Jacob Bronowski), 1987, Women in Love (by D.H. Lawrence), 1988. Mem. Translators Assn. (v.p. Sichuan br. 1984—), Nat. Discipline Com. on Coll. Textbooks and Studies in Fng. Langs. and Lits., 1984—China's Am. Lit. Studies Assn. (bd. dirs. 1985—), MLA. Avocations: travel; classical music; violin playing. Office: Dept Fgn Langs, Sichuan Univ, Chengdu People's Republic of China

ZHUCHENKO, ALEXANDER, geneticist; b. Essentuky, Stavropol, USSR, Sept. 25, 1935; s. Alexander Georgievich and Taisia Alexandrovna (Nikolayeva) Z.; m. Galina Georgievna Khorkva, 1957; children: Alexander, Natalia. D in Biology, Inst. Gen. Genetics, Acad. Scis., Moscow, 1974. Sr. asst. Exptl. Agrl. Sta., Kagul, Moldavia, USSR, 1960-63; mgr. state farm, Kagul, Moldavia, USSR, 1963-66; dir. Inst. of Irrigated Farming and Vegetable Growing, Tiraspol, Moldavia, 1967-76; v.p. Acad. Scis. Moldavia, Kishinev, 1976-77, pres., 1977—; dir. Inst. Ecol. Genetics of Acad. Scis. of Moldavia, 1985-88. Author: Genetics of Tomatoes, 1973, Ecological Genetics, 1980, Adaptive Potential in Cultivated Plants, 1988; contbr. more than 300 articles to profl. jours. Recipient Gold medal Acad. Scis. of Bratislava, Czechoslovakia, 1985. Mem. USSR Acad. Scis., Moldavian Acad. Scis., All-Union Agrl. Acad. (Vavilov Gold medal 1974), German Dem. Rep. Agrl. Acad. Home: Lazo 26 23, 277012 Kishinev USSR Office: Inst Ecol Genetics, Lesnaya 20, 277018 Kishinev USSR

ZHU RONGJI, mayor; b. Changsha, People's Republic of China, 1928. Grad. electrical engring., Qinghua U., Beijing, 1951. Dir. Tech. Transformation Bur. State Econ. Commn., 1982, vice minister, 1983-88; dep. sec. mcpl. com. Chinese Communist Party, 1988; mayor City of Shanghai, 1988—. Mem. Indsl. Econs. Soc. (v.p. 1984). Office: Office of Mayor, Shanghai People's Republic of China *

ZIA-UL-HAQ, MOHAMMED, president of Pakistan; b. Jullundur, East Punjab, India, Aug. 12, 1924; student Dehra Doon Mil. Acad.; grad. Command and Staff Coll., Queta Pakistan, 1955; attended U.S. Command and Gen. Staff Coll. Ft. Leavenworth; married; 2 sons, 3 daus. Served as lt. col. Pakistani Army; instr. Command and Staff Coll., 1964-66; comdr. cav. regt., 1966-68, comdr. armored brigade, 1969, comdr. armored div., 1972; corps comdr. Pakistan Army, 1976-77, gen., chief Army staff, 1976-88; chief martial law adminstr., 1977-78; pres. of Pakistan, 1978-88; minister of Cabinet Affairs, CMLA Secretariat and Establishment Div.; minister of Sci. and Tech., from 1981; minister of States and Frontier Regions, from 1981. Adv. to the Royal Jordanian Army, 1969-81. Decorated by King Hussein of Jordan. Died Aug. 17, 1988. Address: Office of Pres, Islamabad Pakistan *

ZICHEK, MELVIN EDDIE, retired clergyman, educator; b. Lincoln, Nebr., May 5, 1918; s. Eddie and Agnes (Varga) Z.; A.B., Nebr. Central Coll., 1942; M.A., U. Nebr., 1953; D.Litt., McKinley-Roosevelt Ednl. Inst., 1955; m. Dorothy Virginia Patrick, May 28, 1942; 1 dau., Shannon Elaine. Ordained to ministry Christian Ch., 1942; minister Christian chs., Brock, Nebr., 1941, Ulysses, Nebr., 1942-43, Elmwood, Nebr., 1943-47, Central City, Nebr., 1947-83, ret., 1983; rural tchr., Merrick County, Nebr., 1937-40; prin. Alvo (Nebr.) Consol. High Sch., 1943-47; supt. Archer (Nebr.) Pub. Schs., 1948-57; head dept. English and speech Central City (Nebr.) High Sch., 1957-63; supt. Marquette (Nebr.) Consol. Schs., 1963-79. Served as chaplain's asst. AUS, 1942. Mem. Internat. Platform Assn., Disciples of Christ Hist. Soc., Nat. Sch. Adminstrs. Assn. Club: Buffy. Home: 2730 North Rd Grand Island NE 68803

ZICK, LEONARD OTTO, accountant, manufacturing executive, financial consultant; b. St. Joseph, Mich., Jan. 16, 1905; s. Otto J. and Hannah (Heyn) Z.; student Western State U., Kalamazoo; m. Anna Essig, June 27, 1925 (dec. May 1976); children—Rowene (Mrs. A. C. Neidow), Arlene (Mrs. Thomas Anton), Constance Mae (Mrs. Hilary Snell), Shirley Ann (Mrs. John Vander Ley) (dec.); m. 2d, Genevieve Evans, Nov. 3, 1977. Sr. ptnr. firm Zick, Campbell & Rose Accts., South Bend, Ind., 1928-48; sec.-treas. C. M. Hall Lamp Co., Detroit, 1948-51, pres. 1951-54, chmn. bd., 1954-56; pres., treas., dir. Allen Electric & Equipment Co. (now Allen Group, Inc.), Kalamazoo, 1954-57, pres., treas., dir. The Lithibar Co., Holland, Mich., 1957-61; fin. v.p., treas., dir. Crampton Mfg. Co., 1961-63; mgr. corp. fin. dept. Manley, Bennett, McDonald & Co., Detroit, 1963-68; mgr. Leonard O. Zick & Assocs., Holland, 1968-88; former dir. Eberhard's Foods, Inc., Grand Rapids. Former mem. Mich. Republican Central Com.; trustee YMCA Found., Clearwater, Fla. Mem. Nat. Assn. Accts. (past nat. v.p., dir.), Mich. Self Insurers Assn. (past pres.), Fin. Execs. Inst., Stuart Cameron McLeod Soc. (past pres.). Lutheran. Clubs: Peninsular (Grand Rapids); Holland (Mich.) Country; Union League (Chgo.); Macawtawa Yacht; East Bay Country (Largo, Fla.). Home: 1609 F-225 Country Club Dr Largo FL 34641-2245 also: 99 W 11th St Holland MI 49423

ZIEGLER, EDWARD NELSON, chemical engineer, educator; b. Bronx, N.Y., Aug. 15, 1938; s. Louis S. and Elsie H. (Soupowitz) Z.; B.Chem. Engring., CCNY, 1960; M.S., Northwestern U., 1962, Ph.D., 1964; m. Phyllis Marion Dean, May 25, 1974; children—Kenneth Louis, Kaitlin Elizabeth. Faculty mem. Poly. U., 1965—, asso. prof. chem. engring.,

1969—; with Argonne (Ill.) Nat. Lab., 1962-63, Exxon Research & Engring. Co., Linden, N.J. 1964-65, Brookhaven Nat. Lab., Upton, N.Y., summers 1974-80, Consol. Edison Co. N.Y., 1980—; cons. to govt., industry, 1969—. Mem. Bklyn. Clean Air Com., 1968-75. Mem. Am. Inst. Chem. Engrs., Air Pollution Control Assn., Sigma Xi. Recipient G. Edwin White award, 1960; Omega Chi Epsilon Service award, 1979. Contbr. numerous articles to profl. jours. Editor: Comtex Sci. Research Report Series-Environmental Engineering, 1981-83, (with J.R. Pfafflin) Ency. Environ. Sci. and Engring., 1975, 2d edit., 1983, Advances in Environ. Sci. and Engring., 1979-80; editorial bd. Water Air Soil Pollution, 1972—. Home: 2 Pierrepont St Brooklyn NY 11201 Office: Poly U Dept Chem Engring 333 Jay St Brooklyn NY 11201

ZIEGLER, JAMES RUSSELL, computer consultant; b. Warren, Pa., Oct. 10, 1922; s. LeRoy Curtis and Daisy (Gesin) Z.; B.S. in Elec. Engring., Pa. State U., 1943, M.A. in Math., 1948; m. Maxine Evelyn Hogue, Feb. 10, 1952 (dec. Nov. 1968); children—Evalinde Aurelia, Charlotte Elaine, Curtis Wayman, Bruce Allan; m. 2d, Florence M. Bowler, 1969 (div. 1975); 1 son, Scott. UHF wave guide research Norden Corp., N.Y.C., 1943-44; instr. math. Pa. State Coll., 1946-48; instr. math. U. Calif. at Los Angeles, 1948-54, research asso., statistician tchrs. characteristics study sponsored by Am. Council on Edn., 1951-54; mgr. programming services electronic computers Nat. Cash Register Co., Hawthorne, Calif., 1954-68; pres. Turn-Key Computer Applications, 1968-75; dir. So. Fed. Savs. & Loan Assn., Los Angeles, 1968-69; adv. dir. Coast Fed. Savs. & Loan Assn., Los Angeles, 1969-74; sr. cons. analyst NCR Co., San Diego, 1975-78, San Diego Cash Register Co., 1978-80; computer cons. Yemen Arab Republic Nat. Water and Sewerage Authority, 1980-87; tech. cons. Office Naval Research Study; data processing cons. psychol. research projects U. So. Calif., also U. Utah. Served with USMCR, 1944-46; PTO. Mem. Tau Beta Pi, Sigma Tau, Eta Kappa Nu. Republican. Methodist. Mason. Author: Time Sharing Data Processing Systems, 1967; also numerous articles. Home: 1050 Pinecrest Ave Escondido CA 92025 Office: PO Box 1709, Sana'a Yemen Arab Republic

ZIEGLER, MARCUS NIKOLAUS, cameraman; b. Vienna, Austria, Sept. 23, 1963; s. Hanns and Anna (Goetz) Z. Grad., Chemistry Sch., Vienna, 1982. Freelance camera asst. Fed. Republic Germany, 1983-87, freelance cameraman, 1987—. Dir. photography film Faith and Greed, 1985, Bad Luck, 1988; dir. photography, dir. film Oder Wie Auch Immer, 1987. Home: Leopoldstrasse 69, 8000 Munich 40 Federal Republic Germany

ZIEMANN, ROBERT LEWIS, accountant; b. Southwick, Idaho, Jan. 23, 1927; s. Gus H. and Wilda (Keeney) Z.; student Oreg. State Coll., 1945-46, U. Idaho, 1948-49; B.B.A., U. Houston, 1952. Accountant, Briscoe, House & Stovall, C.P.A.s, Houston, 1954, Mattison & Riquelmy, C.P.A.s, Houston, 1954-61, Harris, Kerr, Forster & Co., C.P.A.s, Houston, 1961-65; self-employed as C.P.A., Houston, 1965—. Served with USAAF, 1946-47. Elk. Home: 14803 Cypress Meadow Cypress TX 77429 also: PO Box 66681 Houston TX 77266 Office: 7709 Long Point Houston TX 77055

ZIERDT, CHARLES HENRY, microbiologist; b. Pitts., Apr. 24, 1922; s. Conrad Henry and Nancy Leora (Harshberger) Z.; m. Margaret May Wise, June 1, 1942 (div. 1962); children—Charles Henry, Jr., Carolyn, Douglas, Richard; m. Willadene Smith, Sept. 30, 1967. B.S., Pa. State U., 1943; M.S., U. Mich., 1945; Ph.D., George Washington U., 1967. Research assoc. Parke-Davis & Co., Detroit, 1945-48; microbiologist Henry Ford Hosp., Detroit, 1948-53, USPHS, Detroit, 1953-56; staff microbiologist NIH, Bethesda, Md., 1956—. Scientist sponsor U. Md., 1975—; instr. Found. Advanced Edn. Scis., Bethesda, 1978—. Author: Glucose Nonfermenting Gram Negative Bacteria in Clinical Microbiology, 1978; Non-fermentative Gram Negative Rods: Laboratory Identification and Clinical Aspects, 1985; McGraw-Hill Yearbook of Science and Technology, 1986; Diagnostic Procedures for Bacterial Infections, 1987; contbr. over 100 articles to profl. jours. Patentee in field. Active PTA. Fellow Am. Acad. Microbiology; mem. Am. Soc. Microbiology (chpt. pres. 1976), U.S. Fedn. Culture Collections (membership chmn. 1985), Mensa. Republican. Club: Model A Ford Am. (chpt. pres. 1985) (Fairfax, Va.). Avocations: gardening; antique car restoration. Home: 4100 Norbeck Rd Rockville MD 20853 Office: NIH Bethesda MD 20892

ZIESENISS, HUBERT FREDERICK, publishing company executive; b. N.Y.C., Apr. 16, 1941; s. Charles O. and Claude (David) Z.; 3 children: Christopher, Peter, Caroline. Grad. Ecole des Hautes Etudes Commerciales, Paris, 1964; M.B.A., U. Pa., 1966. Cons. Arthur D. Little, Inc., Cambridge, Mass., 1966-71; mng. dir. Levi Strauss Belgium, Brussels, 1971-74; mng. dir. Groupe Expansion SA, Paris, 1974—. Mem. Fedn. Nat. de la Presse Specialisee (pres. 1981-87), Fedn. Nat. De La Presse Francaise (v.p. 1980-87). Roman Catholic. Clubs: St. Cloud Country, Automobile Club de France (Paris). Office: Groupe Expansion SA, 67 Ave Wagram, 75017 Paris France

ZIFF, LLOYD RICHARD, lawyer; b. N.Y.C., Mar. 9, 1942; s. George and Lillian (Gisnet) Z.; m. M. Morrow Cox, Jan. 28, 1967; children: Tina Marie, M. Courtney, Robert G. Grad., Peekskill Mil. Acad.; BA, U. Pa., 1968, JD magna cum laude, 1971. Bar: Pa. 1971, U.S. Supreme Ct. 1975. Assoc. Pepper, Hamilton & Scheetz, Phila., 1971-77, ptnr., 1977—; teaching fellow U. Pa. Sch. Law, 1971, lectr., 1981-82; faculty Acad. Advocacy, 1980—; mem. Devitt implementation com. U.S. Dist. Ct. (ea. dist.) Pa., 1980-84, mem. continuing legal edn. com., 1985—; co-chmn. Seminar on Complex Litigation, 1983. Contbr. articles to legal jours. Mem. Kent State U. Task Force, Pres.'s Commn. on Campus Unrest, (Ohio), 1970; mem. Inter-disciplinary Com. on Child Abuse S.E. Pa., 1973-75; mem. adv. com. Family Resources Ctr., St. Christopher's Hosp. for Children, Phila., 1976; chmn. Phila. Bail Project, 1969; counsel Phila. Vietnam Vets. Meml. Fund, 1985—. Served with U.S. Army, 1965-67. Warwick Found. scholar U. Pa., 1971; Salzburg Seminar fellow Am. Studies-Am. Law and Legal Instns., (Austria), 1978. Mem. ABA, Pa. Bar Assn., Phila. Bar Assn. (chmn. election procedures com. 1976, chmn. spl. com. on admission attys. to fed. practice 1986, chair Fidelity award com. 1987, chair fed. bench bar conf., 1988), Order of Coif, Chapel of the Four Chaplains, Legion of Honor. Office: Pepper Hamilton & Scheetz 3000 Two Logan Sq 18th and Arch Sts Philadelphia PA 19103-2799

ZIFFREN, LESTER, international public relations consultant; b. Rock Island, Ill., Apr. 30, 1906; s. Davis J. and Rose Ziffren; m. Edythe Wurtzel, May 21, 1937 (dec. 1977); 1 dau. B.J., U. Mo., 1927. Various positions UPI, 1927-37; writer, prodn. exec. 20th Century Fox Studios, Beverly Hills, Calif., 1937-42; dir. Office of Coordinator Inter-Am. Affairs, Santiago, Chile, 1942-45; 1st sec., pub. affairs officer USIA, Am. Embassy, Bogota, Colombia, Santiago, Chile, 1951-54; dir. pub. relations Braden Copper Co. subs. Kennecott Copper Corp., Chile, 1954-60; dir. pub. relations, advt. Kennecott Copper Corp., N.Y., 1961-71; internat. pub. relations cons., N.Y., 1971—, v.p. treas., 1985—; ; cons. Kennecott, Peabody Coal Co., Minerec Corp., Cerro Corp. Decorated comdr. Order Merit, Bernardo O'Higgins, Republic of Chile, 1946. Mem. Am. Fgn. Service Assn., Americas Found. (v.p., treas. 1985—), Pub. Relations Soc. Am., Diplomatic and Ret. Officers, Soc. Silurians, Bolivarian Soc. U.S. (treas., v.p.), Pan Am. Soc. U.S. (treas.), N.Am.-Chilean C. of C. (exec. dir.). Clubs: Nat. Press, Army, Navy (Washington); Overseas Press (N.Y.C.). Home and Office: 220 E 81st St New York NY 10028

ZIGGELAAR, AUGUST, physics lecturer, priest; b. Amsterdam, The Netherlands, Jan. 17, 1928; arrived in Denmark, 1952; s. Antoon and Catharina (Lemkes) Z. PhD, U. Copenhagen, 1971. Ordained priest Roman Cath. Ch., 1961. Physics tchr. various schs., Maastricht and Amsterdam, Holland, 1961-63; lectr. U. Aarhus, Denmark, 1964-68; sr. lectr. Kenyatta U. Coll., Nairobi, Kenya, 1975-76; assoc. prof. Sch. Ednl. Studies, Copenhagen, 1968—; mem. editorial bd. European Jour. Physics, Bristol, Eng., 1983-87. Author: Le Physicien I.G. Pardies (1636-1673), 1971; Fr. de Aguilón (1567-1617), 1982; contbr. articles to profl. jours. Mem. Group Internat. Research Edn. of Physics, Soc. History for Exact Scis. (sec. 1983—). Home: Skt Kjeldsgade 3, DK-2100 Copenhagen Denmark Office: Royal Danish Sch Ednl Studies, Emdrupvej 115 B, DK-2400 Copenhagen NV Denmark

ZIGUN, SYLVIA HELENE, psychotherapist, health educator; b. N.Y.C., July 28, 1934; d. David J. and Anna (Felenstein) Moscovitz; m. Charles Zigun, June 9, 1957; children—Jeffrey, Benjamin. B.A., Brown U., 1954; M.N., Yale U., 1957; M.S., U. Bridgeport, 1980; postgrad. Union Grad. Sch., 1981—. R.N., Conn Psychotherapist, Psychotherapy Assocs. of Fairfield, Conn., 1979—; cons. State of Conn. div. ARC health nursing programs, 1974-75; chmn. nursing services Southeastern Fairfield chpt. ARC, 1974-76, childbirth educator, 1974-76. Mem. Internat. Acad. Preventive Medicine, Internat. Acad. Bariatric Medicine, Sigma Xi, Phi Beta Kappa. Office: Psychotherapy Assocs Fairfield 400 Post Rd Fairfield CT 06430

ZIL, JOHN STEPHEN, psychiatrist, physiologist; b. Chgo., Oct. 8, 1947; s. Stephen Vincent and Marilyn Charlotte (Jackson) Zilius; 1 child, Charlene. BS magna cum laude, U. Redlands, 1969; MD, U. Calif., San Diego, 1973; MPH, Yale U., 1977; JD, Jefferson Coll., 1985. Intern, resident in psychiatry and neurology U. Ariz., 1973-75; fellow in psychiatry, advanced fellow in social and community psychiatry, Yale community cons. to State Dept. Corrections, Yale U., 1975-77, instr. psychiatry and physiology, 1976-77; instr. physiology U. Mass., 1976-77; acting unit chief Inpatient and Day Hosp. Conn. Mental Health Ctr., Yale-New Haven Hosp. Inc., 1975-76, unit chief, 1976-77; asst. prof. psychiatry U. Calif., San Francisco, 1977-82, assoc. prof. psychiatry and medicine, 1982-86, vice-chmn. dept. psychiatry, 1983-86; chief psychiatry and neurology VA Med. Ctr., Fresno, Calif., 1977-86, prin. investigator Sleep Research & Physiology Lab., 1980-86; dir. dept. psychiatry and neurology U. Calif.-San Francisco, Fresno-Cen. San Joaquin Valley Med. Edn. Program and Affiliated Hosps. and Clinics, 1983-86; chief psychiatrist State of Calif. Dept. Corrections cen. office, 1986—; chmn. State of Calif. Inter-Agy. Tech. Adv. com. on Mentally Ill Inmates & Parolees, 1986—; mental health rep. med. adv. com. State Personnel Bd., 1986—; invited faculty contbr. and editor Am. Coll. Psychiatrist's Resident in Tng. Exam., 1981—. Assoc. editor Corrective and Social Psychiatry Jour., 1978—, referee, 1980—, reviewer, 1981—; contbr. articles in field to profl. jours. Nat. Merit scholar, 1965; recipient Nat. Recognition award Bank of Am., 1965, Julian Lee Roberts award U. Redlands, 1969, Kendall award Internat. Symposium in Biochemistry Research, 1970. Fellow Royal Soc. Health, Am. Assn. Social Psychiatry; mem. Am. Assn. Mental Health Profls. in Corrections (nat. pres. 1978—), Calif. Scholarship Fedn. (past pres.), AAUP, Am. Psychiat. Assn., Nat. Council on Crime and Delinquency, Am. Pub. Health Assn., Delta Alpha, Alpha Epislon Delta. Office: Met Sta PO Box 511 Sacramento CA 95812-0511

ZILCHA, ITZHAK, educator; b. Bagdad, Iraq, Oct. 26, 1944; arrived in Israel, 1950; s. Joseph and Victoria (Zilcha) Z.; m. Alice Betty Cedar, July 6, 1970; children: Ron, Michal, Ruth. BSc, Hebrew U., Jerusalem, 1967, MSc, 1970, PhD, 1975. Instr. The Hebrew U., Jerusalem, 1973-75; asst. prof. U. Ill., 1975-77; assoc. prof. Cornell U., Ithaca, N.Y., 1977-78; assoc. prof. Tel-Aviv U., Israel, 1978-83, prof., 1985—; assoc. prof. Johns Hopkins U., Balt., 1983-85. Contbr. articles to profl. jours. NSF grantee, 1975-78, 84-86, Ford Found., 1979-80. Mem. Am. Econ. Assn., Econometric Soc. Home: 4 Yehuda Halevy, Herzeliya Israel Office: Tel Aviv U, Ramat Aviv, Tel Aviv Israel

ZILLMANN, ROBERT EDWARD, accountant; b. Evanston, Ill., Mar. 16, 1929; s. Emil R. and Daisy (Greenland) Z.; m. Marie Frances Vranicar, May 24, 1953; children: Barbara Zillmann Park, Eric Robert. Student, Lake Forest Coll., 1948-49; B.S., Northwestern U., 1952. C.P.A., Ill. Pub. accountant H.C. Goettsche & Co., Chgo., 1952-57; financial exec. Abbott Labs., Chgo., 1957-61; operations mgr. Abbott Labs., S.A.R.L., Montreaux, Switzerland, 1962-63; corp. controller G.D. Searle & Co., Chgo., 1964-67; treas. Marsteller, Inc., Chgo., 1968-70; financial v.p. Marsteller, Inc., 1970-73; asst. treas. Apeco Corp., Evanston, 1973-74; corporate controller Apeco Corp., 1974; controller Nat. Assn. Realtors, Chgo., 1974; v.p. finance and adminstrn. Nat. Assn. Realtors, 1975-79; pres. Zillmann & Co. (C.P.A.s), Chgo., 1979—. Served with AUS, 1946-48. Mem. Am. Inst. C.P.A.s, Ill. Soc. C.P.A.s, Financial Execs. Inst., Corp. Controllers Inst., Nat. Conf. CPA Practitioners. Home: 1820 Balmoral Ln Glenview IL 60025 Office: 100 W Monroe St Chicago IL 60603

ZIMMER, ALBERT ARTHUR, educator; b. Pitts., May 20, 1918; s. Albert Peter and Hilda (Volz) Z.; m. Alma Zimmermann, Mar. 7, 1945; children: Alene Lynne, Alyce Lorraine, Alana Leigh. B.S., Pa. State U., 1942, M.Ed., 1947; Ed.D., U. Pitts., 1951. Tchr. pub. schs. State College, Pa., 1941-42; music supr. pub. schs. Ford City and Monongahela, Pa., 1946-49; instr. U. Pitts., 1949-52; head edn. dept. Susquehanna U., 1952-59, dean students, 1959-62; dean, v.p. Bethany Coll., Lindsborg, Kans., 1962-66; acting pres. coll. Bethany Coll., 1966-67; chmn. dept. edn. Thiel Coll., Greenville, Pa., 1967—; vis. lectr. Bucknell U., Rutgers U., Pa. State U., U. Conn.; Del. Gov. Pa. Conf. Edn., 1954. Contbr. articles to profl. jours. Dir. Snyder County Civil Def., 1952-62; mem. Selinsgrove (Pa.) SSS Bd., 1959-62; Nat. del. Luth Ch. Am., 1956, 60, 62; del. Central Pa. Synod, 1956-62, 64, mem. Christian edn. commn., 1958-62, social welfare commn., 1960-62, church councilman, Selinsgrove, 1952-62, Lindsborg, 1963—, City councilman, Selinsgrove, 1960-62, Greenville, 1980—, mem. planning commn., 1960-62; fire warden Pa. Forest Commn., 1958-62; Bd. dirs. Snyder County chpt. Am. Cancer Soc., 1956-60; bd. dirs., fund chmn. Snyder County chpt. A.R.C., 1954; bd. dirs. Monongahela Youth Council, 1946-47, Monongahela Concert Bd., 1946-47, Walnut Acres Found., Pa., 1958-62, Lindsborg Community Vol. Ambulance Service, 1966—, Gettysburg Luth. Theol. Sem., 1974-78. Served with AUS, 1942-46. Mem. Music Educators Nat. Conf., Pa. Assn. Liberal Arts Colls. (pres. 1960-61), Pa. Assn. Student Teaching (v.p. 1958-59), N.E.A., Am. Assn. U. Profs., Nat. Assn. Deans, Phi Delta Kappa, Theta Chi, Phi Mu Alpha, Kappa Phi Kappa, Alpha Phi Omega. Club: Rotarian. Home: 73 N Main St Greenville PA 16125

ZIMMER, ART, publisher, graphics agencies owner; b. New London, Conn., Sept. 21, 1938; s. Carl and Edna (Payton) Z.; m. Shirley Sherburne Zimmer, 1987. Assoc. in Applied Sci., Mohawk Valley Coll., Utica, N.Y., 1961. Salesman Nat. Bisc, Syracuse, N.Y., 1962-65, Brown News, Baldwinsville, N.Y., 1965-69; owner A-Z Real Estate, Syracuse, 1966—; co-owner Rapid Graphics, Syracuse, 1983—; owner Izitart Graphics, Syracuse, 1984—; pub., editor New Times, Syracuse, 1984—; owner Type Express Co., Syracuse, 1987—; pres. Lowry Real Estate, Syracuse, 1978—; pub. Cen. N.Y. Ski Guide, 1979—; owner Austrian Haus Hotel, Mt. Show, Vt., 1980—, Village Edge Apts., Tully, N.Y., 1980—, Vt. Vacations Hotels, Rutland, 1981—; founder, chmn. Syracuse Ski Show, 1970-87. Ski editor Post Standard, Syracuse, 1978-83. Pres. Concerned Citizens for Better Housing, Syracuse, 1974-76. Served with U.S. Army, 1956-59. Recipient Editor of Yr. award U.S. Eastern Ski Assn., 1964, Master's award Onondaga Ski Club, 1982. Mem. U.S. Ski Writers Assn. Club: Onondaga Ski (pres. 1970-74). Home and Office: 1415 W Genesee St Syracuse NY 13204

ZIMMER, JOHN HERMAN, lawyer; b. Sioux Falls, S.D., Dec. 30, 1922; s. John Francis and Veronica (Berke) Z.; student Augustana Coll., Sioux Falls, 1941-42, Mont. State Coll., 1943; LL.B., U. S.D., 1948; m. Deanna Langner, 1976; children by previous marriage—June, Mary Zimmer Levene, Robert Joseph, Judith Maureen Zimmer Rose. Bar: S.D. 1948. Practice law, Turner County, S.D., 1948—; ptnr. Zimmer & Duncan, Parker, S.D.; states atty. Turner County, 1955-58, 62-64; asst. prof. med. jurisprudence U. S.D.; minority counsel S.D. Senate Armed Services Com. on Strategic and Critical Materials Investigation, 1962-63; chmn. Southeastern Council Govts., 1973-75; mem. U. S.D. Law Sch. adv. council, 1973-74. Chmn. Turner County Rep. Com., 1955-56; mem. S.D. Rep. adv. com., 1959-60; alt. del. Rep. Nat. Conv., 1968; pres. S.D. Easter Seal Soc., 1986-87. Served with AUS, 1943-46; PTO. Decorated Bronze Star, Philippine Liberation ribbon. Mem. ABA, Fed., S.D. (commr. 1954-57) Bar Assns., Assn. Trial Lawyers Am., S.D. Trial Lawyers Assn. (pres. 1967-68), VFW, Am. Legion, Phi Delta Phi. Lodges: Elks, Shriners. Home: Rural Rt Parker SD 57053 Office: Zimmer & Duncan Law Bldg PO Box 547 Parker SD 57053

ZIMMERER, CARL GERHARD, business broker; b. Bad Berneck, Ger., Dec. 4, 1926; s. Adam and Hedwig Elsa (Weiss) Z.; Dipl. Volkswirt, Frankfurt U., 1950; Dr. es sc pol., Geneva U., 1952; m. Ruth Hoffmann, Apr. 22, 1954; children—Sabine, Xaver, Carola, Max, Rudolf. Asst. prof. U. Mannheim, 1952-53, U. Cologne, 1953-54; with Commerzbank Group, 1954-59, co-mgr. Duesseldorf br., 1956-59; pres. Interfinanz GmbH, Duesseldorf, 1959—; dir. Agrippina Reins. Corp.; mem. bd. Deutsche Schutzvereinigung Wertpapierbesitz, Deutsche Gesellschaft Betriebswirtschaft-Schmalenbach Gesellschaft, Decorated Iron Cross 2d degree. Club: Duesseldorf Industrial. Author: Wir Wirtschaftswunderknaben Sind Aelter Geworden, 3rd edit., 1988, Bilanzwahrheit, 3d edit., 1981; Industriebilanzen, 6th edit., 1979; Hammersein-nicht Amboss, 3d edit., 1985. Home: 15 Neuhofstrasse, 4044 Kaarst Federal Republic of Germany Office: 86-88 Schadowstrasse, 4000 Duesseldorf Federal Republic of Germany

ZIMMERLI, KURT, machinery manufacturing company executive; b. Zofingen, Switzerland, May 16, 1928; came to U.S., 1956; s. Jakob and Frieda (Widmer) Z.; m. Nelly Bugler, Aug. 21, 1954; children—Kathy Marianne, Mark Jakob. B.S. in Mech. Engring., State Tech. Coll., Bern, Switzerland, 1954; M.B.A., Western New Eng. Coll., 1962. Registered profl. engr., S.C. Chief engr. B.F. Perkins, Holyoke, Mass., 1957-62; v.p. engring. Butterworth Mfg. Co., Bethayres, Pa., 1962-66; v.p. internat. Universal Am. Corp., N.Y.C., 1966-69; pres. Zima Corp., Spartanburg, S.C., 1969—, Kusters Corp., Spartanburg, 1974—; dir. S.C. Nat. Bank, Spartanburg, 1974—. Bd. assocs. Wofford Coll., Spartanburg, 1976—; trustee Converse Coll., Spartanburg, 1984—; consul of Switzerland, Phila., 1965-69; bd. dirs. Arts Council, Spartanburg, 1980—. Mem. ASME, Profl. Engring. Soc. of S.C. Republican. Presbyterian. Club: Carolina Country (chmn. bd.) (Spartanburg). Home: 104 Montgomery Circle Spartanburg SC 29302 Office: Zima Corp Zima Park PO Box 6010 Spartanburg SC 29304

ZIMMERMAN, EUGENE WALTER, developer, investor, owner motor hotels; b. nr. Jenner Twp., Pa., Mar. 23, 1909; s. Robert and Amanda A. (Walter) Z.; grad. pub. schs.; m. Eleanor Witt, Apr. 8, 1930 (div. Oct. 1965); children—Doris Joan (Mrs. James H. Mapes), Ronald E., Rosalie Eleanor (Mrs. Ralph C. Johnson); m. Irene Fabian, May 23, 1966. Developer, owner Zimmerman Motor Co., Somerset, Pa., 1938-45, Roof Garden Motor Hotel, 1941-52, Ella-Gene Apts., Ft. Lauderdale, Fla., 1946-49, Motel Harrisburg, Pa., 1950-57 (now known as Holiday Motor Hotel-East), 1957—; developer, owner Holiday Motor Hotel, West, Harrisburg, Pa., 1952—, Holiday Inn Town, 1962—; owner Gene Zimmerman's Automobilorama and Mus., Holiday West, Ft. Lauderdale, Fla., 1965—; ofcl. staff editor Clissold Pub. Co., Chgo. Cons. to motor hotel industry. Recipient Hall of Fame award Am. Motel Mag., Chgo., 1961, Merit Resolution, Pa. Ho. of Reps., 1968. Mem. Am. Hotel Assn., Pa. Motel Assn. (pres. 1953-54, dir. master hosts 1955—, ambassador master hosts 1961, 62), Am. Motor Hotel Assn., (v.p., dir. 1956), Pa., Central Pa. restaurant assns., Nat. Assn. Travel Orgn., Hotel Sales Mgrs. Assn., Hotel Greeters Am., Inter-Am., Internat. hotel assns., Hammond Organ Soc., Tall Cedars Lebanon, Harrisburg C. of C., Am. Airlines (Admiral), Acacia, Antique Automobile Club Am. (sr. judge), Classic Car Club Am., Horseless Carriage Club, Vets. Motor Car Club, Auburn-Cord-Duesenberg Club, Pierce-Arrow Soc., Rolls Royce Owners Club, S.A.R., Am. Soc. Travel Agts., Richard Nixon Assos., Pa. Soc. Republican. Lutheran. Clubs: T.W.A. Ambassador (life), American Airlines Admiral (life) (N.Y.C.); Matson Mariners' (hon. navigator) (San Francisco) Curved Dash Owners (New Hope, Pa.); Executives, Zembo Luncheon (Harrisburg); Le Club International (Fort Lauderdale); Chub Cay (The Bahamas). Lodges: Masons, Shriners, K.T., Rotary. Internat. editor: Am. Motel mag., 1962—. Office: Automobilorama Inc 1500 SE 1500 SE 17th St Fort Lauderdale FL 33316

ZIMMERMAN, FRANK RAYWORTH, communications executive; b. Ypsilanti, Mich., Aug. 22, 1931; s. Frank B. and Hazel (Rayworth) Z.; m. Barbara Faye Marie Kellogg, June 30, 1951; children: Deborah, Paul, Judith, John. BS, Ea. Mich. U., 1955. Mgr. traffic Mich. Bell Telephone Co., Detroit, 1955-74, gen. mgr. operator services, 1974-76, asst. v.p. revenues, 1976-78, v.p. pub. relations/revenues, 1978-83, exec. v.p., chief operating officer, 1983; sr. v.p. corp. affairs Ameritech, Chgo., 1983-87; pres., chief exec. officer Ill. Bell Telephone Co., Chgo., 1987—, also bd. dirs.; co-chair, bd. dirs. NCCJ, Chgo. and No. Ill. region, 1985—, also bd. dirs.; bd. dirs. Dearborn Park Corp., Chgo., 1987—; mem. bus. adv. council Chgo. Urban League, 1987—; bd. dirs. Prin. Chgo. United. Bd. dirs. Protestant Found. of Greater Chgo., 1987—, Chgo. Central Area Com., 1988—; mem. fin. research and adv. com. City of Chgo., 1987—; trustee Ill. Inst. Tech., 1987—; mem. Met. Chgo. Info. Ctr. Project Policy Com., 1987—; mem. Econ. Devel. Commn. of Chgo. Strategic Planning Com., 1988—; mem. governing bd. Ill. Council on Econ. Edn., 1988—; mem. exec. bd., mem. commissioning com. USS Abraham Lincoln, 1988—; trustee Ravinia Festival Assn., Chgo., 1988—, Shedd Aquarium, Chgo., 1988—. Recipient Bronze award Jr. Achievement, Detroit, 1982, Silver award, 1983, Disting. Alumnus award Ea. Mich. U., 1986. Republican. Methodist. Club: The Chgo. Avocations: swimming, boating. Office: Ill Bell Telephone Co 225 W Randolph St Chicago IL 60606

ZIMMERMAN, HYMAN JOSEPH, internist, educator; b. Rochester, N.Y., July 14, 1914; s. Philip and Rachel (Marine) Z.; m. Kathrin J. Jones, Feb. 28, 1943; children: Philip M., David J., Robert L., Diane E. A.B., U. Rochester, 1936; M.A., Stanford U., 1938, M.D., 1942. Diplomate Am. Bd. Internal Medicine. Intern Stanford U. Hosp., 1942-43; asst. resident in medicine Gallinger Mcpl. Hosp. div. George Washington U., Washington, 1946-47, chief resident in medicine Gallinger Mcpl. Hosp. med. div., 1947-48, clin. instr. medicine, 1948-51, prof. of medicine, Sch. of Medicine, 1965-68, 71—, prof. of medicine, dir. of gastroenterology Sch. of Medicine, 1980-84; asst. chief of med. services VA Hosp., Washington, 1949-51; chief of med. services VA Hosp., Omaha, 1951-53, Chgo., 1953-57; chief of liver and metabolic research lab. VA Hosp., Washington, 1965-68; chief of med. services VA Hosp., Boston, 1968-71; chief of med. services VA Hosp., Washington, 1971-78, sr. clinician, 1978-80, disting. physician, 1984—; asst. prof. of medicine Coll. of Medicine U. Neb., Omaha, 1951-53; assoc. prof. of medicine Coll. of Medicine U. Ill., Chgo., 1953-57; chmn. dept. of medicine Mt. Sinai Hosp., Chgo., 1957-65; prof. of medicine Sch. of Medicine Boston U., 1968-71; clin. prof. Sch. of Medicine Georgetown U., Washington, 1971-78; clin. prof. of medicine uniformed services U. Health Scis., Bethesda, Md., 1978-84; sr. clinician VA Hosp., Washington, 1978—; clin. prof. medicine Georgetown U., Washington, 1971-78, Howard U., 1971-78, Uniformed Services U. Health Scis., 1978—; cons. Clin. Ctr. NIH, Bethesda, 1965—, USN Med. Ctr., Bethesda, 1965—; visiting prof. and lectr. numerous hosps. and univs. Author: Hepatotoxicity, 1978; contbr. numerous articles to med. jours.; contbg. editor numerous med. pubs. Served to maj. AUS, 1943-46. Recipient Wm. Beaumont award for Clin. Research, 1981. Fellow ACP; mem. AMA (council on drugs, gastroenterology panel 1968-70), AAAS, AAUP, Am. Soc. Clin. Pharmacology and Therapeutics, Am. Fedn. for Clin. Research, Am. Diabetes Assn., Endocrine Soc., Asian-Pacific Assn. for Study Liver Diseases, Am. Soc. Clin. Investigation, N.Y. Acad. Scis., Cen. Soc. Clin. Research, Soc. for Exptl. Biology and Medicine, Am. Gastroenterol. Assn., Drug Info. Assn., Cosmos Club, Sigma Xi, Alpha Omega Alpha. Jewish. Home: 7913 Charleston Ct Bethesda MD 20817 Office: VA Med Ctr 50 Irving St NW Suite 151-L Washington DC 20422

ZIMMERMAN, JEAN, lawyer; b. Berkeley, Calif., Dec. 3, 1947; d. Donald Schiller Zimmerman and Phebe Jean (Reed) Doan; m. Gilson Berryman Gray III, Nov. 25, 1982; children: Charles Donald Buffum, Catherine Elisabeth Phebe (twins); stepchildren: Alison Travis, Laura Rebecca, Gilson Berryman. BSBA, U. Md., 1970; JD, Emory U., 1975. Bar: Ga. 1975, D.C. 1976, N.Y. 1980. Asst. mgr. investments FNMA, Washington, D.C., 1970-73; assoc. counsel Fuqua Industries Inc., Atlanta, 1976-79; assoc. Sage Gray Todd & Sims, N.Y.C., 1979-84; assoc. counsel J. Henry Schroder Bank & Trust Co., N.Y.C., 1984-85, asst. gen. counsel, 1985-86; assoc. gen. counsel, asst. sec. IBJ Schroder Bank & Trust Co., N.Y.C., 1988—. Founder, officer ERA Ga., Atlanta, 1977-79; bd. dirs. Ct. Apptd. Spl. Advs., 1988—. Mem. ABA, N.Y. State Bar Assn., Ga. Assn. Women Lawyers (bd. dirs. 1977-79), LWV, DAR, Democrat. Office: IBJ Schroder Bank & Trust Co One State St New York NY 10004

ZIMMERMAN, JOSEPH FRANCIS, political scientist, educator; b. Keene, N.H., June 29, 1928; s. John Joseph and May Veronica (Gallagher) Z.; m. Margaret Bernardette Brennan, Aug. 2, 1958; 1 dau., Deirdre Ann. B.A., U. N.H., 1950; M.A., Syracuse U., 1951, Ph.D., 1954. Instr. govt. Worcester Poly. Inst., 1954-55, asst. prof., 1955-57, assoc. prof., 1957-62, prof., 1962-65; lectr. Clark U., Worcester, Mass., 1957-65; prof. polit. sci. SUNY, Albany, 1965—; staff dir. N.Y. State Joint Legis. Com. Mass. Transp., 1967-68, research dir., 1968-73; research dir. N.Y. State Select Legis. Com. Transp., 1973-77, N.Y. State Senate Com. on Transp., 1977-82, Legis. Commn. on Critical Transp. Problems, 1982—. Author: State and Local Government, 1962, The Massachusetts Town Meeting: A Tenacious Institution, 1967, The Federated City: Community Control in Large Cities,

1972, Pragmatic Federalism, The Reassignment of Functional Responsibility, 1976, (with Frank W. Prescott) The Politics of the Veto of Legislation in New York, 1980, The Government and Politics of the Empire State, 1981, Local Discretionary Authority, 1981, (with Deirdre A. Zimmerman) The Politics of Subnational Governance, 1983, State-Local Relations: A Partnership Approach, 1983 (CHOICE award as outstanding acad. book 1984), Participatory Democracy: Populism Revived, 1986; contbr. articles to profl. publs. Pres. Citizens' Plan E Assn., Worcester, 1960-62, Citizens for Neighborhood Improvement Worcester, 1957-59. Served to capt. USAF, 1951-53. Named 1 of 3 Outstanding Young Men Worcester Jr. C. of C., 1959, 61, 1 of 3 Outstanding Young Men Mass. Jr. C. of C., 1961, disting. citizen award Nat. Conf. on Govt., 1986. Mem. Am. Polit. Sci. Assn., Am. Soc. Public Adminstrn., Nat. Mcpl. League. Roman Catholic. Club: German-Am. Social. Home: 82 Greenock Rd Delmar NY 12054 Office: SUNY Grad Sch Public Affairs 135 Western Ave Albany NY 12222

ZIMMERMAN, JOSEPH THEODOOR FRANS, physical oceanographer, educator; b. Arnhem, Gelderland, Netherlands, Sept. 9, 1946; s. Joseph Clemens Marie and Petronella (Nielsen) Z.; m. Sidonie Diana Escher, Dec. 30, 1946. BSc, U. Utrecht, 1968; MSci, Free U., Amsterdam, 1971, PhD, 1976. Sr. scientist Netherlands Inst. for Sea Research, Texel, 1971—; prof. phys. oceanography U. Utrecht (Netherlands), 1981—. Contbr. articles to sci. publs. Recipient AKZO award for phys. scis. Hollandsche Maatschappy der Wetenschappen, Haarlem, 1984. Home: Pijpersdijk 20, 1796 MJ De Koog Texel The Netherlands Office: Netherlands Inst Sea Research, PO Box 59, 1790 AB Den Burg Texel The Netherlands

ZIMMERMAN, RICHARD ALBERT, educator; b. Long Island City, N.Y., Mar. 11, 1930; s. Albert Julius and Elsie Marie (Schoelch) Z.; B.S., U. Mo., 1957, M.S., 1959, Ph.D., 1965; m. Johanna Auguste Matilde Staufer, July 14, 1967; children—David, Carl-Ulrich, Corinna. Teaching asst. U. Mo., Rolla, 1957-64; research scientist U. Heidelberg, 1965—. Served with USAF, 1948-52. Fellow Geol. Soc. Am.; mem. Mineral. Soc. Am., Soc. Geology Applied to Mineral Deposits, Internat. Assn. Sedimentologists, Soc. Mining Engrs., N.Y. Acad. Scis., Sigma Xi. Methodist. Contbr. articles to profl. jours. Home: 677 Im Neuenheimer Feld, 6900 Heidelberg Federal Republic of Germany Office: 236 Im Neuenheimer Feld, 6900 Heidelberg Federal Republic of Germany

ZIMMERMAN, ROBERT RAYMOND, management consultant; b. N.Y.C., Jan. 24, 1919; s. Isador and Nettie (Shulman) Z.; m. Helen Eugenie Sperry, Oct. 8, 1949; children—Laurence Irving, Marc Sperry. B.A. in Econs. and Indsl. Psychology, U. Minn., 1941; M.B.A. with honors in Indsl. Relations, U. Chgo., 1947. Indsl. relations mgr. Continental Can Co., Chgo., 1948-54; personnel and orgn. planning cons. to sr. assoc. Booz, Allen & Hamilton, Chgo., 1954-65; personnel v.p. Sanger Harris Dept. Store, Dallas, 1965-66; operating v.p. orgn. and key manpower planning Federated Dept. Stores, Cin., 1966-79; sr. v.p. human resources Central Bancorp., Cin., 1979-84; pres. Zimmerman Cons., Inc., also sr. v.p. Schonberg Assocs., Inc., 1984—; former lectr. mgmt. and orgn. planning Indsl. Relations Ctr. of U. Chgo.; lectr., forum leader Am. Mgmt. Assn., Conf. Bd.; mem. Orgn. Planning Council, Conf. Bd., 1975-79. Bd. dirs. South Suburban Mental Health and Family Counseling Service, Ill., 1960-65. Served to capt. Adj. Gen. Dept., U.S. Army, 1941-46. Mem. Beta Gamma Sigma. Club: Indian Hill (Ohio). Author: Auditing the Organization Structure, 1965. Office: Zimmerman Cons Inc 6340 Miami Rd Cincinnati OH 45253 Office: Schonberg Assocs Inc 2368 Victory Pkwy Cincinnati OH 45206

ZIMMERMAN, RUSSELL RICHARD, aerospace engineer; b. Pitts., Oct. 12, 1942; s. Elwood Booth and Lois Hileman (Shultz) Z. BS, Rochester Inst. Tech., 1965. Engr. Data Corp., Dayton, 1965-67; mgr. precision lab. Data Corp., Manned Spacecraft Ctr., Tex., 1967-71; mgr. photographic engring. Mead Tech. Labs., Dayton, 1971-76, div. dir. imaging scis., 1976-78, v.p. imaging systems, 1978-81; v.p., gen. mgr. MTL Systems, Inc., Dayton, 1981-87, pres., chief exec. officer, 1987—, also bd. dirs.; cons. NASA, Houston, 1967-75, USAF, Dayton, 1971—; trustee Engring and Sci. Found. of Dayton, 1987—. Contbr. various tech. papers and articles to profl. jour. Mem. Soc. Photographic Scis. and Engrs., Am. Soc Photogrammetry and Remote Sensing. Methodist. Club: Engineers. Home: 415 N Park Pl Yellow Springs OH 45387

ZIMMERMANN, JOHN JOSEPH, lawyer; b. Chgo., Apr. 30, 1939; s. John Joseph and Ernestine Elizabeth (Leuver) Z.; m. Alice Rose Farrell, July 4, 1964; children—John, Michael, Thomas, Margaret, Kathleen. A.B., DePaul U., 1962, J.D., 1967. Bar: Ill. 1967, U.S. Dist. Ct. (no. dist.) Ill. 1967, U.S. Ct. Appeals (7th cir. 1967. Ptnr. Bradtke & Zimmermann, Mt. Prospect, Ill., 1979—; village atty. Village of Mt. Prospect, 1968-79, acting village mgr., 1969, 70-71; city atty. City of Wood Dale, Ill., 1975—; spl. corp. counsel City of Highland Park, Ill., 1979—; atty. Mt. Prospect Pub. Library, 1982—; village atty. Village of Mettawa, Ill., 1983—; dir. Joe Mitchell Buick, Inc., Mt. Prospect, 1979—; lectr. Ill. Inst. for Continuing Legal Edn., 1979—, Ill. State Bar Assn., 1988—. Mem. St. Paul of the Cross Sch. Bd. of Edn., Park Ridge, 1972-75, pres., 1974-75; mem. sponsoring com. Ann. Men's Prayer Breakfast, Park Ridge, 1979—. Recipient ofcl. commendation Village of Mt. Prospect, 1971, named hon. citizen, 1974; recipient certs. of appreciation Ill. Inst. Continuing Legal Edn., 1980, Chgo. Bar Assn., 1984, Ill. State Bar Assn., 1988. Mem. Nat. Inst. Mcpl. Law Officers (del., lectr., regional v.p.), Ill. State Bar Assn. (sec. 1983, mem. local govt. sect. council 1981—), Ill. Home Rule Attys. Com. (charter mem., chmn. 1979), Chgo. Bar Assn. (chmn. local govt. com. 1983-84). Roman Catholic. Home: 524 S Vine Ave Park Ridge IL 60068 Office: Bradtke & Zimmermann 1190 S Elmhurst Rd Mount Prospect IL 60056

ZIMMERMANN, ROBERT LAURENCE, marketing professional; b. Mpls., Jan. 1, 1932; s. Lawrence and Bertha Mabel (Foss) Z. BA, U. Minn., 1954, MA, 1965, PhD, 1970. Asst. prof. psychology U. Winnepeg, Man., Can., 1968-69; research assoc. psychiatry research unit U. Minn., Mpls., 1969-75; sr. scientist biometrics lab. George Washington U., Washington, 1975-76; pvt. cons. research design and data analysis Mpls., 1976-84; sr. research mgr. Maritz Market Research, Mpls., 1984—; clin. asst. prof. psychiatry dept. U. Minn., Mpls., 1976—; external rev. officerFDA, Washington, 1974-77. Contbr. numerous articles to profl. jours. Fellow NIMH, 1958, 61, 69-71; merit fellow State of Minn. Mem. AAAS, Am. Psychol. Assn. Democrat. Home: 1920 S First St #1104 Minneapolis MN 55454 Office: Maritz Market Research Inc 6800 France Ave S Minneapolis MN 55435

ZINCKE DOS REIS, ANTONIO MANUEL RODRIGUES, lawyer; b. Lisbon, Portugal, Mar. 26, 1938; s. Eduardo Adolfo and Amelia Maria (Mendes Rodrigues) Zincke dos R.; m. Maria Teresa Pereira Parreira; children: Maria Do Rosario, Maria Paula, Maria Rita, Ana Isabel. JD, U. Lisbon, 1960, Degree in Polit. Economy, 1968. Labor magistrate Lisbon, 1961-67; legal advisor, dir., cons. Tap-Air Portugal, Lisbon, 1967—; chmn. Portuguese Domestic Airline, 1987, Air-Portugal Tours, 1987—, SATA-Air Azores, 1977-79; mem. IATA legal com. Home: Rua Conde Redondo 93-2 DTO, 1100 Lisbon Portugal Office: Lawyers Office, Rua Castilho 75-1 DTO, 1200 Lisbon Portugal

ZINDEL, BONNIE, writer; b. N.Y.C., May 3, 1943; d. Jack and Claire (Bromberg) Hildebrand; m. Paul Zindel, Oct. 25, 1973; children: David, Lizabeth. BA in Psychology, Hofstra U., 1964. Dir. pub. relations The Cleveland Play House, Cleve., 1969-72; producer show Intermission Feature, Boston Symphony, sta. WCLV-FM, Cleve., 1970-72. Author: A Star for the Latecomer, 1980; Hollywood Dream Machine, 1984; playwright I Am A Zoo-Jewish Repetory Theatre-The Troupe Theatre, 1976; Lemons in the Morning, A.M. Back Alley Theatre, 1983, The Latecomer, 1985, Adriana Earthlight-Student Shrink, 1987. Mem. Playwrights Unit-Actors Studio, Women in Film. Office: care Curtis Brown 10 Astor Pl New York NY 10003

ZINKANN, PETER CHRISTIAN, business executive; b. Bremen, Fed. Republic Germany, Sept. 17, 1928; s. Kurt Christian and Edith (Birkolz) Z.; m. Karin Elisabeth Rohe, Feb. 5, 1958; 1 child, Reinhard Christian. M in Engring., Tech. U. Darmstadt, Fed. Republic Germany, 1954, PhD in Econs., 1956. Co-ptnr. Miele & Cie, GmbH & Co. KG, Güterloh, Fed. Republic Germany, 1957—; bd. dirs. Krupp Stahl AG, Bochum, Mannesmann-Kienzle, Villingen, Zanders Feinpapiere AG, Bergisch-Gladbach, all Fed. Republic Germany. Mem. Technischer Überwachungsverein (bd. dirs. 1973—). Lodge: Rotary (Gütersloh). Home: Thesings Allee 11a, D4830 Gutersloh Federal Republic of Germany Office: Miele & Cie, PO Box 2400, D4830 Gutersloh Federal Republic of Germany

ZINMAN, JACQUES, former insurance agency executive; b. Phila., Nov. 7, 1922; B.S., U. Va., 1943; postgrad. U. Pa., 1945-46. Chmn., The Zinman Group, Ins. Agy., 1950-82. Mem. exec. com. Pa. state Republican fin. com.; mem. Presdl. Electoral Coll. from Pa., 1972; bd. dirs. Pop Warner Nat. Football League. Served to ensign USNR, 1943-44. Recipient Outstanding Young Man Phila. award Jewish Nat. Fund, 1961. Mem. Ins. Soc. Phila., Variety Club, Theta Delta Chi. Lodge: Masons. Contbr. articles to profl. jours. Office: Lakes Agy of Florida 629 E Atlantic Blvd Pompano Beach FL 33060

ZINN, ELIAS PAUL, electronic, entertainment marketing executive; b. Houston, Nov. 7, 1954; s. Julius and Harriett (Dubinski) Z.; student U. Tex., 1972-74; m. Janis Ann Turboff, Aug. 7, 1977. Salesman, Custom Hi Fi Discount Center, Houston, 1971-72, mgr., 1972-73, v.p. sales, 1974—, v.p. sales and operation, 1974-75, pres., 1975-76, pres., chief exec. officer, chief operating officer, 1976-81; formed Entertainment Mktg. Sales Reps., chmn., chief exec. officer, 1981-88, pres., chief exec. officer Crazy Eddie Inc., 1987—. advisor Better Bus. Bur., Houston, 1976-79. Mem. Electronic Reps. Assn., C. of C., Houston Jaycees. Republican. Jewish. Club: Beth Yeshrun Brotherhood. Home: 1480 Sugar Creek Blvd Sugarland TX 77478 Office: 10310 Harwin Houston TX 77036

ZINN, WILLIAM, violinist, composer, business executive; b. N.Y.C., Nov. 19, 1924; s. Philip and Anna (Miller) Z.; m. Sophia Kalish, July 11, 1948; children: Karen Louise Swaine, David Benjamin. Student, SUNY, 1952-54. Violinist Balt. Symphony, 1944-45, Indpls. Symphony, 1945-46, Ft. Wayne Philharm., 1946-47, Pitts. Symphony, 1947-49, Mpls. Symphony, 1950-51; concertmaster New Britain (Conn.) Symphony, 1968—, Queens Symphony, 1969-71, Ridgefield (Conn.) Symphony, 1973-76, Chappaqua (N.Y.) Symphony, 1976; soloist with orchs. on records, on radio and in recitals; founder Masterwork Piano Trio, Masterwork Piano Quartet, Classical String Quartet, Zinn's Ragtime String Quartet, Excelsior String Quartet, Queens Festival Orch., Bayside, N.Y., 1965, Assn. Musical William Zinn, Caracas, Venezuela, 1968, Vitametrics of Am., 1976, Internat. Symphony for World Peace, 1978, Big Apple Chamber Pops, 1983, Excelsior Composer's Festival Competition, 1984; tchr. mech. drafting Mondell Inst., 1956; coach ensembles for Chamber Music Assocs., 1973—; engr. N.Y.C. Bd. Edn. 1951-57, Bodin-Zinn Corp., 1957-58, Chem. Constrn. Corp., 1958-59; pres. Zinn Originals, Inc., 1959-68, Sparx, Inc., Trademark Hall of Fame, Inc., Nice Realty Corp., MFW Restaurant Corp.; co-founder Excelsior Music Pub. Co., Visionary Music Pub. Co., Nat. Music Promotion Agy., Telecommunication Services, 1982, Assoc. Sci. Publs., 1985, Barclay House Pubs., 1985, Excelsior Typographers and Engravers Unltd., 1985, Empco Recs. Internat., 1985, Imperial Editions, 1986, Missing Link Publs., 1986, Krazy Klassics Kompany, 1986, New Age Publs., 1987; sec.-treas. Spark Industries, Inc.; adj. prof. NYU, 1987. Author: (with Edward Gordon) Themography, 1947,, (with George S. Grosser) Vitametrics I, The Human Formula for Self-Evaluation, 1976, Vitametrics II, The Human Formula for Self-Improvement, 1978, (with George S. Grosser) The Lost Chord, 1981; composer: (perpetual movement for woodwinds, strings and percussion) Chromatique, 1946, Piccolo Concerto, 1948, Violin Concerto, 1950, String Quartet, 1963, (piano solo) Chopinesque, 1965, (ballet) Night Creatures, 1966, Andante for Strings, 1967, Concerto for Octahorn, 1976, The International Anthem For World Peace, 1977, String Symphony, 1977, Romance for French Horn or Viola and Piano, 1981, Concerto for Violin/Viola/Cello/Double Bass and Orch., 1985, Kol Nidrei Meml. for String Quartet or String Orchestra, 1985, six concert duos for violin and viola, 1988, also songs; arranger numerous operatic arias for string quartet or string orch.; originator Musiphonics, 1981; pioneer multi-styles of music for string quartet and string orch.; composer over 300 works; developer numerous products for home, personal, automobile and novelty use. Chmn. bd. dirs. Let Us Remember to Remember, 1984. Mem. ASCAP, Internat. Platform Assn., Nat. Council Women of U.S., Am. Fedn. Musicians, N.Y. Humanist Assn. Home: 35-19 215th Pl Bayside NY 11361

ZINZOW, JOHN ROBERT, publisher; b. Milw., Nov. 6, 1929; s. John Benjamin and Roselle Barbara (Gerrits) Z.; B.A., U. Chgo., 1952, M.B.A., 1954, M.A. in Econs., 1955. Mem. mfg. mgmt. staff Procter & Gamble, Chgo. and Quincy, Mass., 1957-64; pres. Poole Clarinda Co., Chgo., 1969-71, Programmed Printing Corp., Woodstock, Ill., 1972—, Windward Pub., Inc., Miami, Fla. Active, People for the Am. Way., Washington, 1982-83. Served with U.S. Army, 1955-57. Recipient Spl. Recognition award Burnham Club, 1970. Clubs: Union League, Chgo. Yacht (both Chgo.); Ocean Reef (Key Largo, Fla.). Author: Sportfisherman's Handbook, 1975; Magic of Sea Shells, 1976; Savory Shellfish of North America, 1977; The Shark Book, 1983. Office: 105 NE 25th St Miami FL 33137 also: 1160 NE 87th St Miami FL 33138

ZIOGAS, CHRISTOS CONSTANTIN, construction company executive; b. Greece, June 15, 1931; s. Constantin Christos and Metaxia (Papathanassiou) Z.; B.S., Purdue U., 1954, M.S., 1956; m. Helen Papadakis, July 27, 1969. Engr. in charge materials and methods control Hellenic AF Public Works Dept., Athens, 1956-60; chief engr. Archirodon J.V., Benghazi Harbour Reconstrn. and Benina Airport Improvements, Benghazi, Libya, 1961-65; chief engr. Kastraki J.V., Kastraki Hydroelectric project, Greece, 1966-69; dir. Archimedes Constrn. Co., Athens, 1970-73, Archirodon Constrn., Athens, Arabian Gulf, Saudi Arabia, 1973-77; gen. mgr., mng. dir. Archirodon Hellenic Engring. and Constrn. Co., Athens, 1976-83; sr. v.p. Archirodon Group, Inc., Athens, 1977—; chmn., chief exec. officer Delphinance Devel. Corp., Dallas, 1983—. Served with Greek Air Force, 1956-59. Mem. ASCE, Am. Concrete Inst., Tech. Chamber Greece, Greek Orthodox. Club: Jockey. Home: 4 Ithakis Politia-Kifisia, 14562 Athens Greece Office: 357 Messoghion Ave, Aghia Paraskevi, Athens Greece

ZIPF, ROBERT EUGENE, JR., legal medicine consultant, pathologist; b. Dayton, Ohio, Sept. 18, 1940; s. Robert Eugene and Meriam (Murr) Z.; m. Nancy J. Gaskell, Sept. 11, 1965; children—Karin Lorene, Marjorie Kristine. B.A., DePauw U., 1962; M.D., Ohio State U., 1966. Diplomate Am. Bd. Pathology. Intern, Miami Valley Hosp., Dayton, Ohio, 1966-67; dir. forensic pathology Duke U. Med. Ctr., Durham, N.C., 1967-72; dir. radioisotope pathology Riverside Meth. Hosp., Columbus, 1974-78; dep. coroner, forensic pathologist Franklin County, Columbus, 1974-78; regional forensic pathologist State of N.C., Rocky Mount, 1978—; chmn. pathology Nash Gen. Hosp., Rocky Mount, 1978—; clin. asst. prof. East Caroline U. Med. Sch., Greenville, N.C., 1979—; adj. prof. Atlantic Christian Coll., Wilson, N.C., 1980—, dir. Sch. Med. Tech., 1983—; cons. in field. Contbr. articles to profl. jours. Trustee, United Fund, 1979-84; mem. Mayor's Com. on Drug and Substance Abuse, 1987—. Served to maj. USAF, 1972-74. Fellow Am. Soc. Clin. Pathologist, Am. Acad. Forensic Scientists; mem. Assn. Clin. Scientists, Am. Coll. Nuclear Medicine, N.C. Med. Soc., N.Y. Acad. Scis. Home: 120 Newby Ct Rocky Mount NC 27804 Office: Nash Gen Hosp Pathology Lab Rocky Mount NC 27804

ZLATEV, ZAHARI, mathematician, educator, researcher; b. Tolbouhin, Bulgaria, June 15, 1939; s. Ivan Petrov and Stanka (Janakieva) Z.; m. Ida Margrethe Beck, July 15, 1970; children: Tanja Margrethe, Anna Irina. MSc, U. Sofia, Bulgaria, 1963; PhD, U. Leningrad, USSR, 1969. Research fellow Tech. U. Denmark, Lyngby, 1974-77; asst. prof. U. Copenhagen, 1978-79; assoc. prof. U. Arhus, Denmark, 1979-80; research fellow Air Pollution Lab., Risø, Denmark, 1980—. Author: (with others) Solving Large and Sparse Systems of Linear Algebraic Equation, 1981, Direct Methods for Sparse Matrices, transl. into Russian. Fellow Inst. Math. Eng., Am. Soc. Indsl. Applied Math.; mem. Am. Math. Soc., Am. Assn. Computing Machinery, Danish Math. Soc., Danish Ctr. Applied Math. Mechanics. Home: Hagens Allé 28, DK-2900 Hellerup Denmark Office: Air Pollution Lab, Danish Agy, Environ Protection, Risø Nat Lab, DK-4000 Roskilde Denmark

ZLATOFF-MIRSKY, EVERETT IGOR, violinist; b. Evanston, Ill., Dec. 29, 1937; s. Alexander Igor and Evelyn Ola (Hill) Z.-M.; m. Janet Dalbey, Jan. 28, 1976; children from previous marriage—Tania, Laura. B.Mus., Chgo. Mus. Coll., Roosevelt U., 1960; M.Mus., Roosevelt U., 1961. Mem. faculty dept. music Roosevelt U., Chgo., 1961-66. Violinist orch., Lyric Opera of Chgo., 1974—; concert master, personnel mgr., 1974—, violinist, violist, Contemporary Chamber Players, U. Chgo., 1964-82, solo violinist, Bach Soc., 1966-83; violist, violinist, Lexington String Quartet, 1966-81; rec. artist numerous recs., radio-TV and films; solo violinist appearing throughout U.S. Recipient Olive Ditson award Franklin Honor Soc., 1961. Mem. Nat. Acad. Rec. Arts and Scis. Republican. Roman Catholic. Home: 240 Green Bay Rd Glencoe IL 60022 Office: Lyric Opera Chgo 20 N Wacker Dr Chicago IL 60606

ZLOTOWITZ, BERNARD M., rabbi; b. N.Y.C., July 11, 1925; s. Aron and Fannie (Pasternak) Z.; B.A., Bklyn. Coll., 1948; M.A., Columbia U., 1965; B.H.L., Hebrew Union Coll.-Jewish Inst. Religion, N.Y.C., 1953, rabbi, M.H.L., 1955 D.H.L., 1974, DD (hon.), 1980; Editor One People, 1982; book rev. editor Reform Judaism. 1980; m. Shirley Masef, June 12, 1949; children—Debra, Robin, Richard C., Alice R. Rabbi congregations in N.Y., N.C. and N.J., 1955-75; regional dir. N.J. council Union Am. Hebrew Congregations, N.Y.C., 1975-80, N.Y. Fedn., 1980—; lectr. Bible, Hebrew Union Coll.-Jewish Inst. Religion, 1962-72; adj. asst. prof. religion C.W. Post Coll., 1968-72, U. N.C., Charlotte, 1973-74; lectr. Bibl. archaeology Jewish Museum, N.Y.C., 1972, Charlotte Mus., 1973; lectr. Hebrew Union Coll., 1977—, N.Y.U. Sch. of Continuing Edn., 1985—. Bd. dirs. Nyack (N.Y.) Hosp., 1959-61. Mem. Internat. Orgn. Masoretic Studies (treas. 1972—), Central Conf. Am. Rabbis, N.J. Assn. Reform Rabbis, N.Y. Bd. Rabbis (exec. com. 1957-62, 80—), Am. Schs. Oriental Research, Soc. Bib. Lit., N.Y. Acad. Scis., Am. Oriental Soc., AAUP, Asssn. Reform Rabbis N.Y.C. and Vicinity. Clubs: Masons, KP, Rotary. Author: Folkways and Minhagim, 1970; Art in Judaism, 1975; The Septuagint Translation of the Hebrew Terms in Relation to God in the Book of Jeremiah, 1980; columnist Reform Judaism Jewish Question and Answer; contbg. editor Keeping Posted; book rev. editor Reform Judaism. Home: 15 Aberdeen Pl Fair Lawn NJ 07410 Office: 838 Fifth Ave New York NY 10021

ZLOTOWSKI, MARTIN, psychologist; b. Lodz, Poland, Aug. 10, 1934; s. Pawel and Helen Z.; B.A., N.Y. U., 1955; M.A., Mich. State U., 1958, Ph.D., 1960; m. Judith Ann Lifschitz, May 17, 1974; children—David, Steven, Laura. Research assoc. Grad. Sch. Public Health, U. Pitts., 1960-61; research assoc., lectr. Boston U., 1961-62; staff psychologist VA Hosp., Coatesville, Pa., 1962-65, unit chief, 1965-73; clin. dir. St. Mary Providence, 1966-70; assoc. prof. spl. edn. West Chester (Pa.) U., 1973—; dir. Counseling Assocs., Paoli, Pa., 1973-85, exec. dir., 1985—. Vice-pres., Victim Witness Services Chester County, 1976-77. Fellow Pa. Psychol. Assn., Phila. Soc. Clin. Psychologists (pres. 1978-79, sec. human services ctr. 1982, fellow), Am. Orthopsychiat. Assn.; mem. Am. Psychol. Assn., Am. Orthopsychiat. Assn., Mental Health Assn. S.E. Pa.. Democrat. Jewish. Home: 605 Eagle Rd Wayne PA 19087

ŽMEGAČ, VIKTOR, German literature educator; b. Podravaska Slatina, Croatia, Yugoslavia, Mar. 21, 1929; s. Eduard and Margita (Just) ž; m. Cvjeta Tutovic, Oct. 12, 1955; children: Aleksandra, Andrej. BA, Faculty of Letters, Zagreb, Yugoslavia, 1954, PhD, 1959. Lectr. Faculty of Letters, Göttingen, Fed. Republic Germany, 1955-57; asst. prof. Faculty of Letters, Zagreb, 1960-66, full prof., 1967—; vis. prof. Univ. Berlin, 1970, Graz (Austria) Univ., 1981; head Zagreb Univ. Inst. Lit., 1982. Author: Die Musik im Schaffen Thomas Manns, 1959, Krležini Evropski Obzori, 1986 (Nazor prize 1987); editor, co-author Geschichte der Deutschen Literatur vom. 18 Jahrhundert bis zur Gegenwart, 3 vols. 1978-84. Recipient Goethe medaille Goethe Inst., 1974, City of Zagreb award City Council, 1977, Gundolf prize Deutsche Akademie, 1987; Alexander von Humboldt grantee, 1964-65. Mem. Saxonian Acad. Sci. and Letters. Home: Rapska 37A, 41000 Zagreb Yugoslavia Office: Faculty of Letters, Dure Salaja 3, 41000 Zagreb Yugoslavia

ZMORA, OHAD, publisher; b. Tel-Aviv, July 23, 1933; s. Israel and Ada Olga (Kremianski) Z.; m. Zehara Poznanski, Sept. 9, 1952; children: Eran, Shachar, Hillay. Student, Hebrew U., Jerusalem, 1954-56. Journalist 1955-86; mng. editor D'var Hashavva mag., 1956-64, editor in chief, 1964-86; mng. editor Davar (daily newspaper), 1970-71, dep. chief editor, 1985-86; pub. Zmora, Bitan Pubs., 1973—, Dvir, 1986—. Mem. Labour party. Jewish. Office: Zmora Bitan Pubs, 32 Schoken St, Tel Aviv Israel

ZOLA, MICHAEL S., lawyer; b. Madison, Wis., Dec. 15, 1942; s. Emanuel and Harriet (Sher) Z.; 1 son, Emanuel David. B.S. cum laude, U. Wis., 1964; LL.B., Columbia U., 1967. Bar: D.C. 1968, Wis. 1968, Calif. 1969, Hawaii 1981, U.S. Dist. Ct. Hawaii 1981, U.S. Dist. Ct. (we. dist.) Wis. 1968, U.S. Dist. Ct. (no. dist.) Calif. 1969, U.S. Ct. Appeals (9th cir.) 1969. Law clk. to judge U.S. Dist. Ct. (we. dist.) Wis., 1967-68; mng. atty. San Francisco Neighborhood Legal Assistance Found., San Francisco, 1968-70; sole practice, Calistoga, Calif., 1970-73; directing atty. Mendocino Legal Services, Ukiah, Calif., 1973 76; state chief of legal services State of Calif., Sacramento, 1976-78, dep. state pub. defender, State of Calif., 1978-79; sole practice, Kailua-Kona, Hawaii, 1980—. Chmn. Mendocino County Dem. Cen. Com., Ukiah, 1975-76; pres. Sacramento Waldorf Sch. Parent Council, Sacramento, 1976-77; v.p. Kailua Village Assn., 1983-84. Reginald Heber Smith Poverty Law fellowship, 1968-70. Mem. ABA, Hawaii Assn. Criminal Def. Lawyers, Nat. Assn. Criminal Def. Lawyers, Legal Aid Soc. Hawaii (bd. dirs. 1985-86). Office: 223 Kona Inn Village 75-5744 Alii Dr Kailua-Kona HI 96740

ZÖLD, FERENC LAJOS, professional society administrator; b. Kiskunhalas, Hungary, Dec. 20, 1942. Diploma in Edn., U. Budapest, 1971. Bookseller Györ, Hungary, 1961-73; sr. referent Hungarian Ministry of Culture, Budapest, 1973-78; sec.-gen. Hungarian Pubs'. and Booksellers' Assn., Budapest, 1978—. Author: Studies in the Publishing Activity in the Hungarian County Gy'38r-Sporon, 1980; editor: Publishers and Booksellers in Hungary, 1986, 87; contbr. numerous articles to profl. jours. Fellow Hungarian UNESCO Com. Home: Sziv u 30 II 8, H-1064 Budapest Hungary Office: Magyar Konyvkiadok Konyftrjesztok, Vorosmarty Ter 1, H-1051 Budapest Hungary

ZOLLINGER, HEINRICH FRITZ, chemistry educator; b. Aarau, Switzerland, Nov. 29, 1919; s. Fritz and Helene Marie (Prior) Z.; m. Marie Lina Heidi Frick, Oct. 9, 1948; children: Fritz Ernst, Ruedi Alfred, Hans Jürg. PhD, Swiss Fed. Inst. Tech., Zurich, 1944; PhD (hon.), U. Stuttgart, Fed. Republic of Germany, 1977, Tokyo Inst. Tech., 1983. Research chemist Ciba Co., Basle, Switzerland, 1945-60; lectr. U. Basle, 1952-60; prof. chemistry Swiss Fed. Inst. Tech., 1960-87, prof. emeritus, 1987—; rector Swiss Fed. Inst. Tech., 1973-77. Author: Chemie der Azofarbstoffe, 1958, Diazo and Azo Chemistry, 1961, Leitfaden der Farbstoffchemie, 1970, Chemie und Hochschule, 1979, Color Chemistry, 1987. Served to capt. Swiss Mil., 1955-60. Recipient Alfred Werner award Swiss Chem. Soc., 1959, Ruzicka prize Swiss Univ. Bd., 1960, Herbert Lewinstein award British Soc. Chem. Industry, 1964, Conrad prize Swiss Soc. of Dyers and Colourists, 1970, numerous other awards. Fellow Royal Swedish Acad. of Eng., Acad. Wissenschaften Göttingen; mem. Internat. Union Pure and Applied Chemistry (pres. organic chemistry div. 1975-77, union pres. 1979-81), Swiss Nat. Sci. Found. (pres. 1979-82). Office: ETH, ETH-Zentrum, CH-8092 Zurich Switzerland

ZOLTAK, JOHN LOUIS, electronics company executive; b. Hazleton, Pa., Jan. 3, 1939; s. John George and Mary (Luschak) Z.; student Pa. State U., 1956-57; B.S.E.E., Milw. Sch. Engring., 1961; m. Margaret Mary Bellezza, Sept. 12, 1964; children—John, Mary. With Autonetics div. Rockwell Internat., Downey, Calif., 1962-65, PRD Electronics, div. Harris Corp., Syosset, N.Y., 1966-69; founder, pres., chief exec. officer Support Systems, Assos., Inc., Hauppauge, N.Y., 1969—. Mem. IEEE. Clubs: Northport Yacht, Johns Island, Stratton Mountain, Huntington Crescent. Office: 1300 Veterans Memorial Hwy Hauppauge NY 11788-3025

ZONDERVAN, PETER JOHN (PAT ZONDERVAN), publisher, religious organization executive; b. Paterson, N.J., Apr. 2, 1909; s. Louis and Nellie Petronella (Eerdmans) Z.; m. Mary Swier, May 21, 1934; children: Robert Lee, Patricia Lucille, William J., Mary Beth. Student. pub. schs., Grandville, Mich.; D.Litt. (hon.), John Brown U., 1969; Litt.D., Lee Coll., 1972; LL.D., Campbellsville Coll., Ky., 1985; L.H.D. (hon.), Taylor U, Upland, Ind.,

1985. Co-founder Zondervan Pub. House, Grandville, Mich., 1931, Grand Rapids, Mich., 1932—; co-founder Zondervan Corp., Grand Rapids, 1955—; pres. Grand Rapids Camp of Gideons, 1938-41, chaplain, 1944-46, pres., 1947-48; pres. internat. trustee, 1950-52; v.p. Gideons Internat., 1952-55, pres., 1956-59, treas., 1972-75, chaplain, 1975-78; Bd. dirs. Christian Nationals Evangelism Commn., San Jose, Calif.; bd. dirs. Winona Lake Christian Assembly, Ind., 1937—, sec., 1961—; b. dir. Marantha Bible and Missionary Conf., Muskegon, Mich., 1961; organizer, 1st chmn. Christian Businessmen's Com., Grand Rapids, 1942; chmn. com. for city-wide Evangelistic meeting, 1946. Honored with declaration of P.J. Zondervan Day in Grand Rapids, Dec. 1973. Mem. Internat. Platform Assn. Clubs: Lotus (Grand Rapids) (pres. 1949, 65-67); Peninsular of Grand Rapids, Blythefield Country and Golf; Boca Golf (Boca Raton, Fla.). Office: Zondervan Corp 1415 Lake Dr SE Grand Rapids MI 49506

ZONGOLOWICZ, HELEN MICHAELINE, school principal; b. Kenosha, Wis., July 22, 1936; d. Edmund S. and Helen (Ostrowski) Z.; Ed.B., Dominican Coll., 1966; M.A., Cardinal Stritch Coll., 1973; Ed.D., U. No. Colo., 1977. Tchr. elem. schs. Kenosha, 1956-58, Center Line, Mich., 1958-59, Taft, Calif., 1960-61, Lake Wales, Fla., 1962-63, Albuquerque, 1963-65; tchr., asst. prin. St. Mary's Sch., Taft, 1965-69; asst. sch. supt. Diocese of Fresno, Calif., 1969-70; tchr. primary grades Greasewood Boarding Sch., Ganado, Ariz., 1970-72, coordinator spl. projects, 1972-75, liaison to parent adv. council, 1972-75, tchr. supr., 1972-76; ednl. specialist Ft. Defiance Agy., Navajo Area, Ariz., 1974-75, ednl. diagnostician, 1979-80; vis. asst. prof. U. Colo., 1976; asst. prof. Auburn (Ala.) U., 1977-79, U. N.Mex.-Gallup, 1981—; prin. Chuska Sch., 1980—. Recipient Spl. Achievement award U.S. Dept. Interior, 1971, 73, Superior Performance award, 1982. Mem. Am. Assn. Mental Deficiency, Assn. for Supervision and Curriculum Devel., Council for Exceptional Children, Council for Basic Edn., Am. Ednl. Research Assn., Nat. Assn. Female Execs., Internat. Reading Assn., Assn. for Children with Learning Disabilities Nat. Council Tchrs. of English. Navajo Nation North Cen. Assn. (chmn.), Kappa Delta Pi, Phi Delta Kappa. Address: Chuska Sch Box 321 Tohatchi NM 87325

ZORN, ROBERT LYNN, educator; b. Youngstown, Ohio, Mar. 22, 1938; s. Robert S. and Frances L. Zorn; B.S. Ed., Kent State U., 1959; M.Ed., Westminster Coll., 1964; Ph.D., U. Pitts., 1970; m. Joan M. Wilkos, Apr. 26, 1957; children—Deborah Lynn, Patricia Lynn. Tchr., West Branch (Ohio) Schs., 1961-62; elem. prin. Poland (Ohio) Schs., 1962-67, supt. schs., 1976—; high sch. unit prin. Boardman (Ohio) Schs., 1967-70; dir. adminstrv. services Mahoning County (Ohio) Schs., 1970-73, asst. supt., 1973-76; adj. prof. edn. Youngstown State U., 1970—; chmn. Ohi Adv. Com. to State Dept. Edn.; chmn. McGuffey Hist. Soc. Nat. Educator's Hall of Fame. Chmn. Mahoning County chpt. Am. Cancer Soc.; pres. bd. trustees Poland Methodist Ch.; trustee Mahoning County chpt. Am. Heart Assn. Served to lt. USAF, 1959-61. Mem. Doctoral Assn. Educators (life), Am. Assn. Sch. Adminstrs., Ohio PTA (life; Educator of Yr. 1980-81), Phi Delta Kappa. Republican. Clubs: Fonderlac County, Rotary, Protestant Men's. Author books, the most recent being: Speed Reading, 1980; contbr. articles to profl. jours. Home: 7341 Oak Dr Poland OH 44514 Office: 53 College St Poland OH 44514

ZORN, WILLIAM ALLEN, psychologist; b. Rochester, N.Y., Mar. 2, 1947; s. Richard and Dorothy (Hoffman) Z.; A.A.S., SUNY, Alfred, 1968; B.S., U. Ga., 1970; M.S., SUNY, Albany, 1977; Ph.D., SUNY, Buffalo, 1980; m. Susan Hack, Nov. 1, 1970. Diplomate med. psychotherapist, Am. Bd. Med. Pschotherapists; cert. Nat. Bd. Counselors, counselor. Rehab. counselor Assn. Blind of Rochester, N.Y., 1973-75; intern SUNY at Buffalo Mental Health Clinic, Childrens Hosp. Buffalo, 1978-80; staff psychologist Childrens Hosp. intensive care nursery, 1978-80, dir. intensive care nursery family services, 1980—; asst. prof. pediatrics SUNY, Buffalo, 1980—, adj. asst. prof. psychology, 1980—; cons. N.Y. State Early Childhood Direction Ctrs., 1980—; parent care cons., Maternal Infant Care Project, 1980. Bd. dirs. child and youth services, Medaille Coll., 1980, Sta. WBFO-FM Nat. Pub. Radio, 1980; chmn. We. N.Y. task force on Bereavement, 1985. Mem. Am. Psychol. Assn., Assn. for Care Children's Health, Western N.Y. Psychol. Assn., Am. Assn. Counseling and Devel. Home: 2838 Main St Buffalo NY 14214 Office: 219 Bryant St Buffalo NY 14222

ZORNER, KARL-HEINZ, measuring instruments manufacturing company executive; b. Gispersleben, Germany, Feb. 2, 1936; s. Walter and Ilse (Ritter) Z.; m. Eva Maria Gobel, June 3, 1960; children—Heike, Lars. Diploma Ingenieur, Technische Hochschule, 1962; Doktor Ingenieur, Kernforschungszentrum, 1965; Engr. Siemens Ag, Karlsruhe, Fed. Republic Germany, 1960-62; scientist Kernforschungszentrum, Karlsruhe, 1962-65; research and devel. exec. Meihak Ag, Hamburg, 1966-73, chief exec., 1973—; chmn. analytical instrument dept. Zentralverband Elektroindustrie, Frankfurt, Fed. Republic Germany, 1970—; bd. dirs. Verein Deutscher Ingenieure, Hamburg, 1983—. Cons. editor: Jour. Measuring Technic. Mem. Deutsche Physikalische Gesellschaft, Instrument Soc. Am.

ZORNOW, WILLIAM FRANK, historian, educator; b. Cleve., Aug. 13, 1920; s. William Frederick Emil and Viola (Schulz) Z. A.B., Western Res. U., 1942, A.M., 1944, Ph.D., 1952. Vice pres., treas. Glenville Coal & Supply Co., Real Value Coal Corp., Zornow Coal Corp., 1941-45; dep. clk. Probate Ct., Cuyahoga County, Ohio, 1941-43; prodn. planning engr. Hickok Elec. Instrument Co., Cleve., 1943-46; teaching asst. Western Res. U., 1944-47; instr. U. Akron, 1946-47, Case Inst. Tech., 1947-50, Washburn U., 1950-51; lectr. Cleve. Coll., 1948-49; asst. prof. Kans. State U., 1951-58; asst. prof. history Kent (Ohio) State U., 1958-61, asso. prof., 1961-66, prof. history, 1966—; collection corr. Berkshire Loan and Fin. Co., Painesville (Ohio) Security Credit Acceptance Corp., Mentor, O., 1951-60; cons. Karl E. Mundt Library, Dakota State Coll., Madison, S.D. Author: Lincoln and the Party Divided, 1954, rev. edit., 1972, Kansas: A History of the Jayhawk State, 1957, America at Mid-Century, 1959; contbr.: Abraham Lincoln: A New Portrait, 1959, Kansas: The First Century, 1956; articles to encys. and profl. jours.; editor: Shawnee County (Kans.) Hist. Bull, 1950-51; abstractor: America: History and Life: Historical Abstracts, 1964—. Mem. AAUP, Am. Acad. Polit. and Social Sci., Am. Assn. State and Local History (award of merit 1958), Am. Hist. Assn., Orgn. Am. Historians, Ohio Acad. History (chmn. awards com.), Ohio Hist. Soc. (library advisory com. 1969—), Ohio Soc. N.Y., Center for Study of Presidency, Acad. Polit. Sci., Sierra Club of San Francisco, Delta Tau Delta, Pi Gamma Mu, Phi Alpha Theta, Phi Delta Kappa. Home: 7893 Middlesex Rd Mentor OH 44060 Office: Kent State U 305 Bowman Hall Kent OH 44242

ZOU JIAHUA, government official; b. Shanghai, People's Republic of China, 1927; s. Zou Caofen. Former dep. dir., chief engr. Fengman Power Plant; former del. chief engr. Northeast Electric Power Adminstrn.; former dir. Beijing Power Adminstrn.; alt. mem. Chinese Communist Party Cen. Com., 1977; dep. dir. State Office Nat. Def. Industry, from 1979; vice-minister Commn. Sci., Technology and Industry for Nat. Def., 1983-85; minister of ordnance industry from 1985; mem. Chinese Communist Party 12th Cen. Com., 1985; state councilor, minister of machine bldg. and electronics industry 1988—. Address: State Council, Beijing Peoples Republic of China *

ZOUNGRANA, PAUL CARDINAL, archbishop of Ouagadougou; b. Ouagadougou, Upper Volta, Sept. 3, 1917. Ordained priest Roman Cath. Ch., 1942; archbishop of Ouagadougou, 1960—; elevated to Sacred Coll. Cardinals, 1965; titular ch. St. Camillus de Lellis; mem. Congregation Evangelization of Peoples, Commn. Revision Code of Canon Law. Address: BP 1472, Ouagadougou Burkina Faso *

ZOUPANOS, THEODORE S., diplomat; b. Corfu, Greece, Sept. 19, 1935; s. Spyridon and Evelina (Tsaussi) Z.; m. Aristea Pialopoulos; 1 child: Evangelia-Evelina. BS, Cornell U., 1958; MA, Princeton U., 1962, postgrad. Instr. internat. relations, internat. law Vassar Coll., Poughkeepsie, N.Y., 1961-63; advisor to mission of Cyprus UN, N.Y.C., 1964-66, with div. of human rights, 1966—; chief external relations, inter-agy. affairs UN, Geneva, 1984—; chmn. joint appeals bd. UN, Geneva, 1980—. Active Cornell U. Council, Ithaca, N.Y., 1987—. Mem. Diplomatic Club of Geneva. Greek Orthodox. Home: 18 Ave du Bouchet, 1209 Geneva Switzerland Office: UN Office at Geneva, Palais des Nations, 1211 Geneva 10, Switzerland

ZRAKET, CHARLES ANTHONY, systems research and engineering company executive; b. Lawrence, Mass., Jan. 9, 1924; s. Habib and Martha Z.; m. Shirley Ann Camus, Oct. 13, 1961; children: David, Suzanne, Elizabeth, Caroline. B.S. in Elec. Engring, Northeastern U., Boston, 1951; S.M.E.E., M.I.T., 1953; PhD in Engring. (hon.), Northeastern U., 1988. Mem. research staff digital computer lab., group leader M.I.T., 1951-53; group leader Lincoln Lab., 1953-58; tech. dir., then sr. v.p. MITRE Corp., Bedford, Mass. and McLean, Va., 1958-76; exec. v.p., chief operating officer MITRE Corp., 1976-86, pres., chief exec. officer, 1986—, also trustee; bd. overseers Ctr. Naval Analyses; bd. dirs. Bank of Boston. Trustee Hudson Inst.; chmn. Gov. Mass. Com. Info. Systems, 1978—; mem. Northeastern U. Corp. Council. Served with AUS, 1943-46. Decorated Bronze Star, Purple Heart with oak leaf cluster, Combat Inf. badge. Fellow IEEE, AIAA, AAAS; mem. Council on Fgn. Relations, N.Y. Acad. Scis., Sigma Xi, Tau Beta Pi, Eta Kappa Nu. Home: 71 Sylvan Ln Weston MA 02193 Office: MITRE Corp Burlington Rd Bedford MA 01730

ZSCHAU, JULIUS JAMES, lawyer; b. Peoria, Ill., Apr. 1, 1940; s. Raymond Johann Ernst and Rosamond Lillian (Malicoat) Z.; m. Leila Joan Krueger, Aug. 7, 1971; children—Kristen Elisabeth, Kimberly Erna, Kira Jamie, Karla Johanna. B.S., U. Ill., Champaign, 1964, J.D., 1966; LL.M., John Marshall Law Sch., 1978. Bar: Ill. 1966, Fla. 1975. Atty., Ill. Central Gulf R.R. Co., Chgo., 1966-68; assoc. Coin & Sheerin, Chgo., 1968-70, Snyder, Clarke, Dalziel, Holmquist & Johnson, Waukegan, Ill., 1970-72; csl. Ill. Center Corp., Chgo., 1972-74; v.p., gen. csl., sec. Am. Agronomics Corp., Tampa, Fla., 1974-76; pres. Sorota & Zschau, Clearwater, Fla., 1976—; bd. dirs. Attys. Title Ins. Fund, Inc.; dir. Pinellas Review, Inc., Attys. Title Services, Inc.; chmn. com. on land trusts, exec. com. real property sect., mem. grievance com. Fla. Bar, chair leadership conf. 1987. Bd. dirs. Fla. Gulf Coast Symphony; mem. Pinellas County Exec. Com.; bd. dirs. Attys. Title Ins. Fund. Served to capt. USNR, 1962—. Mem. ABA (vice chmn. condo com., editor newsletter, co-chmn. com. on role of lawyers in real estate transactions, chmn. vol. bar liaison com. Fla. bar), Ill. Bar Assn., Chgo. Bar Assn., Clearwater Bar Assn. (past pres.), Fla. Council Bar Assn. Pres. (bd. dirs., v.p., pres.), Clearwater C. of C. (bd. govs., exec. com.). Republican. Lutheran. Clubs: Harborview, Countryside Country (Clearwater, Fla.); Masons, Scottish Rite, Shriners. Editor Res Ipsa Loquitur, 1982-84. Home: 1910 Saddlehill Rd N Dunedin FL 34698

ZSIDÓ, LÁSZLÓ, mathematics educator, researcher; b. Brasov, Romania, Feb. 22, 1946; came to Fed. Republic Germany, 1978, naturalized, 1979; s. Donat Zsido and Elisabeth Zsido-Nagy; m. Eva Csutak, June 16, 1988. Diploma, Faculty Math., Bucharest, Romania, 1968, Ph.D., 1973. Researcher Math. Inst., Bucharest, 1968-77, Nat. Inst. Sci. and Tech. Creation, Bucharest, 1977-78; asst. Faculty Math., U. Munster, Fed. Republic Germany, 1978-80; prof. math. U. Stuttgart, Fed. Republic Germany, 1980—. Author: (with S. Stratila) Lectures on von Neumann Algebras, 1975 (Romanian Acad. prize 1975); also numerous research articles, 1966—. Mem. Deutsche Mathematiker-Vereinigung, Am. Math. Soc., Societe Mathematique de France, Math. Assn. Am. Roman Catholic. Avocation: swimming. Home: Gotthold-Ege-Strasse 20, 7250 Leonberg Federal Republic of Germany Office: Math Inst A, Pfaffenwaldring 57, 7000 Stuttgart 80 Federal Republic of Germany

ZUBAIR, HABEEBA HUSSAIN HABEEB, librarian; b. Male, Republic of Maldives, Sept. 9, 1930; d. Hussain Habeeb and Shahima Shamsuddin; m. Abdulla Zubair, Mar. 7, 1923; children: Ibrahim, Shafeea, Shahida. Grad. High Sch. Urdu Medium, Hyderabad, India, 1948; Grad. High Sch. English Medium, Colombo, Sri Lanka, 1952. Cert. librarian. Asst. prin. Govt. Service, Male, Maldives, 1956-62; sec. Prime Minister's Office, Male, 1962-67, Foreign Affairs, Male, 1968-70, Transp. Dept. Govt. Service, Male, 1974-78, Aid Dept. Govt. Service, Male, 1974-75; librarian Nat. Library, Male, 1978-86, deputy dir., 1986—. Editor: Jour. Adabi-Shu-Oor; translator: Niru, Wafa, 1982. Home: Mandoovilla 8 Janavary Str, Male, Machchangolhi 20-03, Republic of Maldives Office: Nat Library, Billoorijehige, 59 Majeedi Magu Galolhu Male 20-04, Republic of Maldives

ZUBRINICH, JOHN ANTHONY, marketing manager; b. Port Pirie, South Australia, Australia, June 16, 1945; s. Leslie Bernard and Kathleen Mary (Flinn) Z.; m. Julienne Mary Curtin, May 13, 1970; children: Celia, Kieran, Kathryn, Paul. Grad., South Australian Inst. Tech., 1967; MS in Engring., London U., 1972; diploma, Imperial Coll., London, 1972; MBA, Monash U., Melbourne, Victoria, Australia, 1986. Metall. cadet Broken Hill Associated Smelters, Port Pirie, 1963-68; asst. reseach officer R.T.Z., Bristol, Eng., 1968-69; project metallurgist Western Mining Corp., Perth and Kalgoorlie, Western Australia, 1969-74; prodn. supt. Queensland Alumina Ltd., Gladstone, Australia, 1974-80; mktg. mgr. Fluor Daniel Australia Ltd., Melbourne, 1980—. Nat. exec. mem. Australian Jaycees, Galdstone, 1980. Mem. Instn. Mining and Metallurgy, Australian Inst. Mining and Metallurgy (chmn. Melbourne br. 1987—). Roman Catholic. Club: Minerals and Energy (Brisbane, Queensland), Melbourne South Rotary. Office: Fluor Daniel Australia Ltd, 616 Saint Kilda Rd, Melbourne, Victoria 3004, Australia

ZUBROFF, LEONARD SAUL, surgeon; b. Minersville, Pa., Mar. 27, 1925; s. Abe and Fannie (Freedline) Z.; B.A., Wayne State U., 1945, M.D., 1949. Intern Garfield Hosp., Washington, 1949-50, resident in surgery, 1951-55, chief resident surgery, 1954-55; practice medicine specializing in surgery, 1958-76; med. dir. Chevrolet Gear and Axle Plant, Chevrolet Forge Plant, Gen. Motors Corp., Detroit, 1977-78, divisional med. dir. Detroit Diesel Allison div., 1978-87, regional med. dir. Gen. Motors Corp, 1987—; mem. staff Hutzel Hosp., Detroit Meml. Hosp. Served with USAF, 1956-58. Diplomate Am. Bd. Surgery. Fellow A.C.S.; mem. AMA, Mich. State, Wayne County med. socs., Acad. Surgery Detroit, Am. Occupational Med. Assn., Mich. Occupational Med. Assn., Detroit Occupational Physicians Assn., NAACP, Phi Lambda Kappa. Lodge: Masons (33 deg.). Home: 16233 Nine Mile Rd Apt 201 Southfield MI 48075 Office: 13400 W Outer Dr Detroit MI 48239

ZUBRZYCKI, JERZY, retired sociology educator; b. Krakow, Poland, Jan. 12, 1920; arrived in Australia, 1955.; s. Jozef and Zofia (Madeyska) Z.; m. Alexandra Krolikowska, Oct. 23, 1943; children: Thomas, Anna, John, Joanna. BS in Econs., Sch. Econs. U. London, 1948, MS in Econs., 1952; PhD, Polish U. Abroad, London, 1954. Asst. lectr. sociology U. London, 1949-52; research fellow Australian Nat. U., Canberra, 1955-58, sr. sociology fellow, 1959-64, profl. fellow, 1965-70, found. prof. sociology, 1970-86, prof. emeritus, 1986—. Served to capt. spl. ops. exec., Brit. army, 1941-46. Decorated Polish Cross of Valor, mem. Order of Brit. Empire, comdr. Order of Brit. Empire, officer Order of Australia. Fellow Acad. Social Scis. in Australia.

ZUCK, ALFRED CHRISTIAN, consulting mechanical engineer; b. Ridgefield, N.J., Dec. 16, 1924; s. Frederick William and Margaret Christine (Umland) Z.; m. Vilma Hudson, May 6, 1951; children: Allyson, Jon, Randall. M.E., Poly. Inst. Bklyn., 1960. Registered profl. engr., 21 states including N.Y.; lic. profl. planner, N.J. From designer to sr. v.p. Syska & Hennessy, Inc., N.Y.C., 1946-78; prin. Edwards & Zuck (P.C.), N.Y.C., 1978—; mem. nat. panel Am. Arbitration Assn, Nat. Council Engring. Examiners. Served with AUS, 1943-46; to 1st lt. USAF, 1951-52; to capt. N.J. Air N.G., 1947-56. Decorated Bronze Star (2). Fellow Am. Cons. Engrs. Council (past mem. Nat. Ethical Practices Com.); mem. NSPE, N.Y. State Soc. Profl. Engrs. (past chmn. profl. engrs. in pvt. practice program), Am. Soc. Mil. Engrs., Nat. Council Engring. Examiners, N.Y. Assn. Cons. Engrs. (past v.p., bd. dirs.), ASHRAE, N.Y. Bldg. Congress. (bd. govs.). Lutheran. Club: N.Y. Athletic. Home: 444 Weymouth Dr Wyckoff NJ 07481 Office: Edwards & Zuck PC 330 W 42d St New York NY 10036

ZUCKER, ALFRED JOHN, educator, sch. adminstr.; b. Hartford, Sept. 25, 1940; s. Samuel and Rose (Zucker) Z.; A.A., Los Angeles Valley Coll., 1960; B.A., U. Calif. at Los Angeles, 1962, M.A., 1963, Ph.D., 1966; m. Sallie Lea Friedheim, Dec. 25, 1966; children—Mary Anne, John James, James Patrick, Patrick Jonathan, Anne-Marie Kathleen, Kathleen Mary. Lectr. English, Los Angeles City Coll., 1963-68; prof. English, philosophy, chmn. div. humanities Los Angeles Southwest Coll., 1968-72, chmn. English dept., 1972-74, asst. dean instruction, 1974—; prof. English El Camino Coll., 1985—. Mem. Los Angeles Jr. Coll. Dist. Senate, 1969—. Mem. Los Angeles Coll. Tchrs. Assn. (dir.), Calif. Jr. Coll. Assn., Calif. Tchrs. Assn., AAUP, Phi Beta Kappa, Phi Delta Kappa (pres. U. Calif. at Los Angeles chpt. 1966-67, v.p. 1967-68). Lodge: KC. Contbr. articles to profl. jours. Office: 1600 W Imperial Hwy Los Angeles CA 90047

ZUCKER, DAVID CLARK, lawyer, army officer; b. St. Louis, July 29, 1946; s. Clark S. and Georgia L. (Sellers) Z.; m. Karin Wells Waugh, July 10, 1971 (div. Sept. 1985); 1 child, William W.; m. Charlotte Denton, Feb. 8, 1986. B.A., U. Mo., 1968, J.D., 1971; postgrad. Judge Advocate Gen.'s Sch., Charlottesville, Va., 1977-78, Armed Forces Staff Coll., 1981-82. Bar: Mo. 1971, U.S. Ct. Mil. Appeals 1971, U.S. Ct. Appeals (fed. cir.) 1983, U.S. Supreme Ct, 1974. Commd. 2d lt. U.S. Army, 1968, advanced through grades to col., 1988; chief mil. justice, Ft. Leavenworth, Kans., 1971-74; trial atty. Office of Army Chief Trial Atty., Falls Church, Va., 1974-77; dep. chief adminstrv. law Hdqrs. U.S. Army Europe, Heidelberg, W. Ger., 1978-80, internat. logistics atty. contract law, U.S. Army, Heidelberg, Fed. Rep. of Germany, 1980-81; litigation atty. Office of Judge Advocate Gen., Washington, 1982; chief trial team III, Office of Chief Trial Atty. Hdqrs. Dept. Army, Falls Church, 1982-86; chief, contract law div., Gilbert A. Cuneo prof. govt. contract law, U.S. Army JAG Sch., Charlottesville, Va., 1986—. Mem. ABA, Am. Trial Lawyers Assn., Assn. U.S. Army, Judge Advocates Assn. (bd. dirs. 1983-86), Mo. Bar Assn., Phi Alpha Delta (chpt. vice justice 1969-70). Home: 2116 Morris Rd Charlottesville VA 22903 Office: JAG Sch Contract Law Div 600 Massie Rd Charlottesville VA 22903

ZUCKER, STEFAN, tenor, writer, editor, radio broadcaster; b. N.Y.C. BS, Columbia U., 1967; postgrad., NYU, 1967-72. Freelance tenor concerts and operas in U.S. and Europe, 1965—; tenor RCA Records, N.Y.C., 1972-77; guest singer radio and TV programs, U.S. and Europe, 1975—; radio producer, host WKCR-FM, N.Y.C., 1980—; opera critic N.Y. Tribune, 1983-84; producer, adminstr. Harlem Civic Opera, N.Y.C., 1967; philosophy lectr. Coll. Ins., N.Y.C., 1972; record producer, 1979—; singer, producer, stage dir., adminstr. various operas. Editor Opera Fanatic mag., 1986—; contbr. articles to Opera News, The Opera Quar., Am. Record Guide, Opera Fanatic, News World, others. Pres. Bel Canto Soc., Inc., 1985—. Named Worlds Highest Tenor Guinness Book of World Records, 1979-88; subject of record Stefan Zucker: The World's Highest Tenor, 1981. Mem. NYU Philosophy Assn. (pres. 1969-72, v.p. 1968), NYU Grad. Sch. Arts and Scis. Student Council, Assn. Furtherment Bel Canto (pres. 1967-80). Home: 11 Riverside Dr New York NY 10023

ZUCKERMAN, IRA LAURENCE, lawyer; b. N.Y.C., Apr. 14, 1947; s. William J. and Lillian (Skolnick) Z.; m. Ginger Senatore, Sept. 17, 1982; children: David S., Jonathan S., Lauren J.; stepchildren: Jonathan C. Hunt, Jeffrey R. Hunt. B.B.A., Temple U., 1968; J.D., St. John's U., Jamaica, N.Y., 1974; LL.M. in Taxation, U. Miami, 1978. Bar: N.Y. 1975, U.S. Tax Ct. 1975, Fla. 1984, U.S. Ct. Appeals (11th cir.) 1987. Tax acct. Hanigsberg, Delson & Broser, N.Y.C., 1973-75; tax atty. Nabisco, Inc., East Hanover, N.J., 1975-76; tax mgr. Coulter Electronics, Hialeah, Fla., 1976-79; asst. controller-taxes Storage Tech., Louisville, Colo., 1979-83; dir. internat. tax Touche Ross & Co., Miami, Fla., 1983-85; mgr. internat. tax Ernst & Whinney, Miami, 1985-86; sole practice, Sunrise, Fla., 1986—; frequent speaker, chmn. various profl. seminars, symposia, 1981—. Contbr. articles to profl. jours., 1975—. Mem. ABA (tax com.), Fla. Bar Assn. (internat. tax com.), Internat. Fiscal Assn., N.Y. State Bar Assn. (tax sect.), Internat. Trade Forum (pres.), French-Am. C. of C. Office: Atrium W Suite 205 7771 W Oakland Pk Blvd Sunrise FL 33351

ZUCKERMAN, LINDA ELISE, publishing executive; b. N.Y.C., Oct. 9, 1950; d. Arthur and Claire (Roth) Zuckerman. Student Manhattan Community Coll., 1967-68, H.H. Lehman Coll., 1968-72. Adminstrv. mgr. J.B. Kass & Co., N.Y.C., 1972-74; asst. personnel dir. Morningside House Aging in Am., N.Y.C., 1974-78; outplacement Cons. Re-Placements Unltd., N.Y.C., 1978-80; profl. edn. supr. Coopers & Lybrand, N.Y.C., 1980-81; cons. Tng. Systems Design, N.Y.C., 1982-86; pres. In-Queries Unltd., N.Y.C., 1986—. Contbr. articles to profl. jours. Bronx student coordinator Ottinger for U.S. Senator, N.Y., 1970. Mem. Am. Soc. for Tng. and Devel., Am. Soc. Personnel Adminstrn., Nat. Assn. Female Execs. Democrat. Office: In-Queries Unltd 200 Park Ave Suite 303 E New York NY 10166

ZUHDI, MOHAMED NAZIH, physician; b. Beirut, Lebanon, May 19, 1925; s. Omar and Lutfiye (Atef) Z.; came to U.S., 1950; B.A., Am. U., Beirut, Lebanon, 1946, M.D., 1950; children by previous marriage—Omar, Nabil; m. 2d, Annette McMichael; children—Adam, Leyla, Zachariah. Intern St. Vincent's Hosp., S.I., N.Y., 1950-51, Presbyn.-Columbia Med. Center. N.Y.C., 1951-52; resident Kings County State U. N.Y. Med. Center, N.Y.C., 1952-56; fellow State U. N.Y. Downstate Med. Ctr., Brklyn., 1953-54; resident U. Hosp., Mpls., 1956, Oklahoma City, 1957-58; practice medicine specializing in cardivocascular and thoracic surgery, Oklahoma City, 1958—; dir. Transplantation Inst. Med. Ctr., 1984—, surgeon in chief Bapt. Hosp., Oklahoma City; active cardiac surgery Bapt. Hosp., St. Anthony's Hosp.; chmn. Okla. Cardiovascular Inst., Oklahoma City, 1983-84, Okla. Heart Ctr., Oklahoma City, 1984-85; Named Hon. Citizen Brazil. Diplomate Am. Bd. Surgery, Am. Bd. Thoracic Surgery. Fellow ACS; mem. Am. Thoracic Soc., Okla. Thoracic Soc., AMA, So. Med. Assn., Okla. Med. Assn., Internat., Coll. Angiology, Am. Coll. Chest Physicians, Oklahoma City C. of C., Oklahoma County Med. Soc., Oklahoma City Clin. Soc., Okla. Surg. Assn., Oklahoma City Surg. Soc., Southwestern Surg. Congress, Am. Coll. Cardiology, Am. Soc. Artificial Internal Organs, Soc. Thoracic Surgeons (founder mem.), Am. Assn. for Thoracic Surgery, Internat. Cardiovascular Soc., Okla. State Heart Assn., Osler Soc., So. Thoracic Surg. Assn., Lillehei Surg. Soc., Internat. Soc. Heart Transplantation, Dwight Harken's Founder's Group Cardiac Surgery. Contbg. author Cardiac Surgery, 1967, 2d edit., 1972. Contbr. articles to profl. jours.; developer numerous med. devices and techniques.Club: Oklahoma City Golf and Country. Home: 7305 Lancet Ct Oklahoma City OK 73120 Office: 3400 NW Expressway Oklahoma City OK 73112

ZUKERMAN, PINCHAS, concert violinist, violist, conductor; b. Tel Aviv, July 16, 1948; came to U.S., 1962; s. Yehuda and Miriam (Lieberman) Z.; m. Eugenia Rich, May 26, 1968 (div.); children: Natalia, Arianna; m. Tuesday Weld, 1985. Student, Juilliard Sch. Music, 1965-68. Ind. concert violinist 1968—. With impresario, Sol Hurok, 1967-76; condr., soloist English Chamber Orch., 1974, Mostly Mozart Festival, N.Y.C., 1975; guest condr., soloist Los Angeles Philharm., Boston Symphony, Phila. Orch., N.Y. Philharm.; music dir. South Bank Festival, London, 1978-80, St. Paul Chamber Orch., 1980-87; toured with Isaac Stern; mem. trio with Daniel Barenboim and Jacqueline du Pre; (rec. artist) CBS, EMI, Philips Classics labels. Winner Internat. Levintritt Competition, 1967. Office: care Shirley Kirshbaum & Assocs 711 West End Ave New York NY 10025

ZUKROWSKI, WOJCIECH, author; b. Cracow, Apr. 14, 1916; s. Zygmunt Zukrowski and Jadwiga Wojtowicz; m. Maria Woltersdorf, 1945; 1 child. Ed. Wroclaw U., Jagiellonian U. War corr. North Viet-nam, 1954; counsellor, Polish Embassy, New Delhi, 1956-58; dep. to Seym, 1972—; co-editor Widnokregi (monthly) and Nowe Ksiazki; mem. All Poland Peace Com., Chief Council of Union Fighters for Freedom and Democracy; chmn. Soc. for Polish Spanish Friendship, 1978—. Author short stories: Zkraju milczenia (Fron the Land of Silence), Piorkiem flaminga (With a Flamingo's Quil), Corecka (Little Daughter), Okruchy weselnego tortu (Crumbs from the Wedding Cake), Reka ojca (Father's Hand); novels include: Days of Defeat (Ministry of Def. prize), 1961; The Stone Tables, 1966; The Lucky Devil; Styx Beach, 1976; Zapach psiejsiersci, 1979; House Without Walls; Wanderings with my Guru; In the Kingdom of a Million Elephants; Chinese Legends; Inside Miror, 1973; Collisions, 1973; films include: Bathed in Fire, Direction Berlin, The Last Days, Lotna, Potop. Recipient State prize 1st class, 1953, 78, decorated award of Minister of Nat. Def., 1961, Prize of Minister of Culture and Art, 1963, 65, 69, Pietrzak Prize, 1967, Prize of Prime Minister for lit. prodn. for children and youth, 1977; knight's and officer's cross Order Polonia Restiuta; Order of Banner of Labour, 1st and 2d class, Order of Builders of People's Poland, 1976, named Meritorious Activist of Culture, 1978, others. Mem. Polish Union Writers, PEN Club. Home: Karowa 14/16 m 22, 00-324 Warsaw Poland *

ZULETA-ALVAREZ, ENRIQUE JULIO MAURICIO, Latin American thought educator, librarian; b. Buenos Aires, July 1, 1923; s. Enrique Zuleta and Silvia Alvarez; m. Emilia Puciero, Apr. 12, 1947; children: Enrique,

Ignacio, Graciana, Angela, Javier. Grad., Colegio Nat., Mendoza, Argentina, 1943. Prof. U. Nat. Cuyo, Mendoza, Argentina, 1959, head librarian, 1962-64, prof. history of Latin Am. thought, 1964-68, prof., 1968—, rector, pres., 1981-83; vis. prof. Latin Am. Lit. U. Nat. Chile, Santiago, 1959, Latin Am. U. N. Mex., Albuquerque, 1961-62. Author: Introducción a Maurras, 1965, El Nacionalismo Argentiono, 1975, Lengua y Cultura en Caro, 1977, P. Henriquez Ureñn y su Tiempo, 1985. Sub dir. Nat. Edn. Sec., buenos Aires, 1958; dir. Cultural Sec., Mendoza, 1959-61. Univ. scholar Ministry Fgn. Affairs, Madrid, 1954-55; research grantee Ministry Nat. Edn., Madrid, 1977-78. Mem. Hist. Studies Junta, History Nat. Acad. Miguel Lillo Found. (hon.), Argentine Historians Soc., Cuyano Inst. Hispanic Culture (hon.). Mem. Partido Autonomio Soberania. Roman Catholic. Home: Lamadrid 753 Dpt 2, 5500 Mendoza Argentina Office: U Nat Cuyo, University Ctr, 5500 Mendoza Argentina

ZU LOEWENSTEIN-WERTHEIM-FREUDENBERG, PRINCE RUPERT LOUIS FERDINAND, financial consultant; b. Palma, Majorca, Aug. 24, 1933; s. Prince Leopold and Countess Bianca H-M Fischler von Treuberg L.; M.A., Magdalen Coll., Oxford, 1953; m. Josephine Lowry-Corry, July 18, 1957; children—Rudolf, Konrad, Theodora. With Bache & Co., London, 1953-62; with Leopold Joseph & Sons, Mcht. Bankers, Ltd., London, 1963-81, sr. mng. dir., 1966-81; ind. fin. cons., London, 1981—. Decorated knight of honor and devotion Sovereign Mil. Order of Malta; Constantine Order of St. George; Knight Grand Cross of Justice. Conservative. Roman Catholic. Clubs: Bucks, Boodles, Whites, Portland, Pratt's, Beefsteak; Regency (N.Y.C.). Address: Petersham Lodge, River Ln, Richmond, Surrey England

ZULU, ALEXANDER GREY, Zambian politician; b. Chipata, Eastern Province, Sept. 3, 1924; s. Agrippa and Tionenji Zulu; m. 1952; 8 children. Ed. Mafuta Lower Primary Sch. and Munali Secondary Sch. Water Devel. asst. No. Rhodesia, 1950-53; bookkeeper/mgr. Kabwe Co-operative Soc., 1953-62; parliamentary sec. No. Rhodesia, 1963; Minister of Commerce and Industry, 1964, Minister of Transport and Works, 1964, Minister of Mines and Co-operative, 1965-67, Minister of Home Affairs, 1967-70, Minister of Defence, 1970-73; sec. of State (subsequently chmn. sub-com.) For Defence and Security, 1979-85; sec-gen. United Nations Independence Party (UNIP) 1973-79, 1985—; mem. parliament of Zambia, 1979—. Address: United Nat Ind Party, Private Bag RW 17X, Lusaka Zambia *

ZUMBERGE, JAMES HERBERT, university president, geologist; b. Mpls., Dec. 27, 1923; s. Herbert Samuel and Helen (Reich) Z.; m. Marilyn Edwards, June 21, 1947; children: John Edward, JoEllen, James Frederick, Mark Andrew. Student, Duke, 1943-44; BA, U. Minn., 1946, PhD, 1950; LLD, Grand Valley State Coll., 1970, Kwansei Gakuin U., Japan, 1979; LHD, Nebr. Wesleyan U., 1972, Hebrew Union Coll.-Jewish Inst. Religion, 1987; DSc, Chapman Coll., 1982. Instr. Duke U., 1946-47; mem. faculty U. Mich., 1950-62, prof. geology, 1960-62; pres. Grand Valley State Coll., Allendale, Mich., 1962-68; prof. geology, dean U. Ariz. Coll. Earth Sci., Tucson, 1968-72; chancellor U. Nebr. at Lincoln, 1972-75; pres. So. Meth. U., Dallas, 1975-80, U. So. Calif., Los Angeles, 1980—; cons. geologist ground water and non-metallic minerals, 1950-62; chief glaciologist Ross Ice Shelf Project, IGY, 1957-58; dir. Litton Industries, Pacific Lighting Corp., Security Pacific Nat. Bank; U.S. del., 1970-86; pres. Sci. Com. on Antarctic Research, 1982-86; chmn. Ross Ice Shelf Project NSF, 1970-73, also mem. steering group Greenland Ice Sheet Program, 1971-82; del. numerous internat. confs. on polar research, Moscow, 1958, Chamonix, 1958, Helsinki, 1960, Obergurgl, Austria, 1962, Poland, 1967, Oslo, 1970, Sydney, Australia, 1972, Mendoza, Argentina, 1976, Warsaw, 1978, New Zealand, 1980; mem. Nat. Sci. Bd., 1974-80. Author: The Lakes of Minnesota, 1952, Laboratory Manual for Physical Geology, 1967, 7th edit., 1988, Elements of Geology, 1963, 72, Elements of Physical Geology, 1976; numerous jour. articles and papers. Bd. overseers Hoover Instn. on War, Revolution and Peace, 1978-84; chmn. U.S. Arctic Research Commn., 1984-87. Recipient Antarctic Service medal, 1966; Distinguished Alumni award U. Minn., 1972; James H. Zumberge Library, Grand Valley State Coll., named, 1968; Cape Zumberge, Antarctica named, 1960; Zumberge Coast, Antartica, named 1986. Mem. Geol. Soc. Am., Am. Geophys. Union, Soc. Econ. Geologists, Internat. Glaciological Soc., AAAS, Mich. Acad. Scis. (pres. 1967); Conf. Bd.; Mem. Sigma Xi (nat. lectr. 1978-80). Clubs: Cosmos (Washington); Calif; University (N.Y.C.), Explorers (N.Y.C.); Bohemian (Los Angeles), One Hundred (Los Angeles). Office: U So Calif Office of Pres Univ Park Los Angeles CA 90089-0012

ZUNDE, PRANAS, information science educator, researcher; b. Kaunas, Kithuania, Nov. 26, 1923; came to U.S., 1960, naturalized, 1964; s. Pranas and Elzbieta (Lisajevic) Z.; m Alge R. Bizauskas, May 29, 1945; children: Alge R., Audronis K., Aurelia R., Aidis L., Gytis J. Dipl. Ing., Hannover Inst. Tech., 1947; MS, George Washington U., 1965; PhD, Ga. Inst. Tech., 1968. Dir. project Documentation Inc., Bethesda, Md., 1961-64; mgr. mgmt. info. system Documentation Inc., Bethesda, 1964-65; sr. research scientist Ga. Inst. Tech., Atlanta, 1965-68, assoc. prof., 1968-72, prof. dept. computer sci., 1973—; cons. UNESCO, Caracas, Venezuela, 1970-72, Esquela Polit. Nacional, Quito, Ecuador, 1974-75, State of Ga., Atlanta, 1976-78; Fulbright prof. Nat Acad. Schi., 1975; vis. prof. Simon Bolivar U., Caracas, 1976, J. Kepler U., Austria, 1981; vis. scientist Riso Nat. Lab., Roskilde, Denmark, 1983. Author: Agriculture in Soviet Lithuania, 1962, National Science Information Systems in Eastern Europe, 1972; editor: Procs. Information Utilities, 1974, Procs. Foundations of Information and Software Schience, 1983-86; contbr. articles to tech. and sci. jours. NSF grantee Office of Edn., U.S. Army Research Office, 1968—. Mem. Am. Soc. Info. Sci., Semitic Soc. Am., Soc. Sigma Xi. Roman Catholic. Home: 1808 Timothy Dr NE Atlanta GA 30329 Office: GA Inst Tech North Ave Atlanta GA 30332

ZUNG, THOMAS TSE-KWAI, architect; b. Shanghai, China, Feb. 8, 1933; s. Bate and Rose Yu-Sun (Fong) Z.; came to U.S., 1937, naturalized, 1954; student Drew U., 1950-51, (Rose scholar) Va. Poly. Inst., 1951-53, Columbia U., 1955-57; B.Arch., U. Mich., 1960; M.S. in Design Sci. (student R. Buckminster Fuller), Internat. Coll., 1982; 1 son, Thomas Ba-Tse. Project architect Edward Durell Stone, architect, N.Y.C., 1958, 60-65; architect, Cleve., 1967—; pres. Buckminster Fuller, Sadao and Zung, architects, 1979—; prin. archtl. works include City Cleve. Pub. Utilities Bldg., Cleve. State U. Sports Center Dome, Mayfran, Inc., Sawmill Creek Lodge, U. Akron Guzzetta Hall, music, speech and theater arts center, Alumni Center Bowling Green State U., U. Akron Master Plan-West, City of East Cleveland, Superior Euclid beautification plan, student recreation center at Bowling Green State U., Glenville Public Library, campus bldg. Tex. Wesleyan Coll., recreation, health and phys. edn. bdg. Wittenberg U., Medina Res. Park Office, arena, health, phys. edn. complex U. Akron, Dyke Coll., Lima State Prison, Cleve. Children's Christian Home, State of Ohio Pre-Release Ctr. Cleve., Lorain-Grafton State Prison, Mayfiled High Sch., Asian Village Project, Cleve. Metroparks Tropical Rainforest Bldg., Student Union Wittenberg U., YWCA Salem Ohio, China Internat. Trade Ctr. People's Rep. China, additions to Cleve. Hopkins Internat. Airport. Task force chmn. Greater Cleve. Growth Assn., 1970; mem. Council Human Relations, 1972, Leadership Cleve. Class '77; cubmaster local Boy Scouts Am., 1977-79; bd. dirs. Buckminster Fuller Inst., 1983—; trustee Pace Assn., 1970-73, Karamu House, 1974-80, Cleve. Inst. Music, 1979—, Ohio Arts Council, 1982-84, Chinese Cultural Assn., 1980-84. Served with Signal Corps, U.S. Army, 1953-55. Decorated 4 medals; recipient Design award Cleve. chpt. AIA, 1972, Korean Inst. Constrn. Tech., 1984; Anicka Design award U. Mich., 1959, Sr. design prize, 1960; Public Works award State of Ohio, 1971, others. Mem. AIA (dir. Cleve. chpt. 1980), Am. Soc. Planning Ofcls., English Speaking Union (trustee 1972-75), Ohio Soc. Architects, Ohio Assn. Minority Architects and Engrs. (trustee 1982—); vestryman St. Christopher-by-River, 1980-83. Clubs: Hermit, City (dir. 1972-74, v.p. 1974) (Cleve.). Lodge: Rotary. Patentee in field. Office: 1303 Prospect Ave Cleveland OH 44115

ZUNKER, WILLIAM FREDERICK, III, insurance executive; b. Milw., Aug. 15, 1945; s. William F. and June M. (Henke) Z.; m. Pam Scherer, Apr. 26, 1969 (div. May 1972); m. Denise M. Zunker, Apr. 2, 1977. B.S., U. Wis.-Milw., 1968. Group rep. Equitable Life Ins. Co., Chgo., 1969-78; ind. ins. broker, Chgo., 1978-80; v.p. Kehe, Foy & Snelten, Arlington Heights, Ill., 1980-83; pres. Kaddatz, Zunker, Snelten & Assocs., Arlington Heights, 1983—. Republican. Home: 1914 E Avon Ln Arlington Heights IL 60004

ZUPSIC, MATTHEW MICHAEL, insurance company executive; b. Pitts., Aug. 30, 1950; s. Joseph Matthew and Antoinette (Birsic) Z.; m. Vicki Jean Quinn, Oct. 8, 1982; children: Tina Elizabeth, Matthew Quay. BA, Marietta Coll., 1972. Mktg. rep. Hartford Ins., Pitts., 1972-76; ins. agt. Githens Ins. Ctr., Belle Vernon, Pa., 1976-77; v.p., ptnr. Burchill Ins. Agy., Inc., Pitts., 1977—. Mem. Pa. Assn. Ind. Ins. Agts. (bd. dirs. 1980-88), Ind. Ins. Agts. Pitts. (treas. 1983, 1st v.p. 1984-86, pres. 1986-88), B & S Investment Club (pres 1985-87). Democrat. Roman Catholic. Avocations: sailing, skiing, boating, gardening.

ZU PUTLITZ, GISBERT, physics educator; b. Rostock, Germany, Feb. 14, 1931; s. Waldemar and Annalies (von Wolffersdorff) u. P.; m. Haide Beckers, July 9, 1960; children: Jasper, York, Julian. Diploma in physics, U. Heidelberg, Fed. Republic of Germany, 1961, D Rer. Nat., 1962, D Rer. Nat. Habilitation, 1966; LLD (hon.), Boston U., 1986; DSc (hon.), U. Md., 1986. Prof. physics U. Heidelberg, Fed. Republic Germany, 1972, rektor, 1983-87; chmn. sci. directorat GSI for Schwerionenforschung, Darmstadt, Fed. Republic Germany, 1978-83; hon. prof. U. Rio Grande do Sul, Porto Allegre, Brazil, 1987; chmn. Assn. German Nat. Labs., Bonn, Fed. Republic of Germany, 1981-83, Daimler Benz Found., Ladenburg, Fed. Republic of Germany, 1986—; apptd. to fed. ministries and sci. assns.; assoc. Yale U., New Haven, Conn. Contbr. over 130 articles on physics to profl. jours. Fellow Am. Phys. Soc.; mem. European Phys. Soc., Deutsche Physikalische Gesellschaft, Deutsche Gesellschaft for Naturforscher u. Ärzte, Max Planck Inst. for Nuclear Phys., Heidelberg Acad. Scis., World Acad. Art and Sci., Berlin Acad. Sci., N.Y. Acad. Arts and Sci. Office: Physikalisches Inst, U Heidelberg, Philosophenweg 12, 6900 Heidelberg Federal Republic of Germany

ZUR, LOIS, marketing executive; b. Milw., Aug. 14, 1938; d. LeRoy Earl and Ruth (Plotkin) Michel; m. James Plous, Aug. 18, 1957 (div. 1976); children: Scott, Wendy; m. Levy Zur, Dec. 16, 1984. BS, U. Wis., 1966; MS, U. Wis., Milw., 1973. Tchr. learning disabilities Shorewood (Wis.) Pub. Schs., 1973-75; tchr. learning disabilities Milw. Pub. Schs., 1975-76, supr., 1976-80; state rep. State of Wis., Milw., 1980-85; internat. mktg. pres. Lexim Ltd., Milw., 1985—; mktg. cons. Medogar Med. Supplies, Ltd., Tel-Aviv, 1985—. Bd. dirs. Dems. Abroad, Israel, 1985-86; dir. fund-raising and fgn. relations Child in Placement, Israel, 1987—. Jewish. Home: 6 Antokolsky St #6, Tel Aviv 64044, Israel Office: Lexim Ltd 425 Willow Ct Milwaukee WI 53217

ZURAIK, SAMY, import export executive, b. Beyrouth, Liban, Sept. 29, 1940; s. Salim and Victoria (Kawas) Z.; m. Renée Chery, Aug. 10, 1971; children: Phadya, Samia, Fahim. Grad., Coll. Max Penette, Port-Au-Prince, 1961. Cert. Bus. Adminstrn. Owner mgr. Retail Textile Store, Port-Au-Prince, Haiti, 1963-67, Import and Wholesale Textile, Port-Au-Prince, 1968-71; gen. mgr. Import and Distbn. Electronics and Appliances, Port-Au-Prince, 1971-88; dir. Kaliko Beach Hotle, Port-Au-Prince, 1981—, Land Devel. SAIDA, Port-Au-Prince, 1983—. Officer Nat. Order Labor Haitian Gov. Mem. Interam. Bus. Assn., Haiti C. of C., ASHRAE. Club: Petion-Ville (Port-Au-Prince). Office: Sanyo Ctr, 11 Rue Bonne Foi Box 1670, Port-au-Prince Haiti

ZURAKOWSKI, BOGUSLAW, writer, literary critic; b. Stanislawow, Poland, July 9, 1939; s. Michal and Janina (Kij) Z.; M of Philology, Wyzsza Szkola Pedagogiczna, Opole, Poland, 1961, Dr. Humanities and Philology, 1975; children—Krzysztof, Bozena. Librarian, Pedagogiczna Biblioteka Wojewodzka, Opole, 1962-69; acad. lectr. Wyzsza Szkola Pedagogiczna, Opole, 1969-82, Uniwersytet Jagiellonski, Krakow, 1981—; author: (poetry) Taniec bez ludzi, 1962; Grudy ziemi, 1966; Piesn, 1971; Slowa czasu kazdego, 1975; Cialo i swiatlo, 1978; Narzecze nadziei, 1980; Wybor poezji, 1981; Koncert ciszy, 1984; (sci. books) W swiecie poezji dla dzieci, 1981; Paradoks poezji, 1982. Recipient distinction Internat. Poetry Competition, PEN Club, London, 1965; lit. award Town Pres. of Opole, 1977; Pietak award, Poland, 1979; Periodical award Opole, 1980; Premio Internat., Pinocchio, 1983, Italy, 1983. Mem. PEN, SEC, Union Polish Writers. Roman Catholic. Home: 22 Krupnicza, 31-123 Krakow Poland

ZUSSMAN, BERNARD MAURICE, physician; b. N.Y.C., Apr. 26, 1906; s. Julius and Ida (Finkelstein) Z.; B.S., CUNY, 1925; M.A., Columbia U., 1926; M.D., NYU, 1930; m. Jane Erdman, Feb. 10, 1945. Intern, St. Mark's Hosp., N.Y.C., 1930-31, Coney Island Hosp., Bklyn., 1931-32; resident Montefiore Hosp. & Research Center, Bronx, and Mt. Sinai Hosp., N.Y.C., 1932; sr. clin. asst. medicine Beth Israel Hosp. & Research Center, 1932-41, adj. in medicine, 1933-41; practice internal medicine, N.Y.C., 1932-41; practice internal medicine specializing in allergy, Memphis, 1944—; sr. clin. prof. dept. medicine U. Tenn. Center for Health Scis., Memphis; cons. Bapt. Meml. Hosp., USPHS Hosp., LeBonheur Children's Hosp., Meth. Hosp. Bd. dirs. Memphis Arts Council; trustee, regional co-chmn. Nat. Jewish Hosp./Nat. Asthma Center, Denver, Nat. Jewish Ctr. for Immunology and Respiratory Medicine. Served to 1st lt. M.C., U.S. Army and Med. Reserve Corps, 1939-41, 41-44. Recipient Merit award Am. Coll. Allergists, 1977; Philanthropic Service award Nat. Jewish Hosp. & Research Center/Nat. Asthma Center, 1979. Fellow Am. Acad. Allergy and Immunology, Am. Coll. Allergists, Am. Geriatrics Assn.; mem. Am. Bd. Internal Medicine (diplomate), Am. Bd. Allergy and Immunology (diplomate), Royal Soc. Health, Internat. Assn. Allergology, N.Y. Acad. Sci., AAAS, Cert. Allergists Assn., NYU Alumni Assn. (pres. Memphis chpt.). Clubs: Petroleum, Ridgeway Country, Sertoma (dir., spl. award of merit 1981), Pres.'s of U. Tenn., Pres.'s of Memphis State U. Contbr. articles to profl. jours. Home: 321 Greenway Rd Memphis TN 38117 Office: 40 N Pauline St Memphis TN 38105

ZWAENEPOEL, JOZEF CAMILLE, planning consultant; b. Assebroek, Belgium, May 30, 1922; s. Cyrille Albert and Agnes (Pil) Z.; m. Simonne Van Der Kelen, June 20, 1950; children: Luc, Anne, Johan. Degree in law, Cath. U. Louvain, Belgium, 1947; PhD, U. Brussels, 1951. Asst. A.C.W. Trade Union, Brussels, 1946-54; mgr. C.C.H. Housing Corp., Brussels, 1955-59; exec. pres. M&R Study Group, Brussels, 1960-77; chmn., gen. mgr. M&R Internat. Cons., Brussels, 1977-87, chmn., 1987—; prof. Higher Insts. for Architecture and Town Planning, Brussels and Ghent, Belgium, 1962—; chmn. Commn. of Experts in Gen. Adminstrn. of Town and Regional Planning, Brussels, 1965—; bd. dirs. Mass Design and Assocs., Lagos, Nigeria; chmn. Eigen Huis com. Regional Mortgage Corp., Bruges, Belgium, 1969—, chmn. De Volkshuisvesting C.S., 1977—, bd. dirs. Interbrugse C.S., 1969—; fgn. trade advisor Belgian Govt., 1985—. Author: Housing Legislation and Institution, 1970; contbr. articles on housing, town and regional planning land use policies. Mem. Nat. Housing Inst. (vice chmn. 1964—), Urban Land Inst. (assoc.), Com. of Belgium Cons. Firms (chmn. 1984), European Com. of Cons. Firms (bd. dirs. 1984). Lodges: Order of Leopold (knight), Order of Crown (knight), Order of St. Sylvester (knight). Home: Hovestraat 169 POB11, Edegem Belgium Office: M&R Internat Cons, Ad Lacomblelaan 52, Brussels Belgium

ZWANGER, JEROME, physician; b. N.Y.C., Apr. 4, 1923; s. Benjamin and Evelyn Z.; m. Bernice E. Lomazov, May 22, 1955; children: Susan, Roberta, Melissa, Betsy. AB, U. Pa., 1943; MD, Chgo. Med. Sch., 1947. Diplomate Am. Bd. Radiology. Intern Wyckoff Heights Hosp., Bklyn., 1947-49; resident L.I. Coll. Hosp., Bklyn., 1949-52; practice medicine specializing in radiology; asst. dir. dept. radiology L.I. Coll. Hosp., N.Y., 1953-54; radiologist L.I. Jewish Hosp., 1955-60; dir. radiology Cen. Gen. Hosp., Plainview, N.Y., 1961—, also bd. dirs.; asst. prof. clin. radiology SUNY, Stony Brook, 1974-80. Bd. dirs. Nassau Physicians Rev. Orgn., 1975-78; governing bd. Nassau-Suffolk Health Systems Agy.; mem. N.Y. State Bd. Medicine. Mem. vis. com. Met. Mus. Art, Phila. Art Mus.; bd. overseers Sch. Arts and Scis., U. Pa. Fellow Am. Coll. Radiology (councilor 1975—), Nassau Acad. Medicine (founder); mem. AMA, Med. Soc. N.Y., Nassau County Med. Soc. (pres.), Radiol. Soc. N.Am., N.Y. State Radiol. Soc. (pres. 1986-87), L.I. Radiol. Soc. (past pres.), U. Pa. Alumni Assn. (trustee 1977—). Office: 126 Hicksville Rd Massapequa NY 11758

ZWASS, VLADIMIR, computer scientist, educator; b. Lvov, USSR, Feb. 3, 1946; came to U.S., 1970, naturalized, 1979; s. Adam and Friderike (Getzler) Z.; m. Alicia Kogut, Apr. 24, 1977; 1 child, Joshua Jonathan. M.S., Moscow Inst. Energetics, 1969; M.Ph., Columbia U., 1974, Ph.D., 1975. Mem. profl. staff IAEA, Vienna, Austria, 1970; asst. prof. computer sci. Fairleigh Dickinson U., 1975-79, assoc. prof., 1979-84, prof., 1984—, chmn. com. computer sci., 1976—; cons. U.S. Govt., Met. Life Ins. Co., Citibank, Diebold Group; seminar assoc. Columbia U., 1986—. Author: An Introduction to Computer Science, 1981, Programming in Fortran, 1981, Programming in Pascal, 1985, Programming in Basic, 1986; editor-in-chief Jour. Mgmt. Info. Systems, 1983—; contbr. articles to profl. jours., Ency. Britannica, chpts. to books. Columbia U. fellow, 1970-71; Helena Rubinstein Found. scholar, 1971-75. Mem. Assn. Computer Machinery, IEEE, Sigma Xi, Eta Kappa Nu. Home: 538 Churchill Rd Teaneck NJ 07666 Office: Fairleigh Dickinson U Teaneck NJ 07666

ZWEIG, JOSEPH, reinsurance company executive; b. Glasgow, Scotland, May 19, 1938; came to U.S., 1952; naturalized, 1958; s. Peter and Bessie Z.; B.B.A., Coll. of Ins., N.Y.C., 1970; M.B.A., Fairleigh Dickinson U., 1977; m. Irene Katz, Nov. 27, 1965; children—Lisa, Jennifer, Jill. Mgr. Prudential Reinsurance Co., 1975-78; prin. cons. Ebasco Risk Mgmt. Cons. Inc., N.Y.C., 1978-79; asst. v.p., home office facultative casualty dir. N. Am. Reins. Corp., N.Y.C., 1979-81; sr. v.p., gen. mgr. B.R.I. Internat. Agy. Inc., N.Y.C., 1981—; sr. v.p., dir. Unisea Ins. Co. Ltd., Internat. Gen. Ins. Co. Ltd., Atlantic Security (Cayman) Ltd. Served with U.S. Army, 1961-67. Mem. Soc. Chartered Property and Casualty Underwriters, Soc. Ins. Research. Office: 156 William St New York NY 10038